■ S C H O O L ■
DICTIONARY 3

M A C M I L L A N / M c G R A W - H I L L

Macmillan/McGraw Hill School Publishing Company
New York   Chicago   Columbus

Macmillan/McGraw-Hill School Division
10 Union Square East
New York, New York 10003

Printed in the United States of America

ISBN 0-02-195019-9

1 2 3 4 5 6 7 8 9 RRW 99 98 97 96 95 94 93

STAFF

Editor in Chief	Judith S. Levey
Managing Editor	Helen Chumbley
Senior Editors	Deirdre Dempsey, Peter R. Margolin (science), Gloria Mihályi Solomon (pronunciation), Vesta Urband, Mary Louise Byrd (copy editing), Archie Hobson, Paul G. Lagassé
Editors	Robert K. Haycraft, Susan R. Norton (art), Patricia Clements Shuldiner, John Elliott, Irene Gunther, Bonny R. Hart, John Mariano, Robert Schleifer
Contributing Editors	Kenneth R. Greenhall, Rosalie H. Lipsett, Kay E. Radtke, Irene Smith, Georg Zappler, Kathleen Derzipilski, Eden Eskin, Lora Goldman
Proofreading and Research	Peter Brydges, Robert Gampert, Sara C. Butte, Frederick V. Cisterna, Robin Fleisig, Ezra Maurer
Keyboarding	Margot A. Bonelli, Joan F. Ginsberg, David A. Ackley, John Vinton
Data Processing	Casey Kwang-Chong Lee (systems manager), Fred C. Richardson, Robert L. Keefe, Jackie Dickens
Assistant	Christopher M. Montpetit
Consultants	*Botany:* Susan J. Lacerte, Brooklyn Botanic Garden; *Etymologies:* David L. Gold, Cecil P. Golann; *Law:* Hal B. Grossman; *Medicine:* William S. Beckett, M.D., M.P.H.; *Physics, Computer Science:* Dr. Alan Oppenheim; *Library Research:* Dr. George Lowy; *Biographies, Geography, Sciences, Social Sciences:* Bernard Johnston, Judith Bloch, Patrick J. Quigley, Theodore Zinn, Frank G. Manning, *Collier's Encyclopedia*, and Robert Famighetti, *Collier's Year Book*; *Design:* Mary Ann Albanese
Art Director	Murray Belsky
Designers	Lee Goldstein, Anna Sabin
Photo Research	Photosearch, Inc.; Susan Kaprov
Artists	Howard S. Friedman, Ruth Soffer, Ruth Adam, Erni Barth, Bertrick Associates, Ann Brewster, Eva Cellini, Ken Longtemps, Maria Mizzaro, Judy Skorpil
Front/Back Matter	*Design:* MKR Design; *Art:* Ruth Soffer, Don Daily, Chet Jezierski, Chris Duke; *Maps:* R. R. Donnelley Cartographic Services
Cover	*Design:* BB&K Design, Inc.; *Art:* Dickran Palulian; *Photo:* NASA/ Phototake, NYC

Contents

*R*eference Section

WRITING AND RESEARCH

HISTORICAL REFERENCES AND ATLAS

SCIENTIFIC AND MATHEMATICAL RESOURCES

TAKING TESTS

PRESENTING YOURSELF IN WRITING — R70

CREDITS — R73

*S*ample Pages

MAIN ENTRY	**cairn** (kârn) *n.* a mound of stones piled up as a memorial or landmark. [Gaelic *carn* heap of stones.]
SYLLABLE DIVISION	**cal·cite** (kal′sīt) *n.* a translucent white or transparent mineral, calcium carbonate, the chief constituent of limestone, chalk, and marble. It is one of the most common minerals.
PRONUNCIATION	**cal·cu·la·ble** (kal′kyə lə bəl) *adj.* **1.** capable of being calculated. **2.** able to be relied on; dependable. —**cal′cu·la·bil′i·ty,** *n.* —**cal′cu·la·bly,** *adv.*
PARTS OF SPEECH	**cal·lous** (kal′əs) *adj.* **1.** thickened and hardened, as a callus on the skin. **2.** hardened in mind or feelings; unfeeling; insensitive. —*v.t., v.i.* to make or become callous. [Latin *callōsus* hard-skinned.] —**cal′lous·ly,** *adv.* —**cal′lous·ness,** *n.*
INFLECTED FORMS **RUN-ON ENTRIES**	**can·ny** (kan′ē) *adj.* **-ni·er, -ni·est. 1.** cautiously shrewd in one's behavior or dealings; prudent; wary. **2.** frugal in money matters; thrifty. —**can′ni·ly,** *adv.* —**can′ni·ness,** *n.* [CAN[1] + -Y[1].]
VARIANT SPELLING	**car·ou·sel** (kar′ə sel′, kar′ə sel′) *also,* **carrousel.** *n.* merry-go-round *(def. 1).* [French *carrousel,* from Italian *carosello;* of uncertain origin.]
	cat·a·ma·ran (kat′ə mə ran′) *n.* **1.** any of various boats having two hulls connected by poles or by a platform that serves as a deck. Most catamarans are sailboats. **2.** a raft made of logs lashed together in the shape of a boat hull. [Tamil *kattumaram* bound wood.]
DEFINITIONS	**cay·enne** (kī en′, kā-) *n.* a hot, biting spice made from the ground seeds and pods of any of several hot red peppers, esp. a variety of *Capsicum annuum.* Also,
VARIANT TERM	**red pepper.** [Modification (influenced by *Cayenne,* a city in French Guiana) of Tupi-Guarani *kyinha* this spice.]
COMPOUND ENTRY	**Celtic cross,** a Latin cross having a circle behind the intersection of the cross-piece. For illustration, see **cross.**
HOMOGRAPHS	**chaff**[1] (chaf) *n.* **1.** husks of wheat, oats, rye, and other grains, separated from the seed by threshing and winnowing. **2.** finely cut hay or straw used as feed for livestock. **3.** any worthless matter; refuse. [Old English *ceaf* husks of grain.] **chaff**[2] (chaf) *v.t., v.i.* to tease or make fun (of) in a good-natured way. —*n.* good-natured teasing; raillery. [Possibly a form of CHAFE.]
SUBJECT LABELS	**cha·la·za** (kə lā′zə) *n., pl.* **-zae** (-zē) or **-zas. 1.** *Zoology.* one of the twisted cords of dense albumen, extending from either side of the yolk to the shell, that keep the yolk suspended near the center of the egg. **2.** *Botany.* the basal end of a plant ovule, opposite the point where the pollen tube penetrates. [Modern Latin *chalaza,*
ETYMOLOGY	from Greek *chalaza* hail, lump.] —**cha·la′zal,** *adj.*

catamaran

GUIDE WORDS

cairn / -cy

USAGE LABELS

CROSS-REFERENCE

chees·y (chē′zē) *adj.*, **chees·i·er, chees·i·est. 1.** of or like cheese. **2.** *Slang.* of inferior quality; poorly made; cheap. —**chees′i·ness**, *n.*

cheq·uers (chek′ərz) *British.* checkers.

ci·lan·tro (sə lan′trō) *n.* coriander *(def. 2).*

coax (kōks) *v.t.* **1.** to persuade or try to persuade by flattery, pleasant manners, or soft, gentle speech; wheedle. **2.** to obtain by coaxing: *He coaxed extra money from his mother.* —*v.i.* to use flattery, pleasant manners, or soft, gentle speech in trying to persuade. [From earlier *cokes* a fool; of uncertain origin.] —**coax′-er**, *n.*

SYNONYM STUDY

> **Synonyms** **Coax, cajole,** and **wheedle** mean to persuade or attempt to persuade through flattery, pleasant or reassuring words, or similar means. **Coax** suggests any kind of gentle appeal: *to coax an animal to come closer, to coax someone to join in a game.* **Cajole** more strongly implies a seductive tone or tactic: *to cajole a child to go to bed by promising to read a story.* **Wheedle** suggests an obvious, often obsequious, kind of approach: *The caller tried to wheedle me into buying a magazine subscription.*

PREFIX

com- *prefix* in association with; together: *combine.* [Latin *com-,* form of *cum* with, together.]

ILLUSTRATIVE EXAMPLES

con·sen·sus (kən sen′səs) *n.* **1.** a general agreement: *to reach a consensus.* **2.** the opinion of all or most; collective opinion: *The consensus of the townspeople was to build a new school.* [Latin *consensus* from *consentīre.* See CONSENT.]

USAGE NOTES

> **Usage** **Consensus** by itself always refers to a general opinion; therefore, the phrases *consensus of opinion* and *general consensus of opinion* are redundant and should be avoided in speech and writing.

con·vex (kon veks′, kən-, kon′veks) *adj.* curved outward, as the outside of a circle or sphere: *a convex lens.* ➡ opposed to **concave.** [Latin *convexus* vaulted, arched.]

SCIENTIFIC NAME

co·ri·an·der (kôr′ē an′dər) *n.* **1.** the sweet, aromatic seed of a plant, *Coriandrum sativum,* of the parsley family, used mainly as a seasoning. **2.** the plant itself, bearing these seeds, edible aromatic leaves, and small white, pink, or lavender flowers. Also *(def. 2),* **cilantro.** [Old French *coriandre,* from Latin *coriandrum,* from Greek *koriannon.*]

CHEMICAL SYMBOL

Cr, the symbol for chromium.

SUBENTRY

cram·pon (kram′pən) *n.* **1.** an iron bar bent in the form of a hook, used esp. in hinged pairs to lift heavy objects. **2. crampons.** spiked iron plates attached to the soles of shoes or boots to prevent slipping while climbing mountains or walking on ice. [French *crampon* grappling iron, calk²; of Germanic origin.]

craw (krô) *n.* **1.** the crop of a bird or insect. **2.** the stomach of any animal. [Probably from an unrecorded Old English word.]

IDIOM

·to stick in (one's) craw. to upset or annoy: *The unfair treatment really stuck in my craw.*

ABBREVIATION

CST, Central Standard Time.

SUFFIX

-cy *suffix* (used to form nouns) **1.** the quality, state, condition, or fact of being: *bankruptcy, accuracy, secrecy.* **2.** the office, position, or rank of: *captaincy, curacy.* [Latin *-cia, -tia,* and Greek *-keiā, -kiā, -teiā, -tiā,* often through French *-cie, -tie.*]

PRONUNCIATION KEY

a	at	e	end	o	hot	u	up	hw	white		about
ā	ape	ē	me	ō	old	ū	use	ng	song		taken
ä	far	i	it	ô	fork	ü	rule	th	thin	ə	pencil
âr	care	ī	ice	oi	oil	u̇	pull	th	this		lemon
		îr	pierce	ou	out	ûr	turn	zh	measure		circus

*H*ow to Look Up a Word

To help you find what you want quickly, the *Macmillan/McGraw-Hill School Dictionary 3* is divided into three sections:

- **A to Z** (pages 1-1395). In the A to Z section, you will find all the words that are defined in the dictionary except the names of people and places.
- **Biographical Names** (pages 1396-1419). The section of Biographical Names follows the A to Z section and contains the names of important people, their birth and death dates, nationality, and occupation or major contribution.
- **Geographical Names** (pages 1420-1464). The section of Geographical Names follows Biographical Names and contains the names of countries, states, provinces, important cities, bodies of water, mountains, and the like. Each entry provides important information and statistics.

At the front and back of the book are two additional special sections. **Using the Dictionary,** the part of the dictionary you are now reading, explains all the different parts of the dictionary and how to use them. At the back of the book, following the Geographical Names, is the **Reference Section** (pages R1-R72), which includes information on how to become a better writer; researching and compiling a research paper; literary, historical, and scientific facts and figures; an atlas; and a guide to taking tests.

MAIN ENTRY WORDS

The words that a dictionary defines are called **main entries.** A main entry may be a word, a combination of words, a chemical symbol, a word part, or an abbreviation. Main entries are printed in heavy **boldface** type at the left-hand margin of each column. The following examples are main entries in this dictionary:

aerobics	**greenhouse effect**	**pre-**
counterculture	**Pb**	**supt.**

The information about the main entry follows and is printed in lighter type. This information, together with the main entry itself, is called the **entry.** An example of an entry is shown below:

> **cor·net** (*def. 1*, kôr net′; *def. 2*, kôr′nit, kôr net′) *n.* **1.** a brass musical instrument that is similar to the trumpet but has a mellower sound. **2.** a paper cone twisted at one end, used as a holder for candy, nuts, or other small items. [Old French *cornet* little horn, diminutive of *corn* horn, going back to Latin *cornū*].

ALPHABETICAL ORDER

The entries in this dictionary are arranged in **alphabetical order.** Whether they consist of a single word, a combination of words, or a hyphenated word, entries are listed alphabetically, letter by letter. This means that only the letters are considered in alphabetizing, starting with the first letter, then the second, and so on. If a main entry is inverted and has a comma, such as **Bulge, Battle of the,** only the word up to the comma is considered.

Bulgarian	**bulletin board**	**bullring**
bulge	**bulletproof**	**bull session**
Bulge, Battle of the	**bullet train**	**bull's-eye**
bulgur	**bullfight**	**bullsnake**

USING INDEX TABS TO LOCATE A LETTER

In the A to Z section, each letter of the alphabet begins on a new page. Along the side of right-hand pages are colored **tabs** indicating the letters of the alphabet to assist you in locating a word within a given letter. By their color and position these tabs will guide you to the letter you want, even when the book is closed. The sections on Biographical Names and Geographical Names immediately follow the A to Z section.

GUIDE WORDS

Once you have found the letter of the alphabet you are looking for, **guide words** are given to help you find the particular word you are looking for. Guide words are the words that appear in large boldface type in the box at the top of each page above the outside column. Separated by a slash, the guide words indicate the alphabetical range of the main entries on each page. The first guide word is the first main entry on the page, and the second is the last. For example, the word **detour** is on the page whose guide words are **detective / detrimental.**

VERIFYING SPELLINGS

All of the features discussed thus far can help you find a word that you know how to spell. But what happens if you want to find a word that you know how to pronounce but do not know how to spell? The **Table of English Spellings** on page A28 can help. To use the table, you first have to think about how each part of the word sounds. Then try to match the sounds to those given in the table. Suppose you want to look up the word **gyroscope.** It is pronounced "jiroskope," so you would look under the letter *j* in the table. There you would find that the first sound can be spelled *g, j, dg, d, gg, di.* You would then look for the second sound, the long *i,* and list the possible spellings. You now know that the beginning of the word may be spelled in one of several ways: *gi, ji, dgi, gy, jy, djy, gigh, jigh, dgie, dgei.* If you look up each of these beginning spellings in the dictionary, you will find the right one for the word **gyroscope.**

Kinds of Main Entries

There are several kinds of main entries in a dictionary. Most of them are single words, such as **beneath, buffalo, demure, investigate, mimicry,** and **sinewy.** But some main entries are combinations of words (compounds), such as **American Revolution, apartment house,** and **word processing,** and some are only parts of words, such as the prefix **non-** and the suffix **-tion.** The main entries in this dictionary can be categorized in the following way: single words, compound entries, homographs, parts of words (prefixes, suffixes, combining forms), abbreviations, symbols, and names of people and places.

COMPOUND ENTRIES

A **compound** is a word that is a combination of two or more words. Each word in a compound usually has its own main entry in the dictionary. When the meaning of the compound cannot be understood by knowing the meaning of each of the words in it, the compound is entered as a main entry in the dictionary. For example, the compound entries **hard copy, hot line,** and **jet lag** cannot be understood simply by knowing the meaning of the individual words. Thus, these and many other compounds are main entries in the dictionary.

HOMOGRAPHS

Many words in English are spelled alike but do not have the same meaning and origin. Such words are called **homographs. Hamper** meaning "to obstruct the action or progress" and **hamper** meaning "a large basket or other receptacle" are examples of homographs. Homographs are entered as separate main entries in this dictionary, and they are identified by a small superscript number above and to the right of the main entry word.

> **ham·per¹** (ham′pər) *v.t.* to obstruct the action or progress of; impede: *Stalled cars hampered snow-removal efforts.* [Middle English *hamperen* to surround, enclose, harass.]
> **ham·per²** (ham′pər) *n.* a large basket or other receptacle, usually with a cover: *a picnic hamper, a hamper for laundry.* [Earlier *hanaper,* from Middle English *haniper,* from Old French *hanapier* basket for cups, from *hanap* cup; of Germanic origin.]

PREFIXES, SUFFIXES, AND COMBINING FORMS

Some main entries are not actually words. They are word parts that are used in forming words. There are three kinds of word parts: **prefixes,** which appear at the beginning of a word; **suffixes,** which appear at the end; and **combining**

forms, which may appear in either place. The word **postwar** is composed of the prefix **post-** plus the root word **war.** The words **creation, creative,** and **creator** are formed by adding various suffixes to the root word **create.** The combining form **para-** is used in **parachute** and **parasol.**

In this dictionary, prefixes and combining forms that appear at the beginning of a word are identified by a hyphen after the entry form.

---

retro- *prefix* backward, back, or behind . . .
proto- *combining form* first in time; earliest; original . . .

Suffixes and combining forms that appear at the end of a word are identified by a hyphen before the entry form.

-ative *suffix* . . . **1.** tending to . . .
-cide[1] *combining form* killing off . . .

Many new words are created by adding a prefix, suffix, or combining form to a word that already exists. In your reading you may find certain formations of this type that do not appear in your dictionary but which you can usually understand by using the information given in the dictionary about the word part and the root word, or the word to which it is attached. For example, even though the word **osteosarcoma** does not appear in this dictionary, if you look up the entry for the combining form **osteo-,** which means "of or relating to bone," and combine it with the information given under the entry for the word **sarcoma** ("any of various highly malignant tumors . . ."), you can understand the meaning of **osteosarcoma.** The word means "a malignant tumor arising from bone tissue."

Prefix Lists. This dictionary includes lists of undefined words made with certain prefixes. The lists include commonly used words whose meanings can be easily understood by combining the meaning of the prefix with that of the root word. The lists are helpful in determining the correct spelling for such words. The following prefixes include lists: **anti-, co-, mis-, multi-, non-, over-, pre-, re-, un-, well-.**

ABBREVIATIONS

This dictionary includes **abbreviations** that occur frequently in writing. Many abbreviations have more than one correct form. Since it is not possible to record all possibilities, only the most commonly used forms are entered. The definitions for abbreviations are arranged alphabetically.

A few words are more commonly known by their abbreviations than their spelled-out form, for example, **VCR, DNA,** and **PCB.** The information for these words is given under the abbreviation, rather than the spelled-out form.

BIOGRAPHICAL ENTRIES

On pages 1396-1419 of this dictionary there is a section of **Biographical Entries.** Each main entry is listed alphabetically according to the last name. If the entry is inverted and has a comma, only the word up to the comma is considered.

> **Aus·ten, Jane**...1775-1817, English novelist.
> **Aus·tin, Stephen Fuller**...1793-1836, U.S. colonizer of Texas.
> **A·ver·ro·ës**...1126-1198, Spanish-Arabian philosopher and physician.

GEOGRAPHICAL ENTRIES

On pages 1420-1464 of this dictionary there is a section of **Geographical Entries.** Each main entry is listed alphabetically according to its proper name. If the entry is inverted and has a comma, only the word up to the comma is considered.

> **Ev·er·est, Mount**... the highest mountain in the world, located in the Himalayas on the border between Nepal and Tibet. Height, 29,028 ft (8,848 m).
> **Ev·er·glades**...**1.** an extensive region of marshlands and swamps in southern Florida.

Kinds of Secondary Entries

Even if the word or phrase you are looking for does not appear as a main entry, it is still very likely to be explained in the dictionary. Many words are included as **secondary entries.** Secondary entries are printed in **secondary,** or small, **boldface** type within the body of material following a main entry. They appear with the main entry to which they are most closely related.

> **flee** (flē) *v.*, **fled, flee·ing.**...**—fle′er,** *n.*
> **lac·y** (lā′sē) *adj.*, **lac·i·er, lac·i·est.**...**—lac′i·ness,** *n.*

The different kinds of secondary entries, including inflected forms, variants, subentries, run-on entries, and idioms are described below.

INFLECTED FORMS

In English, a change in the form of a word often signals a change in the meaning of the word. These changes in form are called **inflected forms.** They give such information as the tense of the word **(go, going, went, gone),** its

number **(woman, women; am, are)**, or its degree **(much, more, most).** Inflected forms are printed in **secondary boldface** and follow the label for the appropriate part of speech to which they belong.

> **free** (frē) *adj.*, **fre·er, fre·est. 1.** having personal liberty or rights . . . —*v.t.*, **freed, free·ing. 1.** to release, as from burden, constraint, or obligation . . .

Syllable division is shown for inflected forms. Pronunciation is not shown unless the pronunciation of the inflected form cannot be clearly understood from that of the main entry. When an irregular inflected form is very different from the main entry, it has its own separate main entry and is given a pronunciation there.

> **take** (tāk) *v.*, **took, tak·en, tak·ing.** . . .
> **took** (tu̇k) the past tense of **take.**

Nouns.   The inflected form for a **noun** is its plural. Most English nouns form their plural by adding the letter **-s (pencil, pencils; loop, loops)** or the letters **-es** when the singular ends in **-s, -ss, -ch, -x,** or **-z (loss, losses; lunch, lunches; fox, foxes; buzz, buzzes).** Inflected forms that follow this regular **-s** or **-es** pattern are not shown. Only plurals of nouns that depart from this regular pattern, as by a change in spelling or pronunciation, are shown.

> **half** (haf) *n.*, *pl.* **halves.**
> **house** (hous) *n.*, *pl.* **hous·es** (hou′ziz).
> **ba·sis** (bā′sis) *n.*, *pl.* **ba·ses** (bā′sēz).
> **stim·u·lus** (stim′yə ləs) *n.*, *pl.* **-li** (-lī′).

Plurals are also shown for words whose singular form ends in **-o,** since some of these nouns form their plurals by adding **-s** and others by adding **-es.**

> **ra·di·o** (rā′dē ō′) *n.*, *pl.* **-di·os.**
> **he·ro** (hir′ō) *n.*, *pl.* **-roes.**

Plurals are also shown when there might be confusion about the plural.

> **mon·goose** (mong′güs′) *n.*, *pl.* **-goos·es.**
> **pass·er·by** (pas′ər bī′) *n.*, *pl.* **pass·ers·by.**
> **court-mar·tial** (kôrt′mär′shəl) *n.*, *pl.* **courts-mar·tial** or **court-mar·tials.**

Adjectives and Adverbs.   The inflected forms for **adjectives** and **adverbs** are the **comparative** and **superlative** degrees. Usually the comparative and superlative are formed by adding **-er** and **-est** to the root word **(small, smaller, smallest; dark, darker, darkest).** Inflected forms that follow this regular pattern are not shown. Only those inflected forms that depart from the regular **-er, -est** pattern, as by a change in spelling or complete change in form, are shown.

> **fit¹** (fit) *adj.*, **fit·ter, fit·test.**
> **speed·y** (spē′dē) *adj.*, **speed·i·er, speed·i·est.**
> **bad¹** (bad) *adj.*, **worse, worst.**

Comparative and superlative degrees of adjectives and adverbs can also be formed by using **more** and **most (sillier** or **more silly; silliest** or **most silly).** This style and the **-er, -est** style are both correct. Usage will depend on which one sounds more natural to you. There are certain words, however, for which the **-er, -est** pattern sounds awkward, for example, ''more courteous,'' not ''courteouser.'' For such words the comparative and superlative degrees are formed by using **more** and **most.**

Verbs. The inflected forms for **verbs** usually shown are the **past tense** (The soprano *sang* an aria), the **past participle** (She has *sung* that role many times), and the **present participle** (She is *singing* very well this evening). This is also the order in which they are listed in the entry.

> **go¹** (gō) *v.*, went, gone, go·ing.
> **give** (giv) *v.*, gave, giv·en, giv·ing.

The past tense and the past participle often have the same form (He *taught* history for many years. He has *taught* at our school since last fall). When this occurs, the form is given only once.

> **lose** (lüz) *v.*, lost, los·ing.

Most English verbs form their past tense and past participle by adding the letters **-ed** to the root word, and they form their present participle by adding the letters **-ing** to the root word. These are regular verbs, and their inflections are not shown.

> **con·sid·er** (kən sid′ər) *v.t.* **1.** . . .

Some verbs, however, do not follow this regular pattern and have a change in spelling or a complete change in form. These are irregular verbs, and their inflections are shown.

> **con·spire** (kən spīr′) *v.i.*, -spired, -spir·ing.
> **for·bore** (fôr bôr′) the past tense of **forbear¹.**
> **caught** (kôt) the past tense and past participle of **catch.**

Variants

Variant Spellings. The English language has many words that have more than one acceptable spelling. **Theater, theatre** and **vermilion, vermillion** are but two examples. When **variant spellings** fall close alphabetically, the main entry appears under the spelling that is more commonly used or generally preferred. The variant spelling or spellings appear in alphabetical order after the pronunciation and are preceded by the word *also.* The syllable division of a variant is shown if the variant does not have its own main entry.

> **judg·ment** (juj′mənt) *also,* **judge·ment.**

A variant spelling is given a separate pronunciation if it is different from that of the main entry. If a variant has its own main entry, it is not pronounced.

> **squa·mous** (skwā′məs) *also,* **squa·mose** (skwā′mōs).
> **hur·rah** (hə rä′, -rô′) *also,* **hoo·ray, hur·ray** (hə rā′).

A variant spelling has its own main entry if it does not fall close alphabetically to the preferred form.

> **czar** (zär) *also,* **tsar, tzar.**
> **tsar** (zär, tsär) czar.
> **tzar** (zär, tsär) czar.

The fact that one spelling of a word is given as a main entry and another spelling appears as a variant does not mean that the variant is incorrect. It simply means that the first spelling is generally preferred in American usage.

Variant Terms.   Sometimes two or more words have the same meaning. For example, **German shepherd, police dog,** and **Alsatian** are all words for the same kind of dog. The main entry appears under the word that is used most commonly. The other word or words, which are called **variant terms,** appear at the end of the entry. A variant term is preceded by ''Also'' and is printed in secondary boldface type. Variant terms are syllabicated and given pronunciations only if they do not have separate main entries.

> **cou·gar** (kü′gər) *n.* a tawny or grayish brown wildcat... Also, **catamount, mountain lion, panther, puma.**
> **tid·dly·winks** (tid′lē wingks′) *n.* a game in which... Also, **tid·dle·dy·winks** (tid′əl dē wingks′).

If a variant term does not fall close alphabetically to the preferred term, it has its own separate main entry with a cross-reference to the preferred term.

> **an·gi·o·sperm** (an′jē ə spûrm′) *n.* flowering plant.
> **sea lily,** crinoid.

Subentries

A **subentry** is a word or phrase that is closely related to a main entry word but has a slightly different form. It appears under the main entry in **secondary boldface** type. There are a number of different kinds of subentries. A subentry may be the plural of a singular main entry, the capitalized form of a main entry that begins with a lowercase letter, or the main entry preceded by an article.

> **clas·sic** ... —*n.* **1.** an author, artist, or artistic work of acknowledged excellence and endurance. **2. the classics.** the literature of ancient Greece and Rome.
> **reb·el** (*n., adj.,* reb′əl; *v.,* ri bel′) *n.* **1.** a person who joins in an armed resistance against the legal government of his or her own country. **2.** a person who resists or refuses to obey any law or authority. **3. Rebel.** a person who fought on the side of the Confederacy in the American Civil War.

Another type of subentry is a word or phrase so closely related to the main entry word that the explanation is more appropriate within the entry than as a separate entry.

> **e·clipse** ... *n.* **1.** an apparent partial or total darkening of one celestial body by its passage through the shadow of another. In a **solar eclipse** the moon passes between the sun and the earth ... In a **lunar eclipse** the earth moves between the sun and the moon ...

Run-on Entries

Many words in English are formed by adding a suffix to a root word. The adverb **thoughtfully** and the noun **thoughtfulness** are formed by adding suffixes to the adjective **thoughtful.** A word formed in this way is called a **derived word.** It usually has the same essential meaning as its root word, but a different grammatical form. The noun **dampness** is formed from the adjective **damp** and the suffix **-ness,** which means "quality, state, or condition of being." When the meaning of a derived word equals the meaning of the root word plus the meaning of the suffix, there is no separate main entry for the derived word. Such derived words appear as **run-on entries**—they are "run on" in alphabetical order at the end of the entry for the root word. Run-on entries are set in **secondary boldface** type and are introduced by a dash. Run-ons are divided into syllables, and stress is shown by accent marks. The part of speech of a run-on is indicated following the form.

> **av·id** (av′id) *adj.* **1.** having or showing enthusiasm; ardent; eager: *an avid reader.* **2.** having a great desire ... [Latin *avidus* greedy.] —**av′id·ly,** *adv.* —**av′id·ness,** *n.*

A run-on is not given a pronunciation unless its pronunciation cannot be understood from that of the main entry.

> **con·cen·tric** (kən sen′trik) *adj.* ... —**con·cen·tric·i·ty** (kon′sen tris′i tē), *n.*

A derived word is not run on unless all its meanings can be understood from the definitions for the root word plus those for the suffix. The word **catcher** is a main entry because it has a specialized sense (the player in baseball) that is not fully covered by **catch** + the suffix **-er.**

Idioms

An **idiom** is a group of words whose meaning cannot be understood from the meanings of the individual words. For example, **from the horse's mouth** means "from the original or most reliable source," a meaning that cannot be understood from the individual words defined singly. Idioms are entered in alphabetical order in **secondary boldface** type under the main entry of their key, or most important, word. Thus, **from the horse's mouth** would appear under **horse.**

Some idioms have more than one form. In such a case, the variant word (or words) is put in parentheses indicating that it may be substituted in the idiom. For example, under **petard** appears the idiom **"to be hoist with (or by) one's own petard.** to be caught or victimized by one's own actions.'' This idiom has two forms: **to be hoist with one's own petard** or **to be hoist by one's own petard.**

*D*ictionary Features

SYLLABLE DIVISION

Most main entry words are divided into **syllables** by centered black dots.

> **pre·ten·tious**
> **vid·e·o·cas·sette**

These dots show where to divide a word in writing or printing if space requires that a word begun on one line be completed on the next. If you were using the word **pretentious,** for example, and had to complete it on the next line, you could break it after *pre-* or *preten-*.

Not all main entry words are divided into syllables. The individual words of a compound entry are not syllabicated if they have their own separate main entries. For example, the entry **artificial intelligence** is not divided because each word is syllabicated at its own entry. Words pronounced as one syllable, such as **friend,** are never divided.

PRONUNCIATION

The pronunciation of a word is enclosed in parentheses and follows the boldface spelling of the entry. Pronunciations are shown by respellings of main entries. A special system of letter symbols is used. These symbols represent the sounds of American English. The system is presented in the **Pronunciation Key** on page A30, along with words that show how each symbol is sounded. A shorter pronunciation key is printed at the bottom of each right-hand page of the dictionary. The syllables of the pronunciation are divided by a space. Some syllables of a word are spoken with more stress, or force, than others. An **accent mark** follows a syllable that is stressed. Primary, or strong, stress indicates a syllable spoken with a great degree of force and is represented by a heavy mark ('). Secondary, or weak, stress indicates a syllable spoken with less force and is represented by a lighter mark ('). Syllables that are spoken with no stress at all have no accent mark. Unstressed syllables are separated by a space.

> **gen·er·ous** (jen′ər əs) . . .
> **frag·men·ta·tion** (frag′mən tā′shən) . . .

The syllables of the pronunciation are not always the same as the syllables of the main entry word. The pronunciation syllables are divided according to the way the word is spoken to make it easy to sound out the pronunciation given. **Rhythm** has one syllable in its written form and two in its spoken form. **Sensationalism** has five syllables in its written form but six in its spoken form. Remember that the syllable division of the boldface main entry word applies only to the way the word is written. The syllables of the pronunciation apply to the way the word is spoken. Therefore, the two sets of syllables may not always agree.

> **rhythm** (rith′əm) . . .
> **sen·sa·tion·al·ism** (sen sā′shə nə liz′əm) . . .

You often will find that an entry has more than one pronunciation. Each pronunciation is given in complete form once, but often alternate pronunciations do not appear in full. When a part of an alternate pronunciation does not change from the first pronunciation, that part may be omitted and replaced by a hyphen. The hyphen indicates that you should apply the missing part from the first pronunciation in sounding the second pronunciation. In the case of **magnesium,** for example, the second pronunciation would be (mag nē′zhəm).

> **a·dult** (ə dult′, ad′ult) . . .
> **mag·ne·si·um** (mag nē′zē əm, -zhəm) . . .

Sometimes a pronunciation is preceded by an italicized label that limits the pronunciation to particular definitions or to one or more parts of speech.

> **ap·prox·i·mate** (*adj.*, ə prok′sə mit; *v.*, ə prok′sə māt′) . . .
> **suite** (swēt; *def. 2, also* süt) . . .

Any pronunciation without a label applies to all the definitions of the word. Each one-word main entry is given a pronunciation, no matter how short or how simple the word may be.

> **hut** (hut) . . .

Some main entries that consist of more than one word are not followed by a pronunciation because the individual words of the compound entry are pronounced in their own entries.

> **frame of mind,** . . .

This dictionary has entries for the words **frame, of,** and **mind.** The pronunciations given in those entries tell you how to pronounce the compound **frame of mind.**

A word in a compound entry is given a pronunciation only if it does not have a pronunciation anywhere else in the book.

> **Rich·ter scale** (rik′tər) . . .

Even if part of a compound has its own entry, the word may be given a pronunciation to avoid confusion.

> **wind¹** (wind) . . .
> **wind²** (wīnd) . . .
> **wind³** (wīnd, wind) . . .
> **wind instrument** (wind) . . .

Because our language is spoken in different ways in different parts of the United States, many words have more than one acceptable pronunciation. These alternate pronunciations may reflect either a regional pronunciation or a pronunciation used by some speakers in all regions of the country. The first pronunciation shown for a word is often the most common, but frequently the other pronunciations are used just as often. The first pronunciation is not necessarily considered to be more correct than the others. All the pronunciations given in the *Macmillan/McGraw-Hill School Dictionary 3* are an accepted part of American English as it is actually spoken today.

Parts of Speech

This dictionary uses the traditional **parts of speech** in classifying words. The names of the parts of speech are indicated by the following abbreviations.

n.	noun	*v.t.*	transitive verb	*prep.*	preposition
pl.n.	plural noun	*v.i.*	intransitive verb	*conj.*	conjunction
pron.	pronoun	*adj.*	adjective	*interj.*	interjection
v.	verb	*adv.*	adverb		

There is only one main entry for each word, no matter how many parts of speech it may have. All the definitions of a word that have the same part of speech are grouped together. The first part-of-speech label appears after the pronunciation, or the variant spelling if there is one. If an entry has more than one part of speech, subsequent part-of-speech labels appear before the first definition to which they apply, preceded by a dash.

> **ax** (aks) *also,* **axe.** *n., pl.* **ax·es.** a tool with a bladed metal head . . . —*v.t.* **1.** to chop or cut with an ax . . . .

The different parts of speech of any word are given in order of frequency. The part of speech that occurs most commonly is defined first, the one that occurs second most frequently is defined second, and so on.

> **round** (round) *adj.* **1.** shaped like a sphere . . . —*n.* **1.** something round in shape; that which is spherical, circular, or cylindrical . . . —*v.t.* **1.** to make round in shape . . . —*v.i.* **1.** to become round in shape . . . —**adv. 1.** around . . . —*prep.* **1.** around . . .

A compound entry does not have a part-of-speech label.

> **Irish moss,** a reddish or purple seaweed . . .

The parts of speech assigned to a word in the dictionary do not cover all the possible uses of the word. A word may function as a certain part of speech in a sentence without actually belonging to that part of speech. Most nouns may also be used as adjectives, for example, "a *world* record," "*insect* repellent," or "an *airline* terminal." Verbs may also be used as adjectives or nouns. Present and past participles are often used as adjectives: "an *exhausting* exercise class," "a *printed* invitation." Participles are often used as nouns: "*Walking* is very good exercise." Such forms are not entered separately unless their meaning is not explained by the definitions given for the verb.

DEFINITIONS

The **definitions** of an entry are grouped according to part of speech. They are numbered consecutively, starting with the most common meaning first. The other definitions follow according to their frequency.

> **soft** (sôft, soft) *adj.* **1.** readily yielding to touch or pressure; easily shaped or worked; not hard: *soft clay, a soft bed.* **2.** not hard for its kind; not as hard as is normal or desirable: *soft wood.* **3.** smooth or fine to the touch; having a delicate texture; not rough or coarse: *soft skin.* **4.** not loud or harsh; quiet and melodious; gentle: *a soft tone of voice.* . . .

Related senses of one basic meaning are grouped under one number and lettered.

> **o·pen** (ō′pən) *adj.* . . . **11.a.** receptive, as to new ideas, facts, or views; agreeable (often with *to*): *open to suggestions.* **b.** having no prejudices or biases; unprejudiced: *an open mind.*

A definition may have more than one part to describe the same basic meaning. These parts are separated by semicolons.

> **so·cia·ble** . . . *adj.* **1.** liking to associate with others; fond of company; friendly; affable . . . .

SCIENTIFIC NAMES

In definitions of plants and animals, in addition to the other information, the *Macmillan/McGraw-Hill School Dictionary 3* gives the **scientific name** of a plant or animal in the definition.

> **mal·lard** (mal′ərd) *n., pl.* **-lards** or **-lard.** a wild duck, *Anas platyrhynchos,* of freshwater ponds and marshes throughout temperate northern regions. The male has a green head, a white band around the neck, a reddish brown breast, and a grayish back. Length: 28 inches (71 centimeters).

If the entry refers to a grouping that is more general than a species, the designation of the grouping (such as genus, family, or order) is indicated.

> **floun·der²** (floun′dər) *n., pl.* **-der** or **-ders.** a flatfish of either of two families, Bothidae and Pleuronectidae, valued as both a food and a game fish.

When the genus name of a particular species has been mentioned previously in the definition, the full name is not repeated. The genus is abbreviated after the first letter, followed by the full species name.

> **elephant seal,** either of two species of large, earless seals, genus *Mirounga*, having a trunklike proboscis: *M. angustirostris*, found off the California coast, and *M. leonina*, of subantarctic waters. Length: 14-20 feet (4.3-6.1 meters). Weight: to 3½ tons (3.1 metric tons). Also, **sea elephant.** [Because its long proboscis resembles an elephant's trunk.]

Scientific names are especially helpful in identifying an organism when it is known by several different common names, as in various regions. The animal defined under **cougar,** for example, is also known as the **puma, mountain lion,** or **catamount,** as well as by various other names. But it is known by only one scientific name, *Felis concolor.*

LABELS

Labels are used in this dictionary to provide additional information about a word or definition. The labels used fall into two basic categories: **subject labels** and **usage labels.**

Subject Labels. Subject labels, such as *Chemistry, Sports,* and *Music,* indicate a particular field of knowledge to which a word belongs. They are given when it may not be obvious from a definition that it applies to a particular field.

> **fam·i·ly** . . . **8.** *Biology.* in taxonomic classification, a group of related living things forming a category ranking below an order and above a genus. Zebras, asses, and horses belong to the horse family. **9.** *Linguistics.* a group of related languages descended from a common parent language. The English language belongs to the Indo-European family.

When a word has many definitions, the presence of a subject label makes a specialized definition easier to locate.

> **hit** . . . **13.** *Baseball.* to make (a specified base hit): *to hit a home run.*

Usage Labels. There are many words or meanings of words in English that are not used universally. Some are restricted to only a part of the English-speaking world; others rarely appear in modern speech and writing; still others are restricted to a certain area or level of language. Usage labels help you distinguish between these kinds of words. The absence of a usage label indicates that a word or meaning may be used in any kind of speech and writing.

Informal: The label *Informal* indicates that a word or meaning is not suitable for use in a formal context, such as a research paper, lecture, or legal contract. The label does not mean that a word or definition is incorrect, but simply that it is more appropriate for an informal context than for a formal one.

Slang: The label *Slang* is applied to extremely informal words or meanings. Most slang words are new words or unusual uses of existing words. Slang is usually used to produce a certain effect, such as humor or exaggeration. New slang words are constantly being added to the language, and many existing slang words pass out of use after a brief period of popularity.

British: The label *British* indicates that a word, meaning, or spelling is more common in British English than in American English.

Archaic: The label *Archaic* indicates that a word or meaning was once frequently used but is no longer common. Archaic words or meanings are used by modern speakers or writers who wish to achieve an old-fashioned effect. They are included in this dictionary because you will find them in your reading, especially in the works of writers of the past, such as William Shakespeare and John Milton.

Foreign language: In this dictionary a word or phrase occasionally has a foreign language label, such as *Latin, French,* or *Spanish.* These labels indicate that the entry, although actually part of a foreign language, is used often enough in English contexts to justify its inclusion in an English-language dictionary.

Trademark: This label is used before a definition to indicate that a word is the official registered name for a product of a particular company. The label appears at the end of a definition when the name is no longer restricted to the product of a particular company.

Py·rex . . . *n. Trademark.* a heat-resistant glass used in ovenware, laboratory glassware, and telescope mirrors.

hov·er·craft . . . *n.* a vehicle that can hover or travel over land or water on a thin cushion of high-pressure air created beneath the craft by means of fans or rotors . . . Trademark: **Hovercraft.**

ILLUSTRATIVE SENTENCES AND PHRASES

Many definitions are followed by sentences or phrases printed in italic type. They show the meaning of the word in context and help clarify meanings in several ways. **Illustrative sentences and phrases** may clarify a meaning by showing it in a familiar use.

---

old . . . **10.** experienced, skilled, or practiced: *an old hand at sailing.*

They may also distinguish between two slightly different senses of the same meaning.

> **new** ... **1.** having existed only a short time; recently grown or made: *The tree has new buds. Have you been to the new mall?*

They may also show that in a certain meaning, a word is used in a particular way, such as figuratively:

> **mur·der** ... **3.** to abuse, mangle, or mar: *to murder the English language.*

Usage Notes

Usage notes provide information about the way a particular word or expression is used in current English by educated speakers and writers. Long usage notes deal with words that are often confused and provide information on points of grammar or diction. They appear at the end of an entry and are introduced by a blue color bar and the word **Usage.**

> **bad·ly** *adv.* ...
>
> **Usage** In formal speech and writing, the adjective **bad,** not the adverb **badly,** has traditionally been used after linking verbs such as *look, smell,* and *feel: Those tomatoes smell bad. The whole team feels bad about losing the game.* However, many people now consider it acceptable to use **badly** as an adjective, especially when used after *feel* to mean "sad" or "regretful": *I felt badly about hurting your feelings.*

Short usage notes provide many different kinds of information. Some tell you that a word is used to form other words or is distinguished from or opposed to another word. Others restrict the use of a word or indicate a special use of a word. Short usage notes follow the definition or definitions to which they apply and are introduced by a blue arrow.

> **ex·tro·vert** ... ➡ opposed to **introvert.**
> **his·tri·on·ics** ... *n.* **1.** overemotional or theatrical behavior. **2.** a dramatic representation; acting; dramatics. ➡ used as plural in def. 1, as singular in def. 2.
> **toed** ... *adj.* having toes, esp. a specific number or kind of toes. ➡ usually used in combination: *a three-toed sloth, square-toed shoes.*

Etymologies

An **etymology** is the history of a word tracing it back from its present form to its original source, including changes in spelling and meaning that have taken place. Etymologies are placed between square brackets following the definitions. The words from which an English word comes—sources, or ancestors—are printed in italic type. Names of languages, explanatory material, and translations or explanations of the meaning of a foreign word are in roman type.

> **par·tial** ... [Middle French *partial* biased, incomplete, from Late Latin *partiālis* relating to a part, incomplete, from Latin *pars* share, portion.]

If the first source word has basically the same meaning as the main entry, no gloss, or translation, is given. Glosses are furnished only if the meanings differ significantly. When a source word in an etymology has precisely the same meaning as the word that precedes it, the gloss is not repeated.

> **clan·des·tine** . . . [Latin *clandestīnus*.]
> **plank** . . . [Dialectal Old French *planke* board, from Latin *planca*.]

The name of a language is shown only before its first appearance in an etymology and is not repeated for stages of development in that language.

> **mo·rose** . . . [Latin *mōrōsus* peevish, particular, from *mōs* manner, custom.]

A plus sign (+) is used to connect two or more words or word elements that make up a word.

> **pol·ter·geist** . . . [German *Poltergeist*, from *poltern* to make a noise + *Geist* ghost.]

Sometimes a word in an etymology is printed in small capital letters. This means that the word is a cross-reference to the main entry word from which it or a part of it is formed.

> **pol·y·es·ter** . . . [POLY(MER) + ESTER.]

If a cross-reference in an etymology is preceded by the word "See," it means that a portion of the entry's etymology is identical to that of another main entry. The shared information is given only once (at the other entry).

> **in·tox·i·cate** . . . [Medieval Latin *intoxicatus*, past participle of *intoxicare* to poison, from Latin *in* in + *toxicum* poison. See TOXIC.]
> **tox·ic** . . . [Medieval Latin *toxicus* poisonous, from Latin *toxicum* poison, from Greek *toxikon (pharmakon)* (poison) for arrows, from *toxon* bow[2].]

When a word has an interesting history, full information about its origin is provided in the form of an anecdote. Very often the current meaning of a main entry is clarified by the etymology.

> **mav·er·ick** (mav′ər ik) *n.* **1.** an unbranded animal, esp. a calf, traditionally belonging to the first person to find and brand it. **2.** *Informal.* a person who takes an unorthodox stand, esp. in politics. [From Samuel A. *Maverick*, 1803-70, Texan who decided not to brand his calves because his ranch was on an island.]

Not every entry has an etymology. When the elements of a derived word, compound, or phrase are easy to recognize, an etymology is not necessary. You can simply look up the separate elements where they are entered. For example, since there is an etymology for **extreme,** no etymology is needed for **extremely, extremism,** or **extremist.** You can find sufficient information in the etymologies given for the root word, **extreme,** and the various suffixes, **-ly, -ism,** and **-ist.**

CROSS-REFERENCES

Often, information about an entry is provided under another main entry. In such cases it is necessary to refer you to another part of the dictionary. This is done by means of a **cross-reference.** There are many kinds of cross-references in this dictionary. Some are references to preferred spellings or terms.

> **ar·che·ol·o·gy** (. . .) archaeology.
> **puma** (. . .) *n.* cougar.
> **giant panda,** panda *(def. 1).*
> **deoxyribonucleic acid** (. . .) see **DNA.**

Cross-references also indicate where to find synonym studies and usage notes.

> **pro·voke** (. . .) *v.* . . . For Synonyms, see **incite.**
> **will** (. . .) *auxiliary verb.* . . . For Usage Note, see **shall.**

They also indicate where art, tables, and other information may be found.

> **breast·plate** (. . .) *n.* . . . For illustration, see **armor.**
> **Pa·le·o·zo·ic** (. . .) *n.* . . . For table, see **geologic time.**

SYNONYMS

Because the English language draws its words from many different sources, it has an unusually large number of **synonyms.** Although several words may mean almost the same thing, usually each has particular characteristics that set it off slightly from its synonyms. The purpose of a synonym study is to show subtle distinctions among words that are close in meaning. Such distinctions enable a careful writer or speaker to choose the word most appropriate for the particular context. The synonym study appears as a separate paragraph at the end of the main entry. It is introduced by a red color bar and the word **Synonyms.** If a synonym study applies to a particular part of speech, the part of speech is given.

> **base¹** *n.* . . .
>
> **Synonyms** *n.* **Base¹, basis,** and **foundation** mean something that supports something else. **Base** suggests a bottom part or underlying substance or object on which something rests: *the base of a column.* **Basis** conveys the same idea of support but is usually used of concepts rather than physical things: *The basis of the recycling program is community support.* **Foundation,** used either of physical structures or of concepts, emphasizes the work that has gone into constructing a solid support: *to lay the foundations of a house, a theory with a clearly demonstrated foundation.*

In general, the synonym study appears under the most common or comprehensive word in the group of synonyms being discussed. The other words in the synonym study have a cross-reference to the study at the end of their own entry.

> **foun·da·tion** (. . .) *n.* . . . For Synonyms, see **base¹.**

ILLUSTRATIONS

Illustrations serve to provide a fuller understanding of a word than is possible through the use of definitions alone. Often a fact, idea, or principle that would require a long and complicated written explanation can be expressed more clearly by a photograph or drawing. The photographs and many of the drawings in this dictionary are in full color, giving greater depth and detail than would otherwise be possible.

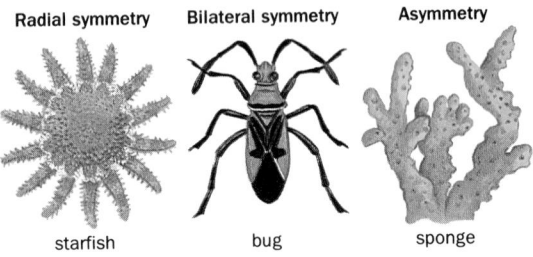

Radial symmetry   Bilateral symmetry   Asymmetry

starfish   bug   sponge

symmetry and asymmetry

TABLES

This dictionary includes many tables and charts that offer more comprehensive information than would be possible within a dictionary definition. These include lists of English words derived from other languages; tables on language-related topics, such as diacritical marks and figures of speech; a table on the derivation of U.S. state names; and tables on scientific and mathematical topics, such as the elements, geologic time, and trigonometric functions. Following is an alphabetical list of entries under which tables and charts can be found:

abbreviation	figure of speech	numeral
adjective	French	Old English
African	Gaelic	Persian
alphabet	geologic time	Portuguese
American Indian	German	proofread
Americanism	Greek	Richter scale
Arabic	Hawaiian	Russian
binary system	Hebrew	Sanskrit
blood group	Hindi	Scandinavian
braille	Italian	Spanish
British English	Japanese	spelling
Chinese	Latin	state
combining form	Malay	taxonomy
diacritical mark	manual alphabet	trigonometry
Dutch	meter^2	Turkish
element	misspelling	weight
eponym	national park	Yiddish

Languages of the World

There are many hundreds of languages spoken throughout the world. Linguists have classified these languages into groups called "families," according to their shared characteristics. Those in the same language family are thought to be derived from a single common parent language. One of the largest is the Indo-European language family, shown below in detail because it is the language group containing English and because half the population of the world speaks one or more of these languages. Some of the world's other languages, which are spoken predominantly in Africa, the Middle East, Asia, and the Pacific, and by native peoples of the Americas, are shown in the second section.

INDO-EUROPEAN LANGUAGE FAMILY

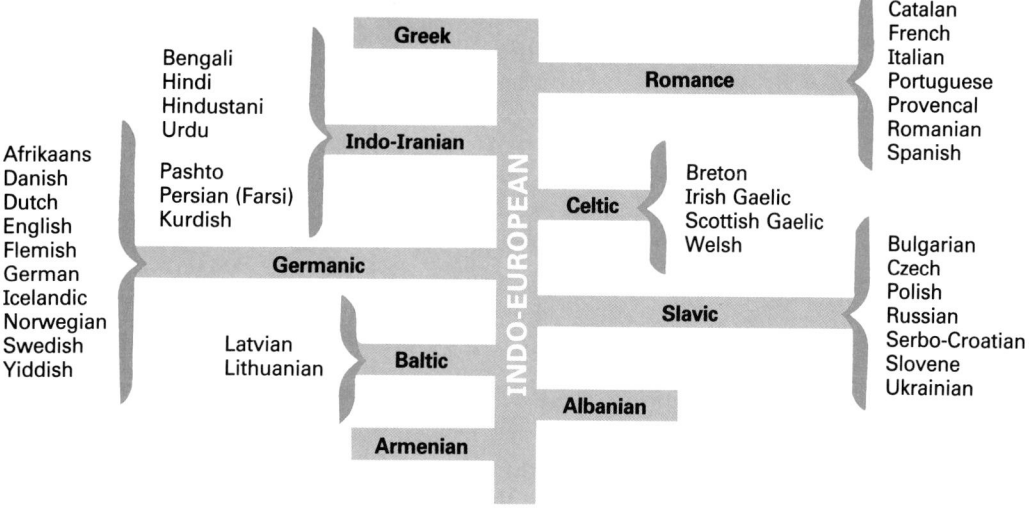

OTHER MAJOR LANGUAGES SPOKEN AROUND THE WORLD

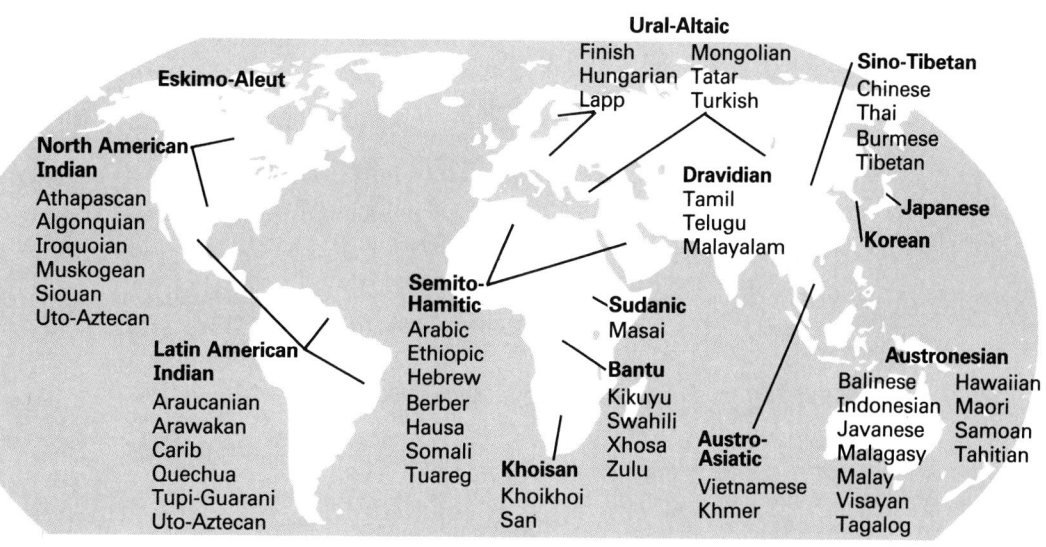

Table of English Spellings

SOUND	SPELLING	EXAMPLE
a	a, au, ai	hand, laugh, plaid
ä	a, e, ea, ua	father, sergeant, heart, guard
ā	a, a-consonant-e, ai, ay, eigh, et, ea, ei, ey, au	paper, rate, rain, pay, eight, ballet, steak, veil, obey, gauge
âr	are, air, ayer, ere, ear, eir	care, fair, prayer, there, bear, heir
b	b, bb	bit, rabbit
ch	ch, t, tch, ti, c	chin, nature, batch, mention, cello
d	d, dd, ed	dive, ladder, failed
e	e, ea, a, ai, ie, eo, u, ae, ay, ei, ue	met, weather, many, said, friend, jeopardy, bury, aesthetic, says, heifer, guess
ē	e, y, ee, ea, e-consonant-e, i-consonant-e, ie, ei, ey, ae, ay, oe, eo	he, city, bee, beach, cede, machine, field, deceive, key, Caesar, quay, amoeba, people
f	f, ph, ff, gh	fine, physical, off, laugh
g	g, gg, gue, gh	go, stagger, catalogue, ghost
h	h, wh	how, whole
hw	wh	wheel
i	i, i-consonant-e, a-consonant-e, y, ie, ui, ei, ia, e, ee, u, o	sit, give, damage, myth, sieve, build, counterfeit, carriage, pretty, been, busy, women
ī	i-consonant-e, i, y, igh, ie, ei, eigh, uy, ai, ey, ye, eye	fine, tiger, try, high, tie, stein, height, buy, aisle, geyser, dye, eye
îr	ear, eer, ere, er, ier, ir, yr	near, deer, here, imperial, fierce, delirious, Syria
j	g, j, dg, d, gg, di	magic, jump, ledger, graduate, exaggerate, soldier
k	c, k, ck, ch, cc, qu, q, cq, cu, que	cat, key, tack, chord, account, liquor, Iraq, acquaint, biscuit, bisque
l	l, ll	line, hall
m	m, mm, mb, mn	mine, hammer, climb, hymn
n	n, nn, kn, gn, pn	nice, funny, knee, gnome, pneumonia
ng	ng, n, ngue	sing, link, tongue
o	o, a	lock, watch
ō	o, o-consonant-e, oa, ow, ou, ough, oe, au, eau, oo, ew, oh	so, bone, boat, know, soul, though, foe, mauve, beau, brooch, sew, oh
ô	o, a, au, aw, ough, augh, oa	toss, fall, author, jaw, bought, caught, broad
ôr	or, ore, orr, oar, aur, our	order, more, horrible, soar, aural, four
oi	oi, oy, uoy	foil, toy, buoy
ou	ou, ow, ough	out, now, bough

SOUND	SPELLING	EXAMPLE
p	p, pp	pill, happy
r	r, rr, wr, rh	ray, parrot, wrong, rhyme
s	s, ss, c, sc, ps, st, sch	song, mess, city, scene, psychology, listen, schism
sh	ti, sh, ci, ssi, si, ss, ch, s, sci, ce, sch	nation, shin, special, mission, expansion, tissue, machine, sugar, conscience, ocean, schist
t	t, tt, ed, pt, th	ten, bitter, topped, ptomaine, thyme
th	th	thin
<u>th</u>	th	them, bathe
u	u, o, ou, o-consonant-e, oo, oe	sun, son, touch, come, flood, does
u̇	u, oo, ou, o	full, look, should, wolf
ü	oo, u, o, u-consonant-e, ou, ew, ue, o-consonant-e, ui, eu, oe	tool, luminous, who, flute, soup, jewel, true, lose, fruit, maneuver, canoe
ū	u, u-consonant-e, ew, eu, ue, iew, eau, ieu, ueue	music, use, new, feud, cue, view, beautiful, adieu, queue
ûr	er, or, ur, ir, yr, our, ear, err, eur, yrrh	fern, worst, turn, thirst, myrtle, courage, earth, err, amateur, myrrh
v	v, f	vine, of
w	w, u, o	we, queen, choir
y	i, y, j	onion, yes, hallelujah
z	s, z, x, zz, ss	has, zoo, xylophone, fuzz, scissors
zh	si, s, g, z, zi	division, treasure, mirage, azure, brazier
ə	o, a, i, e, ou, u, y, ai	lemon, about, pencil, taken, furious, circus, analysis, bargain

*A*bbreviations Used in the Dictionary

A.D.	Anno Domini (after Christ)		m	meters
adj.	adjective		mi	miles
adv.	adverb		n.	noun
b.	born		pl.	plural
B.C.	(before Christ)		Pop.	population
c.	circa		prep.	preposition
conj.	conjunction		pron.	pronoun
contr.	contraction		sing.	singular
d.	died		sq km	square kilometers
def(s).	definition(s)		sq mi	square miles
esp.	especially		St.	Saint
fl.	flourished		U.S.	United States
ft	feet		v.	verb
interj.	interjection		v.i.	intransitive verb
km	kilometers		v.t.	transitive verb

*P*ronunciation Key

a	at, bad
ā	ape, pain, day, break
ä	father, car, heart
âr	care, pair, bear, their, where
e	end, pet, said, heaven, friend
ē	equal, me, feet, team, piece
i	it, big, English, hymn
ī	ice, fine, lie, my
îr	ear, deer, here, pierce
o	odd, hot, watch
ō	old, oat, toe, low
ô	coffee, fork, all, taught, law, fought
oi	oil, toy
ou	out, now
u	up, mud, love, double
ū	use, mule, cue, feud, few
ü	rule, true, food
u̇	put, wood, should
ûr	burn, hurry, term, bird, word, courage
ə	about, taken, pencil, lemon, circus
b	bat, above, job
ch	chin, such, match
d	dear, soda, bad
f	five, defend, leaf, off, cough, elephant
g	game, ago, fog, egg
h	hat, ahead
hw	white, whether, which
j	joke, enjoy, gem, page, edge
k	kite, bakery, seek, tack, cat
l	lid, sailor, feel, ball, allow
m	man, family, dream
n	not, final, pan, knife
ng	long, singer, pink
p	pail, repair, soap, happy
r	ride, parent, wear, more, marry
s	sit, aside, pets, cent, pass
sh	shoe, washer, fish, mission, nation
t	tag, pretend, fat, button, dressed
th	thin, panther, both
<u>th</u>	this, mother, smooth
v	very, favor, wave
w	wet, weather, reward
y	yes, onion
z	zoo, lazy, jazz, rose, dogs, houses
zh	vision, treasure, seizure
KH	ch as in German ach, ich
N	as in French bon, enfant: indicates that the vowel preceding N is nasalized
œ	eu as in French feu; ö as in German schön: rounding the lips for ō, pronounce ā.
Y	u as in French une, tu; ü as in German über: rounding the lips for ō, pronounce ē.
R	any non-English trilled or rolled r-sound

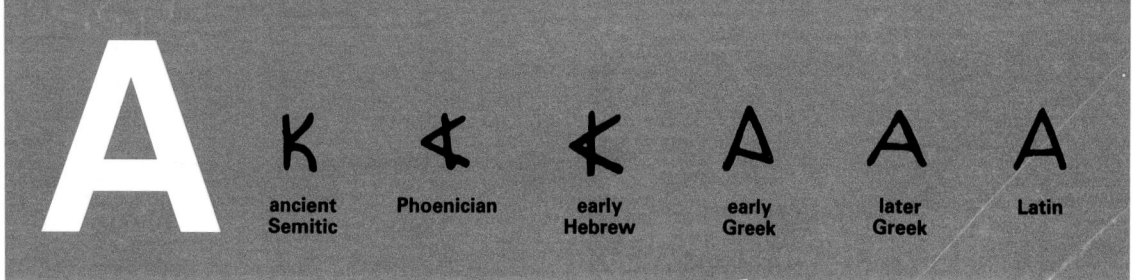

| ancient Semitic | Phoenician | early Hebrew | early Greek | later Greek | Latin |

An alphabet is a series of letters used to represent the sounds of a language in writing. All alphabets are believed to be descended from an ancient Semitic writing system that dates back about 4,000 years. Today, with a few exceptions, including Chinese and Japanese, languages throughout the world use alphabets consisting most commonly of between 20 and 30 letters. The English alphabet uses two forms of letters: capital, or majuscule, letters and lower-case, or minuscule, letters. The capital letters closely resemble the Latin capital letters used in ancient Rome, from which modern letters are descended. The lower-case letters, which also have their roots in the Latin capital letters, developed in the Middle Ages, when scribes began to simplify the capitals by rounding them, joining them together, or omitting some of the loops. In addition to representing sounds, modern English letters are used in many different ways, including as symbols in mathematical and scientific formulas, as musical keys, to indicate a rank or grade, and for numerous technical abbreviations.

A The earliest ancestor of the letter **A** was the symbol used to represent the first letter of the ancient Semitic alphabets. In the Phoenician and early Hebrew alphabets, this letter was a consonant called *aleph*, meaning "ox." The Greeks modified the design of *aleph* and used it to represent their vowel *alpha*. By the eighth century B.C., the Greek *alpha* had assumed the form of the modern capital letter **A**. The letter came into Latin about 2,700 years ago, and from it English and other European languages derived their initial letter. Because it is the first letter of the alphabet, **A** is often used to show the first or highest quality or rank. The English word *alphabet* comes from combining *alpha* with *beta*, the second letter of the Greek alphabet.

a, A (ā) *n., pl.* **a's, A's. 1.** the first letter of the English alphabet. **2.** the shape of this letter or something having this shape. **3.** the first item in a series or group.
· **from a to z** (or **A to Z**). from beginning to end.
a[1] (ə; stressed ā) *indefinite article* **1.** one of a type or class: *The elm is a tree.* **2.** one; no matter which; any: *A child could understand this problem.* **3.** one. ➡ used with numbers or quantities: *a bushel of grain, a hundred dollars.* **4.** one single: *There was not a person in sight! We picked a flower.* [Short for Old English *an*, *one*, *an*.]
a[2] (ə; stressed ā) *prep.* to, in, or for each; per: *three times a year, two dollars a pound.* [Short for Old English *an*, *on* on, to.]
A (ā) *n., pl.* **A's. 1.** *Music.* **a.** the sixth note or tone of the diatonic scale of C major. For illustration, see **do**[2]. **b.** a scale or key that has this note or tone as its tonic. **2.** a grade or rating indicating excellence: *an A in math.* **3.** one of the four principal blood groups. For table, see **blood group**.
A, former symbol for argon.
a-[1] *prefix* in; on; to; at: *atop, apart, aboard, afoot.* [From Old English preposition *an, on* on, to.]
a-[2], form of **ab-**[1] before *m, p, v,* as in *avert*.
a-[3], form of **ad-** before *sc, sp, st,* as in *ascend*.
a-[4], form of **an-**[1] before consonants except *h,* as in *asexual, amorphous*.
a *also,* **a.** acre; acres.
a. 1. about. **2.** adjective. **3.** *Sports.* assist; assists.
A 1. answer. **2.** artillery. **3.** *also,* **Å.** angstrom.
A. 1. April. **2.** August.
AA 1. Alcoholics Anonymous. **2.** antiaircraft.

AAA 1. Agricultural Adjustment Administration. **2.** American Automobile Association.
AAAS, American Association for the Advancement of Science.
aard·vark (ärd'värk') *n.* a burrow-dwelling mammal, *Orycteropus afer,* of southern and east-central Africa, that has a long, sticky tongue and powerful claws and feeds on ants and termites. It constitutes the only genus of the order Tubulidentata. Average length: 6 feet (1.8 meters), including tail. For illustration, see **anteater.** [Afrikaans *aardvark,* from Dutch *aarde* earth + *vark* pig.]
aard·wolf (ärd'wŭlf') *n., pl.* **-wolves** (-wŭlvz'). a carnivorous mammal, *Proteles cristatus,* of southern and east-central Africa, related to the hyena. It feeds mainly on termites and other insects. Average length: 2½ feet (0.8 meter), including tail. [Afrikaans *aardwolf,* from Dutch *aarde* earth + *wolf* wolf.]
AB (ā'bē') *n., pl.* **AB's.** one of the four principal blood groups. For table, see **blood group.**
ab-[1] *prefix* from; departing from; away from: *abnormal, abduct, abjure.* [Latin *ab* from, away.]
ab-[2], form of **ad-** before *b,* as in *abbreviate.*
a.b., able-bodied seaman.
AB, the postal abbreviation for Alberta.
A.B., Bachelor of Arts. Also, **B.A.**
ab·a·ca (ab'ə kä') *n.* **1.** a treelike tropical plant, *Musa textilis,* of the banana family, from whose leaves Manila hemp is made. **2.** Manila hemp. [Spanish *abacá,* from Tagalog *abaká* this plant.]
a·back (ə bak') *adv. Archaic.* at the back; backward. [Old English *on bæc.*]
· **taken aback.** suddenly surprised or startled.

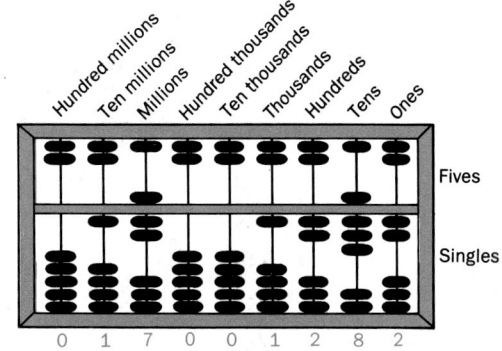

abacus
with beads representing the number 017001282

ab·a·cus (ab'ə kəs, ə bak'əs) *n., pl.* **ab·a·cus·es** or **ab·a·ci** (ab'ə sī'). **1.** a counting device consisting of a frame with balls or beads that slide back and forth in grooves or on wires. **2.** a flat slab forming the top of the capital of a column. [Latin *abacus* counting board, slab, from Greek *abax,* probably from Hebrew *'ābāq* dust. The Greco-Roman abacus was a board covered with

a	at	e	end	o	hot	u	up	hw	white		about
ā	ape	ē	me	ō	old	ū	use	ng	song		taken
ä	far	i	it	ô	fork	ü	rule	th	thin	ə	pencil
âr	care	ī	ice	oi	oil	u̇	pull	th	this		lemon
		îr	pierce	ou	out	ûr	turn	zh	measure		circus

dust or sand, on which figures could be drawn and then brushed away.

a·baft (ə baft′) *prep.* in the stern or rear of; behind. —*adv.* at or toward the stern. [A-¹ + Middle English *baft* behind, from Old English *beæftan.*]

ab·a·lo·ne (ab′ə lō′nē) *n.* any of a group of edible marine mollusks, genus *Haliotis,* in which the ear-shaped shell is lined with mother-of-pearl and perforated along part of the outer rim. The **red abalone,** *H. rufescens,* of Californian and Mexican Pacific waters, is the largest species and is valued for its meat. [Spanish *abulón.*]

a·ban·don (ə ban′dən) *v.t.* **1.** to leave and not intend to return; forsake completely; desert: *to abandon a child, to abandon ship.* **2.** to give up (something) completely: *The castaways abandoned all hope of rescue.* **3.** to give over control of; yield; surrender: *The king abandoned the city to the conquering army.* **4.** to yield (oneself) without restraint, as to an emotion or influence: *to abandon oneself to grief.* —*n.* complete surrender to one's emotions or impulses; freedom from constraint: *The child cried with abandon.* [Old French *abandoner* to give up, from *(mettre) a bandon* (to put) in the power of (someone

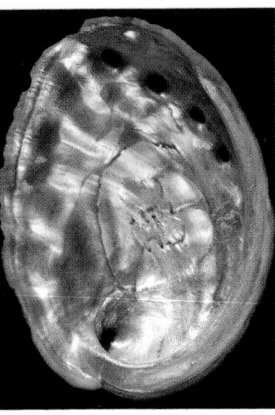

abalone shell

else), from *bandon* power; of Germanic origin.] —**a·ban′don·er,** *n.* —**a·ban′don·ment,** *n.* —For Synonyms *(v.t.),* see **desert².**

a·ban·doned (ə ban′dənd) *adj.* **1.** left without support or care; deserted; forsaken: *an abandoned house, an abandoned child.* **2.** having given up moral behavior; wicked.

a·base (ə bās′) *v.t.,* **a·based, a·bas·ing.** to lower in rank, condition, or esteem; humiliate; humble: *They refused to abase themselves by begging.* [Old French *abaisser* to lower, going back to Latin *ad* to + Late Latin *bassus* low.] —**a·base′ment,** *n.*

a·bash (ə bash′) *v.t.* to make self-conscious or ashamed; disconcert. [Anglo-Norman *abaiss-,* form of Old French *esbaiss-,* a stem of *esbair* to astound.] —**a·bash′ment,** *n.*

a·bate (ə bāt′) *v.,* **a·bat·ed, a·bat·ing.** —*v.i.* to become less in force, intensity, or amount; subside: *The hurricane winds abated.* —*v.t.* **1.** to lessen or reduce in force, intensity, or amount: *Nothing could abate the mob's rage.* **2.** *Law.* to put a stop to or nullify: *to abate a nuisance, to abate a suit.* [Old French *abat(t)re* to beat down, going back to Latin *ad* to + *battuere* to strike, beat.] —**a·bat′a·ble,** *adj.* —**a·bat′er,** *n.*

a·bate·ment (ə bāt′mənt) *n.* **1.** the act or process of lessening or reducing. **2.** *Law.* the act of putting a stop to or annulling. **3.** an amount by which something is abated; reduction.

ab·at·toir (ab′ə twär′) *n.* a slaughterhouse. [French *abattoir,* from Old French *abat(t)re.* See ABATE.]

ab·ba·cy (ab′ə sē) *n., pl.* **-cies.** the office, term of office, or jurisdiction of an abbot. [Late Latin *abbātia,* from *abbās.* See ABBOT.]

ab·bé (ab′ā, a bā′) *n. French.* **1.** a member of the clergy, esp. a priest. ➡ used as a title of respect. **2.** an abbot.

ab·bess (ab′is) *n.* the female superior of a convent. [Old French *ab(b)esse,* from Late Latin *abbātissa,* feminine of *abbās.* See ABBOT.]

ab·bey (ab′ē) *n., pl.* **-beys. 1.a.** a monastery under the rule of an abbot. **b.** a convent under the rule of an abbess. **2.** the church of an abbey. **3.** a church or other building, as the residence of an abbot or abbess, that was originally part of an abbey. [Old French *abbaie* monastery, from Late Latin *abbātia* abbacy, from *abbās.* See ABBOT.]

ab·bot (ab′ət) *n.* the male superior of a monastery. [Old English *abbad,* from Late Latin *abbās,* from Late Greek *abbas,* from Aramaic *abbā* father.]

abbr. 1. abbreviated. **2.** abbreviation. Also, **abbrev.**

ab·bre·vi·ate (ə brē′vē āt′) *v.t.,* **-at·ed, -at·ing. 1.** to shorten (a word or phrase) so that one or more characters stand for the whole, as *Feb.* for *February, no.* for *number,* and *mph* for *miles per hour.* **2.** to reduce in length, size, or duration; shorten: *to abbreviate a speech.* [Late Latin *abbreviātus,* past participle of *abbreviāre* to shorten, from *ab* from + *brevis* short.] —**ab·bre′vi·a′tor,** *n.*

ab·bre·vi·a·tion (ə brē′vē ā′shən) *n.* **1.** one or more letters representing the whole of a word or phrase. **2.** the act of abbreviating or the state of being abbreviated.

ABC's (ā′bē′sēz′) *also,* **ABC** (ā′bē′sē′). *pl. n.* **1.** the alphabet. **2.** the basic principles (of a subject); rudiments.

Ab·di·as (ab dī′əs) *n.* in the Douay Bible, Obadiah.

ab·di·cate (ab′di kāt′) *v.,* **-cat·ed, -cat·ing.** —*v.t.* to renounce or relinquish power, rights, or responsibility formally. —*v.i.* to renounce or relinquish power or a position of power, as a throne; step down formally: *In 1936, King Edward VIII of Great Britain abdicated.* [Latin *abdicātus,* past participle of *abdicāre* to renounce.] —**ab′di·ca′tion,** *n.* —**ab′di·ca′tor,** *n.*

ab·do·men (ab′də mən, ab dō′-) *n.* **1.** the largest of the body cavities of a mammal, situated between the diaphragm and the pelvis, containing many vital organs such as the stomach, the intestines, the kidneys, and the liver; belly. **2.** a corresponding body region or cavity in other vertebrates. **3.** the hindmost section of the body of an insect, spider, or crustacean, situated behind the thorax or cephalothorax. [Latin *abdōmen* belly.]

ab·dom·i·nal (ab dom′ə nəl) *adj.* of, in, on, or relating to the abdomen. —**ab·dom′i·nal·ly,** *adv.*

ab·duct (ab dukt′) *v.t.* **1.** to carry off (someone) unlawfully by force or fraud; kidnap. **2.** to move (a limb) away from the median axis of the body or (a digit) away from the hand or foot. ➡ opposed to **adduct.** [Latin *abductus,* past participle of *abdūcere* to lead away.] —**ab·duc′tion,** *n.* —For Synonyms, see **kidnap.**

ab·duc·tor (ab duk′tər) *n.* **1.** a person who abducts; kidnapper. **2.** a muscle that abducts. ➡ opposed to **adductor.**

a·beam (ə bēm′) *adv.* **1.** alongside a ship, esp. directly opposite the middle of a ship's side. **2.** at right angles to a ship's keel.

a·bed (ə bed′) *adv.* in bed.

Ab·er·deen Angus (ab′ər dēn′) any of a breed of beef cattle originating in Scotland, having a stocky body, black hair, and no horns. Also, **Angus.**

ab·er·rant (ə ber′ənt, ab′ər-) *adj.* **1.** differing or deviating from what is usual, normal, or correct: *aberrant behavior.* **2.** differing or deviating from an ordinary or normal type; atypical: *an aberrant rock formation.* [Latin *aberrāns,* present participle of *aberrāre* to stray from.] —**ab·er′rance, ab·er′ran·cy,** *n.* —**ab·er′rant·ly,** *adv.*

ab·er·ra·tion (ab′ə rā′shən) *n.* **1.** a deviation or differing from the usual, normal, or correct course or mode of action. **2.** a deviation or differing from a normal or ordinary type; abnormal structure or development. **3.** a slight mental disorder or lapse. **4.** the failure of a lens or mirror to focus the light rays from a single point on an object at a corresponding single point on its image, causing the formation of a blurred or otherwise imperfect image. **5.** a displacement in the apparent position of a heavenly body, caused by the motion of the earth. [Latin *aberrātiō* a wandering, from *aberrāre* to stray from.]

a·bet (ə bet′) *v.t.,* **a·bet·ted, a·bet·ting.** to encourage or assist, esp. in wrongdoing. [Old French *abeter* to excite, arouse, from *a* to (from Latin *ad* to) + *beter* to bait (a bear), from Old Norse *beita* to cause to bite.] —**a·bet′ment,** *n.* —**a·bet′tor;** *also,* **a·bet′ter,** *n.*

a·bey·ance (ə bā′əns) *n.* **1.** temporary inactivity or suspension: *We will hold the matter in abeyance until later.* **2.** *Law.* a state of

A

undetermined or unsettled ownership, as of an estate without a legal heir. [Old French *abeance* suspension; literally, gaping at, from *abaer* to gape.]

ab·hor (ab hôr′) *v.t.*, **-horred, -hor·ring.** to feel repugnance, disgust, or hatred for; loathe: *Many people abhor spiders.* [Latin *abhorrēre* to shrink back, from *ab* from, away + *horrēre* to have one's hair stand on end, bristle.] —**ab·hor′rer,** *n.* —For Synonyms, see **hate.**

ab·hor·rence (ab hôr′əns, -hor′-) *n.* **1.** a feeling of disgust, repugnance, or loathing. **2.** something repugnant or loathsome. —For Synonyms, see **disgust.**

ab·hor·rent (ab hôr′ənt, -hor′-) *adj.* **1.** causing disgust, repugnance, or loathing; detestable: *abhorrent criminal acts.* **2.** in opposition; contrary (with *to*): *Lying was abhorrent to the teacher.* **3.** feeling abhorrence (with *of*): *abhorrent of violence.* —**ab·hor′rent·ly,** *adv.*

a·bide (ə bīd′) *v.*, **a·bode** or **a·bid·ed, a·bid·ing.** —*v.i.* **1.** to continue to live in a place; reside; dwell. **2.** to continue to exist; endure: *What was, and is, and will abide* (Wordsworth, 1819). **3.** to continue to stay; remain: *Abide with me from morn till eve* (John Keble, 1827). —*v.t.* **1.** to put up with; bear patiently; tolerate: *The critic could not abide a bad performance.* ➡ used with a negative. **2.** *Archaic.* to await; wait for. [Old English *abīdan* to remain on.] —**a·bid′er,** *n.*

　• **to abide by. a.** to comply with: *You must abide by the rules.* **b.** to live up to; carry out; fulfill: *The store failed to abide by its guarantee.*

a·bid·ing (ə bī′ding) *adj.* continuing; enduring: *an abiding love.*

a·bil·i·ty (ə bil′i tē) *n., pl.* **-ties.** **1.** the condition of being able; capacity; power: *the ability to walk, the ability to learn.* **2.** a natural or acquired skill in doing a particular job or activity; talent: *to show great ability as a carpenter, to have athletic ability.* [Old French *abilité* aptitude, from Latin *habilitās*, from *habēre* to have.]

Synonyms Ability, aptitude, talent, and skill refer to personal power or capacity to do something well. **Ability** is the broadest of these terms, describing a capacity that has been shown, whether innate or acquired: *Your essays demonstrate your writing ability.* **Aptitude** suggests a likelihood of gaining in ability: *With her aptitude for science, Jane will go far.* **Talent** suggests an innate ability, particularly for artistic or mechanical work: *I didn't know you had such a talent for drawing.* **Skill** is the only one of these terms that implies a capacity acquired from practice or experience: *Tom's skill on the guitar comes from years of study.*

-ability *suffix* (used to form nouns) capability or likelihood of being or causing: *movability, irritability.*

ab in·i·ti·o (ab′i nish′ē ō′) *Latin.* from the beginning.

a·bi·o·gen·e·sis (ā′bī ō jen′ə sis) *n.* spontaneous generation. [A-⁴ + BIOGENESIS.] —**a·bi·o·ge·net·ic** (ā′bī ō jə net′ik), *adj.* —**a′bi·o·ge·net′i·cal·ly,** *adv.*

a·bi·ot·ic (ā′bī ot′ik) *adj.* of, relating to, or characterized by the absence of life or living things: *an abiotic environment.*

ab·ject (ab′jekt, ab jekt′) *adj.* **1.** so bad as to be utterly miserable or hopeless: *to live in abject poverty.* **2.** deserving of scorn; contemptible: *abject cruelty, an abject liar.* [Latin *abjectus,* past participle of *abicere* to throw away.] —**ab·jec′tion, ab′ject·ness,** *n.* —**ab′ject·ly,** *adv.*

ab·jure (ab jùr′) *v.t.*, **-jured, -jur·ing.** **1.** to give up on oath; renounce: *The new citizens abjured all allegiance to any other country.* **2.** to abandon or reject (a belief or opinion), esp. formally or publicly; recant. [Latin *abjūrāre* to deny on oath.] —**ab′jur·a′tion,** *n.* —**ab·jur′er,** *n.*

abl., ablative.

ab·late (ab lāt′) *v.*, **-lat·ed, -lat·ing.** —*v.t.* to subject (the nose cone of a spacecraft) to ablation. —*v.i.* to be removed by ablation. [From ABLATION.]

ab·la·tion (ab lā′shən) *n.* a process in which a special protective coating on the nose cone of a spacecraft reentering the earth's atmosphere slowly melts away in order to carry off excessive heat. [Latin *ablātiōn-,* stem of Church Latin *ablātiō* a taking away, from *ablātus.* See ABLATIVE.]

ab·la·tive (ab′lə tiv) *n.* **1.** a grammatical case in Latin and certain other Indo-European languages that indicates movement, direction, source, or cause. **2.** a word or construction in this case. —*adj.* of, relating to, or designating this case. [Latin *ablātīvus* this case, from *ablātus* taken away; with reference to its frequent use to express something taken away.]

a·blaze (ə blāz′) *adj.* **1.** in flames. **2.** brilliantly lit; gleaming: *a Christmas tree ablaze with colored lights.* **3.** in a state of excitement, anger, or desire: *to be ablaze with jealousy.*

a·ble (ā′bəl) *adj.*, **a·bler, a·blest.** **1.** having sufficient power, skill, or qualifications: *able to read and write.* **2.** having or showing unusual competence or intelligence; talented; skillful: *an* **able politician, an able performance.** [Old French *able,* from Latin *habilis* easy to handle, apt, skillful.] —**a′bly,** *adv.*

Synonyms Able, capable, and competent refer to powers of the person or thing described. **Able** indicates a power to accomplish something: *We were able to persuade our guests to stay an extra day.* **Capable** may suggest the limits of the power: *This ship is capable of a speed of 30 knots.* **Competent,** unlike the other two terms, is used almost exclusively in reference to people and always points to some effectiveness already shown: *This mechanic is competent enough to repair your car.* It is also used to imply limits to such effectiveness: *The chef at that restaurant is competent but not great.*

-able *suffix* **1.** (used to form adjectives from verbs) **a.** able to be or capable of being: *eatable, tolerable.* **b.** worthy of being: *laudable, commendable, believable.* **c.** likely to: *perishable.* **2.** (used to form adjectives from nouns) **a.** worthy of or able to cause: *objectionable, comfortable.* **b.** tending toward: *peaceable.* [French *-able,* from Latin *-ābilis.*]

a·ble-bod·ied (ā′bəl bod′ēd) *adj.* having a strong, healthy body; capable of doing physical work.

able-bodied seaman, an experienced and certified sailor in the merchant marine. Also, **able seaman.**

a·bloom (ə blüm′) *adj.* **1.** in bloom; flowering. **2.** filled with blooms: *The garden is abloom.*

ab·lu·tion (ə blü′shən) *n.* **1.** *also,* **ablutions.** a washing or cleansing, esp. of one's body: *one's morning ablutions.* **2.a.** a ceremonial washing as part of a religious rite or observance. **b.** the liquid used for this. [Late Latin *ablūtiō* washing, from Latin *abluere* to wash away.]

ABM, antiballistic missile.

ab·ne·gate (ab′ni gāt′) *v.t.*, **-gat·ed, -gat·ing.** to deny (something) to oneself; forgo: *to abnegate the pleasures of wealth.* [Latin *abnegātus,* past participle of *abnegāre* to refuse, deny.] —**ab′ne·ga′tion,** *n.* —**ab′ne·ga′tor,** *n.*

ab·nor·mal (ab nôr′məl) *adj.* deviating from the normal, usual, or average; not conforming to a type or standard; irregular: *abnormal structure of a plant, an abnormal situation.* [Modification of French *anormal* abnormal, going back to Latin *abnōrmis* irregular, from *ab* away + *nōrma* carpenter's square, rule.] —**ab·nor′mal·ly,** *adv.*

ab·nor·mal·i·ty (ab′nôr mal′i tē) *n., pl.* **-ties.** **1.** the state or quality of being abnormal. **2.** something that is abnormal.

a·board (ə bôrd′) *adv.* **1.** in, on, or into a ship, train, bus, or airplane. **2.** *Nautical.* alongside (of a ship or shore). —*prep.* in, on, or into (a ship, train, or other vehicle).

　• **all aboard.** get in or get on. ➡ a call used to warn passengers that a ship, train, or bus is about to depart.

a·bode (ə bōd′) *n.* the place where one lives; dwelling; home. —*v.* a past tense and past participle of **abide.** [Middle English *abad* remaining, stay, from *abiden* to abide, from Old English *abīdan* to remain on.] —For Synonyms, see **home.**

a·bol·ish (ə bol′ish) *v.t.* to put an end to; do away with completely: *to abolish segregation.* [Middle French *aboliss-,* a stem of *abolir,* from Latin *abolēre* to destroy.] —**a·bol′ish·a·ble,** *adj.* —**a·bol′ish·er,** *n.* —**a·bol′ish·ment,** *n.*

ab·o·li·tion (ab′ə lish′ən) *n.* **1.** the act or process of abolishing or the state of being abolished. **2.** the abolishing of slavery in the United States. [Latin *abolitiō* an annulling, from *abolēre* to destroy.]

ab·o·li·tion·ism (ab′ə lish′ə niz′əm) *n.* the principles or measures of those who advocated the abolition of slavery in the United States.

ab·o·li·tion·ist (ab′ə lish′ə nist) *n.* **1.** a person who advocates abolishing some law, institution, or practice. **2.** a person who advocated the abolition of slavery in the United States.

ab·o·ma·sum (ab′ə mā′səm) *n., pl.* **-sa** (-sə). the fourth and true digestive stomach of a cud-chewing animal, as a cow or camel. For illustration, see **ruminant.** [Latin *ab* away from + *omasum* bullock's tripe.] —**ab′o·ma′sal,** *adj.*

A-bomb (ā′bom′) *n.* atomic bomb. —*v.t.* to attack with an atomic bomb.

a·bom·i·na·ble (ə bom′ə nə bəl) *adj.* **1.** deserving or causing disgust or hatred; loathsome; detestable: *abominable crimes.* **2.** very unpleasant, disagreeable, or distasteful: *abominable manners, abominable decor.* [Latin *abōminābilis* abhorrent, from Latin *abōminārī* to abhor. See ABOMINATE.] —**a·bom′i·na·bly,** *adv.*

a	at	e	end	o	hot	u	up	hw	white		about
ā	ape	ē	me	ō	old	ū	use	ng	song		taken
ä	far	i	it	ô	fork	ü	rule	th	thin	ə	pencil
âr	care	ī	ice	oi	oil	u̇	pull	th	this		lemon
		îr	pierce	ou	out	ûr	turn	zh	measure		circus

abominable snowman, a legendary creature of the Himalayas, variously believed to resemble a bear, ape, or primitive human. Also, **yeti.**

a·bom·i·nate (ə bom′ə nāt′) *v.t.,* **-nat·ed, -nat·ing. 1.** to feel disgust or hatred for; loathe; abhor; detest. **2.** to dislike strongly. [Latin *abōminātus,* past participle of *abōminārī* literally, to turn away from a bad omen.] —**a·bom′i·na′tor,** *n.*

a·bom·i·na·tion (ə bom′ə nā′shən) *n.* **1.** something that is disgusting or loathsome; detestable action or practice: *They feel that cruelty to animals is an abomination.* **2.** an intense feeling of disgust, hatred, or loathing.

ab·o·rig·i·nal (ab′ə rij′ə nəl) *adj.* **1.** existing in a place from the earliest known time; native; indigenous: *aboriginal people.* **2.** of, relating to, or characteristic of aborigines: *aboriginal tools.* —*n.* an aboriginal person. —**ab′o·rig′i·nal·ly,** *adv.*

Australian **aboriginal** painting

ab·o·rig·i·ne (ab′ə rij′ə nē) *n.* one of the original or earliest known inhabitants of a country. [Latin *aborīginēs* original inhabitants of a country, from *ab orīgine* from the beginning.]

a·bort (ə bôrt′) *v.i.* **1.** to give birth to a fetus before it has developed well enough to be able to live outside the womb; miscarry. **2.** to terminate something, as a mission or project, before completion: *The pilots were given orders to abort.* —*v.t.* **1.** to cause an abortion of. **2.** to terminate before completion: *The Navy aborted the test.* [Latin *abortus,* past participle of *aborīrī* to miscarry, disappear.]

a·bor·tion (ə bôr′shən) *n.* **1.** the artificially induced termination of a pregnancy before a fetus is developed enough to survive outside the womb. **2.** miscarriage *(def. 2).* **3.** the product of a prematurely terminated pregnancy. **4.** something that fails to develop properly or succeed: *The experiment was an abortion.*

a·bor·tion·ist (ə bor′shə nist) *n.* a person who performs an abortion or abortions, esp. one who does so illegally.

a·bor·tive (ə bôr′tiv) *adj.* **1.** failing to succeed; unsuccessful; fruitless: *Until 1953 all attempts to climb Mount Everest were abortive.* **2.** *Medicine.* **a.** causing an abortion: *abortive drugs.* **b.** checking the progress of a disease. **3.** not fully or properly formed or developed; rudimentary. —**a·bor′tive·ly,** *adv.* —**a·bor′tive·ness,** *n.*

a·bound (ə bound′) *v.i.* **1.** to exist in great quantity or large numbers; be plentiful: *Buffalo used to abound in the western United States.* **2.** to be filled or well supplied: *The jungle abounds with birds. The English language abounds in idioms.* [Old French *abonder,* from Latin *abundāre* to overflow, going back to Latin *ab* from + *unda* wave.]

a·bout (ə bout′) *prep.* **1.** having to do with; regarding; concerning: *to know about a plan, a story about friendship.* **2.** attached to as an attribute; connected with: *There is something strange about that place.* **3.** in the vicinity of; somewhat near: *There's a pump about the barn somewhere.* **4.** on every side of; around: *There is a fence about the property.* **5.** on or near (one's person); on hand; with: *She kept her wits about her.* **6.** on the point of; ready. ➡ followed by an infinitive: *The cat is about to jump.* **7.** around or over the parts of; here and there; in or on: *Wind scattered the leaves about the yard.* **8.** concerned or occupied with: *to go about one's business.* —*adv.* **1.** close to; approximately: *About a thousand people attended the rally.* **2.** all but; almost: *We are about*

ready to go. **3.** in several directions; all around: *to look about.* **4.** here and there; to and fro: *to wander about.* **5.** in or to the opposite direction or reversed position: *Hearing her name, she turned about.* —*adj.* **1.** on the move; astir: *He was up and about early this morning.* **2.** in the area; somewhere near: *Is your brother about?* [Old English *ābūtan* on the outside of, around.]

a·bout-face (*n.,* ə bout′fās′; *v.,* ə bout′fās′) *n.* **1.** the action of turning around and facing the opposite direction. **2.** a command to perform this action. **3.** a sudden reversal, as of attitude or opinion. —*v.i.,* **-faced, -fac·ing.** to turn around and face the opposite direction.

a·bove (ə buv′) *adv.* **1.** in, at, or to a higher place; overhead: *The stars glittered above.* **2.** in an earlier part of a book or other piece of writing: *See the examples given above.* ➡ hyphenated in combination, as in *above-mentioned* and *above-cited.* **3.** in a higher rank or position: *Take your complaint to the powers above.* **4.** (of temperature) higher than zero: *It was three above this morning at six o'clock.* **5.** in heaven. —*prep.* **1.** on top of; over: *The fog hung above the tall buildings.* **2.** higher than; rising beyond: *a voice heard above the noise, a building towering above the city.* **3.** superior to the influence of; not liable to stoop to: *to be above pettiness.* **4.** superior to in rank, position, degree, or quality: *A general is above a captain.* **5.** in preference to: *I chose this dress above the others.* **6.** more than; in excess of: *Anything above fifty dollars will be too expensive.* **7.** beyond, esp. farther north than: *Canada is above the United States.* **8.** upstream from: *above the falls.* —*adj.* placed, written, or mentioned earlier: *the above explanation.* —*n.* **the above.** something that is placed, written, or mentioned earlier: *The importance of the above will soon be clear.* [Old English *abufan* over, higher up, above.]

a·bove·board (ə buv′bôrd′) *adv., adj.* without deception, dishonesty, or concealment: *The company's business dealings were open and aboveboard.* [ABOVE + BOARD; from playing cards with the hands above the table to prevent cheating by changing cards under the table.]

ab o·vo (ab ō′vō) *Latin.* from the beginning. [Literally, from the egg.]

abp., archbishop.

ab·ra·ca·dab·ra (ab′rə kə dab′rə) *n.* **1.** a secret word once supposed to have magic power when used in incantations or on amulets or charms, now used in performing magic tricks: *The magician said "abracadabra," and the rabbit disappeared.* **2.** a magical spell or incantation. **3.** foolish or meaningless talk; gibberish. [Late Latin *abracadabra* a magic word.]

a·brade (ə brād′) *v.t.,* **a·brad·ed, a·brad·ing. 1.** to wear off or away by rubbing or scraping: *The breaking waves abraded the rocks over the years.* **2.** to make rough or irritated by rubbing or scraping: *The stones on the path abraded the soles of our bare feet.* [Latin *abrādere,* from *ab* away + *rādere* to scratch.]

a·bra·sion (ə brā′zhən) *n.* **1.** a wearing off or away by rubbing or scraping. **2.** an abraded area or spot: *painful skin abrasions.* [Medieval Latin *abrasio* a scraping off, going back to Latin *abrādere* to scrape off.]

a·bra·sive (ə brā′siv, -ziv) *n.* any of a group of natural or synthetic substances used for cleaning, grinding, or polishing. Corundum, emery, and sand are abrasives. —*adj.* **1.** causing or capable of causing abrasion: *an abrasive polishing powder.* **2.** causing irritation or annoyance; provoking: *abrasive humor.* —**a·bra′sive·ly,** *adv.* —**a·bra′sive·ness,** *n.*

a·breast (ə brest′) *adv., adj.* **1.** side by side and facing or moving in the same direction; parallel: *They walked two abreast.* **2.** up with; informed about (usually used with *of* or *with*): *Grandmother likes to keep abreast of the news.* **3.** parallel to or alongside of (used with *of*): *The ship was abreast of the shore.*

a·bridge (ə brij′) *v.t.,* **a·bridged, a·bridg·ing. 1.** to shorten (a written work) by leaving out less important parts; condense. **2.** to lessen or restrict; curtail: *The Magna Carta abridged the king's powers.* **3.** *Archaic.* to keep from having; deprive. [Old French *abregier* to shorten, from Late Latin *abbreviāre.* See ABBREVIATE.] —**a·bridg′a·ble;** also, **a·bridge′a·ble,** *adj.*

a·bridg·ment (ə brij′mənt) also, **a·bridge·ment.** *n.* **1.** the act of abridging or the state of being abridged: *The new law was an abridgment of the citizens' rights.* **2.** a shortened version of a written work; condensation: *an abridgment of a long novel.*

a·broad (ə brôd′) *adv.* **1.** out of one's country; in or into foreign lands: *to travel abroad.* **2.** in circulation; current; prevalent: *Rumors of victory were abroad.* **3.** out-of-doors: *to walk abroad on a nice evening.* **4.** over a large area; far and wide: *The good news spread abroad quickly.*

ab·ro·gate (ab′rə gāt′) *v.t.,* **-gat·ed, -gat·ing.** to abolish or repeal by authority; annul: *to abrogate a law.* [Latin *abrogātus,* past participle of *abrogāre* to repeal.] —**ab′ro·ga′tion,** *n.* —**ab′ro·ga′tor,** *n.*

a·brupt (ə brupt′) *adj.* **1.** happening suddenly or without warning; unexpected: *an abrupt change in plans, an abrupt departure.* **2.** short and rude in manner or speech; unceremonious; brusque: *an abrupt reply.* **3.** having a sharp incline; steep; precipitous: *an abrupt drop down a trail.* **4.** lacking continuity or smooth transitions; disconnected: *an abrupt writing style.* [Latin *abruptus,* past participle of *abrumpere* to break off, interrupt, from *ab-* from, away + *rumpere* to break.] —**a·brupt′ly,** *adv.* —**a·brupt′ness,** *n.*

> **Synonyms** Abrupt, short, brusque, and curt, in reference to speech or conduct, mean without embellishment and taking no more time than necessary. **Abrupt** suggests an unexpected quickness: *His abrupt reply startled the interviewer.* **Short** carries a suggestion of annoyance, even anger, at having to take time: *I was very short with my sister when she interrupted my nap.* **Brusque** suggests a characteristic roughness or lack of social polish: *The clerk's brusque manner drove customers away.* **Curt** suggests intentional discourtesy, perhaps from one who feels superior: *Their polite appeal for a loan from their rich relatives met with a curt refusal.*

abs-, form of **ab-**[1] before *c* and *t*, as in *abscond, abstract.*

ab·scess (ab′ses) *n.* a localized collection of pus resulting from infection in the tissues of some part of the body. [Latin *abscessus* literally, a going away.] —**ab′scessed,** *adj.*

ab·scis·ic acid (ab sis′ik) a growth hormone that causes aging, abscission, and dormancy in plants. Formula: $C_{15}H_{20}O_4$

ab·scis·sa (ab sis′ə) *n., pl.* **-scis·sas** or **-scis·sae** (-sis′ē). **1.** on a line graph, the distance of a point from the vertical axis measured parallel to the horizontal axis, used to define the point in the system of Cartesian coordinates and commonly referred to as the *x* coordinate. ➡ distinguished from **ordinate.** **2.** a line, number, or algebraic expression representing this distance. [Latin *(linea) abscissa* (line) cut off, from *abscindere* to cut off.]

abscissa

ab·scis·sion (ab sizh′ən) *n.* **1.** the act of cutting off. **2.** the dropping of leaves, flowers, fruits, or other parts by a plant. [Middle English *abscisioun,* from Latin *abscissionis,* genitive of *abscissio.* See ABSCISSA.]

ab·scond (ab skond′) *v.i.* to flee secretly and conceal oneself, esp. to avoid the law: *The treasurer absconded with the company's funds.* [Latin *abscondere* to hide, put away.] —**ab·scond′er,** *n.*

ab·sence (ab′səns) *n.* **1.** the state of being away or not present. **2.** a period of being away: *an absence of a year.* **3.** the condition of being without; lack: *Cold is the absence of heat.*
• **absence of mind.** the state or condition of being absent-minded; absent-mindedness.

ab·sent (*adj.,* ab′sənt; *v.,* ab sent′) *adj.* **1.** not in a certain place at a given time; not present; away: *She was absent because of illness.* **2.** not existing; lacking: *Iron is absent in this rock.* **3.** not showing interest or attention; preoccupied: *She had an absent look on her face.* —*v.t.* to take or keep (oneself) away: *He absented himself from the conference.* [Old French *absent* away, from Latin *absēns,* present participle of *abesse* to be away.]

ab·sen·tee (ab′sən tē′) *n.* a person who is absent. —*adj.* designating an absentee; by an absentee: *absentee ownership.*

absentee ballot, a ballot that enables a voter who cannot be present at the polls to vote by mail.

ab·sen·tee·ism (ab′sən tē′iz əm) *n.* habitual or repeated absence, as from work or school.

absentee landlord, a person who owns land or buildings in a place or country but does not reside there.

ab·sent·ly (ab′sənt lē) *adv.* in an absent-minded manner; inattentively.

ab·sent-mind·ed (ab′sənt mīn′did) *adj.* **1.** unaware of one's immediate surroundings or actions; lost in thought; preoccupied: *to wander around in an absent-minded daze.* **2.** likely to forget; chronically forgetful. —**ab′sent-mind′ed·ly,** *adv.* —**ab′sent-mind′ed·ness,** *n.*

ab·sinthe (ab′sinth) *also,* **ab·sinth.** *n.* a bitter, green liqueur with a licorice taste, flavored with wormwood and anise. [French *absinthe,* going back to Greek *apsinthion* wormwood.]

ab·so·lute (ab′sə lüt′, ab′sə lüt′) *adj.* **1.** free from imperfection; complete; utter: *absolute purity.* **2.** free from all restrictions or qualifications; unconditional: *absolute power.* **3.** established as true; not to be doubted or questioned; certain; positive: *absolute proof.* **4.** having power that is not limited by constitutional or other restraints; despotic; arbitrary: *absolute monarchy, an absolute ruler.* **5.** without reference to anything else; not relative or comparative: *the absolute merits of a case.* **6.** *Grammar.* **a.** not connected to the rest of the sentence by the usual relations of syntax. In the sentence *It being Sunday, we slept late,* the phrase *It being Sunday* is an absolute construction. **b.** (of a verb that is usually transitive) having an object implied but not expressed. In the sentence *The violinist played well,* the word *played* is an absolute verb. **c.** (of an adjective or pronoun) standing alone with the noun understood but not stated. In the phrase *their ideas and mine,* the word *mine* is an absolute pronoun. **7.a.** of or relating to absolute temperature. **b.** relating to or derived from the fundamental notions or units of time, space, and mass: *absolute units of velocity.* —*n.* **1. the Absolute.** in philosophy, ultimate reality thought of as a single, all-inclusive system of being. **2.** something that exists independently of all relations and conditions and has reality or validity in and of itself. [Latin *absolūtus,* past participle of *absolvere* to loosen, free.] —**ab′so·lute′ness,** *n.*

ab·so·lute·ly (ab′sə lüt′lē, ab′sə lüt′-) *adv.* **1.** to the fullest extent or highest degree; completely: *absolutely beautiful.* **2.** without doubt or reservation; positively; definitely: *Are you absolutely sure?*

absolute pitch 1. the pitch of a tone as determined by its rate of vibration. **2.** the ability to identify the pitch of any tone heard, or to sing a given tone without reference to any previously sounded pitch. Also *(def. 2),* **perfect pitch.**

absolute temperature, temperature measured from absolute zero.

absolute value, the positive value of a real number. The absolute value of negative 3, written | − 3|, is 3.

absolute zero, the theoretical temperature at which substances would have no molecular motion and no heat. Absolute zero is zero on the Kelvin temperature scale and is equal to − 273.15 degrees Celsius or − 459.67 degrees Fahrenheit. For illustration, see **Fahrenheit.**

ab·so·lu·tion (ab′sə lü′shən) *n.* **1.a.** in some Christian churches, formal remission of sins and the accompanying penalties, esp. as pronounced by a priest in the sacrament of penance. **b.** a formula declaring this remission. **2.** release or freedom from obligation, guilt, or penalty.

ab·so·lut·ism (ab′sə lü tiz′əm) *n.* a system or principles of government in which the power of the ruler is unlimited; despotism. —**ab′so·lut′ist,** *n., adj.* —**ab′so·lu·tis′tic,** *adj.*

ab·solve (ab zolv′, -solv′) *v.t.* **-solved, -solv·ing. 1.** to free from guilt or blame: *The robber's confession absolved all the other suspects.* **2.** to set (someone) free, as from an obligation, duty, or responsibility. **3.** to give absolution to; forgive the sins of: *The priest absolved the penitent.* [Latin *absolvere* to loosen, free. Doublet of ASSOIL.]

> **Synonyms** Absolve, exonerate, and acquit mean to free from blame. **Absolve** is the most general term and refers to any accusation or implication of wrongdoing: *The report absolved the pilot of any responsibility for the crash.* **Exonerate,** on the other hand, refers to a specific charge, often in a legal context, and suggests evidence proving innocence: *The defendant was exonerated when someone else confessed to starting the fire.* **Acquit** refers specifically to the action of a jury or trial judge in finding a defendant not guilty of a charge. Unlike the other two terms, it does not necessarily suggest actual or moral innocence: *The evidence was not sufficient to convict, and the jury acquitted them.*

ab·sorb (ab sôrb′, -zôrb′) *v.t.* **1.** to soak up (liquid): *A sponge absorbs water.* **2.** to engage completely: *The book absorbed my attention.* **3.** to take in and incorporate: *The Roman Empire absorbed many territories.* **4.** to take up and retain (energy) without reflection or echo: *Acoustic tile absorbs sound.* **5.** to take up (a substance) by chemical or molecular action: *Water absorbs oxygen.* ➡ distinguished from **adsorb.** [Latin *absorbēre* to soak up, swallow.] —**ab·sorb′a·bil′i·ty,** *n.* —**ab·sorb′a·ble,** *adj.* —**ab·sorb′er,** *n.*

> **Synonyms** Absorb and assimilate mean to take in thoroughly or completely. **Absorb** does not necessarily suggest a change in what is taken in, but **assimilate** indicates that it becomes like, or part of, the taker: *The United States has absorbed millions of immigrants. Some of them became assimilated into American life more quickly than others.*

ab·sorbed (ab sôrbd′, -zôrbd′) *adj.* having the attention entirely; taken up; preoccupied; rapt: *an absorbed look.*

a	at	e	end	o	hot	u	up	hw	white		about
ā	ape	ē	me	ō	old	ū	use	ng	song	ə	taken
ä	far	i	it	ô	fork	ü	rule	th	thin		pencil
âr	care	ī	ice	oi	oil	u̇	pull	th̲	this		lemon
		îr	pierce	ou	out	ûr	turn	zh	measure		circus

ab·sorb·ent (ab sôr′bənt, -zôr′-) *adj.* absorbing or capable of absorbing: *absorbent cotton.* —*n.* a material that absorbs: *Blotting paper is an absorbent.* —**ab·sor′ben·cy**, *n.*

ab·sorb·ing (ab sôr′bing, -zôr′-) *adj.* taking all the attention; engrossing: *an absorbing play.* —**ab·sorb′ing·ly**, *adv.* —For Synonyms, see **interesting.**

ab·sorp·tion (ab sôrp′shən, -zôrp′-) *n.* **1.** the act or process of absorbing or the state of being absorbed. **2.** entire engrossment or engagement: *absorption in one's work.* **3.** a process by which a substance, as a gas or liquid, is taken up and made a part of another substance by chemical or molecular action. In absorption the substance taken up is distributed throughout the material or substance that receives it. For illustration, see **adsorption. 4.** a process by which energy is received by a substance without reflection or echo: *the absorption of light rays.* **5.** a process by which substances are taken across or into tissues, as the uptake of fluids and nutrients from the intestinal cavity into the cells, blood capillaries, and lymphatic vessels. [Late Latin *absorptiō* a swallowing, from Latin *absorbēre* to swallow.] —**ab·sorp′tive**, *adj.*

ab·stain (ab stān′) *v.i.* **1.** to hold oneself back voluntarily (with *from*): *A teetotaler abstains from drink.* **2.** to refrain voluntarily from voting: *In the UN voting, three countries abstained.* [Middle French *abstenir* to refrain from, from Latin *abstinēre* to withhold, from *ab* from + *tenēre* to hold.] —**ab·stain′er**, *n.*

ab·ste·mi·ous (ab stē′mē əs) *adj.* moderate or sparing, esp. in the use of food and drink. [Latin *abstēmius*, from *abs* away from + *tēmētum* intoxicating drink.] —**ab·ste′mi·ous·ly**, *adv.* —**ab·ste′mi·ous·ness**, *n.*

ab·sten·tion (ab sten′shən) *n.* the act or an instance of abstaining: *There were two abstentions on the vote.* [Late Latin *abstentiō* holding back, from Latin *abstentus*, past participle of *abstinēre.* See ABSTAIN.] —**ab·sten′tious**, *adj.*

ab·sti·nence (ab′stə nəns) *n.* **1.** the act or practice of abstaining from the indulgence of certain foods, drink, or pleasures, often for religious reasons. **2.** the practice of abstaining from alcoholic beverages. [Latin *abstinentia* self-restraint, from *abstinens*, present participle of *abstinēre.* See ABSTAIN.] —**ab′sti·nent**, *adj.*

ab·stract (*adj.,* ab′strakt, ab strakt′; *v., defs. 1, 3-5,* ab strakt′; *v., def. 2,* ab′strakt; *n.,* ab′strakt) *adj.* **1.** considered apart from matter, material objects, or particular examples; not concrete: *the abstract concepts of geometry.* **2.** expressing a quality or attribute without relation to a particular object or example: *The words "goodness" and "purity" are abstract nouns.* ➡ distinguished from **concrete. 3.** theoretical or ideal, as distinguished from real or

abstract sculpture by Barbara Hepworth

practical: *an abstract sense of duty.* **4.** difficult to understand; abstruse. **5.** of, relating to, or characteristic of a style in the arts that does not imitate reality directly, but uses lines, geometric forms, and colors to express emotion or an aesthetic idea. —*v.t.* **1.** to isolate (a quality or attribute) from particular objects or instances; derive as a general idea from a specific instance or group of instances: *to abstract common qualities from individual examples.* **2.** to make a brief account of; summarize: *The student abstracted the report.* **3.** to take away secretly or dishonestly; purloin. **4.** to withdraw or divert the attention of. **5.** to take away; remove: *to abstract water from a solution.* —*n.* **1.** a brief account of something; summary; epitome. **2.** something that concentrates in itself the essential qualities of something more extensive or more general; essence: *An individual is an abstract of humanity.* **3.** something that is abstracted; abstract idea or term. [Latin *abstractus*, past participle of *abstrahere* to draw away, from *abs* away from + *trahere* to draw.] —**ab·stract′er**, *n.* —**ab·stract′ly**, *adv.* —**ab·stract′ness**, *n.* —For Synonyms (*n.*), see **summary.**

· **in the abstract.** without reference to the concrete; in theory rather than in practice: *to know poverty only in the abstract.*

ab·stract·ed (ab strak′tid) *adj.* lost in thought; preoccupied. —**ab·stract′ed·ly**, *adv.* —**ab·stract′ed·ness**, *n.*

abstract expressionism, a nonrepresentational style of painting, first developed in the United States around 1945, characterized esp. by the spontaneous and impulsive application of paint and the free use of accidental effects.

ab·strac·tion (ab strak′shən) *n.* **1.** the process of isolating an attribute or quality from particular objects or instances; formation of a general concept from specific instances. **2.** a concept thus formed; abstract idea: *The idea of redness is an abstraction.* **3.** the state of being lost in thought; preoccupation. **4.** a work of art that is partly or totally abstract. **5.** the act of withdrawing or removing; separation: *The abstraction of heat from a surface will make that surface cold.*

ab·struse (ab strüs′) *adj.* hard to understand; recondite. [Latin *abstrūsus*, past participle of *abstrūdere* to thrust away, conceal.] —**ab·struse′ly**, *adv.* —**ab·struse′ness**, *n.*

ab·surd (ab sûrd′, -zûrd′) *adj.* so contrary to reason, common sense, or truth as to be laughable; irrational; ridiculous. [Latin *absurdus* out of tune, senseless.] —**ab·surd′ly**, *adv.* —**ab·surd′ness**, *n.*

ab·surd·i·ty (ab sûr′di tē, -zûr′-) *n., pl.* -ties. **1.** the state or quality of being absurd. **2.** something absurd: *For a serious movie, it was filled with absurdities.*

a·bun·dance (ə bun′dəns) *n.* **1.** a plentiful or overflowing supply; number or amount that is more than enough: *an abundance of food.* **2.** plentiful money or possessions; wealth; affluence: *to live in abundance.* [Old French *abundance* plenty, from Latin *abundantia*, from *abundāns*, present participle of *abundāre* to overflow. See ABOUND.]

a·bun·dant (ə bun′dənt) *adj.* **1.** more than sufficient; plentiful: *an abundant supply.* **2.** well-supplied; abounding (usually with *in*): *an island abundant in tropical birds.* —**a·bun′dant·ly**, *adv.* —For Synonyms, see **plentiful.**

a·buse (*v.,* ə būz′; *n.,* ə būs′) *v.t.,* a·bused, a·bus·ing. **1.** to use improperly or wrongly; misuse: *to abuse the privileges of a library by damaging books.* **2.** to hurt by treating wrongly; mistreat; injure: *to abuse an animal.* **3.** to attack with coarse or insulting language; revile. —*n.* **1.** wrong or improper use; misuse: *abuse of power.* **2.** ill-treatment that causes damage or injury: *Our car has taken much abuse.* **3.** a corrupt practice or custom: *the abuses of a dictatorship.* **4.** insulting, rude, or maligning language. [Old French *abuser* to misuse, from Latin *abūsus*, past participle of *abūtī* to use up, misuse.] —**a·bus′er**, *n.*

a·bu·sive (ə bū′siv, -ziv) *adj.* **1.** characterized by, containing, or using verbal abuse: *an abusive slander, an abusive article.* **2.** wrongly or improperly used; corrupt: *an abusive exercise of power.* **3.** involving ill-treatment; injurious: *Abusive handling can ruin the camera.* —**a·bu′sive·ly**, *adv.* —**a·bu′sive·ness**, *n.*

a·but (ə but′) *v.,* a·but·ted, a·but·ting. —*v.i.* to touch at one end or side; adjoin; border (usually with *on, upon,* or *against*): *Our land abuts on the forest. The two buildings abut.* —*v.t.* to border on; touch: *The garage abuts our neighbor's wall.* [Old French *aboter* to border on, from *a* to (from Latin *ad* to) + *boter* to thrust (of Germanic origin).]

a·but·ment (ə but′mənt) *n.* **1.** a supporting part designed to withstand thrust or lateral pressure, as one of the end supports of an arch or bridge or the part of a bridge pier against which the water flows. **2.** something that abuts on something else. **3.** a point or place where abutting parts meet; junction. **4.** the act of abutting.

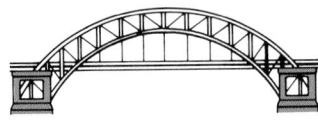

abutments

a·buzz (ə buz′) *adv., adj.* **1.** filled with the sound of buzzing: *a crowded room abuzz with voices.* **2.** filled with noisy activity: *The store was abuzz during the sale.*

a·bysm (ə biz′əm) *n.* abyss. [Old French *abisme*, going back to Latin *abyssus.* See ABYSS.]

a·bys·mal (ə biz′məl) *adj.* **1.** too deep or great to be measured; immeasurable; profound: *abysmal sorrow.* **2.** wretched; so poor or bad as to be pitiful; miserable: *abysmal living conditions, an abysmal time.* —**a·bys′mal·ly**, *adv.*

a·byss (ə bis′) *n.* **1.** an immeasurably deep or seemingly bottomless opening or space; chasm. **2.** anything unfathomable or immeasurable: *the abyss of time.* [Latin *abyssus* bottomless pit, from Greek *abyssos* bottomless.]

a·bys·sal (ə bis′əl) *adj.* **1.** of, relating to, or resembling an abyss. **2.** (of the ocean) so deep that light cannot penetrate. An **abyssal plain** is a flat, deep area of an ocean basin.

Ab·ys·sin·i·an cat (ab′ə sin′ē ən) a breed of domestic cat having short, silky hair with reddish brown tips, a rounded, wedge-shaped head, and a long, tapering tail. [From *Abyssinia,* where this cat may have originated.]

Ac, the symbol for actinium.

ac-, form of **ad-** before *c* and *q,* as in *accent, acquire.*

-ac *suffix* **1.** affected by or having: *hypochondriac.* **2.** of, relating to, or characteristic of: *cardiac, elegiac.*

A

AC, alternating current. *Also,* **ac, a.c., A.C.**

a·ca·cia (ə kā′shə) *n.* **1.** any of a group of trees or shrubs, genus *Acacia,* of the mimosa subfamily, found in warm regions throughout the world, many of which bear delicate, fernlike leaves and clusters of white, yellow, or orange flowers. Some species yield useful products, such as gum arabic or tannic acid. **2.** any of several other trees, esp. certain locusts. **3.** gum arabic. [Latin *acācia* acacia tree, from Greek *akakiā* thorny Egyptian acacia.]

acad. 1. academic. **2.** academy.

ac·a·deme (ak′ə dēm′) *n.* **1.** the academic world; scholarly life. **2.** **Academe.** academy (*def. 4*).

ac·a·de·mi·a (ak′ə dē′mē ə) *n.* the world of scholars; academic life. [Modern Latin, going back to Greek *akadēmeia* Plato's Academy. See ACADEMY.]

ac·a·dem·ic (ak′ə dem′ik) *adj.* **1.** of or relating to an academy or institution of higher education or to advanced study in general; scholarly: *academic pursuits, academic robes.* **2.** relating to liberal or general education rather than technical or vocational, esp. as preparatory for college. **3.** without practical application; theoretical; speculative: *What came before time?* is an academic question. **4.** conforming to set rules and traditions; conventional: *an academic style of painting.* Also, **ac′a·dem′i·cal.** —*n.* a person involved in higher education, as a teacher or student. —**ac′a·dem′i·cal·ly,** *adv.*

academic freedom, the freedom of persons at educational institutions to study, teach, or discuss any subject without fear of interference or dismissal.

a·cad·e·mi·cian (ə kad′ə mish′ən, ak′ə də-) *n.* **1.** a member of an academy for advancing literature, science, or the arts. **2.** a person who rigidly adheres to the formalized rules or traditions of a school of thought.

a·cad·e·my (ə kad′ə mē) *n., pl.* **-mies. 1.** a private secondary or high school. **2.** a school for instruction in a particular subject: *a military academy, an academy of music.* **3.** a society or institution for the cultivation and advancement of literature, science, or the arts. **4. the Academy. a.** a place for sports and leisure activities near ancient Athens, at which Plato established his school. **b.** the school itself. **c.** Plato's followers or their philosophy. [French *académie,* going back to Greek *akadēmeia* Plato's Academy, from *Akadēmia* a grove near Athens which became the site of the Academy.]

Academy Award, any of a group of awards given annually in the United States for achievement in acting, direction, cinematography, and other areas of film production.

A·ca·di·an (ə kā′dē ən) *adj.* of or relating to Acadia, its people, or their culture. —*n.* **1.** an inhabitant of Acadia. **2.** see **Cajun.**

a·can·thus (ə kan′thəs) *n., pl.* **-thus·es** or **-thi** (-thī). **1.** any of a group of thistlelike plants, genus *Acanthus,* native to the Mediterranean region, Africa, and Asia, bearing large spiny or sharply notched leaves and clusters of pink, red, white, or purple flowers. **2.** a conventionalized ornamental representation of the acanthus leaf, used on the capitals of Corinthian columns. The Greeks patterned their decoration after the spiny or toothed leaves of the *A. spinosus;* the Romans copied the fuller leaves of the *A. mollis.* [Latin *acanthus* acanthus plant, from Greek *akanthos,* from *akantha* thorn.]

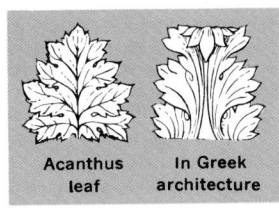

Acanthus leaf — In Greek architecture

acanthus

a cap·pel·la (ä′kə pel′ə) (of vocal music) without instrumental accompaniment. [Italian *a cappella* (music) in the chapel style, from Latin *ad* to + Late Latin *cappella* cloak. See CHAPEL.]

acc. 1. account. **2.** accusative.

ac·cede (ak sēd′) *v.i.,* **-ced·ed, -ced·ing. 1.** to give one's agreement or adherence; assent; yield (with *to*): *to accede to demand, to accede to a treaty.* **2.** to gain and take control or possession of (an office, dignity, or position): *Queen Elizabeth II acceded to the throne in 1952.* [Latin *accēdere* to go to, approach.] —For Synonyms, see consent.

accel., accelerando.

ac·ce·le·ran·do (ak sel′ə rän′dō) *adv., adj. Music.* gradually increasing in speed. [Italian *accelerando,* going back to Latin *accelerāre* to hasten.]

ac·cel·er·ate (ak sel′ə rāt′) *v.,* **-at·ed, -at·ing.** —*v.t.* **1.** to increase the speed of; cause to move faster: *to accelerate the tempo, to accelerate a bicycle.* **2.** to cause to happen sooner; hasten: *The bad weather accelerated our departure.* **3.** to cause to move ahead or develop faster: *to accelerate a bright student.*

4. *Physics.* to change the velocity of (a moving body); cause to undergo acceleration. —*v.i.* to go faster; increase in speed: *The bicycle accelerated as the rider went downhill.* [Latin *accelerātus,* past participle of *accelerāre* to hasten.] —**ac·cel·er·a·tive** (ak-sel′ər ə tiv), *adj.*

ac·cel·er·a·tion (ak sel′ə rā′shən) *n.* **1.** the act or process of accelerating or the state of being accelerated. **2.** *Physics.* **a.** change in the velocity of movement. **Positive acceleration** causes an increase in speed; **negative acceleration** causes a decrease. **b.** the rate of such change per unit of time.

acceleration of gravity, the acceleration experienced by a freely falling body subject to the force of the earth's gravity, equal at sea level to approximately 32 feet (9.8 meters) per second per second.

accelerator *(def. 2)*
inside a particle accelerator

ac·cel·er·a·tor (ak sel′ə rā′tər) *n.* **1.** a device for increasing the speed of a machine, esp. the foot throttle of an automobile. **2.** *Physics.* any of various devices that accelerate subatomic particles to high velocities and high energies, as a cyclotron or synchrotron. Also, **atom smasher, particle accelerator. 3.** anything that causes an increase in speed.

ac·cel·er·om·e·ter (ak sel′ə rom′i tər) *n.* a device that is used to measure acceleration, as in an aircraft or spacecraft.

ac·cent (*n.* ak′sent; *v.* ak′sent, ak sent′) *n.* **1.** a stress given to a particular syllable or word in speech. In the sentence *I heard you,* the accent could be on *I, heard,* or *you.* The meaning of the sentence would vary according to the position of the accent. **2.** a mark (as ′ or ′) used to indicate a stressed syllable. Also, **accent mark, stress mark. 3.** any one of various marks used in certain languages to indicate variant pronunciations or meanings. In French, the accents are acute (′), grave (`), and circumflex (^). **4.** the characteristic mode of pronunciation peculiar to a particular region or group within a single language or to individuals speaking a language not their own: *a British accent, a Southern accent, to speak English with a German accent.* **5.** stress or importance given something; emphasis (with *on*): *a biology course with an accent on laboratory work.* **6.** stress on certain words or syllables marking the rhythm of verse, usually occurring at fixed intervals; ictus. In the line *While joy gave clouds the light of stars,* the words *joy, clouds, light,* and *stars* have the accent. **7.** *Music.* **a.** a stress given to certain notes or chords. **b.** a mark used to indicate this. **8. accents.** *Archaic.* speech; language. **9.** a small ornamental detail or part: *a green room with accents of blue.* —*v.t.* **1.** to pronounce (a syllable, word, or words) with particular stress. **2.** to emphasize; accentuate. **3.** to mark with a written or printed accent. [French *accent* intonation, from Latin *accentus* accentuation of a word, tone, from *ac-,* for *ad* to + *cantus* song; literally, a song added to (speech).] —For Synonyms (*n.*), see **emphasis.**

ac·cen·tu·al (ak sen′chü əl) *adj.* of, relating to, or formed by accent or accents: *accentual verse.* —**ac·cen′tu·al·ly,** *adv.*

ac·cen·tu·ate (ak sen′chü āt′) *v.t.,* **-at·ed, -at·ing. 1.** to heighten the effect of; emphasize; stress: *Your height accentuates your thinness.* **2.** to mark or pronounce with an accent. —**ac·cen′tu·a′tion,** *n.*

a	at	e	end	o	hot	u	up	hw	white		about
ā	ape	ē	me	ō	old	ū	use	ng	song	ə	taken
ä	far	i	it	ô	fork	ü	rule	th	thin		pencil
âr	care	ī	ice	oi	oil	u̇	pull	th	this		lemon
		îr	pierce	ou	out	ûr	turn	zh	measure		circus

ac·cept (ak sept′) *v.t.* **1.** to agree to take (something offered); receive willingly: *to accept a present.* **2.** to receive with favor or approval: *The students quickly accepted their new classmate.* **3.** to give one's agreement to; assent to: *to accept the terms of a contract, to accept a referee's decision.* **4.** to respond affirmatively to: *to accept an invitation.* **5.** to make oneself content with; accommodate oneself to: *to accept a situation.* **6.** to receive as true, just, or proper; acknowledge: *to accept the evidence.* **7.** to take on the responsibility of; to undertake formally: *to accept an office.* **8.** to acknowledge by signature and undertake to pay (a bill or draft). —*v.i.* to take something offered; respond affirmatively. [Latin *acceptāre* to receive, going back to *ad* to + *capere* to take, grasp.] —**ac·cept′er,** *n.* —For Synonyms *(v.t.),* see **receive.**

ac·cept·a·ble (ak sep′tə bəl) *adj.* **1.** worthy or capable of being accepted: *None of the alternatives seem acceptable.* **2.** barely meeting a standard; adequate: *The actor gave an acceptable performance.* —**ac·cept′a·bil′i·ty, ac·cept′a·ble·ness,** *n.* —**ac·cept′a·bly,** *adv.*

ac·cept·ance (ak sep′təns) *n.* **1.** the act of accepting or the state of being accepted. **2.** a favorable reception; approval: *The proposed law gained wide acceptance among the legislators.* **3.** a belief in; assent: *the acceptance of a new theory.* **4.** *Law.* **a.** a written agreement to pay a draft or bill according to contracted terms. **b.** an accepted draft or bill of exchange. **5.** *Law.* agreement to the terms of an offer, forming a contract.

ac·cep·ta·tion (ak′sep tā′shən) *n.* **1.** the generally accepted meaning (of a word, expression, or statement). **2.** *Archaic.* a favorable reception.

ac·cep·tor (ak sep′tər) *n.* a person or institution that accepts a draft or bill of exchange.

ac·cess (ak′ses) *n.* **1.** the right or permission to approach, enter, or use; admittance: *We had access to the author's private library.* **2.** a way of approaching; means of approach: *The only access to the farm was a dirt road.* **3.** the act of going to or reaching: *Access to the mountain lodge was difficult during the winter.* **4.** a sudden outburst or onset: *an access of grief.* **5.** *Computers.* the ability to retrieve data from a file or from memory. —*v.t.* to gain access to, esp. to retrieve (data) from a computer file or memory. [Latin *accessus* approach, from *accedere* to go to, approach.]

access code, a combination of letters, numbers, or other symbols that a person must enter into a computer or other device so that it will respond to further commands.

ac·ces·si·ble (ak ses′ə bəl) *adj.* **1.** capable of being approached or entered; easy to reach: *The airport is accessible from all directions.* **2.** able to be obtained; attainable: *Such information is not readily accessible.* **3.** open to the influence of (usually with *to*): *accessible to bribery.* —**ac·ces′si·bil′i·ty,** *n.* —**ac·ces′si·bly,** *adv.*

ac·ces·sion (ak sesh′ən) *n.* **1.** the act of coming to and taking control or possession of (an office, dignity, or position): *accession to the throne.* **2.** increase by something added; addition: *The library collection was enlarged by the accession of fifty volumes.* **3.** something added: *The new books were a valuable accession.* **4.** the act of agreeing; assent: *accession to a proposal.* [Latin *accessiō* a going to, addition, going back to *accedere* to go to, approach.]

ac·ces·so·ry (ak ses′ə rē) *also,* **ac·ces·sa·ry.** *n., pl.* **-ries.** **1.** something subordinate that aids or adds to a general effect or effectiveness; additional device or object: *clothing accessories, new car accessories.* **2.** *Law.* a person who, without being present at the commission of a felony, assists or instigates the offense. Also, **accessory before the fact. b.** a person who knowingly conceals a felon from the law. Also, **accessory after the fact.** —*adj.* **1.** contributing subordinately; additional; supplemental. **2.** *Law.* giving help as an accessory.

access time, the interval between the time when information is called from storage in a computer and the time when it is delivered.

ac·ci·dence (ak′si dəns) *n.* the part of grammar that deals with the inflection of words.

ac·ci·dent (ak′si dənt) *n.* **1.** something that happens unexpectedly or without apparent cause or reason: *The discovery was a happy accident.* **2.** an unfortunate event that is unexpected or caused unintentionally, usually involving harm or injury; mishap: *a traffic accident.* **3.** chance; fortune: *We met by accident.* **4.** a nonessential quality or characteristic. [Latin *accidēns* chance, happening, going back to *ad* to + *caedere* to fall.]

ac·ci·den·tal (ak′si den′təl) *adj.* **1.** happening by chance; unexpected; unintentional. **2.** not essential; subsidiary; incidental. —*n.* **1.** a nonessential or incidental feature or quality. **2.** *Music.* **a.** a sign, as a flat, sharp, or natural, appearing outside the key signature, altering the pitch of the note or notes it precedes. **b.** a note so altered. —**ac·ci·den·tal·ly** (ak′si den′tə lē, -dent′lē) *adv.*

ac·ci·dent-prone (ak′si dənt prōn′) *adj.* tending to have or

likely to cause accidents: *an accident-prone driver.* —**ac′ci·dent-prone′ness,** *n.*

ac·cip·i·ter (ak sip′i tər) *n.* any of a group of woodland hawks of the genus *Accipiter,* characterized by short, rounded wings and a long tail. [Latin *accipiter,* from earlier *acupeter* swift-winged.]

ac·claim (ə klām′) *v.t.* **1.** to greet or salute with loud or enthusiastic approval; hail; applaud: *Parisians acclaimed Lindbergh when he landed.* **2.** to announce or declare with strong approval: *The judges acclaimed her the winner.* —*n.* emphatic or enthusiastic praise or welcome: *His book was greeted with critical acclaim.* [Latin *acclamāre* to shout applause.]

ac·cla·ma·tion (ak′lə mā′shən) *n.* **1.** an enthusiastic demonstration of approval. **2.** an enthusiastic or unanimous vote of approval by cheering, applause, or the like rather than by formal ballot: *The motion was passed by acclamation.*

ac·cli·mate (ak′lə māt′, ə klī′mit) *v.t., v.i.,* **-mat·ed, -mat·ing.** to adjust or adapt to a new climate, environment, or situation. [French *acclimater* to adapt to a climate, going back to Latin *ad* to + *clima.* See CLIMATE.] —**ac·cli·ma·tion** (ak′lə mā′shən), *n.*

ac·cli·ma·tize (ə klī′mə tīz′) *v.t., v.i.,* **-tized, -tiz·ing.** to acclimate. —**ac·cli′ma·ti·za′tion,** *n.*

ac·cliv·i·ty (ə kliv′i tē) *n., pl.* **-ties.** an upward or ascending slope. ➠ opposed to **declivity.** [Latin *acclīvitās* steepness, going back to *ad* to + *clivus* slope.]

ac·co·lade (ak′ə lād′, -läd′) *n.* **1.** a token or expression of praise; award or honor. **2.** a ceremony used in conferring knighthood, formerly an embrace or kiss and now a light tap on the shoulder with the flat side of a sword. [French *accolade* accolade of knighthood, going back to Latin *ad* to, at + *collum* neck.]

ac·com·mo·date (ə kom′ə dāt′) *v.,* **-dat·ed, -dat·ing.** —*v.t.* **1.** to have or make room or facilities for: *The car can accommodate five passengers.* **2.** to furnish or supply with lodgings or with room and board. **3.** to do a favor or service for; oblige; help: *When we asked for help, they accommodated us.* **4.** to supply or provide (with *with*): *We accommodated the stranger with directions.* **5.** to make suitable; adapt (with *to*): *to accommodate oneself to a new situation.* **6.** to bring into agreement; reconcile: *to accommodate differences of opinion.* —*v.i.* to adjust or come into adjustment: *The lens of the eye accommodates to distance.* [Latin *accommodātus,* past participle of *accommodāre* to adapt, going back to *ad* to + *commodus* appropriate, convenient.] —For Synonyms, see **adapt, contain.**

ac·com·mo·dat·ing (ə kom′ə dā′ting) *adj.* willing to help; readily obliging; helpful. —**ac·com′mo·dat′ing·ly,** *adv.*

ac·com·mo·da·tion (ə kom′ə dā′shən) *n.* **1.** the act or process of accommodating or the state of being accommodated. **2.** *also,* **accommodations.** facilities for passage or lodging, often with food: *tourist accommodations on a boat, motel accommodations.* **3.** aid, comfort, or convenience: *The information booth is for the accommodation of travelers.* **4.** willingness to help; obligingness; complaisance. **5.** something that fills a need or is helpful, such as a loan. **6.** *Physiology.* the automatic adjustment of the lens of the eye for focusing at different distances. **7.** a settling of differences; reconciliation: *The two parties arrived at an accommodation.*

ac·com·pa·ni·ment (ə kum′pə ni mənt) *n.* **1.** something that accompanies; complement or concomitant. **2.** *Music.* a subordinate part or parts, instrumental or vocal, providing a background or complement for a principal part.

ac·com·pa·nist (ə kum′pə nist) *n.* a person who plays or sings a musical accompaniment.

ac·com·pa·ny (ə kum′pə nē) *v.,* **-nied, -ny·ing.** —*v.t.* **1.** to go along or in company with; be a companion or escort for: *I'll accompany you to the theater.* **2.** to exist or occur in association or combination; be an adjunct to: *Slides accompanied the lecture.* **3.** to cause (something) to be supplemented or associated (with *with*): *to accompany a speech with gestures.* **4.** to play or sing a musical accompaniment for or to. —*v.i.* to perform a musical accompaniment. [Old French *acompaigner* to associate with, from *a* to + *compaignon* comrade. See COMPANION.] —**ac·com′pa·ni·er,** *n.*

ac·com·plice (ə kom′plis) *n.* a person who helps another in a crime; associate in wrongdoing. [Earlier *a complice* a confederate, from Middle French *complice,* from Latin *complex* literally, woven together. See COMPLEX.]

ac·com·plish (ə kom′plish) *v.t.* to succeed in completing or carrying out; perform: *to accomplish a task.* [Old French *acompliss-,* a stem of *acomplir* to complete, going back to Latin *ad* to, at + *complēre* to fulfill, complete.] —**ac·com′plish·er,** *n.*

Synonyms Accomplish, achieve, and effect mean to carry something through to the end. **Accomplish** stresses the result rather than the process: *What will all your complaints accomplish?* **Achieve** implies the overcoming of obstacles or difficulties: *For them to achieve so much after growing*

up in such poverty is remarkable. **Effect** emphasizes the application of energy or effort toward a specified goal, and is often used of impersonal forces: *The legislation effected important changes in welfare policies.*

ac·com·plished (ə kom′plisht) *adj.* **1.** successfully completed; done; effected. **2.** skilled; proficient; expert: *an accomplished skier.* **3.** skilled or trained in social arts and graces; polished: *an accomplished diplomat.*

ac·com·plish·ment (ə kom′plish mənt) *n.* **1.** the act or process of accomplishing or the state of being accomplished; completion. **2.** something done successfully; achievement. **3.** *usually,* **accomplishments.** skill, art, or facility, esp. one that is acquired through training or practice.

ac·cord (ə kôrd′) *n.* **1.** a state of agreement; conformity: *They acted in accord with our wishes.* **2.** an agreement between parties, esp. one between nations. **3.** correspondence or harmony, as of color, pitch, or tone. —*v.t.* **1.** to grant as due; concede: *Her colleagues accorded her praise for her achievements in research.* **2.** *Archaic.* to bring into agreement or harmony; reconcile. —*v.i.* to be consistent or in harmony; agree (with *with*): *Our actions accorded with their wishes.* [Old French *acorder* to agree, going back to Latin *ad* to, at + *cor* heart.]
 •**of** (or **on**) **one's own accord.** by one's own choice or will; voluntarily.
 •**with one accord.** with complete agreement; with unanimity.

ac·cord·ance (ə kôr′dəns) *n.* **1.** the state of being in agreement; conformity: *in accordance with one's wishes.* **2.** the act of according, granting, or giving.

ac·cord·ant (ə kôr′dənt) *adj.* in harmony; agreeing; corresponding (with *with*): *accordant with one's principles.* —**ac·cord′ant·ly,** *adv.*

ac·cord·ing (ə kôr′ding) *adj.* in harmony; agreeing.
 •**according to. a.** in agreement or conformity with: *Everything went according to plan.* **b.** in proportion to; in relation to: *We were paid according to the time we spent working.* **c.** on the authority of; as stated by: *According to the weather forecaster, it's going to rain all day.*

ac·cord·ing·ly (ə kôr′ding lē) *adv.* **1.** in agreement with what is expected or appropriate; correspondingly; conformably. **2.** as a result; consequently; therefore.

ac·cor·di·on (ə kôr′dē ən) *n.* a portable musical wind instrument with keys, metallic reeds, and a bellows, which produces tones when the player squeezes or expands the bellows, forcing air through the reeds. —*adj.* resembling the folds of the bellows of an accordion: *a skirt with accordion pleats.* [German *Akkordion,* from *Akkord* chord, from French *accord,* going back to Latin *ad* to, at + *chorda.* See CHORD².]

Bellows

Piano keyboard   Button keyboard

accordion

ac·cost (ə kôst′) *v.t.* to approach and speak to, often in a challenging or aggressive way: *The reporters accosted the city officials as soon as they walked out of the meeting.* [French *accoster,* going back to Latin *ad* to, at + *costa* side, rib.]

ac·couche·ment (ə küsh′mənt; *French* ä küsh män′) *n.* the state or time of being confined for childbirth; childbirth. [French *accouchement,* from *accoucher* to give birth; literally, to be brought to bed, going back to Latin *ad* to + *collocāre* to lay together.]

ac·count (ə kount′) *n.* **1.** an oral or written statement; report or description: *a detailed account of a meeting.* **2.** a statement of reasons, causes, or grounds; explanation: *Give an account of your behavior.* **3.** a record or statement of business or financial transactions: *household accounts.* **4.** bank account. **5.** charge account. **6.** a customer or client with whom one has regular dealings: *Each sales representative has five accounts.* **7.** worth; importance: *a minor official of no account.* —*v.i.* to be responsible to; report to: *Our department read accounts to the president of the company.* —*v.t.* to consider to be; deem; value. [Old French *acompter* to count up, reckon, from *a* to (from Latin *ad* to) + *compter.* See COUNT¹.]
 •**on account. a.** as part of a final payment. **b.** on credit.
 •**on account of. a.** because of. **b.** for the sake of; in consideration of.
 •**on no account.** under no circumstances; never.
 •**on (someone's) account.** for (someone's) sake or benefit.
 •**to account for. a.** to provide an account of; be responsible for: *We must account for the money spent on supplies.* **b.** to give or be a satisfactory reason or cause for; explain: *The bad weather*

accounted for their lateness. *How do you account for your rudeness?* **c.** to cause the death, capture, or destruction of.
 •**to call (someone) to account. a.** to demand an explanation from. **b.** to reprimand; rebuke.
 •**to give (a good** or **poor) account of oneself.** to behave or perform (well or poorly).
 •**to take account of** or **take into account. a.** to take into consideration; allow for. **b.** to take note of.
 •**to turn to account.** to make advantageous, useful, or profitable.

n. **Account, version, story,** and **report** mean a description of events. **Account** usually refers to a description based on personal experience: *The anthropologist gave a fascinating account of her research.* **Version** refers to one of two or more conflicting accounts of the same events: *Now we would like to hear your version of the accident.* **Story** may also suggest conflicting accounts and often implies untruth: *I was skeptical of his story about why he was late.* **Report** indicates an account delivered to a superior or a group: *The committee listened with interest to the president's report on the conference.*

ac·count·a·ble (ə koun′tə bəl) *adj.* **1.** liable to be called to account; responsible: *to be held accountable for one's actions.* **2.** capable of being explained. —**ac·count′a·bil′i·ty, ac·count′a·ble·ness,** *n.* —**ac·count′a·bly,** *adv.*

ac·count·an·cy (ə koun′tən sē) *n.* the work or profession of an accountant.

ac·count·ant (ə koun′tənt) *n.* a person who has charge of or verifies business records and accounts; one trained in accounting.

ac·count·ing (ə koun′ting) *n.* **1.** the principles, procedures, or profession concerned with the systematic recording, analyzing, and verifying of business and financial transactions. **2.** a formal report or statement of transactions by one responsible for property, money, or the execution of some task.

ac·cou·ter (ə kü′tər) *also,* **accoutre.** *v.t.* to attire, equip, or outfit, esp. for military service. [French *accoutrer,* from Old French *acostrer* to prepare, arrange, going back to Latin *ad* to, at + *cōnsuere* to sew together.]

ac·cou·ter·ments (ə kü′tər mənts) *also,* **ac·cou·tre·ments.** *pl. n.* personal equipment or accessories, esp. the equipment of a soldier other than arms and clothing; trappings.

ac·cou·tre (ə kü′tər) *v.t.,* **-tred, -tring.** accouter.

ac·cred·it (ə kred′it) *v.t.* **1.** to give credit to: *Many people accredit the mayor with having ended the transit strike.* **2.** to consider (something) as belonging; attribute: *Scientists accredit the discovery of radium to Pierre and Marie Curie.* **3.** to certify as meeting certain official standards or requirements: *to accredit a college.* **4.** to send or provide with authorization or credentials: *to accredit a diplomat.* **5.** to accept as true; believe: *We accredited their account of the accident.* **6.** to provide authority for; vouch for. [French *accréditer,* from *à* to + *crédit.* See CREDIT.] —**ac·cred′i·ta′tion,** *n.*

ac·cre·tion (ə krē′shən) *n.* **1.** an increase in size by natural growth or external addition. **2.** the product of such a process. **3.** something that is added; external addition. **4.** the growing together of separate parts. [Latin *accrētiō* increase, increment, from *accrēscere* to increase. See ACCRUE.] —**ac·cre′tive,** *adj.*

ac·cru·al (ə krü′əl) *n.* **1.** the act or process of accruing. **2.** something accruing or accrued; amount accrued.

ac·crue (ə krü′) *v.,* **-crued, -cru·ing.** —*v.i.* **1.** to come as a result of natural growth or addition (with *to*): *Benefits accrued to the community from the new construction.* **2.** to grow in amount; accumulate: *Interest on savings accrues from the day of deposit.* —*v.t.* to accumulate (something): *The savings account accrues interest daily.* [Middle French *accrue* increase, from Old French *accreistre* to increase, from Latin *accrēscere* to increase, from *ad* to + *crēscere* to grow.] —**ac·crue′ment,** *n.*

acct. 1. account. **2.** accountant.

ac·cul·tur·a·tion (ə kul′chə rā′shən) *n.* the process or result of adopting traits or patterns of another culture.

ac·cu·mu·late (ə kū′myə lāt′) *v.,* **-lat·ed, -lat·ing.** —*v.t.* to gather or pile up (something); collect; amass: *to accumulate a large collection of books.* —*v.i.* to grow in size, quantity, or number; increase gradually: *A pile of work accumulated on my desk during my absence.* [Latin *accumulātus,* past participle of *accumulāre* to pile up.]

a	at	e	end	o	hot	u	up	hw	white		about
ā	ape	ē	me	ō	old	ū	use	ng	song	ə	taken
ä	far	i	it	ô	fork	ü	rule	th	thin		pencil
âr	care	ī	ice	oi	oil	ů	pull	th	this		lemon
		îr	pierce	ou	out	ûr	turn	zh	measure		circus

Accumulate and **amass** mean to gather together some amount. **Accumulate** suggests addition, by small amounts over a period of time, to a pile or collection that is not necessarily large: *The detectives accumulated evidence piece by piece over several months.* **Amass** emphasizes the large amount gathered rather than the process of gathering: *The couple amassed an art collection that filled their mansion.*

ac·cu·mu·la·tion (ə kū′myə lā′shən) *n.* **1.** the action or process of accumulating or the state of being accumulated. **2.** something that is accumulated or has accumulated; mass; collection: *Accumulations of snow blocked the roads.* —**ac·cu·mu·la·tive** (ə kū′myə lā′tiv, -lə tiv), *adj.*

ac·cu·mu·la·tor (ə kū′myə lā′tər) *n.* **1.** a person or thing that accumulates. **2.** *British.* a storage battery.

ac·cu·ra·cy (ak′yər ə sē) *n.* the state or quality of being accurate; freedom from error; correctness.

ac·cu·rate (ak′yər it) *adj.* **1.** making few or no errors; careful; exact: *an accurate typist.* **2.** conforming exactly to the truth; without error; correct: *an accurate report.* **3.** conforming exactly or closely to a standard: *an accurate scale.* [Latin *accūrātus,* past participle of *accūrāre* to take care of, take care of, from *ad* to + *cura* care.] —**ac′cu·rate·ly,** *adv.* —**ac′cu·rate·ness,** *n.* —For Synonyms, see **correct.**

ac·curs·ed (ə kûr′sid, ə kûrst′) *also,* **ac·curst** (ə kûrst′). *adj.* **1.** under a curse; ill-fated; doomed. **2.** worthy of curses; damnable; hateful.

accus., accusative.

ac·cu·sa·tion (ak′yə zā′ shən) *n.* **1.** a charge of wrongdoing: *to deny an accusation.* **2.** a crime, offense, or error charged: *The accusation is treason.* **3.** the act of accusing or the state of being accused.

ac·cu·sa·tive (ə kū′zə tiv) *n.* **1.** a grammatical case in Latin, Greek, and other Indo-European languages that indicates the direct object of a verb or the object of certain prepositions. It corresponds to the objective case in English. **2.** a word or construction in this case. —*adj.* of, relating to, or designating this case.

ac·cu·sa·to·ry (ə kū′zə tôr′ē) *adj.* containing an accusation; accusing: *an accusatory tone of voice.*

ac·cuse (ə kūz′) *v.t.,* **-cused, -cus·ing. 1.** to bring formal charges against (with *of*): *The police accused them of murder.* **2.** to find at fault or in error; blame. [Old French *acuser,* from Latin *accūsāre* to blame.] —**ac·cus′er,** *n.* —**ac·cus′ing·ly,** *adv.*

Accuse, denounce, and **charge** mean to state that someone is at fault or to blame. **Accuse** is the general term, implying a direct indication of the person blamed: *I accused my classmate of taking my pencil.* **Denounce** usually suggests open, public condemnation: *The speaker denounced the prime minister.* It sometimes, however, refers to just the opposite, a blaming done in secret: *The students who were opposed to the regime were denounced to the police by an informer.* **Charge** usually refers to a formal, sometimes legal, statement of blame: *Three people were charged with disturbing the peace.*

ac·cused (ə kūzd′) *adj.* subjected to an accusation. —*n.* **the accused.** a person or persons charged with an offense, esp. the defendant or defendants in a criminal case.

ac·cus·tom (ə kus′təm) *v.t.* to make (someone) familiar with something by use, custom, or habit; habituate (with *to*): *We have accustomed ourselves to getting up early.* [Old French *acostumer,* from *a* to (from Latin *ad* to) + *costume* custom. See CUSTOM.]

Accustom and **habituate** mean to make used to new circumstances. **Accustom** simply implies repeated exposure to something or enough exposure to make one familiar with it: *Working in this job has accustomed me to using a computer.* **Habituate** implies a certain deadening as a result of such exposure: *Living on a busy street, I have become habituated to traffic noise.*

ac·cus·tomed (ə kus′təmd) *adj.* established by custom or habit; customary; habitual: *We all sat in our accustomed places.* •**accustomed to.** in the habit of; used to: *to be accustomed to rising with the dawn.*

ace (ās) *n.* **1.a.** a playing card having a single symbol of the suit it represents. **b.** a face of a die having one spot. **2.** a person who excels at something; expert: *tennis ace.* **3.** a fighter pilot who has shot down five or more enemy planes. **4.a.** in tennis and similar games, a served ball that the opponent fails to touch. **b.** in golf, a hole in one. —*v.t.,* **aced, ac·ing. 1.** to make (a golf hole) in one stroke. **2.** to score a point by an ace, as in tennis. **3.** *Informal.* to do very well on or in, esp. by receiving a grade of A: *I aced the history exam.* —*adj.* of the highest quality; expert: *an ace performance.* [Old French *as* face of a die having one spot, from Latin *ās* unit, coin.]

•**ace in the hole.** *Slang.* a hidden advantage not revealed until needed.

•**to ace out.** *Slang.* to beat or surpass (someone): *to ace out an opponent.*

•**within an ace of.** to the very point of: *I came within an ace of winning the game.*

a·cel·lu·lar (ā sel′yə lər) *adj.* **1.** without cells. **2.** not composed of cells or not made up of separate cells, although having more than one nucleus, as certain kinds of tissue or organisms. [A-[4] + CELLULAR.]

a·cer·bic (ə sûr′bik) *adj.* **1.** harsh, bitter, or severe in temper, manner, or expression: *an acerbic wit, an acerbic comment.* **2.** sour, bitter, or acid in taste. [Latin *acerbus* sour + -IC.]

a·cer·bi·ty (ə sûr′bi tē) *n., pl.* **-ties. 1.** harshness, bitterness, or severity of temper or manner. **2.** sourness, bitterness, or acidity of taste. [French *acerbité,* from Latin *acerbitās,* from *acerbus* sour, bitter.]

ac·e·tab·u·lum (as′i tab′yə ləm) *n., pl.* **-la** (-lə). a cup-shaped socket in the hipbone into which the head of the thighbone fits. [Latin *acētābulum* a small cup, originally for vinegar, from *acētum* vinegar.]

ac·et·al·de·hyde (as′i tal′də hīd′) *n.* a colorless flammable liquid with a pungent, fruity odor, widely used in the making of organic compounds and as an organic solvent. Formula: C_2H_4O

a·ce·ta·min·o·phen (ə sē′tə min′ə fən, as′i tə-) *n.* a white, crystalline compound used to relieve mild pain and reduce fever. Formula: $C_8H_9O_2$

ac·et·an·i·lide (as′i tan′ə līd′, -lid) *also,* **ac·et·an·i·lid** (as′i tan′ə lid). *n.* a white, crystalline compound, formerly used as a drug to relieve mild pain and reduce fever. Formula: C_8H_9NO

ac·e·tate (as′i tāt′) *n.* **1.** a salt or ester of acetic acid. **2.** cellulose acetate or any of its products, esp. a cellulose acetate fabric, fiber, or yarn.

a·ce·tic (ə sē′tik, ə set′ik) *adj.* of, relating to, like, or producing vinegar or acetic acid. [Latin *acētum* vinegar + -IC.]

acetic acid, a colorless compound having a pungent odor and sour taste. It is the acid in vinegar and is used widely in the production of textile fibers, plastics, and drugs. Formula: $C_2H_4O_2$

a·ce·ti·fy (ə sē′tə fī′, ə set′ə-) *v.t., v.i.,* **-fied, -fy·ing.** to make or become acetic; turn into vinegar. —**a·ce′ti·fi·ca′tion,** *n.*

ac·e·tone (as′i tōn′) *n.* a colorless, volatile, flammable liquid with a minty odor, used widely as a solvent for fats, cellulose compounds, and other organic substances. Formula: C_3H_6O

a·ce·tyl (ə sē′təl, as′i təl) *n.* the univalent radical of acetic acid. Formula: CH_3CO

a·ce·tyl·cho·line (ə sē′təl kō′lēn, as′i təl-) *n.* an organic compound that is derived from choline and whose release at nerve endings is instrumental in the transmission of nerve impulses. Formula: $C_7H_{17}NO_3$ [ACETYL + CHOLINE.]

a·cet·y·lene (ə set′ə lēn′, -lin) *n.* a colorless, highly flammable gas of the alkyne series, used in the synthesis of many organic compounds and, in combination with oxygen, in the cutting and welding of metals. Formula: C_2H_2

a·ce·tyl·sal·i·cyl·ic acid (ə sē′təl sal′ə sil′ik, as′i təl-) aspirin.

A·chae·an (ə kē′ən) *also,* **A·cha·ian** (ə kā′ən, ə kī′-). *adj.* of or relating to Achaea or its people or culture. —*n.* **1.** an inhabitant of Achaea. **2.** a member of one of the four major Greek tribes of antiquity. The Achaeans settled in the Peloponnesus, establishing the Mycenaean civilization, and later fled to Asia Minor during the Dorian invasion.

A·cha·tes (ə kā′tēz) *n.* **1.** in Roman legend, the faithful companion and friend of Aeneas. **2.** any loyal friend.

ache (āk) *v.i.,* **ached, ach·ing. 1.** to have or be in pain, esp. dull or continuous pain. **2.** to feel compassion or sympathy: *Our hearts ached for the victims of the earthquake.* **3.** *Informal.* to be eager; long; yearn: *The weary travelers ached for home.* —*n.* a continuous, usually dull pain. [Old English *acan* to ache.] —**ach′ing·ly,** *adv.* —For Synonyms (*n.*), see **pain.**

a·chene (ā kēn′) *also,* **akene.** *n.* a small, dry, one-seeded fruit,

Achaean gold mask

as of a dandelion or sunflower, whose thin outer covering does not burst open at maturity. [A-[4] + Greek *chainein* to gape.] —**a·che′ni·al,** *adj.*

Ach·er·on (ak′ə ron′) *n.* **1.** in Greek and Roman mythology, one of the rivers of the lower world. **2.** the lower world; Hades; hell.

a·chieve (ə chēv′) *v.,* **a·chieved, a·chiev·ing.** —*v.t.* **1.** to carry out or do successfully; accomplish. **2.** to succeed in gaining; attain: *to achieve fame, to achieve a goal.* —*v.i.* to be successful in something; bring about an intended result: *to achieve in school because of hard work.* [Old French *achever* to bring to an end, accomplish, from a phrase *a chief* to a head, to an end, from Latin phrase *ad caput* to a head.] —**a·chiev′a·ble,** *adj.* —**a·chiev′er,** *n.* —For Synonyms, see **accomplish.**

a·chieve·ment (ə chēv′mənt) *n.* **1.** something achieved, esp. by great exertion or skill; feat; accomplishment. **2.** the act of achieving.

achievement test, a test that is used to measure how much a person has learned in a particular subject over a certain amount of time.

A·chil·les (ə kil′ēz) *n.* the greatest Greek warrior in the Trojan War. Achilles was killed by Paris, who wounded him in his only vulnerable spot, his heel.

Achilles′ heel, one's most vulnerable or weakest point. [From *Achilles,* legendary Greek warrior who was invulnerable except for his heel.]

Achilles′ tendon *also,* **Achilles tendon.** the tendon that joins the muscles of the calf to the bone of the heel.

a·chon·dro·pla·sia (ā kon′drə plā′zhə, -zhē ə, -zē ə) *n.* a congenital disorder of bone formation that results in dwarfism, characterized by shortened limbs and other skeletal deformities. [A-[4] + Greek *chondros* cartilage + Modern Latin *-plasia* growth, development, change (from Greek *plasis* a molding).] —**a·chon·dro·plas·tic** (ā kon′drə plas′tik), *adj.*

ach·ro·mat·ic (ak′rə mat′ik) *adj.* **1.** refracting white light without separating it into the colors of the spectrum. **2.** without hue; colorless. [Greek *achrōmatos* colorless, from *a-* a-[4] + *chrōma* color.] —**ach′ro·mat′i·cal·ly,** *adv.*

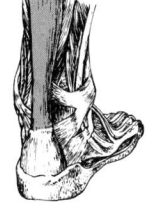

Achilles′ tendon

ach·y (ā′kē) *adj.,* **ach·i·er, ach·i·est.** having or feeling an ache: *I was achy all over when I had the flu.* —**ach′i·ness,** *n.*

ac·id (as′id) *n.* **1.** *Chemistry.* **a.** a compound containing hydrogen and having a sour taste in water solution. Acids react with bases to form salts. **b.** a compound that gives up protons to a base. **c.** a compound capable of accepting an unshared pair of electrons from a base. **2.** any sour substance. **3.** *Slang.* LSD. —*adj.* **1.** of, relating to, yielding, or like an acid. **2.** sharp and biting to the taste; sour. **3.** sharp, as in tone or manner; ill-tempered; biting: *acid remarks.* [Latin *acidus* sour.] —**ac′id·ly,** *adv.* —**ac′id·ness,** *n.*

a·cid·ic (ə sid′ik) *adj.* **1.** forming acid. **2.** (of rock) containing a large percentage of silica. **3.** containing acid: *an acidic substance.*

a·cid·i·fy (ə sid′ə fī′) *v.t., v.i.,* **-fied, -fy·ing. 1.** to make or become acid or sour. **2.** to change into an acid. —**a·cid′i·fi′a·ble,** *adj.* —**a·cid′i·fi·ca′tion,** *n.* —**a·cid′i·fi′er,** *n.*

a·cid·i·ty (ə sid′i tē) *n., pl.* **-ties. 1.** the state or quality of being acid; sourness; tartness. **2.** the degree of being acid: *low acidity.* **3.** hyperacidity.

ac·i·do·sis (as′i dō′sis) *n.* an abnormal condition of the body resulting from increased acidity or reduced alkalinity in the blood and tissues. [ACID + -OSIS.]

acid rain, rain, sleet, or other precipitation polluted with acidic chemicals, esp. as released by combustion of coal, gasoline, and other fossil fuels.

acid rock, a type of rock music characterized by a hypnotic beat and long, slow instrumental solos. The music and lyrics sometimes suggest the taking of drugs or psychedelic experiences.

acid test, something that tests the real or essential quality, character, or worth of a person or thing. [Because acid is used as a test for gold.]

a·cid·u·late (ə sij′ə lāt′) *v.t.,* **-lat·ed, -lat·ing.** to make somewhat acid or sour. —**a·cid′u·la′tion,** *n.*

a·cid·u·lous (ə sij′ə ləs) *adj.* **1.** slightly acid or sour. **2.** harsh or sharp in tone or manner: *an acidulous remark.* Also, **a·cid·u·lent** (ə sij′ə lənt).

ack-ack (ak′ak′) *n. Slang.* antiaircraft fire; antiaircraft gun. [British signalman's code for *AA,* abbreviation of *antiaircraft.*]

ac·knowl·edge (ak nol′ij) *v.t.,* **-edged, -edg·ing. 1.** to admit the truth or fact of; confess: *to acknowledge an error.* **2.** to accept the authority, validity, or claims of: *The government acknowledged our right to petition.* **3.** to express appreciation or gratitude for: *to acknowledge a favor.* **4.** to make known the receipt or arrival of: *She acknowledged the letter.* **5.** to express recognition of; take notice of: *He acknowledged our arrival by waving.* **6.** *Law.* to recognize as valid or true; certify legally: *to acknowledge a deed.* [Probably blend of obsolete *aknow* to recognize (from Old English *oncnāwan*) and obsolete *knowledge* to confess, admit (going back to Old English *cnāwan* to know).] —**ac·knowl′edge·a·ble,** *adj.* —**ac·knowl′edg·er,** *n.* —For Synonyms, see **admit.**

ac·knowl·edged (ak nol′ijd) *adj.* generally accepted; recognized: *She is the acknowledged authority on Renaissance painters.* —**ac·knowl′edged·ly,** *adv.*

ac·knowl·edg·ment (ak nol′ij mənt) *also,* **ac·knowl·edge·ment.** *n.* **1.** the act of admitting or confessing; avowal. **2.** an acceptance of authority, validity, or claims: *acknowledgment of a court's jurisdiction.* **3.** a thing done or given to indicate the arrival or receipt of something: *Their letter was an acknowledgment of the shipment.* **4.** an expression of gratitude, recognition, or appreciation. **5.** *Law.* a sworn declaration of the truth or validity of an action or fact; certificate of such a declaration.

ACLU, American Civil Liberties Union.

ac·me (ak′mē) *n.* the highest point; peak: *the acme of a performer's career.* [Greek *akmē* point, highest point.]

ac·ne (ak′nē) *n.* a skin disorder characterized by pimples or other blemishes on the face, back, or chest resulting from clogged and inflamed pores of the sebaceous glands. [Modern Latin *acne,* mistaken reading of Greek *akmē* point, pimple.]

ac·o·lyte (ak′ə līt′) *n.* **1.** a person who assists a minister or priest at certain religious services. **2.** an assistant or follower. [Medieval Latin *acolythus* follower, attendant, from Greek *akolouthos* follower.]

ac·o·nite (ak′ə nīt′) *n.* **1.** any of a group of mostly poisonous plants, genus *Aconitum,* of the Northern Hemisphere, bearing blue, white, purple, or yellow hood-shaped flowers. Also, **wolfsbane, monkshood. 2.** a drug obtained from any of several species of these plants, esp. from *A. napellus,* formerly used to reduce fever and relieve pain. [French *aconit* the plant, from Latin *aconitum* from Greek *akoniton.*]

a·corn (ā′kôrn, ā′kərn) *n.* the nut, or fruit, of the oak, the base of which is surrounded by a woody cup. [Old English *æcern* fruit of the field.]

acorn squash, an acorn-shaped winter squash having a ridged green or yellow skin and sweet yellow to orange flesh.

Fruit

acorn and oak leaves

a·cous·tic (ə küs′tik) *adj.* **1.** relating to the sense or organs of hearing, to sound, or to the science of sound. **2.** serving to absorb and deaden sound: *acoustic tile.* **3.** (of musical instruments) not using or requiring electronic modification of sound: *an acoustic piano.* Also, **a·cous′ti·cal.** [Greek *akoustikos* relating to hearing, from *akouein* to hear.] —**a·cous′ti·cal·ly,** *adv.*

acoustic feedback, the usually unintended feedback of sound from a loudspeaker to a microphone in an audio system, resulting in the production of a whistling or howling noise. Also, **feedback.**

a·cous·tics (ə küs′tiks) *n.* **1.** the properties, as of a room, theater, or auditorium, that determine how well sound is carried and heard in it. **2.** the science that deals with the production, transmission, effects, and reception of sound. ➡ used as plural in def. 1, as singular in def. 2.

ac·quaint (ə kwānt′) *v.t.* **1.** to make (someone) familiar; cause to know: *I must acquaint myself with the rules of the game.* **2.** to make known to; inform (with *with*): *Shall we acquaint them with our decision before going on?* [Old French *acointier,* from Late Latin *adcognitāre* to make known, going back to Latin *ad* to + *cognitus,* past participle of *cognōscere* to know.]

ac·quaint·ance (ə kwān′təns) *n.* **1.** a person whom one knows, but who is not a close friend. **2.** a relationship between people who are not close friends; state of being acquainted: *We had a brief acquaintance over the summer.* **3.** knowledge of something, esp. as a result of much experience or contact; familiarity (with

a	at	e	end	o	hot	u	up	hw	white		about
ā	ape	ē	me	ō	old	ū	use	ng	song	ə	taken
ä	far	i	it	ô	fork	ū	rule	th	thin		pencil
âr	care	ī	ice	oi	oil	u̇	pull	th	this		lemon
				ou	out	ûr	turn	zh	measure		circus
		îr	pierce								

with): *Long and careful study gave me a thorough acquaintance with the facts.* —ac•quaint′ance•ship′, *n.*

• to make someone's acquaintance. to get to know someone.

ac•quaint•ed (ə kwān′tid) *adj.* **1.** known to someone, or each other, but not intimately: *Are you two acquainted?* **2.** having knowledge or familiarity; familiar: *I'm acquainted with the new rules.*

• to get (or become) acquainted. to come to know (someone or each other): *Let's get acquainted.*

ac•qui•esce (ak′wē es′) *v.i.,* -esced, -esc•ing. to consent or agree tacitly; comply without protest (with *in* or *to*): *They acquiesced to our proposal.* [Latin *acquiēscere* to rest, repose in, assent.] —For Synonyms, see **consent.**

ac•qui•es•cence (ak′wē es′əns) *n.* the act of acquiescing; tacit agreement; silent submission.

ac•qui•es•cent (ak′wē es′ənt) *adj.* acquiescing or disposed to acquiesce; submissive. —ac′qui•es′cent•ly, *adv.*

ac•quire (ə kwīr′) *v.t.,* -quired, -quir•ing. **1.** to get possession of; gain or obtain: *to acquire wealth and property, to acquire an education.* **2.** to come to have; develop: *We acquired an accent while living in England.* [Latin *acquīrere* to obtain, get in addition, from *ad* to + *quaere* to seek.] —ac•quir′a•bil′i•ty, *n.* —ac•quir′a•ble, *adj.* —For Synonyms, see **gain.**

acquired immune deficiency syndrome, see **AIDS.**

ac•quire•ment (ə kwīr′mənt) *n.* **1.** the act of acquiring. **2.** something that is acquired; attainment: *a young person with many social acquirements.*

ac•qui•si•tion (ak′wə zish′ən) *n.* **1.** the act of acquiring: *the acquisition of wealth.* **2.** something that is received or acquired: *The museum displayed its recent acquisitions.* [Latin *acquīsītiō,* from *acquīrere* to obtain. See ACQUIRE.]

ac•quis•i•tive (ə kwiz′i tiv) *adj.* eager or tending to acquire, esp. to acquire and own; grasping: *a greedy and acquisitive person.* —ac•quis′i•tive•ly, *adv.* —ac•quis′i•tive•ness, *n.*

ac•quit (ə kwit′) *v.t.,* -quit•ted, -quit•ting. **1.** to free or clear from an accusation or charge of crime; declare not guilty; exonerate: *The jury acquitted the defendant.* **2.** to relieve or release, as from a duty or obligation: *to acquit someone of responsibility.* **3.** to conduct (oneself); behave: *The team acquitted itself well in its first game.* [Old French *aquiter* to set free, save, going back to Latin *ad* to + *quiētāre* to quiet.] —ac•quit′ter, *n.* —For Synonyms, see **absolve.**

ac•quit•tal (ə kwit′əl) *n.* **1.** a setting free from a criminal charge by a verdict or other legal process. **2.** the act of acquitting or the state of being acquitted.

ac•quit•tance (ə kwit′əns) *n.* **1.** a discharge from or settlement of a debt or obligation. **2.** a written statement confirming this settlement or discharge; receipt in full.

a•cre (ā′kər) *n.* **1.** a measure of land equal to 43,560 square feet (4,051 square meters) or 160 square rods. **2. acres. a.** lands; estate. **b.** *Informal.* a large quantity or amount. [Old English *æcer* originally, field; later, a measure of land.]

a•cre•age (ā′kər ij) *n.* an area of land measured in acres; acres collectively: *How much acreage does the state own?*

a•cre-foot (ā′kər fŭt′) *n.* the volume of irrigation water that would cover an acre of land to a depth of 1 foot, equal to 43,560 cubic feet (1,220 cubic meters).

ac•rid (ak′rid) *adj.* **1.** burning, biting, or irritating to the taste or smell; bitterly pungent: *the acrid smell of smoke.* **2.** biting or cutting in manner, temper, or tone: *acrid comments.* [Alteration of Latin *ācer* sharp; possibly influenced by ACID.] —a•crid•i•ty (ə krid′i tē), ac′rid•ness, *n.* —ac′rid•ly, *adv.*

ac•ri•mo•ni•ous (ak′rə mō′nē əs) *adj.* caustic, bitter, or sarcastic in disposition, manner, or tone: *an acrimonious critic, an acrimonious debate.* —ac′ri•mo′ni•ous•ly, *adv.* —ac′ri•mo′ni•ous•ness, *n.*

ac•ri•mo•ny (ak′rə mō′nē) *n., pl.* -nies. sharpness or bitterness in disposition, manner, or tone. [Latin *ācrimōnia,* from *acer* sharp.]

ac•ro•bat (ak′rə bat′) *n.* a person skilled in performing feats of agility requiring great muscular coordination and control, as a trapeze artist, tightrope walker, or tumbler. [French *acrobate,* from Greek *akrobatēs,* from *akrobatos* walking on tiptoe, from *akros* high point + *bainein* to go.] —ac′ro•bat′ic, *adj.* —ac′ro•bat′i•cal•ly, *adv.*

ac•ro•bat•ics (ak′rə bat′iks) *pl. n.* **1.** the feats or skills of an acrobat. **2.** any display of great skill or agility: *The pianist performed musical acrobatics.*

ac•ro•gen (ak′rə jən) *n.* a plant having a perennial stem that grows only at the tip. Ferns and mosses are acrogens. [Greek *akros* topmost + -GEN.] —ac•ro•gen•ic (ak′rə jen′ik), a•crog•e•nous (ə kroj′ə nəs), *adj.*

ac•ro•me•gal•ic (ak′rō mə gal′ik) *adj.* relating to or afflicted with acromegaly. —*n.* a person afflicted with acromegaly.

ac•ro•meg•a•ly (ak′rə meg′ə lē) *n.* a disease of adults characterized by a permanent enlargement of the bones of the face and of the extremities, caused by oversecretion of growth hormone by the pituitary gland. [French *acromégalie,* from Greek *akros* at the end + *megas* big.]

ac•ro•nym (ak′rə nim′) *n.* a word formed by combining the first letters or syllables of other words. *Radar* is an acronym for *ra(dio) d(etecting) a(nd) r(anging).* [Greek *akros* at the end + *onyma* (dialectal form) name, word.]

ac•ro•pho•bi•a (ak′rə fō′bē ə) *n.* an abnormal, excessive fear of being in a high place.

a•crop•o•lis (ə krop′ə lis) *n.* **1.** a strongly fortified place or citadel in an ancient Greek city, usually built on the highest hill. **2. the Acropolis.** the ancient citadel on the highest hill of Athens, Greece, famous for its temples and monuments. [Greek *akropolis,* from *akros* topmost + *polis* city.]

a•cross (ə krôs′) *adv.* **1.** from one side to the other: *We came across in a boat.* **2.** on or to the other side: *We'll soon be across.* **3.** in a crossed position; crosswise: *The guard stood with arms across.* —*prep.* **1.** from one side of to the other; over: *We drove across the border.* **2.** on the other side of; beyond: *One of my cousins lives across the street.* **3.** in a direction so as to cross: *The cat walked across our path.*

a•cross-the-board (ə krôs′thə bôrd′) *adj.* **1.** including or affecting everyone or everything in a category; general: *an across-the-board pay raise.* **2.** designating a combination bet in which equal amounts of money are placed on several possibilities, as for a horse to win, place, or show in a race: *an across-the-board bet.*

a•cros•tic (ə krôs′tik) *n.* a poem or other arrangement of words in which the first, last, or certain other letters in each line, taken in order, form a word, phrase, or sequence of the alphabet. [French *acrostiche,* from Greek *akrostichis,* from *akros* at the end + *stichos* line of verse.] —a•cros′ti•cal•ly, *adv.*

The two types of acrostics shown below are formed from words relating to the Olympic games.

Olympics	can**O**eing
Luge	pentath**L**on
Yachting	c**Y**cling
Medals	gy**M**nastics
Pentathlon	Water **P**olo
Ice skating	tenn**I**s
Canoeing	field ho**C**key
Skiing	**S**occer

acrostics

---

a•cryl•ic (ə kril′ik) *n.* **1.** acrylic fiber. **2.** acrylic resin. **3.** a paint that contains an acrylic resin. —*adj.* of or containing an acrylic fiber or resin. [Latin *acer* sharp + Greek *hylē* matter + -IC.]

acrylic fiber, any of a group of synthetic textile fibers made from acrylic resins. When woven, they make a long-wearing, lightweight fabric that resists wrinkling, used for such items as sweaters, blankets, and carpets.

acrylic resin, any one of a group of synthetic, thermoplastic, polymeric compounds used esp. in paints and textiles.

ac•ry•lo•ni•trile (ak′rə lō nī′trəl) *n.* a toxic, flammable liquid used in making polymeric products, such as acrylic rubber, fibers, and the clear plastic used to make soda bottles. Formula: C_3H_3N

act (akt) *n.* **1.** something done; deed: *an act of courage.* **2.** the process of doing something: *The smugglers were caught in the act.* **3.** a formal decision or law, as of a legislative body or sovereign: *an act of Congress.* **4.** one of the main divisions of a dramatic or theatrical work: *a play with five acts.* **5.** a short theatrical performance, usually one of several on a program: *The magician's act follows the acrobats.* **6.** a display of feigned or insincere behavior: *Their concern was just an act.* —*v.t.* **1.** to behave in a manner befitting: *Act your age.* **2.** to play the part of; perform: *to act the lead role in a play.* **3.** to pretend to be; behave like: *to act the fool.* —*v.i.* **1.** to do or perform something: *The emergency crew acted quickly to help the accident victims.* **2.** to conduct oneself in a certain way: *to act like a spoiled child.* **3.** to be an actor; perform: *He has acted on television and on the stage.* **4.** to produce an effect: *Wait until the drug acts.* **5.** to assume the appearance of; pretend to be: *She acted calm, although she was very worried.*

6. to function in a certain way; serve: *The chemical acted as a catalyst. Who will act as president in my absence?* **7.** to serve as an agent; substitute: *We will appoint a spokesperson to act for us.* [Partly from Latin *āctus* a doing, partly from Latin *āctum* a thing done; both forms are noun uses of the past participle of *agere* to do.]
  • **to act on** (or **upon**). to behave in accordance with; follow: *Act on my orders.*
  • **to act up.** *Informal.* **a.** to behave mischievously or playfully: *The children were acting up.* **b.** to cause trouble: *My stomach acted up after dinner.*

Synonyms *n.* **Act, deed,** and **action,** when they mean something done, have slightly different uses. **Act** refers to an isolated occurrence, complete in itself and with limited purpose: *Giving money to the beggar was an act of generosity.* **Deed,** a more formal word, usually implies a rewarding act, possibly involving great effort or special skill or courage: *We must not forget the heroic deeds of our firefighters.* **Action** usually refers to something taking more time or to a sequence of acts, each contributing to the whole: *The conductor's action in stopping the train, making an announcement, and opening the doors allowed the passengers to escape safely.*

Ac·te·on (ak tē′ən) *also,* **Ac·tae·on.** *n.* in Greek legend, a hunter who accidentally saw Artemis bathing and was changed by her into a stag, then torn to pieces by his own dogs.

ACTH, a hormone that is produced by the pituitary gland and stimulates the cortex of the human adrenal gland to secrete its hormones. It is manufactured synthetically or obtained from animals for use in treatment of certain diseases, as arthritis, rheumatic fever, and asthma. Also, **corticotropin, corticotrophin.** [Abbreviation of *a(dreno)-c(ortico)-t(rophic) h(ormone).*]

ac·tin (ak′tin) *n.* a muscle protein that in conjunction with myosin produces muscular contraction. [Latin *āctus* a doing, (from *agere* to do) + -IN[1].]

act·ing (ak′ting) *adj.* **1.** performing certain duties or functions, esp. temporarily: *the acting mayor.* **2.** of, relating to, or suitable for theatrical performance: *an acting company, an acting script.* —*n.* the art or occupation of an actor; act of performing on the stage or before cameras.

ac·tin·ic (ak tin′ik) *adj.* of, relating to, or having actinism. [Greek *aktīs* ray + -IC.]

ac·ti·nide (ak′tə nīd′) *n.* any of a series of radioactive elements, atomic numbers 89 through 103, starting with actinium and ending with lawrencium. [ACTIN(IUM) + -IDE.]

ac·tin·ism (ak′tə niz′əm) *n.* the property of visible light, ultraviolet rays, X rays, and other forms of radiant energy that produces chemical changes.

ac·tin·i·um (ak tin′ē əm) *n.* a rare, silver-white, poisonous, radioactive metallic element found in pitchblende and other uranium ores. Symbol: **Ac** For tables, see **element.** [Modern Latin *actinium,* going back to Greek *aktis* ray; because the radioactivity of actinium causes it to glow in the dark.]

ac·tin·o·my·cete (ak tin′ō mī′sēt, -mī sēt′) *n.* any of an order, Actinomycetales, of filamentous or rod-shaped bacteria having branchlike structures, esp. members of the family Actinomycetaceae, some of which cause diseases in humans and animals. [Greek *aktinos,* genitive of *aktis* ray + Modern Latin *mycetes* fungi (from Greek *mykētes,* plural of *mykēs* fungus). So called because their branchlike structures resemble fungi.] —**ac·tin′o·my·ce′tous,** *adj.*

ac·tion (ak′shən) *n.* **1.** the process of acting or doing; operation: *the action of throwing a ball.* **2.** something done; act; deed: *Actions speak louder than words.* **3. actions.** way of behaving; behavior; conduct: *He couldn't explain his actions.* **4.** force or influence exerted by something: *The rocks were eroded by the constant action of the waves.* **5.** a manner of moving or operating: *a washing machine with gentle action.* **6.** a tendency to act quickly and decisively: *a person of action.* **7.** a mechanism by which something operates: *the action of a rifle.* **8.** battle; combat. **9.** the events or progress of events in a story or play; plot. **10.** a suit in a court of law. **11.** great activity or excitement: *to be where the action is.* [French *action* process of doing, motion, battle, lawsuit, from Latin *āctiō* a doing, going back to *agere* to do.] —**ac′tion·less,** *adj.* —For Synonyms, see **act.**
  • **in action.** in a state of activity; at work; in operation.
  • **to see action.** to engage in military combat.
  • **to take action. a.** to become active; start to act: *My insurance company took action as soon as I reported the accident.* **b.** to start a lawsuit.

ac·tion·a·ble (ak′shə nə bəl) *adj.* giving grounds for a lawsuit.

action verb, a verb that expresses action, rather than state or being. An action verb can be transitive, as *start* in *She started the car,* or intransitive, as *nap* in *He naps every afternoon.*

ac·ti·vate (ak′tə vāt′) *v.t.* **-vat·ed, -vat·ing. 1.** to cause to work or operate; make active. **2.** *Physics.* to make radioactive. **3.** *Chemistry.* to accelerate a reaction in; make more reactive. **4.** *Military.* **a.** to create (a unit or installation) officially so that it can be organized to function in its assigned capacity. **b.** to mobilize (an inactive unit or installation). —**ac′ti·va′tion,** *n.*

activation analysis *Chemistry.* a method of qualitative analysis that identifies the elements in a sample by the gamma rays emitted when the sample is bombarded with neutrons. Also, **neutron activation analysis.**

ac·ti·va·tor (ak′tə vā′tər) *n.* **1.** a person or thing that activates. **2.** *Chemistry.* a catalyst.

ac·tive (ak′tiv) *adj.* **1.** full of or characterized by much energy, action, or movement; busy: *an active person, an active life.* **2.** moving or acting quickly; vigorous: *an active mind, active trading on the stock market.* **3.** requiring the exertion of energy: *active participation, active sports.* **4.** acting or capable of acting; functioning or effective: *an active volcano, active ingredients in a chemical formula.* **5.** *Grammar.* **a.** relating to or designating the voice of a verb whose subject is represented as performing the action expressed by the verb. In the sentence *The boy called his sister,* the verb *called* is in the active voice. ➡ opposed to **passive. b.** designating verbs expressing action rather than state or being. *Throw, run,* and *jump* are active verbs. —*n.* **1.** the active voice. **2.** a verb form in this voice. [Old French *actif,* from Latin *āctīvus* practical, denoting the active voice, from *agere* to do.] —**ac′tive·ly,** *adv.* —**ac′tive·ness,** *n.*

active duty, full-time military service.

active immunity, the immunity to disease possessed by an individual as a result of having already produced antibodies in response to infection or inoculation. ➡ distinguished from **passive immunity.**

active transport *Biology.* the transport of material across a cell membrane from a region of low concentration to a region of higher concentration by a process that uses metabolic energy.

ac·ti·vism (ak′tə viz′əm) *n.* the policy or practice of taking vigorous, direct action to achieve an end or in support of a cause.

ac·ti·vist (ak′tə vist) *n.* a person who believes in and uses vigorous, direct action in support of a cause: *a civil rights activist.* —*adj.* of or relating to activists or activism. —**ac·ti·vis′tic,** *adj.*

ac·tiv·i·ty (ak tiv′i tē) *n., pl.* **-ties. 1.** the state or quality of being active; movement: *The doctor told her to curtail all physical activity until she was better.* **2.** brisk or vigorous action; liveliness: *There was little activity on the stock market today.* **3.** a specific action or thing to do: *He is involved in many fundraising activities.*

act of God, a natural occurrence, as lightning or an earthquake, that is beyond human control and could not reasonably have been foreseen or prevented.

ac·tor (ak′tər) *n.* **1.** a person who plays a role or performs, as in a play or motion picture. **2.** a person who acts; doer.

ac·tress (ak′tris) *n.* a woman who plays a role or performs, as in a play or motion picture.

Acts (akts) *n.* a book of the New Testament, attributed to the Evangelist Luke. Also, **Acts of the Apostles.** ➡ used as singular.

ac·tu·al (ak′chü əl) *adj.* **1.** existing as a fact; not imagined or made-up; real: *The actual result differed from our predictions.* **2.** existing at the moment; present: *the actual state of affairs.* [Old French *actuel* active, from Late Latin *āctuālis,* from Latin *āctus* a doing. See ACT.] —**ac′tu·al·ness,** *n.* —For Synonyms, see **real[1].**

ac·tu·al·i·ty (ak′chü al′i tē) *n., pl.* **-ties. 1.** the state or quality of being actual; reality. **2.** an actual condition or circumstance; fact.

ac·tu·al·ize (ak′chü ə līz′) *v.t.* **-ized, -iz·ing.** to make actual; realize in action or fact. —**ac′tu·al·i·za′tion,** *n.*

ac·tu·al·ly (ak′chü ə lē) *adv.* according to the facts; really.

ac·tu·ar·i·al (ak′chü âr′ē əl) *adj.* **1.** of actuaries or their work. **2.** determined by actuaries: *actuarial tables.* —**ac′tu·ar′i·al·ly,** *adv.*

ac·tu·ar·y (ak′chü er′ē) *n., pl.* **-ar·ies.** a person skilled in the mathematics and statistics of insurance. An actuary computes insurance risks and determines premiums, rates, and dividends. [Latin *āctuārius* keeper of accounts, from *āctus* a doing. See ACT.]

ac·tu·ate (ak′chü āt′) *v.t.* **-at·ed, -at·ing. 1.** to put into action or motion: *A spring actuates the lock.* **2.** to incite or influence to

a	at	e	end	o	hot	u	up	hw	white		about
ā	ape	ē	me	ō	old	ū	use	ng	song	ə	taken
ä	far	i	it	ô	fork	ü	rule	th	thin		pencil
âr	care	ī	ice	oi	oil	u̇	pull	th	this		lemon
		îr	pierce	ou	out	ûr	turn	zh	measure		circus

act; motivate: *The desire for new trade routes actuated the explorers.* [Medieval Latin *actuatus,* past participle of *actuare* to perform, put in action, from Latin *āctus* a doing. See ACT.] —**ac′tu·a′tion,** *n.* —**ac′tu·a′tor,** *n.*

a·cu·i·ty (ə kū′i tē) *n.* the quality of being sharp or keen; acuteness: *acuity of vision.* [French *acuité,* going back to Latin *acūtus* sharp. See ACUTE.]

a·cu·men (ə kū′mən) *n.* keenness of insight or judgment; mental sharpness: *business acumen.* [Latin *acūmen* sharpness.]

a·cu·mi·nate (ə kū′mə nit) *adj. Botany.* tapering to a point; pointed: *acuminate leaves.* [Latin *acūminātus,* past participle of *acūmināre* to make pointed.]

a·cu·punc·ture (ak′yù pungk′chər) *n.* the practice, originally Chinese, of inserting needles into certain points on the body in order to treat diseases or to serve as an anesthetic during surgery. [Latin *acus* needle + PUNCTURE.]

a·cute (ə kūt′) *adj.* **1.** having or exhibiting keenness of discernment or insight; penetrating: *an acute mind.* **2.** particularly sensitive to impressions or stimuli: *acute hearing.* **3.** of a very high degree; intense; poignant: *acute jealousy, acute pain.* **4.** (of a disease) having a rapid onset and short duration: *acute pleurisy.* ➡ distinguished from **chronic. 5.** of utmost importance; severe; crucial: *an acute need for medical supplies.* **6.** ending in a sharp point; pointed. **7.** high in pitch: *Dogs can hear acute sounds that people cannot hear.* **8.** marked or pronounced with an acute accent ′ . **9.** (of a triangle) consisting of only acute angles. [Latin *acutus,* past participle of *acuere* to sharpen, from *acus* needle.] —**a·cute′ly,** *adv.* —**a·cute′ness,** *n.*

acute accent, a mark (′) indicating the stress, quality, length, or pitch of a vowel, as in French *lycée,* or a corresponding difference in meaning, as between Spanish *quien* (relative) and *quién* (interrogative).

acute angle, an angle whose measure is between 0 and 90 degrees. For illustration, see **angle**[1].

ad[1] (ad) *n.* **1.** advertisement. **2.** advertising.

ad[2] (ad) *n. Tennis.* advantage.

ad- *prefix* used to express direction or motion toward or nearness to: *address.* [Latin *ad* to.]

A.D., also, **AD** anno Domini; in the year of the Lord. ➡ used before a number to indicate a date occurring since the birth of Jesus: *Attila the Hun died in A.D. 453.*

ad·age (ad′ij) *n.* a familiar saying expressing popular wisdom; proverb. [French *adage,* from Latin *adagium.*] —For Synonyms, see **proverb.**

a·da·gi·o (ə dä′zhē ō′, -jē ō′) *adv. Music.* slowly; leisurely and gracefully. —*adj. Music.* slow. —*n., pl.* **-gi·os. 1.** *Music.* a composition, movement, or part in adagio tempo. **2.** a ballet dance in slow tempo. [Italian *ad agio* at ease, *agio* going back to Latin *adjacēns* nearby place (suggesting ease of access). See ADJACENT.]

ad·a·mant (ad′ə mənt, -mant′) *adj.* unwilling to change position; totally unyielding: *The judge was adamant in refusing to admit the evidence.* —*n.* a legendary substance so hard that it could not be cut or broken. [Old French *adamant* diamond, hardest metal, going back to Greek *adamās,* from *a-* not + *damân* to tame.] —**ad′a·mant·ly,** *adv.*

ad·a·man·tine (ad′ə man′tin, -tēn, -tīn) *adj.* **1.** totally unyielding; inflexible; adamant. **2.** like diamond in hardness or luster.

Ad·am's apple (ad′əmz) a projection in the throat just below the chin, formed by the largest cartilage of the larynx. [From the belief that a piece of the apple of the tree of knowledge stuck in Adam's throat.]

a·dapt (ə dapt′) *v.i.* to become accustomed to or altered in response to new circumstances or surroundings or environmental change: *They adapted easily to their new neighborhood.* —*v.t.* **1.** to change to meet new requirements or new uses: *The playwright adapted the play for television.* **2.** to make (oneself) accustomed to new circumstances or surroundings. [French *adapter* to adjust, fit, from Latin *adaptāre.*]

> **Synonyms** **Adapt, adjust,** and **accommodate** mean to change so as to fit with other persons or things. **Adapt** suggests relative ease in changing something to make it fit new conditions: *A new part was not available, so the mechanic adapted one from another engine.* **Adjust** suggests closeness of fit and the skill that may be required in obtaining it: *It took the plumber an hour to adjust the pipe to the right specifications.* **Accommodate** implies a compromise or less than perfect fit, often between markedly different things: *Accommodating the old school to use as a nursing home resulted in an inconvenient floor plan.*

a·dapt·a·ble (ə dap′tə bəl) *adj.* **1.** capable of being adapted. **2.** capable of adapting. —**a·dapt′a·bil′i·ty, a·dapt′a·ble·ness,** *n.*

ad·ap·ta·tion (ad′əp tā′shən) *n.* **1.** the act or process of adapt-

ing or the state of being adapted. **2.** something produced by adapting: *The movie is an adaptation of a play.* **3.a.** genetic modification of a species as a result of which it is better suited to survive in its environment. **b.** an instance of such modification.

a·dapt·ed (ə dap′tid) *adj.* change in response to new or different conditions; suited; fitted.

a·dapt·er (ə dap′tər) *n.* **1.** a person or thing that adapts. **2.a.** a device for modifying an apparatus for a new use. **b.** a device for connecting unmatched parts of an apparatus.

a·dapt·ive (ə dap′tiv) *adj.* **1.** characterized by or showing adaptation: *adaptive behavior, adaptive coloration.* **2.** tending or able to adapt: *the adaptive power of the mind.*

add (ad) *v.t.* **1.** to put (something) with another or others of the same kind: *to add a coin to a collection.* **2.** to join or combine (something) with something else: *to add herbs to a sauce, to add a porch to a house.* **3.** to combine (mathematical quantities) into a single sum; find the sum of (often with *up*): *to add up numbers.* **4.** to say or write further. **5.** to include; put in: *to add 8% tax to a bill.* —*v.i.* **1.** to find the sum of numbers; perform addition. **2.** to make or serve as an addition; augment (with *to*): *The balloons added to the festive atmosphere.* [Latin *addere* to put with, augment.] —**add′a·ble;** also, **add′i·ble,** *adj.*

• **to add up. a.** to equal an established or desired total: *These figures don't add up.* **b.** to be meaningful or consistent: *The facts don't add up in this case.*

• **to add up to.** to amount to or mean: *Their actions added up to a deliberate violation of the rules.*

ad·dax (ad′aks) *n.* an antelope, *Addax nasomaculatus,* of the desert regions of Arabia, Syria, and North Africa. [Latin *addāx;* of African origin.]

add·ed-val·ue tax (ad′id-val′ū) value-added tax.

ad·dend (ad′end, ə dend′) *n.* a number or algebraic expression to be added to another.

ad·den·dum (ə den′dəm) *n., pl.* **-da. 1.** something added; addition. **2.** an appendix to a written work. [Latin *addendum* something to be added, from *addere* to add.]

addax

ad·der (ad′ər) *n.* **1.** a poisonous snake, *Vipera berus,* of northern Europe and Asia, brown with black markings. Length: 2 feet (0.6 meter). **2.** the North American hognose snake. **3.** any of various snakes of Africa, esp. the puff adder. [Middle English *naddre* viper, from Old English *nædre.* The Middle English phrase *a naddre* was mistakenly divided as *an adder.*]

ad·der's-tongue (ad′ərz tung′) *n.* **1.** a fern, genus *Ophioglossum,* whose spike resembles a snake's tongue. **2.** dogtooth violet.

ad·dict (*n.,* ad′ikt; *v.,* ə dikt′) *n.* **1.** a person who is dependent on something, as a drug. **2.** a person who is strongly devoted to some activity or pastime: *a sports addict.* —*v.t.* **1.** to cause (someone) to become compulsively dependent or devoted. **2.** to allow (oneself) to become obsessive or compulsive about something. ➡ usually used in the passive: *to be addicted to watching television.* [Latin *addictus,* past participle of *addīcere* to assign to, sentence.]

ad·dict·ed (ə dik′tid) *adj.* **1.** physically or psychologically dependent on something, as a drug: *addicted to cocaine.* **2.** so devoted to something as to seem physically or psychologically dependent: *addicted to baseball.*

ad·dic·tion (ə dik′shən) *n.* the condition of being addicted, esp. to drugs; compulsive dependence.

ad·dic·tive (ə dik′tiv) *adj.* **1.** causing or tending to cause addiction: *an addictive drug.* **2.** easily addicted: *an addictive personality.*

adding machine, a machine that can add and often subtract, multiply, and divide numbers. It consists of a set of keys that, when struck, print numbers on a roll of paper. Adding machines have largely been replaced by electronic calculators.

Ad·di·son's disease (ad′ə sənz) a medical condition characterized by anemia, weakness, hypotension, and bronzing of the skin, stemming from deterioration of the cortex of the adrenal glands. [From Thomas *Addison,* 1793-1860, the English physician who first described it.]

ad·di·tion (ə dish′ən) *n.* **1.** the act or process of adding or joining. **2.** the process of combining numbers into one sum. The symbol for the process is +. **3.** something added: *The porch is a new addition.* [Latin *additiō* an adding to, from *addere* to add to.]

• **in addition.** besides; moreover.

• **in addition to.** as well as.

ad·di·tion·al (ə dish′ə nəl) *adj.* added; further. —**ad·di′tion·al·ly**, *adv.* —For Synonyms, see **extra**.

ad·di·tive (ad′i tiv) *n.* a substance used in relatively small quantities to improve or alter another substance or thing: *a fuel additive, a food additive.* —*adj.* involving or characterized by addition: *an additive compound.*

additive identity, a number that, when added to another number, produces a sum equal to that other number. Zero is the additive identity since $0 + 5 = 5$ and $3/4 + 0 = 3/4$.

additive inverse, a number, that when added to a given number, equals zero. The additive inverse of 5 is -5.

ad·dle (ad′əl) *v.t., v.i.,* **-dled, -dling. 1.** to make or become confused. **2.** (of an egg) to make or become rotten. [Middle English *adel egg* rotten egg (from Old English *adela* urine), mistranslation of Latin *urinum* (*ovum*) unhatched (egg), from Greek *ourion* (*ōion*) literally, wind egg.]

ad·dle·brained (ad′əl brānd′) *adj.* confused or absent-minded.

add-on (ad′ôn′, -on′), *n.* something added on, such as an accessory or attachment: *television add-ons.* —*adj.* added on, additional; extra: *hidden add-on costs.*

ad·dress (*n.,* ə dres′, ad′res; *v.,* ə dres′) *n.* **1.** a formal speech, usually given on a special occasion or to a particular group of people: *a commencement address.* **2.** the location of a building or a place at which a person or organization can be reached: *Our address is 105 Town Street.* **3.** the inscription on a letter, package, or other item to be delivered indicating its destination. **4.** personal manner in conversation; deportment: *the poise and address of an experienced politician.* **5.** skill in dealing with people or situations; adroitness: *to accomplish a job with address.* **6. addresses.** acts of courteous attention, esp. in courtship. **7.** a place in the memory of a computer where a particular piece of information may be found. —*v.t.* **1.** to speak formally to: *to address a convention.* **2.** to direct (writing or speech) toward (with *to*): *Both lawyers addressed closing remarks to the jury.* **3.** to direct (oneself) in speech or writing (with *to*): *Address yourself to the class.* **4.** to write the destination on (something to be delivered). **5.** to use proper forms in speaking or writing to: *How should one address a senator?* **6.** to direct the energies or attention of; apply (oneself): *to address oneself to a task.* **7.** in golf, to assume a preparatory position in order to hit (the ball). [Old French *adrecier* to straighten, direct, convey, going back to Latin *ad* to, at + *dīrēctus* straight, direct. See DIRECT.]

ad·dress·ee (ad′re sē′, ə dre sē′) *n.* a person or organization to which anything is addressed.

ad·duce (ə dūs′, ə düs′) *v.t.,* **-duced, -duc·ing.** to present as proof, reason, or example in argument. [Latin *addūcere* to lead to.]

ad·duct (ə dukt′) *v.t.* to move (a limb) toward the median axis of the body or (a finger or toe) toward the axis of the hand or foot. ➡ opposed to **abduct**. [Latin *adductus,* past participle of *addūcere* to lead to.]

ad·duc·tion (ə duk′shən) *n.* **1.** the act of adducing; presenting as evidence. **2.** the act of adducting or the state of being adducted.

ad·duc·tor (ə duk′tər) *n.* a muscle that adducts. ➡ opposed to **abductor**.

ad·e·nine (ad′ə nēn′, -nin′) *n.* a purine base that is one of the essential constituents of DNA and RNA. Formula: $C_5H_5N_5$ For illustration, see **double helix**.

ad·e·noid (ad′ə noid′) *n. usually,* **adenoids.** lymphoid tissue in the upper part of the throat, behind the nose, that is present at birth and generally shrinks in childhood. —*adj.* of or relating to adenoids. [Greek *adenoeidēs* glandular, from *adēn* gland.]

ad·e·noi·dal (ad′ə noi′dəl) *adj.* **1.** adenoid. **2.** of inflamed or enlarged adenoids or the nasal speech and obstructed breathing caused by them.

a·den·o·sine (ə den′ə sēn′, -sin) *n.* an organic compound composed of adenine and ribose from which ADP, AMP, and ATP are derived. Formula: $C_{10}H_{13}N_5O_4$ [Blend of ADENINE and *-os-* of RIBOSE.]

adenosine di·phos·phate (dī fos′fāt) see **ADP**.

adenosine mon·o·phos·phate (mon′ə fos′fāt) see **AMP**.

adenosine tri·phos·phate (trī fos′fāt) see **ATP**.

ad·e·no·vi·rus (ad′ə nō vī′rəs) *n.* any of a group of DNA-bearing viruses that can cause diseases of the respiratory tract and mucous membranes of the eye.

a·dept (*adj.,* ə dept′; *n.,* ad′ept) *adj.* highly skilled; proficient: *adept in one's work.* —*n.* a person who is proficient in some field or art; an expert: *an adept in music.* [Medieval Latin *adeptus* a title given to alchemists who supposedly had achieved the transmutation of lesser metals into gold, from Latin *adeptus,* past participle of *adipīscī* to attain.] —**a·dept′ly,** *adv.* —**a·dept′ness,** *n.* —For Synonyms *(adj.),* see **expert**.

ad·e·qua·cy (ad′i kwə sē) *n.* the state or quality of being adequate.

ad·e·quate (ad′i kwit) *adj.* **1.** providing as much as is required or needed; sufficient; suitable: *A small car is adequate for our family.* **2.** just passable; mediocre. [Latin *adaequātus,* past participle of *adaequāre* to make equal.] —**ad′e·quate·ly,** *adv.* —**ad′e·quate·ness,** *n.* —For Synonyms, see **enough**.

ad·here (ad hir′) *v.i.,* **-hered, -her·ing. 1.** to stick or hold fast: *This glue adheres to wood.* **2.** to remain bound by; observe or follow closely (with *to*): *They adhered to the terms of the contract.* **3.** to give support or loyalty: *to adhere to a political doctrine.* [Latin *adhaerēre* to stick to.]

ad·her·ence (ad hir′əns) *n.* **1.** firm attachment; faithful support: *adherence to a cause.* **2.** close observance: *adherence to procedural rules.* **3.** the act or state of adhering; adhesion.

ad·her·ent (ad hir′ənt) *n.* a firm supporter; advocate: *an adherent of free trade.* —*adj.* **1.** sticking or able to stick. **2.** bound, as by contract: *parties adherent to the agreement.*

ad·he·sion (ad hē′zhən) *n.* **1.** the act or state of sticking or holding fast. **2.** faithful attachment; adherence. **3.a.** an abnormal growing together of separate tissues or organs, as after an operation, inflammation, or injury, esp. in the abdomen. **b.** the fibrous tissue by which such parts are connected. **4.** an attraction, and the result of the attraction, between dissimilar surfaces in contact that causes them to cling to each other. [Latin *adhaesiō* a sticking to, from *adhaerēre* to stick to.]

ad·he·sive (ad hē′siv, -ziv) *adj.* **1.** tending to stick or hold fast; clinging: *Wet snow has adhesive properties.* **2.** having a sticky surface that will hold fast to something; gummed: *adhesive labels.* —*n.* **1.** an adhesive substance: *Glue is an adhesive.* **2.** adhesive tape. —**ad·he′sive·ly,** *adv.* —**ad·he′sive·ness,** *n.*

adhesive tape, tape coated on one side with a sticky substance.

ad hoc (ad hok′) for a specific and limited purpose: *an ad hoc committee.* [Latin *ad hoc* literally, to this.]

ad ho·mi·nem (ad hom′ə nem′) **1.** attacking a person who holds opposing views rather than dealing with those views on their own merit. **2.** appealing to prejudices or personal feelings rather than to intellect. [Latin *ad hominem* literally, to the man.]

ad·i·a·bat·ic (ad′ē ə bat′ik) *adj. Physics.* (of a thermodynamic process) occurring without a loss or gain of heat, as in the cylinder of a steam engine or air compressor. [Greek *adiabatos* which cannot be crossed (from *a-* not + *dia* through + *bainein* to cross) + -IC.] —**ad′i·a·bat′i·cal·ly,** *adv.*

a·dieu (ə dü′, ə dū′) *n., pl.* **a·dieus** or **a·dieux** (ə düz′, ə dūz′) *interj.* good-bye; farewell. [Old French *adieu,* standing for *à Dieu* (I commend you) to God, going back to Latin *ad Deum* to God.]

ad in·fi·ni·tum (ad′in′fə nī′təm) without limit; endlessly. [Latin *ad infīnītum* literally, to the infinite.]

ad in·ter·im (ad in′tər im) Latin. in the meantime.

a·di·os (ä′dē ōs′, ad′ē-) *n., interj.* good-bye; farewell. [Spanish *adiós,* standing for *a Dios* (I commend you) to God, going back to Latin *ad Deum* to God.]

ad·i·pose (ad′ə pōs′) *adj.* composed of or relating to animal fat; fatty. [Modern Latin *adiposus,* from Latin *adeps* fat.]

adipose tissue, loose connective tissue in which fat cells are deposited.

ad·i·pos·i·ty (ad′ə pos′i tē) *n.* **1.** fatness; obesity. **2.** a tendency to become obese.

ad·it (ad′it) *n.* a nearly horizontal tunnel leading from the surface into a mine. [Latin *aditus* approach.]

adj. 1. adjective. **2.** adjourned. **3.** adjunct. **4.** adjustment.

ad·ja·cen·cy (ə jā′sən sē) *n., pl.* **-cies. 1.** the state of being adjacent; nearness; proximity: *the adjacency of the land to water.* **2.** something that lies near.

ad·ja·cent (ə jā′sənt) *adj.* lying next to or near; neighboring: *The fire spread to the adjacent field.* [Latin *adjacēns,* present participle of *adjacēre* to lie near, from *ad* to, at + *jacēre* to lie still.] —**ad·ja′cent·ly,** *adv.*

Synonyms **Adjacent, adjoining,** and **contiguous** refer to physical closeness. **Adjacent** is used of things that are near each other but do not necessarily touch: *The bride and groom come from adjacent towns.* **Adjoining** usually implies direct contact or very slight separation, as by a wall or fence: *The terrace and adjoining lawn overlook the sea.* **Contiguous** suggests continuing contact between two things, as along a line: *The United States and Canada are contiguous for thousands of miles.*

a	at	e	end	o	hot	u	up	hw	white		about
ā	ape	ē	me	ō	old	ū	use	ng	song		taken
ä	far	i	it	ô	fork	ü	rule	th	thin	ə	pencil
âr	care	ī	ice	oi	oil	u̇	pull	th	this		lemon
		îr	pierce	ou	out	ûr	turn	zh	measure		circus

adjacent angles, two angles having the same vertex and a common side.

ad·jec·ti·val (aj'ik tī'vəl) *adj.* **1**. of, belonging to, or resembling an adjective: *an adjectival suffix.* **2**. functioning as an adjective: *an adjectival phrase.*

ad·jec·ti·val·ly (aj'ik tī'və lē) *adv.* as an adjective: *a noun used adjectivally.*

ad·jec·tive (aj'ik tiv) *n.* any of a class of words that modify nouns or pronouns. An adjective may describe the word it modifies (*red* car, *sad* boy) or may limit the word (*that* pen, *her* bat, *many* books, *three* dogs). —*adj.* **1**. having the quality of or functioning as an adjective. **2**. depending on something else; secondary. [Late Latin *adjectīvum (verbum)* added (word), going back to Latin *adjectus,* past participle of *adicere* to cast beside, place beside.]

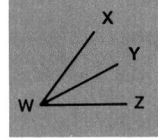

adjacent angles: *XWY* and *YWZ*

ad·join (ə join') *v.t.* **1**. to be next to; touch on; be contiguous to: *The garage adjoins the house.* **2**. to attach by joining; affix. —*v.i.* to be close together or touching: *Their farms adjoin.* [Old French *ajoindre* to join, from Latin *adjungere* to join to.]

ad·join·ing (ə joi'ning) *adj.* located next to or near; adjacent. —For Synonyms, see **adjacent.**

ad·journ (ə jûrn') —*v.t.* **1**. to put off to a later time; postpone; defer: *The hearing was adjourned until next week.* **2**. to suspend the work or proceedings of (a group or formal body). —*v.i.* **1**. to suspend work or proceedings: *The senate adjourned for the summer.* **2**. to go from one place to another: *Let's adjourn to the dining room.* [Old French *ajorner* to postpone (to an appointed day), going back to Latin *ad* to + Late Latin *diurnum* day, from Latin *diurnus* daily.]

ad·journ·ment (ə jûrn'mənt) *n.* **1**. the act of adjourning: *The chairperson called for a vote on adjournment.* **2.a**. the state of being adjourned: *The adjournment of the case lasted for two weeks.* **b**. an interval during which a group or formal body is adjourned: *a month's adjournment.*

ad·judge (ə juj') *v.t.,* **-judged, -judg·ing. 1**. to decide or settle judicially; adjudicate. **2**. to pronounce or decree judicially; rule: *to adjudge a contract as invalid.* **3**. to condemn or sentence (with *to*): *adjudged to life in prison.* **4**. to award or grant judicially: *to adjudge a sum of money to a plaintiff.* **5**. to judge to be; deem; consider. [Old French *ajuger* to bring to trial, sentence, decide, from Latin *adjūdicāre* to award, assign, going back to *ad* to, at + *judex* judge.]

ad·ju·di·cate (ə jū'di kāt') *v.,* **-cat·ed, -cat·ing.** —*v.t.* to consider and decide or settle judicially: *to adjudicate a case.* —*v.i.* to act as judge; pronounce judgment: *to adjudicate in a dispute.*

[Latin *adjūdicātus,* past participle of *adjūdicāre* to award, assign. See ADJUDGE.] —**ad·ju'di·ca'tor,** *n.*

ad·ju·di·ca·tion (ə jū'di kā'shən) *n.* **1**. the act or process of adjudicating. **2**. a decision or decree of a judge or court.

ad·junct (aj'ungkt) *n.* **1**. something that is secondary or auxiliary to another, less important thing. **2**. a person acting as a subordinate or assistant to someone else. **3**. a dependent word or phrase added to another word or phrase as a modifier. —*adj.* joined or associated in a secondary role: *an adjunct professor.* [Latin *adjūnctus,* past participle of *adjungere* to join to.]

ad·ju·ra·tion (aj'ə rā'shən) *n.* **1**. a solemn charge or order. **2**. an earnest request or appeal.

ad·jure (ə jūr') *v.t.,* **-jured, -jur·ing. 1**. to order or charge solemnly, esp. on oath or threat of penalty: *to adjure a witness to testify truthfully.* **2**. to urge seriously; request earnestly: *My friends adjured me to be careful when surfing.* [Latin *adjūrāre* to swear to.]

ad·just (ə just') *v.t.* **1**. to arrange or alter to fit or accommodate a need or requirement: *to adjust one's position for a clearer view.* **2**. to arrange properly or regulate for proper functioning: *to adjust one's clothes, to adjust the lens of a camera.* **3.a**. to arrange satisfactory terms of agreement or settlement of: *to adjust an insurance claim.* **b**. to make correct, as records; rectify: *to adjust an account to reflect a credit.* —*v.i.* to adapt oneself; become accustomed: *to adjust to a new climate.* [Old French *adjuster* to adjust, gauge.] —**ad·just'a·ble,** *adj.* —For Synonyms, see **adapt.**

ad·just·er (ə jus'tər) *also,* **ad·jus·tor.** *n.* **1**. a thing or part used to make an adjustment, as a mechanical device. **2**. someone who rectifies or settles: *an insurance claims adjuster.*

ad·just·ment (ə just'mənt) *n.* **1**. the process of adjusting; adaptation: *a slow adjustment to new surroundings.* **2**. the state of being adjusted for proper functioning: *perfect adjustment of an instrument.* **3**. a method or device by which something is adjusted or regulated: *the adjustments on a microscope.* **4.a**. the process of determining the amount to be paid in settling a claim. **b**. the amount paid. **5**. a change made to meet new conditions; modification: *to make adjustments on the basis of new data.*

ad·ju·tant (aj'ə tənt) *n.* **1**. a military staff officer who acts as administrative assistant to a commanding officer. **2**. an aide; assistant. [Latin *adjūtāns,* present participle of *adjūtāre* to assist, from *adjuvāre* to help.] —**ad'ju·tan·cy,** *n.*

adjutant general *pl.* **adjutants general. 1**. the chief officer of the administrative branch of the U.S. Army. **2**. the adjutant of any U.S. Army unit having a general staff.

adjutant stork, marabou. Also, **adjutant bird.**

ad·ju·vant (aj'ə vənt) *n.* a person or thing that helps or assists, esp. a substance added to a drug to facilitate its action. —*adj.*

Adjectives

Many pairs of adjectives and nouns are related both in meaning and spelling, for example *shade* and *shady*. Others, however, are closely related in meaning but differ in spelling, because each word developed from a different language of origin, or came into English at a different time or through one or more other languages. Many of these adjectives came into English from a foreign language, such as Latin or French, and became associated with an English noun of similar meaning. Although many are in common use today (e.g., *canine* for dog, *dental* for tooth, *visual* for sight), some continue to be used primarily in literature, (e.g., *verdant* for green) or in science (e.g., *igneous* for fire). Below are some nouns and their related adjectives.

NOUN — ADJECTIVE	NOUN — ADJECTIVE	NOUN — ADJECTIVE	NOUN — ADJECTIVE
ape — simian	farewell — valedictory	law — legal	sight — visual
bear — ursine	father — paternal	lung — pulmonary	skin — dermal
birth — natal	finance — fiscal	machine — mechanical	skull — cranial
brother — fraternal	finger — digital	moon — lunar	smell — olfactory
cat — feline	fire — igneous	mother — maternal	sound — acoustic
chest — pectoral	flesh — carnal	mouth — oral	spine — vertebrate
child — filial	flood — diluvial	nerve — neural	spring — vernal
church — ecclesiastical	forest — sylvan	night — nocturnal	stamp — philatelic
city — urban	governor — gubernatorial	nose — nasal	star — stellar
coin — numismatic	green — verdant	noun — nominal	stomach — gastric
commerce — mercantile	hand — manual	number — numerical	sun — solar
cooking — culinary	head — cephalic	pig — porcine	tooth — dental
cow — bovine	hearing — acoustic	poison — toxic	touch — tactile
day — diurnal	heart — cardiac	pope — papal	tree — arboreal
devil — diabolic	heat — thermal	pottery — ceramic	two — binary
dog — canine	home — domestic	punishment — penal	uncle — avuncular
ear — aural	horse — equine	royalty — regal	vein — venous
earth — terrestrial	inheritance — hereditary	salt — saline	voice — vocal
earthquake — seismic	kidney — renal	sea — marine	war — martial
education — scholastic	kitchen — culinary	ship — naval	water — aquatic
eye — optic	language — linguistic	side — lateral	year — annual

A

1. serving as an aid; helping; auxiliary. **2.** using drugs or other treatment to supplement cancer surgery: *adjuvant therapy.* [Latin *adjūvāns,* present participle of *adjūvāre* to help, assist.]

ad-lib (ad′lib′) *v.t., v.i.,* **-libbed, -lib·bing.** to say or do something without previous preparation; improvise: *to ad-lib a speech, to ad-lib a song.* —*n.* something improvised, esp. repartee on the stage. —*adj.* done or said without preparation; improvised. [From AD LIBITUM.]

ad lib, in an improvised way; spontaneously.

ad lib., ad libitum.

ad lib·i·tum (ad lib′i təm) *Music.* as one wishes. ➡ used to indicate that the performer is free to vary, expand, or omit a passage. [Modern Latin *ad libitum* at (one's) pleasure.]

adm. 1. administrative. **2.** administrator.

Adm. 1. Admiral. **2.** Admiralty.

Ad·me·tus (ad mē′təs) *n.* in Greek legend, a king of Thessaly and the husband of Alcestis.

ad·min·is·ter (ad min′ə stər) —*v.t.* **1.** to control the operation of; manage; direct: *to administer the sales department.* **2.** to give or apply, esp. while controlling the use or amount of: *The doctor administered the medication to the patient.* **3.** to give out; dispense or deliver: *to administer aid in a disaster area, to administer a blow.* **4.** to give or offer formally: *to administer an oath of office.* **5.** *Law.* to manage or settle (an estate). —*v.i.* **1.** to be of beneficial service; minister; contribute (with *to*): *to administer to the well-being of the community.* **2.** to act as an administrator or executor. [Old French *aministrer* to take care of, manage, from Latin *administrāre* to manage.] —For Synonyms *(v.t.),* see **manage.**

ad·min·is·trate (ad min′ə strāt′) *v.t., v.i.,* **-trat·ed, -trat·ing.** to administer.

ad·min·is·tra·tion (ad min′ə strā′shən) *n.* **1.** the act or method of managing or directing a business, organization, or the like. **2.** a group of persons empowered to manage and direct; officials: *the school's administration.* **3.** operation and execution of governmental affairs. **4.a.** the executive branch of a government, esp. one in power for a certain period. **b.** *also,* **Administration.** the president of the United States, the cabinet, and other executive officers. **5.** the period during which a chief executive holds office. **6.** the act of administering something to others, as an oath, medicine, or justice.

ad·min·is·tra·tive (ad min′ə strā′tiv) *adj.* of or relating to administration or management. —**ad·min·is·tra′tive·ly,** *adv.*

ad·min·is·tra·tor (ad min′ə strā′tər) *n.* **1.** a person who administers. **2.** a person appointed by a law court to manage or settle the estate of someone who has died. ➡ distinguished from **executor.**

ad·min·is·tra·trix (ad min′ə strā′triks) *n., pl.* **-is·tra·tri·ces** (-ə strā′trə sēz′, -ə strə trī′sēz). a woman who is administrator of an estate.

ad·mi·ra·ble (ad′mər ə bəl) *adj.* **1.** deserving admiration. **2.** excellent. [French *admirable,* from Latin *admīrābilis,* from *admīrārī* to marvel at.] —**ad′mi·ra·ble·ness,** *n.* —**ad′mi·ra·bly,** *adv.*

ad·mi·ral (ad′mər əl) *n.* **1.** the commander in chief of a fleet. **2.** *U.S. Navy.* **a.** an officer of the second highest rank, below a fleet admiral. **b.** fleet admiral, vice admiral, or rear admiral. **3.** either of two species of brightly colored butterflies: the **red admiral,** *Vanessa atalanta,* or the **white admiral,** *Limenitis arthemis.* [Middle French *amiral* high-ranking naval officer, going back to Arabic *amīr-al-* commander of the (as in *amīr-al-bahr* commander of the sea).]

ad·mi·ral·ty (ad′mər əl tē) *n., pl.* **-ties. 1.a.** the branch of law that deals with matters involving ships and shipping. **b.** the court that administers it. **2.** *also,* **Admiralty.** formerly, the department or officials of the British government appointed to administer naval affairs.

ad·mi·ra·tion (ad′mə rā′shən) *n.* **1.** a feeling of high regard or esteem: *She earned the admiration of all who knew her.* **2.** the act of viewing something with appreciation and delight: *admiration of a beautiful painting.* **3.** an object of appreciation or respect: *He is the admiration of his friends.* **4.** *Archaic.* wonder; awe. [Latin *admīrātiō* an admiring, from *admīrārī* to marvel at.]

ad·mire (ad mīr′) *v.t.,* **-mired, -mir·ing. 1.** to feel high regard or esteem for. **2.** to regard with delight and pleasurable appreciation. **3.** *Archaic.* to marvel at. [Latin *admīrārī* to marvel at.] —**ad·mir′ing·ly,** *adv.*

ad·mir·er (ad mīr′ər) *n.* **1.** a person who admires. **2.** a man who is in love with, or courts, a woman; suitor.

ad·mis·si·bil·i·ty (ad mis′ə bil′i tē) *n.* the state or quality of being admissible.

ad·mis·si·ble (ad mis′ə bəl) *adj.* **1.** that can be properly al-

lowed or considered, as in a legal proceeding: *an admissible argument.* **2.** qualifying for admission to something: *New states are admissible by a vote in Congress.* —**ad·mis′si·ble·ness,** *n.* —**ad·mis′si·bly,** *adv.*

ad·mis·sion (ad mish′ən) *n.* **1.a.** the act of granting or the state or fact of being granted entrance or formal acceptance: *The small school's admission of students is limited to fifty applicants. We celebrated my admission to the college.* **b.** permission to function, as in some professional capacity: *admission to medical practice.* **2.** the privilege or right to enter or use: *to have admission to a club.* **3.** a fee required for entrance: *Admission is two dollars.* **4.** the act of admitting the truth or relevance of something: *The suspect's admission provided a break in the case.* **5.** something admitted: *an admission of guilt, the admission of an argument in debate.* [Latin *admissiō* a letting in.]

> **Synonyms** **Admission** and **admittance,** meaning right of entry to a place, differ in use. **Admission** is the more general term, and implies privileges and duties that go along with entry: *The ticket provides admission to the park and has the rules printed on the back.* **Admittance** refers specifically to physical entry: *I went all the way around the building but could not gain admittance at any door.*

ad·mit (ad mit′) *v.,* **-mit·ted, -mit·ting.** —*v.t.* **1.a.** to grant entrance to; let in: *to admit one person at a time, to admit fresh air.* **b.** to allow to function, as in some professional capacity: *to admit an attorney to practice before the Supreme Court.* **2.** to agree to the truth or relevance of; acknowledge; confess: *to admit one's guilt, to admit that someone else is right.* **3.** to accept or recognize as valid or relevant: *to admit evidence in a trial.* **4.** to be the means of entrance for: *This pass will admit you to the show.* **5.** to have the room to hold; accommodate: *The room admits 500 people.* —*v.i.* **1.** to allow the possibility (with *of*): *Your outrageous behavior admits of no apology.* **2.** to provide access to; open on (with *to*): *The hatchway admits to the engine room.* [Latin *admittere* to let in.]

> **Synonyms** **Admit, acknowledge,** and **confess** mean to tell the truth that one had not wanted to reveal about something. **Admit** suggests a force, usually external but sometimes from within oneself, compelling the revelation: *Your arguments are so logical I'll have to admit that you must be right.* **Acknowledge** stresses that one has known something but has kept it concealed: *Sam acknowledged that he was behind the joke.* **Confess** usually implies that one knows the thing concealed to be wrong or at least that one has trouble revealing it: *Ingrid finally summoned up the courage to confess to breaking the vase.*

ad·mit·tance (ad mit′əns) *n.* **1.** permission to enter; privilege of entrance. **2.** the act of admitting or the state of being admitted. —For Synonyms, see **admission.**

ad·mit·ted·ly (ad mit′id lē) *adv.* by common acknowledgment or one's own admission: *The witness was admittedly confused.*

ad·mix (ad miks′) *v.t., v.i.* to mix into something else; blend.

ad·mix·ture (ad miks′chər) *n.* **1.** something added in mixing; additive, alloy, or adulterant. **2.** the act of mixing. **3.** something formed by mixing; mixture. [Latin *admixtus,* past participle of *admiscēre* to mix with.]

ad·mon·ish (ad mon′ish) *v.t.* **1.** to caution, as against a specific action; warn: *We were admonished not to cut class again.* **2.** to reprimand mildly: *The lifeguard admonished the children for splashing water at each other.* **3.** to advise strongly. [Old French *amonester* to warn, going back to Latin *admonēre* to remind, warn.] —**ad·mon′ish·er,** *n.* —**ad·mon′ish·ment,** *n.*

ad·mo·ni·tion (ad′mə nish′ən) *n.* **1.** the act of admonishing; warning. **2.** a mild reprimand. [Latin *admonitiō* a calling to mind, from *admonēre* to remind.]

ad·mon·i·to·ry (ad mon′i tôr′ē) *adj.* expressing admonition; cautioning; warning: *an admonitory tone of voice.* —**ad·mon′i·to′ri·ly,** *adv.*

ad nau·se·am (ad nô′zē əm) to a disgusting extent. [Latin *ad nauseam* to the point of nausea.]

a·do (ə dü′) *n.* excitement or bother; fuss; to-do: *much ado about nothing.* [Middle English *at do* to do.]

a·do·be (ə dō′bē) *n.* **1.** sun-dried brick, used as a building material. **2.** the clay or soil from which these bricks are made.

a	at	e	end	o	hot	u	up	hw	white		about
ā	ape	ē	me	ō	old	ū	use	ng	song	ə	taken
ä	far	i	it	ô	fork	ü	rule	th	thin		pencil
âr	care	ī	ice	oi	oil	ù	pull	th	this		lemon
		îr	pierce	ou	out	ûr	turn	zh	measure		circus

17

adobe house

3. a building made of such bricks. —*adj.* constructed of adobe: *an adobe house.* [Spanish *adobe* sun-dried brick, from Arabic *at-tōb* the brick, from Coptic *tōb* brick.]

ad·o·les·cence (ad′ə les′əns) *n.* **1.** the period or process of human development from puberty to adulthood. **2.** the state or condition of being adolescent.

ad·o·les·cent (ad′ə les′ənt) *n.* a person between puberty and adulthood. —*adj.* **1.** in the stage of human development from puberty to adulthood. **2.** characteristic of or having to do with adolescence or an adolescent; youthful; immature: *adolescent skin problems, adolescent behavior.* [Latin *adolēscēns,* present participle of *adolēscere* to grow up.]

A·don·is (ə don′is, ə dō′nis) *n.* **1.** in classical mythology, a handsome youth who was loved by Aphrodite and Persephone. **2.** any handsome young man. [Latin *Adōnis,* through Greek, from Phoenician *adōn* lord, a title given to one of the Phoenicians′ gods.]

a·dopt (ə dopt′) *v.t.* **1.** to accept and take as one′s own; embrace: *to adopt a faith.* **2.** to accept by formal vote: *The board adopted the proposal after much debate.* **3.** to take (a child of other parents) into one′s family, esp. by a formal legal act. **4.** to select, esp. a textbook, for required use in a U.S. school system. [Latin *adoptāre* to adopt a child, from *ad* to + *optāre* to choose.] —**a·dopt′a·bil′i·ty,** *n.* —**a·dopt′a·ble,** *adj.* —**a·dopt′er,** *n.*

> **Synonyms** **Adopt, assume,** and **embrace** mean to take something as one′s own. **Adopt** is the general term: *The band adopted red uniforms.* **Assume** often implies pretense or the taking of something undeserved: *The escaped convict assumed a new identity. They had the nerve to assume the role of hosts at our party.* **Embrace** emphasizes the enthusiasm or completeness with which something is adopted: *Many young artists eagerly embraced the new style.*

a·dop·tee (ə dop tē′) *n.* a person who has been adopted.

a·dop·tion (ə dop′shən) *n.* **1.** the act of adopting or the state of being adopted. **2.** the legal act of assuming parenthood of a child who is not one′s own.

a·dop·tive (ə dop′tiv) *adj.* **1.** related by adoption: *adoptive parents.* **2.** associated with adoption: *adoptive procedures.* —**a·dop′tive·ly,** *adv.*

a·dor·a·ble (ə dôr′ə bəl) *adj.* **1.** very pleasing; delightful; charming: *an adorable child.* **2.** worthy of adoration. —**a·dor′a·bly,** *adv.*

ad·o·ra·tion (ad′ə rā′shən) *n.* **1.** the act of honoring or worshiping or of being honored or worshiped as divine: *the adoration of idols.* **2.** reverent love and devotion.

a·dore (ə dôr′) *v.t.,* **a·dored, a·dor·ing. 1.** to have love and admiration for; idolize: *They adored their teacher.* **2.** to honor as divine; worship. **3.** *Informal.* to have a great liking for: *I adore your hat.* [Latin *adōrāre* to address, worship, going back to *ad* to + *ōs* (stem *ōr-*) mouth (in the sense of using the mouth, or kissing, in religious observance).] —**a·dor′er,** *n.* —**a·dor′ing·ly,** *adv.*

a·dorn (ə dôrn′) *v.t.* **1.** to add or lend beauty, honor, or distinction to; enhance: *That model′s face has adorned many magazine covers.* **2.** to make beautiful or decorate: *to adorn a room with flowers.* [Old French *adorner* to provide, decorate, from Latin *adōrnāre.*] —**a·dorn′er,** *n.* —For Synonyms, see **decorate.**

a·dorn·ment (ə dôrn′mənt) *n.* **1.** something that adorns; ornament: *adornments for one′s hair.* **2.** the act of adorning or the state of being adorned.

a·down (ə doun′) *adv., prep. Archaic.* down.

ADP 1. adenosine diphosphate, a nucleotide that stores energy while being converted to ATP by combination with a phosphate group. Formula: $C_{10}H_{15}N_5O_{10}P_2$ **2.** automatic data processing.

ad·re·nal (ə drē′nəl) *adj.* **1.** near or on the kidneys. **2.** relating

to or from the adrenal glands. —*n.* an adrenal gland. [Latin *ad* at + Late Latin *rēnālis* of the kidneys, from Latin *rēnēs* kidneys.]

adrenal gland, one of a pair of small ductless glands that are located above the kidneys and that secrete several hormones, including adrenaline. Also, **suprarenal gland.**

ad·ren·a·line (ə dren′ə lin) *also,* **ad·ren·a·lin.** *n.* **1.** a hormone secreted by the medulla of the adrenal glands, esp. under conditions of excitement, danger, or stress, that affects the body as a stimulant, producing changes that enable it to deal more effectively with an emergency. **2.** a synthetic drug used as a stimulant, esp. for the heart. *Trademark:* **Adrenalin.** Also, **epinephrine.**

ad·ren·er·gic (ad′rə nûr′jik) *adj.* of, producing, or activated by adrenaline or a similar substance, as certain kinds of nerve fibers. ➡ distinguished from **cholinergic.**

a·dre·no·cor·ti·cal (ə drē′nō kôr′ti kəl) *adj.* of, relating to, or secreted by the cortex of the adrenal glands: *adrenocortical hormones.*

a·drift (ə drift′) *adv., adj.* **1.** (of a ship or other floating object) without being moored or steered; drifting with the current. **2.** without direction or purpose.

a·droit (ə droit′) *adj.* smoothly skillful; deft: *adroit in the use of tools.* [French *adroit,* from *à droit* rightly, properly, going back to Latin *ad* to + *dīrēctus* straight, right.] —**a·droit′ly,** *adv.* —**a·droit′ness,** *n.* —For Synonyms, see **clever.**

ad·sorb (ad sôrb′, -zôrb′) *v.t.* to retain (a gas, liquid, or dissolved substance) in a thin layer on the surface of a solid substance. ➡ distinguished from **absorb.** [Latin *ad* to + *sorbēre* to suck.]

ad·sor·bate (ad sôr′bāt, -bit, -zôr′-) *n.* a solid, liquid, or gas that is adsorbed.

ad·sor·bent (ad sôr′bənt, -zôr′-) *adj.* able to adsorb. —*n.* a liquid or solid that adsorbs.

ad·sorp·tion (ad sôrp′shən, -zôrp′-) *n.* the process of adsorbing or the state of being adsorbed.

ad·sorp·tive (ad sôrp′tiv, -zôrp′-) *adj.* **1.** relating to adsorption. **2.** able to adsorb.

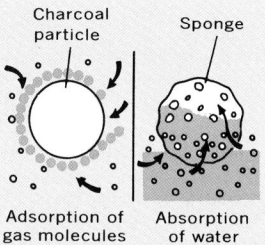

Charcoal particle   Sponge

Adsorption of gas molecules   Absorption of water

adsorption

ad·u·late (aj′ə lāt′) *v.t.,* **-lat·ed, -lat·ing.** to praise or admire excessively: *fans adulating a celebrity.* [Latin *adūlātus,* past participle of *adūlārī* to flatter.] —**ad′u·la′tor,** *n.*

ad·u·la·tion (aj′ə lā′shən) *n.* excessive praise or flattery.

ad·u·la·to·ry (aj′ə lə tôr′ē) *adj.* excessively praising or flattering.

a·dult (ə dult′, ad′ult) *n.* **1.** a grown man or woman; mature person. **2.** a plant or animal that has reached full growth. **3.** a person who is legally of age. ➡ opposed to **minor.** —*adj.* **1.** having attained maturity; fully grown. **2.** of, characteristic of, or for adults. [Latin *adultus* grown up, past participle of *adolescere* to grow up.] —**a·dult′ness,** *n.*

adult education, continuing education *(def. 1).*

a·dul·ter·ant (ə dul′tər ənt) *n.* a substance or element that adulterates.

a·dul·ter·ate (ə dul′tə rāt′) *v.t.,* **-at·ed, -at·ing.** to lessen the quality or purity of (something) by including in it inferior or inappropriate substances or elements. [Latin *adulterātus,* past participle of *adulterāre* to corrupt, literally, to change to something other (for the worse), going back to Latin *ad* to + *alter* other.] —**a·dul′ter·a′tor,** *n.*

a·dul·ter·a·tion (ə dul′tə rā′shən) *n.* **1.** the act or process of adulterating or the fact of being adulterated. **2.** an adulterated substance or product.

a·dul·ter·er (ə dul′tər ər) *n.* a person who commits adultery, esp. a man.

a·dul·ter·ess (ə dul′tər is, -tris) *n.* a woman who commits adultery.

a·dul·ter·ous (ə dul′tər əs) *adj.* **1.** inclined to or guilty of adultery. **2.** characterized by or concerning adultery. —**a·dul′ter·ous·ly,** *adv.*

a·dul·ter·y (ə dul′tə rē) *n., pl.* **-ter·ies.** voluntary sexual intercourse of a married person with anyone except his or her spouse. [Modification of Old French *avouterie,* influenced by Latin *adulterium,* both going back to Latin *ad* to + *alter* other.]

a·dult·hood (ə dult′hùd′) *n.* **1.** the state or condition of being an adult; maturity: *to reach adulthood.* **2.** the time of being an adult.

ad·um·brate (a dum′brāt, ad′əm brāt′) *v.t.,* **-brat·ed, -brat·ing. 1.** to suggest faintly or sketchily. **2.** to suggest beforehand;

A

foreshadow. **3.** to cast a shadow over; obscure; overshadow. [Latin *adumbrātus,* past participle of *adumbrāre* to overshadow, cast a shadow over.] —**ad·um·bra'tion,** *n.* —**ad·um'bra·tive,** *adj.* —**ad·um'bra·tive·ly,** *adv.*

adv. 1. adverb. **2.** adverbial. **3.** advertisement.

ad val., ad valorem.

ad va·lo·rem (ad'və lôr'əm) (of merchandise) in proportion to the value: *an ad valorem tax.* [Latin *ad valorem* (according to) value.]

ad·vance (ad vans') *v.,* **-vanced, -vanc·ing.** —*v.t.* **1.** to bring or move (something) forward: *to advance the hands on a clock.* **2.** to help the growth or progress of; further: *to advance the cause of justice.* **3.** to put forward for consideration; offer; propose: *to advance a theory.* **4.** to raise to a higher or more favorable position or rank: *The recording advanced the pianist to stardom.* **5.** to raise the rate or amount of; increase: *to advance the price of beef.* **6.** to make earlier, as a time, date, or event: *to advance a wedding from June 30 to June 12.* **7.** to pay (money) before it is earned or due: *to advance an author money against royalties.* **8.** to give on condition of repayment; lend: *to advance a friend money until payday.* —*v.i.* **1.** to move forward; proceed: *They advanced through the crowd.* **2.** to make progress; improve; grow. **3.** to move up (in position, rank, or esteem): *to advance rapidly in a job.* **4.** to increase in price, rate, or value: *Railroad stocks advanced this week.* **5.** (of color) to appear to move toward the viewer: *Red advances while black recedes.* —*n.* **1.** movement forward in space. **2.** movement toward a better or higher state of development; progress; improvement: *advances in medical knowledge.* **3.** an increase in price, value, or amount. **4. advances.** attempts to establish friendship, accord, or understanding; personal overtures. **5.a.** a payment or provision given before due or without immediate return of goods, services, or other repayment. **b.** money given on condition of repayment; loan. —*adj.* **1.** ahead of time; early: *an advance sale, advance notice.* **2.** situated in front; preceding: *an advance scout, an advance position.* [Old French *avancier* to set out before (someone), going back to Latin *abante* away before.]
• **in advance. a.** ahead of time: *to pay in advance.* **b.** in front: *I walked in advance and my friends followed.*

Synonyms *v.i.* **Advance, proceed,** and **progress** mean to move forward. **Advance** implies movement toward some definite goal or over a measured course: *to advance toward one's destination, to advance through school.* **Proceed** does not necessarily imply a goal but suggests the presence or possibility of stops or difficulties: *The meeting proceeded after the demonstrators were removed.* **Progress** suggests a goal and adds the implication of regular, methodical movement toward it: *The repairs on the bridge progressed slowly from month to month.*

ad·vanced (ad vanst') *adj.* **1.** ahead of others; modern; progressive: *an advanced society, advanced social concepts.* **2.** past the elementary; not primary: *an advanced skier, advanced algebra.* **3.** near the end in development or time: *at an advanced age.* **4.** situated in front; moved forward: *an advanced position.*

advanced standing, credit given to a student by a college or school for work done in another school.

advance guard, a body of troops going before the main force.

ad·vance·ment (ad vans'mənt) *n.* **1.** movement toward a higher or better state; progress; improvement. **2.** promotion to a higher rank or position: *a job with opportunities for advancement.* **3.** movement forward in space.

ad·van·tage (ad van'tij) *n.* **1.** a useful or beneficial circumstance, factor, or event; asset: *Not having to own a car is an advantage of living in the city.* **2.** benefit; gain: *More practice will be to your advantage.* **3.** a better position; superiority (often with *of* or *over*): *The invaders had an overwhelming advantage over the natives.* **4.** *Tennis.* the first point after deuce. —*v.t.,* **-taged, -tag·ing.** to be of aid to; benefit. [Old French *avantage* advance, head start, going back to Latin *abante* away before.]
• **to advantage.** favorably; effectively: *to display a painting to advantage.*
• **to take advantage of. a.** to use profitably. **b.** to exploit unfairly. —For Synonyms, see **benefit.**

ad·van·ta·geous (ad'vən tā'jəs) *adj.* affording an advantage; favorable; beneficial. —**ad·van·ta'geous·ly,** *adv.* —**ad'van·ta'geous·ness,** *n.*

ad·vec·tion (ad vek'shən) *n.* the horizontal movement of an atmospheric property, as temperature or humidity, by air currents. [AD- + (CON)VECTION.]

ad·vent (ad'vent) *n.* **1.** an arrival; coming: *the advent of old age, the advent of spring.* **2. Advent. a.** the birth of Jesus. **b.** a period of religious observance including the four Sundays before Christmas. **c.** Second Coming. [Latin *adventus* arrival, from *advenire* to happen.]

Ad·vent·ist (ad'ven tist, ad ven'-) *n.* a member of a Christian

denomination believing that the Second Coming will soon occur. —**Ad'vent·ism,** *n.*

ad·ven·ti·tious (ad'ven tish'əs) *adj.* **1.** added by accident from another source; not essential or intrinsic. **2.** (of part of a plant or animal) appearing out of the usual or normal place, as buds growing from the roots of a plant. [Latin *adventīcius* coming from abroad, foreign.] —**ad'ven·ti'tious·ly,** *adv.* —**ad'ven·ti'tious·ness,** *n.*

ad·ven·tive (ad ven'tiv) *adj.* (of plants or animals) in a new environment; not native or not yet naturalized; exotic.

Advent Sunday, the first Sunday in Advent.

ad·ven·ture (ad ven'chər) *n.* **1.** a difficult and perilous undertaking involving risk; hazardous venture. **2.** a liking for dangerous or exciting activity: *The first airplane pilots had a great spirit of adventure.* **3.** a thrilling or unusual experience: *A day in the city is always an adventure for us.* **4.** a business venture involving risk; speculative undertaking. —*v.,* **-tured, -tur·ing.** —*v.i.* **1.** to take risks; venture. **2.** to seek hazardous or thrilling experiences. —*v.t.* to venture; risk. [Old French *aventure* chance, mischance, from Latin *(rēs) adventūra* (thing) about to happen, feminine future participle of *advenīre* to happen.]

ad·ven·tur·er (ad ven'chər ər) *n.* **1.** a person who engages in or seeks adventures. **2.** soldier of fortune. **3.** a person who uses questionable or deceitful means to make money or get ahead.

ad·ven·ture·some (ad ven'chər səm) *adj.* eager for adventure; adventurous.

ad·ven·tur·ess (ad ven'chər is) *n.* a female adventurer, esp. a woman who schemes or uses her charms to obtain wealth or social position.

ad·ven·tur·ous (ad ven'chər əs) *adj.* **1.** eager for adventure; willing to encounter danger: *an adventurous explorer.* **2.** full of danger; hazardous. —**ad·ven'tur·ous·ly,** *adv.* —**ad·ven'tur·ous·ness,** *n.*

ad·verb (ad'vûrb') *n.* any of a class of words that modify verbs, adjectives, other adverbs, or phrases or clauses, indicating such ideas as time, place, degree, or manner. [Latin *adverbium.*]

ad·ver·bi·al (ad vûr'bē əl) *adj.* **1.** of or belonging to an adverb: *an adverbial suffix.* **2.** functioning as an adverb: *an adverbial clause.* —**ad·ver'bi·al·ly,** *adv.*

ad·ver·sar·y (ad'vər ser'ē) *n., pl.* **-sar·ies.** a person or group that is hostile or competing; opponent; enemy. [Old French *adversarie,* from Latin *adversārius.*] —For Synonyms, see **opponent.**

ad·ver·sa·tive (ad vûr'sə tiv) *adj.* (of words or propositions) expressing opposition or antithesis. *But* is an adversative conjunction. —*n.* an adversative word or proposition. —**ad·ver'sa·tive·ly,** *adv.*

ad·verse (ad vûrs', ad'vûrs) *adj.* **1.** unfavorable to one's interests or what is desired: *adverse circumstances.* **2.** not friendly; antagonistic; hostile: *an adverse attitude.* **3.** acting in an opposite or contrary direction, esp. so as to hinder; opposite: *adverse winds.* **4.** causing harm or being harmful; injurious: *the adverse effects of a drug.* [Old French *advers* opposite, hostile, from Latin *adversus* opposite, hostile, past participle of *advertere* to turn to.] —**ad·verse'ly,** *adv.* —**ad·verse'ness,** *n.*

Synonyms **Adverse** and **averse** refer to a state of being against someone or something. **Adverse** suggests opposition and often hostility, especially in opinion: *The committee's adverse reaction to my proposal was obvious.* **Averse** suggests reluctance or disinclination, to suggested actions: *The travelers were averse to trying to cross the swollen stream.*

ad·ver·si·ty (ad vûr'si tē) *n., pl.* **-ties.** a condition or instance of misfortune, hardship, or suffering.

ad·vert (ad vûrt') *v.i.* to call or direct attention; refer (with *to*): *The author adverted in passing to some of the problems of city living.* [Middle French *advertir* to call attention to, going back to Latin *advertere* to turn to.]

ad·vert·ent (ad vûr'tənt) *adj.* paying attention; attentive; heedful. —**ad·vert'ence, ad·vert'en·cy,** *n.*

ad·ver·tise (ad'vər tīz') *v.,* **-tised, -tis·ing.** —*v.t.* to make known publicly, as through communications media, esp. to publicize (a product or service) in a way that makes it seem attractive and promotes its sale or use. —*v.i.* **1.** to inquire or seek by public notice (with *for*): *to advertise for a car.* **2.** to issue or pay for advertisements: *That company advertises nationally.* [Middle French *advertir* to turn to, call attention to, going back to Latin *advertere* to turn to.] —**ad·ver'tis·er,** *n.*

ad·ver·tise·ment (ad'vər tīz'mənt, ad vûr'tiz-, -tis-) *n.* **1.** a

a	at	e	end	o	hot	u	up	hw	white		about
ā	ape	ē	me	ō	old	ū	use	ng	song		taken
ä	far	i	it	ô	fork	u	rule	th	thin	ə	pencil
âr	care	ī	ice	oi	oil	u	pull	th	this		lemon
		îr	pierce	ou	out	ûr	turn	zh	measure		circus

public announcement, usually printed or broadcast, esp. one promoting a product or service. **2.** the act of advertising.

ad·ver·tis·ing (ad′vər tī′zing) *n.* **1.** the act of using public announcements, esp. to promote a product or service. **2.** the business of preparing and placing advertisements, esp. in print, on television, or on the radio. **3.** advertisements collectively: *The magazine contains a lot of advertising.*

ad·vice (ad vīs′) *n.* **1.** an opinion, esp. knowledgeable, offered as guidance; counsel: *I was acting on my lawyer's advice.* **2.** *also,* **advices.** news; information: *We received daily advices from our embassy during the coup.* [Old French *avis* opinion, earlier *a vis* according to one's view, from Latin *ad* according to + *vīsus* something seen.]

ad·vis·a·ble (ad vī′zə bəl) *adj.* that can be recommended; wise; fitting. —**ad·vis′a·bil′i·ty,** *n.* —**ad·vis′a·bly,** *adv.*

ad·vise (ad vīz′) *v.,* **-vised, -vis·ing.** —*v.t.* **1.** to give advice to; counsel. **2.** to suggest as a sound or expedient course; recommend: *They advised caution to all those entering the game preserve.* **3.** to give notice to; notify; inform: *The letter advised us that our lease was up for renewal.* —*v.i.* **1.** to give advice: *I'll do as you advise.* **2.** to meet with and get advice; consult; confer (with *with*): *I'll advise with my friends before making a decision.* [Old French *aviser* to be of the opinion, give an opinion, from Old French *avis* opinion. See ADVICE.]

Synonyms	Advise and counsel mean to express one's views for the guidance of someone else. Advise is more general and often implies nothing about the value of the views: *Without knowing the facts, I would advise caution in blaming anyone for the mix-up.* Counsel implies wisdom or knowledge from experience and is usually used in more serious situations: *You should get someone with expertise in the field to counsel you about your legal responsibilities in the case.*

ad·vised (ad vīzd′) *adj.* thought out; considered. ➡ usually used in combination, as in *ill-advised, well-advised.*

ad·vis·ed·ly (ad vī′zid lē) *adv.* by design; deliberately. ➡ often used ironically: *In describing the landfill, I use the term "scenic" advisedly.*

ad·vise·ment (ad vīz′mənt) *n.* serious consideration or consultation: *to take a matter under advisement.*

ad·vis·er (ad vī′zər) *also,* **ad·vi·sor.** *n.* **1.** a person who advises, esp. one appointed to advise: *The president has several economic advisers.* **2.** a teacher or professor who advises students about their studies, career choices, and the like.

ad·vis·o·ry (ad vī′zə rē) *adj.* **1.** empowered to advise: *an advisory committee.* **2.** giving advice: *an advisory opinion.* —*n.,* *pl.* **-ries.** a warning, esp. one issued by the National Weather Service concerning the progress or development of a potentially dangerous storm or weather conditions: *a hurricane advisory.* —**ad·vi′so·ri·ly,** *adv.*

ad·vo·ca·cy (ad′və kə sē) *n.* the act of advocating; support.

ad·vo·cate (*v.,* ad′və kāt′; *n.,* ad′və kit, -kāt′) *v.t.,* **-cat·ed, -cat·ing.** to plead in favor of; urge or support: *The council advocated a change of policy.* —*n.* **1.** a person who publicly urges or supports; proponent: *an advocate of free trade.* **2.** a person who pleads the cause of another, esp. a lawyer. [Latin *advocātus* witness, attorney; from the past participle of *advocāre* to summon, call to (the bar).]

advt., advertisement.

adz (adz) *also,* **adze.** *n.* a tool for trimming and shaping timber, having a blade set at right angles to the handle and curving inward. [Old English *adesa* ax, hatchet.]

a·e·des (ā ē′dēz) *also,* **a·ë·des.** *n., pl.* **-des.** any of a group of mosquitoes of the genus *Aëdes,* esp. the species *A. aegypti,* which carries the viruses responsible for yellow fever and dengue. [Modern Latin *aedes,* from Greek *aēdēs* unpleasant, from *a-* not + *hēdys* sweet.]

ae·dile (ē′dīl) *also,* **edile.** *n.* a magistrate in ancient Rome in charge of municipal functions and public works, such as buildings, games, streets, and markets. [Latin *aedīlis,* from *aedēs* building.]

ae·gis (ē′jis) *also,* **egis.** *n.* **1.** protection; guard. **2.** sponsorship; patronage;

adz

guidance: *a study issued under the aegis of the university.* [Latin *aegis* shield of Jupiter, from Greek *aigis* goatskin shield of Zeus, possibly from Greek *aix* goat.]

Ae·gis·thus (i jis′thəs) *n.* in Greek legend, the nephew of Atreus and lover of Clytemnestra. Aegisthus and Clytemnestra murdered Agamemnon and were in turn killed by Orestes.

-aemia, -emia.

Ae·ne·as (i nē′əs) *n.* in classical legend, a Trojan warrior who

was the hero of Vergil's *Aeneid* and whose descendants are said to have founded Rome.

Ae·ne·id (i nē′id) *n.* a Latin epic poem by Vergil, describing the adventures of Aeneas.

Ae·o·li·an¹ (ē ō′lē ən) *adj.* **1.** of or relating to Aeolus. **2.** aeolian. eolian. [From *Aeolus.*]

Ae·o·li·an² (ē ō′lē ən) *also,* **Eolian.** *adj.* of, relating to, or characteristic of Aeolis or its people or culture. —*n.* a native or inhabitant of Aeolis; member of one of the four major Greek tribes of antiquity. The Aeolians settled in Thessaly, Boeotia, Lesbos, and along the northwestern coast of Asia Minor. [From Greek *Aiolis* an ancient region of Asia Minor.]

aeolian harp, an instrument over whose opening are stretched strings or wires that produce musical sounds when a current of air passes over them.

Ae·ol·ic (ē ol′ik) *also,* **Eolic.** *adj.* Aeolian².

Ae·o·lus (ē′ə ləs) *n.* **1.** in classical mythology, the god of the winds. **2.** in Greek legend, a king of Thessaly and ancestor of the Aeolians.

ae·on (ē′ən, ē′on) eon.

aer·ate (âr′āt) *v.t.,* **-at·ed, -at·ing.** **1.** to mix with or expose to air: *to aerate drinking water, to aerate soil by plowing.* **2.** to charge or fill (a liquid) with gas: *Soda water is aerated with carbon dioxide.* **3.** to expose to the chemical action of oxygen; oxygenate: *The blood is aerated in respiration.* [AER(O)- + -ATE¹.] —**aer·a′tion,** *n.* —**aer′a·tor,** *n.*

aer·i·al (*adj.,* âr′ē əl, ā ir′ē əl; *n.,* âr′ē əl) *adj.* **1.** of or in the air: *aerial acrobatics.* **2.** like air; light and thin; ethereal: *an aerial being.* **3.** imaginary; fanciful; unsubstantial: *aerial dreams.* **4.** high in the air; lofty: *aerial spires.* **5.** of, for, or from aircraft or spacecraft: *aerial photography.* **6.** growing in the air rather than in soil or water: *aerial roots.* —*n.* antenna *(def. 1).* [Latin *āerius* relating to air, from Greek *āerios* + -AL¹.] —**aer′i·al·ly,** *adv.*

aerial view of an atoll

aer·i·a·list (âr′ē ə list) *n.* an entertainer who performs in the air, as on a trapeze or high wire.

ae·rie (âr′ē, ir′ē, īr′ē) *also,* **ae·ry, eyrie, eyry.** *n.* **1.** a nest built high on a cliff or mountainside by an eagle, hawk, or other bird of prey. **2.** the brood of a bird of prey. **3.** a dwelling or stronghold in a high, remote place. [Medieval Latin *aerea* nest of a bird, from Old French *aire,* from Latin *ārea* open space.]

aero- combining form **1.** of the air; air: *aeroplane.* **2.** of gas or gases: *aeromechanics.* **3.** of aircraft or flying: *aeronautics.* [Greek *aēr* air.]

aer·o·bat·ics (âr′ə bat′iks) *pl. n.* **1.** the performance of feats or stunts with an aircraft in flight. ➡ used as singular. **2.** the feats or stunts performed.

aer·obe (âr′ōb) *n.* a microorganism that requires free oxygen for life. ➡ distinguished from **anaerobe.**

aer·o·bic (â rō′bik) *adj.* **1.** requiring or living in the presence of free oxygen: *aerobic bacteria.* **2.** having to do with or produced by microorganisms requiring oxygen. **3.** of or relating to aerobics. **4.** of or relating to a form of exercise that strengthens the heart and lungs, as jogging and swimming. ➡ distinguished from **anaerobic.** [AERO- + BI(O)- + -IC.] —**aer·o′bi·cal·ly,** *adv.*

aer·o·bics (â rō′biks) *pl. n.* a system of endurance exercises, as jogging, swimming, cycling, and calisthenics, that condition the heart and lungs by increasing the efficiency of the body's consumption and utilization of oxygen. ➡ used as singular or plural.

aer·o·drome (âr′ə drōm′) *British.* airdrome.

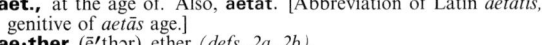

aer·o·dy·nam·ic (âr′ō dī nam′ik) *adj.* relating to or based on aerodynamics: *aerodynamic analysis, an automobile with aerodynamic lines.* —**aer′o·dy·nam′i·cal·ly,** *adv.*

aer·o·dy·nam·ics (âr′ō dī nam′iks) *n.* **1.** the branch of physics that deals with the laws of motion of gases, esp. the atmosphere, and with the forces exerted by such gases on bodies moving in them. **2.** the characteristic behavior of an object moving through air: *the aerodynamics of a small plane.* ➡ used as singular in def. 1, as plural in def. 2.

aer·ol·o·gy (â rol′ə jē) *n.* the branch of meteorology that studies the upper atmosphere. [AERO- + -LOGY.] —**aer·o·log·ic** (âr′ə loj′ik), *adj.* —**aer·ol′o·gist,** *n.*

aer·o·mag·net·ic (âr′ō mag net′ik) *adj.* of or relating to the charting, observation, or study of the earth's magnetic field by means of magnetometers carried aloft by aircraft: *an aeromagnetic survey.* [AERO- + MAGNETIC.]

aer·o·me·chan·ics (âr′ō mi kan′iks) *n.* the science of air and other gases in motion (aerodynamics) and in equilibrium (aerostatics). ➡ used as singular.

aer·o·naut (âr′ə nôt′) *n.* the pilot of a lighter-than-air craft. [French *aéronaute,* from Greek *āēr* air + *nautēs* sailor.]

aer·o·nau·tic (âr′ə nô′tik) *adj.* of or relating to aeronautics or aeronauts. Also, **aer′o·nau′ti·cal.** —**aer′o·nau′ti·cal·ly,** *adv.*

aer·o·nau·tics (âr′ə nô′tiks) *pl. n.* **1.** the science or art of flight. **2.** the branch of engineering concerned with creating and flying aircraft. ➡ used as singular in both defs.

aer·o·pause (âr′ō pôz′) *n.* the region where outer space is considered to begin and where the atmosphere will not support aircraft.

aer·o·plane (âr′ə plān′) *British.* airplane.

aer·o·sol (âr′ə sôl′) *n.* **1.** a colloidal suspension of a solid or liquid in a gas. **2.** aerosol can.

aerosol can, a container fitted with a spray and filled with an aerosol under pressure. Aerosol cans are used for spreading insecticide, paint, and other materials. Also, **aerosal, aerosal bomb, spray can.**

aer·o·space (âr′ō spās′) *n.* the earth's atmosphere and outer space, considered as the region in which aircraft or spacecraft are operated. —*adj.* having to do with aerospace and all aspects of human activity in or relating to this region: *aerospace engineering, the aerospace industry.*

aer·o·stat·ics (âr′ō stat′iks) *pl. n.* the branch of physics that deals with the equilibrium of air and other gases and of solid objects immersed in them. ➡ used as singular.

ae·ry (âr′ē, îr′ē, īr′ē) *n., pl.* -ries. aerie.

Aes·cu·la·pi·us (es′kyə lā′pē əs) *n.* in Roman mythology, the god of medicine and healing. His Greek counterpart is Asclepius.

aes·thete (es′thēt) *also,* esthete. *n.* **1.** a person who is particularly sensitive to and appreciative of beauty. **2.** a person who affects a sensitivity to art and beauty. [Greek *aisthētēs* one who perceives.]

aes·thet·ic (es thet′ik) *also,* esthetic. *adj.* **1.** of or relating to the principles of art or the sense of the beautiful: *aesthetic standards, an aesthetic point of view.* **2.** highly sensitive to or preoccupied with art and beauty. **3.** of or relating to aesthetics. Also, **aes·thet′i·cal.** [German *ästhetisch,* going back to Greek *aisthētikos* pertaining to sense perception, from *aisthanesthai* to perceive.]

aes·thet·i·cal·ly (es thet′i klē) *also,* esthetically. *adv.* **1.** according to aesthetic standards: *The venture was aesthetically rather than financially satisfying.* **2.** in an aesthetic manner: *a room decorated aesthetically.*

aes·thet·i·cism (es thet′ə siz′əm) *also,* estheticism. *n.* **1.** the belief in the supreme importance of aesthetic values. **2.** a strong appreciation of and devotion to art and beauty.

aes·thet·ics (es thet′iks) *also,* esthetics. *pl. n.* **1.a.** the branch of philosophy that studies beauty in art and nature to formulate principles and criteria for its evaluation. **b.** a particular theory or principle of beauty or art. **2.** the theory and description of emotional and intellectual responses to beauty, esp. as studied by psychology. ➡ used as singular.

aes·ti·val (es′tə vəl, es tī′-) estival.

aes·ti·vate (es′tə vāt′) estivate.

Cap

Valve

Spring

Gas

Solution

Container

aerosol can

aet., at the age of. Also, **aetat.** [Abbreviation of Latin *aetātis,* genitive of *aetās* age.]

ae·ther (ē′thər) ether *(defs. 2a, 2b).*

ae·the·re·al (i thîr′ē əl) ethereal.

ae·ti·ol·o·gy (ē′tē ol′ə jē) etiology.

af-, form of ad- before *f,* as in *affront.*

AF, audio frequency.

a·far (ə fär′) *adv.* from, at, or to a distance; far away.

a·feard (ə fîrd′) *also,* a·feared. *adj. Archaic.* afraid.

af·fa·ble (af′ə bəl) *adj.* **1.** easy to approach and speak to; pleasant; friendly. **2.** appearing friendly or gracious: *an affable manner.* [Latin *affābilis* courteous, easily spoken to, from *affārī* to speak to.] —**af′fa·bil′i·ty,** *n.* —**af′fa·bly,** *adv.*

af·fair (ə fâr′) *n.* **1.** a matter or business done or to be done: *Packing and moving can be a tiring affair.* **2.** **affairs.** the practical matters with which a person or group is involved: *Administrative affairs left the teacher no time for scholarly pursuits.* **3.** a private or personal concern: *That's not your affair.* **4.** a thing or object. ➡ often used with a qualifier: *My first soufflé was a sad affair.* **5.** a romantic relationship, esp. a temporary one. **6.** a public controversy or scandal. **7.** a social gathering or party. [Old French *afaire* matter, concern, thing, from *à faire* to do, to be done, from Latin *ad* to + *facere* to do.]

af·fect¹ (*v.,* ə fekt′; *n.,* af′ekt, ə fekt′) *v.t.* **1.** to act upon; produce an effect in: *This drug may affect the central nervous system.* **2.** to influence the emotions; move: *The loss of our dog affected us deeply.* —*n.* **1.** the emotional content of an idea as opposed to the intellectual. **2.** *Psychology.* feeling; emotion. [Latin *affectus,* past participle of *afficere* to influence, produce an effect upon.]

af·fect² (ə fekt′) *v.t.* **1.** to put on a pretense or show of; pretend to have or feel; feign: *to affect boldness although frightened.* **2.** to have a liking for; be partial to; favor: *Some people affect faddish clothes.* [Latin *affectāre* to aim at, pretend to have.]

af·fec·ta·tion (af′ek tā′shən) *n.* **1.** artificiality of manner or conduct, usually to impress others: *Her Southern accent is pure affectation.* **2.** a studied show or pretense: *His affectation of innocence fooled no one.*

af·fect·ed¹ (ə fek′tid) *adj.* **1.** acted upon; influenced: *The affected neighbors protested the building of the fence.* **2.** influenced emotionally; moved. **3.** impaired; afflicted: *an affected limb.* [From AFFECT¹.]

af·fect·ed² (ə fek′tid) *adj.* **1.** assumed for show; artificial: *affected behavior, an affected British accent.* **2.** assuming or displaying artificial behavior: *an affected person.* [From AFFECT².] —**af·fect′ed·ly,** *adv.* —**af·fect′ed·ness,** *n.*

af·fect·ing (ə fek′ting) *adj.* emotionally moving; stirring. —For Synonyms, see **touching.**

af·fec·tion (ə fek′shən) *n.* **1.** tender feeling or fondness; warm attachment. **2.** *Psychology.* the element of emotion or feeling in conscious mental processes. **3.** a disease or diseased condition. [Latin *affectiō* feeling.]

af·fec·tion·ate (ə fek′shə nit) *adj.* full of, expressing, or displaying affection; loving; tender. —**af·fec′tion·ate·ly,** *adv.*

af·fec·tive (ə fek′tiv) *adj.* **1.** having to do with or acting upon the feelings; emotional. **2.** *Psychology.* having to do with or caused by the emotions: *an affective disorder.* —**af·fec′tive·ly,** *adv.*

af·fer·ent (af′ər ənt) *adj.* leading or conducting to a central organ or point, as the nerve fibers that transmit impulses to the central nervous system. ➡ opposed to **efferent.** [Latin *afferēns,* present participle of *afferre* to bring to.]

af·fi·ance (ə fī′əns) *v.t.,* -anced, -anc·ing. to pledge (someone, esp. oneself) to be married; betroth. —*n. Archaic.* a pledge of faith; betrothal. [Old French *afiancer* to promise, from Medieval Latin *affidare* to pledge one's faith, going back to Latin *ad* to + *fidēs* faith.]

af·fi·da·vit (af′i dā′vit) *n.* a written declaration sworn to or affirmed, usually before a judge or other recognized authority. [Medieval Latin *affidavit* he has made an oath (used as the first word in certain legal documents), from *affidare.* See AFFIANCE.]

af·fil·i·ate (*v.,* ə fil′ē āt′; *n.,* ə fil′ē it, -āt′) *v.,* -at·ed, -at·ing. —*v.t.* **1.** to join in close association; unite: *The merger affiliates two large companies.* **2.** to associate (oneself) as a member or supporter (with *with*): *I chose not to affiliate myself with any particular political party.* **3.a.** *Law.* to determine the paternity of. **b.** to trace the origins and connections of. —*v.i.* to join or

a	at	e	end	o	hot	u	up	hw	white		about
ā	ape	ē	me	ō	old	ū	use	ng	song		taken
ä	far	i	it	ô	fork	ü	rule	th	thin	ə	pencil
âr	care	ī	ice	oi	oil	ü	pull	th	this		lemon
		î	pierce	ou	out	ûr	turn	zh	measure		circus

associate oneself. —*n.* **1.** an organization or group that is closely connected with, but subordinate to, a larger organization: *The national television network has many local affiliates.* **2.** a person who is affiliated; associate. [Medieval Latin *affiliatus,* past participle of *affiliare* to adopt, from Latin *ad* to + *fīlius* son.]

af·fil·i·a·tion (ə fil′ē ā′shən) *n.* the act or condition of being affiliated; alliance; connection.

af·fin·i·ty (ə fin′i tē) *n., pl.* **-ties. 1.** a natural attraction or liking. **2.** a close relation or similarity. **3.** a relationship by marriage rather than by birth. ➡ distinguished from **consanguinity. 4.** a resemblance in the structure or physiology of organisms indicating a common origin. **5.** *Chemistry.* a property or force of attraction by which the atoms of certain elements unite with those of certain others to form compounds. [Old French *afinite* proximity, relationship, from Latin *affīnitās* relationship.]

af·firm (ə fûrm′) *v.t.* **1.** to state positively; declare firmly: *to affirm one's approval, to affirm the validity of something.* **2.** to give formal approval to; confirm; ratify; uphold: *The club members affirmed the appointment of the interim treasurer by voting "aye."* —*v.i.* to state solemnly, but not under oath; declare by affirmation. [Old French *afermer,* from Latin *affirmāre,* from *ad* to + *firmāre* to make firm.]

af·fir·ma·tion (af′ər mā′shən) *n.* **1.** the act of affirming: *Public affirmation of the president's policy is very evident in the polls. A show of hands indicates the club members' affirmation of the new bylaw.* **2.** a statement that affirms; positive declaration: *The newspaper editorial contains an affirmation of the zoning restriction.* **3.** *Law.* a solemn declaration in place of an oath made by a person who conscientiously objects to taking oaths.

af·firm·a·tive (ə fûr′mə tiv) *adj.* **1.** asserting or agreeing that something is true or valid; assenting: *an affirmative reply.* **2.** positive, as in manner or tone: *an affirmative outlook.* —*n.* **1.** a word or expression of assent or agreement, such as *yes.* **2.** the side that argues in favor of the proposition in a debate. —**af·firm′a·tive·ly,** *adv.*

• **in the affirmative.** agreeing; responding positively: *to answer in the affirmative.*

affirmative action, an employment or education policy or program designed to compensate for past discrimination against minority groups and women.

af·fix (*v.,* ə fiks′; *n.,* af′iks) *v.t.* **1.** to fix to a surface; attach; fasten: *to affix stamps to an envelope.* **2.** to add; append: *They affixed their names to the document.* —*n.* **1.** a syllable or group of syllables attached to the beginning or end of a word, root, or stem so as to modify the meaning; prefix or suffix. **2.** something that is added or attached. [Medieval Latin *affixare* to fasten onto, going back to Latin *ad* to + *fīgere* to fasten.]

af·fla·tus (ə flā′təs) *n.* inspirational impulse, as of a poet or a prophet. ➡ rare except in the phrase *divine afflatus.* [Latin *afflātus* a breathing on, inspiration.]

af·flict (ə flikt′) *v.t.* to cause great suffering and pain to; distress severely. [Latin *afflīctāre* to injure, torment.]

af·flic·tion (ə flik′shən) *n.* **1.** the state of being afflicted; misery; suffering. **2.** any cause of pain or suffering; misfortune.

af·flic·tive (ə flik′tiv) *adj.* causing pain or distress. —**af·flic′tive·ly,** *adv.*

af·flu·ence (af′lü əns) *n.* **1.** abundant material wealth. **2.** any abundant supply; profusion. **3.** the act of flowing toward something; influx. [Old French *affluence* abundance, from Latin *affluentia* a flow, abundance, going back to *affluere* to flow toward, abound in.]

af·flu·ent (af′lü ənt) *adj.* **1.** materially wealthy; prosperous: *an affluent society.* **2.** abundant; copious; profuse: *affluent praise.* **3.** flowing freely. —*n.* a tributary stream. [Latin *affluēns,* present participle of *affluere* to flow toward, abound in.]

af·ford (ə fôrd′) *v.t.* **1.** to be able to bear the expense of; have the money for. **2.** to be able to spare or give: *I can't afford the time to help you right now.* **3.** to be able to do without risk or harm: *We can afford to try a new sales approach.* **4.** to be a source of; yield; provide: *The garden affords some peace and quiet.* [Old English *geforthian* to further, accomplish.]

af·for·est (ə fôr′ist, ə for′-) *v.t.* to convert (unwooded land) into forest. —**af·for′es·ta′tion,** *n.*

af·fray (ə frā′) *n.* a noisy brawl or quarrel; public disturbance. [Old French *esfrei* assault, attack.]

af·fri·cate (af′ri kit) *n.* a speech sound composed of a stop followed by a fricative. The affricates in English are *ch* as in *chew* and *j* as in *jaw.* [Latin *affricātus,* past participle of *affricāre* to rub against.] —**af′fri·ca′tion,** *n.*

af·fright (ə frīt′) *Archaic. v.t.* to frighten. —*n.* a sudden fear; terror. [Old English *āfyrht,* past participle of *āfyrhtan* to terrify.]

af·front (ə frunt′) *n.* an insulting act or remark, esp. one that is

open and deliberate. —*v.t.* **1.** to insult openly; offend deliberately. **2.** to face defiantly; confront. [Old French *afronter* to strike in the face, insult, going back to Latin *ad frontem* to the face.] —For Synonyms *(v.t.),* see **offend.**

Af·ghan (af′gan, -gən) *n.* **1.a.** a native or citizen of Afghanistan. **b.** a member or close descendant of the people of Afghanistan. **2.** Pashto. **3.** a long-headed dog of a breed originally from Afghanistan, having a coat of long, silky, usually tan hair, large, drooping ears, and a long tail. Height: 27 inches (69 centimeters) at the shoulder. **4. afghan.** a knitted or crocheted wool blanket or shawl, made in colored squares, stripes, or other, usually geometric, patterns. —*adj.* of, relating to, or characteristic of Afghanistan or its people, language, or culture.

Afghan (def. 3)

af·ghan·i (af gan′ē, -gä′nē) *n., pl.* **-is.** the monetary unit of Afghanistan.

a·fi·ci·o·na·do (ə fēs′yə nä′dō, ə fish′ē ə-) *n., pl.* **-dos.** a devotee or fan, as of a sport or art. [Spanish *aficionado;* noun use of past participle of *aficionar* to inspire affection, going back to Latin *affectiō* feeling.]

a·field (ə fēld′) *adv.* **1.** off an intended or usual course; astray. **2.** away from home; abroad. **3.** on, in, or to the field.

a·fire (ə fīr′) *adv., adj.* on fire; burning.

AFL, 1. American Federation of Labor. Also, **AF of L. 2.** American Football League.

a·flame (ə flām′) *adv., adj.* **1.** in flames; flaming. **2.** as if on fire; very excited: *eyes aflame.*

af·la·tox·in (af′lə tok′sin) *n.* any of several poisonous substances produced by molds of the genus *Aspergillus,* esp. *A. flavus,* that may contaminate stored agricultural products, esp. peanuts. [Modern Latin *A(spergillus) fla(vus)* scientific name of the fungus + TOXIN.]

AFL-CIO, the American Federation of Labor and the Congress of Industrial Organizations, which merged in 1955.

a·float (ə flōt′) *adv., adj.* **1.** floating on or as if on water: *to set a boat afloat.* **2.** out of difficulty, esp. financial difficulty: *to keep a business afloat.* **3.** on board ship; at sea. **4.** in circulation: *There are strange rumors afloat.* **5.** covered by water; flooded; awash. **6.** without guidance or direction; adrift.

a·flut·ter (ə flut′ər) *adv., adj.* **1.** fluttering. **2.** nervously confused or agitated: *The cast was all aflutter before the curtain went up.*

a·foot (ə fŭt′) *adv., adj.* **1.** on foot: *We proceeded afoot.* **2.** in progress or motion; stirring: *Plans for a party are afoot.*

a·fore (ə fôr′) *adv., prep., conj.* before. [Old English *onforan* in front, in advance.]

a·fore·men·tioned (ə fôr′men′shənd) *adj.* mentioned before.

a·fore·said (ə fôr′sed′) *adj.* said or mentioned before.

a·fore·thought (ə fôr′thôt′) *adj.* considered or planned beforehand; premeditated. ➡ rare except in the phrase *malice aforethought.*

a for·ti·o·ri (ā fôr′shē ôr′ī) *Latin.* with still stronger reason; all the more.

a·foul (ə foul′) *adv., adj.* in collision or entangled; snarled: *a sailboat with its lines afoul.*

• **to run (or fall) afoul of.** to become entangled with; get into trouble with: *to run afoul of the law.*

Afr., Africa; African.

a·fraid (ə frād′) *adj.* **1.** feeling fear or apprehension; frightened. **2.** not willing or wanting to do something; averse; wary: *afraid of physical work, afraid to inconvenience anyone.* **3.** *Informal.* regretful; sorry. ➡ often used to moderate a statement that might otherwise sound harsh: *I'm afraid you'll have to give up your seat.* [Middle English *affraied,* past participle *affraien* to frighten, from Anglo-Norman *afrayer.*]

| **Synonyms** | **Afraid** and **frightened** mean feeling fear or being aware of imminent danger. **Afraid** implies that both thought and action are affected by fear, perhaps over a period of time: *I've always wanted to see the view from the tower, but I'm afraid of heights.* **Frightened** indicates an immediate and usually short-lived physical reaction: *The noise caused the frightened horse to bolt.* |

A-frame (ā′frām′) *n.* a house with triangular front and rear walls and having steeply angled sides that meet at the top to form the roof.

A

a·fresh (ə fresh′) *adv.* as from the beginning; anew.

Af·ri·can (af′ri kən) *adj.* of, relating to, or characteristic of Africa or its peoples, esp. its black peoples, languages, or cultures. —*n.* a native or inhabitant of Africa, esp. a black African.

Words from Languages Spoken in Africa

Below is a selection of words derived or borrowed from languages spoken exclusively or primarily in Africa. Many of the words borrowed from these languages refer to plants and animals native to Africa.

AFRICAN LANGUAGES

English has borrowed words from many of the languages indigenous to Africa. The first group of words shown below were borrowed from Bantu. Words in the second group were borrowed from various western African languages.

baobab	gumbo	mamba
basenji	impala	marimba
goober	Kwanza	tsetse
banana	gnu	okapi
chimpanzee	jukebox	okra
cola	kudu	yam

AFRIKAANS

Afrikaans, a language spoken in South Africa, is a Germanic language derived from Dutch. It has contributed the following words to English.

aardvark	eland	springbok
apartheid	hartebeest	trek
commandeer	kraal	veld
commando	rand	wildebeest

Af·ri·can-A·mer·i·can (af′ri kən ə mer′i kən) *adj.* of or relating to American blacks of African descent or their culture. —*n.* an American black of African descent.

African violet, any of a group of tropical east African plants, genus *Saintpaulia*, esp. *S. ionantha*, widely grown as houseplants for their colorful flowers and velvety leaves.

Af·ri·kaans (af′ri käns′) *n.* an official language of South Africa, a dialect of Dutch developed from that of seventeenth-century Dutch settlers. For table of words borrowed from Afrikaans, see **African**. [Afrikaans *afrikaans* African, going back to Latin *Africānus.*]

Af·ri·ka·ner (af′ri kä′nər) *n.* a descendant of Dutch settlers in South Africa.

Af·ro (af′rō) *n., pl.* -**ros.** a hair style in which naturally wiry hair is worn in a high, rounded mass. [Short for *Afro-American.*]

Afro- *combining form* **1.** African and: *Afro-Asian.* **2.** of African background: *Afro-American.*

Af·ro-A·mer·i·can (af′rō ə mer′i kən) African-American.

Af·ro-A·sian (af′rō ā′zhən, -shən) *adj.* of or made up of Africans and Asians or the countries of Africa and Asia: *the Afro-Asian bloc.*

aft (aft) *adv., adj.* at, near, or toward the stern of a ship or the tail of an aircraft. [Old English *æftan* behind.]

af·ter (af′tər) *prep.* **1.** in or at the rear of; behind: *The cubs trailed after their mother.* **2.** in search or pursuit of; with desire for: *to seek after success.* **3.** subsequent to or following; later than: *after dark.* **4.** as a consequence of; because of: *After that remark, you'll have to apologize.* **5.** despite; notwithstanding; regardless of: *After all we told them, they still got lost.* **6.** in repeated succession to: *time after time.* **7.** concerning; about: *They inquired after your health.* **8.** in imitation of; in the style of: *a building designed after the Parthenon.* **9.** in honor of; with a name like; for: *to be named after a grandparent.* **10.** in agreement with the nature of: *a man after my own heart.* **11.** below in rank, order, or importance: *After the star come a number of lesser talents.* **12.** (of time) past: *half after one.* —*adv.* **1.** in the rear; behind: *We will follow after.* **2.** later; subsequently: *two days after.* —*conj.* subsequent to the time that: *It happened after you left.* —*adj.* **1.** later; subsequent: *in after years.* **2.** toward the stern; farther aft. **3.** farthest to the rear; hindmost. [Old English *æfter* behind in place or time.] —For Synonyms *(prep.),* see **behind**.

af·ter·birth (af′tər bûrth′) *n.* the placenta and other matter expelled from the uterus after childbirth.

af·ter·brain (af′tər brān′) *n.* in vertebrates, the portion of the hindbrain consisting of the cerebellum and pons. [AFTER + BRAIN.]

af·ter·burn·er (af′tər bûr′nər) *n.* a device that injects fuel into the hot exhaust of a jet engine, thereby creating additional thrust.

af·ter·deck (af′tər dek′) *n.* a deck or part of a deck at a ship's stern.

af·ter·ef·fect (af′tər i fekt′) *n.* an effect that occurs some time after its cause or as a secondary effect: *the aftereffects of a drug.*

af·ter·glow (af′tər glō′) *n.* **1.** a glow remaining after a source of brightness has gone, as in the western sky after sunset. **2.** a good feeling lingering after a pleasant experience: *The afterglow I felt from winning the award lasted all week.*

af·ter·im·age (af′tər im′ij) *n.* the persistence or recurrence of a retinal image or other sensation after withdrawal of, or end of exposure to, an external stimulus.

af·ter·life (af′tər līf′) *n.* **1.** a life believed to follow death. **2.** the later part of a person's life, or the part following some definite time or event: *the afterlife of a famous college athlete.*

af·ter·math (af′tər math′) *n.* **1.** a resulting situation, esp. of something unpleasant or disastrous: *Many people were left homeless as an aftermath of the hurricane.* **2.** the period of time following an unpleasant or disastrous event: *The country's economy had to be rebuilt in the aftermath of the war.* **3.** a second mowing of grass for hay from the same land in the same season. [AFTER + earlier *math* a mowing, cutting of grass, from Old English *mæth,* from *māwan* to mow.]

af·ter·most (af′tər mōst′) *adj.* **1.** nearest the stern of a ship; farthest aft. **2.** nearest the end; last.

af·ter·noon (af′tər nün′) *n.* the part of the day from noon until evening. —*adj.* in, for, or characteristic of the afternoon: *afternoon light.*

af·ter·shock (af′tər shok′) *n.* **1.** an earthquake that occurs shortly after and in the same place as a major earthquake but is less intense. **2.** something that results from an earlier action or condition; resulting situation; consequence: *the aftershock of a divorce.* [AFTER + SHOCK[1].]

af·ter·taste (af′tər tāst′) *n.* **1.** a taste that remains after what caused it is gone; taste occurring after the initial one. **2.** a sensation left after an experience, esp. an unpleasant one.

af·ter·thought (af′tər thôt′) *n.* **1.** a later or second thought or statement. **2.** a thought that comes too late for what it was intended. **3.** something not thought of originally that is added to a planned or completed whole.

af·ter·ward (af′tər wərd) *also,* **af·ter·wards.** *adv.* at a later time; subsequently.

Ag, the symbol for silver. [Abbreviation of Latin *argentum* silver.]

ag-, form of **ad-** before *g,* as in *aggression.*

ag., agriculture.

a·gain (ə gen′, ə gān′) *adv.* **1.** once more; another time: *Please play that song again.* **2.** looking at it another way; on the other hand: *We might go, and again we might not.* **3.** in addition; moreover; furthermore: *Again, I'd like to point out the risks involved.* **4.** back into a former position or state: *Here we go again.* [Old English *ongēan* against, back.]
 •**again and again.** many times.
 •**as much again.** a quantity equal to the original.
 •**now and again.** occasionally; sometimes.

a·gainst (ə genst′, ə gānst′) *prep.* **1.** in opposition to; contrary to: *They voted against the reform. I drove in the snowstorm against my better judgment.* **2.** in the opposite direction to; meeting head-on: *to swim against the current.* **3.a.** in contact with: *I leaned against the tree.* **b.** toward so as to strike or come into contact with: *The wind banged the loose shutter against the side of the house.* **4.** on a background of; in contrast with: *The artist painted a blue vase against a yellow wall.* **5.** in preparation for; as a provision for: *to save against an emergency.* **6.** as a defense or protection from: *Shade trees help against the heat.* **7.** in competition with: *The doctors were in a race against time to come up with the antidote.* **8.** as a charge on: *to ask for an advance against next week's salary.* **9.** expressing hostility toward: *Many people in town are against the new owners of the plant.* [Going back to Old English *ongēan* opposite, back.]

Ag·a·mem·non (ag′ə mem′non) *n.* in Greek legend, the king of Mycenae who led the Greeks in the Trojan War. He was later murdered by his wife, Clytemnestra, and her lover Aegisthus.

a·gape (ə gāp′, ə gap′) *adv., adj.* **1.** with the mouth wide open, esp. expressing wonder or disbelief. **2.** wide open.

a·gar (ä′gär, ag′ər) *also,* **a·gar-a·gar** (ä′gär ä′gär, ag′ər ag′ər). *n.* **1.** a gelatinous product obtained from certain seaweeds, used esp. for growing bacterial cultures and also to thicken food, as ice cream. **2.** a culture medium containing agar.

---

a	at	e	end	o	hot	u	up	hw	white		about
ā	ape	ē	me	ō	old	ū	use	ng	song		taken
ä	far	i	it	ô	fork	ü	rule	th	thin	ə	pencil
âr	care	ī	ice	oi	oil	u̇	pull	th	this		lemon
		îr	pierce	ou	out	ûr	turn	zh	measure		circus

23

ag·a·ric (ag′ə rik, ə gar′ik) *n.* any fungus of the family Agaricaceae, including the common edible mushroom and the shelflike fungus that grows on trees. [Latin *agaricum* a tree fungus, from Greek *agarikon,* possibly from *Agaria,* a settlement in Sarmatia (now part of Poland and Russia), where it abounded.]

ag·ate (ag′it) *n.* **1.** a semiprecious variety of quartz (chalcedony), typically with varicolored layers or bands. **2.** a playing marble made of or resembling agate. **3.** a small size of printing type (5½ point). [Middle French *agate* this stone, from Latin *achātēs,* from Greek *achátēs;* supposedly because it was found near the Sicilian river *Achates.*]

ag·ate·ware (ag′it   wâr′) *n.* **1.** steel ware or ironware for kitchen use, enameled to resemble agate. **2.** pottery with a surface made to resemble agate.

a·ga·ve (ə gä′vē) *n.* any of a group of desert plants, genus *Agave,* of the agave family, having long flower stalks and thick fleshy leaves, typically found in warm, dry regions of the Western Hemisphere. The most familiar is the century plant. [Modern Latin *agave,* from Greek *Agauē,* a mythical queen of Thebes.]

agate (cross section)

age (āj) *n.* **1.** the length of existence since coming into being: *What is the age of this building? My grandfather lived to the age of eighty.* **2.** an average duration of existence; probable life span. **3.** a particular period or stage of life: *My aunt spent her old age by the sea.* **4.** a particular period of life that, naturally or conventionally, qualifies or disqualifies: *She is under the age for a driver's license.* **5.** the state of being old; latter part of life: *weary with age.* **6.a.** a particular period of history or development of civilization: *the computer age.* **b.** the people who live in a particular period; generation: *Dad's age does not understand today's young people.* **7.** a period or epoch in the earth's history: *the age of mammals.* **8.** *also,* **ages.** *Informal.* a very long time. —*v.,* **aged, ag·ing** or **age·ing** —*v.t.* **1.** to cause to seem or look old: *Hard work aged my parents.* **2.** to allow to ripen with time: *to age cheese, to age wood.* —*v.i.* **1.** to become ripe or mature. **2.** to appear older: *I have aged since my illness.* [Old French *age* lifetime, majority, going back to Latin *aetas* time period, time of life.] —For Synonyms *(n.),* see **period.**
• **of age.** at an age, usually eighteen or twenty-one, when certain rights or responsibilities become applicable.

-age *suffix* (used to form nouns) **1.** a collection of: *baggage.* **2.** something that relates to the act of: *tutelage.* **3.** a condition of: *wreckage.* **4.** a home or place of: *orphanage.* **5.** a fee for or cost of: *wharfage.* **6.** an amount of: *acreage.* [Old French *-age,* from Late Latin *-āticum* related to.]

a·ged *(adj., defs. 1, 3, n.,* ā′jid; *adj., defs. 2, 4* ājd) *adj.* **1.** grown old; old. **2.** of the age of: *My cousin is aged three.* **3.** characteristic of old age: *an aged walk.* **4.** having a desired quality as the result of aging: *aged cheese.* —*n.* **the aged.** old people as a group: *medical care for the aged.* —**a′ged·ness,** *n.* —For Synonyms, see **old.**

age·ism (ā′jiz əm) *n.* discrimination or prejudice against a particular age group, esp. older people, often with respect to employment or housing.

age·less (āj′lis) *adj.* **1.** not growing old or showing the effects of age. **2.** not ending; eternal: *the ageless majesty of the mountains.* —**age′less·ly,** *adv.* —**age′less·ness,** *n.*

age·long (āj′lông′) *adj.* lasting a very long time.

a·gen·cy (ā′jən sē) *n., pl.* **-cies. 1.** a company or business empowered to act or conduct business for others: *an insurance agency, a modeling agency.* **2.** the location in which the business of an agency or agent takes place. **3.** an administrative department of government. **4.** the means, action, or power by or through which something is done: *The hostages were freed through the agency of our embassy.*

a·gen·da (ə jen′də) *n.* a list of things to be done: *The reading of the minutes was the first item on the agenda.* [Latin *agenda* things to be done, from *agere* to do.] —For Synonyms, see **program.**

a·gent (ā′jənt) *n.* **1.** a person or organization that has the authority to represent or act for another or others: *The actor's agent represented him during the contract negotiations.* *She is our insurance agent.* **2.** an officer or representative of a government agency, esp. one engaged in law enforcement: *an agent of the CIA.* **3.** something that produces or is used to produce an effect: *a cleansing agent.* **4.** a person or thing through which something is or may be accomplished; means; instrument. **5.** *Informal.* a person who acts or has the power to act. **6.** *Informal.* a salesperson. [Latin *agēns,* present participle of *agere* to do.]

Agent Orange, a herbicide and defoliant containing traces of dioxin, used during the Vietnam War and suspected of causing genetic damage and birth defects.

a·gent pro·vo·ca·teur (ā′jənt prə vok′ə tûr′; *French* ä zhän-prô vô kä tœr′) *pl.* **a·gents pro·vo·ca·teurs** (ā′jənts prə vok′ə-tûr′; *French* ä zhän prô vô kä tœr′). *French.* someone secretly placed in an opponent organization or group, such as a political party or labor union, to provoke illegal or reprehensible acts for which that group can then be prosecuted or blamed.

age-old (āj′ōld′) *adj.* having existed for a long time; of great age; very old: *age-old customs, an age-old question.*

ag·er·a·tum (aj′ə rā′təm, ə jer′ə-) *n.* **1.** an ornamental plant, genus *Ageratum,* of the composite family, having clustered flower heads of blue, white, or pink. **2.** any of several similar plants of the genus *Eupatorium.*

Ag·ge·us (a gē′əs) *n.* in the Douay Bible, Haggai.

ag·glom·er·ate (*v.,* ə glom′ə rāt′; *n., adj.,* ə glom′ər it, -ə rāt′) *v.i., v.t.,* **-at·ed, -at·ing.** to gather in a mass or cluster. —*n.* **1.** things gathered together in a mass or cluster. **2.** a rock formed of a mass of angular volcanic fragments in ash. —*adj.* gathered together in a mass or cluster: *an agglomerate whole.* [Latin *agglomerātus,* past participle of *agglomerāre* to mass together, going back to *ad-* to, at + *glomus* ball.]

ag·glom·er·a·tion (ə glom′ə rā′shən) *n.* **1.** the act or process of agglomerating or the state of being agglomerated. **2.** a collection of things gathered indiscriminately.

ag·glu·tin·ant (ə glü′tə nənt) *n.* a substance causing agglutination —*adj.* tending to cause agglutination.

ag·glu·ti·nate (*v.,* ə glü′tə nāt′; *adj.,* ə glü′tə nit, -nāt′) *v.i., v.t.,* **-nat·ed, -nat·ing. 1.** to unite with or as with glue; stick together. **2.** to form (words) by agglutination. **3.** to clump or cause to clump together, as bacteria or blood cells. —*adj.* joined by or as by glue. [Latin *agglūtinātus,* past participle of *agglūtināre* to glue to, going back to *ad* to + *glūten* glue.]

ag·glu·ti·na·tion (ə glü′tə nā′shən) *n.* **1.** the process of sticking together or the state of being stuck together. **2.** a process by which words or word elements are combined to form new words in which the constituent parts remain apparent without loss of meaning. **3.** a clumping together of bacteria or blood cells in the body due to the presence of an antibody. **4.** a collection of parts stuck together.

ag·glu·ti·na·tive (ə glü′tə nā′tiv) *adj.* **1.** tending to agglutinate. **2.** forming words by agglutination: *an agglutinative language.*

ag·glu·tin·in (ə glü′tə nin) *n.* a substance, as an antibody, that causes agglutination

ag·glu·tin·o·gen (ag′lü tin′ə jən) *n.* an antigen that, when present in the body, causes the formation of agglutinins.

ag·gran·dize (ə gran′dīz, ag′rən dīz′) *v.t.,* **-dized, -diz·ing. 1.** to make greater, larger, or more important, as in power, influence, or wealth: *They began the war to aggrandize their empire.* **2.** to cause to appear greater: *to aggrandize a mediocre subject.* [French *agrandir* to enlarge, increase, going back to Latin *ad-* to + *grandīre* to increase, grow.] —**ag·gran·dize·ment** (ə gran′diz mənt), *n.* —**ag·gran·diz·er** (ə gran′dī zər, ag′rən dī′-), *n.*

ag·gra·vate (ag′rə vāt′) *v.t.,* **-vat·ed, -vat·ing. 1.** to make worse or more severe. **2.** to annoy; irritate. [Latin *aggravātus,* past participle of *aggravāre* to make heavier. Doublet of AG-GRIEVE.] —**ag′gra·vat′ing·ly,** *adv.* —**ag′gra·va′tor,** *n.*

ag·gra·va·tion (ag′rə vā′shən) *n.* **1.** the act of aggravating, esp. by making worse. **2.** the state or condition of being aggravated: *I understand your aggravation at the delay.* **3.** something that aggravates.

ag·gre·gate (*v.,* ag′ri gāt′; *n., adj.,* ag′ri git, -gāt′) *v.,* **-gat·ed, -gat·ing.** —*v.t.* **1.** to collect or gather (something) into a mass or group. **2.** to amount to; total: *Admission charges aggregated $250.* —*v.i.* **1.** to come together; collect. —*n.* **1.** a whole composed of distinguishable parts. **2.** a sum total. **3.** a mixture of sand and gravel used in concrete. —*adj.* **1.** composed of parts gathered together. **2.** *Botany.* **a.** consisting of densely clustered florets: *an aggregate flower.* **b.** (of a fruit) composed of a cluster of ripened ovaries of a single flower. [Latin *aggregātus,* past participle of *aggregāre* to add to a flock, going back to Latin *ad-* to + *grex* flock.] —**ag′gre·gate·ly,** *adv.* —**ag′gre·gate·ness,** *n.*
• **in the aggregate.** taken together; as a whole.

ag·gre·ga·tion (ag′ri gā′shən) *n.* **1.** the collecting of distinguishable things into or as into a single mass or whole. **2.** such a mass or whole.

ag·gres·sion (ə gresh′ən) *n.* **1.** an offensive or unprovoked assault or attack. **2.** the habitual practice of making assaults or attacks; hostile behavior. [Latin *aggressiō* a going toward, attack.]

ag·gres·sive (ə gres′iv) *adj.* **1.** of or characterized by aggression. **2.** characterized by force or energy: *an aggressive publicity campaign.* **3.** bold in an offensive manner; pushy: *an aggressive salesperson.* —**ag·gres′sive·ly,** *adv.* —**ag·gres′sive·ness,** *n.*

ag·gres·sor (ə gres′ər) *n.* a person or group, esp. a nation, that engages in aggression.

ag·grieve (ə grēv′) *v.t.,* -**grieved,** -**griev·ing. 1.** to cause grief or trouble to; distress. **2.** *Law.* to cause to suffer loss or injury without just cause. [Old French *agrever* to make heavier, render more severe, going back to Latin *aggravāre* to make heavier. Doublet of AGGRAVATE.]

ag·grieved (ə grēvd′) *adj.* **1.** feeling troubled or distressed. **2.** treated unjustly; wronged.

a·ghast (ə gast′) *adj.* stricken with fear, horror, or amazement. [Middle English *agast,* past participle of *agasten* to terrify, from Old English *ā-* (for emphasis) + *gæstan* to terrify.]

ag·ile (aj′əl, -īl) *adj.* able to move or think quickly and easily; nimble. [French *agile,* from Latin *agilis.*] —**ag′ile·ly,** *adv.* —**ag′ile·ness,** *n.*

a·gil·i·ty (ə jil′i tē) *n.* quickness and ease in motion or thought; nimbleness.

ag·i·tate (aj′i tāt′) *v.,* -**tat·ed,** -**tat·ing.** —*v.t.* **1.** to move or shake roughly or irregularly; stir up: *The wind agitated the trees.* **2.** to move to and fro with a regular motion: *The washing machine agitates the clothes.* **3.** to stir up the feelings of; perturb; disturb; excite: *The unruliness of the crowd agitated the police.* —*v.i.* to seek to arouse or maintain public interest, as in an effort to bring about change: *The strikers were agitating for safer working conditions.* [Latin *agitātus,* past participle of *agitāre* to move to and fro, drive.] —**ag′i·tat′ed·ly,** *adv.* —For Synonyms, see **disturb.**

ag·i·ta·tion (aj′i tā′shən) *n.* **1.** the act of agitating or the state of being agitated. **2.** a state of being emotionally upset or shaken. **3.** action or argument that seeks to arouse or maintain public interest in some matter.

ag·i·ta·tor (aj′i tā′tər) *n.* **1.** a person who agitates for change, esp. political or social change. **2.** a device for shaking or stirring.

A·gla·ia (ə glā′ə) *n.* in Greek mythology, one of the three Graces.

a·gleam (ə glēm′) *adv., adj.* gleaming.

a·gley (ə glē′, ə glī′) *adv. Scottish.* out of line; awry.

a·glit·ter (ə glit′ər) *adv., adj.* glittering.

a·glow (ə glō′) *adv., adj.* glowing.

ag·nos·tic (ag nos′tik) *n.* a person who holds that nothing can be known about the existence of God or about anything that is not material. —*adj.* relating to or characteristic of agnostics or their beliefs. [Coined in 1869 by the English biologist Thomas Huxley, 1825-95, from Greek *agnōstos* unknown, unknowing; modified by GNOSTIC.] —**ag·nos′ti·cal·ly,** *adv.*

Ag·nus De·i (ag′nəs dē′ī, ä′nyūs de′ē) **1.** a prayer in the Mass starting with the words "Agnus Dei" or "O Lamb of God." **2.** the music for this prayer. **3.** an image of a lamb, esp. one with a halo and the banner of the Cross, emblematic of Jesus. [Latin *Agnus Deī* Lamb of God.]

a·go (ə gō′) *adj.* before now; past. ➡ always placed after the noun: *long ago.* —*adv.* in the past. ➡ used only in *long ago.* [Middle English *ago,* past participle of *agon* to go away, from Old English *āgān.*]

a·gog (ə gog′) *adj., adv.* in a state of excitement or eager expectation. [French phrase *en gogues* lively, in a merry mood.]

ag·o·nist (ag′ə nist) *n.* **1.** *Anatomy.* a muscle whose contraction on a joint is checked by the action of another muscle, the antagonist. **2.** *Medicine.* a substance capable of stimulating an appropriate cellular receptor to trigger a physiological response. [From ANTAGONIST.]

ag·o·nize (ag′ə nīz′) *v.,* -**nized,** -**niz·ing.** —*v.i.* **1.** to feel great pain or anguish; suffer greatly. **2.** to strive painfully; struggle. —*v.t.* to cause to suffer great pain or agony; torture. [French *agoniser* to be in agony, be dying, through Late Latin *agōnizāre* to strive, contend, suffer, from Greek *agōnizesthai* to contend for a prize, struggle, from *agōnia* anguish, struggle.] —**ag′o·niz′ing·ly,** *adv.*

ag·o·ny (ag′ə nē) *n., pl.* -**nies. 1.** great pain, suffering, or anguish of mind or body. **2.** the often unconscious movements of the body, resembling a struggle, that sometimes precede death. **3.** any intense emotion: *an agony of indecision.* [Late Latin *agōnia* anguish, from Greek *agōnia* anguish, struggle, contest.]

ag·o·ra[1] (ag′ər ə, ə gôr′ə) *n., pl.* **ag·o·rae** (ag′ə rē′, ə gôr′ē). the marketplace of an ancient Greek city, usually the center of civic and commercial life. [Greek *agorā* assembly, marketplace.]

a·go·ra[2] (ä gôr′ə) *n., pl.* **a·go·rot** (ä gô rōt′). a unit of currency of Israel, equal to 1/100 of a shekel. [Modern Hebrew *agora,* from Hebrew *agora* a unit of weight.]

ag·o·ra·pho·bi·a (ag′ər ə fō′bē ə) *n.* an abnormal, excessive fear of being in open spaces or public places. [AGORA + PHOBIA.] —**ag′o·ra·pho′bic,** *adj.*

a·gou·ti (ə gü′tē) *n., pl.* -**tis** or -**ties.** a West Indian and South American rodent, genus *Dasyprocta,* related to the guinea pig, about the size of a rabbit. [French *agouti* or Spanish *aguti,* from Tupi-Guarani *aguti.*]

a·grar·i·an (ə grâr′ē ən) *adj.* **1.** concerning agricultural land, its cultivation, or its ownership. **2.** concerning or involved in the furthering of the interests of farmers: *agrarian reforms.* —*n.* a person who favors agrarianism. [Latin *agrārius* relating to land, from *ager* land, field.]

agouti

a·grar·i·an·ism (ə grâr′ē ə niz′əm) *n.* **1.** a doctrine advocating the equal or more equal distribution of agricultural land. **2.** political activity aimed at securing such redistribution.

a·gree (ə grē′) *v.,* **a·greed, a·gree·ing.** —*v.i.* **1.** to have the same opinion; concur. **2.** to be in harmony; coincide: *Your description of the stolen car agrees with that of the one found abandoned.* **3.** to consent (with *to*): *We can agree to that proposal.* **4.** to reach an understanding; come to terms, esp. in ending a dispute: *The negotiators finally agreed on every point.* **5.** *Grammar.* to correspond in case, number, gender, or person (with another word or phrase in a sentence): In the sentence *These books are new,* the words *these* and *are* agree with the subject *books.* **6.** to produce a good effect on; suit (with *with*): *A week by the sea would agree with me.* —*v.t.* to acknowledge or accept; grant (with a noun clause as object): *I agree that the terms of the contract are most generous.* [Old French *agreer* to please, from phrase *a gre* to (one's) pleasure, going back to Latin *ad* to + *grātus* pleasing.]

a·gree·a·ble (ə grē′ə bəl) *adj.* **1.** to one's liking; pleasant: *an agreeable climate.* **2.** willing to consent: *Are you agreeable to my plan?* **3.** agreeing with; suitable (with *to*): *a suggestion agreeable to our plans.* **4.** that can be accepted; satisfactory: *The terms of the sale are agreeable to both the buyer and seller.* —**a·gree′a·bil′i·ty, a·gree′a·ble·ness,** *n.* —**a·gree′a·bly,** *adv.*

a·greed (ə grēd′) *adj.* settled by common consent: *to stick to the agreed route.*

a·gree·ment (ə grē′mənt) *n.* **1.** an understanding reached by two or more parties, such as a treaty or contract. **2.** a state of agreeing; harmony; accord: *We are in agreement on the itinerary.* **3.** *Grammar.* the agreeing of words in a phrase or sentence.

ag·ri·busi·ness (ag′rə biz′nis) *n.* farming combined with businesses connected with farming, such as the manufacturing of farm equipment and the processing and distribution of farm products.

agric., agriculture.

ag·ri·cul·tur·al (ag′ri kul′chər əl) *adj.* relating to farms or farming; of agriculture. —**ag′ri·cul′tur·al·ly,** *adv.*

ag·ri·cul·ture (ag′ri kul′chər) *n.* **1.** the business or practice of raising crops and livestock; farming. **2.** the science of farming, esp. with regard to improving the amount or quality of yield. [Latin *agrīcultūra,* from *agrī cultūra* cultivation of the land.]

ag·ri·cul·tur·ist (ag′ri kul′chər ist) *n.* **1.** farmer. **2.** an expert in the science of agriculture. Also, **ag′ri·cul′tur·al·ist.**

ag·ri·mo·ny (ag′rə mō′nē) *n., pl.* -**nies.** any of a group of plants, genus *Agrimonia,* of the rose family, bearing aromatic, bitter leaves, yellow flowers, and burrs. [Latin *agrimōnia,* a false reading of Latin *argemōnia* a plant, from Greek *argemōnē* poppy.]

ag·ro·nom·ic (ag′rə nom′ik) *adj.* relating to agronomy.

a·gron·o·mist (ə gron′ə mist) *n.* a student of or expert in agronomy.

a·gron·o·my (ə gron′ə mē) *n.* the branch of agriculture concerned with all aspects of field-crop production, including the cultivation of farmland and the conservation and improvement of soil. [Greek *agros* field + *-nomia* management.]

a·ground (ə ground′) *adv., adj.* with the bottom stuck, as in shallow water: *We ran the boat aground on the sandbar.*

agt., agent.

a·gue (ā′gū) *n.* **1.** a fever, often malarial, marked by regularly recurring cold, hot, and sweating stages. **2.** any fit of shivering; chill. [Old French *aguë* sharp fever, from Latin *acūta (febris)* sharp or severe (fever).]

a	at	e	end	o	hot	u	up	hw	white	⎧	about
ā	ape	ē	me	ō	old	ū	use	ng	song		taken
ä	far	i	it	ô	fork	ü	rule	th	thin	ə ⎨	pencil
âr	care	ī	ice	oi	oil	u̇	pull	<u>th</u>	this		lemon
		îr	pierce	ou	out	ûr	turn	zh	measure	⎩	circus

a·gu·ish (ā′gū ish) *adj.* **1.** having the qualities of ague. **2.** tending to cause ague. **3.** subject to ague.

ah (ä) *interj.* used to show any of various feelings from pain or sorrow *(Ah, how pitiful!)* to joy or admiration *(Ah, how beautiful!).*

a·ha (ä hä′) *interj.* used variously, but esp. to indicate discovery: *Aha! You had my book!*

A·hab (ā′hab) in Herman Melville's novel *Moby Dick,* a whaling captain intent on his pursuit of a white whale.

a·head (ə hed′) *adv.* **1.** in or to the front: *The American runner was now ahead.* **2.** onward: *They went ahead with their plans.* **3.** toward the future; in advance: *to plan ahead.* **4.** having as a profit or advantage: *The business is a few dollars ahead this month.*
  • **ahead of.** in advance of; earlier than; before: *We left ahead of them.*
  • **to get ahead.** to advance one's position socially or professionally.
  • **to get ahead of.** to do better than; surpass; overtake.

a·hem (ə hem′) *interj.* used esp. to attract attention or give warning, as by clearing the throat.

-aholic *combining form* describing a person who is addicted to or obsessed with some thing or activity: *workaholic.* ➡ sometimes used in humorous coinages: *I'm such a shopaholic, it's a wonder I can pay the rent!* [From WORKAHOLIC.]

a·hoy (ə hoi′) *interj.* used to greet or catch the attention, esp. by sailors in hailing another ship.

Ah·ri·man (är′i mən) *n.* in the Zoroastrian religion, the spirit of evil opposing Ahura Mazda.

A·hu·ra Maz·da (ä′hŭr ə maz′də) in the Zoroastrian religion, the spirit of goodness, light, and truth, in ceaseless conflict with Ahriman. Also, **Ormazd.**

AI, artificial intelligence.

aid (ād) *v.t.* to give help or support to; assist. —*v.i.* to be of help or assistance. —*n.* **1.** help or support; assistance: *to walk with the aid of a cane.* **2.** a person or thing that helps or is helpful: *A dictionary is a good aid in writing well.* [Old French *aïder* to help, assist, going back to Latin *adjūtāre.*] —For Synonyms *(v.t.),* see **help.**

aide (ād) *n.* **1.** aide-de-camp. **2.** an assistant; helper.

aide-de-camp (ād′də kamp′) *n., pl.* **aides-de-camp.** an officer who serves as an assistant to a superior officer. [French *aide-de-camp* literally, camp assistant.]

AIDS (ādz) *n.* a disease that severely damages the body's immune system, making the body more susceptible to other infections and diseases. Caused by a retrovirus, AIDS is transmitted by the introduction of an infected person's bodily fluids, such as blood or semen, into the bloodstream, as by sexual contact, contaminated hypodermic needles, or transfusion of infected blood. An infected pregnant woman can transmit the virus to the fetus. [Short for *a(cquired) i(mmune) d(eficiency) s(yndrome).*]

AIDS-re·lat·ed complex (ādz′ri lā′tid) a medical condition characterized by fever, weight loss, and the enlargement of lymph nodes, associated with the development of AIDS in certain cases.

ai·grette (ā′gret, ā gret′) *also,* **ai·gret.** *n.* **1.** an ornamental plume or tuft of feathers worn on the head. **2.** the plume or feathers of the egret. **3.** ornamental jewelry imitating such feathers. [French *aigrette* egret, plume, from Provençal *aigreta* from *aigron* heron; of Germanic origin.]

ai·ki·do (ī kē′dō) *n.* a Japanese system of unarmed self-defense that uses various holds and throws to unbalance and overcome an opponent.

ail (āl) *v.t.* to cause illness, trouble, or discomfort to: *What ails you?* —*v.i.* to be ill or indisposed, esp. chronically. [Old English *eglan* to trouble, pain.]

ai·lan·thus (ā lan′thəs) *n., pl.* **-thus·es.** any tree of the genus *Ailanthus,* bearing pinnate leaves and clusters of small, greenish flowers, valued esp. as a shade tree. The best-known species is *A. altissima,* the tree of heaven. [Moluccan *ai lanto* tree of heaven; spelling influenced by Greek *anthos* flower.]

ai·le·ron (ā′lə ron′) *n.* a movable section in the trailing edge of an airplane wing used to control movement of the airplane about its nose-to-tail axis, as in banking or rolling. [French *aileron* bird's wing, diminutive of *aile* wing, from Latin *āla.*]

ailanthus

ail·ment (āl′mənt) *n.* an illness or affliction, esp. a mild or chronic one.

aim (ām) *v.t.* to point, as a weapon, or direct, as a remark or blow, for the purpose of hitting a target. —*v.i.* **1.** to point or direct a weapon or blow: *to aim at a target.* **2.** to have as a purpose or goal (with *at* or *to*): *The immigrants aimed at a better life. The Congress aims to get that bill passed.* —*n.* **1.** the act of pointing or directing something at a target. **2.** the ability to hit a target: *to have a good aim.* **3.** direction in which something is aimed; line of fire. **4.** a person or thing aimed at; target. **5.** something to be attained; purpose or goal. [Old French *aesmer* to estimate, intend, going back to Latin *ad* to + *aestimāre* to value.] —For Synonyms *(n.),* see **purpose.**

aim·less (ām′lis) *adj.* without purpose or direction: *aimless wanderings, aimless remarks.* —**aim′less·ly,** *adv.* —**aim′less·ness,** *n.*

ain't (ānt) **1.** am not. **2.** is not; are not. **3.** has not; have not.

> **Usage** The use of **ain't** is generally considered to be nonstandard English. However, it is sometimes used in informal contexts in both speech and writing where the aim is deliberately to show departure from standard usage. In such cases, **ain't** is used for humorous effect or in dialogue for characterization.

Ai·nu (ī′nü) *n., pl.* **-nu** or **-nus. 1.** a member of an aboriginal race of northern Japan, having light skin and hairy bodies. **2.** the language of the Ainu, not known to be related to any other language.

air (âr) *n.* **1.** the mixture of gases that surrounds and envelops the earth, forming its atmosphere. **2.** the space surrounding and above the earth's surface; sky. **3.a.** a moving current of air; breeze; light wind. **b.** fresh air: *Open the window and let in some air.* **4.** public exposure; circulation: *to give air to grievances.* **5.** an impression, mood, or feeling as imparted by exterior appearance or surroundings: *an air of opulence, an air of expectation.* **6.** a person's appearance, manner, or conduct; bearing; demeanor: *The stranger had a furtive air.* **7.** *usually,* **airs.** pretentious or affected manner: *to put on airs.* **8.** the medium through which radio waves are transmitted. **9.a.** melody; tune. **b.** the main part of a harmonized musical composition. **10.** travel or transport by aircraft: *The package will go by air.* —*v.t.* **1.** to freshen, ventilate, or dry by exposing to fresh air. **2.** to expose to public notice; publicize. **3.** to broadcast by radio or television: *to air a new program.* [Old French *air* atmospheric air, from Latin *āēr,* from Greek *āēr* atmospheric air, mist.]
  • **in the air. a.** in circulation: *rumors in the air.* **b.** not certain; undecided.
  • **off the air.** not broadcasting or being broadcast.
  • **on the air.** broadcasting or being broadcast.
  • **to clear the air.** to remove disagreements or tension.
  • **to take the air.** to go outside; take a walk or ride.
  • **to vanish** (or **disappear**) **into thin air.** to vanish quickly and completely.
  • **to walk on air.** to be elated; be very happy.
  • **up in the air.** undecided; unsettled.

air bag, a plastic bag mounted under an automobile dashboard or in front of a passenger, designed to inflate automatically in a collision to protect the driver or passenger from injury.

air base, a place from which military airplanes operate.

air bladder, a sac filled with air, esp. as found in most fish. It aids in maintaining equilibrium in the water. For illustration, see **fish.** Also, **swim bladder, swimming bladder.**

air·boat (âr′bōt′) *n.* a small, flat-bottomed boat with a shallow draft, driven by an airplane propeller, used for travel in swamps and shallow waters.

air·borne (âr′bôrn′) *adj.* **1.** carried by the air: *airborne pollen.* **2.** transported by airplanes or gliders: *airborne artillery.* **3.** off the ground; in flight: *By midnight we were airborne.*

air brake 1. a mechanical braking system in which compressed air drives a piston or pistons. **2.** the flaps on airplane wings that are used to reduce speed in the air.

air·brush (âr′brush′) *n.* an atomizer operated by compressed air, used to spray paint or other liquids on a surface. —*v.t.* to paint, alter, or embellish with an airbrush.

air·bus (âr′bus′) *n.* a short-range commercial passenger airplane, esp. one used for shuttle service between two popular destinations.

air chamber, a compartment or part filled with air, esp. one used to equalize the flow of a liquid in a hydraulic device.

air coach, coach *(def. 3).*

air cock, a valve to control air flow.

air-con·di·tion (âr′kən dish′ən) *v.t.* **1.** to provide (a room or building) with apparatus for air conditioning. **2.** to treat (the air in an enclosed space) by means of such apparatus.

air-con·di·tioned (âr′kən dish′ənd) *adj.* equipped with air conditioning.

air conditioner, a machine used for air conditioning.

A

air conditioning, a system or process for controlling the temperature, humidity, purity, and circulation of the air in some enclosed area, such as a building, room, or vehicle.
air-cool (âr′kül′) *v.t.* **1.** to reduce heat in (a mechanical device, as an automobile engine) by air circulation. **2.** to blow air into (a room) and cool by causing the air to circulate. —**air′-cooled′,** *adj.*
air corridor, a route followed by an aircraft in flight, esp. one established by international agreement.
air·craft (âr′kraft′) *n., pl.* **-craft. 1.** a machine for flight in air designed to be supported by buoyancy (lighter-than-air craft) or by aerodynamic action (heavier-than-air craft). **2.** such vehicles collectively.
aircraft carrier, a warship with a large open top deck, used as a floating air base.
air cushion vehicle, hovercraft.
air·drome (âr′drōm′) *n.* airport. Also, *British,* **aerodrome.**
air·drop (âr′drop′) *v.t.,* **-dropped, -drop·ping.** to drop (food, supplies, or personnel) by parachute from aircraft. —*n.* the act of airdropping.
Aire·dale (âr′dāl′) *n.* the largest breed of terrier, having a wiry tan coat with dark markings on the back and shoulders. [From the valley or DALE of the *Aire* River in Yorkshire, England.]
air express, a system of shipping packages by air, esp. for overnight delivery.
air·fare (âr′fâr′) *n.* passenger fare on a commercial airliner.
air·field (âr′fēld′) *n.* **1.** the landing field of an airport. **2.** an airport, esp. a small one.
air·foil (âr′foil′) *n.* **1.** any part, such as a wing, aileron, or rudder, designed to help lift or control an aircraft by controlling the flow of air over or

aircraft carrier

around its surface. **2.** any body or surface that serves to control the direction of a flow of air.
air force 1. the air branch of a country's armed forces. **2. Air Force.** the air force of the United States. Before July 26, 1947, it was part of the U.S. Army.
air·frame (âr′frām′) *n.* the framework and external covering of an aircraft or rocket.
air gun 1. a rifle or pistol using compressed air as propellant. **2.** a hand tool operating by the force of compressed air, used to spray paint or apply grease.
air hammer, an automatic hammer driven by compressed air.
air hole 1. a hole through which air is permitted to pass in or out. **2.** a natural opening in the ice on a river, pond, or the like. **3.** air pocket.
air·i·ly (âr′ə lē) *adv.* in an airy manner; lightly; gaily.
air·i·ness (âr′ē nis) *n.* the state or quality of being airy.
air·ing (âr′ing) *n.* **1.** exposure to air for the purpose of drying or freshening. **2.** exposure to public knowledge or discussion. **3.** a walk or ride in the open air.
air lane, a route used by aircraft, esp. on a regular basis. Also, **skyway.**
air·less (âr′lis) *adj.* **1.** without air, esp. fresh air; stuffy. **2.** without any wind; still.
air letter 1. a letter sent by airmail. **2.** a lightweight sheet of paper designed to fold into the form of an envelope, used for writing a letter to be sent by airmail.
air·lift (âr′lift′) *n.* an emergency system of transporting people, supplies, or animals by aircraft when surface routes are closed. —*v.t.* to transport by airlift.
air·line (âr′līn′) *n.* **1.** a system and equipment for transporting people and goods by air. **2.** a business organization owning and managing such a system. **3.** a route used by such a system. **4.** the shortest distance between two places.
air·lin·er (âr′lī′nər) *n.* a large passenger plane operated by an airline.
air lock 1. an airtight chamber in which air pressure can be varied, affording passage between two places having differing air

pressures. **2.** a hindrance to the flow of a liquid in a system caused by the pressure of an air bubble; vapor lock.
air·mail (âr′māl′) *n.* **1.** mail carried by airplane between cities. **2.** a system of transporting mail by airplane. —*v.t.* to send by airmail. —*adj.* sent by or relating to airmail. —*adv.* by airmail: *We sent the package airmail.*
air·man (âr′mən) *n., pl.* **-men** (-mən). **1.** the pilot of an aircraft; aviator. **2.** an enlisted person in the U.S. Air Force.
airman first class, in the U.S. Air Force, an enlisted person ranking below a sergeant and above an airman.
air mass, a widespread body of air that is approximately uniform in its horizontal extent, particularly with reference to its temperature and moisture distribution.
air mattress, an inflatable mattress made of rubber, plastic, or other airtight material.
air mile, a unit of distance in air navigation equal to about 6,076 feet (1,852 meters).
air·mind·ed (âr′mīn′did) *adj.* interested in things connected with airplanes, air travel, aviation, and the like. —**air′-mind′ed·ness,** *n.*
air piracy, the act of hijacking an airplane in flight; skyjacking. —**air pirate.**
air·plane (âr′plān′) *n.* a heavier-than-air craft that has fixed or movable wings, is supported in flight by the action of air on its wings, and is driven by one or more engines. Also, *British,* **aeroplane.**
air plant, epiphyte.
air pocket, a downward current of air that can cause an airplane to drop suddenly.
air pollution, atmospheric contamination by gas, smoke, or vapor produced in the combustion of wood and fossil fuels, and waste gas released from industrial processes.
air·port (âr′pôrt′) *n.* an area equipped with facilities necessary for the landing, takeoff, maintenance, and storage of aircraft and for the loading and discharge of passengers and cargo.
air pressure 1. atmospheric pressure. **2.** the force of compressed air.
air pump, a machine for exhausting air from, or compressing it in, a container or for forcing it through pipes or other apparatus.
air raid, an attack by aircraft, esp. by flights of bombers.
air-raid shelter (âr′rād′) a place intended to provide cover during an air raid.
air rifle, a rifle powered by compressed air, esp. one that shoots BB's.
air rights, the legal rights to own and use the space above a tract of land or any piece of property.
air sac 1. one of a number of membranous sacs of air in the body of a bird that are connected with the lungs. **2.** alveolus *(def. 3).*
air shaft, a passage, usually vertical, to permit fresh air to reach into a mine, building, or the like.
air·ship (âr′ship′) *n.* any lighter-than-air craft, commonly made buoyant by a gas such as helium, that is driven by motor and can be steered, such as a blimp or dirigible.
air·sick (âr′sik′) *adj.* nauseated and dizzy as a result of the motion of an aircraft. —**air′sick′ness,** *n.*
air·space (âr′spās′) *n.* the space above a country, or some part of it, esp. such space considered as subject to national or local laws.
air speed, the speed of an aircraft relative to the air through which it is moving. ➡ distinguished from **groundspeed.**
air·stream (âr′strēm′) *n.* the flow of air around an object, as an airplane, in flight.
air·strip (âr′strip′) *n.* a paved or cleared area where planes can land and take off.
air·tight (âr′tīt′) *adj.* **1.** so tight as to prevent air or gas from entering or escaping. **2.** free of weak points that could easily be criticized or refuted: *an airtight legal case.*
air·time (âr′tīm′) *n.* **1.** the time at which a radio or television broadcast begins or is scheduled to begin. **2.a.** the time during which a radio or television station broadcasts or a particular program is broadcast. **b.** a portion of this time: *to purchase airtime for a commercial.*
air-to-air (âr′tü âr′, -tə-) *adj.* launched from aircraft at an airborne target: *air-to-air missiles.*
air traffic control, a government service whose role is to manage the movement and ensure the safety of aircraft in, near, and

a	at	e	end	o	hot	u	up	hw	white		about
ā	ape	ē	me	ō	old	ū	use	ng	song		taken
ä	far	i	it	ô	fork	ü	rule	th	thin	ə	pencil
âr	care	ī	ice	oi	oil	ů	pull	th	this		lemon
		îr	pierce	ou	out	ûr	turn	zh	measure		circus

between airports, using radar and other instruments and radio communication with pilots. —**air traffic controller.**

air·waves (âr′wāvz′) *pl. n.* the media of radio or television broadcasting: *the highest-paid broadcaster of the airwaves, to take to the airwaves.*

air·way (âr′wā′) *n.* **1.** an air route along which beacons and other aids to navigation are maintained. **2.** a passage used for ventilation, as in a mine.

air·wor·thy (âr′wûr′thē) *adj.* (of an aircraft) in good or safe condition for flying. —**air′wor′thi·ness,** *n.*

air·y (âr′ē) *adj.*, **air·i·er, air·i·est. 1.** lacking material essence; unsubstantial; unreal; imaginary: *an airy being.* **2.** light as air in appearance and movement; thin; delicate. **3.** lighthearted; vivacious; buoyant: *His charmingly airy manner lifted her spirits.* **4.** open to the flow of air; breezy: *an airy apartment.* **5.** high in the air; lofty. **6.** taking place in the air; aerial.

aisle (īl) *n.* **1.** a passage between sections of seats in a place of assembly, such as a theater or stadium. **2.** any similar passageway: *a department store aisle.* **3.** a wing or side division of a church alongside the nave, choir, or transept, set off by pillars or arches. [Old French *ele* wing, from Latin *āla* wing; later influenced by French *aile* wing, wing of a building.]
  ·**to roll in the aisles.** to laugh uproariously and uncontrollably.
  ·**to walk down the aisle.** to get married.

a·jar¹ (ə jär′) *adj., adv.* partly open: *The door was left ajar.* [Middle English *on char* slightly open, literally, on the turn, from Old English *on cerre* on the turn.]

a·jar² (ə jär′) *adv., adj.* out of harmony; shaken up; unsettled: *My nerves are all ajar.* [A-¹ + JAR².]

A·jax (ā′jaks) *n.* **1.** in Greek legend, the son of Telamon, second only to Achilles as a warrior in the Trojan War. Also, **Ajax the Greater. 2.** another warrior in the Trojan War, one of the swiftest of the Greeks. Also, **Ajax the Lesser.**

AK, the postal abbreviation for Alaska.

a.k.a. *also,* **aka** also known as.

a·kim·bo (ə kim′bō) *adj., adv.* (of arms) with the hands on the hips and elbows out. [Middle English *in kenebowe* in a sharp curve; of uncertain origin.]

a·kin (ə kin′) *adj.* **1.a.** related by blood: *Your uncle and my mother are akin.* **b.** of the same class or family: *The dog is akin to the wolf.* **2.** similar in character or properties: *Love and friendship are akin.* [Contraction of OF KIN.]

Ak·ka·di·an (ə kā′dē ən, ə kä′-) *also,* **Accadian.** *n.* **1.** a member of an ancient Semitic people who inhabited the region of Akkad. The Akkadians conquered the Sumerians of Mesopotamia and established one of the first empires of history. **2.** the extinct Semitic language of these people from which the Babylonian and Assyrian languages were derived. —*adj.* of, relating to, or characteristic of the Akkadians, their empire, language, or culture.

Al, the symbol for aluminum.

al-, form of ad- before *l,* as in *allegation, alliteration.*

-al¹ *suffix* (used to form adjectives) of, relating to, or characterized by: *medicinal, historical.* [Latin *-ālis* relating to.]

-al² *suffix* (used to form nouns from verbs) the act, process, or result: *recital, denial, arrival.* [Latin *-ālia,* neuter plural of *-ālis* relating to.]

AL, the postal abbreviation for Alabama.

a·la (ā′lə) *n., pl.* **a·lae.** a wing or winglike part or structure, as of a stem, seed, or bone. [Latin *āla* wing.]

a la (ä′lə, ä′lä) *also,* **à la.** in the manner of: *The author's vivid descriptions are a la Dickens.* [Shortened from A LA MODE.]

ALA, American Library Association.

Ala., Alabama.

al·a·bas·ter (al′ə bas′tər) *n.* **1.** a smooth, whitish stone used esp. in sculpture, a fine-grained, translucent variety of gypsum. **2.** a semitranslucent variety of calcite, often having bandlike markings. —*adj.* resembling alabaster; smooth, translucent, and pale: *alabaster arms.* [Old French *alabastre* these minerals, going back to Greek *alabastron.*]

a la carte (ä′lə kärt′) *also,* **à la carte.** with a separate price for each item on the menu. ➡ distinguished from **table d'hôte.** [French *à la carte* literally, according to the menu.]

a·lack (ə lak′) *interj. Archaic.* an exclamation expressing regret, dismay, or disappointment. Also, **a·lack·a·day** (ə lak′ə dā′).

a·lac·ri·ty (ə lak′ri tē) *n.* **1.** eager willingness: *I accepted the opportunity with alacrity.* **2.** quickness; swiftness; celerity: *to move with alacrity.* [Latin *alacritās* liveliness.]

A·lad·din (ə lad′in) *n.* in the *Arabian Nights,* a youth who obtains a magic lamp and a magic ring with which he is able to summon a genie to obey his commands.

a·lae (ā′lē) the plural form of **ala.**

a la king (ä′lə king′) *also,* **à la king.** cooked in cream sauce with mushrooms and pimentos or green peppers. [A LA + KING.]

al·a·me·da (al′ə mē′də, -mä′-) *n.* a shaded public walk lined with poplars or other trees.

a·la·mo (al′ə mō′, ä′lə-) *n., pl.* **-mos.** a poplar tree, esp. a cottonwood. [Spanish *álamo* poplar.]

Al·a·mo (al′ə mō′) *n.* a fortified mission in San Antonio, Texas, besieged and taken by Mexican troops in 1836.

a la mode (ä′lə mōd′) *also,* **à la mode. 1.** *Cooking.* **a.** served with ice cream: *pie a la mode.* **b.** braised with vegetables and served with a rich brown sauce: *beef a la mode.* **2.** in style; fashionable. [French *à la mode* in the manner or fashion of.]

al·a·nine (al′ə nēn′, -nin) *n.* a nonessential amino acid present in many animal and plant proteins, produced synthetically for biochemical research. Formula: $C_3H_7NO_2$ [German *alanin,* from *aldehyd* ALDEHYDE.]

a·lar (ā′lər) *adj.* **1.** of or relating to an ala or wing. **2.** having alae or wings. **3.** winglike or wing-shaped. [Latin *alāris* relating to a wing, from *āla* wing.]

A·lar (ā′lär, al′är) *n. Trademark.* a growth-retarding chemical used to lengthen the shelf life of apples and to enhance their redness, under investigation because of reported carcinogenic effects. Formula: $C_6H_{12}N_2O_3$

a·larm (ə lärm′) *n.* **1.** sudden fear and excitement, esp. caused by a sense or realization of danger: *The sound of breaking glass filled them with alarm.* **2.** a warning of danger: *Give the alarm.* **3.** a device or signal that warns, rouses, or calls to action: *a burglar alarm.* **4.** *Archaic.* alarum. —*v.t.* **1.** to cause to feel fear, anxiety, or apprehension. **2.** to warn of danger. [Old French *alarme* warning of danger, from Old Italian *all'arme!* to arms! going back to Latin *ad to* + *ille* that + *arma* weapons.]

alarm clock, a clock that has an alarm that can be set to go off at a given time.

a·larm·ing (ə lär′ming) *adj.* causing sudden fear and excitement; disturbing. —**a·larm′ing·ly,** *adv.*

a·larm·ist (ə lär′mist) *n.* a person who is inclined to alarm others or become alarmed needlessly or on slight grounds. —*adj.* of or like an alarmist. —**a·larm′ism,** *n.*

a·lar·um (ə lar′əm, ə lär′-) *n. Archaic.* a call to action or to arms.

a·las (ə las′) *interj.* an exclamation expressing disappointment, sorrow, or regret. [Old French *a las* ah wretched, ah weary, from *a ah* + *las* weary (from Latin *lassus*).]

Alas., Alaska.

A·las·kan malamute (ə las′kən) a wolflike dog of a breed native to northwestern Alaska, having a thick, coarse coat and large, bushy tail, originally raised to pull sleds. Height: 25 inches (64 centimeters) at the shoulder.

A·las·ka Pipeline (ə las′kə) a pipeline, completed in 1977, that carries oil from wells on Alaska's Prudhoe Bay south to the port of Valdez, on the Gulf of Alaska.

Alaska Standard Time, the local time used in all of Alaska except the western Aleutian Islands. It is 9 hours behind Greenwich Time.

a·late (ā′lāt) *adj.* having wings or winglike parts. [Latin *ālātus,* from *āla* wing.]

Alaskan malamute

alb (alb) *n.* a floor-length white linen robe with narrow sleeves, worn girded at the waist by Roman Catholic and some Anglican priests at the Mass and other ceremonies. [Old English *albe,* from Late Latin *alba (vestis)* white (garment), from Latin *albus* white.]

al·ba·core (al′bə kôr′) *n., pl.* **-core** or **-cores.** an important food and game fish, *Thunnus alalunga,* of the tuna family, found mostly in temperate seas and distinguished from other tunas by its long pectoral fin. Weight: under 40 pounds (18 kilograms). [Portuguese *albacora,* from Arabic *al* the + *bakūrah* tuna.]

Al·ba·ni·an (al bā′nē ən, -bān′yən) *adj.* of, relating to, or characteristic of Albania or its people, language, or culture. —*n.* **1.** a native or citizen of Albania. **2.** a person of Albanian ancestry. **3.** the language of the Albanians, a branch of the Indo-European language family.

al·ba·tross (al′bə trôs′, -tros′) *n.* **1.** any of various web-footed seabirds, family Diomedeidae, found chiefly in the southern oceans, having a long hooked beak and capable of prolonged flight. One species, the **wandering albatross,** has a wingspan of up

albatross

to 11 feet (3.4 meters), the largest of any living bird. Length: 28-53 inches (71-135 centimeters). Also, **gooney. 2.** something that is difficult to bear or is a cause of suffering or anxiety: *The unfinished dissertation became an albatross around my neck.* [Modification (influenced by Latin *albus* white) of earlier *alcatras* pelican, from Portuguese *alcatraz* pelican; *(def. 2)* from the *albatross* in *The Rime of the Ancient Mariner* by Samuel Taylor Coleridge, 1772-1834, in which a mariner kills an albatross and has to wear it around his neck as a sign of his guilt.]

al·be·do (al bē′dō) *n., pl.* **-dos** or **-does**. the power of a surface to reflect sunlight, expressed as the ratio of the light reflected by the surface to the light falling on it: *the albedo of the moon.* [Late Latin *albēdō* whiteness, from Latin *albus* white.]

al·be·it (ôl bē′it) *conj.* even though; although; notwithstanding. [Short for *although it be that.*]

Al·ber·ich (al′bər ik) *n.* in Germanic legend, the king of the dwarfs and chief of the Nibelungs.

Al·bi·gen·ses (al′bi jen′sēz) *pl. n.* members of a religious sect existing in southern France from the eleventh to the thirteenth centuries, suppressed for heresy. —**Al′bi·gen′si·an,** *adj., n.*

al·bi·nism (al′bə niz′əm) *n.* the condition of being deficient in normal skin pigmentation; state of being an albino. —**al′bi·nis′- tic,** *adj.*

al·bi·no (al bī′nō) *n., pl.* **-nos. 1.** a person with a congenital deficiency in the pigment melanin, characterized by pale, milky skin, very light hair, and pink eyes. **2.** any plant or animal with deficient coloration. [Spanish *albino,* from *albo* snow white, from Latin *albus* white.]

Al·bi·on (al′bē ən) *n.* England. ➡ used primarily in literature.

al·bite (al′bīt) *n.* a sodic variety of the mineral plagioclase, used esp. as a glaze in ceramics. Moonstone, an opalescent variety, is used as a gemstone. Formula: $NaAlSi_3O_8$

al·bum (al′bəm) *n.* **1.** a book with blank pages or transparent envelopes in which to keep collected items: *an autograph album, a photograph album.* **2.** a holder for a phonograph record or records. **3.** a single long-playing phonograph record. **4.** a set of records or tape recordings sold as a unit. [Latin *album* blank tablet on which notices were recorded.]

al·bu·men (al bū′mən) *n.* **1.** the white of an egg. **2.** albumin. **3.** endosperm. [Latin *albūmen* white of an egg.]

al·bu·min (al bū′mən) *n.* any of a group of water-soluble proteins found in many plant and animal tissues and fluids. Albumin occurs in its purest natural form in the white of an egg. [French *albumine,* from Latin *albūmen* white of an egg.]

al·bu·mi·nous (al bū′mə nəs) *adj.* of, like, or containing albumin.

al·bur·num (al bûr′nəm) *n.* sapwood.

al·caide (al kād′) also, **al·cayde.** *n.* **1.** the governor of a Spanish, Portuguese, or Moorish fortress. **2.** the jailer or warden of a Spanish prison. [Spanish *alcaide* governor of a castle, from Arabic *al-qā′īd* the leader.]

al·cal·de (äl käl′dē) *n.* a mayor of a Spanish or Spanish-American town who has judicial as well as administrative powers and functions. [Spanish *alcalde,* from Arabic *al-qādī* the judge.]

the **Alcazar**

al·ca·zar (al kaz′ər, al′kə zär′) *n.* **1.** a castle or fortress of the Moors in Spain. **2. the Alcazar.** the palace of the Moorish kings

in Seville, Spain, later occupied by the Spanish royal family. [Spanish *alcázar,* from Arabic *al* the + *qaçr* castle, from Latin *castrum* fortified place.]

Al·ces·tis (al ses′tis) *n.* in Greek legend, a Thessalian queen who sacrificed her life to save that of her husband, King Admetus. She was later rescued from Hades by Hercules.

al·che·mist (al′kə mist) *n.* a person who studied or practiced alchemy. —**al′che·mis′tic;** *also,* **al′che·mis′ti·cal,** *adj.*

al·che·my (al′kə mē) *n.* **1.** a form of chemistry of the Middle Ages, concerned primarily with attempts to transmute base metals into gold and with the search for an elixir of life. **2.** any seemingly magical power or process of transforming one thing into another. [Old French *alchemie, alquemie,* from Medieval Latin *alchemia,* from Arabic *al-kīmiyā,* from *al* the + *kīmīā,* presumably from Late Greek *chēmīā* transmutation of metals, chemistry.] —**al·chem·ic** (al kem′ik); *also,* **al·chem′i·cal,** *adj.* —**al·chem′i·cal·ly,** *adv.*

Al·ci·des (al sī′dēz) *n.* Hercules.

Alc·me·ne (alk mē′nē) *n.* in Greek legend, the mother of Hercules.

al·co·hol (al′kə hôl′, -hol′) *n.* **1.a.** an odorless, flammable, volatile liquid that is produced synthetically or by the fermentation of grain, fruit, or other starchy or sugary substances. It is the intoxicating agent in liquor and is used widely in the manufacture of drugs and other chemicals. Formula: C_2H_5OH Also, **ethanol, ethyl alcohol, grain alcohol. b.** any of the group of colorless, flammable, organic compounds to which this liquid belongs, distinguished by the presence of one or more hydroxyl groups. The simplest alcohol is methyl alcohol, or wood alcohol, CH_3OH. **2.** any beverage containing alcohol. [Modern Latin *alcohol* distilled liquid, from Medieval Latin *alcohol* powder for decorating the eyelids, from Arabic *al-koh′l* the powdered antimony used to stain the eyelids.]

al·co·hol·ic (al′kə hô′lik, -hol′ik) *adj.* **1.** of or relating to alcohol. **2.** containing or using alcohol: *an alcoholic drink.* **3.** caused by alcohol: *an alcoholic stupor.* **4.** suffering from alcoholism. —*n.* a person who suffers from alcoholism.

Alcoholics Anonymous, an organization of men and women who suffer from alcoholism and who meet regularly to support each other in their efforts to recover.

al·co·hol·ism (al′kə hô liz′əm, -ho-) *n.* **1.** a chronic disease characterized by the compulsive and excessive use of alcoholic beverages. **2.** a diseased condition of the body caused by the excessive or prolonged use of alcoholic beverages.

Al·co·ran (al′kô răn′, -ran′) *n.* Koran.

al·cove (al′kōv) *n.* **1.** a small room or recess opening off a larger room. **2.** any recessed space or secluded bower: *an alcove in the garden.* [French *alcove* recess, from Spanish *alcoba,* from Arabic *al* the + *qobbah* vaulted area.]

Ald., Aldm. for Alderman. See **Aldm.**

Al·deb·a·ran (al deb′ər ən) *n.* a giant red star, one of the brightest in the sky and the brightest in the constellation Taurus.

al·de·hyde (al′də hīd′) *n.* **1.** any of a group of organic compounds, obtained by oxidation of certain kinds of alcohol, that yield acids when oxidized, as formaldehyde. General formula: R—CHO **2.** acetaldehyde. [Short for Modern Latin *al(cohol) dehyd(rogenatum)* alcohol deprived of its hydrogen.]

al dente (al den′tā, -tē, äl) *Italian.* cooked to remain firm: *spaghetti al dente.* [Italian *al dente* to the tooth.]

al·der (ôl′dər) *n.* any of a group of trees or shrubs, genus *Alnus,* found in cool, moist regions of the Northern Hemisphere, most of which have scaly bark and saw-toothed oval leaves and bear both male and female catkins. [Old English *alor.*]

alder

al·der·man (ôl′dər mən) *n., pl.* **-men** (-mən). **1.** in the United States, a member of a municipal governing body, often representing a certain ward or district. **2.** in England and Ireland, one of the members of a municipal or borough council. **3.** in Anglo-

a	at	e	end	o	hot	u	up	hw	white		about
ā	ape	ē	me	ō	old	ū	use	ng	song		taken
ä	far	i	it	ô	fork	ü	rule	th	thin	ə	pencil
âr	care	ī	ice	oi	oil	u̇	pull	th	this		lemon
				îr	pierce	ou	out	ûr	turn	zh	measure		circus

29

Saxon England, the chief magistrate of a county or group of counties. [Old English *ealdorman* high-ranking nobleman, official, member of a council, from *ealdor* head of a family, elder, chief + MAN.] —**al·der·man·ic** (ôl′dər man′ik), *adj.*

al·dol·ase (al′də lās′) *n.* an enzyme present in muscles and the liver that is instrumental in converting glycogen into lactic acid.

al·dos·te·rone (al dos′tə rōn′, al′dō sti rōn′) *n.* a steroid hormone secreted by the adrenal cortex that acts on the kidneys to regulate the body's balance of water and salt. [ALD(EHYDE) + STER(OL) + -ONE.]

al·drin (ôl′drin) *n.* an insecticide derived from naphthalene, effective in controlling termites and once widely used against soil pests. Formula: $C_{12}H_8Cl_6$ [From Kurt *Alder*, 1902-58, German chemist.]

ale (āl) *n.* a fermented beverage made from hops and malt, similar to beer, but heavier and more bitter. [Old English *ealu*.]

a·lee (ə lē′) *adv., adj.* on or toward the lee side of a ship; away from the wind; leeward. [A[1] + LEE.]

ale·house (āl′hous′) *n., pl.* **-hous·es** (-hou′ziz). **1.** a tavern where ale is served. **2.** any tavern.

a·lem·bic (ə lem′bik) *n.* **1.** a gourd-shaped glass or metal container with a beaked top, formerly used in distilling. **2.** anything that purifies, refines, or transforms. [French *alambic*, going back to Arabic *al* the + *anbīq* still[2], from Greek *ambīx* cup.]

a·lert (ə lûrt′) *adj.* **1.** watchful and prepared to respond quickly, as to danger; vigilant: *an alert sentinel.* **2.** quick to act or learn; lively; active: *an alert mind.* **3.** aware; conscious (with *to*): *to be alert to all the possibilities.* —*n.* **1.** a warning of possible danger; alarm: *an air alert.* **2.** the length of time an alert lasts: *They were quiet during the alert.* **3.** a signal to be ready: *The captain gave the alert an hour before sailing.* —*v.t.* **1.** to notify to be ready; warn: *to alert a town before a hurricane.* **2.** to make aware of; inform: *The government alerted the citizens to the fuel shortage.* [French *alerte* to arms, from Italian *all'erta* on the watch.] —**a·lert′ly**, *adv.* —**a·lert′ness**, *n.*

• **on alert.** on notice to be ready: *The troops were on alert during the crisis.*

• **on the alert.** on the lookout; vigilant: *to be on the alert for any sign of danger.*

A·leut (ə lūt′) *n., pl.* **A·leut** or **A·leuts**. **1.** a member of the Mongolid race of people living in southwestern Alaska, the Aleutian Islands, and islands off the coast of Siberia. **2.** the language spoken by these people, related to Eskimo. —*adj.* of, relating to, or characteristic of the Aleut or their language or culture. Also, **A·leu·tian** (ə lū′shən).

ale·wife[1] (āl′wīf′) *n., pl.* **-wives** (-wīvz′). a small bony fish, *Alosa pseudoharengus*, of the herring family, abundant along the Atlantic coast of the United States. It swims upstream in large numbers to spawn and has survived in landlocked waters, esp. the Great Lakes. Length: 6-15 inches (15-38 centimeters). [Of uncertain origin.]

ale·wife[2] (āl′wīf′) *n., pl.* **-wives** (-wīvz′). a woman who runs an alehouse.

Al·ex·an·dri·an (al′ig zan′drē ən) *adj.* **1.** of or relating to Alexandria, Egypt. **2.** of or relating to the Alexandrian school or its influence. **3.** of Alexander the Great or his reign. **4.** Alexandrine.

Alexandrian school, a school of literature, science, and philosophy that flourished in Alexandria, Egypt, during the first few centuries A.D.

Al·ex·an·drine (al′ig zan′drin, -drēn) *n.* a line of poetry having six iambic feet. —*adj.* designating or composed of an Alexandrine or Alexandrines. [French *alexandrin*, referring to its use in Old French poems about *Alexander* the Great, 356-323 B.C., king of Macedonia.]

al·ex·i·a (ə lek′sē ə) *n.* a form of aphasia marked by the inability to recognize or understand written or printed words. [Modern Latin *alexia*, from Greek *a-* without + *lexis* speech (confused with Latin *legere* to read).]

al·fal·fa (al fal′fə) *n.* any of a group of bushy, cloverlike plants, genus *Medicago*, several varieties of which are widely cultivated as forage and fodder crops. [Spanish *alfalfa*, from Arabic *al-façfaçah* the best kind of fodder.]

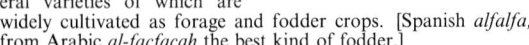
alfalfa

al fi·ne (äl fē′nā) *Italian. Music.* to the end.

al·fres·co (al fres′kō) *also,* **al fres·co.** *adv., adj.* in the open air; outdoors: *to lunch alfresco.* [Italian.]

alg., algebra.

al·gae (al′jē) *pl. n., sing.* **-ga** (-gə). a large group of primitive organisms, including pond scums and most seaweeds, that contain chlorophyll but have none of the vascular tissue (roots, stems, or leaves) of plants. Now classified as protists, algae range from microscopic, one-celled organisms, such as diatoms, to giant marine seaweeds and kelps. The best-known kinds of algae are aquatic. [Latin *algae*, plural of *alga* seaweed.] —**al·gal** (al′gəl), *adj.*

Irish moss
Brown alga
algae

al·ge·bra (al′jə brə) *n.* the branch of mathematics in which the relationships and properties of numbers are expressed and analyzed in terms of letters, numerals, and abstract symbols. [Italian *algebra*, from Arabic *al-jebr* the reduction.]

al·ge·bra·ic (al′jə brā′ik) *adj.* of, used in, or involving algebra: *an algebraic equation.* Also, **al′ge·bra′i·cal.** —**al′ge·bra′i·cal·ly**, *adv.*

al·ge·bra·ist (al′jə brā′ist) *n.* a person who is skilled in algebra.

-algia *combining form* pain: *neuralgia.*

al·gin (al′jin) *n.* a mucilaginous polysaccharide obtained from brown algae, used as a stabilizer in food and as a thickener in food and paints. [ALG(AE) + -IN[1].]

Al·gol (al′gol, -gôl) *n.* a multiple-star system in the constellation Perseus, including an eclipsing double star. [Arabic *al-ghūl* literally, the demon, the ghoul; because its periodic variation in brightness may have suggested the existence of an evil force.]

ALGOL (al′gol, -gôl) a computer coding system used for scientific purposes. [Short for *algo(rithmic) l(anguage)*.]

Al·gon·qui·an (al gong′kē ən, -kwē ən) *n., pl.* **-qui·ans** or **-qui·an.** **1.** one of the most widespread of North American Indian language families, including Cree, Delaware, Shawnee, Ojibwa, Blackfoot, and Cheyenne. **2.** a member of any Algonquian-speaking tribe. —*adj.* of or relating to this linguistic family.

Al·gon·quin (al gong′kin, -kwin) *n., pl.* **-quin** or **-quins.** **1.** a member of a group of Algonquian-speaking Indian tribes formerly living along the Ottawa River and in the region of the St. Lawrence River. **2.** the Algonquian language spoken by these tribes. **3.** any Algonquian-speaking Indian. [Possibly from Micmac *algoomeaking* at the place to spear fish.]

al·go·rithm (al′gə rith′əm) *n.* a method or set of rules that is applied to obtain the solution to a problem in a finite number of steps, as in finding the square root of a number to a specified number of decimal places. [Modification (influenced by ARITHMETIC) of *algorism*, the act or skill of computing numbers, going back to *al-Khwārizmī*, a ninth-century mathematician.] —**al′go·rith′mic**, *adj.*

Al·ham·bra (al ham′brə) *n.* a palace in Granada, Spain, built by Moorish princes in the thirteenth century, an outstanding example of Moorish architecture.

a·li·as (ā′lē əs) *n., pl.* **-as·es.** a false name used to hide one's real identity; assumed name; other name: *William H. Bonney's alias was Billy the Kid.* —*adv.* also known as; under the assumed name of: *Brown alias Bell.* [Latin *alias* otherwise, from *alius* another.] —For Synonyms, see **pseudonym.**

A·li Ba·ba (ä′lē bä′bä, al′ē bab′ə) in a story of the *Arabian Nights*, the poor woodcutter who found the treasure of the forty thieves. He opened the door of the cave by saying "open sesame."

al·i·bi (al′ə bī′) *n., pl.* **-bis. 1.** a claim or proof by an accused person of having been elsewhere at the time an act or offense was committed. **2.** an excuse. —*v.i.* **-bied, -bi·ing.** to offer an excuse (with *for*): *My cousin alibied for me.* [Latin *alibi* elsewhere.]

al·ien (āl′yən, ā′lē ən) *n.* **1.** a foreign-born person who is not a naturalized citizen of the country in which he or she lives. **2.** a person who was born in another country; foreigner; stranger. **3.** in science fiction, a creature who lives in or is from outer space; extraterrestrial. —*adj.* **1.** of or belonging to a foreign-born person living in a country of which he or she is not a citizen: *alien rights.* **2.** of or belonging to another country or people; foreign:

to land on alien shores. **3.** differing from one's own; strange; unfamiliar: *alien patterns of behavior.* **4.** incompatible or inconsistent with; opposed or hostile (with *to*): *actions alien to our democratic traditions.* **5.** in science fiction, living in or from outer space: *alien beings.* [Latin *aliēnus* strange, stranger.]

al·ien·a·ble (āl′yə nə bəl, ā′lē ə-) *adj.* capable of being transferred to another owner.

al·ien·ate (āl′yə nāt′, ā′lē ə-) *v.t.,* **-at·ed, -at·ing. 1.** to cause (someone) to feel unfriendly, indifferent, or hostile: *The manager's rudeness alienated most people.* **2.** to cause to be estranged or withdrawn, as from society: *The repressive government policies alienated many of the country's young people.* **3.** to transfer or convey to another owner: *to alienate property.*

al·ien·a·tion (āl′yə nā′shən, ā′lē ə-) *n.* **1.** the act of alienating or the state of being alienated. **2.** a transfer of property to another owner.

al·ien·ist (āl′yə nist, ā′lē ə-) *n.* a psychiatrist who specializes in giving legal testimony. [French *aliéniste,* going back to Latin *aliēnāre* to estrange, make insane.]

al·i·form (al′ə fôrm′, ā′lə-) *adj.* having the shape of a wing; wing-shaped.

a·light[1] (ə līt′) *v.i.,* **a·light·ed** or **a·lit, a·light·ing. 1.** to step or come down; get off: *The passengers alighted from the plane.* **2.** to come to rest from flight; land: *The bee alighted on the flower.* **3.** *Archaic.* to see or find by chance; discover (with *on* or *upon*). [Old English *ālīhtan* to descend, come down, from *līhtan* to remove a weight from.]

a·light[2] (ə līt′) *adv., adj.* **1.** brightly illuminated; aglow: *a church alight with candles.* **2.** on fire; burning. [Past participle of obsolete *alight* to light up, from Old English *ālīhtan* to enlighten; light up, from *lēoht* light.]

a·lign (ə līn′) also, **aline.** *v.t.* **1.** to bring into a straight line: *The golfer aligned the putter with the ball.* **2.** to ally (oneself) with others for a common cause: *The Republican senators aligned themselves with the president.* **3.** to adjust (the wheels of a vehicle) to the proper position. **4.** to adjust (parts of an electric circuit or a mechanical device) for proper functioning. —*v.i.* **1.** to come or fall into line. **2.** to join in a common cause. [French *aligner* to line up, from *à* to (from Latin *ad-*) + *ligne* line (from Latin *linea*).]

a·lign·ment (ə līn′mənt) also, **alinement.** *n.* **1.** the act of aligning or the state of being aligned. **2.** a line or lines formed by aligning. **3.** the state or condition of having joined with others.

a·like (ə līk′) *adv.* in the same manner; equally; similarly: *The twins sometimes dress alike. The teacher was respected by parents and students alike.* —*adj.* like one another; having resemblance; similar: *No two fingerprints are alike.* [Old English *onlīc.*]

al·i·ment (al′ə mənt) *n.* something that nourishes; food. [Latin *alimentum.*] —**al·i·men′tal,** *adj.*

al·i·men·ta·ry (al′ə men′tə rē, -trē) *adj.* **1.** of or relating to food and nutrition. **2.** providing nourishment; nourishing.

alimentary canal, a continuous tube extending from the mouth to the anus, through which food passes as it is digested, absorbed, and then eliminated as waste matter.

al·i·men·ta·tion (al′ə men tā′shən) *n.* **1.** the act or process of nourishing or the state of being nourished. **2.** something that nourishes; nourishment.

al·i·mo·ny (al′ə mō′nē) *n.* a court-ordered allotment of part of one spouse's estate or income to be paid for the other spouse's support after a couple is divorced or while they are legally separated or awaiting settlement of their case. [Latin *alimōnia* nourishment, support.]

a·line (ə līn′) *v.t., v.i.,* **a·lined, a·lin·ing.** align.

a·line·ment (ə līn′mənt) *n.* alignment.

al·i·phat·ic (al′ə fat′ik) *adj.* (of a hydrocarbon) consisting of a straight or branched chain of carbon atoms, rather than a ring. Aliphatic hydrocarbons occur in three principal series: alkanes, alkenes, and alkynes.

al·i·quant (al′i kwənt) *adj.* contained in but not dividing evenly into another number. The number three is an aliquant part of seven. ➡ distinguished from **aliquot.** [Latin *aliquantum* in some degree.]

al·i·quot (al′i kwət) *adj.* contained in and dividing evenly into another number. The number two is an aliquot part of four. ➡ distinguished from **aliquant.** [French *aliquote* proportionate, from Latin *aliquot* several.]

a·lit (ə lit′) a past tense and past participle of **alight**[1].

a·live (ə līv′) *adj.* **1.** having life; living; animate. **2.** in force or operation; active: *The war memorial will keep alive the memory of those who died.* **3.** full of life; animated; lively: *alive with excitement.* **4.** of all living: *the proudest person alive.* [Old English *on līfe* having life.] —**a·live′ness,** *n.*

• **alive to.** having knowledge or awareness of; sensitive to: *to be alive to changes around one.*

• **alive with.** filled or swarming with: *The station was alive with rushing commuters.*

• **to look alive.** to be alert; move quickly.

a·liz·a·rin (ə liz′ər in) *n.* an orange-red or red compound prepared from aniline, used in making dyes. It was formerly obtained from madder. Formula: $C_{14}H_8O_4$ [French *alizarine,* from *alizari* madder, going back to Arabic *al-'açarah* the extract.]

al·ka·li (al′kə lī) *n., pl.* **-lis** or **-lies. 1.** any of a group of strong, water-soluble bases or their salts. Most alkalis are compounds of the alkali metals. **2.** any water-soluble mineral salt or mixture of such salts. Alkalis are found in soils, esp. desert soils. [Middle English *alkaly,* from Arabic *alqili* the ashes (of the saltwort plant), from *al* the + *qili* ashes, from *qalai* to roast.]

alkali metal, any of the soft, univalent metallic elements of the group comprising lithium, sodium, potassium, rubidium, cesium, and francium.

al·ka·line (al′kə līn′, -lin) *adj.* of or like an alkali; having the properties of an alkali. —**al·ka·lin·i·ty** (al′kə lin′i tē), *n.*

alkaline earth, an oxide of any of the alkaline-earth metals.

al·ka·line-earth metal (al′kə līn′ûrth′, -lin-) any of the bivalent metallic elements of the group comprising beryllium, magnesium, calcium, strontium, barium, and radium.

al·ka·lize (al′kə līz′) *v.t., v.i.,* **-lized, -liz·ing.** to make or become alkaline.

al·ka·loid (al′kə loid′) *n.* any of a large group of organic alkaline substances, including atropine, morphine, caffeine, and quinine, obtained chiefly from higher plants and widely used in medicine. —**al′ka·loi′dal,** *adj.*

al·kane (al′kān) *n.* any saturated member of one of the three principal series of aliphatic hydrocarbons. General formula: C_nH_{2n+2} Also, **paraffin.**

al·kene (al′kēn) *n.* any unsaturated member of one of the three principal series of aliphatic hydrocarbons whose molecules contain one or more double bonds. Ethylene is an alkene. General formula: C_nH_{2n} Also, **olefin.**

Al·ko·ran (al′kô rän′, -ran′) *n.* Koran.

al·kyd (al′kid) *n.* any of a group of thermoplastic resins used in adhesives and paints. Also, **alkyd resin.** [ALKY(L) + (ACI)D.]

al·kyl (al′kəl) *n.* a univalent radical formed when one of the hydrocarbons of the alkane series loses a hydrogen atom. General formula: C_nH_{2n+1} [ALK(ALI) + Greek *hylē* matter.]

al·kyne (al′kīn) *n.* any unsaturated member of one of the three principal series of aliphatic hydrocarbons whose molecules contain one or more triple bonds. General formula: C_nH_{2n-2}

all (ôl) *adj.* **1.** the whole of; every part of: *My friend worked late all week.* **2.** not excluding any; the entire number of: *Delegates from all nations attended the conference.* **3.** the greatest possible: *in all honesty, with all due speed.* **4.** any whatever; any: *beyond all hope.* **5.** nothing but; only: *This is all fantasy.* **6.** including a great variety; very many: *all sorts of people.* ➡ used chiefly in the phrases all sorts of, all kinds of, all manner of. —*n.* **1.** everything one has: *to give one's all.* **2.** all things; everything: *All is lost.* —*pron.* **1.** the whole quantity, amount, or number: *All of the cake is gone.* **2.** every one; each: *All of us went to the zoo.* —*adv.* **1.** without exception; wholly; entirely: *The measurements were all wrong.* **2.** each; apiece: *a score of seven all.* [Old English *eall.*]

• **above all.** before everything else; most of all.

• **after all.** all things considered; despite everything.

• **all but.** not quite completely; almost; nearly.

• **all in.** *Informal.* exhausted; weary.

• **all in all.** everything considered; on the whole.

• **all of.** no less than; no more than: *That child is all of six years old.*

• **all out.** *Informal.* with the greatest effort possible: *We went all out to help our new neighbors get settled.*

• **all over. a.** finished; ended. **b.** many places; everywhere: *We looked for them all over.* **c.** *Informal.* in every way; typically: *That's Chris all over.*

• **at all. a.** in any degree: *no luck at all.* **b.** in any way: *He can't sing at all.* **c.** under any circumstances: *She refuses to drive at all.*

a	at	e	end	o	hot	u	up	hw	white		⟨ about
ā	ape	ē	me	ō	old	ū	use	ng	song		taken
ä	far	i	it	ô	fork	ü	rule	th	thin	ə	pencil
âr	care	ī	ice	oi	oil	u̇	pull	th	this		lemon
		îr	pierce	ou	out	ûr	turn	zh	measure		⟨ circus

• **for all (that).** **a.** in spite of; notwithstanding: *For all their hard work, their business failed.* **b.** as far as: *For all we know, they are lying.*

• **in all.** everyone or everything included; altogether: *In all, about fifty attended.*

al·la bre·ve (ä′lə brā′vā, al′ə brev′ā, brev′) *Music.* in a tempo in duple time in which the rhythmic beat is on the half note, rather than the quarter note, causing the notes to be played twice as fast. Symbol: ¢ [Italian *alla breve* literally, according to the breve.]

Al·lah (al′ə, ä′lə) *n.* the one God of Islam. [Arabic *allāh.*]

all-A·mer·i·can (ôl′ə mer′i kən) *adj.* **1.** representative or typical of the United States: *an all-American teenager.* **2.** selected as the best or composed of the best of its type in the United States: *an all-American halfback, an all-American football team.* **3.** made up entirely of Americans or American parts: *an all-American rescue operation.* —*n.* an all-American player or athlete.

al·lan·to·is (ə lan′tō is) *n., pl.* **al·lan·to·i·des** (al′an tō′i dēz′). a membranous, saclike outgrowth from the gut in the embryos of higher vertebrates. In the incubating eggs of reptiles and birds, it is an organ of respiration and excretion; in mammals, it helps form the placenta. [Modern Latin *allantois,* from Greek *allantoēidis,* sausage-shaped, from *allas* sausage + -*oeidēs* -oid.]

al·lar·gan·do (ä′lär gän′dō) *adj., adv. Music.* gradually slower and more dignified, with the same or greater volume. [Italian *allargando* literally, making slow.]

all-a·round (ôl′ə round′) *adj.* **1.** good at many things: *an all-around athlete.* **2.** good for many purposes; versatile: *an all-around education.* Also, **all-round.**

al·lay (ə lā′) *v.t.,* -**layed,** -**lay·ing.** **1.** to put at rest; quiet; calm: *The doctor allayed the patient's fears about the operation.* **2.** to make less severe; relieve: *The ice pack allayed the pain in the gymnast's sprained ankle.* [Old English *ālecgan* to suppress.]

all clear, a signal indicating that an air raid or other danger is over.

al·le·ga·tion (al′i gā′shən) *n.* **1.** an assertion, esp. one made without proof. **2.** an assertion to be proven in a court of law. [French *allégation* assertion, from Latin *allegatio* alleging.]

al·lege (ə lej′) *v.t.,* -**leged,** -**leg·ing.** **1.** to assert or declare, esp. without proof: *The writer alleged that members of the city council had accepted bribes.* **2.** to give as an excuse or defense. [Anglo-Norman *alegier* to clear at law, going back to Latin *ex* out of + *lītigāre* to sue; influenced by Middle French *alleguer* to urge, from Latin *allēgāre* to bring forward.] —**al·lege′a·ble,** *adj.* —**al·leg′er,** *n.*

al·leged (ə lejd′) *adj.* thought to be true or real; supposed: *The alleged ringleader was shown not to have been involved.* —**al·leg·ed·ly** (ə lej′id lē), *adv.*

al·le·giance (ə lē′jəns) *n.* **1.** the obligation of loyalty to a government, country, or sovereign. **2.** loyalty or devotion to a person, cause, or thing. **3.** *Archaic.* the obligation of a vassal to his feudal lord. [Anglo-Norman *alligeaunce, from Old French a-* (from Latin *ad* to) + *ligeance* homage, from *lige.* See LIEGE.]

al·le·gor·i·cal (al′i gôr′i kəl) *adj.* of, relating to, or containing allegory; figurative. Also, **al′le·gor′ic.** —**al′le·gor′i·cal·ly,** *adv.*

al·le·go·rize (al′i gə rīz′) *v.,* -**rized,** -**riz·ing.** —*v.t.* to make allegorical; treat as an allegory. —*v.i.* to use or make allegory.

al·le·go·ry (al′i gôr′ē) *n., pl.* -**ries.** **1.** a literary device of presenting abstract ideas or moral principles in the form of symbolic characters, events, or objects, used to teach or explain something. **2.** a narrative form in which allegory is used extensively. [Latin *allēgoria,* from Greek *allēgoriā.*]

al·le·gret·to (al′i gret′ō) *Music. adj., adv.* faster than andante but slower than allegro; rather lively. —*n., pl.* -**tos.** a piece, movement, or passage in such tempo. [Italian *allegretto,* diminutive of *allegro* fast. See ALLEGRO.]

al·le·gro (ə lā′grō, ə leg′rō) *Music. adj., adv.* faster than allegretto but slower than presto; lively; fast. —*n., pl.* -**gros.** a piece, movement, or passage in such tempo. [Italian *allegro* fast, from Latin *alacer* lively.]

al·lele (ə lēl′) *n.* any of the possible forms of a gene that determines a particular inherited trait, such as hair or eye color. —**al·le·lic** (ə lē′lik, ə lel′ik), *adj.*

al·le·lu·ia (al′ə lü′yə) hallelujah.

al·le·mande (al′ə mand′) *n.* **1.** any of various German processional dances of the seventeenth and eighteenth centuries. **2.** the music for any of these dances. **3.** a piece of music resembling this in rhythm, formerly used as the movement preceding the prelude in a suite. [French *allemande,* feminine of *allemand* German, from Latin *Alemannī* ancient German tribe; of Germanic origin.]

al·ler·gen (al′er jən) *n.* any substance that induces an allergic reaction, as pollen and certain foods or medicines.

al·ler·gen·ic (al′er jen′ik) *adj.* inducing allergy.

al·ler·gic (ə lûr′jik) *adj.* **1.** of or produced by allergy: *an allergic reaction.* **2.** having an allergy. **3.** *Informal.* having a strong distaste or aversion (with *to*): *allergic to homework.*

al·ler·gist (al′ər jist) *n.* a physician who specializes in treating allergies. [ALLERG(Y) + -IST.]

al·ler·gy (al′ər jē) *n., pl.* -**gies.** **1.** a hypersensitivity of the body tissues to a specific substance, such as pollen, dust, or certain fruits, resulting in various reactions affecting the skin, respiratory system, and the like, including hives, rashes, sneezing, and asthma. **2.** a hypersensitivity to a substance following its reintroduction into the blood; anaphylaxis. **3.** *Informal.* a strong distaste or aversion. [Modern Latin *allergia* from Greek *allos* other + *ergon* work.]

al·le·vi·ate (ə lē′vē āt′) *v.t.,* -**at·ed,** -**at·ing.** to make easier to bear; relieve; lessen: *to alleviate pain.* [Late Latin *alleviātus,* past participle of *alleviāre* to lighten.] —**al·le′vi·a′tion,** *n.*

al·le·vi·a·tive (ə lē′vē ā′tiv) *adj.* capable of alleviating.

al·ley[1] (al′ē) *n., pl.* -**leys.** **1.** a narrow street or passageway between buildings, esp. one giving access to rear entrances or garages. **2.** a bowling alley. **3.** a path or walk, as in a garden or park, bordered by trees or shrubbery. [Old French *alee* passage, walk, from *aler* to go, going back to Latin *ambulare* to walk.]

• **up one's alley.** *Slang.* to one's liking or suited to one's talents.

al·ley[2] (al′ē) *n., pl.* -**leys.** a large playing marble, esp. a white one, used to shoot at other marbles. [Short for ALABASTER; because the best marbles were originally made from alabaster.]

alley cat, a stray, mongrel cat.

al·ley·way (al′ē wā′) *n.* a narrow or short passageway between buildings.

All Fools′ Day, April Fools′ Day.

all hail *Archaic.* used as a greeting or welcome.

All·hal·lows (ôl hal′ōz) *n.* All Saints′ Day.

al·li·ance (ə lī′əns) *n.* **1.a.** a union of nations by formal agreement for mutual cooperation in a common cause, such as a war. **b.** the agreement for such a union. **2.** any union, association, or close connection between people or groups for a common cause: *an alliance between government and industry.* **3.** a joining of families through marriage. **4.** the nations, groups, or persons joined in such a union. **5.** the state of being allied. **6.** a close relationship or similarity; affinity: *the alliance between math and physics.* [Old French *aliance* connection, from *alier* to bind to, going back to Latin *alligāre* to bind, tie.]

> **Synonyms** **Alliance, league,** and **coalition** mean an association of persons or groups for a common purpose. **Alliance** refers to an association whose members have the same interests at stake and pool their resources: *an alliance of civil rights organizations.* **League** is often more formal, usually refers to an association with more limited goals, and may have negative connotations: *a league of writers, a league of criminals.* **Coalition** refers to a temporary alliance of people or groups who are usually or at other times rivals or opponents: *a coalition of political parties, a coalition of business and labor leaders.*

al·lied (ə līd′, al′īd) *adj.* **1.** united by treaty, agreement, or common cause: *allied railroad unions, allied by marriage.* **2.** related or similar: *Painting and sculpture are allied arts.* **3.** **Allied.** of or relating to the Allies of World War I or II: *the Allied Expeditionary Forces.*

Al·lies (al′īz, ə līz′) *pl. n.* **1.** the nations allied against Germany and the other Central Powers in World War I, esp. the nations of the Triple Entente (Great Britain, Russia, and France). **2.** the nations allied against the Axis Powers in World War II, esp. the United States, Great Britain, and the Soviet Union.

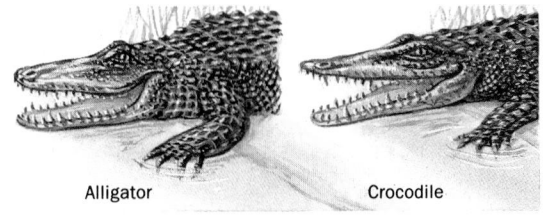

Alligator   Crocodile

al·li·ga·tor (al′i gā′tər) *n.* **1.** a large aquatic reptile related to the crocodile, but having a broader, rounder snout. One species, *Alligator mississippiensis,* is native to the southern United States. Another, *A. sinensis,* found near Shanghai, China, is almost ex-

tinct. Length: 9 feet (2.7 meters). Weight: 250 pounds (113 kilograms). **2.** leather made from the alligator's skin. **3.** caiman. [Spanish *el lagarto* the lizard, going back to Latin *lacertus* lizard.]
alligator pear, avocado.
all·im·por·tant (ôl′im pôr′tənt) *adj.* very important; essential; indispensable.
all·in·clu·sive (ôl′in klü′siv) *adj.* including or covering everything; comprehensive.
al·lit·er·ate (ə lit′ə rāt′) *v.,* -at·ed, -at·ing. —*v.i.* **1.** to display alliteration. **2.** to use alliteration. —*v.t.* to write with or cause to have alliteration.
al·lit·er·a·tion (ə lit′ə rā′shən) *n.* the repetition of the same initial letter, sound, or group of sounds in a series of words, for example: *The furrow followed free* (Samuel Taylor Coleridge, 1798). [AL- + Latin *littera* letter + -ATION.]
al·lit·er·a·tive (ə lit′ə rā′tiv) *adj.* of or characterized by alliteration. —**al·lit′er·a′tive·ly,** *adv.* —**al·lit′er·a′tive·ness,** *n.*
all-night (ôl′nīt′) *adj.* **1.** continuing through the night: *an all-night party.* **2.** open all night: *an all-night coffee shop.*
al·lo·cate (al′ə kāt′) *v.t.,* -cat·ed, -cat·ing. to set aside, as for a specific purpose; designate: *to allocate funds for public housing.* [Medieval Latin *allocatus,* past participle of *allocare* to allot, from Latin *ad* to + *locare* to place.]
al·lo·ca·tion (al′ə kā′shən) *n.* **1.** a thing or amount that is allocated. **2.** the act of allocating or the state of being allocated.
al·lo·morph (al′ə môrf′) *n.* any of the variant forms of a particular morpheme. The *s* in *cats* and the *es* in *glasses* are two allomorphs of the English morpheme indicating a plural. —**al′lo·mor′phic,** *adj.*
al·lo·path (al′ə path′) *n.* a person who practices or advocates allopathy. Also, **al·lop·a·thist** (ə lop′ə thist).
al·lop·a·thy (ə lop′ə thē) *n.* the method of treating a disease by using remedies to produce effects differing from or incompatible with those of the disease being treated. ➡ opposed to **homeopathy.** [German *Allopathie,* from Greek *allos* other + *pathos* suffering.] —**al·lo·path·ic** (al′ə path′ik), *adj.* —**al′lo·path′i·cal·ly,** *adv.*
al·lo·phone (al′ə fōn′) *n.* any of the variant forms of a particular phoneme. Two allophones of *d* are the *d* sound in *down* and the *d* sound in *ladder.* [Greek *allos* other + PHONE².]
al·lot (ə lot′) *v.t.,* -lot·ted, -lot·ting. **1.** to distribute or parcel out; apportion: *to allot shares of stock.* **2.** to set aside; appropriate: *to allot funds for a new library.* [Old French *aloter,* from *à* to + *loter* to divide by lot (of Germanic origin).] —For Synonyms, see **assign.**
al·lot·ment (ə lot′mənt) *n.* **1.** the act of allotting. **2.** something that is allotted; share; portion.
al·lo·trope (al′ə trōp′) *n.* an allotropic form.
al·lo·trop·ic (al′ə trop′ik, -trō′pik) *adj.* of, relating to, or exhibiting allotropy: *Graphite and diamond are allotropic forms of carbon.* Also, **al′lo·trop′i·cal.** —**al′lo·trop′i·cal·ly,** *adv.*
al·lot·ro·py (ə lot′rə pē) *n.* the existence of a chemical element in two or more forms that have different molecular or crystalline structures. Also, **al·lot′ro·pism.** [Greek *allotropia* variation.]
all-out (ôl′out′) *adj.* using all one's efforts or resources; complete; total: *all-out war.*
all·o·ver (ôl′ō′vər) *adj.* covering the whole extent or surface: *an allover pattern of checks.*
al·low (ə lou′) *v.t.* **1.** to grant permission to or for; permit: *His parents allow him to drive the car. They do not allow swimming in the pond.* **2.** to let have; give: *She is allowed five dollars a week for lunch money.* **3.** to permit through oversight or neglect: *to allow a prisoner to escape.* **4.** to take into account or make provision for; set aside: *We should allow extra time for traveling because of the snow.* **5.** to accept as true or valid; acknowledge; concede: *The tax agent allowed the deduction.* **6.** *Informal.* to say or admit: *I allow they'll be late again.* [Old French *alouer* to grant, from Medieval Latin *allocare* to allot. See ALLOCATE.]
• **to allow for.** to make provision or concession for: *to allow for errors.*
• **to allow of.** to have as possible; permit: *The problem allows of only one solution.* —For Synonyms, see **let¹.**
al·low·a·ble (ə lou′ə bəl) *adj.* that can be allowed; legitimate; permissible. —**al·low′a·ble·ness,** *n.* —**al·low′a·bly,** *adv.*
al·low·ance (ə lou′əns) *n.* **1.** a quantity granted or set apart, esp. a sum of money given regularly or for a specific purpose: *an officer's clothing allowance, a child's weekly allowance.* **2.** compensation made for contingencies or modifying circumstances: *a depreciation allowance.* **3.** a deduction or discount given in return for something: *a trade-in allowance on a used car.* **4.** the act of

allowing; concession; acceptance: *allowance of a claim.* **5.** *Archaic.* tolerance; sanction.
• **to make allowance** (or **allowances**) **for.** to take into consideration; allow for: *They made allowance for the new employee's inexperience.*
al·loy (*n.,* al′oi, ə loi′; *v.,* ə loi′) *n.* **1.** a metallic substance formed by adding to a pure metallic element, called the base, some proportion of another metal or metals or, sometimes, nonmetallic elements. Alloys tend to be harder or more malleable or heat resistant than the base metal. **2.** a less valuable metal mixed with a finer one. **3.** something that debases or reduces quality; adulterant. —*v.t.* **1.** to mix (metals) so as to form an alloy. **2.** to reduce the purity of (a metal) by mixture with a less valuable metal. **3.** to debase or modify by mixture with something inferior; adulterate. [French *aloi* standard, (earlier) a joining, from Middle French *aloier* to ally, join, going back to Latin *alligāre* to join together.]
all-pur·pose (ôl′pûr′pəs) *adj.* useful for many things: *all-purpose detergent.*
all-right (ôl′rīt′) *adj. Slang.* good; dependable; admirable: *an all-right guy.*
all right 1. worthy of being accepted; satisfactory: *The carpenter's work was all right. It's all right with me.* **2.** without injury; safe; well: *Are you all right?* **3.** yes; agreed: *All right, I'll do it.* **4.** satisfactorily: *She's doing all right.* **5.** without doubt; certainly: *I'll be there, all right.*
all-round (ôl′round′) all-around.
All Saints' Day, a Christian festival celebrated in honor of all the saints, observed on November 1. Also, **Allhallows.**
All Souls' Day, in the Roman Catholic Church, a day of services and prayer for the souls in purgatory, observed on November 2.
all·spice (ôl′spīs′) *n.* **1.** an aromatic spice made from whole or ground dried berries of the evergreen pimento tree, *Pimenta dioica,* of the myrtle family, native to the West Indies and Central America. **2.** the berry or tree itself. [ALL + SPICE; because it was thought to have the flavors of cloves, cinnamon, and nutmeg.]
all-star (ôl′stär′) *adj.* composed of exceptional or star players or performers: *an all-star cast.* —*n.* an athlete who is a member of an all-star team.
all-time (ôl′tīm′) *adj.* never surpassed: *The temperature today reached an all-time high.*
al·lude (ə lüd′) *v.i.,* -lud·ed, -lud·ing. to mention casually and in passing; refer indirectly (with *to*): *The teacher alluded to the students' absence without actually mentioning their names.* [Latin *allūdere* to touch on.]
al·lure (ə lûr′) *v.t., v.i.,* -lured, -lur·ing. to fascinate or attract with something desirable; entice. —*n.* the power to attract; fascination: *the allure of traveling in outer space.* [Old French *alurer* to attract, from *à* to + *lure* bait (of Germanic origin).] —**al·lur′er,** *n.*
al·lure·ment (ə lûr′mənt) *n.* **1.** something that allures; enticement: *The large reward was a powerful allurement.* **2.** attractiveness; fascination; charm. **3.** the act or process of alluring.
al·lur·ing (ə lûr′ing) *adj.* very tempting or attractive; enticing: *an alluring prospect.*
al·lu·sion (ə lü′zhən) *n.* an indirect or casual reference; incidental mention: *The newspaper article made allusions to the mayor's possible misconduct.* [Late Latin *allūsiō* a touching on.]
al·lu·sive (ə lü′siv) *adj.* containing, using, or characterized by allusions.
al·lu·vi·al (ə lü′vē əl) *adj.* of, relating to, or composed of alluvium: *an alluvial deposit.*
al·lu·vi·um (ə lü′vē əm) *n., pl.* -vi·ums or -vi·a (-vē ə). an accumulation of mud, sand, or other material carried and deposited by flowing water. [Latin *alluvium* alluvial, going back to *ad*-to, at + *luere* to wash.]
al·ly (*v.,* ə lī′; *n.,* al′ī, ə lī′) *v.,* -lied, -ly·ing. —*v.t.* **1.** to unite or associate (oneself) for a common purpose: *The United States allied itself with England and the USSR during World War II.* **2.** to connect by some similarity or common feature; relate: *Domestic cats are allied to tigers.* —*v.i.* to become allied; join an alliance; unite. —*n., pl.* -lies. **1.** a person, nation, or group united or in league with another for a common purpose. **2.** a person who helps or supports; supporter: *His older brother was his greatest ally all*

a	at	e	end	o	hot	u	up	hw	white	(	about
ā	ape	ē	me	ō	old	ū	use	ng	song		taken
ä	far	i	it	ô	fork	ü	rule	th	thin	ə	pencil
âr	care	ī	ice	oi	oil	u̇	pull	th	this		lemon
		îr	pierce	ou	out	ûr	turn	zh	measure	(	circus

through school. **3.** a plant or animal related to another by descent or similar to another in structure. [Old French *alier* to bind to, from Latin *alligāre* to join together.]

al·ma ma·ter (äl′mə mä′tər, mā′tər, al′mə) *also,* **Al·ma Ma·ter. 1.** the school, college, or other institution of learning that a person has attended. **2.** the official anthem of such an institution. [Latin *alma māter* nourishing mother. Students thought of their school as a mother who brought them up and nourished them.]

al·ma·nac (ôl′mə nak′) *n.* **1.** a reference book of statistical and general information compiled annually. **2.** a book arranged by days, weeks, and months, containing astronomical and meteorological data and tables of other useful information. [Medieval Latin *almanach* diary, account, from Arabic *al-manākh* the almanac.]

al·might·y (ôl mī′tē) *adj.* **1.** having limitless power; omnipotent. **2.** *Informal.* great; inordinate: *an almighty bore.* —*n.* **the Almighty.** God. —**al·might′i·ly,** *adv.* —**al·might′i·ness,** *n.*

al·mond (ä′mənd, am′ənd) *n.* **1.** the edible, nutlike seed of the fruit of a tree, *Prunus dulcis,* of the rose family, the sweet variety of which is widely used in desserts, candy, and cooking. **2.** the tree that bears this fruit, found in the Mediterranean region and cultivated in California and other areas for the seeds and as an ornamental. [Old French *almande,* from Medieval Latin *amandula,* modification of Latin *amygdala,* from Greek *amygdalē.*]

al·mond-eyed (ä′mənd īd′, am′ənd-) *adj.* having oval-shaped eyes with tapering ends.

al·mon·er (al′mə nər, ä′mə-) *n.* a person who distributes alms as an official duty, as for a church or royal court. [Old French *almosnier,* from *almosne* alms, from Late Latin *eleēmosyna* alms. See ALMS.]

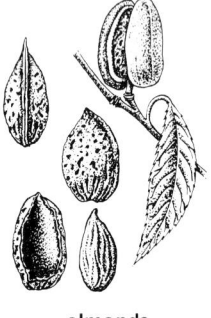

almonds

al·mon·ry (al′mən rē, ä′mən-) *n., pl.* **-ries. 1.** a place where alms are distributed. **2.** the residence of an almoner.

al·most (ôl′mōst, ôl mōst′) *adv.* very nearly but not completely or totally. [Old English *ealmǣst.*]

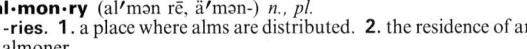

Synonyms **Almost, nearly,** and **practically** indicate the state of being very close to something. **Almost** may imply effort that comes just short of success or completion, or a deficiency of some sort: *I've almost finished my essay. They've saved almost enough money for their trip.* **Nearly** indicates mere closeness in space or time: *We're nearly there. It's nearly ten o'clock.* **Practically** suggests closeness that makes something, in effect, the same: *The two houses are practically identical.*

alms (ämz) *n.* money or gifts for the poor; charity. ➡ used as singular or plural. [Old English *ælmesse,* from Late Latin *eleēmosyna,* from Greek *eleēmosynē* pity.]

alms·giv·ing (ämz′giv′ing) *n.* the giving of alms. —**alms′·giv′er,** *n.*

alms·house (ämz′hous′) *n., pl.* **-hous·es** (-hou′ziz). a publicly supported home for the poor; poorhouse.

al·ni·co (al′ni kō′) *n.* any of several alloys used to make powerful permanent magnets, consisting of iron combined with aluminum, nickel, cobalt, and small amounts of copper or titanium. [Short for *al(uminum) ni(ckel) co(balt).*]

al·oe (al′ō) *n., pl.* **-oes. 1.** any of a group of succulent plants, genus *Aloe,* of the lily family, native chiefly to dry parts of Africa, most of which have thick, fleshy leaves edged with spines and red or yellow tube-shaped flowers that grow at the top of tall, leafless stalks. **2. aloes.** a bitter drug made from the juice of the leaves of certain aloe plants, formerly used as a purgative. ➡ used as singular. **3.** the century plant of North America. [Late Latin *aloē* the cactuslike plant, from Greek *aloē.*]

a·loft (ə lôft′) *adv.* **1.** in or to a place far above the ground; high up. **2.** in, at, or into the rigging of a ship; far above the deck. [Old Norse *ā lopt* in the air.]

a·lo·ha (ə lō′ə, ä lō′hä) *n., interj.* **1.** greetings; hello. **2.** goodbye; farewell. [Hawaiian *aloha* literally, love.]

a·lone (ə lōn′) *adj.* **1.** without other persons or things; unaccompanied; solitary: *She was alone in the room.* **2.** without anyone or anything else; only; solely: *You cannot live by bread alone. He alone can do it. The jacket alone costs fifty dollars.* —*adv.* without or exclusive of anyone or anything else: *The horse stood alone in the field. They were motivated by money alone.* [Middle English *al one* all one; wholly one. See ALL, ONE.]

　•**let alone.** not to mention: *I can't sew on a button, let alone make a dress.*

　•**to leave** (or **let**) **alone.** to refrain from bothering or interfering with: *It's best to leave him alone when he's busy.*

　•**to leave** (or **let**) **well enough alone.** to be content with things the way they are.

　•**to stand alone.** to be unique or without equal: *She stands alone as a conductor of modern French music.*

Synonyms *adj.* **Alone, lone,** and **solitary** mean separated from others. **Alone,** which comes after the word it modifies, may suggest a lack of companions, with the suggestion of cheerlessness: *The orphan felt alone in the world.* But it may have the same sense as **lone,** which comes before the noun and does not ordinarily suggest any mood: *A lone pedestrian was standing on the corner.* **Solitary** implies physical or emotional distance, often deliberately sought: *Even in the heart of the city, the artist lived a solitary life.*

a·long (ə lông′) *prep.* through or by the whole length of; from one end to the other of; following the line of: *We walked along the river's edge.* —*adv.* **1.** progressively onward; forward: *We walked along swiftly. They worked along diligently.* **2.** near or on one's person; with one: *She brought her umbrella along. Bring your friends along.* **3.** advanced in its course: *The party was well along when we arrived.* [Old English *andlang* from end to end, following the line of.]

　•**all along.** from the start; all the time; throughout: *He knew about the plan all along.*

　•**along about** (or **toward**). somewhere near or approaching a certain time: *along about midnight.*

　•**along with. a.** in company or association with; together with: *Let the children go along with you to the market.* **b.** in addition to: *There was a letter along with the present.*

a·long·shore (ə lông′shôr′) *adv.* near, beside, or parallel to the shore.

a·long·side (ə lông′sīd′) *adv.* at, close to, or by the side: *They brought the rescue boat alongside.* —*prep.* by or at the side of; beside: *The car was parked alongside the curb.*

　•**alongside of.** side by side with; next to: *The soldiers stood at attention alongside of each other. The boat docked alongside of the wharf.*

a·loof (ə lüf′) *adv.* at a distance physically or emotionally: *We stood aloof from the demonstrators. They kept aloof from their family. adj.* reserved and disinterested; unfriendly: *The senator had an aloof manner toward reporters.* [A-¹ + *loof,* form of LUFF, probably from Dutch *te loef* to windward.] —**a·loof′ly,** *adv.* —**a·loof′ness,** *n.*

a·loud (ə loud′) *adv.* **1.** in a voice that can be heard; audibly: *Please read the story aloud.* **2.** in a loud voice; loudly.

alp (alp) *n.* a high mountain or mountain peak. [Latin *Alpēs* the Alps.]

al·pac·a (al pak′ə) *n.* **1.** a cud-chewing mammal, *Lama pacos,* of the camel family, closely related to and resembling the llama and guanaco, raised in the Andes for its fine, silky wool. Height: about 3 feet (0.9 meter) at the shoulder. **2.** the wool of this animal. **3.** a silky lightweight fabric woven from or containing this wool, used esp. for coats and suits. [Spanish *alpaca;* of Quechuan origin.]

al·pen·horn (al′pən hôrn′) *n.* a long, slightly curved, wooden horn, used by herdsmen in the Alps, often ranging from 7 to 15 feet (2.1 to 4.6 meters) in length. [German *Alpenhorn,* going back to Latin *Alpes* the Alps + German *Horn* horn.]

al·pen·stock (al′pən stok′) *n.* a strong staff with an iron point, used in mountain climbing. [German *Alpenstock,* going back to Latin *Alpes* the Alps + German *Stock* staff.]

alpaca

al·pha (al′fə) *n.* **1.** the first letter of the Greek alphabet (A, a), corresponding to the English letter *A, a.* **2.** the first in a group or series, esp. in scientific classification; beginning. **3. Alpha.** *Astronomy.* the main or brightest star in a constellation.

alpha and omega, the beginning and the end; the first and the last.

al·pha·bet (al′fə bet′, -bət) *n.* **1.** a series of letters or characters used to write a language, esp. as arranged in a customary order. **2.** any system of characters or symbols representing sounds or words: *a phonetic alphabet.* **3.** the basic principles of something;

Alphabets

Shown below are the Roman and four important non-Roman alphabets. The Roman, or Latin, alphabet is derived, with minor modifications, from the alphabet of the ancient Romans. It is used to write many modern languages, including English. Many of the letters in the non-Roman alphabets have no direct Roman equivalent, and various systems of transliteration have been developed to represent them. In Greek, the third form of sigma is used at the end of a word. The Arabic characters are those used when the letters occur by themselves; other forms may be substituted when the letters are combined in words. The Russian alphabet is a form of Cyrillic. In the Hebrew alphabet, the alternative forms shown with the letters *kaf, mem, nun, pe,* and *sadhe* are those used when the letters occur at the end of a word.

ROMAN	GREEK		ARABIC		RUSSIAN	HEBREW	
A a	A α	alpha	ا	alif	A a	א	aleph
B b	B β	beta	ب	bā	Б б	ב	beth
C c	Γ γ	gamma	ت	tā	В в	ג	gimel
D d	Δ δ	delta	ث	thā	Г г	ד	daleth
E e	E ε	epsilon	ج	jīm	Е е Ё ё	ה	he
F f	Z ζ	zeta	ح	ḥā	Ж ж	ו	vav
G g	H η	eta	خ	khā	З з	ז	zayin
H h	Θ θ	theta	د	dāl	И и Й й	ח	het
I i	I ι	iota	ذ	dhāl	К к	ט	teth
J j	K κ	kappa	ر	rā	Л л	י	yod
K k	Λ λ	lambda	ز	zāy	М м	כ ך	kaf
L l	M μ	mu	س	sīn	Н н	ל	lamed
M m	N ν	nu	ش	shīn	О о	מ ם	mem
N n	Ξ ξ	xi	ص	ṣād	П п	נ ן	nun
O o	O o	omicron	ض	ḍād	Р р	ס	samekh
P p	Π π	pi	ط	ṭā	С с	ע	ayin
Q q	P ρ	rho	ظ	ẓā	Т т	פ ף	pe
R r	Σ σ ς	sigma	ع	'ayn	У у	צ ץ	sadhe
S s	T τ	tau	غ	ghayn	Ф ф	ק	koph
T t	Y υ	upsilon	ف	fā	Х х	ר	resh
U u	Φ φ	phi	ق	qāf	Ц ц	שׂ	sin
V v	X χ	chi	ك	kāf	Ч ч	שׁ	shin
W w	Ψ ψ	psi	ل	lām	Ш ш	ת	tav
X x	Ω ω	omega	م	mīm	Щ щ		
Y y			ن	nūn	Ъ ъ		
Z z			ه	hā	Ы ы		
			و	wāw	Ь ь		
			ى	yā	Э э		
					Ю ю		
					Я я		

rudiments. [Late Latin *alphabētum* the letters of a language, from Greek *alphabētos,* from *alpha* A + *bēta* B, the first two letters of the Greek alphabet.]

al·pha·bet·i·cal (al′fə bet′i kəl) *adj.* **1.** in the order of the letters of the alphabet. **2.** of, relating to, or using an alphabet. Also, **al′pha·bet′ic.** —**al′pha·bet′i·cal·ly,** *adv.*

al·pha·bet·ize (al′fə bə tīz′) *v.t.,* **-ized, -iz·ing. 1.** to arrange in alphabetical order. **2.** to express by or furnish with an alphabet. —**al·pha·bet·i·za·tion** (al′fə bet′ə zā′shən), *n.* —**al′pha·bet·i′zer,** *n.*

Al·pha Cen·tau·ri (al′fə sen tôr′ē) a triple-star system, appearing to the naked eye as a single star, one of the brightest in the sky and the brightest in the constellation Centaurus. It consists of the three stars **Proxima Centauri,** the closest star to our solar system, **Alpha Centauri A,** and **Alpha Centauri B.**

al·pha·nu·mer·ic (al′fə nü mer′ik, -nū-) *adj.* of, relating to, or consisting of a set of symbols, esp. computer characters, that include letters of the alphabet and numerals, and sometimes other symbols such as punctuation marks: *an alphanumeric code.* Also, **al′pha·nu·mer′i·cal.**

alpha particle, a positively charged particle, equivalent to the nucleus of the helium atom, consisting of two protons and two neutrons. Alpha particles are emitted from certain radioactive substances.

alpha ray, a stream of alpha particles.

Al·phe·us (al fē′əs) *n.* in Greek mythology, a river god who pursued the nymph Arethusa and changed into an underground river to be near her after she was turned into a spring by Artemis.

al·pine (al′pīn) *adj.* **1.** of or like high mountains; very high. **2.** Alpine. of, relating to, or characteristic of the Alps. **3.** growing on or situated in high mountains: *alpine flowers.* **4.** of or relating to downhill skiing or slalom events. [Latin *alpinus,* from *Alpes* the Alps.]

al·read·y (ôl red′ē) *adv.* **1.** before or by this or that time; previously: *It's already been done. We had already eaten.* **2.** so soon: *Are you finished already?* [Middle English *al redy.* See ALL, READY.]

al·right (ôl rīt′) **1.** *Informal.* all right. **2.** all-right.

Al·sa·tian (al sā′shən) *adj.* of, relating to, or characteristic of Alsace or its people or culture. —*n.* **1.** a native or inhabitant of Alsace. **2.** a person of Alsatian ancestry. **3.** a German shepherd dog.

al·so (ôl′sō) *adv.* in addition; as well; too. [Old English *ealswā* wholly so.]

al·so-ran (ôl′sō ran′) *n. Informal.* **1.** a horse that fails to finish in first, second, or third place in a race. **2.** any unsuccessful competitor; loser.

alt. 1. alternate. **2.** altitude. **3.** alto.

Alta., Alberta.

Al·tair (al′tār) *n.* one of the brightest stars in the sky and the brightest in the constellation Aquila.

al·tar (ôl′tər) *n.* **1.** a consecrated, usually raised, structure where religious services or rites are performed. In Christian churches, the altar is the table where Communion services are held. **2.** a place where sacrifices and other sacred rites are performed. [Old English *altar,* going back to Latin *altāria* part of an altar used to hold burnt offerings.]

·**to lead to the altar.** to marry.

altar boy, a boy or man who assists the priest during religious services, as during Mass.

al·tar·piece (ôl′tər pēs′) *n.* a decorative hanging or panel attached to an altar, ornamenting the space behind and above it.

al·ter (ôl′tər) *v.t.* **1.** to make different in some way; modify: *to alter a suit.* **2.** to castrate or spay (an animal). —*v.i.* to become different; change: *My attitude toward my work has altered in the past year.* [Middle French *altérer* to change, from Medieval Latin *alterare,* from Latin *alter* other.] —**al′ter·a·ble,** *adj.* —**al′ter·a·bly,** *adv.* —For Synonyms, see **change.**

al·ter·a·tion (ôl′tə rā′shən) *n.* **1.** a change; modification: *There's been an alteration in our plans.* **2.** the act or process of altering or the state of being altered.

al·ter·cate (ôl′tər kāt′, al′-) *v.i.,* **-cat·ed, -cat·ing.** to argue in a noisy or angry manner; wrangle. [Latin *altercātus,* past participle of *altercārī.*]

al·ter·ca·tion (ôl′tər kā′shən, al′-) *n.* a noisy or heated dispute. [Old French *altercation,* going back to Latin *altercārī* to dispute with another.]

al·ter e·go (ôl′tər ē′gō, eg′ō, al′tər) **1.** a person who is an extension of oneself; another self. **2.** a constant companion; intimate friend. [Latin *alter ego* literally, another I.]

al·ter·nate (*v.,* ôl′tər nāt′, al′-; *adj., n.,* ôl′tər nit, al′-) *v.,* **-nat·ed, -nat·ing** —*v.i.* **1.** to succeed each other by turns; take turns: *They alternated at waxing the floor.* **2.** to happen or appear in turn: *Day alternates with night. Red and white stripes alternate on the flag.* **3.** to pass back and forth from one condition, action, or place to another: *The parents of the lost child alternated between hope and despair.* **4.** *Electricity.* (of current) to reverse direction regularly. —*v.t.* **1.** to do or perform by turns: *The performer alternated singing and dancing.* **2.** to cause to follow one another by turns; interchange successively: *The designer alternated blue lines with red.* —*adj.* **1.** occurring or following by turns: *alternate layers of rock and sand.* **2.** every other: *to sit in alternate rows.* **3.** taking the place of another; substitute: *alternate jurors, an alternate plan.* **4.** *Botany.* arranged on different sides and at different places along an axis (such as a stem), as leaves, buds, or

a	at	e	end	o	hot	u	up	hw	white	{	about
ā	ape	ē	me	ō	old	ū	use	ng	song		taken
ä	far	i	it	ô	fork	ü	rule	th	thin		pencil
âr	care	ī	ice	oi	oil	u̇	pull	th	this		lemon
		îr	pierce	ou	out	ûr	turn	zh	measure		circus

35

branches. ➡ distinguished from **opposite**. —*n.* a person who takes the place of another; substitute. [Latin *alternātus,* past participle of *alternāre* to do a thing by turns.] —**al′ter·nate·ly,** *adv.*

alternate angles, two nonadjacent angles formed on opposite sides of a line that crosses two other lines.

alternating current, an electric current in which the flow of electrons reverses direction in regular cycles. ➡ distinguished from **direct current**.

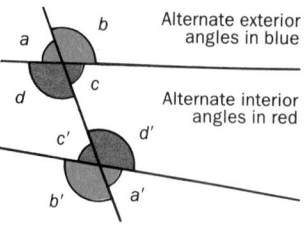

Alternate exterior angles in blue

Alternate interior angles in red

al·ter·na·tion (ôl′tər-nā′shən, al′-) *n.* the act of alternating or the state of being alternated.

alternation of generations, the life cycle of any organism that reproduces first sexually and then asexually.

alternate angles:
a, a′; b, b′; c, c′; d, d′

al·ter·na·tive (ôl tûr′nə tiv, al-) *adj.* providing or being something to do instead: *an alternative solution.* —*n.* **1.** a possibility of selecting between two or more things: *You have the alternative of fixing your car or buying a new one.* **2.** one of the things that may be selected: *The buyer chose the less costly alternative.* **3.** other or remaining thing that may be selected; choice: *no alternative but to sue.* —**al′ter·na·tive·ly,** *adv.* —For Synonyms, see **choice.**

al·ter·na·tor (ôl′tər nā′tər, al′-) *n.* a generator for producing alternating electric current.

al·thae·a (al thē′ə) *also,* **al·the·a.** *n.* **1.** rose of Sharon. **2.** any plant of the genus *Althaea,* including the marsh mallow. [Latin *althaea* marsh mallow, from Greek *althaiā.*]

alt·horn (alt′hôrn′) *n.* the alto member of the saxhorn class, used in some bands in place of the French horn. Also, **alto horn.**

al·though (ôl thō′) *also,* **al·tho.** *conj.* in spite of the fact that; even though; though. [Middle English *although.*]

al·tim·e·ter (al tim′i tər, al′tə mē′-) *n.* an instrument for measuring altitude above sea level or above the ground, esp. an aneroid barometer calibrated for that purpose, used in aircraft. [Latin *altus* high + -METER.]

al·ti·tude (al′ti tüd′, -tūd′) *n.* **1.a.** height above sea level: *The pilot flew the plane at an altitude of 8,000 feet.* **b.** height above the ground: *The balloon rose to an altitude of 2,000 feet over the field.* **2. altitudes.** great heights; elevated regions: *mountain altitudes.* **3.** *Geometry.* the perpendicular distance from the base of a figure to its highest point, or a line segment representing this. **4.** *Astronomy.* (of a celestial body) the angle of elevation, or number of degrees, above the horizon. [Latin *altitudo* height.] —**al′ti·tu′di·nal,** *adj.* —For Synonyms, see **height.**

al·to (al′tō) *n., pl.* **-tos. 1.** the lowest female voice; contralto. **2.** the highest male voice; countertenor. **3.** a singer who has such a voice. **4.** an instrument having the second highest range in a family of musical instruments, as the viola or althorn. **5.** a musical part for such a voice or instrument. —*adj.* **1.** able to sing alto: *an alto voice.* **2.** for the alto: *an alto score.* **3.** having the second highest range in a family of instruments: *an alto saxophone.* [Italian *alto* high, from Latin *altus* high.]

al·to·cu·mu·lus (al′tō kū′myə ləs) *n., pl.* **-lus** or **-li** (-lī′). a middle-level cloud, grayer on the bottom, consisting of large, oval-shaped masses often separated by clear sky. For illustration, see **cloud.**

al·to·geth·er (ôl′tə geth′ər) *adv.* **1.** entirely; wholly; completely: *You missed the bull's-eye altogether.* **2.** with everything included; in all: *There were twelve of us altogether.* **3.** on the whole; everything considered: *Altogether, it was a good paper.* [Middle English *al* all + *togedere* together.]
    • **in the altogether.** *Informal.* nude.

alto horn, althorn.

al·to-re·lie·vo (al′tō ri lē′vō) *n., pl.* **-vos.** high relief. [Italian *altorilievo,* going back to Latin *altus* high + *relevāre* to raise.]

al·to·stra·tus (al′tō strā′təs, -strat′əs) *n., pl.* **-stra·tus** or **-stra·ti** (-strā′tī, -strat′ī). a middle-level cloud appearing as a bluish or grayish white, uniform sheet and covering all or most of the sky. For illustration, see **cloud.**

al·tri·cial (al trish′əl) *adj.* of or relating to birds whose newly hatched young, blind and helpless, are confined to the nest until adequately developed. [Modern Latin *altricialis,* from *altrix* nurse, going back to *alere* to feed.]

al·tru·ism (al′trü iz′əm) *n.* an unselfish concern for or devotion to the welfare of others. [French *altruisme,* term created by Auguste Comte from French *autrui* another; influenced by Latin *alter* other.]

al·tru·ist (al′trü ist) *n.* a person who professes or exhibits altruism. —**al′tru·is′tic,** *adj.* —**al′tru·is′ti·cal·ly,** *adv.*

ALU, arithmetic-logic unit.

al·um (al′əm) *n.* **1.** any of a group of hydrated double salts with the general formula $M^+M^{+++}(SO_4)_2 \cdot 12H_2O$, where M^+ represents a univalent positive ion and M^{+++} represents a trivalent positive ion. **2.** a hydrated double salt of potassium and aluminum, used esp. as a medical astringent and in dyeing and water purification. Formula: $KAl(SO_4)_2 \cdot 12H_2O$ Also, **potash alum.** [Old French *alum,* from Latin *alūmen.*]

a·lu·mi·na (ə lü′mə nə) *n.* an oxide of aluminum, occurring in pure form as the mineral corundum and also widely found in clays and bauxite. Formula: Al_2O_3 [Modern Latin *alumina,* from Latin *alūmen* alum.]

a·lu·mi·nize (ə lü′mə nīz′) *v.t.,* **-nized, -niz·ing.** to treat or coat with aluminum. [ALUMIN(UM) + -IZE.]

a·lu·mi·nous (ə lü′mə nəs) *adj.* of or containing alum or aluminum.

a·lu·mi·num (a lü′mə nəm) *n.* a light, soft, silver-white metallic element obtained from bauxite. The most abundant metallic element in the earth's crust, aluminum is corrosion resistant and has a wide range of uses. Symbol: **Al** Also, *British,* **al·u·min·i·um** (al′yə min′ē əm) For tables, see **element.** [Modern Latin *aluminum,* from *alūmin-,* stem of *alūmen* alum + *-ium* suffix used to form neuter nouns.]

aluminum foil, aluminum in very thin sheets, used esp. to wrap foods or to line pans when baking or broiling.

aluminum oxide, alumina.

a·lum·na (ə lum′nə) *n., pl.* **-nae** (-nē). a female graduate or former student of an educational institution. [Latin *alumna,* feminine of *alumnus* foster child, pupil.]

a·lum·nus (ə lum′nəs) *n., pl.* **-ni** (-nī). a graduate or former student of an educational institution. [Latin *alumnus* foster child, pupil.]

al·ve·o·lar (al vē′ə lər) *adj.* **1.** of, relating to, or having an alveolus or alveoli. **2.** *Phonetics.* formed by placing the tip of the tongue on the ridge just behind the teeth. In English, *s, z, t, d, n,* and *l* are alveolar sounds. —*n.* an alveolar sound.

al·ve·o·late (al vē′ə lit, -lāt′) *adj.* filled with small cavities, or alveoli; resembling a honeycomb. Also, **al·ve′o·lat′ed.** [Latin *alveolatus* hollowed out, from *alveolus.* See ALVEOLUS.]

al·ve·o·lus (al vē′ə ləs) *n., pl.* **-li** (-lī′). **1.** a small cavity or pit, such as one of the cells of a honeycomb. **2.** *Anatomy.* a socket in the jawbone in which a tooth fits. **3.** *Anatomy.* one of the small air sacs of the lungs in which gas exchange occurs between inhaled air and the blood. [Latin *alveolus,* diminutive of *alveus* cavity.]

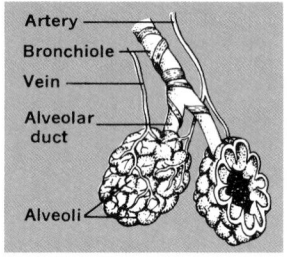

Artery
Bronchiole
Vein
Alveolar duct
Alveoli

alveolus *(def. 3)*

al·way (ôl′wā) *adv. Archaic.* always.

al·ways (ôl′wāz, -wēz) *adv.* **1.** at all times; on every occasion; invariably: *Why are you always late?* **2.** all the time; continuously: *It's always hot in the tropics.* **3.** throughout all time; forever: *I'll remember you always.* **4.** *Informal.* in any case; as a last resort: *If there are no seats left, we can always stand.* [Originally ALL + WAY.]

a·lys·sum (ə lis′əm) *n.* **1.** any of a group of low, branching plants, genus *Alyssum,* of the mustard family, found chiefly in the Mediterranean region, bearing clusters of small white or yellow flowers. **2.** sweet alyssum. [Modern Latin *alyssum,* from Latin *alysson* plant used to cure rabies, from Greek *alysson,* from a- not + *lyssa* rabies.]

Alz·hei·mer's disease (älts′hī mərz, ôlts′-) a progressive, degenerative disease of the brain cells that causes confusion and progressive loss of memory and mental ability. [From the German physician Alois *Alzheimer,* 1864-1915, who described this disease.]

am (am, *unstressed* əm) the first person singular present tense of **be.** [Old English *eom.*]

Am, the symbol for americium.

Am 1. America. **2.** American.

AM 1. a method of radio broadcasting by which a signal is transmitted over radio carrier waves by altering the amplitude of the waves. **2.** a broadcasting system using this method. **3.** of, relating to, or using an AM broadcasting system: *an AM radio, an AM station.* ➡ distinguished from **FM**. [Abbreviation of *amplitude modulation.*]

A.M. 1. *also,* **a.m., AM** before noon; in the time from midnight

to noon. [Abbreviation of *a(nte) m(eridiem)*.] **2.** Master of Arts. Also, **M.A.**

AMA, American Medical Association.

a·mah (ä′mə, am′ə) *n.* in the Orient, a female servant or nurse, esp. a wet nurse. [Portuguese *ama,* from Medieval Latin *amma.*]

a·main (ə mān′) *adv. Archaic.* **1.** with full force. **2.** at full speed. **3.** hastily. [A-[1] + MAIN force.]

a·mal·gam (ə mal′gəm) *n.* **1.** an alloy of mercury with another metal or metals. Silver amalgam is used for filling teeth. **2.** any mixture or combination. [Medieval Latin *amalgame* alloy of mercury.]

a·mal·ga·mate (ə mal′gə māt′) *v.,* **-mat·ed, -mat·ing.** —*v.t.* **1.** to unite so as to form a combination; merge: *to amalgamate several school districts into one.* **2.** to combine (a metal or metals) with mercury. —*v.i.* **1.** to unite together; combine; merge: *The two unions amalgamated.* **2.** to combine with another metal.

a·mal·gam·a·tion (ə mal′gə mā′shən) *n.* **1.** the act of amalgamating or the state of being amalgamated. **2.** the result of amalgamating; combination; blend. **3.** a merger, as of two or more business firms.

am·a·ni·ta (am′ə nī′tə) *n.* any of a group of mushrooms with gills on the underside of the cap and usually with a cup at the base of the stalk. Some amanitas are deadly poisonous, but the edibility of most species is not known.

a·man·u·en·sis (ə man′ū en′sis) *n., pl.* **-ses** (-sēz). a person who is employed to take dictation or copy manuscript; secretary. [Latin *āmanuēnsis* secretary, from *(servus) ā manū* (servant) for writing + *-ēnsis* belonging to.]

am·a·ranth (am′ə ranth′) *n.* **1.** any of a group of weeds and garden plants, genus *Amaranthus,* several species of which are cultivated for their colorful leaves or showy blossoms. **2.** an imaginary flower that never fades or wilts. [Alteration (influenced in spelling by Greek *anthos* flower) of Latin *amarantus* never-fading flower, from Greek *amarantos* never-fading, everlasting.]

am·a·ran·thine (am′ə ran′thin, -thīn) *adj.* **1.** of or resembling the amaranth. **2.** never-fading; everlasting.

am·a·ryl·lis (am′ə ril′is) *n.* **1.** any of a group of plants, genus *Hippeastrum,* native chiefly to tropical America, bearing large, bright-colored, lilylike flowers. **2.** any of various related plants, esp. of the genus *Amaryllis,* as **A. belladonna,** the belladonna lily, native to South Africa. [Modern Latin *amaryllis* from Latin *Amaryllis* country girl in the poems of the Roman poets Vergil, 70-19 B.C., and Ovid, 43 B.C.-A.D. 17?, from Greek *Amaryllis* country girl in the poems of Theocritus, Greek poet of the third century B.C.]

a·mass (ə mas′) *v.t.* to collect (a great quantity); accumulate: *to amass great wealth.* [Old French *amasser* to gather, heap, going back to Latin *ad* to + *massa* mass (from Greek *maza* lump).] —**a·mass′er,** *n.* —**a·mass′ment,** *n.* —For Synonyms, see **accumulate.**

amaryllis

am·a·teur (am′ə chər, -tər, am′ə tûr′) *n.* **1.** a person who does something as a pastime or for pleasure rather than as a profession or for money. **2.** an athlete who has never competed for money or earned money through athletic skill. **3.** a person who does something with less than professional skill. —*adj.* **1.** done by or relating to an amateur or amateurs: *amateur sports.* **2.** being an amateur or composed of amateurs; nonprofessional: *an amateur golfer, an amateur cast.* **3.** characteristic of amateurs; amateurish. [French *amateur* lover of something, dilettante, from Latin *amātor* lover, from *amare* to love.]

am·a·teur·ish (am′ə chûr′ish, -tûr′-, -tûr′-) *adj.* performed as though by an amateur or amateurs; lacking skill; inexpert: *an amateurish performance.* —**am′a·teur′ish·ly,** *adv.* —**am′a·teur′ish·ness,** *n.*

am·a·teur·ism (am′ə chə riz′əm, am′ə tə-, -tyə-) *n.* an amateurish method or character.

A·ma·ti (ä mä′tē) a violin made by Nicolò Amati or a member of his family.

am·a·to·ry (am′ə tôr′ē) *adj.* of, relating to, or expressing love: *amatory poetry.* [Latin *amātōrius* loving, from *amātor* lover.]

a·maze (ə māz′) *v.t.,* **a·mazed, a·maz·ing.** to overwhelm with

sudden wonder or surprise; astound. —*n. Archaic.* amazement; wonder. [Old English *āmasian* to bewilder.] —**a·maz·ed·ly** (ə mā′zid lē), *adv.*

a·maze·ment (ə māz′mənt) *n.* sudden, overwhelming wonder or surprise; astonishment.

a·maz·ing (ə mā′zing) *adj.* causing amazement; wonderful; astonishing. —**a·maz′ing·ly,** *adv.*

Am·a·zon (am′ə zon′, -zən) *n.* **1.** in Greek legend, one of a race of female warriors said to have lived in Scythia, near the Black Sea. **2.** *also,* **amazon.** any woman of notable size or strength. [Latin *Amāzon* woman warrior, from Greek *Amazōn,* river so called because of South American Indian women warriors who fought in a battle near it in 1541.]

Am·a·zo·ni·an (am′ə zō′nē ən) *adj.* **1.** of or relating to the Amazon River or the region it drains. **2.** *also,* **amazonian.** of, like, or characteristic of an Amazon.

Amb., Ambassador.

am·bas·sa·dor (am bas′ə dər) *n.* **1.** a diplomat of the highest rank. An **ambassador extraordinary and plenipotentiary** is accredited to a foreign country or government and is his or her own government's ranking diplomat residing in that country. Other ambassadors can be given special, often temporary, assignments, as to the United Nations or other international bodies. **2.** any representative or messenger. [Old French *ambassadeur,* from Old Italian *ambasciatore,* going back to Medieval Latin *ambactia* mission, embassy, from Latin *ambactus* servant; of Celtic origin.] —**am·bas·sa·dor·i·al** (am bas′ə dôr′ē əl), *adj.* —**ambas′sa·dor·ship′,** *n.*

am·bas·sa·dor-at-large (am bas′ə dər at lärj′, -ət-) *n., pl.* **am·bas·sa·dors-at-large.** an ambassador assigned to no particular country or specific task.

am·bas·sa·dress (am bas′ə dris) *n.* **1.** a female ambassador. **2.** the wife of an ambassador.

am·ber (am′bər) *n.* **1.** a hard, translucent fossil resin from pine trees, yellow to brown in color, used esp. for carvings, jewelry, and electrical insulation. **2.** a yellowish orange or yellowish brown color. —*adj.* **1.** made of amber. **2.** having the color amber. [Old French *ambre* this resin, ambergris, from Arabic *'anbar* ambergris.]

am·ber·gris (am′bər grēs′, -gris) *n.* a grayish, waxy substance formed in the intestines of sperm whales, usually found floating on tropical seas or washed ashore, used in making perfume. [French *ambre gris* literally, gray amber, from *ambre* (see AMBER) + *gris* gray (of Germanic origin).]

am·ber·jack (am′bər jak′) *n., pl.* **-jack** or **-jacks.** any of a group of edible, yellowish fish having deeply forked tails, genus *Seriola,* esp. *S. dumerili,* found off the eastern coasts of North and South America. Average weight: 12 pounds (5.4 kilograms). [So called because of its amber color.]

ambi- *combining form* around; both: *ambience, ambidextrous.* [Latin *ambi-* about, around, both.]

am·bi·ance (am′bē əns) ambience.

am·bi·dex·ter·i·ty (am′bi dek ster′i tē) *n.* the state or quality of being ambidextrous.

am·bi·dex·trous (am′bi dek′strəs) *adj.* **1.** able to use both hands with equal ease. **2.** very skillful or versatile; adroit. **3.** double-dealing; deceitful. [Medieval Latin *ambidexter,* from Latin *ambi-* both + *dexter* right hand.] —**am′bi·dex′trous·ly,** *adv.* —**am′bi·dex′trous·ness,** *n.*

am·bi·ence (am′bē əns) *also,* **ambiance.** *n.* pervading atmosphere; surroundings; milieu: *a restaurant with a cheerful ambience.* [French *ambiance,* going back to Latin *ambire* to go around.]

am·bi·ent (am′bē ənt) *adj.* completely surrounding; encompassing: *ambient temperature.* [Latin *ambiēns,* present participle of *ambīre* to go around.]

am·bi·gu·i·ty (am′bi gū′i tē) *n., pl.* **-ties.** **1.** something that is open to more than one interpretation; unclear, uncertain, or equivocal instance or feature: *The document was filled with ambiguities.* **2.** doubtfulness or uncertainty of purpose or meaning; vagueness: *The president's ambiguity about plans for the company worried the board of directors.*

am·big·u·ous (am big′ū əs) *adj.* **1.** open to more than one interpretation or meaning; equivocal: *an ambiguous statement.* **2.** lacking clarity or certainty; unclear; vague: *an ambiguous attitude.* [Latin *ambiguus* uncertain, from *ambigere* to dispute, to be uncertain.] —**am·big′u·ous·ly,** *adv.* —**am·big′u·ous·ness,** *n.*

a	at	e	end	o	hot	u	up	hw	white	⎧	about
ā	ape	ē	me	ō	old	ū	use	ng	song		taken
ä	far	i	it	ô	fork	ü	rule	th	thin	ə	pencil
âr	care	ī	ice	oi	oil	u̇	pull	th	this		lemon
		îr	pierce	ou	out	ûr	turn	zh	measure	⎩	circus

am·bi·tion (am bish′ən) *n.* **1.** a strong desire or drive to succeed or to achieve something. **2.** the object of such desire: *The sprinter's ambition was to break the track record.* [Latin *ambitiō* going around (to solicit votes).]

Synonyms Ambition and aspiration mean a desire to improve one's position. **Ambition** suggests that desire is coupled with effort or drive. It may or may not imply reaching beyond what is reasonable: *a job change motivated by ambition.* **Aspiration** usually has no negative connotation but may suggest goals too high to reach. It is generally used in the plural: *The young artist's aspirations would require years to achieve.*

am·bi·tious (am bish′əs) *adj.* **1.** full of, guided by, or showing ambition: *an ambitious politician.* **2.** strongly desirous; eager for (with *of* or the infinitive): *ambitious of power, ambitious to win first prize.* **3.** requiring great ability or effort; arduous; demanding: *an ambitious program for helping the homeless.* —**am·bi′tious·ly,** *adv.* —**am·bi′tious·ness,** *n.*

am·biv·a·lence (am biv′ə ləns) *n.* the state or quality of being ambivalent. [AMBI- + VALENCE.]

am·biv·a·lent (am biv′ə lənt) *adj.* having or showing simultaneous conflicting feelings or attitudes toward a person, object, or idea. —**am·biv′a·lent·ly,** *adv.*

am·ble (am′bəl) *v.i.,* **-bled, -bling. 1.** to walk at a relaxed, leisurely pace. **2.** (of a horse) to walk at a slow easy pace by lifting both legs on the same side together. —*n.* **1.** a slow, leisurely pace in walking: *moving at an amble.* **2.** a leisurely stroll or walk: *We decided to take an amble down the boardwalk.* **3.** the slow easy pace of a horse ambling. [Old French *ambler* to amble, from Latin *ambulāre* to walk.] —**am′bler,** *n.*

am·bro·sia (am brō′zhə) *n.* **1.** in classical mythology, the food of the gods, capable of imparting immortality. **2.** something particularly delicious or delightful to taste or smell. [Latin *ambrosia* food of the gods, from Greek *ambrosiā,* from *ambrotos* immortal.]

am·bro·sial (am brō′zhəl) *adj.* **1.** of or like ambrosia; especially delicious or fragrant. **2.** belonging to or worthy of the gods; divine. Also, **am·bro·sian** (am brō′zhən).

am·bu·lance (am′byə ləns) *n.* a specially equipped vehicle for carrying persons who are sick, wounded, or injured. [French *ambulance,* for earlier *(hôpital) ambulant* literally, walking or moving (hospital), going back to Latin *ambulāre* to walk.]

am·bu·lant (am′byə lənt) *adj.* able to move about; ambulatory.

am·bu·late (am′byə lāt′) *v.i.,* **-lat·ed, -lat·ing.** to move or walk about. [Latin *ambulātus,* past participle of *ambulāre.*] —**am′bu·la′tion,** *n.*

am·bu·la·to·ry (am′byə lə tôr′ē) *adj.* **1.** able to move or walk about; not bedridden: *an ambulatory patient.* **2.** of or fitted for walking: *ambulatory exercise.* **3.** moving from place to place; itinerant. **4.** *Law.* capable of being changed or revoked; alterable: *an ambulatory will.* —*n., pl.* **-ries.** a sheltered place for walking in a building, as the cloisters of a monastery.

am·bus·cade (am′bə skād′) *n.* an ambush. —*v.t.,* **-cad·ed, -cad·ing.** to ambush. [French *embuscade* an ambush, from Italian *imboscata,* going back to Latin *in* in + Late Latin *boscus* wood.] —**am′bus·cad′er,** *n.*

am·bush (am′bŏŏsh) *n.* **1.** a surprise attack from a concealed position: *The enemy did not anticipate our ambush.* **2.** a concealed position for surprise attack. **3.** the act of lying in wait for a surprise attack. —*v.t.* to make a surprise attack on from a concealed position. [Old French *embuscher* to place in ambush, going back to Latin *in* in + Late Latin *boscus* wood.] —**am′bush·er,** *n.*

a·me·ba (ə mē′bə) *also,* **amoeba.** *n., pl.* **-bas** or **-bae** (-bē) any of a group of protozoans of the class Sarcodina that move and feed by sending out temporary projections, or pseudopods. Amebas reproduce by binary fission and may be found in fresh or salt water, in moist soils, or as parasites in animals. [Greek *amoibē* change; because it is continually changing shape.]

Contractile vacuole
Pseudopod
Ectoplasm
Nucleus
Endoplasm
Food vacuole
Cell membrane
Pseudopod

ameba

am·e·bi·a·sis (am′ə bī′ə sis) *also,* **amoebiasis.** *n.* a disorder, as amebic dysentery, caused by amebas, esp. by *Entamoeba histolytica,* which is parasitic in the intestines and liver of humans. [Modern Latin *amoebiasis.*]

a·me·bic (ə mē′bik) *also,* **amoebic.** *adj.* **1.** of, like, or relating to an ameba. **2.** caused by an ameba or amebas.

amebic dysentery, a severe intestinal disorder characterized by bloody diarrhea, abdominal cramps, and fever, produced by the parasitic ameba *Entamoeba histolytica.*

a·me·boid (ə mē′boid) *also,* **amoeboid.** *adj.* resembling an ameba, esp. in its flowing movement or change of shape.

a·meer (ə mîr′) amir.

a·mel·io·rate (ə mēl′yə rāt′) *v.,* **-rat·ed, -rat·ing.** —*v.t.* to make better; improve: *The new owners promised to ameliorate working conditions in the factory.* —*v.i.* to grow or become better. [Modification (influenced by French *améliorer* to make better) of MELIORATE (ə mēl′yər ə bəl), *adj.* —**a·mel′io·ra·ble** (ə mēl′yə rə bəl), *adj.* —**a·mel′io·rant,** *n.* —**a·mel′io·ra′tive,** *adj.* —**a·mel′io·ra′tor,** *n.*

a·mel·io·ra·tion (ə mēl′yə rā′shən) *n.* the act of ameliorating or the state of being ameliorated; improvement.

a·men (ā′men′, ä′men′) *interj.* may it be so; so be it. ➡ used to express assent or approval, esp. after a prayer. —*n.* **1.** an uttering of this word. **2.** any expression of assent or approval. —*adv.* verily; truly. [Old English *amen,* from Church Latin *amen,* from Greek *amēn,* from Hebrew *āmēn* verily, truly.]

A·men (ä′mən) *also,* **Amon, Ammon.** *n.* in Egyptian mythology, a local god of fertility, represented as having a ram's head;

Words from American Indian Languages

Below is a selection of words borrowed in English from some of the American Indian languages spoken in the Western Hemisphere. The language of origin is listed in parentheses following each word. The languages spoken in the Arctic are listed as North American. Languages of the Caribbean are listed under Central and South American.

NORTH AMERICAN

anorak (Eskimo)	igloo (Eskimo)	pecan (Algonquian)	succotash (Algonquian)
bayou (Choctaw)	kayak (Eskimo)	persimmon (Algonquian)	tepee (Dakota)
caribou (Algonquian)	malamute (Eskimo)	powwow (Algonquian)	terrapin (Algonquian)
catalpa (Creek)	menhaden (Narragansett)	quahog (Algonquian)	tomahawk (Algonquian)
chinook (Chinook)	moccasin (Algonquian)	raccoon (Algonquian)	tomato (Nahuatl)
chipmunk (Ojibwa)	moose (Algonquian)	sequoia (Cherokee)	tupelo (Creek)
hickory (Algonquian)	mukluk (Eskimo)	skunk (Algonquian)	umiak (Eskimo)
hominy (Algonquian)	opossum (Algonquian)	squash² (Algonquian)	wampum (Algonquian)
husky (Eskimo)	papoose (Algonquian)	squaw (Algonquian)	wigwam (Algonquian)
			woodchuck (Cree)

CENTRAL AND SOUTH AMERICAN

caiman (Carib)	cougar (Tupi)	maguey (Taino)	petunia (Tupi)	tanager (Tupi)
cannibal (Carib)	hammock (Carib)	maize (Taino)	piranha (Tupi)	tapioca (Tupi)
canoe (Carib)	hurricane (Carib)	mangrove (Taino)	potato (Taino)	tobacco (Taino)
cassava (Taino)	iguana (Carib)	mesquite (Nahuatl)	puma (Quechua)	toboggan (Taino)
chocolate (Nahuatl)	jaguar (Tupi)	ocelot (Nahuatl)	quinine (Quechua)	tomato (Nahuatl)
coca (Quechua)	llama (Quechua)	papaya (Carib)	savanna (Taino)	toucan (Tupi)
condor (Quechua)	macaw (Tupi)	peccary (Carib)	tamale (Nahuatl)	yucca (Carib)

later identified with the sun god Ra as the supreme deity and called **Amen-Ra.**

a·me·na·ble (ə mē′nə bəl, ə men′ə-) *adj.* **1.** receptive, as to new ideas, suggestions, or views; agreeable: *amenable to a change in plans.* **2.** liable to be called to account; answerable to some authority or rule: *All citizens are amenable to the law.* [Old French *amener* to lead to, going back to Latin *ad* to + Late Latin *mināre* to drive out, from Latin *minārī* to threaten.] —**a·me′na·bil′i·ty, a·me′na·ble·ness,** *n.* —**a·me′na·bly,** *adv.*

a·mend (ə mend′) *v.t.* **1.** to alter formally by modification, addition, or deletion: *to amend the Constitution.* **2.** to change for the better; improve; correct: *Amend your ways.* **3.** to make changes in; modify; revise: *to amend a manuscript.* [Old French *amender* to make better, from Latin *emendare* to correct, from *ex* out of + *menda* fault.] —**a·mend′a·ble,** *adj.* —**a·mend′er,** *n.*

a·mend·a·to·ry (ə men′də tôr′ē) *adj.* tending or serving to amend; corrective.

a·mend·ment (ə mend′mənt) *n.* **1.** the act of amending or the state of being amended. **2.** the result of amending or being amended; change. **3.a.** a formal change or revision, as by parliamentary or constitutional procedure: *The senator proposed an amendment to the statute.* **b.** the text of such a change.

a·mends (ə mendz′) *pl. n.* **to make amends.** to compensate (for loss, injury, or insult); recompense: *The students made amends for their rude behavior with a sincere apology.*

a·men·i·ty (ə men′i tē, ə mē′ni-) *n., pl.* **-ties. 1.** amenities. **a.** polite social acts, esp. certain standard or accepted ones; civilities. **b.** agreeable or pleasant features or circumstances: *The rustic cabin had few of the amenities of home.* **2.** the quality of being agreeable or pleasant; pleasantness of climate or situation. [Latin *amoenitās* pleasantness.]

am·ent (am′ənt, ā′mənt) *n.* catkin. [Latin *amentum* thong.]

Amer. **1.** America. **2.** American.

Am·er·a·sian (am′ə rā′zhən) *n.* a person of mixed American and Asian parentage. —*adj.* of mixed American and Asian parentage: *an Amerasian child.* [AMER(ICAN) + ASIAN.]

a·merce (ə mûrs′) *v.t.,* **a·merced, a·merc·ing.** to punish with an arbitrary fine or other penalty. [Anglo-Norman *amercier* to fine, from phrase *à merci* at the mercy of, going back to Latin *ad* to + *mercēs* cost.] —**a·merce′a·ble,** *adj.* —**a·merce′ment,** *n.* —**a·merc′er,** *n.*

A·mer·i·can (ə mer′i kən) *adj.* **1.** of, relating to, or characteristic of the United States or its people or culture: *the American flag, American food.* **2.** of, relating to, or characteristic of the Americas or their people or cultures. —*n.* **1.** a native or citizen of the United States. **2.** a person of American ancestry. **3.** a native or citizen of one of the Americas. **4.** American English.

A·mer·i·ca·na (ə mer′i kan′ə, -kä′nə, -kā′nə) *n.* **1.a.** books, documents, and other artifacts relating to America, its history, and its culture. **b.** a collection of such artifacts. ➡ used as singular or plural. **2.** a custom, item, or the like that is typical of American culture: *Fourth of July picnics are pure Americana.*

American Beauty, a variety of red rose.

American cheese, any of several mild, white or yellow cheddar or processed cheeses, popular in the United States.

American Dream, the opportunity to attain personal freedom and material success that is supposed to be available to all Americans.

American eagle, the North American bald eagle, shown on the coat of arms of the United States.

American English, the English language as spoken and written in the United States. ➡ distinguished esp. from **British English.**

American Indian 1. a member of any of the tribes of original inhabitants of North and South America. **2.** of or relating to American Indians or their culture: *American Indian jewelry, American Indian religion.* Also, **Amerind, Amerindian, Indian, Native American.**

A·mer·i·can·ism (ə mer′i kə niz′əm) *n.* **1.** a word, phrase, or usage originating in the United States or peculiar to American English. *Cowcatcher* is an Americanism. **2.** a custom, trait, or belief characteristic of and peculiar to the United States and its people. **3.** devotion to or support of the United States and its institutions.

A·mer·i·can·ize (ə mer′i kə nīz′) *v.,* **-ized, -iz·ing.** —*v.t.* to cause to conform to or acquire American traits or beliefs. —*v.i.* to conform to or acquire American characteristics. —**A·mer′i·can·i·za′tion,** *n.*

American larch, tamarack.

American Legion, an organization of veterans of the U.S. armed forces, founded in 1919.

American plan, in hotels, a system of charging at a fixed rate that includes both room and meals. ➡ distinguished from **European plan.**

American Revolution, a war fought from 1775 to 1783 between England and thirteen of its American colonies, in which the colonies gained their independence. Also, **Revolutionary War.**

American Staf·ford·shire terrier (staf′ərd shir′, -shər) a short-haired, broad-chested mix of bulldog and terrier, having erect pointed ears, bred for courage and agility and formerly used in dog fighting pits. Height: 18 inches (46 centimeters) at the shoulder. Also, **pit bull.**

American Standard Version, a revised form of the King James version of the Bible, prepared by American members of the commission that produced the Revised Version, and published in 1901.

am·er·i·ci·um (am′ə rish′ē əm) *n.* a radioactive metallic element of a silver-white color, produced by the bombardment of uranium and plutonium by high-energy helium ions. Symbol: **Am** For tables, see **element.** [Modern Latin *americium,* from *America.*]

Am·er·ind (am′ə rind) *n., adj.* American Indian. Also, **Am′er·in′di·an.** [AMER(ICAN) + IND(IAN).]

am·e·thyst (am′ə thist) *n.* **1.** a purple or violet quartz, used as a gem. For illustration, see **semiprecious. 2.** a purple or violet color. —*adj.* **1.** containing or made with an amethyst or amethysts. **2.** having the color amethyst. [Latin *amethystus* this gem or stone, from Greek *amethystos* literally, not drunken; because this stone was believed to remedy drunkenness.] —**am·e·thys·tine** (am′ə this′tin), *adj.*

a·mi·a·ble (ā′mē ə bəl) *adj.* **1.** (of persons) having or showing a pleasing and kindly disposition; good-natured; friendly: *The amiable grocer gave us six oranges for the price of five.* **2.** to one's liking; agreeable; pleasant: *amiable surroundings.* [Old French *amiable,* from Late Latin *amīcābilis, from Latin amīcus* friend. Doublet of AMICABLE.] —**a′mi·a·bil′i·ty,** *n.* —**a′mi·a·bly,** *adv.*

am·i·ca·ble (am′i kə bəl) *adj.* characterized by friendliness and goodwill; peaceable: *an amicable settlement of a dispute.* [Late

---

apartment house	fundamentalism	painkiller
automobile	gangster	panhandle
baby-sit	gasoline	parking meter
baking powder	gerrymander	parkway
ballpark	girlfriend	patent leather
basketball	grouch	peanut
bifocals	gulch	peanut butter
billboard	hamburger	pocketbook
bleachers	highbrow	poison ivy
blizzard	hijack	postage
bobsled	hindsight	prom
bookstore	hitchhike	proofread
boyfriend	homestretch	racketeer
brainstorm	hot dog	rattlesnake
bulldozer	ice cream	runway
campsite	immigrant	sagebrush
campus	installment plan	sharecrop
canyon	itemize	sidewalk
chain saw	jackknife	skyscraper
cheerleader	jaywalk	slapstick
chewing gum	jazz	snowplow
cocktail table	jeep	spelling bee
credit card	jump rope	stereo
custom-made	junior college	sundae
department store	junkyard	telephone
district attorney	kerosene	timberline
donate	know-how	tractor
drugstore	landslide	tuna
electrician	maple syrup	tuxedo
escalator	maverick	typewriter
firecracker	overalls	workout

---

a	at	e	end	o	hot	u	up	hw	white	⟨	about
ā	ape	ē	me	ō	old	ū	use	ng	song		taken
ä	far	i	it	ô	fork	ū	rule	th	thin	ə	pencil
âr	care	ī	ice	oi	oil	u̇	pull	th	this		lemon
		ir	pierce	ou	out	ûr	turn	zh	measure	⟨	circus

Latin *amīcābilis.* Doublet of AMIABLE.] —**am′i·ca·bil′i·ty,** *n.* —**am′i·ca·bly,** *adv.*

am·ice (am′is) *n.* a vestment worn under the alb by a priest at Mass, made of an oblong piece of white linen that falls around the neck and shoulders. [Old French *amis,* going back to Latin *amictus* cloak.]

a·mi·cus cu·ri·ae (ə mē′kəs kyŭr′ē ī′) someone not party to a lawsuit who advises or offers arguments to the court regarding issues of law involved. An individual, group, or institution can act as an amicus curiae. [Modern Latin *amicus curiae* friend of the court.]

a·mid (ə mid′) *prep.* in the middle or midst of; surrounded by; among. Also, **amidst.** [Old English *on middan* in the middle.]

am·ide (am′īd) *n.* any of a group of organic and inorganic compounds that contain the radical —NH₂ and are derived from ammonia. [AM(MONIA) + -IDE.]

a·mid·ships (ə mid′ships′) *adv.* in or toward the middle of a ship, either halfway between the bow and stern or between the sides. Also, **midships.**

a·midst (ə midst′) *prep.* amid.

a·mi·go (ə mē′gō) *n., pl.* **-gos.** a friend. [Spanish *amigo,* from Latin *amicus.*]

a·mine (ə mēn′, am′in) *n.* any of a class of organic compounds containing nitrogen, formed from ammonia by replacing hydrogen atoms with organic radicals.

a·mi·no (ə mē′nō, am′ə nō′) *adj.* of, relating to, containing, or designating the group —NH₂.

amino acid, any of a group of organic acids found in plant and animal cells, essential for protein synthesis.

a·mir (ə mîr′) *also,* **ameer.** *n.* a commander, native ruler, or prince in a Muslim country. [Arabic *amīr* commander.]

Am·ish (ä′mish, am′ish) *pl. n.* a Protestant denomination, closely related to the Mennonites, founded in Switzerland in the seventeenth century. The Amish, most of whom live in the United States, are required to live in plain and simple fashion in an agrarian economy. —*adj.* of, belonging to, or relating to this sect. [From the Swiss preacher Jacob *Ammann,* 1644?-1730?, founder of the sect.]

a·miss (ə mis′) *adj.* not as it should be; faulty; wrong: *We knew that something was amiss as soon as we saw their faces.* —*adv.* out of proper course or order; improperly; wrongly. [A-¹ + MISS¹ failure.]
  ·**to take (something) amiss.** to take offense at; resent or misunderstand.

a·mi·to·sis (ā′mī tō′sis, am′i-) *n.* direct cell division by simple division of the nucleus without formation of chromosomes. [A-⁴ + MITOSIS.] —**a·mi·tot·ic** (ā′mī tot′ik, am′i-), *adj.*

am·i·ty (am′i tē) *n., pl.* **-ties.** peaceful, friendly relations; friendship: *amity among nations.* [Middle French *amitié,* going back to Latin *amicus* friend.]

am·me·ter (am′mē′tər, am′ē-) *n.* an instrument used for measuring the strength of an electric current in amperes. [AM(PERE) + -METER.]

am·mo (am′ō) *n. Informal.* ammunition.

Am·mon (am′ən) *n.* Amen.

am·mo·nia (ə mōn′yə, ə mō′nē ə) *n.* **1.** a colorless, gaseous compound of nitrogen and hydrogen having a highly pungent odor. Ammonia is used in fertilizers and in the production of other chemicals. Formula: NH₃ **2.** a water solution of ammonia, used as a cleaning agent. Formula: NH₄OH Also *(def. 2),* **ammonia water, ammonium hydroxide.** [From SAL AMMONIAC, from which ammonia was first isolated.]

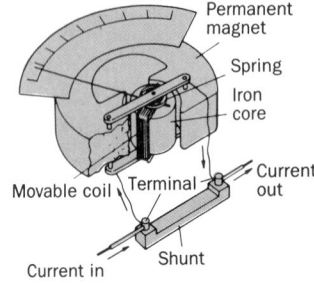

Permanent magnet
Spring
Iron core
Movable coil
Terminal
Current out
Shunt
Current in

ammeter

am·mo·ni·ac (ə mō′nē ak′) *n.* a pungent gum resin used in medicine and in plasters and cements. Also, **gum ammoniac.** [Latin *ammoniacum* (gum) of Amen; because the gum had the same strong-smelling, medicinally useful properties as the salt. See SAL AMMONIAC.]

am·mo·ni·ate (ə mō′nē āt′) *v.t., v.i.,* **-at·ed, -at·ing.** ammonify. [AMMONI(A) + -ATE¹.]

ammonia water, ammonia *(def. 2).*

am·mon·i·fi·ca·tion (ə mon′ə fi kā′shən, ə mō′nə-) *n.* **1.** the act or process of ammonifying. **2.** the release of ammonia through

bacterial decay of nitrogenous organic matter, as in the nitrogen cycle. [AMMONI(A) + -FICATION.]

am·mon·i·fy (ə mon′ə fī′, ə mō′nə-) *v.t., v.i.,* **-fied, -fy·ing.** to combine or become combined with ammonia. Also, **ammoniate.** [AMMONI(A) + -FY.]

am·mo·nite (am′ə nīt′) *n.* an extinct mollusk with a coiled, chambered shell, fossils of which are found in rocks of the Paleozoic and Mesozoic eras. [Modern Latin *Ammonites,* from Medieval Latin *cornu Ammonis* horn of Amen; because of its resemblance to the horns of this ram-headed Egyptian god.]

am·mo·ni·um (ə mō′nē əm) *n.* a univalent radical that acts as an alkali metal in chemical reactions. Formula: NH₄

ammonium chloride, a colorless or white crystalline compound, a salt of ammonia, used esp. in medicine, dry cells, and dyes. Formula: NH₄Cl Also, **sal ammoniac.**

ammonium hydroxide, ammonia *(def. 2).*

ammonium nitrate, a colorless, water-soluble crystalline compound used esp. in fertilizers, explosives, and propellants. Formula: NH₄NO₃

ammonium sulfate, a white, crystalline compound manufactured for use as fertilizer. Formula: (NH₄)₂SO₄

am·mu·ni·tion (am′yə nish′ən) *n.* **1.** bullets, shells, and other projectiles with their fuses, charges, and propellants for use in firearms and artillery. **2.** any type of explosive weapon, as a bomb. **3.** resources for any type of attack or defense: *The scandal provided new ammunition for the senator's foes.* [Obsolete French *amunition* provisions for an army, modification of *munition,* from Latin *mūnītiō* defense.]

am·ne·sia (am nē′zhə) *n.* a partial or total loss of the faculty of memory, esp. as caused by brain injury, mental illness, disease, or shock. [From Greek *amnēsiā* forgetfulness.]

am·ne·si·ac (am nē′zhē ak′, -zē) *n.* a person suffering from amnesia. —*adj.* amnesic.

am·ne·sic (am nē′zik) *adj.* of, relating to, or suffering from amnesia. Also, **amnesiac, am·nes·tic** (am nes′tik). —*n.* amnesiac.

am·nes·ty (am′nə stē) *n., pl.* **-ties.** a general pardon, esp. for political offenses, given by a government to prisoners, outlaws, or rebels, often before prosecution has begun. —*v.t.,* **-tied, -ty·ing.** to grant amnesty to; pardon. [Latin *amnēstia* forgetfulness, from Greek *amnēstiā* forgetfulness.]

am·ni·o·cen·te·sis (am′nē ō sen tē′sis) *n.* the insertion of a hollow needle into the uterus of a pregnant woman to obtain a sample of the fetal cells contained in the amnion, used for detecting genetic disorders in the fetus.

am·ni·on (am′nē ən) *n., pl.* **-ni·ons** or **-ni·a** (-nē ə). a membrane forming the fluid-filled sac surrounding the embryo in reptiles, birds, and mammals. [Greek *amnion* caul, diminutive of *amnos* lamb.] —**am·ni·ot·ic** (am′nē ot′ik), *adj.*

a·moe·ba (ə mē′bə) *n., pl.* **-bas** or **-bae** (-bē). ameba.

am·oe·bi·a·sis (am′ə bī′ə sis) amebiasis.

a·moe·bic (ə mē′bik) amebic.

a·moe·boid (ə mē′boid) ameboid.

a·mok (ə muk′, ə mok′) *also,* **amuck.** *n.* a violent, sometimes homicidal, frenzy often followed by a period of exhaustion and amnesia. [Malay *amok* frenzied to the point of killing.]
  ·**to run** (or **go**) **amok.** to lose control of oneself and rush about wildly, esp. with intent to attack or kill.

A·mon (ä′mən) Amen.

a·mong (ə mung′) *prep.* **1.** in the midst of; surrounded by. **2.** in association with; in the company of: *She lived among the poor.* **3.** in the number or class of: *the best among the new playwrights.* **4.** by, with, or through many or all of: *popular among college students.* **5.** in shares for each of: *He divided the prize money among the winners.* **6.** by the concerted or joint action of: *Among us, we can raise the money.* **7.** mutually between: *They quarreled among themselves.* Also, **amongst.** [Old English *on gemang* in a crowd.]

a·mongst (ə mungst′) *prep.* among.

a·mon·til·la·do (ə mon′tə lä′dō, -tē ä′-) *n., pl.* **-dos.** a pale, medium-dry sherry. [Spanish *amontillado* literally, from Montilla (a town in Spain).]

a·mor·al (ā môr′əl, a môr′-, ā mor′-, a mor′-) *adj.* **1.** not subject to or involving moral considerations; neither moral nor immoral. **2.** not having or concerned with moral standards; incapable of distinguishing between right and wrong. [A-⁴ + MORAL.] —**a·mor·al·i·ty** (ā′mə ral′i tē, am′ə-), *n.* —**a·mor′al·ly,** *adv.* —For Synonyms, see **immoral.**

am·o·rous (am′ər əs) *adj.* **1.** inclined to love or to fall in love: *an amorous nature.* **2.** produced by or exhibiting love: *an amorous glance.* **3.** of or relating to love: *amorous poetry.* **4.** enamored or

A

fond (with *of*): *They have been amorous of each other since childhood.* [Old French *amorous* in love, from Medieval Latin *amōrōsus* full of love, from Latin *amor* love.] —**am'o·rous·ly**, *adv.* —**am'o·rous·ness**, *n.*

a·mor pa·tri·ae (ā'môr pā'trē ē', ä'môr pä'trē ī') *Latin.* love of one's country; patriotism.

a·mor·phous (ə môr'fəs) *adj.* **1.** without definite form or shape; shapeless: *We barely glimpsed an amorphous figure in the fog.* **2.** of no particular kind or character; unorganized: *an amorphous writing style.* **3.** *Chemistry.* without crystalline form. [Greek *amorphos* shapeless.] —**a·mor'phous·ly**, *adv.* —**a·mor'phous·ness**, *n.*

am·or·ti·za·tion (am'ər tə zā'shən, ə môr'-) *n.* **1.** the act of amortizing or the state of being amortized. **2.** money used for this purpose.

am·or·tize (am'ər tīz', ə môr'tīz) *v.t.,* **-tized, -tiz·ing.** to pay (a debt) gradually by periodic payments, usually in equal installments at equal intervals of time. [Old French *amortiss-,* stem of *amortir* to bring to death, going back to Latin *ad* to + *mors* death.]

am·or·tize·ment (am'ər tīz'mənt, ə môr'tiz-) amortization.

A·mos (ā'məs) *n.* a book of the Old Testament, attributed to the Hebrew prophet Amos.

a·mount (ə mount') *n.* **1.a.** a numerical quantity; sum: *What is the amount owed?* **b.** any quantity: *The typist had a large amount of work to do. No amount of argument will change their decision.* **2.** full effect, significance, or extent. —*v.i.* **1.** to be equal in number or quantity; add up (with *to*): *The bill amounts to ten dollars.* **2.** to be equivalent in value, significance, or effect (with *to*): *That remark amounts to a threat.* **3.** (of a person) to develop into; become (with *to*): *Neither of them will ever amount to anything.* [Old French *amonter* to amount to, from *à mont* toward a mountain, going back to Latin *ad* to + *mōns* mountain.]

> **Usage** Amount and number are both used when referring to a quantity. **Amount** is usually used when dealing with a quantity whose parts are considered as a whole: *A large amount of grain was shipped as part of the famine relief effort.* **Number** is preferred when dealing with a quantity whose parts can be counted: *a large number of books.*

a·mour (ə mür') *n.* a love affair, esp. one of an illicit or secret nature. [Old French *amour* love, from Latin *amor.*]

a·mour-pro·pre (ä mür PRô'PRə) *n. French.* self-love; self-esteem.

amp (amp) *n.* **1.** ampere. **2.** amplifier.

amp. 1. amperage. **2.** ampere; amperes.

AMP, adenosine monophosphate, an organic compound vital to the metabolic activity of all living cells. Formula: $C_{10}H_{14}N_5O_7P$

am·per·age (am'pər ij, am pîr'-) *n.* the strength of an electric current measured in amperes.

am·pere (am'pîr) *n.* the meter-kilogram-second unit for measuring the strength of an electric current, equal to the amount of current produced by one volt acting through a resistance of one ohm. [From the French physicist André Marie *Ampère,* 1775-1836.]

am·pere-hour (am'pîr our') *n.* the quantity of electricity delivered in one hour by a current of one ampere, equal to 3,600 coulombs.

am·per·sand (am'pər sand') *n.* a character (&) representing the word *and.* [Modification of the phrase *and per se and* and by itself means and (used in hornbooks).]

am·phet·a·mine (am fet'ə mēn', -min) *n.* any of a group of potentially addictive drugs that stimulate the central nervous system, used medically to treat depression and obesity. [Short for *a(lpha)-m(ethyl)-ph(enyl)-et(hyl)-amine.*]

amphi- *combining form* **1.** around: *amphitheater.* **2.** on two or all sides; at both ends: *amphistylar.* **3.** of two kinds: *amphibian.* [Greek *amphi* on both sides, around.]

am·phib·i·an (am fib'ē ən) *n.* **1.a.** any animal of the class Amphibia, of cold-blooded vertebrates, including frogs, toads, and salamanders, usually living in or near water and typically having moist, scaleless skin. Generally, their eggs are laid in water or moist places and hatch into gilled, legless larvae that develop into adults with lungs and two pairs of limbs. **b.** any amphibious organism. **2.** an aircraft designed to take off from and land on either land or water. **3.** a tank or other vehicle that can travel on both land and water. —*adj.* **1.** of, relating to, or characteristic of the class Amphibia. **2.** amphibious. [Formed from Greek *amphibios* living a double life, from *amphi* both + *bios* life.]

am·phib·i·ous (am fib'ē əs) *adj.* **1.** capable of living on land and in water: *an amphibious plant.* **2.** adapted or suitable for use on land or water: *an amphibious plane.* **3.** carried out by the

action of both land and naval forces: *an amphibious attack.* [Greek *amphibios,* from *amphi* both + *bios* life.] —**am·phib'i·ous·ly,** *adv.* —**am·phib'i·ous·ness,** *n.*

am·phi·bole (am'fə bōl') *n.* any of a group of common rock-forming minerals, including hornblende and varieties of asbestos, that are complex hydrous silicates containing different proportions of sodium, calcium, iron, magnesium, and aluminum. [French *amphibole,* from Late Latin *amphibolus,* ambiguous (because of its many varieties), from Greek *amphibolos,* from *amphiballein* to throw around, doubt, from *amphi-* (see AMPHI-) + *ballein* to throw.]

am·phi·ox·us (am'fē ok'səs) *n., pl.* **-ox·i** (-ok'sī) or **-us·es.** any of a subphylum, Cephalochordata, of small, fishlike lower chordates characterized by a notochord extending the length of the body and a row of gill slits on either side of the pharynx. Also, **lancelet.** [AMPHI- + Greek *oxys* sharp.]

am·phi·pod (am'fə pod') *n.* any member of the crustacean order Amphipoda, such as the sand flea, characterized by a lack of a carapace and three sets of legs, the middle set adapted to make its flealike jumping movements. [Modern Latin *amphipod,* from AMPHI- + *pous* (stem *pod-*) foot.]

am·phi·sty·lar (am'fə stī'lər) *adj.* having columns on both ends or on both sides. [AMPHI- + Greek *stȳlos* pillar.]

am·phi·the·a·ter (am'fə thē'ə tər) *also,* **am·phi·the·a·tre.** *n.* **1.** an elliptical or circular structure with rising tiers of seats around a central open space. **2.** a room having rising tiers of seats arranged around a central area, used for lectures or for observing medical procedures in a school or hospital. **3.** a level area of ground surrounded by rising slopes. [Latin *amphitheātrum,* from Greek *amphitheātron.*]

Am·phi·tri·te (am'fi trī'tē) *n.* in Greek mythology, one of the Nereids, goddess of the sea and wife of Poseidon.

am·pho·ra (am'fər ə) *n., pl.* **-pho·rae** (-fə rē') or **-pho·ras.** a two-handled jar or vase with a narrow neck, broad body, and tapering base, used by the ancient Greeks and Romans for storage. [Latin *amphora,* from Greek *amphoreus,* short for *amphiphoreus,* from *amphi-* on both sides + *phoreus* bearer.]

amphora

am·pho·ter·ic (am'fə ter'ik) *adj.* (of a chemical compound) capable of acting as both an acid and a base. [Greek *amphoteros,* comparative form of *amphō* both + -IC.]

am·pi·cil·lin (am'pi sil'in) *n.* an oral antibiotic, synthesized from penicillin, that is especially effective against certain bacteria. Formula: $C_{16}H_{19}N_3O_4S$ [Probably short for *am(inobenzyl)-p(en)icillin* an alternate chemical name.]

am·ple (am'pəl) *adj.* **-pler, -plest. 1.** of great size, extent, or capacity; roomy: *The car has an ample trunk.* **2.** more than enough; abundant: *an ample supply of paper; ample time in which to finish the job.* **3.** as much as is needed; sufficient; enough: *an income ample for one's needs.* [French *ample* full, wide, from Latin *amplus* large.] —**am'ple·ness,** *n.* —**am'ply,** *adv.* —For Synonyms, see **enough.**

am·pli·fi·ca·tion (am'plə fi kā'shən) *n.* **1.** the act of amplifying or the state of being amplified; expansion. **2.** something that is used to amplify; additional matter: *The footnotes were an amplification of the treatise.* **3.** something so expanded. **4.** an increase in the strength of an electronic signal.

am·pli·fi·er (am'plə fī'ər) *n.* **1.** any of various devices for increasing the strength of an electronic signal by the use of power from a source other than the signal. **2.** the part of a sound-reproduction system that contains such a device. **3.** a person or thing that amplifies.

am·pli·fy (am'plə fī') *v.,* **-fied, -fy·ing.** —*v.t.* **1.** to add to or expand, as speech or thought; enlarge on: *He amplified his statement with various illustrations.* **2.** to increase the strength of (an electronic signal). **3.** to increase in scope, significance, or power; extend. —*v.i.* to make additions to speech or writing; expatiate:

a	at	e	end	o	hot	u	up	hw	white	⎧	about
ā	ape	ē	me	ō	old	ū	use	ng	song	⎪	taken
ä	far	i	it	ô	fork	u̇	rule	th	thin	⎬	pencil
âr	care	ī	ice	oi	oil	u̇	pull	th	this	⎪	lemon
		îr	pierce	ou	out	ûr	turn	zh	measure	⎩	circus

She amplified for the sake of clarity. [Old French *amplifier* to enlarge, develop, from Latin *amplificāre* to enlarge.]

am·pli·tude (am′pli tüd′, -tūd′) *n.* **1.** the state or quality of being ample; greatness of size; largeness; breadth. **2.** an ample amount; abundance; fullness. **3.** the distance that a vibrating or oscillating body moves from its central or rest position. **4.** the highest value reached by an electromagnetic or other kind of wave during a complete cycle, as measured from the average value. [Latin *amplitūdō* breadth.]

amplitude modulation, see AM.

am·pule (am′pūl, -pül) *also,* **am·pul, am·poule.** *n.* a small container, usually of glass and hermetically sealed, holding one dose of a sterile preparation intended for injection, as by hypodermic syringe.

am·pul·la (am pul′ə) *n., pl.* **-pul·lae** (-pul′ē). *Anatomy.* an expanded ending of a tube or canal, as in a mammary duct. [Latin *ampulla,* diminutive of *ampora,* form of *amphora* a two-handled, narrow-necked jar. See AMPHORA.] —**am·pul′lar,** *adj.*

am·pu·tate (am′pyə tāt′) *v.t.,* **-tat·ed, -tat·ing.** to cut off, esp. to remove (all or part of a limb or extremity) surgically. [Latin *amputātus,* past participle of *amputāre* to cut around, prune.] —**am′pu·ta′tion,** *n.* —**am′pu·ta′tor,** *n.*

am·pu·tee (am′pyə tē′) *n.* a person who has had all or part of a limb or extremity amputated.

amt., amount.

amu *also,* **AMU** atomic mass unit.

a·muck (ə muk′) amok.

am·u·let (am′yə lit) *n.* an object worn or placed in a house to bring good fortune or to protect against disease, bad luck, or evil; charm. [Latin *amulētum.*]

a·muse (ə mūz′) *v.t.,* **a·mused, a·mus·ing.** **1.** to please the sense of humor of; make laugh or smile: *The comedienne's jokes amused all of us.* **2.** to keep pleasantly occupied or interested; entertain; divert: *He amused himself by reading.* [Old French *amuser,* from *à* to (from Latin *ad* to) + *muser* to ponder. See MUSE.] —**a·mus′er,** *n.*

a·mused (ə mūzd′) *adj.* **1.** feeling mirth or enjoyment: *an amused spectator.* **2.** expressing mirth or enjoyment: *an amused smile.* —**a·mus·ed·ly** (ə mū′zid lē), *adv.*

a·muse·ment (ə mūz′mənt) *n.* **1.** the state of being amused; enjoyment: *The clown made faces for the amusement of the children.* **2.** something that amuses or entertains; diversion.

> **Synonyms** Amusement, entertainment, diversion, pastime, and recreation mean pleasant ways of spending time. **Amusement** implies conscious involvement in or attention to something pleasant: *We got great amusement from playing with the kittens.* **Entertainment** suggests being passive while others perform: *Two singers provided entertainment for the hospital patients.* **Diversion** emphasizes the turning of one's attention away from daily cares: *The phone call was a pleasant diversion from work.* **Pastime** suggests doing something to use up leisure hours: *Television seemed to be their only pastime.* **Recreation** emphasizes being invigorated by a pursuit: *Fishing is my favorite recreation because it brings me close to nature.*

amusement park, a commercially operated area with various games, rides, and entertainment devices, such as a Ferris wheel, merry-go-round, and shooting gallery.

a·mus·ing (ə mū′zing) *adj.* **1.** causing laughter or enjoyment: *an amusing story.* **2.** entertaining; diverting. —**a·mus′ing·ly,** *adv.* —For Synonyms, see humorous.

a·myg·da·lin (ə mig′də lin) *n.* a glycoside present in certain almonds that is the principal component of laetrile. Formula: $C_{20}H_{27}NO_{11}$

am·yl (am′əl) *n.* a univalent alcohol radical derived from pentane. Formula: C_5H_{11} [Latin *amylum* starch (from Greek *amylon* starch) + Greek *hylē* substance.]

amyl alcohol, a colorless, oily liquid that is the principal ingredient in fuel oil, used as a solvent. Formula: $C_5H_{12}O$

am·yl·ase (am′ə lās′) *n.* any of a large class of enzymes that convert starch to sugar in digestion.

am·y·lop·sin (am′ə lop′sin) *n.* an amylase secreted by the pancreas that converts starch to sugar in the intestines. [AMYL + (TRY)PSIN.]

an¹ (an; *unstressed* ən) *indefinite article* form of *a* before words with an initial vowel sound: *an artichoke, an hour.* [Old English *ān.*]

an² (an; *unstressed* ən) *conj. Archaic.* if. [Form of AND.]

an-¹ *prefix* not; without: *anemia, anarchy, anhydrous.* [Greek *a-, an-.*]

an-² form of *ad-* before *n,* as in *annul.*

-an *suffix* **1.** (used to form nouns) **a.** a person who is a native or citizen of: *Mexican, Texan.* **b.** a person who belongs to or is associated with: *Lutheran, Republican.* **c.** a person who specializes or is skilled in: *mathematician, magician.* **2.** (used to form adjectives) of, relating to, or characteristic of: *Elizabethan, authoritarian.* [Old French *-ien, -ain, -en* belonging to, relating to, from Latin *-anus.*]

ana- *prefix* **1.** up; upward: *anadromous.* **2.** back; backward; against: *anachronism.* **3.** again; anew: *Anabaptist.* **4.** throughout; thoroughly: *analysis.* [Greek *ana* on, up, again.]

An·a·bap·tist (an′ə bap′tist) *n.* any of a group of radically fundamentalist Protestants in Switzerland, Germany, and Holland in the sixteenth century who rejected infant baptism and advocated communal property and separation of church and state. [Modern Latin *anabaptista* literally, one who baptizes again, going back to Greek *ana* again + *baptistēs* one that dips or baptizes.]

an·a·bat·ic (an′ə bat′ik) *adj. Meteorology.* moving upward, as an air current or wind. ➡ opposed to **katabatic.** [Greek *anabatikos,* from *anabasis* a stepping up, from *anabainein* to go up, from *ana-* up + *bainein* to go.]

a·nab·o·lism (ə nab′ə liz′əm) *n.* the phase of metabolism in which food molecules and energy are utilized in repairing body tissue and building proteins such as antibodies and enzymes; constructive metabolism. ➡ distinguished from **catabolism.** [ANA- + (META)BOLISM.] —**an·a·bol·ic** (an′ə bol′ik), *adj.*

a·nach·ro·nism (ə nak′rə niz′əm) *n.* **1.** something out of its proper time. **2.** the placement of something in a time to which it does not belong; chronological error. To say that Benjamin Franklin flew in an airplane is an anachronism. [Greek *anachronismos,* from *ana* back + *chronos* time.]

a·nach·ro·nis·tic (ə nak′rə nis′tik) *adj.* containing or involving an anachronism. Also, **a·nach′ro·nis′ti·cal.** —**a·nach′ro·nis′ti·cal·ly,** *adv.*

a·nach·ro·nous (ə nak′rə nəs) *adj.* anachronistic. —**a·nach′ro·nous·ly,** *adv.*

an·a·co·lu·thon (an′ə kə lü′thon) *n., pl.* **-tha** (-thə) or **-thons.** an interruption in a sentence followed by a change from one grammatical construction to another. The sentence *I wanted to go to—never mind, there's no use in saying it* contains an anacoluthon. [Greek *anakolouthon* inconsistency, from *anakolouthos* inconsistent.]

an·a·con·da (an′ə kon′də) *n.* **1.** a constrictor snake, genus *Eunectes,* native to tropical South America, feeding mostly on fish, water birds, and small mammals. The **giant anaconda,** *E. murinus,* probably the largest snake in the world, may grow to a length of more than 30 feet (9.1 meters). **2.** any large constrictor, such as the python or boa. [Possibly Singhalese *henakandayā* large snake of Sri Lanka.]

anaconda *(def. 1)*

a·nad·ro·mous (ə nad′rə məs) *adj.* (of fish) swimming upstream from the sea to spawn. ➡ distinguished from **catadromous.** [Greek *anadromos* running upward, from *ana* up + *dromos* a running.]

a·nae·mi·a (ə nē′mē ə) anemia.

a·nae·mic (ə nē′mik) *adj.* anemic. —**a·nae′mi·cal·ly,** *adv.*

an·aer·obe (an âr′ōb, an′ə-rōb′) *n.* a microorganism that can live in an environment lacking free oxygen. ➡ distinguished from **aerobe.** [AN¹ + Greek *āēr* air + *bios* life.]

an·aer·o·bic (an′â rō′bik, an′ə-) *adj.* **1.** able to live or grow where free oxygen is lacking: *anaerobic bacteria.* **2.** of or caused by anaerobes: *an anaerobic infection.* **3.** occurring in or caused by the absence of air or oxygen. **4.** of or relating to a form of exercise designed to strengthen the muscles rather than the cardiovascular system. ➡ distinguished from **aerobic.** —**an′aer·o′bi·cal·ly,** *adv.*

an·aer·o·bics (an′â rō′biks, an′ə-) *pl. n.* a system of exercise that is intended to strengthen and build up the muscles rather than the cardiovascular system. ➡ used as singular or plural.

an·aes·the·sia (an′əs thē′zhə, -zē ə) anesthesia.

an·aes·the·si·ol·o·gist (an′əs thē′zē ol′ə jist) anesthesiologist.

an·aes·the·si·ol·o·gy (an′əs thē′zē ol′ə jē) anesthesiology.

an·aes·thet·ic (an′əs thet′ik) *n., adj.* anesthetic. —**an′aes·thet′i·cal·ly,** *adv.*

an·aes·the·tist (ə nes′thi tist) anesthetist.

an·aes·the·tize (ə nes′thi tīz′) *v.t.* anesthetize. —**an·aes′the·ti·za′tion,** *n.*

an·a·gram (an′ə gram′) *n.* **1.** a word or phrase created by transposing the letters of another word or phrase. The word *veil* is an anagram of the word *evil.* **2. anagrams.** a game in which the players form words by rearranging given letters or by arranging letters taken in turn from a pile of cards or tiles. ➡ used as singular. [French *anagramme,* going back to Greek *ana-* backwards + *gramma* letter.]

a·nal (ā′nəl) *adj.* of, relating to, or near the anus.

anal fin, an unpaired fin in fish, located on the underside of the body, between the anus and the tail.

an·al·ge·si·a (an′əl jē′zē ə, -sē ə) *n.* an insensibility to pain without the loss of consciousness. [Greek *analgēsiā,* from *an-*[1] without + *algēsis* sense of pain.]

an·al·ge·sic (an′əl jē′zik, -sik) *adj.* relating to or causing analgesia. —*n.* a remedy used to relieve or remove pain. Aspirin is a common analgesic.

an·a·log (an′ə lôg′, -log′) *adj.* **1.a.** processing or representing data by means of a continuously variable quantity or device. **b.** of or relating to an analog device. **2.** (of a timepiece) displaying the time by means of hands rather than by a digital display. —*n.* analogue. [From French *analogue* something similar, going back to Greek *analogos* in proper proportion.]

analog computer, a computer that represents data using physical entities of analogous value. A slide rule is a simple analog computer, with scales that represent numerical quantities. An electronic analog computer utilizes such things as voltage, current, or electric impulses to represent the given quantities. ➡ distinguished from **digital computer.**

an·a·log·i·cal (an′ə loj′i kəl) *adj.* using, expressing, or based on analogy: *analogical reasoning.* —**an′a·log′i·cal·ly,** *adv.*

a·nal·o·gous (ə nal′ə gəs) *adj.* **1.** alike or similar in certain respects; comparable: *The eye and a camera are analogous.* **2.** *Biology.* having the same function, but differing in structure and origin. The gills of a fish and the lungs of a mammal are analogous. ➡ distinguished from **homologous** in def. 2. —**a·nal′o·gous·ly,** *adv.* —**a·nal′o·gous·ness,** *n.*

an·a·logue (an′ə lôg′, -log′) *also,* **analog.** *n.* **1.** something analogous to something else. **2.** *Biology.* an organ, part, or system that is analogous to one in another organism.

a·nal·o·gy (ə nal′ə jē) *n., pl.* **-gies. 1.** a similarity in certain respects between things otherwise unlike; partial resemblance: *the analogy between the heart and a pump.* **2.** any similarity or correspondence: *There's no analogy between my position and yours.* **3.** *Biology.* a similarity in function of parts dissimilar in structure and origin. **4.** *Logic.* a form of reasoning in which similarities are inferred from others that are already known and observed. **5.** *Linguistics.* the process by which words or phrases are created or changed based on existing patterns in the language. *Computerese* was formed by analogy with words such as *Japanese* and *Portuguese.* [Latin *analogia* resemblance, from Greek *analogiā* resemblance, proportion.]

an·a·lyse (an′ə līz′) *v.t.* **-lysed, -lys·ing.** *British.* analyze.

a·nal·y·sis (ə nal′ə sis) *n., pl.* **-ses** (-sēz′). **1.** a method of determining the nature and essential features of something by separating it into its parts; critical examination: *Analysis of the paint showed that the portrait was a fake.* **2.** a statement or presentation of the results of such an examination. **3.** the separation of a whole into its constituent parts or elements. ➡ distinguished from **synthesis. 4.** psychoanalysis. **5.** *Chemistry.* **a.** the intentional separation or decomposition of a substance into its constituent compounds or elements. **Quantitative analysis** determines the amount of the ingredients; **qualitative analysis** determines their identity. **b.** the determination of the identity or amount of one or more constituents of a substance, whether obtained in separate form or not. **6.** the solution of mathematical problems by means of algebra or calculus, rather than group or number theory. [Modern Latin *analysis,* from Greek *analysis* releasing, solution, from *ana-* ana- + *lyein* to loosen.]

an·a·lyst (an′ə list) *n.* **1.** a person who analyzes or is skilled in analysis: *The journalist was a skilled political analyst.* **2.** psychoanalyst.

an·a·lyt·i·cal (an′ə lit′i kəl) *adj.* of, relating to, or using analysis. Also, **an′a·lyt′ic.** —**an′a·lyt′i·cal·ly,** *adv.*

analytic geometry, a branch of mathematics in which geometric figures are described and analyzed in algebraic terms and plotted in two or three dimensions by means of coordinates.

an·a·lyt·ics (an′ə lit′iks) *n.* a branch of logic concerned with analysis. ➡ used as singular.

an·a·lyze (an′ə līz′) *also, British,* **analyse.** *v.t.* **-lyzed, -lyz·ing. 1.** to separate into constituent parts, esp. so as to determine the nature or essential features of the whole: *to analyze a sentence grammatically.* **2.** to examine critically or in detail: *She tried to analyze his reasons for refusing to help in the campaign.* **3.** to psychoanalyze. **4.** to subject to chemical or mathematical analysis. —**an′a·lyz′a·ble,** *adj.* —**an′a·ly·za′tion,** *n.* —**an′a·lyz′er,** *n.*

An·a·ni·as (an′ə nī′əs) *n.* liar. [From *Ananias,* in the New Testament, a man who was struck dead for lying.]

an·a·pest (an′ə pest′) *also,* **an·a·paest.** *n.* **1.** a metrical foot in verse consisting of two unaccented or short syllables followed by an accented or long syllable. The line *And the sheen′ / of their spears′ / was like stars′ / on the sea′* / (Byron, 1815) contains four anapests. **2.** a line of verse made up of such feet. [Latin *anapaestus* anapest *(def. 1),* from Greek *anapaistos (pous)* reversed (metrical foot); because it is the opposite of a dactyl.] —**an′a·pes′tic;** *also,* **an′a·paes′tic,** *adj.*

an·a·phase (an′ə fāz′) *n. Biology.* a stage in ordinary cell division during which the divided chromosomes separate and move toward opposite poles. In mitosis, there is one such stage; in meiosis, there are two. For illustration, see **mitosis.** [ANA- + PHASE.]

a·naph·o·ra (ə naf′ər ə) *n.* the repetition of a word or phrase at the beginning of two or more successive clauses, verses, or sentences. [Latin *anaphora,* from Greek *anaphorā* repetition.]

an·a·phy·lac·tic (an′ə fə lak′tik) *adj.* relating to, having, or causing anaphylaxis or anaphylactic shock. —**an′a·phy·lac′ti·cal·ly,** *adv.*

anaphylactic shock, a serious and sometimes fatal allergic reaction to a foreign substance, esp. a drug or bee or other venom, following previous exposure, characterized by respiratory difficulties and rapid swelling.

an·a·phy·lax·is (an′ə fə lak′sis) *n.* **1.** a hypersensitivity to a foreign substance following its reintroduction into the blood. **2.** anaphylactic shock. [Modern Latin *anaphylaxis,* from ANA- + Greek *phylaxis* guarding.]

an·arch (an′ärk) *n. Archaic.* anarchist.

an·ar·chic (an är′kik) *adj.* **1.** of, like, or involving anarchy. **2.** advocating anarchy. **3.** causing or provoking anarchy. Also, **an·ar′chi·cal.** —**an·ar′chi·cal·ly,** *adv.*

an·ar·chism (an′ər kiz′əm) *n.* **1.** a political theory that all forms of government and governmental restraint are morally wrong and must be abolished if absolute individual and social liberty is to be achieved. **2.** the advocacy of this theory or practices characteristic of its advocates.

an·ar·chist (an′ər kist) *n.* **1.** a person who promotes, believes in, or advocates anarchy or anarchism, esp. by the violent overthrow of the established political and social order. **2.** a person who promotes disorder or incites revolt against any kind of established rule and order. —**an′ar·chis′tic,** *adj.*

an·ar·chy (an′ər kē) *n.* **1.** the absence of government and law. **2.** lawless confusion and political disorder due to the absence of governmental authority. **3.** general disorder and confusion; chaos. [Medieval Latin *anarchia,* from Greek *anarchia* lack of a ruler, lawlessness.]

A·na·sa·zi (ä′nə sä′zē) *n., pl.* **-zi** or **-zis.** a member of an extinct North American Indian tribe that settled in the southwestern United States around A.D. 100. The modern Pueblo are descendants of this tribe. —*adj.* of or relating to the Anasazi or their culture.

an·a·stig·mat·ic (an′ə stig mat′ik) *adj.* free from or corrected for astigmatism, as a compound lens consisting of diverging and converging elements designed to neutralize each other's astigmatic effects. [AN-[1] + ASTIGMATIC.]

a·nas·to·mose (ə nas′tə mōz′, -mōs′) *v.,* **-mosed, -mos·ing.** —*v.t.* to form by anastomosis. —*v.i.* to divide, subdivide, and rejoin repeatedly. [French *anastomoser,* going back to Modern Latin *anastomosis.* See ANASTOMOSIS.]

a	at	e	end	o	hot	u	up	hw	white		about
ā	ape	ē	me	ō	old	ū	use	ng	song		taken
ä	far	i	it	ô	fork	ü	rule	th	thin	ə	pencil
âr	care	ī	ice	oi	oil	ù	pull	<u>th</u>	this		lemon
				îr	pierce	ou	out	ûr	turn	zh	measure		circus

a·nas·to·mo·sis (ə nas′tə mō′sis) *n.,* *pl.* **-ses** (-sēz).
1. *Anatomy.* an interconnection of blood or lymph vessels or an intermingling of fibers from two nerves. **2.** *Medicine.* a surgical joining of blood vessels, nerves, or tubular organs, as to bypass a diseased or injured section. **3.** a connection between parts of any branching system. [Modern Latin *anastomasis,* from Greek *anastomōsis* an opening, from *ana* again + *stoma* mouth + *-ōsis* (see -OSIS).] —**a·nas·to·mot·ic** (ə nas′tə mot′ik), *adj.*

a·nas·tro·phe (ə nas′trə fē) *n.* inversion of the usual order of words or parts of a sentence, for example: *echoed the hills.* [Greek *anastrophē* inversion.]

a·nath·e·ma (ə nath′ə mə) *n.,* *pl.* **-mas. 1.** in the Roman Catholic and Orthodox churches, the formal denunciation of a person or the condemnation of a practice or doctrine. **2.** any strong denunciation or imprecation; curse. **3.** a person or thing that is accursed or denounced. **4.** a person or thing that is detested or abhorred. [Late Latin *anathema* accursed person, curse, from Greek *anathema* thing devoted (to evil).]

a·nath·e·ma·tize (ə nath′ə mə tīz′) *v.t.,* **-tized, -tiz·ing.** to pronounce an anathema against; denounce; curse.

an·a·tom·i·cal (an′ə tom′i kəl) *adj.* of or relating to anatomy or its study. Also, **an′a·tom′ic.** —**an′a·tom′i·cal·ly,** *adv.*

a·nat·o·mist (ə nat′ə mist) *n.* a person skilled in anatomy or dissection.

a·nat·o·mize (ə nat′ə mīz′) *v.t.,* **-mized, -miz·ing. 1.** to dissect (an animal or plant) in order to study or display the position, structure, and relationships of its parts. **2.** to analyze (something) closely. —**a·nat′o·mi·za′tion,** *n.*

a·nat·o·my (ə nat′ə mē) *n.,* *pl.* **-mies. 1.** the science of the physical structure of plants and animals and the interrelationships of their parts. **2.** the physical structure of a plant or animal or any of its parts. **3.** the dissection of a plant or animal to study the position, structure, and relationship of its parts. **4.** a detailed examination; analysis: *the anatomy of a crime.* **5.** an anatomical model or cast. **6.** *Informal.* a human body. [French *anatomie* science of the physical structure of organisms, dissection, from Late Latin *anatomia* dissection, from Greek *anatomē* cutting up.]

anc., ancient.

-ance *suffix* **1.** (used to form nouns directly from verbs) **a.** the process or action of: *continuance, utterance.* **b.** the state, quality, or condition of: *resemblance, complaisance.* **c.** the result of an action: *inheritance, contrivance.* **d.** an agent of: *conveyance.* **2.** (used to form nouns from adjectives ending in *-ant*) the state, quality, or condition of being: *ignorance, brilliance, vigilance.* [Often through French *-ance,* from Latin *-antia, -entia.*]

an·ces·tor (an′ses tər) *n.* **1.** a person from whom one is descended; forebear. ➡ usually used to designate one more remote than a grandparent. **2.** something that precedes or influences the development (of something else); forerunner; prototype: *The calculator is the ancestor of the modern computer.* **3.** an organism from which higher or later organisms have evolved. [Old French *ancestre* forefather, from Latin *antecessor* one who goes before, predecessor.]

an·ces·tral (an ses′trəl) *adj.* of, relating to, or inherited from ancestors: *an ancestral estate.* —**an·ces′tral·ly,** *adv.*

an·ces·tress (an′ses tris) *n.* a female from whom one is descended.

an·ces·try (an′ses trē) *n., pl.* **-tries. 1.** family lineage or descent: *She is of English ancestry.* **2.** ancestors collectively: *His ancestry was among the first settlers in this area.* **3.** honorable or aristocratic descent: *They were possessed of wealth and ancestry.*

An·chi·ses (an kī′sēz) *n.* in Greek and Roman legend, a prince of Troy and the father of Aeneas.

an·chor (ang′kər) *n.* **1.** a device for preventing a boat or other floating structure from drifting. An anchor usually grips the bottom under water and is attached to the boat by a chain or cable. **2.** any device that holds something in place. **3.** a source or means of support, stability, or security: *Hope was his anchor.* **4.** a person who acts as an anchorman or anchorwoman. —*v.t.* **1.** to hold (a floating

structure) in place by an anchor. **2.** to fasten in place; secure firmly: *Anchor the shelf to the wall.* **3.** to act as an anchorman or anchorwoman: *She anchors the six o'clock news.* **4.** *Informal.* to position or fix (oneself) firmly: *Don't anchor yourself near the door.* —*v.i.* to lower the anchor overboard and remain held fast: *We anchored in the bay.* [Old English *ancor* mooring device, from Latin *ancora,* from Greek *ankyra.*]

• **at anchor.** held fast by an anchor.
• **to drop** (or **cast**) **anchor.** to lower an anchor overboard.
• **to ride at anchor.** to be held fast by an anchor.
• **to weigh anchor.** to take up an anchor.

an·chor·age (ang′kər ij) *n.* **1.** a place for anchoring. **2.** a fee charged for anchoring. **3.** the act of anchoring or the state of being anchored. **4.** something that fastens or holds securely: *The ropes were used as anchorage.*

an·cho·ress (ang′kə ris) *n.* a female who lives in seclusion, esp. for religious reasons.

an·cho·rite (ang′kə rīt′) *also,* **an·cho·ret** (ang′kər it, -kə ret′). *n.* a person who lives in seclusion, esp. for religious reasons; hermit. [Medieval Latin *anachorita,* from Late Latin *anachoreta,* from Greek *anachōrētēs* literally, one who has withdrawn.]

an·chor·man (ang′kər man′) *n., pl.* **-men** (-men′). **1.** the last runner or swimmer in a relay race. **2.** a man who is the principal announcer and coordinator of a television or radio newscast.

an·chor·per·son (ang′kər pûr′sən) *n.* an anchorman or anchorwoman on a newscast.

an·chor·wom·an (ang′kər wŭm′ən) *n., pl.* **-wom·en** (-wim′ən). a woman who is the principal announcer and coordinator of a television or radio newscast.

an·cho·vy (an′chō vē, an chō′-) *n., pl.* **-vies.** any of various saltwater and freshwater fish, family Engraulidae, closely related to the herring. The European anchovy, *Engraulis encrasicholus,* is caught commercially, esp. in the Mediterranean area, and canned as fillets or processed into a paste. Length: 3-4 inches (8-10 centimeters). [Spanish *anchova.*]

an·cienne no·blesse (äṉ syen nô bles′) *French.* the old nobility, esp. that of France before the revolution of 1789.

an·cien ré·gime (äṉ syaṉ Rā zhēm′) *French.* the old political and social system, esp. that of France before the revolution of 1789.

an·cient[1] (ān′shənt, -chənt) *adj.* **1.** of or relating to times long past, esp. before the fall of the Western Roman Empire in A.D. 476: *ancient ruins, the ancient philosophers.* **2.** of great age; very old: *Baptism is an ancient rite.* —*n.* **1.** an aged or venerable person. **2. the ancients. a.** the civilized peoples of antiquity, esp. the Greeks and Romans: *Slavery was common among the ancients.* **b.** the authors, artists, and philosophers of ancient Greece and Rome: *Cicero, Livy, and the other ancients.* [Old French *ancien* old, going back to Latin *ante* before.] —**an′cient·ly,** *adv.* —**an′cient·ness,** *n.*

an·cient[2] (ān′shənt, -chənt) *n. Archaic.* **1.** a flag or banner; ensign. **2.** the bearer of a flag or banner; standardbearer. [Modification of ENSIGN.]

ancient history 1. history from the beginning of recorded events to the fall of the Western Roman Empire in A.D. 476. **2.** *Informal.* recent information or a recent event that is commonly known or is no longer pertinent or interesting.

an·cil·lar·y (an′sə ler′ē) *adj.* serving to help or support; supplementary or subsidiary; auxiliary. [Latin *ancillāris* relating to a maidservant, from *ancilla* maidservant.]

an·con (ang′kon) *n., pl.* **an·co·nes** (ang kō′nēz). a projection used to support a cornice or other structure; console. [Latin *ancōn* projecting stone support, from Greek *ankōn* bend, elbow.] —**an·co·nal** (ang kō′nəl), **an·co·ne·al** (ang kō′nē əl), *adj.*

-ancy, form of **-ance,** as in *vacancy.*

and (and; *unstressed* ənd, ən) *conj.*
1. as well as; moreover: *paper, pen, and ink, a dog both big and strong.* **2.** added to; plus: *Two and two make four.* **3.** as a result or consequence: *She felt tired and sat down. Give him an inch and he'll take a mile.* **4.** immediately or soon afterward; then: *The tired children drank some warm milk and went to bed.* **5.** *Informal.* to: *Come and see us sometime.* **6.** *Archaic.* if: *and it please you.* [Old English *and* also, plus.]

and., andante.

Ring
Stock
Shank
Fluke

Common anchor

Grapnel
anchor
Stockless
anchor
Mushroom
anchor

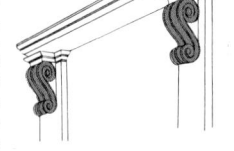

ancons

an·dan·te (än dän′tā, an dan′tē) *Music. adv., adj.* slower than moderato but faster than adagio; moderately slow. —*n.* a composition, movement, or part in such a tempo. [Italian *andante* literally, going.]

an·dan·ti·no (än′dän tē′nō, an′dan-) *Music. adv., adj.* slightly faster than andante. —*n., pl.* **-nos.** a composition, movement, or part in such a tempo. [Italian *andantino,* diminutive of *andante* slow. See ANDANTE.]

an·des·ite (an′də zīt′) *n.* a dark volcanic rock rich in plagioclase feldspar. [From the *Andes,* South American mountain system where it is found, + -ITE¹.] —**an·de·sit·ic** (an′də zit′ik), *adj.*

and·i·ron (and′ī′ərn) *n.* either of two metal supports for holding wood in a fireplace. Also, **firedog.** [Old French *andier,* influenced by *iron.*]

and/or, one or the other or both.

> **Usage** **And/or** is used to indicate that either *and* or *or* may connect two words, phrases, or clauses, depending on what is meant. It should be reserved for situations that offer three distinct possibilities involving two elements: *The railroad is authorized to carry freight and/or passengers.* **And/or** is used mostly in legal and business writing, but in general writing it is usually preferable to spell out all three possibilities: *In Hong Kong, we bought souvenirs with American dollars, Hong Kong dollars, or both.*

An·dro·cles (an′drə klēz′) *also,* **An·dro·clus** (an′drə kləs). *n.* in Roman legend, a slave spared in the arena by a lion because he had once removed a thorn from its paw.

an·droe·ci·um (an drē′shē əm) *n., pl.* **-ci·a** (-shē ə). the stamens of a flower, considered as a unit. [Modern Latin *androecium,* from *andr-,* stem of *anēr* man, male + *oikion,* diminutive of *oikos* house.]

an·dro·gen (an′drə jən) *n.* any of various hormones, as testosterone, that control and stimulate the development of masculine characteristics. —**an·dro·gen·ic** (an′drə jen′ik), *adj.*

an·drog·y·nous (an droj′ə nəs) *adj.* 1. having the characteristics of both sexes; hermaphroditic. 2. (of a flower cluster) having both male and female flowers. [Latin *androgynus* hermaphrodite, from Greek *androgynos,* from *andr-,* stem of *anēr* man + *gynē* woman.] —**androg′y·ny,** *n.*

an·droid (an′droid) *n.* in science fiction, a robot that is human in form or appearance. [Greek *aner* man, male + *-oeidēs* (see -OID).]

An·drom·a·che (an drom′ə kē′) *n.* in Greek legend, the wife of Hector and mother of Astyanax. She was captured by the Greeks after the fall of Troy.

An·drom·e·da (an drom′i də) *n.* 1. in Greek mythology, an Ethiopian princess whom Perseus rescued from a sea monster and then took as his wife. 2. a constellation in the northern sky, conventionally depicted as a woman with outstretched arms.

-ane *suffix* designating a hydrocarbon compound of the alkane, or paraffin, series: *methane.* [Form of -ENE, -INE, or -ONE.]

an·ec·do·tal (an′ik dōt′əl) *adj.* relating to, consisting of, or resembling anecdotes: *an anecdotal writing style.* —**an′ec·do′tal·ly,** *adv.*

an·ec·dote (an′ik dōt′) *n.* a short amusing or interesting account of some incident or event, usually personal or biographical: *They related several anecdotes about their first years in America.* [French *anecdote,* from Greek *anekdota* things unpublished (suggesting a private story or gossip).]

an·ec·dot·ist (an′ik dō′tist) *n.* a person who tells or is given to telling anecdotes.

an·e·cho·ic (an′e kō′ik) *adj.* tending not to reverberate or to reflect sound; not giving rise to echoes. An anechoic chamber, used in acoustic research, has walls covered with small pyramids of an absorbent material, as foam rubber. [AN-¹ + ECHOIC.]

a·ne·mi·a (ə nē′mē ə) *also,* **anaemia.** *n.* an abnormal condition in which there is a deficiency in the number of red corpuscles or the amount of hemoglobin in the blood, characterized by pallor, weakness, and fatigue. [Modern Latin *anaemia,* from Greek *anaimia* lack of blood.]

a·ne·mic (ə nē′mik) *also,* **anaemic.** *adj.* 1. of, having, or characteristic of anemia. 2. lacking vitality or spirit; bloodless: *an anemic attempt.* —**a·ne′mi·cal·ly,** *adv.*

an·e·mom·e·ter (an′ə mom′i tər) *n.* an instrument for measuring the velocity of the wind. [Greek *anemos* wind + -METER.] —**an′e·mo·met′ric** (an′ə mō met′rik); *also,* **an′e·mo·met′ri·cal,** *adj.*

a·nem·o·ne (ə nem′ə nē) *n.* 1. any plant of the genus *Anemone,* usually having slender stems, lobed or notched leaves, and small

flowers. Also, **wind-flower.** 2. sea anemone. [Latin *anemone* wind-flower, from Greek *anem-ōnē.*]

a·nent (ə nent′) *prep. Archaic.* in regard to; concerning. [Old English *on efen* near.]

an·er·oid (an′ə roid′) *adj.* not using or containing liquid. —*n.* aneroid barometer. [French *anér-oïde,* from Greek *a-* without + *nēros* of water + -OID.]

anemone *(def. 1)*

aneroid barometer, a barometer in which a flexible metal box containing a partial vacuum contracts and expands in response to changes in air pressure. When the box expands, it pushes a spring attached to a pointer, which registers the change.

an·es·the·sia (an′əs thē′zhə, -zē ə) *also,* **anaesthesia.** *n.* a loss of physical sensation, with or without a loss of consciousness, esp. the loss of the sensation of pain, induced by drugs or other means to allow the performance of surgery or other painful procedures. [Modern Latin *anaesthesia,* from Greek *anaisthēsiā* lack of feeling.]

an·es·the·si·ol·o·gist (an′əs thē′zē ol′ə jist) *also,* **anaesthesiologist.** *n.* a physician who specializes in the field of anesthesiology.

an·es·the·si·ol·o·gy (an′əs thē′zē ol′ə jē) *also,* **anaesthesiology.** *n.* the branch of medicine that deals with anesthesia and the administration of anesthetics.

an·es·thet·ic (an′əs thet′ik) *also,* **anaesthetic.** *n.* a substance that produces anesthesia. —*adj.* 1. producing anesthesia. 2. of, relating to, or characteristic of anesthesia. —**an′es·thet′i·cal·ly,** *adv.*

an·es·the·tist (ə nes′thi tist) *also,* **anaesthetist.** *n.* a person who is trained and licensed to administer anesthetics, esp. a registered nurse.

an·es·the·tize (ə nes′thi tīz′) *v.t.,* **-tized, -tiz·ing.** *also,* **anaesthetize.** to make insensible, esp. to pain; produce anesthesia in. —**an·es′the·ti·za′tion,** *n.*

an·eu·rysm (an′yə riz′əm) *also,* **an·eu·rism.** *n.* a sac formed by the dilation of the wall of an artery, a vein, or the heart, usually caused by atherosclerosis and hypertension. If an aneurysm ruptures, serious hemorrhaging may result. [Greek *aneurysma* dilation.] —**an·eu′rys·mal;** *also,* **an·eu·ris′mal,** *adj.*

a·new (ə nü′, ə nū′) *adv.* 1. in a new or different way: *The prisoner vowed to begin life anew once released.* 2. over again; once more: *We began the song anew.* [Old English *of-niowe* over again.]

an·gel (ān′jəl) *n.* 1. in various religions, one of the group of immortal, spiritual beings who serve as the attendants and messengers of God. 2. a conventional representation of any of these beings, usually a human form with wings and a halo. 3. a guardian spirit or guiding influence: *Her good angel watched over her.* 4. a person regarded as resembling an angel in goodness, innocence, beauty, or kindliness. 5. *Informal.* a person who provides funds for something, esp. a theatrical production; financial backer. 6. an English gold coin minted between 1465 and 1634, having on its face the archangel Michael defeating Satan. [Old French *angele* divine messenger and spirit (replacing Old English *engel*), from Latin *angelus* messenger, divine messenger, from Greek *angelos* messenger.]

an·gel·fish (ān′jəl fish′) *n., pl.* **-fish** or **-fish·es.** 1. any of various saltwater and freshwater tropical fish that have filamentous extensions on their fins and often have striking markings or coloration. Two freshwater angelfish, *Pterophyllum scalare* and *P. eimekei,* have flattened silver bodies, vertical black bands, and fan-shaped rear fins, and are popular aquarium fish. 2. any of several sharks, genus *Squatina,* found in warm and temperate

a	at	e	end	o	hot	u	up	hw	white		about
ā	ape	ē	me	ō	old	ū	use	ng	song		taken
ä	far	i	it	ô	fork	ü	rule	th	thin	ə	pencil
âr	care	ī	ice	oi	oil	u̇	pull	th	this		lemon
		î	pierce	ou	out	ûr	turn	zh	measure		circus

angelfish *(def. 1)*

shore waters and having large, winglike pectoral fins and a flat body.

an·gel·ic (an jel′ik) *adj.* **1.** like or characteristic of an angel; good, pure, and beautiful; saintly: *an angelic temperament.* **2.** of, relating to, or belonging to the angels. Also, **an·gel′i·cal.** —**an·gel′i·cal·ly,** *adv.*

an·gel·i·ca (an jel′i kə) *n.* **1.** any of a large group of plants, genus *Angelica,* of the parsley family, native to the Northern Hemisphere, esp. *A. archangelica,* some parts of which are used in medicine and in cooking. **2.** the young stems and leafstalks of *A. archangelica,* cooked in sugar syrup and used as a confection, esp. to decorate cakes and cookies. [Medieval Latin *(herba) angelica* angelic (herb); because of its medicinal uses.]

An·ge·lus (an′jə ləs) *also,* **an·ge·lus.** *n.* **1.** in the Roman Catholic Church, a prayer said in commemoration of the Annunciation. **2.** a bell rung at morning, noon, and night to announce the time for saying this prayer. Also, **Angelus bell.** [Latin *angelus* angel; the first word of the prayer.]

an·ger (ang′gər) *n.* a feeling of great displeasure, annoyance, or irritation, often accompanied by antagonism; ire. —*v.t.* to make angry. —*v.i.* to become angry. [Old Norse *angr* grief.]

Synonyms *n.* **Anger, indignation, wrath,** and **ire** mean the emotion experienced when one is greatly displeased or offended. **Anger** is the general term: *My mother expresses anger by clenching her teeth.* **Indignation** suggests moral displeasure, a reaction to something one finds improper or worthy of blame: *The acquittal of the defendants aroused indignation in the city.* **Wrath** implies a desire to punish: *The outlaws fled the wrath of the citizens.* **Ire** is now chiefly a literary word, although it may also be used humorously: *The dripping faucet aroused my grandfather's ire.*

An·ge·vin (an′jə vin) *also,* **An·ge·vine** (an′jə vin, -vīn′) *adj.* **1.** of, relating to, or characteristic of Anjou, its people, or their culture. **2.** of or relating to the Plantagenet line of English kings or the period of their rule. —*n.* **1.** a native or inhabitant of Anjou. **2.** a member of the Plantagenet royal house.

an·gi·na (an jī′nə, an′jə nə) *n.* **1.** angina pectoris. **2.** any disease characterized by attacks of spasmodic suffocation, esp. with an inflammation of the throat or chest. [Latin *angina* quinsy; literally, choking.]

angina pec·to·ris (pek′tər is) a sudden, severe pain spreading across the chest and down the left arm, resulting from a temporarily inadequate flow of blood to the heart muscle, and often caused by heart disease. [Modern Latin *angina pectoris* angina of the chest.]

an·gi·o·gram (an′jē ə gram′) *n.* an X ray on which blood vessels are clearly outlined as a result of the prior injection of a substance that blocks the passage of X rays.

an·gi·o·sperm (an′jē ə spûrm′) *n.* flowering plant.

an·gle¹ (ang′gəl) *n.* **1.a.** a figure formed by two lines extending from a common point or by two planes extending from a common straight line. **b.** the space between these lines or planes. **c.** the amount of divergence between these lines or planes, measured in degrees: *The tree stood at a 90-degree angle to the ground.* **2.** a pointed projection or sharp corner, as of a building: *The sculpture consisted of contrasting angles and curves.* **3.** a point of view; as-

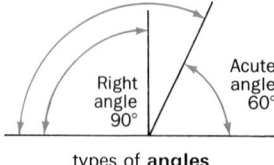

types of **angles**

pect: *Let's look at the problem from every angle.* **4.** *Informal.* a motive or interest: *What's your angle in all this? v.,* **-gled, -gling.** —*v.t.* **1.** to move, turn, or direct at an angle: *to angle a billiard ball into a corner pocket.* **2.** to present from a particular or prejudiced point of view; slant: *The newspaper was accused of angling the news against the mayor's campaign for reelection.* —*v.i.* to move or bend at an angle: *The road angles to the left.* [Old French *angle,* from Latin *angulus* corner.]

an·gle² (ang′gəl) *v.i.,* **-gled, -gling.** to fish with a hook and line. [Old English *angel* fishhook.]

· **to angle for.** to use tricks or schemes to obtain (something): *The employee angled for a promotion.*

angle iron, a piece of metal in the form of an angle, esp. a right angle, used to join or strengthen structural members, as beams, girders, or the like.

angle of incidence, the angle that a ray, as of light, striking a surface forms with a line that is perpendicular to the surface at the point where the ray strikes.

angle of reflection, the angle that a ray, as of light, reflected from a surface forms with a line that is perpendicular to the surface at the point where the ray is reflected.

angle of refraction, the angle that a ray, as of light, makes with a line perpendicular to the surface at which it is refracted when the ray passes from one medium into another, as from air to water.

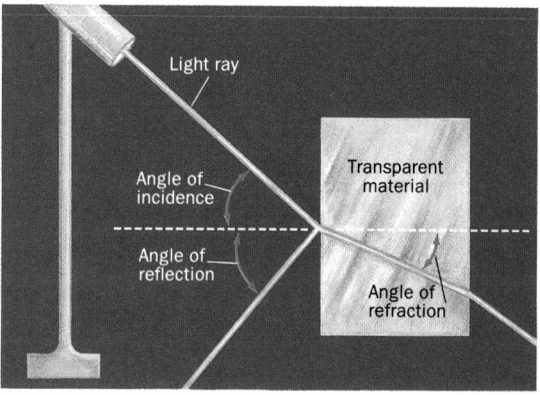

angles of refraction, reflection, and incidence

an·gler (ang′glər) *n.* **1.** a person who fishes with a hook and line. **2.** a person who schemes to gain an objective. **3.** anglerfish.

an·gler·fish (ang′glər fish′) *n., pl.* **-fish** or **-fish·es.** any of various saltwater fish, family Lophiidae, having a wide mouth and a large head with a rod extending from it that is used for luring prey. Length: to 4 feet (1.2 meters).

An·gles (ang′gəlz) *pl. n.* a Germanic tribe that settled in Britain in the fifth and sixth centuries A.D.

an·gle·worm (ang′gəl wûrm′) *n.* earthworm.

An·gli·a (ang′glē ə) *n. Latin.* England.

An·gli·an (ang′glē ən) *adj.* of or relating to the Angles or to their language or culture. —*n.* **1.** one of the Angles. **2.** Old English as spoken by the Angles.

An·gli·can (ang′gli kən) *adj.* of or relating to the Church of England or a church affiliated with it. —*n.* a member of the Church of England or a church affiliated with it.

An·gli·can·ism (ang′gli kə niz′əm) *n.* the body of doctrines and practices of the Church of England.

An·gli·cism (ang′glə siz′əm) *n.* **1.** a word, phrase, or usage peculiar to British English; Briticism. **2.** the state or quality of being English. **3.** a custom or characteristic peculiar to the English.

An·gli·cize (ang′glə sīz′) *also,* **an·gli·cize.** *v.,* **-cized, -ciz·ing.** —*v.t.* **1.** to adopt (a foreign word or phrase) into English, sometimes with a slight change in pronunciation, form, or meaning. *Chauffeur* is a French word that has been Anglicized. **2.** to cause to adapt to or acquire English traits, institutions, or beliefs. —*v.i.* to conform to or acquire English characteristics or institutions. —**An′gli·ci·za′tion;** *also,* **an′gli·ci·za′tion,** *n.*

an·gling (ang′gling) *n.* the act or art of fishing with a hook and line.

An·glo (ang′glō) *n., pl.* **-glos.** a white inhabitant of the United States who is not of Hispanic descent. —*adj.* of, relating to, or characteristic of Anglos. [From ANGLO-.]

Anglo- *combining form* **1.** English: *Anglo-Norman, Anglophobia.*

A

2. English and: *Anglo-American relations.* [From Latin *Anglī* the Angles.]

An·glo-A·mer·i·can (ang′glō ə mer′i kən) *n.* an American citizen or inhabitant who is of English birth or descent. —*adj.* **1.** English and American: *Anglo-American trade.* **2.** of or relating to Anglo-Americans.

An·glo-French (ang′glō french′) *adj.* English and French. —*n.* Anglo-Norman *(def. 2).*

An·glo·ma·ni·a (ang′glə mā′nē ə) *n.* an excessive admiration for or imitation of English institutions, manners, or customs. —**An′glo·ma′ni·ac,** *n.*

An·glo-Nor·man (ang′glō nôr′mən) *n.* **1.** one of the Normans who settled in England after the Norman Conquest in 1066. **2.** a dialect of Old French brought into England by the Norman conquerors and spoken by the upper classes in England from the Norman Conquest through the fourteenth century. Also *(def. 2),* **Anglo-French.** —*adj.* of or relating to the Anglo-Normans, their language, or their culture.

An·glo·phile (ang′glə f īl′) *n.* a person who is extremely fond of England, its people, traditions, manners, or customs. —*adj.* extremely fond of England or the English.

An·glo·pho·bi·a (ang′glə fō′bē ə) *n.* an intense hatred or fear of England or of what is English. —**An′glo·phobe′,** *n.* —**An′glo·pho′bic,** *adj.*

An·glo-Saxon (ang′glō sak′sən) *n.* **1.** a member or descendant of one of the Germanic tribes that invaded England in the fifth and sixth centuries A.D. **2.** any English person of the period from the fifth century to the Norman Conquest in 1066. **3.** a person of English nationality or descent. **4.** Old English. **5.** direct, plain English. —*adj.* **1.** of or relating to the Anglo-Saxons, their language, or their culture. **2.** of or relating to their descendants; English.

An·go·ra (ang gôr′ə) *n.* **1.a.** Angora cat. **b.** Angora goat. **c.** Angora rabbit. **2.** *also,* **angora. a.** mohair. **b.** yarn or knitted fabric made from the hair of the Angora rabbit or Angora goat.

Angora cat 1. any domestic cat with long, silky hair. The Angora cat, in this sense, is not a distinct breed. **2.** a cat of a former breed, originally from Turkey, having a long body, pointed head, and bushy tail.

Angora goat, a goat of a breed that originated in Asia Minor, raised for its long, silky hair, which is called mohair.

Angora rabbit, a domestic rabbit bred for its long, silky hair.

an·gos·tu·ra (ang′gə stŭr′ə, -styŭr′ə) *n.* the aromatic, bitter bark of certain South American citrus trees, used esp. for making a kind of bitters. [From *Angostura* (now Ciudad Bolívar), town in Venezuela.]

an·gry (ang′grē) *adj.,* **-gri·er, -gri·est. 1.** feeling or showing anger; irate. **2.** resulting from or expressing anger: *an angry look, an angry tone of voice.* **3.** threatening and raging, as if in anger: *an angry sea.* **4.** painfully inflamed: *an angry rash.* [From ANGER.] —**an′gri·ly,** *adv.* —**an′gri·ness,** *n.*

angst (angst, ängst) *n.* a deep feeling of dread or apprehension; profound anxiety. [Danish *angst* anxiety, from German *Angst.*]

ang·strom (ang′strəm) *also,* **Ang·strom.** *n.* a unit of measurement equal to one hundred millionth of a centimeter, used to express the wavelength of light or other kinds of radiation. Symbol: Å Also, **angstrom unit.** [From the Swedish physicist Anders J. *Ångström,* 1814-74.]

an·guish (ang′gwish) *n.* extreme mental or physical suffering; agony: *the look of anguish on their faces.* [Old French *anguisse,* from Latin *angustia* narrowness.]

an·guished (ang′gwisht) *adj.* **1.** having or affected by anguish: *an anguished conscience.* **2.** resulting from or exhibiting anguish: *an anguished cry.*

an·gu·lar (ang′gyə lər) *adj.* **1.** having or forming an angle or angles; sharp-cornered: *an angular drawing, an angular piece of rock.* **2.** measured by an angle: *angular distance.* For Weights and Measures table, see **weight. 3.** having prominent bones; bony; gaunt: *a face with angular features.* **4.** (of movement) not smooth or flowing; stiff; jerky. [Latin *angulāris* having corners or angles, from *angulus* corner, angle.] —**an′gu·lar·ly,** *adv.*

an·gu·lar·i·ty (ang′gyə lar′i tē) *n., pl.* **-ties. 1.** the quality or state of being angular. **2. angularities.** angular parts or forms; sharp corners.

angular momentum, *Physics.* the momentum possessed by a rotating body, which is determined by its angular velocity multiplied by its mass and by the square of the distance from the axis of rotation.

angular velocity, the rate at which a body rotating about an axis moves through a given angular distance, esp. as measured in radians per second.

An·gus (ang′gəs) *n.* **1.** in Celtic mythology, the god of love. **2.** Aberdeen Angus.

an·hy·dride (an hī′drīd, -drid) *n.* **1.** an oxide that forms an acid or base when it is added to water. A nonmetal oxide that so reacts forms an acid and is called an **acid anhydride,** and a metal oxide that so reacts forms a base and is called a **basic anhydride. 2.** any compound from which water has been removed.

an·hy·drite (an hī′drīt) *n.* the anhydrous sulfate of calcium, occurring naturally with other evaporites as a colorless or blue or violet mineral that changes to gypsum when it absorbs water. Formula: $CaSO_4$ [Greek *anydros* (see ANHYDROUS) + -ITE^2.]

an·hy·drous (an hī′drəs) *adj.* (of a chemical compound) having no water, esp. water of crystallization. [Greek *anydros* waterless, from *an-* without + *hydōr* water.]

an·il (an′əl) *n.* a deep violet-blue color; indigo. [French *anil,* from Arabic *an-nīl* the indigo, from Persian *nīl,* from Sanskrit *nīlī* indigo plant, from *nēla* dark blue.]

an·ile (an′īl, ā′nīl) *adj.* like a doddering old woman; foolish; feeble-minded. [Latin *anīlis,* from *anus* old woman.] —**a·nil′i·ty,** *n.*

an·i·line (an′ə lin, -līn′) *also,* **an·i·lin** (an′ə lin) *n.* a toxic, oily liquid derived chiefly from nitrobenzene and used in making rubber, dyes, and drugs. Formula: $C_6H_5NH_2$ —*adj.* made of, derived from, or relating to aniline. [German *Anilin,* from *Anil* indigo. See ANIL.]

aniline dye 1. any of a number of dyes made from aniline. **2.** any synthetic dye.

an·i·ma (an′ə mə) *n.* a vital principle; life; soul. [Latin *anima* life, breath.]

an·i·mad·ver·sion (an′ə mad vûr′zhən, -shən) *n.* **1.** a critical or unfavorable remark: *to make animadversions on someone's behavior.* **2.** the act of criticizing; criticism. [Latin *animadversiō* observation, censure.]

an·i·mad·vert (an′ə mad vûrt′) *v.i.* to comment unfavorably or critically (with *on* or *upon*). [Latin *animadvertere* to observe, censure.]

an·i·mal (an′ə məl) *n.* **1.** any of a large kingdom (Animalia) of living organisms distinguished from plants by their ability to move about in their environment or move some parts of their bodies, their inability to produce their own food by photosynthesis, and the presence of sense organs. **2.** any such animal except a human being; beast. **3.** a mammal, as distinguished from a fish, bird, reptile, or the like. **4.** a bestial or brutish human being. —*adj.* **1.** of, relating to, or derived from animals: *animal research, animal fats.* **2.** relating to the physical or sensual rather than the spiritual or intellectual nature of human beings; carnal: *animal appetites.* [Latin *animal* living creature, from *anima* breath, life.]

Synonyms *n.* **Animal, beast,** and **brute** mean a creature considered lower in the scale of living beings than humans. **Animal** is the broadest of these words: *I want to see every animal in the zoo.* **Beast** is usually applied to a four-legged animal, as distinguished from birds, fish, or snakes, for example. **Brute** stresses the lack of human abilities like reason and speech, and often suggests strength: *The preacher classified humanity as below the angels but above the brutes.*

an·i·mal·cule (an′ə mal′kūl) *n.* a minute or microscopic animal. [Modern Latin *animalculum,* diminutive of Latin *animal* living creature.]

animal husbandry, the branch of agriculture dealing with the breeding, raising, and care of livestock.

an·i·mal·ism (an′ə mə liz′əm) *n.* **1.** qualities regarded as typical of animals, esp. vigorous health and uninhibited vitality. **2.** a preoccupation with physical appetites; sensuality. **3.** the doctrine that a human being is a mere animal, having no soul or spiritual qualities. —**an′i·mal·ist,** *n.* —**an′i·mal·is′tic,** *adj.*

an·i·mal·i·ty (an′ə mal′i tē) *n.* the animal nature of humans, as distinguished from their moral and spiritual natures.

animal spirits, exuberant liveliness and vigor; vivacity.

an·i·mate (v., an′ə māt′; adj., an′ə mit) *v.t.,* **-mat·ed, -mat·ing. 1.** to give liveliness, vividness, or interest to; enliven: *Their disagreement animated the discussion. Delight animated her face.* **2.** to move to action; inspire; incite: *The touchdown animated the team to score again.* **3.** to give life to; make alive: *The soul animates the body.* **4.** to produce as an animated cartoon: *to animate a children's book.* —*adj.* having life; alive: *animate beings and inanimate objects.* [Latin *animātus,* past participle of *animāre* to give life to, from *anima* breath, life.]

an·i·mat·ed (an′ə mā′tid) *adj.* **1.** full of life, activity, or spirit;

a	at	e	end	o	hot	u	up	hw	white		about
ā	ape	ē	me	ō	old	ū	use	ng	song	ə	taken
ä	far	i	it	ô	fork	ü	rule	th	thin		pencil
âr	care	ī	ice	oi	oil	u̇	pull	<u>th</u>	this		lemon
		îr	pierce	ou	out	ûr	turn	zh	measure		circus

lively; vivacious: *an animated debate.* **2.** made to appear alive: *animated puppets.* —**an'i·mat'ed·ly,** *adv.*

animated cartoon, a motion picture consisting of a series of drawings, each of which shows a successive stage of movement. When the drawings are photographed and projected in rapid succession, an illusion of movement is created.

an·i·ma·tion (an'ə mā'shən) *n.* **1.** the quality of being full of life, activity, or spirit; liveliness; vivacity: *a story told with great animation.* **2.** the act of animating or the state of being animated. **3.a.** the process and technique of preparing animated cartoons. **b.** the result of this.

a·ni·ma·to (ä'nə mä'tō, an'ə-) *Music. adj.* full of life or spirit; lively; animated. —*adv.* in a spirited, lively manner. [Italian *animato* enlivened, brisk, going back to Latin *animāre* to quicken. See ANIMATE.]

an·i·ma·tor (an'ə mā'tər) *n.* an artist who prepares the drawings for animated cartoons.

an·i·mism (an'ə miz'əm) *n.* **1.** the belief that inanimate objects and natural phenomena possess living souls. **2.** the belief in the existence of the soul as independent of matter. [Latin *anima* life, breath + -ISM.] —**an'i·mist,** *n.* —**an'i·mis'tic,** *adj.*

an·i·mos·i·ty (an'ə mos'i tē) *n., pl.* -**ties.** open or vehement hostility or hatred; enmity. [Late Latin *animōsitās* vehemence, going back to Latin *animus* spirit.] —For Synonyms, see **antagonism.**

an·i·mus (an'ə məs) *n.* **1.** a feeling of hostility or hatred; enmity; animosity. **2.** an animating spirit or purpose; intention. [Latin *animus* spirit.]

an·i·on (an'ī'ən) *n.* **1.** a negatively charged ion of an electrolyte, attracted to the anode in electrolysis. ➡ opposed to **cation.** **2.** any negatively charged atom or group of atoms. [Greek *anion* (thing) going up, neuter present participle of *anienai* to go up.] —**an·i·on·ic** (an'ī on'ik), *adj.*

an·ise (an'is) *n.* **1.** an aromatic herb, *Pimpinella anisum,* of the parsley family, widely cultivated in the Mediterranean region, India, and South America. **2.** aniseed. [Old French *anis,* from Latin *anesum* anise plant, from Greek *anēson.*]

an·i·seed (an'i sēd', an'is-) *n.* the seed of anise, having a spicy, licoricelike taste, used as a flavoring in cookies, pastries, and other food. Aniseed oil is used in some medicines and perfumes and as a flavoring in some candies and liqueurs.

an·i·sog·a·my (an'ī sog'ə mē) *n. Biology.* a process of sexual reproduction, in green algae and other microorganisms, in which one gamete is larger than the other and both are motile. [Greek *anisos* unequal (from *an-* not + *isos* equal) + -GAMY.] —**an'i·sog'a·mous,** *adj.*

ankh (angk) *n.* a simple cross with a loop at the top, an ancient Egyptian symbol of life. [Egyptian *'nh.*]

an·kle (ang'kəl) *n.* **1.** the joint that connects the foot and the leg. **2.** the part of the leg at and just above this joint. [Old English *anclēow.*]

an·kle·bone (ang'kəl bōn') *n.* the bone of the ankle. Also, **talus.**

an·klet (ang'klit) *n.* **1.** a short sock reaching just above the ankle. **2.** an ornamental band or chain worn around the ankle.

an·ky·lo·sis (ang'kə lō'sis) *n.* **1.** a fusion or consolidation of bones of a joint or the different parts of a bone. **2.** the immovability of a joint, caused by disease, injury, or surgical procedure. [Modern Latin *ankylosis,* from Greek *ankylōsis* stiffening of the joints, from *ankyloun* to bend, stiffen.] —**an·ky·lot·ic** (ang'kə lot'ik), *adj.*

an·na (an'ə) *n.* a former coin of India equal to one sixteenth of a rupee. [Hindustani *ānā.*]

an·nal·ist (an'ə list) *n.* a person who writes annals; chronicler.

an·nals (an'əlz) *pl. n.* **1.** a written account of events in chronological order recorded year by year. **2.** any historical record; chronicle: *the annals of medicine.* **3.** a periodical publication of an organization or learned society containing accounts of its activities and articles pertinent to its interests. [Latin *annālēs (librī)* yearly (books), chronicles, from *annus* year.]

an·neal (ə nēl') *v.t.* **1.** to heat and then slowly cool (metal or glass) to reduce brittleness and increase toughness. **2.** to toughen or temper, as the mind or will. [Old English *onǣlan* to burn.]

an·ne·lid (an'ə lid) *n.* any of various segmented worms of the phylum Annelida, including earthworms, marine worms, and leeches. For illustration, see **worm.** [French *annélide,* going back to Old French *annel* ring, going back to Latin *ānulus* ring.]

an·nex (*v.,* ə neks'; *n.,* an'eks) *v.t.* **1.** to add or attach to something larger or more important: *to annex a province to a kingdom.* **2.** to attach as an attribute, condition, or consequence: *to annex an addendum to a document.* —*n.* **1.** a building used as an addition to another; supplementary wing of a building: *the annex of a hospital.* **2.** an addition to a document; addendum.

[Middle French *annexer* to join, from Latin *annexus,* past participle of *annectere* to bind to.]

an·nex·a·tion (an'ek sā'shən) *n.* **1.** the act of annexing or the state of being annexed. **2.** something annexed.

an·ni·hi·late (ə nī'ə lāt') *v.t.,* -**lat·ed, -lat·ing. 1.** to reduce to nothing; destroy totally; obliterate: *The bombers annihilated the city.* **2.** to defeat completely; rout: *Their players annihilated our team.* [Latin *annihilātus,* past participle of *annihilāre* to bring to nothing.] —**an·ni·hi·la'tion,** *n.* —**an·ni·hi·la'tive,** *adj.* —**an·ni·hi·la'tor,** *n.*

an·ni·ver·sa·ry (an'ə vûr'sə rē) *n., pl.* -**ries. 1.** a yearly recurring date of some past event: *the anniversary of the founding of the republic.* **2.** a celebration of this date. —*adj.* of or relating to an anniversary: *an anniversary gift.* [Latin *anniversārius* returning every year, from *annus* year + *versus,* past participle of *vertere* to turn.]

an·no Dom·i·ni (an'ō dom'ə nī') *Latin.* in the year of the Lord. ➡ used to indicate a date occurring since the birth of Jesus.

an·no·tate (an'ə tāt', an'ō-) *v.t., v.i.,* -**tat·ed, -tat·ing.** to provide with or make critical or explanatory notes. [Latin *annotātus,* past participle of *annotāre* to note down.] —**an'no·ta'tor,** *n.*

an·no·ta·tion (an'ə tā'shən, an'ō-) *n.* **1.** a critical or explanatory note or comment. **2.** the act of annotating or the state of being annotated.

an·nounce (ə nouns') *v.,* -**nounced, -nounc·ing.** —*v.t.* **1.** to make known publicly or officially; proclaim: *The mayor held a press conference to announce her bid for reelection.* **2.** to make known the approach, arrival, or presence of: *The butler announced each guest.* **3.** to make obvious; manifest; indicate: *Gathering clouds announced the oncoming storm.* **4.** to serve as a radio or television announcer of: *He announces the local news.* —*v.i.* **1.** to serve as a radio or television announcer. **2.** to make known one's candidacy (with *for*): *She announced for mayor.* [Old French *anoncier* to proclaim, from Latin *annūntiāre.* Doublet of ANNUNCIATE.] —For Synonyms, see **declare.**

an·nounce·ment (ə nouns'mənt) *n.* **1.** the act of announcing or the state of being announced. **2.** a public statement or notice. **3.** a printed or written notice or declaration: *engraved wedding announcements.*

an·nounc·er (ə noun'sər) *n.* **1.** a person on radio or television who introduces programs and people, identifies the station, or presents advertisements, bulletins, or news items. **2.** a person who announces anything.

an·noy (ə noi') *v.t.* to be troublesome or irritating to; vex; bother: *His thoughtlessness annoyed her.* [Old French *anoier,* from *anoi* vexation, going back to Latin *in odiō* in hatred.] —**an·noy'er,** *n.*

an·noy·ance (ə noi'əns) *n.* **1.** a person or thing that annoys; nuisance. **2.** the state or feeling of being annoyed; vexation: *We couldn't hide our annoyance at the delay.* **3.** the act of annoying.

an·noy·ing (ə noi'ing) *adj.* causing annoyance; irritating; vexing: *annoying interruptions.* —**an·noy'ing·ly,** *adv.*

an·nu·al (an'ū əl) *adj.* **1.** relating to or measured by the year: *annual growth, annual income.* **2.** occurring or returning once a year: *an annual stockholders' meeting, an annual sale.* **3.** performed during a year: *the earth's annual course around the sun.* **4.** (of a plant) living or lasting for only one year or growing season. —*n.* **1.** a publication issued once a year. **2.** a plant that sprouts, flowers, produces seeds, and dies within one year or growing season. [Old French *annuel,* from Late Latin *annuālis,* from Latin *annus* year.] —**an'nu·al·ly,** *adv.*

annual ring, any of the rings of wood visible in the cross section of a stem, or trunk, of a tree or shrub. Each ring represents a year's growth.

an·nu·i·tant (ə nü'i tənt, ə nū'-) *n.* a person who receives, or is entitled to, an annuity.

an·nu·i·ty (ə nü'i tē, ə nū'-) *n., pl.* -**ties. 1.** a specified amount of money paid yearly or at other fixed intervals. **2.** the right to receive or the obligation to pay such an amount. **3.** an investment, usually made with an insurance company, guaranteeing an annual income during the investor's lifetime or for a contracted number of years. [French *annuité* annual payment, from Medieval Latin *annuitas,* from Latin *annuus* yearly.]

annual rings

an·nul (ə nul') *v.t.,* -**nulled, -nul·ling.** to make void or of no effect; declare invalid: *to annul a law, to annul a marriage.* [Old

A

French *anuller* to regard as nothing, from Late Latin *annūllāre* to make into nothing, going back to Latin *ad* to + *nūllus* none.]

an·nu·lar (an′yə lər) *adj.* relating to, consisting of, or shaped like a ring or rings. [Latin *anulāris* relating to a ring, from *anulus* ring.] —**an′nu·lar′i·ty,** *n.* —**an′nu·lar·ly,** *adv.*

annular eclipse, a solar eclipse in which a portion of the sun is visible as a ring surrounding the dark body of the moon.

an·nu·let (an′yə lit) *n.* **1.** a little ring. **2.** a narrow, ringlike molding encircling a column.

an·nul·ment (ə nul′mənt) *n.* **1.** the act of annulling or the state of being annulled. **2.** a formal declaration stating that a marriage was invalid from the beginning.

an·nu·lus (an′yə ləs) *n., pl.* **-li** (-lī′) or **-lus·es.** a ring or ringlike part, space, or marking. [Latin *anulus* ring.]

an·num (an′əm) *n. Latin.* year.

an·nun·ci·ate (ə nun′sē āt′) *v.t.,* **-at·ed, -at·ing.** to make known; announce. [Late Latin *annuntiatus,* past participle of *annuntiare* to proclaim. Doublet of ANNOUNCE.]

an·nun·ci·a·tion (ə nun′sē ā′shən) *n.* **1. the Annunciation.** the announcement brought by the angel Gabriel to the Virgin Mary that she was to give birth to Jesus. **2. Annunciation.** the church festival commemorating this announcement, observed on March 25. Also, **Lady Day. 3.** an announcement.

an·nun·ci·a·tor (ə nun′sē ā′tər) *n.* **1.** a device used to register electrical signals and indicate their source. **2.** a person or thing that announces; announcer.

an·ode (an′ōd) *n.* **1.** an electrode through which electrons leave an electrical device or medium. When electricity is used to produce a chemical reaction, the positive electrode is the anode; when a chemical reaction is used to produce electricity, the negative electrode is the anode. **2.** in electrolysis, the electrode with a comparative lack of electrons and a positive charge. Negatively charged ions are oxidized at the anode. **3.** in an electron tube, an electrode or plate that attracts electrons. ➡ opposed to **cathode** in all defs. [Greek *anodos* way up.] —**an·od·ic** (an od′ik), *adj.*

an·o·dize (an′ə dīz′) *v.t.,* **-dized, -diz·ing.** to coat (a metal, esp. magnesium or aluminum) with a protective film by making it the anode of an electrolytic cell. [ANODE + -IZE.]

an·o·dyne (an′ə dīn′) *n.* **1.** a medicine that relieves or removes pain; analgesic. **2.** anything that soothes or calms: *Time is often an anodyne for sorrow.* —*adj.* **1.** relieving or removing pain. **2.** soothing; calming. [Latin *anōdynos* (drug) relieving pain, from Greek *anōdynos* painless.] —**an·o·dyn·ic** (an′ə din′ik), *adj.*

a·noint (ə noint′) *v.t.* **1.** to cover or smear with oil or any oily substance; apply ointment to. **2.** to put oil on as an act of consecration. [Old French *enoint,* past participle of *enoindre,* from Latin *inunguere* to cover with oil.] —**a·noint′er,** *n.* —**a·noint′- ment,** *n.*

anointing of the sick, *also,* **Anointing of the Sick.** a sacrament of the Roman Catholic Church given by a priest to a person who is very ill or dying, intended to absolve the person of his or her sins. Also, **extreme unction.**

a·nom·a·lous (ə nom′ə ləs) *adj.* differing from the usual or normal; irregular; abnormal. [Late Latin *anōmalus,* from Greek *anōmalos* uneven, irregular.] —**a·nom′a·lous·ly,** *adv.* —**a·nom′a·lous·ness,** *n.*

a·nom·a·ly (ə nom′ə lē) *n., pl.* **-lies. 1.** a person or thing that is anomalous. **2.** a deviation from the usual or normal; irregularity; abnormality: *Snow in the desert is an anomaly.*

an·o·mie (an′ə mē′) *n.* a lack or breakdown of values or standards in a society or individual: *the anomie of a community torn apart by war, the anomie of teenagers without goals or role models.* [French *anomie,* from Greek *anomia* lawlessness, from *anomous* lawless, from *a-* not, without + *nomos* law.] —**a·nom·ic** (ə nom′ik), *adj.*

a·non (ə non′) *adv. Archaic.* **1.** in a little while; soon. **2.** at another time; again. [Old English *on āne* in one.]

· **ever and anon.** again and again; now and then.

anon., anonymous.

a·non·y·mous (ə non′ə məs) *adj.* **1.** of unknown or unacknowledged authorship or origin: *an anonymous book, an anonymous phone call.* **2.** having a name that is not known or given: *an anonymous author.* **3.** lacking individuality, personality, or distinction: *The audience was a sea of anonymous faces.* [Late Latin *anonymus,* from Greek *anōnymos* nameless.] —**an·o·nym·i·ty** (an′ə nim′i tē), *n.* —**a·non′y·mous·ly,** *adv.*

a·noph·e·les (ə nof′ə lēz′) *n., pl.* **-les.** a mosquito, genus *Anopheles,* the female of which can transmit malaria by its bite. [Modern Latin *Anopheles,* from Greek *anōphelēs* hurtful.]

an·o·rak (an′ə rak′) *n.* a heavy outer jacket of skin or cloth, often having a hood of fur, worn esp. by Eskimo in cold weather. [Eskimo *ânorâq* parka.]

an·o·rec·tic (an′ə rek′tik) *adj., n.* anorexic. Also, **an·o·ret·ic** (an′ə ret′ik).

an·o·rex·i·a (an′ə rek′sē ə) *n.* **1.** a lack of appetite. **2.** anorexia nervosa. [Greek *anorexia* lack of appetite, from prefix *a-* not + *orexis* appetite.]

anorexia ner·vo·sa (nər vō′sə) an eating disorder marked by a profound aversion to food and obsession with weight loss, sometimes leading to serious nutritional deficiencies, esp. in young women.

an·o·rex·ic (an′ə rek′sik) *adj.* **1.** lacking an appetite for food. **2.** having anorexia nervosa. —*n.* a person who has anorexia nervosa. Also, **anorectic, anoretic.** [ANOREX(IA) + -IC.]

an·or·thite (an ôr′thīt) *n.* a white or gray variety of plagioclase especially rich in calcium. Formula: $CaAl_2Si_2O_8$ [Greek *an-* not + *orthos* straight + -ITE[1], because of its oblique crystals.]

an·oth·er (ə nuth′ər) *adj.* **1.** one more; an additional: *I would like another piece of pie.* **2.** not being the same; different: *She has moved to another city.* **3.** similar or the same in character or achievements: *He thinks he's another Einstein.* —*pron.* **1.** one more; an additional one. **2.** a different person or thing. **3.** a similar or identical one: *I made one copy of the report for you and another for myself.* [Middle English *an other.* See AN[1], OTHER.]

an·ox·i·a (an ok′sē ə, ə nok′-) *n.* a condition in which the body cells fail either to receive or to use a sufficient amount of oxygen; hypoxia. —**an·ox′ic,** *adj.*

ans., answer.

An·schluss (än′shlůs) *n.* a political and economic union of two countries, esp. that of Germany and Austria in 1938. [German *Anschluss* union.]

an·ser·ine (an′sə rīn′, -sər in) *adj.* **1.** of, resembling, or related to a goose or geese. **2.** not showing or having good sense; stupid; foolish. [Latin *ānserīnus,* from *ānser* goose.]

an·swer (an′sər) *n.* **1.a.** something spoken or written as a reply: *The editorial was an answer to the reader's angry letter.* **b.** a correct reply: *She always knows the answer.* **2.** something done in reply or return: *Further bombing was the enemy's answer to the peace offerings.* **3.a.** the solution to a mathematical problem: *To find the answer, multiply by two.* **b.** any solution or explanation: *The answer to our well problem was to buy a new pump.* **4.** something that is an equivalent or the same. **5.** *Law.* the statement of a defendant in response to the charges made by a plaintiff. —*v.t.* **1.** to speak or write in reply to: *She answered my letter. Can you answer that question?* **2.** to act in response to: *He ran to answer the phone.* **3.** to be suitable or sufficient for; serve: *This money should answer your needs.* **4.** to conform or correspond to: *He answers the description of the missing child.* —*v.i.* **1.** to speak or write in reply: *Answer in a loud and clear voice.* **2.** to act in response; respond: *She answered with a wink.* **3.** to be responsible or accountable: *You will have to answer to me if you're late.* **4.** to correspond or conform: *You answer to their description.* **5.** to make amends; atone: *The prisoner has answered for his crime.* **6.** to be sufficient or satisfactory; serve: *This rock will answer for a table.* [Old English *andswaru* sworn statement in reply (to an accusation), from *and-* in reply + *swerian* to swear.]

· **to answer back.** *Informal.* to reply impertinently or rudely; talk back.

Synonyms *n.* **Answer, reply,** and **response** mean something said or written in reaction to something else. **Answer** is the general term, indicating a reaction directly corresponding to what produced it: *Do you know the answer to that question?* **Reply** may be used of a more formal or carefully considered answer: *We wrote to reserve a room and waited for the hotel's reply.* **Response** suggests something predictable, or merely the reaction to a stimulus: *The company's response to the charges of fraud was a flat denial.*

an·swer·a·ble (an′sər ə bəl) *adj.* **1.** liable to be called to account; accountable; responsible: *The committee is answerable for its expenses.* **2.** capable of being answered.

answering machine, a tape recorder that automatically answers the telephone with a message and records messages from callers.

answering service, a company that accepts telephone calls and takes messages for its clients when they do not answer their telephones.

ant (ant) *n.* any of numerous social insects of the family Formicidae, found in all temperate and tropical regions. They live in

a	at	e	end	o	hot	u	up	hw	white		about
ā	ape	ē	me	ō	old	ū	use	ng	song	ə	taken
ä	far	i	it	ô	fork	ū	rule	th	thin		pencil
âr	care	ī	ice	oi	oil	ů	pull	th	this		lemon
		ir	pierce	ou	out	ûr	turn	zh	measure		circus

colonies of from several dozen to over a million. [Old English *æmete.*]

ant-, form of **anti-** before vowels and *h,* as in *antacid.*

-ant *suffix* **1.** (used to form adjectives) doing or being (what is indicated by the stem): *defiant, radiant.* **2.** (used to form nouns) person or thing that does (what is indicated by the stem): *servant, lubricant.* [Old French *-ant,* from Latin *-āns,* present participial ending used as a suffix.]

ant., antonym.

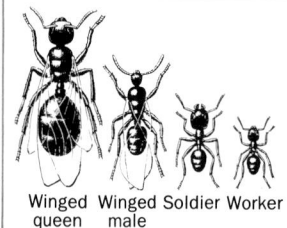

Winged Winged Soldier Worker
queen male

types of **ants**

ant·ac·id (ant as′id) *n.* a chemical substance that neutralizes acids, esp. a remedy for excessive stomach acidity. —*adj.* neutralizing acids.

An·tae·us (an tē′əs) *n.* in Greek mythology, a giant who was invincible as long as he was touching the earth. He was finally killed by Hercules, who crushed him while holding him in the air.

an·tag·o·nism (an tag′ə niz′əm) *n.* active opposition or a feeling of strong dislike; antipathy; enmity; hostility.

Synonyms Antagonism, hostility, enmity, and animosity mean a feeling of strong dislike or opposition bordering on hatred. **Antagonism** may be felt toward a person or a thing, such as an idea: *The playwright could barely conceal his antagonism toward the critic. We must expect that our plan will create antagonism among some of the townspeople.* **Hostility** is often used of antagonism that has come into the open: *Her hostility to the proposal and its author was easy to see.* **Enmity** may be concealed or open and suggests a deep-seated feeling that someone or something is an actual enemy: *Enmity toward its neighbors ran through the country's history.* **Animosity** most strongly suggests bitterness and a desire to hurt someone: *The mass executions reflected the revolutionaries' animosity toward certain classes of society.*

an·tag·o·nist (an tag′ə nist) *n.* **1.** a person who opposes, fights, or competes with another; adversary. **2.** a muscle that acts in opposition to another. —For Synonyms, see **opponent.**

an·tag·o·nis·tic (an tag′ə nis′tik) *adj.* acting or being in opposition; contending; hostile. —**an·tag·o·nis·ti·cal·ly,** *adv.*

an·tag·o·nize (an tag′ə nīz′) *v.t.,* **-nized, -niz·ing.** to provoke dislike or hostility in; make unfriendly: *a boastful manner that antagonized everyone present.* [Greek *antagōnizesthai* to struggle against, going back to *anti-* opposite and *agōn* struggle.]

ant·arc·tic (ant ärk′tik, -är′tik) *adj.* of or relating to the South Pole or to the south polar regions. [Latin *antarcticus* southern, from Greek *antarktikos* opposite to the north, from *anti-* opposite + *arktikos* northern. See ANTI-, ARCTIC.]

Antarctic Circle *also,* **antarctic circle.** an imaginary line around the earth at 66°33′ south latitude, or about 1,600 miles (2,574 kilometers) from the South Pole.

An·tar·es (an târ′ēz) *n.* a giant red star, one of the brightest and largest in the sky, and the brightest in the constellation Scorpio.

ant bear, a gray anteater, *Myrmecophaga tridactyla,* of tropical Central and South America. It is the largest of the anteaters. Length: to 8 feet (2.4 meters), including tail. For illustration, see **anteater.**

an·te (an′tē) *n.* **1.** in poker, a stake that each player must put up before receiving a hand or drawing new cards. **2.** *Slang.* any amount required as a share. —*v.t., v.i.,* **-ted** or **-teed, -te·ing. 1.** in poker, to put up (one's ante). **2.** *Slang.* to pay one's share (often with *up*). [Latin *ante* before.]

ante- *prefix* **1.** previous in time; prior to: *antebellum, antenatal.* **2.** before in position; in front of: *antepenult, antechamber.* [Latin *ante* before.]

ant·eat·er (ant′ē′tər) *n.* **1.** any of various toothless mammals, family Myrmecophagidae, of tropical Central and South America,

Aardvark   Ant bear

anteaters

that feed on ants and termites. They have long narrow heads, long, sticky tongues, and powerful front claws. **2.** any of various other animals that feed on ants, as the aardvark, pangolin, and echidna.

an·te·bel·lum (an′tē bel′əm) *adj.* before the war, esp. before the U.S. Civil War: *the antebellum South.* [Latin *ante bellum* before the war.]

an·te·ced·ence (an′tə sē′dəns) *n.* **1.** the act of going before or the state of being before; precedence. **2.** the apparent retrograde motion of a planet.

an·te·ced·ent (an′tə sē′dənt) *n.* **1.** a thing, event, or circumstance that goes before: *the antecedents of the war.* **2.** *Grammar.* a substantive to which a pronoun refers. In the sentence *He found a dime but lost it later,* the noun *dime* is the antecedent of the pronoun *it.* **3. antecedents. a.** previous events or influences in a person's life. **b.** a person's ancestors; ancestry. **4.** *Mathematics.* the first term of a ratio; first or third term of a proportion. —*adj.* going or being before; preceding; prior: *the conditions antecedent to the Industrial Revolution.* [Latin *antecēdēns,* present participle of *antecēdere* to go before, from *ante-* before + *cedere* to move, go.] —**an′te·ced′ent·ly,** *adv.* —For Synonyms, see **cause.**

an·te·cham·ber (an′tē chām′bər) *n.* anteroom.

an·te·date (an′ti dāt′) *v.t.,* **-dat·ed, -dat·ing. 1.** to be or occur earlier than; precede in time: *The horse and buggy antedated the automobile.* **2.** to give (something) a date earlier than the correct one: *to antedate a check.*

an·te·di·lu·vi·an (an′tē də lü′vē ən) *adj.* **1.** of or relating to the period before the biblical Flood. **2.** very old or old-fashioned; antiquated: *antediluvian ideas.* —*n.* **1.** a person who lived before the biblical Flood. **2.** a very old or old-fashioned person. [ANTE- + Latin *dīluvium* flood.]

an·te·lope (an′tə lōp′) *n., pl.* **-lope** or **-lopes. 1.** any of various cud-chewing mammals, family Bovidae, closely related to goats, having unbranched horns and cloven hoofs. Antelopes are native to Africa and southern Asia. Height: 10 inches to 6 feet (25 centimeters to 1.8 meters) at the shoulder. **2.** pronghorn. [Old French *antelop* savage mythical beast with sawlike horns.]

an·te me·rid·i·em (an′tē mə rid′ē əm) between midnight and noon. [Latin *ante* before + *merīdiēs* noon.]

an·te·na·tal (an′tē nā′təl) *adj.* of, relating to, or occurring before birth; prenatal.

an·ten·na (an ten′ə) *n., pl.* **-ten·nas** *(def. 1)* or **-ten·nae** (-ten′ē) *(def. 2).* **1.** a metal structure, wire, or set of wires used to receive or transmit electromagnetic waves, as in television or radio; aerial. **2.** one of two or four jointed sense organs, or feelers, on the heads of centipedes, millipedes, insects, crustaceans, and some other arthropods. [Medieval Latin *antenna* horn (of an insect), from Latin *antenna* yard for a sail.]

an·ten·nule (an ten′ūl) *n. Zoology.* a small antenna, esp. one of the second, smaller pair of feelers on the head of a crustacean. [ANTENNA + -*ule,* a diminutive suffix.]

an·te·pe·nult (an′tē pē′nult, -pi nult′) *n.* a syllable that is third from the last syllable in a word. In the word *port·fo·li·o,* the syllable *fo* is the antepenult.

an·te·pe·nul·ti·mate (an′tē pi nul′tə mit) *adj.* third from the last. —*n.* antepenult.

an·te·ri·or (an tîr′ē ər) *adj.* **1.** at or toward the front or head; fore: *the anterior lobe of the brain.* ➡ opposed to **posterior. 2.** preceding in time; prior; earlier. [Latin *anterior* former, comparative of *ante* before.]

an·te·room (an′tē rüm′, -rùm′) *n.* a room serving as a waiting room or entranceway to a larger or main room. Also, **antechamber.**

an·them (an′thəm) *n.* **1.** a song of gladness, praise, devotion, or patriotism: *a country's national anthem.* **2.** a piece of sacred choral music with words usually taken from a biblical passage. [Old English *antefn* antiphon, from Late Latin *antiphōna,* going back to Greek *antiphōnos* responsive. See ANTIPHON.]

an·ther (an′thər) *n.* in a flower, the pollen-bearing part of the stamen. For illustration, see **flower.** [Modern Latin *anthera,* from Latin *anthēra* medicine composed of flowers, going back to Greek *anthēros* flowery, from *anthos* flower.] —**an′ther·al,** *adj.*

an·ther·id·i·um (an′thə rid′ē əm) *n., pl.* **-i·a** (-ē ə). the male sex organ of nonflowering plants, such as mosses and ferns. [Modern Latin *antheridium,* diminutive of *anthera.* See ANTHER.] —**an′ther·id′i·al,** *adj.*

ant·hill (ant′hil′) *n.* a mound of dirt or other material heaped up by ants around the entrance to their underground nest.

an·tho·cy·a·nin (an′thə sī′ə nin) *n.* any of a number of glycoside pigments that produce the red, purple, or blue colors found in flowers, fruits, and other plant parts. Also, **an·tho·cy·an** (an′thə sī′ən).

an·thol·o·gist (an thol′ə jist) *n.* a person who compiles an anthology.

an·thol·o·gize (an thol′ə jīz′) *v.,* **-gized, -giz·ing.** —*v.i.* to compile an anthology. —*v.t.* to put in an anthology.

an·thol·o·gy (an thol′ə jē) *n., pl.* **-gies. 1.** a collection of written works or passages, usually by different authors, within a single book or set: *an anthology of French poetry, a folk song anthology.* **2.** a similar collection of recorded materials: *an anthology of baroque concertos.* [Greek *anthologia* a gathering of flowers, going back to *anthos* flower + *legein* to gather, speak.]

an·tho·zo·an (an′thə zō′ən) *n.* any polyp of the class Anthozoa, including sea anemones and corals. Unlike other coelenterates, anthozoans are exclusively polypoid, having no free-swimming jellyfish stage. —*adj.* belonging or pertaining to the anthozoans. [Greek *anthos* flower + *zōion* animal.]

an·thra·cene (an′thrə sēn′) *n.* a crystalline hydrocarbon obtained from coal tar, used in making dyes. Formula: $C_{14}H_{10}$ [Greek *anthrax* coal + -ENE.]

an·thra·cite (an′thrə sīt′) *n.* a lustrous black coal with a high carbon content that burns with a low smokeless flame. Also, **hard coal.** [Greek *anthrakītis* a type of coal, from *anthrax* coal.] —**an·thra·cit·ic** (an′thrə sit′ik), *adj.*

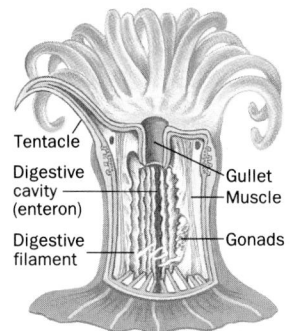

Tentacle
Digestive cavity (enteron)
Digestive filament
Gullet
Muscle
Gonads

sea anemone, a representative **anthozoan**

an·thrax (an′thraks) *n.* a highly infectious disease of animals, esp. hoofed animals, that may be transmitted to humans through contact with infected raw meat or other animal products. It is caused by a spore-forming bacterium, *Bacillus anthracis,* that produces inflamed pustules in humans and often fatal blood poisoning in animals. [Late Latin *anthrax* carbuncle, from Greek *anthrax* coal, carbuncle.]

anthropo- *combining form* human being; human: *anthropomorphic, anthropoid.* [Greek *anthrōpos* human being.]

an·thro·po·cen·tric (an′thrə pō sen′trik) *adj.* **1.** regarding or explaining the universe in terms of human values. **2.** regarding humans and their welfare as the central fact of the universe. —**an·thro·po·cen′tri·cal·ly,** *adv.*

an·thro·poid (an′thrə poid′) *adj.* **1.** (of certain apes) resembling human beings; humanlike. **2.** resembling an ape; apelike: *anthropoid facial features.* —*n.* any of the large, tailless apes, including the chimpanzee, gorilla, gibbon, and orangutan. [Greek *anthrōpoeidēs* of human form, from *anthrōpos* human being.]

an·thro·pol·o·gist (an′thrə pol′ə jist) *n.* a person who is a specialist in anthropology.

an·thro·pol·o·gy (an′thrə pol′ə jē) *n.* the science of the physical, cultural, and social development of human beings and their evolution, behavior, and geographic distribution from prehistoric times to the present. [ANTHROPO- + -LOGY.] —**an·thro·po·log·i·cal** (an′thrə pə loj′i kəl); also, **an·thro·po·log′ic,** *adj.;* also, —**an′thro·po·log′i·cal·ly,** *adv.*

an·thro·pom·e·try (an′thrə pom′i trē) *n.* the science of the measurement of the dimensions and proportions of the human body, esp. as a basis for comparing races or individuals. —**an·thro·po·met·ric** (an′thrə pə met′rik); also, **an′thro·po·met′ri·cal,** *adj.*

The following list contains a selection of compounds that can be formed with the prefix anti-. The meaning of a word on the list can be understood by combining the appropriate sense of the prefix with the root word.

antianxiety	antidandruff	antimonopoly
antiauthoritarian	antidiabetic	antinoise
antibureaucratic	antiemetic	antipollutant
antiburglary	antierosion	antipsychotic
anticancer	antifascist	antireform
anticarcinogenic	antifog	antirevolutionary
anticholesterol	antiglare	antitheft
anticolonial	antigovernment	antitobacco
anticrime	anti-inflationary	antiulcer
	anti-intellectual	antiviolence

an·thro·po·mor·phic (an′thrə pə môr′fik) *adj.* of or characterized by anthropomorphism: *The ancient Greeks worshiped anthropomorphic gods.* —**an′thro·po·mor′phi·cal·ly,** *adv.*

an·thro·po·mor·phism (an′thrə pə môr′fiz əm) *n.* the attribution of human form or characteristics to gods, animals, or inanimate objects.

an·thro·po·mor·phize (an′thrə pə môr′f īz) *v.t., v.i.,* **-phized, -phizing.** to attribute human form or characteristics to a god, animal, or inanimate object.

an·thro·po·mor·phous (an′thrə pə môr′fəs) *adj.* having or resembling human form. [Greek *anthrōpomorphos* of human form, from *anthrōpos* human + *morphē* form, shape.]

an·ti (an′tī, -tē) *n., pl.* **-tis.** *Informal.* a person opposed to something, as a policy, action, or political party. [From ANTI-.]

anti- *prefix* **1.** opposed to; against: *antitrust, anticlerical.* **2.** expressing the opposite or reverse of: *anticlimactic.* **3.** operating against; counteracting: *antifreeze, antiaircraft.* **4.** rival; false: *antipope, antichrist.* **5.** *Medicine.* preventing, curing, or neutralizing: *antipyretic, antitoxin.* [Greek *anti* opposite, against.]

an·ti·a·bor·tion (an′tē ə bôr′shən, an′tī-) *adj.* opposed to or prohibiting induced abortions: *antiabortion demonstrators, antiabortion laws.* —**an′ti·a·bor′tion·ist,** *n.*

an·ti·air·craft (an′tē âr′kraft′, an′tī-) *adj.* for use against aircraft in flight: *antiaircraft gun.*

an·ti·bac·te·ri·al (an′tē bak tir′ē əl, an′tī-) *adj.* destroying bacteria or preventing their growth. —*n.* an antibacterial drug or substance.

an·ti·bal·lis·tic missile (an′tē bə lis′tik, an′tī-) a guided missile launched to search out and destroy a ballistic missile before it reaches its target.

an·ti·bi·o·sis (an′tē bī ō′sis, an′tī-) *n., pl.* **-ses** (-sēz) *Biology.* an antagonistic association between organisms that is harmful to one of them, as a fungus producing an antibiotic against a neighboring bacterium. [Modern Latin *antibiosis,* from *anti-* against + Greek *biōsis* way of life (from *bios* life).]

an·ti·bi·ot·ic (an′tē bī ot′ik, -bē-, an′tī-) *n.* any of a group of substances, as penicillin or streptomycin, produced by molds, bacteria, and other microorganisms and used in medicine to kill or slow the growth of disease-causing organisms, as bacteria, fungi, and amebas. —*adj.* **1.** of or relating to antibiotics. **2.** having the ability to destroy or inhibit living organisms.

an·ti·bod·y (an′tī bod′ē) *n., pl.* **-bod·ies.** any of numerous protein molecules produced by lymphocytes in the blood, usually in response to the presence of foreign, disease-producing antigens. Antibodies combine with antigens to disable or destroy them and can give immunity against certain diseases.

an·tic (an′tik) *n.* **1.** *also,* **antics.** a silly or comical act or action; caper; prank: *the antics of a clown, the antics of a puppy.* **2.** *Archaic.* a clown; buffoon. —*adj.* **1.** silly or comical; funny: *antic behavior.* **2.** grotesque; bizarre; ludicrous: *To put an antic disposition on* (Shakespeare, *Hamlet.*) [Italian *antico* old, grotesque, from Latin *antīquus* old. Doublet of ANTIQUE.]

An·ti·christ (an′ti krīst′) *n.* **1.** the antagonist of Christ, expected to fill the world with wickedness until he is vanquished by Christ on Judgment Day. **2.** *also,* **antichrist.** a person who denies or opposes Christ or Christianity. **3.** *also,* **antichrist.** a person who falsely claims to be Christ.

an·tic·i·pate (an tis′ə pāt′) *v.t.,* **-pat·ed, -pat·ing. 1.** to look forward to; expect: *I do not anticipate any trouble. I anticipate his arrival at four o'clock.* **2.** to foresee and deal with in advance: *She anticipated my next question. The hotel staff anticipated its guest's needs.* **3.** to act so as to prevent or counter; forestall: *to anticipate the enemy's tactics.* **4.** to cause to happen before the proper time; precipitate: *Your question anticipates the material to be covered later.* **5.** to be before (another) in doing or achieving something; precede: *The Vikings are reputed to have anticipated Columbus in the discovery of America.* **6.** to use or expend (funds) in advance of actual possession: *to anticipate an inheritance.* [Latin *anticipātus,* past participle of *anticipāre* to take before.] —**an·tic′i·pa′tor,** *n.* —For Synonyms, see **expect.**

an·tic·i·pa·tion (an tis′ə pā′shən) *n.* **1.** the act of anticipating or the state of being anticipated. **2.** a feeling of excited expectation: *We awaited their arrival with eager anticipation.*

an·tic·i·pa·tive (an tis′ə pā′tiv) *adj.* characterized by, resulting from, or exhibiting anticipation.

a	at	e	end	o	hot	u	up	hw	white		about
ā	ape	ē	me	ō	old	ū	use	ng	song		taken
ä	far	i	it	ô	fork	ü	rule	th	thin	ə	pencil
âr	care	ī	ice	oi	oil	u̇	pull	th	this		lemon
		îr	pierce	ou	out	ûr	turn	zh	measure		circus

an·tic·i·pa·to·ry (an tis′ə pə tôr′ē) *adj.* anticipative: *anticipatory dread.* —**an′tic′i·pa·to′ri·ly,** *adv.*

an·ti·cler·i·cal (an′tē kler′i kəl, an′tī-) *adj.* opposed to the influence and activities of the church or clergy. —**an′ti·cler′i·cal·ism,** *n.* —**an′ti·cler′i·cal·ist,** *n.*

an·ti·cli·mac·tic (an′ti klī mak′tic) *adj.* of, having, or like an anticlimax. —**an′ti·cli·mac′ti·cal·ly,** *adv.*

an·ti·cli·max (an′ti klī′maks) *n.* **1.** an unexpected, often ludicrous, change from the important or dignified to the trivial or absurd in speech and writing, for example: *My car was stolen, my house burned down, and I forgot to tie my shoes.* **2.** anything that is much less important or interesting than what has preceded it; letdown after a high point: *The film's last scene was an anticlimax.*

an·ti·cline (an′ti klīn′) *n.* an archlike fold of stratified rock having the layers sloping downward from the crest in opposite directions. ➡ opposed to **syncline.** [ANTI- + Greek *klīnein* to lean; influenced in form by INCLINE.] —**an′ti·cli′nal,** *adj.*

an·ti·co·a·gu·lant (an′tē kō ag′yə lənt, an′tī-) *adj.* preventing or delaying clotting of the blood. —*n.* an anticoagulant drug or substance.

an·ti·cy·clone (an′ti sī′klōn) *n.* an atmospheric condition consisting of a mass of air currents rotating about a center of high barometric pressure; high pressure area. The winds of an anticyclone

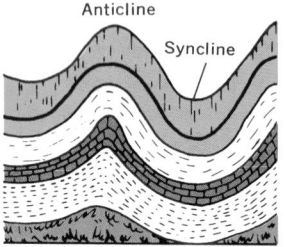

Anticline

Syncline

anticline
cross section of
stratified rock

circle clockwise in the Northern Hemisphere, counterclockwise in the Southern. ➡ distinguished from **cyclone.** —**an·ti·cy·clon·ic** (an′tē sī klon′ik), *adj.*

an·ti·de·pres·sant (an′tē di pres′ənt, an′tī-) *adj.* preventing or relieving psychic depression. —*n.* any drug used for the treatment of depression.

an·ti·do·tal (an′ti dō′təl) *adj.* of, like, or acting as an antidote.

an·ti·dote (an′ti dōt′) *n.* **1.** a medicine or other remedy to counteract the effects of a poison. **2.** any counteracting remedy: *Work is an antidote to boredom.* [Latin *antidotum,* from Greek *antidoton* literally, (thing) given against.]

an·ti·es·tab·lish·ment (an′tē e stab′lish mənt, an′tī-) *adj.* opposed to or hostile to the social, political, and economic structure of a country or society, or to its members.

An·ti·fed·er·al·ist (an′tē fed′ər ə list, an′tī-) *n.* **1.** a member of the political party that opposed the adoption and ratification of the U.S. Constitution and later opposed the creation of a strong central government. **2. antifederalist.** an opponent of federalism. —**An′ti·fed′er·al,** *adj.* —**An′ti·fed′er·al·ism,** *n.*

an·ti·freeze (an′ti frēz′, -frē′) *n.* a substance added to a liquid, esp. the water in the radiator of an automobile, to prevent it from freezing at given temperatures by lowering its freezing point.

an·ti·fric·tion (an′tē frik′shən) *adj.* tending to prevent or reduce friction: *an antifriction compound.*

an·ti·gen (an′ti jən) *n.* a substance usually harmful to the body, such as a toxin or bacterium, that stimulates the body to produce antibodies. [ANTI- + -GEN.] —**an·ti·gen·ic** (an′ti jen′ik), *adj.*

An·tig·o·ne (an tig′ə nē) *n.* in Greek legend, the daughter of Oedipus who was condemned to death for giving her brother a proper burial against the command of her uncle Creon.

an·ti·grav·i·ty (an′tē grav′i tē) *n.* a hypothetical force that would, if it existed, counteract or neutralize gravity.

an·ti·he·ro (an′tē hîr′ō) *n., pl.* **-roes.** a main character, as in a play, motion picture, or novel, who lacks the positive characteristics traditionally associated with a hero.

an·ti·her·o·ine (an′tē her′ō in) *n.* a main character, as in a play, motion picture, or novel, who lacks the positive characteristics traditionally associated with a heroine.

an·ti·his·ta·mine (an′ti his′tə mēn′, -min) *n.* any of several drugs that neutralize the effect of histamine in the body and are used chiefly in the treatment of allergic reactions and colds.

an·ti·in·flam·ma·to·ry (an′tē in flam′ə tôr′ē, an′tī-) *adj.* counteracting or reducing inflammation. —*n., pl.* **-ries.** an anti-inflammatory drug or substance.

an·ti·knock (an′tē nok′, an′tī-) *n.* a chemical substance added to gasoline to reduce knocking in the engine.

an·ti·log·a·rithm (an′ti lô′gə rith′əm, -log′ə-) *n.* the number corresponding to a given logarithm. —**an′ti·log′a·rith′mic,** *adj.*

an·ti·ma·cas·sar (an′ti mə kas′ər) *n.* a small ornamental covering put over the back or arms of a chair, originally to prevent soiling. [ANTI- + earlier *macassar* nineteenth century hair oil from *Macassar,* a district of Celebes.]

an·ti·mag·net·ic (an′tē mag net′ik) *adj.* **1.** resisting magnetization. **2.** (of a watch, gyroscope, or the like) made of or containing parts that are resistant to magnetization so that their operation is not affected by a magnetic field.

an·ti·ma·lar·i·al (an′tē mə lâr′ē əl, an′tī-) *adj.* preventing or suppressing malaria. —*n.* an antimalarial drug or substance.

an·ti·mat·ter (an′tē mat′ər, an′tī-) *n. Physics.* a theoretical form of matter consisting of antiparticles.

an·ti·mi·cro·bi·al (an′tē mī krō′bē əl, an′tī-) *adj.* destroying microbes or preventing their growth. —*n.* an antimicrobial drug or substance.

an·ti·mis·sile (an′tē mis′əl, an′tī-) *adj.* designed or used for defense against ballistic and guided missiles.

an·ti·mo·ny (an′tə mō′nē) *n.* a crystalline metallic element with a silver or bluish white luster, used chiefly as an alloying element to increase hardness. Symbol: **Sb** For tables, see **element.** [Medieval Latin *antimonium.*] —**an′ti·mo′ni·al,** *adj.*

an·ti·neu·tri·no (an′tē nü trē′nō, -nū-, an′tī-) *n., pl.* **-nos.** the antiparticle of the neutrino.

an·ti·neu·tron (an′tē nü′tron, -nū′-, an′tī-) *n.* the antiparticle of the neutron.

an·ti·node (an′tə nōd′) *n. Physics.* any point in a wave where the amplitude is at maximum. —**an′ti·nod′al,** *adj.*

an·ti·nu·cle·ar (an′tē nü′klē ər, -nū′-, an′tī-) *adj.* **1.** opposed to the use of nuclear energy to generate electric power. **2.** opposed to the use or development of atomic weapons.

an·ti·ox·i·dant (an′tē ok′si dənt, an′tī-) *n.* a substance that prevents or delays oxidation, used to retard deterioration of foods, drugs, plastics, rubbers, and the like.

an·ti·par·ti·cle (an′tē pär′ti kəl, an′tī-) *n.* any of a group of subatomic particles, each of which corresponds to another subatomic particle in mass and magnitude of spin but is its opposite in direction of spin and, in the case of charged particles, in electric charge. When a particle and its antiparticle collide, they annihilate each other and their mass is converted into energy.

an·ti·pas·to (an′ti pas′tō, än′tē päs′tō) *n., pl.* **-tos** or **-ti** (-tē). an Italian dish served as an appetizer or first course consisting of small portions of various foods. [Italian *antipasto,* going back to Latin *ante* before + *pastus* food.]

an·ti·pa·thet·ic (an′ti pə thet′ik, an tip′ə-) *adj.* having an aversion; opposed in nature or disposition: *a group composed of people antipathetic to each other.* Also, **an′ti·pa·thet′i·cal.** —**an′ti·pa·thet′i·cal·ly,** *adv.*

an·tip·a·thy (an tip′ə thē) *n., pl.* **-thies. 1.** a feeling of strong dislike; distaste; aversion. **2.** a person or thing that arouses such a feeling. [Latin *antipathīa,* from Greek *antipatheia* literally, a feeling against, from *anti-* opposite + *pathos* emotion.]

an·ti·per·spi·rant (an′tē pûr′spər ənt, an′tī-) *n.* an astringent preparation, applied to the skin, esp. the armpits, to reduce perspiration. [ANTI- + PERSPIR(E) + -ANT.]

an·ti·phon (an′tə fon′) *n.* **1.** a verse of a psalm, hymn, or prayer sung or chanted in alternation or in response to one another. **2.** any composition consisting of passages for responsive singing or chanting. [Late Latin *antiphōna* sacred song sung responsively, going back to Greek *antiphōnos* responsive, from *anti-* opposite, against + *phōnē* sound.]

an·tiph·o·nal (an tif′ə nəl) *n.* a book of antiphons. Also, **an·tiph·o·nar·y** (an tif′ə ner′ē). —*adj.* of or like an antiphon or antiphony; responsive. —**an·tiph′o·nal·ly,** *adv.*

an·tiph·o·ny (an tif′ə nē) *n., pl.* **-nies. 1.** the singing or playing of music by two groups in alternation or in response to one another. **2.** the music so performed; antiphon.

an·tip·o·dal (an tip′ə dəl) *adj.* **1.** of or relating to antipodes; situated on opposite sides of the earth. **2.** diametrically opposed or opposite: *antipodal points of view.*

an·ti·pode (an′ti pōd′) *n.* an exact or direct opposite. [From ANTIPODES.]

an·tip·o·des (an tip′ə dēz′) *pl. n.* **1.** two places on the earth's surface diametrically opposite one another: *The Antarctic and the Arctic are antipodes.* **2.** two opposite or contrary things: *Love and hate are antipodes.* **3.** *British.* Australia and New Zealand. [Latin *antipodēs* geographic antipodes, from Greek *antipodes* people having their feet opposite.] —**an·tip′o·de′an,** *adj.*

an·ti·pol·lu·tion (an′tē pə lü′shən, an′tī-) *adj.* intended or

designed to prevent, lessen, or remove environmental pollution, as a law, mechanical device, or chemical substance.

an·ti·pope (an′ti pōp′) *n.* a person elected as or claiming to be pope in opposition to a pope canonically chosen.

an·ti·pov·er·ty (an′tē pov′ər tē, an′tī-) *adj.* intended to relieve or eliminate poverty: *governmental antipoverty programs.*

an·ti·pro·ton (an′tē prō′ton, an′tī-) *n.* the antiparticle of the proton.

an·ti·py·ret·ic (an′tē pī ret′ik, an′tī-) *adj.* reducing or preventing fever. —*n.* a drug or other agent for reducing or preventing fever.

an·ti·quar·i·an (an′ti kwâr′ē ən) *adj.* of or relating to antiquities. —*n.* antiquary.

an·ti·quar·y (an′ti kwer′ē) *n., pl.* **-quar·ies.** a person who collects, studies, or deals in antiquities. [Latin *antīquārius,* from *antīquus* old.]

an·ti·quate (an′ti kwāt′) *v.t.,* **-quat·ed, -quat·ing.** to cause to become old-fashioned; make obsolete. [Latin *antīquātus,* past participle of *antīquāre* to make old, from *antīquus* old.]

an·ti·quat·ed (an′ti kwā′tid) *adj.* **1.** old-fashioned; out-of-date: *antiquated ideas, an antiquated style of dress.* **2.** no longer in use or usable: *an antiquated manual typewriter.*

an·tique (an tēk′) *adj.* **1.** of, belonging to, or in the style of an earlier period: *antique furniture, an antique watch.* **2.** of, belonging to, or in the style of classical antiquity; of ancient Greece or Rome. **3.** *Archaic.* old-fashioned; antiquated: *an antique custom.* —*n.* **1.** an object of an earlier period that is valued for its age, scarcity, craftsmanship, or historical significance. **2.** *Informal.* any object of great age; relic: *That jalopy is an antique.* **3. the antique.** the style of ancient Greco-Roman art. **4.** *Printing.* a style of type in which all lines are of equal thickness. —*v.t.,* **-tiqued, -tiquing.** to make (something) appear old: *to antique a chair.* [Latin *antīquus* old. Doublet of ANTIC.] —**an·tique′ly,** *adv.* —**an·tique′ness,** *n.*

Usage   United States customs law defines an **antique** as an object that has been made at least 100 years before the date of sale. However, some people prefer to restrict the term to refer to objects that were made by hand before 1830, the advent of the machine age.

an·tiq·ui·ty (an tik′wi tē) *n., pl.* **-ties. 1.** the early ages of history, esp. the period preceding the Middle Ages; ancient times: *Archaeologists study ruins surviving from antiquity to learn about ancient civilizations.* **2.** the people and cultures of ancient times collectively: *the heritage left to us by antiquity.* **3.** the quality of being ancient; great age: *a ring valued for its antiquity.* **4. antiquities.** objects belonging to or remaining from ancient times; ancient relics.

an·ti·ra·chit·ic (an′tē rə kit′ik, an′tī-) *adj.* relieving or curing rickets. —*n.* a remedy for rickets. [ANTI- + RACHIT(IS) + -IC.]

an·ti·scor·bu·tic (an′tē skôr bū′tik, an′tī-) *adj.* relieving or curing scurvy. —*n.* a remedy for scurvy, such as vitamin C, or ascorbic acid.

an·ti·Se·mit·ic (an′tē sə mit′ik, an′tī-) *adj.* prejudiced or discriminating against Jews: *anti-Semitic laws.* —**an′ti·Se·mit′i·cal·ly,** *adv.*

an·ti·Sem·i·tism (an′tē sem′i tiz′əm, an′tī-) *n.* prejudice or discrimination against, or persecution of, Jews. —**an·ti·Sem·ite** (an′tē sem′īt, an′tī-), *n.*

an·ti·sep·sis (an′ti sep′sis) *n.* **1.** prevention of the growth of microorganisms. **2.** procedures that achieve this.

an·ti·sep·tic (an′ti sep′tik) *adj.* **1.** preventing infection, putrefaction, or decay by inhibiting the growth of microorganisms: *an antiseptic ointment.* **2.** like or caused by an antiseptic: *an antiseptic odor.* **3.** free from harmful bacteria or other microorganisms; sterile: *an antiseptic wound.* **4.** lacking warmth or interest; coldly impersonal: *The all-white living room was very antiseptic.* —*n.* a substance that inhibits the growth of harmful bacteria and other microorganisms, esp. in or on living tissue. [ANTI- + SEPTIC.] —**an′ti·sep′ti·cal·ly,** *adv.*

an·ti·se·rum (an′ti sîr′əm) *n., pl.* **-se·rums** or **-se·ra** (-sîr′ə). a serum containing antibodies specific for one or more antigens, obtained from the blood of an animal injected with the antigens.

an·ti·slav·er·y (an′tē slā′və rē, an′tī-) *adj.* opposed to slavery: *antislavery leaders, antislavery oratory.*

an·ti·smok·ing (an′tē smō′king, an′tī-) *adj.* opposed to the smoking of tobacco: *an antismoking campaign.* —**an′ti·smok′er,** *n.*

an·ti·so·cial (an′tē sō′shəl, an′tī-) *adj.* **1.** not liking or wanting companionship or the society of others; unsociable. **2.** opposed to the general good or basic principles of society: *Murder is an antisocial act.*

an·ti·spas·mod·ic (an′tē spaz mod′ik, an′tī-) *adj.* preventing or relieving spasms. —*n.* a drug or other agent that prevents or relieves spasms.

an·ti·stat·ic (an′tē stat′ik, an′tī-) *adj.* of, relating to, or designating a material, technique, or the like that prevents buildup of static electricity, as on textiles or phonograph records.

an·tis·tro·phe (an tis′trə fē) *n.* **1.a.** the part of an ancient Greek choral ode sung in answer to the preceding strophe by a play's chorus when returning from left to right of the stage. **b.** the movement made by the chorus while singing this. **2.** the stanza in a Pindaric ode that follows a strophe. It usually has the same metrical form as the strophe. [Latin *antistrophē,* from Greek *antistrophḗ* literally, a turning about.]

an·ti·tank (an′tē tangk′, an′tī-) *adj.* designed for or used against tanks or other armored vehicles.

an·ti·ter·ror·ist (an′tē ter′ər ist, an′tī-) *adj.* used against or designed to combat terrorists or terrorism: *antiterrorist measures, an antiterrorist treaty.* —*n.* a person or group that opposes or combats terrorism. —**an′ti·ter′ror·ism,** *n.*

an·tith·e·sis (an tith′ə sis) *n., pl.* **-ses** (-sēz′). **1.** the exact opposite: *Hope is the antithesis of despair.* **2.** the state of being opposed to the opposite; contrast: *the antithesis of bravery and cowardice.* **3.** *Rhetoric.* **a.** the opposition or contrast of ideas, esp. by means of parallel arrangements of words, clauses, or sentences, for example: *Ask not what your country can do for you—ask what you can do for your country* (John F. Kennedy, 1961). **b.** the second part of such an expression. [Greek *antithesis* opposition; literally, a setting against.]

an·ti·thet·i·cal (an′ti thet′i kəl) *adj.* **1.** directly opposed; strongly contrasted: *Rudeness is antithetical to my nature.* **2.** of, characterized by, or containing antithesis: *an antithetical construction.* Also, **an′ti·thet′ic.** —**an′ti·thet′i·cal·ly,** *adv.*

an·ti·tox·ic (an′ti tok′sik, an′tē-) *adj.* **1.** counteracting the effects of toxins. **2.** of, relating to, or serving as an antitoxin.

an·ti·tox·in (an′ti tok′sin, an′tē-) *n.* **1.** an antibody formed in the body that provides protection against a specific poison released by invading bacteria. **2.** a serum containing such an antibody, obtained from the blood of horses or other animals that have been injected with a toxin, used to cure or prevent certain diseases.

an·ti·trades (an′ti trādz′) *pl. n.* winds that blow above, and in a direction opposite to, the trade winds.

an·ti·trust (an′tē trust′, an′tī-) *adj.* opposed to or regulating monopolies, trusts, or other business combinations or practices that cause unlawful restraint of trade: *antitrust laws.*

an·ti·ven·in (an′tē ven′in, an′tī-) *n.* a serum containing antitoxins that mitigate the toxic effects of animal venom, esp. an antiserum used to treat snakebite.

an·ti·vi·ral (an′tē vī′rəl, an′tī-) *adj.* destroying or checking the reproduction or effects of a virus. —*n.* an antiviral drug.

ant·ler (ant′lər) *n.* **1.** one of the branched horns of various members of the deer family. Antlers are shed each year and replaced by new ones. **2.** any of the branches of such a horn. [Old French *antoillier,* going back to Latin *ante* before + *oculus* eye.] —**ant′lered,** *adj.*

ant lion 1. any of a group of insects, family Myrmeleontidae, whose larva feeds on ants and other wingless insects that it traps by digging a pit into which the prey falls. **2.** the larva of the ant lion; doodlebug.

an·to·nym (an′tə nim′) *n.* a word having a meaning opposite to another word. *Young* is an antonym of *old.* ➡ opposed to **synonym.** [Greek *antōnymia* interchange of names.]

an·trum (an′trəm) *n., pl.* **-tra** (-trə) or **-trums.** *Anatomy.* a cavity or enlargement, esp. a sinus in a bone. [Latin *antrum,* from Greek *antron* cave.]

ants·y (ant′sē) *adj.,* **ants·i·er, ants·i·est.** *Informal.* very eager, anxious, or restless: *It was the last day of school, and the children were antsy to leave.* [From *ants* (plural of ant) + -Y¹.]

A·nu·bis (ə nü′bis, ə nū′-) *n.* in Egyptian mythology, the son of Osiris and a god of the underworld, represented as a man with the head of a jackal. His Greek counterpart is Hermes.

A number 1, A-1.

a·nu·ran (ə nûr′ən, ə nyûr′-) *n.* any member of the order Anura,

a	at	e	end	o	hot	u	up	hw	white		about
ā	ape	ē	me	ō	old	ū	use	ng	song		taken
ä	far	i	it	ô	rule	ū	rule	th	thin	ə	pencil
âr	care	ī	ice	oi	oil	u̇	pull	th	this		lemon
		îr	pierce	ou	out	ûr	turn	zh	measure		circus

which includes all frogs and toads. —*adj.* of or relating to the anurans. [Greek *an-* not + *oura* tail + *-AN.*]

a·nus (ā′nəs) *n., pl.* **a·nus·es.** the opening at the lower end of the alimentary canal, through which solid waste products are eliminated from the body. [Latin *ānus.*]

an·vil (an′vəl) *n.* **1.** an iron or steel block on which metals that have been heated until soft are hammered into desired shapes. **2.** incus. [Old English *anfilte* block for shaping metals.]

anx·i·e·ty (ang zī′i tē) *n., pl.* **-ties.** **1.** a feeling of fearful uneasiness or apprehension over what may happen; worry: *Your anxiety about your health is unfounded.* **2.** something that causes this feeling: *Lack of money is one of his chief anxieties.* **3.** earnest, intense desire; eagerness: *Her anxiety to succeed hindered her performance.* **4.** an abnormal, intense state of apprehension, tension, and fear, accompanied by physiological symptoms, such as rapid pulse and sweating. —For Synonyms, see **apprehension.**

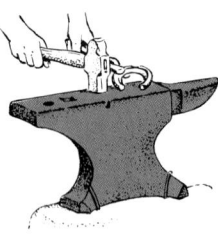

anvil

anx·ious (angk′shəs, ang′-) *adj.* **1.** fearful about what may happen; uneasy; apprehensive: *I'm anxious about our safety on these snowy roads.* **2.** exhibiting, causing, or full of anxiety: *We spent an anxious day waiting for the test results.* **3.** eagerly or earnestly desiring; wanting very much: *anxious to please.* [Latin *anxius* distressed.] —**anx′ious·ly,** *adv.* —**anx′ious·ness,** *n.* —For Synonyms, see **eager.**

> **Usage** Some people make a distinction between **anxious** and **eager,** preferring to limit the use of **anxious** to indicate fear or worry about an anticipated event or outcome, as in *anxious about test results,* and to use **eager** in referring to something pleasant or desirable, as in *eager to make friends.*

an·y (en′ē) *adj.* **1.** one, no matter which: *Take any seat.* **2.** some, whatever quantity or quality: *Have you any apples? Any information will help.* **3.** each without exception; every: *Any child knows the answer.* **4.** at all: *Has a coward any courage? I haven't any change.* —*pron.* any one or ones; any quantity or quality: *We haven't any left. He scored better than any of the others.* —*adv.* to any extent or degree: *Stop before you go any farther.* [Old English *ǣnig* no matter which, at all.]

an·y·bod·y (en′ē bod′ē, -bud′ē) *pron., pl.* **-bod·ies.** any person whatever; anyone: *Has anybody seen him?* —*n.* a person of importance: *Everybody who is anybody was at the wedding.*

> **Usage** The words **anybody, anyone, each, either, everybody, everyone, neither, nobody, no one, somebody,** and **someone** are generally used as singular: *Anybody in the class knows that. Either of the candidates is qualified for the office.* Although plural pronouns are often used to refer to these words, as in *Somebody left their algebra book on the bus,* many people consider this usage unacceptable in formal speech and writing unless the pronoun clearly refers to more than one person and is in a different clause: *The boss told everyone that they could leave early.* Traditionally, a masculine pronoun was used to refer to a word that might refer to either a male or a female or to both sexes: *Somebody left his algebra book on the bus. Everybody served himself.* Today, however, many people consider this tradition derogatory to women and prefer to use both a masculine and a feminine pronoun or to reword the sentence to eliminate the pronoun and the awkwardness of using two pronouns: *Somebody left his or her algebra book on the bus. Somebody left an algebra book on the bus.*

an·y·how (en′ē hou′) *adv.* **1.** in any case; at any rate; nevertheless: *We told them not to go, but they went anyhow. Anyhow, that is beside the point.* **2.** in any way whatever: *You can do it anyhow you want.*

an·y·more (en′ē môr′) *adv.* at the present time or from this time forward: *They don't work here anymore.*

an·y·one (en′ē wun′, -wən) *pron.* any person whatever; anybody: *Has anyone seen my coat?* —For Usage Note, see **anybody.**

an·y·place (en′ē plās′) *adv. Informal.* anywhere.

an·y·thing (en′ē thing′) *pron.* any thing whatever: *I'll accept anything you say.* —*n.* a thing of any sort. —*adv.* to any extent; at all. ➡ now used only in the expression *anything like,* as in *Is this glove anything like the one you lost?*

• **anything but.** by no means; not at all: *The salesperson was anything but polite.*

an·y·time (en′ē tīm′) *adv.* at any time; whenever.

an·y·way (en′ē wā′) *adv.* **1.** in any case; at any rate; nevertheless: *Anyway, I am glad it happened. It was snowing, but we went for a walk anyway.* **2.** in any manner or way: *Anyway you look at it, we're lost.* ➡ for def. 2, now usually written as two separate words, as in *I'll accept it any way it's done.*

an·y·where (en′ē hwâr′, -wâr′) *adv.* **1.** in, at, or to any place: *Put the box down anywhere.* **2.** *Informal.* to any extent; at all: *Did I come anywhere near the right answer?*

• **to get** (or **go**) **anywhere.** to achieve success: *You'll never get anywhere with that attitude.*

an·y·wise (en′ē wīz′) *adv.* in any way; to any degree; at all.

A-OK (ā′ō kā′) *adj., adv., interj.* also, **A-o·kay.** *Informal.* excellent; perfect.

A-1 (ā′wun′) *also,* **A-one, A number 1.** *adj. Informal.* of first quality or in top condition; first-class; excellent: *The lawn is in A-1 shape.* [From the rating *A-1* used in an annual registry of ships published by the London insurers Lloyd's, to indicate that a ship is in first-class condition as to seaworthiness.]

a·o·rist (ā′ər ist) *n.* a tense of Greek verbs expressing action, usually past, without reference to its duration or completion. [Greek *aoristos* indefinite.]

a·or·ta (ā ôr′tə) *n., pl.* **-tas** or **-tae** (-tē). the main artery or trunk of the arterial system. It carries the blood from the left ventricle of the heart to all parts of the body except the lungs. [Modern Latin *aorta,* from Greek *aortē.*] —**a·or′tal, a·or′tic,** *adj.*

aou·dad (ou′dad) *n.* a wild sheep, *Ammotragus lervia,* of northern Africa, that has a tawny coat, fringes of long hair on its neck, forelegs, and chest, and long, curving horns. Height: 40 inches (102 centimeters) at the shoulder. Also, **Barbary sheep.** [French *aoudad,* from Berber *audad.*]

aoudad

ap-¹, form of **ad-** before *p,* as in *approbation.*

ap-², form of **apo-** before vowels and *h,* as in *aphorism.*

AP, Associated Press, U.S.-based cooperative agency that gathers and distributes news stories and pictures throughout the world.

a·pace (ə pās′) *adv.* swiftly; quickly; rapidly: *Great weeds do grow apace* (Shakespeare, *Richard III*). [Old French *à pas* at a (fast) pace, going back to Latin *ad* to, at + *passus* step, pace.]

a·pache (ə päsh′, ə pash′) *n.* a ruffian, gangster, or thug of Paris. [French *apache,* from *Apache* (in the sense of a fierce, ruthless fighter).]

A·pach·e (ə pach′ē) *n., pl.* **A·pach·e** or **A·pach·es.** **1.** a member of a group of Indian tribes of Athapascan linguistic stock, inhabiting the southwestern United States. **2.** any of the Athapascan languages spoken by these people. —*adj.* of or relating to the Apache, their language, or their culture. [Spanish *apache* Apache Indian, from Zuñi *ápachu* enemy.]

ap·a·nage (ap′ə nij) appanage.

a·part (ə pärt′) *adv.* **1.** away from one another; separated in space or time: *Their houses are two miles apart. They left three hours apart.* **2.** into two or more parts; in or to pieces: *The dogs tore the bag of food apart. The old book is falling apart.* **3.** at or to the side; aside: *He sat apart from the others. She always kept some money apart for emergencies.* **4.** as a separate consideration; independently: *Let's consider this problem apart from the others.* —*adj.* having separate or unique features or characteristics; distinct: *a breed apart.* [French *à part* aside, singly, from *à* to (from Latin *ad* to) + *part* part, from Latin *pars* part.] —**a·part′ness,** *n.*

• **apart from.** other than; besides: *Apart from the terrible weather, our vacation was fun.*

• **to take apart. a.** to separate into component parts; disassemble: *to take an engine apart.* **b.** to criticize or upbraid severely: *The critic really took that movie apart.*

• **to tell apart.** to distinguish between: *We couldn't tell the triplets apart.*

a·part·heid (ə pär′tīd, ə pärt′hāt) *n.* an official policy of racial segregation, esp. as practiced in South Africa. [Afrikaans *apart-*

heid separateness, from *apart* separate (from French *à part* aside) + *-heid* -hood. See APART.]

a·part·ment (ə pärt′mənt) *n.* a housing unit consisting of a room or set of rooms, usually in a building that contains other such units. [French *appartement*, from Italian *appartamento* separation, apartment, going back to Latin *ad* to + *pars* part + *-mentum* -ment.]

apartment house, a building divided into a number of apartments. Also, **apartment building.**

ap·a·thet·ic (ap′ə thet′ik) *adj.* **1.** having or showing little interest, concern, or desire to act; indifferent: *apathetic voters who fail to go to the polls.* **2.** having or showing little or no feeling or emotion; unemotional. Also, **ap′a·thet′i·cal.** —**ap′a·thet′i·cal·ly,** *adv.*

ap·a·thy (ap′ə thē) *n.* **1.** a lack of interest, concern, or desire to act; indifference. **2.** a lack of feeling or emotion. [French *apathie* lack of feeling, from Latin *apathīa*, from Greek *apatheia*, from *a-* without + *pathos* emotion.]

ap·a·tite (ap′ə tīt′) *n.* any of a group of calcium phosphate minerals found in rocks such as phosphorite, in bones and teeth, and as pale green or yellow hexagonal crystals in pegmatite. [German *apatit*, from Greek *apatē* deceit; because of its having been mistaken for other minerals.]

ap·a·to·sau·rus (ap′ə tō sôr′əs) *n.*, *pl.* **-rus.** brontosaurus.

ape (āp) *n.* **1.** any of the several large, tailless primates belonging to two families, Pongidae and Hylobatidae, that are structurally similar to humans and capable of standing or walking nearly erect, including the chimpanzee, gibbon, gorilla, and orangutan. **2.** any monkey. **3.** a person who imitates; mimic. —*v.t.,* **aped, ap·ing.** to imitate; mimic. [Old English *apa* ape, monkey.] —**ape′like′,** *adj.* —**ap′er,** *n.* —For Synonyms *(v.t.),* see **imitate.**

ape-man (āp′man′) *n.*, *pl.* **-men** (-men′). any of various extinct hominids, as the australopithecines, with anatomical characteristics intermediate between those of apes and modern humans.

a·pe·ri·ent (ə pîr′ē ənt) *n.* a mild laxative. —*adj.* acting as a mild laxative. [Latin *aperiēns,* present participle of *aperīre* to open.]

a·pe·ri·tif (ə per′i tēf′, ä per′-) *n.* an alcoholic drink taken before a meal as an appetizer. [French *apéritif* appetizer, going back to Latin *aperīre* to open.]

ap·er·ture (ap′ər chər) *n.* **1.** a hole, gap, or other opening. **2.** *Optics.* **a.** an opening in a lens through which light passes into a camera or other optical instrument. **b.** the size of this opening. [Latin *apertūra* opening. Doublet of OVERTURE.]

a·pet·al·ous (ā pet′ə ləs) *adj. Botany.* having no petals.

a·pex (ā′peks) *n.*, *pl.* **a·pex·es** or **ap·i·ces. 1.** the highest point; tip; vertex: *the apex of a triangle.* **2.** the highest accomplishment; culmination; climax: *Playing before the queen was the apex of the pianist's career.* [Latin *apex* point, summit.]

a·pha·sia (ə fā′zhə) *n.* a total or partial loss of the ability to use or understand spoken or written language. It is a symptom of brain disease or injury. [Greek *aphasiā* speechlessness.]

a·pha·sic (ə fā′zik) *adj.* of, relating to, or having aphasia. —*n.* a person who has aphasia. Also (n.), **a·pha·si·ac** (ə fā′zē ak′).

a·phe·li·on (ə fē′lē ən) *n.*, *pl.* **-li·ons** or **-li·a** (-lē ə). the point in the orbit of a planet or other heavenly body at which it is farthest away from the sun. ➡ opposed to **perihelion.** [Modification of Modern Latin *aphelium,* from Greek *apo* off, from + *hēlios* sun.] —**a·phe′li·an,** *adj.*

a·phid (ā′fid, af′id) *n.* any of a group of small insects, family Aphididae, that live by sucking juices from plants. They are often nurtured by ants, which obtain a honeylike substance from them. Also, **plant louse.** [Modern Latin *aphis.*]

a·phis (ā′fis, af′is) *n.*, *pl.* **aph·i·des** (af′i dēz′). aphid.

aph·o·rism (af′ə riz′əm) *n.* a short, pithy statement expressing a general truth or doctrine, for example: *A little learning is a dangerous thing* (Pope, 1711). [Late Latin *aphorismus,* from Greek *aphorismos* definition, short sentence, going back to *apo* from + *horos* limit.] —For Synonyms, see **proverb.**

aph·o·rist (af′ər ist) *n.* a person who writes or uses aphorisms.

aph·o·ris·tic (af′ə ris′tik) *adj.* of, like, or containing aphorisms. —**aph′o·ris′ti·cal·ly,** *adv.*

aph·ro·dis·i·ac (af′rə diz′ē ak′) *n.* a drug or other agent that stimulates or increases sexual desire. —*adj.* stimulating or increasing sexual desire. [Greek *aphrodisiakos* sexual, going back to *Aphroditē* Aphrodite.]

Aph·ro·di·te (af′rə dī′tē) *n.* in Greek mythology, the goddess of love and beauty. Her Roman counterpart is Venus. [Greek *Aphroditē,* said to mean "foam-born."]

a·pi·a·rist (ā′pē ər ist) *n.* a person who raises bees; beekeeper.

a·pi·ar·y (ā′pē er′ē) *n.*, *pl.* **-ar·ies.** a place where bees are kept; collection of beehives. [Latin *apiārium,* from *apis* bee.]

ap·i·cal (ap′i kəl, ā′pi-) *adj.* of, at, or forming the apex.

ap·i·ces (ap′ə sēz′, ā′pə-) a plural of **apex.**

a·pi·cul·ture (ā′pi kul′chər) *n.* the raising of bees for honey or wax; beekeeping. [Latin *apis* bee + CULTURE.] —**a′pi·cul′tur·al,** *adj.* —**a′pi·cul′tur·ist,** *n.*

a·piece (ə pēs′) *adv.* for or to each one; each: *The bags of fertilizer weigh fifty pounds apiece. Give them an apple apiece.*

A·pis (ā′pis) *n.* in Egyptian mythology, a sacred bull worshiped by the ancient Egyptians as representing the soul of their god Osiris.

ap·ish (ā′pish) *adj.* **1.** having the appearance, qualities, or mannerisms of an ape. **2.** stupidly or foolishly imitative. —**ap′ish·ly,** *adv.* —**ap′ish·ness,** *n.*

a·plen·ty (ə plen′tē) *adj. Informal.* enough or more than enough: *There was food aplenty.* [A-[1] + PLENTY.]

a·plomb (ə plom′, ə plum′) *n.* complete self-possession or assurance; poise. [French *aplomb* literally, perpendicularity, from *à plomb* according to the plummet, from *à* to + *plomb* lead. See PLUMB.]

apo- *prefix* away from; from; off: *apogee.* [Greek *apo* off, from.]

APO, Army Post Office.

a·poc·a·lypse (ə pok′ə lips′) *n.* **1.** a prophecy or revelation, esp. about the end of the world. **2. the Apocalypse.** the last book of the New Testament, attributed to Saint John. Also, **Revelation. 3.** the cataclysmic end of the world; doomsday. [Late Latin *apocalypsis* revelation, from Greek *apokalypsis* uncovering, revelation, from *apo* off, from + *kalyptein* to cover.]

a·poc·a·lyp·tic (ə pok′ə lip′tik) *adj.* **1.** of, like, or containing an apocalypse: *an apocalyptic vision.* **2.** of or relating to the Apocalypse. Also, **a·poc′a·lyp′ti·cal.** —**a·poc′a·lyp′ti·cal·ly,** *adv.*

a·poc·o·pe (ə pok′ə pē) *n.* the cutting off or elision of the final sound, syllable, or letter of a word, as in *th'* for *the.* [Late Latin *apocopē,* from Greek *apokopē* cutting off.]

A·poc·ry·pha (ə pok′rə fə) *pl. n.* **1.** fourteen books included in the Septuagint and Vulgate as an appendix to the Old Testament, but rejected as uncanonical by Protestants and Jews. **2.** a collection of early Christian writings of uncertain origin, rejected as additions to the New Testament. **3. apocrypha.** writings or statements of doubtful authorship or authenticity. [Late Latin *apocrypha* not canonical, not authentic, neuter plural of *apocryphus* hidden, from Greek *apokryphos,* going back to *apo* off, from + *kryptos* hidden.]

a·poc·ry·phal (ə pok′rə fəl) *adj.* **1.** of doubtful authenticity; false; spurious. **2.** having no ecclesiastical authority; not canonical. **3. Apocryphal.** of or relating to the Apocrypha.

ap·o·gee (ap′ə jē′) *n.* **1.** the point in the orbit of the moon or any other earth-orbiting object at which it is farthest from the earth. ➡ opposed to **perigee. 2.** the highest or culminating point; climax. [French *apogée,* going back to Greek *apogaios* far from earth, from *apo* from + *gē* earth.] —**ap′o·ge′al, ap′o·ge′an,** *adj.*

a·po·lit·i·cal (ā′pə lit′i·kəl) *adj.* **1.** having no concern with or interest in politics or political issues. **2.** having no political significance: *apolitical writings.* —**a′po·lit′i·cal·ly,** *adv.* [A-[4] + POLITICAL.]

apogee and perigee

A·pol·lo (ə pol′ō) *n.*, *pl.* **-los. 1.** in Greek and Roman mythology, the god of manly beauty, poetry, music, prophecy, and healing. He was also considered god of the sun and, as such, was god of light and truth. **2.** *also,* **apollo.** any handsome or beautiful young man.

Ap·ol·lo·ni·an (ap′ə lō′nē ən) *adj.* **1.** of, like, or relating to Apollo. **2. apollonian.** rational, ordered, or disciplined in character or form.

a	at	e	end	o	hot	u	up	hw	white		about
ā	ape	ē	me	ō	old	ū	use	ng	song		taken
ä	far	i	it	ô	fork	ü	rule	th	thin	ə	pencil
âr	care	ī	ice	oi	oil	u̇	pull	th	this		lemon
		îr	pierce	ou	out	ûr	turn	zh	measure		circus

A·pol·lyon (ə pol′yən) *n.* the angel of the bottomless pit; devil.

a·pol·o·get·ic (ə pol′ə jet′ik) *adj.* **1.** making an apology or excuse; expressing or feeling regret: *They were very apologetic about being late.* **2.** speech or writing offered as a defense. Also, **a·pol′o·get′i·cal.** —*n.* a formal defense made in speech or writing of a belief, cause, or the like. —**a·pol′o·get′i·cal·ly,** *adv.*

a·pol·o·get·ics (ə pol′ə jet′iks) *n.* the branch of theology that deals with the defense and proof of Christianity. ➡ used as singular.

ap·o·lo·gi·a (ap′ə lō′jē ə) *n.* a formal defense or justification in speech or writing.

a·pol·o·gist (ə pol′ə jist) *n.* a person who writes or speaks in defense of a belief, cause, idea, or the like.

a·pol·o·gize (ə pol′ə jīz′) *v.i.,* **-gized, -giz·ing. 1.** to acknowledge and express regret for a fault, error, or offense. **2.** to make a formal defense in speech or writing. —**a·pol′o·giz′er,** *n.*

ap·o·logue (ap′ə lôg′, -log′) *n.* an allegorical narrative or tale with a moral; fable. [French *apologue,* from Latin *apologus,* from Greek *apologos,* from *apo* from + *logos* speech.]

a·pol·o·gy (ə pol′ə jē) *n., pl.* **-gies. 1.** an expression of regret for a fault, error, or offense. **2.** a formal defense or justification in speech or writing. **3.** a poor substitute; makeshift: *The raft was a sad apology for a boat.* [Late Latin *apologia* defense, from Greek *apologiā* speech in defense, from *apo* from + *logos* speech.]

ap·o·phthegm (ap′ə them′) apothegm.

ap·o·plec·tic (ap′ə plek′tik) *adj.* **1.** of, relating to, or causing apoplexy: *an apoplectic stroke.* **2.** suffering from apoplexy: *an apoplectic patient.* **3.** liable to have or showing symptoms of apoplexy; violently excited: *to be apoplectic with rage.* —*n.* a person suffering from or liable to have apoplexy. Also, **ap′o·plec′ti·cal.** —**ap′o·plec′ti·cal·ly,** *adv.*

ap·o·plex·y (ap′ə plek′sē) *n., pl.* **-plex·ies.** a sudden weakness or paralysis, with or without loss of consciousness, caused by rupture or blockage of blood vessels in the brain; stroke. [Old French *apoplexie,* from Late Latin *apoplēxia,* from Greek *apoplēxiā.*]

a·pos·ta·sy (ə pos′tə sē) *n., pl.* **-sies.** a desertion or renunciation of one's religion, cause, political party, or principles. [Late Latin *apostasia* desertion of one's religion, from Late Greek *apostasiā* literally, standing away from, from Greek *apo* from + *histenai* to set.]

a·pos·tate (ə pos′tāt, -tit) *n.* a person who commits apostasy. —*adj.* guilty of apostasy.

a·pos·ta·tize (ə pos′tə tīz′) *v.i.,* **-tized, -tiz·ing.** to commit apostasy; become an apostate.

a pos·te·ri·o·ri (ā′pos tîr′ē ôr′ī) **1.** proceeding from the particular to the general or from effect to cause; inductive: *a posteriori reasoning.* **2.** based on or derived from actual experience; empirical: *a posteriori knowledge.* ➡ opposed to **a priori** in both defs. [Latin *ā posteriorī* from what comes after.]

a·pos·tle (ə pos′əl) *n.* **1. Apostle.** an early disciple of Jesus, esp. one of the twelve originally chosen by Jesus to preach his gospel. **2.** any early Christian leader or missionary. **3.** the first or foremost Christian missionary to a country or other region. **4.** a leader or early advocate of a movement or cause. **5.** one of the twelve members of the administrative council of the Mormon Church. [Old English *apostol* Apostle, from Late Latin *apostolus,* from Greek *apostolos* messenger; literally, one sent forth.]

Apostles' Creed, a formal statement of Christian faith that affirms the apostolic teachings. It begins with the statement *I believe in God the Father Almighty.*

ap·os·tol·ic (ap′ə stol′ik) *adj.* **1.** of or relating to the Apostles, their times, doctrines, or teachings. **2.** of or relating to an apostle. **3.** *also,* **Apostolic.** of or relating to the pope; papal. Also, **ap′os·tol′i·cal.**

Apostolic See, the see of the pope, the Roman Catholic Church, considered to have been founded at Rome by Saint Peter.

apostolic succession, the belief that the spiritual authority of the clergy, esp. the bishops, has been handed down in direct and unbroken succession from Jesus' Apostles.

a·pos·tro·phe¹ (ə pos′trə fē) *n.* **1.** a punctuation mark (') used to indicate the omission of one or more letters in a word, as in *you're* for *you are* or *e'er* for *ever.* **2.** to indicate the possessive case of nouns or indefinite pronouns, as in *Paul's desk, anyone's concern, the boys' club.* **3.** to indicate the plural of letters and figures, as in *the three R's, five 6's.* [French *apostrophe,* from Late Latin *apostrophus* mark of omission, from Greek *apostrophos* literally, turned away, left out.]

a·pos·tro·phe² (ə pos′trə fē) *n.* a figure of speech in which an

object, abstract quality, or person, often absent or imaginary, is directly addressed as if present, for example: *O liberty, what crimes are committed in your name!* (Mme. Jeanne-Marie Roland, 1793). [Latin *apostrophē,* from Greek *apostrophē* turning away, from *apostrephein* to turn away.]

a·pos·tro·phize (ə pos′trə fīz′) *v.,* **-phized, -phiz·ing.** —*v.t.* to speak or write an apostrophe to. —*v.i.* to use an apostrophe.

apothecaries' measure, a system of liquid measure used in pharmacy. For Weights and Measures table, see **weight.**

apothecaries' weight, a system of weights used in pharmacy. For Weights and Measures table, see **weight.**

a·poth·e·car·y (ə poth′ə ker′ē) *n., pl.* **-car·ies. 1.** a person who is licensed to prepare and sell drugs and medicines; druggist; pharmacist. **2.** drugstore; pharmacy. [Late Latin *apothēcārius* storekeeper, from Latin *apothēca* storehouse, from Greek *apothēkē.*]

ap·o·thegm (ap′ə them′) *also,* **apophthegm.** *n.* a terse, instructive, practical saying; maxim, for example: *A stitch in time saves nine.* [Greek *apophthegma.*]

ap·o·them (ap′ə them′) *n. Geometry.* a perpendicular drawn from the center of a regular polygon to any one of its sides. [Apo- + Greek *thema* something placed.]

a·poth·e·o·sis (ə poth′ē ō′sis, ap′ə thē′ə-) *n., pl.* **-ses** (-sēz, -sēz′) **1.** the raising or exaltation of a human being to the rank of a god; deification. **2.** a glorified ideal; perfect example: *the apotheosis of goodness.* [Latin *apotheōsis* deification, from Greek *apotheōsis,* going back to *apo* from + *theos* god.]

a·poth·e·o·size (ə poth′ē ə sīz′, ap′ə thē′ə-) *v.t.,* **-sized, -siz·ing. 1.** to make a god of; deify. **2.** to glorify; exalt.

app. 1. apparent. **2.** apparently. **3.** appendix. **4.** appointed.

ap·pall (ə pôl′) *also,* **ap·pal.** *v.t.,* **-palled, -pall·ing.** to fill with horror or consternation; dismay; shock: *The news reports of the earthquake appalled us.* [Old French *apallir* to make pale, from *a* to (from Latin *ad* to) + *pale* pale, from Latin *pallidus* pale.]

ap·pall·ing (ə pô′ling) *adj.* causing horror or consternation; shocking; dreadful. —**ap·pall′ing·ly,** *adv.*

Ap·pa·loo·sa (ap′ə lü′sə) *n. also,* **ap·pa·loo·sa.** any of a breed of western riding horses characterized by black and white spotted markings on the hindquarters. [From *Palouse,* North American Indian tribe who bred the horse or the *Palouse* River, near which the horses were raised.]

ap·pa·nage (ap′ə nij) *also,* **ap·a·nage.** *n.* **1.** land, money, or other provisions set aside for the support of members of royal or noble families. **2.** a natural or necessary accompaniment or attribute: *Success is not always the appanage of intelligence.* [French *apanage,* from *apaner* to nourish, give bread to, going back to Latin *ad* to + *pānis* bread.]

ap·pa·rat·chik (ä′pə rä′chik) *n., pl.* **-chiks** or **-chi·ki** (-chi kē). a member of a bureaucracy, esp. a bureaucracy in a Communist country. [Russian *apparátchik,* from *apparát* apparatus, political organization (going back to Latin *apparatus* preparation) + *-chik* one who is, has to do with.]

ap·pa·rat·us (ap′ə rat′əs, -rā′təs) *n., pl.* **-us** or **-us·es. 1.** a device or appliance used for a particular purpose: *an underwater breathing apparatus.* **2.** an organized set of instruments, materials, or equipment designed for a particular use: *surgical apparatus.* **3.** the method or means by which an organized activity is carried out; system: *the apparatus of government.* **4.** *Physiology.* a group of organs operating together to perform a particular function: *respiratory apparatus.* [Latin *apparātus* preparation, from *ad* to + *parare* to prepare.]

ap·par·el (ə par′əl) *n.* articles worn on the body; clothing; garments; attire. —*v.t.,* **-eled, -el·ing;** *also, British,* **-elled, -elling.** to put clothes on; clothe; dress. [Old French *apareiller* to clothe, from *a* to + *pareiller* to put like with like, going back to Latin *ad* to + *pār* equal.]

ap·par·ent (ə par′ənt) *adj.* **1.** easily seen or understood; plainly visible: *It was apparent that he was joking. The damage from the storm was apparent everywhere in town.* **2.** appearing or seeming real or true, although not necessarily so: *an apparent contradiction.* [Old French *aparant,* present participle of *aparoir* to appear, from Latin *appārēre* to appear.] —**ap·par′ent·ly,** *adv.* —**ap·par′ent·ness,** *n.*

ap·pa·ri·tion (ap′ə rish′ən) *n.* **1.** a supernatural being; ghost; specter; phantom. **2.** something strange, startling, or unexpected that comes suddenly into view. [Late Latin *appāritiō* appearance, from Latin *appārēre* to appear.] —For Synonyms, see **ghost.**

ap·peal (ə pēl′) *n.* **1.** an earnest request or call, as for aid or sympathy; entreaty: *an appeal for mercy, a television appeal for information on a missing person.* **2.** the power or ability to attract,

A

charm, or interest: *an actor with great audience appeal.* **3.** a resort to some higher authority for proof, aid, or corroboration. **4.** *Law.* **a.** the action of bringing a case before a higher court for review or retrial. **b.** a request for this. —*v.i.* **1.** to make an earnest request; entreat. **2.** to arouse a favorable response; be attractive or interesting: *This menu doesn't appeal to me.* **3.** to turn to a higher authority for a decision or settlement. **4.** *Law.* to bring a case, or request that a case be brought, before a higher court for review or retrial. —*v.t.* *Law.* to institute proceedings for the appeal of (a case). [Old French *apeler* to call, from Latin *appellāre* to accost, call upon, from *ad* to + *pellere* to push, drive.]

ap·peal·ing (ə pē′ling) *adj.* **1.** producing a pleasing response; attractive; charming. **2.** earnestly imploring; entreating. —**ap·peal′ing·ly,** *adv.*

ap·pear (ə pîr′) *v.i.* **1.** to come into view; be visible or perceivable: *He appeared in the doorway. The theme appears throughout the book.* **2.** to give the impression of being; seem: *She appeared interested in the lecture but was not.* **3.** to be or become clear or obvious to the mind: *It does not appear that you are right.* **4.** to come or be placed before the public: *The author's newest book appeared in June. That movie actor has also appeared on the stage.* **5.** to come formally before an authoritative body: *to appear as a witness in a trial.* [Old French *aparoir* to show oneself, from Latin *appārēre* to come into sight, appear.]

ap·pear·ance (ə pîr′əns) *n.* **1.** the act of appearing or coming into view: *the appearance of the sun above the horizon.* **2.** external look or aspect: *She has the appearance of a model.* **3.** outward show as opposed to actual state; semblance: *In spite of his troubles, he gave the appearance of being happy.* **4.** a coming before the public: *The band's first appearance was a sellout.* **5.** **appearances.** circumstances or outward indications: *By all appearances, they seem to like their new neighborhood.* **6.** *Law.* a coming into court as a party or attorney in a suit. **7.** something seen or perceived; phenomenon: *strange appearances in the evening sky.*
  • **to keep up appearances.** to maintain the outward signs of what is normal, conventional, or proper.
  • **to put in an appearance.** to appear briefly; attend for a short time.

ap·pease (ə pēz′) *v.t.,* **-peased, -peas·ing. 1.** to placate by giving in to demands or making concessions: *to refuse to appease an aggressive enemy.* **2.** to bring to a state of peace or quiet; calm: *to appease someone's anger.* **3.** to cause to be satisfied; allay: *to appease one's hunger.* [Old French *apaisier* to pacify, from *a* to (from Latin *ad* to) + *pais* peace. See PEACE.] —**ap·peas′er,** *n.* —**ap·peas′ing·ly,** *adv.*

> **Synonyms** **Appease, pacify,** and **soothe** mean to make calm or quiet. **Appease** is used of satisfying someone angry or demanding, and also of appetites or desires: *to appease a creditor, to appease one's hunger.* **Pacify** emphasizes the averting of an open fight or quarrel, often without addressing the underlying causes: *The speaker managed to pacify the mob for the moment.* **Soothe** suggests returning someone or something from an agitated to a calm state: *to soothe a crying baby with a song.*

ap·pease·ment (ə pēz′mənt) *n.* **1.** the act of appeasing or the state of being appeased; pacification; satisfaction. **2.** a policy of making territorial or other concessions to a hostile or aggressive power in order to maintain peace.

ap·pel·lant (ə pel′ənt) *n.* a person who appeals, esp. to a higher court. —*adj.* of or relating to judicial appeals; appellate.

ap·pel·late (ə pel′it) *adj.* **1.** relating to legal appeals. **2.** having the power to hear and rule on legal appeals: *an appellate court.* [Latin *appellātus,* past participle of *appellāre* to call upon. See APPEAL.]

appellate court, a court that has the power to hear legal appeals and to review the decisions of lower courts. The Supreme Court is the highest appellate court in the federal court system of the United States.

ap·pel·la·tion (ap′ə lā′shən) *n.* **1.** a descriptive name or title; designation. **2.** the act of naming.

ap·pel·la·tive (ə pel′ə tiv) *n.* **1.** a descriptive name, as *Lion-Hearted* in *Richard the Lion-Hearted.* **2.** a common noun. —*adj.* **1.** of or designating a common noun. **2.** of or relating to the giving of names.

ap·pend (ə pend′) *v.t.* to add as a supplemental or subordinate part: *to append explanatory notes to a text.* [Latin *appendere* to hang on, from *ad* to + *pendere* to hang.]

ap·pend·age (ə pen′dij) *n.* **1.** something that is appended; adjunct. **2.** a subordinate part of a plant or animal, attached to and extending from a larger part or the main body.

ap·pend·ant (ə pen′dənt) *adj.* added as an appendage. —*n.* something appended.

ap·pen·dec·to·my (ap′ən dek′tə mē) *n., pl.* **-mies.** surgical removal of the appendix, esp. because of appendicitis. [APPENDIX + Greek *ek* out of + *tomē* cutting.]

ap·pen·di·ci·tis (ə pen′də sī′tis) *n.* an inflammation of the appendix, esp. when accompanied by swelling, severe abdominal pain, and the danger of a ruptured appendix, which can bring on peritonitis. [APPENDIX + -ITIS.]

ap·pen·dix (ə pen′diks) *n., pl.* **-dix·es** or **-di·ces** (-də sēz′). **1.a.** a thin, saclike structure attached to the beginning of the large intestine. In humans it is about 3 to 6 inches (8 to 15 centimeters) in length, is located in the lower right abdomen, and has no apparent function. Also, **vermiform appendix. b.** any of various outgrowths or projections of bodily organs. **2.** a section of additional related material supplementing a book or other piece of writing. [Latin *appendix* appendage, from *appendere* to hang on. See APPEND.]

ap·per·ceive (ap′ər sēv′) *v.t.,* **-ceived, -ceiv·ing.** to comprehend (new experiences or ideas) with the help of past knowledge or experience.

ap·per·cep·tion (ap′ər sep′shən) *n.* **1.** the act or process of apperceiving. **2.** full and conscious perception. [French *aperception* clear perception, from Old French *apercevoir* to apperceive, from *a* to (from Latin *ad*) + *percevoir* to perceive. See PERCEIVE.] —**ap′per·cep′tive,** *adj.*

ap·per·tain (ap′ər tān′) *v.i.* to belong as a part, function, or attribute; pertain; relate (with *to*): *Many responsibilities appertain to the office of president.* [Old French *apartenir,* from Late Latin *appertinēre,* from Latin *ad-* to + *pertinēre* to belong, concern. See PERTAIN.]

ap·pe·tite (ap′i tīt′) *n.* **1.** a desire for food. **2.** a natural or strong desire; craving: *to have an appetite for adventure.* [Old French *apetit* desire, from Latin *appetītus* desire for, literally, assault upon, going back to *ad* to + *petere* to seek, attack.]

ap·pe·tiz·er (ap′i tī′zər) *n.* **1.** food or drink served as a first course or before a meal, usually to stimulate the appetite. **2.** anything that arouses interest in or desire for what is to follow.

ap·pe·tiz·ing (ap′i tī′zing) *adj.* appealing to the appetite; savory: *an appetizing dinner.* —**ap′pe·tiz′ing·ly,** *adv.*

Ap·pi·an Way (ap′ē ən) an ancient Roman road, begun in 312 B.C., that extended more than 350 miles (560 kilometers), from Rome to the Adriatic. Part of it exists today. [From the Roman censor *Appius* Claudius Caecus (flourished late fourth century and early third century B.C.), who ordered its construction.]

ap·plaud (ə plôd′) —*v.t.* **1.** to express approval or enjoyment of (something) by clapping the hands: *The audience applauded the cast's performance.* **2.** to express a favorable opinion of; commend; praise: *The newspaper editorial applauded the mayor's efforts to help the city's poor.* —*v.i.* to express approval or enjoyment by clapping the hands: *They kept applauding long after the curtain came down.* [Latin *applaudere* to clap the hands, from *ad* to + *plaudere* to applaud.] **ap·plaud′er,** *n.*

ap·plause (ə plôz′) *n.* **1.** approval or enjoyment expressed by clapping the hands. **2.** any expression of approval or appreciation; praise: *The author's latest novel received the critics' applause.* [Latin *applausus,* past participle of *applaudere.* See APPLAUD.]

ap·ple (ap′əl) *n.* **1.** a roundish fruit with usually red, yellow, or green skin and a firm, edible outer part surrounding a core with small seeds. It is the most widely cultivated fruit. **2.a.** any of thousands of varieties of cultivated trees, genus *Malus,* of the rose family, bearing this fruit and growing in temperate regions. **b.** any tree of the genus *Malus.* **3.** any of certain other plants, fruits, or fruitlike growths, as the custard apple or oak gall. [Old English *æppel* fruit of the apple tree.]
  • **apple of (one's) eye.** a person or thing that is most precious or dear.

apple butter, thick, brown, spiced applesauce used as a spread for bread.

ap·ple·cart (ap′əl kärt′) *n.* a pushcart for peddling apples.
  • **to upset the (or someone's) applecart.** to spoil plans or disrupt the established situation.

ap·ple·jack (ap′əl jak′) *n.* a brandy distilled from hard cider. [APPLE + JACK.]

a	at	e	end	o	hot	u	up	hw	white		about
ā	ape	ē	me	ō	old	ū	use	ng	song		taken
ä	far	i	it	ô	fork	ü	rule	th	thin	ə	pencil
âr	care	ī	ice	oi	oil	u̇	pull	th	this		lemon
		îr	pierce	ou	out	ûr	turn	zh	measure		circus

apple of discord 1. in Greek legend, a golden apple inscribed "For the fairest," thrown among the gods by Eris. It was claimed by Aphrodite, Athena, and Hera, but Paris, who acted as judge, awarded it to Aphrodite, because she promised him Helen. **2.** any cause of envy or dispute.

ap·ple-pie order (ap′əl pī′) *Informal.* a condition of perfect neatness; perfect order.

apple polisher *Slang.* a person who seeks favor by insincere flattery; bootlicker.

ap·ple·sauce (ap′əl sôs′) *n.* **1.** a food made of apples that have been stewed to a pulp and sweetened. **2.** *Slang.* nonsense; bunk.

ap·pli·ance (ə plī′əns) *n.* **1.** a device or piece of equipment for a particular use, esp. one for household use. **2.** the act of applying; application.

ap·pli·ca·ble (ap′li kə bəl, ə plik′ə-) *adj.* capable of being applied; relevant; suitable: *Your argument is not applicable in this case.* —**ap′pli·ca·bil′i·ty,** *n.* —**ap′pli·ca·bly,** *adv.*

ap·pli·cant (ap′li kənt) *n.* a person who asks or applies (for something); candidate: *an applicant for a job.*

ap·pli·ca·tion (ap′li kā′shən) *n.* **1.** the act of putting to use: *the application of science to industry.* **2.** the act of putting on: *the application of ointment to a burn.* **3.** something put on or applied: *This application will soothe the sore area.* **4.** capacity of being usable or suitable; relevance: *Her testimony has no application to the case.* **5.** a way of being used or applied: *This computer program has a number of applications.* **6.** a request made personally or in writing: *His application for a transfer was denied.* **7.** a written form used in making such a request: *Fill out this application.* **8.** close or diligent attention: *application to one's studies.* [Latin *applicātiō* a joining to, from *applicāre* to join to. See APPLY.]

ap·pli·ca·tor (ap′li kā′tər) *n.* a device for applying something, such as shoe polish, paint, or medicine.

ap·plied (ə plīd′) *adj.* used to work out actual problems; put to practical use: *applied science, applied mathematics.*

ap·pli·qué (ap′li kā′) *n.* a design or decoration made separately and then sewed or otherwise fastened to the background. —*adj.* decorated in this way. —*v.t.,* -**quéd,** -**qué·ing.** to decorate with or apply as appliqué. [French *appliqué,* past participle of *appliquer* to fasten to, from Latin *applicāre* to join to. See APPLY.]

ap·ply (ə plī′) *v.,* -**plied,** -**ply·ing.** —*v.t.* **1.** to put into use or practice; employ: *Learn how to apply your knowledge. He applied pressure on the other committee members to make them vote against the proposal.* **2.** to bring into contact with something; put on: *to apply a bandage to a wound, to apply paint to a wall.* **3.** to use (a word or statement) to refer to a particular person or thing: *That term is rarely applied to animals.* **4.** to devote (oneself) diligently; use (one's resources) fully: *She applied herself to her studies.* —*v.i.* **1.** to make a request; ask (with *for*): *to apply for a loan.* **2.** to have relevance or reference; be suitable; fit: *That principle doesn't apply here.* [Old French *aplier* to bring to, present, from Latin *applicāre* to join to, turn toward, from *ap-* ap-[1] + *plicare* to double up, fold[1].] —**ap·pli′er,** *n.*

ap·pog·gia·tu·ra (ə poj′ə tur′ə, -tyur′ə) *n.* a musical note that precedes and ornaments an essential note of a melody. The **long appoggiatura** takes away a portion of the time value of the note it precedes, while the **short appoggiatura** does not. [Italian *appoggiatura* literally, support, from *appoggiare* to lean on, going back to Latin *ad-* to + *podium* elevated place. See PODIUM.]

ap·point (ə point′) *v.t.* **1.** to name or select for an office or position: *He was just appointed chairman of the committee.* **2.** to arrange or determine by agreement or authority; fix: *The judge appointed the trial date. The secretary appointed a meeting place.* **3.** to furnish; equip. ➡ now commonly used chiefly in combination in the past participle: *a well-appointed ship, beautifully appointed lodgings.* [Old French *apointier* to fix, arrange, going back to Latin *ad* to + *pūnctum* point. See POINT.]

ap·point·ee (ə poin tē′, ap′oin tē′) *n.* a person named to an office or position: *a political appointee.*

ap·poin·tive (ə poin′tiv) *adj.* of or filled by appointment rather than election: *an appointive office.*

ap·point·ment (ə point′mənt) *n.* **1.** a naming or selecting for an office or position: *The vacancy on the finance committee was filled by appointment.* **2.** an office or position so filled: *a high appointment in government.* **3.** an arrangement to meet someone or to be somewhere; engagement: *I have an appointment at six o'clock.* **4. appointments.** furnishings; equipment.

Synonyms Appointment, engagement, rendezvous, and date mean an agreement to meet another or others, especially at a given place and time. **Appointment** emphasizes preciseness of scheduling and generally refers to time rather than place: *I have an appointment with the doctor at noon.* En-

gagement stresses the obligation to meet or attend: *I'd love to come to dinner, but I have another engagement.* **Rendezvous** emphasizes place rather than time and often implies secrecy: *They arranged a rendezvous in a restaurant where no one would recognize them.* **Date** is quite informal and suggests entertainment or romance rather than business or necessity: *We made a date to see a movie Thursday.*

ap·por·tion (ə pôr′shən) *v.t.* to divide and distribute proportionally or according to a rule or plan; allot. [Middle French *apportionner,* from *a-* to (from Latin *ad* to) + *portionner* to share (going back to Latin *portiō* a share).] —For Synonyms, see **assign.**

ap·por·tion·ment (ə pôr′shən mənt) *n.* **1.** the act of apportioning or the state of being apportioned. **2.** the assignment, based upon the proportionate share of the population, of the number of representatives that a state may have in the U.S. House of Representatives or that any other political division may have in its legislative body.

ap·pose (ə pōz′) *v.t.,* -**posed,** -**pos·ing. 1.** to arrange side by side or close together; juxtapose. **2.** *Archaic.* to put or apply (one thing) to another. [Middle French *aposer* to set beside, modification (influenced by Old French *poser* to place, put) of Latin *appōnere* to place to, apply.]

ap·po·site (ap′ə zit, ə poz′it) *adj.* well-suited or adapted; appropriate; pertinent: *an apposite remark.* [Latin *appositus,* past participle of *appōnere* to place to, apply, from *ad* to + *ponere* to place, put.] —**ap′po·site·ly,** *adv.* —**ap′po·site·ness,** *n.*

ap·po·si·tion (ap′ə zish′ən) *n.* **1.** *Grammar.* **a.** the placing of a noun or a noun phrase near another noun or noun phrase so that the second explains or supplements and has the same grammatical construction as the first. **b.** the syntactical relationship between such words. In the sentence *Susy, my sister, lives next door,* the word *Susy* and the phrase *my sister* are in apposition. **2.** the act of apposing or the state of being apposed; juxtaposition. —**ap′po·si′tion·al,** *adj.* —**ap′po·si′tion·al·ly,** *adv.*

ap·pos·i·tive (ə poz′i tiv) *n.* a word, phrase, or clause in apposition. —*adj.* of, relating to, or placed in apposition. —**ap·pos′i·tive·ly,** *adv.*

ap·prais·al (ə prā′zəl) *n.* **1.** the act of appraising or the state of being appraised. **2.** a price or value assigned, esp. by an expert; valuation; estimate. Also, **ap·praise′ment.**

ap·praise (ə prāz′) *v.t.,* -**praised,** -**prais·ing. 1.** to estimate the monetary value of; fix a price for: *to appraise land for taxation, to appraise a diamond for insurance purposes.* **2.** to evaluate the quality or significance of; judge: *to appraise a person's character, to appraise a situation.* —**ap·prais′er,** *n.* —**ap·prais′ing·ly,** *adv.*

ap·pre·ci·a·ble (ə prē′shə bəl) *adj.* enough to be felt or noticed; perceptible: *Your work has shown an appreciable improvement.* —**ap·pre′cia·bly,** *adv.*

ap·pre·ci·ate (ə prē′shē āt′) *v.,* -**at·ed,** -**at·ing.** —*v.t.* **1.** to recognize the worth or quality of; value or regard highly: *The artist's work was not appreciated by his own generation.* **2.** to be grateful for: *I appreciate your kindness.* **3.** to be keenly sensitive to or sensible of: *She's incapable of appreciating the subtleties of your argument.* **4.** to perceive the full nature or effect of; be fully conscious of: *I appreciate all the dangers involved in such an experiment.* **5.** to raise in value. —*v.i.* to rise in value: *This stock has appreciated 20%.* [Late Latin *appretiātus,* past participle of *appretiāre* to value at a price, appraise, from Latin *ad* to + *pretium* value, reward.]

ap·pre·ci·a·tion (ə prē′shē ā′shən) *n.* **1.** the act of recognizing the worth or quality of: *The response of the audience showed an appreciation of the pianist's talent.* **2.** a sensitive or discriminating understanding: *to have a keen appreciation of classical literature.* **3.** gratitude. **4.** an increase in value.

ap·pre·ci·a·tive (ə prē′shə tiv, -shē ā′tiv) *adj.* feeling or showing appreciation: *an appreciative audience.* —**ap·pre′cia·tive·ly,** *adv.* —**ap·pre′cia·tive·ness,** *n.* —For Synonyms, see **grateful.**

ap·pre·hend (ap′ri hend′) *v.t.* **1.** to seize (someone) on legal or other authority; capture; detain: *The police apprehended the burglar.* **2.** to grasp mentally; be aware of; understand: *Do you apprehend the meaning of what was said?* **3.** to anticipate with fear; dread: *I sometimes apprehend that our institutions may perish* (Nathaniel Hawthorne, 1868). [Latin *apprehendere* to seize, grasp mentally, from *ad* to + *prehendere* to seize, take.]

ap·pre·hen·sion (ap′ri hen′shən) *n.* **1.** fear of what may happen; anxiety; foreboding. **2.** a seizure on legal or other authority; capture. **3.** the act of grasping mentally; understanding. [Late Latin *apprehēnsiō* seizing upon, understanding, from Latin *apprehendere.* See APPREHEND.]

Synonyms Apprehension, anxiety, and worry mean a state of troubled concern. **Apprehension** suggests a continuing state of fear over what may happen: *I spent the weeks before the flight in apprehension.* **Anxiety** stresses the nervous discomfort involved and does not necessarily indicate an object of concern: *inability to concentrate on work because of a vague anxiety.* **Worry** suggests fear for or about someone or something specific: *The blizzard that began after they left increased our worry for them.*

ap·pre·hen·sive (ap′ri hen′siv) *adj.* fearful about what may happen; uneasy. —**ap′pre·hen′sive·ly,** *adv.* —**ap′pre·hen′sive·ness,** *n.*

ap·pren·tice (ə pren′tis) *n.* **1.a.** a person who was bound by contract to serve a medieval guild or master for a specified time, in return for instruction in a craft or trade. **b.** a person who is learning a trade or art. An apprentice is usually so classified for a specified period of time, during which he or she works with skilled workers for reduced pay. **2.** any person lacking skill or experience; beginner. —*v.t.,* **-ticed, -tic·ing.** to take on or place as an apprentice. [Old French *aprentis* one who learns a trade, from *aprendre* to learn, from Latin *apprehendere* to seize, grasp mentally. See APPREHEND.]

ap·pren·tice·ship (ə pren′tis ship′) *n.* **1.** the condition or state of being an apprentice. **2.** the time period during which one works as an apprentice.

ap·prise (ə prīz′) *v.t.,* **-prised, -pris·ing.** to give notice to; inform; notify. [French *appris,* past participle of *apprendre* to inform, teach, learn, from Old French *aprendre* to learn. See APPREHEND.]

ap·proach (ə prōch′) *v.i.* to come near in space or time: *The racehorses approached the starting gate. The hour of attack is approaching.* —*v.t.* **1.** to come near or near to: *We heard singing as we approached the house.* **2.** to come near to, as in quality, time, or condition: *to approach adulthood, to approach perfection.* **3.** to go to with a proposal or request; make overtures to: *We approached them about making a large donation to the charity.* **4.** to deal with; try to understand: *We should approach the problem from this angle.* —*n.* **1.** the act of coming or drawing near: *the approach of a car, the approach of fall.* **2.** a method used for dealing with or doing something: *We will try a different approach if this one fails.* **3.** a way of reaching; access: *The approach to the house was blocked.* **4.** a stroke in golf intended to place the ball on the putting green. [Old French *aprochier* to come near to, going back to Latin *ad* to + *prope* near.]

ap·proach·a·ble (ə prō′chə bəl) *adj.* **1.** possible to approach; accessible: *The town was approachable from only one direction.* **2.** easy to approach or talk to; friendly; affable. —**ap·proach′a·bil′i·ty,** *n.*

ap·pro·ba·tion (ap′rə bā′shən) *n.* **1.** the expression of a favorable opinion; praise; commendation. **2.** official approval: *The Senate gave its approbation to the bill.* [Latin *approbātiō* an approving, from *approbare* to approve. See APPROVE.]

ap·pro·pri·a·ble (ə prō′prē ə bəl) *adj.* capable of being appropriated.

ap·pro·pri·ate (*adj.,* ə prō′prē it; *v.,* ə prō′prē āt′) *adj.* particularly well-suited; fitting: *an appropriate remark, a dress appropriate for the occasion.* —*v.t.,* **-at·ed, -at·ing.** **1.** to set apart or assign for a particular use: *Congress appropriated funds for education.* **2.** to take for oneself, esp. without permission. [Late Latin *appropriātus,* past participle of *appropriāre* to make one's own, from Latin *ad* to + *proprius* one's own.] —**ap·pro′pri·ate·ly,** *adv.* —**ap·pro′pri·ate·ness,** *n.* —For Synonyms *(adj.),* see fit[1], proper.

ap·pro·pri·a·tion (ə prō′prē ā′shən) *n.* **1.** something appropriated, esp. a sum of public money set aside for a particular use. **2.** the act of appropriating or the state of being appropriated.

ap·prov·al (ə prü′vəl) *n.* **1.** favorable opinion; acceptance: *While the young people danced, their parents looked on with approval.* **2.** official consent; sanction: *We can't print your article without the editor's approval.*
   •**on approval.** subject to a customer's trial or examination before final sale.

ap·prove (ə prüv′) *v.,* **-proved, -prov·ing.** —*v.t.* **1.** to consider (something) satisfactory or acceptable; be favorable toward: *I can't approve the use of such business tactics.* **2.** to confirm officially; sanction: *Congress approved the budget.* —*v.i.* to have or give a favorable opinion (often with *of*): *I don't approve of their behavior.* [Old French *aprover* from Latin *approbāre,* from *ad* to + *probare* to test, try, prove.] —**ap·prov′er,** *n.* —**ap·prov′ing·ly,** *adv.*

Synonyms *v.t.* **Approve, endorse,** and **sanction** mean to favor or accept. **Approve** is the broadest of the three terms and may refer to either active or passive acceptance: *My friends approved the plan by their silence.* **Endorse** is more formal and implies an open statement of approval: *The voters endorsed the proposal in a referendum.* **Sanction** implies giving official or moral authority to something: *The church supported the protest but would not sanction violence.*

approx. 1. approximate. **2.** approximately.

ap·prox·i·mate (*adj.,* ə prok′sə mit; *v.,* ə prok′sə māt′) *adj.* **1.** nearly accurate or exact: *What is the approximate length of that table?* **2.** near to; close together. **3.** very similar; resembling. —*v.,* **-mat·ed, -mat·ing.** —*v.t.* **1.** to come close to (something) in quality, quantity, or degree: *Wind-tunnel conditions approximate those of actual flight.* **2.** to estimate: *Approximate the time it will take you to finish the job.* **3.** to bring close together. —*v.i.* to come close in quality, quantity, degree, or condition; be almost the same. [Late Latin *approximātus,* past participle of *approximāre* to come near to, from *ad* to + *proximare* to approach. See PROXIMATE.] —**ap·prox′i·mate·ly,** *adv.*

ap·prox·i·ma·tion (ə prok′sə mā′shən) *n.* **1.** the act or process of approximating. **2.** something approximate; estimate. **3.** a value that is not exact, but is accurate enough for a specified purpose: *The figure 3.14 is an approximation of the value of pi.*

ap·pur·te·nance (ə pûr′tə nəns) *n.* **1.** something added and subordinate; accessory. **2.** a subordinate right, privilege, or improvement attached to a property and passing with it, as by sale. [Anglo-Norman *apurtenance* accessory, from Old French *apartenir* to belong to, going back to Latin *ad* to + *pertinēre* to belong. See PERTAIN.]

ap·pur·te·nant (ə pûr′tə nənt) *adj.* appertaining or belonging, as a legal right. —*n.* appurtenance.

Apr., April.

a·pri·cot (ā′pri kot′, ap′ri-) *n.* **1.** the orange-colored fruit of a tree, *Prunus armeniaca,* resembling a small peach but with a distinct aromatic flavor. **2.** the tree itself, native to eastern Asia and cultivated in mild climates. **3.** a pale orange-yellow color. [French *abricot* this fruit, from Portuguese *albricoque,* from Arabic *al-birqūq* the apricot, going back to Latin *(prūnum) praecoquum* early-ripe (plum), form of *praecox* early ripe; because it ripened before certain other fruits.]

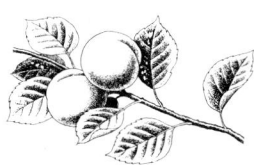

apricot leaves and fruit

A·pril (ā′prəl) *n.* the fourth month of the year, containing thirty days. [Modification of Middle English *Avril,* from Old French *avrill,* from Latin *aprilis.*]

April Fool, a person at whose expense a trick or joke is played on April Fools' Day.

April Fools' Day, the first day of April, traditional day for playing tricks and practical jokes. Also, **All Fools' Day.**

a pri·o·ri (ā′prī ôr′ī) **1.** proceeding from the general to the particular, or from cause to effect; deductive. **2.** innate in the mind, rather than resulting from experience. ➡ opposed to **a posteriori** in defs. 1 and 2. **3.** made or arrived at prior to investigation or analysis: *an a priori judgment.* [Latin phrase *ā priorī* from (something) before.]

a·pron (ā′prən) *n.* **1.** a garment worn over the front of the body, for protection of one's clothes or person or as decoration. **2.** any of various things resembling an apron in use, position, or shape, as a protective metal plate covering machine parts. **3.** the hard-surfaced area in front of an airplane hangar. **4.** the part of a stage in front of the curtain. [Earlier *napron,* from Old French *naperon* napkin, diminutive of *nape* tablecloth, modification of Latin *mappa* cloth. The phrase *a napron* came to be divided incorrectly as *an apron.* For a similar development, see ADDER.]

apron string, one of two strings of an apron, used for tying it on.
   •**tied to (someone's) apron strings.** dependent on or dominated by someone, as a mother or wife.

ap·ro·pos (ap′rə pō′) *adj.* suited to an occasion; pertinent; fitting: *an apropos remark.* —*adv.* to the purpose; pertinently. [French phrase *à propos* to the purpose, going back to Latin *ad* to + *prōpositum* plan, purpose.]

a	at	e	end	o	hot	u	up	hw	white		about
ā	ape	ē	me	ō	old	ū	use	ng	song	ə	taken
ä	far	i	it	ô	fork	u	rule	th	thin		pencil
âr	care	ī	ice	oi	oil	u	pull	th	this		lemon
		îr	pierce	ou	out	ûr	turn	zh	measure		circus

•**apropos of.** with regard to; in relation to: *My question is apropos of the letter I received.*

apse (aps) *n.* **1.** in a building, esp. at the east end of a church, a recess, usually semicircular, with a domed or vaulted ceiling. **2.** apsis *(def. 1).* [Latin *apsis* arch, vault. See APSIS.]

ap·sis (ap′sis) *n., pl.* **-si·des** (-si dēz′). **1.** either of two points in an astronomical orbit. At the **lower apsis** the orbiting body is nearest to the center of attraction; at the **higher apsis** it is farthest away. **2.** apse *(def. 1).* [Latin *apsis* arch, vault, from Greek *hapsis,* from *haptein* to fasten.]

apt (apt) *adj.* **1.** having a tendency; predisposed; inclined: *The baby is apt to cry when tired.* **2.** having a good chance; likely: *The store is apt to be closed.* **3.** to the point; appropriate: *an apt quotation.* **4.** quick to learn; gifted: *an apt student.* [Latin *aptus* fitted, suited.] —**apt′ly,** *adv.* —**apt′ness,** *n.*

apt. *pl.,* **apts.** apartment.

ap·ter·ous (ap′tər əs) *adj.* (of an insect) lacking wings. [Greek *apteros* wingless, from *a-* A-[4] + *pteron* wing.]

ap·ter·yx (ap′tər iks) *n.* kiwi *(def. 1).*

ap·ti·tude (ap′ti tüd′, -tyüd′) *n.* **1.** a natural ability or capacity; talent: *an aptitude for languages.* **2.** quickness in learning or understanding: *a music student of great aptitude.* [Late Latin *aptitūdō* fitness, from Latin *aptus* fit, suited. Doublet of ATTITUDE.] —For Synonyms, see **ability.**

aptitude test, a test given to determine a person's capacity for learning or doing any of a number of specified types of work.

aq·ua[1] (ak′wə, ä′kwə) *n., pl.* **aq·uae** (ak′wē, ä′kwē) or **aq·uas.** **1.** water. **2.** a solution formed of some substance dissolved in water. [Latin *aqua* water.]

aq·ua[2] (ak′wə, ä′kwə) *n.* a light greenish blue color. —*adj.* having the color aqua. [Short for AQUAMARINE.]

aq·ua·cul·ture (ak′wə kul′chər, ä′kwə-) *also,* **aquiculture.** *n.* the raising of aquatic animals and plants, such as shellfish and seaweed, for human use and consumption; underwater agriculture.

aqua for·tis (fôr′tis) nitric acid. [Latin *aqua* water + *fortis* strong.]

aq·ua·lung (ak′wə lung′, ä′kwə-) *n.* a device for breathing underwater, having a valve that supplies air according to demand; scuba. *Trademark:* **Aqua-Lung.**

aq·ua·ma·rine (ak′wə mə rēn′, ä′kwə-) *n.* **1.** transparent beryl of a pale blue or bluish green variety, used as a gem. **2.** a bluish green color. —*adj.* having the color aquamarine. [Latin *aqua marīna* seawater.]

aq·ua·naut (ak′wə nôt′, ä′kwə-) *n.* a person who lives in an underwater chamber for the purpose of conducting oceanographic research and experiments. [Latin *aqua* water + Greek *nautēs* sailor.]

aq·ua·plane (ak′wə plān′, ä′kwə-) *n.* a board on which a person can stand and ride across the surface of the water while being towed by a motorboat. —*v.i.,* **-planed, -plan·ing.** to ride an aquaplane. —**aq′ua·plan′er,** *n.*

aqua re·gi·a (rē′jē ə) a mixture of one part nitric acid and three parts hydrochloric acid, used to dissolve gold and platinum. [Latin *aqua regia* literally, royal water, because it dissolves "royal" metals.]

a·quar·i·um (ə kwâr′ē əm) *n., pl.* **-i·ums** or **-i·a** (-ē ə). **1.** a tank, bowl, or similar container, partly of glass or other transparent material, in which aquatic animals and plants can be kept alive and easily observed. **2.** an establishment where aquatic life is kept for exhibition or study. [Latin *aquārium* (thing) having to do with water, from *aqua* water.]

A·quar·i·us (ə kwâr′ē əs) *n.* **1.** a constellation near the celestial equator, conventionally depicted as a man pouring water out of a vase. **2.** the eleventh sign of the zodiac. [Latin *aquārius* water bearer, from *aqua* water.]

a·quat·ic (ə kwat′ik, ə kwot′-) *adj.* **1.** of, in, or relating to water: *an aquatic environment.* **2.** (of a plant or animal) growing or living in or near water. **3.** performed in or on water: *Swimming and skin diving are aquatic sports.* —*n.* **aquatics.** performances on or in water; water sports. [Latin *aquāticus* having to do with water, from *aqua* water.] —**a·quat′i·cal·ly,** *adv.*

aq·ua·tint (ak′wə tint′, ä′kwə-) *n.* **1.** a process in which spaces are etched on copperplate with acid so as to produce a print resembling an ink or wash drawing. **2.** a print or plate made in this way. —*v.t.* to etch by this process. [French *aquatinte* this kind of print, from Italian *acqua tinta,* going back to Latin *aqua* water + *tincta,* feminine past participle of *tingere* to dye.]

aqua vi·tae (vī′tē) **1.** alcohol. **2.** strong liquor, as brandy or whiskey. [Medieval Latin *aqua vitae* water of life; possibly so called because strong liquor was used medicinally.]

aq·ue·duct (ak′wə dukt′) *n.* **1.** an artificial channel, pipe, or other conduit for carrying water, esp. over long distances. **2.** a

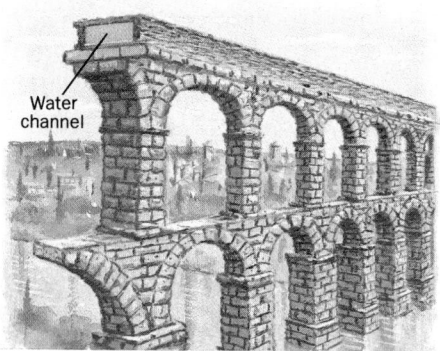

Roman **aqueduct**

structure supporting such a conduit. **3.** a canal or passage for conducting fluids in the body. [Latin *aquae ductus* conveyance of water.]

a·que·ous (ā′kwē əs, ak′wē-) *adj.* **1.** of, like, or containing water; watery: *an aqueous solution.* **2.** (of rock) sedimentary. [Medieval Latin *aqueus* relating to water, from Latin *aqua* water.]

aqueous humor, in the eye, the clear watery fluid filling the space between the cornea and the lens. For illustration, see **eye**[1].

aq·ui·cul·ture (ak′wə kul′chər, ä′kwə-) aquaculture.

aq·ui·fer (ak′wə fər) *n.* an underground bed of rock, sand, or gravel that holds ground water or conducts it elsewhere, esp. to springs or wells. [Modern Latin *aquifer,* from Latin *aqua* water + *-fer* bearing, from *ferre* to bear.]

Aq·ui·la (ak′wə lə) *n.* a constellation in the northern sky containing the bright star Altair, conventionally depicted as a flying eagle, sometimes carrying a boy in its talons. [Latin *aquila* eagle.]

aq·ui·le·gi·a (ak′wə lē′jē ə) *n.* columbine. [Modern Latin *aquilegia,* from Medieval Latin *aquileia,* from Latin *aquila* eagle; because of its spurred flower.]

aq·ui·line (ak′wə līn′, -lin) *adj.* **1.** (of the nose) curved, sharply defined, and prominent, like an eagle's beak. **2.** of or like an eagle. [Latin *aquilīnus* relating to the eagle, from *aquila* eagle.]

a·quiv·er (ə kwiv′ər) *adj.* trembling; quivering: *all aquiver with excitement.*

Ar, the symbol for argon.

ar-, form of ad- before *r,* as in *array.*

-ar[1] *suffix* (used to form adjectives) of, like, or having the nature of (the stem): *lunar, angular, similar.* [Latin *-āris* belonging to, having the form of.]

-ar[2] *suffix* (used to form nouns) a person or thing connected with (the stem): *vicar, scholar, pillar, collar.* [Latin *-ārius* relating to.]

-ar[3] form of -er[1] or -or, as in *liar, beggar.*

AR, the postal abbreviation for Arkansas.

Ar·ab (ar′əb) *n.* **1.a.** a member or close descendant of a Semitic people inhabiting southwestern Asia and North Africa. **b.** before the Islamic expansion, a tribal people inhabiting Arabia and the Syrian Desert. **2.** a native or inhabitant of Arabia. **3.** Bedouin. **4.** Arabian horse. —*adj.* of or relating to Arabia or the Arabs or their culture. [Latin *Arabs* Arabian, from Greek *Araps,* from Arabic *'arab* Arabia.]

ar·a·besque (ar′ə besk′) *n.* **1.** a design consisting of elaborately intertwined patterns of scrollwork, flowers, leaves, or other figures. **2.** a position in ballet in which the dancer stands with one leg lifted in full extension backward and, usually, with one arm extended forward and the other back. **3.** a short musical piece in rondo form. —*adj.* **1.** relating to or done in the style of arabesque. **2.** resembling arabesque; full of ornamentation; fanciful. [French *arabesque,* from Italian *arabesco* in the Arabian manner, going back to Latin *Arabs.* See ARAB.]

arabesque *(def. 1)*

A·ra·bi·an (ə rā′bē ən) *adj.* of or relating to Arabia or its people or culture. —*n.* **1.** a member or close descendant of the people of Arabia. **2.** Arab.

Arabian horse, any of a breed of graceful saddle horses, originally bred in Arabia, noted for their speed.

Arabian Nights, a collection of tales from Arabia, Persia, and India, dating from the tenth century A.D.

Ar·a·bic (ar'ə bik) *adj.* of, relating to, or characteristic of the Arabs, their language, or their culture. —*n.* the Semitic language predominant in most of the Middle East and North Africa, originally spoken by the Arabs of the Arabian peninsula but extended to its present extent by the Islamic conquests. For alphabet table, see **alphabet.**

Words from Arabic

Arabic, a Semitic language spoken primarily in the Middle East and northern Africa, has contributed many important words to English. Key terms in mathematics and astronomy, as well as in science and technology, have come into English from or through Arabic. Long used as a language of trade, Arabic has also contributed many other words to English, including names of foods and spices.

admiral	caraway	jar	saffron
albatross	carmine	jasmine	sahib
alcalde	carob	jennet	salaam
alcazar	casaba	kismet	sash
alchemy	cipher	kohl	satin
alcohol	coffee	Koran	sequin
alcove	cotton	lilac	sheik
alembic	couscous	lime	sherbet
alfalfa	crimson	lute	shrub
algebra	dragoman	magazine	sirocco
Algol	elixir	marabou	sofa
alkali	emir	marcasite	spinach
Allah	fakir	mask	sugar
amber	fellah	massage	sultan
apricot	gazelle	minaret	sultana
arsenal	genie	mohair	sumac
artichoke	ghoul	monsoon	syrup
assassin	giraffe	mosque	tabby
attar	harem	muezzin	talc
azimuth	hashish	mufti	talisman
Bedouin	hazard	mummy	tamarind
caliber	Hegira	nadir	tariff
caliph	henna	popinjay	tuna
camphor	hookah	ream	vizier
candy	houri	roc	wadi
carafe	imam	safari	zenith
carat	Islam	safflower	zero

Arabic numerals, the symbols 1, 2, 3, 4, 5, 6, 7, 8, 9, and 0. Also, **Hindu-Arabic numerals.**

ar·a·ble (ar'ə bəl) *adj.* (of land) fit for plowing or cultivation. [Latin *arābilis,* from *arāre* to plow.] —**ar'a·bil'i·ty,** *n.*

Arab League, an organization of independent Arab states, formed in 1945 to promote Arab cultural, political, and economic cooperation.

Ar·a·by (ar'ə bē) *n. Archaic.* Arabia.

A·rach·ne (ə rak'nē) *n.* in Greek legend, a Lydian maiden changed into a spider by Athena for daring to challenge the goddess to a weaving contest. [Greek *arachnē* spider.]

a·rach·nid (ə rak'nid) *n.* any of a large group of air-breathing arthropods, class Arachnida, characteristically having four pairs of legs, no wings or antennas, and a body divided into two parts, an abdomen and a cephalothorax. Spiders, mites, scorpions, and ticks are arachnids. [Greek *arachnē* spider + -ID².] —**a·rach'ni·dan,** *adj., n.*

a·rach·noid (ə rak'noid) *adj.* **1.** of or resembling the arachnids. **2.** designating the membrane covering the brain and the spinal cord that lies between the dura mater and the pia mater. **3.** (of a plant) covered with or consisting of long, slender hairs or fibers. —*n.* **1.** the arachnoid membrane. **2.** an arachnid. [Greek *arachnoeidēs* like a spider's web, from *arachnē* spider.]

a·rag·o·nite (ə rag'ə nīt', ar'ə gə-) *n.* a translucent, white mineral that, like calcite, is a polymorphous form of crystalline calcium carbonate and is found in coral reefs, pearls, and some seashells. Formula: $CaCO_3$ [From *Aragon,* Spain, where it was first found.]

Ar·a·ma·ic (ar'ə mā'ik) *n.* an ancient Semitic language, or group of dialects, widely used in the ancient Middle East, 600? B.C.-A.D. 800?, as a language of trade and government. It was the language of Jesus.

ar·a·mid (ar'ə mid) *n.* any of a group of synthetic polymer fibers that are esp. suited for making products that combine great strength with light weight, used in radial tires and bulletproof vests.

A·rap·a·ho (ə rap'ə hō') *n., pl.* -**ho** or -**hos. 1.** a member of a North American Indian tribe that lived in Wyoming and Colorado. **2.** the Algonquian language of this tribe. —*adj.* of, relating to, or characteristic of the Arapaho or their language or culture.

Ar·au·ca·ni·an (ar'ô kä'nē ən) *n.* **1.** a member of a group of South American Indian tribes living predominantly in Chile. **2.** any of the several closely related languages spoken by these people and constituting a separate language family. —*adj.* of, relating to, or characteristic of the Araucanians or their languages or culture. [Spanish *araucano* relating to the Araucanians, from *Arauco,* province in Chile.]

Ar·a·wak (ar'ə wak') *n., pl.* -**wak** or -**waks. 1.** a member of a Central American and South American Indian tribe that lived in the West Indies, Venezuela, and Colombia. **2.** the language of this tribe.

A·ra·wa·kan (ar'ə wak'ən) *n.* **1.** a widespread family of South American Indian languages, including Arawak and Taino. **2.** a member of a tribe speaking one of these languages. —*adj.* of or relating to this family of languages.

ar·ba·lest (är'bə ləst) *also,* **ar·ba·list.** *n.* a medieval crossbow having a bow so strong that a special mechanism was needed to bend it. [Old French *arbaleste* crossbow, from Late Latin *arcubal lista* ballista with a bow, from Latin *arcus* bow + *ballista.* See BALLISTA.]

ar·bi·ter (är'bi tər) *n.* **1.** a person or organization whose opinion or decision is authoritative or final: *an arbiter of taste.* **2.** a person chosen to settle a dispute; arbitrator. [Old French *arbitre,* from Latin *arbiter* judge; literally, one who goes to see (in order to judge).]

ar·bi·tra·ble (är'bi trə bəl) *adj.* capable of being arbitrated; suitable for arbitration.

ar·bi·trage (är'bi träzh') *n.* the simultaneous purchase and sale of currency, securities, or commodities in two different financial markets in order to profit from price discrepancies. —*v.i.,* -**traged,** -**traging.** to engage in arbitrage. [French *arbitrage,* from *arbitrer* to judge + -*age.* See -AGE.]

ar·bi·tral (är'bi trəl) *adj.* of or relating to an arbiter or arbitration.

ar·bit·ra·ment (är bit'rə mənt) *n.* **1.** arbitration. **2.** the decision or award made by an arbitrator. **3.** *Archaic.* the power of absolute and final decision.

ar·bi·trar·y (är'bi trer'ē) *adj.* **1.** based on individual will, choice, or judgment; discretionary: *an arbitrary interpretation.* **2.** not limited or controlled by law; having unlimited power; despotic: *harsh and arbitrary government.* **3.** based on whim or chance, rather than calculation or reason: *an arbitrary choice.* **4.** subject to a judge's decision; not fixed by law. [Latin *arbitrārius* relating to arbitration, uncertain, from *arbiter* judge (reflecting the uncertainty of judges' decisions).] —**ar'bi·trar'i·ly,** *adv.* —**ar'bi·trar'i·ness,** *n.*

ar·bi·trate (är'bi trāt') *v.,* -**trat·ed,** -**trat·ing.** —*v.t.* **1.** to decide as arbitrator; settle: *Who is arbitrating this dispute?* **2.** to settle by or submit to arbitration: *Both parties decided to arbitrate their disagreement.* —*v.i.* **1.** to act as arbitrator. **2.** to submit a dispute to arbitration. [Latin *arbitrātus,* past participle of *arbitrārī* to give judgment, from *arbiter* judge.]

ar·bi·tra·tion (är'bi trā'shən) *n.* the hearing and settlement of a dispute by an arbitrator or arbitrators.

ar·bi·tra·tor (är'bi trā'tər) *n.* **1.** a person chosen by parties in a dispute to settle or decide their differences. **2.** a person who has the power to make final decisions; arbiter.

ar·bor¹ (är'bər) *also, British,* **arbour.** *n.* an area covered over and partly enclosed on the sides by trees, shrubs, or a vine-covered trellis, esp. such an area in a garden. [Anglo-Norman *erber* place where grass or herbs are grown, going back to Latin *herba* grass, herb.]

---

a	at	e	end	o	hot	u	up	hw	white
ā	ape	ē	me	ō	old	ū	use	ng	song
ä	far	i	it	ô	fork	ü	rule	th	thin
âr	care	ī	ice	oi	oil	u̇	pull	th	this
		îr	pierce	ou	out	ûr	turn	zh	measure

ə { about, taken, pencil, lemon, circus }

ar·bor² (är′bər) *n.* the main shaft or beam of a machine; axle; spindle. [Latin *arbor* tree, pole.]

Arbor Day, a day set aside in many states of the United States for planting trees. The date varies from state to state but is usually in the spring.

ar·bo·re·al (är bôr′ē əl) *adj.* **1.** of or relating to trees; treelike. **2.** living in trees or adapted for living in trees. Squirrels and monkeys are arboreal animals. —**ar·bo′re·al·ly,** *adv.*

ar·bo·res·cent (är′bə res′ənt) *adj.* treelike in structure, appearance, or growth; branching. —**ar′bo·res′cence,** *n.*

ar·bo·re·tum (är′bə rē′təm) *n., pl.* **-tums** or **-ta** (-tə). a botanical garden devoted primarily to trees and shrubs. [Latin *arborētum* place grown with trees, from *arbor* tree.]

ar·bor·vi·tae (är′bər vī′tē) *n.* any of various evergreen shrubs or trees, genus *Thuja,* of the cypress family, characterized by scalelike aromatic leaves. Many varieties are used as ornamental trees, as hedges, or as windbreaks. [Latin *arbor* tree + *vītae* of life.]

ar·bour (är′bər) *British.* arbor¹.

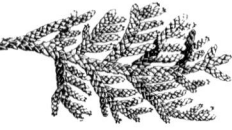

arborvitae leaves

ar·bo·vi·rus (är′bə vī′rəs) *n.* any of a group of RNA-bearing viruses that are transmitted by bloodsucking arthropods, as mosquitoes and ticks. Among the arboviruses are those that cause yellow fever and viral encephalitis. [Short for *ar(thropod) bo(rne)* virus.]

ar·bu·tus (är bū′təs) *n., pl.* **-tus·es. 1.** a trailing evergreen plant, *Epigaea repens,* found in North America, that bears fragrant pink or white flowers in early spring. Also, **mayflower, trailing arbutus. 2.** any of various evergreen shrubs or trees, genus *Arbutus,* of the heath family, bearing clusters of white or pink flowers and scarlet or orange berries. [Latin *arbūtus* strawberry tree.]

arc (ärk) *n.* **1.** a continuous curved line between any two points on a circle; part of the circumference of a circle. **2.** a curved line or shape. **3.** an intensely hot and bright electric current flowing in the gap between two electrodes, used in arc lamps. **4.** part of the circular course that the sun or other heavenly body seems to follow as the earth rotates. —*v.i.,* **arced** or **arcked, arc·ing** or **arck·ing. 1.** to form an electric arc. **2.** to move in a curved line. [Old French *arc,* from Latin *arcus* bow, arch.] —**arc′like′,** *adj.*

ARC (ärk) AIDS-related complex.

ar·cade (är kād′) *n.* **1.** a passageway covered by an arched roof. **2.** any covered passageway, street, or area opening onto a street, esp. one with shops along both sides. **3.** a row of arches with their supporting columns and piers. An arcade may be ornamental, as a **blind arcade,** or it may function as an architectural support. **4.** a building, room, or space filled with coin-operated game machines. —*v.t.,* **-cad·ed, -cad·ing.** to provide with or form into an arcade. [French *arcade* arch, from Italian *arcata* arch, span, going back to Latin *arcus* bow, vault.]

Ar·ca·di·a (är kā′dē ə) *also,* **arcadia.** *n.* a rural region of ideal calm, pleasantness, and simplicity. [From *Arcadia,* region of ancient Greece traditionally known for the simple lifestyle of its inhabitants.]

Ar·ca·di·an (är kā′dē ən) *adj.* **1.** of, relating to, or characteristic of Arcadia or its people or culture. **2.** *also,* **arcadian.** rustically simple, pleasant, and calm; pastoral. —*n.* **1.** a native or inhabitant of Arcadia. **2.** *also,* **arcadian.** a person who favors a simple and pleasant rural way of life.

Ar·ca·dy (är′kə dē) *n. Poetry.* Arcadia.

ar·cane (är kān′) *adj.* known or understood by only a few; secret; mysterious; obscure. [Latin *arcānus* hidden, secret.]

ar·ca·num (är kā′nəm) *n., pl.* **-na** (-nə). **1.** a secret or mystery: *the arcana of political intrigue.* **2.** a secret remedy; elixir. [Latin *arcānum* a secret, from *arcanus* hidden, secret.]

Arc de Tri·omphe (ärk də trē ônf′) a monumental arch in Paris built by Napoleon Bonaparte to commemorate the victories of his troops. Also, **Arch of Triumph.**

arch¹ (ärch) *n.* **1.** a structural feature, esp. a curved one, that rests on its two extremities and spans a space. It is usually constructed to support the weight of material above it, but may be merely ornamental. The traditional masonry arch consists of wedge-shaped blocks fitted together in a semicircle or similar shape. **2.** a monument consisting of an arch or arches. **3.a.** a

curved line or shape: *the arch of an eyebrow.* **b.** something like an arch in shape or function. **4.** the raised, curved part of the foot between the ball and the heel. **5.** archway. —*v.t.* **1.** to form (something) into an arch; curve: *The cat arched its back.* **2.** to cover or span with or as if with an arch: *The bridge arched the stream.* —*v.i.* to have the form of an arch: *The tree branches arched overhead.* [Old French *arche* vault, chest, going back to Latin *arcus* bow, vault.]

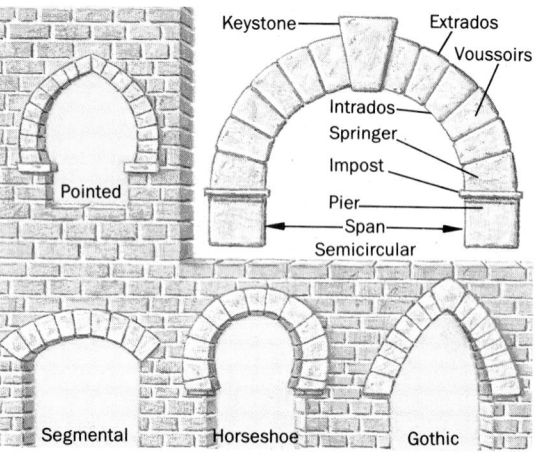

arch¹ *(def. 1)*

arch² (ärch) *adj.* **1.** playfully mischievous; roguish: *an arch smile.* **2.** most eminent; chief; leading: *an arch villain.* [From ARCH-.] —**arch′ly,** *adv.* —**arch′ness,** *n.*

arch- *prefix* **1.** chief; principal: *archbishop, archangel, archenemy.* **2.** original; primitive: *archenteron.* **3.** most extreme or characteristic of its kind: *archconservative.* [Often through Latin *arch(i)-,* from Greek *arch(i)-,* from *archos* chief, from *arche* beginning, from *archein* to begin, take the lead, rule.]

arch. **1.** archaic. **2.** archaism. **3.** archery. **4.** archipelago. **5.** architect. **6.** architectural. **7.** architecture.

Arch., Archbishop.

Ar·chae·an (är kē′ən) Archean.

archaeo- *combining form* ancient; primitive: *archaeology, archaeopteryx.* [Greek *archaios* ancient, from *arche* beginning.]

ar·chae·o·log·i·cal (är′kē ə loj′i kəl) *also,* **archeological.** *adj.* of or relating to archaeology. —**ar′chae·o·log′i·cal·ly,** *adv.*

ar·chae·ol·o·gist (är′kē ol′ə jist) *also,* **archeologist.** *n.* a specialist in archaeology.

ar·chae·ol·o·gy (är′kē ol′ə jē) *also,* **archeology.** *n.* the scientific study of the human past through excavation of former dwelling sites or other places of activity and examination of the physical remains thus discovered, such as tools, artifacts, or architecture. [Greek *archaiologia* study of antiquity.]

ar·chae·op·ter·yx (är′kē op′tər iks) *n.* an extinct primitive bird, genus *Archaeopteryx,* that had many reptilian characteristics, such as teeth, in addition to wings and feathers, found in German fossils from the Jurassic period. [Modern Latin *archaeopteryx,* from ARCHAEO- + Greek *pteryx* wing, bird.]

Ar·chae·o·zo·ic (är′kē ə zō′ik) *also,* **Archeozoic.** *n.* Archean.

ar·cha·ic (är kā′ik) *adj.* **1.** no longer in common use in speech or writing. *Thou* and *thy* are archaic forms of *you* and *your.* **2.** out-of-date; antiquated; old-fashioned. **3.** belonging to an earlier period; ancient. [Greek *archaïkos* old-fashioned, from *archaios* ancient.] —**ar·cha′i·cal·ly,** *adv.*

ar·cha·ism (är′kē iz′əm, är′kā-) *n.* **1.** something archaic, esp. an archaic word or phrase. **2.** the use of something archaic, esp. in language or art. —**ar′cha·ist,** *n.* —**ar′cha·is′tic,** *adj.*

arch·an·gel (ärk′ān′jəl) *n.* an angel of a high rank. [Old French *archangele,* from Late Latin *archangelus* chief angel, from Greek *archangelos,* from *arch-* arch- + *angelos* divine messenger.]

arch·bish·op (ärch′bish′əp) *n.* a bishop of the highest rank. An archbishop can be the chief bishop of an archdiocese or one holding an equivalent honorary rank. [Old English *arcebiscop,* from Church Latin *archiepiscopus,* from Greek *archiepiskopos* literally, chief overseer, from *arch-* arch- + *episkopos* overseer. See BISHOP.]

arch·bish·op·ric (ärch′bish′ə prik) *n.* **1.** archdiocese. **2.** the office, rank, or jurisdiction of an archbishop.

A

arch·con·serv·a·tive (ärch′kən sûr′və tiv) *adj.* extremely conservative. —*n.* an extremely conservative person.

arch·dea·con (ärch′dē′kən) *n.* a member of the clergy in the Anglican or Episcopal Church who serves as chief administrative officer in a diocese.

arch·dea·con·ate (ärch′dē′kə nit) *n.* archdeaconry *(def. 1).*

arch·dea·con·ry (ärch′dē′kən rē) *n., pl.* **-ries. 1.** the office, rank, or jurisdiction of an archdeacon. **2.** an archdeacon's residence.

arch·di·o·cese (ärch′dī′ə sis, -sēz′) *n., pl.* **-ces·es** (-sēz′, -sis′iz). a church district consisting of several dioceses. An archdiocese is governed by an archbishop. —**arch·di·oc·e·san** (ärch′dī os′ə sən), *adj.*

arch·du·cal (ärch′dü′kəl, -dū′-) *adj.* of or relating to an archduke or an archduchy.

arch·duch·ess (ärch′duch′is) *n.* **1.** the wife or widow of an archduke. **2.** a princess of the former royal family of Austria.

arch·duch·y (ärch′duch′ē) *n., pl.* **-duch·ies.** the territory ruled by an archduke or archduchess.

arch·duke (ärch′dük′, -dūk′-) *n.* **1.** a duke of superior authority or power. **2.** a prince of the former royal house of Austria. [Old French *archiduc,* going back to Latin *archi-* chief + *dux* leader.]

Ar·che·an (är kē′ən) *also,* **Archaean.** *n.* the earlier of the two geologic divisions (Proterozoic is the other) of the Precambrian era, during which the earth was formed and life began. Also, **Archeozoic, Archaeozoic.** —*adj.* of, relating to, or characteristic of the Archean. [Greek *archaios* ancient + *-AN*.]

arched (ärcht) *adj.* **1.** having the form of an arch. **2.** covered with or having an arch or arches.

ar·che·go·ni·um (är′ki gō′nē əm) *n., pl.* **-ni·a** (-nē ə). the female reproductive organ in ferns and mosses. [Modern Latin *archegonium,* diminutive of Greek *archegonos* original, primal, from *archein* to begin + *gonos* race.] —**ar′che·go′ni·al,** *adj.*

arch·en·e·my (ärch′en′ə mē) *n., pl.* **-mies.** a chief enemy.

ar·chen·ter·on (är ken′tə ron′) *n.* the digestive cavity of an animal embryo, formed during the gastrula stage. [ARCH- + Greek *enteron* intestine.]

archeo-, form of **archaeo-,** as in *archeology.*

ar·che·o·log·i·cal (är′kē ə loj′i kəl) *adj.* archaeological. —**ar′che·o·log′i·cal·ly,** *adv.*

ar·che·ol·o·gist (är′kē ol′ə jist) archaeologist.

ar·che·ol·o·gy (är′kē ol′ə jē) archaeology.

Ar·che·o·zo·ic (är′kē ə zō′ik) *also,* **Archaeozoic.** *n.* Archean. [ARCHEO- + Greek *zōē* life + -IC.]

arch·er (är′chər) *n.* **1.** a person who shoots with a bow and arrow. **2. the Archer.** Sagittarius. [Anglo-Norman *archer,* from Late Latin *arcārius,* from Latin *arcus* bow.]

arch·er·fish (är′chər fish′) *n., pl.* **-fish** or **-fish·es.** any of a group of fish, family Toxotidae, esp. *Toxotes jaculatrix,* found in the waters of southeastern Asia, that shoot down their insect prey with a stream of water ejected from the mouth.

arch·er·y (är′chə rē) *n.* **1.** the practice, skill, or sport of shooting with a bow and arrow. **2.** a group or company of archers.

ar·che·typ·al (är′ki tī′pəl) *adj.* of, relating to, or having the nature of an archetype. Also, **ar·che·typ·i·cal** (är′ki tip′i kəl).

ar·che·type (är′ki tīp′) *n.* **1.** the original or ideal model or pattern from which all things of the same type are derived or copied; prototype. **2.** in the psychology of Carl Jung, an unconscious way of thinking inherited from primitive ancestors. [Latin *archetypum* original pattern, from Greek *archetypon.*]

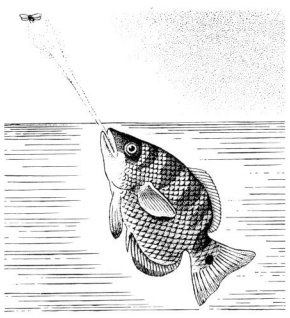

archerfish

arch·fiend (ärch′fēnd′) *n.* **1.** a chief fiend. **2. the archfiend.** Satan.

archi-, form of **arch-,** as in *archiepiscopal.*

ar·chi·di·ac·o·nal (är′ki dī ak′ə nəl) *adj.* of or relating to an archdeacon or the office of an archdeacon. [Late Latin *archidiācōnus,* from Late Greek *archidiakonos,* from *arch-* arch- + *diakonos* servant.]

ar·chi·e·pis·co·pal (är′kē i pis′kə pəl) *adj.* of or relating to an archbishop or the office of an archbishop. [Late Latin *archiepiscopus* archbishop. See ARCHBISHOP.]

Ar·chi·me·de·an screw (är′kə mē′dē ən, -mə dē′ən) an ancient device for raising water, consisting of a spiral tube around or within an inclined cylinder. Also, **Ar·chi·me·des′ screw** (är′kə mē′dēz). [From *Archimedes,* 287?-212 B.C., Greek mathematician, physicist, and inventor.]

ar·chi·pel·a·go (är′kə pel′ə gō′) *n., pl.* **-goes** or **-gos. 1.** a large group of islands. **2.** a large body of water with many islands. [Italian *arcipelago,* going back to Greek *archi-* chief + *pelagos* sea; referring to the Aegean Sea with its many islands.] —**ar·chi·pe·lag·ic** (är′kə pə laj′ik), *adj.*

ar·chi·tect (är′ki tekt′) *n.* **1.** a person whose profession is to design, draw plans for, and supervise the construction of buildings or other structures. **2.** a creator, maker, or designer of anything: *Lenin was one of the chief architects of the Russian Revolution.* [French *architecte,* from Latin *architectus,* from Greek *architektōn* chief builder.]

ar·chi·tec·ton·ic (är′ki tek ton′ik) *adj.* **1.** of, relating to, or according to the principles of architecture. **2.** having the organized design or structural qualities of architecture: *an architectonic poem.*

ar·chi·tec·ton·ics (är′ki tek ton′iks) *n.* **1.** the science of architecture. **2.** structural design, as of a work of art. **3.** the science of systematic classification of knowledge. ➡ used as singular in all defs.

ar·chi·tec·tur·al (är′ki tek′chər əl) *adj.* of, relating to, or characteristic of architecture: *an architectural effect.* —**ar′chi·tec′tur·al·ly,** *adv.*

ar·chi·tec·ture (är′ki tek′chər) *n.* **1.** the science, art, or profession of planning, designing, and supervising the construction of buildings or other structures. **2.** a style or method of building: *Byzantine architecture.* **3.** an architectural work or works: *We saw some impressive church architecture on the trip.* **4.** the construction or design of anything: *the architecture of a novel.*

ar·chi·trave (är′ki trāv′) *n.* **1.** the lowest part of an entablature, resting directly on the capital of a column. For illustration, see **entablature. 2.** the ornamental molding around a door or window. [French *architrave,* from Italian *architrave,* from *archi-* chief + *trave* beam, from Latin *trabs* beam.]

ar·chive (är′kīv) *n.* **1. archives.** public records, papers, or documents, as of a government or institution. **2. archives.** the place where such records, papers, or documents are kept. **3.** a collection of documents. [Possibly from French *archives,* from Late Latin *archīvum,* from Greek *archeion* public building; or from obsolete French *archive,* from *archives.*] —**ar·chi′val,** *adj.*

ar·chi·vist (är′kə vist, -kī-) *n.* a person who is in charge of archives. [French *archiviste,* from *archives* archives + *-iste* -ist. See ARCHIVE, -IST.]

Arch of Triumph, Arc de Triomphe.

ar·chon (är′kon) *n.* **1.** one of the nine chief magistrates in ancient Athens. **2.** ruler. [Greek *archōn* ruler, from *archein* to begin, rule.]

arch·way (ärch′wā′) *n.* **1.** an entrance or passage under an arch. **2.** an arch over a passage.

-archy *combining form* rule; government: *monarchy.* [Greek *-archiā* rule, from *archos* ruler, often through Latin *-archia.*]

arc lamp, a lamp in which high-intensity light is produced by an electric arc between carbon rods. Also, **arc light.**

arc·tic (ärk′tik, är′tik) *adj.* **1.** *also,* **Arctic.** of, relating to, characteristic of, or near the North Pole, or the north polar regions. **2.** extremely cold; frigid. —*n.* **arctics.** warm, waterproof overshoes. [Latin *arcticus* northern, from Greek *arktikos,* from *arktos* bear, with reference to the northern constellation of the Great Bear.]

Arctic Circle *also,* **arctic circle.** an imaginary line around the earth at 66°33′ north latitude, or about 1,600 miles (2,575 kilometers) from the North Pole.

arctic fox, a North American and Eurasian fox, *Alopex lagopus,* of arctic regions. There are two color phases: the white phase, brown in summer and white in winter, and the blue phase, dark bluish gray in summer and pale bluish gray in winter. Average length: 3 feet (0.9 meter), including tail.

Arc·tu·rus (ärk tûr′əs, -tyûr′-) *n.* a giant orange star, one of the brightest stars in the sky and the brightest in the constellation Boötes.

a at	e end	o hot	u up	hw white	⎧ about
ā ape	ē me	ō old	ū use	ng song	⎪ taken
ä far	i it	ô fork	ü rule	th thin	⎨ pencil
âr care	ī ice	oi oil	u̇ pull	th this	⎪ lemon
	îr pierce	ou out	ûr turn	zh measure	⎩ circus

arc welding

arc welding, welding by using the heat of an electric arc.

-ard *suffix* (used to form nouns) a person who does or is something to excess: *drunkard, coward.*

ar·dent (är′dənt) *adj.* characterized by intensity of feeling; full of passion; passionate: *ardent love.* **2.** characterized by enthusiasm or devotion; zealous: *an ardent golfer.* **3.** shining brightly, as with spirit or passion: *ardent eyes.* **4.** hot or burning; fiery. [Old French *ardant* burning, from Latin *ārdēns,* present participle of *ārdēre* to burn.] —**ar′den·cy,** *n.* —**ar′dent·ly,** *adv.* —For Synonyms, see **passionate.**

ardent spirits, strong, distilled alcoholic liquors.

ar·dor (är′dər) *also, British,* **ar·dour.** *n.* **1.** intensity of feeling; fervor; passion: *revolutionary ardor.* **2.** earnest enthusiasm or devotion; zeal. **3.** burning heat; fire. [Old French *ardour,* from Latin *ardor* heat, from *ardēre* to burn.]

ar·du·ous (är′jü əs) *adj.* requiring great exertion or endurance; difficult; strenuous: *an arduous effort, an arduous task.* [Latin *arduus* steep, difficult.] —**ar′du·ous·ly,** *adv.* —**ar′du·ous·ness,** *n.* —For Synonyms, see **hard.**

are[1] (är; *unstressed* ər) the plural and second person singular present indicative of **be.** [Old English (Northumbrian dialect) *aron* are.]

are[2] (âr, är) *n.* in the metric system, a unit of surface measure equal to 100 square meters. [French *are,* from Latin *ārea* open space.]

ar·e·a (âr′ē ə) *n.* **1.** the amount of surface within given limits, esp. as measured in square units: *the area of a triangle.* **2.** a particular surface, space, or tract; region: *the coastal areas of a country.* **3.** a section or place set aside for a particular use: *an industrial area, a picnic area.* **4.** a division or segment of activity, thought, or interest; field: *My education was weak in the area of math until I took an algebra course.* **5.** *British.* areaway *(def. 1).* [Latin *ārea* open space.]

area code, a combination of three numbers that represents any of the various areas into which the United States and Canada are divided for purposes of telephone communication. This combination is dialed before the local number in calling from one area to another.

area rug, a rug that covers only part of the floor.

ar·e·a·way (âr′ē ə wā′) *n.* **1.** a sunken space or passage in front of the windows or entrance of a cellar or basement. **2.** a passageway, as between buildings.

a·re·na (ə rē′nə) *n.* **1.** in ancient Rome, the central part of an amphitheater, used for gladiatorial contests or other performances. **2.** any similar place, usually in a building, used for public meetings or entertainment: *a boxing arena, a circus arena.* **3.** a scene or sphere of conflict or activity: *the arena of politics.* [Latin *arēna* sand, sandy place. Sand was used to cover the ground of Roman amphitheaters.]

ar·e·na·ceous (ar′ə nā′shəs) *adj.* consisting of or containing sand; sandy. [Latin *arēnāceus* sandy, from *arēna* sand.]

arena theater, theater-in-the-round.

aren't (ärnt, är′ənt) *contr.* **1.** are not. **2.** am not. ➡ used in the interrogative in def. 2: *Aren't I allowed to come along?*

a·re·o·la (ə rē′ə lə) *n., pl.* **-lae** (-lē′) or **-las.** *Biology.* **1.** a small space, as between the veins of a leaf or an insect's wing. **2.** a ring of color, as around a vesicle or a nipple. [Latin *āreola* small open place, diminutive of *ārea* open place.] —**a·re′o·lar,** *adj.*

Ar·e·op·a·gus (ar′ē op′ə gəs) *n.* a court of ancient Athens, which met on a hill of the same name. [Latin *Areopagus* this hill, from Greek *Areiopagos* literally, hill of Ares.]

Ar·es (âr′ēz) *n.* in Greek mythology, the god of war. His Roman counterpart is Mars.

a·rête (ə rāt′) *n.* a sharp, rocky ridge in rugged, glaciated mountains, formed at the upper end of a cirque. [French *arête,* literally, skeleton (of a fish), awn (of sharp wheat), ridge, from Old French *areste.*]

Ar·e·thu·sa (ar′ə thü′zə) *n.* in Greek mythology, a nymph who was transformed into a spring by Artemis to save her from her pursuer, the river god Alpheus.

ar·ga·li (är′gə lē) *n., pl.* **-li** or **-lis.** a wild sheep, *Ovis ammon,* of central Asia, noted for its long, thick, curved horns. It is the largest of all sheep. Height: 4 feet (1.2 meters) at the shoulder. [Of Mongol origin.]

ar·gent (är′jənt) *Archaic. n.* silver. —*adj.* made of or like silver; silvery. Also, **ar·gen·tine** (är′jən tin, -tīn′). [French *argent* this metal, from Latin *argentum.*]

ar·gen·tite (är′jən tīt′) *n.* a dark gray sulfide mineral mined as an ore of silver. Formula: Ag_2S [Latin *argentum,* silver + -ITE[1].]

ar·gil (är′jəl) *n.* clay, esp. potter's clay. [Latin *argilla,* from Greek *argillos,* from *arges* shining.]

ar·gil·la·ceous (är′jə lā′shəs) *adj.* of, relating to, or composed of clay or clay minerals: *Shale is an argillaceous rock.* [Latin *argillaceus,* from *argilla* clay (from Greek *argos* white) + -aceus like, related to.]

ar·gi·nine (är′jə nēn′, -nīn′, -nin) *n.* an amino acid that occurs in proteins and is an essential part of the diet of growing children. Formula: $C_6H_{14}N_4O_2$ [German *arginin,* from Greek *arginoesis* white, shining (the earliest known salts of this acid are silvery) + -*in* -INE.]

Ar·give (är′jīv, -gīv) *adj.* **1.** of, relating to, or characteristic of Argos or Argolis or the people or culture of Argos or Argolis. **2.** Greek. —*n.* **1.** a native or inhabitant of Argos or Argolis. **2.** any Greek.

Ar·go (är′gō) *n.* in Greek legend, the ship in which Jason and the Argonauts sailed in quest of the Golden Fleece.

ar·gon (är′gon) *n.* a colorless, inert gaseous element that forms approximately 1 percent of the earth's atmosphere and is the most abundant of the noble gases. It is esp. noted for its use in electric light bulbs. Symbol: **Ar** For tables, see **element.** [Greek *argon,* neuter of *argos* idle, from *a-* not + *ergon* work.]

Ar·go·naut (är′gə nôt′) *n.* **1.** in Greek legend, one of the people who sailed with Jason in search of the Golden Fleece. **2.** a person who went to California in 1848-49 to search for gold. **3.** **argonaut.** paper nautilus. [Latin *Argonauta* Argonaut (of Greek legend), from Greek *Argonautēs,* from *Argō* ARGO + *nautēs* sailor.] —**Ar′go·nau′tic,** *adj.*

ar·go·sy (är′gə sē) *n., pl.* **-sies. 1.** a large merchant ship. **2.** a fleet of such ships. [Modification of Italian *ragusea* ship of Ragusa, former name of the seaport Dubrovnik, Yugoslavia.]

ar·got (är′gō, -gət) *n.* the specialized vocabulary or idiom used by a particular group or class, as the secret language of thieves. [French *argot.*]

ar·gu·a·ble (är′gü ə bəl) *adj.* open to argument; questionable. —**ar′gu·a·bly,** *adv.*

ar·gue (är′gü) *v.,* **-gued, -gu·ing.** —*v.i.* **1.** to have a discussion and disagree; dispute: *to argue about politics.* **2.** to give reasons for or against something: *The attorney argued against the motion.* —*v.t.* **1.** to give reasons for or against; debate: *Let's not argue the matter.* **2.** to persuade (someone) by giving reasons (with *into* or *out of*): *We argued him out of selling his car.* **3.** to try to establish or prove by giving reasons; maintain; contend: *to argue that someone is wrong.* **4.** to give evidence of; indicate; prove: *Her accent argues that she was born abroad.* [Middle French *arguer* to reason, from Latin *argūtāre* to prattle, going back to *arguere* to prove, make clear.] —**ar′gu·er,** *n.*

ar·gu·ment (är′gyə mənt) *n.* **1.a.** a discussion of a disputed topic; controversy; debate. **b.** a heated disagreement; quarrel: *They had an argument about whose turn it was to do the dishes.* **2.** a reason or reasons given to support or oppose something: *What are the arguments for accepting the proposal?* **3.** a process or line of reasoning: *I couldn't follow your argument.* **4.** a summary of the major points of a literary work.

Synonyms **Argument, dispute,** and **controversy** mean a disagreement about which there is discussion. **Argument** suggests two sides trying to convince each other by appealing to reason: *The argument continued until we realized neither of us was going to change our mind.* **Dispute** implies that emotion rather than reason dominates: *After their dispute over the will the brother and sister stopped talking to each other.* **Controversy** is now used of disagreements involving more than two sides or parties or of general disagreement on some issue: *The controversy over the nuclear waste dump brought out many different points of view.*

ar·gu·men·ta·tion (är′gyə men tā′shən) *n.* **1.** the process of

A

forming and presenting reasons and of developing conclusions from them. **2.** argument; debate.

ar·gu·men·ta·tive (är′gyə men′tə tiv) *adj.* **1.** inclined to argue; quarrelsome. **2.** containing argument; controversial. —**ar′gu·men′ta·tive·ly,** *adv.* —**ar′gu·men′ta·tive·ness,** *n.*

Ar·gus (är′gəs) *n.* **1.** in Greek mythology, a giant with a hundred eyes that were put in the peacock's tail after he was killed by Hermes. **2.** an extremely observant or watchful person.

Ar·gus-eyed (är′gəs īd′) *adj.* extremely observant; vigilant.

ar·gyle (är′gīl) *also,* Argyle. *n.* **1.** a diamond-shaped pattern of contrasting colors, used esp. in knitting. **2.** a sock having this pattern. —*adj.* having this pattern. [From *Argyll,* a branch of the Campbell clan of Scotland, whose tartan inspired the design.]

ar·gy·rol (är′jə rôl′) *n.* a compound of silver and a protein, used as an antiseptic in treating inflammation of the mucous membrane. *Trademark:* Argyrol. [Greek *argyros* silver.]

a·ri·a (är′ē ə, âr′ē ə) *n.* an elaborate musical composition for solo voice with instrumental accompaniment, as in an opera. [Italian *aria* air (in all senses), from Latin *āēr* (see AIR).]

Ar·i·ad·ne (ar′ē ad′nē) *n.* in Greek legend, the daughter of King Minos, who gave Theseus the ball of thread by which he found his way out of the Labyrinth of the Minotaur.

Ar·i·an (âr′ē ən, ar′-) *adj.* of or relating to the doctrine of Arius that stated that Jesus was not of the same substance as God, but was created by and subordinate to God. —*n.* a believer in this doctrine. [Latin *Ariānus* relating to Arius.] —**Ar′i·an·ism,** *n.*

-arian *suffix* (used to form nouns) **1.** a person who believes in: *humanitarian.* **2.** a person whose work deals with: *grammarian.* **3.** a person who is an advocate of: *disciplinarian.* **4.** a person who is of the age of: *octogenarian.* [-ARY¹ + -AN.]

ar·id (ar′id) *adj.* **1.** lacking rainfall; dry; parched: *an arid wasteland.* **2.** uninteresting; lifeless. [Latin *āridus* dry, from *arēre* to be dry.] —**a·rid·i·ty** (ə rid′i tē), **ar′id·ness,** *n.* —**ar′id·ly,** *adv.* —For Synonyms, see **dry.**

Ar·i·el (âr′ē əl) *n.* **1.** an airy spirit who used magic to help Prospero in Shakespeare's play *The Tempest.* **2.** a moon of the planet Uranus.

Ar·ies (âr′ēz, -ē ēz′) *n.* **1.** a constellation in the northern sky, conventionally depicted as a ram. **2.** the first sign of the zodiac. [Latin *ariēs* ram.]

a·right (ə rīt′) *adv.* correctly; rightly.

ar·il (ar′əl) *n.* the outer, sometimes pulpy, covering or appendage of certain seeds. [Modern Latin *arillus,* from Medieval Latin *arillus* raisin.]

a·rise (ə rīz′) *v.i.,* **a·rose, a·ris·en** (ə riz′ən), **a·ris·ing. 1.** to come into being or notice; appear; originate: *Questions often arise as we read. We dealt with each problem as it arose.* **2.** to result or proceed (with *from*): *Accidents often arise from carelessness.* **3.** to get up; stand up: *The audience arose and clapped loudly.* **4.** to move upward; ascend: *Smoke arose from the fire.* [Old English *ārīsan.*]

ar·is·toc·ra·cy (ar′ə stok′rə sē) *n., pl.* **-cies. 1.** a privileged upper class that has inherited its wealth and social position; nobility. **2.** government by an upper-class minority or the nobility. **3.** a state having this form of government. **4.** any outstanding or superior group: *the cultural aristocracy of a country.* [French *aristocratie* rule of the nobly born, going back to Greek *aristokratiā* rule of the best, from *aristos* best + *kratos* power.]

a·ris·to·crat (ə ris′tə krat′, ar′ə stə-) *n.* **1.** a member of an aristocracy; nobleman or noblewoman. **2.** a person who has the tastes, manners, and attitudes associated with the aristocracy. **3.** a person who favors government by the aristocracy.

a·ris·to·crat·ic (ə ris′tə krat′ik, ar′ə stə-) *adj.* **1.** characteristic of or befitting an aristocrat: *aristocratic bearing.* **2.** of or belonging to the aristocracy. **3.** of, relating to, or supporting government by aristocracy. —**a·ris′to·crat′i·cal·ly,** *adv.*

Ar·is·to·te·li·an (ar′ə stə tē′lē ən, -tēl′yən, ə ris′tə-) *adj.* of, relating to, or characteristic of the Greek philosopher Aristotle or his philosophy. —*n.* **1.** a follower of Aristotle or his philosophy. **2.** a person whose thinking or method tends to be deductive or empirical rather than intuitive or idealistic. —**Ar′is·to·te′li·an·ism,** *n.*

Aristotelian logic 1. the deductive logic of Aristotle, characterized by the syllogism. **2.** the formal symbolic logic developed from that of Aristotle, dealing with the relations between the forms, rather than the content, of the propositions.

arith. 1. arithmetic. **2.** arithmetical.

a·rith·me·tic (*n.,* ə rith′mə tik′; *adj.,* ar′ith met′ik) *n.* the science and technique of computing with positive, real numbers. Arithmetic deals with the four basic operations of addition, subtraction, multiplication, and division. —*adj. also,* **ar′ith·met′i·cal.** of, relating to, or according to the rules of arithmetic. [Old French *arismetrique,* from Latin *arithmētica* science of numbers,

from Greek *arithmētikē,* from *arithmos* number.] —**ar′ith·met′i·cal·ly,** *adv.*

a·rith·me·ti·cian (ə rith′mə tish′ən) *n.* a student or expert in arithmetic.

ar·ith·met·ic-log·ic unit (ar′ith met′ik loj′ik) the component of a computer's central processing unit that performs all arithmetic operations as well as nonarithmetic, decision-making operations.

arithmetic mean, average *(n., def. 1).*

arithmetic progression, a series in which the difference between any two terms is a constant quantity. 1, 3, 5, 7 and 3, 1, −1, −3 are arithmetic progressions. ➡ distinguished from **geometric progression.**

Ariz., Arizona.

ark (ärk) *n.* **1.** in the Bible, the large boat built by Noah. **2.** any large, flat-bottomed, clumsy boat, esp. one formerly used for transport on American rivers. **3.** Ark of the Covenant *(def. 2).* [Old English *arc,* from Latin *arca* chest, box.]

Ark., Arkansas.

Ark of the Covenant 1. in the Bible, the sacred chest that held the two stone tablets containing the Ten Commandments. **2.** a repository in a synagogue for the scrolls of the Torah and other sacred books.

arm¹ (ärm) *n.* **1.** either of the two upper limbs of the human body, esp. the part between the shoulder and wrist. **2.** the forelimb of any vertebrate animal. **3.** something used to support or cover the human arm: *the arm of a chair, the arm of a coat.* **4.** anything branching out from a larger body: *an arm of the sea, the arm of a phonograph.* **5.** a division of an organization: *an arm of government.* **6.** an extension of authority; power: *the arm of the law.* [Old English *earm* upper limb of the human body.] —**arm′like′,** *adj.*

• **an arm and a leg.** a large amount of money: *A new car will cost an arm and a leg.*

• **arm in arm.** with arms interlinked.

• **at arm's length.** so as to prevent friendship or familiarity.

• **to twist someone's arm.** to convince or try to convince someone by persuasion or by using or threatening to use force.

• **with open arms.** with an eager welcome; cordially.

arm² (ärm) *n.* **1.** a weapon, esp. a firearm. **2.** a combat branch of the armed forces. —*v.t.* **1.** to provide with or as if with weapons or tools: *Arm the populace.* **2.** to provide with something that protects or strengthens; fortify: *The porcupine is armed with quills.* **3.** to make ready for a particular occasion, event, or undertaking; prepare: *The attorneys armed themselves with all the facts before the trial.* **4.** to set or prepare to explode or detonate: *to arm a missile.* —*v.i.* to prepare for war or conflict, esp. by equipping oneself with weapons. [Middle English *armes* (plural), from Old French *armes,* from Latin *arma* tools, weapons.]

ar·ma·da (är mä′də, -mä′-) *n.* **1.** a fleet of warships. **2. the Armada.** Spanish Armada. **3.** any large group of vehicles: *an armada of limousines.* [Spanish *armada* fleet, from *armar* to arm, from Latin *armāre* to furnish with weapons.]

ar·ma·dil·lo (är′mə dil′ō) *n., pl.* **-los.** any of several insect-eating, burrowing mammals, order Edentata, that range from South America to the southern United States, having an armorlike shell composed of bony plates; a long snout; strong, sharp claws; and a long tail. Length: 5 inches to 5 feet (13 centimeters to 1.5 meters). [Spanish *armadillo* literally, little armed creature, from *armado,* past participle of *armar* to arm,

armadillo

from Latin *armāre* to furnish with arms, from *arma* weapons.]

Ar·ma·ged·don (är′mə ged′ən) *n.* **1.** the site of the world's great and final battle between the forces of good and evil, as prophesied in the Bible. **2.** any great and decisive battle. [Going back to Hebrew *Har Megiddō* literally, mountain of Megiddo, a district in ancient Israel where a number of important battles were fought in biblical times.]

ar·ma·ment (är′mə mənt) *n.* **1. armaments.** military forces, equipment, and supplies, esp. considered as the entire military strength of a nation. **2.** *also,* **armaments.** weapons with which

a	at	e	end	o	hot	u	up	hw	white	⎧	about
ā	ape	ē	me	ō	old	ū	use	ng	song		taken
ä	far	i	it	ô	fork	ü	rule	th	thin	ə	pencil
âr	care	ī	ice	oi	oil	u̇	pull	th	this		lemon
		îr	pierce	ou	out	ûr	turn	zh	measure	⎩	circus

a military unit, ship, or plane is equipped. **3.** the process of arming: *The country's armament took two months.*

ar·ma·ture (är′mə chər) *n.* **1.** the rotating member of an electric motor or dynamo, consisting of a laminated iron core with wire coiled around it. **2.** a piece of soft iron placed across the poles of a magnet to preserve magnetic power. **3.** the vibrating iron part of an electric buzzer or relay. **4.** a part or organ of an animal or plant used for offense or defense, such as teeth, shells, or thorns. **5.** a protective covering; armor. **6.** a framework used as a support around which clay or some other substance is modeled in sculpture. [Latin *armātūra* armor. Doublet of ARMOR.]

arm·band (ärm′band′) *n.* a band worn around the upper part of the arm as a badge or symbol: *The deceased's family wore black armbands as a sign of mourning.*

arm·chair (ärm′châr′) *n.* a chair with supports at each side for one's arms or elbows. —*adj.* dealing with problems indirectly or without actual experience: *an armchair general, an armchair quarterback.*

armed (ärmd) *adj.* **1.** having, bearing, or supported by arms or weapons: *armed neutrality, an armed garrison.* **2.** having an arm or arms. ➡ usually used in combination in def. 2: *one-armed, long-armed.*

armed forces, all of the military forces of a nation taken as a whole. The armed forces of the United States include the Army, Navy, Marine Corps, Air Force, and Coast Guard.

Ar·me·ni·an (är mē′nē ən, -mēn′yən) *adj.* of, relating to, or characteristic of Armenia or its people, language, or culture. —*n.* **1.** a native or citizen of Armenia. **2.** a person of Armenian ancestry. **3.** the Indo-European language of the Armenians.

arm·ful (ärm′fʊl′) *n., pl.* **-fuls. 1.** as much as both arms can hold. **2.** something that a person holds in both arms, esp. something large or heavy: *That baby is getting to be quite an armful.*

arm·hole (ärm′hōl′) *n.* an opening in a garment for the arm.

Ar·min·i·an (är min′ē ən) *adj.* of or relating to the Dutch theologian Jacobus Arminius or his doctrines, esp. those that opposed the Calvinist doctrine of predestination. —*n.* a believer in the doctrines of Arminius. —**Ar·min′i·an·ism,** *n.*

ar·mi·stice (är′mə stis) *n.* a temporary suspension of fighting by mutual agreement; truce. [French *armistice,* going back to Latin *arma* weapons + *sistere* to stop.] —For Synonyms, see **truce.**

Armistice Day, see **Veterans Day.**

arm·let (ärm′lit) *n.* **1.** an ornamental band worn around the upper arm. **2.** a small arm or inlet of the sea.

ar·moire (ärm wär′, ärm′wär) *n.* a large, movable cabinet or wardrobe with full-length doors.

ar·mor (är′mər) *also, British,* **armour.** *n.* **1.** a defensive covering, as of metal, for the body. **2.** a protective metal covering used on tanks, warships, or other military vehicles and equipment. **3.** armored military vehicles. **4.** any protective covering, as that of an armadillo. —*v.t., v.i.* to cover or furnish with armor. [Old French *armeüre* defensive covering for the body, from Latin *armātūra,* from *armāre* to furnish with weapons. Doublet of ARMATURE.] —**ar′mor·like′,** *adj.*

ar·mor·bear·er (är′mər bâr′ər) *n.* a person who carries a warrior's armor or weapons.

ar·mored (är′mərd) *also, British,* **armoured.** *adj.* **1.** protected by armor: *an armored ship.* **2.** equipped with armored vehicles: *armored troops.*

armored car 1. a vehicle covered with armor plate, used to transport money or other valuable cargo. **2.** a military vehicle sheathed in armor plate and usually equipped with a machine gun, used esp. for reconnaissance.

ar·mor·er (är′mər ər) *also, British,* **ar·mour·er.** *n.* **1.** *Military.* an enlisted person in charge of small arms. **2.** a person who makes or repairs armor. **3.** a person or company that makes weapons.

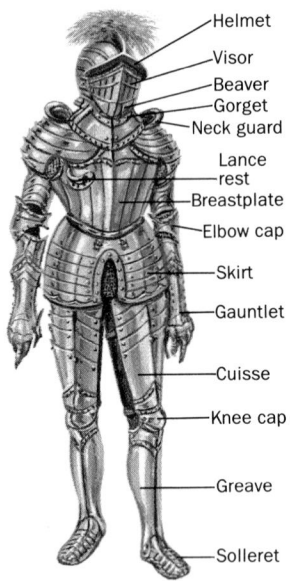

Helmet
Visor
Beaver
Gorget
Neck guard
Lance rest
Breastplate
Elbow cap
Skirt
Gauntlet
Cuisse
Knee cap
Greave
Solleret

armor

ar·mo·ri·al (är môr′ē əl) *adj.* relating to heraldry or coats of arms.

armor plate, specially hardened steel used for protective covering, as on a tank or other vehicle. —**ar′mor-plat′ed,** *adj.*

ar·mor·y (är′mə rē) *n., pl.* **-mor·ies. 1.** a building that is the headquarters and training center of a National Guard or other military reserve unit. **2.** a place where arms are kept; arsenal. **3.** a place where arms are manufactured.

ar·mour (är′mər) *British.* armor.

arm·pit (ärm′pit′) *n.* the hollow under the arm at the shoulder.

arm·rest (ärm′rest′) *n.* a support for the arm or elbow, as on a chair.

arms (ärmz) *pl. n.* **1.** weapons, esp. firearms, considered collectively. **2.** coat of arms. [Old French *armes* weapons, from Latin *arma.*]
•**to arms.** prepare to fight!
•**to bear arms. a.** to possess or carry weapons. **b.** to serve in the armed forces.
•**to take up arms.** to prepare for battle.
•**under arms.** furnished with weapons; ready for war: *The number of soldiers under arms has reached a postwar high.*
•**up in arms.** aroused to fight; indignant: *Congress was up in arms about federal spending.*

ar·my (är′mē) *n., pl.* **-mies. 1.** a large, organized body of soldiers armed and trained for combat on land. **2.** *also,* **Ar·my.** the branch of the military forces of a nation trained primarily for land operations. In some countries it includes the air force. **3.** in the U.S. Army, the largest military unit, consisting of two or more corps. **4.** a large body of persons organized for a common cause: *an army of political protesters.* **5.** any large group; multitude: *an army of holiday shoppers.* [Old French *armee* armed forces, from *armer* to arm, from Latin *armāre* to furnish with weapons.]

army ant, any of a group of nomadic social ants, subfamily Dorylinae, found in Africa and tropical America, that kill their prey by stinging. Hunting and migrating in huge swarms, army ants consume all vegetation and nearly all the small animals in their path. Also, **driver ant.**

Army Post Office, see APO.

ar·my·worm (är′mē wûrm′) *n.* the voracious larva of a brown moth, *Cirphis unipuncta,* that travels in vast numbers, destroying grass, grain, and other crops.

ar·ni·ca (är′ni kə) *n.* **1.** any of a group of plants, genus *Arnica,* of the composite family, bearing clusters of yellow flower heads. **2.** a tincture prepared from the dried flowers and roots of a species of this plant, *A. montana.* [Modern Latin *Arnica.*]

a·ro·ma (ə rō′mə) *n.* **1.** a distinctive, agreeable odor, as of a food, wine, or plant; fragrance. **2.** a distinctive or subtle quality; atmosphere or flavor. [Old French *aroma,* from Late Latin *arōma* spice, fragrance, from Greek *arōma.*] —For Synonyms, see **smell.**

ar·o·mat·ic (ar′ə mat′ik) *adj.* **1.** having an aroma; fragrant: *the aromatic leaves of the clove tree.* **2.** of or relating to a group of organic compounds, including benzene and its derivatives, that contain at least one unsaturated benzene ring and generally have a pleasant odor. —*n.* an aromatic plant, chemical, or other substance. —**ar′o·mat′i·cal·ly,** *adv.*

a·rose (ə rōz′) the past tense of **arise.**

a·round (ə round′) *prep.* **1.** so as to form a circle about: *in orbit around the earth.* **2.** along the circumference or outer edge of: *The blouse has lace around the collar.* **3.** so as to surround or envelop: *She put her arms around the child.* **4.** on all sides of: *Around us lay the ruins of a city.* **5.** here and there in or through: *We wandered around the town.* **6.** somewhere in or near: *The dog always stays around our yard.* **7.** somewhat near as in time or amount; about: *around six o'clock.* **8.** on another side of: *The dock is around the bend of the river.* **9.** so as to avoid: *to find a way around a regulation.* —*adv.* **1.** in a circle or circular course. **2.** in circumference: *The tree measures 4 feet around.* **3.** on all sides; in various directions: *with people all around.* **4.** here and there; about: *We spread the word around. We will drive around until you get back.* **5.** *Informal.* somewhere near: *Stay around awhile.* **6.** to a (particular) place: *Come around again tomorrow.* **7.** in or to the opposite direction: *He spun around quickly.* **8.** close to in number; approximately: *Around a hundred people signed the petition.* [A-¹ + ROUND.]
•**to have been around.** *Informal.* to be experienced or sophisticated.

a·round-the-clock (ə round′thə klok′) *adj.* continuing throughout the twenty-four hours of the day; continuous: *around-the-clock negotiations to settle a strike.* Also, **round-the-clock.**

a·rous·al (ə rou′zəl) *n.* the act of arousing or the state of being aroused.

a·rouse (ə rouz′) *v.,* **a·roused, a·rous·ing.** —*v.t.* **1.** to stir up; excite: *a speech that aroused the crowd, to arouse curiosity.* **2.** to

awaken (someone): *The noise aroused me from sleep.* —*v.i.* to wake up. [A-[1] + ROUSE.]

ar·peg·gi·o (är pej′ē ō′, -pej′ō) *n., pl.* **-gi·os. 1.** the playing of the notes of a chord in succession instead of simultaneously. **2.** a chord played in this way. [Italian *arpeggio,* from *arpeggiare* to play on the harp, from *arpa* harp, of Germanic origin.]

ar·que·bus (är′kwə bəs) harquebus.

ar·raign (ə rān′) *v.t.* **1.** to formally state the charge against (someone) before a judge and record an answer to the charge. **2.** to charge with or criticize for something: *The newspaper's editorial arraigned the polluters.* [Anglo-Norman *arainer,* going back to Latin *ad* to + *ratiō* reason, account.] —**ar·raign′er,** *n.*

ar·raign·ment (ə rān′mənt) *n.* the act of arraigning or the state of being arraigned.

ar·range (ə rānj′) *v.,* **-ranged, -rang·ing.** —*v.t.* **1.** to put in proper, convenient, or pleasing order: *to arrange names in alphabetical order, to arrange the furniture in a room.* **2.** to help to bring about; prepare for; plan: *The negotiators arranged a settlement of the strike.* **3.** to make certain or formal; settle; determine: *to arrange the terms of a contract.* **4.** to adapt or change (a musical composition) while preserving its essential nature, esp. by scoring it for instruments or voices for which it was not originally written. —*v.i.* **1.** to make plans or preparations: *I'll arrange for us to meet them at the restaurant.* **2.** to come to an agreement: *I'll arrange with them about the tickets.* [Old French *arengier* to put into a rank, from *à* to (from Latin *ad* to) + *rengier* to put in order, from *renge* line, row, of Germanic origin.] —**ar·range′a·ble,** *adj.* —**ar·rang′er,** *n.*

ar·range·ment (ə rānj′mənt) *n.* **1.** the act of putting in order or the state of being put in order: *The arrangement of the new furniture took two hours.* **2.** the result of arranging or ordering: *a flower arrangement.* **3.** the style or manner in which something is ordered: *The book has a diagram of the arrangement of electrons in an atom.* **4.** *also,* **arrangements.** something done in preparation; plan: *to make arrangements for a dance.* **5.** the act of settling or the state of being settled; settlement; adjustment: *The arrangement of the dispute pleased us all.* **6.a.** the adaptation or changing of a musical composition, esp. by scoring it for instruments or voices for which it was not originally written. **b.** a work so adapted.

ar·rant (ar′ənt) *adj.* out-and-out; unmitigated; downright: *an arrant fool.* [Form of ERRANT.] —**ar′rant·ly,** *adv.*

ar·ras (ar′əs) *n.* **1.** a type of richly designed tapestry. **2.** a tapestry screen or wall hanging. [From *Arras,* a city in northern France where the tapestry was produced.]

ar·ray (ə rā′) *n.* **1.** an orderly grouping or arrangement, as of troops for battle. **2.** a large, imposing collection; display: *an array of jewels.* **3.** persons or things on display or in order. **4.** clothing, esp. fine clothing; finery: *to dress in rich array.* **5.** an arrangement of mathematical elements, as numbers or symbols, in rows or columns. —*v.t.* **1.** to place in order; marshal: *to array troops for battle.* **2.** to dress, esp. in fine clothing; adorn. [Anglo-Norman *arayer* to prepare, arrange.]

ar·rear·age (ə rîr′ij) *n.* **1.** the state of being in arrears. **2.** an amount in arrears; debt.

ar·rears (ə rîrz′) *pl. n.* an amount of money that is due but unpaid. [Old French *arere* backward, going back to Latin *ad* toward + *retrō* backward.]
· **in arrears.** behind in payments, duties, or obligations.

ar·rest (ə rest′) *v.t.* **1.** to seize or take into custody by legal authority. **2.** to put a stop to; check: *to arrest the progress of a disease.* **3.** to catch and hold; engage: *The newscast arrested my attention.* —*n.* **1.** a seizure by legal authority; taking into custody. **2.** the act of stopping or the state of being stopped; check. **3.** a device for stopping or checking motion. [Old French *arester* to stay, from Latin *ad* to + *restāre* to stop. See REST[2].] —**ar·rest′er;** *also,* **ar·res′tor,** *n.*
· **under arrest.** held by legal authority.

ar·rest·ing (ə res′ting) *adj.* demanding the attention; striking.

ar·rhyth·mi·a (ə rith′mē ə, ā rith′-) *n.* any change or abnormality in the normal rhythm of the heartbeat. [Modern Latin *arrhythmia,* from Greek *arrhythmia* lack of rhythm, from *a-* without + *rhythmos* a measure.] —**ar·rhyth′mic,** *adj.*

ar·ris (ar′is) *n., pl.* **-ris** or **-ris·es.** a sharp ridge or edge formed by the meeting of two surfaces at an angle, as between two flutings on the shaft of a Doric column. [Old French *areste* fish bone, from Latin *arista* ear of corn, fish bone.]

ar·riv·al (ə rī′vəl) *n.* **1.** the act of arriving: *the arrival of a plane, arrival at a decision.* **2.** a person or thing that arrives or has arrived.

ar·rive (ə rīv′) *v.i.,* **-rived, -riv·ing. 1.** to reach a destination; appear at a place. **2.** (of time) to come: *The holiday season has arrived.* **3.** to attain to success or fame: *After years of struggle, the*

actor finally arrived. [Old French *ariver* to come to land, going back to Latin *ad* to + *rīpa* shore.]
· **to arrive at. a.** to come to or reach by traveling: *to arrive at home.* **b.** to come to or reach by any process or effort: *to arrive at a conclusion.*

ar·ri·ve·der·ci (ä′rē və där′chē) *interj. Italian.* until we meet again; good-bye for now.

ar·ri·viste (ar′ē vēst′) *n.* a person who has recently gained status, and often wealth, and behaves in an arrogant and vulgar way; parvenu. [French *arriviste,* from *arriver* to arrive + *-iste* -ist.]

ar·ro·gance (ar′ə gəns) *n.* overbearing pride or confidence in oneself and disdain for others; conceit; haughtiness.

ar·ro·gant (ar′ə gənt) *adj.* full of or proceeding from arrogance; conceited and haughty: *an arrogant person, arrogant claims.* [Latin *arrogāns* insolent, present participle of *arrogāre* to claim for oneself, from *ad* to + *rogāre* to ask, request.] —**ar′ro·gant·ly,** *adv.* —For Synonyms, see **proud.**

ar·ro·gate (ar′ə gāt′) *v.t.,* **-gat·ed, -gat·ing. 1.** to claim or seize presumptuously or without right: *to arrogate judicial powers to oneself.* **2.** to ascribe to another without good reason. [Latin *arrogātus,* past participle of *arrogāre* to claim for oneself. See ARROGANT.]

ar·ro·ga·tion (ar′ə gā′shən) *n.* **1.** the act of arrogating. **2.** something that is arrogated; assumption.

ar·ron·disse·ment (ə ron′dis mənt; *French* a rôN dēs män′) *n., pl.* **-ments** (-mənts; *French* -män′). **1.** the largest administrative division of a department in France. **2.** an administrative district of a city, as in Paris. [French *arrondissement* literally, a rounding, going back to Latin *ad* to + *rotundus* round.]

ar·row (ar′ō) *n.* **1.** a slender shaft, usually pointed at one end and feathered at the other, made to be shot from a bow. **2.** a symbol in the shape of an arrow, used to indicate direction or position, as on a road sign. **3.** anything resembling an arrow in form or function. [Old English *arwe* this shaft.]

ar·row·head (ar′ō hed′) *n.* **1.** the pointed tip of an arrow. **2.** any of a group of aquatic plants, genus *Sagittaria,* found in temperate and tropical regions, bearing arrow-shaped leaves and whorls of white flowers on a separate stem.

ar·row·root (ar′ō rūt′, -rut′) *n.* **1.** a nutritious starch made from the roots of a tropical American plant, *Maranta arundinacea,* used as a thickening agent in cooking. **2.** the plant itself, widely cultivated in the West Indies and other tropical regions, bearing long, pointed leaves and small, white flowers.

ar·row·wood (ar′ō wůd′) *n.* any of several North American trees or shrubs, genus *Viburnum,* having slender, straight shoots that were used by Indians for making shafts, esp. *V. dentatum,* a tree often cultivated as an ornamental, bearing clusters of tiny, white flowers.

ar·row·worm (ar′ō wûrm′) *n.* chaetognath.

ar·roy·o (ə roi′ō) *n., pl.* **-roy·os. 1.** the bed of a stream; gully. **2.** a small river or stream. [Spanish *arroyo* stream, gutter.]

ar·se·nal (är′sə nəl) *n.* **1.** a place for storing or manufacturing arms and munitions. **2.** a collection or accumulation of firearms or other weapons. **3.** a store or collection; storehouse: *Our country is . . . the arsenal of democracy* (Franklin Roosevelt, 1941). [Italian *arsenale,* going back to Arabic *dār as sinā 'ah* house of manufacture.]

ar·se·nate (är′sə nāt′, -nit) *n.* a salt or ester of arsenic acid.

ar·se·nic (*n.,* är′sə nik, ärs′nik; *adj.,* är sen′ik) *n.* **1.** a metalloid chemical element, usually in the form of silver-gray or blackish crystals with a metallic luster, used esp. in alloys and poisonous compounds. Symbol: **As** For tables, see **element. 2.** a white, tasteless, highly poisonous compound, used esp. in rat, insect, and weed poisons. Formula: As_2O_3 or As_4O_6 —*adj.* relating to or containing arsenic, esp. with a valence of five. [Middle English *arsenic,* from Old French *arsenic,* from Latin *arsenicum,* from Greek *arsenikon* yellow arsenic, modification of Arabic *az-zernīkh* the yellow arsenic, from Persian *zarnīk* yellow arsenic from *zar* gold.]

arsenic acid, a colorless, water-soluble, crystalline compound, used to derive arsenates. Formula: H_3AsO_4

ar·sen·i·cal (är sen′i kəl) *adj.* relating to or containing arsenic. —*n.* any preparation, as an insecticide or medicine, containing arsenic.

ar·se·no·py·rite (är′sə nō pī′rīt) *n.* a silvery white sulfide

a	at	e	end	o	hot	u	up	hw	white		about
ā	ape	ē	me	ō	old	ū	use	ng	song	ə	taken
ä	far	i	it	ô	fork	ü	rule	th	thin		pencil
âr	care	ī	ice	oi	oil	ů	pull	th	this		lemon
				îr	pierce	ou	out	ûr	turn	zh	measure		circus

mineral mined as an ore of arsenic. Formula: FeAsS [*Arseno-,* combining form of ARSENIC + PYRITE.]

ar·se·nous (är′sə nəs) *adj.* relating to or containing arsenic, esp. with a valence of three. Also, **ar·se·ni·ous** (är sē′nē əs).

ar·sine (är sēn′, är′sēn) *n.* a toxic, flammable gas with a strong odor similar to that of garlic, used in chemical weapons. Formula: AsH₃ [ARS(ENIC) + -INE².]

ar·son (är′sən) *n.* the crime of setting fire intentionally to a building or property. [Old French *arson,* going back to Latin *arsus,* past participle of *ardēre* to burn.] —**ar′son·ist,** *n.*

ars po·e·ti·ca (ärz′ pō et′i kə) the art of poetry. [Latin *ars poētica.*]

art¹ (ärt) *n.* **1.** the application or exhibition of skill, aesthetic principles, and creative imagination in the production of the beautiful or the meaningful, as in painting, music, literature, dance, or drama. **2.** a form of activity characterized by such application or exhibition. Dance, music, literature, drama, painting, sculpture, and architecture are all forms of art. **3.** the works produced by creative activity, esp. in the fine arts: *modern art.* **4.** a special skill; knack: *the art of dressing well.* **5.a.** a system of rules guiding any form of endeavor: *the art of self-defense.* **b.** a skilled craft, occupation, or pursuit: *the navigator's art, the art of diplomacy.* **6. the arts. a.** the several forms of creative activity considered together. **b.** the liberal arts. **7.** a branch of learning or study. **8.** human skill or endeavor, as distinguished from the work of nature. **9.** deceptive behavior; cunning; artifice: *More matter with less art* (Shakespeare, *Hamlet*). [Old French *art* skill, from Latin *ars.*]

art² (ärt) *Archaic.* a second person singular present indicative of *be.* ➡ used with *thou.* [Old English *eart* (thou) art.]

-art, form of **-ard,** as in *braggart.*

art. 1. article. **2.** artificial. **3.** artillery. **4.** artist.

art de·co (dek′ō) *also,* **Art De·co.** a style of decorative design introduced in the 1920s, characterized by geometric shapes and bold colors and by the use of new materials, such as chrome and plastic. [French *Art Déco,* from *Exposition Internationale des Arts Décoratifs et Industriels Modernes,* an exposition of modern arts held in Paris in 1925.]

ar·te·fact (är′tə fakt′) artifact.

Ar·te·mis (är′tə mis) *n.* in Greek mythology, the virgin goddess of the hunt and of the moon and twin sister of Apollo. Her Roman counterpart is Diana.

ar·te·ri·al (är tîr′ē əl) *adj.* **1.** of, relating to, or resembling an artery or arteries. **2.** of, relating to, or designating blood, esp. in the arteries, that has become bright red from oxygenation in the lungs or gills. **3.** serving as a main channel or route with many branches: *an arterial road.* —**ar·te′ri·al·ly,** *adv.*

ar·te·ri·ole (är tîr′ē ōl′) *n.* any of the small arterial branches that serve to connect arteries with capillaries. [Modern Latin *arteriola,* diminutive of Latin *arteria.* See ARTERY.] —**ar·te′ri·o′lar,** *adj.*

ar·te·ri·o·scle·ro·sis (är tîr′ē ō sklə rō′sis) *n.* a chronic disorder, esp. of old age, in which the walls of the arteries thicken and harden, thereby hampering the flow of blood. [Modern Latin *arteriosclerosis,* from Greek *artēria* windpipe, artery + *sklerōsis* hardening.] —**ar·te·ri·o·scle·rot·ic** (är tîr′ē ō sklə rot′ik), *adj.*

ar·ter·y (är′tə rē) *n., pl.* **-ter·ies. 1.** one of the muscular elastic tubes that carry blood away from the heart to all parts of the body. **2.** a main channel of communication or transportation: *Traffic is slow on all major arteries out of the city.* [Latin *artēria* this blood vessel, from Greek *artēria.*]

ar·te·sian well (är tē′zhən) a well from which water rises as a result of underground water pressure. [French *artésien* of Artois, northern French province, where wells of this kind were first constructed.]

art·ful (ärt′fəl) *adj.* **1.** showing cunning or deceit; crafty: *an artful ruse.* **2.** skillful or clever; ingenious: *an artful invention.* **3.** done with or showing art or skill: *an artful piano recital.* —**art′ful·ly,** *adv.* —**art′ful·ness,** *n.*

ar·thrit·ic (är thrit′ik) *adj.* of, relating to, or affected with arthritis. —*n.* a person who has arthritis.

ar·thri·tis (är thrī′tis) *n.* an inflammation of a joint or joints characterized by pain and swelling. [Latin *arthrītis* gout, from Greek *arthrītis,* from *arthron* joint.]

ar·thro·pod (är′thrə pod′) *n.* any of a large group of invertebrates, phylum Arthropoda, including crustaceans, insects, myriapods, and arachnids, characterized by jointed legs and segmented bodies. [Greek *arthron* joint + *pous* foot.] —**ar·throp·o·dal** (är throp′ə dəl), *adj.*

ar·thro·scope (är′thrə skōp′) *n.* a medical instrument that is inserted inside a joint to examine or treat injuries and abnormalities. —**ar·thro·scop·ic** (är′thrə skop′ik), *adj.*

Ar·thur (är′thər) *n.* a legendary king of ancient Britain and the leader of the Knights of the Round Table. The character of King Arthur was probably based on a military chieftain who led the Britons against the Saxons early in the sixth century A.D.

Ar·thu·ri·an (är thûr′ē ən) *adj.* of or relating to King Arthur or the legends connected with him and his knights.

ar·ti·choke (är′ti chōk′) *n.* **1.** the immature yellowish green flower head of a plant, *Cynara scolymus,* of the composite family, cooked and eaten as a vegetable. **2.** the hardy, thistlelike plant itself, widely cultivated in Mediterranean countries, Belgium, and the United States. **3.** Jerusalem artichoke. [Dialectal Italian *articiocco,* going back to Arabic *al-kharshūf* the artichoke.]

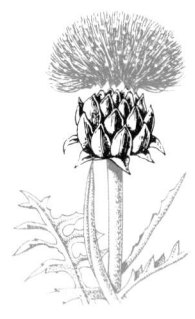

artichoke

ar·ti·cle (är′ti kəl) *n.* **1.** a piece of writing on a particular subject, forming an independent part of a larger publication, as of a periodical or encyclopedia: *The professor wrote an article on solar energy for the magazine.* **2.a.** an individual item (of a group or class): *an article of clothing.* **b.** a particular thing or object; item: *Several articles were stolen from the house.* **3.** a separate clause, provision, or division in a formal document, as in a treaty, constitution, or contract. **4.** one of the words *a, an,* or *the* or their equivalents in other languages, used as modifiers for nouns. *A* and *an* are **indefinite articles** and *the* is the **definite article.** —*v.t.,* **-cled, -cling.** to bind by articles of an agreement: *to article an apprentice.* [Old French *article* clause, joint, from Latin *articulus* division, little joint, diminutive of *artus* joint.]

Articles of Confederation, the first constitution of the United States, adopted by the thirteen original colonies in 1781, superseded by the present Constitution in 1788.

ar·tic·u·lar (är tik′yə lər) *adj.* of or affecting a joint or the joints. [Latin *articulāris,* from *articulus* little joint. See ARTICLE.]

ar·tic·u·late (*adj.,* är tik′yə lit; *v.,* är tik′yə lāt′) *adj.* **1.a.** spoken in distinct syllables and words. **b.** able to speak. **2.** able to express oneself well or effectively: *The senator was an articulate advocate of civil rights.* **3.** expressed or presented clearly and coherently: *an articulate discussion.* **4.** *Anatomy.* composed of jointed segments. Also *(def. 4),* **ar·tic′u·lat′ed.** —*v.,* **-lat·ed, -lat·ing.** —*v.t.* **1.** to pronounce distinctly; enunciate clearly. **2.** to put into words; express effectively: *to articulate one's feelings.* **3.** to unite by means of a joint; connect. —*v.i.* **1.** to pronounce distinct syllables and words; enunciate. **2.** to form a joint or connection: *The bones of the arm articulate at the elbow.* [Latin *articulātus,* past participle of *articulāre* to pronounce distinctly, divide into joints, from *articulus* division. See ARTICLE.] —**ar·tic′u·late·ly,** *adv.* —**ar·tic′u·late·ness,** *n.*

ar·tic·u·la·tion (är tik′yə lā′shən) *n.* **1.** the manner or process of articulating sounds; enunciation. **2.** an articulated sound, esp. a consonant. **3.** the act or manner of jointing or connecting or the state of being connected: *the articulation of bones.* **4.** *Anatomy.* a joint, as the movable segments of an arthropod. **5.** *Botany.* a joint between two parts that separate naturally or easily, as at the base of a leafstalk. —**ar·tic′u·la·tive, ar·tic·u·la·to·ry** (är tik′yə lə tôr′ē), *adj.* —For Synonyms, see **pronunciation.**

ar·tic·u·la·tor (är tik′yə lā′tər) *n.* an organ of speech, as the tongue, lips, or hard palate.

ar·ti·fact (är′tə fakt′) *also,* **artefact.** *n.* anything made or altered by human beings, esp. a tool, weapon, or other object used in the daily life of an ancient civilization. [Latin *ars* skill + *factus,* past participle of *facere* to make.]

ar·ti·fice (är′tə fis) *n.* **1.** a clever or ingenious device; contrivance. **2.** deceptive behavior; trickery; cunning. [French *artifice* skill, cunning, from Latin *artificium* cunning, handicraft. See ARTIFICIAL.]

ar·tif·i·cer (är tif′ə sər) *n.* **1.** a person who is skilled in a craft or trade; craftsman or craftswoman. **2.** a person who creates or devises; inventor.

ar·ti·fi·cial (är′tə fish′əl) *adj.* **1.** made by human beings; not natural: *an artificial lake, artificial light.* **2.** made in imitation of something natural or real; simulated: *artificial flowers.* **3.** not sincere or genuine; pretended; feigned: *artificial politeness.* **4.** (of a person) not natural in manner or conduct; affected. [Latin *artificiālis* relating to art, from *artificium* handicraft, cunning, from *ars* skill, art + *facere* to make.] —**ar′ti·fi′cial·ly,** *adv.* —**ar′ti·fi′cial·ness,** *n.*

A

Synonyms Artificial and synthetic refer to things manufactured rather than occurring naturally. **Artificial** is used of things fashioned by art or skill, often in imitation of natural things: *artificial flowers.* **Synthetic** suggests production by a scientific process, often one involving combining natural substances to make something not found in nature: *synthetic fibers.*

artificial insemination, the injection of semen into the female reproductive organs by artificial means, to induce pregnancy.

artificial intelligence 1. the ability of a computer to perform operations that imitate human reasoning and logic in such applications as designing objects, analyzing problems, or diagnosing illnesses. **2.** a branch of computer science concerned with studying and developing this ability in computer systems.

ar·ti·fi·ci·al·i·ty (är′tə fish′ē al′i tē) *n., pl.* **-ties. 1.** an artificial quality. **2.** something that is artificial.

artificial respiration, the forcing of air into and out of the lungs to restore or maintain proper breathing, as by mouth-to-mouth breathing.

artificial selection, a process of controlled breeding of plants or animals, to create unique genotypes that embody some desired trait or characteristic, as color, size, or temperament, by choosing the parents of each succeeding generation.

ar·til·ler·ist (är til′ər ist) artilleryman.

ar·til·ler·y (är til′ə rē) *n.* **1.** firearms, as cannons, howitzers, and mortars, that fire projectiles and are mounted on stationary or movable emplacements. ➡ distinguished from **small arms. 2.** the branch of a military force utilizing these weapons. [Old French *artillerie* war equipment, from *artiller* to fortify.]

ar·til·ler·y·man (är til′ə rē mən) *n., pl.* **-men** (-mən). a soldier in the artillery; gunner. Also, **artillerist.**

ar·ti·o·dac·tyl (är′tē ō dak′təl) *n.* any of a group of hoofed mammals, order Artiodactyla, having an even number of toes and including swine, hippopotamuses, camels, deer, giraffes, antelope, sheep, goats, and cattle. [Modern Latin *artiodactyl,* from Greek *artios* even + *daktylos* finger, toe.] **—ar′ti·o·dac′tyl·ous,** *adj.*

ar·ti·san (är′tə zən) *n.* a person who is skilled in a particular craft; craftsman or craftswoman. [French *artisan,* from Italian *artigiano,* going back to Latin *artītus* cunning, skilled in arts, from *ars* art.]

art·ist (är′tist) *n.* **1.** a person who is skilled in or whose profession is one of the fine arts, esp. a painter or sculptor. **2.** a skilled public performer. **3.** a person who exhibits artistry and skill in his or her work or occupation: *an artist at repairing cars.* [French *artiste,* from Italian *artista,* from Latin *ars* art, skill.]

ar·tiste (är tēst′) *n.* **1.** artist *(def. 2).* **2.** a person who does anything with skill. ➡ used ironically. [French *artiste.* See ARTIST.]

ar·tis·tic (är tis′tik) *adj.* **1.** relating to or characteristic of art or artists. **2.** skillfully and tastefully done; aesthetically pleasing: *an artistic arrangement.* **—ar·tis′ti·cal·ly,** *adv.*

art·ist·ry (är′tə strē) *n., pl.* **-ries.** artistic quality, methods, skill, or workmanship.

art·less (ärt′lis) *adj.* **1.** without guile or deceit; naive: *the artless questions of a child.* **2.** not artificial; simple; natural: *artless grace.* **3.** lacking skill or knowledge; ignorant. **—art′less·ly,** *adv.* **—art′-less·ness,** *n.*

art nou·veau (ärt′ nü vō′) *also,* Art Nou·veau. a style of decorative art, design, and architecture that originated in the 1890s, characterized by elaborately curving patterns based on natural forms.

art·sy (ärt′sē) *adj.,* **-si·er, -si·est.** *Informal.* **1.** arty: *an artsy magazine full of lavish color prints.* **2.** not genuinely artistic: *The shop was full of artsy little figurines and other trinkets.*

art·work (ärt′wûrk′) *n.* **1.** the production of works of art or craft, esp. when done by hand. **2.** a work of art or craft. **3.** the decorative or

art nouveau cup

illustrative material found in a book or other printed matter.

art·y (är′tē) *adj.,* **art·i·er, art·i·est.** *Informal.* pretentiously pursuing or interested in the arts. **—art′i·ness,** *n.*

a·ru·gu·la (ə rü′gə lə) *n.* any of several plants of the mustard family, esp. *Eruca vesicaria sativa,* grown as a salad herb for its strong-tasting leaves.

ar·um (âr′əm) *n.* **1.** any of a group of small, Eurasian plants, genus *Arum,* bearing a cluster of tiny flowers on a spike surrounded by a showy spathe. **2.** any of various related plants, as the calla lily. **—adj.** designating a family, Araceae, of chiefly tropical plants, typically having many tiny flowers clustered on a spike surrounded by a showy spathe, including the calla lily and the jack-in-the-pulpit. [Latin *arum,* from Greek *aron.*]

-ary¹ *suffix* **1.** (used to form nouns) **a.** a place dealing with: *library, granary.* **b.** a person doing or connected with: *functionary, antiquary.* **c.** a thing or group of things relating to: *dictionary, formulary.* **2.** (used to form adjectives) being or characterized by: *secondary, honorary.* [Latin *-ārius* relating to.]

-ary² *suffix* (used to form adjectives) like; relating to; connected with: *military, exemplary.* [Latin *-aris* having the form of.]

Ar·y·an (âr′ē ən, âr′yən, ar′-) *n.* **1.** a member or descendant of a group of prehistoric nomadic people who spoke an Indo-European language. **2.** formerly, an alternative term for the Indo-European family of languages. **3.** in the doctrine of the Nazis: **a.** a member of the Nordic race, supposedly superior to other racial groups. **b.** any non-Jewish Caucasian. **—adj.** of or relating to Aryans. [Sanskrit *ārya* noble.]

as¹ (az; *unstressed* əz) *adv.* **1.** to the same amount or degree; equally: *Both movies were good, but the second was not as exciting.* **2.** for example; for instance: *The scarf comes in several colors, as red and blue.* **—conj. 1.** to the same degree or extent that: *She was proud as she could be.* **2.** in the same way or manner that: *Speak as I speak.* **3.** at the same time that; while: *They arrived as we were leaving.* **4.** because; since: *As you are not ready yet, we will wait.* **5.** that the result is; with the intent (with *so* and an infinitive): *He told the story so as to entertain everyone. You were so insulting as to offend everyone present.* **6.** though: *Late as it was, we left for the play.* **—prep.** in the manner, function, or role of: *I speak as a friend.* **—pron. 1.** a fact that; which: *It is true, as you can plainly see.* **2.** that; which (after *same* and *such*): *such a night as I had.* [Old English *ealswā* just so, just as.]

  •**as for** (or **to**). with respect to; concerning.

  •**as if** (or **though**). as it would be if.

  •**as is.** in the present condition; just as it is.

  •**as it were.** as if it were so; so to speak.

  •**as of.** beginning at or on (a certain time or date).

  •**as yet.** up to this time; so far.

as² (as) *n., pl.* **as·ses** (as′iz). **1.** a copper or copper alloy coin of ancient Rome, originally weighing about 12 ounces. **2.** a unit of weight in ancient Rome, equal to 12 ounces. [Latin *ās.*]

As, the symbol for arsenic.

as-, form of ad- before *s,* as in *assume.*

AS, the postal abbreviation for American Samoa.

as·a·fet·i·da (as′ə fet′i də) *also,* **as·a·foet·i·da, as·sa·fet·i-da, as·sa·foet·i·da.** *n.* a brown gum resin that smells like garlic, obtained from the roots of various central Asian plants, genus *Ferula,* of the parsley family, formerly used medicinally. [Medieval Latin *asafetida,* going back to Persian *azā* a gum resin + Latin *fetidus* stinking.]

as·bes·tos (as bes′təs, az-) *also,* **as·bes·tus.** *n.* any of several fibrous minerals, as chrysotile, whose fibers may be woven or pressed into material that is incombustible and chemically resistant and does not conduct electricity. The use of such material for insulation and fireproofing is declining because the fibers have been found to cause cancer and other diseases. [Latin *asbestos,* from Greek *asbestos* unquenchable, mistakenly applied by Pliny the Elder, A.D. 23?-79, to the incombustible fiber of a lamp wick used to keep an "unquenchable" eternal light burning in a temple of Athena.]

as·bes·to·sis (as′be stō′sis, az′-) *n.* an irreversible, chronic lung disease caused by long-term inhalation of asbestos dust. [Modern Latin *asbestosis,* from Latin *asbestos* (see ASBESTOS) + *-osis* (see -OSIS).]

as·ca·rid (as′kə rid) *n.* any parasitic roundworm of the family Ascaridae, infesting the intestines of vertebrates. [Modern Latin *ascarid,* from Greek *rides,* genitive of *askaris* intestinal worm.]

as·cend (ə send′) *v.i.* **1.** to move upward physically; rise: *The elevator ascended slowly.* **2.** to move upward from a lower degree or level, as in the musical scale. **—v.t. 1.** to go up; move upward

a	at	e	end	o	hot	u	up	hw	white		about
ā	ape	ē	me	ō	old	ū	use	ng	song		taken
ä	far	i	it	ô	fork	ü	rule	th	thin	ə	pencil
âr	care	ī	ice	oi	oil	u̇	pull	th	this		lemon
				ou	out	ûr	turn	zh	measure		circus
				îr	pierce						

along; climb: *to ascend a mountain.* **2.** to come to occupy; succeed to: *to ascend the throne.* [Latin *ascendere* to climb, rise.] —**as·cend'a·ble**; *also,* **as·cend'i·ble,** *adj.* —For Synonyms, see **climb.**

as·cend·ance (ə sen'dəns) *also,* **ascendence.** *n.* ascendancy.

as·cend·an·cy (ə sen'dən sē) *also,* **ascendency.** *n.* the quality or state of being in a superior position; domination.

as·cend·ant (ə sen'dənt) *also,* **ascendent.** *adj.* **1.** moving upward; ascending; rising. **2.** holding power; superior; dominant: *an ascendant position in public life.* —*n.* **1.** a state or position of being a dominant power or influence: *to gain the ascendant.* **2.** *Astrology.* any sign of the zodiac or other influence that is rising above the eastern horizon, as at the time of one's birth.

as·cend·ence (ə sen'dəns) ascendance.

as·cend·en·cy (ə sen'dən sē) ascendancy.

as·cend·ent (ə sen'dənt) ascendant.

as·cen·sion (ə sen'shən) *n.* **1.** the act or process of ascending. **2.** *Ascension.* **a.** in Christian belief, the passing of Jesus from earth to heaven after his resurrection. **b.** Ascension Day. [Latin *ascēnsiō* ascending, from *ascendere* to rise, ascend.]

Ascension Day, in Christian belief, the day on which Jesus passed from earth to heaven, now observed annually on the fortieth day after Easter. Also, **Ascension Thursday.**

as·cent (ə sent') *n.* **1.** a movement upward in space; rise: *the ascent of a balloon.* **2.** a rise in status; advancement: *a rapid ascent to high office.* **3.** the act of climbing or going up: *Snow made ascent of the mountain impossible.* **4.** a place or way that one ascends; upward slope: *a steep ascent.* [From ASCEND, formed to parallel DESCENT.]

as·cer·tain (as'ər tān') *v.t.* to find out with certainty; determine. [Old French *acertener* to certify, from *à* to (from Latin *ad* to) + *certain* sure. See CERTAIN.] —**as'cer·tain'a·ble,** *adj.* —**as'cer·tain'a·bly,** *adv.* —**as'cer·tain'ment,** *n.*

as·cet·ic (ə set'ik) *n.* **1.** a person who, for religious reasons, practices rigorous self-discipline by leading a life of meditation and self-denial. **2.** a person who leads an austerely abstinent and self-disciplined life. —*adj.* **1.** relating to or characteristic of ascetics or asceticism. **2.** severely abstinent; austere. Also, **as·cet'i·cal.** [Greek *askētikos* laborious, ascetic, from *askētēs* hermit, exerciser, from *askein* to exercise.] —**as·cet'i·cal·ly,** *adv.*

as·cet·i·cism (ə set'ə siz'əm) *n.* **1.** the way of life of an ascetic; extreme self-denial. **2.** the doctrine that one can attain conformity with the will of God through rigorous self-discipline, self-denial, and meditation.

as·cid·i·an (ə sid'ē ən) *n.* any of various saltwater invertebrates, class Ascidiacea, having a leathery, saclike outer covering, as the sea squirts. Ascidians attach themselves to rocks and ship bottoms.

as·cid·i·um (ə sid'ē əm) *n., pl.* **-i·a** (-ē ə). a baglike or flask-shaped part of a plant, the leaf of the pitcher plant. [Modern Latin *ascidium,* from Greek *askidion,* diminutive of *askos* leather bag.]

ASCII (as'kē) a standard computer code of binary numbers that correspond to a standard set of letters, numbers, and other characters. [Abbreviation of *A(merican) S(tandard) C(ode) for I(nformation) I(nterchange).*]

As·cle·pi·us (ə sklē'pē əs) *n.* in Greek mythology, the god of medicine and healing, son of Apollo. His Roman counterpart is Aesculapius.

as·co·my·cete (as'kə mī sēt') *n.* any of a large group of fungi, class Ascomycetes, including yeasts, molds, and mildews, characterized by sexual spores formed in saclike cells. Also, **sac fungus.** [Greek *askos* wineskin, bladder + *mykēs* fungus.] —**as'co·my·ce'tous,** *adj.*

a·scor·bic acid (ə skôr'bik) a crystalline, water-soluble vitamin compound that aids in the formation of connective tissues, increases resistance to infection, and prevents scurvy. It is found in citrus fruits and green vegetables and is made synthetically. Formula: $C_6H_8O_6$ Also, **vitamin C.** [A-[4] + SCORB(UT)IC.]

as·co·spore (as'kə spôr') *n.* a spore of an ascomycete fungus, produced within an ascus.

as·cot (as'kət, -kot) *n.* a scarf worn tied around the neck with one end placed over the other. [From *Ascot,* a racetrack in England, where this neckwear was fashionable.]

as·cribe (ə skrīb') *v.t.,* **-cribed, -crib·ing. 1.** to attribute (something), as to a cause or source: *They ascribed the forest fire to carelessness.* **2.** to regard or allege (a quality or attribute) as belonging to: *to ascribe selfishness to others.* [Latin *ascrībere* to add to a writing, attribute to, from *ad* to + *scribere* to write.] —**as·crib'a·ble,** *adj.* —For Synonyms, see **attribute.**

as·crip·tion (ə skrip'shən) *n.* **1.** the act of ascribing. **2.** an expression or statement that ascribes. [Latin *ascriptiō* an addition in writing, from *ascrībere.* See ASCRIBE.]

as·cus (as'kəs) *n., pl.* **as·ci** (as'ī, -kī). in an ascomycete fungus, a specialized saclike cell in which ascospores develop. [Modern Latin *ascus,* from Greek *askos* wineskin, bladder.]

-ase *suffix* (used to form nouns) an enzyme: *amylase.* [From (DIAST)ASE; because it was the first enzyme isolated.]

a·sep·sis (ə sep'sis, ā sep'-) *n.* **1.** the state or condition of being aseptic. **2.** the use of sterilized medical instruments or materials to prevent infection or inhibit microorganisms that cause decay or disease. [A-[4] + SEPSIS.]

a·sep·tic (ə sep'tik, ā sep'-) *adj.* free from or inhibiting decay or disease-causing microorganisms. [A-[4] + SEPTIC.] —**a·sep'ti·cal·ly,** *adv.*

a·sex·u·al (ā sek'shü əl) *adj. Biology.* **1.** without sex or distinct sexual organs. **2.** not involving the union of male and female germ cells. The simple cell division of amebas is a form of asexual reproduction. —**a·sex'u·al·ly,** *adv.*

As·gard (as'gärd', az'-) *also,* **As·garth** (äs'gärth'), **As·gar·dhr** (äs'gär'thər). *n.* in Norse mythology, the home of the gods and of heroes slain in battle.

ash[1] (ash) *n.* **1.** a gray-white powdery residue left after a substance has burned completely. Also, **ashes. 2.** fine particles of lava, as erupted by a volcano. [Old English *asce* the powdery residue.]

ash[2] (ash) *n.* **1.** any of a group of hardwood trees, genus *Fraxinus,* of the olive family, found chiefly in temperate regions of the Northern Hemisphere, usually bearing pinnate leaves and winged seeds. **2.** the tough, economically valuable wood of any of these trees. —*adj.* relating to or made of the wood of an ash. [Old English *æsc* ash tree.]

a·shamed (ə shāmd') *adj.* **1.** feeling shame, as through the recognition that one's actions or thoughts are foolish or improper: *I was ashamed that I lost my temper.* **2.** unwilling or deterred through fear of shame: *to be ashamed to admit a mistake in public.* [Old English *āscamod,* past participle of *āscamian* to feel shame, to make ashamed.] —**a·sham·ed·ly** (ə shā'mid lē), *adv.*

A·shan·ti (ə shan'tē, ə shän'-) *n., pl.* **-ti** or **-tis. 1.** a native or inhabitant of Ashanti. **2.** the language of the Ashanti.

ash·can (ash'kan') *n.* **1.** a can or similar receptacle for ashes or trash. **2.** *Slang.* depth charge.

ash·en[1] (ash'ən) *adj.* **1.** ash-colored; pale. **2.** of or resembling ashes. [ASH[1] + -EN[2].]

ash·en[2] (ash'ən) *adj.* **1.** of or relating to an ash tree. **2.** made from the wood of an ash tree. [ASH[2] + -EN[2].]

ash·es (ash'iz) *pl. n.* **1.a.** ash[1] *(def. 1).* **b.** the burned remnants, as of logs in a fireplace. **2.** the remains of a dead body after cremation or decomposition. **3.** the remains of something that has been destroyed; ruins.

Ash·ke·naz·i (äsh'kə nä'zē) *n., pl.* **-naz·im** (-nä'zim). a member or descendant of the group of Jews who settled in eastern or central Europe. ➡ distinguished from **Sephardi.** [Hebrew *Ashkenazzīm,* plural of *Ashkenaz,* a biblical name applied in the Middle Ages as a term for Germany.] —**Ash'ke·naz'ic,** *adj.*

ash·lar (ash'lər) *also,* **ash·ler.** *n.* **1.** a square, hewn stone used in building. **2.** a thin slab of stone used for facing a wall. **3.** a masonry wall made of ashlars. [Old French *aisseler* crossbeam.]

a·shore (ə shôr') *adv., adj.* **1.** on or to the shore. **2.** on land.

ash·ram (äsh'rəm) *n.* **1.** a Hindu religious retreat, esp. one associated with a guru. **2.** any place for religious or spiritual meditation. [Sanskrit *āsrama* ashram, religious community.]

Ash·to·reth (ash'tə reth') Astarte.

ash·tray (ash'trā') *n.* a receptacle for smokers' tobacco ashes.

Ash Wednesday, the first day of Lent, observed on the seventh Wednesday before Easter. [From the custom of placing *ashes* on the forehead of churchgoers as a symbol of penitence on this day.]

ash·y (ash'ē) *adj.,* **ash·i·er, ash·i·est. 1.** of, resembling, or covered with ashes. **2.** ash-colored; pale.

A·sian (ā'zhən, ā'shən) *adj.* of, relating to, or characteristic of Asia or its peoples or cultures. —*n.* **1.** a native or citizen of an Asian country. **2.** a person of Asian ancestry.

Asian flu, influenza caused by a strain of virus first recognized in Asia in 1957. Also, **Asian influenza.**

A·si·at·ic (ā'zhē at'ik, ā'shē-) *n., adj.* Asian. ➡ now generally considered offensive; **Asian** is preferred.

Asiatic cholera, cholera.

a·side (ə sīd') *adv.* **1.** on or to one side; out of the way; away: *Step aside, please.* **2.** out of or apart from consideration or use: *Mountain climbing can be enjoyable if you put aside your fear of heights.* **3.** in reserve; in keeping: *Please hold that book aside for me.* —*n.* **1.** a remark not intended to be heard by all those who

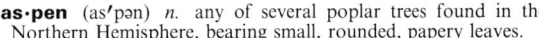

are present, esp. an actor's remark intended for the audience but not the other characters. **2.** a departure from a main theme; digression.

· **aside from. a.** apart from; independent of: *Your comments are aside from the point.* **b.** except for: *I have done all my housework aside from folding the laundry.*

as·i·nine (as′ə nīn′) *adj.* stupid; silly. [Latin *asinīnus* of an ass, from *asinus* ass.] —**as′i·nine′ly,** *adv.*

as·i·nin·i·ty (as′ə nin′i tē) *n., pl.* -**ties. 1.** the quality of being asinine; silliness. **2.** something that is asinine, as a remark.

ask (ask) *v.t.* **1.** to put a question about; inquire about: *We asked the way to the park.* **2.** to put a question to; inquire of: *Ask me if you're not sure.* **3.** to call for the answer to: *to ask a question.* **4.a.** to make a request of: *Let's ask that person for directions.* **b.** to make a request for: *I'd like to ask a favor of you.* **5.** to invite: *to ask someone to dinner.* **6.** to set (as a price); demand: *to ask a high price for an old car.* **7.** to demand; require: *The company asks too much from its workers.* —*v.i.* **1.** to make inquiries (with *for, after,* or *about*): *Everyone asked about you when you were sick.* **2.** to make a request (with *for*): *The customer asked for more bread.* [Old English *āscian* to question.]

· **to ask for.** *Informal.* to invite or provoke (punishment or retaliation).

Synonyms *v.t.* **Ask, question,** and **query** mean to attempt to get information from. **Ask** is the general term: *We stopped to ask a pedestrian directions. The letter asked me for my opinion about the senator.* **Question** implies systematic and continual asking: *The police questioned the suspect for hours.* **Query,** a more formal word, is used of an attempt to get an authoritative answer on some doubtful point: *The editor queried the author on the spelling of a name.*

a·skance (ə skans′) *also,* **a·skant** (ə skant′). *adv.* **1.** with a side glance; sideways. **2.** with suspicion, distrust, or disapproval. [Of uncertain origin.]

a·skew (ə skū′) *adv., adj.* to one side; out of the proper position; awry. [A-¹ + SKEW.]

a·slant (ə slant′) *adv.* in a slanting direction; on a slant. —*adj.* slanting. —*prep.* slantingly across or over.

a·sleep (ə slēp′) *adj.* **1.** in a state of sleep; sleeping. **2.** (of an arm, leg, or other body part) lacking feeling; numb. **3.** not active; sluggish. **4.** dead. —*adv.* into a sleeping condition: *to fall asleep.* [Old French *on slæpe* literally, in sleep.]

a·slope (ə slōp′) *adv., adj.* at a slant; sloping.

a·so·cial (ā sō′shəl) *adj.* **1.** having or showing no interest in the laws or customs of society: *Littering is asocial behavior.* **2.** not desiring the company of others; unsociable: *A hermit is an asocial recluse.*

asp (asp) *n.* **1.** a cobra, *Naja haje,* native to Egypt, worshiped by the ancient Egyptians and said to have been used by Cleopatra to kill herself. **2.** any of several venomous snakes, esp. a viper of central Europe and the Mediterranean. [Latin *aspis,* from Greek *aspis.*]

as·par·a·gus (ə spar′ə gəs) *n.* **1.** the young, green or white spears of the plant *Asparagus officinalis,* of the lily family, cooked and eaten as a vegetable. **2.** the plant itself, native to the Old World but raised in most parts of the world. The spears grow from horizontal, underground stems, called rhizomes, and bear scalelike leaves at the tip. [Latin *asparagus,* from Greek *asparagos.*]

as·par·tame (as′pər tām′, ə spär′tām) *n.* a sweet-tasting white powder manufactured from amino acids and used as a low-calorie sweetener.

as·par·tic acid (ə spär′tik) a nonessential amino acid esp. abundant in beets, young sugarcane, and asparagus. Formula: $C_4H_7NO_4$

ASPCA, American Society for the Prevention of Cruelty to Animals.

as·pect (as′pekt) *n.* **1.a.** the ways in which something appears or presents itself to the mind; facet: *The attorney examined all aspects of the case.* **b.** a way in which to regard something; viewpoint: *From their aspect, we were wrong.* **2.** an appearance presented to the eye; look: *the striking aspect of the mountains.* **3.** the way in which someone appears; countenance; mien: *a face with a fierce aspect.* **4.** a side or surface facing a given direction: *dorsal aspect.* **5.** *Astrology.* the relative positions of the planets, thought to have favorable or unfavorable influence on human affairs. **6.** the direction in which something faces; exposure: *a house with a southern aspect.* [Latin *aspectus* look, sight, going back to *ad* to + *specere* to look, behold.]

asparagus spears

as·pen (as′pən) *n.* any of several poplar trees found in the Northern Hemisphere, bearing small, rounded, papery leaves.

as·per·i·ty (a sper′i tē) *n., pl.* -**ties. 1.** harshness of manner or temper; bitterness. **2.** a condition of difficulty or suffering; hardship; severity; rigor: *the asperities of life on the frontier.* **3.** roughness, as of surface; unevenness. [Latin *asperitās,* from *asper* rough.]

aspen leaves

as·perse (ə spûrs′) *v.t.* -**persed, -pers·ing.** to spread false or damaging accusations against; slander. [Latin *aspersus,* past participle of *aspergere* to sprinkle, bespatter, from *ad* to + *spargere* to scatter.] —**as·pers′er,** *n.* —**as·per′sive,** *adj.*

as·per·sion (ə spûr′zhən, -shən) *n.* **1.** a damaging or false statement; slander: *to cast aspersions on someone's character.* **2.** the act of slandering; defaming.

as·phalt (as′fôlt; *also, British,* as′falt) *n.* **1.** a brown or black bituminous substance, occurring in nature and also obtained as a by-product of petroleum refining. **2.** a mixture of this with gravel, sand, or both of these, used esp. for paving. Also, **as·phal·tum** (as fôl′təm; *also, British,* as fal′təm). —*v.t.* to pave or cover with asphalt. [Late Latin *asphaltus* this bituminous substance, from Greek *asphaltos;* possibly of Semitic origin.] —**as·phal·tic** (as-fôl′tik; *also, British,* as fal′tik), *adj.*

as·pho·del (as′fə del′) *n.* any of several plants of the lily family, bearing showy, trumpet-shaped, pink, white, or yellow flowers on a spike. [Latin *asphodelus,* from Greek *asphodelos.*]

as·phyx·i·a (as fik′sē ə) *n.* suffocation or unconsciousness resulting from a lack of oxygen and an increase of carbon dioxide in the blood and body tissues. [Greek *asphyxiā* stopping of the pulse, from *a-* not, without + *sphyxis* pulse.]

as·phyx·i·ate (as fik′sē āt′) *v.,* -**at·ed, -at·ing.** —*v.t.* to cause asphyxia in; suffocate. —*v.i.* to undergo asphyxia. —**as·phyx′i·a′tion,** *n.* —**as·phyx′i·a′tor,** *n.*

as·pic (as′pik) *n.* a jelly made from meat, poultry, fish, or vegetable juices, chilled, and often served as a molded salad dish. [French *aspic* asp from Latin *aspis* from Greek *aspis;* possibly from the French proverb *froid comme un aspic* cold as an asp.]

as·pi·dis·tra (as′pi dis′trə) *n.* any of several plants, genus *Aspidistra,* of the lily family, bearing large, glossy, evergreen leaves, esp. *A. elatior,* widely cultivated as a houseplant. [Formed from Greek *aspis* shield; because of its shield-shaped leaves.]

as·pi·rant (as′pər ənt, ə spīr′ənt) *n.* a person who aspires to or seeks advancement or honors. —*adj.* aspiring.

as·pi·rate (*v.,* as′pə rāt′; *adj., n.,* as′pər it) *v.t.,* -**rat·ed, -rat·ing. 1.** to precede the pronunciation of (a word or syllable) with a puff of breath or with an *h* sound. In the pronunciation of the word *when,* when the *wh* is aspirated, the word is pronounced *hwen.* **2.** to follow (the pronunciation of certain initial consonants) with a puff of breath. The first *p* in *paper* is aspirated, whereas the second *p* is not. **3.** to remove (fluids or tissue) from a body cavity with an aspirator. —*n.* **1.** the sound of the letter *h.* **2.** a consonant whose pronunciation is followed by a puff of breath. —*adj.* pronounced with an aspirate or followed by a puff of breath. Also, **as′pi·rat·ed.** [Latin *aspīrātus,* past participle of *aspīrāre* to breathe upon, from *ad* to + *spirare* to breath.]

as·pi·ra·tion (as′pə rā′shən) *n.* **1.a.** a strong desire for attainment, as of something good or lofty; high ambition. **b.** the object of this desire or ambition. **2.** the act of breathing; a breath. **3. a.** the articulation of an aspirate. **b.** an aspirate. **4.** the removal of fluids or tissue from a body cavity with an aspirator. —For Synonyms, see **ambition.**

as·pi·ra·tor (as′pə rā′tər) *n.* **1.** any apparatus or device employing suction. **2.** an instrument for the removal of fluids or tissue from a body cavity by the use of suction.

as·pire (ə spīr′) *v.i.,* -**pired, -pir·ing. 1.** to seek ambitiously to attain something; be earnestly desirous; aim: *to aspire after glory, to aspire to the presidency.* **2.** *Archaic.* to rise up; ascend. [Latin *aspīrāre* to breathe upon, desire to obtain. See ASPIRATE.] —**as·pir′er,** *n.* —**as·pir′ing·ly,** *adv.*

as·pi·rin (as′pər in) *n.* **1.** a white, crystalline derivative of salicylic acid, used in tablet form for the relief of pain and fever. Formula: $C_9H_8O_4$ Also, **acetylsalicylic acid. 2.** a tablet of

a	at	e	end	o	hot	u	up	hw	white		about
ā	ape	ē	me	ō	old	ū	use	ng	song		taken
ä	far	i	it	ô	fork	ü	rule	th	thin	ə	pencil
âr	care	ī	ice	oi	oil	u̇	pull	th	this		lemon
		îr	pierce	ou	out	ûr	turn	zh	measure		circus

aspirin. [A(CETYL) + *spir(aeic acid)* (former name of SALICYLIC ACID) + -IN¹.]

ass (as) *n.* **1.** any of several long-eared mammals of the genus *Equus* of the horse family, native to Asia and Africa, esp. the domesticated ass, *Equus asinus,* used as a beast of burden; donkey. **2.** any of several similar mammals of Asia and the Middle East. **3.** a stupid person; fool. [Old English *assa* donkey, possibly from Old Irish *assan,* from Latin *asinus.*]

as·sa·fet·i·da (as′ə fet′i də) *also,* **assafoetida.** asafetida.

as·sa·gai (as′ə gī′) *also,* **assegai.** *n., pl.* **-gais.** a slender spear of hard wood, used by some tribes of southern Africa. [Portuguese *azagaia* javelin, from Arabic *az-zaghāyah,* from *al* the + Berber *zaghāyah* javelin.]

as·sail (ə sāl′) *v.t.* **1.** to attack with physical violence. **2.** to attack vigorously with arguments or abuse. [Old French *asaillir,* going back to Latin *ad* to, at + *salīre* to leap.] —**as·sail′a·ble,** *adj.* —**as·sail′er,** *n.* —**as·sail′ment,** *n.* —For Synonyms, see **attack.**

as·sail·ant (ə sā′lənt) *n.* a person who assails; attacker: *The police rescued the couple from their assailant.*

as·sas·sin (ə sas′in) *n.* a murderer, esp. of a public figure. [French *assassin,* from Arabic *hashshāshīn* eaters of hashish; originally a Muslim society, members of which, under the influence of hashish, killed Christian crusaders.]

as·sas·si·nate (ə sas′ə nāt′) *v.t.,* **-nat·ed, -nat·ing. 1.** to murder, esp. a public figure; kill treacherously. **2.** to destroy or damage maliciously: *to assassinate someone's character.* —**as·sas′si·na′tion,** *n.* —**as·sas′si·na′tor,** *n.* —For Synonyms, see **kill¹.**

as·sault (ə sôlt′) *n.* **1.** a violent or vigorous physical or verbal attack. **2.** *Law.* an unlawful attempt or threat to do physical violence to another without the actual accomplishment of the intended attack. ➤ distinguished from **battery. 3.** *Military.* the last stage of an attack; closing with the enemy in hand-to-hand fighting. **4.** rape. —*v.t., v.i.* to make an assault (on); attack. [Old French *asaut* an attack, going back to Latin *ad* to, at + *saltus* leap.] —**as·sault′er,** *n.* —**as·saul′tive,** *adj.* —For Synonyms *(v.t.),* see **attack.**

assault and battery *Law.* an assault followed by the actual infliction of physical violence upon the person assaulted.

as·say (*v.,* ə sā′; *n.,* ə sā′, as′ā) *v.t.* **1.** to perform chemical analysis to determine the metal content of (an ore, alloy, or the like). **2.** to put to trial; test; evaluate. **3.** to try to do; attempt. —*v.i.* to be shown by analysis to contain a certain amount of a particular metal: *The ore sample assayed low in uranium.* —*n.* **1.** a chemical analysis, as of an ore, mineral, or alloy, to determine metal content. **2.** the substance analyzed. **3.** a report or results of an assaying. **4.** any analysis or examination; test. [Old French *asaier,* form of *essaier* to try, test, from *essai* a test, from Late Latin *exagium* a weighing.] —**as·say′er,** *n.*

as·se·gai (as′ə gī′) assagai.

as·sem·blage (ə sem′blij) *n.* **1.** a group of persons or things brought together; collection. **2.** the act of putting or fitting together, as of parts of something to be constructed. **3.** the act of assembling or the state of being assembled.

as·sem·ble (ə sem′bəl) *v.,* **-bled, -bling.** —*v.t.* **1.** to gather or bring (a group) together; collect. **2.** to put or fit together, as the parts of something to be constructed. —*v.i.* to meet or come together; convene: *The tour group will assemble in front of the museum.* [Old French *assembler* to gather, going back to Latin *ad* to + *simul* together.] —**as·sem′bler,** *n.* —For Synonyms *(v.t.),* see **gather.**

as·sem·bly (ə sem′blē) *n., pl.* **-blies. 1.** a group of people gathered together for a common purpose. **2.** a body of lawmakers. **3. Assembly.** in certain states of the United States, the lower house of the legislature. **4.** the act or process of fitting together (parts) to make a whole: *the assembly of airplane parts.* **5.** a group of parts that fit or work together: *to check the assembly of a machine.* **6.** the act of assembling or the state of being assembled. **7.** a signal for troops to fall in. —For Synonyms, see **meeting.**

assembly language, a low-level computer programming language similar to machine language but using decimal numbers and easily memorized two- or three-letter codes.

assembly line, an arrangement of tools, machines, and workers, past which an unfinished product is moved. Each worker or machine performs a specialized operation on the product until it is completely assembled.

as·sem·bly·man (ə sem′blē mən) *n., pl.* **-men** (-mən). a member of a legislative assembly, esp. of the lower house of a state or provincial legislature.

as·sem·bly·wom·an (ə sem′blē wùm′ən) *n., pl.* **-wom·en** (-wim′ən). a woman who is a member of a legislative assembly, esp. of the lower house of a state or provincial legislature.

as·sent (ə sent′) *v.i.* to express agreement; concur (with *to*): *I* assent to your proposals. —*n.* the act of assenting; agreement; consent. [Old French *assentir* to assent, from Latin *assentīre.*] —For Synonyms *(v.i.),* see **consent.**

as·sert (ə sûrt′) *v.t.* **1.** to state positively; affirm: *to assert that something is true.* **2.** to put forward or maintain insistently; put into effect: *Assert your rights.* [Latin *assertus,* past participle of *asserere* claim, affirm.] —**as·sert′er;** *also,* **as·ser′tor,** *n.*

· **to assert oneself.** to present or defend one's own position or rights in a bold manner.

as·ser·tion (ə sûr′shən) *n.* **1.** a positive statement; declaration: *Their assertion was proved false.* **2.** the act of putting forward or maintaining.

as·ser·tive (ə sûr′tiv) *adj.* characterized by self-assertion; positive; aggressive: *an assertive person, an assertive tone of voice.* —**as·ser′tive·ly,** *adv.* —**as·ser′tive·ness,** *n.*

as·sess (ə ses′) *v.t.* **1.** to set the official value of (property) for taxation. **2.** to determine the amount of (a tax, fine, or damages). **3.** to tax or charge (a person or property): *Assess each member of the club fifty dollars for the building fund.* **4.** to make a judgment of; evaluate: *The judges carefully assessed each contestant.* [Old French *assesser* to determine, tax, from Late Latin *assessāre* to fix a tax, from Latin *assessus,* past participle of *assidēre* to sit beside, assist a judge.] —**as·sess′a·ble,** *adj.*

as·sess·ment (ə ses′mənt) *n.* **1.** the act of assessing. **2.** the amount or value assessed. **3.** a judgment; evaluation: *What is your assessment of the situation?*

as·ses·sor (ə ses′ər) *n.* a person who assesses property for taxation.

as·set (as′et) *n.* **1.** something valuable or useful; advantage: *Speaking several languages can be a great asset.* **2.** anything owned having a money value. **3. assets. a.** the property and resources of a business or person as listed on a balance sheet. ➤ opposed to **liabilities. b.** property or effects applicable for payment of the owner's debts. [Anglo-Norman *assets,* earlier *asetz,* going back to Latin *ad* toward + *satis* enough (in the sense of "enough for payment of debts").]

as·sev·er·ate (ə sev′ə rāt′) *v.t.,* **-at·ed, -at·ing.** to declare solemnly or positively; affirm. [Latin *asseverātus,* past participle of *asseverāre* to affirm strongly.]

as·sev·er·a·tion (ə sev′ə rā′shən) *n.* **1.** the act of asseverating. **2.** an emphatic or solemn assertion.

as·si·du·i·ty (as′i dü′i tē, -dū′-) *n., pl.* **-ties.** the quality or condition of being assiduous; perseverance; diligence.

as·sid·u·ous (ə sij′ü əs) *adj.* characterized by persistence and diligence: *an assiduous student.* [Latin *assiduus* sitting by, busy, constant.] —**as·sid′u·ous·ly,** *adv.* —**as·sid′u·ous·ness,** *n.*

as·sign (ə sīn′) *v.t.* **1.** to give out; distribute; allot: *Work will be assigned daily.* **2.** to select for a duty or office; appoint: *A new principal was assigned to the school.* **3.** to set or fix definitely; designate: *to assign a date for a meeting.* **4.** to ascribe, as to a period of time: *The ruins are assigned to the tenth century.* **5.** *Law.* to transfer (a right, property, or interest). —*n. also,* **assigns.** assignee. [Old French *assigner,* from Latin *assignāre.*] —**as·sign′a·ble,** *adj.* —**as·sign′er,** *n.*

Synonyms *v.t.* Assign, allot, and **apportion** mean to give as a share. **Assign** suggests that shares are distributed on the basis of a plan or conscious decision: *The boss assigned heavier tasks to the young worker than to senior employees.* **Allot** suggests a distribution based on chance: *The team allotted lockers to members in the order that they came through the door.* **Apportion** suggests an attempt at fairness in distribution, if not at equal shares: *The food was apportioned among the refugees according to need.*

as·sig·nat (as′ig nat′) *n.* paper money issued by the French Revolutionary government from 1789 to 1796, based on the security of confiscated lands. [French *assignat,* from Latin *assignātus,* past participle of *assignāre* to allot.]

as·sig·na·tion (as′ig nā′shən) *n.* **1.** the arrangement of a time and place for a meeting, esp. a secret or illicit one between lovers; tryst. **2.** the act of assigning.

as·sign·ee (ə sī nē′, as′ə nē′) *n.* a person to whom a right, property, or interest is legally transferred.

as·sign·ment (ə sīn′mənt) *n.* **1.** something that is assigned; task; job: *Her assignment is to write a report on the company's financial situation.* **2.** the act of assigning or the state of being assigned: *His assignment to the new post was still not official.* **3.** *Law.* **a.** the transfer of a right, property, or interest. **b.** a document by which the transfer is made.

as·sign·or (ə sī′nər, as′ə nôr′) *n.* a person who legally assigns a right, property, or interest.

as·sim·i·la·ble (ə sim′ə lə bəl) *adj.* capable of being assimilated. —**as·sim′i·la·bil′i·ty,** *n.*

as·sim·i·late (ə sim′ə lāt′) *v.,* **-lat·ed, -lat·ing.** —*v.t.* **1.** to take in and incorporate as one's own: *to assimilate knowledge.*

2. to absorb and convert into living tissue: *Food is assimilated in the small intestine.* **3.** to absorb a minority or immigrant group into a prevailing culture: *The United States has assimilated immigrants from many nations.* **4.** to alter phonetically by assimilation. —*v.i.* **1.** to be absorbed by or incorporated into a system or culture. **2.** to become similar to; come to resemble. [Latin *assimilātus,* past participle of *assimilāre* to make like.] —**as·sim′i·la′tor,** *n.* —For Synonyms, see **absorb.**

as·sim·i·la·tion (ə sim′ə lā′shən) *n.* **1.** the act of assimilating or the state of being assimilated. **2.** the process whereby a minority or immigrant group is absorbed into an existing culture through contact. **3.** the absorption and transformation of digested food into living tissue. **4.** the process in which a sound becomes similar to or the same as an adjacent sound, as when *grandma* is pronounced *gramma.*

as·sim·i·la·tive (ə sim′ə lā′tiv) *adj.* capable of or causing assimilation.

As·sin·i·boin (ə sin′ə boin′) *also,* **As·sin·i·boine.** *n., pl.* -**boin** or -**boins;** *also,* -**boine** or -**boines.** **1.** a member of a North American Indian tribe formerly living in the northern Great Plains. **2.** the Siouan language of this tribe. —*adj.* of or relating to the Assiniboin or their language or culture.

as·sist (ə sist′) *v.t.* **1.** to give help or aid to. **2.** to be associated with as an assistant: *The nurses assisted the surgeon.* —*v.i.* **1.** to be of help; aid; support: *to assist in selecting a building site.* **2.** to be present; participate: *to assist at an operation.* —*n.* **1.** *Baseball.* **a.** a play that aids a teammate in making an out. **b.** credit given for such a play. **2.** *Basketball, Ice Hockey.* **a.** the action of passing the ball or puck to a teammate who scores. **b.** credit given for such a play. [French *assister* to help, from Latin *assistere* to stand by, aid.] —For Synonyms *(v.t.),* see **help.**

as·sis·tance (ə sis′təns) *n.* the act of assisting; aid or support.

as·sist·ant (ə sis′tənt) *n.* a person who assists; subordinate; helper. —*adj.* assisting: *present in an assistant capacity only.*

assistant professor, a teacher in a college or university who ranks above an instructor and below an associate professor.

as·size (ə sīz′) *n.* **1.** *Archaic.* a session of a court of law or legislative assembly. **2. assizes. a.** court sessions held periodically in the counties of England to try criminal and civil cases by jury. **b.** the time or place of such sessions. [Old French *assise* sitting, from *asseoir* to sit at, from Latin *assidēre* to sit beside, assist a judge.]

assn., association.

assoc. 1. associate. **2.** association.

as·so·ci·ate (*v.,* ə sō′shē āt′, -sē-; *n., adj.,* ə sō′shē it, -āt′, -sē-) *v.,* -**at·ed,** -**at·ing.** —*v.t.* **1.** to connect in one's mind: *We often associate darkness with danger.* **2.** to join or connect (oneself) as a companion, partner, or friend: *I associated myself with the tenants' organization.* **3.** to join together; combine; connect: *the misery that is always associated with poverty.* —*v.i.* **1.** to keep certain company, as a friend, companion, or partner: *I don't associate with them much anymore.* **2.** to form a union or combination; unite: *Water molecules associate because of hydrogen bonds.* —*n.* **1.** a person who is frequently in the company of another; companion; friend. **2.** a person who is connected with another or others in some enterprise or action; partner; colleague: *business associates.* **3.** a member of a society, institution, or organization having partial rights or privileges. **4.** anything usually accompanying or connected with another. **5.** a person who has received an associate's degree. —*adj.* **1.** having secondary membership, status, or privileges: *an associate judge, an associate partner.* **2.** connected; concomitant. [Latin *associātus,* past participle of *associāre* to join, from *ad* to + *socius* companion.]

associate professor, a teacher in a college or university who ranks above an assistant professor and below a professor.

as·so·ci·a·tion (ə sō′sē ā′shən, -shē-) *n.* **1.** an organized group of people with common interests or purposes; society. **2.** the act of associating or the state of being associated; relationship; connection. **3.a.** a connection of or between thoughts, feelings, images, or sensations, such that one brings the other to mind: *the association between "red" and "blood."* **b.** one of the thoughts or sensations so connected. —**as·so′ci·a′tion·al,** *adj.*

association football, soccer.

as·so·ci·a·tive (ə sō′shē ā′tiv, -sē-, -shə tiv) *adj.* **1.** relating to, characterized by, or resulting from association, esp. of thoughts, feelings, images, or sensations: *associative images.* **2.** *Mathematics.* relating to or designating a law stating that the sum or product of two or more quantities will be the same regardless of the way in which they are grouped. For example, $(6 + 12) + 5$ is the same as $6 + (12 + 5)$.

as·soil (ə soil′) *v.t. Archaic.* **1.** to absolve. **2.** to atone for. [Old French *assoil,* present indicative of *assoldre* to absolve, from Latin *absolvere* to free. Doublet of ABSOLVE.]

as·so·nance (as′ə nəns) *n.* **1.** similarity or repetition of sounds,

as in poetry. **2.** a poetic device in which stressed vowel sounds are alike but consonant sounds are different. In the line *And grassy barrows of the happier dead,* the *a*'s in *grassy, barrows,* and *happier* are examples of assonance. [French *assonance,* from Latin *assonāre* to respond to.]

as·sort (ə sôrt′) *v.t.* to put into like groups or categories; classify: *Assort these cards by color.* —*v.i.* **1.** to fall into a category; be matched. **2.** to consort; associate (with *with*). [Old French *assorter* to match, going back to Latin *ad* to + Latin *sors* lot, share.] —**as·sort′er,** *n.*

as·sort·ed (ə sôr′tid) *adj.* **1.** of various kinds: *a pound of assorted cookies.* **2.** sorted according to kind; classified. **3.** matched; suited. —For Synonyms, see **miscellaneous.**

as·sort·ment (ə sôrt′mənt) *n.* **1.** a varied or diversified collection. **2.** the act of assorting or the state of being assorted.

asst., assistant.

as·suage (ə swāj′) *v.t.,* -**suaged,** -**suag·ing. 1.** to lessen in intensity; mitigate: *to assuage pain.* **2.** to calm; mollify; pacify: *The angry customer was difficult to assuage.* **3.** to satisfy; appease: *to assuage one's hunger.* [Old French *assouagier* to soften, appease, going back to Latin *ad* to + *suāvis* sweet.] —**as·suage′ment,** *n.* —**as·suag′er,** *n.*

as·sume (ə süm′) *v.t.,* -**sumed,** -**sum·ing. 1.** to take for granted; suppose as a fact. **2.** to take upon oneself; undertake: *to assume a position of great responsibility.* **3.** to take on; adopt: *The fugitive assumed a new name.* **4.** to take for oneself; seize; arrogate; usurp: *The dictator assumed absolute power.* **5.** to put on the guise of; pretend: *Assume a virtue if you have it not* (Shakespeare, *Hamlet*). [Latin *assūmere* to take to oneself, adopt.] —**as·sum′a·ble,** *adj.* —**as·sum′er,** *n.* —For Synonyms, see **adopt.**

as·sumed (ə sümd′) *adj.* **1.** pretended; fictitious: *an assumed name.* **2.** taken for granted as true: *an assumed fact.*

as·sum·ing (ə sü′ming) *adj.* taking too much for granted; presumptuous; arrogant.

as·sump·tion (ə sump′shən) *n.* **1.** the act of assuming or the state of being assumed. **2.** something taken for granted; supposition: *Your assumption proved to be wrong.* **3.** presumption; effrontery; arrogance. **4. the Assumption. a.** in Roman Catholicism, the taking up into heaven of the body and soul of the Virgin Mary after her death. **b.** in Roman Catholicism, a church festival celebrating this event. It is observed on August 15. [Latin *assūmptio* a taking.]

as·sur·ance (ə shùr′əns) *n.* **1.** the act of assuring or the state of being assured. **2.** a positive declaration intended to give confidence; guarantee: *We had their assurance that they would help us if needed.* **3.** freedom from doubt; certainty: *to have assurance of someone's loyalty.* **4.** confidence in oneself; aplomb. **5.** impudence; effrontery. **6.** *British.* insurance. —For Synonyms, see **confidence.**

as·sure (ə shùr′) *v.t.,* -**sured,** -**sur·ing. 1.** to declare positively to; tell with certainty: *I assure you that they will come.* **2.** to make certain (the occurrence or accomplishment of something); guarantee: *Their agreement assured passage of the bill.* **3.** to make (someone) certain; convince: *I can assure you of their honesty.* **4.** to give confidence to; reassure: *to assure a frightened child.* **5.** to make secure; ensure: *Closing the deal assured my position in the firm.* **6.** *British.* insure. [Old French *aseürer* to make sure, going back to Latin *ad* to + *sēcūrus* sure.] —**as·sur′er,** *n.*

as·sured (ə shùrd′) *adj.* **1.** made certain; undoubted; guaranteed: *an assured victory.* **2.** self-possessed; confident: *an assured manner.* **3.** *British.* insured. —*n.* **1.** a person who is the beneficiary of an insurance policy. **2.** a person whose life or property is insured. —**as·sur·ed·ly** (ə shùr′id lē, ə shùrd′-), *adv.* —**as·sur′ed·ness,** *n.*

As·syr·i·an (ə sir′ē ən) *adj.* of or relating to Assyria or its people, language, or culture. —*n.* **1.** a native or citizen of ancient Assyria. **2.** the Semitic language of the Assyrians.

As·tar·te (as tär′tē) *also,* **Ashtoreth.** *n.* the Syrian and Phoenician goddess of fertility and love, identified with the Babylonian and Assyrian Ishtar and later with the Greek Aphrodite.

as·ta·tine (as′tə tēn′) *n.* a radioactive chemical element, heaviest of the halogen family, produced by bombarding bismuth with alpha particles. Traces of it occur in nature as radioactive decay products. Symbol: At For tables, see **element.** [Greek *astatos* unstable (from *a-* not and *histanai* to stand) + -INE[2]; because the element is radioactive and has no stable isotopes.]

a	at	e	end	o	hot	u	up	hw	white		about
ā	ape	ē	me	ō	old	ū	use	ng	song		taken
ä	far	i	it	ô	fork	ü	rule	th	thin	ə	pencil
âr	care	ī	ice	oi	oil	ù	pull	th	this		lemon
		îr	pierce	ou	out	ûr	turn	zh	measure		circus

as·ter (as'tər) *n.* **1.** the daisylike flower head of any of a large group of plants of the genus *Aster,* consisting of many ray flowers around a disk of tubular flowers. **2.** a plant bearing such flower heads, usually in clusters, found in most temperate regions of the world. **3.** any other plant of the genus *Aster,* of the composite family, such as the daisy. **4.** *Biology.* a starlike arrangement of fibers radiating from the centriole of a cell. [Latin *astēr* star, from Greek *astēr;* because the arrangement of its petals suggests a star.]

as·ter·isk (as'tə risk') *n.* a star-shaped mark (*) used in printing or writing to indicate a reference, footnote, or omission. —*v.t.* to mark with an asterisk; star. [Late Latin *asteriscus* a typographical mark, from Greek *asteriskos* literally, little star.]

as·ter·ism (as'tə riz'əm) *n.* **1.** a small group of stars; constellation. **2.** a starlike luminous effect displayed by certain gems and minerals, such as varieties of sapphire and ruby.

asters *(def. 1)*

a·stern (ə stûrn') *adv., adj.* **1.** at or toward the rear of a ship. **2.** behind a ship. **3.** backward.

as·ter·oid (as'tə roid') *n.* **1.** any of thousands of minor planets that revolve around the sun, chiefly between the orbits of Mars and Jupiter. Also, **planetoid. 2.** starfish. [Greek *asteroeidēs* starlike, from *astēr* star.]

as·then·o·sphere (as then'ə sf îr') *n.* a zone deep beneath the earth's surface in which rock is hot and can slowly flow, acting as a cushion on which the rigid, overriding plates of the earth's crust can move about, as in continental drift. For illustration, see **earth.** [Greek *asthenēs* weak + -*sphere,* as in ATMOSPHERE.]

asth·ma (az'mə) *n.* a chronic or recurrent respiratory disease characterized by sudden and severe attacks of difficult breathing, wheezing, and coughing, accompanied by a feeling of suffocation. It is often caused by an allergy. [Greek *asthma* panting.]

asth·mat·ic (az mat'ik) *adj.* of, relating to, or having asthma. —*n.* a person who has asthma. —**asth·mat'i·cal·ly,** *adv.*

as·tig·mat·ic (as'tig mat'ik) *adj.* **1.** of, relating to, or having astigmatism. **2.** correcting astigmatism. —*n.* a person who has astigmatism. —**as'tig·mat'i·cal·ly,** *adv.*

a·stig·ma·tism (ə stig'mə tiz'əm) *n.* **1.** a defect of the cornea or lens of an eye causing blurred vision because the light rays from a single point do not converge at one point on the retina. **2.** a similar defect in any type of lens. [A-⁴ + Greek *stigma* mark + -ISM.]

a·stir (ə stûr') *adj.* **1.** in motion; stirring; active. **2.** out of bed.

as·ton·ish (ə ston'ish) *v.t.* to surprise greatly; amaze. [Modification of Middle English *astonen* to stun, from Old French *estoner,* going back to Latin *ex* out + *tonāre* to thunder.]

as·ton·ish·ing (ə ston'i shing) *adj.* causing astonishment; amazing. —**as'ton'ish·ing·ly,** *adv.*

as·ton·ish·ment (ə ston'ish mənt) *n.* **1.** a state of being astonished; amazement or surprise: *You can imagine our astonishment when we heard the news.* **2.** something that causes amazement or surprise.

as·tound (ə stound') *v.t.* to overwhelm with sudden surprise or amazement; stun. [Middle English *astoned,* past participle of *astonen* to stun. See ASTONISH.] —**as·tound'ing·ly,** *adv.*

a·strad·dle (ə strad'əl) *adv., adj., prep.* astride.

as·tra·gal (as'trə gəl) *n.* **1.** a small, convex molding shaped like a string of beads, used in classical architecture around the top of columns. **2.** any small, plain, convex molding. [Latin *astragalus* molding on a column, from Greek *astragalos* molding on a column, anklebone.]

as·trag·a·lus (ə strag'ə ləs) *n., pl.* **-li** (-lī'). talus. [Greek *astragalos* anklebone, molding on a column.] —**as·trag'a·lar,** *adj.*

as·tra·khan (as'trə kən, -kan') *also,* **as·tra·chan. 1.** the curly fur of young lambs, originally from the region of Astrakhan. It is a grade of karakul. **2.** a woolen cloth woven to resemble this.

as·tral (as'trəl) *adj.* **1.** of, relating to, resembling, or from the stars; starry. **2.** *Biology.* of or relating to an aster; star-shaped. [Late Latin *astrālis* relating to the stars, from Latin *astrum* star, from Greek *astron.*]

a·stray (ə strā') *adj., adv.* **1.** off the right path; wandering. **2.** into error or evil.

a·stride (ə strīd') *adj., adv.* **1.** with one leg on each side. **2.** with legs far apart. —*prep.* with one leg on each side of. Also, **astraddle.**

as·trin·gent (ə strin'jənt) *n.* a substance that contracts the tissues of the body. Astringents are used to stop the flow of blood from a wound or cut. —*adj.* **1.** tending to contract the tissues of the body: *an astringent lotion.* **2.** harsh or severe; stern; austere: *an astringent manner of speaking.* [Latin *astringēns,* present participle of *astringere* to bind together.] —**as·trin'gen·cy,** *n.* —**as·trin'gent·ly,** *adv.*

astro- *combining form* of or relating to the stars, space, spacecraft, or space flight: *astrophysics, astronautics.* [Greek *astron* a star.]

as·tro·dome (as'trə dōm') *n.* a dome-shaped window on top of an aircraft that provides the navigator with a view of the stars for the purpose of celestial navigation. [ASTRO- + DOME.]

as·tro·ge·ol·o·gy (as'trō jē ol'ə je) *n.* the science that uses geologic principles and techniques in studying the solid celestial bodies of the solar system, as the planets, moons, and asteroids. [ASTRO- + GEOLOGY.] —**as'tro·ge·ol'o·gist,** *n.* —**as·tro·ge·o·log·ic** (as'trō jē'ə loj'ik), *adj.*

as·tro·labe (as'trə lāb') *n.* an instrument formerly used for measuring the altitudes of the heavenly bodies, replaced by the sextant. [Old French *astrelabe,* from Medieval Latin *astrolabium,* from Greek *astrolabos.*]

as·trol·o·gy (ə strol'ə jē) *n.* the study and interpretation of the influence that the heavenly bodies supposedly exert on people and events. [Old French *astrologie,* from Latin *astrologia* astronomy, from Greek *astrologiā.*] —**as·trol'o·ger,** *n.* —**as·tro·log·i·cal** (as'trə loj'i kəl), *adj.* —**as'tro·log'i·cal·ly,** *adv.*

astron. 1. astronomer. **2.** astronomical. **3.** astronomy.

as·tro·naut (as'trə nôt') *n.* a person who flies in or navigates a spacecraft. [Greek *astron* star + *nautēs* sailor.]

as·tro·nau·ti·cal (as'trə nô'ti kəl) *adj.* of or relating to astronautics or astronauts. Also, **as'tro·nau'tic.** —**as'tro·nau'ti·cal·ly,** *adv.*

as·tro·nau·tics (as'trə nô'tiks) *n.* the science that deals with the design, construction, and operation of spacecraft. ➡ used as singular.

as·tron·o·mer (ə stron'ə mər) *n.* an expert in astronomy.

as·tro·nom·i·cal (as'trə nom'i kəl) *adj.* **1.** of or relating to astronomy. **2.** immensely or unbelievably large: *They spent an astronomical amount of money on their new house.* Also, **as'tro·nom'ic.** —**as'tro·nom'i·cal·ly,** *adv.*

astronomical unit, a unit of length used to measure distances in astronomy, equal to the average distance between the center of the earth and the center of the sun, or about 93 million miles (150 million kilometers).

astronomical year, solar year.

as·tron·o·my (ə stron'ə mē) *n.* the science that deals with the planets, stars, and other heavenly bodies, including the study of their physical characteristics, relative positions, and motions. [Old French *astronomie,* from Latin *astronomia,* from Greek *astronomiā.*]

as·tro·phys·ics (as'trō fiz'iks) *n.* the branch of astronomy dealing with the physical and chemical nature of heavenly bodies, esp. through analysis of the light and other forms of energy they emit. ➡ used as singular. [Greek *astron* star + PHYSICS.] —**as'·tro·phys'i·cal,** *adj.* —**as·tro·phys'i·cist,** *n.*

As·tro·turf (as'trō tûrf') *n. Trademark.* an artificial ground cover of green vinyl and nylon made to resemble grass, used esp. on the playing fields of sports stadiums.

as·tute (ə stūt', ə stut') *adj.* having or showing a keen mind; discerning; shrewd: *an astute businessperson, an astute observation.* [Latin *astūtus,* from *astus* craft, cunning.] —**as·tute'ly,** *adv.* —**as·tute'ness,** *n.*

As·ty·a·nax (as tī'ə naks') *n.* in Greek legend, the young son of Hector and Andromache, hurled from the walls of Troy by the victorious Greeks, so that he would not grow up and avenge the Trojan defeat.

a·sun·der (ə sun'dər) *adv.* **1.** into pieces or separate parts: *The wall was torn asunder by the beast.* **2.** apart in position or direction: *The leaves were scattered asunder by the wind.* [Old English *on sundran* apart.]

As·wan High Dam (as'wän) a large dam in southeastern Egypt, on the Nile.

a·sy·lum (ə sī'ləm) *n.* **1.** an institution providing shelter and care, as for the mentally ill or orphaned. **2.a.** shelter or protection provided as a refuge: *The fugitives were given asylum in the church.* **b.** shelter or protection from punishment or extradition granted by a foreign country to fugitives or political refugees. Also, **political asylum. 3.** an inviolable place of refuge, as a church; sanctuary.

[Latin *asylum* sanctuary, from Greek *asylon,* from *a-* not, without + *syle* right of seizure.]

a·sym·met·ri·cal (ā′si met′ri kəl, as′i-) *adj.* not symmetrical. Also, **a′sym·met′ric.** —**a′sym·met′ri·cal·ly,** *adv.*

a·sym·me·try (ā sim′ə trē) *n.* lack of symmetry. [Greek *asymmetriā* lack of proportion.]

as·ymp·tote (as′im tōt′) *n.* a straight line continually approached by a given curve but never met by it within a finite distance. [Greek *asymptōtos* not falling together.] —**as·symp·tot·ic** (as′im-tot′ik), *adj.*

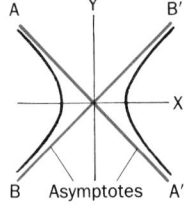

Asymptotes

at (at; *unstressed* ət) *prep.* **1.** in, on, or by; near: *at the top, at the door.* **2.** to or toward: *Look at the scenery.* **3.** in a place, state, or condition of: *at peace, at home.* **4.** on, near, or during the age or time of: *Let's meet at noon. The poet died at seventy.* **5.** occupied with; engaged in: *at play, at dinner.* **6.** because of; resulting from: *We are sad at the thought of leaving.* **7.** in the rate, degree, order, or position of: *at first, at ten miles per hour.* **8.** in the amount of; for: *The dress was sold at half price.* **9.** in the method or manner: *at ease, at random.* **10.** according to: *Proceed at your own risk.* **11.** present during the occurrence of; attending: *at the opera, at the birth.* **12.** from: *Get the book at the library. We warmed our hands at the fire.* **13.** through; by way of: *I entered at the back door.* [Old English *æt* in, near.]

At, the symbol for astatine.

at-, form of **ad-** before *t,* as in *attract.*

at. **1.** atmosphere. **2.** atomic.

At·a·lan·ta (at′ə lan′tə) *n.* in Greek legend, a maiden famed as a runner and as a huntress. After agreeing to wed any suitor who could beat her in a footrace, Atalanta was defeated by Hippomenes.

at·a·man (at′ə mən) *n., pl.* **-mans.** hetman.

at·a·vism (at′ə viz′əm) *n.* **1.** reversion to an earlier or primitive type of behavior. **2.** the reappearance, usually after many generations, of a physical trait possessed by ancestors. Also, **reversion.** [French *atavisme,* from Latin *atavus* remote ancestor.] —**at′a·vist,** *n.* —**at′a·vis′tic,** *adj.* —**at′a·vis′ti·cal·ly,** *adv.*

a·tax·i·a (ə tak′sē ə) *n.* **1.** an impairment of coordination of the voluntary muscles, resulting from disorders affecting the cerebellum, cerebrum, or spinal cord. **2.** locomotor ataxia. [Modern Latin *ataxia,* from Greek *ataxiā* disorder.] —**a·tax′ic,** *adj., n.*

ate (āt) the past tense of **eat.**

A·te (ā′tē) *n.* in Greek mythology, the goddess personifying and instigating reckless and ruinous impulses in humans. [Greek *atē.*]

-ate¹ *suffix* **1.** (used to form adjectives from nouns) of, relating to, or having: *collegiate, vertebrate.* **2.** (used to form verbs from certain stems) **a.** to become: *antiquate.* **b.** to cause to become: *validate, aggravate.* **c.** to produce: *substantiate.* **d.** to combine, impregnate, or treat with: *sulfurate.* **3.** used to form adjectives from certain verbs whose past participle ends in *-ed: separate.* [Latin *-ātus, -āta, -ātum.*]

-ate² *suffix* used to form the names of salts made from an acid ending in *-ic: nitrate, acetate.* [Special use of -ATE¹.]

-ate³ *suffix* (used to form nouns) **1.** a function, office, rule, or agent: *episcopate, magistrate.* **2.** the object or result of an action: *delegate, mandate.* [Latin *-ātus.*]

at·el·ier (at′əl yā′) *n.* a workshop or studio, esp. of an artist. [French *atelier,* from Old French *astelier* carpenter's shop, pile of wood, from *astele* piece of wood, going back to Latin *astula* splinter, wood chip.]

a tem·po (ä tem′pō) *Music.* resuming the original rate of speed. [Italian *a tempo* in time, going back to Latin *ad* to + *tempus* time.]

Ath·a·pas·can (ath′ə pas′kən) *n.* **1.** a North American Indian language family, including languages of Alaska and northwestern Canada, the Pacific coast, and the southwestern United States. The Apache and the Navaho are Athapascan-speaking tribes. **2.** a member of a tribe speaking an Athapascan language. —*adj.* of or relating to this language family.

a·the·ism (ā′thē iz′əm) *n.* the belief that there is no God. [French *athéisme,* from Greek *atheos* without God, denying the gods.]

a·the·ist (ā′thē ist) *n.* a person who does not believe in the existence of God or gods.

a·the·is·tic (ā′thē is′tik) *adj.* of, relating to, or characteristic of atheism or atheists. Also, **a′the·is′ti·cal.** —**a′the·is′ti·cal·ly,** *adv.*

A·the·na (ə thē′nə) *also,* **A·the·ne** (ə thē′nē). *n.* in Greek mythology, the goddess of wisdom and the arts and crafts, and the daughter of Zeus. Her Roman counterpart is Minerva. Also, **Pallas, Pallas Athena.**

ath·e·nae·um (ath′ə nē′əm) *also,* **ath·e·ne·um.** *n.* **1.** A-thenaeum. **a.** a temple dedicated to Athena, esp. the one in ancient Athens where poets and scholars met to discuss their works. **b.** a school founded in ancient Rome by Hadrian for the study of poetry, law, rhetoric, grammar, and philosophy. **2.** a scientific or literary club. **3.** a room for reading; library. [Latin *Athēnaeum* temple of Athena, from Greek *Athēnaion,* from *Athēnē* Athena.]

ath·er·o·scle·ro·sis (ath′ə rō skli rō′sis) *n.* a form of arteriosclerosis characterized by the formation of localized fatty deposits on the inner walls of the arteries. [Modern Latin *atherosclerosis* from Greek *athērōma* tumor filled with grainy matter + SCLEROSIS.] —**ath·er·o·scler·ot·ic** (ath′ə rō sklə rot′ik), *adj.*

a·thirst (ə thûrst′) *adj.* **1.** having a strong desire; eager; longing: *athirst for adventure.* **2.** *Archaic.* thirsty.

ath·lete (ath′lēt) *n.* **1.** a person who is trained for sports, games, or other competitive activities requiring physical strength, skill, agility, and stamina. **2.** a person who has an aptitude for such activities. [Latin *athlēta,* from Greek *athlētēs* contestant in sports, going back to *athlos* contest and *athlon* prize.]

athlete's foot, a contagious fungus infection commonly occurring on the feet, particularly between the toes; ringworm of the foot.

ath·let·ic (ath let′ik) *adj.* **1.** of, relating to, characteristic of, or suited to an athlete or athletics. **2.** physically active and strong; vigorous. —**ath·let′i·cal·ly,** *adv.*

ath·let·ics (ath let′iks) *n.* **1.** athletic games, sports, or activities. ➡ usually used as plural. **2.** the practice or principles of athletic activities or training. ➡ used as singular.

athletic supporter, jockstrap.

at-home (at hōm′) *n.* an informal reception given at one's home, usually in the afternoon.

a·thwart (ə thwôrt′) *adv.* from side to side; crosswise. —*prep.* **1.** from side to side of; across. **2.** in opposition to; against. **3.** *Nautical.* across the line or course of: *The boat was athwart our bow.* [A-¹ + THWART (adverb).]

a·tilt (ə tilt′) *adj., adv.* **1.** in a tilted position; at an angle. **2.** in the manner of a person tilting with a lance.

-ation *suffix* (used to form nouns) **1.** the action or process of: *compilation.* **2.** the condition or state of being: *isolation.* **3.** the result of: *commendation.* [Latin *-ātiō,* genitive *-ationis.*]

-ative *suffix* (used to form adjectives) **1.** tending to: *demonstrative.* **2.** of or relating to: *authoritative.* [Latin *-ātivus.*]

At·lan·te·an (at′lan tē′ən) *adj.* **1.** of or like Atlas; strong. **2.** of or relating to Atlantis.

At·lan·tic (at lan′tik) *adj.* **1.** of, relating to, or designating the Atlantic Ocean. **2.** on, along, or near the coast of the Atlantic Ocean.

Atlantic salmon, a North Atlantic salmon, *Salmo salar,* now rare, valued for sport and as food. It ascends North American and European rivers for several spawnings during its lifetime. Average weight: 15 pounds (6.8 kilograms), but sometimes exceeding 50 pounds (22.7 kilograms).

Atlantic Standard Time, the local time used in the 60th meridian west of Greenwich, England, used in Puerto Rico, the U.S. Virgin Islands, and much of eastern coastal Canada. It is 4 hours behind Greenwich Time.

At·lan·tis (at lan′tis) *n.* a legendary island or continent in the Atlantic which had an advanced civilization but which supposedly sank into the sea. [Latin *Atlantis,* from Greek *Atlantis.*]

at·las (at′ləs) *n.* **1.** a bound collection of maps. **2.** any similar collection containing illustrations, tables, or explanatory material relating to a particular subject. **3.** Atlas. in Greek mythology, a Titan condemned by Zeus to bear the weight of the heavens on his shoulders forever. [Greek *Atlās* the Titan. Collections of maps printed in the sixteenth century often contained a picture of Atlas holding up the earth.]

ATM, automated teller machine.

at·man (ät′mən) *n.* **1.** in Hinduism, the eternal portion of Brahman that exists in every living thing; soul. **2.** Atman. the universal supreme soul from which individual souls arise and with which they reunite; Brahman. [Sanskrit *ātman* breath, soul.]

at·mos·phere (at′məs fir′) *n.* **1.a.** the envelope of air that surrounds the earth. **b.** an envelope of gases surrounding some other planet or moon. **2.** the air in a particular place: *The crowded room had a suffocating atmosphere.* **3.** the pervading or surrounding environment or influence: *There was an atmosphere*

a	at	e	end	o	hot	u	up	hw	white		about
ā	ape	ē	me	ō	old	ū	use	ng	song		taken
ä	far	i	it	ô	fork	ü	rule	th	thin	ə	pencil
âr	care	ī	ice	oi	oil	u̇	pull	th	this		lemon
				îr	pierce	ou	out	ûr	turn	zh	measure		circus

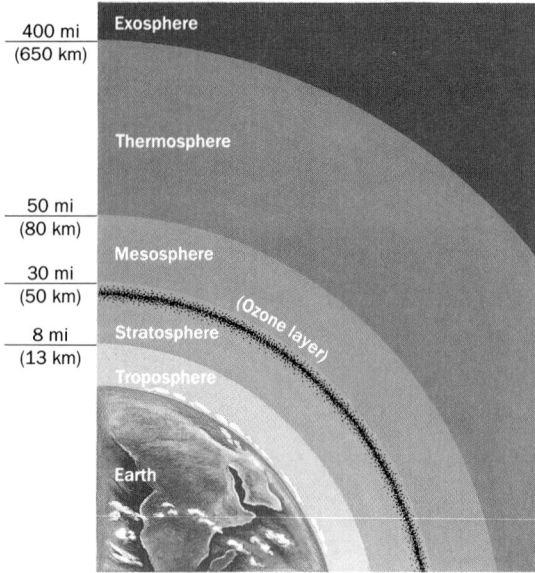

400 mi (650 km)

Exosphere

Thermosphere

50 mi (80 km)

30 mi (50 km)

Mesosphere

(Ozone layer)

8 mi (13 km)

Stratosphere

Troposphere

Earth

layers of the earth's **atmosphere**

of excitement in the locker room before the game. *The house had a gloomy atmosphere.* **4.** a mood or impression conveyed by a play, novel, or other work of art. **5.** a distinctive or interesting character or quality: *a restaurant with atmosphere.* **6.** a unit of pressure equal to atmospheric pressure at sea level, or 14.69 pounds per square inch (1.03 kilograms per square centimeter). [Modern Latin *atmosphaera,* from Greek *atmos* vapor + *sphaira* sphere.]

at·mos·pher·ic (at′məs fer′ik) *adj.* **1.** of, in, relating to, or consisting of the atmosphere. **2.** caused or influenced by the atmosphere. Also, **at′mos·pher′i·cal.** —**at′mos·pher′i·cal·ly,** *adv.*

atmospheric pressure, the pressure exerted by the weight of the earth's atmosphere; barometric pressure. At sea level it is equal to 14.69 pounds per square inch (1.03 kilograms per square centimeter).

at·mos·pher·ics (at′məs fer′iks) *n.* **1.** electrical disturbances in the atmosphere. **2.** radio interference caused by such disturbances; static. Also, **sferics.** ➡ used as singular in both defs.

at. no. *also,* **at no** atomic number.

at·oll (at′ôl, ə tôl′, at′ôl, ə tōl′) *n.* a circular or nearly circular coral reef or string of reefs rising above and surrounding a lagoon. For illustration, see **aerial.** [Malayalam *atolu* the Maldives (which are typical atolls); literally, reef.]

at·om (at′əm) *n.* **1.** the smallest particle of a chemical element that has the chemical properties of that element, composed of a positively charged central nucleus around which one or more negatively charged electrons are in motion. **2.** any extremely small particle; tiny bit; iota: *There is not an atom of truth in that statement.* [Latin *atomus* smallest particle, from Greek *atomos* indivisible, from *a-* not + *temnein* to divide; from the early belief that atoms could not be split.]

atom bomb, atomic bomb.

a·tom·ic (ə tom′ik) *adj.* **1.** of, relating to, or consisting of an atom or atoms: *atomic particles.* **2.** powered by nuclear energy. **3.** involving or produced by nuclear weapons: *atomic fallout.* **4.** extremely minute; microscopic. —**a·tom′i·cal·ly,** *adv.*

atomic age, the period of history characterized by the existence

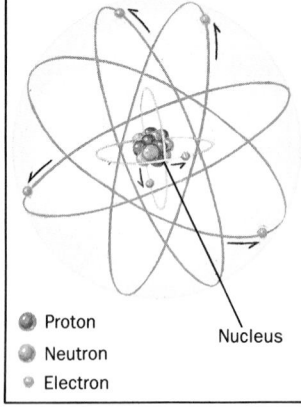

Proton

Neutron

Electron

Nucleus

carbon **atom**

of the atomic bomb and the use of atomic energy; the present age.

atomic bomb, a nuclear bomb whose great destructive power is derived from the sudden release of energy by nuclear fission, as when atoms of heavy elements, such as uranium or plutonium, are split into atoms of lighter elements. Also, **A-bomb, atom bomb.**

atomic clock, an electric clock regulated by atomic vibrations. Atomic clocks are the most accurate devices for keeping time yet developed.

atomic energy, nuclear energy.

atomic mass, the mass of an atom, usually expressed in atomic mass units.

atomic mass unit, a unit of mass equal to one twelfth of the mass of the most common kind of carbon atom. Also, **dalton.**

atomic number, the number of protons in the nucleus of an atom of an element. The atomic number determines the place of an element in the periodic table.

atomic pile, nuclear reactor.

atomic power, nuclear power.

atomic reactor, nuclear reactor.

atomic theory 1. the general theory that all matter is composed of atoms. **2.** the theory that atoms are composed of a nucleus surrounded by electrons.

atomic weight, the average weight or mass of an atom of a chemical element, measured in terms of units equal to one twelfth the mass of an atom of carbon-12.

at·om·ize (at′ə mīz′) *v.t.,* -**ized, -iz·ing. 1.** to reduce to atoms. **2.** to reduce (a liquid) to a fine spray. **3.** to destroy in a nuclear explosion or with nuclear weapons. —**at′om·i·za′tion,** *n.*

at·om·iz·er (at′ə mī′zər) *n.* a device for reducing a liquid to a fine spray.

atom smasher, accelerator *(def. 2).*

a·ton·al (ā tō′nəl) *adj. Music.* characterized by the absence of tonal center or key and by the giving of equal emphasis to all twelve tones of the chromatic scale. —**a·to·nal·i·ty** (ā′tō nal′i tē), *n.* —**a·ton′al·ly,** *adv.*

a·tone (ə tōn′) *v.i.,* **a·toned, a·ton·ing.** to make amends, as for wrongdoing: *to atone for a crime.* [Back formation from ATONE-MENT.]

a·tone·ment (ə tōn′mənt) *n.* **1.** reparation for a wrong or injury; expiation. **2. the Atonement.** in Christianity, the reconciliation of God with humankind through the life, sufferings, and esp. the death of Jesus. [From *at one* (as in "to be at one with") + -MENT.]

a·top (ə top′) *prep.* on the top of. —*adv.* on or at the top.

ATP, adenosine triphosphate, an organic compound found in living cells whose conversion to ADP releases energy used to fuel biochemical processes. Formula: $C_{10}H_{16}N_5O_{13}P_3$

A·tre·us (ā′trē əs, ā′trūs) *n.* in Greek legend, a king of Mycenae and the father of Agamemnon and Menelaus. Atreus brought a curse upon his house when he killed his brother's children and served them to him at a banquet.

a·tri·o·ven·tri·cu·lar (ā′trē ō ven trik′yə lər) *adj. Anatomy.* of, relating to, or situated between the atria and ventricles of the heart: *an atrioventricular valve.*

a·tri·um (ā′trē əm) *n., pl.* **a·tri·a** (ā′trē ə) or **a·tri·ums. 1.** the principal room or entrance hall of an ancient Roman house, having an opening in the center of the roof directly over a pool or fountain. **2.** a colonnaded courtyard in front of the entrance of early Christian churches. **3.** an open or glassed-in court in a house or large building. **4.** either of the two upper chambers of the heart that receive blood from the veins and send it to the ventricles. For illustration, see **heart.** [Latin *ātrium* principal room in a Roman house.] —**a′tri·al,** *adj.*

a·tro·cious (ə trō′shəs) *adj.* **1.** extremely cruel, brutal, or wicked; heinous; despicable: *an atrocious crime.* **2.** *Informal.* very bad; distasteful or offensive: *an atrocious speech.* [Latin *atrox* terrible, frightful.] —**a·tro′cious·ly,** *adv.* —**a·tro′cious·ness,** *n.*

a·troc·i·ty (ə tros′i tē) *n., pl.* **-ties. 1.** the state or quality of being atrocious: *the atrocity of a crime.* **2.** any outrageously cruel act. **3.** *Informal.* something that is distasteful or offensive: *The book is an atrocity.* [Latin *atrōcitās* cruelty.]

at·ro·phy (at′rə fē) *n.* **1.** a wasting away of the body or its tissues or organs. **2.** a withering away; decay; degeneration: *the atrophy of a nation.* —*v.,* **-phied, -phy·ing.** —*v.i.* to waste or wither away. —*v.t.* to cause to waste or wither away. [Late Latin *atrophia* lack of food, from Greek *atrophia.*] —**a·troph·ic** (ə trof′ik, ə trō′fik), *adj.*

at·ro·pine (at′rə pēn′, -pin) *n.* a poisonous, white crystalline alkaloid obtained from belladonna and similar plants or made synthetically, used to relieve muscle spasms, to dilate the pupil of the eye, and to treat Parkinson's disease. Formula: $C_{17}H_{23}NO_3$ [Modern Latin *atropa* belladonna, from Greek *Atropos* Atropos.]

At·ro·pos (at′rə pos′) *n.* in Greek mythology, one of the three Fates. She cuts the thread of life, which is spun and measured by the other two Fates. [Greek *Atropos* literally, inflexible.]

at·tach (ə tach′) *v.t.* **1.** to join one thing to another; connect; affix; fasten: *to attach a luggage tag to a suitcase.* **2.** to join as an associate or part of: *The local chapter attached itself to the national committee.* **3.** to bind by personal ties, as of affection or loyalty: *He is very attached to his cat.* **4.** to consider as an attribute; ascribe: *Don't attach any significance to that story.* **5.** to appoint or assign in an official capacity: *The diplomat is attached to the American Embassy.* **6.** to add at the end; append: *We attached our names to the petition.* **7.** to take (a person or property) by legal authority: *His creditors attached his salary.* **8.** to place units or personnel under the command of a military organization on a temporary basis. —*v.i.* to belong; adhere. [Old French *attachier* to fasten, from *a* (from Latin *ad* to) + Low German *takk* pointed thing. Doublet of ATTACK.] —**at·tach′a·ble,** *adj.*

at·ta·ché (at′ə shā′; *British* ə tash′ā) *n.* **1.** a person who is attached to the official staff of a diplomatic mission to act in a specialized capacity: *a commercial attaché.* **2.** attaché case. [French *attaché,* from past participle of *attacher* to attach, from Old French *attachier.* See ATTACH.]

attaché case, a slim briefcase, usually having rigid sides.

at·tach·ment (ə tach′mənt) *n.* **1.** the act of attaching or the state of being attached. **2.** a binding feeling of affection or loyalty; devotion. **3.** a part that can be connected to an appliance or other machine for a special purpose: *vacuum cleaner attachments.* **4.** something that attaches things together; fastening; connection. **5.a.** the act of taking a person or property by legal authority, esp. the taking of property as security for debts. **b.** a writ or other process authorizing this.

at·tack (ə tak′) *v.t.* **1.** to go against with force or arms; begin combat against; assault. **2.** to write or speak against vehemently; censure. **3.** to start to work on vigorously; undertake energetically: *to attack a problem realistically.* **4.** to begin to act on or to affect destructively: *A fungus attacked the hemlock trees.* —*v.i.* to begin combat: *The enemy attacked at daybreak.* —*n.* **1.** the act of attacking. **2.** a sudden occurrence, as of a disease: *an attack of asthma.* [French *attaquer* to attack, from Italian *attaccare (battaglia)* to join (battle), from Latin *ad* to + Low German *takk* pointed thing. Doublet of ATTACH.] —**at·tack′er,** *n.*

Synonyms *v.t.* **Attack, assault,** and **assail** mean to use violence against someone or something. **Attack,** the most general of these terms, suggests sudden force and often lack of warning: *The guerrillas attacked the base while the defenders' attention was diverted.* **Assault** stresses the force used in attacking and may imply great damage done: *An entire army assaulted the town.* **Assail** suggests repeated blows rather than overwhelming force and may imply failure: *The city withstood the siege despite being assailed for weeks by cannon fire.*

at·tain (ə tān′) *v.t.* **1.** to gain (something) through effort; achieve: *to attain success.* **2.** to come to or reach (a condition) over time by living, growing, or the like: *Both my grandparents attained the age of ninety.* —*v.i.* to succeed in reaching or achieving (with *to*): *to attain to great power.* [Old French *ataindre* to reach, convict, going back to Latin *attingere* to touch upon, reach.]

at·tain·a·ble (ə tā′nə bəl) *adj.* capable of being attained. —**at·tain′a·bil′i·ty, at·tain′a·ble·ness,** *n.*

at·tain·der (ə tān′dər) *n.* the loss of civil rights that occurs when a person convicted of a felony or treason is sentenced to death or declared an outlaw. [Old French *ataindre* to attain, convict. See ATTAIN.]

at·tain·ment (ə tān′mənt) *n.* **1.** the act or process of attaining. **2.** something attained; accomplishment.

at·taint (ə tānt′) *v.t.* **1.** to condemn to attainder. **2.** *Archaic.* to disgrace; dishonor. —*n. Archaic.* a stain upon honor or purity; disgrace. [Old French *ataint,* past participle of *ataindre* to attain, convict; sense in English influenced by confusion with *taint.* See ATTAIN.]

at·tar (at′ər) *n.* a fragrant essential oil obtained from the petals of flowers, esp. roses, used in the making of perfume. [Persian *'atar,* Arabic *'itr* perfume.]

at·tempt (ə tempt′) *v.t.* to make an effort to do or accomplish (something); try. —*n.* **1.** a putting forth of effort to do or accomplish something; endeavor; effort. **2.** an assault or attack: *to make an attempt on a person's life.* [Old French *atempter* to try, from Latin *attemptāre.*] —For Synonyms *(v.t.),* see **try.**

at·tend (ə tend′) *v.t.* **1.** to be present at: *to attend a meeting.* **2.** to take care of; minister to: *The doctor attended the patient.* **3.** to go or be with so as to provide service or companionship: *Two maids attend the queen.* **4.** to accompany as a circumstance or consequence: *Fever attends many diseases.* **5.** to listen to; pay heed to: *Attend my words.* —*v.i.* **1.** to be present: *We belong to the club but don't attend often.* **2.** to devote one's energy; apply oneself (with *to*): *Attend to your duties.* **3.** to give care or attention; minister (with *to*): *The nurse attended to the patients.* **4.** to give careful thought and consideration; pay or give attention (with *to*): *Attend to the speech.* [Old French *atendre* to wait, from Latin *attendere* to give heed to.]

at·ten·dance (ə ten′dəns) *n.* **1.** the act of attending or the state of being present. **2.a.** the persons or number of persons present. **b.** a record of this. **c.** the number of times attending: *That student has perfect attendance.*

at·ten·dant (ə ten′dənt) *n.* **1.** a person who waits on or performs a service for another: *a gas station attendant.* **2.** a person who is present. **3.** an accompanying circumstance; consequence. —*adj.* **1.** following as a result; accompanying: *attendant circumstances.* **2.** being present; in attendance: *attendant crowds.* **3.** providing care or service to another. —**at·tend′ant·ly,** *adv.*

at·ten·tion (ə ten′shən) *n.* **1.** the active focusing of the mind; giving heed: *The speaker had our undivided attention.* **2.** the power or faculty of mental concentration: *My attention was distracted.* **3.** thoughtful care or consideration: *This matter will receive our immediate attention. The parents give equal attention to each child.* **4. attentions.** acts of courtesy, thoughtfulness, or devotion, esp. those of a suitor. **5.** a regulation military stance, characterized by stiff, erect posture, esp. with arms at the sides and eyes front: *The soldiers snapped to attention.* —*interj.* a command to assume the stance of attention. [Latin *attentiō* attentiveness, application.]

at·ten·tive (ə ten′tiv) *adj.* **1.** paying attention; observant; heedful. **2.** showing care for the needs of others; considerate; thoughtful: *an attentive host.* —**at·ten′tive·ly,** *adv.* —**at·ten′tive·ness,** *n.*

at·ten·u·ate (ə ten′ū āt′) *v.,* **-at·ed, -at·ing.** —*v.t.* **1.** to make thin or slender. **2.** to lessen or reduce, as in size, severity, or force. **3.** to reduce in density or consistency; dilute. **4.** to make (a microorganism) less capable of infecting or causing disease. —*v.i.* to become slender, thin, or less. —*adj.* **1.** slender or thin; lessened. **2.** *Botany.* tapering gradually to a slender point. [Latin *attenuātus,* past participle of *attenuāre* to make thin.] —**at·ten′u·a′tion,** *n.*

at·test (ə test′) *v.t.* **1.** to affirm to be correct, true, or genuine, esp. by oath or signature: *The witness attested the truth of the evidence.* **2.** to be proof or evidence of; show clearly: *Her success attests her hard work.* **3.** to put on oath. —*v.i.* to bear witness; certify (with *to*): *He attested to the truth of the statement.* [Latin *attestārī* to bear witness to.] —**at·test′er;** also, **at·tes′tor,** *n.* —For Synonyms, see **certify.**

at·tes·ta·tion (at′ə stā′shən) *n.* **1.** the act of attesting. **2.** something used as proof; testimony; evidence.

at·tic (at′ik) *n.* a space or story directly below the roof of a building. [French *attique* referring to the space or story beneath the roof, which was usually decorated in a simple, elegant style, like the architecture of ancient Athens, from Latin *Atticus* pertaining to Attica or Athens, from Greek *Attikos.*]

At·tic (at′ik) *adj.* **1.** of or relating to Attica. **2.** of, relating to, or characteristic of Athens or its people or culture; Athenian. **3.** *also,* **attic.** characterized by simplicity, elegance, and refinement. —*n.* the Ionic dialect of ancient Greek spoken predominantly in Attica. It was the major literary dialect of ancient Greece.

at·tire (ə tīr′) *v.t.,* **-tired, -tir·ing.** to clothe, esp. in fine garments; dress; array. —*n.* **1.** clothes, esp. fine garments; apparel; dress. **2.** *Heraldry.* the horns of a deer. [Old French *atirier* to arrange, dress, from the phrase *a tire* in order.]

at·ti·tude (at′i tüd′, -tūd′) *n.* **1.** a manner of thinking, acting, or feeling: *to have a positive attitude toward life.* **2.** a position of the body implying or indicating an action or mental state; posture: *to assume a combative attitude.* **3.** the orientation of an aircraft or spacecraft in relation to some frame of reference, as the horizon. [Italian *attitudine* disposition, posture, from Late Latin *aptitūdō* fitness. Doublet of APTITUDE.]

at·tor·ney (ə tûr′nē) *n., pl.* **-neys. 1.** a person whose profession is representing clients in lawsuits and advising them in legal matters; lawyer. **2.** a person legally authorized to act in another's place. [Old French *atorné* literally, one appointed, from *atorner* to appoint, turn to, going back to Latin *ad* to + *tornāre* to turn. See TURN.] —For Synonyms, see **lawyer.**

attorney at law *pl.* **attorneys at law.** lawyer.

a	at	e	end	o	hot	u	up	hw	white		about
ā	ape	ē	me	ō	old	ū	use	ng	song		taken
ä	far	i	it	ô	fork	ü	rule	th	thin	ə	pencil
âr	care	ī	ice	oi	oil	u̇	pull	<u>th</u>	this		lemon
		îr	pierce	ou	out	ûr	turn	zh	measure		circus

attorney general *pl.* **attorneys general** or **attorney generals.** **1.** the chief law officer of a national, state, or provincial government. The attorney general advises the chief executive and appears on behalf of the government in court. **2. Attorney General.** the chief law officer of the United States.

at·tract (ə trakt′) *v.t.* **1.** to be appealing to; draw the attention or interest of; fascinate: *This beach attracts many tourists.* **2.** to draw to oneself or itself by physical force: *A magnet attracts iron.* —*v.i.* to exert attraction; be attractive. [Latin *attractus,* past participle of *attrahere* to draw to.] —**at·tract′er;** *also,* **at·trac′tor,** *n.*

at·trac·tion (ə trak′shən) *n.* **1.** an appealing quality or feature; allurement; charm: *The crowded beach held little attraction for me.* **2.** the act or power of attracting: *the attraction of a magnet.* **3.** someone or something that attracts: *The juggler was the main attraction.* **4.** *Physics.* **a.** the force exerted by bodies on one another, tending to draw them together. **b.** the effect of this force; tendency of bodies to draw together.

at·trac·tive (ə trak′tiv) *adj.* **1.** having an appealing quality or feature; alluring; pleasing. **2.** having the power or property of attracting. —**at·trac′tive·ly,** *adv.* —**at·trac′tive·ness,** *n.*

attrib. 1. attribute. **2.** attributive.

at·trib·ute (*v.,* ə trib′ūt; *n.,* at′rə būt′) *v.t.,* **-ut·ed, -ut·ing.** to designate or consider (something) as belonging to, produced by, or resulting from; assign: *The partners attribute their success to hard work. Art historians attribute the sculpture to Praxiteles.* —*n.* **1.** a quality or characteristic considered as belonging to a person or thing. **2.** an object considered as a characteristic or symbol: *The moon was the attribute of the goddess Diana.* [Latin *attribūtus,* past participle of *attribuere* to assign.] —**at·trib′ut·a·ble,** *adj.*

Synonyms *v.t.* **Attribute, ascribe,** and **impute** mean to believe (something) to have been caused by someone or something else. **Attribute** is the general term, suggesting that the result is appropriate to the assumed cause: *The damage was attributed to the storm.* **Ascribe** suggests a more tentative belief, as though the evidence is only circumstantial and doubt remains: *At first the campers ascribed the chirping sounds to insects.* **Impute** implies an unfavorable judgment of the assumed cause: *I impute this problem to your negligence.* For other Synonyms (*n.*), see **characteristic.**

at·tri·bu·tion (at′rə bū′shən) *n.* **1.** the act of attributing: *The painting is a Rembrandt by attribution.* **2.** a quality or thing attributed; attribute.

at·trib·u·tive (ə trib′yə tiv) *adj.* **1.** of, relating to, or like an attribute. **2.** of, relating to, or being an adjective, or a noun used as an adjective, that modifies a noun and usually precedes it. In the phrase *school bus,* the noun *school* is an attributive word. —*n.* an attributive word. —**at·trib′u·tive·ly,** *adv.*

at·tri·tion (ə trish′ən) *n.* **1.** a wearing away by friction; abrasion. **2.** any gradual wearing down or weakening, as by continued abuse or attack: *a war of attrition.* **3.** the gradual loss of personnel or membership due to death, retirement, or resignation. [Latin *attrītiō* friction.] —**at·tri′tion·al,** *adj.*

at·tune (ə tün′, ə tūn′) *v.t.,* **-tuned, -tun·ing. 1.** to bring into harmony or accord. **2.** to make aware: *to attune oneself to the changes in computer technology.* —**at·tune′ment,** *n.*

atty., attorney.

at. wt. *also,* **at wt** atomic weight.

a·typ·i·cal (ā tip′i kəl) *adj.* not conforming to a standard or type; not typical. —**a·typ′i·cal·ly,** *adv.*

Au, the symbol for gold. [Abbreviation of Latin *aurum.*]

AU 1. angstrom unit. **2.** astronomical unit.

au·burn (ô′bərn) *n.* a reddish brown color. —*adj.* having the color auburn. [Old French *auborne* light-colored, from Late Latin *alburnus* whitish, from *albus* white.]

au cou·rant (ō kü rän′) informed about what is going on, esp. public affairs; up-to-date. [French *au courant* literally, in the current.]

auc·tion (ôk′shən) *n.* **1.** a public sale at which articles or property are sold to the highest bidder. **2.** bidding in certain card games, as bridge. **3.** auction bridge. —*v.t.* to sell by or at auction. [Latin *auctiō* such a public sale, increase, from *augēre* to increase; because it is a sale in which buyers keep increasing their offers.]

auction bridge, a type of bridge differing from contract bridge only in the number of points given, as for tricks or honors, and requiring only thirty points for game.

auc·tion·eer (ôk′shə nîr′) *n.* a person who conducts sales by auction. —*v.t.* to sell by or at auction.

au·da·cious (ô dā′shəs) *adj.* **1.** not showing any fear; very bold or daring; intrepid: *an audacious undertaking.* **2.** unrestrained, as by decorum or morality; insolent: *audacious behavior.* —**au·da′cious·ly,** *adv.* —**au·da′cious·ness,** *n.*

au·dac·i·ty (ô das′i tē) *n.* **1.** great courage; daring; boldness.

2. offensive rudeness or arrogance; impudence. [Latin *audāx* bold + -ITY.]

au·di·ble (ô′də bəl) *adj.* capable of being heard; loud enough to be heard. [Late Latin *audībilis,* from Latin *audīre* to hear.] —**au′di·bil′i·ty,** *n.* —**au′di·bly,** *adv.*

au·di·ence (ô′dē əns) *n.* **1.** an assembled group of listeners or spectators. **2.** a group of people reached or intended to be reached, as by a performance, broadcast, or publication. **3.** a formal meeting, hearing, or interview with a person of rank or position: *an audience with the pope.* **4.** an opportunity to be heard; hearing. [Old French *audience* hearing, from Latin *audientia,* going back to *audīre* to hear.]

au·di·o (ô′dē ō′) *adj.* **1.** of or relating to sound or audio frequencies. **2.** of or relating to the reproduction of sound or audio frequencies, esp. in high-fidelity reproduction. **3.** of, relating to, or used in the transmission or reception of sound or audio frequencies. —*n.* the audio part of television. ➡ distinguished from **video.** [From AUDIO-.]

audio- *combining form* **1.** relating to hearing: *audiovisual.* **2.** sound: *audiophile.* [From Latin *audīre* to hear.]

audio frequency, any frequency at which a sound wave is normally audible, from about 15 hertz to 20,000 hertz.

au·di·ol·o·gy (ô′dē ol′ə jē) *n.* the study or science of hearing, esp. the diagnosis and treatment of hearing defects. [AUDIO- + -LOGY.] —**au·di·o·log·i·cal** (ô′dē ə loj′i kəl), *adj.* —**au′di·ol′o·gist,** *n.*

au·di·om·e·ter (ô′dē om′i tər) *n.* a machine that produces controlled sounds, used for measuring a person's hearing. [AUDIO- + -METER.] —**au·di·o·met·ric** (ô′dē ə met′rik), *adj.* —**au′di·om′e·try,** *n.*

au·di·o·phile (ô′dē ə fīl′) *n.* a person who is very interested in, and usually knowledgeable about, high-fidelity sound reproduction.

au·di·o·vis·u·al (ô′dē ō vizh′ü əl) *adj.* **1.** of or relating to hearing and sight. **2.** of, relating to, or using educational materials directed at both hearing and sight, such as films, recordings, television, and photographs. —*n. also,* **audiovisuals.** audiovisual teaching materials.

au·dit (ô′dit) *v.t.* **1.** to examine and verify (financial accounts and records) officially. **2.** to attend (a college course) as a listener without obligation to do required work or intention of receiving formal credit for attendance. —*v.i.* **1.** to examine and verify financial accounts and records officially. **2.** to attend a college course as an auditor. —*n.* **1.** an official investigation and verification of financial accounts and records. **2.** a final statement, prepared by an auditor, of the financial accounts and records that have been examined and verified. [Latin *audītus* a hearing. In earlier times, audits were made by hearing an oral presentation of accounts rather than by examining written statements.]

au·di·tion (ô dish′ən) *n.* **1.** a test performance of the abilities of a singer, musician, actor, or other performer. **2.** the act or sense of hearing. —*v.t.* to give an audition to (a performer). —*v.i.* to perform in an audition: *to audition for a role.* [Latin *audītiō* hearing.]

au·di·tor (ô′di tər) *n.* **1.** a person who audits financial records and accounts. **2.** a person who audits a college course. **3.** a hearer; listener.

au·di·to·ri·um (ô′di tôr′ē əm) *n., pl.* **-to·ri·ums** or **-to·ri·a** (-tôr′ē ə). **1.** a large room, as in a church or school, in which an audience may assemble, usually with a stage or platform at one end. **2.** a building used for public gatherings. [Latin *audītōrium* place where something is heard, going back to *audīre* to hear.]

au·di·to·ry (ô′di tôr′ē) *adj.* **1.** of or relating to the sense or organs of hearing: *auditory nerve.* **2.** perceived through the sense of hearing.

auf Wie·der·seh·en (ouf vē′dər zā′ən, -zān′) *German.* until we meet again; good-bye for now.

Aug., August.

Au·ge·an stables (ô jē′ən) in Greek legend, the stables of King Augeas that sheltered 3,000 oxen and had not been cleaned for thirty years. Hercules cleaned them by changing the course of two rivers so that they flowed through the stables.

Au·ge·as (ô′jē əs, ô jē′-) *n.* in Greek legend, the king whose stables Hercules cleaned.

au·ger (ô′gər) *n.* **1.** a tool for boring holes in wood. **2.** a drill for boring holes in the earth. [Earlier *nauger,* from Old English *nafugār* auger, a tool used to bore the nave of a wheel; in Middle English, *a nauger* was incor-

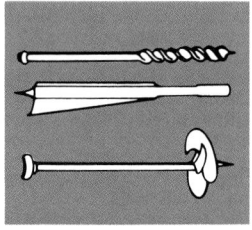

augers

rectly written later as *an auger.* For a similar development, see ADDER.]

aught¹ (ôt) *also,* **ought.** *n.* anything whatever; all: *for aught I care.* —*adv. Archaic.* in any way; at all. [Old English *āwiht* anything; literally, ever a thing, from *ā* ever + *wiht* thing.]

aught² (ôt) *also,* **ought.** *n.* **1.** zero; cipher. **2.** *Archaic.* nothing; naught. [Earlier *naught,* from Old English *nāwiht* nothing, from *nā* no + *wiht* thing; *a naught* being incorrectly written later as *an aught.* For a similar development, see ADDER.]

au·gite (ô′jīt) *n.* a dark variety of the mineral pyroxene, common in many basic igneous rocks, such as basalt. [Latin *augites,* from Greek *augitēs* a precious stone, from *augē* sunlight, brightness + *-ītēs* (see -ITE¹).]

aug·ment (ôg ment′) *v.t.* to make greater, as in size or amount; increase; enlarge: *to augment a salary by working overtime.* —*v.i.* to become greater; increase; grow. [Latin *augmentāre* to increase.] —**aug·ment′a·ble,** *adj.* —**aug·ment′er,** *n.* —For Synonyms *(v.t.),* see **increase.**

aug·men·ta·tion (ôg′men tā′shən) *n.* **1.** the act of augmenting or the state of being augmented. **2.** something that augments; addition. —**aug·men·ta·tive** (ôg men′tə tiv), *adj.*

au gra·tin (ō grat′ən, ō grä′tən) covered with bread crumbs or grated cheese and cooked until brown. [French *au gratin.*]

au·gur (ô′gər) *n.* **1.** any of a group of priests of ancient Rome who made predictions based on the interpretations of various omens. **2.** any soothsayer; diviner; fortuneteller. —*v.t.* **1.** to predict (something) from signs or omens; prophesy. **2.** to be a sign or omen of; give promise of: *The light breeze augured a good day for sailing.* —*v.i.* to predict from signs or omens. [Latin *augur* soothsayer.]
· **to augur ill.** to be a bad sign or omen.
· **to augur well.** to be a good sign or omen.

au·gu·ry (ô′gyə rē) *n., pl.* **-ries.** **1.** the art or practice of prophesying by means of signs or omens; divination. **2.** an indication of something to come; sign or omen. **3.** a rite or ceremony carried out by an augur.

au·gust (ô gust′) *adj.* **1.** inspiring awe, reverence, or admiration; magnificent; majestic; imposing: *the august beauty of the Grand Canyon.* **2.** deserving respect; venerable; dignified; eminent: *an august assembly of scientists.* [Latin *augustus* venerable.] —**au·gust′ly,** *adv.* —**au·gust′ness,** *n.*

Au·gust (ô′gəst) *n.* the eighth month of the year, containing thirty-one days. [Old English *August,* from Latin *Augustus* title of the first Roman emperor, from *augustus* venerable.]

Au·gus·tan (ô gus′tən) *adj.* **1.** of, relating to, or characteristic of the Roman emperor Augustus, his times, or his reign. **2.** of, relating to, or characteristic of the late seventeenth to the middle eighteenth centuries in England, esp. the reign of Queen Anne. —*n.* a writer during an Augustan age.

Augustan age **1.** the period of Latin literature during the reign of Augustus, in which such writers as Horace, Vergil, and Ovid flourished. **2.** any similar period of literary productivity and excellence, esp. in England from the late seventeenth to the middle eighteenth centuries.

Au·gus·tin·i·an (ô′gə stin′ē ən) *adj.* of or relating to Saint Augustine, his religious doctrines, or the religious orders following his rule. —*n.* **1.** an adherent of the doctrines of Saint Augustine. **2.** a member of any of several religious orders that follow the rule of Saint Augustine.

au jus (ō jüs′, ō zhüs′; *French* ō zhy′) (of meat) served with the gravy that forms naturally from the juices of the meat while it is cooking. [French *au jus* literally, in its juice.]

auk (ôk) *n.* any of several web-footed diving birds, family Alcidae, found chiefly in coastal waters of the Northern Hemisphere, resembling the penguin, and having a heavy body, short tail, and short wings. Length: up to 18 inches (46 centimeters). [Old Norse *ālka.*]

au lait (ō lā′) *adj. French.* with milk.

auld lang syne (ôld′ lang zīn′, sīn′, ōld′) the days of long ago, esp. the happy times. [Scottish *auld lang syne* literally, old long ago.]

au na·tu·rel (ō nach′ə rel′; *French* ō na-TY REL′) *French.* **1.** cooked plainly or served without garnish. **2.** in the natural state. **3.** without clothes; nude.

aunt (ant, änt) *n.* **1.** the sister of one's father or mother. **2.** the wife of one's uncle. [Old French *ante,* from Latin *amita* father's sister.]

auk

au pair (ō pâr′) a young person, usually a foreign girl, who does housework or cares for children in a home in exchange for room and board. [French *au pair* even¹, equal.]

au·ra (ôr′ə) *n., pl.* **au·ras** or **au·rae** (ôr′ē). **1.** a distinctive character or atmosphere arising from and surrounding a person or thing: *There was an aura of peace in the cathedral.* **2.** a subtle emanation: *An aura of incense filled the room.* [Latin *aura* breath, breeze, from Greek *aurā.*]

au·ral (ôr′əl) *adj.* of or relating to the ear or the sense of hearing. [Latin *auris* ear + -AL¹.] —**au′ral·ly,** *adv.*

au·re·ate (ôr′ē it, -āt′) *adj.* **1.** having a golden color; gilded. **2.** brilliant or splendid, esp. in literary or rhetorical style. [Late Latin *aureātus* decorated with gold, from Latin *aurum* gold.]

au·re·ole (ôr′ē ōl′) *also,* **au·re·o·la** (ô rē′ō lə). *n.* **1.** *Art.* a ring of light emanating from and encircling the head or body of a sacred figure; halo. **2.** a ring of light or bright region surrounding the sun or moon, as seen through fog. [Latin *aureola (corōna)* golden (crown), from *aurum* gold.]

Au·re·o·my·cin (ôr′ē ō mī′sin) *n. Trademark.* chlortetracycline, a yellow crystalline antibiotic used to treat a variety of infections caused by bacteria, protozoans, and fungi. [Latin *aureus* golden + Greek *mykēs* fungus; name suggested by its color.]

au re·voir (ō′rə vwär′; *French* ō rə vwär′) *French.* until we meet again.

au·ric (ôr′ik) *adj.* of, containing, or derived from gold. [Latin *aurum* gold.]

au·ri·cle (ôr′i kəl) *n.* **1.** atrium *(def. 4).* **2.** the external ear; pinna. **3.** an ear-shaped part. [Latin *auricula* the external ear, diminutive of *auris* ear.]

au·ric·u·lar (ô rik′yə lər) *adj.* **1.** of or relating to the ear or the sense of hearing. **2.** spoken into or perceived by the ear. **3.** shaped like an ear. **4.** of or relating to an auricle of the heart. —**au·ric′u·lar·ly,** *adv.*

au·rif·er·ous (ô rif′ər əs) *adj.* containing or yielding gold. [Latin *aurifer,* from *aurum* gold + *ferre* to bear.]

Au·ri·ga (ô rī′gə) *n.* a constellation near the northern celestial pole containing the bright star Capella, conventionally depicted as a charioteer kneeling in his chariot. [Latin *aurīga* charioteer.]

au·rist (ôr′ist) *n.* a doctor who specializes in treating diseases of the ear; otologist. [Latin *auris* ear + -IST.]

au·rochs (ôr′oks) *n., pl.* **-rochs.** **1.** an extinct wild ox, *Bos primigenius,* that once inhabited Europe and North Africa. The aurochs is probably the direct ancestor of modern domesticated cattle. Also, **urus.** **2.** the European bison, *Bison bonasus,* which resembles the American buffalo. [Obsolete German *Aurochs.*]

Au·ro·ra (ə rôr′ə) *n., pl. (def. 2)* **-ro·ras** or **-ro·rae** (-rôr′ē). **1.** in Roman mythology, the goddess of the dawn. Her Greek counterpart is Eos. **2. aurora. a.** a luminous display appearing in the night sky in various forms, as in bands, streamers, or arches, esp. in polar regions, produced by interaction of the upper atmosphere with the solar wind. **b.** the dawn. [Latin *aurora* dawn, Roman goddess of the dawn.]

au·ro·ra aus·tra·lis (ə rôr′ə ôs trā′lis) the aurora seen in the Southern Hemisphere. Also, **southern lights.** [Modern Latin *aurora australis* literally, southern aurora, from Latin *aurōra* dawn + *austrālis* southern, from *Auster* south wind.]

aurora bo·re·al·is (bôr′ē al′is) the aurora seen in the Northern Hemisphere. Also, **northern lights.** [Modern Latin *aurora borealis* literally, northern aurora, from Latin *aurōra* dawn + *boreālis* northern, from *Boreas* north wind.]

au·ro·ral (ə rôr′əl) *adj.* **1.** relating to or resembling the dawn; dawning; roseate. **2.** relating to an aurora.

aus·cul·tate (ôs′kəl tāt′) *v.t., v.i.* **-tat·ed, -tat·ing.** to examine by auscultation. [Latin *auscultātus,* past participle of *auscultāre* to listen to.]

aus·cul·ta·tion (ôs′kəl tā′shən) *n.* the practice of listening, as with a stethoscope, to sounds arising from various organs, esp. the heart and lungs, to help determine their condition. [Latin *auscultātiō* a listening, from *auscultare* to listen to.]

aus·pice (ôs′pis) *n., pl.* **-pic·es** (-pə siz, -sēz′). **1.** an omen or sign. **2.** a divination or prophecy, esp. one made on the basis of the flight of birds. **3.** *also,* **auspices.** a circumstance or condition, esp. one that indicates success. [Latin *auspicium* divination by observing the actions of birds, from *avis* bird + *specere* to look.]
· **under the auspices of.** under the patronage or guidance of; with the approval and support of: *a tour conducted under the auspices of the school board.*

aus·pi·cious (ô spish′əs) *adj.* **1.** promising success; propitious; favorable. **2.** having good fortune; fortunate; prosperous.

a	at	e	end	o	hot	u	up	hw	white		about
ā	ape	ē	me	ō	old	ū	use	ng	song	ə	taken
ä	far	i	it	ô	fork	ü	rule	th	thin		pencil
âr	care	ī	ice	oi	oil	ů	pull	th	this		lemon
		îr	pierce	ou	out	ûr	turn	zh	measure		circus

—aus·pi'cious·ly, *adv.* —aus·pi'cious·ness, *n.* —For Synonyms, see **favorable.**

aus·tere (ô stîr') *adj.* **1.** stern or unyielding, as in manner or appearance; severe: *an austere master.* **2.** marked by solemnity; grave; serious; sober: *an austere occasion.* **3.** morally strict; ascetic. **4.** severely simple; unadorned: *an austere room.* **5.** providing for only the most basic needs; without excess or luxury: *an austere budget.* [Latin *austērus* harsh, from Greek *austēros;* originally, making the tongue dry.] —aus·tere'ly, *adv.* —aus·tere'ness, *n.* —For Synonyms, see **severe.**

aus·ter·i·ty (ô ster'i tē) *n., pl.* **-ties. 1.** the quality or condition of being austere. **2.** *also,* **austerities.** severe or ascetic practices.

aus·tral[1] (ou strǎl'; *Spanish* ous trǎl') *n., pl.* **-trals** or **-tra·les** (*Spanish* -trǎ'les). the monetary unit of Argentina. [Argentine Spanish *austral,* from Latin *australis* southern, from *auster* south wind.]

aus·tral[2] (ôs'trəl) *adj.* southern. [Middle English *austral,* from Latin *australis,* from *auster* south wind.]

Aus·tra·lian (ô strāl'yən) *adj.* of or relating to Australia or its people, language, or culture. —*n.* **1.** a native or citizen of Australia. **2.** an Australian aborigine. **3.** any of the languages of the aborigines of Australia.

Australian ballot, a ballot containing the names of all candidates and any proposals to be voted on. It is marked in secrecy by the voter.

aus·tra·lo·pith·e·cine (ô strā'lō pith'ə sēn', ôs'trə lō-) *adj.* of or relating to the extinct genus *Australopithecus* of early, but fully bipedal hominids, living from about 4 to 1 ½ million years ago in southern and eastern Africa. —*n.* an australopithecine hominid. [Modern Latin *Australopithecus,* from Latin *australis* southern + Greek *pithēkos.*]

Aus·tro·ne·sian (ôs'trə nē'zhən, -shən) *n.* a family of languages spoken predominantly in the Pacific islands and in some islands in the Indian Ocean. —*adj.* of or relating to this family of languages. Also, **Malayo-Polynesian.**

aut-, form of **auto-** before vowels and *h,* as in *autarchy.*

au·tar·chy (ô'tär kē) *n., pl.* **-chies. 1.** absolute rule by one person, or a country so ruled; despotism; autocracy. **2.** autarky. [Greek *autarchiā,* going back to *autos* self + *archein* to rule.] —au·tar'chic; *also,* au·tar'chi·cal, *adj.*

au·tar·ky (ô'tär kē) *n., pl.* **-kies. 1.** national economic self-sufficiency. **2.** a policy under which a nation supplies all of its own needs, independent of imports. Also, **autarchy.** [Greek *autarkeia* self-sufficiency, going back to *autos* self + *arkein* to suffice.] —au·tar'kic; *also,* au·tar'ki·cal, *adj.*

au·teur (ō tûr') *n.* a motion-picture director, esp. one whose films are felt to display a distinctive personal style. [French *auteur* author, originator, from Old French *autor* creator. See AUTHOR.]

au·then·tic (ô then'tik) *adj.* **1.** deserving of acceptance or belief; reliable; trustworthy: *The eyewitness gave an authentic account of the accident.* **2.** being what it seems or claims to be; genuine; real: *an authentic document.* [Old French *autentique,* from Late Latin *authenticus,* from Greek *authentikos.*] —au·then'ti·cal·ly, *adv.*

au·then·ti·cate (ô then'ti kāt') *v.t.,* **-cat·ed, -cat·ing. 1.** to establish as authentic: *The expert authenticated the painting by testing the pigments.* **2.** to establish as legally valid, as claims or authorship. —au·then'ti·ca'tion, *n.* —For Synonyms, see **confirm.**

au·then·tic·i·ty (ô'then tis'i tē) *n.* the state or quality of being authentic.

au·thor (ô'thər) *n.* **1.** the writer of a book or other literary work. **2.** an author's writings: *Do you read many French authors?* **3.** a person who originates or begins (something); creator: *the author of a plan.* —*v.t.* to be the author of. [Old French *autor* writer, creator, from Latin *auctor* creator.]

au·thor·ess (ô'thər is) *n.* a woman who is an author.

au·thor·i·tar·i·an (ə thôr'i târ'ē ən, ə thor'-) *adj.* advocating or based on total submission to authority, as opposed to individual freedom. —*n.* a person who advocates complete submission to authority. —au·thor'i·tar'i·an·ism, *n.*

au·thor·i·ta·tive (ə thôr'i tā'tiv, ə thor'-) *adj.* **1.** worthy of acceptance or belief; reliable: *The report of the incident came from authoritative sources.* **2.** proceeding from or having acknowledged authority: *an authoritative statement.* **3.** exercising authority; commanding; dictatorial: *authoritative parents.* —au·thor'i·ta'tive·ly, *adv.* —au·thor'i·ta'tive·ness, *n.*

au·thor·i·ty (ə thôr'i tē, ə thor'-) *n., pl.* **-ties. 1.** the power or right to act, command, enforce obedience, or make decisions: *The dictator had ultimate authority.* **2.** *also,* **authorities.** a person or group of persons possessing and exercising such a power or right: *We will report this incident to the military authorities.* **3.** *also,* **Authority.** a public agency or corporation that has the right or power to administer in a specified field: *Housing Authority,*

Transit Authority. **4.** a power or right delegated to another; authorization: *They have our authority to publish the book.* **5.** the power to influence the actions or thoughts of others: *to speak with authority.* **6.** an acknowledged or authoritative source of information or advice. **7.** an expert on a particular subject: *an authority on geology.* **8.** self-assurance and expertise that often result from experience: *The young violinist played with surprising authority.* [Old French *autorite* power, from Latin *auctōritās,* from *auctor* author, one in charge.]

au·thor·i·za·tion (ô'thər ə zā'shən) *n.* **1.** the act of authorizing. **2.** a legal right or power.

au·thor·ize (ô'thə rīz') *v.t.,* **-ized, -iz·ing. 1.** to give authority to; empower. **2.** to approve officially; sanction: *The mayor authorized the appointment of a new police chief.* **3.** to establish by authority or usage; justify: *an interpretation authorized by tradition.*

au·thor·ized (ô'thə rīzd') *adj.* having authority; acknowledged as authoritative: *an authorized agent, an authorized biography.*

Authorized Version, King James Version.

au·thor·ship (ô'thər ship') *n.* **1.** the profession of a writer of books or other literary works. **2.** the origin or source, esp. of a literary work: *a book of unknown authorship.*

au·tism (ô'tiz əm) *n.* a severe developmental disorder of early childhood, characterized by absence of speech or response to it, inability to relate to others, and sometimes rigid, rocking body movements. [Modern Latin *autismus* from Greek *autos* self + -ISM.] —au·tis'tic, *adj.*

au·to (ô'tō) *n., pl.* **au·tos.** automobile.

auto- *combining form* of or by oneself; self-: *autobiography, autocracy.* [Greek *autos* self.]

Au·to·bahn (ô'tō bän') *n., pl.* **-bahns** or **-bahn·en** (-bä'nən). in Germany, a superhighway with a central dividing strip. [German *Autobahn* literally, automobile road.]

au·to·bi·og·ra·phy (ô'tə bī og'rə fē, -bē-) *n., pl.* **-phies.** the story of one's life written or told by oneself. [AUTO- + BIOGRAPHY.] —au·to·bi·og'ra·pher, *n.* —au·to·bi·o·graph·ic (ô'tə bī'ə graf'ik, -bē'-); *also,* au'to·bi'o·graph'i·cal, *adj.* —au'to·bi'o·graph'i·cal·ly, *adv.*

au·toch·thon (ô tok'thən) *n., pl.* **-thons** or **-tho·nes** (-thə nēz'). **1.** an original inhabitant of a place; aborigine. **2.** an indigenous plant or animal. [Greek *autochthōn* sprung from the land itself, native, from *autos* self + *chthōn* earth.]

au·toch·tho·nous (ô tok'thə nəs) *adj.* native to a place; indigenous.

au·to·clave (ô'tə klāv') *n.* an apparatus used for sterilizing by steam under pressure. —*v.t.,* **-claved, -clav·ing.** to sterilize in an autoclave. [French *autoclave* sterilizer; literally, self-locking, from Greek *autos* self + Latin *clāvis* key.]

au·toc·ra·cy (ô tok'rə sē) *n., pl.* **-cies. 1.** a form of government in which one person holds absolute power; the government or power of an autocrat. **2.** a country or community ruled by an autocrat. **3.** the unlimited authority or influence of one person over others.

au·to·crat (ô'tə krat') *n.* **1.** a ruler who has absolute power. **2.** a person who is invested with or assumes unlimited authority over others. **3.** any domineering person. [French *autocrate,* from Greek *autokratēs* ruling by oneself, absolute, from *autos* self + *kratos* power.]

au·to·crat·ic (ô'tə krat'ik) *adj.* relating to or of the nature of an autocrat or autocracy; holding independent and unlimited powers. —au·to·crat'i·cal·ly, *adv.*

au·to·da·fé (ô'tō də fā') *n., pl.* **au·tos-da-fé. 1.** the ceremony accompanying the passing of the final sentence imposed upon heretics by the Spanish Inquisition. **2.** the execution of such a sentence, esp. burning at the stake. [Portuguese *auto-da-fé* act of faith; *auto,* from Latin *āctus* act; *fé,* from Latin *fidēs* faith.]

au·to·e·rot·i·cism (ô'tō i rot'ə siz'əm) *n.* self-induced sexual gratification, as by masturbation. Also, **au·to·er·ot·ism.** [AUTO- + EROTICISM.] —au'to·e·rot'ic, *adj.*

au·tog·a·my (ô tog'ə mē) *n.* **1.** *Botany.* self-fertilization in which a flower is pollinated by its own pollen. **2.** *Biology.* conjugation, as among certain protists and fungi, between closely related cells or nuclei within the same cell. [AUTO- + -GAMY.] —au·tog'a·mous, *adj.*

au·to·gi·ro (ô'tō ji'rō) *n., pl.* **-ros.** *also,* **autogyro.** an airplane that is lifted and supported in air by a large aerodynamically driven rotor and is moved forward by an engine-driven propeller. It differs from a helicopter, which has an engine-driven rotor and no propeller. *Trademark:* **Autogiro.** [Spanish *autogiro* helicopter, from Greek *autos* self + *gyros* circle.]

au·to·graph (ô'tə graf') *n.* **1.** a person's own distinctive signature. **2.** something in a person's own handwriting; original manuscript. —*v.t.* **1.** to write one's signature in or on. **2.** to write (something) in one's own handwriting. [French *autographe* one's

own signature or manuscript, from Latin *autographus* written with one's own hand, from Greek *autographos*, from *autos* self + *graphein* to write.] —**au′to·graph′ic**; *also,* **au′to·graph′i·cal,** *adj.*

au·to·gy·ro (ô′tə jī′rō) *n.* autogiro.

au·to·hyp·no·sis (ô′tō hip nō′sis) *n.* self-hypnosis. —**au′to·hyp·not′ic,** *adj.*

au·to·im·mune (ô′tō i mūn′) *adj.* of or relating to the production by an organism of antibodies that attack the organism's own tissues or cells.

au·to·in·tox·i·ca·tion (ô′tō in tok′si kā′shən) *n.* poisoning by toxic substances formed within the body.

au·to·mat (ô′tə mat′) *n.* a cafeteria in which food is obtained from small compartments whose doors open when the proper coins are deposited in the slots. [Short for AUTOMATIC.]

au·to·mate (ô′tə māt′) *v.t.,* **-mat·ed, -mat·ing.** to convert to or operate by automation.

automated teller machine *also,* **automatic teller machine.** a computerized machine that allows bank customers to deposit or withdraw money and make other transactions without the help of a teller. Also, **cash machine.**

au·to·mat·ic (ô′tə mat′ik) *adj.* **1.** moving or acting from forces within itself; self-regulating; mechanical: *an automatic washing machine.* **2.** done without deliberate or conscious effort; reflex: *Blinking is an automatic reaction of the eye to a foreign particle.* **3.** (of firearms) using either the recoil or the gas from a fired cartridge to eject the empty cartridge, reload, and fire continuously until the trigger is released. —*n.* an automatic weapon. [Greek *automatos* self-acting + -IC.] —**au′to·mat′i·cal·ly,** *adv.*

Synonyms *adj.* **Automatic, involuntary,** and **spontaneous,** used of an action or reaction, refer to a lack of control by the conscious mind. **Automatic** suggests quickness and a mechanical quality, as if the same cause will bring the same reaction again and again: *to get an automatic chill each time one sees a spider.* **Involuntary** stresses the lack of volition or will: *I tried to suppress an involuntary shudder at the gruesome sight.* **Spontaneous** stresses the naturalness of the reaction and the lack of forethought or plan: *The crowd burst into a spontaneous cheer when the surprise winner was announced.*

automatic pilot, a device that guides the course of an aircraft, ship, or other vehicle automatically by means of a computer controlled by one or more gyroscopes. Also, **autopilot.**

automatic teller machine, automated teller machine.

au·to·ma·tion (ô′tə mā′shən) *n.* the development and use of mechanical equipment in combination with automatic control systems. It involves the replacement of machines controlled by human operators with machines that are self-regulating or operated by other machines. [Greek *automatos* self-acting + -ION.]

au·tom·a·tism (ô tom′ə tiz′əm) *n.* the state or quality of being automatic or like an automaton; automatic or involuntary action.

au·tom·a·tize (ô tom′ə tīz′) *v.t.,* **-tized, -tiz·ing. 1.** to make automatic. **2.** automate. [AUTOMAT(IC) + -IZE.] —**au·tom′a·ti·za′tion,** *n.*

au·tom·a·ton (ô tom′ə ton′, -tən) *n., pl.* **-tons** or **-ta** (-tə). **1.** a machine or other device that appears to function by itself through the use of concealed motive power; robot. **2.** a person or animal whose behavior is purely mechanical. [Greek *automaton,* neuter of *automatos* self-acting.]

au·to·mo·bile (ô′tə mə bēl′, ô′tə mə bēl′, ô′tə mō′bēl) *n.* a passenger vehicle, propelled by an engine, and usually having four wheels; car. —*adj.* automotive. [French *automobile,* from Greek *autos* self + Latin *mobilis* movable.] —**au′to·mo·bil′ist,** *n.*

au·to·mo·tive (ô′tə mō′tiv) *adj.* **1.** of, relating to, or for an automobile or automobiles. **2.** moving by itself; self-propelled; self-moving.

au·to·nom·ic (ô′tə nom′ik) *adj.* **1.** of, relating to, or controlled by the autonomic nervous system. **2.** autonomous *(def. 1).* **3.** *Botany.* produced by internal causes: *autonomic movement.* —**au′to·nom′i·cal·ly,** *adv.*

autonomic nervous system, the part of the nervous system of vertebrates consisting of the sympathetic and parasympathetic nervous systems. It controls and regulates the involuntary functions of the body, such as the activities of involuntary muscles that control the heart, lungs, or intestines.

au·ton·o·mous (ô ton′ə məs) *adj.* **1.** self-governing; independent. **2.** *Botany.* autonomic. —**au·ton′o·mous·ly,** *adv.*

au·ton·o·my (ô ton′ə mē) *n., pl.* **-mies. 1.** the quality or condition of being self-governing. **2.** the power or right of self-government. **3.** a self-governing state or community. [Greek *autonomia* independence.]

au·to·pi·lot (ô′tō pī′lət) *n.* automatic pilot.

au·top·sy (ô′top sē, ô′təp-) *n., pl.* **-sies.** the dissection and examination of a dead body in order to discover the cause of death or the nature and extent of the cause; postmortem. [Modern Latin *autopsia,* from Greek *autopsia* seeing with one's own eyes.]

au·to·some (ô′tə sōm′) *n.* a chromosome that is neither an X chromosome nor a Y chromosome. [AUTO- + (CHROMO)SOME.] —**au′to·so′mal,** *adj.*

au·to·sug·ges·tion (ô′tō səg jes′chən, -sə jes′-) *n.* the act or process of influencing one's own attitudes, behavior, or bodily functions by subconscious mental processes, as in self-hypnosis. [AUTO- + SUGGESTION.]

au·tot·o·my (ô tot′ə mē) *n.* the reflex breaking off of a part of the body at a joint, occurring in some animals when this part is damaged or seized. The part later regenerates. [AUTO- + -tomy, a combining form meaning "a dividing," from Modern Latin -tomia, from Greek *tomē* a cutting, from *temnein* to cut.] —**au·to·tom·ic** (ô′tə tom′ik) *adj.*

au·to·troph (ô′tə trof′) *n.* an organism, such as a plant or alga, that is able to synthesize all the nutritive substances it needs from inorganic substances in its environment, as by photosynthesis. ➡ distinguished from **heterotroph.** [German *autotroph,* from Greek *autotrophus* supplying one's own food, from *autos* self + *trephein* to nourish.] —**au′to·troph′ic,** *adj.* —**au′to·troph′i·cal·ly,** *adv.*

au·tumn (ô′təm) *n.* **1.** the season of the year coming between summer and winter; fall. In the Northern Hemisphere it extends from the autumnal equinox, about September 23, to the winter solstice, about December 22. **2.** a time of maturity, mellowing, and beginning decline: *the autumn of one's life.* —*adj.* of, like, characteristic of, or occurring in autumn: *autumn haze.* [Latin *autumnus.*]

au·tum·nal (ô tum′nəl) *adj.* **1.** of, relating to, or characteristic of autumn. **2.** maturing or gathered in autumn: *autumnal fruits.* **3.** past maturity or the middle stage of one's life. —**au·tum′nal·ly,** *adv.*

autumnal equinox, the equinox that occurs on or about September 23. It marks the beginning of autumn in the Northern Hemisphere. For illustration, see **solstice.**

aux·il·ia·ry (ôg zil′yə rē, -zil′ə rē) *adj.* **1.** giving aid or support; helping: *auxiliary firefighters.* **2.** kept or used as a reserve; supplementary: *an auxiliary generator.* **3.** in addition to the regular; subsidiary; secondary: *an auxiliary branch of a library.* —*n., pl.* **-ries. 1.** a person or thing that aids or supports; helper. **2.** a subsidiary group or organization: *ladies' auxiliary.* **3.** auxiliary verb. **4. auxiliaries.** foreign or allied troops in the service of a nation at war. [Latin *auxiliārius* aiding, from *auxilium* aid.]

auxiliary verb, a verb used in addition to the main verb to express the tense, mood, or voice. In the sentence *They will go,* the word *will* is an auxiliary verb. Also, **helping verb.**

aux·in (ôk′sin) *n.* any of a group of substances, esp. indoleacetic acid, produced principally in the tips of plant shoots and promoting lengthwise growth, bud growth, fruit maturation, and the shedding of leaves. [Greek *auxein* to increase + -IN¹.] —**aux·in′ic,** *adj.*

av. 1. *also,* **Av.** avenue. **2.** average. **3.** avoirdupois.

A.V., Authorized Version.

a·vail (ə vāl′) *v.t.* to be of advantage or worth to; assist: *My help will not avail you now.* —*v.i.* to be of use or value; help: *In this matter, force will not avail.* —*n.* a source of help or support; use; advantage: *Your effort would be of no avail.* [A-³ + obsolete *vail* to prevail, from Old French *valoir* to be of value, from Latin *valēre* to be strong.]

• **to avail oneself of.** to take advantage of; make use of: *Please avail yourself of our library during your visit.*

a·vail·a·ble (ə vā′lə bəl) *adj.* **1.** able to be obtained, gotten, or reached; obtainable; accessible: *That sweater is available in all sizes and colors.* **2.** able to be used; at one's disposal: *The telephone is now available.* —**a·vail′a·bil′i·ty, a·vail′a·ble·ness,** *n.* —**a·vail′a·bly,** *adv.*

av·a·lanche (av′ə lanch′) *n.* **1.** a swift, sudden fall of a mass of snow, ice, earth, or rocks down a mountain slope. **2.** anything like an avalanche, as in size or suddenness: *There was an avalanche of mail in response to the editorial.* —*v.,* **-lanched, -lanch·ing.** —*v.i.* to fall in or like an avalanche. —*v.t.* to overwhelm with an abundance of something. [French *avalanche* snowslide, partly from dialectal French *lavanche* (of uncertain origin); partly from French *avaler* to descend, from Old French *a val* to the valley, from the Latin phrase *ad vallem* to the valley.]

Av·a·lon (av′ə lon′) *n.* in Arthurian legend, the island to which King Arthur was carried after being mortally wounded in battle.

a·vant-garde (ä vänt′gärd′, ə vänt′-) *n.* a group of people who

a	at	e	end	o	hot	u	up	hw	white		about
ā	ape	ē	me	ō	old	ū	use	ng	song		taken
ä	far	i	it	ô	fork	ü	rule	th	thin	ə	pencil
âr	care	ī	ice	oi	oil	u̇	pull	th	this		lemon
		îr	pierce	ou	out	ûr	turn	zh	measure		circus

81

are considered in the forefront in experimenting with or accepting new, daring, or extreme styles or ideas, esp. in the arts. —*adj.* **1.** new, daring, or extreme in styles or ideas: *an avant-garde movie.* **2.** of or belonging to the avant-garde: *an avant-garde poet.* [French *avant-garde* literally, advance guard.]

av·a·rice (av′ər is) *n.* an inordinate desire for wealth or possessions; greed; cupidity. [Old French *avarice,* from Latin *avāritia.*]

av·a·ri·cious (av′ə rish′əs) *adj.* greedy for wealth or possessions; covetous; grasping. —**av′a·ri′cious·ly,** *adv.* —**av′a·ri′cious·ness,** *n.* —For Synonyms, see **greedy.**

a·vast (ə vast′) *interj. Nautical.* stop; stay; cease. [Dutch *houd vast* hold fast.]

av·a·tar (av′ə tär′) *n.* **1.** in Hinduism, an incarnation of a god. Krishna is an avatar of Vishnu. **2.** any incarnation or embodiment. [Sanskrit *avatāra* descent.]

avatars of the Hindu god Vishnu

a·vaunt (ə vônt′, ə vänt′) *interj. Archaic.* go away; begone. [Anglo-Norman *avaunt* before, from Latin *abante* from in front of.]

a·ve (ä′vā) *interj.* hail or farewell. —*n.* Ave Maria. [Latin *avē* hail, farewell.]

Ave., avenue. Also, **ave.**

A·ve Ma·ri·a (ä′vā mə rē′ə) **1.** the Latin version of the Hail Mary. **2.** a salutation to the Virgin Mary, the first two words of the Latin version of the Hail Mary. **3.** any of several musical compositions based on the Latin version of the Hail Mary. [Medieval Latin *Ave Maria* hail Mary, its opening words.]

a·venge (ə venj′) *v.t.,* **a·venged, a·veng·ing.** to get revenge for or on behalf of: *She swore to avenge her father's murder.* [Old French *avengier,* from *a* to (from Latin *ad* to) + *vengier* to take vengeance, from Latin *vindicāre* to punish.] —**a·veng′er,** *n.* —For Synonyms, see **revenge.**

a·ven·tu·rine (ə ven′chə rēn′, -rin) *n.* a semiprecious stone that is a sparkling red, iridescent variety of feldspar, composed of sodium aluminum silicate.

av·e·nue (av′ə nū′ -nü′) *n.* **1.** a street or thoroughfare, esp. a wide one. **2.** a means of accomplishing or attaining something: *an avenue to success.* **3.** a road or walk, often lined with trees. [French *avenue* approach, avenue, from *avenir* to come to, from Latin *advenīre.*]

a·ver (ə vûr′) *v.t.,* **a·verred, a·ver·ring. 1.** to declare positively; affirm; assert. **2.** *Law.* to assert or declare formally in a plea. [French *avérer,* going back to Latin *ad* to + *vērus* true.]

av·er·age (av′rij, -ər ij) *n.* **1.** a single number that describes or typifies a set of numbers, found by dividing the sum of two or more quantities by the number of quantities: *The average of 2, 4, 6, and 8 is 5.* Also, **arithmetic mean. 2.** a typical, ordinary, or usual quantity, rate, kind, or quality; anything approaching the norm: *This year's rainfall came close to the average.* —*adj.* **1.** arrived at by calculating the arithmetic mean; resembling or constituting an average: *average yield, average speed.* **2.** not unusual or exceptional; typical; ordinary: *average height, an average American.* —*v.,* **-aged, -ag·ing.** —*v.t.* **1.** to find the arithmetic mean of: *She averaged their test scores for the week.* **2.** to do, take, yield, have, or amount to on the average: *His salary averages 200 dollars a week.* **3.** to share or divide equally: *The partners averaged their profits.* —*v.i.* to be or amount to an average. [French *avarie* damage to ship or cargo, from Italian *avaria* damage at sea, from Arabic *'awārīya* damaged goods, from *'awār* damage; insurance on such damage was calculated and paid on the basis of an

average.] —**av′er·age·a·ble,** *adj.* —**av′er·age·ly,** *adv.* —**av′er·age·ness,** *n.*

•**on the** (or **an**) **average.** considered on the basis of an average; typically: *On the average, we get 40 inches of rain a year.*

•**to average out.** to amount to an average: *Dinner averaged out to thirty dollars per couple.*

a·ver·ment (ə vûr′mənt) *n.* **1.** an act of averring. **2.** something that is averred; assertion.

A·ver·nus (ə vûr′nəs) *n.* in Roman mythology, the lower world; hell. [Latin *(lacus) Avernus* (Lake) Avernus, from Greek *aornos* without birds; this lake was regarded by the ancients as the entrance to the lower world.]

a·verse (ə vûrs′) *adj.* having strong feelings against; opposed (usually with *to*): *averse to a change in plans.* [Latin *āversus,* past participle of *āvertere* to turn away.] —**a·verse′ly,** *adv.* —**a·verse′ness,** *n.* —For Synonyms, see **adverse.**

a·ver·sion (ə vûr′zhən, -shən) *n.* **1.** a deep-rooted opposition or dislike; antipathy: *an aversion to insects.* **2.** a cause or object of opposition or dislike. —For Synonyms, see **disgust.**

a·vert (ə vûrt′) *v.t.* **1.** to turn away or aside: *to avert one's attention, to avert one's eyes.* **2.** to keep from happening; ward off; prevent; avoid: *to avert disaster.* [Latin *āvertere* to turn away.] —**a·vert′i·ble;** also, **a·vert′a·ble,** *adj.*

A·ves·ta (ə ves′tə) *n.* the sacred scriptures of Zoroastrianism.

avg., average.

a·vi·an (ā′vē ən) *adj.* of or relating to birds. [Latin *avis* bird + -AN.]

a·vi·ar·y (ā′vē er′ē) *n., pl.* **-ar·ies.** a large cage, building, or enclosure in which birds are kept. [Latin *aviārium* place for birds, from *avis* bird.] —**a·vi·a·rist** (ā′vē ə rist), *n.*

a·vi·a·tion (ā′vē ā′shən, av′ē-) *n.* **1.** the science or art of flight in heavier-than-air aircraft. **2.** the production and design of heavier-than-air aircraft. [French *aviation,* from Latin *avis* bird.]

a·vi·a·tor (ā′vē ā′tər, av′ē-) *n.* a person who flies an airplane or other heavier-than-air aircraft.

a·vi·a·trix (ā′vē ā′triks, av′ē-) *n., pl.* **-tri·ces** (-ā′trə sēz′, -ə trī′sēz). a woman who flies an airplane or other heavier-than-air aircraft. Also, **a·vi·a·tress** (ā′vē ā′tris).

av·id (av′id) *adj.* **1.** having or showing enthusiasm; ardent; eager: *an avid reader.* **2.** having a great desire; greedy: *to be avid for wealth.* [Latin *avidus* greedy.] —**av′id·ly,** *adv.* —**av′id·ness,** *n.*

a·vid·i·ty (ə vid′i tē) *n.* intense desire, extreme greed, or eagerness.

a·vi·on·ics (ā′vē on′iks) *n.* the branch of electronics concerned with the aerospace applications of electronic devices. ➡ used as singular. [Short for AVI(ATION) + (ELECTR)ONICS.]

av·o·ca·do (av′ə kä′dō, ä′və-) *n., pl.* **-dos. 1.** the pulpy fruit of a tree, *Persea americana,* of the laurel family, having a large single seed and pulp with a buttery texture and a nutty flavor, eaten raw in salads, desserts, and other dishes. Also, **alligator pear. 2.** the evergreen tree bearing this fruit, having dark green, oval-shaped leaves and clusters of small greenish flowers, widely cultivated in California and Florida. [Spanish *aguacate,* from Nahuatl *ahuacatl* testicle.]

av·o·ca·tion (av′ə kā′shən) *n.* **1.** an interest or pastime that a person has in addition to his or her regular occupation; hobby: *Our doctor's avocation is sculpturing.* **2.** a person's usual occupation; vocation. ➡ rarely used in def. 2 because of confusion with **vocation.** [Latin *āvocātiō* diverting of attention.] —**av′o·ca′tion·al,** *adj.*

av·o·cet (av′ə set′) *n.* any of several long-legged wading birds, genus *Recurvirostra,* having webbed feet and a long, slender beak. Length: 15-18 inches (38-46 centimeters) from bill to tail. [French *avocette,* from Italian *avocetta* storklike bird.]

A·vo·ga·dro's law (ä′və gä′drōz) a law stating that equal volumes of gases at the same temperature and pressure contain the same number of molecules, regardless of the gases involved. [From Count Amadeo *Avogadro,* 1776-1856, Italian physicist who formulated it.]

avocet

a·void (ə void′) *v.t.* **1.** to keep away from; shun; evade: *to avoid someone, to avoid a traffic jam.* **2.** to keep from happening; prevent: *She agreed to the plan in order to avoid an argument.* **3.** *Law.* to make void, useless, or of no effect; annul. [Anglo-Norman *avoider,* from Old French *esvuidier* to

empty, from *es-* out (from Latin *ex*) + *vuide* empty.] —a·void′a·ble, *adj.* —a·void′a·bly, *adv.*

Synonyms Avoid, evade, elude, dodge, and shun mean to stay away from. Avoid, the general term, usually implies caution or deliberation in not encountering something undesirable or dangerous: *We drove three miles out of our way to avoid the traffic jam.* Evade suggests avoiding something threatening that is coming after one: *The counterfeiters evaded the law for years.* Elude implies trickiness in evading: *The thieves eluded the police by slipping through an open window.* Dodge suggests sidestepping something coming directly at one: *I dodged the runaway horse by stepping behind the fence.* Shun suggests persistent or habitual avoidance, often because of moral or physical distaste: *The crowd shunned the beggar. The community shunned the defendants during the trial.*

a·void·ance (ə voi′dəns) *n.* **1.** the act of avoiding. **2.** *Law.* a making void; annulment.

av·oir·du·pois (av′ər də poiz′) *n.* **1.** avoirdupois weight. **2.** *Informal.* body weight or heaviness. [Anglo-Norman *aveir de peis* goods of weight; *aveir* goods, from Latin *habēre* to have; *de* of, from Latin *dē*; *peis* weight, from Latin *pensum*.]

avoirdupois weight, a system of weights based on a pound that contains 16 ounces (454 grams). It is used in Great Britain, the United States, and Canada for weighing all goods except drugs or precious metals. For Weights and Measures table, see **weight**.

a·vouch (ə vouch′) *v.t.* **1.** to declare positively; assert; affirm. **2.** to vouch for; guarantee. **3.** to acknowledge; admit; confess. [Old French *avochier* to call upon, from Latin *advocāre* to call to, summon. Doublet of AVOW.] —a·vouch′ment, *n.*

a·vow (ə vou′) *v.t.* to declare frankly or openly; admit; acknowledge. [Old French *avouer*, from Latin *advocāre*. Doublet of AVOUCH.]

a·vow·al (ə vou′əl) *n.* a frank or open declaration, admission, or acknowledgment: *an avowal of one's beliefs.*

a·vowed (ə voud′) *adj.* openly declared or acknowledged: *avowed enemies.* —a·vow·ed·ly (ə vou′id lē, ə voud′-), *adv.*

a·vun·cu·lar (ə vung′kyə lər) *adj.* of, relating to, like, or characteristic of an uncle. [Latin *avunculus* mother's brother + -AR[1].]

a·wait (ə wāt′) *v.t.* **1.** to look forward to; wait for; anticipate: *She had long awaited their reunion. We await your reply.* **2.** to be ready or in store for: *Good fortune awaits him.* [Anglo-Norman *awaitier* to watch for, from *a-* (from Latin *ad* to) + *waitier* to watch (of Germanic origin).] —For Synonyms, see **expect**.

a·wake (ə wāk′) *v.,* a·woke or a·waked, a·waked or a·wok·en or a·woke, a·wak·ing. —*v.t.* **1.** to rouse from sleep; wake. **2.** to make active; stir up or excite: *The company hoped that advertising would awake new interest in their product.* —*v.i.* **1.** to cease to sleep. **2.** to become active or aroused. **3.** to become aware or alert (with *to*): *The accident made him awake to the danger involved in driving too fast.* —*adj.* **1.** not asleep. **2.** informed of something; alert; aware. [Blend of Old English *awācnian* and *onwæcnan* to waken.]

a·wak·en (ə wā′kən) *v.t., v.i.* to awake. —a·wak′en·er, *n.*

a·wak·en·ing (ə wā′kə ning) *n.* **1.** the act of waking. **2.** a becoming aware; awareness; realization. —*adj.* arousing; stirring: *an awakening sense of obligation.*

a·ward (ə wôrd′) *v.t.* **1.** to give as merited or due: *to award a good conduct medal.* **2.** to grant or bestow by judicial determination; adjudge: *The jury awarded damages to the plaintiff.* —*n.* **1.** something that is awarded, as a medal. **2.** a decision or finding, as of a judge or arbitrator. [Anglo-Norman *awarder* to observe, decide, from *es* out (from Latin *ex* out) + *warder* to observe (of Germanic origin).] —a·ward′a·ble, *adj.* —a·ward′er, *n.* —For Synonyms *(n.),* see **prize**[1].

a·ward·ee (ə wôr dē′, ə wôr′dē) *n.* a person or group that receives an award.

a·ware (ə wâr′) *adj.* knowing or being conscious; in possession of information; cognizant; informed (often with *of*): *They were aware of our plans.* [Old English *gewær*.] —a·ware′ness, *n.*

Synonyms Aware, conscious, and cognizant mean recognizing the existence of or knowing something. Aware refers to knowing anything either through the senses or by being told: *to be aware of a noise in the bushes, to be aware of a deadline.* Conscious is used similarly, but perhaps more often of sensory or emotional perception: *to be conscious of increasing tension in a meeting.* It often suggests the threshold at which something becomes known: *to become conscious of one's age for the first time.* Cognizant implies that particular information has been brought to one's attention: *The accident made me cognizant of the dangers of diving into shallow water.*

a·wash (ə wôsh′, ə wosh′) *adv., adj.* **1.** covered with water: *The deck of the boat was awash during the storm.* **2.** level with or just above the surface of the water so that the water washes over it. **3.** tossed or washed about by water; floating.

a·way (ə wā′) *adv.* **1.** from this or that place; off: *to sail away.* **2.** at a distance: *They stood several paces away from us.* **3.** in or to another place: *He was called away from his desk.* **4.** in another direction; aside: *Look away.* **5.** from or out of one's possession, attention, or use: *to put away a coat.* **6.** at or to an end; out of existence: *to wither away.* **7.** without interruption; continuously: *She pounded away at her typewriter.* **8.** without hesitation or delay; directly: *Fire away!* —*adj.* **1.** apart in space; distant: *Our house is five miles away from town.* **2.** not present in a place; absent; gone. **3.** *Sports.* played on an opponent's field, court, or the like: *an away game.* **4.** *Baseball.* out: *There's one batter away in the bottom of the ninth.* [Old English *onweg* literally, on the way.]

·**away back.** *Informal.* far back in time; long ago: *My ancestors arrived in this country away back in the nineteenth century.*

·**away with. a.** take (someone or something) away: *Away with him!* **b.** go away; depart: *Away with all of you!*

·**to do away with. a.** to put an end or stop to; get rid of: *The club did away with many of its requirements for membership.* **b.** to eliminate by killing: *The queen did away with her enemies.*

awe (ô) *n.* an overwhelming sense of wonder combined with fear or reverence: *The children were in awe of the huge shark at the aquarium.* —*v.t.,* awed, aw·ing. to inspire or fill with awe: *We were awed by the fury of the storm.* [Old Norse *agi* terror.]

a·wea·ry (ə wîr′ē) *adj.* extremely tired; weary.

a·weigh (ə wā′) *adj. Nautical.* (of an anchor) raised clear of the bottom.

awe·some (ô′səm) *adj.* **1.** inspiring awe: *an awesome creature.* **2.** expressive of awe: *an awesome glance.* —awe′some·ly, *adv.* —awe′some·ness, *n.*

awe-struck (ô′struk′) *adj.* filled with awe. Also, awe-strick·en (ô′strik′ən).

aw·ful (ô′fəl) *adj.* **1.** causing fear, alarm, or dread; terrible; frightening; appalling: *an awful fire.* **2.** excessively bad, distasteful, or ugly: *an awful movie.* **3.** very great: *They took an awful risk driving in this storm.* **4.** worthy of or commanding respect and reverence: *his awful holiness.* **5.** inspiring awe: *the awful beauty of the Sistine Chapel.* —*adv. Informal.* extremely; terribly: *to be awful glad.* [AWE + -FUL.] —aw′ful·ness, *n.*

aw·ful·ly (ô′fə lē, ôf′lē) *adv.* **1.** in a bad or unpleasant way: *to sing awfully.* **2.** to an extreme degree; very: *It's awfully hot. She's awfully pretty.*

a·while (ə hwīl′, ə wīl′) *adv.* for a short time; for a little.

Usage Because awhile is an adverb meaning for a short time, it should not be used after a preposition such as *for,* *after,* or *in.* These prepositions should be followed instead by the two words *a while.* Thus either *Rest awhile* or *Rest for a while* is acceptable, but not *Rest for awhile.*

awk·ward (ôk′wərd) *adj.* **1.** lacking ease or grace in bearing; ungainly: *an awkward child.* **2.** lacking dexterity or skill: *The dancer gave an awkward performance.* **3.** causing or marked by embarrassment or uneasiness: *an awkward laugh, an awkward silence.* **4.** ill-adapted for use or handling; unwieldy: *an awkward box to carry.* **5.** hard to manage or deal with; requiring skill or caution; difficult: *Your decision to quit puts us in an awkward position.* [Obsolete *awk* perverse, clumsy (from Old Norse *öfugr* turned the wrong way) + WARD.] —awk′ward·ly, *adv.* —awk′ward·ness, *n.*

Synonyms Awkward, clumsy, and ungainly mean lacking grace or skill. Awkward is the general term, applying to either physical or social skills: *an awkward swimmer, to be awkward at parties.* Clumsy implies heaviness, stiffness, or blundering: *The clumsy customer broke the delicate figurine. My clumsy effort to apologize made things worse.* Ungainly stresses a lack of physical adroitness, as if limbs or joints are out of control, especially in youth: *The ungainly teenager kept bumping into the furniture.*

awl (ôl) *n.* a pointed tool used for making small holes or for

a	at	e	end	o	hot	u	up	hw	white		about
ā	ape	ē	me	ō	old	ū	use	ng	song	ə	taken
ä	far	i	it	ô	fork	ü	rule	th	thin		pencil
âr	care	ī	ice	oi	oil	u̇	pull	th	this		lemon
		îr	pierce	ou	out	ûr	turn	zh	measure		circus

working designs into the surface of leather or wood. [Old Norse *alr*.]

awn (ôn) *n.* a bristlelike part that constitutes the beard in some grasses, as on a spike of barley or wheat. [Old Norse *ögn* chaff.] —**awned**, *adj.* —**awn′less**, *adj.*

aw·ning (ô′ning) *n.* a rooflike cover of canvas or other material, as over or before a door, window, or patio, used as a shelter from the sun or rain. [Of unknown origin.]

a·woke (ə wōk′) a past tense and past participle of **awake**.

a·wok·en (ə wō′kən) a past participle of **awake**.

AWOL (ā′wôl′) *also,* **a·wol, a.w.o.l., A.W.O.L.** *adv., adj. Military.* absent from one's post or duties without official leave but without intent to desert. —*n.* a member of the armed forces who is AWOL. [Short for *a(bsent) w(ith)o(ut) l(eave).*]

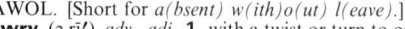

awl

a·wry (ə rī′) *adv., adj.* **1.** with a twist or turn to one side; askew. **2.** out of the right course; wrong; amiss. [A-¹ + WRY.]

ax (aks) *also,* **axe.** *n., pl.* **ax·es.** a tool with a bladed metal head on a handle, used esp. for felling trees and chopping wood. —*v.t.* **1.** to chop or cut with an ax. **2.** *Informal.* to dismiss from a job. **3.** *Informal.* to get rid of: *The new president axed half of the budget for advertising.* [Old English *æx* this tool.]
  • **to have an ax to grind.** *Informal.* **a.** to have a special purpose or end to attain. **b.** to have a grievance.
  • **to get the ax.** *Informal.* to be dismissed from one's job.

axe (aks) *n. & v.* —*v.t.,* **axed, ax·ing.** ax.

ax·es¹ (ak′siz) the plural of **ax**.

ax·es² (ak′sēz) the plural of **axis**.

ax·i·al (ak′sē əl) *adj.* **1.** of, relating to, or forming an axis. **2.** situated on, around, or along an axis. —**ax′i·al·ly,** *adv.*

ax·il (ak′səl) *n.* the upper angle formed where a leafstalk or stem joins the stem on which it is borne. [Latin *axilla* armpit.]

ax·il·la (ak sil′ə) *n., pl.* **ax·il·lae** (ak sil′ē). **1.** the armpit. **2.** an axil. [Latin *axilla* armpit.]

ax·il·lar·y (ak′sə ler′ē) *adj.* **1.** of, relating to, or near the armpit. **2.** of, relating to, situated in, or growing from an axil.

ax·i·om (ak′sē əm) *n.* **1.** a statement or principle accepted as true without proof, as a postulate in logic or mathematics; self-evident or universally accepted truth. **2.** an established principle, rule, or law. [Latin *axiōma* principle, from Greek *axiōma*.]

ax·i·o·mat·ic (ak′sē ə mat′ik) *adj.* **1.** of, relating to, or like an axiom; self-evident. **2.** full of axioms or maxims; aphoristic. —**ax′i·o·mat′i·cal·ly,** *adv.*

ax·is (ak′sis) *n., pl.* **ax·es** (ak′sēz). **1.** a real or imaginary straight line passing through an object or body, as the earth, and around which it rotates or seems to rotate. **2.** a straight, central line around which the parts of a plane or solid figure are symmetrically arranged. The axis of a cylinder is the line segment joining the center of the two bases. **3.** number line. **4.** *Anatomy.* **a.** any central line of a bodily structure, esp. the spinal column, that is an axis of symmetry. **b.** the second cervical vertebra, which acts as a pivot on which the head turns. **5.** the main stem of a plant. **6.** a central line around which the parts of anything are arranged. **7.** a political and military alliance between two or more nations. **8. the Axis.** a World War II alliance between Germany and Italy that ultimately included Japan and several smaller countries. Also, **Axis Powers.** [Latin *axis* axis (of the earth), axle.]

axis of symmetry, a straight line that divides a geometric figure symmetrically.

ax·le (ak′səl) *n.* a shaft or bar on which or with which a pair of wheels or one wheel turns. [Old Norse *öxull*.]

ax·le·tree (ak′səl trē′) *n.* a fixed axle, usually wooden, connecting a pair of wheels, as on a cart or wagon. Each end of the axletree has a spindle or bearings on which the wheel turns.

Ax·min·ster (aks′min stər) *n.* a carpet of a type in which the tufts are individually inserted in order to achieve an almost unlimited variety of colors and intricate designs. [From *Axminster*, England, where originally made.]

ax·o·lotl (ak′sə lot′əl) *n.* any of several salamanders of Mexico and the western United States that usually do not metamorphose into an adult form, remaining and breeding in the larval stage. Length: 6-10 inches (15-25 centimeters). [Nahuatl *axolotl* literally, water spirit.]

ax·on (ak′son) *also,* **ax·one** (ak′sōn). *n.* a nerve fiber that extends from a neuron and conducts impulses away from the body of the cell. For illustration, see **neuron.** [Modern Latin *axon*, from Greek *axōn* axis, axle.]

ay¹ (ā) *also,* **aye.** *adv.* always; ever. [Old Norse *ei* ever.]

ay² (ī) aye¹.

a·yah (ä′yə) *n.* a native nursemaid or maid in India. [Hindi *āyā*, from Portuguese *aia* nurse, governess, from Latin *avia* grandmother.]

a·ya·tol·lah (ä′yə tō′lə) *n.* among Shiite Muslims, a religious leader of the highest rank. ➡ used as a title of respect. [Persian *ayatollah* literally, sign of God, from Arabic *āyat* sign + *Allah* Allah.]

aye¹ (ī) *also,* **ay².** *n.* an affirmative vote or voter. —*adv.* yes; yea. [Of uncertain origin.]

aye² (ā) ay¹.

aye-aye (ī′ī′) *n.* a squirrel-like nocturnal lemur of Madagascar, *Daubentonia madagascariensis,* having brown fur, a long, bushy tail, rodentlike teeth, and sharp claws. It is about the size of a house cat. [French *aye-aye*, from Malagasy *aiay*.]

Ay·ma·ra (ī′mä rä′) *n., pl.* **-ra** or **-ras. 1.** a member of a South American Indian people living in Bolivia and southern Peru. **2.** the language spoken by these people. —**Ay′ma·ran′,** *adj.*

Ayr·shire (âr′shir, -shər) *n.* one of a breed of dairy cattle that originated in Scotland, varying in color from red to dark brown with white blotches. [From the county of *Ayr,* Scotland, where originally bred.]

AZ, the postal abbreviation for Arizona.

a·za·lea (ə zāl′yə) *n.* any of a group of shrubs, genus *Rhododendron,* found in cool and temperate regions of the Northern Hemisphere, bearing clusters of funnel-shaped flowers. [Modern Latin *azalea*, from Greek *azalea*, feminine of *azaleos* dry; possibly because it was thought to thrive in dry soil.]

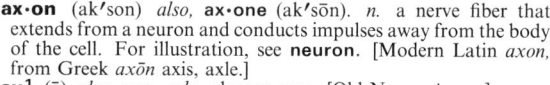

azimuth

az·i·muth (az′ə məth) *n.* **1.** a measurement of angular distance of bearing. In astronomy, it is used to plot the position of a celestial body; in navigation, to plot the position of an aircraft or ship. **2.** *Military.* the angular distance that a weapon must be moved to the left or right in order to give it greater accuracy. [Going back to Arabic *as-sumūt* the azimuth, from *as* the + *samt* way, direction.]

az·o (az′ō, ā′zō) *adj.* of, relating to, or containing the radical —N═N—, as a large class of dyes in which one or more of these radicals are found.

Az·tec (az′tek) *n.* **1.** a member of a large group of Indian tribes having a well-developed civilization and controlling an empire in central Mexico until the Spanish conquest in 1519. **2.** Nahuatl. —*adj.* of or relating to the Aztecs or their language, culture, or civilization. —**Az′tec·an,** *adj.*

Aztec mosaic pendant

az·ure (azh′ər) *n.* **1.** a clear sky-blue color. **2.** *Archaic.* the unclouded sky. —*adj.* having the color azure. [Old French *azur* blue, going back to Arabic *lāzward* lapis lazuli, blue, from Persian *lāzhward*.]

az·u·rite (azh′ə rīt′) *n.* an azure-blue copper carbonate mineral, often used to make jewelry or decorative objects. Formula: $2CuCO_3 \cdot Cu(OH)_2$

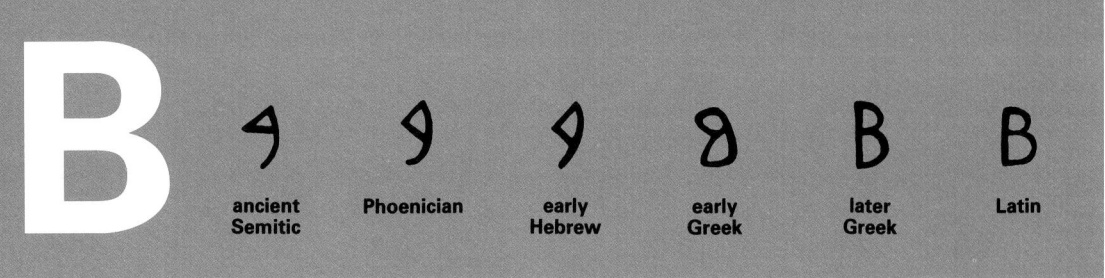

| ancient Semitic | Phoenician | early Hebrew | early Greek | later Greek | Latin |

B The earliest ancestor of the letter **B** was a symbol used as the second letter of the ancient Semitic alphabets. In the Phoenician and early Hebrew alphabets, this letter was called *beth*, meaning "house." The Greek letter *beta* was a modification of *beth*, and by about 800 B.C. it had assumed the form of a backward capital **B**. Several hundred years later, the Greeks reversed *beta*, and it was in this form that the letter passed into the Latin alphabet and eventually into English. The English word *alphabet* comes from a combination of *alpha* and *beta*, the first two letters of the Greek alphabet.

b, B (bē) *n., pl.* **b's, B's. 1.** the second letter of the English alphabet. **2.** the shape of this letter or something having this shape. **3.** the second item in a series or group.

B (bē) *n., pl.* **B's. 1.** *Music.* **a.** the seventh note or tone of the diatonic scale of C major. For illustration, see **do**[2]. **b.** the scale or key that has this note or tone as its tonic. **2.** a grade or rating indicating good or above-average performance: *a B in math.* **3.** one of the four principal blood groups. For table, see **blood group.**

B, the symbol for boron.

b. 1. *Baseball.* **a.** base[1]. **b.** baseman. **2.** bass[1]. **3.** book. **4.** born.

B *Chess.* bishop.

B. 1. Bay. **2.** Bible. **3.** British.

Ba, the symbol for barium.

B.A., Bachelor of Arts. Also, **A.B.**

baa (bä) *v.i.,* **baaed, baa·ing.** to cry, as a sheep; bleat. —*n.* the cry of a sheep; bleat. [Imitative.]

Ba·al (bā'əl, bāl) *n., pl.* **Ba·al·im** (bā'ə lim) or **Ba·als. 1.** the chief god of the ancient Semites, esp. the Canaanites and Phoenicians. He served primarily as the god of fertility and was worshiped under various local names. **2.** *also,* **baal.** a false god; idol. [Hebrew *ba'al* lord.]

Bab·bitt (bab'it) *also,* **bab·bit.** *n.* a person who conforms to provincial, American middle-class ideas of respectability and success in business. [From George F. *Babbitt,* title character of the satirical novel by Sinclair Lewis, 1885-1951, U.S. author.] —**Bab'bitt·ry,** *n.*

Babbitt metal, any of various alloys having a lead or tin base and smaller amounts of antimony or copper, used to reduce friction, as in bearings. Also, **bab'bitt.** [From the American inventor Isaac *Babbitt,* 1799-1862.]

bab·ble (bab'əl) *v.,* **-bled, -bling.** —*v.i.* **1.** to make indistinct or meaningless sounds; prattle: *The baby gurgled and babbled.* **2.** to talk foolishly or excessively; chatter. **3.** to make a continuous, murmuring sound: *The brook babbled.* —*v.t.* **1.** to utter incoherently or with meaningless repetition: *The dazed victim babbled a name and an address.* **2.** to say without thinking; blab: *to babble gossip.* —*n.* **1.** a confused or continuous murmur: *a babble of voices.* **2.** incoherent, unintelligible speech. **3.** foolish or pointless talk; chatter. [Imitative.] —**bab'bler,** *n.*

babe (bāb) *n.* **1.** a baby or young child. **2.** a naive, inexperienced, or helpless person. **3.** *Slang.* a girl or woman. [Of uncertain origin.]

Ba·bel (bā'bəl, bab'əl) *n.* **1.** in the Old Testament, a city in the land of Shinar, identified with Babylon. The **Tower of Babel** was a tower begun in Babel by the descendants of Noah in order to reach heaven. God punished its builders and prevented the completion of the tower by changing their language into many different ones. **2.** *also,* **babel.** a confused mixture of many voices or languages; tumult. [Hebrew *Bābel* Babylon; possibly for Assyrian *bābilu* gate of God.]

ba·bies'-breath (bā'bēz breth') baby's-breath.

bab·i·ru·sa (bab'ə rü'sə, bä'bə-) *also,* **bab·i·rous·sa, bab·i·**

rus·sa. *n.* a wild hog, *Babirussa babirussa,* of the East Indies and Southeast Asia. The male of the species has two pairs of upward-curving tusks. Height: 2.5 feet (0.8 meter) at the shoulder. [Malay *bābīrūsa* hog like a deer, from *bābī* hog + *rūsa* deer.]

Ba·bism (bä'biz əm) *n.* a religious movement founded in 1844 in Persia. Babism stresses abstinence from alcoholic liquors and forbids polygamy and slavery.

bab·ka (bäb'kə) *n.* a cake leavened with yeast and containing raisins, often glazed and flavored with rum. [Polish *babka,* from *baba* old woman.]

ba·boo (bä'bü) babu.

ba·boon (ba bün') *n.* any of several large, social African monkeys, family Cercopithecidae, that have long doglike muzzles, cheek pouches for storing food, front and back legs of almost equal length, and usually a short tail. Length: to 6 feet (1.8 meters), including tail. [Old French *babouin* simpleton, ape, possibly from *baboue* grimace.]

ba·bu (bä'bü) *also,* **baboo.** *n.* **1.** a Hindu gentleman. ➡ used as a Hindu form of address equivalent to *sir* or *Mr.* **2.** in India, a native clerk who can write English. [Hindi *bābū* father.]

ba·bush·ka (bə bùsh'kə) *n.* a kerchief, often made or folded in a triangular shape, worn over the head and tied under the chin. [Russian *babushka* grandmother, diminutive of *baba* old woman; because frequently worn by old women.]

baboon

ba·by (bā'bē) *n., pl.* **-bies. 1.** a newborn or very young child. **2.** the youngest member of a family or group. **3.** a person who behaves like a child; childish or immature person. **4.** a newborn or very young animal. **5.** *Slang.* an object of special affection or pride: *This product is the company's newest baby.* —*adj.* **1.** for a baby: *a baby blanket.* **2.** of or like a baby; childish: *a baby face.* **3.** young: *a baby rabbit.* **4.** small for its kind; comparatively little: *baby artichokes.* —*v.t.,* **-bied, -by·ing. 1.** to treat as a baby; pamper; coddle. **2.** *Informal.* to handle or operate with great care: *to baby an antique car.* [Diminutive of BABE.]

baby boom, an unusual increase in a population's birthrate, esp. in the United States after World War II.

baby boom·er (bü'mər) a person born during a baby boom. [BABY BOOM + -ER[1].]

baby carriage, a small, four-wheeled carriage for a baby, usually with a folding top. Also, **baby buggy.**

ba·by·hood (bā'bē hùd') *n.* **1.** the state of being a baby. **2.** the time during which a person is a baby.

ba·by·ish (bā'bē ish) *adj.* like a baby; childish; infantile. —**ba'by·ish·ly,** *adv.* —**ba'by·ish·ness,** *n.*

Bab·y·lon (bab'ə lon') *n.* a city or place of great wealth, luxury, or vice. [From *Babylon,* ancient city noted for its wealth, magnificence, and wickedness.]

Bab·y·lo·ni·an (bab'ə lō'nē ən) *adj.* of, like, relating to, or characteristic of Babylon or Babylonia or their people, language, or culture. —*n.* **1.** a native or citizen of Babylonia. **2.** the Semitic language of Babylonia.

ba·by's-breath (bā'bēz breth') *also,* **babies'-breath.** *n.* a garden plant, *Gypsophila paniculata* or *G. elegans,* native to Eur-

a	at	e	end	o	hot	u	up	hw	white		about
ā	ape	ē	me	ō	old	ū	use	ng	song		taken
ä	far	i	it	ô	fork	ü	rule	th	thin	ə	pencil
âr	care	ī	ice	oi	oil	ù	pull	th	this		lemon
		îr	pierce	ou	out	ûr	turn	zh	measure		circus

85

ope and northern Asia, bearing thick clusters of tiny white or pink flowers.

ba·by-sit (bā'bē sit') *v.i.,* **-sat** (-sat'), **-sit·ting.** to take care of (children) during the temporary absence of their parents. —**ba'·by-sit'ter,** *n.*

baby tooth *pl.* **baby teeth.** in humans, a milk tooth.

bac·ca·lau·re·ate (bak'ə lôr'ē it) *n.* **1.** a bachelor's degree given by a college or university. **2.** a sermon or address delivered to a graduating class at commencement. Also *(def. 2),* **baccalaureate sermon.** [Medieval Latin *baccalaureatus* rank of holder of a bachelor's degree, from *baccalaureus* bachelor, advanced student, modification of *baccalarius* young man, farmer; of Celtic origin.]

bac·ca·rat (bä'kə rä', bak'ə-) *also,* **bac·ca·ra.** *n.* a card game in which one player acts as banker and two or more players bet against the banker. [French *baccara;* of uncertain origin.]

Bac·chae (bak'ē) *pl. n.* **1.** the female attendants or worshipers of Bacchus, esp. those taking part in the Bacchanalia. **2.** the priestesses of Bacchus.

bac·cha·nal (bä'kə näl', bak'ə nal') *adj.* **1.** of or relating to Bacchus or his worship. **2.** indulging in or characterized by drunken revelry; carousing. —*n.* **1.** a worshiper of Bacchus. **2.** a drunken reveler; carouser. **3.** a drunken revelry or carousal; orgy. **4. Bacchanals.** Bacchanalia. [Latin *bacchānālis* of Bacchus, from *Bacchus* Bacchus, from Greek *Bacchos.*]

Bac·cha·na·li·a (bak'ə nā'lē ə, -nāl'yə) *n.* **1.** an ancient Roman festival in honor of Bacchus. ➡ sometimes used as plural. **2. bacchanalia.** drunken revelry or carousal; orgy. ➡ usually used as singular. —**bac·cha·na'li·an,** *adj., n.*

bac·chant (bak'ənt, bə kant', -känt') *n., pl.* **bac·chants** or **bac·chan·tes** (bə kan'tēz) **1.** a priest or male worshiper of Bacchus. **2.** a drunken reveler; carouser. [Latin *bacchāns,* present participle of *bacchārī* to celebrate the festival of Bacchus, from Greek *bacchān.*] —**bac·chan·tic** (bə kan'tik), *adj.*

bac·chan·te (bə kan'tē, bə kant', bak'ənt) *n.* a priestess or female worshiper of Bacchus; maenad. [French *bacchante,* from Latin *bacchāns.* See BACCHANT.]

Bac·chic (bak'ik) *adj.* **1.** of or relating to Bacchus or his worship. **2.** *also,* **bacchic.** wildly or merrily drunken; riotous.

Bac·chus (bak'əs) *n.* in classical mythology, the god of wine. He was more commonly known to the Greeks as Dionysus.

bach·e·lor (bach'ə lər, bach'lər) *n.* **1.** an unmarried man. **2.** a person who has received a bachelor's degree. **3.** a young knight serving under another's banner. Also *(def. 3),* **bach'e·lor-at-arms'.** [Old French *bacheler* young man, squire, from Medieval Latin *baccalarius.* See BACCALAUREATE.] —**bach'e·lor·hood',** *n.*

Bachelor of Arts **1.** a bachelor's degree awarded by a college or university to a person who has completed an undergraduate course of study in the liberal arts or social sciences. **2.** a person who has been awarded this degree.

Bachelor of Science **1.** a bachelor's degree awarded by a college or university to a person who has completed an undergraduate course of study in science or mathematics. **2.** a person who has been awarded this degree.

bach·e·lor's-but·ton (bach'ə lərz but'ən, bach'lərz-) *n.* a hardy field plant, *Centaurea cyanus,* of the aster family, bearing many slender branching stems and showy, usually blue, flower heads that are used as boutonnieres.

bachelor's degree, an undergraduate degree that represents completion of a four-year college program or its equivalent. The most commonly awarded forms of this degree are Bachelor of Arts and Bachelor of Science. Also, **baccalaureate.**

bac·il·lar·y (bas'ə ler'ē, bə sil'ə rē) *adj.* **1.** (of bacteria) rod-shaped. **2.** relating to, caused by, or characterized by bacilli. Also, **ba·cil·lar** (bə sil'ər, bas'ə lər).

ba·cil·lus (bə sil'əs) *n., pl.* **-cil·li** (-sil'ī). **1.** any rod-shaped or cylindrical, spore-forming bacterium of the genus *Bacillus.* For illustration, see **bacteria.** **2.** any bacterium, esp. a pathogenic variety. [Late Latin *bacillus* small rod, diminutive of Latin *baculus* rod.]

bac·i·tra·cin (bas'i trā'sin) *n.* an antibiotic obtained from a strain of the bacterium *Bacillus subtilis,* used for treating various bacterial infections, esp. of the skin. [BACI(LLUS) + Margaret *Tracy,* American girl from whose tissue the strain was isolated + -IN[1].]

back[1] (bak) *n.* **1.** the rear part of the human body, esp. from the neck to the end of the spine. **2.** the part of the body of animals corresponding to the human back. **3.** the backbone: *Be careful, or you'll break your back.* **4.** the part opposite to or farthest from the front; rear or posterior part: *the back of a room, the back of the head.* **5.** the farther or other side; the reverse: *the back of a door, the back of a check.* **6.** the part opposite to or behind the part that is normally used: *the back of the hand, the back of a spoon.* **7.** the

part of an object that protects, covers, or supports the human back: *the back of a shirt, the back of a bench.* **8.** *Sports.* **a.** a player whose regular position is behind that of players making initial contact with the opposing team. **b.** the position occupied by such a player. —*v.t.* **1.** to approve, aid, or strengthen; help or support (often with *up*): *to back a candidate, to back up an argument with facts.* **2.** to cause to move backward; reverse the action of (often with *up*): *The driver backed up the truck.* **3.** to furnish with a back or backing; strengthen at the back: *to back a book with cardboard.* **4.** to bet in favor of: *to back a horse in a race.* **5.** to lie at the back of; form a background for: *Cliffs backed the house.* —*v.i.* **1.** to move backward (often with *up*): *I backed up to get a better view.* **2.** to have the back facing or extending in a certain direction (often with *up*): *The farm backs up to the railroad.* —*adj.* **1.** at or in the rear: *a back door, back stairs.* **2.** belonging to the past; not current: *back files.* **3.** in an outlying or remote location: *the back areas of a country.* **4.** in arrears; overdue: *back pay, back taxes.* **5.** going or moving in a backward direction; reversed: *a back thrust.* **6.** *Phonetics.* pronounced with the back part of the tongue arched toward the palate: *a back vowel.* [Old English *bæc* human and animal back.]

· **behind someone's back.** without someone's knowledge or consent; in secret.

· **in back of.** behind.

· **to back and fill.** **a.** to handle the sails of a boat so that the wind pushes alternately against the front and back, esp. in order to move along with the current in a channel. **b.** to waver in one's actions; keep changing one's mind.

· **to back down.** to give up a position, opinion, or claim.

· **to back off.** **a.** to withdraw or retreat a short distance. **b.** to give up a position, opinion, or claim; back down. **c.** *Informal.* to refrain from or stop bothering or pursuing.

· **to back out (of).** to withdraw from an engagement, undertaking, or commitment.

· **to back up.** **a.** to make or become congested: *Heavy rains backed up the sewers. Traffic backed up for miles behind the accident.* **b.** to make a copy of (a computer file or other data) in case the original is damaged or erased.

· **to be (flat) on one's back.** to be sick or helpless.

· **to get off someone's back.** *Informal.* to stop bothering or finding fault with someone.

· **to get one's back up.** *Informal.* **a.** to become angry. **b.** to be stubborn.

· **to get (or put) someone's back up.** *Informal.* to make someone angry.

· **to have one's back to the wall.** to be in a difficult or desperate situation.

· **to turn one's back on.** to ignore, neglect, or abandon.

back[2] (bak) *adv.* **1.** at, to, or toward the rear; backward: *Please step back so that I may pass.* **2.** in, to, or toward a previous place or position: *Put the book back on the shelf.* **3.** in, to, or toward a previous condition or state: *to nurse someone back to health.* **4.** in or into the past: *The earthquake happened back in 1950.* **5.** in reply or return: *to answer back.* **6.** so as to retain or restrain: *to hold back payment, to hold back angry words.* **7.** at a distance; away: *The police asked the crowd to move back.* [Short for ABACK.]

· **back and forth.** first in one direction and then in the other; to and fro.

· **back of.** *Informal.* behind. *The orchard is back of the barn.*

· **to go back on.** *Informal.* to refuse to fulfill; fail to keep: *to go back on a promise.*

back·ache (bak'āk') *n.* an ache or pain in one's back, esp. in the lower back.

back·bite (bak'bīt') *v.t., v.i.,* **-bit** (-bit') **-bit·ten** (-bit'ən) or **-bit·ing.** to speak maliciously about (someone who is not present); slander. —**back'bit'er,** *n.*

back·board (bak'bôrd') *n.* **1.** a board forming or supporting the back of something. **2.** *Basketball.* a flat surface of wood, glass, or other material to which the basket is attached.

back·bone (bak'bōn') *n.* **1.** the spinal or vertebral column; the spine. **2.** something resembling a backbone in shape, position, or function; the strongest or most important part: *The courts are the backbone of our judicial system.* **3.** strength of character; resoluteness: *The settlers had a lot of backbone.* **4.** in bookbinding, the reinforced part of a book to which the pages are attached; spine.

back·break·ing (bak'brā'king) *adj.* requiring much strength and effort; physically exhausting.

back burner. **on the back burner.** in a state of temporary delay or suspension: *The building of the library was put on the back burner until the money became available.*

back·door (bak'dôr') *adj.* underhanded; clandestine.

back·drop (bak'drop') *n.* **1.** a curtain hung at the back of a stage, often painted to represent a scene. **2.** the background of an event; setting.

back·er (bak′ər) *n.* a person who supports another person or an undertaking with money or influence; patron.

back·field (bak′fēld′) *n. Sports.* **1.** the players whose regular positions are behind the linebackers or offensive linemen in football or behind the forwards in soccer. **2.** the area where these players play.

back·fire (bak′fīr′) *n.* **1.** an explosion in the cylinder of an internal-combustion engine resulting from a premature ignition of the fuel. **2.** a fire lit to check an advancing forest or prairie fire by burning off an area in its path, thus depriving it of fuel. —*v.i.,* **-fired, -fir·ing. 1.** to undergo a backfire: *The truck backfired.* **2.** to bring results opposite to those planned; boomerang: *The scheme backfired.* **3.** to light or use a backfire.

back-for·ma·tion (bak′fôr mā′shən) *n.* **1.** the derivation of a new word from an existing word assumed to be its derivative, as *sculpt* from *sculptor.* **2.** a word so derived.

back·gam·mon (bak′gam′ən, bak′gam′-) *n.* a game for two played on a special board with dice and fifteen pieces for each player, the throw of the dice determining where the pieces can be moved. [BACK[2] + *gammon,* earlier form of GAME[1]; because sometimes the pieces must go back to start again.]

back·ground (bak′ground′) *n.* **1.** the part of a picture or scene that is, or appears to be, farthest from the viewer's eye. ➡ opposed to **foreground. 2.** the surroundings or surface behind something seen or represented: *The fabric had red roses on a white background.* **3.** information or past circumstances that help to explain some later event or situation: *the background of the Civil War.* **4.** the conditions or environment in which something occurs; setting: *The general assumed power against a background of civil war.* **5.** a person's origin, experience, and education considered as a whole: *to have the right background for a job.* **6.** a position that is less conspicuous, prominent, or important: *Their shady dealings were kept in the background.*

background music, music or sound effects used as accompaniment to dialogue or action in a play, movie, or broadcast.

background radiation 1. *Physics.* natural, low-level, ionizing radiation normally present in the environment, as from cosmic rays and from radioactive minerals in soil and rock. **2.** *Astronomy.* microwave radiation traveling in every direction throughout the universe and representing, according to the big-bang theory, a residue of the radiation that was present at the creation of the universe.

back·hand (bak′hand′) *n.* **1.** in sports, a stroke made with the arm drawn across the body, the palm of the hand facing the body, and the back of the hand turned outward. ➡ distinguished from **forehand. 2.** handwriting that slants toward the left. —*adj.* backhanded. —*adv.* with a backhand stroke. —*v.t.* to perform, hit, or catch in a backhanded manner: *to backhand a tennis ball over the net.*

back·hand·ed (bak′han′did) *adj.* **1.** performed or made with the back of the hand, or with the back of the hand turned outward: *a backhanded blow, a backhanded stroke.* **2.** slanting to the left: *backhanded handwriting.* **3.** critical or sarcastic while seeming to praise; insincere: *a backhanded compliment.* **4.** not straightforward; devious; indirect: *to use backhanded methods to get information.* —**back′hand·ed·ly,** *adv.* —**back′hand·ed·ness,** *n.*

back·hoe (bak′hō′) *n.* a tractorlike power-driven excavator having a bucket or scoop that is at the end of a hinged boom and is drawn toward the machine during operation.

backhoe

back·ing (bak′ing) *n.* **1.** approval or assistance; support: *We will need financial backing for our new business.* **2.** supporters or backers collectively. **3.** something used to support, form, or strengthen a back.

back·lash (bak′lash′) *n.* **1.** an opposing action or trend in reaction to some force or event; sharp recoil: *a reactionary backlash against liberal reforms.* **2.** a jarring recoil of loose or worn parts in a machine.

back·log (bak′lôg′, -log′) *n.* **1.** an accumulation, esp. of unfinished work or unfilled orders. **2.** a reserve supply of something. **3.** a large log placed at the back of a fireplace to sustain the fire and concentrate the heat.

back number 1. an out-of-date issue of a magazine or newspaper. **2.** *Informal.* an old-fashioned person or thing.

back-or·der (bak′ôr′dər) *v.t.* to treat as a back order: *The company will have to back-order the table.*

back order, an order for goods or services not available when the order is placed but that will be provided at a later date.

back·pack (bak′pak′) *n.* a pack for hiking or camping supplies, equipment, or the like, carried on the back and usually supported by a metal frame. —*v.t.* to carry (supplies) in a backpack. —*v.i.* to go on a hike or a camping trip using a backpack. —**back′pack·er,** *n.*

back·ped·al (bak′ped′əl) *v.i.,* **-aled, -al·ing;** *also, British,* **-alled, -al·ling. 1.** to press backward on the pedals of a bicycle or tricycle so as to stop or move backward. **2.** to move backward quickly in order to avoid an opponent, as in boxing. **3.** *Informal.* to change an earlier statement or qualify an opinion or policy.

back·rest (bak′rest′) *n.* a support for the back.

back·seat (bak′sēt′) *also,* **back seat.** *n.* a seat in the back, esp. of a vehicle.
·**to take a backseat.** *Informal.* to occupy a less important position: *Everyday problems took a backseat during the crisis.*

backseat driver *Informal.* a person who offers unwanted advice, esp. a passenger in a car who tells the driver how to handle the car.

back·side (bak′sīd′) *n.* **1.** the back or rear part. **2.** the rump; buttocks.

back·slide (bak′slīd′) *v.i.,* **-slid** (-slid′), **-slid** or **-slid·den** (-slid′ən), **-slid·ing.** to return to bad habits or practices, esp. in religious matters. —**back′slid·er,** *n.*

back·spin (bak′spin′) *n.* a spin given to a moving object that tends to slow, stop, or reverse its forward motion.

back·stage (bak′stāj′) *n.* the part of a theater behind the curtain line, esp. that part behind the stage. —*adj.* **1.** relating to, located, or occurring backstage: *A backstage accident delayed the play.* **2.** occurring in private; secret: *backstage negotiations for a merger.* —*adv.* in, to, or toward the backstage.

back·stay (bak′stā′) *n.* **1.** a rope or wire that extends aft from the top of a mast to the side or stern of a boat. **2.** *Mechanics.* a piece or device used to strengthen or support something at the back.

back·stitch (bak′stich′) *n.* a stitch made by doubling the thread back on the preceding stitch. —*v.t., v.i.* to sew with backstitches.

back·stop (bak′stop′) *n.* **1.** a fence, screen, or wall used in sports to stop the ball from going too far beyond the normal playing area. **2.** *Baseball.* the catcher. **3.** a person or thing that supports or bolsters.

back·stretch (bak′strech′) *n.* the straight part of a racetrack after the first turn and opposite the home stretch.

back·stroke (bak′strōk′) *n.* a stroke in swimming done while lying on the back, esp. one made by moving the arms alternately up and back into the water while kicking the legs rapidly.

back·swim·mer (bak′swim′ər) *n.* any of a group of aquatic bugs, family Notonectidae, having oarlike legs that are used for swimming on its keeled back. *Notonecta undulata* is a common North American species. Length: ½ inch (1 centimeter).

back talk, a rude or disrespectful reply.

back-to-back (bak′tə bak′) *adj.* **1.** (of two or more things in a sequence) coming or following closely or without interruption; consecutive: *back-to-back victories in a tournament, back-to-back sunny days.* **2.** in a position with the backs touching or facing each other: *back-to-back seats on a train.*

back·track (bak′trak′) *v.i.* **1.** to return by the same route or

a	at	e	end	o	hot	u	up	hw	white		about
ā	ape	ē	me	ō	old	ū	use	ng	song	ə	taken
ä	far	i	it	ô	fork	ü	rule	th	thin		pencil
âr	care	ī	ice	oi	oil	ů	pull	th	this		lemon
		ir	pierce	ou	out	ûr	turn	zh	measure		circus

path; retrace one's course: *We backtracked because I had lost my hat.* **2.** to reverse a position or stand: *The suspects backtracked on their earlier statements.*

back·up (bak'up') *also,* **back-up.** *n.* **1.** a person or thing kept in reserve to be used if necessary; standby or reserve: *The hospital installed a generator in the basement as a backup in case of power failures.* **2.** a backing up; buildup: *The clog in the pipe caused a backup of drainage water.* **3.a.** the copying of a file or other set of computer data onto another tape, diskette, or the like, to provide a reserve copy of the information in case the original is lost or damaged. **b.** a file copy made as a backup. —*adj.* **1.** serving as a standby or reserve: *a backup supply of food, a backup pilot.* **2.** of or relating to a backup of data: *a backup file.*

back·ward (bak'wərd) *also,* **back·wards.** *adv.* **1.** toward the back; to the rear: *Swing your arms backward.* **2.** with the back first: *I was walking backward and fell.* **3.** opposite to the usual or right way; in reverse: *to count backward.* **4.** toward or into the past: *to look backward over the past year.* **5.** toward a worse or less advanced state or condition: *Under this administration, the city has moved backward.* —*adj.* **1.** directed or turned toward the back or rear: *a backward glance, backward movement.* **2.** behind or slower in growth or development: *a backward learner, backward nations.* **3.** done or performed with the back first: *a backward dive.* **4.** directed to or toward a previous point or position: *a backward journey.* **5.** done in a reverse or incorrect way: *backward rotation.* **6.** shy; bashful. [Middle English *bakward* toward the back, from *bak* BACK² + -WARD.] —**back'ward·ly,** *adv.* —**back'ward·ness,** *n.*

• **to bend over backward** (or **backwards**). to go beyond what is usual or expected in trying to please or accommodate someone.

back·wash (bak'wôsh', -wosh') *n.* **1.** water moved backward by the propelling force of a moving object. **2.** a backward current of air from an airplane propeller. **3.** the result of an event or condition; aftermath.

back·wa·ter (bak'wô'tər, -wot'ər) *n.* **1.** water turned or held back by an obstruction, tide, or opposing current: *the backwater created by a dam.* **2.** a place or condition regarded as sluggish, stagnant, or backward. —*adj.* like a backwater; stagnant; backward.

back·woods (bak'wudz') *pl. n.* **1.** wild, heavily wooded, or thinly settled areas that are remote from centers of population. **2.** an area regarded as crude, provincial, or culturally backward. ➡ used as singular or plural in both defs. —*adj.* **1.** of, in, or relating to the backwoods: *a backwoods settlement.* **2.** characteristic of the inhabitants of the backwoods; crude; provincial; backward: *a backwoods approach.*

back·woods·man (bak'wudz'mən) *n., pl.* **-men** (-mən). a person who lives in or comes from the backwoods.

back·yard (bak'yärd') *n.* the yard behind a house or other building, esp. one put to some domestic use. —*adj.* of or in a backyard: *a backyard fence.*

ba·con (bā'kən) *n.* salted and smoked meat from the back and sides of a hog. [Old French *bacon;* of Germanic origin.]
• **to bring home the bacon.** *Informal.* **a.** to earn a living. **b.** to succeed.

bac·te·ri·a (bak tîr'ē ə) *pl. n., sing.* **-ri·um.** any of numerous one-celled microorganisms comprising a moneran phylum, Schizomycota. They may be beneficial, harmless, or pathogenic and are classified according to shape and to whether or not they need oxygen: *anaerobic bacteria, aerobic bacteria.* [Modern Latin *bacteria,* plural of *bacterium,* from Greek *baktērion,* diminutive of *baktron* stick. When these microorganisms were first seen under the microscope, they appeared to resemble little rods or bars.]

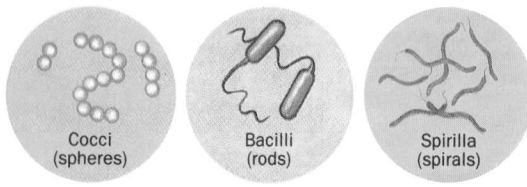

Cocci
(spheres)

Bacilli
(rods)

Spirilla
(spirals)

types of **bacteria**

bac·te·ri·al (bak tîr'ē əl) *adj.* relating to or produced by bacteria: *a bacterial infection, bacterial activity.*

bac·te·ri·cide (bak tîr'ə sīd') *n.* an agent that destroys bacteria. [BACTERI(A) + -CIDE².] —**bac·te'ri·cid'al,** *adj.*

bac·te·ri·o·chlo·ro·phyll (bak tîr'ē ō klôr'ə fil) *n.* a pale gray pigment produced by certain anaerobic bacteria that is closely related to the chlorophyll in green plants.

bac·te·ri·o·log·i·cal (bak tîr'ē ə loj'ə kəl) *adj.* of or relating to bacteriology: *a bacteriological study of water samples.* Also, **bac·te'ri·o·log'ic.** —**bac·te'ri·o·log'i·cal·ly,** *adv.*

bac·te·ri·ol·o·gist (bak tîr'ē ol'ə jist) *n.* a person who studies or specializes in bacteriology.

bac·te·ri·ol·o·gy (bak tîr'ē ol'ə jē) *n.* the branch of microbiology concerned with the characteristics and activities of bacteria.

bac·te·ri·o·phage (bak tîr'ē ə fāj') *n.* any of a group of viruses that destroy bacteria. [BACTERI(A) + -PHAGE.]

bac·te·ri·o·sta·tic (bak tîr'ē ō stat'ik) *adj.* inhibiting or arresting the growth or multiplication of bacteria without actually destroying them.

bac·te·ri·um (bak tîr'ē əm) the singular of **bacteria.**

Bac·tri·an camel (bak'trē ən) a two-humped camel, *Camelus bactrianus,* of central Asia.

bad¹ (bad) *adj.,* **worse, worst. 1.** having little quality or worth; below standard; poor: *The painter did a bad job.* **2.a.** full of or marked by wickedness; immoral; evil: *a bad influence.* **b.** mischievous; disobedient; naughty: *bad behavior.* **3.** severe or intense: *a bad cold, a bad storm.* **4.** containing errors; incorrect; faulty: *bad grammar.* **5.** not pleasant; disagreeable; offensive: *a bad odor, bad manners.* **6.** having

Bactrian camel

a harmful effect; damaging; injurious: *Too much fat in your diet may be bad for your health.* **7.** showing or marked by anger or irritation: *a bad mood, a bad temper.* **8.** not satisfactory or sufficient for use; inadequate: *bad lighting.* **9.** not genuine; worthless: *a bad check.* **10.** not sensible or sound: *bad advice, a bad decision.* **11.** causing pain or suffering; disturbing; distressing: *bad news.* **12.** lacking talent or skill: *a bad actor.* **13.** not working properly; malfunctioning; defective: *bad wiring, a bad telephone connection.* **14.** full of regret; sorry; distressed: *We felt bad about causing such trouble.* **15.** in poor health; sick: *I've felt bad all week.* **16.** not fresh; rotten or spoiled: *The milk is bad.* **17.** *Slang.* very good; excellent. —*n.* something that is bad: *The good outweighed the bad in the mayor's record.* —*adv. Informal.* badly. [Middle English *badde* wicked.] —**bad'ness,** *n.*
• **not** (**so** or **half** or **too**) **bad.** *Informal.* fairly good; acceptable.
• **to be in bad.** *Informal.* to be in trouble or disfavor: *I'm in bad with him because of our argument.*
• **to go bad.** *Informal.* to become spoiled, rotten, or corrupt.
• **too bad.** unfortunate; disappointing: *It's too bad she had to work tonight.*

Synonyms *adj.* **Bad¹, evil,** and **wicked** mean wrong or contrary to moral or ethical standards. **Bad** has the widest use, being applicable to moral transgression of any degree: *Lying to your friend was a bad thing to do.* **Evil** refers to serious or extreme wrong and often suggests corruption or depravity: *Evil ambitions drove the dictator to murder any possible rivals.* **Wicked,** now chiefly a literary word, stresses the willful nature of evildoing: *The people continued their wicked behavior despite the prophet's warnings.*

bad² (bad) *Archaic.* a past tense of **bid.**

bad blood, mutual or long-standing hostility; enmity.

bade (bad, bād) a past tense of **bid.**

badge (baj) *n.* **1.** a distinctive emblem or device worn to indicate rank, membership, or achievement: *a sheriff's badge, a merit badge.* **2.** a symbol or sign; token: *The soldier wore the scar as a badge of courage.* [Anglo-Norman *bage* the emblem; of uncertain origin.]

badg·er (baj'ər) *n.* **1.** any of a group of burrowing mammals of the weasel family, having a wide flat body, short legs, long claws, and a short, thick tail. Length: 2.5 feet (0.8 meter), including tail. **2.** the fur of a badger, often used in making brushes. —*v.t.* to annoy or harass persistently; torment; pester: *The attorney was badgering the witness with questions.* [Possibly from BADGE, with reference to the white mark on its head.]

bad·i·nage (bad'ə näzh', bad'ə nij) *n.* good-natured teasing or raillery; banter. [French *badinage,* from *badiner* to joke, from *badin* roguish, silly, going back to Late Latin *badāre* to gape. See BAY².]

bad·lands (bad'landz') *also,* **Badlands**. *pl. n.* any barren region characterized by numerous ridges, buttes, and gullies created by the erosion of soft sedimentary materials.

bad·ly (bad'lē) *adv.* **1.** in a bad manner. **2.** very much; greatly: *I need new shoes badly.*

> **Usage** In formal speech and writing the adjective **bad,** not the adverb **badly,** has traditionally been used after linking verbs such as *look, smell,* and *feel: Those tomatoes smell bad. The whole team feels bad about losing the game.* However, many people now consider it acceptable to use **badly** as an adjective, especially when used after *feel* to mean "sad" or "regretful": *I felt badly about hurting your feelings.*

bad·min·ton (bad'min'tən) *n.* a game in which players use light rackets to hit a shuttlecock back and forth over a high net. [From *Badminton,* estate of the English Duke of Beaufort, where the game was introduced.]

bad-mouth (bad'mouth', -mouth') *also,* **bad·mouth.** *v.t., v.i. Informal.* to speak ill of someone; malign; slander.

bad-tem·pered (bad'tem'pərd) *adj.* having a cross or quarrelsome disposition; irritable.

baf·fle (baf'əl) *v.t.,* **-fled, -fling. 1.** to bewilder or puzzle greatly; confuse; perplex: *The murder case baffled the police.* **2.** to control or change the progress or flow of. —*n.* a rigid structure, as a wall or screen, for controlling or deflecting the flow of fluids or the movement of sound waves. [Probably from Scottish *bauchle* to dishonor.] —**baf'fle·ment,** *n.* —**baf'fler,** *n.*

bag (bag) *n.* **1.** a container made of paper, cloth, leather, or other flexible material: *a shopping bag, a mail bag.* **2.** something that hangs loosely or resembles a bag in shape: *bags under the eyes, trousers with bags at the knees.* **3.** a purse; handbag. **4.** a suitcase or satchel; valise: *Pack your bags.* **5.** the amount contained in a bag. **6.** a sac or pouchlike part in various animals, as the udder of a cow. **7.** the quantity of game killed or captured in hunting; the legal limit on this. **8.** *Baseball.* a base. **9.** *Slang.* a slovenly, unattractive woman. **10.** *Slang.* something that a person is interested in or does well: *Tennis is not my bag.* —*v.,* **bagged, bag·ging.** —*v.t.* **1.** to kill or capture (game) in hunting: *She bagged three birds.* **2.** *Informal.* **a.** to seize or capture; trap: *The police bagged the thief.* **b.** to shoot down: *to bag three enemy planes.* **3.** to put into a bag: *to bag groceries.* **4.** *Slang.* to make off with; steal: *The robbers bagged a million dollars in furs.* —*v.i.* **1.** to hang loosely; sag: *His jacket bagged at the elbow.* **2.** to swell; bulge. [Old Norse *baggi* pack, bundle.] —**bag'ger,** *n.*

• **bag and baggage.** *Informal.* **a.** with all one's possessions: *The suspect was gone, bag and baggage.* **b.** entirely; completely: *The thieves emptied the vault, bag and baggage.*

• **in the bag.** *Slang.* assured; certain: *My raise is in the bag.*

• **holding the bag.** *Informal.* taking full blame or responsibility when it should be shared.

ba·gasse (bə gas') *n.* crushed sugarcane or sugar beet from which the juice has been extracted, used as a fuel and in the manufacture of paper. [French *bagasse,* from Spanish *bagazo,* from *baga* husk, pod, from Latin *bāca* berry.]

bag·a·telle (bag'ə tel') *n.* **1.** something of little value or importance; trifle. **2.** a game somewhat similar to billiards. **3.** a short and easy piece of music, usually for the piano. [French *bagatelle* trifle, from Italian *bagatella.*]

ba·gel (bā'gəl) *n.* a doughnut-shaped roll made of yeast dough, cooked in simmering water and then baked. [Yiddish *beygl;* of Middle High German origin.]

bag·gage (bag'ij) *n.* **1.** luggage and other belongings that a traveler takes on a trip. **2.** the portable equipment and supplies of an army. **3.** ideas, emotions, circumstances, or other things that interfere with one's ability to develop, adapt, or otherwise get along in life. [Old French *bagage* collection of bundles, from *bague* bundle.]

bag·ging (bag'ing) *n.* a coarse cloth used for making bags; sacking.

bag·gy (bag'ē) *adj.,* **-gi·er, -gi·est.** hanging loosely; bulging. —**bag'gi·ly,** *adv.* —**bag'gi·ness,** *n.*

bag lady, a homeless, usually older, woman who carries her possessions with her in a shopping bag or bags. Also, **shopping-bag lady.**

bag·man (bag'man') *n., pl.* **-men** (-men'). *Slang.* a person who collects illegally obtained money, as from bribes, extortion, or protection, and delivers it to another person: *a bagman working for a gangster.*

bagn·io (ban'yō, bän'-) *n., pl.* **-ios.** a house of prostitution; brothel. [Italian *bagno* bath, from Latin *balneum,* from Greek *balaneion.*]

bag·pipe (bag'pīp') *also,* **bag·pipes.** *n.* a shrill-toned, wind musical instrument, commonly identified with Scotland, consisting of a leather windbag, a chanter or melody pipe, and three drone pipes. —**bag'pip'er,** *n.*

ba·guette (ba get') *n.* **1.** a faceted gem cut in a narrow, rectangular shape. **2.** a long, narrow loaf of bread. [French *baguette,* literally rod, from Italian *bacchetta* small stick, from *bacchio* stick (from Latin *baculus* a stick) + diminutive suffix *-etta* (from Late Latin *-ita*).]

bah (bä) *interj.* an exclamation of contempt or disbelief.

Ba·ha'i (bə hī', bə hä'ē) *also,* **Ba·ha·i.** *n., pl.* **-ha'is. 1.** a follower of Baha'ism. **2.** Baha'ism. —*adj.* of or relating to Baha'is or Baha'ism.

Ba·ha'ism (bə hī'iz əm, -hä'-) *also,* **Ba·ha·ism.** *n.* a religion that developed from Babism in the nineteenth century and teaches that all reli-

bagpipe

gions are one and that all races and individuals are equal. The faith rejects ritual and monasticism and has no official clergy.

baht (bät) *n., pl.* **baht.** the monetary unit of Thailand.

bail¹ (bāl) *n.* **1.** security, esp. money, deposited with a court to obtain the temporary release of a person under arrest and to guarantee that person's appearance for trial at a designated time. **2.** a temporary release obtained with this security. **3.** a person or persons providing bail. —*v.t.* to obtain the temporary release of (a person under arrest) by providing bail (often with *out*). [Middle French and Old French *bail* custody, from *baillier* to have in charge, from Latin *bājulāre* to carry.]

• **to bail out.** to assist (a person or thing) in a financial crisis or other emergency: *Government loans bailed out the failing company.*

• **to go** (or **stand**) **bail.** to supply bail.

• **to jump bail.** to flee or go into hiding while free on bail.

bail² (bāl) *n.* **1.** the arched handle of a kettle, pail, or similar container. **2.** a hooplike piece of sturdy material used for support, as that used for the top of a covered wagon. **3.** a hinged bar on a typewriter or printer that holds the paper against the roller. [Probably of Scandinavian origin.]

bail³ (bāl) *v.t.* **1.** to remove (water) from a boat with a pail or similar container. **2.** to clear (a boat) of water with a pail or similar container (often with *out*). —*v.i.* to bail water: *We bailed desperately for an hour.* [Middle English and Old French *baille* bucket, possibly from Late Latin *bacula,* diminutive of *baca* trough.]

• **to bail out.** to parachute from an aircraft, esp. in an emergency.

bail⁴ (bāl) *n.* in cricket, either of two wood crossbars that form the top of a wicket. [Old French *bail* crossbeam; of uncertain origin.]

bail·a·ble (bā'lə bəl) *adj.* **1.** capable of being bailed. **2.** allowing the possibility of bail: *a bailable offense.*

bail·er (bā'lər) *n.* something used as a container to scoop water out of a boat.

bail·ie (bā'lē) *n.* in Scotland, a municipal officer or magistrate, corresponding to an alderman in England. [Old French *bailli,* form of *baillif* magistrate. See BAILIFF.]

bail·iff (bā'lif) *n.* **1.** a court officer who guards the prisoners and the jurors in a courtroom. **2.** an assistant to a sheriff, who serves processes, writs, and warrants of arrest. **3.** *British.* a person who oversees an estate for the owner; steward. **4.** in certain English towns, a local administrative official or chief magistrate. [Old French *baillif* magistrate, from *bail* custody. See BAIL¹.]

bail·i·wick (bā'lə wik') *n.* **1.** the office, jurisdiction, or district of a bailiff. **2.** a field in which a person has special or superior competence, interest, or authority: *Corporate law is my bailiwick.*

a	at	e	end	o	hot	u	up	hw	white		about
ā	ape	ē	me	ō	old	ū	use	ng	song		taken
ä	far	i	it	ô	fork	ū	rule	th	thin	ə	pencil
âr	care	ī	ice	oi	oil	u	pull	th	this		lemon
		îr	pierce	ou	out	ûr	turn	zh	measure		circus

[Bailie + obsolete English *wick* town, going back to Latin *vīcus* village.]

bail·out (bāl′out′) *n.* **1.** the act of parachuting from an aircraft, esp. in an emergency. **2.** a rescue, as of a corporation or city, from a financial crisis: *a government bailout of a city.*

bails·man (bālz′mən) *n., pl.* **-men** (-mən). a person who gives bail or serves as security for another.

bairn (bârn) *n. Scottish.* a son or daughter; child. [Old English *bearn.*]

bait (bāt) *n.* **1.** something, esp. food, used to attract fish or other animals so that they may be caught. **2.** anything that tempts or attracts; enticement. —*v.t.* **1.** to put bait on or in: *to bait a hook, to bait a trap.* **2.** to persecute or goad, esp. with insulting or exasperating remarks; torment; harass. **3.** to tempt; entice; lure. **4.** to set dogs upon (an animal) for sport. [Partly from Old Norse *beit* pasture; partly from Old Norse *beita* to cause to bite.] —**bait′er,** *n.*

baize (bāz) *n.* a woolen or cotton fabric with a finish like that of felt, used esp. to cover billiard tables. [French *baies,* feminine plural of *bai* the color bay; possibly because the fabric was originally of this color. See BAY⁵.]

bake (bāk) *v.,* **baked, bak·ing.** —*v.t.* **1.** to cook (food) by dry, indirect heat, esp. in an oven. **2.** to dry or harden by heating: *to bake bricks.* —*v.i.* **1.** to prepare food by baking: *I bake only on weekends.* **2.** to become baked or hardened by heat: *The cake baked too long.* —*n.* **1.** the act or process of baking. **2.** a social gathering where the main food is baked and served. [Old English *bacan* to cook by dry heat.]

Baked Alaska, a dessert consisting of a piece of cake covered with ice cream and topped with meringue, baked briefly to brown the meringue.

Ba·ke·lite (bā′kə līt′, bāk′līt′) *n. Trademark.* any of a group of very hard, heat-resistant plastics made from formaldehyde and phenol and used esp. as a protective coating for appliances and floors and in a wide variety of commercial products.

bak·er (bā′kər) *n.* **1.** a person who makes or sells bread and other baked goods. **2.** a small portable oven.

baker's dozen, thirteen. [From a former custom among bakers of giving an excess (thirteen for a dozen) as a safeguard against the penalties for short weights.]

bak·er·y (bā′kə rē) *n., pl.* **-er·ies.** a place where bread and other baked goods are made or sold. Also, **bake·shop** (bāk′shop′).

bak·ing (bā′king) *n.* **1.** the act of a person or thing that bakes. **2.** the amount or batch baked at one time.

baking powder, a powder used as a leavening agent in baking, composed of sodium bicarbonate, an acid-producing chemical, and starch. When moistened, it releases carbon dioxide, which causes dough or batter to rise.

baking soda, sodium bicarbonate.

ba·kla·va (bä′klə vä′, bä′klə vä′) *n.* a dessert made of many thin layers of dough, chopped nuts, and honey. [Turkish *baklava* lozenge.]

bal., balance.

bal·a·lai·ka (bal′ə lī′kə) *n.* a Russian stringed musical instrument resembling a guitar and having a triangular body, three strings, and a fretted neck. [Russian *balalaika.*]

bal·ance (bal′əns) *n.* **1.** a condition of equality between opposing or contrasting forces or elements; equilibrium: *to maintain a balance between work and play.* **2.** the ability to keep one's body in a steady, upright position; physical equilibrium: *to lose one's balance and fall.* **3.** mental or emotional stability; sound mental condition: *a person possessed of judgment, sanity, and balance.* **4.** something that counteracts or makes up for (something else): *The comic highlights were a balance to the play's tragic ending.* **5.** an aesthetically pleasing arrangement of elements or component parts; proportion; harmony: *There is a nice balance between light and shade in the painting.* **6.** *Bookkeeping.* **a.** an equality between the debit and credit sides of an account. **b.** the difference between these sides: *We had a debit balance of ten dollars after the purchase.* **c.** an amount in excess on either side of an account. **7.** any of several instruments for determining the weight of an object, esp. by balancing it against known weights or forces, consisting in its simplest form of a horizontal bar having a pan suspended from each end, that pivots on a central point as weights are placed in the pans. **8.** balance wheel. **9.** something that is left over; remainder: *I'll complete the balance of the work later.* **10.** the power or ability to change or influence something, as a situation or decision: *The undecided voters still hold the balance in this election.* —*v.,* **-anced, -anc·ing.** —*v.t.* **1.** to bring into or keep in a steady state, condition, or position; poise: *The seal balanced the ball on its nose.* **2.** to estimate the relative value, weight, or importance of; compare: *to balance the pros and cons of a situation.* **3.** to counteract the effect of; compensate for; offset: *The good grade balances the poor one.* **4.** to place or keep in

proportion; equalize: *to balance equations.* **5.** to be equal or in proportion to: *The white balances the black in the painting.* **6.** to weigh in a balance. **7.** *Bookkeeping.* **a.** to compute the difference between the credit and debit sides of an account. **b.** to equalize these sides. **c.** to settle (an account) by paying the amount due. —*v.i.* **1.** to be in or come into equilibrium: *The acrobat balanced on the tightrope.* **2.** to be equal: *Income and expenditures exactly balance.* **3.** (of an account) to have the debit and credit sides equal to each other: *My checking account doesn't balance.* [Old French *balance* weighing instrument, going back to Late Latin *bilanx* having two scales, from Latin *bi-* two + *lanx* plate.] —For Synonyms, see remainder.
· **in the balance.** in an uncertain or undetermined, often critical state: *The fate of the defendant hung in the balance.*
· **to strike a balance.** to find or assume an intermediate position; compromise.

balance beam 1. a long, narrow wooden beam raised about 4 feet (1.2 meters) from the floor, used to demonstrate balancing feats in gymnastics. **2.** a competitive event in which the balance beam is used.

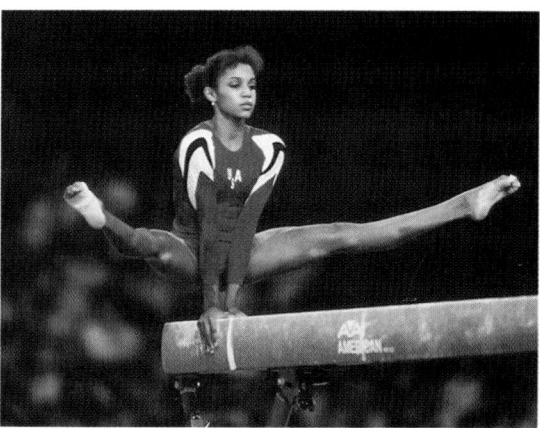

balance beam

balanced diet, a diet that includes the proper amounts of vitamins, minerals, carbohydrates, fats, and proteins needed for the body to grow or remain healthy.

balance of payments, the difference between the total payments made by one country to all foreign countries and its receipt of payments from foreign countries in a given period. Also, **international balance of payments.**

balance of power 1. an equilibrium of military or economic power among nations or groups of nations, maintained to prevent domination by any one nation or group of nations. **2.** the power or ability of one nation or group to influence the outcome of a conflict between equally dominant opposing forces by allying itself with one of them.

balance of trade, the difference in value between the exports and imports of a nation in a given period.

balance sheet 1. an itemized statement that shows the financial condition of a business at a given date by providing a summary of its assets, liabilities, and net worth. **2.** any overall summary or evaluation.

balance wheel, a wheel that regulates the rate of motion of a mechanism, as the works of a watch or clock.

bal·a·ta (bal′ə tə) *n.* **1.** a nonelastic rubberlike gum obtained from the latex of several tropical trees, esp. *Manilkara bidentata,* used in machinery belting, golf ball covers, and other products. **2.** the tree itself. [Spanish *balata;* of Carib origin.]

bal·bo·a (bal bō′ə) *n.* the monetary unit of Panama. [From Vasco de *Balboa,* 1475?-1517, Spanish conquistador.]

bal·brig·gan (bal brig′ən) *n.* a knitted cotton cloth, chiefly used for hosiery or underwear. [From *Balbriggan,* Irish port where it was first made.]

bal·co·ny (bal′kə nē) *n., pl.* **-nies. 1.** a platform projecting from the wall of a building and enclosed by a low wall or railing of some kind. **2.** a projecting gallery in a theater, auditorium, or other place of assembly. [Italian *balcone;* of Germanic origin.]

bald (bôld) *adj.* **1.** partly or completely without hair on the scalp. **2.** without the usual or natural covering: *a bald mountain.* **3.** plain and simple; undisguised; unadorned; bare: *a bald lie.* **4.** (of animals) having white on the face or head. [Middle English *balled,* possibly from *bal* ball¹.] —**bald′ness,** *n.*

B

bald cypress 1. a deciduous, cone-bearing tree, *Taxodium distichum,* native to swamps of southeastern North America, having conical root projections when growing in water. **2.** the hard, durable wood of this tree.

bald eagle, a large eagle of North America, *Haliaeetus leucocephalus,* which, in the adult stage, is brown with a white head, neck, and tail; American eagle. Average wingspan: 6 feet (1.8 meters).

Bal·der (bôl′dər) *also,* **Bal·dr.** *n.* in Norse mythology, the god of light, happiness, and peace; son of Odin and Frigg. His death was caused by the treachery of Loki.

bal·der·dash (bôl′dər dash′) *n., interj.* nonsense; foolishness.

bald·ing (bôl′ding) *adj.* becoming bald.

bald·pate (bôld′pāt′) *n.* **1.** a person who has a bald head. **2.** a migratory widgeon, *Mareca americana,* of Canada and the northern United States, which flies as far south as Central America in the winter.

bal·dric (bôl′drik) *n.* a belt, often richly ornamented, worn over one shoulder and across the chest to support a sword or bugle. [Partly from Old French *baudre* belt; partly from Middle High German *balderich* girdle.]

Bald·win (bôld′win) *n.* a red American winter apple.

bale[1] (bāl) *n.* a large bundle of bulky merchandise compressed, corded, or otherwise prepared for transportation or storage: *a bale of hay.* —*v.t.,* **baled, bal·ing.** to make into a bale or bales. [Old French *bale* round bundle; of Germanic origin.] —**bal′er,** *n.*

bale[2] (bāl) *n. Archaic.* **1.** something that causes ruin or sorrow; evil. **2.** sorrow; misery. [Old English *bealu* woe, evil.]

ba·leen (bə lēn′) *n.* whalebone. [Old French *baleine,* from Latin *balaena* whale, from Greek *phallaina.*]

baleen whale, any whale belonging to the cetacean suborder Mysticetes, which lack teeth and have instead fringed plates of baleen which filter their food from the water.

bale·ful (bāl′fəl) *adj.* **1.** harmful or evil; malignant; sinister. **2.** *Archaic.* sorrowful; miserable; wretched. —**bale′ful·ly,** *adv.* —**bale′ful·ness,** *n.*

Ba·li·nese (bä′lə nēz′, -nēs′) *n., pl.* **-nese. 1.** a native or inhabitant of Bali. **2.** a person of Balinese ancestry. **3.** the language of Bali. —*adj.* of, relating to, or characteristic of Bali or its people, language, or culture.

balk (bôk) *also,* **baulk.** *v.i.* **1.** to stop short and refuse to proceed or act (often with *at*): *My horse balked at the high jump.* **2.** *Baseball.* (of a pitcher) to make an illegal motion, esp. to fail to complete a pitching motion when a runner is on base. —*v.t.* **1.** to hinder or check; thwart. —*n.* **1.** something that hinders or checks; defeat. **2.** a ridge between furrows; strip of unplowed land. **3.** a large beam or timber; tie beam. **4.** *Baseball.* an instance of balking. [Old English *balca* ridge, beam.] —**balk′er,** *n.*

Bal·kan (bôl′kən) *adj.* **1.** of or relating to the Balkan Peninsula. **2.** of or relating to the Balkan States or their people. **3.** of or relating to the Balkan Mountains.

bal·kan·ize (bôl′kə nīz′) *also,* **Bal·kan·ize.** *v.t., v.i.,* **-ized, -iz·ing.** to break up into small, often hostile political units or states. [In allusion to the fragmentation of the Balkans in the late nineteenth and early twentieth centuries.] —**bal′kan·i·za′tion;** *also,* **Bal′kan·i·za′tion,** *n.*

balk·y (bô′kē) *also,* **baulky.** *adj.,* **balk·i·er, balk·i·est.** given to balking: *a balky horse.* —**balk′i·ness,** *n.*

ball[1] (bôl) *n.* **1.** any round or spherical body; globe: *a ball of yarn, the blazing ball of the sun.* **2.** a round or egg-shaped object used in playing various sports and games. **3.** any game played with such an object, esp. baseball. **4.** a ball put into motion or play in a specified manner: *a high ball, a curve ball.* **5.** a rounded, protruding part of something: *the ball of the foot.* **6.** *Baseball.* a pitch that fails to pass through the strike zone and is not swung at by the batter. **7.** a solid, usually round projectile that is fired from a cannon or other firearm and is larger than shot. —*v.t., v.i.* to form, wind, or gather into a ball or balls. [Old Norse *böllr* globe.]
 •**to ball up.** *Slang.* to make or become hopelessly confused; muddle.
 •**to be** (or **have something**) **on the ball.** *Slang.* to be alert, efficient, or capable.
 •**to get the ball rolling.** *Informal.* to begin a certain action.
 •**to keep the ball rolling.** *Informal.* to continue a certain action.
 •**to play ball. a.** to begin or resume a ballgame or other activity. **b.** *Informal.* to work together; cooperate.

ball[2] (bôl) *n.* **1.** a large, formal dance. **2.** *Slang.* a very enjoyable time. [Old French *bal,* from *baler* to dance, from Late Latin *ballāre,* from Greek *ballizein.*]

bal·lad (bal′əd) *n.* **1.** a poem or song written in simple verse and short stanzas that tells a dramatic or exciting story. Ballads of popular origin were usually altered as they were passed along orally through generations. **2.** the music for such a song. **3.** a slow, sentimental or romantic song of two or more verses, each sung to the same melody. [Old French *balade* dancing song, from Provençal *balada,* from *balar* to dance, going back to Late Latin *ballāre.* See BALL[2].] —**bal′lad·ry,** *n.*

bal·lade (bə läd′) *n.* **1.** a verse form having three stanzas of eight, ten, or twelve lines each, an envoy of four, five, or six lines, and the same rhyme scheme repeated throughout. The last lines of the three stanzas and of the envoy are the same. **2.** a short, musical composition on the pattern of a ballad, for piano and orchestra. [Old French *balade.* See BALLAD.]

ball-and-sock·et joint (bôl′ən sok′it) a joint formed by a ball or knob in a socket, permitting limited rotary movement in every direction.

bal·last (bal′əst) *n.* **1.** weighty material placed in a floating or airborne vessel to maintain stability or control altitude. **2.** something lending stability or weight, as to a person's character. **3.** gravel or crushed rock used as a bed for the ties of a railroad. —*v.t.* **1.** to fill or furnish with ballast: *to ballast a ship, to ballast a railroad bed.* **2.** to steady with ballast; stabilize. [Probably from Low German.]

ball bearing 1. a bearing consisting of a number of metal balls on which the moving parts of a machine turn. **2.** any of these metal balls.

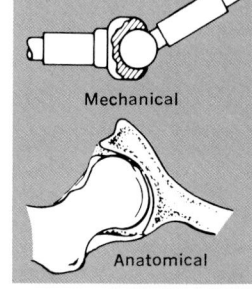

Mechanical

Anatomical

ball-and-socket joints

bal·le·ri·na (bal′ə rē′nə) *n., pl.* **-nas.** a female ballet dancer, esp. one who is a principal dancer in a ballet company. [Italian *ballerina,* from *ballare* to dance, from Late Latin *ballāre.* See BALL[2].]

bal·let (ba lā′, bal′ā) *n.* **1.** a form of dancing that combines conventionalized steps and positions in continuous, flowing movement. **2.** a theatrical presentation in which a story or mood is conveyed by such dancing. **3.** a company of dancers who perform ballet. **4.** music for a ballet. [French *ballet* literally, little dance, from Italian *balletto,* diminutive of *ballo* dancing, from *ballare* to dance. See BALLERINA.]

ballet master, a man who trains and rehearses the dancers of a ballet company.

ballet mistress, a woman who trains and rehearses the dancers of a ballet company.

ball·game (bôl′gām′) *also,* **ball game.** *n.* **1.** a game played with a ball, such as baseball. **2.** *Informal.* a set of conditions or circumstances; situation: *With the sudden rise in prices, consumers found themselves in a whole new ballgame.*

bal·lis·ta (bə lis′tə) *n., pl.* **-tae** (-tē) a weapon used in ancient and medieval times to hurl stones, javelins, and other projectiles. [Latin *ballista,* going back to Greek *ballein* to throw.]

bal·lis·tic (bə lis′tik) *adj.* **1.** of, relating to, or used in ballistics. **2.** of or relating to projectiles. —**bal·lis′ti·cal·ly,** *adv.*

ballistic missile, a self-propelled missile that is controlled during the upward portion of its trajectory, but is a free-falling object in its descent.

bal·lis·tics (bə lis′tiks) *n.* the study of the motion and impact of projectiles and the conditions that affect their motion. **Interior ballistics** studies a projectile's movement within the barrel of a weapon. **Exterior ballistics** studies the flight of a projectile after it has left the barrel and is also used to calculate the path of rockets and ballistic missiles. **Terminal ballistics** studies the impact of projectiles. ➡ used as singular. —**bal·lis·ti·cian** (bal′ə stish′ən), *n.*

bal·lo·net (bal′ə net′) *n.* a flexible air-filled or gas-filled compartment inside a balloon or airship for maintaining and controlling buoyancy and shape. [French *ballonnet* small balloon, diminutive of *ballon.* See BALLOON.]

bal·loon (bə lün′) *n.* **1.** an inflatable, often brightly colored, rubber bag, used as a toy or decoration. **2.** an airtight bag made of tough, light material, filled with heated air or with a gas lighter than air, and designed to rise and float in the atmosphere. A basket or container is often attached to its bottom for carrying scientific instruments or passengers. **3.** an outline enclosing words represented as spoken by a character, as in a cartoon or comic strip.

a	at	e	end	o	hot	u	up	hw	white		about
ā	ape	ē	me	ō	old	ū	use	ng	song	ə	taken
ä	far	i	it	ô	fork	ü	rule	th	thin		pencil
âr	care	ī	ice	oi	oil	u̇	pull	th	this		lemon
		îr	pierce	ou	out	ûr	turn	zh	measure		circus

—*v.i.* **1.** to go up or travel in a balloon. **2.** to swell out or expand like a balloon: *The sails ballooned in the wind.* **3.** to increase or grow rapidly: *The town's population has ballooned.* —*v.t.* to inflate or distend (something) like a balloon; fill with air. —*adj.* swelled or puffed out like a balloon. [French *ballon* child's air balloon, from Italian *ballone* large ball, from *balla* ball; of Germanic origin.]

bal·loon·ist (bə lü′nist) *n.* a person who operates or rides in balloons as a sport.

balloon tire, a pneumatic tire, containing air under low pressure.

bal·lot (bal′ət) *n.* **1.** a written or printed form used to cast a vote. **2.** the total number of votes cast in an election: *The ballot was recorded.* **3.** the list of candidates running in an election or of propositions in a referendum: *There are three proposals on the ballot.* **4.** the system of secret voting by ballots or voting machines. **5.** the right to vote. —*v.i.*, **-lot·ed, -lot·ing.** to cast a ballot or ballots; vote. [Italian *ballotta* little ball used in voting, diminutive of *balla* ball; of Germanic origin; from the ancient Greek method of voting by using small white and black balls to indicate approval and disapproval respectively.]

ballot box, a box into which ballots are put.

ball·park (bôl′pärk′) *n.* a park or stadium in which ballgames, esp. baseball, are played. —*adj. Informal.* not exact; approximate: *The mechanic gave me a ballpark figure on the cost of repairing my car.*
 · **in the ballpark.** *Informal.* within a reasonable or acceptable range: *That price is high, but it's still in the ballpark.*

ball·play·er (bôl′plā′ər) *n.* a person who plays any of various ballgames, esp. baseball.

ball·point pen (bôl′point′) a pen whose point is a small metal ball that rolls the ink from a cartridge onto the writing surface. Also, **ball·point.**

ball·room (bôl′rüm′, -rüm′) *n.* a large room for dances or other social gatherings.

bal·ly·hoo (*n.,* bal′ē hü′; *v.,* bal′ē hü′, bal′ē hü′) *Informal. n., pl.* **-hoos. 1.** exaggerated or sensational advertising or publicity. **2.** noisy uproar; clamor. —*v.t., v.i.,* **-hooed, -hoo·ing.** to advertise or promote with ballyhoo. [Said to be named after *Ballyhooly,* an Irish village famous for its noisy quarrels.]

balm (bäm) *n.* **1.** a fragrant gum resin obtained from certain trees or shrubs and used as salve; balsam. **2.** any fragrant ointment or oil. **3.** anything that heals or soothes: *Sleep was a balm to my troubled mind.* **4.** a sweet or pleasing fragrance. **5.** any of various aromatic plants of the mint family, esp. lemon balm. [Old French *basme* balsam, from Latin *balsamum,* from Greek *balsamon;* probably of Semitic origin. Doublet of BALSAM.]

balm of Gil·e·ad (gil′ē əd) **1.** a fragrant gum from a tree, formerly used as a soothing and healing ointment. **2.** a small evergreen tree, *Commiphora opobalsamum,* of Asia and Africa, from which this gum was obtained. **3.** balsam fir *(def. 1).* [From *Gilead,* ancient region of Palestine known for its balm, as mentioned in the Old Testament (Jeremiah 8:22).]

balm·y¹ (bä′mē) *adj.,* **balm·i·er, balm·i·est. 1.** mild and soothing: *balmy spring weather.* **2.** fragrant like balm. [BALM + -Y¹.] —**balm′i·ly,** *adv.* —**balm′i·ness,** *n.*

balm·y² (bä′mē) *adj.,* **balm·i·er, balm·i·est.** *British. Slang.* crazy; foolish. [Form of BARMY.]

ba·lo·ney (bə lō′nē) *n.* **1.** bologna. **2.** *Slang.* nonsense; foolishness.

bal·sa (bôl′sə, bäl′-) *n.* **1.** a strong, lightweight wood used esp. for making models and in rafts and floats. **2.** any of a group of tropical American trees, genus *Ochroma,* from which this wood comes. **3.** a raft, esp. one made of cylindrical floats attached to a framework. [Spanish *balsa* raft.]

bal·sam (bôl′səm) *n.* **1.** any of a group of aromatic oily or gummy oleoresins used in cough drops, candies, and medicine. **2.** a tree yielding such a substance, as the balsam fir. **3.** a bushy plant, *Impatiens balsamina,* widely cultivated in tropical and subtropical gardens for its showy blossoms. Its mature pods burst open at a slight touch, scattering the seeds for several feet. Also, **garden balsam. 4.** something that heals or soothes. [Latin *balsamum* resin, resin-yielding tree. See BALM.] —**bal·sam·ic** (bôl sam′ik), *adj.*

balsam fir 1. an evergreen tree, *Abies balsamea,* of the pine family, found in North America, having resinous blisters on its bark from which a kind of balsam is made. Also, **balm of Gilead. 2.** the wood of this tree, used esp. to make boxes, crates, and paper pulp.

Bal·tic (bôl′tik) *adj.* **1.** of or relating to the Baltic Sea. **2.** of or relating to the Baltic States or their inhabitants. **3.** of or relating to the branch of the Indo-European language family that includes Lithuanian and Latvian. —*n.* the Baltic branch of the Indo-European language family.

Bal·ti·more oriole (bôl′tə môr′) a North American songbird,

Icterus galbula, closely related to the meadowlark and blackbird. The male of the species has brilliant markings of orange and black. [From the family coat of arms of Lord *Baltimore,* which is orange and black.]

bal·us·ter (bal′ə stər) *n.* an upright support for the railing of a staircase, parapet, or similar structure. [French *balustre,* from Italian *balaustro* baluster, small pillar, going back to Latin *balaustium* pomegranate flower, from Greek *balaustion;* from its resemblance to the flower's shape.]

bal·us·trade (bal′ə strād′) *n.* a row of balusters and the handrail that they support. [French *balustrade,* from Italian *balaustrata,* from *balaustro* small pillar. See BALUSTER.]

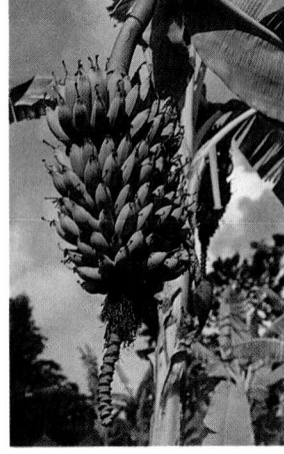

Baluster   Balustrade

bam·bi·no (bam bē′nō, bäm-) *n., pl.* **-nos** or **-ni** (-nē). **1.** a baby or child. **2.** a figure of the baby Jesus. [Italian *bambino* baby, diminutive of *bambo* childlike; literally foolish; of imitative origin.]

bam·boo (bam bü′) *n., pl.* **-boos. 1.a.** the hollow, jointed woody stem or piece of a stem of any of a large group of tropical and semitropical plants, genus *Bambusa* and related genera, of the grass family. **b.** such stems collectively, esp. those used for furniture, shades, utensil handles, and similar items. **2.** the tall, fast-growing plant itself, having slender branches and sword-shaped leaves. Some may reach a height of 120 feet (36.6 meters). [Malay *bambū* this plant.]

bam·boo·zle (bam bü′zəl) *v.t.,* **-zled, -zling.** *Informal.* to deceive or cheat by trickery; hoodwink: *to bamboozle a person into buying a worthless car.* [Of uncertain origin.] —**bam·boo′zle·ment,** *n.* —**bam·boo′zler,** *n.*

ban (ban) *v.t.,* **banned, ban·ning. 1.** to forbid officially; prohibit. **2.** to pronounce an ecclesiastical ban upon; condemn. —*n.* **1.** a formal or official prohibition: *a ban on the testing of nuclear weapons.* **2.** a denunciation or prohibition by public opinion. **3.** an official denunciation by the church; excommunication. **4.** a sentence of outlawry or banishment. [Partly from Old English *bannan* to summon; partly from Old French *ban* edict, prohibition; of Germanic origin.]

ba·nal (bā′nəl, bə nal′, -näl′) *adj.* dull or boring from having been used or said too often; commonplace; trite. [French *banal,* from Old French *banal* relating to compulsory service to a feudal lord; hence, for everybody, commonplace, from *ban* edict; of Germanic origin.] —**ba′nal·ly,** *adv.*

ba·nal·i·ty (bə nal′i tē) *n., pl.* **-ties. 1.** a banal remark or idea: *Her conversation is full of clichés and other banalities.* **2.** the quality of being banal: *The banality of his ideas bored me.*

ba·nan·a (bə nan′ə) *n.* **1.** the pulpy, crescent-shaped edible fruit of any of a group of large plants, genus *Musa,* found in nearly all tropical regions of the world. The most popular species in the United States is the yellow-skinned *M. paradisiaca,* variety *sapientum.* **2.** the tree-like plant bearing this fruit, having a high, thick stalk and large palmlike leaves. [Spanish *banana* this fruit; of West African origin.]

banana oil, a colorless, liquid ester that smells like bananas, used as a solvent and to flavor food products. Formula: $C_7H_{14}O_2$

band¹ (band) *n.* **1.** a group of persons or animals; troop: *a band of gypsies, a band of sheep.* **2.** a group of musicians organized to play together: *a marching band, a dance band.* —*v.t., v.i.* to unite in a group (usually with *together*): *The residents of the town banded together to oppose the new highway. The troops banded together for the attack.* [Middle French *bande* band, group; of Germanic origin.] —For Synonyms (*n.*), see company.

band² (band) *n.* **1.** a flat strip of material used for binding, trimming, or some other purpose: *I tied my hair back with a red cloth band.* **2.** a strip of contrasting color or material; stripe; bar:

banana tree

The cat had bands of brown and gray in its coat. **3.** a plain or simply decorated ring: *a gold band.* **4.** a range of wavelengths or frequencies between two specified limits. Also, **wave band.** **5. bands.** a pair of strips hanging from the front of the collar on certain clerical, legal, or academic garments. **6.** *Archaic.* something that ties, binds, or restrains, esp. morally or legally. —*v.t.* to mark, decorate, or furnish with a band or bands: *to band the leg of a bird, to band a box with tape before mailing it.* [Old French *bande* bond, tie; of Germanic origin.]

band·age (ban′dij) *n.* a strip of cloth or other material used in covering or binding part of the body, esp. an injured part. —*v.t.,* **-aged, -ag·ing.** to bind or cover with a bandage. [French *bandage* strip of material, from *bande* band[2]; of Germanic origin.] —**band′ag·er,** *n.*

band-aid (band′ād′) *n.* a small, adhesive bandage with a gauze pad in the center. *Trademark:* **Band-Aid.**

ban·dan·na (ban dan′ə) *also,* **ban·dan·a.** *n.* a large handkerchief, often brightly colored or patterned. [Hindi *bāndhnū* method of dyeing cloth in which certain parts of the cloth do not receive the dye.]

band·box (band′boks′) *n.* a box of cardboard or other light material, used for holding hats and other articles of apparel.

ban·deau (ban dō′, ban′dō) *n., pl.* **-deaux** (-dōz′, -dōz) or **-deaus.** **1.** a narrow band, esp. one worn about the hair; headband. **2.** a narrow brassiere. [French *bandeau* headband, diminutive of *bande* band[2]; of Germanic origin.]

ban·de·ril·la (ban′də rē′ə, -rēl′yə) *n.* a long, decorated barbed dart, customarily thrust into the hump behind the bull's head at the beginning of a bullfight. [Spanish *banderilla,* diminutive of *bandera* banner, going back to Late Latin *bandum.* See BANNER.]

ban·de·ril·le·ro (ban′də rē âr′ō, -rēl yâr′ō) *n.* the person who thrusts the banderillas into the bull's hump during a bullfight. [Spanish *banderillero,* from *banderilla.* See BANDERILLA.]

ban·de·role (ban′də rōl′) *also,* **ban·de·rol.** *n.* a small flag or streamer; pennant. [French *banderole,* from Italian *banderuola,* diminutive of *bandiera* flag, banner, going back to Late Latin *bandum.* See BANNER.]

ban·di·coot (ban′di küt′) *n.* **1.** a large rat, *Mus* or *Nesokia bandicota,* of India and Sri Lanka, which may grow to over 1 foot (0.3 meter) in length and often destroys gardens and rice fields. **2.** any of various marsupial mammals, family Peramelidae, native to Australia and neighboring islands, which resemble rats. They have large hind feet and slender forefeet with long, sharp claws. [Telugu *pandikokku* pig-rat.]

ban·dit (ban′dit) *n., pl.* **ban·dits** or **ban·dit·ti** (ban dit′ē). **1.** a robber, esp. one who is a member of a gang that robs travelers. **2.** a person who cheats or steals from others. [Italian *bandito,* noun use of past participle of *bandire* to banish; of Germanic origin.] —**ban′dit·ry,** *n.*

band·mas·ter (band′mas′tər) *n.* the conductor of a musical band.

ban·do·leer (ban′də lîr′) *also,* **ban·do·lier.** *n.* a broad belt worn over the shoulder and across the chest, with loops or small pockets for carrying ammunition and other small articles. [French *bandoulière,* from Spanish *bandolera,* from *banda* band; of Germanic origin.]

band saw, a saw consisting of an endless serrated steel belt running over and driven by pulleys.

band shell, a bandstand with a shell-like, concave back.

bands·man (bandz′mən) *n., pl.* **-men** (-mən). a member of a musical band.

band·stand (band′stand′) *n.* a platform for musical concerts, often roofed when outdoors.

band·wag·on (band′wag′ən) *n.* a decorated wagon that carries a musical band in a parade or similar procession.
· **to climb** (or **jump**) **on the bandwagon.** *Informal.* to be on the successful or popular side, as of a cause, movement, or candidacy: *The candidate's victory in the primary was so impressive that everyone climbed on the bandwagon.*

band·width (band′width′, -with′) *n.* the range of frequencies within a band alloted to a specific purpose, as the broadcast of a radio or television signal.

ban·dy (ban′dē) *v.t.,* **-died, -dy·ing.** **1.** to give and take; exchange: *to bandy blows, to bandy words.* **2.** to discuss freely or carelessly (often with *about*): *to bandy a rumor about.* **3.** to throw or knock back and forth: *to bandy a ball over a net.* —*adj.* (of legs) bent or curved outward; bowed. [Middle French *bander* to toss back and forth, bend; of uncertain origin.]

ban·dy-leg·ged (ban′dē leg′id, -legd′) *adj.* with the legs bent or curved outward; bowlegged.

bane (bān) *n.* **1.** a source or cause of death, ruin, or injury: *Drought is the bane of farmers.* **2.** *Archaic.* ruin; woe. [Old English *bana* murderer.]

bane·ber·ry (bān′ber′ē, -bə rē) *n., pl.* **-ries.** **1.** any of a group of

hardy woodland plants, genus *Actaea,* bearing showy clusters of small white flowers and white or red berries. **2.** one of these berries.

bane·ful (bān′fəl) *adj.* causing death, ruin, or injury; pernicious. —**bane′ful·ly,** *adv.* —**bane′ful·ness,** *n.*

bang[1] (bang) *n.* **1.** a loud, sudden, or explosive noise: *The door shut with a bang.* **2.** a heavy, noisy blow; thump; whack: *I fell and gave my head a good bang on the floor.* **3.** *Informal.* a sudden burst of energy or activity: *The racers started off with a bang.* **4.** *Slang.* a feeling of pleasure or excitement; thrill: *He gets a bang out of skiing.* —*v.t.* **1.** to strike violently or noisily: *She banged her elbow on the chair.* **2.** to produce a loud noise by slamming (something): *to bang a window shut.* —*v.i.* **1.** to make a loud, sudden, or explosive noise: *The loose shutter banged against the side of the house.* **2.** to strike or bump noisily or violently: *to bang into a chair.* —*adv. Informal.* suddenly and violently: *The bicyclist rode bang into the wall.* [Of Scandinavian origin.]
· **to bang up.** to do damage to (something): *to bang up a car in a crash.*

bang[2] (bang) *v.t.* to cut (the hair) short and straight across the forehead. —*n. usually,* **bangs.** hair worn over or across the forehead. [Short for *bangtail* racehorse with a short tail.]

ban·gle (bang′gəl) *n.* **1.** an ornamental circular band worn around the wrist, arm, or ankle. **2.** a small, loosely hanging ornament, as on a bracelet. [Hindi *bangrī* bracelet.]

bang-up (bang′up′) *adj. Slang.* exceptionally good; excellent: *You did a bang-up job of waxing the car.*

ban·ian (ban′yən) *n.* **1.** banyan. **2.** a Hindu trader or merchant of a caste that eats no meat. [Portuguese *banian* trader, from Gujarati *vāniyo* member of the merchant caste, from Sanskrit *vānija* merchant.]

ban·ish (ban′ish) *v.t.* **1.** to force by official decree to leave a country. **2.** to send or drive away; dismiss; expel: *Your reassuring words helped to banish my fears.* [Old French *baniss-,* a stem of *banir* to expel; of Germanic origin.] —**ban′ish·er,** *n.* —**ban′-ish·ment,** *n.*

Synonyms Banish, exile, and **deport** mean to force a person to leave a place. **Banish** is the most general term, usually suggesting only a sending away: *The rebellious nobles were banished from the city.* **Exile** more commonly suggests a place one is banished to: *Russian governments traditionally exiled their opponents to Siberia.* **Deport** refers to sending noncitizens out of a country: *to deport illegal immigrants, to deport foreign agents.*

ban·is·ter (ban′ə stər) *also,* **bannister.** *n.* **1.** a handrail and its upright supports along the edge of a staircase, parapet, or other elevated structure. **2.** the handrail itself. **3.** a baluster. [Modification of BALUSTER.]

banjo

ban·jo (ban′jō) *n., pl.* **-jos** or **-joes.** a stringed musical instrument, usually having five strings, with a long fretted neck and a round, tambourinelike body. The strings are plucked or strummed with the fingers or a plectrum. [Probably of African origin.] —**ban′jo·ist,** *n.*

a	at	e	end	o	hot	u	up	hw	white	ə	about
ā	ape	ē	me	ō	old	ū	use	ng	song		taken
ä	far	i	it	ô	fork	ü	rule	th	thin		pencil
âr	care	ī	ice	oi	oil	u̇	pull	th	this		lemon
		îr	pierce	ou	out	ûr	turn	zh	measure		circus

bank¹ (bangk) *n.* **1.** a long pile, mound, or mass: *a cloud bank, a bank of leaves.* **2.** the rising ground bordering a body of water or any cut or hollow: *a river bank, a road bank.* **3.** a slope. **4.** an elevation in the sea floor or bed of a river; shoal: *banks of Dunkirk.* **5.** a controlled tilt to one side made by an airplane in a turn. —*v.t.* **1.** to border with or as with a bank; raise a bank around; embank: *They banked the river with sandbags during the flood.* **2.** to form into a bank; pile (often with *up*): *The plow banked the snow along the side of the road.* **3.** to cover (a fire) with ashes, earth, or fuel so that it will burn slowly. **4.** to give a sideways slope to: *The engineers banked the highway.* **5.** to tilt (an airplane) to one side when making a turn. —*v.i.* **1.** to lie or form in banks: *Snow banked all along the road.* **2.** to tilt an airplane to one side when turning: *The pilot banked too sharply.* [Of Scandinavian origin.]

bank² (bangk) *n.* **1.a.** a business that safeguards, lends, exchanges, and issues money and conducts a variety of other financial transactions. **b.** a building or offices housing such a business. **2.** a small closed container, often with a slot, used for saving money. **3.** the money held by the dealer or banker in some gambling games, out of which the winners are paid. **4.** any reserve supply. **5.** a place of storage or safekeeping, as for a reserve supply. —*v.t.* to deposit in a bank: *I banked twenty dollars this week.* —*v.i.* **1.** to do business or have an account with a bank: *We bank downtown.* **2.** to keep the bank in a game: *You deal, he'll bank.* [Italian *banca* bench (of a banker); of Germanic origin.]
• **to bank on** (or **upon**). *Informal.* to depend on; be sure about: *You can bank on her going.*

bank³ (bangk) *n.* **1.** a group of objects arranged in a line or in tiers: *a bank of spotlights, a bank of elevators.* **2.** *Nautical.* **a.** a bench for rowers in a galley. **b.** a row or tier of oars. **3.** a row of keys on an organ. —*v.t.* to arrange in a bank. [Old French *banc* bench, from Late Latin *bancus;* of Germanic origin.]

bank account, money deposited in a bank to the credit of, and subject to withdrawal by, the depositor.

bank·book (bangk′bŭk′) *n.* a book held by a depositor in which the transactions relating to his or her bank account are recorded. Also, **passbook.**

bank·card (bangk′kärd′) *also,* **bank card.** *n.* **1.** a credit card issued by a bank. **2.** a coded card used for identification at an automated teller machine: *to use a bankcard for making deposits or withdrawing cash.*

bank·er (bang′kər) *n.* **1.** an owner, officer, or executive of a bank. **2.** the keeper of the bank in certain gambling games.

bank holiday, any day, except Saturday or Sunday, when banks are closed for a legal holiday.

bank·ing (bang′king) *n.* the business carried on by a bank or a banker.

bank note, a promissory note issued by a bank, payable to bearer on demand and serving as currency.

bank·roll (bangk′rōl′) *n.* a supply of money; funds. —*v.t.* to provide money for; finance: *to bankroll a new business.* [BANK² + ROLL.]

bank·rupt (bangk′rupt′, -rəpt) *n.* **1.** a debtor who is legally declared unable to pay his or her debts and whose property is distributed among or administered for the benefit of creditors under bankruptcy laws. **2.** a person who is without resources or unable to pay his or her debts. **3.** a person who lacks a particular quality or thing: *an intellectual bankrupt.* —*adj.* **1.** subject to legal process because of an inability to pay debts; insolvent. **2.** lacking or destitute (often with *in* or *of*): *morally bankrupt.* **3.** having failed to work or be useful. —*v.t.* to make bankrupt. [Italian *bancarotta* bankruptcy; literally, broken bench (from medieval custom of breaking the bench of an insolvent moneychanger), from *banca* bench (of Germanic origin) + *rotta* feminine past participle of *rompere* to break, from Latin *rumpere* to break.]

bank·rupt·cy (bangk′rupt′sē, -rəp sē) *n., pl.* **-cies. 1.** the state of being bankrupt; financial ruin. **2.** total ruin, failure, destitution, or the like: *a corrupt mayor's political bankruptcy.*

ban·ner (ban′ər) *n.* **1.** a piece of cloth bearing some emblem or motto: *Marchers in the parade carried colorful banners.* **2.** a flag. **3.** something regarded or displayed as a symbol. **4.** a headline extending across a newspaper page. Also (*def. 4*), **banner headline.** —*adj.* leading or outstanding; foremost: *The business had a banner first year.* [Old French *baniere* standard, flag, going back to Late Latin *bandum;* of Germanic origin.]

ban·nis·ter (ban′ə stər) banister.

ban·nock (ban′ək) *n. Scottish.* a round, flattened cake made of oatmeal or barley meal. [Old English *bannuc* a cake, from Gaelic *bonnach.*]

banns (banz) *also,* **bans.** *pl. n.* the public announcement in church of an intended marriage. [Plural of *bann,* a form of BAN.]

ban·quet (bang′kwit) *n.* **1.** a large, elaborate meal; lavish feast. **2.** a formal or ceremonial dinner, often followed by speeches. —*v.t.,* **-quet·ed, -quet·ing.** to entertain at a banquet. —*v.i.* **1.** to attend a banquet. **2.** to eat sumptuously; feast. [Middle French *banquet* feast, from Italian *banchetto* literally, little bench (as at a feast table), diminutive of *banco* bench; of Germanic origin.] —For Synonyms (*n.*), see **feast.**

ban·quette (bang ket′) *n.* **1.** an upholstered bench, as along a wall in a restaurant. **2.** a platform along the inside of a parapet or trench for soldiers to stand on when firing. [French *banquette* bench, platform, from Provençal *banqueta,* diminutive of *banc* bench; of Germanic origin.]

bans (banz) banns.

ban·shee (ban′shē) *also,* **ban·shie.** *n.* in Celtic folklore, a female spirit whose wails mean that a member of the family will soon die. [Irish *bean sidhe* woman of the fairies.]

ban·tam (ban′təm) *n.* **1.** *also,* **Bantam.** any of various miniature domestic fowl. **2.** a small person who is cocky or quarrelsome. —*adj.* diminutive; small. [From *Bantam,* city of Java, from which the fowl was supposedly imported.]

ban·tam·weight (ban′təm wāt′) *n.* a boxer competing in the weight class of up to 118 pounds (54 kilograms), or a competitor, as a wrestler, in a similar class.

ban·ter (ban′tər) *n.* good-natured, witty teasing or joking; repartee. —*v.i.* to exchange good-natured, playful remarks. [Of uncertain origin.] —**ban′ter·er,** *n.* —**ban′ter·ing·ly,** *adv.*

Ban·tu (ban′tü) *n., pl.* **-tu** or **-tus. 1.** a member of any of various Negroid tribes in central and southern Africa. **2.** the family of languages spoken by these tribes and allied with the Sudanese-Guinean family. It includes Swahili and Zulu. —*adj.* of or relating to the Bantu or their languages or culture.

ban·yan (ban′yən) *also,* **banian.** *n.* any of several large trees, genus *Ficus,* of Asia, whose branches send down aerial roots that enter the ground and develop into new trunks. One tree will often cover a large expanse of ground. [Originally applied to a tree of this family, under which Hindu merchants (sometimes known as *banians*) had erected a temple. See BANIAN.]

banyan

ban·zai (bän′zī′) *interj.* **1.** used by the Japanese as a battle cry. **2.** used by the Japanese as a cheer to wish the emperor long life. [Japanese *banzai* (may you live) ten thousand years.]

ba·o·bab (bā′ō bab′, bä′-) *n.* a broad-trunked tree, *Adansonia digitata,* found mostly in tropical Africa, having thick spreading branches and large white flowers that develop into an edible gourdlike fruit. The fibers of its bark are used for making rope, cloth, and paper. [Of central African origin.]

Bapt., Baptist. Also, **Bap.**

bap·tism (bap′tiz əm) *n.* **1.** the act of baptizing, esp. the ceremonial initiation into the Christian church through a ritualized use of water. **2.** any experience that purifies, initiates, or tests. —**bap·tis′mal,** *adj.* —**bap·tis′mal·ly,** *adv.*

baptism of fire 1. the first time that a soldier is engaged in actual combat or under enemy fire. **2.** any severe ordeal that tests one's endurance for the first time.

Bap·tist (bap′tist) *n.* **1.** a member of a Protestant denomination holding that baptism should be given by immersion and only to consenting believers. **2.** **baptist.** a person who baptizes. **3. the Baptist.** John the Baptist. —*adj.* of or relating to the Baptists, their doctrines, or their practices.

bap·tis·ter·y (bap′tə strē) *also,* **bap·tis·try.** *n., pl.* **-ter·ies;** *also,* **-tries. 1.** the part of a church, or a separate building, in which baptism is performed. **2.** a tank used for baptism by immersion.

bap·tize (bap tīz′, bap′tīz) *v.,* **-tized, -tiz·ing.** —*v.t.* **1.** to ceremonially initiate (a person) into the Christian church by immersing in water or pouring or sprinkling water upon. **2.** to purify or initiate. **3.** to give a name to; christen. —*v.i.* to administer baptism. [Old French *baptiser,* from Late Latin *baptizāre,* from Greek *baptizein,* from *baptein* to dip.] —**bap·tiz′er,** *n.*

bar¹ (bär) *n.* **1.** a piece of metal, wood or other sturdy material, longer than it is wide or thick, used as a barrier, fastening, lever, or support: *The cage has metal bars.* **2.** an oblong piece of solid material: *a bar of soap, a bar of gold, a bar of candy.* **3.** anything that obstructs or hinders; obstacle; barrier: *Lack of education can be a bar to advancement.* **4.** a stripe or band: *The painting consisted of bars of red and gold.* **5.a.** a counter where food or drinks, esp. alcoholic drinks, are served. **b.** an establishment containing such a counter. **6.a.** the legal profession: *a member of the bar.* **b.** lawyers collectively. **7.** the railing in a courtroom that encloses the area occupied by judges, attorneys, defendants, and witnesses. **8.** a law court or system of law courts. **9.** any tribunal or place of judgement: *before the bar of divine justice.* **10.** a bank of deposited sand or other material forming an obstruction to navigation or to the flow of water, as in a river. **11.** *Music.* **a.** a vertical line placed on a staff to mark the division between two measures. **b.** a unit of music contained between two such lines; measure. **c.** two parallel vertical lines marking the end of a composition or section of a composition. Also *(def. 11c.),* **double bar. 12.** barre. **13.** a narrow metal or cloth strip worn by members of the military to show rank or service. **14.** a horizontal stripe covering one fifth or less of a heraldic shield or device. —*v.t.,* **barred, bar·ring. 1.** to fasten with or as with a bar: *Bar the windows.* **2.** to block or hinder; obstruct: *Armed guards barred the way into the building.* **3.** to prevent or prohibit: *Smoking was barred.* **4.** to keep out; exclude: *to be barred from membership in a club.* **5.** to mark with bars, as of different colors. —*prep.* except; excluding: *Many think Shakespeare the greatest playwright, bar none.* [Old French *barre* rod, from Late Latin *barra;* of uncertain origin.]

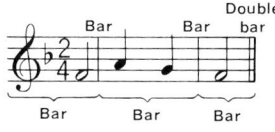

bar *(def. 11)*

bar² *n.* a centimeter-gram-second unit of pressure, equal to 1 million dynes per square centimeter. [German *bar,* from Greek *baros* weight.]

bar. 1. barometer. **2.** barometric. **3.** barrel.

barb¹ (bärb) *n.* **1.** a point or hook extending out and backward from the main part or tip: *the barb of a fishhook.* **2.** any sharp pointed projection: *My sleeve ripped on the barbs of the wire.* **3.** a sharp or sarcastic remark. **4.** one of the hairlike projections growing from the shaft of a bird's feather. For illustration, see **feather. 5.** a thin, beardlike growth near the mouth of certain animals. —*v.t.* to furnish with a barb or barbs: *to barb an arrow.* [Old French *barbe* beard, from Latin *barba.*]

barb² (bärb) *n.* **1.** any saddle horse of a breed native to northern Africa, noted for endurance and gentleness, and introduced into Spain by the Moors. **2.** any pigeon of a breed similar to that of a carrier pigeon, but with a shorter beak and more naked skin around the eyes. **3.** any of a group of brightly colored, tropical aquarium fish, genus *Barbus.* [French *barbe* a horse from Barbary, from Italian *barbero,* from Arabic *Barbar* Berber. See BERBER.]

bar·bar·i·an (bär bâr′ē ən) *n.* **1.** a person who belongs to a people, group, or tribe considered primitive or uncivilized. **2.** a crude, coarse, or brutal person; brute. **3.** a person who lacks understanding or appreciation of literature or the arts; philistine. **4.** in ancient or medieval times, a foreigner, esp. one who was not Greek, Roman, or Christian, and therefore considered to be uncivilized. —*adj.* **1.** characteristic of or resembling a barbarian; uncivilized; savage. **2.** of or relating to a people or culture differing from one's own, esp. in a way regarded as inferior; foreign; alien. —**bar·bar′i·an·ism,** *n.*

Synonyms *adj.* Barbarian, barbaric, barbarous, and savage all mean uncivilized or only partly civilized. **Barbarian** is the general term, suggesting that those referred to remain outside the civilized world or outside some group that regards itself as superior: *Barbarian nomads lived at the edge of the empire.* **Barbaric** emphasizes the crudeness and coarseness attributed to uncivilized peoples and sometimes suggests cruelty: *The missionaries tried to do away with the tribe's barbaric customs.* **Barbarous** is similar to *barbaric* but is more likely to suggest cruelty or ferocity than more civilized people find horrifying: *barbarous tortures.* **Savage** is sometimes simply equivalent to *barbarian* but more often refers to people considered more primitive or to the violence and brutality attributed to them.

bar·bar·ic (bär bar′ik) *adj.* **1.** of, relating to, or characteristic of barbarians; uncivilized or savage: *barbaric tribes, barbaric rites.* **2.** crude or unrestrained in style or manner; having a primitive or

unsophisticated quality. [Latin *barbaricus* foreign, uncivilized, from Greek *barbarikos,* from Greek *barbarikos* foreign, uncivilized.] —**bar·bar′i·cal·ly,** *adv.* — For Synonyms, see **barbarian.**

bar·ba·rism (bär′bə riz′əm) *n.* **1.** an uncivilized or primitive state or condition. **2.** an act, custom, or trait characteristic of people in such a condition. **3.** the use of words or forms not approved or current in the usage of a language. **4.** such a word or form.

bar·bar·i·ty (bär bar′i tē) *n., pl.* **-ties. 1.** savage or merciless cruelty. **2.** an act of savage or merciless cruelty. **3.** crudeness or coarseness, as in taste, style, or manner.

bar·ba·rize (bär′bə rīz′) *v.t., v.i.,* **-rized, -riz·ing.** to make or become barbarous. —**bar′ba·ri·za′tion,** *n.*

bar·ba·rous (bär′bər əs) *adj.* **1.** not civilized; primitive or savage. **2.** brutally harsh or cruel: *barbarous living conditions in a slum.* **3.** lacking refinement; crude or coarse. **4.** characterized by or using words or forms not approved or current in the usage of a language. [Latin *barbarus* foreign, uncivilized, from Greek *barbaros* foreign.] —**bar′ba·rous·ly,** *adv.* —**bar′ba·rous·ness,** *n.* —For Synonyms, see **barbarian.**

Bar·ba·ry ape (bär′bə rē) a tailless monkey, *Macaca sylvana,* of northern Africa and Gibraltar. Average length: 2½ feet (0.8 meter).

Barbary sheep, aoudad.

bar·be·cue (bär′bi kū′) *also,* **barbeque.** *n.* **1.** a gathering, usually outdoors, at which meat or other foods are roasted over an open fire and served. **2.** a spit, grill, or pit used for roasting food over an open fire. **3.** a whole animal carcass or other meat or food roasted over an open fire or direct heat, esp. with a highly seasoned sauce. —*v.t.,* **-cued, -cu·ing.** to cook (meat or other foods) over an open fire or by direct heat, esp. with a highly seasoned sauce. [Spanish *barbacoa* frame for roasting an animal, from native West Indian word.]

barbed (bärbd) *adj.* **1.** having a barb or barbs. **2.** sharp or sarcastic; biting; cutting: *a barbed remark.*

barbed wire, a wire or set of twisted wires to which barbs are attached at short intervals.

bar·bel (bär′bəl) *n.* **1.** one of the threadlike feelers hanging from the mouths of certain fish, as the catfish. **2.** any of various freshwater fish, genus *Barbus,* of the carp family, having such feelers, esp. *B. barbus,* a European game fish that may grow to 3 feet (0.9 meter) in length. [Old French *barbel* barbel fish, going back to Latin *barba* beard.]

bar·bell (bär′bel′) *n.* a bar to which one or more weights may be attached at each end, used for exercise and in weightlifting.

bar·be·que (bär′bi kū′) *n.* barbecue. —*v.t.,* **-qued, -qu·ing.** barbecue.

bar·ber (bär′bər) *n.* a person whose business or trade is cutting or dressing hair, shaving or trimming beards, and providing related services. —*v.t.* to trim or dress the hair or beard of. —*v.i.* to work as a barber. [Old French *barbour* a barber, from *barbe* beard, from Latin *barba.*]

bar·ber·ry (bär′ber′ē, -bə rē) *n., pl.* **-ries. 1.** any of a group of spiny shrubs, genus *Berberis,* having small, fragrant yellow to red flowers and inedible red or purple berries. **2.** the berry itself. [Old French *barbarim* the barberry shrub, from Arabic *barbārīs.*]

bar·ber·shop (bär′bər shop′) *n.* a barber's place of business. —*adj.* of or relating to a type of American vocal music characterized by the performance of traditional or popular songs in close, four-part harmony.

barber's itch, inflammation of the hair follicles of the beard associated with bacterial infection.

bar·bette (bär bet′) *n.* a platform in a fort that allows guns to shoot over the walls. [French *barbette,* diminutive of *barbe* beard, from Latin *barba.*]

bar·bi·can (bär′bi kən) *n.* a defensive tower or other fortification at a bridge or gate leading into a castle or city. [Old French *barbacane* battlement; of uncertain origin.]

bar·bi·cel (bär′bə sel′, -səl) *n.* any of the tiny extensions growing from the barbule of a feather that serves to hook adjacent barbules together. [Modern Latin *barbicella,* diminutive of *barba* beard.]

bar·bi·tal (bär′bi tôl′) *n.* a long-acting, white, crystalline, barbiturate used as a sedative. Formula: $C_8H_{12}N_2O_3$

bar·bi·tu·rate (bär bich′ər it, -ə rāt′) *n.* any of a group of barbituric acid derivatives, used as sedatives and hypnotics. They are often addictive.

a	at	e	end	o	hot	u	up	hw	white	(about
ā	ape	ē	me	ō	old	ū	use	ng	song	taken
ä	far	i	it	ô	fork	ü	rule	th	thin	ə pencil
âr	care	ī	ice	oi	oil	ù	pull	th	this	lemon
		îr	pierce	ou	out	ûr	turn	zh	measure	(circus

bar·bi·tu·ric acid (bär′bi tûr′ik, -tyûr′-) a crystalline acid used chiefly as the basis of barbiturates. Formula: $C_4H_4O_3N_2$

bar·bule (bär′būl) *n.* any of the interlocking parallel projections growing from the barb of a feather. [Latin *barbula,* diminutive of *barba* beard.]

bar·ca·role (bär′kə rōl′) *also,* **bar·ca·rolle.** *n.* **1.** a song sung by Venetian gondoliers. **2.** a musical composition similar in style and rhythm to this song. [French *barcarolle* boatman's song, from Italian *barcarola,* from *barcarolo* gondolier, from *barca* boat. See BARK[3].]

bar chart, bar graph.

bar code, a machine-readable code in which parallel bars of different widths each represent a letter or binary number. Printed on a product, shipping container, or other object, bar codes contain information such as the name of a product or an address, which can be read by using a computerized scanner.

bard (bärd) *n.* **1.** in ancient times, a poet and musician who composed and sang verses, esp. of heroes and heroic achievements. **2.** any poet. [Of Celtic origin.] —**bard′ic,** *adj.*

Bard of A·von (ā′vən, ā′von) William Shakespeare. [From his birthplace, Stratford-on-*Avon.*]

bare[1] (bâr) *adj.,* **bar·er, bar·est. 1.a.** without the natural or usual covering: *a bare light bulb, the bare trees of winter.* **b.** without clothing; naked: *bare arms.* **2.** lacking or without furnishings, contents, or decoration; empty: *bare walls, a bare cupboard.* **3.** without disguise or ornament; unadorned; plain: *bare facts.* **4.** just sufficient or no more than; mere: *the bare necessities of life, the bare minimum.* **5.** without tools, weapons, or other means.
➡ obsolete except as in the phrase *to work with one's bare hands.*
—*v.t.,* **bared, bar·ing.** to make bare; uncover; expose: *The poet bared her thoughts in her verse. The dog bared its fangs.* [Old English *bær* without covering.] —**bare′ness,** *n.*
• **to lay bare.** to open to view; uncover or expose: *The investigator laid bare an official conspiracy in his report.*

bare[2] (bâr) *Archaic.* a past tense of **bear[1].**

bare·back (bâr′bak′) *adj.* on the unsaddled back of a horse or other animal: *a bareback rider.* —*adv.* without a saddle: *to ride bareback.*

bare·bones (bâr′bōnz′) *adj.* concerning or including only the most essential elements, parts, or facts; basic: *Our rooms in the college dorm are bare-bones.*

bare·faced (bâr′fāst′) *adj.* **1.** without shame or embarrassment; brazen: *barefaced disrespect.* **2.** not concealed; open: *barefaced tyranny.* **3.** with the face uncovered. —**bare·fac·ed·ly** (bâr′fā′sid lē, -fāst′lē), *adj.* —**bare′fac′ed·ness,** *n.*

bare·foot (bâr′fŏt′) *also,* **bare′foot′ed.** *adj., adv.* with the feet bare.

bare·hand·ed (bâr′han′did) *adj., adv.* **1.** with hands uncovered. **2.** without tools, weapons, or other means; with the hands alone.

bare·head·ed (bâr′hed′id) *adj., adv.* with the head uncovered.

bare·leg·ged (bâr′leg′id) *adj., adv.* with the legs bare.

bare·ly (bâr′lē) *adv.* **1.** almost not; hardly; scarcely: *barely enough food to go around.* **2.** in a bare or scanty way; poorly: *a barely furnished room.*

bar·gain (bär′gin) *n.* **1.** something bought, sold, or offered at a price advantageous to the buyer. **2.** an agreement on the terms of a business transaction or other arrangement: *We made a bargain that I would help him cut wood if he would help me rake.* **3.** the terms of such an agreement, esp. as affecting one of the parties: *She made a bad bargain.* —*v.i.* **1.** to negotiate the terms of a bargain; haggle, esp. over a purchase price. **2.** to make or try to make a bargain: *to bargain for a wage increase.* —*v.t.* to achieve or arrange through bargaining; negotiate: *to bargain a new contract.* [Old French *bargaignier* to haggle; probably of Germanic origin.] —**bar′gain·er,** *n.*
• **in** (or **into**) **the bargain.** in addition; besides: *to break a leg and lose a ski in the bargain.*
• **to bargain for** (or **on**). to be prepared for; expect: *There was more work than I bargained for.*
• **to strike a bargain.** to reach an agreement.

bargaining chip, some advantage that a person may give up, concede, or trade to another person or persons during negotiations.

barge (bärj) *n.* **1.** a flat-bottomed boat for transporting freight on inland waterways; lighter. **2.** a large boat, often highly ornamented, used for recreation, pageants, or formal ceremonies. **3.** a large launch used by the commanding officer of a flagship. —*v.,* **barged, barg·ing.** —*v.i.* **1.** to move clumsily and abruptly: *to barge out of a room.* **2.** to enter or intrude rudely or heedlessly: *to barge into a meeting, to barge in on a conversation.* **3.** to collide

with; bump (with *into*): *I barged into an old friend as I came out of the store.* —*v.t.* to transport by barge. [Old French *barge* flat boat, from Late Latin *barca.*]

bar·gel·lo (bär jel′ō) *n., pl.* **-los. 1.** a needlepoint work or design consisting of patterns of zigzag or oblique lines. **2.** the upright stitch used in this needlework. —*v.,* **-loed, -lo·ing.** —*v.t.* to produce a bargello pattern on: *to bargello a pillow.* —*v.i.* to produce a bargello pattern. [Probably from the *Bargello,* a museum in Florence, Italy, containing chairs embroidered with this stitch.]

bargello sampler

barge·man (bärj′mən) *n., pl.* **-men** (-mən). a person who operates or works aboard a barge.

bar graph, a graph in which different quantities are represented by rectangles of lengths that are proportional to the quantities. Also, **bar chart.** For illustration, see **graph.**

bar·ite (bâr′īt, bar′-) *n.* a mineral composed of barium sulfate, the main source of barium. Formula: $BaSO_4$ [Greek *barytēs* weight, from *baryos* heavy.]

bar·i·tone (bar′i tōn′) *also,* **barytone.** *n.* **1.** a male voice lower than tenor and higher than bass. **2.** a singer who has a baritone voice. **3.** any of several brass or wind instruments with a similar range. **4.** a musical part for a baritone. —*adj.* **1.** able to sing or play baritone: *a baritone voice.* **2.** for the baritone: *a baritone score.* [Italian *baritono* this male voice, from Greek *barytonos* deep-toned, from *barys* heavy, deep + *tonos* tone.]

bar·i·um (bar′ē əm) *n.* a soft, silver-white metallic element extracted from barite, used esp. in alloys, paints, and in electron tubes. Symbol: **Ba** For tables, see **element.** [Modern Latin *barium,* from Greek *barys* heavy; because its mineral compounds are dense and heavy.]

barium sulfate, a white, solid compound used in making pigments for paint and printing ink, occurring naturally as the mineral barite. Because of its insolubility, it is safely ingested as part of a procedure for taking X rays of the gastrointestinal system.

bark[1] (bärk) *n.* the outer covering of the branches, stems, trunks, and roots of trees and other woody plants. —*v.t.* **1.** to rub the skin off of; scrape: *to bark one's shins.* **2.** to strip the bark off of. **3.** to treat or tan with an infusion of bark. [Old Norse *börkr.*]

bark[2] (bärk) *n.* **1.** a sharp, abrupt cry made by a dog or other animal, as a seal. **2.** any similar cry or sound: *the bark of a gun.* —*v.i.* **1.** to utter or give forth a bark. **2.** to speak loudly and sharply; snap: *The sergeant barked at the private.* **3.** *Informal.* to advertise by lively, persistent talking or shouting. —*v.t.* to utter or advertise in a sharp, loud tone: *She barked orders at her staff. The street vendor barked his wares.* [Old English *beorcan* to utter a bark.]
• **to bark up the wrong tree.** *Informal.* to mistake one's object or the means of attaining it.

bark[3] (bärk) *also,* **barque.** *n.* **1.** a ship with three or more masts, all square-rigged except for the aftermost one, which is fore-and-aft-rigged. **2.** *Archaic.* a sailing vessel, esp. a small one. [Middle French *barque* small ship, from Italian *barca* boat, from Late Latin *barca* small ship.]

bar·keep·er (bär′kē′pər) *n.* a person who owns, manages, or tends a bar where alcoholic liquors are served. Also, **bar′keep′.**

bar·ken·tine (bär′kən tēn′) *also,* **barquentine.** *n.* a ship with three or more masts, the foremast square-rigged and the other masts fore-and-aft-rigged. [BARK[3] + ending *-entine,* suggested by BRIGANTINE.]

bark·er[1] (bär′kər) *n.* **1.** a person, animal, or thing that makes a barking sound. **2.** a person who stands outside a show and at-

tracts customers by lively, persistent talking: *a barker at a carnival.* [BARK² + -ER¹.]

bark·er² (bär′kər) *n.* a person or thing that strips the bark off trees or logs. [BARK¹ + -ER¹.]

bar·ley (bär′lē) *n.* **1.** the grain of any of several hollow-stemmed plants of the genus *Hordeum,* esp. *H. vulgare,* of the grass family. It is used mainly as animal feed, but is often made into malt and used for flavoring cereals and beverages. **2.** the plant itself, bearing short spear-shaped leaves and spikes with tightly packed rows of grain. [Old English *bærlic.*]

bar·ley·corn (bär′lē kôrn′) *n.* a grain of barley.

barm (bärm) *n.* a foamy yeast that forms on top of fermenting malt liquors. [Old English *beorma.*]

bar magnet, an elongated permanent magnet, shaped like a bar or rod.

bar·maid (bär′mād′) *n.* a woman who serves customers in a bar.

bar·man (bär′mən) *n., pl.* **-men** (-mən). a man who serves customers in a bar.

Bar·me·cid·al (bär′mə sī′dəl) *adj.* giving an illusion of abundance. Also, **Bar′me·cide′.**

Bar·me·cide feast (bär′mə sīd′) an illusory or false show of hospitality or abundance. [From *Barmecide,* a Persian prince in *The Arabian Nights,* who served a beggar empty dishes, pretending they were an elaborate feast.]

bar mitz·vah (bär mits′və) **1.** a ceremony marking a Jewish boy's assumption of religious responsibilities upon his reaching the age of thirteen. **2.** a boy for whom this ceremony is held. —*v.t.,* **-vahed, -vah·ing.** to confirm in the ceremony of bar mitzvah. [Yiddish *bar-mitsve,* from Hebrew *bar-mitsva,* from Aramaic *bar* son of + Hebrew *mitsva* commandment (from *tsiva* to order, command).]

barm·y (bär′mē) *adj.,* **barm·i·er, barm·i·est. 1.** containing or resembling barm; frothy. **2.** *British. Slang.* crazy; idiotic. [BARM + -Y¹.]

barn (bärn) *n.* **1.** a building for storing farm produce and equipment and for sheltering cows, horses, and other livestock. **2.** a large building for housing vehicles, such as buses or trucks. [Old English *bereærn* literally, place for storing barley, from *bere* barley + *ærn* place.]

bar·na·cle (bär′nə kəl) *n.* any of various small marine crustaceans, order Cirripedia, that attach themselves to underwater objects and secrete a hard, cup-shaped shell. The **rock barnacle,** *Balanus balanoides,* is found on such objects as wharves or ship bottoms; the **goose barnacle,** *Lepas fascicularis,* on floating objects such as seaweed, attached by a long, fleshy stalk. [Of Celtic origin.] —**bar′na·cled,** *adj.*

barn dance, a social gathering, esp. one held in a barn, with square dances or other folk dances, and hoedown music.

barn owl, any of a group of owls, family Tytonidae, having a heart-shaped facial disk and long, feathered legs, esp. *Tyto albans,* the **common barn owl,** having rusty brown plumage above and light-colored below, found worldwide in hollow trees and barns. Length: 16 inches (41 centimeters).

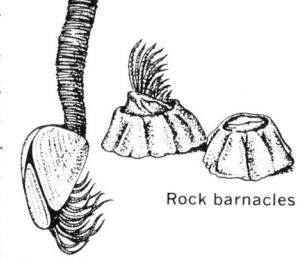

Rock barnacles

Goose barnacle

barn·storm (bärn′stôrm′) *v.i.* **1.** to tour rural or outlying areas, making brief stops, esp. to give campaign speeches or lectures or to present plays: *The presidential candidate barnstormed through five states.* **2.** to tour such areas as a stunt flyer or pilot. [When theatrical companies made tours in nineteenth-century America, they would *storm* through country districts, often performing their plays in *barns.*] —**barn′storm′er,** *n.*

barn swallow, a fork-tailed swallow, *Hirundo rustica,* of North America and Eurasia, that usually builds a mud nest in chimneys or on the rafters inside barns.

barn·yard (bärn′yärd′) *n.* the yard surrounding or adjoining a barn, often fenced in to hold poultry or livestock.

bar·o·gram (bar′ə gram′) *n.* a record traced by a barograph.

bar·o·graph (bar′ə graf′) *n.* an aneroid barometer that automatically records its readings. [Greek *baros* weight + -GRAPH.]

ba·rom·e·ter (bə rom′i tər) *n.* **1.** an instrument for measuring atmospheric pressure, used in weather forecasting and to determine height above sea level. **2.** anything that indicates changes: *The stock market is a barometer of business activity.* [Greek *baros* weight + -METER.]

bar·o·met·ric (bar′ə met′rik) *adj.* of or indicated by a barometer. Also, **bar′o·met′ri·cal. —bar′o·met′ri·cal·ly,** *adv.*

barometric pressure, atmospheric pressure.

bar·on (bar′ən) *n.* **1.a.** a British nobleman of the lowest rank. **b.** a nobleman of certain European countries or of Japan having a similar rank. **2.** in the Middles Ages, a feudal lord who held lands as a vassal of a king or other higher-ranking lord. **3.** a person who wields great power or dominates, esp. in business or industry: *an oil baron; a cattle baron.* [Old French *baron* man, warrior; probably of Germanic origin.]

bar·on·age (bar′ə nij) *n.* **1.** the entire body of barons or nobles collectively. **2.** the rank, title, or territory of a baron.

bar·on·ess (bar′ə nis) *n.* **1.** the wife or widow of a baron. **2.** a noblewoman having baronial rank in her own right, as by inheritance.

bar·on·et (bar′ə nit, -net′) *n.* a member of the lowest hereditary order of honor in Great Britain. Although a baronet is not a nobleman, he is addressed as *Sir,* and may write *Bart.* after his name; for example: *Sir Thomas Beecham, Bart.*

bar·on·et·age (bar′ə ni tij, -net′ij) *n.* **1.** the entire body of baronets collectively. **2.** the rank or title of a baronet.

bar·on·et·cy (bar′ə nit sē, -net′-) *n., pl.* **-cies. 1.** the rank or title of a baronet. **2.** a document conferring such rank or title.

ba·ro·ni·al (bə rō′nē əl) *adj.* **1.** of or relating to a baron, barony, or the entire body of barons. **2.** befitting a baron; stately; magnificent: *a baronial mansion.*

bar·o·ny (bar′ə nē) *n., pl.* **-nies. 1.** the territory of a baron. **2.** the rank or title of a baron.

baroque wall hanging

ba·roque (bə rōk′) *adj.* **1.** of, characteristic of, or like a style of art and architecture that was prevalent in Europe from about 1550 to the end of the eighteenth century, distinguished by elaborate ornamentation and the use of curved rather than straight lines. **2.** of, characteristic of, or like a style of music that was prevalent in Europe from about 1600 to 1750, distinguished by elaborate ornamentation, strong rhythm, polyphony, and a figured bass. **3.** showy or ornate in an exaggerated or grotesque way. **4.** (of pearls) irregular in shape. —*n.* a baroque style or period. [French *baroque,* from Italian *barocco,* probably from Provençal *barroca* irregular, mountainous terrain.]

ba·rouche (bə rüsh′) *n.* a large four-wheeled carriage with two double seats facing each other and covered by a folding top, with a box seat in front for the driver. [German *barutsche,* from Italian *biroccio* two-wheeled cart, going back to Latin *birotus* two-wheeled.]

barque (bärk) bark³.

bar·quen·tine (bär′kən tēn′) barkentine.

bar·rack (bar′ək) *n.* barracks. —*v.t.* to house in barracks.

bar·racks (bar′əks) *n.* **1.** a building or set of buildings for housing soldiers or other military personnel, esp. at a permanent base. **2.** any plain, usually temporary housing for many people in close quarters: *refugee barracks, workers' barracks.* ➡ used as singular or plural in both defs. [French *baraque* hut, from Spanish *barraca;* of uncertain origin.]

bar·ra·cu·da (bar′ə kü′də) *n., pl.* **-da** or **-das.** any of a group of long-bodied, predatory fish, genus *Sphyraena,* found in warm seas throughout the world and often caught for food. The **great barracuda** of the southern United States and West Indies, with its

a	at	e	end	o	hot	u	up	hw	white		about
ā	ape	ē	me	ō	old	ū	use	ng	song		taken
ä	far	i	it	ô	fork	ü	rule	th	thin	ə	pencil
âr	care	ī	ice	oi	oil	u̇	pull	th	this		lemon
		îr	pierce	ou	out	ûr	turn	zh	measure		circus

large mouth, strong teeth, and aggressive nature, is known to attack swimmers. [Spanish *barracuda;* of uncertain origin.]

bar·rage¹ (bə räzh′) *n.* **1.** a heavy, curtainlike concentration of artillery fire for protecting one's own troops or halting an enemy advance. **2.** any heavy concentration or massive outpouring: *The reporters met the president with a barrage of questions.* — *v.t.,* **-raged, -rag·ing.** to subject to a barrage: *The star was barraged with requests for autographs.* [From French *tir de barrage* curtain fire, from *barrage* barrier. See BARRAGE².]

bar·rage² (bär′ij) *n.* an artificial barrier in or across a watercourse; dam. [French *barrage* barrier, dam, from *barrer* to bar, from Old French *barre.* See BAR.]

bar·ra·try (bar′ə trē) *n., pl.* **-tries. 1.** fraud or negligence by captain or crew against the interest of the owner or insurer of a ship or its cargo, esp. destruction of the ship or cargo in order to collect insurance. **2.** the crime of repeatedly inciting quarrels or lawsuits. **3.** the act or practice of selling or buying positions of honor or profit, esp. in the church. [Old French *baraterie* deception, from *barater* to cheat. See BARTER.] —**bar′ra·trous,** *adj.*

barre (bär) *also,* **bar.** *n.* a round, horizontal bar used by ballet dancers for support during exercises. [French *barre,* from Medieval Latin *barra* rod, bar.]

barred (bärd) *adj.* **1.** having bars: *a barred cell.* **2.** having stripes: *barred feathers.*

bar·rel (bar′əl) *n.* **1.a.** a cylindrical wooden container having bulging sides and round, flat ends. It is made of staves bound by hoops. **b.** any of various other cylindrical containers: *an oil barrel, a trash barrel.* **2.** the capacity of a barrel, esp. a standard capacity used as a measure of weight or quantity, varying by country or commodity. **3.** the tube-shaped part of a gun through which a bullet or shell is shot. **4.** any of various cylindrical parts or casings, esp. of mechanical devices: *a fountain-pen barrel, the barrel of a winch.* **5.** the hard, hollow part at the base of a feather. **6.** *Informal.* a large quantity: *a barrel of laughs, a barrel of fun, a barrel of money.* — *v.,* **-reled, -rel·ing;** *also, British,* **-relled, -rel·ling.** — *v.t.* to put or pack in barrels. — *v.i. Informal.* to travel or move rapidly: *The train was barreling along.* [Old French *baril* cask, possibly from *barre* bar; in the sense that a barrel is constructed with "bars" of wood. See BAR¹.]

  •**over a barrel.** *Informal.* in an awkward position; in a dilemma or quandary.

bar·rel·head (bar′əl hed′) *n.* either round, flat end of a barrel.
  •**on the barrelhead.** immediately and in full: *to pay for something with cash on the barrelhead.*

barrel organ, a musical instrument in which organ pipes are played by air released through valves controlled by a pin-studded cylinder similar to that in a music box.

bar·ren (bar′ən) *adj.* **1.** having little or no vegetation; producing poor crops: *barren soil, barren desert wastes.* **2.** not producing or able to produce offspring; sterile: *a barren cow, a barren fruit tree.* **3.** not leading to any gain; fruitless; unprofitable: *barren endeavors, barren prospects.* **4.** without interest, charm, or hopefulness; empty; dreary: *Life seemed barren to the friendless misfit.* **5.** devoid; lacking (with *of*): *barren of interest, barren of any charm.* — *n. usually,* **barrens.** an area of barren land. [Anglo-Norman *barai(g)ne* sterile; of uncertain origin.] —**bar′ren·ly,** *adv.* —**bar′ren·ness,** *n.*

adj. **Barren, sterile,** and **infertile** mean not capable of producing, or not having produced, offspring. **Barren,** used of females or of couples, indicates that no offspring may have been produced, although the possibility may remain: *a woman barren for fifteen years.* **Sterile,** used of males or females, indicates the scientific certainty that no offspring can be produced: *Most hybrid animals are sterile.* **Infertile,** also a scientific term, is capable of barrenness that may be reversible: *New treatments are helping many previously infertile couples to have children.*

bar·rette (bə ret′, bä-) *n.* a clasp or clip, often in the shape of a bar, for holding the hair in place. [French *barrette,* diminutive of *barre.* See BAR.]

bar·ri·cade (bar′i kād′) *n.* **1.** a hastily built rampart of makeshift materials, as in revolutionary street fighting: *to storm the barricades.* **2.a.** a temporary or hastily erected barrier of any kind: *The police made a barricade of trucks across the highway to block the bank robbers' escape.* **b.** any barrier. — *v.t.,* **-cad·ed, -cad·ing. 1.** to block; obstruct: *Fallen trees barricaded the road.* **2.** to prevent access to with or as with a barricade: *The terrorists barricaded themselves on the top floor of the building.* [French *barricade* barrier, obstacle, from *barrique* barrel, from Spanish *barrica,* from *barril* cask, probably from *barra* bar; from the early use of *barrels* filled with earth and stones as makeshift ramparts in revolutionary street fighting in Paris. See BARREL.]

bar·ri·er (bar′ē ər) *n.* **1.** something that blocks the way, as a fence or wall. **2.** something that restricts, hinders, or separates:

The disagreements within the political party were a barrier to progress. [Anglo-Norman *barrere* obstacle, from *barre.* See BAR.]

barrier reef 1. an offshore coral reef roughly parallel to the shoreline, usually acting as a breakwater that leaves the landward channel, or lagoon, relatively still. It is the high outer edge of a coral shelf which, in turn, extends underwater from the shore. **2.** any similar offshore reef, as of rock, usually acting as a breakwater.

bar·ring (bär′ing) *prep.* **1.** excluding the possibility of: *Barring any problems, the ship will be docking here next week.* **2.** with the exception of: *No one, barring the parties to the agreement, is to know of these plans.*

bar·ri·o (bar′ē ō′, bär′-) *n., pl.* **-ri·os. 1.** in the United States, a neighborhood or section of a city or town inhabited mainly by Spanish-speaking people. **2.** in Spanish-speaking countries, a district of a city or town. [Spanish *barrio,* from Arabic *barrī* open country.]

bar·ris·ter (bar′ə stər) *n.* in England, a lawyer who argues cases in court. ➡ distinguished from **solicitor.** [BAR (the legal profession) + -STER.]

bar·room (bär′rūm′, -rùm′) *n.* a room or establishment having a bar where alcoholic drinks are sold.

bar·row¹ (bar′ō) *n.* **1.** wheelbarrow. **2.** handbarrow. [Middle English *barwe,* from Old English *bearwe* wheelbarrow.]

bar·row² (bar′ō) *n.* a mound of earth or stones marking a prehistoric grave. [Middle English *berwe,* from Old English *beorg* mound, hill.]

bar·row³ (bar′ō) *n.* a male pig castrated before reaching sexual maturity. [Middle English *barow,* from Old English *bearg.*]

bar sinister, a diagonal stripe on a coat of arms, erroneously supposed to indicate illegitimate descent.

Bart., Baronet.

bar·tend·er (bär′ten′dər) *n.* a person who makes and serves alcoholic drinks at a bar.

bar·ter (bär′tər) *v.t.* to trade (goods or services) without using money. — *v.i.* to engage in bartering goods or services. — *n.* **1.** the act or practice of bartering. **2.** something bartered. [Old French *barater* to exchange, cheat, from *barat* an exchange, cheating; possibly of Celtic origin.]

  •**to barter away.** to trade (something) in return for something of less value: *to barter away one's happiness for wealth.*

bar·ti·zan (bär′tə zən, bär′tə zan′) *n.* a small overhanging turret on a wall or tower. [Modification of Old French *bretesque;* of uncertain origin.]

Bart·lett pear (bärt′lit) a pear of a variety that is usually large, yellow, and juicy. [From Enoch *Bartlett,* 1779-1806, merchant who popularized it in the United States.]

Bar·uch (bâr′ək) *n.* a book of the Apocrypha.

bar·y·on (bar′ē on′) *n.* any subatomic particle whose weight is equal to or greater than that of a proton. [Greek *barys* heavy.]

bar·y·tone (bar′i tōn′) *n.* baritone.

ba·sal (bā′səl, -zəl) *adj.* **1.** of or at the base; forming part or·all of the base. **2.** forming the basis; fundamental; basic: *a basal English textbook.*

basal metabolic rate, a measure of basal metabolism, usually determined as the rate at which heat is given off by a resting individual 12 to 18 hours after eating.

basal metabolism, the minimal amount of energy expended by an organism to maintain basic body functions, as circulation and respiration.

ba·salt (bə sôlt′, bā′sôlt) *n.* a dark, usually fine-grained volcanic rock, often found in striking columnar formations. [Latin *basaltēs* a kind of marble, form of *basanītēs (lapis)* touchstone, going back to Greek *basanos* touchstone.]

ba·sal·tic (bə sôl′tik) *adj.* of or like basalt.

bas·cule bridge (bas′kūl) a drawbridge hinged at the bank so that it may be raised to allow ships to pass under it. For illustration, see **bridge.** [French *bascule* seesaw.]

base¹ (bās) *n.* **1.a.** the part on which a thing rests or stands: *The statue has a marble base.* **b.** the underlying or fundamental part that gives support: *a broad political base, a country's industrial base.* **c.** a guiding principle; basis. **2.** the lowest part; bottom: *the base of a tree, the base of a mountain.* **3.** the main element or ingredient: *a paint having an oil base.* **4.a.** a military area and facilities, esp. one used for a particular purpose or activity; installation: *a training base, a supply base, a missile base.* **b.** any center of operations; headquarters. **5.** *Chemistry.* **a.** any compound that reacts with an acid to form a salt. Dissolved in water, such compounds yield hydroxyl ions and turn red litmus paper blue. **b.** a compound capable of receiving protons from an acid. **c.** a compound able to give up an unshared pair of electrons to an acid. **6.** *Mathematics.* a fixed number from which all numbers in a numerical or logarithmic system are derived. Simple arithmetic is usually done in the decimal system, whose base is 10. Computers

B

use the binary system, whose base is 2. **7.a.** the station, goal, or safety area in certain games. **b.** any of the four corners of a baseball diamond. For illustration, see **infield**. **8.** the lower part of a column, building, or wall as a distinct architectural feature. **9.** the part of an organ in a plant or animal that is closest to the point of attachment to a larger or more central part: *the base of the thumb, the base of the skull.* **10.a.** the line or plane in a geometrical figure upon which it is considered to be resting: *the base of a triangle.* **b.** in a trapezoid, either of the two parallel sides. **11.** baseline *(def. 4).* **12.** the form of a word to which affixes are added. **13.** a primary coat or layer, as of paint. —*v.t.,* **based, bas·ing. 1.** to place on a basis or foundation: *to base opinions on facts.* **2.** to derive from; model after: *to base a movie on a bestseller.* **3.** to locate; station: *to base troops in Europe.* [Old French *base,* from Latin *basis* foundation, base, from Greek *basis* pedestal, base, from *bainein* to go.]
· **off base.** *Informal.* not accurate; mistaken: *Your guess was really off base.*
· **to touch base (with).** *Informal.* to communicate or make contact (with): *Let's touch base in a week.*

Synonyms *n.* **Base¹, basis,** and **foundation** mean something that supports something else. **Base** suggests a bottom part or underlying substance or object on which something rests: *the base of a column.* **Basis** conveys the same idea of support but is usually used of concepts rather than physical things: *The basis of the recycling program is community support.* **Foundation,** used either of physical structures or of concepts, emphasizes the work that has gone into constructing a solid support: *to lay the foundations of a house, a theory with a clearly demonstrated foundation.*

base² (bās) *adj.,* **bas·er, bas·est. 1.** low in standards of decency or morality; without honor or worth: *a base person, base motives.* **2.** low in status; menial; degrading: *base labor.* **3.** (of coin) having little or no value; debased. **4.** *Archaic.* baseborn. [Middle French *base* from Medieval Latin *bassus* low, short.] —**base′ly,** *adv.* —**base′ness,** *n.*

base·ball (bās′bôl′) *n.* **1.a.** a game played with ball and bat between two teams, officially of nine players each, on a field having four bases that form a diamond. A player of the team at bat must hit the ball and reach at least first base without being put out by the opposing team. To score, the player must then reach home base by way of second and third bases before being put out. For illustration, see **infield. b.** any game played on a similar field with similar rules. **2.** the ball used in any of these games.

base·board (bās′bôrd′) *n.* a strip of board, molding, or the like at the bottom of a wall, for covering the line where the wall meets the floor.

base·born (bās′bôrn′) *adj.* **1.** of humble birth or origin. **2.** born out of wedlock; illegitimate.

base·burn·er (bās′bûr′nər) *n.* a coal stove or furnace fed automatically from above as the fuel below is consumed.

base hit, the hitting of a pitched baseball by a batter in a way that enables the batter to get on base without benefit of an opponent's error and without forcing out a runner already on base.

base·less (bās′lis) *adj.* having no basis in fact: *a baseless claim to fame.* —For Synonyms, see **unfounded.**

base·line (bās′līn′) *n.* **1.** a line serving as or representing a base. **2.** *Baseball.* an area within which a base runner must stay while running from one base to another. **3.** a line marking either end of a tennis or basketball court. **4.** (in surveying) the measured base of a triangle established by triangulation.

base·man (bās′mən) *n., pl.* **-men** (-mən). a baseball player stationed near first, second, or third base. ➡ now used only in the specific terms *first baseman, second baseman,* and *third baseman.*

base·ment (bās′mənt) *n.* **1.** the floor of a building below the ground floor. **2.** the lowest or fundamental portion of a structure, as a wall, that serves as its support.

base metal, a metal, such as iron or lead, that is not a precious metal.

ba·sen·ji (bə sen′jē) *n.* a short-haired hound of a breed that originated in central Africa, usually having a reddish brown or black coat with white markings. It does not bark but makes a chortling whine. Height: 17 inches (43 centimeters) at the shoulder. [Of Bantu origin.]

basenji

base on balls *Baseball.* a walk.

base runner *Baseball.* a member of the team at bat who is on base or attempting to reach a base.

bas·es¹ (bā′siz) the plural of **base¹.**

bas·es² (bā′sēz) the plural of **basis.**

bash (bash) *v.t. Informal.* to strike with a smashing blow (often with *in*). —*n.* **1.** *Informal.* such a blow. **2.** *Slang.* an exciting, lively party. **3.** *British.* an attempt; try: *Have a bash at it.* [Of uncertain origin.]

ba·shaw (bə shô′) *n.* **1.** pasha. **2.** an important or pretentious person. [Form of PASHA.]

bash·ful (bash′fəl) *adj.* easily embarrassed; extremely modest; shy. [Short for ABASH + -FUL.] —**bash′ful·ly,** *adv.* —**bash′-ful·ness,** *n.*

ba·sic (bā′sik) *adj.* **1.** of, at, or constituting the base; fundamental. **2.** *Chemistry.* **a.** of or containing a base. **b.** alkaline. **3.** (of rock) containing a relatively low percentage of silica. —*n. usually,* **basics.** something basic. —**ba′si·cal·ly,** *adv.* —**ba·sic·i·ty** (bā sis′i tē), *n.* —For Synonyms, see **elementary.**

BASIC (bā′sik) *n.* a computer programming language that uses simple English words to represent commands designed especially for beginners. [Short for *B(eginner's) A(ll-purpose) S(ymbolic) I(nstruction) C(ode).*]

basic training, the initial period of military training for a person who has been inducted into the armed forces.

ba·sid·i·o·my·cete (bə sid′ē ō mī′sēt, -mī sēt′) *n.* any of a large group of fungi, division Basidiomycota, including the mushrooms, puffballs, rusts, and smuts, that produce and bear sexual spores on a basidium. [BASIDIUM + Modern Latin *mycetes* fungi (from Greek *mykētes,* plural of *mykēs* fungus).]

ba·sid·i·o·spore (bə sid′ē ō spôr′) *n.* a sexual spore of a basidiomycete fungus, produced and borne on a basidium. [BASIDIUM + SPORE.]

ba·sid·i·um (bə sid′ē əm) *n., pl.* **-sid·i·a** (-sid′ē ə). a specialized, clublike structure of a basidiomycete fungus on which sexual spores, usually four, are produced and borne. [Modern Latin *basidium,* from Latin *basis.* See BASIS.]

bas·il (baz′əl, bā′zəl) *n.* **1.** any of several aromatic plants, genus *Ocimum,* of the mint family, esp. the common cooking herb sweet basil. **2.** the leaves themselves. [Old French *basile* the plant, from Late Latin *basilicum,* from Greek *basilikon (phyton)* literally, royal (plant).]

bas·i·lar (bas′ə lər) *adj.* of or at the base, esp. of the skull.

ba·sil·i·ca (bə sil′i kə) *n.* **1.** in ancient Rome, a rectangular building composed of a broad central aisle ending in a semicircular area and separated from two or more side aisles by rows of columns. Basilicas were used chiefly for the transaction of business and the deciding of legal matters. **2.** an early Christian church built on the model of the Roman structure. [Latin *basilica* the building, from Greek *basilikē (oikia)* royal (house), palace.]

bas·i·lisk (bas′ə lisk′, baz′-) *n.* **1.** a mythical monster that was supposedly hatched by a serpent from a rooster's egg and whose breath or gaze was deadly. Also, **cockatrice. 2.** any of a group of lizards of tropical America related to the iguanas and characterized by an inflatable sac upon the head, an erectile crest along the back and tail, and the ability to run upright on the hind legs. [Latin *basiliscus* the mythical monster, from Greek *basiliskos* literally, little king (supposedly because it had a spot on its head resembling a crown).]

basilisk *(def. 2)*

ba·sin (bā′sin) *n.* **1.a.** a shallow container that is usually round with a wide, flat bottom and sloping sides, used esp. for holding liquids. **b.** a bathroom sink. **2.** the contents or capacity of a basin. **3.** the entire region drained by a river and its tributaries. **4.** a depression in the earth usually holding water, as a pond. **5.** an enclosed or partially enclosed place containing water: *a boat basin.* [Old French *bacin* bowl, going back to Late Latin *bacca* water container.]

bas·i·net (bas′ə net′) *n.* an iron skullcap worn under the helmet in feudal Europe. It gradually developed into a large headpiece with a movable visor. [Old French *bacinet,* diminutive of *bacin* bowl. See BASIN.]

a	at	e	end	o	hot	u	up	hw	white		about
ā	ape	ē	me	ō	old	ū	use	ng	song		taken
ä	far	i	it	ô	fork	ū	rule	th	thin	ə	pencil
âr	care	ī	ice	oi	oil	u̇	pull	th	this		lemon
		îr	pierce	ou	out	ûr	turn	zh	measure		circus

ba·sis (bā′sis) *n., pl.* **ba·ses** (bā′sēz). **1.** a fundamental supporting element; foundation: *the basis of an argument.* **2.** an underlying or guiding principle, as of a system of beliefs; premise. **3.** the main element or ingredient; base. **4.** an established or accepted standard: *to be paid on a weekly basis.* [Latin *basis* foundation, pedestal, from Greek *basis* step, pedestal.] —For Synonyms, see **base¹.**

bask (bask) *v.i.* **1.** to lie and enjoy a pleasant warmth: *to bask in the sun.* **2.** to take pleasure in favorable treatment or circumstances: *to bask in the glow of a smile.* [Possibly of Scandinavian origin.]

bas·ket (bas′kit) *n.* **1.a.** a container woven out of thin wooden strips, rods, or other flexible material: *a willow basket, a rope basket.* **b.** a container made of thin wooden slats in which fruit, vegetables, or certain other foodstuffs are packed and shipped: *a bushel basket of peaches, a pint basket of strawberries.* **2.** something resembling a basket in shape or function: *the basket in a clothes dryer, a wire bicycle basket.* **3.** the amount contained in a basket. **4.a.** *Basketball.* the metal hoop and circular net through which the ball is thrown in order to score. **b.** any passing of the ball through the hoop. **c.** a score, esp. the two-point score made when the ball is in open play. [Of Anglo-Norman origin.]

bas·ket·ball (bas′kit bôl′) *n.* **1.** a game played with a large, air-filled ball on a hard-surface court between two teams, officially of five players each (for men) and six each (for women). To score, a player on one team must toss the ball through a raised basket at the opponent's end of the court. **2.** the ball used in this game.

basket case *Slang.* **1.** a person whose four limbs have all been amputated. ➡ considered offensive. **2.** a completely incapable person.

bas·ket·ful (bas′kit fûl′) *n., pl.* **-fuls.** the amount that a basket holds.

bas·ket·ry (bas′ki trē) *n.* **1.** the art or trade of weaving baskets. **2.** baskets collectively.

basket weave, a loose weave in cloth made by interlacing two or more threads at the same time. It resembles the weave in a basket.

bas·ket·work (bas′kit wûrk′) *n.* wickerwork.

bas mitz·vah (bäs mits′və) bat mitzvah. [Yiddish *bas-mitsve,* from Hebrew *bat-mitsva.* See BAT MITZVAH.]

ba·so·phil (bā′sə fil) *also,* **ba·so·phile** (bā′sə fīl′, -fil). *n.* any cell, substance, or tissue element susceptible to staining by basic dyes, esp. certain white blood cells. [BAS(IC) + -PHILE.] —**ba′so·phil′ic,** *adj.*

Basque (bask) *n.* **1.** a member of a people of uncertain origin living in the Pyrenees in southwestern France and in northern Spain. **2.** the language of the Basque people, apparently having no relation to any other known language. **3.** **basque.** a woman's close-fitting bodice that extends over the hips to form a short overskirt. —*adj.* of, relating to, or characteristic of the Basques or their language or culture.

bas-re·lief (bä′ri lēf′, bas′-) *n.* a carving or sculpture on a flat surface, as a wall, in which the figures stand out only slightly from the background. Also, **low relief.** [French *bas-relief,* from Italian *bassorilievo,* going back to Late Latin *bassus* low + Latin *relevāre* to raise up.]

bas-relief from the palace of Darius, king of Persia

bass¹ (bās) *n., pl.* **bass·es.** **1.a.** the lowest part in harmonic music. **b.** the lower half of the audio frequency range. ➡ opposed to **treble.** **2.** the lowest male singing voice. **3.** a singer having such a voice. **4.** an instrument having the lowest range in a class of instruments, as a guitar or bass viol. —*adj.* **1.** able to sing or play bass: *a bass voice.* **2.** for the bass: *a bass score.* **3.** having the lowest range in a class of instruments: *a bass trombone.* **4.** deep or low in sound: *the bass rumble of thunder.* [Form of BASE²; influenced in spelling by Italian *basso* low.]

bass² (bas) *n., pl.* **bass** or **bass·es.** any of various edible species of freshwater or saltwater fish, esp. of the families Serranidae, Percichthyidae, and Centrarchidae, having spiny-rayed fins. [Modification of earlier *barse* perch, from Old English *bærs.*]

bass³ (bas) *n.* **1.** basswood or linden. **2.** bast. [Modification of BAST.]

bass clef (bās) the clef placed on the fourth line of the staff, indicating that the line corresponds to the note F below middle C. Also, **F clef.** For illustration, see **clef.**

bass drum (bās) a drum of the largest type. It gives off a deep, booming sound and is usually held so that both sides can be beaten. For illustration, see **percussion instrument.**

bas·set (bas′it) *n.* a short-legged breed of hound with a long body and drooping ears. Height: 14 inches (36 centimeters) at the shoulder. Also, **basset hound.** [French *basset,* from *bas* low; possibly referring to its low height.]

bass fiddle (bās) double bass.

bass horn (bās) tuba.

bas·si·net (bas′ə net′) *n.* **1.** a basketlike cradle, often on legs and hooded at one end, used esp. for newborn babies. **2.** a perambulator resembling this. [French *bassinet* small basin, diminutive of *bassin* basin, from Old French *bacin.* See BASIN.]

bass·ist (bā′sist) *n.* **1.** a person who plays a bass instrument, as the bass viol. **2.** a singer with a bass voice.

bas·so (bas′ō, bä′sō) *n., pl.* **bas·sos.** a bass singer, voice, or part. [Italian *basso* low, from Late Latin *bassus.*]

bas·soon (bə sün′) *n.* a wind instrument with a low range, the bass of the woodwind family, having a wooden tube so long that it doubles back on itself. It is played from the side through a curved metal mouthpiece containing the reed. [French *basson,* from Italian *bassone,* from *basso* low, from Late Latin *bassus.*]

bass vi·ol (bās′ vī′əl) double bass.

bass·wood (bas′wûd′) *n.* **1.** any of the several species of linden, genus *Tilia,* that grow in North America, esp. *T. americana.* **2.** the wood of such a tree, widely used in cabinetmaking and millwork. Also, **bass³.** [BASS³ + WOOD.]

bast (bast) *n.* **1.** the strong, flexible fibers obtained from the inner bark of several trees and from the stems or leaves of certain plants, used esp. in making cloth, rope, and heavy paper. **2.** phloem. Also, **bass³.** [Old English *bæst* inner bark.]

bas·tard (bas′tərd) *n.* **1.** an illegitimate child. **2.** something irregular, inferior, or counterfeit. —*adj.* **1.** illegitimate in birth. **2.** not genuine or standard; inferior or counterfeit: *to speak a bastard French.* **3.** abnormal or irregular in shape, size, or proportion. [Old French *bastard* illegitimate child, equivalent to Old French *fils de bast* child of a packsaddle (implying not of the marriage bed), from *bast* packsaddle, from Late Latin *bastum;* of uncertain origin.] —**bas′tard·ly,** *adj.* —**bas′tard·y,** *n.*

bas·tard·ize (bas′tər dīz′) *v.,* **-ized, -iz·ing.** —*v.t.* **1.** to lower or corrupt in condition or worth; debase. **2.** to declare (someone) to be of illegitimate birth. —*v.i.* to become debased. —**bas′tard·i·za′tion,** *n.*

baste¹ (bāst) *v.t.,* **bast·ed, bast·ing.** to apply melted butter, gravy, or other liquid to (food) while cooking: *The cook used a large spoon to baste the turkey.* [Of uncertain origin.] —**bast′er,** *n.*

baste² (bāst) *v.t.,* **bast·ed, bast·ing.** to sew with temporary stitches: *to baste a hem.* [Middle English *basten,* from Old French *bastir* to sew loosely; of Germanic origin.]

baste³ (bāst) *v.t.,* **bast·ed, bast·ing.** *Informal.* **1.** to beat soundly; thrash. **2.** to scold or abuse vigorously; berate. [Old Norse *beysta* to beat.]

Bas·tille (bas tēl′) *n.* **1.** a fortress in Paris used as a prison before the French Revolution. Its destruction on July 14, 1789, was one of the opening acts of the revolution. The anniversary of this date, **Bastille Day,** is celebrated as a national holiday in France. **2.** **bastille.** *also,* **bas·tile.** *Archaic.* a prison. [Old French *bastille* fortress, from Provençal *bastida* building, from *bastir* to build; of Germanic origin.]

bas·ti·na·do (bas′tə nā′dō) *n., pl.* **-does. 1.** a blow or beating with a stick, esp. on the soles of the feet. **2.** a stick; cudgel. —*v.t.,* **-doed, -do·ing.** to beat with a stick, esp. on the soles of the feet. [Spanish *bastonada* blow with a cudgel, from *baston* cudgel, from Late Latin *bastum* stick. See BATON.]

bast·ing¹ (bās′ting) *n.* **1.** the application of melted butter, gravy, or other liquid to food being cooked. **2.** the liquid used.

bast·ing² (bās′ting) *n.* **1.** the act of sewing with long, loose, temporary stitches. **2.** the thread used to make such stitches. **3.** **bastings.** the stitches made in basting. [From *baste².*]

bas·tion (bas′chən, -tē ən) *n.* **1.** the part of a rampart or fortification projecting from the main body and forming an irregular pentagon. For illustration, see **curtain. 2.** any fortified or firmly established place or position; stronghold: *a bastion of academic freedom.* [French *bastion,* from *bastille.* See BASTILLE.] —**bas′tioned,** *adj.*

bat¹ (bat) *n.* **1.** a wooden stick or club, esp. one used for hitting

the ball in baseball and other games. **2.** the act of batting. **3.** the right or turn to bat. **4.** *Informal.* a blow. **5.** *Slang.* a spree; binge. —*v.,* **bat·ted, bat·ting.** —*v.i.* **1.** to use a bat in baseball and other games. **2.** to take a turn at bat: *to bat next.* —*v.t.* **1.** to hit with or as with a bat. **2.** to have a batting average of (a certain figure): *to bat .319 for the season.* [Old English *batt* cudgel, club.]
- **at bat.** in the act or position of batting.
- **right off the bat.** *Informal.* at once; immediately: *I knew the answer right off the bat.*
- **to bat around.** *Slang.* **a.** to travel or go about without any particular purpose or destination: *The two friends batted around all summer.* **b.** to talk about in a free and easy way: *We batted around some ideas for a party.*
- **to go to bat for.** *Informal.* to give support to; defend: *My best friend went to bat for me when I was in trouble.*

bat² (bat) *n.* any of numerous mouselike mammals, with wing-like membranes supported by elongated forelimbs, order Chiroptera. They are mostly nocturnal and are the only flying mammals. Many bats guide themselves by echolocation, using the echo of their ultrasonic cries to judge the size and position of obstacles or insect prey. Others, such as fruit bats, orient visually. Wingspan: 2 inches to 5 feet (5 centimeters to 1.5 meters). [Middle English *bakke;* of Scandinavian origin.]

bat²

- **blind as a bat.** having very poor vision; nearly totally blind.
- **to have bats in one's (or the) belfry.** *Slang.* to be crazy or have crazy ideas.

bat³ *v.t.* **bat·ted, bat·ting.** *Informal.* to flutter; wink: *to bat one's eyelashes.* [Earlier *bate* to flap, beat one's wings, from Middle English *baten,* from Old French *batre* to beat, from Latin *battuere.*]
- **not bat an eye (or eyelash).** to fail to show any emotion or surprise.

bat., battery.

batch (bach) *n.* **1.** a number of persons or things taken together; group: *a batch of newspapers, a batch of recruits.* **2.** a quantity produced or done at one time: *The instructor just finished grading a batch of papers.* **3.** a quantity of material prepared or required for one operation: *a batch of dough, a batch of cement.* **4.** an amount baked at one time. **5.** a group of computer operations processed as a unit. [Middle English *bacche* a baking.]

bate (bāt) *v.t., v.i.* **bat·ed, bat·ing.** *Archaic.* to diminish or lessen; abate. [Short for ABATE.]
- **with bated breath.** with the breath checked or held because of anticipation, fear, or excitement: *Everyone waited for the astronauts' landing with bated breath.*

ba·teau (ba tō′) *n., pl.* **-teaux** (-tōz′). any of various light-weight, flat-bottomed boats used chiefly in the United States and Canada, esp. one having flaring sides and a pointed bow and stern. [French *bateau* boat, going back to Old English *bāt.*]

bat·fish (bat′fish′) *n., pl.* **-fish** or **-fish·es. 1.a.** any of a group of broad, flat marine fish, having pectoral fins at the end of a muscular base, that resemble flying bats when swimming. **b.** a batlike ray, *Myliobatis californica,* of the eastern Pacific. **2.** gurnard. [BAT² + FISH.]

bath (bath) *n., pl.* **baths** (bathz, baths). **1.** the washing or immersing of something, esp. the body, in water or other liquid. **2.** water or other liquid used for bathing: *The bath was too hot.* **3.** a container for such liquid, as a bathtub: *Clean out the bath when you're done.* **4.** a room equipped for bathing; bathroom: *a room and bath.* **5.** a set of rooms or a building for bathing: *the public baths of ancient Rome.* **6.** *also,* **baths.** a resort where bathing is part of a medical treatment; spa. **7.** a solution or other preparation in which something is immersed for chemical treatment: *an electrolytic bath.* [Old English *bæth* washing of the body, liquid for bathing.]

bathe (bāth) *v.,* **bathed, bath·ing.** —*v.i.* **1.** to take a bath. **2.** to go into a body of water, as the ocean, to swim for pleasure or to cool oneself; go swimming. **3.** to become covered or enveloped as if with liquid. —*v.t.* **1.** to immerse in liquid to clean; give a bath to: *to bathe a baby.* **2.** to wash or moisten with water or other liquid to cleanse or heal: *to bathe the eyes, to bathe a wound.* **3.** to make wet; moisten. **4.** to cover or envelop as if with liquid: *The stagehand pulled a switch, and the stage was bathed in light.* [Old English *bathian* to wash.] —**bath′er,** *n.*

ba·thet·ic (bə thet′ik) *adj.* characterized by bathos.

bath·house (bath′hous′) *n., pl.* **-hous·es** (-hou′ziz). **1.** a building equipped for bathing. **2.** a building having dressing rooms for swimmers.

bathing suit, a garment worn while swimming; swimsuit.

bath mat, 1. a mat or rug used to stand on when getting in or out of a shower or bathtub. **2.** a mat, usually rubber, placed on the bottom of a bathtub to prevent slipping.

bath·o·lith (bath′ə lith) *n.* a large mass of plutonic rock, up to hundreds of square miles in extent, whose roots lie deeply buried within the earth's crust. [Greek *bathos* depth + -LITH.]

ba·thos (bā′thos) *n.* **1.** a sudden and ludicrous descent from the lofty to the commonplace in speech or writing; anticlimax. For example: *The senator pledged to oppose war, fight poverty, protect individual freedom, and name a new state flower.* **2.** triteness or dullness. **3.** insincere or excessive pathos; sentimentality. [Greek *bathos* depth.]

bath·robe (bath′rōb′) *n.* a loose, coatlike garment worn before and after bathing or for lounging.

bath·room (bath′rüm′, -rùm′) *n.* a room usually equipped with a toilet, sink, and a bathtub or shower.

bath salts, crystals or flakes of a salt used in bath water to perfume and soften the skin.

bath·tub (bath′tub′) *n.* a tub in which to bathe, esp. one permanently fixed in a bathroom.

bath·y·al (bath′ē əl) *adj.* of or relating to ocean depths of from 700 to 9,800 feet (213 to 2,987 meters) or creatures inhabiting these depths. [Greek *bathys* deep + -AL¹.]

bath·y·scaphe (bath′ə skāf′, -skaf′) *also,* **bath·y·scaph** (bath′ə skaf′). *n.* a craft for deep-sea exploration, consisting of a thick-walled steel sphere suspended beneath a large hull. The crew and scientific instruments are carried in the sphere, and the hull is filled with gasoline, which makes it buoyant. A bathyscaphe has electric motors that enable it to move horizontally. [Greek *bathys* deep + *skaphē* light boat.]

bath·y·sphere (bath′ə sfir′) *n.* a hollow, watertight steel globe having heavy quartz observation windows and made to withstand great pressure, used for undersea exploration. A bathysphere is suspended by cable from a surface vessel and cannot move independently. [Greek *bathys* deep + *sphaira* ball, globe.]

ba·tik (bə tēk′, bat′ik) *n.* **1.** a method of hand printing colored designs on cloth by putting a wax coating on those parts that are not to be dyed. **2.** cloth decorated by this method. [Javanese *'mbatik* wax painting.]

ba·tiste (bə tēst′) *n.* any of several fine, soft, sheer fabrics of plain weave, made of cotton or other fibers. [French *batiste;* probably from *Baptiste* of Cambrai, a thirteenth-century French weaver believed to have invented the fabric.]

bat mitz·vah (bät mits′və) **1.** a ceremony signifying a Jewish girl's assumption of religious responsibilities upon reaching the age of thirteen. **2.** a girl for whom this ceremony is held. Also, **bas mitzvah.** [Hebrew *bat-mitsva,* from *bat* daughter of + *mitsva* commandment (from *tsiva* to order, command).]

ba·ton (bə ton′, ba-) *n.* **1.** a wand with which a conductor directs a musical performance. **2.** a rod with a knob at one or both ends, as used by a drum majorette or drum major. **3.** a short staff or truncheon used as a symbol of office, command, or authority: *a field marshal's baton.* **4.** a band on an escutcheon, used as a mark of illegitimacy in English heraldry. Also, **baton sinister. 5.** a short stick that is handed from one runner to the next in a relay race. [French *bâton,* from Old French *baston,* going back to Late Latin *bastum* stick.]

baton *(def. 4)*

ba·tra·chi·an (bə trā′kē ən) *n.* a frog or toad. —*adj.* of or relating to amphibians, esp. frogs and toads. [Greek *batrachos* frog + -IAN.]

bats·man (bats′mən) *n., pl.* **-men** (-mən). a batter, esp. in cricket.

bat·tal·ion (bə tal′yən) *n.* **1.** a military unit composed of two or more companies or comparable units and a headquarters company and forming part of a brigade or regiment. **2.** any large group or force; host: *a battalion of protesters, battalions of ants.* [French *battaillon,* from Italian *battaglione* unit of an army, from *battaglia* battle, going back to Late Latin *battuālia.* See BATTLE.]

a	at	e	end	o	hot	u	up	hw	white		(about
ā	ape	ē	me	ō	old	ū	use	ng	song		taken
ä	far	i	it	ô	fork	ü	rule	th	thin	ə	pencil
âr	care	ī	ice	oi	oil	ù	pull	th	this		lemon
		îr	pierce	ou	out	ûr	turn	zh	measure		(circus

bat·ten¹ (bat′ən) *Archaic. v.i.* to grow fat by or as by feeding; thrive. —*v.t.* to make fat. [Old Norse *batana* to get better.]

bat·ten² (bat′ən) *n.* **1.** a piece of sawed timber used esp. for flooring. **2.** a light strip of wood used in construction, esp. to cover or reinforce a joint between boards. **3.** *Nautical.* a long, narrow strip of wood or metal used for various purposes, as to secure a tarpaulin over a hatch. —*v.t.* **1.** to fasten, furnish, or strengthen with battens. **2.** *Nautical.* to fasten tarpaulins over (a ship's hatches), esp. in preparation for bad weather. [French *baton* small stick, from Late Latin *bastum* stick.]

bat·ter¹ (bat′ər) *v.t.* **1.** to strike or beat with heavy, repeated blows. **2.** to subject to rough, bruising usage; damage greatly: *The hurricane battered the coastal towns.* —*v.i.* to deal heavy, repeated blows; pound; hammer. [From BAT¹ + -ER⁴.]

bat·ter² (bat′ər) *n.* a mixture of flour, liquid, and other ingredients beaten together, prepared for use in cooking and thin enough to be poured or stirred. [Probably from BATTER¹.]

bat·ter³ (bat′ər) *n.* a player who is batting or whose turn it is to bat in baseball, softball, or cricket. [BAT¹ + -ER¹.]

battering ram, an ancient military machine, esp. a long, massive beam, used for battering down walls or gates.

bat·ter·y (bat′ə rē) *n., pl.* **-ter·ies. 1.** *Electricity.* a cell or group of cells producing and storing direct current by means of a chemical reaction. **2.** a group of things that are similar or related to one another and are assembled or used as a unit: *a battery of stage lights, a battery of blood tests.* **3.** *Military.* **a.** two or more guns or other weapons operating as a unit. **b.** these guns or other weapons together with the soldiers and equipment for them. **c.** the soldiers operating these weapons. **4.** *Law.* an unlawful beating, touching, or physical constraint of another person. ➡ distinguished from **assault. 5.** *Baseball.* a team's pitcher and catcher, considered as a unit. **6.** *Archaic.* a platform or fortification on which artillery is mounted. [French *batterie* beating, from *battre* to beat, from Latin *battuere.*]

bat·ting (bat′ing) *n.* **1.** the act or manner of using a bat, esp. in a game of ball. **2.** cotton or wool fibers that have been pressed into sheets or layers, used esp. in bandaging wounds or as padding for upholstery or quilts.

batting average, a mathematical average indicating the hitting ability of a baseball player, obtained by dividing the number of base hits by the number of official times at bat and carrying the result to three decimal places.

bat·tle (bat′əl) *n.* **1.** a fight between opposing armed forces, on land, at sea, or in the air. **2.** armed conflict; warfare; combat: *to die in battle.* **3.** any fight or conflict; struggle: *There was a battle between the two teams for first place.* —*v.,* **-tled, -tling.** —*v.i.* **1.** to engage in fighting: *The armies battled on the beach.* **2.** to struggle; contend: *to battle against temptation.* —*v.t.* to fight or struggle against: *The ship battled the waves.* [Old French *bataille* a fight, going back to Late Latin *battuālia* fighting exercises, from Latin *battuere* to beat.] —**bat′tler,** *n.*

bat·tle-ax (bat′əl aks′) *also,* **bat·tle-axe.** *n.* **1.** a wide-bladed ax, formerly used as a weapon in war. Also, **broadax. 2.** *Slang.* a quarrelsome, domineering woman.

battle cruiser, cruiser *(def. 1).*

battle cry 1. a shout or cry of troops in battle; war cry. **2.** a motto or slogan used in any contest or conflict: *"Down with poverty" was their battle cry.*

bat·tle·dore (bat′əl dôr′) *n.* a small racket used to hit a shuttlecock in the game of battledore and shuttlecock. [Middle English *batyldore,* from Provençal *batedor* implement for beating laundry, from *batre* to beat, from Latin *battuere;* influenced by BATTLE.]

battledore and shuttlecock, an ancient game from which the modern game of badminton was developed.

battle fatigue, a type of hysteria or psychoneurosis arising during combat and often marked by depression, loss of self-control, and great anxiety. Also, **combat fatigue.**

bat·tle·field (bat′əl fēld′) *n.* **1.** the scene of a battle. **2.** any area of conflict or struggle. Also, **bat′tle·ground′.**

bat·tle·front (bat′əl frunt′) *n.* a place where a battle is being fought; front.

bat·tle·ment (bat′əl mənt) *n.* a parapet having a series of indentations along its upper edge, used originally for defense and later for ornamentation. —**bat·tle·ment·ed** (bat′əl men′tid), *adj.* [Old French *batailler* to fortify with battlements, from *bataille.* See BATTLE.]

battle royal 1. a severe fight or struggle involving many people: *The police and the pickets had quite a battle royal.* **2.** a vehement, heated argument: *The discussion soon became a battle royal.*

bat·tle-scarred (bat′əl skärd′) *adj.*

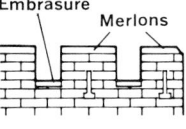

battlement

1. scarred from wounds received in or as in battle: *a battle-scarred boxer.* **2.** showing the effects of many trying experiences or much hard usage: *a battle-scarred desk.*

bat·tle·ship (bat′əl ship′) *n.* any of a class of heavily armored warships having the most powerful guns afloat.

battle wagon *Slang.* battleship.

bat·tue (ba tü′, -tū′) *n.* **1.** the act of beating the bushes and making loud noises to drive game out toward hunters. **2.** the hunt in which this is done. **3.** wholesale slaughter, esp. of defenseless crowds. [French *battue* beating, from *battre* to beat, going back to Latin *battuere.*]

bat·ty (bat′ē) *adj.,* **-ti·er, -ti·est.** *Slang.* crazy. [From *to have bats in one's belfry.* See BAT².]

bau·ble (bô′bəl) *n.* **1.** a showy, worthless trinket; trifle: *cheap bracelets and other baubles.* **2.** *Archaic.* a jester's staff. [Old French *ba(u)bel* toy.]

Bau·cis (bô′sis) *n.* in Greek mythology, an aged Phrygian woman who, along with her husband Philemon, was rewarded for showing hospitality to the disguised gods Zeus and Hermes.

baud (bôd) *n.* a unit for measuring the speed of data transmission, defined for microcomputers as 1 bit per second: *a modem that transmits data at 300 baud.* [From J.M.E. *Baudot,* 1845-1903, French inventor.]

baulk (bôk) *n.* balk.

baulk·y (bô′kē) *adj.* balky.

baux·ite (bôk′sīt, bō′zīt) *n.* a clayey sedimentary rock composed of several hydrous aluminum oxides. It is the chief ore of aluminum. [French *bauxite;* from Les *Baux,* the town in southeastern France where it was first found.]

baw·bee (bô bē′, bô′bē) *n. Scottish.* halfpenny.

bawd (bôd) *n.* **1.** a prostitute. **2.** *Archaic.* a person who runs a brothel. [Possibly from Old French *baud* licentious.]

bawd·ry (bô′drē) *n. Archaic.* obscenity or lewdness, esp. in language.

bawd·y (bô′dē) *adj.,* **bawd·i·er, bawd·i·est.** indecent or lewd; obscene. —**bawd′i·ly,** *adv.* —**bawd′i·ness,** *n.*

bawd·y·house (bô′dē hous′) *n., pl.* **-hous·es** (-hou′ziz). a brothel.

bawl (bôl) *v.i.* **1.** to weep or sob loudly; wail. **2.** to shout or yell; bellow: *The boss bawled at the worker for coming in late.* —*v.t.* to call out or proclaim noisily; shout: *The sergeant bawled commands to the recruits.* —*n.* a loud shout or outcry: *to let out a bawl of rage.* [Possibly of Scandinavian origin.] —**bawl′er,** *n.* **·to bawl out.** *Informal.* to scold or reprimand severely.

bay¹ (bā) *n.* an arm of a sea or lake extending into the land; broad inlet. [Old French *baie,* from Spanish *bahia.*]

bay² (bā) *n.* **1.** *Architecture.* **a.** a space or section of a wall or building that separates the whole into corresponding parts, as that between two columns. **b.** an internal recessed space forming an outward projection in a wall and containing a window or set of windows. **2.** a compartment or area in a ship or aircraft that is used for a particular purpose, as for carrying bombs or cargo. **3.** a compartment in a barn for storing hay or grain. **4.** a space or area for a car, as in a garage. [Old French *baée* opening, from *baer* to stand open.]

bay³ (bā) *n.* **1.** the deep, prolonged barking of a dog or other canine animal. **2.** the position of or as of a cornered animal that is forced to turn and confront its pursuers: *The boar stood at bay. The police brought the convict to bay.* **3.** the state of being held off by or as by one's quarry: *The bronco kept the cowboys at bay.* —*v.i.* to bark with a deep, prolonged howl: *hounds baying at their prey.* —*v.t.* **1.** to bark at: *The wolf bayed at the moon.* **2.** to utter or express by or as by barking: *The dogs bayed their anger.* [Old French *abaiier* to bark.]

bay⁴ (bā) *n.* **1.** a small, ornamental tree, *Laurus nobilus,* of the laurel family, widely cultivated in Europe and the Americas, having stiff lance-shaped leaves, purple berries, and yellowish flowers; laurel. **2.** any of various shrubs or trees resembling the laurel. [Middle French *baie* berry, from Latin *bāca.*]

bay⁵ (bā) *n.* **1.** a reddish brown color. **2.** a horse or other animal of this color. —*adj.* having the color bay. [Old French *bai* bay-colored, from Latin *badius.*]

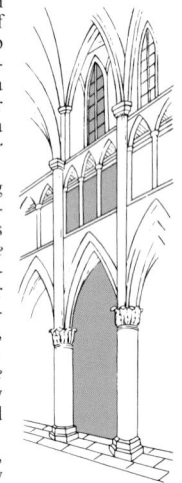

bay² *(def. 1a)*

bay·ber·ry (bā′ber′ē, -bə rē) *n., pl.* **-ries. 1.** a North American shrub, *Myrica pensylvanica,* having fragrant oblong leaves and pale blue, wax-coated berries. **2.** the small, round berry itself, used for making scented soaps and fragrant candles. **3.** a tropical American tree, *Pimenta racemosa,* of the myrtle family, having large leathery leaves that yield an oil that was once used in making bay rum.

Ba·yeux Tapestry (bā ū′, bä-) a medieval embroidery, probably made during the eleventh century, that depicts events leading to and including the Norman conquest of England. [From *Bayeux,* the French town in which it is kept.]

Bayeux Tapestry (detail)

bay leaf, the dried, spicy leaf of the bay tree, used as a seasoning in cooking.

bay·o·net (bā′ə nit, -net′) *n.* a large knife or dagger that can be attached to the muzzle of a rifle and used for stabbing or slashing in hand-to-hand fighting. —*v.t.,* **-net·ed, -net·ing.** to stab or slash with or as with a bayonet. [French *baïonnette* such a knife, from *Bayonne,* the French city where bayonets were first made.]

bay·ou (bī′ü, bī′ō) *n., pl.* **-ous.** a marshy, sluggish, sometimes stagnant inlet, branch, or overflowing of a river or gulf, esp. in the southern United States. [Louisiana French *bayou,* from Choctaw *bayuk* stream.]

bay rum, a fragrant liquid used in cosmetics and medicines, originally distilled from the leaves of the bayberry tree, but now prepared from a mixture of essential oils, alcohol, and water.

bay window 1. a window or set of windows projecting outward from the wall of a building and forming a recess within. **2.** *Slang.* a large protruding belly, esp. of a man; paunch.

ba·zaar (bə zär′) *also,* **ba·zar.** *n.* **1.** a sale of miscellaneous articles for some special purpose: *a charity bazaar.* **2.** a place for the sale of a variety of goods. **3.** in Middle and Far Eastern countries, a marketplace or street lined with shops or stalls. [Persian *bāzār* market.]

ba·zoo·ka (bə zü′kə) *n.* a portable tube-shaped weapon used for firing armor-piercing rockets, esp. against tanks.

BB *n., pl.* **BB′s** small shot, 0.18 inch (0.5 centimeter) in diameter, used esp. in a type of air rifle.

BBC, British Broadcasting Corporation.

BB gun, an air rifle that uses BB′s.

bbl *also,* **bbl.** *pl.* **bbls** barrel.

BC, the postal abbreviation for British Columbia.

B.C. *also,* **BC 1.** before Christ. ➡ used after a number to indicate a date occurring before the birth of Jesus. **2.** British Columbia.

B cell, any of the lymphocytes that secrete antibodies when activated by T cells. [Abbreviation of *B(ursa of Fabricius),* an organ in chickens analogous to the human thymus in which this cell was discovered.]

B complex, vitamin B complex.

bd. 1. board. **2.** bond. **3.** bound.

bd. ft., board foot; board feet.

bdl., bundle.

be (bē) *v.i.,* **been, being.** Present indicative: *sing.,* first person, **am**; second, **are** or *(archaic)* **art**; third, **is**; *pl.* **are.** Past indicative: *sing.,* first person, **was**; second, **were** or *(archaic)* **wast** or **wert**; third, **was**; *pl.* **were.** Present subjunctive: **be.** Past subjunctive: **were. 1.a.** to live or exist: *There are 120 tenants in that apartment building. There is much evidence against you.* **b.** to take place; happen; occur: *My birthday was last month. It had to be.* **c.** to occupy a place, situation, or position: *Your coat is on the chair. I am in debt.* **d.** to remain or continue as before: *Let me be.* **e.** *Archaic.* to belong or attend; befall: *Peace be with you.* **2.a.** used to link the subject with its predicate adjective or nomina-

tive to describe, identify, or amplify the subject: *John is tall. Let x be 10. She was president last year.* **b.** used to form or introduce interrogative or imperative sentences: *Is that true? Be still!* **c.** used to form participial and infinitive phrases: *the sorrow of being lonely, to be to blame.* **3.a.** used with the present participle of another verb to express continuous or progressive action: *He is talking. They are building a dam.* **b.** used with the past participle of a transitive verb to form the passive voice: *It is being washed. The book was found by the librarian.* **c.** used with the infinitive or participle of another verb to express future time, duty, possibility, or purpose: *The defendants were to appear before the judge. I am visiting them tomorrow.* **d.** used with the past participles of intransitive verbs to form the perfect tense: *I am done. They were gone.* [Old English *bēon.*]

Be, the symbol for beryllium.

be- *prefix* **1.** all around; all over; throughout: *besiege, besprinkle.* **2.** about: *bemoan.* **3.** cause to be; make: *betroth, bedazzle.* **4.** furnish with: *bejewel, bespeckled.* [Old English *be-* about, unstressed form of *bi* BY.]

beach (bēch) *n.* the gently sloping shore of an ocean or other body of water, esp. that part covered by sand or pebbles. —*v.t., v.i.* to run or haul (a boat) up onto a beach. [Of uncertain origin.]

beach buggy, dune buggy.

beach·comb·er (bēch′kō′mər) *n.* **1.a.** a vagrant or loafer who lives on the seashore. **b.** a person who collects shells and other salable objects on the seashore as a means of livelihood. **2.** a long wave that rolls in from the ocean and onto the beach; comber.

beach flea, sand flea *(def. 2).*

beach·head (bēch′hed′) *n.* **1.** an area on an enemy shore first seized and held to secure further operations. **2.** an initial advance position or foothold; breakthrough: *The new vaccine established a beachhead in the fight against the disease.*

beach plum 1. a shrubby plum, *Prunus maritima,* that grows in sandy coastal areas of northeastern North America, bearing showy white flowers and purple to yellow fruit. **2.** the edible fruit of this shrub, often used in preserves.

bea·con (bē′kən) *n.* **1.** a guiding or warning signal, esp. a light or fire. **2.** a lighthouse, buoy, or other object placed so as to guide or warn mariners. **3.** a radio beacon. **4.** anything that warns, signals, or guides. —*v.t.* **1.** to furnish or mark with beacons. **2.** to guide or warn by or as by beacons. —*v.i.* to serve or shine as a beacon. [Old English *bēacen* sign, signal.]

bead (bēd) *n.* **1.** a small, pierced ball or piece of wood, glass, or other material that can be strung on a thread or wire, used for decoration or other purposes: *the beads of a necklace, the beads of an abacus.* **2. beads. a.** a necklace of beads; a rosary. **3.** any small, roundish body, as of a liquid: *Beads of sweat formed on my brow.* **4.** a small, metal knob used as the front sight of a gun. **5.** *Architecture.* a small, convex molding, often cut in the form of a string of beads. —*v.t.* to furnish or decorate with beads or beading: *The dressmaker beaded the jacket.* —*v.i.* to collect in beads or drops: *Water beaded on the side of the glass.* [Middle English *bede* prayer, from Old English *gebed* prayer; later applied to rosary beads used in prayer and then to small balls or jewels strung together as ornaments.]

• **to draw a bead on.** to aim carefully at.

• **to say** (or **count** or **tell**) **one′s beads.** to say prayers with a rosary.

bead·ing (bē′ding) *n.* **1.** decorative work made of or with beads. **2.** material consisting of or decorated with beads. **3.** lace or embroidery having openwork through which ribbon may be run. **4.** *Architecture.* a narrow, convex molding.

bea·dle (bē′dəl) *n.* **1.** in the Church of England, a lay officer having such duties as ushering and keeping order during services. **2.** a minor official in a synagogue. [Middle English *bedel* herald, partly from Old English *bydel* minor church official; and partly from Old French *bedel;* of Germanic origin.]

bead·work (bēd′wûrk′) *n.* **1.** decorative work made of or with beads. **2.** *Architecture.* beads collectively.

bead·y (bē′dē) *adj.,* **bead·i·er, bead·i·est. 1.** (of eyes) small, round, and glittering. **2.** covered with or full of beads.

bea·gle (bē′gəl) *n.* a small, smooth-coated breed of hound having short legs, drooping ears, and usually white, tan, and black markings. Height: 9-15 inches (23-38 centimeters) at the shoulder. [Of uncertain origin.]

a	at	e	end	o	hot	u	up	hw	white	ə	{	about
ā	ape	ē	me	ō	old	ū	use	ng	song			taken
ä	far	i	it	ô	fork	ü	rule	th	thin			pencil
âr	care	ī	ice	oi	oil	u̇	pull	th	this			lemon
		îr	pierce	ou	out	ûr	turn	zh	measure			circus

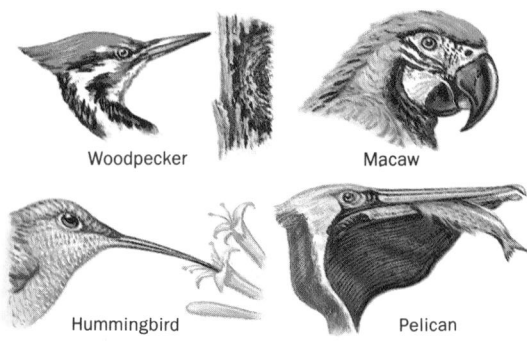

Woodpecker   Macaw

Hummingbird   Pelican

beaks

beak (bēk) *n.* **1.** the horny, projecting mouthpart of a bird; bill. **2.** a similar rigid, projecting part in other animals, as the horny jaws of turtles and certain cephalopods. **3.** something resembling a bird's beak, as the spout of a pitcher or the pointed end of an anvil. **4.** a pointed projection at the prow of an ancient warship, used to ram or pierce enemy ships. **5.** *Slang.* a person's nose, esp. if large or prominent. [Old French *bec* bird's bill, from Latin *beccus;* of Celtic origin.] —**beaked, beak′y,** *adj.* —For Synonyms, see **bill².**

beak·er (bē′kər) *n.* **1.** a cylindrical vessel of glass or other material, often having a lip for pouring, used esp. in laboratories. **2.** a large drinking cup or goblet with a wide mouth. **3.** the contents of a beaker. [Old Norse *bikarr* cup, from Late Latin *bīcārium* goblet.]

beam (bēm) *n.* **1.a.** a large, heavy piece of wood, steel, or other material, used in construction. **b.** one of the main horizontal supports of a building. **2.a.** a ray or shaft of light: *We saw the beam of headlights through the fog.* **b.** a narrow stream of subatomic particles or radiation: *a particle beam, a laser beam.* **3.** *Nautical.* **a.** one of the heavy pieces of timber stretching across a ship to support the decks and stay the sides. **b.** the greatest width of a ship. **c.** the side of a ship, or the direction at right angles to the keel. **4.** a continuous radio signal transmitted in one direction to guide pilots. **5.** a suggestion or hint; gleam: *a beam of hope.* **6.** the transverse bar of a balance, from which the scales are suspended. **7.** the horizontal part of a plow to which the handles and share are attached and by which it is pulled. **8.** *Slang.* the hips or buttocks. —*v.t.* **1.** to emit (light) in beams or rays: *The headlights beamed in the eyes of the oncoming drivers.* **2.** to direct or transmit (a broadcast or radio signal). **3.** to guide (an airplane) by radio beams: *The air-traffic controllers beamed the plane down safely.* —*v.i.* **1.** to shine brightly; radiate: *The sun beamed down.* **2.** to smile radiantly or joyfully: *The members of the debating team beamed with pride as they accepted the award.* [Old English *bēam* tree, ray.]
· **off the beam. a.** not following the course indicated by a radio beam. **b.** *Informal.* not correct; wrong: *The weather report was certainly off the beam to predict heavy rains for such a bright, sunny day.*
· **on the beam. a.** following the course indicated by a radio beam. **b.** *Nautical.* at right angles with a ship's keel. **c.** *Informal.* correct; right.

Synonyms *n.* **Beam, shaft,** and **ray** mean a column of light. **Beam** suggests enough width to be visible as more than a line: *a beam of moonlight coming through the window.* **Shaft** also suggests visible width but appears more often in literary or general than in scientific contexts: *Shafts of sunlight warmed the valley.* **Ray** suggests a central point from which the light emanates and is used of even the narrowest column: *The sun's rays extend in all directions. A ray of the setting sun penetrated the crack in the wall.*

beam-ends (bēm′endz′) *n.* the ends of a ship's beams.
· **on her** (or **the**) **beam-ends.** (of a ship) tipped so far over that the beams are almost vertical; almost capsizing.

beam·ing (bē′ming) *adj.* bright; shining; radiant: *a beaming smile, a beaming face.* —**beam′ing·ly,** *adv.*

bean (bēn) *n.* **1.** the seed of any of various plants of the pea family, some varieties of which are edible, esp. the genera *Phaseolus* and *Vicia.* **2.** the elongated pod containing several such seeds. The pods of some varieties are cooked and eaten as a vegetable with the seed still inside. **3.** the plant that produces these pods. **4.** a beanlike seed of various other unrelated plants, as the coffee bean and the cacao bean. **5.** *Slang.* the head. —*v.t. Slang.* to hit on the head, esp. with a pitched baseball. [Old English *bēan* common leguminous plant or its seed.]
· **full of beans.** *Informal.* full of energy; active; vigorous.
· **to spill the beans.** *Informal.* to reveal a secret, esp. unintentionally.

bean·bag (bēn′bag′) *n.* a small cloth bag filled with beans and used in certain games.

bean·ball (bēn′bôl′) *n.* a baseball deliberately pitched at or near the batter's head.

bean curd, tofu.

bean·er·y (bē′nə rē) *n., pl.* **-er·ies.** a cheap restaurant. [BEAN + -ERY.]

bean·ie (bē′nē) *n.* a small, brimless cap.

bean·pole (bēn′pōl′) *n.* **1.** a tall pole for a growing bean plant to climb on. **2.** *Slang.* a tall, thin person.

bean sprout, the sprout of certain beans, especially the mung bean, used as a vegetable in salads and in cooking.

bean·stalk (bēn′stôk′) *n.* the main stem of a bean plant.

bear¹ (bâr) *v.,* **bore** or *(archaic)* **bare, borne** or **born, bearing.** —*v.t.* **1.** to hold up; support: *Beams bear the weight of the roof.* **2.** to possess as a feature, characteristic, or attribute; show; display: *The letter bears his signature. She bears a striking resemblance to her cousin.* **3.** to carry; transport: *The elevator bore us to the top floor. My friends always bear gifts when they visit.* **4.** to suffer or endure; undergo: *He bore the brunt of the punishment. I can't bear her rudeness.* **5.** to bring forth or give birth to; produce: *to bear fruit, to bear young.* **6.** to hold in the mind; entertain: *to bear a grudge.* **7.** to accept or acknowledge; assume: *to bear the blame, to bear the expense.* **8.** to conduct or guide; escort: *They bore their sick friend to the hospital.* **9.** to communicate or spread; convey: *to bear tidings.* **10.** to move or push by pressing against; thrust: *The crowd bore us along.* **11.** to be fit for or worthy of; demand; require: *That new actor bears watching. The case bears investigating.* **12.** to give; render: *to bear testimony.* **13.** to carry or conduct (oneself): *The dancers bore themselves gracefully.* **14.** to be able to withstand; allow: *This evidence won't bear scrutiny.* **15.** to have or stand in (a relationship): *Demand bears a relation to supply.* **16.** *Archaic.* to exercise; wield: *to bear sway.* —*v.i.* **1.** to lean or press; weigh: *Financial worries bear heavily upon them.* **2.** to lie or move in a particular direction: *to bear east.* **3.** to bring forth young or fruit. [Old English *beran* to carry, support.]
· **to bear down. a.** to press or weigh down: *The heavy bundle bore me down.* **b.** to make a strong effort; exert oneself: *The runner bore down during the last lap of the race.*
· **to bear down on** (or **upon**). **a.** to make a great effort toward; strive harder at: *to bear down on the task at hand.* **b.** to exert pressure on; press hard: *to bear down on a pencil and break the point.* **c.** to approach rapidly: *The police bore down on the getaway car.*
· **to bear on** (or **upon**). to affect or relate to; be relevant to: *This evidence bears on the testimony.*
· **to bear out.** to confirm or support; corroborate: *The facts bear out my story.*
· **to bear up.** to undergo stress or strain without yielding; endure: *to bear up under hardship.*
· **to bear with.** to be patient or tolerant toward: *Bear with my faults.*
· **to bring to bear.** to apply or exert; employ: *to bring experience to bear, to bring pressure to bear.*

Synonyms *v.t.* **Bear¹, stand,** and **endure** mean to undergo and survive something painful or difficult. **Bear** suggests the strength or capacity to carry a burden or sustain a blow: *The news of her son's death was almost too much for the woman to bear.* **Stand** has almost the same meaning, except that it is used more often of matters of taste than of physical or emotional suffering: *I can't stand any more of that music!* **Endure** emphasizes the time through which one has to withstand something: *The patient endured great pain for hours.* For other Synonyms *(v.t.),* see **carry.**

bear² (bâr) *n.* **1.** any of various thickset mammals, family Ursidae, of North and South America, Asia, Europe, and the Arctic, having coarse, thick fur, powerful legs and claws, and a short, stumpy tail. Bears, the largest carnivorous land animals, range in size from 3 to 9 feet (0.9 to 2.7 meters) long. **2.** any of various animals thought to resemble the bear, as the ant bear and the koala bear. **3.** a gruff, surly, or clumsy person. **4.** a speculator, esp. one in the stock market, who attempts to bring down prices or who anticipates a decline in prices and sells in order to be able to buy back at a lower rate. ➡ opposed to **bull.** —*adj.* marked by or relating to falling prices, as of stocks: *to lose money in a bear market.* [Old English *bera,* mammal of the family Ursidae.]

bear·a·ble (bâr′ə bəl) *adj.* capable of being borne or endured; tolerable. —**bear′a·bly,** *adv.*

bear·bait·ing (bâr′bā′ting) *n.* the former sport of setting dogs on a chained bear.

bear·ber·ry (bâr′ber′ē, -bə rē) *n., pl.* **-ries.** any of several hardy, trailing evergreen shrubs of the genus *Arctostaphylos* of the heath family, esp. *A. uva-ursi,* found on sandy or rocky soils in northern regions, having branched stems, clusters of small white flowers, and red fruit or *A. alpina,* found in Arctic regions and mountains of the Northern Hemisphere, having black fruit.

beard (bîrd) *n.* **1.** a growth of hair on the cheeks, chin, and throat, esp. of a man. **2.** a growth or appendage resembling a beard, as the hair on the chin of a goat or the bristles near the beak of certain birds. **3.** a tuft or covering of awns or other hairlike growths, as on the head of a stalk of wheat. For illustration, see **wheat.** —*v.t.* **1.** to furnish with a beard. **2.** to confront or defy (an opponent or difficulty) resolutely. [Old English *beard* hair on the face.]

beard·ed (bîr′did) *adj.* having a beard.

beard·less (bîrd′lis) *adj.* having no beard.

bear·er (bâr′ər) *n.* **1.** a person or thing that carries, supports, or brings: *a flag bearer, a bearer of good news.* **2.** a person who holds or presents a check or other order for payment of money. **3.** a pallbearer. **4.** a tree or plant that yields fruit or flowers.

bearer bond, a bond that is not registered to any specific person and may be presented for payment by whoever holds it.

bear hug, a tight, vigorous hug. [From *bear²*.]

bear·ing (bâr′ing) *n.* **1.** a manner of carrying or conducting oneself; carriage; behavior: *a regal bearing.* **2.** relevance or relation; connection: *Your comments have no bearing on the matter.* **3. bearings.** an awareness or comprehension of one's environment, situation, or relative position: *We lost our bearings in the snowstorm.* **4.** a direction or position in relation to another point or to the points of a compass. **5.** a part of a machine that holds or supports moving parts and reduces friction and wear, as a ball bearing or a roller bearing. **6.** the act or capacity of enduring; endurance: *That person's insolence is beyond bearing.* **7.** the act, capacity, or period of producing or bringing forth: *a tree past bearing.* **8.** any single device in a coat of arms.

bear·ish (bâr′ish) *adj.* **1.** rough or cross; gruff. **2.** marked by, tending toward, or expecting a decline in the price of stocks. —**bear′ish·ly,** *adv.* —**bear′ish·ness,** *n.*

bear·skin (bâr′skin′) *n.* **1.** the skin of a bear. **2.** a tall, black fur cap, as that worn by Buckingham Palace guards.

beast (bēst) *n.* **1.** any animal other than a human being, esp. a four-footed mammal: *the beasts of the forest.* **2.** a coarse, brutal, or contemptible person. [Old French *beste* animal, going back to Latin *bēstia.*] —For Synonyms, see **animal.**

beast·ly (bēst′lē) *adj.,* **-li·er, -li·est. 1.** brutal or coarse; bestial. **2.** *Informal.* very unpleasant; disagreeable; nasty: *beastly weather.* —*adv. Informal.* very: *It's beastly hot today.* —**beast′·li·ness,** *n.*

beast of burden, an animal used for carrying or pulling loads, as an ox or a mule.

beat (bēt) *v.,* **beat, beat·en** or **beat, beat·ing.** —*v.t.* **1.** to deal repeated blows to so as to hurt; thrash. **2.** to strike or hit repeatedly; pound: *to beat a drum.* **3.** to dash against: *The waves beat the shore.* **4.** to drive or force by or as by blows: *The soldiers beat back the invaders.* **5.** to defeat or outdo: *I always beat my friend at checkers.* **6.** to flap repeatedly or vigorously: *The bird beat its wings against the cage.* **7.** to form, shape, or flatten by hammering: *to beat a horseshoe into shape.* **8.** to stir vigorously: *Beat the yolks and whites separately.* **9.** to sound or signal, as on a drum: *to beat a steady rhythm.* **10.** to mark or measure (time or rhythm), as with a baton or by tapping the foot. **11.** to hunt through in order to flush or locate quarry; scour: *to beat the bushes for game.* **12.** to surpass or be superior to: *That product certainly beats the competition. This book beats all others in length. Ordering merchandise by telephone beats shopping in a crowded store.* **13.** to make (a path) by frequent treading or passage. **14.** to offset, avoid, or circumvent the effects of: *The children beat the heat by going swimming.* **15.** *Informal.* to bewilder or perplex; baffle: *It beats me how you get such high grades without studying.* —*v.i.* **1.** to strike repeatedly: *The rain beat against the windows.* **2.** to throb; pulsate: *The heart beats rhythmically.* **3.** to strike as if with blows: *The sun beat into my face.* **4.** to sound upon being struck: *The drums beat in time to the march.* **5.** to strike a drum. **6.** to permit beating: *The cake batter doesn't beat smoothly.* **7.** *Nautical.* to move against the wind by tacking: *to beat to windward.* —*n.* **1.** a stroke or blow. **2.** a rhythmic sequence of sounds or movements; pulsation: *the beat of the drums, the beat of the heart.* **3.** an assigned or regular course; habitual round: *a police officer's beat, a reporter's beat.* **4.** *Music.* an accent or unit of time. **5.** a pattern of recurrence of stressed syllables in a line or stanza of poetry; rhythm. **6. beats.**

Physics. the regularly recurring pulsation heard when sound waves of slightly different frequencies combine. **7.** *Slang.* the reporting of a news story ahead of one's competitors; scoop. —*adj. Informal.* **1.** worn out; weary; exhausted. **2.** of, like, or relating to beatniks or to the beat generation. [Old English *bēatan* to strike repeatedly.]

• **to beat a retreat.** to withdraw quickly.

• **to beat around** (or **about**) **the bush.** *Informal.* to approach a matter or subject in a roundabout way; avoid coming to the point.

• **to beat down.** *Informal.* to cause (a seller) to lower the price.

• **to beat it.** *Slang.* to leave in a hurry; leave at once.

• **to beat up.** *Informal.* to give a beating to; thrash.

Synonyms	*v.t.* **Beat** and **pound** mean to hit or strike repeatedly. **Pound,** having a heavier sound, is used to suggest particularly heavy and noisy blows: *I beat the door with my fists for a while, but it wasn't until I really started pounding it that someone heard me.*

beat·en (bē′tən) *v.* a past participle of **beat.** —*adj.* **1.** formed or shaped by blows; hammered: *beaten gold.* **2.** worn by use; commonly used: *a beaten path.* **3.** thwarted or vanquished; defeated: *a beaten enemy.* **4.** mixed or whipped by vigorous stirring: *Add a beaten egg.*

beat·er (bē′tər) *n.* **1.** a person or thing that beats, esp. an implement or device used for beating: *a rug beater.* **2.** a person who flushes game during a hunt.

beat generation, a group of people belonging to the generation that reached adulthood after the Korean War, who expressed disillusionment with middle-class values. They were characterized by their unconventional dress and their interest in the arts, esp. jazz and poetry. [Supposedly coined by Jack Kerouac, 1922-70, U.S. novelist.]

be·a·tif·ic (bē′ə tif′ik) *adj.* imparting or expressing bliss or blessedness; blissful: *a beatific smile.* —**be′a·tif′i·cal·ly,** *adv.*

be·at·i·fi·ca·tion (bē at′ə fi kā′shən) *n.* **1.** the act of beatifying or the state of being beatified. **2.** in the Roman Catholic Church, the act whereby the pope declares a deceased person to be one of the blessed in heaven and entitled to public reverence within a certain locality or group. It is one of the steps toward canonization.

be·at·i·fy (bē at′ə fī′) *v.t.,* **-fied, -fy·ing. 1.** to make extremely happy. **2.** in the Roman Catholic Church, to declare the beatification of. [Late Latin *beātificāre* to make happy, from Latin *beātus* happy + *facere* to make.]

beat·ing (bē′ting) *n.* **1.** the act of a person or thing that beats. **2.** a series of forceful blows; thrashing. **3.** throbbing; pulsation: *the beating of the heart.* **4.** a severe loss or defeat: *The speculator took a beating on the stock market. The opposing team gave us quite a beating.* **5.** rough or damaging treatment: *The car took a beating on those unpaved roads.*

be·at·i·tude (bē at′i tūd′, -tōōd′) *n.* **1.** extreme happiness or blessedness; bliss. **2. the Beatitudes.** in the New Testament, the pronouncements made by Jesus in the Sermon on the Mount blessing those who possess particular virtues. Each Beatitude begins with "Blessed are." [Latin *beātitūdō* happiness.]

beat·nik (bēt′nik) *n.* a member of the beat generation. [BEAT + -NIK.]

Be·a·trice (bē′ə tris) *n.* the idealized and symbolic figure in Dante's *Divine Comedy* who was based on the woman he loved.

beat-up (bēt′up′) *adj. Informal.* worn out from overuse or abuse; shabby: *We threw out our beat-up sofa with the broken springs.*

beau (bō) *n., pl.* **beaux** (bōz) or **beaus. 1.** a sweetheart or lover of a girl or woman; boyfriend. **2.** a man who is overly concerned about his clothes and appearance; dandy. [French *beau* fine, handsome, from Latin *bellus.*]

Beau Brum·mell (bō′ brum′əl) a fop; dandy. [From George Bryan *(Beau) Brummell,* 1778-1840, English leader of society and men's fashion.]

Beau·fort scale (bō′fərt) the internationally used scale of wind velocities, ranging from 0 for speeds of less than 1 mile (1.6 kilometers) per hour (calm) to 12 for speeds above 75 miles (120.7 kilometers) per hour (hurricane). [From Sir Francis *Beaufort,* 1774-1857, British admiral who originated it.]

beau geste (bō zhest′) *pl.* **beaux gestes** (bō zhest′). **1.** a gracious or noble gesture. **2.** such an act or gesture when made

a	at	e	end	o	hot	u	up	hw	white		about
ā	ape	ē	me	ō	old	ū	use	ng	song		taken
ä	far	i	it	ô	fork	ū	rule	th	thin	ə	pencil
âr	care	ī	ice	oi	oil	u̇	pull	th	this		lemon
		î	pierce	ou	out	ûr	turn	zh	measure		circus

105

only for selfish reasons or for effect. [French *beau geste* handsome gesture, from Latin *bellus* handsome + *gestus* gesture.]

beau ideal *pl.* beau ideals or beaux ideals. an ideal of excellence or beauty; perfect type or model. [French *beau idéal,* from Latin *bellus* handsome + Late Latin *ideālis.* See IDEAL.]

beau monde (bō′ mond′) the fashionable world; society. [French *beau monde,* from Latin *bellus* handsome + *mundus* world.]

beau·te·ous (būˈtē əs) *adj.* beautiful. —**beau′te·ous·ly,** *adv.* —**beau′te·ous·ness,** *n.*

beau·ti·cian (bū tishˈən) *n.* a hairdresser or cosmetologist.

beau·ti·ful (būˈtə fəl) *adj.* possessing qualities that please the mind or senses; full of beauty. —**beau′ti·ful·ly,** *adv.* —**beau′ti·ful·ness,** *n.*

> **Synonyms** **Beautiful, lovely, pretty,** and **handsome** mean pleasing or delightful to the senses or to the aesthetic function of the mind. **Beautiful** has the widest application, suggesting a standard of perfection: *a beautiful piece of music, a beautiful evening, a beautiful cat.* **Lovely** suggests an emotional reaction rather than an intellectual judgment: *I could hardly bear to leave such a lovely place.* **Pretty** stresses such characteristics as grace, delicacy, and charm and may imply superficial or transient rather than deep or lasting appeal: *a pretty face that coarsened with age.* When used of people, *beautiful, lovely,* and *pretty* are almost always applied to females. **Handsome** suggests excellence of form, and sometimes dignity, stateliness, or impressiveness: *The architect designed a handsome mahogany-paneled courtroom.* When used of people, it is applied most often to males but sometimes to stately females.

beau·ti·fy (būˈtə fī′) *v.t.,* **-fied, -fy·ing.** to make beautiful or add beauty to. —**beau′ti·fi·ca′tion,** *n.* —**beau′ti·fi′er,** *n.*

beau·ty (būˈtē) *n., pl.* **-ties. 1.** a quality or combination of qualities that pleases the senses or mind: *the beauty of a sunset.* **2.** a person or thing that is beautiful: *Our grandchild is quite a beauty. That yacht is a beauty.* **3.** an outstanding or particularly pleasing feature or part: *The beauty of these pots is that they need never need scouring.* [Middle English *beaute,* from Old French *biauté,* going back to *bellus* pretty.]

beauty mark, a mole or other small mark on the skin.

beauty parlor, an establishment offering hair care, manicures, and the like, esp. to women. Also, **beauty salon, beauty shop.**

beauty spot, a beauty mark, esp. a patch put on the face to set off its whiteness.

beaux (bōz) a plural of **beau.**

beaux-arts (bō zär′) *n. French.* the fine arts.

bea·ver[1] (bēˈvər) *n.* **1.** an aquatic rodent, genus *Castor,* having sharp incisors, webbed hind feet, grayish fur, and a broad, flat tail. It builds its lodge in or on the banks of shallow streams and constructs a dam of branches, stones, and mud to protect it. There are two species, the American beaver, *C. canadensis,* and the Eurasian beaver, *C. fiber.* Length: 3-4 feet (0.9-1.2 meters), including tail. **2.** the fur of this animal. **3.** a heavy woolen cloth finished with a thick nap. **4.** a man's top hat, originally made of beaver fur. [Old English *beofor* this animal.]

beaver[1]

bea·ver[2] (bēˈvər) *n.* the movable part of a helmet in a suit of armor, used to protect the mouth and chin. For illustration, see **armor.** [Old French *baviere* beaver of a helmet, bib.]

bea·ver·board (bēˈvər bôrd′) *n.* a thin, stiff material made of compressed wood fibers, used for partitions, ceilings, and temporary structures.

be·bop (bēˈbop′) *n.* a style of jazz developed in the 1940s, characterized by complex harmony, extreme variation in rhythmic pattern, and very rapid tempos. [Imitative of a staccato two-beat phrase typical of this music.]

be·calm (bi käm′) *v.t.* **1.** to keep motionless by a lack of wind. **2.** to make calm or still; quiet. —**be·calmed′,** *adj.*

be·came (bi kām′) the past tense of **become.**

be·cause (bi kôz′, -kuz′) *conj.* **1.** due to the fact that; since: *I was cold because I forgot my sweater.* **2.** the fact that; that: *The reason we're late is because there was a lot of traffic on the road.* [Middle English *bi cause* literally, by cause. See BY, CAUSE.]
• **because of.** by reason of; on account of: *I went swimming because of the heat.*

be·chance (bi chans′) *v.t., v.i.,* **-chanced, -chanc·ing.** to befall.

beck (bek) *n. Archaic.* a nod or other gesture given as a summons or command. —*v.t., v.i. Archaic.* to beckon. [Short for BECKON.]
• **at one's beck and call.** subject to a person's slightest wish; ready to do a person's bidding.

beck·on (bekˈən) *v.t., v.i.* **1.** to signal, summon, or direct by a sign or gesture: *She beckoned me aside. He beckoned for the waiter with his hand.* **2.** to be inviting or enticing (to); attract: *The smell of bread beckoned the hungry child. The pool beckoned on such a hot day.* [Old English *bīecnan,* to indicate, signify.]

be·cloud (bi kloud′) *v.t.* to obscure with or as with clouds: *to becloud an issue with unrelated arguments.*

be·come (bi kum′) *v.,* **-came** (-kām′), **-come, -com·ing.** —*v.i.* to come to be; grow to be: *The tired child became cranky. Tadpoles become frogs.* —*v.t.* **1.** to look attractive or well on; suit: *Blue becomes you.* **2.** to be appropriate for; befit: *Rudeness does not become him.* [Old English *becuman* to happen.]
• **to become of.** to be the condition or fate of; happen to: *Whatever became of your childhood friend? What has become of my umbrella?*

be·com·ing (bi kumˈing) *adj.* **1.** looking well on; attractive; flattering: *a becoming hat.* **2.** suitable; appropriate: *conduct not becoming to an officer.* —**becom′ing·ly,** *adv.*

bed (bed) *n.* **1.** a piece of furniture upon which to sleep or rest, often consisting of a mattress and springs in a bedstead. **2.** any place or thing used for sleeping or resting: *The hayloft was the cat's bed.* **3.** something resembling a bed in shape or function: *a bed of leaves.* **4.** sleeping accommodations for the night; lodging. **5.** a piece of ground used for planting: *beds of roses and tulips.* **6.** the ground at the bottom of a body of water, as the seabed: *the bed of a stream, a lake bed.* **7.** a part or surface serving as a foundation or support: *a railroad bed.* **8.** layer; stratum: *The miners dug through beds of sand and clay.* —*v.,* **bed·ded, bed·ding.** —*v.t.* **1.** to provide with a place to sleep: *to bed guests in a spare room.* **2.** to put or take to bed. **3.** to set or plant in the ground: *to bed rose bushes.* **4.** to fix or set firmly; embed: *to bed cobblestones in mortar.* **5.** to lay flat or arrange in layers: *to bed oysters.* —*v.i.* **1.** to go to bed. **2.** to form a layer; stratify. [Old English *bed* couch to sleep on, ground for planting.]
• **bed and board.** sleeping accommodations and meals: *Day students at the school live at home, whereas resident students pay for bed and board.*
• **to bed down. a.** to provide with a place to sleep: *to bed down cattle in a barn.* **b.** to go to bed; sleep: *I told my friend I would bed down on the sofa.*
• **to get up on the wrong side of the bed.** to be irritable or cross.
• **to make one's bed and lie in it.** to create a situation and suffer the consequences.
• **to put to bed.** *Slang.* to complete work on (a newspaper or other publication).
• **to take to one's bed.** to go to bed because of illness.

bed-and-break·fast (bedˈən brekˈfəst) *n.* an inn, private home, or hotel that provides lodging and breakfast for one price. —*adj.* of, relating to, or designating such accommodations: *a bed-and-breakfast place.*

be·daub (bi dôb′) *v.t.* to smear with something dirty.

be·daz·zle (bi dazˈəl) *v.t.,* **-zled, -zling. 1.** to impress or charm greatly; overwhelm: *I was bedazzled by the child's smile.* **2.** to blind, as by excessive light.

bed·bug (bedˈbug′) *n.* any of a widespread group of wingless, bloodsucking insects, family Cimicidae, esp. *Cimex lectularius,* that often infests beds and upholstery.

bed·cham·ber (bedˈchām′bər) *n.* bedroom.

bed·clothes (bedˈklōz′, -klōthz′) *pl. n.* coverings, as sheets and blankets, used on a bed.

bed·ding (bedˈing) *n.* **1.** bedclothes. **2.** materials for a bed: *The farmer used straw for the oxen's bedding.* **3.** a bottom layer; foundation: *a bedding of gravel for a road.* **4.** *Geology.* stratification.

be·deck (bi dek′) *v.t.* to cover with ornaments; adorn.

be·dev·il (bi devˈəl) *v.t.,* **-iled, -il·ing;** *also, British,* **-illed, -il·ling. 1.** to worry or harass; plague; torment. **2.** *Archaic.* to possess with or as with a devil; bewitch. —**be·dev′il·ment,** *n.*

be·dew (bi dü′, -dü′) *v.t. Archaic.* to moisten with or as with dew.

bed·fast (bedˈfast′) *adj. Archaic.* bedridden.

bed·fel·low (bedˈfel′ō) *n.* **1.** a person who shares a bed with another. **2.** a companion or ally; associate: *Politics makes strange bedfellows.*

Bed·ford cord (bedˈfərd) a heavy durable cloth having lengthwise ribs, used for such items as coats, uniforms, and riding habits.

be·dight (bi dīt′) *v.t.,* **-dight, -dight** or **-dight·ed, -dight·ing.** *Archaic.* to dress or adorn; array. [BE- + DIGHT.]

be·dim (bi dim′) *v.t.,* -**dimmed, -dim·ming.** to make dim; obscure.

Bed·i·vere (bed′ə vîr′) *n.* in Arthurian legend, the loyal knight who brought the dying King Arthur to the barge that then bore Arthur to Avalon.

be·di·zen (bi dī′zən, -diz′ən) *v.t. Archaic.* to dress or adorn gaudily. [BE- + DIZEN.]

bed jacket, a short, loose robe for the upper part of the body, usually worn over a nightgown.

bed·lam (bed′ləm) *n.* **1.** a scene or situation marked by wild uproar and confusion: *It was bedlam at the department store during the sale.* **2. Bedlam.** the Hospital of Saint Mary of Bethlehem in London, used since 1547 as an insane asylum. **3.** *Archaic.* an insane asylum; madhouse. [Modification of *Bethlehem* in Hospital of Saint Mary of Bethlehem.]

bed·lam·ite (bed′lə mīt′) *n. Archaic.* an insane person; lunatic.

bed linen, bedclothes, esp. sheets and pillowcases.

Bed·ling·ton terrier (bed′ling tən) *n.* any of an English breed of rough-coated, medium-sized terriers, bluish or brownish in color, resembling a lamb. [From *Bedlington,* England.]

Bed·ou·in (bed′ü in, bed′win) *n.* **1.** a member of a large group of nomadic Arab tribes who inhabit the desert regions of North Africa and the Middle East. **2.** a wanderer; nomad. —*adj.* of, relating to, or characteristic of the Bedouins. [French *bédouin,* from Arabic *badāwīn* literally, desert dwellers.]

bed·pan (bed′pan′) *n.* a pan used as a toilet by someone confined to bed.

bed·post (bed′pōst′) *n.* one of the vertical supports at the corners of certain beds.

be·drag·gle (bi drag′əl) *v.t.,* -**gled, -gling.** to make wet, soiled, or disheveled, as with rain or dirt.

be·drag·gled (bi drag′əld) *adj.* **1.** wet, soiled, and limp, as though drenched by rain. **2.** messy or soiled, as though dragged through mire.

bed·rid·den (bed′rid′ən) *adj.* confined to bed: *Pneumonia kept the patient bedridden for weeks.* Also, **bed′rid′.** [Old English *bedreda* paralyzed person, from *bed* bed + *rida* rider.]

bed·rock (bed′rok′) *n.* **1.** the solid rock underlying the looser materials of the earth's surface. **2.** a firm foundation; basis: *The medical theory was built on a bedrock of years of research.* **3.** the lowest point or level; bottom.

bed·roll (bed′rōl′) *n.* a sleeping bag, blankets, or other bedding that can be rolled up and carried, usually used for sleeping outdoors.

bed·room (bed′rüm′, -rùm′) *n.* a room for sleeping.

bed·side (bed′sīd′) *n.* the side of a bed, esp. of a sick person.

bedside manner, the attitude or manner that a doctor assumes toward patients.

bed·sore (bed′sôr′) *n.* a skin ulceration caused by prolonged pressure against a bed, occurring among persons bedridden for long periods.

bed·spread (bed′spred′) *n.* a covering placed on a bed for protective or decorative purposes.

bed·stead (bed′sted′) *n.* the framework that supports the springs and mattress of a bed.

bed·straw (bed′strô′) *n.* any of a group of plants of the madder family, Rubiaceae, esp. *Galium saxatile,* having a square, slender stem, whorled leaves, and clusters of tiny yellow or white flowers. It was formerly used as a mattress stuffing.

bed·time (bed′tīm′) *n.* the time for going to bed.

bed-wet·ting (bed′wet′ing) *n.* uncontrolled urination in bed, usually during sleep; enuresis.

bee (bē) *n.* **1.a.** any of a great variety of relatively thick-bodied, hairy, winged insects, superfamily Apoidea, that feed on nectar and pollen and are related to wasps and ants. The best-known bees, the honeybees and bumblebees, of the family Apidae, live in colonies and may sting, but most kinds of bees are not social and many bees, esp. in the tropics, are stingless. **b.** the common honeybee, *Apis mellifera,* that lives in colonies, or hives, of many thousands and is widely domesticated for the honey and beeswax it produces. **2.** a gathering or meeting combining work, pleasure, and often, competition: *a spelling bee, a quilting bee.* [Old English *bēo* the insect.]

• **to have a bee in one's bonnet.** to be overly concerned about or preoccupied with some idea or notion.

bee balm, a North American plant, *Monarda didyma,* of the mint family, that grows in moist soils and bears aromatic leaves and showy flower heads that are usually bright red or pink in color.

bee·bread (bē′bred′) *n.* a mixture of pollen and honey or nectar, made by bees to feed their young.

beech (bēch) *n.* **1.** any of a group of ornamental trees, genus *Fagus,* found in cooler regions of the Northern Hemisphere, having light gray bark and bearing small, edible nuts. **2.** the close-grained wood of this tree. Also, **beechwood. 3.** any of a family,

Fagaceae, of trees and shrubs chiefly of the temperate regions of the Northern Hemisphere, including important timber and ornamental trees, as the beech, oak, and chestnut. [Old English *bēce* beech tree.] —**beech′en,** *adj.*

beech·nut (bēch′nut′) *n.* the small, edible, triangular nut of the beech tree, used to make cooking oil and flavorings.

beech·wood (bēch′wùd′) *n.* beech.

bee eater, any of various colorful, insect-eating birds, family Meropidae, of the warmer regions of Europe, Africa, Asia, and Australia, having a slender, curved bill. Length: 6-14 inches (15-36 centimeters).

bee eater

beef (bēf) *n., pl. (def. 2)* **beeves** (bēvz) or **beefs;** *(def. 4)* **beefs. 1.** the meat of a mature steer, cow, or bull. **2.** a fully grown steer, cow, or bull that is raised for meat. **3.** *Informal.* muscle; brawn. **4.** *Slang.* a complaint. —*v.i. Slang.* to complain. [Middle English *beef,* from Old French *bæf, buef* ox, beef, from Latin *bōs* ox.]

• **to beef up.** *Informal.* to add force or vigor to; strengthen: *to beef up an army with new recruits.*

beef cattle, cattle raised for meat.

beef·eat·er (bēf′ē′tər) *n.* a yeoman of the English royal guard or a warder of the Tower of London.

beefeaters at the Tower of London

beef·steak (bēf′stāk′) *n.* a slice of beef suitable for broiling or frying.

beef tea, a broth made from beef extract or by boiling lean beef in water.

beef·y (bē′fē) *adj.,* **beef·i·er, beef·i·est.** strong and muscular; brawny. —**beef′i·ness,** *n.*

bee·hive (bē′hīv′) *n.* **1.** a hive for a colony of bees, either artificially made or natural. **2.** a busy, crowded place: *The office was a beehive of activity.*

bee·keep·er (bē′kē′pər) *n.* a person who raises bees.

bee·keep·ing (bē′kē′ping) *n.* the raising of bees for honey or wax.

bee·line (bē′līn′) *n.* **1.** the direct course a honeybee follows to its hive after collecting nectar or pollen. **2.** any direct line or course.

• **to make a beeline for.** to go directly to.

Be·el·ze·bub (bē el′zə bub′) *n.* **1.** the devil; Satan. **2.** the fallen angel ranking second to Satan in *Paradise Lost,* by the English poet John Milton. [Latin *Beelzebūb,* transliteration of Hebrew *ba'al-z'būb* Philistine god of pestilence and flies mentioned in the Old Testament; literally, lord of flies; also, transliteration of Greek *Beelzeboub* Satan in the New Testament.]

been (bin) the past participle of **be.**

beep (bēp) *n.* a brief sound, as that made by the horn of an

a	at	e	end	o	hot	u	up	hw	white		about
ā	ape	ē	me	ō	old	ū	use	ng	song		taken
ä	far	i	it	ô	fork	ù	rule	th	thin	ə	pencil
âr	care	ī	ice	oi	oil	ù	pull	th	this		lemon
		îr	pierce	ou	out	ûr	turn	zh	measure		circus

automobile or by an electronic device, used as a warning or signal. —*v.i., v.t.* to make or cause to make such a sound. [Imitative.]

beep·er (bē′pər) *n.* **1.** a small electronic device that beeps a signal to summon the person carrying it. It is controlled by radio from some central location. Also, **pager. 2.** an electronic device that emits a beep, often built into watches, clocks, telephones, or computers to alert the user to the time, a message, an error, or the like.

beer (bîr) *n.* **1.** an alcoholic beverage usually made from malt and hops. **2.** any of various carbonated or fermented beverages flavored with the roots or leaves of a plant, as ginger. [Old English *bēor*.]

bees·wax (bēz′waks′) *n.* the yellow wax secreted by honeybees to make their honeycombs, used commercially in candles, cosmetics, floor wax, and other products.

beet (bēt) *n.* **1.** the fleshy root of any of a group of leafy plants, genus *Beta,* esp. the common red beet, a variety of *B. vulgaris,* cooked and eaten as a vegetable. **2.** the plant itself, having leaves that may be eaten either cooked or raw. **3.** sugar beet. [Old English *bēte,* from Latin *bēta.*]

bee·tle[1] (bē′təl) *n.* **1.** any insect of the order Coleoptera, having biting mouthparts and hard, sheathlike front wings that, when folded back, cover the membranous hind wings. The order is the largest in the insect class, containing some 300,000 species, and includes the boll weevil and Japanese beetle. **2.** any insect resembling a beetle. [Old English *bitela* literally, biting insect, from *bītan* to bite.]

bee·tle[2] (bē′təl) *n.* **1.** a heavy hammering implement, usually with a wooden head, used for driving wedges, pounding paving stones, and for other similar purposes. **2.** a wooden mallet used for household purposes, as mashing. —*v.t.,* **-tled, -tling.** to use a beetle on. [Old English *bīetel* hammer.] —**bee′tler,** *n.*

bee·tle[3] (bē′təl) *v.i.,* **-tled, -tling.** to project or jut out; overhang: *The cliffs beetled over the shore.* —*adj.* (of eyebrows) protruding; prominent. [From BEETLE-BROWED.]

bee·tle-browed (bē′təl broud′) *adj.* **1.** having protruding eyebrows. **2.** scowling; frowning. [Middle English *bitel-browed,* from *bitel* projecting (of uncertain origin) + BROW + -ED[2].]

beet sugar, sugar obtained from the sugar beet.

beeves (bēvz) a plural of **beef.**

be·fall (bi fôl′) *v.,* **-fell** (-fel′), **-fall·en, -fall·ing.** —*v.t.* to happen to: *An awful misfortune befell my friend.* —*v.i.* to come to pass, as by chance; happen: *No matter what befalls, our plan will succeed.* [Old English *befeallan* to fall.]

be·fit (bi fit′) *v.t.,* **-fit·ted, -fit·ting.** to be suitable or appropriate for: *to expect to be treated with the dignity that befits one's rank.*

be·fit·ting (bi fit′ing) *adj.* suitable; appropriate; proper. —**be·fit′ting·ly,** *adv.* —**be·fit′ting·ness,** *n.*

be·fog (bi fôg′, -fog′) *v.t.,* **-fogged, -fog·ging.** to envelop in or as if in a fog; obscure; confuse: *Mist befogged the skyline. All their arguments befogged the real issue.*

be·fool (bi fūl′) *v.t.* to fool; delude; dupe.

be·fore (bi fôr′) *prep.* **1.** in front of; in advance of; ahead of: *The fox ran before the baying hounds. The cheerleaders marched before the band.* **2.** previous to; earlier than: *We awoke before dawn.* **3.** in preference to; rather than: *death before dishonor.* **4.** in the presence, notice, or sight of: *The lawyer stood before the jury.* **5.** in precedence of development, importance, or rank: *Put the child's welfare before all else. The letter "A" comes before "B."* **6.** under the consideration or cognizance of; occupying: *Let's consider the problem before us.* **7.** in store for; awaiting: *His best years were still before him.* —*adv.* **1.** in front; in advance; ahead: *Several soldiers went before to scout.* **2.** in time preceding; previously: *She has more money than she had before.* **3.** earlier; sooner: *I'll phone at six o'clock, not before.* —*conj.* **1.** previous to the time when: *I hope to see them before I leave.* **2.** rather than; sooner than: *I would walk away before I would fight with those bullies.* [Old English *beforan* ahead (of), in the presence of.]

be·fore·hand (bi fôr′hand′) *adv., adj.* ahead of time; in advance.

be·foul (bi foul′) *v.t.* to make dirty or foul; soil.

be·friend (bi frend′) *v.t.* to act as a friend to; assist: *to befriend a stranger.*

be·fud·dle (bi fud′əl) *v.t.,* **-dled, -dling.** to confuse or bewilder utterly: *The complicated directions befuddled me.*

beg (beg) *v.,* **begged, beg·ging.** —*v.t.* **1.** to ask for as charity: *to beg food.* **2.** to ask for or of earnestly; entreat: *to beg a favor, to beg someone's pardon.* —*v.i.* **1.** to ask alms or charity; be a beggar. **2.** to ask humbly or earnestly: *The prisoner begged for mercy.* [Possibly from Anglo-Norman *begger* to ask for alms, from Old French *begard.* See BEGGAR.]

• **to beg off.** to ask to be excused from a promise or duty: *They said they would go, but then begged off.*

• **to beg the question. a.** to assume the truth of the very matter in dispute: *By insisting that the behavior of the derelict is not deranged but solely the result of homelessness, you are begging the question.* **b.** to evade an issue.

• **to go begging.** to go unwanted, unclaimed, or unused.

Synonyms *v.t.* **Beg, beseech, entreat,** and **implore** mean to earnestly ask someone for something. **Beg** implies abasing oneself to some degree and is the only one of the four terms regularly used to describe asking for money, food, or other material objects: *He was forced to beg a meal from a friend.* **Beseech** stresses urgency and anxiety about the response: *The passenger beseeched the cabdriver to get him to the station on time.* **Entreat,** a more formal word, implies persuasion or an ingratiating approach to overcome resistance: *After listing her accomplishments, the candidate entreated the suspicious voters to forgive her mistakes and reelect her.* **Implore** has the strongest emotional connotation of these words, implying desperation or great anxiety: *The prisoners' families implored the governor to spare their lives.*

be·gan (bi gan′) the past tense of **begin.**

be·get (bi get′) *v.t.,* **-got** or *(archaic)* **-gat** (-gat′), **-got·ten** or **-got, -get·ting. 1.** to be the father of; sire; father: *Abraham begat Isaac.* **2.** to give rise to; produce: *Jealousy begets hatred.* [Old English *begitan* to get.] —**be·get′ter,** *n.*

beg·gar (beg′ər) *n.* **1.** a person who asks for alms, esp. one who does so for a living. **2.** a very poor person; pauper. **3.** a fellow; rascal. —*v.t.* **1.** to reduce to poverty; impoverish. **2.** to exhaust the resources of; surpass: *That family's wealth beggars comparison.* [Possibly from Old French *begard* a person who begs, going back to Middle Dutch *beggaert.*]

beg·gar·ly (beg′ər lē) *adj.* fit for or like a beggar; poor; inadequate; mean. —**beg′gar·li·ness,** *n.*

beg·gar's-lice (beg′ərz līs′) *also,* **beg·gar-lice.** *n.* **1.** any of two groups of plants, genus *Cynoglossum* or *Hackelia,* with bristly fruit. **2.** the bristly fruit itself.

beg·gar's-ticks (beg′ərz tiks′) *also,* **beg·gar-ticks.** *n.* **1.** any of two groups of plants, genus *Bidens* or *Desmodium,* bearing barbed fruit that stick to clothing and to animal fur. **2.** the dry, bristly fruit itself. ➡ used as singular or plural in def. 1, as plural in def. 2.

beg·gar·y (beg′ə rē) *n.* **1.** extreme poverty. **2.** beggars collectively.

be·gin (bi gin′) *v.,* **-gan, -gun, -gin·ning.** —*v.i.* **1.** to set about (doing or being something); take the first step; start: *Where should I begin?* **2.** to come into existence; arise: *The epidemic began last month. The highway begins at the border.* **3.** to do or be in the slightest degree: *The author's second book doesn't begin to compare with the first.* **4.** to have the first part undertaken, performed, or the like: *The movie begins soon.* —*v.t.* **1.** to do the first act or part of; start to do: *They began their homework.* **2.** to bring into existence; create; originate: *The commercial air industry began in earnest after World War II.* [Old English *beginnan* to start.]

Synonyms *v.i.* **Begin, start,** and **commence** mean to take the first step on a course of action. **Begin** is the general term, used whether or not there is an end in view: *Begin at the front door and search the whole house. I have so much to do that I don't know where to begin.* **Start,** a more informal word, suggests a definite point from which one is taking a step and implies that there has been or will be a stop: *After two days in Cleveland the tourists started for Chicago. Today we will start on page 36.* **Commence** is more formal and is often used of processes or other impersonal things: *The drive for funds commences on September 12.*

be·gin·ner (bi gin′ər) *n.* **1.** a person who is just beginning to do or learn something; novice: *That welding class is only for beginners.* **2.** a person who begins or originates anything; founder.

be·gin·ning (bi gin′ing) *n.* **1.** the first part: *The beginning of the trip was dull.* **2.** the point at which something begins: *The starter signaled the beginning of the race.* **3.** the act of starting: *A ceremony was held to commemorate the beginning of the library's construction.* **4.** the first cause; source; origin: *The beginning of the dispute is unknown.* **5.** *also,* **beginnings.** the initial or rudimentary stage: *the beginnings of medical science.*

be·gird (bi gûrd′) *v.t.,* **-girt** (-gûrt′) or **-gird·ed, -gird·ing.** to gird; encircle; surround.

be·gone (bi gôn′, -gon′) *v.i. Archaic.* to go away; depart. ➡ used most frequently in the imperative.

be·gon·ia (bi gōn′yə, -gō′nē ə) *n.* **1.** the large showy flower of certain plants, genus *Begonia,* now widely cultivated in temperate zones. The flowers may be white, yellow, red, orange, or pink. **2.** the plant bearing this flower. **3.** any other flowering or nonflowering plant of the genus *Begonia.* [From Michel *Bégon,* 1638-1710, a French botanist.]

be·got (bi got′) a past tense and past participle of **beget.**

be·got·ten (bi got′ən) a past participle of **beget.**

be·grime (bi grīm′) *v.t.,* **-grimed,** **-grim·ing.** to make grimy; soil.

be·grudge (bi gruj′) *v.t.,* **-grudged,** **-grudg·ing.** **1.** to envy (someone) the possession or pleasure of something: *Don't begrudge them their good fortune.* **2.** to give or allow reluctantly: *to begrudge a beggar a few pennies.* —**be·grudg′ing·ly,** *adv.*

be·guile (bi gīl′) *v.t.,* **-guiled,** **-guil·ing.** **1.** to influence by guile; mislead; deceive. **2.** to amuse or delight; charm. **3.** to pass (time) pleasantly. —**be·guile′ment,** *n.* —**be·guil′er,** *n.*

be·guine (bə gēn′) *n.* **1.** a social dance similar to the rumba. **2.** the music for this dance.

be·gum (bē′gəm) *n.* a Muslim woman of high rank. [Urdu *begam* lady; of Turkic origin.]

be·gun (bi gun′) the past participle of **begin.**

be·half (bi haf′) *n.* **1. in** (or **on**) **behalf of. a.** in the interest of; for the benefit of: *A charity bazaar was planned in behalf of the church.* **b.** in the name of; as a representative of: *The minister accepted the contribution on behalf of the congregation.* **2. in** (or **on**) **someone's behalf.** in the interest of or aid of (someone): *The lawyer spoke in the defendant's behalf.* [From Middle English phrase *on behalve* on the side of, from blend of Old English *on healfe* on the side of and *be healfe* by the side of.]

be·have (bi hāv′) *v.,* **-haved,** **-hav·ing.** —*v.i.* **1.** to act in a particular way: *to behave admirably under stress.* **2.** to conduct oneself properly: *Did the children behave while I was out?* **3.** to perform, function, or react in a particular way: *This substance behaves like mercury.* —*v.t.* **1.** to conduct (oneself) in a particular way: *They behaved themselves badly.* **2.** to conduct (oneself) in a proper manner: *Sit up and behave yourself.*

be·hav·ior (bi hāv′yər) *also, British,* **behaviour.** *n.* **1.** a manner of behaving or acting; conduct; deportment: *That person's behavior was disgraceful.* **2.** the manner in which something acts under given circumstances: *the behavior of coal under pressure.* **3.** *Psychology.* the actions or responses of an organism. —**be·hav′ior·al,** *adj.* —**be·hav′ior·al·ly,** *adv.*

Synonyms Behavior and **conduct** mean the manner in which one acts or manages oneself. **Behavior** refers to any acts by either people or animals: *The behavior of cats suggests their hunting heritage. The children's behavior improved after their parents arrived.* **Conduct** suggests the existence of duties or obligations against which behavior can be measured and is thus used only of human beings, especially adults: *the dignified conduct of ushers at a funeral.*

behavioral science, any discipline, as psychology, cultural anthropology, or sociology, that uses observation and experiment to study human conduct in the context of the physical and social environment.

be·hav·ior·ism (bi hāv′yə riz′əm) *n.* a system of psychology emphasizing openly observable behavior, rather than mental activity, as a valid source of scientific data. —**be·hav′ior·ist,** *n.,* *adj.* —**be·hav′ior·is′tic,** *adj.*

behavior modification, a psychological conditioning technique that seeks to change the behavior of humans or animals, establishing desired habits through a system of rewards or punishments.

be·hav·iour (bi hāv′yər) *British.* behavior.

be·head (bi hed′) *v.t.* to cut off the head of; decapitate.

be·held (bi held′) the past tense and past participle of **behold.**

be·he·moth (bi hē′məth, bē′ə môth′) *n.* **1.** in the Bible, an enormous animal, assumed to be the hippopotamus. **2.** any creature or thing of monstrous size or power. [Medieval Latin *Behemoth* mythical biblical animal, from Hebrew *b'hēmōth,* plural of *b'hēmāh* beast.]

be·hest (bi hest′) *n.* an authoritative or insistent request; command; bidding: *They agreed to help at our behest.* [Old English *behǣs* vow, promise.]

be·hind (bi hīnd′) *prep.* **1.** at or toward the back of; in the rear of: *I sat behind a very tall man. Look behind you.* **2.** at or on the farther side of; beyond: *The path runs behind these hedges.* **3.** not on or up to: *Production was running behind schedule.* **4.** later than; after: *Our bus came ten minutes behind the first one.* **5.** less advanced than; inferior to: *a nation far behind its neighbors in technology.* **6.** hidden by: *Fear lay behind their show of bravery.* **7.** causing or contributing to: *What were the reasons behind your resignation?* **8.** in support of; supporting; backing: *The president is fully behind the senator's welfare policy.* **9.** remaining after: *Leave your cares behind you.* —*adv.* **1.** in a place or condition departed from: *The poet left a great legacy behind. The child wished to remain behind.* **2.** at or toward the back; in the rear: *They grabbed the angry dog from behind. Unable to keep up with the others, I dropped behind.* **3.** not on time; slow: *They are behind in their work.* **4.** in or into arrears; overdue: *The customer fell behind*

in the car payments. —*n. Informal.* buttocks. [Old English *behindan* in the rear (of).]

Synonyms *prep.* **Behind** and **after** mean following in space or time. **Behind** is generally used of position in space: *The garden is behind the house.* When used in position in time, it may imply delay or backwardness: *The train arrived two hours behind schedule.* **After** is generally used of position in time but sometimes of position in space: *After dinner we went to a movie.* Abbreviations like M.D. and Ph.D. are used after a name.

be·hind·hand (bi hīnd′hand′) *adv., adj.* behind schedule; late.

be·hind-the-scenes (bi hīnd′thə sēnz′) *adj.* not public; private; secret: *behind-the-scenes negotiations.*

be·hold (bi hōld′) *v.t.,* **-held,** **-hold·ing.** to look at; gaze upon; see. —*interj.* look; see. [Old English *behealdan* to hold, see.] —**be·hold′er,** *n.*

be·hold·en (bi hōl′dən) *adj.* obligated; indebted.

be·hoof (bi hüf′) *n.* advantage; benefit. [Old English *behōf.*]

be·hoove (bi hüv′) *v.t.,* **-hooved,** **-hoov·ing.** to be necessary, fitting, or advantageous for: *It would behoove you to apologize for your bad behavior.* [Old English *behōfian* to need.]

beige (bāzh) *n.* a pale brown or grayish tan color. —*adj.* having the color beige. [French *beige.*]

be·ing (bē′ing) *n.* **1.** existence; life: *to come into being.* **2.a.** a living creature, esp. a human being. **b.** something that is thought to exist: *beings from outer space, celestial beings.* **3.** the essential nature of something; essence: *The essay examined the very being of literature.* **4.** *Philosophy.* something that exists or is logically conceivable.

•**one's whole being.** all of one's capacities: *They put their whole being into the project.*

be·jew·el (bi jü′əl) *v.t.,* **-eled, -el·ing;** *also, British,* **-elled, -el·ling.** to adorn with or as with jewels.

bel (bel) *n. Physics.* a unit expressing the ratio of the values of two amounts of power, used to measure sound intensity. A bel is equal to 10 decibels. [From Alexander Graham Bell, 1847-1922, U.S. inventor of the telephone.]

Bel (bāl, bel) *n.* in Assyrian and Babylonian mythology, the god of the earth and of nature. [Akkadian *Belu* literally, master, lord.]

be·la·bor (bi lā′bər) *also, British,* **be·la·bour.** *v.t.* **1.** to beat soundly; thrash. **2.** to attack with words: *The store manager constantly belabored and nagged the clerks.* **3.** to deal with (something) for an excessive amount of time: *The speaker belabored the point long after the audience had lost interest.*

be·lat·ed (bi lā′tid) *adj.* delayed; late: *a belated arrival, a belated birthday present.* —**be·lat′ed·ly,** *adv.* —**be·lat′ed·ness,** *n.*

be·lay (bi lā′) *v.t., v.i.,* **-layed, -lay·ing.** *Nautical.* **1.** to secure (a rope) by winding around a belaying pin, cleat, or similar object. **2.** *Informal.* to stop; hold. ➡ used chiefly in the imperative: *Belay there!* [Old English *beleagan.*]

belaying pin *Nautical.* a removable pin around which running rigging is made fast.

belch (belch) *v.i.* **1.** to expel gas noisily from the stomach through the mouth. **2.** to issue forth in violent spasms; gush: *Flames belched from the windows of the burning house.* **3.** to expel or explode contents violently: *The geyser rumbled and belched.* —*v.t.* to send forth in violent spasms: *The chimney belched smoke and sparks.* —*n.* the act of belching. [Old English *bealcan* to eructate, give vent to.]

bel·dam (bel′dəm) *also,* **bel·dame** (bel′dəm, -dām′). *n.* an old woman, esp. one who is ugly; hag. [Middle English *beldam,* from *bel-* grand (going back to Latin *bellus* handsome) + *dam* mother, lady (going back to Latin *domina* lady).]

belaying pins

be·lea·guer (bi lē′gər) *v.t.* **1.** to surround or shut in with troops; besiege: *to beleaguer an enemy camp.* **2.** to surround or harass; beset: *The celebrity was beleaguered by reporters.* [Dutch *belegeren* to besiege with troops; literally, to camp beside, from *be-* by + *leger* camp.]

a	at	e	end	o	hot	u	up	hw	white
ā	ape	ē	me	ō	old	ū	use	ng	song
ä	far	i	it	ô	fork	u̇	rule	th	thin
âr	care	ī	ice	oi	oil	u̇	pull	th	this
		îr	pierce	ou	out	ûr	turn	zh	measure

ə { about, taken, pencil, lemon, circus }

bel·em·nite (bel′əm nīt′) *n.* the cigar-shaped, fossilized, internal shell of a member of an extinct order of squidlike cephalopods, Belemnoidea. [Greek *belemnon* dart, arrow.]

bel·fry (bel′frē) *n.*, *pl.* **-fries. 1.** a bell tower, esp. one attached to a church or other structure. **2.** that part of a steeple or tower in which a bell or bells are hung. [Old French *belfroi,* form of *berfrei,* from Middle High German *bercfrit* protecting tower. A *berfrey,* originally a movable tower used in attacks, was later used as a watchtower and had an alarm *bell.*]

Belg. 1. Belgian. **2.** Belgium.

Bel·gian hare (bel′jən) a reddish brown domestic rabbit, raised in Europe for meat.

Belgian sheepdog, any of a hardy breed of large working dogs, developed mainly for herding, including a long-haired, black-coated variety and a short-haired, fawn-colored variety.

Be·li·al (bē′lē əl, bēl′yəl) *n.* **1.** in the New Testament, a figure thought of as representing evil; the devil. **2.** one of the fallen angels in *Paradise Lost,* by the English poet John Milton. [Hebrew *b'liya'al* Satan, literally, worthlessness.]

be·lie (bi lī′) *v.t.,* **-lied, -ly·ing. 1.** to give a false idea of; misrepresent; disguise: *Her smile belied her sadness.* **2.** to show to be false; contradict: *The thief's trembling hands belied his profession of innocence.* **3.** to fail to come up to; disappoint: *to belie expectations.* [Old English *belēogan* to deceive by lies.]

belfry

be·lief (bi lēf′) *n.* **1.** acceptance of the truth or reality of: *a belief in life on other planets.* **2.** something believed; opinion; conviction: *We must uphold our democratic beliefs.* **3.** confidence, esp. in another person; faith; trust: *I have great belief in your ability to succeed.* [Middle English *bileafe* faith, opinion, from Old English *gelēafa* faith (with substitution of BE- for ge-).]

Synonyms **Belief** and **faith** mean acceptance of the truth or validity of something. **Belief,** the more general term, is used of acceptance with or without proof or the use of reasoning: *My belief in his intelligence was confirmed by what he said. Many societies have been characterized by a belief in witchcraft.* **Faith** has stronger connotations of a lack of questioning or a belief for which there is no rational basis: *Her naive faith in human goodness was rarely shaken by events.* For other Synonyms, see **opinion.**

be·lieve (bi lēv′) *v.,* **-lieved, -liev·ing.** —*v.t.* **1.** to accept as true or real: *I believe your story.* **2.** to credit (somebody) with truthfulness: *I don't believe you.* **3.** to be of the opinion; think; suppose: *I believe they went out shopping.* —*v.i.* to have religious faith. [Old English *bīleven.*] —**be·liev′a·bil′i·ty, be·liev′a·ble·ness,** *n.* —**be·liev′a·ble,** *adj.* —**be·liev′a·bly,** *adv.* —**be·liev′er,** *n.*

• **to believe in. a.** to be convinced of the truth, existence, or worth of something: *to believe in ghosts, to believe in freedom of speech.* **b.** to have confidence or faith in: *We believe in our government.*

• **to make believe.** to imagine; pretend: *The two young friends made believe they were on a spaceship.*

be·like (bi līk′) *adv. Archaic.* perhaps; probably.

be·lit·tle (bi lit′əl) *v.t.,* **-tled, -tling.** to cause to seem small or less important; disparage: *to belittle an opponent's arguments in a debate.* —**be·lit′tler,** *n.* —For Synonyms, see **disparage.**

bell[1] (bel) *n.* **1.** a hollow, metallic instrument, usually cup-shaped, that rings when struck by a clapper, hammer, or similar object. **2.** the sound produced by a bell. **3.** something resembling a bell in shape or function, as the flared lower end of a musical instrument or a doorbell. **4.** *Nautical.* **a.** the stroke of a bell sounded aboard ship to mark intervals during the watches, which begin at 4:00, 8:00, and 12:00. One bell signals the end of the first half hour of a watch, and an additional bell is struck for each succeeding half hour, so that eight bells signal the end of each four-hour watch. **b.** the half-hour interval thus indicated. —*v.t.* **1.** to put a bell on. **2.** to cause to swell out like a bell. —*v.i.* to swell out like a bell; flare. [Old English *belle* hollow metallic instrument that rings when struck.]

• **to bell the cat.** to perform a dangerous or daring feat.

• **to ring a bell.** to evoke a feeling of recognition; remind one of something: *That name rings a bell.*

bell[2] (bel) *v.i.* to bellow or cry, as a stag or hound. —*n.* a bellow; cry. [Old English *bellan* to make a loud noise.]

bel·la·don·na (bel′ə don′ə) *n.* **1.** a poisonous plant, *Atropa belladonna,* of the nightshade family, native to the Mediterranean

areas of Europe and Asia, having bell-shaped, dull purple-brown flowers and black berries. Also, **deadly nightshade. 2.** a drug derived from this plant, containing atropine and other alkaloids, chiefly used to dilate the pupil of the eye, to stimulate the heart, and to relieve spasms. [Italian *bella donna* literally, beautiful lady, going back to Latin *bellus* handsome + *domina* lady.]

belladonna lily, an ornamental plant, *Amaryllis belladonna,* of the amaryllis family, widely cultivated throughout the world, having long strap-shaped leaves and bearing large fragrant red, white, or purple flowers.

bell-bot·tom (bel′bot′əm) *also,* **bell-bot·tomed.** *adj.* (of trousers) gradually flaring from below the knee to the bottom of each leg.

bell-bot·toms (bel′bot′əmz) *n.* bell-bottom trousers.

bell·boy (bel′boi′) *n.* a man or boy employed, as in a hotel or club, to carry luggage, attend to guests, and run errands.

bell buoy, a buoy with a bell mounted on it that is rung by the motion of the sea or by electric batteries.

bell captain, an employee, as in a hotel, who supervises the bellboys.

belle (bel) *n.* **1.** a beautiful woman or girl. **2.** the most beautiful, popular, or admired woman or girl (in a certain place or situation): *the belle of the ball.* [French *belle,* feminine of *beau* handsome. See BEAU.]

Bel·ler·o·phon (bə ler′ə fon′) *n.* in Greek legend, the Corinthian hero who killed the monstrous Chimera with the help of the winged horse Pegasus.

belles-let·tres (bel′let′rə) *pl. n.* literature, including fiction, drama, poetry, and criticism, having artistic rather than didactic value or appeal. ➡ used as singular. [French *belles-lettres* (plural). See BELLE, LETTER.]

bell-flow·er (bel′flou′ər) *n.* **1.** a bell-shaped flower of any of a large group of plants, genus *Campanula,* found throughout the Northern Hemisphere and ranging in color from lavender to blue, white, or pink. **2.** the plant bearing this flower, having narrow, scalloped or toothed leaves.

bell glass, bell jar.

bell·hop (bel′hop′) *n. Informal.* bellboy.

bel·li·cose (bel′i kōs′) *adj.* exhibiting a tendency or eagerness to fight; warlike: *a bellicose people, a bellicose disposition.* [Latin *bellicōsus.*] —**bel′li·cose·ly,** *adv.* —**bel′li·cose·ness, bel·li·cos·i·ty** (bel′i kos′i tē), *n.*

bel·lig·er·ence (bə lij′ər əns) *n.* **1.** the state or quality of being belligerent: *That country's belligerence frightened its peaceful neighbors.* **2.** fighting; warfare.

bel·lig·er·en·cy (bə lij′ər ən sē) *n.* **1.** the status of a belligerent country; state of being at war. **2.** belligerence.

bel·lig·er·ent (bə lij′ər ənt) *adj.* **1.** eager or willing to fight; hostile: *a belligerent attitude, a belligerent person.* **2.** engaged in warfare; at war: *belligerent countries.* —*n.* a country or person engaged in warfare or fighting. [Latin *belligerāns,* present participle of *belligerāre* to wage war.] —**bel·lig′er·ent·ly,** *adv.*

bell jar, a bell-shaped glass vessel used to cover objects, to contain gases, or to create a vacuum. Also, **bell glass.**

bell·man (bel′mən) *n.*, *pl.* **-men** (-mən). **1.** town crier. **2.** bellboy.

bel·low (bel′ō) *v.i.* **1.** to emit a loud, hollow sound: *The bull bellowed.* **2.** to cry out in a loud, deep voice; roar: *The injured person bellowed with pain.* —*v.t.* to utter (words or sounds) loudly and deeply. —*n.* a loud, hollow sound; roar: *the bellow of a bull, the bellow of a foghorn.* [Old English *bylgian* to roar like a bull.]

bel·lows (bel′ōz, -əz) *pl. n.* **1.** a device for producing an air current, as for making a fire burn faster or for sounding a musical instrument, consisting of an expansible air chamber into which air is drawn and from which it is expelled under pressure. **2.** anything that resembles a bellows, as the collapsible connection between the lens and body of a folding camera. ➡ used as singular or plural in both defs. [Old English *belga,* plural of *belig* bag, belly.]

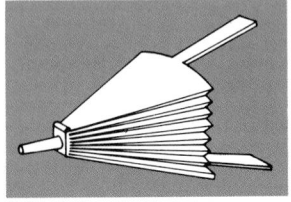

bellows

bell pepper, sweet pepper.

bell·weth·er (bel′weth′ər) *n.* **1.** a male sheep that leads the flock, usually having a bell around its neck. **2.** a person or thing that leads or signifies a trend: *That city is a bellwether in state elections.*

bel·ly (bel′ē) *n.*, *pl.* **-lies. 1.** abdomen *(def. 1).* **2.** the underside of the body of an animal. **3.** the stomach, esp. in its capacity or

B

appetite for food. **4.** an internal cavity; interior: *the belly of a ship.* **5.** a curved or bulging surface or part: *the belly of a laboratory flask.* **6.** the front or underside of anything: *The plane landed on its belly.* —*v.t., v.i.,* **-lied, -ly·ing.** to swell or bulge. [Old English *belig* bag.]

bel·ly·ache (bel′ē āk′) *n.* a pain in the abdomen, esp. the stomach. —*v.i.,* **-ached, -ach·ing.** *Slang.* to complain peevishly; whine.

bel·ly·band (bel′ē band′) *n.* a strap running under an animal's belly forming part of a harness.

bel·ly·but·ton (bel′ē but′ən) *n. Informal.* navel.

belly dance, an Oriental dance performed by women, often as a solo performance, making use of abdominal and pelvic movements.

bel·ly·flop (bel′ē flop′) *Informal. n.* a dive in which the front of the diver's body lands flat against the surface of the water. —*v.i.,* **bel·ly·flopped, bel·ly·flop·ping.** to make a bellyflop.

bel·ly·ful (bel′ē fûl′) *n., pl.* **-fuls. 1.** enough to fill the stomach or satiate the appetite. **2.** *Informal.* enough or more than enough: *We've had a bellyful of their antics.*

bel·ly·land (bel′ē land′) *v.i., v.t. Informal.* to land (an aircraft) without using the landing gear.

belly laugh 1. a hearty laugh. **2.** the cause of such a laugh.

be·long (bi lông′) *v.i.* to have a proper or fitting place: *The lamp belongs on that table. You don't belong in the beginners' class.* [Middle English *belongen,* from BE- + *longen* to concern, pertain, going back to Old English *langian* to desire.]
• **to belong to. a.** to be the property of: *This book belongs to me.* **b.** to be part of: *That vest belongs to the new suit.* **c.** to be a member of: *to belong to a club.*

be·long·ings (bi lông′ingz) *pl. n.* personal property; possessions.

be·lov·ed (bi luv′id, -luvd′) *adj.* much loved. —*n.* a person who is dearly loved.

be·low (bi lō′) *adv.* **1.** in or to a lower place: *in the valley below.* **2.** on or to a lower floor or deck: *The sailors stowed the gear below.* **3.** in a lower rank. **4.** in a later part of a book or other piece of writing: *A detailed description is given below.* **5.** on earth. **6.** less than zero on the temperature scale: *It was five below this morning.* **7.** in or to hell. —*prep.* **1.** in a lower place or position than: *This year, hems are below the knee.* **2.** lower in rank, degree, or amount than; less than: *five dollars below cost.* **3.** unworthy of; beneath: *It was below them to be so rude.* [*Be,* form of BY + LOW¹.]

belt (belt) *n.* **1.** a strip or band of leather or other pliant material worn around the body as a support for clothing or tools, as an ornament or identification, or for safety. **2.** any strip or band that encircles something: *The city had a belt of highways.* **3.** a region or zone characterized by or noted for something distinctive: *a wheat belt.* **4.** *Mechanics.* **a.** an unbroken flexible band passing around two or more wheels or pulleys, used to transmit power or motion. **b.** a conveyor belt. **c.** a wide, stiff layer or layers of fabric or metal placed beneath the tread of a tire to strengthen it and give it greater traction. **5.** *Informal.* a strong or powerful blow. —*v.t.* **1.** to encircle or fasten with a belt. **2.** to beat or strike with a belt or strap. **3.** *Informal.* to strike forcefully. **4.** *Informal.* to sing in a loud, forceful style: *The jazz singer belted out a blues song.* [Old English *belt* girdle, going back to Latin *balteus.*]
• **below the belt. a.** in boxing, below the waist. **b.** unfair; unfairly: *Attacking the candidate's family was below the belt. He was accused of dealing below the belt.*
• **to tighten one's belt.** to live in a thriftier way; spend less.
• **under one's belt.** as part of one's experience or knowledge: *She has ten years with the company under her belt.*

belt·ing (bel′ting) *n.* **1.** material used for belts. **2.** belts collectively. **3.** *Informal.* a beating; thrashing.

belt·way (belt′wā′) *n.* a highway that encircles the outskirts of a city or other urban area.

be·lu·ga (bə lü′gə) *n.* **1.** a freshwater sturgeon, *Huso huso,* of the Black Sea, Caspian Sea, and Volga River, whose roe is processed as caviar. **2.** a white whale, *Delphinapterus leucas,* of the shallow coastal waters of Arctic seas. Length: 18 feet (5.5 meters). [Russian *byeluga* sturgeon, and Russian *byelukha* white whale; both from *belyi* white.]

be·mire (bi mīr′) *v.t.* **-mired, -mir·ing. 1.** to sink in mud or mire. **2.** to cover or make dirty with mud.

be·moan (bi mōn′) *v.t.* to grieve over; bewail; lament: *to bemoan one's fate.*

be·muse (bi mūz′) *v.t.* **-mused, -mus·ing. 1.** to occupy all the attention of; preoccupy; engross. **2.** to confuse completely; bewilder; confound.

be·mused (bi mūzd′) *adj.* **1.** lost in thought; preoccupied. **2.** confused; bewildered.

bench (bench) *n.* **1.** a long seat, with or without a back. **2.** a sturdy worktable: *a cobbler's bench.* **3.a.** a seat for judges in a law

court. **b.** the office or position of a judge: *The governor appointed the distinguished lawyer to the bench.* **c.** a judge or judges who sit in a law court. **4.** a strip of elevated, relatively level land on a slope or along a coast. **5.** a platform used for exhibiting animals, esp. dogs, at a show. —*v.t.* **1.** to keep (a player) from participating in a game or games: *The coach benched the player for the rest of the season.* **2.** to exhibit (cats or dogs) on or as on a bench: *to bench a dog.* **3.** to seat (someone) on a bench. [Old English *benc* long seat.]
• **on the bench. a.** serving as judge in a law court. **b.** *Sports.* (of a player) not participating in the game.

bench·er (ben′chər) *n. British.* a person who sits on an official bench, as a judge or a member of Parliament.

bench·mark (bench′märk′) *n.* something that serves as a standard or reference by which something else can be measured or compared.

bench mark, an identifying mark made on a fixed point of known elevation, used as a reference point in surveying or tidal observation.

bench warrant, a warrant issued by a judge or a court of law for the apprehension or arrest of a person.

bend¹ (bend) *v.,* **bent, bend·ing.** —*v.t.* **1.** to change the shape of, esp. by making curved or crooked. **2.** to cause to yield; make submissive: *to bend someone to one's will.* **3.** to direct or apply: *to bend all one's energies toward building a business.* **4.** to direct or turn from a straight line; deflect. **5.** *Nautical.* to tie; secure: *to bend a sail to the mast.* —*v.i.* **1.** to become curved or crooked: *The branch bent under the weight of its fruit.* **2.** to assume a stooping posture; bow: *He bent over to tie his shoe.* **3.** to turn in a particular direction: *The river bends westward.* **4.** to bow in submission or deference; yield: *She bent to her parents' wishes.* —*n.* **1.** a thing or part of a thing that is curved or bent; crook: *a bend in the river.* **2.** the act of bending or the state of being bent. **3.** *Nautical.* **a.** any of several knots used to join two ropes or to fasten a rope to something else. **b.** the wales of a ship. **4. the bends.** a painful condition resulting from a rapid decrease in external pressure on the body, as when a deep-sea diver surfaces too quickly, causing nitrogen gas bubbles to form in the blood. Also, **caisson disease, decompression sickness.** [Old English *bendan* to stretch a bow, bind.]
• **to bend over backward** (or **backwards**). to make a determined effort; do one's best: *to bend over backward to help a needy friend.*

bend² (bend) *n.* a diagonal band on a heraldic shield. [Old French *bende* band, heraldic band; of Germanic origin.]

bend·er (ben′dər) *n.* **1.** a person or thing that bends. **2.** *Slang.* a drinking spree.

be·neath (be nēth′) *prep.* **1.** lower than; below: *We stood beneath the stars.* **2.** directly under; underneath: *The earth was firm beneath my feet.* **3.** not fitting the dignity of; unworthy of: *Lying is beneath me.* **4.** under the influence or pressure of: *The citizens suffered beneath the yoke of oppression.* **5.** less important or inferior to, as in rank or quality: *A sergeant is beneath a captain.* —*adv.* below; underneath. [Old English *beneothan* below.]

ben·e·di·ci·te (ben′i dis′i tē) *n.* **1.** the invocation of a blessing, esp. one said before a meal. **2. Benedicite.** the canticle that begins *Benedicite omnia opera Domini* in Latin and *O all ye works of the Lord, bless ye the Lord* in English. —*interj.* bless you. [Latin *benedīcite,* plural imperative of *benedīcere* to bless, praise.]

ben·e·dict (ben′i dikt′) *n.* a newly married man, esp. one who had seemed to be a confirmed bachelor. [From *Benedick,* a character in Shakespeare's *Much Ado About Nothing,* a bachelor who eventually marries.]

Ben·e·dic·tine (*n. def. 1,* ben′i dik′tin, -tēn; *n. def. 2, adj.,* ben′i dik′tēn) *n.* **1.** a monk or nun following the rules of the order founded by Saint Benedict in the sixth century. **2.** a liqueur containing herbs and spices. —*adj.* of or relating to Saint Benedict or to his religious order. [French *bénédictin* monk of the order of Saint Benedict, from Late Latin *Benedictus* (Saint) Benedict.]

Benedictine rule, a set of rules stressing useful employment and frugality that governs life in Benedictine monasteries.

ben·e·dic·tion (ben′i dik′shən) *n.* **1.** the invocation of a divine blessing upon a person or persons, esp. at the close of a church service. **2.** the blessing so invoked. **3.** the result of a blessing; blessedness. [Late Latin *benedictiō,* from Latin *benedicere* to speak well of, praise, from *bene* well and *dicere* to speak.]

a	at	e	end	o	hot	u	up	hw	white	ə	{ about
ā	ape	ē	me	ō	old	ū	use	ng	song		taken
ä	far	i	it	ô	fork	ü	rule	th	thin		pencil
âr	care	ī	ice	oi	oil	ù	pull	th	this		lemon
		îr	pierce	ou	out	ûr	turn	zh	measure		circus

Ben·e·dic·tus (ben′i dik′təs) *n.* **1.** the canticle of praise beginning *Benedictus qui venit in nomine Domini* in Latin and *Blessed is He that cometh in the name of the Lord* in English. **2.** the canticle of thanksgiving beginning *Benedictus Dominus Deus Israel* in Latin and *Blessed be the Lord God of Israel* in English. **3.** a musical setting of either of these canticles. [Latin *benedictus* blessed, past participle of *benedīcere* to bless.]

ben·e·fac·tion (ben′ə fak′shən) *n.* **1.** the act of conferring a benefit; kind or generous act. **2.** the benefit conferred; charitable gift, etc.

ben·e·fac·tor (ben′ə fak′tər) *n.* a person who gives help or financial aid; patron. [Latin *benefactor,* going back to *bene* well + *facere* to do.]

ben·e·fice (ben′ə fis) *n.* an endowed church office, esp. that of a rector or vicar. [Old French *benefice,* from Latin *beneficium* kindness.]

be·nef·i·cence (bə nef′ə səns) *n.* **1.** active kindness or generosity; doing good. **2.** a charitable gift or act. [Latin *beneficentia* kindness.]

be·nef·i·cent (bə nef′ə sənt) *adj.* **1.** doing or bringing about good; being charitable. **2.** resulting in good: *a beneficent gift.*

ben·e·fi·cial (ben′ə fish′əl) *adj.* having a good effect; advantageous; helpful: *Some insects are harmful, others are beneficial.* —**ben′e·fi′cial·ly,** *adv.*

ben·e·fi·ci·ar·y (ben′ə fish′ē er′ē, -fish′ə rē) *n., pl.* **-ar·ies. 1.** a person who receives anything as a benefit: *to be the beneficiary of a generous scholarship.* **2.** a person named to receive the money or proceeds from a will, trust, or insurance policy.

ben·e·fit (ben′ə fit) *n.* **1.** something that helps or betters a person or thing; advantage. **2.a.** money or other services given by an insurance company, government agency, or other institution, as to the sick, disabled, or aged: *Social Security benefits.* **b.** a fringe benefit. **3.** a social or theatrical event held to raise money for some charity or cause. **4.** *Archaic.* an act of kindness; good deed. —*v.t.* to be useful, profitable, or helpful to: *Rain will benefit the crops.* —*v.i.* to gain or profit; receive help: *We can all benefit from the great scholar's knowledge.* [Anglo-Norman *benfet* good deed, from Latin *benefactum.*]

Synonyms *n.* **Benefit, advantage,** and **profit** all mean a gain or increase to the good. **Benefit** stresses the idea of improvement: *The benefits of not watering the plants too often became obvious.* **Advantage** may imply that the gain puts one person or thing in a better position than others: *The extra training will be to your advantage in competing for a job.* **Profit** is used especially where material gain is implied: *There's no real profit in saving a little money if in doing so we waste a lot of time.*

benefit of clergy 1. a former privilege allowing a member of the clergy accused of serious crimes to be tried in ecclesiastic rather than secular courts. **2.** the services administered or sanction given by a church.

Ben·e·lux (ben′ə luks′) *n.* the economic union of Belgium, the Netherlands, and Luxembourg.

be·nev·o·lence (bə nev′ə ləns) *n.* **1.** a disposition to do good; kindliness; generosity. **2.** a forced loan or contribution formerly levied by some English kings on their subjects. **3.** *Archaic.* an act of kindness. [Old French *benevolence* goodwill, from Latin *benevolentia* kindness.]

be·nev·o·lent (bə nev′ə lənt) *adj.* doing or desiring to do good; kindly: *a benevolent despot, benevolent acts.* —**be·nev′o·lent·ly,** *adv.* —For Synonyms, see **kind**[1].

Ben·ga·li (ben gô′lē, beng-) *adj.* of, relating to, or characteristic of Bengal, its people, their language, or culture. —*n., pl.* **Bengali. 1.** a native or inhabitant of Bengal. **2.** a modern Indic language of the Indo-European family spoken predominantly in Bengal.

ben·ga·line (beng′gə lēn′) *n.* a durable corded fabric made of silk or rayon combined with wool or cotton. [French *bengaline,* from *Bengal,* source of a fabric it resembles.]

be·night·ed (bi nī′tid) *adj.* **1.** morally or intellectually unaware; unenlightened; ignorant. **2.** overtaken by darkness or night. [Past participle of obsolete *benight* to be overtaken by night, from BE- + NIGHT.]

be·nign (bi nīn′) *adj.* **1.** having a kindly or gentle disposition; gracious: *a benign monarch.* **2.** exhibiting gentleness or kindness: *a benign smile.* **3.** having a good effect; favorable; beneficial: *a benign climate.* **4.** *Medicine.* not threatening life or health; not malignant: *a benign tumor.* [Old French *benigne* kind, from Latin *benīgnus* kind; literally, wellborn.] —**be·nign′ly,** *adv.*

be·nig·nant (bi nig′nənt) *adj.* **1.** kindly or gracious: *a benignant sovereign.* **2.** having a good effect or influence; favorable; beneficial: *the sun's benignant rays.* —**be·nig′nan·cy,** *n.* —**be·nig′nant·ly,** *adv.*

be·nig·ni·ty (bi nig′ni tē) *n., pl.* **-ties. 1.** the quality or condition of being benign. **2.** a kind or gracious act.

ben·i·son (ben′ə zən, -sən) *n.* a blessing; benediction. [Old French *beneison,* from Latin *benedictiō.* See BENEDICTION.]

Ben·ja·min (ben′jə min) *n.* in the Old Testament, one of the tribes of Israel.

bent[1] (bent) *v.* the past tense and past participle of **bend**[1]. —*adj.* **1.** having a turn or other deviation; not straight. **2.** having the mind set to do something; determined (with *on*): *bent on going camping.* —*n.* an inclination or ability: *a bent for dancing, a natural bent for fixing things.*

bent[2] (bent) *n.* any of various grasses that make up the genus *Agrostis,* found esp. in the north temperate zone. Certain varieties are cultivated as lawn and pasture grasses. Also, **bent grass.** [Old English *beonot-* (found only in compounds) stiff grass.]

ben·thic (ben′thik) *adj.* **1.** of, relating to, or inhabiting the ocean bottom. **2.** of or relating to the benthos. Also, **ben·thon′ic.**

ben·thos (ben′thos) *n.* **1.** all the organisms that occupy both shallow and deep bottom environments in bodies of water, esp. in the oceans. **2.** the bottom of any body of water, esp. the ocean. [Modern Latin *benthos,* from Greek *benthos* depth of the sea.]

ben·ton·ite (ben′tə nīt′) *n.* a light-colored clay, formed from volcanic ash by weathering, that swells when wet, used in a wide variety of industrial processes, often interchangeably with fuller's earth. [From Fort *Benton,* Montana, where it is found + -ITE[1].]

bent·wood (bent′wŏd′) *n.* **1.** wood that is steamed and then bent or pressed into curved forms for use in making furniture. **2.** furniture made with such wood. —*adj.* of, relating to, or made with such wood: *a bentwood chair.*

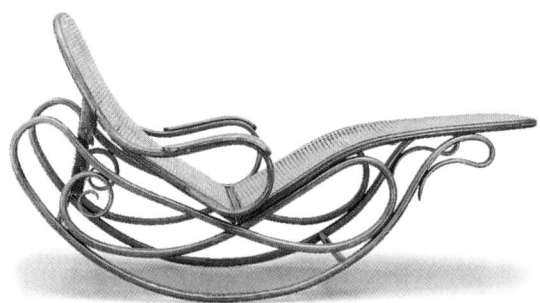

bentwood rocking chair

be·numb (bi num′) *v.t.* **1.** to make numb; deprive of sensation. **2.** to cause to become inactive; dull; stupefy. [Old English *benumen,* past participle of *beniman* to deprive.]

Ben·ze·drine (ben′zi drēn′, -drin) *n. Trademark.* a brand of amphetamine.

ben·zene (ben′zēn, ben zēn′) *n.* a colorless liquid hydrocarbon that is toxic, volatile, and flammable. It is obtained from coal tar and the refining of petroleum and is used as a solvent for waxes and oils and in the manufacture of other chemicals and synthetic products. Formula: C_6H_6 Also, **benzol.** [BENZ(OIC ACID) + -ENE.]

benzene ring, a representation of the molecular structure that exists in benzene and other aromatic compounds. In benzene, the structure consists of six carbon atoms linked in a six-sided ring, with a hydrogen atom attached to each carbon atom. Different atoms or groups replace the hydrogen atoms to form different aromatic compounds.

ben·zine (ben′zēn, ben zēn′) *n.* a colorless, volatile, flammable mixture of hydrocarbons obtained in petroleum distillation, used as a solvent and as a motor fuel. [BENZ(OIC ACID) + -INE[2].]

ben·zo·ate (ben′zō āt′, -it) *n.* a salt or ester of benzoic acid.

benzoate of soda, sodium benzoate.

ben·zo·ic acid (ben zō′ik) a colorless or white crystalline organic acid occurring in certain plants and produced commercially, used esp. in flavoring tobacco, fixing dyes, and in certain antiseptics and pharmaceuticals. Formula: $C_7H_6O_2$ [BENZO(IN)[1] + -IC + ACID.]

ben·zo·in[1] (ben′zō in, -zoin) *n.* **1.** a fragrant resin obtained from the tree *Styrax benzoin* of southeast Asia, used esp. in medicine and perfume. **2.** any plant of a genus, *Lindera,* of the laurel family, including the spicebush. [French *benjoin* the resin, going back to Arabic *lubān jāwī* frankincense of Java.]

ben·zo·in[2] (ben′zō in, -zoin) *n.* a white or yellowish crystalline compound with an odor like camphor, used esp. as an antiseptic and food flavoring. [BENZO(IC ACID) + -IN[1].]

ben·zol (ben′zôl) *n.* **1.** benzene. **2.** a crude form of benzene

consisting of about 70 percent benzene and 20 to 30 percent other hydrocarbons.

Be·o·wulf (bā′ə wŭlf′) *n.* **1.** an Old English epic in alliterative verse, composed by an unknown poet, probably early in the eighth century. **2.** the hero of this epic.

be·queath (bi kwēth′, -kwēth′) *v.t.* **1.** to give or leave (property) by will. **2.** to hand down; transmit: *to bequeath a heritage of independence to future generations.* [Old English *becwethan* to leave by will.] —**be·queath′al, be·queath′ment,** *n.*

be·quest (bi kwest′) *n.* **1.** something bequeathed; legacy: *The will contained a bequest for each relative.* **2.** the act of bequeathing. [Middle English *biqueste,* going back to Old English *bī* by + *-cwiss* saying.]

be·rate (bi rāt′) *v.t.,* **-rat·ed, -rat·ing.** to speak to sharply and usually at length; scold severely; upbraid. —For Synonyms, see **scold.**

Ber·ber (bûr′bər) *n.* **1.** a member of one of a group of Muslim tribes living in northern Africa. **2.** any of several languages spoken by the Berbers. —*adj.* of, relating to, or characteristic of the Berbers, their culture, or their language. [Arabic *Barbar* one of the people of Barbary, possibly from Greek *barbaros* foreign, uncivilized. See BARBARIC.]

ber·ceuse (bɛʀ sœz′) *n., pl.* **-ceuses** (-sœz′). **1.** lullaby. **2.** a musical composition having a soothing or gentle quality. [French *berceuse,* literally woman who rocks to sleep, from *bercer* to rock to sleep, from *berceau* cradle, of Vulgar Latin origin.]

be·reave (bi rēv′) *v.t.,* **-reaved** or **-reft** (-reft′) **-reav·ing. 1.** to keep from having something, as hope; deprive. **2.** to make desolate or forlorn, esp. by the death of a loved one. [Old English *berēafian* to rob.]

be·reaved (bi rēvd′) *adj.* having suffered the death of a loved one. —*n.* **the bereaved.** a bereaved person or persons.

> **Usage** Bereaved rather than **bereft,** is usually used when referring to the death of a loved one: *We offered our sympathy to the bereaved family.* **Bereft** is more commonly used when referring to the loss or lack of something and is usually used with *of: The fire left them bereft of all their belongings.*

be·reave·ment (bi rēv′mənt) *n.* the condition of being bereaved, esp. by the death of a loved one.

be·reft (bi reft′) *v.* a past tense and past participle of **bereave.** —*adj.* deprived of or without something. —For Usage Note, see **bereaved.**

be·ret (bə rā′, ber′ā) *n.* a soft, round cap, usually without a brim. [French *béret,* from Provençal *berret,* from Late Latin *birrus* hooded cloak.]

berg (bûrg) *n.* iceberg.

ber·ga·mot (bûr′gə mot′) *n.* **1.** a round, yellow fruit of a tree, *Citrus aurantium* subspecies *bergamia,* related to the lemon and orange, widely cultivated in Italy and southern Europe for the oil extracted from its thin peel. **2.** the honey-colored oil so extracted, used in making perfume. **3.** the small, spiny evergreen tree that bears this fruit. **4.** any of various aromatic plants of the mint family, native to northern temperate areas, esp. the genera *Monarda* and *Mentha.* [French *bergamote* this fruit, from Italian, *bergamotta;* of Turkic origin.]

be·rib·boned (bi rib′ənd) *adj.* decorated with ribbons.

ber·i·ber·i (ber′ē ber′ē) *n.* a disease affecting the nervous system, muscles, and heart, caused by a deficiency of thiamine (vitamin B₁). It occurs mainly in Asia and in areas where white rice is the staple, and is treated by administering thiamine or by improving the diet. [Singhalese *beriberi,* repetition of *beri* weakness.]

ber·ke·li·um (bər kē′lē əm) *n.* a radioactive element produced artificially by bombarding americium with alpha particles. Symbol: **Bk** For tables, see **element.** [From *Berkeley,* California, site of the University of California where it was first isolated.]

ber·lin (bər lin′, bûr′lin) *n.* **1.** a closed, four-wheeled, two-seated carriage with a suspended body, a rear platform for footmen, and a raised front seat for the driver. **2.** a soft woolen yarn. Also *(def. 2),* **Berlin wool.** [From *Berlin,* Germany, where this type of coach flourished in the seventeenth century.]

berlin

berm (bûrm) *n.* **1.** an almost level part of a beach, back from the part near the water, formed of sand deposited by waves. **2.** a bank of earth pushed up against a building to protect it from extreme temperatures. [French *berme,* from Dutch *berm* strip of land alongside a dike.]

Ber·mu·da grass (bər mū′də) any of several perennial grasses, genus *Cynodon,* with creeping stolons or rhizomes, esp. *C. dacty-*

lon, commonly grown in pastures and lawns in the southern United States. [Because it is commonly grown in *Bermuda.*]

Bermuda onion, a large, flattened onion with a mild, slightly sweet taste, grown mostly in Bermuda, Texas, and California. Bermuda onions may be red, yellow, or white.

Bermuda shorts, shorts reaching almost to the knees. Also, **Bermu′das.** [From *Bermuda,* where American tourists in the 1920s had local tailors adapt for civilian wear the regulation army shorts of British soldiers stationed there.]

Ber·noul·li effect (bər nü′lē) *Physics.* the decrease in the pressure exerted by a moving fluid as the fluid moves faster. [From Daniel *Bernoulli,* 1705-82, Swiss physicist.]

ber·ry (ber′ē) *n., pl.* **-ries. 1.** any of several small, pulpy fruits with numerous seeds, such as raspberries and strawberries. **2.** *Botany.* any fleshy, indehiscent fruit that develops from a single pistil and contains one or more seeds, such as tomatoes, grapes, and cranberries. **3.** the dry seed or kernel of various plants, as the bean of the coffee plant. **4.** an individual egg of a fish or lobster. —*v.i.,* **-ried, -ry·ing. 1.** to look for and gather berries. **2.** to bear berries. [From Old English *berie* small pulpy fruit with seeds, grape.] —**ber′ry·like′,** *adj.*

ber·serk (bər sûrk′, -zûrk′) *adj., adv.* in or into a crazed, violent rage; frenzied. [See BERSERKER.]

ber·serk·er (bər sûr′kər, -zûr′-) *n.* in Norse legend, a warrior known for frenzied fury in battle and reputed to be invulnerable. [Old Norse *berserkr* literally bear shirt; referring to the bearskins often worn by Norse warriors.]

berth (bûrth) *n.* **1.** a built-in bed or bunk on a ship, train, or other vehicle. **2.** *Nautical.* **a.** a place for a ship to moor, esp. a slip at a dock. **b.** enough space to maneuver a ship safely. **3.** a position or job: *The team gained a berth in the play-offs.* —*v.t.* **1.** to bring (a ship) into a berth. **2.** to provide with a berth. —*v.i.* to come into or occupy a berth: *The ship berthed in the harbor.* [Possibly from BEAR¹.]

·**to give a wide berth to.** to keep away from; avoid: *to give a wide berth to an unfriendly dog.*

ber·tha (bûr′thə) *n.* a wide collar, usually made of lace, worn by women to cover the shoulders. [French *berthe,* from *Berthe,* died 783, mother of Charlemagne, known for her modesty.]

Ber·til·lon system (bûr′tə lon′) a system of identifying persons, esp. criminals, by recording their body measurements and other distinguishing physical characteristics. It was later replaced by fingerprinting. [From the French police official Alphonse *Bertillon,* 1853-1914, who introduced it.]

ber·yl (ber′əl) *n.* a hard, opaque or transparent mineral occurring in various colors, but usually green, blue, or light yellow. Beryl is a silicate of beryllium and aluminum and the principal ore of beryllium. Emeralds and aquamarines are varieties of beryl. [Latin *bēryllus,* from Greek *bēryllos,* going back to a Dravidian word.]

be·ryl·li·um (bə ril′ē əm) *n.* a strong, light, poisonous, silver-white metallic element, used chiefly in alloys and as a moderator in nuclear reactors. Symbol: **Be** For tables, see **element.** [Modern Latin *beryllium,* from Greek *bēryllion* little beryl, from *bēryllos* beryl.]

be·seech (bi sēch′) *v.t.,* **-sought** or **-seeched, -seech·ing. 1.** to ask (someone) earnestly; beg; implore: *I beseech you, help us.* **2.** to ask for earnestly; plead for: *I beseech your mercy.* [Middle English *bisechen,* from BE- + *sechen* to SEEK.] —**be·seech′ing·ly,** *adv.* —For Synonyms, see **beg.**

be·seem (bi sēm′) *v.t. Archaic.* to be appropriate for; suit: *Your behavior does not beseem a person of your rank.*

be·set (bi set′) *v.t.,* **-set, -set·ting. 1.** to attack from all sides; besiege: *The campers were beset by mosquitoes.* **2.** to hem in; surround: *The enemy troops beset the soldiers' camp.* **3.** to trouble or worry constantly; harass: *Many difficulties beset the city's new mayor.* **4.** to cover with or as with ornaments; stud: *a gown beset with jewels.* [Old English *besettan* to set near, surround.]

be·set·ting (bi set′ing) *adj.* constantly attacking or harassing.

be·shrew (bi shrü′) *v.t. Archaic.* to wish evil upon; curse: *Beshrew me, if I would do such a wrong* (Shakespeare, *Othello*). [BE- + SHREW.]

be·side (bi sīd′) *prep.* **1.** at or by the side of; near: *Sit beside me.* **2.** in comparison with: *My work seems poor beside yours.* **3.** not relevant to; not connected with: *Your comments are beside the point.* —*adv. Archaic.* besides. [Old English *be sīdan* by the side.]

a	at	e	end	o	hot	u	up	hw	white	⎧	about
ā	ape	ē	me	ō	old	ū	use	ng	song	⎪	taken
ä	far	i	it	ô	fork	ü	rule	th	thin	⎨	pencil
âr	care	ī	ice	oi	oil	ü	pull	th	this	⎪	lemon
		îr	pierce	ou	out	ûr	turn	zh	measure	⎩	circus

•**beside oneself.** extremely agitated or excited; beyond self-control: *to be beside oneself with worry.*

be·sides (bi sīdz′) *adv.* **1.** moreover; furthermore: *I don't want to go; besides, it's too late.* **2.** in addition; as well; also: *I brought two others besides.* **3.** otherwise; else: *Whatever you do besides, keep my advice in mind.* —*prep. also,* **beside. 1.** in addition to; other than: *Besides the piano, I play the trumpet.* **2.** except: *Besides you, no one else is qualified.*

be·siege (bi sēj′) *v.t.,* **-sieged, -sieg·ing. 1.** to surround with armed forces in order to capture: *to besiege a fort.* **2.** to crowd around; hem in: *Autograph seekers besieged the singer.* **3.** to attack from all sides; overwhelm: *The community besieged the newspaper with letters about its recent editorial.* —**be·sieg′er,** *n.*

be·smear (bi smîr′) *v.t.* to smear; soil.

be·smirch (bi smûrch′) *v.t.* to make dirty with or as with mud; soil; sully: *to besmirch someone's reputation.*

be·som (bē′zəm) *n.* a broom, esp. one made of twigs. [Old English *besma.*]

be·sot (bi sot′) *v.t.,* **-sot·ted, -sot·ting. 1.** to make into a sot; stupefy with alcoholic drink. **2.** to make foolish, esp. by infatuation.

be·sought (bi sôt′) a past tense and past participle of **beseech.**

be·spake (bi spāk′) *Archaic.* a past tense of **bespeak.**

be·span·gle (bi spang′gəl) *v.t.,* **-gled, -gling.** to adorn or cover with or as with spangles.

be·spat·ter (bi spat′ər) *v.t.* to spatter with or as with mud; soil; sully.

be·speak (bi spēk′) *v.t.,* **-spoke** or *(archaic)* **-spake, -spo·ken** or **-spoke, -speak·ing. 1.** to give evidence of; indicate: *a house that bespeaks great wealth.* **2.** to be an omen of; foreshadow: *events that bespeak coming danger.* **3.** *Archaic.* to speak to. [Old English *besprecan* to speak to, complain.]

be·spec·ta·cled (bi spek′tə kəld) *adj.* wearing eyeglasses.

be·spoke (bi spōk′) *v.* a past tense and past participle of **bespeak.** —*adj. British.* made to order; custom-made: *a bespoke overcoat.*

be·spread (bi spred′) *v.t.,* **-spread, -spread·ing.** to spread over or cover thickly: *Daffodils bespread the field.*

be·sprent (bi sprent′) *adj. Archaic.* sprinkled over. [Middle English *bespreynt,* going back to Old English *besprengan* to besprinkle.]

be·sprin·kle (bi spring′kəl) *v.t.,* **-kled, -kling.** to sprinkle or scatter (something) over: *grass besprinkled with dew.*

Bes·se·mer converter (bes′ə mər) a pear-shaped steel vessel with air inlets at the bottom, used in the Bessemer process. [From Sir Henry *Bessemer,* 1813-98, English inventor and industrialist.]

Bessemer process, a method of making steel in which a blast of air blown through molten iron oxidizes and removes the carbon and impurities in the iron. [From Sir Henry *Bessemer,* 1813-98, English inventor and industrialist.]

best (best) *adj.* the superlative of **good. 1.** of the highest quality or excellence; superior to all others: *the best speaker in the class.* **2.** most advantageous, desirable, or appropriate: *the best approach to the problem.* **3.** largest; most: *It took the best part of a day to get there.* —*adv.* the superlative of **well¹. 1.** in the most excellent way; most successfully or advantageously: *I work best when I'm by myself.* **2.** in or to the highest degree; to the fullest extent; most fully: *according to those best qualified.* —*n.* **1.** something of the highest quality or excellence: *This camera is the best on the market.* **2.** a person or persons of the highest repute or capability: *The heart surgeon is one of the best in the field.* **3.** a person's greatest effort or degree of excellence: *Do your best on the exam.* **4.** a person's finest clothes: *my Sunday best.* —*v.t.* to do better than; outdo or defeat. [Old English *betst* of highest excellence, in the most excellent way.]

•**all for the best.** having a result more favorable than could have been expected.

•**at best.** under the most favorable or advantageous circumstances.

•**at one's best.** at one's highest degree of excellence, as of health, mood, or appearance.

•**had best.** would be wise to; ought to; should: *We had best leave.*

•**to get** (or **have**) **the best.** to defeat in or as in a contest; overcome.

•**to make the best of.** to deal with as well as possible: *to make the best of an unpleasant situation.*

be·stead (bi sted′) *v.t.,* **-stead·ed, -stead·ed** or **-stead, -stead·ing.** *Archaic.* to help; serve; avail. —*adj.* placed; situated. [BE- + STEAD.]

bes·tial (bes′chəl, bēs′-) *adj.* **1.** having the qualities of a beast; savage; brutish; inhuman. **2.** of or relating to beasts. [Latin *bēstiālis* like a beast, from *bēstia* beast.] —**bes′tial·ly,** *adv.*

bes·ti·al·i·ty (bes′chē al′i tē, bēs′-) *n., pl.* **-ties. 1.** bestial quality, character, or nature. **2.** bestial act or behavior.

bes·ti·ar·y (bes′chē er′ē, bēs′-) *n.* a collection of allegorical fables and stories about animals, particularly popular during the Middle Ages. [Medieval Latin *bestiarium,* going back to Latin *bēstia* beast.]

be·stir (bi stûr′) *v.t.,* **-stirred, -stir·ring.** to rouse to action or activity: *to bestir oneself early in the morning.*

best man, the chief attendant of the bridegroom at a wedding.

be·stow (bi stō′) *v.t.* **1.** to present as a gift or honor; confer: *to bestow medals on a hero.* **2.** to apply or devote: *to bestow time to the study of medicine.* **3.** *Archaic.* to deposit for safekeeping. **4.** *Archaic.* to provide quarters for. [BE- + STOW.] —**be·stow′al,** *n.*

be·strew (bi strü′) *v.t.,* **-strewed, -strewed** or **-strewn** (-strün′), **-strew·ing. 1.** to scatter or strew over (something): *The onlookers bestrewed the motorcade with confetti.* **2.** to scatter (something) around: *The children bestrewed toys all over the floor.* **3.** to lie scattered over or about: *Fallen leaves bestrewed the ground.* [Old English *bestrēowian* to cover.]

be·stride (bi strīd′) *v.t.,* **-strode** (-strōd′) or **-strid** (-strid′), **-strid·den** (-strid′ən) or **-strid, -strid·ing. 1.** to mount, sit on, or stand over (something) with one leg on each side; straddle. **2.** *Archaic.* to stride over or across. [Old English *bestrīdan* to sit astride.]

best·sell·er (best′sel′ər) *also,* **best seller, best-sell·er.** *n.* a book or other article that sells or has sold in very large quantities.

bet (bet) *n.* **1.** an agreement, usually between two parties, that one will pay money or give some other specified thing to the other, based on the outcome of a contest or other uncertain event; wager: *My cousin and I made a small bet on who would win the election.* **2.** something risked or wagered: *a bet of one dollar.* **3.** something on which a wager is or can be made: *That horse is a good bet in the first race.* —*v.,* **bet** or **bet·ted, bet·ting.** —*v.t.* **1.** to agree to pay or give (money or some other specified thing) in a bet. **2.** to assert confidently: *I bet he won't be surprised.* **3.** to make a bet with (someone): *I'll bet you she won't come.* —*v.i. Informal.* to make a bet: *Yesterday we bet on a horse that lost.* [Of uncertain origin.]

•**you bet.** of course; certainly.

be·ta (bā′tə, bē′-) *n.* **1.** the second letter of the Greek alphabet (B, β). **2.** the second in a group or series, esp. in scientific classification.

beta blocker *also,* **be·ta-block·er** (bā′tə blok′ər). any of a group of drugs that block some of the regulatory effects of the sympathetic nervous system on the heart and other organs, used to slow the heartbeat, relieve angina pectoris, and reduce high blood pressure.

be·take (bi tāk′) *v.t.,* **-took** (-tůk′), **-tak·en, -tak·ing. 1.** to cause (oneself) to go: *They betook themselves on a long voyage.* **2.** *Archaic.* to apply (oneself).

beta particle, an electron or positron ejected from an unstable atomic nucleus as part of a process of radioactive decay.

beta ray, a stream of beta particles.

be·ta·tron (bā′tə tron′, bē′-) *n.* a particle accelerator in which electrons are accelerated to high speeds by a varying magnetic field. [BETA (RAYS) + (ELEC)TRON.]

be·tel (bē′təl) *n.* a climbing plant, *Piper betle,* of the pepper family, native to Eastern tropic regions. Its dark green, heart-shaped leaves are chewed with betel nuts. [Portuguese *betel,* from Malayalam *vettila.*]

Be·tel·geuse (bē′təl jüz′, bet′əl jœz′) *n.* a giant red star that varies in size and brightness in a regular cycle and is the brightest star in the constellation Orion. [French *Bételgeuse,* apparently from Arabic *bīt al-jauzā'* shoulder of the giant (Orion), with reference to its position in the constellation Orion.]

betel nut, the red or orange fruit of the betel palm, having a mottled brown, fibrous husk. Betel nuts are wrapped in leaves from the betel plant and chewed for their mild narcotic effect.

betel palm, a tall Asian tree, *Areca catechu,* of the palm family, native to India and Malaya and widely cultivated for its nuts.

bête noire (bāt′ nwär′) *pl.* **bêtes noires** (bāt′ nwärz′). a person or thing that is particularly dreaded or disliked; bugbear. [French *bête noire* literally, black beast, going back to Latin *bēstia* beast + *niger* black.]

beth·el (beth′əl) *n.* **1.** a hallowed place. **2.** a place of worship for seamen. [Hebrew *bēth Ēl* house of God.]

be·think (bi thingk′) *v.t.,* **-thought** (-thôt′), **-think·ing. 1.** to cause (oneself) to consider; reflect. **2.** to remind (oneself): *The elderly couple bethought themselves of their younger days.* [Old English *bithencan* to consider.]

be·tide (bi tīd′) *v.t., v.i.,* **-tid·ed, -tid·ing.** to happen (to); befall. [BE- + TIDE².]

be·times (bi tīmz′) *adv.* **1.** early: *to wake betimes.* **2.** *Archaic.* in a short time; soon; quickly. [Earlier *betime,* from *be* BY + TIME.]

be·to·ken (bi tō′kən) *v.t.* **1.** to be a sign or token of: *a gift that betokens affection.* **2.** to indicate beforehand; foreshadow: *Cloudy skies betoken rain.*

be·tray (bi trā′) *v.t.* **1.** to aid the enemy of; be a traitor to: *to betray one's country.* **2.** to be unfaithful or false to; fail to live up to: *to betray a friend's trust.* **3.** to make known (something secret or confidential); reveal; disclose. **4.** to show unintentionally or unknowingly: *A blush betrayed the child's embarrassment.* **5.** to be a sign of; indicate: *Footprints betrayed the presence of an intruder.* **6.** to lead astray; deceive; seduce: *to be betrayed by one's own ambitions.* [BE- + Middle English *traien* to be a traitor, from Old French *traïr* to hand over, from Latin *trādere.*] —**be·tray′al,** *n.* —**be·tray′er,** *n.*

be·troth (bi trōth′, -trôth′) *v.t.* to promise to give in marriage. [Middle English *betreuthien,* from BE- + *treuthe* troth, from Old English *trēowth.*]

be·troth·al (bi trō′thəl, -trô′thəl) *n.* the act of betrothing or the state of being betrothed; engagement.

be·trothed (bi trōthd′, -trôtht′) *n.* a person who is engaged to be married. —*adj.* engaged to be married.

bet·ta (bet′ə) *n.* any brightly colored, long-finned, tropical freshwater fish of the genus *Betta,* native to southeast Asia, esp. *B. splendens,* the **Siamese fighting fish,** often kept in aquariums. [Modern Latin *betta.*]

bet·ter[1] (bet′ər) *adj.* the comparative of **good. 1.** of higher quality or excellence: *a better brand of oil.* **2.** more advantageous, desirable, or appropriate: *Copper is a better conductor of heat than iron.* **3.** improved in health: *I feel much better today.* **4.** more than half; larger; greater: *to spend the better part of one's salary on rent.* —*adv.* the comparative of **well**[1]. **1.** in a more excellent way; more advantageously or successfully: *The child was better behaved today than yesterday. Cactuses grow better in a hot, dry climate.* **2.** in or to a higher degree; to a fuller extent: *Your dog is better trained than mine.* **3.** more: *The trip took better than two hours.* —*n.* **1.** something more desirable or of greater excellence: *I voted for the better of the two candidates.* **2.** also, **betters.** a person's superior, as in rank, skill, or power. —*v.t.* **1.** to make better; improve: *You can better yourself by taking this new job.* **2.** to improve on; outdo; surpass; excel: *The team bettered last year's record.* [Old English *betera* of greater excellence, improved in health.]

• **better off. a.** in a better condition or position: *We'd be better off staying right here until the rain stops.* **b.** in an improved financial position; wealthier: *We are better off this year than we were last year.*

• **had better.** would be wise to; ought to.

• **to get (or have) the better of.** to gain or have an advantage over; outdo; defeat.

• **to go (someone) one better.** to do or achieve more than; outdo; surpass.

• **to think better of.** to reconsider and reach a wiser or more favorable conclusion about.

bet·ter[2] (bet′ər) *n.* bettor. [BET + -ER[1].]

bet·ter·ment (bet′ər mənt) *n.* **1.** the act of bettering or the condition of being bettered; improvement. **2.** improvement, other than by mere repairs, that enhances the value of real property.

bet·tor (bet′ər) *also,* **bet·ter.** *n.* a person who bets. [BET + -OR.]

be·tween (bi twēn′) *prep.* **1.** in the space, time, or range separating: *We camped between the river and the hill. I try not to eat snacks between meals. They live between one and two miles down the road.* **2.** from one to the other of; joining; connecting: *a bridge between the island and mainland.* **3.** involving (two or more parties): *a discussion between students and teachers.* **4.** by the joint action of: *Between them, they can finish in an hour.* **5.** commonly shared or possessed by: *They had three dollars between them.* **6.** one or the other of: *to choose between two books.* —*adv.* in the space, time, or range separating: *two houses with a vacant lot between.* [Old English *betwēonum* among, in the middle of, from *be-* BY + *twēonum,* dative plural of *twēone* double.]

• **between you and me.** in confidence; confidentially.

• **in between. a.** in an intermediate position: *I'm neither a liberal nor a conservative; I'm somewhere in between.* **b.** placed in the middle: *two rooms with a hall in between.*

> **Usage** In general, **between** is used when referring to two persons or things and **among** when referring to three or more: *The estate was divided equally between the twins. A spirit of cooperation developed among the team members.* **Between** can also be used when three or more items are considered individually or in pairs rather than collectively: *The teacher explained the difference between ducks, geese, and swans. The police recorded various telephone conversations between the four defendants.*

be·twixt (bi twikst′) *prep., adv.* between. [Old English *betweox.*]

• **betwixt and between.** in an intermediate position; neither one nor the other.

Bev (bev) *also,* **bev, BeV, BeV.** *n.* a billion electron volts. [Short for *b(illion) e(lectron) v(olts).*]

bev·a·tron (bev′ə tron′) *n.* a high-speed synchrotron that accelerates protons to energies in the billions of electron volts. [BEV + (CYCLO)TRON.]

bev·el (bev′əl) *n.* **1.a.** a slanting edge or surface formed by two lines or surfaces meeting at anything other than a right angle. **b.** the angle formed by such an edge or surface. **2.** an adjustable tool used for plotting angles or for adjusting the angle of surfaces to be set at a slant. Also *(def. 2),* **bevel square.** —*v.,* **-eled, -el·ing;** *also, British,* **-elled, -el·ling.** —*v.t.* to cut or shape to a bevel. —*v.i.* to incline or slope at a bevel. —*adj.* oblique; sloping. [Probably from an unrecorded Old French word.]

bevel gear, a gear fitting into another so that the shafts would intersect if extended.

bevel square, bevel *(n., def. 2).*

bev·er·age (bev′ər ij, bev′rij) *n.* a drink, hot or cold, usually consisting of something other than plain water. [Old French *bevrage,* from *bevre* to drink, from Latin *bibere.*]

bev·y (bev′ē) *n., pl.* **bev·ies. 1.** a group, esp. of girls or women. **2.** a group of birds or animals, esp. a flock of quail. [Middle English *bevey* group; possibly from an earlier meaning "a drinking company," from Anglo-Norman *bevée* flock.]

be·wail (bi wāl′) *v.t.* to express or feel deep sorrow for; mourn; lament: *to bewail the death of a loved one.*

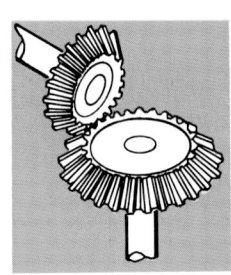

bevel gears

be·ware (bi wâr′) *v.i.* to be wary or careful: *Beware of the dog!* —*v.t.* to be wary or careful of: *Beware the oncoming storm!* [From *be ware* be wary; from *be,* imperative of *to* BE + WARE[2].]

be·wil·der (bi wil′dər) *v.t.* to confuse completely; perplex; confound. [BE- + archaic *wilder* to lead astray, perplex.] —**be·wil′dered·ly,** *adv.* —**be·wil′der·ing·ly,** *adv.* —For Synonyms, see **puzzle.**

be·wil·der·ment (bi wil′dər mənt) *n.* **1.** the state of being bewildered. **2.** a confusing or perplexing situation; tangle.

be·witch (bi wich′) *v.t.* **1.** to affect by witchcraft or magic; cast a spell over. **2.** to affect as if by magic; enchant; charm.

be·witch·ing (bi wich′ing) *adj.* fascinating; enchanting; charming: *a bewitching smile.* —**be·witch′ing·ly,** *adv.*

bey (bā) *n.* **1.** in the Ottoman Empire, a governor of a province or district. ➡ formerly used as a title of respect in Turkey. **2.** formerly, a native ruler of Tunis. [Turkish *beg* prince, gentleman.]

be·yond (bē ond′, bi yond′) *prep.* **1.** on or to the other or far side of; farther on than: *The camp is beyond those hills.* **2.** later than: *to be up beyond one's bedtime.* **3.** out of the reach, scope, or understanding of: *That story is beyond belief.* **4.** to a greater degree or amount than; more than: *gems priced far beyond their worth.* —*adv.* farther on or away: *Beyond is the ocean.* [Old English *begeondan* farther away, farther on than.]

• **the (great) beyond.** life after death.

bez·ant (bez′ənt, bi zant′) *n.* a gold coin widely circulated in Europe during medieval times; solidus. [Old French *besant,* from Medieval Latin *bȳzantius (nummus)* Byzantine (coin), from *Byzantium,* where it was first struck.]

bez·el (bez′əl) *n.* **1.** the sloping edge of a cutting tool, such as a chisel. **2.** the oblique sides or faces of a cut jewel, esp. those on the upper portion. **3.** a groove and flange by which a jewel or watch crystal is held in place. [Old French *bisel* sloping edge.]

be·zique (bə zēk′) *n.* a card game, similar to pinochle, played with two or more decks of cards using only the cards above the six.

bf *also,* **b.f.** *Printing.* boldface.

bg. *pl.* **bgs.** bag.

BHA, a synthetic antioxidant used to preserve foods containing fats or oils. Formula: $C_{11}H_{16}O_2$ [Abbreviation of *b(utylated) h(ydroxy)a(nisole).*]

Bha·ga·vad-Gi·ta (bug′ə vəd gē′tä) *n.* a sacred Hindu text in

a	at	e	end	o	hot	u	up	hw	white		about
ā	ape	ē	me	ō	old	ū	use	ng	song		taken
ä	far	i	it	ô	fork	ū	rule	th	thin	ə	pencil
âr	care	ī	ice	oi	oil	u̇	pull	th	this		lemon
		îr	pierce	ou	out	ûr	turn	zh	measure		circus

the Sanskrit epic Mahabharata, consisting of a dialogue that relates the philosophy of Krishna. [Sanskrit *Bhagavadgītā* song of the Blessed One.]

bhang (bang) *n.* **1.** the hemp plant of India. **2.** dried hemp leaves and flowers, used as a narcotic and intoxicant. It is related to marijuana and hashish. [Hindi *bhāng* hemp, from Sanskrit *bhangā.*]

BHT, a synthetic antioxidant used to preserve food and prevent deterioration of plastics, rubbers, and fuels. Formula: $C_{15}H_{24}O$ [Abbreviation of *b(utylated) h(ydroxy)t(oluene)*.]

Bi, the symbol for bismuth.

bi- *prefix* **1.a.** having two; two: *bicameral, bicycle.* **b.** involving two: *bilateral.* **2.** twice; doubly: *biconvex.* **3.a.** coming or occurring every two: *bimonthly, biweekly.* **b.** coming or occurring twice each: *biannual.* **4.** *Chemistry.* **a.** having proportionally twice as much. For example, a molecule of sodium bicarbonate has proportionally twice as much carbonate as a molecule of sodium carbonate. **b.** indicating the doubling and linkage of an organic radical or molecule: *bisulfate* [Latin *bi-* twice, doubly, two.]

bi·a·ly (bē ä′lē) *n.* a flat roll covered with onion flakes, usually with a slight depression in the center of one side. [Short for earlier *Bialystok roll,* translation of Yiddish *byalestoker pletsl;* because originally made in *Bialystok,* Poland.]

bi·an·nu·al (bī an′ū əl) *adj.* occurring twice a year; semiannual. —**bi·an′nu·al·ly,** *adv.*

bi·as (bī′əs) *n.* **1.** a mental or emotional inclination or tendency to favor one side or point of view; prejudice. **2.** a slanting line cutting diagonally across the threads of a fabric. **3.a.** an unevenness in the shape of a ball used in lawn bowling, causing it to swerve when rolled. **b.** the swerved course taken by such a ball. —*adj.* slanting across the threads of the fabric; diagonal; oblique. —*adv.* in a diagonal manner; diagonally; obliquely. —*v.t.,* **bi·ased, bi·as·ing;** *also,* British, **bi·assed, bi·as·sing.** to cause to have a bias; influence; prejudice. [French *biais* slant.] —For Synonyms *(n.),* see **prejudice.**

bi·ath·lon (bī ath′lon) *n.* an athletic competition that combines cross-country skiing and rifle marksmanship. [BI- + Greek *athlon* contest.]

bi·ax·i·al (bī ak′sē əl) *adj.* having two axes.

bib (bib) *n.* **1.** a piece of cloth or plastic tied under the chin, esp. of an infant, to protect the clothing from spilled food or drink. **2.** the upper front part of an apron or overalls. [From earlier *bib* to drink, from Latin *bibere.*]

Bib. 1. Bible. **2.** Biblical.

bib and tucker *Informal.* clothes.

Bibb lettuce (bib) a type of lettuce forming a loose head of soft, tender leaves that have a buttery taste. [From Jack *Bibb,* 1789-1884, Kentucky horticulturist who developed it.]

bib·cock (bib′kok′) *n.* a faucet with the nozzle bent downward.

bi·be·lot (bib′lō, bē blō′) *n.* a small decorative object valued for its beauty or rarity. [French *bibelot* trinket.]

Bi·ble (bī′bəl) *n.* **1.** the sacred writings of the Christian religion, including the Old and New Testaments and, in some cases, all or part of the Apocrypha. **2.** the sacred writings of the Jewish religion corresponding to the Christian Old Testament. **3.** a book or writings sacred to any religion. **4. bible.** any book used or accepted as an authority: *This book is a bible for baseball fans.* [Old French *bible* the Bible, from Medieval Latin *biblia,* going back to Greek *biblos* book, papyrus scroll.]

Bible Belt, an area, esp. in the southern and midwestern United States, noted for its avid religious fundamentalism.

bib·li·cal (bib′li kəl) *also,* **Bib·li·cal.** *adj.* of, relating to, or found in the Bible: *a biblical scholar, biblical names.* —**bib′li·cal·ly;** *also,* **Bib′li·cal·ly,** *adv.*

bib·li·og·ra·pher (bib′lē og′rə fər) *n.* a person who compiles bibliographies; expert in bibliography.

bib·li·og·ra·phy (bib′lē og′rə fē) *n., pl.* **-phies. 1.a.** a list of books or other literature on a particular subject or person, including such information as the title of the work, author, publisher, and publication date. **b.** a similar list of works of a particular author or publishing house. **2.** the study of the description, comparison, and history of books and other written material. **3.** a list of books or other sources referred to in a text or used by an author in the preparation of a text. [Greek *bibliographiā* the writing of books, from *biblion* literally, little book + *graphein* to write.] —**bib′li·o·graph′ic;** *also,* **bib′li·o·graph′i·cal,** *adj.* —**bib′li·o·graph′i·cal·ly,** *adv.*

bib·li·o·ma·ni·a (bib′lē ō mā′nē ə) *n.* a passion for collecting books. [Greek *biblion* literally, little book + *maniā* madness.] —**bib′li·o·ma′ni·ac′,** *n.* —**bib′li·o·ma·ni·a·cal** (bib′lē ō mə nī′ə kəl), *adj.*

bib·li·o·phile (bib′lē ə fīl′) *n.* a person who loves books, esp.

someone who enjoys collecting them. [French *bibliophile,* from Greek *biblion* literally, little book + *philos* friend.]

bib·u·lous (bib′yə ləs) *adj.* **1.** fond of or given to drinking alcoholic beverages. **2.** very absorbent; spongy. [Latin *bibulus* drinking freely.] —**bib′u·lous·ly,** *adv.* —**bib′u·lous·ness,** *n.*

bi·cam·er·al (bī kam′ər əl) *adj.* having or consisting of two legislative chambers or houses: *The United States Congress is a bicameral legislature.* ➡ distinguished from **unicameral.** [BI- + Latin *camera* chamber, from Greek *kamarā* vault.]

bi·car·bo·nate (bī kär′bə nit, -nāt′) *n.* any salt containing the radical HCO_3-, as sodium bicarbonate, $NaHCO_3$.

bicarbonate of soda, sodium bicarbonate.

bi·cen·te·nar·y (bī′sen ten′ə rē, bī sen′tə ner′ē) *adj., n., pl.* **-nar·ies.** bicentennial.

bi·cen·ten·ni·al (bī′sen ten′ē əl) *adj.* **1.** occurring every 200 years. **2.** consisting of or lasting 200 years. —*n.* a 200th anniversary or its celebration.

bi·ceps (bī′seps) *n., pl.* **-ceps** or **-ceps·es. 1.** a large muscle in the front of the upper arm. **2.** a large muscle in the back of the thigh. [Latin *biceps* two-headed; because these muscles have two heads or origins.]

bi·chlo·ride (bī klôr′īd) *n.* **1.** dichloride. **2.** bichloride of mercury.

bichloride of mercury, a very poisonous white crystalline compound, used esp. in photography, tanning, and metallurgy. Formula: $HgCl_2$

bi·chro·mate (bī krō′māt) *n.* dichromate.

bick·er (bik′ər) *v.i.* **1.** to quarrel noisily, esp. over something unimportant; squabble. **2.** to move quickly and irregularly with a bubbling sound; babble; gurgle. **3.** to shine with flashes of light; flicker; twinkle. —*n.* a petty quarrel; altercation. [Middle English *bikeren* to skirmish; perhaps of Dutch origin.]

bi·con·cave (bī′kon kāv′, bī kon′kāv) *adj.* concave on both sides.

bi·con·vex (bī′kon veks′, bī kon′veks) *adj.* convex on both sides.

bi·cus·pid (bī kus′pid) *adj.* having two cusps, or points. —*n.* a bicuspid tooth, as a premolar. [BI- + Latin *cuspis* point.]

bicuspid valve, mitral valve.

bi·cy·cle (bī′si kəl, -sik′əl) *n.* a vehicle consisting of a frame suspended between two wheels, one behind the other, a saddle, or seat, for the rider, handlebars for steering, and two foot pedals for propulsion. —*v.i.,* **-cled, -cling.** to ride a bicycle. [French *bicycle* this vehicle, from *bi-* (from Latin *bi-*) + Greek *kyklos* wheel.] —**bi′cy·cler, bi′cy·clist,** *n.*

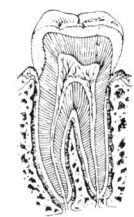

bicuspid

bid (bid) *v.* *(v.t.,* defs. *1, 2, 5, 6)* **bade** or **bid** or *(archaic)* **bad, bid·den** or **bid, bid·ding;** *(v.t.,* defs. *3, 4; v.i.)* **bid, bid·ding.** —*v.t.* **1.** to request, esp. with authority; command; order: *The captain bids you to join him on deck.* **2.** to say or express, as a greeting: *The children bade good-bye to their friends.* **3.** to offer (an amount of money) as the price or terms: *The company that bids the lowest price will win the contract.* **4.** in certain card games, to state (the number of points or tricks) one will attempt to make in return for declaring what is trump. **5.** to issue an invitation to join. **6.** to state openly; declare: *to bid defiance.* —*v.i.* to offer an amount of money for something: *We bid on the table at the auction.* —*n.* **1.** an offer or proposal, as of a price for an object or fees for services: *We received three bids for the contract.* **2.** the amount offered. **3.** an attempt to win or achieve something: *to make a bid for the presidency.* **4.a.** the number of tricks or points a player tries to make in certain card games. **b.** a player's turn to bid. **5.** an invitation to join: *The club sent out three bids.* [Partly from Old English *biddan* to ask, order; partly from Old English *bēodan* to offer, command.] —**bid′der,** *n.*

· **to bid fair.** to seem likely or probable: *Her candidacy bids fair to succeed.*

· **to bid in.** at an auction, to offer a higher final bid when other bids are considered too low, in order to retain ownership.

· **to bid up.** at an auction, to raise the price of something by offering successively higher bids.

bid·da·ble (bid′ə bəl) *adj.* **1.** worth enough or suitable to bid on: *a biddable bridge hand.* **2.** willing to do as asked; obedient; docile.

bid·den (bid′ən) a past participle of **bid.**

bid·ding (bid′ing) *n.* **1.** the act of bidding; request or invitation. **2.** the making of a bid or bids: *The bidding at the auction is slow. The bidding in this game is hard to follow.*

· **to do someone's bidding.** to obey or carry out the commands of another.

B

bid·dy¹ (bid′ē) *n., pl.* **-dies.** a chicken, esp. a hen. [Possibly imitative.]

bid·dy² (bid′ē) *n., pl.* **-dies.** *Informal.* a fussy old woman. [Familiar form of *Bridget* feminine proper name.]

bide (bīd) *v.,* **bid·ed** or **bode, bid·ed, bid·ing.** —*v.t. Archaic.* to endure; suffer; withstand. —*v.i.* **1.** to wait: *Bide here awhile.* **2.** *Archaic.* to dwell; abide. [Old English *bīdan* to wait.]
· **to bide one's time.** to wait patiently for a good opportunity.

bi·den·tate (bī den′tāt) *adj.* having two teeth or toothlike projections.

bi·det (bē dā′, bi det′) *n.* a low bathroom fixture with a shallow porcelain bowl connected to a water supply, used to wash the lower part of the torso. [French *bidet* literally, pony, from Old French *bider* to trot.]

bi·en·ni·al (bī en′ē əl) *adj.* **1.** occurring once every two years: *biennial elections.* **2.** living for two years: *a biennial plant.* —*n.* **1.** a plant that lives two years, usually producing flowers, fruit, and seeds in the second year. **2.** an event that occurs once every two years. [Latin *biennālis* of two years; English spelling influenced by Latin *biennium* period of two years.] —**bi·en′ni·al·ly,** *adv.*

bier (bir) *n.* **1.** a movable stand on which a corpse or the coffin containing it is placed before burial. **2.** a coffin together with its stand. [Old English *bǣr* this stand.]

biff (bif) *Slang. n.* a blow; hit. —*v.t.* to strike; hit. [Imitative.]

bi·fid (bī′fid) *adj. Botany, Anatomy.* divided into two equal parts by a cleft; forked: *a bifid foot, a bifid leg.* [Latin *bifidus.*] —**bi′fid·ly,** *adv.*

bi·fo·cal (bī fō′kəl) *adj.* having two focal lengths. —*n.* **1.** a lens ground with two focal lengths, one for focusing on distant objects, the other for close ones. **2.** *also,* **bifocals.** a pair of eyeglasses having bifocal lenses.

Bif·rost (biv′rost) *n.* in Norse mythology, the rainbow bridge between Asgard, home of the gods, and Midgard, the earth.

bi·fur·cate (bī′fər kāt′, bī fûr′kāt; *adj., also* bī′fər kit, bī fûr′-) *v.i., v.t.,* **-cat·ed, -cat·ing.** to divide into two branches. —*adj.* divided into two branches. [Medieval Latin *bifurcatus,* past participle of *bifurcari* to divide into two parts, from Latin *bifurcus* having two prongs.] —**bi·fur·cate·ly** (bī′fər kāt′lē, bī fûr′kāt-), *adv.*

bi·fur·ca·tion (bī′fər kā′shən) *n.* **1.** the act of bifurcating or the state of being bifurcated; division into two parts. **2.** the point at which the division occurs.

big (big) *adj.,* **big·ger, big·gest. 1.** of great size, amount, capacity, intensity, or extent; large: *a big city, a big dinner, a big car.* **2.** having great importance, prominence, or influence: *a big executive in the company, a big name in the entertainment business.* **3.** full grown; mature: *Our children are all big now.* **4.** having a full, rich sound: *a big operatic voice.* **5.** pregnant (with with): *big with child.* **6.** about to overflow; full; brimming: *eyes big with tears.* **7.** filled with self-importance; boastful; haughty; pretentious: *a big talker.* **8.** generous in character; magnanimous: *a person with a big heart.* **9.** *Informal.* known or liked by many or most people; popular: *That hair style was big last year.* —*adv. Informal.* in a boastful way; haughtily; pompously: *to talk big.* [Middle English *big* large, strong, rich; of uncertain origin.] —**big′gish,** *adj.* —**big′ness,** *n.*

Synonyms **Big, large,** and **great** mean above average in extent or size, especially in physical dimensions. **Big** is the least formal of these words and generally suggests bulk or mass: *a big car, a big dog, a big football player.* **Large** is more formal and is used more commonly than *big* in reference to nonphysical things: *a large university, a large salary, a large ambition.* **Great** is even more formal and suggests impressiveness: *a great ocean, a great empire.*

big·a·mist (big′ə mist) *n.* a person who commits bigamy.

big·a·mous (big′ə məs) *adj.* **1.** guilty of bigamy. **2.** involving bigamy. —**big′a·mous·ly,** *adv.*

big·a·my (big′ə mē) *n.* the crime of willfully marrying a second time while a first marriage is still legal. [Old French *bigamie,* from *bigame* bigamist, from Late Latin *bigamus* twice married, from Latin *bi-* twice + Greek *gamos* marriage.]

big bang theory, the theory that the universe began billions of years ago as the result of a huge cosmic explosion of a dense mass of material.

Big Ben (ben) **1.** the bell in the clock tower of the House of Commons in London, England. **2.** the clock itself.

Big Brother, a person, government, or organization that keeps individuals under a tyranny of surveillance and thought control. [From *Big Brother,* representative of the totalitarian state in the novel *1984* by George Orwell, 1903-50, English novelist.]

Big Dipper, a group of seven stars in the constellation Ursa Major, which forms the outline of a dipper.

big·foot (big′fут) *also,* **Big Foot.** *n.* a large, hairy creature somewhat like a human being, said to inhabit forests of the Pacific Northwest. Also, **Sasquatch.** [From the large footprints it supposedly makes.]

big game 1. large animals or fish sought by hunters or fishermen for sport. **2.** an important objective, esp. one involving risk.

big·gie (big′ē) *n. Slang.* an important or influential person or thing: *That company is a biggie in computer technology.*

big·heart·ed (big′här′tid) *adj.* having or showing a generous nature; charitable.

big·horn (big′hôrn′) *n., pl.* **-horn** or **-horns.** a wild sheep, *Ovis canadensis,* of the Rocky Mountains, having a coarse, grayish brown coat. The male has horns that are tightly curled and grow to as much as 50 inches (127 centimeters) long. It is the largest wild sheep in North America. Height: 3½ feet (1.1 meters) at the shoulder. Also, **Rocky Mountain sheep.**

bighorn

bight (bīt) *n.* **1.** a bend or curve, as in a river, coastline, or mountain chain. **2.** a bay bounded by such a bend. **3.** a part of a rope between the ends; loop of a rope. [Old English *byht* bending.]

big league 1. major league. **2.** *also,* **big leagues.** *Informal.* a group made up of the leading people or organizations engaged in a particular activity: *Our computer company has grown a lot, and now it's in the big leagues.* —**big′-league′,** *adj.*

big·no·ni·a (big nō′nē ə) *n.* a climbing, woody vine, *Bignonia capreolata,* native to warm southern and eastern regions of the United States, having trumpet-shaped, brilliant scarlet flowers that grow in large clusters. Also, **cross vine.** [From Abbé J. P. Bignon, 1662-1743, librarian at the court of Louis XV.]

big·ot (big′ət) *n.* a person who is excessively intolerant of any race, religion, belief, or opinion other than his or her own; a narrow-minded, prejudiced person. [French *bigot,* possibly from Old French *bigot,* term used by the medieval French to insult the Normans.]

big·ot·ed (big′ə tid) *adj.* characteristic of a bigot; intolerant; prejudiced.

big·ot·ry (big′ə trē) *n., pl.* **-ries.** a belief, attitude, or action characteristic of a bigot.

big shot *Informal.* a person of importance or influence. Also, **big wheel.**

big time *Informal.* the highest level of achievement, as in some profession or activity: *an actor who hasn't yet made the big time.*

big toe, the large inner toe of the foot in humans and other primates.

big top 1. the main tent of a circus. **2.** a circus.

big tree, sequoia *(def. 1).*

big·wig (big′wig′) *n. Informal.* a person of importance or influence. [BIG + WIG; from the large wigs formerly worn by men of importance.]

bi·jou (bē′zhü) *n., pl.* **-joux** (-zhüz). **1.** a jewel. **2.** a small, finely made object. [French *bijou,* from Breton *bizou* ring, from *biz* finger.]

bike (bīk) *Informal. n.* **1.** a bicycle. **2.** a motorcycle. **3.** a motorbike. —*v.i.,* **biked, bik·ing.** to ride a bicycle, motorcycle, or motorbike.

bik·er (bī′kər) *n.* **1.** a person who rides a bicycle. **2.** a motorcyclist, esp. one who belongs to a gang of motorcyclists.

bi·ki·ni (bi kē′nē) *n.* **1.** a scanty two-piece bathing suit for women or girls. **2.** very brief swimming trunks for men or boys. **3.** very brief underpants for women or men.

bi·la·bi·al (bī lā′bē əl) *adj.* **1.** (of a consonant) formed by both lips touching or almost touching. *B, p, m,* and *w* are bilabial consonants. **2.** having two lips; bilabiate. —*n.* a bilabial speech sound.

bi·la·bi·ate (bī lā′bē it) *adj. Botany.* having two lips, such as a corolla.

a	at	e	end	o	hot	u	up	hw	white		about
ā	ape	ē	me	ō	old	ū	use	ng	song		taken
ä	far	i	it	ô	fork	ü	rule	th	thin	ə	pencil
âr	care	ī	ice	oi	oil	ů	pull	<u>th</u>	this		lemon
		îr	pierce	ou	out	ûr	turn	zh	measure		circus

bi·lat·er·al (bī lat′ər əl) *adj.* **1.** affecting or influencing two sides or parties; reciprocal: *a bilateral treaty.* **2.** arranged on two sides of an axis. **3.** having two sides. —**bi·lat′er·al·ly,** *adv.*

bilateral symmetry, the arrangement of similar body parts along opposite sides of a median plane, so that one half of the body is the mirror image of the other.

bil·ber·ry (bil′ber′ē, -bə rē) *n., pl.* **-ries. 1.** the blue-black fruit of any of several low shrubs of the heath family, related to the blueberry, native to the Northern Hemisphere and growing as far north as the Arctic Circle. **2.** the shrub bearing this fruit. [Probably of Scandinavian origin.]

bil·bo (bil′bō) *n., pl.* **-boes. 1.** an ankle fetter consisting of a long metal bar with a lock and sliding shackles, formerly used on sailing ships for confining prisoners. **2.** *Archaic.* a finely tempered sword. [From *Bilbao,* Spain, noted for its swords.]

bilbo *(def. 1)*

bile (bīl) *n.* **1.** a bitter yellow or greenish liquid secreted by the liver and poured into the duodenum, where it aids in digestion, esp. in emulsifying fats. **2.** bad temper; nastiness. [French *bile,* from Latin *bīlis* the humor thought to cause anger.]

bile duct, the tube that empties bile into the small intestine, formed by the merging of the tubes that drain the liver and the gallbladder.

bilge (bilj) *n.* **1.** the bottom part of the hull of a boat or ship, esp. the lowest interior part. **2.** bilge water. **3.** the bulging part of a cask or barrel. **4.** *Informal.* foolish talk or writing; nonsense; foolishness. —*v.,* **bilged, bilg·ing.** —*v.t.* to damage the bottom of (a boat or ship) so that it takes in water. —*v.i.* **1.** to take in water in the bilge. **2.** to bulge; swell out. [Probably form of BULGE.]

bilge water, stagnant water that collects in the bilge of a ship.

bil·i·ar·y (bil′ē er′ē) *adj.* **1.** of or relating to bile. **2.** carrying bile. **3.** bilious *(def. 3).*

bi·lin·e·ar (bī lin′ē ər) *adj.* of, relating to, or having reference to two straight lines.

bi·lin·gual (bī ling′gwəl) *adj.* **1.** capable of speaking a foreign language as fluently or almost as fluently as one's native language. **2.** expressed in, using, or containing two languages: *a bilingual dictionary.* [Latin *bilinguis* speaking two languages + -AL[1].] —**bi·lin′gual·ism,** *n.* —**bi·lin′gual·ly,** *adv.*

bil·ious (bil′yəs) *adj.* **1.** bad-tempered; nasty; cross. **2.** of, relating to, or characteristic of bile. **3.** caused by or having some disorder of the liver, esp. an excess secretion of bile. [French *bilieux,* from Latin *bīliōsus,* from *bīlis* the humor thought to cause anger.] —**bil′ious·ly,** *adv.* —**bil′ious·ness,** *n.*

bil·i·ru·bin (bil′ə rü′bin) *n.* a reddish yellow organic compound found in bile, blood, urine, and gallstones. High concentrations of bilirubin in the blood result in the yellowish skin typical of jaundice. Formula: $C_{33}H_{36}N_4O_6$ [Latin *bilis* bile + *ruber* red + -IN[1].]

bilk (bilk) *v.t.* **1.** to deprive by dishonest means of something rightfully due; defraud; cheat; swindle: *to bilk a company of thousands of dollars.* **2.** to prevent the accomplishment or achievement of; thwart. —*n.* **1.** a dishonest person; cheater; swindler. **2.** a hoax; fraud. [Possibly a form of BALK.] —**bilk′er,** *n.*

bill[1] (bil) *n.* **1.** a statement of money owed for goods supplied or services performed: *a telephone bill, a grocery bill.* **2.** a piece of paper money; bank note: *a dollar bill.* **3.** a written or printed advertisement or public notice; poster or handbill: *Do not post bills on the walls of this building.* **4.** an itemized statement or list of items, such as a playbill or menu. **5.** a performance or presentation offered by a theater or concert hall: *What's this week's bill at the Bijou?* **6.** the draft of a proposed law. **7.a.** a bill of exchange. **b.** a promissory note. **8.** a formal, written statement of charges against a defendant, esp. a statement of complaint filed in court. —*v.t.* **1.a.** to send to (someone) a statement of money owed: *The store billed us for the furniture we bought.* **b.** to charge or enter in a bill: *Please bill my purchases to my charge account.* **2.** to announce or advertise by bills or posters. [Anglo-Norman *bille,* from Medieval Latin *billa,* form of *bulla* seal, document with seal, from Latin *bulla* bubble, knob.]
  •**to fill the bill.** to satisfy or meet the requirements.
  •**to foot the bill.** *Informal.* to pay.

bill[2] (bil) *n.* **1.** the horny beak of a bird. **2.** a mouthpart shaped like a bird's bill: *the bill of a turtle.* **3.** anything resembling the shape of a bird's bill, such as the visor of a cap. —*v.i.* (of birds) to join or touch bills. [Old English *bile* beak.]
  •**to bill and coo.** to kiss, caress, and speak softly, as lovers do.

n. **Bill**[2] and **beak** mean the horny parts of the mouth or jaws of a bird. **Bill** is the more general term but is used specifically when the shape is elongated and flattened, and often relatively straight. **Beak** is used of a downward-curving bill in which the upper part fits over the lower, and suggests a powerful structure used to pierce things and pull them apart.

bill[3] (bil) *n.* **1.** a spear having a hook-shaped blade with a spike at the back, formerly used as a military weapon; halberd. **2.** bill-hook. [Old English *bil* sword.]

bil·la·bong (bil′ə bong′) *n. Australian.* a branch of a river flowing away from the main stream but not leading to any other body of water.

bill·board (bil′bôrd′) *n.* a large panel usually placed outdoors, on which advertisements or announcements are posted.

bil·let[1] (bil′it) *n.* **1.** an official order to provide lodging for a member of the armed forces, as in a private home. **2.** the quarters assigned by such an order. **3.** a job; position; appointment. —*v.t.* **1.** to provide lodging for; quarter. **2.** to assign (soldiers) to lodging. [Old French *billette* letter of safe conduct, going back to Medieval Latin *billa* document with seal. See BILL[1].]

bil·let[2] (bil′it) *n.* **1.** a small thick stick of wood, esp. one used for fuel. **2.** a small bar of iron or steel. [Old French *billette* billet of wood, diminutive of *bille* log of wood; of Celtic origin.]

bil·let-doux (bil′ā dü′) *n., pl.* **bil·lets-doux** (bil′ā düz′). a love letter. [French *billet doux* literally, sweet letter, going back to Medieval Latin *billa* document + Latin *dulcis* sweet. See BILL[1].]

bill·fold (bil′fōld′) *n.* a flat folding case, usually made of leather, for money, cards, photographs, and the like; wallet.

bill·head (bil′hed′) *n.* **1.** a sheet of paper with a business letterhead, used for billing. **2.** the letterhead on such a sheet.

bill·hook (bil′huk′) *n.* a hook-shaped tool used for pruning or cutting.

bil·liard (bil′yərd) *adj.* of or for billiards: *a billiard ball.* —*n.* carom.

bil·liards (bil′yərdz) *n.* **1.** a game played with three hard balls and a cue on a cloth-covered rectangular table having cushions along the edges. **2.** any of several similar games, such as pool. ➤ used as singular in both defs. [French *billard* the game, billiard cue, from *bille* log. See BILLET[2].]

bil·ling (bil′ing) *n.* **1.** the relative position that a performer or act occupies in an advertisement or program for a show: *That actor always gets top billing.* **2.** publicity or advertising, as for a show or product: *The new play received a lot of advance billing.*

bil·lings·gate (bil′ingz gāt′) *n.* vulgar, abusive language. [From *Billingsgate,* fish market at a London gate, notorious for vulgar language.]

bil·lion (bil′yən) *n.* **1.a.** in the United States, the cardinal number that is one thousand times one million. **b.** a symbol representing this number; 1,000,000,000. **2.a.** in Great Britain, the cardinal number that is one million times one million. **b.** a symbol representing this number; 1,000,000,000,000. —*adj.* numbering one billion. [French *billion,* from *bi-* BI- + *(mi)llion* MILLION.]

bil·lion·aire (bil′yə nâr′) *n.* a person who has a billion or more units of a particular currency, such as dollars, pounds, or francs.

bil·lionth (bil′yənth) *adj.* **1.** (the ordinal of billion) being last in a series of one billion. **2.** being one of a billion equal parts. —*n.* **1.** that which is last in a series of one billion. **2.** one of a billion equal parts.

bill of attainder, a legislative act sentencing an accused person to death and attainder without a trial. Bills of attainder are prohibited in the United States by the Constitution.

bill of exchange, a written order to pay to a designated person a certain sum of money at a specified time.

bill of fare, a list of the foods served at a restaurant; menu.

bill of health, a certificate given to the captain of a ship stating whether or not there are infectious diseases on a ship or in a port at the time of a ship's departure.
  •**clean bill of health.** *Informal.* a favorable recommendation or report.

bill of lading, a written acknowledgment given by a carrier representing both a receipt and contract for goods being shipped.

bill of rights 1. Bill of Rights. the first ten amendments to the Constitution of the United States guaranteeing fundamental rights and liberties, such as freedom of speech and freedom of religion. **2.** any declaration or summary of the fundamental rights and liberties guaranteed to, or felt to be essential to, a group of people.

bill of sale, a written statement transferring ownership of property from the person selling it to the person buying it.

bil·low (bil′ō) *n.* **1.** a great wave or swell of a body of water. **2.** any great wave or surging mass: *Billows of smoke engulfed the firefighters.* —*v.i.* **1.** to rise or roll in billows; surge; swell. **2.** to

B

swell out: *The sail billowed in the wind.* —*v.t.* to cause to swell out: *The wind billowed the curtains.* [Old Norse *bylgja* a wave.]

bil·low·y (bil′ō ē) *adj.*, **-low·i·er**, **-low·i·est.** full of or characterized by billows; swelling; surging.

bill·post·er (bil′pōs′tər) *n.* a person hired to post advertisements or notices.

bil·ly (bil′ē) *n., pl.* **-lies.** a short, heavy club or stick, esp. one carried by a police officer. Also, **billy club.** [Probably from *Billy*, nickname of *William*.]

billy goat *Informal.* a male goat.

bi·lo·bate (bī lō′bāt) *adj.* divided into or having two lobes, as a leaf, feather, or organ. Also, **bi·lo′bat·ed, bi·lobed** (bī′lōbd′).

bim·bo (bim′bō) *n., pl.* **-bos** or **-boes.** *Slang.* a stupid or inept person. [Perhaps from Italian *bimbo* baby.]

bi·met·al (bī met′əl) *n.* a bimetallic material. —*adj.* bimetallic. [Possibly from BI- + METAL, or from BIMETALLIC.]

bi·me·tal·lic (bī′mə tal′ik) *adj.* **1.** made of, containing, or relating to two metals. **2.** relating to, based on, or using bimetallism. [BI- + METALLIC.]

bi·met·al·lism (bī met′ə liz′əm) *n.* a monetary system in which two metals, usually gold and silver, are used as the standard of currency. The relative value of the metals is fixed by law.

bi·month·ly (bī munth′lē) *adj.* **1.** occurring every two months. **2.** occurring twice a month; semimonthly. —*n., pl.* **-lies.** a bimonthly publication. —*adv.* **1.** every two months. **2.** twice a month; semimonthly.

> **Usage** | **Bimonthly** can be used to refer to something that occurs either once every two months or twice a month. However, for clarity, it is usually preferable to restrict its use to mean "occurring once every two months" and to use **semimonthly** when "occurring twice a month" is meant.

bin (bin) *n.* a receptacle or enclosed place for holding or storing something, such as grain or coal. —*v.t.*, **binned, bin·ning.** to store in a bin [Old English *binn* manger, crib.]

bin-, form of **bi-** used before a vowel, as in *binary*.

bi·na·ry (bī′nə rē) *adj.* **1.** consisting of, involving, or characterized by two things or parts. **2.** using or based on the binary system: *the binary digits 0 and 1.* —*n.* binary star. [Late Latin *bīnārius* consisting of two, from Latin *bīnī* two each.]

binary compound, a chemical compound composed of two elements, as water, which consists of hydrogen and oxygen.

binary fission, a process of asexual reproduction whereby a cell divides into two halves that are roughly equal in size.

binary star, a pair of stars revolving around a common center of gravity.

binary system, a number system with a base of two, in which any number can be expressed by 0 or 1 or a combination of these.

Binary System

All fundamental computer operations are based on the binary system. The numbers in this system are written from right to left and double in value as they move one place to the left. Following the rule that $0 + 0 = 0$, $0 + 1 = 1$, $1 + 0 = 1$, and $1 + 1 = 0$ carry 1, digital computers use binary numbers written as follows to process all information:

0001 = 1	0111 = 7	1101 = 13	10011 = 19
0010 = 2	1000 = 8	1110 = 14	10100 = 20
0011 = 3	1001 = 9	1111 = 15	11001 = 25
0100 = 4	1010 = 10	10000 = 16	11110 = 30
0101 = 5	1011 = 11	10001 = 17	110010 = 50
0110 = 6	1100 = 12	10010 = 18	1100100 = 100

Examples

$$10100 = 20$$
$$+ \ 0101 = \ 5$$
$$11001 = 25$$

$$1001 = 9$$
$$\times \ 0100 = 4$$
$$100100 = 36$$

bi·nate (bī′nāt) *adj. Botany.* growing in pairs; double: *a binate leaf.*

bin·au·ral (bī nôr′əl) *adj.* **1.** relating to or involving the use of both ears. **2.** stereophonic: *binaural recording.* **3.** having two ears. [Latin *bīnī* two at a time + AURAL.] —**bin·au′ral·ly,** *adv.*

bind (bīnd) *v.*, **bound, bind·ing.** —*v.t.* **1.** to tie, as with a rope; fasten together; secure: *to bind a sail to the mast, to bind newspapers into bundles.* **2.** to fasten or wrap around with something; encircle: *to bind one's hair with a ribbon.* **3.** to put a bandage on (often with *up*): *to bind up a wound.* **4.** to obligate or compel, as by a promise or duty: *Her sense of loyalty bound her to help her friend.* **5.** to place under a definite legal obligation: *The contract*

binds him to stay with the company for a year. **6.** to confine or restrict: *This tight collar binds me around the neck.* **7.** to cause to stick together: *Water binds particles of dirt to form mud.* **8.** to bring or hold together, as by ties of love, gratitude, or loyalty: *Strong family sentiment binds all their children.* **9.** to fasten or enclose between covers: *to bind a book.* **10.** to strengthen or ornament by a border or edge: *to bind the hem of a dress.* **11.** to constipate. —*v.i.* **1.** to be obligatory or compelling: *a promise that binds.* **2.** to confine or restrict someone or something: *My jeans shrank so much that they bind.* **3.** to stick together; cohere. —*n.* **1.** something that binds or ties. **2.** *Music.* a tie or slur between notes. **3.** *Informal.* a difficult situation. [Old English *bindan* to tie fast, tie together, cause to cohere.]

· **to bind over.** *Law.* to put (a person) under legal bond to do a particular act, such as to appear in court or pay a debt.

bind·er (bīn′dər) *n.* **1.** a person who binds, esp. a bookbinder. **2.** anything that binds, such as string or glue. **3.** a removable cover that holds sheets of paper or other material together. **4.** a machine that reaps grain and ties it into bundles. **5.** a temporary agreement binding parties until the completion of a formal contract, used esp. in real estate transactions.

bind·er·y (bīn′də rē, -drē) *n., pl.* **-er·ies.** a place where books are bound.

bind·ing (bīn′ding) *n.* **1.** anything that binds. **2.** a cloth tape used to protect or finish raw edges, as of a garment, carpet, or blanket. **3.** a cover and backing holding together and enclosing the pages of a book. **4.** the act of binding. **5.** a set of fasteners on a ski used to secure the ski to a boot. —*adj.* **1.** having the power to obligate or compel; obligatory: *a binding agreement to pay back a loan.* **2.** able to bind in any way.

binding energy, the quantity of energy required to break a particular molecule, atom, or nucleus into its constituent parts.

bind·weed (bīnd′wēd′) *n.* any of various trailing or climbing herbaceous plants, esp. genus *Convolvulus*, found in most temperate and tropical regions, bearing showy, trumpet-shaped flowers.

bine (bīn) *n.* a twining stem of a climbing plant, as the hop. [Dialectal form of BIND.]

binge (binj) *n. Informal.* a period of unrestrained or extreme indulgence in some activity, such as eating, drinking, or spending money; spree. [From English dialect *binge* to drink heavily.]

bin·go (bing′gō) *n.* a game in which each player covers numbers on a card as they are called out. The winner is the first player to cover a row of five numbers.

bin·na·cle (bin′ə kəl) *n.* a case or stand containing a ship's compass, usually placed near the helm. [Modification of obsolete *bittacle*, from Spanish *bitácula*, from Latin *habitāculum* dwelling.]

bi·noc·u·lar (bə nok′yə lər, bī-) *adj.* using or for both eyes: *binocular vision, a binocular microscope.* —*n.* **binoculars.** an optical instrument designed for use with both eyes, as field glasses or opera glasses, used to magnify distant objects. [Latin *bīnī* two each + *oculus* eye.]

bi·no·mi·al (bī nō′mē əl) *adj.* **1.** *Algebra.* consisting of two terms: *a binomial equation.* **2.** *Botany, Zoology.* consisting of two names. Binomial nomenclature is used to classify plants and animals. The genus name is given first, followed by the species designation, as in the taxonomic name for the wolf, *Canis lupus.* —*n.* a mathematical expression consisting of two terms joined by a plus or minus sign. The expressions $3x + 7y$ and $8 + 2$ are binomials. [Late Latin *binōmius* having two names, going back to Latin *bi-* two + *nōmen* name.]

binomial theorem *Mathematics.* a rule for raising a binomial to any power without writing out the actual multiplication.

bi·nu·cle·ate (bī nü′klē it, -āt′, -nū′-) *adj. Biology.* having two nuclei or central structures. Also, **bi·nu·cle·ar** (bī nü′klē ər, -nū′-), **bi·nu′cle·at·ed.**

bio- *combining form* of life or living things: *biology, biography.* [Greek *bios* life.]

bi·o·as·say (bī′ō as′ā) *n.* a method of determining the potency of a substance, as a drug or hormone, by comparing its effects on living organisms or tissues with the effects of a standard preparation. [BIO- + ASSAY.]

bi·o·as·tro·nau·tics (bī′ō as′trə nô′tiks) *n.* the study of the effects of space flight on living things. ➡ used as singular.

bi·o·chem·is·try (bī′ō kem′ə strē) *n.* the science dealing with the chemical structure, products, and processes of living things.

a	at	e	end	o	hot	u	up	hw	white		(	about
ā	ape	ē	me	ō	old	ū	use	ng	song		{	taken
ä	far	i	it	ô	fork	ü	rule	th	thin	ə	{	pencil
âr	care	ī	ice	oi	oil	u̇	pull	th	this		{	lemon
		îr	pierce	ou	out	ûr	turn	zh	measure		(	circus

119

[BIO- + CHEMISTRY.] —**bi′o·chem′i·cal,** *adj.* —**bi′o·chem′-ist,** *n.*

bi·o·de·grad·a·ble (bī′ō di grā′də bəl) *adj.* capable of decaying by the action of natural processes: *Paper is biodegradable, but most plastics are not.* [BIO- + DEGRADE + -ABLE.]

bi·o·de·grade (bī′ō di grād′) *v.t.,* -grad·ed, -grad·ing. to break down (garbage, detergents, or the like) by the action of natural processes, as bacteria or sunlight. [From BIODEGRADABLE.]

bi·o·e·lec·tric·i·ty (bī′ō i lek tris′i tē) *n.* electricity occurring naturally in living organisms, as in the electric eel.

bi·o·en·er·get·ics (bī′ō en′ər jet′iks) *n.* the study of how organisms convert food, sunlight, and chemicals into usable energy and of how they use this energy. ➡ used as singular. —**bi′o·en′er·get′ic,** *adj.*

bi·o·en·gi·neer·ing (bī′ō en′jə nîr′ing) *n.* the use of engineering principles and equipment to understand and solve problems in biology and medicine, as in the development of artificial organs and limbs. Also, **biomedical engineering.**

bi·o·eth·ics (bī′ō eth′iks) *n.* a field of study concerned with ethical questions raised by new biological and medical procedures, such as prolonging life by artificial means and organ transplants. ➡ used as singular. —**bi′o·eth′i·cal,** *adj.*

bi·o·feed·back (bī′ō fēd′bak′) *n.* a method of learning to control a normally involuntary body function, such as blood pressure or heart rate, by using electronic equipment to monitor the function.

bi·o·fla·vo·noid (bī′ō flā′və noid′) *n.* any of a group of biologically active plant substances, present in citrus fruits and other plant foods, that strengthen the body's capillary walls and help prevent hemorrhaging.

biog. 1. biographer. 2. biographical. 3. biography.

bi·o·gen·e·sis (bī′ō jen′ə sis) *n.* 1. the theory that life develops only from living organisms. 2. such development itself. [BIO- + GENESIS.] —**bi·o·ge·net·ic** (bī′ō jə net′ik), *adj.*

bi·o·ge·og·ra·phy (bī′ō jē og′rə fē) *n.* a biological science dealing with the geographical distribution of living organisms. —**bi·o·ge·og′ra·pher,** *n.* —**bi·o·ge·o·graph·ic** (bī′ō jē′ə-graf′ik), *adj.*

bi·og·ra·pher (bī og′rə fər, bē-) *n.* a person who writes biographies.

bi·o·graph·i·cal (bī′ə graf′i kəl) *adj.* 1. of or relating to a person's life: *biographical information.* 2. of, relating to, or containing biography: *a biographical section of a book.* Also, **bi′o·graph′ic.** —**bi′o·graph′i·cal·ly,** *adv.*

bi·og·ra·phy (bī og′rə fē, bē-) *n., pl.* -phies. 1. an account of a person's life. 2. such accounts collectively, considered as a form of literature or history. [Late Greek *biographiā* a writing of lives, from Greek *bios* life + *graphein* to write.]

bi·o·log·i·cal (bī′ə loj′i kəl) *adj.* 1. of or relating to biology: *a biological experiment.* 2. used in or resulting from applied biology: *biological pest control.* Also, **bi′o·log′ic.** —**bi′o·log′i·cal·ly,** *adv.*

biological clock, an internal timing mechanism in plants and animals that directs certain natural rhythms and cycles of behavior, such as sleep and wakefulness.

biological warfare, warfare using bacteria, viruses, and other toxic biological products against people, livestock, or crops. Also, **germ warfare.**

bi·ol·o·gy (bī ol′ə jē) *n.* the science of living organisms. Its two major divisions are botany, the science of plants, and zoology, the science of animals. [French or German *biologie;* going back to BIO- + -LOGY.] —**bi·ol′o·gist,** *n.*

bi·o·lu·mi·nes·cence (bī′ō lü′mə nes′əns) *n.* the emission of light from living organisms, as from fireflies and certain types of bacteria. —**bi′o·lu′mi·nes′cent,** *adj.*

bi·o·mass (bī′ō mas′) *n.* 1. *Ecology.* the weight or volume of living material, including plants, animals, and bacteria, in a certain habitat: *The scientists carefully measured the biomass of the pond.* 2. organic material, especially discarded matter such as cornstalks or scrap paper, that can be used as fuel or as a source of fuel: *Biomass may be an important source of energy in the future.*

bi·ome (bī′ōm) *n.* 1. a type of ecosystem in which a complex community of plants and animals inhabits a particular geographical area with a particular climate: *Deserts and rain forests are two vastly different biomes.* 2. the area occupied by such a community. [From *bio-* + the Latin suffix *-oma* meaning "a mass."]

bi·o·me·chan·ics (bī′ō mi kan′iks) *n.* the application of mechanical principles to problems of human and animal movement. [BIO- + MECHANICS.]

bi·o·med·i·cal engineering (bī′ō med′i kəl) bioengineering.

bi·o·med·i·cine (bī′ō med′ə sin) *n.* the branch of medicine that incorporates the biological and physical sciences, esp. as a means of determining the modifications necessary for human survival in hostile environments, such as outer space. [BIO- + MEDICINE.] —**bi′o·med′i·cal,** *adj.*

bi·o·met·rics (bī′ō met′riks) *n.* the use of statistical methods in the study of biological problems. ➡ used as singular. Also, **bi·om·e·try** (bī om′i trē). [BIO- + -METRY.]

bi·on·ic (bī on′ik) *adj.* 1. of or relating to bionics. 2. of or relating to a mechanical device used to replace or reinforce a part of a person's body: *a bionic leg.*

bi·on·ics (bī on′iks) *n.* the study of the mechanisms and systems of humans and animals as a basis for designing new or improved electronic devices. The designs of computers and artificial limbs are based on bionics. ➡ used as singular.

bi·o·nom·ics (bī′ə nom′iks) *n.* ecology *(def. 1).* ➡ used as singular. [BIO- + Greek *nomos* law + -ICS.] —**bi′o·nom′i·cal,** *adj.*

bi·o·phys·ics (bī′ō fiz′iks) *n.* the application of the concepts and methods of physics to the study of biological organisms and processes. ➡ used as singular. —**bi′o·phys′i·cal,** *adj.* —**bi·o·phys·i·cist** (bī′ō fiz′ə sist), *n.*

bi·op·sy (bī′op sē) *n., pl.* -sies. the surgical removal of a small amount of living tissue for microscopic examination, used in the diagnosis of disease, esp. cancer. [BI(O)- + Greek *opsis* sight.]

bi·o·rhythm (bī′ō rith′əm) *n.* natural inherent rhythm that initiates or controls various biological processes and functions of organisms.

bi·o·sphere (bī′ə sfîr′) *n.* 1. the part of the earth and its atmosphere where life is found. 2. the ecosystem that includes the earth and all living organisms inhabiting it.

bi·o·syn·the·sis (bī′ō sin′thə sis) *n.* the formation of complex chemical substances from simpler substances by enzymatic reactions in the cells of living organisms. [BIO- + SYNTHESIS.] —**bi′o·syn·thet′ic,** *adj.*

bi·o·ta (bī ō′tə) *n.* the plants, animals, and other living things of a region. [Modern Latin *biota.*]

bi·o·tech·nol·o·gy (bī′ō tek nol′ə jē) *n.* the use of living organisms, esp. microorganisms, to produce materials useful in medicine and industry, as in genetic engineering.

bi·ot·ic (bī ot′ik) *adj.* 1. of, relating to, or characterized by life: *a biotic environment.* 2. of, relating to, or caused by living organisms. Also, **bi·ot′i·cal.** [Greek *biōtikos* relating to life, from *bios* life.]

biotic potential, the capacity of a species of organism to reproduce and survive, expressed in terms of the size of the population that could be produced under optimal environmental conditions.

bi·o·tin (bī′ə tin) *n.* a crystalline acid that, as part of the vitamin B complex, is necessary for metabolism and growth. Biotin is synthesized by intestinal bacteria, so there is no known deficiency disease. Formula: $C_{10}H_{16}N_2O_3S$ Formerly, **vitamin H.** [Greek *biotos* life, substance (from *bios* life) + -IN [1].]

bi·o·tite (bī′ə tīt′) *n.* mica of a black, dark brown, or dark green variety, containing potassium, magnesium, and iron, and found in igneous and metamorphic rock. [From the French scientist Jean B. *Biot,* 1774-1862.]

bi·par·ti·san (bī pär′tə zən) *adj.* composed of, representing, or supported by two parties, esp. the Republican and Democratic parties: *bipartisan legislation.*

bi·par·tite (bī pär′tīt) *adj.* 1. consisting of two parts, esp. two corresponding parts, one for each party: *a bipartite business contract.* 2. involving or shared by two groups, nations, or the like: *a bipartite trade agreement.* 3. *Botany.* divided into two parts, almost to the base, as in a leaf. [Latin *bipartītus,* past participle of *bipartīre* to divide into two parts.]

bi·ped (bī′ped′) *n.* an animal having two feet. —*adj.* two-footed. [Latin *bipēs* two-footed.] —**bi·ped·al** (bī′ped′əl), *adj.*

bi·pin·nate (bī pin′āt) *adj.* (of a pinnate leaf) having pinnate leaflets.

bi·plane (bī′plān′) *n.* an airplane with two sets of wings, one above the other.

bi·po·lar (bī pō′lər) *adj.* 1. having or relating to two poles. 2. of, characteristic of, or found at both polar regions. —**bi·po·lar·i·ty** (bī′pō lar′i tē), *n.*

bi·ra·mous (bī rā′məs) *adj. Biology.* having or consisting of two branches, as certain appendages in crustaceans. [BI- + RAMOUS.]

birch (bûrch) *n.* 1. any of a group of shrubs or trees, genus *Betula,* found in temperate regions and bearing saw-toothed leaves. The pale or white bark of many species is easily peeled in thin papery strips and was used by American Indians to make canoes. 2. the hard, close-grained wood of any of these trees. 3. a birch rod or a bundle of birch twigs, used as a whip. —*v.t.* to beat with or as with a birch; whip. [Old English *beorc* birch tree.] —**birch′en,** *adj.*

bird (bûrd) *n.* **1.** any of a class, Aves, of warm-blooded, egg-laying vertebrates that have feathers and wings. **2.** game bird. **3.** shuttlecock. **4.** clay pigeon. **5.** *Informal.* a person: *Our neighbor is an odd bird.* **6.** *Informal.* a sound of derision; hiss; jeer. ➡ usually used in the phrases *to give (someone) the bird* and *to get the bird.* **7.** *Informal.* an aircraft, spacecraft, guided missile, or rocket. —*v.i.* **1.** to observe or identify wild birds in their natural environments. **2.** to trap or shoot birds. [Old English *bridd* young bird.] —**bird′like′**, *adj.*
  • **birds of a feather.** people who share the same interests, opinions, or characteristics.
  • **for the birds.** *Slang.* unappealing or worthless.

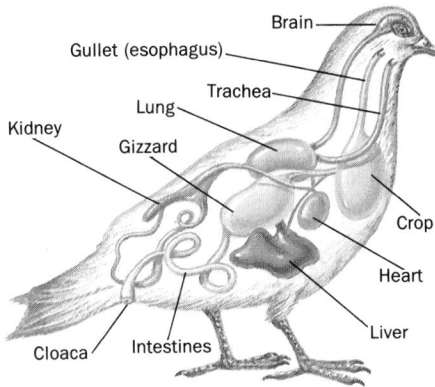

internal view of a **bird**

bird·bath (bûrd′bath′) *n., pl.* **-baths** (-ba<u>th</u>z′, -baths′). a decorative basin, usually on a pedestal, placed outdoors for birds to bathe in and drink from.
bird·brain (bûrd′brān′) *n. Informal.* a foolish, absent-minded person.
bird call 1. the sound made by a bird; song of a bird. **2.a.** an imitation of the sound made by a bird. **b.** an instrument for imitating this sound.
bird dog, any of various dogs specially trained to hunt and retrieve game birds.
bird·er (bûr′dər) *n.* bird watcher.
bird·house (bûrd′hous′) *n., pl.* **-hous·es** (-hou′ziz). **1.** an aviary. **2.** a small box, usually resembling a house, in which birds may nest.
bird·ie (bûr′dē) *n.* **1.** a small bird. **2.** in golf, a score of one under par on a hole.
bird·ing (bûr′ding) *n.* bird-watching.
bird·lime (bûrd′līm′) *n.* a sticky substance that is smeared on twigs to catch small birds. —*v.t.,* **-limed, -lim·ing.** to smear or catch with birdlime.
bird·man (bûrd′man′, -mən) *n., pl.* **-men** (-men′, -mən) **1.** *Informal.* an aviator. **2.** a person who deals with birds, such as an ornithologist.
bird of paradise, any of numerous songbirds, family Paradiseaidae, native to Australia, New Guinea, and neighboring islands. The male of the species is noted for its colorful, variegated plumage.
bird of passage 1. a migratory bird. **2.** a person who does not stay in one locality for long; transient.
bird of prey, any of various flesh-eating birds, as eagles, hawks, owls, and vultures.
bird·seed (bûrd′sēd′) *n.* a mixture of small seeds fed to caged birds and wild birds.
bird's-eye (bûrdz′ī′) *adj.* **1.** seen from above: *We got a bird's-eye view of the town from the airplane.* **2.** general; overall: *a bird's-eye view of the problem.* **3.** having markings resembling birds' eyes: *a desk of bird's-eye maple.* —*n.* **1.** a fabric, usually cotton or linen, woven with a pattern resembling birds' eyes. **2.** any of various plants with small, bright-colored flowers, as the primrose or speedwell.
bird shot, a small-sized metal shot, used esp. for hunting game birds.
bird watcher, a person who observes and studies wild birds in their natural environments. Also, **birder.**
bird-watch·ing (bûrd′woch′ing) *n.* the observation and study of wild birds in their natural environments. Also, **birding.**

bi·re·fring·ence (bī′ri frin′jəns) *n.* the separation of a ray of light into two components having perpendicular polarizations and different velocities, as by transparent calcite or certain other crystals. Also, **double refraction.** —**bi′re·fring′ent,** *adj.*
bi·reme (bī′rēm) *n.* a ship with two rows or tiers of oars on each side, used in ancient times. [Latin *birēmis* having two rows of oars.]
bi·ret·ta (bə ret′ə) *n.* a stiff, square cap with three or four projections on top, worn by the Roman Catholic clergy and some members of the Anglican clergy. Its color is black for priests, purple for bishops, and red for cardinals. [Italian *berretta,* going back to Late Latin *birrus* hooded cloak; possibly of Celtic origin.]
birth (bûrth) *n.* **1.a.** the act or fact of being born; nativity. **b.** the act of bearing or bringing forth offspring; childbirth; parturition. **2.** the beginning of anything; origin: *the birth of civilization.* **3.a.** descent; lineage; extraction: *to be Italian by birth.* **b.** noble lineage; good family. **4.** a natural or inherited bent or ability: *an artist by birth.* [Old Norse *byrth.*]
  • **to give birth to. a.** to bring forth (offspring). **b.** to bring forth (anything); be the cause of.
birth control, the control of the number of offspring born, esp. by the use of contraceptive methods or devices.
birth·day (bûrth′dā′) *n.* **1.** the day of a person's birth. **2.** the anniversary of this day.
birth defect, any physical or mental deformity or disorder present at birth.
birth·mark (bûrth′märk′) *n.* a mark or blemish on the skin present at birth.
birth·place (bûrth′plās′) *n.* **1.** the place of a person's birth. **2.** any place of origin: *Greece is often considered to be the birthplace of democracy.*
birth·rate (bûrth′rāt′) *also,* **birth rate.** *n.* the number of births occurring in a given population per year.
birth·right (bûrth′rīt′) *n.* a right, privilege, or possession to which a person is entitled by birth: *Freedom of religion is the birthright of everyone born in the United States.*
birth·stone (bûrth′stōn′) *n.* a gem associated with a particular month of the year, supposed to bring good luck when it is worn by a person whose birthday falls in that month.
bis·cuit (bis′kit) *n., pl.* **-cuits** or **-cuit. 1.** a small, raised, baked cake made of a type of bread dough, usually raised with baking powder or soda. **2.** *British.* a cracker or thin cookie. **3.** pottery after the first firing and before painting or glazing. Also *(def. 3),* **bisque².** [French *biscuit,* from Old French *bescoit,* shortening of *pain bescoit* twice-baked bread (from the practice of baking bread twice to preserve it for long sea voyages), from *bis* twice (from Latin *bis*) + *cuit* cooked, past participle of *cuire* to cook (from Latin *coquere*).]
bi·sect (bī sekt′, bī′sekt) *v.t.* **1.** to divide (a geometrical figure) into two equal parts. **2.** to cut in two. —*v.i.* to divide in two; fork: *The road bisects up ahead.* [BI- + Latin *sectus,* past participle of *secāre* to cut.] —**bi·sec′tion,** *n.*
bi·sec·tor (bī sek′tər, bī′sek-) *n.* a line or plane that bisects an angle or a line segment.
bi·sex·u·al (bī sek′shü əl) *adj.* **1.** having both male and female organs; hermaphroditic. **2.** of or relating to both sexes. —*n.* **1.** a hermaphrodite. **2.** a person who is sexually attracted by both sexes. —**bi·sex′u·al·ism, bi·sex·u·al·i·ty** (bī′sek shü al′i tē), *n.* —**bi·sex′u·al·ly,** *adv.*
bish·op (bish′əp) *n.* **1.** a high-ranking member of the clergy in any of various churches, usually the administrative head of a diocese. **2.** a chess piece that may be moved diagonally across any number of squares. [Old English *bisceop* church bishop, going back to Church Latin *episcopus* overseer, church bishop, from Greek *episkopos.*]
bish·op·ric (bish′ə prik) *n.* **1.** the office, rank, or jurisdiction of a bishop. **2.** a church district administered by a bishop; diocese. [Old English *bisceoprīce* diocese, from *bisceop* BISHOP + *rīce* realm.]
bis·muth (biz′məth) *n.* a brittle, crystalline, gray-white metallic element with a reddish

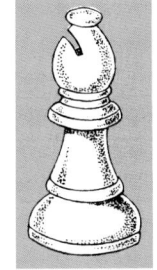

bishop
(def. 2)

a	at	e	end	o	hot	u	up	hw	white		about
ā	ape	ē	me	ō	old	ū	use	ng	song		taken
ä	far	i	it	ô	fork	ü	rule	th	thin	ə	pencil
âr	care	ī	ice	oi	oil	u̇	pull	th	this		lemon
		îr	pierce	ou	out	ûr	turn	zh	measure		circus

tinge, used esp. in low-melting-point alloys for fire alarms and sprinkler systems and in some drugs. Symbol: **Bi** For tables, see **element**. [Modern Latin *bismutum,* from German *Bismuth,* form of *Wismut,* from *Wesemut;* of unknown origin.]

bi·son (bī′sən, -zən) *n., pl.* **-son. 1.** a cud-chewing mammal, *Bison bison,* of North America, having a large head, short, permanent horns, humped shoulders, and a thick brown coat. Height: 5½ feet (1.7 meters) at the shoulder. Also, **buffalo. 2.** aurochs *(def. 2).* [Latin *bison* wild ox; of Germanic origin.]

bisque¹ (bisk) *n.* **1.a.** a thick, creamy soup made of fish or meat, esp. shellfish or game. **b.** any thick, creamy soup, esp. one made of pureed vegetables. **2.** ice cream containing crushed macaroons or nuts. [French *bisque* soup made of shellfish or fish; of uncertain origin.]

bisque² (bisk) *n.* in ceramics, biscuit. [Short for BISCUIT *(def. 3).*]

bis·ter (bis′tər) *also,* **bis·tre.** *n.* **1.** an orange-yellow to brown-black pigment made from the soot of burnt wood. **2.** a yellowish to grayish brown color. [French *bistre;* of uncertain origin.]

bis·tro (bis′trō, bēs′-) *n.* a small bar, nightclub, or café. [French *bistro, bistrot* literally wine shop, wine seller, from *bistraud* shepherd, from *biste* goat.]

bi·sul·fate (bī sul′fāt) *also,* **bi·sul·phate.** *n.* an acid salt of sulfuric acid, containing the radical —HSO₄.

bi·sul·fide (bī sul′fīd) *also,* **bi·sul·phide.** *n.* disulfide.

bi·sul·fite (bī sul′fīt) *also,* **bi·sul·phite.** *n.* an acid salt of sulfurous acid, containing the radical —HSO₃.

bit¹ (bit) *n.* **1.** the metal piece of a bridle that goes into a horse's mouth. **2.a.** a boring or drilling part that fits into a brace, drill, or similar tool. **b.** the cutting or end part of a tool. **3.** the part of a key that enters the lock and acts on the bolt and tumblers. —*v.t.,* **bit·ted, bit·ting. 1.** to put a bit in the mouth of (a riding animal); train to the bit. **2.** to curb or restrain with or as with a bit. [Old English *bite* bite.]

bit² (bit) *n.* **1.** a small piece, part, or quantity: *bits of broken glass, a bit of bread.* **2.** a short while; moment: *Please wait a bit.* **3.** some amount, degree or extent: *He is a bit of an artist.* **4.** *Informal.* an amount equivalent to twelve and a half cents, originally a Spanish or Mexican coin used as currency in the southwestern United States. ➡ now used only in multiples of two, as *two bits, four bits.* **5.** *Informal.* a typical set of actions or pattern of behavior: *We did the whole tourist bit on our vacation.* **6.** a short performance or routine: *a song and dance bit.* —*adj.* of little importance; small; insignificant: *a bit part in a play.* [Old English *bita* morsel, small piece bitten off.]

•**a bit.** to some degree or extent; somewhat; rather: *I am a bit tired.*

•**bit by bit.** a little at a time; gradually:

•**every bit.** without exception; entirely; completely: *She is every bit as talented as her sister.*

Synonyms Bit² and **particle** mean a small piece or amount of something. **Bit** is more general and is more likely to be used of abstract as well as concrete things: *a bit of fabric, a bit of salt, a bit of luck.* **Particle** suggests a bit just large enough to be distinguished, implies a larger whole more strongly than *bit* does, and is more restricted to reference to concrete things: *When I swept the room I found several particles of the broken glass still under the table.*

bit³ (bit) the past tense and a past participle of bite.

bit⁴ (bit) *n.* **1.** a unit of information recording the decision made by a computer between two alternatives, as "yes" or "no." **2.** a digit, either 0 or 1, in the binary system. **3.** a unit of information storage in a computer. A group of 8 bits makes up a byte. [BI(NARY) + (DIGI)T.]

bitch (bich) *n.* the female of the dog or other canine. [Old English *bicce* female dog.]

bite (bīt) *v.,* **bit, bit·ten** or **bit, bit·ing.** —*v.t.* **1.** to cut, pierce, or seize with the teeth: *to bite on a sandwich.* **2.** to remove with the teeth; cut or tear (with *off* or *out*): *to bite off a piece of an apple.* **3.** to pierce the skin of with teeth, fangs, or similar parts: *The horsefly bit me.* **4.** to cut or pierce with or as with a sharp weapon. **5.** to cause to smart or sting: *The winter wind bit our faces.* **6.** to eat into; corrode: *Acid bites metal.* **7.** to take a firm hold on; grip: *The chains enabled the tires to bite the snow.* —*v.i.* **1.** to cut, pierce, seize, or grip something: *The teeth of the saw bit into the wood.* **2.a.** to cut or pierce with teeth, fangs, or similar parts: *to bite into an apple.* **b.** to have a tendency to do this: *Does the dog bite?* **3.** to cause smarting or stinging. **4.** (of fish) to take the bait. **5.** to be tricked. —*n.* **1.** the act of biting. **2.** a wound made by biting or stinging: *a mosquito bite.* **3.** a piece bitten off; mouthful; morsel. **4.** *Informal.* a small meal; snack: *We stopped for a bite*

before the show. **5.** the effect or quality of biting; sting: *the bite of spicy food.* **6.** a grip or hold on a surface: *the extra bite of snow tires.* **7.** the manner in which the upper and lower teeth meet. [Old English *bītan* to cut into with the teeth, pierce.] —**bit′er,** *n.*

•**to bite off more than one can chew.** to undertake something beyond one's capabilities.

bit·ing (bī′ting) *adj.* **1.** causing sharp pain; stinging: *biting cold.* **2.** intending to hurt someone's feelings; sarcastic; cutting; caustic: *biting wit.* —**bit′ing·ly,** *adv.*

bitt (bit) *n.* a post on a ship's deck to which ropes are secured. —*v.t.* to put (a rope) around a bitt. [Possibly from Old Norse *biti* beam.]

bit·ten (bit′ən) a past participle of bite.

bit·ter (bit′ər) *adj.* **1.** having a sharp, biting, unpleasant taste. **2.** emotionally or intellectually unpleasant; hard to accept or bear: *the bitter truth.* **3.** harsh or biting; sarcastic: *bitter humor.* **4.** causing or showing pain, misery, or discomfort: *bitter cold, bitter tears.* **5.** having or showing intense animosity: *a bitter quarrel, bitter enemies.* **6.** full of resentment; unforgiving: *to be bitter about losing a job.* —*n.* something bitter; bitter quality or thing. —*adv.* much more than usual; extremely: *a bitter cold morning.* [Old English *biter* severe, not sweet.] —**bit′ter·ly,** *adv.* —**bit′ter·ness,** *n.*

•**to the bitter end. a.** until the very end, however painful or unpleasant. **b.** to death itself.

bit·tern (bit′ərn) *n.* any of several marsh birds, family Ardeidae, closely related to, but smaller than, the heron, and having a loud, booming cry. [Old French *butor,* going back to Latin *būtiō* bittern + *taurus* bull; possibly because it "bellows" like a bull.]

bit·ter·root (bit′ər rüt′, -rŭt′) *n.* a low-growing plant, *Lewisia rediviva,* found in the northern Rocky Mountain region, bearing a circle of fleshy leaves at its base and a single white or rose-colored flower at the top. [So called because of its bitter taste.]

bit·ters (bit′ərz) *pl. n.* a liquid, usually alcoholic, made from bitter herbs and roots or angostura bark, used to flavor mixed drinks or as an ingredient in medicine.

bit·ter·sweet (bit′ər swēt′) *n.* **1.** a poisonous climbing, woody plant, *Solanum dulcamara,* of the nightshade family, native to Europe, northern Africa, and Asia, bearing drooping clusters of violet flowers that ripen into scarlet berries. **2.** a climbing shrub, genus *Celastrus,* bearing clusters of small, greenish flowers that ripen into yellow and orange fruit. —*adj.* **1.** containing a small amount of sweetener; moderately sweet: *bittersweet chocolate.* **2.** both pleasant and painful: *bittersweet memories.*

bi·tu·men (bī tü′mən, -tū′-, bi-) *n.* any of various dark-colored solid or liquid hydrocarbons, such as asphalt, bituminous coal, or crude petroleum, all of which are flammable. [Latin *bitūmen.*]

bi·tu·mi·nous (bī tü′mə nəs, -tū′-, bi-) *adj.* made of, containing, or like bitumen.

bituminous coal, a dull to shiny black coal, rich in volatile hydrocarbons, that burns with a smoky flame. Also, **soft coal.**

bi·va·lence (bī vā′ləns, biv′ə-) *n. Chemistry.* the quality or state of being bivalent. Also, **bi·va′len·cy.**

bi·va·lent (bī vā′lənt, biv′ə-) *adj. Chemistry.* having a valence of plus or minus two. [BI- + Latin *valēns,* present participle of *valēre* to be strong.]

bi·valve (bī′valv′) *n.* a mollusk whose shell consists of two parts, or valves, hinged together, as the oyster or clam. For illustration, see **shell.** —*adj.* **1.** having two shells united by a hinge. **2.** having two valves, as a seedcase.

biv·ou·ac (biv′ü ak′, biv′wak) *n.* a temporary encampment, esp. one made by soldiers in the field, with or without shelter. —*v.i.,* **-acked, -ack·ing.** to camp out in a bivouac. [French *bivouac* temporary encampment, probably from Low German *biwake* literally, additional watch or guard (with reference to a watch by citizens to aid the regular watch).]

bi·week·ly (bī wēk′lē) *adj.* **1.** occurring every two weeks. **2.** occurring twice a week; semiweekly. —*n., pl.* **-lies.** a biweekly publication. —*adv.* **1.** every two weeks. **2.** twice a week; semiweekly.

Usage Biweekly can be used to refer to something that occurs either once every two weeks or twice a week. However, for clarity, it is usually preferable to restrict its use to mean "occurring once every two weeks" and to use **semiweekly** when "occurring twice a week" is meant.

bi·year·ly (bī yîr′lē) *adj.* **1.** occurring twice a year; semiannually. **2.** occurring every two years. —*adv.* **1.** twice a year; semiannually. **2.** every two years.

bi·zarre (bi zär′) *adj.* strikingly odd, as in manner or appearance; eccentric; fantastic; grotesque. [French *bizarre,* from Italian *bizzaro* capricious.] —**bi·zarre′ly,** *adv.* —**bi·zarre′ness,** *n.* —For Synonyms *(adj.),* see **grotesque.**

Bk, the symbol for berkelium.

bk. **1.** bank. **2.** book.

bkg., banking.

bkt. *pl.* **bkts.** basket.

bl. **1.** bale. **2.** barrel.

b.l., bill of lading. Also, **B/L.**

blab (blab) *v.,* **blabbed, blab·bing.** —*v.t.* to tell or reveal thoughtlessly or indiscreetly. —*v.i.* **1.** to chatter foolishly or excessively. **2.** to reveal a secret; talk indiscreetly. —*n.* **1.** foolish or excessive talk; idle chatter. **2.** a person who blabs. [Imitative.]

blab·ber (blab′ər) *v.i.* to chatter foolishly or excessively. —*n.* **1.** a person who blabs. **2.** foolish or excessive chatter. [Imitative.]

blab·ber·mouth (blab′ər mouth′) *n., pl.* **-mouths** (-mou<u>th</u>z′, -mouths′). *Informal.* a person who blabs.

black (blak) *adj.* **1.** absorbing all light; having the darkest of all colors; having the color of coal. ➡ opposed to **white.** **2.** having or reflecting no light; in darkness; dark: *a black room, the black depths of the ocean.* **3.a.** *also,* **Black.** of, relating to, or belonging to a dark-skinned people, esp. of African descent. **b.** dark-skinned. **4.** full of sadness or gloom: *It was a black day when the factory closed.* **5.** full of anger; hostile: *a black mood.* **6.** dirty; soiled: *clothes black with grime.* **7.** emphasizing that which is morbid or grotesque: *black humor.* **8.** full of evil; wicked: *black deeds.* **9.** indicating disgrace or discredit: *Cheating is a black mark on one's record.* **10.** without milk or cream: *black coffee.* —*n.* **1.** the total absorption of light. Although technically black is the complete absorption of light, it is perceived as a color and as the darkest of all colors; it is the color of coal. ➡ opposed to **white.** **2.** a black dye, paint, or the like. **3.** something black, such as a black piece in the game of checkers. **4.** *also,* **Black.** a member of a dark-skinned people, esp. of African descent. **5.** dark clothes, esp. those worn for mourning. —*v.t.* **1.** to make black; blacken. **2.** to clean and polish with blacking. —*v.i.* to become black. [Old English *blæc* opposite of white.] —**black′ish,** *adj.* —**black′ly,** *adv.* —**black′ness,** *n.*

 · **in the black.** making a profit; prospering financially. ➡ opposed to **in the red.**

 · **to black out.** **a.** to lose vision, memory, or consciousness temporarily. **b.** to interrupt the normal operations of: *The storm blacked out the electricity in town.* **c.** to turn off or cover lights in, esp. as a protection against enemy air raids: *to black out a city.* **d.** to suppress or prevent coverage of by censorship: *The new rebel government blacked out all the news from the country.*

black·a·moor (blak′ə mûr′) *n. Archaic.* a dark-skinned person, esp. a black African. [BLACK + MOOR.]

black-and-blue (blak′ən blü′) *adj.* discolored as a result of ruptured blood vessels under the skin; bruised.

Black and Tan, a member of the British recruits sent to Ireland in June 1920 to aid the royal Irish constabulary in putting down the Sinn Fein rebellion. [From the *black and tan* uniforms worn by these recruits.]

black and white **1.** writing; print: *Give us your opinion of the matter in black and white.* **2.** a photograph or picture in which black, white, and gray are the only colors.

black angus *also,* **Black Angus.** *pl.* **angus.** Aberdeen Angus.

black art, black magic.

black·ball (blak′bôl′) *v.t.* **1.** to vote against, esp. to vote against admitting into an organization. **2.** to exclude (someone) from a social group; ostracize. —*n.* a vote rejecting a person or thing. [From the ancient Greek method of indicating a negative vote by putting a small *black ball* in a container.]

black bass (bas) any of several freshwater game fish, genus *Micropterus,* found in eastern and central North America. Length: to 28 inches (71 centimeters).

black bear, any of various bears, genus *Euarctos,* native to North America and Mexico, having fur ranging from black to cinnamon-colored.

black belt **1.** the highest rank awarded in judo and karate. **2.** a person who has attained such a rank.

black·ber·ry (blak′ber′ē, -bə rē) *n., pl.* **-ries.** **1.** the sweet black fruit of any of several bramble bushes, genus *Rubus,* of the rose family, esp. *R. allegheniensis,* of the northeastern United States and Canada. **2.** the thorny bush that bears this fruit.

black·bird (blak′bûrd′) *n.* **1.** any of various New World birds, family Icteridae, that are all or mostly black or dark in color, as the red-winged blackbird, cowbird, and grackle. **2.** a black or dark brown thrush, *Turdus merula,* native to Europe. Also *(def. 2),* merle.

black·board (blak′bôrd′) *n.* a hard, smooth, usually dark surface of slate or other material for writing or drawing on with chalk.

black·bod·y, (blak′bod′ē) *n., pl.* **-bod·ies.** a hypothetical surface or body capable of absorbing all radiation falling on it and reflecting none.

black book, a book containing a blacklist.

black box **1.** a mechanical or electronic device for performing intricate automatic functions, especially one that can be installed or removed as a unit. **2.** any device or system whose function is known but whose structure or workings are not known or understood. **3.** flight recorder.

black bread, pumpernickel.

black·cap (blak′kap′) *n.* **1.** black raspberry. **2.** any of several birds having a black crown, as the European warbler, *Sylvia atricapilla,* or the chickadee.

black·cock (blak′kok′) *n., pl.* **-cocks** or **-cock.** the male of the black grouse.

black·damp (blak′damp′) *n.* a suffocating gaseous mixture consisting mostly of carbon dioxide, produced esp. by explosions or fires in mines. Also, **chokedamp.**

Black Death, an epidemic of bubonic plague that spread through Europe, Africa, and Asia in the fourteenth century. By 1352 it had wiped out one quarter of the total population of Europe. [From the *black* spots on the body caused by the disease.]

black diamond **1.** **black diamonds.** mineral coal. **2.** carbonado.

black·en (blak′ən) *v.t.* **1.** to make black; darken. **2.** to speak badly of; sully; defame: *to blacken someone's reputation.* —*v.i.* to become black or dark: *The sky blackened.* —**black′en·er,** *n.*

Black English, any of the dialects of English spoken by American blacks.

black eye **1.** a discoloration of the skin around the eye, usually caused by a blow. **2.** *Informal.* a damaged or bad reputation: *The rumors about corruption gave the mayor a black eye.*

black-eyed pea (blak′īd′) a kind of cowpea.

black-eyed Su·san (sü′zən) the showy, daisylike flower head of a plant, *Rudbeckia hirta,* of the composite family, having yellow petallike rays surrounding a dark brown center, native to eastern Canada and the United States.

black·face (blak′fās′) *n.* **1.** formerly, makeup used by performers playing Negro stereotypes, esp. in minstrel shows. **2.** a performer playing a Negro role in this makeup. **3.** *Printing.* boldface.

black·fish (blak′fish′) *n., pl.* **-fish** or **fish·es.** **1.** any of various dark-colored saltwater fish, as the sea bass and the tautog. **2.** either of two freshwater fish, genus *Dallia,* of the swamps and bogs of Alaska and Siberia that can survive freezing water temperatures for a short time and is valued as a food fish.

black flag, Jolly Roger.

black·fly (blak′flī′) *n.* a dark-colored biting fly, family Simuliidae, common to North American forests.

Black·foot (blak′fût′) *n., pl.* **-feet** or **-foot.** **1.** a member of any of three tribes of Plains Indians of Algonquian linguistic stock who lived east of the Rocky Mountains in Saskatchewan and Montana. **2.** the Algonquian language of the Blackfeet. [Translation of Blackfoot *Siksika;* said to refer to their custom of blackening their moccasins.]

Black Friar, a Dominican friar. [From the *black* color of his mantle.]

black grouse, a large grouse of Europe and northern Asia, *Lyrurus tetrix,* the male of which is black with white markings.

black·guard (blag′ärd, -ərd) *n.* a low, dishonest person; scoundrel. —*v.t.* to attack with abusive language; revile; vilify. [Originally used contemptuously to refer to kitchen servants, who were soiled by their work.]

black·head (blak′hed′) *n.* **1.** a small, black, oily plug formed in a pore in the skin, usually occurring on the face, shoulders, and back. **2.** any of various birds whose heads are partially or totally black.

black·heart (blak′härt′) *n.* a disease of trees and other plants, such as the potato, characterized by a blackening and decay of the internal tissues.

black hole, the hypothetical final stage in the life cycle of a huge star, which forms when the star burns out, loses the energy to withstand the force of its own gravity, and collapses. Matter in a black hole is compressed so densely that gravity prevents the escape of anything within its influence, including visible light.

B

a	at	e	end	o	hot	u	up	hw	white		about
ā	ape	ē	me	ō	old	ū	use	ng	song		taken
ä	far	i	it	ô	fork	ü	rule	th	thin	ə	pencil
âr	care	ī	ice	oi	oil	u̇	pull	<u>th</u>	this		lemon
		îr	pierce	ou	out	ûr	turn	zh	measure		circus

black humor, a form of humor that treats pain and unhappiness as absurd or ironic rather than as tragic, esp. in drama and literature.

black·ing (blak′ing) n. a black polish or coating, as for shoes or stoves.

black·jack (blak′jak′) n. **1.** a small, flexible-handled club covered with leather, used as a weapon. **2.** a pirate's black flag. **3.** a card game in which the players play against the dealer, the winner being the one whose cards bear numbers adding up to twenty-one or to the closest number below that. Also, **twenty-one. 4.** an oak tree, *Quercus marilandica,* found in the eastern United States, having a heavy black bark. —*v.t.* to strike with a blackjack.

black lead, graphite.

black·leg (blak′leg′) n. **1.** *Informal.* a gambler who cheats, esp. at cards. **2.** *British.* someone who takes a striking worker's job; strikebreaker; scab. **3.** a bacterial disease of cattle and sheep that is usually fatal. **4.** any of several bacterial or fungous diseases causing a blackening of the base of plant stems, esp. in cabbages or potatoes.

black letter, a heavy, angular, elaborate form of Gothic type.

black light 1. invisible light, esp. ultraviolet radiation, used to cause fluorescence. **2.** a lamp emitting such light.

black·list (blak′list′) n. a list of persons or organizations to be regarded as suspect, or to be boycotted or punished in some way. —*v.t.* to place on a blacklist.

black lung, an irreversible, chronic disease of the lungs that affects coal miners, caused by the long-term inhalation of coal dust.

black magic, magic used for evil purposes; witchcraft.

black·mail (blak′māl′) n. **1.** the act of obtaining money or something else of value from a person by threat, esp. the threat to reveal information that would harm him or her in some way. **2.** something of value obtained in this way. —*v.t.* **1.** to subject (someone) to blackmail. **2.** to make do something by threats or intimidation (with *into*). [BLACK + Scottish *mail* rent, tribute, from Old English *māl* agreement, payment, from Old Norse *māl* agreement, speech; from the tribute formerly extorted by bandits and freebooters from Scottish and English farmers for protection against pillage.] —**black′mail′er,** n.

Black Ma·ri·a (mə rī′ə) *Informal.* patrol wagon.

black market 1. the selling of goods illegally, esp. in violation of price controls or rationing. **2.** a place where such selling is going on.

Black Muslim, a member of a chiefly black American sect of Islam.

black oak 1. any of several oaks of North America having dark leaves and bark, esp. *Quercus velutina,* of the eastern United States, whose inner bark is used in making dye. **2.** the wood of any of these trees.

black·out (blak′out′) n. **1.** a temporary loss of vision, consciousness, or memory. **2.** the temporary stoppage or interruption of electric service in a certain area. **3.** the turning out or covering of lights as a protection against enemy air raids. **4.** a turning off of all stage lights, esp. to indicate a separation between scenes in a play. **5.** (of news) a deliberate suppression or noncoverage of news or other information.

black pepper, see pepper.

black power also, **Black Power.** a movement among American blacks aimed at exerting political, social, and economic pressure to achieve racial equality.

black racer, blacksnake *(def. 1).*

black raspberry, a raspberry, *Rubus occidentalis,* or any of its cultivars, grown for their purplish black fruits.

black sheep 1. a sheep that is black. **2.** a person who is regarded as a disgrace or embarrassment to other members of the person's family or group because he or she does not conform to the standards or level of success espoused by the group.

Black Shirt 1. formerly, a member of the Italian Fascist corps of armed guards. **2.** a member of any similar fascist organization. [A *black shirt* was part of their uniform.]

black·smith (blak′smith′) n. **1.** a person who makes horseshoes and shoes horses. **2.** a person who works with iron by heating it in a forge and then hammering it into shape on an anvil. [From their working with iron, a *black* metal.]

black·snake (blak′snāk′) n. **1.** a nonpoisonous snake, *Coluber constrictor,* of the eastern United States, having dull black scales. Length: 4-5 feet (1.2-1.5 meters). Also, **black racer. 2.** any of various other snakes having black or dark-colored skins. **3.** a heavy, flexible whip of braided leather or rawhide.

black studies, courses in the history, literature, and culture of American blacks as taught in high schools, colleges, or universities.

black tea, a tea made from tea leaves that have withered and fermented before being subjected to the drying process.

black·thorn (blak′thôrn′) n. **1.** a thorny shrub, *Prunus spinosa,* of the rose family, found in Europe and parts of Asia, bearing white flowers and deep blue, plumlike fruit. Also, **sloe. 2.** a walking stick made from the wood of this shrub. **3.** a hawthorn of North America, *Crataegus calpodendron.*

black tie 1. a black bow tie, worn with a formal jacket or a tuxedo. **2.** semiformal evening wear. ➡ distinguished from **white tie.**

black·top (blak′top′) n. **1.** a bituminous material, such as asphalt, used to pave roads. **2.** a road paved with such a material. —*v.t.,* -**topped,** -**top·ping.** to pave with blacktop.

black walnut 1. the strong, dark brown wood of a North American tree, *Juglans nigra,* used chiefly for furniture and gun stocks. **2.** the tree itself. **3.** the oily, edible nut of this tree.

black widow, a small, glossy black spider, *Latrodectus mactans,* commonly found in Central America and in southern and western parts of the United States. The female is poisonous, has a red hourglass-shaped marking on the underside of its abdomen, and is more than twice the size of the male. [From its color and its practice of eating its mate.]

black widow spider

black willow, see willow *(def. 1).*

blad·der (blad′ər) n. **1.** an elastic, membranous sac in the body that stores or receives a liquid or gas, esp. the bladder in the pelvic cavity, which stores urine received from the kidneys. **2.** something resembling a bladder in shape, use, or inflatability, such as the inflatable inner bag of a football. **3.** an inflated sac in certain plants, esp. one that acts as a food trap or as a float on an aquatic plant. [Old English *blædre* membranous sac in the body.]

blad·der·wort (blad′ər wûrt′) n. any of various insect-eating plants growing in marshes or in water, genus *Utricularia,* found in temperate and tropical regions, having small bladders on their leaves.

blade (blād) n. **1.** the flat, sharp-edged part of a tool, instrument, or weapon that cuts: *the blade of a knife, the blade of a sword.* **2.** a leaf, as of grass. **3.** the broad part of a leaf or petal. For illustration, see leaf. **4.** a broad, flat part or surface, as on an oar, propeller, or fan. **5.** a sword. **6.** the sharp runner of an ice skate. **7.** a broad, flat bone or part of a bone. **8.** the foremost part of the tongue. **9.** a dashing, rakish young man. [Old English *blæd* leaf, broad flat part of an implement.] —**blad′ed,** adj. —**blade′-like′,** adj.

blah (blä) *Informal. adj.* not interesting; boring or dull: *a blah personality.* —*n.* senseless chatter; nonsense. [Imitative.]
• **the blahs.** a feeling of boredom, discomfort, or depression: *The rainy morning gave me the blahs.*

blain (blān) n. an inflamed swelling. [Middle English *bleine,* from Old English *blegen* a blister.]

blam·a·ble (blā′mə bəl) also, **blame·a·ble.** adj. deserving blame; reprehensible. —**blam′a·bly;** also, **blame′a·bly,** adv.

blame (blām) *v.t.,* **blamed, blam·ing. 1.** to find fault with; censure: *I can't blame you for trying.* **2.** to accuse or hold (someone or something) responsible: *I blame you for this mistake.* **3.** to fix responsibility for (something): *They blamed the damage on the storm.* —*n.* **1.** the responsibility for something wrong: *to take the blame for an error.* **2.** the act of finding fault; censure; condemnation: *Such serious misbehavior is deserving of blame.* [Old

B

French *blasmer* to accuse, censure, going back to Latin *blasphēmāre* to speak ill of. See BLASPHEME.]
· **to be to blame.** to be at fault: *It was an accident, so no one is to blame.*

Synonyms *v.t.* **Blame, censure, criticize,** and **reproach** mean to express disapproval of or find fault with someone or something. **Blame** implies assuming the role of judge of right and wrong and is the only one of these terms that may indicate unexpressed disapproval: *Although I blame them for starting the argument, I didn't say anything.* **Censure** strengthens the sense of competence or authority in judging and suggests formal public expression: *The city council censured the project manager for negligence.* **Criticize** often suggests making distinctions based on standards: *His parents criticized his taste in music. Her boss criticized her for an inadequate job performance.* **Reproach** indicates a direct accusation and suggests an emotional reaction: *We reproached our friends for not letting us in on the secret.*

blame·less (blām′lis) *adj.* not deserving blame; innocent. —**blame′less·ly,** *adv.* —**blame′less·ness,** *n.*

blame·wor·thy (blām′wûr′thē) *adj.* deserving blame: *Everyone who was involved in the affair is blameworthy.*

blanch (blanch) *v.i.* to become white; turn pale: *to blanch with fear.* —*v.t.* **1.** to remove color from; bleach. **2.** to make pale, as from fear or sickness. **3.a.** to remove the skin of by scalding: *to blanch almonds.* **b.** to scald or parboil, as in preparation for further cooking. [Old French *blanchir* to whiten, from *blanc* white. See BLANK.]

blanc·mange (blə mänj′, -mänzh′) *n.* a sweet gelatinous dessert that is shaped in a mold and made of milk that is thickened and flavored. [Old French *blancmanger* literally, white food, from *blanc* white (of Germanic origin) + *manger* food (going back to Latin *mandūcāre* to eat.)]

bland (bland) *adj.* **1.** lacking individual interest or excitement; uninteresting; vapid; dull: *a bland movie, a bland personality.* **2.** not irritating; mild; soothing: *a bland diet, a bland climate.* **3.** smoothly agreeable or pleasant: *a bland smile.* [Latin *blandus* soft.] —**bland′ly,** *adv.* —**bland′ness,** *n.*

blan·dish (blan′dish) *v.t.* to coax with flattery; cajole. [Old French *blandiss-*, a stem of *blandir* to flatter, from Latin *blandīrī.*]

blan·dish·ment (blan′dish mənt) *n.* a coaxing or flattering speech or action; coaxing; flattery.

blank (blangk) *adj.* **1.** not written or printed upon; unmarked: *a blank sheet of paper, a blank canvas.* **2.** having spaces to be filled out: *a blank questionnaire.* **3.** lacking interest or thought; empty: *His mind is blank.* **4.** showing a lack of interest or thought; expressionless; vacant: *a blank gaze.* **5.** showing confusion; bewildered: *a blank look.* **6.** lacking some finishing feature or characteristic: *a blank cartridge, a blank key.* **7.** to the fullest extent; complete; utter; absolute: *a blank denial.* —*n.* **1.** an empty space to be filled out, as in a printed form. **2.** a form or document containing such spaces. **3.** an empty place or time; void: *My mind is a blank.* **4.** a partially completed object, such as a piece of metal, ready to be finished by a further operation. **5.** a cartridge containing powder, but no bullet. —*v.t.* **1.** to obscure or delete (often with *out*). **2.** to keep (an opponent) from scoring in a game. [Old French *blanc* white; of Germanic origin.] —**blank′ly,** *adv.* —**blank′ness,** *n.*
· **to draw a blank.** to be unsuccessful in an attempt, esp. to be unable to think of a solution or an answer.

blank check 1. a signed check without the amount filled in. **2.** the freedom to act without control; carte blanche.

blan·ket (blang′kit) *n.* **1.** a covering made of wool or other woven fabric, used esp. for warmth, as in bed. **2.** something that covers like a blanket: *a blanket of fog.* —*v.t.* to cover with or as with a blanket: *Snow blanketed the town.* —*adj.* applicable to or covering a wide range of conditions or items: *blanket approval.* [Old French *blankete* woolen covering; originally, white wool cloth, from *blanc* white; of Germanic origin.]

blank verse 1. unrhymed verse written in iambic pentameter. Much of Shakespeare's work is in blank verse. **2.** unrhymed verse having any regular meter.

blare (blâr) *v.,* **blared, blar·ing.** —*v.i.* to make a loud, harsh sound: *The bugles blared.* —*v.t.* to proclaim loudly and harshly: *The radio blared the news.* —*n.* a loud, harsh sound. [Middle English *bleren* to bellow, from an unrecorded Old English word.]

blar·ney (blär′nē) *n.* smooth, flattering talk. —*v.t.* to influence or try to influence with blarney; coax; cajole. [From the BLARNEY STONE.]

Blarney Stone, a stone block in a wall of a castle in Ireland, said to endow those who kiss it with skill in flattery and cajolery.

bla·sé (blä zā′, blä′zā) *adj.* indifferent to pleasure or excitement,

as from overindulgence; jaded; world-weary. [French *blasé*, past participle of *blaser* to weary by indulgence; of uncertain origin.]

blas·pheme (blas fēm′, blas′fēm) *v.,* **-phemed, -phem·ing.** —*v.t.* to speak of (God or anything sacred) with contempt or disrespect. —*v.i.* to speak with contempt or disrespect. [Old French *blasfemer*, from Latin *blasphēmāre* to speak ill of, from Greek *blasphemein.* Doublet of BLAME.] —**blas·phem′er,** *n.*

blas·phe·mous (blas′fə məs) *adj.* characterized by or using blasphemy; irreverent: *a blasphemous statement.* [Late Latin *blasphēmus*, from Greek *blasphēmos.*] —**blas′phe·mous·ly,** *adv.*

blas·phe·my (blas′fə mē) *n., pl.* **-mies.** an expression of contempt or irreverence for God or anything sacred.

blast (blast) *n.* **1.** a strong rush of wind; gust: *The chilling blasts swept over the lake.* **2.** a loud, explosive sound, such as that made by a horn: *the blast of trumpets, the blast of the radio.* **3.** a strong current of air produced artificially. **4.a.** an explosion, as of dynamite. **b.** the charge set off in such an explosion. **5.** a current of compressed air directed into a blast furnace to promote combustion during smelting. **6.** *Informal.* a violent attack or denunciation. **7.** *Informal.* a good time, esp. a wild party. **8.** a destructive influence; blight. —*v.t.* **1.** to blow up or shatter with or as with an explosive. **2.** to bring damage or blight to; ruin; wither: *Losing this game blasts our hopes for the championship. Frost blasted the blossoms.* **3.** to cause to sound loudly. **4.** *Informal.* to criticize or denounce vigorously. —*v.i.* to sound loudly or harshly: *The loudspeakers blasted.* [Old English *blæst* gust of wind.] —**blast′er,** *n.*
· **(at) full blast.** at maximum speed, capacity, or volume.
· **to blast off.** (of a rocket or missile) to take off; begin flight.

blast·ed (blas′tid) *adj.* **1.** characterized by destruction; withered; blighted. **2.** condemned as bad; damned; confounded.

blast furnace, a vertical smelting furnace in which the heat is maintained by a blast of preheated air, used esp. in the reduction of iron ore.

blas·to·coele (blas′tə sēl′) *also,* **blas·to·coel,** **blas·to·cele.** *n.* the cavity of a blastula.

blas·to·cyst (blas′tə sist) *n.* the blastula of a mammal; a stage in embryonic development.

blas·to·derm (blas′tə dûrm′) *n.* a layer of germinal cells arising from the segmentation of the fertilized ovum and later forming the wall of the blastula. [Greek *blastos* germ + *derma* skin.] —**blas′to·der′mic,** *adj.*

blast-off (blast′ôf′, -of′) *also,* **blast·off.** *n.* the launching of a rocket or missile.

blas·to·mere (blas′tə mîr′) *n.* one of the cells produced during the cleavage of the fertilized ovum. —**blas·to·mer′ic** (blas′tə-mer′ik), *adj.*

blas·to·pore (blas′tə pôr′) *n.* the opening of the archenteron on the surface of a gastrula.

blas·tu·la (blas′chə lə) *n., pl.* **-lae** (-lē′). an early stage in the development of an animal embryo, usually consisting of a single layer of cells forming a sphere around a central cavity, the blastocoele. [Modern Latin *blastula*, diminutive of Greek *blastos* germ.] —**blas′tu·lar,** *adj.*

blat (blat) *v.i., v.t.,* **blat·ted, blat·ting.** to bleat. —*n.* a bleat. [A form of BLEAT.]

bla·tant (blā′tənt) *adj.* **1.** impossible to overlook; conspicuously evident; obtrusive: *blatant negligence.* **2.** noisy in a coarse or offensive manner. [Coined by the English poet Edmund Spenser, 1552-99, to describe a noisy beast symbolizing slander; possibly from Latin *blatīre* to babble.] —**bla′tan·cy,** *n.* —**bla′tant·ly,** *adv.*

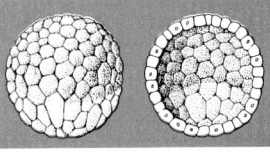

blastula
exterior and cross section

blath·er (blath′ər) *also,* **blether.** *n.* foolish talk; nonsense. —*v.t., v.i.* to speak foolishly. [Old Norse *blathra* to talk foolishly.]

blath·er·skite (blath′ər skīt′) *n.* a talkative, foolish person.

blaze¹ (blāz) *n.* **1.** a bright, intense flame or fire. **2.** a bright, intense light or glow: *the blaze of the sun.* **3.** a brilliant or striking display: *a blaze of color.* **4.** a strong, sudden outburst: *a blaze of*

a	at	e	end	o	hot	u	up	hw	white		about
ā	ape	ē	me	ō	old	ū	use	ng	song		taken
ä	far	i	it	ô	fork	ü	rule	th	thin	ə	pencil
âr	care	ī	ice	oi	oil	ù	pull	th	this		lemon
		îr	pierce	ou	out	ûr	turn	zh	measure		circus

fury. **5.** blazes. *Slang.* hell. —*v.i.,* **blazed, blaz·ing. 1.** to burn brightly. **2.** to shine brilliantly; be bright: *The city streets blazed with light.* **3.** to display strong feeling: *eyes that blaze with anger.* [Old English *blæse* flame, torch.]
•**to blaze away. a.** to work at vigorously or enthusiastically. **b.** to keep on shooting a gun or guns.

blaze² (blāz) *n.* **1.** a light-colored marking on the face of an animal, as a horse or cow. **2.** a mark made on a tree, as by chipping off a piece of bark, to indicate a trail or boundary. —*v.t.,* **blazed, blaz·ing. 1.** to mark (a tree) with blazes. **2.** to indicate (a trail) by marking trees: *to blaze a path through the forest.* **3.** to open up or take the lead in; pioneer: *The diplomat's efforts blazed the way for future negotiations.* [Probably from Middle Low German *bles* white spot.]

blaze³ (blāz) *v.t.,* **blazed, blaz·ing.** to make known; proclaim; publicize: *Blaze forth the news.* [Old Norse *blāsa* to blow.]

blaz·er (blā′zər) *n.* a sports jacket, often solid-colored, with metal buttons, originally having the identifying insignia of a particular school, club, or other group on the breast pocket.

bla·zon (blā′zən) *v.t.* **1.** to make public; proclaim. **2.** to decorate or embellish, as with blazonry; adorn. **3.** to describe or illustrate (a coat of arms) according to the rules of heraldry. —*n.* **1.** a coat of arms; heraldic shield or banner; armorial bearings. **2.** a description or the art of describing or illustrating armorial bearings. **3.** an ostentatious display; show. [Middle French *blason* coat of arms, from Old French *blason* shield; of uncertain origin.]

bla·zon·ry (blā′zən rē) *n.* **1.** the art of describing or illustrating armorial bearings. **2.** a coat of arms; armorial bearings. **3.** a brilliant display; spectacle.

bldg. *pl.* **bldgs.** building.

bleach (blēch) *v.t., v.i.* to make or become white, colorless, or pale, as by exposing to chemicals. —*n.* **1.** a substance used as a bleaching agent. **2.** the act or process of bleaching. **3.** the degree of whiteness or paleness obtained from bleaching. [Old English *blǣcan* to whiten, fade.]

bleach·er (blē′chər) *n.* **1.** a person or thing that bleaches. **2. bleachers. a.** the roofless section of tiered seats or benches in a stadium, usually low-priced, unreserved, and, in baseball, past the outfield. **b.** any similar group of tiered seats or the structure that contains them: *Wooden bleachers were set up for the parade.*

bleaching powder 1. a powder that bleaches. **2.** chloride of lime.

bleak (blēk) *adj.* **1.** exposed, barren, and windswept; desolate: *bleak stretches of deserted farmland.* **2.** cold; chilling: *a bleak December.* **3.** causing sadness or gloom; dreary; depressing: *a bleak outlook.* [Old Norse *bleikr* white, pale.] —**bleak′ly,** *adv.* —**bleak′ness,** *n.*

blear (blîr) *adj.* dim or blurred; indistinct. —*v.t.* **1.** to dim or blur (the eyes or vision). **2.** to make dim or blurred; obscure. [Middle English *bleren* to dim the eyes; probably from an unrecorded Old English word.]

blear-eyed (blîr′īd′) *adj. Archaic.* bleary-eyed.

blear·y (blîr′ē) *adj.,* **blear·i·er, blear·i·est. 1.** (of the eyes or vision) dimmed or blurred. **2.** groggy or dazed from exhaustion: *We were bleary after the long drive home.* **3.** vague or indistinct: *bleary, distant shapes in the haze.* —**blear′i·ly,** *adv.* —**blear′i·ness,** *n.*

blear·y-eyed (blîr′ē īd′) *adj.* **1.** having bleared eyes. **2.** groggy or dazed from exhaustion.

bleat (blēt) *n.* **1.** the cry of a sheep, goat, or calf. **2.** any similar sound. —*v.i.* **1.** to utter the cry of a sheep, goat, or calf. **2.** to make a similar sound. **3.** to whine or complain. —*v.t.* to utter with or as with a bleat or a similar sound. [Old English *blǣtan* to cry, as a sheep, goat, or calf.] —**bleat′er,** *n.* —**bleat′ing·ly,** *adv.*

bleb (bleb) *n.* **1.** a skin blister that is filled with fluid. **2.** an air bubble, as in liquid or glass. [Probably a form of BLOB.]

bleed (blēd) *v.,* **bled, bleed·ing.** —*v.i.* **1.** to lose or shed blood: *The cut started to bleed.* **2.** to suffer wounds or die: *those who bled for the cause.* **3.** to feel anguish, sympathy, or pity: *My heart bled for the homeless family.* **4.** to ooze sap or other fluid. **5.** (of a dye or paint) to run or become diffuse. **6.** *Printing.* to extend to, or seem to run off, the edge or edges of a page. —*v.t.* **1.** to draw blood from, esp. as a remedy for illness. **2.** to lose or exude: *to bleed sap.* **3.** to drain or extract (air, liquid, sap, or other substance) from. **4.** *Informal.* to extort money or something valuable from. **5.** *Printing.* **a.** to permit (an illustration or ornamentation) to extend to the edge of the page. **b.** to trim (a book or sheet) so closely as to mutilate the text or illustration. —*n. Printing.* **1.** an illustration that bleeds. **2.** a page that has been bled. —*adj. Printing.* having printed matter that bleeds: *a bleed page.* [Old English *blēdan* to lose blood.]

bleed·er (blē′dər) *n.* **1.** a person who bleeds excessively, esp. a hemophiliac. **2.** a person who bleeds patients as a remedy for illness.

bleeding heart 1. any of several plants, genus *Dicentra,* esp. *D. spectabilis,* the common bleeding heart, widely cultivated for its drooping clusters of red, pink, or white, heart-shaped flowers. **2.** *Informal.* a person who displays excessive pity and concern for others.

bleep (blēp) *n.* a brief, high-pitched sound used as a signal or warning or to censor words in a broadcast. —*v.i.* to make such a sound. —*v.t.* to censor (words), as in a broadcast. [Imitative.] —**bleep′er,** *n.*

blem·ish (blem′ish) *n.* **1.** a physical flaw or defect, esp. a mark on the skin. **2.** any imperfection, flaw, or stain: *a blemish in an otherwise perfect crystal goblet, a moral blemish.* —*v.t.* to spoil the beauty or perfection of; mar; sully. [Old French *blemiss-,* a stem of *blesmir* to stain; of Germanic origin.]

Synonyms *n.* **Blemish, defect,** and **flaw** mean something that spoils the perfection of a concrete object or abstract quality. **Blemish** suggests something external or superficial: *This cream will conceal skin blemishes. A "B" in calculus was the only blemish on his otherwise perfect academic record.* **Defect,** on the other hand, suggests something more serious, possibly essential to functioning, although it may not be immediately apparent: *A defect in the structure of the building caused it to collapse. Snobbery was the major defect in her character.* **Flaw,** which may be used of either something essential or something more superficial, suggests a break in cohesion or consistency: *a flaw in an argument, a flaw in the glaze on a bowl.*

blench¹ (blench) *v.i. Archaic.* to shrink away; flinch. [Old English *blencan* to deceive.]

blench² (blench) *v.t., v.i.* to make or become pale; whiten. [Form of BLANCH.]

blend (blend) *v.,* **blend·ed** or **blent, blend·ing.** —*v.t.* **1.** to mix together thoroughly; combine so as to make separate components indistinguishable: *The cook blended flour and milk to make pancake batter.* **2.** to mix (varieties) so as to produce a desired quality: *to blend tobacco.* —*v.i.* **1.** to mix; mingle; unite: *voices blended in song.* **2.a.** to pass or shade gradually into each other: *Sea and sky seemed to blend in the hazy distance.* **b.** to be or become indistinguishable from (with *into*): *The black coat blended into the surrounding darkness.* **3.** to fit together; harmonize: *The rug blends well with the decor.* —*n.* **1.** a result or product of blending; mixture: *a new blend of coffee.* **2.** a word formed by combining separate words or parts of separate words. The word *telecast* is a blend of *television* and *broadcast.* [Probably from *blend-,* a stem of Old Norse *blanda* to mix.] —For Synonyms *(v.t.),* see mix.

blende (blend) *n.* any of several sulfide minerals, such as sphalerite. [German *Blende* sphalerite, from *blenden* to deceive; because sphalerite resembles an ore rich in lead, but contains none.]

blended whiskey, a whiskey consisting of either a blend of whiskeys or a blend of whiskey and neutral spirits.

blend·er (blen′dər) *n.* **1.** a machine with high-speed rotary blades for mixing drinks and soft foods and chopping or liquefying solid foods. **2.** a person or thing that blends.

blen·ny (blen′ē) *n.,* **pl. -nies.** any of various small, saltwater fish, family Blenniidae, having an elongated body and a large dorsal fin. [Latin *blennius* a saltwater fish, from Greek *blennos* a type of fish.]

bless (bles) *v.t.,* **blessed** (blest) or **blest, bless·ing. 1.** to make or pronounce holy; consecrate: *And God blessed the seventh day* (Genesis 2:3). **2.** to invoke divine favor or protection for: *The minister blessed the congregation.* **3.** to endow or favor (with *with*): *to be blessed with good health.* **4.** to confer good or happiness upon (with *with*): *She blessed us with her presence.* **5.** to extol; praise; glorify: *Bless His holy name* (Psalms 103:1). **6.** to make the sign of the cross over. **7.** to guard or protect (with *from*). [Old English *blētsian* originally, to consecrate with blood, from *blōd* blood.]

bless·ed (bles′id, blest) *also,* **blest.** *adj.* **1.** consecrated by a religious rite; holy: *blessed water.* **2.** worthy of adoration or worship: *the blessed Trinity.* **3.** enjoying great happiness; fortunate. **4.** bringing happiness or pleasure. **5.** enjoying the bliss of heaven; beatified. **6.** cursed; damned: *a blessed nuisance.* ➡ used as a euphemism. —*n.* **the blessed. a.** people who are blessed. **b.** in Roman Catholicism, the dead who are beatified. —**bless′ed·ly,** *adv.* —**bless′ed·ness,** *n.*

blessed event *Informal.* the birth of a child.

Blessed Virgin, the Virgin Mary.

bless·ing (bles′ing) *n.* **1.** a prayer for divine favor, esp. at the close of a church service; benediction. **2.** the act of a person who

blesses. **3.** a prayer of thanksgiving, usually made before or after a meal. **4.** something that provides happiness or prosperity; boon: *We enjoy the blessings of a happy home.* **5.** approval: *The family gave its blessing to the marriage.* **6.** a wish for good fortune or success: *blessings for the New Year.*

blest (blest) *v.* a past tense and past participle of **bless.** —*adj.* blessed.

bleth·er (bleth′ər) blather.

blew (blü) the past tense of **blow²** and **blow³.**

blight (blīt) *n.* **1.** any of several plant diseases that cause sudden and severe damage, esp. to leaves or fruit. **2.** a bacteria, fungus, or virus that causes such a disease. **3.** something that damages, spoils, or frustrates: *the blight of corruption.* **4.** the state of being blighted; ruined condition. —*v.t.* **1.** to cause to wither or decay; blast: *Rain blighted the corn.* **2.** to spoil; frustrate; ruin: *Financial ruin blighted their hopes for a secure future.* [Of uncertain origin.]

blimp (blimp) *n.* a small, nonrigid airship, used chiefly for observation. [Of uncertain origin.]

blind (blīnd) *adj.* **1.** unable to see; sightless. **2.** lacking in insight or perception: *to be blind to someone's needs.* **3.** independent of reason or intelligence: *blind faith.* **4.** without rational direction or control; random: *blind chance.* **5.** lacking thought, control, or good judgment; reckless: *blind fury, blind tenacity.* **6.** not directed or governed by sight: *blind flying, blind groping in the dark.* **7.** closed at one end: *a blind roadway.* **8.** not easily seen; hidden: *a blind corner.* **9.** unconscious; insensible: *a blind stupor.* **10.** *Informal.* drunk. **11.** without openings for light or passage: *a blind wall, a blind hedge.* **12.** of, relating to, or for the sightless. **13.** *Archaic.* hard to make out; illegible: *blind writing.* —*n.* **1.** something that obstructs vision or keeps out light. **2.** Venetian blind. **3.** a person, thing, or action used to mislead; pretext; decoy. **4.** a place of concealment; ambush: *The hunter ducked into his blind.* —*v.t.* **1.** to make blind; render sightless. **2.** to deprive of sight temporarily; dazzle: *The glare of the sunlight blinded us.* **3.** to deprive of the power to discern or judge: *blinded by jealousy.* **4.** to darken; obscure; conceal: *Ivy blinded the windows of the old house.* —*adv.* **1.** without sight or the aid of vision: *to fly blind.* **2.** without guidance or reason: *to be working blind.* **3.** to the point of being unconscious or insensible: *blind drunk.* [Old English *blind* sightless, lacking in perception.] —**blind′ly,** *adv.* —**blind′ness,** *n.*

blind alley 1. a passageway shut off at one end. **2.** any position or activity that leads nowhere.

blind date *Informal.* **1.** a date between two persons who have never met, arranged by a third party. **2.** either of the two persons.

blind·er (blīn′dər) *n.* either of a pair of flaps attached to a horse's bridle to prevent the horse from seeing sideways. Also, **blinker.**

blind·fold (blīnd′fōld′) *v.t.* **1.** to cover the eyes of, esp. with a cloth. **2.** to obstruct the understanding or judgment of; mislead; deceive. —*n.* a cover for the eyes, esp. one of cloth. [Middle English *blindfellen* to strike blind, from BLIND + *fellen* to strike down, FELL²; altered by confusion with FOLD¹.] —**blind′fold′ed,** *adj.*

blind·man's buff (blīnd′manz′ buf′) a game in which a blindfolded player tries to catch and identify another player. Also, **blindman's bluff.**

blind spot 1. a small area of the retina that is not sensitive to light because the optic nerve enters the eye there. For illustration, see **eye. 2.** an area or subject about which a person is ignorant or unable to form unbiased judgments: *to have a blind spot about racial matters.* **3.** an area in which radio or television reception is poor. **4.** an area where sight or detection is obstructed: *a blind spot in a car's rearview mirror.*

blind trust, a trust fund established to provide the independent management of stocks, bonds, and other investments of an individual in public office in order to avoid a conflict of interest.

blind·worm (blīnd′wûrm′) *n.* **1.** a small, limbless, snakelike lizard, *Anguis fragilis,* of Europe and Africa, having very tiny eyes. Length: 1 foot (0.3 meter). Also, **slowworm. 2.** a caecilian found in Sri Lanka that wraps itself around its eggs. [It was erroneously believed to have no eyes at all.]

blink (blingk) *v.i.* **1.** to close and open the eyelids rapidly, often unintentionally: *The photographers' flashbulbs made them blink.* **2.** to look with winking or half-shut eyes; squint. **3.** to flash on and off; glimmer; twinkle: *A star blinked in the sky.* —*v.t.* **1.** to close and open (one's eyes) rapidly. **2.** to cause to flash on and off: *We blinked the car lights as a signal.* —*n.* **1.** a rapid closing and opening of the eyes. **2.** a twinkle; glimmer. **3.** a glance of the eye; glimpse. [Middle English *blenchen* to jerk, turn one's eyes; probably of Scandinavian origin.]

• **on the blink.** *Slang.* not working properly; out of order: *The old radio is on the blink.*

• **to blink at.** to overlook or ignore deliberately: *The employer blinked at the new clerk's mistakes.*

blink·er (bling′kər) *n.* **1.** blinder. **2.a.** a flashing light signal. **b.** a device that flashes a light on and off. **3.** *Slang.* eye.

blintze (blints, blint′sə) *also,* **blintz** (blints). *n.* a thin pancake rolled around a filling, as of cheese or fruit, and fried. [Yiddish *blintse,* from Ukrainian *blynci* plural taken as singular.]

blip (blip) *n.* a spot of light on a radar screen that indicates the presence of an object within range of the radar transmitter. [Imitative.]

bliss (blis) *n.* **1.** supreme happiness or joy; rapture. **2.** spiritual joy, esp. the joy of the blessed in heaven. [Old English *bliss,* joy.]

bliss·ful (blis′fəl) *adj.* full of, characterized by, or causing bliss. —**bliss′ful·ly,** *adv.* —**bliss′ful·ness,** *n.*

blis·ter (blis′tər) *n.* **1.** a bubblelike swelling of the skin, filled with watery matter and usually caused by rubbing or by a burn. **2.** any similar swelling, as on a plant, painted surface, or molded plastic. **3.** a domelike, transparent structure on the fuselage of certain aircraft. —*v.t.* **1.** to raise blisters on: *The sun blistered my face.* **2.** to subject to harsh, scathing criticism. —*v.i.* to have or develop blisters. [Old French *blestre* a swelling; of Germanic origin.] —**blis′ter·y,** *adj.*

blister beetle, any of various beetles of the family Meloidae, as the Spanish fly, many of which secrete a substance that can blister the skin.

blis·ter·ing (blis′tər ing) *adj.* **1.** causing blisters: *blistering heat.* **2.** harsh; withering; scathing: *a blistering reply.* **3.** severe; intense: *a blistering attack on the fort.* —**blis′ter·ing·ly,** *adv.*

B.Lit. 1. Bachelor of Letters. **2.** Bachelor of Literature.

blithe (blīth, blīth) *adj.* **1.** full of joy or gaiety; lighthearted; cheerful. **2.** showing no concern, interest, or responsibility; heedless: *blithe indifference to a problem.* [Old English *blīthe* joyous.] —**blithe′ly,** *adv.* —**blithe′ness,** *n.*

blith·er·ing (blith′ər ing) *adj.* given to silly, aimless talk; jabbering: *a blithering fool.*

blithe·some (blīth′səm, blīth′-) *adj.* full of joy or gaiety; lighthearted; cheerful. —**blithe′some·ly,** *adv.* —**blithe′some·ness,** *n.*

blitz (blits) *n.* blitzkrieg. —*v.t.* to subject to or overwhelm by a blitz. [Short for BLITZKRIEG.]

blitz·krieg (blits′krēg′) *n.* **1.a.** a method of offensive warfare based on sudden, swift, and massive attacks designed to overwhelm the enemy quickly. **b.** an attack or campaign using this method. **2.** any sudden, overwhelming attack. [German *Blitzkrieg* lightning war, from *blitz* lightning + *krieg* war.]

bliz·zard (bliz′ərd) *n.* **1.** a severe windstorm characterized by wind-driven snow and intense cold. **2.** a severe, heavy snowstorm marked by a very strong wind. **3.** a great quantity arriving, happening, or the like at one time. [Of uncertain origin.]

B.LL., Bachelor of Laws. Also, **LL.B.**

bloat (blōt) *v.i.* to become swollen or puffed up; swell. —*v.t.* **1.** to cause to swell or expand; inflate. **2.** to cure (fish) by salting, smoking, and partial drying. —*n.* in domestic cattle, sheep, and horses, a gassy intestinal disorder caused by eating green forage. [From Middle English *blote* soft, probably from Old Norse *blautr* soft, wet.]

bloat·er (blō′tər) *n.* a herring or mackerel that has been bloated, or cured.

blob (blob) *n.* **1.** a drop or lump of a thick, soft, or sticky substance: *a blob of paint.* **2.** *Informal.* a shapeless thing. [Of uncertain origin.]

bloc (blok) *n.* a collection of persons, groups, or nations formed to pursue a common purpose: *the farm bloc, the Asian bloc in the United Nations.* [French *bloc* the whole collection; see BLOCK.]

block (blok) *n.* **1.** a solid piece of matter, often having one or more flat surfaces: *a block of wood, a block of ice.* **2.** a heavy slab of wood on which cutting or chopping is done: *a butcher's block.* **3.** something that obstructs or hinders; obstacle; hindrance; stoppage. **4.a.** an area or group of buildings enclosed by streets: *Walk around the block.* **b.** the length of a side of such an area: *I*

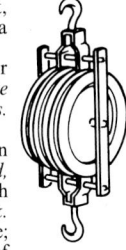

block
(def. 12)

walked six blocks. **5.** a cubelike child's toy, used for building. **6.** a piece of wood on which the head of a person about to be beheaded is placed. **7.** a number of things of the same kind, dealt with as a unit: *a block of tickets, a block of stock shares.* **8.** a hollow brick used for construction. **9.** a platform or stand from which something is auctioned. **10.a.** a piece of wood or other solid material used as a support: *a mounting block.* **b.** a mold or form upon which an object is shaped or displayed: *a hat block.* **11.** a piece of wood or linoleum with engraved or raised images, used to form impressions when inked. **12.** a pulley or system of pulleys mounted in a casing. **13.** *Sports.* an action that hinders, interferes with, or stops an opponent's movement or play. **14.** *Psychology.* an interruption in thought or action produced by emotional rather than physical causes: *a mental block.* **15.** a section of railroad track controlled by signals. **16.** *Medicine.* an interruption or obstruction of normal physiological functioning. **17.** a group of four or more attached stamps in the shape of a square or rectangle: *The collector bought a block of the new commemorative stamp.* —*v.t.* **1.** to obstruct passage through (something): *Debris blocked the chimney. Uprooted trees blocked the road.* **2.** to stand in the way of; be an obstacle to; hinder: *to block the enactment of a law.* **3.** to shape or stamp with or as with a block: *to block a sweater.* **4.** to strengthen, support, or fit with blocks. **5.** *Sports.* to hinder (an opponent's or the ball's movement). **6.** *Psychology.* to interrupt or suppress (something) by the action of or as a result of emotional forces. **7.** *Medicine.* to prevent the transmission of impulses in (a nerve). —*v.i.* **1.** *Sports.* to hinder an opponent's actions. **2.** to experience a psychological block: *to block on an exam.* [Old French *bloc* log, mass, the whole collection; from Middle Dutch *blok* a mass.] —**block′er,** *n.*
  • **to block in** (or **out**). to plan or outline roughly: *The artist blocked in the figures with charcoal before starting the painting. The board members blocked out a schedule for introducing the new product.*
  • **to go to the block.** to be beheaded.
block·ade (blo kād′) *n.* **1.** the shutting off of a port, city, or coast by enemy troops or ships to prevent people or supplies from going in or out. **2.** the forces that carry on a blockade. **3.** something that shuts off or obstructs; obstacle. —*v.t.,* **-ad·ed, -ad·ing.** to subject to a blockade. —**block·ad′er,** *n.*
  • **to run the blockade.** to go through a blockade successfully.
block·ade-run·ner (blo kād′run′ər) *n.* a person or ship that is engaged in slipping back and forth through a blockade.
block·age (blok′ij) *n.* obstruction.
block and tackle, an arrangement of pulley blocks and ropes, used for lifting or hauling.
block·bust·er (blok′bus′tər) *n. Informal.* **1.** an aerial bomb weighing two or more tons and having great demolition power. **2.** a person or thing that is remarkably impressive or successful: *The latest film in the series was a veritable blockbuster.*
block·head (blok′hed′) *n.* a stupid or foolish person; dolt.
block·house (blok′hous′) *n., pl.* **-hous·es** (-hou′ziz). **1.** a fortified building having loopholes from which to fire, originally made of timber and later of concrete. **2.** a heavily reinforced building serving as an observation and control center near a launch pad.

blockhouse

block·ish (blok′ish) *adj.* stupid; dull. —**block′ish·ly,** *adv.* —**block′ish·ness,** *n.*
block letter 1. a letter or lettering without serifs. **2.** a printing type that is cut from wood.
block plane, a small plane used chiefly for smoothing ends of wood across the grain.
block printing, printing from wood or linoleum blocks that have engraved or raised images.
block signal, a railway signal controlling the movement of trains into and within a block.
block system, a control system in which a railroad track is divided into blocks, the movement of trains into each block being regulated by an automatic signal.
bloke (blōk) *n. British. Slang.* a fellow; guy.
blond (blond) *adj.* **1.** (of hair) having some shade of light yellow as its main color. **2.** (of a person) having such hair, often with light-colored skin and eyes. **3.** light-colored: *blond furniture, a blond complexion.* —*n.* a blond person. used for both sexes in all defs. [Old French *blond* fair, fair-haired; probably of Germanic origin.] —**blond′ness,** *n.* —**blond′ish,** *adj.*

blonde (blond) *adj.* (of a female) having blond hair, often with light-colored skin and eyes. —*n.* a blonde woman or girl. —**blonde′ness,** *n.*
blood (blud) *n.* **1.** the fluid circulated by the heart through the bodies of vertebrates and many invertebrates, consisting in human beings of red blood cells, white blood cells, platelets, and other substances suspended in plasma, and functioning chiefly to convey oxygen, nourishment, and waste materials from one part of the body to another. **2.** essential nature; lifeblood. **3.** the shedding of blood; murder: *I am innocent of the blood of this just person* (Matthew 27:24). **4.** descent from a common ancestor; kinship: *a cousin related by blood.* **5.** family; lineage, esp. noble lineage: *of noble blood.* **6.** national or racial extraction: *of Indian blood.* **7.** state of mind or temperament; disposition: *a person of hot blood.* **8.** good breed or pedigree; purebred stock. **9.** a spirited young man; rake. —*v.t.* **1.** to expose (a hunting dog) to the blood of the game it is to hunt. **2.** to give (troops) their first experience in warfare. [Old English *blōd* the fluid circulated by the heart.]
  • **bad blood.** hatred; hostility: *Because of the dispute, there was bad blood between them.*
  • **fresh** (or **new** or **young**) **blood.** people considered as a source of new vigor, energy, or ideas: *We need some new blood in the company.*
  • **in cold blood.** deliberately and without emotion or compassion.
  • **to have (someone's) blood on one's head** (or **hands**). to be responsible for (someone's) death or ruination.
  • **to make one's blood boil.** to make one angry; infuriate.
  • **to make one's blood run cold.** to make one frightened; terrify.
  • **to run** (or **be**) **in one's blood. a.** to be hereditary. **b.** to be natural or important to.
blood bank 1. a place where whole blood or plasma is collected, processed, and stored for future use. **2.** the reserve of blood so stored.
blood bath, the merciless slaughter of many people; massacre.
blood brother 1. a brother by birth. **2.** a person bound to another by a ceremonial intermingling of blood. —**blood brotherhood.**
blood count, the count of the number of red and white blood cells and platelets in a given sample of blood, used chiefly to help diagnose disease and prescribe treatment.
blood·cur·dling (blud′kûrd′ling) *adj.* causing great horror or fear; terrifying.
blood·ed (blud′id) *adj.* **1.** (of horses and other livestock) of good blood or stock; thoroughbred. **2.** having (a specified kind of) blood. **3.** having or exhibiting (a specified) temperament or state of mind. used in combination in defs. 2 and 3, as in *a warm-blooded animal, a cold-blooded murder.*
blood fluke, schistosome.
blood group, one of the groups into which blood is classified according to whether certain agglutinogens and other antigens are present on the surface of the red blood cells. The major human blood group is ABO, and the four types of blood in this group are A, B, AB, and O. Also, **blood type.**

Blood Groups		
Blood Group	**Can Donate To**	**Can Receive From**
A	A, AB	O, A
B	B, AB	O, B
AB	AB	A, B, AB, O
O	A, B, AB, O	O

blood·guilt·y (blud′gil′tē) *adj.* guilty of murder or bloodshed. —**blood′guilt′,** **blood′guilt′i·ness,** *n.*
blood·hound (blud′hound′) *n.* **1.** one of a breed of hunting dogs having a smooth, black-and-tan or red-and-tan coat, noted for its keen sense of smell and skill in tracking. Height: to 26 inches (66 centimeters) at the shoulder. **2.** *Informal.* a keen pursuer; sleuth.
blood·less (blud′lis) *adj.* **1.** without bleeding or bloodshed: *a bloodless revolution, bloodless surgery.* **2.** lacking blood; pale: *bloodless lips.* **3.** lacking vitality; spiritless. **4.** lacking warmth; cold-hearted. —**blood′less·ly,** *adv.* —**blood′less·ness,** *n.*
blood·let·ting (blud′let′ing) *n.* the act or process of removing blood by opening a vein; phlebotomy.
blood·line (blud′līn′) *n.* a line of direct descent, esp. of animals; strain; pedigree.

B

blood·mo·bile (blud′mə bēl′) *n.* a motor vehicle equipped for the collection of blood from donors.

blood money 1. money obtained at the cost of another's life or well-being. **2.** payment to a hired murderer. **3.** compensation paid to next of kin for the killing of a relative.

blood plasma, the liquid part of the blood, without any of its corpuscles. Also, **plasma.**

blood platelet, one of the numerous minute cells found in the blood of all mammals and essential to blood clotting. Blood platelets lack a nucleus, DNA, and hemoglobin. Also, **platelet, thrombocyte.**

blood poisoning, a diseased condition of the blood caused by the presence of toxins or toxic bacteria; toxemia.

blood pressure, the force exerted by the blood against the inner walls of the blood vessels, esp. the arteries, created by the pumping action of the heart. It varies according to age, health, and other conditions.

blood relation, a person related by birth; kinsman. Also, **blood relative.**

blood·root (blud′rūt′, -rŏot′) *n.* a North American plant, *Sanguinaria canadensis,* of the poppy family, having white or rose flowers and a red root that yields an acrid, red sap.

blood serum *(def. 2).*

blood·shed (blud′shed′) *n.* the loss of blood or life: *We won the battle without much bloodshed.*

blood·shot (blud′shot′) *adj.* (of an eye) inflamed or marked with reddish streaks caused by dilation of the blood vessels.

blood sport, any sport that involves the killing of animals, such as fox hunting or bullfighting.

blood·stain (blud′stān′) *n.* a stain produced by blood.

blood·stained (blud′stānd′) *adj.* **1.** soiled or smeared with blood: *bloodstained clothes.* **2.** guilty of bloodshed or slaughter.

blood·stone (blud′stōn′) *n.* a semiprecious stone consisting of dark green chalcedony flecked with spots of red jasper. Also, **heliotrope.** For illustration, see **semiprecious.**

blood·stream (blud′strēm′) *n.* the blood as it flows through the circulatory system.

blood·suck·er (blud′suk′ər) *n.* **1.** an animal that sucks blood, esp. a leech. **2.** *Informal.* a person who takes as much as possible from others; extortionist. —**blood′suck′ing,** *adj.*

blood sugar 1. glucose present in the blood. **2.** the amount or level of glucose present in the blood, which when elevated is symptomatic of diabetes.

blood test, an analysis of the blood for various factors, as blood type or evidence of illness.

blood·thirst·y (blud′thûr′stē) *adj.* eager to shed blood; murderous; brutal. —**blood′thirst′i·ly,** *adv.* —**blood′thirst′i·ness,** *n.*

blood type, blood group.

blood typing, the determination of an individual's blood group by laboratory tests to establish compatibility for a blood transfusion or bone marrow transplant.

blood vessel, any of the flexible tubes, as an artery, vein, or capillary, through which the blood flows.

blood·worm (blud′wûrm′) *n.* **1.** any of various red or reddish annelid worms, some of which are used as bait or feed for fish. **2.** the wormlike, red, aquatic larva of various midges, esp. of the genus *Chironomus.*

blood·y (blud′ē) *adj.,* **blood·i·er, blood·i·est. 1.** stained or covered with blood: *a bloody knife.* **2.** losing blood; bleeding: *a bloody wound.* **3.** of, like, containing, or composed of blood. **4.** involving much bloodshed: *a bloody brawl.* **5.** relishing bloodshed; bloodthirsty. **6.** having the color of blood. **7.** *British. Slang.* damned: *a bloody nuisance.* —*adv. British. Slang.* very; exceedingly: *They're bloody drunk.* —*v.t.,* **blood·ied, blood·y·ing.** to stain or cover with blood. —**blood′i·ly,** *adv.* —**blood′i·ness,** *n.*

bloody mary, a drink made chiefly of vodka and tomato juice.

bloom¹ (blüm) *n.* **1.** a flower of a plant. **2.** the state or time of flowering: *roses in bloom.* **3.** a time or state of flourishing; peak: *an artist whose talent is in bloom.* **4.** a rapid proliferation of aquatic microscopic life: *an algal bloom.* **5.** a rosy glow of the cheeks or skin suggesting health and freshness. **6.** a delicate, waxy, powdery coating on certain fruits, leaves, and stems: *the bloom on a peach.* —*v.i.* **1.** to produce or yield blossoms; flower: *Cherry trees bloom in early April.* **2.** to be at or come to one's peak; flourish: *That person's true self has just begun to bloom.* **3.** to glow with color, health, or beauty. [Old Norse *blōm* flower.] —**bloom′er,** *n.*

bloom² (blüm) *n.* **1.** a spongy mass of wrought iron intended to be further hammered or rolled into bars. **2.** a bar of iron or steel that is obtained from rolling or hammering an ingot. [Old English *blōma* lump of iron.]

bloom·ers (blü′mərz) *pl. n.* **1.** loose, baggy pants gathered at the knee, formerly worn by women or girls chiefly as an athletic costume. **2.** women's underpants resembling these. **3.** *Slang.* any type of women's underpants. **4. bloomer.** a costume for women or girls consisting of a short skirt and loose pants gathered at the ankles. [From Amelia J. *Bloomer,* 1818-94, U.S. feminist who promoted the costume *(def. 4)*.]

bloom·ing (blü′ming) *adj.* **1.** in flower; blossoming. **2.** thriving; flourishing. **3.** *Informal.* complete; utter: *a blooming idiot.* —**bloom′ing·ly,** *adv.*

bloop·er (blü′pər) *n.* **1.** *Informal.* a blunder, esp. one made in public. **2.** *Baseball.* a weakly hit fly ball.

blos·som (blos′əm) *n.* **1.** a flower, esp. one of a fruit-producing plant. **2.** the time or state of flowering; bloom: *a peach tree in blossom.* —*v.i.* **1.** to put forth blossoms; bloom. **2.** to start to flourish; develop; thrive: *to blossom into a beautiful person.* [Old English *blōstm* flower.] —**blos′som·y,** *adj.*

blot (blot) *n.* **1.** a spot or stain, esp. of ink. **2.** a blemish on character or reputation; disgrace. **3.** something that detracts from or mars beauty. —*v.,* **blot·ted, blot·ting.** —*v.t.* **1.** to spot or spatter with or as if with ink. **2.** to dry or absorb with or as with blotting paper. —*v.i.* **1.** to make blots: *The ink blotted.* **2.** to become stained or marked with a blot: *This paper blots easily.* [Of uncertain origin.]

•**to blot out. a.** to hide; obscure: *The clouds blotted out the moon.* **b.** to wipe out completely; destroy: *to blot out a memory.* **c.** to cross out or erase: *to blot out a word.*

blotch (bloch) *n.* **1.** a spot or stain, esp. one that is large and irregular in shape. **2.** a blemished or discolored patch on the skin. —*v.t.* to mark or cover with blotches. [Probably a blend of BLOT and BOTCH.] —**blotch′i·ness,** *n.* —**blotch′y,** *adj.*

blot·ter (blot′ər) *n.* **1.** a piece of blotting paper. **2.** a book in which transactions or events are recorded in the order of their occurrence: *a sales blotter, a police blotter.*

blotting paper, a soft, porous paper used to soak up ink.

blouse (blous, blouz) *n.* **1.** a garment resembling a loose, light shirt that extends to the waist or below. **2.** a smocklike overgarment worn by certain European peasants and workers. **3.** a loose-fitting shirt of a sailor's uniform. **4.** a jacket or tunic worn as part of the U.S. Army uniform. —*v.t., v.i.,* **bloused, blous·ing.** to hang in full, loose folds; drape. [French *blouse* the shirtlike garment; of uncertain origin.]

blow¹ (blō) *n.* **1.** a forceful, heavy stroke with the fist or a weapon: *a blow to the jaw.* **2.** a severe or painful misfortune; calamity; shock: *The news came as a blow.* **3.** a sudden, forceful attack, action, or effort: *Strike a blow for freedom.* [Middle English *blaw;* of Germanic origin.]

•**at one blow** or **at a blow.** by a single action or effort.

•**blow-by-blow.** detailed and complete: *a blow-by-blow description.*

•**to come to blows.** to begin fighting.

blow² (blō) *v.,* **blew, blown, blow·ing.** —*v.i.* **1.** (of wind or air) to be in motion; move with speed or force: *The wind blew against the sails.* **2.** to produce or send forth a current of air: *The fan was blowing.* **3.** to move or be carried by a current of air or wind: *My hat blew off. The curtains blew in the breeze.* **4.** to produce sound by a blast of air: *The whistle blows at noontime.* **5.** to break and expel air; burst (often with *out*): *As we drove down the street, a tire blew out.* **6.** to stop working properly; fail (often with *out*): *The fuse blew.* **7.** to spout water and air: *The whale blew before submerging.* **8.** *Slang.* to go away; depart: *The bored teenagers decided it was time to blow.* —*v.t.* **1.** to drive by a current of air: *The wind blew the leaves across the yard.* **2.** to direct a current of air upon: *The breeze from the open window blew the curtains.* **3.** to cause to sound by directing a blast of air: *to blow a horn, to blow taps on a bugle.* **4.** to form or shape (something) by air pressure: *to blow glass, to blow bubbles.* **5.** to expel from the mouth: *to blow smoke rings.* **6.** to break or destroy, as by a rupture or explosion: *The dynamite blew the rock to pieces.* **7.** to clear or empty by forcing air into or through: *to blow one's nose.* **8.** to melt (a fuse) by overloading. **9.** *Slang.* to spend (money) quickly or recklessly; squander: *to blow a week's pay on a new suit.* **10.** *Slang.* to spend money on; treat (someone) (with *to*): *I'll blow you to dinner.* **11.** *Slang.* to handle wrongly or unsuccessfully; bungle: *to blow one's chances for a job.* **12.** *Slang.*

a	at	e	end	o	hot	u	up	hw	white		about
ā	ape	ē	me	ō	old	ū	use	ng	song	ə	taken
ä	far	i	it	ô	fork	ü	rule	th	thin		pencil
âr	care	ī	ice	oi	oil	ů	pull	th	this		lemon
		î	pierce	ou	out	ûr	turn	zh	measure		circus

to go away from; leave, esp. hurriedly: *to blow town.* **13.** (of insects) to deposit eggs on or in. —*n.* **1.** the act or instance of producing or directing a current of air. **2.** the sound resulting from the production of a blast of air: *with a blow of the whistle.* **3.** a strong wind or storm: *A blow came in from the northeast.* [English *blāwan* to send forth air.]
  • **to blow hot and cold.** to change one's mind between favoring or liking something and opposing or disliking it, esp. frequently or repeatedly; vacillate; waver: *to blow hot and cold on an issue.*
  • **to blow in.** *Slang.* to arrive; appear.
  • **to blow one's stack (fuse, top, cork, or gasket).** *Informal.* to become violently angry; lose self-control.
  • **to blow out. a.** to put out or be put out by a gust of air: *to blow out a flame.* **b.** (of a storm) to dissipate or dispel: *The hurricane blew itself out over land.*
  • **to blow over. a.** to pass by or over; subside: *The storm finally blew over.* **b.** to be forgotten: *The scandal blew over quickly.*
  • **to blow up. a.** to explode or destroy with an explosion: *The building blew up because of a gas leak. The soldiers blew up the bridge.* **b.** to fill with air or gas; inflate. **c.** *Informal.* to lose one's temper. **d.** to exaggerate; magnify. **e.** to arise and increase in intensity: *A storm blew up last night.* **f.** to enlarge (a photograph).
blow³ (blō) *v.t., v.i.,* **blew, blown, blow·ing.** *Archaic.* to blossom or cause to blossom. —*n.* **1.** a display of blossoms or flowers: *a blow of tulips.* **2.** the state of flowering; bloom: *a tree in full blow.* [Old English *blōwan* to bloom.]
blow-by-blow (blō′bī blō′) *adj.* employing precise or minute detail: *a blow-by-blow description of a meeting.* —*n.* a blow-by-blow account or description: *Just give me the main points, not a blow-by-blow.*
blow-dry (blō′drī′) *v.t.,* **-dried, -dry·ing.** to dry or style (hair) with a blow dryer. —*n.* the act or process of using a blow dryer on the hair. [BLOW² + DRY.]
blow dryer, a portable electric device that blows a stream of warmed air, used for drying and styling a person's hair.
blow·er (blō′ər) *n.* **1.** a machine or device for producing a current of air or forcing air into a particular area: *Blowers ventilated the mine shaft.* **2.** a person or thing that blows.
blow·fish (blō′fish′) *n., pl.* **-fish** or **-fish·es.** any of several fish that can swell their bodies, as the puffer and the walleye.

blowfish

blow·fly (blō′flī′) *n., pl.* **-flies.** any of various two-winged flies, family Calliphoridae, that deposit their larvae on the wounds, wastes, or flesh of animals.
blow·gun (blō′gun′) *n.* a tube through which a person may blow darts or other missiles. Also, **blowpipe, blowtube.**
blow·hard (blō′härd′) *n. Slang.* braggart.
blow·hole (blō′hōl′) *n.* **1.** the breathing hole of certain whales and other cetaceans, often situated at the top of the head. **2.** an escape vent for gas or air, as in mines. **3.** a hole in the ice to which animals, as whales or seals, come to breathe. **4.** a defect in cast metal caused by an air or gas bubble.
blown¹ (blōn) *v.* the past participle of **blow².** —*adj.* **1.** inflated; distended; swollen. **2.** made by using a blowpipe or similar device: *colored bottles of blown glass.* **3.** out of breath: *Their horses were blown from the race.* **4.** flyblown.
blown² (blōn) *v.* the past participle of **blow³.** —*adj.* in full bloom. ➡ now used mostly in the hyphenated term *full-blown.*
blow·out (blō′out′) *n.* **1.** a sudden bursting of an automobile tire. **2.** *Informal.* a big, lively party or other social gathering; spree. **3.** a melting of an electric fuse caused by a current overload.

blow·pipe (blō′pīp′) *n.* **1.** blowgun. **2.** a tube for blowing air or gas into a flame to increase its heat. **3.** a long hollow pipe with a knob at one end and a mouthpiece at the other, used to shape molten glass. Also *(def. 3),* **blowtube.**
blows·y (blou′zē) *adj.,* **blows·i·er, blows·i·est.** blowzy. —**blows′i·ly,** *adv.* —**blows′i·ness,** *n.*
blow·torch (blō′tôrch′) *n.* a device that produces and shoots out a hot flame under pressure, used esp. in melting and soldering metals and in removing paint.
blow·tube (blō′tūb′, -tūb′) *n.* **1.** blowpipe *(def. 3).* **2.** blowgun.
blow·up (blō′up′) *n.* **1.** an explosion. **2.** *Informal.* an outburst of temper; quarrel. **3.** an enlargement, as of a snapshot.
blow·y (blō′ē) *adj.,* **blow·i·er, blow·i·est.** windy.
blowz·y (blou′zē) *also,* **blowsy.** *adj.,* **blowz·i·er, blowz·i·est.** **1.** red-faced, fat, and coarse-complexioned. **2.** not neat, clean, or tidy; messy; slovenly. [Dialectal English *blowze* wench, slattern (of uncertain origin) + -Y¹.] —**blowz′i·ly,** *adv.* —**blowz′i·ness,** *n.*
bls. **1.** bales. **2.** barrels.
BLT, a bacon, lettuce, and tomato sandwich.
blub·ber (blub′ər) *n.* **1.** a layer of fat in whales and other cetaceans, used as a source of oil. **2.** profuse, noisy weeping. **3.** *Informal.* fat, esp. in great quantity. —*v.i.* to weep and sob noisily. —*v.t.* to utter with tears and sobs. —*adj.* swollen; thick: *blubber lips.* [Imitative.] —**blub′ber·er,** *n.*
blub·ber·y (blub′ə rē) *adj.* of or like blubber; fat.
blu·cher (bloo′kər, -chər) *n.* **1.** a heavy leather half boot or high shoe. **2.** a shoe in which the tongue and vamp are of one piece, and the quarters extend forward to lace across the tongue. [From the Prussian field marshal Gebhard von *Blücher,* 1742-1819.]
bludg·eon (bluj′ən) *n.* a short club, often weighted or thicker at one end. —*v.t.* **1.** to strike with or as with a bludgeon. **2.** to bully; coerce: *The dictator bludgeoned the country into submission.* [Of uncertain origin.] —**bludg′eon·er,** *n.*
blue (bloo) *n.* **1.** the color between green and violet in the spectrum. **2.** a blue dye or paint. **3.** *also,* **Blue.** a Union soldier in the American Civil War. **4. blues.** *Informal.* the blue uniform of a sailor. **5. the blue. a.** the sky. **b.** the sea. **6.** something, as clothing, having the color blue: *I wore blue to the dance.* —*adj.,* **blu·er, blu·est.** **1.** having the color blue. **2.** depressed or depressing; melancholy: *I've felt blue all day.* **3.** (of skin) of a bluish purple color; discolored: *a face blue from the cold.* **4.** exasperated; enraged; livid: *blue with rage, blue in the face.* **5.** *Slang.* profane; obscene. —*v.t.,* **blued, blu·ing** or **blue·ing.** **1.** to make blue. **2.** to treat with bluing. [Old French *bleu* the color blue, having the color blue; of Germanic origin.] —**blue′ness,** *n.*
  • **once in a blue moon.** very seldom; rarely: *A chance like this comes only once in a blue moon.*
  • **out of the blue.** suddenly and unexpectedly: *They appeared out of the blue.*
blue baby, a newborn infant whose skin has a bluish color because its blood does not receive adequate oxygen from its lungs, usually caused by a congenital heart or lung defect.
blue·beard (bloo′bîrd′) *n.* a person who has murdered his wife or wives. [From *Bluebeard,* a figure in folklore who murdered six of his seven wives.]
blue·bell (bloo′bel′) *n.* any of various plants with blue, bell-shaped flowers, such as the harebell of Scotland, *Campanula rotundifolia.*
blue·ber·ry (bloo′ber′ē, -bə rē) *n., pl.* **-ries. 1.** a small, dark blue, edible berry with tiny seeds, grown on any of several shrubs, genus *Vaccinium,* that grows in many parts of the world. **2.** any of the shrubs producing this berry.
blue·bird (bloo′bûrd′) *n.* any of several small songbirds, genus *Sialia,* of the thrush family, found in North America and having predominantly blue plumage. Length: 7 inches (18 centimeters).
blue-black (bloo′blak′) *adj.* black with a bluish tint; almost black.
blue blood 1. aristocratic or royal descent. **2.** a person of such descent; aristocrat. [Translation of Spanish *sangre azul.* Supposedly, the blood of Spanish aristocrats was thought to have a bluer tint than that of the common people.] —**blue′blood′ed,** *adj.*
blue·bon·net (bloo′bon′it) *n.* **1.** any of several plants, genus *Lupinus,* of the pea family, having clusters of blue, bonnet-shaped flowers, esp. *L. subcarnosus,* native to the prairies of the southwestern United States. **2.** any of various plants with blue flowers, such as the blue cornflower. **3.** a broad, flat, blue-colored cap, often of wool, formerly worn in Scotland. **4.** a person who wears such a cap; Scot.
blue book *also,* **blue·book** (bloo′buk′). **1.** a directory or register

of socially prominent persons. **2.** a booklet with blue paper covers, used for writing examination answers.

blue·bot·tle (blü′bot′əl) *n.* **1.** a large blowfly, genus *Calliphora,* with a steel-blue abdomen and hairy body. **2.** a blue cornflower. **3.** any of various other plants having tubular blue flowers, as the grape hyacinth.

blue cheese, a pungent cheese, veined with blue mold.

blue-chip (blü′chip′) *adj.* **1.** having a good record of dividend payments and price stability: *blue-chip securities.* **2.** most excellent or valuable; best: *blue-chip service.*

blue chip, a high-priced stock in a leading corporation that has a sound financial base and a good record of earnings, considered a safe investment. [From the *blue chips* used in gambling, which have a high value.]

blue-col·lar (blü′kol′ər) *adj.* of or relating to workers who do mostly physical labor. [From the *blue* shirts worn by many workers.]

blue·fin (blü′fin′) *n., pl.* **-fin** or **-fins.** a large tuna, *Thunnus thynnus,* of temperate seas. Length: to 10 feet (3 meters). Weight: to 1,000 pounds (454 kilograms). Also, **bluefin tuna.**

blue·fish (blü′fish′) *n., pl.* **-fish** or **-fishes. 1.** a saltwater food and game fish, *Pomatomus saltatrix,* having a bluish and silver body, found in coastal waters in various parts of the world. **2.** any of various other fishes of a bluish color, as the cunner.

blue flag, an iris with blue or purple flowers, esp. *Iris versicolor.*

blue fox 1. the blue color phase of the arctic fox. **2.** the fur of such a fox.

blue·gill (blü′gil′) *n., pl.* **-gill** or **-gills.** a central and western North American sunfish, *Lepomis macrochirus,* of variable color, usually with faint bars, and dark lobes extending back from the gill covers. Weight: to over 1 pound (0.5 kilogram).

blue·grass (blü′gras′) *n.* any of various grasses, genus *Poa,* with bluish green stems, widely raised as pasturage and lawn grass, esp. **Kentucky bluegrass,** *P. pratensis.*

blue-green algae (blü′grēn′) cyanobacteria.

blue gum, any of a group of eucalyptus trees, *Eucalyptus globulus,* bearing leaves that contain a strong-smelling oil used in medicine as an antiseptic and an expectorant.

blue·ing (blü′ing) bluing.

blue·ish (blü′ish) bluish.

blue·jack·et (blü′jak′it) *n.* an enlisted man in the British or U.S. navy; sailor.

blue jay, a crested jay, *Cyanocitta cristata,* of eastern North America, predominantly blue in color with black-and-white markings. Length: 11-12½ inches (28-32 centimeters).

blue jeans, pants or overalls, usually made of blue denim.

blue jay

blue law 1. one of numerous laws, originating in colonial New England, prohibiting recreation or business on Sunday. **2.** any law regulating Sunday activities.

blue note, a flatted third or seventh note of a scale. It is a characteristic feature of blues and jazz.

blue-pen·cil (blü′pen′səl) *v.t.,* **-ciled, -cil·ing;** *also, British,* **-cilled, -cil·ling.** to correct or modify with or as with a blue-colored pencil: *The editor blue-penciled the manuscript.*

blue·point (blü′point′) *n.* a small oyster, usually eaten raw. [From *Blue Point,* Long Island, where beds of such oysters are located.]

blue·print (blü′print′) *n.* **1.** a photographic print, usually showing white lines on a blue background, used esp. for architectural plans and mechanical drawings. **2.** a detailed outline or plan of action: *a blueprint for democracy.* —*v.t.* to make a blueprint of: *blueprint a floor plan.*

blue racer, a nonpoisonous snake, *Coluber constrictor flaviventris,* of the blacksnake family, that is blue-green in color and is native to the central and south-central United States.

blue-rib·bon (blü′rib′ən) *adj.* having some superior or special characteristic: *a blue-ribbon champion, a blue-ribbon jury.*

blue ribbon, the highest honor or award in a contest or competition; first prize.

blues (blüz) *pl. n.* **1. the blues.** *Informal.* low spirits; melancholy. **2.** *also,* **the blues.** an American musical form originating with the melancholy songs sung by Southern blacks. The blues is an important element in jazz and rock music. [Short for earlier *blue devils,* slang term for the hallucinations or depression often accompanying extreme intoxication.]

blue spruce, a tall spruce, *Picea pungens,* native to the Rocky Mountain region, or any of its cultivars, grown as ornamentals for their blue, silvery, or green needles.

blue·stock·ing (blü′stok′ing) *n.* a woman having literary or intellectual interests. [From *Blue Stocking* Society, a derisive term applied to literary-social gatherings sponsored by a group of women in mid-eighteenth-century London.]

blue·stone (blü′stōn′) *n.* a bluish, fine-grained sandstone commonly used in construction.

blue streak *Informal.* something moving with great speed: *to take off like a blue streak.*

• **to talk a blue streak.** to speak rapidly and at great length.

blu·ets (blü′its) *n., pl.* **blu·ets. 1.** *also,* **blu·et.** a delicate, low-growing plant, *Hedyotis caerulea,* native to North America, bearing light blue, white, or violet flowers with yellowish centers. Also, **innocence, Quaker-ladies.** **2.** any of various plants having blue flowers, as the cornflower. [From BLUE.]

blue vitriol, copper sulfate.

blue whale, a migratory baleen whale, *Balaenoptera musculus,* of the oceans and seas of the Southern Hemisphere, having grayish blue skin with light spots. It grows to a length of 100 feet (30.5 meters) and is the largest mammal ever known. For illustration, see **whale.**

bluff¹ (bluf) *n.* a bold, broad cliff or headland. —*adj.* **1.** rising with or having a flat, broad front: *bluff cliffs.* **2.** outspoken, rough, and hearty; good-natured and blunt. [Possibly from Middle Dutch *blaf* broad, flat.] —**bluff′ly,** *adv.* —**bluff′ness,** *n.*

bluff² (bluf) *v.t.* **1.** to deceive (someone) by putting on a false front: *The fake doctor bluffed the community for years.* **2.** to convince or frighten (someone) by using deception or idle threats. —*v.i.* to use pretense or deception; fake: *I was only bluffing when I said I knew the answer.* —*n.* the act or instance of bluffing. [Possibly from Dutch *bluffen* to boast.] —**bluff′er,** *n.*

• **to call someone's bluff.** to challenge someone's falsely threatening statements or actions; expose a deception.

blu·ing (blü′ing) *also,* **blueing.** *n.* a blue liquid or powder used in laundering to whiten and brighten fabrics.

bluish (blü′ish) *also,* **blueish.** *adj.* somewhat blue.

blun·der (blun′dər) *n.* a careless or stupid mistake. —*v.i.* **1.** to move or act blindly or clumsily; stumble; flounder. **2.** to make a stupid, clumsy, or careless mistake. —*v.t.* to utter (something) thoughtlessly or confusedly (with *out*). [Old Norse *blunda* to shut the eyes.] —**blun′der·er,** *n.* —For Synonyms *(n.),* see **mistake.**

blun·der·buss (blun′dər bus′) *n.* **1.** an old-fashioned gun with a flared muzzle for scattering shot at close range. **2.** a stupid, blundering person. [Modification (influenced by BLUNDER) of Dutch *donderbus* this gun, from *donder* thunder + *bus* gun.]

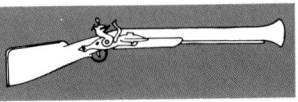

blunderbuss

blunt (blunt) *adj.* **1.** having a dull edge or point; not sharp. **2.** outspoken and honest; without subterfuge: *a blunt manner, a blunt remark.* —*v.t.* to make less sharp or keen; dull. —*v.i.* to become blunt or dull. [Probably from an unrecorded Old English word.] —**blunt′ly,** *adv.* —**blunt′ness,** *n.* —For Synonyms *(adj.),* see **dull, frank¹.**

blur (blûr) *v.t., v.i.,* **blurred, blur·ring. 1.** to make or become less distinct in form or outline: *Fog blurred the skyline. My image blurred as the mirror steamed up.* **2.** to smudge or smear: *to blur the paints in a watercolor.* **3.** to make or become dim: *eyes blurred with tears.* —*n.* something unclear or dim; blurred appearance: *a blur of trees seen from a speeding train.* [Probably a form of BLEAR.] —**blur′ry,** *adj.*

blurb (blûrb) *n.* a brief advertisement or description: *the blurb on a book jacket.* [Coined by Gelett Burgess, 1866-1951, American humorist.]

blurt (blûrt) *v.t.* to say suddenly, by accident, or on impulse (often with *out*): *to blurt out a secret.* [Imitative.]

blush (blush) *v.i.* **1.** to become red in the face from shame, embarrassment, or modesty: *to blush like a shy child.* **2.** to be

a	at	e	end	o	hot	u	up	hw	white	⟨	about
ā	ape	ē	me	ō	old	ū	use	ng	song		taken
ä	far	i	it	ô	fork	ü	rule	th	thin	ə	pencil
âr	care	ī	ice	oi	oil	u̇	pull	th	this		lemon
		îr	pierce	ou	out	ûr	turn	zh	measure	⟨	circus

ashamed or embarrassed (often with *at* or *for*): *I blushed at my ridiculous mistake.* **3.** to be or become rosy; bloom. —*n.* **1.** a reddening of the face from shame, embarrassment, or modesty. **2.** a red or rosy tint. [Old English *blyscan* to redden.] —**blush′er,** *n.*

•**at first blush.** on first glance: *At first blush, the task seemed easy.*

blus·ter (blus′tər) *v.i.* **1.** to blow with noise or stormy violence; be gusty: *The storm blustered outside.* **2.** to be noisy or swaggering; utter loud empty threats: *The bully blustered and raged.* —*v.t.* to utter noisily and violently (often with *out*). —*n.* **1.** noisy, stormy blowing, as of the wind. **2.** noisy, swaggering talk or manner. [Middle Low German *blusteren* to blow violently.] —**blus′ter·er,** *n.* —**blus′ter·y,** *adj.*

blvd., boulevard.

BMR, basal metabolic rate.

B'nai B'rith (bə nā′ brith′) a Jewish service organization that conducts various social, educational, cultural, and charitable programs. [Hebrew *b'nēy b'rīth* sons of the covenant.]

bo·a (bō′ə) *n., pl.* **bo·as. 1.** any of various nonpoisonous, constrictor snakes, family Boidae, found in the tropical and temperate regions, having vestigial hind legs and noted for their great muscular strength. Length: 2-33 feet (0.6-10.1 meters). **2.** a long scarf of fur or feathers. [Latin *boa* large serpent.]

boa constrictor, a nonpoisonous, constrictor snake, *Boa constrictor,* of Mexico, Central and South America, having pale brown skin with dark brown marks on its back. Its loosely hinged jaws enable it to swallow animals much larger than its head. Average length: 10 feet (3 meters).

boar (bôr) *n.* **1.** an uncastrated male swine. **2.** wild boar. [Old English *bār.*]

board (bôrd) *n.* **1.** a thin piece of sawed wood, esp. one much longer than it is wide. **2.** a piece of wood or other material used for some specific purpose: *a board for playing checkers.* **3.** a group of persons who direct or supervise an activity; council: *board of trustees.* **4.a.** food or meals, esp. meals provided regularly for pay: *room and board.* **b.** *Archaic.* a table on which meals are served. ➡ *def.* 4b now chiefly restricted to the phrase *groaning board* to mean a table heavily laden, as at a feast. **5.** a pasteboard or other stiff material used for the covers of books. **6.** the side of a ship. —*v.t.* **1.** to cover or close up with boards (often with *up*): *to board up the windows of an abandoned house.* **2.** to provide with meals, or with lodging and meals, for pay. **3.** to place (someone) where meals and lodging are provided: *The university boarded some of its summer students with local families.* **4.** to get on (a boat, train, or other conveyance). **5.** *Nautical.* to come alongside of and go aboard (a vessel) as a member of a boarding party. —*v.i.* to receive meals, or lodging and meals, for pay. [Old English *bord* plank, table, ship's side.]

•**across the board. a.** (of betting) in equal amounts on several possibilities, as for a horse to win, place, or show. **b.** so as to include everyone or everything in a category: *The company raised salaries across the board.*

•**on board.** on or in a ship, plane, or train; aboard.

•**the boards.** the stage.

•**to go by the board.** to be forgotten, ruined, or ignored.

•**to tread the boards.** to act in the theater.

board·er (bôr′dər) *n.* a person who receives regular meals, or room and board, for a fixed price.

board foot *pl.* **board feet.** a unit of measure for logs and lumber, equal to the volume of a board 1 foot square and 1 inch thick; 144 cubic inches (2,359 cubic centimeters).

board·ing (bôr′ding) *n.* wooden boards collectively.

boarding house, a house at which regular meals, or lodging and meals, are furnished for a fixed price.

boarding party, a group assigned to board a vessel, usually in order to seize or search it.

boarding school, a school where students live during the school year.

board measure, a system of measure whose unit is the board foot.

board of education, a committee responsible for setting the policies of a school system.

board of trade 1. an association of businesspersons to promote and protect business interests. **2. Board of Trade.** a department of the British government supervising commerce and industry.

board·walk (bôrd′wôk′) *n.* a wide walkway, esp. of boards, along a beach.

boar·hound (bôr′hound′) *n.* a large dog used originally for hunting wild boars, esp. the Great Dane.

boast (bōst) *v.i.* **1.** to speak with too much pride about oneself,

one's family, or one's possessions; brag: *to boast about one's accomplishments.* **2.** to be proud: *That's nothing to boast of.* —*v.t.* **1.** to assert with exaggeration; brag about. **2.** to possess with pride; take pride in: *The library boasts 500 new volumes.* —*n.* **1.** a boastful statement; bragging: *Your boast that you are the best player on the team just isn't true.* **2.** something boasted of; cause for pride. [Anglo-Norman *bost* bragging; probably of Germanic origin.] —**boast′er,** *n.*

Synonyms *v.i.* **Boast** and **brag** mean to praise oneself in an offensive way. **Boast** suggests self-praise that is offensive whether justified or not: *She may be the best player, but her teammates resent her boasting about it.* **Brag** suggests a cruder, more insistent boasting, intended to magnify oneself and often stretching or embroidering the truth: *He was always bragging about his family's "estate," which turned out to be an ordinary suburban house.*

boast·ful (bōst′fəl) *adj.* characterized by or given to boasting; bragging: *a boastful account of their team's victory.* —**boast′fully,** *adv.* —**boast′ful·ness,** *n.*

boat (bōt) *n.* **1.** a small vessel for use on water, propelled by oars, sails, or a motor. **2.** a vessel of any size; ship: *The passenger boat left the dock at noon.* **3.** an open, boat-shaped dish, as for gravy. —*v.i.* to travel in a boat. —*v.t.* to place or carry in a boat. [Old English *bāt* small vessel.]

•**in the same boat.** in the same situation or condition.

•**to miss the boat.** to fail to make use of an opportunity: *to miss the boat by not buying a coat during a sale.*

boat hook, a pole with a metal hook on one end, used for pulling or pushing a boat.

boat·house (bōt′hous′) *n., pl.* **-hous·es** (hou′ziz). a building near the water's edge for sheltering or storing boats.

boat·ing (bō′ting) *n.* the act or practice of using a boat, esp. for pleasure: *I enjoy boating on the lake.*

boat·load (bōt′lōd′) *n.* **1.** the amount that a boat can hold or transport. **2.** a load carried by a boat.

boat·man (bōt′mən) *n., pl.* **-men** (-mən). a person who operates, works on, or sells, rents, or services boats.

boat people, people who emigrate in small boats as refugees seeking political asylum in any country.

boat·swain (bō′sən, bōt′swān′) *also,* **bo's'n, bosun.** *n.* a petty officer or warrant officer on a ship who has charge of certain gear, as the rigging or anchors, and whose duties include summoning the crew and directing their work.

bob¹ (bob) *v.,* **bobbed, bob·bing.** —*v.i.* **1.** to move up and down, or to and fro, with a short, jerky motion: *The buoy bobbed in the water.* **2.** *Archaic.* to curtsy briefly. **3.** to try to snatch floating or dangling fruit with the teeth (with *for*): *to bob for apples.* —*v.t.* to move (something) up and down with a short, jerky motion: *to bob one's head.* —*n.* a short, jerking movement. [Middle English *bobben* to move up and down, probably from Old French *bober* to mock.]

•**to bob up.** to appear suddenly and unexpectedly.

bob² (bob) *n.* **1.** a short haircut for a woman or child. **2.** a docked tail, as of a horse. **3.** a small, hanging weight, as at the end of a pendulum or plumb line. **4.** a float or cork for a fishing line. **5.** bobsled. —*v.t.,* **bobbed, bob·bing.** to cut short, as hair or a tail. —*v.i.* to fish with a bob. [Middle English *bobbe* bunch; of uncertain origin.]

bob³ (bob) *n., pl.* **bob.** *British. Informal.* shilling. [Possibly from *Bob,* nickname of *Robert.*]

bob·bin (bob′in) *n.* **1.** the spool around which thread or yarn is wound, used in weaving, machine sewing, or spinning. **2.** something resembling a bobbin in shape or function, as a reel around which wire is coiled, or a small, notched pin used in making lace. [Of uncertain origin.]

bob·bi·net (bob′ə net′) *n.* a machine-made net fabric having hexagonal meshes. [Bobbin + net¹.]

bobbin lace, lace made by hand on a pattern laid out on a pad or pillow, the thread or bobbins being wound around pins showing the pattern. Also, **pillow lace.**

bob·ble (bob′əl) *v.,* **-bled, -bling.** —*v.i.* **1.** to move with a continuous or repeated bobbing. **2.** *Informal.* to make a mistake; blunder. —*v.t. Baseball.* to fumble or mishandle (a ball). —*n.* a mistake; blunder.

bob·by (bob′ē) *n., pl.* **-bies.** *British. Informal.* a police officer. [From Sir *Robert* Peel, 1788-1850, who reorganized the London police force.]

bobby pin, a flat hairpin with prongs that press close together to hold hair tightly.

bobby socks *Informal.* ribbed, often heavy, socks, usually folded just above the ankle.

B

bob·by·sox·er (bob'ē sok'sər) *n. Slang.* a teenage girl, esp. one of the teenagers who followed the fads and fashions popular in the 1940s.

bob·cat (bob'kat') *n.* a North American lynx, *Lynx rufus,* having a reddish brown coat speckled with dark spots. Length: to 3 feet (0.9 meter). Also, **wildcat.**

bob·o·link (bob'ə lingk') *n.* a songbird of North and South America, *Dolichonyx oryzivorus,* having predominantly buff-colored plumage. In early spring the male's plumage turns black with yellow and honey-colored markings. [Imitative of the cry of this bird.]

bob·sled (bob'sled') *n.* **1.** a long racing sled with two sets of runners, a steering wheel, and a brake. **2.a.** a long sled formed by attaching one short sled behind another. **b.** either of the short sleds so joined. —*v.i.,* **-sled·ded, -sled·ding.** to ride on a bobsled. Also, **bob'sleigh'.**

bob·stay (bob'stā') *n. Nautical.* a rope or chain connecting the bowsprit to the cutwater, used to counteract the pull of the forestays.

bob·tail (bob'tāl') *n.* **1.** a tail cut short; short tail. **2.** an animal having such a tail. —*v.t.* to cut the tail of. —*adj.* having a bobtail.

bob·white (bob'hwīt', -wīt') *n.* an American game bird of the eastern and central United States, *Colinus virginianus,* of the quail family, having reddish brown plumage with streakings of white, black, and buff. Length: 10 inches (25 centimeters).

boc·cie (boch'ē) *n.* a game similar to bowls, of Italian origin, played on a narrow court, usually of hard-packed earth and enclosed by low sides. [Italian *boccie* bowls, plural of *boccia* (wooden) ball; of uncertain origin.]

bock beer (bok) a strong, dark beer, usually brewed in the cold months and sold in the spring. Also, **bock.** [Partial translation of German *Bockbier,* short for *Eimbockbier* beer from Eimbeck, a German city.]

bode[1] (bōd) *v.t.,* **bod·ed, bod·ing. 1.** to be an omen or indication of; portend: *This bodes disaster.* **2.** *Archaic.* to foretell; predict. [Old English *bodian* to announce.]
· **to bode ill.** to be a bad omen.
· **to bode well.** to be a good omen: *Your good work bodes well for your future in the business.*

bode[2] (bōd) a past tense of **bide.**

bo·de·ga (bō dā'gə) *n.* in a Spanish-speaking community, a small grocery store. [Spanish *bodega,* from Latin *apotheca* storehouse. See APOTHECARY.]

bod·ice (bod'is) *n.* **1.** that part of a dress from the neckline to the waistline. **2.** a vest worn over a dress or blouse, that laces up the front. [Modification of *bodies,* plural of BODY. For a similar development, see PENCE.]

bod·ied (bod'ēd) *adj.* having a (specified kind of) body. ▶ used in combination, as in *able-bodied, full-bodied.*

bod·i·less (bod'ē lis) *adj.* having no body or material form; incorporeal: *bodiless phantoms.*

bod·i·ly (bod'ə lē) *adj.* of or relating to the body: *bodily harm.* —*adv.* **1.** in the flesh; in person: *They carried him bodily out of the room.* **2.** as a single body: *The audience rose bodily to applaud the singer.*

bod·kin (bod'kin) *n.* **1.** a small, pointed tool for making holes in cloth. **2.** a long, ornamental pin for fastening hair. **3.** a large, blunt needle for pulling tape or other material through a hem. **4.** *Archaic.* dagger. [Middle English *boydekyn* dagger; of Old French origin.]

bod·y (bod'ē) *n., pl.* **bod·ies. 1.** the whole physical structure and material of a human being, animal, plant, or other organism. **2.a.** the main portion of a human being or animal excluding the head and limbs; trunk. **b.** the main stem or trunk of a plant or tree. **3.** the main or central part of anything, as the nave of a church, fuselage of an airplane, or hull of a ship. **4.** a dead person; corpse. **5.** the part of a vehicle that carries the load: *the body of an automobile.* **6.** the main part of a document, excluding the introduction, appendixes, and other supplementary material. **7.** a group of persons or things considered as a whole: *a legislative body, a body of laws.* **8.** the main portion of such a group; majority: *The body of the people voted against the measure.* **9.** a distinct mass; portion of matter: *the force of a body in motion, a body of cold air.* **10.** *Informal.* a person. **11.** solid quality; substance; density: *Wool has more body than organdy.* **12.** that part of a garment that covers the trunk, or the trunk above the waist. **13.** *Printing.* the part of a piece of type on which the letter is cast. —*v.t.,* **bod·ied, bod·y·ing.** *Archaic.* to provide with or as with a body. [Old English *bodig* physical frame of a man or animal, trunk, main part of something.]

· **to keep body and soul together.** to have the barest essentials in order to stay alive; sustain life: *The young artist worked as a carpenter to keep body and soul together.*

bod·y·build·ing (bod'ē bil'ding) *n.* the practice of developing the muscles by exercising, esp. using weights. —**bod'y·build'er,** *n.*

body cavity 1. a space that develops in the embryo of most advanced multicellular animals, in which the digestive tract and other internal organs become suspended; coelom. **2.** any of the subdivisions of the original embryonic body cavity, as the abdominal and thoracic cavities of mammals.

bod·y·guard (bod'ē gärd') *n.* a person or persons responsible for protecting someone from physical danger or attack.

body language, the body movements, gestures, postures, and facial expressions by which a person communicates, often unconsciously, with others.

body louse, see louse *(def. 1).*

body politic, the people of a state, nation, or other political entity considered as a whole.

body snatcher, a person who steals corpses from graves, esp. for dissection.

Boe·o·tian (bē ō'shən) *adj.* **1.** of or relating to Boeotia or its people. **2.** dull; provincial. —*n.* **1.** a native or inhabitant of Boeotia. **2.** any dull or provincial person.

Boer (bôr) *n.* a South African of Dutch descent. —*adj.* of or relating to the Boers. [Dutch *boer* farmer.]

Boer War, the war between Great Britain and the Dutch republics of Transvaal and the Orange Free State, from 1899 to 1902, in which the Boers were defeated.

bog (bog, bôg) *n.* a wet, spongy ground or area composed chiefly of decayed plant material; marsh; mire. —*v.t., v.i.,* **bogged, bog·ging. 1.** to sink or stick in a bog or soggy ground. **2.** to become stuck as if in a bog; be hindered (often with *down*): *to be bogged in financial matters, to be bogged down in petty details.* [Irish or Scottish Gaelic *bogach* marsh, from *bog* soft.] —**bog'gy,** *adj.*

bo·gey[1] (bō'gē) *n., pl.* **-geys.** bogy[1].

bo·gey[2] (bō'gē) *n., pl.* **-geys. 1.** one stroke over par for a hole in golf. **2.** par in golf. —*v.t., v.i.,* **-geyed, -gey·ing.** to use one stroke over par for (a hole in golf). [A form of BOGY[1].]

bo·gey·man (bug'ē man', bü'gē-, bō'-) *n., pl.* **-men** (-men'). a frightful imaginary figure, esp. one used to threaten children.

bog·gle (bog'əl) *v.,* **-gled, -gling.** —*v.i.* **1.** to make a sudden involuntary movement, as from fright or astonishment; start. **2.** to hesitate or shrink from scruples or doubt (with *at*). —*v.t.* to astound; startle; overwhelm: *That boggles the imagination.* [Possibly from BOGLE.]

bo·gie[1] (bō'gē) bogy[1].

bo·gie[2] (bō'gē) *n. also,* **bogy. 1.** (on a truck) a rear-wheel assembly consisting of four wheels on two axles. **2.** one of the wheels supporting the tread of a tractor or tank. [Of uncertain origin.]

bo·gle (bō'gəl) *n.* a hobgoblin; specter. [Scottish *bogle.*]

bo·gus (bō'gəs) *adj.* not genuine; counterfeit; sham. [First found in 1827 as name of a machine coining counterfeit money; possibly related to BOGY[1].]

bo·gy[1] (bō'gē) *n., pl.* **-gies.** *also,* **bogey, bogie. 1.** an evil spirit; goblin; specter. **2.** a frightening or dreaded person or thing; bugbear. **3.** *Military. Slang.* unidentified enemy aircraft. [Possibly modification of BOGLE; possibly from Welsh *bwg* ghost.]

bo·gy[2] (bō'gē) *n., pl.* **-gies.** bogie[2].

Bo·he·mi·an (bō hē'mē ən) *n.* **1.** a native or inhabitant of Bohemia. **2.** the language spoken in Bohemia; Czech. **3.** *also,* **bohemian.** a person who leads a nonconformist life, esp. an artist or writer. **4.** Gypsy. —*adj.* **1.** of, relating to, or characteristic of Bohemia or its people, language, or culture. **2.** *also,* **bohemian.** characteristic of or relating to a bohemian. —**Bo·he'mi·an·ism;** *also,* **bo·he'mi·an·ism,** *n.*

Bohr theory (bôr) *Nuclear Physics.* a theory of atomic structure that assumes that the angular momentum of an electron in orbit around a nucleus can only have certain values, or quanta. The further from the nucleus an electron is in orbit, the greater its angular momentum and the higher its energy level. [From Niels Bohr, 1885-1962, Danish physicist.]

a	at	e	end	o	hot	u	up	hw	white		about
ā	ape	ē	me	ō	old	ū	use	ng	song		taken
ä	far	i	it	ô	old	u̇	rule	th	thin	ə	pencil
âr	care	ī	ice	oi	oil	u̇	pull	th	this		lemon
		îr	pierce	ou	out	ûr	turn	zh	measure		circus

boil¹ (boil) *v.i.* **1.** (of a liquid) to form bubbles that escape as vapor due to the application of heat. **2.** to contain a boiling liquid: *The pot is boiling.* **3.** to reach the boiling point: *Turn off the flame as soon as the water boils.* **4.** to be stirred up or angry: *to boil with rage.* —*v.t.* **1.** to bring to the boiling point: *The cook boiled the water.* **2.** to cook, cleanse, or prepare by boiling: *to boil potatoes.* **3.** to cause to undergo the action of a boiling liquid: *to boil dirty clothes.* **4.** to separate or collect by boiling: *to boil sugar.* —*n.* the act or state of boiling. [Old French *boillir* to form bubbles, be angry, from Latin *bullīre,* from *bulla* bubble.]
• **to boil down. a.** to reduce or lessen by boiling. **b.** to shorten or be shortened: *to boil down a long report to a brief outline.*
• **to boil over. a.** to overflow during boiling. **b.** to lose one's temper; show anger: *I boiled over at the insult.*

boil² (boil) *n.* a painful, pus-filled swelling in the skin, formed around a hard core. It is caused by bacterial infection. [Old English *bȳl.*]

boil·er (boi′lər) *n.* **1.** a large container with a system of tubes in which water or other liquid is transformed into steam or other vapor for heat or power. **2.** a container in which something is heated or boiled. **3.** a tank in which water is heated or hot water is stored.

boiling point 1. the temperature at which a liquid begins to boil. The boiling point of water at sea level is 212 degrees Fahrenheit or 100 degrees Celsius. **2.** *Informal.* the point at which a person loses his or her temper.

bois·ter·ous (bois′tər əs, -trəs) *adj.* noisy and high-spirited; lively and unrestrained: *boisterous merriment, a boisterous party.* [Old French *boisteus* limping, rough.] —**bois′ter·ous·ly,** *adv.* —**bois′ter·ous·ness,** *n.*

bo·la (bō′lə) *also,* **bo·las** (bō′ləs). *n.* a weapon used chiefly in South America, consisting of heavy balls tied to the ends of a cord. It is thrown to entangle the victim. [Spanish and Portuguese *bola* ball, from Latin *bulla* bubble, knob.]

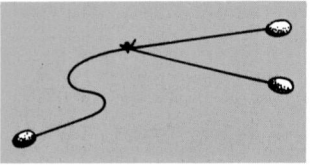

bola

bold (bōld) *adj.* **1.** being without fear when confronted with risk or danger; having courage; fearless; intrepid: *a bold warrior, a bold explorer.* **2.** showing or requiring spirit or courage; daring: *a bold enterprise.* **3.** too free in speech or manner; rashly forward: *The bold youngster went right up to the celebrity and got an autograph.* **4.** standing out prominently; distinct and striking: *bold handwriting.* **5.** steep; abrupt: *a bold cliff.* [Old English *beald* courageous.] —**bold′ly,** *adv.* —**bold′ness,** *n.*
• **to make bold.** to take the liberty; venture: *I made bold to criticize my teacher's opinion.*

bold·face (bōld′fās′) *n.* a type with heavy, thick lines that stands out clearly. **This is printed in boldface.**

bole (bōl) *n.* the trunk of a tree. [Old Norse *bolr.*]

bo·le·ro (bə lâr′ō) *n., pl.* **-ros. 1.** a lively Spanish dance in ¾ time that is usually accompanied by castanets. **2.** the music for this dance. **3.** a short, open jacket ending at or above the waistline. [Spanish *bolero.*]

bol·i·var (bol′i vər, bō lē′vär) *n., pl.* **bol·i·vars** or **bo·li·va·res** (bō′lē vär′ās). the monetary unit of Venezuela. [From Simón Bolívar, 1783-1830, South American revolutionary leader and statesman.]

bo·li·vi·a·no (bō liv′ē ä′nō, bə-) *n., pl.* **-nos** (-nōz). the monetary unit of Bolivia. [Spanish *boliviano,* from *Bolivia.*]

boll (bōl) *n.* the rounded seed pod or capsule of a plant, as of cotton or flax. [Form of BOWL¹.]

bol·lix (bol′əks) *also,* **bol·lox.** *v.t. Informal.* to make a mess of (often with *up*). [From earlier *ballocks* testicles, from Old English *beallucas.*]

boll weevil, a long-beaked beetle, *Anthonomus grandis,* of Central America and the southern United States, that damages cotton bolls.

boll·worm (bōl′wûrm′) *n.* a moth larva that feeds on cotton bolls and ears of corn.

bo·lo (bō′lō) *n., pl.* **-los.** a long, single-edged knife, used in the Philippines. [Spanish *bolo,* from the native Philippine name.]

bo·lo·gna (bə lō′nə, -nē) *also,* **ba·lo·ney, bo·lo·ney.** *n.* a highly seasoned, smoked sausage made of beef, veal, and pork. Also, **bologna sausage.** [From BOLOGNA, Italy.]

Boll weevil

Cotton bud

boll weevil

bo·lom·e·ter (bō lom′i tər) *n.* a highly sensitive electronic instrument used to measure small amounts of radiation, esp. infrared radiation from stellar sources, as in astronomy. [Greek *bolē* ray; literally, something thrown (from *ballein* to throw) + -METER.] —**bo·lo·met·ric** (bō′lə met′rik), *adj.*

Bol·she·vik (bōl′shə vik, bol′-) *also,* **bol·she·vik.** *n., pl.* **-viks** or **-vi·ki** (-vē′kē, vik′ē). **1.** a member of the left-wing majority faction of the Social Democratic Party in czarist Russia that, in 1917, led by V.I. Lenin and Leon Trotsky, overthrew the provisional government of Alexander Kerensky and established the Soviet Union. In 1918 this group changed its name to the Russian Communist Party. **2.** any radical. —*adj.* of or relating to Bolsheviks or Bolshevism. [Russian *bolshevik* member of the majority, from *bolshe* greater.]

Bol·she·vism (bōl′shə viz′əm, bol′-) *also,* **bol·she·vism.** *n.* the doctrines and policies of the Bolsheviks; revolutionary Marxism.

Bol·she·vist (bōl′shə vist, bol′-) *also,* **bol·she·vist.** *n., adj.* Bolshevik. —**Bol′she·vis′tic;** *also,* **bol′she·vis′tic,** *adj.*

bol·ster (bōl′stər) *n.* **1.** a narrow, often cylindrical, pillow, as long as the width of a bed or couch. **2.** any cushion, pad, or pillow. **3.** something resembling a bolster in shape or use; support. —*v.t.* **1.** to uphold or reinforce: *to bolster someone's spirits.* **2.** to support or prop with a cushion: *to bolster a sick child with a pillow.* [Old English *bolster* cushion.]

bolt¹ (bōlt) *n.* **1.** a pin or rod used for holding things together, usually with a head at one end and threads for a nut to be attached on the other end. **2.** a sliding bar for fastening a door or gate. **3.** the part of a lock that is moved out or withdrawn by turning the key. **4.** a sudden swift movement, as a dash or spring: *The burglar made a bolt for the window when the police arrived.* **5.** a stroke of lightning; thunderbolt. **6.** a roll of cloth or paper. **7.** the breaking away or withdrawal of support from (a political party or set of political beliefs). **8.** a sliding rod that may be pushed to load a cartridge case into place in a rifle's chamber and pulled to eject the empty case. —*v.t.* **1.** to fasten or secure with or as with a bolt: *Bolt the door after I leave.* **2.** to swallow (food) quickly or without chewing; gulp: *The puppy bolted its dinner.* **3.** to break away from (a political party or set of political beliefs): *The angry senator bolted the party.* —*v.i.* **1.** to spring or move suddenly (often with *out* or *from*): *to bolt out the door.* **2.** to break away from control; start and run off: *The horse bolted.* **3.** to break away from a political party or set of political beliefs: *The presidential candidate bolted and started a third party movement.* [Old English *bolt* arrow.] —**bolt′er,** *n.*
• **bolt from the blue.** a sudden, unexpected happening: *My promotion and raise in salary came as a bolt from the blue.*
• **bolt upright.** stiffly straight and erect: *At the sound of the explosion I sat bolt upright in bed.*

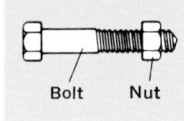

Bolt Nut

bolt¹ *(def.1)*

bolt² (bōlt) *v.t.* to sift through a cloth or sieve. [Old French *buleter;* of Germanic origin.] —**bolt′er,** *n.*

bolt·rope (bōlt′rōp′) *n.* a rope sewn along the edge of a sail to strengthen it.

bo·lus (bō′ləs) *n.* **1.** a small, rounded mass, esp. of chewed food. **2.** a large pill. [Late Latin *bōlus,* from Greek *bōlos* lump.]

bomb (bom) *n.* **1.** a container filled with an explosive, incendiary, or chemical substance that is set off by dropping or throwing, by a fuse, or by a timing device. **2.** a container whose contents are stored under pressure for later release as a fine spray or foam: *an insecticide bomb.* **3.** *Slang.* total failure: *That play was a real bomb.* —*v.t.* to attack or destroy (something) with a bomb or bombs. —*v.i.* **1.** to drop or set off bombs. **2.** *Slang.* to fail completely. [French *bombe* the projectile, going back to Latin *bombus* a booming, from Greek *bombos* deep hollow sound; imitative.]

bom·bard (bom bärd′) *v.t.* **1.** to attack with artillery or bombs. **2.** to subject to a vigorous or persistent attack: *Reporters bombarded the candidate with questions.* **3.** *Physics.* to subject (atomic nuclei) to a stream of high-speed subatomic particles. [French *bombarder,* from *bombarde* cannon, from Medieval Latin *bombarda* weapon for hurling stones, from Latin *bombus.* See BOMB.] —**bom·bard′ment,** *n.*

bom·bar·dier (bom′bər dîr′) *n.* the crew member of a bomber who aims and drops the bombs.

bom·bast (bom′bast) *n.* pretentious speech or writing; pom-

pous language. [Old French *bombace* cotton padding, from Late Latin *bombax* cotton, modification of Latin *bombyx* cotton, silk, from Greek *bombyx* silk.]

bom·bas·tic (bom bas′tik) *adj.* given to or characterized by pompous language; grandiloquent. —**bom·bas′ti·cal·ly**, *adv.*

bom·ba·zine (bom′bə zēn′) *n.* a twilled cloth with a silk warp and worsted filling. [French *bombasin,* from Italian *bambagino* cotton cloth, going back to Late Latin *bombax.* See BOMBAST.]

bomb bay, the section in a bomber in which bombs are carried and from which they are dropped.

bomb·er (bom′ər) *n.* **1.** a military airplane designed for dropping bombs. **2.** a person who drops, plants, or throws bombs.

bomb·proof (bom′prüf′) *adj.* safe from damage by bombs: *a bombproof shelter.*

bomb·shell (bom′shel′) *n.* **1.** a bomb. **2.** a startling, unforeseen, and upsetting occurrence: *The news that the mayor had been bribed was a political bombshell.*

bomb shelter, a place, usually underground, where people may take refuge from an air raid.

bomb·sight (bom′sīt′) *n.* an instrument in a bomber used to sight the target and help the bombardier drop bombs accurately.

bo·na fide (bō′nə fīd′, bon′ə, bō′nə fī′dē) **1.** in good faith; without fraud or deception. **2.** genuine; authentic. [Latin *bonā fidē* in good faith.]

bo·nan·za (bə nan′zə) *n.* **1.** a rich mine or mass of ore. **2.** any source of great profit or wealth. [Spanish *bonanza* fair weather, prosperity, going back to Latin *bonus* good.]

Bo·na·part·ist (bō′nə pär′tist) *n.* an adherent of the French military leader and emperor Napoleon Bonaparte, his policies, or his dynasty.

bon·bon (bon′bon′) *n.* a piece of candy, esp. one with a fondant or chocolate coating and a fondant center. [French *bonbon* literally, good-good, repetition of *bon* good, from Latin *bonus* good.]

bond (bond) *n.* **1.** something that binds, fastens, or holds together: *bonds made of rope.* **2.** a binding or uniting force or influence; tie: *bonds of friendship, bonds of affection.* **3.** a binding assurance or agreement; pledge: *bonds of marriage, one's word is as good as one's bond.* **4.** *Finance.* an interest-bearing certificate of indebtedness issued by a government or corporation that promises to repay a specified sum of money at a fixed future date. **5.** chemical bond. **6.** *Law.* **a.** an obligation to pay or forfeit a specified sum of money if certain acts are or are not committed. **b.** the amount of money so specified; bail. **c.** a person acting as surety or bail. **7.** an insurance policy covering losses suffered through the acts of an employee or other unforeseeable circumstances. **8.** a strong, durable, nonyellowing paper made partly or entirely of rag pulp; bond paper **9.** a substance that causes particles to stick or hold fast. **10.** the storage of imported goods in a warehouse until taxes on them are paid. **11.** in building, a method of arranging bricks, stones, or boards by overlapping them to form a solid whole. —*v.t.* **1.** to place in or under bond; guarantee: *to bond an employee, to bond imported goods.* **2.** to provide a bond for: *to bond a prisoner.* **3.** to place a bonded debt upon; mortgage. **4.** to cause to adhere; unite. —*v.i.* to hold together; join; adhere. [Form of BAND².] —**bond′a·ble,** *adj.* —**bond′er,** *n.*

Synonyms *n.* **Bond** and **tie** mean something that holds people or things together. **Bond** suggests strength and sometimes rigidity, and may imply that those held together become in some sense one: *the bonds of matrimony.* **Tie** is used of connections that are more flexible and allow more individual freedom: *I no longer have many ties to my hometown.*

bond·age (bon′dij) *n.* **1.** involuntary servitude; slavery. **2.** subjection to any binding or dominating influence: *addicts in bondage to their drug habits.*

bond·ed (bon′did) *adj.* **1.** secured or guaranteed by a bond or bonds. **2.** placed in bond; stored in a bonded warehouse.

bonded fabric, a fabric consisting of two layers of material held together by an adhesive medium.

bond·hold·er (bond′hōl′dər) *n.* an owner of a bond or bonds issued by a government or corporation.

bond·ing (bon′ding) *n.* **1.** the forming of a close psychological relationship, esp. as between a mother and her newborn. **2.** the permanent adherence of specialized plastics to a tooth surface that has been chemically treated, esp. for cosmetic repair or recoloring of the tooth. [BOND + -ING¹.]

bond·maid (bond′mād′) *n.* a female bond servant.

bond·man (bond′mən) *n., pl.* -men (-mən). a slave or feudal serf.

bond paper, a strong, durable paper made from rag pulp; bond.

bond servant **1.** a person bound to service without pay. **2.** slave.

bonds·man (bondz′mən) *n., pl.* -men (-mən). **1.** a person who assumes responsibility for another by furnishing a bond; surety. **2.** bondman.

bond·wom·an (bond′wùm′ən) *n., pl.* -wom·en (-wim′ən). a female slave or feudal serf.

bone (bōn) *n.* **1.** one of the parts of the skeleton of a vertebrate animal. **2.** the hard porous tissue of which such parts are composed. **3.** a substance resembling bone, as ivory or whalebone. **4.** a strip of whalebone or other sturdy material used to shape a corset or other garment; stay. **5.** **bones.** **a.** the body, living or dead. **b.** *Slang.* dice. **c.** clappers of bone or wood used as noisemakers or for musical accompaniment. —*v.t.,* **boned, bon·ing.** **1.** to remove the bones from: *to bone chicken.* **2.** to stiffen (a garment) with whalebone or similar material. [Old English *bān* one of the parts of a skeleton.]

· **to bone up on.** *Informal.* to review diligently; study intensely: *The student boned up on algebra before the big test.*

· **to feel in one's bones.** to feel certain of for no apparent reason; know intuitively: *I felt in my bones that my wish would come true.*

· **to have a bone to pick.** to have something to argue or complain about.

· **to make no bones about.** to be direct or blunt about; make no attempt to conceal: *I make no bones about my fear of snakes.*

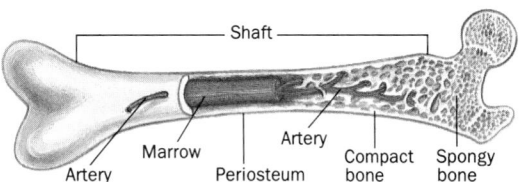

human **bone**

bone ash, the white, porous ash of bones, composed chiefly of calcium phosphate, made by roasting animal bones in the open air, used esp. as a fertilizer and for bone china.

bone·black (bōn′blak′) *n.* a black carbonaceous pigment made by roasting animal bones in closed iron containers.

bone-chilling (bōn′chil′ing) *adj.* very frightening; terrifying.

bone china, a translucent white china made with bone ash.

bone-dry (bōn′drī′) *adj.* very dry.

bone·fish (bōn′fish′) *n., pl.* -fish or -fish·es. any of various silvery fish, family Albulidae, found in warm, shallow ocean waters and having a skeleton made up of many small bones. Length: to 3½ feet (1.1 meters).

bone·less (bōn′lis) *adj.* **1.** without bones; with the bones removed. **2.** cowardly; lacking courage.

bone marrow, marrow *(def. 1).*

bone meal, crushed or ground animal bones, used as fertilizer or feed.

bone of contention, the subject or cause of dispute or disagreement.

bon·er (bō′nər) *n. Informal.* a foolish mistake.

bone·set (bōn′set′) *n.* any of several plants of the genus *Eupatorium,* esp. *E. perfoliatum,* of the family Compositae, bearing clusters of white or grayish flowers and having a strong smell, formerly used medicinally.

bon·fire (bon′fīr′) *n.* a large fire built in the open air. [Middle English *bone fire;* referring to fires built out-of-doors for burning bones.]

bon·go drums (bong′gō) a pair of small, connected drums, each with a different pitch, played with the hands while being held between the knees. Also, **bon′gos.** [American Spanish *bongó.*]

bon·ho·mie (bon′ə mē′, bō′nə-) *also,* **bon·hom·mie.** *n.* good nature; affability. [French *bonhomie,* from *bonhomme* good-natured man, going back to Latin *bonus* good + *homō* man.]

bo·ni·to (bə nē′tō) *n., pl.* -tos. any of various edible saltwater fish, genera *Sarda* and *Euthynnus,* closely related to the tuna and mackerel. [Spanish *bonito,* going back to Latin *bonus* good.]

bon jour (bôN zhür′) *French.* good morning; good day.

a	at	e	end	o	hot	u	up	hw	white		about
ā	ape	ē	me	ō	old	ū	use	ng	song		taken
ä	far	i	it	ô	fork	ü	rule	th	thin	ə	pencil
âr	care	ī	ice	oi	oil	u̇	pull	th	this		lemon
				îr	pierce	ou	out	ûr	turn	zh	measure		circus

bon mot (bon′mō′; *French* bôn mō′) *pl.* **bons mots** (bon′mōz′; *French* bôn mō′). a clever saying or remark. [French *bon mot* literally, good word.]

bonne (bôn) *n.* a nursemaid or housemaid. [French *bonne,* feminine of *bon* good, from Latin *bonus.*]

bon·net (bon′it) *n.* **1.** a hat enclosing both the sides and the back of the head and tied under the chin, worn esp. by women and girls. **2.** any girl's or woman's hat. **3.** a ceremonial headdress of feathers worn by some North American Indians. **4.** a traditional cap worn by men and boys in Scotland. **5.** something resembling a bonnet in shape or function, as the protective hood or cowl of a chimney. **6.** *British.* an automobile hood. —*v.t.* to put a bonnet on. [Old French *bonet* or *bonnet* such a hat; originally, material used for hats.]

bon·ny (bon′ē) *also,* **bon·nie.** *adj.,* **-ni·er, -ni·est.** *Scottish.* **1.** good-looking; comely. **2.** admirable; fine. **3.** healthy-looking; robust. [Possibly from Old French *bon* good, from Latin *bonus.*] —**bon′ni·ly,** *adv.* —**bon′ni·ness,** *n.*

bon·sai (bon sī′, bon′sī) *n., pl.* **-sai. 1.** the art of growing miniature plants that have been dwarfed and shaped by special methods, including pruning roots and stems and wiring branches. **2.** a plant grown this way. [Japanese *bon* basin + *sai* to plant.]

bonsai tree

bon soir (bôn swär′) *French.* good evening; good night.

bo·nus (bō′nəs) *n.* something given in addition to what is usual or due; something extra: *a Christmas bonus.* [Latin *bonus* good.]

bon vi·vant (bôn vē vän′) *pl.* **bons vi·vants** (bôn vē vän′). a person who takes great pleasure in fine foods, wines, and other luxuries. [French *bon vivant* literally, good liver.]

bon vo·yage (bon′voi äzh′; *French* bôn vwä yäzh′) pleasant trip; good-bye. [French *bon voyage* literally, good trip.]

bon·y (bō′nē) *adj.,* **bon·i·er, bon·i·est. 1.** of, relating to, or like bone. **2.** having many bones: *a bony fish.* **3.** having prominent bones; thin; gaunt. —**bon′i·ness,** *n.*

boo (bü) *n., interj.* a sound made to express dislike or disapproval or to frighten. —*v.,* **booed, boo·ing.** —*v.t.* to express disapproval of by making this sound: *The audience booed the last speaker.* —*v.i.* to make this sound. [Imitative.]

boob (büb) *n. Slang.* a stupid or foolish person; dunce. [From BOOBY.]

boo-boo (bü′bü′) *n.* **1.** a bruise or other small hurt. ➡ said of a baby's bruise or in imitation of baby talk. **2.** *Slang.* mistake.

boob tube *Slang.* television.

boo·by (bü′bē) *n., pl.* **-bies. 1.** a stupid or foolish person; dunce. **2.** any of several web-footed seabirds, genus *Sula,* found in tropical and subtropical waters, having a long, straight bill, a heavy, streamlined body, and long, pointed wings. Length: 30 inches (76 centimeters). [Spanish *bobo* fool, from Latin *balbus* stammering.]

booby prize, a prize, often a funny one, given to the person who has done the worst in a competition.

booby trap 1. a bomb or other harmful device camouflaged to appear harmless and designed so that the victim's own movements make it explode. **2.** any trick or device for causing someone harm unexpectedly.

boo·dle (bü′dəl) *n. Slang.* money obtained illegally, esp. bribe money. [Dutch *boedel* property, possessions.]

boog·ie-woog·ie (bùg′ē wùg′ē, bü′gē wü′gē) *n.* a form of jazz music, usually for piano, characterized by repeated bass figures in 8/8 time with melodic and harmonic variations in the treble. [Of uncertain origin.]

boo·hoo (bü′hü′) *v.i.,* **-hooed, -hoo·ing.** to weep noisily; blubber. —*n., pl.* **-hoos.** a noisy sob; loud weeping. [Imitative.]

book (bùk) *n.* **1.** a written or printed work of some length, esp. when on sheets bound together between two protective covers. **2.** a set of blank or ruled sheets of paper bound together: *an address book.* **3.** a section of a literary work or treatise: *the fifth book of the Aeneid.* **4.** a set of items bound together like a book: *a book of matches, a book of stamps.* **5.** the words or text of an opera or musical play; libretto. **6.** the script of a play. **7.** a list or record of bets. **8.** the number of cards or tricks that must be won before a score may be recorded in a card game. **9. books.** business accounts. —*v.t.* **1.** to arrange for; engage; reserve: *to book passage for two, to book a singer for a week's engagement.* **2.** to enter charges against (someone) in a police record. [Old English *bōc* book, writing tablet.]

• **by the book.** according to rule; in the prescribed way.

• **off the books. a.** paid in cash, with no records kept for tax or other purposes: *to be paid off the books.* **b.** not listed on an official or permanent record: *The juvenile's petty crime was kept off the books.*

• **one for the books.** something worthy of special note.

• **on the books. a.** paid by check or other written order, with full records kept for tax or other purposes: *to be paid on the books.* **b.** listed on an official or permanent record.

• **the book.** a set of rules or ideas regarded as authoritative or definitive.

• **the Good Book.** the Bible.

• **to bring to book. a.** to demand an account from. **b.** to scold; reprimand.

• **to know like a book.** to know completely and thoroughly.

• **to make book.** *Informal.* to place a bet or accept bets.

• **to throw the book at.** *Slang.* **a.** to make all possible legal charges against. **b.** to punish severely: *That judge always throws the book at white-collar criminals.*

book·bind·er (bùk′bīn′dər) *n.* a person whose business or trade is the binding of books.

book·bind·er·y (bùk′bīn′də rē) *n., pl.* **-er·ies.** a place where books are bound.

book·bind·ing (bùk′bīn′ding) *n.* the art, trade, or process of binding books.

book·case (bùk′kās′) *n.* a cabinet for holding books.

book club 1. an organization that sells its subscribers selected books, usually at a savings. **2.** a club organized for the reading and discussion of books.

book·end (bùk′end′) *n.* a support placed at the end of a row of books to hold them upright.

book·ie (bùk′ē) *n. Informal.* bookmaker *(def. 1).*

book·ish (bùk′ish) *adj.* **1.** fond of reading or study; scholarly. **2.** better acquainted with books than with practical experience. **3.** too formal or scholarly in writing or speaking; stilted. —**book′ish·ly,** *adv.* —**book′ish·ness,** *n.*

book·keep·er (bùk′kē′pər) *n.* a person who keeps records of business accounts or transactions.

book·keep·ing (bùk′kē′ping) *n.* the art or work of keeping records of business accounts or transactions.

book learning, knowledge derived from books, as distinguished from that gained from practical experience. —**book-learn·ed** (bùk′-lur′nid, -lurnd′), *adj.*

book·let (bùk′lit) *n.* a small, thin book or pamphlet.

book·mak·er (bùk′mā′kər) *n.* **1.** a person who makes a business of taking bets, as on horse races. **2.** a person who composes, prints, or binds books.

book·mark (bùk′märk′) *n.* an object inserted between the pages of a book to mark a place.

book·mo·bile (bùk′mə bēl′) *n.* a motor vehicle equipped to carry books and serve as a traveling library.

Book of Common Prayer, the official book of worship of the Church of England, also used in revised versions by other Anglican churches.

Book of Mormon, see Mormon.

book·plate (bùk′plāt′) *n.* a printed label pasted in a book to show who owns it.

book·rack (bùk′rak′) *n.* **1.** a rack to hold an open book. **2.** a rack or shelf for holding books.

book review, an essay or talk offering a critical appraisal of a book.

book·sell·er (bùk′sel′ər) *n.* a person whose business is selling books.

book·shelf (bùk′shelf′) *n., pl.* **-shelves** (-shelvz′). a shelf for books.

book·stall (bŏŏk′stôl′) *n.* **1.** a stall or stand, often outdoors, where both new and secondhand books are sold. **2.** *British.* a newsstand.

book·stand (bŏŏk′stand′) *n.* **1.** bookstall *(def. 1)*. **2.** bookrack.

book·store (bŏŏk′stôr′) *n.* a store where books are sold. Also, **book shop.**

book value, the value of a business or asset as it appears on the account books. ➡ distinguished from **market value.**

book·worm (bŏŏk′wûrm′) *n.* **1.** a person who devotes much time to reading and studying, often to the exclusion of other activities. **2.** any of various insect larvae that feed on the bindings or pages of books.

Bool·e·an algebra (bü′lē ən) algebra that is based on laws of the relationships among sets, applied esp. to solving problems in logic and to designing electrical switching circuits and digital computers. [From George *Boole,* 1815-64, British mathematician and logician.]

boom¹ (büm) *n.* **1.** a deep, hollow reverberating sound: *the boom of crashing waves.* **2.** a period of rapid economic growth and prosperity: *the boom that followed the depression.* **3.** any great increase or favorable upturn: *a boom in building.* —*v.i.* **1.** to make a deep, hollow, reverberating sound: *The cannon boomed in the distance.* **2.** to increase or develop suddenly and rapidly; flourish: *Business has been booming.* —*v.t.* **1.** to give forth or utter with a booming sound (often with *out*): *The loudspeaker boomed out the announcement.* —*adj.* caused by a boom: *boom prices.* [Imitative.]

boom² (büm) *n.* **1.** a spar used to extend the foot of certain sails or to facilitate cargo handling. For illustration, see **sloop. 2.** a movable arm of a crane or derrick from which the object to be moved is suspended. **3.** a long, adjustable pole used to support a microphone. **4.** a chain, cable, or connection of timbers in a waterway to prevent logs from floating away. [Dutch *boom* tree, pole.]

• **to lower the boom.** to act forcefully to punish, criticize, or defeat.

boom box *Slang.* a large, portable radio, often combined with a cassette player.

boom·er·ang (bü′mə-rang′) *n.* **1.** a flat, curved piece of wood, one type of which can be thrown so as to return to the thrower. It is

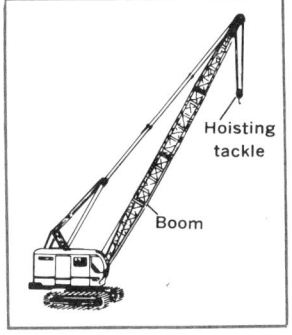

boom² *(def. 2)*

used as a weapon by Australian aborigines and some Africans. **2.** something that recoils upon its originator; something that backfires. —*v.i.* to act as a boomerang: *That plan boomeranged.* [From the native Australian.]

boom town, a town that has grown rapidly because of sudden increased activity in a business or industry: *a mining boom town.* [BOOM¹ + TOWN.]

boon¹ (bün) *n.* **1.** a greatly appreciated benefit; blessing: *Your thoughtful concern was a boon to me.* **2.** *Archaic.* a favor sought; request. [Old Norse *bōn* petition.]

boon² (bün) *adj.* jolly; merry; convivial: *a boon companion.* [Old French *bon* good, from Latin *bonus.*]

boon·docks (bün′dŏks′) *n. Informal.* a poor, unsophisticated, backwoods area. [Tagalog *bundok* mountain; applied by U.S. Marines stationed in the Philippines to the backwoods.]

boon·dog·gle (bün′dôg′əl) *v.i.,* **-gled, -gling.** *Informal.* to do useless or unnecessary work; waste time. —*n.* useless, unnecessary work. [Supposedly coined by Robert H. Link, 1897-1957, American scoutmaster.] —**boon′dog′gler,** *n.*

boor (bŏŏr) *n.* a crude, bad-mannered, or awkward person. [Dutch *boer* farmer, peasant.]

boor·ish (bŏŏr′ish) *adj.* crude, bad-mannered, or awkward. —**boor′ish·ly,** *adv.* —**boor′ish·ness,** *n.* —For Synonyms, see uncouth.

boost (büst) *n.* **1.** an upward shove or push: *a boost over the wall.* **2.** something that aids or advances (a person or thing): *a boost to morale.* **3.** an increase or rise: *a tax boost.* —*v.t.* **1.** to lift by pushing from below. **2.** to advance by speaking well of; promote. **3.** to raise; increase: *to boost prices.* [Of uncertain origin.]

boost·er (bü′stər) *n.* **1.** an enthusiastic supporter. **2.** something

that increases or reinforces power or effectiveness, as a booster shot or an amplifier for a radio or television receiver. **3.a.** the first-stage engine of a rocket, providing thrust for the launching and initial part of the flight. Also, **booster engine. b.** the first stage of a multistage rocket, which contains this engine and its fuel supply. Also, **booster stage.**

booster shot, a supplementary inoculation against a disease, given to prolong or reinforce immunity.

boot¹ (büt) *n.* **1.** a covering for the foot and part or most of the leg. **2.** kick. **3.** something resembling a boot in shape or function, as a sheath on a saddle to hold a rifle or a protective covering for an open vehicle. **4.** a protective covering for the foot and leg of a horse. **5.** *British.* the baggage compartment of an automobile; trunk. **6.** a thick patch for the inner surface of an automobile tire. —*v.t.* **1.** to kick. **2.** *Informal.* to dismiss abruptly. **3.** to put boots on. **4.a.** to start a computer by loading the operating system. **b.** to start a computer by loading the first few instructions. [Old French *bote* covering for the foot and leg; of uncertain origin.]

• **the boot.** *Informal.* an abrupt dismissal: *The store manager gave the dishonest clerk the boot.*

• **to bet your boots.** to be certain of; depend on it.

• **to die with one's boots on.** to die while in action.

• **to lick the boots of.** to flatter or seek favor in a servile way; fawn on.

boot² (büt) *Archaic. n.* remedy; profit; benefit. —*v.t., v.i.* to be of use; be of avail: *It boots us little.* [Old English *bōt* advantage.]

• **to boot.** in addition; besides: *I bought a new shirt and a tie to boot.*

boot·black (büt′blak′) *n.* a person whose work is polishing shoes and boots.

boot camp *Informal.* a military camp for basic training.

boot·ee (bü′tē, bü tē′) *n.* an infant's soft, usually knitted or socklike, shoe.

Bo·ö·tes (bō ō′tēz) *n.* a constellation in the northern sky containing the bright star Arcturus, conventionally depicted as a man holding a crook. [Latin *Boōtes,* from Greek *Boōtēs* literally, plowman.]

booth (büth) *n., pl.* **booths** (büthz, büths). **1.** a small compartment designed for a specific use: *a voting booth, a telephone booth, a ticket booth.* **2.** a seating compartment, as in a restaurant, consisting of a table and a set of seats whose backs serve as partitions. **3.** a stall for the display or sale of goods: *a refreshment booth at a bazaar.* [Of Scandinavian origin.]

boot·jack (büt′jak′) *n.* a device to hold a boot while the foot is pulled out.

boot·leg (büt′leg′) *v.t., v.i.,* **-legged, -leg·ging.** to make, sell, or transport (liquor or other goods) illegally. —*adj.* made, transported, or sold illegally: *bootleg whisky.* —*n.* a bootlegged article, esp. alcoholic liquor. [From the practice of smuggling products, esp. liquor, in the legs of boots.] —**boot′leg′ger,** *n.*

boot·less (büt′lis) *adj.* unprofitable; useless. —**boot′less·ly,** *adv.* —**boot′less·ness,** *n.*

boot·lick (büt′lik′) *v.t., v.i. Slang.* to flatter or seek favor in a servile way; fawn (on). —**boot′lick′er,** *n.*

boots (büts) *n. British.* a servant at an inn or hotel who polishes shoes and boots.

boot·strap (büt′strap′) *n.* **1.** a leather loop at the back of a boot. **2.** *Computers.* a process whereby built-in instructions are used to load application programs.

boot tree, a device inserted in a boot or shoe to stretch it or keep it in shape.

boo·ty (bü′tē) *n., pl.* **-ties. 1.** goods taken from an enemy in combat; spoils of war. **2.** goods seized by violence and robbery; plunder. **3.** any rich prize or gain. [Old French *butin* from Middle Low German *būte* share, distribution; influenced by BOOT².]

booze (büz) *Informal. n.* **1.** alcoholic drink, esp. hard liquor. **2.** a drinking spree. —*v.i.,* **boozed, booz·ing.** to drink excessively. [Form of archaic *bouse* to booze, from Middle Dutch *būzen.*] —**booz′er,** *n.* —**booz′y,** *adj.*

bop¹ (bop) *v.t.,* **bopped, bop·ping.** *Slang.* to hit or punch. —*n.* a blow or punch. [Imitative.]

bop² (bop) *n.* bebop.

bor., borough.

bo·rac·ic (bə ras′ik) *adj.* boric.

a	at	e	end	o	hot	u	up	hw	white	{ about
ā	ape	ē	me	ō	old	ū	use	ng	song	{ taken
ä	far	i	it	ô	fork	ü	rule	th	thin	ə pencil
âr	care	ī	ice	oi	oil	u̇	pull	th	this	{ lemon
		îr	pierce	ou	out	ûr	turn	zh	measure	{ circus

bor·age (bôr′ij) *n.* **1.** the young leaves and flowers of a plant, *Borago officinalis,* used esp. in salads or as a flavoring agent. **2.** the plant itself, native to Europe and North Africa, having hairy oblong or oval-shaped leaves and blue or purple flowers. [Old French *bourage* the plant, from Medieval Latin *borrago,* possibly from Late Latin *burra* rough hair (with reference to the plant's hairy leaves).]

bo·rate (bôr′āt) *n.* a salt or ester of boric acid; any compound containing BO_3.

bo·rat·ed (bôr′ā tid) *adj.* mixed or treated with borax or boric acid.

bo·rax (bôr′aks) *n.* a borate of sodium that occurs as a mineral in the form of white or colorless translucent crystals, used esp. in soaps and cleansing powders. Formula: $Na_2B_4O_7 \cdot 10H_2O$ [Old French *boras,* from Medieval Latin *borax,* from Arabic *būraq,* from Persian *būrah.*]

Bor·deaux (bôr dō′) *n.* any of several red or white wines originally produced in the region around Bordeaux, France.

Bordeaux mixture, a light blue, liquid mixture of copper sulfate, slaked lime, and water, sprayed on trees and plants as a bactericide and fungicide.

bor·der (bôr′dər) *n.* **1.** the boundary line of a territory, country, or state: *You must go through customs in order to pass across the border.* **2.** a strip along an edge, esp. one that is ornamental: *a blue border on a dress, a border of tulips in a garden.* **3.** the edge or the part near it; brink: *a path along the border of a river.* —*v.t.* **1.** to lie on or form the edge of; bound: *The design bordered the page.* **2.** to put a border or edging on. [Old French *bordeüre* an edge, from *border* to edge, from *bort* an edge; of Germanic origin.] —For Synonyms *(n.),* see **edge.**
· **to border on** (or **upon**). **a.** to be next to or adjoining: *Their land borders on ours.* **b.** to come close to; verge on: *That scheme borders on madness.*

bor·der·land (bôr′dər land′) *n.* **1.** the land lying near or at a border. **2.** a vague situation or region; borderline.

bor·der·line (bôr′dər līn′) *n.* **1.** a dividing line; boundary. **2.** an unclear situation or position: *the borderline between passing and failing.* —*adj.* uncertain; indefinite: *a borderline case.*

bore¹ (bôr) *v.,* **bored, bor·ing.** —*v.t.* **1.** to make (a hole or passage), as by drilling, digging, or pushing: *The railroad crew bored a tunnel through the mountain.* **2.** to make a hole in or through, as with a rotating tool: *to bore a plank.* —*v.i.* **1.** to make a hole or passage: *The animal bored into the ground.* **2.** to be drilled or drillable by an instrument: *The wood bored easily.* —*n.* **1.** a hole made by or as if by boring. **2.** a long, hollow interior, as of a tube or gun barrel. **3.** the diameter of a hole or the inside of a tube, as of a gun barrel. [Old English *borian* to make a hole.]

bore² (bôr) *v.t.,* **bored, bor·ing.** to weary by being dull or monotonous. —*n.* a person or thing that bores. [Of uncertain origin.]

bore³ (bôr) a past tense of **bear¹.**

bore⁴ (bôr) *n.* tidal bore. [Possibly from Old Norse *bāra* wave.]

bo·re·al (bôr′ē əl) *adj.* of or characteristic of a northern region or regions or the north wind. [Late Latin *borealis* northern, going back to Greek *Boreas* god of the north wind.]

Bo·re·as (bôr′ē əs) *n.* **1.** the Greek god of the north wind. **2.** the north wind.

bore·dom (bôr′dəm) *n.* the state of being bored; tedium.

bor·er (bôr′ər) *n.* **1.** a tool for boring holes. **2.** any of various insects or their wormlike larvae that do harm by boring into wood, fruit, or other parts of plants.

bo·ric (bôr′ik) *adj.* of or containing boron. Also, **boracic.**

boric acid, a white, crystalline compound derived from borax, used as an external antiseptic, esp. for the eyes, and in various manufacturing processes. Formula: H_3BO_3.

born (bôrn) *adj.* **1.** brought into life or existence. **2.** by birth or nature; innate: *a born politician.* [Past participle of BEAR¹.]

born-a·gain (bôrn′ə gen′, -ə gān′) *adj.* **1.** of, relating to, or being a person who establishes or renews a commitment to faith in Jesus as a personal savior, esp. after an intense religious experience: *a born-again Christian.* **2.** characterized by or having a renewal of interest, conviction, or activity: *a born-again liberal, a born-again jogger.* [From the statement in the Gospel of John that a person "must be born again" (John 3:3).]

borne (bôrn) a past participle of **bear¹.**

born·ite (bôr′nīt) *n.* a dark-colored sulfide mineral with an iridescent, metallic luster, mined as an ore of copper. Formula: Cu_5FeS_4 [From Ignaz von Born, 1742-91, Austrian mineralogist + -ITE¹.]

bo·ron (bôr′on) *n.* a semimetallic element in the form of yellowish brown crystals or dark brown powder, produced from borax

and similar minerals. It is used in alloys and semiconductors and in nuclear reactors. Symbol: **B** For tables, see **element.** [Earlier *boracium,* from BORAX.]

bor·ough (bûr′ō, bur′ō) *n.* **1.** in some states of the United States, an incorporated municipality smaller than a city. **2.** one of the administrative divisions of a city, as in New York City or London. **3.** *British.* **a.** a major city, one of the two principal units of local government. **b.** a former political subdivision having the right to send representatives to Parliament and a royal charter guaranteeing self-government. **4.** a political subdivision, usually smaller than a county, as in Australia and New Zealand. **5.** a division of Alaska, having the same functions as a county in other states. [Old English *burg* fortress, town.]

bor·row (bor′ō, bôr′ō) *v.t.* **1.** to take or obtain (something) with the understanding that it or its equivalent will be returned: *to borrow a book from the library, to borrow ten dollars and repay by check.* **2.** to adopt (from another source) and use as one's own: *Many words in English have been borrowed from French.* **3.** *Mathematics.* in subtraction, to take (a unit) from a position in the minuend and add it, as 10 in the decimal system, to the position of the next lower denomination. —*v.i.* to engage in borrowing, esp. money. [Old English *borgian,* from *borg* pledge.] —**bor′-row·er,** *n.*
· **to borrow trouble.** to create unnecessary difficulties for oneself.

Bors (bôrs) *n.* in Arthurian legend, one of King Arthur's knights and the nephew of Lancelot.

borscht (bôrsht) *also,* **borsch** (bôrsh). *n.* a beet soup of Russian origin, eaten hot or cold. [Russian *borshch.*]

bor·zoi (bôr′zoi) *n.* a hound of a breed originally developed in Russia for hunting wolves, noted for its swiftness, having a narrow head, a long, curving tail, and a coat of long, silky hair. Height: 30 inches (76 centimeters) at the shoulder. Also, **Russian wolfhound.** [Russian *borzoi* swift.]

bos·cage (bos′kij) *n.* shrubbery or trees; thicket; grove. [Old French *boscage,* from *bosc* forest; of Germanic origin.]

bosh (bosh) *n., interj. Informal.* foolish talk; nonsense. [Turkish *bosh* worthless.]

bosk (bosk) *n.* a small wooded area; thicket; grove. [Variant of *busk,* dialectal form of BUSH.]

bosk·y (bos′kē) *adj.,* **bosk·i·er, bosk·i·est. 1.** wooded; bushy. **2.** shaded by trees or shrubs.

bo's'n (bō′sən) boatswain.

bos·om (būz′əm, bü′zəm) *n.* **1.** the upper front part of the human chest, esp. of a woman. **2.** the upper front part of a woman's garment. **3.** the inner or enclosed part, thought of as providing protection, warmth, or privacy: *bosom of the family, lying in the bosom of the earth.* **4.** a broad surface or expanse: *tossed on the bosom of the stormy sea* (William Wordsworth, 1837). **5.** the human breast regarded as the seat of emotions. —*adj.* intimate; dear: *a bosom friend.* —*v.t. Archaic.* to take to or enclose in the bosom. [Old English *bōsm* breast.]

bo·son (bō′son) *n.* any of a class of subatomic particles, such as the photon or pion, whose spin is equal to a whole number or zero. [From Satyendra Nath Bose, 1894-1974, Indian physicist.]

boss¹ (bôs, bos) *Informal. n.* **1.** a person who hires, directs, or supervises others, esp. one who exercises authority over workers; employer or supervisor. **2.** a party politician who controls a political organization, as in a certain locality. —*v.t.* **1.** to order or command, esp. in a domineering fashion: *to boss someone around.* **2.** to direct or supervise: *to boss a work crew.* —*adj.* master; chief. [Dutch *baas* master, from Middle Dutch *baas* person in charge of a ship, as on a dike; of unknown origin.]

boss² (bôs, bos) *n.* **1.** a raised ornamental part on a flat surface, as a knob on silver, ivory, or leather. **2.** a protuberance or projection, as of rock, machine parts, or plants. —*v.t.* to ornament with bosses; emboss. [Old French *boce* protuberance; of uncertain origin.]

bos·sa no·va (bō′sə nō′və, bos′ə) **1.** a music of Brazilian origin, influenced by jazz and rhythmically similar to the samba. **2.** the slow, smooth dance performed to this music. [Portuguese *bossa nova* literally, new tendency, from *bossa* bump (from Old French *boce.* See BOSS²) + *nova* new (going back to Latin *novus.*]

boss·ism (bô′siz əm, bos′iz-) *n.* control by political bosses.

boss·y¹ (bô′sē, bos′ē) *adj.,* **boss·i·er, boss·i·est.** inclined to order others; domineering. [BOSS¹ + -Y¹.] —**boss′i·ly,** *adv.* —**boss′i·ness,** *n.*

bosses on
a Chinese bell

boss·y² (bô′sē, bos′ē) *adj.* having or decorated with bosses. [BOSS² + -Y¹.]

Bos·ton bull (bôs′tən, bos′-) Boston terrier.

Boston cream pie, a rich cake with a creamy filling between its two layers, often topped with chocolate icing or confectioners' sugar.

Boston fern, a fern, *Nephrolepis exaltata,* variety *bostoniensis,* or any of its cultivars, widely grown as houseplants for their graceful, usually drooping fronds.

Boston ivy, a woody, deciduous climbing vine, *Parthenocissus tricuspidata,* of the grape family, having three-lobed leaves, often grown to ornament walls.

Boston Tea Party, a raid on British ships in Boston Harbor on December 16, 1773, in which American colonists, disguised as Indians, threw chests of tea overboard as a protest against British taxation on tea.

Boston terrier, any of a breed of short-haired dogs having a smooth black or brindled coat with white markings. Height: 16 inches (41 centimeters) at the shoulder. Also, **Boston bull.**

bos·un (bō′sən) boatswain.

bot (bot) *also,* **bott.** *n.* the parasitic larva of a botfly. [Of uncertain origin.]

bo·tan·i·cal (bə tan′i kəl) *adj.* of or relating to plants or botany. Also, **bo·tan′ic.** [French *botanique* botanical, botany, from Greek *botanikos* relating to herbs, from *botanē* plant, herb.] —**bo·tan′i·cal·ly,** *adv.*

botanical garden, grounds containing gardens, and sometimes greenhouses and research facilities, for the study and display of plants. Also, **botanic garden.**

Boston terrier

bot·a·nize (bot′ə nīz′) *v.i.,* **-nized, -niz·ing.** to study plant life or collect it for study.

bot·a·ny (bot′ə nē) *n., pl.* **-nies.** the science or study of plants, including the origin, development, structure, function, and distribution of all forms of plant life. [From BOTANICAL.] —**bot′a·nist,** *n.*

botch (boch) *v.t.* to do or make in a poor or inept way; bungle. —*n.* a poor piece of work or inept performance. [Middle English *bocchen* to patch, mend; of uncertain origin.]

botch·y (boch′ē) *adj.,* **botch·i·er, botch·i·est.** poorly made or performed; botched.

bot·fly (bot′flī′) *n., pl.* **-flies.** any of various flies whose larvae are parasites of certain mammals, esp. horses, cattle, and sheep.

both (bōth) *adj.* one and the other: *We got both dogs as puppies.* —*pron.* the one and the other: *Why not invite both of them to dinner? Seeing the two movies, I liked both.* —*conj.* alike; equally: *Both my cousin and I enjoy playing chess.* [Old Norse *bāthir* the two.]

both·er (both′ər) *v.t.* **1.** to give trouble to; pester; annoy: *You bother the neighbors with your loud stereo.* **2.** to make uneasy or anxious: *Meeting new people bothers my shy friend.* —*v.i.* to take trouble; concern oneself: *Don't bother about it.* —*n.* **1.** a person or thing that bothers: *Changing a tire during a trip can be a real bother.* **2.** a state of worry or annoyance: *They always get into a bother.* [Perhaps from Irish Gaelic *bodhar* bothered.]

both·er·a·tion (both′ə rā′shən) *n., interj. Informal.* bother.

both·er·some (both′ər səm) *adj.* causing trouble or worry; annoying.

bott (bot) bot.

bot·tle (bot′əl) *n.* **1.** a container usually made of glass, having a narrow neck or mouth that can be stopped, used esp. for holding liquids. **2.** the amount held by a bottle: *We drank a whole bottle of orange juice.* **3.** milk in a bottle for a baby. —*v.t.,* **-tled, -tling.** to put into a bottle or bottles. [Old French *boteille* container having a neck, from Medieval Latin *butticula,* diminutive of Late Latin *buttis* cask.] —**bot′tler,** *n.*

• **to bottle up.** to hold in or back; restrain: *to bottle up one's feelings.*

• **to hit the bottle.** to drink an intoxicating beverage.

bottled gas, liquefied petroleum gas stored and distributed in transportable steel tanks.

bottle green, dark green.

bot·tle·neck (bot′əl nek′) *n.* **1.** a narrow opening or passageway. **2.** a situation or thing that hinders progress: *The traffic was slowed by a bottleneck in the road.*

bot·tle·nose (bot′əl nōz′) *n.* any dolphin of the genus *Tursiops,*

esp. *T. truncatus,* found in the North Atlantic and Mediterranean, which may be trained to perform tricks. Length: 10-12 feet (3-3.7 meters).

bot·tom (bot′əm) *n.* **1.** the lowest part of anything: *Footnotes are usually found at the bottom of a page.* **2.** a part on which an object rests or stands; underside: *the bottom of a plate.* **3.** the ground beneath a body of water: *The boat capsized and sank to the bottom.* **4.** the cause or source; basis; origin: *The detective tried to get to the bottom of the mystery.* **5.** *Informal.* buttocks. **6.** the second half of a baseball inning: *The player hit a home run in the bottom of the eighth.* **7.** the seat, as of a chair. **8.a.** the part of a boat's or ship's hull that is below the water line. **b.** *Archaic.* a ship, esp. a cargo ship. **9.** low-lying land adjacent to a river, usually rich in alluvial deposits. Also, **bottoms, bottom land. 10. bottoms.** the pants of a pair of pajamas. —*adj.* on or at the bottom; lowest; undermost: *a bottom stair.* —*v.i.* **1.** to reach, rest on, or touch the bottom: *The submarine bottomed to observe the ocean floor.* **2.** *Archaic.* to be founded or based; rest. —*v.t.* **1.** to bring (a submarine) to the ocean floor. **2.** *Archaic.* to found or base (with *on* or *upon*): *The lawyer bottomed the decision on legal precedent.* [Old English *botm* lowest part.] —**bot′tom·most′,** *adj.*

• **at bottom.** on a fundamental level; in reality: *Those political beliefs are at bottom simply an excuse for exploiting people.*

• **bottoms up.** *Informal.* drink up.

bottom dollar *Slang.* last dollar.

bottom land, bottom *(def. 9).*

bot·tom·less (bot′əm lis) *adj.* **1.** having an immeasurable depth; seeming to have no bottom: *a bottomless well.* **2.** having no bottom.

• **the bottomless pit.** hell.

bottom line 1. the line at the end of a financial statement of a business, showing its profit or loss. **2.** a final result or consequence; upshot; outcome: *The other team played very well, but the bottom line was a win for our team.* **3.** the essential point or most important consideration; crux: *The illustrations in a book can be interesting and helpful, but the bottom line is the quality of the text.* —**bot′tom-line′,** *adj.*

bot·u·lism (boch′ə liz′əm) *n.* an often fatal poisoning affecting the nervous system caused by a toxin from certain bacteria that breed rapidly in airless media, esp. improperly canned foods. [Latin *botulus* sausage + -ISM.]

bou·clé (bü klā′) *n.* **1.** a woven or knitted fabric with an irregular surface of small twists and loops. **2.** the yarn used in making this fabric. [French *bouclé* buckled, curled, going back to Old French *boucle* curl, metal ring. See BUCKLE.]

bou·doir (büd′wär, -wôr) *n.* a woman's bedroom, dressing room, or private sitting room. [French *boudoir* lady's private room; literally, place for sulking, from *bouder* to sulk; imitative; with reference to the earlier practice of a lady's withdrawing to her *boudoir* when angry.]

bouf·fant (bü fänt′) *adj.* puffed out: *a bouffant hairdo, a bouffant skirt.* [French *bouffant,* from *bouffer* to swell; imitative.]

bough (bou) *n.* a branch of a tree, esp. a large or main branch. [Old English *bōg* shoulder, arm.] —For Synonyms, see **branch.**

bought (bôt) the past tense and past participle of **buy.**

bouil·la·baisse (bül′yə bās′, bül′yə bās′) *n.* a chowder made of fish and shellfish, vegetables, wine, and seasonings such as garlic and saffron. [French *bouillabaisse,* from Provençal *bouiabaisso* literally, boil and settle, going back to Latin *bullīre* to bubble + *ad* to + Late Latin *bassus* low.]

bouil·lon (bül′yon, -yən) *n.* a clear, thin soup usually made from chicken or beef stock and having a strong flavor. [French *bouillon* broth, from *bouillir* to boil, from Latin *bullīre* to bubble.]

bouillon cube, a cube of dehydrated concentrate of bouillon.

boul·der (bōl′dər) *n.* a large, rounded, rock, esp. one lying on the surface of the ground. [Of Scandinavian origin.] —**boul′der·y,** *adj.*

boul·e·vard (bül′ə värd′, bü′lə-) *n.* a broad city street, often having trees or other greenery. [French *boulevard* originally, rampart, from Middle Dutch *bolwerc* bulwark.]

boulle (bül) buhl.

bounce (bouns) *v.,* **bounced, bounc·ing.** —*v.i.* **1.** to spring back from a surface, as a ball; rebound: *The rubber toy bounced*

a	at	e	end	o	hot	u	up	hw	white		about
ā	ape	ē	me	ō	old	ū	use	ng	song	ə	taken
ä	far	i	it	ô	fork	ü	rule	th	thin		pencil
âr	care	ī	ice	oi	oil	ù	pull	th	this		lemon
		îr	pierce	ou	out	ûr	turn	zh	measure		circus

off the chair. **2.** to move or walk in a springy or energetic manner: *The happy child bounced down the street.* **3.** *Informal.* (of a check) to be rejected for payment by a bank because of insufficient funds in the drawer's account. —*v.t.* **1.** to cause (something) to spring back or rebound: *She bounced the ball. He bounced the child on his knee.* **2.** *Slang.* to force (someone) to leave: *to bounce a disorderly person from a nightclub.* **3.** *Slang.* to dismiss from a job or position. —*n.* **1.** a springing back; rebound: *to hit the ball on the second bounce.* **2.** the capacity to spring back or rebound: *The ball has lost its bounce.* **3.** energetic manner; liveliness; pep. **4.** *British. Informal.* bluster; impudence. [Middle English *bunsen* to beat; probably imitative.]

• **to bounce back.** to recover, as from a blow or defeat: *After losing the first game, the team bounced back to win the second.*

• **to get the bounce.** to be forced to leave abruptly.

• **to give the bounce.** to force (someone) to leave abruptly: *The manager of the restaurant gave the bounce to the drunken customer.*

bounc·er (boun′sər) *n.* **1.** *Informal.* a person employed, as by a nightclub or bar, to force disorderly persons to leave. **2.** something that bounces, esp. in a particular way: *The ball was a good bouncer.*

bounc·ing (boun′sing) *adj.* big or strong; healthy; strapping: *a bouncing baby.*

bounc·y (boun′sē) *adj.,* **bounc·i·er, bounc·i·est. 1.** tending to bounce; bouncing readily: *bouncy cushions, a bouncy ball.* **2.** lively; vivacious; exuberant: *a bouncy personality.* —**bounc′i·ly,** *adv.* —**bounc′i·ness,** *n.*

bound¹ (bound) *v.* the past tense and past participle of **bind.** —*adj.* **1.** made fast by a bond; tied. **2.** certain; sure: *You are bound to fail in school if you don't study.* **3.** under legal or moral obligation; obliged: *A psychiatrist is bound to keep information about a patient confidential.* **4.** having a binding or cover, as a book. **5.** *Informal.* determined; resolved: *bound to have one's way.* **6.** *Chemistry.* held with another element or compound by a chemical bond: *bound water.* [Middle English *bounden,* past participle of *binden* to bind, from Old English *bindan.*]

• **bound up in** or **bound up with. a.** closely connected with. **b.** deeply devoted to: *scientists bound up in their work.*

bound² (bound) *v.i.* **1.** to move by a leap or a series of leaps; spring; jump: *The children bounded over the hill. The young actor bounded onto the stage.* **2.** to spring back from a surface, as a ball; rebound: *The arrow bounded off the target.* —*n.* a long or high leap: *With one great bound the dog cleared the stream.* [Old French *bondir* to rebound; originally, resound, going back to Latin *bombus* deep sound. See BOMB.] —For Synonyms *(v.i.),* see **jump.**

bound³ (bound) *n. also,* **bounds.** ·**1.** limiting line; boundary: *Their love of money knows no bounds.* **2.** an area near or within a boundary: *the outermost bounds of the realm.* —*v.t.* **1.** to form the boundary of. **2.** to have a boundary with; lie adjacent to. [Old French *bodne* boundary, from Medieval Latin *bodina* limit; of uncertain origin.]

• **out of bounds. a.** beyond the boundary or limits, as of a playing field. **b.** not allowed; prohibited.

bound⁴ (bound) *adj.* going or intending to go; on the way (often with *for*): *I am bound for California. They're homeward bound.* [Old Norse *būinn* ready, past participle of *būa* to get ready.]

bound·a·ry (boun′də rē, -drē) *n., pl.* **-ries.** something that limits or marks a separation; border: *the boundary of a ball field, the boundary between illusion and reality.*

bound·en (boun′dən) *adj.* obligatory; binding. ➡ used in the phrase *bounden duty.* [Past participle of BIND.]

bound·er (boun′dər) *n. British. Informal.* an ill-mannered man; cad; rogue.

bound·less (bound′lis) *adj.* having no bounds; limitless; vast: *energy that seems boundless.* —**bound′less·ly,** *adv.* —**bound′less·ness,** *n.*

bounds (boundz) *n.* bound³.

boun·te·ous (boun′tē əs) *adj.* **1.** plentiful; abundant: *a bounteous crop.* **2.** giving or given freely; generous; beneficent: *a bounteous supporter of the hospital fund, bounteous donations.* [Earlier *bountevous,* from Old French *bontif, bontive* kind, from *bonte.* See BOUNTY.] —**boun′te·ous·ly,** *adv.* —**boun′te·ous·ness,** *n.*

boun·ti·ful (boun′tə fəl) *adj.* **1.** plentiful; abundant: *a bountiful supply.* **2.** overflowing with generosity: *a bountiful nature.* —**boun′ti·ful·ly,** *adv.* —**boun′ti·ful·ness,** *n.*

boun·ty (boun′tē) *n., pl.* **-ties. 1.** a reward or premium, esp. one given by a government for the killing of certain animals or the raising of certain crops. **2.** generosity in giving: *Many were dependent on the rich family's bounty.* **3.** a gift generously given: *nature's bounties.* [Old French *bonte* goodness, from Latin *boni tās.*]

bou·quet (bō kā′, bü-) *n.* **1.** a bunch of flowers. **2.** a fragrance or aroma, esp. of a wine. [French *bouquet* bunch, as of flowers; originally, thicket, from Old French *bosc* forest; of Germanic origin.]

bour·bon (bûr′bən) *also,* **Bour·bon.** *n.* a whiskey distilled from a mash of malt, rye, and not less than 51% corn. [From *Bourbon* County, Kentucky, where it was first made.]

Bour·bon (bür′bən, bôr′-) *n.* a person who holds very conservative social and political views; extreme conservative. [From *Bourbon,* a royal family of France, Spain, Naples, and Sicily, noted for its conservative policies.] —**Bour′bon·ism,** *n.*

bour·geois (bür zhwä′, bür′zhwä) *adj.* **1.** of, characteristic of, or belonging to the middle class or bourgeoisie. **2.** conforming to narrow ideas of respectability and success; materialistic and conventional. —*n., pl.* **-geois. 1.** a member of the middle class. **2.** a person who has bourgeois values.

bour·geoi·sie (bür′zhwä zē′) *n.* **1.** the middle class. **2.** in Marxist theory, the capitalist class. [French *bourgeoisie,* from *bourgeois* middle-class person. See BOURGEOIS.]

bourn¹ (bôrn) *also,* **bourne, burn.** *n.* a small stream; brook. [Old English *burna.*]

bourn² (bôrn, bürn) *also,* **bourne.** *n. Archaic.* **1.** boundary; limit. **2.** goal; destination. [French *borne* limit, boundary, from Old French *bodne.*]

bour·rée (bü rā′) *n.* **1.** an old French dance similar to the gavotte, usually in quick time. **2.** the music for this dance. [French *bourrée* the dance.]

Bourse (bürs) *n.* the stock exchange in Paris and in certain other principal cities of continental Europe. [French *bourse* stock exchange, purse, from Medieval Latin *bursa* purse, from Greek *bursā* skin. See BURSA.]

bout (bout) *n.* **1.** a trial of strength or skill; contest; match: *a boxing bout, a fencing bout.* **2.** a period of time; spell: *a bout of influenza, a bout of hot weather.* [Form of obsolete *bought* turn, bend.]

bou·tique (bü tēk′) *n.* a small specialty shop or department, esp. one selling fashionable apparel. [French *boutique,* going back to Greek *apothēkē* storehouse.]

bou·ton·niere (bü′tən yâr′) *n.* a flower or flowers worn in the buttonhole of a lapel. [French *boutonnière* buttonhole, from *bouton* bud, button, from Old French *bouter* to bud; of Germanic origin.]

bou·zou·ki (bü zü′kē) *n., pl.* **-kis.** a stringed musical instrument somewhat like a guitar but with a longer neck and more strings, which produces tones similar to those of a harpsichord or mandolin, used esp. in Greek folk singing and dancing. [Modern Greek *mpouzouki;* of Turkish origin.]

bo·vine (bō′vīn, -vin, -vēn) *adj.* **1.** of, relating to, or characteristic of a cow or ox. **2.** having the characteristics of a cow or ox; dull, sluggish, or stolid. —*n.* any of various mammals that constitute the family Bovidae, including domestic cattle, sheep, goats, and antelopes. [Late Latin *bovīnus* of oxen or cows, from Latin *bōs* ox, cow.]

bow¹ (bou) *v.i.* **1.** to incline the head or upper part of the body forward, as in respect, submission, or greeting. **2.** to give in; submit; yield: *to bow to authority.* **3.** to bend, as under a weight: *The trees bowed in the wind.* —*v.t.* **1.** to cause to stoop or be bent: *Age and hard work had bowed the farmer's once straight back.* **2.** to bend forward, as in respect, submission, or greeting: *to bow one's head.* **3.** to express by bowing: *to bow one's agreement.* **4.** to usher in or out with a bow or bows: *The doorman bowed us into the hotel.* —*n.* a forward inclination of the head or upper part of the body, as in respect, submission, or greeting. [Old English *būgan* to bend.]

• **to bow and scrape.** to be too polite or slavish.

• **to bow out.** to withdraw or resign, as from a job or competition: *Illness forced her to bow out of the campaign for senator.*

• **to take a bow.** to acknowledge praise, applause, or other recognition, as by bowing: *All the members of the committee were asked to stand and take a bow.*

bow² (bō) *n.* **1.** an implement for shooting arrows, consisting of a strip of wood or other flexible material that is bent and held by a taut string connecting the two ends. **2.** a knot with two or more loops extending from it. **3.** a device for playing musical instruments of the violin family, consisting of a slender rod having fibers, usually horsehair, stretched tautly from one end to the other. **4.** a curve; bend. **5.** something curved, esp. a rainbow. **6.** the curved part of a pair of eyeglasses passing over the ear. —*v.t., v.i.* **1.** to curve or cause to curve. **2.** to play by means of a bow. [Old English *boga* this weapon, arch.]

bow³ (bou) *n.* **1.** the forward end of a boat, ship, or airship. ➡ opposed to **stern. 2.** the rower nearest the bow of a boat. [Probably from Middle Low German *boog* or Dutch *boeg.*]

bowd·ler·ize (boud′lə rīz′) *v.t.,* **-ized, -iz·ing.** to edit by removing words and passages considered obscene or otherwise objectionable: *to bowdlerize a book.* [From Dr. Thomas *Bowdler,* 1754-1825, who in 1818 published an expurgated edition of Shakespeare's plays suitable, from his point of view, "to be read aloud in the family."]

bow·el (bou′əl) *n.* **1.** a part of the intestines. **2.** *usually,* **bowels.** intestines; entrails. **3. bowels. a.** the inner part or deep recesses of something: *The well reached to the bowels of the earth.* **b.** *Archaic.* tender emotions, such as pity. [Old French *boel* intestine, from Latin *botellus* sausage, intestine, diminutive of *botulus* sausage.]

bow·er¹ (bou′ər) *n.* **1.** a shelter of leafy branches, often entwined; arbor. **2.** *Archaic.* a rustic dwelling; cottage. **3.** *Archaic.* a private chamber; boudoir. [Old English *būr* dwelling, chamber.]

bow·er² (bou′ər) *n.* an anchor carried at the bow of a ship. [BOW³ + -ER².]

bow·er·bird (bou′ər bûrd′) *n.* any of a group of small- to medium-sized birds, family Ptilonorhynchidae, of Australia and New Guinea, the males of which build structures called bowers or stages, usually on the ground, and ornament them with objects of different colors and shapes to attract females.

bow·er·y (bou′ə rē) *adj.* like a bower; leafy; shady.

bow·fin (bō′fin′) *n.* a mottled, green ganoid fish, *Amia calva,* found in fresh waters of the eastern United States. It is the only surviving species of the order Amiiformes. Length: 2½-3 feet (0.8-0.9 meter).

bow·head (bō′hed′) *n., pl.* **-heads** or **-head.** a rare Arctic right whale, *Balaena mysticetus.* Its huge head and upwardly arched mouth take up about one third of its long, black body. Length: to 60 feet (18.3 meters). [BOW² + HEAD.]

bow·ie knife (bō′ē, bü′ē) a single-edged knife, 10-15 inches (25-38 centimeters) long, with a hilt and crosspiece. The front part of the blunt edge curves concavely to meet the cutting edge in a sharp point. [From Colonel James *Bowie,* 1796-1836, U.S. frontiersman, who used this kind of knife.]

bow·ing (bō′ing) *n.* the act, art, or technique of using a bow in playing a stringed instrument, as a violin. [BOW² + -ING¹.]

bow·knot (bō′not′) *n.* a slipknot having one or two loops, which can be untied by pulling the ends.

bowl¹ (bōl) *n.* **1.** a hollow, rounded, concave vessel used as a container, as for food. **2.** the amount a bowl can hold; contents of a bowl: *a bowl of soup.* **3.** a part shaped like a bowl: *the bowl of a pipe, the bowl of a spoon.* **4.** *Archaic.* a large drinking cup; goblet. **5.** a structure, esp. a stadium or theater, having the shape of a bowl. **6.** a landform having a bowllike shape. **7.** a football game played after the regular season between two specially selected teams. [Old English *bolla* hollow, rounded container.]

bowl² (bōl) *n.* **1.** a wooden ball that is weighted or shaped so that it will curve when rolled, used in the game of bowls. **2.** the act of or a turn at rolling the ball in bowls or bowling. —*v.i.* **1.** to participate in a game of bowls or bowling: *They bowl every Sunday.* **2.** to roll a ball in bowls or bowling. —*v.t.* **1.** to roll (a ball or bowl). **2.** (in bowling) to make a score of: *The winner bowled 175.* **3.** to move with a rapid and easy motion, esp. on wheels. [Middle French *boule* ball, from Latin *bulla* bubble, knob.]
 · **to bowl over. a.** to knock over: *The swimmer was bowled over by the surging waves.* **b.** *Informal.* to confound or confuse; overwhelm: *We were bowled over by the bad news.*

bow·leg (bō′leg′) *n.* **1.** a leg that curves outward at the knee. **2.** an outward curvature of the legs at the knees.

bow·leg·ged (bō′leg′id, -legd′) *adj.* with legs curved outward at the knees; having bowlegs.

bowl·er¹ (bō′lər) *n.* a person who bowls. [BOWL² + -ER¹.]

bowl·er² (bō′lər) *n.* *British.* derby. [From John *Bowler,* nineteenth-century London maker of hats.]

bow·line (bō′lin, -līn′) *n.* **1.** a knot used in making a secure loop. Also, **bowline knot.** **2.** *Nautical.* a rope leading forward from the windward edge of a square sail, used to hold the sail taut when sailing into the wind.

bowl·ing (bō′ling) *n.* **1.** any of several games, esp. tenpins, duckpins, and candlepins, in which a number of wooden pins are set up at one end of a bowling alley and a player standing at the opposite end rolls a ball at the pins in an attempt to knock them all down. **2.** the game of bowls. **3.** the act of playing one of these games.

bowling alley 1. a long, narrow course along which a ball is rolled in bowling. **2.** a building or establishment containing one or more of these alleys.

bowling green, a smooth, level lawn used for the game of bowls.

bowls (bōlz) *n.* a game played on a smooth lawn by rolling a

weighted or slightly flattened wooden ball toward a ball that has come to rest at some distance from the player. The aim is to roll the ball as close as possible to the resting one. Also, **lawn bowling.** [Plural of BOWL².]

bow·man (bō′mən) *n., pl.* **-men** (-mən). a person who shoots with a bow and arrow; archer.

Bow·man's capsule (bō′mənz) a saclike structure at one end of each nephron of a kidney, surrounding a glomerulus. Blood plasma is filtered through the capillaries of the glomerulus into Bowman's capsule during the formation of urine. [From William *Bowman,* 1816-92, English surgeon.]

bow·shot (bō′shot′) *n.* the distance covered by an arrow when shot from a bow.

bow·sprit (bou′sprit′, bō′-) *n.* a large spar projecting forward from the bow of a ship, to which lines steadying or holding sails are attached. [Probably from Middle Low German *bōchsprēt,* from *bōch* bow³ + *sprēt* pole.]

bow·string (bō′string′) *n.* a strong cord connecting the two ends of a bow. —*v.t.,* **-stringed** or **-strung** (-strung′), **-string·ing.** to kill or execute by strangling.

bow tie (bō) a necktie tied in a bowknot.

bow window (bō) a curved bay window.

box¹ (boks) *n.* **1.** any of several types of rigid containers of varying sizes, shapes, and materials, usually with a top or lid. **2.a.** such a container with its contents: *to buy a box of crayons.* **b.** the quantity contained in a box: *to eat a box of crackers.*
3. anything resembling a box in shape, function, or use, as a protective covering or enclosure for a mechanical part or a driver's seat on a carriage. **4.** a compartment or space partitioned off to seat or accommodate a limited number of people: *a jury box, a press box, a theater box.* **5.** a small booth for sheltering one or two persons: *a sentry box.* **6.** *Baseball.* any of several specified areas on the field for batter, pitcher, or coaches. **7.** box stall. **8.** space on a printed page set off by borders, lines, or white spaces. **9.** a small square or rectangular compartment: *a post office box.* **10.** a difficult situation; predicament: *to be in a box about money.* **11. the box.** *Informal.* television. **12.** *British.* a gift in a box, esp. a Christmas gift. —*v.t.* to place or pack in a box. [Old English *box* container made of boxwood, from Latin *buxum* boxwood, something made of boxwood, from Latin *buxus* box tree. See BOX³.] —**box′like′,** *adj.*
 · **to box in. a.** in racing, to prevent (another racer) from getting ahead by blocking a way past. **b.** box up.
 · **to box the compass. a.** to name the thirty-two points of the compass in order. **b.** to take all possible sides of an issue.
 · **to box up.** to surround or confine in or as in a box.

box² (boks) *n.* a blow struck with the open hand or the fist, esp. on the ear or side of the head. —*v.t.* **1.** to strike (someone) with the hand and fist. **2.** to fight (someone) with the fists as a sport: *The challenger boxed the champion with great skill.* —*v.i.* to fight with the fists. [Middle English *box;* possibly imitative.]

box³ (boks) *n.* any of various ornamental evergreen trees or shrubs, genus *Buxus,* most varieties of which have small, oval, leathery leaves and are planted as hedges. [Old English *box* box tree, from Latin *buxus,* from Greek *pyxos.*]

box camera, a simple, box-shaped camera having only one shutter speed and a fixed focus.

box·car (boks′kär′) *n.* a roofed railroad freight car, completely closed, as by a sliding door in the side.

box elder, a rapidly growing North American tree, *Acer negundo,* of the maple family, having low, spreading branches and compound leaves.

box·er¹ (bok′sər) *n.* a person who engages in boxing; prizefighter; pugilist. [BOX² + -ER¹.]

box·er² (bok′sər) *n.* any of a breed of medium-sized, stocky, short-haired dogs having a smooth, tan or brindled coat, often with white markings, and a square, black muzzle. Height: 22-24 inches (56-61 centimeters) at the shoulder. [German *boxer,* from Middle English *boxen* to box² + -ER¹.]

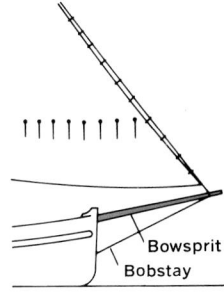

Bowsprit
Bobstay

bowsprit

a	at	e	end	o	hot	u	up	hw	white		about
ā	ape	ē	me	ō	old	ū	use	ng	song		taken
ä	far	i	it	ô	fork	ü	rule	th	thin	ə	pencil
âr	care	ī	ice	oi	oil	u̇	pull	<u>th</u>	this		lemon
				îr	pierce	ou	out	ûr	turn	zh	measure		circus

Box·er (bok′sər) *n.* a member of the Chinese secret society that fomented and led the Boxer Rebellion, an unsuccessful uprising in China in 1899-1900, aimed at expelling foreigners and foreign influence. [From a version of the society's name, *I Ho Ch′üan* literally, righteous harmonious fists, which Westerners changed to Boxers.]

box·ing[1] (bok′sing) *n.* **1.** a sport in which two contestants fight each other with their fists, esp. when wearing padded gloves. **2.** the act of fighting with the fists: *a bout of boxing.* [Box[2] + -ING[1].]

box·ing[2] (bok′sing) *n.* material used for making boxes. [Box[1] + -ING[1].]

Boxing Day, in Great Britain and certain former British colonies, a legal holiday observed on the first weekday after Christmas. [From the British practice of giving *boxes* containing presents to service workers on this day.]

boxing glove, a padded mitten worn for boxing.

box kite, a tailless kite consisting of two or more open-ended paper boxes over a light framework.

box office **1.** a booth or window, as in a theater, where admission tickets are sold. **2.** the receipts of a theatrical performance or sports event.

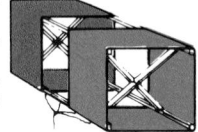

box kite

box pleat, a double pleat with the undersides folded toward each other: *a skirt with box pleats.*

box score, a condensed record of an athletic contest, esp. a baseball game, arranged in the form of a table made up of columns listing a statistical record of each player's performance.

box seat, a seat in a box at a theater, stadium, or similar place of public assembly.

box spring, a rectangular frame containing rows of coiled springs, used as a resilient support for a mattress.

box stall, an enclosed stall for an animal, such as a horse or cow.

box turtle, any of a group of mostly terrestrial North American turtles, genus *Terrapene,* in which the bottom shell is hinged so as to close completely against the domed top shell.

box·wood (boks′wŏŏd′) *n.* **1.** the hard, close-grained wood of the box tree or shrub. **2.** the tree or shrub itself. [Box[3] + WOOD.]

boy (boi) *n.* **1.a.** a male child from birth to physical maturity. **b.** son: *John is our youngest boy.* **c.** an immature youth, esp. one lacking emotional maturity. **2.** any man; fellow: *Dad is playing golf with the boys.* **3.** a male domestic servant. ➡ now generally considered offensive. **4.** a man considered to be of inferior rank. ➡ considered offensive. [Middle English *boi, boy* young male child; of uncertain origin.] —**boy′like′,** *adj.*

bo·yar (bō yär′, boi′ər) *n.* a member of a privileged aristocratic class in czarist Russia, abolished by Peter I. [Russian *boyarin* lord.]

boy·cott (boi′kot) *v.t.* **1.** to combine with others in refusing to patronize, associate with, participate in, or have any dealings with: *to boycott a store, to boycott an election.* **2.** to refuse to buy, sell, or use (a product): *The association agreed to boycott all imported meats.* —*n.* the act or an instance of boycotting. [From Captain Charles *Boycott,* 1832-97, agent for an absentee Irish landlord, who was ostracized and harassed by Irish farmers for his harsh actions against them.]

boy·friend (boi′frend′) *n. Informal.* a male friend, esp. a sweetheart.

boy·hood (boi′hŏŏd′) *n.* **1.** the time or state of being a boy: *Tom spent his boyhood in Virginia.* **2.** boys collectively.

boy·ish (boi′ish) *adj.* **1.** of or relating to boys or boyhood. **2.** characteristic of or fit for a boy; youthful or immature: *a boyish face.* —**boy′ish·ly,** *adv.* —**boy′ish·ness,** *n.*

Boyle's law (boilz) a law of physics that states that the pressure exerted by an ideal gas at a constant temperature varies inversely with the volume occupied by the gas. [From Robert *Boyle,* 1627-91, English scientist.]

boy scout, a member of the Boy Scouts.

Boy Scouts, a worldwide organization for boys and young men that aims to promote physical fitness and outdoor skills, to develop qualities of leadership and good citizenship, and to encourage service to the community.

boy·sen·ber·ry (boi′zən ber′ē, -bə rē) *n., pl.* **-ries. 1.** the soft purple fruit of a cultivated variety of a hybrid plant, *Rubus loganobaccus,* closely related to the blackberry. **2.** the shrub that bears this fruit. [From the American horticulturist Rudolph *Boysen,* died 1950, its developer.]

Bp., Bishop.

BPOE *also,* **B.P.O.E.** Benevolent and Protective Order of Elks, a fraternal organization.

Br, the symbol for bromine.

Br. 1. Britain. **2.** British.

bra (brä) *n.* brassiere.

brace (brās) *n., pl.* **brac·es** or *(def. 2)* **brace. 1.** something that holds parts in place or together or supports parts. **2.** two of the same kind; pair; couple: *a brace of pheasants, a brace of pistols.* **3.** a cranklike device to hold and rotate a bit. **4.** either of the double-curved lines, { }, used in writing or printing to connect two or more items, as lines, words, figures, or musical staves. **5.** a device worn to support a weak body part: *neck brace.* **6.** *also,* **brac·es.** a metal wire or wires used to straighten irregularly aligned teeth. **7. braces.** suspenders. —*v.t.,* **braced, brac·ing. 1.** to make strong, firm, or steady, with or as with a brace; support. **2.** to prepare to meet some form of shock: *Brace yourself for the news.* **3.** to make taut or increase the tension of: *I braced my muscles and lifted the weight.* **4.** to give stimulus to; invigorate: *The cold winter air braces one.* [Old French *brace* the two arms, from Latin *bracchia,* plural of *bracchium* arm, from Greek *brachīōn.*]

·**to brace up.** to rouse one's strength, courage, or resolution.

brace and bit, a tool for drilling or boring, consisting of a bit fitted into a brace.

brace·let (brās′lit) *n.* **1.** an ornamental band or chain worn around the wrist, arm, or ankle. **2.** something resembling a bracelet, esp. a handcuff. [Old French *bracelet* little arm, diminutive of *bracel* armlet, going back to Latin *bracchium* arm. See BRACE.]

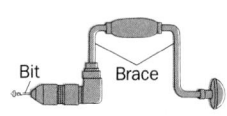

Bit   Brace

brace and bit

brac·er (brā′sər) *n.* **1.** a person or thing that braces. **2.** *Informal.* a drink of liquor taken as a stimulant.

bra·ce·ro (brə sâr′ō) *n., pl.* **-ros.** a Mexican laborer in the southwestern United States, esp. an agricultural worker who is brought in legally under contract to work for a specific employer on a temporary basis. [Spanish *bracero* worker, laborer, from *brazo* arm, from Latin *bracchium.* See BRACE.]

bra·chi·al (brā′kē əl) *adj.* of or resembling the vertebrate arm or an analogous structure, as in a fin or wing. [Latin *brachialis,* from *bracchium* arm, from Greek *brachīōn* arm, upper arm.]

bra·chi·ate (brā′kē āt′, brak′ē-) *v.i.,* **-ated, -ating.** to swing arm over arm from one branch to the next, as an ape or monkey moving through the treetops. [Latin *bracchium* arm, from Greek *brachīōn.*] —**bra′chi·a′tion,** *n.* —**bra′chi·a′tor,** *n.*

brach·i·o·pod (brak′ē ə pod′, brā′kē-) *n.* any of the mollusk-like sea animals constituting the phylum Brachiopoda, characterized by a bivalve shell and a pair of cilia-covered tentacles near the mouth, used in feeding. One genus, *Lingula,* is regarded as a living fossil, having changed very little in the course of 400 million years. Also, **lamp shell.** [Formed from Greek *brachīōn* arm + *pous* foot.]

brach·y·ce·phal·ic (brak′ē sə fal′ik) *adj.* having a relatively short head, from front to back, with a cephalic index of more than 80. Also, **brach·y·ceph·a·lous** (brak′ē sef′ə ləs). —**brach·y·ceph·a·ly** (brak′ē sef′ə lē), *n.*

brac·ing (brā′sing) *adj.* making one feel lively and alert; invigorating; refreshing; stimulating. —*n.* a brace or system of braces. —**brac′ing·ly,** *adv.*

brack·en (brak′ən) *n.* brake[3].

brack·et (brak′it) *n.* **1.** a piece of wood, metal, or stone projecting from a wall and used as a support for a shelf or other object. **2.** a support joined or bent at an angle, esp. a right angle. **3.** a shelf supported by brackets. **4.** a gas or electric fixture projecting from a wall. **5.** either of two symbols, [ ], used to enclose words, letters, or figures, esp. to set them off from a context. **6.** a grouping or classification based on a specific criterion, esp. that of taxable income: *the middle-income bracket.* —*v.t.* **1.** to supply or support with a bracket or brackets: *to bracket a shelf.* **2.** to enclose within brackets, as words or phrases. **3.** to classify together; associate: *The personnel director bracketed job applicants according to years of experience.* **4.** to fire shots on both sides of (a target) to find the correct range. [French *braguette* front flap of breeches, diminutive of *brague* breeches, going back to Latin *brāca;* of Germanic origin.]

brack·ish (brak′ish) *adj.* **1.** somewhat salty; briny: *brackish water, a brackish pond.* **2.** having an unpleasant taste; distasteful; nauseating. [Obsolete *brack* salty (from Dutch *brak*) + -ISH.] —**brack′ish·ness,** *n.*

bract (brakt) *n.* a modified leaf, esp. one at or near the base of a flower or flower head. Some bracts are very prominent and showy and are frequently mistaken for flower petals. [Latin *bractea* thin plate of metal.]

brad (brad) *n.* a small thin nail with a head only slightly wider than the nail's thickness. [Old Norse *broddr* spike.]

brad·awl (brad′ôl′) *n.* an awl with a chisel edge instead of a point, used to make holes for brads.

brae (brā) *n. Scottish.* slope; hillside. [Old Norse *brā* eyelash (suggesting "brow of a hill").]

brag (brag) *v.t., v.i.,* **bragged, brag·ging.** to talk about oneself or one's abilities or possessions in a way that shows too much pride or satisfaction; boast: *He is always bragging about how much money he earns. She bragged that she was the smartest in her class.* —*n.* **1.** boastful talk; boast. **2.** a person who boasts; braggart. [Of uncertain origin.] —**brag′ger,** *n.* —For Synonyms *(v.i.),* see **boast.**

brag·ga·do·ci·o (brag′ə dō′shē ō′) *n., pl.* **-ci·os. 1.** empty boasting or bragging. **2.** boaster; braggart. [From *Braggadocchio,* name created by the English poet Edmund Spenser, 1552-99, for a boastful and cowardly character, from BRAG + -*occhio,* an Italian suffix signifying an increase.]

brag·gart (brag′ərt) *n.* a person who brags a great deal; boaster. —*adj.* bragging; boastful. [Middle French *bragard,* from *braguer* to brag; of uncertain origin.]

Brah·ma[1] (brä′mə, brā′-) *also,* **brah·ma.** *n.* any of an Asian breed of large domestic fowl, having feathered legs and small wings and tail. [Short for *Brahmaputra;* because first imported from a town on this river.]

Brah·ma[2] (brä′mə; *def. 2, also,* brā′mə) *n.* **1.** one of the three principal gods of Hinduism; the creator of the universe. **2.** Brahman *(def. 2).* **3.** Brahman *(def. 3).* [Sanskrit *brahman* prayer, the universal soul, the Absolute.]

Brah·man (brä′mən) *n., pl.* **-mans. 1.** a member of the Hindu priestly caste, the highest of the main castes. Also, **Brahmin. 2.** in Hinduism, the universal spirit or soul with which the atman reunites at the time of salvation. **3.** any of a hardy breed of cattle developed in the United States from the zebu, used esp. for cross-breeding. Also *(defs. 2, 3),* **Brahma.** [Sanskrit *brāhmana* member of the Brahman caste, from *Brahman.* See BRAHMA[2].]

Brah·man·ism (brä′mə niz′əm) *n.* a system of religious and social institutions derived from the Hinduism of pre-Buddhist India.

Brah·min (brä′mən) *n., pl.* **-min. 1.** Brahman *(def. 1).* **2.** a cultivated, intellectual, usually conservative member of the upper class, esp. in New England.

braid (brād) *n.* **1.** a ropelike strip or band in which three or more strands of hair, straw, leather, or the like are woven together. **2.** a band of material woven in this way, used for trimming or binding. Also, **braid′ing.** —*v.t.* **1.a.** to weave or intertwine three or more strands of (hair, straw, leather, or the like). **b.** to form (something) by such weaving: *to braid a belt out of thongs.* **2.** to ornament or trim with braid. [Old English *bregdan* to weave.] —**braid′er,** *n.*

brail (brāl) *n.* one of the ropes fastened to the edge of a fore-and-aft sail, used to take in the sail. —*v.t.* to haul in (a sail) with brails (usually with *up*). [Old French *braiel* belt, from Late Latin *brācāle,* from Latin *brāca* breeches; of Germanic origin.]

braille (brāl) *also,* **Braille.** *n.* **1.** a system of writing and printing for the blind, in which the characters are composed of raised dots in specific patterns that may be recognized and read by touch. **2.** the characters themselves. [From the blind Frenchman Louis *Braille,* 1809-52, who developed the system.]

Braille Alphabet

In braille, the letters of the alphabet are represented by patterns of raised dots based on a grid that is two dots wide by three dots high. In the diagram below, the darker dots show the grid and the lighter dots show the position of the raised dots. Capital letters and numbers are indicated by preceding the lowercase alphabet with special symbols.

a b c d e f g h i

j k l m n o p q r

s t u v w x y z

---

brain (brān) *n.* **1.** the main organ of the nervous system in humans and other vertebrates, located in the cranium at the top of the spinal cord, composed of a complex mass of nerves and supporting tissue, and divided into several parts with varying functions. The brain controls and coordinates all voluntary actions and many involuntary functions; it receives and correlates sensory impulses, initiates responses, and is the seat of thought, memory, and the emotions. **2.** a clump of nerve cells in some invertebrates corresponding to the brain of vertebrates. **3.** *Informal.* a very intelligent person. **4.** *also,* **brains. a.** intelligence: *That student has a lot of brains.* **b.** a person who formulates the plans of action for a group or organization: *The defendant was the brains behind the bank robbery.* **5.** *also,* **brains.** *Informal.* the part of a computer or other machine that controls all of its functions. —*v.t.* **1.** to kill by smashing the skull of. **2.** *Informal.* to hit (someone) on the head. [Old English *brægen* main organ of the nervous system in vertebrates.]

• **to have (something) on the brain.** to be obsessed by (something).

• **to pick someone's brains** (or **brain**). to get information by questioning someone rather than seeking it on one's own: *My friend would rather pick my brains than read the lesson.*

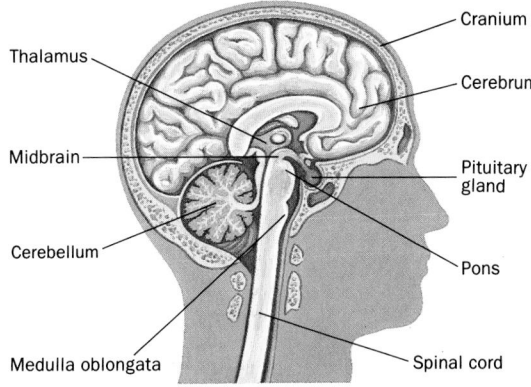

Thalamus — Cranium
— Cerebrum
Midbrain — Pituitary gland
Cerebellum — Pons
Medulla oblongata — Spinal cord

human **brain**

brain·child (brān′chīld′) *n. Informal.* an invention, discovery, or idea regarded as the product of someone's mental effort.

brain-dead (brān′ded′) *adj.* (of a person) judged to be dead because of the absence of any central nervous system activity, esp. the absence of brain waves.

brain·less (brān′lis) *adj.* without intelligence; foolish. —**brain′less·ly,** *adv.* —**brain′less·ness,** *n.*

brain·pan (brān′pan′) *n.* cranium *(def. 2).*

brain·stem (brān′stem′) *n.* the part of the spinal cord that extends into the brain, consisting of the pons, the medulla oblongata, and the midbrain. For illustration, see **nervous system.**

brain·storm (brān′stôrm′) *n.* **1.** *Informal.* a sudden inspiration or idea. **2.** *Archaic.* a sudden, violent mental disturbance. —*v.i.* to take part in brainstorming.

brain·storm·ing (brān′stôr′ming) *n.* the spontaneous and unrestrained offering of ideas by participants in a group discussion.

brain trust, a group of experts whose advice is sought by someone responsible for establishing policy.

brain·wash (brān′wôsh′, -wosh′) *v.t.* **1.** to change the beliefs or behavior patterns of (someone, esp. a prisoner) by using techniques of coercion and manipulation that have a psychological effect. **2.** to persuade (someone) by subtle or high-pressure techniques: *The salesclerk tried to brainwash me into buying the most expensive stereo.*

brain·wash·ing (brān′wô′shing, -wosh′ing) *n.* the action or process by which a person is brainwashed.

brain wave, a series of rhythmic electrical signals produced by

a	at	e	end	o	hot	u	up	hw	white		about
ā	ape	ē	me	ō	old	ū	use	ng	song		taken
ä	far	i	it	ô	fork	ü	rule	th	thin	ə	pencil
âr	care	ī	ice	oi	oil	ů	pull	th	this		lemon
		îr	pierce	ou	out	ûr	turn	zh	measure		circus

brain cells. Recordings of brain waves are used to study brain activity and diagnose brain disorders.

brain·y (brā′nē) *adj.*, **brain·i·er, brain·i·est.** *Informal.* intelligent; scholarly. —**brain′i·ness,** *n.*

braise (brāz) *v.t.*, **braised, brais·ing.** to cook (meat or vegetables) by browning quickly on all sides, then simmering in a covered pot or pan with a little liquid. [French *braiser* to stew, from *braise* live coals; of Germanic origin.]

brake¹ (brāk) *n.* a device for slowing or stopping the motion of a wheel or vehicle, esp. by means of friction. —*v.*, **braked, braking.** —*v.t.* to cause to slow up or stop by applying a brake: *to brake a bicycle.* —*v.i.* to apply a brake: *The driver braked suddenly on seeing the child.* [Probably from Middle Dutch *braeke* device for breaking.]

brake² (brāk) *n.* a clump or thicket, as of cane, brush, or briar. [Middle Low German *brake* thicket.]

brake³ (brāk) *n.* any coarse, hardy fern, genus *Pteridium,* esp. *P. aquilinum,* whose fronds consist of long, sturdy stalks topped by three fanlike blades. It may grow over 3 feet (0.9 meter) in height and is often used for thatch or fodder. Also, **bracken.** [Probably from Middle English *bracken;* possibly of Scandinavian origin.]

brake band, a flexible band with a friction-producing lining, extending partially around a wheel or drum and exerting a braking force when tightened against the wheel or drum.

brake drum, a metal cylinder on the hub of a wheel, to which friction is applied in order to stop the wheel's motion, as on an automobile.

brake·man (brāk′mən) *n.*, *pl.* **-men** (-mən). a member of a train crew who assists the conductor.

brake shoe, shoe *(def. 5).*

bram·ble (bram′bəl) *n.* **1.** any of a large group of shrubs and plants of the rose family, having thorny stems and including the blackberry and raspberry. Many species are cultivated for their small, tasty fruits, and others are grown as ornamentals. **2.** any thorny shrub or stem; brier. [Old English *brēmbel.*]

bram·bly (bram′blē) *adj.*, **-bli·er, -bli·est. 1.** full of brambles. **2.** like a bramble; thorny.

bran (bran) *n.* the ground outer coat of any of several cereal grains, separated from the flour by sifting. Bran is used to feed livestock and in breakfast cereals, breads, and certain other foods. [Old French *bran;* possibly of Celtic origin.]

branch (branch) *n.* **1.** a subdivision of a plant stem, esp. a woody stem of a tree or shrub growing out and away from the trunk or main stem or limb. **2.a.** a physical subdivision resembling a tree branch in growing out and away from a main part: *a branch of an antler, a branch of a railroad line.* **b.** a tributary stream or river: *a branch of the Missouri River.* **c.** a small stream or creek; brook. **3.a.** a subdivision, part, or offshoot of a main body: *Calculus is a branch of mathematics.* **b.** one of two or more lines of descent of a family sharing a common ancestor. **4.** a unit of an organization located apart from the main establishment: *a neighborhood branch of a library, a suburban branch of a store.* —*v.i.* **1.** to put forth branches; spread in branches: *The maple tree branches over the patio.* **2.** to separate or diverge from a main route or body: *Turn left where the path branches.* [Old French *branche* bough, from Late Latin *branca* paw, claw; of uncertain origin.] —**branched,** *adj.* —**branchless,** *adj.* —**branch′y,** *adj.*

• **to branch off. a.** to separate into branches; go in different directions: *The trail branches off west of the pass.* **b.** to go in another direction: *We branched off at the crossroads, but they kept on straight ahead.*

• **to branch out. a.** to give forth branches. **b.** to extend, enlarge upon, or vary, as business or other activities: *I'm going to branch out and learn computer programming.*

Synonyms *n.* **Branch, bough,** and **limb** mean one of the woody members growing out of the trunk of a tree or one of the parts such a member divides into. **Branch** refers to any such member, large or small: *A bird sat on the topmost branch.* **Bough,** used mostly in literature, suggests fullness with leaves, flowers, or fruit: *Boughs covered with pink blossoms tossed in the wind.* **Limb** is used of a large branch, especially one growing directly from the trunk or created by the forking of the trunk: *The house was seriously damaged by a limb that broke off the maple during the storm.*

bran·chi·al (brang′kē əl) *adj.* of, relating to, or located near the gills of an aquatic animal. [Latin *branchia* gill, from Greek *branchion* + -AL¹.]

bran·chi·ate (brang′kē it, -āt′) *adj.* having gills, as a fish or mosquito larva. [Latin *branchia* gill, from Greek *branchion* + -ATE¹.]

bran·chi·o·pod (brang′kē ə pod′) *n.* any of a group of small crustaceans, class Branchiopoda, having leaflike, gill-bearing limbs, such as fairy shrimp and water fleas. [Latin *branchia* gill, from Greek *branchion* + *pous* (stem -*pod*) foot.]

brand (brand) *n.* **1.** a kind, quality, or make of a product, as indicated by the manufacturer's identifying mark: *a good brand of clothing, a new brand of soap.* **2.** the manufacturer's mark itself; trademark. **3.** a mark of ownership applied to the skin of livestock by burning with a hot iron. **4.** the iron used for this purpose. **5.a.** a mark of disgrace; stigma: *to bear the brand of a traitor.* **b.** a mark formerly burned onto the skin of criminals. **6.** a burning or partly burned piece of wood. **7.** *Archaic.* sword. —*v.t.* **1.** to mark with a brand. **2.** to put a mark of disgrace on; stigmatize. [Old English *brand* torch, burning, sword.] —**brand′er,** *n.*

bran·dish (bran′dish) *v.t.* to wave, shake, or swing threateningly, as a weapon; flourish: *The guard brandished a club at the intruders.* —*n.* a threatening wave or shake; flourish. [Old French *brandiss-,* a stem of *brandir* to brandish, from Anglo-Norman *brand* sword; of Germanic origin.]

brand name, trade name *(def. 1).*

brand-new (brand′nü′, -nü′, bran′-) *adj.* entirely new; newly made or acquired; unused.

bran·dy (bran′dē) *n.*, *pl.* **-dies. 1.** an alcoholic beverage distilled from wine. **2.** a similar alcoholic beverage distilled from fermented fruit juice: *peach brandy.* —*v.t.*, **-died, -dy·ing.** to treat, flavor, or preserve with brandy. [Earlier *brandywine,* from Dutch *brandewijn* the beverage, from *branden* to burn, distill + *wijn* wine (from Latin *vīnum*).]

brant (brant) *n.*, *pl.* **brants** or **brant.** any of various wild geese, genus *Branta,* having black and brownish gray feathers. Brants breed in the tundra of northern North America and arctic Eurasia and migrate south in the autumn. Length: about 2 feet (0.6 meter). [Of uncertain origin.]

brant

brash (brash) *adj.* **1.** aggressively forward; impudent; disrespectful: *a brash youth.* **2.** made or done in haste; impetuous; rash: *a brash decision.* [Of uncertain origin.] —**brash′ly,** *adv.* —**brash′ness,** *n.*

Synonyms **Brash** and **brazen,** describing behavior, mean bold and without shame. **Brash** implies impetuousness and a disregard for the claims or feelings of others: *The brash new employee was constantly arguing with his superiors.* **Brazen** more strongly implies arrogance and a defiant attitude: *She was so brazen as to walk right through the door marked "Private."*

bra·sier (brā′zhər) brazier².

brass (bras) *n.* **1.** a yellow alloy of copper whose main added element is zinc. It is valued for durability, ductility, and beauty. **2.** an object or objects made of brass, such as utensils or ornaments: *They polished all the brass in the kitchen.* **3.** *also,* **brasses.** musical wind instruments, of the trumpet, horn, or other related families, made of brass or other kinds of metal, esp. these instruments collectively in an orchestra or band. **4.** *Informal.* extreme boldness or self-assurance; impudence. **5. the brass.** *Informal.* high-ranking officials, esp. military officers. —*adj.* **1.** made or composed of brass. **2.** made up of or composed for brass musical instruments: *a brass ensemble.* [Old English *bræs* alloy of copper and tin.]

bras·sard (bras′ärd, brə särd′) *n.* **1.** a band worn above the elbow, bearing an insignia or identifying mark. **2.** a piece of armor for the upper arm. Also *(def. 2),* **bras·sart** (bras′ärt). [French *brassard* arm guard, armlet, from *bras* arm, from Latin *brachium.* See BRACE.]

brass band, a band in which most or all of the instruments are brasses.

brass hat *Slang.* a high-ranking official, esp. a military officer.

brass·ie (bras′ē) *also,* **brassy.** *n.*, *pl.* **brass·ies.** a golf club having a wooden head, often with a metal plate on the sole, used for low shots; number 2 wood.

bras·siere (brə zîr′) *n.* a woman's undergarment that supports the breasts. Also, **bra.** [French *brassière,* from *bras,* arm, from Latin *bracchium.* See BRACE.]

brass knuckles, a metal bar or set of rings fitting over the knuckles, used in rough fighting.

brass tacks *Informal.* basic or essential facts: *Let's get down to brass tacks.*

brass·ware (bras′wâr′) *n.* articles made of brass.

brass·y (bras′ē) *adj.,* **brass·i·er, brass·i·est. 1.** of, like, or containing brass. **2.** harsh and loud in tone: *a brassy voice.* **3.** cheap and showy: *brassy taste in clothes.* **4.** *Informal.* rude and bold; brazen; impudent. —*n.* brassie. —**brass′i·ly,** *adv.* —**brass′i·ness,** *n.*

brat (brat) *n.* a child, esp. one who misbehaves or is ill-mannered. [Possibly from dialectal English *brat* rag, from Old English *bratt* cloak.] —**brat′tish, brat′ty,** *adj.*

bra·va (brä′vä, brä vä′) *interj.* well done; good; excellent. ➡ used to express enthusiastic approval of a female performer. —*n., pl.* **-vas.** a shout of "brava."

bra·va·do (brə vä′dō) *n.* pretended boldness or daring, esp. an ostentatious display of supposed fearlessness or confidence. [Spanish *bravada* boast, bravado, from *bravo* courageous, savage. See BRAVE.]

brave (brāv) *adj.,* **brav·er, brav·est. 1.** willing to face danger, pain, or difficulty; having or showing courage: *brave pioneers.* **2.** *Archaic.* making a fine appearance; elegant; showy: *brave flags.* **3.** *Archaic.* fine; excellent. —*n.* a North American Indian warrior. —*v.t.,* **braved, brav·ing.** to face without or despite fear; encounter or endure courageously: *The rescuers braved the storm.* [French *brave* courageous, from Italian and Spanish *bravo* courageous, bold, wild, possibly going back to Latin *barbarus.* See BARBAROUS.] —**brave′ly,** *adv.* —**brave′ness,** *n.*

brav·er·y (brā′və rē) *n.* the quality of being brave; courage.

bra·vo[1] (brä′vō, brä vō′) *interj.* well done; good; excellent. —*n., pl.* **-vos.** a shout of "bravo." [Italian *bravo* fine, brave. See BRAVE.]

bra·vo[2] (brä′vō, brä′-) *n., pl.* **-vos** or **-voes.** a reckless, daring fighter, esp. one for hire in sixteenth- or seventeenth-century Europe. [Italian *bravo* villain, bold. See BRAVE.]

bra·vu·ra (brə vyür′ə) *n.* **1.** a musical piece or passage requiring great skill and technical power on the part of the performer. **2.** a display of daring; brilliantly executed performance. [Italian *bravura* bravery, spirit, from *bravo.* See BRAVE.]

braw (brô, brä) *adj. Scottish.* **1.** splendid in appearance. **2.** excellent; fine. [Scottish form of BRAVE.]

brawl (brôl) *n.* **1.** a noisy, rough fight or quarrel. **2.a.** a noisy commotion. **b.** *Informal.* an uproarious party. —*v.i.* **1.** to fight or quarrel noisily. **2.** to babble loudly, as a brook. [Of Low German origin.] —**brawl′er,** *n.*

brawn (brôn) *n.* **1.a.** muscular strength: *all brawn and little brain.* **b.** large, strong muscles. **2.** the flesh of a boar, esp. boiled and pickled. **3.** headcheese. [Old French *braon* fleshy part; of Germanic origin.]

brawn·y (brô′nē) *adj.,* **brawn·i·er, brawn·i·est.** muscular and sturdy; strong. —**brawn′i·ness,** *n.*

bray (brā) *n.* **1.** the loud, harsh cry made by a donkey or mule. **2.** any sound resembling such a cry: *the bray of trumpets.* —*v.i.* to make a loud, harsh cry or sound. —*v.t.* to make (as a cry or sound) in loud, harsh tones (often with *out*): *The sergeant brayed out orders to the troops.* [Old French *braire* to cry; probably of Celtic origin.]

Braz., Brazil; Brazilian.

braze[1] (brāz) *v.t.,* **brazed, braz·ing.** to cover or ornament with brass. [Old English *bræsian,* from *bræs* brass.]

braze[2] (brāz) *v.t.,* **brazed, braz·ing.** to join (metal parts) by a process similar to soldering, using a hard alloy that melts at a high temperature. [French *braser* to solder, from *braise* live coals; of Germanic origin.]

bra·zen (brā′zən) *adj.* **1.** made of brass. **2.** sounding like brass; loud; harsh: *brazen bells.* **3.** forward and without shame; impudent: *brazen behavior.* [Old English *bræsen* of brass, bold, from *bræs* bold.] —**bra′zen·ly,** *adv.* —**bra′zen·ness,** *n.* —For Synonyms *(adj.),* see **brash.**

  • **to brazen it out** (or **through**). to face a situation boldly and without shame; behave defiantly: *The suspect decided to brazen it out and refused to confess despite the evidence.*

bra·zier[1] (brā′zhər) *n.* a metal container to hold burning charcoal or coal, formerly used for heating or lighting or, when fur-

nished with a grill or rack, for cooking food. [French *brasier* brazier, furnace, from *braise* live coals; of Germanic origin.]

bra·zier[2] (brā′zhər) *also,* **brasier.** *n.* an artisan who works in brass. [From BRASS. Compare GLAZIER and GLASS.]

Bra·zil nut (brə zil′) a large nut with a dark, rough shell and triangular, cream-colored kernel, the seed of a tropical evergreen tree, *Bertholletia excelsa,* native to Brazil.

bra·zil·wood (brə zil′wŭd′) *n.* the deep red wood of any of several tropical trees of the pea family, esp. *Caesalpinia echinata,* native to Brazil, yielding red and purple dyes.

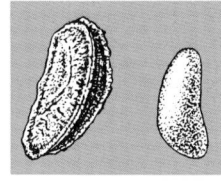

Brazil nut
shell and nut

breach (brēch) *n.* **1.** a gap or break made in something solid, as a wall. **2.** a violation of or failure to live up to a law, promise, or obligation: *a breach of duty, a breach of contract.* **3.** a rupture of friendly relations; quarrel: *a breach between family members.* —*v.t.* to break through; make a gap in: *Our soldiers breached the enemy lines.* —*v.i.* (of a whale) to leap entirely or partially out of the water. [Old English *bryce* breaking.]

breach of promise, a breaking of one's word, esp. of a promise to marry.

breach of the peace, a disturbance of the public peace, as by a riot.

bread (bred) *n.* **1.a.** a food made by mixing flour or meal with liquid and usually a leavening agent, then kneading and baking. **b.** a baked food like bread made of batter containing eggs and fruit, vegetables, or nuts: *cranberry nut bread.* **2.** food in general; sustenance. **3.** a means of supporting oneself; livelihood: *to earn one's bread by writing.* **4.** *Slang.* money. —*v.t.* to cover with or as with bread crumbs before cooking. [Old English *brēad* the food; originally, fragment, morsel.]

  • **to break bread. a.** to eat together; share a meal. **b.** to administer or partake of Holy Communion.

  • **to cast one's bread upon the waters.** to do good without seeking reward; be generous.

  • **to know which side one's bread is buttered on.** to know what is to one's advantage or where that advantage lies.

  • **to take the bread out of someone's mouth.** to deprive someone of the means of self-support.

bread-and-but·ter (bred′ən but′ər) *adj.* **1.** concerning one's livelihood: *Bread-and-butter issues worried the union members.* **2.** seeming suited to everyday life; basic; commonplace: *The company's profits come mainly from its bread-and-butter products.* **3.** giving thanks for hospitality: *to write a bread-and-butter note.*

bread and butter 1. bread spread with butter. **2.** a means of supporting oneself; livelihood.

bread·bas·ket (bred′bas′kit) *n.* **1.** a basket for holding bread or rolls. **2.** a chief grain-supplying region: *the breadbasket of a nation.* **3.** *Slang.* the stomach.

bread·board (bred′bôrd′) *n.* **1.** a board on which dough may be rolled or shaped, bread sliced, or other food prepared. **2.** a board, usually perforated, on which experimental electrical or electronic circuits may be set up quickly.

bread·fruit (bred′früt′) *n.* **1.** the round, starchy fruit of a tropical tree, *Artocarpus altilis,* native to southern Asia and Polynesia. It may be cooked and eaten, or dried and ground into flour. **2.** the tree bearing this fruit, having leathery, glossy green leaves and yellow flowers. [BREAD + FRUIT; because of the fruit's similarity to bread when baked.]

bread line, a line of people waiting to receive food distributed as charity or relief.

bread·stick (bred′stik′) *n.* a long, slender roll of very crisp bread, sometimes covered with sesame seeds.

bread·stuff (bred′stuf′) *n.* **1.** the material for making bread; grain, flour, or meal. **2.** bread.

breadth (bredth, bretth) *n.* **1.** the measure of a surface from side to side; width. **2.** something having a definite and regular width: *a breadth of silk.* **3.** the amount of space something contains; extent; largeness: *My European cousins were overwhelmed by the*

a	at	e	end	o	hot	u	up	hw	white		about
ā	ape	ē	me	ō	old	ū	use	ng	song	ə	taken
ä	far	i	it	ô	fork	ü	rule	th	thin		pencil
âr	care	ī	ice	oi	oil	u̇	pull	th	this		lemon
		îr	pierce	ou	out	ûr	turn	zh	measure		circus

breadth of the United States. **4.** freedom from narrowness in attitude or outlook; liberality; comprehensiveness: *an article of great breadth.* [Earlier *bredethe,* from Middle English *brede* width, from Old English *brǣdu.*]

breadth·wise (bredth′wīz′, bretth′-) *adv., adj.* in the direction of the breadth. Also, **breadth·ways** (bredth′wāz′, bretth′-).

bread·win·ner (bred′win′ər) *n.* a person who earns an income and provides support for his or her family or dependents.

break (brāk) *v.,* **broke, bro·ken, break·ing.** —*v.t.* **1.** to separate or fragment by force; reduce into pieces; shatter: *to break a window.* **2.** to pierce or lay open a surface; wound: *to break ground, to break the skin.* **3.** to destroy or disrupt the completeness, continuity, or order of: *to break formation, to break stride.* **4.a.** to render ineffective or unusable by smashing, crushing, or injuring; make inoperable. **b.** to fracture the bone of: *to break one's arm.* **5.** to act against; violate; transgress: *to break the law, to break one's word.* **6.** to force one's way through or into: *to break the sound barrier.* **7.** to escape from; make one's way out of. **8.** to lessen or destroy the force, intensity, or effect of; weaken: *The matted leaves broke my fall. Jetties broke the waves.* **9.** to interrupt abruptly the uniformity or continuing state or quality of: *A scream broke the silence. We broke the meeting early.* **10.** to sever (a bond or something confining); dissolve; loosen: *to break the chains of slavery.* **11.** to put an end to; stop; overcome: *to break a habit, to break a losing streak.* **12.** *Military.* to reduce in rank; demote: *to break a sergeant to corporal.* **13.** to train to obedience; tame: *to break a mustang to the saddle.* **14.** to crush, impair, or reduce the spirit of; discourage. **15.** to overwhelm the health or strength of; exhaust; wear out. **16.** to go beyond; surpass; excel: *to break the speed record.* **17.** to make known; disclose; inform: *to break the news.* **18.** to cause (someone) to discontinue a habit (with *of*): *to break a child of lying.* **19.** to make bankrupt; ruin financially. **20.** to open and thus stop the flow of electric current in: *to break a circuit.* **21.** to give or obtain change for: *to break a dollar.* **22.** to discover the secret or system of: *to break a code.* —*v.i.* **1.** to come apart; separate into pieces; burst; shatter. **2.** to become inoperable or unusable, as because of damage: *The radio broke.* **3.** to escape or depart forcefully; move away suddenly: *The water broke from the bursting dam. The deer broke from the woods.* **4.** to divide up; disperse; scatter: *The clouds broke and the sun shone again.* **5.** to take place; happen; develop: *Because of the way things broke, the investor made a large profit.* **6.** to come into being or become evident or known, esp. suddenly or violently: *The storm broke. The story broke on Monday.* **7.** to change or fall off suddenly or abruptly: *The child's voice broke. The hot weather finally broke today.* **8.** to decline suddenly in price or value: *The pound broke, but the dollar and franc remained stable.* **9.** to become overwhelmed or crushed with sorrow: *Their hearts broke when they saw the damage done by the earthquake.* —*n.* **1.** the result of breaking; broken place; rupture; crack. **2.** the act of breaking; fracture; shattering. **3.** a sudden rush or dash, as in attempting to escape: *The prisoner made a break for the fence.* **4.** the act of breaking in, out, or forth: *a prison break.* **5.** an opening or start; beginning: *the break of day.* **6.a.** a sudden or marked change or deviation: *a break in the weather.* **b.** a sudden decline or lowering, as of prices or values. **7.** a sudden interruption of continuity or regularity; stoppage; suspension: *a break in diplomatic relations.* **8.** *Slang.* a fortunate chance or opportunity: *a lucky break.* **9.** a brief rest period; pause: *a coffee break.* **10.** an opening or interruption in an electric circuit that renders it incomplete. **11.** *Music.* **a.** the point in the scale where a voice or musical instrument changes from one register or quality to another. **b.** a brief improvised jazz phrase played during a pause between regular phrases of the melody. [Old English *brecan* to shatter, violate, burst.] —For Synonyms (*n.*), see **opportunity.**

  • **to break away. a.** to start before the starting signal is given. **b.** to escape suddenly; free oneself; get away. **c.** to sever connections with (usually with *from*): *to break away from a political party.*
  • **to break camp.** to pack up equipment in preparation for departure.
  • **to break down. a.** to fail to function; stop working. **b.** to become ill through physical or mental collapse. **c.** to give way to emotion. **d.** to analyze or be analyzed or separated into distinct parts. **e.** to crush or overcome, as opposition. **f.** to decompose.
  • **to break ground.** to begin operations; start (something), esp. excavation for building.
  • **to break in. a.** to make comfortable by using or wearing: *to*

break in new shoes. **b.** to give training or instruction to: *to break in a new employee.* **c.** to enter forcibly or suddenly. **d.** to interrupt: *Don't break in while I'm talking.*
  • **to break in on** (or **upon**). **a.** to intrude on. **b.** to interrupt.
  • **to break into. a.** to enter by force. **b.** to interrupt or interfere with. **c.** to burst forth suddenly, as with speech or an action.
  • **to break off. a.** to stop abruptly; discontinue suddenly. **b.** to sever connections or relations; stop being friendly.
  • **to break out. a.** to erupt or become covered with eruptions on the skin. **b.** to escape from restraint or confinement.
  • **to break the ice. a.** to begin something. **b.** to overcome the first awkward moments of a new acquaintance or endeavor.
  • **to break up. a.** to send or go in different directions; disperse; scatter: *The police broke up the crowd. The ice on the pond is breaking up.* **b.** to put an end to; stop: *to break up a fight.* **c.** to make or become upset; become greatly distressed. **d.** to take apart; dismantle. **e.** to sever a relationship. **f.** *Informal.* to laugh or cause to laugh.
  • **to break with. a.** to sever relations or connections with. **b.** to cease conforming to: *to break with tradition.*

break·a·ble (brā′kə bəl) *adj.* capable of being broken. —*n.* an object easily broken.

break·age (brā′kij) *n.* **1.** a breaking or break. **2.** something broken. **3.a.** damage caused by breaking. **b.** compensation allowed for such damage.

break dance, to engage in break dancing.

break dancing, a style of dancing characterized by acrobatic movements, such as spinning and jumping, improvisation, and pantomime.

break·down (brāk′doun′) *n.* **1.** a failure to operate, as of a machine, a system, or an organization. **2.** a collapse of one's physical or emotional health. **3.** a separation into smaller or simpler parts; detailed analysis: *I prepared a breakdown of the household expenses for the month.* **4.** chemical decomposition. **5.a.** a fast, lively country dance. **b.** the music for this dance.

break·er (brā′kər) *n.* **1.** a large wave that foams as it breaks on rocks or the shore. **2.** a person or thing that breaks. **3.** circuit breaker. [BREAK + -ER[1].]

break·fast (brek′fəst) *n.* the first meal of the day, usually eaten in the morning. —*v.i.* to eat breakfast. [BREAK + FAST[2]; because it is the meal that breaks the night's fast.]

break·neck (brāk′nek′) *adj.* extremely dangerous: *The car raced by us at breakneck speed.*

break·through (brāk′thrü′) *n.* **1.** a military attack that penetrates through enemy lines to a rear area. **2.** a major development or discovery helping to further progress in any field of knowledge or activity: *The development of penicillin was a medical breakthrough.* **3.** turning point.

break·up (brāk′up′) *n.* **1.** the act or process of separating into smaller parts: *the breakup of large estates into small farms.* **2.** the stopping or ending of something, as a game or personal relationship.

break·wa·ter (brāk′wô′tər, -wot′ər) *n.* a wall or other structure that protects an area, as a harbor, from the effects of waves.

bream (brēm) *n., pl.* **breams** or **bream.** **1.** any of various European freshwater fish, genus *Abramis,* of the carp family, having a flattened body. **2.** any of various freshwater sunfish of the southeastern United States. **3.** sea bream. [Old French *bresme;* of Germanic origin.]

breast (brest) *n.* **1.** either of the two milk-secreting glands on the chest of a human female, having a nipple for suckling a baby; mammary gland. **2.** the front part of the human body between the neck and the abdomen; chest. **3.** the corresponding upper ventral part of an animal's body. **4.** the upper, front part of a garment, esp. a coat or dress. **5.** something resembling or likened to the breast. **6.** the breast thought of as the center of the emotions. —*v.t.* to struggle against; contend with: *The swimmer breasted the waves.* [Old English *brēost* chest.]
  • **to make a clean breast of.** to make complete confession of; disclose.

breast·bone (brest′bōn′) *n.* the flat, narrow bone in the center of the breast to which the ribs are joined. Also, **sternum.**

breast-feed (brest′fēd′) *v.t.,* **-fed** (-fed′), **-feed·ing.** to feed (a baby) with milk from a mother's breast; nurse; suckle.

breast·pin (brest′pin′) *n.* an ornamental pin worn on the breast or near the throat, esp. to keep a garment closed; brooch.

breast·plate (brest′plāt′) *n.* **1.** a vestlike plate of armor worn to protect the chest. For illustration, see **armor. 2.** an ornamental

cloth worn over the chest by the Jewish high priests of ancient times.

breast·stroke (brest′strōk′) *n.* a stroke made while swimming face down, in which both arms go out in front of the head, then are swept in an arc to the sides and back, accompanied by a frog kick.

breast·work (brest′wûrk′) *n.* a low, hastily constructed defensive wall.

breath (breth) *n.* **1.** air inhaled and exhaled in breathing: *to gasp for breath.* **2.** the act or process of breathing; respiration: *I held my breath and dived.* **3.** a single respiration: *My chest hurt with every breath I took.* **4.** the ability to breathe freely and easily: *to get one's breath back after running.* **5.** air exhaled from the lungs, esp. as made apparent by odor or vapor: *It is so cold that I can see my breath.* **6.** a slight current or whiff (of air): *There's not a breath of air in this heat.* **7.** a whisper or hint; suggestion: *There's a breath of spring in the air.* **8.** life; spirit. **9.** *Phonetics.* a voiceless exhalation of air producing a hiss or similar sound, used in pronouncing such consonants as *h, s,* and *f.* **10.** *Archaic.* the characteristic odor or fragrance of something: *the breath of honeysuckle.* [Old English *brǣth* odor, exhaled air.]
• **in the same** (or **next**) **breath.** almost simultaneously; immediately afterwards.
• **out of breath.** needing to stop to rest and breathe more freely; winded.
• **to catch one's breath. a.** to rest between activities or after an activity; pause; relax. **b.** to check the breath suddenly, as in fear; gasp.
• **to hold one's breath.** to wait in expectation or suspense.
• **to save one's breath.** to remain silent when discussion would be useless.
• **to take one's breath away.** to overwhelm or stun, as with astonishment, awe, or delight.
• **under one's breath.** in a low or barely audible voice.

breathe (brēth) *v.,* **breathed, breath·ing.** —*v.i.* **1.** to draw air into the lungs and force it out; respire. **2.** to be alive; live. **3.** to pause and rest; relax: *We were so busy we never had time to breathe.* **4.** to emit a fragrance or aura: *The ship's galley breathed of the sea.* **5.** (of wine) to be exposed to air after being opened, to enhance flavor and bouquet. **6.** *Archaic.* to blow softly, as wind. —*v.t.* **1.** to inhale and expel from the lungs, as air. **2.** to inject, as if by pumping air in; infuse: *Her enthusiasm breathed new life into the campaign.* **3.** to emit by or as by breathing: *to breathe a sigh of relief, to breathe a minty smell.* **4.** to express or manifest; display: *to breathe confidence.* **5.** to whisper or say confidentially: *He promised not to breathe a word about our secret.* **6.** to allow to rest or recover breath: *The jockey breathed the horse after the race.* **7.** *Phonetics.* to utter with the breath only, without the voice. [From BREATH.] —**breath′a·ble,** *adj.*
• **to breathe again** (or **freely**). to feel relieved or reassured.
• **to breathe one's last.** to die.

breath·er (brē′thər) *n.* **1.** *Informal.* a short rest period. **2.** a person or animal that breathes, esp. in a particular way: *a heavy breather.*

breath·ing (brē′thing) *n.* **1.** respiration. **2.** *Linguistics.* aspiration.

breathing space 1. space or an area in which one can breathe or move about freely. **2.** breathing spell.

breathing spell, a pause in which to rest or think. Also, **breathing space.**

breath·less (breth′lis) *adj.* **1.** out of breath: *The climb left me breathless.* **2.** in a state of fear or excitement; tense: *The children were breathless as they watched the tightrope act.* **3.** without a breath or breeze: *a breathless August evening.* —**breath′less·ly,** *adv.* —**breath′less·ness,** *n.*

breath·tak·ing (breth′tā′king) *adj.* causing extreme excitement or pleasure; thrilling; overwhelming: *breathtaking suspense, breathtaking beauty.* —**breath′tak′ing·ly,** *adv.*

breath·y (breth′ē) *adj.,* **breath·i·er, breath·i·est.** characterized by audible sounds of breathing while singing, playing a wind instrument, or reciting: *a breathy voice.*

brec·ci·a (brech′ē ə) *n.* a sedimentary rock formed of angular fragments that have been cemented together. [Italian *breccia,* from Old High German *brecha* breaking.]

bred (bred) the past tense and past participle of **breed.**

breech (brēch) *n.* **1.** the part of a firearm behind or at the rear of the barrel, in which the projectile is loaded. **2.** the lower or back part of something, as a pulley. **3.** the lower, rear part of the body; buttocks. [Old English *brēc* breeches. See BREECHES.]

breech·cloth (brēch′klôth′) *n., pl.* **-cloths** (-klôthz′, -klôths′). a narrow length of cloth passing between the legs and having its

ends held up at the waist, front and back, by a string or belt; loincloth. Also, **breech·clout** (brēch′klout′).

breech·es (brich′iz) *pl. n.* **1.** any trousers reaching to or just below the knees. **2.** *Informal.* trousers. Also *(def. 2),* **britches.** [Old English *brēc* breeches, plural of *brōc* buttocks, covering for the buttocks.]

breech·es buoy (brē′chiz, brich′iz) an apparatus consisting of canvas shorts attached to a life preserver, hung from a pulley that slides along a rope strung between two ships or between a ship and a shore point. It is used to transfer personnel or rescue people.

breech·ing (brē′ching, brich′ing) *n.* the part of a harness that passes around the rump of a horse or similar draft animal, enabling it to back up with or hold back its load.

breech·load·er (brēch′lō′dər) *n.* a firearm that is loaded at the breech rather than at the muzzle. —**breech′load′ing,** *adj.*

breed (brēd) *v.,* **bred, breed·ing.** —*v.t.* **1.** to cause to reproduce, esp. in order to develop certain qualities; raise: *to breed cattle, to breed roses.* **2.** to give rise to; produce; cause: *War breeds hatred and misery.* **3.** to bring up; train; rear: *They were bred to be politicians.* **4.** to mate: *They bred the stallion with the mare.* **5.** to produce (offspring). **6.** to produce (nuclear fuel) in a breeder reactor. —*v.i.* **1.** to produce offspring: *Trout breed in this pond.* **2.** to be produced; develop: *Crime breeds in slums.* —*n.* **1.** a variety or strain of a species: *Beagles are a breed of dog.* **2.** a kind or sort of anything; type: *The settlers were a hardy breed.* [Old English *brēdan* to hatch, nourish.]

breed·er (brē′dər) *n.* **1.** a person who breeds animals or plants, often as a business: *a dog breeder.* **2.** an animal or plant that produces offspring, esp. one kept for this purpose. **3.** breeder reactor.

breeder reactor, a nuclear reactor that produces at least as much fissionable material as it consumes.

breed·ing (brē′ding) *n.* **1.** the bringing up or training of the young, esp. training in character or deportment. **2.** admirable character and social behavior; good manners. **3.** the production of offspring. **4.** the controlled reproduction of plants or animals, usually to bring about improvements in offspring.

breeze (brēz) *n.* **1.** a light current of air; soft, gentle wind. **2.** *Informal.* something easy to do: *The test was a breeze.* —*v.i.,* **breezed, breez·ing.** *Informal.* to move in a relaxed or jaunty manner: *to breeze into a room.* [Of uncertain origin.]
• **to breeze through.** to do or complete effortlessly and quickly.
• **to shoot** (or **bat**) **the breeze.** *Slang.* to talk or gossip casually; chat.

breeze·way (brēz′wā′) *n.* a roofed passageway, open at the sides, between two structures, such as a house and garage.

breez·y (brē′zē) *adj.,* **breez·i·er, breez·i·est. 1.** swept by gentle winds: *breezy shores.* **2.** lively or carefree; sprightly: *a breezy manner.* —**breez′i·ly,** *adv.* —**breez′i·ness,** *n.*

br'er (brûr, brâr) *n.* brother. ➡ used in parts of the southern United States before a name or noun functioning as a name: *Br'er Rabbit.*

breth·ren (breth′rən) a plural of **brother.** ➡ used chiefly by fellow members of a religion or fraternal society.

Bret·on (bret′ən) *n.* **1.a.** a native or inhabitant of Britanny. **b.** a member of the people who have inhabited Brittany since ancient times and who speak a Celtic language. **2.** the Celtic language spoken by Bretons. —*adj.* of or relating to Brittany or its people, language, or culture. [French *Breton,* from Latin *Brittō* a Breton, a Briton.]

breve (brēv, brev) *n.* **1.** a mark (˘) placed over a vowel or syllable to show that it has a short sound. **2.a.** a musical note equivalent to two whole notes. **b.** the symbol for it. [Italian *breve,* from Latin *brevis* short.]

bre·vet (brə vet′) *n.* formerly, a commission promoting a military officer without a corresponding increase in pay, conferred esp. as an honor. —*v.t.,* **-vet·ted** or **-vet·ed, -vet·ting** or **-vet·ing.** to promote by brevet. [French *brevet* note, diminutive of *bref* document, letter, from Latin *breve* letter, note, from *brevis* short.]

bre·vi·ar·y (brē′vē er′ē, brev′ē-) *n., pl.* **-ar·ies.** in the Roman Catholic and Orthodox churches, a book or books of prayers and ceremonies arranged for each day of the calendar year, which

a	at	e	end	o	hot	u	up	hw	white		about
ā	ape	ē	me	ō	old	ū	use	ng	song	ə	taken
ä	far	i	it	ô	fork	ü	rule	th	thin		pencil
âr	care	ī	ice	oi	oil	u̇	pull	th	this		lemon
		îr	pierce	ou	out	ûr	turn	zh	measure		circus

147

certain members of the clergy and religious orders are required to follow. [Latin *breviārium* summary.]

brev·i·ty (brev′i tē) *n.* shortness, esp. in speech or writing. [Latin *brevitās.*]

brew (brü) *v.t.* **1.** to produce (beer, ale, or a similar beverage) by steeping, boiling, and fermenting malt and hops. **2.** to prepare (a nonalcoholic beverage, as tea or coffee) by steeping, boiling, or mixing. **3.** to plan or devise; concoct: *to brew trouble.* —*v.i.* **1.** to be brewed: *The tea is brewing.* **2.** to begin to develop; be imminent: *There is a storm brewing in the west. Mischief is brewing.* —*n.* **1.** a drink prepared by brewing. **2.** the amount that is brewed at one time. [Old English *brēowan* to make beer or ale by boiling and fermenting.]

brew·er (brü′ər) *n.* a person who brews, esp. one whose business or trade is the preparation of beer or other malt beverages.

brewer's yeast, a type of yeast used in brewing and sometimes as a source of B complex vitamins.

brew·er·y (brü′ə rē) *n., pl.* **-er·ies.** a building or establishment where beer or other malt beverages are brewed.

brew·ing (brü′ing) *n.* **1.** the process by which beer or other malt beverages are produced. **2.** the amount brewed at one time.

bri·ar[1] (brī′ər) *also,* **brier.** *n.* **1.** tree heath. **2.** briarwood *(def. 1).* **3.** a tobacco pipe made from briarwood. Also *(def. 3),* **briarwood.** [French *bruyère* heath, heather; of Celtic origin.]

bri·ar[2] (brī′ər) brier[1].

Bri·a·re·us (brī âr′ē əs) *n.* in Greek mythology, a monster with a hundred arms and fifty heads.

bri·ar·root (brī′ər rüt′, -rŭt′) *also,* **brierroot.** *n.* the root of the tree heath, composed of a fine-grained wood that is used for making tobacco pipes.

bri·ar·wood (brī′ər wŭd′) *also,* **brierwood.** *n.* **1.** the wood of the root of the tree heath, used in making tobacco pipes. Also, **briar.** **2.** briar[1] *(def. 3).*

bribe (brīb) *n.* **1.** something, esp. money, given or offered to a person in a position of trust to induce him or her to act illegally or with special favor toward some person or cause. **2.** anything that influences or persuades; inducement. —*v.t.,* **bribed, bribing.** **1.** to give or offer a bribe to. **2.** to influence or induce with a bribe: *to bribe a child with candy.* [Old French *bribe* gift, scrap of bread given to a beggar; of uncertain origin.] —**brib′a·ble,** *adj.* —**brib′er,** *n.*

brib·er·y (brī′bə rē) *n., pl.* **-er·ies.** the act or practice of giving, offering, or accepting a bribe.

bric-a-brac (brik′ə brak′) *also,* **bric-à-brac.** *n.* small decorative objects; knickknacks. [French *bric-à-brac,* from *de bric et de brac* by hook or by crook; *bric* and *brac* are of uncertain origin.]

brick (brik) *n.* **1.** a molded, usually rectangular, block of clay baked by fire, esp. in a kiln, or by the sun, used in building and paving. **2.** bricks as a material for building: *a fireplace made of brick.* **3.** something shaped like a brick: *a brick of gold.* **4.** *Informal.* a good or admirable person. —*v.t.* **1.** to enclose, cover, or wall with bricks (usually with *up* or *over*): *to brick up a doorway.* **2.** to build or pave with bricks. —*adj.* made of brick: *a brick house.* [Middle Dutch *bricke* a brick.]

brick·bat (brik′bat′) *n.* **1.** a piece of brick or other material, esp. when used as a missile. **2.** *Informal.* an insulting or critical remark.

brick·lay·er (brik′lā′ər) *n.* a person whose business or trade is building with bricks and other masonry materials. —**brick′lay′ing,** *n.*

brick red, any of various shades of a brownish red color. —**brick′-red′,** *adj.*

brick·work (brik′wûrk′) *n.* work of or with bricks.

brick·yard (brik′yärd′) *n.* a place where bricks are made or sold.

brid·al (brī′dəl) *adj.* of or relating to a bride or wedding: *a bridal bouquet, a bridal suite.* —*n. Archaic.* wedding. [Old English *brŷdealu* wedding feast, from *brŷd* bride + *ealu* ale; from the early English custom of drinking ale at a marriage ceremony.]

bridal wreath, any of various white-flowered shrubs, genus *Spiraea,* of the rose family, having oval-shaped, dark green leaves.

bride (brīd) *n.* a woman newly married or about to be married. [Old English *brŷd.*]

bride·groom (brīd′grüm′, -grŭm′) *n.* a man newly married or about to be married. [Old English *brŷdguma* literally, bride man, from *brŷd* bride + *guma* man; influenced in spelling by GROOM *(def. 1).*]

brides·maid (brīdz′mād′) *n.* a woman, usually young and unmarried, who attends a bride at her wedding.

bridge[1] (brij) *n.* **1.** any structure built across a waterway, chasm, or other obstacle to afford passage. **2.** a means of access, transition, or connection; intermediate phase: *The joint venture served as a bridge to full partnership.* **3.** a firm connecting part in the body, esp. the upper, bony ridge of the nose. **4.** the curved part of a pair of eyeglasses that joins the two lenses and rests on the bridge of the nose. **5.** one or more false teeth in a mounting supported by the adjacent natural teeth. **6.** a raised structure on a deck of a ship, from which the ship is navigated and steered. **7.** in certain string instruments, a thin piece of wood or other material over which the strings are stretched, raising them above the soundboard. For illustration, see **violin.** **8.** anything resembling a bridge in shape, position, or function, as a notched piece of wood attached to a long handle, sometimes used in pool and billiards to support the cue in striking a ball. —*v.t.,* **bridged, bridg·ing.** **1.** to build a bridge or bridges over: *to bridge a ravine.* **2.** to go over or across; span: *An overpass bridged the highway.* **3.** to serve as or make a way of passing or overcoming: *The student exchange program may help to bridge the gap in understanding between the two countries.* [Old English *brycg* structure over a waterway.]

• **to burn one's bridges (behind one).** to cut off all means or chances for retreat from a course of action.

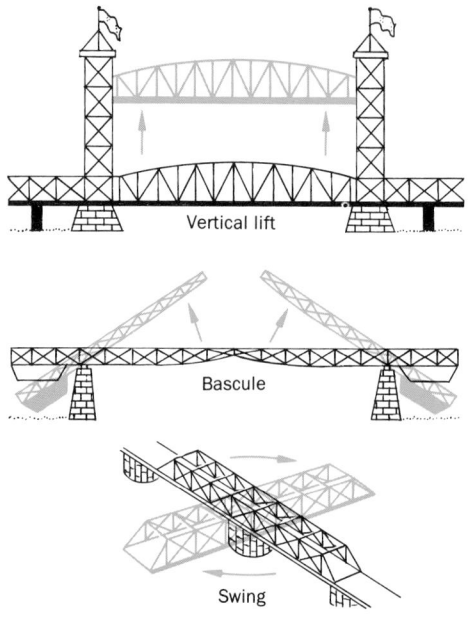

bridge[1]
types of movable **bridges**

bridge[2] (brij) *n.* **1.** contract bridge. **2.** any of various similar card games for up to four hands. [Earlier *biritch* Russian whist, possibly from Russian *birich* literally, announcer.]

bridge crane, a crane mounted on a horizontal bridge, which runs along tracks supported by stationary uprights.

bridge·head (brij′hed′) *n.* **1.** an area secured on the enemy side of an obstacle into which troops and supplies may be funneled so that further advance may be made. **2.** any position taken as a foothold from which to advance further.

bridge table, a square table with folding legs, on which card games are played.

bridge·work (brij′wûrk′) *n.* a mounting for false teeth.

bri·dle (brī′dəl) *n.* **1.** the head part of a riding or draft animal's gear, used to guide or control the animal and usually consisting of a bit, reins, and the headstall. **2.** anything that restrains; curb; control. —*v.,* **-dled, -dling.** —*v.t.* **1.** to put a bridle on. **2.** to restrain, as with a bridle; curb: *to bridle one's anger.* —*v.i.* to show anger, indignation, or scorn, as by throwing back the head and drawing in the chin: *She bridled at his accusations.* [Old English *brīdel* head part of a harness.]

bridle hand, the left hand, in which the reins are usually held.

bridle path, a path for horseback riding.

Brie (brē) *n.* a variety of soft, creamy cheese with a strong aroma and a mild, rich flavor, ripened by mold or bacteria. [From *Brie,* district in France where it was first made.]

brief (brēf) *adj.* **1.** short in duration; quickly ending: *a brief interruption, a brief stay.* **2.** short in expression; using few words; concise; succinct: *I'll be brief and to the point. I gave a brief summary of my proposal.* **3.** short in length: *a brief pair of shorts.* **4.** curt; abrupt: *You were very brief with them.* —*n.* **1.** *Law.* a summary of the facts, the applicable points of law, and other material pertinent to a case, prepared by the counsel as the basis for arguing a case in court. **2. briefs.** short, close-fitting underpants. —*v.t.* **1.** to give all important information or details to; instruct by a briefing: *The commander briefed the crew on the plan of attack.* **2.** *British.* to inform by a legal brief. [Old French *brief* short, from Latin *brevis.*] —**brief′ly,** *adv.* —**brief′ness,** *n.*
 • **in brief.** in a few words.

brief·case (brēf′kās′) *n.* a flat or expansible case, frequently clamped or zippered and having a handle, used esp. for carrying papers and books.

brief·ing (brē′fing) *n.* **1.** a meeting at which the important details of a military operation are outlined for the participants. **2.** the outline itself, esp. one given to the pilots or crew of combat planes before they take off. **3.** any similar discussion of procedure, instructions, or other essential information.

bri·er[1] (brī′ər) *also,* **briar.** *n.* **1.** any thorny shrub or plant, esp. the wild rose; bramble. **2.** a thorny stem or thorn on such a stem. [Old English *brær* this shrub.] —**bri′er·y,** *adj.*

bri·er[2] (brī′ər) briar[1].

bri·er·root (brī′ər rüt′, -rūt′) briarroot.

bri·er·wood (brī′ər wùd′) briarwood.

brig (brig) *n.* **1.** a ship with two square-rigged masts. **2.** a place on a ship for confining prisoners. **3.** a naval prison. [Short for BRIGANTINE.]

Brig. 1. Brigade. **2.** Brigadier.

bri·gade (bri gād′) *n.* **1.** a military unit consisting of from two to five battalions and forming part of a division. **2.** formerly, a military unit consisting of two regiments and forming part of a division. **3.** a group of people organized for a particular purpose: *The town set up a fire brigade.* [French *brigade* troop, from Italian *brigata,* from *brigare* to fight, from *briga* strife; of Celtic origin.]

brig

brig·a·dier (brig′ə dîr′) *n.* brigadier general. [French *brigadier* corporal, from *brigade* troop. See BRIGADE.]

brigadier general *pl.* **brigadier generals.** a commissioned officer in the U.S. Army, Air Force, or Marines, ranking above a colonel and below a major general.

brig·and (brig′ənd) *n.* a robber or bandit, esp. one of a band of roving outlaws. [Old French *brigand,* from Italian *brigante,* from *brigare* to fight. See BRIGADE.]

brig·and·age (brig′ən dij) *n.* the practices of brigands; robbery.

brig·an·tine (brig′ən tēn′) *n.* a two-masted ship with both masts square-rigged, except for a fore-and-aft mainsail. [French *brigantin,* from Italian *brigantino* pirate ship, from *brigante* robber. See BRIGAND.]

bright (brīt) *adj.* **1.** radiating or reflecting much light; filled with light; shining: *a bright and sunny day, a waxed floor with a bright finish.* **2.** of brilliant color; vivid: *a bright yellow dress.* **3.** having or showing much intelligence; quick-witted; clever: *a bright student, a bright idea.* **4.** favorable or hopeful; auspicious: *bright prospects, a bright future.* **5.** full of happiness and good cheer; lively; cheerful: *a bright and gay occasion, bright eyes.* **6.** glorious; splendid: *the brightest period of the empire.* —*adv.* in a bright manner; brightly: *stars shining bright.* [Old English *beorht* shining.] —**bright′ly,** *adv.* —**bright′ness,** *n.*

Synonyms *adj.* Bright, brilliant, radiant, and luminous mean giving off light. **Bright,** the most general of these words, implies strength or intensity: *I was dazzled by the bright reflection from the snow.* **Brilliant** suggests great intensity and usually motion, such as flashing or sparkling: *The brilliant fireworks lit up the sky.* **Radiant** is used of bright light coming from a source, not reflecting from a surface, and suggests an outward effect: *The radiant campfire lit the whole clearing.* **Luminous** also suggests a source rather than a reflecting surface but is used generally of softer, glowing light: *The luminous insects gave off a faint gleam in the twilight.*

bright·en (brī′tən) *v.t., v.i.* to make or become bright or brighter. —**bright′en·er,** *n.*

Bright's disease (brīts) any of various forms of kidney disease characterized by a degeneration of the kidneys and the presence of albumin in the urine. [From Dr. Richard *Bright,* 1789-1858, English physician who studied and wrote about the disease.]

brill (bril) *n., pl.* **brill** or **brills.** a European flatfish, *Scophthalmus rhombus.* [Possibly from Cornish *brilli* mackerel.]

bril·liance (bril′yəns) *n.* the state or quality of being brilliant. Also, **bril′lian·cy.**

bril·liant (bril′yənt) *adj.* **1.** sparkling with light or luster; shining radiantly: *brilliant spotlights, brilliant stars.* **2.** splendid or outstanding; magnificent: *a brilliant career.* **3.** having or showing great intelligence, ability, or talent: *a brilliant mathematician.* **4.** intensely rich or clear in color or sound; vivid: *a peacock's brilliant plumage, a brilliant voice.* —*n.* a gem, esp. a diamond, cut in a particular form with many facets to increase its sparkle. [French *brillant* shining, present participle of *briller* to shine, possibly going back to Latin *bēryllus* beryl (noted for its glassy luster). See BERYL.] —**bril′liant·ly,** *adv.* —For Synonyms, see **bright.**

bril·lian·tine (bril′yən tēn′) *n.* **1.** an oily preparation used to make the hair shine. **2.** a lightweight glossy fabric made of cotton and wool or mohair, used esp. for summer suits or dresses. [French *brillantine,* from *brillant* shining. See BRILLIANT.]

brim (brim) *n.* **1.** the upper edge or rim of a cup, bowl, or similar object. **2.** a projecting edge or rim: *the brim of a hat.* **3.** an edge or margin, as of a canyon; brink. —*v.,* **brimmed, brim·ming.** —*v.i.* to be full to the brim; overflow: *eyes brimming with tears, to brim with happiness.* —*v.t. Archaic.* to fill to the brim. [Middle English *brimme* rim, shore.]

brim·ful (brim′fùl′) *adj.* full to the brim; completely full.

brim·stone (brim′stōn′) *n.* sulfur. [Middle English *brinston* literally, burn stone, from *brinnen* to burn[1] + *ston* stone. See BURN[1], STONE.]

brin·dle (brin′dəl) *adj.* brindled. —*n.* **1.** a brindled color. **2.** a brindled animal. [From BRINDLED.]

brin·dled (brin′dəld) *adj.* gray or tawny with irregular, darker streaks or spots. [Modification of *brinded,* from Middle English *brended,* from *brend,* past participle of *brennen* to burn[1].]

brine (brīn) *n.* **1.** water full of or saturated with salt, esp. used for pickling or preserving food. **2.** the sea or its water: *afloat on the brine.* —*v.t.,* **brined, brin·ing.** to treat with or steep in brine. [Old English *brȳne* salt water.]

brine shrimp, any of a group of fairy shrimp, genus *Artemia,* found in salt lakes and used as tropical fish food.

bring (bring) *v.t.,* **brought, bring·ing. 1.** to carry, convey, or cause (someone or something) to come with oneself from another place: *Bring all your books home. They brought a message from the office.* **2.** to cause to come; attract; draw: *What brings you here? The screams brought the police.* **3.** to cause to come into a particular state or condition: *to bring a fire under control, to bring water to a boil.* **4.** to cause to come about or happen; result in; produce: *Floods bring disaster. The drug brought relief from pain.* **5.** to cause (someone or oneself) to adopt a course of action or belief; persuade; induce: *I couldn't bring myself to lie.* **6.** to sell for: *The car brought a high price.* **7.** *Law.* to present before a court or magistrate: *to bring charges, to bring suit.* [Old English *bringan* to cause to come.]
 • **to bring about.** to make happen; cause; accomplish: *The new job brought about many changes in my life.*
 • **to bring around** (or **round**). **a.** to cause (someone) to adopt an opinion or viewpoint; convince; persuade. **b.** to restore to consciousness; revive.
 • **to bring down.** to fell by wounding or killing: *The hunter brought down four ducks.*
 • **to bring down the house.** to elicit a sustained burst of applause or laughter from an audience, as in a theater: *The duet brought down the house.*
 • **to bring forth. a.** to produce (offspring or fruit). **b.** to disclose or advance; introduce: *to bring forth a proposal, to bring forth new evidence.* **c.** to give rise to; cause: *The proposed closing of the factory brought forth cries of protest from the townspeople.*

a	at	e	end	o	hot	u	up	hw	white		about
ā	ape	ē	me	ō	old	ū	use	ng	song		taken
ä	far	i	it	ô	fork	ü	rule	th	thin	ə	pencil
âr	care	ī	ice	oi	oil	ù	pull	th	this		lemon
				îr	pierce	ou	out	ûr	turn	zh	measure		circus

• **to bring forward. a.** to introduce; present: *to bring arguments forward in support of a plan.* **b.** in bookkeeping, to carry (a figure) over from one page or column to another.

• **to bring in. a.** to yield or produce, as profits. **b.** *Law.* to give or submit (a verdict).

• **to bring off.** to accomplish successfully.

• **to bring on.** to lead to; cause: *The crisis brought on a full-scale war.*

• **to bring out. a.** to cause to be evident; make clear: *That's not the point I want to bring out.* **b.** to introduce or present to the public: *to bring out the fall fashions.*

• **to bring to. a.** to restore to consciousness; revive. **b.** *Nautical.* to cause (a ship) to come to a standstill.

• **to bring up. a.** to rear; educate. **b.** to introduce to notice or consideration: *to bring up a subject in conversation.* **c.** to cause to pause or stop: *The suggestion brought us up short.* **d.** to cough up; vomit.

• **to bring up the rear.** to come last, as in a procession.

brink (bringk) *n.* **1.** the edge or margin of a steep place, as of a precipice or the bank of a river. **2.** the point at which something is likely to begin; verge: *on the brink of disaster, on the brink of tears.* [Middle English *brink;* probably of Scandinavian origin.]

brink·man·ship (brink′mən ship′) *also,* **brinksmanship.** *n.* the policy or practice of manipulating a dangerous situation to the brink of disaster in order to secure some advantage, as used by a country in its foreign affairs.

brin·y (brī′nē) *adj.,* **brin·i·er, brin·i·est.** of or like brine; salty: *a briny taste.* —**brin′i·ness,** *n.*

bri·oche (brē′osh) *n.* a soft, light roll rich in eggs and butter. [Dialectal French *brioche,* from *brier* to knead; of Germanic origin.]

bri·quette (bri ket′) *also,* **bri·quet.** *n.* a molded block of compressed coal dust or other material, used for fuel. [French *briquette,* diminutive of *brique* brick, from Middle Dutch *bricke.*]

Bri·se·is (brī sē′is) *n.* in Greek legend, a beautiful woman captured by Achilles in the Trojan War but taken from him by the Greek king Agamemnon, causing Achilles to withdraw from battle.

brisk (brisk) *adj.* **1.** quick and lively; energetic; vigorous: *a brisk manner, a brisk pace.* **2.** keen; invigorating; bracing: *a brisk wind.* [Probably from French *brusque.* See BRUSQUE.] —**brisk′ly,** *adv.* —**brisk′ness,** *n.*

bris·ket (bris′kit) *n.* **1.** a cut of meat from the breast of an animal, esp. a beef animal. **2.** the breast of an animal. [Middle English *brusket;* of Scandinavian origin.]

bris·ling (briz′ling, bris′-) *n.* a type of small, sardinelike herring of the northeastern Atlantic, canned and used for food.

bris·tle (bris′əl) *n.* **1.** one of the coarse, short, stiff hairs of a hog, often used for making brushes. **2.** something resembling this: *The donkey had bristles on its ears and chin. My toothbrush has nylon bristles.* —*v.,* **-tled, -tling.** —*v.i.* **1.** to raise the hairs on the back, as in fear, anger, or excitement: *The dog bristled at the sight of the stranger.* **2.** to show anger or irritation: *I bristled at the accusation.* **3.** to become stiffly erect: *The cat's hair bristled as the dog approached.* **4.** to be thick with or full of (with *with*): *The shores bristled with crabs. The crowd bristled with excitement.* —*v.t.* **1.** to cause to be stiffly erect: *The porcupine bristled its quills.* **2.** to furnish with bristles. [Middle English *brustel* hog's hair, stiff hair, diminutive of Old English *byrst* hog's hair.]

bris·tle·cone pine (bris′əl kōn′) a slow-growing, sometimes shrubby, pine, *Pinus aristata* or *P. longaeva,* of the western United States that may live for 5,000 years and is among the oldest of living things.

bris·tle·tail (bris′əl tāl′) *n.* any of the wingless insects of the order Thysanura, such as the silverfish, with long bristlelike appendages at the end of the abdomen.

bris·tly (bris′lē) *adj.,* **-tli·er, -tli·est.** **1.** like bristles: *The goat had bristly hairs on its chin.* **2.** easily angered or irritated: *a bristly personality.*

Bris·tol board (bris′təl) a fine pasteboard having a smooth finish.

Brit. **1.** Britain. **2.** British.

Bri·tan·ni·a (bri tan′ē ə, -tan′yə) *n.* **1.** the ancient Roman name for Britain. **2.** the British Empire. **3.** a female figure thought of as representing Great Britain or the British Empire. **4.** Britannia metal. [Latin *Britannia, Britānia* island of Britain, from *Britō.* See BRITON.]

Britannia metal, a pewterlike, white alloy of tin, whose main added element is antimony, with lesser amounts of copper. It is malleable and tarnish-resistant and is used esp. in making tableware.

Bri·tan·nic (bri tan′ik) *adj.* British.

britch·es (brich′iz) *pl. n. Informal.* breeches *(def. 2).*

Brit·i·cism (brit′ə siz′əm) *n.* a word, phrase, or idiom occurring only or mainly in British English. *Lorry* is a Briticism for *truck.*

Brit·ish (brit′ish) *adj.* of, relating to, or characteristic of Great Britain or its people. Also, **Britannic.** —*n.* **1. the British.** the people of Great Britain. **2.** British English. [Old English *Brittisc* relating to the ancient Britons, from *Bret* a Briton; of Celtic origin.]

British English, the English language as spoken and written predominantly in Great Britain. ➡ distinguished esp. from **American English.**

British English

Although there tend to be fewer differences between British English and American English than in the past, some variations still exist. Following are some examples.

AMERICAN TERM — BRITISH EQUIVALENT

apartment — flat
baby carriage — pram
cracker or cookie — biscuit
dessert — sweet
diaper — nappy
electric cord — flex
elevator — lift
flashlight — torch
french fries — chips
garbage can — dustbin
gasoline — petrol
hood (of a car) — bonnet
ice-cream cone — cornet
mail — post
potato chips — crisps
private school — public school
subway — underground
trailer or mobile home — caravan
truck — lorry
trunk (of a car) — boot
two weeks — fortnight
vacation — holiday
windshield — windscreen

Brit·ish·er (brit′i shər) *n.* a native or subject of Great Britain, esp. of England; Briton.

British thermal unit, a unit of measurement equal to the amount of heat needed to raise the temperature of one pound of water one degree Fahrenheit.

Brit·on (brit′ən) *n.* **1.** a native or subject of Great Britain, esp. of England. **2.** a member of an ancient Celtic people inhabiting southern Britain at the time of the Roman invasion. [Old French *Breton* Breton, from Latin *Britō* ancient Briton, Breton; probably of Celtic origin.]

Brit·ta·ny spaniel, (brit′ə nē) any of a French breed of tall, short-tailed bird dogs having a slightly wavy orange and white or liver and white coat, developed in Brittany by interbreeding pointers with local spaniels.

brit·tle (brit′əl) *adj.* **1.** rigid and liable to break or snap; easily broken: *brittle fingernails.* **2.** having or showing a lack of warmth, flexibility, or friendliness: *a brittle manner, a brittle personality, a brittle tone of voice.* [Middle English *britel* easily broken.] —**brit′tle·ness,** *n.*

brittle star, any of a group of echinoderms, class Ophiuroidea, having a central disk surrounded by five long, slender arms that are used for wriggling snakelike along the sea bottom.

bro. *pl.* **bros.** brother.

broach (brōch) *n.* **1.** a cutting tool consisting of a tapered steel shaft with transverse cutting edges, driven or pulled through rough holes to enlarge or shape them. **2.** a spit for roasting. —*v.t.* **1.** to mention or suggest for the first time; introduce: *I hesitated to broach the topic while you were angry.* **2.** to pierce, so as to draw out a liquid; tap: *to broach a keg of wine.* —*v.i.* to come up to and break the surface of water: *The whale broached right in front*

of us. [Old French *broche* a roasting spit, clasp, from Late Latin *brocca* pointed stick, from Latin *broccus* projecting.]

broad (brôd) *adj.* **1.a.** of large extent from side to side; wide: *The broad boulevard had four traffic lanes.* **b.** large in size; spacious: *broad plains, a broad expanse of mountains.* **2.** willing to accept a wide range of views; tolerant; open-minded: *a broad outlook on life.* **3.** having a wide range or application; extensive: *broad interests, a broad rule.* **4.** concerning the main parts or features; not detailed; general: *a broad description.* **5.** easy to understand; clear; obvious: *a broad hint.* **6.** widely diffused; full: *broad daylight.* **7.** coarse; vulgar; earthy: *broad humor.* **8.** strongly marked or dialectal: *a broad accent.* **9.** (of vowel sounds) formed with the mouth open wide and the back portion of the tongue in a low, flat position. The *a* in *father* is broad. [Old English *brād* wide.] —**broad′ly,** *adv.* —**broad′ness,** *n.*

broad-ax (brôd′aks′) *also,* **broad·axe.** *n., pl.* **-ax·es.** **1.** a wide-bladed ax, used esp. to cut logs or to make incisions in trees to obtain turpentine. **2.** battle-ax *(def. 1).*

broad·band (brôd′band′) *adj.* of, relating to, or operating over a wide range of radio or television frequencies.

broad-based (brôd′bāst′) *adj.* based on or involving many different groups or things; having a wide range; not limited or narrow: *a broad-based economy that does not rely only on agriculture.*

broad bean **1.** the edible seed of an Old World vetch, growing in long, broad pods. **2.** the plant, *Vicia faba,* bearing these pods, widely grown for its seeds and as forage. Also, **fava bean.**

broad·brim (brôd′brim′) *n.* **1.** a hat with a wide brim. **2.** *also,* **Broadbrim.** *Informal.* Quaker.

broad·cast (brôd′kast′) *v.,* **-cast** or **-cast·ed,** **-cast·ing.** —*v.t.* **1.** to transmit (information or entertainment) by radio or television. **2.** to make widely known or spread: *They broadcast the story all over town.* **3.** to scatter over a wide area, as seed. —*v.i.* to transmit by radio or television: *This station broadcasts until midnight.* —*n.* **1.** something that is broadcast by radio or television, esp. a program: *The story will appear on tomorrow's broadcast.* **2.** the act of broadcasting, esp. transmission by radio or television. —*adj.* **1.** of, relating to, or transmitted by radio or television broadcasts. **2.** scattered over a wide area: *broadcast seed.* —*adv.* by scattering over a large area: *to sow broadcast.* [BROAD + CAST.] —**broad′cast′er,** *n.*

broad·cloth (brôd′klôth′) *n.* **1.** a smooth, closely woven cotton or cotton polyester fabric, used esp. in making shirts, pajamas, and dresses. **2.** a fabric similar to cotton broadcloth but made of rayon or silk. **3.** a woolen fabric of compact weave, often a twill, used esp. in suits and coats.

broad·en (brô′dən) *v.t., v.i.* to make or become broad or broader: *The workers broadened the road. One's views broaden at college.*

broad-gauge (brôd′gāj′) *adj.* (of railroad tracks) having a width between rails greater than the standard gauge of 56½ inches (144 centimeters).

broad jump, long jump. —**broad jumper.**

broad-leaved (brôd′lēvd′) *adj.* having broad or relatively broad leaves, as any deciduous or evergreen tree or shrub bearing leaves that are not needles. Also, **broad·leaf** (brôd′lēf′).

broad·loom (brôd′lüm′) *n.* a carpet woven on a wide loom, usually in widths ranging from 6 to 18 feet (1.8 to 5.5 meters). Also, **broadloom carpet.**

broad-mind·ed (brôd′mīn′did) *adj.* tolerant of views and behavior that are unconventional or different from one's own; liberal. —**broad′-mind′ed·ly,** *adv.* —**broad′-mind′ed·ness,** *n.*

broad·side (brôd′sīd′) *n.* **1.** the whole side of a boat or ship above the water line. **2.a.** a simultaneous discharge of all the guns on one side of a ship. **b.** all the guns on one side of a ship. **3.** a condemning or abusive written or spoken attack against a person or thing. **4.** a broad surface or side, esp. of a large structure. **5.** a large sheet of paper printed on one or both sides, as with advertisements. —*adv.* with the side turned; on the side; sideward: *The wave caught the boat broadside, almost capsizing it.*

broad-spec·trum (brôd′spek′trəm) *adj.* (of drugs) effective against a wide range of microorganisms: *a broad-spectrum antibiotic.*

broad·sword (brôd′sôrd′) *n.* a sword with a broad, flat blade, made for cutting rather than thrusting.

broad·tail (brôd′tāl′) *n.* the fur from prematurely born karakul lambs, having a wavy surface instead of the tight curls of Persian lamb.

Broad·way (brôd′wā′) *n.* **1.** a street running through New York City, famous for the theaters on and near it. **2.** the commercial theater industry of New York City. —*adj.* of, relating to, or

characteristic of this industry: *a Broadway musical, Broadway style.*

Brob·ding·nag·i·an (brob′ding nag′ē ən) *adj.* of or like Brobdingnag, the land of giants in Jonathan Swift's *Gulliver's Travels,* or its inhabitants; of enormous size; gigantic. —*n.* a person of enormous size; giant.

bro·cade (brō kād′) *n.* an elegant, heavy fabric woven with raised designs. —*v.t.,* **-cad·ed, -cad·ing.** to weave (fabric) with a raised design. [Spanish *brocado* this fabric, from Italian *broccato,* past participle of *broccare* to spur, brocade, going back to Latin *broccus* projecting (like teeth).]

broc·co·li (brok′ə lē) *n.* **1.** the thick branching green stems and unripened flower buds of a variety of cauliflower, cooked and eaten as a vegetable. **2.** the plant itself, widely cultivated in temperate regions. [Italian *broccoli* sprouts, going back to Latin *broccus* projecting (like teeth).]

bro·chette (brō shet′) *n.* a small skewer or spit on which pieces of food are placed for broiling or roasting. [French *brochette,* going back to Old French *broche* a roasting spit. See BROACH.]

bro·chure (brō shùr′) *n.* a pamphlet, esp. one advertising something: *a travel brochure.* [French *brochure* literally, stitching (of the pages), from *brocher* to stitch, from *broche* spindle, spit, going back to Latin *broccus* projecting (like teeth).]

bro·gan (brō′gən) *n.* a coarse, sturdy shoe, one that reaches to the ankle. [Irish and Scottish Gaelic *brōgan,* diminutive of *brōg* shoe. See BROGUE².]

broccoli

brogue¹ (brōg) *n.* **1.** a thick or rough Irish or Scottish accent in the pronunciation of English. **2.** any strong regional or dialectal accent. [Of uncertain origin.]

brogue² (brōg) *n.* **1.** a coarsely made shoe of untanned hide, formerly worn in Ireland and Scotland. **2.** a shoe similar to an oxford, usually decorated with perforations. [Irish and Scottish Gaelic *brōg* shoe, from Old Norse *brōk* hose.]

broil¹ (broil) *v.t.* **1.** to cook by exposing to fire or direct heat; grill. **2.** to make very hot; scorch. —*v.i.* **1.** to be cooked by exposure to direct heat. **2.** to be subjected to great heat; become very hot: *to broil under the sun at the beach.* **3.** to become very angry. —*n.* something broiled, esp. meat. [Anglo-Norman *broiller* to broil, roast; of uncertain origin.]

broil² (broil) *n.* an angry quarrel; tumult; brawl. —*v.i.* to begin or engage in a broil; quarrel. [Old French *brouiller* to confuse; of uncertain origin.]

broil·er (broi′lər) *n.* **1.** any device used for broiling food. **2.** a chicken, usually young and tender, that is suitable for broiling.

broke (brōk) *v.* the past tense of **break.** —*adj. Informal.* having little or no money.

• **to go broke.** *Informal.* to lose all one's money; become bankrupt.

• **to go for broke.** *Slang.* to risk everything in an attempt to win or achieve something.

bro·ken (brō′kən) *v.* the past participle of **break.** —*adj.* **1.** separated by force into parts or pieces; split, burst, or fractured: *a broken window, a broken bone, a broken leg.* **2.** not working properly; damaged: *a broken radio.* **3.** having continuity interrupted as if by breaking: *a broken electrical circuit, broken ground.* **4.** not kept or fulfilled; transgressed; violated: *a broken promise.* **5.** overwhelmed by grief or sorrow; lacking morale; depressed. **6.** reduced to obedience or discipline; tamed: *a broken horse.* **7.** lacking strength; weakened; exhausted: *broken health.* **8.** imperfectly spoken: *The tourists spoke broken English.* **9.** financially ruined; bankrupt. **10.** incomplete; fragmentary: *a broken set of dishes.* **11.** uttered disjointedly or haltingly: *broken sobs.* **12.** in a state of disruption; divided: *a broken home.* —**bro′ken·ly,** *adv.* —**bro′ken·ness,** *n.*

a	at	e	end	o	hot	u	up	hw	white		about
ā	ape	ē	me	ō	old	ū	use	ng	song		taken
ä	far	i	it	ô	fork	ü	rule	th	thin	ə	pencil
âr	care	ī	ice	oi	oil	ù	pull	th	this		lemon
		îr	pierce	ou	out	ûr	turn	zh	measure		circus

bro·ken-down (brō′kən doun′) *adj.* **1.** in poor condition, as from ill health or age: *a broken-down horse, a broken-down house.* **2.** not functioning: *a broken-down car.*

bro·ken·heart·ed (brō′kən här′tid) *adj.* crushed by despair or grief; heartbroken. —**bro′ken·heart′ed·ly,** *adv.*

bro·ker (brō′kər) *n.* an agent who arranges for the purchase or sale of stocks, bonds, commodities, or other property, negotiates contracts, or handles other business affairs for a client, receiving a commission or fee for the services: *an insurance broker, a real estate broker, a ticket broker.* [Anglo-Norman *brocour* agent, originally, seller of wine, one who broached wine barrels, from Old French *broche.* See BROACH.]

bro·ker·age (brō′kər ij) *n.* **1.** the business of a broker; broker's trade. **2.** the fee or commission charged by a broker.

brokerage house, a business establishment that deals in the purchase or sale of commodities and securities for other people.

bro·me·li·ad (brō mē′lē ad′) *n.* any of a large family, Bromeliaceae, of mostly epiphytic, tropical American plants, including the pineapple and Spanish moss, often grown as ornamentals.

bro·mide (brō′mīd) *n.* **1.** a compound consisting of bromine and another element or radical. **2.** potassium bromide, formerly used as a sedative. **3.** *Informal.* **a.** a trite or commonplace statement; platitude. **b.** a person who makes such statements. [BROM-(INE) + -IDE.]

bro·mid·ic (brō mid′ik) *adj. Informal.* commonplace; trite.

bro·mine (brō′mēn) *n.* a reddish brown, nonmetallic liquid element of the halogen group having a disagreeable odor and irritating fumes and causing chemical burns on contact. It is used esp. in gasoline, drugs, dyes, and photographic chemicals. Symbol: **Br** For tables, see **element.** [French *brome* (from Greek *brōmos* stink) + -INE²; referring to its bad odor.]

bronc (brongk) *n. Informal.* bronco. [Short for BRONCO.]

bronch-, a form of **broncho-** before vowels.

bron·chi (brong′kī, -kē) the plural of **bronchus.**

bron·chi·a (brong′kē ə) *pl. n.* bronchial tubes that are branches or subdivisions of the bronchi but are larger than the bronchioles.

bron·chi·al (brong′kē əl) *adj.* of or relating to the bronchi, bronchia, or bronchioles.

bronchial pneumonia, bronchopneumonia.

bronchial tubes, the passages through which air flows to and from the lungs, consisting of the bronchi and their branching tubes. For illustration, see **respiratory system.**

bron·chi·ole (brong′kē ōl′) *n.* the smallest subdivision of a bronchus.

bron·chi·tis (brong kī′tis) *n.* an inflammation of the lining of the bronchial tubes. [BRONCH(O-) + -ITIS.] —**bron·chit·ic** (brong kit′ik), *adj.*

bron·cho (brong′kō) *n., pl.* **-chos.** bronco.

broncho- *combining form* of or relating to a bronchus or the bronchi: *bronchopneumonia.* [Greek *bronchos* trachea.]

bron·cho·pneu·mon·ia (brong′kō nü mōn′yə, -nū-) *n.* an inflammation of the lungs in which the bronchioles become clogged, resulting from a bacterial infection of the upper respiratory system. Also, **bronchial pneumonia.**

bron·cho·scope (brong′kə skōp′) *n.* an illuminated, flexible tube inserted into the trachea through the mouth in order to examine the bronchi.

bron·chus (brong′kəs) *n., pl.* **-chi** (-kī, -kē). either of the two main divisions of the trachea, through which air flows into the lungs. [Modern Latin *bronchus,* from Greek *bronchos* trachea.]

bron·co (brong′kō) *n., pl.* **-cos.** *also,* **broncho.** a small, untamed or partially tamed horse of the western United States. Also, **bronc.** [Spanish *bronco* rough, rude (applied to a wild pony); of uncertain origin.]

bron·co·bust·er (brong′kō bus′tər) *n.* in the western United States, a person who breaks broncos to the saddle.

bron·to·sau·rus (bron′tə sôr′əs) *n., pl.* **-sau·rus·es** or **-sau·ri** (-sôr′ī) or **-sau·rus.** any of various plant-eating dinosaurs, genus *Apatosaurus,* order Saurischia, that lived during the Jurassic period. It was one of the largest land animals, growing to as long as 80 feet (24.3 meters) and weighing up to 35 tons (31.7 metric tons). Also, **apatosaurus, bron·to·saur** (bron′tə sôr′). [Greek *brontē* thunder + *sauros* lizard. The scientific name *Brontosaurus* has been replaced by *Apatosaurus.*]

bronze (bronz) *n.* **1.** an alloy of copper and tin that is hard and malleable and resists corrosion. **2.** an alloy of copper and a metal other than tin, such as manganese or aluminum. **3.** a work of art, as a statue, made of bronze. **4.** a reddish brown color similar to that of bronze. —*adj.* **1.** made of bronze. **2.** having the color bronze. —*v.,* **bronzed, bronz·ing.** —*v.t.* to give a bronzelike color or appearance to; brown. —*v.i.* to become bronze in color;

Chinese **bronze** elephant
from the Zhou dynasty

turn brown; tan. [French *bronze* alloy of copper and tin, from Italian *bronzo;* of uncertain origin.] —**bronz′y,** *adj.*

Bronze Age, a stage in the development of civilization, from the end of the Stone Age to the Iron Age (from approximately 3500 B.C. to approximately 1000 B.C.), characterized by the widespread use of bronze, as in making tools and weapons.

brooch (brōch, brüch) *n.* an ornamental pin usually worn at the neck or breast, fastened by a clasp. [Form of BROACH.]

brood (brüd) *n.* **1.** all of the young of an animal, esp. of a bird, produced or cared for at the same time. **2.** all of the children in one family. **3.** a group of the same kind. —*v.i.* **1.** to meditate moodily and persistently: *to brood over a failure.* **2.** to sit on eggs in order to hatch them; incubate. —*v.t.* to sit on (eggs) until they hatch; incubate. —*adj.* kept for breeding: *a brood hen, a brood mare, a brood cow.* [Old English *brōd* the young of an animal.]

brood·er (brü′dər) *n.* **1.** a structure for keeping newly hatched chicks in a heated, controlled environment, usually for six to eight weeks. **2.** a hen that hatches eggs and cares for newly hatched chicks. **3.** a person who broods.

brook¹ (brŭk) *n.* a small, natural stream. [Old English *brōc.*]

brook² (brŭk) *v.t.* to put up with; endure; tolerate. ➡ usually used with a negative: *The teacher brooks no nonsense.* [Old English *brūcan* to use.]

brook·let (brŭk′lit) *n.* a small brook.

brook trout, an olive-brown game fish of eastern North America, *Salvelinus fontinalis,* having wormlike markings or speckles on its back. Also, **speckled trout.**

broom (brüm, brŭm) *n.* **1.** a brush with a long handle, used for sweeping. **2.** any of several shrubs of the pea family, esp. of the genera *Cytisus* and *Genista.* [Old English *brōm* broom shrub.]

broom·corn (brüm′kôrn′, brŭm′-) *n.* any of a group of grassy plants, genus *Sorghum,* whose grain grows on long, strawlike stems that are used in some regions for making brooms.

broom·stick (brüm′stik′, brŭm′-) *n.* the handle of a broom.

bros., brothers.

broth (brôth) *n., pl.* **broths** (brôths, brôthz). a thin, clear soup made by boiling meat, fish, or vegetables in water, which is then strained. [Old English *broth.*]

broth·el (broth′əl, brô′thəl) *n.* an establishment where prostitutes work. [From Middle English *brothel* prostitute, scoundrel, going back to Old English *brothen* ruined.]

broth·er (bruth′ər) *n., pl.* **broth·ers** or *(defs. 4, 5)* **breth·ren. 1.** a male person having the same parents as another person. **2.** a male person having one parent in common with another person; half brother. **3.** stepbrother. **4.** a person to whom one feels closely associated, as through affection; fellow human being. **5.** a fellow member, as of a church, profession, or fraternal order. **6.** a male member of a religious order who is not a priest. [Old English *brōthor* male child having the same parents as another child, fellow man, member of a Christian order.]

broth·er·hood (bruth′ər hud′) *n.* **1.** the state or quality of being a brother or brothers; brotherly relationship. **2.** the state or quality of being united by beliefs, experiences, or other matters of common interest; fellowship. **3.a.** an association of men, as a fraternal order, joined by common interests. **b.** all the members of such an association.

broth·er-in-law (bruth′ər in lô′) *n., pl.* **broth·ers-in-law.** **1.** the brother of one's husband or wife. **2.** the husband of one's sister. **3.** the husband of one's wife's or husband's sister.

broth·er·ly (bruth′ər lē) *adj.* relating to, characteristic of, or befitting a brother; kind; affectionate. —*adv.* in the manner of a brother. —**broth′er·li·ness,** *n.*

brougham (brüm, brü′əm, brō′-) *n.* **1.** a closed, four-wheeled, horse-drawn carriage having seating for two or four passengers and an uncovered raised seat for the driver. **2.** an automobile having an enclosed passenger compartment and an exposed driver's seat. [From the British statesman Lord *Brougham,* 1778-1868.]

brought (brôt) the past tense and past participle of **bring.**

brou·ha·ha (brü′hä hä′) *n.* a noisy, often angry, disturbance; uproar; commotion. [French *brouhaha,* going back to Hebrew *bârûk habbâ (beshêm âdônai)* Blessed (is) the one coming (in the name of the Lord); from the use of the distortion of this opening of a Hebrew prayer in a sixteenth-century French play.]

brow (brou) *n.* **1.** forehead. **2.** *also,* **brows.** eyebrow. **3.** general expression; countenance. **4.** the edge of a steep place; upper portion of a slope: *the brow of a hill.* [Old English *brū* eyebrow.]

brow·beat (brou′bēt′) *v.t.,* -**beat,** -**beat·en,** -**beat·ing.** to intimidate with stern, overbearing looks or words; bully: *The leader browbeat them until no one dared to disagree.*

brown (broun) *n.* a dull, usually dark color combining red, yellow, and black. —*adj.* **1.** having the color brown. **2.** dark-complexioned; tanned. —*v.t.* to make brown. —*v.i.* to become brown: *The roast browned in the oven.* [Old English *brūn* dusky, dark.] —**brown′ish,** *adj.* —**brown′ness,** *n.*

brown algae, any of a division, Phaeophyta, of mostly marine algae, including many of the large seaweeds, such as kelp, colored brown by a pigment that masks their chlorophyll.

brown-bag (broun′bag′) *v.i., v.t.,* -**bagged,** -**bag·ging.** to take (one's lunch) to work or school, often in a brown paper bag. —**brown′-bag′ger,** *n.*

brown bear, any of various bears, *Ursus arctos,* native to North America, Europe, and Asia, having fur that ranges from yellowish brown to very dark brown. Height: to 9 feet (2.7 meters).

brown bet·ty (bet′ē) a baked pudding of bread crumbs, sugar, spices, butter, and fruit, esp. apples.

brown bread, any bread made of dark flour, as rye bread or whole-wheat bread.

brown coal, lignite.

Brown·i·an movement (brou′nē ən) the rapid, erratic movements of microscopic particles suspended in gas or liquid, caused by impact with molecules of the gas or liquid. Also, **Brownian motion.** [From the British botanist Robert *Brown,* 1773-1858, its discoverer.]

brown·ie (brou′nē) *n.* **1.** in folklore, a good-natured elf or goblin that does good deeds. **2.** a flat, sweet cake, usually chocolate, sometimes made with nuts or topped with frosting. **3. Brownie.** a girl between the ages of seven and nine who belongs to the junior division of the Girl Scouts.

brown lung, byssinosis.

brown·out (broun′out′) *n.* a temporary reduction in electric power, usually caused by a shortage of electricity.

brown rice, rice with the hulls removed but with the layers of bran still intact.

brown·shirt (broun′shûrt′) *n.* **1.** *also,* **Brown Shirt.** storm trooper. **2.** any Nazi.

brown·stone (broun′stōn′) *n.* **1.** a reddish brown sandstone, used as a building material. **2.** a house with a brownstone façade.

brown study, a state of being absorbed in serious thought; meditation.

brown sugar, partially refined sugar retaining traces of molasses, which gives it a dark or golden brown color.

brown thrasher, a large reddish brown songbird, *Toxostoma rufum,* of eastern North America, closely related to the mockingbird, having a slender, curved beak, long tail, and black and white markings. Length: 11 inches (28 centimeters).

brown trout, a yellow-brown, European trout, *Salmo trutta,* marked with large, light-bordered red spots, widely introduced in North America as a game fish. Weight: to 5 pounds (2.3 kilograms).

browse (brouz) *v.,* **browsed, brows·ing.** —*v.i.* **1.** to glance through or look at leisurely or casually, as a book, store, or merchandise. **2.** to feed, as on leaves or twigs: *The deer browsed in the field.* —*v.t.* **1.** to cause to feed on leaves or twigs: *The farmer browsed the cattle.* **2.** to feed on: *The cows browsed the hillside.* —*n.* the tender parts of shrubs or trees on which certain animals, as cattle or deer, feed. [Middle French *broust* bud, shoot; of Germanic origin.] —**brows′er,** *n.*

bru·cel·lo·sis (brü′sə lō′sis) *n.* undulant fever. [Modern Latin *Brucella* (from David *Bruce,* 1855-1931, British doctor) + -OSIS.]

bru·in (brü′in) *n.* a bear, esp. a brown bear. [Dutch *bruin* brown, name (and color) of the bear in a medieval bestiary.]

bruise (brüz) *n.* **1.** an injury, as from a fall or blow, that discolors but does not break the surface of the skin. **2.** a discoloration on the outer surface of a fruit, vegetable, or plant caused by such an injury. —*v.,* **bruised, bruis·ing.** —*v.t.* **1.** to cause a bruise on the surface of: *to bruise one's leg, to bruise a banana.* **2.** to injure or hurt slightly: *The critic's comments bruised the actor's feelings.* **3.** to pound, crush, or grind (drugs or food). —*v.i.* to become bruised. [Partly from Old English *brȳsan* to crush; partly from Old French *bruisier* to break.]

bruis·er (brü′zər) *n. Informal.* **1.** bully. **2.** a tough, husky person.

bruit (brüt) *v.t.* to spread a rumor of; announce; report: *They bruited the victory about.* —*n. Archaic.* **1.** report; rumor. **2.** noise; din; clamor. [Old French *bruit* loud noise, from *bruire* to roar, possibly going back to Latin *rugīre* to roar.]

brum·ma·gem (brum′ə jəm) *Informal. adj.* showy but worthless; sham. —*n.* something showy but worthless or of inferior quality. [Modification of *Birmingham,* English city, at one time noted for cheap, showy products and counterfeit coins.]

brunch (brunch) *n.* a meal eaten late in the morning in lieu of breakfast and lunch. —*v.i.* to eat brunch. [Blend of BR(EAKFAST) and (L)UNCH.]

Bru·nei dollar (brü nī′) the monetary unit of Brunei.

bru·net (brü net′) *adj.* **1.** (of hair) having some shade of brown or brownish black as its main color. **2.** (of a person) having such hair. **3.** dark-colored: *a brunet complexion.* —*n.* a brunet person. ➡ used for both sexes in all defs. [French *brunette,* feminine of *brunet* brownish, diminutive of *brun* brown; of Germanic origin.]

bru·nette (brü net′) *adj.* (of a female) having brunet hair. —*n.* a brunette woman or girl.

brunt (brunt) *n.* the main stress or violence: *The houses on the beach bore the brunt of the hurricane.* [Middle English *bront* a blow, rush; probably of Scandinavian origin.]

brush¹ (brush) *n.* **1.** an implement consisting of bristles, hairs, wires, or similar material, set into a stiff back and often having a handle: *a makeup brush, a clothes brush.* **2.** the act of brushing. **3.** anything resembling a brush, as the bushy tail of an animal. **4.** brushwork. **5.** an electrical conductor that serves to make contact between stationary and moving parts, as of a motor or generator. **6.** a growth of shrubs and bushes; thicket. **7.** cut or broken twigs or branches. **8.** thinly settled country; backwoods. —*v.t.* **1.** to use a brush on, as in painting, cleaning, or smoothing: *to brush one's hair.* **2.** to remove with or as with a brush: *to brush lint from one's clothes, to brush crumbs from a table.* [Middle English *brushe,* from Old French *brosse, broce* brushwood; of uncertain origin.] —**brush′y,** *adj.*

· **to brush aside** (or **away**). to regard as unworthy of consideration; disregard.

· **to brush off.** to dismiss or reject curtly.

· **to brush up. a.** to refresh one's acquaintance with (with *on*): *to brush up on basic Spanish.* **b.** to improve in any way; renovate.

brush² (brush) *n.* **1.** a light, momentary touch: *I felt a brush against my leg when the cat went by.* **2.** a slight encounter: *a brush with the law.* —*v.t.* to graze lightly in passing: *He brushed the wall going around the corner.* —*v.i.* to graze lightly and quickly, as in passing: *She brushed against a chair as she rushed to answer the telephone.* [Middle English *bruschen* to rush, hurry; of uncertain origin but possibly related to BRUSH¹.] —**brush′y,** *adj.*

brush-off (brush′ôf′) *n. Informal.* a curt dismissal or rejection.

brush·wood (brush′wüd′) *n.* brush¹ (*defs. 6, 7*).

brush·work (brush′wûrk′) *n.* **1.** a characteristic manner of applying paint with a brush: *van Gogh's brushwork.* **2.** the quality of the marks made on the surface of a painting by a brush as paint is applied.

brusque (brusk) *adj.* short and rude in manner or speech; blunt. [French *brusque* harsh, from Italian *brusco* rough, sour, from Late Latin *brūcus* heather.] —**brusque′ly,** *adv.* —**brusque′ness,** *n.* —For Synonyms, see **abrupt.**

a	at	e	end	o	hot	u	up	hw	white		about
ā	ape	ē	me	ō	old	ū	use	ng	song		taken
ä	far	i	it	ô	fork	ü	rule	th	thin	ə	pencil
âr	care	ī	ice	oi	oil	u̇	pull	th	this		lemon
		îr	pierce	ou	out	ûr	turn	zh	measure		circus

Brus·sels sprouts (brus′əl, -əlz) **1.** buds, resembling small cabbages, that grow on the stem of a variety of the plant *Brassica oleracea,* and are cooked and eaten as a vegetable. **2.** the leafy plant itself, a member of the mustard family, widely cultivated in temperate regions.

bru·tal (brü′təl) *adj.* characteristic of or like a brute; inhuman; cruel; savage. —**bru′tal·ly,** *adv.*

bru·tal·i·ty (brü tal′i tē) *n., pl.* **-ties. 1.** the quality of being brutal; cruelty; inhumanity. **2.** a brutal act.

bru·tal·ize (brü′tə līz′) *v.,* **-ized, -iz·ing.** —*v.t.* **1.** to make brutal: *Harsh treatment brutalized the prisoners.* **2.** to treat brutally. —*v.i.* to become brutal. —**bru′tal·i·za′tion,** *n.*

brute (brüt) *n.* **1.** any animal except a human being. **2.** a brutal person. **3.** the animal nature in humans: *to bring out the brute in someone.* —*adj.* **1.** without the ability to reason; not human: *a brute creature.* **2.** of the character or quality of a brute; characteristic of animals: *brute strength.* **3.** powerful, but without reason or feeling: *the brute forces of nature.* [French *brut* raw, rude, from Latin *brūtus* heavy, stupid.] —For Synonyms, see **animal.**

brut·ish (brü′tish) *adj.* relating to, like, or characteristic of a brute; stupid and savage. —**brut′ish·ly,** *adv.* —**brut′ish·ness,** *n.*

Bryn·hild (brin′hild′) *n.* in Norse legend, a Valkyrie whom Sigurd tricked into marrying Gunnar.

bry·ol·o·gy (brī ol′ə jē) *n.* the branch of botany that deals with the study of bryophytes. [Greek *bryon* moss + -LOGY.]

bry·o·ny (brī′ə nē) *n., pl.* **-nies.** any of the climbing plants in the genus *Bryonia,* of the gourd family, native to temperate regions of Europe and western Asia, having five-lobed leaves, greenish white flowers, and red or black berries. [Latin *bryōnia,* from Greek *bryōniā.*]

bry·o·phyte (brī′ə fīt′) *n.* any of the mosses or liverworts, two classes of small green plants that constitute a division, Bryophyta, of the plant kingdom. [Modern Latin *Bryophyta,* from Greek *bryon* moss + *phyton* plant.] —**bry·o·phyt·ic** (brī′ə fit′ik), *adj.*

bry·o·zo·an (brī′ə zō′ən) *n.* any of a group of tiny, aquatic, mostly marine animals, phylum Bryozoa, forming branching or matlike colonies, usually made up of interconnected, walled chambers that encrust rocks or seaweed. [Modern Latin *bryozoan,* from Greek *bryon* mass + *zōia* animals + -AN.]

b.s. 1. balance sheet. **2.** bill of sale.

B.S. *also,* **B.Sc.** Bachelor of Science.

btl., bottle.

btry., battery.

BTU, British thermal unit or units.

bu *also,* **bu.** bushel; bushels.

bub·ble (bub′əl) *n.* **1.** a thin globular film of liquid filled with air or other gas: *The children blew bubbles with a bubble pipe.* **2.** a small globule of air or other gas in a solid or liquid: *There are bubbles in carbonated soda.* **3.** the act, process, or sound of bubbling: *the bubble of boiling water.* **4.** something unsubstantial or worthless, esp. an unsuccessful or fraudulent financial scheme. **5.** something shaped like a bubble, hemisphere, or dome: *to build a bubble over tennis courts.* —*v.,* **-bled, -bling.** —*v.i.* **1.** to form or rise in bubbles: *The boiling soup bubbled.* **2.** to flow with or make a gurgling sound. **3.** to show an emotion, as happiness, glee, or enthusiasm, in an effervescent manner: *to bubble with joy.* —*v.t.* to cause to bubble; form bubbles in. [Probably from Middle Dutch *bobbel* a bubble.] —**bub′bly,** *adj.*

• **to bubble over. a.** to overflow: *The boiling soup bubbled over.* **b.** to effervesce, as with great happiness, glee, or enthusiasm: *The proud parents bubbled over with joy.*

bubble bath, a bath covered with a foam of bubbles made by a soap preparation added to the water.

bubble chamber, a vessel filled with a superheated liquid through which accelerated subatomic particles pass, leaving trails of bubbles by which the particles can be identified.

bub·ble·gum (bub′əl gum′) *n.* chewing gum that can be blown into large bubbles.

bub·bler (bub′lər) *n.* a drinking fountain from which bubbling water can be drunk without using a cup.

bu·bo (bū′bō) *n., pl.* **-boes.** an inflammation and swelling of a lymph node, esp. in the groin or armpit. [Late Latin *bubo* swelling, from Greek *boubōn* groin, swollen gland.]

bu·bon·ic (bū bon′ik, bü-) *adj.* relating to or characterized by buboes.

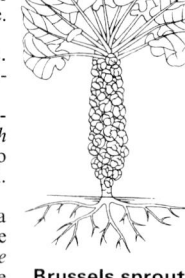

Brussels sprouts

bubonic plague, a serious disease caused by a bacterium, *Yersinia pestis,* and characterized by the formation of buboes and a high fever. It is transmitted to humans by fleas from infected rodents.

buc·cal (buk′əl) *adj.* **1.** of or relating to the cheek. **2.** of or relating to the sides of the mouth or to the mouth; oral. [Latin *bucca* cheek, mouth + -AL¹.]

buc·ca·neer (buk′ə nîr′) *n.* **1.** pirate. **2.** any of certain pirates of the seventeenth and eighteenth centuries who attacked and robbed Spanish ships and settlements in America. [French *boucanier,* originally, one who smokes meat, from *boucan* frame for smoking meat, from Tupi-Guarani *mocaem;* adopted by seventeenth-century French settlers in the West Indies, many of whom became pirates.]

buck¹ (buk) *n.* **1.** the male of certain animals, esp. of deer or antelope. **2.** a man, esp. a young man. ➤ sometimes used disparagingly. **3.** the act of bucking. —*v.i.* **1.** (of certain riding animals) to jump, kick, arch the back, or otherwise contort the body, in order to throw off a rider or load. **2.** *Informal.* to resist obstinately; balk (with *at*): *to buck at authority.* —*v.t.* **1.** to throw off (a rider or load) by bucking. **2.** *Informal.* to resist or oppose stubbornly: *to buck the rules, to buck a trend.* **3.** to charge at and strike with the head; butt. **4.** in football, to make a quick charge into (the opposing line) while carrying the ball. —*adj. Slang.* of the lowest grade of a specific military rank: *buck private, buck sergeant.* [Old English *buc* male deer, and *bucca* male goat.] —**buck′er,** *n.*

• **to buck for.** *Informal.* to strive for (a better position or other gain): *to buck for a raise.*

• **to buck up.** *Informal.* to become more confident or courageous; cheer up.

buck² (buk) *n. Slang.* dollar. [Possibly from BUCKSKIN, referring to the use of deerskins as a unit of exchange on the American frontier in the nineteenth century.]

• **to pass the buck.** *Informal.* to shift the responsibility, duty, or blame to someone else.

buck³ (buk) *n.* **1.** sawhorse. **2.** a padded block on a frame resembling a sawhorse, used in gymnastics. [Short for SAW-BUCK¹.]

buck·a·roo (buk′ə rü′) *also,* **buckeroo.** *n., pl.* **-roos.** cowboy. [Modification of VAQUERO.]

buck·board (buk′bôrd′) *n.* an open, four-wheeled carriage that has a platform of long, flexible boards in place of a body and springs upon which the seat rests.

buck·er·oo (buk′ə rü′) *n., pl.* **-oos.** buckaroo.

buck·et (buk′it) *n.* **1.** a round, hollow container with a flat bottom and usually a curved handle, used for carrying or holding water, sand, or other substances; pail. **2.** anything resembling this, as any of various scooplike devices mounted on or attached to machines such as dredges and steam shovels; dipper; scoop. **3.** the amount that a bucket can hold; bucketful. **4.** a great amount: *The rain came down in buckets.* —*v.,* **-et·ed, -et·ing.** —*v.t.* to lift, draw, or carry in a bucket. —*v.i. Informal.* to move quickly: *We were bucketing down the road.* [Anglo-Norman *buket* pail, possibly from Old English *būc* pitcher.]

buckboard

• **to kick the bucket.** *Slang.* to die.

bucket brigade, a row of people who pass buckets of water from person to person in order to put out a fire.

buck·et·ful (buk′it fůl′) *n., pl.* **-fuls.** as much as a bucket can hold.

bucket seat, a low single seat, usually with a rounded back, used esp. in automobiles.

bucket shop 1. an establishment where highly speculative, worthless, or illegal stocks are sold, frequently by high-pressure or unethical tactics. **2.** formerly, an establishment that purported to be a brokerage house but did not execute the customer's orders, took an opposing position in the market, and thereby gained from the customer's losses. [Originally a cheap bar or liquor store; supposedly because liquor was mixed or sold in buckets.]

buck·eye (buk′ī′) *n.* **1.** any of several North American shrubs or small trees, genus *Aesculus,* of the horse chestnut family, bearing showy clusters of yellow, white, or red flowers and inedible round fruits with one or two seeds in each. **2.** the shiny brown nutlike seed of this tree. [BUCK¹ + EYE; because the seed resembles the eye of a deer.]

B

Buck·ing·ham Palace (buk′ing əm, -ham′) **1.** a palace in Westminster, London, the official residence of British monarchs. **2.** the British royal family or monarchy: *Buckingham Palace released a statement today.*

buck·le (buk′əl) *n.* **1.** a clasp, often with a movable tongue, used to fasten two loose ends, as of a belt or strap. **2.** an ornament that resembles this, as on a shoe. **3.** a bulge, bend, or other distortion in a surface: *a buckle in the road surface.* —*v.,* **-led, -ling.** —*v.t.* **1.** to fasten with a buckle. **2.** to cause (something) to bulge, bend, or kink, esp. from heat or pressure: *The extreme heat buckled the road.* —*v.i.* **1.** to be fastened or joined by a buckle. **2.** to bulge, bend, or kink; give way, as by bending or folding: *A beam supporting the building buckled.* [Old French *boucle* metal ring, boss on a shield, from Latin *buccula* cheek strap of a helmet, diminutive of *bucca* cheek.]
·**to buckle down (to).** to apply oneself with vigor (to): *to buckle down and finish a job.*
·**to buckle under.** to give in or submit; yield: *The president buckled under to pressure to resign.*

buck·ler (buk′lər) *n.* **1.** a small, round shield. **2.** a means of defense; protection. [Old French *bocler* shield with a boss, from *boucle* boss on a shield. See BUCKLE.]

buck-pass·er (buk′pas′ər) *n.* a person who habitually shifts responsibility, duty, or blame to someone else. —**buck′-pass′-ing,** *n.*

buck·ram (buk′rəm) *n.* coarse cloth that has been stiffened with size, used esp. in bookbinding or as interlining in garments. [Old French *boquerant* fine linen, going back to *Bokhara,* central Asian city that was the original source of this linen.]

buck·saw (buk′sô′) *n.* a saw set in an H-shaped frame with one side of the frame extended to form a handle.

buck·shot (buk′shot′) *n.* large, round metal pellets fired from a shotgun.

buck·skin (buk′skin′) *n.* **1.** a strong, soft, yellowish tan leather, made from the skins of deer or sheep. **2. buckskins.** breeches or clothing made of buckskin. **3.** a horse of the color of buckskin.

buck·thorn (buk′thôrn′) *n.* **1.** any of a large group of usually thorny trees or shrubs, genus *Rhamnus,* found generally in temperate regions, bearing pale green clustered flowers and black or red fruits. **2.** a shrub or small tree, *Bumelia lycioides,* often having thorny branches, found esp. in the southern United States. [BUCK¹ + THORN, translation of Modern Latin *cervi spina* stag's thorn.]

buck·tooth (buk′tüth′) *n., pl.* **-teeth** (-tēth′). a projecting upper front tooth. [BUCK¹ + TOOTH.] —**buck′toothed′,** *adj.*

buck·wheat (buk′hwēt′, -wēt′) *n.* **1.** the grain of any of a group of cereal plants, genus *Fagopyrum,* used for animal feed or ground into flour, esp. for pancakes. **2.** flour made from this grain. **3.** any of the plants that bear this grain, widely cultivated throughout the world, having heart-shaped leaves and clusters of small white flowers. [Dialectal English *buck* beech (from Old English *bōc*) + WHEAT; its seeds are shaped like the nuts of the beech.]

buckwheat cake, a pancake made of buckwheat flour.

bu·col·ic (bū kol′ik) *adj.* **1.** of or relating to shepherds; pastoral. **2.** relating to country life; rustic; rural. —*n.* a pastoral poem. [Latin *būcolicus* pastoral, from Greek *boukolikos,* from *boukolos* herdsman.] —For Synonyms, see **rural.**

bud (bud) *n.* **1.** a small swelling on a plant containing a rudimentary branch, stem, leaf, or flower. **2.** a flower that has not completely blossomed. **3.** the act or time of budding: *The trees are in bud.* **4.** a budlike protuberance on certain lower organisms, as the yeast or hydra, that develops into a new individual. For illustration, see **hydra.** —*v.,* **bud·ded, bud·ding.** —*v.i.* **1.** to put forth buds. **2.a.** to begin to grow or develop. **b.** to be at an early or promising stage of development. —*v.t.* **1.** to cause to bud. **2.** to bring or put forth as a bud or buds. **3.** to insert (a bud) from one kind of plant into the stem or bark of another kind. [Of uncertain origin.]
·**to nip in the bud.** to stop something just as it is beginning: *to nip a problem in the bud.*

Bud·dhism (bůd′iz əm, bü′diz-) *n.* a religion based on the teachings of Buddha that originated in India but has spread over much of Asia. It teaches that pain and evil are caused by desire and that to conquer desire is to attain nirvana. —**Bud′dhist,** *adj., n.*

bud·dy (bud′ē) *n., pl.* **-dies.** *Informal.* a pal; companion; comrade.

buddy system, the pairing of two persons engaged in the same outdoor, hazardous, or athletic activity so that each can look out for the other's safety, as in a group of children swimming or police officers on patrol.

budge (buj) *v.,* **budged, budg·ing.** —*v.i.* **1.** to move or stir slightly; give way: *The cow wouldn't budge from the road.* **2.** to change an opinion; give in: *The senator refused to budge on the issue.* —*v.t.* **1.** to cause to move or stir slightly: *The farmer couldn't budge the mule.* **2.** to cause to change an opinion: *No amount of pleading would budge them.* ➡ usually used with a negative in both defs. [French *bouger* to stir, going back to Latin *bullīre* to boil.]

budg·er·i·gar (buj′ər i gär′) *n.* a small, greenish yellow, Australian parakeet, *Melopsittacus undulatus,* now bred in many color varieties as a cage bird. [From a native Australian name.]

budg·et (buj′it) *n.* **1.** an estimate of expected income and specific expenditures for a given period. **2.** an amount of money set aside for a particular purpose or given period of time: *My budget for this week includes new shoes.* —*v.t.* **1.** to plan for the use or expenditure of: *to budget one's salary carefully.* **2.** to plan for in a budget: *The family budgeted $100 a month for a summer vacation.* **3.** to allot or assign for a specific purpose: *to budget time for study.* —*v.i.* to make a budget: *Congress budgeted for the new poverty program. The couple budgeted for a car.* [Old French *bougette* little bag, diminutive of *bouge* leather bag, from Latin *bulga;* of Celtic origin.] —**budg·et·ar·y** (buj′i ter′ē), *adj.*

budg·ie (buj′ē) *n. Informal.* budgerigar.

bud scale, scale² *(def. 3).*

buff¹ (buf) *n.* **1.** a soft, sturdy, yellowish brown or tan leather with a napped surface, usually made from the hide of buffalo or oxen. **2.** formerly, a military jacket made of buff leather. **3.** a medium tan color; yellowish brown. **4.** buffer² *(def. 2).* —*adj.* **1.** made of buff leather. **2.** having the color buff. —*v.t.* to polish or clean with or as with a buff or buffer. [French *buffle* buffalo, wild ox, from Italian *bufalo* ox, from Late Latin *bufalus* wild ox, from Greek *boubalos* antelope, wild ox, from *bous* a head of cattle.]
·**in the buff.** *Informal.* with no clothes on; naked.

buff² (buf) *n.* a person who is a devoted follower of something; enthusiast; devotee; fan: *an opera buff.* [From the *buff* coats often worn by nineteenth-century volunteer firefighters in New York City.]

buf·fa·lo (buf′ə lō′) *n., pl.* **-loes** or **-los** or **-lo. 1.** bison *(def. 1).* **2.** any of various wild or domesticated oxen, subfamily Bovinae, of India, southeastern Asia, and parts of Africa, as the water buffalo. —*v.t.,* **-loed, -lo·ing.** *Slang.* **1.** to fool; bewilder. **2.** to intimidate. [Italian *bufalo* ox, going back to Greek *boubalos* antelope, wild ox.]

buffalo grass, a short, hardy grass, *Buchloë dactyloides,* of central and western North America, having creeping stems, narrow, flat leaves, and short flower spikes. It forms a thick gray green turf that provides a valuable forage for cattle.

buff·er¹ (buf′ər) *n.* **1.** a person or thing that softens or neutralizes the force or impact of a shock or collision. **2.** a chemical substance that, in solution, tends to resist changes in acidity or alkalinity. **3.** a portion of the circuitry of a computer dedicated to the temporary storage of data. [Dialectal English *buff* to strike (from Old French *bu(f)fer* to strike ultimately imitative) + -ER¹.]

buff·er² (buf′ər) *n.* **1.** a person who buffs. **2.** a wheel, stick, or other device covered with a soft material, as chamois, used for polishing. [BUFF¹ (verb) + -ER¹.]

buffer state, a small country lying between two larger ones and regarded as reducing the chance of conflict between them.

buf·fet¹ (buf′it) *v.t.* **1.** to beat or strike with the hand or fist. **2.** to strike repeatedly; knock about: *The rough water buffeted the buoy.* **3.** to fight against; contend with: *The ship buffeted the waves.* —*n.* **1.** a blow with the hand or fist. **2.** something that hits with the force of a blow; violent shock: *the buffet of a hurricane.* [Old French *buffet* blow, diminutive of *buffe;* imitative.]

buf·fet² (bə fā′, bů-) *n.* **1.** a piece of furniture with a flat surface for serving and with cabinets for the storage and display of such items as dishes, silver, glassware, and table linen; sideboard. **2.** a meal laid out on a buffet or on a table or tables, so that people may serve themselves. ➡ often used in combinations such as *buffet supper* and *buffet luncheon.* **3.** a counter where refreshments or light meals are served. [French *buffet* sideboard, light meal, from Old French *buffet* bench.]

buf·fle·head (buf′əl hed′) *n.* a small, mainly North American duck, *Bucephala albeola.* The male is glossy black above, white below, with a large white patch on the back of the head. The coloration of the female is duller. Average length: 13 ½ inches (34

a	at	e	end	o	hot	u	up	hw	white		about
ā	ape	ē	me	ō	old	ū	use	ng	song		taken
ä	far	i	it	ô	fork	ü	rule	th	thin	ə	pencil
âr	care	ī	ice	oi	oil	ů	pull	th	this		lemon
		îr	pierce	ou	out	ûr	turn	zh	measure		circus

centimeters). [Obsolete *buffle* buffalo, from French *buffle* (see BUFF[1]) + HEAD.]

buf·foon (bə fün′) *n.* a person who amuses others with pranks and jokes; clown. [French *bouffon*, from Italian *buffone*, from *buffare* to joke, puff; with reference to the medieval jesters' making noise by puffing out their cheeks and blowing the air out; imitative.] —**buf·foon′er·y**, *n.* —**buf·foon′ish**, *adj.*

bug (bug) *n.* **1.** any of the insects of the order Hemiptera, such as stinkbugs and squash bugs, having beaklike sucking mouthparts. Most have membranous hind wings, with forewings thick at the base and membranous at the tip, though some, such as bedbugs, are wingless and others have vestigial wings. Also, **hemipteran**. **2.** any insect or similar animal. **3.** *Informal.* a disease-causing microorganism. **4.** *Informal.* **a.** a defect or difficulty, as in a machine: *a bug in the television set.* **b.** *Computers.* an error in a program or a malfunction in hardware that prevents a computer from operating or from operating properly. **5.** *Informal.* a fan or hobbyist; buff. **6.** *Informal.* a small, hidden microphone used to overhear conversations. —*v.t.,* **bugged, bug·ging. 1.** *Informal.* to place a hidden microphone in. **2.** *Slang.* to annoy, bother, or worry (someone). [Of uncertain origin.] —**bug′like′**, *adj.*

bug·a·boo (bug′ə bü′) *n., pl.* **-boos.** a real or imaginary object of fear. [Obsolete *bug* bogy[1] (possibly from Welsh *bwg* ghost) + BOO.]

bug·bear (bug′bâr′) *n.* **1.** bugaboo. **2.** an annoying problem. [Obsolete *bug* bogy[1] (possibly from Welsh *bwg* ghost) + BEAR[2].]

bug·gy[1] (bug′ē) *n., pl.* **-gies. 1.** a light, four-wheeled carriage with one large seat and, sometimes, a top. **2.** a baby carriage; perambulator. [Of uncertain origin.]

bug·gy[2] (bug′ē) *adj.,* **-gi·er, -gi·est. 1.** infested or swarming with bugs. **2.** *Slang.* of unsound mind; crazy. [BUG + -Y[1].]

bu·gle[1] (bū′gəl) *n.* a brass wind instrument resembling, but smaller than, a trumpet, usually without keys or valves, used esp. for giving military signals and calls. —*v.,* **-gled, -gling.** —*v.i.* to sound or play a bugle. —*v.t.* to summon by blowing on a bugle. [Short for earlier *bugle horn* musical instrument made from the horn of an ox or buffalo, from Old French *bugle* wild ox, buffalo, from Latin *būculus* steer.] —**bu′gler**, *n.*

bu·gle[2] (bū′gəl) *n.* a tubular bead used to ornament women's clothing. Also, **bugle bead.** [Possibly from BUGLE[1]; because of its resemblance to a horn.]

bu·gloss (bū′glôs′) *n.* any of a group of coarse, hairy Old World plants, genus *Anchusa*, related to borage, grown for their showy flowers. [Middle English and Old French *buglosse*, from Latin *buglossa*, from Greek *bouglōssos* the tongue of an ox, from *bous* ox, cow + *glōssa* tongue.]

buhl (bül) *n.* decoration consisting of such materials as tortoise shell, mother-of-pearl, and metals inlaid in wood, used on furniture. [German *Buhl*, from French *boulle;* from the French cabinetmaker Charles André Boulle, 1642-1732.]

build (bild) *v.,* **built, build·ing.** —*v.t.* **1.** to erect or make by assembling materials or parts; construct. **2.** to form over a period of time; establish and strengthen; develop: *to build a good reputation.* **3.** to form a basis for: *to build an argument on logic.* —*v.i.* **1.** to construct a building or have a building erected. **2.** to use as a basis or foundation for development (with *on* or *upon*): *Let's build on your idea.* **3.** to increase, as in intensity, speed, or size: *The story built to a surprising climax.* **4.** to form groups of cards by denomination or suit. —*n.* the way in which a person or thing is formed; manner of construction; physique: *The football player has a solid build.* [Old English *byldan* to construct (a house), from *bold* dwelling.] —For synonyms *(v.t.),* see **make.**

• **to build up. a.** to make stronger; strengthen: *to build up one's muscles by exercising.* **b.** to form gradually; develop: *to build up an extensive dental practice.* **c.** to fill with buildings or houses: *Speculators have built up all the vacant land around the city.* **d.** to praise so as to enhance the appeal or desirability of: *Advance publicity built up the latest car models.*

build·er (bil′dər) *n.* **1.** a person who builds. **2.** a person whose occupation or profession is building houses or other structures.

build·ing (bil′ding) *n.* **1.** something built; structure; edifice. **2.** the act, process, or business of constructing.

building block 1. one of a set of children's toy blocks. **2.** a fundamental or elementary principle or part: *The right to vote is a building block of democracy.*

build·up (bild′up′) *also,* **build-up.** *n.* **1.** an increase, as in number or strength: *an armament buildup, a troop buildup.* **2.** *Informal.* publicity or praise used to make someone or something famous or more appealing.

built (bilt) the past tense and past participle of **build.**

built-in (bilt′in′) *adj.* **1.** built as a permanent part of something: *a built-in bureau.* **2.** inherent in the nature of a person or thing: *built-in reflexes.* **3.** created as an essential part of something: *a system of government with built-in checks and balances.*

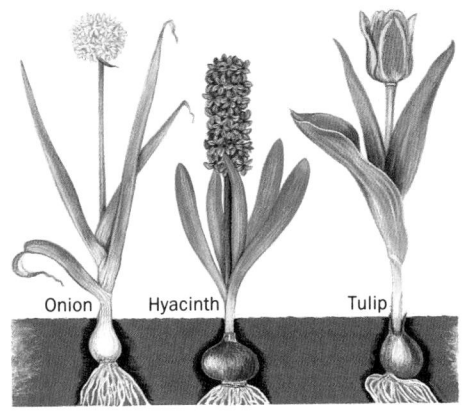

bulbs and their flowers

Onion   Hyacinth   Tulip

bulb (bulb) *n.* **1.** a usually enlarged, underground modified leaf bud of certain plants, as the onion, consisting of a short stem surrounded by scalelike leaves that provide nourishment for the growing plant. **2.** an underground stem resembling a bulb, as a corm or tuber. **3.** any plant that develops from a bulb, as a tulip or daffodil. **4.** any enlarged, rounded object or part: *a thermometer bulb.* **5.** light bulb. [Latin *bulbus* bulbous root, onion, from Greek *bolbos.*]

bulb·ar (bul′bər) *adj.* of or relating to a bulb or bulb-shaped organ, esp. the bulb of the spinal cord, the medulla oblongata: *bulbar paralysis.*

bul·bil (bul′bəl) *n.* a small bulb or bulblike structure growing in a leaf axil in place of a flower or in other places on a flower stalk. [Modern Latin *bulbillus*, diminutive of Latin *bulbus.* See BULB.]

bulb·ous (bul′bəs) *adj.* **1.** of, having, or growing from bulbs. **2.** bulb-shaped; round; swollen.

bul·bul (bùl′bùl′) *n.* **1.** any of various thrushlike songbirds, family Pycnonotidae, native to tropical and subtropical forests of Africa and southern Asia. Length: 6-11 inches (15-28 centimeters). **2.** a songbird mentioned in Persian poetry, believed to have been a nightingale. [Persian *bulbul* Persian songbird; imitative.]

Bul·gar (bul′gär, bùl′-) *n.* Bulgarian.

Bul·gar·i·an (bul gâr′ē ən, bùl-) *adj.* of, relating to, or characteristic of Bulgaria or its people, language, or culture. —*n.* **1.** a native or citizen of Bulgaria. **2.** a person of Bulgarian ancestry. **3.** the Slavic language of the Bulgarians.

bulge (bulj) *n.* a rounded swelling; hump. —*v.,* **bulged, bulging.** —*v.i.* to swell out: *The bag bulged with groceries.* —*v.t.* to cause to swell out. [Old French *bouge, boulge* leather bag, swelling. See BUDGET.]

Bulge, Battle of the (bulj) the last major German counteroffensive of World War II, begun on December 16, 1944, against the Allies in Belgium and repulsed in January 1945.

bul·gur (bul′gər, bùl′-) *n.* cracked wheat that has been parboiled and dried. [Turkish *bulgur*, going back to Persian *burghul.*]

bulg·y (bul′jē) *adj.,* **bulg·i·er, bulg·i·est.** having a bulge; bulging: *bulgy shopping bags, bulgy eyes.* —**bulg′i·ness**, *n.*

bu·lim·i·a (bū lim′ē ə, -lē′mē ə, bü-) *n.* a serious eating disorder, mainly affecting young women, characterized by the consumption of large amounts of food followed by deliberate vomiting or the excessive use of laxatives to prevent weight gain. [Formed from Greek *boulimia* extreme hunger.]

bulk (bulk) *n.* **1.** size, esp. large size; magnitude; volume: *a package of great bulk.* **2.** the main or greater part: *The bulk of the people voted.* —*v.i.* **1.** to have bulk; appear important; loom. **2.** to increase in bulk; swell; grow. —*v.t.* to cause to swell or grow in size. [Old Norse *bulki* heap.]

• **in bulk. a.** not packaged; loose: *to sell peanuts in bulk.* **b.** in large quantities: *The bakery buys flour in bulk.*

bulk·head (bulk′hed′) *n.* **1.** one of the walls that divides a ship or airplane into compartments in order to prevent the spread of flooding or fire or to strengthen the structure. **2.** a retaining wall or partition, designed to protect embankments of earth in a tunnel or along a shore, or to hold back earth or prevent the passage of water or gases, as in a mine. **3.** a boxlike structure built on a roof to cover the top of a staircase or other opening. **4.** a horizontal or inclined door giving access from the outside of a house to cellar stairs.

bulk·y (bul′kē) *adj.,* **bulk·i·er, bulk·i·est. 1.** of great bulk; large. **2.** difficult to manage or handle; unwieldy; clumsy. —**bulk′i·ly**, *adv.* —**bulk′i·ness**, *n.*

bull¹ (bul) *n.* **1.** the mature male of any animal of the cattle family. **2.** the male of certain other large animals, as the elephant, moose, whale, or seal. **3.** a person who believes that prices on a stock, bond, or commodity exchange will rise, esp. one who makes purchases with the hope of selling later at a higher price. ➡ opposed to **bear. 4.** *Slang.* a policeman or detective. **5.** a person resembling a bull, as in size, strength, or aggressiveness. —*v.t.* to make or force, as with the strength of a bull: *to bull one's way into a closed meeting.* —*adj.* **1.** male. **2.** resembling a bull, as in size or strength. **3.** characterized by rising prices on a stock, bond, or commodity exchange: *a bull market in aerospace stocks.* [Old English *bula* male of the cattle family.]

· **bull in a china shop.** a person who is clumsy and causes damage or destruction unintentionally.

· **to take the bull by the horns.** to face and deal courageously with some danger or difficulty.

bull² (bul) *n.* a papal document issued only for pronouncements on matters of great importance, presented according to a prescribed form on parchment with a lead seal attached. [Medieval Latin *bulla* seal, document, from Latin *bulla* knob, bubble.]

bull³ (bul) *n.* a silly, contradictory, or nonsensical mistake in language, for example: *Include me out,* or *I know nothing, but know it well.* [Of uncertain origin.]

bull⁴ (bul) *Slang. n.* foolish, empty talk; nonsense. —*v.t.* to achieve by pretended knowledge; bluff: *to bull one's way through an interview.* [Middle English *bul* deception, lie, probably from Medieval Latin *bulla* game, joking, from Latin *bulla* bubble.]

bul·la (bul′ə) *n., pl.* **bul·lae** (bul′ē, bul′ī). the round lead seal attached to a papal bull. [Medieval Latin *bulla* lead seal attached to an edict. See BULL².]

bull·dog (bul′dôg′) *n.* a heavily built dog, originally bred in England, having a large head, square jaw, short bowed legs, and a smooth coat. It is noted for its courage. Height: 15 inches (38 centimeters) at the shoulder. —*v.t.*, **-dogged, -dog·ging.** to wrestle (a steer) to the ground by taking hold of its horns and twisting its neck. —*adj.* resembling or characteristic of a bulldog; courageous; obstinate. [BULL¹ + DOG; possibly because such dogs were once used to bait bulls.]

bull·doze (bul′dōz′) *v.t.*, **-dozed, -doz·ing. 1.** to move, clear, level, or shape by using a bulldozer. **2.** *Informal.* to intimidate by threats or violence; bully. [Possibly from BULL¹ + modification of DOSE; with the sense of a dose of medicine enough for a bull.]

bull·doz·er (bul′dō′zər) *n.* **1.** a vehicle with a powerful motor that moves on treads like those of a tank and carries a wide, heavy metal blade mounted in front, used for such work as road grading, building demolition, and land clearing. **2.** *Informal.* a person who intimidates others with threats or violence.

bul·let (bul′it) *n.* **1.** a small, cylindrical piece of metal with a rounded or tapered point, used as ammunition in a gun. **2.** cartridge *(def. 1).* **3.** anything resembling a bullet in shape or speed: *The car shot through the intersection like a bullet.* [French *boulet,* diminutive of *boule* ball, from Latin *bulla* bubble, knob.]

· **to bite the bullet.** to make oneself do or endure something difficult or unpleasant.

bul·le·tin (bul′i tin) *n.* **1.** a brief official public report or statement on the current condition of something: *a government bulletin on the progress of a war.* **2.** a short account, statement, or report of news or other matters of public interest, as on television or the radio: *a television bulletin about an airplane crash.* **3.** a periodical publication, as of a society, church, or other organization. —*v.t.* to make known by a bulletin. [French *bulletin* ticket, from Italian *bulletino* pass, going back to Medieval Latin *bulla.* See BULL².]

bulletin board, a board for posting such items as notices, announcements, and pictures.

bul·let·proof (bul′it prüf′) *adj.* capable of resisting the penetration of a bullet or of lessening or absorbing its shock: *a bulletproof vest, bulletproof glass.*

bullet train, a high-speed passenger train, esp. one that operates in Japan.

bull·fight (bul′fīt′) *n.* a spectacle in an arena in which a bull is fought and is usually killed by a matador, popular in Spain, Portugal, and Mexico. In the Portuguese version the bull is not killed. —**bull′fight′er,** *n.* —**bull′fight′ing,** *n.*

bull·finch (bul′finch′) *n.* a Eurasian songbird, *Pyrrhula pyrrhula,* related to the cardinal and grosbeak, the male of which has a gray back, black cap, wings, and tail, and a rose-colored breast.

bull·frog (bul′frôg′, -frog′) *n.* a brownish green frog, *Rana catesbeiana,* the male of which has a loud, bellowing call. The largest frog in the United States, it may grow to 8 inches (20 centimeters) in length.

bull·head (bul′hed′) *n.* any of a group of freshwater catfish, genus *Ictalurus,* native to eastern North America, having a large flat head with four pairs of sensitive feelers around the mouth and no scales. Length: up to 16 inches (41 centimeters).

bull·head·ed (bul′hed′id) *adj.* foolishly stubborn; obstinate; headstrong. —**bull′head′ed·ness,** *n.*

bull·horn (bul′hôrn′) *n.* a portable electric device resembling a megaphone, used to increase or direct the sound of a voice.

bul·lion (bul′yən) *n.* gold, silver, or other precious metal, esp. such metal in the form of bars or ingots. [Partly from Old French *billon* ingot (from *bille* a stick) and partly from Old French *boillon* melted metal, from Latin *bullīre* to bubble.]

bull·ish (bul′ish) *adj.* **1.** of, relating to, or resembling a bull. **2.** tending toward, marked by, or causing rising prices on a stock, bond, or commodity exchange. —**bull′ish·ly,** *adv.* —**bull′ish·ness,** *n.*

bull·mas·tiff (bul′mas′tif) *n.* a heavily built dog of a breed originally developed by crossing a bulldog and a mastiff. It has a blunt, wrinkled muzzle and a tan or brown coat, often marked with white. Height: 26 inches (66 centimeters) at the shoulder.

Bull Moose, a member or supporter of the Progressive Party led by Theodore Roosevelt in the presidential campaign of 1912. [Term first used on several occasions by Theodore Roosevelt, 1858-1919, to denote either a forceful person or himself; later applied to the Progressive Party, whose symbol it became.]

bull·necked (bul′nekt′) *adj.* having a short, thick neck.

bull·ock (bul′ək) *n.* a castrated bull; ox or steer. [Old English *bulluc* bull calf.]

bull·pen (bul′pen′) *n.* **1.** *Baseball.* an area adjacent to or on the playing field where relief pitchers may warm up without interfering with a game in progress. **2.** *Informal.* a room in a jail for the temporary detention of prisoners. **3.** an enclosed area for bulls.

bull·ring (bul′ring′) *n.* an arena for bullfights.

bull session *Informal.* an informal group discussion, usually among close friends.

bull's-eye (bulz′ī′) *n.* **1.** the central circle of a target. **2.** a shot that hits the bull's-eye. **3.** a round piece of thick glass set in a ship's deck or similar structure to admit light. **4.** a convex lens shaped like a half sphere. **5.** a lantern having such a lens. **6.** a small, circular opening or window.

bull·snake (bul′snāk′) *n.* a large, nonpoisonous, North American snake, *Pituophis melanoleucus sayi,* that feeds mainly on rodents. Average length: 60 inches (152 centimeters). [BULL¹ + SNAKE.]

bull terrier, a strong, agile dog of a breed originally developed in England by crossing a bulldog with the now extinct white terrier, having a strong build, a broad pointed snout, and a white or brindled coat. Height: 20 inches (51 centimeters) at the shoulder.

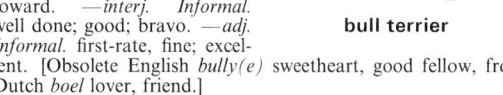

bull·whip (bul′hwip′, -wip′) *n.* a long, heavy rawhide whip, formerly used to drive a large team of horses or oxen.

bul·ly (bul′ē) *n., pl.* **-lies.** a quarrelsome person who browbeats, frightens, or hurts smaller or weaker people. —*v.t.,* **-lied, -ly·ing.** to threaten or intimidate into doing something; act the bully toward. —*interj. Informal.* well done; good; bravo. —*adj. Informal.* first-rate, fine; excellent. [Obsolete English *bully(e)* sweetheart, good fellow, from Dutch *boel* lover, friend.]

bull terrier

bully beef, canned corned beef. [French *bouilli* boiled beef, from *bouillir* to boil, from Latin *bullīre* to bubble.]

bul·ly·rag (bul′ē rag′) *v.t.,* **-ragged, -rag·ging.** to bully; intimidate; abuse.

bul·rush (bul′rush′) *n.* **1.** any of a large group of coarse plants, genus *Scirpus,* having grasslike leaves and small flower-bearing spikelets and growing in wet ground or shallow water. The sturdy stems of one species, *S. lacustris,* are used to weave mats, baskets, and chair seats. **2.** in the Bible, the papyrus plant of Egypt. **3.** *British.* cattail. [Possibly from BULL¹ large (adjective) + RUSH².]

bul·wark (bul′wərk) *n.* **1.** a defensive earthwork; rampart; fortification. **2.** any means of defense or protection; safeguard: *A mighty fortress is our God, a bulwark never failing* (Martin Luther, 1524). **3.** a breakwater for protection against waves. **4.** *also,*

a	at	e	end	o	hot	u	up	hw	white		about
ā	ape	ē	me	ō	old	ū	use	ng	song	ə	taken
ä	far	i	it	ô	fork	ü	rule	th	thin		pencil
âr	care	ī	ice	oi	oil	u̇	pull	th	this		lemon
		îr	pierce	ou	out	ûr	turn	zh	measure		circus

bulwarks. the part of a ship's side above the deck. —*v.t.* to furnish with a bulwark or bulwarks; defend; protect. [Probably from Middle Dutch *bolwerc* fortification, from *bole* plank + *werc* work.]

bum (bum) *n. Informal.* an idle or worthless person; loafer; tramp; vagrant. —*v.*, **bummed, bum·ming.** —*v.i.* **1.** to live or be like a bum; be idle; loaf. **2.** to live off others. —*v.t.* to get (something) by begging: *to bum a ride.* —*adj.*, **bum·mer, bum·mest. 1.** of inferior or poor quality; bad or worthless: *That short story is a bum piece of work.* **2.** in poor physical condition: *a bum leg from a skiing accident.* [Short for earlier *bummer* loafer, from German *Bummler* tramp.] —**bum′mer,** *n.*

• **on the bum. a.** living the life of a bum. **b.** out of order; broken: *The toaster is on the bum again.*

• **to bum around.** *Informal.* to travel or spend time with no particular destination or goal in mind: *The students bummed around Europe for the summer.*

• **to give** (or **get**) **the bum's rush.** *Slang.* to eject or be ejected by force: *The usher gave the disorderly patron the bum's rush.*

bum·ble (bum′bəl) *v.*, **-bled, -bling.** —*v.i.* to act or work in an awkward or clumsy manner. —*v.t.* to handle (something) in an awkward or clumsy manner; bungle. [Form of BUNGLE.] —**bum′bler,** *n.*

bum·ble·bee (bum′bəl bē′) *n.* any of several species of thick-bodied, hairy, black-and-yellow bees, genus *Bombus,* that are closely related to honeybees but live in smaller, more primitive colonies. [From obsolete *bumble* to buzz (imitative) + BEE.]

bump (bump) *v.i.* **1.** to strike suddenly; collide. **2.** to move with a jolt or jolts: *The car bumped along the dirt road.* —*v.t.* **1.** to hit suddenly; knock against. **2.** to cause to strike or knock: *The child bumped the tricycle against the wall.* **3.** *Informal.* to remove or displace, as from a job or a reservation on an airline. —*n.* **1.** a heavy jolt; thump. **2.** a swelling or lump caused by a collision or blow. **3.** any uneven part that rises above or protrudes from a basically even surface: *a bump in the road, a bump on a wall.* [Imitative.]

• **to bump into.** to meet by chance.

• **to bump off.** *Slang.* to kill; murder.

bump·er (bum′pər) *n.* **1.** a protective device, usually in the shape of a horizontal bar, attached to the front and rear ends of a vehicle to absorb the shock of collision. **2.** a cup or glass filled to the brim, esp. when drunk as a toast. —*adj.* unusually large or abundant, as a crop or harvest. [BUMP + -ER¹.]

bumper sticker, a sticker bearing a printed message or slogan, displayed on the bumper of a vehicle.

bump·kin (bump′kin) *n.* an awkward or simple person from the country. [Possibly from Flemish *bommekijn* little cask.]

bump·tious (bump′shəs) *adj.* unpleasantly bold or assertive; forward or aggressive in a conceited, obnoxious manner: *a bumptious youth.* [From BUMP; modeled upon FRACTIOUS.] —**bump′tious·ly,** *adv.* —**bump′tious·ness,** *n.*

bump·y (bum′pē) *adj.*, **bump·i·er, bump·i·est. 1.** having an uneven surface; full of bumps: *a bumpy piece of wood.* **2.** filled with or characterized by bumps or jolts: *a bumpy train ride.* —**bump′i·ly,** *adv.* —**bump′i·ness,** *n.*

bun (bun) *n.* **1.** a small bread roll, sometimes sweetened: *a hamburger bun, a breakfast bun.* **2.** a knot or roll of hair arranged in the shape of a bun. [Of uncertain origin.]

Bu·na (bü′nə, bü′-) *n. Trademark.* a synthetic rubber made from butadiene and styrene or some similar compound; the original and most widely used synthetic rubber. [Bu(TADIENE) + NA, symbol for *sodium.*]

bunch (bunch) *n.* **1.** a number of things of the same kind growing, fastened, grouped, or classified together; collection: *a bunch of bananas, a bunch of letters.* **2.** *Informal.* a group of people: *A bunch of us went to the movies.* —*v.i.* to form a bunch or bunches; gather together. —*v.t.* to group or make into a bunch or bunches; gather. [Of uncertain origin.] —**bunch′y,** *adj.*

bunch·ber·ry (bunch′ber′ē, -bə rē) *n.*, *pl.* **-ries.** a small perennial plant, *Cornus canadensis,* of the dogwood family, found in eastern Asia and North America, bearing clusters of white, petal-like leaves in the spring and clusters of small, bright red berries in the fall.

bunch grass, any of various grasses that grow in clumps or large tufts and are native to the dry soils and prairies of the western United States.

bun·co (bung′kō) *n.*, *pl.* **-cos.** bunko. —*v.t.*, **-coed, -co·ing.** bunko.

bun·combe (bung′kəm) *n.* bunk².

Bun·des·rat (bun′dəs rät′) *n.* the upper house of the federal legislature of Germany or of Austria. [German *Bundesrat,* from *Bundes* (genitive of *Bund* league, federation) + *Rat* council.]

Bun·des·tag (bun′dəs täg′, -täk′) *n.* the lower, popularly

elected house of the federal legislature of Germany. [German *Bundestag,* from *Bundes* + *-tag* meeting, assembly, from Middle High German *tagen* to gather, meet (on a certain day), from *tag* day. See BUNDESRAT.]

Bun·des·wehr (bun′dəs vâr′) *n.* the federal army or defense forces of Germany. [German *Bundeswehr,* from *Bundes* + *wehr* defense. See BUNDESRAT.]

bun·dle (bun′dəl) *n.* **1.** a number of things tied, wrapped, or otherwise bound together; parcel; package. **2.** a group, concentration, or collection; bunch: *a bundle of energy, a bundle of money.* **3.** *Botany.* vascular bundle. **4.** *Physiology.* a number of fibers, as nerve or muscle fibers, grouped together and running in the same direction. —*v.*, **-dled, -dling.** —*v.t.* **1.** to wrap or bind together; make into a bundle. **2.** *Informal.* to send or remove hastily or unceremoniously: *to bundle children off to school.* —*v.i.* **1.** to go hastily; hurry. **2.** in an early New England courting custom, to lie or sleep without undressing in the same bed with one's sweetheart, separated by a board. [Middle Dutch *bundel* sheaf.] —**bun′dler,** *n.*

• **to bundle up.** to dress warmly.

bung (bung) *n.* **1.** a stopper for the hole in a barrel, cask, or similar container. **2.** bunghole. —*v.t.* **1.** to close with a bung (often with *up*): *to bung up a barrel with a large cork.* **2.** to stop up; shut. [Middle Dutch *bonghe* stopper, possibly going back to Latin *puncta* hole.]

bun·ga·low (bung′gə lō′) *n.* a small house or cottage, usually of one or one-and-a-half stories. [Hindi *banglā* relating to Bengal; hence a Bengalese type of house.]

bun·gee cord (bun′jē) an elastic cord with a hook at each end, used as a fastener, as for securing packages to a luggage rack. Also, **bungee.**

bung·hole (bung′hōl′) *n.* a hole in a barrel, cask, or similar container through which it is filled or emptied.

bun·gle (bung′gəl) *v.*, **-gled, -gling.** —*v.i.* to work or act in a clumsy, unskilled way. —*v.t.* to do or make (something) in a clumsy, unskillful manner; botch. —*n.* a clumsy, unskillful performance, job, or piece of work. [Possibly of Scandinavian origin.] —**bun′gler,** *n.* —**bun′gling·ly,** *adv.*

bun·ion (bun′yən) *n.* an inflamed and often painful swelling on the foot, at the base of the big toe. [Of uncertain origin.]

bunk¹ (bungk) *n.* **1.** a shelflike, narrow bed or sleeping berth built in or against a wall. **2.** *Informal.* any bed or other place for sleeping. **3.** *Informal.* a bunkhouse; cabin. —*v.i. Informal.* **1.** to sleep in a bunk. **2.** to sleep anywhere: *We bunked on the floor.* —*v.t.* to provide with a place to sleep. [Possibly from BUNKER.]

bunk² (bungk) *n. Informal.* empty, insincere, or untrue talk; nonsense; humbug. Also, **buncombe, bunkum.** [Shortened from BUNKUM, phonetic spelling of BUNCOMBE, from *Buncombe* County, North Carolina, whose congressman in 1820 explained that a long, irrelevant speech he had made was meant not for Congress but for Buncombe.]

bunk·bed (bungk′bed′) *n.* **1.** a piece of furniture consisting of two or more single beds, one above the other. **2.** one of the beds that make up such a piece of furniture.

bunk·er (bung′kər) *n.* **1.** a military fortification consisting of a chamber built largely below ground, protected by earth or steel and concrete. **2.** an obstacle in or along a golf fairway or close to the green, as a sand trap or barrier of earth. **3.** a storage compartment or bin, as for coal on a ship. [Of uncertain origin.]

bunk·house (bungk′hous′) *n.*, *pl.* **-hous·es** (-hou′ziz). a rough building with sleeping quarters or bunks, as for workers or campers.

bun·ko (bung′kō) *also,* **bunco.** *n.*, *pl.* **-kos.** *Informal.* a confidence game; swindle. —*v.t.*, **-koed, -ko·ing.** *Informal.* to swindle. [Possibly from Spanish *banca* name of a card game, bank, from Italian *banca* bank, bench. See BANK².]

bun·kum (bung′kəm) *n.* bunk².

bun·ny (bun′ē) *n.*, *pl.* **-nies.** *Informal.* a rabbit, esp. a young rabbit. [Dialectal English *bun* rabbit (of uncertain origin) + -Y².]

Bun·sen burner (bun′sən) a gas burner, used esp. in laboratories, consisting of a short metal tube into which gas is fed. Openings at the base allow air to enter and mix with the gas, which, when lighted, burns with a very hot, blue flame. [From the German chemist Robert W. Bunsen, 1811-99, who invented it.]

bunt¹ (bunt) *v.t.*, *v.i.* **1.** to tap (a pitched baseball) so that it goes only a short distance into the infield. **2.** to strike or push with or as with the head or horns; butt. —*n.* **1.a.** the act of bunting. **b.** a hit made by bunting. **c.** a ball hit by bunting. **2.** a push or shove; butt. [Modification of BUTT³.] —**bunt′er,** *n.*

bunt² (bunt) *n.* a smut disease of grains and grasses, esp. wheat, in which the interior of the seed is replaced by a solid mass of spores. [Of uncertain origin.]

bun·ting¹ (bun′ting) *n.* **1.** a sacklike blanket or wrapper for babies, made of wool, cotton, or other soft material. **2.** a worsted

cloth used in making flags. **3.** decorative banners or drapes of cloth printed with the colors or symbols of a national flag. [Possibly from earlier *bunt* to sift; possibly because bunting was used to sift flour.]

bun·ting² (bun'ting) *n.* any of various colorful songbirds, family Fringillidae, of North America and Eurasia, related to and resembling the sparrow in every respect except color, having a short, stout, pointed bill. Length: 5½ inches (14 centimeters). [Of uncertain origin.]

bunt·line (bunt'lin, -līn') *n.* any of the ropes used to haul up a square sail for furling. [*Bunt* middle part of a sail (of uncertain origin) + LINE¹.]

bu·oy (bü'ē, boi) *n.* **1.** a floating marker anchored to the bottom of a waterway, used to warn of an underwater hazard or to indicate a channel. **2.** life buoy. —*v.t.* **1.** to furnish or mark with a buoy or buoys. **2.** to prevent from sinking; keep afloat (often with *up*). **3.** to hold up or raise, as in spirits or hope (often with *up*): *The victory buoyed up the morale of the troops. Scoring first buoyed the team.* [Old French *boie* anchored floating marker, fetter; of Germanic origin.]

buoy·an·cy (boi'ən sē, bü'yən-) *n.* **1.** the power or tendency to float or rise in a liquid or gas: *Cork has great buoyancy.* **2.** the power of a liquid or gas to keep something afloat. **3.** the ability to recover from depression or sadness; lightheartedness; cheerfulness.

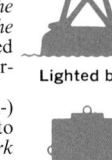

Lighted buoy Spar buoy

Can buoy Nun buoy

buoys

buoy·ant (boi'ənt, bü'yənt) *adj.* having or marked by buoyancy. —**buoy'ant·ly,** *adv.*

bur¹ (bûr) *also,* **burr.** *n.* **1.a.** a prickly seedcase covered with tiny barbs that stick to clothing or fur. **b.** any plant bearing burs, esp. a weed. **2.** a person or thing that clings like a bur. **3.** burr¹. —*v.t.,* **burred, bur·ring.** to remove burs from.

bur² (bûr) *n.* burr² —*v.,* **burred, bur·ring.** burr².

bur·ble (bûr'bəl) *v.i.,* **-bled, -bling.** to make or utter with a bubbling sound; gurgle. [Imitative.]

bur·bot (bûr'bət) *n., pl.* **-bot** or **-bots.** a freshwater fish, *Lota lota,* of the cod family, native to North America, Europe, and Siberia, having a long, slender body and barbels on its chin and snout. Length: 2½-5 feet (0.8-1.5 meters). [French *bourbotte,* from *bourbe* mud; of Celtic origin.]

bur·den¹ (bûr'dən) *n.* **1.** something that is carried or borne; load. **2.** something wearisome, oppressive, or hard to bear. **3.** the cargo capacity of a ship or weight of a ship's cargo. —*v.t.* to put a heavy load on; overload; oppress: *The government burdened the nation with many kinds of taxes.* [Old English *byrthen* load.]

bur·den² (bûr'dən) *n.* **1.** a chief topic, theme, idea, or sentiment: *the burden of an essay.* **2.** a refrain or recurring chorus at the end of the stanzas of a song or ballad. [Old French *bourdon* humming, drone bee, from Late Latin *burdo* drone bee; imitative.]

burden of proof, the obligation of proving a disputed or controversial statement or charge.

bur·den·some (bûr'dən səm) *adj.* wearisome, oppressive, or hard to bear.

bur·dock (bûr'dok) *n.* any of a small group of coarse, bur-bearing plants constituting the genus *Arctium,* of the composite family, esp. the **common burdock,** *A. minus,* and the **great burdock,** *A. lappa,* which are widely distributed as weeds in the eastern United States and Canada. [BUR¹ + DOCK⁴.]

bu·reau (byür'ō) *n., pl.* **bu·reaus** or **bu·reaux** (byür'ōz). **1.** a chest of drawers, esp. for clothes, sometimes with a mirror. **2.** a government division, department, or agency: *the bureau for Far Eastern affairs.* **3.** an office or agency, esp. one where business is transacted or information is given: *a travel bureau, a credit bureau.* **4.** a desk or writing table with drawers. [French *bureau* desk, office; originally, cloth used to cover desks, from Old French *burel* coarse russet cloth, going back to Late Latin *burra* tuft of wool, rough cloth.]

bu·reauc·ra·cy (byü rok'rə sē) *n., pl.* **-cies. 1.** government by bureaus and numerous officials. **2.** government officials collectively. **3.** excessive multiplication of, and concentration of power in, administrative bureaus. **4.** too strict attention to rules and routine, often resulting in delay and inefficiency; governmental red tape. [French *bureaucratie,* from *bureau* desk, office + Greek *-kratiā* power, rule. See BUREAU.]

bu·reau·crat (byür'ə krat') *n.* **1.** an official in a bureaucracy. **2.** an official who follows and insists on strict attention to rules

and routine. —**bu'reau·crat'ic,** *adj.* —**bu'reau·crat'i·cal·ly,** *adv.*

bu·rette (byü ret') *also,* **bu·ret.** *n.* a glass tube marked to measure volume, with a stopcock at the bottom, used for accurately controlling the flow of small amounts of liquid. [French *burette,* diminutive of *buire* bottle, pitcher; of Germanic origin.]

burg (bûrg) *n.* **1.** *Informal.* a small town or city. **2.** *Archaic.* a fortified or walled town. [Old English *burg.*]

bur·geon (bûr'jən) *v.i.* **1.** to grow rapidly; flourish. **2.** to bud or sprout. —*v.t.* to sprout or put forth, as leaves, buds, or shoots. —*n.* a bud or sprout. [Old French *burjon* bud, going back to Late Latin *burra* tuft of wool; because of the hairiness of many buds.]

burg·er (bûr'gər) *n. Informal.* hamburger.

bur·gess (bûr'jis) *n.* **1.** an inhabitant, esp. a citizen or officer, of a British borough of earlier times. **2.** a member of

burette

the popularly elected legislature of colonial Virginia or Maryland. **3.** in Pennsylvania, the mayor of a borough. [Old French *borjois* citizen, going back to *borc* town, from Late Latin *burgus* fortress; of Germanic origin.]

burgh (bûrg) *n.* a chartered town in Scotland. [Form of BOROUGH.]

burgh·er (bûr'gər) *n.* an inhabitant of a city, esp. a merchant city in feudal times.

bur·glar (bûr'glər) *n.* a person who commits burglary. [Anglo-Norman *burgler* thief, from Medieval Latin *burglator,* going back to Late Latin *burgus.* See BURGESS.]

bur·glar·i·ous (bər glâr'e əs) *adj.* of, relating to, or involving burglary. —**bur·glar'i·ous·ly,** *adv.*

bur·glar·ize (bûr'glə rīz') *v.t.,* **-ized, -iz·ing.** to break into (a building) with the intent to steal or commit some other felony.

bur·glar·y (bûr'glə rē) *n., pl.* **-glar·ies.** the breaking into and entering of a dwelling or other building with the intent to steal or commit some other felony. —For Synonyms, see **theft.**

bur·gle (bûr'gəl) *v.t., v.i.,* **-gled, -gling.** *Informal.* to burglarize. [From BURGLAR.]

bur·go·mas·ter (bûr'gə mas'tər) *n.* the mayor or chief magistrate of a town in the Netherlands, Flanders, Germany, or Austria. [Dutch *burgemeester,* from *burg* town + *meester* master, from Latin *magister.*]

Bur·gun·dy (bûr'gən dē) *n., pl.* **-dies.** a red or white wine of a type originally produced in Burgundy, France.

bur·i·al (ber'ē əl) *n.* the act of burying, esp. the interment of a dead body. —*adj.* of or relating to burying: *a burial mound.* [Old English *byrgels* tomb.]

burial ground, graveyard; cemetery.

bur·ied (ber'ēd) the past tense and past participle of **bury.**

bu·rin (byür'in) *n.* a steel cutting tool used by engravers for incising lines in a metal plate. [French *burin,* probably from Italian *burino* (now *bulino*); of Germanic origin.]

burl (bûrl) *n.* **1.** a small knot or lump, as in wool, thread, or cloth. **2.** a knot, lump, or other growth on certain tree trunks, used for ornamental veneering. —*v.t.* to finish (cloth), as by removing burls or loose threads. [Old French *bourle* tuft of wool, going back to Late Latin *burra.*]

bur·lap (bûr'lap) *n.* a coarse fabric, usually made from jute or hemp, used in making such items as sacks, curtains, and wall coverings. [Of uncertain origin.]

bur·lesque (bər lesk') *n.* **1.** a literary or dramatic composition that presents a comical treatment of a serious subject or a mock-serious treatment of an unimportant subject; parody; caricature: *The novel "Don Quixote" is, in part, a burlesque of medieval chivalry and romance.* **2.** a theatrical entertainment with often indecent songs, jokes, and comic skits. —*v.t.,* **-lesqued, -les·quing.** to make ridiculous, as by grotesque parody, imitation, or carica-

a	at	e	end	o	hot	u	up	hw	white		about
ā	ape	ē	me	ō	old	ū	use	ng	song		taken
ä	far	i	it	ô	fork	ü	rule	th	thin	ə	pencil
âr	care	ī	ice	oi	oil	u̇	pull	th	this		lemon
		îr	pierce	ou	out	ûr	turn	zh	measure		circus

ture. —*adj.* **1.** humorously mocking. **2.** of or relating to theatrical burlesque. [French *burlesque* ludicrous, a parody, from Italian *burlesco* comical, from *burla* joke.] —**bur·les′quer,** *n.*

bur·ley (bûr′lē) *also,* **Bur·ley.** *n., pl.* **-leys.** a light brown American tobacco raised mainly in Kentucky, used esp. in pipe tobaccos.

bur·ly (bûr′lē) *adj.,* **-li·er, -li·est.** large in bodily size; strongly built; sturdy. [Probably going back to Old English *borlīce* excellently.] —**bur′li·ness,** *n.*

bur marigold, any of a number of plants, genus *Bidens,* of the daisy family, having yellow flowers and prickly burs that stick to clothing or fur.

Bur·mese (bər mēz′, -mēs′) *adj.* of, relating to, or characteristic of Burma or its people, language, or culture. —*n., pl.* **-mese. 1.** a native or citizen of Burma. **2.** a person of Burmese ancestry. **3.** the language predominantly spoken in Burma, belonging to the Sino-Tibetan family of languages.

burn[1] (bûrn) *v.,* **burned** or **burnt, burn·ing.** —*v.t.* **1.** to cause to be destroyed or consumed by fire: *to burn old newspapers.* **2.a.** to injure or damage by fire or anything resembling fire in its effect: *to burn one's finger on a hot stove.* **b.** to overcook so as to blacken or turn to charcoal: *The cook burned the toast.* **c.** sunburn. **3.** to cause or produce by or as by fire: *An ash burned a hole in the dress. The artist burned an image into the wood.* **4.** to cause or produce a sensation of heat in: *The chili burned my mouth.* **5.a.** to use or consume to produce heat, light, or power: *to burn candles, a car that burns a lot of gasoline.* **b.** to use or expend (energy): *to burn a lot of energy playing football.* **6.** *Informal.* to anger; gall: *That comment really burns me.* **7.** to put to death by fire. **8.** to finish, harden, or glaze by fire or heat; fire: *to burn clay.* **9.** to remove by or as if by fire: *to burn paint off metal with a blowtorch.* **10.** to cauterize; brand. **11.** *Chemistry.* to cause to undergo combustion. **12.** *Slang.* to deceive or cheat. ➡ usually used in the passive voice: *to be burned by a bad check.* **13.** *Slang.* to electrocute. —*v.i.* **1.** to be on fire; flame. **2.a.** to be destroyed, injured, or altered in appearance or texture by or as if by fire: *The steak burned on the outside. The house burned to the ground.* **b.** sunburn. **3.** to give off light or heat; shine; glow: *The street lights burned all night.* **4.** to feel or seem to be hot: *The child burned with a fever.* **5.** to be consumed by strong emotion: *to burn with love.* **6.a.** to undergo combustion; oxidize. **b.** to undergo nuclear fission or fusion. **7.** to be impressed deeply or fixed permanently (with *into*): *The acid burned into the metal plate. The author's stirring words burned into my mind.* **8.** *Slang.* to be electrocuted. —*n.* **1.** an injury, damage, or effect caused by or as if by burning: *a hospital that treats burns.* **2.** the firing of one or more rocket engines of a spacecraft while in flight. [Partly from Old English *beornan* to be on fire; partly from Old English *bærnan* to set on fire.] —**burn′a·ble,** *adj.*

•**to burn.** in large amounts; in abundance: *to have cash to burn.*

•**to burn down.** to destroy or be destroyed by fire.

•**to burn off.** (of mist or fog) to be dissipated by the sun.

•**to burn out. a.** to stop burning because of lack of fuel: *The forest fire burned out when it reached the lake.* **b.** to wear out or stop working: *Hard driving burned out the car's transmission. The street light burned out.* **c.** to drive out or destroy by fire: *The late-night fire burned the family out. All the stores in the block were burned out.* **d.** to exhaust physically, mentally, or emotionally: *Overwork burned the teacher out.*

•**to burn up. a.** to destroy or be destroyed by fire. **b.** to make angry: *Your snide remark really burns me up.*

burn[2] (bûrn) *n.* bourn[1]. [Old English *burn.*]

burn·er (bûr′nər) *n.* **1.** a person or thing that burns. **2.** the part of a stove, furnace, or similar device from which the flame comes.

burn·ing (bûr′ning) *adj.* **1.** on fire; in flames: *a burning log in a fireplace.* **2.** very hot; glowing; scorching: *a burning feeling from too much sun.* **3.** of the utmost importance: *a burning question.* **4.** characterized by intensity of feeling; ardent; vehement: *a burning desire.*

burning glass, a convex lens used to heat or cause something to ignite by focusing the sun's rays on it.

bur·nish (bûr′nish) *v.t.* to polish by friction; make smooth and shiny: *to burnish metal.* —*n.* a polish; luster; gloss. [Old French *burniss-,* a stem of *burnir* to polish, make brown, from *brun* brown; of Germanic origin.]

bur·nish·er (bûr′ni shər) *n.* **1.** a tool, usually with a smooth, rounded head, used for burnishing. **2.** a person who burnishes.

bur·noose (bər nüs′, bûr′nüs′) *also,* **bur·nous.** *n.* a cloak with a hood, as that worn by Moors and Arabs. [French *burnous,* from Arabic *burnus,* from Greek *birros.*]

burn·out (bûrn′out′) *n.* **1.** the termination of combustion in a

rocket engine, after the fuel is exhausted. **2.** mental, emotional, or physical exhaustion caused by stress over a period of time.

burn·sides (bûrn′sīdz′) *n.* side whiskers, often with a mustache; muttonchops. For illustration, see **sideburns.** [From the American Civil War general Ambrose E. *Burnside,* 1824-81, who wore whiskers of this style.]

burnt (bûrnt) a past tense and past participle of **burn**[1].

burnt orange, a brownish orange color.

burnt sienna, see **sienna.**

burnt umber, see **umber.**

burp (bûrp) *Informal. n.* a belch. —*v.i.* to belch. —*v.t.* to cause (a baby) to belch. [Imitative.]

burr[1] (bûr) *also,* **bur.** *n.* **1.** a rough or sharp edge left on metal by a cutting or drilling tool. **2.** any of several small cutting heads used on dentists' drills. **3.** any of various other tools used for cutting or drilling. **4.** bur[1]. —*v.t.,* **burred, bur·ring.** bur[1]. [Possibly of Scandinavian origin.]

burr[2] (bûr) *also,* **bur.** *n.* **1.** a rough, trilled pronunciation of *r,* as heard in Scotland and northern England. **2.** any rough or guttural pronunciation. **3.** a humming or whirring sound. —*v.t.* to pronounce (something) with a burr. —*v.i.* **1.** to speak with a burr. **2.** to make a humming or whirring sound. [Possibly imitative.]

bur·ri·to (bə rē′tō) *n., pl.* **-tos.** a tortilla wrapped around a filling of meat, cheese, or beans. [Spanish *burrito* this food, literally, little donkey, from *burro.* See BURRO.]

bur·ro (bûr′ō, bər′ō) *n., pl.* **-ros.** a small donkey. [Spanish *burro,* from *borrico,* from Late Latin *burrīcus* small horse.]

bur·row (bûr′ō, bər′ō) *n.* **1.** a hole dug in the ground, usually by a small animal, as a rabbit or badger, for refuge or habitation. **2.** any similar passage for shelter, retreat, or refuge. —*v.i.* **1.** to live or hide in a burrow. **2.** to dig a burrow or burrows. **3.** to penetrate or dig. **4.** to hunt; search: *I burrowed into my desk for a pencil.* —*v.t.* **1.** to construct by burrowing. **2.** to dig a burrow or burrows in. [Form of BOROUGH.] —**bur′row·er,** *n.*

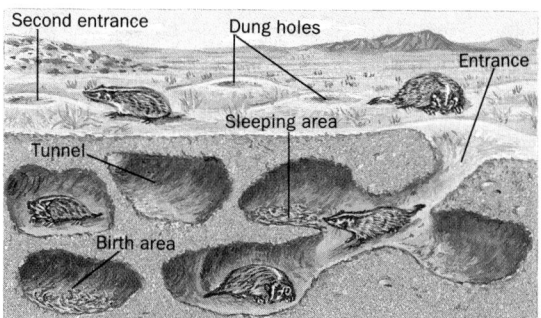

badgers' **burrow**

bur·sa (bûr′sə) *n., pl.* **-sae** (-sē) or **-sas.** a closed, fluid-filled sac that helps prevent friction in certain parts of the body, as at a joint or where a tendon passes over a bone. [Medieval Latin *bursa* purse, from Greek *byrsā* skin. Doublet of BOURSE, PURSE.]

bur·sar (bûr′sər, -sär) *n.* a treasurer, as of a college. [Medieval Latin *bursarius,* from Medieval Latin *bursa* purse. See BURSA.]

bur·sa·ry (bûr′sə rē) *n., pl.* **-ries.** a treasury, as of a college.

bur·si·tis (bər sī′tis) *n.* a severely painful condition resulting from inflammation of a bursa, the most commonly affected areas being the shoulder, elbow, and hip joints. [BURSA + -ITIS.]

burst (bûrst) *v.,* **burst, burst·ing.** —*v.i.* **1.** to break open or fly apart suddenly or as from internal pressure; explode: *Fireworks burst in the sky. The buds on the peach tree were ready to burst into bloom.* **2.** to be full to the point of overflowing: *a full suitcase bursting at the seams, to burst with energy, to burst with pride.* **3.** to come or appear suddenly and with force: *The protesters burst into the room. The gorilla burst out of its cage.* **4.** to give vent suddenly to an action or emotional expression: *to burst into song, to burst into tears.* —*v.t.* **1.** to cause to break open or explode suddenly: *The strong wind burst the door open. The child burst the bubble.* —*n.* **1.** a sudden issuing forth or eruption; outbreak: *a burst of gunfire, a burst of enthusiasm.* **2.** a sudden display of activity or energy; spurt: *a burst of speed.* **3.** the result of bursting; crack; break. **4.a.** a series of shots fired by one continued pressing on the trigger of an automatic weapon. **b.** the explosion of a shell or bomb. [Old English *berstan* to break.]

bur·then (bûr'thən) *Archaic.* burden[1].

bur·y (ber'ē) *v.t.,* **bur·ied, bur·y·ing. 1.** to put (a dead body) in the earth, a tomb, or the sea; inter. **2.** to cover up or hide; conceal: *The pirates buried their treasure.* **3.** to cause to sink, plunge, or lodge: *The lumberjack buried the ax in the tree trunk.* **4.** to interest (oneself) in; engross: *to bury oneself in a newspaper.* **5.** to put out of one's mind; forget; abandon: *to bury one's anger.* [Old English *byrgan* to inter.]

bus (bus) *n., pl.* **bus·es** or **bus·ses. 1.** a motor vehicle with rows of seats to accommodate many passengers, used esp. on a fixed, regular route. **2.** a path for the transmission of data from one part of a computer to another, shared by signals from several components. —*v.,* **bused** or **bussed, bus·ing** or **bus·sing.** —*v.t.* **1.** to carry by bus: *to bus a tour group from city to city.* **2.** to transport by bus to a school outside a neighborhood in order to help the school system maintain a racial balance of students. —*v.i.* to travel by bus: *We bused to the city.* [Short for OMNIBUS.]

bus., business.

bus·boy (bus'boi') *also,* **bus boy.** *n.* a waiter's or waitress's assistant who clears and resets tables, pours water, and performs other duties.

bus·by (buz'bē) *n., pl.* **-bies.** a fur hat with a bag hanging from the top over the right side, worn by hussars, artillerymen, and engineers in the British army. [Apparently from the proper name *Busby,* possibly the name of the manufacturer or a wearer.]

bush (bush) *n.* **1.** a shrub, esp. a thick shrub without a distinct trunk. **2.** a clump of shrubs or trees; thicket; undergrowth. **3.** a wild, uncultivated tract of country covered with scrub: *the Australian bush.* —*v.i.* to be or become thick or bushy; resemble a bush. —*v.t.* to protect (plants, crops, or trees) with bushes set around them; cover or support with bushes. [Possibly from Middle English *busk* shrub, thicket, from Old Norse *buskr.*]

• **to beat around the bush.** to speak or write around a subject without coming to the point.

• **to beat the bushes.** to search all over for (someone or something): *The college administration beat the bushes for a new dean.*

bush baby, any of a group of small, nocturnal prosimian primates, genus *Galago,* with a long, bushy tail and large eyes, native to Africa south of the Sahara. Also, **galago.** [So called because of its bushy tail.]

bushed (busht) *adj. Informal.* thoroughly exhausted or fatigued; worn-out.

bush·el[1] (bush'əl) *n.* **1.** a dry measure equal to 4 pecks or 32 quarts (35.2 liters). **2.** a container holding a bushel. [Old French *boissel* the measure, probably from *boisse* sixth of a bushel; possibly of Celtic origin.]

bush·el[2] (bush'əl) *v.t., v.i.,* **-eled** or **-elled, -el·ing** or **-el·ling.** to repair or alter (clothing). [Possibly from German *bosseln* to patch.]

bu·shi·do (bü'shē dō') *also,* **Bu·shi·do.** *n.* the unwritten code of honor of the samurai warriors of feudal Japan, which prescribed loyalty, courage, self-sacrifice, and death before dishonor, usually by hara-kiri. [Japanese *bushidō* literally, warrior's way.]

bush·ing (bush'ing) *n.* **1.** a removable metal lining used in a machine to lessen friction and wear. **2.** a lining that insulates and prevents abrasion of electric conductors. [From earlier *bush* metal lining, from Middle Dutch *busse* box, from Late Latin *buxis.* See BOX[3].]

bush league 1. a minor league in baseball. **2.** any unimportant or inferior group, organization, or activity. —**bush-league,** *adj.*

bush leaguer 1. a baseball player in a bush league. **2.** a person whose work or performance is mediocre or second-rate.

bush·man (bush'mən) *n., pl.* **-men** (-mən). **1.** a settler or farmer in the Australian bush. **2. Bushman.** San. [BUSH + MAN; influenced by Afrikaans *boschjesman* literally, man of the bush.]

bush·mas·ter (bush'mas'tər) *n.* a deadly tropical pit viper, *Lachesis mutus,* found in Central and South America. It is the longest poisonous snake in the Western Hemisphere, occasionally growing to 12 feet (3.7 meters).

bush pilot, a pilot who flies passengers or cargo in a small plane to and from rugged or remote areas that cannot be easily reached by other means of transportation.

bush·whack (bush'hwak', -wak') *v.t.* to attack from ambush. —*v.i.* **1.** to cut one's way through rough, overgrown terrain. **2.** to fight or attack from ambush.

bush·whack·er (bush'hwak'ər, -wak'-) *n.* **1.** a person who attacks from ambush. **2.** a Confederate guerrilla. **3.** a woodsman. [Originally from the idea of one who "whacks" through the bushes.]

bush·y (bush'ē) *adj.,* **bush·i·er, bush·i·est. 1.** resembling a bush; thick and spreading. **2.** full of or overgrown with bushes. —**bush'i·ness,** *n.*

bus·i·ly (biz'ə lē) *adv.* in a busy manner.

busi·ness (biz'nis) *n.* **1.** a person's occupation, trade, or profession. **2.a.** a commercial or industrial enterprise: *Two new businesses opened on Main Street.* **b.** a building or office where such an enterprise is located: *That clothing business takes up an entire block on Center Street.* **c.** the conducting of such an enterprise: *My cousin went into business right after college.* **3.** the volume of buying and selling; commercial transactions: *Business was bad at the store.* **4.a.** something done or to be done; matter; affair: *Moving can be a tiresome business.* **b.** something to be concerned about: *This business of noisy traffic has the entire neighborhood upset.* **5.** private or personal care or responsibility: *It is none of your business what they do. I made it my business to finish the work on schedule.* **6.** commercial policy or custom: *It's bad business not to advertise.* **7.** any action or gesture by an actor or entertainer. ➡ distinguished from **dialogue** or **lyrics.** —*adj.* of, relating to, connected with, or engaged in business: *business hours, a business card.* [BUSY + -NESS.]

• **to do business with.** to have commercial dealings with.

• **to get down to business.** *Informal.* to settle down and work seriously.

• **to give** (or **get**) **the business.** *Slang.* to treat or be treated harshly: *We got the business for being late.*

• **to go about one's business.** to do without fuss or ceremony what one has to do: *The hotel employees ignored the crowd around the celebrity and went about their business.*

• **to have no business.** to have no right to do or say something: *You have no business interfering in my private affairs.*

• **to mean business.** *Informal.* to be in earnest: *When the coaches say the team must practice every day, they mean business.*

• **to mind one's own business.** to refrain from meddling in other people's work or concerns; attend to one's own affairs.

business college, a school that gives training in skills needed for a career in business or commerce.

busi·ness·like (biz'nis līk') *adj.* having qualities suitable to business; methodical; efficient.

busi·ness·man (biz'nis man') *n., pl.* **-men** (-men'). a person who owns, operates, or works in a business.

busi·ness·per·son (biz'nis pûr'sən) *n.* a person who owns, operates, or works in a business.

business school 1. a school in a college or university that teaches techniques of management, finance, and commerce. **2.** business college.

busi·ness·wom·an (biz'nis wum'ən) *n., pl.* **-wom·en** (-wim'ən). a woman who owns, operates, or works in a business.

bus·ing (bus'ing) *also,* **bus·sing.** *n.* the transportation of children by buses to schools outside their neighborhoods in order to help the schools maintain a racial balance of students.

bus·kin (bus'kin) *n.* **1.** a laced half boot, usually reaching the middle of the calf. **2.** a thick-soled boot worn by actors in tragedies during the Hellenistic and Roman periods. **3.** tragic drama as a genre; tragedy. [Old French *brousequin* the boot; of uncertain origin.]

bus·man's holiday (bus'mənz) a holiday spent by choice in doing something similar to one's regular work.

buss (bus) *n.* a kiss; smack. —*v.t.* to kiss (someone). [Probably from Middle English *bassen* to kiss, from Old French *baisier,* from Latin *basiare.*]

bus·ses (bus'iz) a plural of bus.

bust[1] (bust) *n.* **1.** a piece of sculpture representing the head, shoulders, and breast of a person. **2.** the bosom of a woman. [French *buste,* from Italian *busto,* perhaps from Latin *bûstum* tomb; possibly because tombs were often decorated with a bust of the deceased.]

bust[2] (bust) *Slang.* —*v.t.* **1.** to cause to come apart; burst; break. **2.** to cause to go bankrupt. **3.** to hit; punch; sock. **4.** to reduce in rank, esp. in military rank; demote. **5.** to arrest (someone). **6.** to tame; break: *to bust a mustang.* —*v.i.* **1.** to burst; break. **2.** to become bankrupt. —*n.* **1.** an utter failure; flop: *The play was a bust and closed after two performances.* **2.** a spree. **3.** a blow; hit: *a bust on the chin.* **4.** bankruptcy or economic depression: *a period of boom and bust.* **5.** an arrest: *a drug bust.* [Form of BURST.]

bus·tard (bus'tərd) *n.* any of various game birds of the family

a	at	e	end	o	hot	u	up	hw	white	⟨	about
ā	ape	ē	me	ō	old	ū	use	ng	song		taken
ä	far	i	it	ô	fork	ü	rule	th	thin	ə⟨	pencil
âr	care	ī	ice	oi	oil	ù	pull	th	this		lemon
		îr	pierce	ou	out	ûr	turn	zh	measure	⟨	circus

Otididae, related to the cranes and native to Eurasia, Africa, and Australia, having long legs, a large, heavy body, and a long neck. Height: 4 feet (1.2 meters). [Old French *bistarde,* from Latin *avis tarda* slow bird.]

bus·tle¹ (bus′əl) *v.i., v.t.,* **-tled, -tling.** to move or cause to move quickly or energetically. —*n.* noisy or excited activity; commotion; stir: *the bustle of a city.* [Possibly a modification of obsolete *buskle* to prepare, going back to Old Norse *būask* to get ready.]

bus·tle² (bus′əl) *n.* **1.** a large amount of gathered material worn over the back of a skirt just below the waist. **2.** a pad or frame formerly worn by women to add fullness to the back part of a skirt. [Of uncertain origin.]

bus·y (biz′ē) *adj.,* **bus·i·er, bus·i·est. 1.** actively and attentively doing something: *busy at work, too busy to see someone.* **2.** full of or marked by activity: *Tomorrow is going to be a busy day.* **3.** in use: *When we phoned, the line was busy.* **4.** tending to meddle; prying; officious. **5.** excessively ornamented; fussy: *busy wallpaper.* —*v.t.,* **bus·ied, bus·y·ing.** to make or keep busy; occupy (oneself): *to busy oneself cleaning house.* [Old English *bisig* occupied.] —**bus′y·ness,** *n.*

bus·y·bod·y (biz′ē bod′ē) *n., pl.* **-bod·ies.** a person who pries into other people's affairs; meddler.

bus·y·work (biz′ē wûrk′) *n.* work that has no essential value other than to occupy one's time.

but (but; *unstressed* bət) *conj.* **1.** on the other hand; in contrast: *She is tall, but her brother is short.* **2.** contrary to expectation; yet; nevertheless: *It is early November, but it has begun snowing. I was not invited, but I plan to go anyway.* **3.** other than; except: *There was no direct route but through the center of town. We have no choice but to arrive late.* **4.** that: *There is no doubt but the patient will recover.* **5.** without the result that; unless: *It never rains but it pours.* **6.** that . . . not: *Who knows but we may make a fortune?* —*prep.* other than; except: *Everyone has signed but you.* —*adv.* only; merely; just: *I have but a day to see the sights. I saw them but a few minutes ago.* —*n.* an objection or limitation; exception: *No ifs, ands, or buts about it.* [Old English *būtan* except, without, unless.]

　•**all but.** nearly; almost: *The party was all but over when we arrived.*

　•**but for.** if it were not for; except for: *The poor family would have had no food but for a neighbor's kindness.*

bu·ta·di·ene (bū′tə dī′ēn, -dī ēn′) *n.* a colorless, flammable gas obtained from petroleum by-products, used esp. in making synthetic rubber, nylon, and rocket fuels. Formula: C_4H_{16} [BU-TA(NE) + DI-¹ + -ENE.]

bu·tane (bū′tān) *n.* either of two isomers of a colorless, flammable gas. in the production of liquefied petroleum gas, high-octane gasoline, and synthetic rubber. Formula: C_4H_{10} [Latin *būt(ȳrum)* butter + -ANE. See BUTTER.]

bu·ta·nol (bū′tə nôl′) *n.* butyl alcohol. [BUTAN(E) + -OL.]

butch·er (būch′ər) *n.* **1.** a person who slaughters animals or dresses their flesh for market. **2.** a person who deals in meat. **3.** a person guilty of cruel, bloody, or indiscriminate slaughter. **4.** a person who is clumsy and unskillful; bungler. —*v.t.* **1.** to slaughter or dress (animals) for market or for food. **2.** to slaughter in a cruel, bloody, or indiscriminate manner. **3.** to spoil by bad work; botch: *The pianist butchered the concerto.* [Old French *bochier* originally, seller of goat meat, from *boc* male goat.] —**butch′er·er,** *n.*

butch·er·bird (būch′ər bûrd′) *n.* a shrike of the genus *Lanius,* noted for impaling its prey on thorns for storage.

butcher block, a heavy block of laminated strips of hardwood, as maple, usually unpainted, and made into tops for counters and tables. —**butch′er-block′,** *adj.*

butch·er's-broom (būch′ərz brüm′, -brüm′) *n.* an evergreen shrub, *Ruscus aculeatus,* of the lily family, having small, greenish flowers and red or yellow berrylike fruit.

butch·er·y (būch′ə rē) *n., pl.* **-er·ies. 1.** cruel or wholesale slaughter; carnage. **2.** slaughterhouse. **3.** the trade or business of a butcher.

bu·te·o (bū′tē ō) *n.* any of a group of large, mostly Old World hawks, genus *Buteo,* having broad, usually banded tails and rounded wings. [Modern Latin *buteo,* from Latin *būteō* hawk.]

but·ler (but′lər) *n.* a male servant, usually the head servant in a household. [Old French *botillier* one who carries bottles, from *boteille.* See BOTTLE.]

butler's pantry, a serving pantry, esp. between the kitchen and dining room.

butt¹ (but) *n.* **1.** the end of something, esp. the thicker or larger end: *a rifle butt, the butt of a spear.* **2.** a leftover end, esp. the part

of a cigar or cigarette that remains after smoking; stub. **3.** *Informal.* the buttocks. **4.** *Slang.* a cigarette. [Middle English *botte* end of something.]

butt² (but) *n.* **1.** a person or thing that is the object of ridicule, scorn, criticism, or sarcasm: *The royal family was the butt of the satire.* **2.** a target. **3.** an embankment, ditch, or structure on a range in back of a target, designed to protect the marker or stop the projectile. **4. butts.** a target range. [Probably from Old French *but* goal.]

butt³ (but) *v.i.* to push or strike with or as with the head or horns. —*v.t.* to strike or push (something) with or as with the head or horns; ram. —*n.* a push or blow with or as with the head or horns. [Old French *buter* to push; of Germanic origin.]

　•**to butt in.** *Informal.* to interrupt or meddle.

　•**to butt into.** *Informal.* to interrupt or meddle in: *to butt into a conversation.*

butt⁴ (but) *v.t.* to join or meet the edge or end of (something); abut. —*v.i.* to be joined to the edges or ends; abut. [Partly from BUTT¹; partly from BUTT².]

butt⁵ (but) *n.* **1.** a large cask, as for wine, ale, or beer. **2.** a liquid measure for wine, equal to 126 U.S. gallons (479 liters). [Old French *botte* cask, from Late Latin *buttis.* See BOTTLE.]

butte (būt) *n.* (in the western United States) an isolated, usually flat-topped mountain, hill, or pinnacle. [French *butte* rising ground, from Old French *but* goal.]

butte

but·ter (but′ər) *n.* **1.** a yellow or white, semisolid, fatty substance, derived from cream by churning, used esp. as a spread or in cooking. **2.a.** any of several food preparations used as spreads, such as peanut butter. **b.** any of various vegetable oils that have a solid consistency at ordinary temperatures: *cocoa butter.* —*v.t.* **1.** to spread with butter. **2.** *Informal.* to flatter (usually with *up*): *If we butter the teacher up, we may be able to leave early.* [Old English *butere* the substance derived from cream by churning, from Latin *būtȳrum,* from Greek *boutȳron,* from *bous* cow + *tȳros* cheese.]

　•**to know which side one's bread is buttered on.** to know where one's advantage or security lies.

　•**to look as if butter wouldn't melt in one's mouth.** to look innocent and coy.

but·ter-and-eggs (but′ər ən egz′) *n.* a weedy plant, *Linnaria vulgaris,* related to the figwort, bearing yellow and orange flowers. Also, **toadflax.**

butter bean 1. lima bean. **2.** wax bean.

but·ter·cup (but′ər kup′) *n.* **1.** a cup-shaped flower, usually bright yellow, of any of a large group of plants, genus *Ranunculus,* of the crowfoot family, found throughout the world. **2.** any of the plants bearing this flower, many of which have deeply divided leaves resembling a three-toed crow's foot.

but·ter·fat (but′ər fat′) *n.* the yellowish fat in milk, consisting of a mixture of glycerides of fatty acids, from which butter is made.

but·ter·fin·gers (but′ər fing′gərz) *n. Informal.* a person who drops things easily or frequently.

but·ter·fish (but′ər fish′) *n., pl.* **-fish** or **-fish·es.** a saltwater fish, *Poronotus triacanthus,* of the Atlantic coast of North America, which has a silvery blue body and a deeply forked tail, valued as a food fish. Length: 8-12 inches (20-30 centimeters).

but·ter·fly (but′ər flī′) *n., pl.* **-flies. 1.** any of various insects, order Lepidoptera, characterized by slender bodies and four large,

usually bright-colored wings. **2.** a stroke in swimming face down, similar to the breaststroke, in which both arms are brought forward simultaneously over the water, causing the shoulders to lunge out of the water. The arms are then drawn down and back, accompanied by either a dolphin kick or frog kick. **3.** a person who is interested only in self and pleasure; vain, flighty person. **4. butterflies.** an uneasy feeling, esp. in the stomach, as that caused by anxiety over an upcoming performance or event. [Old English *buterflēoge* this insect; possibly so called because it was once believed that witches took the form of butterflies to steal butter or milk.]

butterfly fish

butterfly fish 1. a brightly colored, flat-bodied saltwater fish, family Chaetodontidae, commonly found in warm coral-reef pools. Length: to 2 feet (0.6 meter). **2.** a silvery freshwater fish, family Pantodontidae, found in the swamps of tropical western Africa, having an enormous mouth and large pectoral fins.

butterfly weed, a wildflower, *Asclepias tuberosa,* of the milkweed family, widely distributed throughout the United States, having lance-shaped, hairy leaves and small, loosely clustered orange or orange-and-yellow flowers.

but·ter·milk (but'ər milk') *n.* **1.** a curdled, sour beverage, similar to yogurt, made from skim milk to which certain bacteria cultures have been added. **2.** the liquid remaining after cream has been churned into butter.

but·ter·nut (but'ər nut') *n.* **1.** the edible, oily nut of the tree *Juglans cinerea,* of the walnut family, found in eastern and central North America. **2.** the tree bearing this nut, having coarse-grained, soft wood that is used for furniture and interiors.

butternut squash, a small, pear-shaped winter squash with a smooth, tan skin and orange flesh.

but·ter·scotch (but'ər skoch') *n.* **1.** a hard, sticky candy made from brown sugar, butter, and corn syrup. **2.** a flavoring made from similar ingredients. —*adj.* made or flavored with butterscotch.

but·ter·y[1] (but'ə rē) *adj.* **1.** having the look or taste of butter. **2.** containing or spread with butter. [BUTTER + -Y[1].]

but·ter·y[2] (but'ə rē, but'rē) *n., pl.* **-ter·ies.** a pantry; larder. [Old French *boterie* place to store bottles and casks, from *botte* butt (cask). See BUTT[5].]

but·tock (but'ək) *n.* **1.** either of the two fleshy parts of the body behind the hips. **2. buttocks.** the part of the body that consists of these parts; seat; rump. [Old English *buttuc* rump.]

but·ton (but'ən) *n.* **1.** a small disk, knob, or other object, used esp. to fasten or ornament clothing. **2.** anything resembling a button: *a campaign button, an elevator button.* **3.** the head of a young mushroom. —*v.t.* to fasten with or as with a button or buttons. —*v.i.* to be capable of being fastened with a button or buttons. [Old French *boton* knob sewn to clothing; originally, bud, from *boter* to bud, thrust; of Germanic origin.] —**but'ton·er,** *n.*

• **on the button.** *Informal.* completely right or precise: *Your analysis of the problem was on the button.*

• **to button one's lip.** *Informal.* to be or become silent.

• **to button up.** *Informal.* to be or become silent.

but·ton·hole (but'ən hōl') *n.* a hole or slit through which a button passes. —*v.t.* **-holed, -hol·ing. 1.** to make buttonholes in. **2.** to sew with a buttonhole stitch. **3.** to detain (a person) in conversation as if by seizing the buttonhole of the coat: *The reporters buttonholed the senator.*

but·ton·hook (but'ən hŭk') *n.* a small, metal hook used for pulling small buttons through buttonholes, esp. in shoes or gloves.

but·ton·wood (but'ən wŭd') *n.* a plane tree of North America; sycamore.

but·tress (but'ris) *n.* **1.** a strong or heavy structure, usually of brick or stone, built against a wall or building to strengthen or support it. **2.** any support or prop. —*v.t.* **1.** to support or strengthen with a buttress. **2.** to prop up; support. [Old French *bouterez* (plural) supports, from Old French *boter* to thrust; of Germanic origin.]

bu·tyl (bū'təl) *n.* a univalent radical derived from butane. Formula: C_4H_9

butyl alcohol, any of four colorless, volatile alcohols that are isomers derived from butane, used as solvents. Formula: C_4H_9OH Also, **butanol.**

bu·tyr·ic acid (bū tir'ik) a colorless liquid compound with an unpleasant odor that occurs in rancid milk fats and is a by-product of hydrocarbon synthesis, used esp. in perfume and flavor ingredients and in solvents. Formula: $C_4H_8O_2$ [Latin *būtȳr(um)* butter + -IC; because found in butter. See BUTTER.]

bux·om (buk'səm) *adj.* (of women) plump and healthy; full-bosomed. [Middle English *buxom* humble, obedient, going back to Old English *būgan* to bend; development of meaning from "pliable" to "plump" in Modern English.]

buttress

buy (bī) *v.,* **bought, buy·ing.** —*v.t.* **1.** to acquire possession of (something) by paying money or its equivalent; purchase: *We bought a house. The candidate bought time on television during the campaign.* **2.** to be a means of purchasing an equivalent price for; obtain: *Money cannot buy everything.* **3.** to obtain by exchange or sacrifice: *to buy approval with good deeds.* **4.** to bribe: *That police officer cannot be bought.* **5.** *Informal.* to accept as true; believe: *They wouldn't buy our excuse.* —*v.i.* to make a purchase; be or become a purchaser. —*n. Informal.* **1.** something bought at a lower price than usual; bargain. **2.** something bought, esp. with reference to its value; purchase: *The used car was a good buy.* [Old English *bycgan* to purchase.]

• **to buy into.** to purchase shares, interest, or membership in: *The wealthy banker tried to buy into the exclusive club.*

• **to buy off.** *to attempt to buy off a judge.*

• **to buy out.** to buy all the shares, rights, or interests of: *to buy out a business partner.*

• **to buy up.** to buy the entire supply of: *to buy up all the fresh strawberries in a store.*

Synonyms	*v.t.* **Buy** and **purchase** mean to get something by paying for it. **Buy** is the more general and less

formal word: *to buy a newspaper, to buy a house.* **Purchase** may be simply more formal, or it may suggest the size or importance of what is acquired or the complicated nature of the transaction: *The developer began negotiating to purchase the land for the shopping mall.*

buy·er (bī'ər) *n.* **1.** a person who buys; purchaser. **2.** a person employed to buy merchandise for a retail store: *a buyer of children's clothing for a department store.*

buyer's market, a market in which supplies of a commodity or product are greater than the demand, resulting in lower prices for the buyer. ➡ opposed to **seller's market.**

buy·out (bī'out') *n.* the purchase of all shares, rights, or interests of a person or persons owning some part of a business.

buzz (buz) *n.* **1.** a continuous humming or sharp, rasping sound resembling that made by some insects. **2.** a low sound, as that made by many people engaged in conversation. **3.** a rumor; report. **4.** *Informal.* a telephone call: *Give me a buzz when you get home.* —*v.i.* **1.** to make a continuous humming or sharp, rasping sound: *A mosquito buzzed in my ear.* **2.** to talk excitedly and continuously, esp. in low tones. **3.** to signal by using a buzzer: *The secretary buzzed, but no one answered.* **4.** to move busily or hastily; scurry: *My friend buzzed around town shopping.* —*v.t.* **1.** to utter or express (something) by buzzing: *to buzz rumors.* **2.** to signal with a buzzer. **3.** to produce a buzzing sound with;

a	at	e	end	o	hot	u	up	hw	white		about
ā	ape	ē	me	ō	old	ū	use	ng	song		taken
ä	far	i	it	ô	fork	ü	rule	th	thin	ə	pencil
âr	care	ī	ice	oi	oil	u̇	pull	th	this		lemon
				îr	pierce	ou	out	ûr	turn	zh	measure		circus

cause to buzz: *to buzz an intercom.* **4.** to fly an airplane fast and low over. **5.** *Informal.* to telephone (someone). [Imitative.]

buz·zard (buz′ərd) *n.* **1.** any of various soaring birds of prey, esp. the buteo. **2.** any of various other birds, as the turkey vulture or condor. [Old French *busart* hawk, going back to Latin *būteō.*]

buzz bomb, a self-propelled guided missile used by the Germans esp. against Great Britain during World War II. Also, **robot bomb.**

buzz·er (buz′ər) *n.* a device that produces a buzzing sound.

buzz saw, a power saw that has a rotating circular blade.

buzz·word (buz′wûrd′) *n.* a word or phrase temporarily in fashion, used as part of the jargon of a particular profession, discipline, or group.

bx. *pl.* **bxs.** box.

by (bī) *prep.* **1.** close to; near; beside: *A tree stands by the house.* **2.** up to and beyond; past: *The bus sped by us.* **3.** through the action, means, agency, or use of: *to take by force, to be destroyed by fire.* **4.** on the evidence or authority of; according to: *to go by the rules.* **5.** on the part of: *The accident was regretted by all concerned.* **6.** by way of; through: *We came by the northern route.* **7.** during the course of: *by day.* **8.** not later than: *Be here by eight o'clock.* **9.** in the direction of; toward: *north by northwest.* **10.** in the presence of; before: *I swear by all that is holy.* **11.** according to (a fixed standard); in terms of: *We buy milk by the gallon. The clerk measured the cloth by the yard.* **12.** in relation to; with respect to; regarding: *The young attorney did well by her family.* **13.** in immediate succession to; after: *piece by piece, one by one.* **14.** in or to the extent or amount of: *older by five years, smaller by a third.* **15.** combined in multiplication or measurement with: *to multiply 3 by 4, to measure 9 by 12 feet.* —*adv.* **1.** at hand; near: *close by.* **2.** alongside and beyond: *to run by.* **3.** past; over: *in years gone by.* **4.** *Informal.* at or into another's house, office, or the like: *I'll stop by on my way to the store.* —*adj.* bye. [Old English *bī* near, according to, through.]

  • **by and by.** in the near future; before long.

  • **by and large.** on the whole: *By and large, you did a good job.*

  • **by oneself.** without the presence or help of anyone else; alone.

  • **by the by** (or **bye**). by the way; incidentally.

by- *prefix* **1.** of less importance; secondary: *by-product, by-election.* **2.** near by: *bystander.* **3.** aside: *byway, bystreet.* [From BY (adverb).]

by-and-by (bī′ən bī′) *n.* a future time: *in the sweet by-and-by.*

bye (bī) *n.* **1.** a right, earned by being seeded or gained by draw, to enter subsequent rounds in an elimination tournament without competing in one or more earlier rounds. **2.** a hole or holes left unplayed after a match-play golf tournament has been won. —*adj.* **1.** *also,* **by.** of secondary importance; incidental. **2.** situated to one side. [Form of BY (preposition).]

  • **by the bye** (or **by**). by the way; incidentally.

bye-bye (bī′bī′) *interj. Informal.* good-bye.

by·e·lec·tion (bī′i lek′shən) *n. British.* a special election held to fill a vacancy in office.

Bye·lo·rus·sian (byel′ō rush′ən) *n.* **1.** a native or inhabitant of Byelorussia (now Belarus). **2.** the Slavic language of these people, closely related to Russian and Ukrainian. —*adj.* of, relating to, or characteristic of Byelorussia or its people, language, or culture. Also, **White Russian.**

by·gone (bī′gôn′, -gon′) *adj.* gone by; past; former. —*n. also,* **bygones.** something gone by or past.

  • **to let bygones be bygones.** to let past disagreements or hatreds be forgotten.

by·law (bī′lô′) *n.* a law or rule regulating the internal affairs of a government body, corporation, or organization. [Middle English *bilawe* literally, town law, going back to Old Norse *bӯr* town + *lög* law.]

by·line (bī′līn′) *n.* the name of the writer of a newspaper or magazine article printed at the beginning or end of the article.

by·name (bī′nām′) *n.* **1.** a secondary name; surname. **2.** a nickname.

by·pass (bī′pas′) *n.* **1.** a road designed to enable a motorist to avoid a congested route or place or an obstruction, as an urban center. **2.** a pipe or channel for temporarily diverting the flow of a liquid or gas from a main pipe. **3.** a surgical operation in which a diseased part, as a blocked artery, is circumvented. **4.** *Electricity.* shunt *(def. 3).* —*v.t.* **1.** to go around or avoid by or as if by a bypass. **2.** to cause (a liquid or gas) to follow a bypass. **3.** to furnish with a bypass.

by·path (bī′path′) *n., pl.* **-paths** (-pathz′, -paths′). a private or side path.

by·play (bī′plā′) *n.* actions or conversations that take place apart from the main action or conversation, esp. in a theatrical production.

by-prod·uct (bī′prod′əkt) *also,* **by·prod·uct.** *n.* something, often useful, that results from the manufacture of something else; secondary or incidental product.

by·road (bī′rōd′) *n.* a road that is out of the way or rarely used; side road.

By·ron·ic (bī ron′ik) *adj.* **1.** of or relating to the English poet Lord Byron or his works. **2.** like or characteristic of Byron or his works, esp. romantic or heroic.

bys·si·no·sis (bis′ə nō′sis) *n.* a lung disease caused by long-term occupational inhalation of dust from unprocessed cotton. Also, **brown lung.**

by·stand·er (bī′stan′dər) *n.* a person who is present but does not take an active part.

by·street (bī′strēt′) *n.* a street that is out of the way or rarely used; side street.

byte (bīt) *n. Computers.* **1.** a group of eight bits treated as a unit. One byte can store a single alphabetical character or numerical symbol. **2.** a memory cell that can store eight bits of information. [Perhaps a form of BITE; influenced by BIT⁴.]

by·way (bī′wā′) *n.* **1.** a secluded or rarely traveled road; side road. **2.** a subordinate, minor, or obscure aspect of an area of interest.

by·word (bī′wûrd′) *n.* **1.** a person or thing that is thought of or spoken of as being representative or typical of a particular quality: *The company's name became a byword for quality.* **2.** a proverbial or common saying. **3.** an object of contempt or scorn: *Genghis Khan became a byword for cruelty and wanton destruction.* **4.** a word or phrase associated with or typical of a person. [Old English *bīword* proverb.]

Byz·an·tine (biz′ən tēn′, -tīn′, bi zan′tin) *adj.* **1.** of or relating to Byzantium, the Byzantine Empire, or its art or culture. **2.** of, relating to, or having the characteristics of a style of architecture developed in the Byzantine Empire during the fifth and sixth centuries. Byzantine architecture is characterized by the use of round arches, domes, rich mosaic decorations, and centralized plans. —*n.* a native, inhabitant, or citizen of ancient Byzantium.

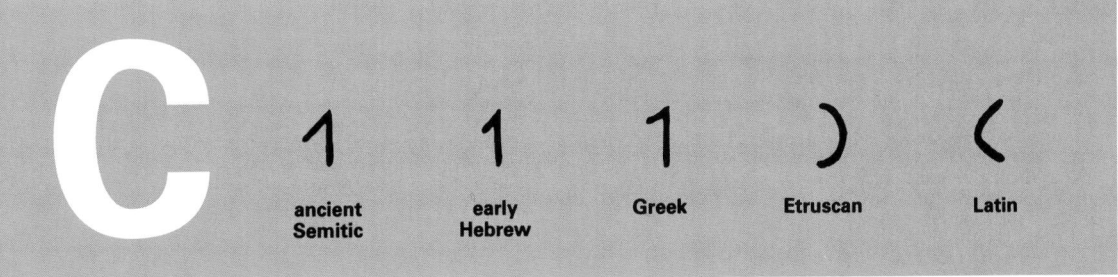

| ancient Semitic | early Hebrew | Greek | Etruscan | Latin |

C

The letter **C** representing the hard *k* sound did not develop until Roman times. Its earliest ancestor was *gimel*, meaning "camel," the third letter of the ancient Semitic alphabets, which stood for the hard *g* sound. The early Hebrew form of *gimel* was borrowed by the Greeks, who called it *gamma*. About 400 B.C., the Etruscans began using a form of *gamma* to stand for both the hard *g* and the hard *k* sound, and this form was adopted by the early Romans for their Latin alphabet. Since in Latin the *k* sound was more common than the hard *g* sound, the letter **C** became more and more identified with the *k* sound. Around the third century B.C., the Romans began to use **C** only for the *k* sound and devised a new letter for the *g* sound. When the Anglo-Saxons adopted the Latin alphabet, they continued to use **C** for the *k* sound. Later, some **C**'s were pronounced *ch*. The sound of *c* in *grace* became part of Middle English when certain French words came into the language. In modern English, **C** can represent all of these sounds.

c, C (sē) *n., pl.* **c's, C's. 1.** the third letter of the English alphabet. **2.** the shape of this letter or something having this shape. **3.** the third item in a series or group.

C (sē) *n., pl.* **C's. 1.** *Music.* **a.** the first note or tone of the diatonic scale of C major. For illustration, see **do**[2]. **b.** the scale or key that has this note or tone as its tonic. **2.** a grade or rating indicating average performance: *a C student.* **3.** *also,* **c** the Roman numeral for 100.

C, the symbol for carbon.

c *also,* **c. 1.** centimeter; centimeters. **2.** cubic.

c. 1. *Baseball.* catcher. **2.** cent; cents. **3.** center. **4.** century. **5.** circa. **6.** copyright.

C 1. Celsius. **2.** centigrade.

C. 1. Cape. **2.** Catholic. **3.** Celtic. **4.** Conservative. **5.** Corps. **6.** Court.

Ca, the symbol for calcium.

ca. *also,* **Ca** circa.

CA, the postal abbreviation for California.

C.A., Central America.

Caa·ba (kä′bə) Kaaba.

cab (kab) *n.* **1.** taxicab. **2.** any of various carriages for hire with a driver, such as a hansom, brougham, or cabriolet. **3.** the enclosed or covered part of a truck, locomotive, steam shovel, or the like, where the controls and operator are housed. [Short for CABRIOLET.]

ca·bal (kə bal′) *n.* **1.** a small group of people secretly united to advance themselves or their aims by scheming and intrigue. **2.** a scheme or intrigue developed by such a group; plot. —*v.i.,* **-balled, -bal·ling.** to form or join in a cabal; conspire. [French *cabale* intrigue, cabala, from Medieval Latin *cab(b)ala* (the cabala having been associated with secrecy and magic in the Middle Ages). See CABALA.]

cab·a·la (kab′ə lə, kə bä′-) *also,* **cab·ba·la, kab·a·la, kab·ba·la.** *n.* **1.** an occult system of religious philosophy developed in the Middle Ages by Jewish rabbis, based on a mystical interpretation of the Scriptures. **2.** any esoteric or occult doctrine. [Medieval Latin *cab(b)ala,* transliteration of Hebrew *qabbālāh* tradition.] —**cab′a·list,** *n.*

cab·al·le·ro (kab′əl yâr′ō, kab′ə lâr′ō) *n., pl.* **-ros. 1.** a Spanish gentleman, knight, or cavalier. **2.** horseman. **3.** a lady's escort or admirer. [Spanish *caballero,* from Late Latin *caballārius.* See CAVALIER.]

ca·ba·na (kə ban′ə, -ban′yə) *n.* **1.** a small shelter at a swimming area, used as a bathhouse. **2.** a summer cottage; cabin. [Spanish *cabaña* hut, from Late Latin *capanna;* of uncertain origin.]

cab·a·ret (kab′ə rā′) *n.* **1.** a restaurant or café providing food and drink, dancing, and entertainment; nightclub. **2.** the entertainment provided by such an establishment. [French *cabaret* tavern, possibly going back to Late Latin *camera.* See CHAMBER.]

cab·bage (kab′ij) *n.* **1.** the leafy head of a plant, *Brassica oleracea capitata,* of the mustard family, having thick, coarsely veined, green or reddish purple leaves, eaten as a vegetable either raw or cooked. **2.** the plant itself, widely cultivated in temperate regions. [Dialectal Old French *caboche* head, probably going back to Latin *caput;* referring to its shape.]

cabbage butterfly, a common butterfly, *Pieris rapae,* with white wings bearing several black spots. Its green larvae feed on cabbage and related plants. Wingspread: 1¾ inches (4 centimeters).

cabbage palm, any of several tropical American palm trees having edible leaf buds.

cab·ba·la (kab′ə lə, kə bä′-) cabala.

cab·by (kab′ē) *also,* **cabbie.** *n., pl.* **-bies.** *Informal.* cabdriver.

cab·driv·er (kab′drī′vər) *n.* the driver of a cab, esp. of a taxicab.

cab·in (kab′in) *n.* **1.** a small, simply constructed house, usually having only one story; cottage. **2.a.** a room or compartment serving as living or working quarters on a ship. **b.** a compartment below the deck of a small boat, providing living quarters or shelter. **3.** an enclosed space for passengers, crew, or cargo in an aircraft or spacecraft. —*v.i.* to live in a cabin. —*v.t.* to confine; cramp. [French *cabane* hut, going back to Late Latin *capanna;* of uncertain origin.]

cabin boy, a boy or man who waits on a ship's officers and passengers.

cabin class, a class of accommodations on a passenger ship, below first class and above tourist class.

cabin cruiser, a powerboat equipped with living facilities.

cab·i·net (kab′ə nit) *n.* **1.** a piece of furniture fitted with shelves or drawers and often having doors, for storing or displaying objects; cupboard: *a kitchen cabinet, a china cabinet.* **2.** *also,* **Cabinet.** an official council that advises the chief executive or sovereign of a nation or state, usually composed of the heads of various departments of the government: *a policy set by a cabinet.* **3.** *Archaic.* a small, private room. —*adj.* **1.** of or relating to a political cabinet. **2.** of such value, size, or beauty as to be kept or displayed in a cabinet. **3.** *Archaic.* private; confidential; secret. [Middle French *cabinet* small room, piece of furniture, diminutive of dialectal Old French *cabine* gambling house; of uncertain origin.]

cab·i·net·mak·er (kab′ə nit mā′kər) *n.* a person who makes or repairs fine furniture and woodwork.

cab·i·net·mak·ing (kab′ə nit mā′king) *n.* the business, craft, or skill of making and repairing fine furniture and woodwork.

cab·i·net·work (kab′ə nit wûrk′) *n.* **1.** any fine furniture or woodwork. **2.** the making of fine furniture or woodwork.

ca·ble (kā′bəl) *n.* **1.** a strong, thick rope, esp. one made of wires twisted together. **2.** *Nautical.* **a.** a heavy rope or

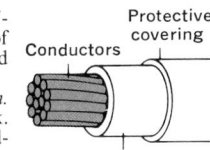

cable
(n., def. 3)

a	at	e	end	o	hot	u	up	hw	white		about
ā	ape	ē	end	ō	old	ū	use	ng	song		taken
ä	far	i	it	ô	fork	ü	rule	th	thin	ə	pencil
âr	care	ī	ice	oi	oil	u̇	pull	th	this		lemon
		îr	pierce	ou	out	ûr	turn	zh	measure		circus

165

chain used to moor a vessel. **b.** cable's length. **3.** an electrical transmission line consisting of one or more conductors enclosed in a protective covering. **4.** cablegram. **5.** cable TV. —*adj.* relating to, providing, or transmitted by cable TV: *cable movies.* —*v.,* -**bled, -bling.** —*v.t.* **1.** to fasten with or as with a cable. **2.** to furnish with a cable or cables. **3.** to transmit (a message) by underwater cable. **4.** to send a cablegram to. —*v.i.* to transmit a message by underwater cable. [Old French *cable* thick rope, from Late Latin *capulum* halter, from Latin *capere* to hold.]

cable car, a car drawn by an overhead cable or pulled along rails by an underground cable, used to carry passengers or cargo up and down steep grades.

ca·ble·cast (kā′bəl kast′) *n.* a program broadcast by cable TV. —*v.t.,* -**cast** or -**cast·ed, -casting.** to broadcast by cable TV.

ca·ble·gram (kā′bəl gram′) *n.* a message sent by underwater telegraph cable. [CABLE + -GRAM¹.]

cable railway, a railway on which cable cars are drawn by an underground cable driven by a stationary engine.

cable's length, a unit of measurement equal to 720 feet (219 meters) or 120 fathoms, in U.S. usage, or 608 feet (185 meters), ¹/₁₀ of a nautical mile, in British usage.

cable TV, a system for transmitting television programs by cable to the individual sets of subscribers who pay for such a service. Also, **cable, cable television.**

cab·man (kab′mən) *n., pl.* -**men** (-mən). cabdriver.

cab·o·chon (kab′ə shon′) *n.* a precious stone polished to a smooth, convex shape without facets. [Old French *cabochon,* from *caboche* head. See CABBAGE.]

ca·boo·dle (kə bü′dəl) *n. Informal.* collection; lot; group. [Possibly contraction of the phrase *whole kit and boodle.* See KIT¹, BOODLE.]

ca·boose (kə büs′) *n.* a railroad car, usually at the rear of a freight train, used by train and railroad workers. [Middle Dutch *kabuys* ship's kitchen or galley, possibly contraction of *kaban huys* cabin house.]

cab·ri·o·let (kab′rē ə lā′) *n.* **1.** a light, one-horse carriage, usually two-wheeled, with a folding top. **2.** an early automobile of the coupe type, with a convertible top. [French *cabriolet* one-horse carriage, diminutive of *cabriole* leap, from Italian *capriola* leap (like that of a goat), going back to Latin *caper* goat; because the light carriage bounced, when in motion, like a goat leaping.]

ca·ca·o (kə kā′ō, -kā′ō) *n., pl.* -**ca·os. 1.** the nutlike seed of an evergreen tree, genus *Theobroma,* cultivated in tropical regions and valued as the source of cocoa, chocolate, and cocoa butter. **2.** the wide, branching tree that produces this seed. [Spanish *cacao,* from Nahuatl *cacauatl* this tree.]

cac·cia·to·re (kach′ə tôr′ē, kä′chə-) *adj.* cooked with tomatoes, herbs and spices, and often dry white wine: *veal cacciatore, chicken cacciatore.* [Italian *cacciatore* hunter; because this was a traditional way a hunter would prepare food.]

cach·a·lot (kash′ə lot′, -lō′) *n.* sperm whale. [French *cachalot,* from Portuguese *cachalote;* of uncertain origin.]

cache (kash) *n.* **1.** a hiding place for storing things, as provisions or treasure. **2.** something hidden or stored in such a place. —*v.t.,* **cached, cach·ing.** to hide or store in a cache. [French *cache* hiding place, from *cacher* to hide, going back to Latin *coāctāre* to force.]

ca·chet (ka shā′) *n.* **1.** a seal or stamp, as on an official letter or document. **2.** a distinguishing mark, feature, or quality, such as one conferring prestige or establishing authenticity. **3.** a design or slogan stamped or printed on mail. [French *cachet* seal, from *cacher* to press, hide. See CACHE.]

ca·chex·i·a (kə kek′sē ə) *n.* a condition of severe generalized weakness, malnutrition, and emaciation, as is often associated with a chronic disease. [Modern Latin *cachexia,* from Greek *kachexia* bad condition of the body, from *kachos* bad + *hexis* condition, habit.] —**ca·chec·tic** (kə kek′tik), **ca·chex′ic,** *adj.*

cach·in·nate (kak′ə nāt′) *v.i.,* -**nat·ed, -nat·ing.** to laugh loudly or with too much vigor. [Latin *cachinnātus,* past participle of *cachinnāre.*] —**cach′in·na′tion,** *n.*

ca·cique (kə sēk′) *n.* a native chief among the Indians of the West Indies, Mexico, and other parts of Latin America. [Spanish *cacique;* of Carib origin.]

cack·le (kak′əl) *v.,* -**led, -ling.** —*v.i.* **1.** to utter a shrill, broken cry, as a hen makes after laying an egg. **2.** to laugh or talk with such a sound: *The children cackled at the funny story.* —*v.t.* to utter or express in a cackling manner: *to cackle one's disapproval.* —*n.* **1.** the act or sound of cackling. **2.** shrill, broken laughter or chatter. **3.** idle talk; chatter. [Imitative.] —**cack′ler,** *n.*

cac·o·mis·tle (kak′ə mis′əl) *n.* a raccoonlike mammal, *Bassariscus astutus,* native to woods and rocky hillsides from Oregon to Mexico, having a pointed muzzle, large eyes, pale yellowish gray fur, and a long tail ringed with black and white bands.

Length: 32 inches (81 centimeters), including tail. [Spanish *cacomiztle,* from Nahuatl *claco* half + *miztli* lion.]

ca·coph·o·ny (kə kof′ə nē) *n., pl.* -**nies.** harsh or unpleasant sound; dissonance; discord. [Greek *kakophōniā* harsh sound.] —**ca·coph′o·nous,** *adj.*

cac·tus (kak′təs) *n., pl.* -**ti** (-tī) or -**tus·es** or -**tus.** any of a large group of succulents, family Cactaceae, including vines, shrubs, and trees, found chiefly in desert regions of North and South America. Cacti usually have a central, woody stem surrounded by thick, pulpy tissue in which water is stored, a leathery skin, and spines or scales. Many species bear beautiful flowers and edible fruits. [Latin *cactus* a prickly plant found in Sicily, from Greek *kaktos.*]

barrel **cactus**

cad (kad) *n.* a boy or man who does not behave like a gentleman; ill-bred or ill-mannered person. [Short for CADDIE.]

CAD, computer-aided design.

ca·dav·er (kə dav′ər) *n.* a dead body, esp. a corpse prepared or used for dissection. [Latin *cadāver.*]

ca·dav·er·ous (kə dav′ər əs) *adj.* of, relating to, or like a corpse; pale; ghastly; gaunt.

cad·die (kad′ē) *also,* **caddy.** *n.* a person who assists a golfer, as by carrying golf clubs. —*v.i.,* -**died, -dy·ing.** to act as a caddy. [French *cadet* younger son, young officer. See CADET.]

cad·dis·fly (kad′is flī′) *n., pl.* -**flies.** a small, mothlike insect, order Trichoptera, whose larva lives in fresh water. [Of uncertain origin.]

cad·dish (kad′ish) *adj.* characteristic of or like a cad; ungentlemanly. —**cad′dish·ly,** *adv.* —**cad′dish·ness,** *n.*

cad·dis·worm (kad′is wûrm′) *n.* the larva of a caddisfly, used as bait by anglers.

Cad·do (kad′ō) *n., pl.* -**do** or -**dos.** a member of an American Indian tribe that lived in what is now southwestern Arkansas, Louisiana, and eastern Texas.

cad·dy¹ (kad′ē) *n., pl.* -**dies.** a small box, can, or chest, esp. one used to hold tea. [Malay *kātī* a weight of 1¹/₃ pounds (0.6 kilogram).]

cad·dy² (kad′ē) *n., pl.* -**dies.** caddie. —*v.i.,* -**died, -dy·ing.** caddie.

ca·dence (kā′dəns) *n.* **1.** a rhythmic flow or pattern, as in poetry, speech, or natural sounds; rhythm. **2.** a measure or beat of any rhythmical movement, such as dancing or marching. **3.** the fall of the voice, as at the end of a sentence. **4.** the rising and falling of sound, esp. modulation of the voice. **5.** *Music.* **a.** a melodic or harmonic sequence that concludes a phrase, passage, movement, or composition. **b.** cadenza. [French *cadence,* from Italian *cadenza,* from Late Latin *cadentia* falling (as of dice), from Latin *cadere* to fall. Doublet of CADENZA, CHANCE.] —**ca′denced,** *adj.*

ca·den·za (kə den′zə) *n. Music.* an elaborate and technically difficult passage for solo voice or instrument, usually occurring near the end of an aria, a movement of a concerto, or other musical composition. [Italian *cadenza,* from Late Latin *cadentia* falling (as of dice), from Latin *cadere* to fall. Doublet of CADENCE, CHANCE.]

ca·det (kə det′) *n.* **1.a.** a student in a military academy in training for service as an officer. **b.** a student in a military school. **2.** a younger son or brother. [French *cadet,* from Gascon dialect *capdet* chief, going back to Late Latin *capitellum* small head, diminutive of Latin *caput* head.] —**ca·det′ship′,** *n.*

cadge (kaj) *Informal. v.,* **cadged, cadg·ing.** —*v.t.* to get by

begging. —*v.i.* to beg; sponge. [Of uncertain origin.] —**cadg′-er,** *n.*

ca·di (kä′dē, kā′-) *n., pl.* **-dis.** a minor Muslim magistrate or judge, usually of a town or village. [Arabic *qādī* judge.]

Cad·me·an (kad mē′ən) *adj.* of, relating to, or like Cadmus.

cad·mi·um (kad′mē əm) *n.* a soft, malleable, ductile, metallic element, with a bluish white luster, obtained as a by-product of zinc refining. Cadmium resembles zinc in appearance and behavior and is used esp. to plate steel and other metals for corrosion resistance. Symbol: **Cd** For tables, see **element.** [Modern Latin *cadmium,* from Latin *cadmīa* calamine (cadmium being found with calamine in zinc ore), from Greek *kadmeiā (gē)* Cadmean (earth), calamine, from *Kadmos* Cadmus, legendary founder of Thebes, where calamine supposedly was first found.]

Cad·mus (kad′məs) *n.* in Greek mythology, a Phoenician prince who founded the Greek city of Thebes, along with five other men. He killed a dragon and sowed its teeth, from which many men sprang who fought each other until only five remained.

cad·re (kad′rē, -rā, kä′drā) *n.* **1.** framework; frame. **2.** a nucleus of military personnel necessary for the establishment and training of a new unit. **3.** the personnel forming the nucleus of a larger group or organization. **4.** a member of a cadre. [French *cadre,* from Italian *quadro* framework, square, painting, from Latin *quadrus* square.]

ca·du·ce·us (kə dū′sē əs, -dū′-) *n., pl.* **-ce·i** (-sē ī′). **1.** a wand or staff carried by an ancient Greek or Roman herald, esp. the winged staff with two snakes twined around it carried by Mercury, or Hermes, as the herald of the gods. **2.** a similar staff used as the emblem of the medical profession. [Latin *cādūceus* herald's staff, from dialectal Greek *kārykeion.*] —**ca·du′ce·an,** *adj.*

cae·cil·i·an (sē sil′ē ən) *n.* any of a group of limbless, burrowing tropical amphibians, order Gymnophiona, resembling earthworms. [Latin *caecilia* lizard + -AN.]

cae·cum (sē′kəm) cecum.

Cae·sar (sē′zər) *n.* **1.** a title used by the Roman emperors from Augustus to Hadrian and also by certain later rulers, as the Holy Roman and Byzantine emperors. **2.** any emperor. **3.** a dictator; tyrant. [From Gaius Julius *Caesar,* 100?-44 B.C., Roman statesman and general.]

Cae·sar·e·an (si zâr′ē ən) *also,* **Cae·sar·i·an, Ce·sar·e·an, Ce·sar·i·an.** *adj.* of or relating to Julius Caesar or the Caesars. —*n.* **caesarean.** cesarean section.

caesarean section, cesarean section.

cae·sar·ism (sē′zə riz′əm) *n.* imperial or military absolutism.

cae·si·um (sē′zē əm) cesium.

caes·tus (ses′təs) cestus.

cae·su·ra (si zhŭr′ə, -zŭr′ə) *also,* **cesura.** *n., pl.* **-su·ras** or **-su·rae** (-zhŭr′ē, -zŭr′ē). a pause or break in a line of verse. In English poetry a caesura is usually linked to a pause or break in the sense of the line. [Latin *caesūra* literally, a cutting off.]

ca·fé (ka fā′, kə-) *also,* **ca·fe.** *n.* **1.** a coffeehouse or restaurant. **2.** a barroom, cabaret, or nightclub. **3.** coffee. [French *café* coffee, coffeehouse, Italian *caffè,* from Turkish *kahveh.* See COFFEE.]

ca·fé au lait (ka fā ō lā′) **1.** coffee with milk or cream, esp. strong coffee with an equal quantity of scalded milk. **2.** a soft, pale brown color.

caf·e·te·ri·a (kaf′i tîr′ē ə) *n.* a restaurant in which customers buy food at a counter and carry it to a table themselves. [Spanish *cafetería* coffee shop, from *café* coffee, from Italian *caffè,* from Turkish *kahveh.* See COFFEE.]

caf·feine (ka fēn′, kaf′ēn, kaf′ē in) *also,* **caf·fein.** *n.* an odorless, bitter white alkaloid that stimulates the central nervous system, found esp. in coffee, tea, and cola. Caffeine is used medicinally to treat migraine headaches and fatigue. Formula: $C_8H_{10}N_4O_2 \cdot H_2O$ [French *caféine,* from *café* coffee. See CAFÉ.]

caf·tan (kaf′tən, käf tän′) *also,* **kaftan.** *n.* **1.** a long, sashed robe that is worn as an outer garment, usually over a shirt and trousers and under a coat, esp. in certain Middle Eastern countries. **2.** a long, usually collarless robe with wide, loose-fitting sleeves, often worn by women in the West for lounging. [Turkish *qaftan* dress.]

cage (kāj) *n.* **1.** a boxlike structure or enclosure for confining birds or animals, usually having openwork of wires or bars. **2.** anything like a cage in form or function, as the enclosed platform of certain elevators or a cashier's window. **3.** anything that confines or imprisons; prison. **4.** *Baseball.* a movable screen placed behind home plate during batting practice or the area enclosed by this screen. **5.** *Hockey.* a framed net structure serving as a goal. **6.** *Basketball.* basket. —*v.t.,* **caged, cag·ing.** to put

or confine in or as in a cage. [Old French *cage* enclosure for animals, from Latin *cavea.*]

cage·ling (kāj′ling) *n.* a caged bird.

cage·y (kā′jē) *also,* **cag·y.** *adj.,* **cag·i·er, cag·i·est.** *Informal.* wary of being tricked; shrewd; cautious. [Of unknown origin.] —**cag′i·ly,** *adv.* —**cag′i·ness,** *n.*

ca·hoots (kə hüts′) *n. Slang.* **1. in cahoots.** in partnership, esp. secretly: *The mayor was in cahoots with some shady developers.* **2. to go cahoots.** to be partners; share equally: *The friends went cahoots in the purchase of the boat.* [Possibly from French *cahute* hut, blend of *cabane* hut (see CABIN) and *hutte* hut (of Germanic origin).]

CAI, computer-aided instruction.

cai·man (kā′mən) *also,* **cayman.** *n., pl.* **-men** (-mən). any of several aquatic reptiles, order Crocodylia, of Central and South America, closely related to and resembling the alligator. Length: to 15 feet (4.6 meters). [Spanish *caimán;* of Carib origin.]

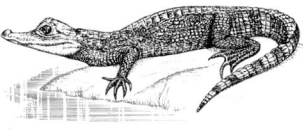
caiman

Cain (kān) *n.* a murderer, esp. of a brother. [From *Cain,* in the Old Testament, the oldest son of Adam and Eve, who murdered his brother Abel.]

•**to raise Cain.** *Slang.* to make a great disturbance; cause a commotion.

ca·ique (kä ēk′) *n.* **1.** a long, narrow rowboat, popular in Turkey. **2.** a sailboat popular in the eastern Mediterranean. [French *caïque,* from Italian *caicco,* from Turkish *qāïq* boat.]

cairn (kârn) *n.* a mound of stones piled up as a memorial or landmark. [Gaelic *carn* heap of stones.]

cairn terrier, a small terrier of a breed originally developed on the Isle of Skye, having a short, wide head, short, pointed ears, and a shaggy coat. Height: 10 inches (25 centimeters) at the shoulder. [Supposedly because it hunts among *cairns.*]

cais·son (kā′sən, -son) *n.* **1.a.** a large, boxlike or cylindrical structure used for laying underwater foundations, as for a bridge. In a **pneumatic caisson** there is an airtight work chamber at the bottom into which compressed air is pumped to force out the water and which workers enter through an air lock. **b.** a similar structure sunk into the ground so that soil can be removed and replaced by concrete to form part of a foundation. **2.** a watertight container that is attached to a sunken ship and filled with air. The buoyancy of the caisson helps to raise the ship to the surface. **3.** a box for ammunition. **4.** *Artillery.* an ammunition wagon composed of a limber and detachable two-wheeled vehicle. [French *caisson* ammunition wagon, coffer, from *caisse* chest, going back to Latin *capsa* box.]

caisson disease, the bends (bend, *def.* 4).

cai·tiff (kā′tif) *n.* a base, despicable, or cowardly person; scoundrel. —*adj.* base, despicable, or cowardly. [Dialectal Old French *caitif* captive, wretched man, going back to Latin *captīvus* captive. Doublet of CAPTIVE.]

ca·jole (kə jōl′) *v.t.,* **-joled, -jol·ing.** to coax or persuade by flattery, soothing words, or false promises; wheedle: *The salesperson tried to cajole the couple into buying a new vacuum cleaner.* [French *cajoler* to coax; originally, to chatter like a bird in a cage, probably modification (influenced by French *cage* CAGE) of Middle French *gaioler* to chatter like a bird in a cage, from dialectal Old French *gaiole* cage, going back to Latin *cavea.*] —**ca·jol′er,** *n.* —**ca·jol′ing·ly,** *adv.* —**ca·jol′ment,** *n.* —For Synonyms, see **coax.**

ca·jol·er·y (kə jō′lə rē) *n., pl.* **-er·ies.** persuasion by flattery, soothing words, or false promises.

Ca·jun (kā′jən) *n.* **1.** a descendant of the French who formerly lived in Acadia and settled in Louisiana in the eighteenth century. **2.** the French dialect spoken by the Cajuns. —*adj.* of, relating to, or characteristic of the Cajuns: *Cajun music, Cajun cooking.* [Modification of ACADIAN.]

cake (kāk) *n.* **1.** a baked mixture of various ingredients, such as flour, sugar, eggs, and flavoring, often covered with icing: *a chocolate cake.* **2.** a flat, thin portion of dough or batter that is baked or fried, as a pancake. **3.** any flat mass of food: *a crab cake.* **4.** a shaped, flattened, or compressed mass: *a cake of soap.* —*v.t., v.i.,*

a	at	e	end	o	hot	u	up	hw	white
ā	ape	ē	me	ō	old	ū	use	ng	song
ä	far	i	it	ô	fork	ü	rule	th	thin
âr	care	ī	ice	oi	oil	u̇	pull	th	this
		îr	pierce	ou	out	ûr	turn	zh	measure

ə { about / taken / pencil / lemon / circus

C

caked, cak·ing. to form into a hardened mass or crust. [Old Norse *kaka* small mass of baked dough.]
  • **a piece of cake.** *Informal.* something done with ease or pleasure.
  • **to take the cake.** *Informal.* **a.** to win first prize. **b.** to surpass others, esp. in some negative quality: *Their stupidity takes the cake.*

cakes and ale, the good things of life; material pleasures.

cake·walk (kāk'wôk') *n.* **1.** formerly, a march or promenade originated by American blacks in which a cake was awarded to the person or couple who performed the most original and intricate steps. **2.** a dance developed from this promenade. **3.** the music for this dance. —*v.i.* to participate in a cakewalk. —**cake'-walk'er,** *n.*

cal. 1. calendar. **2.** caliber.

Cal., California.

cal·a·bash (kal'ə bash') *n.* **1.** gourd. **2.** the dried fruit of a tropical American tree, *Crescentia cujete,* used for bowls, dippers, and water jugs. **3.** something made from this fruit, such as a bowl or tobacco pipe. **4.** the tree bearing this fruit, having large horizontal branches that bear clusters of leaves at intervals. [French *calebasse* gourd, from Spanish *calabaza,* possibly from Persian *kharbuz* melon, or from Arabic *qar*' gourd + *yābis* dry.]

cal·a·boose (kal'ə büs') *n. Informal.* jail; lockup. [Spanish *calabozo* prison, possibly from Arabic *qal'a* castle + *būs* hidden.]

ca·la·di·um (kə lā'dē əm) *n.* any of a group of small tropical plants, genus *Caladium,* of the arum family, having heart-shaped or spade-shaped leaves with red, pink, violet, or yellow patterns, popular as a houseplant. [Modern Latin *Caladium,* from Malay *keladi* a plant of this genus.]

cal·a·mine (kal'ə mīn', -min) *n.* **1.** hemimorphite. **2.** an odorless pink powder made from a mixture of zinc oxide and ferric oxide, used medicinally in lotions and ointments to reduce inflammation of the skin. [French *calamine,* from Medieval Latin *calamina,* modification of Latin *cadmīa,* from Greek *kadmeiā.* See CADMIUM.]

ca·lam·i·tous (kə lam'i təs) *adj.* marked by or causing calamity; disastrous. —**ca·lam'i·tous·ly,** *adv.* —**ca·lam'i·tous·ness,** *n.*

ca·lam·i·ty (kə lam'i tē) *n., pl.* **-ties. 1.** an event that causes great misfortune; disaster. **2.** great suffering or distress; misery. [Latin *calāmitās* misfortune.] —For Synonyms, see **disaster.**

cal·a·mus (kal'ə məs) *n., pl.* **-mi** (-mī'). **1.** sweet flag. **2.** any tropical climbing palm, genus *Calamus,* yielding rattan. **3.** the lower part of the shaft of a feather; quill. [Latin *calamus* reed, from Greek *kalamos.*]

ca·lash (kə lash') *also,* **calèche.** *n.* **1.** a light, low-wheeled carriage, usually having a folding top. **2.** a folding hood or top of a carriage. **3.** a woman's bonnet that folds back like a carriage top, worn esp. in the eighteenth century. [French *calèche,* from German *Kalesche* light carriage, from Polish *kolaska* small carriage, from *kolo* wheel.]

cal·ca·ne·us (kal kā'nē əs) *n., pl.* **-ne·i** (-nē ī'). **1.** the large bone of the ankle that forms the heel in humans. **2.** a corresponding bone in other vertebrates. Also, **cal·ca'ne·um.** [Late Latin *calcaneus,* from Latin *calcaneum,* from *calx* the heel.] —**cal·ca'-ne·al,** *adj.*

cal·car·e·ous (kal kâr'ē əs) *adj.* consisting of or containing calcium, calcium carbonate, or lime; chalky. [Latin *calcārius* relating to lime, from *calx* lime. See CALX.]

cal·ces (kal'sēz) a plural of **calx.**

cal·cic (kal'sik) *adj.* of, derived from, or containing calcium or lime.

cal·cif·er·ol (kal sif'ə rôl', -rōl') *n.* a form of vitamin D, derived from ergosterol by exposing it to ultraviolet light. [CAL-CIF(EROUS) + (ERGOST)EROL.]

cal·cif·er·ous (kal sif'ər əs) *adj.* yielding or containing calcite. [Latin *calc-,* stem of *calx* lime + FERROUS. See CALX.]

cal·ci·fi·ca·tion (kal'sə fi kā'shən) *n.* **1.** the process of calcifying, esp. the depositing of lime salts in organic tissue and bone. **2.** a calcified formation or structure.

cal·ci·fy (kal'sə fī') *v.t., v.i.,* **-fied, -fy·ing.** to harden or become hard or bony by the deposit of lime salts.

cal·ci·mine (kal'sə mīn', -min) *also,* **kalsomine.** *n.* a white or colored wash consisting of whiting or zinc white, water, and glue, used esp. on plastered ceilings and walls. —*v.t.,* **-mined, -min·ing.** to cover with calcimine.

cal·ci·na·tion (kal'sə nā'shən) *n.* the act or process of calcining.

cal·cine (kal'sīn) *v.,* **-cined, -cin·ing.** —*v.t.* to cause (a substance) to lose moisture or impurities or to be oxidized or reduced by heating to a high temperature. Limestone is calcined to make lime. —*v.i.* to undergo calcination. [French *calciner,* going back to *calx* lime. See CALX.]

cal·cite (kal'sīt) *n.* a translucent white or transparent mineral, calcium carbonate, the chief constituent of limestone, chalk, and marble. It is one of the most common minerals.

cal·ci·to·nin (kal'si tō'nin) *n.* a hormone that regulates the balance of calcium and phosphate in the blood, secreted by the thyroid gland.

cal·ci·um (kal'sē əm) *n.* a malleable, ductile, silver-white metallic element that is the most abundant mineral in the human body and is essential for the growth of bones and teeth, as well as for normal functioning of nerves, muscles, and the heart. It is found in chalk, limestone, and marble. Symbol: Ca For tables, see **element.** [Modern Latin *calcium,* from Latin *calx* lime; because it is found in lime. See CALX.]

calcium carbide, a lumpy, grayish black compound produced in an electric furnace from the reaction of coke or anthracite coal with crushed limestone, used to form acetylene gas and calcium cyanamide. Formula: CaC_2

calcium carbonate, a compound of calcium, carbon, and oxygen that is a white powder or colorless crystals in its pure state and occurs in nature as chalk, limestone, marble, and several other mineral forms. It is used in medicines as an antacid and is used in baking powder, tooth powders, and cement. Formula: $CaCO_3$

calcium chloride, a water-absorbing compound of calcium and chlorine in the form of colorless crystals, used esp. as a drying agent and antifreeze. Formula: $CaCl_2$

calcium cyanamide, a grayish black lumpy or powdered compound that decomposes in water to yield ammonia and acetylene, used in fertilizers and weed killers. Formula: $CaCN_2$

calcium cyanide, a poisonous, gray compound, used esp. as a fumigating agent and pesticide. Formula: $Ca(CN)_2$

calcium hydroxide, slaked lime.

calcium oxide, a white, caustic compound, the chief constituent of lime, obtained by calcining limestone. Formula: CaO

calcium phosphate, any of several phosphates of calcium found in some rocks and in various animal tissue, used in various products, as medicines, cleaning agents, and fertilizers.

cal·cu·la·ble (kal'kyə lə bəl) *adj.* **1.** capable of being calculated. **2.** able to be relied on; dependable. —**cal'cu·la·bil'i·ty,** *n.* —**cal'cu·la·bly,** *adv.*

cal·cu·late (kal'kyə lāt') *v.,* **-lat·ed, -lat·ing.** —*v.t.* **1.** to determine by arithmetical methods; compute. **2.** to figure out beforehand by reasoning; estimate: *to calculate the time needed to make a trip.* **3.** to plan; intend: *The speech was calculated to win votes.* **4.** *Informal.* to think; suppose; guess. —*v.i.* **1.** to perform an arithmetical process; compute. **2.** to rely or count (with *on* or *upon*): *The farmer calculated on good spring weather.* [Late Latin *calculātus,* past participle of *calculāre* to compute, reckon, from Latin *calculus* small stone, diminutive of *calx* limestone; reckoning was often done in ancient times with the aid of stones used as counters. See CALX.]

Synonyms *v.t.* **Calculate, estimate, compute,** and **reckon** mean to determine an amount, price, or the like by mathematical operations. **Calculate** is the most general of these words, but often is used specifically of intricate operations that do not yield an exact or easily confirmable result: *The weather bureau calculated the chances that the storm would blow out to sea.* **Estimate** suggests an even less certain result: *The sales director estimates that next year's income will be $3 million, but there are many variables.* **Compute** suggests a mechanical process of arriving at an answer from given figures through the use of standard formulas: *With all this data it should be easy to compute the costs of the project.* **Reckon** is a less formal word than the others, suggesting the use of relatively simple arithmetical means and not necessarily implying an exact result: *The speaker reckoned the odds of the bill's passage as poor.*

cal·cu·lat·ed (kal'kyə lā'tid) *adj.* **1.** done, attempted, or undertaken after estimating the probable results: *a calculated risk.* **2.** done on purpose; deliberate; planned; intended: *the calculated cruelty of a dictator.* **3.** done or ascertained by mathematical calculation.

cal·cu·lat·ing (kal'kyə lā'ting) *adj.* **1.** given to or characterized by careful or shrewd thought and planning: *a calculating defense attorney.* **2.** scheming and selfish: *a calculating embezzler.* **3.** that calculates: *a calculating machine.*

cal·cu·la·tion (kal'kyə lā'shən) *n.* **1.** the act or process of calculating. **2.** a product or result of calculating. **3.** careful or shrewd planning, often for selfish gain: *Their actions were spontaneous and without calculation.* —**cal'cu·la'tive,** *adj.*

cal·cu·la·tor (kal'kyə lā'tər) *n.* **1.** a person who calculates. **2.** a machine for performing mathematical operations mechanically or electronically.

cal·cu·lous (kal'kyə ləs) *adj. Medicine.* having or produced by one or more stony masses, or calculi, such as kidney stones. [Latin *calculosus,* from *calculus* small stone + *-osus* (see -OUS).]

cal·cu·lus (kalʹkyə ləs) *n., pl.* **-li** (-lī′) or **-lus·es**. **1.** any of several systematic methods of calculation in higher mathematics, using a special system of algebraic notation. **Differential calculus** deals with the rates at which quantities change. **Integral calculus** develops methods for finding the areas enclosed by curved boundaries. **2.** an abnormal stonelike mass of mineral matter formed in a duct or organ of the body. Kidney stones are calculi. [Latin *calculus* small stone, calculation. See CALCULATE.]

cal·de·ra (kal därʹə) *n.* a broad crater or basin formed by an unusually powerful volcanic explosion or by the collapse of the flanks of a volcano. [From *Caldera*, a crater in the Canary Islands, from *caldera* pot, cauldron, from Late Latin *caldāria*, from Latin *caldārius* pertaining to warmth.]

cal·dron (kôlʹdrən) cauldron.

ca·lèche (kə leshʹ) calash.

Cal·e·do·ni·a (kalʹi dōʹnē ə) *n.* Scotland. ➡ used chiefly in literature. —**Cal′e·do′ni·an**, *adj., n.*

cal·en·dar (kalʹən dər) *n.* **1.** a table showing the days, weeks, and months of a given year. **2.** a method of dividing time into fixed intervals, esp. with reference to the beginning, length, and division of the year. **3.** a list, register, or schedule, esp. one arranged in chronological order, as a list of cases to be tried in court or of bills to be considered by a legislature. —*v.t.* to enter in a calendar; list. [Medieval Latin *kalendarium*, from Latin *calendārium* account book, from *calendae* calends, the day on which accounts were due for payment in ancient Rome.]

calendar month, month *(def. 1).*

calendar year, year *(def. 1).*

cal·en·der (kalʹən dər) *n.* a machine consisting of a number of rollers through which cloth, paper, or other material is passed in order to produce a desired finish or a uniform thickness. —*v.t.* to press in a calender. [French *calandre* this machine, probably going back to Greek *kylindros* cylinder, roller.]

cal·ends (kalʹəndz) *also,* **kalends.** *pl. n.* the first day of the month in the ancient Roman calendar. ➡ used as singular or plural. [Latin *calendae.*]

ca·len·du·la (kə lenʹjə lə) *n.* any of a group of plants, genus *Calendula,* of the composite family, bearing bright yellow or orange flowers. [Modern Latin *Calendula,* diminutive of Latin *calendae* calends. It supposedly bloomed on the first day of the month.]

cal·en·ture (kalʹən chər) *n.* a tropical fever accompanied by delirium and hallucinations, thought to be caused by excessive heat. [Spanish *calentura* fever, going back to Latin *calēre* to be hot.]

calf[1] (kaf) *n., pl.* **calves. 1.** the young of various bovine animals, esp. of the domestic cow. **2.** the young of various other mammals, as the elephant, whale, and seal. **3.** calfskin. **4.** a silly or awkward youth. [Old English *cealf* young of bovine animals.]
  · **to kill the fatted calf.** to prepare a great feast, celebration, or welcome.

calf[2] (kaf) *n., pl.* **calves.** the fleshy part of the back of the leg between the knee and ankle. [Old Norse *kālfi.*]

calf·skin (kafʹskin′) *n.* **1.** the skin or hide of a calf. **2.** the soft leather made from it.

cal·i·ber (kalʹə bər) *also,* **cal·i·bre.** *n.* **1.** the diameter of a round body, esp. the internal diameter of a hollow tube. **2.a.** the diameter of the bore of a gun. **b.** the diameter of a bullet or shell. **3.** degree of ability, merit, excellence, or worth; quality: *a learned judge of high caliber, to improve the caliber of the schools.* [French *calibre* sort, bore of a gun, through Italian *calibro,* from Arabic *qālib* mold[1], model, probably from Greek *kālopous* shoemaker's last; literally, wooden foot.]

cal·i·brate (kalʹə brāt′) *v.t.,* **-brat·ed, -brat·ing. 1.** to determine, check, or correct the graduations of (a thermometer or similar measuring instrument). **2.** to determine the caliber of. —**cal′i·bra′tion,** *n.* —**cal′i·bra′tor,** *n.*

cal·i·co (kalʹi kō′) *n., pl.* **-coes** or **-cos.** a cotton fabric printed with small, usually brightly colored motifs. —*adj.* **1.** made of calico. **2.** resembling calico; spotted or mottled: *a calico cat.* [From *Calicut,* port of India, from which this fabric was first imported.]

cal·i·co·back (kalʹi kō bak′) *n.* harlequin bug.

ca·lif (kāʹlif, kalʹif) caliph.

Calif., California.

ca·lif·ate (kāʹlə fāt′, -fit, kalʹə-) caliphate.

Cal·i·for·nia condor (kalʹə fôrnʹyə, -fôrʹnē ə) a nearly extinct American vulture, *Gymnogyps californianus,* formerly found in the mountains of southern and central California. It is mostly black with white wing linings and a naked orange head. It feeds on carrion. Average length: 4 feet (1.2 meters); average wingspan: 9 feet (2.7 meters). For illustration, see **condor.**

California poppy 1. the saucer-shaped flower of any of several plants, genus *Eschscholzia,* of the poppy family and esp. *E. califor-*

nica, bearing four petals ranging in color from pale yellow to orange. **2.** the plant itself.

cal·i·for·ni·um (kalʹə fôrʹnē əm) *n.* a radioactive element produced artificially from curium. Symbol: Cf For tables, see **element.** [Modern Latin *californium,* from *California,* where it was discovered.]

cal·i·per (kalʹə pər) *also,* **calliper.** *n.* **1.** *also,* **calipers.** a hinged instrument resembling a pair of tongs, used esp. to measure the internal or external dimensions of a small object. **2.** caliper rule. [Form of CALIBER.]

caliper rule, a graduated rule with one stationary jaw and one sliding jaw.

ca·liph (kāʹlif, kalʹif) *also,* **calif, kaliph, kalif.** *n.* formerly, the successor of Muhammad as the religious and secular head of Islam. ➡ used as a title. [Old French *calife,* from Arabic *khalīfa* successor.]

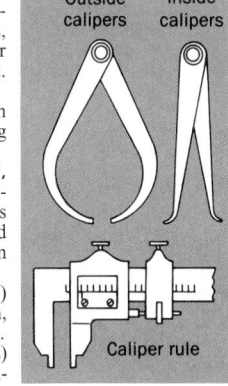

Outside calipers · Inside calipers

Caliper rule

calipers

ca·liph·ate (kāʹlə fāt′, -fit, kalʹə-) *also,* **califate.** *n.* the office, reign, government, or territory of a caliph.

cal·is·then·ics (kalʹəs thenʹiks) *also,* **callisthenics.** *n.* **1.** light gymnastic exercises designed to develop strength and grace and to promote good health. **2.** the science or practice of such exercises. ➡ used as plural in def. 1, as singular in def. 2. [Greek *kallos* beauty + *sthenos* strength + -ICS.] —**cal′is·then′ic,** *adj.*

ca·lix (kāʹliks, kalʹiks) calyx *(def. 2).*

calk[1] (kôk) caulk.

calk[2] (kôk) *n.* **1.** one of the projecting pieces of a horseshoe that grips the ground and prevents the horse from slipping. **2.** a sharp, projecting piece of metal on the bottom of the heel or toe of a shoe or boot to prevent slipping. —*v.t.* furnish with calks. [Short for earlier *calkin,* from Old French *calcain* heel, from Latin *calcāneum.*]

calk·er (kôʹkər) caulker.

call (kôl) *v.t.* **1.** to utter or read in a loud voice: *The teacher called the roll.* **2.** to command or request the presence or attendance of; summon: *to call someone to testify in a case, to call a cab.* **3.** to cause to assemble or begin officially; convene: *to call a meeting.* **4.** to summon to a special duty, office, or activity: *to be called to the army.* **5.** to arouse from sleep; waken: *Call me for breakfast at seven o'clock.* **6.** to make a telephone call to: *I'll call you from the airport when I arrive.* **7.** to attract or lure (birds or animals) by imitating their characteristic sound. **8.** to give a name to; name: *We decided to call the puppy Rover.* **9.** to characterize as or designate in some way: *I call him an honest man.* **10.** to consider or estimate to be: *Although all the votes were not counted, they called it a Republican victory.* **11.** to give an order for; order: *The union called a strike.* **12.** to cause to come; bring: *The photographs called my childhood to mind.* **13.** to announce beforehand or predict: *to call heads or tails, to call a pool shot.* **14.** *Sports.* **a.** to declare (a player, play, or the like) officially to be; rule: *The umpire called the pitch a strike.* **b.** to choose and signal (a particular play): *The quarterback called a short pass.* **15.** *Baseball.* to stop or suspend (a game): *The game was called on account of rain.* **16.** *Poker.* to demand a show of hands by equaling the bet of (another). **17.** to demand payment of: *to call a loan.* **18.** to demand for payment or redemption: *The company will call its bonds April first.* **19.** to utter the directions for (a square dance). —*v.i.* **1.** to speak loudly; shout: *to call for help.* **2.** to make a short visit or stop: *We called at her house yesterday.* **3.** to make a telephone call. **4.** *Poker.* to equal the last bet. —*n.* **1.** an act or instance of calling; shout or cry. **2.a.** the characteristic sound or cry of a bird or animal. **b.** a device that produces an imitation of such a sound, in order to attract or lure birds or animals. **3.** a request or order to go somewhere or do something; invitation or summons: *The speech was a call to revolution.* **4.** a signal or summons as played on a drum or bugle: *Reveille is the first call of the day.* **5.** a claim; demand: *Busy people have many calls on their time.* **6.** a need or cause; reason: *There was no call*

a	at	e	end	o	hot	u	up	hw	white		about
ā	ape	ē	me	ō	old	ū	use	ng	song		taken
ä	far	i	it	ô	fork	ü	rule	th	thin	ə	pencil
âr	care	ī	ice	oi	oil	u̇	pull	t͟h	this		lemon
		îr	pierce	ou	out	ûr	turn	zh	measure		circus

for them to be so rude. **7.** a short, usually formal, visit or stop. **8.** an act or instance of communicating by telephone. **9.** roll call. **10.** a power or force that attracts: *the call of the wild.* **11.** a request for an item, service, or the like: *The company no longer gets any calls for that model.* **12.** a demand for payment or redemption of money. **13.** calling *(def. 2)*. **14.** *Poker.* an act or instance of demanding a show of hands by equaling the bet of another. **15.** *Sports.* a ruling by a game official. **16.** a direction given to square dancers by a caller. [Old English *ceallian* to cry out, shout, from Old Norse *kalla.*]

- **on call. a.** available if summoned: *The doctor was on call all weekend.* **b.** subject to payment or return on demand.
- **to call back. a.** to ask or command (a person) to return. **b.** to telephone again or in return.
- **to call down. a.** to invoke from above: *to call down the wrath of God.* **b.** *Informal.* to scold; rebuke; reprimand.
- **to call for. a.** to go and get; stop to obtain (something or someone): *We called for the packages at the post office.* **b.** to have need of; demand or require: *This crisis calls for action. The recipe calls for butter.* **c.** to be an appropriate occasion or reason for: *Your promotion calls for a celebration.*
- **to call forth.** to summon into action; evoke: *to call forth one's courage in a crisis.*
- **to call in. a.** to demand repayment of, as money or debts. **b.** to withdraw from circulation, as currency. **c.** to summon or invite, as for assistance or consultation: *to call in an expert.*
- **to call into** (or **in**) **question.** to doubt the truth or accuracy of.
- **to call off. a.** to cancel, as something previously scheduled. **b.** to command to withdraw: *The guard called off the dog.* **c.** to read aloud: *He called off the names of the winners.*
- **to call on** (or **upon**). **a.** to make a brief visit to. **b.** to appeal to or demand from: *The police called on the citizens to fight crime.* **c.** to ask (a person) to speak or give an answer: *The teacher called on me.*
- **to call out.** to summon into service; order into action: *The governor called out the National Guard.*
- **to call up. a.** to telephone. **b.** to bring or summon into action or discussion: *to be called up for military duty.* **c.** to bring to mind; remember. **d.** to display on the screen of a computer: *to call up a file.*
- **within call.** within hearing distance; nearby: *She said she would stay within call.*

Synonyms *v.t.* **Call** and **summon** mean to request someone or something to come. **Call** is the general word, used in all contexts: *to call a child in for supper, to call employees to a meeting.* **Summon** is more formal, is used only of persons, and suggests authority or power: *The president summoned the members of the cabinet. I was summoned to the principal's office.*

cal·la (kal′ə) *n.* **1.** any of a group of plants, genus *Zantedeschia,* found in southern Africa, bearing tiny flowers on a spike inside a showy, usually white or yellow spathe. Also, **calla lily.** **2.** a marsh plant, *Calla palustris,* in North America, Europe, and Asia, bearing heart-shaped leaves and tiny flowers in a spike inside a showy white spathe. [Modern Latin *Calla,* from Latin *calla* name of a plant.]

call·back (kôl′bak′) *n.* **1.** the return to work of employees previously laid off. **2.** recall *(def. 3).*

call·boy (kôl′boi′) *n.* **1.** a boy or man who summons actors or other performers when it is time for them to appear on stage. **2.** bellboy.

call·er (kô′lər) *n.* **1.** a person who makes a short visit. **2.** a person or thing that calls. **3.** a person who calls directions to dancers in a square dance.

cal·lig·ra·phy (kə lig′rə fē) *n.* **1.** beautiful or elegant handwriting. **2.** the art of writing beautifully or elegantly. **3.** handwriting; penmanship. [Greek *kalligraphiā* beautiful writing, going back to *kallos* beauty + *graphein* to write.] —**cal·lig′ra·pher, cal·lig′ra·phist,** *n.* —**cal·li·graph·ic** (kal′i graf′ik), *adj.*

call·ing (kô′ling) *n.* **1.** profession; vocation. **2.** a strong impulse toward a course of action, esp. of a religious nature: *a calling to enter the ministry.* Also, **call. 3.** the act of a person or thing that calls, esp. crying or shouting aloud.

calling card, a small card with one's name on it, used for social purposes. Also, **visiting card.**

cal·li·o·pe (kə lī′ə pē′; *def. 1, also* kal′ē ōp′) *n.* **1.** a musical instrument consisting of a series of steam whistles, played by means of a keyboard. **2.** **Calliope.** in Greek mythology, the Muse of eloquence and epic poetry. [Latin *Calliopē* the Muse,

from *Kalliopē* literally, beautiful-voiced, from *kallos* beauty + *ops* voice.]

cal·li·op·sis (kal′ē op′sis) *n.* any of several species of coreopsis.

cal·li·per (kal′ə pər) caliper.

cal·lis·then·ics (kal′əs then′iks) calisthenics.

Cal·lis·to (kə lis′tō) *n.* **1.** in Greek mythology, a nymph loved by Zeus, changed into a bear by the jealous Hera, and set among the constellations as Ursa Major by Zeus. **2.** a moon of Jupiter.

call letters, the letters that identify a radio or television transmitting station.

call loan, a loan that must be repaid on demand.

call number, a number and letter code used in a library to classify a book according to its subject and its location on the shelves.

cal·los·i·ty (kə los′i tē) *n., pl.* **-ties. 1.** callus *(defs. 1, 3).* **2.** the quality or state of being hardened in mind or feeling; insensitivity.

cal·lous (kal′əs) *adj.* **1.** thickened and hardened, as a callus on the skin. **2.** hardened in mind or feelings; unfeeling; insensitive. —*v.t., v.i.* to make or become callous. [Latin *callōsus* hardskinned.] —**cal′lous·ly,** *adv.* —**cal′lous·ness,** *n.*

cal·low (kal′ō) *adj.* **1.** lacking in experience or maturity; immature: *a callow youth.* **2.** (of a young bird) lacking sufficient feathers for flight; unfledged. [Old English *calu* bald.] —**cal′low·ness,** *n.*

call-up (kôl′up′) *n.* **1.** an order to report for active military service, usually issued to reserves. **2.** the total number of reservists or civilians included in such an order.

cal·lus (kal′əs) *n., pl.* **-lus·es. 1.** a hardened and thickened area of the skin. **2.** a new growth of bony tissue that forms between and around the ends of a fractured bone and reunites them. **3.** a hardened, thickened layer of tissue that forms over a wound of a plant. [Latin *callus* hardened skin.]

calm (käm) *adj.* **1.** without or nearly without wind or motion; not stormy: *a calm sea.* **2.** free from excitement, nervousness, or strong emotion; undisturbed by passion; quiet; serene: *The crowd remained calm during the blackout.* —*n.* **1.** the condition or a period of being without motion or wind; stillness. **2.** in meteorology, a state in which the wind velocity is less than 1 mile (1.6 kilometers) per hour or in which there is no wind at all. **3.** freedom from excitement, nervousness, or strong emotion; tranquillity; serenity. —*v.t., v.i.* to make or become calm or quiet (often with *down*): *The mother calmed her child. He calmed down after the argument.* [French *calme* quiet, from Italian *calma* rest, going back to Greek *kauma* heat of the sun or the day (at which time flocks and people rested in the shade).] —**calm′ly,** *adv.* —**calm′ness,** *n.*

Synonyms *adj.* **Calm, tranquil, serene,** and **placid,** when used of persons or personal behavior, mean peaceful and free from agitation or excitement. **Calm** suggests the weathering of a crisis or the exercise of self-control: *The captain remained calm throughout the storm.* **Tranquil** implies more depth than *calm* and may suggest an inner peace that has not been troubled: *Country people seemed tranquil to me when I moved from the city.* **Serene** adds a suggestion of sublime peacefulness, such as may come from religious or philosophical acceptance of things as they are: *In the wisdom gained through a long life, the couple lived a serene old age.* **Placid** suggests a smooth exterior and may imply ignorance or an unwillingness to recognize trouble: *Even the perilous situation did not change the mystic's placid expression.*

cal·o·mel (kal′ə mel′, -məl) *n.* a white, tasteless, crystalline powder, used esp. as an insecticide, antiseptic, or laxative. Formula: Hg_2Cl_2 Also, **mercurous chloride.** [French *calomel,* from Greek *kalos* beautiful + *melās* black.]

ca·lor·ic (kə lôr′ik, -lor′-) *adj.* of or relating to heat or calories. —*n.* formerly, a hypothetical substance to which the sensation and phenomena of heat were attributed.

cal·o·rie (kal′ə rē) *also,* **calory.** *n., pl.* **-ries. 1.** the quantity of heat required to raise the temperature of 1 gram of water 1 degree centigrade. Also, **small** (or **gram**) **calorie. 2.** the quantity of heat, equal to 1,000 gram calories, required to raise the temperature of 1 kilogram of water 1 degree centigrade. Also, **large** (or **kilogram**) **calorie. 3.** a unit equivalent to the large calorie, used to measure the heat output of organisms or the energy-producing value of food. **4.** the quantity of food having such an energy-producing value. [French *calorie* small calorie, from Latin *calor* heat.]

cal·o·rif·ic (kal′ə rif′ik) *adj.* relating to or producing heat.

cal·o·rim·e·ter (kal′ə rim′i tər) *n.* an apparatus for measuring the amount of heat emitted or absorbed by a substance or for determining the specific heat of a substance. —**cal·o·ri·met·ric** (kal′ər ə met′rik), *adj.* —**cal·o·rim′e·try,** *n.*

cal·o·ry (kal′ə rē) *n., pl.* **-ries.** calorie.

cal·u·met (kal′yə met′, kal′yə met′) *n.* peace pipe. [Dialectal French *calumet* herb stem, pipe, going back to Latin *calamus* reed, from Greek *kalamos*.]

ca·lum·ni·ate (kə lum′nē āt′) *v.t.,* **-at·ed, -at·ing.** to utter false and malicious statements or accusations about; slander. [Latin *calumniātus,* past participle of *calumniārī* to slander.] —**ca·lum′ni·a′tion,** *n.* —**ca·lum′ni·a′tor,** *n.*

ca·lum·ni·ous (kə lum′nē əs) *adj.* containing or characterized by calumny; slanderous: *the calumnious rumors being circulated to discredit the candidate.* Also, **ca·lum·ni·a·to·ry** (kə lum′nē ə tôr′ē). —**ca·lum′ni·ous·ly,** *adv.*

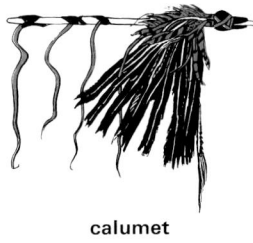

calumet

cal·um·ny (kal′əm nē) *n., pl.* **-nies. 1.** a false and malicious statement or accusation intended to damage the reputation of a person or thing. **2.** the uttering of such statements or accusations. [French *calomnie,* from Latin *calumnia* false accusation. Doublet of CHALLENGE.]

calve (kav) *v.t., v.i.,* **calved, calv·ing.** to give birth to (a calf). [Old English *cealfian,* from *cealf.* See CALF[1].]

calves (kavz) the plural of **calf.**

Cal·vin·ism (kal′və niz′əm) *n.* the religious teachings of the French theologian John Calvin and his followers, which emphasize the omnipotence of God, the base state of human beings, the doctrine of predestination and salvation through God's grace alone, and an austere moral code. —**Cal′vin·ist,** *n., adj.* —**Cal′vin·ist′ic,** *adj.*

calx (kalks) *n., pl.* **calx·es** or **cal·ces.** the ashy powder left after a metal or mineral substance has been calcined. [Latin *calx* lime, limestone, stone, probably from Greek *chalix* pebble.]

cal·y·ces (kal′ə sēz′, kā′lə-) a plural of **calyx.**

ca·lyp·so (kə lip′sō) *n., pl.* **-sos.** an improvised song, originally from the West Indies, usually dealing with subjects that are humorous or of current interest. [Possibly from CALYPSO.]

Ca·lyp·so (kə lip′sō) *n.* in Greek legend, a sea nymph who detained the shipwrecked Odysseus on an island for seven years.

ca·lyx (kā′liks, kal′iks) *n., pl.* **ca·lyx·es** or **cal·y·ces. 1.** the circle of sepals that surrounds an unopened flower and usually folds back beneath the petals when the bud opens. For illustration, see **sepal. 2.** a cup-shaped anatomical feature. Also *(def. 2),* **calix.** [Latin *calyx* covering, calyx, from Greek *kalyx* shell, calyx.]

cal·zo·ne (kal zō′nā, -zōn′) *n.* a large turnover made of pizza dough, with a cheese, meat, or other filling. [Italian *calzone* literally, trouser leg, from *calza* stocking, going back to Latin *calx* heel.]

cam (kam) *n.* a projection on a shaft that changes a rotating motion into a back-and-forth linear motion. [Dutch *kam* cog, comb.]

CAM, computer-aided manufacturing.

ca·ma·ra·de·rie (kam′ə rad′ə rē, kä′mə rä′də rē) *n.* friendliness and loyalty among comrades; fellowship; comradeship. [French *camaraderie,* from *camarade.* See COMRADE.]

cam·ass (kam′əs) *also,* **cam·as.** *n.* any of a group of ornamental plants, genus *Camassia,* of the lily family, esp. *C. quamash,* of the northwestern United States, bearing sword-shaped leaves and clusters of blue or white flowers. [Chinook jargon *kamass.*]

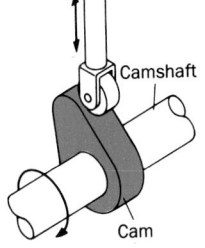

cam

cam·ber (kam′bər) *v.t., v.i.* to bend or curve upward in the middle; arch slightly. —*n.* **1.** a slight arch or convexity of a surface, as of a beam or road. **2.** in aeronautics, the curvature of a line midway between the curving upper and lower surfaces of an airfoil. **3.** the inward or outward tilt of a wheel of an automobile, adjusted so that a pair of wheels are closer together at the bottom than at the top. [Old French *cambre* bent, from Latin *camur* crooked.]

cam·bi·um (kam′bē əm) *n.* a layer of growth tissue between the bark and the wood of trees and woody plants that gives rise to cells for both new bark and new wood. [Late Latin *cambium* exchange, from Latin *cambiāre* to exchange.] —**cam·bi·al** (kam′bē əl), *adj.*

Cam·bo·di·an (kam bō′dē ən) *adj.* of, relating to, or characteristic of Cambodia or its people, language, or culture. Also, **Kampuchean.** —*n.* **1.** a person who is a native or citizen of Cambo-

dia. **2.** a person of Cambodian ancestry. Also *(defs. 1, 2),* **Kampuchean. 3.** Khmer *(def. 2).*

Cam·bri·a (kam′brē ə) *n.* Wales. ➡ used primarily in literature.

Cam·bri·an (kam′brē ən) *n.* **1.** the first geologic period of the Paleozoic era, during which shelled marine invertebrates became common. For table, see **geologic time. 2.** a native or inhabitant of Cambria; Welshman. —*adj.* **1.** of, relating to, or characteristic of the Cambrian period. **2.** of or relating to Cambria; Welsh.

cam·bric (kām′brik) *n.* a soft, lightweight linen or cotton fabric. [From the former Flemish town *Kamerijk* (now *Cambrai,* in France), where this fabric was first made.]

cambric tea, a drink made with hot water, milk, sugar, and usually, a little tea.

Cam·bridge University (kām′brij) a university in Cambridge, England.

cam·cord·er (kam′kôr′dər) *n.* a portable television camera and videotape recorder in a single unit. [CAM(ERA) + (RE)CORDER.]

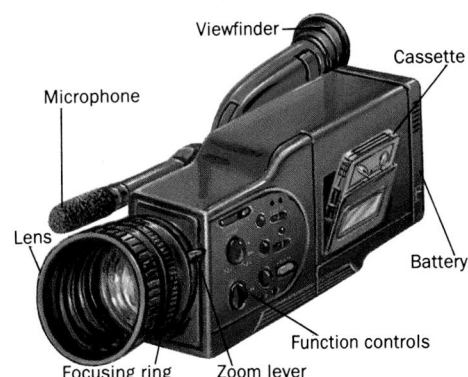

camcorder

came (kām) the past tense of **come.**

cam·el (kam′əl) *n.* **1.** any of various cud-chewing mammals, genus *Camelus,* of the desert regions of Africa, Asia, Asia Minor, and Arabia, having a humped back, a sandy white to deep brown coat, and cloven hoofs, valued for riding, as a beast of burden, and as a source of meat, milk, and leather. There are two species of camels: the dromedary, having one hump, and the Bactrian camel, having two humps. Height: 7 feet (2.1 meters) at the hump. For illustrations, see **Bactrian camel** and **dromedary. 2.** a medium tan color. —*adj.* having the color camel. [Old English *camel,* from Latin *camēlus,* from Greek *kamēlos,* from Hebrew *gāmāl.*]

cam·el·eer (kam′ə lîr′) *n.* a camel driver.

ca·mel·lia (kə mēl′yə, -mē′lē ə) *n.* **1.** the fragrant flower of any of a group of shrubs and trees, genus *Camellia,* of the tea family, widely cultivated in warm, damp regions and having white, red, or pink petals. **2.** the woody plant bearing this flower. [From the seventeenth-century Jesuit missionary G. J. *Kamel* (Latinized form of his name: *Camellus*), 1661-1706, who introduced it to Europe from the East.]

ca·mel·o·pard (kə mel′ə pärd′) *n. Archaic.* giraffe. [Latin *camēlopardālis,* from Greek *kamēlopardālis,* from *kamēlos* camel + *pardalis* leopard; because its head resembles a camel's and its spots, a leopard's. See CAMEL.]

Cam·e·lot (kam′ə lot′) *n.* **1.** the legendary site of King Arthur's court. **2.** a time or place characterized by idyllic aspects associated with King Arthur's court, such as great happiness or beauty.

camel's hair 1. the hair of a camel. **2.** a soft, usually tan-colored fabric made of this hair alone or in combination with wool, used for coats, suits, and sweaters.

Cam·em·bert (kam′əm bâr′) *n.* a rich, creamy soft cheese with a pungent flavor. [From the French village *Camembert,* where it was first made.]

cam·e·o (kam′ē ō′) *n., pl.* **-e·os. 1.** a piece of jewelry made from a precious or semiprecious stone or a shell having a raised design carved on it. The stone often consists of different colored layers, as onyx, so that the darker layer can serve as a background

a	at	e	end	o	hot	u	up	hw	white
ā	ape	ē	me	ō	old	ū	use	ng	song
ä	far	i	it	ô	fork	ü	rule	th	thin
âr	care	ī	ice	oi	oil	ů	pull	th	this
		îr	pierce	ou	out	ûr	turn	zh	measure

ə { about taken pencil lemon circus

for the figure carved in relief from the lighter part. **2.** a brief role in a single scene in a motion picture or television show, esp. when done by a prominent actor or actress. [Italian *cammeo;* of uncertain origin.]

cam·er·a (kam′ər ə, kam′rə) *n., pl. (defs. 1, 2)* **-er·as** or *(def. 3)* **-er·ae** (-ə rē) **1.** a device for taking photographs consisting of a lightproof box with a lens and shutter through which light is admitted and an image focused on a light-sensitive film or plate. **2.** a device that transforms an image into electrical impulses for transmission, as in television. **3.** a judge's private office. [Short for Latin *camera obscura* dark chamber (the name for the forerunner of this device), from Late Latin *camera* room, chamber, from Latin *camera* arch, vault, from Greek *kamarā* vault. Doublet of CHAMBER.]
  · **in camera. a.** in a judge's office in privacy: *a court hearing held in camera.* **b.** privately.
  · **on** (or **off**) **camera.** before (or out of the range of) a camera that is broadcasting or filming: *The senator looked nervous when on camera.*

cam·er·al (kam′ər əl) *adj.* of or relating to a legislature or a judge's chambers.

camera lu·ci·da (lü′si də) an instrument consisting of a glass prism mounted on a stand in such a manner that the image of an object appears as if projected on a flat surface, upon which it can be traced. [Modern Latin *camera lucida* literally, light chamber. See CAMERA, LUCID.]

cam·er·a·man (kam′ər ə man′, -mən, kam′rə-) *n., pl.* **-men** (-men′, -mən). a person whose job is operating a motion-picture or television camera.

camera ob·scu·ra (ob skyůr′ə) a device consisting of a darkened box into which light enters through a small opening or lens in one side and an image is formed on the opposite side and reflected by a mirror onto a wall or screen. It was the forerunner of the modern camera. [Modern Latin *camera obscura* literally, dark chamber. See CAMERA, OBSCURE.]

cam·er·a·shy (kam′ər ə shī′, kam′rə-) *adj.* embarrassed or unwilling to be photographed.

cam·er·a·wom·an (kam′ər ə wům′ən, kam′rə-) *n., pl.* **-wom·en** (-wim′ən). a woman whose job is operating a motion-picture or television camera.

cam·i·on (kam′ē ən) *n.* **1.** a heavy wagon or cart; dray. **2.** a truck, esp. one used for carrying military supplies or artillery. [French *camion;* of uncertain origin.]

cam·i·sole (kam′ə sōl′) *n.* a woman's undergarment that resembles the top of a slip. [French *camisole* woman's jacket, going back to Late Latin *camisia* shirt; of uncertain origin.]

cam·o·mile (kam′ə mīl′, -mēl′) chamomile.

cam·ou·flage (kam′ə fläzh′) *n.* **1.** *Military.* the act, process, or result of disguising or changing the appearance of soldiers, equipment, or installations to conceal them from the enemy, as by using paint, nets, or foliage. **2.** any disguise or behavior that serves to conceal or deceive, as the protective coloration of an animal. —*v.t.*, **-flaged, -flag·ing.** to disguise or conceal by means of camouflage: *to camouflage a trench with branches.* [French *camouflage* disguise, from *camoufler* to disguise, from Italian *camuffare;* of uncertain origin.]

camp (kamp) *n.* **1.** an outdoor site, often with tents, huts, or other structures, where people live or sleep temporarily, esp. while traveling or marching; encampment: *The scouts had their camp by the river.* **2.** a place, usually in the country, that provides supervised activities and is attended for a fixed period of time: *a tennis camp, a camp for musicians.* **3.** a group of permanent structures in which a number of persons may be sheltered or confined: *an army camp, a prisoner-of-war camp, a labor camp, a hunting camp.* **4.** an area used for or occupied by a camp. **5.** the people occupying a camp. **6.** a group of people who support a common theory, policy, or doctrine: *The controversy divided the townspeople into two camps.* —*v.i.* **1.** to set up a temporary camp: *They decided to camp on the ridge.* **2.** to live or sleep in or as in a camp or outdoors (often with *out*): *to camp by a lake for a month.* **3.** to maintain a presence stubbornly, as in protest: *The demonstrators camped outside city hall.* [Old French *camp* field, field of battle, from Italian *campo* field, from Latin *campus.* Doublet of CAMPUS.]
  · **to break camp.** to pack up camping equipment.
  · **to make camp.** to establish a temporary camp.

cam·paign (kam pān′) *n.* **1.** a series of related military operations for accomplishing a common objective, usually conducted in a particular region or period of time and constituting a distinct part of a war. **2.** an organized series of actions conducted to accomplish a particular goal: *an election campaign, a fundraising campaign.* —*v.i.* to conduct or serve in a campaign: *to campaign for president.* [French *campagne* open country, military campaign, from Italian *campagna,* from Late Latin *campānia* open country, from Latin *campus* field.] —**cam·paign′er,** *n.*

cam·pa·ni·le (kam′pə nē′lē, -nēl′) *n., pl.* **-ni·les** or **-ni·li** (-nē′-lē). a bell tower, esp. one that is a separate building. [Italian *campanile,* from *campana* bell, from Late Latin *campāna.*]

cam·pan·u·la (kam pan′yə lə) *n.* **1.** the bell-shaped flower of any of a large group of plants, genus *Campanula;* bellflower. **2.** the plant bearing this flower. [Modern Latin *campanula* little bell, diminutive of Late Latin *campāna* bell.]

camp chair, a light, portable folding chair.

camp·er (kam′pər) *n.* **1.** a person who stays at, goes to, or lives in a camp. **2.** a vehicle or trailer built or adapted for camping.

camp·fire (kamp′fīr′) *n.* **1.** an outdoor fire in a camp, used for warmth or cooking. **2.** a social gathering or meeting, as around a campfire.

Camp Fire, a national organization for girls and boys ages seven through eighteen that encourages participation in outdoor activities, sports, creative arts, and community service. Formerly called Camp Fire Girls, it permitted boys to join beginning in 1975.

camp·ground (kamp′ground′) *n.* a place for a camp or a camp meeting.

cam·phor (kam′fər) *n.* a white, aromatic, flammable, crystalline compound obtained from the wood of the camphor tree or made synthetically, used as a mothproofing agent, in some medicines, and in the manufacture of plastics. Formula: $C_{10}H_{16}O$ [Medieval Latin *camphora,* from Arabic *kāfūr,* either from Sanskrit *karpūra* or from Malay *kāpūr* chalk.] —**cam·phor·ic** (kam fôr′ik, -for′-), *adj.*

cam·phor·ate (kam′fə rāt′) *v.t.*, **-at·ed, -at·ing.** to impregnate or treat with camphor.

camphor ball, mothball.

camphor ice, an ointment made from camphor, white wax, spermaceti, and castor oil, used for chapped skin.

camphor tree, an aromatic Asian tree, *Cinnamomum camphora,* related to the laurel, that is a source of camphor.

camp·ing (kam′ping) *n.* the practice or pastime of living outdoors, at a camp, or in a camper. —*adj.* relating to or used in camping: *camping gear.*

cam·pi·on (kam′pē ən) *n.* any plant of either of the genera *Silene* or *Lychnis,* of the pink family, bearing white, pink, or red flowers. The stems or other parts are sticky, serving to trap insects. [Probably from Latin *campus* field (with the sense of field flower).]

camp meeting, a religious gathering, usually lasting several days, held outdoors or in a tent.

camp·site (kamp′sīt′) *n.* **1.** any location where a temporary camp is established. **2.** an area reserved for camping, as in a park, usually having cooking, eating, sanitary, and other facilities.

camp·stool (kamp′stül′) *n.* a light, portable folding seat.

cam·pus (kam′pəs) *n.* the grounds, including buildings, of a school, college, or university. —*adj.* of or relating to a school, college, or university or to its students: *campus politics.* [Latin *campus* field; possibly because college grounds were originally located in open country. Doublet of CAMP.]

cam·shaft (kam′shaft′) *n.* a shaft on which one or more cams are fastened, as in an internal-combustion engine where it is part of the system that opens and closes the valves. [CAM + SHAFT.]

can¹ (kan; *unstressed* kən) *auxiliary verb* (followed by an infinitive without *to*). Present: **can** or *(archaic second person sing.)* **canst** (kanst). Past: **could** (kůd) or *(archaic second person sing.)* **could·est** or **couldst.** **1.** to be able to: *She can run faster than you. The car can hold five passengers.* **2.** to know how to: *He can speak French. Can you dance the waltz?* **3.** to have the right to: *Only the general can order the attack.* **4.** to have the possibility or be likely to: *No agreement can be reached unless concessions are made.* **5.** *Informal.* to be permitted to; may: *My parents say I can go to the movies.* [Old English *can,* third person singular of *cunnan* to know, know how to, be able.]

Usage Although **can** is often used in speech and writing to mean "to be permitted to," **may** is still generally preferred: *Each student may take one elective.* In negative questions, however, **can't,** not **mayn't,** is used: *Why can't I take French?*

---

can² (kan) *n.* **1.** a container or receptacle, usually made of metal or plastic: *a garbage can, a water can.* **2.** a container, usually made of iron coated with tin or of aluminum, in which food or other products are sealed for preservation. **3.** the contents of a can: *to drink a can of root beer.* **4.** *Slang.* jail. —*v.t.*, **canned, can·ning. 1.** to put or preserve in a can or jar. **2.** *Slang.* to fire from a job; discharge: *The boss canned me for being late too often.* **3.** *Slang.* to put an end to; stop: *Can it!* [Old English *canne* container for liquids, cup.]

Can. 1. Canada. **2.** Canadian.

Ca·naan·ite (kā′nə nīt′) *n.* **1.** a member of the Semitic people who inhabited the land of Canaan prior to its conquest by the Hebrews. **2.** the language of the Canaanites.

Can·a·da balsam (kan′ə də) a yellow oleoresin obtained from the bark of the balsam fir, used as a transparent cement for mounting microscopic specimens on slides and in the manufacture of fine lacquers.

Canada Day, a national holiday of Canada, commemorating the formation of the Dominion of Canada in 1867. Formerly, **Dominion Day.** It is observed on July 1.

Canada goose, a wild goose, *Branta canadensis,* native to Arctic and temperate regions of North America, having a black head and neck, white patches on the face, and a brownish gray body. Length: 22-38 inches (56-97 centimeters).

Ca·na·di·an (kə nā′dē ən) *n.* **1.** a native or citizen of Canada. **2.** a person of Canadian ancestry. —*adj.* of, relating to, or characteristic of Canada or its people or culture.

Canadian bacon, rolled, boneless loin of pork, smoked and cut in slices to be eaten like bacon.

ca·naille (kə nāl′, ka nī′) *n.* the masses; rabble; riffraff. [French *canaille,* from Italian *canaglia,* from *cane* dog, from Latin *canis.*]

ca·nal (kə nal′) *n.* **1.** an inland waterway built to carry water for purposes of navigation, irrigation, drainage, or power. **2.** a tubular passage in a plant or in the body of an animal; duct. **3.** any of the long, faint, narrow markings on the planet Mars, as seen through a telescope. [Latin *canālis* pipe, channel, from *canna* reed, from Greek *kanna;* of Semitic origin. Doublet of CHANNEL.]

canal boat, a long, narrow boat, as a barge, used on canals.

can·a·lic·u·lus (kan′ə lik′yə ləs) *n., pl.* **-lic·u·li** (-lik′yə lī′). a minute anatomical canal, as in bone. [Latin *canaliculus,* diminutive of *canalis,* groove, channel. See CANAL.]

ca·nal·ize (kə nal′īz, kan′əl īz′) *v.t.,* **-ized, -iz·ing. 1.** to convert into or make like a canal: *to canalize a river.* **2.** to furnish with a canal or series of canals. —**ca·nal′i·za′tion,** *n.*

can·a·pé (kan′ə pē, -pā′) *n.* a cracker or thin piece of bread, topped with cheese, meat, or fish or spread with a seasoned mixture and served hot or cold as an appetizer. [French *canapé* sofa, from Medieval Latin *canāpēum,* from Latin *cōnōpēum* mosquito net, from Greek *kōnōpeion* mosquito net, bed with a mosquito net, from *kōnōps* mosquito. Doublet of CANOPY.]

ca·nard (kə närd′) *n.* a false or exaggerated story, report, or rumor, esp. a derogatory one deliberately spread. [French *canard* duck, hoax, from phrase *vendre des canards à moitié* to deceive; literally, to sell ducks by halves, from Old French *caner* to cackle; imitative.]

ca·nar·y (kə nâr′ē) *n., pl.* **-nar·ies. 1.** a small yellow songbird, *Serinus canarius,* of the finch family, widely kept as a pet. **2.** canary yellow. **3.** a sweet white wine from the Canary Islands. —*adj.* having the color canary yellow. [French *canari,* from Spanish *canario,* bird from the Canary Islands, its original habitat.]

canary yellow, a light, bright yellow color.

ca·nas·ta (kə nas′tə) *n.* **1.** a form of rummy for two to six players, usually using two decks of fifty-two cards and four jokers. **2.** in the card game canasta, a set of seven or more cards of a kind. [Spanish *canasta* basket (because many, or a "basketful" of, cards are used), going back to Latin *canistrum.* See CANISTER.]

can·can (kan′kan′) *n.* a dance originated in Paris in the early nineteenth century, performed by female entertainers and characterized by exaggerated high kicking and leaping. [French *cancan* originally, a word for the duck *(canard)* in baby talk; because the dance resembles the waddle of a duck.]

can·cel (kan′səl) *v., -celed, -cel·ing; also, British, -celled, -cel·ling.* —*v.t.* **1.** to do away with, withdraw, or stop (something that has been planned or expected), esp. without the intention of scheduling it again. **2.** to mark or deface, esp. a postage stamp or check, so that it cannot be used again. **3.** to make up for (often with *out*); balance or neutralize; offset: *A vote for and a vote against a candidate cancel each other out.* **4.** to cross out with a line or other mark; delete: *to cancel a name from a list.* **5.** to make null and void; annul: *to cancel a contractual agreement.* **6.** *Mathematics.* to eliminate (a common factor) from the numerator and denominator of a fraction or from both sides of an equation. —*v.i.* to offset each other (with *out*). —*n.* **1.** the act of canceling. **2.** cancellation *(def. 2).* [Middle English *cancellen,* from Norman French *canceler,* from Late Latin *cancellare* to erase, cancel, from Latin *cancelli* to make like a lattice, from *cancelli,* plural of *cancellus* small lattice, diminutive of *cancer* lattice, from *carcer* prison.] —**can′cel·a·ble;** *also, British,* **can′cel·la·ble,** *adj.* —**can′cel·er;** *also, British,* **can′cel·ler,** *n.*

can·cel·la·tion (kan′sə lā′shən) *n.* **1.** the act of canceling or the state of being canceled. **2.** a mark or marks used in canceling. **3.** something that is canceled.

can·cer (kan′sər) *n.* **1.** any of a group of frequently fatal diseases, including carcinoma, sarcoma, and leukemia, characterized by abnormal cellular growth in which new cells revert to a more primitive form, invade surrounding healthy tissue, and tend to spread to other parts of the body. Cancer occurs in most species of animals and in many kinds of plants. **2.** any malignant tumor. **3.** any destructive or spreading evil. **4. Cancer. a.** Tropic of Cancer. **b.** a constellation in the northern sky, conventionally depicted as a crab. **c.** the fourth sign of the zodiac. [Latin *cancer* crab, malignant tumor. Doublet of CANKER, CHANCRE.] —**can′cer·ous,** *adj.*

can·de·la (kan dē′lə) *n.* a unit of luminous intensity equal to ¹/₆₀ of the light emitted by 1 square centimeter of the surface of a black object at the solidification temperature of platinum (1,773.5 degrees centigrade). Also, **candle.**

can·de·la·brum (kan′də lä′brəm, -lā′-) *n., pl.* **-bra** (-brə) or **-brums.** a large ornamental branched candlestick or lamp. Also, **can′de·la′bra.** [Latin *candēlābrum* candlestick from *candēla* candle.]

candelabrum

can·des·cent (kan des′ənt) *adj.* glowing, esp. with heat; incandescent. [Latin *candēscēns,* present participle of *candēscere* to begin to glow.] —**can·des′cence,** *n.* —**can·des′cent·ly,** *adv.*

can·did (kan′did) *adj.* **1.** honest and straightforward; frank; sincere: *a candid opinion.* **2.** not posed; informal: *a candid photograph.* **3.** free from bias; fair; impartial. [Latin *candidus* white, shining, pure.] —**can′did·ly,** *adv.* —**can′did·ness,** *n.* —For Synonyms *(adj.),* see frank[1].

can·di·da·cy (kan′di də sē) *n., pl.* **-cies.** the state or fact of being a candidate. Also, *British,* **candidature.**

can·di·date (kan′di dāt′, -dit) *n.* **1.** a person who seeks, or is put forward by others for, an office or honor. **2.** a person or thing that seems likely to have a certain fate: *This old computer is a candidate for replacement.* **3.** a person applying for a position who has a chance of getting it: *a candidate for a job, a candidate for admission to a college.* **4.** a student who is studying for a degree: *a doctoral candidate.* [Latin *candidātus* a person dressed in white, candidate for office, from *candidus* white; in ancient Rome, those seeking political office would wear spotless white togas to symbolize integrity.]

can·di·da·ture (kan′di də chər) *n. British.* candidacy.

candid camera, a small camera with a fast lens for taking unposed, informal pictures.

can·died (kan′dēd) *adj.* **1.** cooked in or glazed with sugar: *candied yams.* **2.** encrusted or preserved with sugar: *candied ginger.*

can·dle (kan′dəl) *n.* **1.** a mass of wax, tallow, or other solid fat, usually cylindrical, formed around a wick, which is burned to give light or low heat. **2.** anything like a candle in shape or use. **3.** candela. **4.** international candle. —*v.t.,* **-dled, -dling.** to examine (eggs) for signs of fertilization and for freshness and quality, by holding in front of a light. [Old English *candel* light made of wax or tallow around a wick, from Latin *candēla.*]

· **to burn the candle at both ends.** to exhaust one's energy in working or playing too hard; live recklessly.

· **to hold a candle to.** to compare favorably with; be as good as: *I'm a good violinist, but I can't hold a candle to my teacher.*

can·dle·hold·er (kan′dəl hōl′dər) *n.* candlestick.

can·dle·light (kan′dəl līt′) *n.* **1.a.** the light given by a candle or candles. **b.** a similar artificial light. **2.** the time to light candles; dusk; nightfall.

Can·dle·mas (kan′dəl məs) *n.* a church festival celebrating the purification of the Virgin Mary and the presentation of the infant Jesus in the Temple, during which candles for sacred use are blessed, observed on February 2. [Old English *candelmæsse.*]

can·dle·pin (kan′dəl pin′) *n.* **1.** a cylindrical wooden pin, tapering slightly toward top and bottom, used in the game of candlepins. **2. candlepins.** a bowling game using ten of these pins, in which three balls are bowled in each frame and the pins that are knocked down are not removed until the completion of the frame. ➡ used as singular.

can·dle·pow·er (kan′dəl pou′ər) *n.* a measure for the intensity

a	at	e	end	o	hot	u	up	hw	white	{	about
ā	ape	ē	me	ō	old	ū	use	ng	song	{	taken
ä	far	i	it	ô	fork	ū	rule	th	thin	{	pencil
âr	care	ī	ice	oi	oil	u̇	pull	th	this	{	lemon
		îr	pierce	ou	out	ûr	turn	zh	measure	{	circus

of a source of light based on the light emitted in a particular direction from that source and expressed in candelas.

can·dle·stick (kan′dəl stik′) *n.* a holder with a cup or spike for a candle. Also, **candleholder.**

can·dle·wick (kan′dəl wik′) *n.* the wick of a candle.

can·dor (kan′dər) *also, British,* **can·dour.** *n.* **1.** frankness, as of speech; honesty and openness. **2.** freedom from prejudice; fairness; impartiality. [Latin *candor* brightness, whiteness, purity.]

can·dy (kan′dē) *n., pl.* **-dies. 1.** a sweet food made chiefly of sugar or syrup combined with other ingredients, as chocolate, milk, nuts, and fruits. **2.** a piece of this food. —*v.,* **-died, -dy·ing.** —*v.t.* **1.** to cause to form into crystals. **2.** to preserve by cooking or coating with sugar. **3.** to cover or encrust with or as with sugar crystals. **4.** to make sweet, agreeable, or pleasant. —*v.i.* to become crystallized into or covered with sugar. [French *(sucre) candi* (sugar) candy, through Italian, from Arabic *qand* sugar, going back to Sanskrit *khanda* pieces of sugar; originally, fragment.]

can·dy·tuft (kan′dē tuft′) *n.* any of a group of plants, genus *Iberis,* of the mustard family, bearing narrow leaves and clusters of small white, purple, or pink flowers. [From *Candia* earlier name of Crete + TUFT; because it came from Crete.]

cane (kān) *n.* **1.** a stick or staff, usually made of wood, esp. one used to help a person in walking; walking stick. **2.** a stick or rod, esp. one used for beating or flogging. **3.** the slender, woody, jointed stem of certain tall grasses, as bamboo, reed, and rattan. **4.** any plant having such a stem. **5.** a material made of such stems, such as rattan, used in making furniture and wickerwork. **6.** sugarcane. —*v.t.,* **caned, can·ing. 1.** to beat or flog with a cane. **2.** to make or repair with cane, as furniture. [Old French *can(n)e* reed, from Latin *canna,* from Greek *kanna;* of Semitic origin. Doublet of CANNA.] —**can′er,** *n.*

cane·brake (kān′brāk′) *n.* a thicket of cane.

ca·nel·la (kə nel′ə) *n.* **1.** the inner bark of a tree, *Canella winterana,* having a smell resembling cinnamon and a pungent taste, yielding an oil used as a spice and in making perfume. **2.** the evergreen tree from which this bark is obtained, found in the West Indies and the Florida Keys. [Medieval Latin *canella* cinnamon, diminutive of Latin *canna* reed. See CANE.]

cane sugar, sugar obtained from sugarcane.

ca·nine (kā′nīn) *adj.* **1.** of, resembling, or relating to a dog. **2.** of or relating to the dog family, Canidae, which includes dogs, foxes, wolves, and jackals. —*n.* **1.** a domestic dog. **2.** any member of the dog family. **3.** canine tooth. [Latin *canīnus* relating to a dog, from *canis* dog.]

canine tooth, one of the four sharp-pointed teeth situated between the incisors and the bicuspids in the upper and lower jaw. Also, **cuspid.**

Ca·nis Ma·jor (kā′nis mā′jər) a constellation in the southern sky, near the celestial equator, containing the bright star Sirius, conventionally depicted as a dog. [Latin *Canis Mājor* the Greater Dog.]

Ca·nis Mi·nor (kā′nis mī′nər) a constellation in the northern sky, near the celestial equator, containing the bright star Procyon, conventionally depicted as a dog. [Latin *Canis Minor* the Lesser Dog.]

can·is·ter (kan′ə stər) *n.* **1.** a small box, can, or other container for holding coffee, sugar, flour, or other dry foods. **2.** a can filled with musket balls or scrap metal that scatters its contents when fired from a cannon. Also, **canister shot, case shot. 3.** the filtration unit of a gas mask. [Latin *canistrum* basket made of reeds, from Greek *kanastron* wicker basket, from *kanna* reed. See CANE.]

can·ker (kang′kər) *n.* **1.** an ulceration, esp. of the mouth or lip. Also, **canker sore. 2.a.** any of various diseases of trees that cause decay of the bark and underlying tissue. **b.** a lesion caused by such a disease. **3.** anything that corrodes, corrupts, or destroys: *The canker of constant war ruined the nation.* **4.** cankerworm. —*v.t.* **1.** to affect with canker. **2.** to corrode, corrupt, or destroy. —*v.i.* to become infected with or as with canker. [Old English *cancer* cancer and dialectal Old French *cancre* ulcer, both from Latin *cancer* malignant tumor. Doublet of CANCER, CHANCRE.]

can·ker·ous (kang′kər əs) *adj.* **1.** of the nature of canker. **2.** causing canker.

can·ker·worm (kang′kər wûrm′) *n.* a moth larva, family Geometridae, that is very destructive to shade and fruit trees.

can·na (kan′ə) *n.* **1.** the red or yellow flower of any of a group of plants, genus *Canna.* The stamens are broad and petallike and form the showy part of the flower. **2.** the plant bearing this flower, having large, oblong leaves. [Latin *canna* reed, from Greek *kannā;* of Semitic origin. Doublet of CANE.]

can·na·bis (kan′ə bis) *n.* marijuana. [Modern Latin *cannabis,* from Latin *cannabis* hemp, from Greek *kannabis.*]

canned (kand) *adj.* **1.** preserved in a can or jar. **2.** *Informal.* not live; recorded: *The television comedy was broadcast with canned laughter.*

can·nel coal (kan′əl) a black bituminous coal having a uniform and fine-grained compact texture. It is easily ignited and burns with a bright flame. Also, **cannel.** [Form of CANDLE + COAL; because, like a candle, it does not smoke when burning.]

can·ner (kan′ər) *n.* a person or business that cans food.

can·ner·y (kan′ə rē) *n., pl.* **-ner·ies.** a factory where foods are canned.

can·ni·bal (kan′ə bəl) *n.* **1.** a person who eats human flesh. **2.** an animal that eats its own kind. —*adj.* of or relating to cannibals; given to cannibalism. [Spanish *caníbal,* form of *caríbal* human cannibal, Carib; of Carib origin; Modern English meaning from the Carib practice of eating human flesh.]

can·ni·bal·ism (kan′ə bə liz′əm) *n.* the act or practice of eating the flesh of one's own kind. —**can′ni·bal·is′tic,** *adj.*

can·ni·bal·ize (kan′ə bə līz′) *v.t.,* **-ized, -iz·ing. 1.** to take parts from (something) to build, repair, or strengthen one or more other things: *to build a hot rod by cannibalizing cars bought from the junkyard.* **2.** to use (material from another writer, artist, or composer or from an earlier work of one's own) in a current undertaking. —**can′ni·bal·i·za′tion,** *n.*

can·ning (kan′ing) *n.* the act, process, or business of preserving food by sealing it in airtight containers.

can·no·li (kə nō′lē) *n., pl.* **-li.** a tube-shaped pastry filled with sweetened ricotta cheese, often flavored with citron, chocolate, or the like. [Italian *cannoli* literally, little tubes, going back to Latin *canna* reed. See CANE.]

can·non (kan′ən) *n., pl.* **-nons** or **-non. 1.** a large firearm mounted on a base, such as a gun, howitzer, or mortar. **2.** a large caliber, automatic gun mounted on an aircraft. **3.** cannon bone. [French *canon* gun, gun barrel, going back to Latin *canna* reed, tube. See CANE.]

can·non·ade (kan′ə nād′) *n.* **1.** a very heavy or continuous firing of artillery. **2.** an attack with artillery. —*v.,* **-ad·ed, -ad·ing.** —*v.t.* to attack with or as with artillery. —*v.i.* to fire artillery continuously. [French *canonnade* cannon shot, from Italian *cannonata* firing of a cannon, from *cannone* cannon, large tube, going back to Latin *canna* reed, tube. See CANE.]

can·non·ball (kan′ən bôl′) *n.* **1.** a heavy ball, made of iron or other metal, designed to be fired from a cannon. **2.** a jump into water, as from a diving board, with the legs bent and held close to the front of the torso.

cannon bone, the long bone between the hock or knee and the fetlock, in hoofed animals, esp. the horse.

can·non·eer (kan′ə nîr′) *n.* a soldier in the artillery; gunner.

can·non·ry (kan′ən rē) *n., pl.* **-ries. 1.** artillery. **2.** continuous cannon fire.

cannon shot 1. cannon balls or other projectiles for a cannon. **2.** a shot fired from a cannon. **3.** the range of a cannon.

can·not (kan′ot, ka not′) can not.

 ·cannot but. have no choice except to; must: *We cannot but admire their bravery.*

can·ny (kan′ē) *adj.,* **-ni·er, -ni·est. 1.** cautiously shrewd in one's behavior or dealings; prudent; wary. **2.** frugal in money matters; thrifty. —**can′ni·ly,** *adv.* —**can′ni·ness,** *n.* [CAN[1] + -Y[1].]

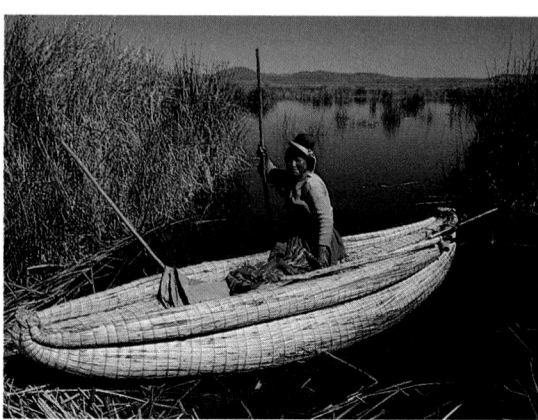

reed **canoe** on Lake Titicaca

ca·noe (kə nü′) *n.* a light, narrow boat, usually pointed at both ends, propelled by hand with a paddle. —*v.,* **ca·noed, ca·noe-**

C

ing. —*v.i.* to paddle or go in a canoe. —*v.t.* to transport by canoe. [Spanish *canoa* Indian boat; of Carib origin; Modern English spelling influenced by French *canoë* Canadian canoe.] —**ca·noe′ist,** *n.*

can of worms *Informal.* a situation that produces unexpected and often troublesome problems.

can·o·la (kə nō′lə) *n.* a variety of rapeseed used in the manufacture of a cooking oil that is low in saturated fatty acids.

can·on¹ (kan′ən) *n.* **1.** a law, rule, or decree of a church, usually enacted by a church council. **2.** a general rule, fundamental principle, or standard: *canons of good behavior.* **3.** a collection or list of the books of the Bible accepted by the church as genuine and divinely inspired. **4.** a list of saints officially recognized by the Roman Catholic Church and certain other churches. **5.** an official or authoritative list or catalog, as of the works of a particular author. **6.** *also,* **Canon.** the portion of the Mass following the Sanctus. **7.** *Music.* a form of contrapuntal composition in which the different vocal or instrumental parts take up the melody in succession at the same or at a different pitch. [Old English *canon* rule, from Latin *canōn,* from Greek *kanōn* rod, carpenter's rule, rule, standard.]

can·on² (kan′ən) *n.* **1.** a member of the clergy serving in a cathedral or collegiate church. **2.** one of a group of Roman Catholic clergymen living according to certain rules, or canons, of the church. [Dialectal Old French *canonie* priest, from Church Latin *canōnicus* clergyman, one belonging to the canon or rule, from Latin *canōn.* See CANON¹.]

ca·ñon (kan′yən) canyon.

ca·non·i·cal (kə non′i kəl) *adj.* **1.** relating to, prescribed by, or conforming to canon law. **2.** of or contained in the canon of the Bible. **3.** recognized as authoritative; accepted: *a canonical source of knowledge.* —*n.* **canonicals.** vestments prescribed by church canon to be worn by the clergy when officiating. —**ca·non′i·cal·ly,** *adv.*

canonical hours, the seven periods of the day fixed by church canon for prayer and devotion.

can·on·ize (kan′ə nīz′) *v.t.,* **-ized, -iz·ing. 1.** to declare (a deceased person) a saint; place in the canon of saints. **2.** to treat as sacred or saintly; glorify. **3.** to admit into the canon of the Bible. **4.** to sanction by the authority of the church. —**can′on·i·za′tion,** *n.*

canon law, in a Christian church, the body of law governing matters of faith and discipline.

Ca·no·pus (kə nō′pəs) *n.* the second brightest star in the sky.

can·o·py (kan′ə pē) *n., pl.* **-pies. 1.** an awning, drapery, or similar covering, often suspended over a bed, throne, or entrance of a building, or supported on poles over a person or sacred object. **2.** anything that acts or seems to act as an overhanging shelter or covering: *the canopy of heaven, a tropical rain forest soaring to a 50-meter canopy.* **3.** a sliding, transparent covering over an airplane cockpit. **4.** the umbrellalike lifting surface of a parachute. —*v.t.,* **-pied, -py·ing.** to cover with or as with a canopy. [Medieval Latin *canapeum* mosquito net, going back to Greek *kōnōpeion* mosquito net, bed with a mosquito net, from *kōnōps* mosquito. Doublet of CANAPÉ.]

canst (kanst) *Archaic.* a second person singular present tense of can¹. ➡ used with thou.

cant¹ (kant) *n.* **1.** trite, pretentious, or insincere talk, esp. the hypocritical expression of religious or moralistic sentiments. **2.** words or language peculiar to a particular class, profession, sect, or other group; jargon. **3.** whining, singsong speech. —*v.i.* to speak in cant; use cant. [Latin *cantus* song and *cantāre* to sing; originally applied to the whining of beggars and probably to the chanting in Christian religious services.]

cant² (kant) *n.* **1.** a slant or slope; tilt. **2.** a sudden movement that tilts or overturns something. **3.** a slanting or sloping surface, as one produced by cutting off a corner or edge. —*v.t.* **1.** to put or set at an angle; tilt, slant, or slope. **2.** to give a sloping edge to; bevel. **3.** to throw with a sudden jerk; pitch; toss. —*v.i.* to tilt, slant, or slope. [Middle Dutch *cant* border, edge, corner, going back to Late Latin *cantus* corner, from Latin *cant(h)us* tire², wheel; of Celtic origin.]

can't (kant) *contr.* cannot.

can·ta·bi·le (kän tä′bə lā′, kän tab′ə lē) *Music. adj., adv.* in a smooth and flowing style. —*n.* a cantabile passage, piece, or style. [Italian *cantabile* singable, from *cantare* to sing, from Latin *cantāre.*]

Can·ta·brig·i·an (kan′tə brij′ē ən) *adj.* of or relating to Cambridge, England, or Cambridge University. —*n.* **1.** a student or graduate of Cambridge University. **2.** a native or inhabitant of Cambridge, England. [Medieval Latin *Cantabrigia* Cambridge + -AN.]

can·ta·loupe (kan′tə lōp′) *also,* **can·ta·loup.** *n.* a variety of muskmelon having a coarse, pale green or yellow rind and sweet,

usually yellowish orange flesh. [French *cantaloup,* from Italian *Cantalupo,* name of a former papal residence, where it was first grown in Europe.]

can·tan·ker·ous (kan tang′kər əs) *adj.* ill-tempered and ready to quarrel or oppose others. [Probably modification of Middle English *contek* strife; influenced by words like *cankerous, rancorous.*] —**can·tan′ker·ous·ly,** *adv.* —**can·tan′ker·ous·ness,** *n.*

can·ta·ta (kən tä′tə) *n.* a musical composition in which a story is sung by soloists and a chorus but not acted. [Italian *cantata,* from *cantare* to sing, from Latin *cantāre.*]

can·teen (kan tēn′) *n.* **1.** a small, usually metal container for carrying water or other liquids. **2.a.** a place run by civilian volunteers where free food, beverages, and, usually, entertainment are provided for members of the armed forces. **b.** post exchange. **3.** a place providing food and beverages, such as a snack bar at a factory. [French *cantine,* from Italian *cantina* cellar (formerly often used as a shop), going back to Late Latin *cantus* corner. See CANT².]

can·ter (kan′tər) *n.* an easy gait, faster than a trot but slower than a full gallop. —*v.i., v.t.* to move or ride at a canter. [Short for *Canterbury pace,* the slow pace used by pilgrims on horseback when approaching the religious shrine at Canterbury, England.]

Can·ter·bur·y bell (kan′tər ber′ē, -bə rē) **1.** a tall stalk of bell-shaped flowers borne by a plant, *Campanula medium,* of the bellflower family, having white, pink, or blue-violet petals. **2.** the plant bearing this flower, widely cultivated as a garden plant, having hairy leaves and stems. [Because of its resemblance to the bells on the horses of pilgrims riding to the religious shrine at *Canterbury,* England.]

cant hook, a pole with a movable hooked arm at or near one end, which loggers use in order to grip and turn over logs or poles.

can·ti·cle (kan′ti kəl) *n.* a song or chant, esp. a short, nonmetrical hymn whose text is usually taken directly from the Bible. [Latin *canticulum* little song, diminutive of *canticum* song.]

Canticle of Canticles, in the Douay Bible, the Song of Solomon.

Can·ti·cles (kan′ti kəlz) *n.* Song of Solomon. ➡ used as singular.

can·ti·le·ver (kan′tə lē′vər, -lev′ər) *n.* a projecting bracket, beam, or slab that is supported at one end only. —*v.t.* to support with cantilevers. [Possibly CANT² + LEVER.]

cantilever bridge, a bridge formed by two cantilevers whose projecting ends meet but do not support each other.

can·ti·na (kan tē′nə) *n.* in the southwestern United States, a saloon or bar. [Spanish *cantina* canteen, from Italian *cantina* cellar. See CANTEEN.]

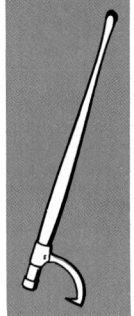

can·tle (kan′təl) *n.* the part at the back of the seat of certain saddles that curves up. For illustration, see **saddle.** [Anglo-Norman *cantel* piece, corner, going back to Late Latin *cantus* corner. See CANT².]

cant hook

can·to (kan′tō) *n., pl.* **-tos.** one of the main divisions of a long poem. [Italian *canto,* from Latin *cantus* song.]

can·ton (kan′tən, -ton) *n.* **1.** a small territorial district or political division of a country, esp. one of the states of the Swiss confederation. **2.** a rectangular section of a flag in the top corner nearest to the staff. —*v.t.* **1.** to divide into cantons or districts. **2.** to quarter (troops). [Old French *canton* corner, portion, going back to Late Latin *cantus* corner. See CANT².] —**can′ton·al,** *adj.*

Can·ton·ese (kan′tə nēz′, -nēs′) *n., pl.* **-ese. 1.** a native or inhabitant of Canton, China, or the surrounding region. **2.** the Chinese dialect spoken in and around Canton. —*adj.* of, relating to, or characteristic of the region around Canton, China, or its people, dialect, or culture.

can·ton·ment (kan tōn′mənt, -ton′-) *n.* **1.** a military installation that includes quarters for soldiers and their families. **2.** temporary housing for troops. **3.** the assignment of troops to such quarters. [French *cantonnement* housing for troops, from *cantonner* to quarter, from *canton* corner, portion. See CANTON.]

can·tor (kan′tər) *n.* **1.** a singer who leads a choir or congregation; precentor. **2.** in a synagogue, the chief singer of the liturgy. [Latin *cantor* singer.]

a	at	e	end	o	hot	u	up	hw	white		about
ā	ape	ē	me	ō	old	ū	use	ng	song	ə	taken
ä	far	i	it	ô	fork	ū	rule	th	thin		pencil
âr	care	ī	ice	oi	oil	ů	pull	th	this		lemon
			ir	pierce	ou	out	ûr	turn	zh	measure		circus

Ca·nuck (kə nuk′) *n. Slang.* **1.** Canadian. **2.** French Canadian. ➡ usually considered offensive. [Modification of CANADIAN.]

can·vas (kan′vəs) *n.* **1.** a strong, heavy cloth made of cotton, flax, or hemp, used to make such items as tents, sails, and awnings. **2.** a piece of canvas on which a painting, esp. an oil painting, is made. **3.** a painting done on canvas: *an artist's favorite canvas.* **4.** *Nautical.* a sail or sails. **5. the canvas.** the floor of a boxing or wrestling ring. **6.** a tent, esp. a circus tent. [Dialectal Old French *canevas* made of hemp, going back to Latin *cannabis* hemp, from Greek *kannabis.*]
• **under canvas. a.** in tents. **b.** with sails spread.

can·vas·back (kan′vəs bak′) *n.* a wild duck, *Aythya valisineria,* of North America, the male of which has black and brown plumage and white feathers on its back. It is valued as a game bird and for its savory flesh. Length: 24 inches (61 centimeters). [Because the markings on its back recall the doublets of certain economical gentlemen of the seventeenth century that had fine, expensive cloth fronts, but cheap canvas on the backs.]

can·vass (kan′vəs) *v.t.* **1.** to go through (a place) or among (people) to solicit votes, opinions, orders, or contributions. **2.** to examine or discuss carefully or thoroughly. —*v.i.* to go about soliciting votes, opinions, orders, or contributions. —*n.* **1.** the act or process of soliciting, as of votes, opinions, orders, or contributions. **2.** an examination or discussion. [From CANVAS, with the idea, originally, of sifting something through canvas; hence, to investigate, discuss, i.e., to "sift" opinions or responses.] —**can′vass·er,** *n.*

can·yon (kan′yən) *also,* **cañon.** *n.* a deep valley with steep sides, usually with a stream running through it. [Spanish *cañon* tube, gorge, going back to Latin *canna* reed, cane. See CANE.]

caou·tchouc (kou chŭk′, -chŭk′) *n.* latex. [French *caoutchouc* rubber, from Carib *cahuchu* sap of a tree.]

cap (kap) *n.* **1.** a soft, close-fitting head covering, usually brimless or with a visor. **2.** a special head covering worn to show rank, membership, or occupation: *a nurse's cap.* **3.** something resembling a cap in shape, position, or use: *a mushroom cap, a bottle cap.* **4.** something that restricts or limits: *a cap on federal spending.* **5.** percussion cap. **6.** a paper wrapping or covering containing a small quantity of explosive, used in toy guns. **7.** an artificial crown for a tooth. —*v.t.,* **capped, cap·ping. 1.** to put a cap on; cover: *to cap a bottle.* **2.** to form or serve as a cap, cover, or top for; lie on top of: *Clouds capped the mountains.* **3.** to follow with something equal to or better than; match or surpass: *to cap a friend's story with an even more exciting one.* **4.** to cause to end on a high point (often with *off*): *We capped off our dinner with a delicious dessert.* **5.** to affix an artificial crown to (a tooth). [Old English *cæppe* hood, close head covering, from Late Latin *cappa* hood, cloak; of uncertain origin.]
• **cap in hand.** in a respectful or humble manner: *to ask for a second chance cap in hand.*
• **to set one's cap for.** to try to win as a lover or spouse.

cap. *pl.* **caps. 1.** capacity. **2.** capital. **3.** capitalize. **4.** capital letter.

ca·pa·bil·i·ty (kā′pə bil′i tē) *n., pl.* **-ties. 1.** the quality of being capable; ability; capacity: *The applicant has little capability for the job.* **2.** a quality or ability that may be used or developed; potentiality: *That politician has the capability to be a great leader.*

ca·pa·ble (kā′pə bəl) *adj.* having or showing ability; able; efficient; competent: *a capable doctor, a capable performance.* [Late Latin *capābilis* able, from Latin *capere* to take, hold.] —**ca′pa·ble·ness,** *n.* —**ca′pa·bly,** *adv.* —For Synonyms, see **able.**
• **capable of. a.** having the capacity, ability, or quality needed for: *to be capable of accomplishing great deeds.* **b.** open to the influence or effect of; susceptible to: *That statement is capable of misinterpretation.* **c.** tending or able to: *capable of murder.*

ca·pa·cious (kə pā′shəs) *adj.* able to hold or contain much; roomy; spacious: *a capacious auditorium.* —**ca·pa′cious·ly,** *adv.* —**ca·pa′cious·ness,** *n.*

ca·pac·i·tance (kə pas′i təns) *n.* the ratio of the amount of electric charge stored in a capacitor to the voltage across its terminals. Also, **capacity.**

ca·pac·i·tor (kə pas′i tər) *n.* a device for receiving and storing an electric charge, consisting usually of pairs of metallic plates or foils separated by a nonconductor, as air. Also, **condenser.**

ca·pac·i·ty (kə pas′i tē) *n.* **1.** the ability to receive or contain: *The auditorium has a seating capacity of 200.* **2.** the maximum amount that can be held or contained in a space; content; volume: *The room is filled to capacity.* **3.** the power of grasping or taking in impressions, ideas, or knowledge; mental ability: *a scholar of great capacity.* **4.** the ability, power, or faculty to do something: *the capacity to do harm.* **5.** the maximum output, as of a factory: *The war required industry to operate at capacity.* **6.** a specific position, occupation, or function: *Who represents the company in the capacity of sales manager?* **7.** *Law.* legal qualification or competency. **8.** capacitance. —*adj.* at or reaching maximum capacity: *a capacity crowd at a stadium.* [Latin *capācitās* ability to hold much.]

cap and bells, a cap trimmed with bells, worn by a court jester.

cap and gown, a mortarboard and loose gown, worn by teachers, students, and other participants at academic functions, esp. at graduation.

ca·par·i·son (kə par′ə sən) *n.* **1.** an ornamental covering for a horse. **2.** rich clothing, equipment, or trappings. —*v.t.* **1.** to cover (a horse) with a caparison. **2.** to dress or adorn richly. [Middle French *caparasson* trappings for a horse, going back to Late Latin *cap(p)a* hood, cape; of uncertain origin.]

caparison *(def. 1)*

cape[1] (kāp) *n.* **1.** an outer garment without sleeves that falls loosely over the shoulders and is worn in place of or attached to a jacket or coat. **2.** the red cloak used by a bullfighter to attract and guide a bull. [French *cape,* from Spanish *capa,* from Late Latin *cap(p)a* hood, cloak; of uncertain origin.]

cape[2] (kāp) *n.* a point of land extending out from the coastline into the sea, a lake, or another large body of water. [Middle French *cap* head, cape[2], from Italian *capoa,* from Latin *caput* head.]

cap·e·lin (kap′ə lin) *n.* a small fish, *Mallotus villosus,* similar to a smelt, found in the North Atlantic and used commercially as bait for cod. [French *capelan* codfish, from Provençal *capelan* codfish, chaplain, from Medieval Latin *cappellanus.* See CHAPLAIN.]

Ca·pel·la (kə pel′ə) *n.* a yellow double star, the brightest star in the constellation Auriga. [Latin *capella* female goat.]

ca·per[1] (kā′pər) *v.i.* to leap or jump about in a playful manner; prance. —*n.* **1.** a playful leap, skip, or jump. **2.** a capricious action; prank; antic. **3.** *Slang.* an illegal act, as a robbery or burglary. [Short for CAPRIOLE.]

ca·per[2] (kā′pər) *n.* **1.** the pickled green flower bud of a shrub, *Capparis spinosa,* used as a condiment. **2.** the spiny, vinelike shrub itself, which grows wild in rocky regions of the Mediterranean. [Latin *cappāris,* from Greek *kapparis.*]

cap·er·cail·lie (kap′ər kāl′yē) *n.* a large grouse, *Tetrao urogallus,* native to the evergreen forests of Eurasia. The male, which is black, is the largest of all grouse. Length: 2-3 feet (0.6-0.9 meter). [Gaelic *capullcoille* great cock of the wood, from *capull* horse (from Latin *caballus* inferior horse) + *coille* forest.]

Ca·pe·tian (kə pē′shən) *adj.* of or relating to Hugh Capet or the French dynasty (987-1328) descended from him.

cap·il·lar·i·ty (kap′ə lar′i tē) *n.* the rising or falling of a liquid where it touches a solid, caused by the forces of adhesion, cohesion, or surface tension. Also, **capillary action.**

cap·il·lar·y (kap′ə ler′ē) *n., pl.* **-lar·ies. 1.** any of the smallest blood vessels of the circulatory system, connecting the arteries and veins. **2.** a tube with a very narrow inside diameter. Also, **capillary tube.** —*adj.* **1.** of, relating to, or resembling hair; fine; slender. **2.** having a very narrow inside diameter, as a tube or vessel. **3.** of, relating to, or taking place in a capillary or capillaries. **4.** of or relating to capillarity: *capillary attraction, capillary repulsion.* [Latin *capillāris* relating to hair, from *capillus* hair.]

capillary action, capillarity.

capillary tube, capillary *(def. 2).*

cap·i·tal[1] (kap′i təl) *n.* **1.a.** a city or town in which is located the official seat of government of a country, state, or other political division. **b.** a town, city, or area that is the leading center of a specified activity or field, such as an industry or art: *This town once was the steel capital of the country.* **2.** capital letter. **3.** the total amount of money or property owned or used by a corporation or individual. **4.** wealth in any form used or available for use in the production of more wealth. **5.** capitalists as a group or class. **6.** any source of profit, power, or advantage; assets. —*adj.* **1.** main, principal, or chief. **2.** containing the official seat of government: *a capital city.* **3.** of or relating to economic capital or wealth. **4.** excellent; first-rate: *a capital idea.* **5.** punishable by or involving the death penalty: *a capital offense.* **6.** most serious; grave; fatal: *a capital error.* [Old French *capital* chief, from Latin *capitālis* chief, relating to the head, from *caput* head.]
• **to make capital of.** to turn or use to one's own advantage; exploit: *Other politicians made capital of the senator's blunder.*

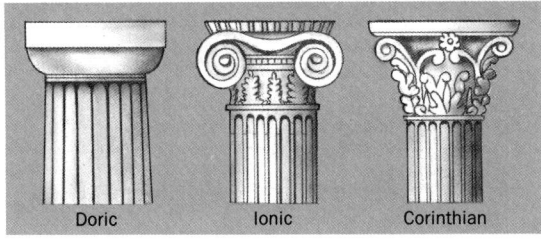

classical Greek **capitals**

cap·i·tal² (kap′i tǝl) *n.* the top part of a column, pilaster, or pillar. [Norman French *capitel,* from Late Latin *capitellum,* diminutive of Latin *caput* head.]

capital gain, the profit realized from the sale of capital investments, such as stocks, bonds, or real estate.

capital goods, goods, such as raw materials, buildings, or machinery, used in the production of other goods. ➡ distinguished from **consumer goods.**

cap·i·tal·ism (kap′i tǝ liz′ǝm) *n.* an economic system in which capital goods and the means of production and distribution are privately owned, the wealth and goods passing freely between producers and consumers, with competition between producers and demand from consumers largely determining the price.

cap·i·tal·ist (kap′i tǝ list) *n.* **1.** a person who has capital, particularly capital that is available for, or in use in, some economic enterprise. **2.** a supporter of capitalism. **3.** any affluent person.

cap·i·tal·is·tic (kap′i tǝ lis′tik) *adj.* **1.** of, relating to, or characteristic of capitalism or capitalists. **2.** based on or favoring capitalism: *a capitalistic system.* —**cap′i·tal·is′ti·cal·ly,** *adv.*

cap·i·tal·i·za·tion (kap′i tǝ lǝ zā′shǝn) *n.* **1.** the act or process of capitalizing or the condition of being capitalized, as a business. **2.** the act or system of using capital letters: *This author doesn't use standard English capitalization.* **3.** the amount resulting from capitalizing. **4.** the total value of the authorized stocks and bonds of a corporation. **5.** the present value of a business or property.

cap·i·tal·ize (kap′i tǝ līz′) *v.,* **-ized, -iz·ing.** —*v.t.* **1.** to write or print with a capital letter or letters, or begin with a capital letter. **2.** to convert into or use as capital. **3.** to provide capital for; finance. **4.** to calculate the present value of (a business or property) on the basis of future earnings or worth. —*v.i.* to use to one's advantage; profit (often with *on*): *to capitalize on an opportunity.*

capital letter, a form of a letter of the alphabet, usually the largest form, used esp. as the initial letter of a sentence or proper noun. Also, **capital.**

cap·i·tal·ly (kap′i tǝ lē) *adv.* in an excellent or first-rate manner; excellently; admirably.

capital punishment, the use of execution to punish a criminal or criminals.

capital ship, a large warship, formerly a heavily armed sailing ship, now usually a battleship or aircraft carrier.

capital stock 1. the total number of shares that a company is authorized to issue. **2.** the total of the par values of the shares that a company is authorized to issue.

cap·i·ta·tion (kap′i tā′shǝn) *n.* a tax or fee imposed uniformly on each individual; per capita or poll tax. [Late Latin *capitātiō* poll tax, from Latin *caput* head.]

Cap·i·tol (kap′i tǝl) *n.* **1.** the building in which the U.S. Congress meets, in Washington, D.C. **2.** *also,* **capitol.** the building in which a state legislature meets; statehouse. **3.** the temple of Jupiter on the Capitoline hill in ancient Rome. [Latin *Capitōlium* ancient temple of Jupiter in Rome, from *caput* head; possibly because a *caput* or man's head was uncovered when the foundation of this Roman temple was laid.]

Capitol Hill, the legislative branch of the U.S. government.

ca·pit·u·late (kǝ pich′ǝ lāt′) *v.i.,* **-lat·ed, -lat·ing. 1.** to surrender or yield on stipulated terms or conditions: *The rebels capitulated with the understanding that they would be granted amnesty.* **2.** to give up; cease resisting: *We capitulated and agreed to go with them.* [Medieval Latin *capitulatus,* past participle of *capitulare* to arrange under separate headings, to arrange terms, going back to Latin *caput* head.] —**ca·pit′u·la′tor,** *n.* —For Synonyms, see **yield.**

ca·pit·u·la·tion (kǝ pich′ǝ lā′shǝn) *n.* **1.** the act of capitulating. **2.** a treaty or document containing the conditions of surrender. **3.** a statement of the main points of a subject; summary.

cap·let (kap′lit) *n.* an oval-shaped tablet of medicine, coated to make it easier to swallow. Trademark: **Caplet.**

ca·po (kä′pō, kap′ō) *n., pl.* **-pos.** the leader of one of the branches of a criminal organization, as in the Mafia. [Italian *capo* literally, head, leader, going back to Latin *caput* head.]

ca·pon (kā′pon, -pǝn) *n.* a young rooster that has been castrated to promote fattening and to improve the flesh for eating. [Old English *capūn,* from Latin *cāpō.*]

cap·puc·ci·no (kä′pǝ chē′nō, kap′ǝ-) *n., pl.* **-nos.** a drink made with espresso and hot milk, usually flavored with cinnamon. [Italian *cappuccino* literally, Capuchin monk; from its color, which resembles the Capuchin habit.]

ca·pric·ci·o (kǝ prē′chē ō′, -chō) *n., pl.* **-ci·os.** a musical composition written in a free, irregular form and usually in a spirited, whimsical style. [Italian *capriccio* whim, shudder (suggesting "head with hair standing on end"), from *capo* head (from Latin *caput*) + *riccio* hedgehog (from Latin *ērīcius*); sense influenced by Italian *capro* goat (with its friskiness).]

ca·price (kǝ prēs′) *n.* **1.** a sudden change of mind without adequate or apparent motivation; whim. **2.** a tendency to change one's mind in this manner; capriciousness. **3.** *Music.* capriccio. [French *caprice,* from Italian *capriccio* shudder, whim. See CAPRICCIO.]

Synonyms Caprice, fancy, whim, and vagary mean an arbitrary, seemingly inexplicable notion or desire. Caprice suggests willfulness leading to often sudden impulse: *The spoiled child's caprices forced her parents to change plans at a moment's notice.* Fancy is often used in reference to a specific desire one develops casually: *For a while I took a fancy to bicycling after dark, until I realized how dangerous it was.* Whim stresses that the notion or desire comes and goes quickly: *It was difficult to keep up with his whims.* Vagary implies an erratic or wayward quality: *The vagaries of public opinion made it difficult to plan a long-term policy.*

ca·pri·cious (kǝ prish′ǝs, -prē′shǝs) *adj.* subject to or characterized by caprice; guided by or as if by whim or fancy; changeable; fickle. —**ca·pri′cious·ly,** *adv.* —**ca·pri′cious·ness,** *n.*

Cap·ri·corn (kap′ri kôrn′) *n.* **1.** Tropic of Capricorn. **2.** a constellation in the southern sky, conventionally depicted as a goat. **3.** the tenth sign of the zodiac. [Latin *Capricornus* a sign of the zodiac; literally, goat-horned, from *caper* goat + *cornu* horn.]

cap·ri·ole (kap′rē ōl′) *n.* **1.** a vertical leap made by a horse, with a backward kick of the hind legs at the top of the jump. **2.** a leap, spring, or caper. —*v.i.* **-oled, -ol·ing.** to perform a capriole. [Middle French *capriole* leap, caper¹, from Italian *capriola* leap (like that of a goat), going back to Latin *caper* goat.]

caps. 1. capitalize. **2.** capital letters.

cap·si·cum (kap′si kǝm) *n.* any of a group of plants, genus *Capsicum,* of the nightshade family, widely cultivated for their red or green pods containing seeds that are usually sharp-tasting. Peppers, pimientos, and chilies are kinds of capsicum. [Modern Latin *capsicum,* probably from Latin *capsa* box; because of its pods.]

cap·size (kap′sīz, kap sīz′) *v.t., v.i.,* **-sized, -siz·ing.** to overturn: *The rough waves capsized the boat. The boat capsized in the storm.* [Of uncertain origin.]

cap·stan (kap′stǝn) *n.* **1.** a device with a vertical spindle that is rotated manually or by motor to wind up rope or cable, as in hoisting an anchor. **2.** *Electronics.* the axle on a tape recorder that turns the reels of tape at a controlled speed. [Provençal *cabestan* device for winding up rope, from *cabestre* halter, from Latin *capistrum.*]

capstan bar, one of the levers by which a ship's capstan is turned.

cap·stone (kap′stōn′) *n.* **1.** the top or finishing stone of a wall or other structure. **2.** the highest point or greatest achievement: *Performing in "Othello" was the capstone of the actor's career.*

cap·su·lar (kap′sǝ lǝr) *adj.* of, in, or resembling a capsule.

cap·sule (kap′sǝl) *n.* **1.** a small soluble case enclosing a dose of medicine. **2.** a sealed, pressurized cabin in a spacecraft, designed to support life during flight and to be recovered after landing. **3.a.** a dry seedcase that develops from a compound carpel and opens when ripe. The seeds of the iris, azalea, and poppy develop in capsules. **b.** a sac or case containing spores. **4.** any membrane or membranous sac enclosing an organ or body part. —*adj.* in a concise form; very brief: *a capsule commentary.* [French *capsule* small container, from Latin *capsula,* diminutive of *capsa* box.]

a	at	e	end	o	hot	u	up	hw	white		about
ā	ape	ē	me	ō	old	ū	use	ng	song		taken
ä	far	i	it	ô	fork	ü	rule	th	thin	ǝ	pencil
âr	care	ī	ice	oi	oil	u̇	pull	th	this		lemon
		îr	pierce	ou	out	ûr	turn	zh	measure		circus

Capt., Captain.

cap·tain (kap′tən) *n.* **1.** a person who is at the head of or has authority over others; leader; chief. **2.** a person in command of a boat or ship. **3.** in the U.S. Navy and Coast Guard, an officer ranking below a commodore or a rear admiral and above a commander. **4.** in the U.S. Army, Air Force, and Marine Corps, an officer ranking below a major and above a first lieutenant. **5.** in a police or fire department, an officer ranking above a lieutenant. **6.** the chief pilot of an aircraft. **7.** the leader of a side or team, as in a sport. **8.** headwaiter. —*v.t.* to act as captain of; lead: *to captain a basketball team.* [Old French *capitaine* commander of a body of troops, from Late Latin *capitāneus* chief, from Latin *caput* head. Doublet of CHIEFTAIN.]

cap·tain·cy (kap′tən sē) *n., pl.* **-cies.** the rank, authority, or period of authority of a captain. Also, **cap·tain·ship** (kap′tən-ship′). [CAPTAIN + -CY.]

cap·tion (kap′shən) *n.* **1.** the title or descriptive material for a picture. **2.** a title or heading, as at the head of a chapter, page, or article. **3.** explanatory or descriptive text, such as a subtitle, projected on a screen along with a film or television program. —*v.t.* to furnish with a caption or captions. [Latin *captiō* a seizing.]

cap·tious (kap′shəs) *adj.* **1.** apt to make much of unimportant faults or defects; difficult to please: *a captious critic.* **2.** designed to entrap or entangle in argument by subtlety: *a captious question.* [Latin *captiōsus* deceptive, sophistical.] —**cap′tious·ly,** *adv.* —**cap′tious·ness,** *n.*

cap·ti·vate (kap′tə vāt′) *v.t.,* **-vat·ed, -vat·ing.** to capture and hold the attention or affection of, as by beauty or excellence; charm; fascinate; enchant: *The singer captivated the audience.* —**cap′ti·va′tion,** *n.* —**cap′ti·va′tor,** *n.*

cap·tive (kap′tiv) *n.* **1.** a person or animal captured and held in confinement; prisoner: *The enemy captives were brought to the commanding officer for questioning.* **2.** a person who is captivated or enthralled, as by beauty, love, or passion. —*adj.* **1.** taken or kept prisoner, as in war: *The captive soldiers were not harmed.* **2.** enthralled, as by beauty, love, or passion; captivated. **3.** kept under control; confined or restrained: *a captive balloon.* **4.** not able to act freely: *a captive nation.* [Latin *captīvus* prisoner, taken prisoner. Doublet of CAITIFF.]

captive audience, any group of people compelled by circumstances to listen to something.

cap·tiv·i·ty (kap tiv′i tē) *n., pl.* **-ties.** the state of being a captive: *Zoo animals live in captivity.*

cap·tor (kap′tər) *n.* a person who captures or holds a captive.

cap·ture (kap′chər) *v.t.,* **-tured, -tur·ing. 1.** to take or seize by force, surprise, or skill: *to capture an enemy stronghold, to capture an opponent's chess piece.* **2.** to attract or catch: *The exciting novel captured my interest.* **3.** to represent in permanent form; reproduce: *The artist captured the sunset on canvas.* —*n.* **1.** the act of capturing. **2.** a person or thing that is captured. [French *capture* act of capturing, what is captured, from Latin *captūra,* from *captus,* past participle of *capere* to take.] —For Synonyms *(v.t.),* see **catch.**

cap·u·chin (kap′yə chin, -shin) *n.* **1.** any of various tree-dwelling Central and South American monkeys, genus *Cebus,* having a long, prehensile tail, black or brown fur, and, in some species, black hair on the head that resembles a monk's cowl. Length: 14-24 inches (36-61 centimeters), without tail. **2. Capuchin.** a member of one of the branches of the Franciscan religious order of the Roman Catholic Church. A Capuchin monk is usually bearded and wears a coarse brown

capuchin

habit with a distinctive long, pointed hood and sandals. [Middle French *capuchin* Capuchin monk, from Italian *cappuccino* Capuchin monk, small hood (as worn by the Capuchins), diminutive of *cappuccio* hood, going back to Late Latin *cappa.* See CAPE¹.]

cap·y·ba·ra (kap′ə bär′ə) *n.* a rodent, *Hydrochoerus hydrochoerus,* native to banks of rivers and streams in South America, resembling a large guinea pig, and having a coarse coat of brownish, bristly hair. It is the largest living rodent. Height: 21 inches (53 centimeters) at the shoulder. [Of Tupi-Guarani origin.]

car (kär) *n.* **1.** automobile. **2.** a vehicle designed to move on rails: *a railroad car.* **3.** any wheeled vehicle. **4.** the cage of an elevator, which carries the passengers or cargo. **5.** the passenger compartment of a lighter-than-air craft. **6.** *Archaic.* chariot.

[Anglo-Norman *carre* wagon, from Late Latin *carra;* of Celtic origin.]

car·a·ba·o (kar′ə bä′ō, kär′-) *n., pl.* **-ba·os.** Philippine water buffalo that is often domesticated as a draft animal. [Spanish *carabao;* from native Philippine word.]

car·a·bi·neer (kar′ə bə nîr′) *also,* **car·a·bi·nier, car·bi·neer.** *n.* formerly, a soldier in the cavalry armed with a carbine.

ca·ra·ca·ra (kär′ə kär′ə, kar′ə kär′ə) *n.* any of certain long-legged birds of prey, family Falconidae, native to Mexico, Central America, and South America, that feed mainly on carrion. [Spanish *caracara,* from Tupi (a South American language) *caracara;* imitative of its cry.]

car·a·cole (kar′ə kōl′) *n.* a half-turn executed by a horse and rider. —*v.i.,* **-coled, -col·ing.** to make a caracole or move in a series of caracoles. [French *caracole* gambol, a caracole, from Spanish *caracol* snail, spiral shell, a caracole; of uncertain origin; from the comparison of the movements of a horse to the spirals on a snail shell.]

car·a·cul (kar′ə kəl) *also,* **karakul.** *n.* the loosely curled wool of young karakul lambs. [Form of KARAKUL.]

ca·rafe (kə raf′) *n.* a bottle, usually made of glass, for holding or serving water, wine, or other beverages. [French *carafe,* from Italian *caraffa,* from Spanish *garrafa,* from Arabic *gharrāf* drinking vessel.]

car·a·ga·na (kar′ə gā′nə, -gä′nə) *n.* any of a number of hardy, deciduous shrubs or small trees, genus *Caragana,* of the pea family, grown as ornamentals for their showy, usually yellow flowers.

car·a·mel (kar′ə məl, -mel′, kär′məl) *n.* **1.** burnt sugar used as a coloring or flavoring agent. **2.** a chewy candy made mainly from sugar, cream, and corn syrup, usually in the form of small squares. [French *caramel,* from Spanish *caramelo;* of uncertain origin.]

car·a·mel·ize (kar′ə mə līz′, kär′mə-) *v.t., v.i.,* **-ized, -iz·ing.** to melt or change into caramel: *to caramelize sugar, the sugar caramelized.* —**car′a·mel·i·za′tion,** *n.*

car·a·pace (kar′ə pās′) *n.* the hard or bony covering on the back of some animals, as turtles or lobsters. [French *carapace,* from Spanish *carapacho;* of uncertain origin.]

car·at (kar′ət) *n.* **1.** a unit of weight equal to $\frac{1}{5}$ of a gram, used chiefly in measuring the weight of gems. **2.** karat. [French *carat,* through Italian and Arabic, from Greek *keration* small weight, seed of the carob tree; literally, small horn. The seeds were used as a unit of weight in ancient times because of their uniform size and weight.]

car·a·van (kar′ə van′) *n.* **1.** a company of travelers, merchants, or pilgrims traveling together for safety and security, esp. through deserts or dangerous regions. **2.** a number of vehicles traveling together: *The caravan of trucks stopped to refuel.* **3.** *British.* a house on wheels; trailer. [French *caravane* convoy, from Persian *kārwān* company of travelers.]

car·a·van·sa·ry (kar′ə van′sə rē) *also,* **car·a·van·se·rai** (kar′-ə van′sə rī′). *n., pl.* **-ries;** *also,* **-rais. 1.** in certain Asian and African countries, an inn with a central court, for accommodating caravans. **2.** any large inn or hotel. [Persian *kārwānsarāi* caravan inn, from *kārwān* caravan + *sarāi* inn.]

car·a·vel (kar′ə vel′) *n.* any of several types of small, fast sailing ships developed in Portugal and Spain in the fifteenth century. Two of Christopher Columbus's ships were caravels. [French *caravelle,* from Portuguese *caravela* going back to Greek *karabos* light ship.]

car·a·way (kar′ə wā′) *n.* **1.** the pungent seeds of a plant, *Carum carvi,* of the parsley family, used as a spice. **2.** the plant itself. [Spanish *alcaravea,* from Arabic *al-karawiyā',* possibly going back to Greek *kareon* cumin.]

car·bide (kär′bīd) *n.* **1.** any of a large group of compounds that contain carbon and one other element. **2.** calcium carbide.

car·bine (kär′bīn, -bēn) *n.* **1.** a lightweight automatic or semiautomatic weapon, shorter and less powerful than a rifle, but with a greater range than a pistol. **2.** formerly, a short rifle or musket used by the cavalry. [French *carabine* short rifle, from *carabin* carabineer; of uncertain origin.]

car·bi·neer (kär′bə nîr′) carabineer.

car·bo·hy·drase (kär′bō hī′drās, -bə-) *n.* any of a group of enzymes that convert complex carbohydrates into simple sugars. [CARBOHYDR(ATE) + -ASE.]

car·bo·hy·drate (kär′bō hī′drāt, -bə-) *n.* a compound of carbon, hydrogen, and oxygen produced by green plants in the process of photosynthesis and used by animals as a source of energy. Cellulose, sugars, and starches are carbohydrates. [CARBO(N) + HYDRATE.]

car·bo·lat·ed (kär′bə lā′tid) *adj.* containing or impregnated with carbolic acid, or phenol.

car·bol·ic acid (kär bol′ik) *n.* phenol *(def. 1).*

car bomb, a bomb that is placed in a car and is set to explode at a specific time, by remote control or when the car is started.

car·bon (kär′bən) *n.* **1.** a common nonmetallic element occurring in crystalline forms, such as diamond and graphite, and in amorphous forms, such as charcoal. Carbon is present in all organic compounds and in many inorganic compounds and is essential to all forms of life. Symbol: **C** For tables, see **element. 2.** a piece of carbon paper. **3.** carbon copy *(def. 1).* [French *carbone* the element, from Latin *carbō* coal.]

carbon 12, the most common isotope of carbon, now used instead of oxygen as the standard for determining the atomic weight of chemical elements.

carbon 14, a radioactive isotope of carbon, widely used as a tracer element and in radiocarbon dating.

car·bo·na·ceous (kär′bə nā′shəs) *adj.* of, relating to, or containing carbon.

car·bo·na·do (kär′bə nā′dō) *n., pl.* **-does.** a very hard crystalline carbon, related to diamond, used in industry for cutting and grinding. [Portuguese *carbonado* literally, carbonated, from *carbone* the element, from French *carbone.* See CARBON.]

carbon arc, an arc or discharge of electricity produced in a gap between electrically charged rods of carbon, employed in welding and as a very bright light source for spotlights and movie projectors.

car·bon·ate (*n.,* kär′bə nāt′, -nit; *v.,* kär′bə nāt′) *n.* a salt or ester containing the radical —CO_3. —*v.t.* **-at·ed, -at·ing.** to charge or impregnate (a substance) with carbon dioxide, esp. to dissolve carbon dioxide in (a liquid) to make it effervescent.

car·bon·a·tion (kär′bə nā′shən) *n.* **1.** impregnation or saturation with carbon dioxide, esp. in manufacturing soda water. **2.** the removal of lime, as in sugar refining, by precipitating it with carbon dioxide.

carbon black, a sooty, powdery form of carbon used as an ink pigment and in the manufacture of rubber.

carbon copy 1. a copy, as of a letter, made by using carbon paper. **2.** a close or exact replica; duplicate: *This house is a carbon copy of the one next door.*

carbon cycle 1. *Biology.* the continual exchange of carbon between living organisms and the earth's atmosphere and water, during which carbon is extracted from the water or air through photosynthesis for use by plants and animals and is eventually returned to the water or air through respiration, decomposition, or combustion. **2.** *Physics.* the series of thermonuclear reactions in stars, such as the sun, by which hydrogen is transformed into helium through the catalytic action of carbon and nitrogen, releasing great amounts of energy.

carbon dating, radiocarbon dating.

carbon dioxide, a colorless, odorless gas, composed of carbon and oxygen, that is present in the atmosphere and used commercially in soft drinks, fire extinguishers, and, in solid form, as a refrigerant. It is exhaled by plants and animals as a waste product and is absorbed by green plants as part of photosynthesis. Formula: CO_2

carbon disulfide, a colorless, flammable, poisonous liquid that is explosive when mixed with air and ignited, used as a solvent and disinfectant. Formula: CS_2

car·bon·ic (kär bon′ik) *adj.* of, containing, or obtained from carbon.

carbonic acid, a weak acid formed when carbon dioxide is dissolved in water. Formula: H_2CO_3

Car·bon·if·er·ous (kär′bə nif′ər əs) *n.* the period of the Paleozoic era that in North America comprises the Mississippian and Pennsylvanian periods, an interval during which most of the coal-forming tropical forests flourished. —*adj.* **1.** of, relating to, or characteristic of this period. **2. carboniferous.** yielding or containing carbon or coal. [CARBON + -FEROUS.]

car·bon·i·za·tion (kär′bə nə zā′shən) *n.* the act of carbonizing or the state of being carbonized, esp. the conversion of organic matter, as wood, into coal or charcoal.

car·bon·ize (kär′bə nīz′) *v.t.* **-ized, -iz·ing. 1.** to reduce (a substance) to carbon, as by charring. **2.** to cover, treat, or combine (something) with carbon.

carbon monoxide, a colorless, odorless, very poisonous gas, formed when carbon burns in an atmosphere lacking sufficient oxygen for complete combustion, as in an automobile engine. Formula: CO

carbon paper, a thin paper coated on one side with a preparation of carbon or other inky or coloring substance, that is placed between two sheets of paper to reproduce on the lower sheet any marks made by pressure, as of writing or typing, on the top sheet.

carbon tet·ra·chlo·ride (tet′rə klôr′īd) a colorless, poisonous, nonflammable liquid, made from carbon and chlorine, used in refrigerants and propellants, as a cleaning fluid, and in fire extinguishers. Formula: CCl_4

car·bon·yl (kär′bə nil) *n.* a radical consisting of a carbon atom joined to an oxygen atom by a double bond, occurring in aldehydes, ketones, and many other classes of compounds.

Car·bo·run·dum (kär′bə run′dəm) *n. Trademark.* any of various abrasives of silicon carbide. [CARBO(N) + (CO)RUNDUM.]

car·box·yl (kär bok′sil) *n.* the radical —COOH, characteristic of organic acids. —**car·box·yl·ic** (kär′bə sil′ik), *adj.*

car·box·yl·ase (kär bok′sə lās′) *n.* any of a group of enzymes that catalyze production of aldehydes by removing carbon dioxide from certain organic acids.

car·boy (kär′boi′) *n.* a large bottle, usually of glass, enclosed in basketwork or a wooden box or crate for protection, used esp. for containing acids and other corrosive liquids. [Persian *qarābah* large flagon.]

car·bun·cle (kär′bung kəl) *n.* **1.** a hard, painful, pus-filled sac resembling a boil, but larger and more severe, caused by bacterial infection and often accompanied by fever, headache, and loss of appetite. **2.** a smooth, deep red garnet cut without facets. [Dialectal Old French *carbuncle* the gem, from Latin *carbunculus* small coal, red gem, tumor, diminutive of *carbō* coal.] —**car·bun·cu·lar** (kär bung′kyə lər), *adj.*

car·bu·ret (kär′bə rāt′, -byə rāt′, -byə ret′) *v.t.* **-ret·ed, -ret·ing;** *also, British,* **-ret·ted, -ret·ting. 1.** to mix (air or gas) with volatile carbon compounds, such as gasoline or benzine. **2.** to combine (a substance) chemically with carbon. [From CARBON.] —**car·bu·re·tion** (kär′bə rā′shən, -byə-), *n.*

car·bu·re·tor (kär′bə rā′tər, -byə-) *also, British,* **car·bu·ret·tor** (kär′byə ret′ər). *n.* a device in an internal-combustion engine that mixes a fine spray of gasoline with air to form a combustible mixture that can be burned in the cylinders.

carburetor

Choke / Air filter / Air / Air mixes with fuel / Fuel / Throttle / To pistons

car·ca·jou (kär′kə jü′) *n.* wolverine. [Canadian French *carcajou;* of Algonquian origin.]

car·cass (kär′kəs) *n.* **1.** the dead body of an animal. **2.** *Informal.* the body of a human being, living or dead. ➡ usually used humorously. **3.** something from which life, essence, or power is gone; decaying or worthless remains, as the ruined framework of a structure: *The carcass of an old barn stood on the hill.* [French *carcasse;* of uncertain origin.]

car·cin·o·gen (kär sin′ə jən) *n.* a substance or agent capable of inducing cancer. —**car·cin·o·gen·ic** (kär′sə nō jen′ik), *adj.*

car·ci·no·ma (kär′sə nō′mə) *n., pl.* **-mas** or **-ma·ta** (-mə tə). any of several types of malignant growths, originating in epithelial tissue, as in the skin, stomach, or breast. Carcinoma is the most frequent type of cancer. [Latin *carcinōma* cancerous ulcer, from Greek *karkinōma,* from *karkinos* cancer.]

card¹ (kärd) *n.* **1.** a flat, usually rectangular piece of stiff paper, thin cardboard, or plastic, used for various purposes, as for containing information: *a business card, a membership card, an index card.* **2.** playing card. **3. cards. a.** a game played with such cards, as bridge or poker. **b.** the playing of such a game: *I beat my roommate at cards.* **4.** a piece of stiff paper or cardboard, usually ornamented, bearing a message or greeting, as for a particular occasion: *an anniversary card, a birthday card.* Also, **greeting card. 5.** postcard *(def. 1).* **6.** a number of articles attached to a piece of cardboard and to be sold as a unit: *a card of buttons.* **7.** credit card. **8.** a program or listing of events or participants, as in racing or boxing. **9.** a large, usually rectangular piece of cardboard on which an advertisement or announcement is printed, as for placing in a window. **10.** something comparable to a playing card held during a game, useful as a resource in obtaining an objective. **11.** compass card. **12.** *Informal.* a person who is amusing or facetious; wag. —*v.t.* to list or put on a card. [Middle French *carte* piece of stiff paper, playing card, from Latin *charta* paper, leaf of papyrus, from Greek *chartēs* leaf of papyrus, writing. Doublet of CHART.]

• **in** (or **on**) **the cards.** likely to happen; impending.

• **to put** (or **lay**) **one's cards on the table.** to reveal something frankly and openly, as one's intentions or resources; be completely straightforward.

card² (kärd) *n.* **1.** a textile machine having wire teeth, for combing or brushing matted or loose fibers, removing short fibers,

a	at	e	end	o	hot	u	up	hw	white		about
ā	ape	ē	me	ō	old	ū	use	ng	song		taken
ä	far	i	it	ô	fork	ü	rule	th	thin	ə	pencil
âr	care	ī	ice	oi	oil	u̇	pull	th	this		lemon
		îr	pierce	ou	out	ûr	turn	zh	measure		circus

and producing a continuous strand, or sliver. **2.** a tool or comb having metal or wire teeth, used to separate, comb, or straighten hairs or fibers. —*v.t.* to use a card on, as in preparing wool for spinning. [Middle French *carde* the implement, going back to Latin *cardu(u)s* thistle (used to make a card).] —**card′er,** *n.*

car·da·mom (kär′də məm) *also,* **car·da·mon** (kär′də mən), **car·da·mum.** —*n.* **1.** the greenish brown, aromatic fruit capsules of a plant, *Elettaria cardamomum,* of the ginger family, used whole or ground as a spice in foods, as curries, in beverages, as wines, in medicines, and for chewing. **2.** the plant itself. [Latin *cardamōmum* the spice, from Greek *kardamōmon.*]

card·board (kärd′bôrd′) *n.* a thin pasteboard or other stiff material made of paper pulp, used to make such items as cartons, boxes, and cards.

card catalog, an alphabetical file of cards indicating the books and other items in a library collection, each card usually identifying a single item by author, title, or subject.

card file, card index.

cardi-, form of **cardio-** before vowels, as in *cardiac.*

car·di·ac (kär′dē ak′) *adj.* **1.** of, relating to, situated near, or affecting the heart: *cardiac disease, a cardiac massage.* **2.** of or relating to the esophageal opening of the stomach. —*n.* a person who has heart disease. [Latin *cardiacus* relating to the heart, from Greek *kardiakos,* from *kardia* heart.]

cardiac arrest, a sudden stoppage of the heart, as from shock, most commonly suffered by patients while undergoing surgery.

cardiac muscle, striated muscle found in the outer wall of the heart.

car·di·gan (kär′di gən) *n.* a sweater that opens down the front like a jacket and usually has no collar. [From the Earl of *Cardigan,* 1797-1868, English army officer who popularized it.]

car·di·nal (kär′də nəl) *n.* **1.** in the Roman Catholic Church, one of a number of prelates forming the chief advisory body of the pope, typically wearing rich red robes. Cardinals rank immediately below the pope; at his death, they meet to elect a new pope. **2.** a crested finchlike bird, *Cardinalis cardinalis,* native to various parts of North, Central, and South America, the male of which has bright red plumage with a black patch around the bill; redbird. **3.** a deep, rich red color. **4.** cardinal number. —*adj.* **1.** of primary or fundamental importance; chief; principal: *a cardinal rule.* **2.** having the color cardinal. [Latin *cardinālis* chief, that on which something hinges, from *cardō* hinge.]

cardinal *(def. 2)*

car·di·nal·ate (kär′də nə lāt′) *n.* **1.** the rank, dignity, or term of office of a cardinal. **2.** College of Cardinals.

cardinal flower 1. the trumpet-shaped, usually bright red flower of any of a group of plants, *Lobelia cardinalis,* that grow wild in damp regions of eastern and central North America. **2.** the plant bearing this flower, having lance-shaped leaves.

cardinal number, a number that indicates a total or how many, as zero, one, two, and so forth. Cardinal numbers express the result of counting or of operations that depend on counting: *Six times two is twelve. There are three kittens in the box.* ➡ distinguished from **ordinal number.**

cardinal points, the four principal directions of the compass; north, south, east, and west.

cardinal sins, seven deadly sins.

cardinal virtues, justice, temperance, prudence (or wisdom), and fortitude (or courage), classified by Plato and considered by ancient philosophers and theologians as the qualities essential to moral excellence. ➡ often distinguished from **theological virtues.**

card index, a file or other systematic arrangement of cards on which records or other data, as a listing, are entered. Also, **card file.**

card·ing (kär′ding) *n.* the process of preparing textile fibers, as wool, cotton, or flax, for spinning, during which the raw material is passed through rollers and brushes to clean, untangle, and align the fibers.

cardio- *combining form* heart: *cardiogram.* [Greek *kardiā* heart.]

car·di·o·gram (kär′dē ə gram′) *n.* electrocardiogram.

car·di·o·graph (kär′dē ə graf′) *n.* electrocardiograph.

car·di·ol·o·gist (kär′dē ol′ə jist) *n.* a doctor who specializes in treating disorders and diseases of the heart.

car·di·ol·o·gy (kär′dē ol′ə jē) *n.* the branch of medicine that studies the heart, its functions, and its diseases.

car·di·o·pul·mo·nar·y resuscitation (kär′dē ō pŭl′mə ner′ē, -pul′-) see CPR.

car·di·o·vas·cu·lar (kär′dē ō vas′kyə lər) *adj.* of or relating to the heart and blood vessels.

car·doon (kär dün′) *n.* a coarse, spiny perennial plant, *Cynara cardunculus,* bearing purple-blue flowers, grown for its edible root and thick leafstalks. [French *cardon,* from Provençal *cardon,* from Late Latin *cardo,* from Latin *carduus* thistle.]

card·sharp (kärd′shärp′) *n.* a person, esp. a professional gambler, who cheats at cards. Also, **card′sharp′er, card·shark** (kärd′shärk′).

care (kâr) *n.* **1.** a troubled state of mind, as that arising from anxiety, doubt, or concern; worry; distress. **2.** a cause of this: *She acts as though she hasn't a care in the world.* **3.** close and serious attention: *Your care in compiling the report is appreciated.* **4.** temporary keeping or charge; supervision; custody: *He is under a doctor's care.* **5.** an object of concern or attention. —*v.,* **cared, car·ing.** —*v.i.* **1.** to have or show interest or solicitude; be anxious or concerned: *to care about one's personal appearance, to care about the feelings of others.* **2.** to have a liking, fondness, or affection: *I don't care for beets. He cares very much for her.* **3.** to have an objection; mind. ➡ used chiefly in questions or with a negative: *Do you care if I use you as a reference? She doesn't care if the appointment is canceled.* **4.** to make provision or look after (with *for*): *to care for the aged.* **5.** to want or wish; like (with *for*): *Do you care for more soup?* —*v.t.* **1.** to have an objection or pay attention to; feel interest, concern, or distress about: *I don't care what people say.* **2.** to have an inclination; wish: *Would you care to dance?* [Old English *caru* grief, trouble, interest.] —**car′er,** *n.*

• **care** (or **in care**) **of.** at the address of.
• **to take care.** to be careful.
• **to take care of. a.** to look after or provide for: *to take care of a patient.* **b.** to attend to; deal with; accomplish: *Will you take care of the problem?*

Synonyms *n.* **Care, concern,** and **solicitude** mean a troubled state of mind arising especially from involvement with the interests or troubles of others. **Care** generally suggests heavy responsibility or anxious affection: *A year in office left the president's face worn by care.* **Concern** implies involvement or interest in something specific: *to feel concern because one hasn't heard from a friend.* **Solicitude** suggests deep concern and sympathetic attentiveness: *The invalid's friends showed their solicitude with daily visits and phone calls.*

CARE, Cooperative for American Relief Everywhere, Inc., a nonprofit, voluntary American agency that distributes food, funds, and goods to the needy in other countries, founded after World War II as the Cooperative for American Remittances to Europe.

ca·reen (kə rēn′) *v.i.* **1.** to sway from side to side while moving, as if out of control; lurch: *The car careened around the corner.* **2.** to list or lean to one side: *The schooner careened in the high wind.* —*v.t.* **1.** to turn (a ship) over on one side in order to clean, caulk, or repair the bottom. **2.** to cause to list or lean to one side. [Middle French *carène* keel of a ship, going back to Latin *carīna.*]

ca·reer (kə rîr′) *n.* **1.** an occupation or profession, esp. as followed as one's lifework; calling; vocation: *a career in medicine.* **2.** the course or progress of a person's life, or some portion of it, esp. as related to a vocation: *I've met many interesting people in my career.* **3.** a swift or rushing movement or course; speed: *The horse stumbled in full career.* —*v.i.* to move or run with a swift, headlong motion; rush or dash along: *The train careered down the tracks.* [French *carrière* racecourse, course, profession, going back to Late Latin *carrāria (via)* (road) for carriages, from Latin *carrus* wagon.]

care·free (kâr′frē′) *adj.* free from care or worry; untroubled; happy-go-lucky; lighthearted.

care·ful (kâr′fəl) *adj.* **1.** acting with or showing thoughtful prudence and attention; watchfully cautious; mindful; wary: *Be careful not to trip. I was careful not to reveal the secret.* **2.** done or made with thought, thoroughness, or attention to detail; painstaking: *careful research, a careful analysis of a problem.* **3.** taking pains with or attentive to one's work; thorough: *Careful writers check their spelling.* **4.** *Archaic.* anxious; worried. —**care′ful·ly,** *adv.* —**care′ful·ness,** *n.*

Synonyms **Careful, meticulous,** and **punctilious** mean taking pains with or being attentive to or thorough in doing something. **Careful** suggests the exercise of caution to avoid errors or sloppiness: *Be careful to check your final draft for misspellings.* **Meticulous** more particularly suggests

carefulness leading to finicky attention to detail: *Don't be so meticulous in painting the window trim that you run out of time to do the walls.* **Punctilious** refers to extreme attention to detail: *The punctilious researcher insisted on checking every date in three sources.*

care·giv·er (kâr′giv′ər) *n.* a person who cares for others who need help in taking care of themselves, such as the very young, the mentally disturbed, and the elderly.

care label, a label attached by the manufacturer to a garment, giving laundering or cleaning instructions.

care·less (kâr′lis) *adj.* **1.** not paying enough attention or exercising enough caution; not watchful: *to be careless in crossing the street.* **2.** resulting from or done with a lack of care, attentiveness, or thoughtfulness: *a careless mistake.* **3.** not caring or troubling; unconcerned; indifferent: *to be careless about one's appearance.* **4.** achieved without effort; artless; unstudied: *careless grace.* **5.** free from care or worry; carefree: *a careless existence.* —**care′less·ly,** *adv.* —**care′less·ness,** *n.*

ca·ress (kə res′) *v.t.* **1.** to touch or stroke gently and lovingly; fondle; pet: *The child caressed her kitten.* **2.** to touch soothingly, as if with affection: *The music caressed his ears.* —*n.* **1.** a gentle, loving touch or stroke. **2.** a light, soothing touch: *the soft caress of a summer breeze.* [French *caresse* stroking, fondling, from Italian *carezza,* going back to Latin *carus* dear.] —**ca·ress′a·ble,** *adj.* —**ca·ress′er,** *n.* —**ca·ress′ing·ly,** *adv.*

car·et (kar′it) *n.* a mark (∧) used, as in editing, to indicate where something should be inserted. [Latin *caret* it is lacking.]

care·tak·er (kâr′tā′kər) *n.* **1.** a person who takes care of a person, place, or thing, esp. the custodian of a building or estate. **2.** a person or persons who temporarily fulfill the duties of an office.

care·worn (kâr′wôrn′) *adj.* showing signs of having undergone anxiety, worry, or distress: *a careworn face.*

car·fare (kär′fâr′) *n.* the cost of riding, as on a streetcar or bus.

car·go (kär′gō) *n., pl.* **-goes** or **-gos.** the goods and merchandise carried by a ship, plane, or vehicle; freight. [Spanish *cargo* load, burden, from *cargar* to load, from Late Latin *carricāre,* from Latin *carrus* two-wheeled wagon; of Celtic origin.] —For Synonyms, see **freight.**

car·hop (kär′hop′) *n.* a waitress or waiter at a drive-in restaurant.

Car·ib (kar′ib) *n.* **1.** a member of one of several Indian tribes who live in the West Indies and northeastern South America. **2.** a family of South American Indian languages spoken predominantly in the West Indies and northeastern parts of South America. [Spanish *caribe;* of Carib origin.]

Car·ib·be·an (kar′ə bē′ən, kə rib′ē-) *adj.* **1.** of or relating to the Caribbean Sea or its islands and their peoples. **2.** of or relating to the Caribs, their language, or their culture.

ca·ri·be (kə rē′bā) *n., pl.* **-bes** or **be.** piranha. [Spanish *caribe* Carib; referring to its voracity and the Carib practice of eating human flesh.]

car·i·bou (kar′ə bü′) *n., pl.* **-bou** or **-bous.** any of a group of large deer, genus *Rangifer,* native to the northern regions of the world, having a coarse, heavy coat and large antlers. The doe, unlike all other female deer, bears antlers. The Eurasian caribou, *R. tarandus,* is commonly called the reindeer. Caribou are valued for their hide, meat, and milk and as draft animals. [French *caribou;* of Algonquian origin.]

car·i·ca·ture (kar′i kə chər, -chūr′) *n.* **1.** a pictorial or descriptive representation that exaggerates or distorts the characteristics, peculiarities, or features of a person or thing. **2.** the art or process of making such representations. **3.** something so distorted or inferior as to seem a ludicrous imitation; poor or inept likeness or copy. —*v.t.,* **-tured, -turing.** to make a caricature of; represent so as to make ridiculous. [French *caricature* satirical picture, from Italian *caricatura* literally, a loading, from *caricare* to load, going back to Latin *carrus* two-wheeled wagon; of Celtic origin; because such a picture was loaded to excess or exaggerated.] —**car′i·ca·tur·ist,** *n.*

car·ies (kâr′ēz, -ē ēz) *n.* decay of a bone or tooth. Dental caries often results in inflammation of the dental pulp if left untreated.
➡ used as singular. [Latin *cariēs* rottenness.]

car·il·lon (kar′ə lon′, -lən) *n.* **1.** a set of stationary bells sounded by means of a keyboard or by machinery. **2.** a melody played on a carillon. **3.** an organ stop that produces a sound like that of a carillon. [French *carillon* chime, musical bells, going back to Late Latin *quaterniō* group of four, from Latin *quater* four times; originally, a group of four bells.]

car·il·lon·neur (kar′ə lə nûr′) *n.* a person who plays a carillon.

car·i·ole (kar′ē ōl′) *also,* **carriole.** *n.* **1.** a small, open carriage designed to be drawn by one horse. **2.** a light, covered cart.

[French *carriole,* from Italian *carriuola* wheelbarrow, from *carro* cart, from Latin *carrus* two-wheeled wagon; of Celtic origin.]

car·i·ous (kâr′ē əs) *adj.* having caries; decayed. [Latin *cariōsus* rotten.]

cark·ing (kär′king) *adj. Archaic.* troublesome; annoying; distressing. [From obsolete *cark* burden, distress (from Anglo-Norman *kark* burden, weight, going back to Late Latin *carricāre* to load, from Latin *carrus* two-wheeled wagon; of Celtic origin) + -ING¹.]

carl (kärl) *also,* **carle.** *n. Archaic.* **1.** boor; churl. **2.** peasant; rustic. [Old Norse *karl* man.]

car·load (kär′lōd′) *n.* the amount that a car, as a railroad freight car, can hold or carry.

Car·lo·vin·gi·an (kär′lə vin′jē ən) *adj., n.* Carolingian.

car·ma·gnole (kär′mən yōl′) *n.* **1.** a lively dance and song popular during the French Revolution of 1789. **2.** a costume worn by French revolutionists, consisting of a short jacket with wide lapels and metal buttons, a red cap, black pantaloons, and a tricolored girdle. [French *carmagnole,* from *Carmagnola,* town in Piedmont, Italy, where the jacket of the costume originated.]

Car·mel·ite (kär′mə līt′) *n.* a member of a religious order of friars and nuns founded in Palestine in the twelfth century. Also, **White Friar.** —*adj.* of or relating to the Carmelites or their order.

car·min·a·tive (kär min′ə tiv, kär′mə nā′-) *n.* a medicine that expels gas from the stomach and intestines. —*adj.* having the power to expel gas from the stomach and intestines. [Latin *carminātus,* past participle of *carmināre* to card wool, purify + -IVE.]

car·mine (kär′min, -mīn) *n.* **1.** a deep red or purplish red color; crimson. **2.** a crimson pigment obtained from the dye cochineal. —*adj.* having the color carmine. [French *carmin,* from Medieval Latin *carminium* the crimson pigment, from blend of Arabic *qirmizī* crimson and Latin *minium* red lead.]

car·nage (kär′nij) *n.* **1.** an extensive and bloody slaughter, as in battle; massacre. **2.** *Archaic.* dead bodies, as of soldiers. [French *carnage* slaughter, going back to Latin *carō* flesh, meat.]

car·nal (kär′nəl) *adj.* **1.** relating to or characterized by bodily or sexual passions and appetites; sensual: *carnal pleasures.* **2.** not spiritual; worldly. [Latin *carnālis,* from *carō* flesh.] —**car·nal·i·ty** (kär nal′i tē), *n.* —**car′nal·ly,** *adv.*

car·na·tion (kär nā′shən) *n.* **1.** the fragrant flower of any of a large group of plants, *Dianthus caryophyllus,* cultivated commercially and as a garden flower. The varieties differ greatly in size, shape, and color. **2.** the plant bearing this flower, having grayish green, grasslike leaves. **3.** a light red color. —*adj.* having the color carnation. [French *carnation,* from Italian *carnagione* flesh, flesh color, going back to Latin *carō* flesh; because the flower was originally flesh-colored.]

carnation

car·nau·ba (kär nou′bə, -nô′bə) *n.* **1.** a Brazilian palm, *Copernicia prunifera,* having wax-covered leaves. **2.** the hard, shiny wax produced by this tree, used esp. in making polishes and floor coatings. [Brazilian Portuguese *carnauba,* from Tupi-Guarani *carnauba.*]

car·nel·ian (kär nēl′yən) *also,* **cornelian.** *n.* a red to reddish orange variety of chalcedony, used as a semiprecious stone. [Modification (influenced by Latin *carō* flesh) of CORNELIAN, from Old French *corneline,* from *corne* a kind of cherry, going back to Latin *cornum;* because of the stone's color.]

car·ni·val (kär′nə vəl) *n.* **1.** an amusement show, usually one that travels, having rides, sideshows, games, and refreshments. **2.** any merrymaking, revelry, or festival, as a program of entertainment or sports: *a winter skiing carnival.* **3.** *also,* **Carnival.** a period of feasting and merrymaking immediately preceding Lent, varying from three days to a few weeks and observed esp. in countries with large Roman Catholic populations. [Italian *carnevale* Shrovetide, from Medieval Latin *carnelevarium* Shrovetide, removal of meat (during Lent), from Latin *carō* flesh + *levāre* to raise, take away.]

car·ni·vore (kär′nə vôr′) *n.* a plant or animal that eats flesh, esp. any of numerous mammals constituting the order Carnivora,

a	at	e	end	o	hot	u	up	hw	white		about
ā	ape	ē	me	ō	old	ū	use	ng	song		taken
ä	far	i	it	ô	fork	ü	rule	th	thin	ə	pencil
âr	care	ī	ice	oi	oil	u̇	pull	th	this		lemon
		îr	pierce	ou	out	ûr	turn	zh	measure		circus

including dogs, cats, bears, and weasels, having long, daggerlike canine teeth and sharp claws.

car·niv·o·rous (kär niv′ər əs) *adj.* **1.** flesh-eating: *Flytraps are carnivorous plants.* **2.** of or relating to carnivores. [Latin *carnivorus* feeding on flesh.] —**car·niv′o·rous·ly,** *adv.* —**car·niv′o·rous·ness,** *n.*

car·no·tite (kär′nə tīt′) *n.* a yellowish uranium mineral found predominantly in southwestern Colorado. [From Adolphe Carnot, 1839-1920, French mining engineer.]

car·ob (kar′əb) *n.* **1.** an evergreen tree, *Ceratonia siliqua,* native to the eastern Mediterranean, but cultivated in many warm regions for its edible pod. **2.** St. John's bread. [Middle French *carobe* this evergreen tree, going back to Arabic *kharrūb* bean pod.]

car·ol (kar′əl) *n.* a song of joy or praise, esp. a Christmas song or hymn. —*v.,* **-oled, -ol·ing**; *also, British,* **-olled, -ol·ling.** —*v.i.* **1.** to sing Christmas carols in a group. **2.** to sing, esp. in a lively, joyous manner; warble. —*v.t.* **1.** to sing (something) joyously. **2.** to celebrate or praise in song. [Old French *carole* round dance, through Latin, from Greek *choraulēs* flute player who accompanied a choral dance.] —**car′ol·er**; *also, British,* **car′ol·ler,** *n.*

Car·o·lin·gi·an (kar′ə lin′jē ən) *adj.* of or relating to the dynasty that ruled in France from A.D. 751 to 987, in Germany from A.D. 751 to 911, and in Italy from A.D. 751 to 887, and that reached its greatest prominence under Charlemagne, king of the Franks. —*n.* a sovereign or member of the Carolingian family or dynasty. Also, **Carlovingian.**

Car·o·lin·i·an (kar′ə lin′ē ən) *adj.* of or relating to North Carolina or South Carolina or both. —*n.* a native or inhabitant of North Carolina or South Carolina.

car·om (kar′əm) *also,* **carrom.** *n.* **1.** *Billiards.* a shot in which the cue ball strikes two other balls in succession. **2.** any strike and rebound, as a ball bouncing off a wall. —*v.i.* **1.** to make a carom. **2.** to strike and rebound. [French *carambole* red ball in billiards, from Spanish *carambola* a round and orange-colored fruit, red ball in billiards; of uncertain origin.]

car·o·tene (kar′ə tēn′) *n.* an orange or yellow hydrocarbon out of which the liver manufactures vitamin A, occurring as a pigment in eggs, butter, and certain vegetables, such as carrots and sweet potatoes; provitamin A. [Latin *carōt(a)* carrot + -ENE. See CARROT.]

ca·rot·e·noid (kə rot′ə noid′) *n.* any of a group of light yellow to purplish red plant and animal pigments, including carotene. —*adj.* **1.** of, relating to, or similar to carotene. **2.** of or relating to the carotenoids. [CAROTEN(E) + -OID.]

ca·rot·id (kə rot′id) *n.* either of two large arteries, one on each side of the neck, that carry blood to the head. Also, **carotid artery.** —*adj.* of, relating to, or near these arteries. [Greek *karōtides* carotid arteries, from *karoun* to stupefy; because compressing them was formerly thought to cause stupor.]

ca·rous·al (kə rou′zəl) *n.* a boisterous or uproarious drinking party; noisy, drunken, jovial banquet or revel.

ca·rouse (kə rouz′) *v.i.,* **-roused, -rous·ing.** to drink freely and heavily; take part in a carousal. —*n.* carousal. [Old French *carous* all out, from German *garaus (trinken)* (to drink) completely out, all out (in the sense of "emptying one's cup").] —**ca·rous′er,** *n.*

car·ou·sel (kar′ə sel′, kar′ə sel′) *also,* **carrousel.** *n.* merry-go-round *(def. 1).* [French *carrousel,* from Italian *carosello;* of uncertain origin.]

carp[1] (kärp) *v.i.* to find fault or complain, esp. petulantly or unreasonably (often with *at*): *My boss carps at even the smallest errors.* [Old Norse *karpa* to brag; meaning probably influenced by Latin *carpere* to pluck.] —**carp′er,** *n.*

carp[2] (kärp) *n., pl.* **carp** or **carps. 1.** a freshwater fish, *Cyprinus carpio,* popular as a food fish, esp. in the Far East and in Europe where it is bred and raised as a delicacy. Length: 2 feet (0.6 meter). **2.** any of a group of similar or related fish, including goldfish, minnows, chub, and dace. [Old French *carpe,* from Late Latin *carpa;* possibly of Germanic origin.]

-carp *combining form* a part of a fruit, or a fruiting body: *pericarp.* [Modern Latin *-carpium,* from Greek *karpos* fruit.]

car·pal (kär′pəl) *adj.* of, relating to, or near the wrist. —*n.* any of the eight bones of the wrist. For illustration, see **hand.** [Modern Latin *carpalis,* from *carpus* wrist.]

car·pe di·em (kär′pē dī′em) *Latin.* take advantage of or make the most of the present; enjoy today.

car·pel (kär′pəl) *n.* a pistil or one unit of a compound pistil. [French *carpelle,* from Greek *karpos* fruit.]

car·pen·ter (kär′pən tər) *n.* a person who builds and repairs wooden parts and structures, as a house or its framework. —*v.i.* to do a carpenter's work; work as a carpenter. —*v.t.* to make or repair by or as if by carpentry. [Old French *carpentier* worker in

wood, from Late Latin *carpentārius* carriage maker, going back to Latin *carpentum* carriage; of Celtic origin.]

car·pen·try (kär′pən trē) *n.* **1.** the business, trade, or work of a carpenter. **2.** the work produced by a carpenter.

car·pet (kär′pit) *n.* **1.** a floor covering made of heavy, often woven or felted, fabric. **2.** the fabric used for it; carpeting. **3.** any covering, surface, or expanse resembling a carpet: *a carpet of leaves, a carpet of flowers.* —*v.t.* to cover or furnish with or as with a carpet: *Snow carpeted the field.* [Medieval Latin *carpita* a thick cloth, probably from Latin *carpere* to pluck, spin (wool).]
· **on the carpet.** before an authority for a reproof or reprimand: *to be called on the carpet for negligence.*

car·pet·bag (kär′pit bag′) *n.* a satchel or bag for traveling, made of carpeting, commonly used in the nineteenth century. —*v.i.,* **-bagged, -bag·ging.** to act as a carpetbagger.

car·pet·bag·ger (kär′pit bag′ər) *n.* **1.** any Northerner who went to the South immediately after the American Civil War in order to gain political or other advantages from the disorganized conditions then prevailing in the Southern states. ➡ used contemptuously. **2.** a person taking up residence in a place and seeking to gain advantages, esp. one who interferes with the politics of a locality with which he or she is thought to have no permanent or genuine connection. [CARPETBAG + -ER[1]; because many of these Northerners came South carrying clothes in *carpetbags.*]

carpet beetle, any of a group of small beetles, order Coleoptera, whose larvae destroy carpets, fur, and woolen fabrics.

car·pet·ing (kär′pi ting) *n.* **1.** fabric used for carpets. **2.** carpets collectively.

carpet sweeper, a mechanical device for cleaning carpets and rugs that, when pushed, rotates a brush that sweeps dirt from the surface into an attached dustpan.

carp·ing (kär′ping) *adj.* tending to carp; overly critical; fault-finding. —**carp′ing·ly,** *adv.*

car·pool (kär′pül′) *v.i.* to be in a car pool. —*v.t.* to drive in a car pool: *We carpool the children to dancing class.*

car pool 1. an arrangement among a group of car owners in which each member of the group takes a turn driving the others or their children, as to and from work or school. Also, **car pooling. 2.** the people belonging to such a group. —**car pooler.**

car·port (kär′pôrt′) *n.* a shelter for an automobile, usually consisting of a roof projecting from the side of a building.

car·pus (kär′pəs) *n., pl.* **-pi** (-pī). the bones of the wrist collectively; wrist. [Modern Latin *carpus* wrist, from Greek *karpos.*]

car·rack (kar′ək) *n.* a large three-masted ship developed in the fourteenth century. [Old French *carraque* small ship, going back to Arabic *qarārqīr* merchant ships.]

car·ra·geen (kar′ə jēn′) *also,* **car·ra·gheen.** *n.* Irish moss. [From *Carragheen,* Ireland.]

car·ra·gee·nan (kar′ə jē′nən) *n.* a colloidal substance extracted from Irish moss, used as a stabilizer and emulsifier in dairy products, cosmetics, and paints. [CARRAGEEN + -an, suffix used to form chemical compounds.]

car·rel (kar′əl) *also,* **car·rell.** *n.* a small enclosure or partitioned area for individual study, near the stacks in a library. [Modification of Middle English *carole* round dance, ring, enclosed place, from Old French *carole* round dance. See CAROL.]

car·riage (kar′ij) *n.* **1.** a wheeled, usually horse-drawn, vehicle designed to carry passengers. **2.** baby carriage. **3.** the manner of carrying or holding the head and body: *a person with a stately carriage.* **4.** a movable part of a machine that carries or supports some other part: *the carriage of a typewriter.* **5.** the act of carrying or transporting; conveyance. **6.** the cost or price of transportation. **7.** *British.* a railroad passenger car. **8.** a wheeled support for a gun or cannon. [Dialectal Old French *cariage* something carried, from *carier* to carry. See CARRY.]

carriage trade, wealthy or upper-class patrons, as of a theater, restaurant, or store. [Because they formerly drove up in private carriages.]

car·ri·er (kar′ē ər) *n.* **1.** a person or organization, as a railroad or shipping line, whose business it is to carry or transport something. **2.** a commercial or military vehicle used to carry or transport something: *a troop carrier.* **3.** a medium or device in or on which something is carried: *The blood serves as a carrier of oxygen to the cells.* **4.** any organism that carries or transmits an infectious disease, often without contracting it. **5.** an individual who has a recessive gene for some defect and although not displaying the defect, can pass it on to offspring. **6.** carrier wave. **7.** aircraft carrier.

carrier pigeon 1. a homing pigeon used to carry messages. **2.** a pigeon of a variety developed in England, having a straight thick beak, long wattles, and plumage that is usually black or grayish brown. Originally bred for its homing instinct, the carrier pigeon is now used only for show purposes.

C

carrier wave, a wave that can be modulated and carries signals to be transmitted, as through a radio system.

car·ri·ole (kar′ē ōl′) cariole.

car·ri·on (kar′ē ən) *n.* dead and putrefying flesh. [Anglo-Norman *caroigne* carcass, going back to Latin *carō* flesh.]

carrion crow 1. a black crow, *Corvus corone,* of Europe that feeds on carrion. **2.** a black vulture, *Coragyps atratus,* of the southern United States.

car·rom (kar′əm) carom.

car·rot (kar′ət) *n.* **1.** the fleshy root of a plant, *Daucus carota,* of the parsley family, eaten as a vegetable. **2.** the plant itself. [Middle French *carote,* from Latin *carōta,* from Greek *karōton.*]

car·rot·y (kar′ə tē) *adj.* resembling a carrot in color; orange red.

car·rou·sel (kar′ə sel′, kar′ə sel′) carousel.

car·ry (kar′ē) *v.,* **-ried, -ry·ing.** *—v.t.* **1.** to move while bearing the weight of; transport: *He carried the child upstairs.* **2.** to serve as a means of conveyance or transmission for: *Air carries sound waves. The pipeline carries crude oil.* **3.** to have on one's person: *She always carries a pen.* **4.** to have as an attribute, property, or mark: *Your opinion carries great weight. The contract carries a guarantee.* **5.** to bear the weight or burden of; sustain: *Pillars carried the roof of the porch.* **6.** to continue or extend (something) in a particular direction or to a certain point: *to carry a highway across marshland, to carry political opinions into one's business life.* **7.** to keep in stock, as for sale; deal in: *That store carries stationery.* **8.** to pass or adopt (a motion or bill): *The bill was carried by a wide margin.* **9.** to be successful or victorious in; win or capture: *The president carried all of the Southern states in the election.* **10.** to transfer and add, as a number or total, from one column or page to another. **11.** to cause to go or come; lead: *The hurricane carried the ship off course. Their sense of adventure carried them to far places.* **12.** to sing (a melody or part) correctly: *to carry a tune.* **13.** to hold (one's body or a part of it) in a certain way: *to carry oneself proudly.* **14.** to have as a consequence or result: *The crime carries a three-year prison term.* **15.** to be pregnant with: *The mare is carrying a foal.* **16.** to maintain (a charge) on one's account books in hope of future payment. **17.** to include in a broadcast or publication: *The network carried the story on the evening news.* *—v.i.* **1.** to go or travel for a distance: *The arrow carried for 20 yards. The speaker's voice carried well.* **2.** to be approved by vote: *The bill carried by a large majority.* **3.** to act as a bearer or carrier. *—n., pl.* **-ries. 1.** the range or distance covered or traveled by something, as a gun or projectile. **2.** a portage, as between navigable bodies of water. **3.** the act of carrying: *The halfback gained 60 yards in ten carries.* [Dialectal Old French *carier* to convey in a vehicle, from Late Latin *carricāre* to load (as a wagon), from Latin *carrus* two-wheeled wagon. Doublet of CHARGE.]

•**to carry away.** to arouse great emotional reaction in; excite or move greatly: *The audience was carried away by the pianist's performance.*

•**to carry forward. a.** to transfer, as a total or item, to another column or page. **b.** to make progress or proceed with.

•**to carry off. a.** to win, as a prize or honor. **b.** to accomplish or do (something): *The thieves succeeded in carrying off the robbery.* **c.** to cause to die; kill: *War and famine carried off half the population.*

•**to carry on. a.** to keep going; continue. **b.** to engage in; manage; conduct: *to carry on a debate.* **c.** *Informal.* to behave in a wild, foolish, or silly manner.

•**to carry out. a.** to obey; execute: *The soldier carried out the order promptly.* **b.** to bring to completion; accomplish.

•**to carry over. a.** to transfer, as an item or total, to another column or page. **b.** to set aside; postpone.

•**to carry through. a.** to accomplish; complete. **b.** to bring through difficulties or trouble; sustain: *Our friends helped carry us through our troubles.*

Synonyms *v.t.* **Carry, bear**[1]**, convey,** and **transport** mean to move objects or people from one place to another. **Carry** is the general term, sometimes used of moving done with a container or vehicle, but also of the action of people or animals: *The train carried 400 passengers. The child was carrying a stick.* **Bear** stresses the importance or dignity of what is carried or the effort involved: *The royal coach bore the king and queen. Two workers bore the heavy beam to the construction site.* **Convey** suggests continuous movement, especially of a substance or mass of material: *These ducts convey heat to the upper floors.* **Transport** applies to the movement of goods or persons in bulk or large numbers, and strongly implies a destination: *The fleet transported the army to the landing site.*

car·ry·all[1] (kar′ē ôl′) *n.* a covered, lightweight, one-horse carriage for several persons. [Modification of CARIOLE.]

car·ry·all[2] (kar′ē ôl′) *n.* a large bag, handbag, or basket. [CARRY + ALL.]

carrying capacity, the maximum population of a species of organism that a given area has the resources to support.

carrying charge 1. interest or any other charge added to the cost of an item or service paid for on an installment plan. **2.** an expense incurred by ownership or use of property, such as taxes.

car·ry-on (kar′ē ôn′, -on′) *adj.* small enough for a passenger to carry aboard an airplane and store beneath a seat or in an overhead compartment: *carry-on luggage.* *—n.* a suitcase or other piece of luggage this small.

car·ry-out (kar′ē out′) *n., adj.* take-out.

car·ry-o·ver (kar′ē ō′vər) *n.* **1.** something retained or remaining: *My interest in stamps is a carry-over from childhood.* **2.** an amount carried forward in an account book.

car·sick (kär′sik′) *adj.* nauseated and dizzy from riding in a car, train, or bus. **—car′sick′ness,** *n.*

cart (kärt) *n.* **1.** a sturdy two-wheeled vehicle, usually drawn by horses or mules, for conveying heavy loads. **2.** a small, wheeled vehicle moved manually; pushcart. **3.** a light two-wheeled carriage. *—v.t.* to carry in or as in a cart. [Partly from Old English *cræt* chariot; partly from Old Norse *kartr* a two-wheeled vehicle.]

•**to put the cart before the horse.** to reverse the proper order; do or say something in reverse order.

cart·age (kär′tij) *n.* **1.** the act of carting. **2.** the rate charged for this.

carte blanche (kärt′ blänch′, blänsh′) *pl.* **cartes blanches** (kärt′ blän′chiz, blänsh′) complete authority or freedom of action or judgment. [French *carte blanche* literally, white card (with a signature above which anything may be written). See CARD[1], BLANK.]

car·tel (kär tel′, kär′təl) *n.* **1.** an international syndicate or trust of commercial enterprises formed to establish a monopoly by controlling prices and production. **2.** a written agreement between warring nations, as for the exchange of prisoners. **3.** *Archaic.* a written challenge to a duel. [French *cartel,* from Italian *cartello* written challenge, placard, diminutive of *carta* sheet of paper, from Latin *c(h)arta* paper. See CARD[1].]

Car·te·sian (kär tē′zhən) *adj.* of or relating to René Descartes, or of his philosophy or mathematical methods. *—n.* a follower of Descartes, or of his philosophy or mathematical methods. [From *Cartesius,* Latinized form of René *Descartes,* 1596-1650, French philosopher and mathematician + -AN.]

Cartesian coordinate, any of the numbers that determine the position of a point in a Cartesian coordinate system.

Cartesian coordinate system, a system that locates a point, in a plane or in space, by its distance from each of two or three axes that intersect, usually at right angles.

Cartesian product, a set that is the collection of all ordered pairs from two given sets such that the first element of each pair is from one set and the second element is from the other set.

Car·thu·sian (kär thü′zhən) *n.* a member of a religious order of monks and nuns, founded in France in 1084. *—adj.* of or relating to this order. [From *Carthusia,* Latinized form of *Chartreuse,* French town where the first monastery of this order was located + -AN.]

car·ti·lage (kär′tə lij) *n.* **1.** the tough, flexible connective tissue in the skeletal structure of human beings and other vertebrates; gristle. **2.** a part or structure formed of cartilage. [French *cartilage* gristle, from Latin *cartilāgō.*]

car·ti·lag·i·nous (kär′tə laj′ə nəs) *adj.* **1.** of or resembling cartilage. **2.** having a skeleton consisting mostly of cartilage, as a shark.

cart·load (kärt′lōd′) *n.* the amount that a cart holds.

car·tog·ra·pher (kär tog′rə fər) *n.* a person who makes or compiles maps or charts.

car·tog·ra·phy (kär tog′rə fē) *n.* the art or science of making or compiling maps or charts. [French *carte* map, card[1] + -GRAPHY. See CARD[1].] **—car·to·graph·ic** (kär′tə graf′ik); *also,* **car′to·graph′i·cal,** *adj.*

car·ton (kär′tən) *n.* **1.** a container made of any of several materials, as cardboard or plastic: *an egg carton, a milk carton.* **2.** the amount that a carton holds: *a carton of milk.* [French *carton* pasteboard, from Italian *cartone,* from *carta* paper, from Latin *charta.* See CARD[1].]

car·toon (kär tün′) *n.* **1.** a sketch or drawing, as in a magazine or periodical, that depicts a humorous situation, satirizes some person or subject of public interest, or illustrates an opinion. **2.** animated cartoon. **3.** comic strip. **4.** a full-size preliminary

a	at	e	end	o	hot	u	up	hw	white		about
ā	ape	ē	me	ō	go	ū	use	ng	song		taken
ä	far	i	it	ô	fork	ü	rule	th	this	ə	pencil
âr	care	ī	ice	oi	oil	u̇	pull	th	this		lemon
		îr	pierce	ou	out	ûr	turn	zh	measure		circus

drawing of a design or picture, to be copied in or transferred to a fresco, mosaic, tapestry, mural painting, or stained glass. —v.i. to draw cartoons. —v.t. to draw a cartoon of. [French *carton* pasteboard. See CARTON.] —**car·toon′ist,** *n.*

car·tridge (kär′trij) *n.* **1.** a cylindrical case, as of metal or paper, usually containing a percussion cap, a propelling charge of gunpowder, and a bullet. **2.** a roll of camera film enclosed in a protective case that fits into a camera as a unit. **3.** a device that holds a phonograph needle and acts as a transducer, converting the vibrations of the needle into an electrical signal as the needle follows a record groove. Also, **pickup. 4.** a small container, designed for easy replacement as a unit, as in a pen or tube. **5.** cassette *(def. 2).* **6.** a small case that holds the electronic circuits that make up a computer program or video game. [Modification of French *cartouche* roll of paper, the cylindrical case for firearms, from Italian *cartoccio,* from *carta* paper, from Latin *charta.* See CARD[1].]

cart·wheel (kärt′hwēl′, -wēl′) *n.* **1.** a sideways handspring. **2.** the wheel of a cart.

car·un·cle (kar′ung kəl, kə rung′-) *n.* **1.** *Zoology.* a naked, fleshy outgrowth, as the comb and wattles of a fowl. **2.** *Botany.* any outgrowth from the covering of a seed, near the point of its attachment to a stalk. [Obsolete French *caruncle,* from Latin *caruncula,* diminutive of *caro* flesh.] —**ca·run′cu·lar, ca·run′-cu·late, ca·run′cu·lous,** *adj.*

carve (kärv) *v.,* **carved, carv·ing.** —v.t. **1.** to cut, esp. meat, into slices or pieces: *to carve a turkey.* **2.** to make or shape by or as by cutting (often with *out*): *to carve a doll from a block of wood, to carve out a career.* **3.** to adorn, as with figures or designs; decorate by cutting: *We carved a pumpkin for Halloween. The chest was carved with many figures.* —v.i. to cut meat into slices or pieces. [Old English *ceorfan* to cut.]

carv·en (kär′vən) *adj. Archaic.* that has been carved.

carv·er (kär′vər) *n.* **1.** a person who carves. **2.** carving knife.

carv·ing (kär′ving) *n.* **1.** a carved work, such as a figure or design. **2.** the act or art of a person who carves.

carving knife, a knife used for carving.

car·wash (kär′wôsh′, -wosh′) *also,* **car wash.** *n.* **1.** a place where automobiles are washed. **2.** the machinery used at such a place. **3.** the act or process of washing an automobile.

car·y·at·id (kar′ē at′id) *n., pl.* **-ids** or **-i·des** (-i dēz′). a statue of a draped female figure serving as a column. [Latin *caryātidēs* (plural), from Greek *Karyātides* (plural).]

caryatids of the Erechtheum in Athens, Greece

car·y·op·sis (kar′ē op′sis) *n., pl.* **-ses** (-sēz) or **-si·des** (-si dēz′). a small, dry seedlike fruit, esp. of a grass, as a grain of wheat or barley.

ca·sa·ba (kə sä′bə) *also,* **cassaba.** *n.* a melon, a cultivated variety of *Cucamis melo,* having a creamy white pulp and a wrinkled rind. Also, **casaba melon.** [From *Kasaba,* Turkey, famous for this kind of melon.]

cas·cade (kas kād′) *n.* **1.** a small waterfall or series of such waterfalls. **2.** anything resembling this: *The blouse had a cascade of ruffles down the front.* —v.i., **-cad·ed, -cad·ing.** to fall or flow in or as in a cascade. [French *cascade* waterfall, from Italian *cascata,* going back to Latin *cāsus* a falling.]

cas·car·a sa·gra·da (kas kâr′ə sə grä′də) *n.* **1.** a North American tree, *Rhamnus purshiana,* of the buckthorn family, bearing black, berrylike fruits and having reddish brown bark, used for making a laxative. **2.** the laxative itself, an extract prepared from dried strips of bark of this tree. Also, **cas·car′a.**

case[1] (kās) *n.* **1.** a specific example or occurrence: *The fire was clearly a case of carelessness.* **2.** the actual state of affairs or circumstances: *If that's the case, then we must go.* **3.** an instance of a disease or injury: *a case of the flu.* **4.** a person who has a disease or injury; patient. **5.** a statement, as of arguments or reasons: *to present a case for proposed legislation.* **6.** a matter or problem, esp. one under investigation: *The bank robbery was a difficult case to solve.* **7.** *Law.* **a.** an action or suit brought before a court for decision. **b.** a statement of facts or circumstances presented for consideration by a court. **8.** *Grammar.* **a.** one of the various inflectional forms of a noun, pronoun, or adjective, used to indicate its syntactical relation to other words in a sentence through word ending or position. **b.** any such relation shown by inflection or other means. **c.** such relationships or forms collectively. **9.** *Informal.* a peculiar or remarkable person. —v.t., **cased, cas·ing.** *Informal.* to look over carefully, esp. with criminal intent: *They cased the store before robbing it.* [Old French *cas* chance, event, from Latin *cāsus* a falling, chance, from *cadere* to fall.]

• **in any case.** no matter what happens; anyhow; regardless.

• **in case.** in the event that; if: *In case anything happens, call me immediately.*

• **in case of.** in the event of: *In case of emergency, use the back exit to get out.*

case[2] (kās) *n.* **1.** something designed to contain, enclose, or protect; box or other container: *a camera case.* **2.** a box and its contents; amount contained in a case: *We ordered three cases of soda for the party.* **3.** a frame, as of a window. **4.** *Printing.* a shallow tray divided into compartments, used for holding type. —v.t., **cased, cas·ing.** to put in or cover with a case; encase. [Norman French *casse* box, chest, from Latin *capsa.*]

case·hard·en (kās′här′dən) *v.t.* **1.** to harden (iron or steel) on the surface, allowing the interior to remain ductile. **2.** to make (someone) callous or unfeeling. —**case′hard′ened,** *adj.*

case history, a record of or report on a person or group, prepared for the purposes of study, diagnosis, or treatment of some physical, mental, or social problem or disorder. Also, **case study.**

ca·sein (kā′sēn, -sē in) *n.* **1.** the chief protein present in milk, which forms, when coagulated by rennet, the basis of cheese, and, when precipitated, is used in the manufacture of paints, plastics, and adhesives. **2.** a paint made from the curd of sour milk, producing a dull finish. [Latin *cāseus* cheese + -IN[1].]

case knife 1. a knife kept in a sheath. **2.** a table knife.

case·load (kās′lōd′) *n.* the total number of cases being handled at any one time, as by a court, clinic, government agency, or member of the staff. [CASE[1] + LOAD.]

case·mate (kās′māt′) *n.* a vaulted chamber in a fortification, or an armored enclosure on a ship, having openings through which guns may be fired. [French *casemate,* from Italian *casamatta,* going back to Greek *chasmata* gaps, chasms.]

case·ment (kās′mənt) *n.* **1.** the frame of a window that opens on hinges on one side. **2.** a window having such a frame.

ca·se·ous (kā′sē əs) *adj.* of or like cheese. [Latin *cāseus* cheese.]

ca·sern (kə zûrn′) *also,* **ca·serne.** *n.* a building for housing soldiers in a fortified town; barracks. [French *caserne,* from Provençal *cazerna* literally, place for four persons, possibly from Latin *quaternī* four each.]

case shot, canister *(def. 2).*

case study 1. an intensive study and detailed analysis of a single case. **2.** the method by which such a study is done, as by research, observation, and interviews. **3.** case history.

case·work (kās′wûrk′) *n.* the work done by a caseworker.

case·work·er (kās′wûr′kər) *n.* a social worker who is assigned to interview and give guidance and advice to an individual or family with social, psychological, or economic difficulties.

cash (kash) *n.* **1.** money in the form of coins or bills. **2.** money or its equivalent, as a check, paid at the time of buying something. —v.t. to give or obtain cash for: *to cash a check.* [Old French *casse* money; originally, money box, from Italian *cassa,* from Latin *capsa* box, chest.]

• **to cash in.** to exchange for cash: *to cash in a savings bond.*

• **to cash in on.** *Informal.* **a.** to make a profit from. **b.** to turn to, or use to, one's advantage.

cash·book (kash′bŭk′) *n.* a book in which a record is kept of money received and paid out.

cash crop, a crop grown for sale rather than for use on the farm where it is produced. Cotton is a cash crop.

cash·ew (kash′ū, kə shū′) *n.* **1.** a kidney-shaped edible nut of a tropical evergreen tree, *Anacardium occidentale.* **2.** the tree producing this nut. [Portuguese *cajú, acajú,* from Tupi-Guarani *acaju.*]

cash·ier[1] (ka shîr′) *n.* a person who is in charge of cash intake and outflow and other monetary transactions, as in a bank or

business. [French *caissier* treasurer, from *caisse* money box, going back to Latin *capsa* box, chest.]

cash·ier² (ka shîr′) *v.t.* to dismiss from service in disgrace, as a military officer. [Dutch *casseren,* from Middle French *casser* to break, revoke, discharge, from Latin *quassāre* to shake violently (influenced by Late Latin *cassāre* to annul).]

cashier's check, a check drawn by a bank on its own funds and signed by its cashier.

cash machine, automated teller machine.

cash·mere (kazh′mîr, kash′-) *n.* **1.** a fine, soft woolen fabric, woven of a mixture of sheep's wool and the hair of the Kashmir goat, used for such items as coats, suits, and sweaters. **2.** the fine, silken hair of the Kashmir goat. **3.** a rare and expensive cloth made solely of this hair, used esp. for shawls. [From KASHMIR, noted for its goats and their fine wool.]

Cashmere goat, Kashmir goat.

cash on delivery, immediate payment in cash upon delivery of merchandise.

cash register, a machine, usually with a money drawer, that automatically shows and records the amount of a sale.

cas·ing (kā′sing) *n.* **1.** something that contains, encloses, or protects. **2.** the outer part of an automobile tire, not including the tread. **3.** a frame, as of a door or window.

ca·si·no (kə sē′nō) *n., pl.* **-nos. 1.** a building or room for public entertainment, esp. for gambling. **2.** *also,* **cassino.** a card game for two, three, or four players using a regular 52-card deck. [Italian *casino* house, gaming house, diminutive of *casa* house, from Latin *casa* cottage.]

cask (kask) *n.* **1.** a large wooden barrel, usually used to hold liquids. **2.** the amount contained in a cask. [Spanish *casco* vat, helmet, from *cascar* to crack, going back to Latin *quassāre* to shake violently.]

cas·ket (kas′kit) *n.* **1.** a wood or metal rectangular box, usually ornamented, in which a corpse is placed for interment; coffin. **2.** a small box or chest, as for jewels. [Modification of French *cassette* small box, from *casse* box, chest, from Latin *capsa.*]

casque (kask) *n.* **1.** a medieval helmet. **2.** *Zoology.* a helmetlike formation on the head of an organism. [French *casque,* from Spanish *casco* skull, helmet, from *cascar* to crack, going back to Latin *quassāre* to shake violently.]

cas·sa·ba (kə sä′bə) casaba.

Cas·san·dra (kə san′drə) *n.* **1.** in Greek legend, a daughter of King Priam of Troy. Apollo, who was in love with her, gave her the gift of prophecy, but when she refused to love him in return, he decreed that no one should believe her prophecies. **2.** a person who prophesies misfortune and disaster, but is not believed.

cas·sa·va (kə sä′və) *n.* **1.** a bushy shrub, *Manihot esculenta,* widely cultivated in tropical regions for its edible roots. **2.** the nutritious starch obtained from its roots, from which tapioca and bread are made. Also, **manioc.** [French *cassave* the shrub, from Spanish *casabe* manioc bread; of Taino origin.]

cas·se·role (kas′ə rōl′) *n.* **1.** a deep baking dish, often of glass or earthenware, in which food can be cooked and served. **2.** any food prepared and served in a casserole. **3.** a small, deep dish with a handle, used in chemical laboratories for heating substances. [French *casserole* saucepan, from Middle French *casse* pan, ladle, from Late Latin *cattia* ladle, from Greek *kyathion* small ladle.]

cas·sette (kə set′) *n.* **1.** cartridge *(def. 2).* **2.** a cartridge designed to hold magnetic tape for easy insertion in a tape deck, recorder, computer, or VCR.

cas·sia (kash′ə, kas′ē ə) *n.* **1.** the aromatic bark of a tree, *Cinnamomum cassia,* of the laurel family, used as a substitute for cinnamon. **2.** the evergreen tree bearing this bark, having glossy oblong leaves and found mainly in China and Indonesia. **3.** any of a large group of plants, shrubs, and trees, genus *Cassia,* of the pea family, found in both tropical and temperate regions. **4.** the sweet edible pulp from the pods of the tree, *Cassia fistula,* that is mildly laxative. [Latin *cassia* tree like cinnamon, from Greek *kasiā* spice like cinnamon, from Hebrew *q'tsī'āh* bark like that of cinnamon.]

cas·si·mere (kas′ə mîr′) *n.* a light- to medium-weight wool fabric, often a serge, used chiefly for men's suits. [Form of CASH-MERE.]

cas·si·no (kə sē′nō) casino *(def. 2).*

Cas·si·o·pe·ia (kas′ē ə pē′ə) *n.* **1.** in Greek legend, the wife of Cepheus and mother of Andromeda. **2.** a constellation in the northern sky that daily orbits the celestial pole, conventionally depicted as the seated figure of Cassiopeia.

Cassiopeia's Chair, a group of five bright stars in the constellation Cassiopeia, which seem to form the outline of a chair.

cas·sit·er·ite (kə sit′ə rīt′) *n.* a brown or black translucent mineral that is the world's major source of tin, found esp. in China and Malaya. Formula: SnO₂ Also, **tinstone.** [Greek *kassiteros* tin + -ITE¹.]

cas·sock (kas′ək) *n.* an ankle-length garment worn by the clergy and certain laity assisting at services in the Roman Catholic, Anglican, and other churches. In the Roman Catholic Church, the cassocks of the priests are black, those of bishops violet, those of cardinals red, and that of the pope white. [French *casaque* long coat, from Persian *kazagand* type of jacket.] —**cas′socked,** *adj.*

cas·so·war·y (kas′ə wer′ē) *n., pl.* **-war·ies.** any of several flightless birds, genus *Casuarius,* of Australia and New Guinea, related to and resembling the ostrich and having black, bristlelike feathers and a bony casque on its bare, brilliantly colored head. Height: 5 feet (1.5 meters). [Malay *kasuārī.*]

cast (kast) *v.,* **cast, cast·ing.** —*v.t.* **1.** to impel through the air; throw: *to cast a stone, to cast a fishing fly.* **2.** to cause to fall over or upon or in a particular direction; project: *The statue cast a shadow on the ground.* **3.** to direct or turn: *She cast an eye in his direction.* **4.** to put or place, as if by throwing: *to cast the blame on others.* **5.** to discard, dismiss, or ignore: *to cast all caution aside.* **6.** to deposit or register, as a ballot or vote. **7.a.** to assign the parts of, as a play or motion picture: *They have cast the movie.* **b.** to select (an actor) for a particular part: *The director cast me in the leading role.* **8.** to compute astrologically: *to cast one's horoscope.* **9.a.** to shape (a substance) by pouring into a mold to harden. **b.** to make by this process: *to cast a statue.* **10.** to shed; molt: *The snake cast its skin.* **11.** to lose or throw away: *The horse cast its shoe.* **12.** to arrange or devise: *to cast a story to appeal to sentiment.* —*v.i.* **1.** to throw something, esp. a fishing line. **2.** to take shape in a mold. —*n.* **1.** the act or manner of throwing. **2.** the distance to which something is thrown. **3.** something that is formed or shaped in a mold. **4.** a group of actors, as in a play or motion picture. **5.** a rigid form, usually made of gauze soaked in plaster of Paris, used to immobilize a broken bone or badly sprained muscle. **6.** an impression formed by molding; mold: *The police made a cast of the footprints.* **7.** a tinge of color: *The sky had a bluish cast.* **8.** the form, appearance, or shape of something, as facial features. **9.** a throw of dice; the number thrown. **10.** kind; sort. **11.** a twist or turn to one side: *to have a cast in one eye.* [Old Norse *kasta* to throw.]

· **to cast about for.** to search for; look for: *to cast about for an explanation.*

· **to cast away.** to shipwreck.

· **to cast off. a.** to let loose; free: *to cast off a boat from its mooring.* **b.** in knitting, to make the last row of stitches.

· **to cast on.** in knitting, to make the first row of stitches.

· **to cast out.** to put or drive out; expel.

· **to cast up.** to cause to appear; turn up.

cas·ta·net (kas′tə net′) *n.* one of a pair of small concave pieces, as of hard plastic or ivory, held in the hand and clicked together rhythmically, esp. as an accompaniment to certain Spanish music and dancing. For illustration, see **percussion instrument.** [Spanish *castañeta,* diminutive of *castaña* chestnut, from Latin *castanea* chestnut tree, from Greek *kastanon* chestnut; because it resembles a chestnut shell.]

cast·a·way (kast′ə wā′) *n.* **1.** a person who is shipwrecked or set adrift at sea. **2.** outcast. —*adj.* **1.** thrown away; discarded. **2.** shipwrecked or set adrift.

caste (kast) *n.* **1.** one of the hereditary social classes into which Hindus are traditionally divided. **2.** any social system or set of principles that divides a society according to class distinctions based on heredity, wealth, position, or religion. **3.** an exclusive social or professional group: *a priestly caste.* [Portuguese *casta* race; originally, a pure stock, from *casto* pure, from Latin *castus.* Doublet of CHASTE.]

· **to lose caste.** to lose social standing or prestige.

cas·tel·lat·ed (kas′tə lā′tid) *adj.* built with turrets and battlements, like a castle.

cast·er (kas′tər) *n.* **1.** a person or thing that casts. **2.** *also,* **castor.** one of a set of swiveling wheels or rollers placed or fitted under furniture or other large, heavy articles to facilitate moving. **3.** *also,* **castor. a.** a bottle for holding condiments, as salt, mustard, or vinegar; cruet. **b.** a stand for such bottles. [CAST + -ER¹.]

cas·ti·gate (kas′ti gāt′) *v.t.,* **-gat·ed, -gat·ing.** to criticize or rebuke severely. [Latin *castīgātus,* past participle of *castīgāre* to correct (in the sense of making pure), from *castus* pure.] —**cas′ti·ga′tion,** *n.* —**cas′ti·ga′tor,** *n.*

Cas·tile soap (kas tēl′) *also,* **castile soap.** a fine, hard soap made from olive oil and caustic soda.

Cas·til·ian (kas til′yən) *adj.* of, relating to, or characteristic of

a	at	e	end	o	hot	u	up	hw	white	{	about
ā	ape	ē	me	ō	old	ū	use	ng	song		taken
ä	far	i	it	ô	fork	ü	rule	th	thin		pencil
âr	care	ī	ice	oi	oil	u̇	pull	th	this		lemon
		îr	pierce	ou	out	ûr	turn	zh	measure		circus

Castile or its people, language, or culture. —*n.* **1.** the standard European form of Spanish, based on the dialect of Castile. **2.** a native or inhabitant of Castile.

cast·ing (kas′ting) *n.* **1.** something that is shaped in a mold; cast. **2.** the act or process of a person or thing that casts: *The casting for the play has been completed. Casting bronze is an ancient art.*

cast-i·ron (kast′ī′ərn) *adj.* **1.** made of cast iron. **2.** unyielding; inflexible: *cast-iron rules.* **3.** like cast iron in strength; hardy: *a cast-iron stomach.*

cast iron, a hard, brittle form of pig iron, having a high carbon content, made by casting.

cas·tle (kas′əl) *n.* **1.** a large fortified building or group of buildings serving as a stronghold or residence, as of a feudal prince or noble. **2.** any large, imposing house. **3.** *Chess.* rook[2]. —*v.,* -tled, -tling. —*v.t. Chess.* to move (the king) two squares to the right or left and move the rook to the square passed over by the king. —*v.i.* to castle the king. [Anglo-Norman *castel* fortress, from Latin *castellum,* diminutive of *castrum* fortified place.]

castle in the sky, something imagined and wished for but not likely to come true; daydream. Also, **castle in the air, castle in Spain.**

cast·off (kast′ôf′, -of′) *adj.* discarded or abandoned. —*n.* a person or thing that has been discarded or abandoned.

cas·tor[1] (kas′tər) caster *(defs. 2, 3).*

cas·tor[2] (kas′tər) *n.* an oily, strong-smelling substance, secreted by certain glands in beavers, used in perfumery and, formerly, in making medicines. [Latin *castor* beaver, from Greek *kastōr.*]

Cas·tor and Pol·lux (kas′tər; pol′əks) **1.** in classical mythology, twin brothers whose mother was Leda and whose father was usually regarded as being Zeus. Castor was traditionally thought to be the mortal twin of the pair and Pollux to be the immortal. **2.** two bright stars in the constellation Gemini. Pollux is the brightest star in the constellation; Castor, a system of six stars, appears as one star to the naked eye.

castor bean, the oval bean of the castor-oil plant.

castor oil, a pale yellow or colorless oil obtained from castor beans, used as a strong laxative, as a low-temperature lubricant, and in the preparation of such products as paints and soaps.

cas·tor-oil plant (kas′tər oil′) the wide-leaved plant *Ricinus communis,* whose beans yield castor oil.

cas·trate (kas′trāt) *v.t.,* -trat·ed, -trat·ing. **1.** to remove the testicles of; emasculate. **2.** to deprive of vitality or strength; make ineffectual. [Latin *castrātus,* past participle of *castrāre.*] —**cas·tra′tion,** *n.*

cast steel, steel that has been formed by casting.

cas·u·al (kazh′ü əl) *adj.* **1.** without special or serious intention or design; offhand: *a casual remark.* **2.** occurring by chance; unexpected; accidental: *a casual meeting.* **3.** (of clothes) designed for informal wear: *Casual dress was suggested for the party.* **4.** without particular concern; indifferent; nonchalant: *a casual attitude.* **5.** temporary or irregular: *The farmer hired casual labor to pick the crops.* **6.** lacking seriousness or intensity: *a casual friendship.* —*n.* **1.** a worker who is employed irregularly or temporarily. **2.** a soldier temporarily assigned to a post or unit while awaiting a permanent assignment. [Late Latin *cāsuālis* accidental, occurring by chance, from Latin *cāsus* a falling, chance.] —**cas′u·al·ly,** *adv.* —**cas′u·al·ness,** *n.*

cas·u·al·ty (kazh′ü əl tē) *n., pl.* -ties. **1.** a member of the armed forces who has been lost to a unit as a result of having been wounded, killed, captured, or missing in action. **2.** a person who is injured or killed in an accident. **3.** a person or thing that is ruined or destroyed: *The house was a casualty of the flood.* **4.** an accident, esp. one involving a death.

cas·u·ist (kazh′ü ist) *n.* **1.** a person who studies or resolves cases of conscience or problems concerning conduct and duty. **2.** a person who reasons cleverly but equivocally about such matters. [French *casuiste,* going back to Medieval Latin *cāsus* case of conscience, from Latin *cāsus* a falling, chance.]

cas·u·is·tic (kazh′ü is′tik) *adj.* **1.** of or relating to casuists or casuistry. **2.** clever but false or misleading; specious; sophistic. —**cas′u·is′ti·cal·ly,** *adv.*

cas·u·ist·ry (kazh′ ə strē) *n., pl.* -ries. **1.** the method or practice of applying moral principles to concrete situations. **2.** clever but false or misleading reasoning; sophistry.

ca·sus bel·li (kā′səs bel′ī) *Latin.* a cause or reason for declaring war.

cat (kat) *n.* **1.** a carnivorous mammal, *Felis catus,* domesticated, and commonly kept as a pet or for catching mice. **2.** any animal of the cat family, Felidae, as the domestic cat, lion, tiger, leopard, or lynx. **3.** a person thought of as resembling a cat in some way, esp. a spiteful or backbiting woman. **4.** catfish. **5.** *Slang.* a man. **6.** cat-o'-nine-tails. **7.** tackle for hoisting an anchor to the cathead. —*v.t.* to hoist (an anchor) to the cathead. [Old English

cat(t) the domesticated animal, possibly going back to Late Latin *cattus;* possibly of Hamitic origin.]

· **to let the cat out of the bag.** to inadvertently reveal a secret.

CAT, CAT scan.

cata- *prefix* down or against: *catacomb, catalyst, catastrophe.* [Greek *kata* down, against, in accordance with.]

ca·tab·o·lism (kə tab′ə liz′əm) *n.* a metabolic process by which complex substances, as glycogen, are broken down by living cells into simpler substances, producing energy, carbon dioxide, and water; destructive metabolism. ➡ distinguished from **anabolism.** [Greek *katabolē* a throwing down + -ISM.] —**cat·a·bol·ic** (kat′ə bol′ik) *adj.*

ca·tab·o·lize (kə tab′ə līz′) *v.t., v.i.,* -lized, -liz·ing. to undergo or to cause to undergo catabolism.

cat·a·chre·sis (kat′ə krē′sis) *n., pl.* -ses (-sēz). any misuse of words, esp. of figures of speech. [Latin *catachrēsis,* from Greek *katachrēsis* misuse.]

cat·a·clysm (kat′ə kliz′əm) *n.* **1.** a violent and extensive change in the ordinary processes of nature, as a flood or earthquake. **2.** any violent change or sudden upheaval, as a revolution or war. [French *cataclysme,* from Latin *cataclysmos* flood, from Greek *kataklysmos.*] —**cat′a·clys′mic,** *adj.*

cat·a·comb (kat′ə kōm′) *also,* **cat·a·combs.** *n.* an underground cemetery consisting of rooms and passages with recesses excavated in the walls for tombs. ➡ **catacombs** is used as plural. [French *catacombe,* from Late Latin *catacumba;* of uncertain origin, but possibly from Latin *cata* by (from Greek *kata* against, down) + Late Latin *tumba* tomb (from Greek *tymbos* tomb).]

ca·tad·ro·mous (kə tad′rə məs) *adj.* of or relating to fish that live in fresh water but go downstream to spawn in the sea. ➡ distinguished from **anadromous.** [CATA- + Greek *dromos* running, course + -OUS.]

cat·a·falque (kat′ə fôk′, -fôlk′, -falk′) *n.* the stand or frame on which a casket rests while a body lies in state or during a funeral service. [French *catafalque,* from Italian *catafalco;* of uncertain origin, but possibly going back to Latin *cata* by (from Greek *kata* down, against) + *fala* scaffold (of Etruscan origin).]

Cat·a·lan (kat′ə lan′, kat′ə lan′) *adj.* of, relating to, or characteristic of Catalonia or its people, language, or culture. —*n.* **1.** a native or inhabitant of Catalonia. **2.** the Romance language of Catalonia, Valencia, Andorra, the Balearic Islands, and some parts of southern France.

cat·a·lase (kat′ə lās′) *n.* a red enzyme found in blood that acts as a catalyst to decompose hydrogen peroxide into oxygen and water. [CATAL(YSIS) + -ASE.]

cat·a·lep·sy (kat′ə lep′sē) *n.* a condition associated with mental disorders in which the muscles become extremely rigid and the limbs remain in any position in which they are placed. [Greek *katalēpsis* seizure.]

cat·a·lep·tic (kat′ə lep′tik) *adj.* of, relating to, or having catalepsy. —*n.* a person who has catalepsy.

cat·a·log (kat′ə lôg′, -log′) *also,* **catalogue.** *n.* **1.** a listing, usually in alphabetical order, that identifies and often describes items, as in a collection. **2.** a publication containing such a listing: *The store sent us a catalog of their merchandise.* **3.** a book or booklet issued by a college or university listing information, as rules, courses offered, or fees. **4.** card catalog. —*v.t.* to make a catalog of or enter in a catalog: *to catalog the paintings in a museum.* [French *catalogue* list, enumeration, from Late Latin *catalogus,* from Greek *katalogos* enrollment, register.] —**cat′a·log′er,** *n.*

cat·a·logue (kat′ə lôg′, -log′) *n.* catalog. —*v.t.,* -logued, -logu·ing. catalog. —**cat′a·logu′er,** *n.*

ca·tal·pa (kə tal′pə) *n.* **1.** any of a group of softwood trees, genus *Catalpa,* found in North America and Asia, having large, heart-shaped leaves, showy white, pink, or yellow flowers, and beanlike pods. **2.** the coarse-grained, durable wood of this tree. [Modern Latin *Catalpa,* said to be from Creek *kutuhlpa* head having wings; because of the shape of its flowers.]

ca·tal·y·sis (kə tal′ə sis) *n., pl.* -ses (-sēz′). the acceleration of a chemical reaction by the presence of a substance that remains unchanged by the reaction. [Greek *katalysis* dissolution.]

cat·a·lyst (kat′ə list) *n.* **1.** a substance that causes catalysis. **2.** a person or thing that brings about or hastens a change: *The petition was the catalyst for reform.*

cat·a·lyt·ic (kat′ə lit′ik) *adj.* of, relating to, or causing catalysis.

catalytic converter, a device on a motor vehicle that converts harmful carbon monoxide and hydrocarbons in the exhaust gases of an internal-combustion engine into carbon dioxide and water vapor.

cat·a·lyze (kat′ə līz′) *v.t.,* -lyzed, -lyz·ing. to submit to, or act upon, by catalysis. —**cat′a·lyz′er,** *n.*

cat·a·ma·ran (kat′ə mə ran′) *n.* **1.** any of various boats having two hulls connected by poles or by a platform that serves as a deck. Most catamarans are sailboats. **2.** a raft made of logs lashed together in the shape of a boat hull. [Tamil *kattumaram* bound wood.]

cat·a·mount (kat′ə-mount′) *n.* any of several wild animals of the cat family, as the cougar, lynx, or mountain lion. Also, **cat·a·moun·tain** (kat′ə-moun′tən), **cat-o′-moun·tain**. [Short for *cat of the mountain.*]

cat·a·pult (kat′ə pult′, -pult′) *n.* **1.** an ancient war machine, similar to a ballista, used to shoot or hurl projectiles. **2.** a track-mounted device used to launch an airplane from the deck of a ship. **3.** *British.* slingshot. —*v.t.* to hurl or shoot (something) from or as from a catapult. —*v.i.* to leap or be ejected suddenly or quickly: *I found myself catapulting out of my chair a split second after I heard an explosion outside.*

catamaran

[Late Latin *catapulta* this war machine, from Greek *katapaltēs*.]

cat·a·ract (kat′ə rakt′) *n.* **1.** a large, steep waterfall. **2.** steep rapids in a river. **3.** a violent flood or downpour of water. **4.** a cloudy or opaque condition in the lens of the eye, or its capsule, resulting in impairment of vision. [Latin *cataracta* waterfall, portcullis, from Greek *katarraktēs.*]

ca·tarrh (kə tär′) *n.* an inflammation of a mucous membrane, esp. that of the nose or throat, causing excessive secretion of mucus. [French *catarrhe,* from Late Latin *catarrhus,* from Greek *katarrhous* literally, a flowing down.] —**ca·tarrh′al,** *adj.*

ca·tas·tro·phe (kə tas′trə fē′) *n.* **1.** a great and sudden disaster or misfortune: *The plane crash was a catastrophe.* **2.** a complete failure; fiasco: *My recital was a catastrophe.* **3.** a culmination or conclusion of a dramatic work, esp. a tragedy. [Greek *katastrophē* overturning.] —For Synonyms, see **disaster.**

cat·a·stroph·ic (kat′ə strof′ik) *adj.* of, resulting from, or resembling a catastrophe. —**cat′a·stroph′i·cal·ly,** *adv.*

cat·a·to·ni·a (kat′ə tō′nē ə) *n.* a syndrome usually associated with schizophrenia, characterized by one or more alternating or fixed symptoms, such as rigidity, stupor, extreme excitability, and an inability to feel or perceive. [German *Katatonie,* from Greek *kata-* cata- + *tonos* a stretching, strain, from *teinein* to stretch.]

cat·a·ton·ic (kat′ə ton′ik) *adj.* **1.** caused by catatonia: *a catatonic stupor.* **2.** suffering from catatonia: *a catatonic patient.*

Ca·taw·ba (kə tô′bə) *n., pl.* -**bas. 1.** a sweet, purplish red variety of grape, grown in the eastern United States. **2.** a dry white wine made from it. [From the *Catawba* River in South Carolina.]

cat·bird (kat′bûrd′) *n.* a slate gray songbird, *Dumetella carolinensis,* of North and Central America, related to the mockingbird and having a black cap and tail and a call like the mewing of a cat.

catbird seat *Informal.* a position of much advantage or power.

cat·boat (kat′bōt′) *n.* a sailboat with a single mast set well forward and a mainsail but no jib.

cat·bri·er (kat′brī′ər) *n.* greenbrier.

cat burglar, a person who burglarizes buildings by entering through an upper story, often after skillful feats of climbing.

cat·call (kat′kôl′) *n.* a shrill cry or whistle expressing disapproval, derision, or impatience. —*v.i.* to make catcalls. —*v.t.* to express disapproval, derision, or impatience with catcalls.

catch (kach) *v.,* **caught, catch·ing.** —*v.t.* **1.a.** to take as a captive, as after a chase or search: *The police caught the thief.* **b.** to take hold of; grasp: *He caught my arm as I was leaving.* **2.** to stop or intercept the motion or passage of: *to catch a ball, to catch water from a leak in a pail.* **3.** to take (animals), as by trapping, netting, or shooting: *to catch salmon, to catch butterflies.* **4.** to be in time for boarding; get aboard: *to catch a train.* **5.** to cause to become stuck, entangled, or hooked: *She caught her sweater on a nail.* **6.** to overtake or detain: *The storm caught us as we left the house. We caught them as they were leaving.* **7.** to hit; strike: *The blow caught me in the stomach.* **8.** to come upon suddenly or unexpectedly; surprise or discover: *The guard caught the thieves in*

the act of breaking into the office. **9.** to check (oneself) suddenly or momentarily, esp. in speaking: *I caught myself before telling the secret.* **10.** to take, get, or perceive suddenly or momentarily: *to catch a glimpse of a person.* **11.** to become affected or infected with: *to catch a cold.* **12.** to attract suddenly or momentarily, as the senses: *The bright dress caught my eye.* **13.** to grasp with the senses or intellect: *I finally caught the gist of the conversation.* **14.** to portray or reproduce accurately: *The artist caught the color of the sea exactly.* **15.** *Informal.* to see, as a motion picture. —*v.i.* **1.** to become stuck, entangled, or hooked: *The fabric caught in the zipper.* **2.** to become fastened or take hold: *The bolt didn't catch.* **3.** to become lighted; ignite. **4.** to act as catcher in baseball. —*n.* **1.** the act of catching: *The outfielder made a great catch.* **2.** something that catches; fastening: *a catch on a door.* **3.** something that is caught; quantity caught: *a good catch of fish.* **4.** a small part; fragment: *catches of a song.* **5.** a round for three or more voices. **6.** a game in which an object, esp. a ball, is thrown and caught. **7.** a break in the voice, esp. as a result of emotion. **8.** *Informal.* a person who is desirable as a prospect for marriage. **9.** *Informal.* a hidden condition; trick or trap: *The plan seems too good; there must be a catch somewhere.* —*adj.* **1.** attracting or intended to attract attention or interest: *a catch phrase.* **2.** intended to deceive; tricky: *a catch question.* [Anglo-Norman *cachier* to hunt, going back to Latin *captāre* to try to catch, chase. Doublet of CHASE[1].]

• **to catch it.** *Informal.* to receive a scolding or punishment.
• **to catch on.** *Informal.* **a.** to understand: *I didn't catch on to the joke at first.* **b.** to become popular or fashionable.
• **to catch up.** **a.** to come up to or overtake. **b.** to grab or pick up suddenly or quickly: *The thief caught up the jewels and ran.*
• **to catch up in.** **a.** to bring or get up to date: *to catch up in one's work.* **b.** to become absorbed or entangled in: *to be caught up in a book.*
• **to catch up on.** to bring or get up to date on: *I have a lot of reading to catch up on. They caught me up on all the latest news in town.*
• **to catch up to.** to come up to or overtake: *I caught up to the leader near the end of the race.*
• **to catch up with.** **a.** to come up to or overtake: *He caught up with his friends even though he left late.* **b.** to bring or get up to date: *She caught up with her correspondence.* **c.** to raise up or fasten in loops with: *The skirt was caught up with bows.*

Synonyms *v.t.* **Catch** and **capture** mean to take hold of or seize people or animals through pursuit or through overcoming resistance. **Catch,** the more general term, is applied to taking persons or animals in any circumstance, but esp. while in motion: *to catch a thief climbing out of a window, to catch a raccoon that has been raiding garbage cans.* **Capture** suggests greater difficulty or resistance, as in military and police contexts: *to capture a fugitive, to capture a fortress.* In reference to animals, it implies taking alive: *After capturing the bird that had flown in the window, I released it outside.*

catch·all (kach′ôl′) *n.* **1.** anything that serves as a receptacle for odds and ends: *The closet was a catchall.* **2.** a word or phrase used to cover various conditions or situations. —*adj.* covering various conditions or situations: *a catchall provision in regulations.*

catch·er (kach′ər) *n.* **1.** a person or thing that catches. **2.** a baseball player who is positioned behind home plate to catch pitched balls not hit by the batter and to guard the plate from runners advancing from third base.

catch·fly (kach′flī′) *n., pl.* -**flies.** any of several flowering plants of the genus *Silene,* as campion, whose sticky blossoms trap insects.

catch·ing (kach′ing) *adj.* **1.** liable to be caught; contagious; infectious: *Some diseases are catching.* **2.** attractive; fascinating.

catch·ment (kach′mənt) *n.* **1.** a reservoir built for collecting and storing water. **2.** drainage basin.

catch·pen·ny (kach′pen′ē) *adj.* made to be sold quickly; cheap and showy. —*n., pl.* -**nies.** a catchpenny article.

catch phrase, catchword *(def. 1).*

catch·pole (kach′pōl′) *also,* **catch·poll.** *n. Archaic.* a sheriff's deputy or bailiff who makes arrests, esp. for debt.

Catch-22 (kach′twen′tē tü′) *also,* **catch-22.** *n.* a problematic situation that cannot be resolved because of some circumstance that is inherent in the situation or because of a paradoxical rule. [From the catch or hidden trick that gives the title to the novel *Catch-22* by Joseph Heller, born 1923, U.S. author.]

a	at	e	end	o	hot	u	up	hw	white		about
ā	ape	ē	me	ō	old	ū	use	ng	song	ə	taken
ä	far	i	it	ô	fork	ù	rule	th	thin		pencil
âr	care	ī	ice	oi	oil	ů	pull	th	this		lemon
		îr	pierce	ou	out	ûr	turn	zh	measure		circus

C

catch·up (kech′əp, kach′-) ketchup.

catch·word (kach′wûrd′) *n.* **1.** a word or phrase used repeatedly for effect; slogan. Also, **catch phrase. 2.** a word placed so as to attract attention, as a word placed at the top of a page in a dictionary.

catch·y (kach′ē) *adj.,* **catch·i·er, catch·i·est. 1.** catching the attention and easy to remember: *a catchy title.* **2.** designed or intended to deceive; tricky: *a catchy question.*

cate (kāt) *n. Archaic.* a choice food; delicacy. [Short for Middle English *acate* purchase, from Anglo-Norman *acat,* from *acater* to buy, going back to Latin *ad* to + *capere* to take.]

cat·e·chet·i·cal (kat′i ket′i kəl) *adj.* relating to oral instruction by questions and answers. Also, **cat′e·chet′ic.**

cat·e·chise (kat′i kīz′) *v.t.,* **-chised, -chis·ing.** catechize.

cat·e·chism (kat′i kiz′əm) *n.* **1.** a small book or manual in which the precepts of a religion, esp. of a Christian denomination, are set forth in question and answer form. **2.** a similar book or manual about any subject. **3.** a series of long or formal questions used as an examination, as of a political candidate.

cat·e·chist (kat′i kist′) *n.* a person who catechizes.

cat·e·chize (kat′i kīz′) *also,* **catechise.** *v.t.,* **-chized, -chiz·ing. 1.** to instruct by questions and answers, esp. in Christian belief. **2.** to question closely and systematically. [Church Latin *catēchizāre* to instruct in religion, going back to Greek *katēchein* to instruct orally, din (something) in.] **—cat′e·chiz′er;** *also,* **cat′e·chis′er,** *n.*

cat·e·chol·a·mine (kat′i kō′lə mēn′) *n.* any of a group of amine neurotransmitters, as adrenaline, norepinephrine, and dopamine, that are directly or indirectly derived from the adrenal gland and are vital to the operation of the sympathetic nervous system.

cat·e·chu (kat′i chü′, -kū′) *n.* a gummy, dark brown substance, most of which is obtained from certain acacia trees. It is used as an ingredient in dyes and certain medicines and as a tanning extract. [Modern Latin *catechu,* from Malay *kāchū.*]

cat·e·chu·men (kat′i kū′mən) *n.* **1.** a person being instructed in the basic principles of Christianity prior to baptism. **2.** a person being instructed in the fundamentals of any subject. [Church Latin *catēchūmenus,* from Greek *katēchoumenos* one being instructed orally, present participle of *katēchein* to instruct orally.]

cat·e·gor·i·cal (kat′i gôr′i kəl) *adj.* **1.** without conditions or qualifications; absolute. **2.** of, relating to, or in a category. Also, **cat′e·gor′ic. —cat′e·gor′i·cal·ly,** *adv.*

cat·e·go·rize (kat′i gə rīz′) *v.t.,* **-rized, -riz·ing.** to put into a category; classify. **—cat′e·go·ri·za′tion,** *n.*

cat·e·go·ry (kat′i gôr′ē) *n., pl.* **-ries.** a group or division in any system of classification; class. [Late Latin *catēgoria* accusation, class (in logic), from Greek *katēgoría.*]

cat·e·nar·y (kat′ə ner′ē) *n., pl.* **-nar·ies.** the curve assumed by a completely uniform cord or chain suspended from its ends. [Latin *catenarius* relating to a chain, from *catena* chain.]

cat·e·nate (kat′ə nāt′) *v.t.,* **-nat·ed, -nat·ing.** to link together like a chain; form into a chain. [Latin *catēnātus,* past participle of *catēnāre* to chain together.] **—cat′e·na′tion,** *n.*

ca·ter (kā′tər) *v.i.* **1.** to provide food, supplies, or other services, as entertainment: *The restaurant caters for large private parties.* **2.** to provide with what is needed or desired (with *to* or *for*): *The shop caters to a small, wealthy clientele.* *—v.t.* to provide with food, supplies, or other services, as entertainment: *to cater a wedding.* [From obsolete *cater* buyer, short for Middle English *acatour* buyer of provisions, from Anglo-Norman *acatour* buyer, from *acater* to buy. See CATE.]

cat·er-cor·ner (kat′ər kôr′nər) *adj.* placed in or having a diagonal position. *—adv.* diagonally. Also, **cat′er-cor′nered, catty-corner, kitty-corner.** [Obsolete *cater* a four-spotted die (from Old French *quatre* four) + CORNER.]

ca·ter·er (kā′tər ər) *n.* a person or business that caters, esp. one that provides food, supplies, or other services, as for a party.

cat·er·pil·lar (kat′ər pil′ər) *n.* **1.** the wormlike larva of a butterfly or moth. **2.** crawler tractor. Trademark: **Caterpillar.** [Dialectal Old French *catepelose* literally, hairy cat, from Late Latin *catta pilōsa* hairy female cat; influenced by obsolete English *piller* robber. See CAT, PILOSE.]

cat·er·waul (kat′ər wôl′) *v.i.* to howl or screech as a cat that is rutting. *—n.* such a howl or screech. [Middle English *caterwawen* to howl like a cat, from CAT + *waw* to howl like a cat (imitative).]

caterpillar

cat·fish (kat′fish′) *n., pl.* **-fish** or **-fish·es.** any of various usually scaleless fish, suborder Siluroidea, found in rivers or tropical lakes in Europe and America, having a large head, sensitive barbels around the mouth, and a characteristic small, fleshy fin on its back.

cat·gut (kat′gut′) *n.* the tough string or cord processed from the dried and twisted intestines of sheep and certain other animals, used for surgical sutures and for stringing musical instruments and tennis rackets.

cath-, form of **cata-** before *h,* as in *cathode.*

Cath., Catholic.

ca·thar·sis (kə thär′sis) *n.* **1.** a purifying or purging of the emotions, esp. through an art medium, as drama. **2.** the act of emptying the bowels; purgation. **3.** *Psychiatry.* a therapeutic discharge of pent-up emotions, as to alleviate tension and anxiety. [Modern Latin *catharsis,* from Greek *katharsis* purification.]

ca·thar·tic (kə thär′tik) *n.* a medicine causing movement of the bowels; laxative. *—adj.* purgative or purifying.

Ca·thay (ka thā′) *n. Archaic.* China.

cat·head (kat′hed′) *n.* a beam that projects from a ship's side at the bow. The anchor is hoisted and secured to it.

ca·the·dra (kə thē′drə, kath′i-) *n.* **1.** a bishop's official throne in the cathedral. **2.** an official chair, as of a professor. [Latin *cathedra* chair, from Greek *kathedrā.* Doublet of CHAIR.]

ca·the·dral (kə thē′drəl) *n.* **1.** the official church of a bishop, containing the bishop's throne. **2.** any large or important church. *—adj.* **1.** relating to or possessing a cathedra, or bishop's throne. **2.** coming as from a bishop's throne; authoritative. **3.** of, relating to, or suggestive of a cathedral. [Medieval Latin *(ecclesia) cathedralis* (church) having a cathedra, or bishop's throne, from Latin *cathedra* chair. See CATHEDRA.]

cathedral at Reims, France

cath·e·ter (kath′i tər) *n.* a slender, hollow, flexible tube for inserting into a cavity of the body to keep a passage open or to drain or inject fluids, esp. one used to remove urine from the bladder. [Late Latin *cathetēr,* from Greek *kathetēr.*]

cath·e·ter·ize (kath′i tə rīz′) *v.t.,* **-ized, -iz·ing.** to put a catheter into. [CATHETER + -IZE.] **—cath′e·ter·i·za′tion,** *n.*

cath·ode (kath′ōd) *n.* **1.** an electrode through which electrons enter an electrical device or medium. When electricity is used to produce a chemical reaction, as in an electrolytic cell, the negative electrode is the cathode, but when a chemical reaction is used to produce electricity, as in a dry cell battery, the positive electrode is the cathode. **2.** in electrolysis, an electrode that has an excess of electrons and is negatively charged. Positively charged ions are reduced at the cathode. **3.** an electrode from which electrons are emitted, as in an electron tube. ➡ opposed to **anode** in all definitions. [Greek *kathodos* a way down, from *kata* down + *hodos* way.] **—ca·thod·ic** (ka thod′ik), *adj.*

cathode ray, a stream of electrons emitted from the cathode in an electron tube.

cath·ode-ray tube (kath′ōd rā′) an electron tube in which a visible glowing pattern is produced on a luminescent screen by a cathode ray emitted from an electron gun at the back of the tube. It is used in television sets, computer monitors, oscilloscopes, and radar sets.

cath·o·lic (kath′ə lik, kath′lik) *adj.* **1.** of universal interest or

use; broad. **2.** having sympathies with or embracing all; liberal, as in tastes or interests. **3. Catholic. a.** of or relating to the Christian church under the authority of the pope; Roman Catholic. **b.** of or relating to the ancient undivided Christian church, or to those churches claiming unbroken descent from it, as the Roman, Orthodox, Eastern, and Anglican. —*n.* **Catholic.** a member of a Catholic Church, esp. the Roman Catholic Church. [Church Latin *catholicus* universal, orthodox, from Greek *katholikos* universal, general.]

Ca·thol·i·cism (kə thol′ə siz′əm) *n.* **1.** the beliefs, practices, and government of the Roman Catholic Church. **2. catholicism.** catholicity.

cath·o·lic·i·ty (kath′ə lis′i tē) *n.* the state or quality of being catholic.

ca·thol·i·cize (kə thol′ə sīz′) *v.t., v.i.,* **-cized, -ciz·ing. 1.** to make or become catholic. **2. Catholicize.** to make or become Catholic.

Catholic Reformation, Counter Reformation.

cat·i·on (kat′ī′ən) *n.* a positively charged ion of an electrolyte, attracted to the cathode in electrolysis. ➡ opposed to **anion.** [Greek *kation* a going down, noun use of neuter present participle of *katienai* to go down.]

cat·kin (kat′kin) *n.* a fuzzy spike of tiny flowers that grows on certain trees, as willows or birches. Also, **ament.** [Obsolete Dutch *katteken* literally, little cat, from *katte* cat + *-ken* diminutive ending; because it resembles a cat's tail.]

cat·nap (kat′nap′) *n.* a short nap. —*v.i.,* **-napped, -nap·ping.** to take a short nap.

cat·nip (kat′nip′) *n.* **1.** the dried leaves and stems of a plant, *Nepeta cataria,* of the mint family, used as a stuffing for cats' toys because cats are stimulated by its strong aroma. **2.** the strongly aromatic plant itself. [CAT + dialectal English *nip* catnip, form of dialectal English *nep,* going back to Latin *nepeta.*]

cat-o′-moun·tain (kat′ə moun′tən) *n.* catamount.

cat-o′-nine-tails (kat′ə nīn′tālz′) *n., pl.* **-tails.** a whip, usually consisting of nine knotted cords fastened to a handle, formerly used in flogging.

cat rig, a rig having one sail and a single mast set well forward, as in a catboat. —**cat′-rigged′,** *adj.*

CAT scan (kat) **1.** an X ray, made by a computerized instrument, that provides three-dimensional images of soft tissues of the body such as the brain and liver. **2.** an examination using such an instrument. Also, **CT scan.** [Short for *c(omputerized) a(xial) t(omography).*]

cat's cradle, a children's game in which a loop of string is intertwined over the fingers of both hands in such a way as to form different patterns.

cat's-eye (kats′ī′) *n.* **1.** any gem that reflects light like a cat's eye. **2.** a playing marble with a pattern like the eye of a cat.

cat's-paw (kats′pô′) *also,* **cats·paw.** *n.* **1.** a person used as a pawn by another person; dupe. **2.** a light breeze that ruffles the surface of calm water.

cat·sup (kat′səp, kech′əp, kach′-) ketchup.

cat·tail (kat′tāl′) *n.* any of various tall marsh plants, genus *Typha,* bearing long, narrow leaves and flowers clustered in a spike that turns velvety brown when mature.

cat·tle (kat′əl) *pl. n.* **1.** domesticated bovine animals, as cows, bulls, and steers, raised primarily for meat or dairy products. **2.** human beings, esp. in a large group. ➡ used contemptuously. [Anglo-Norman *catel* property (cattle being an important early form of property), from Late Latin *capitāle,* from Latin *capitālis* chief, relating to the head, from *caput* head. Doublet of CHATTEL.]

cat·tle·man (kat′əl mən) *n., pl.* **-men** (-mən). a person who owns, raises, or deals in cattle.

cat·ty (kat′ē) *adj.,* **-ti·er, -ti·est.** slyly malicious; spiteful. —**cat′ti·ly,** *adv.* —**cat′ti·ness,** *n.*

cat·ty-cor·ner (kat′ē kôr′nər) *adj.* cater-corner. Also, **cat′ty-cor′nered.**

cat·walk (kat′wôk′) *n.* a narrow walking space, as along a bridge.

Cau·ca·sian (kô kā′zhən, -shən, -kazh′ən) *n.* **1.** Caucasoid. **2.** a native or inhabitant of the Caucasus. —*adj.* **1.** Caucasoid. **2.** of or relating to the Caucasus, its inhabitants, or their languages or cultures. [Latin *Caucasus* Caucasus, from Greek *Kaukasos* + -IAN; first applied to the white race by the German anthropologist Johann Blumenbach, 1752-1840, because he thought it had originated in the Caucasus.]

Cau·ca·soid (kô′kə soid′) *n.* a member of one of the major divisions traditionally used to classify the human race whose physical characteristics vary greatly, ranging from pale pink to dark brown skin color, blond to dark brown hair color, and slender to

stocky build. Caucasoids inhabit Europe, parts of Asia, Africa, and Australia, and the Western Hemisphere. —*adj.* of, relating to, characteristic of, or resembling Caucasoids. [CAUCAS(IAN) + -OID.]

cau·cus (kô′kəs) *n.* **1.** a meeting of all the members of a particular political party or faction to choose party leaders, nominate candidates, or determine the general policies their party or group will advocate. **2.** a faction within a legislative body organized to advocate certain policies or promote certain interests: *the farm caucus.* —*v.i.* to meet in or hold a caucus. [Possibly from Algonquian *cau-cau-as-u* adviser, counselor.]

cau·dal (kô′dəl) *adj.* **1.** of, relating to, or near the tail: *the caudal fin of a fish.* **2.** resembling a tail; taillike. [Modern Latin *caudalis,* from Latin *cauda* tail.] —**cau′dal·ly,** *adv.*

cau·date (kô′dāt) *adj.* having a tail or taillike appendage.

cau·dle (kô′dəl) *n.* a warm drink of gruel mixed with wine, ale, spices, and eggs, usually given to invalids. [Dialectal Old French *caudel* going back to Latin *cal(i)dum.*]

caught (kôt) the past tense and past participle of **catch.**

caul (kôl) *n.* a membrane that encloses a fetus before birth, or a portion of it that sometimes envelops the head at birth, once believed to be a sign that the child would have good luck. [Old French *cale* cap, from *calotte* skullcap, possibly going back to Latin *calautica* type of woman's head covering.]

caul·dron (kôl′drən) *also,* **caldron.** *n.* a large kettle or boiler. [Anglo-Norman *caudron,* from Late Latin *caldāria,* going back to Latin *cal(i)dus* hot.]

cau·li·flow·er (kô′lə flou′ər, kol′ē-) *n.* **1.** the white head of a plant, a variety of *Brassica oleracea,* related to broccoli and cabbage, eaten as a vegetable either raw or cooked. **2.** the low-growing plant itself, a member of the mustard family, probably developed from the wild cabbage of western Europe. [Modification (influenced by Latin *caulis* cabbage + English FLOWER) of earlier *colyflory,* from obsolete French *chou fleuri* literally, flowered cabbage, going back to Latin *caulis* + *flōs* flower.]

cauliflower ear, an ear that has been misshapen by repeated blows or injuries usually received in boxing.

caulk (kôk) *also,* **calk.** *v.t.* to fill up (a seam, crack, or joint) with a substance, as tar or oakum, that stops leaks; make watertight or airtight. —*n.* a substance used for caulking. [Dialectal Old French *cauquer* to tread, press, from Latin *calcāre.*]

caulk·er (kô′kər) *also,* **calker.** *n.* **1.** a person who caulks. **2.** a tool used for caulking.

caulk·ing (kô′king) *n.* a substance, such as tar or oakum, used to fill a seam, crack, or joint, so that it won't leak.

caus·al (kô′zəl) *adj.* **1.** of, indicating, or acting as a cause. **2.** *Grammar.* expressing or implying cause or reason. In the sentence *The mosquitoes are bad this year because it has rained so much,* the word *because* is a causal conjunction. —**caus′al·ly,** *adv.*

cau·sal·i·ty (kô zal′i tē) *n., pl.* **-ties. 1.** the principle that everything requires a cause for its existence; relationship between cause and effect. **2.** a causal quality or agency.

cau·sa·tion (kô zā′shən) *n.* **1.** the act of causing. **2.** something that produces an effect; cause. **3.** the relation of cause and effect; causality.

caus·a·tive (kô′zə tiv) *adj.* **1.** acting as a cause. **2.** *Grammar.* expressing or indicating causation. In *ennoble, en-* is a causative prefix. —*n. Grammar.* a causative word or form. —**caus′a·tive·ly,** *adv.*

cause (kôz) *n.* **1.** something that produces an effect or makes another thing happen: *The hurricane was the cause of great damage along the coast.* **2.** a basis, as for action; reason; motive: *There is no cause for alarm.* **3.** a subject, object, or principle of concern or interest to an individual or group and to which they give their support: *Helping the poor is a worthy cause.* **4.a.** a matter or question to be decided by a court of law; ground of action. **b.** a judicial proceeding; suit. —*v.t.,* **caused, caus·ing.** to result in or make happen; produce or make: *The traffic jam caused me to be late. Negligence causes many accidents.* [Old French *cause* motive, from Latin *causa* reason, lawsuit.] —**caus′a·ble,** *adj.* —**cause′less,** *adj.*

·**to make common cause.** to unite to pursue a common objective.

a	at	e	end	o	hot	u	up	hw	white		about
ā	ape	ē	me	ō	old	ū	use	ng	song		taken
ä	far	i	it	ô	fork	u̇	rule	th	thin	ə	pencil
âr	care	ī	ice	oi	oil	u̇	pull	th	this		lemon
		îr	pierce	ou	out	ûr	turn	zh	measure		circus

189

Synonyms *n.* **Cause, determinant,** and **antecedent** mean something that produces or helps to produce an effect or result. **Cause,** the most general of these terms, implies something necessary to an effect, whether the connection is immediate or not: *The cause of death was a heart attack. One of the major causes of poverty is unemployment.* **Determinant** refers to something that, together with other circumstances, shapes a result: *One determinant of the severity of the disease is age.* **Antecedent** indicates something that comes before and is regarded as influencing a result, sometimes indirectly: *The antecedents of the cold war included the distrust between the Soviet Union and its Western allies in World War II.*

cause·cé·lè·bre (kôz′sə leb′rə, kōz′sə leb′) any controversy or issue, esp. one of a legal nature, that becomes famous. [French *cause célèbre* famous legal case, going back to Latin *causa* lawsuit + *celeber* famous.]

cau·se·rie (kō′zə rē′) *n.* **1.** an informal conversation or discussion; chat. **2.** a short article, essay, or other composition written in an informal, conversational style. [French *causerie,* from *causer* to talk, from Latin *causārī* to plead, discuss.]

cause·way (kôz′wā′) *n.* **1.** a raised road or path, as across a body of water. **2.** highway. [Earlier *causey way,* from dialectal Old French *cauciee* (from Medieval Latin *calciata* paved road, going back to Latin *calx* limestone) + English WAY. See CALX.]

caus·tic (kôs′tik) *adj.* **1.** capable of corroding or destroying animal tissue; corrosive. **2.** sarcastic; cutting; biting: *a caustic remark.* —*n.* a substance, as lye, that is destructive or corrosive to animal tissue. [Latin *causticus* corrosive, from Greek *kaustikos.*]

caus·ti·cal·ly (kôs′ti klē) *adv.* in a caustic manner; sarcastically.

caustic potash, potassium hydroxide.

caustic soda, sodium hydroxide.

cau·ter·ize (kô′tə rīz′) *v.t.,* **-ized, -iz·ing.** to sear with a hot instrument or a caustic substance, esp. to destroy dead tissue or prevent infection. —**cau′ter·i·za′tion,** *n.*

cau·tion (kô′shən) *n.* **1.** care with regard to danger or risk; prudence; wariness: *to use caution in working with chemicals.* **2.** warning. **3.** *Informal.* a very odd or unusual person. —*v.t.* to urge (someone) to be careful; warn. [Latin *cautiō* carefulness, wariness.]

cau·tion·ar·y (kô′shə ner′ē) *adj.* conveying a warning.

cau·tious (kô′shəs) *adj.* characterized by or exhibiting caution; careful. —**cau′tious·ly,** *adv.* —**cau′tious·ness,** *n.*

Synonyms **Cautious** and **wary** mean taking care, in one's words or actions, to avoid risk or danger. **Cautious** is the more general of the terms, suggesting either a pattern of behavior or the attitude one has at a particular moment: *The doctor was cautious not to alarm the patient's family. Be cautious in approaching a strange dog.* **Wary** suggests stronger caution and a suspicious or defensive attitude that may arise from experience: *After being bitten, I am wary of strange dogs.*

cav., cavalry.

cav·al·cade (kav′əl kād′, kav′əl kād′) *n.* **1.** a procession, esp. of people on horseback or in vehicles. **2.** a large, impressive group or gathering: *A cavalcade of movie stars attended the awards ceremony.* **3.** a series, as of events: *a cavalcade of sporting events.* [Middle French *cavalcade* riding on horse, from Italian *cavalcata* band of horsemen, going back to Latin *caballus* nag, inferior horse.]

cav·a·lier (kav′ə lîr′) *n.* **1.** a horseman, esp. one who is armed; knight. **2.** a gallant or courteous gentleman, esp. one serving as the escort of a lady. **3. Cavalier.** a supporter of Charles I of England in his struggles with Parliament from 1641 to 1649. ➡ opposed to **Roundhead.** —*adj.* **1.** having or showing little concern; free and easy; offhand: *She is very cavalier about her possessions.* **2.** haughty; disdainful: *He is cavalier in his attitude toward those he considers his inferiors.* **3. Cavalier.** of or relating to the Cavaliers. [French *cavalier* knight who rides a horse, gentleman, from Italian *cavaliere,* from Late Latin *caballārius* horseman, from Latin *caballus* inferior horse, nag. In Latin the elegant word for horse was *equus,* yet aristocratic English words concerning horses come from *caballus,* a working-class word for the animal. Doublet of CHEVALIER.] —**cav′a·lier′ly,** *adv.*

cav·al·ry (kav′əl rē) *n., pl.* **-ries. 1.** a military unit trained to fight on horseback. **2.** in some countries, a military unit composed of armored vehicles, as tanks. [Middle French *cavallerie* horsemen, from Italian *cavalleria* knighthood, cavalry, from *cavaliere* knight. See CAVALIER.]

cav·al·ry·man (kav′əl rē mən, -man′) *n., pl.* **-men** (-mən, -men′). a member of a cavalry.

cav·a·ti·na (kav′ə tē′nə) *n.* **1.** a short, simple song or melody, usually without a second part or repeat, often found in a larger work, as an oratorio or opera. **2.** a short, lyric, instrumental composition or passage. [Italian *cavatina* melodious air, from *cavata* production of sound, from *cavare* to extract, from Latin *cavāre* to make hollow.]

cave (kāv) *n.* a natural hollow chamber or cavity beneath the earth's surface or in the side of a mountain. —*v.t.,* **caved, cav·ing.** to hollow out: *The children caved out a fort in the hill.* [Old French *cave* den, going back to Latin *cavus* hollow.]

• **to cave in. a.** to fall or cause to fall in or down. **b.** *Informal.* to stop resisting something; give in; surrender.

ca·ve·at (kā′vē at′, kav′ē-, kä′vē ät′) *n.* **1.** a formal notice to a legal authority to prevent some specific action until the notifier can be heard. **2.** warning. [Latin *caveat* let him beware; with reference to the first word of certain legal texts.]

ca·ve·at emp·tor (kā′vē at′ emp′tôr, kav′ē-, kä′vē ät′) *Latin.* let the buyer beware.

cave dweller, a person or animal that lives in a cave, esp. a person who did so during prehistoric times.

cave-in (kāv′in′) *n.* **1.** a collapse or falling in, as of a mine. **2.** the site of such a collapse.

cave man 1. a cave dweller of the Paleolithic period. **2.** *Informal.* a man who behaves in a rough, crude manner, esp. toward women.

cav·ern (kav′ərn) *n.* a cave, esp. one of very great size or extent. [French *caverne,* from Latin *caverna,* from *cavus* hollow.]

cav·ern·ous (kav′ər nəs) *adj.* **1.** like a cavern; large and hollow: *a cavernous auditorium.* **2.** full of or containing caverns or cavities. **3.** deep-set: *cavernous eyes.* **4.** deep-sounding, as though issuing from a cavern: *a cavernous voice.*

cav·i·ar (kav′ē är′) *also,* **cav·i·are.** *n.* the salty processed roe of sturgeon or certain other large fish, served as an appetizer. [French *caviar,* from Italian *caviaro,* going back to Turkish *khāv·yār.*]

cav·il (kav′əl) *v.,* **-iled, -il·ing;** *also, British,* **-illed, -il·ling.** —*v.i.* to find fault unnecessarily; raise trivial objections; quibble (often with *at* or *about*). —*v.t.* to find fault with unnecessarily. —*n.* a captious, quibbling objection; trivial criticism. [Old French *caviller* to wrangle, mock, from Latin *cavillārī* to jeer.] —**cav′il·er;** *also, British,* **cav′il·ler,** *n.*

cav·i·ta·tion (kav′i tā′shən) *n.* the rapid formation and collapse of vapor bubbles in a swiftly moving current in a liquid, as that produced in water by a ship's propeller, often causing structural damage. [Late Latin *cavitationis,* genitive of *cavitas* cavity, from Latin *cavus* hollow.]

cav·i·ty (kav′i tē) *n., pl.* **-ties. 1.** a hollow place; hole. **2.** a hollow space in a tooth, usually caused by decay. **3.** a space within the body or an organ. [Late Latin *cavitās* hollowness, from Latin *cavus* hollow.] —For Synonyms, see **hole.**

ca·vort (kə vôrt′) *v.i. Informal.* to run and jump around playfully; frisk. [Possibly modification of CURVET.]

ca·vy (kā′vē) *n., pl.* **-vies.** any of various rodents, family Caviidae, of South America, having short legs, small ears, and a rounded body, the best known of which is the guinea pig. [Modern Latin *Cavia;* of Carib origin.]

caw (kô) *n.* a harsh cry or call, as of a crow or raven. —*v.i.* to make this cry or call. [Imitative.]

cay (kā, kē) *n.* a low mound or island of sand and, often, coral fragments, built up on a reef slightly above high tide level; key. [Spanish *cayo* rock, shoal, from Taino *cayo* small island.]

cay·enne (kī en′, kā-) *n.* a hot, biting spice made from the ground seeds and pods of any of several hot red peppers, esp. a variety of *Capsicum annuum.* Also, **red pepper.** [Modification (influenced by *Cayenne,* a city in French Guiana) of Tupi-Guarani *kyinha* this spice.]

cay·man (kā′mən) caiman.

Ca·yu·ga (kā ū′gə, kī-) *n., pl.* **-ga** or **-gas.** a member of a tribe of Iroquois Indians formerly living in what is now the state of New York.

cay·use (kī ūs′, kī′ūs) *n.* an Indian pony of the western United States.

Cb, the symbol for columbium.

CB, citizen's band (radio).

cc *also,* **cc.** cubic centimeter; cubic centimeters.

CCD, charge-coupled device.

C clef, in music, a movable clef indicating that the line of the staff on which it is placed represents middle C. There are three C clefs: the **alto clef,** having the symbol on the third line of the staff, the **tenor clef,** having the symbol on the fourth line, and the **soprano**

clef having the symbol on the first line of the staff. For illustration, see **clef**.

Cd, the symbol for cadmium.

cd also, **cd.** cord; cords.

CD 1. certificate of deposit. **2.** civil defense. **3.** compact disc.

CDC, Centers for Disease Control.

cd ft also, **cd. ft.** cord foot; cord feet.

Cdr., Commander.

Ce, the symbol for cerium.

C.E., Civil Engineer.

cease (sēs) v., **ceased, ceas·ing.** —v.i. to come to an end; stop. —v.t. to put an end to; discontinue: *The factory will cease operations next week.* [Old French *cesser* to yield, stop, from Latin *cessāre* to stop, delay.] —For Synonyms *(v.i.),* see **stop.**

cease-fire (sēs'fīr') n. **1.** a temporary halt in hostilities by mutual agreement of the combatants. **2.** an order or signal for such a halt. —For Synonyms, see **truce.**

cease·less (sēs'lis) adj. never stopping; continuous; incessant. —**cease'less·ly,** adv. —**cease'less·ness,** n.

ce·cro·pi·a moth (si krō'pē ə) a large silkworm moth, *Hyalophora cecropia,* native to the eastern United States and having colorful markings.

ce·cum (sē'kəm) also, **caecum.** n., pl. **-ca** (-kə). a pouch or cavity that is open at one end, esp. the blind pouch that is the beginning of the large intestine and to which the vermiform appendix is attached. [Short for Latin *intestīnum caecum* blind intestine.] —**ce'cal,** adj.

ce·dar (sē'dər) n. **1.** any of several evergreen trees, genus *Cedrus,* of the pine family, having rough dark gray bark and numerous branches that bear needle-shaped leaves. One of the best-known species is the **cedar of Lebanon,** *C. libani.* **2.** any of various other trees that have fragrant wood or needle-shaped leaves but are not true cedars, as the **red cedar,** *Juniperus virginiana.* **3.** the durable fragrant wood of the true cedar, used for making chests and cabinets. [Latin *cedrus* cedar tree, from Greek *kedros.*]

cedar waxwing, a crested waxwing, *Bombycilla cedrorum,* native to North America, having brownish gray plumage with yellow, black, and red markings. Also, **ce·dar·bird** (sē'dər-bûrd').

cede (sēd) v.t., **ced·ed, ced·ing.** to give up, as title or possession; surrender; relinquish: *to cede territory.* [Latin *cēdere* to yield, go.]

ce·di (sā'dē) n. the monetary unit of Ghana.

ce·dil·la (si dil'ə) n. a mark (,) placed under certain letters to indicate pronunciation. It is used esp. under *c* coming before a hard vowel to indicate the sound *s,* as in *façade.* [Spanish *cedilla,* diminutive of *ceda* the letter *z,* through Latin, from Greek *zēta* the letter *z;* because a *z* used to be added to *c* to indicate a soft pronunciation of *c,* as in French or Spanish.]

cei·ba (sā'bə) n. silk-cotton tree. [South American Spanish *ceiba,* from Arawakan *ceiba.*]

ceil·ing (sē'ling) n. **1.** the interior, overhead covering or surface of a room. **2.** the maximum height above sea level at which a given aircraft can maintain horizontal flight under standard air conditions. **3.** vertical visibility measured from sea level to the bottom of the lowest cloud bank. **4.** maximum or upper limit set on anything: *The government imposed a ceiling on wages.* [CEIL + -ING[1].]

· **to hit the ceiling.** *Informal.* to lose one's temper.

cel·an·dine (sel'ən dīn', -dēn') n. a plant of the poppy family that grows wild as a weed but is sometimes cultivated as a garden plant because of its clusters of yellow flowers. [Old French *celidoine,* from Late Latin *chelīdonium,* from Greek *chelīdonion,* from *chelīdōn* swallow.]

cel·e·brant (sel'ə brənt) n. **1.** a person who participates in a celebration. **2.** a priest who officiates at a Mass or other liturgical service.

cel·e·brate (sel'ə brāt') v., **-brat·ed, -brat·ing.** —v.t. **1.** to observe or commemorate (an event) with ceremonies or festivities: *We celebrated my cousin's birthday.* **2.** to perform, as a ritual, publicly with the proper ceremonies; solemnize: *The priest celebrated the Mass.* **3.** to honor or make known publicly, esp. with praise; extol: *Their courage was celebrated in all the newspapers.* —v.i. **1.** to observe or commemorate an event with ceremonies or festivities. **2.** *Informal.* to have a merry time. [Latin *celebrātus,* past participle of *celebrāre* to honor, frequent.] —**cel'e·bra'tor,** n.

cel·e·brat·ed (sel'ə brā'tid) adj. widely praised or talked about; well-known; famous. —For Synonyms, see **famous.**

cel·e·bra·tion (sel'ə brā'shən) n. **1.** the act of celebrating. **2.** the ceremonies or festivities with which something is celebrated.

ce·leb·ri·ty (sə leb'ri tē) n., pl. **-ties. 1.** a person who is well-known or much publicized. **2.** the state of being well-known or much publicized.

ce·ler·i·ac (sə ler'ē ak', -lîr'-) n. a variety of celery, *Apium graveolens rapaceum,* grown for its thick, turniplike, edible root. [Modification of CELERY.]

ce·ler·i·ty (sə ler'i tē) n. swiftness; speed. [Latin *celeritās.*]

cel·er·y (sel'ə rē) n. **1.** the thick, crisp green or creamy white leafstalks of a plant, *Apium graveolens,* of the parsley family. **2.** the plant itself. [French *céleri* the plant, from dialectal Italian *selleri* (plural), from Latin *selīnon* parsley, from Greek *selīnon.*]

ce·les·ta (sə les'tə) n. a musical keyboard instrument having steel plates that are struck by hammers to produce a tone similar to that of the glockenspiel. [French *célesta,* from *céleste* heavenly, from Latin *caelestis.*]

ce·les·tial (sə les'chəl) adj. **1.** of or relating to the sky or heavens: *The planets are celestial bodies.* **2.** of or fit for heaven; heavenly; divine: *celestial beauty.* [Old French *celestiel* heavenly, from Latin *caelestis.*] —**ce·les'tial·ly,** adv.

celestial equator, the great circle formed by the intersection of the plane of the earth's equator and the celestial sphere.

celestial latitude, angular distance measured north or south of the ecliptic.

celestial longitude, angular distance measured eastward on the ecliptic from the vernal equinox.

celestial mechanics, the science that deals with the motion of celestial bodies, esp. those under the influence of gravitational fields.

celestial meridian, a great circle on the celestial sphere passing through the north and south celestial poles and the zenith.

celestial navigation, a method of navigation in which position is determined by the observation of celestial bodies with respect to points on the earth that lie beneath those bodies.

celestial pole, either of the two intersections of the earth's axis with the celestial sphere.

celestial sphere, an imaginary sphere surrounding the earth and representing the entire sky and to whose inner surface the stars are apparently attached.

ce·li·ac (sē'lē ak') also, **coeliac.** adj. of, relating to, or situated within the abdominal cavity. [Latin *coeliacus,* from Greek *koiliakos,* from *koiliā* abdomen.]

celiac disease, an intestinal disorder caused by faulty digestion and characterized by diarrhea, malnutrition, and anemia.

cel·i·ba·cy (sel'ə bə sē) n. the state of being unmarried, esp. in accordance with religious vows.

cel·i·bate (sel'ə bit) n. a person who remains unmarried, esp. in accordance with religious vows. —adj. unmarried. [Latin *caelibatus* single life, from *caelebs* unmarried.]

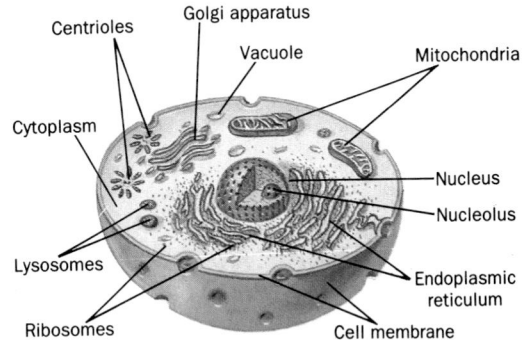

animal **cell**

cell (sel) n. **1.** a small, usually austere, room, as in a prison, convent, or monastery. **2.** the basic unit of all living organisms, consisting of a mass of cytoplasm including organelles, such as ribosomes and mitochondria, plus a nucleus near the center and

a	at	e	end	o	hot	u	up	hw	white	(	about
ā	ape	ē	me	ō	old	ū	use	ng	song		taken
ä	far	i	it	ô	fork	ü	rule	th	thin	ə	pencil
âr	care	ī	ice	oi	oil	u̇	pull	th	this		lemon
		îr	pierce	ou	out	ûr	turn	zh	measure	(	circus

enclosed by a cell membrane or, in plants, a cell wall. **3.** a device that transforms chemical, solar, or light energy into electrical energy. **4.** a local, underground unit of a political organization, esp. of a Communist Party. **5.** a small cavity or compartment, as in a honeycomb. **6.** the area covered by a transmitter in a cellular phone system. **7.** *Computers.* a place for storage, in memory, of a single unit of information. [Latin *cella* small room, storeroom.]

cel·lar (sel'ər) *n.* **1.** a room or group of rooms, either wholly or partly underground, usually under a building and often used as a place for storage. **2.** wine cellar *(def. 1).* **3.** a stock of wines. **4.** *Sports.* last place in the standings of a league. —*v.t.* to store, as wines, in a cellar. [Anglo-Norman *celer* storeroom, from Late Latin *cellārium* pantry, from Latin *cella* small room, storeroom.]

cel·lar·er (sel'ər ər) *n.* a person who is in charge of a cellar and the wines or provisions in it, esp. in a monastery.

cell division, the process in which a cell divides into two new cells, each with the same number of chromosomes as the original.

cel·list (chel'ist) *also,* **'cel·list.** *n.* a person who plays the cello. Also, **violoncellist.**

cell membrane, a thin membrane that surrounds the cell and encloses the cytoplasm. For illustration, see **cell.**

cel·lo (chel'ō) *also,* **'cel·lo.** *n., pl.* **-los.** a tenor instrument of the violin family, intermediate between the viola and double bass in size and pitch. Also, **violoncello.**

cel·lo·phane (sel'ə fān') *n.* a thin, flexible, usually transparent material made from cellulose, used esp. as a wrapping material. [CELLULOSE + Greek *phainein* to show.]

cel·lu·lar (sel'yə lər) *adj.* **1.** of, relating to, or resembling a cell or cells. **2.** consisting of cells. —**cel·lu·lar·i·ty** (sel'yə lar'i tē), *n.*

cellular phone, a mobile telephone, usually used in motor vehicles, that operates within a network of radio transmitters that send and relay signals from one geographical area, or cell, to another. Also, **cellular radio.**

cellular respiration, the process in which oxygen is utilized by living cells to release energy from food molecules.

cel·lu·loid (sel'yə loid') *n.* a strong, transparent, flammable plastic made from nitrocellulose, alcohol, and camphor.

cel·lu·lose (sel'yə lōs') *n.* a white, solid carbohydrate that is insoluble in water. It is the major component of the walls of plant cells and thus makes up the woody part of trees and plants. It is used esp. to make paper, rayon, and other products. Formula: $(C_6H_{10}O_5)_n$ [French *cellulose,* from Latin *cellula* small storeroom, diminutive of *cella* small room, storeroom.]

cellulose acetate, a thermoplastic resin made by treating cellulose with acetic acid and other compounds, used to make synthetic acetate fibers and membranes for removing salt from seawater.

cellulose nitrate, nitrocellulose.

cell wall, in plants, the hard outer layer of cellulose that covers the cell membrane.

Cel·si·us (sel'sē əs, -shəs) *adj.* of, according to, or designating the temperature scale on which the freezing point of water is at 0 degrees and the boiling point is at 100 degrees under standard atmospheric pressure. Also, **centigrade.** For illustration, see **Fahrenheit.** [From Anders *Celsius,* 1701-44, Swedish astronomer who established the centigrade scale.]

Celt (selt, kelt) *also,* **Kelt.** *n.* **1.** a member of a Celtic-speaking people to which the Irish, Highland Scots, Welsh, Cornish, and Bretons belong. **2.** a member of an ancient people of central and western Europe, including the Gauls and Britons. [French *Celte,* from Latin *Celtae* (plural) Celts, from Greek *Keltoi* (plural).]

Celt·ic (sel'tik, kel'-) *also,* **Keltic.** *adj.* of or relating to the Celts, their languages, or their culture. —*n.* a group of languages belonging to the Indo-European language family, including Irish Gaelic, Scottish Gaelic, Breton, Welsh, and Cornish.

Celtic cross, a Latin cross having a circle behind the intersection of the crosspiece. For illustration, see **cross.**

cel·tuce (sel'təs) *n.* **1.** the stems of a plant, *Lactuca sativa asparagina,* of the composite family, cooked like a vegetable and tasting like a mixture of celery and lettuce. **2.** the plant itself. [CEL(ERY) + (LET)TUCE.]

ce·ment (sə ment') *n.* **1.** a construction material made by burning a mixture of limestone, clay or shale, silica, gypsum, and other substances to create a fine powder that when mixed with water forms a slow-hardening paste. It is used to make concrete and mortar. **2.** concrete. **3.** any soft substance, esp. one made of

rubber or synthetic resins, that acts as an adhesive. **4.** anything that joins together or unites; bond: *the cement of family ties.* —*v.t.* **1.** to cause to adhere or fasten together with cement: *to cement bricks, to cement a wing to a model airplane.* **2.** to coat or cover with cement: *to cement a driveway.* **3.** to join together or unite; bind: *The agreement cemented the business partnership.* —*v.i.* to become joined or fastened together. [Old French *ciment* mixture of limestone and crushed bricks, from Latin *caementum* rough stone, stone chips used to make mortar.] —**ce·ment'er,** *n.*

Usage Cement originally referred to the central ingredient of concrete, but now its use has been extended to also mean concrete itself, as in *a cement floor.* Some people prefer to reserve the word for the original meaning because it is more precise.

ce·ment·ite (sə men'tīt) *n.* an iron carbide that is a constituent of steel and cast iron. [CEMENT + -ITE[1].]

ce·men·tum (sə men'təm) *n.* a bony substance that covers the root of a tooth, protecting the dentin and helping to anchor the tooth in the jawbone. [Modern Latin *cementum,* from Latin *c(a)ementum* rough stone.]

cem·e·ter·y (sem'i ter'ē) *n., pl.* **-ter·ies.** a place for burying the dead; graveyard. [Late Latin *coemētērium,* from Greek *koimētērion* literally, sleeping place, from *koimān* to put to sleep.]

cen. 1. central. **2.** century.

ce·no·bite (sē'nə bīt', sen'ə-) *also,* **coenobite.** *n.* a member of a religious order living in a monastery or convent. [Late Latin *coenobita* monk, from *coenobium* monastery, convent, from Greek *koinobion* convent, community life, from *koinos* common + *bios* life.]

cen·o·taph (sen'ə taf') *n.* an empty tomb or monument erected in memory of a deceased person whose body is buried elsewhere. [French *cénotaphe,* from Late Latin *cenotaphium,* from Greek *kenotaphion.*]

Ce·no·zo·ic (sē'nə zō'ik, sen'ə-) *n.* the most recent geologic era, comprising the Tertiary and Quaternary periods; the age of mammals. For table, see **geologic time.** —*adj.* of, relating to, or characteristic of this era. [Greek *kainos* recent, new + *zōē* life + -IC.]

cen·ser (sen'sər) *n.* a container that is used for burning incense. Also, **thurible.** [Old French *censier,* going back to Latin *incēnsum* incense.]

cen·sor (sen'sər) *n.* **1.a.** a person employed by a government or organization to examine material, such as books, news reports, and motion pictures, and suppress what is considered politically or morally objectionable. **b.** a person employed by a government during wartime to examine letters and dispatches and to remove any information considered to be dangerous to national security. **2.** one of two magistrates of ancient Rome who were in charge of taking the census and supervising public morals. **3.** anyone who disapproves, denounces, or otherwise criticizes the behavior or morality of others. —*v.t.* to act as censor of: *to censor books.* [Latin *cēnsor* assessor, critic.] —**cen'sor·a·ble,** *adj.* —**cen·so'ri·al,** *adj.*

cen·so·ri·ous (sen sôr'ē əs) *adj.* tending to or containing censure; severely critical: *A censorious manner wins few friends.* —**cen·so'ri·ous·ly,** *adv.* —**cen·so'ri·ous·ness,** *n.*

cen·sor·ship (sen'sər ship') *n.* **1.** the act or system of censoring. **2.** the office or power held by a censor.

cen·sur·a·ble (sen'shər ə bəl) *adj.* worthy of censure. —**cen'sur·a·bly,** *adv.*

cen·sure (sen'shər) *v.t.,* **-sured, -sur·ing.** to express disapproval of or find fault with; blame; condemn. —*n.* **1.** an expression of disapproval; condemnation. **2.** an official expression of disapproval, as for misconduct in public office. [Latin *cēnsūra* opinion, judgment.] —**cen'sur·er,** *n.* —For Synonyms *(v.t.),* see **blame.**

cen·sus (sen'səs) *n.* an official, usually periodic count of the population of a country or district, made in order to obtain certain statistics, such as age, sex, occupation, or economic status. [Latin *cēnsus* registration of citizens and their property.]

cent (sent) *n.* **1.a.** a unit of currency of the United States and Canada, equal to 1/100 of a dollar. **b.** the coin representing this unit of currency; penny. **2.** 1/100 of any of various monetary units, as of the rand or the guilder. [Contraction of Latin *centēsimus* hundredth, from *centum* hundred.]

cent. 1. centigrade. **2.** central. **3.** century.

cen·tare (sen'târ) *n.* centiare.

cen·taur (sen'tôr) *n.* in Greek mythology, one of a race of creatures having a human head, arms, and torso attached to the

centaurs

body and legs of a horse. [Latin *Centaurus*, from Greek *Kentauros*.]

Cen·tau·rus (sen tôr′əs) *n.* a constellation south of the celestial equator containing the bright star Alpha Centauri.

cen·ta·vo (sen tä′vō) *n., pl.* **-vos.** ¹/₁₀₀ of any of various monetary units, as of the Salvadoran colon or the peso in certain Latin American countries. [Spanish *centavo* hundredth part, from Latin *centum* hundred.]

cen·te·nar·i·an (sen′tə nâr′ē ən) *n.* a person who is 100 years old or older. —*adj.* **1.** of the age of 100 years. **2.** of or relating to a period of 100 years.

cen·te·nar·y (sen ten′ə rē, sen′tə ner′ē) *n., pl.* **-nar·ies. 1.** centennial. **2.** a period of 100 years. —*adj.* **1.** of or relating to a period of 100 years. **2.** recurring once in every 100 years. [Latin *centēnārius* relating to a hundred, going back to Latin *centum* hundred.]

cen·ten·ni·al (sen ten′ē əl) *n.* a 100th anniversary or its celebration. —*adj.* **1.** of, relating to, or marking a period of 100 years or its completion. **2.** of or relating to a 100th anniversary. **3.** 100 years old. [Latin *centum* hundred + BI(ENNIAL).] —**cen·ten′ni·al·ly,** *adv.*

cen·ter (sen′tər) *also, British,* **centre.** *n.* **1.** a point or place equally distant from the sides; middle part, point, or place: *the center of a page, the center of town.* **2.** a place or point around which some interest or activity revolves or is concentrated; pivotal or focal point: *a tourist center, the center of attention.* **3.** a point, line, or axis around which anything, as a wheel, revolves. **4.** *Geometry.* a point within a circle or sphere equally distant from all points on the circumference or surface. **5.** *also,* **Center.** a group holding moderate political views, as between those of conservatives and radicals. **6.** *Sports.* **a.** a football player who is in the middle of the offensive line and snaps the ball back to the quarterback. **b.** in basketball, hockey, and lacrosse, a player in the middle of the forward line who begins play. **7.** nerve center. —*v.t.* **1.** to place or fix in or at the center: *We centered the mirror on the wall.* **2.** to draw or gather toward one point; collect or concentrate around a focal point: *to center one's attention on a problem.* —*v.i.* to be centered or concentrated: *The main action of the story centered around the child.* [Latin *centrum* middle point (of a circle), from Greek *kentron* spike, goad, point around which a compass draws a circle.]

cen·ter·board (sen′tər bôrd′) *n.* a fin-shaped board or plate lowered through a slot in the bottom of a sailboat that does not have a fixed keel, to prevent drifting.

center field *Baseball.* **1.** the middle section of the outfield behind second base, when viewed from home plate. **2.** the position of the player stationed in this area. —**center fielder.**

cen·ter·fold (sen′tər fōld′) *n.* **1.** a magazine illustration that covers two facing central pages and sometimes folds out further from one or both of them. **2.** a person, usually photographed in the nude, appearing in such an illustration.

center of gravity, the point within a body around which the weight of the body is evenly balanced, usually identical with the center of mass.

center of mass, the point at which the mass of a body or system of bodies is theoretically concentrated.

cen·ter·piece (sen′tər pēs′) *n.* an ornamental object placed in the center of a table.

Centers for Disease Control, an agency of the U.S. government concerned with health education, environmental and occupational health, and the spread and control of disease.

cen·tes·i·mal (sen tes′ə məl) *adj.* **1.** hundredth. **2.** relating to or divided into hundredths. [Latin *centēsimus* hundredth (from *centum* hundred) + -AL¹.] —**cen·tes′i·mal·ly,** *adv.*

cen·tes·i·mo (sen tes′ə mō′; *Spanish* sen te′sē mô′; *Italian* chente′zē mô′) *n., pl.* **-mos** (-mōz′; *Spanish* -môs′) *or Italian* **-mi** (-mē′). ¹/₁₀₀ of any of various monetary units, as of the Italian lira or the balboa. [Italian *centesimo* hundredth, from Latin *centēsimus.* See CENT.]

centi- *combining form* a hundredth part of: *centigram, centimeter.* [Latin *centum* hundred.]

cen·ti·are (sen′tē âr′) *n.* a unit of measure equal to 1 square meter. Also, **centare.** [French *centiare,* from Latin *centum* hundred + French *are.* See ARE².]

cen·ti·grade (sen′ti grād′) *adj.* Celsius. [CENTI- + Latin *gradus* step, degree.]

cen·ti·gram (sen′ti gram′) *also, British,* **cen·ti·gramme.** *n.* a unit of metric weight equal to ¹/₁₀₀ of a gram. [French *centigramme,* going back to Latin *centum* hundred + Greek *gramma* small weight.]

cen·ti·li·ter (sen′tə lē′tər) *also, British,* **cen·ti·li·tre.** *n.* a unit of metric measure equal to ¹/₁₀₀ of a liter.

cen·til·lion (sen til′yən) *n.* **1.** in the United States, the cardinal number that is represented by 1 followed by 303 zeros. **2.** in Great Britain, the cardinal number that is represented by 1 followed by 600 zeros. —*adj.* numbering one centillion. [Latin *centum* one hundred; formed on the model of MILLION.]

cen·time (sän′tēm) *n.* any of various monetary units representing ¹/₁₀₀ of the basic unit, as of the franc. [French *centime,* going back to Latin *centēsimus* hundredth.]

cen·ti·me·ter (sen′tə mē′tər) *also, British,* **cen·ti·me·tre.** *n.* a unit of metric measure equal to ¹/₁₀₀ of a meter. [French *centimètre,* going back to Latin *centum* hundred + Greek *metron* measure.]

cen·ti·me·ter-gram-sec·ond (sen′tə mē′tər gram′sek′ənd) *adj.* of, relating to, or being a system of measurement in which the centimeter is the unit of length, the gram is the unit of mass, and the second is the unit of time.

cen·ti·mo (sen′tə mō′) *n., pl.* **-mos.** ¹/₁₀₀ of any of various monetary units, as of the bolivar or the Costa Rican colon. [Spanish *céntimo,* from French *centime.* See CENTIME.]

cen·ti·pede (sen′tə pēd′) *n.* any of a group of small wormlike invertebrates, class Chilopoda, with a flattened, elongated body made up of many segments, each bearing a pair of legs. In some centipedes the foremost pair of legs is modified into poisonous fangs. [Latin *centipeda,* from *centum* hundred + *pēs* foot.]

cen·tral (sen′trəl) *adj.* **1.** in, at, or near the center: *The railroad station has a central location in town.* **2.** of or forming the center: *The post office is in the central part of town.* **3.** being that from which other things come or upon which they depend; principal: *the central issue of a debate, the central character of a book.* **4.** that exercises a controlling or directing influence: *a central office, a central agency of the government.* **5.** operating from a single location: *a central heating system.* —*n.* formerly, the main telephone exchange of a town or city or the telephone operator at such an exchange. [Latin *centrālis* relating to a center, from *centrum* middle point. See CENTER.] —**cen′tral·ly,** *adv.*

central angle, an angle whose sides are the radii and whose vertex is the center of a circle.

cen·tral·i·ty (sen tral′i tē) *n., pl.* **-ties. 1.** the state or quality of being central. **2.** a central position or situation.

cen·tral·i·za·tion (sen′trə lə zā′shən) *n.* **1.** the act of centralizing or the state of being centralized. **2.** the concentration of power in a central group or institution.

cen·tral·ize (sen′trə līz′) *v.,* **-ized, -iz·ing.** —*v.t.* **1.** to bring together at a center; make central. **2.** to bring or organize under one control or central authority. —*v.i.* to come together at a center.

central nervous system, that part of the vertebrate nervous system composed of the brain and the spinal cord.

Central Powers, the countries that fought against the Allies in World War I: Germany and Austria-Hungary, and their allies, Turkey and Bulgaria.

central processing unit, the part of a computer that contains the main memory and hardware for controlling all functions.

Central Standard Time, the local time of the 90th meridian west of Greenwich, England, used in the central United States and Canada. It is 6 hours earlier than Greenwich Time.

cen·tre (sen′tər) *British. n.* center. —*v.t., v.i.,* **-tred, -tring.** center.

centri-, form of **centro-,** as in *centrifugal.*

a	at	e	end	o	hot	u	up	hw	white		about
ā	ape	ē	me	ō	old	ū	use	ng	song		taken
ä	far	i	it	ô	fork	ü	rule	th	thin	ə	pencil
âr	care	ī	ice	oi	oil	ů	pull	<u>th</u>	this		lemon
				îr	pierce	ou	out	ûr	turn	zh	measure		circus

193

cen·tric (sen′trik) *adj.* in or at a center; central. Also, **cen′tri·cal.** —**cen′tri·cal·ly,** *adv.* —**cen·tric·i·ty** (sen tris′i tē) *n.*

cen·trif·u·gal (sen trif′yə gəl, -ə gəl) *adj.* **1.** moving or directed away from a center. ➡ opposed to **centripetal. 2.** using or operating by centrifugal force: *a centrifugal pump.* [Modern Latin *centrifugus* fleeing from the center (from Latin *centrum* middle point + *fugere* to flee) + -AL[1]. See CENTER.] —**cen·trif′u·gal·ly,** *adv.*

centrifugal force

centrifugal force, the force generated when a body is moving in a curved path, tending to move the body away from the center of curvature.

cen·tri·fuge (sen′trə fūj′) *n.* **1.** a device using centrifugal force to separate substances of different densities by spinning them at high speeds. **2.** a large machine that simulates gravitational effects, usually consisting of a capsule or chair spun in a circle at the end of a long support, used chiefly in training astronauts to withstand gravitational pull. —*v.t.,* -**fuged, -fug·ing.** to subject to the action of a centrifuge. [French *centrifuge* centrifugal, from Latin *centrum* middle point + *fugere* to flee. See CENTER.] —**cen·trif·u·ga·tion** (sen trif′yə gā′shən, -trif′ə-), *n.*

cen·tri·ole (sen′trē ōl′) *n.* a tiny cylindrical organelle in all animal cells and many plant cells, usually paired. Centrioles duplicate themselves just before mitosis and move to opposite ends of the cell during mitosis, where they form the poles of the spindle to which the chromosomes move. For illustration, see **cell.** [Latin *centrum* middle point + Latin *-olus,* diminutive suffix. See CENTER.]

cen·trip·e·tal (sen trip′i təl) *adj.* **1.** moving or directed toward a center. ➡ opposed to **centrifugal. 2.** using or operating by centripetal force. [Modern Latin *centripetus* seeking the center (from Latin *centrum* middle point + *petere* to seek) + -AL[1]. See CENTER.] —**cen·trip′e·tal·ly,** *adv.*

centripetal force, the force generated when a body is moving in a curved path, tending to move the body toward the center of curvature.

cen·trist (sen′trist) *n.* a person whose political views are moderate, esp. in certain European countries; member of a center party.

centro- *combining form* center: *centrosome.* [Latin *centrum* middle point. See CENTER.]

cen·troid (sen′troid) *n.* the point of intersection of the medians of a triangle. [CENTRO- + -OID.]

cen·tro·mere (sen′trə mîr′) *n.* the region of constriction in a dividing chromosome to which spindle fibers attach during meiosis or mitosis. [CENTRO- + Greek *meros* a part.]

cen·tro·some (sen′trə sōm′) *n.* an area in the cytoplasm of a cell that contains the centrioles. [Greek *kentron* spike, central point + *sōma* body.] —**cen·tro·som·ic** (sen′trə som′ik), *adj.*

cen·tro·sphere (sen′trə sfîr′) *n.* the protoplasm surrounding the centrosome. [Greek *kentron* spike, central point + *sphaira* ball, globe.]

cen·trum (sen′trəm) *n., pl.* -**trums** or -**tra** (-trə). the central,

solid portion of a vertebra, exclusive of its processes and arches. [Latin *centrum* middle point (of a circle). See CENTER.]

cen·tu·ple (sen′tə pəl, -tyə-) *adj.* multiplied by 100; hundredfold. —*v.t.,* -**pled, -pling.** to multiply by 100; increase a hundredfold. [French *centuple* hundredfold, from Late Latin *centuplus,* from Latin *centum* hundred.]

cen·tu·ri·on (sen tûr′ē ən, -tyûr′-) *n.* a commander of a century in the ancient Roman army. [Latin *centuriō,* going back to *centum* hundred.]

cen·tu·ry (sen′chə rē) *n., pl.* -**ries. 1.** a period of 100 years. **2.** a period of 100 years reckoned forward or backward from some fixed date, esp. from the birth of Jesus: *The American Civil War took place in the nineteenth century* A.D. **3.** in the ancient Roman army, an infantry division originally consisting of 100 men. **4.** one of 193 political divisions of the ancient Roman people, each division having one vote. [Latin *centuria* division of 100 units, from *centum* hundred.]

century plant, a desert plant, *Agave americana,* found in Mexico and the southwestern United States, having thick, spiny-edged leaves and a flower stalk that grows to a height of 20-40 feet (6.1-12.1 meters). [So called because it was mistakenly believed to bloom only once every century; actually, it blooms once after maturing for ten to thirty years and then it dies.]

CEO, Chief Executive Officer.

ce·phal·ic (sə fal′ik) *adj.* **1.** of or relating to the head. **2.** near, on, in, or toward the head. [Latin *cephalicus* relating to the head, from Greek *kephalikos,* from *kephalē* head.] —**ce·phal′i·cal·ly,** *adv.*

cephalic index, the ratio of the greatest width of the human head to its greatest length from front to back, multiplied by 100, used in anthropometry to characterize types of skulls.

ceph·a·lo·pod (sef′ə lə pod′) *n.* any of a group of highly developed mollusks, class Cephalopoda, including the octopus, squid, and cuttlefish, having a clearly defined head with large, well-developed eyes, a sharp beak, and muscular tentacles around the mouth that bear suckers. [Modern Latin *Cephalopoda,* from Greek *kephalē* head + *pous* foot.]

ceph·a·lo·spor·in (sef′ə lō spôr′in) *n.* any of a group of broad-spectrum antibiotics that are derived from certain fungi of the genus *Cephalosporium* and are more effective than penicillin against gram-negative bacilli.

ceph·a·lo·tho·rax (sef′ə lō thôr′aks) *n., pl.* -**tho·rax·es** or -**tho·ra·ces** (-thôr′ə sēz′). the anterior portion of the body in certain crustaceans and arachnids, consisting of the united head and thorax. [Greek *kephalē* head + *thōrāx* chest.]

Ce·phe·id (sē′fē id) *n.* any of a class of variable stars that undergo cyclical changes in brightness associated with contraction and expansion in volume. Also, **Cepheid variable.**

Ce·phe·us (sē′fē əs, sē′fūs) *n.* **1.** in Greek legend, the Ethiopian king who was the father of Andromeda and husband of Cassiopeia. **2.** a large constellation extending to the celestial north pole.

ce·ram·ic (sə ram′ik) *adj.* of or relating to pottery and other articles made of fired and baked clay, such as earthenware or porcelain. —*n.* an object made of baked clay. [Greek *keramikos,* from *keramos* potter's clay, pottery.]

ce·ram·ics (sə ram′iks) *pl. n.* **1.** the art or technique of shaping objects from clay and other inorganic, nonmetallic materials and firing them at high temperatures. **2.** articles made by this technique, as pottery, glass, abrasives, bricks, and tiles. ➡ used as singular in def. 1, as plural in def. 2. —**ce·ram′i·cist, cer·a·mist** (ser′ə mist′, sə-ram′ist), *n.*

Cer·ber·us (sûr′bər əs) *n.* in classical mythology, the monstrous three-headed dog that guarded the entrance to Hades.

cer·cus (sûr′kəs, ker′-) *n., pl.* **cer·ci** (sûr′sī, ker′kē). one of a pair of usually jointed, taillike or pincerlike appendages at the end of the abdomen of certain insects and other arthropods, as earwigs. [Modern Latin *cercus,* from Greek *kerkos* tail.]

Cerberus

cere (sîr) *n.* a fleshy, waxy-looking membrane above the beak of certain birds, as parrots and birds of prey, that contains the nostrils. [French *cire* wax, from Latin *cēra.*]

ce·re·al (sîr′ē əl) *n.* **1.** any of a number of foods made from the processed seeds or seedlike fruits of cereal grains. **2.** the seed or seedlike fruit itself. **3.** any of a number of plants of the grass

family that bear such seeds or seedlike fruits, as wheat or barley. —*adj.* of or relating to edible grain or the plants producing it. [Latin *cereālis* relating to grain, relating to CERES.]

cer·e·bel·lum (ser'ə bel'əm) *n., pl.* **-bel·lums** or **-bel·la** (-bel'ə). the part of the brain that coordinates voluntary muscular activity and is involved with the maintenance of posture and balance. For illustration, see **brain.** [Latin *cerebellum* small brain, diminutive of *cerebrum* brain.] —**cer'e·bel'lar,** *adj.*

cer·e·bral (ser'ə brəl, sə rē'-) *adj.* **1.** of or relating to the cerebrum. **2.** relating to, involving, or appealing to the intellect rather than the emotions; intellectual.

cerebral cortex, the thick, folded outer layer of the cerebrum of the brain. The cerebral cortex is divided into areas responsible for voluntary movement, learning, memory, and interpretation of messages from the senses.

cerebral palsy, a condition characterized by lack of control over the muscles, esp. those involved in the performance of voluntary actions, resulting from damage to the brain before or during birth.

cer·e·brate (ser'ə brāt') *v.i.,* **-brat·ed, -brat·ing.** to use the brain; think. —**cer'e·bra'tion,** *n.*

cer·e·bro·spi·nal (ser'ə brō spī'nəl) *adj.* of or relating to the brain and spinal cord.

cer·e·brum (ser'ə brəm, sə rē'-) *n., pl.* **-brums** or **-bra** (-brə) the main division of the vertebrate brain, in humans, occupying the whole upper portion of the cranium. The cerebrum interprets sensation, controls voluntary muscles, and coordinates mental processes. For illustration, see **brain.** [Latin *cerebrum* brain.]

cere·cloth (sir'klôth') *n., pl.* **-cloths** (-klôthz', -klôths'). a cloth treated with wax or a similar substance, formerly used esp. to wrap a dead body. [Originally *cered cloth,* from obsolete *cere* to wax, from Latin *cērāre.*]

cere·ment (sir'mənt) *also,* **cere·ments.** *n.* **1.** cerecloth. **2.** any burial clothes; shroud. [French *cirement* a waxing, from *cirer* to wax, from Latin *cērāre.*]

cer·e·mo·ni·al (ser'ə mō'nē əl) *adj.* **1.** of, relating to, or characterized by ceremony; formal; ritual: *a ceremonial dinner.* **2.** used in a ceremony: *ceremonial robes.* —*n.* **1.** a set form or system of rites for the performance of a sacred or solemn ceremony: *the ceremonial of a church wedding, the ceremonial of a state funeral.* **2.** the observance of this; rite or ritual: *We attended the elaborate Easter ceremonial at the cathedral.* —**cer'e·mo'ni·al·ism,** *n.* —**cer'e·mo'ni·al·ly,** *adv.*

cer·e·mo·ni·ous (ser'ə mō'nē əs) *adj.* **1.** strictly or carefully attentive to ceremony or formality: *a ceremonious person.* **2.** characterized by ceremony; formal: *a ceremonious occasion.* —**cer'e·mo'ni·ous·ly,** *adv.* —**cer'e·mo'ni·ous·ness,** *n.*

cer·e·mo·ny (ser'ə mō'nē) *n., pl.* **-nies. 1.** a formal act or set of acts performed on a special or important occasion: *a wedding ceremony, a graduation ceremony, an inaugural ceremony.* **2.** a formal or traditional act of courtesy: *the ceremony of introductions at a banquet.* **3.** strict adherence to conventional forms of social behavior; very formal or polite conduct: *The greeting of the dignitaries was conducted with much ceremony. A few guests got up and left without ceremony.* **4.** a routine faithfully followed: *a nightly ceremony of brushing one's hair.* **5.** a rite or act that has lost its meaning; empty ritual or formality. [Old French *ceremonie* rite, from Latin *caerimōnia* sacred rite, sanctity.]

 • **to stand on ceremony.** to behave with or insist on strict formality: *You needn't stand on ceremony with your old friends.*

> **Synonyms** **Ceremony, rite,** and **ritual** mean a formal act or set of acts carried out on special or solemn occasions. **Ceremony** suggests actions, sometimes elaborate, performed as required by religion, custom, or law: *a simple funeral ceremony, graduation ceremonies that lasted three hours.* **Rite** suggests something more closely prescribed or more unvarying, particularly a religious act, and stresses the symbolic significance: *The rite of marriage incorporated many steps so ancient their origin had been forgotten.* **Ritual** emphasizes the preciseness with which procedure is followed and may refer to a set of rites: *New members were expected to memorize every step of the society's ritual.*

Ce·res (sir'ēz) *n.* **1.** in Roman mythology, the goddess of grain and agriculture. Her Greek counterpart is Demeter. **2.** the largest of the asteroids and the first to be discovered, first sighted in 1801.

ce·re·us (sir'ē əs) *n.* **1.** any of a group of large, columnar, usually treelike cactuses, genus *Cereus,* found in South America. **2.** any of various other cactuses, as the night-blooming cereus. [Latin *cēreus* wax candle, from *cēra* wax; because its shape suggests a wax candle.]

ce·rise (sə rēs', -rēz') *n.* a bright red color; cherry. —*adj.* having the color cerise. [French *cerise* cherry, going back to Latin *cerasus* cherry tree, from Greek *kerasos.*]

ce·ri·um (sir'ē əm) *n.* a malleable, grayish metallic element, used esp. in refining processes and alloys. It is the most abundant

of the rare-earth elements. Symbol: **Ce** For tables, see **element.** [Modern Latin *cerium,* from the asteroid *Ceres* (because the asteroid was discovered two years before this element), from Latin *Cerēs* Roman goddess of grain.]

cer·met (sûr'met) *n.* an alloy of a heat-resistant ceramic compound and a metal, used in rocket engines and other applications in which stress and temperatures are extreme. [Short for *cer-(amic) met(al).*]

cer·tain (sûr'tən) *adj.* **1.** free from doubt; fully confident; positive: *I am certain that I am correct.* **2.** beyond doubt or question; indisputable: *It is now certain that the incumbent was reelected.* **3.** bound to happen; inevitable: *Capture meant certain death for the spy.* **4.** agreed upon; settled; determined: *They plan to meet at a certain time.* **5.** that may be depended on; reliable; trustworthy: *a certain cure for a headache.* **6.** known, but not named or specified; particular: *The room has a certain charm about it. Certain people think you are wrong.* **7.** enough to be noticed; some, but not much: *There has been a certain amount of improvement in the patient's health.* [Old French *certain* assured, definite, going back to Latin *certus* sure.] —**cer'tain·ness,** *n.* —For Synonyms, see **sure.**

 • **for certain.** without doubt; positively: *The police never knew for certain who had committed the crime.*

cer·tain·ly (sûr'tən lē) *adv.* without doubt; definitely; surely: *You certainly are sloppy. Certainly, they can come in our car.*

cer·tain·ty (sûr'tən tē) *n., pl.* **-ties. 1.** the quality, state, or fact of being certain: *a feeling of certainty.* **2.** something certain; established fact: *With the score 17-1, our team's victory became a certainty.*

cer·tes (sûr'tēz) *adv. Archaic.* truly; certainly. [Old French *certes,* going back to Latin *certus* sure.]

cer·tif·i·cate (*n.,* sər tif'i kit; *v.,* sər tif'i kāt') *n.* **1.** an official document declaring the truth of certain facts: *a death certificate, a birth certificate, a marriage certificate.* **2.** an official document certifying that a person has met all the qualifications necessary: *a teaching certificate, a graduation certificate, a certificate of merit.* —*v.t.,* **-cat·ed, -cat·ing.** to furnish or declare by a certificate. [Medieval Latin *certificatum* thing certified, from *certificare* to certify. See CERTIFY.]

certificate of deposit, a receipt given by a bank or savings and loan association for a deposit of a specific sum of money at a regulated rate of interest and for a fixed period of time.

cer·ti·fi·ca·tion (sûr'tə fi kā'shən) *n.* **1.** the act of certifying or the state of being certified. **2.** a certified statement; certificate.

cer·ti·fied (sûr'tə fīd') *adj.* **1.** reliably endorsed or guaranteed, as by a certificate. **2.** furnished with or having a certificate: *a certified representative.*

certified check, a check whose payment is guaranteed by the bank upon which it is drawn.

certified mail, uninsured first-class mail requiring a receipt signed by the addressee and returned to the sender as proof of delivery.

certified milk, raw or pasteurized milk produced according to rules and regulations of an authorized medical milk commission.

certified public accountant, an accountant who has received a certificate from a state verifying that he or she has met the requirements of its laws for working as a public accountant.

cer·ti·fy (sûr'tə fī') *v.,* **-fied, -fy·ing.** —*v.t.* **1.** to declare that (something) is true, accurate, or certain, esp. by a signed statement or official document; testify or attest to: *The birth certificate certifies my date of birth. The doctor certified the defendant's mental incompetence.* **2.** to guarantee that (someone) has met all the qualifications necessary. **3.** to guarantee as to quality, value, or validity: *The bank certified the check.* **4.** *Archaic.* to assure or inform with certainty. —*v.i.* to vouch or testify (with *to*). [Old French *certifier* to secure, make sure, guarantee, from Medieval Latin *certificare* to make sure, from Latin *certus* sure + *facere* to make.] —**cer'ti·fi'a·ble,** *adj.* —**cer'ti·fi'er,** *n.*

> **Synonyms** *v.t.* **Certify** and **attest** mean to testify to the truth or authenticity of something. To **certify** something is to declare formally, almost always in writing, that it is what it purports to be. What is certified is also usually in writing: *The hospital certified the birth record.* To **attest** is to state orally or in writing, usually under oath, that one knows something to be true or genuine: *The witness attested that the deed was genuine.*

cer·ti·o·rar·i (sûr'shē ə rär'ē, -rär'ī, -shə-) *n. Law.* **1.** a docu-

a	at	e	end	o	hot	u	up	hw	white		about
ā	ape	ē	me	ō	old	ū	use	ng	song		taken
ä	far	i	it	ô	fork	ü	rule	th	thin	ə	pencil
âr	care	ī	ice	oi	oil	u̇	pull	th	this		lemon
		îr	pierce	ou	out	ûr	turn	zh	measure		circus

ment issued by a higher court of law to a lower court, calling for the record of a case for review or inspection. **2.** permission to present a case for review or inspection. [Late Latin *certiōrārī* to be informed, from Latin *certior,* comparative of *certus* sure; because *certiōrārī* is used in the Latin text of the writ.]

cer·ti·tude (sûr′ti tüd′, -tūd′) *n.* complete assurance or confidence; certainty. [Late Latin *certitūdō,* from Latin *certus* sure.]

ce·ru·le·an (sə rü′lē ən) *n.* a sky-blue color; azure. —*adj.* having the color cerulean. [Latin *caeruleus* dark blue + -AN.]

ce·ru·men (sə rü′mən) *n.* earwax. [Modern Latin *cerumen,* from Latin *cēra* wax.]

ce·rus·site (sə rus′īt, sîr′ə sīt′) *n.* a lustrous, white carbonate mineral mined as an ore of lead. Formula: $PbCO_3$ [German *zerussit,* from Latin *cerussa* white lead, possibly from an unattested Greek word *kēroessa* waxlike, from *kēros* wax.]

cer·vi·cal (sûr′vi kəl) *adj.* of or relating to the cervix.

cer·vine (sûr′vīn) *adj.* of, relating to, or resembling deer. [Latin *cervīnus* relating to deer, from *cervus* deer.]

cer·vix (sûr′viks) *n., pl.* -vix·es or -vi·ces (-və sēz′). **1.** the neck, esp. the back of the neck, connecting the head and the trunk of the body. **2.** the lower, necklike part of the uterus, connecting with the vagina. **3.** any necklike part of an organ, as in the bladder. [Latin *cervīx* neck.]

Ce·sar·e·an (si zâr′ē ən) *also,* **Ce·sar·i·an.** *adj., n.* Caesarean.

cesarean section *also,* **caesarean section.** the delivery of a baby from its mother's uterus by a surgical incision made through the abdomen into the uterus. It is performed when normal delivery is impossible or dangerous. Also, **cesarean birth, cesarean operation.** [Because the Roman statesman and general Julius CAESAR, 100?-44 B.C., or an ancestor of his, was supposedly delivered in this way, though the story probably arose by misidentification of *Caesar* with Latin *caedere* to cut.]

ce·si·um (sē′zē əm) *also,* **caesium.** *n.* a soft, silvery metallic element used esp. in photoelectric cells, infrared devices, spectrometers, and other optical instruments. It is the most reactive and one of the rarest of metals. Symbol: **Cs** For tables, see **element.** [Modern Latin *caesium,* from Latin *caesius* bluish gray; because its spectrum has two blue lines.]

ces·sa·tion (se sā′shən) *n.* a ceasing or halting; stop: *a cessation of hostilities.* [Latin *cessātiō.*]

ces·sion (sesh′ən) *n.* the act of ceding; giving up or surrendering to another: *a cession of territory, a cession of rights.* [Latin *cessiō* a giving up.]

cess·pool (ses′pül′) *n.* **1.** a pit, well, or other underground container connected to plumbing to receive sewage. **2.** any foul or filthy receptacle or place. [Of uncertain origin.]

c'est la vie (sā lä vē′) *French.* such is life; that's life.

ces·tode (ses′tōd) *n.* a flatworm, class Cestoda, esp. a tapeworm. [Greek *kestos* belt.]

ces·tus (ses′təs) *also,* **caestus.** *n.* a covering for the hand, wrist, and forearm, made of leather thongs with metal studs or spikes attached, used by boxers of ancient Rome. [Latin *caestus,* from *caedere* to strike.]

ce·su·ra (si zhùr′ə, -zùr′ə) caesura.

ce·ta·cean (si tā′shən) *adj.* of, relating to, or belonging to an order, Cetacea, of aquatic, fishlike mammals, including whales, dolphins, and porpoises. —*n.* a cetacean mammal.

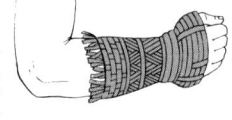

cestus

[Modern Latin *Cetacea* (from Latin *cētus* whale, from Greek *kētos*) + -AN.] —**ce·ta′ceous,** *adj.*

Cf, the symbol for californium.

cf., compare. [Abbreviation of Latin *confer,* from *conferre* to collect, bring together.]

CFC, chlorofluorocarbon.

CFI *also,* **c.f.i., C.F.I.** cost, freight, and insurance.

cg *also,* **cg., cgm.** centigram; centigrams.

cgs *also,* **CGS** centimeter-gram-second.

ch. *also,* **Ch. 1.** chapter. **2.** church.

Cha·blis (sha blē′, shab′lē) *n.* a dry, white Burgundy wine. [From *Chablis,* French town where it was originally made.]

cha-cha (chä′chä′) *n.* **1.** a ballroom dance of Latin American origin, similar to the mambo. Also, **cha′-cha′-cha′.** **2.** the music for this dance. [Spanish *cha-cha-cha* this dance; probably imitative of the beat of this music.]

cha·conne (sha kôn′, -kon′) *n.* a musical composition in slow triple time, having a melodic or harmonic motif that is usually played by the bass and repeated over and over. [French *chaconne,* from Spanish *chacona* slow dance in triple time and its music; of uncertain origin.]

chae·tog·nath (kē′tog nath′, -təg-) *n.* any of the group of small, wormlike, marine invertebrates constituting the phylum Chaetognatha. They have an arrow-shaped, transparent body,

swim near the surface, and feed on plankton. Length: 1 inch (3 centimeters). Also, **arrowworm.** [Modern Latin *chaetognath,* from Greek *chaitē* hair + *gnathos* jaw.]

chafe (chāf) *v.,* **chafed, chaf·ing.** —*v.t.* **1.** to wear away or make sore by friction or rubbing; abrade: *The diaper chafed the baby's skin.* **2.** to make angry; irritate; annoy: *The clerk's rudeness chafed me.* **3.** to restore warmth or sensation to by rubbing: *to chafe numb hands.* —*v.i.* **1.** to be worn away or made sore by friction or rubbing: *My skin chafed from the stiff collar.* **2.** to be irritated or annoyed; fret; fume: *to chafe at needless delay, to chafe under constant criticism.* —*n.* soreness or wear caused by friction or rubbing. [Old French *chaufer* to warm, going back to Latin *calefacere* to make warm.]

· **to chafe at the bit.** to be irritated or annoyed, esp. because of delay.

chaf·er (chā′fər) *n.* any of a group of destructive beetles, family Scarabaeidae, including the June bug and cockchafer. [Old English *ceafor* beetle.]

chaff[1] (chaf) *n.* **1.** husks of wheat, oats, rye, and other grains, separated from the seed by threshing and winnowing. **2.** finely cut hay or straw used as feed for livestock. **3.** any worthless matter; refuse. [Old English *ceaf* husks of grain.]

chaff[2] (chaf) *v.t., v.i.* to tease or make fun (of) in a good-natured way. —*n.* good-natured teasing; raillery. [Possibly a form of CHAFE.]

chaf·fer (chaf′ər) *v.i.* to haggle about price; bargain. [Middle English *chaffare* trade, wares, from Old English *cēap* bargain + *faru* journey, business.] —**chaf′fer·er,** *n.*

chaf·finch (chaf′inch) *n.* a European finch, *Fringilla coelebs,* having a pleasant short song, popular as a pet. [Old English *ceaffinc,* from *ceaf* chaff[1] + *finc* finch; referring to its fondness for chaff.]

chaff·y (chaf′ē) *adj.,* **chaff·i·er, chaff·i·est. 1.** full of chaff. **2.** like chaff; worthless.

chafing dish, a pan or dish with a heating device underneath it, for cooking or keeping food warm at the table.

cha·grin (shə grin′) *n.* a feeling of annoyance, embarrassment, or anxiety caused by failure, disappointment, or humiliation: *to be filled with chagrin on failing a test.* —*v.t.* to cause to feel chagrin; vex or distress: *The loss of the case chagrined the lawyer.* [French *chagrin* grief; of uncertain origin.]

chain (chān) *n.* **1.** a series of connected links or rings, usually of metal, used chiefly to bind, drag, hold, or ornament. **2.** a series connected or following in succession; sequence: *a chain of events, a mountain chain.* **3. chains. a.** shackles; fetters: *The prisoners were led off the boat in chains.* **b.** imprisonment; bondage; confinement: *Moses helped the Hebrews throw off their chains and led them out of Egypt.* **4.** a number of similar business establishments under the same ownership or management: *a chain of movie theaters, a chain of drugstores.* **5.** a series of atoms of the same element linked together. **6.a.** a measuring instrument consisting of 100 links of equal length, used by surveyors and engineers. **b.** its unit of length, equal to either 66 feet (20 meters) in surveying or 100 feet (30 meters) in engineering. —*v.t.* **1.** to fasten, secure, or connect with a chain: *to chain a bicycle to a post, to chain a door.* **2.** to restrain or confine; bind: *All that work chained me to my desk.* [Old French *chaeine* fetter, from Latin *catēna* fetter, series.]

chain gang, a group of convicts chained together, usually while at hard labor outdoors.

chain letter, a letter sent to a number of people, asking each to send a copy in turn to a specific number of other persons.

chain-link fence (chān′lingk′) a fence made from thick wire of galvanized steel, interlinked in a diamond-shaped pattern.

chain mail, flexible body armor made of interlaced metal rings or links.

chain reaction 1. any series of events so related to one another that each is caused by the preceding one and initiates a succeeding one. **2.** a series of self-sustaining nuclear reactions in which the nuclei of radioactive atoms split and release neutrons. Some of these then split other nuclei, releasing more neutrons and continuing the process.

chain saw, a portable power saw with teeth on an endless chain.

chain-smoke (chān′smōk′) *v.,* **-smoked, -smok·ing.** —*v.i.* to smoke one cigarette or cigar after another in almost continuous succession. —*v.t.* to smoke in almost continuous succession.

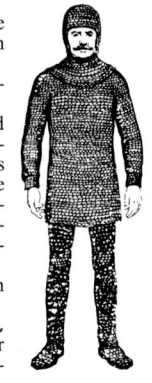

chain mail

chain-smok·er (chān′smō′kər) *also,* **chain smoker.** *n.* a person who smokes one cigarette or cigar after another in almost continuous succession.

chain·stitch (chān′stich′) *v.t.* to sew or crochet with chain stitches.

chain stitch, stitching made by looping each stitch and connecting it to the next one, forming links as in a chain.

chain store, one of a group of retail stores owned and operated by one company and selling similar merchandise.

chair (châr) *n.* **1.** a piece of furniture that has a seat, legs, a backrest, and sometimes arms, usually designed to seat one person. **2.** an office or position of authority or dignity: *a chair of medieval literature at a university.* **3.** a presiding officer; chairman or chairwoman: *The speaker rose to address the chair.* **4.** the position of a player in an orchestra: *to have first chair in the flute section.* **5.** *Slang.* electric chair. —*v.t.* to preside over; act as chairman or chairwoman of: *to chair a panel discussion.* [Old French *chaiere* seat, from Latin *cathedra,* from Greek *kathedrā.* Doublet of CATHEDRA.]
· **to take the chair.** to take the position of chairman or chairwoman; preside at or open a meeting.

chair lift, a conveyor consisting of a series of seats suspended from a moving cable, used to carry people, esp. skiers, up and down a mountain slope.

chair·man (châr′mən) *n., pl.* **-men** (-mən). a person in charge of a meeting, committee, board, or organization.

chair·man·ship (châr′mən ship′) *n.* the position, duties, or term of office of a chairman or chairwoman.

chair·per·son (châr′pûr′sən) *n.* chairman or chairwoman.

chair·wom·an (châr′wŭm′ən) *n., pl.* **-wom·en** (-wim′ən). a woman in charge of a meeting, committee, board, or organization.

chaise (shāz) *n.* **1.** a light, two-wheeled carriage, often with a hood or folding top, usually seating one or two passengers. Also, **shay. 2.** a similar vehicle having four wheels. **3.** chaise longue. [French *chaise* seat, form of *chaire* seat, from Old French *chaiere.* See CHAIR.]

chaise longue (shāz′lông′, chāz′-) a chair with a seat long enough for a person to lie down or sit with legs outstretched. Also, **chaise, chaise lounge.** [French *chaise longue* lounging chair; literally, long chair. See CHAISE.]

> **Usage** Chaise longue, which came into English directly from French, was often mistakenly read and pronounced as **chaise lounge** because it referred to a chair in which one relaxed, or lounged. Although the **lounge** form is widely used, many people consider it unacceptable.

cha·la·za (kə lā′zə) *n., pl.* **-zae** (-zē) or **-zas. 1.** *Zoology.* one of the twisted cords of dense albumen, extending from either side of the yolk to the shell, that keep the yolk suspended near the center of the egg. **2.** *Botany.* the basal end of a plant ovule, opposite the point where the pollen tube penetrates. [Modern Latin *chalaza,* from Greek *chalaza* hail, lump.] —**cha·la′zal,** *adj.*

chal·ced·o·ny (kal sed′ə nē, kal′sə dō′nē) *n., pl.* **-nies.** any of several fine-grained translucent varieties of quartz, as agate and carnelian, having a waxy luster and occurring in various colors. [Latin *chalcēdonius* a precious stone mentioned only in the New Testament, from Greek *chalkēdōn.*] —**chal·ce·don·ic** (kāl′sidon′ik), *adj.*

chal·cid (kal′sid) *n.* any of a group of very small four-winged or wingless insects, family Chalcididae, whose larvae are parasitic on the eggs, larvae, or pupae of other insects. [Greek *chalkos* copper; referring to its color.]

chal·co·cite (kal′kə sīt′) *n.* a gray mineral with a metallic luster, an important ore of copper; cuprous sulfide. Formula: Cu_2S [Modification of French *chalcosine,* from Greek *chalkos* copper.]

chal·co·py·rite (kal′kə pī′rīt) *n.* a yellowish, opaque mineral with a metallic luster, one of the most important sources of copper. Formula: $CuFeS_2$ [Modern Latin *chalcopyrites,* from Greek *chalkos* copper + Latin *pyrités* flint. See PYRITES.]

Chal·de·an (kal dē′ən) *n.* **1.** one of an ancient Semitic people of Chaldea who became dominant in and ruled Babylonia. **2.** the Semitic language of the Chaldeans, a dialect of Aramaic. **3.** a person versed in occult learning, as that of the Chaldeans; astrologer; soothsayer. —*adj.* **1.** of, relating to, or characteristic of Chaldea or its people, language, or culture. **2.** of or relating to astrology or occultism, esp. as first practiced by the Chaldeans. Also, **Chal·da·ic** (kal dā′ik). [Latin *Chaldaeus* (from Greek *Chaldaios;* of Semitic origin) + -AN.]

cha·let (sha lā′) *n.* **1.** a house characterized by wide, sloping roofs with overhanging eaves, commonly found in Switzerland and other Alpine regions of Europe. **2.** any cottage, house, or villa built in this style. **3.** any herdsman's hut or simple cottage in the Alpine regions of Europe, esp. in Switzerland. [Swiss French *chalet* cottage, from a pre-Latin word for "shelter."]

chal·ice (chal′is) *n.* **1.** a drinking cup or goblet. **2.** a cup or vessel containing the wine consecrated at Holy Communion. **3.** a cup-shaped flower. [Old French *c(h)alice* cup, from Latin *calix.*]

chalk (chôk) *n.* **1.** a soft, porous limestone, used esp. to make lime and portland cement, and, sometimes, as a fertilizer. **2.** a piece of this substance or a synthetic substance similar to this, usually in the form of a crayon, used esp. for writing or drawing on a blackboard. —*v.t.* **1.** to mark, write, or draw with chalk: *The director chalked the actors' positions on the stage floor.* **2.** to rub, treat, or prepare with chalk: *to chalk the tip of a billiard cue.* **3.** to whiten with or as with chalk: *The children chalked their faces on Halloween.* —*v.i.* **1.** to become powdery: *The paint chalked.* [Old English *cealc* limestone, plaster, from Latin *calx* limestone. See CALX.] —**chalk′like′,** *adj.*
· **to chalk up. a.** to score or earn: *Our team chalked up two goals in the first ten minutes of the game.* **b.** to charge or credit: *You can chalk up that mistake to ignorance.*

chalk·board (chôk′bôrd′) *n.* blackboard.

chalk·y (chô′kē) *adj.,* **chalk·i·er, chalk·i·est. 1.** resembling or suggesting chalk: *a chalky taste, a chalky consistency.* **2.** of or containing chalk. —**chalk′i·ness,** *n.*

chal·lenge (chal′ənj) *v.,* **-lenged, -leng·ing.** —*v.t.* **1.** to invite or summon defiantly or provocatively, as to combat or to a contest. **2.** to bid or call upon boldly or defiantly: *I challenge you to show your proof.* **3.** to call into question; take exception to (something), esp. as being invalid: *I challenge that interpretation.* **4.** to excite or make demands upon the talents or interests of; arouse; stimulate: *The science project challenged the entire class.* **5.** to stop and demand a countersign or form of identification from: *The sentry challenged anyone approaching the campsite.* **6.** to claim as due; demand; require. **7.** *Law.* to object or take formal exception to: *The defendant's lawyer challenged the prospective juror.* —*v.i.* to make or present a challenge. —*n.* **1.** an invitation or summons, as to combat or to a contest. **2.** a calling into question; demand, as for proof or an explanation. **3.** something that excites or makes demands upon one's talents and interests. **4.** a demand for a countersign or identification, as from a sentry. **5.** *Law.* a formal objection made by counsel, as to the seating of a juror. [Anglo-Norman *chalenge* accusation, claim, from Latin *calumnia* false accusation. Doublet of CALUMNY.] —**chal′lenge·a·ble,** *adj.* —**chal′leng·er,** *n.*

chal·lis (shal′ē) *also,* **chal·lie.** *n.* a lightweight woolen, cotton, or rayon fabric, used esp. for blouses, robes, and scarves. [Of uncertain origin.]

cha·lyb·e·ate (kə lib′ē it) *adj.* **1.** containing salts of iron, as a medicine or mineral spring. **2.** having a taste of iron. —*n.* chalybeate water or medicine. [Latin *chalybs* steel (from Greek *chalyps,* from *Chalybes* the Chalybes, an ancient people of Asia Minor noted for their work in iron and steel) + -ATE².]

cham (kam) *Archaic.* khan¹.

cham·ber (chām′bər) *n.* **1.** a room, esp. a bedroom. **2.** *also,* **chambers.** a room where a judge conducts business when not holding a court session. **3.** a legislative or judicial body, council, or assembly: *The Senate is the upper chamber of the U.S. Congress.* **4.** the hall where such a body meets. **5.** the reception room of a person of authority or rank, such as in a palace. **6.** a cavity or enclosed space in an animal or plant: *The heart has four chambers.* **7.** the rear portion of the barrel of a firearm, into which the ammunition is inserted. **8.** any enclosed compartment, as the spaces between the gates of a canal lock. **9. chambers.** *British.* a suite of rooms; apartment. —*adj.* of or relating to chamber music: *a chamber concert, a chamber orchestra.* —*v.t.* **1.** to provide with a chamber. **2.** to put in or as in a chamber: *to chamber a bullet.* [Old French *chambre* bedroom, dwelling, from Late Latin *camera* room, from Latin *camera* arch, vault, from Greek *kamarā* vault. Doublet of CAMERA.]

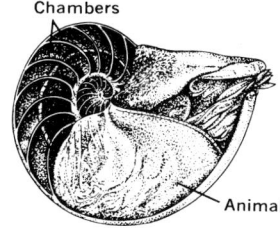

Chambers

Animal

chamber *(def. 6)*
nautilus shell

chambered nautilus, nautilus *(def. 1).*

a	at	e	end	o	hot	u	up	hw	white		about
ā	ape	ē	me	ō	old	ū	use	ng	song		taken
ä	far	i	it	ô	fork	ü	rule	th	thin	ə	pencil
âr	care	ī	ice	oi	oil	u̇	pull	t͟h	this		lemon
		îr	pierce	ou	out	ûr	turn	zh	measure		circus

C

cham·ber·lain (chām′bər lin) *n.* **1.** an officer in charge of a royal or noble household; steward. **2.** a person who receives or keeps funds and revenues; treasurer. **3.** a high official of certain royal courts. [Old French *chamberlenc* high official in a king's service; literally, one who takes care of bedchambers, through German, going back to Late Latin *camera* room (see CHAMBER) + German *-ling* (see -LING¹).]

cham·ber·maid (chām′bər mād′) *n.* a maid who makes beds and cleans rooms, esp. in a hotel or motel.

chamber music, music written for a small instrumental ensemble, suitable for performance in a room or small hall.

chamber of commerce, an association organized to regulate and promote the industrial and commercial interests of a particular locality.

chamber pot, a portable vessel used as a toilet, usually kept in a bedroom.

cham·bray (sham′brā) *n.* a cotton fabric woven with a colored warp and white filling, used esp. for dresses, shirts, and pajamas. [From *Cambrai,* France, where this fabric was first made.]

cha·me·leon (kə mēl′yən, -mē′lē ən) *n.* **1.** any lizard of either of two groups, the family Chamaeleonidae, of Africa and southern Europe and Asia, or the family Iguanidae, found in the southeastern United States, whose skin changes color according to variations in temperature, emotion, and other factors, often serving to camouflage it from its enemies. **2.** a person whose disposition or opinions change quickly or readily; fickle person. [Latin *chamaeleōn* the Old World chameleon, from Greek *chamaileōn,* from *chamai* on the ground, dwarf + *leōn* lion.]

chameleon

cham·fer (cham′fər) *n.* a slanting surface produced by beveling an edge or corner. —*v.t.* **1.** to cut so as to form a slanting surface; bevel. **2.** to cut a furrow in; flute; channel. [Middle French *chanfrain* beveled edge, going back to Old French *chant* edge, from Late Latin *cantus* (see CANT²) + *fraindre* to break, from Latin *frangere.*]

cham·ois (sham′ē) *n., pl.* **-ois** (-ēz). **1.** a goatlike antelope, *Rupicapra rupicapra,* native to the mountains of Europe, the Caucasus, and western Asia, having a long, reddish brown coat that turns dark brown in the winter. Height: 2½ feet (0.8 meter) at the shoulder. **2.** *also,* **cham·my, sham·my.** a soft, pliable leather, originally made from the skin of the chamois, now made from the skins of various animals. **3.** a cotton cloth made to resemble this leather. [French *chamois,* from Late Latin *camox* the antelope; probably of pre-Roman origin.]

cham·o·mile (kam′ə mīl′, -mēl′) *also,* **camomile.** *n.* any of several strongly scented plants of the composite family, found in temperate regions, bearing daisylike flower heads, which in certain species are dried and used to make an herb tea. For illustration, see **herb.**

champ¹ (champ) *v.t.* **1.** to crush and chew vigorously and noisily; munch. **2.** to bite upon restlessly or impatiently: *The horse was champing the bit.* —*v.i.* to make biting or chewing movements with the jaws and teeth: *The burro champed loudly.* —*n.* the act of champing. [Earlier *cham;* probably imitative.]
 • **to champ at the bit.** to show signs of restlessness or impatience.

champ² (champ) *n. Informal.* champion. [Short for CHAMPION.]

cham·pagne (sham pān′) *n.* **1.** a sparkling, effervescent white or light pink wine, originally from Champagne, France. **2.** a pale, brownish yellow color. —*adj.* having the color champagne.

cham·paign (sham pān′) *n.* flat, open country; plain. —*adj.* flat and open. [Old French *champaigne* open country, from Late Latin *campānia,* from Latin *campus* field.]

cham·pi·on (cham′pē ən) *n.* **1.** the winner of first place or first prize in a competition: *a heavyweight boxing champion.* **2.** a person who fights for or defends a person or cause: *a champion of freedom of speech.* **3.** a brave fighter or warrior; hero. —*adj.* having won first place or first prize; superior to all others: *a champion wrestler.* —*v.t.* to fight in behalf of; defend; support: *to champion the underdog.* [Old French *champion* combatant, from Medieval Latin *campio* fighter (in the field), from Latin *campus* field (of combat).]

cham·pi·on·ship (cham′pē ən ship′) *n.* **1.** the position or honor of being a champion: *Our school's football team won the state championship last year.* **2.** the act of championing; advocacy; defense; support: *championship of civil liberties.* **3.** a competition held in order to determine a champion.

chance (chans) *n.* **1.** a favorable or suitable time or occasion; opportunity: *The prisoner saw a chance to escape.* **2.** the likelihood or probability of something happening; possibility: *There is little chance of winning.* **3.** an exposure to loss or harm; risk; gamble: *Don't take any chances.* **4.** the unpredictable or unknown factor influencing the way things happen; luck; fortune: *Everything is subject to chance.* **5.** an unusual or unexpected occurrence; accident: *By some strange chance we discovered the error.* **6.** a ticket in a lottery, raffle, sweepstakes, or similar contest. —*v.,* **chanced, chanc·ing.** —*v.i.* to happen by chance: *If an argument should chance to arise, try to settle it peacefully.* —*v.t. Informal.* to take the chance of; hazard; risk: *Do we dare chance the possibility of being late?* —*adj.* happening by chance; unplanned; accidental: *a chance meeting, a chance remark.* [Old French *cheance* a falling (as of dice), hazard, luck, from Late Latin *cadentia* a falling (as of dice), from Latin *cadere* to fall. Doublet of CADENCE, CADENZA.] —For Synonyms, see **luck, opportunity.**
 • **on the (off) chance.** with the hope (that something is possible): *We'll wait here on the off chance that they are on their way home.*
 • **to chance on** (or **upon**). to find or meet accidentally or unexpectedly: *I chanced on the lost key while looking for my pen.*

chan·cel (chan′səl) *n.* the space around the altar of a church, used by the clergy and the choir. [Old French *chancel* enclosure, from Latin *cancellī* lattice; because it was closed off by a lattice. See CANCEL.]

chan·cel·ler·y (chan′sə lə rē, -slə rē) *also,* **chancellory.** *n., pl.* **-ler·ies. 1.** the position of a chancellor. **2.** the office of a chancellor or the building that houses it. **3.** the office of an embassy, legation, or consulate or the building that houses it. Also *(defs. 2, 3),* **chancery.** [Old French *chancelerie* the position, court of chancery, from *chancelier.* See CHANCELLOR.]

chan·cel·lor (chan′sə lər, -slər) *n.* **1.** the prime minister in certain European countries, as Germany and Austria. **2.** the chief administrative officer or president at certain American universities. **3.** a judge of a court of equity in some states of the United States. **4.** a high official who serves as the chief secretary of a sovereign or embassy. [Old French *chancelier* high official of a king, from Late Latin *cancellārius* secretary; originally, officer in a law court standing near the *cancellī,* or lattice, in front of the judge's seat. See CANCEL.]

Chancellor of the Exchequer, the minister of finance in the British government.

chan·cel·lor·ship (chan′sə lər ship′) *n.* the position or term of office of a chancellor.

chan·cel·lor·y (chan′sə lə rē) *n., pl.* **-lor·ies.** chancellery.

chan·cer·y (chan′sə rē) *n., pl.* **-cer·ies. 1.** a court of equity. Also, **court of chancery. 2.** equity *(defs. 3a, 3b).* **3.** chancellery *(defs. 2, 3).* **4.** a court or office where public records are kept; archives. [Short for CHANCELLERY.]
 • **in chancery. a.** in litigation, in a court of equity. **b.** in wrestling or boxing, with the head encircled by the opponent's arm; in a headlock. **c.** in an embarrassing or helpless situation.

chan·cre (shang′kər) *n.* an ulcer or sore having a hard base and formed at the primary site of infection, esp. the initial lesion of syphilis. [French *chancre,* from Latin *cancer* crab, cancer. Doublet of CANCER, CANKER.] —**chan′crous,** *adj.*

chanc·y (chan′sē) *adj.,* **chanc·i·er, chanc·i·est.** *Informal.* subject to chance; uncertain; risky.

chan·de·lier (shan′də lir′) *n.* a lighting fixture designed to be suspended from the ceiling, usually having several lights arranged on projecting arms or branches. [French *chandelier* candlestick, going back to Latin *candēlābrum,* from *candēla* candle.]

chan·dler (chand′lər) *n.* **1.** a person who makes or sells candles. **2.** a dealer or merchant, esp. one who deals in groceries or ship's supplies. [Old French *chandelier* maker or seller of candles, from Late Latin *candēlārius,* from Latin *candēla* candle.]

chan·dler·y (chand′lə rē) *n., pl.* **-dler·ies. 1.** a place for storing candles. **2.** the business, goods, or shop of a chandler.

change (chānj) *v.,* **changed, chang·ing.** —*v.t.* **1.** to make different; alter; modify: *to change one's attitude.* **2.** to cause to pass from one form, composition, or state to another; transform (often with *into*): *There was a movement in the country to change the monarchy into a republic. The magician appeared to change the scarf into a pigeon.* **3.** to replace with or switch to another or others, often of the same or a similar kind: *to change one's shirt, to change jobs, to change sides during an argument.* **4.** to give and receive reciprocally; exchange: *Change seats with the person sitting next to you.* **5.** to give or receive the equivalent of (money), as in smaller units or foreign currency: *to change a five-dollar bill for five singles.* **6.** to remove and replace the covering or coverings on: *to change a bed, to change a baby.* —*v.i.* **1.** to become different, altered, or modified: *The scenery changed as the train went farther south. The boy's voice changed as he became older.* **2.** to become transformed (often with *into*): *In the story, the coach changed into a pumpkin.* **3.** to put on other clothes (often with *into*): *The actors changed into their costumes. We changed before dinner.* **4.** to make an exchange: *If you're not comfortable in that chair, I'll change with you.* **5.** to transfer from one means of conveyance to another: *We have to change here for an express train.* **6.** (of the moon) to pass from one phase to another. —*n.* **1.** the act or fact of changing: *The schedule is subject to change. This represents a change in our policy. We have to make a change at the next station.* **2.** something that is or may be substituted for another: *We've left a change of towels for you in the guest room.* **3.** something different from the usual; variety; novelty; diversity: *It would be a nice change to go south in the winter.* **4.** money in the form of coins: *I've got lots of change in my pocket.* **5.** an amount returned when money given in payment exceeds the sum due: *The waitress gave us our change.* **6.** money of a lower denomination given in exchange for higher: *to ask for change of one dollar in dimes.* **7.** a clean, fresh, or different set of clothes. [Old French *changier* to alter, from Late Latin *cambiāre* to exchange; probably of Celtic origin.] —**chang′er,** *n.*

Synonyms *v.t.* **Change, alter,** and **modify** mean to make something different. **Change** is the most general of these terms, referring to any difference, great or small: *to change one's attitude from strong opposition to enthusiastic support, to change a seating arrangement slightly by switching two people.* **Alter** suggests difference in detail, but not in substance: *The pilot altered the boat's course to pass closer to the island.* **Modify** suggests alteration to meet some model or standard: *We've modified this part to fit your engine.*

change·a·ble (chān′jə bəl) *adj.* **1.** likely to change; inconstant; variable: *changeable weather, a changeable mood.* **2.** that can be changed; alterable: *a changeable policy.* **3.** changing in color or appearance when looked at from different points of view. —**change′a·bil′i·ty, change′a·ble·ness,** *n.* —**change′a·bly,** *adv.*

change·ful (chānj′fəl) *adj.* full of or given to change; variable; inconstant. —**change′ful·ly,** *adv.* —**change′ful·ness,** *n.*

change·less (chānj′lis) *adj.* that does not change; unchanging; constant; enduring. —**change′less·ly,** *adv.* —**change′less·ness,** *n.*

change·ling (chānj′ling) *n.* **1.** a child secretly substituted for another, esp. in infancy. **2.** in folklore, a strange, stupid, or ugly child left by fairies in place of a child they have stolen.

change of life, menopause.

change·o·ver (chānj′ō′vər) *n.* a shift, transition, or transfer, as from one activity, method, or system to another: *The train stopped for a changeover from diesel to electric power.*

change ringing, the art or practice of ringing a set of bells in an order that permits continuous variation until all possible combinations are rung.

chan·nel (chan′əl) *n.* **1.** the deepest part of a river, harbor, or other waterway, often dredged and maintained as a passage for boats and ships. **2.** the bed of a stream, river, or other waterway. **3.** a wide strait. **4.** the means by which something is directed or conveyed; course through which something passes: *a channel of communication.* **5. channels.** the proper or official route or means, esp. of communication: *All requests must go through channels.* **6.** a furrow or groove. **7.** a tube or tubular passage, as for liquids. **8.a.** a frequency or band of electromagnetic frequencies assigned to a broadcasting station for the transmission and reception of electronic signals. **b.** a frequency or band of frequencies used by certain telecommunications devices, as CB radios and mobile telephones. —*v.t.,* **-neled, -nel·ing;** *also, British,* **-nelled, -nel·ling. 1.** to make or form by or as by erosion; cut out as a channel: *The stream channeled its way over the mountains.* **2.** to direct or convey through or as through a channel: *They channeled the stream onto the neighboring property. I channeled all*

my efforts into solving the problem. **3.** to form or cut one or more channels or grooves in: *to channel a column.* [Old French *chanel* canal, from Latin *canālis* pipe, canal. Doublet of CANAL.]

chan·nel·ize (chan′ə līz′) *v.t.,* **-ized, -iz·ing.** channel. —**chan′nel·i·za′tion,** *n.*

chan·son (shan′sən, shan sôn′; *French* shäN sôN′) *n., pl.* **-sons** (-sənz, -sônz′; *French* -sôN′). *French.* song.

chant (chant) *n.* **1.** a repetitive, monotonous, usually rhythmic utterance or song: *The fans broke into a chant when the team ran out onto the field.* **2.** a simple liturgical melody, usually unaccompanied, in which a number of syllables or words are sung or intoned on one note. **3.** a psalm, canticle, or other nonmetrical sacred text so sung or intoned. —*v.t.* **1.** to recite or shout in a repetitive or rhythmic tone: *to chant a slogan.* **2.** to sing to or like a chant; intone: *to chant a psalm, to chant the litany.* —*v.i.* **1.** to recite or shout a chant: *The protesters chanted in the street.* **2.** to sing or intone a chant or chants: *The choir chanted in the background.* [Old French *chanter* to sing, from Latin *cantāre.*]

chant·er (chan′tər) *n.* **1.** a person who chants, as a cantor. **2.** the pipe of a bagpipe on which the melody is played. [Old French *chanteor* singer, from Latin *cantātor.*]

chan·te·relle (shan′tə rel′, chan′-) *n.* any of several mushrooms, esp. *Cantharellus cibarius,* an edible species having a bright yellow to orange cap. [French *chanterelle,* from Modern Latin *cantharella,* from Latin *cantharus* drinking cup, tankard (from Greek *kántharos*) + *-ella* suffix used to form diminutives.]

chan·teuse (shan tüs′, -tüz′; *French* shäN tœz′) *n., pl.* **-teuses** (-tü′siz, -tü′ziz; *French* -tœz′). *French.* a female singer, esp. one who sings in a nightclub or cabaret.

chan·tey (shan′tē, chan′-) *also,* **chanty, shantey, shanty.** *n., pl.* **-teys.** a sailors' song, originally sung in rhythm with their work. [Modification of French *chanter* to sing, from Latin *cantāre.*]

chan·ti·cleer (chan′tə klîr′) *n.* rooster. ➡ used as a proper name in medieval fables about Reynard the Fox and in other literature. [Old French *Chantecler* the cock in these fables, from *chanter* to sing (from Latin *cantāre*) + *cler* clear (from Latin *clārus*).]

Chan·til·ly (shan til′ē) *n.* a delicate bobbin lace made of silk or other fibers, used chiefly for evening and bridal gowns. Also, **Chantilly lace.** [From *Chantilly,* town in northern France, where it was originally made.]

chan·try (chan′trē) *n., pl.* **-tries. 1.** an endowment for the singing or saying of Masses for the soul of the donor, or for the souls of those specified by the donor. **2.** a chapel or altar so endowed. [Old French *chanterie* singing, from *chanter.* See CHANT.]

chan·ty (shan′tē, chan′-) *n., pl.* **-ties.** chantey.

Cha·nu·kah (hä′nə kə; *Hebrew* KHä nü kä′) Hanukkah.

cha·os (kā′os) *n.* **1.** a state of utter confusion and disorder. **2.** *also,* **Chaos.** infinite space or formless matter out of which the cosmos or ordered universe supposedly evolved. [Latin *chaos* empty space, from Greek *chaos* vast chasm, space.]

cha·ot·ic (kā ot′ik) *adj.* in utter confusion and disorder: *The candidate's headquarters was chaotic on the night of the election.* Also, **cha·ot′i·cal.** —**cha·ot′i·cal·ly,** *adv.*

chap[1] (chap) *v.,* **chapped, chap·ping.** —*v.t.* to cause to split, crack, or become rough or red: *Washing dishes chaps my hands.* —*v.i.* to become split, cracked, roughened, or reddened: *My lips always chap in the winter.* [Middle English *chappen* to cut; of uncertain origin.]

chap[2] (chap) *n. Informal.* a man or boy; fellow. [Short for CHAPMAN.]

chap[3] (chap) *n.* chops. [Of uncertain origin.]

chap., chapter.

cha·pa·ra·jos (shap′ə rä′ōs) *also,* **chaperejos.** *pl. n.* chaps. [Spanish *chaparajos* (because worn as a protection against the thorns of the chaparral), from *chaparral.* See CHAPARRAL.]

chap·ar·ral (shap′ə ral′) *n.* **1.** a dense thicket of low or shrubby trees or thorny, stiff-branched shrubs, usually found in dry, sunny regions. **2.** an ecological community characterized by such vegetation, esp. in the southwestern United States. [Spanish *chaparral* plantation of evergreen oaks, from *chaparro* evergreen oak, from Basque *txapar,* diminutive of *saphar* thicket.]

chap·book (chap′buk′) *n.* a small book or pamphlet containing popular tales, poems, ballads, and similar literature, formerly peddled by chapmen.

a	at	e	end	o	hot	u	up	hw	white		about
ā	ape	ē	me	ō	old	ū	use	ng	song		taken
ä	far	i	it	ô	fork	ü	rule	th	thin	ə	pencil
âr	care	ī	ice	oi	oil	u̇	pull	th	this		lemon
		îr	pierce	ou	out	ûr	turn	zh	measure		circus

cha·peau (sha pō′) *n., pl.* **-peaus** or **-peaux** (-pōz′). hat. [French *chapeau*, going back to Medieval Latin *cappellus* head covering, from Late Latin *cappa* head covering; cloak.]

chap·el (chap′əl) *n.* **1.** a building, smaller than a church, used as a place of worship, as on a school or college campus or a military post. **2.** a room or recess within a church or other public or private building, usually containing an altar, used for religious services. **3.** a religious service conducted in a chapel, esp. at a school or college: *We were late for chapel.* **4.** *British.* a place of worship for Roman Catholics or Protestant Nonconformists. [Old French *chapele* holy place for worship, place for keeping sacred things, from Late Latin *cappella* cloak, shrine where the cloak (or *cappella*) of Saint Martin of Tours was preserved as a sacred relic, diminutive of *cappa* cape, hood; of uncertain origin.]

cha·pe·re·jos (shap′ə rā′ōs) chaparajos.

chap·er·on (shap′ə rōn′) *also,* **chaperone.** *n.* **1.** a mature person who attends and supervises social gatherings of young unmarried people. **2.** a mature woman who accompanies a young unmarried woman in public. —*v.t.* to act as chaperon to. [French *chaperon* protector (compared jokingly to a hood); originally, hood, from Old French *chape* cape, from Late Latin *cappa* hood, cape; of uncertain origin.] —**chap′er·on·age,** *n.*

chap·er·one (shap′ə rōn′) *n.* chaperon. —*v.t.,* **-oned, -on·ing.** chaperon.

chap·fall·en (chap′fô′lən, chop′-) *also,* **chopfallen.** *adj.* dejected; dispirited; crestfallen.

chap·lain (chap′lin) *n.* a member of the clergy who performs religious functions for a group or organization, as the armed forces, a college, or a court. [Middle English *chapelain* from Old French *chapelain,* from Medieval Latin *cappellanus* originally, guardian of the cloak (or *cappella*) of Saint Martin of Tours, from Late Latin *cappella.* See CHAPEL.] —**chap′lain·cy, chap′lain·ship′,** *n.*

chap·let (chap′lit) *n.* **1.** a wreath or garland worn on the head. **2.** a string of beads used to keep count when saying the prayers of the rosary, equal to one third of a complete rosary. **3.** prayers said with such beads. **4.** any string of beads; necklace. [Old French *chapelet* wreath, little hat, from *chapel* hat, wreath, going back to Late Latin *cappa.* See CHAPEL.]

chap·man (chap′mən) *n., pl.* **-men** (-mən). *British.* peddler; hawker. [Old English *cēapman* merchant, from *cēap* trade + *mann* man. See CHEAP.]

chaps (chaps, shaps) *pl. n.* strong leather leggings worn over trousers to protect the legs while riding horseback. [Short for CHAPARAJOS.]

chap·ter (chap′tər) *n.* **1.** any of several main divisions of a book, treatise, or the like. **2.** a main division or part of anything: *a new chapter in one's life.* **3.** a local branch or division of an organization, as of a club, fraternity, or society. **4.** a group composed of members of the clergy who serve a cathedral. —*v.t.* to arrange or divide into chapters. [Old French *chapitre* section of a book, assembly of clerics, from Late Latin *capitulum* meeting of clerics (at which a *chapter* of the Bible was often read), from Latin *capitulum* section of a book, small head, diminutive of Latin *caput* head.]

chapter house 1. a building used for a cathedral chapter's assembly. **2.** a house or meeting room of a college fraternity or sorority.

char¹ (chär) *v.,* **charred, char·ring.** —*v.t.* **1.** to burn slightly or partially; scorch: *The fire charred and blackened many of the trees in the park.* **2.** to reduce to charcoal by burning. —*v.i.* to become charred. —*n.* a charred substance; charcoal. [Probably from CHARCOAL.]

char² (chär) *British. n.* **1.** *also,* **chare.** a chore, esp. a household chore. **2.** charwoman. —*v.i.,* **charred, char·ring.** *also,* **chare.** to do chores, esp. housework; work as a charwoman. [Old English *cierr, cerr* turn of work.]

char³ (chär) *also,* **charr.** *n., pl.* **chars** or **char;** *also,* **charrs** or **charr.** any of a group of trouts, genus *Salvelinus,* characterized by small scales and a reddish belly, as the brook trout. [Gaelic *ceara* red, from *cear* blood.]

char·a·banc (shar′ə bang′, -bangk′) *also,* **char·à·banc.** *n., pl.* **-bancs.** *British.* a long vehicle with rows of transverse seats facing forward, esp. a sightseeing bus. [French *charàbancs* literally, car with benches, going back to Latin *carrus* wagon (see CARGO) + *ad* to + an unrecorded Germanic word meaning "bench."]

char·ac·ter (kar′ik tər) *n.* **1.** all the qualities or features that are typical of or serve to distinguish a person, group, or thing; individual nature: *That author's stories have a gloomy character.* **2.** all the qualities of a person, good or bad, that make up his or her moral nature: *a person with a fine, honest character.* **3.** moral qualities strongly developed or strikingly displayed; moral force or excellence; integrity: *Hard work helps build character.* **4.** a person represented in a novel, play, motion picture, or the like: *Hamlet*

is one of the most famous characters in literature. **5.** *Informal.* a person who is odd, eccentric, amusing, or very different. **6.** a position or function; capacity; status: *I signed the document in my character as president.* **7.** a mark or sign used as a symbol in writing or printing or as one of the components of an alphabet. **8.** a style of writing or printing: *This is not my writing, though, I confess, much like the character* (Shakespeare, *Twelfth Night*). **9.** *Biology.* a distinctive trait, feature, or property that is genetically determined and common to all members of a group. [Latin *charactēr* tool for marking, mark, characteristic, from Greek *charaktēr.*] —**char′ac·ter·less,** *adj.* —For Synonyms, see **disposition.**

• **in character.** in keeping with a person's disposition or usual behavior.

• **out of character.** not in keeping with a person's disposition or usual behavior.

character actor, an actor who is capable of playing a wide variety of roles or who specializes in portraying persons of a certain type.

character actress, an actress who is capable of playing a wide variety of roles or who specializes in portraying women of a certain type.

char·ac·ter·is·tic (kar′ik tə ris′tik) *n.* **1.** something that is typical of, helps to define the identity of, or is thought of as belonging to a person or thing; distinguishing or essential element, property, or trait: *Kindness is my friend's most outstanding characteristic. The specimen can be identified by checking for certain characteristics.* **2.** *Mathematics.* the integral part of a logarithm. —*adj.* relating to or indicating the character of a person or thing; distinctive; typical: *a characteristic gesture, a characteristic taste, formations characteristic of a geological period.* —**char′ac·ter·is′ti·cal·ly,** *adv.*

> **Synonyms** *n.* **Characteristic, quality, trait,** and **attribute** mean an aspect or feature that defines or describes someone or something. **Characteristic** emphasizes an essential aspect: *The nursing of offspring by the female is a basic characteristic of mammals.* **Quality** is used to describe identifying features in general, esp. when a value judgment is being made: *Generosity is an admirable quality.* **Trait** is more neutral and is usually applied to persons or types: *A willingness to compromise is a trait shared by many politicians.* **Attribute** is a quality closely associated with and often deemed essential to a particular person or thing: *Vision is an important attribute of a leader.*

char·ac·ter·i·za·tion (kar′ik tər ə zā′shən) *n.* **1.** the result of characterizing; description; portrayal. **2.** the act of characterizing. **3.** the creation or representation of characters in an art form, as in a play or novel.

char·ac·ter·ize (kar′ik tə rīz′) *v.t.,* **-ized, -iz·ing. 1.** to be a characteristic of; distinguish: *High fever characterizes that illness.* **2.** to describe the character or qualities of (a person or thing); depict; portray: *The author characterizes the central figure as heroic.*

character sketch 1. a short description, esp. in essay form, of a person or particular type of person. **2.** in the theater, a brief portrayal of an individual; short impersonation.

character witness, a person who attests to the moral character and integrity of someone before a court of law.

cha·rade (shə rād′) *n.* **1.** charades. a game in which the participants attempt to guess words or phrases pantomimed by one of the players. ➡ used as singular. **2.** a word or phrase pantomimed in this game. **3.** something thought of as resembling such a game; false show or pretense: *Their friendliness toward each other was a mere charade.* [French *charade* this game, from Provençal *charrado* talk, chat, from *charra* to chatter; of imitative origin.]

char·broil (chär′broil′) *v.t.* to broil over a charcoal fire. [CHAR¹ + BROIL¹.]

char·coal (chär′kōl′) *n.* **1.** a black, brittle, porous form of carbon produced by heating or charring animal or vegetable matter. It is used as fuel and in the manufacture of food and chemicals. **2.** a pencil or crayon made of charcoal. **3.** a drawing made with such a pencil or crayon. —*v.t.* to mark, write, or blacken with charcoal. [Middle English *charcole* the black, porous solid, possibly from *char* turn (from Old English *cierr*) + *cole* coal; in the sense of "turned to coal." See COAL.]

chard (chärd) *n.* Swiss chard.

chare (châr) *British. n.* char² (*def. 1*). —*v.i.,* **chared, char·ing.** char².

charge (chärj) *v.,* **charged, charg·ing.** —*v.t.* **1.** to fix or ask as a price: *The shop charged twenty dollars to repair the radio.* **2.** to require payment from; make financially liable: *The neighbor charged the child's parents for the broken window.* **3.a.** to defer payment for (something) until a bill is received: *I charged the gifts at the store.* **b.** to record the cost of something to; enter as a debt:

Please charge the purchase to my account. **4.** to rush violently upon or toward in an attack: *The infuriated bull charged one of the horses. The troops charged the fortress.* **5.** to bring an accusation against or lay blame upon; accuse: *The police charged them with the theft.* **6.** to give a task, duty, or responsibility to; entrust: *The nursemaid is charged with the care of their young children.* **7.** to fill (something) with a requisite supply: *to charge a furnace with ore.* **8.** to supply with a quantity of electricity or electrical energy: *to charge a storage battery.* **9.** to diffuse or distribute throughout; saturate: *to charge water with carbon dioxide.* **10.** to fill full as if with electricity; make pulsating; suffuse: *The air was charged with excitement.* **11.** to command or order; enjoin: *Satan, avoid! I charge thee, tempt me not!* (Shakespeare, *Comedy of Errors*). **12.** to instruct officially or authoritatively, as on matters or points of law: *The judge charged the jury to disregard the witness's last statement.* —*v.i.* **1.** to rush violently or go quickly in or as in an attack: *The elephant charged. I charged up the stairs after the cat.* **2.** to fix or ask a price: *The shop always charges for delivery.* —*n.* **1.** a required payment; price asked: *There was an hourly charge of $5.00 for cleaning services. The charge for admission was $1.50.* **2.** a charged purchase; debt. **3.** care, custody, or management; superintendence: *He had charge of his brother while their mother went out. She took charge of the situation when she arrived.* **4.** a violent or rushing attack: *The charge was repulsed by the enemy.* **5.** a signal or order for such an attack: *The bugler sounded the charge.* **6.** an accusation; allegation: *The charge was robbery.* **7.** a person or thing under the care, custody, or management of another. **8.** a task, duty, or responsibility: *The orphans' education became the charge of their guardians.* **9.** the quantity that an apparatus or receptacle is fitted to receive and hold: *The charge for the furnace is two tons.* **10.** an electric charge. **11.** the amount of powder or other explosive to be detonated at one time, as in a cartridge or shell. **12.** a command or instruction, esp. one concerning points of law, given by a judge to a jury before it retires to deliberate. **13.** *Heraldry.* a geometric design or other figure used on an escutcheon. **14.** *Slang.* thrill; kick: *We got a big charge out of seeing the pictures of us as children.* [Old French *charger* to load, from Late Latin *carricāre* to load (a wagon), from Latin *carrus* two-wheeled wagon; of Celtic origin. Doublet of CARRY.] —**charge′a·ble;** *also,* **charg′a·ble,** *adj.* —For Synonyms (*v.t.*), see **accuse;** (*n.*), see **price.**
· **in charge.** in the position of authority or responsibility.
· **in charge of.** in control of; responsible for.
charge account, a credit arrangement by which a person may make purchases to be paid for at some future date.
charge card, a small card bearing a person's name, signature, and account number, used for making purchases on a charge account. Also, **charge plate.**
charge-cou·pled device (chärj′kup′əld) a semiconductor chip that converts images into electric signals that can be stored on a computer disk or transmitted by a television camera.
char·gé d'af·faires (shär zhā′ də fâr′) *pl.* **char·gés d'af·faires** (shär shäz′ də fâr′). **1.** a diplomatic official who serves as a temporary substitute for an ambassador or minister. **2.** a diplomatic official sent to a foreign government to which a diplomat of higher standing is not sent. [French *chargé d'affaires* literally, one charged with affairs.]
charg·er[1] (chär′jər) *n.* **1.** a horse trained or suitable for use in battle. **2.** a person or thing that charges. **3.** an electrical device used to recharge storage batteries. [CHARGE + -ER[1].]
charg·er[2] (chär′jər) *n.* a large, flat dish; platter. [Middle English *chargeour;* of uncertain origin.]

chariots in a Roman mosaic (c.1000 B.C.)

char·i·ot (char′ē ət) *n.* a two-wheeled vehicle drawn by two, three, or four horses, all abreast, and driven from a standing position, used chiefly in warfare, processions, and races in ancient times. [Old French *chariot* wagon, from *char* cart, wagon, from Latin *carrus* two-wheeled wagon; of Celtic origin.]

char·i·ot·eer (char′ē ə tîr′) *n.* the driver of a chariot, as in ancient Greece or Rome.
cha·ris·ma (kə riz′mə) *n.* **1.** a unique and magnetic personal quality that attracts the loyalty and devotion of a large following of people: *The presidential candidate had a lot of charisma.* **2.** in Christianity, extraordinary spiritual power, as for healing or prophesying. [Greek *charisma* favor, grace, gift.]
char·is·mat·ic (kar′iz mat′ik) *adj.* **1.** having or showing charisma: *a charismatic actor.* **2.** of or relating to any of various religious groups or sects that emphasize divine inspiration, as in healing or prophesying. —*n.* a member of a charismatic group.
char·i·ta·ble (char′i tə bəl) *adj.* **1.** of or for charity; providing assistance to the poor or needy: *a charitable institution.* **2.** merciful, lenient, or forgiving, esp. in judging others; kindly; tolerant: *It was charitable of you to overlook my thoughtlessness.* **3.** generous in giving help to the poor or needy; beneficent. —**char′i·ta·ble·ness,** *n.* —**char′i·ta·bly,** *adv.*
char·i·ty (char′i tē) *n., pl.* -ties. **1.** the providing of assistance to the poor or needy, esp. on a widespread or organized basis. **2.** money or other help given to the poor or needy: *The old woman refused to accept charity when her husband died.* **3.** a fund, institution, or organization for assisting the poor or needy: *Give generously to your favorite charity.* **4.** mercy, leniency, or forgiveness, esp. in judging others; kindness; tolerance. **5.** love for one's fellow human beings: *And now abideth faith, hope, charity, these three; but the greatest of these is charity* (I Corinthians 13:2). [Old French *charité,* from Late Latin *caritas* Christian love, from Latin *cāritās* dearness, from *carus* dear, beloved.]

Synonyms Charity and philanthropy mean voluntary help extended to the needy. **Charity** simply suggests a kindly desire to relieve distress: *to give charity to a beggar.* **Philanthropy** implies a desire to effect change, as to foster development of the recipients' abilities or skills, and suggests forethought, organization, and aid on a large scale: *The millionaire's philanthropy included endowment of a scholarship program at the university.*

cha·riv·a·ri (shiv′ə rē′, shiv′ə rē, shə riv′ə rē) *n., pl.* -ris. shivaree.
char·la·tan (shär′lə tən) *n.* a person who professes to have knowledge or skill that he or she does not actually possess; quack; impostor. [French *charlatan,* from Italian *ciarlatano* mountebank, babbler; modification (influenced by Italian *ciarlare* to chat) of *cerretano* mountebank; literally, inhabitant of *Cerreto,* Italian town supposedly once regarded as being inhabited by cheats and impostors.] —**char′la·tan·ism, char′la·tan·ry,** *n.*
Charles·ton (chärl′stən) *n.* a lively dance in ⁴/₄ time, popular esp. in the 1920s. —*v.i.* to do this dance. [From *Charleston,* South Carolina.]
char·ley horse (chär′lē) an instance of severe muscular stiffness or soreness, caused by strain, esp. of the thigh. [Possibly from the use of *Charley* as a name for a lame horse.]
char·lock (chär′lək) *n.* a weed, *Brassica kaber,* of the mustard family, bearing yellow flowers and found in grain fields. If it becomes mixed with animal feed and is eaten, it can cause colic and other illnesses. [Old English *cerlic.*]
char·lotte (shär′lət) *n.* a sweet dish consisting of whipped cream, custard, gelatin, or fruit enclosed in a mold of bread, cake, or crumbs. [French *charlotte,* possibly from the feminine proper name *Charlotte.*]
charlotte russe (rüs) a charlotte made of a sponge cake mold filled with whipped cream or custard. [French *charlotte russe* literally, Russian charlotte. See CHARLOTTE.]
charm (chärm) *n.* **1.** the power to fascinate, attract, or delight greatly: *a person of beauty and charm.* **2.** any fascinating, attractive, or delightful quality or feature: *The pond is the property's greatest charm.* **3.** a small ornament or trinket, often worn on a chain bracelet. **4.** something worn to ward off evil or ensure good luck; amulet: *to carry a rabbit's foot as a good luck charm.* **5.a.** any action or formula supposed to have magic power. **b.** the chanting or recitation of such a formula. **6.** *Physics.* a hypothetical property that distinguishes one class of quarks from another. —*v.t.* **1.** to fascinate, attract, or delight greatly; captivate: *The child's sweet disposition charmed everyone.* **2.** to affect by or as by magic; bewitch: *The playing of the flute charmed the cobra.* **3.** to endow with or protect by or as by magic power. —*v.i.* **1.** to be greatly fascinating, attractive, or delightful: *a smile that charms.* **2.** to use spells or enchantments; practice magic. [Old French

a	at	e	end	o	hot	u	up	hw	white		about
ā	ape	ē	me	ō	old	ū	use	ng	song		taken
ä	far	i	it	ô	fork	ü	rule	th	thin	ə	pencil
âr	care	ī	ice	oi	oil	u̇	pull	th	this		lemon
		îr	pierce	ou	out	ûr	turn	zh	measure		circus

charme magical formula, incantation, from Latin *carmen* song, incantation.] —**charm′er,** *n.* —**charm′less,** *adj.*

char·meuse (shär müz′) *n.* a soft lightweight fabric, usually of silk, having a satin finish and used chiefly for evening dresses. [French *charmeuse* literally, female charmer, from *charmer* to enchant, going back to Latin *carmen* song, incantation.]

charm·ing (chär′ming) *adj.* that charms or is full of charm; enchanting; captivating: *a charming host, a charming nature.* —**charm′ing·ly,** *adv.*

char·nel (chär′nəl) *n.* charnel house. —*adj.* of, like, or fit for a charnel house; sepulchral; ghastly. [Old French *charnel* (as noun) cemetery, (as adjective) fleshly, from Late Latin *carnāle* cemetery, noun use of neuter of Latin *carnālis* fleshly.]

charnel house, a building, vault, or other place in which the bones or bodies of the dead are put.

Char·on (kâr′ən, kar′-) *n.* in Greek mythology, the boatman who ferried the souls of the dead across the river Styx to the entrance of Hades.

chart (chärt) *n.* **1.** a sheet showing information in the form of lists, diagrams, tables, or the like: *a chart of geological periods.* **2.** a graphic representation of the fluctuations of any variable, as population, prices, or barometric pressure. **3.a.** a map containing information necessary for navigation, as the location and depth of channels and harbors, or the location of air lanes and airports. **b.** an outline map used to show special conditions or facts: *a chart of the topography of the region, a weather chart.* **4. the charts.** *Informal.* a list of recordings on compact discs, audio cassettes, and phonograph records arranged to show their popularity and sales during a specific week. —*v.t.* **1.** to make a map or chart of: *to chart a coastline.* **2.** to plan or map out: *to chart a course of action.* [Old French *charte* card[1], map, from Latin *charta* paper, leaf of papyrus, from Greek *chartēs* leaf of papyrus, writing. Doublet of CARD[1].] —**chart′less,** *adj.* —For Synonyms *(n.),* see **map.**

char·ter (chär′tər) *n.* **1.** a formal written document issued by a government or a sovereign to a person, group, or corporation, granting the right to organize for carrying on some specified activity and imposing certain obligations. **2.** *also,* **Charter.** a document defining the functions or form of organization of a body, or setting forth its aims and principles; constitution. **3.** written permission from a society or organization authorizing the establishment of a new local chapter or branch. **4.a.** a contract or agreement to lease a carrier for transporting goods or persons. **b.** a leasing under such a contract: *Those planes are available for charter.* —*v.t.* **1.** to lease or hire by charter: *Our school chartered three buses for the trip.* **2.** to grant a charter to; establish by charter: *to charter a bank.* [Old French *chartre* letter, edict registering property, granted privileges, from Latin *chartula* a little paper, diminutive of *charta* paper. See CHART.] —**char′ter·er,** *n.* —For Synonyms *(v.t.),* see **lease.**

charter member, any of the original members of an organization, such as a club, society, or company.

Chart·ist (chär′tist) *n.* a member of a political movement of British workers, active from 1838 to 1849, who supported universal suffrage for men, secret ballots, the elimination of property qualifications for members of Parliament, and other reform measures. [From the *charter* of this movement, which presented its ideas and aims.] —**Chart′ism,** *n.*

char·treuse (shär trüz′, -trüs′) *n.* **1.** a pale yellowish green color. **2.** a pale green, yellow, or white liqueur originally made by Carthusian monks. —*adj.* having the color chartreuse. [French *chartreuse* Carthusian monastery, this liqueur, from *Grande Chartreuse,* mountainous region in southeastern France where the first Carthusian monastery was built.]

char·wom·an (chär′wŭm′ən) *n., pl.* **-wom·en** (-wim′en). a woman hired to clean a home, office, or public building. Also, **char.** [CHAR[2] + WOMAN.]

char·y (châr′ē) *adj.,* **char·i·er, char·i·est. 1.** hesitant and circumspect about dangers or risks; careful; cautious; wary: *to be chary of strangers.* **2.** reluctant in granting or giving; not lavish; sparing; frugal (often with *of*): *He is chary of his time. She was chary of complimenting others.* [Old English *cearig* careful, sorrowful.] —**char′i·ly,** *adv.* —**char′i·ness,** *n.*

Cha·ryb·dis (kə rib′dis) *n.* in Greek mythology, a hideous monster having the form of a raging whirlpool, dwelling in the Strait of Messina opposite the cave of the monster Scylla. Most sailors who were not devoured by Scylla were drowned by Charybdis.

chase[1] (chās) *v.,* chased, chas·ing. —*v.t.* **1.** to go after and try to catch; pursue: *The dog chased the ball. The police chased the thief down the alley.* **2.** to cause to depart or flee; drive: *The cranky neighbor chased the children out of his yard.* **3.** to devote one's attention to or follow in order to win or gain: *to chase a dream.* **4.** to investigate or try to verify; seek out (often with

down): *to chase down a rumor, to chase a lead.* —*v.i.* **1.** to follow in pursuit: *The child chased after the ball that rolled down the hill.* **2.** *Informal.* to rush about; hurry: *She chased all over town looking for a new dress.* —*n.* **1.** the act of chasing; pursuit: *The children caught the puppy after a long chase.* **2. the chase.** the sport of hunting. **3.** something that is chased or hunted; quarry. **4.** *British.* a tract of unenclosed land used as a private game preserve. [Old French *chacier* to hunt, pursue, going back to Latin *captāre* to try to catch, pursue. Doublet of CATCH.] —**chase′a·ble,** *adj.* —For Synonyms *(v.t.),* see **hunt.**

  • **to give chase.** to run or go after; pursue: *When the man saw the thief snatch the woman's purse, he gave chase.*

chase[2] (chās) *v.t.,* **chased, chas·ing.** to decorate (a metal surface) by embossing or engraving. [Short for ENCHASE.]

chase[3] (chās) *n.* **1.** a furrow, groove, or trench. **2.** a rectangular metal frame into which pages of type or plates are locked for printing or plate making. —*v.t.* to groove; indent. [French *châsse* setting, frame, from Latin *capsa* box, chest.]

chas·er (chā′sər) *n.* **1.** a person or thing that chases. **2.** a small, fast ship designed for pursuit. **3.** *Informal.* a drink, as of water or beer, taken after a drink of hard liquor.

chasm (kaz′əm) *n.* **1.** a deep, yawning crack or fissure in the earth's surface. **2.** a break marking a divergence, as in beliefs, interests, or opinion; profound difference: *The chasm between the two political parties was widening.* **3.** a marked interruption of or gap in continuity; hiatus. [Latin *chasma* opening, abyss, from Greek *chasma* opening, gulf.] —**chas′mal,** *adj.*

chas·sé (sha sā′) *n.* a gliding dance step in which the same foot always takes the lead. —*v.i.* to execute this step. [French *chassé* this dance step, from *chasser* to pursue, from Old French *chacier.* See CHASE[1].]

chas·seur (sha sûr′) *n.* **1.** a member of a military unit, esp. a member of a French infantry unit, trained and equipped for rapid movement. **2.** a huntsman; hunter. **3.** a liveried attendant or servant. [French *chasseur* hunter, from Old French *chaceor,* from *chacier* to hunt. See CHASE[1].]

Chas·sid (has′id) *n., pl.* **Chas·si·dim** (has′i dim, hä sē′dim). Hasid. —**Chas·sid·ic** (hə sid′ik), *adj.*

Chas·si·dism (has′i diz′əm) Hasidism.

chas·sis (shas′ē, chas′ē) *n., pl.* **chas·sis** (shas′ēz, chas′ēz) **1.** the skeleton of a motor vehicle, including the wheels, frame, and mechanical parts, on which the body is supported. **2.** a framework on which the parts of a radio or television set are mounted. **3.** the landing gear of an aircraft. **4.** the rails or frame on which a gun carriage moves backward and forward. [French *châssis* frame, from *châsse,* from Latin *capsa* box, chest.]

chaste (chāst) *adj.* **1.a.** not having engaged in unlawful or immoral sexual intercourse; virtuous. **b.** not having engaged in any sexual intercourse; virgin. **2.** free from indecency or offensiveness; modest. **3.** restrained or simple in style; not ornate. [Old French *chaste* pure, from Latin *castus.* Doublet of CASTE.] —**chaste′ly,** *adv.* —**chaste′ness,** *n.*

chas·ten (chā′sən) *v.t.* **1.** to punish or reprimand in order to correct or improve. **2.** to restrain from excess; temper; subdue: *The timely speech chastened the unruly crowd.* **3.** to make chaste in style; purify. [From obsolete *chaste* to correct, from Old French *chastier* to punish, from Latin *castīgāre* to make pure, correct, from *castus* pure.] —**chas′ten·er,** *n.*

chas·tise (chas tīz′, chas′tīz) *v.t.,* **-tised, -tis·ing.** to punish, reprimand, or discipline severely. [Probably from obsolete *chaste* to correct. See CHASTEN.] —**chas·tise′ment,** *n.* —**chas·tis′er,** *n.*

chas·ti·ty (chas′ti tē) *n.* **1.** the state or quality of being chaste. **2.** abstinence from all sexual intercourse; virginity or celibacy.

chastity belt, a beltlike device worn by women in the Middle Ages to prevent sexual intercourse while their husbands were away.

chas·u·ble (chaz′yə bəl, -ə bəl, chas′-) *n.* a sleeveless outer vestment worn over the alb by a priest officiating at Mass. [Old French *chasuble,* from Late Latin *casubula,* going back to Latin *casa* house. It was originally a hooded mantle, resembling a small house.]

chat (chat) *v.i.,* **chat·ted, chat·ting.** to converse in a light, familiar, or informal manner. —*n.* **1.** an informal, friendly conversation. **2.** any of several songbirds, as the stonechat or wheatear, having a chattering cry. [Short for CHATTER.]

cha·teau (sha tō′) *n., pl.* **-teaus** or **-teaux** (-tōz′). **1.** a castle in a French-speaking country. **2.** any large and elaborate country

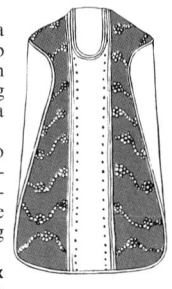

chasuble

house, esp. one resembling a castle. [French *château,* from Old French *chastel* castle, from Latin *castellum* castle, fortress.]

cha·teau·bri·and (shä tō bʀē äɴ′) *n.* a tender, boneless steak cut from the tenderloin of beef, usually served with a sauce. [From François René de *Chateaubriand,* 1768-1848, French author and statesman.]

chat·e·lain (shat′ə lān′) *n.* the keeper of a castle. [French *châtelain* lord of a castle, from Latin *castellānus* occupant of a castle, from *castellum* fortress, castle. See CASTLE.]

chat·e·laine (shat′ə lān′) *n.* **1.** the mistress or lady of a castle. **2.** an ornamental chain or clasp, usually worn at a woman's waist, to which keys, a purse, or other articles may be attached. [French *châtelaine,* feminine of *châtelain.* See CHATELAIN.]

chat·tel (chat′əl) *n.* any article of personal property, as furniture or livestock, as distinguished from real property, as lands or buildings. [Old French *chatel* property, from Late Latin *capitāle,* noun use of neuter of Latin *capitālis* chief, relating to the *caput* or head. Doublet of CATTLE.]

chat·ter (chat′ər) *v.i.* **1.** to talk rapidly and foolishly, esp. about matters of little consequence; jabber: *They chattered on and on about their new clothes.* **2.** to click together rapidly or uncontrollably: *My teeth chattered from the cold.* **3.** to make quick, short sounds: *The magpies chattered in the trees.* **4.** to rattle or vibrate during cutting, as an electric saw. —*v.t.* to say rapidly or foolishly: *to chatter nonsense.* —*n.* **1.** rapid, foolish talk. **2.** the act or sound of chattering. [Imitative.] —**chat′ter·er,** *n.*

chat·ter·box (chat′ər boks′) *n.* a person who talks incessantly.

chatter mark 1. a mark caused by the chattering of a tool or machine. **2.** one of a series of small, curved abrasions on the surface of a glaciated rock.

chat·ty (chat′ē) *adj.,* **-ti·er, -ti·est. 1.** given to chatting; talkative. **2.** full of chat; light, familiar, and informal: *a chatty letter.* —**chat′ti·ly,** *adv.* —**chat′ti·ness,** *n.*

Chau·ce·ri·an (chô sîr′ē ən) *adj.* of, relating to, or characteristic of the English poet Geoffrey Chaucer or his works. —*n.* a scholar specializing in the study of Chaucer and his works.

chauf·feur (shō′fər, shō fûr′) *n.* a person employed as the driver of an automobile, esp. a limousine. —*v.t., v.i.* to act or work as a chauffeur (for); drive. [French *chauffeur* stoker, heater, from *chauffer* to heat, going back to Latin *calefacere* to make warm; because the first automobiles were often powered by steam, the French humorously referred to drivers as "stokers" or *chauffeurs.*]

chau·tau·qua (shə tô′kwə) *also,* **Chau·tau·qua.** *n.* **1.** an educational movement begun in 1874 at Chautauqua, New York, establishing summer programs of instruction in education, religion, and the arts. Also, **Chautauqua movement. 2.** any of various similar programs, esp. those formerly offered by a number of traveling groups that brought information, religious inspiration, and professional entertainment to small towns and cities of the rural United States. [From *Chautauqua,* New York.]

chau·vin·ism (shō′və niz′əm) *n.* **1.** greatly exaggerated and boastful devotion to one's country or its military glory; exaggerated or fanatical patriotism. **2.** exaggerated, unreasoning pride in or attachment to one's own group, race, or sex. [French *chauvinisme,* from Nicolas *Chauvin,* a character in a play noted for his blind patriotism and devotion to Napoleon I, 1769-1821, French emperor.]

chau·vin·ist (shō′və nist) *n.* **1.** a person who has a greatly exaggerated and boastful devotion to his or her country. **2.** a person who has a exaggerated, unreasoning pride in or attachment to his or her own group, sex, or race. —**chau′vin·is′-tic,** *adj.* —**chau′vin·is′ti·cal·ly,** *adv.*

Ch.E., Chemical Engineer.

cheap (chēp) *adj.* **1.** low in price; inexpensive: *Milk is cheap at that supermarket.* **2.** charging low prices: *a cheap dress shop.* **3.** of little value or worth; inferior in quality; shoddy: *a novel printed on cheap paper, cheap furniture that falls apart under normal use.* **4.** unwilling to spend money; ungenerous; stingy; miserly: *to be too cheap to buy a birthday gift for a friend.* **5.** worthy of contempt; not esteemed; vulgar, common, or immoral: *All that makeup makes you look cheap.* **6.** costing little effort or trouble; easily expended or obtained: *Talk is cheap.* **7.** (of money) **a.** obtainable at a low rate of interest. **b.** depreciated in exchange value or buying power: *Cheap dollars are the result of inflation.* —*adv.* at a low price; cheaply: *He went to a wholesaler and got the radio cheap.* [Old English *cēap* bargain, price, trade, going back to Latin *caupō* tradesman.] —**cheap′ness,** *n.*

 • **on the cheap.** without spending much money; cheaply: *to take a vacation on the cheap by staying at old, unfashionable hotels.*

 • **to feel cheap.** to feel ashamed or low in self-esteem.

cheap·en (chē′pən) *v.t.* to lower, as in quality, value, or esteem; make cheap. —*v.i.* to become cheap.

cheap·ly (chēp′lē) *adv.* **1.** at a low price: *to buy something cheaply at a discount store.* **2.** in a low, vulgar, or immoral manner: *to dress cheaply.*

cheap shot, an unfair attack or criticism, esp. one that takes advantage of an opponent's weakness.

cheap·skate (chēp′skāt′) *n. Informal.* a stingy or miserly person. [CHEAP + SKATE[3].]

cheat (chēt) *v.t.* **1.** to defraud or swindle; trick: *They cheated us out of our share of the money.* **2.** to deprive, esp. of something expected: *The rain cheated us of our picnic.* —*v.i.* **1.** to practice fraud or act dishonestly: *to cheat on an exam, to cheat at cards.* **2.** *Slang.* to be unfaithful in a sexual or romantic relationship (often with *on*). —*n.* **1.** a person who is dishonest or unfaithful. **2.** a dishonest act or practice; fraud; trick. [Short for ESCHEAT; from the dishonest practice of those who took care of the *escheats* in feudal times. See ESCHEAT.] —**cheat′er,** *n.* —**cheat′ing·ly,** *adv.*

> **Synonyms** *v.t.* **Cheat, defraud,** and **swindle** mean to gain an advantage over or profit from someone by dishonest means. **Cheat** is the general term, referring to any of various forms of tricking or deceiving: *to cheat customers by selling shoddy goods, to cheat one's opponents at cards.* **Defraud** implies misrepresentation or a scheme of some complexity: *to defraud landowners of their rights by forging deeds.* **Swindle** suggests a particularly ruthless or flagrant action, often by gaining someone's confidence, and may imply that the victim is naive: *A stranger swindled the couple out of their savings by convincing them they could double their money quickly.*

check (chek) *n.* **1.** a person or thing that stops, controls, or limits: *The president's veto acts as a check on the powers of the board.* **2.** a test, examination, or inspection to see if something is as it should be: *The technician ran a check on the equipment.* **3.** a search, inquiry, or investigation: *We made a quick check for the missing files.* **4.** a mark (√) used to indicate that something has been approved, noted, or examined. **5.** control or supervision: *The store manager kept a close check on the employees.* **6.** *also, British,* **cheque.** a written order directing a bank to pay a specified sum. **7.** a slip of paper listing an amount owed, esp. in payment for a meal in a restaurant. **8.** a ticket, tag, or other token showing ownership or used for identification, as in reclaiming something left for temporary safekeeping: *a baggage check.* **9.** a sudden stop; abrupt halt: *Their disapproval put a check on our enthusiasm.* **10.** a square in a checkered surface or pattern. **11.** a checkered pattern. **12.** a fabric having such a pattern. **13.** *Chess.* the position of a king when it is under direct attack from one of the opposing pieces and is subject to mate on the next opposing move. **14.** *Ice Hockey.* a defensive blocking of the opponent in possession of the puck by the use of one's body or stick. —*v.t.* **1.** to halt the course or progress of sharply or forcefully; bring to a sudden stop: *to check the spread of a disease.* **2.** to hold in control or restraint; restrain; curb: *to check one's temper.* **3.** to compare, as with an authority or source of information, for accuracy: *Check the copy against the original. I checked my answers with those in the back of the book.* **4.** to test, investigate, or verify: *to check someone's references.* **5.** to inspect and ascertain the condition of; examine: *The medic checked the injured athlete for broken bones.* **6.** to mark with or as with a check (often with *off*): *Please check the correct answer. I checked each item off as my boss dictated the list.* **7.** to leave (something) for temporary safekeeping or custody, as in a checkroom: *Please check your coat.* **8.** to deposit (baggage) with an airline or other carrier that one is traveling on so as to have it sent along to one's destination. **9.** to mark in or with a pattern of small squares; checker. **10.** *Chess.* to place (an opponent's) king in check. **11.** *Ice Hockey.* to block the progress of the opponent in possession of the puck by the use of one's body or stick. —*v.i.* **1.** to agree on every point; correspond accurately: *My totals check with yours.* **2.** *Chess.* to place the opponent's king in check. **3.** *Ice Hockey.* to block the opponent in possession of the puck by the use of one's body or stick. —*interj.* **1.** agreed; all right. **2.** *Chess.* a call telling an opponent that his or her king is in check and must be moved. [Old French *eschec* check at chess, repulse, loss, through Arabic, from Persian *shāh* king (the most important chesspiece).] —**check′a·ble,** *adj.*

 • **in check. a.** under control or restraint: *to keep one's anger in check.* **b.** *Chess.* (of a king) under direct attack.

a	at	e	end	o	hot	u	up	hw	white		about
ā	ape	ē	me	ō	old	ū	use	ng	song		taken
ä	far	i	it	ô	fork	ü	rule	th	thin	ə	pencil
âr	care	ī	ice	oi	oil	u̇	pull	<u>th</u>	this		lemon
		îr	pierce	ou	out	ûr	turn	zh	measure		circus

•**to check in**. to make known one's arrival, as by registering at a hotel or airline counter: *We have to check in one hour before the flight.*

•**to check on** (or **up on**). to make an examination, inspection, or investigation: *The doctor checked on the bandage on my leg.*

•**to check out**. **a.** to pay one's bill and give up one's hotel or motel room. **b.** to add up prices for payment at a checkout counter of a supermarket or other store. **c.** to take on loan; borrow, as from a rental store or library: *We checked out two books to read over the weekend.* **d.** to examine in order to verify the truth, accuracy, or soundness of: *The editor checked out the dates and names in the manuscript. The mechanic checked out the car's transmission.* **e.** to prove to be true or correct: *The suspect's alibi checked out.*

check·book (chek′bŏk′) *n.* a book of blank checks issued by a bank to a depositor.

checked (chekt) *adj.* marked with squares; checkered: *a checked tablecloth.*

check·er[1] (chek′ər) *n.* **1.** a cashier, esp. in a supermarket. **2.** a person or thing that checks. [CHECK + -ER[1].]

check·er[2] (chek′ər) *also, British,* **chequer.** *n.* **1.** one of the flat, circular, usually red or black pieces used in the game of checkers. **2.** a pattern of squares of alternating colors or shades. **3.** one of the squares of such a pattern. —*v.t.* **1.** to mark with squares of alternating colors or shades, as a checkerboard. **2.** to vary or mottle with patches of different colors or shades; variegate: *The sky was checkered with clouds.* **3.** to vary with contrasting elements or situations; fill with variations. [Old French *eschekier* chessboard, from *eschec* check game.]

check·er·ber·ry (chek′ər ber′ē) *n., pl.* **-ries. 1.** wintergreen *(def. 1).* **2.** the bright red berry of the wintergreen; teaberry.

check·er·board (chek′ər bôrd′) *n.* a square board marked off into sixty-four alternately colored squares, used in playing checkers and chess.

check·ered (chek′ərd) *adj.* **1.** marked with squares of alternating colors or shades: *a checkered scarf.* **2.** marked with patches of different colors or shades: *a landscape checkered by shadows.* **3.** filled with changes of fortune or situations, some good and some bad or dubious: *to have a checkered past.*

check·ers (chek′ərz) *also, British,* **chequers.** *n.* a game for two played on a checkerboard, each player having twelve pieces. The game is won when one of the players cannot make a move because his or her pieces have been captured or blocked. Also, British, **draughts.** ➧ used as singular. [Plural of CHECKER[2].]

checking account, a bank account against which checks may be drawn by the depositor.

check·list (chek′list′) *n.* a list used for reference, verification, or comparison.

check·mate (chek′māt′) *v.t.,* **-mat·ed, -mat·ing. 1.** *Chess.* to put (the opponent's king) in check from which no escape is possible, thus winning the game. **2.** to defeat or thwart, esp. by a shrewd or skillful maneuver. —*n.* **1.** *Chess.* the situation or position of a king when it has been checkmated. **2.** a complete or utter defeat. —*interj. Chess.* an exclamation by a player announcing that his or her opponent's king is checkmated. [Old French *eschec et mat* checkmate (in chess); literally, check and conquered, through Arabic, from Persian *shāh-māt* literally, the king is dead.]

check·off (chek′ôf′, -of′) *n.* a practice whereby an employer deducts union dues from employees' wages and turns these deductions over to the union.

check·out (chek′out′) *n.* **1.** the examination and testing of a machine or machine part to determine if it is in sound condition or good running order. **2.a.** the process of adding up prices for payment in a supermarket or other store. **b.** checkout counter. **3.** the time by which one must give up a hotel or motel room or be charged for remaining in it.

checkout counter, a counter where purchases are paid for, as in a supermarket. Also, **checkout.**

check·point (chek′point′) *n.* a place where vehicles or travelers are stopped for inspection or clearance: *a border checkpoint.*

check·rein (chek′rān′) *n.* **1.** a short rein fastened from the bit to the harness to keep a horse from lowering its head. **2.** a short rein connecting the bit of one horse in a team to the driving rein of the other.

check·room (chek′rüm′, -rüm′) *n.* a room in which personal property, as hats, coats, or packages, may be left temporarily.

checks and balances, a system in which the actions of each branch or part of a government are subject to restraints or vetoes from the others, so that no one branch becomes too powerful. The Constitution of the United States has a system of checks and balances to limit the power of the executive, legislative, and judicial branches.

check·up (chek′up′) *n.* **1.** a complete physical examination. **2.** an examination or inspection: *We took the car for its 1,000-mile checkup.*

Ched·dar (ched′ər) *also,* **ched·dar.** *n.* any of several types of hard, smooth cheese, ranging in color from white to dark yellow and in taste from strong and sharp to mild. Also, **Cheddar cheese.** [From the village of *Cheddar,* England, where it was first made.]

cheek (chēk) *n.* **1.** either side of the face below the eye, esp. that part above the level of the mouth. **2.** something resembling this part of the face in shape or position: *the cheek of a vise.* **3.** saucy or brazen insolence; impudence; effrontery. **4.** a buttock. [Old English *cēce* side of the face below the eye.]

•**cheek by jowl**. side by side; in close proximity or intimacy.

cheek·bone (chēk′bōn′) *n.* the bone that forms the prominence at the upper part of the cheek below the eye of most mammals; zygomatic bone.

cheek pouch, a pouch or bag in the cheek of any of various animals, as the squirrel or monkey, used for holding food.

cheek·y (chē′kē) *adj.,* **cheek·i·er, cheek·i·est.** *Informal.* saucily or brazenly insolent; impudent. —**cheek′i·ly,** *adv.* —**cheek′i·ness,** *n.*

cheep (chēp) *v.t., v.i.* to make or utter with a faint, shrill sound, as does a young bird, mouse, or bat; chirp; peep. —*n.* a faint, shrill, chirping sound. [Imitative.]

cheer (chîr) *n.* **1.** a lively shout of acclamation, encouragement, or joy: *A cheer arose from the crowd when the president appeared.* **2.** a traditional set of words or sounds used by spectators to encourage or show enthusiasm, as for a contestant or athletic team: *a school cheer, our class cheer.* **3.** gladness, gaiety, or animation: *There is a general feeling of cheer as the holiday season nears.* **4.** something that gives joy or gladness; comfort; encouragement: *The doctor spoke words of cheer to the sick child.* **5.** a state of mind or spirits; mood: *to be of good cheer.* **6.** food and drink, as for a feast; provisions; fare. —*v.t.* **1.** to salute or acclaim with cheers: *The audience cheered the cast as they appeared on stage.* **2.** to make hopeful or glad; restore cheer to; comfort or gladden (often with *up*): *The news cheered us up.* **3.** to incite or urge on with or as with cheers; encourage (often with *on*): *to cheer on a team.* —*v.i.* **1.** to utter cheers: *The crowd cheered wildly as the horses neared the finish line.* **2.** to become hopeful or glad (often with *up*): *I cheered up at the thought of seeing my friend again.* —*interj.* **cheers.** good spirits; good health. ➧ used as a toast. [Old French *chere* face (suggesting a glad expression on the face, hence, gladness), from Late Latin *cara,* from Greek *karā* head, face.]

cheer·ful (chîr′fəl) *adj.* **1.** showing or feeling cheer; full of good spirits; happy; joyous: *a cheerful personality, a cheerful smile.* **2.** bringing cheer: *a cheerful fire, cheerful surroundings.* **3.** ready and willing to help; ungrudging: *a cheerful worker.* —**cheer′ful·ly,** *adv.* —**cheer′ful·ness,** *n.*

cheer·i·o (chîr′ē ō′) *interj., pl.* **-i·os.** *British. Informal.* **1.** hello. **2.a.** good-bye. **b.** good luck. ➧ often used as a toast to drinking companions.

cheer·lead·er (chîr′lē′dər) *n.* a person who leads organized cheering, esp. at a sports event.

cheer·less (chîr′lis) *adj.* devoid of cheer; joyless; gloomy. —**cheer′less·ly,** *adv.* —**cheer′less·ness,** *n.*

cheer·y (chîr′ē) *adj.,* **cheer·i·er, cheer·i·est.** bringing or full of cheerfulness; gay: *a cheery hello.* —**cheer′i·ly,** *adv.* —**cheer′i·ness,** *n.*

cheese[1] (chēz) *n.* **1.** a food made from the curds of milk, usually pressed into a mass or cake and aged. **2.** a mass or cake of cheese. **3.** something resembling cheese in shape or consistency. [Old English *cēse* the dairy product, going back to Latin *cāseus.*]

cheese[2] (chēz) *n. Slang.* an important person: *the big cheese around an office.* [Possibly from Urdu *chīz* thing, from Persian *chīz.*]

cheese·burg·er (chēz′bûr′gər) *n.* a hamburger with cheese, usually melted on top of the meat.

cheese·cake (chēz′kāk′) *n.* **1.** a rich, creamy cake made of cream cheese or cottage cheese, eggs, sugar, milk, and various flavorings, often having a bottom crust. **2.a.** *Informal.* a photograph of a woman posed to display her figure and legs. **b.** such photographs collectively.

cheese·cloth (chēz′klôth′) *n.* a thin, loosely woven cotton cloth. [Because first used for wrapping cheese.]

chees·y (chē′zē) *adj.,* **chees·i·er, chees·i·est. 1.** of or like cheese. **2.** *Slang.* of inferior quality; poorly made; cheap. —**chees′i·ness,** *n.*

chee·tah (chē′tə) *also,* **chetah**. *n.* a leopardlike wild mammal, genus *Acinonyx,* of the cat family, native to Africa and southern Asia, having a tawny coat with black spots or blotches, long legs, and claws that are permanently extended. It is capable of attaining speeds up to 70 miles (112.6 kilometers) per hour for short distances. Height: 2 feet (0.6 meter) at the shoulder. [Hindi *chītā* leopard, panther, going back to Sanskrit *chitra* spotted.]

cheetahs

chef (shef) *n.* **1.** the head cook of a restaurant, household, or other establishment. **2.** any cook. [French *chef* chief, master, head (short for *chef de cuisine* head cook), going back to Latin *caput* head. Doublet of CHIEF.]

chef-d'oeu·vre (shā dœ′vrə) *n., pl.* **chefs-d'oeuvre** (shā dœ′-vrə). a masterpiece, esp. in art or literature. [French *chef d'oeuvre* literally, chief piece of work, going back to Latin *caput* head + *dē* from + *opus* work.]

chef's salad, a salad usually consisting of greens, strips of cheese, cold meats, hard-boiled eggs, and garnishes. It is often served as the main dish of a meal.

che·la (kē′lə) *n., pl.* **-lae** (-lē). the pincerlike claw of certain crustaceans, as the lobster or crab, and of certain arachnids, as the scorpion. [Modern Latin *chela,* from Greek *chēlē* claw.]

che·late (kē′lāt) *adj. Zoology.* having or resembling a chela or chelae. —*n. Chemistry.* a compound in which ligands are bound to a metal ion at two or more points to form a complex, ring-shaped ion or molecule with the metal at the center. —*v.t.,* **-lat-ed, -lat·ing.** to combine with (a metal ion) to form a chelate. [CHEL(A) + -ATE[1].] —**che·la′tion,** *n.*

che·lo·ni·an (ki lō′nē ən) *adj.* of or relating to turtles. —*n.* turtle. [Modern Latin *Chelonia* (from Greek *chelōnē* tortoise) + -AN.]

chem-, form of **chemo-** before vowels, as in *chemist.*

chem., **1.** chemical. **2.** chemist. **3.** chemistry.

chemi-, form of **chemo-.**

chem·ic (kem′ik) *adj. Archaic.* **1.** of or relating to alchemy. **2.** chemical.

chem·i·cal (kem′i kəl) *adj.* of, relating to, or produced by chemistry or its phenomena, laws, or operations: *a chemical formula, a chemical reaction, the chemical composition of a substance.* —*n.* a substance obtained by or used in a chemical process. —**chem′i·cal·ly,** *adv.*

chemical bond, the electrical force of attraction that holds together the atoms of a molecule or the ions in a crystal.

chemical engineer, a specialist in chemical engineering.

chemical engineering 1. the application of chemical knowledge and principles to industrial processes. **2.** the profession practicing this application.

Chemical Mace *Trademark.* mace[3].

chemical warfare, the use of chemicals or chemical products, esp. poisonous gases, as weapons.

chem·i·lu·mi·nes·cence (kem′i lü′mə nes′əns) *n.* a form of luminescence in which light is emitted as the result of a chemical reaction that produces no heat, as in bioluminescence. [CHEMI- + LUMINESCENCE.] —**chem′i·lu′mi·nes′cent,** *adj.*

che·mise (shə mēz′) *n.* **1.** a loose, shirtlike undergarment worn as a slip. **2.** shift *(def. 5).* [Old French *chemise* shirt, from Late Latin *camīsia;* of uncertain origin.]

chem·ist (kem′ist) *n.* **1.** a person versed or trained in the science of chemistry; person professionally engaged in making chemical

investigations. **2.** *British.* druggist. [Short for ALCHEMIST. See ALCHEMY.]

chem·is·try (kem′ə strē) *n., pl.* **-tries. 1.** the science that deals with the composition and properties of substances and the changes that take place when they react with other substances. **2.** chemical composition, properties, or processes: *the chemistry of carbon, body chemistry.* **3.a.** a reaction between people characterized by mutual understanding or attraction; rapport. **b.** such a reaction as a cause or characteristic quality or factor of something: *the chemistry of love.* [From CHEMIST. See ALCHEMY.]

chemo- *combining form* of or relating to chemistry, chemicals, or chemical reactions: *chemotherapy.* [Going back to Late Greek *chēmiā* alchemy, chemistry; of uncertain origin.]

che·mo·re·cep·tion (kē′mō ri sep′shən, kem′ō-) *n.* the response of certain cells, such as those sensory cells located in the taste buds and nasal cavity, to specific chemical stimuli. [CHEMO- + RECEPTION.]

che·mo·re·cep·tor (kē′mō ri sep′tər, kem′ō-) *n.* a specialized cell, such as a nerve ending in the tongue or nose, that is capable of reacting to a chemical stimulus thereby triggering the process by which sensations are perceived. [CHEMO- + RECEPTOR.] —**che′mo·re·cep′tive,** *adj.*

chem·o·sphere (kem′ə sf ir′) *n.* the region of the upper atmosphere where photochemical reactions occur, extending from the stratosphere into the ionosphere. [CHEMO- + -*sphere,* as in ATMOSPHERE, STRATOSPHERE.]

che·mo·ster·i·lant (kē′mō ster′ə lənt, kem′ō-) *n.* any chemical substance that produces sterility in organisms, used esp. in insect control.

che·mo·syn·the·sis (kē′mō sin′thə sis, kem′ō-) *n.* the manufacture by certain bacteria of organic compounds from organic and inorganic molecules, using energy from chemical reactions rather than from light. [CHEMO- + SYNTHESIS.] —**che·mo·syn·thet·ic** (kē′mō sin thet′ik, kem′ō-), *adj.* —**che′mo·syn·thet′i·cal·ly,** *adv.*

che·mo·tax·is (kē′mō tak′sis, kem′ō-) *n., pl.* **-tax·es** (-tak′sēz). the movement or orientation toward or away from a chemical stimulus by an organism or by an individual cell. [CHEMO- + TAXIS.] —**che·mo·tac·tic** (kē′mō tak′tik, kem′ō-), *adj.* —**che′mo·tac′ti·cal·ly,** *adv.*

che·mo·ther·a·peu·tic (kē′mō ther′ə pū′tik, kem′ō-) *adj.* of or relating to chemotherapy. —**che′mo·ther′a·peu′ti·cal·ly,** *adv.*

che·mo·ther·a·py (kē′mō ther′ə pē, kem′ō-) *n.* the use of chemical substances to treat certain diseases, esp. to prevent cancer cells from reproducing. [German *chemotherapie,* from CHEMO- + THERAPY.]

che·mot·ro·pism (ki mot′rə piz′əm, ke-; kē′mō trō′piz əm, kem′ō-) *n.* the positive or negative response of a plant or plant part to a chemical substance, as by growth or movement. [CHEMO- + TROPISM.] —**che·mo·trop·ic** (kē′mō trop′ik, -trō′pik, kem′ō-), *adj.*

chem·ur·gy (kem′ər jē) *n.* the branch of chemistry that deals with the development of new industrial uses for plant and animal products. [CHEM(O)- + Greek *ergon* work.]

che·nille (shə nēl′) *n.* **1.** a yarn, often of cotton, silk, or worsted, with a velvety, fuzzy pile, used for embroidery, tassels, and fringes. **2.** a fabric woven from this yarn, used for such items as rugs and bedspreads. [French *chenille* caterpillar, from Latin *canīcula* little dog, diminutive of *canis* dog; because of its furry appearance.]

cheque (chek) *n. British.* check *(def. 6).*

chequ·er (chek′ər) *British.* checker[2].

chequ·ers (chek′ərz) *British.* checkers.

cher·i·moy·a (cher′ə moi′ə) *n.* **1.** the light green edible fruit of a tropical South American tree, *Annona cherimoa,* related to the custard apple. **2.** the tree bearing this fruit. [South American Spanish *chirimoya;* of uncertain origin.]

cher·ish (cher′ish) *v.t.* **1.** to treat with affection; care for tenderly; hold dear: *to cherish one's child.* **2.** to hold or entertain in the mind; cling fondly or steadfastly to: *to cherish the memory of a loved one.* [Old French *cheriss-,* a stem of *cherir* to hold dear, from *cher* dear, from Latin *cārus.*]

| **Synonyms** | **Cherish, treasure,** and **prize**[3] mean to value someone or something highly. **Cherish** suggests |

love or affection and is used of persons or things: *to cherish a close friend, to cherish memories of home.* **Treasure** stresses the value attached to the possession and suggests preserving it or

a	at	e	end	o	hot	u	up	hw	white		about
ā	ape	ē	me	ō	old	ū	use	ng	song	ə	taken
ä	far	i	it	ô	fork	u̇	rule	th	thin		pencil
âr	care	ī	ice	oi	oil	u̇	pull	t͟h	this		lemon
		îr	pierce	ou	out	ûr	turn	zh	measure		circus

guarding against injury or loss: *The woman treasured the vase so much she did not use it.* **Prize** also stresses value but does not imply a defensive or protective attitude so strongly. It may also suggest pride: *The boy prized his stamp collection and liked showing it off to his friends.*

cher·no·zem (chûr′nə zem′; *Russian* cher′nə zyôm′) *n.* a type of soil, dark and rich in humus, found in the temperate grasslands of continental interiors, as the steppes of Russia. [Russian *chernozem,* from *chernyi* black + *zemlya* earth.]

Cher·o·kee (cher′ə kē′) *n., pl.* **-kee** or **-kees.** 1. a member of a tribe of North American Indians, formerly the largest tribe that lived in the southeastern United States, now living mostly in Oklahoma. 2. their language, belonging to the Iroquoian language family. [Modification of *Tsălagi* or *Tsaragi,* Cherokee name for themselves, possibly from Choctaw *chiluk-ki* cave people; because of the many caves in Cherokee territory.]

Cherokee rose 1. the fragrant white flower of a climbing evergreen plant, *Rosa laevigata,* native to China, which now grows in the southern United States, usually having three sharply toothed leaflets. 2. the plant itself.

che·root (shə rüt′) *n.* a cigar cut square at both ends. [Tamil *shuruttu* roll of tobacco.]

cher·ry (cher′ē) *n., pl.* **-ries.** 1. a small, round or heart-shaped fruit of any of several shrubs or trees, genus *Prunus,* of the rose family, cultivated in temperate regions of the world, having a smooth skin and a fleshy pulp enclosing a pit. 2. the tree or shrub bearing this fruit, having clusters of white or pink flowers. 3. its wood. 4. a bright red color. —*adj.* 1. made of or consisting of cherries. 2. having the color cherry; bright red. 3. made of cherry wood. [Dialectal Old French *cherise* fruit of the cherry tree, going back to Latin *cerasus* cherry tree, from Greek *kerasos.*]

cherry picker *Informal.* a movable boom with a bucket or enclosed platform, used to lift a person into the air to perform work, such as repairing or servicing telephone or electric lines or trimming trees. [Possibly because it was originally used to lift people up into cherry trees to pick the fruit.]

cher·ry·stone (cher′ē stōn′) *n.* 1. a quahog clam, when larger than a littleneck clam. 2. the pit of a cherry.

chert (chûrt) *n.* a hard, fine-grained sedimentary rock consisting of microscopic crystals of quartz. —**cher′ty,** *adj.*

cher·ub (cher′əb) *n., pl.* **cher·ubs** or *(defs. 1, 2)* **cher·u·bim** (cher′ə bim′). 1. a member of the second highest order of angels. 2. a conventional representation of a cherub, often a chubby, winged child. 3. a beautiful, innocent, or sweet child. [Hebrew *k′rūb* winged angel.] —**che·ru·bic** (chə rü′bik); *also,* **che·ru′bi·cal,** *adj.* —**che·ru′bi·cal·ly,** *adv.*

cher·vil (chûr′vəl) *n.* the aromatic leaves of a plant, *Anthriscus cerefolium,* of the parsley family, used as a garnish and in salads and soups. [Old English *cærfille* the plant *Anthriscus cerefolium,* through Latin, from Greek *chairephyllon.*]

Ches·a·peake Bay retriever (ches′ə pēk′) any of a breed of large, powerful sporting dogs developed in Maryland by crossing the Newfoundland with local retrievers. The short, dense, slightly waved coat varies from straw-colored to dark brown. Height: to 26 inches (66 centimeters) at the shoulder. Weight: to 75 pounds (34 kilograms).

Chesh·ire cat (chesh′ər, -ir) the grinning cat in the English author Lewis Carroll's *Alice's Adventures in Wonderland,* that gradually faded away until only a grin remained.

chess (ches) *n.* a game for two played on a chessboard, each player having sixteen chess pieces. The players take turns moving their pieces, each with the aim of checkmating the opponent's king. [Old French *esches,* plural of *eschec* check (at chess.) See CHECK.]

chess·board (ches′bôrd′) *n.* a square board marked off into sixty-four alternately colored squares, used in playing chess or checkers.

chess·man (ches′man′, -mən) *n., pl.* **-men** (-men′, -mən). any of the pieces used in playing chess. Each player has a king, a queen, eight pawns, two bishops, two knights, and two rooks. Also, **chess·piece** (ches′pēs′).

chest (chest) *n.* 1.a. the front part of the body in humans and other mammals, extending from the neck to the abdomen. b. the part of the body containing the heart, lungs, and ribs. Also, **thorax.** 2. this part considered as the seat of the emotions: *Get*

whatever is bothering you off your chest. 3. chest of drawers. 4. a box or boxlike container, usually with a hinged lid, for storage, safekeeping, or shipping of articles: *a tool chest.* 5. the contents of such a container: *a chest of clothes, a chest of tea for shipment.* 6. a public fund made up of contributions for charitable purposes, as a community chest. [Old English *cest, cist* box, basket, going back to Latin *cista,* from Greek *kistē.*]

ches·ter·field (ches′tər fēld′) *n.* 1. an overcoat, usually single-breasted, having concealed buttons and a velvet collar. 2. an overstuffed davenport or sofa, usually having upright, upholstered arms. [From one of the earls of *Chesterfield.*]

Ches·ter White (ches′tər) a large, white hog of a breed that originated in Chester County, Pennsylvania.

chest·nut (ches′nut′, -nət) *n.* 1. the edible nut of a tree, genus *Castanea,* of the beech family, cultivated in North America, southern Europe, and Japan, having a shiny, usually mahogany-colored shell. 2. the tree producing this nut, having leathery, oblong leaves and fragrant flowers. 3. the wood of this tree. 4. any of several similar trees, as the horse chestnut or water chestnut. 5. a reddish brown color. Also, **chestnut brown.** 6. a reddish brown horse having mane and tail of the same or a lighter color. 7. *Informal.* something, as a joke or story, that has been repeated or used too often. —*adj.* having the color chestnut. [From obsolete *chesten* chestnut (tree and nut), from Old French *chastaigne,* from Latin *castanea,* from Greek *kastanon* + NUT.]

chest of drawers, a piece of furniture consisting of a frame containing a set of drawers for holding clothing, linens, or other articles.

che·tah (chē′tə) cheetah.

che·val-de-frise (shə val′də frēz′) *n., pl.* **che·vaux-de-frise** (shə vō′də frēz′). 1. an obstacle consisting of a timber or sawhorse covered with projecting spikes or barbed wire, used to close a gap in a defensive position. 2. a protecting line, as a row of spikes or broken glass, on top of a wall. [French *cheval de Frise* literally, horse of Friesland; because first used by the Frisians to offset their lack of cavalry. See CHEVAL GLASS.]

che·val glass (shə val′) a full-length mirror mounted and standing on swivels in a frame. [French *cheval* horse, support, from Latin *caballus* inferior horse, nag + GLASS.]

chev·a·lier (shev′ə lir′) *n.* 1. a member of an order of knighthood or honor, as the French Legion of Honor. 2. a knight or cavalier. [Old French *chevalier* knight, horseman, from Late Latin *caballārius* horseman, from Latin *caballus* inferior horse, nag. Doublet of CAVALIER.]

Chev·i·ot (shev′ē ət, chev′-) *n.* 1. a sheep of a breed valued as meat and for their thick wool. 2. a lustrous, wiry, white wool obtained from these sheep. 3. **cheviot.** a rough fabric made from this wool, woven with a twill and used for such items as suits and overcoats. [From *Cheviot Hills,* a range of hills on the English-Scottish border, where this breed originated.]

chev·ron (shev′rən) *n.* 1. an emblem or insignia, often consisting of stripes meeting at an angle, worn on the sleeve, as by police or the military, to indicate rank, length of service, or some other distinction. 2. an ornamental molding in the shape of an inverted V or zigzag pattern, used esp. in Norman and other Romanesque architecture. 3. *Heraldry.* a charge or bearing formed by two stripes that meet at an angle, like an inverted V. [Old French *chevron* rafter, kid[1], going

chevrons

back to Latin *caper* goat; possibly referring to the resemblance of rafters meeting at an angle to the horns of goats.]

chew (chü) *v.t.* 1. to crush or grind with the teeth: *Chew your food thoroughly.* 2. to damage or tear, as if by chewing (often with *up*): *The broken VCR chewed up the tape.* 3. to make by or as by chewing: *The puppy chewed a hole in the slipper.* 4. to consider or examine carefully; meditate on (often with *over*): *to chew over a problem.* —*v.i.* 1. to perform the action of crushing or grinding with the teeth: *The dog chewed on the bone.* 2. to tear with or as with the teeth: *The goat chewed through the fence.* 3. *Informal.* to chew tobacco. —*n.* 1. the act of chewing. 2. something chewed or for chewing: *a chew of tobacco.* [Old English *cēowan* to grind with the teeth.] —**chew′a·ble,** *adj.* —**chew′er,** *n.*
• **to chew out.** *Informal.* to scold severely; upbraid.

chewing gum, a gummy preparation that is sweetened and flavored for chewing, usually made of chicle.

che·wink (chi wingk′) *n.* towhee. [Imitative.]

chew·y (chü′ē) *adj.,* **chew·i·er, chew·i·est.** soft or sticky and requiring much chewing to be eaten.

Chey·enne (shī en′, -an′) *n., pl.* **-enne** or **-ennes.** a member of a tribe of North American Indians, speaking an Algonquian lan-

Files

Ranks

chessboard

guage, formerly living in the Great Plains, now living mainly in Montana and Oklahoma. [Sioux *Shaiyena* people who speak a strange language.]

chez (shā) *prep. French.* at or in the home of; by; with.

chg., charge.

chi (kī) *n.* the twenty-second letter (X, χ) of the Greek alphabet, represented in English by *ch (k).*

Chi·an·ti (kē än′tē, -an′-) *n.* **1.** a dry, red Italian wine. **2.** any similar wine, esp. a red one.

chi·a·ro·scu·ro (kē är′ə skŭr′ō, -skyŭr′ō) *n., pl.* **-ros.** **1.** the treatment and distribution of light and shade in a painting or drawing. **2.** the manner in which an artist uses or treats light and shade. **3.** a painting or drawing in which only light and shade are represented. [Italian *chiaroscuro* light and shade; literally, clear dark; from *chiaro* clear (from Latin *clārus*) + *oscuro* dark (from Latin *obscūrus*).] —**chi·a′ro·scu′rist,** *n.*

chi·as·mus (kī az′məs) *n., pl.* **-ma·ta** (-mə tə). *Rhetoric.* a reversal in the order of words in one of two otherwise parallel phrases, for example: *Do not live to eat, but eat to live.* [Greek *chīasmos* a placing crosswise, going back to *chi* the Greek letter; with reference to the shape (X) of the letter's symbol.]

Chib·cha (chib′chä) *n., pl.* **-cha** or **-chas.** a member of a South American Indian tribe, formerly living in parts of what are now Colombia and Ecuador, whose highly advanced culture was destroyed by the Spanish conquistadors.

chic (shēk) *adj.* attractive, tasteful, and fashionable in style; stylish; smart. —*n.* tasteful elegance, sophistication, and fashionableness, esp. in dress; style. [French *chic,* possibly from German *Schick* taste.] —**chic′ly,** *adv.* —**chic′ness,** *n.*

Chi·ca·na (chi kä′nə) *n., pl.* **-nas.** a female American of Mexican birth or descent. [Spanish *chicana,* feminine of *chicano.* See CHICANO.]

chi·cane (shi kān′) *v.t., v.i.,* **-caned, -can·ing.** to deceive by chicanery; trick. —*n.* chicanery. [French *chicane* a quibble, from *chicaner* to quibble, wrangle; of uncertain origin.]

chi·can·er·y (shi kā′nə rē) *n., pl.* **-er·ies.** **1.** the use of unfair or deceitful methods; trickery; subterfuge. **2.** an unfair or deceitful method; trick; subterfuge.

Chi·ca·no (chi kä′nō) *n., pl.* **-nos.** an American of Mexican birth or descent. [Shortening of a regional pronunciation of Mexican Spanish *mexicano* Mexican.]

chick (chik) *n.* **1.** a young chicken. **2.** the young of certain birds. **3.** *Slang.* a young woman. ➡ often considered offensive in def. 3. [Short for CHICKEN.]

chick·a·dee (chik′ə dē′) *n.* any of various small North American birds, family Paridae, having a stout body and gray or brown plumage with black, white, or chestnut markings. The most common species is the **black-capped chickadee,** *Parus atricapillus,* having a gray body and a black cap and throat. [Imitative.]

chick·a·ree (chik′ə rē′) *n.* red squirrel. [Imitative.]

Chick·a·saw (chik′ə sô′) *n., pl.* **-saw** or **-saws.** a member of a Muskogean tribe of North American Indians formerly living in what are now Tennessee and northern Mississippi, now living in Oklahoma.

chick·en (chik′ən) *n.* **1.** the common domestic fowl, *Gallus gallus.* **2.** a hen or rooster of any age. **3.** the flesh of a chicken, esp. when prepared for food. **4.** *Slang.* a person who is cowardly. **5.** *Slang.* a young person. —*adj.* **1.** immature: *a chicken lobster.* **2.** *Slang.* chicken-hearted; cowardly. —*v.i. Slang.* to lose one's courage; become cowardly (with *out*). [Old English *cīcen* young fowl.]

chicken hawk, any of various hawks, reputed to prey on chickens and other domestic fowl.

chick·en-heart·ed (chik′ən här′tid) *adj.* cowardly.

chicken pox *also,* **chick·en·pox** (chik′ən poks′). a mild but highly contagious viral disease, generally occurring in children and characterized by a blotchy red rash that develops into blisters and, finally, scabs. Also, **varicella.**

chicken wire, a light wire netting used especially for enclosures for poultry.

chick·pea (chik′pē′) *also,* **chick-pea, chick pea.** *n.* **1.** the large round seed of a plant, *Cicer arietinum,* of the pea family, eaten raw or cooked as a vegetable. **2.** the plant itself, bearing one or two seeds in a short pod. Also, **garbanzo.** [French *chiche* (going back to Latin *cicer*) + PEA.]

chick·weed (chik′wēd′) *n.* a common weed, *Stellaria media,* of the pink family, found throughout the world, having a creeping root, small oval leaves, and tiny white flowers. [Because eaten by chickens.]

chi·cle (chik′əl) *n.* a gum obtained from the milky juice of the sapodilla tree, used chiefly for making chewing gum. [Spanish *chicle,* from Nahuatl *chictli.*]

chic·o·ry (chik′ə rē) *n., pl.* **-ries.** **1.** the leaves of a plant, *Cichorium intybus,* of the composite family, eaten as a vegetable,

either raw or cooked. **2.** the dried, roasted, and ground root of this plant, mixed with or substituted for coffee. **3.** the plant itself. For illustration, see **herb.** [French *chicorée* the plant, from Latin *cichorium,* from Greek *kichorion.*]

chide (chīd) *v.t.,* **chid·ed** or **chid** (chid); **chid·ed** or **chid** or **chid·den** (chid′ən); **chid·ing.** to find fault with; reproach. [Old English *cīdan* to rebuke, quarrel.] —**chid′er,** *n.* —**chid′ing·ly,** *adv.*

chief (chēf) *n.* **1.** a person who is highest in rank or authority, as the leader of a group or tribe. **2.** the upper third of an escutcheon. —*adj.* **1.** highest in rank or authority: *chief cook.* **2.** most important; principal; main: *the chief problem.* [Old French *ch(i)ef* head, going back to Latin *caput.* Doublet of CHEF.] —For Synonyms *(adj.),* see **main.**

· **in chief.** of the highest title, rank, or authority: *editor in chief.*

Chief Executive, the president of the United States.

chief justice 1. the presiding or head judge of a court having several judges. **2. Chief Justice.** the head of the U.S. Supreme Court and chief judicial officer of the United States.

chief·ly (chēf′lē) *adv.* **1.** mainly but not exclusively: *The dish consisted chiefly of meat.* **2.** above all; especially: *We are chiefly interested in seeing the gardens of the house.*

chief of staff *pl.* **chiefs of staff. 1.** *Military.* a senior officer or head of a staff; principal assistant to a commander. **2. Chief of Staff.** the top military officer of the U.S. Army or Air Force.

chief of state, the formal head of a nation, charged with ceremonial duties: *The queen or king of England is the chief of state of the United Kingdom.*

chief·tain (chēf′tən) *n.* a leader or head, esp. of a tribe or clan. [Modification (influenced by CHIEF) of Old French *chevetaine,* from Late Latin *capitāneus* chief, from Latin *caput* head. Doublet of CAPTAIN.] —**chief′tain·cy, chief′tain·ship′,** *n.*

chif·fon (shi fon′, shif′on) *n.* a sheer, lightweight fabric, usually of silk or rayon, used for such items as scarves and dresses. —*adj.* **1.** made of or resembling chiffon. **2.** made partially of beaten egg whites or gelatin and having a light, airy consistency: *lemon chiffon pie.* [French *chiffon* rag, from *chiffe;* of uncertain origin.]

chif·fo·nier (shif′ə nîr′) *n.* a high bureau or chest of drawers, often having a mirror at the top. [French *chiffonnier* literally, place for pieces of cloth, from *chiffon* rag. See CHIFFON.]

chig·ger (chig′ər) *also,* **jigger.** *n.* **1.** the larva of any of various mites, family Trombidiidae. It pierces the skin of humans and other animals and sucks tissue fluids, leaving red spots and causing severe itching. **2.** chigoe *(def. 1).* [Modification of CHIGOE.]

chi·gnon (shēn′yon, shēn yon′) *n.* a twist or knot of hair usually worn at the nape of the neck. [French *chignon* coil of hair; earlier, nape of the neck; literally, little chain (referring to the chain of vertebrae there), going back to Latin *catēna* chain.]

chig·oe (chig′ō) *n.* **1.** a small, bloodsucking sand flea, *Tunga penetrans,* found in tropical America and Africa, the female of which burrows under the skin, causing painful sores and itching. **2.** chigger *(def. 1).* [Of Carib origin.]

Chi·hua·hua (chi wä′wä, -wä′wä) *also,* **chi·hua·hua.** *n.* a dog of a breed originally native to Mexico, having large, pointed ears and a smooth or wavy coat that is usually tan. It is the smallest breed of dog. Height: 5 inches (13 centimeters) at the shoulder. [From *Chihuahua,* the Mexican state where this breed originated.]

chil·blain (chil′blān′) *n.* a mild form of frostbite affecting the hands or feet and characterized by an itching inflammation of the skin. [CHILL + BLAIN.]

child (chīld) *n., pl.* **chil·dren. 1.** the offspring of a human being; son or daughter: *Do you have any children?* **2.** a boy or girl between birth and adolescence. **3.** a descendant: *children of Israel.* **4.** a childish person. **5.** a person who is a product of a certain condition, place, or time: *a child of poverty.* [Old English *cild* young person.] —**child′less,** *adj.*

· **with child.** pregnant.

child abuse, physical or psychological injury, neglect, or mistreatment of a child, as by an adult.

child·bear·ing (chīld′bâr′ing) *n.* the act of giving birth to a child or children. —*adj.* relating to or capable of bearing a child or children: *a woman of childbearing age.*

child·bed fever (chīld′bed′) puerperal fever.

child·birth (chīld′bûrth′) *n.* the act of giving birth to a child or children; parturition.

child·hood (chīld′hŭd′) *n.* the period from birth to adolescence; time of being a child.

a	at	e	end	o	hot	u	up	hw	white		about
ā	ape	ē	me	ō	old	ū	use	ng	song		taken
ä	far	i	it	ô	fork	ü	rule	th	thin	ə	pencil
âr	care	ī	ice	oi	oil	u̇	pull	th	this		lemon
		îr	pierce	ou	out	ûr	turn	zh	measure		circus

child·ish (chīl'dish) *adj.* **1.** of, like, or befitting a child: *a childish dress.* **2.** immature; silly: *childish fears, a childish waste of time.* —**child'ish·ly,** *adv.* —**child'ish·ness,** *n.*

> **Usage** Childish and childlike, which both mean having the qualities of a child, are often confused. **Childish** tends to be derogatory, suggesting emotional immaturity: *a childish tantrum.* **Childlike,** on the other hand, usually indicates positive or admirable traits: *a childlike joy in nature.* Sometimes, however, it hints at vulnerability: *childlike innocence.*

child labor, the employment of children at regular and sustained labor.

child·like (chīld'līk') *adj.* like or befitting a child; innocent: *childlike simplicity.* —For Usage Note, see **childish.**

child·proof (chīld'prōōf') *adj.* that cannot be opened, operated, damaged, or tampered with by children.

chil·dren (chīl'drən) the plural of **child.**

Children's Crusade, a futile attempt to recover the Holy Land from the Muslims, undertaken by thousands of French and German children in 1212.

child's play, anything easily done or accomplished.

Chil·e saltpeter (chīl'ē) sodium nitrate.

chil·i (chīl'ē) *also,* **chil·e, chil·li.** *n., pl.* **chil·ies. 1.** the pod of any of several species of pepper, genus *Capsicum,* used to make a hot spice. **2.** the plant itself. **3.** chili con carne. [Spanish *chile* red pepper, from Nahuatl *chilli.*]

chili con car·ne (kon kär'nē) *also,* **chile con car·ne.** a highly seasoned dish made of meat, red peppers, tomato sauce, and, usually, beans. [Spanish *chili con carne* literally, chili with meat.]

chili powder, a powdered spice consisting of a blend of dried and ground chili pods and other herbs and spices, as oregano, garlic, cloves, and allspice.

chili sauce, a highly spiced sauce used as a condiment, made of red peppers, tomatoes, vinegar, sugar, and onions.

chill (chil) *n.* **1.** coldness, esp. when moderate but penetrating: *There was a slight chill in the air.* **2.** the sensation of cold, esp. when ac-

chili peppers

companied by shivering and fever: *to get a chill.* **3.a.** a lack of warmth or friendliness; icy manner: *a chill in one's voice.* **b.** a depressing or discouraging influence or effect: *The sad news cast a chill over the festivities.* **4.** a disquieting feeling, as of fear or anxiety: *The macabre sight sent a chill through me.* —*v.t.* **1.** to make cold: *to chill wine.* **2.** to cause a sensation of cold in: *The night air chilled me.* **3.** to check, as enthusiasm; depress or discourage. **4.** to harden the surface of (a metal) by sudden cooling. —*v.i.* **1.** to become cold. **2.** to have the sensation of or be affected by cold. **3.** to become hardened on the surface by a sudden cooling, as metal. —*adj.* chilly: *a chill night.* [Old English *c(i)ele* coldness.] —**chill'ness,** *n.*

chill factor, wind-chill factor.

chil·li (chil'ē) *n., pl.* **-lies.** chili.

chill·y (chil'ē) *adj.,* **chill·i·er, chill·i·est. 1.** cold: *chilly night air.* **2.** affected by, sensitive to, or feeling cold: *to be chilly.* **3.** lacking warmth; unfriendly: *a chilly reception.* —**chill'i·ness,** *n.*

Chi·mae·ra (ki mîr'ə, kī-) *n., pl.* **-ras.** Chimera.

chime (chīm) *n.* **1.** *also,* **chimes.** a set of large bells, tuned to a musical scale, that produce tones when swung or struck. **2.** **chimes.** a musical instrument made of a set of metal tubes that sound when struck with a mallet. For illustration, see **percussion instrument. 3.** a single bell, as in a clock. **4.** *also,* **chimes.** a sound or series of musical sounds made by a chime. **5.** accord; harmony. —*v.,* **chimed, chim·ing.** —*v.t.* **1.** to produce a musical sound by striking; ring: *to chime bells.* **2.** to give or announce by ringing: *The clock chimed the hour.* **3.** to recite or repeat mechanically or in cadence. —*v.i.* **1.** to ring: *The clock chimed every hour.* **2.** to be in accord; harmonize (with *with*): *Your plans chime with mine.* [Old French *chimbe, cymbe* cymbal, from Latin *cymbalum,* from Greek *kymbalon.*]

·to chime in. a. to join in or interrupt a conversation: *I wish you wouldn't always chime in with your opinions.* **b.** to be in accord; harmonize: *The new furniture does not chime in with the decor of the room.*

Chi·me·ra (ki mîr'ə, kī-) *also,* **Chimaera.** *n., pl.* **-ras. 1.** in Greek mythology, a fire-breathing monster with a lion's head, a goat's body, and a serpent's tail. It was finally destroyed by Bellerophon. **2.** **chimera. a.** any imaginary monster. **b.** a fantastic or unfounded idea; silly fancy. **c.** *Biology, Botany.* an organism with tissues of differing genetic composition, produced by mutation or grafting. [Latin *chimaera* this mythological monster, from Greek *chimaira* female goat, this mythological monster.]

chi·mer·i·cal (ki mer'i kəl, -mîr'-, kī-) *adj.* **1.** unreal; imaginary. **2.** filled with wild ideas; whimsical; fanciful: *a chimerical mind.* Also, **chi·mer'ic.**

chim·ney (chim'nē) *n., pl.* **-neys. 1.** a vertical structure containing a flue by which smoke or vapor from a fireplace or furnace ascends and escapes. **2.** the part of such a structure rising above a roof. **3.** smokestack. **4.** a cylinder, usually of glass, surrounding the flame of a lamp to protect the flame and promote combustion. **5.** a vent or fissure in a cliff or volcano. [Old French *cheminee* fireplace, from Late Latin *camīnāta,* from Latin *camīnus* furnace, from Greek *kamīnos.*]

chimney piece, mantel *(def. 2).*

chimney pot, a cylindrical pipe, as of earthenware or metal, placed on top of a chimney to increase the draft and prevent smoking.

chimney sweep, a person whose business is cleaning out soot from chimneys.

chimney swift, a North American swift, *Chaetura pelagica,* having narrow, crescent-shaped wings and dull plumage. It often builds its nest in unused chimneys and is capable of rapid and sustained flight.

chimp (chimp) *n. Informal.* chimpanzee. [Short for CHIMPANZEE.]

chim·pan·zee (chim'pan zē', chim pan'zē) *n.* a tree-dwelling anthropoid ape, genus *Pan,* native to western and central Africa, having brownish black hair and protruding ears. It is highly intelligent and smaller and easier to train than a gorilla. [From the native West African name of the ape.]

chin (chin) *n.* **1.** the part of the face below the mouth and above the neck. **2.** the central, front part of the lower jaw. —*v.,* **chinned, chin·ning.** —*v.t.* to lift (oneself) from or as from an overhead horizontal bar by pulling with the arms until the chin is level with or above the hands. —*v.i.* **1.** to chin oneself. **2.** *Informal.* to chat or gossip. [Old English *cin(n)* part of the lower jaw.]

chi·na (chī'nə) *n.* **1.** a fine, vitreous pottery composed principally of clay, feldspar, and flint, believed to have originated in China. China differs from porcelain in that it requires two firings. **2.** objects, esp. dishes, made of this material. **3.** any pottery or dishes.

chi·na·ber·ry (chī'nə ber'ē) *n., pl.* **-ries. 1.** a deciduous Asian tree, *Melia azedarach,* grown in warm regions for its shade, having fragrant purplish flowers and yellow berries. Also, **China tree. 2.** soapberry. [CHINA (the country) + BERRY.]

Chi·na·man (chī'nə mən) *n., pl.* **-men** (-mən). a person of Chinese descent. ➡ now generally considered offensive. **Chinese** is preferred.

Chi·na·town (chī'nə toun') *n.* the Chinese section of any city outside China.

China tree, chinaberry *(def. 1).*

chi·na·ware (chī'nə wâr') *n.* **1.** china *(def. 2).* **2.** pottery or dishes of any kind.

chinch (chinch) *n.* **1.** chinch bug. **2.** any bedbug. [Spanish *chinche,* from Latin *cīmex* bug.]

chinch bug, a small black-and-white insect pest, *Blissus leucopterus,* common in the middle and southwestern United States, very destructive to wheat, corn, and other cereal grasses, esp. in dry weather.

chin·chil·la (chin chil'ə) *n.* **1.** the valuable, very fine, silver or bluish gray fur of any of a group of South American rodents, genus *Chinchilla,* used to make coats and jackets and to trim other apparel. **2.** the squirrellike animal that bears this fur. It has large dark eyes and broad ears rounded at the tip. Some species are raised commercially. Length: 20 inches (51 centimeters), including tail. **3.** a heavy fabric, usually made partially or entirely of wool, characterized by a nubby finish, used for such items as coats and suits. [Spanish *chinchilla* South American rodent; probably of Quechua origin.]

chine (chīn) *n.* **1.** backbone; spine. **2.** a cut of meat including the whole or part of an animal's backbone with the adjoining flesh. [Old French *eschine* spine; of Germanic origin.]

Chi·nese (chī nēz′, -nēs′) *adj.* of, relating to, or characteristic of China or its people, language, or culture. —*n., pl.* **-nese. 1.a.** a native or citizen of China. **b.** a person of Chinese descent. **2.** a language belonging to the Sino-Tibetan language family, consisting of many dialects. Mandarin, the dialect spoken in Beijing, is standard Chinese.

Words from Chinese

Chinese is spoken by approximately a billion people, more than speak any other language. It is a member of the Sino-Tibetan family of languages, which also includes Burmese, Tibetan, and Thai (but not Japanese or Korean). There are many Chinese dialects, the best-known of which are Mandarin, Cantonese, and Pekingese. Below is a selection of loanwords that have come into English from or through Chinese.

chopsticks	kaolin	pidgin	Taoism
chop suey	kowtow	Pinyin	tea
chow	kumquat	pongee	typhoon
chow mein	kung fu	sampan	wok
egg foo yung	litchi	shantung	wonton
fantan	loquat	shogun	yang
ginseng	mah jongg	soy	yen²
gung ho	pekoe	t'ai chi	yin

Chinese cabbage, either of two edible Asian plants related to cabbage but forming a more cylindrical head.
Chinese checkers, a game for two to six players, using marbles on a board shaped like a six-pointed star and containing holes for the marbles. The object is to move the marbles filling one triangle to the opposite triangle.
Chinese gooseberry, kiwi *(defs. 2, 3).*
Chinese lantern 1. a collapsible lantern of thin paper, usually decorated. Also, **Japanese lantern. 2.** winter cherry.
Chinese puzzle 1. a complicated or ingenious puzzle. **2.** anything complicated and hard to solve.
Chinese Wall, Great Wall of China.
chink¹ (chingk) *n.* a narrow crack or fissure: *The chinks in the wall admitted light.* —*v.t.* to fill the chinks in; plug. [Old English *cinu* fissure.]
chink² (chingk) *n.* a short, sharp sound, as of pieces of metal striking together. —*v.t., v.i.* to make or cause to make a chink. [Imitative.]
chi·no (chē′nō) *n., pl.* **-nos. 1.** a strong twill fabric, often made of cotton, used for durable clothing. **2. chinos.** trousers made from this fabric. [Spanish *chino* this fabric; of uncertain origin.]
Chi·nook (shi nŭk′, -nŭk′, chi-) *n., pl.* **-nook** or **-nooks. 1.** a member of a former tribe of North American Indians who lived near the mouth of the Columbia River in what is now the state of Washington. **2.** the language spoken by these people. **3. chinook.** king salmon. **4. chinook. a.** a warm, moist southwest wind that blows from the sea along the coasts of Washington and Oregon. **b.** a warm, dry wind that descends the eastern slopes of the Rocky Mountains, esp. in winter or early spring. In the Alps, a wind of this sort is called a foehn. [From an American Indian name of the tribe, *Tsinūk.*]
Chinook jargon, a language based on Chinook incorporating elements of other Indian languages and French and English, formerly used as a lingua franca in the Pacific Northwest.
chin·qua·pin (ching′kə pin′) *n.* **1.** a deciduous, shrubby North American tree, *Castanea pumila,* of the beech family, closely related to the chestnut. **2.** any of several evergreen shrubs or trees, genus *Castanopsis,* native to Asia and western North America. **3.** the edible nut of either of these trees. [Of Algonquian origin.]
chintz (chints) *n.* a cotton fabric, usually glazed and printed with a colorful pattern, used for such items as curtains and slipcovers. [Earlier *chints,* plural of *chint* used as singular, from Hindi *chīnt* spotted cotton cloth, from Sanskrit *chitra* spotted.]
chintz·y (chint′sē) *adj.,* **chintz·i·er, chintz·i·est.** *Informal.* cheap; tawdry.
chin-up (chin′up′) *n.* an act of chinning oneself: *to do twenty chin-ups.*
chip (chip) *n.* **1.** a small, usually thin, fragment that has been cut or broken off: *a wood chip.* **2.** a place where such a fragment has been cut or broken off: *a chip on the edge of a glass.* **3.** a small, usually thin, slice of food. **4.** *British.* a French fried potato. **5.** a disk or counter used to represent money in certain games, such as poker. **6.** a thin strip, as of wood or straw, used in weaving. **7.a.** the tiny slice of silicon on which an integrated circuit is formed. **b.** integrated circuit. Also, **microchip. 8.** *also,* **chips.** dried dung used for fuel. —*v.,* **chipped, chip·ping.** —*v.t.* **1.** to

cut or break off a fragment or fragments from: *to chip one's tooth.* **2.** to shape or produce by cutting off small fragments: *The stone-cutter chipped the name on the gravestone.* —*v.i.* to break off in small pieces. [Old English *cipp* log, piece cut off a log.]
• **a chip off the old block.** *Informal.* a child who resembles either parent.
• **a chip on one's shoulder.** *Informal.* a belligerent attitude or haughty manner.
• **in the chips.** *Informal.* having money; affluent.
• **to cash in one's chips. a.** in a gambling establishment, to exchange chips for money. **b.** *Slang.* to die.
• **to chip in.** to give one's share, as of money or help; contribute.
• **when the chips are down.** when the moment to act or decide has come; at the point of crisis.
Chip·e·wy·an (chip′ə wī′ən) *n., pl.* **-an** or **-ans. 1.** a member of a North American Indian tribe living in northwestern Canada. **2.** the Athapascan language spoken by this tribe.
chip·munk (chip′mungk′) *n.* any of various rodents of the squirrel family, native to North America and Asia, having brown or gray fur with black and white or buff stripes on the back and tail, round ears, large cheek pouches, and a slender, flattened tail. Length: 10 inches (25 centimeters), including tail. [Earlier *chitmunk,* from Ojibwa *acitamon* red squirrel; literally, headfirst, facedown; referring to its habit of climbing down trees headfirst.]
chipped beef, beef that is sliced thinly and smoked or dried, sometimes served with a cream sauce.
Chip·pen·dale (chip′ən dāl′) *adj.* designating a style of furniture characterized by elegance, intricate carving, and fine proportions. [From Thomas Chippendale, 1718?-79, English furniture designer.]
chip·per (chip′ər) *adj.* feeling or appearing lively and happy. [Possibly form of dialectal English *kipper* frisky, lively; of uncertain origin.]
Chip·pe·wa (chip′ə wä′, -wā′, -wə) *n., pl.* **-wa** or **-was.** Ojibwa.
chipping sparrow, a small sparrow, *Spizella passerina,* of eastern and central North America, having a reddish brown crown.
chiro- *combining form* hand: *chirography.* [From Greek *cheir* a hand.]
chi·rog·ra·phy (kī rog′rə fē) *n.* the art or an individual style of handwriting. [Greek *cheirographos* written with the hand (from *cheir* hand + *-graphos* written) + -Y³.] —**chi·rog′ra·pher,** *n.* —**chi·ro·graph·ic** (kī′rə graf′ik), *adj.*
Chi·ron (kī′ron) *n.* in Greek mythology, a wise centaur, skilled in the arts, medicine, and prophecy. He was the teacher of many Greek heroes, including Jason, Achilles, and Hercules.
chi·rop·o·dist (kə rop′ə dist, kī-, shə rop′-) *n.* podiatrist.
chi·rop·o·dy (kə rop′ə de, kī-, shə rop′-) *n.* podiatry.
chi·ro·prac·tic (kī′rə prak′tik) *n.* a system of manual and mechanical therapy based on the theory that disease results from interference with the normal functioning of the nervous system. Treatment includes massage and manipulation, esp. of the vertebrae, and the use of heat, water, electricity, and other forms of therapy. —*adj.* of, relating to, or involving chiropractic. [Greek *cheir* hand + *praktikos* concerned with action, effective, practical.] —**chi′ro·prac′tor,** *n.*
chi·rop·ter (kī rop′tər) *n.* any mammal of the order Chiroptera, consisting of the bats. [Greek *cheir* hand + *pteron* wing.]
chi·rop·ter·an (kī rop′tər ən) *n.* chiropter. —*adj.* of or relating to a chiropter.
chirp (chûrp) *v.i.* to make a short, sharp sound, as that made by small birds and certain insects. —*v.t.* to utter by or as by chirping. —*n.* a short, sharp sound, as that made by a bird or insect. [Imitative.] —**chirp′er,** *n.*
chirr (chûr) *also,* **churr.** *n.* a sharp, trilling sound, as that made by a grasshopper. —*v.i.* to make such a sound. [Imitative.]
chir·rup (chir′əp, chûr′-) *n.* a lively series of chirps. —*v.i.* to chirp continuously. [Imitative.]
chi·rur·geon (kī rûr′jən) *n. Archaic.* surgeon. [Old French *cirurgien.* See SURGEON.] —**chi·rur′ger·y,** *n.*
chis·el (chiz′əl) *n.* a metal tool with a sharp cutting edge at the end of a blade, used to shape stone, wood, or metal. —*v.,* **-eled, -el·ing;** *also, British,* **-elled, -el·ling.** —*v.t.* **1.** to cut or shape

Chippendale chair

a	at	e	end	o	hot	u	up	hw	white		about
ā	ape	ē	me	ō	old	ū	use	ng	song		taken
ä	far	i	it	ô	fork	ü	rule	th	thin	ə	pencil
âr	care	ī	ice	oi	oil	ů	pull	th	this		lemon
		î	pierce	ou	out	ûr	turn	zh	measure		circus

with or as with a chisel. **2.** *Slang.* **a.** to cheat; swindle: *They chiseled me out of ten dollars.* **b.** to obtain in such a way. —*v.i.* to work with a chisel. [Dialectal Old French *chisel* this tool, from Late Latin *cisellus* forceps; literally, cutting tool, from Latin *caesus,* past participle of *caedere* to cut.] —**chis'el·er;** also, *British,* **chis'el·ler,** *n.*

chi-square (kī'skwâr') *n.* a statistical measure of the discrepancy between an observed frequency distribution and a calculated one, represented by the symbol χ. The larger the value of χ, the greater the discrepancy is.

chit (chit) *n.* a pert young person, esp. a girl. [Probably a form of *kit*², short for KITTEN.]

chit·chat (chit'chat') *n.* **1.** light informal conversation. **2.** gossip. —*v.i.,* **-chat·ted, -chat·ting.** to converse informally. [Repetition of CHAT with vowel change.]

chi·tin (kī'tin) *n.* a horny substance forming the hard outer covering in insects, crustaceans, and arachnids. [French *chitine,* from Greek *chitōn* tunic, covering; of Semitic origin.] —**chi'tin·ous,** *adj.*

chi·ton (kī'tən, -ton) *n.* a tuniclike garment worn by men and women in ancient Greece. [Greek *chitōn;* of Semitic origin.]

chit·ter·lings (chit'linz) also, **chit·lings, chit·lins.** *pl. n.* the small intestines of pigs, prepared as food. [Of uncertain origin.]

chiv·al·ric (shiv'əl rik) *adj.* **1.** of or relating to chivalry. **2.** chivalrous.

chiv·al·rous (shiv'əl rəs) *adj.* **1.** having or exhibiting the qualities characteristic of chivalry, such as gallantry, honor, and courtesy. **2.** of or relating to chivalry. —**chiv'al·rous·ly,** *adv.* —**chiv'al·rous·ness,** *n.*

chiv·al·ry (shiv'əl rē) *n.* **1.** the qualities and conduct of an ideal knight, such as honor, courtesy, generosity, valor, respect for women, protection of the weak, and skill in battle. **2.** the feudal system that embodied these ideals and formed them into a code of behavior. **3.a.** a body of knights: *the chivalry of France.* **b.** gallant gentlemen collectively. [Old French *chevalerie* knighthood, from *chevalier* knight, warrior with a horse, from Late Latin *caballārius* horseman, from Latin *caballus* inferior horse, nag. See CAVALIER.]

chiv·a·ree (shiv'ə rē') shivaree.

chive (chīv) *n.* **1. chives.** the long, slender leaves of a plant, *Allium schoenoprasum,* related to the onion, used as a garnish or seasoning. **2.** the plant itself. For illustration, see **herb.** [Dialectal Old French *chive* this plant, from Latin *cēpa* onion.]

Ch. J., Chief Justice.

chla·myd·i·a (klə mid'ē ə) *n., pl.* **-myd·i·ae** (-mid'ē ē'). **1.** any of a genus, *Chlamydia,* of gram-negative bacteria that includes the causative agents of a sexually transmitted disease, psittacosis, and trachoma. **2.** the sexually transmitted disease caused by one species of these bacteria, the initial symptoms of which resemble those of gonorrhea. [Modern Latin *chlamydia,* from Greek *chlamydis,* genitive of *chlamys* a short mantle clasped at the shoulder worn by men in ancient Greece.] —**chla·myd'i·al,** *adj.*

chla·mys (klā'mis, klam'is) *n.* a short cloak, usually fastened over the shoulder, worn by men in ancient Greece. [Latin *chlamys,* from Greek *chlamys.*]

chlo·ral (klôr'əl) *n.* **1.** a colorless, oily liquid having a strong odor, used esp. in the manufacture of DDT. Formula: C_2Cl_3HO **2.** chloral hydrate.

chloral hydrate, a white, crystalline compound prepared from chlorine, ethyl alcohol, and water, used as a sedative. Formula: $C_2H_3Cl_3O_2$

chlor·am·phen·i·col (klôr'am fen'i kôl') *n.* Chloromycetin.

chlo·rate (klôr'āt) *n.* a salt of chloric acid.

chlor·dane (klôr'dān) *n.* also, **chlor·dan** (klôr'dan) a highly poisonous, oily chemical compound, formerly used as an insecticide. Formula: $C_{10}H_6Cl_8$

chlo·rel·la (klə rel'ə) *n.* any of a genus, *Chlorella,* of unicellular green algae, certain species of which are sources of vitamins and proteins.

chlo·ric (klôr'ik) *adj.* of, relating to, or containing chlorine, esp. in the pentavalent state.

chloric acid, a strong acid that reacts violently with organic compounds. It exists only in solution. Formula: $HClO_3$

chlo·ride (klôr'īd) *n.* a compound of chlorine with another element or radical, esp. a salt of hydrochloric acid.

chloride of lime, a white powder used as a bleaching agent and disinfectant, prepared by treating slaked lime with chlorine. Formula: $CaCl(ClO)$ Also, **bleaching powder, chlorinated lime.**

chlo·rin·ate (klôr'ə nāt') *v.t.,* **-at·ed, -at·ing.** to combine or treat with chlorine. —**chlo·rin·a'tion,** *n.*

chlo·rine (klôr'ēn, -in) *n.* a poisonous, greenish yellow gaseous element with an irritating, pungent odor. Chlorine and its compounds are used in bleaching and disinfecting. The most familiar chlorine compound is table salt, sodium chloride. Symbol: **Cl** For tables, see **element.** [Greek *chlōros* greenish yellow + -INE²; because of its color.]

chlo·rite¹ (klôr'īt) *n.* any of a group of common minerals, formed by alteration of magnesium and iron silicates, usually green in color with a vitreous to pearly luster and often occurring in clusters of thin, flexible scales. [Latin *chlōrītis* a green precious stone, from Greek *chlōrītis.*] —**chlo·rit·ic** (klō rit'ik), *adj.*

chlo·rite² (klôr'īt) *n.* a salt of chlorous acid. [Greek *chlōros* greenish yellow + -ITE².]

chlo·ro·fluor·o·car·bon (klôr'ō flùr'ō kär'bən, -flôr'-) *n.* any of a group of fluorocarbons containing both chlorine and fluorine, widely used as refrigerants. Their use as aerosol propellants has declined because they cause the depletion of ozone from the atmosphere's ozone layer.

chlo·ro·form (klôr'ə fôrm') *n.* a compound of carbon, hydrogen, and chlorine in the form of a colorless volatile liquid with a sweetish smell. Formerly used as an anesthetic, it is now used esp. to extract and purify antibiotics and to dissolve rubber, fats, and other substances. Formula: $CHCl_3$ —*v.t.* to administer chloroform to, as to render unconscious or to kill. [CHLOR(INE) + FORM(IC ACID); because it is able to form potassium *chloride* and *formic* acid.]

Chlo·ro·my·ce·tin (klôr'ə mī sē'tin) *n.* Trademark. chloramphenicol, an antibiotic drug that is very effective in the treatment of certain diseases, esp. typhoid fever, but must be used with care. Formula $C_{11}H_{12}Cl_2N_2O_5$ [Greek *chlōros* greenish yellow + *mykēs* fungus + -IN¹.]

chlo·ro·phyll (klôr'ə fil') also, **chlo·ro·phyl.** *n.* an organic compound of carbon, hydrogen, nitrogen, oxygen, and magnesium that is the green coloring matter of plants and is essential to photosynthesis, the process by which plants manufacture food materials. [French *chlorophylle,* from Greek *chlōros* greenish yellow + *phyllon* leaf.]

chlo·ro·plast (klôr'ə plast') *n.* any of the small chlorophyll-bearing bodies in the cells of plants and algae. [Greek *chlōros* greenish yellow + *plastos* formed.]

chlo·ro·prene (klôr'ə prēn') *n.* a colorless liquid used in making synthetic rubber. Formula: C_4H_5Cl

chlo·ro·quine (klôr'ə kwīn') *n.* a synthetic organic compound used in the treatment of malaria.

chlo·ro·sis (klô rō'sis) *n., pl.* **-ses** (-sēz). **1.** a yellowing or blanching in green plants due to a drop in chlorophyll levels caused by inadequate lighting, viral infection, or mineral deficiencies. **2.** an iron-deficiency anemia, most common in young women, characterized by a greenish skin color, weakness, and menstrual disorders. Also *(def. 2),* **greensickness.** —**chlo·rot·ic** (klô rot'ik), *adj.*

chlo·rous (klôr'əs) *adj.* of, relating to, or containing trivalent chlorine.

chlor·prom·a·zine (klôr prom'ə zēn', -prō'mə-) *n.* a synthetic drug used as a tranquilizer in the treatment of psychosis and to control nausea and vomiting. Formula: $C_{17}H_{19}ClN_2S$

chlor·tet·ra·cy·cline (klôr'tet rə sī'klin) *n.* Aureomycin.

chm. also, **chmn.** chairman.

chock (chok) *n.* **1.** a block or wedge put under or in front of something to keep it from moving, as in front of the wheels of an airplane on the ground. **2.** a metal fitting, as on a boat or ship, having projections at both ends that are curved toward the center and through which cable or rope may pass. —*v.t.* to furnish or secure with a chock or chocks. [Dialectal Old French *chouque* log; possibly of Celtic origin.]

chock·a·block (chok'ə blok') *adj.* **1.** (of a boat or ship's tackle) having the blocks pulled together very tightly. **2.** very crowded; crammed: *The shop was chockablock with furniture.*

chock-full (chok'fùl') also, **chuck-full.** *adj.* as full as can be; crammed.

choc·o·late (chô'kə lit, chok'ə-, chôk'lit, chok'-) *n.* **1.** a food product prepared from ground and roasted cacao beans that still retain the fat. **2.** a beverage made by dissolving chocolate or cocoa in hot milk or water and adding sugar. **3.** a candy made of or coated with chocolate: *a box of chocolates.* **4.** a dark brown color. —*adj.* **1.** made of or flavored with chocolate. **2.** having the color chocolate. [Spanish *chocolate,* from Nahuatl *chocolatl* food made from cacao seeds.]

Choc·taw (chok'tô) *n., pl.* **-taw** or **-taws. 1.** a member of a Muskogean tribe of North American Indians, formerly living in parts of what are now Mississippi, Alabama, and Louisiana, now living in Oklahoma. **2.** the Muskogean language spoken by these

people. [Possibly modification of Spanish *chato* flat, going back to Greek *platys;* with reference to the Choctaw practice of flattening the head.]

choice (chois) *n.* **1.** an act or an instance of choosing: *It was a wise choice.* **2.** the power or an opportunity to choose: *We were given a choice between the two movies.* **3.** a person or thing that is chosen. **4.** a variety from which to choose: *a menu with a wide choice of dishes.* **5.** an alternative: *Our only choice was to go.* **6.** the most preferable part of something; select portion. —*adj.,* **choic·er, choic·est. 1.** worthy of being chosen; select; excellent: *a choice spot for a picnic.* **2.** carefully selected: *The artist exhibited a few choice works.* **3.** indicating a U.S. government grade of meat less tender than prime. [Old French *chois* act of choosing, preference, from *choisir* to choose; of Germanic origin.] —**choice′ly,** *adv.* —**choice′ness,** *n.*

> **Synonyms** *n.* **Choice, alternative,** and **option** mean the power or an opportunity to choose. **Choice** is the broadest of these terms, often implying no limitation on the method of selecting or the possibilities: *a choice of anything on the menu.* **Alternative** literally means a choice between two: *the alternative of a shared room or a slightly more expensive single.* In common usage, however, it has come to refer to a choice among a few or several: *The governor had to decide among half a dozen alternatives for balancing the budget.* **Option** stresses that the power to choose is specifically given: *This plan offers employees the option of three different kinds of coverage.*

choir (kwīr) *n.* **1.** an organized group of singers, esp. one used in a religious service. **2.** that part of a church set apart for the use of such singers. **3.** an organized company or collection, esp. of a particular group of instruments: *a brass choir.* [Old French *cuer* group of singers, the choir of a church, from Latin *chorus* band of singers and dancers, from Greek *choros.* Doublet of CHORUS.]

choir·boy (kwīr′boi′) *n.* a boy who is a member of and sings in a choir.

choir·girl (kwīr′gûrl′) *n.* a girl who is a member of and sings in a choir.

choir·mas·ter (kwīr′mas′tər) *n.* the leader or director of a choir.

choke (chōk) *v.,* **choked, chok·ing.** —*v.t.* **1.** to prevent or hinder the breathing of by or as by squeezing the throat or blocking the windpipe. **2.a.** to obstruct by or as by filling; block; clog: *Dirt choked the drain.* **b.** to fill completely. **3.** to check the growth, progress, or action of: *to choke a fire with water.* **4.** to regulate the amount of air that enters the carburetor in order to enrich the fuel mixture of (an internal combustion engine). —*v.i.* **1.** to be prevented or hindered from breathing: *to choke on a bone.* **2.** to become obstructed, blocked, or clogged. —*n.* **1.** the act or sound of choking. **2.** a valve that regulates the amount of air that enters the carburetor of an internal combustion engine. **3.** choke coil. [Possibly short for obsolete *achoke* to suffocate, from Old English *ācēocian.*]

· **to choke back.** to repress, as a feeling; stifle.
· **to choke off.** to put a stop to; end: *to choke off further discussion.*
· **to choke up. a.** to become speechless, as from sorrow or anger. **b.** to give a poor performance because of tension or nervousness.
· **to choke up on.** to grip (a baseball bat) nearer the striking surface.

choke·bore (chōk′bôr′) *n.* **1.** a bore of a shotgun that is made to narrow toward the muzzle in order to limit the scattering of the shot and to gain longer range. **2.** a shotgun with such a bore.

choke·cher·ry (chōk′cher′ē) *n., pl.* **-ries. 1.** the bitter edible cherrylike fruit of a shrub, genus *Aronia,* of the rose family, used to make jams and jellies. **2.** the shrub itself.

choke coil, a coil of wire that allows direct current to flow while limiting the flow of alternating current.

choke·damp (chōk′damp′) *n.* blackdamp.

chok·er (chō′kər) *n.* **1.** a person or thing that chokes. **2.** a necklace fitting tightly around the throat.

chol·er (kol′ər) *n.* irritability or anger. [Old French *colere,* going back to Greek *cholerā* cholera, from *cholē* bile, the humor thought to cause anger. See HUMOR.]

chol·er·a (kol′ər ə) *n.* an infectious disease of the intestines, characterized by severe vomiting and diarrhea. Also, **Asiatic cholera.** [Latin *cholera* bile, cholera, from Greek *cholerā* cholera, from *cholē* bile.]

chol·er·ic (kol′ər ik) *adj.* **1.** easily irritated or angered; irascible. **2.** indicating or expressing anger: *a choleric speech.* [Old French *coleric* bad-humored, having a surplus of choler. See CHOLER.]

cho·les·ter·ol (kə les′tə rôl′, -rōl′) *n.* a fatty material present in all body tissues, required for the digestion of fats, the production of certain hormones, and the manufacture of vitamin D. Some

authorities believe that the presence of large amounts of this substance in the blood increases the possibility of hardening of the arteries. Formula: $C_{27}H_{45}OH$ [Greek *cholē* bile, gall[1] + *stereos* solid + -OL; referring to its originally having been found in gallstones.]

cho·line (kō′lēn) *n.* a vitamin of the vitamin B complex that is widely distributed in plants and animals and is essential for the metabolism of fats in the body. Formula: $C_5H_{15}NO_2$

cho·lin·er·gic (kō′lə nûr′jik) *adj.* of, producing, or activated by acetylcholine or a similar substance, as certain kinds of nerve fibers. ➡ distinguished from **adrenergic.**

cho·lin·es·ter·ase (kō′lə nes′tə rās′) *n.* an enzyme that catalyzes the reaction in which acetylcholine is broken down into choline and acetic acid, thereby terminating nerve impulses across synapses, used in treating myasthenia gravis. [CHOLIN(E) + ESTERASE.]

chol·la (choi′ə) *n.* any of several usually treelike North American cacti, genus *Opuntia,* having cylindrical stems. [Mexican Spanish *cholla,* from Spanish *cholla* literally, skull, head.]

chomp (chomp) *v.i., v.t. Informal.* to bite or chew noisily. —*n.* the act of chomping.

choose (chüz) *v.,* **chose, cho·sen, choos·ing.** —*v.t.* **1.** to select, esp. by preference, from all that are available: *I chose the largest apples.* **2.** to prefer and decide; think fit (to do something): *We chose to leave the party early.* —*v.i.* **1.** to make a choice: *choose carefully.* **2.** to think fit: *You can go if you choose.* [Old English *cēosan* to select.] —**choos′er,** *n.*

> **Synonyms** *v.t.* **Choose, select,** and **pick** mean to decide what one wants from among two or more possibilities. **Choose** implies taking time or giving thought to the possibilities: *After much discussion we chose yellow paint for the house.* **Select,** a more formal word, is close to *choose* but suggests a more important decision or a larger number of possibilities: *to select a candidate for office, to select a site for a factory.* **Pick,** a less formal word, suggests a less important decision, often based on personal taste rather than careful consideration: *The teacher asked the children to pick their favorite character in the story.*

choos·y (chü′zē) also, **choos·ey.** *adj.,* **choos·i·er, choos·i·est.** *Informal.* inclined to be selective; fussy.

chop¹ (chop) *v.,* **chopped, chop·ping.** —*v.t.* **1.a.** to cut or sever by a quick blow or blows with a sharp instrument, such as an ax: *to chop a tree down.* **b.** to make or form in this way: *The firefighters chopped a hole in the wall.* **2.** to cut into pieces: *to chop onions.* **3.** to shorten in length or duration: *The reporter chopped the story by three paragraphs.* **4.** to hit (a ball) with a short, quick, downward stroke, as in tennis. —*v.i.* to make cutting strokes: *to chop at a ball.* —*n.* **1.** the act of chopping. **2.** a short, quick, downward stroke: *to give a chop to a ball.* **3.** a small cut of meat, as of lamb, pork, or veal, usually including a piece of the rib. **4.** the short, irregular motions of a wave or waves: *There is a chop today that makes swimming difficult.* [Form of CHAP¹.]

chop² (chop) *v.i.,* **chopped, chop·ping.** to change or shift suddenly, as the wind. [Form of obsolete *chap* to exchange, change constantly, from Old English *cēapian* to bargain, trade, from *cēap* bargain, price, trade, going back to Latin *caupō* tradesperson.]

chop·fall·en (chop′fô′lən) chapfallen.

chop·house (chop′hous′) *n., pl.* **-hous·es** (-hou′ziz). a restaurant that specializes in chops and steaks.

cho·pine (chō pēn′, chop′in) *n.* a woman's shoe popular in the sixteenth and seventeenth centuries, having a high, thick platform that served as both a heel and sole. [Middle French *chappin,* from Spanish *chapín* shoe with high cork sole, from *chapa* leather or metal covering; of uncertain origin.]

chop·per (chop′ər) *n.* **1.** a person or thing that chops. **2.** *Slang.* helicopter. **3.** choppers. *Slang.* teeth, esp. false teeth.

chop·py¹ (chop′ē) *adj.,* **-pi·er, -pi·est. 1.** rough with short, irregular, broken waves: *a choppy sea.* **2.** not continuous; jerky; broken: *The dancer's movements were very choppy.* [CHOP¹ + -Y¹.] —**chop′pi·ly,** *adv.* —**chop′pi·ness,** *n.*

chopine

a	at	e	end	o	hot	u	up	hw	white	⎧	about
ā	ape	ē	me	ō	old	ū	use	ng	song	⎨	taken
ä	far	i	it	ô	fork	ū	rule	th	thin	⎬	pencil
âr	care	ī	ice	oi	oil	u̇	pull	th	this	⎨	lemon
		îr	pierce	ou	out	ûr	turn	zh	measure	⎩	circus

chop·py² (chop′ē) *adj.,* **-pi·er, -pi·est.** changing or shifting suddenly, as the wind. [CHOP² + -Y¹.]

chops (chops) *pl. n.* **1.** the jaw or cheek. **2.** mouth. [Of uncertain origin.]

chop·sticks (chop′stiks′) *pl. n.* a pair of eating utensils of a kind first developed in China, consisting of long, slender sticks, usually wood or ivory, that are held between the thumb and fingers. [Pidgin English *chop* quick + STICK¹, translation of Chinese (Mandarin) *k′uai tze* chopsticks; literally, quick ones.]

chop su·ey (chop′ sü′ē) a dish of Chinese-American origin consisting of vegetables, such as bamboo shoots, mushrooms, and onions, cooked with small pieces of meat, fish, or chicken, usually served with rice. [Chinese (Cantonese) *shap sui* odds and ends.]

cho·ral (*adj.,* kôr′əl; *n.,* kə ral′, kô–, kôr′əl) *adj.* **1.** of or relating to a choir or chorus. **2.** performed by or written for a choir or chorus. —*n.* chorale. —**cho′ral·ly,** *adv.*

cho·rale (kə ral′, -räl′, kôr′əl) *also,* **choral.** *n.* **1.** a hymn having a plain melody and stately rhythm, usually sung in unison. **2.** a musical composition based on such a hymn: *a Bach chorale.* **3.** a group of people singing such music; chorus.

chord¹ (kôrd) *n.* a combination of three or more musical tones or notes sounded simultaneously to produce harmony. —*v.i.* to play chords, as on a piano or guitar in accompanying another instrument or a singer. [Earlier *cord,* short for ACCORD.] —**chord′al,** *adj.*

chord² (kôrd) *n.* **1.** a line segment joining any two points on a curve. **2.** a feeling: *to strike a chord of compassion.* **3.** the top or bottom member of a truss, as on a bridge. **4.** *Archaic.* a string of a musical instrument. [Latin *chorda* gut, string of a musical instrument, from Greek *chordē.* Doublet of CORD.]

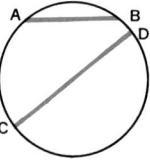

chord²
AB and *CD* are chords

chor·date (kôr′dāt) *n.* any animal of the phylum Chordata, which includes all animals with backbones as well as those with notochords. [Modern Latin *Chordata,* from Latin *chorda.* See CHORD².]

chore (chôr) *n.* **1.** a small or minor job: *I had several chores to do before noon.* **2. chores.** routine duties, esp. those of a domestic nature: *household chores.* **3.** a difficult or unpleasant task: *It's a real chore to mow this lawn.* [Form of CHAR².] —For Synonyms, see **job.**

cho·re·a (kôr′ē ə) *n.* any of a number of diseases affecting the central nervous system, causing involuntary and uncontrollable twitching of the muscles. [Modern Latin *chorea (Sancti Viti)* dance (of Saint Vitus), from Greek *choreiā* dance.]

cho·re·o·graph (kôr′ē ə graf′) *v.t., v.i.* **1.** to create, arrange, or direct (dance movement), as for ballet or modern dance. **2.** to arrange the details of (something). —**cho·re·og·ra·pher** (kôr′ē og′rə fər), *n.*

cho·re·og·ra·phy (kôr′ē og′rə fē) *n.* **1.** the art of creating, arranging, or directing dance movement, as for ballet or modern dance. **2.** the representation of dance movement through a system of notation. **3.** dancing. [Greek *choreiā* dance + -GRAPHY.]

cho·ric (kôr′ik) *adj.* of, relating to, or suitable for the chorus, esp. in ancient Greek drama.

cho·ri·on (kôr′ē on′) *n.* **1.** the membrane that encloses the amnion, surrounding the embryo of reptiles, birds, and mammals. In mammals, its villi penetrate the uterus to take in nutrients for the fetus. **2.** the outer membrane or shell of the eggs of certain invertebrates, esp. insects. [Modern Latin *chorion,* from Greek membrane surrounding the fetus.] —**cho′ri·on·ic,** *adj.*

chor·is·ter (kôr′ə stər) *n.* **1.** a person who sings in a choir. **2.** a choirboy or choirgirl. **3.** a person who leads a choir. [Medieval Latin *chorista* singer in a choir (from Latin *chorus* band of singers and dancers) + -ER¹. See CHOIR.]

cho·roid (kôr′oid) *n.* the membrane forming the middle coat of the eyeball, lying between the sclera and the retina, and joined to the iris by the ciliary body in the front of the eye. Also, **choroid coat.** —*adj.* of or relating to the choroid. [Greek *choroeidēs* like a membrane, from *chorion* membrane.]

chor·tle (chôr′təl) *v.t., v.i.,* **-tled, -tling.** to utter or utter with a low, sonorous chuckle. —*n.* such a chuckle. [Blend of CHUCKLE and SNORT, coined by the English author Lewis Carroll, 1832-98.] —**chor′tler,** *n.*

cho·rus (kôr′əs) *n., pl.* **-rus·es. 1.** a large, organized group of people who sing together. **2.** a group of people who sing, dance, and often play minor parts, as in a musical comedy. **3.** a vocal composition, usually written for four or more parts, to be sung by a large group. **4.** a recurring refrain, esp. of a song. **5.** a group of people who recite or speak simultaneously. **6.** a simultaneous

utterance by a group of people: *There was a chorus of loud laughter from the next room.* **7.** in ancient Greek drama, a group of actors who comment upon and often take part in the main action. **8.** in Elizabethan drama, a single actor who recites the prologue and epilogue and explains or comments upon the action. —*v.t., v.i.,* **-rused, -rus·ing.** to sing or speak simultaneously. [Latin *chorus* band of singers and dancers, dance in a ring, from Greek *choros.* Doublet of CHOIR.]

 • **in chorus.** in unison; simultaneously.

chorus girl, a woman or girl who sings and often dances in the chorus of a musical show.

chose (chōz) *v.* the past tense of **choose.**

cho·sen (chō′zən) *v.* the past participle of **choose.** —*adj.* **1.** taken by preference; select. **2.** in some religions, selected for salvation by God.

chough (chuf) *n.* a glossy, blue-black bird, genus *Pyrrhocorax* of the crow family, native to Europe. It has red feet and a red or yellow beak. [Middle English *choughe* crow.]

chow¹ (chou) *n. Slang.* food. [Possibly from Pekingese *chiao* meat-filled dumpling.]

chow²

chow² (chou) *n.* a dog of a breed originally developed in China, having a compact body, large head, thick, usually brown or black coat, and a bluish black tongue. Height: 20 inches (51 centimeters) at the shoulder. Also, **chow chow.** [From a word in a Chinese dialect akin to Cantonese *kaú* dog.]

chow-chow (chou′chou′) *n.* **1.** a relish of mixed chopped vegetables, esp. pickles, cooked in a highly spiced mustard sauce. **2.** a Chinese dish of mixed fruits preserved in a rich syrup. [Possibly from pidgin English *chow-chow* literally, mixed; of uncertain origin.]

chow·der (chou′dər) *n.* a thick soup usually made of fish or shellfish, esp. clams, with vegetables and, sometimes, milk. [French *chaudière* pot (from Late Latin *caldāria* pot for boiling, going back to Latin *calidus* hot); from the phrase *faire la chaudière* to contribute to a community pot in which a dish of fish and biscuits is prepared.]

chow mein (chou′ mān′, shou′) a dish of Chinese-American origin made of shredded fish or meat and vegetables, as celery, onions, and bean sprouts, usually served with rice and fried noodles. [Pekingese *ch'ao mien* fried dough.]

Chr., Christian.

chres·tom·a·thy (kres tom′ə thē) *n., pl.* **-thies.** a collection of choice literary passages, used esp. as an aid in learning a foreign language. [Greek *chrēstomatheia* desire of learning, book of choice passages.]

chrism (kriz′əm) *n.* consecrated oil, used by some churches in certain sacred rites, as baptism and confirmation. [Old English *crisma,* from Late Latin *chrīsma,* from Greek *chrīsma* unguent.] —**chris·mal** (kriz′məl), *adj.*

Christ (krīst) *n.* the title given Jesus of Nazareth by his followers. [Old English *Crīst,* from Latin *Chrīstus,* from Greek *Chrīstos* literally, anointed, translation of Hebrew *māshīah* anointed, Messiah.]

chris·ten (kris′ən) *v.t.* **1.** to receive into a Christian church by baptism; baptize. **2.** to give a name to at baptism. **3.** to give a name to, as a ship. **4.** *Informal.* to use for the first time. [Old English *cristnian* to make Christian, from *crīsten* Christian, from Latin *Chrīstiānus,* from Greek *Chrīstiānos,* from *Chrīstos.* See CHRIST.]

Chris·ten·dom (kris′ən dəm) *n.* **1.** the countries of the world, collectively, in which Christianity is the predominant religion. **2.** Christians collectively. [Old English *cristendom,* from *cristen* Christian + *dōm* authority, dominion. See CHRISTEN.]

chris·ten·ing (kris′ə ning, kris′ning) *n.* **1.** the act or ceremony of baptizing and naming an infant; baptism. **2.** a public ceremony at which something is formally given a name or used for the first time.

Chris·tian (kris′chən) *n.* **1.a.** a person who believes in and follows the teachings of Jesus. **b.** a member of the religion based on those teachings. **2.** *Informal.* a decent, respectable, or civilized person. —*adj.* **1.** of or relating to Jesus or his teachings. **2.** believing in the divine nature of Jesus and following his teachings or belonging to the religion based on them. **3.** of or relating to Christians or Christianity. **4.** showing character and conduct consistent with discipleship to Jesus, such as love and kindness. **5.** *Informal.* decent, respectable, or civilized.

Christian Church, a Protestant denomination founded in the United States in the early nineteenth century. Also, **Disciples of Christ.**

Christian Era, the era reckoned from the date formerly thought to be that of the birth of Jesus. Dates in this era are denoted A.D., those before it, B.C.

Chris·ti·an·i·ty (kris'chē an'i tē) *n.* **1.** the religion based on the teachings of Jesus; Christian religion. **2.** Christians collectively; Christendom.

Chris·tian·ize (kris'chə nīz') *v.t.,* **-ized, -iz·ing. 1.** to convert to Christianity. **2.** to imbue with Christian principles. —**Chris'·tian·i·za'tion,** *n.* —**Chris'tian·iz'er,** *n.*

Christian name, the name or names given at baptism; first name.

Christian Science, a religion founded by Mary Baker Eddy in 1866 that stresses the use of spiritual means to heal sickness. —**Christian Scientist.**

Christ·like (krīst'līk') *adj.* exhibiting the spirit of Jesus; like Jesus.

Christ·mas (kris'məs) *n.* the yearly celebration commemorating the birth of Jesus, observed on December 25. Also, **Christmas Day.** [Old English *Cristes mæsse* Christ's Mass. See CHRIST, MASS.]

Christmas Eve, the day and evening before Christmas.

Christ·mas·tide (kris'məs tīd') *n.* the season of Christmas.

Christmas tree, a tree, esp. an evergreen, decorated at Christmas time.

chro·ma (krō'mə) *n.* saturation *(def. 3).* [Greek *chrōma* color; originally, skin, color of the skin.]

chro·mate (krō'māt) *n.* a salt of chromic acid.

chro·mat·ic (krō mat'ik, krə-) *adj.* **1.** of, relating to, or containing color or colors. **2.** of, relating to, or designating the use of all the notes of the chromatic scale. ➡ distinguished from **diatonic.** [Greek *chrōmatikos,* from *chrōma* color, chromatic scale.] —**chro·mat'i·cal·ly,** *adv.*

chromatic aberration, the failure of a lens to focus light rays of different colors so that they meet at a common point, a defect resulting in formation of an image with colored fringes.

chro·mat·ics (krō mat'iks, krə-) *n.* the science of colors. ➡ used as singular.

chromatic scale, a twelve-tone musical scale progressing entirely by half tones. ➡ distinguished from **diatonic scale.**

chro·ma·tid (krō'mə tid) *n.* either of two strands of a replicated chromosome, formed during the early stages of cell division. [Greek *chrōmat-,* stem of *chrōma* color + -ID².]

chro·ma·tin (krō'mə tin) *n.* a material in the cell nucleus, made up of RNA, DNA, and protein, that forms chromosomes during cell division. [Greek *chrōmat-,* stem of *chrōma* color + -IN¹.]

chro·mat·o·gram (krō mat'ə gram') *n.* a visual record of a chemical separation produced by chromatography.

chro·ma·tog·ra·phy (krō'mə tog'rə fē) *n.* a process for separating mixtures of related chemical compounds by selective absorption. —**chro·mat·o·graph·ic** (krō mat'ə graf'ik, krō'mə tə-), *adj.*

chro·ma·to·phore (krō mat'ə fôr', krō'mə tə-) *n.* **1.** *Zoology.* a specialized cell, found usually in the skin of lower vertebrates and cephalopods, containing granules of pigment and often capable of contraction and expansion, thereby allowing the animal to change its color to match its surroundings. **2.** *Botany.* any of the pigmented plastids in a plant cell, as a chromoplast or a chloroplast. [Greek *chrōmat-,* stem of *chrōma* color + -*phoros* bearing (from *pherein* to bear).]

chrome (krōm) *n.* **1.** chromium. **2.** chrome yellow. [French *chrome* chromium, from Greek *chrōma* color; from the striking colors of its compounds.]

chrome steel, a tough steel alloy containing chromium. Also, **chromium steel.**

chrome yellow, any of various shades of yellow pigment, ranging from lemon to deep orange and composed of lead chromate.

chro·mic (krō'mik) *adj.* of, relating to, or containing chromium.

chromic acid, an acid that exists only in solution or in the form of chromate salts. Formula: H_2CrO_4

chro·mite (krō'mīt) *n.* a mineral, chromic iron oxide, the chief source of chromium. Formula: $FeCr_2O_4$

chro·mi·um (krō'mē əm) *n.* a hard, brittle, silver-white metallic element that does not tarnish in air. It is used for electroplating and in many alloys to provide strength as well as resistance to corrosion and heat. Symbol: **Cr** For tables, see **element.** [Mod-

ern Latin *chromium,* from Greek *chrōma* color; from the striking colors of its compounds.]

chromium steel, chrome steel.

chro·mo (krō'mō) *n., pl.* **-mos.** chromolithograph.

chro·mo·lith·o·graph (krō'mō lith'ə graf') *n.* a color print produced from a series of metal plates or specially prepared stones. [Greek *chrōma* color + LITHOGRAPH.]

chro·mo·phore (krō'mə fôr') *n.* a chemical group that can absorb light of a particular wavelength, thereby imparting color to a compound, esp. as in a dyestuff.

chro·mo·plast (krō'mə plast') *n. Botany.* a specialized plastid containing pigments other than chlorophyll, usually yellow, red, or orange carotenoids.

chro·mo·some (krō'mə sōm') *n.* a tiny threadlike body in the nuclei of plant and animal cells, composed chiefly of proteins and DNA. Chromosomes carry the genes that determine sex, size, color, and many other characteristics. [Greek *chrōma* color + *sōma* body.] —**chro'mo·so'mal,** *adj.*

chro·mo·sphere (krō'mə sfîr') *n.* **1.** a thick layer of gas, consisting largely of hydrogen, helium, and calcium, that surrounds the photosphere of the sun. For illustration, see **sun. 2.** a similar gaseous layer around any star. [Greek *chrōma* color + SPHERE.]

chron. 1. chronological. **2.** chronology.

Chron., Chronicles.

chron·ic (kron'ik) *adj.* **1.** (of an illness) lasting a long time or recurring: *chronic bronchitis.* ➡ distinguished from **acute. 2.** done or doing by habit; habitual; constant: *a chronic complainer.* **3.** having had an illness or habit for a long time: *a chronic invalid.* [Latin *chronicus* relating to time, from Greek *chronikos,* from *chronos* time.] —**chron'i·cal·ly,** *adv.*

chron·i·cle (kron'i kəl) *n.* a detailed and continuous register of events in order of time or occurrence; history. —*v.t.,* **-cled, -cling.** to record in or as in a chronicle. [Anglo-Norman *chronicle* annals, from Medieval Latin *chronica,* from Greek *chronika,* going back to *chronos* time.] —**chron'i·cler,** *n.*

Chron·i·cles (kron'i kəlz) *n.* either of two books, I Chronicles and II Chronicles, of the Old Testament. ➡ used as singular.

chron·o·graph (kron'ə graf') *n.* **1.** an instrument that measures time intervals, esp. the duration of astronomical events and other natural occurrences, and records them, usually by means of a stylus on a graph carried by a rotating drum. **2.** stopwatch. [Greek *chronos* time + -GRAPH.]

chron·o·log·i·cal (kron'ə loj'i kəl) *adj.* **1.** arranged according to the order of time or occurrence. **2.** relating to or containing chronology. Also, **chron'o·log'ic.** —**chron'o·log'i·cal·ly,** *adv.*

chro·nol·o·gy (krə nol'ə jē) *n., pl.* **-gies. 1.** the arrangement of events according to the order of time or occurrence. **2.** a table or list arranged in this way. **3.** the science of computing periods of time and of arranging and recording the dates and historical order of past events. [Greek *chronos* time + -LOGY.] —**chro·nol'o·ger, chro·nol'o·gist,** *n.*

chro·nom·e·ter (krə nom'i tər) *n.* a clock, specially designed for keeping time at sea, set on Greenwich Time and used to determine longitude. [Greek *chronos* time + -METER.]

chron·o·met·ric (kron'ə met'rik) *adj.* of or relating to a chronometer or chronometry.

chro·nom·e·try (krə nom'i trē) *n.* the science or technology of the accurate and precise measurement of time. [Greek *chronos* time + -METRY.]

chron·o·scope (kron'ə skōp') *n.* an instrument that measures short time intervals. [Greek *chronos* time + -SCOPE.]

chrys·a·lid (kris'ə lid) *n., pl.* **chrys·al·i·des** (kri sal'i dēz'). chrysalis. —*adj.* of or relating to a chrysalis.

chrys·a·lis (kris'ə lis) *n., pl.* **-lis·es. 1.** the pupal stage during which a butterfly or moth undergoes structural changes while enclosed in a cocoon and before emerging as a winged adult. **2.** cocoon. **3.** anything in a stage of development or transition. [Latin *chrȳsallis* gold-colored pupa of the butterfly, from Greek *chrȳsallis,* from *chrȳsos* gold; of Semitic origin.]

chry·san·the·mum (kri san'thə məm) *n.* **1.** the globe-shaped or daisylike flower head of any of a large group of plants, genus *Chrysanthemum,* of the composite family, growing in many colors. **2.** the leafy plant bearing this flower head, widely cultivated as a

a	at	e	end	o	hot	u	up	hw	white		about
ā	ape	ē	me	ō	old	ū	use	ng	song		taken
ä	far	i	it	ô	fork	ü	rule	th	thin	ə	pencil
âr	care	ī	ice	oi	oil	ủ	pull	th	this		lemon
		îr	pierce	ou	out	ûr	turn	zh	measure		circus

213

chrysanthemums

garden plant. [Latin *chrȳsanthemum* marigold, from Greek *chrȳ-santhemon*, from *chrȳsos* gold (of Semitic origin) + *anthemon* flower.]

Chry·se·is (krī sē′is) *n.* in Greek legend, a beautiful young woman captured by the Greeks in a raid near Troy. The Greeks held her captive until Apollo, in answer to her father's prayers, sent a plague upon their camp.

chrys·o·ber·yl (kris′ə ber′əl) *n.* a green or yellow beryllium mineral sometimes used as a gem. Formula: $BeAl_2O_4$ [Latin *chrȳsobēryllus*, from Greek *chrȳsobēryllos* gold-colored beryl, from *chrȳsos* gold (of Semitic origin) + *bēryllos* beryl. See BERYL.]

chrys·o·lite (kris′ə līt′) *n.* a semiprecious variety of olivine. [Old French *crisolite*, from Latin *chrȳsolithus* topaz, from Greek *chrȳsolithos*, from *chrȳsos* gold (of Semitic origin) + *lithos* stone.]

chrys·o·prase (kris′ə prāz′) *n.* a semiprecious apple-green variety of chalcedony. [Latin *chrȳsoprasos* golden-green gem, from Greek *chrȳsoprasos*, from Greek *chrȳsos* gold (of Semitic origin) + *prason* leek.]

chrys·o·tile (kris′ə təl, -tīl′) *n.* a light green or yellow fibrous variety of the mineral serpentine. It is the principal type of asbestos. [Greek *chrȳsos* gold (of Semitic origin) + *tilos* something plucked (as fiber).]

chub (chub) *n., pl.* **chubs** or **chub.** any of several freshwater and saltwater fish, as the **freshwater chub,** or minnow, of the order Cypriniformes, and the **Bermuda chub,** order Perciformes. [Of uncertain origin.]

chub·by (chub′ē) *adj.,* **-bi·er, -bi·est.** round and plump. —**chub′bi·ness,** *n.*

chuck[1] (chuk) *n.* **1.** a gentle or playful pat or tap, esp. under the chin. **2.** a throw; toss. —*v.t.* **1.** to pat or tap gently or playfully, esp. under the chin. **2.** to throw; toss; pitch: *Chuck the ball here.* **3.** *Informal.* to throw away; discard: *We chucked the leftovers.* **4.** *Informal.* to give up; abandon: *I chucked the idea of going skiing this weekend.* [Possibly from Old French *choquer* to knock; of uncertain origin.]

chuck[2] (chuk) *n.* **1.** a device for holding a piece of work or a tool in a machine, as in a lathe or drilling machine. **2.** a cut of beef including parts between the neck and the shoulder blade and first three ribs. [Form of CHOCK.]

chuck-full (chuk′fûl′) chock-full.

chuck·le (chuk′əl) *v.i.,* **-led, -ling.** to laugh in a soft manner, esp. to oneself, as in expressing mild amusement or satisfaction. —*n.* a soft laugh, as expressive of mild amusement or satisfaction. [Imitative.] —**chuck′ler,** *n.*

chuck·le·head (chuk′əl hed′) *n. Informal.* a stupid person.

chuck wagon, a wagon that carries cooking equipment and provisions, as for lumbering or harvesting crews, esp. in the western United States.

chuck·wal·la (chuk′wä′lə) *n.* a lizard, genus *Sauromalus,* related to the iguana, found in the southwestern United States and northwestern Mexico. When frightened it can inflate its lungs, increasing its size by more than half. Length: to 16 inches (41 centimeters). [Modification of Spanish *chacahuala;* of Shoshonean origin.]

chuck of a drill

chug (chug) *n.* a short, dull, explosive sound, as that made by the exhaust of an engine. —*v.i.,* **chugged, chug·ging.** to move with or make such sounds: *The old car chugged along.* [Imitative.]

chuk·ker (chuk′ər) *also,* **chuk·kar.** *n.* any of the eight periods

of play in polo, lasting $7\frac{1}{2}$ minutes each. [Hindi *chakar* a period (of play), from Sanskrit *cakrāh* wheel, circle.]

chum[1] (chum) *n.* a close friend. —*v.i.,* **chummed, chum·ming.** to be close friends. [Probably from earlier *cham,* shortening of *chamber fellow, chamber mate.*]

chum[2] (chum) *n.* pieces of fish or other meat thrown in the water as bait for fish. —*v.i.,* **chummed, chum·ming.** to use chum to attract fish: *to chum for sharks.* [Possibly from Scottish *chum* food.]

chum·my (chum′ē) *adj.,* **-mi·er, -mi·est.** *Informal.* like a chum or chums; friendly; intimate. —**chum′mi·ly,** *adv.* —**chum′mi·ness,** *n.*

chump (chump) *n.* **1.** *Informal.* a person who is easily fooled or deceived; dupe. **2.** a short, heavy chunk of wood. [Possibly blend of CHUNK and LUMP[1].]

chunk (chungk) *n. Informal.* **1.** a thick piece or lump, as of wood, bread, or cheese. **2.** an amount; quantity: *A large chunk of their income was spent on entertainment.* **3.** a solidly built person, esp. a man. [Form of CHUCK[2].]

chunk·y (chung′kē) *adj.,* **chunk·i·er, chunk·i·est.** *Informal.* **1.** solidly built; stocky. **2.** like a chunk. **3.** containing chunks. —**chunk′i·ly,** *adv.* —**chunk′i·ness,** *n.*

church (chûrch) *n.* **1.** a building for public worship, esp. that of a Christian denomination. **2.** public worship; religious services: *to go to church every Sunday.* **3.** Christians collectively. **4.** *also,* **Church.** a particular group of Christians united by similar doctrines, beliefs, and disciplines; denomination. **5.** a locally organized congregation of Christians. **6.** ecclesiastical authority, power, or organization: *the separation of church and state.* **7.** the clerical profession. [Old English *cirice* building for Christian worship, going back to Greek *kȳriakon (dōma)* (house) of the Lord, from *kȳrios* master, lord.]

Church Fathers, Fathers of the Church.

church·go·er (chûrch′gō′ər) *n.* a person who goes to church regularly.

church·go·ing (chûrch′gō′ing) *n.* the practice of attending church regularly. —*adj.* of or relating to regular church attendance.

Church Latin, the form of Latin used by the Roman Catholic Church.

church·ly (chûrch′lē) *adj.* **1.** of, relating to, or suitable for a church. **2.** belonging or devoted to a church. —**church′li·ness,** *n.*

church·man (chûrch′mən) *n., pl.* **-men** (-mən). **1.** a member of the clergy. **2.** a member or supporter of a church.

Church of Christ, Scientist, the official name of the Christian Science Church.

Church of England, the established church in England, headed by the British sovereign and having an episcopal hierarchy. It is the mother church of the Protestant Episcopal Church.

Church of Jesus Christ of Latter-day Saints, the official name of the Mormon Church.

church·war·den (chûrch′wôr′dən) *n.* in the Church of England and the Protestant Episcopal Church, an elected lay official whose duty is the management of secular affairs.

church·wom·an (chûrch′wûm′ən) *n., pl.* **-wom·en** (-wim′ən). a woman who is a member or supporter of a church.

church·yard (chûrch′yärd′) *n.* the ground around or adjoining a church, often used as a cemetery.

churl (chûrl) *n.* **1.** a surly, ill-bred person. **2.** peasant; rustic. [Old English *ceorl* freeman of the lowest rank, man.]

churl·ish (chûr′lish) *adj.* of, like, or characteristic of a churl. —**churl′ish·ly,** *adv.* —**churl′ish·ness,** *n.*

churn (chûrn) *n.* a vessel in which cream or milk is agitated to separate the fat globules in order to make butter. —*v.t.* **1.** to stir or agitate (cream or milk) in a churn. **2.** to make (butter) in a churn. **3.** to stir or agitate with violent or continued motion: *The plow churned up the soil.* —*v.i.* **1.** to work a churn. **2.** to move with violent agitation: *The water churned behind the ship.* **3.** to be or become upset: *My stomach churned before I gave my speech.* [Old English *cyrin* vessel for making butter.] —**churn′er,** *n.*

• **to churn out.** to produce regularly and abundantly, often in a mechanical way: *That novelist churns out books.*

churr (chûr) chirr.

chute (shüt) *n.* **1.** an inclined or vertical trough or passage, usually having a slanted opening, down or through which various things may be passed or conveyed: *a mail chute, a coal chute.* Also, **shoot.** **2.** a waterfall or rapids in a river. **3.** a steep or curving slope, as for toboggans. **4.** *Informal.* parachute. [French *chute* fall, going back to Latin *cadere* to fall; influenced by English SHOOT in meaning.]

chut·ney (chut′nē) *n., pl.* **-neys.** a condiment or relish made of fruits, herbs, and spices. [Hindi *chatnī* relish.]

chutz·pah (KHŭts′pə) *n. Informal.* shameless impudence; nerve; gall. [Yiddish *khutspe*, from Hebrew *chutspa.*]

chyle (kīl) *n.* a milky fluid consisting of emulsified fat and lymph, formed from the chyme in the small intestine and passed into the veins. [Late Latin *chȳlus* juice, from Greek *chȳlos.*] —**chy′lous**, *adj.*

chyme (kīm) *n.* a pulpy, semiliquid mass of partly digested food that passes from the stomach into the small intestine. [Late Latin *chȳmos* fluid of the stomach, from Greek *chȳmos* juice of a plant or animal.] —**chy′mous**, *adj.*

CIA, Central Intelligence Agency, a U.S. government organization established in 1947 to coordinate intelligence activities of all departments of the government and to give advice on policy matters.

ciao (chou) *interj. Italian.* a familiar expression of greeting or parting, equivalent to hello or good-bye. [Italian *ciao* hello, good-bye.]

ci·bo·ri·um (si bôr′ē əm) *n., pl.* **-bo·ri·a** (-bôr′ē ə). **1.** the covered container that holds the bread of the Eucharist. **2.** a canopy over an altar, esp. one that is permanent. [Medieval Latin *ciborium* vessel for the sacrament, from Latin *cibōrium* drinking cup, from Greek *kibōrion* seed vessel of the Egyptian bean, cup made from or resembling it.]

ci·ca·da (si kā′də, -kä′-) *n., pl.* **-das** or **-dae** (-dē). any of a group of large insects, family Cicadidae, with transparent wings, the male of which makes a loud, shrill sound by means of two vibrating plates on its abdomen. The seventeen-year locust is a cicada. [Latin *cicāda.*]

cic·a·trix (sik′ə triks′, si kā′-) *also,* **cic·a·trice** (sik′ə tris). *n., pl.* **cic·a·tri·ces** (sik′ə trī′sēz). **1.** a scar consisting of fibrous connective tissue formed when a wound heals. **2.** a scar left on a tree or plant, as one left when a leaf falls. **3.** hilum. [Latin *cicātrīx* scar.]

cic·a·trize (sik′ə trīz′) *v.t., v.i.,* **-trized, -triz·ing.** to heal or become healed by the formation of a scar.

cic·e·ro·ne (sis′ə rō′nē) *n., pl.* **-nes.** a person who shows and explains points of interest, curiosities, and antiquities to sightseers; guide. [Italian *cicerone,* presumably from Marcus Tullius *Cicero,* 106-43 B.C., Roman orator, writer, and statesman; either in allusion to his learning and eloquence or as an originally pejorative word alluding to the loquacity of guides.]

Cic·e·ro·ni·an (sis′ə rō′nē ən) *adj.* of, relating to, or characteristic of Cicero or his orations and writings.

cich·lid (sik′lid) *n.* any of a group of freshwater fish, family Cichlidae, found in North and South America, including the angelfish and other popular home aquarium fish. [Modern Latin *Cichlidae,* from Greek *kichlē* thrush, wrasse.]

-cide¹ *combining form* killing of: *homicide.* [Latin *-cīdium,* from *caedere* to kill.]

-cide² *combining form* killer of: *regicide.* [Latin *-cīda,* from *caedere* to kill.]

ci·der (sī′dər) *n.* juice pressed from apples or, formerly, from other fruits, used as a beverage and in making certain products, such as vinegar or applejack. [Old French *sidre,* from Late Latin *sīcera* strong drink, from Late Greek *sīkera,* from Hebrew *shēkār.*]

cider press, a machine used to crush and to extract juice from the pulp of apples for making cider.

CIF *also,* **c.i.f., C.I.F.** cost, insurance, and freight.

ci·gar (si gär′) *n.* a compact roll of tobacco leaves prepared for smoking. [Spanish *cigarro,* possibly going back to Mayan *siq* tobacco.]

cig·a·rette (sig′ə ret′, sig′ə ret′) *also,* **cig·a·ret.** *n.* a small roll of finely shredded tobacco leaves, enclosed in thin paper, used for smoking. [French *cigarette,* diminutive of *cigare* cigar, from Spanish *cigarro.* See CIGAR.]

ci·lan·tro (sə lan′trō) *n.* coriander *(def. 2).*

cil·i·a (sil′ē ə) *pl. n., sing.* **-i·um** (-ē əm). **1.a.** the minute hairlike projections that line the trachea, bronchi, and bronchioles, and are constantly in motion, thus filtering the air entering and leaving the lungs. **b.** similar hairlike projections on certain protozoans, as paramecia, which move to and fro, propelling the creature through the water. **2.** eyelashes. [Latin *cilia,* plural of *cilium* eyelid.]

cil·i·ar·y (sil′ē er′ē) *adj.* **1.** of, relating to, or resembling cilia; hairlike. **2.** of or relating to the ciliary body.

ciliary body, the part of the covering of the eye that joins the choroid coat with the iris and whose ligaments and muscles support and adjust the shape of the lens of the eyeball.

cil·i·ate (sil′ē it, -āt′) *adj.* having cilia. Also, **cil·i·at·ed** (sil′ē-ā′tid). —*n.* any of a class of protozoans having cilia that are used in moving about and obtaining food.

cil·i·um (sil′ē əm) the singular of **cilia.**

Cim·me·ri·an (si mîr′ē ən) *n.* in Greek legend, any of a group of

people who lived in eternal darkness and gloom. —*adj.* very dark and gloomy.

cinch (sinch) *n.* **1.** a girth for fastening a saddle or pack on a horse. For illustration, see **saddle. 2.** *Informal.* a firm or tight grip. **3.** *Slang.* something sure or easy: *Passing the test was a cinch.* **4.** *Slang.* a person or thing that is certain to succeed: *This horse is a cinch to win the race.* —*v.t.* **1.** to fasten or bind with or as with a cinch: *to cinch one's waist with a belt.* **2.** *Informal.* to get a firm or tight grip on. **3.** *Slang.* to make sure of: *Our third touchdown cinched the victory.* [Spanish *cincha* saddle girth, from Latin *cingula* belt.]

cin·cho·na (sin kō′nə) *n.* **1.** any of a group of evergreen trees or shrubs found in South America, Asia, and Jamaica. Two species widely cultivated for their bark are the **yellow-barked cinchona,** *C. calisaya,* and the **red-barked cinchona,** *C. pubescens.* **2.** the bark of this tree, from which quinine and other similar drugs are derived. Also *(def. 2),* **Peruvian bark.** [Modern Latin *cinchona;* named in honor of the Spanish Countess *Chinchón,* 1576?-1641.]

cinc·ture (singk′chər) *n.* **1.** belt; girdle. **2.** anything that encompasses; enclosure; border. —*v.t.,* **-tured, -tur·ing.** to encompass with or as with a cincture; gird. [Latin *cinctūra* girdle.]

cin·der (sin′dər) *n.* **1.** a combustible substance, esp. coal, that is burning but has ceased to flame. **2.** a combustible substance, as wood or coal, burned but not reduced to ashes. **3. cinders.** ashes. **4.** slag *(def. 1).* **5.** a speck, as of dirt or ash: *to have a cinder in one's eye.* **6.** scoria *(def. 1).* [Old English *sinder* dross, slag.]

cinder block, a building brick that is partially hollow, made from cinders and cement.

Cin·der·el·la (sin′də rel′ə) *n.* **1.** the heroine in a fairy tale who was forced by her cruel stepmother and stepsisters to work very hard. With the help of her fairy godmother, she eventually married a prince. **2.** any person, esp. a girl, whose worth, beauty, or talent goes for a time unrecognized.

cin·e·aste (sin′ē ast′, sin′ā-) *n.* **1.** a devotee or enthusiast of motion pictures. **2.** a director or writer of motion pictures. [French *cinéaste* film enthusiast, from *ciné(ma)* cinema + *-aste* one connected with, going back to Greek *-astês.*]

cin·e·ma (sin′ə mə) *n.* **1.** a motion-picture theater. **2.** the **cinema. a.** motion pictures collectively. **b.** the art or business of making motion pictures. **3.** motion picture. [Short for earlier *cinematograph* motion-picture camera or projector, from Greek *kīnēmat-,* stem of *kīnēma* motion + -GRAPH.] —**cin′e·mat′ic,** *adj.* —**cin′e·mat′i·cal·ly,** *adv.*

cin·e·ma·tog·ra·phy (sin′ə mə tog′rə fē) *n.* the art and process of photographing motion pictures. —**cin′e·ma·tog′ra·pher,** *n.* —**cin′e·mat·o·graph·ic** (sin′ə mat′ə graf′ik), *adj.*

cin·é·ma vé·ri·té (sin′ə mə ver′i tā′) a style of motion-picture making that strives for documentary realism by filming unrehearsed action, using hand-held cameras, and editing as little footage as possible. [French *cinéma-vérité* truth-cinema.]

cin·e·rar·i·a (sin′ə rár′ē ə) *n.* an ornamental plant, *Senecio cruentus,* of the composite family, having heart-shaped woolly leaves and bearing daisylike flower heads that may be white, blue, pink, or purplish red. [Modern Latin *cineraria,* from Latin *cinerārius* relating to ashes; from *cinis* ashes; from the color of the down on its leaves.]

cin·e·rar·i·um (sin′ə rár′ē əm) *n., pl.* **-rar·i·a** (-rár′ē ə). a place for keeping the ashes of a cremated body. [Latin *cinerārium,* from *cinis* ashes.] —**cin′e·rar′y,** *adj.*

cin·na·bar (sin′ə bär′) *n.* **1.** a red, crystalline mineral, mercuric sulfide, the chief source of mercury. Formula: HgS **2.** an artificial mercuric sulfide, prepared commercially for use as a red paint pigment. **3.** a bright red color; vermilion. —*adj.* having the color cinnabar. [Late Latin *cinnābaris* this mineral, this color, from Greek *kinnabari;* of Oriental origin.]

cin·na·mon (sin′ə mən) *n.* **1.** a reddish brown spice made from the dried, highly aromatic bark of several East Indian trees, genus *Cinnamomum,* of the laurel family. **2.** the bark itself, either ground or rolled into sheets. **3.** a tree yielding this bark. **4.** a light, reddish brown color. —*adj.* having the color cinnamon. [Latin *cinnamōmum* this spice, from Greek *kinnamōmon,* from Hebrew *qinnāmōn.*]

a	at	e	end	o	hot	u	up	hw	white		about
ā	ape	ē	me	ō	old	ū	use	ng	song	ə	taken
ä	far	i	it	ô	fork	ü	rule	th	thin		pencil
âr	care	ī	ice	oi	oil	u̇	pull	th	this		lemon
				ir	pierce	ou	out	ur	turn	zh	measure		circus

cinque·foil (singk′foil′) *n.* **1.** any of a group of plants and shrubs, genus *Potentilla*, of the rose family, found in northern temperate or frigid climates throughout the world, having compound leaves and bearing flat white, yellow, or red flowers consisting of five petals. **2.** an ornament, used esp. in architecture, consisting of five foils or arcs joined by pointed projections. [Latin *quīnquefolium* this plant, from *quīnque* five + *folium* leaf.]

ci·on (sī′ən) scion *(def. 1)*.

ci·pher (sī′fər) *also,* **cypher.** *n.* **1.** zero. **2.** the symbol representing this; 0. **3.** a person or thing that is of no value or importance; nonentity. **4.** a system of writing that renders a message or text unintelligible to those who do not have the prearranged key or pattern; code. **5.** a message written in cipher; cryptogram. **6.** the key or pattern to such a code. **7.** any Arabic numeral. **8.** a combination of letters, esp. the initials of a name; monogram. —*v.t.* **1.** to work (something) out arithmetically. **2.** to write (something) in cipher. —*v.i.* to figure arithmetically. [Old French *cifre* zero, through Spanish, from Arabic *çifr,* noun use of adjective *çifr* empty; applied to code writing because of the earlier use of numbers in devising codes. Doublet of ZERO.]

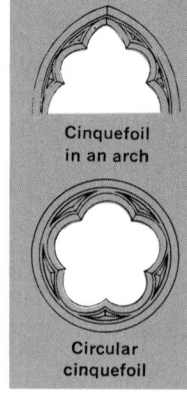

Cinquefoil in an arch

Circular cinquefoil

cinquefoils

cir·ca (sûr′kə) *prep. Latin.* around; about. ➡ used esp. to indicate an approximate date: *circa 500 B.C.*

cir·ca·di·an (sûr kā′dē ən, -kad′ē-, sûr′kə dī′-) *adj.* having a natural rhythm or cycle of approximately 24 hours: *Human beings have a circadian sleep pattern.* [Latin *circa* about, around + *dies* day + -AN.]

Cir·ce (sûr′sē) *n.* in Greek legend, a beautiful enchantress who lived on an island and changed half of Odysseus's men into swine. After he rescued his men, they escaped from her. —**Cir·ce′an,** *adj.*

cir·ci·nate (sûr′sə nāt′) *adj.* **1.** rolled up in a circle; coiled. **2.** curled up from the tip toward the base, as the fronds of certain ferns. [Latin *circinātus,* past participle of *circināre* to make round.] —**cir′ci·nate′ly,** *adv.*

cir·cle (sûr′kəl) *n.* **1.** a continuous curved line, lying in a plane, every point of which is equally distant from the center. **2.** a plane figure bounded by such a line. **3.** anything shaped like a circle, as a halo, crown, or ring. **4.** a group of people united by common interests: *a circle of friends, to join a reading circle.* **5.** a gallery or tier of seats in a theater. **6.** a complete series or course ending at the point where it began and perpetually repeated: *the circle of the seasons.* **7.** an area or sphere in which influence, action, or interest is exerted; realm. **8.** *Logic.* a fallacious form of argument in which the conclusion and premise are used to prove one another. Also *(def. 8),* **vicious circle.** —*v.,* -cled, -cling. —*v.t.* **1.** to surround with or as with a circle; encompass: *The enemy circled the camp.* **2.** to move around in or as in a circle: *The animal circled its prey before attacking.* —*v.i.* to move around in a circle: *The airplane circled for an hour before it could land.* [Latin *circulus* circular figure, small ring, diminutive of *circus* ring.] —**cir′cler,** *n.*

cir·clet (sûr′klit) *n.* **1.** a small circle. **2.** an ornamental ring or band worn about the head, neck, arm, or finger.

cir·cuit (sûr′kit) *n.* **1.** the act of going around; circular course; revolution. **2.** a periodic journey around a set route, as by a judge or preacher. **3.** the district traveled through, or included in, such a journey, esp. the district assigned to a judge for holding court. **4.** the distance around an area; area enclosed. **5.** a system or part of a system of electric or electronic components through which an electric current flows; path of an electric current. **6.** a group of associated theaters or other public establishments at which productions, as movies or plays, or entertainers are presented simultaneously or in turn. —*v.t.* to make a circuit of. —*v.i.* to go in a circuit. [Latin *circuitus* a going about.] —**cir′cuit·al,** *adj.*

circuit board, a flat piece of material, usually fiberglass, on which integrated circuits are mounted.

circuit breaker, a safety switch that automatically interrupts the flow of current through an electric circuit when the current becomes dangerously strong.

circuit court, formerly, a court that sat at intervals in various places within the territory over which it had jurisdiction.

cir·cu·i·tous (sər kū′i təs) *adj.* not direct; roundabout; indirect: *a circuitous route.* —**cir·cu′i·tous·ly,** *adv.* —**cir·cu′i·tous·ness, cir·cu′i·ty,** *n.*

circuit rider, formerly, a Methodist minister who traveled over a circuit to preach.

cir·cuit·ry (sûr′ki trē) *n.* the components or layout of an electric or electronic circuit. [CIRCUIT + -RY.]

cir·cu·lar (sûr′kyə lər) *adj.* **1.** having the form of a circle; round: *a circular driveway.* **2.** moving in or forming a circle: *the circular motion of a merry-go-round.* **3.** of or relating to a circle or its mathematical properties. **4.** circuitous; indirect: *a circular way of approaching a subject.* **5.** sent to several persons or intended for general circulation. —*n.* printed material, as a letter or advertisement, produced in large quantities for general circulation. [Late Latin *circulāris* round, from Latin *circulus.* See CIRCLE.] —**cir·cu·lar·i·ty** (sûr′kyə lar′i tē), **cir′cu·lar·ness,** *n.* —**cir′cu·lar·ly,** *adv.*

cir·cu·lar·ize (sûr′kyə lə rīz′) *v.t.,* -ized, -iz·ing. **1.** to send circulars to. **2.** to make circular.

circular measure, a system for measuring circles and angles, using seconds, minutes, and degrees as units of measure. For Weights and Measures table, see **weight.**

circular saw, a power saw having a thin, metal disk with a toothed edge mounted in a framework and rotated at high speed.

cir·cu·late (sûr′kyə lāt′) *v.,* -lat·ed, -lat·ing. —*v.i.* **1.** to move in a circular course back to the starting point: *Blood circulates in the body.* **2.** to pass from place to place or person to person; move freely: *Air circulates in a room. The rumor circulated throughout the office.* —*v.t.* to cause to pass from place to place or person to person; put into circulation: *to circulate money.* [Latin *circulātus,* past participle of *circulārī* to gather in a circle, from *circulus.* See CIRCLE.] —**cir′cu·la′tor,** *n.* —For Synonyms *(v.t.),* see **spread.**

circulating library, a library from which books may be borrowed or rented. Also, **lending library.**

circulating medium, money in actual use; currency.

cir·cu·la·tion (sûr′kyə lā′shən) *n.* **1.** the act of circulating. **2.** the movement of the blood to and from the heart through the blood vessels of the body. **3.a.** the extent of distribution and sales of a publication, as a newspaper: *The newspaper has a wide circulation that covers three states.* **b.** the number of copies of a newspaper or magazine that are distributed and sold per issue or for a given period: *The circulation of the newspaper is over 30,000.* **4.** the number of items lent by a library.

cir·cu·la·to·ry (sûr′kyə lə tôr′ē) *adj.* of or relating to circulation, esp. of the blood.

circulatory system, the network of tissues involved in transporting fluids throughout an organism. In animals, the circulatory system typically consists of the heart, the blood vessels, the blood, and the lymphatic system.

circum- *prefix* around; about: *circumnavigate.* [Latin *circum.*]

cir·cum·am·bi·ent (sûr′kəm am′bē ənt) *adj.* existing or going all around; surrounding; encompassing. —**cir′cum·am′bi·ence,** *n.*

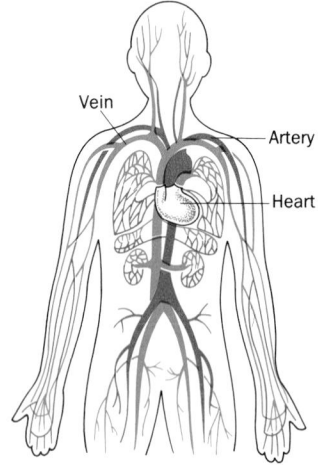

Vein

Artery

Heart

circulatory system

cir·cum·cen·ter (sûr′kəm sen′tər) *n.* the center of a circle that is circumscribed around a polygon.

cir·cum·cise (sûr′kəm sīz′) *v.t.,* -cised, -cis·ing. to remove all or part of the foreskin of. [Latin *circumcīsus,* past participle of *circumcīdere* to cut around.]

cir·cum·ci·sion (sûr′kəm sizh′ən) *n.* **1.** the act or rite of circumcising or being circumcised. **2. Circumcision.** the feast day commemorating the circumcision of the infant Jesus, observed on January 1.

cir·cum·fer·ence (sər kum′fər əns) *n.* **1.** a line bounding any rounded plane figure, esp. a circle. **2.** the measurement of this line; distance around. [Latin *circumferentia* boundary of a circle.] —**cir·cum·fer·en·tial** (sər kum′fə ren′shəl), *adj.* —**cir·cum·fer·en′tial·ly,** *adv.*

cir·cum·flex (sûr′kəm fleks′) *n.* any of various marks, as ^ or ˜, placed over a letter to indicate pronunciation in certain languages or in phonetic transcriptions. Also, **circumflex accent.** —*adj.* **1.** pronounced or marked with a circumflex. **2.** bending or

winding around. —*v.t.* **1.** to pronounce or mark with a circumflex. **2.** to bend or wind around. [Latin *circumflexus,* past participle of *circumflectere* to bend around.]

cir·cum·flu·ent (sər kum′flü ənt) *adj.* flowing around; surrounding. [Latin *circumfluēns,* present participle of *circumfluere* to flow round.]

cir·cum·flu·ous (sər kum′flü əs) *adj.* **1.** circumfluent. **2.** surrounded by or as by water. [Latin *circumfluus.*]

cir·cum·fuse (sûr′kəm fūz′) *v.t.,* **-fused, -fus·ing. 1.** to pour or spread about. **2.** to surround, as with a liquid; suffuse. [Latin *circumfūsus,* past participle of *circumfundere* to pour around.] —**cir′cum·fu′sion,** *n.*

cir·cum·lo·cu·tion (sûr′kəm lō kū′shən) *n.* **1.** a roundabout or indirect way of speaking; use of too many words. **2.** an instance of this; roundabout expression. [Latin *circumlocūtiō.*] —**cir·cum·loc·u·tor·y** (sûr′kəm lok′yə tôr′ē) *adj.*

cir·cum·lu·nar (sûr′kəm lü′nər) *adj.* around, in orbit about, or surrounding the moon: *a circumlunar halo.* [CIRCUM- + LUNAR.]

cir·cum·nav·i·gate (sûr′kəm nav′i gāt′) *v.t.,* **-gat·ed, -gat·ing.** to sail or go completely around. —**cir′cum·nav′i·ga′tion,** *n.* —**cir′cum·nav′i·ga′tor,** *n.*

cir·cum·po·lar (sûr′kəm pō′lər) *adj.* **1.** near or around either of the terrestrial poles: *circumpolar regions.* **2.** near or revolving around either of the celestial poles: *a circumpolar star.*

cir·cum·scribe (sûr′kəm skrīb′) *v.t.,* **-scribed, -scrib·ing. 1.** to draw a line around; form the boundaries of; encircle. **2.** to put restrictions on; limit; confine: *to circumscribe one's activities.* **3.a.** to draw (one geometric figure) around another so that the outer touches the inner at as many points as possible. **b.** to enclose (a geometric figure) in this way: *A circle that circumscribes a pentagon touches it at five points.* [Latin *circumscribere* to draw around, limit, from *circum* circle + *scribere* to draw, write.]

cir·cum·scrip·tion (sûr′kəm skrip′shən) *n.* **1.** the act of circumscribing or the state of being circumscribed. **2.** something that circumscribes. **3.** something, as a space, that is circumscribed. **4.** an inscription around something, such as a coin, medal, or seal. [Latin *circumscrīptiō* boundary, limit.]

cir·cum·so·lar (sûr′kəm sō′lər) *adj.* around, in orbit about, or surrounding the sun: *a circumsolar satellite.* [CIRCUM- + SOLAR.]

cir·cum·spect (sûr′kəm spekt′) *adj.* **1.** examining all sides of a problem carefully before acting or making a decision; cautious; prudent. **2.** showing or involving circumspection. [Latin *circumspectus.*] —**cir′cum·spect′ly,** *adv.* —**cir′cum·spect′ness,** *n.*

cir·cum·spec·tion (sûr′kəm spek′shən) *n.* circumspect behavior or action; caution; prudence.

cir·cum·stance (sûr′kəm stans′) *n.* **1.** a condition, act, or event accompanying and often affecting another condition, act, or event: *Good weather and other circumstances made our picnic a success.* **2.** *also,* **circumstances.** the existing state of affairs surrounding and affecting a person or action; external factors considered as helping or hindering: *Due to circumstances beyond our control, the lecture was canceled.* **3.** an event or fact; occurrence: *Getting the job was a happy circumstance.* **4. circumstances.** financial condition; means: *to be in poor circumstances.* **5.** detail, esp. full detail, as in a narrative: *The scientist explained the theory with great circumstance.* **6.** a formal or splendid ceremony or display: *The coronation was accompanied by much pomp and circumstance.* [Latin *circumstāntia* a surrounding, attribute, condition.]

• **under no circumstances.** under no conditions; never.

• **under (or in) the circumstances.** things being as they are: *Under the circumstances, we must leave immediately.*

> **Synonyms** Circumstance, situation, and condition mean an existing state of affairs. **Circumstance** or **circumstances** suggests the surrounding environment, events, and forces that affect something that happens: *The circumstances under which the accident occurred make it very hard to determine the cause.* **Situation** is more often used of the precise position a person or thing is in, a position that circumstances may have created: *Huge medical bills put the family in a desperate financial situation.* **Condition** or **conditions** is used more broadly of a state of affairs, suggesting both immediate and more enduring or remote elements: *The union called a strike to protest working conditions.*

cir·cum·stan·tial (sûr′kəm stan′shəl) *adj.* **1.** relating to, affected by, or depending on circumstances. **2.** not essential; incidental; secondary: *The report was full of circumstantial details.* **3.** full of details; particular: *The writer gave a circumstantial account of the battle.* —**cir′cum·stan′tial·ly,** *adv.*

circumstantial evidence, evidence of facts or circumstances from which other facts in question can be inferred.

cir·cum·stan·ti·ate (sûr′kəm stan′shē āt′) *v.t.,* **-at·ed, -at·ing.** to confirm or support with facts or particulars. —**cir′cum·stan′ti·a′tion,** *n.*

cir·cum·vent (sûr′kəm vent′) *v.t.* **1.** to go around; avoid: *to circumvent a town to avoid traffic, to circumvent an issue in debate.* **2.** to evade, as by trickery or cleverness: *to circumvent a law.* **3.** to entrap or get the better of, as by craft or fraud. [Latin *circumventus,* past participle of *circumvenīre* to surround, deceive, from *circum* around + *venīre* to come.] —**cir′cum·ven′tion,** *n.*

cir·cus (sûr′kəs) *n.* **1.a.** a traveling show, usually featuring acrobats, clowns, and both trained and wild animals. **b.** all the persons, animals, and equipment associated with such a show. **c.** a performance given by such a show. **2.a.** in ancient Rome, an oval or oblong structure, open at one end, with tiers of seats surrounding an open space, used esp. for horse and chariot races. **b.** an entertainment given in such a structure. **3.** *Informal.* any place or event resembling a circus, as in activity or showiness: *The town was a circus on the day of the big game.* [Latin *circus* ring, round place for games. Doublet of CIRQUE.]

Cir·cus Max·i·mus (sûr′kəs mak′sə məs) the largest circus, or amphitheater, in ancient Rome.

cirque (sûrk) *n.* **1.** a circular space, esp. a bowl-shaped depression, located at the head of a valley and having steep walls. **2.** *Archaic.* a circlet; ring [French *cirque* circus, geological cirque, from Latin *circus* ring. Doublet of CIRCUS.]

cir·rate (sir′āt) *adj. Biology.* having a cirrus or cirri.

cir·rho·sis (si rō′sis) *n.* a chronic disease of the liver marked by the growth of scar tissue, the destruction of normal liver cells, and a distortion in shape. Cirrhosis is usually caused by prolonged consumption of alcohol but may also be caused by poor nutrition and infections such as hepatitis. [Modern Latin *cirrhosis,* from Greek *kirrhos* orange, tawny; from the color of the affected liver.] —**cir·rhot·ic** (si rot′ik), *adj.*

cir·ri (sir′ī) the plural of **cirrus.**

cir·ri·ped (sir′ə ped′) *n.* any of a group of parasitic crustaceans, subclass Cirripedia, as the barnacle, having threadlike appendages. They are free-swimming in the larval stage and become attached to rocks or other organisms in adulthood. [Modern Latin *Cirripedia,* from Latin *cirrus* curl + *ped-,* stem of *pēs* foot.]

cir·ro·cu·mu·lus (sir′ō kū′myə ləs) *n., pl.* **-mu·lus** or **-mu·li** (-myə lī′). a cloud made up of ice crystals appearing in thin layers of ripples or small puffs, formed at an altitude of about 20,000 to 25,000 feet (6,100 to 7,600 meters). For illustration, see **cloud.** [CIRRUS + CUMULUS.]

cir·ro·stra·tus (sir′ō strā′təs, -strat′əs) *n., pl.* **-stra·tus** or **-stra·ti** (-strā′tī, -strat′ī). a thin, veillike cloud of ice crystals formed at about 20,000 to 25,000 feet (6,100 to 7,600 meters). The sun or moon appears to have a halo around it when it shines through such clouds. For illustration, see **cloud.** [CIRRUS + STRATUS.]

cir·rus (sir′əs) *n., pl.* **cir·ri. 1.** a white, thin, fibrous cloud composed of ice crystals in small patches or bands, found at altitudes above 20,000 feet (6,100 meters). For illustration, see **cloud. 2.** *Biology.* **a.** a tendril of a plant. **b.** a threadlike, flexible appendage of an animal, as a feeler or tentacle. [Latin *cirrus* curl.]

cis·al·pine (sis al′pīn, -pin) *adj.* situated on the southern side of the Alps, toward Rome. [Latin *Cisalpīnus,* going back to *cis* on this side of + *Alpēs* Alps.]

cis·co (sis′kō) *n., pl.* **-coes** or **-cos.** any of several whitefish found in the Great Lakes. [Shortened from French *ciscoette,* modification of Ojibwa *pemitewiskawet* fish having oily flesh.]

cis·lu·nar (sis lü′nər) *adj.* of, relating to, or designating the area between the earth and the moon.

Cis·ter·cian (sis tûr′shən) *n.* a member of an order of monks and nuns who live by the Benedictine rule, founded in France in 1098. —*adj.* of or relating to this order. [Medieval Latin *Cistercium* Cîteaux (French village where this order was founded) + -AN.]

cis·tern (sis′tərn) *n.* **1.** an artificial or natural reservoir or tank for storing liquids, esp. rainwater. **2.** a sac or cavity in the body containing some natural fluid. [Old French *cisterne* reservoir, from Latin *cisterna,* from *cista* box. See CHEST.]

cit·a·del (sit′ə dəl, -del′) *n.* **1.** a fortress commanding a city. **2.** any strongly fortified place, esp. one of refuge. [Italian *cittadella* small town, diminutive of earlier Italian *cittade* city, from Latin *cīvitās* city, state.]

ci·ta·tion (sī tā′shən) *n.* **1.** the act of citing or quoting. **2.** a passage or words cited; quotation. **3.** a public commendation or

a	at	e	end	o	hot	u	up	hw	white		about
ā	ape	ē	me	ō	old	ū	use	ng	song		taken
ä	far	i	it	ô	fork	ü	rule	th	thin	ə	pencil
âr	care	ī	ice	oi	oil	u̇	pull	th	this		lemon
		îr	pierce	ou	out	ûr	turn	zh	measure		circus

award, as for bravery or outstanding achievement. **4.** a summons to appear before a court of law. **5.a.** specific mention of a soldier or unit, in an official dispatch, for bravery or meritorious service. **b.** a medal or award given for this.

cite (sīt) *v.t.,* **cit·ed, cit·ing. 1.** to quote, as a passage or author, esp. as an authority. **2.** to refer to as support, proof, or confirmation. **3.** to give a public commendation to, as for bravery or outstanding achievement. **4.** to summon to appear before a court of law. **5.** *Military.* to mention in a citation. [French *citer* to summon, quote, from Latin *citāre.*] —**cit′a·ble;** *also,* **cite′a·ble,** *adj.*

cith·a·ra (sith′ər ə, kith′-) *n.* an ancient Greek stringed instrument somewhat resembling the lyre. [Latin *cithara,* from Greek *kithārā.* Doublet of GUITAR, ZITHER.]

cith·ern (sith′ərn, sith′-) cittern.

cit·ied (sit′ēd) *adj.* **1.** occupied by a city or cities. **2.** made into or resembling a city.

cit·i·fied (sit′ə fīd′) *adj.* having the manners or fashions characteristic of urban life.

cit·i·zen (sit′ə zən, -sən) *n.* **1.** a native or naturalized resident of a nation or state who owes allegiance to it and has the rights, duties, and privileges established by the fundamental law of that nation or state: *a citizen of Canada, a citizen of the Ukraine.* **2.** a permanent resident, esp. of a city or town. **3.** a civilian, as distinguished from a member of the military, a police force, or similar group. [Anglo-Norman *citezein,* modification of Old French *citeain* townsman, from *cite* city, from Latin *cīvitās* city, state.]

> **Synonyms** Citizen, subject, and national mean a person acknowledged to be a member of the people of a country. **Citizen** suggests the rights and privileges of persons who live under a republican government, which in theory derives its authority from them: *citizens of the United States.* **Subject** suggests the domination of a ruler and is used of persons who live under a government headed, at least in theory, by a monarch or other sovereign: *subjects of the British crown.* **National** is used most often of citizens or subjects of one country who are living elsewhere: *French nationals living in Canada.* It may also be used of members of a country who do not yet have full citizenship, or of residents of areas whose sovereignty is not clearly defined.

cit·i·zen·ry (sit′ə zən rē, -sən rē) *n., pl.* **-ries.** citizens collectively.

citizens band, a set of radio frequencies designated by the United States government for private two-way communication over short distances.

cit·i·zen·ship (sit′ə zən ship′, -sən-) *n.* the status or position of being a citizen, including its rights, duties, and privileges.

cit·rate (sit′rāt) *n.* a salt or ester of citric acid.

cit·ric (sit′rik) *adj.* of or derived from citrus fruits.

citric acid, a sour-tasting organic acid, present in almost all plants but esp. in lemons, limes, and other citrus fruits. It is an intermediate in cellular metabolism and is used as a flavoring, in medicine, and in fixing dyes. Formula: $C_6H_8O_7$

cit·rine (sit′rēn, -rin) *n.* a lemon yellow color. —*adj.* having the color citrine. [French *citrin* pale yellow, from Latin *citrus* citron tree.]

cit·ron (sit′rən) *n.* **1.** the large lemonlike fruit of a shrub or small tree, *Citrus medica,* grown in Asia, the Mediterranean regions, and the West Indies, valued mainly for its thick, warty, yellow-green rind, which is used in desserts and in making liqueurs and perfumes. **2.** the shrub or tree bearing this fruit. **3.** the preserved or candied rind of this fruit, used in confections, esp. in fruitcakes. **4.** citron melon. [French *citron* citron fruit, lemon, from Latin *citrus* citron tree.]

cit·ron·el·la (sit′rə nel′ə) *n.* **1.** a pale yellow oil distilled from the leaves of a grass, *Cymbopogon nardus,* having a lemon fragrance and used to make insect repellent and to scent soaps and cosmetics. **2.** the plant itself. [Modern Latin *citronella,* going back to French *citron;* from its scent resembling the citron. See CITRON.]

citron melon, a small round watermelon, *Citrullus lanatus,* variety *citroides,* grown in warm temperate regions and used mainly in pickles and preserves.

cit·rul·line (sit′rə lēn′) *n.* an amino acid serving as an essential link in the process by which the liver forms urea from ammonia and carbon dioxide. Formula: $C_6H_{13}N_3O_3$

cit·rus (sit′rəs) *n.* **1.** any of a group of shrubs and small trees, genus *Citrus,* valued esp. for its fruit, grown in warm regions throughout the world. **2.** citrus fruit. —*adj. also,* **cit·rous.** of or relating to such trees or their fruit. [Latin *citrus* citron tree, citrus tree.]

citrus fruit, the fleshy, juicy fruit of any of a group of shrubs and small trees, genus *Citrus,* as the orange, lemon, lime, or grapefruit.

cit·tern (sit′ərn) *also,* **cithern.** *n.* a musical instrument of the guitar family, used mainly in the sixteenth and seventeenth centuries, having wire strings. [Blend of Latin *cithara* type of guitar or lute, and GITTERN. See CITHARA.]

cit·y (sit′ē) *n., pl.* **cit·ies. 1.** any densely populated center, larger and more important than a town, where people live and engage in commerce and industry. **2.** in the United States, any incorporated municipality, chartered by the state in which it is located and usually having a mayor or city manager. **3.** in Canada, any municipality of the highest class. **4.** the inhabitants of a city collectively. **5.** city-state. **6. the City.** the City of London, the oldest section of the modern city, now the financial district. —*adj.* of or relating to a city; urban. [Old French *cité* large town, body of citizens, from Latin *cīvitās* community, state, citizenship, from *cīvis* citizen.]

cittern

city desk, the department of a newspaper office that receives and edits local news.

city editor, the editor of a newspaper who has charge of collecting and editing local news and of distributing assignments to reporters.

city fathers, the officials of a city, as councilors, aldermen, or magistrates.

city hall 1. the building serving as the administrative headquarters of a city government. **2.** the administrative body of a city: *City hall issued a statement on the rise of crime.* **3.** *Informal.* a bureaucracy or its rules and regulations: *You can't fight city hall.*

city manager, an administrator not publicly elected but appointed by a city council to manage the government of a city.

City of Da·vid (dā′vid) **1.** Bethlehem. **2.** Jerusalem.

City of God, heaven.

City of Seven Hills, Rome.

city planning 1. organized efforts to physically improve cities. **2.** the profession of planning the physical improvement of cities. Also, **urban planning.** —**city planner.**

cit·y-state (sit′ē stāt′) *n.* a self-governing political unit consisting of a city and sometimes the surrounding territory that it controls.

civ·et (siv′it) *n.* **1.** any of various catlike animals related to the mongoose, native to the warmer regions of Africa, Europe, and Asia, having a narrow head, a pointed muzzle, and a slender body. Length: about 4 feet (1.2 meters), including tail. Also, **civet cat. 2.** the fur of any of these animals. **3.** a thick, yellowish substance, having a strong musklike odor, secreted by the anal glands of the civet, used in perfumes. [French *civette* civet perfume, civet cat, through Italian, from Arabic *zabād* civet perfume.]

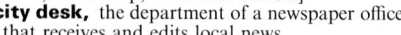

civet

civ·ic (siv′ik) *adj.* **1.** of or relating to a city: *civic improvements.* **2.** of or relating to citizens or citizenship: *I consider serving on a jury an important civic responsibility.* [Latin *cīvicus* relating to a citizen, from *cīvis* citizen.]

civ·ics (siv′iks) *n.* the study of the function, services, and purpose of a government and of the duties, rights, and privileges of citizenship. ➡ used as singular.

civ·il (siv′əl) *adj.* **1.** of or relating to a citizen or citizens. **2.** of or relating to the relations between a government and its citizens: *civil affairs.* **3.** occurring within the boundaries of a nation or among its citizens; domestic; internal: *civil strife.* **4.** not military or ecclesiastical: *a civil wedding ceremony.* **5.a.** polite; courteous: *a civil response.* **b.** polite but without warmth: *They were merely civil.* **6.** having social order and organized government; civilized. **7.** of or in accordance with civil law: *civil court, civil proceedings.* ➡ distinguished from criminal. **8.** of or relating to those divisions of time that are recognized as legal standards: *The civil week goes from Sunday to Saturday.* [Latin *cīvīlis* relating to a citizen, polite, from *cīvis* citizen.]

civil defense, organized plans for the defense and protection of life and property to be carried out by civilians in case of enemy attack or other national emergencies.

civil disobedience, refusal to obey a law or laws as a means of nonviolent protest because of one's moral conviction.

civil engineer, a person whose profession is civil engineering.

civil engineering, the profession of designing and supervising the construction of roads, bridges, and other public works.

ci·vil·ian (si vil′yən) *n.* **1.** a person who is not a member of the

military. **2.** a person who does not belong to a police force, firefighting unit, or similar organization. —*adj.* of or relating to civilians.

ci·vil·i·ty (si vil′i tē) *n., pl.* **-ties. 1.a.** politeness; courtesy. **b.** politeness without warmth. **2.** an act or expression of politeness or courtesy.

civ·i·li·za·tion (siv′ə lə zā′shən) *n.* **1.** a state or stage of human society characterized by a highly organized and complex level of social, economic, cultural, political, and intellectual development. **2.** the countries and peoples that have attained such a stage of development. **3.** the way of life of a particular people, place, or time: *medieval civilization, Greek civilization.* **4.** the act or process of civilizing or of becoming civilized. **5.** *Informal.* the style or way of life that includes those comforts to which one is accustomed: *After camping, it was good to be back in civilization.*

civ·i·lize (siv′ə līz′) *v.t.,* **-lized, -liz·ing. 1.** to bring out of a primitive or savage state and accustom to civilization. **2.** to bring to a socially accepted level of good breeding or culture; refine. [French *civiliser,* going back to Latin *cīvīlis.* See CIVIL.] —**civ′i·liz′er,** *n.*

civ·i·lized (siv′ə līzd′) *adj.* **1.** advanced beyond that which is primitive or savage; being part of civilization: *civilized society.* **2.** of or relating to countries or people so advanced: *a civilized way of life.* **3.** having or exhibiting culture or breeding; polite.

civil law 1. the body of law of a state or country that controls and regulates private rights and duties. ➡ distinguished from **criminal law. 2.** a system of law based on a document or code designed to embrace all possible situations, rather than on judicial decisions. ➡ distinguished from **common law.**

civil liberties, those rights, as specified in a constitution, that guarantee an individual freedom from arbitrary interference by a government.

civ·il·ly (siv′ə lē) *adv.* **1.a.** in a polite manner. **b.** in a coolly polite manner. **2.** in accordance with the civil law.

civil marriage, a marriage performed by a government official instead of by a member of the clergy.

civil rights, individual rights of a citizen, esp. those of personal liberty guaranteed to all U.S. citizens by the Constitution.

civil servant, a person who is employed in the civil service.

civil service 1. a category of governmental service in which individuals are hired on the basis of merit determined through the use of competitive examinations. **2.** the body of employees in all government administrative positions, except those in the military, legislature, or judiciary.

civil war 1. a war between two sections or groups within a country. **2. Civil War.** in the United States, the war between the North and the South from 1861 to 1865.

civil year, calendar year.

civ·vies (siv′ēz) *pl. n. Informal.* civilian clothes, as opposed to a uniform of some group, such as the military, police, or firefighters. [CIV(ILIAN) + -IE + -S¹.]

Cl, the symbol for chlorine.

cl *also,* **cl.** centiliter; centiliters.

cl. 1. claim. **2.** class. **3.** clause. **4.** clearance.

clab·ber (klab′ər) *n.* milk that has curdled in the process of souring. —*v.t., v.i.* to curdle, as milk. [Short for earlier *bonnyclabber* sour curdled milk, from Irish *bainne clabair.*]

clack (klak) *v.i.* **1.** to make a short, sharp sound, as by striking two pieces of wood together. **2.** to talk rapidly and continually; chatter. **3.** to cluck or cackle, as a hen does. —*v.t.* to cause to make a short, sharp sound. —*n.* **1.** a short, sharp sound: *the clack of knitting needles.* **2.** rapid, continual talk; chatter. [Imitative.] —**clack′er,** *n.*

clad (klad) a past tense and past participle of **clothe.**

clad·ding (klad′ing) *n.* **1.** a metal coating bonded to another metal, usually to protect the underlying metal from corrosion. **2.** the act or process of applying such a coating.

clad·o·phyll (klad′ə fil) *n.* a branch resembling a foliage leaf in shape and function.

claim (klām) *v.t.* **1.** to assert or demand possession of or recognition of one's right to: *None of the passengers claimed the suitcase. Both teams claimed a victory.* **2.** to declare as a fact or as true; maintain; contend: *He claimed that he saw the accident.* **3.** to call for; require: *Her work claimed the better part of her waking hours.* —*n.* **1.** the right or title to something: *a claim to an inheritance.* **2.** a declaration of something as a fact or as true; contention: *a claim of innocence.* **3.** a demand for something that is due: *After the robbery, the store's owner filed a claim with the insurance company.* **4.** something that is claimed, as a piece of land. [Old French *cla(i)mer* to call, cry out, lay claim to, from Latin *clāmāre* to call, proclaim.] —**claim′a·ble,** *adj.* —For Synonyms *(v.t.),* see CLAIM.

· **to lay claim to.** to assert one's right to: *to lay claim to property.*

claim·ant (klā′mənt) *n.* a person who makes a claim.

clair·voy·ance (klâr voi′əns) *n.* **1.** an alleged ability to perceive objects or events that are beyond the recognized range of the sense organs. **2.** unusually strong insight or perception. [French *clairvoyance* clear-sightedness, from *clairvoyant.* See CLAIRVOYANT.]

clair·voy·ant (klâr voi′ənt) *adj.* of, relating to, or having clairvoyance. —*n.* a person who is clairvoyant. [French *clairvoyant* clear-sighted, going back to Latin *clārus* clear, bright + *vidēre* to see.]

clam (klam) *n.* **1.** any of a group of bivalve saltwater or freshwater mollusks, many of which are highly valued as seafood, as the quahog and mussel. **2.** the edible part of such a mollusk. —*v.i.* **clammed, clam·ming.** to dig for clams. [Old English *clamm* fetter; with reference to the firm way a clam's shell closes up.]

· **to clam up.** *Slang.* to become or remain silent, esp. in an effort to withhold something; stop talking.

clam·bake (klam′bāk′) *n.* **1.** an outdoor party at which seafood, esp. clams, is prepared and served. **2.** *Informal.* a social gathering, esp. one that is large and noisy.

clam·ber (klam′bər, klam′ər) *v.i., v.t.* to climb by using both the hands and feet, esp. hastily or awkwardly. —*n.* an act or instance of clambering. [From *clamb,* obsolete past tense of CLIMB + -ER⁴.]

clam·my (klam′ē) *adj.,* **-mi·er, -mi·est.** cold and damp. —**clam′mi·ly,** *adv.* —**clam′mi·ness,** *n.*

clam·or (klam′ər) *also, British,* **clamour.** *n.* **1.** a loud, noisy outcry; uproar: *A clamor went up from the audience when they were told the show was canceled.* **2.** a vehement expression, as of protest or dissatisfaction: *a clamor for reform.* **3.** any loud and continuous noise: *the clamor of trumpets.* —*v.i.* to make loud, continuous cries or demands: *to clamor for lower taxes.* —*v.t.* to utter loudly or noisily. [Old French *clamor* cry, appeal, from Latin *clāmor* loud cry.] —**clam′or·er,** *n.*

clam·or·ous (klam′ər əs) *adj.* **1.** loud and noisy; vociferous. **2.** uttering vehement expressions, as of protest or dissatisfaction. —**clam′or·ous·ly,** *adv.* —**clam′or·ous·ness,** *n.*

clam·our (klam′ər) *British.* clamor.

clamp (klamp) *n.* any of several devices that operate on the principle of a vise, having two jaws that can be tightened to hold two or more things firmly together. —*v.t.* to fasten with or place in a clamp or clamps. [Of Germanic origin.]

· **to clamp down on.** *Informal.* to become more strict with; act to control.

clam·shell (klam′shel′) *n.* **1.** the shell of a clam. **2.** a bucket, hinged like the shell of a clam, used for dredging.

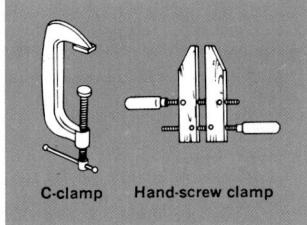

C-clamp   Hand-screw clamp

clamps

clan (klan) *n.* **1.** a group of families in a community who claim descent from a remote common ancestor. **2.** a group of people closely united by a common interest; clique. **3.** *Informal.* family. [Gaelic *clann* family, offspring, from Latin *planta* sprout, scion.]

clan·des·tine (klan des′tin) *adj.* secret, esp. for an illicit purpose; surreptitious; furtive. [Latin *clandestīnus.*] —**clan·des′tine·ly,** *adv.* —**clan·des′tine·ness,** *n.* —For Synonyms, see **secret.**

clang (klang) *n.* a loud, reverberating, ringing sound, as of metal striking metal. —*v.t.* to cause to make a clang: *They clanged the bell at noon.* —*v.i.* to make a clang. [Latin *clangere* to resound; partly imitative.]

clang·or (klang′gər, klang′ər) *also, British,* **clangour.** *n.* a continuous clanging. —*v.i.* to make a clangor. [Latin *clangor* sound.] —**clang′or·ous,** *adj.* —**clang′or·ous·ly,** *adv.*

clank (klangk) *n.* a sharp, abrupt, metallic sound, as the rattling of chains. —*v.i.* to make a clank or a series of clanks. —*v.t.* to cause to clank. [Imitative.]

clan·nish (klan′ish) *adj.* **1.** of, relating to, or characteristic of a clan. **2.** tending to stick closely together in a group; cliquish. —**clan′nish·ly,** *adv.* —**clan′nish·ness,** *n.*

clans·man (klanz′mən) *n., pl.* **-men** (-mən). a member of a clan.

a	at	e	end	o	hot	u	up	hw	white		about
ā	ape	ē	me	ō	old	ū	use	ng	song		taken
ä	far	i	it	ô	fork	ü	rule	th	thin	ə	pencil
âr	care	ī	ice	oi	oil	u̇	pull	th	this		lemon
		îr	pierce	ou	out	ûr	turn	zh	measure		circus

clans·wom·an (klanz′wŭm′ən) *n., pl.* **-wom·en** (-wim′ən). a female member of a clan.

clap (klap) *n.* **1.** a short, sharp sound, as that produced by two surfaces or forces coming together suddenly: *a clap of thunder, a clap of the hands.* **2.** a usually friendly slap: *a clap on the back.* —*v.*, **clapped, clap·ping.** —*v.t.* **1.** to strike (one's hands) together. **2.** to strike together with a clap: *The child clapped the blocks together.* **3.** to strike with the palm of the hand, as in friendship: *He clapped me on the back.* **4.** to put or place, esp. with a sudden or forceful motion: *She clapped her hands to her face. They clapped the prisoner into a cell.* —*v.i.* **1.** to strike one's hands together, esp. as an expression of approval or enjoyment; applaud. **2.** to make a short, sharp sound, by or as by suddenly striking two surfaces together: *The shutters clapped in the breeze.* [Old English *clæppan* to beat.]

clap·board (klab′ərd, klap′bôrd′) *n.* a thin, narrow board, having one thick edge, used as siding by being nailed horizontally in an overlapping manner. —*v.t.* to cover with clapboards. [Partial translation of Low German *klappholt* stave wood, from *klappen* to clap, fit together + *holt* wood.]

clap·per (klap′ər) *n.* **1.** the tongue of a bell. **2.** a person or thing that claps or makes a clapping sound.

clap·trap (klap′trap′) *n.* pretentious, empty talk; bunk; nonsense. [CLAP + TRAP[1]; originally referring to any device, or *trap,* used by actors to obtain applause, or a *clap.*]

claque (klak) *n.* **1.** an individual or organized group hired to applaud a performance, as in a theater. **2.** a group of sycophants or fawners. [French *claque* paid applauders in a theater, from *claquer* to clap; imitative.]

clar·et (klar′it) *n.* **1.** a dry red wine, esp. red Bordeaux wine. **2.** a deep purplish red color. —*adj.* having the color claret. [Old French *claret* wine clarified with honey, diminutive of *cler* clear, bright, from Latin *clārus.*]

clar·i·fi·ca·tion (klar′ə fi kā′shən) *n.* **1.** the act of clarifying or the state of being clarified. **2.** something, as a statement, that clarifies: *The government issued a clarification of policy.*

clar·i·fy (klar′ə fī′) *v.*, **-fied, -fy·ing.** —*v.t.* **1.** to show more intelligibly; explain: *to clarify one's stand on an issue.* **2.** to make pure and clear: *to clarify butter.* —*v.i.* **1.** to become intelligible. **2.** to become clear: *The water gradually clarified.* [Old French *clarifier* to make bright or clear, from Late Latin *clārificāre,* from Latin *clārus* clear, bright + *facere* to make.] —**clar′i·fi′er,** *n.*

clar·i·net (klar′ə net′) *n.* a musical instrument of the woodwind family, having a single-reed mouthpiece and played by means of finger holes and keys. [French *clarinette,* diminutive of *clarine* bell, going back to Latin *clārus* clear.] —**clar′i·net′ist;** *also, British,* **clar′i·net′tist,** *n.*

clar·i·on (klar′ē ən) *adj.* loud and clear. —*n.* **1.** a trumpet having a clear, shrill tone, popular in the seventeenth and eighteenth centuries. **2.** *Archaic.* **a.** the sound of a clarion. **b.** a sound resembling this. [Medieval Latin *clario* type of trumpet, from Latin *clārus* clear.]

clar·i·ty (klar′i tē) *n.* the quality of being clear; lucidity. [Latin *clāritās.*]

clash (klash) *n.* **1.** a loud, harsh, resounding noise, as of the collision of two metal objects: *the clash of cymbals.* **2.** a strong disagreement or conflict, esp. of opposing interests or opinions. —*v.i.* **1.** to come together with a clash. **2.** to be at variance; conflict; disagree: *The two senators clashed on the issue of new taxes.* **3.** to lack harmoniousness: *The orange sweater clashes with the red skirt.* —*v.t.* to cause to strike together with a clash. [Imitative.] —For Synonyms *(v.i.),* see **conflict.**

clarinet

clasp (klasp) *n.* **1.** a fastening, as a hook, used to hold two objects or parts together. **2.** a close or tight grasp or embrace. —*v.t.* **1.** to fasten together or secure with or as with a clasp. **2.** to encompass and hold closely with the arms and hands; embrace. **3.** to take firm hold of; grip with the hand. [Of uncertain origin.] —**clasp′er,** *n.*

clasp knife, a large pocket knife with one or more blades that fold into the handle.

class (klas) *n.* **1.** a number of persons or things grouped together because they are similar in some way; category: *a class of sailboats.* **2.** a group of students taught or studying together: *The biology class took a field trip to the aquarium.* **3.** a meeting of such a group: *I have a nine o'clock history class.* **4.** a group of students in school or college who are ranked together or graduate in the same year: *She was a member of the graduating class. He was in the freshman class.* **5.a.** a rank, section, or division of society, regarded as a unit due to common economic, occupational, or other social characteristics: *the upper classes, the working class.* **b.** the division of society into such units: *Class divided the people of the*

city. **6.** social rank, esp. high rank. **7.** a level, grade, or quality: *third-class mail, reservations in the lowest class on a boat.* **8.** *Biology.* a category of organisms classified below a phylum or division and above an order: *Apes belong to the order of primates and tigers belong to the order of carnivores, but they both belong to the class Mammalia.* **9.** *Slang.* excellence, esp. of style; elegance. —*v.t.* to place or group in a class; classify. [Latin *classis* a division of the Roman people, fleet[1].]

class action, a legal action taken by one or more persons on their own behalf and on behalf of all other persons whom the case affects: *to bring a class action against an industrial polluter.*

clas·sic (klas′ik) *adj.* **1.** serving as a standard, model, or guide because of excellence: *That cathedral is considered a classic example of Gothic design.* **2.** simple, regular, and restrained, as in style or lines: *The suit was in a classic style.* **3.** having all the characteristics typical of its kind: *a classic case of mistaken identity.* **4.** classical *(def. 1).* —*n.* **1.** an author, artist, or artistic work of acknowledged excellence and endurance. **2. the classics.** the literature of ancient Greece and Rome. **3.** a style, or an item executed in such a style, that is simple, restrained, and enduring. **4.** an event that is considered typical or traditional and of great importance: *The World Series is the classic of baseball.* [Latin *classicus* of the highest class, of the first rank, from *classis* a division or class of the Roman people; referring first to people, then to works of literature.]

clas·si·cal (klas′i kəl) *adj.* **1.** of or relating to ancient Greece or Rome or their art, literature, or culture. **2.** learned in or based on the classics: *a classical scholar, classical studies.* **3.** *Music.* **a.** of or relating to music that conforms to certain chiefly European standards of form and style and is held to be of enduring interest and value. Bach's, Beethoven's, and Brahms's compositions are examples of classical music. **b.** of, relating to, or adhering to a musical style of the middle eighteenth through the early nineteenth centuries, characterized by homophony, symmetry, simplicity, formal structure, and emotional restraint. Mozart and Haydn are the most famous classical composers. **4.** thought of as standard and authoritative: *classical economics.* **5.** relating to a course of study based upon the humanities, fine arts, and general sciences, as opposed to the technical fields. **6.** classic *(defs. 2, 3).* —**clas′si·cal·ly,** *adv.*

clas·si·cism (klas′ə siz′əm) *n.* **1.** aesthetic principles derived from the literature and art of ancient Greece and Rome but found as ideals in all ages. Classicism strives for perfect order, harmony, and clarity in form achieved by an emphasis on such elements as symmetry, proportion, technical perfection, simplicity, and restraint. **2.** adherence to these principles. **3.** knowledge or study of these principles; classical scholarship.

clas·si·cist (klas′ə sist) *n.* **1.** a person, as an artist, who adheres to the principles of classicism. **2.** a person who is versed or expert in the classics. **3.** a person who strongly advocates the study of the classics.

clas·si·fi·ca·tion (klas′ə fi kā′shən) *n.* **1.** the act of classifying. **2.** the result of classifying or being classified. **3.** *Biology.* the grouping of plants and animals in categories, as genus or species, on the basis of their structural and evolutionary relationships; taxonomy. —**clas·si·fi·ca·to·ry** (klas′ə fi kə tôr′ē, kla sif′ə-; *British* klas′ə fi kā′tə rē), *adj.*

clas·si·fied (klas′ə fīd′) *adj.* not available for public knowledge, esp. for reasons of national security; secret.

classified ad, a condensed advertisement, usually one arranged in a special section of a newspaper or magazine, as for help wanted or real estate. Also, **classified advertisement.**

clas·si·fy (klas′ə fī′) *v.*, **-fied, -fy·ing.** —*v.t.* **1.** to arrange or group in classes according to a given criterion or criteria. **2.** to designate or label (something) as secret in order to restrict or limit knowledge of its contents. —*v.i.* to qualify for or be in a class. [Latin *classis* class + -FY. See CLASS.] —**clas′si·fi′a·ble,** *adj.* —**clas′si·fi′er,** *n.*

class·mate (klas′māt′) *n.* a member of the same class in school or college.

class·room (klas′rüm′, -rùm′) *n.* a room in which classes are held.

class struggle 1. in Marxist theory, the economic and political struggle for power between capitalists and workers. **2.** any conflict between the social classes of a society.

clas·sy (klas′ē) *adj.*, **class·i·er, class·i·est.** excellent or elegant, esp. in style; having class; smart. —**class′i·ness,** *n.*

clas·tic (klas′tik) *adj.* of, relating to, or designating a rock or sediment composed of fragments of preexisting rock, or the fragments themselves. [Greek *klastos* broken (from *klan* to break) + -IC.]

clat·ter (klat′ər) *n.* **1.** a rattling noise, as of hard objects striking against one another: *the clatter of dishes.* **2.** noisy disorder; commotion: *the clatter of a mob in the streets.* **3.** noisy or idle

talk; chatter: *the clatter at a large party.* —*v.i.* **1.** to make a rattling noise: *The pots and pans clattered as I put them away.* **2.** to move with such a noise: *The wagon clattered over the wooden bridge.* **3.** to talk noisily or idly; chatter: *The children clattered after school.* —*v.t.* to cause to clatter. [Probably from an unrecorded Old English word.]

clause (klôz) *n.* **1.** a group of words containing a subject and predicate, forming part of a complex or compound sentence. The two kinds of clauses are the independent clause and the dependent clause. **2.** a subdivision, as an article, stipulation, or provision, of a formal or legal document. [Old French *clause,* from Medieval Latin *clausa* close of a periodic sentence, section of a law, going back to Latin *claudere* to close.]

claus·tro·pho·bi·a (klôs′trə fō′bē ə) *n.* an abnormal fear of being in small, crowded, or enclosed spaces. [Modern Latin *claustrophobia,* from Latin *claustrum* bolt, enclosure + Greek *-phobiā.* See PHOBIA.] —**claus′tro·pho′bic,** *adj.*

clave (klāv) *Archaic.* a past tense of **cleave**[2].

clav·i·chord (klav′i kôrd′) *n.* a keyboard instrument whose tones were produced by the striking of brass wedges against metal strings. It was a forerunner of the piano. [Medieval Latin *clavichordium* key string, from Latin *clāvis* key + *chorda* string. See CHORD[2].]

clav·i·cle (klav′i kəl) *n.* either of two long slender bones connecting the breastbone and the shoulder blade; collarbone. For illustration, see **skeleton.** [Modern Latin *clavicula,* from Latin *clāvicula* bolt, small key, diminutive of *clāvis* key; referring to its shape.] —**cla·vic·u·lar** (klə vik′yə lər), *adj.*

cla·vier (klə vîr′, klā′vē ər, klav′ē-) *n.* **1.** any stringed keyboard instrument, as the clavichord, harpsichord, or piano. **2.** the keyboard of a musical instrument, esp. of a stringed instrument. [French *clavier,* going back to Latin *clāvis* key.]

claw (klô) *n.* **1.a.** a sharp, usually curved nail on the foot of a bird or animal. **b.** a foot with such a nail or nails. **2.** one of the pincers or pincerlike appendages of certain crustaceans or insects, as of a lobster or scorpion. **3.** anything resembling a claw, as the forked end of the head of a hammer. —*v.t., v.i.* to scratch or tear with or as with claws. [Old English *clawu* nail, foot with such nails, pincers of a shellfish.] —**clawed,** *adj.* —**claw′like′,** *adj.*

claw hammer 1. a hammer having one end of the head forked and curved for pulling out nails. **2.** *Informal.* swallow-tailed coat.

clay (klā) *n.* **1.a.** a fine-grained earthy material, consisting mostly of hydrated aluminum silicates, that can be molded when wet but hardens permanently when fired, as in the making of pottery, sculptured models, bricks, and porcelain. **b.** a synthetic substance similar to this, used esp. for modeling, that does not harden permanently and cannot be fired. Also, **modeling clay. 2.** a person or thing that can be shaped, manipulated, or easily influenced: *The students were clay in the hands of the famous artist.* **3.** the human body, esp. as distinguished from the soul. **4.** earth; soil. [Old English *clæg* sticky earth.] —**clay′like′,** *adj.*
• **feet of clay.** personal weakness or flaw in one considered a hero or model.

clay·ey (klā′ē) *adj.,* **clay·i·er, clay·i·est. 1.** of, like, or containing clay. **2.** covered with clay.

clay·more (klā′môr′) *n.* a broadsword used by Scottish Highland warriors. [Gaelic *claidheamh mōr* broadsword, from *claidheamh* sword + *mōr* great.]

clay pigeon 1. a saucer-shaped clay disk tossed into the air as a target in trapshooting. **2.** *Slang.* a person who can be taken advantage of easily.

-cle *suffix* used to form the diminutive of nouns: *corpuscle.* [French *-cle,* from Latin *-culus.*]

clean (klēn) *adj.* **1.** free from dirt or filth; unsoiled; unstained: *clean clothes.* **2.** free from foreign or extraneous matter; unadulterated: *clean water, clean air.* **3.** characterized by or having moral integrity; honorable: *clean living, a clean record.* **4.** fair or within the rules, as in sports: *a clean fighter, a clean basketball game.* **5.** not obscene or indecent: *a clean joke.* **6.** free from embellishments or irregularities; even: *a clean incision, the clean lines of a new building.* **7.** complete; entire; thorough: *to make a clean break with the past.* **8.** trim; well-proportioned: *the clean limbs of a thoroughbred horse.* **9.** keeping oneself or one's surroundings free from dirt or disorder; neat in habits: *The cat is a clean animal.* **10.** showing skill and ease; adroit; deft: *a clean golf swing.* **11.** empty or blank; bare: *a clean sheet of paper.* **12.** free from obstructions or restrictions: *a clean getaway.* **13.** having few corrections or alterations; easily legible: *to produce clean copy for a printer.* **14.** (of nuclear weapons) producing relatively little or no radioactive fallout: *a clean bomb.* —*adv.* **1.** in a clean manner. **2.** all the way; completely; entirely; wholly: *The arrow passed clean through the target.* —*v.t.* **1.** to make free of dirt, impurities, or extraneous matter: *to clean a car, to clean air with*

a filter. **2.** to remove or get rid of by cleaning: *to clean dishes off a table, to clean grease from a shirt.* **3.** to prepare (food, as fish or fowl) for cooking. —*v.i.* to undergo or perform cleaning: *The raccoon cleaned thoroughly.* [Old English *clǣne* clear, pure.] —**clean′ness,** *n.*
• **to clean out. a.** to remove dirt or trash from. **b.** to make empty or use up; exhaust: *to clean out a supply cabinet, to clean out a store's stock during a sale.* **c.** to take away the money or resources from: *Our last business venture cleaned us out.*
• **to clean up. a.** to clear of dirt, trash, disorder, or other undesirable matter. **b.** *Informal.* to finish; complete: *We'll clean up this project before starting the next.* **c.** to make oneself fresh or clean: *Let's clean up before we eat.* **d.** *Slang.* to make a large profit.
• **to come clean.** *Slang.* to tell the truth; confess.

Synonyms *v.t.* **Clean** and **cleanse** mean to rid something of dirt or other impure substances. **Clean** is the more general term and may or may not suggest methods: *to clean one's shoes with a brush, to clean a closet.* **Cleanse** suggests purification, either by the use of fluids or in an abstract sense: *to cleanse a wound with alcohol, to cleanse the soul of sin.*

clean-cut (klēn′kut′) *adj.* **1.** sharply defined, as in outline or meaning; clear; definite: *a clean-cut statement of the facts.* **2.** having a wholesome appearance or personality: *a clean-cut young person.*

clean·er (klē′nər) *n.* **1.** a person or organization whose work or business is cleaning, esp. dry cleaning. **2.** something that cleans, as a machine or chemical substance.

clean-limbed (klēn′limd′) *adj.* having shapely or well-proportioned limbs.

clean·li·ness (klen′lē nis) *n.* the state of being clean, esp. habitually clean.

clean·ly[1] (klen′lē) *adj.,* **-li·er, -li·est.** carefully and habitually clean or kept clean. [Old English *clǣnic* pure, clean.]

clean·ly[2] (klēn′lē) *adv.* in a clean manner. [Old English *clǣnlīce* purely, entirely.]

clean room, a room in which humidity and temperature are strictly controlled and contaminants, as dust and bacteria, are virtually eliminated, used in hospitals and factories that assemble sensitive parts or materials.

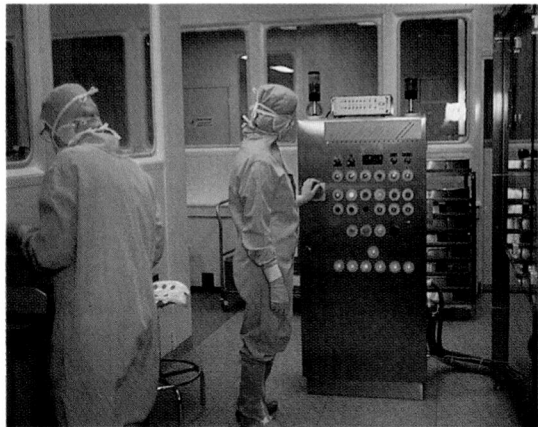

clean room

cleanse (klenz) *v.t.,* **cleansed, cleans·ing. 1.** to free from dirt, filth, or other undesirable matter: *to cleanse a wound.* **2.** to free from moral taint or guilt; purge: *to cleanse one's soul.* [Middle English *clensen,* from Old English *clǣnsian,* from *clǣne* clean.] —For Synonyms, see **clean.**

cleans·er (klen′zər) *n.* a substance, as soap or detergent, that removes dirt or other undesirable matter.

clean-shav·en (klēn′shā′vən) *adj.* having all the facial hair shaved off.

clean·up (klēn′up′) *n.* **1.** the thorough removal of dirt or taint, esp. an elimination of vice or corruption. **2.** *Slang.* an exception-

a	at	e	end	o	hot	u	up	hw	white		about
ā	ape	ē	me	ō	old	ū	use	ng	song		taken
ä	far	i	it	ô	fork	ü	rule	th	thin	ə	pencil
âr	care	ī	ice	oi	oil	u̇	pull	th	this		lemon
		îr	pierce	ou	out	ûr	turn	zh	measure		circus

ally large profit. —*adj.* designating the fourth batter in a baseball batting order.

clear (klîr) *adj.* **1.** free from anything that darkens, dims, or clouds; bright: *a clear morning, a clear sky.* **2.** free from anything impairing transparency or purity of color; not murky: *a clear yellow, clear water.* **3.** free from blemishes: *a clear complexion.* **4.** free from obstructions or hindrances; not blocked; open: *The road is now clear.* **5.** sharply defined and easily seen; not blurred; distinct: *a clear photograph, clear fingerprints.* **6.** easily understood; fully intelligible: *a clear description of an event.* **7.** understood without question; unmistakable; obvious: *It soon became clear we were lost.* **8.** free from confusion, uncertainty, or doubt; not vague; sharp: *a clear head, clear thinking.* **9.** free from entanglement or connection; out of reach or touch; not in contact (often with *of*): *Stand clear of the falling tree. We kept clear of them after the quarrel.* **10.** not feeling or showing signs of feeling disturbed or troubled; serene: *a clear conscience.* **11.** without limitation or qualification; complete; absolute: *a clear defeat.* **12.** without diminution or further cost to be deducted; net: *We made a clear profit of $500.* **13.** free from hoarse or rasping qualities; sounding distinctly or purely; plainly audible: *a clear voice, a clear tone.* **14.** free from knots, roughness, or protrusions: *a clear pine board.* —*adv.* **1.** in a clear manner; plainly; distinctly: *She shouted it loud and clear.* **2.** all the way; completely; entirely: *He climbed clear to the top of the tree.* —*v.t.* **1.** to free from anything that occupies, obstructs, or impedes use or passage (often with *off, of,* or *out*): *Please clear the aisle. The cook cleared off the counter. The police cleared the street of traffic for the parade.* **2.** to remove (a person or thing) that occupies, obstructs, or encumbers (often with *away, off,* or *out*): *The judge ordered the bailiff to clear the spectators from the courtroom. Clear the dishes off the table. We cleared the snow out of the driveway.* **3.** to free from blemishes, impurities, or foreign matter (often with *up*): *This ointment should clear up your skin in a few days.* **4.** to pass by, over, or through without touching: *The runner cleared the hurdle. The plane barely cleared the trees.* **5.** to free of accusations or suspicions of guilt, blame, or responsibility; acquit; vindicate: *His testimony cleared her of the charges.* **6.** to go through or be approved by, esp. without difficulty or hindrance; pass: *The travelers cleared customs and boarded the bus. The bill cleared the Senate.* **7.** to submit for approval and receive authorization or clearance for: *We cleared the budgetary request with the accountant.* **8.** to give approval or clearance to or for; authorize: *The manager cleared them for sensitive research projects. The mechanics cleared the plane for takeoff.* **9.** to remove cloudiness from; brighten: *to clear a mirror.* **10.** to free of confusion, uncertainty, or vagueness: *The cold shower cleared my head.* **11.** to remove accumulated totals or information or previously made settings from: *to clear an adding machine, to clear a cash register.* **12.** to gain as profit beyond expenses or charges; net: *to clear $20,000 annually.* **13.** to charge (a check) to an account having sufficient funds to cover the amount: *The bank cleared the check I wrote for the groceries.* **14.** to pass (checks, notes, or bills) through a clearinghouse in order to settle accounts between different banks. —*v.i.* **1.** to become free of cloudiness, fog, or obscurity; grow bright or become fair, as the weather (often with *up*): *The sky cleared around noon. It finally cleared up after two days of rain.* **2.** to come to an end or vanish; disperse; disappear (often with *away* or *up*): *When the smoke cleared away, we could see the damage from the fire. My rash cleared up in a week.* **3.** to become free of confusion, uncertainty, or vagueness: *His head cleared after he'd eaten some breakfast. Her vision cleared after she'd been up for a while.* **4.** to become free of murkiness: *We watched the solution clear in the test tube.* **5.** to obtain approval or clearance. **6.** (of a check) to be charged to an account having sufficient funds to cover the amount. **7.** to pass checks, notes, or bills through a clearinghouse in order to settle accounts between different banks. **8.** *Informal.* to go away; depart; leave (often with *off* or *out*): *We told the trespassers to clear off or we'd call the police. The spy cleared out of the country.* [Old French *cler* pure, bright, from Latin *clārus* bright, manifest.] —**clear′ly**, *adv.* —**clear′ness**, *n.*

• **in the clear.** *Informal.* free or absolved of guilt; not under suspicion.

• **to clear the air.** to dispel ambiguities or emotional tensions; settle misunderstandings or differences.

• **to clear up.** to clarify or solve: *to clear up a mystery, to clear up a misunderstanding.*

Synonyms *adj.* **Clear, transparent,** and **translucent** mean able to be seen through. **Clear** suggests simply that nothing interferes with vision: *Through the clear water we could see fish on the bottom.* **Transparent** suggests more strongly that nothing visible comes between the viewer and the object: *Most window glass is transparent.* **Translucent** describes the passage of enough light to allow shapes, but not details, to be seen: *The actors' silhouettes were visible through the translucent screen.*

clear·ance (klîr′əns) *n.* **1.** the act of clearing: *the clearance of trees for new construction.* **2.** approval or certification as free from objection, prohibition, or suspicion: *We received budgetary clearance for additional advertising expenses. The research staff got clearance to work on the secret project.* **3.** the disposal of merchandise, esp. discontinued stock, at reduced prices to make room for new goods. Also, **clearance sale. 4.** permission to proceed, as after having satisfied certain requirements: *The plane received clearance from the control tower. The ship and its cargo received clearance to dock.* **5.** an official certificate granting such permission. Also, **clearance papers. 6.** the amount of clear space between two things, as between an overpass and the road underneath it: *This tunnel has a clearance of ten feet.* **7.** the distance by which a moving object clears something: *There was a clearance of two feet between the truck and the walls of the tunnel.* **8.** the process of clearing checks, notes, or bills through a clearinghouse.

clear-cut (klîr′kut′) *adj.* **1.** having a distinct outline: *the clear-cut features of a face, a clear-cut profile.* **2.** completely evident or clear; direct; definite: *It was a clear-cut case of mistaken identity.* —*v.t.,* **-cut, -cut·ting.** to remove all the trees from (an area) by cutting: *The developers clear-cut thirty acres for new houses.*

clear·head·ed (klîr′hed′id) *adj.* having or suggesting a clear head; without confusion; alert; sensible: *The pilot of the small plane remained clearheaded enough to send out a distress call before crashing. The committee suggested a clearheaded approach to the problem.* —**clear′head′ed·ly,** *adv.* —**clear′head′ed·ness,** *n.*

clear·ing (klîr′ing) *n.* **1.** a tract of land, esp. within a densely wooded area, free of trees, brush, or other obstructions. **2.** the exchange between banks of checks, notes, or bills in a clearinghouse to settle differences in accounts.

clear·ing·house (klîr′ing hous′) *also,* **clearing house.** *n., pl.* **-hous·es** (-hou′ziz). **1.** an office maintained by a voluntary association, as of bankers or brokers, where accounts among its members are settled by means of a central computer or the mutual exchange of checks, notes, bills, or stocks. **2.** any central source or headquarters for assignment, collection, or distribution, as of funds or information.

clear-sight·ed (klîr′sī′tid) *adj.* **1.** having or showing acute and accurate perception and sound judgment; discerning. **2.** having keen vision. —**clear′-sight′ed·ly,** *adv.* —**clear′-sight′ed·ness,** *n.*

clear·sto·ry (klîr′stôr′ē) clerestory.

cleat (klēt) *n.* **1.a.** a protruding piece of rubber or metal attached to the sole of a shoe to increase traction. **b. cleats.** sports shoes that grip the ground by means of cleats on the sole, used chiefly in football, baseball, and track. **2.** a wedgelike metal or wood block with projections at both ends, used for controlling or securing ropes, esp. on the spar or rail of a boat. **3.** a piece of wood or iron fastened across a surface as a support or to prevent slipping, as on a ramp. —*v.t.* **1.** to furnish with a cleat or cleats. **2.** to fasten to or with a cleat. [Middle English *clete* wedge, from an unrecorded Old English word.]

cleav·age (klē′vij) *n.* **1.** the process or state of being cleft; fissure; rift: *the cleavage of a tree trunk into branches, a cleavage of opinion.* **2.a.** the series of cell divisions by which a fertilized egg splits into a number of smaller cells, or blastomeres, without increasing in overall size. This process changes the egg into an embryo. **b.** any one of these cell divisions. **3.** the tendency of certain minerals and rocks to split in a way that produces smooth plane surfaces. **4.** *Informal.* the space between a woman's breasts, esp. as emphasized by a low neckline.

cleave¹ (klēv) *v.,* **cleaved** or **cleft** or **clove, cleaved** or **cleft** or **clo·ven, cleav·ing.** —*v.t.* **1.** to split or part by force; rend apart; divide: *The lightning cleaved the tree.* **2.** to pass through; pierce: *The ship's prow cleaved the choppy waters.* **3.** to form by or as by cutting: *to cleave a trail through the forest.* —*v.i.* **1.** to come apart; split. **2.** to advance or penetrate (with *through*): *The ship cleaved through the waves.* [Old English *clēofan* to split.] —**cleav′a·ble,** *adj.*

cleave² (klēv) *v.i.,* **cleaved** or *(archaic)* **clave, cleaved, cleaving. 1.** to stick fast; adhere (with *to*): *Mud cleaved to my shoes.* **2.** to remain attached, devoted, or faithful (with *to*): *to cleave to a principle.* [Old English *cleofian, clifian* to stick, adhere.]

cleav·er (klē′vər) *n.* a heavy, short-handled, broad-bladed implement for chopping meat, used esp. by butchers.

cleav·ers (klē′vərz) *n.* any of several slender New World plants with whorled leaves, genus *Galium,* esp. *G. aparine,* having stems covered with small hooks. ➡ used as singular or plural. [CLEAVE(E)² + -ER¹ + -S¹.]

clef (klef) *n. Music.* a symbol placed on a staff to indicate the name and pitch of the notes on the various lines and spaces. [French *clef* key, key in music, from Latin *clāvis* key.]

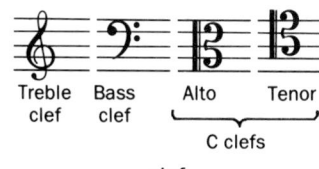

Treble clef   Bass clef   Alto   Tenor

C clefs

clef

cleft¹ (kleft) *n.* **1.** a space or opening made by splitting; crack; fissure: *a cleft in a rock.* **2.** an indentation that is made when the parts of something separate: *the cleft in a horse's hoof.* [Modification of earlier *clift* crack, split, from Old English *(ge)clyft.*]

cleft² (kleft) *v.* a past tense and past participle of **cleave¹.** —*adj.* **1.** appearing to be split; partially or completely divided: *a cleft chin.* **2.** *Botany.* having deep narrow divisions, as a leaf.

cleft palate, a complete or partial split along the length of the palate of the mouth, resulting from faulty embryonic development.

cleis·tog·a·mous (klīs tog′ə məs) *adj.* (of flowers) small, closed, and self-pollinated. [Greek *kleistos* shut + *gamos* marriage.]

clem·a·tis (klem′ə tis, kli mat′is) *n.* any of a group of mostly climbing plants, genus *Clematis,* widely distributed in temperate regions and cultivated for their showy, variously colored flowers. [Latin *clēmatis,* from Greek *klēmatis,* from *klēma* vine branch.]

clem·en·cy (klem′ən sē) *n.* **1.** a disposition to be merciful in punishing or judging; leniency: *The shopkeeper showed clemency in refusing to prosecute the thief.* **2.** mildness of weather or climate. [Latin *clēmentia.*] —For Synonyms, see **mercy.**

clem·ent (klem′ənt) *adj.* **1.** forbearing, forgiving, or merciful in disposition or character; lenient: *a clement judge, a clement use of authority.* **2.** (of weather or climate) temperate; mild. [Latin *clēmēns.*] —**clem′ent·ly,** *adv.*

clench (klench) *v.t.* **1.** to close or press together tensely or tightly: *to clench one's fists, to clench one's teeth.* **2.** to grasp or grip firmly or tensely; clutch: *She clenched her father's hand as the winner of the contest was announced.* **3.** clinch *(defs. 2, 3).* —*n.* **1.** an act or instance of clenching; a firm or tense grasp or grip. **2.** something that clenches or grips. [Old English *(be)clencan* to hold fast.]

clep·sy·dra (klep′si drə) *n., pl.* **-dras** or **-drae** (-drē′). water clock. [Latin *clepsydra,* from Greek *klepsydrā,* from *kleptein* to steal + *hydōr* water; referring to the water's *stealing* out of the vessel.]

clep·to·ma·ni·a (klep′tə mā′nē ə) kleptomania.

clere·sto·ry (klîr′stôr′ē) *also,* **clearstory.** *n., pl.* **-ries.** the highest story or uppermost portion of a wall of a building, esp. a church, having a series of windows for lighting and airing the interior. [Earlier *clere* light, clear + STORY²; referring to its windows. See CLEAR.]

cler·gy (klûr′jē) *n., pl.* **-gies.** a body of persons ordained for religious service, as ministers, priests, or rabbis, collectively. ➡ distinguished from **laity.** [Old French *clergie* clerkship, body of clergymen, from *clerc* clergyman, from Latin *clēricus.* See CLERIC.]

cler·gy·man (klûr′jē mən) *n., pl.* **-men** (-mən). a person ordained as a minister, priest, or rabbi; a member of the clergy.

clerestory

cler·gy·wom·an (klûr′jē-wùm′ən) *n., pl.* **-wom·en** (-wim′ən). a female member of the clergy.

cler·ic (kler′ik) *n.* a member of the clergy. [Latin *clēricus* clergyman, from Greek *clērikos* clergyman, relating to the clergy, from *klēros* clergy; originally, lot; because their lot is the service of God.]

cler·i·cal (kler′i kəl) *adj.* **1.** of or relating to clerks or office workers or their work: *clerical errors, clerical duties.* **2.** of, relating to, or characteristic of the clergy: *clerical robes.* **3.** advocating clericalism. —*n.* **1.** a member of the clergy. **2. clericals.** clerical attire, as a cassock, worn by certain members of the clergy when not officiating at religious services. [Late Latin *clēricālis* relating to the clergy, from Latin *clēricus* clergyman. See CLERIC.] —**cler′i·cal·ly,** *adv.*

clerical collar, a stiff, white, bandlike collar fastened at the back of the neck and worn without a tie by certain members of the clergy.

cler·i·cal·ism (kler′i kə liz′əm) *n.* **1.** the power or influence of the clergy in politics or secular affairs. **2.** belief in the desirability of such power or influence. —**cler′i·cal·ist,** *n.*

clerk (klûrk; *British* klärk) *n.* **1.** a person employed, as in a commercial establishment, to handle correspondence, keep records, accounts, or files, and do other general office work. **2.** a person employed to sell merchandise in a store; salesclerk. **3.** a person whose job involves direct dealing with, or service to, customers or clients: *a room clerk in a hotel, a reservations clerk for an airline.* **4.** an official who keeps records and correspondence and performs routine business, as in a court of law or legislature: *a county clerk, a town clerk.* **5.** an attorney who works as an assistant to a judge after having been admitted to the bar. **6.** a layperson or student of the ministry who assists a parish priest. **7.** *Archaic.* a literate person; scholar. **8.** *Archaic.* a member of the clergy. —*v.i.* **1.** to work or act as a clerk: *to clerk behind the glove counter.* **2.** (of an attorney) to work as an assistant to a judge after having been admitted to the bar. [Partly from Old English *cler(i)c* clergyman, partly from Old French *clerc* clergyman, official in charge of records and correspondence, both from Latin *clēricus* clergyman. The few people who could read and write in the Christian West during the Middle Ages were mostly priests and monks. See CLERIC.] —**clerk′ship′,** *n.*

clerk·ly (klûrk′lē) *adj.,* **-li·er, -li·est. 1.** of, relating to, or characteristic of a clerk. **2.** *Archaic.* learned; scholarly.

clev·er (klev′ər) *adj.* **1.** mentally keen and alert; quick-witted: *a clever lawyer, a clever liar.* **2.** showing skill or mental keenness; shrewd; ingenious: *a clever scheme, a clever remark.* **3.** having or showing skill in performing a physical act, esp. with the hands; adroit. [Of uncertain origin.] —**clev′er·ly,** *adv.* —**clev′er·ness,** *n.*

> **Synonyms** Clever, adroit, and ingenious all mean having or showing mental resourcefulness, as in solving problems or coming up with new ways to do things. **Clever** indicates a general ability to use one's mind quickly and efficiently: *The clever employee saved the company a great deal of money.* **Adroit** suggests an almost physical flexibility or smoothness: *An adroit change of emphasis got the debater out of a difficult corner.* **Ingenious** suggests originality or inventiveness: *The researchers patented an ingenious machine for garbage disposal.*

clev·is (klev′is) *n.* a fastening device consisting of a U-shaped piece of metal into which something, as a shaft, hook, or lever, can be bolted. [Possibly of Scandinavian origin.]

clew (klü) *n.* **1.** *British.* clue *(def. 1).* **2.** *also,* **clue.** a ball of thread, yarn, or cord. **3.** *also,* **clue.** either lower corner of a square sail or the lower aft corner of a fore-and-aft sail. —*v.t. also,* **clue. 1.** to coil or roll into a ball. **2.** to raise or lower (a sail) by the clews. [Old English *cleowen, cliwen* ball of thread. In certain legends, as that of Theseus, a ball of thread served as a means of solving a problem (or *clue*), for it was used in escaping from a labyrinth.]

clew·line (klü′līn′) *n.* a rope attached to the clew of a square sail, used to raise and lower the sail.

cli·ché (klē shā′) *n.* **1.** an expression, phrase, or idea made trite by overuse; for example, *as pretty as a picture.* **2.** a trite or hackneyed plot, theme, or motif, as in art or literature. [French *cliché* stereotype plate, trite expression, from *clicher* to stereotype, imitative of the sound of the die hitting the metal; referring to the repetition of an expression or phrase over and over again in the same way.] —For Synonyms, see **truism.**

click (klik) *n.* **1.** a light, sharp, often metallic sound: *the click of fingernails on typewriter keys, the click of a key in a lock.* **2.** pawl. **3.** a speech sound, esp. characteristic of certain southern African languages, produced by pressing the tongue against some part of the mouth and quickly withdrawing it with a sucking action. Also *(def. 3),* **suction stop.** —*v.t.* to move (something) with a click; cause to make a click or clicks: *He clicked his heels together. She sat there clicking the top of the pen.* —*v.i.* **1.** to move with a click; produce a click or clicks: *Their heels clicked on the sidewalk.* **2.** *Informal.* **a.** to fit or function harmoniously; agree: *We clicked as friends as soon as we met.* **b.** to become comprehensible or intelligible; make sense: *All the clues in the mystery suddenly clicked in my mind.* **3.** *Slang.* to be a success; do or go well: *The new show clicked with the audience.* [Imitative.]

a	at	e	end	o	hot	u	up	hw	white		about
ā	ape	ē	me	ō	old	ū	use	ng	song		taken
ä	far	i	it	ô	fork	ü	rule	th	thin	ə	pencil
âr	care	ī	ice	oi	oil	ù	pull	th	this		lemon
				îr	pierce	ou	out	ûr	turn	zh	measure		circus

click beetle, any of a group of beetles, family Elateridae, that when placed on their backs throw themselves into the air and right themselves while making a loud snapping noise. Also, **elater, snapping beetle.**

cli·ent (klī'ənt) *n.* **1.** a person, group, or company that engages the professional advice or services of another: *an advertising agency with many clients, a lawyer who had many corporations for clients.* **2.** a customer of any business. **3.** a person who receives benefits or services from a government bureau or social service agency. **4.** a person or group under the guardianship and protection of another; dependent. [Latin *cliēns* retainer[1], dependent.]

cli·en·tele (klī'ən tel') *n.* clients or customers collectively: *a business with a loyal clientele.* [French *clientèle,* from Latin *clientēla.*]

cliff (klif) *n.* a high, steep, often perpendicular or overhanging face of rock, earth, or glacial ice. [Old English *clif* rock, steep descent.]

cliff dweller 1. *also,* **Cliff Dweller.** a member of a prehistoric tribe who were the ancestors of the Pueblo Indians of the southwestern United States and built their houses in caves or on ledges of cliff walls. **2.** *Informal.* a person who lives in an apartment house, esp. in a large city.

cliff dwelling in Mesa Verde National Park

cliff dwelling, a dwelling built in a cave or on a ledge of a cliff wall. Ruins of cliff dwellings are found in Arizona, New Mexico, Utah, and Colorado.

cliff-hang·er (klif'hang'ər) *also,* **cliff·hang·er** *n.* **1.** an exciting adventure serial or melodrama, esp. one presented in installments each of which ends in suspense. **2.** any contest or situation having an uncertain and anxiously awaited outcome: *The election was a real cliff-hanger.*

cliff swallow, a migratory swallow, *Petrochelidon pyrrhonota,* that lives in colonies in bottle-shaped mud nests under the eaves of buildings or against cliffs.

cli·mac·ter·ic (klī mak'tər ik, klī'mak ter'-) *n.* **1.** a critical or crucial period or stage, as in a person's life. **2.** the period of life during which the capacity to reproduce decreases, ending for women in menopause. —*adj.* of or relating to a critical period or stage. Also *(adj.),* **cli'mac·ter'·i·cal.** [Latin *clīmactēricus* relating to a critical period, from Greek *klīmaktērikos,* from *klīmaktēr* critical period, rung of a ladder.]

cli·mac·tic (klī mak'tik) *adj.* of, relating to, or constituting a climax: *The third scene in the play was a climactic one.* —**cli·mac'ti·cal·ly,** *adv.*

cli·mate (klī'mit) *n.* **1.** the weather characteristic of or prevailing in an area over an extended period of time, usually considered in terms of average temperature, humidity, precipitation, and wind conditions. **2.** an area or region considered with regard to its characteristic or prevailing weather: *We like living in cooler climates.* **3.** the prevailing temper, trend, or conditions of a group, time, or place: *The political climate was becoming more conservative.* [Late Latin *clīmat-,* stem of *clīma* region, weather of a region, from Greek *klīma.*]

cli·mat·ic (klī mat'ik) *adj.* of or relating to climate. Also, **cli·mat'i·cal.** —**cli·mat'i·cal·ly,** *adv.*

cli·ma·tol·o·gy (klī'mə tol'ə jē) *n.* the science dealing with the study of climate. —**cli·ma·to·log·ic** (klī'mə tə loj'ik); *also,* **cli'ma·to·log'i·cal,** *adj.* —**cli'ma·to·log'i·cal·ly,** *adv.* —**cli'ma·tol'o·gist,** *n.*

cli·max (klī'maks) *n.* **1.** the highest point, as of development, intensity, interest, or excitement; culmination: *His election to the presidency was the climax of his career.* **2.** the turning point or point of highest dramatic tension in the action or theme of a play, book, or the like. **3.** the final stage in the ecological development of a given community in which plant and animal life is stable and

self-perpetuating and will remain so as long as the same ecological conditions persist. Also, **climax community. 4.** in rhetoric, the arrangement of a series of statements or ideas in order of increasing force or interest. **5.** orgasm. —*v.i., v.t.* to reach or bring to a climax: *The play climaxed in the third act. The evening was climaxed by her memorable speech.* [Late Latin *clīmax* ascending series of expressions, from Greek *klīmax* ladder, ascending series of expressions.]

climb (klīm) *v.i.* **1.** to move upward or toward the top of something by using the hands or feet: *We climbed for an hour before we reached a ledge on the mountain. The monkey climbed to the top of the tree.* **2.** to move or proceed by using the hands or feet: *to climb through a window, to climb into bed.* **3.** to go upward or move higher by or as if by climbing; rise: *The plane climbed to an altitude of 12,000 feet. Prices climbed last summer. The family climbed to the top of the social ladder.* **4.** to extend upward: *The building climbs to a height of twenty stories.* **5.** to grow in an upward direction, as certain plants, by twining around or clinging to another object for support: *The vines climbed up the latticework along the door.* —*v.t.* **1.** to move toward the top of or up (something), esp. by using the hands or feet: *I climbed the ladder. The car climbed the hill with difficulty.* **2.** to grow on or over in an upward direction: *The ivy climbed the old brick walls.* —*n.* **1.** the act or process of climbing; ascent: *Their climb to fame and fortune was rapid. Our climb up the hill took an hour.* **2.** a distance to be climbed: *It's only a short climb to the top from here.* **3.** a place or thing to be climbed: *That mountain is quite a treacherous climb.* [Old English *climban* to move upward by using the hands and feet.] —**climb'a·ble,** *adj.*

Synonyms *v.t.* **Climb, ascend, mount**[1], and **scale**[3] mean to move up something, as toward a summit. **Climb** suggests the effort involved: *The patient was too weak to climb stairs.* **Ascend,** on the other hand, may be used of any upward motion: *The skiers ascended the slope by using the lift. Smoke ascended the chimney.* **Mount** stresses reaching a higher level, esp. the top of something: *The speaker mounted the platform and looked down at the audience.* **Scale** especially suggests effort and movement in stages: *The novice climbers took all morning to scale the rock wall.*

climb·er (klī'mər) *n.* **1.** a person or thing that climbs. **2.** a climbing plant, as ivy. **3.** climbing iron. **4.** *Informal.* social climber.

climbing iron, one of a pair of frames with metal spikes or spurs attached, for strapping to the legs or shoes to aid in climbing trees, telephone poles, or the like.

clime (klīm) *n. Archaic.* a country or region, esp. with respect to its climate. [Late Latin *clīma.* See CLIMATE.]

clinch (klinch) *v.t.* **1.** to make final and definite; settle conclusively: *to clinch a deal.* **2.** to fasten and secure firmly, as a driven nail or bolt, by bending over or flattening the protruding point. **3.** to fasten (objects) together, using nails, bolts, or the like secured in this way. Also *(defs. 2, 3),* **clench.** —*v.i.* **1.** to grasp or hold an opponent's or each other's arms or body, esp. in boxing to prevent or hinder punching. **2.** *Slang.* to embrace passionately. —*n.* **1.** the act of clinching, esp. in boxing. **2.** a fastening made by bending or flattening the end of a nail, bolt, or the like. **3.** *Nautical.* a half hitch in which the loose end of the rope is lashed back on the knot it has formed. **4.** *Slang.* a close or passionate embrace. [Form of CLENCH.]

clinch
(n., def. 3)

clinch·er (klin'chər) *n.* **1.** a person or thing that clinches, esp. a nail made for clinching. **2.** *Informal.* something that is deciding or conclusive, as a point made in an argument: *Of all the reasons for not moving there, the high cost of living is the clincher.*

cling (kling) *v.i.,* **clung, cling·ing. 1.** to adhere closely, as if glued; stick: *The wet shirt clung to my back.* **2.** to hold tightly, as by grasping or embracing: *The children clung to each other in fear.* **3.** to remain close or in contact; be or stay near, as if attached: *She clung to her father's side. His car clung to the road as it rounded the curves.* **4.** to remain attached: *to cling to a routine, to cling to outdated ideas.* —*n.* clingstone. [Old English *clingan* to shrink, contract.]

clinging vine *Informal.* a person who displays helpless or excessive dependence on another person.

cling·stone (kling'stōn') *n.* a fruit, esp. a peach, in which the flesh adheres to the stone. ➡ distinguished from **freestone.** Also, **cling.**

clin·ic (klin'ik) *n.* **1.** an institution or building, often connected

with a hospital or medical school, where outpatients are treated, often for free or for a reduced fee. **2.** an institution or part of an institution where specialists cooperate in the study, diagnosis, and treatment of certain types of patients or certain diseases: *a cancer clinic, a maternity clinic.* **3.a.** an organization or institution offering advice, remedial work, repair, or instruction in some specific field: *a marriage clinic, a reading clinic, a doll clinic.* **b.** instruction or a class offered by such an organization or institution. **4.a.** instruction given by doctors to medical students in the presence of a patient, in which the patient is examined, the illness discussed, and treatment recommended. **b.** a meeting in which such instruction takes place. [Latin *clīnicus* doctor treating patients in bed, from Greek *klīnikos* relating to a bed, doctor treating patients in bed, from *klīnē* bed.]

clin·i·cal (klin′i kəl) *adj.* **1.** of or relating to a clinic. **2.** based on or dealing with the direct observation and treatment of patients rather than laboratory experimentation. **3.** coolly scientific or unemotional; detached: *The novel gave a clinical description of the battle.* **4.** relating to the course of a disease or the care of a patient: *Weight loss is a clinical sign of certain illnesses.* —**clin′i·cal·ly,** *adv.*

clinical thermometer, a thermometer used to measure body temperature.

cli·ni·cian (kli nish′ən) *n.* a physician, psychiatrist, or psychologist whose work consists primarily of the diagnosis and treatment of patients rather than laboratory experiments or other research. [CLINIC + -IAN.]

clink[1] (klingk) *v.t., v.i.* to make or cause to make a light, sharp, ringing sound: *They clinked their glasses together in a toast. The coins clinked in my pocket.* —*n.* a light, sharp, ringing or tinkling sound. [Possibly from Middle Dutch *clinken* to sound; imitative.]

clink[2] (klingk) *n. Slang.* jail; prison. [Possibly from *Clink,* an English prison in London; possibly referring to the *clinking* of chains in a prison.]

clink·er (kling′kər) *n.* **1.** a hard residue consisting of impurities that remain after coal is burned. **2.** very hard brick. **3.** slag. **4.** *Slang.* **a.** a mistake; error. **b.** any utter failure, esp. an inferior product. [Earlier *klincard,* from obsolete Dutch *klinkaard* brick that rings when struck; literally, that which clinks, from *klinken* to sound.]

clink·er-built (kling′kər bilt′) *adj.* built or faced with overlapping planks, boards, or plates, as a ship.

cli·nom·e·ter (klī nom′i tər, kli-) *n.* an instrument for measuring angles of inclination or slope. [Greek *klinein* to slope + -METER.]

Cli·o (klī′ō) *n.* in Greek mythology, the Muse of history. [Latin *Clīo,* from Greek *Kleiō* literally, the proclaimer, from *kleiein* to tell of, make famous.]

clip[1] (klip) *v.,* **clipped, clip·ping.** —*v.t.* **1.** to cut, as with shears or scissors; remove or detach by severing: *to clip wool from sheep, to clip off loose strands of thread, to clip an article out of a newspaper.* **2.** to make shorter by cutting; trim: *to clip one's nails, to clip a hedge.* **3.** to trim or cut the hair or fleece of: *to clip a poodle, to clip sheep.* **4.** to cut short; curtail; abridge. **5.** to pronounce rapidly, crisply, and distinctly, often omitting certain sounds: *She clipped her words angrily.* **6.** to pare the edge of (a coin). **7.** *Informal.* to hit with a quick, sharp blow: *to clip someone on the chin.* **8.** *Slang.* to cheat or swindle, esp. by overcharging: *The salesperson clipped the customer by overcharging five dollars.* —*v.i.* **1.** to cut or trim. **2.** *Informal.* to move rapidly: *The horse clipped along.* —*n.* **1.** the act of clipping. **2.** the quantity of wool obtained from sheep at one shearing or during one season. **3.** clips. clippers or shears. **4.** a section or piece clipped from a newspaper, magazine, film, or videotape. **5.** *Informal.* **a.** a rate or pace: *He moved along at a good clip.* **b.** a quick, sharp blow or punch. **c.** a single instance or occasion: *You can play the game at fifty cents a clip.* [Old Norse *klippa* to cut off, cut short; imitative.] —**clip′pa·ble,** *adj.*

clip[2] (klip) *n.* **1.** a device that grips or holds things together: *a money clip, a hair clip.* **2.** a piece of jewelry attached by means of a clip or clasp: *a tie clip, an ear clip.* **3.** a holder for ammunition for certain firearms that fits into the magazine. —*v.t.,* **clipped, clip·ping. 1.** to fasten with or as with a clip: *to clip documents together.* **2.** *Football.* to block (an opposing player not carrying the ball), usually from behind, by illegally throwing one's body across the lower part of the player's legs. [Old English *clyppan* to surround, embrace, grip.]

clip·board (klip′bôrd′) *n.* a board with a spring clip at one end for holding papers, used as a portable writing surface.

clip joint *Slang.* a nightclub, store, or other establishment that cheats or overcharges customers.

clip·per (klip′ər) *n.* **1.** *usually,* **clippers.** a tool or instrument

for clipping, cutting, or shearing: *a barber's clippers.* **2.** a fast-sailing cargo ship developed in the United States in the nineteenth century, having a narrow beam and, usually, three square-rigged masts. **3.** a person who clips.

clip·ping (klip′ing) *n.* something cut off or out, esp. an item cut from a newspaper or magazine.

clique (klēk, klik) *n.* a small, exclusive group of people, often having some aim or interest in common. [French *clique,* possibly from Middle French *clique* latch (in the sense of a secretive group closed, or latched in, together), from *cliquer* to click; imitative.] —**cli′quey;** *also,* **cli′quy,** *adj.*

cli·quish (klē′kish, klik′ish) *adj.* **1.** disposed to form or adhere to a clique. **2.** having the characteristics of a clique; exclusive. —**cli′quish·ly,** *adv.* —**cli′quish·ness,** *n.*

cli·tel·lum (klī tel′əm) *n., pl.* **-tel·la** (-tel′ə). a thick, glandular portion of the body wall of earthworms and certain other annelids that secretes the cocoon in which fertilized eggs are deposited during mating. [Modern Latin *clitellum,* from Latin *clitellae* packsaddle, pair of panniers.]

clit·o·ris (klit′ər is, kli tôr′-) *n., pl.* **clit·o·ris·es** or **clit·o·ri·des** (kli tôr′i dēz′). a small erectile organ at the upper end of the vulva, homologous to the penis. [Greek *kleitoris.*]

clo·a·ca (klō ā′kə) *n., pl.* **-cae** (-sē). **1.** a body chamber found in birds, fish, reptiles, amphibians, and some primitive mammals, into which the intestinal, urinary, and genital tracts open. **2.** a sewer. [Latin *cloāca* sewer, drain.]

cloak (klōk) *n.* **1.** a loose outer garment, with or without sleeves. **2.** something that covers or conceals; disguise: *The treaty was arranged under a cloak of secrecy.* —*v.t.* **1.** to cover with or as with a cloak. **2.** to conceal; disguise: *The meeting was cloaked in mystery.* [Old French *cloque, cloche* cape[1], bell, from Late Latin *clocca;* of Celtic origin; referring to the bell-like shape of a cape. Doublet of CLOCHE, CLOCK[1].] —For Synonyms *(v.t.),* see **mask.**

cloak-and-dag·ger (klōk′ən dag′ər) *adj.* characterized by exaggerated intrigue, as in tales of spies and secret agents: *a cloak-and-dagger movie.*

cloak·room (klōk′rüm′, -rùm′) *n.* a room where wearing apparel, as coats and hats, or articles, as umbrellas, may be left temporarily. Also, **coatroom.**

clob·ber (klob′ər) *v.t. Slang.* **1.** to hit with overwhelming force. **2.** to defeat utterly. [Of uncertain origin.]

cloche (klōsh) *n.* a close-fitting, helmet-shaped hat for women, usually having a deep, rounded crown and brim. [French *cloche* bell, from Late Latin *clocca;* of Celtic origin. Doublet of CLOAK, CLOCK[1].]

clock[1] (klok) *n.* **1.** any of various instruments for measuring and indicating the passage of time, usually with hands that pass over a dial marked to show hours or minutes or with a digital display. **2.** a time clock: *a job where employees have to punch a clock.* —*v.t.* to find out or record the frequency or speed of; time, as with a stopwatch: *to clock a race, to clock a runner.* —*v.i.* to register hours worked on or as if on a time clock (used with *in* or *out*): *What time did you clock in today?* [Old French *cloke* or Middle Dutch *clocke* clock (the instrument), bell, from Late Latin *clocca* bell; of Celtic origin; possibly because many clocks had bells with which to strike the hour. Doublet of CLOAK, CLOCHE.] —**clock′er,** *n.*

· **around the clock.** through all 24 hours of the day; constantly.

clock[2] (klok) *n.* a decorative pattern woven or embroidered on the side of a stocking or sock. [Probably from CLOCK[1]; because originally a bell-shaped ornament.]

clock radio, a radio equipped with a clock and alarm mechanism and designed so that the clock can be set to turn on the radio, with or without the alarm, at any chosen time.

clock·wise (klok′wīz′) *adv., adj.* in the direction in which the hands of a clock rotate.

clock·work (klok′wûrk′) *n.* a mechanism consisting of gears, wheels, and springs, such as that which runs a clock or other mechanical device.

· **like clockwork.** with regularity, precision, and smoothness; perfectly.

clod (klod) *n.* **1.** a lump or mass, esp. of earth or clay. **2.** a dull, awkward, or stupid person; dolt. [Modification of Middle English *clot* lump, clot. See CLOT.] —**clod′dish,** *adj.* —**clod′dish·ness,** *n.*

clod·hop·per (klod′hop′ər) *n.* **1.** *Informal.* a clumsy, awkward boor; bumpkin. **2.** any large, heavy, clumsy-looking shoe or boot.

a	at	e	end	o	hot	u	up	hw	white		about
ā	ape	ē	me	ō	old	ū	use	ng	song		taken
ä	far	i	it	ô	fork	ü	rule	th	thin	ə	pencil
âr	care	ī	ice	oi	oil	ù	pull	th	this		lemon
		îr	pierce	ou	out	ûr	turn	zh	measure		circus

clog (klog) *v.,* **clogged, clog·ging.** —*v.t.* **1.** to stuff or stop up, as with thick or sticky matter; block; obstruct: *Leaves clogged the street drain.* **2.** to hinder the progress or action of: *The snow clogged traffic.* **3.** to fill to or beyond capacity: *Holiday traffic clogged the bridge.* —*v.i.* to become obstructed, stopped up, or impeded. —*n.* **1.** a shoe or sandal with a thick sole of wood or cork. **2.** a block of wood or other weight fastened, as to a horse, to hinder movement or prevent escape. **3.** anything that impedes or encumbers. [Of uncertain origin.]

clog dance, a dance, as any of several folk dances of France or Holland, in which clogs are worn to beat out the rhythm. —**clog dancer.** —**clog dancing.**

cloi·son·né (kloi′zə nā′) *n.* the technique or process of decorating metal objects by applying thin strips of metal in a pattern and filling the spaces with colored enamel. —*adj.* relating to or formed or decorated by this technique. [French *cloisonné* partitioned, past participle of *cloisonner* to partition, from *cloison* partition, going back to Latin *clausus,* past participle of *claudere* to close.]

clois·ter (klois′tər) *n.* **1.** a place of religious seclusion, as a convent or monastery. **2.** the seclusion of a cloister; monastic life. **3.a.** a covered walk or arcade along the wall or walls of a building, having a row of columns on one side and usually built around the courtyard of a monastery, church, or college building. **b.** an open courtyard surrounded by such walks, usually square or rectangular in shape. **4.** any place of quiet seclusion. —*v.t.* to confine in or as if in a cloister; seclude. [Old French *cloistre, clostre* place of religious seclusion, going back to Latin *claustrum* enclosed place, bar.] —**clois′tral,** *adj.*

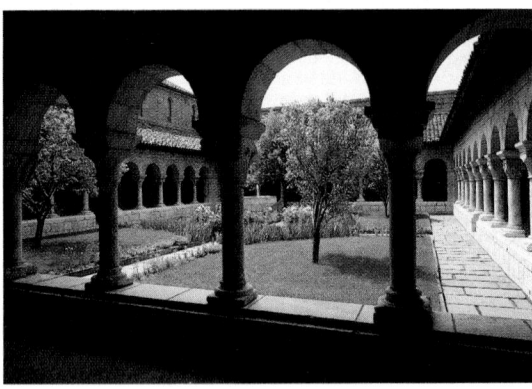

cloister *(def. 3)*

clois·tered (klois′tərd) *adj.* **1.** retired or secluded from the world; sheltered: *a cloistered academic life.* **2.** living in a cloister or cloisters: *cloistered nuns.*

clomp (klomp) *n.* a heavy, dull sound, as of footsteps. —*v.i.* to walk heavily and clumsily. [Probably a form of CLUMP.]

clone (klōn) *n.* **1.** any of a group of genetically identical organisms reproduced asexually from a single ancestor. **2.** a person or thing that closely or exactly resembles another. *v.,* **cloned, cloning.** —*v.t.* **1.** to reproduce asexually. **2.** to make a duplicate or imitation of. —*v.i.* to reproduce asexually. [Greek *klōn* slip[2], twig, from *klan* to break.]

clonk (klongk) *n.* a heavy, dull, thumping sound. —*v.i.* to make such a sound. —*v.t.* to strike with a clonk. [Imitative.]

clo·nus (klō′nəs) *n.* a series of muscular spasms in which rigidity and relaxation alternate rapidly. [Modern Latin *clonus,* from Greek *klonos* violent motion, turmoil.] —**clo·nic** (klō′nik, klon′ik), *adj.*

clop (klop) *n.* a heavy, sharp sound, as of hoofbeats. —*v.i.,* **clopped, clop·ping.** to walk with or make such a sound. [Imitative.]

close (*v., n.* defs. 1, 3, klōz; *adj., adv., n.* def. 2, klōs) *v.,* **closed, clos·ing.** —*v.t.* **1.** to move (something) so as to obstruct or eliminate an opening; shut: *to close a window, to close a drawer, to close one's mouth.* **2.** to bring together the parts of so as to eliminate openings or gaps or to form a whole (often with *up*): *to close a penknife, to close a book, to close one's fist, to close up ranks.* **3.** to fill or obstruct; stop up: *Rocks from the landslide closed the mountain pass.* **4.** to suspend or stop the operations of (often with *up* or *down*): *We closed our account at the store. They closed the schools down because of the blizzard.* **5.** to prevent or limit access to or passage across (often with *off*): *Officials closed the western border to tourists. The workers closed off the street for repairs.* **6.** to

bring to an end; conclude; finish: *to close a deal, to close a lecture with a humorous anecdote.* **7.** to shut in; enclose; confine: *We closed the puppy in the room while we were at work.* **8.** to shut off, as from suggestion or change: *She closed her mind to opposing arguments.* —*v.i.* **1.** to become shut: *The door closed with a bang.* **2.** to suspend or stop operation: *Banks close on legal holidays.* **3.** to come to a conclusion; end; finish: *The sermon closed with a powerful message.* **4.** to come together, as parts of a whole (often with *up*): *The wound closed up after a week.* **5.** to engage in hand-to-hand fighting; grapple (often with *with*): *We closed with the enemy before dark.* **6.** to draw near (often with *on*): *His pursuers closed on him rapidly.* **7.** to be at a certain point or worth a certain amount at the end of a business day: *The market closed at 4.75. That stock closed two points higher today.* **8.** to sign final papers for the sale of real estate. —*adj.,* **clos·er, clos·est. 1.** being near in time or space; with little or no distance between: *The hunter fired at close range. Those holidays follow in close succession.* **2.** not distant in relation, degree, effect, or condition: *He's a close relative. She's close to tears. Spanish is close to Italian.* **3.** having component parts or elements near each other; compact; dense: *a fabric with a close weave, a close formation of troops.* **4.** attached or characterized by strong affection, intimacy, or loyalty: *He is a close friend. My sister and I are very close.* **5.** conforming to or resembling a model or original: *a close translation, a close copy, a close resemblance.* **6.** directed or maintained strictly and carefully; thorough; rigorous: *The police kept the suspect under close surveillance. Please pay close attention to my directions.* **7.** near to the ground, skin, or other surface: *a close haircut.* **8.** established or decided by a narrow margin: *a close race.* **9.** fitting snugly or tightly: *a close cap.* **10.** lacking freely circulating air; oppressive, stifling, or stuffy: *It's very close in this room.* **11.** in strict confinement; carefully guarded: *a close secret.* **12.** marked by a narrow escape; barely avoiding disaster: *That was close—next time they'll catch you.* **13.** secretive in manner; uncommunicative; reticent. **14.** not generous; stingy; miserly: *to be close with money.* **15.** difficult to obtain; scarce, as money or credit. **16.** *Phonetics.* (of a vowel) articulated with the tongue close to or touching the palate, as the vowels in *feet.* —*adv.* in a close manner or position; closely: *The lovers held each other close. You're not parked close enough to the curb.* —*n.* **1.** conclusion; end; finish: *the close of day, to bring the case to a close.* **2.** an enclosed place, esp. enclosed land surrounding or beside a cathedral or other building. **3.** the act of closing. [Old French *clos,* past participle of *clore* to shut, enclose, end, from Latin *claudere.*] —**close·ly** (klōs′lē), *adv.* —**close·ness** (klōs′nis), *n.* —**clos·er** (klō′zər), *n.*

• **to close in (on). a.** to advance upon or surround (something or someone) so as to prevent escape: *The police closed in on the hide-out.* **b.** to envelop or approach (something or someone) from all sides, as if to shut in or entrap: *We were still lost as night closed in.*

• **to close out.** to sell (all or particular merchandise), usually at greatly reduced prices, as to make room for new stock or to liquidate a business: *The store closed out its summer stock.*

Synonyms *adj.* **Close, compact**[1], **crowded,** and **dense** mean having parts or elements very near each other. **Close** implies little space between parts, which usually remain distinguishable: *a close seating arrangement, a close weave.* **Compact** suggests economy or efficiency in placement: *The kitchen was compact, with no space wasted.* **Crowded,** on the other hand, suggests an inefficient or annoying closeness: *The room was so crowded that I could not turn around.* **Dense** is used of a mass of similar things or material, so close that it cannot be seen through or passed through: *dense foliage, a dense fog.* For other Synonyms *(adj.),* see **intimate**[1], **near;** *(v.t.),* see **end.**

close call *Informal.* a narrow escape.

closed (klōzd) *adj.* **1.** not allowing free passage in and out; shut: *a closed door.* **2.** having surrounding barriers or obstructions; enclosed. **3.** blocked by obstructions or hindrances: *a closed bridge.* **4.** drawn, folded, or rolled together: *the closed petals of a flower.* **5.** holding fast to preconceptions or biases; not receptive, as to new ideas, facts, or views: *a closed mind.* **6.** hidden from general or public view or knowledge; secret or private: *a closed meeting.* **7.** not prepared or available to do business: *a closed office.* **8.** *Mathematics.* **a.** having no end points, as a curve that forms an unbroken loop. **b.** (of a set) composed of members that when subjected to a particular operation, produce a result that is a member of the same set, as the set of whole numbers when added or multiplied.

closed-cap·tioned (klōzd′kap′shənd) *adj.* (of a television program) broadcast with captions that are intended for viewers with hearing impairments and are visible only with the aid of a decoding device attached to a television receiver. —**closed′-cap′tion·ing,** *n.*

closed circuit 1. an electric circuit through which current can

flow without interruption. **2.** a television system in which signals are transmitted, usually by a cable, to a limited and predetermined number of receivers. Also *(def. 2)*, **closed-circuit television.** —**closed′-cir′cuit,** *adj.*

closed corporation, a corporation whose stock is owned by a small number of people and is not for sale on the open market.

closed-end investment company (klōzd′end′) an investment company selling a fixed number of shares to the public and not obligated to redeem the holders' shares upon request. ➡ distinguished from **mutual fund.**

closed primary, a direct primary election in which only members of a given political party may vote.

closed shop, an establishment in which only union members in good standing are hired and employed. ➡ distinguished from **open shop** and **union shop.**

closed syllable, a syllable ending in a consonant or consonant cluster, as *hat* and *hatch.*

close·fist·ed (klōs′fis′tid) *adj.* not generous; stingy; miserly.

close-grained (klōs′grānd′) *adj.* having fine and closely arranged fibers or particles; compact and dense in structure or texture, as wood; fine-grained.

close-hauled (klōs′hôld′) *adj., adv.* with sails pulled in tight so as to sail as nearly as possible in the direction from which the wind is blowing.

close-knit (klōs′nit′) *adj.* closely united, as by kinship, friendship, or common purpose: *a close-knit family.*

close·mouthed (klōs′mouthd′, -moutht′) *adj.* not given to talking or disclosing information; secretive. Also, **close′-lipped′.**

close-or·der drill (klōs′ôr′dər) systematic practice in formation marching and the formal handling of arms in which the participants are arranged at close intervals.

close·out (klōz′out′) *also,* **close-out.** *n.* a sale in which all or particular merchandise is to be sold, usually at greatly reduced prices.

close quarters (klōs) **1.** a small, cramped place or position: *to live in close quarters.* **2.** immediate contact or close range: *to fight at close quarters.*

close shave (klōs) *Informal.* a narrow escape.

clos·et (kloz′it) *n.* **1.** a small room or recess, usually with a door, for storing clothing. **2.** a cabinet, enclosed recess, or small room for storing household utensils, food, or other articles: *a china closet.* **3.** a small, private room, esp. one for prayer, study, or consultation. **4.** water closet. —*v.t.* to confine or shut up in a private room, as for a consultation or study: *The president's staff was closeted all day.* —*adj.* **1.** in secret; hidden: *a closet conservative.* **2.** held in secret or private: *closet meetings.* [Old French *closet* small enclosure, diminutive of *close* enclosure, from *clore.* See CLOSE.]

close-up (klōs′up′) *also,* **close·up.** *n.* **1.** a photograph or television or motion-picture shot taken at close range or with a telescopic lens. **2.** a detailed or intimate examination, as of an issue or person.

clos·ing (klō′zing) *n.* **1.** a concluding section, as of a speech. **2.** something that closes a gap, esp. in clothing; fastening. **3.** the final proceeding in a sale of real estate, in which title is transferred from the seller to the buyer.

clos·trid·i·um (klo strid′ē əm) *n., pl.* **clos·trid·i·a** (klo-strid′ē ə). any of a group of anaerobic, rod-shaped, usually toxic bacteria, genus *Clostridium,* including those causing tetanus and botulism, found in soil and in the intestines of humans and animals. [Modern Latin *clostridium* literally, little spindle, from Greek *klōstēr* spindle; because of its shape.]

clo·sure (klō′zhər) *n.* **1.** the act of closing or the state of being closed. **2.** something that closes or shuts. **3.** a bringing to a conclusion; end. **4.** cloture. **5.** *Mathematics.* the property that a set has when it is closed. —*v.t.,* **-sured, -suring.** cloture. [Old French *closure* barrier, from Late Latin *clausūra* bar, bolt, from Latin *clausus,* past participle of *claudere* to close, shut.]

clot (klot) *n.* a semisolid or thickened mass, formed esp. by coagulation: *a clot of blood.* —*v.t., v.i.,* **clot·ted, clot·ting.** to form or cause to form into clots. [Old English *clot, clott* mass, lump.]

cloth (klôth) *n., pl.* **cloths** (klôthz, klôths). **1.** something made by weaving, knitting, braiding, or felting textile fibers; fabric. **2.** a piece of fabric used for a certain purpose, esp. a tablecloth. **3. the cloth.** the clergy: *a member of the cloth.* [Old English *clāth* fabric, garment.]

clothe (klōth) *v.t.,* **clothed** or **clad, cloth·ing. 1.** to put clothes on; dress. **2.** to provide with clothes. **3.** to cover as with clothing: *Snow clothed the field.* **4.** to put into words; couch: *wisdom clothed in simple language.* [Old English *clāthian* to dress.]

clothes (klōz, klōthz) *pl. n.* **1.** articles of clothing for the human body; attire. **2.** bedclothes.

clothes·horse (klōz′hôrs′, klōthz′-) *n.* **1.** a frame on which clothes are hung to dry or air. **2.** *Informal.* a person who takes great pleasure in owning and wearing fashionable clothes.

clothes·line (klōz′līn′, klōthz′-) *n.* a rope or wire on which articles, esp. clothes, are hung to dry or air.

clothes moth, any of various small moths, family Tineidae, whose larvae feed on wool, fur, and other materials made from, or soiled with, animal products.

clothes·pin (klōz′pin′, klōthz′-) *n.* a clamp or forked piece of wood or plastic used to fasten clothes on a line.

clothes pole, a pole used to support a clothesline.

clothes·press (klōz′pres′, klōthz′-) *n.* a place for keeping clothes; wardrobe.

clothes tree, an upright pole with hooks or pegs near the top on which to hang clothes.

cloth·ier (klōth′yər, klō′thē ər) *n.* a person who sells or makes cloth or clothing.

cloth·ing (klō′thing) *n.* **1.** articles worn to protect, cover, or adorn the body; clothes; attire; garments. **2.** any covering.

Clo·tho (klō′thō) *n.* in classical mythology, one of the three Fates, the spinner of the thread of life.

cloth yard, a unit for measuring cloth, equal to the standard yard.

clo·ture (klō′chər) *n.* a method of ending debate in a legislative body in order to bring a question to a vote. —*v.t.,* **-tured, -tur·ing.** to end a debate by cloture. Also, **closure.** [French *clôture* closing, going back to Latin *clausus,* past participle of *claudere* to close.]

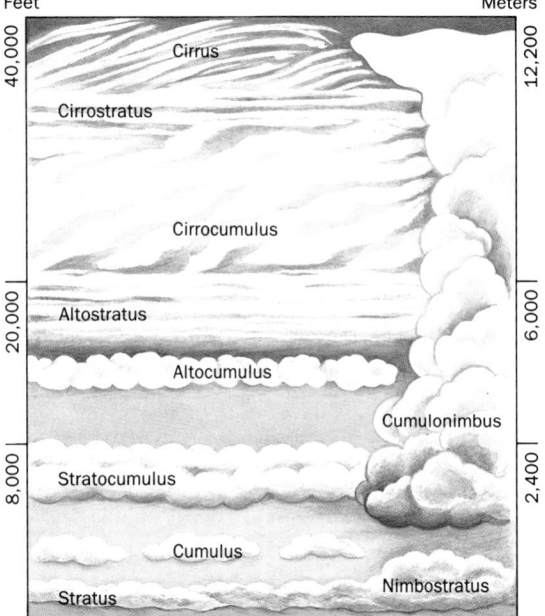

types of **clouds**

cloud (kloud) *n.* **1.** a visible mass of water vapor or ice particles suspended in the atmosphere, usually at a considerable altitude. Low-level clouds, such as cumulus, occur at altitudes up to 8,000 feet (2,400 meters). Middle-level clouds, such as altocumulus, occur at altitudes of 8,000-20,000 feet (2,400-6,000 meters). High-level clouds, such as cirrus, occur at altitudes of 20,000-40,000 feet (6,000-12,200 meters). **2.** any similar mass, as of smoke, dust, or steam. **3.** a great number or mass of persons or things in motion: *a cloud of locusts, a cloud of arrows.* **4.** something that obscures, darkens, or dims: *a cloud of suspicion.* **5.** a dimness or murkiness in something otherwise clear or transparent: *a cloud in the water.* **6.** a streak or spot of different, usually darker, color, as in marble. —*v.t.* **1.** to cover with or as with a cloud or clouds: *Mist clouded*

a	at	e	end	o	hot	u	up	hw	white		about
ā	ape	ē	me	ō	old	ū	use	ng	song		taken
ä	far	i	it	ô	fork	ŭ	rule	th	thin	ə	pencil
âr	care	ī	ice	oi	oil	ù	pull	th	this		lemon
		îr	pierce	ou	out	ûr	turn	zh	measure		circus

227

the mountaintop. Smoke from the fire clouded the lobby of the building. **2.** to obscure, darken, or dim: *The panel's judgment was clouded by selfishness.* **3.** to make gloomy or troubled: *Anxiety clouded their faces.* **4.** to place under suspicion, as a reputation; sully. —*v.i.* to become cloudy (often with *up* or *over*): *The sky clouded up. Their faces clouded with worry.* [Old English *clūd* hill, rock; originally, mass.]
   • **in the clouds.** daydreaming.
   • **under a cloud.** suspected of being wrong, bad, or guilty; distrusted: *The politician's reputation was under a cloud.*
cloud·ber·ry (kloud′ber′ē, -bə rē) *n., pl.* **-ries.** **1.** the edible, orange-yellow fruit of a plant, *Rubus chamaemorus,* a species of raspberry. **2.** the plant itself, found in cold regions of the Northern Hemisphere, bearing rounded, lobed leaves and large white flowers.
cloud·burst (kloud′bûrst′) *n.* a sudden, heavy rainfall.
cloud chamber, an apparatus used to detect the paths of subatomic particles by means of a gas supersaturated with water vapor that condenses as the particles move through it, creating a cloud-like trail.
cloud·less (kloud′lis) *adj.* without clouds; clear; bright. —**cloud′less·ly,** *adv.* —**cloud′less·ness,** *n.*
cloud·let (kloud′lit) *n.* a small cloud. [CLOUD + -LET.]
cloud nine *Informal.* a state of great happiness: *I was on cloud nine when I won a free trip to England.*
cloud seeding, any of various techniques used to produce rain artificially by scattering particles, usually of dry ice or silver iodide, into clouds.
cloud·y (klou′dē) *adj.,* **cloud·i·er, cloud·i·est.** **1.** covered with or obscured by clouds; overcast: *a cloudy sky.* **2.** having little sunshine: *a cloudy day.* **3.** of or resembling clouds. **4.** not clear or transparent: *a cloudy liquid.* **5.** confused or not easily understood; vague: *cloudy ideas.* **6.** gloomy or troubled: *cloudy looks.* **7.** having cloudlike markings; streaked or spotted: *cloudy marble.* —**cloud′i·ness,** *n.*
clout (klout) *n.* **1.** *Informal.* a heavy blow, esp. with the hand; cuff. **2.** *Informal.* influence, force, or power: *That family has a lot of political clout.* **3.** *Baseball.* a long, powerful hit. **4.** a white cloth or other object used as a target in long-distance archery. **5.** *Archaic.* a small piece of cloth, esp. a rag. —*v.t. Informal.* to hit, esp. with the hand. [Old English *clūt* piece of cloth or metal.]
clove[1] (klōv) *n.* **1.** the dried, unopened flower bud of a tree, *Syzygium aromaticum,* of the myrtle family, used as a spice either whole or ground. **2.** the tropical evergreen tree itself, bearing oval, oblong leaves and clusters of small yellow flowers. [Old French *clou (de girofle)* literally, nail (of clove tree), from Latin *clāvus* nail; because the bud resembles a nail.]
clove[2] (klōv) *n.* one of the separable sections of a compound bulb, as garlic. [Old English *clufu.*]
clove[3] (klōv) a past tense of **cleave**[1].
clove hitch, a type of knot used to tie a line, esp. a rope, around something, as a spar. For illustration, see **knot.**
clo·ven (klō′vən) *v.* a past participle of **cleave**[1]. —*adj.* split; divided.
cloven hoof 1. a divided hoof, as of cows, oxen, or deer. For illustration, see **hoof. 2.** such a hoof considered as the symbol of Satan, who was supposed to have such hooves. Also, **cloven foot.**
clo·ven-hoofed (klō′vən hûft′, -hōōft′) *adj.* **1.** having divided hooves. **2.** satanic; devilish. Also, **clo′ven-foot′ed.**
clo·ver (klō′vər) *n.* **1.** any of a group of plants, genus *Trifolium,* of the pea family, bearing compound leaves, usually composed of three leaflets, and dense, rounded heads or spikes of small red, white, yellow, or purple fragrant flowers. Clovers are among the most widely cultivated and important cover and forage crops. **2.** any of various plants of the pea family, as **sweet clover,** genus *Melilotus,* and **bush clover,** genus *Lespedeza.* [Old English *clāfre, clǣfre* plant of the genus *Trifolium.*]
   • **in clover.** living in a prosperous or luxurious manner or situation.
clo·ver·leaf (klō′vər lēf′) *n., pl.* **-leafs** or **-leaves** (-lēvz′). a complex intersection of curving ramps that connect highways crossing each other on different levels.
clown (kloun) *n.* **1.** a professional entertainer, esp. in a circus, who amuses the audience, as by performing tricks or exaggerated pantomiming, and is usually dressed in a ridiculous costume with bizarre makeup. **2.** a person who habitually jokes or acts silly. **3.** an ill-mannered, clumsy person; boor. —*v.i.* to behave like a clown. [Of uncertain origin.]
clown·ish (klou′nish) *adj.* of or resembling a clown: *clownish behavior.* —**clown′ish·ly,** *adv.* —**clown′ish·ness,** *n.*
cloy (kloi) *v.t.* to weary with too much of something that is usually pleasant, as sweet or rich food; satiate. —*v.i.* to become unpleasant through too much of something that is usually pleas-

ant: *The excitement of constant travel soon cloyed.* [Earlier *accloy* to drive a nail into, fill up, from Middle French *encloer* to drive a nail into, going back to Latin *in* in + *clāvāre* to nail.] —**cloy′ing·ly,** *adv.*
club (klub) *n.* **1.** a thick, heavy stick, usually tapered at one end, used esp. as a weapon. **2.** any of various sticks or bats used to hit a ball in certain games, as golf. **3.** a group of people organized for some special purpose: *an athletic club.* **4.** a building or room used or occupied by such a group. **5.** an organization that is usually joined by payment of a membership fee, which offers its members certain purchasing advantages: *a videocassette club, a theater club.* **6.a.** a playing card having black marks in the shape of a trefoil. **b. clubs.** the suit of such cards. **7.** nightclub. *v.,* **clubbed, club·bing.** —*v.t.* **1.** to beat or strike with or as with a club. **2.** to unite, contribute, or combine (persons or things) for a common purpose. —*v.i.* to unite, contribute, or combine for a common purpose (often with *together*): *The golf enthusiasts clubbed together to sponsor a tournament.* [Old Norse *clubba* thick stick.]
club car, a railroad passenger car equipped with lounge chairs, card tables, and usually a bar or buffet.
club·foot (klub′fŏot′) *n., pl.* **-feet** (-fēt′). **1.** a condition in which the foot is deformed or twisted out of position, caused by abnormal development before birth. Also, **talipes. 2.** a foot so deformed. —**club′foot′ed,** *adj.*
club fungus, any basidiomycete of the fungal family Clavariaceae.
club·house (klub′hous′) *n., pl.* **-hous·es** (-hou′ziz). a building used or occupied by a club.
club moss, any of a group of small evergreen plants, genus *Lycopodium,* found in tropical and temperate regions growing along the ground and bearing small, upright branches covered with tiny, dark green leaves that look like pine needles.
club sandwich, a sandwich made with three slices of bread, usually toasted, and a filling of cold meats, lettuce, tomato, and a dressing.
club soda, soda water.
club steak, a small, boneless cut of beef from the loin tip.
cluck (kluk) *n.* **1.** a low, guttural sound made by a hen when brooding or calling its chicks. **2.** any similar sound. **3.** *Slang.* a stupid or dull-witted person. —*v.i.* **1.** to make the low, guttural sound of a hen. **2.** to utter any similar sound: *The driver clucked at the horse to urge it on.* —*v.t.* to call or express by clucking. [Imitative.]
clue (klōō) *n.* **1.** *also, British,* **clew.** a guide or key that aids in finding the solution to a problem or mystery. **2.** clew *(defs. 2, 3).* —*v.t.,* **clued, clu·ing.** clew *(defs. 1, 2).* [Form of CLEW.]
   • **to clue (someone) in.** *Informal.* to make aware of the facts.
clum·ber spaniel (klum′bər) a dog having a long, heavy-boned body, short legs, a very large head, and a thick coat of silky, straight white hair with lemon or orange markings, valued as a hunting dog. Height: 17 inches (43 centimeters) at the shoulder. Also, **clum′ber.** [From *Clumber,* an estate of the Duke of Newcastle in England.]

clumber spaniel

clump (klump) *n.* **1.** a small, closely gathered group of things of the same kind; cluster: *a clump of trees.* **2.** a thick mass; lump: *a clump of clay.* **3.** a heavy, dull sound, as of footsteps. —*v.t.* to gather or form into a clump or clumps. —*v.i.* **1.** to walk heavily and clumsily. **2.** to form a clump or clumps. [Middle Low German *klumpe* shoe made of a lump of wood.] —**clump′y,** *adj.*
clum·sy (klum′zē) *adj.,* **-si·er, -si·est.** **1.** lacking dexterity, grace, or skill; awkward: *a clumsy dancer.* **2.** ungracefully or awkwardly shaped or made; unwieldy: *clumsy boots.* **3.** awkwardly or unskillfully said or done; ill-contrived: *clumsy sentences.* [From obsolete *clumse* to be numb with cold (hence, awkward); probably of Scandinavian origin.] —**clum′si·ly,** *adv.* —**clum′si·ness,** *n.* —For Synonyms, see **awkward.**
clung (klung) the past tense and past participle of **cling.**
clunk (klungk) *n.* a heavy, dull, thumping sound, such as that made by a hard object hitting the ground. —*v.i.* to make such a sound. —*v.t.* to strike with a clunk. [Imitative.]
clunk·y (klung′kē) *adj.,* **clunk·i·er, clunk·i·est.** *Informal.* ungracefully heavy or awkward: *clunky boots, clunky bracelets.*
Clu·ny lace (klōō′nē) bobbin lace made of heavy linen or cotton thread, usually with an open design, used for trimming. [After CLUNY, France.]
clus·ter (klus′tər) *n.* **1.** a group of things of the same kind growing naturally together; bunch: *Grapes grow in a cluster.* **2.** any group of similar persons or things situated or grouped close

together: *The ring had a cluster of pearls.* **3.** oak leaf cluster. —*v.i.* to group or grow in a cluster or clusters: *The children clustered around the Christmas tree.* —*v.t.* **1.** to group or form (something) into a cluster or clusters. **2.** to furnish or cover with clusters: *The hills are clustered with flowers.* [Old English *clyster* bunch.]

clutch¹ (kluch) *v.t.* **1.** to grasp or hold tightly or firmly: *She clutched the money in her hand.* **2.** to seize eagerly with or as with the hand or claws; snatch: *The football player clutched the ball and ran toward the end zone.* —*v.i.* to attempt to grasp or seize (with *at*): *I clutched at the banister as I stumbled down the stairs.* —*n.* **1.** a strong hold; grip. **2.** a claw, paw, or hand that clutches. **3.** **clutches.** control; power: *The spy fell into the clutches of the enemy.* **4.** the act of clutching. **5.a.** a device in a machine that engages or disengages the engine. **b.** a lever or pedal that operates such a device. **6.** a serious or difficult situation or circumstance: *You can depend on him in a clutch.* —*adj. Informal.* **1.** done in a serious or difficult situation; crucial: *a clutch pass interception.* **2.** performing well in such a situation: *a clutch hitter.* [Middle English *clucchen,* from Old English *clyccan* to grasp, grip tightly.]

clutch² (kluch) *n.* **1.** the number of eggs laid or incubated at one time. **2.** a brood of chickens. [Earlier *cletch* a brood, from *cleck* to hatch, from Middle English *clekken* to give birth to, create, from Old Norse *klekja* to hatch.]

clut·ter (klut′ər) *n.* a confused or disorderly state or collection; litter. —*v.t.* to crowd or litter with a confused or disorderly collection of things: *The children cluttered the room with their toys.* [From CLOT.]

Clydes·dale (klīdz′dāl′) *n.* one of a breed of strong, heavy draft horses. [From *Clydesdale,* Scotland, the valley of the Clyde River, where this breed was originally developed.]

Cly·tem·nes·tra (klī′təm nes′trə) *n.* in Greek legend, the wife of Agamemnon, who along with her lover Aegisthus was killed by her son, Orestes, in revenge for Agamemnon's murder.

Cm, the symbol for curium.

cm *also,* **cm.** centimeter; centimeters.

cml., commercial.

cni·dar·i·an (nī dâr′ē ən) *n.* coelenterate. [Modern Latin *Cnidaria,* from Greek *knídē* nettle + Latin *-ārius,* a suffix meaning "relating to" + -AN; because this group of invertebrates is characterized by stinging cells.]

Co, the symbol for cobalt.

co- *prefix* **1.** with; together: *coexist.* **2.** fellow; joint: *copilot.* **3.** equally: *coextend, coeval.* **4.** complement of: *cosine, cosecant.* [Latin *co-,* form of *com-* with. See COM-.]

co. *also,* **Co. 1.** company. **2.** county.

c.o. *also,* **c/o 1.** in care of. **2.** carried over.

CO 1. the postal abbreviation for Colorado. **2.** Commanding Officer. **3.** conscientious objector.

co·ac·er·vate (kō as′ər vāt′) *n.* a colloidal system intermediate between a gel and a sol, in which viscous droplets are held together by electrostatic forces. [Latin *coacervatus,* past participle of *coacervare* to heap together.]

coach (kōch) *n.* **1.** a large, four-wheeled closed carriage with seats inside for passengers and a raised seat outside

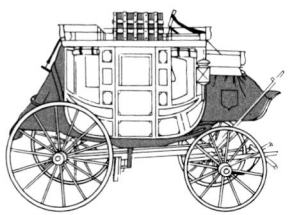

coach *(def. 1)*

for the driver. **2.** a railroad passenger car, esp. one offering low rates. **3.** a class of passenger travel offering the lowest rates for

traveling, as on trains or airplanes. **4.** bus. **5.** a person who trains or teaches an athlete or athletic team. **6.** a person who trains and teaches in speech, dramatics, or voice. **7.** a member of a baseball organization, positioned in either of two coaches' boxes, who gives instructions to batters and base runners. **8.** formerly, a closed two-door automobile like a sedan. —*v.t.* to act as a coach to; train or teach. —*v.i.* **1.** to study with or be trained by a coach. **2.** to act as a coach: *Who coaches for the baseball team?* [French *coche* this carriage, going back to Hungarian *kocsi* literally, of Kocs, Hungarian town where these carriages are said to have originated.]

coach-and-four (kōch′ən fôr′) *n.* a coach drawn by four horses.

coach dog, Dalmatian.

coach·man (kōch′mən) *n., pl.* **-men** (-mən). a person who drives a coach or carriage.

co·ad·ju·tor (kō aj′ə tər, kō′ə jü′-) *n.* **1.** a person who assists or works with another; assistant; helper. **2.** a bishop appointed to assist a diocesan bishop or archbishop with the right to succeed him or her. [Old French *coadjuteur,* going back to Latin *co-* with + *adjūtor* helper.]

co·ag·u·la·ble (kō ag′yə lə bəl) *adj.* capable of being coagulated. —**co·ag′u·la·bil′i·ty,** *n.*

co·ag·u·lant (kō ag′yə lənt) *n.* a substance that promotes coagulation.

co·ag·u·lase (kō ag′yə lās′) *n.* any enzyme that causes coagulation, as thrombin, which coagulates blood, and rennin, which coagulates milk. [COAGUL(ATE) + -ASE.]

co·ag·u·late (kō ag′yə lāt′) *v.t., v.i.,* **-lat·ed, -lat·ing.** to change or become changed from a liquid into a thickened mass; clot; congeal. [Latin *coāgulātus,* past participle of *coāgulāre* to cause to curdle, going back to *co-* with, together + *agere* to drive, do, make.] —**co·ag′u·la′tor,** *n.* —**co·ag′u·la·to·ry** (kō ag′yə lə tôr′ē), *adj.*

co·ag·u·la·tion (kō ag′yə lā′shən) *n.* **1.** the act of coagulating or the state of being coagulated. **2.** a coagulated mass.

coal (kōl) *n.* **1.** a black or dark brown combustible substance widely used as a fuel, formed mostly of vegetable matter that has been buried deep in the earth for millions of years and carbonized under pressure. The three main types of coal are anthracite, bituminous, and lignite. **2.** a piece of this substance. **3.** any piece of fuel, as wood or coal, that is glowing, charred, or burned. **4.** charcoal. —*v.t.* **1.** to provide with coal. **2.** to convert or reduce to charcoal by burning; char. —*v.i.* to take in a supply of coal. [Old English *col* piece of carbon or partly burnt wood.]

• **to carry** (or **bring**) **coals to Newcastle.** to supply something where it is already abundant.

• **to rake** (**haul, drag,** or **call**) **over the coals.** to scold; reprimand.

coal·er (kō′lər) *n.* **1.** something, as a ship or railroad, used for carrying or supplying coal. **2.** a person who sells or supplies coal.

co·a·lesce (kō′ə les′) *v.i.,* **-lesced, -lesc·ing. 1.** to grow together so as to form one body; fuse: *The two parts of the broken bone coalesced.* **2.** to unite, as into one unit or organization; combine: *The opposing factions coalesced to form a new political party.* [Latin *coalēscere.*] —**co′a·les′cence,** *n.* —**co′a·les′cent,** *adj.*

coal·field (kōl′fēld′) *n.* a region where deposits of coal are found.

coal gas 1. a mixture of gases, consisting primarily of hydrogen and methane, produced by heating bituminous coal in the absence of oxygen, used esp. in open-hearth furnaces and as a source of such compounds as ammonia and benzene. **2.** the gas given off by burning coal.

coaling station, a place where coal is supplied to ships or trains.

co·a·li·tion (kō′ə lish′ən) *n.* **1.** a temporary alliance, as of political factions, parties, or nations, for some special purpose. **2.** a union into one mass or body; combination. [Medieval Latin *coalitio* society, meeting, corporation, from Latin *coalēscere* to grow together.] —For Synonyms, see **alliance.**

coal measures, strata, esp. of the Carboniferous period, containing beds of coal.

coal oil, kerosene.

coal scuttle, a pail or other bucketlike container, often with a wide, projecting lip, for carrying or holding coal. Also, **coal hod.**

coal tar, a black, sticky residue left after heating bituminous coal

The following list contains a selection of compounds that can be formed with the prefix co-. The meaning of a word on the list can be understood by combining the appropriate sense of the prefix with the root word.

coaction	cofeature	coprisoner
cocaptain	cofinance	coproduce
cochampion	cofounder	coproducer
cocomposer	coheir	copromoter
coconspirator	cohost	coproprietor
codefendant	coinventor	copublish
codesign	coinvestigator	copublisher
codesigner	coleader	corecipient
codiscoverer	comanage	cotenant
coedit	comanager	cowinner
coeditor	coorganizer	cowrite
coexecutor	copresident	cowriter

a	at	e	end	o	hot	u	up	hw	white		about
ā	ape	ē	me	ō	old	ū	use	ng	song		taken
ä	far	i	it	ô	fork	ü	rule	th	thin	ə	pencil
âr	care	ī	ice	oi	oil	u̇	pull	th	this		lemon
		îr	pierce	ou	out	ûr	turn	zh	measure		circus

in the absence of oxygen, used as a basis for many synthetic products, as dyes, nylon, aspirin, and plastics.

coam·ing (kō′ming) *n.* a raised edge, as around a hatch on a ship, used to keep out water. [Of uncertain origin.]

co·an·chor (kō ang′kər) *n.* a person who serves jointly with another person as anchor of a news broadcast. —*v.t.* to serve as anchor of (a news broadcast) jointly with another person.

coarse (kôrs) *adj.,* **coars·er, coars·est. 1.** lacking refinement or delicacy; crude; vulgar: *coarse behavior, coarse language.* **2.** lacking fineness of texture or structure; thick or rough: *coarse cloth, coarse skin, coarse hair.* **3.** composed of large parts or particles: *coarse sand.* **4.** intended for rough or less delicate work: *a coarse saw.* **5.** of inferior or poor quality or worth; common; base. [Earlier *corse, course;* of uncertain origin.] —**coarse′ly,** *adv.* —**coarse′ness,** *n.*

> **Synonyms** Coarse, gross, and vulgar mean lacking refinement in taste, behavior, or language. **Coarse** is generally opposed to *fine* and suggests a roughness or lack of polish: *One comedian's coarse jokes contrasted with the sophisticated wit of the other.* **Gross** stresses a lack of physical delicacy: *Their gross table manners disgusted the other diners.* **Vulgar** suggests an offensive lack of taste or propriety, often combined with social pretensions: *the unnecessary use of vulgar language, a vulgar display of jewelry.*

coarse-grained (kôrs′grānd′) *adj.* **1.** having a coarse texture or grain. **2.** lacking refinement or delicacy; crude.

coars·en (kôr′sən) *v.t., v.i.* to make or become coarse.

coast (kōst) *n.* **1.** land next to the sea. **2. the Coast.** the region of the United States bordering the Pacific Ocean. **3.a.** a ride or slide down a hill or similar incline, as on a sled. **b.** an incline, as a hill, down which one may slide. —*v.i.* **1.** to ride or slide down an incline by the force of gravity, as on a sled. **2.** to continue to move on acquired momentum after power has been shut off: *The car coasted after she turned off the engine.* **3.** to advance or move along with little or no effort: *He coasted through his senior year in college.* **4.** to sail along or near a coast. —*v.t.* to sail along or near the coast of. [Old French *coste* rib, shore, slope of a hill, from Latin *costa* rib, side.] —For Synonyms *(n.),* see **shore**[1].

· **the coast is clear.** there is no danger or hindrance present.

coast·al (kōs′təl) *adj.* of, at, near, or along a coast.

coastal plain, a low, usually flat land area along a coast.

coast·er (kōs′tər) *n.* **1.** a small mat or shallow tray placed under a glass or bottle to protect the surface beneath. **2.** a ship that engages in trade along a coast. **3.** a sled or toboggan. **4.** roller coaster. **5.** a person or thing that coasts.

coaster brake, a brake on the rear wheel of a bicycle, operated by pushing the pedals backwards.

Coast Guard 1. the military service responsible for preserving safety and order along the coasts and inland waterways of the United States. **2. coast guard. a.** any similar military service. **b.** a member of any such service. —**coast′guards′man,** *n.*

coast·line (kōst′līn′) *n.* the outline or contour of a coast.

coast·ward (kōst′wərd) *adj.* directed toward the coast. —*adv.* also, **coast·wards.** toward the coast.

coast·wise (kōst′wīz′) *adj.* following, or carried on, along the coast. —*adv.* by way of or along the coast. Also *(adv.),* **coast·ways** (kōst′wāz′).

coat (kōt) *n.* **1.** an outer garment with sleeves, usually designed to be worn outdoors over other clothing. **2.** a natural, external covering, as the fur or hair of an animal. **3.** any outer layer that covers a surface: *a coat of paint.* —*v.t.* **1.** to cover with a layer, as of paint: *Grease coated the stove.* **2.** to provide or cover with a coat. [Old French *cote* tunic; of Germanic origin.]

co·a·ti (kō ä′tē) *n., pl.* **-tis.** any of various raccoonlike mammals, genus *Nasua,* of Central and South America, having a long body, yellowish brown, gray, or red fur, a long, striped tail, and a flexible snout. Length: 4 feet (1.2 meters). **co·a·ti·mun·di** (kō ä′tē mun′dē). [Of Tupi-Guarani origin.]

coat·ing (kō′ting) *n.* **1.** a layer covering a surface. **2.** cloth for making coats.

coat of arms *pl.* **coats of arms.** a group of heraldic devices, esp. of a person or family, usually including an escutcheon, a crest, supporters, if any, and a motto. Originally worn as identification, it often contains symbols of the

coati

history or tradition of the bearer. [Translation of French *cotte d'armes* surcoat decorated with heraldic devices worn by medieval knights over their armor.]

coat of mail *pl.* **coats of mail.** a shirt or coat made of chain mail, formerly worn as armor.

coat·room (kōt′rüm′, -rům′) *n.* cloakroom.

coat·tail (kōt′tāl′) also, **coattails.** *n.* the lower back part of a man's coat or jacket, esp. when long and divided, as on a cutaway or swallow-tailed coat.

· **to ride on (someone's) coattails.** to benefit from the popularity, prestige, or influence of someone, esp. someone in politics: *The congressional candidate rode on the president's coattails.*

co·au·thor (kō ô′thər) *n.* a joint author. —*v.t.* to write as a joint author with another or others.

coax (kōks) *v.t.* **1.** to persuade or try to persuade by flattery, pleasant manners, or soft, gentle speech; wheedle. **2.** to obtain by coaxing: *He coaxed extra money from his mother.* —*v.i.* to use flattery, pleasant manners, or soft, gentle speech in trying to persuade. [From earlier *cokes* a fool; of uncertain origin.] —**coax′-er,** *n.*

> **Synonyms** Coax, cajole, and wheedle mean to persuade or attempt to persuade through flattery, pleasant, or reassuring words, or similar means. **Coax** suggests any kind of gentle appeal: *to coax an animal to come closer, to coax someone to join in a game.* **Cajole** more strongly implies a seductive tone or tactic: *to cajole a child to go to bed by promising to read a story.* **Wheedle** suggests an obvious, often obsequious, kind of approach: *The caller tried to wheedle me into buying a magazine subscription.*

co·ax·i·al (kō ak′sē əl) *adj.* **1.** having a common axis. Also, **co·ax′al. 2.** (of a loudspeaker) with two or more speaker elements mounted one inside the other on the same axis, each receiving only a certain range of frequencies. [Co- + AXIS + -AL[1].]

coaxial cable, high-frequency telephone, telegraph, and television cable capable of transmitting thousands of electronic signals simultaneously, composed of a number of parallel wires, each surrounded by insulating material that is encased in a thin sheath of conducting material.

cob (kob) *n.* **1.** corncob *(def. 1).* **2.** a thick-set horse with short legs. **3.** a male swan.

co·balt (kō′bôlt) *n.* a hard silver-white or pinkish metallic element, used esp. in high-temperature steel and magnetic alloys and as a coloring agent for ceramics. Symbol: **Co** For tables, see **element.** [German *Kobalt,* form of *Kobold* goblin; so called by German miners because cobalt ore, which contains arsenic and sulfur, was harmful to their health.]

cobalt blue 1. a deep blue pigment made from cobalt. **2.** a deep blue color.

co·bal·tite (kō′bôl tīt′, kō bôl′tīt) *n.* a silvery white sulfide mineral mined as an ore of cobalt. Formula: CoAsS [COBALT + -ITE[1].]

cobalt 60, a radioactive isotope of cobalt, used in radiology.

cob·ble[1] (kob′əl) *v.t.,* **-bled, -bling. 1.** to mend or make, as shoes or boots. **2.** to mend or put together clumsily or roughly. [Middle English *cobelere* cobbler, with change of part of speech.]

cob·ble[2] (kob′əl) *n.* cobblestone. —*v.t.,* **-bled, -bling.** to pave with cobblestones. [From dialectal *cob* lump (of uncertain origin).]

cob·bler (kob′lər) *n.* **1.** a person whose work is making or mending shoes. **2.** a deep-dish fruit pie having no bottom crust and a thick top crust. **3.** an iced, sweetened fruit drink made with wine or liquor and usually served with a garnish, as lemon or mint. **4.** *Archaic.* a clumsy worker. [Of uncertain origin.]

cob·ble·stone (kob′əl stōn′) *n.* a naturally rounded stone, formerly used in paving.

co·bel·lig·er·ent (kō′bə lij′ər ənt) *n.* a nation that aids or cooperates with another or others in waging war but is not bound by a formal alliance.

COBOL (kō′bôl′) *n.* a computer coding system oriented toward business applications. [Short for *co(mmon) b(usiness) o(riented) l(anguage).*]

co·bra (kō′brə) *n.* any of several large, usually hooded, venomous snakes, family Elapidae, found in Africa and Asia. The king cobra is the world's longest venomous snake. Length: to 18½ feet (5.6 meters). [Short for Portuguese *cobra (de capello)* snake (with a hood); *cobra* from Latin *colubra.*]

cob·web (kob′web′) *n.* **1.** spiderweb. **2.** a single thread of a spiderweb or the material of which it is made. **3.** anything resembling this, as in use or construction. [Short for Old English *āttor-coppe* spider; literally, poison head + WEB.] —**cob′web′by,** *adj.*

co·ca (kō′kə) *n.* **1.** any of several tropical shrubs or small trees, genus *Erythroxylum,* and esp. *E. coca,* of South America. **2.** the

dried leaves of these plants, esp. *E. coca,* which yield alkaloids, as cocaine. [Spanish *coca;* of Quechua origin.]

co·caine (kō kān′, kō′kān) *also,* **co·cain.** *n.* a white, crystal-line alkaloid obtained from coca leaves, used medically as a local anesthetic. It is also used illegally as a stimulant and as such creates a strong physical and psychological dependence. Formula: $C_{17}H_{21}NO_4$ [COCA + -INE².]

coc·cid (kok′sid) *n.* any of a group of small, sap-sucking scale insects, family Coccidae, characterized by the secretion of a soft, waxy, outer covering. Many are agricultural pests, esp. on fruit trees. [Modern Latin *Coccidae,* from Greek *kokkos* seed, berry.]

coc·coid (kok′oid) *adj.* of, relating to, or resembling a coccus. [COCC(US) + -OID.]

coc·cus (kok′əs) *n., pl.* **coc·ci** (kok′sī). any bacterium charac-terized by a spherical or oval shape. For illustration, see **bacte-ria.** [Modern Latin *coccus,* from Greek *kokkos* seed, berry.]

coc·cyx (kok′siks) *n., pl.* **coc·cy·ges** (kok′si jēz′, kok sī′jēz). a small triangular bone at the lower end of the spinal column con-sisting of four rudimentary vertebrae. [Latin *coccyx* cuckoo, from Greek *kókkyx;* because supposedly shaped like a cuckoo's beak.]

co·chin (kō′chin, koch′in) *also,* **Co·chin.** *n.* any of a variety of large domestic fowl having heavily feathered legs. [From COCHIN CHINA, where it originated.]

coch·i·neal (koch′ə nēl′) *n.* a dark red dye prepared from the dried bodies of a female scale insect, *Coccus cacti,* of Mexico and Central America, used chiefly as a coloring in foods, inks, and cosmetics. [Spanish *cochinilla,* from Latin *coccinus* scarlet, going back to Greek *kokkos* variety of berry or gall used to dye scarlet.]

coch·le·a (kok′lē ə) *n., pl.* **-le·ae** (-lē ē′). the tube of the in-ner ear, shaped somewhat like a snail shell, containing the sen-sory ends of the auditory nerve. For illustration, see **ear¹**. [Latin *cochlea* snail, snail shell, from Greek *kochliās* snail with a spiral shell.] —**coch′le·ar,** *adj.*

cock¹ (kok) *n.* **1.** a male chicken; rooster. **2.** the male of various other birds. **3.a.** the hammer of a firearm. **b.** the position into which this hammer is brought when pulled back in preparation for firing. **4.** a device, as a faucet or valve, used to control the flow of a liquid or gas. —*v.t.* to pull back the hammer of (a firearm) to a firing position. [Old English *cocc* male bird.]

cock² (kok) *v.t.* to turn up or upward or tilt to one side, esp. in a jaunty, pert, or inquisitive manner: *The dog cocked its ears. She cocked the hat on her head.* —*n.* an upward turn or tilt to one side. [From COCK¹; with reference to the movement of a cock's head and chest when it crows.]

cock³ (kok) *n.* a small, cone-shaped stack of hay. —*v.t.* to arrange in such stacks. [Possibly of Scandinavian origin.]

cock·ade (ko kād′) *n.* a knot of ribbon, rosette, or similar ornament worn as a badge, insignia, or indication of rank, esp. on a hat. [French *cocarde* rosette on a cap, from Old French *coquard* vain, from *coq* cock¹; imitative.]

Cock·aigne (ko kān′) *n.* an imaginary country of idleness and luxury. [Middle French *(pais de) cocaigne* (land of) plenty, possi-bly from Middle Low German *kōkenje* small sweet cake.]

cock·a·ma·mie (kok′ə mā′mē) *also,* **cock·a·ma·my.** *Slang. adj.* silly, foolish, or absurd: *a cockamamie scheme.* [From earlier dialectal *cockamamie* decal, a form of DECALCOMANIA.]

cock-and-bull story (kok′ən bûl′) an absurd, unlikely story that is told as being the truth.

cock·a·tiel (kok′ə tēl′) *also,* **cock·a·teel.** *n.* a small, gray, Australian parrot, *Nymphicus hollandicus,* with a yellow-crested head and a long tail. Average length: 12 inches (30 centimeters). [Dutch *kaketielje,* diminutive of *kaketoe,* from Malay *kakatua* cockatoo; influenced in spelling by COCK¹.]

cock·a·too (kok′ə tü′) *n., pl.* **-toos.** any of various crested parrots, family Psittacidae, native to Australia, the East Indies, and southwestern Asia, having white plumage that may be tinged with pink or yellow. [Dutch *kaketoe,* from Malay *kakatua;* influ-enced in spelling by COCK¹.]

cock·a·trice (kok′ə tris′) *n.* a fabled serpent, hatched from a cock's egg, whose glance was supposed to cause death. [Old French *cocatris* crocodile, fabled serpent, modification of Late Latin *calcātrīx* literally, treader, from Latin *calcāre* to tread.]

cock·boat (kok′bōt′) *n.* a ship's small rowboat. Also, **cockle-boat.**

cock·chaf·er (kok′chā′fər) *n.* a black-and-brown beetle, fam-ily Scarabaeidae, common in Europe, the destructive larvae of which eat the roots of many kinds of plants.

cock·crow (kok′krō′) *n.* the time when roosters begin to crow; dawn.

cocked hat, a hat with the brim turned up so as to form two or more points; tricorn.

cock·er (kok′ər) *n.* cocker spaniel.

cock·er·el (kok′ər əl, kok′rəl) *n.* a young rooster, less than one year old.

cocker spaniel, a spaniel having a short, compact body, long, silky hair, and drooping ears, kept as a bird dog or house pet. Height: 14 inches (36 centimeters) at the shoulder. [From WOOD-COCK + SPANIEL; with reference to its skill in hunting woodcocks and other game birds.]

cock·eye (kok′ī′) *n.* an eye that squints. [COCK² + EYE.]

cock·eyed (kok′īd′) *adj.* **1.** cross-eyed. **2.** *Slang.* tilted to one side; off-center. **3.** *Slang.* absurd; foolish: *a cockeyed idea.*

cock·fight (kok′fīt′) *n.* a fight between gamecocks, which are usually fitted with steel spurs on their legs. —**cock′fight′ing,** *n.*

cock·horse (kok′hôrs′) *n.* hobbyhorse.

cock·le¹ (kok′əl) *n.* **1.** any of several saltwater mollusks, family Cardiidae, having a brittle, heart-shaped, bivalve shell. **2.** cockle-shell. **3.** a wrinkle; pucker. —*v.t., v.i.,* **-led, -ling.** to wrinkle; pucker. [Old French *coquille* shell, going back to Latin *conchȳlium* shellfish, from Greek *konchylion* little mollusk, from *konchē* conch.]

· **the cockles of one's heart.** the deepest part of one's heart or emotions.

cock·le² (kok′əl) *n.* any of several weeds of the pink family that grow in grain fields. [Old English *coccel.*]

cock·le·boat (kok′əl bōt′) *n.* cockboat.

cock·le·bur (kok′əl bûr′) *n.* any of a group of weeds, genus *Xanthium,* widely distributed in North America and Mexico and bearing spiny burs.

cock·le·shell (kok′əl shel′) *n.* **1.** the shell of a cockle. **2.** a small, light, shallow boat.

cock·ney (kok′nē) *also,* **Cock·ney.** *n., pl.* **-neys. 1.** a native or inhabitant of the old eastern district of London, England. **2.** the dialect peculiar to this district. —*adj.* of, relating to, or resem-bling cockneys or their dialect. [Middle English *cokeney* cock's egg, spoiled child, city dweller, going back to Old English *cocc* cock¹ + *æg* egg.] —**cock′ney·ish,** *adj.* —**cock′ney·ism,** *n.*

cock·pit (kok′pit′) *n.* **1.** an open or enclosed compartment in an airplane where the pilot and copilot sit. **2.** a pit or enclosed area for cockfights. **3.** an open space in a sailboat or other small boat where the pilot and passengers sit. **4.** a place where many contests or battles are or have been fought. **5.** formerly, quarters below the deck of warships used for treating the wounded during battle.

cock·roach (kok′rōch′) *n.* any of a large group of brown or black insects, family Blattidae, with oval, flattened, leathery bod-ies, bristly legs, and long antennas. Some species are common household pests. [Modification of Spanish *cucaracha,* from *cuca* caterpillar; of uncertain origin.]

cocks·comb (koks′kōm′) *n.* **1.** the comb or fleshy red crest on the head of a rooster. **2.** a jester's cap resembling this in shape. **3.** a plant, *Celosia cristata,* having showy red, purple, yellow, or white flower spikes that resemble a rooster's comb or a feath-ery plume.

cock·sure (kok′shûr′) *adj.* **1.** overly confident or sure of oneself. **2.** abso-lutely certain. —**cock′sure′ness,** *n.*

cock·swain (kok′sən, -swān′) cox-swain.

cock·tail (kok′tāl′) *n.* **1.** any of vari-ous, usually iced, alcoholic drinks made by mixing liquor with flavoring ingredi-ents, as bitters, liqueurs, or fruit juices. **2.** any of various appetizers, as fruit juice, a mixture of diced fruits, or seafood.

cockscomb
(def. 1)

cock·y (kok′ē) *adj.* **cock·i·er, cock·i·est.** *Informal.* too sure or confident of oneself; arrogantly self-confident. —**cock′i·ly,** *adv.* —**cock′i·ness,** *n.*

co·co (kō′kō) *n., pl.* **-cos. 1.** coconut. **2.** coconut palm.

co·coa (kō′kō) *n.* **1.** a brown powder made by drying, ferment-ing, roasting, and grinding cacao seeds and removing most of the cocoa butter. It is used esp. in making various chocolate drinks. **2.** a chocolate beverage made by mixing this powder with hot milk or water and, sometimes, sugar. **3.** a light, dull brown color. —*adj.* having the color cocoa. [Form of CACAO.]

cocoa butter, a yellowish white fat obtained from cacao seeds, used in making such items as chocolate, soap, and cosmetics.

co·co·nut (kō′kə nut′, -nət) *also,* **co·coa·nut.** *n.* **1.** the large, oval fruit of the coconut palm, having a smooth outer rind, a

a	at	e	end	o	hot	u	up	hw	white		about
ā	ape	ē	me	ō	old	ū	use	ng	song	ə	taken
ä	far	i	it	ô	fork	ü	rule	th	thin		pencil
âr	care	ī	ice	oi	oil	u̇	pull	th	this		lemon
		îr	pierce	ou	out	ûr	turn	zh	measure		circus

reddish brown fibrous husk, and a hard inner shell lined with edible white meat and containing a milky fluid called **coconut milk**. **2.** coconut palm.

coconut oil, an oil extracted from the dried fruit of coconuts, used in making soap, shampoo, and many other products.

coconut palm, a tall palm tree, *Cocos nucifera,* that bears coconuts and has huge feathery leaves.

co·coon (kə kün′) *n.* **1.** a protective case consisting of silk, leaves, or other materials that encloses the pupa of certain insects, as the silkworm, during the pupal stage. **2.** any similar protective covering, as the egg containers of certain spiders. [French *cocon* the protective case for the pupa of the silkworm, from Provençal *coucoun,* from *coco* shell, from Latin *coccum* berry, from Greek *kokkos* berry, seed.]

cod (kod) *n., pl.* **cod** or **cods**. any of a group of commercially important food fish, family Gadidae, found in the colder northern waters of the Atlantic and Pacific oceans. [Possibly from obsolete *cod* bag, from Old English *codd;* with reference to its shape.]

c.o.d. *also,* **C.O.D. 1.** cash on delivery. **2.** collect on delivery.

co·da (kō′də) *n.* a passage at the end of a musical composition or movement, more or less independent of it and bringing it to a formal, satisfactory close. [Italian *coda,* from Latin *cauda* tail.]

cod·dle (kod′əl) *v.t.,* **-dled, -dling. 1.** to treat tenderly or overindulgently; pamper. **2.** to cook gently in a liquid at or just below the boiling point; simmer: *to coddle eggs.* [Possibly a form of CAUDLE.]

code (kōd) *n.* **1.** a systematic collection of an existing body of law: *a penal code.* **2.** any system or collection of principles and rules of conduct: *a moral code, a code of ethics.* **3.** a system of communication in which sounds, light flashes, flags, or other signals represent numbers, letters, or words, used to send messages, as by telegraph or heliograph. **4.a.** a system of writing using letters, words, numbers, or other symbols that are arbitrarily given certain meanings, used for secrecy or brevity in communication: *The message was written in code.* **b.** a message in code. **c.** a key or pattern to a code. **5.** *Computers.* any system using binary numbers to represent letters, numbers, or other characters. **6.** genetic code. *—v.t.,* **cod·ed, cod·ing.** to put into the form of a code. [Old French *code* code of laws, from Latin *cōdex* wooden tablet for writing, book, code of laws. Doublet of CODEX.]

co·deine (kō′dēn) *also,* **co·dein.** *n.* a habit-forming drug derived from opium, used to relieve pain and cough and to induce sleep. [Greek *kōdeia* poppy head + -INE[2].]

co·de·pen·dent (kō′di pen′dənt) *adj.* of or relating to a psychologically unhealthy condition in which one person becomes dependent upon another dependent, and often addicted, person. *—n.* a person who becomes dependent upon another dependent, and often addicted, person.

co·dex (kō′deks) *n., pl.* **co·di·ces** (kō′də sēz′, kod′ə-). a manuscript volume, esp. of the Scriptures or ancient classics. [Latin *cōdex* wooden tablet for writing, book. Doublet of CODE.]

cod·fish (kod′fish′) *n., pl.* **-fish** or **-fish·es.** cod.

codg·er (koj′ər) *n. Informal.* an odd, eccentric, or grumpy person, esp. one who is old.

cod·i·cil (kod′ə sil) *n.* **1.** a supplement to a will that adds to, changes, or explains something in it. **2.** any supplement or appendix. [Latin *cōdicillus* a writing, addition to a will, diminutive of *cōdex* book. See CODEX.] *—***cod·i·cil·la·ry** (kod′ə sil′ə rē), *adj.*

cod·i·fy (kod′ə fī′, kō′də-) *v.t.,* **-fied, -fy·ing.** to arrange in a systematic way, as laws; reduce to a code. [CODE + -FY.] *—***cod′·i·fi·ca′tion,** *n. —***cod′i·fi′er,** *n.*

cod·ling (kod′ling) *also,* **cod·lin** (kod′lin). *n.* **1.** a variety of apple having an elongated shape, used for cooking. **2.** an unripe apple. [Middle English *querd(e)lynge* hard apple, possibly from Anglo-Norman *quere de lion* heart of lion (with reference to its shape), going back to Latin *cor* heart + *dē* + *leō* lion; influenced in spelling by English *coddle* to cook.]

codling moth, a small moth, *Carpocapsa pomonella,* whose larvae feed on the pulp of apples, pears, and other fruits.

cod-liv·er oil (kod′liv′ər) oil extracted from the livers of cod and certain other fish, used as a source of vitamins A and D.

co·don (kō′don) *n.* a group of three nucleotides that forms the genetic code for a specific amino acid as part of the synthesis of proteins within a cell. [CODE + -on, on the model of *proton.*]

co·ed (kō′ed′) *also,* **co-ed.** *Informal. n.* a female student at a coeducational college or school. *—adj.* **1.** having both male and female students in attendance; coeducational: *a coed class.* **2.** intended for or used by both sexes: *coed dormitories, a coed team.* [Short for COEDUCATIONAL.]

co·ed·u·ca·tion (kō′ej ə kā′shən) *n.* the education of students of both sexes in the same school, college, or classes. [CO- + EDUCATION.]

co·ed·u·ca·tion·al (kō′ej ə kā′shə nəl) *adj.* educating students of both sexes in the same school, college, or classes. *—***co′ed·u·ca′tion·al·ly,** *adv.*

co·ef·fi·cient (kō′i fish′ənt) *n.* **1.** *Mathematics.* a number or algebraic expression put before and multiplying an algebraic expression. In the expression $3x^2y$, 3 is the numerical coefficient of x^2y; in $3x^2(y + z)$, $3x^2$ is the coefficient of $(y + z)$. **2.** *Physics.* a numerical constant determined for a property of a given substance under certain conditions and used to measure or calculate change in that property or substance under other conditions: *coefficient of expansion, coefficient of friction.* [Co- + EFFICIENT.]

coe·la·canth (sē′lə kanth′) *n.* a large, primitive, lobe-fin, bony fish, *Latimeria chalumnae,* long thought to be extinct. First caught in 1938 off the coast of South Africa, it is a marine representative of the group of fish that gave rise to amphibians. [Modern Latin *coelacanthus* literally, having a hollow spine, from Greek *koilos* hollow + *akantha* thorn, spine.]

coe·len·ter·ate (si len′tə rāt′, -tər it) *n.* any of a group of aquatic, largely marine invertebrates, phylum Coelenterata, including coral, jellyfish, and hydras, having a saclike body with numerous tentacles around a single mouth opening. Also, **cni·darian.** *—adj.* relating to, belonging to, or characteristic of this group. [Modern Latin *coelenterata* (plural) literally, having empty intestines, from Greek *koilos* hollow + *enteron* intestine.]

coe·li·ac (sē′lē ak′) celiac.

coe·lom (sē′ləm) *also,* **coe·lome** (sē′lōm), **ce·lom.** *n., pl.* **coe·loms** or **coe·lo·ma·ta** (si lō′mə tə). the main body cavity of higher multicellular animals, lined on the inside, in which most of the internal organs are suspended. [Greek *koiloma,* from *koilos* hollow.] *—***coe·lom·ate** (sē′lə māt′, si lō′mit), **coe·lom·ic** (si lom′ik, -lō′mik), *adj.*

coe·no·bite (sē′nə bīt′, sen′ə-) cenobite.

co·en·zyme (kō en′zīm) *n.* an organic molecule, often derived from a water-soluble vitamin, that forms an active enzyme system when joined to a protein molecule. [Co- + ENZYME.]

co·e·qual (kō ē′kwəl) *adj.* same or equal, as in rank, ability, value, or size. *—n.* a person or thing coequal with another or others. *—***co·e·qual·i·ty** (kō′i kwol′i tē), *n. —***co·e′qual·ly,** *adv.*

co·erce (kō ûrs′) *v.t.,* **-erced, -erc·ing. 1.** to force, as by violence, threats, or authority. **2.** to bring about by force: *to coerce a confession from someone.* **3.** to control or dominate by force. [Latin *coercēre* to shut in, restrain.] *—***co·erc′er,** *n. —***co·er′ci·ble,** *adj.*

co·er·cion (kō ûr′shən) *n.* **1.** the use of force to compel or control; constraint. **2.** government by force.

co·er·cive (kō ûr′siv) *adj.* tending or serving to coerce. *—***co·er′cive·ly,** *adv. —***co·er′cive·ness,** *n.*

co·e·val (kō ē′vəl) *adj.* of, belonging to, or living in the same age, date, time, or duration; contemporary. *—n.* contemporary. [Late Latin *coaevus* of the same age (from Latin *co-* with + *aevum* age) + -AL[1].]

co·ex·ist (kō′eg zist′) *v.i.* **1.** to exist in or at the same place or time as another. **2.** to live together peacefully despite differences in policy or principle. *—***co′ex·ist′ence,** *n. —***co′ex·ist′ent,** *adj.*

co·ex·tend (kō′ek stend′) *v.t., v.i.* to extend to or through the same space or time. *—***co′ex·ten′sion,** *n.*

co·ex·ten·sive (kō′ek sten′siv) *adj.* extending to or through the same space or time; extending equally. *—***co′ex·ten′sive·ly,** *adv.*

cof·fee (kô′fē, kof′ē) *n.* **1.** an aromatic, dark brown beverage prepared from ground or crushed coffee beans and hot or boiling water. **2.** coffee beans collectively, whether whole or ground. **3.** any of a group of tropical evergreen shrubs and small trees, genus *Coffea,* that bear coffee beans. **4.** a rich, dark brown color. *—adj.* having the color coffee. [Italian *caffé,* from Turkish *kahveh* the beverage, from *Kaffa,* region in Ethiopia where the coffee plant originated.]

coffee bean, the seed of the coffee plant, dried, roasted, and ground to make the beverage coffee.

coffee break, a short rest period, usually in the middle of the morning or afternoon, during which one has coffee or other refreshment.

coffee cake, a rich cake or sweetened bread, often containing nuts and fruits, served with coffee or other beverages.

cof·fee·house (kô′fē hous′, kof′ē-) *n., pl.* **-hous·es** (-hou′ziz). an establishment that sells coffee and other refreshments and often functions as an informal social or entertainment center.

cof·fee·pot (kô′fē pot′, kof′ē-) *n.* a container, usually with a cover, for preparing or serving coffee.

coffee shop, an informal restaurant.

coffee table, a low table, usually placed in front of a sofa.

cof·fer (kô′fər, kof′ər) *n.* **1.** a box or chest, esp. one used for

holding money or other valuables; strongbox. **2. coffers.** monetary resources; treasury. **3.** a recessed ornamental panel, usually in a series, in a ceiling, vault, or dome. **4.** cofferdam. [Old French *cofre* chest, from Latin *cophinus* basket, from Greek *kophinos.* Doublet of COFFIN.]

cof·fer·dam (kô′fər dam′, kof′ər-) *n.* **1.** a temporary watertight enclosure built in water and pumped dry to permit construction of foundations, bridge piers, or similar structures in the enclosed area. **2.** any of certain similar, usually watertight, structures.

cof·fin (kô′fin, kof′in) *n.* a box or case into which a corpse is placed for burial; casket. [Old French *cofin* chest, case, from Latin *cophinus* basket, from Greek *kophinos.* Doublet of COFFER.]

coffin bone, the bone in the hoof of a horse, donkey, or zebra. It is equivalent to the bone forming the last joint of the middle toe in five-toed mammals.

coffer *(def. 3)*

co·func·tion (kō′fungk′shən) *n.* the trigonometric function of the complement of a particular angle. Sine and cosine are cofunctions, as are tangent and cotangent, and secant and cosecant.

cog (kog) *n.* **1.** one of a series of teeth on the circumference of a wheel that transmits or receives motion by locking into similar teeth on another wheel or on a track. **2.** cogwheel. **3.** a projection or tenon on the end of a piece of wood that fits into a notch on another piece to form a joint. **4.** *Informal.* a person who plays a minor, but usually necessary, part in a large process or organization. [Of Scandinavian origin.]

co·gen·cy (kō′jən sē) *n.* the state or quality of being cogent.

co·gen·er·a·tion (kō jen′ə rā′shən) *n.* the use of industrial energy by-products, as steam or heat, to generate electricity. [Co- + GENERATION.]

co·gent (kō′jənt) *adj.* having the power to be persuasive; forcible; convincing: *a cogent argument.* [Latin *cōgēns,* present participle of *cōgere* to drive together, compel.] —**co′gent·ly,** *adv.*

cog·i·tate (koj′i tāt′) *v.i.,* -**tat·ed,** -**tat·ing.** to think or consider earnestly and carefully; meditate; ponder. [Latin *cōgitātus,* past participle of *cōgitāre* to think.] —**cog′i·ta·tor,** *n.*

cog·i·ta·tion (koj′i tā′shən) *n.* careful and earnest thought or consideration; meditation; reflection.

cog·i·ta·tive (koj′i tā′tiv) *adj.* capable of or given to cogitation.

co·gnac (kōn′yak, kon′-) *n.* a brandy originally made in the French town of Cognac.

cog·nate (kog′nāt) *adj.* **1.** related through a common origin; derived from the same source: *cognate words, cognate languages.* **2.** having the same ancestor or parentage; related by birth. **3.** allied in nature, quality, or characteristics. —*n.* a person or thing that is cognate. [Latin *cōgnātus* related by blood, kindred.]

cog·ni·tion (kog nish′ən) *n.* **1.** the act or faculty of knowing or perceiving. **2.** something known or perceived. [Latin *cognitiō.*]

cog·ni·tive (kog′ni tiv) *adj.* of, relating to, or involving knowledge or awareness.

cog·ni·za·ble (kog′nə zə bəl, kon′ə-) *adj.* **1.** capable of being known or perceived. **2.** within the jurisdiction of a court of law.

cog·ni·zance (kog′nə zəns, kon′ə-) *n.* **1.** knowledge or awareness; conscious recognition: *We had no cognizance of the facts.* **2.** the limits of knowledge or awareness: *an idea beyond one's cognizance.* **3.a.** the right or power of a court of law to try and settle cases; jurisdiction. **b.** the exercise of jurisdiction. [Old French *conoissance* knowledge, from *conoistre* to know, from Latin *cognōscere.*]

· **to take cognizance of.** to notice or recognize.

cog·ni·zant (kog′nə zənt, kon′ə-) *adj.* having cognizance; aware. —For Synonyms, see **aware.**

cog·no·men (kog nō′mən) *n.* **1.** a family name; surname. **2.** any name, esp. a nickname. **3.** the last of the three names of an ancient Roman. [Latin *cognōmen* family name.]

co·gno·scen·te (kon′yə shen′tā, -tē, kog′nə-) *n., pl.* -**ti** (-tē). a person who has special knowledge or superior taste in a field, esp. the arts, literature, or fashion; connoisseur. [Earlier Italian *cognoscente* wise, from Latin *cognoscens,* present participle of *cognōscere* to know.]

cog railway, a railway that obtains the traction needed to climb steep grades from a cogwheel aboard the engine that meshes with cogs on a center rail.

cog·wheel (kog′hwēl′, -wēl′) *n.* a wheel with teeth on its rim, for transmitting or receiving motion. Also, **gearwheel.**

co·hab·it (kō hab′it) *v.i.* to live together as husband and wife, esp. when not married. [Late Latin *cohabitāre* to dwell together, from Latin *co-* together + *habitāre* to inhabit.] —**co·hab′i·ta′tion,** *n.*

co·here (kō hîr′) *v.i.,* -**hered,** -**her·ing. 1.** to stick or hold together, as parts of a mass: *The cake ingredients cohered when I added milk.* **2.** to be logically connected or consistent: *The points in your argument do not cohere.* [Latin *cohaerēre* to stick together.]

cogwheels

co·her·ence (kō hîr′əns, -her′-) *n.* **1.** logical connection; consistency. **2.** a sticking or holding together. Also, **co·her′en·cy.**

co·her·ent (kō hîr′ənt, -her′-) *adj.* **1.** logically connected; consistent. **3.** sticking or holding together. **3.** capable of expressing oneself intelligibly or articulately. **4.** *Physics.* (of electromagnetic radiation) having waves that are in phase with one another: *A laser emits coherent light.* —**co·her′ent·ly,** *adv.*

co·he·sion (kō hē′zhən) *n.* **1.** the act or state of cohering. **2.** the attraction between molecules of a substance that holds the substance together. [French *cohésion,* going back to Latin *cohaesus,* past participle of *cohaerēre* to stick together.]

co·he·sive (kō hē′siv) *adj.* capable of, having, or causing cohesion. —**co·he′sive·ly,** *adv.* —**co·he′sive·ness,** *n.*

co·ho (kō′hō) *n., pl.* -**hos** or -**ho.** a small, silvery, North Pacific salmon, *Oncorhynchus kisutch.* The males turn red in the spawning season. Weight: 5-8 pounds (2.3-3.6 kilograms). Also, **coho salmon.** [Earlier *co-hue,* from Salish *kwúhw-uth.*]

co·hort (kō′hôrt′) *n.* **1.** a companion, associate, or follower. **2.** any one of ten divisions constituting a legion in the ancient Roman army. **3.** any band, company, or group, esp. of persons. [Latin *cohors* enclosure, company of soldiers. Doublet of COURT.]

coif (*n., def. 1, v., def. 1* koif; *n., def. 2, v., def. 2* kwäf) *n.* **1.** any of various close-fitting caps that conform to the shape of the head. Nuns wore coifs under their veils. Knights wore leather coifs under their helmets. **2.** coiffure. —*v.t.* **1.** to cover with or as with a coif. **2.** to dress or arrange (the hair). [Old French *coif(f)e* headdress, from Late Latin *cofia* helmet, cap; possibly of Germanic origin.]

coif·feur (kwä fœr′) *n. French.* a male hairdresser. [French *coiffeur,* from *coiffer* to arrange the hair, from *coiffe.* See COIF.]

coif·fure (kwä fyûr′) *n.* the style in which one's hair is worn or arranged; hair style. [French *coiffure,* from *coiffer.* See COIF, COIFFEUR.]

coign (koin) *n.* a projecting corner. [Form of COIN corner (obsolete meaning).]

coign of vantage, an advantageous position for observing or acting.

coil[1] (koil) *n.* **1.** anything made up of a series of concentric spirals or rings: *a coil of wire.* **2.** one of the spirals or rings of such a series. **3.** a spiral pipe or series of connected pipes arranged in rows to conduct heat or liquids, as in a radiator. **4.** a spiral wire for conducting electricity, as in the ignition system of some automobile engines. —*v.i.* **1.** to form coils. **2.** to move in a winding course: *The road coiled around the mountain.* —*v.t.* to wind in coils: *The sailor coiled the rope around the anchor.* [Old French *coillir* to collect, from Latin *colligere.*]

coil[2] (koil) *n. Archaic.* disturbance; trouble. [Of uncertain origin.]

coin (koin) *n.* **1.** a piece of metal stamped with official government markings and of fixed weight and value, used as money. **2.** metal money collectively. —*v.t.* **1.** to make (money) by stamping metal. **2.** to make (metal) into coins. **3.** to make up; invent; devise: *to coin a phrase.* [Old French *coin* corner, wedge, die to stamp money, a coin (so called because stamped by a wedge), from Latin *cuneus* wedge.] —**coin′er,** *n.*

coin·age (koi′nij) *n.* **1.** the act, process, or right of making coins. **2.** something coined; metal money. **3.** coins collectively. **4.** the act or process of making up or inventing. **5.** something made up or invented.

co·in·cide (kō′in sīd′) *v.i.,* -**cid·ed,** -**cid·ing. 1.** to occur at the same time: *The football practice coincided with the concert.* **2.** to occupy the same area or place in space: *The two roads coincide*

a	at	e	end	o	hot	u	up	hw	white		about
ā	ape	ē	me	ō	old	ū	use	ng	song		taken
ä	far	i	it	ô	fork	ü	rule	th	thin	ə	pencil
âr	care	ī	ice	oi	oil	u̇	pull	th	this		lemon
		îr	pierce	ou	out	ûr	turn	zh	measure		circus

233

after 50 miles. **3.** to agree exactly; correspond: *Their views coincided.* [Medieval Latin *coincidere* literally, to fall upon together, from Latin *co-* together + *incidere* to fall upon.]

co·in·ci·dence (kō in'si dəns) *n.* **1.** a notable and remarkable occurrence of events, ideas, or circumstances at the same time and apparently by mere chance: *By coincidence we both arrived at the same time.* **2.** the fact or condition of coinciding.

co·in·ci·dent (kō in'si dənt) *adj.* **1.** occurring at the same time. **2.** occupying the same area or place in space. **3.** in exact agreement; corresponding: *an account coincident with the facts.* **—co·in'ci·dent·ly,** *adv.*

co·in·ci·den·tal (kō in'si den'təl) *adj.* characterized by, resulting from, or involving coincidence. **—co·in'ci·den'tal·ly,** *adv.*

co·in·sur·ance (kō'in shùr'əns) *n.* **1.** insurance underwritten jointly by two or more insurers. **2.** a form of property insurance that covers a loss only in proportion to the ratio between the amount of insurance and a fixed percentage of the value of the property.

co·in·sure (kō'in shùr') *v.,* **-sured, -sur·ing.** **—v.t.** to insure with coinsurance. **—v.i.** to take out coinsurance.

coir (koir) *n.* a coarse fiber obtained from the husks of coconuts, used to make such items as rope, mats, and brushes. [Malayalam *kāyar* cord.]

co·i·tus (kō'i təs, kō ē'-) *n.* sexual intercourse. [Latin *coitus* a coming together.] **—co'i·tal,** *adj.*

coke (kōk) *n.* a gray-black solid fuel, obtained by heating bituminous coal in the absence of oxygen, that burns with much heat and little smoke or ash, used esp. in blast furnaces for smelting iron ore. **—v.t., v.i., coked, cok·ing.** to convert into or become coke. [Of uncertain origin.]

col (kol) *n.* a low place along the crest of a mountain ridge that may be used as a pass; saddle. [French *col,* from Latin *collum* neck.]

col-, form of **com-** before *l,* as in *collateral.*

col. **1.** colony. **2.** color; colored. **3.** column.

Col. **1.** Colonel. **2.** Colossians.

co·la[1] (kō'lə) **1.** kola. **2.** a carbonated soft drink flavored with an extract obtained from kola nuts. [Modern Latin *Cola,* from Mandingo *kolo.*]

co·la[2] (kō'lə) a plural of **colon**[2].

col·an·der (kul'ən dər, kol'-) *n.* a container with holes in the bottom and sides, used to rinse or drain liquid from food. [Going back to Medieval Latin *colatorium* strainer, from Latin *cōlāre* to strain.]

cola nut, kola nut.

col·chi·cine (kol'chə sēn') *n.* a poisonous alkaloid extracted from the corms of colchicum, used in medicine to treat gout and in agriculture to produce greater yields by inducing chromosome doubling. Formula: $C_{22}H_{25}NO_6$ [COLCHIC(UM) + -INE[2].]

colander

col·chi·cum (kol'chi kəm) *n.* **1.** any of a group of plants, genus *Colchicum,* of the lily family, found in Europe and Asia and bearing light purple crocuslike flowers. **2.** the dried seeds and corm of *C. autumnale,* from which the drug colchicine is obtained. [Latin *colchicum* plant with a poisonous root, from Greek *Kolchikos* of Colchis, from *Kolchis* Colchis; with reference to Medea, a princess of *Colchis* noted for her skill in poisoning.]

cold (kōld) *adj.* **1.** having a lower temperature than that of the normal human body: *The patient had very cold hands and feet.* **2.** having a relatively low temperature; with little or no warmth: *The fire has gotten cold. My dinner is cold.* **3.** feeling a lack of warmth; chilly: *The children were cold after playing outside.* **4.** not influenced by personal feeling or emotion; objective: *a cold, calculating move.* **5.** lacking in enthusiasm or intensity of feeling; indifferent; apathetic: *They were a cold audience. The story left me cold.* **6.** not friendly or cordial: *The latecomers got a cold reception.* **7.** dispiriting; depressing: *We have to face the cold facts.* **8.** not fresh; stale or weak: *a cold scent.* **9.** dead. **10.** lacking warmth of color; of a bluish tone. **11.** *Informal.* unconscious: *I was knocked cold by the blow on my head.* **12.** *Informal.* far from the person or object sought, as in certain children's games. **—n.** **1.** an absence of warmth or heat. **2.** the sensation produced by the loss or absence of heat. **3.** an acute inflammation of the mucous membranes of the upper respiratory organs, characterized by coughing and sneezing. Also, **common cold.** **—adv.** *Informal.* **1.** thoroughly; completely: *to know something cold.* **2.** without any former knowledge or preparation: *to go into a test cold.* [Old

English *cald, ceald* of cool temperature.] **—cold'ly,** *adv.* **—cold'ness,** *n.*

· **cold feet.** a lack or loss of courage; timidity: *I got cold feet right before it was my turn to speak.*

· **(out) in the cold.** excluded from benefits given to others; ignored or neglected: *The will gave everything to charity and left the children in the cold.*

· **to catch (or take) cold.** to become ill with a cold.

· **to throw cold water on.** to show lack of enthusiasm for; discourage or disparage: *to throw cold water on a suggestion.*

cold-blood·ed (kōld'blud'id) *adj.* **1.** having blood, as fish, reptiles, and amphibians, that varies in temperature with the surrounding air, water, or land. **2.** lacking feeling, sensitivity, or pity; cruel. **3.** sensitive to cold. **—cold·'blood'ed·ly,** *adv.* **—cold-'blood'ed·ness,** *n.*

cold chisel, a chisel of tempered steel, used for cutting cold metal.

cold cream, a creamy preparation used for cleansing and soothing the skin.

cold cuts, cooked meat or fowl, as roast beef, turkey, pastrami, and bologna, that has been sliced and is served cold.

cold frame, a boxlike structure with a transparent cover and no bottom, used to protect plants against cold and wind.

cold front, the forward edge of a mass of cold air advancing into an area of warmer air.

cold-heart·ed (kōld'här'tid) *adj.* without feeling or sympathy; unkind. **—cold'-heart'ed·ly,** *adv.* **—cold'-heart'ed·ness,** *n.*

cold light, light produced by luminescence, as fluorescent light.

cold pack, a cold, wet wrapping, as a towel or an ice pack, used to relieve swelling or reduce pain.

cold-shoul·der (kōld'shōl'dər) *v.t. Informal.* to show deliberate unfriendliness or indifference toward.

cold shoulder *Informal.* deliberate unfriendliness or indifference; slight.

cold sore, a blister in or near the mouth caused by a virus and often accompanying a cold; herpes simplex. Also, **fever blister, fever sore.**

cold storage, the storage of perishable objects in an artificially cooled chamber.

cold sweat, perspiration accompanied by chill, usually caused by fear or shock.

cold turkey *Informal.* **1.** in blunt language; frankly: *to talk cold turkey about a problem.* **2.** the abrupt stopping of a habit or practice, as smoking or the taking of an addictive drug. **3.** without preparation: *to give a speech cold turkey.* **4.** abruptly: *to quit smoking cold turkey.*

cold war 1. *also,* **Cold War.** the state of rivalry and hostility in international relations, stopping short of military conflict, which developed after World War II between the United States and its allies on one side and the Soviet Union and its allies on the other. It ended in 1991 with the breakup of the Soviet Union. **2.** any state of intense political, economic, or ideological rivalry between nations, stopping short of actual warfare. ➡ distinguished from **hot war** in def. 2.

cold wave 1. a period of sudden, unusually cold weather. **2.** a permanent wave using a cold liquid solution instead of heat.

cole (kōl) *n.* any of various plants belonging to the same genus, *Brassica,* as the cabbage, esp. rape. Also, **colewort.** [Old English *cāl, cawel* cabbage, from Latin *caulis.*]

co·le·op·ter·an (kō'lē op'tər ən, kol'ē-) *n.* beetle[1] *(def. 1).* **—co'le·op'ter·ous,** *adj.* [Modern Latin *Coleoptera* (plural), from Greek *koleos* sheath + *pteron* wing + -AN.]

co·le·op·tile (kō'lē op'təl, kol'ē-) *n.* the first leaf above the ground in grasses and other monocotyledonous plants, forming a protective sheath around the shoot tip. [Modern Latin *coleoptilum,* from Greek *koleos* sheath + *ptilon* feather.]

cole·slaw (kōl'slô') *n.* a salad made of sliced, shredded, or grated raw cabbage, mixed with a dressing. Also, **slaw.** [Dutch *koolsla,* from *kool* cabbage (from Latin *caulis*) + *sla,* short for *salade* salad (from French *salade*). See SALAD.]

co·le·us (kō'lē əs) *n.* any of a group of tropical plants or shrubs, genus *Coleus,* of the mint family, having showy leaves which are outlined or patterned in yellow, red, orange, or purple. [Modern Latin *Coleus,* from Greek *koleos* sheath; coleus stamens are joined to form a sheath.]

cole·wort (kōl'wûrt') *n.* **1.** cole. **2.** cabbage with a loosely packed head.

col·ic (kol'ik) *n.* a sudden attack of severe pain in the abdomen, esp. in infants. [French *colique,* from Late Latin *cōlicus* sick with colic, from Greek *kōlikos.*] **—col'ick·y,** *adj.*

co·li·form (kō'lə fôrm', kol'ə-) *adj.* of, relating to, or resembling the aerobic bacilli normally found in the colon or large intestine. A count of coliform bacteria is used as an indicator of fecal contamination of drinking water.

col·i·se·um (kol′ə sē′əm) *n.* **1.** *also,* **colosseum.** a large, usually oval, building or stadium in which athletic contests and other entertainments are presented. **2. Coliseum.** Colosseum. [Form of COLOSSEUM.]

co·li·tis (kə lī′tis) *n.* an inflammatory disease of the colon, often characterized by abdominal cramps and diarrhea containing blood and mucus. [Modern Latin *colitis,* from Greek *kolon* large intestine + -ITIS.]

coll. 1. colleague. **2.** collection. **3.** collector. **4.** college. **5.** colloquial.

col·lab·o·rate (kə lab′ə rāt′) *v.i.,* **-rat·ed, -rat·ing. 1.** to work or cooperate with another or others, esp. in literary or scientific endeavors. **2.** to aid or cooperate with the enemy, esp. an enemy that has occupied one's country; be a collaborationist. [Latin *collabōrātus,* past participle of *collabōrāre* to work together.] —**col·lab′o·ra′tion,** *n.* —**col·lab·o·ra·tive** (kə lab′ə rā′tiv, -ər ə tiv), *adj.* —**col·lab′o·ra′tive·ly,** *adv.* —**col·lab′o·ra′tor,** *n.*

col·lab·o·ra·tion·ist (kə lab′ə rā′shə nist) *n.* a person who collaborates with an enemy invader or occupier. —**col·lab′o·ra′tion·ism,** *n.*

col·lage (kə läzh′) *n.* **1.** an artistic composition emphasizing texture and pattern, made by pasting, gluing, or otherwise fastening objects and paper, cloth, or other materials together on a surface. **2.** the art or technique of producing such compositions. [French *collage,* from *colle* glue, paste, from Greek *kolla.*]

a **collage** by Romare Bearden

col·la·gen (kol′ə jən) *n.* a fibrous protein abundant in the bones, cartilage, and connective tissue of vertebrates, yielding gelatin and glue when boiled. [Greek *kolla* glue + -GEN.] —**col·la·gen·ic** (kol′ə jen′ik), **col·lag·e·nous** (kə laj′ə nəs), *adj.*

col·lapse (kə laps′) *v.,* **-lapsed, -laps·ing.** —*v.i.* **1.** to fall in or together; cave in: *The roof collapsed when the beams gave way.* **2.** to become more compact by being folded or pushed together: *The cot collapses for easy storage.* **3.** to fail completely or suddenly; come to nothing: *Their plans collapsed when they lost financial backing.* **4.** to lose strength or health, as from fatigue or disease. **5.** to fall or drop, as from exhaustion. **6.** to decline sharply, as in value or force: *Stock prices collapsed in 1929.* —*v.t.* to cause to collapse. —*n.* **1.** a falling in or together; cave-in. **2.** any sudden or complete failure. **3.** a breakdown, as from exhaustion or a loss of health. **4.** a sharp decline. [Latin *collapsus,* past participle of *collābī* to fall together, fall in ruins.]

col·laps·i·ble (kə lap′sə bəl) *also,* **col·laps·a·ble.** *adj.* capable of being folded or pushed together: *a collapsible chair.*

col·lar (kol′ər) *n.* **1.** the part of a garment at the neckline, usually sewn on as a separate piece. **2.** a separate band of jewels, cloth, fur, or other material worn to ornament the neckline. **3.** a band, as of leather or metal, placed around the neck of an animal, esp. a dog. **4.** a cushioned band that fits over the base of a horse's neck to bear the strain of the load it pulls. **5.** any of various devices, as a ring or flange on a rod or shaft, that prevent or limit sideward motion. —*v.t.* **1.** to put a collar on. **2.** to seize by the neck or collar. **3.** *Informal.* to lay hold of; capture or seize. [Old French *colier* necklace, collar, from Latin *collāre,* from *collum* neck.]

col·lar·bone (kol′ər bōn′) *n.* either of two bones connecting the breastbone and the shoulder blade; clavicle.

collar cell, one of the flagellated cells lining the internal cavity of a sponge. The collective beating of the flagella keeps water circu-

lating through the sponge. [So called because a collar of protoplasm encircles the base of the flagellum.]

col·lard (kol′ərd) *n.* **1.** a variety of kale grown in the southern United States. **2. collards.** the dark green leaves of this plant, eaten as a vegetable. Also *(def. 2),* **collard greens.** [A form of COLEWORT.]

col·late (kə lāt′, kol′āt, kō′lāt) *v.t.,* **-lat·ed, -lat·ing. 1.** to arrange in proper order: *I collated the pages of the report.* **2.** to compare critically and carefully, as texts or facts. [Latin *collātus* brought together, past participle of *conferre* to bring together.] —**col·la′tor,** *n.*

col·lat·er·al (kə lat′ər əl) *n.* **1.** property, usually something for which there is a stable and immediately available market, as stocks or bonds, given as security for a loan. **2.** a person who is related by blood, other than in the direct line of descent, as a niece. —*adj.* **1.** situated or placed side by side; parallel: *collateral roads.* **2.** accompanying or connected but subordinate in position; secondary: *collateral causes.* **3.** serving to support or confirm; additional: *collateral evidence.* **4.** guaranteed or secured by collateral: *a collateral loan.* **5.** descended from common ancestors, but in a different line of descent: *Children of brothers are collateral cousins.* [Medieval Latin *collateralis* alongside of, from Latin *col-* + *lateralis* lateral. See COL-.] —**col·lat′er·al·ly,** *adv.*

col·la·tion (kə lā′shən, kō-) *n.* **1.** the act, process, or result of collating. **2.** a light, informal meal, usually served cold.

col·league (kol′ēg) *n.* a fellow member, as of a profession; associate. [Middle French *collègue,* from Latin *collēga* partner in office.]

col·lect (*v., adj., adv.,* kə lekt′; *n.,* kol′ekt) *v.t.* **1.** to gather together; assemble: *We collected old clothes for the rummage sale.* **2.** to make a collection of, as a hobby or for study: *to collect coins.* **3.** to request and receive (payments or contributions): *The state collects a toll on that bridge.* **4.** to call for and remove: *They collect the garbage at five o'clock.* **5.** to regain control of or summon up: *to collect one's thoughts.* —*v.i.* **1.** to gather; assemble: *A great crowd collected to hear the speaker.* **2.** to pile up; accumulate: *Dust collected in the unused room.* **3.** to request and receive payments or contributions: *to collect for a charity.* —*n.* a short prayer that varies according to feast day or season, used in certain liturgies, esp. the Roman Catholic and Anglican. —*adj., adv.* with charges to be paid by the recipient: *a collect phone call, to call collect.* [Latin *collēctus,* past participle of *colligere* to gather, bring together.] —For Synonyms *(v.t.),* see **gather.**

col·lect·ed (kə lek′tid) *adj.* in control of oneself; composed. —**col·lect′ed·ly,** *adv.* —**col·lect′ed·ness,** *n.*

col·lect·i·ble (kə lek′tə bəl) *also,* **col·lect·a·ble.** *n.* something collected as a hobby, but having little intrinsic value. —*adj.* suitable for collecting: *Old tobacco tins are very collectible items.*

col·lec·tion (kə lek′shən) *n.* **1.** the act or process of collecting. **2.** things gathered together, esp. as a hobby or for study. **3.a.** the act or process of soliciting and collecting money, as for religious or charitable purposes. **b.** money or the amount of money so collected. **4.** something that has accumulated; mass.

col·lec·tive (kə lek′tiv) *adj.* **1.** of, relating to, characteristic of, or deriving from a group of persons or things; common; united: *The collective effort of the club members made the auction a success.* **2.** formed by collecting; aggregated. **3.** constituting or representing a whole or collection: *the collective needs of a community.* **4.** characterized by collectivism: *a collective farm.* —*n.* **1.** a collective noun. **2.** an organization or enterprise characterized by collectivism. **3.** the group of individuals who make up and work in such an organization or enterprise. —**col·lec′tive·ly,** *adv.*

collective bargaining, negotiation between union representatives and employers for reaching an agreement on terms of employment, as wages, hours, or working conditions.

collective farm, a farm operated and managed jointly by a group of farmers, often under supervision of a government, as in communist countries.

collective noun, a singular noun denoting a group of persons or things. It takes a singular verb if the group acts as a single unit, as in *The jury was locked in for the night;* it takes a plural verb if the group acts as individuals, as in *The jury were divided in their opinions.*

col·lec·tiv·ism (kə lek′tə viz′əm) *n.* **1.** an economic and political system in which the people as a community or the government owns and controls the means of production and distribution.

a	at	e	end	o	hot	u	up	hw	white		about
ā	ape	ē	me	ō	old	ū	use	ng	song	ə	taken
ä	far	i	it	ô	fork	ü	rule	th	thin		pencil
âr	care	ī	ice	oi	oil	u	pull	th	this		lemon
		îr	pierce	ou	out	ûr	turn	zh	measure		circus

2. an economic and political theory advocating such a system. —**col·lec′tiv·ist**, *adj., n.* —**col·lec′tiv·is′tic**, *adj.* —**col·lec·ti·vi·za·tion** (kə lek′tə və zā′shən), *n.*

col·lec·tor (kə lek′tər) *n.* **1.** a person who collects objects of interest or value: *a rare-book collector, a coin collector.* **2.** a person employed to collect money due: *a tax collector, a toll collector.* **3.** any person or thing that collects, as a solar collector. —**col·lec′tor·ship′**, *n.*

col·leen (kol′ēn, ko lēn′) *n.* a girl, esp. an Irish girl. [Irish Gaelic *cailín,* diminutive of *caile* girl.]

col·lege (kol′ij) *n.* **1.** an institution of higher education that grants degrees upon completion of courses of general study in liberal arts and sciences. **2.a.** a division of a university that offers a four-year course of general or specialized study leading to a bachelor's degree, as distinguished from the professional, graduate, or technical schools. **b.** an institution, often part of a university, that offers a course of study leading to a graduate or professional degree: *a medical college.* **3.** an independent institution for vocational or technical instruction that grants no academic degrees: *a barber college.* **4.** higher education in general: *to go to college.* **5.** a group of individuals engaged in a common pursuit and having certain rights, duties, and powers: *a college of surgeons.* **6.** the building or buildings and grounds occupied by a college. [Latin *collēgium* association, society of persons.]

College Boards, a set of standardized national examinations administered by a nonprofit testing service and used by some colleges to rate high school students seeking admission to college in their general aptitude for college work.

College of Cardinals, the cardinals of the Roman Catholic Church, collectively, who elect and advise the pope. Also, **Sacred College, Sacred College of Cardinals.**

col·le·gian (kə lē′jən, -jē ən) *n.* a college student or recent graduate of a college.

col·le·giate (kə lē′jit, -jē it) *adj.* **1.** of, for, or characteristic of college students: *a collegiate program of study.* **2.** of or like a college.

col·lide (kə līd′) *v.i.,* -**lid·ed,** -**lid·ing. 1.** to come together or against with force; crash: *The two cars collided.* **2.** to come into conflict; clash: *Our different political views often collide.* [Latin *collīdere* to clash together.]

col·lie (kol′ē) *n.* a dog originally bred for tending sheep, having a long, narrow head, slender body, and typically, a long-haired coat of white and tan or white, tan, and black. Height: to 2 feet (0.6 meter) at the shoulder. [Of uncertain origin.]

col·lier (kol′yər) *n. British.* **1.** a coal miner. **2.** a ship for transporting coal. [Middle English *colier* charcoal burner, from *col.* See COAL.]

col·lier·y (kol′yə rē) *n., pl.* -**lier·ies.** a coal mine with its buildings and equipment.

col·li·ga·tive (kol′i gā′tiv) *adj. Chemistry.* (of the properties of a solution) dependent on the concentration of the particles of the solute rather than on the nature of the particles.

collie

col·li·mate (kol′ə māt′) *v.t.,* -**mat·ed,** -**mat·ing. 1.** to bring into line; make parallel: *to collimate diverging rays of light.* **2.** to adjust the line of sight of (an instrument): *to collimate a telescope.* [Latin *collimātus,* past participle of *collimāre,* incorrect reading for *collīneāre* to aim, going back to *co-* together + *līnea* line.] —**col′li·ma′tion,** *n.* —**col′li·ma′tor,** *n.*

col·lin·e·ar (kə lin′ē ər, kō-) *adj.* (of points) contained in the same straight line.

col·li·sion (kə lizh′ən) *n.* **1.** the act of colliding; a coming together with force. **2.** a conflict, as of interests or viewpoints; clash. [Late Latin *collīsiō* a dashing together, from Latin *collīdere* to clash together.]

col·lo·cate (kol′ə kāt′) *v.t.,* -**cat·ed,** -**cat·ing.** to place or arrange side by side or in relation to one another. [Latin *collocātus,* past participle of *collocāre* to place together.] —**col′lo·ca′tion,** *n.*

col·lo·di·on (kə lō′dē ən) *n.* a flammable, gluelike solution of pyroxylin in a mixture of alcohol and ether, which leaves a transparent, plastic film upon evaporating, chiefly used to coat minor wounds and to make such items as patent leather and artificial pearls. [Greek *kollōdēs* like glue, from *kolla* glue.]

col·loid (kol′oid) *n.* **1.** a substance evenly dispersed throughout another substance in particles that are larger than ordinary mole-

cules but too small to be visible to the naked eye. Both the particles and the medium in which they are dispersed may be a gas, liquid, or solid. **2.** colloidal system. [Greek *kolla* glue + -OID.] —**col·loi·dal** (kə loi′dəl), *adj.* —**col·loi·dal·ly,** *adv.*

colloidal system, a combination of a colloid and the substance in which it is dispersed. If left undisturbed, the particles of a colloidal system will not precipitate but will remain dispersed. Sols, emulsions, and aerosols are colloidal systems. Also, **colloidal dispersion.**

colloq. 1. colloquial. **2.** colloquialism.

col·lo·qui·al (kə lō′kwē əl) *adj.* (of language) used in, characteristic of, or appropriate for ordinary or familiar conversation, rather than formal speech or writing: *"Movie" is a colloquial term for "motion picture."* —**col′lo′qui·al·ly,** *adv.* —**col·lo′qui·al·ness,** *n.*

col·lo·qui·al·ism (kə lō′kwē ə liz′əm) *n.* **1.** a colloquial word, phrase, or expression. **2.** the use of such words, phrases, or expressions; colloquial style or usage.

col·lo·qui·um (kə lō′kwē əm) *n., pl.* -**qui·ums** or -**qui·a** (-kwē ə). a group discussion or conference. [Latin *colloquium.*]

col·lo·quy (kol′ə kwē) *n., pl.* -**quies. 1.** a conversation, discussion, or conference, esp. one that is formally arranged. **2.** a literary work written in the form of a dialogue or conversation. [Latin *colloquium* conversation, conference.]

col·lude (kə lüd′) *v.i.,* -**lud·ed,** -**lud·ing.** to act in collusion; cooperate secretly; conspire; plot. [Latin *collūdere* to play with, act secretly and deceptively.]

col·lu·sion (kə lü′zhən) *n.* a secret agreement or cooperation for a fraudulent or deceitful purpose, esp. an illegal one. [Latin *collūsiō.*]

col·lu·sive (kə lü′siv) *adj.* characterized by or involving collusion. —**col·lu′sive·ly,** *adv.* —**col·lu′sive·ness,** *n.*

Colo., Colorado.

co·log·a·rithm (kō lô′gə rith′əm, -log′ə-) *n.* the logarithm of the reciprocal of a number.

co·logne (kə lōn′) *n.* a fragrant liquid made from alcohol and scented oils and used as perfume. Also, **eau de Cologne.** [From COLOGNE, Germany, where it was first manufactured.]

co·lon[1] (kō′lən) *n.* a mark of punctuation (:) used chiefly to introduce, set apart, or direct attention to something that follows, as a list or series, a quotation, or an explanation. [Greek *kōlon* limb, clause; because it often separates a clause.]

co·lon[2] (kō′lən) *n., pl.* -**lons** or -**la** (-lə). the lower part of the large intestine, extending from the cecum to the rectum. It absorbs water and nutrients from digested food passing through it. [Latin *colon* large intestine, from Greek *kolon.*] —**co·lon·ic** (kō lon′ik), *adj.*

co·lon[3] (kō lōn′) *n., pl.* **co·lons** or **co·lo·nes** (kō lō′nās). the monetary unit of Costa Rica and El Salvador. [Spanish *colón,* from Cristóbal *Colón,* Spanish for Christopher COLUMBUS, 1451?-1506, Italian explorer.]

colo·nel (kûr′nəl) *n.* a military officer usually ranking above a lieutenant colonel and below a brigadier general. [French *colonel,* from Italian *colonnello* literally, little column (of soldiers led by him), from *colonna* column, from Latin *columna.*] —**colo′nel·cy, colo′nel·ship′,** *n.*

co·lo·ni·al (kə lō′nē əl) *adj.* **1.** of or relating to a colony or colonies: *a colonial government, a colonial empire.* **2.a.** *also,* **Colonial.** of, relating to, or characteristic of the thirteen British colonies that became the United States of America. **b.** of, relating to, or characteristic of the period of these colonies: *colonial architecture.* —*n.* a person who was born or is living in a colony. —**co·lo′ni·al·ly,** *adv.*

co·lo·ni·al·ism (kə lō′nē ə liz′əm) *n.* **1.** the policy of a nation seeking to acquire, extend, or retain its political, economic, and cultural control over other peoples or territories. **2.** the state of being a colony. —**co·lo′ni·al·ist,** *n., adj.*

col·o·nist (kol′ə nist) *n.* **1.** a person who was born or is living in a colony. **2.** a person who helps to found or settle a colony.

col·o·nize (kol′ə nīz′) *v.,* -**nized,** -**niz·ing.** —*v.t.* **1.** to establish a colony or colonies in; send colonists to: *Spain colonized parts of South America.* **2.** to migrate to and settle in; occupy as a colony: *English settlers colonized Plymouth.* —*v.i.* to form or establish a colony or colonies. —**col′o·ni·za′tion,** *n.* —**col′o·niz′er,** *n.*

col·on·nade (kol′ə nād′) *n.* a series of columns, placed at regular intervals, usually supporting an entablature. [French *colonnade,* from Italian *colonnato,* from *colonna* column, from Latin *columna.*] —**col′on·nad′ed,** *adj.*

col·o·ny (kol′ə nē) *n., pl.* -**nies. 1.** any territory politically, economically, and culturally subject to another, usually distant, country. **2.a.** a body of emigrants or their descendants living in an

area or land apart from, but under the control of, the country from which they came. **b.** the area or land so inhabited: *Plymouth was an English colony.* **3. the Colonies.** the thirteen British colonies that became the first states of the United States: New Hampshire, Massachusetts, Rhode Island, Connecticut, New York, New Jersey, Pennsylvania, Delaware, Maryland, Virginia, North Carolina, South Carolina, and Georgia. **4.a.** a group of people living or drawn together in an area because of common nationality, religion, or interests: *the American colony in Paris.* **b.** the area inhabited or occupied by such a group. **5.** a group of animals or plants of the same kind, living or growing together in the same place: *a colony of bees.* [Latin *colōnia* farm, settlement, going back to *colere* to cultivate.]

col·o·phon (kol′ə fon′, -fən) *n.* **1.** an identifying device, as a distinctive emblem or trademark, of a publisher or printer. **2.** an inscription formerly placed at the end of a book, giving the publisher and other information relative to its publication. [Greek *kolophōn* summit, finishing touch.]

col·or (kul′ər) *also, British,* **col·our.** *n.* **1.** a quality of an object or substance, perceived as a visual sensation, resulting from its transmission or reflection of light of any or all of the parts of the spectrum. **2.** one of the constituents of the spectrum, sometimes including black and white; a particular hue, tint, or shade. **3.** two or more of these used as or in a medium of presentation: *That television show is in color. We've got a picture of that mosaic in color.* **4.** something used for coloring, as paint, dye, or pigment. **5.** the rosiness of the skin, esp. the face, characteristic of good health. **6.** the ruddiness or redness of or as if of a blush: *The compliment brought color to her cheeks.* **7.** skin pigmentation or complexion, esp. as regarded as a racial feature: *without regard to race, creed, or color.* **8.** a vivid, lively, or picturesque quality or character; vitality; interest: *The teacher's anecdotes added color to the lecture.* **9.** the general character or variety; nature: *The political scandal changed the whole color of the campaign.* **10.** an outward show or appearance, often concealing an underlying true character; semblance; aspect: *The nonsense the lecturer was speaking had the color of reason.* **11.** a false appearance or pretense; pretext; disguise: *a tyrant who carried out crimes against the people under the color of justice.* **12. colors. a.** any distinctive color or pattern of colors, as of a badge or uniform, worn or used as a symbol or for identification: *My school colors are yellow and green.* **b.** a flag, ensign, or standard, as of a regiment or school, esp. the national flag: *They raised the colors over the captured fort.* **c.** personality; characteristics; attitude: *to show one's true colors.* **13.** *Music.* a timbre or distinguishing quality of tone. **14.** *Physics.* a hypothetical characteristic of quarks that governs how they combine with each other. **15.** a particle of metal, esp. gold, found in soil, rock, or other material, usually indicating the quality of the ore in which it is contained. —*v.t.* **1.** to give or apply color to, as by painting, dyeing, or staining: *The child colored the picture with a yellow crayon. She colors her hair.* **2.** to cause to appear different from reality; misrepresent, as by distorting or exaggerating: *The witness colored his testimony to favor the defendant.* **3.** to modify or change in character or nature; affect; influence: *Your emotions are coloring your judgment.* —*v.i.* **1.** to become red in the face; blush; flush. **2.** to take on or change color. [Old French *color* complexion, hue, appearance, from Latin *color.*] —**col′or·er,** *n.*

Col·o·rad·o potato beetle (kol′ə rad′ō, -rä′dō) a small, oval yellow beetle with black stripes, *Leptinotarsa decemlineata,* found throughout North America and Europe, that feeds on the leaves of potato plants and attacks such plants as tomatoes and eggplants. Also, **potato beetle, potato bug.**

col·or·a·tion (kul′ə rā′shən) *n.* an arrangement of colors; appearance as to color; coloring.

col·or·a·tu·ra (kul′ər ə tùr′ə, -tyùr′ə, kol′-) *n.* **1.** florid ornamentations, such as trills or runs, in vocal music. **2.** music characterized by such ornamentations. **3.a.** a high soprano voice having a wide range and great flexibility, trained for performing coloratura. **b.** a singer with such a voice. Also *(def. 3),* **coloratura soprano.** —*adj.* characterized by or suitable for coloratura. [Italian *coloratura* ornamental musical passages; literally, coloring, from *colorare* to color, from Latin *colōrāre.*]

col·or·bear·er (kul′ər bâr′ər) *n.* a person who carries the colors or flag, as in a ceremony or parade.

col·or-blind (kul′ər blīnd′) *adj.* affected with color blindness.

color blindness, an impairment in the ability to perceive colors. It is most often a difficulty in distinguishing between certain colors, as between red and green, but sometimes it is a total inability to distinguish anything but black, white, and gray.

col·or·cast (kul′ər kast′) *n.* a television program broadcast in color. —*v.t., v.i.,* **-cast, -cast·ing.** to broadcast (a television program) in color.

col·or-code (kul′ər kōd′) *v.t.,* **-cod·ed, -cod·ing.** to color

(something) in order to distinguish it from others like it; key (a group of things) with different colors: *to color-code the insulation on wires in a telephone cable.*

col·ored (kul′ərd) *adj.* **1.** having color, esp. other than solid black or white: *The book has colored illustrations.* **2.** of or relating to peoples other than the Caucasoid, esp. black peoples. ➡ now usually considered offensive. **3.** influenced, as by prejudice or emotion; distorted; slanted: *The witness gave a highly colored account of what had occurred.*

col·or·fast (kul′ər fast′) *adj.* (of fabrics) having color that is resistant to fading or running.

color film, film for taking color photographs and slides.

col·or·ful (kul′ər fəl) *adj.* **1.** abounding or rich in color. **2.** vivid, lively, or picturesque: *a colorful speaker.* —**col′or·ful·ly,** *adv.* —**col′or·ful·ness,** *n.*

color guard, persons who carry and escort the colors, as in a ceremony.

col·or·im·e·ter (kul′ə rim′i tər) *n.* an instrument used to measure the hue, purity, and brightness of a color. —**col·or·i·met·ric** (kul′ər ə met′rik); *also,* **col′or·i·met′ri·cal,** *adj.* —**col′or·i·met′ri·cal·ly,** *adv.* —**col′or·im′e·try,** *n.*

col·or·ing (kul′ər ing) *n.* **1.** the way in which a thing is colored; complexion or appearance as to color: *a fawn's mottled coloring.* **2.** a substance used to give color: *food coloring.* **3.** the act or technique of applying color. **4.** a false appearance or semblance: *flattery with a coloring of sincerity.*

coloring book, a book of outline drawings for coloring with crayons or other materials.

col·or·ist (kul′ər ist) *n.* a person who uses or works with color, esp. an artist who uses colors skillfully or a hairdresser who specializes in coloring hair.

Col·or·i·za·tion (kul′ər ə zā′shən) *n. Trademark.* the process of adding computer-generated colors, as to a motion picture originally produced in black and white.

col·or·ize (kul′ər rīz′) *v.t.,* **-ized, -izing.** to add computer-generated colors to (a motion picture or the like).

col·or·less (kul′ər lis) *adj.* **1.** lacking liveliness or distinctive character; not vivid or interesting; dull: *a colorless personality.* **2.** without color: *a colorless liquid.* **3.** dull in or empty of color; pallid: *The sick child's face was colorless.* —**col′or·less·ly,** *adv.* —**col′or·less·ness,** *n.*

color wheel, a circular schematic chart showing the relations among colors, used as a tool by artists and designers.

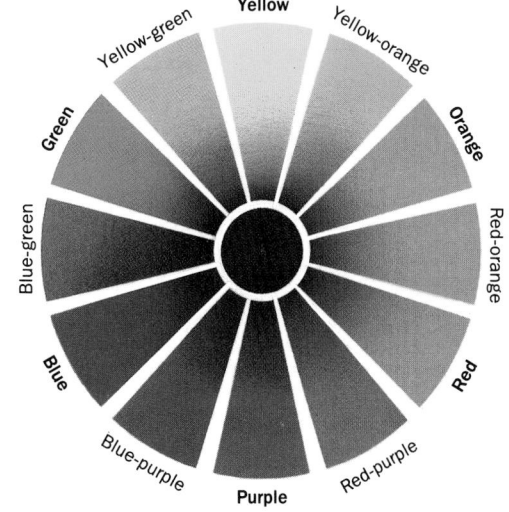

color wheel

co·los·sal (kə los′əl) *adj.* **1.** extraordinarily or awesomely large; immense; gigantic; vast. **2.** *Informal.* to an extraordinary or astonishing degree: *The show was a colossal success.* —**co·los′sal·ly,** *adv.*

a	at	e	end	o	hot	u	up	hw	white		about
ā	ape	ē	me	ō	old	ū	use	ng	song	ə	taken
ä	far	i	it	ô	fork	ü	rule	th	thin		pencil
âr	care	ī	ice	oi	oil	u̇	pull	th	this		lemon
				îr	pierce	ou	out	ûr	turn	zh	measure		circus

Col·os·se·um (kol′ə sē′əm) *n.* **1.** *also,* **Coliseum.** an oval amphitheater in Rome, built between A.D. 72 and 82, that was the site of games and gladiatorial fights in ancient times. **2. colosseum.** coliseum *(def. 1).* [Late Latin *colossēum,* noun use of neuter of Latin *colossēus* gigantic, from *colossus.* See COLOSSUS.]

Co·los·sians (kə lō′shəns) *n.* a book of the New Testament, consisting of an Epistle written by the Apostle Paul to the Christian community of Colossae, a city in Asia Minor. ➡ used as singular.

co·los·sus (kə los′əs) *n., pl.* **-los·si** (-los′ī) or **-los·sus·es. 1.** a gigantic statue. **2.** a person or thing of awesome or immense size or power. [Latin *colossus* gigantic statue, from Greek *kolossos.*]

Colossus of Rhodes, a bronze statue of the sun god Helios that stood at the entrance to the harbor of Rhodes. It was built about 280 B.C. and was more than 100 feet (30 meters) high.

co·los·to·my (kə los′tə mē) *n., pl.* **-mies.** the surgical procedure of forming an artificial excretory opening in the body wall after part of the colon has been removed. [COLO(N) + Greek *stoma* mouth, opening.]

co·los·trum (kə los′trəm) *n.* a milky fluid, high in antibodies, secreted by the female mammary gland just before and after parturition. [Latin *colostrum.*]

col·our (kul′ər) *British.* color.

col·por·teur (kol′pôr′tər) *n.* a person who travels about selling or distributing Bibles and religious literature. [French *colporteur* peddler, from *colporter* to peddle; literally, to carry on the neck; modification (influenced by French *col* neck) of Old French *comporter* to transport, from Latin *comportāre* to bring together.]

colt (kōlt) *n.* **1.** a male horse, or other male member of the horse family, under four years old. **2.** *Informal.* foal. **3.** a young or inexperienced person. [Old English *colt* young camel, young ass.]

col·ter (kōl′tər) *also,* **coulter.** *n.* a sharp blade or disk attached to a plow to cut the earth ahead of the plowshare. [Old English *culter,* from Latin *culter* knife, plowshare.]

colt·ish (kōl′tish) *adj.* **1.** not trained or disciplined; awkward; unruly. **2.** having the liveliness of a colt; frisky; playful. **3.** of, relating to, or resembling a colt. —**colt′ish·ly,** *adv.* —**colt′ish·ness,** *n.*

colts·foot (kōlts′fût′) *n., pl.* **-foots.** a plant bearing yellow flower heads, *Tussilago farfara,* of the composite family, having large leaves whose shape suggests a horse's footprint.

Co·lum·bi·a (kə lum′bē ə) *n.* the United States of America, often personified as a woman. [From Christopher *Columbus,* 1451?-1506, Italian explorer.]

Co·lum·bi·an (kə lum′bē ən) *adj.* **1.** of or relating to Columbia. **2.** of or relating to the Italian explorer Christopher Columbus.

col·um·bine (kol′əm bīn′) *n.* **1.** a showy, usually drooping flower of any of a group of plants, genus *Aquilegia,* growing in a variety of colors and having five petals that extend backward to form hollow, tubelike projections. **2.** the plant bearing this flower. [Late Latin *columbīna* the plant, from Latin *columbīnus* like a dove, from *columba* dove; because its flower was thought to resemble a group of doves.]

Col·um·bine (kol′əm bīn′) *n.* a stock character from commedia dell'arte, the sweetheart of Harlequin, usually costumed in a tutu. [Italian *Colombina,* diminutive of *colomba* dove, from Latin *columba.*]

co·lum·bi·um (kə lum′bē əm) *n.* niobium. [Modern Latin *columbium,* from *Columbia* the United States, where it was first found. See COLUMBIA.]

Co·lum·bus Day (kə lum′bəs) a legal holiday commemorating the discovery of America by the Italian explorer Christopher Columbus on October 12, 1492, observed in most states on the second Monday in October.

col·umn (kol′əm) *n.* **1.** a written or printed group of items arranged one above the other; vertical row: *to add a column of figures.* **2.** one of two or more vertical sections of printed or written matter on a sheet or page, separated by a line or blank space: *This book has two columns.* **3.** a feature article that appears regularly or at intervals in a newspaper, magazine, or periodical, written by a particular writer or writers or devoted to a particular subject: *a gossip column, a sports column.* **4.** an upright structure, usually cylindrical and longer than it is wide, consisting of a base, shaft, and capital, and serving as a support or ornament, as for part of a building, or standing alone as a monument. **5.** something resembling such a structure: *a*

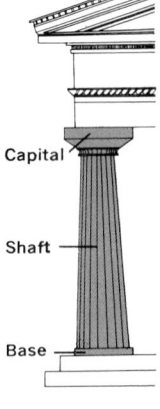

Capital

Shaft

Base

column *(def. 4)*

column of smoke. **6.** a military formation in which the units, as soldiers, vehicles, or ships, are arranged one behind the other in one or more rows. ➡ distinguished from **line**[1]. **7.** something resembling such a formation: *a column of ants.* [Latin *columna* pillar.] —**col′umned,** *adj.*

co·lum·nar (kə lum′nər) *adj.* **1.** relating to or resembling a column. **2.** made of, with, or arranged in columns.

co·lum·ni·a·tion (kə lum′nē ā′shən) *n.* the use or arrangement of columns in a structure.

co·lum·nist (kol′əm nist, -ə mist) *n.* a person who writes a column in a newspaper, magazine, or periodical.

col·za (kol′zə) *n.* **1.** rape. **2.** rapeseed. [French *colza* rapeseed, going back to Dutch *kool* cabbage (from Latin *caulis*) + *zaad* seed.]

com- *prefix* in association with; together: *combine.* [Latin *com-,* form of *cum* with, together.]

com. 1. comedy. **2.** commerce. **3.** common. **4.** commonly.

Com. 1. Commission. **2.** Commissioner. **3.** Committee.

co·ma[1] (kō′mə) *n., pl.* **-mas. 1.** a state of unconsciousness from which a person cannot be aroused by an external stimulus, caused by disease, injury, or poison. It may last for hours, days, or months, or, in rare cases, for years. **2.** *Informal.* a state of mental distraction or apathy; stupor. [Modern Latin *coma,* from Greek *kōma* deep sleep.]

co·ma[2] (kō′mə) *n., pl.* **-mae** (-mē). **1.** the gaseous, luminous envelope surrounding the nucleus of a comet. **2.** *Botany.* **a.** a tuft of leaves, bracts, or branches. **b.** a tuft of long silky hairs on the end of a seed. [Latin *coma* hair (of the head), from Greek *komē.*]

Co·man·che (kə man′chē) *n., pl.* **-che** or **-ches. 1.** a member of a tribe of North American Indians formerly of the southern part of the Great Plains, now living in Oklahoma. **2.** the language of this tribe, belonging to the Uto-Aztecan language family. [Spanish *Comanche* member of this tribe, probably from Ute *komanchi* stranger.]

co·ma·tose (kō′mə tōs′, kom′ə-) *adj.* **1.** relating to, characterized by, or in a coma. **2.** *Informal.* in a state of distraction or apathy; lethargic; torpid. [Greek *kōma* deep sleep + -OSE[1].]

comb[1] (kōm) *n.* **1.** a toothed implement of plastic, bone, metal, or other sturdy material, for smoothing, arranging, or fastening the hair. **2.** something resembling a comb in shape or function, as a card for cleaning and separating fibers. **3.** a thick, usually reddish, fleshy growth on the head of domestic fowl and certain other birds, most fully developed in the male. **4.** something resembling this, as the crest of a wave. **5.** honeycomb. **6.** currycomb. —*v.t.* **1.** to smooth or arrange (the hair) with a comb. **2.** to remove with or as with a comb: *I combed the knots out of my hair.* **3.** to search (something) extensively and with care; look everywhere in or through: *They combed the woods looking for the lost child.* **4.** to card, as fibers. —*v.i.* **1.** to search extensively and with care (usually with *through*): *I combed through the house looking for the keys.* **2.** (of waves) to roll over or break at the crest. [Old English *cāmb* implement for arranging the hair, cock's crest.]

comb[2] (küm, kōm) combe.

com·bat (*n.,* kom′bat; *v.,* kəm bat′, kom′bat) *n.* **1.** military struggle with an enemy: *a soldier wounded in combat.* **2.** any fight, contest, or struggle, esp. a direct physical struggle between two persons. —*v.,* **-bat·ed, -bat·ing;** *also, British,* **-bat·ted, -bat·ting.** —*v.t.* **1.** to take measures or struggle against; oppose vigorously; resist: *to combat inflation.* **2.** to fight with; oppose in battle. —*v.i.* to fight; struggle. [Old French *combatre* to fight, going back to Latin *com-* with + *battuere* to beat, strike.] —**com·bat′er,** *n.* —For Synonyms *(n.),* see **fight.**

com·bat·ant (kəm bat′ənt, kom′bə tənt) *n.* a person or thing that is engaged in or ready for combat or hostilities; fighter. —*adj.* **1.** ready or disposed to fight. **2.** fighting: *combatant military forces.*

combat boot, a heavy, laced leather boot designed to be worn by military personnel.

combat fatigue, battle fatigue.

com·bat·ive (kəm bat′iv, kom′bə tiv) *adj.* ready or eager to fight; quarrelsome; pugnacious. —**com·bat′ive·ly,** *adv.* —**com·bat′ive·ness,** *n.*

combe (küm, kōm) *also,* **coomb, comb.** *n. British.* a deep narrow valley or deep hollow. [Old English *cumb;* of Celtic origin.]

comb·er (kō′mər) *n.* **1.** a long, rolling wave that curls over or breaks at the crest. **2.** a person or thing that combs, as a carder.

com·bi·na·tion (kom′bə nā′shen) *n.* **1.** something that is formed by combining; mixture; union: *Green is a combination of yellow and blue.* **2.a.** a series of numbers or letters dialed in a set sequence or direction to open a combination lock. **b.** the mechanism of a combination lock. **3.** the act of combining; being combined. **4.** the act or process of combining to form a chemical compound or the state of being combined in this way. **5.** an

alliance or association of persons or groups to further some common purpose. **6.** a one-piece undergarment consisting of an undershirt or chemise and drawers. **7.** *Mathematics.* any of the possible arrangements of a certain number or of all the elements of a set, in which the order is immaterial. Some possible combinations of *x, y,* and *z* are *xy, xz,* and *yz.* —**com′bi·na′tion·al,** *adj.*

combination lock, a lock opened by turning one or more dials to a series of numbers or letters in a set sequence or direction.

com·bi·na·to·ri·al (kəm bīˈnə tôrˈē əl, komˈbə-) *adj.* **1.** of, relating to, or involving the combination of elements. **2.** *Mathematics.* of or relating to the permutations and combinations of elements in finite sets.

com·bine (*v.,* kəm bīn′; *n.,* komˈbīn) *v.,* **-bined, -bin·ing.** —*v.t.* **1.** to bring into close relationship; join together; unite: *We combined forces to finish the job faster.* **2.** to cause to mix together; mingle; blend: *Combine eggs, flour, and milk to make the batter.* **3.** to possess or exhibit simultaneously or in union. —*v.i.* **1.** to become one; constitute a whole; merge: *The colonies combined to form the United States.* **2.** to associate or unite for a common purpose; form an alliance; act together: *The rival factions combined to oppose the new legislation.* **3.** to unite to form a chemical compound. One atom of carbon combines with two atoms of oxygen to form a molecule of carbon dioxide, CO_2. —*n.* **1.** an alliance of persons or groups for business or political purposes or to further personal interests. **2.** a farm machine, either tractor-drawn or self-propelled, that combines the functions of a harvester and a thresher by cutting, threshing, and cleaning grains and other field crops. [Late Latin *combīnāre* to unite, from Latin *com-* together + *bīnī* two each, two at a time.] —**com·bin′a·ble,** *adj.* —**com·bin′er,** *n.*

comb·ings (kōˈmingz) *pl. n.* hairs, wool, or other material removed by or from a comb.

combining form, a linguistic form, usually a stem of a word, often of Greek or Latin origin, that may be combined with a word, another combining form, or an affix to form a compound word or derivative, such as *psycho-* in *psychoanalysis, -graphy* in *biography,* and *cyan(o)-* in *cyanic.*

Combining Forms

A combining form can be the first, a middle, or the last element in a word, and it is sometimes separated from the rest of a word by a hyphen. If you look up the words listed below and the combining forms that have been underlined within them, you can determine how the words have arrived at their present meaning.

astrogeology	ecosystem	omnipresent
audiophile	equidistant	pan-American
autobiography	hydroelectric	paratroops
cardiovascular	lactose	pterodactyl
childproof	megalith	pyrotechnic
counteract	microwave	retrorocket
double-decker	monogamy	speedometer
dysfunctional	neoclassicism	turbocharger

---

comb jelly (kōm) any of a group of saltwater invertebrates, phylum Ctenophora, that move by means of cilia arranged lengthwise along the body like the teeth on a comb and that often have two trailing tentacles with sticky cells for capturing food. Length: from 3/4 inch to 3 feet (2 centimeters to 0.9 meter). Also, **ctenophore.**

com·bo (komˈbō) *n.* **1.** a small jazz or dance band, usually consisting of three or four musicians. **2.** *Informal.* combination *(def. 1).* [Modification and shortening of COMBINATION.]

com·bust (kəm bust′) *v.t., v.i.* burn. [Middle English *combust,* from Latin *combustus,* past participle of *combūrere* to burn up. See COMBUSTION.]

com·bus·ti·ble (kəm busˈtə bəl) *adj.* **1.** capable of catching fire and burning. **2.** easily aroused or excited; fiery. —*n.* a substance capable of catching fire and burning. —**com·bus′ti·bil′i·ty,** *n.* —**com·bus′ti·bly,** *adv.*

comb jelly

com·bus·tion (kəm busˈchən) *n.* **1.** the act or process of burning. **2.a.** rapid oxidation of a substance, accompanied by the release of considerable heat and sometimes light. **b.** any chemical reaction attended by the release of heat or light. **c.** slow oxidation

accompanied by lesser amounts of heat and no light, as of food in the body. **3.** a violent agitation or disturbance. [Late Latin *combustiō* a burning, from Latin *combustus,* past participle of *combūrere* to burn up.]

com·bus·tor (kəm busˈtər) *n.* the chamber in a jet engine or gas turbine in which combustion takes place. [COMBUST(ION) + -OR.]

Comdr., Commander.

Comdt., Commandant.

come (kum) *v.i.,* **came, come, com·ing. 1.** to move or advance to or toward the speaker or a particular place; draw near; approach: *Will you please come here? They're coming down the street now.* **2.** to advance or arrive as the result of motion or progress: *The horse and rider came to the first barrier and jumped over it. Now we come to the interesting part.* **3.** to arrive or occur in time, in due course, or in orderly progression: *Easter comes late this year. Wait till your turn comes.* **4.** to move, pass, or be brought into a particular state, condition, or position: *to come into prominence, to come to a boil, to come to a sudden stop.* **5.** to exist or occur in a particular place or position or at a particular point: *Five comes before six.* **6.** to reach as far as; extend: *Her hair comes to her shoulders. His dog barely comes up to his knees.* **7.** to be derived; originate; emanate: *Paper pulp comes from trees. I can't believe those words came from your mouth.* **8.** to be or have been a native or resident (with *from):* *My family comes from California.* **9.** to make progress; manage; fare (often with *on* or *along):* *The seedlings are coming on nicely. The project's coming along well.* **10.** to be born or issue; descend: *They come from a well-known family.* **11.** to take place; happen; occur: *They said no harm would come to us. Come what may, I'll be there.* **12.** to exist or happen as a result: *This comes of your carelessness. No good will come of your deception.* **13.** to be available, offered, sold, or produced: *This dress comes in several colors. This car comes with or without a convertible top.* **14.** to prove or turn out to be: *The prediction came true.* **15.** to be passed along, as by tradition or inheritance (often with *down):* *These traditions have come down through generations of my family.* **16.** to occur to the mind: *An idea just came to me.* **17.** to be within one's range of possible activities or talents: *Skiing comes easily to some people.* **18.** to have to do with; relate; concern; involve: *When it comes to details, I'm not very helpful.* **19.** *Informal.* **a.** to chance; happen: *How'd you come to know that? How'd they come to meet her?* **b.** to exist: *He's as mean as they come.* [Old English *cuman* to go toward, happen.]

• **come again.** *Informal.* used to ask someone to repeat something: *Come again? I didn't hear.*

• **to come about. a.** to take place; occur; happen. **b.** *Nautical.* to shift to another tack.

• **to come across. a.** to find or meet with by chance. **b.** to be clear, convincing, or understandable; be communicated, as to an audience: *The speaker's point just didn't come across.* **c.** *Slang.* to do or give what is demanded or expected of one, esp. to pay money; make good one's promise.

• **to come around** (or **round**). **a.** to recover consciousness; revive. **b.** to change one's opinion, attitude, or stance so as to agree with another's; be persuaded.

• **to come at. a.** to rush toward; attack. **b.** to approach, as a problem: *Try coming at it from another angle.*

• **to come back.** to occur to the mind again: *It all comes back to me now.*

• **to come back (at).** *Informal.* to retort or answer (someone) sharply: *He came back at her with a nasty remark. She came back with a question just as cutting.*

• **to come between.** to cause bad feeling; estrange; separate: *Don't let a little thing like that come between you two.*

• **to come by.** to get; obtain; acquire: *This money is honestly come by. How did you come by such wealth?*

• **to come down on** (or **upon**). *Informal.* to criticize severely; take to task; upbraid; scold: *The principal came down hard on them for being disrespectful.*

• **to come down with.** *Informal.* to become ill with: *to come down with the flu.*

• **to come forward.** to offer or present oneself, as for work or duty; volunteer.

• **to come in.** to be brought into use or fashion.

• **to come in for.** to be eligible to receive or be subjected to; get; acquire: *He came in for a share of the blame.*

a	at	e	end	o	hot	u	up	hw	white	⎧	about
ā	ape	ē	me	ō	old	ū	use	ng	song		taken
ä	far	i	it	ô	fork	ü	rule	th	thin	ə	pencil
âr	care	ī	ice	oi	oil	u̇	pull	th	this		lemon
		îr	pierce	ou	out	ûr	turn	zh	measure	⎩	circus

239

• to come into. a. to inherit. **b.** to get; obtain; acquire: *How did you come into your present job?*

• to come off. to take place; occur; happen: *The party came off successfully.*

• to come on. *Informal.* to give the impression of being; appear to be: *She comes on like a big executive.*

• to come out. a. to become known or evident; be disclosed or revealed: *The truth has come out at last.* **b.** to declare oneself; express or reveal one's opinions: *The candidate came out for community control of schools.* **c.** to be published or released; be presented to the public: *The magazine comes out once a month.* **d.** to emerge; end; result: *Everything will come out all right.* **e.** to make a formal social debut.

• to come out with. a. to give vent to; declare openly; utter: *to come out with a clever remark.* **b.** to make available or offer to the public: *The car company came out with a new sportier model.*

• to come over. to take possession of; happen to; seize: *A strange feeling came over me. What's come over you?*

• to come through. a. to endure or finish successfully; survive. **b.** *Informal.* to perform or do what is expected or anticipated: *I always try to come through for my friends when they need help.*

• to come to. a. to recover consciousness; revive. **b.** to be equal or equivalent to; amount to: *The bill comes to five dollars. It all comes to the same thing.* **c.** *Nautical.* to anchor.

• to come under. to be classified or included under: *That budget item comes under administrative expenses.*

• to come up. to be presented as the subject of attention; arise: *The bill came up for debate. The question came up during our discussion.*

• to come upon (or on). a. to find or meet with by chance. **b.** to attack, esp. suddenly.

• to come up to. to compare with, as to excellence or quantity; rival, as a standard; equal: *His work didn't come up to that of his classmates. The results did not come up to our anticipation.*

• to come up with. to think of or produce; present; propose: *She came up with the answer.*

come·back (kum′bak′) *n.* **1.** a return to or recovery of a former prosperity, condition, or position: *The ex-champion made a remarkable comeback and won the title.* **2.** *Informal.* a clever or effective retort.

co·me·di·an (kə mē′dē ən) *n.* **1.** a professional entertainer, as in a nightclub or on a television show, who tells jokes, does amusing impersonations, or performs comic routines. **2.** an actor who specializes in comic roles. **3.** *Informal.* a person who continually amuses or attempts to amuse others. [French *comédien* actor, from *comédie.* See COMEDY.]

co·me·di·enne (kə mē′dē en′) *n.* **1.** a woman who is a professional comic entertainer. **2.** an actress who specializes in comic roles.

come·down (kum′doun′) *n.* a change for the worse in one's circumstances; descent in position or status, esp. a humiliating one.

com·e·dy (kom′i dē) *n., pl.* **-dies. 1.** a play in which life is viewed or treated humorously and which usually has a happy ending. **2.** the branch of drama composed of such plays. ➡ distinguished from **tragedy. 3.** any piece of literature or presentation on stage, screen, television, or radio of a humorous nature. **4.** the art of writing, acting, or producing a comedy or comedies. **5.** a situation or series of events having humorous or comic qualities. **6.** a humorous or comic state, quality, or effect. [Old French *comedie* play, humorous play, from Latin *cōmoedia* humorous play, from Greek *kōmōidia*, going back to *kōmos* revel + *aeidein* to sing; because comedies in ancient Greece were originally festive performances with singing.] —**co·me·dic** (kə mē′dik, -med′ik); *also,* **co·me′di·cal,** *adj.*

come-hith·er (kum′hith′ər) *adj.* inviting or alluring; seductive: *a come-hither look.*

come·ly (kum′lē) *adj.,* **-li·er, -li·est. 1.** pleasing in appearance; good-looking; attractive. **2.** suited to the occasion; proper; becoming. [Old English *cȳmlīc* beautiful.] —**come′li·ness,** *n.*

come-on (kum′on′, -on′) *n. Slang.* a person or thing offered to allure or attract; lure; inducement.

com·er (kum′ər) *n.* **1.** a person who comes or arrives, as in response to a challenge or invitation: *The challenger was willing to take on all comers.* **2.** *Informal.* a person or thing that shows great promise or potential.

co·mes·ti·ble (kə mes′tə bəl) *n. also,* **co·mes·ti·bles.** food. ➡ **comestibles** is used as plural. —*adj.* edible; eatable. [Late Latin *comestibilis,* from Latin *comestus,* past participle of *comedere* to eat up.]

com·et (kom′it) *n.* a bright celestial body, traveling in a long, eccentric orbit around the sun, consisting largely of ice, frozen

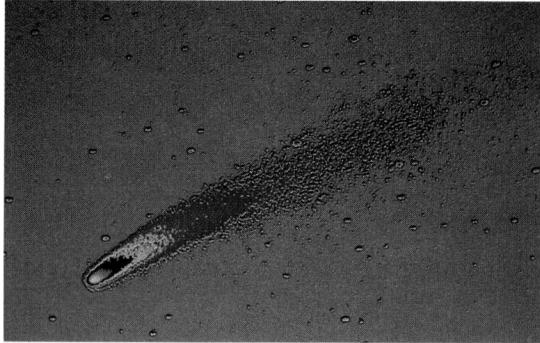

comet (color-enhanced)

gases, and dust particles, and usually having one or more long, gaseous, visible tails that point away from the sun. [Old English *cometa,* from Old French *comete,* from Latin *cometa,* from Greek *komētes (astēr)* literally, long-haired (star); referring to its tail.]

come·up·pance (kum′up′əns) *also,* **come·up·ance.** *n. Informal.* one deserved punishment or retribution one deserves.

com·fit (kum′fit, kom′-) *n.* a piece of candy or sweetmeat; confection. [Old French *confit* literally, preserved, past participle of *confire* to candy, preserve, from Latin *conficere* to prepare.]

com·fort (kum′fərt) *n.* **1.** a state of ease, well-being, and satisfaction of bodily wants, with freedom from pain or anxiety: *With our savings, we'll be able to retire in comfort.* **2.** relief or support in affliction or sorrow; consolation; solace: *to bring comfort to the sick.* **3.** a person or thing that gives or provides this: *Jack was a comfort to his father after his mother's death.* **4.** *also,* **comforts.** anything that gives physical ease, well-being, or cheer. **5.** the ability to give physical ease and well-being. **6.** a cause or matter of satisfaction or relief: *It's no comfort to me that the exam was postponed for only one day.* **7.** acts or statements that encourage or aid; support: *to give aid and comfort to the enemy.* —*v.t.* to ease the grief or sorrow of; bring solace or cheer to; console. [Old French *conforter* to console, urge, from Late Latin *confortāre* to strengthen, from Latin *con-* together + *fortis* strong.]

Synonyms *v.t.* **Comfort** and **console**[1] mean to ease or help to ease distress caused by sorrow or trouble. **Comfort** is the more general term, suggesting the bringing of cheer or support: *to comfort victims of a disaster, to comfort a lost child.* **Console** more specifically refers to the soothing of grief or disappointment over a loss: *to console a friend over the death of a parent, to console the loser of a game.* For other Synonyms (*n.*), see **ease.**

com·fort·a·ble (kumf′tə bəl, kum′fər tə-) *adj.* **1.** providing physical ease or comfort: *a comfortable chair.* **2.** free from mental or physical distress; at ease: *I felt very comfortable with them even though we'd just met.* **3.** adequate or more than adequate: *a comfortable salary.* **4.** *Informal.* having more than enough money; well-off; well-to-do. —**com′fort·a·ble·ness,** *n.* —**com′fort·a·bly,** *adv.*

com·fort·er (kum′fər tər) *n.* **1.** a person or thing that comforts. **2.** a quilted blanket or covering for a bed. **3. the Comforter.** Holy Ghost.

com·fort·ing (kum′fər ting) *adj.* offering or giving comfort; consoling; reassuring; cheering: *comforting words.* —**com′fort·ing·ly,** *adv.*

comfort station, a public toilet or rest room.

com·fy (kum′fē) *adj.,* **-fi·er, -fi·est.** *Informal.* comfortable. [COMF(ORTABLE) + -Y[1].] —**com′fi·ly,** *adv.*

com·ic (kom′ik) *adj.* **1.** of, relating to, or connected with comedy. **2.** causing laughter or mirth; amusing; funny. **3.** of or relating to comic strips. —*n.* **1.** comedian. **2. comics.** comic strips or a section of a newspaper in which they appear. **3.** comic book. [Latin *cōmicus* relating to comedy, from Greek *kōmikos,* from *kōmos* revel. See COMEDY.]

com·i·cal (kom′i kəl) *adj.* causing laughter or mirth; amusing; funny; ludicrous. —**com′i·cal·i·ty** (kom′i kal′i tē), **com′i·cal·ness,** *n.* —**com′i·cal·ly,** *adv.* —For Synonyms, see **humorous.**

comic book, a booklet or small magazine consisting of comic strips.

comic opera, an opera or operetta of a light or humorous nature, usually having a happy ending, and often having some spoken dialogue.

comic relief, a comic episode in a play, film, or other dramatic production that provides relief from the buildup of dramatic tension in the plot.

comic strip, a sequence of cartoon drawings relating a story or presenting a situation, usually having captions or dialogue enclosed in balloons pointing to the speaker, esp. when printed in a newspaper or similar publication on a regular or serialized basis.

com·ing (kum′ing) *adj.* **1.a.** nearer and nearer, esp. in time: *the coming holiday season.* **b.** next: *this coming Monday.* **2.** *Informal.* **a.** deserving; due: *You'll get what's coming to you.* **b.** showing promise or on the way to importance or popularity: *a dance that is the coming thing.* —*n.* approach; arrival: *We anxiously await their coming.*

com·ing-out (kum′ing out′) *n. Informal.* a formal social debut.

Com·in·tern (kom′in tûrn′) *n.* an international organization of Communist parties, created in Moscow in 1919 to establish Communism as a worldwide force, dissolved in 1943. [Short for *Com(munist) Intern(ational).*]

com·i·ty (kom′i tē) *n., pl.* **-ties.** mutual respect or courtesy; civility; politeness. [Latin *cōmitās.*]

com·ma (kom′ə) *n.* a punctuation mark (,) chiefly used to indicate a slight separation of ideas, to separate items in a series, and to set off certain grammatical constructions, as a main clause. [Late Latin *comma,* from Latin *comma* clause of a sentence, from Greek *komma* piece cut off, clause.]

comma bacillus, the bacterium *Vibrio comma* or *cholerae* that is shaped like a comma and causes cholera.

com·mand (kə mand′) *v.t.* **1.** to give an order to, esp. with authority: *The general commanded the troops to retreat.* **2.** to have authority, power, or influence over; control: *The British once commanded the seas.* **3.** to be worthy of and get: *to command respect and admiration.* **4.** to dominate by reason of position or location; overlook: *The tower commanded the small town.* **5.** to have at one's disposal or use: *This writer commands a large vocabulary.* —*v.i.* to be in a position of authority, power, or influence; be in control: *The admiral was born to command.* —*n.* **1.** the act of ordering; bidding. **2.** something that is commanded; order. **3.** the possession or exercise of authority or power to command: *She assumed complete command of the project.* **4.** ability to use; control or mastery: *He has a good command of Italian.* **5.** power to dominate by reason of position or location: *The guns had command of the enemy position.* **6.** range of vision; outlook: *The telescope provided command of the valley.* **7.** the troops, equipment, or area under a commander. **8.** an officer or officers in command. **9.** *Computers.* a signal used to generate a particular kind of operation. [Old French *comander* to order, entrust, from Late Latin *commandāre* to order, commit to another, from Latin *com-* together + *mandāre* to order, entrust.]

| **Synonyms** | *v.t.* **Command, direct,** and **order** mean to tell someone to do something. **Command** implies |

that one has formal authority to do so: *to command troops to advance.* **Direct** suggests guidance more than insistence, though the one directing may also be in a position of authority: *The sales manager directed the staff to be more polite to customers.* **Order** suggests power rather than authority: *The robber ordered the store owner to open the safe.*

com·man·dant (kom′ən dant′, -dänt′) *n.* an officer in command of a military or naval installation or district. [French *commandant,* noun use of present participle of *commander.* See COMMAND.]

com·man·deer (kom′ən dîr′) *v.t.* **1.** to seize (private property), esp. for military use. **2.** *Informal.* to take by force or coercion. **3.** *Archaic.* to force (someone) into military service. [Afrikaans *kommandeeren* to command, requisition, from French *commander.* See COMMAND.]

com·mand·er (kə man′dər) *n.* **1.** an officer in command of a military unit. **2.** in the U.S. Navy or Coast Guard, an officer ranking above a lieutenant commander and below a captain. **3.** a person who is officially in command. **4.** a member of high rank or merit, as in certain orders of knighthood or fraternal societies.

commander in chief *pl.* **commanders in chief. 1.** *also,* **Commander in Chief.** the supreme commander of the armed forces of a country. **2.** an officer commanding armed forces in a particular theater of operations.

com·mand·ing (kə man′ding) *adj.* **1.** demanding or compelling attention or respect; arresting. **2.** (of a view or position) unobstructed, overlooking, or dominating. **3.** exercising command; controlling.

commanding officer, an officer having command of a unit of the armed forces or of the police.

com·mand·ment (kə mand′mənt) *n.* **1.** something given as a command; order; dictate. **2.** *also,* **Commandment.** any one of the Ten Commandments.

com·man·do (kə man′dō) *n., pl.* **-dos** or **-does. 1.** a member of a military unit specially trained for scouting, sabotage, and hit-and-run raids in enemy territory. **2.** a unit made up of such personnel. **3.** a member of a military or police unit trained to act quickly, as by assault, in dangerous situations, as when hostages are being held. [Afrikaans *kommando* party of militia, from Portuguese *commando* party commanded, from *commandar* to command, going back to Latin *com-* together + *mandāre* to command, entrust.]

command performance, a performance of a play, film, ballet, or other entertainment given before royalty or other rulers by order or request.

com·me·di·a dell'ar·te (kə mä′dē ə del är′tē, är′tā) a traditional comedy based upon improvisation of dialogue and action revolving around various stock characters, such as Harlequin and Columbine. It originated in Italy in the sixteenth century. [Italian *commedia dell'arte* literally, comedy of art.]

comme il faut (kô mēl fō′) *French.* as it should or must be; proper.

com·mem·o·rate (kə mem′ə rāt′) *v.t.,* **-rat·ed, -rat·ing. 1.** to serve as a memorial to; memorialize: *The town commissioned a statue to commemorate the battle.* **2.** to honor the memory of; celebrate: *Every year the country commemorates the revolution with a parade.* [Latin *commemorātus* past participle of *commemorāre* to call to mind.] —**com·mem′o·ra′tor,** *n.*

com·mem·o·ra·tion (kə mem′ə rā′shən) *n.* **1.** the act of commemorating. **2.** something that serves to commemorate, as a memorial or ceremony.

com·mem·o·ra·tive (kə mem′ə rā′tiv, -ər ə tiv) *adj.* serving to commemorate. —*n.* a postage stamp or coin that commemorates a person or thing.

U.S. **commemorative** stamps

com·mence (kə mens′) *v.i., v.t.,* **-menced, -menc·ing.** to begin; start. [Old French *com(m)encier,* going back to Latin *com-* together + *initiāre* to initiate.] —For Synonyms *(v.i.),* see **begin.**

com·mence·ment (kə mens′mənt) *n.* **1.** the act or fact of commencing; beginning; start; inception. **2.a.** a day on which a college, university, or other school confers degrees upon, and gives diplomas to, qualified students. **b.** the ceremonies that are conducted on such a day; graduation exercises.

com·mend (kə mend′) *v.t.* **1.** to express admiration for or a very favorable opinion of; praise: *The general commended the sergeant for bravery.* **2.** to present as worthy of attention or regard; recommend. **3.** to deliver to one's care or keeping; commit; entrust. [Latin *commendāre* to entrust, recommend.] —For Synonyms, see **praise.**

com·mend·a·ble (kə men′də bəl) *adj.* worthy of praise; laudable. —**com·mend′a·bly,** *adj.*

a	at	e	end	o	hot	u	up	hw	white	⟨	about
ā	ape	ē	me	ō	old	ū	use	ng	song		taken
ä	far	i	it	ô	fork	ü	rule	th	thin	ə	pencil
âr	care	ī	ice	oi	oil	u̇	pull	<u>th</u>	this		lemon
		îr	pierce	ou	out	ûr	turn	zh	measure		circus

com·men·da·tion (kom′ən dā′shən) *n.* **1.** the act of commending; praise; recommendation. **2.** something that expresses approval or praise; citation. —**com·men·da·to·ry** (kə men′də tôr′ē), *adj.*

com·men·sal (kə men′səl) *adj.* of, relating to, or participating in commensalism. —*n.* a plant or animal living in commensalism.

com·men·sal·ism (kə men′sə liz′əm) *n.* a relationship between two organisms in which one is benefited and the other, the host, is neither benefited nor harmed.

com·men·su·ra·ble (kə men′sər ə bəl, -shər-) *adj.* **1.** measurable by the same standards, values, or units; having a common divisor. **2.** proportionate; commensurate. —**com·men′su·ra·bly,** *adv.*

com·men·su·rate (kə men′sər it, -shər-) *adj.* **1.** corresponding or suitable in measure or degree; proportionate: *The increase in price was commensurate with the increase in demand.* **2.** having the same measure; of equal size; coextensive: *Their expenses were commensurate with their income.* **3.** measurable by the same standards, values, or units; commensurable. [Late Latin *commēnsūrātus* equal in measure, going back to Latin *com-* together + *mēnsūra* a measure.] —**com·men′su·rate·ly,** *adv.* —**com·men′su·rate·ness,** *n.*

com·ment (kom′ent) *n.* **1.** a brief statement that explains, criticizes, or expands on something; remark: *She angered him with her sarcastic comments.* **2.** gossip or discussion: *the subject of much comment.* **3.** observation or revelation; commentary: *The new film provides an interesting comment on our times.* —*v.i.* to make a comment or comments. [Late Latin *commentum* interpretation, from Latin *commentum* invention.]

com·men·tar·y (kom′ən ter′ē) *n., pl.* **-tar·ies. 1.** a series of notes or remarks explaining, describing, or expanding on material presented: *a commentary at the back of a book, slides accompanied by a commentary.* **2.** anything that reveals, points out, or serves to illustrate: *The need for tanks to keep order was a frightening commentary on conditions in the city.* **3.** also, **commentaries.** a historical narrative or record; memoirs.

com·men·tate (kom′ən tāt′) *v.,* **-tat·ed, -tat·ing.** —*v.t.* to give a commentary on. —*v.i.* to serve as a commentator. [From COMMENTATOR.]

com·men·ta·tor (kom′ən tā′tər) *n.* **1.** a radio or television reporter who analyzes news. **2.** anyone who describes, reports, or comments, esp. on social mores or history. [Latin *commentātor* inventor, interpreter.]

com·merce (kom′ərs) *n.* **1.** the exchanging or buying and selling of commodities or services, esp. on a large scale; trade. **2.** social interaction. [Latin *commercium* trade, intercourse.]

com·mer·cial (kə mûr′shəl) *adj.* **1.** of, relating to, or engaged in commerce or trade. **2.** designed for or oriented toward monetary gain. **3.** supported by revenues from advertisers: *a commercial radio station.* —*n.* a paid advertising message on radio or television. —**com·mer′cial·ly,** *adv.*

commercial bank, a bank that offers most or all banking services, esp. demand deposits and the granting of loans.

com·mer·cial·ism (kə mûr′shə liz′əm) *n.* **1.** an overemphasis on monetary gain. **2.** the methods, principles, and spirit of commerce. —**com·mer′cial·is′tic,** *adj.*

com·mer·cial·ize (kə mûr′shə līz′) *v.t.,* **-ized, -iz·ing. 1.** to put on a commercial basis; run as a business for profit. **2.** to exploit for profit: *Some people feel that many holidays have been commercialized.* —**com·mer′cial·i·za′tion,** *n.*

commercial paper, short-term negotiable papers, such as bills of exchange, used in business transactions.

commercial traveler, traveling salesperson.

Com·mie (kom′ē) *n. Informal.* a member of a Communist Party or a person who supports communism. ➡ usually considered offensive or derogatory. [COMM(UNIST) + -IE.]

com·mi·na·tion (kom′ə nā′shən) *n.* **1.** in the Church of England, a recital of divine threats against sinners, used esp. on Ash Wednesday. **2.** a threat or denunciation. [Latin *comminātiō* a threatening.]

com·min·gle (kə ming′gəl) *v.t., v.i.,* **-gled, -gling.** to mix together; mingle.

com·mi·nute (kom′ə nüt′, -nūt′) *v.t.,* **-nut·ed, -nut·ing.** to break down into minute particles; pulverize. [Latin *comminūtus,* past participle of *comminuere.*] —**com′mi·nu′tion,** *n.*

com·mis·er·ate (kə miz′ə rāt′) *v.,* **-at·ed, -at·ing.** —*v.i.* to feel or express sympathy: *to commiserate with someone over a loss.* —*v.t.* to feel or express sympathy for; pity; condole. [Latin *commiserātus,* past participle of *commiserārī,* going back to *com-* with + *miser* wretched.] —**com·mis′er·a′tive,** *adj.* —**com·mis′er·a′tor,** *n.*

com·mis·er·a·tion (kə miz′ə rā′shən) *n.* a feeling or expression of sympathy; compassion.

com·mis·sar (kom′ə sär′) *n.* **1.** until 1946, the head of a government department in the Soviet Union. **2.** an official of the Communist Party whose duties included political indoctrination and the enforcement of party loyalty, as in a military unit. [Russian *komissar,* from German *Kommissar* commissioner, from Medieval Latin *commissarius.* See COMMISSARY.]

com·mis·sar·i·at (kom′ə sâr′ē it) *n.* **1.** a military department that provides food, supplies, and equipment for soldiers. **2.** until 1946, any government department in the Soviet Union. [Russian *kommissariat* and Modern Latin *commissariatus,* both from Medieval Latin *commissarius.* See COMMISSARY.]

com·mis·sar·y (kom′ə ser′ē) *n., pl.* **-sar·ies. 1.** a store that sells food and supplies, esp. in a military camp. **2.** a place to eat, as a cafeteria, esp. in a motion-picture or television studio. **3.** a person who is entrusted with a special duty or commission by a higher authority; deputy; representative. **4.** formerly, a military officer in charge of supplying provisions. [Medieval Latin *commissarius* person in charge, commissioner, from Latin *commissus,* past participle of *committere* to put together, entrust.]

com·mis·sion (kə mish′ən) *n.* **1.** a group of persons who have been appointed or elected to perform certain duties: *a commission investigating crime.* **2.** a fee paid for services or work done, often based on a percentage of the total amount of business transacted: *The salesclerk received a commission on the sale.* **3.a.** in the United States, a document issued by the president, giving military rank and authority. **b.** the rank and authority granted by such a document. **4.** the act of committing; performance; perpetration: *the commission of a crime.* **5.** an assignment or appointment to do something, as a work of art. **6.a.** a giving of authority to act for, or in behalf of, another. **b.** the authority given. **c.** the thing for which authority is given. **7.** an order; command. **8.** a written warrant or document granting certain powers, privileges, and duties. —*v.t.* **1.** to give military rank and authority to, as an officer. **2.** to give authority to; empower: *The company commissioned a private detective to investigate the theft.* **3.** to hire or appoint (someone) to do something: *We commissioned the sculptor to do a bust.* **4.** to put (a ship) in commission. [French *commission* mandate, charge, from Late Latin *commissiō,* from Latin *commissiō* a bringing together in contest.]

· **in commission.** ready for service or use; in working order: *The battleship was in commission in the Pacific.*

· **out of commission.** not in service or use; not in working order.

commissioned officer, in the United States, an officer of the armed forces who receives a commission from the president.

com·mis·sion·er (kə mish′ə nər) *n.* **1.** a member of a commission. **2.** an official appointed as the head of a government department: *a parks commissioner, a highway commissioner.* **3.** a member of a group of individuals elected or appointed to the governing body of a city or county. **4.** an official appointed by a sports league to act as an administrator and arbitrator: *a baseball commissioner.*

commission merchant, a person who buys or sells goods on a commission.

com·mis·sure (kom′ə shûr′) *n. Anatomy.* **1.** any area where two corresponding parts, as the lips or eyelids, come together. **2.** any band or strand of nerve fibers connecting like structures on the right and left sides of the brain or spinal cord. [Middle English *commissure,* from Old French *commissure,* from Latin *commissura,* from *commissus,* past participle of *committere* to put together, join.]

com·mit (kə mit′) *v.t.,* **-mit·ted, -mit·ting. 1.** to do (something wrong): *to commit an error, to commit murder.* **2.** to put into the charge or keeping of another; entrust. **3.** to put into official custody, as of a prison or mental institution. **4.** to devote or pledge; bind (with *to*): *She was fully committed to the plan.* **5.** to state the position of: *He wouldn't commit himself on any issue.* **6.** to refer, as a legislative bill or report, to a committee for consideration. **7.** to place or consign so as to preserve, for future use: *to commit an address to memory, to commit one's thoughts to paper.* [Latin *committere* to put together, entrust, perpetrate.] —**com·mit′ta·ble,** *adj.*

com·mit·ment (kə mit′mənt) *n.* **1.** the act of committing or the state of being committed. **2.** an obligation; pledge. **3.** a court order directing that a person be confined, as in a prison or mental institution. Also, **com·mit′tal.**

com·mit·tee (kə mit′ē) *n.* **1.** a group of persons appointed or elected to perform certain duties or to investigate, report, or act on a particular matter. **2.** a group of persons who organize to pursue a common goal. [COMMIT + -EE.]

com·mit·tee·man (kə mit′ē mən, -man′) *n., pl.* **-men** (-mən, -men′). a member of a committee.

committee of the whole, all the attending members of a legislative assembly or similar body, who have constituted themselves as a group to consider proposals under modified, usually less formal, rules of debate.

com·mit·tee·wom·an (kə mit′ē wŭm′ən) *n., pl.* **-wom·en** (-wim′ən). a woman who is a member of a committee.

com·mode (kə mōd′) *n.* **1.** toilet *(def. 1)*. **2.** a small piece of furniture, as a cabinet or chair, containing a chamber pot. **3.** a movable, usually covered, washstand. **4.** a chest or cabinet of drawers. [French *commode* chest of drawers, from *commode* convenient, from Latin *commodus.*]

com·mo·di·ous (kə mō′dē əs) *adj.* having or containing ample room; roomy; spacious. [Medieval Latin *commodiosus* useful, from Latin *commodus* convenient.] —**com·mo′di·ous·ly,** *adv.* —**com·mo′di·ous·ness,** *n.*

com·mod·i·ty (kə mod′i tē) *n., pl.* **-ties. 1.a.** an article of trade or commerce; ware or product. **b. commodities.** basic, usually unprocessed goods, as grains, fruits, or metals, traded in a stock market. **2.** something whose usefulness is exploited or turned to advantage or profit. [Latin *commoditās* advantage, convenience.]

com·mo·dore (kom′ə dôr′) *n.* **1.** in the U.S. Navy, an officer ranking above a captain and below a rear admiral. ➡ used as a rank only in time of war. **2.** formerly, a captain who holds a temporary command of a squadron in the U.S. Navy or Merchant Marine. **3.** the president or head of a yacht club. [Earlier *commandore,* from Dutch *commandeur* commander of a town, from French *commandeur* commander, from *commander.* See COMMAND.]

com·mon (kom′ən) *adj.* **1.** of frequent or habitual occurrence; appearing frequently; usual: *a common mistake.* **2.** widely distributed; general; widespread: *common knowledge, a word in common use.* **3.** belonging equally to two or more; shared by all alike: *common property, common interests.* **4.** relating or belonging to the community as a whole; public: *the common good.* **5.** undistinguished by special or superior characteristics; average; standard: *It is common courtesy to reply to an invitation.* **6.** not distinguished by rank, station, or special status: *the common people.* **7.** of the most familiar, widely known, or frequently occurring kind of species: *the common bluebird, the common pea.* **8.** of mediocre or inferior quality; not rare or costly. **9.** not refined or distinguished; coarse; vulgar: *common manners.* **10.** *Mathematics.* bearing the same relation to two or more terms or quantities: *a common ratio.* —*n. also,* **commons.** a tract of land, as a pasture or park, owned or used by the public. [Old French *comun* general, mutual, from Latin *commūnis* general, universal.] —**com′mon·ness,** *n.*

  • **in common.** shared jointly or equally: *a couple who have many interests in common.*

Synonyms *adj.* **Common, familiar,** and **ordinary** mean occurring or encountered frequently, so as to be expected in given circumstances. **Common** suggests that the thing in question is encountered every day or with great regularity and does not have distinguishing characteristics: *Acne is a common problem among adolescents.* **Familiar** emphasizes a sense of knowledge or expectation of the thing: *This food is familiar to those who have traveled in Africa.* **Ordinary** suggests closeness to an average or rule: *An ordinary car has the trunk in the rear.* For other Synonyms *(adj.),* see **general.**

com·mon·age (kom′ə nij) *n.* **1.** formerly, the right to pasture animals on a common, as during feudal times in England. **2.** the land on which this right was held.

com·mon·al·ty (kom′ə nəl tē) *n., pl.* **-ties. 1.** the common people, as opposed to royalty or the nobility or upper classes. **2.** the members of a corporation or the corporation itself. Also, **com·mon·al·i·ty** (kom′ə nal′i tē).

common carrier, an individual or company, as a railroad or steamship line, engaged in transporting goods or people for a fee.

common cold, cold *(n., def. 3)*.

common denominator, any number that can be divided by each of the denominators of a given group of fractions without leaving a remainder. The number 18 is a common denominator of ⅓, ⅚, and 2/9.

common divisor, any number or algebraic expression that divides two or more other numbers or algebraic expressions without leaving a remainder. The number 3 is a common divisor of 6*x*, 9*x²y*, and 21. Also, **common factor.**

com·mon·er (kom′ə nər) *n.* a member of the common people, esp. a person who is not of noble rank.

common fraction, a fraction whose numerator and denominator are integers, as ¼ or ⅗.

common law, a body or system of law based on custom, usage, and court decisions, as distinct from law enacted by statute. ➡ distinguished from **civil law** *(def. 2)*.

com·mon-law marriage (kom′ən lô′) a marriage in which the parties agree to live together as man and wife without having undergone a religious or civil ceremony.

common logarithm, a logarithm to the base 10.

com·mon·ly (kom′ən lē) *adv.* **1.** in many or most cases; generally; ordinarily. **2.** in a common manner.

Common Market, European Economic Community.

common multiple, any number or algebraic expression that is divisible by two or more other numbers or algebraic expressions without leaving a remainder. The number 20 is a common multiple of 2, 4, 5, and 10.

common noun, a noun that names any one or all of the members of a class rather than any one particular person, place, or thing, as *dog, dogs, street, streets.* ➡ distinguished from **proper noun.**

com·mon·place (kom′ən plās′) *adj.* not original, remarkable, or interesting; ordinary. —*n.* **1.** a customary or obvious remark; platitude. **2.** anything ordinary, uninteresting, or generally accepted and taken for granted; everyday thing. —**com′mon·place′ness,** *n.*

com·mons (kom′ənz) *pl. n.* **1.** a hall or building for dining, esp. at a college or university. **2.** food served in such a hall or building. **3. Commons.** House of Commons. **4.** the common people; commonalty. **5.** common. ➡ used as singular in defs. 1, 2, and 5, as singular or plural in defs. 3 and 4.

common sense, understanding independent of specialized knowledge; sound, practical judgment. —**com′mon-sense′;** *also,* **com′mon·sense′,** *adj.* —**com′mon·sen′si·cal,** *adj.*

common stock, stock representing the basic ownership of a corporation, carrying voting rights with it, and receiving dividends only after those due the holders of preferred stock have been paid. ➡ distinguished from **preferred stock.**

com·mon·weal (kom′ən wēl′) *also,* **common weal.** *n.* **1.** the general or public welfare; common good. **2.** *Archaic.* commonwealth.

com·mon·wealth (kom′ən welth′) *n.* **1.** the whole body of people of a nation or state; body politic. **2.** a nation or state in which supreme power is held by the people; republic or democratic country or state. **3.** any of certain states of the United States that use *commonwealth* rather than *state* as an official designation: Kentucky, Massachusetts, Pennsylvania, and Virginia. **4. the Commonwealth.** Commonwealth of Nations. **5. Commonwealth.** the government established in England by Oliver Cromwell, lasting from 1649 to 1653 or, in some views, to 1660. [COMMON + WEALTH.]

com·mo·tion (kə mō′shən) *n.* **1.** a noisy or turbulent disturbance, excitement, or disorder; agitation; turmoil. **2.** bustle or stir, as of a busy place. [Latin *commōtiō.*]

com·mu·nal (kə mū′nəl, kom′yə-) *adj.* **1.** of, relating to, or characteristic of a commune or community. **2.** belonging to the people of a community; public. —**com·mu′nal·ly,** *adv.*

com·mu·nal·ism (kə mū′nə liz′əm, kom′yə-) *n.* **1.** a theory or system of government in which each commune is virtually an independent state, and the nation is merely a federation of such states. **2.** the belief in or practice of communal ownership of goods and property. —**com·mu′nal·ist,** *n.* —**com·mu′nal·is′tic,** *adj.*

com·mu·nal·ize (kə mū′nə līz′, kom′yə-) *v.t.,* **-ized, -iz·ing.** to make communal; make community property. —**com·mu′nal·i·za′tion,** *n.*

com·mune¹ (kə mūn′) *v.i.,* **-muned, -mun·ing. 1.a.** to confer or converse intimately (with *with*): *to commune with an old friend.* **b.** to experience a profound feeling of unity and receptivity (with *with*): *to commune with nature.* **2.** to receive Holy Communion. [Old French *comuner* to share, have in common, from *comun.* See COMMON.]

com·mune² (kom′ūn) *n.* **1.** a society or community, often rural, in which property is owned and used in common and work and facilities, as living quarters or nurseries, are usually shared. **2.** the smallest unit of local government in France, Italy, Belgium, and certain other European countries. **3. the Commune. a.** the revolutionary committee in Paris that governed France from July

a	at	e	end	o	hot	u	up	hw	white		about
ā	ape	ē	me	ō	old	ū	use	ng	song	ə	taken
ä	far	i	it	ô	fork	ü	rule	th	thin		pencil
âr	care	ī	ice	oi	oil	u̇	pull	th	this		lemon
		ir	pierce	ou	out	ûr	turn	zh	measure		circus

1792 to 1794. **b.** the radical coalition that governed Paris from March 18 to May 28, 1871. [French *commune* township, parish, from Medieval Latin *communia* group sharing a common life, from Latin *communis* general, universal.]

com·mu·ni·ca·ble (kə mū′ni kə bəl) *adj.* capable of being communicated or transmitted: *a communicable disease.* —**com·mu′ni·ca·bil′i·ty, com·mu′ni·ca·ble·ness,** *n.* —**com·mu′ni·ca·bly,** *adv.*

com·mu·ni·cant (kə mū′ni kənt) *n.* **1.** a person who receives Holy Communion. **2.** a person who communicates. —*adj.* communicating.

com·mu·ni·cate (kə mū′ni kāt′) *v.,* **-cat·ed, -cat·ing.** —*v.t.* **1.** to make known or understood; impart or transfer knowledge or information of: *You communicate your ideas very well in this essay.* **2.** to pass on or along; transmit, as a disease. —*v.i.* **1.** to exchange or share feelings, thoughts, or information: *The couple communicated without words. We've been communicating by mail.* **2.** to be connected or form a connecting passage: *This passageway communicates with the tunnel leading to the mine.* **3.** to receive Holy Communion. [Latin *communicātus,* past participle of *communicāre* to impart, share.] —**com·mu′ni·ca·tor,** *n.*

> **Synonyms** **Communicate** and **impart** mean to transfer something such as feelings or information. **Communicate** emphasizes that what is transferred is thus shared: *to communicate good news, to communicate one's concern about something.* **Impart** suggests that what is given remains somehow in the possession of the giver: *to impart a little of one's special knowledge.*

com·mu·ni·ca·tion (kə mū′ni kā′shən) *n.* **1.** the transfer of information, as facts, wishes, or emotions. **2.** something that is communicated; message. **3.** the act or process of communicating. **4. communications. a.** a system or systems for communicating, esp. one involving telephone, telegram, radio, television, and similar advanced technology. **b.** the science, study, or technology of communicating. **5.** a connecting passage or opening; channel.

communications satellite, an earth-orbiting device that relays radio, television, telephone, or other electromagnetic signals between ground stations on earth or satellites in space.

com·mu·ni·ca·tive (kə mū′ni kā′tiv, -kə tiv) *adj.* inclined to communicate or disclose information readily; talkative. —**com·mu′ni·ca′tive·ly,** *adv.* —**com·mu′ni·ca′tive·ness,** *n.*

com·mun·ion (kə mūn′yən) *n.* **1.** a sharing of feelings or thoughts; sympathetic and intimate intercourse. **2.** an association or fellowship, esp. a religious or spiritual fellowship. **3.** a group of churches having a common religious creed. **4. Communion. a.** Holy Communion. **b.** that part of a church service during which Holy Communion

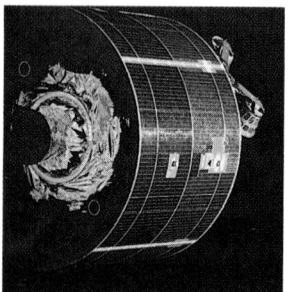

communications satellite
in orbit

is received by members of the congregation. [Late Latin *communiō* Holy Communion, from Latin *communiō* fellowship, mutual participation.]

com·mu·ni·qué (kə mū′ni kā′, -mū′ni kā′) *n.* an official communication, announcement, or bulletin. [French *communiqué,* from *communiquer* to communicate, from Latin *communicāre* to impart, share.]

com·mu·nism (kom′yə niz′əm) *n.* **1.** a theory of social and economic organization, advanced chiefly by the German socialist Karl Marx, advocating public ownership of the means of production, as factories and resources, the sharing of the products of labor, and the establishment of a society in which hostile, competitive social classes disappear. **2.** *also,* **Communism. a.** a revolutionary political movement advocating this theory and the establishment of an international classless society in which productive resources would be owned in common and used for the benefit of all. **b.** a system of government based on this theory. **3.** a social system characterized by the communal sharing of goods and services. [French *communisme,* from *commun* general, universal, from Latin *communis.*]

com·mu·nist (kom′yə nist) *also,* **Com·mu·nist.** *n.* **1.** a member of a Communist Party. **2.** a person who supports or advocates communism. —*adj.* relating to, characteristic of, or resembling communism, communists, or a Communist Party. —**com′mu·nis′tic,** *adj.* —**com′mu·nis′ti·cal·ly,** *adv.*

Communist Party, a political party that supports or advocates communism.

com·mu·ni·ty (kə mū′ni tē) *n., pl.* **-ties. 1.** a number of people living in the same locality, as a district or town, and under the same government. **2.** the locality itself. **3.** a number of people considered as a group or unit because of some similarity or commonly held characteristic, as identical religion, occupation, or interests: *The new zoning law will affect the entire local business community.* **4.** society as a whole or in general; the public. **5.** a holding in common; joint possession; sharing: *a community of ownership.* **6.** similar character; agreement; identity: *community of interests.* **7.** all the plants, animals, and other organisms that live together in the same area and either interact with each other or in some way influence each other's lives, considered as a group. [Old French *comunete* society of people, from Latin *communitās* fellowship.]

community center, a meeting place used by a community for recreational, social, and cultural activities.

community chest, a fund formed by voluntary contributions from the people and businesses of a community and drawn upon by various charitable organizations for local welfare activities.

community college, a junior college, esp. one partially supported by the community it serves.

community property, in certain states of the United States, property acquired during a marriage, by either partner, that is considered to be owned equally by both partners.

com·mu·nize (kom′yə nīz′) *v.t.,* **-nized, -niz·ing. 1.** to place under community control or ownership. **2.** to make communist. —**com′mu·ni·za′tion,** *n.*

com·mu·ta·tion (kom′yə tā′shən) *n.* **1.** regular travel, esp. over a considerable distance, to and from work. **2.** a substitution, as of one type of payment for another. **3.** a reduction or change, as of a prison sentence or penalty. **4.** reversal of an electric current by a commutator.

commutation ticket, a transportation ticket, sold at a reduced rate, that entitles the holder to travel over a given route a given number of times or during a specified period.

com·mu·ta·tive (kə mū′tə tiv, kom′yə tā′-) *adj. Mathematics.* relating to or designating a law stating that the sum or product of two or more quantities will be the same regardless of the order in which they appear.

com·mu·ta·tor (kom′yə tā′tər) *n.* a split ring that revolves with the armature of an electric generator or motor and causes a periodic reversal of the generated or supplied current.

com·mute (kə mūt′) *v.,* **-mut·ed, -mut·ing.** —*v.i.* to travel regularly, esp. over a considerable distance, between one's place of business and one's home. —*v.t.* **1.** to substitute, as one type of payment for another; interchange. **2.** to reduce or change, as a prison sentence or penalty. —*n.* the distance or time involved in such travel: *I have a short commute.* [Latin *commūtāre* to exchange.] —**com·mut′a·ble,** *adj.*

com·mut·er (kə mū′tər) *n.* a person who regularly travels a relatively long distance to and from work, as from a suburb to a city. —*adj.* used by or designed for commuters: *a commuter railroad.*

comp. 1. companion. **2.** comparative. **3.** compare. **4.** composer. **5.** composition. **6.** compositor. **7.** compound.

com·pact¹ (*adj.,* kəm pakt′, *def. 4, also* kom′pakt; *v.,* kəm pakt′; *n.,* kom′pakt) *adj.* **1.** closely and firmly united; tightly packed together. **2.** occupying a relatively small space or area. **3.** using few words; expressed succinctly; concise; terse. **4.** (of an automobile) smaller and more economical to operate than the standard size. **5.** solid and firm: *The bulldog has a compact build.* **6.** *Archaic.* composed; made (with *of*). —*v.t.* to press together closely and firmly; pack. —*n.* **1.** a small case containing face powder and a mirror, designed to be carried in a purse. **2.** a compact car. [Latin *compactus* joined together, past participle of *compingere* to join or put together, from *com-* with, together + *pangere* to fix, set.] —**com·pact′ly,** *adv.* —**com·pact′ness,** *n.* —For Synonyms *(adj.),* see **close.**

com·pact² (kom′pakt) *n.* an agreement or contract. [Latin *compactum,* from *compacīscī* to make an agreement.]

compact disc (kom′pakt) *also,* **compact disk.** an optical disk about 4 ¾ inches (12 centimeters) in diameter, carrying a digital sound recording that can be read and played by means of a laser beam. Also, **CD**

com·pac·tor (kom pak′tər, kom′pak-) *also,* **com·pact·er.** *n.* a device that presses garbage into a small compact mass for easy disposal. [COMPACT¹ + -OR.]

com·pan·ion (kəm pan′yən) *n.* **1.** a person who associates with or accompanies another or others. **2.** a person employed to live

with, accompany, or assist another. **3.** anything that matches, or forms a pair with, another: *I've lost the companion to this glove.* **4.** a member of the lowest rank in orders of knighthood. —*v.t.* to be a companion to; accompany. [Old French *compaignon* comrade, from Late Latin *compāniō* literally, bread-sharer, from Latin *com-* with + *pānis* bread.]

com·pan·ion·a·ble (kəm pan′yə nə bəl) *adj.* suitable as a companion; sociable. —**com·pan′ion·a·bil′i·ty,** *n.* —**com·pan′ion·a·bly,** *adv.*

companion cell, a specialized cell adjacent to a sieve tube in the phloem of flowering plants, believed to regulate flow within the sieve tube.

com·pan·ion·ship (kəm pan′yən ship′) *n.* the state of being companions; friendship; fellowship.

com·pan·ion·way (kəm pan′yən wā′) *n.* **1.** a stairway leading from the deck of a ship to the cabin or deck below. **2.** the space where such a stairway is located.

com·pa·ny (kum′pə nē) *n., pl.* **-nies. 1.** a guest or guests: *We had company for dinner.* **2.** a business establishment: *an oil company.* **3.** a group of entertainers or all those associated with a theatrical presentation; troupe: *a dance company, a repertory company.* **4.** companionship; fellowship: *We enjoy their company. He provides pleasant company for me.* **5.** a person or persons with whom one habitually associates. **6.** a group or gathering of persons, as for social purposes. **7.** *also,* **Company.** a partner or partners not named, as in the title of a firm: *She works for Wells and Company.* **8.** a military unit composed of a headquarters and two or more platoons, forming part of a battalion. **9.** a ship's crew, including the officers. [Old French *compagnie* association, body of troops, from Late Latin *compāniēs* body of soldiers dwelling together, army mess, from Latin *com-* with + *pānis* bread.]

• **to keep company.** to be involved romantically: *They've been keeping company for about six months.*

• **to keep (someone) company.** to be with (someone).

• **to part company. a.** to separate and go in different directions. **b.** to end an association or friendship.

company union, a labor union with membership limited to workers in one company, usually organized and dominated by the employer.

compar., comparative.

com·pa·ra·ble (kom′pər ə bəl) *adj.* **1.** capable of being compared: *These radios are of comparable value.* **2.** worthy of comparison: *Our school orchestra is not comparable to a professional one.* —**com′pa·ra·bly,** *adv.* —For Synonyms, see **like**[1].

com·par·a·tive (kəm par′ə tiv) *adj.* **1.** involving, based on, or relating to comparison: *a comparative study of human and animal anatomy.* **2.** as estimated by comparison; not absolute; relative: *I was a comparative stranger to them.* **3.** denoting the second of the three degrees of quantity, quality, or relation that can be expressed by an adjective or adverb. *Faster* is the comparative degree of the adjective *fast.* ➡ distinguished from **positive** and **superlative.** —*n.* **1.** the comparative degree of an adjective or adverb. **2.** a word or group of words that expresses this degree. —**com·par′a·tive·ly,** *adv.* —**com·par′a·tive·ness,** *n.*

com·par·a·tor (kəm par′ə tər, kom′pə rā′-) *n.* an instrument for comparing a measurement, as of length or brightness, with an established standard.

com·pare (kəm pâr′) *v.,* **-pared, -par·ing.** —*v.t.* **1.** to examine in order to find or show similarities and differences: *The police compared the fingerprints on the gun with the ones on the door.* **2.** to represent or speak of as similar, analogous, or alike; parallel; liken (with *to*): *The lecturer compared the human brain to a computer.* **3.** to form the comparative and superlative degrees of (an adjective or adverb). —*v.i.* **1.** to be worthy of being compared; be considered as alike or similar (with *with*): *Did your trip compare with the last one?* [Old French *comparer* to put persons or things in comparison, from Latin *comparāre* to match, pair together.] For Usage Note, see **contrast.**

• **beyond** (or **without**) **compare.** without equal.

com·par·i·son (kəm par′ə sən) *n.* **1.** the act of comparing or the state of being compared. **2.** a comparable quality or character; likeness; similarity: *There is no comparison between the two.* **3.** a change in form of an adjective or adverb to indicate the positive, comparative, or superlative degree. [Old French *comparaison* a comparing, from Latin *comparātiō.*]

com·par·i·son-shop (kəm par′ə sən shop′) *v.i.,* **-shopped, -shop·ping. 1.** to compare prices, as of competing brands of an item or of the same item in different stores, to find the best available values. **2.** to act or serve as a comparison shopper.

comparison shopper 1. an employee of a store whose job is to shop in competing stores to check on their prices and quality and selection of merchandise. **2.** any person who shops in different stores looking for the best prices on merchandise.

com·part·ment (kəm pärt′mənt) *n.* **1.** any of the divisions or separate sections into which an enclosed space is divided: *The wallet has a separate compartment for change. The drawer was partitioned into four compartments.* **2.** a separate room, chamber, or similarly enclosed space: *sleeping compartments on a train.* [French *compartiment* partition, from Italian *compartimento,* from *compartire* to divide, share, going back to Latin *com-* together + *partīre* to divide.]

com·part·men·tal·ize (kəm pärt men′tə līz′) *v.t.,* **-ized, -iz·ing.** to divide into separate compartments or categories. —**com·part·men′tal·i·za′tion,** *n.*

com·pass (kum′pəs, kom′-) *n.* **1.** an instrument for determining and showing directions, consisting of a magnetized needle freely suspended on a pivot to allow it to point to the north magnetic pole. **2.** the circumference or boundary of an enclosed area. **3.** the range or extent within limits; reach; scope: *within the compass of one's capabilities.* **4.** the range of tones of a voice or musical instrument. **5.** *also,* **compasses.** an instrument for drawing circles and measuring distances, consisting of two straight and equal legs connected at one end. **6.** *Archaic.* a circular course; circuit. —*v.t.* **1.** to make a circuit of; go around: *a voyage that compassed the globe.* **2.** to circle around; encircle; surround; encompass: *The mountains compassed the valley.* **3.** to grasp mentally; comprehend: *We could not compass such a difficult concept.* **4.** to accomplish or gain; achieve; obtain: *to compass one's goals.* **5.** to plot (something evil); scheme; contrive. [Old French *compas* pair of compasses, circle, measure, from *compasser* to measure, go round, going back to Latin *com-* together + *passus* step.] —For Synonyms *(n.),* see **scope.**

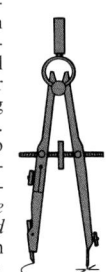

compass
(n.,
def. 5)

compass card, a dial on a mariner's compass marked for every two degrees between 0 and 360 degrees, and for the thirty-two points of the compass.

com·pas·sion (kəm pash′ən) *n.* a feeling of pity or sorrow for another's suffering or misfortune combined with a desire to help; sympathy. [Old French *compassion,* from Late Latin *compassiō,* going back to Latin *com-* with + *patī* to suffer.] —For Synonyms, see **sympathy.**

com·pas·sion·ate (kəm pash′ə nit) *adj.* feeling or expressing compassion; sympathetic. —**com·pas′sion·ate·ly,** *adv.*

compass rose, a circle divided into thirty-two points of the compass, esp. one printed on a map for use in navigation.

compass saw, a tool with a small, tapering blade for sawing in circles or cutting wood in patterns. Also, **fret saw, keyhole saw.**

com·pat·i·ble (kəm pat′ə bəl) *adj.* **1.** capable of existing or functioning together in harmony; congenial; consistent: *She and*

a	at	e	end	o	hot	u	up	hw	white		about
ā	ape	ē	me	ō	old	ū	use	ng	song		taken
ä	far	i	it	ô	fork	ü	rule	th	thin	ə	pencil
âr	care	ī	ice	oi	oil	u̇	pull	th	this		lemon
		îr	pierce	ou	out	ûr	turn	zh	measure		circus

her roommate were not compatible. His testimony was not compatible with that of the first witness. **2.** *Electronics.* **a.** in computers, capable of processing data and programs devised for some other type of system. **b.** in television, capable of receiving or being received in both black and white and in color. [French *compatible,* going back to Latin *compatī* to suffer with.] —**com·pat′i·bil′i·ty,** *n.* —**com·pat′i·bly,** *adv.*

com·pa·tri·ot (kəm pā′trē ət, -pat′rē-) *n.* a person from one's own country; fellow citizen. [Middle French *compatriote,* going back to Latin *com-* with + *patriōta* countryman (from Greek *patriōtēs* fellow countryman).]

com·peer (kəm pîr′, kom′pîr) *n.* **1.** a person of equal rank or standing; equal; peer. **2.** a close friend or associate; comrade; companion. [Old French *comper* equal, from Latin *compār* equal, comrade.]

com·pel (kəm pel′) *v.t.,* **-pelled, -pel·ling. 1.** to drive or urge irresistibly; constrain; oblige: *The transit strike compelled many people to drive to work.* **2.** to obtain or bring about by force; exact; command: *The army compelled obedience to the dictatorship.* [Latin *compellere* to drive together, force.] —**com·pel′la·ble,** *adj.* —**com·pel′ler,** *n.* —**com·pel′ling·ly,** *adv.* —For Synonyms, see **force.**

com·pend (kom′pend) *n.* compendium.

com·pen·di·ous (kəm pen′dē əs) *adj.* brief but comprehensive; concise. [Latin *compendiōsus* abridged, short.] —**com·pen′di·ous·ly,** *adv.* —**com·pen′di·ous·ness,** *n.*

com·pen·di·um (kəm pen′dē əm) *n., pl.* **-di·ums** or **-di·a** (-dē ə). a brief summary covering a subject comprehensively. Also, **compend.** [Latin *compendium* saving, abridgment; literally, that which is weighed together.]

com·pen·sate (kom′pən sāt′) *v.,* **-sat·ed, -sat·ing.** —*v.t.* **1.** to make suitable or equal return or payment to; recompense; reimburse; remunerate: *The company compensated me for the extra hours I worked.* **2.** to make up for; counterbalance; offset. —*v.i.* to provide or be an equivalent; make up (often with *for*): *The band tried to compensate for lack of skill by playing louder.* [Latin *compēnsātus,* past participle of *compēnsāre* to weigh one thing against another.] —**com′pen·sa′tive, com·pen·sa·to·ry** (kəm pen′sə tôr′ē), *adj.* —**com′pen·sa′tor,** *n.*

com·pen·sa·tion (kom′pən sā′shən) *n.* **1.** the act of compensating. **2.** something that compensates, as payment given or received as an equivalent for services, loss, or damage. **3.** payment given for services; salary; wages. **4.** increased activity or development of an organ or function to make up for loss or weakness of another.

com·pete (kəm pēt′) *v.i.,* **-pet·ed, -pet·ing.** to contend with another or others for or as if for a prize; vie: *The two students competed with each other for the highest mark.* [Latin *competere* to strive for (in competition) with another; be suitable.]

| **Synonyms** | **Compete, vie,** and **contend** mean to struggle against a rival or rivals. **Compete** usually suggests that a goal or prize is involved: *to compete for a trophy, to compete for a job.* **Vie** focuses more on the rivalry itself: *The new company vied successfully with much larger competitors.* **Contend** suggests effort or maneuvering and the closeness of the struggle: *The runners strained every muscle as they contended for the finish line.* |

com·pe·tence (kom′pi təns) *n.* **1.** the state of being competent; ability; fitness. **2.** a sufficient income or other means to provide a comfortable living. **3.** the condition of being legally qualified or admissible: *competence to testify.* Also, **com′pe·ten·cy.**

com·pe·tent (kom′pi tənt) *adj.* **1.** having sufficient ability; capable: *a competent swimmer.* **2.** sufficient or adequate for the purpose: *Although they were inexperienced, they did a competent job.* **3.** legally qualified or admissible: *a competent witness.* [Latin *competēns,* present participle of *competere* to be suitable, compete.] —**com′pe·tent·ly,** *adv.* —For Synonyms, see **able.**

com·pe·ti·tion (kom′pi tish′ən) *n.* **1.** the act of competing; rivalry. **2.** a trial or match for determining relative skill or ability; contest. **3.** a business rivalry between two or more persons or firms competing for the same customers or market. **4.** *Biology.* the struggle among organisms, populations, or species, esp. to consume the same food or occupy the same place. **5.** the competition. one's competitors or rivals.

com·pet·i·tive (kəm pet′i tiv) *adj.* of, involving, or characterized by competition: *a competitive examination, competitive prices, a competitive spirit.* —**com·pet′i·tive·ly,** *adv.* —**com·pet′i·tive·ness,** *n.*

com·pet·i·tor (kəm pet′i tər) *n.* a person or thing that competes.

com·pi·la·tion (kom′pə lā′shən) *n.* **1.** the act of compiling. **2.** something that is compiled, as an anthology, list, or report.

com·pile (kəm pīl′) *v.t.,* **-piled, -pil·ing. 1.** to collect and put together (various material or data), as for a report: *to compile*

statistics. **2.** to make or form, as a book or report, by collecting and organizing material or data from various sources: *to compile an anthology of poems.* [Old French *compiler* to put together, collect, from Latin *compīlāre* to gather together, rob.]

com·pil·er (kəm pī′lər) *n.* **1.** a person who compiles. **2.** *Computers.* a program that translates a high-level language into the binary digits of machine language.

com·pla·cen·cy (kəm plā′sən sē) *n.* a feeling of contentment or satisfaction, esp. self-satisfaction. Also, **com·pla′cence.**

com·pla·cent (kəm plā′sənt) *adj.* feeling or showing satisfaction, esp. self-satisfaction. [Latin *complacēns,* present participle of *complacēre* to please.] —**com·pla′cent·ly,** *adv.*

com·plain (kəm plān′) *v.i.* **1.** to express dissatisfaction or displeasure; find fault: *The class complained that the exam was too hard.* **2.** to talk about one's pains or ills. **3.** to make a formal accusation or charge: *We complained to the police about the noisy party next door.* [Old French *complaindre* to lament, going back to Latin *com-* with + *plangere* to lament.] —**com·plain′er,** *n.* —**com·plain′ing·ly,** *adv.*

com·plain·ant (kəm plā′nənt) *n.* a person who files a complaint in a legal action or proceeding.

com·plaint (kəm plānt′) *n.* **1.** an expression of dissatisfaction or displeasure. **2.** a cause for complaining; grievance. **3.** an illness; ailment. **4.** *Law.* the first pleading filed in a civil suit, in which the plaintiff states the wrong or harm allegedly done and demands a specific form of relief.

com·plai·sance (kəm plā′səns, -zəns, kom′plə zans′) *n.* a willingness to please or oblige others; agreeableness; graciousness.

com·plai·sant (kəm plā′sənt, -zənt, kom′plə zant′) *adj.* characterized by complaisance; obliging; agreeable; courteous. [French *complaisant,* present participle of *complaire* to please, from Latin *complacēre.*] —**com·plai′sant·ly,** *adv.*

com·plect·ed (kəm plek′tid) *adj.* complexioned. ➡ used in combination, as in *dark-complected.* [From a form of COMPLEXION.]

com·ple·ment (*n.,* kom′plə mənt; *v.,* kom′plə ment′) *n.* **1.** something that completes or makes perfect: *The new table is just the right complement for the room.* **2.** a quantity or amount that completes or is required to complete something: *The football team now has its full complement of players.* **3.** the total number of officers and other personnel constituting the crew of a ship. **4.** either of two parts that together form a whole. **5.** *Geometry.* the measure of an angle or arc that must be added to the measure of a given angle or arc to produce a sum equal to 90 degrees. **6.** *Grammar.* a word or phrase used to complete a construction, esp. in the predicate. The **subjective complement** describes or identifies the subject, and the **objective complement** describes or identifies the object. —*v.t.* to add or be a complement to; complete. [Latin *complēmentum* that which completes, from *complēre* to fill up, complete. Doublet of COMPLIMENT.]

com·ple·men·ta·ry (kom plə men′tə rē, -trē) *adj.* **1.** serving as a complement; completing. **2.** mutually supplying each other's needs. Also, **com·ple·men·tal** (kom′plə men′təl).

complementary angle, either of two angles whose sum is 90 degrees.

complementary color 1. a color of the spectrum whose reflected light, when combined with that of a certain other color, produces white or gray light. Yellow and blue are one of the pairs of complementary colors. **2.** *Art.* either of a pair of colors that are opposed to each other, as shown on a color wheel. Examples of complementary colors are green and red, orange and blue, and yellow and purple.

com·plete (kəm plēt′) *adj.* **1.** having all its parts or elements; whole; entire. **2.** having been ended; finished: *The job is complete.* **3.** realized to the fullest extent; total; thorough: *a complete success.* **4.** *Archaic.* expert; accomplished; skilled. —*v.t.,* **-plet·ed, -plet·ing. 1.** to make whole; include all parts of. **2.** to bring to an end; finish. **3.** to make perfect; make entirely satisfactory: *The delicious dinner completed a wonderful day.* [Latin *complētus,* past participle of *complēre* to fill up, finish.] —**com·plete′ly,** *adv.* —**com·plete′ness,** *n.*

| **Synonyms** | *adj.* **Complete, entire, total,** and **whole** mean having all the appropriate or necessary parts or elements. **Complete** refers to having all the parts needed to function, meet a requirement, or be what is desired: *a complete overhaul of an engine, a complete set in tennis.* **Entire** stresses the size or extent of the thing involved: *an entire prairie covered with wheat.* **Total** suggests the numbering or measurement of parts: *the total inventory of a store.* **Whole** is close to *entire* but suggests the unbroken or undivided nature of the thing in question: *We didn't go out once the whole day.* |

com·ple·tion (kəm plē′shən) *n.* the act of completing or the state of being completed.

com·plex (*adj.*, kəm pleks′, kom′pleks; *n.*, kom′pleks) *adj.*
1. difficult to understand, analyze, or execute; intricate; complicated: *a complex theory, a complex problem.* **2.** consisting of a
combination of related elements or parts: *complex machinery.*
3. (in biochemistry) arising from the combination of simpler substances: *a complex protein.* —*n.* **1.** a whole made up of a
combination of related parts: *The new industrial complex consists
of ten manufacturing companies.* **2.** *Psychiatry.* a group of related
ideas, emotions, memories, or desires that have been partially or
totally repressed, but can influence a person's thoughts and actions to an abnormal degree. **3.** *Informal.* an excessive or unreasonable concern or fear; obsession: *to have a complex about being
late.* **4.** *Chemistry.* coordination compound. [Latin *complexus*
entwined around; hence, complicated, past participle of *complectī*
to embrace, entwine around.] —**com·plex′ly**, *adv.* —**com·
plex′ness**, *n.*

Synonyms Complex, complicated, and intricate mean
having many parts that are not easily distinguished from one another or whose relationship is not easily
understood. **Complex** is used especially in scientific and technical contexts and suggests that careful examination or study is
necessary to determine detail and relationship: *a complex geologic structure, a complex social system.* **Complicated** is less
formal and less technical and stresses the difficulty of understanding or use: *Many students were confused by the complicated
registration process.* **Intricate** suggests elaborate small detail,
difficult to trace one's way through: *an intricate geometric pattern.*

complex fraction, any fraction with a common fraction, mixed
number, or algebraic expression in the numerator, in the denominator, or in both. The fractions $1/2 / 21/8$ and $3/4 / 12/9$ are complex
fractions. Also, **compound fraction.**
com·plex·ion (kəm plek′shən) *n.* **1.** the natural color, texture,
and general appearance of the skin, esp. of the face. **2.** a general
appearance or character; aspect: *The testimony of the witness gave
a new complexion to the case.* [Old French *complexion* appearance,
nature, from Late Latin *complexiō* physical constitution, temperament, from Latin *complexiō* combination, association.]
com·plex·ioned (kəm plek′shənd) *adj.* having a (specified kind
of) complexion. ➡ used in combination, as in *fair-complexioned.*
com·plex·i·ty (kəm plek′si tē) *n., pl.* **-ties. 1.** the state or
quality of being complex. **2.** something that is complex.
complex number, any number written $a + bi$ in which i is the
positive square root of -1 and a and b are real numbers.
complex sentence, any sentence that consists of one independent clause and one or more dependent clauses, for example: *After
we had played tennis for an hour, we decided to go for a swim.*
com·pli·ance (kəm plī′əns) *n.* **1.** the act of complying or
yielding; acquiescence. **2.** a tendency to yield to others. Also,
com·pli′an·cy.
 ·in compliance with. complying with; in accordance with:
They acted in compliance with our request.
com·pli·ant (kəm plī′ənt) *adj.* complying or tending to comply;
yielding; submissive. —**com·pli′ant·ly**, *adv.* —For Synonyms,
see **obedient.**
com·pli·cate (kom′pli kāt′) *v.t.*, **-cat·ed, -cat·ing.** to make
difficult to understand, analyze, or do; make complex. [Latin
complicātus, past participle of *complicāre* to fold together, from
com- with, together + *plicāre* to fold.]
com·pli·cat·ed (kom′pli kā′tid) *adj.* difficult to understand,
analyze, or do; intricate. —**com′pli·cat′ed·ly**, *adv.* —**com′·
pli·cat′ed·ness**, *n.* —For Synonyms, see **complex.**
com·pli·ca·tion (kom′pli kā′shən) *n.* **1.** the act or process of
complicating. **2.** a complicated state or condition; complexity.
3. something that complicates, as an element, detail, or condition.
4. a secondary disease or condition that occurs with and aggravates the primary disease.
com·plic·i·ty (kəm plis′i tē) *n.* the state of being an accomplice,
esp. in wrongdoing: *complicity in fraud.* [French *complicité* conspiracy, participation, going back to Latin *complex* confederate,
participant.]
com·pli·ment (*n.*, kom′plə mənt; *v.*, kom′plə ment′) *n.* **1.** an
expression of admiration or praise; flattering comment: *to receive
compliments on one's cooking.* **2.** **compliments.** an expression of
regard, greeting, or good wishes: *Extend my compliments to your
family. The dessert came with the compliments of the management.*
—*v.t.* **1.** to pay a compliment to. **2.** to present (someone) with
something as a mark of courtesy. [French *compliment* commendation, through Italian and Spanish, going back to Latin *complēmentum* that which completes. Doublet of COMPLEMENT.]
com·pli·men·ta·ry (kom′plə men′tə rē, -trē) *adj.* **1.** containing, expressing, or of the nature of a compliment. **2.** given without
charge; free: *a complimentary ticket to a game.* —**com′pli·men′·
ta·ri·ly**, *adv.* —**com′pli·men′ta·ri·ness**, *n.*

com·plin (kom′plin) *also*, **com·pline** (kom′plin, -plīn). *n.* the
last of the seven canonical hours or the service for it. [Old French
complie this hour, from Late Latin *complēta (hōra)* literally, completed (hour) (because it completed the hours of the service), feminine of Latin *complētus* complete.]
com·ply (kəm plī′) *v.i.*, **-plied, -ply·ing.** to act in accordance,
as with a request, wish, rule, or command. [Italian *complire* to
fulfill,‚suit, from Spanish *cumplir* to accomplish, from Latin *complēre* to fill up, finish.] —**com·pli′er**, *n.*
com·po·nent (kəm pō′nənt) *n.* **1.** a constituent part or element;
ingredient: *the components of a chemical, the components of one's
personality.* **2.** one of the devices, as an amplifier or speaker, that
makes up a hi-fi or video system. —*adj.* being an essential part or
ingredient; serving to constitute: *component parts.* [Latin *com-
pōnēns,* present participle of *compōnere* to put together, arrange.]
—For Synonyms (*n.*), see **ingredient.**
com·port (kəm pôrt′) *v.t.* to behave or conduct (oneself). —*v.i.*
to suit, befit, or agree (with *with*): *The store manager's rude attitude does not comport with the responsibility of the position.* [Late
Latin *comportāre* to behave, from Latin *comportāre* to carry together.]
com·port·ment (kəm pôrt′mənt) *n.* the manner of comporting
oneself; behavior; conduct.
com·pose (kəm pōz′) *v.*, **-posed, -pos·ing.** —*v.t.* **1.** to be the
parts of; make up; constitute: *Twelve jurors compose a jury. The
fabric was composed of synthetic fibers.* **2.** to make or form from
parts or elements: *The debater composed the argument
from four logical statements.* **3.** to create (a musical or literary
work). **4.** to make tranquil or quiet; calm: *It was hard to compose
myself after such a shock.* **5.** to arrange artistically, as the elements
in a painting. **6.** *Printing.* **a.** to set (type). **b.** to set the type for:
The printer composed the page. —*v.i.* to create an artistic work,
esp. a piece of music: *to compose for the piano.* [French *composer*
to make up, form, fashion; alteration (influenced by French *poser*
to place, put) of Latin *compōnere* to put together, arrange.]
com·posed (kəm pōzd′) *adj.* having or showing control of
one's emotions; calm; tranquil. —**com·pos·ed·ly** (kəm pō′zid-
lē), *adv.* —**com·pos′ed·ness**, *n.*
com·pos·er (kəm pō′zər) *n.* a person who composes something, esp. music.
composing stick, a small adjustable tray used by compositors
to gather and assemble type.

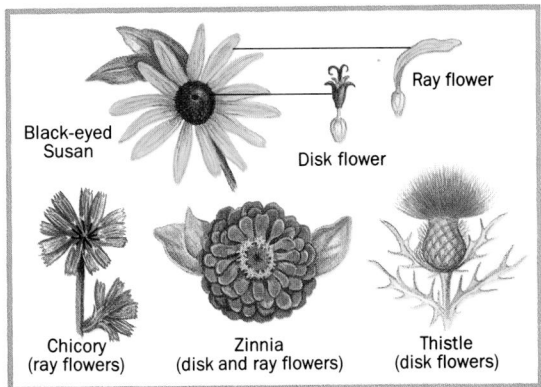

composite flowers

com·pos·ite (kəm poz′it) *adj.* **1.** made up of various parts or
elements. **2.** belonging to the family Compositae, one of the
largest and most highly evolved groups of flowering plants. Composite plants bear dense flower heads composed of many tiny disk
flowers, ray flowers, or both. Daisies and chrysanthemums are
composite flowers. —*n.* **1.** something that is composed of various parts or elements. **2.** a composite plant. **3.** composite photograph. [Latin *compositus,* past participle of *compōnere* to put
together, arrange. Doublet of COMPOST.] —**com·pos′ite·ly**, *adv.*

a	at	e	end	o	hot	u	up	hw	white		about
ā	ape	ē	me	ō	old	ū	use	ng	song		taken
ä	far	i	it	ô	fork	ü	rule	th	thin		pencil
âr	care	ī	ice	oi	oil	u̇	pull	th	this		lemon
		îr	pierce	ou	out	ûr	turn	zh	measure		circus

composite number, a number that can be divided without a remainder by one or more numbers as well as by itself and 1. The numbers 4, 6, 8, 9, and 10 are composite numbers.

composite photograph, a photograph made by combining two or more photographs.

com·po·si·tion (kom′pə zish′ən) *n.* **1.** the act of combining parts or elements in order to form a whole. **2.** the manner in which something is composed; makeup; ingredients: *The chemist analyzed the substance to determine its composition.* **3.** a substance formed by a mixture of various ingredients. **4.** the act, process, or art of creating a musical, literary, or artistic work. **5.** a musical, literary, or artistic work. **6.** a short essay, esp. one written as an exercise for school. **7.** *Printing.* the setting of type. [Old French *composition* a making, framing, from Latin *compositiō* a putting together, connection.] —**com′po·si′tion·al,** *adj.*

com·pos·i·tor (kəm poz′i tər) *n.* typesetter *(def. 1).*

com·post (kom′pōst) *n.* **1.** a mixture of decaying organic matter, soil, and manure used to fertilize and condition soil. **2.** a mixture; compound. —*v.t.* **1.** to use in making compost: *to compost grass clippings.* **2.** to improve (soil) with compost. [Old French *composte* a composition, and *compost* mixture, both going back to Latin *compositus* mixed, past participle of *compōnere* to put together. Doublet of COMPOSITE.]

com·po·sure (kəm pō′zhər) *n.* the state of being calm and in control of oneself; tranquility.

com·pote (kom′pōt) *n.* **1.** a fruit that is stewed or preserved in syrup, usually served as a dessert. **2.** a shallow bowl or dish having a stem, usually used for fruit or candy. [French *compote* stewed fruit, going back to Latin *composita,* feminine past participle of *compōnere* to put together.]

com·pound[1] (*adj.,* kom′pound, kom pound′; *v.,* kəm pound′; *n.,* kom′pound) *adj.* composed of or produced by the union of two or more parts or elements. —*v.t.* **1.** to mix (parts, elements, or ingredients) to form a compound substance: *Early builders compounded water, sand, and soil to form bricks.* **2.** to make by combining various parts, elements, or ingredients: *A pharmacist compounds drugs from prescribed ingredients.* **3.** to compute (compound interest). **4.** to add to; intensify: *She compounded the insult by walking away as he started to speak.* —*n.* **1.** a combination of two or more parts, elements, or ingredients; mixture. **2.** a substance formed by chemical combination of two or more elements in a fixed proportion. A compound has properties different from the elements of which it is made, is held together by chemical bonds, and can be separated into its component parts only by chemical processes. **3.** compound word. [Middle French *compondre* to put together, arrange, from Latin *compōnere,* from *com*-with, together + *pōnere* to put.] —**com·pound′a·ble,** *adj.* —**com·pound′er,** *n.*

• **to compound a felony** (or **crime**). to commit the illegal act of agreeing not to prosecute or disclose a crime, in return for payment or other consideration.

com·pound[2] (kom′pound) *n.* **1.** in eastern Asia, an enclosed area containing a residence, factory, or other buildings owned by Europeans. **2.** any similar enclosed area: *a prison compound.* [Malay *kampong* gathering, enclosure.]

com·pound-com·plex sentence (kom′pound kom pleks′) a sentence that consists of two or more independent clauses and one or more dependent clauses, for example: *One afternoon the tour group divided up, and Catherine and Mike, who have studied archaeology, decided to go to the Egyptian collection at the museum.*

compound eye, an eye, as in many insects, consisting of numerous units, each of which has a lens system and nerve fibers connecting it to the central nervous system.

compound fraction, complex fraction.

compound fracture, a fracture in which the broken bone pierces the flesh and projects through the wound.

compound interest, interest computed on the sum of the principal and previously accrued interest.

compound leaf, a leaf having two or more leaflets on a common leafstalk.

compound microscope, the most common type of optical microscope, having two or more lenses, as an eyepiece and several objectives.

compound eye of a housefly

compound number, a quantity expressed in two or more units or denominations, for example: 5 feet, 10 inches; 7 pounds, 10 ounces; and 4 hours, 17 minutes.

compound sentence, a sentence that consists of two or more independent clauses, usually connected by a conjunction or conjunctions, for example: *We went to the beach on Friday, and we went to the movies on Saturday.*

compound word, a word composed of two or more words that are written as one word, joined together by a hyphen, or written separately. The words *blueberry, fair-haired,* and *elementary school* are compound words.

com·pre·hend (kom′pri hend′) *v.t.* **1.** to grasp mentally; understand fully. **2.** to take in or contain; include; embrace: *The topic I was assigned comprehended all of the major political developments of the year.* [Latin *comprehendere* to grasp, perceive.] —For Synonyms, see **know.**

com·pre·hen·si·ble (kom′pri hen′sə bəl) *adj.* capable of being comprehended; understandable. Also, **com·pre·hen·di·ble** (kom′pri hen′də bəl). —**com′pre·hen·si·bil′i·ty,** *n.* —**com′pre·hen′si·bly,** *adv.*

com·pre·hen·sion (kom′pri hen′shən) *n.* **1.** the act, fact, or power of grasping mentally; understanding. **2.** the act or fact of containing or including; inclusion. [Latin *comprehēnsiō* a seizing, perception.]

com·pre·hen·sive (kom′pri hen′siv) *adj.* **1.** large in scope or content; including much; extensive: *a comprehensive study of the animal life in a region.* **2.** capable of understanding many things: *a comprehensive mind.* —**com′pre·hen′sive·ly,** *adv.* —**com′pre·hen′sive·ness,** *n.*

com·press (*v.,* kəm pres′; *n.,* kom′pres′) *v.t.* to press or squeeze together so as to make more compact; condense. —*n.* **1.** a pad or cloth used to apply cold, heat, moisture, medication, or pressure to some part of the body. **2.** an apparatus for pressing cotton into bales. [Late Latin *compressāre* to press, oppress, from Latin *comprimere* to press together.] —**com·press′i·bil′i·ty,** *n.* —**com·press′i·ble,** *adj.*

com·pressed (kəm prest′) *adj.* **1.** pressed or squeezed together, made more compact. **2.** narrow or flattened laterally or lengthwise, as the body of certain fish or parts of certain plants.

compressed air, air that has been reduced in volume by compression to a pressure greater than that of the atmosphere. The force it exerts upon release can be harnessed to drive machinery, as paint sprayers, pneumatic drills, and the brakes on a train.

com·pres·sion (kəm presh′ən) *n.* **1.** the act or process of compressing or the state of being compressed. **2.** the process by which the volume of a confined gas or vapor mixture is reduced by the application of pressure, as in an internal combustion engine.

com·pres·sive (kəm pres′iv) *adj.* compressing or tending to compress. —**com·pres′sive·ly,** *adv.*

com·pres·sor (kəm pres′ər) *n.* **1.** a machine that compresses a gas so that its expansion may be used as a source of power. **2.** a person or thing that compresses. **3.** a surgical instrument for applying pressure to a part of the body, as to an artery. [Latin *compressor* one who compresses.]

com·prise (kəm prīz′) *also,* **comprize.** *v.t.,* -prised, -pris·ing. to consist of; be composed of; include; contain: *These two books comprise all of the author's published poetry.* [French *compris,* past participle of *comprendre* to include, understand, from Latin *comprehendere* to grasp, perceive.]

com·prize (kəm prīz′) *v.t.* -prized, -priz·ing. comprise.

com·pro·mise (kom′prə mīz′) *n.* **1.** the settlement of a dispute by the partial surrender by each side of claims or demands; adjustment of differences by mutual concessions. **2.** the result of such a settlement. **3.** something intermediate between or combining the characteristics of two different things. —*v.,* -mised, -mis·ing. —*v.i.* to make a compromise: *to compromise on an issue.* —*v.t.* **1.** to settle or adjust (a dispute or differences) by making mutual concessions. **2.** to expose to disrepute, suspicion, or danger: *Their dishonest practices compromised the company's reputation.* [French *compromis* mutual agreement, from Latin *comprōmissum* mutual promise to accept arbitration.] —**com′pro·mis′er,** *n.*

comp·trol·ler (kən trō′lər) *n.* controller *(def. 2).* —**comptrol′ler·ship,** *n.*

com·pul·sion (kəm pul′shən) *n.* **1.** the act of compelling; coercion. **2.** the state of being compelled. **3.** *Psychology.* an irresistible or irrational impulse to perform a particular act. [Late Latin *compulsiō* a driving, urging, from Latin *compellere* to drive together, compel.]

com·pul·sive (kəm pul′siv) *adj.* **1.** of, relating to, or caused or characterized by compulsion: *a compulsive liar, compulsive gambling.* **2.** compulsory; coercive. —**com·pul′sive·ly,** *adv.* —**com·pul′sive·ness,** *n.*

com·pul·so·ry (kəm pul'sə rē) *adj.* **1.** imposed as a requirement or duty; required; obligatory; mandatory. **2.** involving or using force; coercive. —**com·pul'so·ri·ly,** *adv.*

com·punc·tion (kəm pungk'shən) *n.* an uneasiness of mind caused by feelings of remorse or guilt; twinge of conscience; qualm. [Late Latin *compūnctiō* pricking (of conscience), remorse, from Latin *compungere* to prick severely.]

com·pu·ta·tion (kom'pyə tā'shən) *n.* **1.** the act, process, or method of computing. **2.** a result of computing; amount computed. —**com'pu·ta'tion·al,** *adj.*

com·pute (kəm pūt') *v.,* **-put·ed, -put·ing.** —*v.t.* to determine, as an amount or number, by mathematical calculation; calculate. —*v.i.* **1.** to make a computation; reckon. **2.** to use a computer. **3.** *Informal.* to be logical or consistent: *The evidence against the suspect doesn't compute.* [Latin *computāre.* Doublet of COUNT[1].] —**com·put'a·bil'i·ty,** *n.* —**com·put'a·ble,** *adj.* —For Synonyms, see **calculate.**

com·put·er (kəm pū'tər) *n.* **1.** a high-speed electronic device that performs complex mathematical and logical operations, using information and instructions it receives and stores, and then displaying the results on a video screen or on paper. **2.** any device or person that computes.

com·put·er-aid·ed design (kəm pū'tər ā'did) the automated process of generating designs that can be displayed on the screen of a computer.

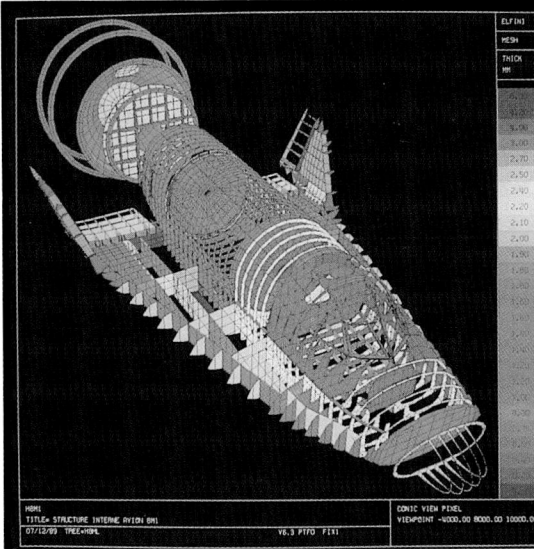

computer-aided design of a spacecraft

computer-aided instruction, the use of computers as a teaching tool.

computer-aided manufacture, the process of manufacturing with machinery that has been programmed to operate by computer.

computer graphics, pictures, charts, diagrams, and other graphic material produced with the aid of a computer.

com·put·er·ize (kəm pū'tə rīz') *v.t.,* **-ized, -iz·ing. 1.** to adapt to, control by, or store in an electronic computer. **2.** to equip with electronic computers: *The company computerized its sales division.* —**com·put'er·i·za'tion,** *n.*

computer language, a set of symbols, such as letters, numerals, and punctuation marks, together with rules for using them, used to communicate instructions to a computer.

computer literacy, understanding of the basic principles of computer hardware and software, together with the ability to use them for practical purposes.

computer science, the study of the theory, design, and application of computer hardware and software.

com·rade (kom'rad, -rəd) *n.* **1.** a close friend or companion. **2.** a person who participates with another or others in a common interest, activity, occupation, or other concern; associate. **3.** a fellow member, as of a political party, esp. the Communist Party. [French *camarade* roommate, companion, from Spanish *camarada,* from *camara* room, from Late Latin *camera.* See CAMERA.] —**com'rade·ly,** *adj.* —**com'rade·ship',** *n.*

Com·sat (kom'sat') *n. Trademark.* communications satellite. [Short for COM(MUNICATIONS) SAT(ELLITE).]

comte (kôNT) *French. n.* count[2].

Co·mus (kō'məs) *n.* in classical mythology, a youthful god of drunken revelry and entertainment.

con[1] (kon) *adv.* against: *The senator weighed the arguments pro and con before voting.* —*n.* a reason, argument, or person against something. [Short for Latin *contrā* against.]

con[2] (kon) *v.t.,* **conned, con·ning. 1.** to peruse, examine, or study carefully. **2.** to learn by such study: *to con a part in a play.* [Old English *cunnian* to try (to know), test.]

con[3] (kon) *also,* **conn.** *Nautical. v.t.,* **conned, con·ning.** to direct the steering of (a vessel). —*n.* the act or post of a person who cons. [Short for obsolete *cond, condue* to conduct, from Old French *conduire* to lead, from Latin *condūcere* to lead to.]

con[4] (kon) *Slang. v.t.,* **conned, con·ning. 1.** to cheat, swindle, or defraud: *The crook conned us out of all our money.* **2.** to trick or dupe: *My friends conned me into buying lunch for everyone.* —*n.* swindle; fraud. —*adj.* involving or using deception or fraud. [From CONFIDENCE.]

con[5] (kon) *n. Slang.* convict. [Short for CONVICT.]

con- *prefix* form of **com-** before all consonants except *b, h, l, m, p, r,* and *w,* as in *concentrate, connote, congenial.*

con. 1. against. **2.** conclusion.

con a·mo·re (kôn ä mô'Rā) *Italian.* **1.** *Music.* tenderly. **2.** with enthusiasm or zeal.

con artist *Informal.* a person who swindles by means of confidence games.

con·cat·e·nate (kon kat'ə nāt') *v.t.,* **-nat·ed, -nat·ing.** to link or join together; connect in a series or chain. —*adj.* joined or linked together. [Late Latin *concatēnātus,* past participle of *concatēnāre* to link together, connect, from Latin *con-* together + *catēna* chain.]

con·cat·e·na·tion (kon kat'ə nā'shən) *n.* **1.** a series of interconnected or interdependent things or events: *a concatenation of causes and effects.* **2.** the act of concatenating or the state of being concatenated.

con·cave (*adj.,* kon kāv', kon'kāv; *n.,* kon'kāv) *adj.* hollow and curving inward like the inside of a circle or bowl. ➡ opposed to **convex.** —*n.* a concave surface. [Latin *concavus* hollow, curved.] —**con·cave'ly,** *adv.* —**con·cave'ness,** *n.*

con·cav·i·ty (kon kav'i tē) *n., pl.* **-ties. 1.** the state of being concave. **2.** a concave surface or space; hollow.

con·ca·vo-con·vex (kon kā'vō kon veks') *adj.* **1.** concave on one side and convex on the other. **2.** of or designating a lens in which the concave face has a greater degree of curvature than the convex face, making the lens thinnest in the middle.

con·ceal (kən sēl') *v.t.* **1.** to put or keep out of sight; hide: *I concealed the key under a flowerpot.* **2.** to keep from the knowledge or observation of others; keep secret: *She concealed her displeasure by smiling. He concealed the truth about the incident.* [Old French *conceler* to hide, from Latin *concēlāre.*] —**con·ceal'a·ble,** *adj.* —**con·ceal'er,** *n.* —For Synonyms, see **hide**[1].

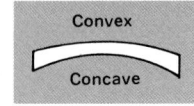

concavo-convex lens

con·ceal·ment (kən sēl'mənt) *n.* **1.** the act of concealing or the state of being concealed. **2.** a means or place for hiding.

con·cede (kən sēd') *v.,* **-ced·ed, -ced·ing.** —*v.t.* **1.** to acknowledge as true, just, or proper; admit: *I'll concede the point you're making. The candidate conceded defeat.* **2.** to acknowledge as won by an opponent before the results have been determined: *to concede an election.* **3.** to grant or yield, as a right or privilege. —*v.i.* to make a concession; yield. [Latin *concēdere* to retire, yield.] —For Synonyms (*v.t.*), see **grant.**

con·ceit (kən sēt') *n.* **1.** a very high opinion of oneself or of one's accomplishments; personal vanity or pride. **2.** a fanciful, ingenious, or witty thought or expression. **3.** an elaborate or extended poetic device, esp. a metaphor. [From CONCEIVE, on the model of the pair *deceit, deceive.*]

con·ceit·ed (kən sē'tid) *adj.* having or showing an excessively high opinion of oneself or of one's accomplishments; vain. —**con·ceit'ed·ly,** *adv.* —**con·ceit'ed·ness,** *n.*

a	at	e	end	o	hot	u	up	hw	white		about
ā	ape	ē	me	ō	old	ū	use	ng	song	ə	taken
ä	far	i	it	ô	fork	th	thin			pencil
âr	care	ī	ice	oi	oil	u̇	pull	th	this		lemon
		îr	pierce	ou	out	ûr	turn	zh	measure		circus

249

con·ceiv·a·ble (kən sē′və bəl) *adj.* capable of being thought of, imagined, or believed; imaginable. —**con·ceiv′a·bil′i·ty,** *n.* —**con·ceiv′a·bly,** *adv.*

con·ceive (kən sēv′) *v.,* **-ceived, -ceiv·ing.** —*v.t.* **1.** to form or develop mentally; plan; devise: *The coach conceived the strategy that won the game for us.* **2.** to have or form a mental image or idea of; imagine: *We could not conceive that they would do such a silly thing.* **3.** to become pregnant with (a child). —*v.i.* **1.** to form a mental image or idea; think (with *of*): *I could not conceive of failure.* **2.** to become pregnant. [Old French *conceveir* to become pregnant, perceive, from Latin *concipere.*] —**con·ceiv′er,** *n.*

con·cen·trate (kon′sən trāt′) *v.,* **-trat·ed, -trat·ing.** —*v.t.* **1.** to bring, draw, or direct to a common center or objective; focus: *The team concentrated its efforts on winning the game.* **2.** to increase the strength, density, or purity of by reducing the amount of or removing that which is undesirable or unnecessary: *to concentrate a fluid.* —*v.i.* **1.** to direct all of one's efforts or attention: *I could not concentrate on my reading because the room was so noisy.* **2.** to come to or toward a common center; converge. **3.** to become stronger, denser, or purer. —*n.* a substance, such as a chemical solution, that has been concentrated. [CON- + Latin *centrum* center + -ATE¹.] —**con′cen·tra′tor,** *n.*

con·cen·tra·tion (kon′sən trā′shən) *n.* **1.** the act or process of concentrating or the state of being concentrated. **2.** close or complete attention fixed on a particular subject or goal: *The successful solution of the problem required patience and concentration.* **3.** something that is concentrated. **4.** the relative strength or amount of a substance, as a solute, per unit volume.

concentration camp, a prison camp used to confine persons considered dangerous or undesirable by a government or military ruler.

con·cen·tric (kən sen′trik) *adj.* (of circles) having a common center. Also, **con·cen′tri·cal.** —**con·cen′tri·cal·ly,** *adv.* —**con·cen·tric·i·ty** (kon′sen tris′i tē), *n.*

con·cept (kon′sept) *n.* a thought or notion, esp. a generalized idea or image formed on the basis of knowledge or experience: *Those bullies have no concept of fair play. The sketch will give you a concept of how the room will look after we rearrange the furniture.* [Late Latin *conceptus* thought, from Latin *conceptus* a collecting, conceiving.] —For Synonyms, see **idea.**

con·cep·tion (kən sep′shən) *n.* **1.** the act or power of forming concepts. **2.** a mental image or idea; concept. **3.** a design; plan. **4.** the act of conceiving or the state of being conceived, as in the womb; fertilization. **5.** something that is so conceived; embryo; fetus.

con·cep·tu·al (kən sep′chü əl) *adj.* of or relating to conception or concepts. —**con·cep′tu·al·ly,** *adv.*

conceptual art, a work of art intended to represent an idea or concept in the mind of the artist rather than a particular object. —**conceptual artist.**

con·cep·tu·al·ize (kən sep′chü ə līz′) *v.,* **-ized, -iz·ing.** —*v.t.* to form a concept or conception of: *It is difficult to conceptualize life on another planet.* —*v.i.* to form a concept or conception.

con·cern (kən sûrn′) *v.t.* **1.** to be of interest or importance to: *Conservation concerns us all.* **2.** to relate to; have to do with: *My question concerns the finances of the group.* **3.** to cause to worry; trouble or distress: *His illness concerns me very much.* **4.** to involve or occupy: *Don't concern yourself about other people's affairs.* ➡ used reflexively or in the passive. —*n.* **1.** something that relates to, interests, or affects someone; affair: *International sales are her special concern. What you do is no concern of mine.* **2.** a feeling of worry or care; solicitude; anxiety: *Concern for the accident victims was expressed by everyone.* **3.** a business organization or establishment; company; firm: *They own the largest manufacturing concern in the area.* [Medieval Latin *concernere* to relate to, from Late Latin *concernere* to mix, from Latin *con-* together + *cernere* to sift, see.] —For Synonyms (*n.*), see **care.**

con·cerned (kən sûrnd′) *adj.* **1.** having or feeling involvement or interest: *I am not concerned in their business affairs.* **2.** having or showing worry; troubled; anxious: *a concerned look.*

con·cern·ing (kən sûr′ning) *prep.* having to do with; relating to; regarding.

con·cert (*n., adj.,* kon′sərt; *v.,* kən sûrt′) *n.* **1.** a public performance of vocal or instrumental music: *a jazz concert, a piano concert.* **2.** accord or harmony, as in plan or action. —*adj.* of, relating to, performing in, or intended for concerts: *a concert pianist, a concert hall.* —*v.t.* to plan or arrange (something) by mutual agreement. —*v.i.* to plan or arrange by mutual agreement. [French *concert* musical performance, harmony, from Italian *concerto,* from *concertare* to bring into harmony; of uncertain origin.]

·in concert. in agreement or accord; all together.

con·cert·ed (kən sûr′tid) *adj.* **1.** involving or carried out by all: *The workers made a concerted effort to finish the job on time. The two armies launched a concerted attack on the enemy.* **2.** *Music.* arranged in parts for voices or instruments. —**con·cert′ed·ly,** *adv.*

con·cer·ti·na (kon′sər tē′nə) *n.* a musical instrument resembling a small accordion, having a bellows and buttonlike keys. [From CONCERT.]

con·cert·mas·ter (kon′sərt mas′tər) *n.* the leader of the first violin section of an orchestra, who serves as assistant to the conductor.

con·cer·to (kən cher′tō) *n., pl.* **-tos** or **-ti** (-tē). a musical composition for a solo instrument or instruments accompanied by an orchestra, usually in three movements. [Italian *concerto* concert, harmony. See CONCERT.]

con·cer·to gros·so (kən cher′tō grō′sō) *pl.* **con·cer·ti gros·si** (kən cher′tē grō′sē). a musical composition for a small group of solo instruments and an orchestra.

con·ces·sion (kən sesh′ən) *n.* **1.** the act of granting or conceding: *Management's concession of a wage increase satisfied the union.* **2.** something granted or conceded: *The workers demanded a number of concessions.* **3.** something, as a grant of land or a business franchise, conceded by a government or other authority. **4.a.** the privilege of operating a business within certain premises. **b.** the business itself or the space it occupies: *The concessions are near the park entrance.* [Latin *concessiō* granting, yielding.]

con·ces·sion·aire (kən sesh′ə nâr′) *n.* a merchant who owns or operates a concession or who has been granted a concession.

con·ces·sive (kən ses′iv) *adj.* **1.** characteristic of or tending toward concession. **2.** *Grammar.* expressing concession. The word *although* is a concessive conjunction.

conch (kongk, konch) *n., pl.* **conchs** (kongks) or **conch·es** (kon′chiz). **1.** any of various tropical saltwater mollusks, having large spiral shells, esp. *Strombus gigas* of the Florida Keys and the West Indies. **2.** the shell of this animal, esp. when used as a horn or to make buttons or cameos. [Latin *concha* shell, mussel, from Greek *konchē.*]

con·choi·dal (kong koi′dəl) *adj. Mineralogy.* smoothly curved, as a freshly broken surface of a substance that has no cleavage, such as quartz or obsidian.

con·chol·o·gy (kong kol′ə jē) *n.* the branch of zoology comprising the study of mollusk shells. [Greek *konchē* shell + -LOGY.] —**con·cho·log·i·cal** (kong′kə loj′i kəl), *adj.*

con·ci·erge (kon′sē ârzh′; *French* kôn syerzh′) *n., pl.* **-ci·erges** (-sē âr′zhiz; *French* -syerzh′). **1.** a person who lives in and takes care of a building, esp. in France, and also checks people entering or leaving. **2.** an employee of a hotel who is in charge of seeing to the special needs of its guests, such as obtaining theater tickets or making dinner reservations. **3.** an employee of an apartment building who checks people entering or leaving and is in charge of certain services for tenants, such as accepting deliveries. [French *concierge,* going back to Latin *conservus* fellow servant.]

con·cil·i·ate (kən sil′ē āt′) *v.t.,* **-at·ed, -at·ing.** **1.** to overcome the hostility or mistrust of; win over; placate: *The only thing that would conciliate the angry customer was a full refund.* **2.** to gain (goodwill or favor) by friendly or pleasing acts. **3.** to make compatible; reconcile. [Latin *conciliātus,* past participle of *conciliāre* to combine, bring together.] —**con·cil′i·a′tion,** *n.* —**con·cil′i·a′tor,** *n.*

con·cil·i·a·to·ry (kən sil′ē ə tôr′ē) *adj.* meant to or tending to conciliate. Also, **con·cil·i·a·tive** (kən sil′ē ā′tiv, -ə tiv).

con·cise (kən sīs′) *adj.* expressing much in few words; terse; compact. [Latin *concīsus* divided, short, past participle of *concīdere* to cut to pieces, from *com-* with, together + *caedere* to cut.] —**con·cise′ly,** *adv.* —**con·cise′ness,** *n.*

> **Synonyms** Concise, succinct, and terse mean brief in expression or using few words. **Concise** suggests the cutting away or removing of all that is not essential: *The article gave all the necessary facts in two concise pages.* **Succinct** implies compressing what is said into the smallest space possible: *How many words would it take to give a succinct summary of the plot?* **Terse** suggests a polished style as well as directness and simplicity: *a writer noted for terse descriptions of characters.*

con·clave (kon′klāv, kong′-) *n.* **1.a.** a private meeting. **b.** a group holding such a meeting. **2.a.** a meeting of the cardinals of the Roman Catholic Church to elect a pope. **b.** the private chamber where the cardinals meet for this purpose. [Medieval Latin *conclave* assembly of cardinals, from Latin *conclāve* room that can be locked, from *con-* together + *clāvis* key.]

con·clude (kən klüd′) *v.,* **-clud·ed, -clud·ing.** —*v.t.* **1.** to bring to an end; finish: *to conclude a speech.* **2.** to arrange or settle

finally: *The two countries concluded a treaty.* **3.** to reach a decision or come to an opinion about: *What do you conclude from the facts?* —*v.i.* **1.** to come to an end; close; terminate: *The campaign concluded with a mass meeting.* **2.** to reach a decision; come to an opinion. [Latin *concludĕre* to shut up, close.] —**con·clud′er,** *n.*

Synonyms *v.t.* **Conclude** and **deduce** mean to come to a realization or decision by thinking logically. **Conclude** stresses arriving at a final judgment: *On studying all the data, the researchers concluded that their hypothesis was incorrect.* **Deduce,** on the other hand, focuses on the reasoning process or the basis for a judgment: *From the darkening sky and increased winds, I deduced that a storm was coming.* For other Synonyms (*v.t.*), see **end.**

con·clu·sion (kən klü′zhən) *n.* **1.** the final part of something; end; termination: *The audience cheered at the conclusion of the speech.* **2.** the closing portion of a discourse, usually containing a summary and opinion of what preceded. **3.** a final arrangement or result; settlement: *The conclusion of the sale took place in the lawyer's office.* **4.** a final decision or opinion arrived at through reasoning: *Our conclusion is that the problem is insoluble.* **5.** *Logic.* the proposition that may be logically inferred from the premises of a syllogism. See **syllogism.** [Latin *conclūsiō* a shutting up, end.]

• **in conclusion.** as a final statement; to sum up.

con·clu·sive (kən klü′siv) *adj.* serving to conclude or decide; ending all doubt; definitive; final. —**con·clu′sive·ly,** *adv.* —**con·clu′sive·ness,** *n.*

con·coct (kon kokt′, kən-) *v.t.* **1.** to prepare by mixing several ingredients: *to concoct a stew with beef, potatoes, and carrots.* **2.** to put together; devise: *We concocted a plan for a surprise party.* [Latin *concoctus,* past participle of *concoquere* to devise; literally, to cook together.] —**con·coct′er;** also, **con·coc′tor,** *n.* —**con·coc′tive,** *adj.*

con·coc·tion (kon kok′shən) *n.* **1.** the act or process of concocting. **2.** something concocted.

con·com·i·tance (kon kom′i təns, kən-) *n.* the state or fact of being concomitant; accompaniment.

con·com·i·tant (kon kom′i tənt, kən-) *adj.* happening together; accompanying; attendant: *concomitant circumstances.* —*n.* an accompanying or attendant state, quality, or circumstance. [Late Latin *concomitāns,* present participle of *concomitārī* to accompany, from Latin *con-* together + *comitārī* to accompany.] —**con·com′i·tant·ly,** *adv.*

con·cord (kon′kôrd, kong′-) *n.* **1.** agreement between persons, nations, or things; accord. **2.** a treaty establishing a state of peace and harmony, esp. between countries. **3.** *Music.* a harmonious combination of tones; consonance. ➡ opposed to **discord.** **4.** *Grammar.* agreement in number, person, gender, or case. [Old French *concorde* agreement, from Latin *concordia* agreement, harmony, going back to *con-* together + *cor* heart.]

con·cord·ance (kon kôr′dəns, kən-) *n.* **1.** the state or fact of being in concord; agreement; harmony. **2.** an alphabetical index of the important words of a book or an author's works, indicating the passages in which the words occur.

con·cord·ant (kon kôr′dənt, kən-) *adj.* being in concord; agreeing; harmonious. —**con·cord′ant·ly,** *adv.*

con·cor·dat (kon kôr′dat) *n.* **1.** a formal agreement; compact; covenant. **2.** a treaty between the Vatican and a secular government concerning the regulation of church affairs. [Medieval Latin *concordatum* agreement, from Latin *concordāre* to agree.]

Con·cord grape, (kong′kərd) a North American grape, a variety of *Vitis labrusca,* having a blue-black color. [From *Concord,* Massachusetts, where it was found.]

con·course (kon′kôrs, kong′-) *n.* **1.** a large, open place where crowds gather, as in a park or a railroad station or other public building. **2.** a large gathering; crowd. **3.** a moving or coming together: *a concourse of ideas.* **4.** a wide street; boulevard. [Old French *concours* meeting, from Latin *concursus* a running together, meeting.]

con·cres·cence (kən kres′əns, kon-) *n.* a growing together of parts, esp. the growing together of cells of an embryo. [Latin *concrēscentia* a growing together.] —**con·cres′cent,** *adj.*

con·crete (*adj., n., v.t., def. 1* kon′krēt, kong′-, kon krēt′, kong′-; *v.t.i., def. 2, v.i.,* kon krēt′, kong-) *adj.* **1.** of or relating to things or events that can be seen, felt, or experienced rather than merely thought about: *A chair is a concrete object.* **2.** of or relating to a specific person, thing, or event; not general; particular: *concrete facts, concrete evidence.* **3.** naming something perceptible or tangible: *The word "soap" is a concrete noun.* ➡ distinguished from **abstract. 4.** made of concrete: *a concrete driveway.* **5.** formed

by the union of particles into a mass; solid. —*n.* a mixture of such substances as crushed stone, gravel, sand, or pebbles cemented together and used for building or paving. —*v.,* **-cret·ed, -cret·ing.** —*v.t.* **1.** to make of or cover with concrete. **2.** to form (something) into a mass; harden. —*v.i.* **1.** to form into a mass; harden. [Latin *concrētus,* past participle of *concrēscere* to grow together, harden.] —**con·crete′ly,** *adv.* —**con·crete′ness,** *n.*

con·cre·tion (kon krē′shen, kong-) *n.* **1.** the act or process of growing together or forming into a mass. **2.** a solidified mass. **3.** *Geology.* a rounded mass of mineral matter formed around a fossil or other nucleus, found in sedimentary rock. **4.** a mass of inorganic matter found in a tissue or cavity of a human body.

con·cu·bi·nage (kon kū′bə nij, kong-) *n.* **1.** cohabitation of a woman with a man out of wedlock. **2.** the state of being a concubine.

con·cu·bine (kong′kyə bīn′, kon′-) *n.* **1.** a woman who cohabits with a man out of wedlock. **2.** in certain polygamous societies, a wife of secondary or inferior rank. [Old French *concubine* woman who lives in concubinage, from Latin *concubīna,* from *con-* with + *cubāre* to lie.]

con·cu·pis·cence (kon kū′pə səns, kong-) *n.* abnormally strong desire, esp. sexual desire. [Late Latin *concupīscentia* great longing, from Latin *concupīscere* to desire greatly.] —**con·cu′pis·cent,** *adj.*

con·cur (kən kûr′) *v.i.,* **-curred, -cur·ring. 1.** to hold the same opinion; agree: *They rarely concur on any issue.* **2.** to act together or cooperate toward the same end: *Scientists from two countries concurred in developing the vaccine.* **3.** to happen at the same time or place; coincide. [Latin *concurrere* to run together, join.]

con·cur·rence (kən kûr′əns) *n.* **1.** the sharing of an opinion; agreement; accord. **2.** an acting together toward the same end; cooperation. **3.** a simultaneous happening; coincidence. **4.** *Geometry.* a point where three or more lines meet.

con·cur·rent (kən kûr′ənt) *adj.* **1.** existing or happening simultaneously: *concurrent events.* **2.** acting in cooperation. **3.** *Law.* being equal in authority to deal with the same matter. **4.** in agreement; harmonious: *concurrent viewpoints.* **5.** coming toward or meeting at the same point. —*n.* something that concurs. —**con·cur′rent·ly,** *adv.*

con·cuss (kən kus′) *v.t.* to cause to have a concussion. [From CONCUSSION.]

con·cus·sion (kən kush′ən) *n.* **1.** a violent shaking or shock. **2.** an injury produced by a severe blow to the brain or spinal cord. [Latin *concussiō* a shaking.] —**con·cus·sive** (kən kus′iv) *adj.*

con·demn (kən dem′) *v.t.* **1.** to express strong disapproval of; censure. **2.** to show or declare the guilt of; convict. **3.** to pronounce the punishment of; sentence: *The judge condemned the criminal to ten years in jail.* **4.** to declare unfit for use: *The building was condemned and torn down.* **5.** *Law.* to appropriate (private property) for public use under the right of eminent domain. [Latin *condemnāre* to sentence, censure.] —**con·dem·na·ble** (kən dem′nə bəl, -dem′ə-), *adj.* —**con·demn′er,** *n.*

con·dem·na·tion (kon′dem nā′shən, -dəm-) *n.* **1.** the act of condemning or the state of being condemned. **2.** strong disapproval or censure. **3.** a cause or reason for condemning. —**con·dem·na·to·ry** (kən dem′nə tôr′ē), *adj.*

con·den·sate (kon′dən sāt′, kən den′sāt) *n.* the liquid formed when a gas or vapor condenses; distillate.

con·den·sa·tion (kon′den sā′shən, -dən-) *n.* **1.** the act or process of condensing or the state of being condensed. **2.** a product of condensing. **3.a.** the reduction of a gas or vapor to a liquid or solid form: *the condensation of steam into water.* **b.** a product of this process, as dew; condensate. **4.** *Chemistry.* a reaction between two or more molecules, in which a larger molecule is formed, often with the elimination of a simple molecule, as water.

con·dense (kən dens′) *v.,* **-densed, -dens·ing.** —*v.t.* **1.** to make denser or more compact; reduce the volume of: *to condense a sauce by boiling it.* **2.** to make more concise; abridge: *to condense a report into a series of recommendations.* **3.** to reduce (a gas or vapor) to a liquid or solid form. **4.** to make (light rays) more intense; concentrate. —*v.i.* to become condensed. [Latin *condēnsāre* to make very dense.] —**con·den·sa·bil·i·ty;** also, **con·den′si·bil′i·ty,** *n.* —**con·den′sa·ble;** also, **con·den′si·ble,** *adj.*

condensed milk, cow's milk thickened by evaporating part of the water content and sweetened with sugar, used esp. in cooking.

a	at	e	end	o	hot	u	up	hw	white		about
ā	ape	ē	me	ō	old	ū	use	ng	song	ə	taken
ä	far	i	it	ô	fork	ü	rule	th	thin		pencil
âr	care	ī	ice	oi	oil	u̇	pull	<u>th</u>	this		lemon
				îr	pierce	ou	out	ûr	turn	zh	measure		circus

con·dens·er (kən den′sər) *n.* **1.** a person or thing that condenses. **2.** capacitor. **3.** an apparatus for changing a gas or vapor into a liquid. For illustration, see **distillation**. **4.** a lens, lens system, or mirror that concentrates light upon a small area, used as in viewing something under a microscope.

con·de·scend (kon′di send′) *v.i.* **1.** to lower oneself to do something beneath one's dignity or position, esp. willingly or graciously: *The physicist condescended to explain the theory to the audience in simple language.* **2.** to assume a superior or patronizing manner in dealing with those one considers inferior. [French *condescendre* to yield, grant, from Late Latin *condēscendere* to grant, stoop, from Latin *con-* together + *dēscendere* to come down.]

con·de·scend·ing (kon′di sen′ding) *adj.* characterized by condescension. —**con′de·scend′ing·ly,** *adv.*

con·de·scen·sion (kon′di sen′shən) *n.* **1.** an act or instance of condescending. **2.** a superior or patronizing attitude or manner. [Late Latin *condēscēnsiō,* from *condēscendere.* See CONDESCEND.]

con·dign (kən dīn′) *adj.* (esp. of punishment) deserved; adequate; fitting. [Old French *condigne* very worthy, from Latin *condignus.*]

con·di·ment (kon′də mənt) *n.* something added to food to make it more flavorful, such as a seasoning, spice, or sauce. [Latin *condīmentum.*]

con·di·tion (kən dish′ən) *n.* **1.** the particular manner of existence of a person or thing; state of being: *The condition of the land is poor for planting. My old coat is in shabby condition.* **2.** a state of health: *The accident victim's condition was described as serious.* **3.** a state of physical fitness: *Athletes must be in top condition.* **4.** something essential to the existence of something else; prerequisite: *Oxygen and hydrogen are conditions of life on earth.* **5.** something that restricts, limits, or modifies something else; qualification: *You may go only under certain conditions.* **6. conditions.** circumstances that affect or influence a mode of existence or activity: *Road conditions were hazardous after the ice storm.* **7.** something required for the fulfillment or effectiveness of an agreement; provision; stipulation: *We bought the house with the condition that it would be repainted.* **8.** a social position or status; rank. **9.** *Grammar.* a dependent clause of a conditional sentence. **10.** a requirement that a student with an unsatisfactory grade do special work to receive credit for a course. **11.** *Informal.* disease; ailment: *a heart condition.* —*v.t.* **1.** to put in a fit or proper state: *Regular exercise conditions the body.* **2.** to make conditional; limit (with *on* or *upon*): *She conditioned her acceptance of the favor on his coming to dinner next week.* **3.** *Psychology.* to develop behavior patterns in by repeatedly exposing to certain conditions or stimuli with which responses become associated. **4.** to accustom (someone) to something: *Living in Alaska soon conditioned us to cold weather.* **5.** to give a condition to (a student): *I was conditioned in geometry.* [Old French *condicion* physical or moral state, Latin *condiciō, conditiō* agreement, situation.] —For Synonyms *(n.),* see **circumstance.**

·on condition that. given a certain circumstance or circumstances; if: *You may go on condition that you come home early.*

con·di·tion·al (kən dish′ə nəl) *adj.* **1.** depending on, subject to, or implying a condition or conditions; not absolute: *The sale of the painting was conditional on the expert's agreement that it was by Rembrandt.* **2.** expressing a condition, as the clause *If you go* in the sentence *If you go, I will go too.* —*n.* a tense, word, clause, or mood expressing a condition. —**con·di′tion·al·ly,** *adv.*

con·di·tioned (kən dish′ənd) *adj.* **1.** having or subject to a condition or conditions: *Their answers to the question were tentative and conditioned.* **2.** in good physical condition; fit. **3.** *Psychology.* having developed specific responses or reflexes through conditioning.

conditioned reflex, any automatic response to a stimulus that did not originally evoke the response, developed through a process of psychological conditioning that links the two stimuli.

con·di·tion·er (kən dish′ə nər) *n.* **1.** a person or thing that conditions. **2.** a substance added or applied to something to maintain or improve its condition: *The shampoo contains a conditioner for dry hair.*

con·do (kon′dō) *n., pl.* **-dos.** *Informal.* condominium *(def. 1).*

con·dole (kən dōl′) *v.i.,* **-doled, -dol·ing.** to express sympathy; mourn (with *with*): *We condoled with them over their loss.* [Late Latin *condolēre* to suffer with, from Latin *con-* with + *dolēre* to grieve.]

con·do·lence (kən dō′ləns) *n.* **1.** sympathy with someone suffering grief or sorrow. **2.** an expression of sympathy: *They sent their condolences when my father died.*

con·dom (kon′dəm) *n.* a sheath used to cover the penis during sexual intercourse to help prevent the spread of sexually transmitted diseases and sometimes as a method of birth control. Also, **prophylactic.** [Of uncertain origin.]

con·do·min·i·um (kon′də min′ē əm) *n., pl.* **-i·ums. 1.a.** an apartment house in which apartments are owned by the individual tenants. **b.** an apartment in such a building. **2.** joint control or sovereignty, esp. by two or more countries. **3.** a dominion or territory governed jointly. [Modern Latin *condominium,* from Latin *con-* with + *dominium* lordship, rule.]

con·done (kən dōn′) *v.t.,* **-doned, -don·ing.** to accept or excuse (something) that one does not approve of without offering protest or criticism: *By not punishing them, it appears that you condone their behavior.* [Latin *condōnāre* to give up, forgive.] —**con·don′a·ble,** *adj.* —**con·do·na·tion** (kon′dō nā′shən, -də-), *n.* —**con·don′er,** *n.* —For Synonyms, see **excuse.**

con·dor (kon′dər, -dôr) *n.* **1.** a South American vulture that is the largest extant flying bird, *Vultur gryphus,* native to the Andes and having black-and-white plumage, a white ruff, and a bare, dark gray head and neck. Wingspan: to 10 feet (3 meters). **2.** California condor. [Spanish *cóndor,* from Quechua *cuntur.*]

California **condor**

con·duce (kən düs′, -dūs′) *v.i.,* **-duced, -duc·ing.** to help bring about; lead (with *to* or *toward*): *Your pleasant manner will conduce to a good working relationship.* [Latin *condūcere* to lead to, bring together.]

con·du·cive (kən dü′siv, -dū′-) *adj.* helping bring about; contributing; leading (with *to*): *A brisk walk is conducive to good appetite.* —**con·du′cive·ness,** *n.*

con·duct (*n.,* kon′dukt; *v.,* kən dukt′) *n.* **1.** the way that a person behaves; personal behavior; deportment: *The children's conduct at the party was very good.* **2.** administration or management, esp. of a business. **3.** the act of leading; guidance. —*v.t.* **1.** to take charge of; manage: *The treasurer conducted the financial affairs of the company.* **2.** to direct or lead (an orchestra, chorus, or other musical group): *Who will conduct the orchestra next season?* **3.** to behave or comport (oneself): *to conduct oneself in a gracious manner.* **4.** to act as an escort; lead; guide: *My cousin conducted us to the station.* **5.** to serve as a medium for; transmit, as heat, electricity, or sound: *The drainpipe conducts water from the gutters.* —*v.i.* to act as a conductor. [Latin *conductus,* past participle of *condūcere* to lead to, bring together.] —**con·duct′i·bil′i·ty,** *n.* —**con·duct′i·ble,** *adj.* —For Synonyms *(n.),* see **behavior.**

con·duct·ance (kən duk′təns) *n.* the property that allows a material to conduct electric current; the reciprocal of resistance, expressed in siemens or mhos.

con·duc·tion (kən duk′shən) *n.* **1.** the flow, as of heat, electricity, or sound, in a medium by the transmission of energy from one particle of the medium to another. **2.** the act of conveying; transmission.

con·duc·tive (kən duk′tiv) *adj.* **1.** having conductivity. **2.** characteristic of or resulting from conduction.

con·duc·tiv·i·ty (kon′duk tiv′i tē) *n.* **1.** the ability of a material to conduct heat, electricity, or sound. **2.** a measure of the conductance of a given material.

con·duc·tor (kən duk′tər) *n.* **1.** a person who conducts; director; guide; leader. **2.** the director of an orchestra, chorus, or other musical group, who is responsible for interpreting the music, rehearsing the musicians, and leading the performance. **3.** a person employed to collect tickets or fares and announce stops on a railroad train, streetcar, or bus. **4.** a material or object that conducts or can conduct energy, as electricity, heat, or sound. —**con·duc·to·ri·al** (kon′duk tôr′ē əl), *adj.*

con·duit (kon′dit, -dü it, -dū-) *n.* **1.** a channel, pipe, or tube

used to convey liquids. **2.** a tube or similar structure that serves as a protective passage for electrical wires or cables. [Old French *conduit* thing that conducts, escort, from Medieval Latin *conductus* escort, canal, from Latin *condūcere* to lead to.]

con·dy·larth (kon′də lärth′) *n.* any of a group of extinct primitive ungulates, order Condylarthra, of early Tertiary geologic time, from which modern hoofed mammals are believed to have evolved. [Modern Latin *Condylarthra,* from Greek *kóndylos* a knuckle + *árthra,* plural of *árthron* joint.]

con·dyle (kon′dīl, -dil) *n. Anatomy.* any rounded knob at the end of a bone, often forming a joint with the concave part of another bone. [French *condyle,* from Latin *condylus* knuckle, from Greek *kóndylos.*]

cone (kōn) *n.* **1.** *Geometry.* **a.** a solid whose base is a circle, whose vertex is a point in another plane, and whose surface consists of all the straight lines between the vertex and the circumference of the base. **b.** a surface generated by a straight line passing through the vertex and traced along any simple closed curve in another plane. **c.** any solid with such a surface and a base formed by the intersection of the surface and a plane. **2.** an object or mass shaped like a cone: *an ice-cream cone, a volcanic cone.* **3.** a generally cone-shaped reproductive structure of a gymnosperm, as most evergreen trees, consisting of a mass of symmetrically arranged scales bearing seeds or pollen. **4.** a cell in the retina of the eye that is sensitive to color and bright light. [French *cône,* from Latin *cōnus,* from Greek *kōnos.*]

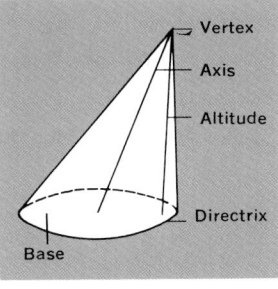

cone

cone·nose (kōn′nōz′) *n.* any of a group of bloodsucking bugs, family Reduviidae, of the southern United States and tropical America, having a conelike base on the sucking beak. Some, esp. members of the genus *Triatoma,* transmit diseases to humans.

Con·es·to·ga wagon (kon′ə stō′gə) a covered wagon with an arched canvas top and broad wheels, formerly used for transportation across the prairies. For illustration, see **covered wagon.** [From *Conestoga,* Pennsylvania, where it was first made.]

co·ney (kō′nē) *n., pl.* **-neys. 1.** a fish of the sea bass family, *Epinephelus fulvus,* found in the seas of tropical America. **2.** cony.

con·fab (*n.,* kon′fab; *v.,* kən fab′, kon′fab) *Informal. n.* chat. —*v.i.,* **-fabbed, -fab·bing.** to chat; confabulate.

con·fab·u·late (kən fab′yə lāt′) *v.i.,* **-lat·ed, -lat·ing.** to talk together casually and informally; chat. [Latin *confābulātus,* past participle of *confābulārī,* from *con-* together + *fābula* story.] —**con·fab′u·la′tion,** *n.* —**con·fab′u·la′tor,** *n.* —**con·fab·u·la·to·ry** (kən fab′yə lə tôr′ē), *adj.*

con·fect (kən fekt′) *v.t.* to make by mixing or putting together various elements: *to confect a cake, to confect a story.*

con·fec·tion (kən fek′shən) *n.* **1.** any sweet mixture or delicacy, as a pastry or preserve. **2.** a frilly or stylish article of women's clothing. [Latin *confectiō* preparation.]

con·fec·tion·er (kən fek′shə nər) *n.* a person or business that makes or sells confections, as candy or sweet pastry.

confectioners' sugar, finely powdered sugar to which cornstarch has been added, made by pulverizing granulated sugar.

con·fec·tion·er·y (kən fek′shə ner′ē) *n., pl.* **-er·ies. 1.** a place where confections are made or sold, esp. an ice-cream or candy shop. **2.** candies or sweets; confections collectively. **3.** the work of a confectioner.

con·fed·er·a·cy (kən fed′ər ə sē) *n., pl.* **-cies. 1.** a union of countries, states, or persons joined to further a mutual aim; league; alliance. **2. the Confederacy.** Confederate States of America. **3.** a group joined together for evil or unlawful purpose; conspiracy.

con·fed·er·ate (*n., adj.,* kən fed′ər it; *v.,* kən fed′ə rāt′) *n.* **1.** an individual or group associated with another for a mutual purpose; ally. **2. Confederate.** a citizen or supporter of the Confederate States of America. **3.** a person in league with another in a plot; accomplice. —*v.t., v.i.,* **-at·ed, -at·ing.** to unite in a confederacy. —*adj.* **1.** united in a league or alliance. **2. Confederate.** having to do with the Confederate States of America. [Latin *confoederātus,* past participle of *confoederāre* to unite in a league.]

Confederate States of America, the political union formed by the eleven Southern states that seceded from the United States in 1860-61 and included Alabama, Arkansas, Florida, Georgia, Louisiana, Mississippi, North Carolina, South Carolina, Tennessee, Texas, and Virginia.

con·fed·er·a·tion (kən fed′ə rā′shən) *n.* **1.** the act of confederating or the state of being confederated. **2.** an association for a mutual purpose, esp. a group of states joined in a relatively permanent alliance. **3. the Confederation.** the union of the thirteen American states from 1781 to 1789, under the Articles of Confederation.

con·fer (kən fûr′) *v.,* **-ferred, -fer·ring.** —*v.i.* to consult together; deliberate: *The committee conferred for three hours before taking a vote.* —*v.t.* to grant, esp. as an honor; bestow (with *on* or *upon*): *The university conferred its highest degree on the author.* [Latin *conferre.*] —**con·fer′ment, con·fer′ral,** *n.* —**con·fer′rer,** *n.* —For Synonyms, see **consult, give.**

con·fer·ee (kon′fə rē′) *n.* **1.** a person who takes part in a conference. **2.** a person on whom something is conferred.

con·fer·ence (*defs. 1-3* kon′fər əns, -frəns; *def. 4* kən fûr′əns) *n.* **1.** a meeting of persons for the purpose of deliberating or discussing something: *The conference on international economic problems met in Geneva.* **2.** a meeting of members from the two houses of a legislature to resolve differences, as between similar bills from each house. **3.** an association of organized groups, as of schools, churches, or athletic teams. **4.** the act of conferring.

conference call, a telephone call, as among business people, in which several people talk with each other on the same line at the same time.

con·fess (kən fes′) *v.t.* **1.** to disclose, esp. something personal that has been kept secret. **2.** to acknowledge as being true; concede; admit: *I must confess that I was wrong.* **3.** to declare (one's faith or belief). **4.a.** to disclose (one's sins) to a priest so as to be absolved. **b.** (of a priest) to hear the confession of (someone wishing to be absolved of a sin or sins); act as a confessor to. —*v.i.* **1.** to admit or disclose one's guilt. **2.a.** to disclose one's sins to a priest. **b.** to act as a confessor. [Old French *confesser* to acknowledge, confess sins, from Late Latin *confessāre,* from Latin *confitērī.*] —For Synonyms, see **admit.**

con·fess·ed·ly (kən fes′id lē) *adv.* by confession or admission; avowedly.

con·fes·sion (kən fesh′ən) *n.* **1.** the act of confessing; acknowledgment, esp. of guilt. **2.** something that is confessed, esp. a written statement of what is confessed. **3.** the act of telling one's sins to a priest so as to be absolved of them. **4.a.** confession of faith. **b.** a religious group adhering to a common confession of faith; denomination.

con·fes·sion·al (kən fesh′ə nəl) *n.* a small compartment in a church where a priest hears confessions. —*adj.* of or relating to confession.

confession of faith 1. an affirmation of religious belief, esp. as accompanying or preceding a sacrament. **2.** a declaration of the beliefs of a church; creed.

con·fes·sor (kən fes′ər) *n.* **1.** a priest who hears confessions and grants absolution. **2.** a person who confesses. **3.** a person persecuted but not martyred for professing adherence to Christianity.

con·fet·ti (kən fet′ē) *n.* small bits or strips of paper that may be thrown about as a sign of celebration. [Italian *confetti,* plural of *confetto* confection, candy, from Medieval Latin *confectum,* going back to Latin *conficere* to prepare, from *com-* with, together + *facere* to make. Originally at carnival time in Italy confections, or small candies, were tossed about; later applied to bits of colored paper.]

con·fi·dant (kon′fi dant′, -dänt′, kon′fi dant′, -dänt′) *n.* a person to whom one's most private affairs or secrets are disclosed and entrusted.

con·fi·dante (kon′fi dant′, -dänt′, kon′fi dant′, -dänt′) *n.* a female confidant.

con·fide (kən fīd′) *v.,* **-fid·ed, -fid·ing.** —*v.t.* **1.** to disclose with the expectation of secrecy: *She confided her fears to him.* **2.** to give into another's care; entrust for safekeeping. —*v.i.* **1.** to disclose private affairs or secrets (with *in*): *to confide in a friend.* **2.** to put trust or have faith (with *in*): *I confide in your good judgment.* [Latin *confīdere* to trust in, rely on.] —**con·fid′er,** *n.*

con·fi·dence (kon′fi dəns) *n.* **1.** firm trust or reliance: *to have confidence in someone's honesty.* **2.** a feeling of certainty; assurance: *Knowing they were willing to help gave me confidence.*

a	at	e	end	o	hot	u	up	hw	white		about
ā	ape	ē	me	ō	old	ū	use	ng	song		taken
ä	far	i	it	ô	fork	ü	rule	th	thin	ə	pencil
âr	care	ī	ice	oi	oil	ु	pull	th	this		lemon
		îr	pierce	ou	out	ûr	turn	zh	measure		circus

253

3. faith in one's own competence; self-assurance. **4.** something disclosed in trust; secret. [Latin *confīdentia* firm trust in something.]
• **in confidence.** privately and with reliance on another's good faith in keeping one's secrets.

Synonyms **Confidence** and **assurance** mean belief or faith in oneself or one's abilities. **Confidence** is the broader term, suggesting belief but not necessarily certainty: *I have confidence that I'll pass the test, but I'm still planning to study for it.* **Assurance** implies a stronger belief, to the point of complete absence of doubt, and sometimes suggests arrogance: *Your assurance that you know all the answers is hard to put up with.* For other Synonyms, see **trust.**

confidence game, a swindle carried out by gaining the confidence of the victim.
confidence man, a swindler who carries out a confidence game.
con·fi·dent (kon′fi dənt) *adj.* **1.** firmly assured; certain; sure: *I'm confident that we will get the contract for the job.* **2.** having faith in one's own competence; self-assured. —*n.* confidant. —**con′fi·dent·ly,** *adv.*
con·fi·den·tial (kon′fi den′shəl) *adj.* **1.** originated or maintained in strict secrecy or privacy: *confidential files.* **2.** indicating intimacy or readiness to disclose matters of a secret nature: *a confidential tone.* **3.** entrusted with secret or private matters: *a confidential secretary.* —**con′fi·den′ti·al′i·ty, con′fi·den′tial·ness,** *n.* —**con′fi·den′tial·ly,** *adv.*
con·fid·ing (kən fī′ding) *adj.* tending to confide; trusting. —**con·fid′ing·ly,** *adv.*
con·fig·u·ra·tion (kən fig′yə rā′shən) *n.* **1.** the relative arrangement of the parts of something. **2.** the form or shape resulting from such an arrangement: *The miners examined the configuration of the southern plateau.* [Late Latin *configūrātiō* conformation, from Latin *configūrāre* to fashion after something.] —**con·fig′u·ra′tion·al, con·fig·u·ra·tive** (kən fig′yər ə tiv), *adj.*
con·fine (*v.,* kən fīn′; *n.,* kon′fīn) *v.t.,* **-fined, -fin·ing. 1.** to keep within limits; restrict: *Please confine your discussion to that particular book.* **2.** to restrict to a particular place; keep or shut in: *Illness confined me to bed. The criminal was confined to prison.* —*n.* usually, **confines.** limit; boundary; border: *The dog was not permitted within the confines of the house.* [French *confiner* to border on, imprison, from *confin* border, going back to Latin *confīne.*] —**con·fin′er,** *n.*
con·fine·ment (kən fīn′mənt) *n.* **1.** the act of confining or the state of being confined. **2.** imprisonment. **3.** the state or time of being confined to bed because of childbirth; lying-in.
con·firm (kən fûrm′) *v.t.* **1.** to determine the validity of; verify: *I telephoned to confirm the train schedule.* **2.** to make binding by formal or authoritative approval; ratify: *The Senate confirmed the judge's nomination to the Supreme Court.* **3.** to make firm or firmer; strengthen, as a belief, resolution, or desire: *The experience confirmed my opinion.* **4.** to admit to full membership in a church or synagogue by administering the ceremony of confirmation to. [Old French *confermer* to make firm, from Latin *confirmāre.*] —**con·firm′a·ble,** *adj.*

Synonyms **Confirm, corroborate, substantiate,** and **authenticate** mean to establish the truth or genuineness of something. **Confirm** generally suggests removing all doubt: *The rash confirmed the diagnosis of measles.* **Corroborate** suggests agreement with or the strengthening of existing evidence or a theory, rather than the final confirmation of it: *The new testimony corroborated the defendant's account.* **Substantiate** is used of information that strongly supports or proves some theory, belief, or statement: *The figures substantiate my claim.* **Authenticate** is used of establishing something questionable, especially a physical object, as genuine: *Exhibits in a court case must be authenticated by a witness.*

con·fir·ma·tion (kon′fər mā′shən) *n.* **1.** the act of confirming or the state of being confirmed. **2.** something that confirms; proof. **3.a.** a Christian rite whereby a baptized person, usually at a specified age, is admitted to full membership in a church. **b.** a ceremony formally admitting a person to full membership in the Jewish community, performed esp. among Reform Jews.
con·firm·a·to·ry (kən fûr′mə tôr′ē) *adj.* serving to confirm; confirming. Also, **con·firm′a·tive.**
con·firmed (kən fûrmd′) *adj.* **1.** firmly established; verified or proved: *We have confirmed hotel reservations.* **2.** firmly settled in a habit or condition; steadfast: *a confirmed bachelor.* **3.** having undergone the religious rite of confirmation. —**con·firm·ed·ly** (kən fûr′mid lē), *adv.*
con·fis·cate (kon′fis kāt′) *v.t.,* **-cat·ed, -cat·ing. 1.** to seize for the public use or treasury, esp. as a penalty: *The authorities confiscated the smuggled goods.* **2.** to seize by or as by authority: *The teacher confiscated all the water pistols from the students.*

—*adj.* seized by or as by authority. [Latin *confiscātus,* past participle of *confiscāre* to put in a chest, place in the treasury, appropriate, from *con-* together + *fiscus* chest, treasury.] —**con′fis·ca′tion,** *n.* —**con′fis·ca′tor,** *n.*
con·fis·ca·to·ry (kən fis′kə tôr′ē) *adj.* having to do with or characterized by confiscation: *a confiscatory tax.*
con·fla·gra·tion (kon′flə grā′shən) *n.* a very large and destructive fire. [Latin *conflagrātiō.*]
con·flict (*n.,* kon′flikt; *v.,* kən flikt′) *n.* **1.** a struggle between two forces; battle; war. **2.** a clash or opposition of ideas, views, or interests; disagreement: *a conflict between two accounts of a car accident.* **3.** an emotional disturbance caused by the struggle of opposing impulses or desires within an individual: *to have a conflict about one's career aims.* —*v.i.* **1.** to be directly opposed or incompatible; clash. **2.** *Archaic.* to struggle; battle; contend. [Latin *conflīctus* a striking together, fight.]

Synonyms *v.i.* **Conflict** and **clash** mean to disagree or oppose one another. **Conflict** is used generally of direct contradiction or inconsistency: *The transcript of the interview conflicts with the tape recording. The meeting conflicts with my work schedule.* **Clash** suggests a lack of harmony: *The two countries' interests clashed in the Middle East. The couple's tastes clashed so strongly that they could not agree on what furniture to buy. The skirt clashes with the blouse.* It is also used of a single incident within a conflict: *The longtime rivals clashed once more in the championship game.* For other Synonyms *(n.),* see **fight.**

conflict of interest, a conflict that may arise between the duties of an office or position and the opportunities that go with that office or position. For example, a legislator who holds stock in a corporation may face a conflict between the public good and his or her own financial interests if a law affecting that corporation's business is to be voted on.
con·flu·ence (kon′flü əns) *n.* **1.a.** the flowing together of two or more bodies of water: *a confluence of streams.* **b.** the point at which this occurs. **c.** the body of water resulting from this flowing together. **2.** a coming together of people or things; crowd; throng.
con·flu·ent (kon′flü ənt) *adj.* flowing or running together; blending into one: *confluent rivers.* —*n.* a confluent stream. [Latin *confluēns,* present participle of *confluere* to flow together.]
con·flux (kon′fluks) *n.* confluence.
con·form (kən fôrm′) *v.i.* **1.** to act in accordance with an established rule or standard: *to conform to fashion.* **2.** to be the same or very similar; correspond: *The house conformed to the architect's plans.* **3.** to be in accord; comply (with *to*): *to conform to the terms of a contract.* **4.** in English history, to comply with the principles and requirements of the Church of England. —*v.t.* to bring into agreement; make the same: *to conform a copy with the original.* [Old French *conformer* to fit with, comply with, from Latin *conformāre* to fashion, form.] —**con·form′er,** *n.*
con·form·a·ble (kən fôr′mə bəl) *adj.* **1.** corresponding; similar. **2.** in agreement; harmonious. **3.** tending or willing to conform; obedient; submissive. —**con·form′a·ble·ness,** *n.* —**con·form′a·bly,** *adv.*
con·for·mal (kən fôr′məl) *adj.* **1.** relating to, designating, or using a cartographic projection that shows the true shape of small areas: *a conformal map.* **2.** *Mathematics.* of or relating to a transformation of one set of curves to another in which corresponding angles remain equal.
con·form·ance (kən fôr′məns) *n.* conformity.
con·for·ma·tion (kon′fôr mā′shən) *n.* **1.** the way in which the parts of something are arranged; shape or structure. **2.** a symmetrical arrangement of the parts of something. **3.** the act of conforming or the state of being conformed.
con·form·ism (kən fôr′miz əm) *n.* the belief or practice of a conformist.
con·form·ist (kən fôr′mist) *n.* **1.** a person who conforms. **2.** in English history, a person who complies with the usages of the Church of England.
con·form·i·ty (kən fôr′mi tē) *n., pl.* **-ties. 1.** the state of agreeing in form or manner; correspondence. **2.** action or thought in accordance with an established rule or standard. **3.** in English history, compliance with the usages of the Church of England. Also, **conformance.**
con·found (kən found′, kon-) *v.t.* **1.** to cause to feel confused, as to be unable to act; bewilder; disconcert: *The conflicting news reports about the extent of the damage from the earthquake confounded us.* **2.** to mistake (one thing) for another; fail to distinguish between; confuse: *to confound a dream for reality.* **3.** to damn. ➡ used as a mild oath: *Confound it!* **4.** *Archaic.* to put to shame; abash. **5.** *Archaic.* to defeat or overthrow; destroy. [Old French *confondre* to overturn, destroy, from Latin *confundere* to pour together, mix, overwhelm.]

con·found·ed (kən foun′did, kon-) *adj.* **1.** confused; bewildered. **2.** damned. ➡ used as a mild oath. —**con·found′ed·ly,** *adv.*

con·fra·ter·ni·ty (kon′frə tûr′ni tē) *n., pl.* **-ties. 1.** a group of men united for a common purpose or in a common profession. **2.** a lay brotherhood united for some religious or charitable purpose. [Medieval Latin *confraternitas* brotherhood, going back to Latin *con-* together + *frāter* brother.]

con·frere (kon′frâr) *n.* a fellow member, as of a professional group; colleague. [Old French *confrere* member of the same society or association, from Medieval Latin *confrater,* from Latin *con-* together + *frāter* brother.]

con·front (kən frunt′) *v.t.* **1.** to come face to face with; stand facing: *Turning the corner, we found ourselves confronting a wall.* **2.** to face boldly or with defiance: *to confront an enemy.* **3.** to bring face to face: *The police officer confronted the speeder with a summons.* **4.** to place together for comparison. [French *confronter,* going back to Latin *con-* together + *frōns* forehead.] —**con·fron·ta·tion** (kon′frun tā′shən), *n.* —**con·fron·ta′·tion·al,** *adj.*

Con·fu·cian (kən fū′shən) *adj.* of or having to do with the Chinese philosopher Confucius, his teachings, or his followers. —*n.* an adherent of Confucianism.

Con·fu·cian·ism (kən fū′shə niz′əm) *n.* an ethical system based on the teachings of the Chinese philosopher Confucius and his followers, emphasizing maintenance of peace, harmony, and justice through an elaborate social etiquette and through duties toward ancestors, family, and friends. —**Con·fu′cian·ist,** *n., adj.*

con·fuse (kən fūz′) *v.t.,* **-fused, -fus·ing. 1.** to create uncertainty in the mind of; bewilder; perplex: *The maze of highways confused me, and I took the wrong road.* **2.** to throw into disorder; mix; jumble: *to confuse the issues of an argument.* **3.** to mistake one thing or person for another: *Even the family confused the twins.* **4.** to cause to lose composure or concentration; disconcert: *The applause confused me, and I forgot my next line.* [Middle English *confusen* to perplex, from *confus* perplexed, from Latin *confūsus,* past participle of *confundere* to pour together, mix, overwhelm.] —**con·fus·ed·ly** (kən fū′zid lē) *adv.* —**con·fus′ing,** *adj.* —**con·fus′ing·ly,** *adv.*

con·fu·sion (kən fū′zhən) *n.* **1.** the state of being confused; disorder; disarray: *The false fire alarms created a lot of confusion in the school.* **2.** the act of confusing one person or thing for another. **3.** a state of mental uncertainty; bewilderment. **4.** a loss of composure; embarrassment.

Synonyms Confusion, disorder, and disarray mean a lack of order or correct relationship in arrangement. **Confusion** is the most general of these terms and does not imply any previously existing order: *The meadow displayed a confusion of wildflowers.* **Disorder,** on the other hand, implies that something has disturbed a proper order: *The records were in disorder, with those from 1990 filed next to those from 1983.* **Disarray** suggests even more strongly the breaking up of order or arrangement: *The army turned and ran in disarray. After the free-for-all, the whole house was in disarray.*

con·fu·ta·tion (kon′fyū tā′shən) *n.* **1.** the act of confuting. **2.** something that confutes. —**con·fu·ta·tive** (kən fū′tə tiv), *adj.*

con·fute (kən fūt′) *v.t.,* **-fut·ed, -fut·ing.** to prove to be incorrect; refute; disprove: *The doctors soundly confuted the diagnosis on the basis of the X rays.* [Latin *confūtāre* to check, refute.] —**con·fut′a·ble,** *adj.* —**con·fut′er,** *n.*

Cong. 1. Congregational. **2.** Congress. **3.** Congressional.

con·ga (kong′gə) *n.* **1.** a dance of Cuban origin consisting of three steps forward followed by an exaggerated kick, performed by dancers in a single line. **2.** the fast music for this dance. **3.** a tall, narrow bass drum that is played with the hands. Also, **conga drum.** —*v.i.,* **-gaed, -ga·ing.** to dance the conga. [Spanish *conga* this dance, from *congo* of the Congo.]

con game *Informal.* confidence game.

con·gé (kon′zhā, -jā; *French* kôN zhe′) *also,* **congee.** *n., pl.* **-gés** (-zhāz, -jāz; *French* -zhe′). **1.** formal permission to leave. **2.** an abrupt or sudden dismissal. [French *congé,* going back to Latin *commeātus* going to and fro, leave of absence.]

con·geal (kən jēl′) *v.t., v.i.* **1.** to change from a fluid to a solid state by or as by cooling or freezing. **2.** to thicken; coagulate: *Oil congeals in cold weather.* [Old French *congeler* to cause to freeze, from Latin *congelāre.*] —**con·geal′a·ble,** *adj.* —**con·geal′er,** *n.* —**con·geal′ment,** *n.*

con·gee (kon′jē) congé.

con·ge·ner (kon′jə nər) *n.* a member of the same kind, class, or genus. [Latin *congener* of the same kind.] —**con·ge·ner·ic** (kon′jə ner′ik), **con·gen·er·ous** (kən jen′ər əs), *adj.*

con·gen·ial (kən jēn′yəl) *adj.* **1.** having similar tastes and interests; compatible. **2.** to a person's liking; agreeable; pleasant: *congenial work, a congenial host.* [CON- + GENIAL.] —**con·ge·ni·al·i·ty** (kən jē′nē al′i tē), *n.* —**con·gen′ial·ly,** *adv.*

con·gen·i·tal (kən jen′i təl) *adj.* (of a condition or disease) present at the time of birth, whether due to heredity or to development in the uterus: *a congenital heart defect, a congenital birth defect.* [Latin *congenitus* born with + -AL[1].] —**con·gen′i·tal·ly,** *adv.*

con·ger (kong′gər) *n.* any of a group of saltwater eels, family Congridae, found in warm waters, esp. *Conger conger,* of European coastal waters, that is valued as food. Length: up to 6 feet (1.8 meters). Also, **conger eel.** [Old French *congre,* from Latin *congrus, conger,* from Greek *gongros.*]

con·ge·ries (kən jir′ēz, kon′jə rēz′) *n., pl.* **-ries.** a collection of things in one mass; aggregate; heap. ➡ used as singular or plural. [Latin *congeriēs* heap.]

con·gest (kən jest′) *v.t.* **1.** to fill beyond capacity; overcrowd: *On weekends, automobiles congest the highways near the city.* **2.** to cause an abnormal amount of blood, mucus, or other matter to collect in (an organ or part of the body). —*v.i.* to become congested. [Latin *congestus,* past participle of *congerere* to bring together.]

con·ges·tion (kən jes′chən) *n.* **1.** an overcrowded condition: *traffic congestion.* **2.** an excessive or abnormal amount of blood, mucus, or other matter in an organ or part of the body. —**con·ges·tive** (kən jes′tiv), *adj.*

con·glom·er·ate (*v.,* kən glom′ə rāt′; *adj., n.,* kən glom′ər it) *v.t., v.i.,* **-at·ed, -at·ing.** to collect together into a mass or heap. —*adj.* **1.** made up of unlike parts massed together. **2.** clustered into or forming a dense, irregular mass. —*n.* **1.** a mass formed of diverse parts. **2.** a sedimentary rock composed of rounded, worn fragments of rocks cemented together by a substance such as clay. **3.** a corporation composed of many different companies in varied fields. [Latin *conglomerātus,* past participle of *conglomerāre* to roll together, heap together, going back to *con-* together + *glomus* ball.]

con·glom·er·a·tion (kən glom′ə rā′shən) *n.* **1.** a cohesive mass, esp. of unlike parts. **2.** the act of conglomerating.

Con·go·lese (kong′gə lēz′, -lēs′) *n., pl.* **-lese. 1.** a person who was born in or is a citizen of the Congo. **2.** a person who was a citizen of the Democratic Republic of the Congo, now called Zaire. —*adj.* of or relating to either the Congo or the former Democratic Republic of the Congo, their people, or their culture.

con·go snake (kong′gō) an eellike salamander, *Amphiuma means,* common in swampy regions of the southeastern United States, having two pairs of weak, rudimentary legs. Length: to 40 inches (102 centimeters). Also, **congo eel.**

con·grat·u·late (kən grach′ə lāt′) *v.t.,* **-lat·ed, -lat·ing.** to express happiness or pleasure to (a person) on account of the person's success or good fortune. [Latin *congrātulātus,* past participle of *congrātulārī* to wish joy.] —**con·grat·u·la·to·ry** (kən grach′ə lə tôr′ē), *adj.*

con·grat·u·la·tion (kən grach′ə lā′shən) *n.* **1.** the act of congratulating. **2. congratulations.** an expression of happiness or pleasure for another's good fortune or success.

con·gre·gate (*v.,* kong′gri gāt′; *adj.,* kong′gri git) *v.t., v.i.,* **-gat·ed, -gat·ing.** to bring or come together in a crowd or mass; assemble. —*adj.* gathered together; assembled. [Latin *congregātus,* past participle of *congregāre* to assemble, going back to *con-* together + *grex* flock.]

con·gre·ga·tion (kong′gri gā′shən) *n.* **1.** the act of assembling in a crowd or mass. **2.a.** an assembly of people for religious worship or instruction. **b.** a group of people who regularly worship together. **3.** a gathering of people or things; assemblage. **4.** *Roman Catholic Church.* **a.** a religious community under a common rule or simple vows. **b.** a permanent committee of cardinals and other officials charged with administering a department of church affairs. **5.** in the Old Testament, the entire body of Hebrews.

con·gre·ga·tion·al (kong′gri gā′shə nəl) *adj.* **1.** of or relating to a congregation. **2. Congregational.** of or relating to Congregationalism or Congregationalists.

Con·gre·ga·tion·al·ism (kong′gri gā′shə nə liz′əm) *n.* **1.** a Protestant denomination holding that the Bible is the only author-

a	at	e	end	o	hot	u	up	hw	white	⎧	about
ā	ape	ē	me	ō	old	ū	use	ng	song	⎪	taken
ä	far	i	it	ô	fork	ü	rule	th	thin	ə	pencil
âr	care	ī	ice	oi	oil	u̇	pull	th	this	⎪	lemon
				îr	pierce	ou	out	ûr	turn	zh	measure	⎩	circus

itative guide to doctrine and worship and that each local congregation is responsible only to Jesus. **2. congregationalism.** a form of church government in which each local church is independent and self-governing. —**Con′gre·ga′tion·al·ist,** *n., adj.*

con·gress (kong′gris) *n., pl.* **-gress·es. 1.** the legislative body of any of various countries, esp. of a republic. **2. Congress. a.** the federal legislature of the United States, consisting of the Senate and the House of Representatives. **b.** a specific group of legislators making up Congress during one approximately two-year term from the January following elections to the House of Representatives until Congress adjourns, usually shortly after the next such election: *the 100th Congress.* **3.** a formal meeting of representatives, as of several nations or interested groups, gathered to discuss a subject of common concern. **4.** the act of coming together. **5.** sexual intercourse.

con·gres·sion·al (kən gresh′ə nəl) *adj.* **1.** of or relating to a congress. **2. Congressional.** of or relating to Congress.

Congressional Medal of Honor, Medal of Honor.

con·gress·man (kong′gris mən) *also,* **Con·gress·man.** *n., pl.* **-men** (-mən). a member of Congress, esp. of the House of Representatives.

con·gress·wom·an (kong′gris wùm′ən) *also,* **Con·gress·wom·an.** *n., pl.* **-wom·en** (-wim′ən). a female member of Congress, esp. of the House of Representatives.

con·gru·ence (kong′grü əns, kən grü′-) *n.* the state of being congruent; agreement; harmony. Also, **con·gru·en·cy** (kong′grü ən sē, kən grü′-).

con·gru·ent (kong′grü ənt, kən grü′-) *adj.* **1.** agreeing in every way; harmonious; congruous: *My opinion of the matter is congruent with yours.* **2.** *Geometry.* exactly alike in shape and size; coinciding exactly if placed one on the other. Symbol: ≅ **3.** *Algebra.* (of two quantities) leaving the same remainder when divided by a modulus. [Latin *congruēns,* present participle of *congruere* to agree, correspond.] —**con′gru·ent·ly,** *adv.*

con·gru·i·ty (kən grü′i tē, kon-) *n., pl.* **-ties. 1.** the state of being congruous; agreement; harmony. **2.** *Geometry.* exact similarity in size and shape. **3.** a point of agreement: *a congruity of opinions.*

con·gru·ous (kong′grü əs) *adj.* **1.** harmoniously related; agreeing; concordant: *congruous architectural elements.* **2.** suited to the purpose or needs; fitting; appropriate. **3.** congruent *(def. 2).* [Latin *congruus.* See CONGRUENT.] —**con′gru·ous·ly,** *adv.* —**con′gru·ous·ness,** *n.*

con·i·cal (kon′i kəl) *adj.* **1.** shaped like a cone. **2.** of or relating to a cone. Also, **con′ic.** —**con′i·cal·ly,** *adv.*

conic section *Geometry.* a curve formed by the intersection of a plane with a right circular cone, or the plane section described by such a curve. Circles, ellipses, parabolas, and hyperbolas are conic sections.

co·nid·i·um (kō nid′ē əm, kə-) *n., pl.* **-di·a.** an asexual spore not contained within a sporangium, produced by certain fungi, esp. ascomycetes. [Modern Latin *conidium,* from Greek *konis* dust.]

co·ni·fer (kon′ə fər, kō′nə-) *n.* any of a large group of trees and shrubs that bear cones. Most conifers, such as the pines, spruces, and cedars, are evergreen and bear needle-shaped leaves. [Latin *cōnifer* bearing cones, from *cōnus* cone (from Greek *kōnos*) + *ferre* to bear [1].]

co·nif·er·ous (kō nif′ər əs, kə-) *adj.* **1.** bearing cones. **2.** of or relating to the conifers.

conj. 1. conjugation. **2.** conjunction.

con·jec·tur·al (kən jek′chər əl) *adj.* **1.** based on or involving conjecture. **2.** tending to make conjectures. —**con·jec′tur·al·ly,** *adv.*

con·jec·ture (kən jek′chər) *n.* **1.** the act of forming an opinion not based on complete or definite evidence or proof. **2.** an opinion or conclusion so formed; guess. —*v.t., v.i.,* **-tured, -tur·ing.** to form an opinion not based on complete or definite evidence or proof; guess. [Latin *conjectūra* guess, conclusion.] —**con·jec′tur·a·ble,** *adj.* —**con·jec′tur·er,** *n.* —For Synonyms *(v.t.),* see **guess.**

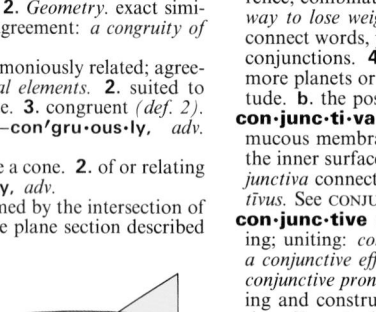
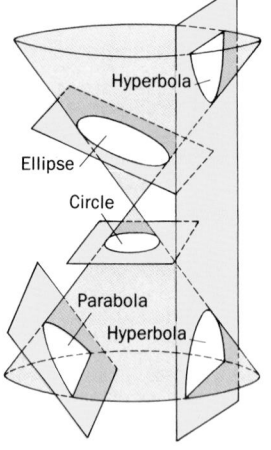

Hyperbola

Ellipse

Circle

Parabola

Hyperbola

conic sections

con·join (kən join′) *v.t., v.i.* to join together; unite; combine. [Old French *conjoindre,* from Latin *conjungere.*] —**con·join′er,** *n.*

con·joint (kən joint′) *adj.* **1.** joined together; united; combined. **2.** being made by or involving two or more in combination; joint. [French *conjoint,* past participle of *conjoindre.* See CONJOIN.] —**con·joint′ly,** *adv.*

con·ju·gal (kon′jə gəl) *adj.* of or relating to marriage or marital relations. [Latin *conjugālis,* going back to *con-* together + *jugum* yoke; with reference to marriage as a yoking together as a team.] —**con′ju·gal·ly,** *adv.*

con·ju·gant (kon′jə gənt) *n.* either of a pair of one-celled organisms or gametes that temporarily fuse in the process of biological conjugation. [CONJUG(ATE) + -ANT.]

con·ju·gate (*v.* kon′jə gāt′; *adj., n.,* kon′jə git, -gāt′) *v.,* **-gat·ed, -gat·ing.** —*v.t.* to give the inflections of (a verb). —*v.i. Biology.* to fuse in conjugation. —*adj.* **1.** joined together, esp. in pairs; coupled. **2.** (of words) derived from a common root. —*n.* a conjugate word. [Latin *conjugātus,* past participle of *conjugāre* to join together, marry, from *con-* with, together + *jugāre* to join.]

con·ju·ga·tion (kon′jə gā′shən) *n.* **1.** the act of conjugating or the state of being conjugated. **2.** *Grammar.* **a.** the inflections of a verb, indicating tense, person, number, and mood. **b.** an arrangement of the inflections of a verb. **c.** a group of verbs having the same inflections. **3.** *Biology.* a form of sexual reproduction in which the temporary fusion of two similar cells is accompanied by a transfer of hereditary material, occurring among some protozoans and algae. —**con′ju·ga′tion·al,** *adj.* —**con′ju·ga′tion·al·ly,** *adv.*

con·junct (kən jungkt′, kon′jungkt) *adj.* joined together; associated; combined. [Latin *conjūnctus,* past participle of *conjungere* to join together.]

con·junc·tion (kən jungk′shən) *n.* **1.** the act of joining together or the state of being joined together. **2.** a simultaneous occurrence; combination: *Dieting in conjunction with exercise is a good way to lose weight.* **3.** any of a class of words that are used to connect words, phrases, clauses, or sentences. *And, but,* and *if* are conjunctions. **4.** *Astronomy.* **a.** an apparent meeting of two or more planets or other heavenly bodies at the same celestial longitude. **b.** the position or condition of such bodies.

con·junc·ti·va (kon′jungk tī′və) *n., pl.* **-vas** or **-vae** (-vē). the mucous membrane that covers the front of the eyeball and lines the inner surface of the eyelids. [Modern Latin *(membrana) conjunctiva* connective (membrane), feminine of Late Latin *conjunctīvus.* See CONJUNCTIVE.]

con·junc·tive (kən jungk′tiv) *adj.* **1.** joining together; connecting; uniting: *conjunctive tissue.* **2.** joined together; joint; united: *a conjunctive effort.* **3.** like or functioning like a conjunction: *a conjunctive pronoun.* **4.** uniting parts of a sentence in both meaning and construction. —*n.* a conjunctive word, esp. a conjunction. [Late Latin *conjūnctīvus* connective, from Latin *conjūnctus.* See CONJUNCT.] —**con·junc′tive·ly,** *adv.*

con·junc·ti·vi·tis (kən jungk′tə vī′tis) *n.* an inflammation of the conjunctiva; pinkeye. [CONJUNCTIVA + -ITIS.]

con·junc·ture (kən jungk′chər) *n.* a combination of events or circumstances, esp. as related to or producing a critical situation.

con·ju·ra·tion (kon′jə rā′shən, kun′-) *n.* **1.** a set of words used in conjuring; spell; incantation. **2.** the practice or performance of magic. **3.** an invocation using a sacred name. **4.** *Archaic.* a solemn appeal or entreaty, esp. to a deity.

con·jure (kon′jər, kun′-; *v.t., def. 3,* kən jùr′) *v.,* **-jured, -jur·ing.** —*v.t.* **1.** to summon or cause (a demon or spirit) to appear by using magic words. **2.** to bring about by or as by magic. **3.** *Archaic.* to make a solemn appeal to. —*v.i.* **1.** to summon demons or spirits by means of spells; practice sorcery. **2.** to perform tricks by illusion or sleight of hand. [Old French *conjurer* to adjure, exorcise, from Latin *conjūrāre* to swear together, conspire.]

 •**to conjure up.** to cause to appear or bring into existence by or as by supernatural means: *The chef conjured up a delicious sauce. The pictures conjured up happy thoughts.*

con·jur·er (kon′jər ər, kun′-) *also,* **con·ju·ror.** *n.* **1.** a person who practices magic; wizard; sorcerer. **2.** a person who practices tricks involving sleight of hand; magician.

conk (kongk) *Slang. n.* a blow, esp. to the head. —*v.t.* to hit or strike, esp. on the head. [Of uncertain origin.]

 •**to conk out.** *Slang.* **a.** to break down suddenly; stall: *The car conked out halfway up the hill.* **b.** to go to sleep: *The tired hikers conked out early.*

conn (kon) con [3].

Conn., Connecticut.

con·nate (kon′āt) *adj.* **1.** existing from birth; congenital; inborn. **2.** allied in origin or nature; cognate. **3.** *Botany, Zoology.*

congenitally or firmly united. **4.** *Geology.* (of fluids in sedimentary rocks) entrapped at the time of deposition: *connate water.* [Late Latin *connātus,* past participle of *connāsci* to be born with, from Latin *con-* with + *nāscī* to be born.]

con·nect (kə nekt′) *v.t.* **1.** to join or fasten together; unite; link: *The workers connected the boxcar to the freight train.* **2.** to think of as having a close relationship; associate mentally: *We often connect clowns with circuses.* **3.** to put on the same telephone line (with *with*): *The operator will connect you with our sales department.* **4.** to place in a relationship or association: *The police can connect the suspect with the crime.* **5.** to link in an electric circuit. —*v.i.* **1.** to be or become joined; meet: *This wire connects with that one.* **2.** (of buses, trains, or airplanes) to be scheduled so that passengers can transfer from one route to another: *This plane connects in Chicago.* **3.** to meet or contact someone for social or professional reasons: *The reporter wanted to connect with someone in the police department for an interview.* **4.** to be successful in hitting or meeting what is aimed at: *to connect for a home run.* [Latin *connectere* to tie together.] —**con·nect′er;** also, **con·nec′tor,** *n.* —**con·nect′i·ble;** also, **con·nect′a·ble,** *adj.*

con·nect·ed (kə nek′tid) *adj.* **1.** joined or fastened together; linked. **2.** joined or linked in sequence: *connected thoughts.* **3.** related by blood or marriage: *That couple is connected with the governor's family.* **4.** having a social or professional relationship. —**con·nect′ed·ly,** *adv.* —**con·nect′ed·ness,** *n.*

connecting rod, a rod that connects a rotating part of a machine with a reciprocating part, esp. one that connects a piston to the crankshaft in an automobile engine.

con·nec·tion (kə nek′shən) *also, British,* **connexion.** *n.* **1.** the act of connecting; union; linking up. **2.** the state of being connected; relationship or association: *The report studied the connection between poverty and crime.* **3.** something that unites, relates, or joins; connecting part; link: *The fire was caused by a faulty connection in the wiring.* **4.a.** the relation or association of a word or idea with the surrounding text: *It is interesting to note the connection in which this word is used.* **b.** a relation with something else due to or based on sequence, cause, or involvement: *I no longer have any connection with that company.* **5.** a person with whom one has a useful association, esp. in business or politics: *The senator has many important connections.* **6.** a related person, esp. by marriage or distant kinship. **7.a.** a scheduling of trains, buses, or airplanes that permits the passenger to transfer from one route to another without undue delay. **b.** a specific means of transportation that is part of such scheduling: *The plane that just left was our connection for Dallas.* **8.** a religious denomination or sect. **9.** a line of communication between two points: *a bad telephone connection.*
·**in connection with. a.** together with. **b.** with reference or regard to.

con·nec·tive (kə nek′tiv) *adj.* tending or serving to connect. —*n.* **1.** something that connects. **2.** a word used to connect words, phrases, and clauses. Conjunctions and relative pronouns are connectives.

connective tissue, any of several kinds of fibrous tissue found throughout the body that serve to unite and support other tissues and organs.

con·nex·ion (kə nek′shən) *British.* connection.

con·ning tower (kon′ing) **1.** an armored pilothouse on the deck of a warship. **2.** a structure on the deck of a submarine in which the housing for the periscope and other equipment is located and which serves as a bridge and as an entrance when the submarine is surfaced. Also (def. 2), **sail.** For illustration, see **submarine.** [*Conning,* present participle of CON³.]

con·nip·tion (kə nip′shən) *n. Informal.* a fit of rage or hysteria. [Of uncertain origin.]

con·niv·ance (kə nī′vəns) *n.* the act or an instance of conniving.

con·nive (kə nīv′) *v.i.,* **-nived, -niv·ing. 1.** to permit or encourage wrongdoing by overlooking or pretending ignorance (with *at*): *Some government officials connive at graft.* **2.** to cooperate secretly; conspire (with *with*): *He connived with his sister to take over the company.* [Latin *connīvēre* to shut the eyes, wink at.] —**con·niv′er,** *n.*

con·nois·seur (kon′ə sûr′) *n.* a person who, because of expert knowledge and discriminating taste, is qualified to pass critical judgment on something, esp. the fine arts, wine, or food. [Obsolete French *connoisseur* literally, one who knows, from Old French *connoistre* to know, from Latin *cognōscere* to know, understand.]

con·no·ta·tion (kon′ə tā′shən) *n.* an implied meaning or association of a word or expression in addition to the literal meaning. ➡ distinguished from **denotation.**

con·note (kə nōt′) *v.t.,* **-not·ed, -not·ing. 1.** to imply or call to mind a meaning in addition to the literal meaning: *The word*

"red" denotes a color, but it connotes danger. ➡ distinguished from **denote. 2.** to involve in direct association: *Smoke connotes fire.* [Medieval Latin *connotare* to mark in addition, from Latin *con-* together + *notāre* to mark.] —**con′no·ta′tive,** *adj.*

con·nu·bi·al (kə nü′bē əl, -nū′-) *adj.* relating to or characteristic of marriage; matrimonial. [Latin *connūbiālis,* from *connūbium* marriage.]

co·noid (kō′noid) *adj.* resembling a cone in shape. Also, **co·noi·dal** (kō noi′dəl). —*n.* something cone-shaped. [Greek *kōnoeidēs* cone-shaped, from *kōnos* cone + *eidos* form.]

con·quer (kong′kər) *v.t.* **1.** to acquire or secure by force, as in a war: *to conquer a country.* **2.** to overcome by force; defeat; vanquish: *to conquer an enemy.* **3.** to overcome a mental, emotional, or moral obstacle by one's own effort: *to conquer a habit, to conquer shyness.* —*v.i.* to be victorious; win. [Old French *conquerre* to win, achieve, going back to Latin *conquīrere* to seek together, win.] —**con′quer·a·ble,** *adj.* —**con′quer·or,** *n.* —For Synonyms, see **defeat.**

con·quest (kon′kwest, kong′-) *n.* **1.** the act or an instance of conquering. **2.** something that is conquered, esp. something acquired or subdued by force: *Spain had many conquests in the New World.* **3.a.** a person whose love or favor has been won. **b.** the winning of that person's love or favor. **4. the Conquest.** Norman Conquest. [Old French *conqueste* acquisition, from *conquerre.* See CONQUER.]

con·quis·ta·dor (kon kēs′tə dôr′, -kwis′-) *n., pl.* **-dors** or **-do·res** (-dôr′ās, -ēz). any of the Spanish conquerors in the Americas, esp. in Mexico and Peru during the sixteenth century. [Spanish *conquistador* conqueror, from *conquistar* to conquer, going back to Latin *conquīrere* to seek together, win, from *com-* with, together + *quaerere* to seek.]

17th-century painting of a **conquistador** in Mexico

con·san·guin·e·ous (kon′sang gwin′ē əs) *adj.* of the same ancestor; akin. Also, **con·san·guine.** [Latin *consanguineus,* going back to *con-* together + *sanguis* blood.] —**con′san·guin′e·ous·ly,** *adv.*

con·san·guin·i·ty (kon′sang gwin′i tē) *n.* kinship by descent from the same ancestor; relationship by blood.

con·science (kon′shəns) *n.* **1.** the mental or emotional faculty that prompts one to do right and by which right and wrong are distinguished, esp. with regard to one's own behavior or motives. **2.** conformity to one's own moral principles; conscientiousness. [Old French *conscience* consciousness of good and evil, from Latin *conscientia* consciousness, knowledge.] —**con′science·less,** *adj.*
·**in all conscience. a.** in all reason or honesty; in truth. **b.** surely; certainly.
·**on one's conscience.** causing feelings of guilt or remorse: *The lie that I told was on my conscience.*

conscience money, money paid to relieve one's conscience for some wrongdoing.

a	at	e	end	o	hot	u	up	hw	white		about
ā	ape	ē	me	ō	old	ū	use	ng	song		taken
ä	far	i	it	ô	fork	ü	rule	th	thin	ə	pencil
âr	care	ī	ice	oi	oil	u̇	pull	th	this		lemon
		îr	pierce	ou	out	ûr	turn	zh	measure		circus

con·science-strick·en (kon'shəns strik'ən) *adj.* feeling remorseful because of real or imaginary wrongdoing.

con·sci·en·tious (kon'shē en'shəs) *adj.* **1.** guided by one's conscience: *to be conscientious in one's dealings with people.* **2.** capable of or showing much thought and care; painstaking: *a conscientious student, to do conscientious work.* —**con'sci·en'tious·ly,** *adv.* —**con'sci·en'tious·ness,** *n.*

conscientious objector, a person whose religious or moral convictions will not allow fighting in a war.

con·scious (kon'shəs) *adj.* **1.** having a feeling or knowledge; perceiving; aware (with *of* or *that*): *to be conscious of someone's presence.* **2.** aware of the external world; physically and mentally awake: *Despite the blow on the head, I remained conscious.* **3.** felt by or known to oneself: *conscious anger.* **4.** done on purpose; deliberate; intentional: *a conscious insult, a conscious effort.* **5.** self-conscious. [Latin *conscius* aware.] —**con'scious·ly,** *adv.* —For Synonyms, see **aware.**

con·scious·ness (kon'shəs nis) *n.* **1.** the state of being conscious; awareness. **2.** the totality of thoughts and feelings of a person or group.

con·scious·ness-raising (kon'shəs nis rā'zing) *n.* a process aimed at helping members of a group, such as women or minorities, become more aware of discrimination against them as a group and reevaluate their position in society.

con·script (*v.,* kən skript'; *adj., n.,* kon'skript) *v.t.* to compel (someone) by law to serve in the armed forces; draft. —*adj.* compelled to serve in the armed forces; conscripted; drafted. —*n.* a person compelled by law to serve in the armed forces; draftee. [Latin *conscriptus* enrolled, chosen, past participle of *conscrībere* to enroll, write together.]

con·script fathers (kon'skript) **1.** the senators of ancient Rome. **2.** any legislators.

con·scrip·tion (kən skrip'shən) *n.* **1.** compulsory enrollment in a nation's armed services by an act of law; draft. **2.** forced enrollment in or contribution to any organization or group under government control: *conscription for labor battalions.*

con·se·crate (kon'si krāt') *v.t.,* -**crat·ed,** -**crat·ing. 1.** to set apart as sacred; make or declare holy: *to consecrate a shrine.* **2.** to dedicate or devote, as to a particular purpose: *to consecrate one's life to the dance.* **3.** to elevate to a sacred or exalted office, esp. to crown (a king) or ordain (a bishop). —*adj. Archaic.* consecrated. [Latin *consecrātus,* past participle of *consecrāre* to dedicate, make sacred.] —**con'se·cra'tion,** *n.* —**con'se·cra'tor,** *n.*

con·sec·u·tive (kən sek'yə tiv) *adj.* **1.** following one after another in an uninterrupted sequence; successive: *The numbers 1, 2, 3, and 4 are in consecutive order.* **2.** marked by a logical progression from one idea or event to another: *to tell a consecutive story.* [French *consécutif,* going back to Latin *consequī* to follow.] —**con·sec'u·tive·ly,** *adv.* —**con·sec'u·tive·ness,** *n.* —For Synonyms, see **successive.**

con·sen·su·al (kən sen'shü əl) *adj.* **1.** binding by or involving mutual consent: *a consensual contract.* **2.** caused by sympathetic reflex to some stimulus on the body, as of the lids of the eyes closing when an object is caught in only one eye. [Latin *consensus* agreement + -AL[1].] —**con·sen'su·al·ly,** *adv.*

con·sen·sus (kən sen'səs) *n.* **1.** a general agreement: *to reach a consensus.* **2.** the opinion of all or most; collective opinion: *The consensus of the townspeople was to build a new school.* [Latin *consensus* from *consentīre.* See CONSENT.]

> **Usage** **Consensus** by itself always refers to a general opinion; therefore, the phrases *consensus of opinion* and *general consensus of opinion* are redundant and should be avoided in speech and writing.

con·sent (kən sent') *v.i.* to give one's permission; agree; permit (often with *to*): *The patient consented to the operation.* —*n.* **1.** agreement with what is done or proposed by another; acquiescence: *With my consent, my neighbor trimmed the hedge between our houses.* **2.** agreement in opinion or sentiment: *consent of the governed.* [Old French *consentir* to agree, approve, from Latin *consentīre* to agree, from *con-* together + *sentīre* to feel.]

> **Synonyms** *v.i.* **Consent, accede, assent,** and **acquiesce** mean to agree to what someone has said or proposed. **Consent** implies agreement by someone in authority, but not necessarily with approval: *The mayor consented to see the protesters.* **Accede** suggests giving in to a proposal, perhaps against one's wishes: *I acceded without enthusiasm to my friend's request for a loan.* **Assent,** on the other hand, implies approval or agreement without hesitation: *The board assented to the proposal with no debate.* **Acquiesce** suggests simply failing to oppose something, even though one may have reservations: *They acquiesced in the group's plans because an argument would have been futile.*

con·se·quence (kon'si kwens', -kwəns) *n.* **1.** something that results from an earlier action or condition; effect: *You will have to*

suffer the consequences if you lie to the police. **2.a.** the quality of having great relevance; importance; significance: *a subject of no consequence.* **b.** social distinction or importance, as in rank or position: *a family of great consequence.* **3.** a logical conclusion arrived at through the process of reasoning; inference. —For Synonyms, see **outcome.**

· **in consequence of.** as a result of; because of.

con·se·quent (kon'si kwent', -kwənt) *adj.* **1.** following as a result or effect: *a heavy rainfall and consequent flood.* **2.** following as a logical conclusion: *The consequent answer must definitely be negative.* **3.** characterized by logic. —*n.* **1.** anything that follows something else; result. **2.** *Mathematics.* the second term of a ratio. [Latin *consequēns,* present participle of *consequī* to follow.]

con·se·quen·tial (kon'si kwen'shəl) *adj.* **1.** following as a result or effect; resultant. **2.** of consequence; important. **3.** self-important. —**con'se·quen'tial·ly,** *adv.* —**con'se·quen'tial·ness,** *n.*

con·se·quent·ly (kon'si kwent'lē, -kwənt-) *adv.* as a result; therefore: *I didn't study, and consequently I failed.*

con·serv·an·cy (kən sûr'vən sē) *n., pl.* -**cies. 1.** conservation, esp. of natural resources. **2.** an organization specifically created to conserve natural resources or historical sites. [Medieval Latin *conservantia* conservation, from *conservatia,* from Latin *conservatio.*]

con·ser·va·tion (kon'sər vā'shən) *n.* **1.** the act of preserving or protecting, as from loss, harm, or waste. **2.** the public protection and care of natural resources, such as forests, rivers, and wildlife.

con·ser·va·tion·ist (kon'sər vā'shə nist) *n.* a person who advocates and works toward the conservation of natural resources.

conservation of energy, the principle of physics stating that energy can neither be created nor destroyed, but can only be changed from one form to another.

conservation of mass and energy, the principle of physics stating that the total amount of mass and energy in a closed system remains constant, although mass may be converted into energy and energy converted into mass within the system.

conservation of momentum, a law of physics stating that the total momentum of moving bodies that collide or otherwise interact within a closed system remains constant.

con·serv·a·tism (kən sûr'və tiz'əm) *n.* **1.** a disposition to have things continue as they are or have been; opposition to change. **2.** the principles and practices of conservative people or groups.

con·serv·a·tive (kən sûr'və tiv) *adj.* **1.** characterized by or tending toward opinions favoring the status quo; opposed to change. ➡ distinguished from **liberal.** **2.** *also,* **Conservative.** of or belonging to a political party that supports existing social, political, and economic institutions. **3.** avoiding risks; cautious; moderate: *a conservative estimate, a conservative business venture.* **4.** avoiding novelties and fads; traditional: *conservative taste in clothes.* **5. Conservative.** of, relating to, or practicing Conservative Judaism. —*n.* **1.** a conservative person, esp. in politics or religion. **2. Conservative.** a member of a conservative political party, esp. the Conservative Party in Great Britain. —**con·serv'a·tive·ly,** *adv.* —**con·serv'a·tive·ness,** *n.*

Conservative Judaism, the branch of Judaism that preserves many traditional Jewish religious practices but adopts change when necessary to accommodate modern circumstances.

Conservative Party 1. one of the three major political parties in Great Britain. Traditionally it is opposed to radical change in existing social, political, and economic institutions. **2.** any of several similar political parties in other countries.

con·ser·va·toire (kən sûr'və twär') *n.* conservatory *(def. 1).*

con·ser·va·tor (kon'sər vā'tər, kən sûr'və-) *n.* **1.** a person who protects or preserves; guardian. **2.** a person whose profession is preserving, restoring, and repairing works of art: *a paper conservator.*

con·serv·a·to·ry (kən sûr'və tôr'ē) *n., pl.* -**ries. 1.** a school for instruction in music or the fine arts. Also, **conservatoire. 2.** a small greenhouse or glass-enclosed room for growing and displaying plants. [Medieval Latin *conservatorium* place for preserving, from Latin *conservāre* to save, protect.]

con·serve (*v.,* kən sûrv'; *n.,* kon'sûrv, kən sûrv') *v.t.,* -**served,** -**serv·ing. 1.** to protect from loss, harm, or waste; keep safe: *Conserve your strength for the game.* **2.** to preserve with sugar: *to conserve fruit.* —*n. also,* **conserves.** preserves, esp. a type made of two or more fruits stewed in sugar, often with raisins and nuts added. [Old French *conserver* to preserve, from Latin *conservāre* to preserve, protect.]

con·sid·er (kən sid'ər) *v.t.* **1.** to think about carefully or seriously, esp. in order to decide; deliberate upon: *The company gave me three days to consider the job offer.* **2.** to think to be; regard as:

We consider this the finest view of the valley. **3.** to allow for; take into account; keep in mind: *This car is in good shape, when you consider its age.* **4.** to have regard for (others and their feelings); treat thoughtfully: *You never consider anyone else.* **5.** to think of as possible or acceptable: *Would you consider selling your car?* —*v.i.* to think carefully or seriously; deliberate: *Take time to consider before you rush into anything.* [Old French *considerer* to observe closely, from Latin *considerāre* originally, to observe the stars, from *con-* with + *sīdus* star; from the ancient astrological practice of consulting the stars when trying to make a decision.]

Synonyms Consider, contemplate, study, and weigh mean to think about something carefully, so as to make a decision or to learn more. **Consider** is the broadest term: *to consider a theory in light of new research, to consider the best approach to solving a problem.* **Contemplate** implies closer attention to a subject, without necessarily seeking a result or a decision: *to contemplate a philosophical question, to contemplate the intricate workings of the brain.* **Study** implies purposeful examination in detail: *to study patterns of use in a transportation system.* **Weigh** is used of a process of evaluating or placing something in relation to other things: *to weigh the merits of performing surgery against treating the patient with medication.*

con·sid·er·a·ble (kən sid′ər ə bəl) *adj.* **1.** worth considering; important: *a person of considerable stature in the community.* **2.** great in amount or extent: *That pianist has considerable talent.* —*n. Informal.* a great amount; much. —**con·sid′er·a·bly,** *adv.*

con·sid·er·ate (kən sid′ər it) *adj.* **1.** characterized by a regard for others and their feelings; thoughtful. **2.** characterized by careful thought. —**con·sid′er·ate·ly,** *adv.* —**con·sid′er·ate·ness,** *n.*

con·sid·er·a·tion (kən sid′ə rā′shən) *n.* **1.** the act of considering; careful thought: *I will give consideration to your objections in making my decision.* **2.** something that is or should be considered; reason. **3.** thoughtful or appreciative regard for others; respect: *You can show consideration for others by being polite.* **4.** an opinion or thought arrived at carefully; reflection. **5.** a claim to notice or regard; importance; consequence: *The storekeeper is a person of some consideration in the community.* **6.** something given as payment; recompense; fee: *The carpenter will do the extra work for a small consideration.* —For Synonyms, see **respect.**

• **in consideration of. a.** because of; in view of. **b.** in return for: *I received a gold watch in consideration of my many years with the company.*

• **to take into consideration.** to make allowances for; take into account: *In passing sentence, the judge took into consideration the fact that it was the youth's first offense.*

• **under consideration.** being considered: *Several people were under consideration for the job.*

con·sid·ered (kən sid′ərd) *adj.* **1.** carefully thought out: *a considered reply.* **2.** highly regarded; respected.

con·sid·er·ing (kən sid′ər ing) *prep.* taking into account; in view of: *Considering the snow, the roads aren't too bad.* —*conj.* taking into account (often with *that*): *Considering that we've been driving all day, I feel remarkably fresh.* —*adv. Informal.* keeping all things in mind: *I feel much better today, considering.*

con·sign (kən sīn′) *v.t.* **1.** to hand over formally; transfer: *They consigned the business to their children.* **2.** to put into the care or charge of another; entrust. **3.** to send or deliver, esp. merchandise to be sold or cared for: *The dealer consigned the books to an agent for sale.* [French *consigner* to present, deliver, from Latin *consignāre* to seal, record.] —**con·sign′a·ble,** *adj.*

con·sign·ee (kon′sī nē′) *n.* a person or company to whom merchandise is consigned.

con·sign·ment (kən sīn′mənt) *n.* **1.** the act of consigning or the state of being consigned. **2.** a shipment of goods sent to a company or individual for sale or safekeeping: *The store received a large consignment of Japanese silks.*

• **on consignment.** (of goods) sent to a retailer with the understanding that the retailer will pay only for what is sold and may return whatever is not sold.

con·sign·or (kən sī′nər, kon′sī nôr′) *also,* **con·sign·er** (kən sī′nər). *n.* a person or company that consigns merchandise to another.

con·sist (kən sist′) *v.i.* **1.** to be made up or composed (with *of*): *Bricks consist mostly of clay.* **2.** to be inherent; exist (with *in*): *Good health consists partly in eating properly.* [Latin *consistere* to stand still, exist.]

con·sist·en·cy (kən sis′tən sē) *n., pl.* **-cies. 1.** the degree of firmness or density: *Flour will give the dough a thicker consistency.* **2.** agreement or conformity between things: *There is no consistency between the movie and the book.* **3.** agreement between current thoughts or courses of action and ones preceding them: *There*

has been consistency in the senator's voting record on environmental issues over the years. Also, **con·sist′ence.**

con·sist·ent (kən sis′tənt) *adj.* **1.** characterized by adherence to the same thoughts or courses of action: *He remained consistent in his support of various charities throughout his life.* **2.** in agreement or conformity; compatible: *Her story is not consistent with the facts.* —**con·sist′ent·ly,** *adv.*

con·sis·to·ry (kən sis′tə rē) *n., pl.* **-ries. 1.** *Roman Catholic Church.* **a.** a meeting of the College of Cardinals presided over by the pope for the transaction of church business, esp. for the naming of new cardinals. **b.** the cardinals attending such a meeting. **c.** the place where the meeting occurs. **2.** *Church of England.* a spiritual court of a diocesan bishop presided over by the chancellor. Also, **consistory court. 3.** the lowest court in various reformed churches, consisting primarily of the ministers and elders of an individual church. [Late Latin *consistōrium* place of assembly, from Latin *consistere* to stand still, exist.]

con·so·la·tion (kon′sə lā′shən) *n.* **1.** the act of consoling. **2.** someone or something that consoles. —**con·sol·a·to·ry** (kən sol′ə tôr′ē), *adj.*

consolation prize, an award given to someone who competes in a contest but does not win.

con·sole[1] (kən sōl′) *v.t.,* **-soled, -sol·ing.** to comfort or cheer (someone) in grief, sorrow, or disappointment; solace. [French *consoler,* from Latin *consōlārī.*] —**con·sol′a·ble,** *adj.* —**con·sol′er,** *n.* —For Synonyms, see **comfort.**

con·sole[2] (kon′sōl) *n.* **1.** the cabinet of a radio, television set, or phonograph that rests on the floor. **2.** the desklike case or frame of an organ, containing the keyboard, stops, and pedals. **3.** the control or instrument panel used for operating an electronic or mechanical system, as of a computer or an airplane. **4.** an ornamental bracket that supports a cornice, shelf, or other structure. **5.** console table. [French *console* bracket, console table, possibly blend of *consoler* to comfort and *consolider* to strengthen (from Latin *consolidāre*). See CONSOLE[1], CONSOLIDATE.]

con·sole table (kon′sōl) a table placed against a wall, supported by bracketlike legs that are often elaborately carved or decorated.

console[2] *(def. 4)*

con·sol·i·date (kən sol′i dāt′) *v.,* **-dat·ed, -dat·ing.** —*v.t.* **1.** to join together; unite; combine: *The couple consolidated their earnings.* **2.** to make secure or strong; strengthen: *The team consolidated their position in first place by winning the last two games.* **3.** *Military.* to organize and strengthen (a newly captured position) so that it can be used against the enemy. —*v.i.* to become united. [Latin *consolidātus,* past participle of *consolidāre* to strengthen, make solid.]

consolidated school, a school, usually rural, formed by uniting several smaller schools, attended by students from several school districts.

con·sol·i·da·tion (kən sol′i dā′shən) *n.* **1.** the act of consolidating or the state of being consolidated. **2.** something that has been consolidated.

con·sols (kon′solz, kən solz′) *pl. n.* government securities of Great Britain. [Short for *consol(idated annuitie)s.*]

con·som·mé (kon′sə mā′) *n.* a clear soup made of meat, poultry, or vegetable stock. [French *consommé,* from *consommer* to finish, from Latin *consummare;* because its making used to require a very long time.]

con·so·nance (kon′sə nəns) *n.* **1.** agreement among various parts or elements; accordance. **2.** *Music.* simultaneous sounding of tones in harmony. ➡ distinguished from **dissonance. 3.** *Poetry.* a correspondence or agreement of the final consonants but not the vowels of stressed syllables, as in *bill* and *wall,* and *furnished* and *varnished.* Also, **con′so·nan·cy.**

con·so·nant (kon′sə nənt) *n.* **1.** a speech sound produced by blocking the passage of air through the mouth with the lips, teeth, or tongue. ➡ distinguished from **vowel. 2.** any letter of the alphabet representing such a sound, such as *t, m,* or *p.* —*adj.* **1.** in agreement; in accord. **2.** harmonious in sound. **3.** conso-

a	at	e	end	o	hot	u	up	hw	white
ā	ape	ē	me	ō	old	ū	use	ng	song
ä	far	i	it	ô	fork	ü	rule	th	thin
âr	care	ī	ice	oi	oil	u̇	pull	th	this
		î	pierce	ou	out	ûr	turn	zh	measure

ə { about / taken / pencil / lemon / circus }

nantal. [Latin *consonāns (littera)* this sound or letter; literally, (letter) sounding with (a vowel), from *consonāre* to sound together; harmonize; because it normally has to be *sounded with* a vowel.] —**con′so·nant·ly,** *adv.*

con·so·nan·tal (kon′sə nan′təl) *adj.* relating to or having one or more consonants.

con·sort (*n.,* kon′sôrt; *v.,* kən sôrt′) *n.* **1.** a husband or wife; spouse. **2.** a constant companion; partner. **3.** a ship accompanying another. —*v.i.* **1.** to keep company; associate (with *with*): *They were suspected of consorting with known criminals.* **2.** to be in accord; agree (with *with*). [Latin *consort-,* stem of *consors* sharer, partner.]

con·sor·ti·um (kən sôr′shē əm) *n., pl.* **-ti·a** (-shē ə). **1.** an international agreement or coalition of banks, businesses, or individuals to raise and invest large sums of money for a common purpose: *The consortium was formed to develop African oil fields.* **2.** any partnership or association. [Latin *consortium* partnership.]

con·spe·cif·ic (kon′spi sif′ik) *adj.* belonging to the same species: *conspecific organisms.*

con·spec·tus (kən spek′təs) *n.* **1.** a general or overall view. **2.** a short summary; synopsis; digest; résumé. [Latin *conspectus* a looking at, sight.]

con·spic·u·ous (kən spik′ū əs) *adj.* **1.** easily seen or noticed; obvious: *conspicuous courage, a conspicuous stain on a rug.* **2.** attracting attention: *That bright red jacket is conspicuous in the crowd. You were conspicuous by your absence.* [Latin *conspicuus* visible.] —**con·spic′u·ous·ly,** *adv.* —**con·spic′u·ous·ness,** *n.*

conspicuous consumption, overt, lavish consumption of expensive goods or services, designed to show off one's wealth or social status. [Coined by the U.S. sociologist Thorstein Veblen, 1857-1929, in *The Theory of the Leisure Class* (1899).]

con·spir·a·cy (kən spir′ə sē) *n., pl.* **-cies. 1.** the act of secretly planning together to perform some evil or illegal act. **2.** a plan so devised; plot. **3.** a group devising such a plan. —**con·spir′a·tor,** *n.* —**con·spir·a·to·ri·al** (kən spir′ə tôr′ē əl), *adj.* —For Synonyms, see **plot.**

con·spire (kən spīr′) *v.i.* **-spired, -spir·ing. 1.** to plan a conspiracy; plot. **2.** to work or act together to effect something: *All things conspired to make their wedding day memorable.* [Latin *conspīrāre* to breathe together, agree, plot.] —**con·spir′er,** *n.*

con·sta·ble (kon′stə bəl, kun′-) *n.* **1.** a public officer, esp. in a small, local jurisdiction. **2.** a chief officer of the household, court, or military forces of a medieval ruler. **3.** a keeper or warden of a royal fortress or castle. **4.** *British.* police officer. [Old French *conestable* officer of the Frankish kings in charge of the stable, from Late Latin *comes stabulī* literally, count of the stable. See COUNT², STABLE¹.]

con·stab·u·lar·y (kən stab′yə ler′ē) *n., pl.* **-lar·ies. 1.** all the constables of a district. **2.** a district under the jurisdiction of a particular constable. **3.** a police force organized along military lines, but not part of the regular army. —*adj.* of or relating to constables or constabularies.

con·stan·cy (kon′stən sē) *n.* **1.** the condition of remaining unchanged; steadiness: *The constancy of good weather made our vacation enjoyable.* **2.** unchanging devotion or loyalty; steadfastness; faithfulness: *to show constancy in friendships.*

con·stant (kon′stənt) *adj.* **1.** remaining the same; invariable; unchanging: *Careful control ensures that the quality of the product remains constant.* **2.** continuing without a break; happening all the time; continual: *constant chatter.* **3.** steadfast in loyalty or devotion; faithful: *a constant friend.* —*n.* **1.** something that does not change. **2.a.** a value that remains unchanged, such as pi, or a value that is believed never to change, as the speed of light. **b.** a value that remains or is held unchanged under the specific circumstances of an investigation or within the limits of an experiment. [Old French *constant* lasting, continuous, from Latin *constāns,* present participle of *constāre* to stand firm.] —**con′stant·ly,** *adv.* —For Synonyms *(adj.),* see **regular.**

con·stan·tan (kon′stən tan′) *n.* an alloy of copper and nickel, used in the manufacture of thermocouples and electric resistors. [Because its resistance remains *constant* as its temperature changes.]

con·stel·la·tion (kon′stə lā′shən) *n.* **1.** any of eighty-eight groups of stars, many of which traditionally represent characters and objects in ancient mythology. **2.** an area or division of the heavens occupied by such a group. **3.** *Astrology.* a relative grouping of the planets and stars, esp. at the time of one's birth, which is said to influence one's character and fate, or world events. **4.** a brilliant or distinguished group of people or things. [Middle English *constellacion,* from Middle French *constellation,* from *constellation-,* stem of Late Latin *constellatio,* from *constellatus* starry, from Latin *com-* with, together + *stellatus,* past participle of *stellare* to shine, from *stella* star.]

con·ster·na·tion (kon′stər nā′shən) *n.* a feeling of alarm or amazement leading to confusion or fear: *We discovered to our consternation that the house was on fire.* [Latin *consternātiō.*]

con·sti·pate (kon′stə pāt′) *v.t.* **-pat·ed, -pat·ing.** to cause constipation in. [Latin *constīpātus,* past participle of *constīpāre* to press together.]

con·sti·pa·tion (kon′stə pā′shən) *n.* a condition of the bowels marked by infrequent or difficult evacuation.

con·stit·u·en·cy (kən stich′ü ən sē) *n., pl.* **-cies. 1.** all the voters in a district who elect a legislator to represent them. **2.** the district represented. **3.** any group of supporters.

con·stit·u·ent (kən stich′ü ənt) *adj.* **1.** serving to form or make up a whole; component: *Hydrogen and oxygen are the constituent parts of water.* **2.** empowered to establish or elect a government, or to create or amend a constitution: *a constituent assembly.* —*n.* **1.** a necessary part; element; component. **2.** a person who elects another as a representative; resident of a constituency; voter. **3.** *Grammar.* any of the forms making up a sentence, clause, or phrase. [Latin *constituēns,* present participle of *constituere* to cause to stand, establish.] —For Synonyms *(n.),* see **ingredient.**

con·sti·tute (kon′sti tüt′, -tūt′) *v.t.,* **-tut·ed, -tut·ing. 1.** to make up; compose; form: *Four quarts constitute a gallon.* **2.** to appoint to an office or function; empower: *The committee constituted one representative as its chairperson.* **3.** to set up; establish; found: *The city council constituted new traffic regulations.* **4.** to give legal form to: *There is a definite procedure by which the legislature constitutes itself.* [Latin *constitūtus,* past participle of *constituere* to cause to stand, establish.]

con·sti·tu·tion (kon′sti tü′shən, -tū′-) *n.* **1.** the way in which something is made up or put together: *The constitution of a primitive society is not necessarily simple.* **2.** the physical makeup of the human body, esp. as to strength or resistance to disease: *The athlete has a strong constitution.* **3.a.** the system of fundamental principles by which a nation, state, or other organization is governed. **b.** a written document containing these principles. **c. the Constitution.** the supreme law and plan of government of the United States, in effect since 1789. **4.** the act of constituting or setting up; establishment.

con·sti·tu·tion·al (kon′sti tü′shə nəl, -tū′-) *adj.* **1.** of, relating to, or inherent in the constitution of a person or thing: *a constitutional weakness of the heart.* **2.** of, in, regulated by, or in agreement with a constitution, esp. of a nation, state, or private organization: *constitutional amendments, constitutional rights.* —*n.* an exercise, esp. a walk, taken for one's health. —**con′sti·tu′tion·al·ly,** *adv.*

con·sti·tu·tion·al·i·ty (kon′sti tü′shə nal′i tē, -tū′-) *n.* conformity with a constitution, esp. a political constitution: *The constitutionality of the law was questioned.*

constitutional monarchy, a monarchy in which the powers of the monarch are defined and limited by a constitution.

con·sti·tu·tive (kon′sti tü′tiv, -tū′-) *adj.* **1.** forming a constituent part; essential. **2.** having the power to enact or establish. —**con′sti·tu′tive·ly,** *adv.*

con·strain (kən strān′) *v.t.* **1.** to force (someone) to do something; compel; oblige: *Conscience constrained me to do the right thing.* **2.** to confine or secure, as by holding in or binding: *The police constrained the prisoner with handcuffs.* **3.** to hold back or repress; restrain: *to constrain one's anger.* [Old French *constraindre,* from Latin *constringere* to draw together, restrain.] —**con·strain·ed·ly** (kən strā′nid lē, -strānd′-), *adv.* —**con·strain′er,** *n.* —For Synonyms, see **force.**

con·straint (kən strānt′) *n.* **1.** a holding back or restraining of natural feelings; forced or unnatural manner. **2.** the state of being confined; restriction. **3.** the act of forcing or compelling; coercion: *The horse slowed under constraint from the reins.* **4.** something that constrains. [Old French *constreinte* binding, coercion, from *constreindre.* See CONSTRAIN.]

con·strict (kən strikt′) *v.t.* **1.** to make narrower or smaller by squeezing or binding together; contract: *to constrict a blood vessel with a tourniquet.* **2.** to slow the growth of; limit: *Narrow-mindedness constricted their intellectual growth.* —*v.i.* to become constricted. [Latin *constrictus,* past participle of *constringere* to draw together, restrain.]

con·stric·tion (kən strik′shən) *n.* **1.** the act of constricting or the state of being constricted. **2.** tightness or a feeling of tightness: *a constriction in one's chest.* **3.** something that constricts or is constricted. —**con·stric′tive,** *adj.*

con·stric·tor (kən strik′tər) *n.* **1.** any of various snakes, such as the python, boa, and anaconda, that kill by squeezing their prey in their coils. **2.** a muscle that causes a cavity or organ of the body to contract.

con·struct (*v.*, kən strukt′; *n.*, kon′strukt) *v.t.* **1.** to make by putting parts or elements together; build. **2.** *Geometry.* to draw a geometrical figure according to given conditions. —*n.* something put together or formulated: *a mathematical construct.* [Latin *constructus,* past participle of *construere* to pile up, build, make.] —**con·struc′tor,** *n.* —For Synonyms (*v.t.*), see **make.**

con·struc·tion (kən struk′shən) *n.* **1.a.** the act or process of constructing or being constructed. **b.** the trade or business of constructing: *to work in construction.* **2.** the way in which something is constructed. **3.** something constructed; structure. **4.** the way in which something is understood; explanation; interpretation: *to put the wrong construction on someone's comments.* **5.** *Grammar.* the arrangement or relation of words to form a sentence, clause, or phrase. —**con·struc′tion·al,** *adj.* —**con·struc′tion·al·ly,** *adv.*

con·struc·tion·ist (kən struk′shə nist) *n.* a person who interprets such things as laws or documents in a particular way: *A strict constructionist emphasizes the literal wording.*

con·struc·tive (kən struk′tiv) *adj.* **1.** serving to improve, aid, or build: *constructive criticism.* **2.** of or relating to construction; structural. **3.** indirectly stated or inferred by interpretation: *constructive consent.* —**con·struc′tive·ly,** *adv.* —**con·struc′tive·ness,** *n.*

con·struc·tiv·ism (kən struk′tə viz′əm) *n.* a movement in art and architecture in which wood, paper, wire, and glass are used as mediums of expression in contrast to paint, watercolor, stone, and other materials. —**con·struc′tiv·ist,** *adj., n.*

con·strue (kən strü′) *v.*, **-strued, -stru·ing.** —*v.t.* **1.** to explain or understand the meaning of; interpret: *I construed your words as a compliment.* **2.** to analyze (a sentence, clause, or phrase) for its grammatical structure. **3.** to use syntactically: *Is the word "group" construed as a singular or plural?* **4.** to translate, esp. orally. —*v.i.* to analyze grammatical structure, esp. in translating. [Latin *construere* to pile up, build, make.] —**con·stru′a·ble,** *adj.*

con·sul (kon′səl) *n.* **1.** an official appointed by a government to live in a foreign city to protect and represent his or her country's citizens or commercial interests there. **2.** either of the two annually elected magistrates who jointly exercised supreme authority in the ancient Roman republic. **3.** any of the three chief magistrates of the French republic from 1799 to 1804. [Latin *consul* the Roman magistrate.] —**con′su·lar,** *adj.* —**con′sul·ship′,** *n.*

con·su·late (kon′sə lit) *n.* **1.** the official residence or headquarters of a consul. **2.** the position, term of office, or authority of a consul. **3.a.** a government by consuls. **b. Consulate.** the government of France from 1799 to 1804.

consul general *pl.* **consuls general.** the highest ranking consular official of a country, stationed in another country in an important city and often supervising other consuls.

con·sult (kən sult′) *v.t.* **1.** to refer to for information or advice: *to consult a physician, to consult an encyclopedia.* **2.** to have consideration or regard for before acting; think of: *I wish you had consulted my feelings in the matter.* —*v.i.* **1.** to meet in order to ask advice or exchange ideas or opinions; confer together (with *with*): *We would like to consult with our lawyer before making a decision.* **2.** to give advice as an authority; serve as a consultant. [Latin *consultāre* to take counsels, reflect.]

> **Synonyms** *v.i.* **Consult** and **confer** mean to meet in order to get or exchange advice or opinions. **Consult** suggests discussion with someone who has special knowledge or wisdom: *The defendant consulted with a lawyer. Before registering for the course, the student consulted with someone who had already taken it.* **Confer** implies discussion among equals: *The board members conferred before electing a new chair.*

con·sult·ant (kən sul′tənt) *n.* **1.** a person who gives professional or technical advice. **2.** a person who seeks advice or information, as from another person or a reference work.

con·sul·ta·tion (kon′səl tā′shən) *n.* **1.** the act of consulting. **2.** a meeting to confer about something: *The doctors held a consultation before the operation.* —**con·sult′a·tive,** *adj.*

con·sume (kən süm′) *v.*, **-sumed, -sum·ing.** —*v.t.* **1.** to use up: *An automobile consumes gasoline.* **2.** to eat or drink up. **3.** to destroy, esp. by fire. **4.** to squander or waste, as time or money. **5.** to occupy all the attention of; engross; absorb: *to be consumed with curiosity.* —*v.i.* to waste away. [Latin *consūmere* to take completely, devour, destroy.] —**con·sum′a·ble,** *adj.*

con·sum·ed·ly (kən sü′mid lē) *adv.* to a great extent; extremely; excessively.

con·sum·er (kən sü′mər) *n.* **1.** a person who uses up an article of production, as contrasted with its producer or seller. **2.** a person or thing that consumes. **3.** an organism, usually an animal, that feeds on those lower than it in the food chain.

consumer credit, credit given to customers of a business enabling them to pay for goods or services over a period of time, either by an installment plan or by monthly billing.

consumer goods, goods for directly satisfying people's wants, as food or clothing, rather than for use in further production. ➡ distinguished from **capital goods.**

con·sum·er·ism (kən sü′mə riz′əm) *n.* **1.** a movement to protect consumers from such things as inferior or dangerous products, misleading labeling and advertising, and unfair prices. **2.** the theory that an ever-increasing consumption of consumer goods is beneficial to the economy.

consumer price index, an index that indicates any rise or fall in the prices of a number of basic items in a typical family budget.

con·sum·mate (*v.*, kon′sə māt′; *adj.*, kən sum′it, kon′sə mit) *v.t.*, **-mat·ed, -mat·ing.** **1.** to complete or make perfect; finish or fulfill: *The artist consummated a life's work in a magnificent fresco.* **2.** to complete or fulfill (a marriage) by sexual intercourse. —*adj.* **1.** of the highest degree; complete or perfect: *consummate skill.* **2.** skilled or accomplished; expert: *a consummate liar.* [Latin *consummātus,* past participle of *consummāre* to complete, perfect, from *con-* together + *summus* highest.] —**con·sum′mate·ly,** *adv.*

con·sum·ma·tion (kon′sə mā′shən) *n.* the act of consummating or the state of being consummated.

con·sump·tion (kən sump′shən) *n.* **1.** the act of consuming or the state of being consumed. **2.** the amount consumed: *The consumption of gasoline is greater in some cars than in others.* **3.** a wasting disease, esp. tuberculosis of the lungs. [Latin *consūmptiō* a consuming, wasting.]

con·sump·tive (kən sump′tiv) *adj.* **1.** of, relating to, or having consumption, esp. tuberculosis of the lungs. **2.** tending to consume; destructive; wasteful: *a consumptive disease.* —*n.* a person affected with consumption.

cont. 1. containing. **2.** contents. **3.** continent. **4.** continental. **5.** continue. **6.** continued.

Cont., Continental.

con·tact (kon′takt) *n.* **1.** the act or an instance of touching; coming together. **2.** the state of being in communication: *The expedition was completely out of contact with civilization for months.* **3.** a potentially useful association: *a business contact.* **4.** contact lens. **5.a.** a junction of conductors that permits an electrical current to pass. **b.** a device creating such a connection. —*v.t.* **1.** to bring into contact; touch. **2.** to communicate with: *I'll contact you tomorrow by telephone.* —*v.i.* to be in or come into contact. [Latin *contāctus* a touching.]

contact flying, the flying of an aircraft at an altitude that enables the pilot to navigate by watching the ground or water below.

contact lens, a thin plastic lens worn to correct a defect in vision, individually shaped to a prescription and fitted to the cornea. Also, **contact.**

contact print, a photographic print made by placing a negative in direct contact with photosensitive paper and exposing them to light.

con·ta·gion (kən tā′jən) *n.* **1.** the spreading of disease by direct or indirect contact. **2.** a disease spread in this manner; contagious disease. **3.** an agent or substance by which disease is spread. **4.** the spreading of any idea or state of mind or emotion: *No one remained untouched by the contagion of hysteria.* **5.** an influence that spreads rapidly, esp. an evil or corrupting one. [Latin *contāgiō* a touching, contact, infection.]

con·ta·gious (kən tā′jəs) *adj.* **1.** spread by contact, as a disease. **2.** carrying or capable of spreading disease. **3.** readily spread from one person to another; catching: *Fear can be contagious.* —**con·ta′gious·ly,** *adv.* —**con·ta′gious·ness,** *n.*

con·tain (kən tān′) *v.t.* **1.** to have in it; hold inside itself: *The jar contains flour.* **2.** to have the capacity to hold: *That car comfortably contains six passengers.* **3.** to be made up of or have as a part; consist of: *A quart contains two pints. This sculpture contains bronze as well as other metals.* **4.** to keep under control or within limits; restrain: *I tried to contain my anger at the insult.* **5.** to be divisible by without a remainder: *The number 12 contains 3, 4, 2, and 6.* [Old French *contenir* to confine, subdue, going back to Latin *continēre* to hold together, restrain.] —**con·tain′a·ble,** *adj.*

a	at	e	end	o	hot	u	up	hw	white		about
ā	ape	ē	me	ō	old	ū	use	ng	song		taken
ä	far	i	it	ô	fork	th	rule	th	thin	ə	pencil
âr	care	ī	ice	oi	oil	u̇	pull	th	this		lemon
		îr	pierce	ou	out	ûr	turn	zh	measure		circus

Contain, accommodate, and hold[1] mean to have or be capable of having a quantity inside. Contain may be used in stating capacity but more often refers to actual contents: *A quart contains two pints. This basket contains all the vegetables I picked today.* Accommodate indicates a containing with ease, as when the container is designed for a certain amount or number: *Each cabin accommodates six campers.* Hold is less formal than the other two words and is often used of less exact quantities: *I think these shelves will hold all our books. A commercial hive holds up to 30,000 bees.*

con·tain·er (kən tā′nər) *n.* a box, jar, can, or the like that contains or may contain something; receptacle.

con·tain·er·ize (kən tā′nə rīz′) *v.t.,* -ized, -iz·ing. to pack in large containers, often of several tons in capacity, suitable for shipping by boat, train, or truck. —con·tain′er·i·za′tion, *n.*

containerize
containerized cargo

con·tain·ment (kən tān′mənt) *n.* **1.** the policy of preventing the expansion of a hostile political, military, or economic power. **2.** the act or process of containing something or the state of being contained: *Containment of the forest fire was our first aim.* **3.** a structure or system designed to contain a hazardous process, as nuclear fission.

con·tam·i·nant (kən tam′ə nənt) *n.* something that contaminates or makes impure: *The beaches were closed when contaminants were found in the water.*

con·tam·i·nate (kən tam′ə nāt′) *v.t.,* -nat·ed, -nat·ing. to make impure by contact; defile; pollute. [Latin *contāminātus,* past participle of *contāmināre* to bring into contact, defile.] —con·tam′i·na′tive, *adj.* —con·tam′i·na′tor, *n.* —For Synonyms, see **pollute.**

con·tam·i·na·tion (kən tam′ə nā′shən) *n.* **1.** the act or process of contaminating or the state of being contaminated; pollution: *Food should be kept covered to avoid contamination.* **2.** something that contaminates; impurity.

contd., continued.

con·temn (kən tem′) *v.t.* to treat or view with contempt; despise; scorn. [Latin *contemnere.*] —con·tem·ner (kən tem′ər, -tem′nər), *n.*

con·tem·plate (kon′təm plāt′) *v.,* -plat·ed, -plat·ing. —*v.t.* **1.** to give prolonged or intense attention to; consider carefully: *The graduates contemplated the future.* **2.** to have in mind, as a plan of action; intend: *I'm contemplating going for a ride.* —*v.i.* to be absorbed in thought; meditate; ponder: *I go to the park every day to sit and contemplate.* [Latin *comtemplātus,* past participle of *contemplārī* to observe, from *con-* with + *templum* space marked out in the sky for observation, temple[1]; with reference to the practice of ancient Roman priests of observing a *templum* for omens.] —For Synonyms, see **consider.**

con·tem·pla·tion (kon′təm plā′shən) *n.* **1.** the act of looking at or thinking about something long and intensely. **2.** meditation, esp. spiritual or religious meditation. **3.** expectation or intention: *We bought new clothes in contemplation of our trip.*

con·tem·pla·tive (kon′təm plā′tiv, kən tem′plə-) *adj.* of, relating to, or characterized by contemplation: *a contemplative person, a contemplative afternoon.* —con′tem·pla′tive·ly, *adv.* —con′tem·pla′tive·ness, *n.*

con·tem·po·ra·ne·ous (kən tem′pə rā′nē əs) *adj.* belonging to or occurring during the same period of time: *The American Civil War and the rise of the Republican Party were contemporaneous.* [Latin *contemporaneus.*] —con·tem′po·ra′ne·ous·ly, *adv.* —con·tem′po·ra′ne·ous·ness, *n.*

con·tem·po·rar·y (kən tem′pə rer′ē) *adj.* **1.** belonging to or living at the same time: *Much of my research on the Renaissance was based on contemporary accounts.* **2.** of the same age or date. **3.** belonging to the present time; current; modern: *contemporary art, contemporary furniture.* —*n., pl.* -rar·ies. **1.** a person who belongs to or lives at the same time as another or others: *Queen Victoria and Abraham Lincoln were contemporaries.* **2.** a person or thing that is of the same age or date. [Latin *con-* together + *temporarius* relating to time.] —For Synonyms, see **modern.**

con·tempt (kən tempt′) *n.* **1.** a feeling that a person or thing is low, mean, or worthless; scorn; disdain. **2.** the state of being scorned or despised; disgrace: *to be held in contempt by everyone for dishonesty.* **3.** willful disobedience to or open disrespect for a law court or lawmaking body: *They were fined for contempt of court.* [Latin *contemptus* scorn.]

con·tempt·i·ble (kən temp′tə bəl) *adj.* deserving of or held in contempt or scorn; despicable. —con·tempt′i·ble·ness, *n.* —con·tempt′i·bly, *adv.*

con·temp·tu·ous (kən temp′chü əs) *adj.* showing contempt; scornful: *a contemptuous remark.* —con·temp′tu·ous·ly, *adv.* —con·temp′tu·ous·ness, *n.*

con·tend (kən tend′) *v.i.* **1.** to vie in a contest; compete: *The two teams contended for first place.* **2.** to engage in debate; argue; dispute. —*v.t.* to assert or maintain as a fact: *They contend that their plan will work.* [Latin *contendere* to stretch out, fight.] —con·tend′er, *n.* —For Synonyms *(v.i.),* see **compete.**

· **to contend with.** to deal with in or as in struggle: *The Eskimo have to contend with harsh weather.*

con·tent[1] (kon′tent) *n.* **1.a.** *usually,* contents. all that is contained inside: *the contents of a box.* **b.** the facts or topics dealt with in a written work; subject matter: *the content of an essay, a table of contents for a book.* **2.** essential meaning; substance: *The papers will be graded on form as well as content.* **3.** the amount of a specific substance contained: *the water content of an apple.* [Latin *contentum* that which is contained; originally, neuter of *contentus,* past participle of *continēre* to hold together, contain, from *com-* with, together + *tenēre* to hold.]

con·tent[2] (kən tent′) *adj.* wanting nothing else; free of desire for more; satisfied: *I am content to eat only two meals a day.* —*v.t.* to make content; satisfy: *A word of praise will content me.* —*n.* the state of being content; satisfaction. [Middle French *content* satisfied, from Latin *contentus* restrained, satisfied, from *continēre* to hold together, contain.]

con·tent·ed (kən ten′tid) *adj.* enjoying or feeling contentment; satisfied. —con·tent′ed·ly, *adv.* —con·tent′ed·ness, *n.*

con·ten·tion (kən ten′shən) *n.* **1.** a state or instance of disagreement or dispute; argument: *There was always contention between them.* **2.** a point maintained in an argument: *It is my cousin's contention that dogs are smarter than cats.* **3.** the act of contending; struggle; contest: *The two teams were in contention for the championship.* [Old French *contention* strife, dispute, from Latin *contentiō* a stretching, strife.]

con·ten·tious (kən ten′shəs) *adj.* **1.** fond of arguing; quarrelsome; argumentative: *People often try to avoid a contentious person.* **2.** apt to cause or characterized by contention: *a contentious act, a contentious issue.* —con·ten′tious·ly, *adv.* —con·ten′tious·ness, *n.*

con·tent·ment (kən tent′mənt) *n.* the state of being happy and content; satisfaction. —For Synonyms, see **satisfaction.**

con·ter·mi·nous (kən tûr′mə nəs) *adj.* **1.** having a common boundary. **2.** contained within the same boundaries; coextensive. Also, **coterminal, coterminous.** [Latin *conterminus* bordering on.] —con·ter′mi·nous·ly, *adv.*

con·test (*n.,* kon′test; *v.,* kən test′) *n.* **1.** something, such as a race or a game, that tests or proves skill or ability; competition for a prize, honor, or position. **2.** a struggle for superiority or victory; conflict: *a contest between nations.* —*v.t.* **1.** to struggle in order to win (something); fight for: *The soldiers contested every bit of ground.* **2.** to challenge the validity of; dispute: *The pitcher contested the decision of the umpire.* —*v.i.* to enter into competition; vie (with *with* or *against*): *Only a fool would contest against those odds.* [Latin *contestārī* to call to witness, introduce a lawsuit.] —con·test′a·ble, *adj.*

con·test·ant (kən tes′tənt) *n.* **1.** a person who takes part in a contest. **2.** a person who contests the legality or validity of something, such as an election or decision: *to be the chief contestant of a will.*

con·text (kon′tekst) *n.* **1.** the words, phrases, or sentences that surround a word, sentence, or passage and help determine its meaning: *to quote a passage out of context.* **2.** the conditions or circumstances in which a particular thing or event exists or occurs; environment. [Latin *contextus* a joining together, connection, going back to *con-* together + *texere* to weave.]

con·tex·tu·al (kən teks′chü əl) *adj.* relating to or depending on the context. —**con·tex′tu·al·ly,** *adv.*

con·ti·gu·i·ty (kon′ti gū′ i tē) *n., pl.* **-ties. 1.** the state of being contiguous; contact or proximity. **2.** a continuous extent; unbroken series.

con·tig·u·ous (kən tig′ū əs) *adj.* **1.** in actual contact; touching: *Michigan, Indiana, and Ohio are contiguous states.* **2.** near in time or space; close: *contiguous events.* [Latin *contiguus* bordering on, touching.] —**con·tig′u·ous·ly,** *adv.* —**con·tig′u·ous·ness,** *n.* —For Synonyms, see **adjacent.**

con·ti·nence (kon′tə nəns) *n.* self-restraint or moderation, esp. with regard to sexual desires. Also, **con′ti·nen·cy.**

con·ti·nent[1] (kon′tə nənt) *n.* **1.** one of the seven great land areas of the earth, traditionally including Asia, Africa, North America, South America, Antarctica, Europe, and Australia. **2. the Continent.** the mainland of Europe, as distinguished from the British Isles. **3.** *Archaic.* mainland. [Latin *(terra) continēns* mainland; literally, (land) holding together, from *continēns,* present participle of *continēre* to hold together, contain, from *com-* with, together + *tenēre* to hold.]

con·ti·nent[2] (kon′tə nənt) *adj.* practicing self-restraint or moderation, esp. with regard to sexual desires. [Latin *continēns,* present participle of *continēre* to hold together, restrain.]

con·ti·nen·tal (kon′tə nen′təl) *adj.* **1.** *also,* **Continental.** of, on, or characteristic of the mainland of Europe; European: *continental cuisine.* **2. Continental.** of or relating to the American colonies during and immediately after the American Revolution: *the Continental army.* **3.** of, characteristic of, or resembling a continent: *a continental landmass.* —*n.* **1.** *also,* **Continental.** an inhabitant of the mainland of Europe; European. **2.** a currency note issued by the Continental Congress during the American Revolution, which became worthless after the war. **3. Continental.** a soldier in the American army established by the Continental Congress on June 14, 1775.

  ·not worth a continental. worthless.

Continental Congress, either of two assemblies of delegates from the American colonies that met from 1774 to 1781. The Second Continental Congress convened in 1775, issued the Declaration of Independence in 1776, and governed the colonies until the Articles of Confederation were ratified in 1781.

continental divide 1. the elevation of land that separates river systems flowing toward one side of a continent from those flowing toward the other side. **2. Continental Divide.** in North America, such an elevation formed by the various peaks of the Rocky Mountains, separating rivers flowing eastward from those flowing westward. Also, **Great Divide.**

continental drift, the slow movement of the continental landmasses over millions of years, and the changes in geography that this has produced.

continental shelf, the broad edge of a continent that forms a shelf extending underwater from the shore and sloping down to a depth of approximately 600 feet (200 meters).

con·tin·gen·cy (kən tin′jən sē) *n., pl.* **-cies. 1.** an event that can possibly take place; chance happening: *A mountain climber tries to prepare for every contingency.* **2.** the quality or condition of being contingent; subject to chance; uncertain.

con·tin·gent (kən tin′jənt) *adj.* **1.** dependent on an uncertain condition or occurrence; conditional: *Our trip to Europe is contingent on making enough money*

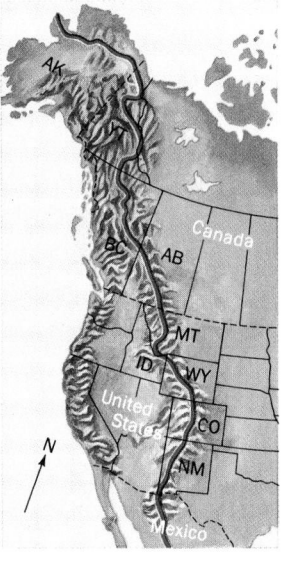

the **Continental Divide**

this summer. **2.** likely to happen, but not certain; possible: *A contingent result of our trip to the city is that we might see our grandparents.* **3.** happening by chance or by an unknown or unforeseen cause; accidental. **4.** *Logic.* (of a proposition) possibly true; logically possible. —*n.* **1.** a group, as of troops or delegates, contributed by another group as a part or share of a larger body. **2.** an accident or unforeseen event; contingency. [Latin *contingēns,* present participle of *contingere* to happen.] —**con·tin′gent·ly,** *adv.*

con·tin·u·al (kən tin′ū əl) *adj.* **1.** continuing without interruption; continuous: *the continual noise of traffic in the city.* **2.** occurring over and over again; repeated frequently and regularly: *The continual chiming of the clock kept me awake all night.* —**con·tin′u·al·ly,** *adv.*

con·tin·u·ance (kən tin′ū əns) *n.* **1.** the act of continuing or the state of being continued. **2.** the time during which something lasts; duration: *a famine of long continuance.* **3.** *Law.* an adjournment or postponement of a pending court action to a future date. **4.** anything that continues something already started; continuation.

con·tin·u·a·tion (kən tin′ū ā′shən) *n.* **1.** the act or fact of continuing, remaining, or extending without interruption: *The voters supported a continuation of the present city administration.* **2.** a continuing after an interruption; resumption: *the continuation of telephone service after the flood.* **3.** anything added to continue something already started: *This television program is a continuation of last week's.*

con·tin·ue (kən tin′ū) *v.,* **-tin·ued, -tin·u·ing.** —*v.i.* **1.** to keep on in a condition or course of action; go on; persist: *Continue until you reach the stop sign, then turn left.* **2.** to remain in effect or existence; last; endure: *The snowfall continued for two days.* **3.** to remain in a place or position: *She chose to continue as head nurse.* **4.** to proceed after an interruption; resume: *The meeting will continue after lunch.* —*v.t.* **1.** to go on with; keep on with; persist in: *to continue work despite illness.* **2.** to go on with (after an interruption); resume: *The professor will continue the lecture tomorrow.* **3.** to extend or prolong (something) in space, time, or development: *to continue a magazine subscription for another year.* **4.** to cause to remain in a place or position; retain: *The team continued him as manager.* **5.** *Law.* to adjourn or postpone (a pending court action) to a future date. [Old French *continuer* to proceed, go on, from Latin *continuāre* to make continuous, connect.] —**con·tin′u·a·ble,** *adj.*

Synonyms *v.i.* **Continue, endure** and **last**[2] mean to remain in existence. **Continue** implies unbroken existence: *The party continued until midnight.* **Endure** implies withstanding wear or some opposing force: *The town endured through fires and floods.* **Last** stresses the length of time passed: *The cold spell lasted ten days.*

continuing education 1. any program of usually part-time educational courses for adults, not designed as steps toward a degree, and offered in various settings. Also, **adult education. 2.** educational courses designed to refresh and update the knowledge or skills of workers in a given occupation or place of work.

con·ti·nu·i·ty (kon′tə nü′i tē, -nū′-) *n., pl.* **-ties. 1.** the state or quality of being continuous: *the continuity of time.* **2.** a logical connection, as of ideas; coherence: *The jury appreciated the continuity of the lawyer's argument.* **3.** a detailed plan giving the events, sequence of scenes, or script, as of a motion picture or television program. **4.** transitional comments or announcements between parts of a television or radio program.

con·tin·u·ous (kən tin′ū əs) *adj.* continuing without interruption in space, time, or development; unbroken: *a continuous curve.* —**con·tin′u·ous·ly,** *adv.* —**con·tin′u·ous·ness,** *n.*

con·tin·u·um (kən tin′ū əm) *n., pl.* **-tin·u·a** (-tin′ū ə). a continuous whole, having no discernible parts or separations. [Latin *continuum,* neuter of *continuus* continuous.]

con·tort (kən tôrt′) *v.t.* to twist or bend out of the usual shape or appearance; distort: *The patient's face was contorted with pain.* [Latin *contortus,* past participle of *contorquēre* to twist together.]

con·tor·tion (kən tôr′shən) *n.* **1.** the act of contorting or the state of being contorted. **2.** a twisted or bent shape: *the amazing contortions of the acrobat's body.*

con·tor·tion·ist (kən tôr′shə nist) *n.* a person who contorts, esp. a performer who twists and bends the body into unusual positions.

a	at	e	end	o	hot	u	up	hw	white		about
ā	ape	ē	me	ō	old	ū	use	ng	song	ə	taken
ä	far	i	it	ô	fork	ü	rule	th	thin		pencil
âr	care	ī	ice	oi	oil	u̇	pull	th	this		lemon
				ir	pierce	ou	out	ûr	turn	zh	measure		circus

con·tour (kon′tür) *n.* the shape of an object, figure, or body, or the line representing this: *The contour of the earth can be seen from an orbiting spacecraft. —adj.* **1.** following contour lines of hilly land when plowing and planting, thereby creating terraces that help prevent erosion: *contour farming.* **2.** made to fit the shape of something: *contour sheets for a bed. —v.t.* to shape or construct (something) to fit the contour of something else, as a road around a mountain. [French *contour* circuit, outline, from Italian *contorno,* going back to Latin *con-* together + *tornāre* to turn. See TURN.] —For Synonyms (*n.*), see **outline.**

contour line, a line, as on a map, connecting points of equal elevation above sea level.

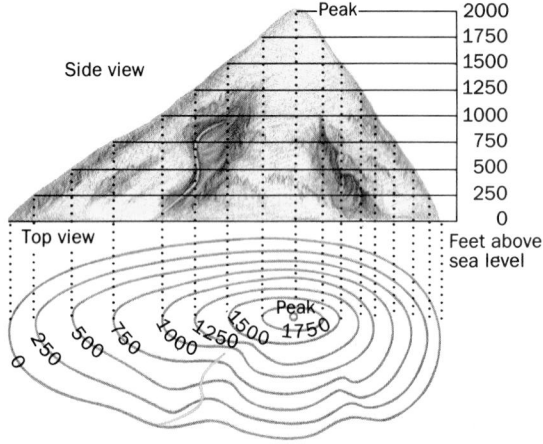

contour map

contour map, a map that shows the relative elevations of a land surface by means of contour lines; topographic map.

contr. 1. contract. **2.** contracted. **3.** contraction.

contra- *prefix* **1.** against; opposite: *contravene, contradiction.* **2.** *Music.* lower in pitch: *contrabass.* [Latin *contrā.*]

con·tra·band (kon′trə band′) *n.* **1.** goods prohibited by law from being imported or exported; smuggled goods: *The weapons were seized as contraband.* **2.** unlawful trade in such goods; smuggling: *The government tried to prevent the contraband in drugs.* **3.** goods, usually arms and ammunition, that, according to international law, when furnished by a neutral country to a country at war, may be rightfully seized by an opposing country. Also, **contraband of war.** *—adj.* prohibited by law from being imported or exported: *contraband goods.* [Spanish *contrabando,* from Italian *contrabbando,* from *contra* against (from Latin *contra*) + *bando* ban (of Germanic origin).]

con·tra·bass (kon′trə bās′) *n.* any of a family of musical instruments having a range below the bass, esp. the double bass of the violin family. *—adj.* pitched an octave lower than the normal bass.

con·tra·bas·soon (kon′trə ba sün′) *n.* a large bassoon, the largest and deepest toned member of the oboe family, pitched an octave lower than the ordinary bassoon; double bassoon.

con·tra·cep·tion (kon′trə sep′shən) *n.* the prevention of conception, esp. by chemical or mechanical means; birth control. [CONTRA- + (CON)CEPTION.]

con·tra·cep·tive (kon′trə sep′tiv) *adj.* relating to or used for contraception: *a contraceptive device. —n.* a chemical substance or mechanical device for preventing conception.

con·tract (*v.,* kən trakt′; *v.t.,* def. 3, *v.i.,* def. 2, also kon′trakt; *n.,* kon′trakt) *v.t.* **1.** to draw together (the parts of a thing) so as to shorten or make smaller: *A frightened hedgehog contracts its body into a ball.* **2.** to get or acquire: *to contract pneumonia, to contract a debt.* **3.** to establish by formal agreement: *The two businesses contracted a merger.* **4.** to shorten (a word, syllable, or phrase) by omitting or combining sounds or letters. *Are not* can be contracted to *aren't.* **5.** to hire under contract: *We contracted them to paint our house. —v.i.* **1.** to draw together so as to become shorter or smaller: *The leather strap contracted as it dried.* **2.** to make or enter into a formal agreement: *The farmer contracted for summer help. —n.* **1.** a formal agreement between two or more parties to do or not to do something; compact: *a marriage contract between two families.* **2.** *Law.* **a.** a formal agreement that is legally binding. **b.** a document containing the terms of this agreement. **3.** *Bridge.* **a.** an undertaking by the declarer to take the number of tricks in the final bid plus six tricks. **b.** the final bid itself. **c.** the number

of tricks specified in the bid. [Latin *contractus,* past participle of *contrahere* to draw together, make smaller, make an agreement.] —**con·tract′i·ble,** *adj.*

contract bridge, a card game played by four players in teams of two with a 52-card deck, in which only the number of tricks bid count toward game. ➡ distinguished from **auction bridge.**

con·tract·ed (kən trak′tid) *adj.* drawn together; shortened or made smaller: *a contracted muscle.*

con·trac·tile (kən trak′təl) *adj.* having the ability to contract or cause contraction: *contractile tissue, the contractile force of cold.* —**con·trac·til·i·ty** (kon′trak til′i tē), *n.*

contractile vacuole, a small cavity found in many one-celled organisms that pumps excess water and waste from the organism. For illustration, see **ameba.**

con·trac·tion (kən trak′shən) *n.* **1.** the act or process of contracting or the state of being contracted: *the contraction of a disease.* **2.** a shortening and thickening of muscle tissue. **3.** a shortened form of a word, syllable, or phrase made by an omission or combination of letters. *Wouldn't* is a contraction of *would not.*

con·trac·tive (kən trak′tiv) *adj.* contractile.

con·trac·tor (kon′trak tər, kən trak′-) *n.* **1.** a person who agrees to supply goods or do a job for a fixed price. **2.** one of the parties that makes a contract. **3.** something that contracts, esp. a muscle.

con·trac·tu·al (kən trak′chü əl) *adj.* of, relating to, or having the force of a contract: *contractual agreements.*

con·tra·dance (kon′trə dans′) contredanse.

con·tra·dict (kon′trə dikt′) *v.t.* **1.** to assert the opposite of or deny (a statement); declare to be untrue: *The eyewitness contradicted earlier testimony.* **2.** to assert the opposite of or deny what is stated by (someone): *They contradicted each other.* **3.** to be opposed to or inconsistent with: *Your words contradict your behavior. —v.i.* to speak in opposition; oppose. [Latin *contradictus,* past participle of *contradicere* to speak against, from *contra* against, opposite + *dicere* to say, speak.] —**con·tra·dict′a·ble,** *adj.* —**con·tra·dict′er;** *also,* **con·tra·dic′tor,** *n.*

con·tra·dic·tion (kon′trə dik′shən) *n.* **1.** a statement that contradicts another: *That speech contains many contradictions.* **2.** the act of contradicting. **3.** opposition or disagreement; inconsistency: *There seems to be contradiction between the two newspapers about what caused the fire.* **4.** a person or thing that contains inconsistent elements, esp. a self-contradictory statement. The statement *A circle is square* is a contradiction.

con·tra·dic·to·ry (kon′trə dik′tə rē) *adj.* **1.** involving or constituting a contradiction; inconsistent: *contradictory accounts of an accident.* **2.** inclined to contradict: *a contradictory person.* —**con·tra·dic′to·ri·ly,** *adv.* —**con·tra·dic′to·ri·ness,** *n.*

con·tra·dis·tinc·tion (kon′trə dis tingk′shən) *n.* a distinction by contrast or opposition. —**con·tra·dis·tinc′tive,** *adj.* —**con·tra·dis·tinc′tive·ly,** *adv.*

con·trail (kon′trāl) *n.* a trail of vapor that forms behind an airplane or rocket flying at high altitude. Also, **vapor trail.** [CON(DENSATION) + TRAIL.]

con·tra·in·di·cate (kon′trə in′di kāt′) *v.t.,* -cat·ed, -cat·ing. *Medicine.* to make (a procedure, drug, course of treatment, or the like) inadvisable. [CONTRA- + INDICATE.] —**con·tra·in·di·ca′tion,** *n.* —**con·tra·in·dic·a·tive** (kon′trə in dik′ə tiv), *adj.*

con·tral·to (kən tral′tō) *n., pl.* -tos. **1.** the lowest female voice. **2.** the part sung by a contralto. **3.** a singer having a contralto voice. *—adj.* of, relating to, or for a contralto: *a contralto voice.* [Italian *contralto* lowest female voice, singer having a contralto voice, going back to Latin *contrā* against + *altus* high.]

con·trap·tion (kən trap′shən) *n. Informal.* a mechanical device; contrivance; gadget. [Possibly blend of CONTRIVE, APT, and -ION.]

con·tra·pun·tal (kon′trə pun′təl) *adj.* **1.** of, relating to, or characterized by counterpoint: *contrapuntal theory.* **2.** composed according to the rules or principles of counterpoint: *contrapuntal music.* [Italian *contrappunto* counterpoint (going back to Latin *contrā* against + *pūnctus* point) + -AL¹.] —**con·tra·pun′tal·ly,** *adv.*

con·tra·pun·tist (kon′trə pun′tist) *n.* a person skilled in the composing of counterpoint.

con·tra·ri·e·ty (kon′trə rī′i tē) *n., pl.* -ties. **1.** the state or quality of being contrary: *contrariety of opinion.* **2.** something that is contrary: *the many contrarieties of human nature.*

con·trar·i·wise (kon′trer ē wīz′, kən trâr′ē-) *adv.* **1.** in the opposite direction. **2.** on the contrary. **3.** perversely.

con·trar·y (kon′trer ē; *adj.,* def. 3, also kən trâr′ē) *adj.* **1.** opposite in nature or tendency; entirely different; opposed: *contrary ideas, contrary statements.* **2.** opposite in position or direction: *contrary motion.* **3.** tending to oppose or contradict; unaccommodating; perverse: *a contrary person.* **4.** not what is wanted or needed; unfavorable; adverse: *Contrary winds put us off our course. —n., pl.* -trar·ies. **1.** a fact, quality, or condition that is

the opposite of something else; the opposite: *I believe the contrary to be the case.* **2.** one of a pair of opposites: *Hot and cold are contraries.* —*adv.* in opposition; contrarily: *Many people act contrary to what they think.* [Anglo-Norman *contrarie* directly opposed, from Latin *contrārius* opposite, opposed.] —**con·trar·i·ly** (kon′trer ə lē, kən trâr′-), *adv.* —**con′trar·i·ness,** *n.*
 • **on the contrary.** just the opposite: *On the contrary, we are not going to go.*
 • **to the contrary.** to the opposite effect: *Did you hear any rumors to the contrary?*
con·trast (*v.,* kən trast′; *n.,* kon′trast) *v.t.* to examine or set in opposition in order to show differences: *The lecturer contrasted two primitive cultures.* —*v.i.* to show differences when compared: *The white hat contrasted sharply with the black dress. The colors in that painting contrast nicely.* —*n.* **1.** the act of contrasting or the state of being contrasted: *The rich and poor sections of that city are in sharp contrast with each other.* **2.** a difference shown by contrasting: *the contrast between darkness and light.* **3.** a person or thing that shows differences: *This new car is quite a contrast to the one you used to own.* [French *contraster* to be or to put in contrast, from Italian *contrastare* to stand out against, going back to Latin *contrā* against + *stāre* to stand.] —**con·trast′a·ble,** *adj.*

> **Usage** The verbs to **contrast** and **compare,** and their derivative nouns **contrast** and **comparison,** are used for examining things side by side and showing their similarities and differences. **Contrast,** as both verb and noun, is used when emphasizing differences: *The students were asked to contrast the views of the two main characters in the novel. This year's clothes are bright in color, in contrast to last year's browns and grays.* **Compare** and **comparison** are broader in scope, used to focus on both the differences and the likenesses between things: *How do the views of the presidential candidates compare with your own? A comparison of the structure of these two flowers shows that they come from completely different plant families. A comparison of these two artists shows many similarities in their style.*

con·tra·vene (kon′trə vēn′) *v.t.* -**vened,** -**ven·ing. 1.** to go against; come in conflict with; violate; transgress: *Slavery contravenes the principles of justice.* **2.** to oppose in argument; contradict: *to contravene a proposal.* [Late Latin *contrāvenīre,* from Latin *contrā* against + *venīre* to come.]
con·tra·ven·tion (kon′trə ven′shən) *n.* the act of contravening; opposition; violation.
con·tre·danse (kon′trə dans′; *French* kôn trə däns′) *also,* **con·tra·dance, con·tre·dance.** *n.* **1.** a type of dance for several couples in which the dancers face each other in two opposing lines. **2.** a piece of music written for such a dance. [French *contredanse* quadrille, from English COUNTRY-DANCE; influenced by French *contre* against, opposite (with reference to the two opposing lines of dancers).]
con·tre·temps (kon′trə tän′; *French* kôn trə tän′) *n., pl.* -**temps** (-tänz′; *French* -tän′). an embarrassing or awkward incident or situation; mishap. [French *contre-temps* mishap, out of time (in music), going back to Latin *contrā* against + *tempus* time.]
con·trib·ute (kən trib′ūt, -yut) *v.,* -**ut·ed,** -**ut·ing.** —*v.t.* **1.** to give or furnish (something) along with others to a common fund or for a common purpose: *to contribute money to charity.* **2.** to furnish (an article, story, or the like), as to a newspaper or magazine. —*v.i.* **1.** to give along with others; make a contribution: *to contribute to a discussion.* **2.** to furnish an article, story, or the like to a publication: *to contribute to a literary journal.* **3.** to have a part in bringing about a result: *Good weather contributed to the success of the fair.* [Latin *contribūtus,* past participle of *contribuere* to bring together, add, collect, going back to *con-* together + *tribus* tribe; originally with reference to payments made by the ancient Roman *tribes.*] —**con·trib′u·tive,** *adj.* —**con·trib′u·tive·ly,** *adv.* —For Synonyms (*v.t.*), see **donate.**
con·tri·bu·tion (kon′trə bū′shən) *n.* **1.** the act of contributing: *A political campaign depends largely on the contribution of money and time by supporters.* **2.** something that is contributed: *The invention of the typewriter was a great contribution to communication and printing.*
con·trib·u·tor (kən trib′yə tər) *n.* **1.** a person who contributes: *All contributors to the fund drive will meet today.* **2.** a person who furnishes writings to a publication.
con·trib·u·to·ry (kən trib′yə tôr′ē) *adj.* having a part in bringing about a result; contributing: *Adequate rain was a contributory factor in the large harvest.*
con·trite (kən trīt′, kon′trīt) *adj.* **1.** deeply sorry for one's faults or wrongdoings; remorseful; penitent: *I felt contrite about my rude behavior.* **2.** showing or arising from sorrow or remorse: *a contrite apology.* [Old French *contrit* repentant, from Late Latin *contrītus,* from Latin *contrītus,* ground up, bruised, past participle

of *conterere* to grind, bruise.] —**con·trite′ly,** *adv.* —**con·trite′ness,** *n.*
con·tri·tion (kən trish′ən) *n.* sorrow or remorse for one's faults or wrongdoings; penitence. For Synonyms, see **penitence.**
con·triv·ance (kən trī′vəns) *n.* **1.** something contrived, such as a plan, scheme, or mechanical device. **2.** the act of contriving or the ability to contrive: *beyond the reach of human contrivance.*
con·trive (kən trīv′) *v.,* -**trived,** -**triv·ing.** —*v.t.* **1.** to devise or plan in a clever or ingenious way; scheme; plot: *The prisoners of war contrived an escape route.* **2.** to bring about, esp. with difficulty: *They contrived to keep their plan a secret.* **3.** to create in a clever or ingenious way; invent; design: *to contrive a new lock, to contrive a new accounting system.* —*v.i.* to form schemes or plots. [Old French *controver* to imagine, invent, going back to Latin *con-* with + *tropus* figure of speech. See TROPE.] —**con·triv′a·ble,** *adj.* —**con·triv′er,** *n.* —For Synonyms, see **devise.**
con·trived (kən trīvd′) *adj.* obviously planned; not natural; artificial.
con·trol (kən trōl′) *n.* **1.** the power to direct or regulate; authority: *The dictator had absolute control over the country.* **2.** the power or ability to hold in check; restraint: *to lose control of one's temper.* **3.** a method or means of restraint; check: *The government imposed controls to combat inflation.* **4.** *also,* **controls.** a device or system for operating, regulating, or guiding a mechanism, such as an airplane. **5.** a standard of comparison, esp. one used to measure or verify the results of an experiment. **6.** in spiritualism, a spirit that acts as an intermediary between a medium and the spirit to be contacted. —*v.t.,* -**trolled,** -**trol·ling. 1.** to have power to direct or regulate; exercise authority over: *The federal government controls interstate commerce.* **2.** to hold in check; curb; restrain: *to control one's temper.* **3.** to use a control in (an experiment), esp. for verifying results. [Old French *contrerolle* duplicate register kept as a check on the original, going back to Latin *contrā* against + Medieval Latin *rotulus* roll of paper, from Latin *rotulus* little wheel.] —**con·trol′la·bil′i·ty,** *n.* —**con·trol′la·ble,** *adj.*
controlled substance, a drug, esp. a narcotic, whose possession and use is restricted by law.
con·trol·ler (kən trō′lər) *n.* **1.** a person or thing that controls. **2.** *also,* **comptroller.** an officer, as in a bank or corporation, in charge of the bookkeeping, accounting, and auditing procedures and reports. —**con·trol′ler·ship′,** *n.*
control rod, a rod made of a material, such as boron or cadmium, that absorbs neutrons. It is lowered into a nuclear reactor to control the rate of fission.
control stick, a lever by which the pilot of an airplane controls the movement of the ailerons and elevators and thereby controls the direction of flight. Also, **control column.**
control tower, a structure on an airfield that controls communication with aircraft and air traffic.

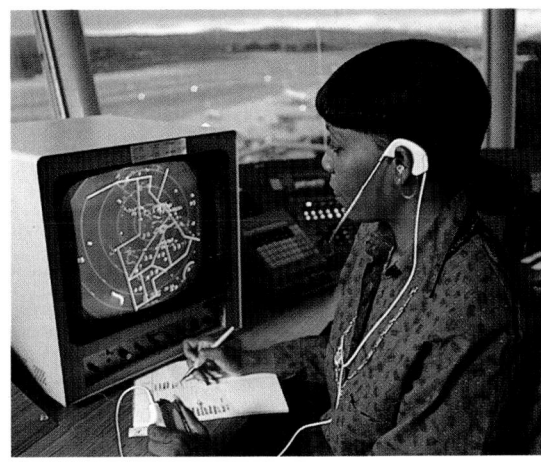

control tower

a	at	e	end	o	hot	u	up	hw	white	(	about
ā	ape	ē	me	ō	old	ū	use	ng	song		taken
ä	far	i	it	ô	fork	u	rule	th	thin	ə	pencil
âr	care	ī	ice	oi	oil	u̇	pull	th	this		lemon
		ir	pierce	ou	out	ûr	turn	zh	measure	(	circus

265

con·tro·ver·sial (kon'trə vûr'shəl) *adj.* **1.** causing or characterized by controversy: *a controversial issue.* **2.** given to controversy; argumentative: *a controversial person.* —**con'tro·ver'sial·ly,** *adv.*

con·tro·ver·sial·ist (kon'trə vûr'shə list) *n.* a person who engages in or enjoys controversy.

con·tro·ver·sy (kon'trə vûr'sē) *n., pl.* **-sies.** a dispute or disagreement, esp. one that leads to much debate: *The new tax caused widespread controversy.* [Latin *contrōversia.*] —For Synonyms, see **argument.**

con·tro·vert (kon'trə vûrt', kon'trə vûrt') *v.t.* **1.** to argue against; oppose; deny; contradict: *The facts controvert the testimony of the witness.* **2.** to argue about; dispute; debate. [From CONTROVERSY.] —**con'tro·vert'er,** *n.* —**con'tro·vert'i·ble,** *adj.*

con·tu·ma·cious (kon'tù mā'shəs, -tyù-) *adj.* obstinately and willfully disobedient; insubordinate; rebellious.

con·tu·ma·cy (kon'tù mə sē, -tyù-) *n., pl.* **-cies.** obstinate and willful disobedience of, or resistance to, authority; insubordination. [Latin *contumācia* obstinacy.]

con·tu·me·li·ous (kon'tù mē'lē əs, -tyù-) *adj.* rude in a scornful or haughty way; humiliating and insolent. —**con'tu·me'li·ous·ly,** *adv.*

con·tu·me·ly (kon'tù mə lē, -tyù-) *n., pl.* **-lies. 1.** rudeness in manner or speech; scornful or haughty insolence. **2.** an instance of such insolence; humiliating insult. [Latin *contumēlia* reproach, insult.]

con·tuse (kən tüz', -tyüz') *v.t.,* **-tused, -tus·ing.** to injure without breaking the skin; bruise. [Latin *contūsus,* past participle of *contundere* to bruise.]

con·tu·sion (kən tü'zhən, -tū'-) *n.* an injury in which the skin is not broken; bruise.

co·nun·drum (kə nun'drəm) *n.* **1.** a riddle whose answer involves a pun, for example: *What would an elephant bring on a trip? Its trunk.* **2.** any puzzling or difficult problem. [Of uncertain origin.]

con·va·lesce (kon'və les') *v.i.,* **-lesced, -lesc·ing.** to regain health and strength gradually after illness; recover. [Latin *convalēscere.*]

con·va·les·cence (kon'və les'əns) *n.* **1.** gradual recovery of health and strength after illness. **2.** the period of this recovery.

con·va·les·cent (kon'və les'ənt) *adj.* **1.** recovering from illness: *a convalescent patient.* **2.** for or related to convalescence: *a convalescent home.* —*n.* a person who is convalescing.

con·vec·tion (kən vek'shən) *n.* the transfer of heat from one part of a gas or liquid to another by heated currents of the gas or liquid. [Late Latin *convectiō* a carrying together, from Latin *convehere* to carry together.] —**con·vec'tive,** *adj.*

con·vec·tor (kən vek'tər) *n.* a device for heating a room or space by convection, as by warming the air that passes over or through it.

con·vene (kən vēn') *v.,* **-vened, -ven·ing.** —*v.i.* to come together, esp. for a meeting; assemble: *Congress will convene again in the fall.* —*v.t.* to cause to assemble; convoke: *The club president convened the members.* [Latin *convenīre* to come together.] —**con·ven'er,** *n.*

con·ven·ience (kən vēn'yəns) *n.* **1.** the quality of being convenient; serviceability: *the convenience of frozen foods.* **2.** freedom from effort or difficulty; comfort; ease: *an information service for the convenience of visitors.* **3.** something that gives comfort or ease; something convenient: *A washing machine is one of the many modern conveniences.*

  ·at one's convenience. at a time or place, or under conditions, suitable to one's needs or wishes: *We will meet at your convenience.*

con·ven·ien·cy (kən vēn'yən sē) *n., pl.* **-cies.** *Archaic.* convenience.

con·ven·ient (kən vēn'yənt) *adj.* **1.** favorable to one's needs or purposes; giving comfort or ease: *It is convenient to have a dishwasher if you have a large family.* **2.** within easy reach; near: *a home convenient to all public transportation.* **3.** not requiring effort or causing difficulty; easy to do: *Is it convenient to meet at noon?* [Latin *conveniēns,* present participle of *convenīre* to come together, suit.] —**con·ven'ient·ly,** *adv.*

con·vent (kon'vent, -vənt) *n.* **1.** a society of nuns. **2.** the building or buildings occupied by such a society; nunnery. **3.** formerly, any group of persons living together under strict religious discipline. [Latin *conventus* assembly; literally, a coming together.]

con·ven·ti·cle (kən ven'ti kəl) *n.* **1.** a secret meeting, esp. for religious worship, such as that of the dissenters from the Church of England in the sixteenth and seventeenth centuries. **2.** the place of such a meeting. [Latin *conventīculum* small assembly, diminutive of *conventus* assembly.]

con·ven·tion (kən ven'shən) *n.* **1.** a formal meeting of delegates or members for a particular purpose: *a medical convention, a political convention.* **2.** the delegates or members at such a meeting: *The convention voted on a new constitution.* **3.** the generally accepted practices or standards of a society: *They ignored convention and lived exactly as they wanted.* **4.** a generally accepted rule, practice, or custom: *Saying "How are you?" when you meet someone is a social convention.* **5.** an international agreement, as between countries, usually covering specific matters. [Latin *conventiō* meeting, agreement.]

con·ven·tion·al (kən ven'shə nəl) *adj.* **1.** conforming to traditional or generally accepted practices or standards; not original or new: *a conventional approach to a problem.* **2.** established by, or in accordance with, accepted custom or usage; customary: *conventional rules of etiquette.* **3.** not involving or using nuclear weapons or energy: *conventional warfare.* **4.** following accepted models, standards, or traditions; unimaginative: *a conventional person, a conventional work of art.* —**con·ven'tion·al·ly,** *adv.*

con·ven·tion·al·ism (kən ven'shə nə liz'əm) *n.* **1.** adherence to, or regard for, that which is conventional. **2.** something that is conventional, as an idea, custom, or practice.

con·ven·tion·al·i·ty (kən ven'shə nal'i tē) *n., pl.* **-ties. 1.** the quality or character of being conventional: *The conventionality of their opinions often becomes boring.* **2.** conventional behavior or opinion; adherence to convention. **3.** a conventional rule, practice, or custom: *the conventionalities of society.*

con·ven·tion·al·ize (kən ven'shə nə līz') *v.t.,* **-ized, -iz·ing. 1.** to make conventional. **2.** to represent in a conventional manner, as in art. —**con·ven'tion·al·i·za'tion,** *n.*

conventional wisdom, a generally accepted belief or attitude; widely held opinion.

con·ven·tu·al (kən ven'chü əl) *adj.* of, relating to, or belonging to a convent. —*n.* a member of a convent.

con·verge (kən vûrj') *v.,* **-verged, -verg·ing.** —*v.i.* **1.** to come together or tend to come together at a place or point: *The roads converged at the stadium.* **2.** to come together, as in a common interest or conclusion: *All attention converged on the center ring at the circus.* —*v.t.* to cause to converge. [Late Latin *convergere* to incline together, from Latin *con-* together + *vergere* to incline.]

con·ver·gence (kən vûr'jəns) *n.* **1.** the act or process of converging or the state of being converged. **2.** the degree or point of converging. **3.** *Biology.* the tendency of unrelated organisms to develop similar structures because they live in the same type of environment, as the wings of birds and insects and the fins of whales and fish.

con·ver·gen·cy (kən vûr'jən sē) *n., pl.* **-cies.** convergence.

con·ver·gent (kən vûr'jənt) *adj.* coming or tending to come to a point; converging.

converging lens, a lens that is thicker in the middle than at the edges, causing light rays to converge and focus on a point.

con·vers·a·ble (kən vûr'sə bəl) *adj.* **1.** easy or pleasant to talk with; affable. **2.** inclined to converse; fond of talking. **3.** *Archaic.* relating to or proper for conversation. —**con·vers'a·bly,** *adv.*

con·ver·sant (kən vûr'sənt, kon'vər-) *adj.* familiar or acquainted, esp. by study or experience: *to be conversant with the law.* —**con·ver'sant·ly,** *adv.*

con·ver·sa·tion (kon'vər sā'shən) *n.* informal or friendly talk between people, or an instance of such talk.

con·ver·sa·tion·al (kon'vər sā'shə nəl) *adj.* **1.** of or characteristic of conversation: *a conversational tone.* **2.** given to or good at conversation. —**con'ver·sa'tion·al·ly,** *adv.*

con·ver·sa·tion·al·ist (kon'vər sā'shə nə list) *n.* a person who is fond of or good at conversation.

con·verse[1] (*v.,* kən vûrs'; *n.,* kon'vûrs) *v.i.,* **-versed, -vers·ing.** to talk in an informal or friendly way; engage in or hold a conversation: *Although they were strangers, they conversed with ease.* —*n.* informal or friendly talk; conversation. [Old French *converser* to associate with, from Latin *conversārī* to live with, keep company with.] —**con·vers'er,** *n.*

con·verse[2] (*adj.,* kən vûrs', kon'vûrs; *n.,* kon'vûrs) *adj.* opposite in order, direction, or action; reversed; contrary. —*n.* **1.** something that is opposite or contrary to something else: *Day is the converse of night.* **2.** a proposition in logic that is derived from another by interchanging the subject and predicate terms. The statement *Some Mondays are holidays* is the converse of the statement *Some holidays are Mondays.* [Latin *conversus,* past participle of *convertere* to turn about, from *com-* with, together + *vertere* to turn.] —**con·verse'ly,** *adv.*

con·ver·sion (kən vûr'zhən, -shən) *n.* **1.** the act or process of converting or the state of being converted; change in character, condition, or function; transformation: *the conversion of water*

into ice, the conversion of an attic into a bedroom. **2.a.** a change by which one adopts a different belief, opinion, or course of action. **b.** the adoption of a religion or religious way of life. **3.** an unlawful appropriation and use of another person's property. **4.** the exchange of one thing into another of equivalent value, as currency or units of measurement. **5.** an interchange of the subject and predicate terms of a proposition in logic. **6.** a play in football by which a team that has just scored a touchdown makes an extra point or points when the ball is kicked between the goal posts or carried or passed into the end zone.

con·vert (*v.,* kən vûrt′; *n.,* kon′vûrt) *v.t.* **1.** to change in character, condition, or function; transform: *to convert salt water to fresh water.* **2.a.** to cause (someone) to change a belief, opinion, or course of action: *We'll soon convert you to our way of thinking.* **b.** to cause (someone) to adopt a religion or religious way of life. **3.** to exchange for an equivalent: *to convert Swiss francs into dollars, to convert feet into meters.* **4.** to appropriate and use (another person's property) unlawfully. **5.** to transpose the subject and predicate terms of (a proposition) in logic. —*v.i.* to change one's beliefs, course of action, or conduct. —*n.* a person who has been converted, as from one religious belief to another. [Old French *convertir* to turn, going back to Latin *convertere* to turn about, change, from *com-* with, together + *vertere* to turn.]

con·vert·er (kən vûr′tər) *n.* **1.** a person or thing that converts. **2.** a machine for changing alternating electric current to direct current or vice versa. **3.** any of various other machines or devices used to change the form of energy. **4.** Bessemer converter. **5.** catalytic converter.

con·vert·i·ble (kən vûr′tə bəl) *adj.* **1.** capable or being converted: *This convertible sofa also serves as a bed.* **2.** (of an automobile) having a roof that may be folded back or removed. —*n.* an automobile with a roof that is convertible. —**con·vert′i·bil′i·ty,** *n.* —**con·vert′i·bly,** *adv.*

con·vex (kon veks′, kən-, kon′veks) *adj.* curved outward, as the outside of a circle or sphere: *a convex lens.*
➠ opposed to **concave.** [Latin *convexus* vaulted, arched.]

Convex   Concave

convex and concave surfaces

con·vex·i·ty (kən vek′si tē) *n., pl.* **-ties. 1.** the quality or condition of being convex. **2.** a convex surface or thing.

con·vex·o·con·cave (kən vek′sō kon kāv′) *adj.* convex on one side and concave on the other, with the convex side having a greater degree of curvature.

con·vey (kən vā′) *v.t.* **1.a.** to take or carry from one place to another; transport: *The train conveyed the supplies to the warehouse.* **b.** to serve as the medium or path for; transmit; conduct: *Pipes convey water from the reservoir to the city.* **2.** to make known; express; impart; communicate: *to convey the impression of being calm, to convey an idea through a painting.* **3.** to transfer the ownership of, as real property, from one person to another. [Anglo-Norman *conveier* to conduct, going back to Latin *cum* with + *via* road, way.] —**con·vey′a·ble,** *adj.* —For Synonyms, see **carry.**

con·vey·ance (kən vā′əns) *n.* **1.** the act of conveying. **2.** something that transports or carries, esp. a vehicle: *Buses are a public conveyance.* **3.a.** the transfer of the ownership of real property from one person to another. **b.** the document by which such a transfer is made.

con·vey·anc·er (kən vā′ən sər) *n.* a lawyer who is engaged in conveyancing.

con·vey·anc·ing (kən vā′ən sing) *n.* the act or business of dealing with the transfer of ownership of real property, including the preparation of documents and the investigation of titles to land.

con·vey·or (kən vā′ər) *also,* **con·vey·er.** *n.* **1.** a person or thing that conveys. **2.** conveyor belt.

conveyor belt *also,* **conveyer belt.** a mechanical device for transporting objects over generally short distances, usually designed as a continuous belt or series of rollers.

con·vict (*v.,* kən vikt′; *n.,* kon′vikt) *v.t.* **1.** to prove (someone) guilty: *to be convicted by the evidence.* **2.** to find (someone) guilty of a criminal charge: *The jury convicted the defendant of robbery.* **3.** to arouse a sense of guilt in (someone): *convicted by one's own conscience.* —*n.* **1.** a person serving a prison sentence, esp. for an extended period of time. **2.** a person who has been convicted by a court of law. [Latin *convictus,* past participle of *convincere* to prove clearly, refute, overcome.]

con·vic·tion (kən vik′shən) *n.* **1.a.** the act of finding or pronouncing (someone) guilty of a criminal charge. **b.** the state of being found or pronounced guilty. **2.** a firmly established opinion or belief: *It is my conviction that all people are equal.* **3.** the state of being convinced; certainty: *to act with conviction.*

con·vince (kən vins′) *v.t.,* **-vinced, -vinc·ing.** to cause (some-

one) to believe or feel certain; persuade by argument or evidence: *I convinced them that I was right.* [Latin *convincere* to prove clearly.] —**con·vin′ci·ble,** *adj.* —For Synonyms, see **persuade.**

con·vinc·ing (kən vin′sing) *adj.* having power to convince; able to be believed; persuasive: *a convincing speech, a convincing performance.* —**con·vinc′ing·ly,** *adv.* —**con·vinc′ing·ness,** *n.*

con·viv·i·al (kən viv′ē əl) *adj.* **1.** fond of merriment and good company; jovial; sociable. **2.** relating to or characteristic of a feast or jovial party; festive: *a convivial atmosphere.* [Latin *convīviālis* festive, from *convīvium* feast.] —**con·viv·i·al·i·ty** (kən viv′ē al′i-tē), *n.* —**con·viv′i·al·ly,** *adv.*

con·vo·ca·tion (kon′və kā′shən) *n.* **1.** a group of persons assembled by summons; assembly: *There was a convocation of the students before the graduation exercises.* **2.** a calling together of such a group; summons to assemble. —**con′vo·ca′tion·al,** *adj.*

con·voke (kən vōk′) *v.t.,* **-voked, -vok·ing.** to call together; summon to meet or assemble: *to convoke a legislature.* [Latin *convocāre.*] —**con·vok′er,** *n.*

con·vo·lute (kon′və lüt′) *v.t., v.i.,* **-lut·ed, -lut·ing.** to coil up or twist intricately; wind in and out. —*adj.* convoluted. [Latin *convolūtus,* past participle of *convolvere* to roll together.]

con·vo·lut·ed (kon′və lü′tid) *adj.* **1.** turned in or wound up upon itself; intricately twisted, wound, or coiled. **2.** difficult to understand, analyze, or do; intricate; complicated: *a convoluted plot for a story.*

con·vo·lu·tion (kon′və lü′shən) *n.* **1.** one of the windings, twists, or coils of something convoluted. **2.** any of the irregular folds on the surface of the brain. **3.** the act of convoluting or the state of being convoluted.

con·vol·vu·lus (kən vol′vyə ləs) *n., pl.* **-lus·es** or **-li** (-lī′). bindweed. [Latin *convolvulus,* from *convolvere* to roll together; with reference to its twining runners.]

con·voy (*n.,* kon′voi; *v., also* kən voi′) *n.* **1.** a group, as of ships or vehicles, traveling with a protective escort: *a convoy of tankers.* **2.** a group, as of warships, troops, or aircraft, that acts as a protective escort: *A convoy of submarines escorted the battleship out of the harbor.* **3.** any group of persons or vehicles traveling together: *A convoy of trucks passed us on the highway.* **4.** the protection provided by an escort: *to sail under the convoy of a large fleet.* —*v.t.* to accompany or escort in order to afford protection. [Old French *convoier* to accompany on the way, going back to Latin *cum* with + *via* road, way.]

con·vulse (kən vuls′) *v.t.,* **-vulsed, -vuls·ing. 1.** to cause violent shaking, agitation, or disturbance in: *The earthquake convulsed the city. A revolution convulsed the country.* **2.** to cause to shake with strong emotion or violent fits of laughter: *convulsed in rage.* **3.** to cause violent, involuntary muscular contractions. —*v.i.* to experience violent, involuntary muscular contractions. [Latin *convulsus,* past participle of *convellere* to tear up, wrench.]

con·vul·sion (kən vul′shən) *n.* **1.** a violent, involuntary contraction or series of contractions of the muscles; spasm. **2.** a violent fit of laughter. **3.** a violent shaking or disturbance; agitation; upheaval.

con·vul·sive (kən vul′siv) *adj.* **1.** of, like, or producing a convulsion or convulsions. **2.** having or characterized by convulsions: *a convulsive medical disorder.* —**con·vul′sive·ly,** *adv.*

co·ny (kō′nē) *n., pl.* **-nies.** *also,* **coney. 1.** rabbit fur. **2.** a rabbit. **3.** pika. **4.** in the Old Testament, a small rabbitlike animal, probably a hyrax. [Anglo-Norman *conil, conin* rabbit, from Latin *cunīculus;* possibly of Iberian origin.]

coo (kü) *n.* a soft, murmuring sound, such as that made by a pigeon or dove. —*v.,* **cooed, coo·ing.** —*v.i.* **1.** to make a soft, murmuring sound. **2.** to speak softly and lovingly; murmur in gentle, loving tones. —*v.t.* to express or utter with a coo: *He cooed his answer to her.* [Imitative.] —**coo′er,** *n.*

cook (kŭk) *v.t.* **1.** to prepare (food) for eating by the application of heat, as by roasting, boiling, baking, or frying. **2.** to apply heat or fire to (something). —*v.i.* **1.** (of food) to undergo cooking; be cooked. **2.** to prepare food for eating. **3.** *Informal.* to undergo preparation: *How long has that plan been cooking?* **4.** *Informal.* to take place; occur; happen: *Let's go see what's cooking with them.* —*n.* a person who prepares food for eating. [Old English *cōc* a cook, from Late Latin *cocus,* from Latin *coquus.*]
·to cook up. *Informal.* **a.** to prepare; concoct: *to cook up trouble.* **b.** to devise or invent, esp. in order to deceive: *to cook up a good excuse.*

a	at	e	end	o	hot	u	up	hw	white		about
ā	ape	ē	me	ō	old	ū	use	ng	song		taken
ä	far	i	it	ô	fork	ü	rule	th	thin	ə	pencil
âr	care	ī	ice	oi	oil	u̇	pull	th	this		lemon
				îr	pierce	ou	out	ûr	turn	zh	measure		circus

cook·book (kŭk′bŭk′) *n.* a book containing recipes and other information about food and its preparation.

cook·er (kŭk′ər) *n.* an apparatus or utensil for cooking food: *a steam cooker for vegetables.*

cook·er·y (kŭk′ə rē) *n., pl.* **-er·ies. 1.** the art or practice of preparing and cooking food. **2.** a place for cooking and serving food.

cook·house (kŭk′hous′) *n., pl.* **-hous·es** (-hou′ziz). a separate building or other place for cooking and preparing meals.

cook·ie (kŭk′ē) *also,* **cooky.** *n.* **1.** a small, usually flat cake baked from sweetened dough. **2.** *Slang.* a person: *a smart cookie.* [Dutch *koekje* small cake.]

cook·out (kŭk′out′) *n.* an outdoor gathering at which food is cooked and eaten.

cook·stove (kŭk′stōv′) *n.* a stove, usually large and having more than one oven, used for cooking.

cook·y (kŭk′ē) *n., pl.* **cook·ies.** cookie.

cool (kül) *adj.* **1.** lacking warmth but not extremely cold; moderately cold: *a cool breeze.* **2.** giving protection or relief from heat: *a cool summer dress.* **3.** not excited; calm; rational; composed: *to remain cool in the face of danger.* **4.** lacking enthusiasm or warmth; not cordial: *The play received a cool response from the critics.* **5.** having or showing boldness or a deliberate lack of respect; impudent: *a cool look, a cool reply.* **6.** (of color) suggesting coolness or serenity: *Blue and green are usually considered cool colors.* **7.** *Slang.* excellent; fabulous; great. **8.** *Informal.* without exaggeration; actual: *a cool million dollars.* *—adv. Informal.* in a cool manner; with coolness: *to play it cool.* *—n.* **1.** a cool time, place, or thing: *We took a walk in the cool of the evening.* **2.** *Slang.* composure; rationality; calmness: *to keep one's cool.* *—v.t.* **1.** to make less warm. **2.** to lessen the intensity of; moderate; calm: *The price cooled my eagerness to buy a new car.* *—v.i.* **1.** to become less warm. **2.** to lessen in intensity or excitement; become calmer. [Old English *cōl* moderately cold.] **—cool′ly,** *adv.* **—cool′ness,** *n.*

• **to cool one's heels.** *Informal.* to wait or be kept waiting at great length.

cool·ant (kü′lənt) *n.* a substance, usually a liquid, used to cool machinery, such as an automobile engine or a dentist's drill.

cool·er (kü′lər) *n.* **1.** a container or apparatus for keeping or making something cool. **2.** something that cools, such as an iced drink. **3.** *Slang.* jail.

cool-head·ed (kül′hed′id) *adj.* not easily excited or disturbed; calm.

coo·lie (kü′lē) *n.* formerly, an unskilled Asian laborer, esp. one working for low wages. *—adj.* of or characteristic of a coolie: *coolie wages.* [Hindi *kūli* laborer; of uncertain origin.]

cooling tower

cooling tower, a large concrete structure designed to remove heat from water used for cooling, as in a nuclear reactor.

coomb (küm, kōm) combe.

coon (kün) *n.* raccoon.

coon·skin (kün′skin′) *n.* the skin of a raccoon, esp. one cured to make a hat or coat. *—adj.* made from the skin of a raccoon: *a coonskin cap.*

coop (küp, kŭp) *n.* **1.** a cage, pen, or enclosure for fowl or small animals: *a rabbit coop.* **2.** *Slang.* any place of confinement; jail. *—v.t.* to confine in or as in a coop (often with *in* or *up*): *We were cooped up in the house because of the weather.* [Latin *cūpa* cask.]

• **to fly the coop.** *Slang.* to escape, as from jail or confinement.

co-op (kō′op) *n.* cooperative.

coop., cooperative.

coop·er (kü′pər, kŭp′ər) *n.* a person who makes or repairs barrels, casks, and similar containers. *—v.t., v.i.* to make or repair (barrels, casks, and similar containers). [Middle Dutch *cūper* a cooper, from *cūpe* cask, from Latin *cūpa.*]

coop·er·age (kü′pər ij, kŭp′ər-) *n.* **1.** the work or business of a cooper. **2.** a place where a cooper works. **3.** a fee charged for a cooper's work.

co·op·er·ate (kō op′ə rāt′) *also,* **co-op·er·ate.** *v.i.,* **-at·ed, -at·ing.** to work or act with another or others for a common purpose; unite in action: *The three clubs cooperated in planning a party.* [Late Latin *cooperātus,* past participle of *cooperārī* to work together, from Latin *co-* together + *operārī* to work.] **—co·op′er·a′tor,** *n.*

co·op·er·a·tion (kō op′ə rā′shən) *also,* **co-op·er·a·tion.** *n.* **1.** the act or process of cooperating; working with another or others for a common purpose. **2.** the association of a group of people for mutual economic benefit.

co·op·er·a·tive (kō op′ər ə tiv, -op′rə-, -op′ə rā′-) *also,* **co-op·er·a·tive.** *adj.* **1.** willing to work together with others: *a cooperative child.* **2.** of or characterized by cooperation: *It took a cooperative effort to paint the kitchen.* **3.** of, relating to, or designating a business enterprise, such as a food store or farm produce distributor, that is owned and operated by its members, who share its profits or benefits. *—n.* **1.** a cooperative business enterprise. **2.** a place where such an enterprise is located. **3.a.** an apartment building or complex in which each resident owns a share of the whole building or complex, occupies an apartment, and pays a share of the total costs. **b.** an apartment in such a building or complex. Also, **co-op.** **—co·op′er·a·tive·ly,** *adv.* **—co·op′er·a·tive·ness,** *n.*

co·or·di·nate (*v.,* kō ôr′də nāt′; *adj., n.,* kō ôr′də nit, -nāt′) *also,* **co-or·di·nate.** *v.,* **-nat·ed, -nat·ing.** *—v.t.* to bring into proper order, esp. so as to be harmonious and work well together: *to coordinate the functions of various government agencies.* *—v.i.* to act in harmony and work well together. *—n.* **1.** a person or thing that is equal in rank or importance to another. **2.** *Mathematics.* one of a set of numbers that define the position of a point in a line, in a plane, or in three-dimensional space. *—adj.* **1.** of equal rank or importance; of the same order: *coordinate clauses.* **2.** of, relating to, or using coordination or coordinates. [From COORDINATION.] **—co·or′di·nate·ly,** *adv.* **—co·or′di·nate·ness,** *n.* **—co·or′di·na′tive,** *adj.* **—co·or′di·na′tor,** *n.*

coordinate axis, a line along which coordinates are measured, as the x-axis or y-axis in the Cartesian coordinate system.

coordinate bond *Chemistry.* a covalent bond in which both of the electrons shared by a pair of adjacent atoms are supplied by just one of the atoms.

coordinating conjunction, a conjunction used to join two or more words or groups of words of the same type, such as nouns or independent clauses. In the sentence *Bill and Mary like to ski, but Jane and Mike prefer to swim or jog,* the conjunctions *and, but,* and *or* are coordinating conjunctions.

co·or·di·na·tion (kō ôr′də nā′shən) *also,* **co-or·di·na·tion.** *n.* **1.** the act of coordinating or the state of being coordinated. **2.** harmonious, integrated action or functioning: *to have good muscular coordination.* [Late Latin *coōrdinātiō* arrangement in the same order, from Latin *co-* with + *ōrdinātiō* arrangement.]

coot (küt) *n., pl.* **coots** or (*def 1.*) **coot. 1.** any of various water birds, genus *Fulica,* of temperate and tropical marshlands, resembling small, plump ducks and having short wings, lobed toes, and usually black or gray plumage, esp. the **American coot,** *F. americana,* or **mud hen.** Length: 16 inches (41 centimeters). **2.** scoter. **3.** *Informal.* a foolish person; simpleton. [Possibly of Low German origin.]

coot·ie (kü′tē) *n. Slang.* louse.

cop¹ (kop) *n. Informal.* police officer. [Short for COPPER².]

cop² (kop) *v.t.,* **copped, cop·ping.** *Slang.* **1.** to steal. **2.** to capture or seize. [Northern British dialectal *cop,* from earlier *cap* to grab, seize, probably from Old French *caper,* from Latin *capere* to take.]

• **to cop a plea.** *Slang.* **a.** to plead guilty so as to receive a lighter sentence, as by pleading guilty to a lesser charge. **b.** to admit wrongdoing or guilt and plead for mercy.

• **to cop out.** *Slang.* to withdraw from or back out of, as a promise or commitment (often with *of* or *on*): *to cop out on a promise.*

co·pa·cet·ic (kō′pə set′ik) *also,* **copesetic, copasetic.** *adj.* *Slang.* in good shape; fine. [Of uncertain origin.]

co·pal (kō′pəl, -pal) *n.* any of a group of hard resins obtained from various tropical trees or from their fossil remains. Copals have a high melting point and are used chiefly in making varnish. [Spanish *copal,* from Nahuatl *copalli* resin.]

co·part·ner (kō pärt′nər, kō′pärt′-) *n.* partner. —**co·part′·ner·ship′,** *n.*

co·pa·set·ic (kō′pə set′ik) copacetic.

cope[1] (kōp) *v.i.,* **coped, cop·ing. 1.** to be able to handle, esp. with success; contend (with *with*): *We don't have enough help to cope with all the work.* **2.** to deal with problems, responsibilities, difficulties, or the like: *to be overwhelmed and unable to cope.* [Old French *co(l)per* to strike, from *co(l)p* a blow, going back to Latin *colaphus,* from Greek *kolaphos.*]

cope[2] (kōp) *n.* **1.** a long cape worn by bishops, priests, and other members of the clergy during processions and certain religious services. **2.** something resembling a cope in shape or function, as a canopy, a vaulted roof, or the sky. **3.** coping. —*v.t.,* **coped, cop·ing.** to cover or furnish with a cope or coping. [Late Latin *cap(p)a* hood, cape; of uncertain origin.]

co·peck (kō′pek) kopeck.

co·pe·pod (kō′pə pod) *n.* any of a large group of tiny marine or freshwater crustaceans, order Copepoda, having six pairs of limbs and without compound eyes or a shell. Some copepods are parasites of fish, and others live on plankton.

Co·per·ni·can (kə pûr′ni kən) *adj.* of or relating to the Polish astronomer Nikolaus Copernicus or to his theory that the earth, like the other planets, revolves around the sun and that the apparent movement of the stars is due to the earth's rotation on its axis.

co·pe·set·ic (kō′pə set′ik) copacetic.

cope·stone (kōp′stōn′) *n.* **1.** the top stone of a wall or building; stone used for or in a coping. **2.** a finishing touch; crowning point. [COPE[2] + STONE.]

cop·i·er (kop′ē ər) *n.* **1.** a person or thing that makes copies, esp. an office machine that makes copies of letters, documents, or other materials. **2.** a person who imitates.

co·pi·lot (kō′pī′lət) *n.* the second pilot in an aircraft who assists and relieves the pilot.

cop·ing (kō′ping) *n.* a layer of brick or stone on the top of a wall, usually with a slope for shedding water. Also, **cope.** [COPE[2] + -ING[1].]

coping saw, a narrow-bladed saw in a U-shaped frame, used for very fine work, such as cutting sharp angles or curves.

co·pi·ous (kō′pē əs) *adj.* **1.** large in quantity; plentiful; abundant: *copious notes, copious tears.* **2.** yielding or containing a plentiful amount or supply: *a copious harvest.* **3.** using or containing many words or full of information: *a copious speaker, a copious report.* [Latin *cōpiōsus,* from *cōpia* abundance.] —**co′pi·ous·ly,** *adv.* —**co′pi·ous·ness,** *n.* —For Synonyms, see **plentiful.**

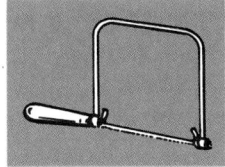

coping saw

co·pla·nar (kō plā′nər) *adj.* Geometry. contained in the same plane.

co·pol·y·mer (kō pol′ə mər) *n.* a compound formed by the polymerization of two or more dissimilar molecules, used in making plastics and synthetic rubber. —*v.t.* to make into a copolymer.

co·pol·y·mer·ize (kō pol′ə mə rīz′) *v.i.,* **-ized, -iz·ing.** to change into a copolymer. —**co·pol′y·mer·i·za′tion,** *n.*

cop-out (kop′out′) *n. Slang.* **1.** the act or an instance of copping out: *The senators' refusal to vote on the bill they claimed to support was a cop-out.* **2.** a person who cops out.

cop·per[1] (kop′ər) *n.* **1.** a lustrous, reddish metallic element that is highly ductile and malleable and an excellent conductor of heat and electricity. The widespread use of copper in alloys, esp. in brass and bronze, makes it the most useful nonferrous metal. Symbol: **Cu** For tables, see **element. 2.** a lustrous reddish brown color. **3.** a coin made of copper or bronze, such as a penny. **4.** a large boiler or cauldron, used esp. on ships. —*adj.* **1.** made of or containing copper. **2.** having the color copper; reddish brown. —*v.t.* to cover or coat with copper. [Old English *copor* this metal, going back to Late Latin *cuprum,* from Latin *(aes) Cyprium* (metal) of Cyprus, going back to Greek *Kypros* Cyprus, one of the main sources of copper in ancient times.] —**cop′per·y,** *adj.*

cop·per[2] (kop′ər) *n. Informal.* cop[1]. [Probably from COP[2] + -ER[1].]

cop·per·as (kop′ər əs) *n.* a greenish crystalline sulfate of iron, used in medicine, in photography, and in making inks and dyes.

Formula: FeSO₄·7H₂O [Old French *co(u)perose,* from Late Latin *cuprī rosa* rose of copper. See COPPER[1], ROSE[1].]

cop·per·head (kop′ər hed′) *n.* **1.** a pit viper, *Agkistrodon contortrix,* usually inhabiting rocky and overgrown areas of the eastern United States, having a copper-colored head and a light brown body with dark brown markings. Length: to 4½ feet (1.4 meters). **2. Copperhead.** a Northerner who sympathized with the Confederacy during the American Civil War.

cop·per·plate (kop′ər plāt′) *n.* **1.** a thin sheet of copper etched or engraved with a picture, design, or writing. **2.** a print made from such a plate. **3.** a printing process using such plates.

cop·per·smith (kop′ər smith′) *n.* a person who works with copper, esp. one who makes objects from copper.

copper sulfate, a copper salt occurring in the form of blue powder or efflorescent crystals, used as a fungicide and wood preservative and in electroplating and dyeing. When dehydrated, it becomes white. Formula: CuSO₄·5H₂O Also, **blue vitriol.**

cop·pice (kop′is) *n.* copse.

cop·ra (kop′rə) *n.* the dried meat of the coconut, the source of coconut oil. [Portuguese *copra,* from Malayalam *koppara* coconut, possibly going back to Sanskrit *kharparah* skull.]

copse (kops) *n.* a thicket or grove of small trees or bushes. Also, **coppice.** [Old French *copeïz* cut wood, from *co(l)per* to strike. See COPE[1].]

Copt (kopt) *n.* **1.** a native Egyptian descended from the ancient Egyptians. **2.** a member of the Coptic Church. [Modern Latin *Coptus,* through Arabic and Coptic, from Greek *Aigyptios* Egyptian.]

cop·ter (kop′tər) *n. Informal.* helicopter.

Cop·tic (kop′tik) *adj.* **1.** of or relating to the Copts, their language, or their culture. **2.** of or relating to the Coptic Church. —*n.* an ancient language of the Hamitic family, descended from Egyptian, and formerly spoken by the Copts. It is now used only as the liturgical language of the Coptic Church.

Coptic Church, a Christian church of Egypt and formerly of Ethiopia, adhering to the doctrine of Monophysitism and governed by a patriarch.

cop·u·la (kop′yə lə) *n., pl.* **-las** or **-lae** (-lē′). linking verb. [Latin *cōpula* bond, connection.]

cop·u·late (kop′yə lāt′) *v.i.,* **-lat·ed, -lat·ing.** to unite in sexual intercourse. [Latin *cōpulātus,* past participle of *cōpulāre* to bind together.]

cop·u·la·tion (kop′yə lā′shən) *n.* **1.** sexual intercourse. **2.** the act of coupling or the state of being coupled; union.

cop·u·la·tive (kop′yə lā′tiv, -lə tiv) *adj.* **1.** serving to link subject and predicate words or phrases. In the sentence *The cousins were also friends,* were is a copulative verb. **2.** joining coordinate words, phrases, or clauses. The word *or* is a copulative conjunction. —*n.* a copulative word. —**cop′u·la·tive·ly,** *adv.*

cop·y (kop′ē) *n., pl.* **cop·ies. 1.** a reproduction of an original; duplicate; imitation. **2.** one of a number of reproductions of the same work: *The poet gave me an autographed copy of his new book. She bought two copies of the magazine.* **3.a.** written, illustrative, or other material to be set for reproduction in a newspaper, advertisement, or the like. **b.** written or printed matter for use in a book, advertisement, or the like, as distinguished from illustrative material. **c.** the subject of an article, story, or book: *Election campaigns always make good copy.* —*v.,* **cop·ied, cop·y·ing.** —*v.t.* **1.** to make a copy or copies of (something); reproduce. **2.** to make or do something in imitation of (something or somebody else); imitate. **3.** *Informal.* to give a copy of something to (someone): *Please copy me on the memo.* —*v.i.* **1.** to make a copy or copies. **2.** to undergo copying. [Old French *copie* transcript, plenty, going back to Latin *cōpia* plenty; the meaning "transcript" developed from the sense of a plentiful supply of copies.] —For Synonyms *(v.t.),* see **imitate.**

cop·y·book (kop′ē bŭk′) *n.* a book containing examples of handwriting for students to copy. —*adj.* commonplace, conventional, or trite: *copybook phrases, copybook morality.*

cop·y·cat (kop′ē kat′) *n.* a person who constantly imitates others.

copy desk, a central desk in a newspaper office where stories, editorials, and other material undergo final editing and preparation for publication.

cop·y·ed·it (kop′ē ed′it) *v.t.* to prepare (written material) for typesetting and publishing by correcting errors and styling.

copy editor, an editor who styles written material and corrects it

a	at	e	end	o	hot	u	up	hw	white		about
ā	ape	ē	me	ō	old	ū	use	ng	song		taken
ä	far	i	it	ô	fork	ü	rule	th	thin	ə	pencil
âr	care	ī	ice	oi	oil	u̇	pull	<u>th</u>	this		lemon
		îr	pierce	ou	out	ûr	turn	zh	measure		circus

C

269

for errors in grammar, spelling, punctuation, and the like in preparation for typesetting and publishing.

cop·y·ist (kop′ē ist) *n.* **1.** a person who makes copies, esp. of documents or manuscripts. **2.** a person who imitates.

cop·y·right (kop′ē rīt′) *n.* the exclusive right to produce, publish, or sell a literary or artistic work, granted by law for a certain number of years. —*v.t.* to obtain copyright for; protect by copyright. —*adj.* relating to or protected by copyright.

cop·y·writ·er (kop′ē rī′tər) *n.* a person who writes copy, esp. for advertisements.

co·quet (kō ket′) *also,* **coquette.** *v.i.,* **-quet·ted, -quet·ting. 1.** to play the coquette; flirt. **2.** to deal with something without seriousness; trifle; toy. [French *coqueter* to flirt; literally, to act like a cock, from *coquet* little cock, flirt, diminutive of *coq* cock [1]; of imitative origin.]

co·quet·ry (kō′ki trē, kō ket′rē) *n., pl.* **-ries.** the behavior or actions of a coquette; flirtation.

co·quette (kō ket′) *n.* a woman who tries to interest men by pretending affection or attraction; flirt. —*v.i.* **-quet·ted, -quet·ting.** coquet. [French *coquette,* feminine of *coquet. See* COQUET.] —**co·quet′tish,** *adj.* —**co·quet′tish·ly,** *adv.* —**co·quet′tish·ness,** *n.*

co·qui·na (kō kē′nə) *n.* **1.** a small clam, *Donax variabilis,* common along sandy beaches of the east coast of the United States and Mexico, and distinguished by thin, colorful shells. **2.** a soft, whitish limestone made up of fragments of seashells and corals, used for building. [Spanish *coquina* shellfish, probably going back to Latin *concha* shell, mussel.]

cor-, form of **com-** before *r,* as in *corrupt.*

cor. 1. corner. **2.** coroner. **3.** corrected **4.** correction. **5.** corresponding.

Cor. 1. Corinthians. **2.** Coroner.

cor·a·cle (kôr′ə kəl, kor′-) *n.* a small, light boat made by stretching animal skins or other waterproof material over a basketlike framework. [Welsh *corwgl.*]

cor·a·coid (kôr′ə koid′, kor′-) *n.* **1.** a bone that extends from the shoulder blade to the breastbone in birds, reptiles, and monotremes. **2.** a rudimentary bony process that projects from the shoulder blade toward the breastbone in humans and other higher mammals. —*adj.* of, relating to, or designating either of these bones. [Modern Latin *coracoides,* from Greek *korakoeidēs* like a crow; because its shape resembles a crow's beak.]

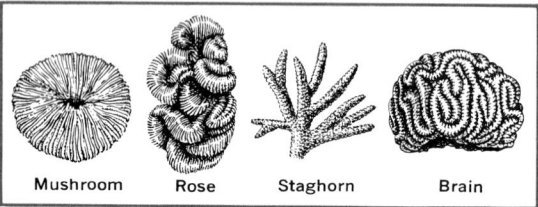

types of **coral**

cor·al (kôr′əl, kor′-) *n.* **1.** a hard, skeletal substance, chiefly calcium carbonate, secreted by certain polyps, usually found in tropical waters. **2.** any of the polyps that secrete this substance. **3.** a mass or structure formed by the skeletons of these animals, such as a reef. **4.** a pinkish red color. —*adj.* **1.** made of coral. **2.** having the color coral; pinkish red. [Old French *coral* the substance, from Latin *corallium,* from Greek *korallion;* probably of Semitic origin.]

cor·a·line (kôr′ə lin, -līn′, -lēn′) *n.* **1.** any animal similar to or related to the corals. **2.** any of a group of lime-forming red algae, family Corallinaceae. —*adj.* **1.** resembling coral in color or shape. **2.** made up of coral or corallines. [Modern Latin *corallina,* from Late Latin *corallinus* coral-red from *corallium* (see CORAL) + -INE [1].]

coral reef, a reef formed chiefly by the gradual buildup into a large mass of the calcareous skeletons of certain species of coral.

coral snake, any of several narrow-headed, venomous, snakes, family Elapidae, found in many parts of the world. Only two spe-

coral snake

cies are found in the United States: *Micrurus fulvius,* the common or eastern coral snake, having wide red and black bands, and *M. euryxanthus,* a rare species of Arizona and New Mexico. Length: to 3 feet (0.9 meter).

cor·bel (kôr′bəl) *n.* a bracketlike architectural feature, usually of stone, projecting from the side of a wall and supporting an overhanging structure; ancon; console. —*v.t.,* **-beled** or **-belled, -bel·ing** or **-bel·ling.** to provide with or support by a corbel or corbels. [Old French *corbel* corbel, raven, going back to Latin *corvus* raven; because of its resemblance to a raven's beak.]

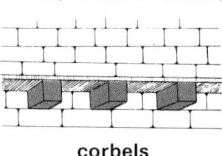

corbels

cord (kôrd) *n.* **1.** a string or thin rope made of several strands twisted or woven together. **2.** electric wires encased in rubber or other insulating material, used to connect an appliance to an outlet or to make other electrical connections. **3.** an anatomical structure resembling a cord. **4.a.** a rib or ridge on the surface of a fabric. **b.** a fabric having such ribs or ridges, as corduroy. **c. cords.** slacks made of such fabric, esp. corduroys. **5.** a quantity of wood, usually sawed, equaling 128 cubic feet (3.6 cubic meters), usually arranged in a pile 4 feet (1.2 meters) wide, 4 feet (1.2 meters) high, and 8 feet (2.4 meters) long. —*v.t.* **1.** to bind or fasten with cord; furnish with a cord. **2.** to pile (wood) in cords. [Old French *corde* rope, string, from Latin *chorda* gut, string of a musical instrument, from Greek *chordē.* Doublet of CHORD [2].]

cord·age (kôr′dij) *n.* **1.** cords or ropes collectively, esp. those in a ship's rigging. **2.** the quantity of cut wood, measured in cords, in a given area.

cor·date (kôr′dāt) *adj.* heart-shaped: *a cordate shell, a cordate leaf.* [Modern Latin *cordatus,* from Latin *cor* heart.] —**cor′date·ly,** *adv.*

cord·ed (kôr′did) *adj.* **1.** fastened with cord. **2.** having ridges or twills; ribbed. **3.** (of timber) piled in cords.

cor·dial (kôr′jəl) *adj.* genuinely warm and friendly; hearty: *a cordial greeting.* —*n.* **1.** a strong, sweet alcoholic drink; liqueur. **2.** a stimulant, such as a drink or medicine. [Medieval Latin *cordialis* relating to the heart, from Latin *cor* heart.] —**cor′dial·ly,** *adv.* —**cor′dial·ness,** *n.*

cor·dial·i·ty (kôr jal′i tē, kôr′jē al′-) *n., pl.* **-ties. 1.** a genuinely warm or friendly feeling or quality. **2.** an expression of such feeling, such as a friendly greeting.

cor·dil·le·ra (kôr′dəl yâr′ə, kôr dil′ər ə) *n.* an extensive series of mountain ranges, usually constituting the main mountain chain of a large land area. [Spanish *cordillera,* from *cordilla,* diminutive of *cuerda* string, chain, from Latin *chorda.* See CORD.] —**cor′dil·le′ran,** *adj.*

cord·ite (kôr′dīt) *n.* a smokeless gunpowder consisting of nitroglycerin, nitrocellulose, and petroleum jelly. [CORD + -ITE [1]; because of its resemblance to cord.]

cord·less (kôrd′lis) *adj.* powered by a battery, esp. a rechargeable one; not requiring the use of an electric cord when operating: *a cordless razor.*

cor·do·ba (kôr′də bə) *n.* the monetary unit of Nicaragua.

cor·don (kôr′dən) *n.* **1.** a line, as of police, ships, or barricades, set up to guard or close off an area. **2.a.** a cord or ribbon worn, usually diagonally across the chest, as a badge of honor or rank. **b.** any cord or ribbon worn as an ornament. —*v.t.* **1.** to form or place a cordon around (usually with *off*): *to cordon off an area for a parade, to cordon off a village to search for enemy soldiers.* [French *cordon* ribbon, from *corde.* See CORD.]

cor·don bleu (kôr dôn blœ′) *pl.* **cor·dons bleus** (kôr dônblœ′). **1.** an emblem of high distinction or achievement. **2.** a person of great distinction in a certain field, esp. a master chef. **3.** stuffed or layered with ham and cheese, breaded, and then sautéed: *chicken cordon bleu.* [French *cordon bleu* literally, blue ribbon; from the blue ribbon worn by the highest order of knighthood in France under the Bourbons.]

cor·do·van (kôr′də vən) *n.* **1.a.** a soft, fine-grained leather usually made of split horsehide, originally made of goatskin in Córdoba, Spain. **b.** a shoe made of this leather. **2.** a dark grayish brown or red color. —*adj.* **1.** of, relating to, or made of cordovan. **2.** having the color cordovan. [Spanish *cordobán* this leather, from *Córdoba,* Spain.]

cor·du·roy (kôr′də roi′, kôr′də roi′) *n.* **1.** a fabric, usually made of cotton, with a velvety, ribbed surface, used for clothing and upholstery. **2. corduroys.** slacks made of corduroy. —*adj.* made of corduroy. [Possibly from French *corde du roi* literally, cord of the king, said to have been made originally of silk and used for hunting clothes by French kings.]

corduroy road, a road constructed of logs laid side by side transversely, as over low, marshy ground.

cord·wain·er (kôrd'wā'nər) *n. Archaic.* **1.** a person who works in cordovan leather. **2.** shoemaker. [Old French *cordoanier,* from *cordoan* cordovan leather, going back to Spanish *cordobán.* See CORDOVAN.]

cord·wood (kôrd'wŏd') *n.* wood sold by the cord or cut for piling in cords.

core (kôr) *n.* **1.** the hard or papery central part of certain fruits, such as apples and pears, containing the seeds. **2.** the central or essential part; essence: *an argument built around a core of fact, to get to the core of a discussion.* **3.** the innermost part of anything, as a piece of wood to which veneer is glued or a central strand of wire around which other strands are twisted. **4.** a mass of ferromagnetic material forming the central part of an electromagnet, induction coil, or armature. **5.** the hot, metallic, central mass of the earth, underlying the mantle. —*v.t.,* **cored, cor·ing.** to remove the core of: *to core an apple.* [Of uncertain origin.] —**cor'er,** *n.* —For Synonyms *(n.),* see **heart.**

CORE (kôr) Congress of Racial Equality.

co·re·op·sis (kôr'ē ŏp'sĭs) *n.* **1.** the daisylike flower head of any of a group of plants, genus *Coreopsis,* of the composite family, usually yellow, orange, or red in color. **2.** the plant bearing this flower head, having lobed or blade-shaped leaves and small, dry fruit. Also, **tickseed.** [Modern Latin *coreopsis,* from Greek *koris* bedbug + *opsis* appearance; because of the resemblance of its seed to an insect.]

co·re·spond·ent (kō'rĭ spŏn'dənt) *n.* a joint defendant, esp. one charged in a divorce suit with having committed adultery with the defendant.

cor·gi (kôr'gē) *n.* Welsh corgi. [Welsh *corgi,* from *corr* dwarf + *ci* dog.]

co·ri·an·der (kôr'ē ăn'dər) *n.* **1.** the sweet, aromatic seed of a plant, *Coriandrum sativum,* of the parsley family, used mainly as a seasoning. **2.** the plant itself, bearing these seeds, edible aromatic leaves, and small white, pink, or lavender flowers. Also *(def. 2),* **cilantro.** [Old French *coriandre,* from Latin *coriandrum,* from Greek *koriannon.*]

Co·rin·thi·an (kə rĭn'thē ən) *adj.* **1.** of, relating to, or characteristic of Corinth, Greece, or its people or culture. **2.** of or relating to the most elaborate of the three orders of classical Greek architecture, characterized by columns having bell-shaped capitals decorated with carved acanthus leaves and small volutes. —*n.* **1.** a native, inhabitant, or citizen of ancient or modern Corinth, Greece. **2. Corinthians.** either of two books, I Corinthians and II Corinthians, of the New Testament, composed of Epistles written by the Apostle Paul to the Christians of Corinth. ➡ used as singular.

Co·ri·o·lis effect (kôr'ē ō'lĭs) the apparent deflection of a moving object or current of air or water owing to the rotation of the earth. An object or current appears to be deflected to the right in the Northern Hemisphere and to the left in the Southern Hemisphere. [From G. G. de *Coriolis,* 1792-1843, French mathematician who explained the phenomenon in 1835.]

co·ri·um (kôr'ē əm) *n., pl.* **co·ri·a** (kôr'ē ə). dermis. [Latin *corium* skin.]

cork (kôrk) *n.* **1.** the light, thick, porous outer bark of the cork oak, used esp. as insulating material and for floats. **2.a.** something made of cork, esp. a stopper for a bottle or other container. **b.** a stopper, as for a bottle, made of another material, such as rubber. **3.** the tissue forming the outer bark of woody plants, acting as a protective covering. —*v.t.* **1.** to stop or furnish with cork or a cork. **2.** to blacken with burnt cork. **3.** to hold in check; restrain (often with *up*): *to keep one's feelings corked up inside.* [Spanish *alcorque* cork shoe, through Arabic, probably going back to Latin *cortex* rind, bark of the cork oak.]

corked (kôrkt) *adj.* **1.** stopped with a cork. **2.** corky *(def. 2).* **3.** blackened with burnt cork.

cork·er (kôr'kər) *n. Slang.* a person or thing that is outstanding or remarkable.

cork oak, an evergreen oak tree, *Quercus suber,* found widely throughout the Mediterranean region, from whose bark cork is obtained.

cork·screw (kôrk'skrü') *n.* a device for removing corks from bottles, usually consisting of a pointed, metal spiral set in a handle. —*adj.* shaped like a corkscrew; spiral; winding. —*v.t., v.i.* to move in a spiral or zigzag course; wind; twist.

cork·y (kôr'kē) *adj.,* **cork·i·er, cork·i·est. 1.** of or like cork. **2.** (of wine) tasting of cork; spoiled, esp. by poor corking. Also *(def. 2),* **corked.**

corm (kôrm) *n.* a thick, fleshy underground stem that functions like a bulb but differs from it in structure, consisting mainly of stem rather than leafy tissue. The crocus and gladiolus are two common plants that develop from corms. [Modern Latin *cormus,* from Greek *kormos* trimmed tree trunk.]

cor·mo·rant (kôr'mər ənt) *n.* **1.** any of various swimming and diving birds, family Phalacrocoracidae, having webbed feet, a hooked bill, and a pouch under the beak for holding fish. Usually its plumage is black tinged with bronze or green. Length: to 3 feet (0.9 meter). **2.** a greedy or rapacious person. [Old French *cormaren* this bird, from *corp* raven (from Latin *corvus*) + *marenc* of the sea (from Latin *marīnus*).]

cormorant

corn[1] (kôrn) *n.* **1.** a kernel or grain that grows in rows on the large spikes or ears of a tall, coarse grass, *Zea mays,* used for food; esp. variety *rugosa,* sweet corn. **2.** the plant itself, having a jointed stalk and broad, lance-shaped leaves and bearing both male and female flowers on the same plant. Also *(defs. 1, 2),* **maize, Indian corn. 3.** an ear of this plant. **4.a.** a major edible grain crop of a particular region, as wheat in England and oats in Scotland and Ireland. **b.** *British.* any food grain or the plant it grows on. **5.** *Informal.* something considered old-fashioned, trite, or overly sentimental. —*v.t.* to preserve or season (meat) in strong brine or with coarse, dry salt. [Old English *corn* seed, grain.]

corn[2] (kôrn) *n.* a small, conical hardening and thickening of the skin caused by friction or pressure, esp. on a toe. [Middle French *corne* horn, horny swelling, from Old French *corn,* from Latin *cornū* horn.]

Corn Belt, a region in the Middle West of the United States, consisting of the chief corn-growing states, extending from Ohio to Kansas and Nebraska.

corn borer, any of several moth larvae, family Pyraustidae or Pyralididae, that destroy corn and other crops.

corn bread, bread made from cornmeal.

corn·cob (kôrn'kŏb') *n.* **1.** the almost woody core of an ear of corn, on which the kernels grow in rows. **2.** corncob pipe.

corncob pipe, a tobacco pipe with a bowl made from a hollowed, dried corncob.

corn cockle, a whitish, hairy weed, *Agrostemma githago,* commonly found in wheat fields. Its red-purple flowers bear poisonous seeds.

corn crake, a short-billed bird, *Crex crex,* of the rail family, common in the grain fields of Europe.

corn·crib (kôrn'krĭb') *n.* a structure for storing husked cobs of corn, built with slats that are spaced for ventilation.

cor·ne·a (kôr'nē ə) *n.* the transparent outer covering or wall of the front of the eyeball, lying over the iris and the pupil. For illustration, see **eye.** [Latin *cornea (tēla)* horny (web), going back to Latin *cornū* horn.] —**cor'ne·al,** *adj.*

corned (kôrnd) *adj.* (of meat) preserved or seasoned in strong brine or with coarse, dry salt.

cor·nel (kôr'nəl) *n.* any of a group of mostly hardwood trees or shrubs, genus *Cornus,* of the dogwood family. [Middle Dutch *kornelle* fruit of the cornel, going back to Latin *cornus* the cornel.]

cor·nel·ian (kôr nēl'yən) carnelian.

cor·ne·ous (kôr'nē əs) *adj.* of, like, or consisting of horn; horny. [Latin *corneus,* from *cornū* horn.]

cor·ner (kôr'nər) *n.* **1.a.** a point or place where converging lines or surfaces meet; angle: *the sharp corners of a table.* **b.** a place where two streets meet. **2.** the space between converging lines or surfaces near their meeting place: *The table stood in the far corner of the room.* **3.** a place that is secluded, private, or secret: *The children played in their own little corner of the woods.* **4.** a region, part, or quarter: *The politician campaigned in every corner of the state.* **5.** a place or position that is awkward or threatening, esp. one from which escape is difficult: *The fugitive was driven into a corner by the police.* **6.** the purchase or control of enough of a particular stock or commodity to raise the price: *to have a corner on silver.* **7.** a piece used to protect, ornament, or form a corner: *These paper corners will hold that photograph in the scrapbook.* —*adj.* **1.** at or near a corner: *a corner store.* **2.** designed for or used in a corner: *a corner cabinet.* —*v.t.* **1.** to force, drive into, or catch in an awkward or threatening place or position, esp. one from which escape is difficult: *The reporters cornered the mayor*

a	at	e	end	o	hot	u	up	hw	white		about
ā	ape	ē	me	ō	old	ū	use	ng	song		taken
ä	far	i	it	ô	fork	ü	rule	th	thin	ə	pencil
âr	care	ī	ice	oi	oil	ů	pull	th	this		lemon
				îr	pierce	ou	out	ûr	turn	zh	measure		circus

271

and asked about the new budget. **2.** to form or get a corner on (a stock or commodity, or its trading): *to corner the wheat market.* **3.** to place in a corner. —*v.i.* to turn at a corner: *Our new sports car corners beautifully.* [Anglo-Norman *cornere* angle¹, recess, nook, from Late Latin *cornēria* angle¹, going back to Latin *cornū* horn, point, end.]

· **around the corner.** in the near future; ahead: *The frustrated inventor believed success was just around the corner.*

· **to cut corners.** to reduce the time, effort, or expense needed to do something; economize: *to cut corners in building by using cheaper materials.*

· **to turn the** (or **a**) **corner**: to pass a point, as in an illness, where the worst is behind.

cor·ner·stone (kôr′nər stōn′) *n.* **1.a.** a stone that lies at the corner of a building, serving to unite two walls. **b.** any such stone, used to mark the actual or nominal starting point in building. It is often inscribed and made a repository of historical documents or objects. **2.** a fundamental principle or part; foundation; basis: *Freedom is the cornerstone of democracy.*

cor·ner·wise (kôr′nər wīz′) *adv.* **1.** with the corner facing forward. **2.** from corner to corner; diagonally. Also, **cor·ner·ways** (kôr′nər wāz′).

cor·net (*def. 1,* kôr net′; *def. 2,* kôr′nit, kôr net′) *n.* **1.** a brass musical instrument that is similar to the trumpet but has a mellower sound. **2.** a paper cone twisted at one end, used as a holder for candy, nuts, or other small items. [Old French *cornet* little horn, diminutive of *corn* horn, going back to Latin *cornū.*]

cor·net·ist (kôr net′ist) *also,* **cor·net·tist.** *n.* a person who plays a cornet.

corn·fed (kôrn′fed′) *adj.* **1.** fed, raised, or fattened on corn: *cornfed beef.* **2.** *Informal.* healthy and robust, but unsophisticated.

corn·field (kôrn′fēld′) *n.* a field in which corn is grown.

corn·flakes (kôrn′flāks′) *pl. n.* small crisp flakes made from corn and served cold, usually with milk, as a breakfast cereal.

corn·flow·er (kôrn′flou′ər) *n.* **1.** the daisylike blue, purple, pink, or white flower of a plant, *Centaurea cyanus,* of the composite family, native to the Old World but now widely cultivated in North America. **2.** the plant itself. Also, **bachelor's button.** [Because it is commonly found growing in grain fields.]

cornflowers

corn·husk (kôrn′husk′) *n.* the coarse leaves or husk enclosing an ear of corn.

cor·nice (kôr′nis) *n.* **1.** the uppermost projecting part of an entablature. For illustration, see **entablature. 2.** any projecting horizontal molding, as along the top of a building or along the walls of a room just below the ceiling. **3.** an ornamental frame or molding used to conceal curtain rods and other fixtures. —*v.t.,* **-niced, -nic·ing.** to furnish or decorate with or as with a cornice. [Middle French *cornice* pillar, part of a wall, from Italian *cornice* part of a wall, ledge, possibly going back to Greek *korōnis* wreath, something curved.]

Cor·nish (kôr′nish) *adj.* of or relating to Cornwall, its people, their culture, or their now extinct language. —*n.* a Celtic language formerly spoken in Cornwall but extinct since the late eighteenth century.

Corn Laws, a series of laws, in force between 1436 and 1846, that severely limited the import and export of wheat and other grains to and from Great Britain.

corn·meal (kôrn′mēl′) *also,* **corn meal.** *n.* meal made from coarsely ground corn.

corn oil, a yellow, fatty oil obtained from the germ of corn kernels, used as a salad oil, in margarine, and in soft soaps.

corn pone, a simple corn bread that is baked or fried, usually made without milk or eggs. Also, **pone.**

corn silk 1. the long, silky fibers projecting from the top of the husk on an ear of corn. **2.** any one of these fibers.

corn smut, a smut disease of corn, characterized by large whitish boils that rupture to reveal a mass of dark spores. For illustration, see **fungus.**

corn·stalk (kôrn′stôk′) *n.* a stalk of corn.

corn·starch (kôrn′stärch′) *n.* a white, powdery starch extracted from corn kernels, used in cooking as a thickening agent.

corn sugar, dextrose made from cornstarch.

corn syrup, a syrup made from cornstarch, used as a sweetener and in making candies and jellies.

cor·nu·co·pi·a (kôr′nə kō′pē ə, kôrn′yə-) *n.* **1.** a curved, twisted horn overflowing with fruit, grain, and vegetables, used as a symbol of abundance and prosperity. Also, **horn of plenty. 2.** any container or ornament shaped like a horn or cone. **3.** a great store or supply; abundance. [Late Latin *cornūcōpia* horn of plenty, from Latin *cornū cōpiae;* in Greek mythology, the horn of the goat Amalthea, which nourished the infant Zeus.]

corn·y (kôr′nē) *adj.,* **corn·i·er, corn·i·est. 1.** *Informal.* old-fashioned, overly sentimental, or trite. **2.** of corn or abounding in corn. [CORN¹ + -Y¹; said to refer to the supposedly unsophisticated taste of the CORN BELT.]

co·rol·la (kə rol′ə) *n.* the petals of a flower, considered collectively as a flower part. [Latin *corolla* garland, diminutive of *corōna.* See CORONA.] —**co·rol·late** (kə rol′āt, -it), *adj.*

cor·ol·lar·y (kôr′ə ler′ē, kor′-) *n., pl.* **-lar·ies. 1.** a proposition that follows obviously from an already proven proposition and therefore requires no separate proof. **2.** an easily drawn inference or deduction. **3.** anything that naturally follows from something else; natural consequence or result. [Late Latin *corollārium* deduction, from Latin *corollārium* garland given as a gift, additional gift, from *corolla.* See COROLLA.]

corona during total solar eclipse

co·ro·na (kə rō′nə) *n., pl.* **-nas** or **-nae** (-nē). **1.a.** a luminous region seen closely surrounding a heavenly body, esp. the sun or moon, caused by the diffraction of light through the earth's atmosphere. **b.** the outer atmosphere of the sun, made up of free electrons, protons, and fine dust particles, usually seen during an eclipse. **2.** a crownlike part, as the top of the head or the structure on the inner side of the corolla in such flowers as the daffodil. [Latin *corōna* crown, garland, from Greek *korōnē* something bent. Doublet of CROWN.]

Corona Aus·tra·lis (ôs trā′lis) a constellation in the southern sky.

Corona Bo·re·al·is (bôr′ē al′is) a constellation in the northern sky.

cor·o·nach (kôr′ə nəкн, kor′-) *n.* in Scotland or Ireland, a lamentation for the dead; dirge.

cor·o·nal (*n.,* kôr′ə nəl, kor′-; *adj.,* kə rō′nəl, kôr′ə nəl, kor′-) *n.* an ornamental band for the head; crown, coronet, or garland. —*adj.* of or relating to a crown or corona.

cor·o·nar·y (kôr′ə ner′ē, kor′-) *adj.* **1.a.** of, relating to, or designating either of two arteries that branch from the aorta and supply blood to the muscular tissue of the heart. **b.** encircling like a crown, as certain vessels or nerves. **2.** of or relating to the heart. **3.** relating to or resembling a crown. —*n., pl.* **-nar·ies.** coronary occlusion or coronary thrombosis. [Latin *corōnārius* relating to a crown, from *corōna.* See CORONA.]

coronary artery disease, disease of the blood vessels that supply blood to the muscle of the heart. It often occurs when fatty substances clog the inside of the arteries, making it difficult for blood to pass through them.

coronary occlusion, a blockage of one of the coronary arteries.

coronary thrombosis, a blockage in one of the coronary arteries caused by formation of a blood clot.

cor·o·na·tion (kôr′ə nā′shən, kor′-) *n.* the act, occasion, or ceremony of crowning, esp. the crowning of a sovereign or the consort of a sovereign.

cor·o·ner (kôr′ə nər, kor′-) *n.* a local official whose chief duty is to determine by an inquest the cause of any suspicious or violent death. [Anglo-Norman *cor(o)uner* English officer of justice (orig-

inally charged with watching over property belonging to the crown), from *coro(u)ne* crown, from Latin *corōna.* See CORONA.]

coroner's inquest, a legal investigation into the cause of a death that has occurred suddenly or under suspicious or violent circumstances.

cor·o·net (kôr′ə net′, kor′-, kôr′ə net′, kor′-) *n.* **1.** a small crown denoting a noble rank lower than that of sovereign. **2.** a crownlike head ornament, esp. one made with precious metals, jewels, or flowers. [Old French *coronete,* diminutive of *corone* crown, from Latin *corōna.* See CORONA.]

Corp. 1. Corporal. **2.** *also,* **corp.** Corporation.

cor·po·ral[1] (kôr′pər əl, -prəl) *adj.* of or relating to the human body; physical: *corporal punishment.* [Old French *corporal,* from Latin *corporālis,* from *corpus* body.] —**cor′po·ral·ly,** *adv.*

cor·po·ral[2] (kôr′pər əl, -prəl) *n.* the lowest noncommissioned officer in the U.S. Army or Marine Corps, ranking below a sergeant. [Obsolete French *corporal,* form of *caporal,* from Italian *caporale,* from *capo* head, chief, from Latin *caput* head.]

cor·po·rate (kôr′pər it, -prit) *adj.* **1.** of, relating to, belonging to, or forming a corporation: *corporate policy, a corporate meeting.* **2.** of or relating to a united group of individuals; joint; collective: *The corporate action of the townspeople led to a referendum on the proposed ordinance.* **3.** united or combined into a whole. [Latin *corporātus,* past participle of *corporāre* to make into a body, from *corpus* body.] —**cor′po·rate·ly,** *adv.*

cor·po·ra·tion (kôr′pə rā′shən) *n.* **1.** an organization that exists as a legal entity independent of the individuals that establish, own, or manage it. A corporation is created by a government charter and, within the limits imposed by the charter and the law, has the rights and liabilities of an individual, including the right to buy and sell property and to enter into contracts. **2.** any group of persons authorized to act as a single body. **3.** *Informal.* a protruding abdomen; paunch.

cor·po·re·al (kôr pôr′ē əl) *adj.* **1.** of or for the body or of the nature of the body; not spiritual. **2.** having substance; material; tangible. [Latin *corporeus* of the body (from *corpus* body) + -AL[1].] —**cor·po·re·al·i·ty** (kôr pôr′ē al′i tē), **cor·po′re·al·ness,** *n.* —**cor·po′re·al·ly,** *adv.*

corps (kôr) *n., pl.* **corps** (kôrz). **1.a.** a unit of a military service with a specialized function: *a medical corps.* **b.** a tactical military unit consisting of a headquarters, two or more divisions, and additional support units and forming part of a field army. **2.** a group of persons acting or working together: *the press corps, a corps of volunteers.* [French *corps* body, from Latin *corpus.* Doublet of CORPSE, CORPUS.]

corps de bal·let (kôr′də ba lā′) the dancers in a ballet company who generally perform as a group rather than as soloists.

corpse (kôrps) *n.* **1.** a dead body, esp. of a human being. **2.** something that has lost its life or usefulness: *the corpse of a wrecked boat.* [Old French *cor(p)s* body, from Latin *corpus.* Doublet of CORPS, CORPUS.]

corps·man (kôr′mən) *n., pl.* **-men** (-mən). an enlisted member of the armed forces trained to give medical assistance.

cor·pu·lence (kôr′pyə ləns) *n.* fatness or fleshiness of the body; obesity. Also, **cor′pu·len·cy.**

cor·pu·lent (kôr′pyə lənt) *adj.* having a fat or fleshy body; obese. [Latin *corpulentus,* from *corpus* body.]

cor·pus (kôr′pəs) *n., pl.* **-po·ra** (-pər ə). **1.** a large or complete collection of writings of a particular kind or on a particular subject. **2.** *Archaic.* a body, esp. a dead one. **3.** the main part or body of an anatomical organ. [Latin *corpus* body. Doublet of CORPS, CORPSE.]

Corpus Chris·ti (kôr′pəs kris′tē) in the Roman Catholic Church, a feast in honor of the Eucharist, held on the first Thursday after Trinity Sunday. [Medieval Latin *corpus Christi* literally, body of Christ. See CORPUS, CHRIST.]

cor·pus·cle (kôr′pus′əl, -pə səl) *n.* **1.** a living cell, esp. a red or white cell in the blood or lymph of vertebrates. **2.** any minute particle. [Latin *corpusculum* little body, atom, diminutive of *corpus* body.] —**cor·pus·cu·lar** (kôr pus′kyə lər), *adj.*

cor·pus de·lic·ti (kôr′pəs di lik′tī) **1.** the physical object upon which a crime has been committed, esp. the victim's body in a murder case. **2.** the essential fact or facts proving that a crime has been committed. [Modern Latin *corpus delicti* literally, body of the crime, from Latin *corpus* body + *dēlictum* crime.]

cor·pus ju·ris (kôr′pəs jŭr′is) a complete collection of laws of a nation, state, or the like. [Late Latin *corpus jūris* literally, body of law.]

Corpus Juris Ci·vi·lis (si vī′lis, -vil′is) the body of Roman civil law compiled between A.D. 528 and 534, during the reign of Justinian I.

cor·pus lu·te·um (kôr′pəs lü′tē əm) *n., pl.* **cor·por·a lu·te·a** (kôr′pər ə lü′tē ə). a mass of yellowish tissue formed in the ovary from the remaining cells of the ruptured follicle following dis-

charge of the ovum. It secretes estrogen and progesterone to maintain the lining of the uterus during pregnancy. [Modern Latin *corpus luteum,* literally, saffron-colored body.]

corr. 1. correspondence. **2.** correspondent. **3.** corresponding.

cor·ral (kə ral′) *n.* **1.** a fenced enclosure for cattle, horses, or other livestock. **2.** a circular enclosure formed by wagons for defense against attack. —*v.t.* **-ralled, -ral·ling. 1.** to drive into or enclose in a corral: *to corral a herd of horses.* **2.** to capture by surrounding or gathering together: *The police corralled the entire gang.* **3.** to get hold of or corner: *Reporters corralled the senator in the hall.* **4.** *Informal.* to gather together; collect: *to corral votes.* **5.** to arrange (wagons) into a corral. [Spanish *corral* enclosure, from *corro* ring, from *correr* to run, from Latin *currere.*]

cor·rect (kə rekt′) *adj.* **1.** agreeing with fact or truth; free from error; accurate: *a correct address, a correct spelling.* **2.** conforming to an acknowledged or approved standard; proper: *correct dress for a banquet, correct behavior.* —*v.t.* **1.** to bring into agreement with or change to what is right, accurate, or true; set right: *to correct a mistake in pronunciation.* **2.** to note or mark the errors or faults in: *I corrected the spelling tests.* **3.** to counteract, remove, or end (something harmful or undesirable); rectify: *The new battery should correct the problem with my car.* **4.** to punish or rebuke so as to remove faults or improve; discipline: *to correct an unruly child.* **5.** to adjust to or bring into conformity with a standard; remove a fault from: *to correct poor eyesight with glasses.* —*v.i.* to make adjustments in order to compensate (with *for*): *to correct for the effects of air currents.* [Latin *correctus,* past participle of *corrigere* to make straight, reform.] —**cor·rect′a·ble,** *adj.* —**cor·rect′ly,** *adv.* —**cor·rect′ness,** *n.* —**cor·rec′tor,** *n.*

Synonyms *adj.* **Correct, accurate,** and **exact** mean agreeing with fact or truth and without error. **Correct** is the general term: *the correct answer, correct information.* **Accurate** suggests care taken to avoid errors: *The reporter used a tape recorder to ensure that quotations were accurate.* **Exact** implies that no detail is wrong or lacking: *The figures in this balance sheet must be exact to satisfy the auditors.*

cor·rec·tion (kə rek′shən) *n.* **1.a.** the act of correcting or the state of being corrected. **b.** a change made to correct an error: *There were many spelling corrections on the paper.* **2.** the act or process of punishing or rebuking; corrective discipline: *Ideally, correction should rehabilitate a criminal.* **3.** a quantity added or subtracted in order to ensure accuracy: *a correction for the thickness of a lens.* —**cor·rec′tion·al,** *adj.*

correctional facility, a prison, esp. for criminals with long sentences. —For Synonyms, see **prison.**

correctional officer, prison guard.

cor·rec·tive (kə rek′tiv) *adj.* tending or intended to correct or improve: *corrective lenses, corrective eye exercises.* —*n.* something that corrects or tends to correct. —**cor·rec′tive·ly,** *adv.*

cor·re·late (*v.,* kôr′ə lāt′, kor′-; *n., adj.,* kôr′ə lit, -lāt′, kor′-) *v.,* **-lat·ed, -lat·ing.** —*v.t.* to place in or bring into a mutual or reciprocal relationship; show a meaningful connection between: *to correlate fact with theory.* —*v.i.* to have a mutual or reciprocal relationship; be meaningfully connected: *These facts seem to correlate.* —*n.* either of two things mutually or reciprocally related, esp. so that one necessarily implies the other: *Good is the correlate of evil.* —*adj.* correlated. [From CORRELATION.]

cor·re·la·tion (kôr′ə lā′shən, kor′-) *n.* **1.** a mutual or reciprocal relationship: *the correlation between poor sanitation and disease.* **2.** the act or process of correlating or the state of being correlated. **3.** *Statistics.* the extent or degree to which two sets of data correspond to one another. [Medieval Latin *correlatio* mutual relation, from Latin *cum* with + *relātiō* a carrying back, report, reference.]

cor·rel·a·tive (kə rel′ə tiv) *adj.* **1.** having or involving a mutual or reciprocal relationship, esp. so that one thing necessarily implies the other: *to have correlative interests in psychology and the chemistry of the brain.* **2.** *Grammar.* complementing one another and commonly used together. *Either* and *or* are correlative conjunctions. —*n.* **1.** either of two correlative things; correlate. **2.** *Grammar.* a correlative word or term. —**cor·rel′a·tive·ly,** *adv.* —**cor·rel′a·tive·ness, cor·rel′a·tiv′i·ty,** *n.*

cor·re·spond (kôr′ə spond′, kor′-) *v.i.* **1.** to be in agreement or conformity; match (often with *with* or *to*): *Their words do not correspond with their actions. Your answer corresponds to mine.* **2.** to be similar, analogous, or equivalent, as in character or function (with *to*): *Our state assembly corresponds to the U.S. House of*

a	at	e	end	o	hot	u	up	hw	white		about
ā	ape	ē	me	ō	old	ū	use	ng	song	ə	taken
ä	far	i	it	ô	fork	ü	rule	th	thin		pencil
âr	care	ī	ice	oi	oil	ủ	pull	th	this		lemon
		îr	pierce	ou	out	ûr	turn	zh	measure		circus

Representatives. **3.** to communicate by exchanging letters. [Medieval Latin *correspondere* to answer to each other, from Latin *cum* together + *respondēre* to answer.]

cor·re·spon·dence (kôr′ə spon′dəns, kor′-) *n.* **1.a.** communication by exchange of letters: *The boys continued their correspondence throughout the summer.* **b.** letters written or exchanged: *The senator tried to personally read all her correspondence.* **2.** the act of corresponding or the state of being correspondent; agreement or similarity: *the correspondence of a theory with the facts, a close correspondence between Greek and Roman gods.* Also, **cor′re·spon′den·cy. 3.** *Mathematics.* a relationship between sets such that each member of one set can be paired with a member of another set.

correspondence course, a course of instruction offered by a correspondence school.

correspondence school, any of various schools offering courses of study by mail in vocational, professional, or academic subjects.

cor·re·spon·dent (kôr′ə spon′dənt, kor′-) *n.* **1.** a person who communicates with another by letter. **2.** a person employed, as by a newspaper or television network, to report news and commentary from a particular place or area. **3.** a person or firm, esp. one located in a distant place, having regular business dealings with another. **4.** something that corresponds to something else. —*adj.* corresponding.

cor·re·spond·ing (kôr′ə spon′ding, kor′-) *adj.* **1.** matching or identical: *The two chairs have a corresponding design.* **2.** having a similar function, position, form, or the like: *corresponding ranks in the army and navy.* **3.** exchanging or handling written correspondence: *a corresponding secretary.*

cor·re·spond·ing·ly (kôr′ə spon′ding lē, kor′-) *adv.* **1.** in an identical or similar manner: *The challenger taunted the champion, who replied correspondingly.* **2.** of a similar nature; with similar characteristics: *War and disaster survivors have witnessed correspondingly horrifying events.*

cor·ri·dor (kôr′i dər, -dôr′, kor′-) *n.* **1.** a long hallway or passageway in a building, often having rooms opening onto it. **2.** a narrow strip of land used as a passageway, esp. through foreign territory, and often providing access to the sea. **3.** air corridor. [French *corridor* passage, from Italian *corridore* long passage; literally, runner, going back to Latin *currere* to run.]

cor·ri·gen·dum (kôr′i jen′dəm, kor′-) *n., pl.* **-da** (-də). **1.** an error to be corrected, esp. in a book after it has been printed; erratum. **2. corrigenda.** a list of such errors and their corrections included in a published work. [Latin *corrigendum* literally, (thing) to be corrected, from *corrigere* to make straight, reform.]

cor·ri·gi·ble (kôr′i jə bəl, kor′-) *adj.* **1.** capable of being corrected, improved, or reformed. **2.** open to correction or reform. [Medieval Latin *corrigibilis,* from Latin *corrigere* to make straight, reform.] —**cor′ri·gi·bil′i·ty,** *n.* —**cor′ri·gi·bly,** *adv.*

cor·rob·o·rate (kə rob′ə rāt′) *v.t.,* **-rat·ed, -rat·ing.** to strengthen or support, as by giving additional proof or evidence; confirm: *The evidence given by several witnesses corroborated the defendant's story.* [Latin *corrōborātus,* past participle of *corrōborāre* to strengthen, going back to Latin *cum* together + *rōbur* oak, strength.] —**cor·rob′o·ra′tive, cor·rob·o·ra·to·ry** (kə rob′ər ə tôr′ē), *adj.* —**cor·rob′o·ra′tive·ly,** *adv.* —**cor·rob′o·ra′tor,** *n.* —For Synonyms, see **confirm.**

cor·rob·o·ra·tion (kə rob′ə rā′shən) *n.* **1.** the act of corroborating or the state of being corroborated. **2.** something that corroborates.

cor·rode (kə rōd′) *v.,* **-rod·ed, -rod·ing.** —*v.t.* **1.** to eat or wear away gradually, esp. by chemical action: *That acid corrodes metal.* **2.** to weaken or destroy: *Frequent criticism corrodes one's self-confidence.* —*v.i.* to become corroded: *Some substances corrode easily.* [Latin *corrōdere* to gnaw to pieces.] —**cor·rod′i·ble,** *adj.*

cor·ro·sion (kə rō′zhən) *n.* **1.** the act or process of corroding or the state of being corroded. **2.** the product or result of corroding. [Late Latin *corrōsiō* a gnawing to pieces, from *corrōdere* to gnaw to pieces.]

cor·ro·sive (kə rō′siv) *adj.* **1.** capable of producing corrosion: *a corrosive acid.* **2.** tending to weaken; destructive: *the corrosive effect of corruption.* **3.** tending to be biting or cutting; harshly sarcastic. —*n.* something that corrodes, esp. a chemical agent. —**cor·ro′sive·ly,** *adv.* —**cor·ro′sive·ness,** *n.*

cor·ru·gate (kôr′ə gāt′, kor′-) *v.,* **-gat·ed, -gat·ing.** —*v.t.* to shape or contract (something, as a sheet of metal) into parallel ridges or folds; wrinkle. —*v.i.* to become corrugated. —*adj.* corrugated. [Latin *corrūgātus,* past participle of *corrūgāre* to wrinkle.]

cor·ru·gat·ed (kôr′ə gā′tid, kor′-) *adj.* shaped or contracted into parallel ridges or folds; wrinkled.

corrugated iron, iron or steel, usually galvanized, shaped into sheets with parallel ridges and troughs and used chiefly in making roofs and walls.

corrugated paper, heavy paper or cardboard shaped into parallel ridges, used for packaging.

cor·ru·ga·tion (kôr′ə gā′shən, kor′-) *n.* **1.** the act of corrugating or the state of being corrugated. **2.** one of a series of parallel ridges or folds; wrinkle.

cor·rupt (kə rupt′) *adj.* **1.** marked by dishonesty or other improper conduct: *corrupt practices at election time.* **2.** acting dishonestly or improperly; influenced by bribery: *a corrupt judge.* **3.** immoral or wicked; depraved: *a corrupt life.* **4.** made inferior to the original or correct form or version, as by additions or errors: *a corrupt form of German, a corrupt translation.* **5.** rotten; decayed. —*v.t.* **1.** to cause to act dishonestly, as by bribery; destroy the integrity of: *The lure of money corrupted the judge.* **2.** to pervert the morality of; make morally wicked: *Socrates was accused of corrupting the youth of his time.* **3.** to make inferior to an original or correct form or version: *to corrupt the text of a manuscript.* **4.** to make rotten; cause to decay. —*v.i.* to become corrupt. [Latin *corruptus,* past participle of *corrumpere* to ruin, seduce, bribe; literally, to break to pieces.] —**cor·rupt′er;** also, **cor·rup′tor,** *n.* —**cor·rupt′ly,** *adv.* —**cor·rupt′ness,** *n.*

cor·rupt·i·ble (kə rup′tə bəl) *adj.* capable of being corrupted. —**cor·rupt′i·bil′i·ty, cor·rupt′i·ble·ness,** *n.* —**cor·rupt′i·bly,** *adv.*

cor·rup·tion (kə rup′shən) *n.* **1.** the act or process of corrupting or the state of being corrupted. **2.** bribery, dishonesty, or other improper conduct or practices. **3.** morally wicked conduct or practices; depravity. **4.** a corrupted form or incorrect version, as of a text or language. **5.** something that corrupts; corruptive influence. **6.** rot; decay.

cor·rup·tive (kə rup′tiv) *adj.* tending to corrupt; causing corruption: *a corruptive influence.*

cor·sage (kôr säzh′) *n.* a flower or small bouquet of flowers to be worn by a woman, usually at the shoulder or waist or on the wrist. [Old French *corsage* bodice, chest, from *cors* body, from Latin *corpus.*]

cor·sair (kôr′sâr) *n.* **1.** a privateer or pirate, esp. of the Barbary Coast. **2.** a privateering vessel or pirate ship. [French *corsaire* pirate, going back to Late Latin *cursārius,* from *cursus* plunder, from Latin *cursus* course. Doublet of HUSSAR.]

corse (kôrs) *n. Archaic.* corpse. [Form of CORPSE.]

cor·se·let (*def. 1,* kôr′sə let′; *def. 2,* kôrs′lit) *n.* **1.** a woman's undergarment similar to a corset but made with less reinforcing material. **2.** *also,* **corslet.** a plate of body armor, esp. the breastplate and back plate considered as one part. [French *corselet* literally, little body, diminutive of Old French *cors.* See CORSET.]

cor·set (kôr′sit) *n.* **1.** an undergarment reinforced with stitching and stiffening material, worn chiefly by women to shape and support the body, and usually extending from the midriff to below the hips. **2.** a similar garment worn to support the muscles of the back or abdomen, esp. for medical reasons. —*v.t.* to fit with or dress in a corset. [French *corset* little body, stays, diminutive of Old French *cors* body, from Latin *corpus.*]

cors·let (kôrs′lit) corselet (*def. 2*).

corselet (*def. 2*)

cor·tege (kôr tezh′, -tāzh′) *also,* **cor·tège.** *n.* **1.** a ceremonial procession, esp. a funeral procession. **2.** a train of followers or attendants; retinue. [French *cortège* procession, from Italian *corteggio,* from *corte* court, from Latin *cohors.* See COHORT.]

Cor·tes (kôr′tiz, kôr′tes) *n.* the national legislature of Spain or Portugal.

cor·tex (kôr′teks) *n., pl.* **-ti·ces** (-tə sēz′). **1.** the outer portion of an internal organ, esp. the wrinkled gray matter covering most of the brain. **2.** the zone of tissue in a plant beneath the epidermis, whose outer layers manufacture sugar, contain chlorophyll, and store nutrients. [Latin *cortex* rind, bark.]

cor·ti·cal (kôr′ti kəl) *adj.* **1.** of, relating to, or consisting of a cortex. **2.** of or involving the cortex of the brain. —**cor′ti·cal·ly,** *adv.*

cor·ti·cate (kôr′ti kit, -kāt′) *adj.* having a cortex. Also, **cor′ti·cat′ed.** [Latin *corticātus* covered with bark, from *cortex* bark.]

cor·ti·co·ster·oid (kôr'ti kō ster'oid, -stîr'-) *n.* any of a group of steroid hormones, as cortisone, hydrocortisone, or aldosterone, that are secreted by the cortex of the adrenal glands and are also produced synthetically for medicinal use. Also, **cor·ti·coid** (kôr'ti koid').

cor·ti·co·tro·pin (kôr'ti kō trō'pin) *also*, **cor·ti·co·tro·phin** (kôr'ti kō trō'fin). *n.* ACTH.

cor·ti·sol (kôr'tə sôl') *n.* hydrocortisone. [CORTIS(ONE) + -OL.]

cor·ti·sone (kôr'tə zōn', -sōn') *n.* a hormone produced by the cortex of the adrenal gland that affects the metabolism of carbohydrates, proteins, and fats. It is also made synthetically and used to treat various allergic and inflammatory conditions.

co·run·dum (kə run'dəm) *n.* a mineral consisting of aluminum oxide, second to diamond in hardness. The dark, opaque variety is used for polishing and grinding; colored, transparent crystals include the gem varieties sapphire and ruby. Formula: Al_2O_3 [Tamil *kurundam,* possibly going back to Sanskrit *kuruvinda* ruby.]

cor·us·cate (kôr'ə skāt', kor'-) *v.i.* -cat·ed, -cat·ing. to give off flashes of light; sparkle; glitter. [Latin *coruscātus,* past participle of *coruscāre* to vibrate, glitter.]

cor·us·ca·tion (kôr'ə skā'shən, kor'-) *n.* **1.a.** the act of giving off flashes of light: *the coruscations of a star.* **b.** a flash of light; sparkle. **2.** a brilliant display of intellect or wit.

cor·vée (kôr vā') *n.* **1.** unpaid work owed by a vassal to a feudal lord and usually performed by the vassal's serfs. **2.** forced labor exacted by a government instead of taxes or for little or no pay, esp. for the construction and repair of public works. [French *corvée,* from Late Latin *corrogāta (opera)* requisitioned (work), from Latin *corrogāre* to collect.]

cor·vette (kôr vet') *also*, **cor·vet.** *n.* **1.** a fast ship, smaller than a destroyer, armed with antisubmarine and antiaircraft guns and depth charges, used esp. to escort convoys. **2.** a sailing warship smaller than a frigate and having one tier of guns. [French *corvette* sloop of war, from Middle Dutch *korf* small ship, basket, from Latin *corbis* basket.]

cor·vine (kôr'vīn, -vin) *adj.* of or like a crow. [Latin *corvīnus,* relating to the raven, from *corvus* raven.]

Cor·vus (kôr'vəs) *n.* a constellation in the southern sky, conventionally depicted as a crow. [Latin *corvus* raven.]

Cor·y·bant (kôr'ə bant, kor'-) *n., pl.* **Cor·y·bants** or **Cor·y·ban·tes** (kôr'ə ban'tēz, kor'-). **1.** in classical mythology, one of the attendants of the ancient Phrygian goddess Cybele, who worshiped her with wild, frenzied music and dancing. **2.** a priest of Cybele. —**Cor'y·ban'tic,** *adj.*

cor·ymb (kôr'imb, -im, kor'-) *n.* a form of inflorescence in which each small stemmed flower grows individually at different levels on a main stem, but develops so that the flowers reach approximately the same height, forming a flat-topped cluster, as in cherry blossoms. For illustration, see **inflorescence.** [Latin *corymbus* cluster of fruit or flowers, from Greek *korymbos* top, head, cluster.] —**co·rymb'ose,** *adj.*

co·ry·za (kə rī'zə) *n.* an acute inflammation of the nose, characterized by sneezing and nasal congestion, as in a cold. [Modern Latin *coryza,* from Late Latin, from Greek *koryza* catarrh.]

cos (kôs, kos) *n.* romaine. [From the name of the Greek island from which it first came.]

cos, cosine.

Co·sa Nos·tra (kō'zə nōs'trə) a secret organization of criminals in the United States, said to be related to or the same as the Mafia. [Italian *cosa nostra* literally, our affair.]

cosec, cosecant.

co·se·cant (kō sē'kənt, -kant) *n.* (of an acute angle in a right triangle) the trigonometric function that is the ratio of the hypotenuse to the side opposite the angle.

co·sign (kō'sīn', kō sīn') *v.t.* **1.** to sign jointly with another or others: *Three countries cosigned the treaty.* **2.** to add one's signature to (a document, as a loan, contract, or lease) and take responsibility for fulfilling the obligation if the person who signed the document fails to do so. —**co'sign'er,** *n.*

co·sig·na·to·ry (kō sig'nə tôr'ē) *adj.* signing or having signed jointly with another or others. —*n., pl.* -ries. a person, nation, corporation, or the like that signs or has a representative sign something jointly with another or others: *the cosignatories of a peace treaty.*

co·sine (kō'sīn) *n.* (of an acute angle in a right triangle) the trigonometric function that is the ratio of the angle's adjacent side to the hypotenuse.

cos·met·ic (koz met'ik) *n.* a preparation designed chiefly to beautify various parts of the human body, such as the face or hair. —*adj.* **1.** used or done to improve the appearance of something, such as the body: *cosmetic skin treatment.* **2.** of or relating to improving the appearance of something: *surgery done for cosmetic reasons.* [Greek *kosmētikos* relating to adornment, going back to *kosmos* order, ornament.] —**cos·met'i·cal·ly,** *adv.*

cos·me·ti·cian (koz'mi tish'ən) *n.* a person whose profession is making, selling, or applying cosmetics.

cos·me·tol·o·gist (koz'mi tol'ə jist) *n.* a person whose profession is applying cosmetic preparations to the body.

cos·me·tol·o·gy (koz'mi tol'ə jē) *n.* the skill or profession of applying cosmetic preparations to the body, as in a beauty shop. [French *cosmétologie,* from *cosmétique* cosmetic (from Greek *kosmētikos*) + *-logie* -logy. See COSMETIC.]

cos·mic (koz'mik) *adj.* **1.** of or relating to the cosmos as a whole: *cosmic law, cosmic order.* **2.** having immense or immeasurable extent or effect; vast: *a disaster of cosmic proportions.* **3.** of or from outer space. [Greek *kosmikos* relating to the world, from *kosmos* order, world.] —**cos'mi·cal·ly,** *adv.*

cosmic dust, matter in fine particles falling on the earth from outer space.

cosmic rays, high-frequency radiation that has great penetrating power, consisting mainly of positively charged high-energy particles that come to the earth from all directions in outer space.

cos·mog·o·ny (koz mog'ə nē) *n., pl.* -nies. a theory, description, or account of the origin of the universe. [Greek *kosmogoniā* origin of the world, from *kosmos* world, order + *gonos* offspring.] —**cos·mog'o·nist,** *n.*

cos·mog·ra·phy (koz mog'rə fē) *n.* **1.** the science dealing with the description of the general physical features and structure of the universe, embracing astronomy, geography, and geology. **2.** a description of the general physical features of the universe. [Greek *kosmographiā* description of the world, from *kosmos* world, order + *graphein* to write.] —**cos·mog'ra·pher,** *n.* —**cos·mo·graph·ic** (koz'mə graf'ik), *adj.*

cos·mol·o·gy (koz mol'ə jē) *n.* **1.** a theory of the origin and nature of the universe: *the cosmologies of early philosophers.* **2.** a branch of astronomy dealing with such theories. [Greek *kosmos* world, order + -LOGY.] —**cos·mo·log·i·cal** (koz'mə loj'i kəl), *adj.* —**cos·mol'o·gist,** *n.*

cos·mo·naut (koz'mə nôt') *n.* an astronaut, esp. a Soviet astronaut. [Adaptation of Russian *kosmonaut,* from Greek *kosmos* world + *nautēs* sailor.]

cos·mo·pol·i·tan (koz'mə pol'i tən) *adj.* **1.** composed of or having elements, characteristics, or people from many different countries: *a cosmopolitan city.* **2.** free from national, provincial, or other limiting attitudes or attachments: *an adventurous traveler with a cosmopolitan outlook.* **3.** marked by or exhibiting sophistication; worldly: *cosmopolitan tastes, cosmopolitan manners.* **4.** (of a plant or animal) distributed widely throughout the world. —*n.* a cosmopolitan person; cosmopolite. —**cos'mo·pol'i·tan·ism,** *n.*

cos·mop·o·lite (koz mop'ə līt') *n.* a person who is worldly or cosmopolitan in attitude or outlook. [Greek *kosmopolitēs* citizen of the world.]

cos·mos (koz'məs, -mōs) *n., pl.* -mos or -mos·es. **1.** the universe considered as an ordered and harmonious system. **2.** any ordered and harmonious system. **3.a.** the large daisylike flower head of any of a group of plants, genus *Cosmos,* of the composite family, widely cultivated in temperate regions and found in a variety of colors. **b.** the plant bearing this flower head, having slender stems and feathery leaves. [Greek *kosmos* order, world.]

Cos·sack (kos'ak, -ək) *n.* a member of a people living mainly in the southwestern border regions of Russia, noted as horsemen and cavalry soldiers. [Russian *kazak,* from Turkic *quzzak* nomad, adventurer.]

cos·set (kos'it) *v.t.* to treat as a pet; pamper; fondle. —*n.* a pet, esp. a pet lamb. [Possibly from Old English *cot-sǣta* cottage dweller; referring to a pet kept in the house.]

cost (kôst) *n.* **1.** the amount of money, or its equivalent, paid or charged for something; price; expense: *the cost of education.* **2.** a loss, penalty, or sacrifice: *The war was won at a cost of many lives.* **3. costs.** money for legal expenses awarded at the discretion of the court to the winning party in a lawsuit, usually based on statutory limits. —*v.,* **cost, cost·ing.** —*v.t.* **1.** to be acquired at the price of; require the expenditure of: *This book cost me ten dollars.* **2.** to involve the loss or sacrifice of: *The accident cost two lives.* —*v.i. Informal.* to require great expenditure: *That sofa really costs.* [Old French *couster* to be of a certain price, cause pain, from Latin *cōnstāre* to stand together, consist.] —For Synonyms *(n.),* see **price.**

• **at all costs** (or **any cost**). regardless of the cost.

a	at	e	end	o	hot	u	up	hw	white		about
ā	ape	ē	me	ō	old	ū	use	ng	song		taken
ä	far	i	it	ô	fork	ü	rule	th	thin	ə	pencil
âr	care	ī	ice	oi	oil	ù	pull	th	this		lemon
		îr	pierce	ou	out	ûr	turn	zh	measure		circus

cos·tal (kos′təl) *adj.* of, relating to, or near a rib or the ribs. [Modern Latin *costalis*, from Latin *costa* rib.]

co·star (*n.,* kō′stär′; *v.,* kō′stär′) *n.* **1.** an actor or actress sharing star billing with another or others. **2.** an actor or actress having less prominent billing than the star or stars. —*v.,* -starred, -star·ring. —*v.t.* to feature or use as a costar. —*v.i.* to be a costar.

cos·tard (kos′tərd) *n.* a type of large English apple. [Modification of Old French *coste* rib, from Latin *costa;* with reference to its riblike markings.]

cost-ef·fec·tive (kôst′i fek′tiv) *adj.* producing the best results in relation to the money spent: *The city sought cost-effective measures to reduce pollution.*

cos·ter·mon·ger (kos′tər mung′gər, -mong′gər) *n. British.* a person who sells food, such as fruit, vegetables, or fish, in the street. Also, **cos·ter** (kôs′tər). [Earlier *costardmonger,* from COS-TARD + MONGER.]

cos·tive (kos′tiv) *adj.* constipated. [Middle French *costivé,* from Latin *cōnstīpātus,* past participle of *cōnstīpāre* to press together.]

cost·ly (kôst′lē) *adj.,* -li·er, -li·est. **1.** requiring or involving great expense, loss, or sacrifice; costing much: *a costly expedition, a costly mistake.* **2.** of great value; splendid; sumptuous. —cost′li·ness, *n.*

cost of living, the average cost of basic goods and services in a typical family budget in a given area during a given period of time.

cost-of-liv·ing allowance (kôst′əv liv′ing) a provision in a labor agreement that specifies a raise in the pay scale of workers comparable to the rate of inflation during the time of the agreement. Also, **cost-of-living adjustment.**

cost-of-living index, a rating of the prices of goods and services needed to support wage earners in a given area, calculated in a given period of time and compared with the same prices for a previous period of time.

cos·tume (*n.,* kos′tüm, -tüm; *v.,* kos tüm′, -tüm′) *n.* **1.** an outfit worn to portray someone or something else, as by an actor or a person at a masquerade: *a Halloween costume, costumes for a play.* **2.** a style of dress, including accessories and hair style, belonging to a particular region, time, or class: *Roman costume, peasant costume.* **3.** special clothing and accessories for a particular occasion or activity: *a riding costume.* —*v.t.,* -tumed, -tum·ing. to provide with a costume. —*adj.* characterized by or requiring the wearing of costumes: *a costume party.* [French *costume* style of dress, from Italian *costume* dress, fashion; originally, custom, going back to Latin *cōnsuētūdō* custom. Doublet of CUSTOM.]

costume jewelry, jewelry made with glass and other inexpensive materials rather than with precious stones.

cos·tum·er (kos tü′mər, -tū′-, kos′tü-, -tü-) *n.* a person or business that makes or deals in costumes. Also, **cos·tum·i·er** (kos tü′mē ər, -tū′-, kos′tü myä′).

co·sy (kō′zē) *adj.,* -si·er, -si·est. cozy. —*n., pl.* -sies. cozy. —co′si·ly, *adv.* —co′si·ness, *n.*

cot[1] (kot) *n.* a narrow, usually collapsible bed, esp. one made of canvas stretched on a folding frame. [Hindi *khat* bed, couch, going back to Sanskrit *khatvā.*]

cot[2] (kot) *n.* **1.** a small house; cottage. **2.** a small structure for shelter or protection, esp. for animals. **3.** a protective covering or sheath, as for a sore finger. [Old English *cot* cottage, dwelling.]

cot, cotangent.

co·tan·gent (kō tan′jənt, kō′tan′-) *n.* (of an acute angle in a right triangle) the trigonometric function that is the ratio of the angle's adjacent side to the side opposite.

cote (kōt) *n.* a small shelter for animals or birds. [Old English *cote* dwelling.]

co·te·rie (kō′tə rē) *n.* a small, often exclusive group of people who share a particular interest and usually meet socially. [French *coterie* clique, circle, from Old French *coterie* an association of tenants holding land together; of Germanic origin.]

co·ter·mi·nous (kō tûr′mə nəs) *adj.* conterminous. Also, **co·ter·mi·nal** (kō tûr′mə nəl).

co·tid·al (kō tī′dəl) *adj.* of or relating to a coincidence in time of tides: *a cotidal line on a map.*

co·til·lion (kə til′yən) *also,* **co·til·lon.** *n.* **1.** an elaborate ballroom dance popular in the nineteenth century, usually led by one couple, and characterized by great complexity of steps and figures and frequent changing of partners. **2.** the music for such a dance. **3.** a formal ball, esp. one at which debutantes are presented. [French *cotillon* dance accompanied by games; literally, petticoat, diminutive of *cotte* coat; of Germanic origin.]

co·to·ne·as·ter (kə tō′nē as′tər, kot′ə nēs′-) *n.* any of a group of woody shrubs, genus *Cotoneaster,* of the rose family, having white or pink flowers and red to purple-red fruit, widely grown as ornamentals.

Cots·wold (kots′wōld, -wəld) *n.* a sheep of a breed having long, coarse hair, originally from the Cotswold Hills, England.

cot·tage (kot′ij) *n.* **1.** a small house, usually in a suburban or rural area. **2.** a small house, as in a resort area, used for vacationing or as a summer house. [COT[2] + -AGE.]

cottage cheese, unripened, soft, white cheese made of strained and seasoned curds of sour skim milk.

cottage industry, an industry or system of production in which the workers manufacture goods, such as jewelry or clothing, at home.

cottage pudding, plain cake covered with a hot, sweet sauce, esp. a fruit sauce.

cot·tag·er (kot′i jər) *n.* **1.** a person who lives or vacations in a cottage. **2.** *British.* a rural laborer.

cot·ter[1] (kot′ər) *also,* **cot·tar.** *n.* **1.** *Scottish.* a tenant farmer. **2.** cottager *(def. 2).* [COT[2] + -ER[1].]

cot·ter[2] (kot′ər) *n.* **1.** a pin, bolt, wedge, or other mechanical part fitting into a hole or slot and holding other parts together. **2.** cotter pin. [Of uncertain origin.]

cotter pin, a pin-shaped cotter split lengthwise so that the ends may be bent to keep it in place after it is inserted in a hole or slot, used to hold parts of a machine or device together.

cot·ton (kot′ən) *n.* **1.** soft white, gray, or brown fibers that grow in a fluffy mass in large seed pods (or bolls) of certain plants and that are used in making textiles and other products. **2.** any of the woody, branching shrubs bearing these fibers, constituting the genus *Gossypium,* certain species of which are widely cultivated in warm areas. **3.** cotton plants collectively. **4.** a crop of such plants. **5.** thread made of cotton fibers. **6.** any fabric woven of cotton. **7.** any downy substance resembling cotton fibers, growing around the seeds on other plants. —*adj.* relating to or made of cotton. [Old French *coton* cotton fiber, cotton cloth, from Arabic *qutn* cotton fiber.]

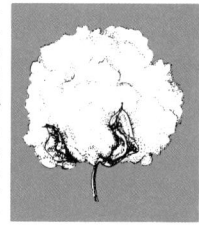

cotton boll

· **to cotton to. a.** to take a liking to; become friendly with: *Our dog doesn't cotton to strangers.* **b.** to agree with; approve of: *to cotton to an idea.*

Cotton Belt, the region of the southern United States where much cotton is grown.

cotton candy, a light, fluffy candy consisting of threadlike fibers of melted sugar spun or wound around a cone or stick.

cotton flannel, flannel *(def. 1).*

cotton gin, gin[2].

cot·ton·mouth (kot′ən mouth′) *n., pl.* -mouths (-mouthz′). water moccasin.

cot·ton·seed (kot′ən sēd′) *n., pl.* -seeds or -seed. the seed of cotton, from which cottonseed oil is extracted. The residue, a protein-rich meal, is used chiefly as a fertilizer or as livestock feed.

cottonseed oil, an oil extracted from cottonseed, refined for use as a cooking and salad oil and in the manufacture of lard substitutes, margarine, and various other products.

cot·ton·tail (kot′ən tāl′) *n.* any of various rabbits, genus *Sylvilagus,* of North America, having brown or grayish fur and a short, fluffy tail that is white underneath. Length: 12-17 inches (30-43 centimeters).

cot·ton·wood (kot′ən wood′) *n.* **1.** any of several fast-growing trees, genus *Populus,* of the willow family, esp. *P. deltoides,* found in moist regions of North America, having leathery, triangular leaves with toothed edges and tiny brown seeds covered with silky white hairs. **2.** the light, soft wood of this tree.

cotton wool, raw cotton.

cot·ton·y (kot′ə nē) *adj.* resembling cotton in texture or color; soft, downy, or white.

cot·y·le·don (kot′ə lē′dən) *n.* a seed leaf or rudimentary leaf that forms part of a plant embryo. In many plants the cotyledon develops into the first leaf or one of the first pair of leaves to grow above the ground. [Greek *kotylēdōn* cup-shaped hollow, from *kotylē* hollow, small cup.] —cot′y·le′don·ous, *adj.*

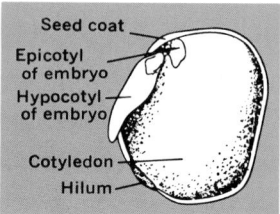

cotyledon

cot·y·lo·saur (kot′ə lə sôr′) *n.* any of an extinct group of

primitive ancestral reptiles, order Cotylosauria, of Pennsylvanian through Triassic geologic time, consisting of short-legged, stocky, or massive forms. —**cot′y·lo·sau′ri·an,** *n., adj.*

couch (kouch) *n.* **1.** a piece of furniture, usually upholstered, designed for several people to sit on or for one person to recline on; sofa. **2.** any place for sleeping or resting. —*v.t.* **1.** to put into words; express: *The diplomat couched the reply in vague terms.* **2.** to lower or bring down, esp. to lower (a spear, gun, or other weapon) to the position of attack. **3.** to lay down on or as if on a bed or couch. —*v.i.* **1.** to lie at rest or in a resting place. **2.** to lie in ambush; be hidden; lurk. [Old French *couche* a lying down, place for lying down, from *coucher* to lay down, put to bed, from Latin *collocāre* to place together, lay in its place.]

couch·ant (kou′chənt) *adj.* **1.** lying down. **2.** *Heraldry.* lying down with the head raised. [French *couchant,* present participle of *coucher* to lay down, put to bed. See COUCH.]

couch grass, quack grass.

couch potato *Slang.* a person who habitually spends free time watching television instead of engaging in more active, social, or intellectually challenging pursuits.

cou·gar (kü′gər) *n.* a tawny or grayish brown wild cat, *Felis concolor,* of North, Central, and South America, having a small round head, long limbs, and a slender, muscular body. Length: 6-8 feet (1.8-2.4 meters), including tail. Also, **catamount, mountain lion, panther, puma.** [French *couguar,* going back to Tupi-Guarani *suasuarana* literally, false deer.]

cough (kôf) *v.i.* to expel air from the lungs suddenly with effort and noise. —*v.t.* to expel by coughing: *to cough blood.* —*n.* **1.** the act or sound of coughing. **2.** an illness or condition that causes frequent coughing. [From an unrecorded Old English word.]
 •**to cough up. a.** to expel from the lungs or throat by coughing. **b.** *Slang.* to hand over or produce, usually reluctantly and as a result of pressure: *to cough up money owed to someone.*

cough drop, a small medicated lozenge, usually flavored and sweetened, for relieving coughs, hoarseness, sore throat, and the like.

cough syrup, a liquid, often containing a medicine, used to suppress the urge to cough or loosen phlegm or mucus from the respiratory tract.

could (kud) *auxiliary verb.* **1.** a past tense of **can¹. 2.** used to express possibility: *What you say could be true, but I'm not sure.* **3.** used to express ability: *Many countries could do more to reduce pollution.* **4.** used to make polite requests: *Could you help us move this desk?* **5.** used to ask permission: *Could I use your phone?* **6.** used to offer a suggestion: *You could paint the house blue instead of white.*

could·n't (kud′ənt) *contr.* could not.

couldst (kudst) *Archaic.* a second person singular past tense of **can¹.** ➡ used with **thou.**

cou·lee (kü′lē) *n.* **1.** in the western United States, a deep gulch or ravine, often dry, that has been formed by running water. **2.** a stream of lava, either flowing or solidified. [French *coulée* a flow, from *couler* to flow, from Latin *cōlāre* to strain.]

cou·lomb (kü′lom, -lōm, kü lom′, -lōm′) *n.* a unit of measure of electric charge. It is the amount of charge that in 1 second passes a given point in a wire carrying a current of 1 ampere. [From the French physicist Charles A. de *Coulomb,* 1736-1806.] —**cou·lom·bic** (kü lom′bik, -lōm′-) *adj.*

coul·ter (kōl′tər) colter.

coun·cil (koun′səl) *n.* **1.** an assembly or meeting convened for consultation, deliberation, or advice: *a family council.* **2.** a body of persons elected or appointed to serve in an administrative, legislative, or advisory capacity, as in a city, town, or borough. **3.** any assembly or representative body, as of church officials. **4.** an organization, society, or federation of a group of organizations. **5.** deliberation or discussion that takes place in a council. [Old French *concile* assembly, from Latin *concilium* assembly, gathering.]

coun·cil·lor (koun′sə lər, -slər) *n. British.* councilor. —**coun′·cil·lor·ship′,** *n.*

coun·cil·man (koun′səl mən) *n., pl.* **-men** (-mən). a member of a council, esp. of a city or town.

coun·ci·lor (koun′sə lər, -slər) *also, British,* **councillor.** *n.* a member of a council; councilman or councilwoman. —**coun′ci·lor·ship′,** *n.*

coun·cil·wom·an (koun′səl wum′ən) *n., pl.* **-wom·en** (-wim′ən). a woman who is a member of a council, esp. of a city or town.

coun·sel (koun′səl) *n., pl.* **-sels** or *(def. 3)* **-sel. 1.** a mutual

exchange of ideas, opinions, or advice; consultation; deliberation: *The leaders of the government met for counsel.* **2.** advice, direction, or opinion given esp. as the result of consultation: *In time of stress, people often fail to heed moderate counsel.* **3.** a lawyer or group of lawyers engaged in giving legal advice or in preparing or conducting a case in court: *to refuse to testify on advice of counsel.* **4.** someone one turns to for advice. **5.** a deliberate purpose or plan; intent. —*v.,* **-seled, -sel·ing** or **-selled, -sel·ling.** —*v.t.* **1.** to give advice to; advise. **2.** to urge the adoption of; recommend. —*v.i.* **1.** to give or take advice. [Old French *conseil* advice, plan, from Latin *cōnsilium* deliberation, advice.] —For Synonyms *(v.t.),* see **advise.**
 •**to keep one's own counsel.** to keep one's opinions, intentions, or plans secret.
 •**to take counsel.** to seek or exchange ideas, advice, or opinions; consult; deliberate.

coun·sel·ing (koun′sə ling, -sling) *n.* professional advice in solving educational, career, emotional, or medical problems: *marriage counseling, genetic counseling.*

coun·se·lor (koun′sə lər, -slər) *also, British,* **coun·sel·lor.** *n.* **1.** a person who gives counsel or advice; adviser. **2.** a lawyer, esp. one who conducts cases in court. Also, **coun·se·lor-at-law** (koun′sə lər ət lô′, -slər-). **3.** a person employed to supervise activities and campers at a camp. —**coun′se·lor·ship′;** *also, British,* **coun′sel·lor·ship′,** *n.* —For Synonyms, see **lawyer.**

count¹ (kount) *v.t.* **1.** to list or recite numbers by name in sequence up to and including (a certain number): *The referee counted ten over the fallen boxer.* **2.** to list or check, one by one, all (people or things in a group) to ascertain the total number; enumerate: *to count the eggs in a carton.* **3.** to include in reckoning; take into account: *There were forty people in the bus, counting the driver.* **4.** to believe to be; consider: *The survivors counted themselves lucky. Great Britain counts France among its allies.* —*v.i.* **1.** to list or recite numbers in units or groups in sequence: *to count to five.* **2.** to be of value; have importance or significance; matter: *Good manners count with some people. Every moment counts.* **3.** to be included in counting; be taken into account: *Your experience will count when promotions are given.* **4.** to depend, rely, or plan (with *on* or *upon*): *We're counting on your help.* —*n.* **1.** the act of counting; reckoning; numbering: *I made a rapid count of those present.* **2.** a number obtained by counting; total. **3.** *Law.* each distinct charge in an accusation: *to plead innocent to all counts.* **4.** *Boxing.* **a.** the counting of seconds, up to ten, by the referee, during which a fallen boxer must rise or be declared the loser. **b.** ten seconds, the maximum time a fallen boxer has to rise before being declared the loser. **5.** *Baseball.* the number of balls and strikes that a batter has accumulated. [Old French *co(u)nter* to reckon, tell, from Latin *computāre* to reckon, calculate, from *com-* with, together + *putāre* to think, consider. Doublet of COM-PUTE.] —**count′a·ble,** *adj.*
 •**to count for.** to be equal to; be worth: *Empty promises count for little.*
 •**to count in.** to include: *Count me in!*
 •**to count off.** to divide into equal groups by counting: *The coach told the students to count off by fours.*
 •**to count out. a.** to exclude; omit: *You can count me out if you've planned anything illegal.* **b.** to declare (a fallen boxer) the loser if unable to rise before a count of ten seconds is completed.

count² (kount) *n.* a nobleman of certain European countries having a rank corresponding to that of a British earl. [Old French *conte,* from Late Latin *comes* member of the emperor's court, from Latin *comes* companion.]

count·down (kount′doun′) *n.* **1.a.** the process of steps leading to a launching, as of a space vehicle or missile, marked by a count in reverse numerical order from a given time to zero, at which time the launching takes place. **b.** any similar process, as before the real or mock test of a nuclear weapon or other device. **c.** the time during which such a process takes place. **2.** the act of counting in reverse numerical order, esp. in the last stage of such a process.

coun·te·nance (koun′tə nəns) *n.* **1.** the facial features; face: *a handsome countenance.* **2.** an expression of the face; look. **3.** approval; support; encouragement: *We could not give countenance to such an illegal act.* **4.** calmness; composure. —*v.t.,* **-nanced, -nanc·ing.** to give countenance to;

a	at	e	end	o	hot	u	up	hw	white		about
ā	ape	ē	me	ō	old	ū	use	ng	song		taken
ä	far	i	it	ô	fork	ü	rule	th	thin	ə	pencil
âr	care	ī	ice	oi	oil	u̇	pull	th	this		lemon
		îr	pierce	ou	out	ûr	turn	zh	measure		circus

approve; support; encourage: *We countenanced their appeal for justice.* [Old French *contenance* look, visage, behavior, from Late Latin *continentia* demeanor, from Latin *continentia* a holding back, moderation.]
• **out of countenance.** embarrassed, disconcerted, or confused.
count·er¹ (koun′tər) *n.* **1.a.** a long table or case across which sales are made, business is conducted, or food is served, as in a store, bank, or restaurant. **b.** any long shelf or similar flat working area, as in a kitchen. **2.** something used in counting, esp. a piece of metal, ivory, or other material used for keeping score in certain games. **3.** an imitation coin; token. [Anglo-Norman *counteour* counting table, counting house, from Medieval Latin *computatorium* literally, place for counting, from Latin *computāre* to reckon, calculate, from *com-* with, together + *putāre* to think, consider.]
• **over the counter. a.** through a stockbroker's office instead of through a stock exchange: *to sell shares over the counter.* **b.** without a doctor's prescription: *That medicine can now be sold over the counter.*
• **under the counter.** in a secret manner, esp. illegally.
count·er² (koun′tər) *n.* a person or thing that counts, esp. a mechanical device for counting. [Middle French *conteor* person who counts, probably from Latin *computator,* from *computāre* to reckon, calculate; see COUNTER¹.]
coun·ter³ (koun′tər) *adv.* in an opposite or different direction or manner; in opposition; contrary: *The new rules ran counter to tradition.* —*adj.* acting or moving in an opposite or different manner or direction; opposing; contrary. —*v.t.* **1.** to go or act counter to; oppose or check: *The witness's testimony countered that of the defendant.* **2.** to offer as a response or defense: *The politician countered that the tax was fair.* **3.** in boxing, to deal a blow in return for (an opponent's blow). —*v.i.* **1.** to make an opposing move: *The defenders countered by attacking the enemy's flank.* **2.** to respond; reply: *The debater countered with another argument.* **3.** in boxing, to deal a blow while parrying or receiving one: *The champ countered with a left to the head.* —*n.* **1.** something that is opposite or contrary. **2.** a boxing blow in return for an opponent's blow. **3.** a stiff piece on the inside of the heel of a shoe. **4.** the sloping underside of a ship's stern above the water line. [Old French *contre* against, from Latin *contrā* against, opposite.]
counter- *combining form* **1.** in opposition to; against: *countermeasure.* **2.** in return; reciprocal: *counterattack.* **3.** corresponding: *counterpart.* [Old French *contre-, contre* against, towards, from Latin *contrā* against, opposite, in return.]
coun·ter·act (koun′tər akt′) *v.t.* to neutralize the action or force of; act in opposition to; check: *This drug will counteract the effects of poison.* —**coun′ter·ac′tion,** *n.* —**coun′ter·ac′tive,** *adj.*
coun·ter·at·tack (*n.,* koun′tər ə tak′; *v.,* koun′tər ə tak′, koun′tər ə tak′) *n.* an attack made to counter another attack: *a counterattack against an invading force, a counterattack against persistent critics.* —*v.t.* to make a counterattack against. —*v.i.* to make a counterattack.
coun·ter·bal·ance (*n.,* koun′tər bal′əns; *v.,* koun′tər bal′əns, koun′tər bal′-) *n.* **1.** a weight used to balance another weight. **2.** any aspect, power, or influence that balances a contrary one: *Your easygoing nature is a counterbalance to your partner's quick temper.* —*v.,* **-anced, -anc·ing.** —*v.t.* to act as a counterbalance to; offset. —*v.i.* to act as a counterbalance.
coun·ter·check (*n.,* koun′tər chek′; *v.,* koun′tər chek′, koun′tər chek′) *n.* **1.** something that stops, restrains, or opposes something else. **2.** a check made to confirm an earlier check; double check. —*v.t.* **1.** to stop, restrain, or oppose by a counteraction; check. **2.** to confirm by a second check; double-check.
coun·ter·claim (*n.,* koun′tər klām′; *v.,* koun′tər klām′, koun′tər klām′) *n.* an opposing claim, esp. an action by the defendant against the plaintiff in a lawsuit. —*v.i.* to make or put in a counterclaim. —*v.t.* to make a counterclaim against (the plaintiff or a prior claim). —**coun′ter·claim′ant,** *n.*
coun·ter·clock·wise (koun′tər klok′wīz) *adv., adj.* in the direction opposite to the movement of a clock's hands.
coun·ter·cul·ture (koun′tər kul′chər) *n.* a subculture, esp. one shared by young people, that is opposed to the standards and traditions of society.
coun·ter·cur·rent (koun′tər kûr′ənt, -kur′-) *n.* a current moving in a direction opposite to that of another current; opposing current.
coun·ter·es·pi·o·nage (koun′tər es′pē ə näzh′, -nij) *n.* operations and measures designed to prevent and counteract espionage.

coun·ter·feit (koun′tər fit′) *v.t.* **1.** to make an unauthorized copy of, as money, documents, or handwriting, with intent to deceive or defraud: *It is a crime to counterfeit money.* **2.** to be an imitation of; resemble closely. **3.** to make a pretense of; pretend; feign: *to counterfeit sympathy.* —*v.i.* **1.** to make an unauthorized copy with intent to deceive or defraud. **2.** to practice deceit; pretend; feign. —*n.* a copy or imitation made with intent to deceive or defraud; forgery. —*adj.* **1.** made in imitation of an original, with intent to deceive or defraud; not genuine: *counterfeit postage stamps.* **2.** pretended; feigned: *counterfeit kindness.* [Old French *contrefait,* past participle of *contrefaire* to copy, imitate, going back to Latin *contrā* against, opposite + *facere* to make.] —**coun′ter·feit′er,** *n.*
coun·ter·foil (koun′tər foil′) *n.* the part of a check, money order, ticket, or similar document kept by the issuer as a record or receipt; stub. [COUNTER- + FOIL².]
coun·ter·in·sur·gen·cy (koun′tər in sûr′jən sē) *n., pl.* **-cies.** military or political action taken against guerrillas or other insurgents.
coun·ter·in·sur·gent (koun′tər in sûr′jənt) *n.* a person who engages in counterinsurgency. —*adj.* of, involving, or engaged in counterinsurgency.
coun·ter·in·tel·li·gence (koun′tər in tel′i jəns) *n.* **1.** actions carried on by a government to counteract enemy intelligence, espionage, and sabotage activities. **2.** a group or organization that carries out such actions.
coun·ter·ir·ri·tant (koun′tər ir′i tənt) *n.* an agent used to produce mild inflammation, esp. of the skin, in order to reduce a more deep-seated inflammation.
coun·ter·man (koun′tər man′) *n., pl.* **-men** (-men′). a person who waits on customers at a counter, esp. in a cafeteria or other eating place.
coun·ter·mand (*v.,* koun′tər mand′, koun′tər mand′; *n.,* koun′tər mand′) *v.t.* **1.** to cancel or reverse (an order or command). **2.** to recall or order back by a contrary order. —*n.* an order or command canceling or reversing a previous one. [Old French *contremander* to contradict an earlier command, going back to Latin *contrā* against + *mandāre* to command.]
coun·ter·march (*n.,* koun′tər märch′; *v.,* koun′tər märch′, koun′tər märch′) *n.* **1.** a march back or in the opposite direction; return march. **2.** a drill maneuver in which marchers reverse direction but retain their original order and positions. —*v.i., v.t.* to perform or cause to perform a countermarch.
coun·ter·meas·ure (koun′tər mezh′ər) *n.* an action taken to counteract another.
coun·ter·move (koun′tər müv′) *n.* a move made to counter or retaliate for the move of another.
coun·ter·of·fen·sive (koun′tər ə fen′siv) *n.* an offensive undertaken by a military force to turn back the enemy's offensive and seize the initiative.
coun·ter·of·fer (koun′tər ô′fər) *n.* an offer or proposal made in response to another offer, esp. one made as a substitute for an offer or proposal rejected as unsatisfactory.
coun·ter·pane (koun′tər pān′) *n.* a quilt or coverlet for a bed; bedspread. [Modification of obsolete *counterpoint* quilt, from Middle French *contrepointe,* going back to Latin *culcita pūncta* literally, stitched quilt.]
coun·ter·part (koun′tər pärt′) *n.* **1.** a person or thing corresponding to or closely resembling another; equivalent: *The U.S. Congress is the counterpart of the British Parliament.* **2.** a person or thing that completes or complements another. **3.** a copy; duplicate: *a counterpart of a lease.*
coun·ter·plot (*n.,* koun′tər plot′; *v.,* koun′tər plot′, koun′tər plot′) *n.* a plot designed to defeat another plot. —*v.,* **-plot·ted, -plot·ting.** —*v.i.* to devise a counterplot; plot in opposition. —*v.t.* to plot against (a plot or plotter); defeat by a counterplot.
coun·ter·point (koun′tər point′) *n. Music.* **1.** the art or practice of having one or more distinct melodies occur simultaneously with a given basic melody according to certain rules of harmony. **2.** one or more melodies added to a principal melody in this way. [Old French *contrepoint* music arranged in counterpoint, from Medieval Latin *(cantus) contrapunctus* literally, (song) pointed against, from Latin *contrā* against, opposite + *pūnctus* point; because the notes of the additional melody (originally represented by *points*) were formerly marked *opposite* (or *against*) the corresponding notes in the basic melody.]
coun·ter·poise (*n.,* koun′tər poiz′; *v.,* koun′tər poiz′, koun′tər poiz′) *n.* **1.** counterbalance. **2.** any aspect, influence, or power that balances or offsets a contrary one. **3.** the state of being in balance. —*v.t.,* **-poised, -pois·ing.** to act in opposition to with equal weight, power, or effect; counterbalance. [Old French *con-*

trepois equal weight, going back to Latin *contrā* against, opposite + *pēnsum* something weighed.]

coun·ter·pro·duc·tive (koun′tər prə duk′tiv) *adj.* tending to defeat one's purpose, as by producing a result opposite to what is intended: *Too much training in sports can be counterproductive.*

Counter Reformation, a reform movement in the Roman Catholic Church during the sixteenth century, aimed at revitalizing Catholicism in Europe and meeting the political and religious challenge of Protestantism. Also, **Catholic Reformation.**

coun·ter·rev·o·lu·tion (koun′tər rev′ə lü′shən) *n.* **1.** a revolution opposed to a previous one and seeking to reverse its effects. **2.** political activity undertaken to combat a revolutionary movement. —**coun′ter·rev′o·lu′tion·ist,** *n.*

coun·ter·rev·o·lu·tion·ar·y (koun′tər rev′ə lü′shə ner′ē) *adj.* relating to or of the nature of a counterrevolution. —*n., pl.* **-ar·ies.** a person who takes part in or advocates a counterrevolution.

coun·ter·shaft (koun′tər shaft′) *n.* a shaft receiving motion from the main shaft of an engine or machine and transmitting it to a working part.

coun·ter·sign (*n.,* koun′tər sīn′; *v.,* koun′tər sīn′, koun′tər sīn′) *n.* **1.** a secret sign or signal given in answer to another, esp. a military password given in answer to the challenge of a guard or sentry. **2.** a signature added to a previously signed check or other document to confirm or authenticate it. Also *(def. 2),* **coun·ter·sig·na·ture** (koun′tər sig′nə chər). —*v.t.* to sign a document (already signed by another) in order to confirm or authenticate it: *The treasurer of the company countersigned the checks.* [French *contresigner* to sign in addition, attest, going back to Latin *contrā* against + *signāre* to mark, sign.]

coun·ter·sink (*v.,* koun′tər singk′, koun′tər singk′; *n.,* koun′tər-singk′) *v.t.,* **-sunk** (-sungk′, -sungk′), **-sink·ing. 1.** to enlarge the upper part of (a hole or cavity) to receive the head of a screw, bolt, or similar bonding device. **2.** to set (a screw, bolt, or rivet) in a countersunk hole. —*n.* **1.** a countersunk hole. **2.** a tool, esp. a bit, for enlarging the upper end of a drilled hole.

coun·ter·spy (koun′tər spī′) *n., pl.* **-spies.** a spy who is employed to detect and counteract the activities of enemy spies.

coun·ter·ten·or (koun′tər ten′ər) *Music. n.* **1.** the highest adult male voice. **2.** a singer who has a countertenor voice. **3.** a musical part for a countertenor voice. —*adj.* **1.** able to sing countertenor. **2.** for countertenor: *The countertenor part was difficult to sing.*

coun·ter·vail (koun′tər vāl′) *v.t.* **1.** to act against with equal force, power, or effect; counteract. **2.** to compensate or make up for; offset. —*v.i.* to be of equal force in opposition (with *against*). [Old French *contrevaloir* to be effective against, going back to Latin *contrā* against + *valēre* to be worth.]

coun·ter·weigh (koun′tər wā′) *v.t., v.i.* counterbalance.

coun·ter·weight (koun′tər wāt′) *n.* counterbalance.

count·ess (koun′tis) *n.* **1.** the wife or widow of a count or, in Great Britain, of an earl. **2.** a woman holding in her own right a rank equal to that of an earl or count. [Old French *contesse,* feminine of *conte.* See COUNT².]

counting house *also,* **count·ing·house** (koun′ting hous′). a building, office, or room used for such purposes as bookkeeping, correspondence, or business transactions. Also, **counting room.**

counting number, a number used in counting the numbers of a set; any whole number except 0; natural number.

count·less (kount′lis) *adj.* too many to be counted; innumerable: *There are countless trees in the forest.*

coun·tri·fied (kun′tri fīd′) *also,* **countryfied.** *adj.* having the appearance, manner, or characteristics associated with the country or country life; rural; rustic.

coun·try (kun′trē) *n., pl.* **-tries. 1.a.** a tract or expanse of land; territory: *This is lovely country.* **b.** any district or region, esp. one considered as having a distinguishing characteristic: *We went camping in the hill country.* **2.a.** a nation or independent state: *Fifty-one countries signed the United Nations Charter.* **b.** the territory of a nation. **c.** the people of a nation or independent state: *Half the country voted in the last election.* **3.** the land where a person was born, resides, or is a citizen. **4.** any region outside of cities or towns; rural area. —*adj.* **1.** of, relating to, or characteristic of rural areas: *a country road.* **2.** of, relating to, or performing country music: *country records, country entertainers.* [Old French *contree* region, district, from Medieval Latin *contrata* land lying opposite, landscape, from Latin *contrā* against, opposite.] —For Synonyms, see **state.**

country and western, country music.

country club, a private social club usually located in a suburb,

equipped with a clubhouse and various recreational facilities, such as a golf course, swimming pool, or tennis courts.

country cousin, a person from the country who finds city life bewildering and confusing.

coun·try-dance (kun′trē dans′) *n.* a folk dance of English origin, esp. one in which partners form two lines facing each other.

coun·try·fied (kun′tri fīd′) countrified.

coun·try·folk (kun′trē fōk′) *n., pl.* **-folk** or **-folks.** people who live in rural areas.

country gentleman, a man of wealth or position who lives on his country estate.

coun·try·man (kun′trē mən) *n., pl.* **-men** (-mən). **1.** a native, citizen, or inhabitant of one's own country; compatriot. **2.** a native or inhabitant of a particular country or region. **3.** a person who lives in the country; rustic.

country mile *Informal.* a long distance; very far.

country music, a kind of popular music derived from the folk music of the southern and western United States, typically played on stringed instruments such as the guitar, fiddle, and banjo. Also, **country and western.**

coun·try·seat (kun′trē sēt′) *n.* a mansion or estate in the country, esp. one belonging to a country gentleman or noble.

coun·try·side (kun′trē sīd′) *n.* **1.** a rural region or district. **2.** its inhabitants.

coun·try·wom·an (kun′trē wùm′ən) *n., pl.* **-wom·en** (-wim′ən). **1.** a woman who is a native, citizen, or inhabitant of one's own country. **2.** a woman who is a native, citizen, or inhabitant of a particular country or region. **3.** a woman who lives in the country.

coun·ty (koun′tē) *n., pl.* **-ties. 1.** the political division next below a state in most of the United States. It is the largest unit for local government within a state. **2.** the most important territorial division for administrative, judicial, and political purposes in Great Britain and Ireland; shire. **3.** the people of a county. **4.** formerly, the area governed by a count or earl. [Old French *conté* territory ruled by a count, from Late Latin *comitātus,* from *comes.* See COUNT².]

county agent, a government official employed chiefly to advise and assist farmers and rural people, esp. in matters of agriculture and home economics.

county seat, a town or city that is the center of county government.

coup (kü) *n., pl.* **coups** (küz). **1.** a sudden, brilliant action; unexpected, clever stratagem; master stroke. **2.** coup d'etat. [French *coup* stroke, blow, from Medieval Latin *colpus,* from Vulgar Latin *colapus,* from Latin *colaphus* blow, from Greek *kolaphos.*] —For Synonyms, see **revolt.**

coup de grâce (kü də grās′) *French.* **1.** a death blow or shot, esp. one that ends the suffering of a mortally wounded animal or person. **2.** a decisive or finishing stroke. [French *coup de grâce* finishing stroke; literally, stroke of grace.]

coup d'e·tat (kü′dä tä′) *pl.* **coups d'e·tat** (kü′dä täz′). a sudden seizure, usually forcible, of government control by a person or group, esp. one previously holding some official authority. Also, **coup.** [French *coup d'état* literally, stroke of state.]

coupe (küp, kü pā′) *also,* **cou·pé** (kü pā′). *n.* **1.** a two-door automobile seating two to six people. **2.** a short, four-wheeled closed carriage that carries two passengers and has a seat outside for the driver. [French *coupé,* short for *(carrosse) coupé* literally, (carriage) cut off, noun use of the past participle of *couper* to cut, from *coup.* See COUP.]

cou·ple (kup′əl) *n.* **1.** two things of the same kind joined or considered together; pair. **2.** two people who are married or engaged or are partners in a dance, game, or other activity. ➡ used as singular or plural. **3.** *Informal.* a small number; several; few: *We walked a couple of miles.* **4.** something joining two things together; link; coupler. —*v.,* **-pled, -pling.** —*v.t.* to join, link, or fasten together in a pair or pairs. —*v.i.* to join or unite in a pair or pairs. [Old French *co(u)ple* a pair, from Latin *cōpula* bond, connection.]

cou·pler (kup′lər) *n.* **1.** a person or thing that couples. **2.** a device in a pipe organ for connecting two or more keys or key-

a	at	e	end	o	hot	u	up	hw	white	⎧	about
ā	ape	ē	me	ō	old	ū	use	ng	song		taken
ä	far	i	it	ô	fork	ü	rule	th	thin	ə	pencil
âr	care	ī	ice	oi	oil	ù	pull	th	this		lemon
		îr	pierce	ou	out	ûr	turn	zh	measure	⎩	circus

boards so they can be played together. **3.** an interlocking device used to connect two railroad cars. Also *(def. 3),* **coupling.**

cou·plet (kup′lit) *n.* two successive lines of verse, usually rhyming and in the same meter, that form a unit, for example: *Know then thyself, presume not God to scan; / The proper study of mankind is man* (Alexander Pope). [Old French *couplet,* diminutive of *couple* a pair. See COUPLE.]

cou·pling (kup′ling) *n.* **1.** the act of someone or something that couples; joining together. **2.** any of various devices for joining parts of machinery. **3.** coupler *(def. 3).* **4.** an arrangement for transferring electrical energy from one circuit to another, in one or both directions.

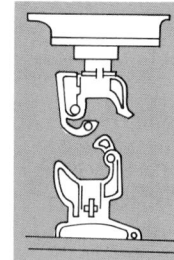

coupler *(def. 3)* (top view)

cou·pon (kü′pon, kū′-) *n.* **1.** a detachable part of a ticket, certificate, or printed advertisement, entitling the holder to something, as a gift or discount. **2.** a printed form that can be used for ordering or obtaining something, such as an item or information. **3.** a detachable printed statement on a bond representing the amount of interest accrued on the bond during a specific period. It is clipped by the bondholder and presented for payment on the due date. [French *coupon* literally, piece cut off, from *couper* to cut, from *coup.* See COUP.]

cour·age (kûr′ij, kur′-) *n.* a quality that enables a person to face danger or difficulties without fear; bravery; boldness. [Old French *corage* state of mind, feelings, going back to Latin *cor* heart.]

•**to have the courage of one's convictions.** to have the courage to do what one believes is right.

cou·ra·geous (kə rā′jəs) *adj.* having or marked by courage; brave; fearless. —**cou·ra′geous·ly,** *adv.* —**cou·ra′geous·ness,** *n.* —For Synonyms, see **brave.**

cour·i·er (kûr′ē ər, kur′-) *n.* a messenger, esp. one carrying an important or urgent message. [Middle French *courier,* from Italian *corriere,* from *correre* to run, from Latin *currere.*]

course (kôrs) *n.* **1.** a moving from one point to the next; onward movement; progress; advance: *the course of history, in the course of human events.* **2.** the line in which anything moves; direction taken: *a westward course.* **3.** a continuous passage in time; duration: *in the course of a year.* **4.** a sequential advance through progressive stages or conditions: *the course of the seasons.* **5.** a natural or regular advance, order, or development: *the course of a disease.* **6.** a line of conduct or action; way of acting or doing: *The diplomat took a conciliatory course.* **7.a.** a way, path, or channel over which something moves: *the course of a river.* **b.** an area arranged for certain sports or games: *a race course.* **8.** an ordered sequence or group of similar things: *a course of lectures, a course of medical treatment.* **9.** a complete prescribed series of studies in a school, college, or university; curriculum: *a liberal arts course.* **10.** one unit of study in such a curriculum: *a course in biology, a psychology course.* **11.** part of a meal served at one time: *The main course was chicken.* **12.** a single continuous row or layer of building materials, as bricks, stones, or wood, on the face or wall of a structure. **13.a.** the lowest square sail on any mast of a square-rigged ship. **b.** a point of the compass toward which a ship proceeds. —*v.,* **coursed, cours·ing.** —*v.t.* **1.** to run or move through or over: *The deer coursed the open field.* **2.** to chase; pursue: *The cavalry coursed the fleeing troops.* **3.** to hunt (game) with dogs: *to course rabbits.* **4.** to cause (dogs) to run in a hunt: *The hunters coursed their hounds after the fox.* —*v.i.* **1.** to move swiftly; run; flow: *The tears coursed down the child's cheeks.* **2.** to take or follow a particular course: *The boats coursed along the east bank of the river.* **3.** to hunt game with dogs. [Old French *cours* a running, from Latin *cursus* a running, place for running.]

•**in due course.** at the proper time or in the natural order of events: *The damage will be fixed in due course.*

•**of course. a.** certainly; undoubtedly: *Of course that's a photo of me.* **b.** as is or might be expected; naturally: *My parents were angry, of course, when I lied.*

•**off course.** traveling or moving in an unintended direction; on an unintended course.

•**on course.** traveling or moving in the intended direction; on the planned or intended course.

cours·er (kôr′sər) *n.* a swift or spirited horse. [Old French *corsier* racehorse, from *cours* a running, course. See COURSE.]

course·ware (kôrs′wâr′) *n.* computer programs designed to help students learn specific subjects, esp. for use in a classroom.

court (kôrt) *n.* **1.** an open space partially or wholly enclosed by walls or buildings; courtyard. **2.** a short street or wide alley. **3.** a special section of a large building, as a hotel or museum, usually roofed with glass. **4.** a level space or area marked off for certain games: *a basketball court, a tennis court.* **5.** the residence of a sovereign or other high dignitary; palace. **6.** the family, councilors, and retinue of a sovereign, collectively: *the court of the Medici.* **7.** a sovereign together with officials and advisers, considered as a ruling power: *He served as U.S. ambassador at the court in Oslo.* **8.** any formal assembly held by a sovereign: *She was presented at court.* **9.** a place where justice is judicially administered; courtroom; courthouse. **10.** one or several persons appointed to hear, investigate, and determine legal cases and administer justice; judge or judges: *a criminal court.* **11.** a judicial assembly of such persons. **12.** a session of a judicial assembly: *This court will adjourn for lunch.* **13.** flattering attention paid to win favor. **14.** courtship; wooing. —*v.t.* **1.** to seek the love or affection of; woo. **2.** to pay flattering attention to (a person) to win favor. **3.** to attempt to get or gain; seek: *to court flattery, to court favor.* **4.** to act so as to invite: *to court defeat, to court danger.* —*v.i.* to carry on a courtship: *They courted for a year.* [Old French *cort*[1], royal court, court of justice, from Latin *cohors* enclosure, company of soldiers. Doublet of COHORT.]

•**out of court.** without a trial: *They settled the claim out of court.*

•**to pay court to. a.** to try to win the love of; woo. **b.** to pay attention to (a person) to win favor.

cour·te·ous (kûr′tē əs) *adj.* **1.** having or marked by good manners; polite. **2.** considerate of others. [Old French *corteis* courtly, well-bred, from *cort.* See COURT.] —**cour′te·ous·ly,** *adv.* —**cour′te·ous·ness,** *n.*

cour·te·san (kôr′tə zən, kûr′-) *n.* a prostitute, esp. one who associates with clients of wealth and rank. [French *courtisane* strumpet; earlier, lady of the court, court mistress, from Italian *cortigiana,* from *corte* court, from Latin *cohors* enclosure.]

cour·te·sy (kûr′tə sē) *n., pl.* **-sies. 1.** courteous behavior; politeness. **2.** a courteous act or remark. **3.** generosity, help, or cooperation: *Two musicians play on this recording through the courtesy of their record companies.* **4.** a polite usage or act that honors, compliments, or shows respect: *to be called "colonel" by courtesy.* [Old French *cortoisie* polite behavior, from *corteis.* See COURTEOUS.]

•**courtesy of.** without charge by; through the generosity of: *The actors' outfits were provided courtesy of a well-known Hollywood store.*

court·house (kôrt′hous′) *n., pl.* **-hous·es** (-hou′ziz). **1.** a building in which courts of law are held. **2.** a building housing the principal offices of a county government.

cour·ti·er (kor′tē ər) *n.* **1.** a person who frequents or attends the court of a sovereign. **2.** a person who seeks favor by flattery.

court·ly (kôrt′lē) *adj.,* **-li·er, -li·est. 1.** suitable for a monarch's court; refined; elegant; polished: *courtly manners.* **2.** flattering, esp. in an insincere or fawning way. —**court′li·ness,** *n.*

court-mar·tial (kôrt′mär′shəl) *n., pl.* **courts-mar·tial** or **court-mar·tials. 1.** a military court that tries persons subject to military law. **2.** a trial by such a court. **3.** a conviction by such a court. —*v.t.,* **-tialed, -tial·ing;** *also, British,* **-tialled, -tial·ling. 1.** to try by a court-martial. **2.** to find guilty in a court-martial: *The discharged soldier had been court-martialed.*

court of law, a court that hears and rules on cases in accordance with the common law.

Court of St. James's (sānt jām′ziz) the royal court of Great Britain.

court plaster, a cloth with an adhesive substance on one side, used for covering slight wounds. [Because ladies of royal *courts* used to wear black patches of this material on their faces and shoulders as beauty spots.]

court·room (kôrt′rüm′, -rum′) *n.* a room in which a court of law is regularly held.

court·ship (kôrt′ship′) *n.* the act, process, or period of courting or wooing.

court tennis, a form of tennis played on an indoor court having high cement walls, off which the ball may be played.

court·yard (kôrt′yärd′) *n.* an open area surrounded by walls or buildings, in or next to a large building.

cous·cous (küs′küs) *n.* a North African dish made of coarsely ground wheat flour, esp. semolina, usually steamed and served with meat or vegetables. [French *couscous,* from Arabic *kuskus,* from Berber *seksu* this dish.]

cousin (kuz′in) *n.* **1.** a son or daughter of one's uncle or aunt.

2. any kinsman or kinswoman; specifically, a relative with whom one shares a common ancestor. First cousins are descended from the same pair of grandparents; second cousins have great-grandparents in common. The children of one's first (or second) cousins are first (or second) cousins once removed; grandchildren of one's first cousins are first cousins twice removed. **3.** a person or a kindred race or nation. **4.** a title of address used by a sovereign to a fellow sovereign or to a noble. [Old French *cousin* son of an uncle or aunt, going back to Latin *consōbrīnus* child of a mother's sister.] —**cous′in·ly,** *adj.*

cous·in-ger·man (kuz′in jûr′mən) *n., pl.* **cous·ins-ger·man.** cousin *(def. 1).* [Old French *cousin-germain.* See COUSIN, GERMAN.]

couth (kūth) *n.* good manners; refinement; polish: *a person with no couth.* —*adj.* well-mannered; refined; polished. ➡ used humorously. [Old English *cūth* familiar.]

cou·ture (kü tur′) *n.* the work of a couturier; dressmaking or fashion designing. [French *couture* sewing, going back to Latin *consuere* to sew together.]

cou·tu·ri·er (kü tur′ē ā′, -ē ər, -tür′yā) *n.* **1.** a dressmaker or fashion designer. **2.** a business engaged in dressmaking or fashion designing. [French *couturier,* from *couture.* See COUTURE.]

cou·tu·ri·ere (kü tur′ē ər, -ē âr′) *n.* a female dressmaker or fashion designer. [French *couturière,* feminine of *couturier.* See COUTURIER.]

co·va·lence (kō vā′ləns) *n. Chemistry.* the number of pairs of electrons that an atom can share with adjacent atoms. [Co- + VALENCE.] —**co·va′lent,** *adj.* —**co·va′lent·ly,** *adv.*

co·va·lent bond (kō vā′lənt) a chemical bond formed by the sharing of pairs of electrons by adjacent atoms.

cove (kōv) *n.* **1.** a small, sheltered recess in a shoreline. **2.** a sheltered hollow, as in hills, mountains, or a wood. [Old English *cofa* chamber.]

cov·en (kuv′ən) *n.* a gathering or group of witches. [Old French *covine* band, going back to Latin *convenīre* to come together.]

cov·e·nant (kuv′ə nənt) *n.* **1.** an agreement, usually formal, between two or more persons or parties; compact. **2. Covenant. a.** an agreement between Scottish Presbyterians and members of the English Parliament in 1643 that attempted to establish the Presbyterian Church as the state church of England, Scotland, and Ireland. Also, **Solemn League and Covenant. b.** an agreement signed by Scottish Presbyterians in 1638 as a testament of their faith. Also, **National Covenant. 3.a.** in the Bible, the solemn promises made by God to the human race. **b.** the compact between God and the people of ancient Israel, in which God promised them protection if they were faithful. **4.** *Law.* a written agreement, usually under seal, such as a contract. —*v.i.* to enter into a covenant. —*v.t.* to promise by or in a covenant. [Old French *covenant* a coming together, promise, from *covenir* to agree, meet together, from Latin *convenīre* to come together.]

cov·e·nant·er (kuv′ə nən tər; *def. 2, also* kuv′ə nan′tər) *n.* **1.** a person who makes a covenant. **2. Covenanter.** a person who signed or supported either of the Scottish Presbyterian Covenants.

Cov·en·try (kuv′ən trē, kov′-) *n.* **to send to Coventry.** to refuse to associate with; ignore and snub. [Probably originally referred to Cavaliers sent to prison in *Coventry,* a Roundhead stronghold.]

cov·er (kuv′ər) *v.t.* **1.** to put something over or upon, as to protect, conceal, or enclose; overlay: *to cover a table with a tablecloth, to cover an injured person with a blanket.* **2.** to extend over or coat the surface of; spread over: *Snow covered the ground. The dog was covered with mud.* **3.** to wrap up; clothe: *He covered the children with heavy clothing.* **4.** to conceal from view or knowledge; hide; screen: *Darkness covered their escape.* **5.** to give protection or shelter to; shield: *The flood victims were without a roof to cover them.* **6.** to travel or pass over: *We covered the distance in fifteen minutes.* **7.** to deal with; include; encompass: *The memorandum covers the subject of the meeting.* **8.** to be sufficient to pay for or provide security or protection against: *Our insurance covered the cost of the damages.* **9.a.** to aim directly at, as with a firearm: *The sheriff covered the thief with a pistol.* **b.** to protect by shooting or being ready to shoot at an enemy: *The air force covered the infantry's retreat.* **10.** to put or hold within range; command: *The fortress on the hill covered the harbor area below.* **11.a.** to have as a journalistic assignment; report on, review, photograph, film, or videotape: *She will cover the trial for the paper.* **b.** to publish or broadcast reports, reviews, or the like concerning: *This television network covers sports thoroughly.* **12.** to have responsibility for, as a territory, route, sphere of work, or the like: *The company's Illinois office covers the entire Midwest.* **13.** to equal the bet of (an opponent); accept the conditions of (a bet). **14.** *Sports.* **a.** to guard or defend against (an opposing player): *to cover a pass receiver.* **b.** to be responsible for defending

(an area or position): *to cover first base on a bunt.* **15.** to brood or sit on (eggs or chicks); incubate. **16.** to put or wear a hat or cap on (one's head): *You may cover your head after the flag passes.* —*v.i.* **1.** to envelop or spread over something in order to overlay or conceal it: *This paint covers in one coat.* **2.** to act as a substitute or replacement for another. **3.** to provide an excuse or alibi (often with *up*): *to cover up for a friend.* —*n.* **1.** something that covers: *the cover of a box, the cover of a book.* **2.** something that shelters or protects, esp. from attack: *The troops fought under the cover of the airplanes.* **3.** something that shelters or conceals game or wild animals. **4.** a quilt, blanket, or the like: *The sleeping child had pushed the covers aside.* **5.** a table setting, esp. for one person, including utensils and linens. **6.** something that disguises or conceals; pretense: *The spy obtained their confidence under the cover of friendship.* **7.** cover charge. [Old French *covrir* to hide, put something over something, from Latin *cooperīre* to cover entirely.] —**cov′er·a·ble,** *adj.* —**cov′er·er,** *n.* —**cov′er·less,** *adj.*

•**to blow one's or someone's cover.** to expose one's or someone's true identity.

•**to break cover.** to come out from hiding: *The approach of the dog caused the grouse to break cover.*

•**to cover up. a.** to cover completely: *Falling leaves had covered up the path.* **b.** to conceal from view or knowledge; keep from becoming known: *The prosecutor covered up her son's crime.*

•**to take cover.** to seek protective or concealing shelter: *The soldiers quickly took cover when the bombing began.*

•**under cover.** secret or secretly: *Plans for the attack were made under cover.*

cov·er·age (kuv′ər ij, kuv′rij) *n.* **1.** the extent or degree to which something covers or is covered. **2.** all the risks covered or the extent of protection under the terms of an insurance policy. **3.** the act, manner, or extent of gathering and reporting news: *comprehensive coverage of an election.*

cov·er·all (kuv′ər ôl′) *also,* **cov·er·alls.** *n.* a one-piece work garment, usually combining a long-sleeved shirt and trousers, designed to be worn over regular clothing. ➡ **Coveralls** is used as plural.

cover charge, an amount added to the check in addition to the cost of the food and drink served by a restaurant or nightclub, esp. as a charge for entertainment. Also, **cover.**

cover crop, a crop, such as clover or rye, sown in a field or orchard to protect the soil from erosion or to enrich it between plantings of other crops.

covered wagon, a large wagon with a removable, arched canvas cover that is supported by hoops or similar devices, used by American pioneers in the West.

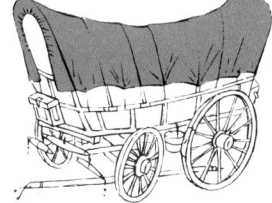
covered wagon

cover glass, coverslip.

cov·er·ing (kuv′ər ing) *n.* something that covers.

cov·er·let (kuv′ər lit) *n.* an outer covering for a bed; bedspread; counterpane. [Anglo-Norman *covrelit* from Old French *covrir* to cover + *lit* bed (from Latin *lectus*). See COVER.]

cov·er·slip (kuv′ər slip) a very thin piece of glass used to lay over a specimen on a slide to view under a microscope. Also, **cover glass.**

cov·ert (kuv′ərt, kō′vərt) *adj.* **1.** concealed from general view or knowledge; secret; disguised, or hidden: *a covert glance, a covert attempt to communicate with the prisoner.* **2.** covered over; sheltered. —*n.* **1.** a hiding place; shelter. **2.** a thicket that gives shelter to wild animals or game. **3.** covert cloth. **4.** one of the small feathers that cover the point of attachment of a bird's wing or tail feathers. [Old French *covert,* past participle of *covrir* to cover. See COVER.] —**cov′ert·ly,** *adv.* —**cov′ert·ness,** *n.* —For Synonyms *(adj.),* see **secret.**

covert cloth, twilled fabric, usually of wool and woven with two colors of yarn in the warp.

cov·er·ture (kuv′ər chŭr′, -chər) *n.* a covering, esp. for shelter, disguise, or concealment.

cov·er-up (kuv′ər up′) *n.* an attempt to conceal or a means of concealing something, esp. something dishonest or illegal.

cov·et (kuv′it) *v.t.* to desire (something belonging to another person) eagerly or inordinately. —*v.i.* to feel eager or inordinate

a	at	e	end	o	hot	u	up	hw	white		about
ā	ape	ē	me	ō	old	ū	use	ng	song		taken
ä	far	i	it	ô	fork	ü	rule	th	thin	ə	pencil
âr	care	ī	ice	oi	oil	ů	pull	th	this		lemon
		îr	pierce	ou	out	ûr	turn	zh	measure		circus

desire for something belonging to another. [Old French *coveitier* to desire, going back to Latin *cupiditās* desire.] —**cov′et·er,** *n.*

cov·et·ous (kuv′i təs) *adj.* eagerly or inordinately desiring something, esp. something belonging to another person. —**cov′-et·ous·ly,** *adv.* —**cov′et·ous·ness,** *n.*

cov·ey (kuv′ē) *n., pl.* **-eys. 1.** a small flock of birds, esp. partridge or grouse. **2.** any small group; bevy; company. [Old French *covee* flock of birds, especially of partridges, from *cover* to hatch, sit on, from Latin *cubāre* to lie down.]

cow[1] (kou) *n., pl.* **cows** or *(archaic)* **kine. 1.** a mature female of any bovine animal, genus *Bos,* esp. the domestic bovine. **2.** a mature female of various other large mammals, as the elephant, whale, or seal. [Middle English *cou,* from Old English *cū* female of the bovine family.]

cow[2] (kou) *v.t.* to frighten with threats or a display of force; intimidate; overawe. [Old Norse *kūga* to tyrannize over.]

cow·ard (kou′ərd) *n.* a person who lacks courage; person who flees from danger, difficulty, or pain. —*adj.* cowardly. [Old French *coart* (also *Coart* the timid hare in the medieval tales about Reynard the Fox), from *coe, coue* tail, from Latin *cauda;* because a frightened animal turns tail or has its tail between its legs.]

cow·ard·ice (kou′ər dis) *n.* a lack of courage; shameful fear of danger, difficulty, or pain.

cow·ard·ly (kou′ərd lē) *adj.* **1.** lacking courage; easily made afraid; shamefully fearful. **2.** of, characteristic of, or befitting a coward. —*adv.* like a coward. —**cow′ard·li·ness,** *n.*

cow·bane (kou′bān′) *n.* **1.** any of several plants, genus *Cicuta,* of the carrot family that are extremely poisonous. **2.** any of several related plants that are poisonous to cattle.

cow·bell (kou′bel′) *n.* a small bell hung around a cow's neck to ring and indicate the cow's whereabouts.

cow·ber·ry (kou′ber′ē) *n., pl.* **-ries. 1.** a low cranberry, *Vaccinium vitis-idaea,* with white or pink flowers and purple to purple-red fruit. **2.** the edible fruit of this plant. Also *(defs. 1, 2),* **lingonberry. 3.** a deciduous North American viburnum, *Viburnum lentago,* bearing white flowers and blue-black fruit.

cow·bird (kou′bûrd′) *n.* any of several songbirds of the family Icteridae, native to North and South America, often found with cattle. Length: 7-8 inches (18-20 centimeters).

cow·boy (kou′boi′) *n.* **1.** a person who herds and tends cattle on a ranch, usually riding on horseback to perform the work. **2.** a person, as in a rodeo, who participates in competitions or performs feats requiring the skills of a cowboy. **3.** *Informal.* a person who acts recklessly or irresponsibly, esp. in a dangerous, complicated, or sensitive situation.

cow·catch·er (kou′kach′ər) *n.* a metal frame on the front of a locomotive or streetcar for clearing the tracks of obstructions.

cow·er (kou′ər) *v.i.* to crouch or cringe, as in fear or shame. [Of Scandinavian origin.]

cow·fish (kou′fish′) *n., pl.* **-fish** or **-fish·es. 1.** any of several species of trunkfish having long, bony, hornlike projections over the eyes. **2.** any of various marine mammals, as the dugong, manatee, or dolphin.

cow·girl (kou′gûrl′) *n.* **1.** a woman who herds or tends cattle on a ranch, usually riding on horseback to perform the work. **2.** a woman, as in a rodeo, who participates in competitions or performs feats requiring the skills of a cowgirl.

cow·hand (kou′hand′) *n.* a person who works on a cattle ranch; cowboy or cowgirl.

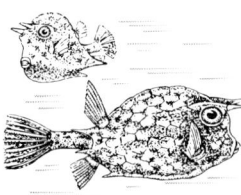

cowfish

cow·herd (kou′hûrd′) *n.* a person who herds or tends cattle.

cow·hide (kou′hīd′) *n.* **1.** the hide of a cow or leather made from it. **2.** a strong, flexible whip made of braided leather or rawhide. —*v.t.,* **-hid·ed, -hid·ing.** to whip with a cowhide; flog.

cowl (koul) *n.* **1.** a hood attached to a monk's robe. **2.** a monk's robe with a hood. **3.** the top front part of an automobile body to which the windshield, the instrument board, and the rear end of the hood are attached. **4.** cowling. **5.** a covering, usually shaped like a hood, placed on the top of a chimney or vent to increase the draft. —*v.t.* **1.** to cover with or as with a cowl. **2.** to put a monk's cowl on. **3.** to make a monk of. [Old English *cūle, cug(e)le* monk's hood, going back to Latin *cucullus* hood.]

cow·lick (kou′lik′) *n.* a tuft of hair that grows in a different direction from the rest of the hair and will not lie flat.

cowl·ing (kou′ling) *n.* a streamlined metal covering for a section of an airplane, esp. one designed to cover an engine. Also, **cowl.**

cow·man (kou′mən) *n., pl.* **-men** (-mən). **1.** a person who owns cattle; rancher. **2.** cowherd.

co-work·er (kō′wûr′kər, kō′wûr′-) *n.* a fellow worker.

cow·pea (kou′pē′) *n.* **1.** a bushy or trailing vine, *Vigna unguiculata,* widely planted as a forage or cover crop, bearing long pods that contain edible kidney-shaped seeds. **2.** the seed of this plant.

cow·poke (kou′pōk′) *n. Informal.* cowboy.

cow pony, a horse used in herding cattle.

cow·pox (kou′poks′) *n.* a mild but very contagious eruptive disease of cows caused by a strain of the virus that causes smallpox in humans. Smallpox vaccine is prepared from the cowpox virus.

cow·punch·er (kou′pun′chər) *n. Informal.* cowhand.

cow·rie (kour′ē) *also,* **cow·ry.** *n., pl.* **-ries. 1.** the small glossy shell of any of various sea snails, family Cypraeidae, commonly found in warm shallow waters of the Pacific and Indian oceans. The shell of the **money cowrie,** *Cypraea moneta,* is used as money by certain tribes of Africa and southern Asia. **2.** one of these snails. [Hindi *kaurī* small shell used as money, from Sanskrit *kaparda;* of Dravidian origin.]

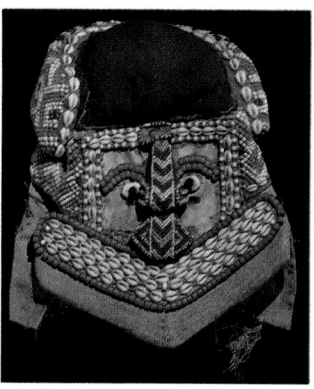

cowrie shells and colored beads on an African mask

cow·slip (kou′slip′) *n.* **1.** a wild plant, *Primula veris,* of the primrose family, having fragrant yellow flowers. **2.** a common marsh marigold, *Caltha palustris,* having deep yellow flowers. **3.** the flower of either of these plants. [Old English *cūslyppe* the plant *Primula veris,* from *cū* cow[1] + *slyppe* slime; probably because the flower grows profusely in well-manured cow pastures.]

cox (koks) *n. Informal.* coxswain. —*v.t.* to act as coxswain to (a boat or crew). —*v.i.* to be coxswain.

cox·a (kok′sə) *n., pl.* **cox·ae** (kok′sē). **1.** the hip joint or hip. **2.** in insects and other arthropods, the segment of the leg that attaches to the body. [Latin *coxa* hip.] —**cox′al,** *adj.*

cox·comb (koks′kōm′) *n.* **1.** a vain and pretentious fellow; conceited dandy. **2.** cockscomb. [Earlier *cockscombe* jester's cap resembling a rooster's crest; hence, fool, fop. See COCK[1], COMB.]

cox·comb·ry (koks′kōm′rē) *n., pl.* **-ries.** the action, behavior, or manner characteristic of a coxcomb; foppery; vanity.

cox·swain (kok′sən, -swān′) *n. also,* **cockswain.** a person who steers a boat and has charge of the crew, esp. the crew member who steers and gives directions to oarsmen in a racing shell. [Earlier *cockswain,* from obsolete *cock* cockboat (from Old French *coque,* from Late Latin *caudica* canoe; literally, boat made from the trunk of a tree, from Latin *caudex* trunk of a tree) + SWAIN.]

coy (koi) *adj.* **1.** shy or modest; bashful. **2.** pretending to be shy or modest, esp. in a flirtatious manner. **3.** showing unwillingness to discuss one's plans, views, or the like, esp. when done as a ploy. [Old French *coi,* earlier *quei* calm, quiet, going back to Latin *quiētus.* Doublet of QUIET.] —**coy′ly,** *adv.* —**coy′ness,** *n.*

coy·o·te (kī ō′tē, kī′ōt) *n., pl.* **-tes** or **-te.** a wolflike mammal, *Canis latrans,* native to the prairies of central and western North America, known for its howling at night. Height: 21 inches (53 centimeters) at the shoulder. Also, **prairie wolf.** [Spanish *coyote,* from Nahuatl *coyotl.*]

coy·pu (koi′pü) *n., pl.* **-pus** or **-pu.** nutria *(def. 1).* [Spanish *coipú,* from Araucanian *kóypu.*]

coz·en (kuz′ən) *v.t.* to cheat; dupe; deceive. —*v.i.* to act dishonestly or deceitfully; cheat. [Possibly from obsolete Italian *cozzonare* to act like a horse trader, cheat, from *cozzone* horse trader, from Latin *coctiō* broker.] —**coz′en·er,** *n.*

coz·en·age (kuz′ə nij) *n.* the act or practice of cozening; fraud.

co·zy (kō′zē) *adj.,* **-zi·er, -zi·est.** *also,* **cosy. 1.** warm and comfortable; snug: *a cozy spot by the fire.* **2.** marked by friendliness and emotional warmth: *a restaurant with a cozy atmosphere.* **3.** marked by opportunism, corruption, or conniving: *a cozy relationship between the mayor and the company building city hall.* —*n., pl.* **-zies.** a padded cloth or knitted cover for keeping the contents of a teapot warm. [Possibly from Norwegian *koselig* snug.] —**co′zi·ly,** *adv.* —**co′zi·ness,** *n.*

• **to cozy up to.** to try to become well liked by, esp. in the hope of obtaining benefit.

cp 1. candle power. **2.** chemically pure.

cp., compare.

C.P. 1. Common Prayer. **2.** Communist Party.
CPA also, **C.P.A.** Certified Public Accountant.
cpd., compound.
Cpl., Corporal.
CPR, a sequence of emergency procedures aimed at restoring normal breathing and circulation of the blood when a person's heart has stopped beating. It includes mouth-to-mouth resuscitation and massage of the heart by applying rhythmic pressure on the breastbone. [Short for *c(ardio)p(ulmonary) r(esuscitation).*]
cps 1. characters per second. **2.** cycles per second.
CPU, central processing unit.
Cr, the symbol for chromium.
cr. 1. credit. **2.** creditor. **3.** crown.
crab[1] (krab) *n.* **1.** any of a widespread group of usually saltwater crustaceans, suborder Brachyura, having a broad, flat body with the abdomen tightly curled under the body, four pairs of legs, and a pair of pincer claws. Many kinds of crabs are highly valued as food. **2.** any of various similar arthropods, such as the horseshoe crab. **3.** crab louse. **4.** a machine or apparatus for hoisting or hauling heavy weights. **5.** a cross, ill-tempered person. —*v.,* **crabbed, crab·bing.** —*v.i.* **1.** to fish for

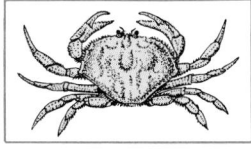
crab[1] *(def. 1)*

or catch crabs. **2.** *Informal.* to find fault; complain. —*v.t. Informal.* to spoil; ruin. [Old English *crabba* the crustacean.] —**crab′ber,** *n.* —**crab′like′,** *adj.*
  · **to catch a crab.** to make a faulty stroke in rowing either by dipping the oar into the water on the recovery or by missing the water on the stroke.
crab[2] (krab) *n.* crab apple. [Of uncertain origin.]
crab apple 1. the small, hard, sour apple of any of several trees, genus *Malus,* of the rose family, growing wild or cultivated. Some varieties are pickled or used for making jelly. **2.** the tree bearing this fruit, having oval leaves and small, fragrant pink, white, or red flowers.
crab·bed (krab′id) *adj.* **1.** characterized by or showing bad temper; cross; peevish; crabby. **2.** hard to understand; involved; perplexing. **3.** (of handwriting) hard to read or decipher; cramped. [CRAB[1] + -ED[2].] —**crab′bed·ly,** *adv.* —**crab′bed·ness,** *n.*
crab·by (krab′ē) *adj.,* **-bi·er, -bi·est.** ill-tempered; peevish; cross. —**crab′bi·ly,** *adv.* —**crab′bi·ness,** *n.*
crab grass, any of several hardy, creeping grasses, genus *Digitaria,* having fuzzy, sword-shaped leaves, and bearing spikes of purple flowers. Crab grass spreads rapidly and is a common lawn and agricultural weed.
crab louse, a louse, *Phthirus pubis,* that infests humans, esp. the coarse hairs of the pubic area and armpits. With its wide body and three pairs of stoutly clawed legs, it resembles a crab. Also, **crab.**
Crab Nebula *Astronomy.* an expanding cloud of gas in the constellation Taurus, identified as the remnant of a supernova observed in A.D. 1054. [Because the nebula is crab-shaped.]
crab tree, any of various species of trees that bear crab apples.
crack (krak) *n.* **1.** a break that does not cause separation into parts: *a crack in a mirror.* **2.** a sudden, sharp noise, as that made by something breaking: *the crack of a rifle.* **3.** *Informal.* a sharp, heavy, resounding blow: *I got a crack on the head going through the low doorway.* **4.** a narrow opening; fissure: *Open the window a crack.* **5.** *Informal.* an instant; moment: *to get up at the crack of dawn.* **6.** *Slang.* a try; attempt: *Let me have a crack at opening that jar.* **7.** *Slang.* a witty, often sarcastic comment. **8.** *Slang.* a highly addictive form of the drug cocaine. —*v.i.* **1.** to break without completely separating into parts; become split or fissured: *The mirror cracked when I dropped it on the floor.* **2.** to break with or make a sudden, sharp noise: *The branch cracked under my weight. The green log cracked loudly in the fire.* **3.** to become harsh, shrill, or dissonant; change suddenly in tone or register: *The radio announcer's voice cracked.* **4.** *Informal.* to break down; fail: *The soldier cracked under the pressure of combat.* —*v.t.* **1.** to cause to make a sudden, sharp noise; snap: *The wild animal trainer cracked the whip above the lion's head.* **2.** to cause to split or fissure; break partially: *The boiling water cracked the glass.* **3.** to break, as into pieces, with a sudden, sharp noise: *to crack a coconut with a hammer.* **4.** *Informal.* to hit or strike with a sharp blow: *The branch sprang back and cracked me on the knee.* **5.** *Informal.* to break into; force open: *to crack a safe.* **6.** *Informal.* to find the solution to; puzzle out: *The police finally cracked the case.* **7.** to cause (the voice) to become harsh, shrill, or dissonant. **8.** to undermine or destroy: *to crack a person's self-confidence.* **9.** to subject (petroleum) to the process of cracking. **10.** *Informal.* to open a little: *to crack a window.* —*adj. Informal.* excellent;

first-rate: *The hunter was a crack shot.* [Old English *cracian* to make a sharp noise in breaking, resound.]
  · **cracked up to be.** *Informal.* claimed or believed to be.
  · **to crack a book.** to open a book, esp. a textbook, to read or study.
  · **to crack a joke.** to tell a joke; make a witty remark.
  · **to crack a smile.** to begin to smile.
  · **to crack down on.** to become strict or stricter with or take severe measures against.
  · **to crack up.** *Informal.* **a.** to suffer a mental or physical breakdown. **b.** to crash or cause to crash: *to crack up a car.* **c.** to be or cause to become overwhelmed by laughter.
  · **to get cracking.** *Informal.* **a.** to start doing something, as a job. **b.** to begin working harder or more intently.
crack·brained (krak′brānd′) *adj.* extremely foolish; crazy: *a crackbrained scheme.*
crack·down (krak′doun′) *n.* a sudden, strict enforcement of laws or rules: *a crackdown on illegal gambling.*
cracked (krakt) *adj.* **1.** having a crack or cracks; broken without a separation of parts; fractured. **2.** broken into small pieces; crushed: *We put cracked ice in the drinks.* **3.** (of the voice) harsh, shrill, or dissonant; changing in tone. **4.** *Informal.* crazy; deranged.
crack·er (krak′ər) *n.* **1.** a thin, crisp biscuit. **2.** a person or thing that cracks. **3.** firecracker. **4.** a small paper roll used as a party favor, containing candy, a toy, or another surprise, that makes a popping sound when it is pulled sharply at both ends. **5.** *Informal.* an impoverished white person in parts of the southeastern United States, esp. rural areas of Georgia and Florida.
➡ usually considered offensive in def. 5.
crack·er·jack (krak′ər jak′) *Informal. n.* a person or thing of exceptional ability or quality. —*adj.* of exceptional ability or quality.
crack·ing (krak′ing) *n.* the use in a refinery of heat, pressure, or catalysis to decompose complex hydrocarbons, esp. petroleum, into simpler hydrocarbons with lower boiling points. In producing gasoline, the yield from fractional distillation of petroleum is increased by cracking.
crack·le (krak′əl) *v.,* **-led, -ling.** —*v.i.* **1.** to make a succession of slight, sharp sounds: *The dry leaves crackled when we walked on them.* **2.** to develop a network of very fine cracks on the surface. —*v.t.* **1.** to crush or break with slight, sharp sounds. **2.** to cause to develop a network of very fine cracks on the surface: *The extreme heat crackled the glaze on the pottery.* —*n.* **1.** a series or one of a series of slight, sharp sounds. **2.** a network of very fine cracks in the glazed surface of certain types of ceramics, glassware, and painted finishes. **3.** ceramics or glassware having such a surface. Also *(def. 3),* **crack′le·ware′.** [CRACK + -LE.]

crackle *(n., def. 2)*

crack·ling (krak′ling) *n.* **1.** a rapid succession of slight, sharp sounds. **2.** the crisp, browned skin of roasted pork. **3.** **cracklings.** *Informal.* crisp residues left after lard has been rendered from hog or poultry fat.
crack·ly (krak′lē) *adj.* tending to crackle or making a crackling sound.
crack·nel (krak′nəl) *n.* **1.** a small, hard, brittle biscuit. **2. cracknels. a.** small pieces of crisply fried fat pork. **b.** cracklings. [Modification of French *craquelin* a crisp biscuit, from Middle Dutch *krākelinc,* from *krāken* to crack.]
crack of doom 1. the signal announcing Judgment Day. **2.** the end of the world; Doomsday.
crack·pot (krak′pot′) *n. Informal.* an eccentric or deranged person. —*adj.* eccentric; crazy; foolish.
cracks·man (kraks′mən) *n., pl.* **-men** (-mən). *Slang.* a burglar or safecracker.
crack·up (krak′up′) *n.* **1.** a crash, as of a car or airplane. **2.** *Informal.* a mental or physical breakdown.

a	at	e	end	o	hot	u	up	hw	white		about
ā	ape	ē	me	ō	old	ū	use	ng	song		taken
ä	far	i	it	ô	fork	ü	rule	th	thin	ə	pencil
âr	care	ī	ice	oi	oil	u̇	pull	th	this		lemon
		îr	pierce	ou	out	ûr	turn	zh	measure		circus

crad·le (krā′dəl) *n.* **1.** a small bed for an infant, usually on rockers. **2.** a place or region where something starts or begins to develop: *a cradle of industry, the cradle of civilization.* **3.** a framework supporting something large, as a ship, while it is being constructed or repaired. **4.** a frame used to keep bedclothes from touching an injured part of the body. **5.** a low frame set on rollers or casters, used by mechanics while working under an automobile. **6.** the part of some kinds of telephone that is electrically connected to the wall outlet and holds the handset. **7. the cradle.** the time of infancy; babyhood: *from the cradle to the grave.* **8.** a box on rockers used to separate gold from gold-bearing earth. **9.a.** a frame with several long, curved prongs, attached to a scythe to collect stalks of grain as they are cut. **b.** a scythe equipped with such a frame. Also, **cradle scythe.** —*v.t.,* **-dled, -dling. 1.** to put, rock, or hold in or as in a cradle: *to cradle a child in one's arms.* **2.** to nurture, shelter, or train in infancy or the earliest stages of development. **3.** to support in or on a cradle, as a ship. **4.** to wash (earth containing gold) in a cradle. **5.** to cut (grain) using a cradle. [Old English *cradol* baby's bed.]
   · **to rob the cradle.** to take as one's spouse or sweetheart someone much younger than oneself.
cra·dle·song (krā′dəl sông′) *n.* lullaby.
craft (kraft) *n., pl.* **crafts** or *(def. 5)* **craft. 1.** special skill, dexterity, or ability: *The cabinetmaker worked with precision and craft.* **2.** skill in deceiving; deceit; guile; cunning. **3.** a trade or occupation requiring special skill, dexterity, or ability, esp. manual dexterity, acquired through training that may include apprenticeship. **4.** the members of a trade collectively. **5.** a boat, ship, or aircraft. **6.** boats, ships, or aircraft collectively. ➡ used as plural: *Small craft fill the harbor in the summer.* [Old English *craft* strength, skill, trade.]
crafts·man (krafts′mən) *n., pl.* **-men** (-mən). **1.** a person who has skill in a craft; artisan. **2.** an artist, esp. one who is technically proficient.
crafts·man·ship (krafts′mən ship′) *n.* the skill or work of a craftsman.
crafts·per·son (krafts′pûr′sən) *n.* a person who has skill in a craft; craftsman or craftswoman; artisan.
crafts·wom·an (krafts′wùm′ən) *n., pl.* **-wom·en** (-wim′ən). a woman who has skill in a craft; female artisan.
craft union, a labor union that limits membership to workers in a single craft or occupation or a few very closely related ones. ➡ distinguished from **industrial union.**
craft·y (kraf′tē) *adj.,* **craft·i·er, craft·i·est.** skillful or showing skill in deceiving; wily; cunning. —**craft′i·ly,** *adv.* —**craft′i·ness,** *n.* —For Synonyms, see **sly.**
crag (krag) *n.* a steep, rugged, or projecting rock or cliff. [Of Celtic origin.]
crag·gy (krag′ē) *adj.,* **-gi·er, -gi·est. 1.** having many crags; steep and rugged: *Northern Scotland is a craggy region.* **2.** rough and uneven: *a face with craggy features.* Also, **crag·ged** (krag′id). —**crag′gi·ness,** *n.*
crake (krāk) *n.* any of various birds of the rail family, esp. those having short bills and long legs. [Old Norse *krāka* crow²; of imitative origin.]
cram (kram) *v.,* **crammed, cram·ming.** —*v.t.* **1.** to fill (a space or receptacle) with more than it normally or conveniently holds: *We managed to cram the suitcase with all our clothes for the weekend.* **2.** to force or crowd (something) into a space or receptacle: *We crammed all our books into one box.* **3.** to fill to excess with food; stuff: *We crammed ourselves at dinner.* **4.** *Informal.* to prepare (a person) or study (a subject) for an examination or the like, hastily and intensely. —*v.i.* **1.** to eat greedily or to excess; stuff. **2.** to study hastily and intensely for an examination or similar purpose: *I crammed all day for the history exam.* [Old English *crammian* to stuff.]
cramp¹ (kramp) *n.* **1.** a painful contraction occurring suddenly in a muscle or group of muscles. **2.** a spasm or temporary paralysis of particular muscles as a result of having been used too much, as in writing. **3. cramps.** sharp abdominal pains. —*v.t.* to affect with or as with a cramp. —*v.i.* to suffer a cramp: *My leg cramped.* [Middle English *crampe,* from Middle French *crampe,* from Old French *crampe;* of Germanic origin.]
cramp² (kramp) *n.* **1.** a metal bar bent at the ends, for holding together pieces of stone, timber, or masonry. **2.** clamp. **3.** anything that confines or hinders. **4.** a confined or hindered condition or part. —*v.t.* **1.** to fasten or hold with a cramp. **2.** to put restrictions on; confine; hamper: *Lack of money cramped us.* [Middle Dutch *crampe* hook.]
   · **to cramp someone's style.** *Slang.* to hamper someone's normal efforts, skill, or confidence.
cram·pon (kram′pən) *n.* **1.** an iron bar bent in the form of a hook, used esp. in hinged pairs to lift heavy objects. **2. crampons.** spiked iron plates attached to the soles of shoes or boots to

prevent slipping while climbing mountains or walking on ice. [French *crampon* grappling iron, calk²; of Germanic origin.]
cran·ber·ry (kran′ber′ē, -bə rē) *n., pl.* **-ries. 1.** the red, sour-tasting berry of any of several low, creeping shrubs, genus *Vaccinium,* of the heath family, grown in bogs and widely used for sauce, juice, and other dishes. **2.** the shrub bearing this fruit. [Low German *kraanbere* literally, crane berry; because its stamens are shaped like beaks.]
crane (krān) *n.* **1.** any of various mobile machines having a long boom equipped with hoisting tackle for lifting and moving heavy loads. **2.** a metal arm pivoted on the wall of a fireplace and used to swing a kettle or a pot over the fire. **3.** any of a group of large wading birds, family Gruidae, having very long legs, a long neck, a short, wide tail, long, broad wings, and gray, brown, or white plumage. **4.** any of various similar birds, as the great blue heron. —*v.t.* **1.** to stretch out (the neck) in order to see something better. **2.** to hoist, lower, or move by or as if by a crane. —*v.i.* to stretch out the neck: *The people in the back row had to crane to see the stage.* [Old English *cran* the bird; with reference to the resemblance of the machine's boom to the long neck of the bird.]
crane fly, any of a group of harmless, slender, long-legged flies, family Tipulidae, resembling giant mosquitos. [Because its long legs resemble those of a crane.]
cranes·bill (krānz′bil′) *also,* **crane's-bill.** *n.* any geranium, esp. the common wild American geranium.
cra·ni·al (krā′nē əl) *adj.* of, from, or relating to the cranium or skull: *a cranial suture.* —**cra′ni·al·ly,** *adv.*
cranial nerve, any of the paired nerves arising from the brainstem of vertebrates. In mammals, there are twelve such paired nerves, including the olfactory, optic, facial, and acoustic nerves.
cra·ni·ol·o·gy (krā′nē ol′ə jē) *n.* the science dealing with the variations in size, shape, and other characteristics of skulls, esp. human skulls. [Greek *krānion* skull + -LOGY.]
cra·ni·om·e·try (krā′nē om′i trē) *n.* the science of measuring skulls; measurement of skulls and the relations between their parts. [Greek *krānion* skull + -METRY.]
cra·ni·um (krā′nē əm) *n., pl.* **-ni·ums** or **-ni·a** (-nē ə). **1.** the skull of a vertebrate. **2.** the part of the skull that encloses the brain. For illustration, see **brain.** Also *(def. 2),* **brainpan.** [Medieval Latin *cranium* skull, from Greek *krānion.*]
crank (krangk) *n.* **1.** a device that transmits motion, esp. an arm attached at right angles to a shaft for transmitting rotary motion. **2.** *Informal.* a person given to peculiar ideas or behavior; eccentric. **3.** *Informal.* a grouchy, ill-tempered person. **4.** an eccentric notion or action; caprice; whim. **5.** a fanciful turn of speech. —*v.t.* **1.** to start or operate with a crank (often with *up*): *It was necessary to crank the engine of the antique car.* **2.** to bend into the shape of a crank. —*v.i.* to turn a crank, as in starting an engine. —*adj.* characteristic of the behavior of a crank; eccentric: *a crank telephone call.* [Old English *cranc-,* as in *crancstæf* weaver's instrument.]

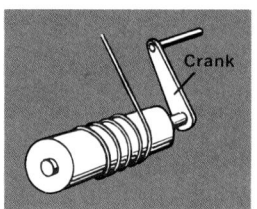

Crank

crank·case (krangk′kās′) *n.* a metal case enclosing the crankshaft of an engine.
crank·pin (krangk′pin′) *n.* a pin or cylinder by which a connecting rod is attached to a crank.
crank·shaft (krangk′shaft′) *n.* a shaft driven by or driving a crank.
crank·y (krang′kē) *adj.,* **crank·i·er, crank·i·est. 1.** ill-tempered; irritable. **2.** peculiar; eccentric. —**crank′i·ly,** *adv.* —**crank′i·ness,** *n.*
cran·ny (kran′ē) *n., pl.* **-nies.** a small, narrow opening; crack; crevice; fissure. [Old French *cran* notch, from *crener* to notch; of Celtic origin.] —**cran′nied,** *adj.*
crap (krap) *n.* **1.** craps. **2.** a losing throw in a game of craps. —*v.i.* to make a losing throw in a game of craps: *to crap on the first throw.*
   · **to crap out. a.** in craps, to roll a 7 when trying to make a point. **b.** *Slang.* to run out of power or energy; come to a halt; fail.
crape (krāp) *n.* **1.** crepe *(def. 1).* **2.** *also,* **crepe.** a band of black crepe worn or hung as a sign of mourning.
crape myrtle, a deciduous shrub or small tree, *Lagerstroemia indica,* grown in warm regions for its showy white, pink, or purple flowers. [Because its flowers are crinkled like crepe.]
crap·pie (krap′ē) *n.* a North American sunfish of either of two species, the **black crappie,** *Pomoxis nigromaculatus,* found in clear, quiet lakes and ponds, or the **white crappie,** *P. annularis,* found in swiftly running waters. Both are valued as food fish. [French *crapet* a freshwater fish; of uncertain origin.]

craps (kraps) *n.* a gambling game played with two dice. On the first throw, a roll of 2, 3, or 12 loses; a 7 or 11 wins. If a 4, 5, 6, 8, 9 or 10 is rolled, the same number must be rolled again before a 7 is rolled in order to win the bet.

crap·shoot·er (krap′shü′tər) *n.* a person who plays craps.

crash[1] (krash) *n.* **1.** a sudden, loud noise, as of something shattering or breaking: *There was a crash when the ball went through the window.* **2.** a heavy fall or breaking with force, as of something solid: *the crash of a falling tree.* **3.a.** a sudden decline, collapse, or ruin, esp. of a commercial enterprise: *The crash of the great railroad empire was unexpected.* **b.** a sudden general financial or business crisis and decline of values: *the Wall Street crash of 1929.* **4.** a violent, destructive collision or fall, as of a car or airplane. **5.** a sudden failure or breakdown in a computer operation. —*v.i.* **1.** to make a sudden, loud noise: *Thunder crashed overhead.* **2.** to fall, strike, or break into pieces forcefully with a loud noise; smash: *The cup crashed to the floor.* **3.** to move, strike, or go with much violence and noise: *to crash through the bushes, to crash into a wall.* **4.** to suffer sudden decline, collapse, or ruin: *Their business crashed last year.* **5.** to land, fall, or be driven abnormally so as to be damaged or destroyed: *The plane crashed short of the runway.* **6.** (of a computer operation) to fail or stop suddenly. —*v.t.* **1.** to cause to break noisily and violently; smash; shatter: *to crash a glass on the floor.* **2.** to force or drive with violence and noise: *to crash one's foot through a door.* **3.** to cause to be damaged or destroyed, as an automobile or airplane. **4.** *Informal.* to enter, as a party or theater, either without paying admission or without an invitation. —*adj.* characterized by or carried out with extreme speed, intense effort, and assignment of all necessary resources: *a crash course in French, a crash program to build new housing.* [Middle English *crashen* to smash, be shattered, probably from Old French *crasir* to shatter, crush.] —**crash′er,** *n.*

crash[2] (krash) *n.* a cotton or linen cloth, made from uneven and irregular yarns, used for towels, tablecloths, curtains, and the like. [Short for Russian *krashenina* colored linen, from *krashenie* coloring.]

crash-dive (krash′dīv′) *v.i., v.t.,* **-dived, -div·ing.** to make or cause to make a crash dive.

crash dive, a sudden rapid dive made by a submarine, esp. to avoid attack by an enemy aircraft or surface vessel.

crash helmet, a padded helmet for protection against head injury, worn esp. by motorcyclists, automobile racers, and aviators.

crash-land (krash′land′) *v.t.* to land (an aircraft), esp. with damage to the craft, under conditions that make normal landing impossible. —*v.i.* to crash-land an aircraft. —**crash landing,** *n.*

crass (kras) *adj.* **1.** grossly dull or stupid; insensitive. **2.** *Archaic.* thick; coarse. [Latin *crassus* gross, thick, fat.] —**crass′ly,** *adv.* —**crass′ness,** *n.*

crate (krāt) *n.* **1.** a box, case, or framework, usually of wooden slats, for protecting things during shipping or storage: *an orange crate, a furniture crate.* **2.** *Slang.* a battered or decrepit automobile or airplane. —*v.t.,* **crat·ed, crat·ing.** to pack in a crate or crates. [Latin *crātis* wickerwork, hurdle.]

a **crater** in Arizona 600 feet (183 meters) deep and 1/2 mile (0.8 kilometer) wide

cra·ter (krā′tər) *n.* **1.** a bowl-shaped depression at the mouth of a volcano. For illustration, see **volcano.** **2.** any depression resembling this, as one caused by the explosion of a bomb on earth or by the impact of a meteorite on the earth or moon. **3.** a vessel or bowl used in ancient Greece for mixing wine and water. —*v.t.*

to form craters in: *Meteorites have cratered the moon's surface.* [Latin *crātēr* bowl, mouth of a volcano, from Greek *krātēr.*]

cra·vat (krə vat′) *n.* **1.** necktie. **2.** a scarf of silk or other fine material worn as a neckcloth. [French *cravate* necktie, from *Cravate* Croatian, going back to Serbo-Croatian *Hrvat;* with reference to the linen scarf worn around the neck by Croatians in the French army in the seventeenth century.]

crave (krāv) *v.,* **craved, crav·ing.** —*v.t.* **1.** to long or yearn for; eagerly desire: *The artist craved recognition.* **2.** to need greatly; require: *The wound craved medical attention.* **3.** to ask for earnestly; beg: *to crave forgiveness.* —*v.i.* to eagerly desire; long; yearn (with *for* or *after*): *to crave after the unknown.* [Old English *crafian* to demand.]

cra·ven (krā′vən) *adj.* characterized by or showing extreme cowardice; extremely cowardly. —*n.* coward. [Middle English *cravant* vanquished, from Old French *cravant,* present participle of *craver, crever* to burst, break, from Latin *crepāre* to burst.] —**cra′ven·ly,** *adv.* —**cra′ven·ness,** *n.*

crav·ing (krā′ving) *n.* an intense or eager desire; longing; yearning.

craw (krô) *n.* **1.** the crop of a bird or insect. **2.** the stomach of any animal. [Probably from an unrecorded Old English word.]
   •**to stick in (one's) craw.** to upset or annoy: *The unfair treatment really stuck in my craw.*

craw·dad (krô′dad′) *n. Informal.* crayfish. Also, **crawdaddy.** [Modification of CRAWFISH.]

craw·dad·dy (krô′dad′ē) *n., pl.* **-dies.** *Informal.* crayfish.

craw·fish (krô′fish′) *n., pl.* **-fish** or **-fish·es.** crayfish. —*v.i. Informal.* to retreat from a position, opinion, or plan; back out; back down. [Form of CRAYFISH.]

crawl[1] (krôl) *v.i.* **1.** to move slowly by dragging the body along the ground. **2.** to move slowly on hands and knees: *The baby crawled across the room.* **3.** to move slowly: *Traffic crawled through the city.* **4.** to move or behave in a sneaky or servile manner. **5.** to swarm or be alive with or as with crawling things: *The picnic table was crawling with ants. The resort crawled with tourists.* **6.** to feel as if covered with crawling things: *The ghost story made my skin crawl.* —*n.* **1.** the act of crawling; slow crawling motion: *Traffic slowed to a crawl.* **2.** any of several swimming strokes combining an overarm motion with a flutter kick. The **American crawl** consists of six flutter kicks to each overarm cycle. The **Australian crawl** consists of eight flutter kicks to each overarm cycle. [Old Norse *krafla* to paw, creep.] —**crawl′er,** *n.*

crawl[2] (krôl) *n.* an enclosure of stakes set upright in shallow water, used esp. to confine turtles, fish, or shellfish. [Afrikaans *kraal* enclosure, village, from Portuguese *curral* cattle pen, enclosure. See KRAAL.]

crawler tractor, a tractor with two continuous tracks or belts rather than wheels.

crawl space, a narrow or shallow space under a roof or floor, usually one that gives access to wiring or plumbing.

crawl·y (krô′lē) *adj.,* **crawl·i·er, crawl·i·est.** *Informal.* having or causing the sensation of things crawling over one's skin; creepy.

cray·fish (krā′fish′) *n., pl.* **-fish** or **-fish·es.** any of several lobsterlike crustaceans found in fresh water in most parts of the world, valued as a food source, esp. in Europe and the southeastern United States. Also, **crawfish, crawdad, crawdaddy.** [Earlier *crevis,* from Old French *crevice,* from Old High German *krebiz;* influenced by FISH.]

cray·on (krā′on, -ən) *n.* **1.a.** a stick of a colored waxlike substance used for drawing, coloring, or writing. **b.** a stick of chalk, charcoal, or clay, sometimes mixed with pigment, used as an artist's drawing implement. **2.** a drawing made with a crayon or crayons. —*v.t., v.i.* to draw, color, or mark with a crayon or crayons. [French *crayon* pencil, drawing made with a crayon, from *craie* chalk, from Latin *crēta.*] —**cray′on·ist,** *n.*

craze (krāz) *n.* **1.a.** a sudden and temporary feeling of great enthusiasm for something; mania. **b.** something suddenly and temporarily very popular; fad; rage. **2.** a minute crack in the glazed surface of ceramics or glassware. —*v.,* **crazed, craz·ing.** —*v.t.* **1.** to make insane; derange. **2.** to make or cause minute

a	at	e	end	o	hot	u	up	hw	white		about
ā	ape	ē	me	ō	old	ū	use	ng	song		taken
ä	far	i	it	ô	fork	ü	rule	th	thin	ə	pencil
âr	care	ī	ice	oi	oil	ů	pull	th	this		lemon
		îr	pierce	ou	out	ûr	turn	zh	measure		circus

cracks in the glazed surface of (ceramics or glassware). —*v.i.* **1.** to become insane. **2.** to become minutely cracked, as the glaze on the surface of pottery. [Of Scandinavian origin.]

cra·zy (krā′zē) *adj.,* **-zi·er, -zi·est. 1.** of unsound or deranged mind; insane; demented. **2.** caused by, marked by, or showing mental derangement. **3.** not practical or sensible; foolish: *What a crazy idea!* **4.** *Informal.* extremely enthusiastic or excited: *The kids were crazy about cars.* **5.** not usual or ordinary: *The hut stood at a crazy angle.* —**cra′zi·ly,** *adv.* —**cra′zi·ness,** *n.*

crazy bone, funny bone.

crazy quilt, a quilt made of pieces of cloth of various materials, shapes, colors, and sizes that are sewed together without any regular pattern.

creak (krēk) *v.i.* **1.** to make a sharp, grating, or squeaking sound: *My new shoes creak when I walk.* **2.** to move with such a sound: *The gate creaked open.* —*v.t.* to cause to creak. —*n.* a sharp, grating, or squeaking sound. [Imitative.]

creak·y (krē′kē) *adj.,* **creak·i·er, creak·i·est.** creaking or likely to creak. —**creak′i·ly,** *adv.* —**creak′i·ness,** *n.*

cream (krēm) *n.* **1.** the fatty, yellowish part of milk, which contains butterfat and rises to the top of milk that is not homogenized. **2.** a food made from, containing, or resembling this substance: *chocolate creams, cream of tomato soup.* **3.** a soft preparation put on the skin to cleanse or protect: *shaving cream.* **4.** the choicest part of anything: *the cream of the crop, the cream of society.* **5.** the yellowish white color of cream. —*v.t.* **1.** to remove the cream from; skim: *to cream milk.* **2.** to cook with cream, milk, or a cream sauce: *to cream onions.* **3.** to blend into a creamy consistency: *to cream butter and sugar.* **4.** to allow or cause (milk) to form cream. **5.** to add cream to: *to cream coffee.* **6.** to use cream on: *to cream one's face.* **7.** to take the best or choicest part from. **8.** *Slang.* to defeat soundly; beat decisively. —*v.i.* to form cream or a creamy substance on the top; foam; froth. —*adj.* **1.** containing or made of cream or milk. **2.** having the color cream. [Old French *cresme* holy oil, fatty part of milk, from blend of Late Latin *crāmum* fatty part of milk (of Celtic origin) and Latin *chrīsma* holy oil (from Greek *chrīsma* unguent).]

cream cheese, a soft, smooth, unripened cheese made from a mixture of milk and cream.

cream·er (krē′mər) *n.* **1.** a small pitcher used for serving cream. **2.** a powder or liquid used as a substitute for cream or milk in coffee or tea, but containing no dairy products.

cream·er·y (krē′mə rē) *n., pl.* **-er·ies. 1.** a place where butter, cheese, and other dairy products are made. **2.** a place where milk, cream, and dairy products are sold.

cream of tartar, a white crystalline, powdery salt, used esp. in baking powder, and also in medicine and the tinning of metals. Formula: $C_4H_5KO_6$ Also, **potassium bitartrate.**

cream·puff (krēm′puf′) *n.* a very light pastry shell filled with custard or whipped cream.

cream sauce, a sauce made of cream or milk cooked with flour and butter.

cream·y (krē′mē) *adj.,* **cream·i·er, cream·i·est. 1.** containing cream. **2.** resembling cream in appearance, color, or consistency: *creamy skin.* —**cream′i·ly,** *adv.* —**cream′i·ness,** *n.*

crease[1] (krēs) *n.* **1.** a line or mark produced by folding, wrinkling, or pressing cloth, paper, or the like: *a crease in a pair of trousers.* **2.** any similar line or mark: *a face with many creases.* —*v.,* **creased, creas·ing.** —*v.t.* **1.** to make a crease or creases on or in. **2.** to graze, as if to leave a crease mark: *The bullet creased her arm.* —*v.i.* to become creased: *This fabric creases easily.* [Earlier *creast* ridge, form of CREST.] —**creas′er,** *n.*

crease[2] (krēs) kris.

cre·ate (krē āt′) *v.t.,* **-at·ed, -at·ing. 1.** to bring into being; cause to exist: *to create a new government.* **2.** to give rise to; bring about; occasion: *Their rudeness created much ill will.* **3.** to produce by one's own thought or imagination: *That author has created many famous characters.* **4.** to invest with new office, rank, or function: *The crown created many new peers.* **5.** (of an actor) to be the first to portray (a character or role). [Latin *creātus,* past participle of *creāre* to make, produce.]

cre·a·tine (krē′ə tēn′, -tin) *n.* an amino acid found primarily in muscle tissues which combines with phosphorus to furnish the energy that is needed for voluntary muscle contractions. Formula: $C_4H_9N_3O_2$ [Greek *kreatis,* genitive of *kreas* flesh + -INE[2].]

cre·a·tion (krē ā′shən) *n.* **1.** the act of creating or the state or time of being created. **2.** something that is created, esp. something that is a product of human intelligence, imagination, or power. **3.** the world and everything in it; universe. **4. the Creation.** in the Bible, God's act of creating the universe.

cre·a·tion·ism (krē ā′shə niz′əm) *n.* **1.** the belief that the universe, and everything in it, was created by God in its present form and did not slowly evolve or develop. **2.** the doctrine that the universe was created by God in the exact way described in Genesis. —**cre·a′tion·ist,** *n., adj.*

cre·a·tive (krē ā′tiv) *adj.* **1.** having the power or quality of creating: *a creative mind.* **2.** marked by or showing originality of thought, presentation, or performance: *a creative solution to a problem.* —**cre·a′tive·ly,** *adv.* —**cre·a′tive·ness,** *n.*

cre·a·tiv·i·ty (krē′ā tiv′i tē) *n.* the quality of being creative; artistic or intellectual ability to create: *The painting showed the artist's creativity.*

cre·a·tor (krē ā′tər) *n.* **1.** a person or thing that creates: *This writer is the creator of a famous detective.* **2. the Creator.** God.

cre·a·ture (krē′chər) *n.* **1.** a living being, esp. an animal as distinct from a human: *the small creatures of the forest.* **2.** a human being. **3.** a person who is completely dependent upon or under the influence of someone or something; puppet; tool: *to be a creature of habit.* **4.** anything created; creation. [Old French *creature* animal, person, from Late Latin *creātūra* thing created, creation, from Latin *creāre* to make, produce.]

creature comforts, physical comforts, esp. food, clothing, and shelter.

crèche (kresh, krāsh) *n.* **1.** a representation of the Nativity scene, usually including figures of the infant Jesus, Mary, Joseph, the shepherds, the Three Wise Men, and the animals at the manger, often displayed at Christmas. **2.** *British.* a day nursery. [French *crèche* manger, crib, day nursery; of Germanic origin.]

cre·dence (krēd′əns) *n.* belief, esp. in the reports or statements of others: *I don't give credence to rumors.* [Old French *credence,* from Medieval Latin *credentia,* from Latin *crēdere* to believe.]

cre·den·tial (kri den′shəl) *n.* **1.** anything that entitles a person to status, confidence, authority, or credit. **2.** a document or documents establishing the identity, authority, or the right to confidence or accreditation of the bearer.

cre·den·za (kri den′zə) *n.* a buffet or sideboard, esp. one without legs. [Italian *credenza* literally, belief, trust, from Medieval Latin *credentia,* from Latin *crēdere* to believe; because in earlier times a nobleman's food was placed on such a sideboard to be tested for poison before the meal.]

credibility gap 1. a lack of trust, esp. by the public, in the claims or statements made by a person or group, as a government, corporation, or public official. **2.** a discrepancy between actual fact and what a person or group wants others to believe or what is reported to have happened: *There was a credibility gap between the government's declared foreign policy and its implementation.*

cred·i·ble (kred′ə bəl) *adj.* capable of being believed; believable; reliable: *a credible witness, a credible account.* [Latin *crēdibilis,* from *crēdere* to believe.] —**cred′i·bil′i·ty, cred′i·ble·ness,** *n.* —**cred′i·bly,** *adv.*

cred·it (kred′it) *n.* **1.** belief in or reliance on the truth of something; faith; trust: *We gave credit to their story.* **2.a.** a favorable estimation of one's character; good reputation; esteem: *Civic service brings credit to a citizen.* **b.** influence or authority derived from this. **3.** honor or commendation due for some action or quality; praise: *You deserve credit for the success of the party.* **4.** a person or thing that brings honor, approval, or praise: *to be a credit to one's school.* **5. credits.** acknowledgments for work done or assistance given, as in a motion picture: *The costume designer's name appeared in the credits.* **6.a.** trust or confidence in a person's or firm's ability and intention to meet financial obligations when due: *The store extended me credit.* **b.** the time allowed for payment of a debt: *thirty days' credit.* **7.** reputation in financial matters: *Your credit is no longer good at the store because you don't pay your bills.* **8.** an amount of money against which a person or firm may draw, as from a bank. **9.** *Bookkeeping.* **a.** the entry of an amount in an account in payment of an existing or future debt: *Carry that payment as a credit against next month's billing.* **b.** the right-hand side of an account where such entries are made. **c.** the sum of the entries, or any one entry, on this side of the account. **10.** a balance in one's favor, as in a bank account. **11.a.** an official entry on a student's record certifying satisfactory completion of a course of study: *to receive credit for a course.* **b.** a unit of such study: *to take three credits of math.* **12.** the state or quality of being worthy of belief or trust. —*v.t.* **1.** to give financial credit to: *The bank credited the deposit to my account.* **2.** to believe in the truth or validity of; trust: *Do you expect me to credit that absurd story?* **3.** *Bookkeeping.* to enter on the credit side of an account. **4.** to give educational credits to (a student). [French *crédit* trust, reputation, from Latin *crēditum* thing entrusted, loan, from *crēdere* to believe.]

·on credit. with the understanding that one will pay at a future time.

·to credit (something) to. to think of as being caused by; attribute to: *They credit the defeat to poor planning by the general.*

·to credit with. to consider or believe (someone or something) to be responsible for: *History credits the Chinese with inventing gunpowder.*

·to do credit to. to bring honor, approval, or praise to.

·to give credit to. to accept or believe as true; have faith in; trust.

·to give someone credit for. a. to believe that one has: *I'll give him credit for sincerity.* **b.** to praise someone for: *We gave her credit for her contribution to the project's success.*

cred·it·a·ble (kred′i tə bəl) *adj.* bringing honor or approval; praiseworthy: *a creditable performance.* —**cred′it·a·bil′i·ty, cred′it·a·ble·ness,** *n.* —**cred′it·a·bly,** *adv.*

credit bureau, an agency that acts as a clearinghouse for credit information on individuals and businesses.

credit card, a card entitling its holder to make purchases or obtain services on credit from commercial establishments recognizing the validity of the card.

credit line 1. a printed acknowledgment of the original source of a newspaper article, motion picture, photograph, or the like. **2.** line of credit.

cred·i·tor (kred′i tər) *n.* a person or firm that gives credit; one to whom payment of a debt is owed.

credit union, a cooperative association able to make loans to its members at low interest rates by common pooling of the members' savings.

cred·it·wor·thy (kred′it wûr′thē) *adj.* qualified to receive financial credit: *The bank considered the small company creditworthy because it had repaid all its previous loans.*

cre·do (krē′dō, krā′-) *n., pl.* **-dos. 1.** creed. **2.** Credo. Apostles' Creed or Nicene Creed. **3.** a musical setting for either of these Creeds. **4.** the portion of the Mass in which the Nicene Creed is said or sung. [Latin *crēdō* I believe; first word in the Latin texts of the Apostles' Creed and the Nicene Creed.]

cre·du·li·ty (kri dū′li tē, -dū′-) *n.* a readiness to believe, trust, or accept on weak or insufficient evidence; gullibility.

cred·u·lous (krej′ə ləs) *adj.* **1.** tending to believe readily; gullible. **2.** characterized by or arising from credulity: *credulous superstitions.* [Latin *crēdulus* easy of belief, from *crēdere* to believe.] —**cred′u·lous·ly,** *adv.* —**cred′u·lous·ness,** *n.*

Cree (krē) *n., pl.* **Cree** or **Crees. 1.** a member of a tribe of North American Indians, formerly living in eastern and central Canada, now living mainly in Manitoba. **2.** the Algonquian language of this tribe.

creed (krēd) *n.* **1.** a formal and authoritative statement of religious belief; confession of faith. **2.** any formal statement of belief, principles, or opinions: *a political creed.* **3.** Creed. Apostles' Creed or Nicene Creed. [Old English *crēda* belief, from Latin *crēdō* I believe. See CREDO.] —**creed′al,** *adj.*

creek (krēk, krik) *n.* **1.** a small stream, usually larger than a brook and smaller than a river. **2.** a narrow inlet, going farther inland than a cove. [Old Norse *kriki* bay, nook.]

·up the creek. *Informal.* in a difficult situation.

Creek (krēk) *n., pl.* **Creek** or **Creeks. 1.** a member of a confederation of North American Indian tribes, formerly living in Alabama, Georgia, and northern Florida, now living in Oklahoma. **2.** the Muskogean language of these tribes.

creel (krēl) *n.* **1.** an angler's basket for holding fish. **2.** a basketlike wickerwork trap for catching fish, crabs, lobsters, or the like. [Possibly from French *creil* wickerwork, going back to Latin *crātis.*]

creep (krēp) *v.i.,* **crept, creep·ing. 1.** to move with the body prone or close to the ground, esp. on hands and knees; crawl: *The child crept across the room.* **2.** to move slowly, imperceptibly, timidly, or stealthily: *The thief crept into the room through the open window. Traffic was creeping over the bridge.* **3.** to move or behave in a humble or servile manner: *The rejected applicant crept from the room.* **4.** to have a sensation as of things crawling over the skin; shiver in fear or repugnance: *The howling of the wolves made my flesh creep.* **5.** (of a plant) to grow along a surface by sending out small tendrils or roots along the length of the stem. **6.** to slip gradually out of position. —*n.* **1.** the act of creeping; slow movement. **2.** a slow but continuous deformation of metal, concrete, or other materials under prolonged stress or steady load. **3.** *Slang.* a repugnant or contemptible person. **4. the creeps.** *Informal.* a sensation as of things crawling over one's skin; aversion; uneasiness. [Old English *crēopan* to crawl.]

creep·age (krē′pij) *n.* a gradual movement.

creep·er (krē′pər) *n.* **1.** a person or thing that creeps. **2.** any plant that grows along a surface by sending out small tendrils or roots along the length of the stem; climber. **3.** any small, brown bird, family Certhiidae, of wooded regions of the Northern Hemisphere, that climbs tree trunks to find the insects on which it feeds. **4. creepers. a.** a one-piece garment, combining shirt and pants, worn by infants. **b.** a set of spiked attachments worn on the legs or shoes to prevent slipping, as in climbing a pole.

creep·y (krē′pē) *adj.,* **creep·i·er, creep·i·est. 1.** having or causing a sensation of aversion or uneasiness, as of things crawling over one's skin. **2.** moving slowly; creeping. —**creep′i·ly,** *adv.* —**creep′i·ness,** *n.*

creese (krēs) kris.

cre·mate (krē′māt, kri māt′) *v.t.,* **-mat·ed, -mat·ing. 1.** to reduce (a dead body) to ashes by burning, esp. as a funeral rite. **2.** to consume by fire; burn up. [Latin *cremātus,* past participle of *cremāre* to burn.] —**cre·ma′tion,** *n.*

cre·ma·tor (krē′mā tər, kri mā′-) *n.* **1.** a person who cremates. **2.** a crematory furnace. [Late Latin *cremātor* burner, from Latin *cremāre* to burn.]

cre·ma·to·ri·um (krē′mə tôr′ē əm, krem′ə-) *n., pl.* **-to·ri·ums** or **-to·ri·a** (-tôr′ē ə). crematory.

cre·ma·to·ry (krē′mə tôr′ē, krem′ə-) *n., pl.* **-ries.** a furnace or establishment for cremating. —*adj.* of or relating to cremation.

crème (krem, krēm; *French* krɛm) *n. French.* **1.** cream. **2.** a thick, sweet liqueur.

crème de ca·ca·o (krem′ də kä kä′ō, krēm′də kō′kō) a sweet brown or white liqueur flavored with cacao and vanilla. [French *crème de cacao* literally, cream of cacao.]

crème de menthe (krem′ də menth′, mint′, krēm′) a sweet green or white liqueur flavored with mint. [French *crème de menthe* literally, cream of mint.]

cre·nate (krē′nāt) *adj.* having a notched or scalloped margin or edge, as a leaf; crenulate. Also, **cre′nat·ed.** [Modern Latin *crenatus,* from Late Latin *crēna* notch; of uncertain origin.]

cre·na·tion (kri nā′shən) *n.* **1.** a crenate formation. **2.** the state of being crenate.

cren·el (kren′əl) *also,* **cre·nelle** (krə nel′). *n.* an indentation in a battlement through which defenders may fire on attackers; embrasure. [Old French *crenel* battlement. See CRENELATE.]

cren·el·ate (kren′ə lāt) *also, British,* **cren·el·late.** *v.t.,* **-at·ed, -at·ing.** to furnish with crenels. [French *créneler* to embattle[2], notch, from Old French *crenel* battlement, going back to Late Latin *crēna* notch; of uncertain origin.] —**cren′el·a′tion;** *also, British,* **cren′el·la′tion,** *n.*

cren·u·late (kren′yə lāt′, -lit) *adj.* having tiny, rounded scallops or notches, as certain leaves or seashells. Also, **cren′u·lat′ed.** [Modern Latin *crenulatus,* from *crenula,* diminutive of Vulgar Latin *crena* notch, groove + -ATE[1].]

cre·o·dont (krē′ə dont′) *n.* any of an order, Creodonta, of extinct, primitive, carnivorous mammals whose evolutionary development ended in early Tertiary geologic time, including a variety of weasellike, hyenalike, and bearlike animals. [Modern Latin *Creodonta* (plural), from Greek *kreas* flesh + *odous* tooth.]

Cre·ole (krē′ōl) *n.* **1.a.** a direct descendant of the original French and Spanish settlers of the Gulf Coast, esp. Louisiana. **b.** a person of European descent, esp. Spanish or French, born in the West Indies or Latin America. **2.a.** the dialect of French spoken by Creoles in Louisiana. **b.** Haitian Creole. **c.** the dialect of French spoken in Martinique. **3. creole.** a person who has both Negro and Creole ancestors. —*adj.* **1.** of, relating to, or characteristic of Creoles. **2. creole.** (of food) prepared with sweet peppers and onions and highly seasoned, usually served with rice. [French *créole* white person of European origin born in the West Indies, from Spanish *criollo* one born in America or the West Indies, from Portuguese *crioulo* one born in the colonies; literally, one brought up, from *criar* to bring up, nourish, from Latin *creāre* to make, produce.]

Cre·on (krē′on) *n.* in Greek legend, a king of Thebes, the successor to Oedipus and uncle of Antigone.

cre·o·sol (krē′ə sôl′) *n.* a colorless, oily, aromatic liquid used as an antiseptic. Formula: $C_8H_{10}O_2$ [CREOS(OTE) + -OL.]

cre·o·sote (krē′ə sōt′) *n.* **1.** a colorless or yellowish oily liquid obtained by distilling wood tar and used in medicines and antiseptics. **2.** a similar liquid obtained from coal tar and used as a wood preservative. —*v.t.,* **-sot·ed, -sot·ing.** to treat with creosote.

a	at	e	end	o	hot	u	up	hw	white		about
ā	ape	ē	me	ō	old	ū	use	ng	song	ə	taken
ä	far	i	it	ô	fork	ū	rule	th	thin		pencil
âr	care	ī	ice	oi	oil	ů	pull	th	this		lemon
		îr	pierce	ou	out	ûr	turn	zh	measure		circus

287

[German *Kreosot* the liquid distilled from wood tar, from Greek *kreas* flesh + *sōtēr* savior, preserver; because it preserves flesh owing to its antiseptic qualities.]

creosote bush, an evergreen shrub, *Larrea tridentata,* found in hot, dry regions in the southwestern United States and Mexico, whose small, olive-green leaves have a strong, tarlike odor.

crepe (krāp; *def. 5, also* krep) *n.* **1.** *also,* **crape, crêpe.** any of various fabrics, made of silk, cotton, rayon, or wool, characterized by a crinkled surface. **2.** crape *(def. 2).* **3.** crepe paper. **4.** crepe rubber. **5.** *also,* **crêpe.** a thin, light pancake, usually spread or rolled up with a filling and served as an hors d'oeuvre or dessert. [French *crêpe* the fabric, pancake, from Old French *crespe* curly, from Latin *crispus* curled, crinkled.]

crepe de Chine (krāp′ də shēn′) a soft, medium-weight, silk crepe. [French *crêpe de Chine* literally, crepe of China.]

crepe paper, a thin paper with a crinkled surface like that of crepe.

crepe rubber, a crude or synthetic rubber with a crinkled texture, used esp. for the soles of shoes.

crêpe su·zette (krāp′ sü zet′, krep′) *pl.* **crêpes su·zette** (krāps′sü zet′, kreps′) or **crêpe su·zettes** (krāp′sü zets′, krep′). a very thin dessert pancake rolled and heated in a sweet sauce flavored with orange or lemon juice and a liqueur, often served in flaming cognac. [French *crêpe* pancake + *Suzette* female proper name. See CREPE.]

crep·i·tate (krep′i tāt′) *v.i.,* **-tat·ed, -tat·ing.** to make repeated crackling sounds; crackle; rattle. [Latin *crepitātus,* past participle of *crepitāre* to crackle, rattle.] —**crep′i·tant,** *adj.* —**crep′i·ta′tion,** *n.*

crept (krept) the past tense and past participle of **creep.**

cre·pus·cu·lar (kri pus′kyə lər) *adj.* **1.** of, relating to, or resembling twilight; dim; obscure. **2.** (of animals) appearing, active, or flying at twilight. [Latin *crepusculum* twilight + -AR.]

cresc., crescendo.

cre·scen·do (kri shen′dō) *adj., adv.* with a gradual increase in loudness or force. —*n., pl.* **-dos. 1.** a gradual increase in loudness or force. **2.** *Music.* a crescendo passage. [Italian *crescendo,* present participle of *crescere* to increase, grow, from Latin *crescere.*]

cres·cent (kres′ənt) *n.* **1.** the shape of the visible part of the moon in its first or last quarter, having one convex edge and one concave edge. For illustration, see **moon. 2.** anything having this shape: *We rolled the cookies into crescents.* **3.a.** an emblem appearing on the flags of Turkey and of various Muslim countries. **b. the Crescent.** Turkish or Muslim power or the Muslim religion. —*adj.* **1.** shaped like the moon in its first or last quarter. **2.** increasing; growing. [Old French *creissant* crescent of the moon, originally present participle of *creistre* to grow, from Latin *crescere.*]

cre·sol (krē′sôl) *n.* any of three isomeric liquid or crystalline organic compounds derived principally from coal tar, used esp. as an antiseptic. Formula: C_7H_8O [Form of CREOSOL.]

cress (kres) *n.* **1.** the pungent leaves of any of several plants of the mustard family, esp. watercress, used as a garnish or in salads. **2.** any of these plants. [Old English *cresse, cærse* watercress.]

cres·set (kres′it) *n.* a metal container mounted on a pole or suspended from above, containing burning pitch-covered rope, oil, grease, wood, or other fuel for illumination. [Old French *cresset, craisset,* from *craisse* oil, grease (with which a cresset was filled), going back to Latin *crassus* thick, fat.]

Cres·si·da (kres′i də) *n.* in medieval legend, a Trojan woman who is unfaithful to her lover, Troilus.

crest (krest) *n.* **1.** a comb, tuft, ridge, or other natural growth on the head, neck, or back of a bird or other animal. **2.** a plume or similar ornament on the top of a helmet. **3.** a heraldic device placed above the escutcheon in a coat of arms. It is sometimes used separately and put on such personal articles as china or writing paper. **4.** the highest point or stage; summit; apex: *the crest of a hill, the crest of a wave, the crest of a politician's popularity.* —*v.i.* to reach the highest point or stage: *The river crested late Sunday night. The waves crest far from the beach.* —*v.t.* to reach the crest of: *The marchers crested the hill.* [Old French *creste* tuft, from Latin *crista.*]

crest·ed (kres′tid) *adj.* having a crest.

crest·fall·en (krest′fô′lən) *adj.* feeling hurt, humiliated, or without hope; dejected; disheartened.

Cre·ta·ceous (kri tā′shəs) *n.* the last geologic period of the Mesozoic era, during which thick beds of chalk were deposited and the dinosaurs became extinct. For table, see **geologic time.** —*adj.* **1.** of, relating to, or characteristic of this period. **2. creta·ceous.** containing, abounding in, or resembling chalk; chalky. [Latin *crētāceus* chalky, from *crēta* chalk.]

cre·tin (krē′tən) *n.* a person afflicted with cretinism. [French *crétin,* from Swiss French *crestin* deformed idiot, human being,

Christian (with reference to the humanity even of a deformed person), from Latin *Chrīstiānus* Christian, from Greek *Chrīstiānos,* from *Chrīstos.* See CHRIST.] —**cre′tin·ous,** *adj.*

cre·tin·ism (krē′tə niz′əm) *n.* a condition present at birth or developing in infancy characterized by stunted physical and mental development, caused by a severe deficiency of thyroxin.

cre·tonne (krē′ton, kri ton′) *n.* a strong, medium-weight cotton fabric in bold print patterns, used for curtains, draperies, and slipcovers. [French *cretonne,* from *Creton,* Norman village where the fabric was first made.]

cre·vasse (kri vas′) *n.* **1.** a deep fissure or crevice, esp. in a glacier. **2.** a break in a levee, dike, or dam. [French *crevasse,* from Old French *crevace.* See CREVICE.]

crev·ice (krev′is) *n.* a narrow crack into or through something; fissure; chink. [Old French *crevace* fissure, ravine, from *crever* to split, from Latin *crepāre* to rattle, crack.]

crew¹ (krü) *n.* **1.a.** all those who operate a ship, aircraft, or spacecraft. **b.** all of these except the officers. **2.** a group of people assigned to or working together on a specific job: *a cleaning crew, a wrecking crew.* **3.** any group of people; crowd; company; gang. **4.a.** the sport of competitive rowing, esp. in eight-oared shells. **b.** the rowers and coxswain who operate a shell in this sport. [Old French *creue* increase, reinforcement, from *creistre* to grow, from Latin *crēscere.*]

crew² (krü) a past tense of **crow¹.**

crew cut, a style of haircut in which the hair is closely cropped.

crew·el (krü′əl) *n.* **1.** a loosely twisted worsted yarn, used for embroidery. **2.** crewelwork. [Of uncertain origin.]

crew·el·work (krü′əl wûrk′) *n.* embroidery done with crewel on linen, cotton, or other fabric, often with floral designs.

crewelwork

crew·man (krü′mən) *n., pl.* **-men** (-mən). a member of a crew, as of a ship or spacecraft.

crew neck, a round, closely fitting neckline without a collar, as on a sweater.

crib (krib) *n.* **1.** a baby's small bed with high sides, usually composed of slats. **2.** a manger or rack for fodder. **3.** a small building or bin for storing corn, grain, salt, or the like. **4.** a stall or pen for cattle. **5.** a small room or house; shack. **6.** a framework of wood or metal used to strengthen or support, as in a mine shaft. **7.** *Informal.* **a.** a petty theft. **b.** a taking as one's own of another's words or ideas; plagiarism. **8.** *Informal.* an unauthorized aid, as notes or a translation of a foreign text, used dishonestly by students in doing schoolwork or during examinations. —*v.,* **cribbed, crib·bing.** —*v.t.* **1.** to enclose in or as in a crib; confine. **2.** to provide with a crib or cribs. **3.** *Informal.* to plagiarize (another's words or ideas). **4.** *Informal.* to steal; pilfer: *The pickpocket cribbed the wallet.* —*v.i. Informal.* to use unauthorized notes or other aids; employ a crib: *to crib on an examination.* [Old English *cribb* manger, rack for fodder.] —**crib′ber,** *n.*

crib·bage (krib′ij) *n.* a card game, usually for two players, in which points are counted during the play of the hand and then for cards held. Score is kept on a small board by advancing pegs along the length of a series of holes.

crib death, sudden infant death syndrome.

crick (krik) *n.* a painful muscular spasm, esp. of the neck or back, limiting movement of the part affected. —*v.t.* to cause a spasm in (a muscle or part). [Of uncertain origin.]

crick·et¹ (krik′it) *n.* a hopping insect, family Gryllidae, related

to the grasshopper, having strong hind legs and long slender antennae. The male of the species makes a chirping noise by rubbing the bases or edges of its forewings together. [Old French *criquet,* from *criquer* to rattle, crackle; imitative.]

crick·et² (krik′it) *n.* **1.** a game played on a grass field with a ball, flattened bats, and two wickets by two teams of eleven players each, popular in Great Britain and other countries. **2.** *Informal.* fair play; good sportsmanship. —*v.i.* to play cricket. [Old French *criquet* wicket, stick, probably a diminutive of Middle Dutch *cricke* crutch, stick.] —**crick′et·er,** *n.*

crick·et³ (krik′it) *n.* a low wooden stool for the feet while sitting; footstool. [Of uncertain origin.]

cried (krīd) the past tense and past participle of **cry.**

cri·er (krī′ər) *n.* **1.** a person who cries. **2.** an official who makes public announcements. **3.** a person who shouts out announcements about wares for sale; hawker.

crime (krīm) *n.* **1.** an act forbidden by law, or the omission of a duty prescribed by law, for which the offender is liable to punishment by the state. **2.** any grave offense against morality; iniquity; sin. **3.** criminal activity; violation of law: *There is much crime in that neighborhood.* **4.** *Informal.* an unfortunate, regrettable, or shameful act; shame: *It's a crime to stay inside on such a beautiful day.* [Old French *crime* offense, fault, from Latin *crīmen* accusation, offense.]

crim·i·nal (krim′ə nəl) *n.* a person guilty or convicted of a crime. —*adj.* **1.** of the nature of or involving crime: *criminal negligence.* **2.** of or in accordance with criminal law: *a criminal court, criminal charges.* ➡ distinguished from **civil. 3.** engaged in crime: *the criminal element of society.* **4.** *Informal.* unfortunate, regrettable, or shameful. [Late Latin *crīminālis* relating to crime, from Latin *crīmen* accusation, offense.] —**crim′i·nal·ly,** *adv.*

crim·i·nal·i·ty (krim′ə nal′i tē) *n., pl.* **-ties. 1.** the state or quality of being criminal. **2.** a criminal act or practice.

crim·i·nal·ize (krim′ə nə līz′) *v.t.,* **-ized, -iz·ing.** to make criminal. —**crim′i·nal·i·za′tion,** *n.*

criminal law, a body of law defining crimes and establishing punishments for those who are guilty. ➡ distinguished from **civil law** *(def. 1).*

crim·i·nate (krim′ə nāt′) *v.t.,* **-nat·ed, -nat·ing. 1.** to show the guilt of; incriminate. **2.** to accuse of a crime. —**crim·i·na·to·ry** (krim′ə nə tôr′ē) *adj.*

crim·i·nol·o·gy (krim′ə nol′ə jē) *n.* the scientific study and investigation of crime and criminals. [Latin *crīmen* accusation, offense + -LOGY.] —**crim′i·no·log′i·cal** (krim′ə nə loj′i kəl) *adj.* —**crim′i·no·log′i·cal·ly,** *adv.* —**crim′i·nol′o·gist,** *n.*

crimp¹ (krimp) *v.t.* **1.** to press into small, regular ridges, folds, or pleats: *to crimp paper to make a fan.* **2.** to give waves or curls to (hair): *to crimp hair with a curling iron.* —*n.* **1.** something that has been or appears to have been crimped; ridge; fold. **2.** *usually,* **crimps,** waved or curled hair. [Middle Low German *krimpen* to wrinkle, shrink.] —**crimp′er,** *n.*

• **to put a crimp in.** *Informal.* to make difficult or complicated; hinder; obstruct.

crimp² (krimp) *n.* a person who procures men to serve as soldiers or sailors by decoying or entrapping them. —*v.t.* to decoy or entrap (men) to serve as soldiers or sailors. [Of uncertain origin.]

crim·ple (krim′pəl) *v.i., v.t.,* **-pled, -pling.** *Informal.* to wrinkle, crumple, or curl. [CRIMP¹ + -LE.]

crimp·y (krim′pē) *adj.,* **crimp·i·er, crimp·i·est.** having a crimped appearance; ridged; pleated; wavy. —**crimp′i·ness,** *n.*

crim·son (krim′zən, -sən) *n.* a deep red color. —*adj.* **1.** having the color crimson. **2.** bloody. —*v.t., v.i.* to make or become crimson. [Obsolete Spanish *cremesin* deep red color, from Arabic *qirmizī,* from *qirmiz* insect from which a red dye was obtained, going back to Sanskrit *krmi* insect, worm.]

cringe (krinj) *v.i.,* **cringed, cring·ing. 1.** to shrink, flinch, or crouch, as in fear, pain, horror, or servility. **2.** to behave in an obsequious, servile manner; fawn. —*n.* the act of cringing. [Old English *cringan* to fall in battle, yield.] —**cring′er,** *n.*

crin·gle (kring′gəl) *n.* one of a set of small loops or eyes of rope or metal along the edge of a sail. The sail can be fastened to the boom or yard by ropes running through the cringles. [Low German *kringel* ring, diminutive of *kring* ring, circle.]

crin·kle (kring′kəl) *v.,* **-kled, -kling.** —*v.i.* **1.** to form numerous wrinkles or ripples; wrinkle. **2.** to make a rustling or crackling sound; crackle. —*v.t.* **1.** to cause to form numerous wrinkles or ripples. **2.** to cause to rustle or crackle. —*n.* **1.** wrinkle; ripple. **2.** a rustling sound; crackle. [Old English *crincan* to yield, bend + -LE.] —**crin′kly,** *adj.*

cri·noid (krī′noid, krin′oid) *n.* any of a group of colorful, flowerlike echinoderms, having branched, radiating arms around a single mouth opening, found anchored to the sea bottom by a slender, segmented stalk, usually in deeper tropical waters. Also, **sea lily, feather star.** —*adj.* of or relating to crinoids. [Greek *krinoeidēs* like a lily, from *krinon* lily.]

crin·o·line (krin′ə lin) *n.* **1.** a stiff petticoat worn to give fullness to a skirt or dress. **2.** a stiff fabric, originally made with horsehair, used as a lining for skirts, millinery, or the like. **3.** hoop skirt. [French *crinoline* haircloth, stiff petticoat once made of haircloth, going back to Latin *crīnis* hair + *līnum* flax.]

crip·ple (krip′əl) *n.* a person or animal that is lame or otherwise physically disabled. ➡ sometimes considered offensive. —*v.t.,* **-pled, -pling. 1.** to make a cripple of. **2.** to impair the power or efficiency of; disable; weaken: *The air attack crippled the enemy's supply lines.* [Old English *crypel* disabled or lame person.] —**crip′pler,** *n.*

cri·sis (krī′sis) *n., pl.* **-ses** (-sēz). **1.** a decisive or extremely important point in a course of events. **2.** a condition or period of difficulty, insecurity, or suspense: *The closing of the aircraft plant caused an economic crisis in the town.* **3.** a turning point in an acute disease, toward recovery or death. [Latin *crisis* decision, from Greek *krisis* decision, turning point of a disease.] —For Synonyms, see **emergency.**

crisis center, an organization or service that assists people in an emergency, as in the aftermath of an earthquake, or provides information and counseling to those in need of immediate assistance for emotional problems, for example, runaways or individuals suffering from severe depression.

crisp (krisp) *adj.* **1.** easily crumbled or crushed; brittle: *crisp potato chips.* **2.** firm and fresh: *crisp lettuce.* **3.** brisk; bracing; invigorating: *a cool, crisp autumn day.* **4.** fresh and clean: *a crisp apron.* **5.** clear and terse: *The statement was crisp and decisive.* **6.** lively; sparkling: *crisp conversation.* **7.** (of hair) curly, wavy, or wiry. —*v.t., v.i.* to make or become crisp. —*n.* something crisp, esp. a thin cookie: *ginger crisps.* [Old English *crisp* curly, from Latin *crispus.*] —**crisp′ly,** *adv.* —**crisp′ness,** *n.*

crisp·y (kris′pē) *adj.,* **crisp·i·er, crisp·i·est.** brittle or firm; crisp. —**crisp′i·ness,** *n.*

criss·cross (kris′krôs′) *adj.* arranged in or marked with crossed lines; crossed; crossing. —*adv.* crosswise. —*n.* **1.** intersecting lines. **2.** a mark or pattern made by intersecting lines. —*v.t.* **1.** to mark with intersecting lines. **2.** to cross repeatedly: *We crisscrossed the neighborhood looking for our dog.* —*v.i.* to form a crisscross; intersect frequently: *The trails of the skiers crisscrossed in the snow.* [Modification of archaic *christcross* a symbol of the cross placed in front of the alphabet in a hornbook. See CHRIST, CROSS.]

cris·ta (kris′tə) *n., pl.* **cris·tae** (kris′tē). *Biology.* any of the folds or projections of the inner membrane of a mitochondrion upon which a variety of metabolic reactions take place. [Latin *crista,* crest, comb.]

cri·te·ri·on (krī tîr′ē ən) *n., pl.* **-te·ri·a** (-tîr′ē ə) or **-te·ri·ons.** a rule, standard, principle, or test by which something can be judged or measured: *In ancient Greece, symmetry and balance were the criteria of artistic beauty.* [Greek *kritērion* means for judging, from *kritēs* judge.] —For Synonyms, see **standard.**

crit·ic (krit′ik) *n.* **1.** a person who judges books, plays, films, music, paintings, television programs, or the like, reviewing them for their merits and faults, esp. one who reports professionally for publication or broadcast. **2.** a person who analyzes or evaluates anything: *The author was an astute critic of the international social scene.* **3.** a person who judges severely or unfavorably; faultfinder. [Latin *criticus* able to judge, from Greek *kritikos* able to judge, literary critic, from *kritēs* judge.]

crit·i·cal (krit′i kəl) *adj.* **1.** inclined to find fault or judge severely or unfavorably. **2.** exercising, involving, or marked by careful analysis, judgment, and evaluation; judicial: *a critical evaluation.* **3.** of or relating to critics or criticism. **4.** of, relating to, or of the nature of a crisis or turning point; crucial: *The*

crinoid

C

a	at	e	end	o	hot	u	up	hw	white	⎧	about
ā	ape	ē	me	ō	old	ū	use	ng	song	⎪	taken
ä	far	i	it	ô	fork	ü	rule	th	thin	ə ⎨	pencil
âr	care	ī	ice	oi	oil	u̇	pull	th	this	⎪	lemon
		îr	pierce	ou	out	ûr	turn	zh	measure	⎩	circus

patient's condition is now critical. The peace talks have reached a critical stage. **5.** (of supplies, labor, or resources) of vital importance but in current or anticipated short supply: *Water became critical during the drought.* **6.** (of a nuclear bomb or reactor) able to sustain a chain reaction: *a critical mass.* —**crit′i·cal·ly,** *adv.* —**crit′i·cal·ness,** *n.*

critical angle *Optics.* the angle of incidence beyond which total reflection of a light ray takes place.

crit·i·cism (krit′ə siz′əm) *n.* **1.** the act of criticizing, esp. unfavorably. **2.** a critical comment or unfavorable judgment. **3.** the art or profession of judging the quality of artistic or literary work. **4.** a comment, article, or review expressing such judgment; critique. **5.** a detailed investigation of the origin, history, accuracy, or the like of a document, esp. an effort to determine the original text of a literary work or, specifically, of the Bible or its parts.

Synonyms **Criticism, critique,** and **review** mean analysis or evaluation of a work or performance, esp. in the arts. **Criticism** is the least specific of these terms, implying only that the writer or speaker claims some expertise and is using some standard or standards: *Her literary criticism was based on her studies of the modern novel.* **Critique** suggests a formal analytical essay: *The journal carried a brief critique of staging techniques in the play.* A **review** is usually a relatively short evaluation of a performance or production, designed to inform a potential consumer or spectator: *He looked in the paper to see the movie reviews.*

crit·i·cize (krit′ə sīz′) *v.,* **-cized, -ciz·ing.** —*v.t.* **1.** to find fault with: *They criticized my work.* **2.** to discuss, judge, or examine critically: *to criticize a poem.* —*v.i.* **1.** to judge disapprovingly; censure. **2.** to act as a critic; pass judgment. —**crit′i·ciz′er,** *n.* —For Synonyms, see **blame.**

cri·tique (kri tēk′) *n.* **1.** a critical comment, article, or review. **2.** the art or practice of criticism. —*v.t.,* **-tiqued, -tiqu·ing.** to discuss, judge, or examine critically: *to critique a motion picture.* [French *critique,* from Greek *kritikē* the critical art.] —For Synonyms *(n.),* see **criticism.**

crit·ter (krit′ər) *n. Informal.* a creature; animal.

croak (krōk) *n.* a deep, hoarse sound like that made by a frog or raven. —*v.i.* **1.** to make a deep, hoarse sound. **2.** to speak in a deep, hoarse voice. **3.** to prophesy evil or misfortune; grumble. **4.** *Slang.* die. —*v.t.* to utter with a croak. [Imitative.]

croak·er (krō′kər) *n.* **1.** any of a group of saltwater fish, family Sciaenidae, that are found in warm, coastal waters and characteristically produce a loud, croaking sound. **2.** a person or thing that croaks.

Cro·at (krō′at) *n.* **1.a.** a native or citizen of Croatia; Croatian. **b.** a person of Croatian descent. **2.** the language of the Croats; Serbo-Croatian as it is written and spoken in Croatia; Croatian.

Cro·a·tian (krō ā′shən) *adj.* of or relating to Croatia or to its people, language, or culture. —*n.* **1.** Croat. **2.** Serbo-Croatian.

cro·chet (krō shā′) *v.,* **-cheted** (-shād′) **-chet·ing** (-shā′ing). —*v.i.* to make interlocking loops or stitches using a single needle with a hook at one end. —*v.t.* to make by crocheting. —*n.* needlework done or produced by crocheting; crocheting. [French *crochet* little hook, diminutive of *croc* hook; of Scandinavian origin.] —**cro·chet′er,** *n.*

cro·chet·ing (krō shā′ing) *n.* **1.** a piece of crocheted work. **2.** the action of a person or thing that crochets.

crock (krok) *n.* an earthenware pot, jar, or other small vessel. [Old English *crocca* earthenware pot, pitcher.]

crock·er·y (krok′ə rē) *n.* pots, dishes, and the like made of earthenware.

croc·o·dile (krok′ə dīl′) *n.* any of several large, lizardlike, aquatic reptiles, family Crocodylidae, of both fresh and salt water, in swampy areas of tropical and semitropical Asia, Africa, and America, esp. along the Nile. They are covered with bony protective plates, have elongated, pointy snouts, and usually grow 6-10 feet (1.8-3 meters) in length. For illustration, see **alligator.** [Latin *crocodīlus,* from Greek *krokodeilos* lizard, alligator, possibly from *krokē* pebble + *drilos* worm; with reference to the habit of reptiles of lying on stones in the sun.]

crocodile tears, pretended or insincere tears; hypocritical show of grief. [From the ancient belief that crocodiles shed tears while consuming their victims.]

croc·o·dil·i·an (krok′ə dil′ē ən) *adj.* of, relating to, or like a crocodile. —*n.* any reptile of the order Crocodylia, including crocodiles, alligators, caimans, and gavials.

cro·cus (krō′kəs) *n., pl.* **-cus·es** or **-ci** (-sī). **1.** the cup-shaped flower of any of a group of plants, genus *Crocus,* of the iris family, widely cultivated as a garden flower of various colors. Most crocuses bloom in early spring, but some bloom in autumn, as the saffron. **2.** the plant bearing this flower, having a single flower stalk and grasslike leaves, growing directly from a bulblike stem or corn. [Latin *crocus* saffron, from Greek *krokos;* of Semitic origin.]

Croe·sus (krē′səs) *n.* any very rich man. [From *Croesus,* king of Lydia, died 546? B.C., noted for his great wealth.]

croft (krôft, kroft) *n. British.* **1.** a small field for farming, esp. one next to a house. **2.** a small rented farm. [Old English *croft* field.]

croft·er (krôf′tər) *n. British.* a tenant farmer working a croft, esp. in Scotland or northern England.

crois·sant (krə sänt′; *French* krwä sän′) *n., pl.* **-sants** (-sänts′, -sänz′; *French* -sän′) a rich, flaky roll in the shape of a crescent. [French *croissant* literally, crescent, from Old French *creissant* crescent moon. See CRESCENT.]

Croix de Guerre (krwä də ger′) a French military decoration awarded for distinguished service in war. [French *croix de guerre* literally, cross of war.]

Cro-Mag·non (krō mag′non, -man′yən) *n.* a member of a prehistoric group of humans living in Europe who were distinguished by a well-developed brain, tall, erect stature, and their use of stone and bone implements. —*adj.* relating or belonging to this group. [Because bones of this form of human were found in the *Cro-Magnon* cave in southern France.]

crom·lech (krom′lek) *n.* **1.** a prehistoric monument of upright stones or monoliths arranged in a circle. Stonehenge is the best-known example of a cromlech. **2.** dolmen. [Welsh *cromlech* incumbent flagstone, from *crom* bowed + *llech* flat stone.]

crone (krōn) *n.* a withered old woman. [Middle Dutch *croonje* carcass, old sheep, from dialectal Old French *carogne* carcass, going back to Latin *carō* flesh.]

Cro·nus (krō′nəs) *also,* **Kronos.** *n.* in Greek mythology, the youngest of the Titans, who overthrew his father, Uranus, to become ruler of the universe and was in turn overthrown by his son Zeus. His Roman counterpart is Saturn.

cro·ny (krō′nē) *n., pl.* **-nies.** a close friend; pal. [Greek *chronios* lasting.]

crook (krŭk) *n.* **1.** a shepherd's staff with a hooklike curve at one end. **2.** crosier. **3.** any bent, curved, or angular thing or part: *the crook of the arm.* **4.** any bend, curve, or turn: *The captain knew the crooks of the river by heart.* **5.** *Informal.* a person not to be trusted; thief; swindler. —*v.t.* to bend into an angular or curved form: *to beckon someone by crooking one's finger.* —*v.i.* to be or become crooked; bend; curve. [Old Norse *krōkr* hook, curve.]

crook·ed (krŭk′id) *adj.* **1.** not straight; bent; twisted. **2.** dishonest. —**crook′ed·ly,** *adv.* —**crook′ed·ness,** *n.*

crook·neck (krŭk′nek′) *n.* any of several varieties of squash having a long curved neck.

croon (krün) *v.i.* **1.** to sing or hum in a soft, low tone: *I crooned to the baby.* **2.** to sing in a soft and sentimental manner. —*v.t.* **1.** to sing or hum (a song or melody) in a soft, low tone. **2.** to sing (a popular song) in a soft and sentimental manner. —*n.* a soft, low singing or humming. [Middle Low German *krōnen* to mourn, groan; imitative.] —**croon′er,** *n.*

crop (krop) *n.* **1.** any agricultural product growing or gathered for use, as wheat, corn, or cotton. **2.** the entire yield (of any product) in one place or season: *The winter wheat crop was not large this year.* **3.** a group or collection of anything appearing or produced together: *a crop of new graduates, a crop of memos.* **4.** the act or result of cropping. **5.a.** a short haircut. **b.** a style of cutting the hair in this way. **6.** a mark made in clipping the ear of an animal. **7.** a pouchlike enlargement of a bird's gullet in front of the stomach in which preliminary preparation for digestion occurs; craw. For illustration, see **bird. 8.** a short whip with a leather loop in place of a lash. **9.** the handle of a whip. —*v.,* **cropped, crop·ping.** —*v.t.* **1.** to cut or bite off the top end of: *Sheep crop grass very short. The gardener cropped the hedges.* **2.** to grow or reap as a crop. **3.** to cut short; trim; clip: *The barber cropped my hair.* **4.** to cause to bear a crop; raise crops on: *We cropped several acres with barley.* —*v.i.* **1.** to feed by grazing: *The sheep cropped in the field.* **2.** to yield a crop or crops. [Old English *cropp* bird's craw, sprout, ear of corn.]

 •**to crop up** (or **out**). **a.** to come up or appear unexpectedly: *Something cropped up and I had to cancel my plans.* **b.** to come to or appear on the surface; sprout: *Trees cropped out from several places along the cliff.*

crop-dust (krop′dust′) *v.t., v.i.* to spray pesticides (on) from an airplane. —**crop′-dust′ing,** *n.*

crop duster 1. a person who crop-dusts. **2.** an airplane used by such a person.

crop·land (krop′land′) *n.* land used for or suitable for the growing of crops.

crop·per (krop′ər) *n.* **1.** a person or thing that crops. **2.** *Informal.* a heavy fall, as from a horse. **3.** *Informal.* a failure in an undertaking; collapse.

 •**to come a cropper.** *Informal.* **a.** to fall heavily or headlong. **b.** to fail miserably; collapse.

crop·pie (krop′ē) *n., pl.* **-pies** or **-pie.** crappie. [Form of CRAPPIE.]

crop rotation, a method of farming in which crops grown in the same ground are changed, or rotated, in an orderly sequence. Crop rotation helps to replace soil nutrients used up by some crops and to control diseases and pests.

cro·quet (krō kā′) *n.* an outdoor game in which each player uses a mallet to drive a ball through small, bent wickets arranged in a particular order to form a course. [Dialectal French *croquet,* form of French *crochet* little hook. See CROCHET.]

cro·quette (krō ket′) *n.* a small rounded or cone-shaped mass of chopped food, as meat, fish, or vegetables, coated with beaten egg and bread crumbs and fried in deep oil. [French *croquette,* from *croquer* to crunch; imitative.]

cro·sier (krō′zhər) *also,* **crozier.** *n.* an ornamental staff carried by or before bishops, archbishops, and certain abbots and abbesses, during religious ceremonies as a symbol of office. [Old French *crossier* bearer of a bishop's staff, from *crosse* bishop's staff; of Germanic origin.]

cross (krôs) *n.* **1.** an upright stake with a transverse bar, used esp. by the ancient Romans as an instrument of torture and execution. **2. the Cross.** the cross on which Jesus was crucified. **3.a.** a representation of the cross upon which Jesus died, considered as the symbol of Christianity. **b.** this representation mounted with the figure of Jesus; crucifix. **c.** *also,* **the Cross.** Christianity; Christendom. **4.** any of various similar representations, conventionally used as a symbol, badge, or ornament. **5.a.** any object, figure, or mark formed by the intersection of two lines. **b.** such a mark made as a signature by a person who cannot write. **6.** sign of the cross. **7.** any obstruction, misfortune, or affliction that tries one's patience or virtue. **8.** a person or thing that combines the characteristics of two or more individuals or things: *A motorcycle is a cross between a bicycle and an automobile.* **9.a.** an instance of crossbreeding. **b.** a product of crossbreeding; hybrid. —*v.t.* **1.** to move or pass from one to the other side of; go across: *to cross a room, to cross the ocean in seven days.* **2.** to place or lay one thing or part over another: *Cross one lace over the other, then tie them.* **3.** to pass so as to intersect: *That street crosses the railroad tracks. The paths cross each other.* **4.** to draw a line or lines through or across: *Cross all your "t's" neatly.* **5.** to extend across; span: *The bridge crosses the river.* **6.** to pass while going in different directions; meet (each other) in passing: *Your letter must have crossed mine in the mail.* **7.** to interfere with; oppose; thwart: *Cross me, and you'll regret it.* **8.** to make the sign of the cross upon or over: *The worshipers crossed themselves as they entered the church.* **9.** to crossbreed (animals or plants.) —*v.i.* **1.** to move, pass, or extend across: *We crossed at the corner. The trail crosses through the woods.* **2.** to pass each other so as to intersect; lie or be crosswise: *The friends met where the two roads crossed.* **3.** to meet in passing: *Our paths have not yet crossed.* **4.** crossbreed. —*adj.* **1.** feeling or showing irritability; ill-tempered; peevish: *Hunger made the children cross.* **2.** resulting from or exhibiting irritability: *a cross word, a cross look.* **3.** lying or passing across or crosswise: *cross streets, cross ventilation.* **4.** having been crossbred; hybrid. [Old English *cros* horizontal post crossed by a vertical post, from Old Norse *kross,* from Old Irish *cros,* from Latin *crux.* Doublet of CRUX.] —**cross′ly,** *adv.* —**cross′ness,** *n.*

• **to cross off** (or **out**). to mark out or over, as by drawing a line across; cancel: *Cross your name off the list.*
• **to cross one's fingers.** to hope for luck or success, as by placing one's middle finger over the index finger.
• **to cross one's heart.** to make a promise or affirm the truth of a statement, as by making the sign of the cross over one's heart.
• **to cross one's mind.** to occur to one suddenly or momentarily.
• **to cross someone's palm.** to give (someone) money or a bribe.
• **to take (up) the cross.** to join a crusade; become a crusader.

cross- *combining form* **1.** lying or passing across: *crossbeam, crosspiece.* **2.** running counter; opposing; opposite: *cross-purposes, crosscurrent.* **3.** resembling or forming a cross: *cross-stitch.* **4.** involving interchange or reciprocal action: *cross-reference.* [From CROSS.]

cross·bar (krôs′bär′) *n.* **1.** a bar fixed across a structure or joining upright members. **2.** a transverse line: *the crossbar on the letter "H."*

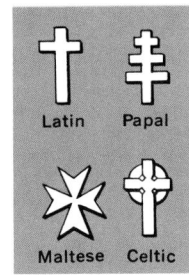

Latin   Papal

Maltese   Celtic

crosses

cross·beam (krôs′bēm′) *n.* any large beam that crosses another or extends from wall to wall.

cross·bill (krôs′bil′) *n.* any of a group of finchlike songbirds, genus *Loxia,* of the evergreen forests of North America, Europe, and Asia.

cross·bones (krôs′bōnz′) *pl. n.* see **skull and crossbones.**

cross·bow (krôs′bō′) *n.* a weapon widely used in the Middle Ages, consisting of a bow mounted crosswise at the front of a grooved stock along which arrows, stones, or other missiles are released.

crossbow

cross·bred (krôs′bred′) *adj.* (of a plant or animal) produced by crossbreeding; hybrid.

cross·breed (krôs′brēd′) *v.,* **-bred,** **-breed·ing.** —*v.t.* to breed (plants or animals) with different varieties or lines, or sometimes different species, in order to produce hybrids; hybridize. —*v.i.* to undergo such breeding. —*n.* an individual or type produced by crossbreeding; hybrid.

cross-coun·try (krôs′kun′trē) *adj., adv.* **1.** across open country or fields instead of following roads: *cross-country racing, to race cross-country.* **2.** from one end of a country to the other: *a cross-country flight, to fly cross-country.*

cross-country skiing, the sport or recreation of skiing across generally flat or gently varying countryside, using narrow skis and light, flexible boots.

cross·cur·rent (krôs′kûr′ənt, -kur′-) *n.* **1.** a current, as in a stream, flowing across the main current. **2.** a contrasting or contradictory tendency or movement: *crosscurrents of opinion.*

cross·cut (krôs′kut′) *adj.* **1.** adapted or used for cutting crosswise: *a crosscut blade.* **2.** cut across the grain or transversely. —*n.* **1.** a cut across. **2.** a course or path across. —*v.t., v.i.,* **-cut,** **-cut·ting.** to cut across.

crosscut saw, a saw having beveled teeth shaped like knives, used for cutting wood across the grain.

crosse (krôs) *n.* lacrosse stick. [See LACROSSE.]

cross-ex·am·ine (krôs′eg zam′in, -ig-) *v.t.,* **-ined,** **-in·ing.** **1.** to question (a witness who has already testified for the opposing side) to determine the reliability of his or her testimony or character. **2.** to question (someone) again to check the reliability of previous answers; question closely. —**cross′-ex·am′i·na′tion,** *n.* —**cross′-ex·am′in·er,** *n.*

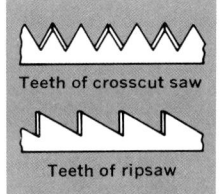

Teeth of crosscut saw

Teeth of ripsaw

crosscut saw

cross-eye (krôs′ī′) *n.* a strabismus in which one or both eyes turn inward toward the nose.

cross-eyed (krôs′īd′) *adj.* having one or both eyes turning inward toward the nose.

cross-fer·ti·li·za·tion (krôs′fûr′tə lə zā′shən) *n.* **1.** fertilization in which a reproductive cell from a female individual unites with a reproductive cell from a separate male individual. **2.** cross-pollination.

cross-fer·ti·lize (krôs′fûr′tə līz′) *v.t.,* **-lized,** **-liz·ing.** **1.** to subject to cross-fertilization. **2.** to cross-pollinate.

cross·fire (krôs′fīr′) *n.* **1.** intersecting lines of fire, esp. gunfire, from two or more positions: *The photographer was caught in the crossfire between the police and the bank robber.* **2.** a rapid or animated exchange of words or opinions: *a crossfire of insults.*

cross-grained (krôs′grānd′) *adj.* **1.** having the grain running transversely or irregularly; having a gnarled grain: *cross-grained wood.* **2.** stubborn; contrary.

cross hairs, a crossed network of fine strands inside a telescope, microscope, surveying instrument, or the like, positioned at the focus of the eyepiece to permit pinpoint location of the line of sight, as in aiming a rifle with a telescopic sight.

cross·hatch (krôs′hach′) *v.t.* to mark or shade with sets of parallel lines that cross each other. —**cross′hatch′ing,** *n.*

cross·ing (krô′sing) *n.* **1.** the act of going across: *The ship made an Atlantic crossing.* **2.** a place or point of intersection, as of

a	at	e	end	o	hot	u	up	hw	white	⌠	about
ā	ape	ē	me	ō	old	ū	use	ng	song		taken
ä	far	i	it	ô	fork	ŭ	rule	th	thin	ə ⟨	pencil
âr	care	ī	ice	oi	oil	u̇	pull	th	this		lemon
		îr	pierce	ou	out	ûr	turn	zh	measure	⌡	circus

roads. **3.** a place where something, as a street, may be crossed. **4.** the act of crossbreeding.

cross·ing·o·ver (krô′sing ō′vər) *n. Biology.* an exchange of segments, or of genes in the segments, between chromosomes during meiosis.

cross·jack (krôs′jak′, krô′jik) *n.* a square sail on the lower yard of a mizzenmast.

cross-leg·ged (krôs′leg′id, -legd′) *adj., adv.* with the ankles crossed and the knees out.

cross·let (krôs′lit) *n.* a small cross, esp. one used as a heraldic device.

cross·o·ver (krôs′ō′vər) *n.* **1.** crossing-over. **2.** a short secondary railroad track for switching trains from one main track to another. **3.** a means or place for crossing over something, as a footbridge over a railway. **4.** the act of crossing over from one place or part to another.

cross·patch (krôs′pach′) *n. Informal.* a cross, ill-tempered person; grouch.

cross·piece (krôs′pēs′) *n.* a piece of any material placed or lying across something else.

cross·pol·li·nate (krôs′pol′ə nāt′) *v.t.* -nat·ed, -nat·ing. to subject to cross-pollination.

cross·pol·li·na·tion (krôs′pol′ə nā′shən) *n.* the transfer of pollen from the anther of one flower to the stigma of another by wind, water, insects, or birds. ➡ distinguished from **self-polli- nation**.

cross product 1. either of the two products obtained by multiplying the means or extremes of a proportion. In the ratio *a/b* and *c/d*, the products *a × d* and *b × c* are cross products. **2.** vector product.

cross·pur·pose (krôs′pûr′pəs) *n.* an opposing or conflicting purpose.
   · **at cross-purposes.** unintentionally opposing or hindering each other's efforts.

cross·ques·tion (krôs′kwes′chən) *v.t.* to question closely or repeatedly; cross-examine. —*n.* a question asked in cross-examining.

cross·re·fer (krôs′ri fûr′) *v.,* -ferred, -fer·ring. —*v.t.* to refer (a reader) from one part to another, as in a book or catalog. —*v.i.* to make a cross-reference.

cross·ref·er·ence (krôs′ref′ər əns) *n.* a reference from one part, as in a book or index, to another part for additional information.

cross·road (krôs′rōd′) *n.* **1.** a road crossing another or a secondary road leading from one main road to another. **2. cross- roads. a.** a place where roads intersect. **b.** in rural areas, a small community at such a place. **c.** a central meeting place or center of activity, as of people or cultures. **d.** a point where an important decision must be made. ➡ used as singular in defs. 2b and 2c, as either singular or plural in 2a and 2d.

cross·ruff (krôs′ruf′) *n.* in bridge or whist, a play in which each of two partners alternately leads a card that the other will be able to trump. —*v.i.* to engage in such a play.

cross·sec·tion (krôs′sek′shən) *v.t.* to make or cut into a cross section: *to cross-section an apple.* —**cross′-sec′tion·al,** *adj.*

cross section 1. a plane section produced by cutting an object, esp. at right angles to an axis. **2.** a piece cut in this manner. **3.** a diagram or representation of such a cut. **4.** a sampling considered representative or typical of the whole: *a cross section of public opinion.*

cross-stitch (krôs′stich′) *n.* **1.** a stitch made by crossing one stitch over another, forming an X. **2.** needlework made with this stitch. —*v.t., v.i.* to embroider or sew with a cross-stitch.

cross street, a street that crosses another, esp. one crossing a main thoroughfare.

cross·town (krôs′toun′) *adj.* going across a town or city: *a crosstown bus, crosstown traffic.* —*adv.* across a town or city: *We traveled crosstown on a slow, old bus.*

cross·trees (krôs′trēz′) *pl. n.* two horizontal bars attached near the top of a mast on a sailing ship to spread the rigging and support a work platform.

cross vine, bignonia.

cross·walk (krôs′wôk′) *n.* a lane marked off for use by pedestrians in crossing a street.

cross·way (krôs′wā′) *n.* crossroad.

cross·wind (krôs′wind′) *n.* a wind blowing across the course or path of a vessel, esp. an aircraft.

cross·wise (krôs′wīz′) *adv.* **1.** so as to cross; across; transversely. **2.** *Archaic.* in the form of a cross. Also, **cross·ways** (krôs′wāz′).

cross·word puzzle (krôs′wûrd′) a puzzle in which words or phrases are filled in on a pattern of numbered squares in answer to a list of correspondingly numbered clues. The words usually

intersect each other in such a way that they read both across and down.

crotch (kroch) *n.* **1.a.** the region of the human body where the legs fork from the pelvis. **b.** the corresponding place in a piece of clothing. **2.** a fork or angle formed by two diverging parts, as by the branches of a tree. **3.** a forked pole used as a support. [Old French *croche* hook, from *croc*; of Scandinavian origin.]

crotch·et (kroch′it) *n.* **1.** a peculiar, whimsical, or perverse notion. **2.** a small hook or hooked instrument. **3.** *British.* quarter note, in music. [Old French *crochet* small hook, diminutive of *croc* hook; of Scandinavian origin.]

crotch·et·y (kroch′i tē) *adj.* full of perverse or eccentric notions; cantankerous. —**crotch′et·i·ness,** *n.*

cro·ton (krō′tən) *n.* **1.** any tropical herb, shrub, or tree of the genus *Croton,* of the spurge family, one species of which was formerly cultivated for its seeds, which yield a purgative oil. **2.** any tropical evergreen tree or shrub, of the related genus *Codiaeum,* cultivated for its bright, attractive foliage. [Modern Latin *Croton,* from Greek *krotōn* tick, castor-oil plant; probably because its seed resembles a tick.]

Cro·ton bug (krō′tən) a small cockroach, *Blattella germanica,* that is a common household pest. [From *Croton* Aqueduct and *Croton* River, part of the water-supply system for New York City; because these bugs became numerous in the city after the opening of the aqueduct in 1842.]

crouch (krouch) *v.i.* **1.** to stoop or bend low, esp. with the knees bent, as an animal preparing to spring or trying to hide. **2.** to cringe or cower humbly or servilely. —*v.t. Archaic.* to bend (something) low. —*n.* **1.** the act of crouching. **2.** a crouching posture. [Old French *crochir* to become bent, from *croc* hook; of Scandinavian origin.]

croup¹ (krüp) *n.* an inflammation of the throat and windpipe, esp. in children, characterized by a high-pitched, barking cough and difficult breathing, caused by infection or allergy. [From obsolete or dialectal *croup* to speak in a hoarse voice; of imitative origin.] —**croup′y,** *adj.*

croup² (krüp) *n.* the highest part of the rump of a horse or other animal. [Middle English *croupe,* from Old French *croupe, crope;* of Germanic origin.]

crou·pi·er (krü′pē ər, krü′pē ā′) *n.* an attendant at a gambling table, as in roulette, who rakes in chips or other lost bets and pays winners or, in many cases, has charge of the entire game. [French *croupier* originally, one who rides (behind another) on the rump; hence assistant, from *cro(u)pe* rump of a horse. See CROUP².]

crou·ton (krü′ton, krü ton′) *n.* a small cube of toasted or fried bread, often served in soup or salads. [French *croûton* bit of crust, diminutive of *croûte* crust, from Latin *crusta* crust, shell.]

crow¹ (krō) *v.i.,* **crowed** or *(def. 1)* **crew, crowed, crow·ing. 1.** to utter the shrill cry of a rooster. **2.** to utter a delighted, happy cry, as a baby does. **3.** to boast in triumph; exult. —*n.* **1.** the cry of a rooster. **2.** a delighted, happy cry, as that made by a baby. [Old English *crāwan* to utter the cry of a rooster.]

crow² (krō) *n.* **1.** any of various omnivorous birds, genus *Corvus,* having glossy black plumage, a heavy, black bill, and a harsh, croaking cry or caw. Length: 17-21 inches (43-53 centimeters). **2.** any of various similar birds, as the raven, magpie, or jay. **3.** crowbar. [Old English *crāwe* bird of the genus *Corvus.*]
   · **as the crow flies.** in a straight line.
   · **to eat crow.** *Informal.* to be forced to humble oneself, as by admitting a mistake.

Crow (krō) *n., pl.* **Crow** or **Crows. 1.** a member of a tribe of North American Indians formerly living along the Missouri River in the Great Plains. **2.** the language of the Crow, a member of the Siouan language family. [Translation of Crow *Absaroke* crow², bird people.]

crow·bar (krō′bär′) *n.* a bar of iron or steel with a wedge-shaped end that is sometimes slightly bent and forked, used as a lever or pry.

crow·ber·ry (krō′ber′ē, -bə rē) *n., pl.* -ries. **1.** any of several trailing or low evergreen plants, genus *Empetrum,* having black fruit. **2.** the edible berrylike fruit of any of these plants. [Possibly a translation of German *krähenbeere.*]

crowd (kroud) *n.* **1.** a large number of people gathered together; throng: *We tried to make our way through the crowd. The comedian's act drew a large crowd.* **2.** *Informal.* a particular group of people; set; clique: *That crowd is too old for you.* **3.** people in general; the masses. **4.** a large number of things collected or grouped together. —*v.t.* **1.a.** to push or shove: *Please don't crowd me.* **b.** to force (with *off* or *out*): *They crowded me off the bus.* **2.a.** to fill to excess, as by pressing or thronging: *I crowded the shelves with my books. Swimmers crowded the float.* **b.** to press or force into a close space; cram: *I crowded everything into the trunk and then could not close it.* —*v.i.* **1.** to gather or congregate closely or in large numbers: *We crowded around the table to serve*

ourselves. **2.** to press forward; advance by pushing: *to crowd into a bus.* [Old English *crūdan* to press.]

•**to crowd (on) sail.** to raise as many sails as possible in order to achieve maximum speed.

crowd·ed (krou′did) *adj.* **1.** filled with a crowd; packed: *crowded sidewalks.* **2.** gathered, pressed, or clustered uncomfortably close together: *the crowded conditions of the city's ghettos.* —For Synonyms, see **close.**

crow·foot (krō′fŏot′) *n., pl. (def. 1)* -**foots** or *(def. 2)* -**feet** (-fēt′). **1.** any of various flowering plants, esp. one of the genus *Ranunculus,* as the buttercup or peony, whose leaves are often deeply divided into three lobes, thus resembling a crow's foot. **2.** *Nautical.* a device consisting of a number of small cords passed through a long block and used for various purposes, as to suspend an awning. —*adj.* of or designating a family, Ranunculaceae, of herbs and woody plants of the temperate and arctic regions of the Northern Hemisphere, including the buttercup, anemone, and peony.

crown (kroun) *n.* **1.** a covering for the head, often of jewels and precious metal, worn as a symbol of sovereignty. **2.** a wreath, band, or other circular ornament for the head: *a crown of flowers.* **3.** something resembling a crown in shape, as the corona of a flower. **4.** the power or authority of a monarch. **5.** *also,* **the Crown.** a sovereign ruler; monarch. **6.a.** the highest part of something; top: *the crown of a hill.* **b.** the head. **c.** the upper part of a hat or other head covering. **7.** an exalting attribute; chief ornament: *Their grandchildren were the crown of the couple's old age.* **8.** the highest or most perfect state or form of anything; culmination. **9.** a distinction for achievement or victory, as in an athletic contest; honor; reward: *the middleweight boxing crown.* **10.a.** the portion of a tooth that projects from the gum. **b.** an artificial substitute for this portion, usually made of gold, porcelain, or plastic. **11.** the crest of an animal, esp. of a bird. **12.** the uppermost part of a tree or shrub, formed by the branches and foliage. **13.** any of various coins, often stamped with a crown or crowned head, as the krona of Sweden. **14.** a former British silver coin, worth five shillings. **15.** the point at the top of the root of a plant, at or just below ground level, where the stem begins. —*v.t.* **1.a.** to make a monarch of; invest with royal power and dignity; enthrone. **b.** to place a crown or wreath on (someone's) head). **2.** to be the top part of; surmount: *Whipped cream crowned the dessert.* **3.** to add the finishing touch to; complete; consummate: *The award crowned the writer's career.* **4.** to recognize officially as: *The league crowned our team champion.* **5.** to endow with honor or dignity. **6.** to make a king of in checkers. **7.** to put an artificial crown on (a tooth). **8.** *Informal.* to hit on the head: *One clown crowned the other with the rubber bat.* [Old French *corone* crown (as of a monarch), from Latin *corōna* wreath, crown, from Greek *korōnē* something bent. Doublet of CORONA.]

crown colony, a colony under the authority of the British Crown and largely administered by the British government.

crown glass **1.** a hard glass of low refraction, used in optical instruments. **2.** a window glass blown and whirled into flat, circular sheets with a lump left in the center by the blower's rod.

crown prince, the male heir apparent to a throne, esp. the eldest son of a ruling monarch.

crown princess **1.** the wife of a crown prince. **2.** the female heir apparent to a throne.

crow's-foot (krōz′fŏot′) *n., pl.* -**feet** (-fēt′). **1.** crow's-feet. wrinkles near the outer corners of the eyes. **2.** a three-pointed embroidered design, sometimes used to finish the ends of seams or the corners of pockets.

crow's-nest (krōz′nest′) *n.* **1.** a small enclosed platform or other structure near the top of a ship's mast, used for maintaining a lookout. **2.** any similar structure ashore.

cro·zier (krō′zhər) crosier.

CRT, cathode-ray tube.

cru·ces (krü′sēz) a plural of **crux.**

cru·cial (krü′shəl) *adj.* **1.** likely to determine a contest or conflict or be a turning point; of utmost importance; critical; decisive: *a crucial decision, a crucial battle.* **2.** very difficult to endure; trying; severe. [French *crucial* cross-shaped, decisive, from Latin *crux* cross; referring to the choosing of a road at a crossroad.] —**cru′cial·ly,** *adv.*

cru·ci·ate (krü′shē it, -āt′) *adj.* **1.** shaped like a cross. **2.** *Botany.* having leaves or petals arranged in the form of a cross. [Modern Latin *cruciatus* cross-shaped, from Latin *crux* cross.]

cru·ci·ble (krü′sə bəl) *n.* **1.** a hard, heat-resistant vessel for melting chemicals, metals, and ores. **2.** a severe test or trial.

crow's-foot
(def. 2)

[Medieval Latin *crucibulum* melting pot, night lamp (possibly placed before a crucifix), from Latin *crux* cross.]

crucible steel, a high-grade cast steel prepared in crucibles that distribute carbon content uniformly, formerly in widespread use for tools and cutlery.

cru·ci·fix (krü′sə fiks′) *n.* **1.** a cross with the crucified figure of Jesus upon it. **2.** any cross considered as a Christian symbol. [Old French *crucefis,* going back to Latin *crucī fīxus* fixed to a cross.]

cru·ci·fix·ion (krü′sə fik′shən) *n.* **1.** the act of crucifying or the state of being crucified. **2. Crucifixion. a.** the execution of Jesus on the Cross. **b.** a picture, statue, or other representation of this.

cru·ci·form (krü′sə fôrm′) *adj.* in the form of a cross; cross-shaped. [Latin *cruc-,* stem of *crux* cross + -FORM.]

cru·ci·fy (krü′sə fī′) *v.t.,* -**fied,** -**fy·ing. 1.** to put to death by nailing or otherwise affixing to a cross. **2.** to treat cruelly; persecute; torment. [Old French *crucifier* to nail to a cross, going back to Latin *crucī fīgere* to fix to a cross.] —**cru′ci·fi′er,** *n.*

crud (krud) *n. Slang.* **1.** a deposit or accumulation of filth or grease. **2.** an obnoxious or contemptible person or thing. [Earlier form of CURD.] —**crud′dy,** *adj.*

crude (krüd) *adj.,* **crud·er, crud·est. 1.** lacking skill, finish, or completeness; rough; unpolished: *a crude drawing, a crude theory.* **2.** lacking tact, taste, or refinement; uncultured; rude: *crude behavior.* **3.** in a natural or raw state; unrefined: *crude rubber.* **4.** coarse; vulgar: *crude jokes.* **5.** *Archaic.* immature; unripe. [Latin *crūdus* raw.] —**crude′ly,** *adv.* —**crude′ness,** *n.* —For Synonyms, see **uncouth.**

crude oil, oil as it comes from the ground in its natural state, before refining.

cru·di·ty (krü′di tē) *n., pl.* -**ties. 1.** the state or quality of being crude. **2.** something crude, as a remark.

cru·el (krü′əl) *adj.,* **cru·el·er, cru·el·est;** *also, British,* **cru·el·ler, cru·el·lest. 1.** willing or inclined to inflict suffering; indifferent to or enjoying the pain or distress of others. **2.** causing grief, pain, or suffering: *a cruel winter, cruel punishment.* **3.** willing to watch others suffer; callous. [Old French *cruel* severe, harsh, from Latin *crūdēlis.*] —**cru′el·ly,** *adv.* —**cru′el·ness,** *n.*

cru·el·ty (krü′əl tē) *n., pl.* -**ties. 1.** the state or quality of being cruel. **2.** an action or occurrence that is cruel. **3.** *Law.* intentional actions, as toward a spouse, that cause mental or physical suffering.

cru·et (krü′it) *n.* a small glass bottle for holding vinegar, oil, or other dressings. [Anglo-Norman *cruet,* diminutive of Old French *cruie* earthen pot; of Germanic origin.]

cruise (krüz) *v.,* **cruised, cruis·ing.** —*v.i.* **1.** to sail about unhurriedly, usually without a specific destination, as for pleasure or in search of something. **2.** to ride or move about in a similar way: *The police car cruised through the neighborhood. The taxi cruised along the street looking for a fare.* **3.** to move at the speed of maximum efficiency, as an aircraft or automobile. —*v.t.* to cruise over or around in: *The pleasure boat cruised the Mediterranean. We cruised the park looking for our lost dog.* —*n.* the act of cruising, esp. a sea voyage taken for pleasure. [Dutch *kruisen* to cross, to sail to and fro, from *kruis* cross, from Latin *crux.*]

cruet

cruise control, an electronic system that enables the speed of an automobile or other vehicle to be maintained automatically by means of the accelerator.

cruise missile, a winged guided missile with an onboard computer, programmed to fly at low altitudes and at subsonic speeds in order to evade detection by enemy radar, launched by airplanes, submarines, and ships.

cruis·er (krü′zər) *n.* **1.** a warship less heavily armed than a battleship, having a long cruising radius and designed for speed and maneuverability. **2.** a power-driven boat, as a motorboat or cabin cruiser. **3.** squad car. **4.** a person or thing that cruises.

cruising radius, the maximum distance that an aircraft or ship can travel and then return at cruising speed before its fuel is exhausted.

cruising speed, the speed at which an aircraft, powered boat, or vehicle operates at maximum efficiency.

crul·ler (krul′ər) *also,* **kruller.** *n.* a small cake made of sweet-

a	at	e	end	o	hot	u	up	hw	white		about
ā	ape	ē	me	ō	old	ū	use	ng	song		taken
ä	far	i	it	ô	fork	ü	rule	th	thin	ə	pencil
âr	care	ī	ice	oi	oil	u̇	pull	th	this		lemon
		îr	pierce	ou	out	ûr	turn	zh	measure		circus

293

ened dough cut into strips that are twisted together and fried in deep fat. [Dutch *krulle* literally, curled cake, from *krullen* to curl.]

crumb (krum) *n.* **1.** a tiny fragment, as of bread, cake, or similar food. **2.** a small bit of something; scrap: *crumbs of information.* **3.** the soft inner part of bread. **4.** *Slang.* a contemptible person. —*v.t.* **1.** to break into crumbs. **2.** to prepare for cooking by covering or dressing with crumbs. **3.** to clear the crumbs from: *to crumb a table.* [Old English *cruma* fragment.]

crum·ble (krum′bəl) *v.,* **-bled, -bling.** —*v.t.* to break into small fragments: *to crumble bread to feed pigeons.* —*v.i.* **1.** to fall into small fragments: *The yellowed pages of the book crumbled at a touch.* **2.** to fall apart or be destroyed; disintegrate: *Our hopes for winning the game crumbled when our quarterback was injured.* [Modification (influenced by CRUMB) of earlier *crimble,* going back to Old English *cruma* fragment.]

crum·bly (krum′blē) *adj.,* **-bli·er, -bli·est.** liable to crumble; easily crumbled; friable. —**crum′bli·ness,** *n.*

crumb·y (krum′ē) *adj.,* **crumb·i·er, crumb·i·est. 1.** full of crumbs. **2.** soft, like the inner part of bread. **3.** *Slang.* crummy.

crum·my (krum′ē) *adj.,* **crum·mi·er, crum·mi·est.** *Slang.* inferior, shabby, or miserable: *a crummy movie, a crummy apartment, to feel crummy.* [Possibly obsolete *crum* crooked (from Old English *crumb*) + -Y¹.] —**crum′mi·ness,** *n.*

crum·pet (krum′pit) *n.* a soft, unsweetened batter cake that is first baked on a griddle, then usually toasted and buttered. [Probably from Middle English *crompid (cake)* literally, curled up (cake), going back to Old English *crump* crooked.]

crum·ple (krum′pəl) *v.,* **-pled, -pling.** —*v.t.* to press or crush (something) into irregular folds or creases: *to crumple paper.* —*v.i.* **1.** to become wrinkled or shriveled: *The fender crumpled when it hit the wall.* **2.** to fall as though being folded; collapse: *The wounded soldier crumpled to the ground.* —*n.* an irregular fold or crease. [Obsolete *crump* to curl up (going back to Old English *crump* crooked) + -LE.]

crunch (krunch) *v.t.* **1.** to chew or bite with a crushing or crackling sound; chew noisily: *to crunch carrots.* **2.** to crush or grind noisily: *The wheels crunched the gravel.* —*v.i.* **1.** to chew noisily: *to crunch on some celery.* **2.** to produce or emit a crunching or crackling sound: *The dry leaves crunched under our feet.* **3.** to move or proceed with such a sound: *The ship crunched through the ice.* —*n.* **1.** the sound of crunching. **2.** the act of crunching. **3.** a difficult or critical time or situation: *My friends always come through in a crunch.* [Imitative.]

crunch·y (krun′chē) *adj.,* **crunch·i·er, crunch·i·est.** making a crunching sound: *crunchy potato chips.*

crup·per (krup′ər, krŏŏp′-) *n.* **1.** a leather strap attached to the back of a saddle and passing over the horse's back and around its tail to prevent the saddle from sliding forward. **2.** the rump of a horse; croup. [Old French *cropière* saddle strap, from *crope* rump. See CROUP².]

cru·ral (krŏŏr′əl) *adj. Anatomy.* of or relating to a leg or thigh: *a crural artery.* [Latin *crūrālis,* from *crūs* leg.]

cru·sade (krōō sād′) *n.* **1.** *also,* **Crusade.** any of the military expeditions that were undertaken by European Christians between 1096 and 1270 to capture the Holy Land from the Muslims. **2.** any war or military expedition undertaken under papal sanction, esp. during the Middle Ages. **3.** any vigorous campaign for the advancement of a cause, esp. for reform or improvement: *a crusade for clean government.* —*v.i.,* **-sad·ed, -sad·ing.** to engage in a crusade. [Blend of French *croisade* and Spanish *cruzada,* from Medieval Latin *cruciata,* from *cruciatus,* past participle of *cruciare* to mark with the sign of a cross, from Latin *crux* cross.] —**cru·sad′er,** *n.*

cruse (krōōz, krōōs) *n.* an earthenware jug, pot, or bottle, esp. one used to hold oil. [Middle Dutch *cruyse* pot.]

crush (krush) *v.t.* **1.** to press or squeeze with such force as to damage, deform, or destroy. **2.** to break into fragments or small particles, as by grinding or pounding: *to crush ice.* **3.** to subdue completely; put down; quell: *to crush an uprising.* **4.** to depress or burden grievously; overwhelm: *to be crushed by bad news.* **5.** to forcibly press: *The crowd crushed me against the building as the motorcade went by.* **6.** to extract by pressing or squeezing: *to crush oil from olives.* —*v.i.* to become crushed. —*n.* **1.** the act of crushing or the state of being crushed. **2.** a thick or closely pressed crowd: *I was caught in the crush at the parade.* **3.** *Informal.* **a.** infatuation. **b.** the object of an infatuation. [Old French *cruis(s)ir* to break, crack; of Germanic origin.] —**crush′er,** *n.*

crust (krust) *n.* **1.a.** the outer, often hard or crisp, part of bread. **b.** a piece of this. **c.** any dry, hard piece of bread. **2.** the outer coating or layer of certain foods: *pie crust, the crust on fried chicken.* **3.** any hard or brittle outer coating; surface layer: *The lake was covered with a thin crust of ice.* **4.** the cold, solid outer layer of the earth, overlying the mantle. **5.** *Slang.* insolence; audacity. —*v.t., v.i.* **1.** to cover or become covered with a crust.

2. to form or harden into a crust. [Old French *crouste* crust of bread, from Latin *crusta* crust of bread, rind, shell.]

crus·ta·cean (krus tā′shən) *n.* any of a diverse, widely distributed group of chiefly aquatic arthropods, class Crustacea, including lobsters, crabs, shrimp, crawfish, barnacles, and wood lice, which live on land. Crustaceans breathe through gills, have two pairs of antennae, and in the most familiar species have shells that are hard and limy. —*adj.* of or relating to crustaceans. [Modern Latin *Crustacea,* going back to Latin *crusta* rind, shell + -AN.]

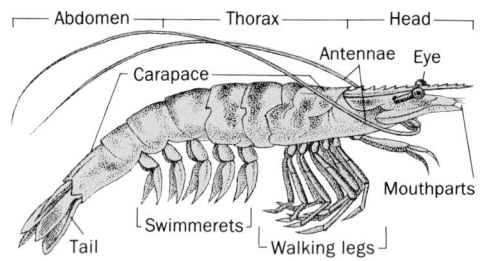

shrimp, a representative **crustacean**

crus·ta·ceous (krus tā′shəs) *adj.* **1.** of or like a crust or shell. **2.** having a crust or shell. **3.** crustacean.

crus·tal (krus′təl) *adj.* of or relating to a crust, esp. the earth's or moon's crust. [CRUST + -AL¹.]

crust·y (krus′tē) *adj.,* **crust·i·er, crust·i·est. 1.** having or resembling a crust. **2.** ill-tempered and harsh in manner or speech. —**crust′i·ly,** *adv.* —**crust′i·ness,** *n.*

crutch (kruch) *n.* **1.** a staff used by a lame person as a support in walking, esp. one having a grip for the hand and either a crosspiece that fits under the armpit or a curved piece that fits around the forearm. **2.** anything resembling a crutch in shape or function, as a forked support for the leg on a sidesaddle. **3.** anything that gives support. [Old English *crycc* staff.]

crux (kruks) *n., pl.* **crux·es** or **cru·ces. 1.** the most important, fundamental, or decisive point or part: *the crux of the matter, the crux of an argument.* **2.** **Crux.** *Astronomy.* Southern Cross. **3.** a difficult or perplexing problem. [Latin *crux* cross, torture, trouble. Doublet of CROSS.]

cru·za·do (krōō zä′dō) *n., pl.* **-does** or **-dos.** the monetary unit of Brazil.

cru·zei·ro (krōō zâr′ō) *n.* the former monetary unit of Brazil.

cry (krī) *v.,* **cried, cry·ing.** —*v.i.* **1.** to shed tears, esp. as an expression of emotion; weep: *The children cried when they had to leave their friends.* **2.** to call loudly; shout: *We accidentally overturned our boat in the lake and cried for help. The injured child cried out in pain.* **3.** (of an animal) to make its characteristic call: *The sea gulls cried as they flew overhead.* —*v.t.* **1.** to utter loudly; exclaim; shout. **2.** to affect (oneself) in a specified way by weeping: *to cry oneself to sleep.* **3.** to announce or advertise publicly: *The sidewalk vendors cried their wares.* —*n., pl.* **cries. 1.** a loud call or shout, esp. one expressing emotion: *a cry of joy.* **2.** a fit of weeping: *to feel better after a good cry.* **3.** entreaty; appeal: *a cry for mercy.* **4.** a public proclamation or advertisement: *a street vendor's cry.* **5.** a public outcry; clamor; demand: *a cry for justice.* **6.** a rallying call; slogan; watchword. **7.** (of an animal) a characteristic call. **8.** (of hounds) a pack. [Old French *crier* to cry out, shout, from Latin *quirītāre* to cry out, shriek; literally, to call for the assistance of the *Quirītēs,* or Roman citizens.]

· **a far cry. a.** a long way: *Europe is a far cry from here.* **b.** something very different: *The published book is a far cry from the early manuscript.*

· **in full cry.** in full pursuit, as a pack of hounds.

· **to cry down.** to deprecate; disparage.

· **to cry off.** to withdraw from an agreement or undertaking.

· **to cry one's eyes** (or **heart**) **out.** to weep inconsolably or profusely.

· **to cry (out) for.** to be in urgent need of; demand: *The situation cries out for attention.*

· **to cry up.** to praise highly; extol.

· **to cry wolf.** to give a false alarm.

cry·ba·by (krī′bā′bē) *n., pl.* **-bies.** a person, esp. a child, who cries or complains often.

cry·ing (krī′ing) *adj.* **1.** that cries. **2.** requiring immediate attention or remedy: *a crying need for a kidney transplant.*

cryo- *combining form* cold; freezing; frost: *cryogen.* [Greek *kryos* frost.]

cry·o·gen (krī′ə jən) *n.* a mixture that causes freezing; refrigerant. [CRYO- + -GEN.]

cry·o·gen·ics (krī′ə jen′iks) *n.* the branch of physics dealing with the structure and properties of materials at very low temperatures. ➡ used as singular. [CRYO- + -GEN + -ICS.] —**cry′o·gen′ic,** *adj.*

cry·o·lite (krī′ə līt′) *n.* a natural or synthetic fluoride of sodium and aluminum, used chiefly in making aluminum. Formula: Na_3AlF_6 [CRYO- + Greek *lithos* stone.]

cry·o·sur·ger·y (krī′ə sûr′jə rē) *n.* surgery using the application of extremely low temperatures to destroy diseased or damaged tissue. [CRYO- + SURGERY.]

cry·o·ther·a·py (krī′ə ther′ə pē) *n.* the use of extremely low temperatures in medical treatment. [CRYO- + THERAPY.]

crypt (kript) *n.* an underground chamber or vault used chiefly as a burial place, esp. one beneath the main floor of a church. [Latin *crypta* vault, cave, from Greek *kryptē,* from *kryptos* hidden. Doublet of GROTTO.]

cryp·tic (krip′tik) *adj.* **1.** having an ambiguous or hidden meaning; enigmatic: *a cryptic remark.* **2.** *Zoology.* serving to conceal; protective: *cryptic coloring.* Also, **cryp′ti·cal.** [Late Latin *crypticus* concealed, from Greek *kryptikos* obscuring, from *kryptos* hidden.] —**cryp′ti·cal·ly,** *adv.* —For Synonyms, see **vague.**

crypto- *combining form* hidden; secret: *cryptogram.* [Greek *kryptos.*]

cryp·to·gam (krip′tə gam′) *n.* a plant, as a fern, alga, fungus, or moss, that does not bear flowers or seeds. [Modern Latin *cryptogamia,* from Greek *kryptos* hidden + *gamos* marriage.]

cryp·to·gram (krip′tə gram′) *n.* a message written in cipher or code. [CRYPTO- + -GRAM[1].] —**cryp′to·gram′mic,** *adj.*

cryp·to·graph (krip′tə graf′) *n.* **1.** cryptogram. **2.** a system of cipher writing; cipher. [CRYPTO- + -GRAPH.]

cryp·tog·ra·phy (krip tog′rə fē) *n.* the art or science of writing and deciphering cryptograms. [CRYPTO- + -GRAPHY.] —**cryp·tog′ra·pher, cryp·tog′ra·phist,** *n.* —**cryp·to·graph·ic** (krip′tə graf′ik), *adj.*

crys·tal (kris′təl) *n.* **1.** rock crystal. **2.** a solid bounded by plane surfaces, whose atoms, molecules, or ions are arranged in an orderly and repeated pattern: *crystals of salt.* **3.a.** glass having a high degree of transparency and brilliance. **b.** drinking glasses, bowls, vases, or other objects made of this glass. **4.** a transparent covering over the face of a watch. Also, **watch glass. 5.** a crystalline substance, as quartz, galena, or silicon, that either acts as a semiconductor or displays special electrical properties, used esp. in radios and other communications devices. —*adj.* **1.** made of crystal: *a crystal goblet.* **2.** resembling crystal; clear; transparent: *crystal waters.* [Old French *cristal* rock crystal, from Latin *crystallum* ice, rock crystal (because it resembles ice), from Greek *krystallos.*]

crystal ball, a ball of transparent glass, crystal, or similar material supposed to reveal future or distant events when gazed into.

crystal detector, a solid-state electronic device that uses a crystal semiconductor to separate a radio or TV signal from its carrier wave.

crystal gazing, the act or practice of gazing into a crystal ball, supposedly to discover future events. —**crystal gazer.**

crystal lattice *Mineralogy.* lattice (def. 3).

crys·tal·line (kris′tə lin, -līn′, -lēn′) *adj.* **1.** consisting of crystal or crystals. **2.** having the structure of a crystal. **3.** resembling crystal; clear; pure: *a crystalline lake.*

crystalline lens, the lens of the eye in vertebrates.

crys·tal·lize (kris′tə līz′) *v.,* **-lized, -liz·ing.** —*v.t.* **1.** to cause to form crystals or become crystalline: *The chemist crystallized salt as part of the experiment.* **2.** to give a definite or fixed form to: *I crystallized my ideas before beginning to write.* **3.** to coat or cover with sugar. —*v.i.* **1.** to form into crystals; become crystalline. **2.** to assume a definite or fixed form: *Our suspicions crystallized into certainty.* —**crys′tal·liz′a·ble,** *adj.* —**crys′tal·li·za′tion,** *n.*

crys·tal·log·ra·phy (kris′tə log′rə fē) *n.* the science of the form, structure, and physical and chemical properties of crystals. [Greek *krystallos* ice, rock crystal + -GRAPHY.] —**crys′tal·log′ra·pher,** *n.* —**crys·tal·lo·graph·ic** (krist′ə lə graf′ik); *also,* **crys′tal·lo·graph′i·cal,** *adj.*

crys·tal·loid (kris′tə loid′) *n.* a substance, usually capable of crystallization, that, when dissolved in liquid, will diffuse readily through a membrane. —*adj. also,* **crys′tal·loi′dal.** resembling a crystal or a crystalloid. [Greek *krystalloeidēs* like ice, like crystal, from *krystallos* ice, rock crystal.]

crystal set, a radio receiver with a crystal detector rather than vacuum tubes or transistors.

Cs, the symbol for cesium.

CS 1. Christian Science. **2.** Civil Service.

CSC, Civil Service Commission.

CST, Central Standard Time.

ct. *pl.,* **cts.** cent.

Ct., Connecticut.

CT, the postal abbreviation for Connecticut.

cten·o·phore (ten′ə fôr′, tē′nə-) *n.* comb jelly. [Modern Latin *Ctenophora,* from Greek *kten-,* stem of *kteis* comb + *-phoros* bearing.]

CT scan, CAT scan.

Cu, the symbol for copper. [Late Latin *cuprum.* See COPPER.]

cu *also,* **cu.** cubic.

cub (kub) *n.* **1.** a young animal of certain species, as bears, foxes, wolves, lions, or tigers. **2.** an awkward, coarse, or inexperienced youth. **3.** a beginner or apprentice, esp. in the newspaper business. **4.** cub scout. [Of uncertain origin.]

cub·by·hole (kub′ē hōl′) *n.* a small, enclosed space, esp. one used to store or conceal something. Also, **cub′by.** [Obsolete English *cub* stall, shed (from Middle Dutch *cubbe*) + -Y[2] + HOLE.]

cube (kūb) *n.* **1.** a solid figure with six equal, square faces. **2.** something resembling this figure in shape: *a cube of sugar.* **3.** the product of a number or quantity and its square; third power of a number. The cube of 2 is 8, that is, $2^3 = 2 \times 2 \times 2 = 8.$ —*v.t.,* **cubed, cub·ing. 1.** to cut or form into cubes or cubelike shapes: *to cube potatoes.* **2.** to raise (a number or quantity) to the third power by multiplying it by its square. [Latin *cubus* solid square, die, cubic number, from Greek *kybos.*]

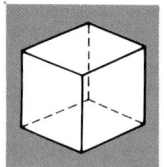
cube

cu·beb (kū′beb) *n.* **1.** the dried, unripe berry of a tropical plant, *Piper cubeba,* of the pepper family. It was formerly thought that smoking a cigarette made from these berries would relieve respiratory ailments. **2.** the climbing, woody evergreen plant bearing these berries, cultivated in Java and Sumatra. [Middle French *cubèbe* this berry, going back to Arabic *kabābah.*]

cube root, the number or quantity that, when multiplied by its square, produces a given number or quantity. The cube root of 8 is 2.

cu·bic (kū′bik) *adj.* **1.** of or having three dimensions, length, breadth, and width: *cubic inch, cubic centimeter.* **2.** relating to or involving the cube of a number; of the third power: *a cubic equation.* **3.** cubical.

cu·bi·cal (kū′bi kəl) *adj.* shaped like a cube. —**cu′bi·cal·ly,** *adv.*

cu·bi·cle (kū′bi kəl) *n.* a small room, compartment, or partitioned area. [Latin *cubiculum* bedroom, from *cubāre* to recline, sleep.]

cubic measure, a unit or system of units for measurement of volume. For Weights and Measures table, see **weight.**

cubism
a painting by Juan Gris

cub·ism (kū′biz əm) *n.* a movement in art, esp. painting, begun in the early twentieth century, characterized by abstract representations of objects using geometric forms and overlapping planes. —**cu′bist,** *adj., n.* —**cu·bis′tic,** *adj.*

a	at	e	end	o	hot	u	up	hw	white		about
ā	ape	ē	me	ō	old	ū	use	ng	song		taken
ä	far	i	it	ô	fork	ü	rule	th	thin	ə	pencil
âr	care	ī	ice	oi	oil	u̇	pull	th	this		lemon
		îr	pierce	ou	out	ûr	turn	zh	measure		circus

cu·bit (kū′bit) *n.* an ancient unit of measure based on the length of the forearm from the elbow to the fingertips. Its value varied from one area to another but usually ranged between 18 and 22 inches (46-56 centimeters). [Latin *cubitum* elbow, cubit.]

cu·boid (kū′boid) *adj.* shaped like a cube. Also, **cu·boi′dal.** —*n.* the outermost of the tarsal bones of the foot.

cub reporter, a young and inexperienced newspaper reporter.

cub scout, *also,* **Cub Scout.** a member of the Cub Scouts.

Cub Scouts, the junior division of the Boy Scouts, for boys from eight to ten years of age.

Cu·chu·lain (kü kul′in, -KHŭl′-) *n.* a legendary Irish hero of almost supernatural courage and strength who single-handedly defended Ulster against invaders.

cuck·old (kuk′əld) *n.* the husband of an unfaithful wife. —*v.t.* to make a cuckold of. [Old French *cucuault* a cuckold, from *cucu* cuckoo; because the female cuckoo frequently changes her mate. See CUCKOO.] —**cuck′old·ry,** *n.*

cuck·oo (kū′kü, kŭk′ü) *n., pl.* **-oos. 1.** any bird of the family Cuculidae, found in tropical and temperate regions throughout the world, esp. the European cuckoo, *Cuculus canorus,* which, like various other species of the family, lays its eggs in the nests of other birds. **2.** the call of the cuckoo or an imitation of it. —*adj. Informal.* crazy; silly. [Old French *cucu* this bird; imitative of the bird's call.]

cuckoo clock, a clock with a toy cuckoo that pops out on the hour, or at shorter intervals, and announces the time by a sound similar to a cuckoo's call.

cuckoo spit 1. the frothy secretion of spittlebugs, produced on plant stems and grasses, made by females to protect their eggs and by young nymphs as a covering. **2.** spittlebug.

cu cm *also,* **cu. cm.** cubic centimeter; cubic centimeters.

cu·cum·ber (kū′kum bər) *n.* **1.** the fleshy, green-skinned fruit of a climbing plant, *Cucumis sativus,* of the gourd family, usually eaten in salads or pickled. **2.** the plant itself. [Old French *coucombre* the plant, going back to Latin *cucumis.*]
 • **cool as a cucumber.** entirely self-possessed; calm.

cu·cur·bit (kū kûr′bit) *n.* any plant of the gourd family. [Middle English *cucurbite* gourd, from Latin *cucurbita,* probably related to biblical Hebrew *kikayon* (Jonah 4:6).]

cud (kud) *n.* partially digested, barely chewed food that cattle and other ruminants regurgitate from the first stomach back into the mouth for a thorough second chewing. [Old English *cudu.*]
 • **to chew the** (or **one's**) **cud.** to think about something; ruminate; meditate.

cud·dle (kud′əl) *v.,* **-dled, -dling.** —*v.i.* to lie close and snug; nestle; snuggle. —*v.t.* to hold (someone or something) closely in one's arms, esp. to make warm and snug; hug and caress fondly. —*n.* a warm or fond embrace. [Of uncertain origin.] —**cud′dly,** *adj.*

cud·dy (kud′ē) *n., pl.* **-dies. 1.** a small cabin on a boat or ship. **2.** a small room, closet, or cupboard. [Of uncertain origin.]

cudg·el (kuj′əl) *n.* a short, thick club. —*v.t.,* **-eled, -el·ing;** *also, British,* **-elled, -el·ling.** to beat with or as with a cudgel. [Old English *cycgel* a club.]
 • **to cudgel one's brains.** to think hard.
 • **to take up the cudgels (for).** to enter into a contest or controversy (in defense of someone).

cue¹ (kū) *n.* **1.** a signal, before or during a stage performance, for an actor or other participant to begin some action: *The slamming of a door was my cue to run on stage.* **2.** any similar signal to begin: *The candidate's appearance in the hall was the band's cue to play.* **3.** a guiding suggestion as to what to do or how to behave; hint: *Take a cue from me and stand when I do.* **4.** *Archaic.* a prescribed or necessary course of action. **5.** *Archaic.* a frame of mind; mood. —*v.t.,* **cued, cu·ing.** to give a cue to. [Earlier *q, Q,* abbreviation of Latin *quando* when or *qualis* in what way; originally, a guide to actors in written copies of plays to direct them when to come in.]

cue² (kū) *n.* **1.** a long, tapering stick used in billiards and pool. **2.** queue *(def. 2).* [Old French *coe, cue* tail, stalk ¹, going back to Latin *cōda,* form of *cauda* tail.]

cue ball, in billiards and pool, a white ball intended to be hit by the cue and in turn to strike and move one or more of the other balls.

cuff¹ (kuf) *n.* **1.** a band, fold, or similar piece at the bottom of a sleeve, usually at the wrist. **2.** a turned-up fold on the bottom of a trouser leg. **3.** a sheathlike part or fold on a glove that covers the wrist or lower arm. **4.** a detachable piece of material designed to be worn over the wrist end of a sleeve for decoration or protection. **5.** handcuff. [Middle English *cuffe* glove; possibly from Medieval Latin *cuphia* headdress.]
 • **off the cuff.** *Informal.* with little or no preparation; spontaneously.
 • **on the cuff.** *Slang.* on credit.

cuff² (kuf) *v.t.* to strike with or as with the side or back of the hand. —*n.* a blow, esp. with the side or back of the hand. [Possibly from Middle English *cuffe* glove (suggesting "a striking with a glove"). See CUFF¹.]

cuff link, one of a pair of linked buttons or ornamental buttons with a device for fastening the two sides of a French cuff of a shirt.

cu ft *also,* **cu. ft.** cubic foot; cubic feet.

cui bo·no (kwē′bō′nō, kī′) *Latin.* **1.** for whose benefit. **2.** to what use or good purpose.

cu in. *also,* **cu. in.** cubic inch; cubic inches.

cui·rass (kwi ras′) *n.* **1.** a piece of armor consisting of a breastplate and a back plate. **2.** the breastplate alone. [Middle French *cuirasse,* from *cuir* leather, from Latin *corium;* with reference to the earlier use of leather for breastplates.]

cui·ras·sier (kwîr′ə sîr′) *n.* a mounted soldier wearing a cuirass.

cuish (kwish) cuisse.

cui·sine (kwi zēn′) *n.* **1.** a manner or style of cooking or preparing food: *the cuisine of Spain.* **2.** prepared food, as that offered at a restaurant: *The cuisine here is excellent.* [French *cuisine,* from Late Latin *coquīna* kitchen, cookery, from Latin *coquere* to cook.]

Cuirass

cuisse (kwis) *also,* **cuish.** *n.* the part of a suit of plate armor used to protect the thigh. For illustration, see **armor.** [Old French (plural) *cuisseaux* armor for the thighs, going back to Latin *coxa* hip.]

cuirass

cul-de-sac (kul′də sak′, -sak′, kŭl′-) *n., pl.* **cul-de-sacs** or **culs-de-sac. 1.** a street or passage closed at one end; blind alley; dead end. **2.** a situation in which further progress or advance is impossible; impasse. **3.** a pouch or cavity in the body that is open only at one end. [French *cul-de-sac* blind alley; literally, bottom of a sack; *cul* bottom, from Latin *cūlus* backside; *sac* sack ¹, from Latin *saccus.* See SACK¹.]

cu·lex (kū′leks) *n., pl.* **-li·ces** (-lə sēz′). any mosquito of the genus *Culex,* esp. *C. pipiens,* the most common mosquito of North America and Europe. [Latin *culex* gnat.]

cu·li·nar·y (kū′lə ner′ē, kul′ə-) *adj.* of, relating to, or used in cooking or the kitchen: *culinary skills, culinary herbs.* [Latin *culīnārius* relating to a kitchen, from *culīna* kitchen.]

cull (kul) *v.t.* **1.** to pick out from a group; select: *We culled the oldest books from the library shelves.* **2.** to pick, as flowers; gather. **3.** to examine for quality and make a selection from; pick over: *to cull a basket of blueberries.* —*n.* something selected, esp. to be put aside as inferior. [Old French *coillir* to collect, from Latin *collīgere.*]

culm¹ (kulm) *n.* coal dust; refuse of coal; slack. [Middle English *culme, colme,* possibly from Old English *col* coal.]

culm² (kulm) *n.* the stem of certain grasses, usually hollow except at the nodes. [Latin *culmus* stalk ¹.]

cul·mi·nate (kul′mə nāt′) *v.,* **-nat·ed, -nat·ing.** —*v.i.* to reach the highest or most decisive point; come to a climax or final result (with *in*): *The border clashes culminated in the outbreak of war.* —*v.t.* to bring to a close or to the highest point; complete; climax: *The attorney culminated the summation with a call for justice.* [Late Latin *culmināˌtus,* past participle of *culmināre* to crown, exalt, from Latin *culmen* top, summit.]

cul·mi·na·tion (kul′mə nā′shən) *n.* the point at which something culminates; highest point; climax.

cu·lotte (kü′lot, kü lot′, kū-) *also,* **cu·lottes.** *n.* women's wide trousers that may be short or long, designed to look like a skirt. [French *culottes,* from *cul* bottom, backside, from Latin *cūlus* backside.]

cul·pa·ble (kul′pə bəl) *adj.* deserving blame or censure. [Old French *culpable,* from Latin *culpābilis,* from *culpāre* to blame.] —**cul′pa·bil′i·ty, cul′pa·ble·ness,** *n.* —**cul′pa·bly,** *adv.*

cul·prit (kul′prit) *n.* **1.** a person or thing guilty of some offense or crime: *The police caught the culprit in the bank robbery.* **2.** a person who has been charged with a crime. [Anglo-Norman *cul. pri(s)t,* short for *culpable—prist* guilty—ready: *culpable* (CUL-PABLE) + *prist* ready, going back to Latin *praestō* ready, at hand. In the law courts of medieval England, when the accused pleaded "not guilty," the prosecutor replied "guilty—ready" for "He is guilty; I am ready (to prove the accusation)."]

cult (kult) *n.* **1.** a particular form or system of religious worship. **2.** the enthusiastic devotion of a group to a particular person, thing, or idea. **3.** the object of such devotion. **4.** the followers of a cult; devoted adherents. [Late Latin *cultus* cultivation, reverence.] —**cult′ish,** *adj.* —**cult′ism,** *n.* —**cult′ist,** *n.*

cul·ti·gen (kul′ti jən) *n.* a cultivated plant or group of plants

whose wild ancestor is unknown, such as the pumpkin. [CUL-TI(VATED) + -GEN.]

cul·ti·va·ble (kul′tə və bəl) *adj.* capable of being cultivated. Also, **cul·ti·vat·a·ble** (kul′tə vā′tə bəl).

cul·ti·var (kul′tə vär′) *n.* a variety of plant produced and maintained by cultivation. [CULTI(VATED) + VAR(IETY).]

cul·ti·vate (kul′tə vāt′) *v.t.,* **-vat·ed, -vat·ing. 1.** to prepare and use (land) for growing crops; till. **2.** to promote or improve the growth of (a plant or crop) by labor or attention: *to cultivate roses.* **3.** to loosen the soil around (growing plants) in order to uproot the weeds, aerate the soil, and reduce water loss. **4.** to promote the growth or advancement of; foster; develop: *to cultivate good habits.* **5.** to improve, as by study, training, or exercise; refine: *to cultivate one's mind.* **6.** to seek familiarity with; court the acquaintance or friendship of: *The lobbyist cultivates politicians.* [Medieval Latin *cultivatus,* past participle of *cultivare* to till[2], going back to Latin *cultus,* past participle of *colere.*]

cul·ti·vat·ed (kul′tə vā′tid) *adj.* **1.** (of soil) prepared for growing crops. **2.** produced or improved by cultivation. ➡ distinguished from **wild. 3.** improved by education or training; cultured; refined.

cul·ti·va·tion (kul′tə vā′shən) *n.* **1.** the act of cultivating soil or plants. **2.** the improvement or development of something, as by study or training. **3.** culture; refinement.

cul·ti·va·tor (kul′tə vā′tər) *n.* **1.** a person who cultivates. **2.** a farm or garden implement for uprooting weeds and loosening the ground around growing plants.

cul·tur·al (kul′chər əl) *adj.* of, relating to, or tending to develop culture: *cultural activities.* —**cul′tur·al·ly,** *adv.*

cultural anthropology, the branch of anthropology that studies all aspects of human culture, including language, customs, and social structure. ➡ distinguished from **physical anthropology.**

cultural lag, the failure of one aspect of a culture to develop or progress as rapidly as another: *the cultural lag of ethics in relation to science and technology.* Also, **culture lag.**

cultural revolution 1. a change in the nature of a society and its culture. **2. Cultural Revolution.** a movement in China from 1966 to 1971 to restore the strict ideology and leadership of Mao Zedong.

cul·ture (kul′chər) *n.* **1.** the way of life of a group of people at a particular time, including their common language, social institutions, customs, beliefs, and arts: *the culture of the ancient Maya.* **2.** the shared beliefs, behavior, and manner of speech and dress of a particular subgroup: *teenage culture.* **3.** a knowledge of intellectual and artistic accomplishments and of what is considered to be fine in taste and manners. **4.** the improvement or refinement of the mind or body, as by education and training: *physical culture.* **5.** the cultivation of the soil. **6.a.** the development of microorganisms or living cells in a prepared medium favorable to their growth. **b.** a product of such development. **7.a.** the care and raising of plants or animals, esp. with an interest in improving the species. **b.** the result of this. —*v.t.,* **-tured, -tur·ing. 1.** to grow (microorganisms or living cells) in a prepared medium. **2.** to inoculate with a prepared culture: *to culture milk.* [Latin *cultūra* cultivation, care, agriculture.]

cul·tured (kul′chərd) *adj.* **1.** having or exhibiting culture; educated; refined: *a cultured person, cultured speech.* **2.** produced or raised by cultivation or under controlled, artificial conditions: *a cultured virus, a cultured pearl.*

culture lag, cultural lag.

culture medium, a substance or preparation in which microorganisms or living cells may be grown for research or testing.

culture shock, the confusion and uncertainty a person feels when first experiencing a different way of life or a foreign culture.

cul·tus (kul′təs) *n., pl.* **-tus·es** or **-ti** (-tī) a religious cult. [Latin *cultus.* See CULT.]

cul·ver·in (kul′vər in) *n.* **1.** a long, heavy cannon of the sixteenth and seventeenth centuries. **2.** a crude musket used in medieval times. [Old French *couleuvrine,* from *couleuvre* snake, going back to Latin *colubra;* with reference to the snakelike shape.]

cul·vert (kul′vərt) *n.* a drain or other structure that provides for the free flow of water under a sidewalk, road, or other surface passage.

culvert

cum·ber (kum′bər) *v.t.* **1.** to hinder the motion or action of; hamper: *to be cumbered by bulky clothing.* **2.** to weigh down; trouble; burden. [Possibly from Old French *combrer* to hinder, from Late Latin *cumbrus* barrier; of uncertain origin.]

cum·ber·some (kum′bər səm) *adj.* not easily managed or carried; clumsy; unwieldy. —**cum′ber·some·ly,** *adv.* —**cum′-ber·some·ness,** *n.*

cum·brous (kum′brəs) *adj.* cumbersome. —**cum′brous·ly,** *adv.* —**cum′brous·ness,** *n.*

cum·in (kum′in, kûm′-, kūm′in) *also,* **cummin.** *n.* **1.** the aromatic, hot-tasting, seedlike fruit of an herb, *Cuminum cyminum,* of the parsley family, used in curry powder and in flavoring such foods as cheese, meat, and pickles. **2.** the small, delicate herb itself, widely cultivated in southern Europe and India. [Old English *cymen* this herb, from Latin *cumīnum,* from Greek *kymīnon;* of Semitic origin.]

cum lau·de (kŭm lou′dē, kum lô′də) with honors or praise. ➡ used to signify graduation with honors from a college or university. [Modern Latin *cum laude.*]

cum·mer·bund (kum′ər bund′) *n.* a broad sash worn around the waist, esp. with a tuxedo. [Hindi *kamar-band* sash, loin band, going back to Persian *kamar* waist, loins + *band* band.]

cum·min (kum′in, kûm′-) cumin.

cum·quat (kum′kwot) kumquat.

cu·mu·late (*v.,* kū′myə lāt′; *adj.,* kū′myə lit, -lāt′) *v.t., v.i.,* **-lat·ed, -lat·ing.** accumulate. —*adj.* gathered or piled up; accumulated. [Latin *cumulātus,* past participle of *cumulāre* to heap.]

cu·mu·la·tion (kū′myə lā′shən) *n.* **1.** the act of accumulating. **2.** something accumulated; heap; mass.

cu·mu·la·tive (kū′myə lə tiv, -lā′tiv) *adj.* **1.** increasing in size, strength, or value, as by accumulation or successive additions: *the cumulative effect of pollution.* **2.** arising or gained from accumulation: *cumulative knowledge.* **3.** (of unpaid interest or dividends) accumulating and due to be paid in the future. —**cu′mu·la·tive·ly,** *adv.* —**cu′mu·la·tive·ness,** *n.*

cu·mu·lo·cir·rus (kū′myə lō sir′əs) *n., pl.* **-rus.** a small, filmy cumulus cloud. [CUMULUS + CIRRUS.]

cu·mu·lo·nim·bus (kū′myə lō nim′bəs) *n., pl.* **-bus.** a cumulus cloud billowing upward in the shape of a mountain or tower, often producing thunderstorms. For illustration, see **cloud.** [CU-MULUS + NIMBUS.]

cu·mu·lo·stra·tus (kū′myə lō strā′təs, -strat′əs) *n., pl.* **-stra·ti** (-strā′tī, -strat′ī) or **-stra·tus.** a cumulus cloud whose base has the stretched-out form of a stratus cloud. [CUMULUS + STRATUS.]

cu·mu·lous (kū′myə ləs) *adj.* (of clouds) of or resembling a cumulus.

cu·mu·lus (kū′myə ləs) *n., pl.* **-lus** or **-li** (-lī′). **1.** a dense, low-level cloud made up of rounded mounds or heaps billowing upward from a flat base. For illustration, see **cloud. 2.** a heap; pile; accumulation. [Latin *cumulus* heap.]

cu·ne·ate (kū′nē it, -āt′) *adj.* wedge-shaped; narrowly triangular, with the narrow part near the stem, as a leaf. [Latin *cuneātus,* from *cuneus* wedge.]

cu·ne·i·form (kū nē′ə fôrm′) *n.* **1.** a system of writing distinguished by wedge-shaped characters, used in ancient times by the Sumerians, Babylonians, Assyrians, and Persians. **2.** any of the wedge-shaped bones located next to the metatarsal bones of the foot. —*adj.* **1.** wedge-shaped: *cuneiform characters.* **2.** written in wedge-shaped characters: *a cuneiform text.* [Latin *cuneus* wedge + -FORM.]

cun·ner (kun′ər) *n.* a saltwater fish, *Tautogolabrus adspersus,* commonly found off the North Atlantic coast of the United States. [Of uncertain origin.]

cuneiform

cun·ning (kun′ing) *adj.* **1.** artfully shrewd or crafty; sly: *a cunning opponent.* **2.** characterized by skill or cleverness; ingenious. **3.** cute or appealing; charming: *a cunning toy.* —*n.* **1.** skill in deception; craftiness; slyness: *The plan for the fraudulent scheme showed a good deal of cunning.* **2.** skill in performance or workmanship; expertness. [Middle English *cunning* knowing, present participle of *cunnen* to know, from Old English *cunnan* to know, be able.] —**cun′ning·ly,** *adv.* —**cun′ning·ness,** *n.* —For Synonyms *(adj.),* see **sly.**

cup (kup) *n.* **1.** a small, open vessel, often with a handle, used chiefly for drinking. **2.** the amount contained in a cup; contents of a cup: *I'd like a cup of soup.* **3.** a unit of capacity equal to 8 fluid ounces or half a pint (0.24 liter). **4.** the part of a drinking vessel that contains the liquid. **5.** an ornamental cup-shaped vessel given

a	at	e	end	o	hot	u	up	hw	white		about
ā	ape	ē	me	ō	old	ū	use	ng	song		taken
ä	far	i	it	ô	fork	ü	rule	th	thin	ə	pencil
âr	care	ī	ice	oi	oil	ù	pull	th	this		lemon
		îr	pierce	ou	out	ûr	turn	zh	measure		circus

as a prize, esp. in sports. **6.** something resembling a cup in shape, as the calyx of a flower. **7.** a person's lot or fate; share: *bitter cup of humiliation.* **8.** *also,* **cups.** an intoxicating drink, or the habit of drinking: *The jolly prince . . . loving his cups and ease* (William Makepeace Thackeray, 1861). **9.a.** the chalice used in Communion. **b.** the consecrated wine used in Communion. **10.a.** the metal container in a hole on a golf course. **b.** the hole itself. —*v.t.,* **cupped, cup·ping. 1.** to shape like a cup: *She cupped her hands under the running water.* **2.** to place in or as in a cup: *He cupped his chin in his hand.* **3.** *Medicine.* to subject to cupping. [Old English *cuppe* drinking vessel, from Late Latin *cuppa,* form of Latin *cūpa* vat, cask.] —**cup′like′,** *adj.*

· **cup of tea.** *Informal.* a person or thing that is suitable or to one's taste or liking: *That pianist isn't exactly my cup of tea.*
· **in one's cups.** drunk.

cup·bear·er (kup′bâr′ər) *n.* a person who fills and serves cups of wine, as at a royal banquet.

cup·board (kub′ərd) *n.* **1.** a closet or cabinet with shelves, esp. for dishes or food. **2.** any small closet or cabinet.

cup·cake (kup′kāk′) *n.* a small cake baked in a cup-shaped container.

cu·pel (kū′pəl, kū pel′) *n.* a small, shallow, porous container, usually made of bone ash, used in assaying gold. —*v.t.,* **-peled** or **-pelled, -pel·ing** or **-pel·ling.** to assay or refine in a cupel. [French *coupelle,* from Medieval Latin *cupella,* diminutive of Latin *cūpa* vat, cask.]

cup·ful (kup′fūl′) *n., pl.* **-fuls.** the amount that a cup holds.

Cu·pid (kū′pid) *n.* **1.** in Roman mythology, the god of love and son of Venus, usually represented as a winged boy with bow and arrows. His Greek counterpart is Eros. **2.** *also,* **cupid.** any representation of a naked winged boy, esp. with bow and arrows, considered as a symbol of love. [Latin *Cupīdō* the god of love, personification of *cupīdō* desire, from *cupere* to desire.]

cu·pid·i·ty (kū pid′i tē) *n.* eager desire for possession, esp. of wealth; avarice; greed. [Latin *cupiditās* desire.]

cu·po·la (kū′pə lə) *n.* **1.** a small structure like a dome or tower rising above a roof. **2.** a rounded roof or ceiling; dome. [Italian *cupola* dome, from Late Latin *cūpula* little cask, diminutive of Latin *cūpa* vat, cask.]

cup·ping (kup′ing) *n.* a former method of drawing blood to the surface of the skin by applying a heated glass cup that creates a partial vacuum as it cools.

cu·pre·ous (kū′prē əs, kū′-) *adj.* of, containing, or resembling copper; coppery. [Late Latin *cupreus* of copper, from *cuprum* copper. See COPPER.]

cu·pric (kū′prik, kū′-) *adj.* of, relating to, or containing copper, esp. copper with a valence of 2: *cupric chloride.*

cu·prite (kū′prīt, kū′-) *n.* a red, lustrous, translucent mineral that is an important copper ore. Formula: Cu_2O [Late Latin *cuprum* copper + -ITE[1]. See COPPER.]

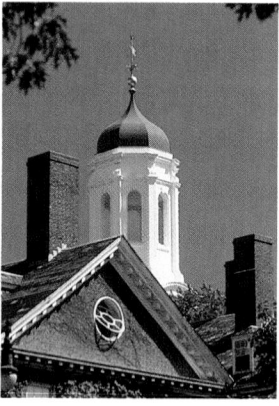

cupola

cu·prous (kū′prəs, kū′-) *adj.* of, relating to, or containing copper, esp. copper with a valence of 1: *cuprous oxide.*

cu·pule (kū′pūl) *n.* any of various cuplike structures, esp. at the base of certain fruit, as the acorn. [Middle English *cupule,* from Late Latin *cūpula.* See CUPOLA.]

cur (kûr) *n.* **1.** a worthless or bad-tempered dog; mongrel. **2.** a despicable person. [Possibly from Old Norse *kurr* grumbling; because of the growling of such a dog.]

cur. 1. currency. **2.** current.

cur·a·ble (kyūr′ə bəl) *adj.* capable of being cured. —**cur′a·bil′i·ty, cur′a·ble·ness,** *n.* —**cur′a·bly,** *adv.*

cu·ra·çao (kyûr′ə sō′, kûr′ə sou′) *also,* **cu·ra·çoa.** *n.* a sweet liqueur flavored with the dried peel of bitter oranges. [From *Curaçao;* because originally made with oranges from Curaçao, an island in the Caribbean.]

cu·ra·cy (kyūr′ə sē) *n., pl.* **-cies.** the position, duties, or term of office of a curate.

cu·ra·re (kyū rär′ē) *n.* any of various poisons obtained as a dark brown resinous extract from certain South American plants, used by natives as an arrow poison, formerly used in medicine as a muscle relaxant. [Spanish *curare;* of Carib origin.]

cu·ras·sow (kyûr′ə sō′, kyū ras′ō) *n.* any of several large, arboreal, turkeylike birds, family Cracidae, native to mountainous

regions of South and Central America, having a crest of stiff, curled feathers and a long tail. Length: 20-40 inches (51-102 centimeters). [Form of *Curaçao,* Caribbean island where the bird was first found.]

cu·rate (kyûr′it) *n.* a member of the clergy who assists the pastor, rector, or vicar of a parish. [Medieval Latin *curatus* one having a spiritual charge, priest, going back to Latin *cūra* care.]

cur·a·tive (kyûr′ə tiv) *adj.* **1.** having the power to cure or remedy: *curative treatment, curative measures.* **2.** of, relating to, or used in the cure of disease: *curative medicine.* —*n.* something that cures; remedy.

cu·ra·tor (kyū rā′tər, kyûr′ā-) *n.* a person in charge of all or part of the collection or exhibits at a museum, art gallery, zoo, or the like. [Latin *cūrātor* guardian, overseer.] —**cu·ra·to·ri·al** (kyûr′ə tôr′ē əl), *adj.* —**cu·ra′tor·ship′,** *n.*

curb (kûrb) *n.* **1.** *also, British,* **kerb.** a border of concrete, stone, or other material along the edge of a street or sidewalk. **2.** something that restrains or controls; check: *The budget committee recommended a curb on spending.* **3.** a chain or strap fastened to a horse's bit and passed under its lower jaw, used to check the horse when the reins are pulled. **4.** an enclosing, confining, or reinforcing framework or border, as that around the top of a well. —*v.t.* **1.** to restrain or control with or as with a curb; check: *to curb a horse, to curb one's appetite.* **2.** to provide with a curb. **3.** to walk (a dog) along the edge of a street rather than on the sidewalk for the elimination of its waste matter. [Old French *courber* to bend, from Latin *curvāre.*]

curb bit, a horse's bit designed so that a slight pull on the reins will exert great pressure on the horse's tongue or jaw, causing the horse to stop quickly.

curb·ing (kûr′bing) *n.* material forming a curb or used for making one.

curb market, a market for trading in securities not listed on an organized stock exchange; over-the-counter market. Also, **curb exchange.** [CURB + MARKET; because it was originally conducted on the sidewalk or street.]

curb roof, a roof consisting of two slopes on each side, the lower one steeper than the upper.

curb·stone (kûrb′stōn′) *also, British,* **kerbstone.** *n.* a stone or row of stones along the edge of a street or sidewalk.

cur·cu·li·o (kûr kū′lē ō′) *n., pl.* **-li·os.** any of various weevils of Eurasia and North America that cause damage to fruit and nuts. [Latin *curcūliō* weevil.]

curd (kûrd) *n.* **1.** *also,* **curds.** the coagulated portion of milk, produced by natural or artificial souring, used in making cheese. ➡ distinguished from **whey. 2.** any substance resembling this. —*v.t., v.i.* to form into or become curd. [Of uncertain origin.]

cur·dle (kûr′dəl) *v.,* **-dled, -dling.** —*v.t.* to change into curd; coagulate; thicken. —*v.i.* to become curd; coagulate; thicken. [CURD + -LE.]

· **to make one's blood curdle.** to fill (one) with horror or fear.

cure (kyūr) *n.* **1.** restoration to a healthy or sound condition; recovery. **2.** something that restores health; remedy. **3.** a particular method or course of remedial or medicinal treatment. **4.** something that corrects an undesirable condition or situation. —*v.,* **cured, cur·ing.** —*v.t.* **1.** to restore to a healthy or sound condition; make well. **2.** to get rid of; remedy: *to cure a sore throat.* **3.** to rid of something that is harmful or undesirable: *She could never cure him of his habit of always being late.* **4.** to prepare for preservation or use, as by drying, smoking, or chemically treating: *to cure fish, to cure hay, to cure hides.* —*v.i.* **1.** to bring about a cure. **2.** to be or become preserved or processed by curing: *The meat was hung up in the smokehouse to cure.* [Old French *curer* to take care of, heal, from Latin *cūrāre.*] —**cur′er,** *n.*

Synonyms **Cure, heal,** and **remedy** mean to correct or eliminate an unhealthy or troublesome condition. **Cure** is used in disease or diseaselike conditions: *to cure hepatitis, to cure inflation.* **Heal** is used more of injuries, with the suggestion of returning the sufferer to wholeness: *to heal a broken arm, to heal racial divisions.* **Remedy** implies a particular treatment: *To remedy your itch, try this ointment. My friends tried to remedy my bad mood with jokes.*

cu·ré (kyū rā′, kyûr′ā; *French* kY rā′) *n. French.* a parish priest, esp. in France. [French *curé,* from Medieval Latin *curatus.* See CURATE.]

cure-all (kyûr′ôl′) *n.* something that supposedly will cure all diseases or evils; panacea.

cu·ret·tage (kyûr′i täzh′, kyū ret′ij) *n.* the surgical procedure of scraping the inside of a body cavity, as the uterus. [French *curetage,* from *curette* curet (from *curer* to cleanse, heal, from Latin *cūrāre*) + *-age* (see -AGE).]

cur·few (kûr′fū) *n.* **1.** an order or rule requiring certain persons to be indoors or at home before a fixed time, esp. at night. **2.a.** the hour at which such an order or rule becomes effective. **b.** the

period during which it is in effect. **3.a.** the sounding of a bell or other signal at evening time. **b.** the bell or other signal so used. [Anglo-Norman *coeverfu* signal for putting out or covering fires at night (a medieval practice); literally, cover fire, from Old French *covrir* to cover (from Latin *cooperīre*) + *feu* fire (going back to Latin *focus* hearth).]

cu·ri·a (kyŭr′ē ə) *n., pl.* **cu·ri·ae** (kyŭr′ē ē′). **1.** one of the thirty divisions into which the three ancient Roman tribes were divided. **2.** a building where such a division met. **3.** *also,* **Curia.** Curia Romana. **4. Curia.** the building where the senate of ancient Rome met. **5.** a medieval council, assembly, or court of justice. [Latin *cūria* division of the Roman tribes, Roman senate house.]

Cu·ri·a Ro·ma·na (kyŭr′ē ə rō mä′nə) the body of officials who assist the pope in the government of the Roman Catholic Church.

cu·rie (kyŭr′ē) *n.* a unit of measurement of radioactivity, equal to 3.70 × 10^{10} disintegrations per second. [From Marie *Curie*, 1867-1934, Polish-French chemist and physicist.]

cu·ri·o (kyŭr′ē ō′) *n., pl.* **cu·ri·os.** an object valued as a curiosity or for its quaintness: *I collect old china figurines and other curios.* [Short for CURIOSITY.]

cu·ri·os·i·ty (kyŭr′ē os′i tē) *n., pl.* **-ties.** **1.** the desire for knowledge of something, esp. of something new, strange, or unknown. **2.** a person or thing that is strange, rare, or unusual and arouses interest. [Latin *cūriōsitās* desire of knowledge.]

cu·ri·ous (kyŭr′ē əs) *adj.* **1.** eager to know or learn. **2.** arousing interest because of rarity or strangeness; unusual: *There were curious markings on the walls of the cave.* **3.** showing too much interest in the affairs of others; nosy. [Latin *cūriōsus* careful, inquisitive, from *cūra* care.] —**cu′ri·ous·ly,** *adv.* —**cu′ri·ous·ness,** *n.*

cu·ri·um (kyŭr′ē əm) *n.* a radioactive element first produced artificially by bombardment of plutonium 239 with helium ions. Symbol: **Cm** For tables, see **element.** [Modern Latin *curium*, from Pierre, 1859-1906, and Marie, 1867-1934, *Curie*, French physicists and chemists.]

curl (kûrl) *v.t.* **1.** to twist or form into ringlets or coils, as the hair. **2.** to bend or form into a curved or spiral shape: *to curl one's lips in disdain.* —*v.i.* **1.** to take the form of ringlets or coils. **2.** to assume a curved or spiral shape. **3.** to play the game of curling. —*n.* **1.** a coiled or curved lock of hair; ringlet. **2.** something having a curved or spiral shape. **3.** the act of curling or the state of being curled. [Possibly from Middle Dutch *krul* curly.]

·**to curl up.** to sit or lie down in a comfortable position, as with the back curved and the legs drawn up.

curl·er (kûr′lər) *n.* **1.** a person or thing that curls, esp. a device on which hair is wound to make it curl. **2.** a person who plays the game of curling.

cur·lew (kûr′lŭ) *n.* any of various migratory wading birds, family Scolopacidae, native to arctic and temperate regions, having long legs, a long, slender bill that curves downward, and, usually, brown plumage. [Old French *courlieu;* imitative of the bird's call.]

curl·i·cue (kûr′li kū′) *also,* **curlycue.** *n.* a fancy curve, twist, or flourish, as in handwriting. [CURLY + CUE².]

curl·ing (kûr′lĭng) *n.* a game played on the ice, in which curling stones are slid toward a circular target, the object being to come as close as possible to the target.

curlew

curling iron, a metal rod or other device that is heated and used for curling the hair.

curling stone, a large, rounded block of granite or other heavy material, having a handle on one side, used in the game of curling.

curl·pa·per (kûrl′pā′pər) *n.* a strip of paper designed to hold a lock of hair that is being curled.

curl·y (kûr′lē) *adj.* **curl·i·er, curl·i·est. 1.** tending to curl. **2.** having curls. —**curl′i·ness,** *n.*

curl·y·cue (kûr′li kū′) curlicue.

cur·mudg·eon (kər muj′ən) *n.* a surly, bad-tempered, or stingy person, esp. an old man. [Of uncertain origin.]

cur·rant (kûr′ənt, kur′-) *n.* **1.a.** a tart, edible berry of any of several shrubs, genus *Ribes*, used esp. for making jelly, syrup, and wine. **b.** the shrub on which this berry grows. **2.** a small, seedless raisin used esp. in baked goods. [Anglo-Norman *(raisin de) Corauntz* (raisin of) Corinth, going back to Greek *Korinthos* Corinth, from which such raisins were first exported.]

cur·ren·cy (kûr′ən sē, kur′-) *n., pl.* **-cies. 1.** the current medium of exchange in a country; money in actual use. **2.** general use or acceptance; prevalence: *That custom has little currency in this*

country. **3.** a passing from person to person; circulation: *The rumor gained wide currency.*

cur·rent (kûr′ənt, kur′-) *adj.* **1.a.** of or belonging to the present time; in progress: *current fashions, the current year.* **b.** most recent; newest: *the current issue of a magazine.* **2.** generally used or accepted; prevalent: *a current practice.* **3.** passing from person to person; widely circulated: *current rumors.* —*n.* **1.** a continuous movement, as of water; flow: *a river with a rapid current.* **2.** a portion of a body of water or of air flowing continuously in a definite direction: *an ocean current.* **3.** a noticeable course, movement, or tendency; trend: *one current of modern political thought.* **4.a.** the flow of electricity in an electric circuit or through any conducting body or medium. **b.** the rate of such a flow, measured in amperes. [Old French *corant*, present participle of *courre*, to run, from Latin *currere*.] —**cur′rent·ly,** *adv.* —**cur′rent·ness,** *n.* —For Synonyms *(adj.),* see **modern.**

current density, the amount of electric current passing through a given area in a conductor.

cur·ri·cle (kûr′i kəl) *n.* an open, two-wheeled carriage drawn by two horses. [Latin *curriculum* course, racecourse, chariot.]

cur·ric·u·lar (kə rik′yə lər) *adj.* of or relating to a curriculum.

cur·ric·u·lum (kə rik′yə ləm) *n., pl.* **-la** (-lə) or **-lums. 1.** all the courses of study offered at a school, college, or university. **2.** a group or sequence of courses leading to a particular degree, certificate, or license. [Latin *curriculum* course, racecourse, chariot; with reference to a course of study.]

curriculum vi·tae (vī′tē, vē′tī) *pl.* **curricula vitae.** a brief summary of one's educational or professional background, often used in applying for a job; résumé. [Latin *curriculum vitae* course of life.]

cur·rish (kûr′ish) *adj.* like a cur; bad-tempered. —**cur′rish·ly,** *adv.* —**cur′rish·ness,** *n.*

cur·ry¹ (kûr′ē, kur′ē) *v.t.,* **-ried, -ry·ing. 1.** to rub down and clean (a horse or other animal) with a brush or currycomb. **2.** to treat (hides or leather) with grease, oil, or wax. [Middle English *curraien*, from Anglo-Norman *curreier* to prepare, arrange, from Old French *correier*, going back to Latin *cum* with, together + an unrecorded German word.] —**cur′ri·er,** *n.*

·**to curry favor.** to try to win favor, as by flattery; attempt to ingratiate oneself: *to curry favor with those in power.*

cur·ry² (kûr′ē, kur′ē) *n., pl.* **-ries. 1.** a condiment prepared from various dried, ground spices. Also, **curry powder. 2.** a sauce or food flavored with this. —*v.t.,* **-ried, -ry·ing.** to flavor or prepare with curry. [Tamil *kari* sauce.]

cur·ry·comb (kûr′ē kōm′, kur′-) *n.* a brush with rows of teeth rather than bristles for currying a horse or similar animal. —*v.t.* to rub down or groom with a currycomb.

curse (kûrs) *n.* **1.** an invoking of evil or harm on someone or something. **2.** the evil or harm invoked. **3.a.** a word or words used in making such an invocation. **b.** a word or words used in swearing. **4.** something that brings or causes evil or harm. **5.** something cursed. —*v.,* **cursed** or **curst, curs·ing.** —*v.t.* **1.** to call down evil or harm upon; damn. **2.** to use profane language against; swear at. **3.** to cause evil, harm, or suffering to; torment; afflict: *to be cursed with poor health.* —*v.i.* to utter curses; swear. [Old English *curs* invocation of harm.]

curs·ed (kûr′sid, kûrst) *adj. also,* **curst** (kûrst). **1.** deserving a curse; detestable; abominable. **2.** under a curse; damned. —**curs′ed·ly,** *adv.* —**curs′ed·ness,** *n.*

cur·sive (kûr′siv) *adj.* (of writing or type) having the letters joined together with flowing strokes. —*n.* **1.** a cursive letter or character. **2.** *Printing.* a type resembling cursive handwriting. [Medieval Latin *cursivus* running, from Latin *cursus*, past participle of *currere* to run.] —**cur′sive·ly,** *adv.*

cur·sor (kûr′sər) *n.* the movable square, bar, or other symbol on a computer screen that indicates where the operator is working or where the next keyboarded character will appear. [Latin *cursor* runner.]

cur·so·ri·al (kûr sôr′ē əl) *adj.* **1.** adapted for running. **2.** having limbs adapted for running: *The ostrich is a cursorial bird.*

cur·so·ry (kûr′sə rē) *adj.* not thorough; rapid and superficial; hasty: *to give a letter a cursory reading.* [Late Latin *cursōrius* hasty, from Latin *cursor* runner.] —**cur′so·ri·ly,** *adv.* —**cur′so·ri·ness,** *n.*

curst (kûrst) *v.* a past tense and past participle of **curse.** —*adj.* cursed.

curt (kûrt) *adj.* rudely brief or abrupt: *a curt nod, a curt greeting.*

a	at	e	end	o	hot	u	up	hw	white		about
ā	ape	ē	me	ō	old	ū	use	ng	song		taken
ä	far	i	it	ô	fork	ü	rule	th	thin	ə	pencil
âr	care	ī	ice	oi	oil	ů	pull	th	this		lemon
		îr	pierce	ou	out	ûr	turn	zh	measure		circus

[Latin *curtus* cut short.] —**curt′ly,** *adv.* —**curt′ness,** *n.* —For Synonyms, see **abrupt.**

cur·tail (kər tāl′) *v.t.* to cut short or cut down; shorten in duration or extent; reduce: *to curtail a speech, to curtail expenses.* [Modification (influenced by TAIL) of obsolete *curtal* horse with a docked tail, from Middle French *courtault,* from *court* short, from Latin *curtus* cut short.] —**cur·tail′ment,** *n.*

cur·tain (kûr′tin) *n.* **1.** a piece or pieces of cloth or other material hung as a decoration or screen, as at a window. **2.** *Theater.* **a.** the screen used to conceal the major part of the stage from the view of the audience. **b.** the beginning or end of a performance, act, or scene, usually indicated by opening or closing the curtain. **3.** anything that screens or covers like a curtain: *a curtain of fog.* **4.a.** that part of a wall which connects two bastions, towers, or similar structures in a fortification. **b.** curtain wall. **5. curtains.** *Slang.* death; disaster. —*v.t.* to provide, shut off, or cover with or as with a curtain. [Old French *curtine* a cloth hanging, as for a bed, from Late Latin *cortīna* small enclosure, a hanging around a small enclosure, from Latin *cōrs* enclosure.]

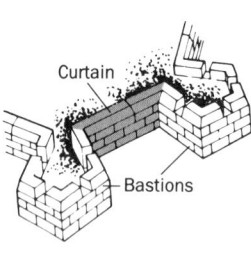

Curtain

Bastions

curtain *(def. 4a)*

curtain call, the reappearance of a performer or performers on the stage to acknowledge the applause of the audience, usually at the end of a performance.

curtain raiser 1. a short entertainment given before the main performance, as a short play before a full-length one. **2.** any introductory event.

curtain wall, an exterior, enclosing, nonbearing wall, as of a skyscraper, often consisting largely of glass.

cur·te·sy (kûr′tə sē) *n., pl.* -**sies.** in common law, the right of a husband to hold for life the real property left by his dead wife, provided they have had children capable of inheriting. Curtesy has been abolished or altered in most states. [Form of COURTESY.]

curt·sy (kûrt′sē) *also,* **curt·sey.** *n., pl.* -**sies.** a gesture of respect or greeting made by women and girls, by bending the knees and lowering the body slightly. —*v.i.* -**sied, -sy·ing.** to make a curtsy. [Form of COURTESY.]

cu·rule chair (kyûr′ül) the official seat reserved for the highest magistrates of ancient Rome, originally resembling a folding stool with curved legs. [Latin *curūlis* relating to a chariot or to the Roman official seat (which originally was placed on a chariot), from *currus* chariot.]

cur·va·ceous (kûr vā′shəs) *adj.* (of a woman) having a full figure; shapely.

cur·va·ture (kûr′və chər) *n.* **1.** the act of curving or the state or condition of being curved. **2.** something curved. **3.** the amount of curving, esp. the rate of deviation of an arc from a plane or a straight line. **4.** abnormal curving, as of a bodily structure or part, esp. the spine.

curule chair

curve (kûrv) *n.* **1.** a continuously bent line having no straight parts or angles, as the arc of a circle. **2.** something having the shape of a curve: *a curve in the road.* **3.** a baseball or softball pitched so that it veers from a straight path. **4.** *Mathematics.* a set of points whose coordinates are determined by an equation: *A sine curve is the graph of $y = \sin x$.* **5.** *Statistics.* any line that is plotted from coordinates and represents the changing value of a given variable: *population curve, production curve.* —*v.,* **curved, curv·ing.** —*v.i.* **1.** to have or assume the form of a curve: *The road curves just before you reach my house.* **2.** to move in the course of a curve: *The ball curved to the right.* —*v.t.* to cause to curve. [Latin *curvus* bent, crooked.]

cur·vet (*n.,* kûr′vit; *v.,* kər vet′, kûr′vit) *n.* a leap made by a horse in which first the forelegs and then the hind legs are raised so that all four legs are briefly off the ground at the same time. —*v.,* -**vet·ted** or -**vet·ed,** -**vet·ting** or -**vet·ing.** —*v.i.* **1.** to make a curvet. **2.** to leap about; prance; frisk. —*v.t.* to cause to curvet. [Italian *corvetta* leap, diminutive of *corvo* curve, going back to Latin *curvus* bent, crooked.]

cur·vi·lin·e·ar (kûr′vi lin′ē ər) *adj.* consisting of or enclosed by a curved line or lines. Also, **cur′vi·lin′e·al.**

cush·ion (kŭsh′ən) *n.* **1.** a bag or casing filled with soft or resilient material, used for resting, sitting, or kneeling on. **2.** something resembling a cushion in shape or function, esp. a device used to absorb shock, as padding or a layer of air. **3.** anything that lessens severity or protects against harm, loss, or need;

buffer: *to diversify financial investments as a cushion against possible losses.* **4.** the resilient padding around the inside rim of a billiard table. —*v.t.* **1.** to absorb the shock or effect of: *The pile of leaves cushioned his fall.* **2.** to place or seat on or as on a cushion; support: *She cushioned the baby's head in her lap.* **3.** to furnish with a cushion or cushions. [Old French *coissin, coussin* cushion (for sitting on), going back to Latin *coxa* hip (which a cushion supports).]

Cush·it·ic (kū shit′ik) *also,* **Kushitic.** *n.* a group of Hamitic languages, including Somali, spoken chiefly in Ethiopia and eastern Africa.

cush·y (kŭsh′ē) *adj.,* **cush·i·er, cush·i·est.** *Slang.* not difficult; comfortable; easy: *a nice, cushy job.* [Modification of Hindi *khush* pleasant, from Persian *khūsh.*]

cusk (kusk) *n., pl.* **cusks** or **cusk. 1.** a saltwater food fish, *Brosme brosme,* related to the cod and found in the northern Atlantic. **2.** burbot. [Possibly modification of earlier *tusk* the saltwater food fish; of Scandinavian origin.]

cusp (kusp) *n.* **1.** a point or pointed end; apex; peak. **2.** either point of a crescent moon. **3.** a rounded or pointed part on the grinding surface or crown of a tooth. [Latin *cuspis* point.]

cus·pid (kus′pid) *n.* a canine tooth. [Latin *cuspid-,* stem of *cuspis* point.]

cus·pi·dal (kus′pi dəl) *adj.* **1.** of or relating to a cusp. **2.** ending in a point.

cus·pi·date (kus′pi dāt′) *adj.* having a cusp or cusps; ending in a point.

cus·pi·dor (kus′pi dôr′) *n.* spittoon. [Portuguese *cuspidouro* place for spitting, from *cuspir* to spit, going back to Latin *cōnspuere* to spit on.]

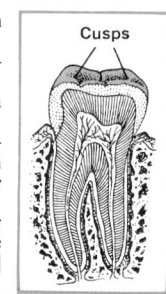

Cusps

cuss (kus) *Informal. v.t., v.i.* to swear or swear at; curse. —*n.* **1.** an odd or perverse person or animal. **2.** curse. [Form of CURSE.]

cuss·ed (kus′id) *adj. Informal.* **1.** cursed. **2.** stubborn; perverse; mean. —**cuss′ed·ness,** *n.*

cus·tard (kus′tərd) *n.* a sweet dessert made from eggs, sugar, milk, and flavoring, either baked or boiled. [Middle English *crustade* pie made with crust, from Old French *croustade,* going back to Latin *crusta* rind, shell, crust.]

custard apple 1. the fleshy, edible fruit of any of a large group of shrubs and small trees, genus *Annona,* esp. of *A. cherimola,* grown in tropical and subtropical regions of the Americas. **2.** the shrub or tree bearing this fruit. **3.** any of several other tropical American trees or shrubs cultivated for their fruits.

cus·to·di·al (kə stō′dē əl) *adj.* of or relating to custody or custodians.

cus·to·di·an (kə stō′dē ən) *n.* **1.** a person who has care or custody of another person or thing; guardian; keeper. **2.** a person responsible for the maintenance and care of a building; janitor. —**cus·to′di·an·ship′,** *n.*

cus·to·dy (kus′tə dē) *n., pl.* -**dies. 1.** the act or right of supervising and caring for another: *The grandparents gained custody of their grandchild after the parents died.* **2.** the state of being kept by or in the charge of officers of the law: *to take a thief into custody.* [Latin *custōdia* watching, guard.]

cus·tom (kus′təm) *n.* **1.** an established social habit or practice of a group, transmitted from one generation to another; convention. **2.** a usual manner of doing or acting; habitual practice; habit: *We went to the park on Sunday, as is our custom.* **3.** habitual patronage of a business establishment. **4. customs. a.** taxes or duties levied by a government on goods imported from foreign countries. **b.** the governmental agency responsible for inspecting imported goods and for assessing and collecting duties on them. **5.** *Law.* an established usage or practice of a group that has acquired the force of law. **6.** a tax, rent, tribute, or service regularly given to a feudal lord by his tenants. —*adj.* **1.** dealing or specializing in made-to-order goods: *a custom tailor.* **2.** custom-made: *a custom suit.* [Old French *custume* usage, going back to Latin *cōnsuētūdō* usage, habit. Doublet of COSTUME.] —For Synonyms *(n.),* see **habit.**

cus·tom·ar·y (kus′tə mer′ē) *adj.* based on custom; usual; habitual. —**cus′tom·ar′i·ly,** *adv.* —**cus′tom·ar′i·ness,** *n.*

cus·tom·built (kus′təm bilt′) *adj.* built to individual specifications.

cus·tom·er (kus′tə mər) *n.* **1.** a person who is shopping or who buys, esp. one who deals regularly at a given establishment. **2.** *Informal.* anyone with whom a person has to deal: *a tough customer.*

cus·tom·house (kus′təm hous′) *also,* **cus·toms·house.** *n., pl.* -**hous·es** (-hou′ziz). a government office or building where customs are collected and where ships or their cargoes are cleared.

cus·tom·ize (kus′tə mīz′) *v.t.,* **-ized, -iz·ing.** to build or alter according to individual requirements: *to customize a car.* [CUS-TOM custom-made + -IZE.]

cus·tom-made (kus′təm mād′) *adj.* made to individual order.

cut (kut) *v.,* **cut, cut·ting.** —*v.t.* **1.** to separate or divide into parts with a sharp-edged instrument; sever; slice: *He cut the meat into cubes.* **2.** to penetrate, slit, or wound with a sharp edge; make an incision in; pierce (often with *open*): *I cut my arm on the jagged glass. She cut the bag of dog food open.* **3.** to remove or detach with or as with a sharp-edged instrument (often with *out* or *off*): *to cut branches from a tree, to cut out pictures from a magazine.* **4.** to make shorter by removing a portion with a sharp-edged instrument; trim; clip: *to cut one's nails, to cut one's hair.* **5.** to cause to fall by sawing; hew; fell (often with *down*): *to cut timber, to cut down a tree.* **6.** to make, form, or shape with or as with a sharp-edged instrument: *to cut gems, to cut a pattern for a dress.* **7.** to reduce in amount; make smaller or less; decrease (often with *down*): *to cut prices, to cut expenses down.* **8.** to take out; omit or eliminate; remove: *The actor's part was cut from the play. The coach cut two players from the team.* **9.** to put an end to; discontinue or stop: *The driver cut the motor and removed the key. Let's cut the nonsense.* **10.** to shorten, abridge, or edit by removing parts: *The editor cut the lengthy article.* **11.** to go across or through; intersect: *This road cuts the field at one corner.* **12.** to cause to break down; dissolve: *a detergent that cuts grease.* **13.** to reduce the concentration or strength of; weaken; dilute: *to cut wine with water.* **14.** to cause emotional pain or distress to; hurt the feelings of: *Her sarcasm cut me deeply.* **15.** to hit or strike sharply, as with a whip. **16.** to perform; present: *to cut a caper.* **17.** to break (a deck of cards) at random into two or more parts and put them back together in a different order, as before dealing. **18.** to grow (a tooth or teeth) through the gum: *The baby is cutting her first tooth.* **19.a.** to make (a song popular): *The band cut the hit song last year.* **b.** to make (a recording): *to cut an album.* **20.a.** in television or motion pictures, to suspend or end the filming of (a scene). **b.** to edit (film) by removing or rearranging scenes. **21.** *Informal.* to be absent from: *to cut a class.* **22.** *Informal.* to pretend not to recognize or be acquainted with; snub: *He cut us in the street without a word.* —*v.i.* **1.** to act or function as a sharp-edged instrument; make an incision: *This saw cuts well.* **2.** to use a sharp-edged instrument: *The barber cut with a deft hand.* **3.** to be separated into parts with a sharp-edged instrument: *Silk cuts easily.* **4.** to go, proceed, or move by the shortest or most direct route: *The child cut through the playground on the way home. The tugboat cut across the harbor.* **5.** to cross or pass obliquely or diagonally: *The road cuts through the swamp.* **6.** to change direction sharply or suddenly; veer; swerve: *The driver cut to the right to avoid hitting the dog.* **7.** to penetrate like a sharp-edged instrument: *The bitter wind cut through my jacket. This soap cuts through grease.* **8.** to divide a deck of cards, as before dealing. **9.** to shift, esp. abruptly or suddenly, from one shot or scene to another in television or motion pictures: *The cameras cut to the front of the house.* —*n.* **1.** a slice, blow, or stroke with or as with a sharp-edged instrument: *to sever a rope with one cut of a knife.* **2.** an opening or wound made by such a movement: *I bandaged the cut on my arm.* **3.** a piece or part cut or cut off: *a cut of tobacco, a fine cut of beef.* **4.** a reduction in amount; decrease: *The workers took a cut in salary.* **5.** the manner or shape in which a thing is cut; style; fashion: *The cut of that jacket becomes you.* **6.** the omission or removal of a part: *The editor made several cuts in the manuscript.* **7.** a remark or action that hurts the feelings. **8.** a cut of a deck of cards. **9.** a passage or channel made by cutting, digging, or blasting. **10.** a stroke or swing at the ball, as in baseball. **11.** *Informal.* an absence: *You're allowed four cuts per semester.* **12.** *Informal.* a percentage, commission, or share, as of profits or loot: *The sales representative got a 7% cut on all sales.* **13.** *Printing.* **a.** an engraved block or plate from which a picture is printed. **b.** the picture so printed. **14.** a shortcut: *We took a cut through the woods to save time.* —*adj.* **1.** that has been cut: *a cut finger, freshly cut flowers.* **2.** formed, shaped, or finished by or as by cutting: *cut diamonds, a face with finely cut features.* [Middle English *cutten, kitten* to make an incision into, sever, trim, reap, divide; of uncertain origin.]

· **a cut above.** a degree better than; superior to: *The politician's honesty showed she was a cut above the others.*

· **cut and dried. a.** arranged or settled beforehand; not open to discussion: *a cut and dried matter.* **b.** lacking freshness or spontaneity; dull: *a cut and dried speech, a cut and dried meeting.*

· **to cut back. a.** to prune (a plant) by removing the ends of branches or shoots. **b.** in football, to reverse or change direction suddenly. **c.** to reduce in size or amount; decrease: *to cut back staff.*

· **to cut down.** to strike or kill with or as with a sword: *The young soldier was cut down in the prime of his life.*

· **to cut in. a.** to break or move into suddenly or out of turn: *It is rude to cut in at the head of a line.* **b.** to interrupt: *The announcer cut in with a news bulletin.* **c.** to interrupt a dancing couple in order to take the place of one partner. **d.** *Slang.* to include (someone) in the distribution of profits or loot: *The burglars cut in the bank guard who had helped them.*

· **to cut loose.** *Informal.* to act or speak without restraint or inhibition.

· **to cut off. a.** to separate, as by cutting; isolate: *The explorers were cut off from civilization for days.* **b.** to stop the passage or movement of; interrupt or intercept: *The naval blockade cut off food and supplies to the enemy. The posse cut the outlaws off at the pass.* **c.** to disinherit: *to be cut off without a dime.*

· **to cut out. a.** to plan or prepare; arrange: *You have your work cut out for you.* **b.** to be suited or fit for: *I am not cut out to be a doctor.* **c.** to oust and take the place of: *to cut out a rival.* **d.** *Informal.* to leave, esp. suddenly or hastily: *The students cut out as soon as the three o'clock bell sounded.* **e.** *Informal.* to cease doing something; stop: *Please cut out the noise.*

· **to cut short.** to stop before the end: *The fire drill cut short our meeting.*

· **to cut up. a.** to separate into pieces with a cutting tool: *to cut up a steak, to cut up a magazine.* **b.** *Informal.* to injure the feelings of; distress or hurt: *Your harsh words cut me up greatly.* **c.** *Informal.* to behave in a mischievous or boisterous way: *The unruly students cut up in class.*

cu·ta·ne·ous (kū tā′nē əs) *adj.* of or relating to the skin. [Modern Latin *cutaneus,* from Latin *cutis* skin.]

cut·a·way (kut′ə wā′) *n.* a man's formal coat for daytime wear, cut so as to slope back from the waistline to the tails. —*adj.* having or showing parts or sections removed, as in a drawing: *The cutaway drawing showed the inner parts of the camera.*

cut·back (kut′bak′) *n.* a reduction: *a cutback in production, a cutback in government spending.*

cute (kūt) *adj.,* **cut·er, cut·est.** *Informal.* **1.** charmingly pretty or attractive; adorable; appealing: *a cute baby, a cute dress.* **2.** clever; shrewd: *a cute trick.* **3.** flippant or impudent; obnoxious. [Short for ACUTE.] —**cute′ly,** *adv.* —**cute′ness,** *n.*

cu·tey (kū′tē) cutie.

cut glass, glass that is shaped or decorated by cutting and polishing with an abrasive wheel.

cu·ti·cle (kū′ti kəl) *n.* **1.** the tough skin surrounding the base and sides of a fingernail or toenail. **2.** the outer skin; epidermis. **3.** *Botany.* the waxy layer covering the outer surface of epidermal cells on the leaves and stems of plants. It retards moisture loss and gives leaves their shiny appearance. [Latin *cutīcula* skin, diminutive of *cutis* skin.]

cu·tie (kū′tē) *also,* **cutey.** *n. Informal.* a person or thing that is very cute. [CUTE + -IE.]

cu·tin (kū′tin) *n.* the waxy substance present in the epidermis of plant cells that form the cuticle. [Latin *cut(is)* skin + -IN[1].]

cu·tis (kū′tis) *n.* the part of the skin containing the dermis and epidermis. [Latin *cutis* skin.]

cut·lass (kut′ləs) *also,* **cut·las.** *n.* a short sword with a flat, wide, slightly curved blade designed for slashing rather than thrusting. [French *coutelas,* going back to Latin *cultellus* little knife, diminutive of *culter* knife.]

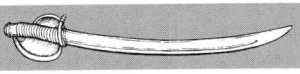
cutlass

cutlass fish *also,* **cut·lass·fish** (kut′ləs fish′). any of various saltwater fish, family Trichiuridae, usually found in tropical seas, having large sharp teeth and a dorsal fin that runs the length of its body and gradually tapers to form a thin tail. [CUTLASS + FISH; with reference to its shape.]

cut·ler (kut′lər) *n.* a person who makes, sharpens, repairs, or deals in cutlery. [Old French *cotelier* maker of knives, from *coutel* knife, from Latin *cultellus* little knife. See CUTLASS.]

cutlass fish

a	at	e	end	o	hot	u	up	hw	white		about
ā	ape	ē	me	ō	old	ū	use	ng	song		taken
ä	far	i	it	ô	fork	ü	rule	th	thin	ə	pencil
âr	care	ī	ice	oi	oil	u̇	pull	th	this		lemon
		îr	pierce	ou	out	ûr	turn	zh	measure		circus

cut·ler·y (kut′lə rē) *n.* **1.** cutting instruments collectively, esp. those used in eating or serving food. **2.** the business or trade of a cutler.

cut·let (kut′lit) *n.* **1.** a thin slice of meat or poultry cut from the leg, ribs, or breast: *veal cutlet.* **2.** a flat mass of chopped meat, fish, or other food having a shape similar to such a slice of meat: *a vegetable cutlet.* [French *côtelette* literally, small rib, diminutive of *côte* rib, from Latin *costa* rib, side.]

cut·off (kut′ôf′, -of′) *n.* **1.** a stopping or cutting off, esp. of the flow of steam or fluid into the cylinder of an engine. **2.** the point at which this is done. **3.** a mechanism or device for cutting off the flow of steam or fluid. **4.** a shorter road or route; shortcut. **5.** a new and shorter channel formed when a stream cuts across a bend in its course. **6. cutoffs.** shorts made by cutting short the legs of trousers, esp. jeans. —*adj.* at or during which something ends or expires: *The cutoff date for contest entries is September 30.*

cut·out (kut′out′) *n.* something cut out or designed to be cut out: *The book has paper cutouts of animals.*

cut·o·ver (kut′ō′vər) *adj.* (of land) having most or all of the trees cut down.

cut·purse (kut′pûrs′) *n.* pickpocket. [CUT + PURSE; referring to the theft of purses in earlier times by cutting them from belts or girdles.]

cut-rate (kut′rāt′) *adj.* **1.** offering merchandise or services at reduced or cheap prices: *a cut-rate drugstore.* **2.** sold or selling at reduced or cheap prices: *cut-rate appliances.*

cut·ter (kut′ər) *n.* **1.** a person who cuts, esp. one whose job entails cutting: *a glass cutter, a dress cutter, a cutter of diamonds.* **2.** something that cuts; device or machine for cutting. **3.** a single-masted sailboat, usually carrying a mainsail and two sails forward of the mast, similar to a sloop but having its mast set nearer the center of the boat. **4.** any ship used by the Coast Guard. **5.** a small boat carried on a ship, used to take people to and from the ship. **6.** a small, light sleigh, usually made to be drawn by one horse.

cut·throat (kut′thrōt′) *n.* a murderer or murderous thug. —*adj.* ruthless; merciless: *cutthroat competition.*

cut·ting (kut′ing) *adj.* **1.** adapted to cut; sharp: *a cutting edge.* **2.** that hurts the feelings; sarcastic: *a cutting reply.* **3.** piercingly chilling; penetrating: *a cutting wind.* —*n.* **1.** the act of a person or thing that cuts. **2.** something made or obtained by cutting, esp. a recording. **3.** a small shoot or other part cut from a plant and used to grow a new plant. **4.** a newspaper or magazine clipping. —**cut′ting·ly,** *adv.*

cut·tle (kut′əl) *n.* **1.** cuttlefish. **2.** cuttlebone. [Old English *cudele* cuttlefish.]

cut·tle·bone (kut′əl bōn′) *n.* the hard internal shell or plate of cuttlefish, used for making polishing powder and often placed in cages to provide birds with lime and with something on which to peck and sharpen their beaks.

cut·tle·fish (kut′əl fish′) *n., pl.* -**fish** or -**fish·es.** any of a group of squidlike mollusks, genus *Sepia,* found in warm, shallow waters of the Atlantic and Indian oceans, having arms that bear suckers and a limy internal shell covered by a muscular mantle. When in danger, it may release an inky fluid. [CUTTLE + FISH.]

cut·up (kut′up′) *n. Informal.* a person who clowns, plays tricks, or behaves in a mischievous or boisterous way.

cut·wa·ter (kut′wô′tər, -wot′ər) *n.* **1.** the forward edge of a ship's prow. **2.** the angular edge of a bridge pier, designed to resist the effects of moving water or ice.

cut·worm (kut′wûrm′) *n.* **1.** the larva or caterpillar of any of several moths, family Noctuidae, that feed at night on the leaves and stems of most cultivated crops and garden plants. **2.** any of several caterpillars, as the armyworm.

cwt., hundredweight.

-cy *suffix* (used to form nouns) **1.** the quality, state, condition, or fact of being: *bankruptcy, accuracy, secrecy.* **2.** the office, position, or rank of: *captaincy, curacy.* [Latin *-cia, -tia,* and Greek *-keiā, -kiā, -teiā, -tiā,* often through French *-cie, -tie.*]

cy·an·a·mide (sī an′ə mīd, -mid′, sī′ə nam′īd, -id) *also,* **cy·an·a·mid.** (sī an′ə mid, sī′ə nam′id). *n.* **1.** calcium cyanamide, used in making ammonia. **2.** a highly reactive compound, available as colorless crystals or in water solution, prepared from calcium cyanamide. Formula: CH_2N_2

cy·a·nate (sī′ə nāt′) *n.* a salt or ester of cyanic acid. [CYAN(O-) + -ATE[2].]

cy·an·ic (sī an′ik) *adj.* **1.** of, relating to, or containing cyanogen. **2.** blue. [CYAN(O) + -IC.]

cyanic acid, an unstable, colorless, poisonous liquid. Formula: HOCN

cy·a·nide (sī′ə nīd′, -nid) *also,* **cy·a·nid** (sī′ə nid). *n.* any of several very poisonous compounds containing the cyanogen radical, CN, combined with a metal or another radical, esp. **potassium cyanide,** KCN, and **sodium cyanide,** NaCN. They are

used esp. as pesticides and in the extraction of metal from ore. —*v.t.* to treat (gold ore or the like) with cyanide.

cyano- *combining form* **1.** characterized by bluish coloring; blue: *cyanosis.* **2.** *Chemistry.* of or containing the cyanogen radical, CN. [Greek *kyanos* dark blue color.]

cy·a·no·bac·te·ri·a (sī′ə nō bak tîr′ē ə) *pl. n., sing.* -**te·ri·um** (-tîr′ē əm). any of a number of photosynthetic one-celled organisms, formerly classified as algae but now regarded as monerans, some of which can fix nitrogen, occurring in diverse and often extremely inhospitable environments. Also, **blue-green algae.** [CYANO- + BACTERIA.]

cy·an·o·gen (sī an′ə jən) *n.* **1.** a compound of carbon and nitrogen in the form of a colorless, poisonous gas with a sharp, penetrating odor, used in synthesizing organic compounds. Formula: C_2N_2 **2.** the univalent radical CN, contained in all cyanide compounds. [CYANO- + -GEN literally, producing blue, with reference to the dark blue pigment, Prussian blue, in which it was first found.]

cy·a·no·phyte (sī′ə nō fīt′, sī an′ə-) *n.* a member of the phylum (Cyanophyta) of lower organisms that comprises the cyanobacteria, or blue-green algae. [CYANO- + -PHYTE.]

cy·a·no·sis (sī′ə nō′sis) *n.* blueness of the skin or mucous membranes, caused by a lack of oxygen in the blood. [Modern Latin *cyanosis,* from Greek *kyanōsis* dark blue color.] —**cy′a·not′ic,** *adj.*

Cyb·e·le (sib′ə lē′) *n.* a fertility goddess of ancient Asia Minor, whose worship later spread to Greece and Rome.

cy·ber·nate (sī′bər nāt′) *v.t.,* -**nat·ed, -nat·ing.** to automate. [CYBERN(ETICS) + -ATE[1].] —**cy′ber·na′tion,** *n.*

cy·ber·net·ics (sī′bər net′iks) *n.* the science dealing with the similarities between communication and control processes in the brain and in electronic machines. ➡ used as singular. [Greek *kybernētēs* pilot (from *kybernān* to steer) + -ICS.] —**cy′ber·net′ic,** *adj.*

cy·cad (sī′kad) *n.* any of a group of primitive evergreen plants, family Cycadaceae, that grow in tropical and subtropical climates. The separate male and female plants resemble palms and have cones, the female bearing seeds. [Modern Latin *Cycas,* from Greek *kykas,* incorrect recording of *koïkas,* accusative plural of *koïx* palm[2].]

cy·cla·mate (sī′klə māt′) *n.* the synthetic sodium or calcium salt of an organic acid, having an extremely sweet taste and formerly used as a sweetener but now banned as a suspected carcinogen. [Short for *cycl(ohexylsulf)amate.*]

cyc·la·men (sī′klə mən, sik′lə-) *n.* **1.** the showy flower of any of a group of plants, genus *Cyclamen,* of the primrose family, having pink, purple, rose, or white petals. **2.** the widely cultivated plant bearing this flower, having heart-shaped leaves that are often patterned with silver. [Modern Latin *cyclamen,* from Greek *kyklamīnos,* from *kyklos* circle; because of its bulbous roots.]

cy·cle (sī′kəl) *n.* **1.** a complete course or series of events or phenomena that recur regularly in a definite sequence. **2.** the period of time during which such a course or series occurs and completes itself. **3.** a unicycle, bicycle, tricycle, or motorcycle. **4.** a group of stories, poems, or plays about a central figure, event, or theme: *The Arthurian cycle deals with the adventures of King Arthur and his knights.* **5.** *Physics.* a complete round or series of changes in a quantity that varies periodically, as alternating current. **6.** a long period of time; age. —*v.i.,* -**cled, -cling. 1.** to ride a cycle, esp. a bicycle: *We cycled through the park.* **2.** to pass through a cycle. [Late Latin *cyclus* circle, recurring period, from Greek *kyklos* circle, wheel.]

cyclamen

cy·clic (sī′klik, sik′lik) *adj.* **1.** moving or occurring in cycles: *the cyclic changing of the seasons.* **2.** of or relating to a cycle. **3.** *Chemistry.* of, relating to, or characterized by a molecular structure in which the atoms are arranged in a ring or closed chain. Also, **cyclical.**

cy·cli·cal (sī′kli kəl, sik′li-) *adj.* **1.** cyclic. **2.** of, relating to, or caused by economic cycles: *cyclical industries, cyclical stocks,*

cyclical poverty. —*n.* the stock of a company, as a steel, chemical, or paper manufacturer, whose profits fluctuate in a manner particularly sensitive to changes in the economic cycle. —**cy′cli·cal·ly,** *adv.*

cy·clist (sī′klist) *n.* a person who rides a cycle. Also, **cy′cler.**

cy·cloid (sī′kloid) *adj.* resembling a circle; having a circular shape. —*n.* a curve traced by a point on the circumference of a circle when the circle is rolled along a straight line in its plane. —**cy·cloi′dal,** *adj.*

cy·clom·e·ter (sī klom′i tər) *n.* **1.** an instrument for recording the revolutions of a wheel, often used to measure the distance traveled by a wheeled vehicle. **2.** an instrument for measuring circular arcs. [Greek *kyklos* circle, wheel + -METER.]

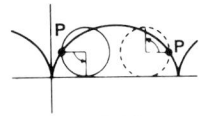

cycloid

cy·clone (sī′klōn) *n.* **1.** an atmospheric disturbance in which winds rotate around a moving center of low atmospheric pressure. Cyclone winds circle counterclockwise in the Northern Hemisphere, clockwise in the Southern. ▶ distinguished from **anticyclone. 2.** any violent windstorm, as a hurricane or a tornado. [Modification of Greek *kyklōma* wheel, coil of a snake, from *kyklos* circle, wheel.] —**cy·clon·ic** (sī klon′ik); *also,* **cy·clon′i·cal,** *adj.* —**cy·clon′i·cal·ly,** *adv.*

Cy·clo·pe·an (sī′klə pē′ən) *adj.* **1.** of, relating to, or characteristic of the Cyclopes. **2.** *also,* **cyclopean.** huge or massive; gigantic.

cy·clo·pe·di·a (sī′klə pē′dē ə) *also,* **cy·clo·pae·di·a.** *n.* encyclopedia. [Short for ENCYCLOPEDIA.]

cy·clo·pe·dic (sī′klə pē′dik) *also,* **cy·clo·pae·dic.** *adj.* encyclopedic.

Cy·clops (sī′klops) *n., pl.* **Cy·clo·pes** (sī klō′pēz). in Greek mythology, one of a group of one-eyed giants having the eye located in the middle of the forehead. [Latin *Cyclops,* from Greek *Kyklōps* literally, round-eyed, from *kyklos* circle + *ōps* eye.]

cy·clo·ram·a (sī′klə ram′ə, -rä′mə) *n.* **1.** a large picture or series of pictures represented on the wall of a circular room so as to appear in natural perspective to a spectator standing in the center. **2.** a large, often curved, piece of scenery used to surround the back of a stage. [Greek *kyklos* circle + *horama* view.] —**cy′clo·ram′ic,** *adj.*

cy·clo·sis (sī klō′sis) *n., pl.* **-ses** (-sēz). the circulation of cytoplasm in a cell, esp. the streamlike flow of cytoplasm in plant cells. [Modern Latin *cyclosis,* from Greek *kyklōsis* an enveloping, encircling, from *kykloun* to encircle, from *kyklos* a circle.]

cy·clo·spo·rine (sī′klə spôr′ēn, -in, sik′lə-) *n.* a drug derived from various fungi, esp. *Tolypocladium inflatum,* used in organ transplantation to suppress the T cells that reject foreign tissue. Formula: $C_{62}H_{111}N_{11}O_{12}$

cy·clo·stome (sī′klə stōm′, sik′lə-) *n.* any of various primitive, jawless, eellike freshwater or saltwater vertebrates, class Agnatha, that have a large, round, sucking mouth, as the lamprey and hagfish. [Greek *kyklos* circle, wheel + STOMA mouth.] —**cy·clos·to·mate** (sī klos′tə māt′, si-), **cy·clo·stom·a·tous** (sī′klə stom′ə təs, -stō′mə-, sik′lə-), *adj.*

cy·clo·thy·mi·a (sī′klə thī′mē ə, sik′lə-) *n.* a mild emotional disorder in which periods of liveliness and excitement alternate with periods of depression. [Modern Latin *cyclothymia,* going back to Greek *kyklos* circle, wheel + *thŷmos* spirit, soul, mind.] —**cy′clo·thy′mic,** *adj.*

cy·clo·tron (sī′klə tron′, sik′lə-) *n.* a device that accelerates elementary particles and ions in a flat, spiral orbit of increasing radius by means of an alternating electric field. [Greek *kyklos* circle + -*tron* means, device; referring to the spiral motion produced.]

cyg·net (sig′nit) *n.* a young swan. [Diminutive of French *cygne* swan, going back to Latin *cygnus,* from Greek *kyknos.*]

Cyg·nus (sig′nəs) *n.* a constellation in the northern sky, conventionally depicted as a swan. [Latin *cygnus* swan. See CYGNET.]

cyl., cylinder.

cyl·in·der (sil′ən dər) *n.* **1.** a solid bounded by two equal, parallel circles and a curved surface that is generated by a straight line moving parallel to itself with its ends always on the circumferences of the circles. **2.** something resembling a cylinder in shape. **3.** the rotating part of a revolver that contains chambers for cartridges. **4.** the piston chamber of

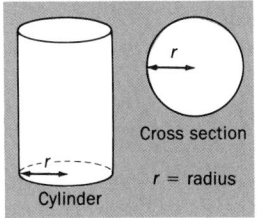

cylinder *(def. 1)*

an engine or pump. [Latin *cylindrus* the solid, from Greek *kylindros* literally, roller, from *kylindein* to roll.]

cy·lin·dri·cal (sə lin′dri kəl) *adj.* **1.** having the form of a cylinder; shaped like a cylinder. **2.** of or relating to a cylinder. Also, **cy·lin′dric.** —**cy·lin′dri·cal·ly,** *adv.*

cym·bal (sim′bəl) *n.* a musical percussion instrument consisting of a circular, slightly concave metal plate that produces a ringing sound when clashed against another cymbal or struck, as with a drumstick. For illustration, see **percussion instrument.** [Old English *cymbal* and Middle French *cymbale,* both from Latin *cymbalum,* from Greek *kymbalon,* from *kymbē* hollow of a vessel, cup.]

cym·bid·i·um (sim bid′ē əm) *n.* any of a number of tropical epiphytic orchids, genus *Cymbidium,* bearing stalks of showy flowers. [Modern Latin *Cymbidium,* from Latin *cymba* boat, skiff (from Greek *kymbē* boat, hollow of a vessel).]

cyme (sīm) *n.* an inflorescence characterized by a broad, flat-topped cluster in which the central flowers open first. For illustration, see **inflorescence.** [Latin *cȳma* young sprout of a cabbage, from Greek *kŷma* something swollen, wave, young sprout of a plant.]

cy·mose (sī′mōs, sī mōs′) *adj.* relating to, bearing, or resembling a cyme.

Cym·ric (kim′rik, sim′-) *adj.* of or relating to the Welsh people or their language. —*n.* the Welsh language.

Cym·ry (kim′rē) *pl. n.* the Welsh people.

cyn·ic (sin′ik) *n.* **1.** a person who disbelieves in or doubts the sincerity, goodness, or selflessness of human motives and actions. **2. Cynic.** a member of a group of Greek philosophers of the fourth century B.C. who held that virtue was the goal of life and that it could be achieved by living a natural and simple life, disdaining possessions and social conventions. —*adj.* **1. Cynic.** of or relating to the Cynics or their doctrines. **2.** cynical. [Latin *cynicus* a Cynic philosopher, from Greek *kynikos* literally, doglike, from *kyōn* dog; because of the currish behavior attributed to the Cynic philosophers.]

cyn·i·cal (sin′i kəl) *adj.* having or showing disbelief in or doubt about the sincerity, goodness, or selflessness of human motives and actions: *a cynical person, a cynical attitude.* —**cyn′i·cal·ly,** *adv.*

cyn·i·cism (sin′ə siz′əm) *n.* **1.** a cynical disposition, character, or quality. **2.** the expression of such a disposition, character, or quality; cynical remark, act, or opinion. **3. Cynicism.** the doctrines or practices of the Cynics.

cy·no·sure (sī′nə shŭr′, sin′ə-) *n.* a person or thing that attracts attention; center or object of attraction, interest, or admiration. [Latin *Cynosūra* constellation of the Little Bear (which served as a guide to navigators), from Greek *kynosoura* literally, dog's tail.]

Cyn·thi·a (sin′thē ə) *n.* **1.** in Greek mythology, Artemis. **2.** the moon. [Latin *Cynthia,* from Greek *Kynthiā* literally, (goddess) of *Kynthos,* a mountain of Delos, where Apollo and Artemis were born.]

cy·pher (sī′fər) cipher.

cy·press (sī′prəs) *n.* **1.** any of a group of evergreen trees or shrubs, genus *Cupressus,* found in southern Europe, Asia, and North America, having closely overlapping, scalelike leaves and woody cones. **2.** bald cypress. **3.** the wood of any of these trees. [Old French *cypres* the European cypress or its wood, from Latin *cupressus,* from Greek *kyparissos.*]

Cyp·ri·an (sip′rē ən) *n.* Cypriot.

cyp·ri·noid (sip′rə noid′) *n.* any of a group of freshwater fish, family Cyprinidae, including carp, barbels, goldfish, chubs, breams, and most freshwater minnows. —*adj.* resembling or belonging to any of the fish of this group. Also, **cyp·ri·nid** (sip′rə nid). [Latin *cyprīnus* carp (from Greek *kyprīnos*) + -OID.]

Cyp·ri·ot (sip′rē ət) *also,* **Cyp·ri·ote** (sip′rē ōt′, -ət). *n.* **1.** a native or citizen of Cyprus. **2.** the ancient or modern Greek dialect of Cyprus. —*adj.* of or relating to Cyprus or its people, language, or culture. Also, **Cyprian.**

cyp·ri·pe·di·um (sip′rə pē′dē əm) *n., pl.* **-di·a** (-dē ə). lady's slipper. [Modern Latin *cypripedium,* probably from Greek *Kypris* Aphrodite + *pedīlon* slipper; with reference to the shape of the flower.]

a at	e end	o hot	u up	hw white	⟨ about
ā ape	ē me	ō old	ū use	ng song	taken
ä far	i it	ô fork	ü rule	th thin	ə pencil
âr care	ī ice	oi oil	u̇ pull	th this	lemon
	îr pierce	ou out	ûr turn	zh measure	⟨ circus

Cy·ril·lic alphabet (si ril′ik) an alphabet based on the Greek alphabet, dating from the ninth century A.D., used for Russian, Bulgarian, Serbian, and certain other languages. [From Saint *Cyril*, ninth-century Greek Christian missionary to the Slavs, said to be its inventor.]

cyst (sist) *n.* **1.** an abnormal sac in the body encased by a distinct membrane and usually containing liquid or semisolid substances. **2.a.** a protective outer membrane formed around an organism, such as a protozoan, during reproduction or in response to unfavorable environmental conditions. **b.** such a membrane and the organism so enclosed. **3.** any of various saclike structures in plants or animals. [Modern Latin *cystis*, from Greek *kystis* bladder, pouch.]

cys·te·ine (sis′tē ēn′, -in) *n.* a sulfur-containing nonessential amino acid derived from cystine that is present in nearly all proteins. Formula: $C_3H_7NO_2S$ [Modification of CYSTINE.]

cyst·ic (sis′tik) *adj.* **1.** of, relating to, or resembling a cyst. **2.** having or containing a cyst or cysts. **3.** of or relating to the gallbladder or to the urinary bladder.

cystic fibrosis, an inherited disease of infants, children, and young adults, affecting the exocrine glands, esp. the pancreas, and causing digestive disorders and respiratory problems.

cys·tine (sis′tēn, -tin) *n.* a sulfur-containing nonessential amino acid, found esp. in keratin. Formula: $C_6H_{12}N_2O_4S_2$

cys·ti·tis (si stī′tis) *n.* an inflammation of the urinary bladder.

cys·to·scope (sis′tə skōp′) *n.* an instrument used to examine the urinary bladder. —**cys·to·scop·ic** (sis′tə skop′ik), *adj.*

Cyth·er·e·a (sith′ə rē′ə) *n.* in classical mythology, Aphrodite or Venus. [Latin *Cytherea* Venus, from Greek *Kythereia* Aphrodite; literally, (goddess) of *Kythēra*, Greek island in the Aegean Sea where the goddess was worshiped.] —**Cyth′e·re′an,** *adj.*

cyto- *combining form* cell: *cytoplasm.* [Greek *kytos* hollow vessel.]

cy·to·chrome (sī′tə krōm′) *n.* any of several iron-containing proteins whose oxidation and reduction are essential to the cellular respiration of plants and animals.

cy·to·gen·e·sis (sī′tō jen′ə sis) *n.* the origin and development of cells. [CYTO- + GENESIS.]

cy·to·ge·net·ics (sī′tō jə net′iks) *n.* the branch of genetics that deals with the study of those parts of cells that contribute to heredity, as chromosomes and genes. ➡ used as singular. [CYTO- + GENETICS.] —**cy′to·ge·net′ic;** *also,* **cy′to·ge·net′i·cal,** *adj.* —**cy′to·ge·net′i·cal·ly,** *adv.* —**cy·to·ge·net·i·cist** (sī′tō jə net′ə sist), *n.*

cy·to·ki·nin (sī′tə kī′nin) *n.* any of a group of plant hormones, closely related to adenine, that promote cell division and differentiation in roots, shoots, leaves, and other growing parts. Also, **kinin.** [CYTO- + KININ.]

cy·tol·o·gy (sī tol′ə jē) *n.* the branch of biology that deals with the study of cells, including such aspects as their formation, structure, and function. [CYTO- + -LOGY.] —**cy·to·log·ic** (sī′tə loj′ik); *also,* **cy′to·log′i·cal,** *adj.* —**cy′to·log′i·cal·ly,** *adv.* —**cy·tol′o·gist,** *n.*

cy·to·plasm (sī′tə plaz′əm) *n.* the substance of a cell exclusive of the cell membrane and the nucleus, consisting of a watery gel in which the organelles and other structures are suspended. For illustration, see **cell.** [CYTO- + -PLASM.] —**cy′to·plas′mic,** *adj.*

cy·to·sine (sī′tō sēn′, -zēn′) *n.* a pyrimidine base that is an essential constituent of DNA and RNA. Formula: $C_4H_5N_3O$ For illustration, see **double helix.**

CZ, the postal abbreviation for the Canal Zone.

C.Z., Canal Zone.

czar (zär) *also,* **tsar, tzar.** *n.* **1.** any of the emperors of Russia before the Revolution of 1917. **2.** a person having great or absolute power or authority, as a dictator or magnate. [Russian *tsar* emperor, going back to Latin *Caesar.* See CAESAR.] —**czar′dom,** *n.*

czar·das (chär′däsh) *n.* **1.** a Hungarian dance consisting of a slow, melancholy introduction followed by a rapid and spirited section. **2.** the music for such a dance. [Magyar *csárdás,* from *csárda* tavern.]

czar·e·vitch (zär′ə vich′) *also,* **tsarevitch, tzarevitch.** *n.* the eldest son of a Russian czar. [Russian *tsarevich,* from *tsar.* See CZAR.]

cza·rev·na (zä rev′nə) *also,* **tsarevna, tzarevna.** *n.* **1.** the wife of a czarevitch. **2.** the daughter of a Russian czar. [Russian *tsarevna,* from *tsar.* See CZAR.]

cza·ri·na (zä rē′nə) *also,* **tsarina, tzarina.** *n.* the wife of a Russian czar; empress of Russia. [German *Zarin,* feminine of *Zar* czar, from Russian *tsar.* See CZAR.]

czar·ism (zär′iz əm) *also,* **tsarism, tzarism.** *n.* an autocratic or absolute government or rule, esp. the government of Russia under the czars. [CZAR + -ISM.]

czar·ist (zär′ist) *also,* **tsarist, tzarist.** *adj.* of, relating to, or characteristic of a czar or czarism. —*n.* a follower or supporter of a czar or of czarism. [CZAR + -IST.]

Czech (chek) *n.* **1.a.** a member of the most westerly branch of the Slavs, including the Bohemians and Moravians. **b.** Czechoslovak. **2.** a language belonging to the western division of the Slavic languages, spoken chiefly in Czechoslovakia; Bohemian. —*adj.* of or relating to Czechoslovakia or its people, language, or culture.

Czech·o·slo·vak (chek′ə slō′vak, -väk) *n.* a native or citizen of Czechoslovakia. —*adj.* of or relating to Czechoslovakia or its people, language, or culture. Also, **Czech·o·slo·va·ki·an** (chek′ə slə vä′kē ən, -vak′ē ən).

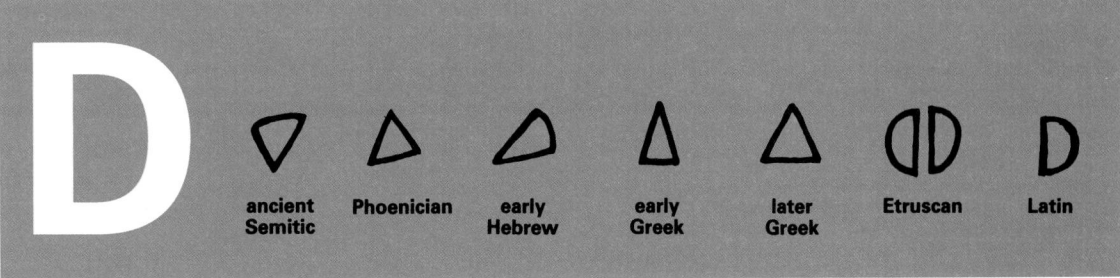

ancient Semitic | Phoenician | early Hebrew | early Greek | later Greek | Etruscan | Latin

D The ancient Semitic letter *daleth*, meaning "door," is the earliest graphic symbol that corresponds to our modern letter **D**. This letter and its triangular shape were adopted into Phoenician and Hebrew. Around the ninth century B.C., the Greeks borrowed *daleth*, making only slight changes in its shape, and called it *delta*. In later centuries, *delta* was written by the Greeks in the form of an equilateral triangle. The Etruscans changed the shape of *delta* by rounding two sides of the triangle to form a semicircle. This form was used, with only slight changes, in the Latin alphabet and is the forerunner of the English capital **D**.

---

d, D (dē) *n., pl.* **d's, D's. 1.** the fourth letter of the English alphabet. **2.** the shape of this letter or something having this shape. **3.** the fourth item in a series or group.
D (dē) *n., pl.* **D's. 1.** *Music.* **a.** the second note or tone of the diatonic scale of C major. For illustration, see **do**[2]. **b.** the scale or key that has this note or tone as its tonic. **2.** a grade or rating indicating poor performance: *a D on an exam.* **3.** *also,* **d** the Roman numeral for 500.
D, a symbol for deuterium.
-'d *suffix* (used in contractions) **1.** had: *I'd already seen the movie.* **2.** would: *I'd have said it differently.*
d. 1. date. **2.** daughter. **3.** day; days. **4.** dead. **5.** degree. **6.** delete. **7.** diameter. **8.** died. **9.** dime. **10.** dollar. **11.** drachma. **12.** pence: *3d.*
D *Physics.* density.
D. 1. day. **2.** December. **3.** Democrat. **4.** Department. **5.** Doctor. **6.** Duchess. **7.** Duke. **8.** Dutch.
D.A. *also,* **DA** district attorney.
dab[1] (dab) *v.,* **dabbed, dab·bing.** —*v.t.* **1.** to pat with something soft or moist: *A nurse dabbed the wound with cotton.* **2.** to apply with a light, quick touch: *The artist dabbed green paint on the canvas.* —*v.i.* to pat or stroke, as with something soft or moist: *The boy dabbed at the stain on his shirt.* —*n.* **1.** a small, moist mass of something: *a dab of clay.* **2.** a little bit. **3.** a light, quick pat: *She gave her nose a dab with a powder puff.* [Possibly imitative.] —**dab'ber,** *n.*
dab[2] (dab) *n.* any of various flounders, order Pleuronectiformes. [Possibly from DAB[1].]
dab·ble (dab'əl) *v.,* **-bled, -bling.** —*v.i.* **1.** to do something superficially or occasionally (with *in* or *at*): *to dabble in politics, to dabble at painting.* **2.** to splash or play gently, as in water. —*v.t.* to splash or dip (something) gently, as in water. —**dab'bler,** *n.*
da ca·po (dä kä'pō) *Music.* from the beginning. ➡ used as a direction to repeat a passage.
dace (dās) *n., pl.* **dace** or **dac·es.** any of various minnows found in small streams of North America and Europe, esp. the **black-nose dace,** *Rhinichthys atratulus,* the most abundant of American minnows, and the **European dace,** *Leuciscus leuciscus.* [Old French *dars,* from Late Latin *dardus* javelin; of Germanic origin.]
da·cha (dä'chə) *n.* a Russian country house. [Russian *dacha* literally, a giving.]
dachs·hund (däks'-hůnt', -hůnd', dash'ənd) *n.* a small dog of a breed of German origin, having a long body, very short legs, a long, tapered head,

dachshund

drooping ears, and a red, tan, or black-and-tan coat. Height: 9 inches (23 centimeters) at the shoulder. [German *Dachshund,* from *Dachs* badger + *Hund* dog; because it was bred for hunting badgers.]
Da·cron (dā'kron, dak'ron) *n. Trademark.* **1.** a polyester textile fiber that is long-wearing, wrinkle-resistant, stretch-resistant, and quick-drying, used for many items, esp. clothing. **2.** a yarn or fabric made of this fiber.
dac·tyl (dak'təl) *n.* **1.a.** in modern English verse, a metrical foot consisting of one accented syllable followed by two unaccented syllables. The line *Think' of her mourn'fully, gent'ly and hu'manly* contains four dactyls. **b.** in classical verse, a metrical foot consisting of one long syllable followed by two short syllables. **2.** a line of verse made up of such feet. **3.** a finger or toe; digit. [Latin *dactylus* the classical meter, from Greek *daktylos* finger, toe, the classical meter; because its three metrical feet suggest the three joints of a finger.] —**dac·tyl·ic** (dak til'ik), *adj.*
dactylo- *also,* **dactyl-.** *combining form* finger or toe; digit: *dactylography.* [Greek *daktylos.*]
dac·tyl·o·gram (dak til'ə gram') *n.* fingerprint. [DACTYLO- + -GRAM[1].]
dac·ty·log·ra·phy (dak'tə log'rə fē) *n.* the scientific study of fingerprints, used as a technique of identification in crime detection. [DACTYLO- + -GRAPHY.]
dad (dad) *n. Informal.* father. [Said to be derived from baby talk.]

Dada art
fur-lined teacup by Meret Oppenheim

Da·da (dä'dä, -də) *also,* **da·da.** *n.* a movement in art and literature during the early twentieth century characterized by the use of ridicule, nonsense, and deliberate irrationality to reflect what was considered to be the meaninglessness of the modern world and all of human culture, esp. the arts. Also, **Da'da·ism.** [French *dada* hobby, hobbyhorse (used arbitrarily as a name for their movement by the Dadaists), from baby talk.] —**Da'da·ist,** *n.* —**Da'da·is'tic,** *adj.*
dad·dy (dad'ē) *n., pl.* **-dies.** *Informal.* father.
dad·dy-long·legs (dad'ē lông'legz') *n., pl.* **-legs.** any of a

a	at	e	end	o	hot	u	up	hw	white		about
ā	ape	ē	me	ō	old	ū	use	ng	song		taken
ä	far	i	it	ô	fork	ü	rule	th	thin	ə	pencil
âr	care	ī	ice	oi	oil	ů	pull	th	this		lemon
		îr	pierce	ou	out	ûr	turn	zh	measure		circus

group of harmless arachnids, order Phalangida, that are related to the spider and have long, slender legs but do not spin webs. Also, **harvestman.**

da·do (dā′dō) *n., pl.* **-does** or **-dos. 1.** the portion of a pedestal between the base and the cornice. **2.** the lower part of an interior wall if decorated differently from the rest of the wall, as with paneling or ornamentation. [Italian *dado* cube, pedestal, from Latin *datum* thing given, noun use of neuter of *datus,* past participle of *dare* to give.]

Daed·a·lus (ded′ə ləs) *n.* in Greek legend, a skillful artisan and inventor who designed the Labyrinth in Crete and was later imprisoned in it with his son Icarus. Daedalus then invented artificial wings, with which they escaped.

dae·mon (dē′mən) demon *(defs. 5, 6).*

daf·fo·dil (daf′ə dil′) *n.* **1.** the trumpet-shaped flower of any of several plants, genus *Narcissus,* of the amaryllis family, commonly having yellow petals that surround the base of a central tube of any of various colors. **2.** the plant bearing this flower, cultivated throughout the world, having tall, stiff, bladelike leaves and growing from a bulb. **3.** a brilliant yellow color. [Probably from Dutch *(de) affodil* (the) asphodel, from Old French *affrodile, asphodile* asphodel, through Latin, from Greek *asphodelos.*]

daff·y (daf′ē) *adj.,* **daff·i·er, daff·i·est.** *Informal.* **1.** silly; foolish. **2.** crazy; insane. [Obsolete English *daff* fool (of uncertain origin) + -Y¹.] —**daff′i·ness,** *n.*

daft (daft) *adj.* **1.** having or showing a lack of mental balance; crazy; insane. **2.** having or showing a lack of good sense; silly; foolish. [Middle English *daffte* gentle, foolish, from Old English *gedæfte* mild, gentle.] —**daft′ly,** *adv.* —**daft′ness,** *n.*

dag·ger (dag′ər) *n.* **1.** a small, swordlike weapon having a pointed blade, used for thrusting and stabbing. **2.** a mark (†) used in printing to indicate a reference to a supplementary note or to indicate a death or death date. [Possibly from obsolete *dag* to stab; of uncertain origin.]

·**to look daggers at.** to look at with hatred or anger.

Da·gon (dā′gon) *n.* the chief god of the Philistines and the Phoenicians, represented as half man and half fish.

da·guerre·o·type (də gâr′ə tīp′, -ē ə tīp′) *n.* **1.** an early photographic process in which light-sensitized, silvered copper plates were exposed to light and then developed with mercury vapor. **2.** a picture produced by this process. [French *daguerréotype,* from Louis *Daguerre,* 1789-1851, French inventor of the process.]

dahl·ia (dal′yə, däl′-) *n.* **1.** the flower head of any of a group of leafy plants, genus *Dahlia,* of the composite family, growing in various bright colors. **2.** the leafy plant bearing this flower head, cultivated throughout the world from seeds or from cuttings of the tuberous roots. [Modern Latin *Dahlia,* from the Swedish botanist Anders *Dahl,* d. 1789.]

Dail Eir·eann (dôl âr′ən, doil) the lower house of the National Parliament of the Republic of Ireland. [Irish *Dáil Éireann* literally, assembly of Ireland.]

dai·ly (dā′lē) *adj.* relating to or happening every day or every weekday: *a daily routine, daily pay.* —*n., pl.* **-lies.** a newspaper appearing every day or every weekday. —*adv.* day after day; every day: *That column is published daily.* [Old English *dæglīc,* from *dæg* day.]

daily double, a system of betting on horse races in which a better, in order to win, must select the winner in each of two specified races on the same day.

dai·myo (dī′myō) *also,* **dai·mio.** *n., pl.* **-myo** or **-myos;** *also,* **-mio** or **-mios.** one of the chief territorial barons or feudal nobles of Japan who were vassals of the emperor. [Japanese *daimyō,* from *dai* great + *mio* name.]

dain·ty (dān′tē) *adj.,* **-ti·er, -ti·est. 1.** delicately beautiful or graceful: *a dainty porcelain vase.* **2.** having delicate tastes or fastidious habits; refined: *Few children are dainty eaters.* **3.** pleasing to the palate; delicious: *dainty cakes.* —*n., pl.* **-ties.** a delicious bit of food; delicacy. [Old French *daintie* pleasure, tidbit, from Latin *dignitās* worth, from *dignus* worthy.] —**dain′ti·ly,** *adv.* —**dain′ti·ness,** *n.*

dai·qui·ri (dī′kə rē, dak′ə rē) *n.* a cocktail made of rum, lime or lemon juice, and sugar. [From *Daiquirí,* Cuban town from which the rum for this cocktail originally came.]

dair·y (dâr′ē) *n., pl.* **dair·ies. 1.** a business establishment that produces and distributes milk and milk products. **2.** a room or building where milk and milk products are processed and stored. **3.** the business of producing milk and milk products; dairying. **4.** a store that sells milk and milk products. **5.** dairy farm. —*adj.* relating to, containing, or designating milk and milk products. [Middle English *deierie* place where milk and milk products are processed and stored, from *deie* dairymaid, from Old English *dæge* (female) maker of bread.]

dairy cattle, cows bred and raised for milk production.

dairy farm, a farm where dairy cattle are raised and milk is produced. Also, **dairy.**

dair·y·ing (dâr′ē ing) *n.* the business of a dairy.

dair·y·maid (dâr′ē mād′) *n.* a girl or woman who works in a dairy; milkmaid.

dair·y·man (dâr′ē mən) *n., pl.* **-men** (-mən). a person who owns or is employed by a dairy or dairy farm.

da·is (dā′is, dās) *n.* a slightly raised platform, as for a throne, speaker's desk, or seats for guests of honor. [Old French *deis* high table, from Late Latin *discus* table, from Latin *discus* quoit, dish, from Greek *diskos* round plate, quoit. Doublet of DESK, DISCUS, DISH, DISK.]

dai·sy (dā′zē) *n., pl.* **-sies. 1.** the flower head of any of various plants of the composite family, having petallike rays surrounding a yellow disk. The **oxeye daisy,** *Chrysanthemum leucanthemum,* bears white and yellow flowers. **2.** the plant bearing such flowers. [Old English *dægesēage* literally, day's eye; named partly for its round yellow center resembling the sun, partly for its closing at night and opening in the day.]

daisy wheel, a printing element used in some computer printers and electric typewriters that resembles the hub and spokes of a wheel, with a raised character at the end of each spoke. [Because of its resemblance to a daisy.]

Da·ko·ta (də kō′tə) *n.* **1.** a member of a Siouan tribe of North American Indians formerly living on the Great Plains. Also, **Sioux. 2.** the language of the Dakotas, a member of the Siouan family of languages. [Dakota *dakota* literally, allies.]

Da·lai La·ma (dä lī′ lä′mə) the spiritual and political leader of Lamaism. Also, **Grand Lama.**

dale (dāl) *n.* valley. [Old English *dæl.*]

dal·li·ance (dal′ē əns) *n.* **1.** a wasting of time; loitering. **2.** flirtation or playfulness.

dal·ly (dal′ē) *v.,* **-lied, -ly·ing** —*v.i.* **1.** to waste time; linger; delay: *If you dally any longer, we will be late.* **2.a.** to toy or play; trifle: *to dally with danger.* **b.** to flirt. —*v.t.* to waste (time) (with *away*): *to dally the morning away.* [Old French *dalier* to converse, chat; possibly of Germanic origin.]

Dal·ma·tian (dal mā′shən) *n.* **1.** a large dog of a breed believed to have been developed in Dalmatia, having a short-haired white coat speckled with small black or brown spots. Height: 21 inches (53 centimeters) at the shoulder. Also, **coach dog. 2.** a native or inhabitant of Dalmatia. —*adj.* of, relating to, or characteristic of Dalmatia or its people.

Dalmatian

dal·ton (dôl′tən) *n.* atomic mass unit. [From John *Dalton,* 1766-1844, English physicist.]

dam¹ (dam) *n.* **1.** a structure made of concrete, earth, or other material, erected across a stream or river to hold back water. **2.** any similar barrier. **3.** the body of water held back by a dam. —*v.t.,* **dammed, dam·ming. 1.** to hold back by a dam; furnish with a dam: *damming the river's lower branch.* **2.** to restrain or confine, as if with a dam (usually with *up*): *to dam up one's anger.* [Probably from Middle Low German *dam* the structure.]

dam¹

dam² (dam) *n.* **1.** the female parent of a four-footed animal, such as a horse. **2.** *Archaic.* mother. [Old French *dame* lady. Doublet of DAME.]

dam·age (dam′ij) *n.* **1.** harm or injury causing loss, as in value or usefulness: *The earthquake caused great damage.* **2. damages.** *Law.* money claimed or allowed as compensation for injury or loss. **3.** *also,* **damages.** *Informal.* cost or price. —*v.,* **-aged, -ag·ing.** —*v.t.* to cause damage to: *to damage a car, to damage a person's reputation.* —*v.i.* to suffer damage: *This cloth damages easily.* [Old French *damage* harm, from *dam* loss, from Latin *damnum.*] —**dam′age·a·ble,** *adj.* —For Synonyms *(v.t.),* see injure.

dam·a·scene (dam′ə sēn′, dam′ə sēn′) *v.t.,* **-scened, -scen·ing. 1.** to ornament (metal) with wavy patterns. **2.** to ornament (metal) with designs etched into the surface and inlaid with gold or silver. —*n.* **1.** work produced by damascening. **2. Dama·scene.** a native or inhabitant of Damascus. —*adj.* **1.** of or relating to damask or to the art of damascening. **2. Damascene.** of, relating to, or characteristic of Damascus or its people. [Latin *Damascēnus* of Damascus (once famous for such work), from Greek *Damaskēnos.* See DAMASCUS STEEL.]

Da·mas·cus steel (də mas′kəs) a tough steel whose surface is decorated with a wavy pattern resembling watermarks, originally made at Damascus. It was used for sword blades during the Middle Ages. Also, **damask, damask steel.**

dam·ask (dam′əsk) *n.* **1.** a reversible fabric made of various fibers woven with elaborate patterns or designs, used for such items as tablecloths and napkins. **2.a.** Damascus steel. **b.** the patterns on Damascus steel. **3.** a deep pink or rose color. —*adj.* **1.** made of or resembling damask. **2.** having the color damask. **3.** of or from Damascus. —*v.t.* **1.** damascene. **2.** to ornament or weave with the elaborate pattern or design of damask fabric. [Medieval Latin *damascus* fabric of Damascus (where such cloth was first made), going back to Hebrew *d'meseq* fabric of Damascus, and also to Hebrew *Dammeseq* Damascus.]

damask rose, a variety of rose, *Rosa damascena,* having fragrant pink or red flowers, cultivated in Europe as a source of perfume.

damask steel, Damascus steel.

dame (dām) *n.* **1.** *British.* **a.** a woman upon whom an honorary rank equivalent to that of a knight has been conferred. **b.** the wife or widow of a knight or baronet. **2.** formerly, a woman of rank or authority; lady. **3.** an elderly woman. **4.** *Slang.* any woman or girl. [Old French *dame* lady, from Latin *domina* lady, mistress. Doublet of DUENNA, DAM².]

damn (dam) *v.t.* **1.** to declare (something) to be bad, worthless, or a failure: *The critics damned the play.* **2.** to curse or swear at. **3.** to be the ruin of; cause to fail: *Their greed damned them.* **4.** to condemn to eternal punishment in hell. —*v.i.* to swear; curse. —*n.* **1.** the utterance of "damn" as an expression of anger, disappointment, or annoyance. **2.** a negligible amount; slightest bit: *That's not worth a damn.* —*adj., adv. Informal.* very; damned. —*interj.* an expression of anger, disappointment, or annoyance. [Old French *damner* to harm, condemn, from Latin *damnāre* to condemn.]
  • **to damn with faint praise.** to praise so grudgingly as to imply condemnation.
  • **to give a damn.** *Informal.* to care; be concerned. ➡ used chiefly with a negative: *I don't give a damn what you think.*

dam·na·ble (dam′nə bəl) *adj.* deserving condemnation; outrageous; detestable. —**dam′na·bly,** *adv.*

dam·na·tion (dam nā′shən) *n.* **1.** the act of damning or the state of being damned. **2.** condemnation to eternal punishment in hell. —*interj.* damn.

dam·na·to·ry (dam′nə tôr′ē) *adj.* conveying, imposing, or causing condemnation; damning.

damnd·est (dam′dist) *also,* **damnedest.** *Informal. adj.* **1.** most abominable or outrageous: *That story contained some of the damndest lies.* **2.** most exceptional or extraordinary: *We had the damndest experience yesterday.* —*n.* utmost; best: *I will certainly try my damndest to be there.*

damned (damd) *adj.* **1.** condemned as bad, worthless, or a failure. **2.** *Informal.* outrageous: *The flies are a damned nuisance.* **3.** condemned to eternal punishment in hell. —*adv. Informal.* very; utterly: *That's a damned clever idea.*

damned·est (dam′dist) damndest.

damn·ing (dam′ing, -ning) *adj.* tending to damn or condemn; condemnatory: *damning testimony.*

dam·oi·selle (dam′ə zel′) *also,* **dam·o·sel, dam·o·zel.** *n. Archaic.* damsel.

Da·mon and Pythias (dā′mən) in classical legend, two Greek youths celebrated for their devoted friendship. Damon pledged his life as security that his friend Pythias, who had been condemned to death, would return from settling his affairs. When he did return, both were pardoned.

damp (damp) *adj.* slightly wet; moist: *a damp cloth, a damp cellar, damp weather.* —*n.* **1.** the quality or condition of being wet; moisture; humidity. **2.** something that checks or discourages.

3. a harmful gas found esp. in mines, such as firedamp. —*v.t.* **1.** to dampen. **2.** to reduce in intensity; check; dull: *to damp a fire, to damp a sound, to damp one's spirits.* [Middle Dutch or Middle Low German *damp* vapor.] —**damp′ly,** *adv.* —**damp′ness,** *n.*

damp·en (dam′pən) *v.t.* **1.** to make damp; moisten. **2.** to diminish the force or intensity of; check; depress: *The rain dampened our enthusiasm for a picnic.* —*v.i.* to become damp. —**damp′en·er,** *n.*

damp·er (dam′pər) *n.* **1.** a person or thing that depresses or checks: *The loss put a damper on our hopes for the championship.* **2.** a movable plate in a flue, used for regulating the draft, as in a fireplace, stove, or furnace. **3.** a device for deadening vibration, as of piano strings, or oscillations, as of a magnetic needle.

damp·ing-off (dam′ping ôf′, -of′) *n.* a disease of young plants, esp. seedlings and cuttings, caused by any of several parasitic fungi that attack roots or stems, causing them to decay and die.

dam·sel (dam′zəl) *n.* a young unmarried woman; maiden. [Old French *dameisele,* going back to Latin *domina* lady, mistress.]

dam·sel·fly (dam′zəl flī′) *n., pl.* **-flies.** any of a group of brightly colored insects, suborder Zygoptera, closely related to the dragonfly, but distinguished by a more slender body and the folded position of the wings when at rest.

dam·son (dam′zən, -sən) *n.* **1.** the small, round, dark purple fruit of a plum tree, *Prunus insititia,* having a tart flavor and used mainly in preserves. **2.** the tree bearing this fruit, originally cultivated in Asia Minor. [Latin *(prūnum) Damascēnum* (plum) of Damascus.]

damselfly

Dan. 1. Daniel. **2.** Danish.

Dan·a·e (dan′ā ē′) *also,* **Dan·a·ë.** *n.* in Greek mythology, the mother of Perseus by Zeus, who appeared to her in the form of a shower of gold.

Da·na·i·des (də nā′i dēz′) *also,* **Dan·a·i·des.** *n.* in Greek legend, the fifty daughters of Danaus, who, with one exception, killed their husbands on their wedding night at their father's command. Their punishment was to draw water with broken vessels forever in Hades.

Dan·a·us (dan′ā əs) *also,* **Dan·a·üs.** *n.* in Greek legend, a king of Argos and father of the Danaides.

dance (dans) *v.,* **danced, danc·ing.** —*v.i.* **1.** to move the body or feet rhythmically in a prescribed or improvised pattern, usually in time to music. **2.** to move about in a lively or excited way; leap about: *We all danced with joy when we heard the news.* **3.** to bob up and down: *The sunlight danced on the water's surface.* —*v.t.* **1.** to perform or take part in (a dance): *to dance the polka.* **2.** to cause to dance: *He danced her around the room.* —*n.* **1.** a definite series of rhythmical steps or movements, usually done to music: *The waltz is a well-known dance.* **2.** the act or an instance of dancing. **3.** *also,* **the dance.** the art of dancing. **4.** a social gathering for dancing: *There will be a dance Friday night at the club.* **5.** one round of dancing: *He was her partner for the last dance.* **6.** a piece of music written for dancing: *Strauss composed many dances.* [Old French *danser* to move rhythmically with steps; possibly of Germanic origin.]
  • **to dance attendance on.** to wait on constantly and obsequiously.

dance of death, an allegory popular in medieval art, in which a skeleton representing Death leads people in a dance to the grave. Also, **danse macabre.**

danc·er (dan′sər) *n.* a person who dances, esp. one whose profession is dancing.

dan·de·li·on (dan′də lī′ən) *n.* **1.** a yellow flower of any of a group of plants, genus *Taraxacum,* of the composite family, esp. *T. officinale,* the common dandelion. **2.** the plant bearing this flower, having a cluster of leaves around the base of a hollow stalk and found growing wild in temperate regions throughout the world. [Middle English *dentdelyon,* from Old French *dent de lion* literally, tooth of the lion (from the shape of its toothlike leaves), going back to Latin *dēns* tooth + *dē* from, of + *leō* lion.]

dan·der (dan′dər) *n.* loose flakes or scales shed by the skin: *I'm allergic to cat dander.* [Of uncertain origin.]
  • **to get one's** (or **someone's**) **dander up.** to get (or make) angry.

a	at	e	end	o	hot	u	up	hw	white		about
ā	ape	ē	me	ō	old	ū	use	ng	song		taken
ä	far	i	it	ô	fork	ü	rule	th	thin	ə	pencil
âr	care	ī	ice	oi	oil	u̇	pull	th	this		lemon
		îr	pierce	ou	out	ûr	turn	zh	measure		circus

Dan·die Din·mont terrier (dan′dē din′mont) a small, long-bodied terrier of a breed originally developed in Scotland for hunting small game, having hind legs longer than the front legs, a curly topknot, and a shaggy coat. Height: 8-11 inches (20-28 centimeters) at the shoulder. [From *Dandie Dinmont*, a character who owned two such terriers in the novel *Guy Mannering*, by the Scottish novelist Sir Walter Scott, 1771-1832.]

Dandie Dinmont terrier

dan·dle (dan′dəl) *v.t.*, **-dled, -dling. 1.** to move (a person) up and down on one's knees or in one's arms: *to dandle a child.* **2.** to handle or stroke affectionately; fondle; pet. [Of uncertain origin.] —**dan′dler,** *n.*

dan·druff (dan′drəf) *n.* small white or grayish scales of dead skin shed from the scalp. [Possibly from dialectal English *dander* scales on the skin + Middle English *roufe* scab (of Scandinavian origin).]

dan·dy (dan′dē) *n.*, *pl.* **-dies. 1.** a man who is excessively concerned about the neatness and elegance of his dress and appearance; fop. **2.** *Informal.* a very fine example of its class: *That mystery novel is a dandy.* —*adj.*, **-di·er, -di·est. 1.** characteristic of or resembling a dandy; foppish. **2.** *Informal.* very good; excellent. [Possibly from a nickname for *Andrew*, or a shortened form of earlier *jack-a-dandy* fop.] —**dan′dy·ish,** *adj.*

Dane (dān) *n.* **1.** a native or citizen of Denmark. **2.** a person of Danish ancestry.

Dane·law (dān′lô′) also, **Dane·lagh.** *n.* **1.** a region in east and northeast England ruled by the Danes during the ninth and tenth centuries. **2.** the body of laws enforced by the Danes in this region. [Old English *Dena lagu* Danes' law; of Scandinavian origin.]

dan·ger (dān′jər) *n.* **1.** exposure or liability to harm, injury, evil, or loss; risk; peril: *There is danger in skating on thin ice.* **2.** an instance or cause of harm, risk, or peril: *Narrow, winding roads are a danger to drivers.* [Old French *dangier* power (hence, power to harm), jurisdiction, going back to Latin *dominium* power, sovereignty.]

Synonyms **Danger, hazard, peril,** and **risk** denote a threat of damage or harm. **Danger** is the general term, with no implication of extent, immediacy, or inevitability: *the danger of drowning, the danger of losing one's wallet.* **Hazard** suggests that there is chance of harm, while **peril** suggests a high probability of harm: *Driving on these roads at night is a hazard, but if you wait, you are in peril of being caught in the blizzard.* **Risk,** like *hazard,* suggests chance, and implies accepting the odds: *Are you willing to live with the risk of not having insurance?*

dan·ger·ous (dān′jər əs) *adj.* **1.** full of danger; risky; hazardous: *Mining is a dangerous occupation.* **2.** likely to cause harm: *A tiger is a dangerous animal.* —**dan′ger·ous·ly,** *adv.* —**dan′ger·ous·ness,** *n.*

dan·gle (dang′gəl) *v.*, **-gled, -gling.** —*v.i.* **1.** to hang or swing loosely: *The broken branch dangled from the tree.* **2.** to follow a person longingly or closely, as for a favor; be a hanger-on (often with *after*): *to dangle after a celebrity.* —*v.t.* **1.** to make (something) swing loosely. **2.** to hold out as an incentive: *to dangle the prospect of a raise to an employee.* [Possibly from Danish *dangle* to bob[1].] —**dan′gler,** *n.*

dangling participle, a participle that does not agree logically with the word it is supposed to modify. In the sentence *After working all morning, the lunch was brought out to us, working* is a dangling participle because it appears to modify the word *lunch.*

Dan·iel (dan′yəl) *n.* a book of the Old Testament, containing the story of the Hebrew prophet Daniel and his prophecies.

Dan·ish (dā′nish) *adj.* of, relating to, or characteristic of Denmark or its people, language, or culture. —*n.* **1.** the North Germanic language spoken by the people of Denmark, a member of the Indo-European family of languages. **2.** *Informal.* Danish pastry.

Danish pastry, a sweet, rich pastry made with raised dough.

dank (dangk) *adj.* disagreeably damp; moist and cold. [Probably of Scandinavian origin.] —**dank′ly,** *adv.* —**dank′ness,** *n.*

danse ma·ca·bre (däns mä kä′br) dance of death.

dan·seur (dän sœr′) *n.*, *pl.* **-seurs** (-sœr′). a male ballet dancer. [French *danseur* male dancer, going back to Old French *danser.* See DANCE.]

dan·seuse (dän sœz′) *n.*, *pl.* **-seuses** (-sœz′). a female ballet dancer. [French *danseuse* female dancer, from *danseur.* See DANSEUR.]

Daph·ne (daf′nē) *n.* in Greek mythology, a nymph who escaped from her pursuer, Apollo, by being changed into a laurel tree.

daph·ni·a (daf′nē ə) *n.* any of a group of tiny, transparent crustaceans, genus *Daphnia,* that inhabit freshwater ponds and puddles throughout the world. [Modern Latin *Daphnia,* possibly from DAPHNE.]

dap·per (dap′ər) *adj.* **1.** smart in dress or appearance; neat; trim. **2.** small and active. [Dutch *dapper* brave, quick.] —**dap′per·ly,** *adv.* —**dap′per·ness,** *n.*

dap·ple (dap′əl) *adj.* marked with spots; spotted; variegated: *a dapple horse.* Also, **dap′pled.** —*n.* **1.** a spot or dot, as on an animal's skin or coat. **2.** an animal having a spotted coat. —*v.t., v.i.* **-pled, -pling.** to mark or become marked with spots. [Of uncertain origin.]

dap·ple-gray (dap′əl grā′) *adj.* gray marked with spots of a darker shade. —*n.* a dapple-gray horse.

DAR, Daughters of the American Revolution, a society of women descended from Americans who fought on or gave aid to the Colonial side in the American Revolution.

Dar·by and Joan (där′bē; jōn′) any happily married elderly couple. [From a couple so named and described in an eighteenth-century English ballad.]

dare (dâr) *v.*, **dared** or *(archaic)* **durst, dar·ing.** —*v.t.* **1.** to make or issue a challenge to (someone) to do something, esp. as proof of courage or ability: *I dared him to climb the wall.* **2.** to be courageous or impudent enough to attempt or undertake: *to dare the ascent of a mountain, to dare to challenge authority.* **3.** to meet boldly and defiantly: *We dared the elements by going out in the storm.* —*v.i.* to have the courage or impudence to do or try something: *Several people were skating on the thin ice, but I didn't dare.* —*auxiliary verb.* to be courageous or impudent enough to. ➡ used chiefly in questions or with the negative. In the present tense, the form **dare** rather than **dares** is used in the third person singular: *How dare she do such a thing? He dare not speak.* —*n.* a challenge: *I took the dare and rode the horse bareback.* [Old English *dear,* first person singular of *durran* to venture.] —**dar′er,** *n.*

dare·dev·il (dâr′dev′əl) *n.* a recklessly daring person. —*adj.* **1.** daring; fearless: *daredevil stunts.* **2.** reckless; rash. —**dare′dev′il·ry, dare′dev′il·try,** *n.*

dare·say (dâr′sā′) also, **dare say.** *v.t., v.i.* to think or suppose: *I daresay the mayor's speech will cause controversy.* ➡ used only in the present tense and only with the pronoun *I.*

dar·ing (dâr′ing) *n.* adventurous courage; boldness. —*adj.* courageous and adventurous; fearless. —**dar′ing·ly,** *adv.*

Dar·jee·ling (där jē′ling) *n.* a very fine variety of black tea from the mountainous regions of northern India. [From *Darjeeling,* district in India where this tea is grown.]

dark (därk) *adj.* **1.** having little or no light: *a dark night, a dark room.* **2.** reflecting or radiating little light: *a dark color.* **3.a.** of a deep shade: *a dark blue.* **b.** nearly black: *dark eyes, dark hair.* **4.** not light-complexioned or fair; swarthy: *dark skin.* **5.** gloomy; cheerless; dismal: *Don't always look on the dark side of things.* **6.** having a morose appearance or character; sullen: *a face dark with anger, a dark mood.* **7.** hidden from view or knowledge; mysterious: *a dark scheme.* **8.** spiritually or mentally blind; unenlightened; ignorant: *a dark era of superstition and bigotry.* **9.** difficult to comprehend or explain; obscure in meaning: *a dark subject, a dark passage in a book.* **10.** evil; wicked; heinous: *a dark purpose, dark deeds.* —*n.* **1.** a partial or total absence of light: *The child was afraid of the dark.* **2.** the part of a day when there is no sunlight or when sunlight ends; night; nightfall: *The thieves crept away after dark.* **3.** a dark color or shade: *There are many lights and darks in that painting.* [Old English *deorc* devoid of light, gloomy, wicked.] —**dark′ly,** *adv.* —**dark′ness,** *n.*

·**in the dark. a.** in concealment, obscurity, or secrecy: *The senator kept his political intentions in the dark.* **b.** in a state of ignorance; uninformed: *We were in the dark about her vacation plans.*

Synonyms *adj.* **Dark, dim,** and **gloomy** mean lacking light. **Dark** may describe anything from a complete absence of light to insufficient illumination: *the dark interior of a box lined with black velvet, trying to find one's way on a dark night.* **Dim** implies a lack of clarity because of too little light: *I could not make out his face in the dim room.* **Gloomy** may describe a much less dark condition, but suggests a mood established by lack of light: *An overcast sky made the afternoon gloomy.*

Dark Ages also, **dark ages. 1.** the period in European history from about A.D. 476 to about A.D. 1000, between the fall of the Western Roman Empire and the rise of medieval civilization. ➡ so called because it has traditionally been thought of as a time when learning and culture were neglected and civilization did not advance. **2.** formerly, the Middle Ages as a whole, from about A.D. 476 to about A.D. 1450.

Dark Continent, Africa. ➡ used esp. during the nineteenth century when the rest of the world knew very little about it.

dark·en (där′kən) *v.t., v.i.* to make or become dark or darker. —**dark′en·er,** *n.*

dark horse 1. a winner, esp. in a horse race, about whom little is known and whose chances of success had been considered small. **2.a.** a person who is mentioned as a possible nominee for political office but is considered unlikely to receive the nomination. **b.** a person who unexpectedly receives a nomination for political office.

dark·ish (där′kish) *adj.* somewhat dark.

dark lantern, a lantern whose light can be concealed by a dark slide or cover.

dark·ling (därk′ling) *Archaic. adv.* in the dark. —*adj.* **1.** characterized or obscured by darkness; dim: *And we are here as on a darkling plain* (Matthew Arnold, "Dover Beach"). **2.** taking place in the dark.

dark·room (därk′rüm′, -ru̇m′) *n.* a room in which photographs are developed, arranged so that all actinic light is excluded.

dark·some (därk′səm) *adj. Archaic.* **1.** dark; darkish. **2.** gloomy; cheerless.

dar·ling (där′ling) *n.* **1.** a person who is very dear or much loved. ➡ often used as an affectionate form of address. **2.** a favorite: *That actress was once the darling of movie audiences.* —*adj.* **1.** dearly loved; cherished: *a darling son.* **2.** *Informal.* charmingly attractive; cute: *What a darling child!* [Old English *dēorling* one dearly loved, from *dēore* dear.]

darn¹ (därn) *v.t., v.i.* to mend, as a tear or hole in clothing, by sewing interlacing stitches across the gap. —*n.* **1.** a place mended by darning. **2.** the act of darning. [Middle French *darner,* from Breton *darn,* a piece.]

darn² (därn) *Informal.* damn. ➡ used as a euphemism. [Milder form of DAMN.]

dar·nel (där′nəl) *n.* an annual rye grass, *Lolium temulentum,* often found in grain fields. It is a weed pest and its seeds may become poisonous. [Of uncertain origin.]

darn·er (där′nər) *n.* **1.** a person who darns. **2.** darning needle *(def. 1).* **3.** a hard, round device of wood or other material placed under a hole to be darned. Also *(def. 3),* **darning ball.**

darn·ing (där′ning) *n.* **1.a.** the act of mending with interlaced stitches. **b.** the result of such a process. **2.** articles darned or to be darned.

darning needle 1. a long needle with a large eye, used for darning. Also, **darner. 2.** dragonfly.

dart (därt) *n.* **1.a.** a slender, oblong projectile with a short metal point in front and feathers or featherlike projections in the rear, used in playing certain games. **b. darts.** a game in which such projectiles are thrown at a target. **2.** a slender, pointed weapon to be thrown or shot, such as that used in blowguns by some Indian tribes of North and South America. **3.** a sudden, swift movement. **4.** a tapered tuck sewn in a garment to give it a better fit. **5.** the stinger of an insect. —*v.i.* to spring or move suddenly and swiftly: *The rabbit darted from the bushes.* —*v.t.* **1.** to throw or emit suddenly and rapidly: *The lizard darted its tongue at the insect.* **2.** to send suddenly: *to dart a glance at a person.* [Old French *dart,* accusative of *dars* javelin, from Late Latin *dardus;* of Germanic origin.]

dart·er (där′tər) *n.* **1.** a person or thing that moves suddenly and swiftly. **2.** any of several small freshwater fish, family Percidae, closely related to the perch, that swim in quick, darting movements and are found in North America east of the Rockies. Length: to 8 inches (20 centimeters). **3.** snakebird.

Dar·win·i·an (där win′ē ən) *adj.* of or relating to Charles Darwin or his theory of evolution. —*n.* an advocate of Darwinism.

Dar·win·ism (där′wə niz′əm) *n.* the theory of evolution propounded by the English naturalist Charles Darwin, which states that all species of plants and animals developed by inheriting slight variations from earlier forms, and that those organisms having traits best suited to their environment survive through the process of natural selection. —**Dar′win·ist,** *adj., n.*

dash (dash) *v.i.* **1.** to move with speed and violence; rush: *The dog dashed after the ball I threw.* **2.** to strike or hit with violence; smash: *Waves dashed against the ship.* —*v.t.* **1.** to strike violently against: *The waves dashed the shore.* **2.** to shatter or break with force or violence; smash: *The storm dashed the ship against the rocks.* **3.** to throw, knock, or thrust violently and suddenly: *The angry man dashed the chair against the door.* **4.** to wet by throwing liquid; splash; spatter: *The girls dashed each other with water.* **5.** to ruin or frustrate: *The bad news dashed our hopes of getting the contract.* **6.** to daunt; depress. **7.** to put to shame; abash. **8.** to mix with a small quantity of something else: *to dash juice with water.* —*n.* **1.** a sudden rush or movement: *The prisoner made a dash for freedom.* **2.** a small quantity added or mixed in: *a dash of pepper.* **3.** a short race that is run or swum at top speed: *the 50-yard dash.* **4.** a hasty stroke, as of a pen. **5.a.** a splashing of water or other liquid on or against something. **b.** the sound of splashing. **6.** spirited energy and style: *The dancer has dash and verve.* **7.** a short horizontal line (—) used in writing or printing, as for showing a pause or break in a sentence or indicating an omission. **8.** *Telegraphy.* a long signal used in conjunction with a shorter one to represent numbers or letters, as in Morse code. ➡ distinguished from DOT¹. **9.** dashboard *(def. 1).* [Probably imitative.]

· **to dash off. a.** to hurry away; leave quickly. **b.** to make, write, or complete quickly or hastily: *I dashed off a letter to my cousin.*

dash·board (dash′bôrd′) *n.* **1.** a panel equipped with instruments and gauges, located in front of the driver in an automobile or similar vehicle. Also, **dash. 2.** a screen placed on the front of an open vehicle, as a buggy or buckboard, to prevent mud or water from being splashed into it.

dash·er (dash′ər) *n.* **1.** a person or thing that dashes. **2.** the plunger of a churn.

dash·ing (dash′ing) *adj.* **1.** full of dash; lively; spirited: *the dashing young star of a movie.* **2.** showy or stylish: *a dashing outfit.* —**dash′ing·ly,** *adv.*

das·tard (das′tərd) *n.* a mean, base coward; sneak. —*adj.* dastardly. [Of uncertain origin.]

das·tard·ly (das′tərd lē) *adj.* mean and despicably cowardly. —**das′tard·li·ness,** *n.*

dat., dative.

DAT, digital audio tape.

da·ta (dā′tə, dat′ə) *pl. n., sing.* **-tum. 1.** information from which inferences or conclusions can be drawn; facts and figures. **2.** information processed by a computer. ➡ used as singular or plural: *The data indicate that our theory is wrong. The data for the project has been collected.* [Plural of DATUM.]

da·ta·base (dā′tə bās′, dat′ə-) *also,* **data base.** *n.* a collection of data that is organized by categories so that information can be retrieved logically and easily, as by a computer. Also, **data bank.**

data processing, the rapid organization and analysis of large amounts of information by machines, esp. digital computers.

date¹ (dāt) *n.* **1.** a day of the month or year: *Today's date is May 15.* **2.** the specific point or period of time when something occurs or is to occur: *The date of his death is uncertain. She set a date for the wedding.* **3.** an inscription, as on a coin or statue, stating when something was written or made: *The cornerstone on the building bears the date 1954.* **4.** *Informal.* an appointment or social engagement for a specified time or place: *The friends made a date for next Tuesday.* **5.** *Informal.* a person with whom such an engagement is made: *John and his date went to a play. Do you have a date for lunch?* **6.** the period of time or age to which something belongs: *The chariot is of Roman date.* **7.** the time during which something lasts; duration. —*v.,* **dat·ed, dat·ing.** —*v.t.* **1.** to furnish or mark with a date: *The secretary dated the letter.* **2.** to determine or fix the time of; assign a date to: *Archaeologists dated the fossil after much study.* **3.** *Informal.* to have a date or dates with. **4.** to show to be old-fashioned: *Your style of dress dates you.* —*v.i.* **1.** to belong to, or have origin in, a particular time or era (often with *from*): *This custom dates from the seventeenth century.* **2.** *Informal.* to go out on dates: *We've been dating a year.* [Middle English *date* date (in time), from Middle French *date,* going back to Latin *data,* feminine of *datus* given, past participle of *dare* to give; from the expression used to date a letter in ancient Rome: *(epistola) data Romae* (letter) given at Rome (as on a specified date).] —For Synonyms *(n.),* see **appointment.**

· **out of date.** no longer in vogue or use; old-fashioned: *Bustles are out of date.*

· **to date.** up to and including the present time: *I have received only three replies to date.*

· **up to date.** so as to agree with the latest facts or information: *The accountants brought all their records up to date.*

date² (dāt) *n.* **1.** the oval-shaped edible fruit of the date palm, having thick, sweet flesh. **2.** date palm. [Middle English *date* this fruit, from Old French *date,* from Latin *dactylus,* from Greek *daktylos* this fruit; literally, finger (from the supposed resemblance of its shape to a finger); of Semitic origin.]

dat·ed (dā′tid) *adj.* **1.** marked with a date. **2.** out-of-date; old-fashioned: *dated ideas.*

date·less (dāt′lis) *adj.* **1.** without a date; bearing no date: *The letter was dateless.* **2.** old but retaining permanent interest or

a	at	e	end	o	hot	u	up	hw	white		about
ā	ape	ē	me	ō	old	ū	use	ng	song		taken
ä	far	i	it	ô	fork	u̇	rule	th	thin	ə	pencil
âr	care	ī	ice	oi	oil	u̇	pull	th	this		lemon
		îr	pierce	ou	out	ûr	turn	zh	measure		circus

309

worth: *a dateless novel.* **3.** so old as to be undatable; immemorial. **4.** having no limit or end.

date·line (dāt′līn′) *n.* a line in a piece of printed material, as an article or newspaper, that supplies its place and date of origin. —*v.t.,* **-lined, -lin·ing.** to provide with a dateline.

date line, International Date Line.

date palm, a tall tropical tree, *Phoenix dactylifera,* of the palm family, having a straight, shaggy trunk topped with divided leaves and bearing thick clusters of fruit. Also, **date².**

date palm trees

da·tive (dā′tiv) *n.* **1.** the grammatical case in Latin, Russian, and several other Indo-European languages that indicates the indirect object of a verb. In English this case is usually denoted by the use of *to* or *for* preceding the object or by word order: *Please hand that book to me. Please hand me that book.* **2.** a word in this case. —*adj.* of, designating, or belonging to the dative. [Latin *dativus* of giving, as in the grammatical term *cāsus datīvus* literally, case of giving.]

da·tum (dā′təm, dat′əm) *n., pl.* **data.** **1.** a single piece of information; a single fact. **2.** a known or assumed fact from which a conclusion can be inferred. **3.** something used as a basis for measurements or calculations. [Latin *datum* something given, from neuter of *datus,* past participle of *dare* to give.]

dau., daughter.

daub (dôb) *v.t.* **1.** to coat, cover, or smear with a soft adhesive substance, as plaster, grease, or clay: *to daub a wall with plaster.* **2.** to spread (a soft adhesive substance) on something: *to daub paint on a canvas.* **3.** to paint (something) coarsely or inartistically. —*v.i.* to paint something coarsely or inartistically. —*n.* **1.** a smear or smudge: *The children had daubs of mud on their legs.* **2.** a substance used for daubing, as plaster or clay. **3.** a crudely painted picture. **4.** the act of daubing. [Old French *dauber* to whitewash, plaster, from Latin *dēalbāre,* going back to *dē* down + *albus* white.] —**daub′er,** *n.*

daugh·ter (dô′tər) *n.* **1.** a female offspring considered in relationship to one or both of her parents. **2.** a female descendant: *Ruth was a daughter of Abraham.* **3.** a female considered in relation to something that functions in a way similar to a parent: *a daughter of Scotland.* **4.** anything considered as female in relation to its source or origin: *The Romance languages are daughters of Latin.* [Old English *dohtor* female offspring or descendant.]

daughter cell *Biology.* a cell that results from division or replication.

daugh·ter-in-law (dô′tər in lô′) *n., pl.* **daugh·ters-in-law.** the wife of one's son.

daugh·ter·ly (dô′tər lē) *adj.* of, relating to, or proper for a daughter.

daunt (dônt) *v.t.* to cause to lose hope or courage; frighten or discourage: *The explorers were not daunted by the dangers involved in their expedition.* [Old French *danter* to tame, subdue, from Latin *domitāre.*]

daunt·less (dônt′lis) *adj.* having or showing no fear; fearless; courageous; daring. —**daunt′less·ly,** *adv.*

dau·phin (dô′fin, dō′-; *French* dō faN′) *n.* the oldest son of the king of France. ➡ used as a title from 1349 to 1830. [Old French *daulphin, dauphin* literally, dolphin; originally referring to the three *dolphins* in the coat of arms of a noble French family that, in 1349, gave the province *Dauphiné* to the king of France on condition that the oldest son of the king of France would thereafter have the title *dauphin.* See DOLPHIN.]

dau·phin·ess (dô′fi nis, dō′-) *n.* the wife of a dauphin. Also, **dau·phine** (dô′fēn, dō′-).

dav·en·port (dav′ən pôrt′) *n.* **1.** a large upholstered sofa, esp. one that is convertible into a bed. **2.** a writing desk or table, often with drawers. [Supposedly named after the first maker of the desk.]

dav·it (dav′it, dā′vit) *n.* **1.** one of a pair of movable or curved arms that can project over the stern or side of a boat or ship, used esp. to carry a small boat or to raise it from or lower it into the water. **2.** a similar device used for raising or lowering the anchor of a ship. [Earlier *david;* an example of the use of a name for a tool, as in BILLY, JACK.]

Da·vy Jones (dā′vē jōnz′) the spirit of the sea.

Davy Jones's locker, the bottom of the ocean, esp. regarded as the grave of those who drown at sea.

daw (dô) *n.* jackdaw. [Probably from an unrecorded Old English word.]

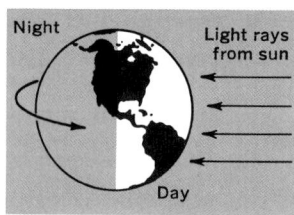

davits

daw·dle (dô′dəl) *v.t., v.i.,* **-dled, -dling.** to waste (time); idle; linger (often with *away*): *to dawdle the afternoon away, to dawdle over breakfast.* [Of uncertain origin.] —**daw′dler,** *n.*

dawn (dôn) *n.* **1.** the first appearance of light in the morning; daybreak. **2.** the beginning or first appearance: *the dawn of a new era, the dawn of civilization.* —*v.i.* **1.** to begin to grow light in the morning; become day. **2.** to begin to be clear, understood, or perceived (with *on* or *upon*): *It suddenly dawned on us that we were being deceived.* **3.** to begin to appear, develop, or open: *The space age dawned in the twentieth century.* [From earlier *dawning* daybreak; probably of Scandinavian origin.]

dawn redwood, a deciduous conifer, *Metasequoia glyptostroboides,* first discovered as fossil remains and later found growing in China, now grown as an ornamental. Also, **metasequoia.**

day (dā) *n.* **1.** the period of light between the rising and setting of the sun: *June 21 is the longest day of the year.* **2.** the light of day; daylight. **3.a.** the length of time required for the earth to complete one rotation on its axis, approximately 24 hours. Also, **solar day. b.** the length of time required by another planet or moon to complete one rotation on its axis. **4.a.** the part of a day passed in a particular way or place: *a school day.* **b.** the hours of a day devoted to work: *They worked a seven-hour day.* **5.** a day regarded as a point or unit of time when something happens or which fixes a date: *She came on the third day and left on the fifth.* **6.** *also,* **Day.** a specific day set aside for a particular purpose or observance: *election day, a wedding day.* **7.** a period of existence, power, action, success, or influence: *Knighthood has had its day.* **8.** *also,* **days.** a particular time or period; era: *in King Arthur's day, in those days.* **9.** *usually,* **days.** a span of existence; lifetime: *The settlers spent their days eking out a living.* **10.** chance; opportunity: *Your day will come soon.* **11.** contest or struggle: *The runner carried the day by winning three races.* [Old English *dæg* period between the rising and setting of the sun, length of time required for the earth to complete one rotation on its axis.]

• **day after day.** every day.
• **day by day.** each day; daily.
• **day in, day out.** every day.
• **from day to day. a.** without foresight or provision for the future: *They lived from day to day.* **b.** from one day to the next: *The situation changed from day to day.*
• **the other day.** in the recent past; not long ago.
• **to call it a day.** *Informal.* to stop engaging in an activity.

Day·ak (dī′ak, -ək) Dyak.

day·bed (dā′bed′) *also,* **day bed.** *n.* a sofa that can be converted into a bed.

day·book (dā′bŏŏk′) *n.* **1.** in bookkeeping, a book in which business transactions are recorded chronologically. **2.** a diary or journal.

day·break (dā′brāk′) *n.* the time each morning when daylight first appears; dawn.

day care, daytime care, including supervision, medical services, and the providing of meals, for preschool children or elderly people. —**day′-care′,** *adj.*

day and **night**

day-care center (dā′kâr′) a facility for the care of small children during the day. Also, **day nursery.**

day coach, a railroad passenger car equipped only with seating facilities, as distinguished from sleeping, dining, or other specialized cars.

day·dream (dā′drēm′) *n.* an imaginary fancy experienced while awake, esp. one of happy, pleasant thoughts, hopes, or ambitions. —*v.i.* to indulge in or have daydreams. —**day′dream′er,** *n.*

day laborer, a worker who is paid by the day, esp. an unskilled worker.

day letter, a telegram sent during the day, which is cheaper but slower than a regular telegram.

day·light (dā′līt′) *n.* **1.** the light of day. **2.** daytime. **3.** dawn: *The farmer was up before daylight.* **4.** public view: *The committee brought the matter out into the daylight.* **5. daylights.** *Informal.* wits; sense: *to scare the daylights out of someone.*
• **to see daylight.** *Informal.* **a.** to understand. **b.** to near the end or conclusion of a difficult task.

daylight saving time, the system of time in which clocks are set one or more hours ahead of standard time, used esp. during summer months to provide more daylight hours at the end of the working day.

day·lil·y (dā′lil′ē) *n., pl.* **-lil·ies. 1.** the yellow, orange, red, or purple flower of any of a group of plants, genus *Hemerocallis,* of the lily family. The flowers live for only one day. **2.** the long-leaved plant that bears these flowers.

day·long (dā′lông′) *adj.* lasting all day. —*adv.* through all the whole day.

day nursery, day-care center.

Day of Atonement, Yom Kippur.

Day of Judgment, Judgment Day.

days (dāz) *adv.* regularly during the daytime: *to work days.*

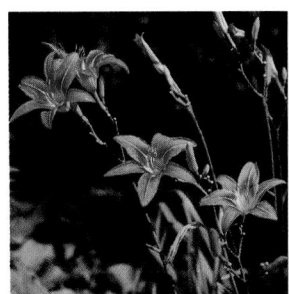

daylilies

➤ distinguished from **boarding**

day school 1. a school that holds classes only during the day. **2.** a private school whose students live at home.
school.

days of grace, an extension of time given for payment of a note or bill of exchange after its due date.

day·star (dā′stär′) *n.* **1.** morning star. **2.** *Archaic.* sun.

day student, a student at a preparatory school or college who lives at home.

day·time (dā′tīm′) *n.* the period of time between the rising and setting of the sun.

day-to-day (dā′tə dā′) *adj.* **1.** of, relating to, or happening every day; daily: *Brushing your teeth is an important part of a day-to-day routine.* **2.** dealing with things one day at a time, with little thought for the future: *to run a business on a day-to-day basis.*

daze (dāz) *v.t.,* **dazed, daz·ing.** to stun or stupefy, as by a blow; bewilder; confuse: *The blow to his head dazed the boxer.* —*n.* a dazed state or condition: *The accident left her in a daze.* [Of Scandinavian origin.]

daz·zle (daz′əl) *v.,* **-zled, -zling.** —*v.t.* **1.** to dim or overpower the vision of with an excess of light: *The bright morning sun dazzled him.* **2.** to overpower, confound, or impress, as by brilliance, splendor, or ostentation: *The tennis star's outstanding play dazzled her opponent.* —*v.i.* **1.** to be overpowered or blinded by light. **2.** to excite admiration by brilliance or showiness. —*n.* the act of dazzling or the state of being dazzled. [DAZE + -LE.] —**daz′zler,** *n.* —**daz′zling·ly,** *adv.*

dB, decibel.

dbl., double.

DC 1. direct current. *also,* **dc, d.c. 2.** the postal abbreviation for the District of Columbia.

D.C. 1. direct current. **2.** District of Columbia.

D.C.L., Doctor of Civil Law.

D.D., Doctor of Divinity.

D-day (dē′dā′) *n.* **1.** the day on which the Allied forces invaded France during World War II; June 6, 1944. **2.** the day on which any operation commences or is to commence: *Monday is D-day for the new sales campaign.* [D abbreviation of day + DAY.]

D.D.S., Doctor of Dental Surgery.

DDT, a white or cream-colored powdery compound with a faint odor, poisonous to humans and animals upon contact, formerly widely used as an insecticide. [Abbreviation of *d(ichloro)d(i-phenyl)t(richloroethane).*]

de- *prefix* **1.** removed from; away; off: *deport, delay, dethrone.* **2.** down: *demote, degrade.* **3.** to do the opposite of, reverse, or undo: *demoralize, decompose.* **4.** thoroughly; completely: *deplore, declaim.* [Either Latin *dē* from, away, down, or Latin *dis* apart, away, un-², exceedingly.]

DE, the postal abbreviation for Delaware.

dea·con (dē′kən) *n.* **1.** in some Christian churches, a cleric or layperson who assists the priest or minister in the services or who helps administer the business affairs of the church. **2.** *Roman Catholic Church.* **a.** a cleric who helps conduct worship for a year before becoming a priest. **b.** a priest who assists the celebrant at a Solemn High Mass. [Old English *deacon* servant or minister of the Christian church, from Latin *diāconus,* from Greek *diākonos* originally, servant.]

dea·con·ess (dē′kə nis) *n.* a woman who is a church assistant, esp. one who does medical or social work.

dea·con·ry (dē′kən rē) *n., pl.* **-ries. 1.** the position or office of a deacon. **2.** deacons collectively.

dead (ded) *adj.* **1.** no longer living; having died; lifeless. **2.** resembling death; still: *a dead faint, a dead sleep.* **3.** not endowed with life; inanimate: *dead matter.* **4.** lacking sensation; numb: *The anesthetic will make the nerve dead.* **5.** lacking sensitivity; unresponsive: *He was dead to all sense of shame.* **6.** destitute of spiritual life or energy. **7.** lacking significance, usefulness, or interest: *a dead issue, the dead past.* **8.** lacking power, force, or effectiveness: *dead laws.* **9.** lacking social or intellectual activity or interest; dull; quiet: *a dead town.* **10.** lacking resilience or elasticity: *a dead tennis ball.* **11.** (of colors) lacking luster or brightness. **12.** having ceased to burn; extinguished: *a dead fire, a dead cigar.* **13.** commercially inactive, useless, or unprofitable: *dead capital.* **14.** not operating or functioning: *The telephone is dead.* **15.** no longer active or in existence: *a dead volcano.* **16.** no longer in use: *a dead language.* **17.** lacking fertility; barren; unproductive: *dead soil.* **18.** *Electricity.* not connected to a source for charge or current: *a dead battery.* **19.** without exception or interruption; complete; absolute: *a dead silence.* **20.** without error; sure; certain: *a dead shot.* **21.** exact; direct: *a dead certainty.* **22.** characterized by a complete and sudden cessation of action or motion; abrupt: *a dead stop.* **23.** *Informal.* very tired; exhausted. **24.** *Informal.* destined for disaster; doomed: *We're dead if we get caught.* **25.** *Sports.* out of play; not in the game. **26.** (of sounds) without resonance; muffled. —*adv.* **1.** to the greatest extent possible; completely; absolutely; entirely: *dead tired, dead sure.* **2.** directly; straight: *dead ahead.* —*n.* **1. the dead.** dead persons collectively. **2.** a time of greatest intensity, as of coldness, darkness, or quiet: *the dead of night, the dead of winter.* [Old English *dēad* no longer living, lifeless.] —**dead′ness,** *n.*

dead·beat (ded′bēt′) *n. Slang.* **1.** a person who avoids paying bills. **2.** an idle person; loafer.

dead center 1. in mechanics, the position of a crank at which it is in a direct line with the connecting rod. Also, **dead point. 2.** the exact center.

dead·en (ded′ən) *v.t.* **1.** to lessen the activity, force, or intensity of; weaken: *to deaden sound.* **2.** to lessen the sensitivity of; numb; dull: *The dentist deadened the nerve with an anesthetic.* **3.** to make soundproof: *to deaden a ceiling.* —*v.i.* to become dead; lose force or sensitivity.

dead-end (ded′end′) *adj.* having or being a dead end: *a dead-end street.*

dead end 1. a street, alley, or passage closed at one end. **2.** a situation or point from which no progress can be made.

dead·eye (ded′ī′) *n.* **1.** a round, laterally flattened wooden block, encircled by a rope or iron band and pierced with three holes, used esp. to extend the shrouds and stays of a ship. **2.** *Informal.* a person who has expert aim with a weapon.

dead·fall (ded′fôl′) *n.* **1.** a trap constructed so that a weight falls upon and kills or holds down an animal. **2.** a tangled mass of fallen trees and underbrush.

dead·head (ded′hed′) *n. Informal.* **1.** a dull, spiritless person. **2.** a nonpaying spectator or passenger, esp. a passenger who rides on a public conveyance free of charge. **3.** a commercial vehicle, as a truck or boat, traveling with no passengers or freight. —*v.i.* **1.** to travel, esp. back to a terminal, with no passengers or freight. **2.** to be a nonpaying spectator or passenger. —*v.t.* **1.** to drive or pilot (a commercial vehicle) with no passengers or freight. **2.** to

a	at	e	end	o	hot	u	up	hw	white		about
ā	ape	ē	me	ō	old	ū	use	ng	song		taken
ä	far	i	it	ô	fork	ü	rule	th	thin	ə	pencil
âr	care	ī	ice	oi	oil	u̇	pull	th	this		lemon
		îr	pierce	ou	out	ûr	turn	zh	measure		circus

carry (someone) as a nonpaying passenger. —*adv.* with no passengers or freight.

dead heat, a race or contest in which two or more competitors are considered winners; tie.

dead letter **1.** a letter that lies unclaimed or cannot be delivered, esp. because of a wrong address. **2.** something that has lost its former importance, as a law or ordinance that is no longer enforced or valid but has not been formally repealed.

dead-letter office (ded′let′er) the department of the post office that receives and handles dead letters.

dead·line (ded′līn′) *n.* a predetermined time by which something must be completed; time limit: *The deadline for the first edition of the paper was 5:00 A.M.*

dead·lock (ded′lok′) *n.* a standstill resulting from the exertion of force by opposing factions: *A compromise broke the deadlock between labor and management.* —*v.t., v.i.* to bring or come to a deadlock.

dead·ly (ded′lē) *adj.*, **-li·er, -li·est. 1.** causing or tending to cause death; fatal: *a deadly blow.* **2.** aiming to kill or destroy; mortal: *deadly enemies.* **3.** extremely effective or dangerous: *deadly sarcasm, deadly aim.* **4.** resembling that of death: *a deadly pallor.* **5.** very great; extreme; excessive: *a deadly hush.* **6.** *Informal.* extremely boring: *a deadly speech.* —*adv.* **1.** in a manner resembling death: *deadly pale.* **2.** *Informal.* very; extremely: *deadly serious.* —**dead′li·ness,** *n.*

Synonyms Deadly, mortal, fatal, and lethal mean causing or capable of causing death. Deadly generally implies great likelihood of death: *a deadly poison, a deadly combination of circumstances.* Mortal is used in reference to individuals, when death has occurred or is going to occur: *The soldier suffered a mortal wound and died five days later.* Fatal is similar to *mortal,* but is more widely used, and may suggest a chain of events between death and its cause: *Locking the gate was a fatal mistake, since it left the victims no escape.* Lethal connotes inevitable death from the nature or purpose of something: *a lethal dose of a drug, a lethal weapon.*

deadly nightshade, belladonna *(def. 1).*

deadly sins, seven deadly sins.

dead·man's float (ded′manz′) a floating position in swimming, face down with the arms stretched out in front.

dead·pan (ded′pan′) *Informal. n. also,* **dead pan. 1.** an expressionless face; poker face. **2.** a person who has or assumes such a face. —*adj., adv.* with a blank or expressionless face. —*v.,* **-panned, -pan·ning.** —*v.i.* to act or speak in an emotionless and expressionless manner. —*v.t.* to do or say (something) in an emotionless and expressionless manner.

dead point, dead center *(def. 1).*

dead reckoning, the calculation of the present position of a boat, ship, or aircraft without astronomical observations, by using the records of its speed and last known position and the compass readings of the course steered.

Dead Sea Scrolls, ancient manuscripts, dating from 100 B.C. to A.D. 100, found in caves near the western shore of the Dead Sea and including some of the oldest known copies of several books of the Old Testament.

dead weight **1.** a heavy, oppressive weight, as of an inert body. **2.** an oppressive burden: *the dead weight of debt.* **3.** the weight of a ship, truck, or other vehicle when not loaded.

dead·wood (ded′wŏŏd′) *n.* **1.** the dead branches of a tree or a dead tree itself. **2.** anything useless or valueless.

deaf (def) *adj.* **1.** wholly or partly unable to hear. **2.** unwilling to hear or listen; heedless: *He was deaf to her warning.* —*n.* **the deaf.** deaf persons collectively. [Old English *dēaf* unable to hear.] —**deaf′ly,** *adv.* —**deaf′ness,** *n.*

deaf·en (def′ən) *v.t.* **1.** to make deaf. **2.** to stun or overwhelm with noise. —**deaf′en·ing,** *adj., n.* —**deaf′en·ing·ly,** *adv.*

deaf-mute (def′mūt′) *n.* a person who cannot hear or speak.

deal¹ (dēl) *v.,* **dealt, deal·ing.** —*v.i.* **1.** to be engaged or concerned; have to do (with *with* or *in*): *This book deals with dogs. Science deals in facts.* **2.** to act or conduct business (often with *with*): *Our principal always deals fairly with students. Mounted police dealt with the rioters.* **3.** to take action with regard to; consider (with *with*): *I will deal with the problem now.* **4.** to do business; trade (with *in* or *with*): *to deal in antiques, to deal with the local butcher.* **5.** to distribute cards to the players of a card game: *It's your turn to deal.* —*v.t.* **1.** to distribute (cards) among the players of a card game: *I dealt seven cards.* **2.** to give as a share; distribute (often with *out*): *She dealt out cookies to the children.* **3.** to give or deliver: *The boxer dealt his opponent a heavy blow.* **4.** *Slang.* to sell (illegal drugs). —*n.* **1.** *Informal.* **a.** a business transaction: *to close the deal for a merger.* **b.** bargain: *to get a good deal on a used car.* **2.** *Informal.* a private or secret arrangement, esp. in commerce or politics, entered into for mutual advantage. **3.** *Informal.* treatment, arrangement, or plan: *a fair deal, a*

dirty deal. **4.** *Card Games.* **a.** the act of distributing cards to the various players; deal. **b.** the cards so distributed; hand. **c.** a player's right or turn to distribute the cards: *It's your deal.* **d.** a single round of playing cards; hand. **5.** *Archaic.* an indefinite quantity, degree, or extent. [Old English *dælan* to divide.]
• **a great** (or **good**) **deal. a.** a large amount or quantity: *You've spent a good deal of time writing that report.* **b.** to a great extent or degree; very much: *to travel a great deal.*
• **big deal.** *Informal.* an important person or thing. ➡ often used ironically as an exclamation.
• **to deal (someone) in. a.** to include in a card game. **b.** *Informal.* to include: *When I heard about their plan to start a business, I asked them to deal me in.*

deal² (dēl) *n.* **1.** a plank of pine or fir wood of any of several standard sizes. **2.** pine or fir wood used for these planks. —*adj.* made of deal. [Middle Low German or Middle Dutch *dele* plank, floor.]

deal·er (dē′lər) *n.* **1.** a person who is engaged in buying and selling: *an antique dealer.* **2.** a person who distributes the cards in a card game.

deal·er·ship (dē′lər ship′) *n.* **1.** authorization to sell a particular commodity in a certain area. **2.** an individual distributor or agency having such authorization.

deal·ing (dē′ling) *n.* **1.** the act of distributing. **2. dealings.** relations, transactions, or communications with others, esp. in business.

dealt (delt) the past tense and past participle of **deal¹.**

de·am·i·nate (dē am′ə nāt′) *v.t.,* **-nat·ed, -nat·ing.** to remove the amino group from (a chemical compound), resulting in the liberation of ammonia, as occurs in the metabolism of amino acids by enzymes in the liver. —**de·am′i·na′tion,** *n.*

dean (dēn) *n.* **1.** an administrator of a college or university who is in charge of the discipline, activities, studies, and guidance of the students or a particular group of students: *the academic dean, the dean of women.* **2.** the head of a faculty or division of a school, college, or university: *dean of the graduate school.* **3.** the chief official of a cathedral. **4.** the senior member in length of service, as of an association or group: *the dean of American literary critics.* [Old French *deien* head of a cathedral, mayor's deputy, from Late Latin *decānus* leader of ten persons, from Latin *decem* ten.] —**dean′ship′,** *n.*

dean·er·y (dē′nə rē) *n., pl.* **-er·ies. 1.** the office, position, or jurisdiction of a dean. **2.** the place of residence of a dean.

dean's list, a list published regularly, as at the end of each semester, of students at a college or university who have achieved a certain high academic rank.

dear (dîr) *adj.* **1.** held in tender affection; beloved: *a dear friend.* **2.** highly esteemed. ➡ used as a salutation in letters: *Dear Sir.* **3.** having a high price; costly; expensive. **4.** heartfelt; earnest: *our dearest congratulations.* —*n.* a beloved person; darling. ➡ often used as an affectionate form of address. —*adv.* **1.** affectionately; fondly: *She held them very dear.* **2.** at a high price. —*interj.* an exclamation of emotion, as surprise, astonishment, or distress. [Old English *dēore* beloved, costly.] —**dear′ly,** *adv.* —**dear′ness,** *n.*

dearth (dûrth) *n.* **1.** a scant supply; scarcity; lack. **2.** *Archaic.* a scarcity of food; famine. [Middle English *derthe,* from *dere* costly, dear, from Old English *dēore.*] —For Synonyms, see **scarcity.**

dear·y (dîr′ē) *also,* **dear·ie.** *n., pl.* **dear·ies.** *Informal.* dear one; darling. ➡ often used humorously or ironically.

death (deth) *n.* **1.** the permanent cessation of all vital functions in a plant or animal; end of life; dying. **2.** the state or condition of being dead. **3.** the ending or destruction of anything; extinction: *the death of feudalism, the death of silent movies.* **4.** *usually,* **Death.** a figure thought of as representing death, usually symbolized by a skeleton carrying a scythe. **5.** a cause of dying: *This cold will be the death of me.* **6.** a manner of dying: *a martyr's death.* **7.** wholesale slaughter; bloodshed: *The empire fell amidst death and destruction.* [Old English *dēath.*]
• **at death's door.** close to death; dying.
• **to death.** to the extreme: *You scared me to death.*
• **to put to death.** to execute.

death·bed (deth′bed′) *n.* the bed on which a person dies. —*adj.* done or made during the last hours of life: *a deathbed wish.*
• **on one's deathbed.** in the last hours of life.

death·blow (deth′blō′) *n.* **1.** a blow that causes death. **2.** the cause of the end or destruction of something.

death cup, any of several poisonous mushrooms, genus *Amanita,* characterized by a cuplike swelling at the base of the stem. Also, **destroying angel.**

death duty *British.* inheritance tax.

death house, death row.

death·less (deth′lis) *adj.* never dying; immortal; eternal. —**death′less·ness,** *n.*

death·like (deth'līk') *adj.* characteristic of or resembling death.

death·ly (deth'lē) *adj.* **1.** characteristic of or resembling death: *a deathly pallor.* **2.** causing death; deadly: *a deathly blow.* —*adv.* **1.** in a deathlike manner. **2.** to an extreme degree; extremely; very: *deathly ill.*

death mask, a cast, usually made of plaster, of the face of a dead person.

death penalty, the sentence of death given to a criminal or criminals.

death rate, the number of deaths occurring in a given population within a specific period, usually stated in terms of the number of deaths per thousand per year.

death row, a building or part of a prison where prisoners condemned to death await execution. Also, **death house.**

death's-head (deths'hed') *n.* a human skull, or a figure representing it, used to symbolize death.

death's-head moth, a large Old World moth, *Acherontia atropos,* having markings on its thorax that resemble a human skull.

death squad, a group of persons organized to murder people, esp. the political opponents of a dictatorship or other government.

death·trap (deth'trap') *n.* **1.** a structure or place where there is great risk of death, as from fire: *The old theater was a deathtrap.* **2.** any extremely dangerous situation.

death's-head moth

death·watch (deth'woch') *n.* **1.** a vigil kept beside a dying or dead person. **2.** a guard set over a condemned prisoner prior to his or her execution. **3.** any of several destructive beetles, family Anobiidae, that burrow into wood. The deathwatch makes a ticking sound that was once believed to be an omen of death. Also *(def. 3),* **deathwatch beetle.**

de·ba·cle (di bä'kəl, -bak'əl) *n.* **1.** a sudden and complete downfall or collapse; rout; ruin. **2.** the breaking up of ice in a river. [French *débâcle* collapse, from *débâcler* to unbar, free, going back to Latin *dis-* un-[2] + *baculum* stick.]

de·bar (di bär') *v.t.,* **-barred, -bar·ring. 1.** to shut or keep out; exclude; bar: *The club debarred anyone who was not a graduate of the university.* **2.** to prohibit; prevent. [French *débarrer* to unbar, from *de-* un-[2] (from Latin *dis-*) + *barrer* to bar, from Old French *barre* bar. See BAR.] —**de·bar'ment,** *n.*

de·bark (di bärk') *v.t.* to bring to land or unload from a ship or airplane. —*v.i.* to land; disembark: *We debarked in Atlanta.* [French *débarquer* to land, from *dé-* away (from Latin *dis-*) + *barque* ship. See BARK[3].] —**de·bar·ka·tion** (dē'bär kā'shən), *n.*

de·base (di bās') *v.t.,* **-based, -bas·ing.** to lower in quality, value, or character; adulterate: *to debase coinage, to debase oneself by lying.* [DE- + BASE[2].] —**de·base'ment,** *n.* —**de·bas'er,** *n.*

de·bat·a·ble (di bā'tə bəl) *adj.* open to discussion or dispute; capable of being debated; questionable; moot.

de·bate (di bāt') *n.* **1.** a discussion or argument; dispute: *There was much debate over the statement.* **2.** a formal discussion of the arguments for and against a question or issue, esp. a public contest in which two people or teams argue opposite sides of a given topic. —*v.,* **-bat·ed, -bat·ing.** —*v.t.* **1.** to argue about or discuss, as at a public meeting. **2.** to deliberate upon; consider: *I debated whether to eat before or after the movie.* **3.** to discuss or dispute in a formal debate. —*v.i.* **1.** to discuss or argue a matter by giving opposing viewpoints. **2.** to deliberate; consider: *I debated about buying a new car.* **3.** to participate in a formal debate. [Old French *debatre* to argue, fight, going back to Latin *dē-* down + *battuere* to beat.] —**de·bat'er,** *n.*

de·bauch (di bôch') *v.t.* to lead away from morality; pervert; deprave. —*v.i.* to indulge in debauchery; dissipate. —*n.* **1.** debauchery. **2.** an act or instance of debauchery. [Old French *desbaucher* to lead away from; literally, to roughhew (timber for a beam), from *des-* (from Latin *dis-* away from) + *bauch* beam (of Germanic origin).] —**de·bauch'er,** *n.* —**de·bauch'ment,** *n.*

deb·au·chee (deb'ô chē', -shē') *n.* a person who indulges in debauchery; lewd or depraved person.

de·bauch·er·y (di bô'chə rē) *n., pl.* **-er·ies.** excessive indulgence in eating, drinking, and other sensual pleasures.

de·ben·ture (di ben'chər) *n.* a bond backed by the general credit of the issuer, but not by a lien on any specific property. [Latin *dēbentur* there are owing, from *dēbēre* to owe; probably at one time the first word of documents concerning debt.]

de·bil·i·tate (di bil'i tāt') *v.t.,* **-tat·ed, -tat·ing.** to impair the strength of; weaken: *Disease debilitated the patient.* [Latin

dēbilitātus, past participle of *dēbilitāre* to weaken.] —**de·bil'i·ta'tion,** *n.*

de·bil·i·ty (di bil'i tē) *n., pl.* **-ties.** a lack of strength or vigor; feebleness. [Old French *debilite,* from Latin *dēbilitās.*]

deb·it (deb'it) *n.* **1.** the entry of a debt in an account. **2.** an item entered in an account as a debt. **3. debits.** the sum total of such entries. **4.** the left-hand side or column of an account, where such entries are recorded. **5.** a charge against a bank account. **6.** a fault or deficiency; shortcoming. —*v.t.* **1.** to enter (a debt) in an account. **2.** to charge with a debt: *to debit an account with $300.* [Latin *dēbitum* debt, what is owing. See DEBT.]

deb·o·nair (deb'ə nâr') *also,* **de·bo·naire.** *adj.* **1.** characterized by sophisticated courtesy and charm; urbane. **2.** lighthearted; gay; cheerful. [Old French *debonaire* genial, from *de bon aire* of good stock or disposition, going back to Latin *dē* of + *bonus* good + *ārea* open space.] —**deb'o·nair'ly,** *adv.* —**deb'o·nair'ness,** *n.*

de·bouch (di büsh', -bouch') *v.i.* **1.** to march out from a narrow or confined area into the open, as a body of soldiers. **2.** to come forth or emerge; issue. —*v.t.* to cause to come forth or emerge. —*n.* an opening, esp. in military fortifications, for the passage of troops. [French *déboucher* to emerge; literally, to come out of the mouth, going back to Latin *dis-* away + *bucca* mouth.]

de·bouch·ment (di büsh'mənt, -bouch'-) *n.* **1.** the act or process of debouching. **2.** a mouth or outlet, as of a river.

de·bride·ment (di brēd'mənt, dā-) *n.* the removal of dead tissue or foreign material from a wound, either by surgery or by use of enzymatic preparations, in order to prevent infection. [French *débridement,* from *débrider* to remove tissue; literally, to take off the bridle of, from *de-* de- + *bride* bridle.]

de·brief (dē brēf') *v.t.* to question or instruct (someone, as a pilot, spy, or diplomat) at the end of a mission or term of service. —**de·brief'ing,** *n.*

de·bris (də brē', dā'brē) *also,* **dé·bris.** *n.* **1.** scattered remains, as of something broken or destroyed; rubbish. **2.** an accumulation of rock fragments: *The landslide left massive debris.* [French *débris* rubbish, from Old French *debrisier* to shatter, from *de-* down (from Latin *dē*) + *brisier* to break (of Celtic origin).]

debt (det) *n.* **1.** something that is owed to another: *a debt of $1,000.* **2.** a liability or obligation to pay or render something to another. **3.** the state or condition of owing or being obligated: *to be in debt, to get out of debt.* **4.** a moral wrong; sin; trespass. [Old French *dete* what is owing, from Latin *dēbitum,* from *dēbēre* to owe. Doublet of DEBIT.]

debt of honor, a debt, as in gambling, that is not legally enforceable but depends for its payment on the honor of the debtor.

debt·or (det'ər) *n.* a person who owes something to another.

de·bug (dē bug') *v.t.,* **-bugged, -bug·ging. 1.** to find and correct errors or eliminate malfunction in (a computer program or system). **2.** to remove a concealed electronic listening device, as a microphone or wiretap, from. [DE- + BUG.]

de·bunk (di bungk') *v.t.* to expose or ridicule as false, pretentious, or exaggerated: *to debunk the claims made in an advertisement.* [DE- + BUNK[2].] —**de·bunk'er,** *n.*

de·but (dā bū', dē'bū) *also,* **dé·but.** *n.* **1.** a first public appearance, as of a performer on stage. **2.** the formal introduction of a young woman into society. **3.** a beginning, as of a career or course of action. —*v.i.* to appear for the first time: *The dancer debuted in last night's performance.* —*v.t.* to present for the first time: *The company debuted its new ballet last night.* [French *début* a first play (in a game), first appearance, from *débuter* to play first, make one's début, from *dé-* from (from Latin *dis-* apart) + *but* aim (of Germanic origin).]

deb·u·tante (deb'yù tänt', -yə tant') *also,* **dé·bu·tante.** *n.* a young woman who is making her formal entrance into society.

dec *also,* **dec.** decimeter.

dec. 1. deceased. **2.** declaration. **3.** decrease.

Dec., December.

deca- *also,* **dec-.** *combining form* ten: *decagon.* [Greek *deka.*]

dec·ade (dek'ād) *n.* **1.** a period of ten years. **2.** a group, series, or set of ten. [French *décade,* from Late Latin *decas,* from Greek *dekas* group of ten, from *deka* ten.]

dec·a·dence (dek'ə dəns) *n.* **1.** a process of decay; deterioration: *the gradual decadence of an empire.* **2.** a period or condition

a	at	e	end	o	hot	u	up	hw	white		about
ā	ape	ē	me	ō	old	ū	use	ng	song		taken
ä	far	i	it	ô	fork	ü	rule	th	thin	ə	pencil
âr	care	ī	ice	oi	oil	ủ	pull	th	this		lemon
			îr	pierce	ou	out	ûr	turn	zh	measure		circus

D

of decline, as in morals, art, or literature. [French *décadence* decay, from Medieval Latin *decadentia*, going back to Latin *dē* away + *cadere* to fall (in the sense of falling away from what is good).]

dec·a·dent (dek′ə dənt) *adj.* **1.** characterized by or undergoing deterioration. **2.** *also,* **Decadent.** of, relating to, or characteristic of a group of French and English writers of the late nineteenth century whose work reflected a morbid outlook on life and an extreme concern with purity of style and form. —*n.* **1.** a person who is decadent. **2.** *also,* **Decadent.** a member of the decadent group of writers. —**dec′a·dent·ly,** *adv.*

de·caf·fein·at·ed (dē kaf′ə nā′tid) *adj.* having had all or most of the caffeine removed: *decaffeinated coffee.* [DE- + CAFFEIN(E) + -AT(E)[1] + -ED[2].]

dec·a·gon (dek′ə gon′) *n.* a plane figure having ten sides and ten angles. [Modern Latin *decagonum,* from Greek *dekagōnon,* from *deka* ten + *gōnia* corner, angle[1].]

dec·a·gram (dek′ə gram′) *also,* **dec·a·gramme, dek·a·gram.** *n.* a metric unit of weight, equal to 10 grams. [French *décagramme,* going back to Greek *deka* ten + *gramma* small weight.]

dec·a·he·dron (dek′ə hē′drən) *n., pl.* **-drons** or **-dra** (-drə). a solid figure bounded by ten plane surfaces. [DECA- + Greek *hedra* base[1], seat.]

de·cal (dē′kal, di kal′) *n.* a design or picture prepared for transfer from specially treated paper to glass, wood, or other surfaces. Also, **decalcomania.**

de·cal·ci·fy (dē kal′sə fī′) *v.t.,* **-fied, -fy·ing.** to remove calcium or calcium compounds from (soil, bone, or the like). [DE- + CALCIFY.] —**de·cal′ci·fi·ca′tion,** *n.*

de·cal·co·ma·ni·a (di kal′kə mā′nē ə) *n.* **1.** the art or process of transferring designs or pictures from specially treated paper to glass, wood, or other surfaces. **2.** decal. [French *décalcomanie,* from *décalquer* to transfer a tracing (going back to Latin *dē* from, off + *calcāre* to trample) + *manie* craze (from *mania* madness).]

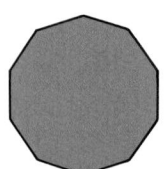

Regular decagon

Concave decagon

decagons

dec·a·li·ter (dek′ə lē′tər) *also,* **dec·a·li·tre, dek·a·li·ter.** *n.* a metric measure of volume, equal to 10 liters. [French *décalitre,* from Greek *deka* ten + *lītra* pound[1].]

Dec·a·logue (dek′ə lôg′, -log′) *also,* **Dec·a·log.** *n.* Ten Commandments. [Late Latin *decalogus,* from Greek *dekalogos,* from *deka* ten + *logos* speech, word.]

dec·a·me·ter (dek′ə mē′tər) *also,* **dec·a·me·tre, dek·a·me·tre.** *n.* a metric measure of length, equal to 10 meters. [French *décamètre,* from Greek *deka* ten + *metron* measure.]

de·camp (di kamp′) *v.i.* **1.** to leave an encampment; break camp. **2.** to depart quickly or secretly; run away. [French *décamper* to make off; literally, to leave the field, going back to Latin *dis-* away + *campus* field.] —**de·camp′ment,** *n.*

dec·a·nal (dek′ə nəl, di kā′-) *adj.* of or relating to a dean or deanery. [Late Latin *decānus* dean + -AL[1]. See DEAN.]

de·cant (di kant′) *v.t.* **1.** to pour off (a liquid) gently without disturbing the sediment: *to decant wine.* **2.** to pour from one container into another. [Medieval Latin *decanthare* to pour out, from *de* down + *canthus* edge of a jug, going back to Greek *kanthos* corner of the eye.]

de·cant·er (di kan′tər) *n.* a decorative bottle with a stopper, used for serving wine or other liquids.

de·cap·i·tate (di kap′i tāt′) *v.t.,* **-tat·ed, -tat·ing.** to cut off the head of; behead. [Late Latin *dēcapitātus,* past participle of *dēcapitāre,* from Latin *dē* off + *caput* head.] —**de·cap′i·ta′tion,** *n.*

dec·a·pod (dek′ə pod′) *n.* **1.** any crustacean, order Decapoda, having ten legs or arms, as a lobster or crab. **2.** any mollusk, order Decapoda, having ten arms or tentacles, as a squid or cuttlefish. —*adj.* having ten legs or arms. [Modern Latin *Decapoda,* from Greek *deka* ten + *pod-,* stem of *pous* foot.]

dec·a·stere (dek′ə stîr′) *also,* **dekastere.** *n.* a unit of volume equal to 10 steres. [DECA- + STERE.]

dec·a·syl·la·ble (dek′ə sil′ə bəl) *n.* a line of verse or a word having ten syllables. —**dec′a·syl·lab′ic,** *adj.*

de·cath·lon (di kath′lon) *n.* an athletic contest consisting of ten different track and field events. The contestant scoring the most total points for all events is the winner. [DECA- + Greek *athlon* contest.]

de·cay (di kā′) *n.* **1.** destructive decomposition, as of organic tissue; rot: *bacterial decay, tooth decay.* **2.** gradual deterioration, as in strength or quality: *a decay in health, the decay of an empire.* **3.** a product of decay. **4.** the spontaneous transformation of an atomic nucleus of a radioactive element into another isotope of the same element or into a nucleus of a different element. —*v.i.* **1.** to break down; rot; decompose. **2.** to undergo a gradual loss, as in quality or strength. **3.** to undergo radioactive decay. —*v.t.* to cause to decay. [Dialectal Old French *decair* to fall off, decline, going back to Latin *dē* away + *cadere* to fall.]

Synonyms *v.i.* **Decay, decompose,** and **disintegrate** mean to break down from a whole or sound state. **Decay** suggests a gradual breakdown: *Some fallen leaves decay faster than others. The decay of the neighborhood followed the closing of the automobile plant.* **Decompose** connotes separation into elemental parts, or into a simpler state: *This material will decompose into water and several simple chemicals if we leave it in a warm place.* **Disintegrate** suggests a complete falling apart: *Flood waters caused the dike to disintegrate.*

de·cease (di sēs′) *n.* death. —*v.i.,* **-ceased, -ceas·ing.** to die. [Old French *deces* death, from Latin *dēcessus* departure, death.]

de·ceased (di sēst′) *adj.* dead. —*n.* **the deceased.** a dead person or persons.

de·ce·dent (di sē′dənt) *n. Law.* a deceased person. [Latin *dēcēdēns,* present participle of *dēcēdere* to depart, die.]

de·ceit (di sēt′) *n.* **1.** the act or practice of concealing or misrepresenting the truth; lying. **2.** something intended to deceive; artifice; trick. **3.** the quality of being deceitful; deception. [Old French *deceite* act of deceiving, deception, from *deceveir* to deceive. See DECEIVE.]

Synonyms **Deceit, deception,** and **guile** mean the deliberate misrepresentation of facts or truth. **Deceit** implies that the use of untruth may be habitual as well as intentional: *He lived by deceit, forging signatures on checks.* **Deception** may be used of misrepresentation that is not habitual nor for a bad purpose: *The story about the phone call was part of her deception to keep the surprise party secret.* **Guile** suggests the use of skill or subtlety, and sometimes treachery: *the guile of a magician, the guile of a swindler.*

de·ceit·ful (di sēt′fəl) *adj.* **1.** given to deceiving; lying: *a deceitful person.* **2.** tending or meant to deceive; false: *a deceitful act.* —**de·ceit′ful·ly,** *adv.* —**de·ceit′ful·ness,** *n.*

de·ceive (di sēv′) *v.,* **-ceived, -ceiv·ing.** —*v.t.* to make (someone) believe something that is false; mislead; delude. —*v.i.* to use deceit; lie. [Old French *deceveir,* from Latin *dēcipere.*] —**de·ceiv′er,** *n.* —**de·ceiv′ing·ly,** *adv.*

de·cel·er·ate (dē sel′ə rāt′) *v.t., v.i.,* **-at·ed, -at·ing.** to decrease the speed or rate (of); slow down. [DE- + (AC)CELERATE.] —**de·cel′er·a′tion,** *n.* —**de·cel′er·a′tor,** *n.*

De·cem·ber (di sem′bər) *n.* the twelfth and last month of the year, containing thirty-one days. [Old French *Decembre,* from Latin *December* name of the tenth month in the early Roman calendar (in which March was the first month), from *decem* ten.]

de·cem·vir (di sem′vər) *n., pl.* **-virs** or **-vi·ri** (-və rī′). **1.** in ancient Rome, a member of either of two councils of ten men, one elected in 451 B.C., the other in 450 B.C., whose duties were to codify and publish the laws. **2.** a member of any council of ten. [Latin *decemvir* one of ten men, going back to *decem* ten + *vir* man.]

de·cem·vi·rate (di sem′vər it, -və rāt′) *n.* **1.** a body of decemvirs. **2.** a government of decemvirs.

de·cen·cy (dē′sən sē) *n., pl.* **-cies. 1.** the quality or condition of being decent; conformity to standards of propriety or good taste, as in speech, behavior, or dress: *They had the decency to admit their error.* **2.** decencies. **a.** socially accepted or proper acts or observances. **b.** requirements for a respectable or comfortable manner of living.

de·cen·ni·al (di sen′ē əl) *adj.* **1.** of or continuing for ten years. **2.** occurring every ten years. —*n.* a tenth anniversary or its celebration. [Latin *decennium* period of ten years + -AL[1].] —**de·cen′ni·al·ly,** *adv.*

de·cen·ni·um (di sen′ē əm) *n., pl.* **-cen·ni·ums** or **-cen·ni·a** (-sen′ē ə). a period of ten years; decade. [Latin *decennium,* going back to Latin *decem* ten + *annus* year.]

de·cent (dē′sənt) *adj.* **1.** conforming to or satisfying approved standards of society, as in moral character or social conduct; respectable. **2.** in accordance with standards of good taste; proper: *It is not decent to pry into other people's business.* **3.** not obscene; modest; chaste: *decent language.* **4.** kind; generous: *It was very decent of you to help me.* **5.** fairly good; passable; satisfactory: *to earn a decent salary, to do a decent job.* **6.** *Informal.* adequately clothed; dressed: *Before entering, they knocked and asked, "Are you decent?"* [Latin *dēcens,* present participle of

decēre to be fitting, suitable.] **—de′cent·ly,** *adv.* **—de′cent·ness,** *n.*

de·cen·tral·ize (dē sen′trə līz′) *v.,* **-ized, -iz·ing.** *—v.t.* **1.** to redistribute centralized power or authority, as of a government body or industry, by giving it to smaller groups or units: *to decentralize a school system.* **2.** to break up a centralized concentration of by redistributing from urban centers to outlying areas: *Suburban complexes have helped to decentralize the business community.* *—v.i.* to be or become decentralized. **—de·cen′tral·i·za′tion,** *n.*

de·cep·tion (di sep′shən) *n.* **1.** the act of deceiving or the state of being deceived. **2.** something that deceives or is intended to deceive; trick. [Late Latin *dēceptiō* a deceiving, from Latin *dēcipere* to deceive.] **—For Synonyms, see deceit.**

de·cep·tive (di sep′tiv) *adj.* characterized by deception; meant to deceive. **—de·cep′tive·ly,** *adv.* **—de·cep′tive·ness,** *n.* —For Synonyms, see **misleading.**

deci- *combining form* one tenth of: *deciliter, decimeter.* [Latin *decimus* tenth, from *decem* ten.]

dec·i·bel (des′ə bel′, -bəl) *n.* a unit for measuring the intensity of sound. [DECI- + BEL.]

de·cide (di sīd′) *v.,* **-cid·ed, -cid·ing.** *—v.i.* **1.** to make up one's mind: *We could not decide between the two alternatives.* **2.** to make a judgment; come to a conclusion: *The judge decided in favor of the plaintiff.* *—v.t.* **1.** to make up one's mind (to do something); resolve: *We decided to take the bus.* **2.** to determine or settle, as a dispute or question: *I will decide who goes first.* **3.** to determine the result of: *The last touchdown decided the game.* **4.** to cause (someone) to come to a decision: *What decided you against buying a new car?* [Latin *dēcīdere* to cut off, determine.]

| **Synonyms** | **Decide, determine, resolve,** and **settle**[1] mean to make a judgment or draw a conclusion regarding an issue or a dispute. **Decide** implies that some time has been spent in logical consideration: *to decide a complex issue.* **Determine** suggests firmness in decision: *to determine who was the winner of the contest.* **Resolve** suggests clearing up what has been confused: *to resolve the issue of who owns the property.* **Settle** implies the end of wavering or doubt: *Let's settle the question of payment so we can proceed.* |

de·cid·ed (di sī′did) *adj.* **1.** leaving no doubt; definite; unquestionable: *a decided advantage, a decided improvement in grades.* **2.** showing decisiveness; determined; unwavering: *to speak in a decided tone of voice.* **—de·cid′ed·ly,** *adv.* **—de·cid′ed·ness,** *n.*

de·cid·u·ous (di sij′ü əs) *adj.* **1.** (of trees, shrubs, and other plants) shedding leaves annually. ➡ distinguished from **evergreen. 2.** falling off or shed at a particular season or stage of growth: *deciduous petals, deciduous antlers.* **3.** not permanent or enduring; transitory. [Latin *dēciduus* falling down.]

dec·i·gram (des′i gram′) *also,* **dec·i·gramme.** *n.* a metric unit of weight, equal to ¹/₁₀ of a gram. [French *décigramme,* from Latin *decimus* tenth + Greek *gramma* small weight.]

dec·i·li·ter (des′ə lē′tər) *also,* **dec·i·li·tre.** *n.* a metric measure of volume, equal to ¹/₁₀ of a liter. [French *décilitre,* from Latin *decimus* tenth + Greek *lītrā* pound[1].]

de·cil·lion (di sil′yən) *n.* **1.** in the United States, the cardinal number that is represented by 1 followed by 33 zeros. **2.** in Great Britain, the cardinal number that is represented by 1 followed by 60 zeros. [Latin *decem* ten + (M)ILLION.] **—de·cil′lionth,** *adj., n.*

dec·i·mal (des′ə məl) *adj.* relating to or based on the number 10; proceeding by tens. *—n.* a decimal fraction or a number containing one. [Latin *decimus* tenth (from *decem* ten) + -AL[1].]

decimal fraction, a fraction whose denominator is equal to 10 or a power of 10. The fractions ⁵/₁₀ and ⁷⁵/₁₀₀ expressed as decimal fractions are 0.5 and 0.75.

decimal point, a period placed before a decimal fraction, which indicates, by the number of figures following it, the size of the denominator.

decimal system, a system of computation having the number 10 as its base.

dec·i·mate (des′ə māt′) *v.t.,* **-mat·ed, -mat·ing. 1.** to destroy or kill a large number or proportion of: *The final battle decimated the enemy's ranks.* **2.** to select by lot and execute one out of every ten of. [Latin *decimātus,* past participle of *decimāre* to select every tenth man for punishment. In ancient Rome an army revolt was punished by taking every tenth soldier and executing them.] **—dec·i·ma′tion,** *n.* **—dec′i·ma′tor,** *n.*

| **Usage** | **Decimate** means to destroy a large number or proportion of a group. However, because it can also be used to refer specifically to the killing of every tenth member of a group, chosen by lot, it should not be used with a fraction or percentage, as in the sentence *The plague decimated a fourth of the population.* |

dec·i·me·ter (des′ə mē′tər) *also,* **dec·i·me·tre.** *n.* a metric measure of length, equal to ¹/₁₀ of a meter. [French *décimètre,* from Latin *decimus* tenth + Greek *metron* measure.]

de·ci·pher (di sī′fər) *v.t.* **1.** to make out the meaning of (something illegible, obscure, or difficult to understand): *to decipher messy handwriting, to decipher a riddle.* **2.** to interpret or translate (something written in code) by using a key; decode: *to decipher a message.* [DE- + CIPHER.] **—de·ci′pher·a·ble,** *adj.* **—de·ci′pher·er,** *n.* **—de·ci′pher·ment,** *n.*

de·ci·sion (di sizh′ən) *n.* **1.** the act of making up one's mind: *He hesitated because of the difficulty of the decision.* **2.** the act of deciding something, as a controversy or question, by reaching a conclusion or making a judgment: *The decision will be left to the court.* **3.** a judgment or conclusion reached or given as a result of deciding: *The umpire's decision was final. What is your decision?* **4.** the quality of being decided; firmness; determination: *a woman of decision.* **5.** in boxing, a victory determined by points instead of by a knockout or a technical knockout. [Latin *dēcīsiō* a cutting down, settlement.]

de·ci·sive (di sī′siv) *adj.* **1.** settling controversy or uncertainty; conclusive: *a decisive victory.* **2.** having or showing determination, as in making a choice or adhering to a course of action; resolute: *a decisive person.* **—de·ci′sive·ly,** *adv.* **—de·ci′sive·ness,** *n.*

dec·i·stere (des′ə stîr′) *n.* a unit of volume equal to ¹/₁₀ of a stere. [DECI- + STERE.]

deck (dek) *n.* **1.a.** a platform or other horizontal surface serving as the floor in a boat or ship. **b.** a space between any two such surfaces, or an uncovered area, as on an upper deck, constituting one of the levels of a ship. **2.** any similar horizontal surface. **3.** a complete set of playing cards, usually fifty-two. **4.** a component in an audio or video system in which a tape is recorded or played. *—v.t.* **1.** to dress or adorn; ornament: *We decked the mantel with pine boughs for the holiday.* **2.** to provide with a deck. **3.** *Slang.* to knock down. [Middle Dutch *dec* roof, covering.]
 • **on deck.** *Informal.* **a.** on hand and ready for use or action. **b.** ready and waiting for one's turn: *The next batter was on deck.*
 • **to clear the deck** (or **decks**). to remove obstacles or impediments in preparation for action, as combat.
 • **to hit the deck.** *Slang.* **a.** to fall into a prone position so as to avoid injury. **b.** to get out of bed. **c.** to get ready for action.

deck chair, a folding chair with a canvas or wooden seat, armrests, and usually a leg rest, used for lounging, as on ship decks.

-decker *combining form* having a specified number of decks, layers, floors, or levels: *a double-decker bus, a triple-decker sandwich.*

deck·hand (dek′hand′) *n.* a sailor who performs general tasks either above or below deck.

deck·house (dek′hous′) *n., pl.* **-hous·es** (-hou′ziz). a cabin or room built on the upper deck of a ship.

deck·le (dek′əl) *n.* deckle edge. [German *Deckel,* diminutive of *Decke* cover.]

deckle edge, the rough, raw edge of untrimmed paper.

deck·le-edged (dek′əl ejd′) *adj.* having a deckle edge.

de·claim (di klām′) *v.i.* **1.** to speak or recite publicly; give an oration. **2.** to speak in a loud, pretentious or oratorical manner. **3.** to make an impassioned verbal attack; inveigh: *to declaim against political corruption.* *—v.t.* to utter or recite loudly and pretentiously or oratorically. [Latin *dēclāmāre* to cry aloud, deliver a speech.] **—de·claim′er,** *n.*

dec·la·ma·tion (dek′lə mā′shən) *n.* **1.** the act of declaiming. **2.** the art of speaking or reciting publicly; public speaking. **3.** a formal, prepared public speech or recitation. **4.** a loud, pretentious or oratorical talk; harangue.

de·clam·a·to·ry (di klam′ə tôr′ē) *adj.* **1.** of or relating to declamation. **2.** loud and pretentious or oratorical.

dec·la·ra·tion (dek′lə rā′shən) *n.* **1.** the act of declaring. **2.** something that is declared; announcement. **3.** a formal statement, or a document containing such a statement: *a declaration of war.* **4.** a statement of goods liable to taxation, or a document containing such a statement. **5.** in bridge, a contract.

Declaration of Independence, the document declaring the thirteen American colonies independent of Great Britain, written chiefly by Thomas Jefferson and adopted on July 4, 1776, by the Second Continental Congress.

a	at	e	end	o	hot	u	up	hw	white		about
ā	ape	ē	me	ō	old	ū	use	ng	song		taken
ä	far	i	it	ô	fork	ü	rule	th	thin	ə	pencil
âr	care	ī	ice	oi	oil	ủ	pull	<u>th</u>	this		lemon
		îr	pierce	ou	out	ûr	turn	zh	measure		circus

de·clar·a·tive (di klar′ə tiv) *adj.* making a statement or affirmation. Also, **de·clar·a·to·ry** (di-klar′ə tôr′ē). —**de·clar′a·tive·ly,** *adv.*

de·clare (di klâr′) *v.,* **-clared, -clar·ing.** —*v.t.* **1.** to make known publicly or formally; announce; proclaim: *The governor declared a new state holiday.* **2.** to state emphatically; assert: *The suspects declared that they had nothing to hide.* **3.** to make a full statement or account of (goods for taxation). **4.** to reveal or prove. **5.** in bridge, to make (the final bid); announce (the contract). —*v.i.* to announce, as an opinion or choice: *The newspaper declared for the Republican candidate.* [Latin *dēclārāre* to make clear, going back to *dē* thoroughly + *clārus* clear.] —**de·clar′er,** *n.*

> **Synonyms** **Declare, proclaim,** and **announce** mean to make known publicly. **Declare** connotes any explicit statement of something significant: *I declared my intention to leave the company. The government declared a change of economic policy.* **Proclaim** implies a large audience, and suggests an official, perhaps autocratic, speaker: *The emperor proclaimed a holiday to celebrate the victory.* **Announce** suggests making something important known for the first time: *to announce the opening of a store, to announce wedding plans.*

de·clas·si·fy (dē klas′ə fī′) *v.t.,* **-fied, -fy·ing.** to remove from a secret or restricted classification, as government documents.

de·clen·sion (di klen′shən) *n.* **1.** the inflection of nouns, pronouns, and adjectives with regard to case, gender, and number. **2.** a class of words whose inflections are the same. **3.** a downward slope or bend; descent. **4.** a sinking or declining into a lower or inferior condition; deterioration. [Old French *declinaison* grammatical declension, decline, from Latin *dēclīnātiō* turning aside, inflection.]

de·clin·a·ble (di klī′nə bəl) *adj.* capable of being grammatically declined.

dec·li·na·tion (dek′lə nā′shən) *n.* **1.** a leaning, bending, or sloping downward; inclination. **2.** the angular difference between the direction in which a magnetic compass points and the direction of the true North Pole. Also, **magnetic declination. 3.** the angular distance, as of a star or planet, from the celestial equator in a system of coordinates used to state the position of celestial objects. It is similar to geographic latitude. **4.** a polite refusal.

de·cline (di klīn′) *v.,* **-clined, -clin·ing.** —*v.t.* **1.** to refuse politely: *to decline an invitation.* **2.** to give the inflected forms of (a noun, pronoun, or adjective). **3.** to cause to bend or slope downward; incline. —*v.i.* **1.** to refuse politely. **2.** to fall into an inferior or impaired condition; weaken: *Her health was declining. The nation declined as a world power.* **3.** to fall or become less: *Prices on the stock market declined.* **4.** to bend or slope downward or aside. **5.** to draw to a close or end; wane: *The day declined.* **6.** to stoop, as to an unworthy object; condescend. —*n.* **1.** a decrease, as in influence, strength, value, or amount: *the decline of the nobility, a decline in population, a decline in the nation's influence abroad.* **2.** a falling; sinking. **3.** a downward bend or slope. **4.** a period during which something is drawing to a close or weakening: *He was approaching the decline of his life.* [Old French *decliner* to turn aside, inflect grammatically, from Latin *dēclīnāre.*] —For Synonyms *(v.t.),* see **refuse**[1].

de·cliv·i·ty (di kliv′i tē) *n., pl.* **-ties.** a downward slope. ➡ opposed to **acclivity.** [Latin *dēclīvitās* sloping place.]

de·coct (di kokt′) *v.t.* to extract the essence or flavor of by boiling, usually in water. [Latin *dēcoctus,* past participle of *dēcoquere* to boil down.]

de·coc·tion (di kok′shən) *n.* **1.** the act or process of boiling something, usually in water, to extract the soluble properties. **2.** an extract obtained by such a process.

de·code (dē kōd′) *v.t.,* **-cod·ed, -cod·ing.** to convert from code into ordinary language by using a key: *to decode a secret message.* —**de·cod′er,** *n.*

dé·colle·tage (dā′kol tazh′, dek′ə lə-) *n.* a low-cut neckline, as of a dress or blouse.

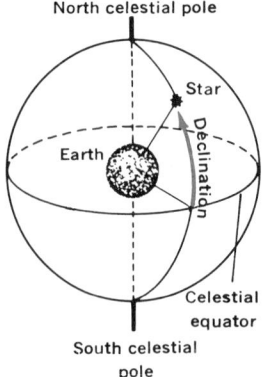

North celestial pole

Star

Declination

Earth

Celestial equator

South celestial pole

declination *(def. 3)*

dé·colle·té (dā′kol tā′, dek′ə lə-) *adj.* **1.** having a low-cut neckline. **2.** having the neck and shoulders exposed; wearing a low-necked garment. [French *décolleté,* past participle of *décolleter* to uncover the neck and shoulders, going back to Latin *dē* away + *collum* neck.]

de·col·or·ize (dē kul′ə rīz′) *v.t.,* **-ized, -iz·ing.** to deprive of color; bleach. —**de·col′or·i·za′tion,** *n.* —**de·col′or·iz′er,** *n.*

de·com·mis·sion (dē′kə mish′ən) *v.t.* **1.** to take out of commission: *to decommission a ship.* **2.** to take away the military commission of, as an officer.

de·com·pose (dē′kəm pōz′) *v.t., v.i.,* **-posed, -pos·ing. 1.** to putrefy; rot. **2.** to separate into constituent parts or elements. —**de·com·po·si·tion** (dē′kom pə zish′ən), *n.* —For Synonyms *(v.i.),* see **decay.**

de·com·pos·er (dē′kəm pō′zər) *n.* an organism, such as a bacterium, that breaks down dead plant and animal matter into simpler substances that can be used as food by other organisms.

de·com·press (dē′kəm pres′) *v.t.* to cause to undergo decompression.

de·com·pres·sion (dē′kəm presh′ən) *n.* the reduction or removal of pressure, esp. of high atmospheric pressure on the human body.

decompression chamber, a chamber of special construction in which pressure on the body is gradually reduced, esp. one used to prevent caisson disease by slowly bringing a person back to normal atmospheric pressure.

decompression sickness, the bends (**bend,** *def. 4*).

de·con·ges·tant (dē′kən jes′tənt) *n.* a medicine that relieves congestion in the nose or nasal sinuses. [DE- + CONGEST + -ANT.]

de·con·struc·tion (dē′kən struk′shən) *n.* an approach to the analysis of literature, originating in France in the 1960s, that assumes that a text can have no fixed meaning, because all language refers to other language rather than to reality. [French *déconstruction,* going back to Latin *dis-*[1] apart + *constructus,* past participle of *construere* to build up.] —**de′con·struc′tion·ist,** *adj., n.*

de·con·tam·i·nate (dē′kən tam′ə nāt′) *v.t.,* **-nat·ed, -nat·ing. 1.** to rid of contamination. **2.** to make (a contaminated area or object) safe by removing harmful materials, as poison gas, bacteria, or radioactive wastes. —**de′con·tam′i·na′tion,** *n.*

de·con·trol (dē′kən trōl′) *v.t.,* **-trolled, -trol·ling.** to remove controls, esp. government controls, from: *to decontrol rents.* —*n.* the removal of controls.

dé·cor (dā kôr′, dā′kôr) *also,* **de·cor.** *n.* **1.** a decorative plan or style, as of a room. **2.** scenery, as in a theatrical or television presentation. [French *décor,* from *décorer* to adorn, from Latin *decorāre.*]

dec·o·rate (dek′ə rāt′) *v.t.,* **-rat·ed, -rat·ing. 1.** to furnish with ornaments; adorn; embellish: *We decorated the room for the party.* **2.** to plan and execute the style and design of (a room or rooms), as by selecting and arranging furniture, choosing fabrics, paint, or wallpaper, or adding ornamentation. **3.** to honor, as with a medal: *to decorate a soldier for valor.* [Latin *decorātus,* past participle of *decorāre* to adorn.]

> **Synonyms** **Decorate, adorn,** and **embellish** mean to make something more appealing or beautiful by adding something to it. **Decorate** is the most general of these terms: *to decorate a Christmas tree, to decorate an apartment.* **Adorn** suggests that what is added is beautiful in itself: *Flowering shrubs adorned the entrance.* **Embellish** may be used to emphasize the act rather than the result: *The artisan spent hours embellishing the cup with gold inlay.*

dec·o·ra·tion (dek′ə rā′shən) *n.* **1.** the act or process of decorating. **2.** something used to decorate; ornament; adornment. **3.** a mark of honor, as a medal or ribbon.

Decoration Day, Memorial Day.

dec·o·ra·tive (dek′ər ə tiv) *adj.* relating, tending, or serving to decorate; ornamental. —**dec′o·ra·tive·ly,** *adv.* —**dec′o·ra·tive·ness,** *n.*

dec·o·ra·tor (dek′ə rā′tər) *n.* a person who decorates, esp. an interior decorator.

dec·o·rous (dek′ər əs, di kôr′-) *adj.* characterized by decorum; proper; suitable. [Latin *decōrus.*] —**dec′o·rous·ly,** *adv.* —**dec′o·rous·ness,** *n.*

de·co·rum (di kôr′əm) *n.* **1.** conformity to the approved standards of good taste; propriety, as in behavior or speech. **2.** *also,* **decorums.** proprieties. [Latin *decōrum* that which is seemly.]

dé·cou·page (dā′kü päzh′) *also,* **dé·cou·page.** *n.* **1.** the art or technique of decorating objects or surfaces, usually with paper cutouts, and then applying coats of varnish or lacquer. **2.** a work produced by this technique. [French *découpage* a cutting out,

from *découper* to cut out; literally, to divide by a blow, going back to Latin *dē* away + *colaphus* blow[1] (from Greek *kolaphos*).]

decoupage box

de·coy (*n.*, dē′koi, di koi′; *v.*, di koi′) *n.* **1.** an artificial bird used to lure birds into a trap or within gunshot. **2.** a person or thing that lures, as into danger or deception: *The police officer was used as a decoy to trap the murderer.* **3.** trick; deception. —*v.t.* **1.** to lure (wildfowl or other animals) into a trap or within gunshot. **2.** to lure by or as by a decoy. —*v.i.* to be lured by or as by a decoy. [Dutch *de kooi* literally, the cage, from *de* the + *kooi* cage (from Latin *cavea*).]

de·crease (*v.*, di krēs′; *n.*, dē′krēs, di krēs′) *v.*, **-creased,** **-creas·ing.** —*v.i.* to become less; diminish; abate: *The number of traffic accidents decreased last year.* —*v.t.* to cause to become less; reduce: *to decrease speed, to decrease crime.* —*n.* **1.** the act or process of decreasing; lessening. **2.** the amount by which something decreases or is decreased. [Anglo-Norman *decreis-,* a stem of *decreistre* to grow less, going back to Latin *dēcrēscere.*] —**de·creas′ing·ly,** *adv.*

> **Synonyms** *v.i.* **Decrease, diminish,** and **dwindle** mean to become less. **Decrease** suggests a gradual lessening, but implies nothing about the proportion by which something is reduced: *Because of the mild winter the demand for boots decreased.* **Diminish** suggests a perceptible reduction, putting the focus on the resulting state: *The wind diminished, leaving the sea calm.* **Dwindle** implies a gradual lessening toward a vanishing point: *Food supplies dwindled as the blockade continued.*

de·cree (di krē′) *n.* **1.** *Law.* a decision or order issued by a court: *a divorce decree.* **2.** an official decision or order; edict. —*v.*, **-creed, -cree·ing.** —*v.t.* to order, decide, or appoint by decree: *to decree a national holiday.* —*v.i.* to issue a decree. [Old French *decre, decret* decision, ordinance, from Latin *dēcrētum,* from *dēcernere* to decide.] —For Synonyms (*n.*), see **verdict.**

dec·re·ment (dek′rə mənt) *n.* **1.** the act or process of decreasing. **2.** the amount lost by decrease. **3.** *Mathematics.* the amount by which the value of a variable decreases. [Latin *dēcrēmentum* decrease.]

de·crep·it (di krep′it) *adj.* broken down or feeble because of old age or overuse. [Latin *dēcrepitus* literally, making no noise (in the sense of "moving about quietly like an old person"), from *dē* away + *crepitus,* past participle of *crepare* to make noise.] —**de·crep′it·ly,** *adv.*

de·crep·i·tude (di krep′i tüd′, -tūd′) *n.* a decrepit state or condition; feebleness, as from old age.

decresc., decrescendo.

de·cre·scen·do (dē′krə shen′dō, dā′-) *n., pl.* **-dos.** *Music.* **1.** a gradual decrease in loudness or force; diminuendo. **2.** a passage in which such a decrease occurs. —*adj., adv.* with a gradual decrease in loudness or force. [Italian *decrescendo* decreasing, from *decrescere* to decrease, from Latin *dēcrēscere.*]

de·cre·tal (di krē′təl) *n.* **1.** a papal decree or letter determining some question of ecclesiastical law, esp. a papal response to an appeal. **2. Decretals.** a collection of such decrees or letters, forming part of the canon laws. —*adj.* of, relating to, or containing a decree. [Medieval Latin *decretale* decree, from Late Latin *dēcrētālis* relating to a decree, from Latin *dēcrētum* decree.]

de·cri·al (di krī′əl) *n.* the act of decrying; condemnation.

de·crim·i·nal·ize (dē krim′ə nə līz′) *v.t.*, **-ized, -iz·ing.** to eliminate criminal penalties for: *to decriminalize possession of certain substances.* —**de·crim′i·nal·i·za′tion,** *n.*

de·cry (di krī′) *v.t.*, **-cried, -cry·ing. 1.** to denounce or disparage; condemn publicly: *The defendant's lawyer decried capital punishment.* **2.** to depreciate officially: *The government decried the foreign coins.* [Old French *descrier* to cry down, disparage, going back to Latin *dis-* un-[2] + *quirītāre* to cry out.] —**de·cri′er,** *n.*

de·cum·bent (di kum′bənt) *adj.* **1.** (of stems or branches) lying or trailing on the ground with the end tending to climb. **2.** lying down; reclining. [Latin *dēcumbēns,* present participle of *dēcumbere* to lie down.] —**de·cum′ben·cy,** *n.*

de·cur·rent (di kûr′ənt, -kur′-) *adj.* extending down and growing along the stem, as the base of certain leaves. [Latin *dēcurrēns,* present participle of *dēcurrere* to run down.]

de·cus·sate (*v.*, dek′ə sāt′, di kus′āt; *adj.*, dek′ə sāt′, di kus′it) *v.t., v.i.,* **-sat·ed, -sat·ing.** to cross or cut in the form of an X. —*adj.* **1.** having the form of an X. **2.** (of leaves or branches) arranged in pairs, each of which is at right angles to the pair above and below it. [Latin *decussātus,* past participle of *decussāre* to divide crosswise (in the form of an X), from *decussis* the number ten (for which the symbol was X).] —**de·cus·sate·ly** (di kus′it·lē), *adv.*

ded·i·cate (ded′i kāt′) *v.t.*, **-cat·ed, -cat·ing. 1.** to set apart for or devote to a deity or a sacred purpose; consecrate: *The ancient Greeks dedicated the Parthenon to Athena.* **2.** to set apart for or devote to a special purpose or use: *Part of the building was dedicated to chemical research.* **3.** to give or devote (oneself) entirely or earnestly to some person or purpose: *The researchers dedicated themselves to finding a cure for the disease.* **4.** to inscribe (a book or other artistic composition) to someone as a testimony, as of affection, respect, or gratitude. **5.** to open or unveil formally to the public: *The mayor dedicated the new city hall.* [Latin *dēdicātus,* past participle of *dēdicāre* to proclaim, consecrate.]

ded·i·ca·tion (ded′i kā′shən) *n.* **1.** the act of dedicating or the state of being dedicated. **2.** an inscription in a book or other artistic work, dedicating it to someone.

ded·i·ca·tive (ded′i kā′tiv) *adj.* dedicatory.

ded·i·ca·to·ry (ded′i kə tôr′ē) *adj.* of the nature of, constituting, or serving as a dedication.

de·dif·fer·en·ti·a·tion (dē dif′ə ren′shē ā′shən) *n. Biology.* a process in which cells, tissues, or organs lose specialized features and revert to a more generalized state, esp. as preparatory to certain kinds of cell development in plants.

de·duce (di düs′, -dūs′) *v.t.*, **-duced, -duc·ing. 1.** to derive or draw as a conclusion from something known or assumed; infer. **2.** to trace, as the course, descent, or derivation of. [Medieval Latin *dēducere* to infer logically, from Latin *dēdūcere.* See DE-DUCT.] —**de·duc′i·ble,** *adj.* —For Synonyms see **conclude.**

de·duct (di dukt′) *v.t.* to take away or subtract from a total. [Latin *dēductus,* past participle of *dēdūcere* to lead down, lead away, subtract, from *de* from + *ducere* to lead.] —**de·duct′i·ble,** *adj.*

de·duc·tion (di duk′shən) *n.* **1.** the act of deducting; subtraction. **2.** something that is deducted. **3.** reasoning from one or more principles or premises to a conclusion that necessarily or logically follows; reasoning from the general to the particular. ➠ distinguished from **induction. 4.** something that is deduced; inference; conclusion.

de·duc·tive (di duk′tiv) *adj.* of, employing, or based on deduction. —**de·duc′tive·ly,** *adv.*

deed (dēd) *n.* **1.** something done; act. **2.** a worthy or notable act; feat; exploit. **3.** a sealed document signifying or proving the transfer of real estate. **4.** action or performance, esp. in contrast to words. —*v.t.* to convey or transfer (real estate) by deed. [Old English *dæd* act, action.] —For Synonyms (*n.*), see **act.**
  ·in deed. in fact or reality.

dee·jay (dē′jā′) *n. Informal.* disc jockey.

deem (dēm) *v.t., v.i.* to think; believe; judge: *The employee deemed it wise to accept the new position.* [Old English *dēman.*]

deep (dēp) *adj.* **1.** extending far downward from the surface or top: *a deep well, deep water, a deep hole, a deep cut, a deep box.* **2.** great in degree; intense; extreme: *deep love, deep differences, deep distress, a deep sleep.* **3.** extending far inward or backward from the front or outer edge: *a deep shelf, a deep room.* **4.** difficult to understand or penetrate: *Philosophy is too deep for me.* **5.** completely occupied; absorbed; engrossed: *She was deep in thought.* **6.** coming from or extending to a depth: *a deep sigh, a deep plunge.* **7.** intellectually penetrating; profound: *a deep thinker, a deep insight.* **8.** to a large extent: *deep in debt.* **9.** going beyond that

a	at	e	end	o	hot	u	up	hw	white		about
ā	ape	ē	me	ō	old	ū	use	ng	song		taken
ä	far	i	it	ô	fork	ü	rule	th	thin	ə	pencil
âr	care	ī	ice	oi	oil	u̇	pull	th	this		lemon
		îr	pierce	ou	out	ûr	turn	zh	measure		circus

which is obvious or understood: *The statement had deep signifi-cance.* **10.** dark and rich in color: *a deep brown.* **11.** low in pitch: *a deep voice, the deep tones of an organ.* **12.** having a specified dimension downward, inward, or backward: *a pool 12 feet deep, a shelf 24 inches deep, a line of troops four deep.* **13.** closely guarded: *a deep, dark secret.* **14.** tall and dense: *deep grass.* **15.** sly; cunning. —*adv.* **1.** in, at, to, or with a great depth; deeply: *We went deep into the jungle. I reached deep into the bowl.* **2.** far on (in time); late: *The emergency meeting continued deep into the night.* —*n.* **1.** the part of greatest intensity: *the deep of winter, the deep of night.* **2.** an exceptionally deep area of the ocean. **3. the deep.** the sea. [Old English *dēop* extending far downward or inward; profound.] —**deep′ly,** *adv.* —**deep′ness,** *n.*
 • **to go off the deep end.** to act irrationally.

deep-dish pie (dēp′dish′) a pie, usually containing fruit, baked in a deep dish and having only a top crust.

deep•en (dē′pən) *v.t., v.i.* to make or become deep or deeper.

deep fat, fat used in deep-frying.

deep-freeze (dēp′frēz′) *v.t.,* **-froze** or **-freezed, -fro•zen** or **-freezed, -freez•ing.** quick-freeze. —*n.* freezer *(def. 1).*

deep-fry (dēp′frī′) *v.t.,* **-fried, -fry•ing.** to fry in a deep pan of fat or oil.

deep-laid (dēp′lād′) *adj.* made with great cunning, care, or secrecy: *a deep-laid plot.*

deep-root•ed (dēp′rü′tid, -rut′id) *adj.* **1.** firmly fixed or estab-lished; deep-seated: *a deep-rooted hatred.* **2.** having roots that extend far below the surface.

deep-sea (dēp′sē′) *adj.* of, in, or relating to the deeper parts of the ocean: *deep-sea fishing.*

deep-seat•ed (dēp′sē′tid) *adj.* firmly fixed or established; deeply implanted: *a deep-seated fear.*

deep-set (dēp′set′) *adj.* placed deeply: *deep-set eyes.*

deer (dîr) *n., pl.* **deer.** any of numerous cloven-hoofed, cud-chewing mammals, family Cervidae, typically having deciduous paired antlers in the male, as the white-tailed deer, the moose, the elk, and the rein-deer. Height: 13 inches to 6 feet (33 centimeters to 1.8 me-ters) at the shoulder. [Old English *dēor* wild animal, deer.]

deer•hound (dîr′hound′) *n.* a large, shaggy-haired dog of a breed originally developed in Scotland, formerly used for hunting deer. Height: 31 in-ches (79 centimeters) at the shoulder. Also, **Scottish deerhound.**

deer mouse, any of various nocturnal mice, genus *Pero-myscus,* of North and Central America, having buff or brown fur with white markings on the underside and legs. Length: 7½ inches (19 centimeters).

deer

deer•skin (dîr′skin′) *n.* **1.** the hide of a deer. **2.** leather made from this hide.

de•es•ca•late (dē es′kə lāt′) *v.t., v.i.,* **-lat•ed, -lat•ing.** to diminish by stages, as in size, scale, or intensity: *Calm talk de-escalated the quarrel to a difference of opinion.*

def. 1. defective. **2.** defendant. **3.** defense. **4.** deferred. **5.** de-fined. **6.** definite. **7.** definition.

de•face (di fās′) *v.t.,* **-faced, -fac•ing.** to spoil or destroy the surface or appearance of: *to deface a monument with graffiti.* [Old French *desfacier* to disfigure, going back to Latin *dis-* away, apart + *faciēs* face.] —**de•face′ment,** *n.* —**de•fac′er,** *n.*

Synonyms **Deface, mar,** and **disfigure** mean to damage the appearance of someone or something. **Deface** ap-plies to damage, which may be minor or temporary, to the face or surface of something: *Someone defaced the poster with a crayon.* **Mar** is used of more permanent damage: *Water stains marred the surface of the table.* **Disfigure** is used of injuries that cannot be easily repaired or hidden: *Scars from the accident disfigured the model's face.*

de fac•to (dē fak′tō) existing in reality, with or without legal right or sanction; actual: *de facto segregation, the de facto ruler.* ➡ distinguished from **de jure.** [Latin *dē factō* literally, from the fact.]

de•fal•cate (di fal′kāt, -fôl′-) *v.i.,* **-cat•ed, -cat•ing.** to misap-propriate money entrusted to one's care; embezzle. [Medieval Latin *defalcatus,* past participle of *defalcare* to take away, to cut

off with a sickle, going back to Latin *dē* away + *falx* sickle.] —**de•fal′ca•tor,** *n.*

de•fal•ca•tion (dē′fal kā′shən, -fôl-) *n.* **1.** the misappropria-tion of money entrusted to one's care; embezzlement. **2.** the amount misappropriated.

def•a•ma•tion (def′ə mā′shən, dē′fə-) *n.* the act or an instance of defaming or being defamed; slander or libel.

de•fam•a•to•ry (di fam′ə tôr′ē) *adj.* injurious to the reputation; slanderous or libelous.

de•fame (di fām′) *v.t.,* **-famed, -fam•ing.** to injure the reputa-tion of (a person) by false and malicious statements; slander or libel. [Old French *diffamer, defamer,* from Latin *diffāmāre,* from *dis-* apart, away + *fama* rumor, reputation.] —**de•fam′er,** *n.*

de•fault (di fôlt′) *n.* **1.** a failure to do something required. **2.** a failure to meet a financial obligation. **3.** a failure to take part in or complete a scheduled game or contest. **4.** a failure to take a required step in a legal action, esp. to appear in court. **5.** an alternative action that a computer will take automatically when not instructed to take a particular action. —*v.i.* **1.** to fail or neglect to do something required. **2.** to fail to meet a financial obligation. **3.a.** to fail to take part in or complete a scheduled game or contest. **b.** to lose a game or contest by default. **4.a.** to fail to take a required step in a legal action at the specified time, esp. to fail to appear in court. **b.** to lose an action by default. [Old French *defaute* lack, fault, going back to Latin *dē* from, away + Late Latin *fallita* deficiency (from Latin *fallere* to fail).] —**de•fault′er,** *n.*
 • **in default.** in a condition of having failed or neglected to do something required.
 • **in default of.** in the absence of; through lack of.

de•feat (di fēt′) *v.t.* **1.** to overcome in a contest or conflict of any kind; win a victory over; beat: *to defeat an opponent in tennis, to defeat an enemy in battle.* **2.** to prevent the success of; thwart; frustrate: *to defeat a purpose, to defeat someone's hopes.* —*n.* **1.** the act of overcoming or fact of being overcome in a contest or conflict. **2.** the act of thwarting or the state of being thwarted; frustration. [Old French *de(s)fait,* past participle of *desfaire* to undo, going back to Latin *dis-* un-[2] + *facere* to do.]

Synonyms **Defeat, conquer, overcome,** and **vanquish** mean to win a victory or gain control over. **De-feat** implies a clear decision: *to defeat an opponent in a game, to defeat a political initiative.* **Conquer** connotes getting control, and may imply a long or strenuous effort: *to conquer a disease, to conquer an empire.* **Overcome** suggests surmounting an ob-stacle or difficulty: *to overcome shyness, to overcome unfavorable odds.* **Vanquish** is a more formal word, suggesting a definitive victory, usually over a human adversary: *to vanquish the foe.*

de•feat•ist (di fē′tist) *n.* a person who expects defeat or prema-turely accepts it as inevitable. —*adj.* characteristic of a defeatist. —**de•feat′ism,** *n.*

def•e•cate (def′i kāt′) *v.i.,* **-cat•ed, -cat•ing.** to excrete waste from the bowels. [Latin *dēfaecātus,* past participle of *dēfaecāre* to remove the dregs from.] —**def′e•ca′tion,** *n.*

de•fect (*n.,* dē′fekt, di fekt′; *v.,* di fekt′) *n.* **1.** an imperfection, flaw, or weakness; fault; blemish: *a defect in a glass bowl.* **2.** a lack of something essential to completeness; deficiency: *a defect in eyesight.* —*v.i.* to leave a group, country, or cause, esp. for another of opposing policies or principles. [Latin *dēfectus* a want, failure.] —**de•fec′tor,** *n.* —For Synonyms *(n.),* see **blemish.**

de•fec•tion (di fek′shən) *n.* the act of leaving a group, country, or cause, esp. for another of opposing policies or principles.

de•fec•tive (di fek′tiv) *adj.* **1.** having a defect or defects; imper-fect; incomplete: *a house with defective wiring.* **2.** *Grammar.* lacking one or more of the usual forms of conjugation or other inflection. *Ought* and *must* are defective verbs. **3.** having less than normal physical or mental ability. —*n.* a person who has less than normal physical or mental ability. —**de•fec′tive•ly,** *adv.* —**de•fec′tive•ness,** *n.*

de•fence (di fens′) *British.* defense.

de•fend (di fend′) *v.t.* **1.** to guard against attack, injury, or danger; protect: *The troops defended the city.* **2.** to support, justify, or maintain by word or deed: *to defend one's rights.* **3.** *Law.* **a.** to plead the case or cause of (an accused person). **b.** to contest (a charge or suit). —*v.i.* to make a defense. [Old French *defendre* to protect, from Latin *dēfendere* to ward off.] —**de•fend′a•ble,** *adj.* —**de•fend′er,** *n.*

Synonyms **Defend, guard, protect,** and **shield** mean to keep someone or something safe from injury, dan-ger, or attack. **Defend** implies action taken to resist some threat: *to defend a fort against attackers, to defend a theory against critics.* **Guard** connotes standing watch against danger: *The sen-try guarded the entrance all night.* **Protect** implies the use of some kind of covering or screen against a potential attack: *Net-ting protected us from insects. A high wall protected the mansion*

from intruders. **Shield** makes the idea of a screen even more explicit: *The sandbags shielded them from the bombardment. An awning shielded the children from the sun.*

de·fend·ant (di fen′dənt) *n.* a person against whom a civil or criminal action is brought in a court of law.

de·fense (di fens′) *also, British,* **defence.** *n.* **1.** the act of guarding against attack, injury, or danger; protection: *to be engaged in the defense of a city.* **2.** a person or thing that protects; means of protection: *The dike was the town's only defense against flooding.* **3.** support or justification by word or deed: *The governor spoke in defense of the proposed new tax.* **4.** an argument, speech, or writing that so supports or justifies: *The historian's defense of the thesis lacked clarity.* **5.a.** the act or method of defending oneself, one's side, or one's goal, as in a sport or game. **b.** the defending team, players, or side in a sport or game. **6.a.** arguments presented in court by a defendant or his or her lawyer or lawyers. **b.** a defendant and his or her lawyer or lawyers collectively. [Old French *defense* act of protecting, means of protecting, from Latin *dēfensa* a defending.]

de·fense·less (di fens′lis) *adj.* having no defense; helpless; unprotected. —**de·fense′less·ly,** *adv.* —**de·fense′less·ness,** *n.*

defense mechanism **1.** a reaction or mental process unconsciously adopted by a person to limit his or her awareness of painful or unpleasant feelings, such as guilt or anxiety. Rationalization and repression are defense mechanisms. **2.** a self-protective reaction of an organism to stimuli, as the production of antitoxins.

de·fen·si·ble (di fen′sə bəl) *adj.* **1.** capable of being defended in argument; justifiable: *a defensible action.* **2.** capable of being defended against attack, injury, or danger: *a defensible coastline.* —**de·fen′si·bil′i·ty, de·fen′si·ble·ness,** *n.* —**de·fen′si·bly,** *adv.*

de·fen·sive (di fen′siv) *adj.* **1.** serving to defend; protective: *defensive armor.* **2.** formed or carried on for the purpose of resisting attack or aggression: *defensive warfare.* **3.** having or using defenses: *a defensive attitude, a defensive person.* —*n.* a position or attitude of defense. —**de·fen′sive·ly,** *adv.* —**de·fen′sive·ness,** *n.*

• **on the defensive.** assuming or forced to assume a protective or self-justifying attitude.

de·fer¹ (di fûr′) *v.,* **-ferred, -fer·ring.** —*v.t.* **1.** to hold (an action or decision) for a future time; put off; postpone: *to defer judgment on a matter.* **2.** to postpone the induction of (a person) into the armed forces. —*v.i.* to put off action; delay. [Middle English *differen,* from Old French *differer,* from Latin *differre* to delay, disperse. Doublet of DIFFER.] —**de·fer′ra·ble,** *adj.* —**de·fer′rer,** *n.*

Synonyms **Defer¹, delay,** and **postpone** mean to put off for the time being. **Defer** implies that something will take place but not necessarily at a specified time: *to defer action on a piece of legislation.* **Delay** connotes keeping something from happening at the expected time: *Heavy traffic delayed our arrival. Rain delayed the game.* **Postpone** usually implies a definite rescheduling: *The opening has been postponed until Thursday.*

de·fer² (di fûr′) *v.i.,* **-ferred, -fer·ring.** to submit in judgment or opinion; yield respectfully: *I deferred to my friend's conclusion.* [Middle English *deferen,* from Old French *deferer* to yield, from Late Latin *deferre* to yield, pay respect to, from Latin *deferre* to carry away, grant, allow, from *de-* away + *ferre* to carry.]

def·er·ence (def′ər əns) *n.* courteous respect or regard, as for the authority or position of someone: *to have deference for one's elders.*

• **in deference to.** in respectful acknowledgment of the authority or position of; out of respect for: *In deference to our grandparents, we were not noisy in the mornings.*

def·er·en·tial (def′ə ren′shəl) *adj.* characterized by or showing deference; respectful: *a deferential attitude.* Also, **def·er·ent** (def′ər ənt). —**def·er·en′tial·ly,** *adv.*

de·fer·ment (di fûr′mənt) *n.* a putting off or delay; postponement: *a deferment of jury duty.* Also, **de·fer·ral** (di fûr′əl).

de·ferred (di fûrd′) *adj.* **1.** put off for a time; postponed. **2.** with payments or benefits put off until a certain date: *deferred stock.* **3.** classified as temporarily exempt from military draft.

de·fi·ance (di fī′əns) *n.* **1.** bold or open resistance to authority, an adversary, or an opposing force; contempt of opposition or authority. **2.** a challenge to meet in a fight or contest.

• **in defiance of.** in spite of.

• **to bid defiance to.** to defy.

de·fi·ant (di fī′ənt) *adj.* characterized by or showing defiance; openly or boldly resisting. [French *défiant,* present participle of *défier* to defy, from Old French *defier.* See DEFY.] —**de·fi′ant·ly,** *adv.*

de·fib·ril·late (dē fib′rə lāt′, -fī′brə-) *v.t.,* **-lat·ed, -lat·ing.** to stop fibrillation of (the heart), as by electric shock. [DE- + *fibrillate* (from FIBRILLATION).] —**de·fib′ril·la′tion,** *n.* —**de·fib′ril·la′tor,** *n.*

de·fi·cien·cy (di fish′ən sē) *n., pl.* **-cies.** **1.** the state of being deficient; lack of something essential: *a vitamin deficiency.* **2.** the amount of shortage or lack; deficit: *a deficiency of ten dollars.*

deficiency disease, a disease, as scurvy or rickets, caused by a lack of some essential element in the diet.

de·fi·cient (di fish′ənt) *adj.* **1.** not adequate in quantity or supply; insufficient: *a diet deficient in vitamins.* **2.** lacking something essential; incomplete; imperfect: *mentally deficient.* [Latin *deficient-,* stem of *deficiens,* the present participle of *deficere* to lack something necessary, fail, from *de-* from + *facere* to do, make.] —**de·fi′cient·ly,** *adv.*

def·i·cit (def′ə sit) *n.* **1.** the amount by which something, esp. a sum of money, falls short of what is due, required, or expected; shortage. **2.** a loss in business operations: *The store has been running at a deficit for a year.* [French *déficit* deficiency, shortage in keeping accounts, from Latin *dēficit* it is wanting, from *dēficere* to be wanting.]

deficit spending, a government fiscal policy of spending beyond tax receipts by borrowing funds from public banks and expanding the public debt. Also, **deficit financing.**

de·fi·er (di fī′ər) *n.* a person who defies.

de·file¹ (di fīl′) *v.t.,* **-filed, -fil·ing.** **1.** to spoil the purity or sacredness of; profane; taint: *to defile a temple.* **2.** to make filthy, dirty, or impure; pollute: *to defile a stream with garbage.* [Middle English *defoulen,* partly from Old French *defouler* to trample on, violate (going back to Latin *dē* down + *fullō* fuller; with reference to treading cloth to full it), and partly going back to Old English *fȳlan* to make foul.] —**de·file′ment,** *n.* —**de·fil′er,** *n.* —For Synonyms, see **pollute.**

de·file² (di fīl′, dē′fīl) *v.i.,* **-filed, -fil·ing.** to march in a line or by files. —*n.* a narrow passage in a mountain region, esp. one that permits travel only in a narrow line. [French *défiler* to march in a column; earlier, to unravel, from *dé* away, from (from Latin *dis-* apart) + *fil* thread, line (from Latin *filum* thread).]

de·fine (di fīn′) *v.,* **-fined, -fin·ing.** —*v.t.* **1.** to state the meaning or meanings of (a word or phrase): *Can you define the word "cafeteria"?* **2.** to describe the essential nature or characteristics of; explain: *to define the concepts used in an argument.* **3.** to fix or set forth precisely or authoritatively: *The U.S. Constitution defines the powers of the president.* **4.** to determine or constitute the limits or extent of: *Rivers define the country's borders.* **5.** to make clear or distinct in outline or shape: *The contrast in color helped to define the forms in the painting.* —*v.i.* to formulate a definition or definitions. [Old French *definer* to determine, limit, from Latin *dēfīnīre* to limit, determine, going back to *dē* down + *fīnis* end, boundary.] —**de·fin′a·ble,** *adj.* —**de·fin′er,** *n.*

def·i·nite (def′ə nit) *adj.* **1.** clearly defined; precise; exact: *I have definite ideas on that subject.* **2.** having been settled; positive; certain; sure: *It is definite that school will be closed today.* **3.** having precise limits: *a definite boundary.* **4.** *Botany.* determinate. [Latin *dēfīnītus,* past participle of *dēfīnīre* to limit, determine. See DEFINE.] —**def′i·nite·ly,** *adv.* —**def′i·nite·ness,** *n.* —For Synonyms, see **precise.**

definite article, the article *the,* which limits or specifies the noun it modifies. ➡ distinguished from **indefinite article.**

def·i·ni·tion (def′ə nish′ən) *n.* **1.** a statement of the meaning of a word or phrase. **2.** a statement of the essential nature or characteristics of a thing. **3.** the act of stating the meaning of a word or phrase, or the essential nature or characteristics of a thing. **4.** the act of making or being made clear in outline or form. **5.** the power of a lens to produce clear, sharp images. **6.** sharpness of outline, as of a photograph; distinctness; clearness. **7.** in radio and television, the accuracy with which sound or images are reproduced by a receiver. —**def′i·ni′tion·al,** *adj.*

de·fin·i·tive (di fin′i tiv) *adj.* **1.** most nearly accurate and complete: *the definitive edition of a poet's works.* **2.** ending any question or confusion; conclusive; final; decisive: *a definitive answer.* **3.** serving to limit or define. —**de·fin′i·tive·ly,** *adv.* —**de·fin′i·tive·ness,** *n.*

de·flate (di flāt′) *v.,* **-flat·ed, -flat·ing.** —*v.t.* **1.** to reduce in size by releasing air or gas from: *to deflate a tire.* **2.** to reduce in self-confidence or importance, esp. something exaggerated: *to deflate someone's ego, to deflate a rumor.* **3.** to reduce in amount, size, level, or value: *to deflate prices.* —*v.i.* to collapse or con-

a	at	e	end	o	hot	u	up	hw	white		about
ā	ape	ē	me	ō	old	ū	use	ng	song		taken
ä	far	i	it	ô	fork	ü	rule	th	thin	ə	pencil
âr	care	ī	ice	oi	oil	u̇	pull	t͟h	this		lemon
		îr	pierce	ou	out	ûr	turn	zh	measure		circus

tract, as through loss of air or gas: *The balloon deflated.* [DE- + (IN)FLATE.] —**de·fla′tor,** *n.*

de·fla·tion (di flā′shən) *n.* **1.** the act of deflating or the state of being deflated. **2.** a decline in the general level of prices, resulting from a reduction in money supply or spending.

de·fla·tion·ar·y (di flā′shə ner′ē) *adj.* relating to, causing, or characterized by deflation.

de·flect (di flekt′) *v.t., v.i.* to turn or cause to turn aside; bend or deviate from a straight course. [Latin *dēflecter* to bend aside.] —**de·flec′tive,** *adj.* —**de·flec′tor,** *n.*

de·flec·tion (di flek′shən) *also, British,* **de·flex·ion.** *n.* **1.** the act of deflecting or the state of being deflected; turning away; deviation. **2.** the amount of such turning or deviation. **3.** the amount an indicator on a measuring instrument moves or deviates from the zero reading on its scale.

def·lor·a·tion (def′lə rā′shən, dē′flə-) *n.* the act of deflowering or the state or occasion of being deflowered.

de·flow·er (dē flou′ər) *v.t.* **1.** to take away the virginity of (a woman). **2.** to spoil the beauty or purity of; ravish; violate. **3.** to strip of flowers. —**de·flow′er·er,** *n.*

de·fo·li·ant (dē fō′lē ənt) *n.* a chemical agent for defoliating plants, chiefly used in farming to remove unwanted leaves and in warfare to destroy crops or plant life.

de·fo·li·ate (dē fō′lē āt′) *v.,* -**at·ed,** -**at·ing.** —*v.t.* **1.** to strip of leaves. **2.** to destroy (a forest, jungle, or other area of vegetation) by stripping of leaves, esp. with a defoliant. —*v.i.* to lose leaves. [Late Latin *dēfoliātus,* past participle of *dēfoliāre* to strip off leaves, from Latin *dē* from + *folium* leaf.] —**de·fo′li·a′tion,** *n.* —**de·fo′li·a′tor,** *n.*

de·for·est (dē fôr′ist, -for′-) *v.t.* to clear or strip of forests or trees. —**de·for′est·a′tion,** *n.*

de·form (di fôrm′) *v.t.* **1.** to spoil the form of; make misshapen: *The heat from the fire deformed the plastic.* **2.** to make ugly; mar the beauty of; disfigure. [Latin *dēformāre* to disfigure.]

de·for·ma·tion (dē′fôr mā′shən, def′ər-) *n.* **1.** the act of deforming or the state of being deformed. **2.** a result or instance of being deformed; deformity.

de·formed (di fôrmd′) *adj.* **1.** misshapen, esp. in body or limbs; distorted. **2.** ugly; offensive.

de·form·i·ty (di fôr′mi tē) *n., pl.* -**ties.** **1.** an improperly formed or distorted part of the body. **2.** the condition of being deformed. **3.** moral disfigurement or defect; depravity.

de·fraud (di frôd′) *v.t.* to deprive (someone) by fraud of something rightfully held or due; cheat; swindle: *to defraud a person of property.* [Latin *dēfraudāre.*] —**de·fraud·a·tion** (dē′frô dā′shən), *n.* —**de·fraud′er,** *n.* —For Synonyms, see **cheat.**

de·fray (di frā′) *v.t.* to pay (costs or expenses): *The college raised its tuition to help defray expenses.* [French *défrayer,* from *de-* (see DE-) + *frai* cost (of Germanic origin).] —**de·fray′a·ble,** *adj.* —**de·fray′al, de·fray′ment,** *n.*

de·frock (dē frok′) *v.t.* unfrock.

de·frost (di frôst′) *v.t., v.i.* **1.** to make or become free of frost or ice: *to defrost a refrigerator.* **2.** to thaw.

de·frost·er (di frôs′tər) *n.* a device that removes or prevents the formation of ice or frost, as in a refrigerator or on an automobile windshield.

deft (deft) *adj.* having or showing skill and nimbleness; dexterous; adroit: *deft fingers, deft handling of a difficult situation.* [Old English *gedæfte* gentle.] —**deft′ly,** *adv.* —**deft′ness,** *n.* —For Synonyms, see **dexterous.**

de·funct (di fungkt′) *adj.* no longer existing or active; dead; extinct: *a defunct organization.* [Latin *dēfūnctus,* past participle of *dēfungī* to have done with, die[1].]

de·fuse (dē fūz′) *v.t.,* -**fused,** -**fus·ing.** **1.** to remove the fuse from: *to defuse an unexploded bomb.* **2.** to lessen the danger or intensity of: *to defuse political tensions.*

de·fy (di fī′) *v.t.,* -**fied,** -**fy·ing.** **1.** to face (opposition or authority) with contempt; resist openly or boldly: *to defy the law.* **2.** to resist completely or successfully; withstand: *That problem defies solution.* **3.** to present with a challenge; dare: *I defy you to beat my score.* [Middle English *defien,* from Old French *defier* to defy; earlier, to renounce faith in God, going back to Latin *dis-* apart + *fidus* faithful.]

deg. *also,* **deg** degree; degrees.

de·gas (dē gas′) *v.t.,* -**gassed,** -**gas·sing.** to remove gas from (a device, area, or the like); rid of gas. [DE- + GAS.]

de·gauss (dē gous′) *v.t.* to neutralize the magnetic field of (an object, as a television receiver or ship) by the use of special coils that produce a magnetic field equal but opposite to that of the object; demagnetize. [From Karl F. *Gauss,* 1777-1855, German scientist.]

de·gen·er·a·cy (di jen′ər ə sē) *n., pl.* -**cies.** **1.** the state of being degenerate, esp. in moral character. **2.** the process of degenerat-

ing; deterioration. **3.** degenerate behavior, esp. immoral behavior.

de·gen·er·ate (*v.,* di jen′ə rāt′; *adj., n.,* di jen′ər it) *v.i.* -**at·ed,** -**at·ing.** **1.** to become worse or inferior in condition, character, or quality; deteriorate. **2.** (of an organism) to regress to a less complex or less developed form. —*adj.* having become worse or inferior in condition, character, or quality, esp. with regard to moral character; degraded. —*n.* **1.** a person who is morally degraded. **2.** a person who has deteriorated or regressed, as from a higher physical or cultural standard. [Latin *dēgenerātus,* past participle of *dēgenerāre* to deteriorate, going back to *dē-* down, from + *genus* race, kind.] —**de·gen′er·ate·ly,** *adv.* —**de·gen′er·ate·ness,** *n.*

de·gen·er·a·tion (di jen′ə rā′shən) *n.* **1.** the process of degenerating. **2.** the state of being degenerate. **3.** a progressive deterioration of tissue caused by disease or injury and leading to structural or functional impairment of an organ or other body part.

de·gen·er·a·tive (di jen′ər ə tiv, -ə rā′tiv) *adj.* **1.** relating to, characterized by, or causing degeneration: *a degenerative disease.* **2.** tending to degenerate.

de·glu·ti·tion (dē′glü tish′ən, deg′lü-) *n.* the act, power, or process of swallowing. [French *déglutition* swallowing, from Latin *dēglūtīre* to swallow down.]

deg·ra·da·tion (deg′rə dā′shən) *n.* **1.** the act of degrading or the state of being degraded. **2.** the state of being lowered in character, quality, or estimation.

de·grade (di grād′) *v.t.,* -**grad·ed,** -**grad·ing.** **1.** to lower in character or quality, esp. moral character; debase; corrupt: *Lying degrades a person.* **2.** to bring into contempt or low esteem; dishonor. **3.** to reduce in rank or position, esp. as a punishment. **4.** to wear down by erosion. [Old French *degrader* to deprive of rank, going back to Latin *dē-* down + *gradus* grade, rank, step.] —**de·grad′a·ble,** *adj.* —**de·grad′er,** *n.*

de·grad·ed (di grā′did) *adj.* lowered in character or quality; corrupt; debased.

de·grad·ing (di grā′ding) *adj.* tending to degrade; debasing; humiliating.

de·gree (di grē′) *n.* **1.** one of a series of stages or steps in a process or course: *The child learned to walk by degrees.* **2.** intensity, amount, or extent considered as on a scale: *a high degree of intelligence, a low degree of privacy.* **3.** relative social or official rank or position: *townspeople of low degree.* **4.** relative condition, manner, or respect: *A dog and a flower may be equally beautiful, each in its own degree.* **5.** a unit of temperature measurement, varying according to the scale used. ➡ The symbol for degrees (°) is often used with figures: *70° Fahrenheit.* **6.** a rank or title given by an academic institution for completion of a course of study or as an honorary distinction: *a master's degree in history.* **7.** a step in a line of genealogical descent: *A grandparent and grandchild are two degrees removed from each other.* **8.** *Mathematics.* a unit of measurement for angles or arcs, equal to 1/360 of the circumference of a circle. **9.** a unit of angular distance on the earth's surface measured from a specified meridian or the equator. **10.** *Law.* the relative seriousness of a particular crime: *murder in the first degree.* **11.** *Algebra.* **a.** a rank of a monomial term as determined by the sum of the exponents of the variables. The terms x^4 and xy^3 are both of the fourth degree. **b.** the rank of a polynomial as determined by the sum of the exponents of the term of the highest degree. The equation $xy^4 + yz$ is of the fifth degree. **12.** *Grammar.* one of the three forms of comparison of adjectives or adverbs. For the adjective *good,* the positive degree is *good,* the comparative degree is *better,* and the superlative degree is *best.* **13.** *Music.* **a.** a note or tone of a scale. **b.** the interval between consecutive notes or tones of a scale. **c.** a line or space on a staff. [Old French *degré* step, stage, rank, going back to Latin *dē-* down + *gradus* step, grade, rank.]

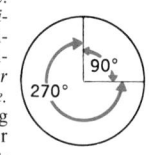

degree
(def. 8)

·**to a degree. a.** somewhat. **b.** to a great extent or amount; exceedingly.

de·gree-day (di grē′dā′) a unit representing one degree of difference in the average temperature for a given day from a standard, usually 65 degrees Fahrenheit, used for estimating fuel requirements.

de·hisce (di his′) *v.i.,* -**hisced,** -**hisc·ing.** to burst open, as the capsule or seed pod of a plant. [Latin *dēhīscere* to gape.]

de·his·cence (di his′əns) *n.* the act or process of bursting open, as of certain ripe fruits or anthers when the seeds or pollen grains are discharged. —**de·his′cent,** *adj.*

de·horn (dē hôrn′) *v.t.* to remove the horns from.

de·hu·man·ize (dē hū′mə nīz′, dē ū′-) *v.t.,* -**ized,** -**iz·ing.** to deprive of human qualities; make inhuman or mechanical. —**de·hu′man·i·za′tion,** *n.*

de·hu·mid·i·fi·er (dē′hū mid′ə fī′ər, dē′ū-) *n.* a device for removing moisture from the air.

de·hu·mid·i·fy (dē′hū mid′ə fī′, dē′ū-) *v.t.,* **-fied, -fy·ing.** to remove moisture from: *to dehumidify air, to dehumidify a room.* —**de′hu·mid′i·fi·ca′tion,** *n.*

de·hy·drate (dē hī′drāt) *v.,* **-drat·ed, -drat·ing.** —*v.t.* **1.** to remove water or its chemical equivalents from (a chemical compound). **2.** to remove water from; dry: *to dehydrate foods.* —*v.i.* to lose water; become dry. —**de′hy·dra′tion,** *n.* —**de′hy·dra·tor,** *n.*

de·hy·dro·gen·ase (dē hī′drə jə nās′) *n.* any of a group of enzymes that act as catalysts in the removal of hydrogen during the oxidation of metabolites in living tissues. [DE- + HYDROGEN + -ASE.]

de·hy·dro·gen·ate (dē hī′drə jə nāt′, dē′hī droj′ə-) *v.t.,* **-at·ed, -at·ing.** to remove hydrogen from (a molecule or compound). —**de·hy′dro·gen·a′tion,** *n.*

de·ice (dē īs′) *v.t.,* **-iced, -ic·ing.** to remove ice from or prevent ice from forming on.

de·ic·er (dē ī′sər) *n.* a device or substance that prevents ice from forming or removes it, as on an airplane wing.

de·i·fi·ca·tion (dē′ə fi kā′shən) *n.* **1.** the act of deifying or the state of being deified. **2.** a person or thing that has been deified.

de·i·fy (dē′ə fī′) *v.t.,* **-fied, -fy·ing. 1.** to make a god of. **2.** to worship as a god; regard as an object of worship: *to deify an emperor.* **3.** to glorify, idealize, or worship as though a god: *to deify wealth.* [Old French *deifier* to make a god of, from Late Latin *deificāre,* going back to Latin *deus* a god + *facere* to make.] —**de′i·fi′er,** *n.*

deign (dān) *v.i.* to think it worthy of oneself; condescend: *She would not deign to accept our offer of help.* —*v.t.* to condescend to grant or give: *He deigned no reply to our invitation.* [Old French *deignier* to think worthy, from Latin *dignārī.*]

de·in·sti·tu·tion·al·ize (dē in′sti tü′shə nə līz′, -tū′-) *v.t.,* **-ized, -iz·ing. 1.** to release from an institution, such as a mental hospital, to be cared for under supervision through community facilities, such as halfway houses. **2.** to divest or free (an institution) from its institutional quality or character. —**de·in′sti·tu′tion·al·i·za′tion,** *n.*

de·i·on·ize (dē ī′ə nīz′) *v.t.,* **-ized, -iz·ing.** to remove ions from (a substance, esp. water). —**de·i′on·i·za′tion,** *n.*

de·ism (dē′iz əm) *n.* **1.** the belief that the universe and its natural laws were created by God, but that the natural laws govern its operation, not the will of God. **2.** the belief in God as the source of existence, stressing dependence upon reason rather than revelation and rejecting the rituals of organized religion. [Latin *deus* a god + -ISM.] —**de′ist,** *n.* —**de·is′tic;** *also,* **de·is′ti·cal,** *adj.* —**de·is′ti·cal·ly,** *adv.*

de·i·ty (dē′i tē) *n., pl.* **-ties. 1.** a god or goddess; divine being. **2.** the state or attributes of being a god; divine nature; divinity. **3. the Deity.** God. [Old French *deite* divinity, divine nature, from Late Latin *deitās,* from Latin *deus* a god.]

dé·jà vu (dā′zhä vü′) the illusion of having already experienced something that is actually being experienced for the first time. [French *déjà vu* literally, already seen.]

de·ject (di jekt′) *v.t.* to make low in spirits; dishearten; depress. [Latin *dējectus,* past participle of *dēicere* to throw down.]

de·ject·ed (di jek′tid) *adj.* low in spirits; disheartened; depressed. —**de·ject′ed·ly,** *adv.* —**de·ject′ed·ness,** *n.*

de·jec·tion (di jek′shən) *n.* lowness of spirits; depression; sadness.

de ju·re (dē jūr′ē) according to law: of right; legitimate; *a de jure ruler, de jure segregation.* ➡ distinguished from **de facto.** [Latin *dē jūre* according to law.]

deka-, variant of **deca-.**

dek·a·gram (dek′ə gram′) decagram.

dek·a·li·ter (dek′ə lē′tər) decaliter.

dek·a·me·ter (dek′ə mē′tər) decameter.

dek·a·stere (dek′ə stîr′) decastere.

del. 1. delegate. **2.** delete.

Del., Delaware.

de·lam·i·na·tion (dē lam′ə nā′shən) *n.* a separation or splitting apart into layers.

Del·a·ware (del′ə wâr′) *n., pl.* **-ware** or **-wares. 1.** a member of a North American Indian tribe formerly living in the Delaware River valley. **2.** the Algonquian language of this tribe.

de·lay (di lā′) *v.t.* **1.** to put off to a future time; postpone: *The umpire delayed the start of the game because of the rain.* **2.** to make late; hinder the progress of; detain: *Heavy traffic delayed us.* —*v.i.* to put off or slow down action; linger; procrastinate: *You'll be late if you delay any longer.* —*n.* **1.** the act of delaying or the state of being delayed: *The delay was caused by a derailment.* **2.** the amount of time something is delayed: *a two-day delay.* [Old

French *delaier* to postpone, from *de-* (see DE-) + *laier* to leave (of uncertain origin).] —**de·lay′er,** *n.* —For Synonyms *(v.t.),* see **defer**[1].

de·le (dē′lē) *v.t.,* **-led, -le·ing.** to cross out or take out; delete. ➡ usually used in the imperative as a direction in printing and represented by the symbol ⌒ . —*n.* the mark used to give this direction. [Latin *dēlē,* imperative singular of *dēlēre* to destroy, wipe out.]

de·lec·ta·ble (di lek′tə bəl) *adj.* highly pleasing or delightful, esp. to the taste; delicious. [Latin *dēlectābilis* delightful.] —**de·lec′ta·bil′i·ty, de·lec′ta·ble·ness,** *n.* —**de·lec′ta·bly,** *adv.*

de·lec·ta·tion (dē′lek tā′shən) *n.* delight, esp. of the senses; pleasure; enjoyment.

del·e·ga·cy (del′i gə sē) *n., pl.* **-cies. 1.** the act of delegating or the state of being delegated. **2.** the position or authority of a delegate. **3.** a body or committee of delegates.

del·e·gate (*n.,* del′i git, -gāt′; *v.,* del′i gāt′) *n.* **1.** a person given authority to represent or act for another or others; representative; deputy. **2.** a representative of a territory in the U.S. House of Representatives. A delegate may speak, but not vote. **3.** a member of the lower house of the state legislature in Maryland, Virginia, or West Virginia. —*v.t.,* **-gat·ed, -gat·ing. 1.** to commit or entrust (power, authority, or responsibility) to another or others. **2.** to appoint or send as a delegate: *The club delegated three members to attend the national convention.* [Latin *dēlēgātus,* past participle of *dēlēgāre* to send, assign.]

del·e·ga·tion (del′i gā′shən) *n.* **1.** a group of persons authorized to represent others: *A delegation from our district presented a petition to the school board.* **2.** the act of delegating or the state of being delegated.

de·lete (di lēt′) *v.t.,* **-let·ed, -let·ing.** to cross out or take out (something written or printed); omit; cancel. [Latin *dēlētus,* past participle of *dēlēre* to destroy, wipe out.] —For Synonyms, see **erase.**

del·e·te·ri·ous (del′i tîr′ē əs) *adj.* causing harm; injurious; hurtful: *a deleterious drug.* [Medieval Latin *dēlētērius* noxious, from Greek *dēlētērios.*] —**del′e·te′ri·ous·ly,** *adv.* —**del′e·te′ri·ous·ness,** *n.*

de·le·tion (di lē′shən) *n.* **1.** the act of deleting or the state of being deleted. **2.** something deleted.

delft (delft) *n.* glazed earthenware usually decorated with a blue and white glaze in patterns inspired by Chinese porcelains, originally made in Delft, the Netherlands. Also, **delft′ware′.**

del·i (del′ē) *n. Informal.* delicatessen.

de·lib·er·ate (*adj.,* di lib′ər it; *v.,* di lib′ə rāt′) *adj.* **1.** carefully thought out or planned; intentional; studied: *The writer made a deliberate attempt to misrepresent the facts.* **2.** careful and slow in deciding; not hasty or rash: *I am deliberate in all my financial decisions.* **3.** unhurried in action or movement; slow: *the deliberate steps of someone with a broken foot.* —*v.,* **-at·ed, -at·ing.** —*v.i.* **1.** to consider or reflect carefully: *I deliberated whether or not to accept the job offer.* **2.** to confer in order to consider and decide something: *The council deliberated behind closed doors.* —*v.t.* to think over or debate carefully; weigh: *The Senate has been deliberating the question for three days.* [Latin *dēlīberātus,* past participle of *dēlīberāre* to weigh well, reflect, consult, going back to *dē* thoroughly + *lībra* a pair of scales.] —**de·lib′er·ate·ly,** *adv.* —**de·lib′er·ate·ness,** *n.* —**de·lib′er·a′tor,** *n.*

delft plate

Synonyms *adj.* **Deliberate** and **intentional** mean done or designed by choice rather than by accident or because of some external force that cannot be resisted. **Deliberate** connotes more forethought, implying that the consequences have been weighed: *The president made a deliberate decision to use force after all other options were exhausted.* **Intentional** suggests a premeditated attempt to achieve a purpose: *My sarcasm was an intentional effort to get the audience stirred up.*

de·lib·er·a·tion (di lib′ə rā′shən) *n.* **1.** careful consideration with the aim of reaching a decision. **2.** discussion and consideration by a group of the reasons for and against something: *the*

a	at	e	end	o	hot	u	up	hw	white		about
ā	ape	ē	me	ō	old	ū	use	ng	song		taken
ä	far	i	it	ô	fork	ü	rule	th	thin	ə {	pencil
âr	care	ī	ice	oi	oil	u	pull	th	this		lemon
			ir	pierce	ou	out	ûr	turn	zh	measure	circus

deliberations of a jury. ➡ usually used in the plural. **3.** slowness and care in decision or action: *to speak with deliberation.*

de·lib·er·a·tive (di lib′ə rā′tiv, -ər ə tiv) *adj.* **1.** relating to deliberation or having the function of deliberating: *Congress is a deliberative assembly.* **2.** characterized by deliberation or careful consideration: *a deliberative attempt to get the facts.* —**de·lib′·er·a′tive·ly,** *adv.* —**de·lib′er·a′tive·ness,** *n.*

del·i·ca·cy (del′i kə sē) *n., pl.* **-cies. 1.** exquisite fineness of structure, texture, quality, or form; daintiness; frailty: *the delicacy of lace.* **2.** a rare or choice food: *caviar and other delicacies.* **3.** susceptibility to disease or injury; physical weakness. **4.** the quality or condition of requiring tact, skill, or care in treatment or handling: *a problem of great delicacy.* **5.** fineness of perception, taste, or skill; sensitivity: *the delicacy of an epicure's palate.* **6.** sensitivity in measurement or response; accuracy: *the delicacy of a galvanometer.* **7.** sensitivity to what is becoming, proper, or modest: *a person of some delicacy.*

del·i·cate (del′i kit) *adj.* **1.** intricately detailed or dainty in structure, quality, texture, or form: *a delicate piece of lace, a delicate pattern of shadows and light.* **2.** pleasing to the senses in a soft, mild, or subtle way: *a delicate perfume, a delicate color, a delicate flavor.* **3.** easily damaged; fragile: *a delicate flower, a delicate wine glass.* **4.** extremely susceptible to disease or injury: *a delicate child.* **5.** requiring tact in handling; ticklish: *a delicate topic of conversation.* **6.** requiring great skill and precision in execution: *a delicate brain operation.* **7.** finely sensitive in measurement or response; minutely accurate: *A barometer is a delicate instrument.* **8.** scarcely perceptible; subtle: *a delicate shade of meaning.* **9.** finely skilled or sensitive: *a delicate touch, a delicate palate.* **10.** sensitive to or in accord with what is becoming, proper, or modest: *delicate manners.* **11.** having or showing tact or care; considerate. [Latin *dēlicātus* dainty, charming, luxurious.] —**del′i·cate·ly,** *adv.* —**del′i·cate·ness,** *n.*

| **Synonyms** | **Delicate, fragile,** and **frail** can all mean easy to break. **Delicate** connotes fineness of structure |

that makes an object susceptible to damage or a person susceptible to disease or injury: *delicate porcelain figurines, a delicate child.* **Fragile** suggests that the substance of which a thing is made leaves it vulnerable: *The shipment of crystal was marked "fragile" to help avoid breakage in transport.* **Frail** suggests a weakness in construction or because of age: *The frail wooden bridge cracked and swayed in the heavy winds.*

del·i·ca·tes·sen (del′i kə tes′ən) *n.* **1.** a store that specializes in prepared foods, as cooked meats. Also, **deli. 2.** such foods collectively, usually served cold. ➡ used as plural in def. 2. [German *Delikatessen,* plural of *Delikatesse* choice food, through French, going back to Latin *dēlicātus* dainty, charming, luxurious.]

de·li·cious (di lish′əs) *adj.* highly pleasing or delightful, esp. to the taste or smell: *delicious fruit, a delicious meal.* —*n.* **Delicious,** a sweet red or yellow variety of apple. [Old French *delicieus* fine, delicate, from Late Latin *dēliciōsus* pleasant, from Latin *dēlicia* delight, pleasure.] —**de·li′cious·ly,** *adv.* —**de·li′cious·ness,** *n.*

de·light (di līt′) *n.* **1.** a high degree of pleasure or joy, esp. as experienced through the senses. **2.** something that gives great pleasure or joy: *The dance was a delight to watch.* —*v.t.* to give great pleasure or joy to; please highly: *The play delighted the children.* —*v.i.* to have or take great pleasure: *The gourmet delighted in eating good food.* [Old French *delitier* to rejoice, please, from Latin *dēlectāre* to charm.] —For Synonyms *(v.t.),* see **please.**

de·light·ed (di lī′tid) *adj.* highly pleased; gratified: *I'd be delighted to go with you.* —**de·light′ed·ly,** *adv.* —**de·light′ed·ness,** *n.* —For Synonyms, see **glad¹.**

de·light·ful (di līt′fəl) *adj.* highly pleasing; giving delight. —**de·light′ful·ly,** *adv.* —**de·light′ful·ness,** *n.*

de·light·some (di līt′səm) *adj. Archaic.* delightful.

De·li·lah (di lī′lə) *n.* any treacherous, seductive woman. [From *Delilah,* in the Old Testament, the mistress of Samson who betrayed him.]

de·lim·it (di lim′it) *v.t.* to mark or fix the limits of; bound; demarcate. —**de·lim′i·ta′tion,** *n.* —**de·lim′i·ta′tive,** *adj.*

de·lin·e·ate (di lin′ē āt′) *v.t.,* **-at·ed, -at·ing. 1.** to draw or indicate the outline of; sketch out: *The map clearly delineated the boundaries of the farm.* **2.** to represent by a drawing or sketch. **3.** to depict in words; describe; portray: *The poet delineated a summer evening.* [Latin *dēlineātus,* past participle of *dēlineāre* to sketch out, going back to *dē* down + *līnea* line¹.] —**de·lin·e·a·tive** (di lin′ē ā′tiv, -ē ə tiv), *adj.* —**de·lin′e·a′tor,** *n.* —For Synonyms, see **portray.**

de·lin·e·a·tion (di lin′ē ā′shən) *n.* **1.** the act or process of delineating or the state of being delineated. **2.** something that delineates, as a drawing or description.

de·lin·quen·cy (di ling′kwən sē) *n., pl.* **-cies. 1.** failure in or neglect of a law, duty, or obligation. **2.** an offense or misdeed, esp. through neglect of a duty. **3.** juvenile delinquency. **4.** something delinquent, as an unpaid debt.

de·lin·quent (di ling′kwənt) *adj.* **1.** failing in or neglectful of a law, duty, or obligation: *to be delinquent in renewing one's driver's license.* **2.** due and unpaid, as taxes or accounts. —*n.* a person who is delinquent, esp. a juvenile delinquent. [Latin *dēlinquēns,* present participle of *dēlinquere* to fail, offend.] —**de·lin′quent·ly,** *adv.*

del·i·quesce (del′i kwes′) *v.i.,* **-quesced, -quesc·ing. 1.** *Chemistry.* to melt or become liquid by absorbing moisture from the air. **2.** to melt away. **3.** *Botany.* **a.** to become soft or liquid upon maturing, as certain fungi. **b.** to branch out into many small subdivisions. [Latin *dēliquēscere* to melt.] —**del′i·ques′cence,** *n.*

del·i·ques·cent (del′i kwes′ənt) *adj.* **1.** *Chemistry.* able to melt and form a solution by absorbing moisture directly from the air. Some salts are deliquescent. **2.** *Botany.* branching out into many small subdivisions, as the elm or oak.

de·lir·i·ous (di lîr′ē əs) *adj.* **1.** affected with delirium. **2.** characteristic of or caused by delirium: *delirious fantasies.* **3.** wildly excited: *delirious with joy.* —**de·lir′i·ous·ly,** *adv.* —**de·lir′i·ous·ness,** *n.*

de·lir·i·um (di lîr′ē əm) *n., pl.* **-lir·i·ums** or **-lir·i·a** (-lîr′ē ə). **1.** a temporary mental disturbance that may occur during high fevers, intoxication, and metabolic and nutritional disorders. Delirium is characterized by confusion, restlessness, disorientation, excitement, and illusions or hallucinations. **2.** wild excitement or emotion. [Latin *dēlīrium* madness; literally, a going out of the furrow (in plowing), going back to *dē* from + *līra* furrow.]

delirium tre·mens (trē′mənz) a violent form of delirium, occurring as a withdrawal symptom in chronic alcoholics, characterized by restlessness, muscular tremors, and terrifying hallucinations. Also, **d.t.'s.** [Modern Latin *delirium tremens* literally, trembling delirium.]

de·liv·er (di liv′ər) *v.t.* **1.** to carry or take to a particular place or person: *to deliver mail, to deliver groceries.* **2.** to give forth in words or sound; utter; pronounce: *to deliver a speech.* **3.** to give or send forth; emit or yield: *The offshore well delivers fifty barrels of oil a day.* **4.a.** to strike: *to deliver a blow.* **b.** to throw; pitch: *The pitcher delivered a curve ball.* **5.** to surrender or hand over; transfer: *to deliver a town into the hands of the enemy.* **6.a.** to assist in the birth of: *The veterinarian delivered the puppies.* **b.** to assist in giving birth: *to deliver a woman of triplets.* **c.** to give birth to. **7.** to set free; liberate; rescue; save: *to deliver a city from a siege.* **8.** *Informal.* to bring or supply (something needed or promised): *to deliver votes in an election.* —*v.i.* **1.** to give birth. **2.** to make deliveries: *Does that supermarket deliver?* **3.** *Informal.* to bring or supply something needed or promised. [Old French *delivrer* to set free, from Late Latin *dēlīberāre,* going back to Latin *dē* from + *līber* free.] —**de·liv′er·a·ble,** *adj.* —**de·liv′er·er,** *n.*

• **to be delivered of.** to give birth to.

• **to deliver oneself of.** to express in words; utter.

de·liv·er·ance (di liv′ər əns) *n.* **1.** the act of setting free or the fact of being set free; liberation; rescue. **2.** a judgment or opinion expressed formally or publicly.

de·liv·er·y (di liv′ə rē) *n., pl.* **-er·ies. 1.a.** the act of carrying or taking something to a particular place or person: *The laundry makes deliveries on Tuesdays.* **b.** something that is delivered: *Two items were missing from the delivery.* **2.** the act or manner of speaking, singing, or giving something forth in sound: *The singer's delivery was too weak for such a rousing song.* **3.** the act or manner of sending forth, discharging, or striking something: *a pitcher with an awkward delivery.* **4.** the act of giving birth. **5.** a giving up; handing over; surrender. **6.** a setting free or saving; release or rescue.

dell (del) *n.* a small, usually wooded, secluded glen or valley. [Old English *dell* deep hollow, valley.]

de·louse (dē lous′, -louz′) *v.t.,* **-loused, -lous·ing.** to remove lice from.

Del·phic (del′fik) *adj.* **1.** relating to Delphi, the oracle of Apollo at Delphi, or Apollo himself. **2.** obscure in meaning; ambiguous. Also, **Del·phi·an** (del′fē ən).

Delphic oracle, the oracle or prophetess of Apollo at Delphi, famed for giving ambiguous advice or prophecies.

del·phin·i·um (del fin′ē əm) *n.* any of a large group of plants, genus *Delphinium,* of the crowfoot family, bearing dense spikes of

showy flowers, usually blue or purple. Also, **larkspur.** [Modern Latin *Delphinium,* from Greek *delphīnion,* from *delphīs* dolphin; from the dolphinlike shape of its flowers.]

del·ta (del′tə) **1.** the fourth letter of the Greek alphabet (Δ, δ), corresponding to English *D, d.* **2.** anything shaped like a triangle. **3.** an area of land formed by deposition of sediment at the mouth of a river. —**del·ta·ic** (del tā′ik), *adj.*

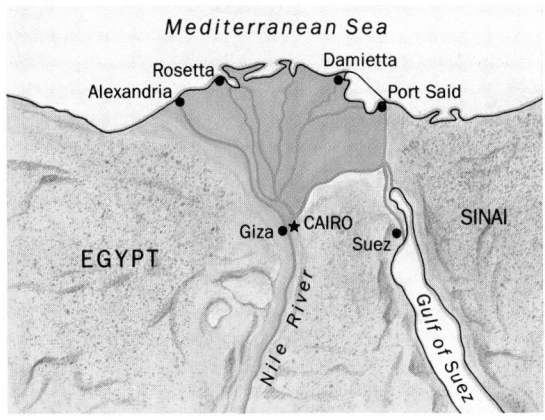

delta of the Nile River

delta wing, a broadly triangular aircraft wing. —**del′ta-wing′;** *also,* **del′ta-winged′,** *adj.*

del·toid (del′toid) *n.* a broad, triangular muscle covering the shoulder joint and serving to flex and extend the arm and to raise it away from the side of the body. —*adj.* **1.** shaped like a delta; triangular. **2.** relating to the deltoid. [Greek *deltoeidēs* delta-shaped, from *delta* the Greek letter; of Semitic origin. See DELTA.]

de·lude (di lüd′) *v.t.,* **-lud·ed, -lud·ing.** to mislead the mind or judgment of; deceive; trick: *The campaign advertising attempted to delude the voters.* [Latin *dēlūdere.*] —**de·lud′er,** *n.* —**de·lud′ing·ly,** *adv.*

del·uge (del′ūj) *n.* **1.** an overflowing of water; great flood; inundation. **2.** a heavy rainfall; downpour. **3.** anything that overwhelms or rushes like a flood: *a deluge of tourists during the holiday season.* **4. the Deluge.** in the Old Testament, the great flood in the time of Noah. —*v.t.,* **-uged, -ug·ing. 1.** to flood with water; inundate. **2.** to overwhelm by any great rush: *The network was deluged with irate letters from viewers.* [Old French *deluge* flood, from Latin *dīluvium.*]

de·lu·sion (di lü′zhən) *n.* **1.** a false impression or belief: *the delusion that wealth always leads to happiness.* **2.** a false belief held despite evidence to the contrary, characteristic of certain types of mental illness. **3.** the act of deluding or the state of being deluded. [Latin *dēlūsiō* a deceiving.] —**de·lu′sion·al,** *adj.*

de·lu·sive (di lü′siv) *adj.* **1.** apt or tending to delude; misleading; deceptive. **2.** like a delusion; false; unreal. Also, **de·lu·so·ry** (di lü′sə rē). —**de·lu′sive·ly,** *adv.* —**de·lu′sive·ness,** *n.*

de·luxe (di luks′, -lůks′) *adj.* exceptionally fine in quality or elegance: *deluxe accommodations.* —*adv.* in a deluxe fashion: *to travel deluxe.* [French *de luxe* literally, of luxury, from Late Latin *dē* of + Latin *luxus* luxury.]

delve (delv) *v.i.,* **delved, delv·ing. 1.** to make careful investigation or examination; search for information: *The board of inquiry delved into the question of possible fraud.* **2.** *Archaic.* to dig. [Old English *delfan* to dig.]

Dem., Democrat; Democratic.

de·mag·net·ize (dē mag′ni tīz′) *v.t.,* **-ized, -iz·ing.** to deprive of magnetic properties; degauss. —**de·mag′net·i·za′tion,** *n.* —**de·mag′net·iz′er,** *n.*

dem·a·gog·ic (dem′ə goj′ik, -gog′-, -gô′jik, -gik) *adj.* of, relating to, or characteristic of a demagogue. Also, **dem′a·gog′i·cal.** —**dem′a·gog′i·cal·ly,** *adv.*

dem·a·gogue (dem′ə gog′, -gôg′) *also,* **dem·a·gog.** *n.* a public leader or agitator who appeals to the passions and prejudices of the people in order to obtain power or to further his or her own interests. [Greek *dēmagōgos* popular leader, from *dēmos* people + *agōgos* leader.]

dem·a·gogu·er·y (dem′ə gog′ə rē, -gô′gə rē) *n.* the actions, practices, or principles of a demagogue. Also, **dem·a·gog·y** (dem′ə gog′ē, -gog′ē, -gô′jē).

de·mand (di mand′) *v.t.* **1.** to ask for with insistence or urgency: *The customer demanded entrance even though the store was closed.*

2. to ask for with authority or as a right: *The judge demanded silence in the courtroom.* **3.** to ask to know; request to be told: *to demand the truth.* **4.** to call for as necessary or useful; require; need: *This work demands careful attention.* —*v.i.* to make a demand or demands. —*n.* **1.** the act of demanding. **2.** something that is demanded: *We obeyed the fire department's demand that the street be cleared.* **3.** something necessary or called for; requirement: *the demands of one's job.* **4.** an expressed or existing desire; call: *There is a great demand for the author's latest book.* **5.a.** the desire for a commodity or service combined with the ability to purchase it. **b.** the quantity of a commodity that buyers are willing to purchase at a certain price at a given time. **6.** *Archaic.* inquiry; question. [Old French *demander* to ask, ask for, from Late Latin *dēmandāre* to ask, from Latin *dēmandāre* to entrust.] —**de·mand′a·ble,** *adj.* —**de·mand′er,** *n.*

• **in demand.** sought after; wanted: *That author is in great demand as a lecturer.*

• **on demand.** when presented; on being requested: *a note payable on demand.*

Synonyms *v.t.* **Demand, claim,** and **require** can all mean to state that one wants or needs something. **Demand** suggests an arbitrary manner: *They walked in and demanded service immediately. The child demanded attention.* **Claim** implies a belief that one has a right to what is wanted: *to claim the best seat at the table because of one's age.* **Require** implies the force of authority: *The employer required three references.*

demand deposit, a bank deposit that can be withdrawn by the depositor without advance notice. Checking accounts are demand deposits.

de·mand·ing (di man′ding) *adj.* requiring or calling for much care, attention, time, or effort; making demands: *demanding work, a demanding child.* —**de·mand′ing·ly,** *adv.*

de·mar·cate (di mär′kāt, dē′mär kāt′) *v.t.,* **-cat·ed, -cat·ing. 1.** to mark or fix the limits or boundaries of; delimit. **2.** to separate or distinguish. [From DEMARCATION.]

de·mar·ca·tion (dē′mär kā′shən) *n.* **1.** the marking or fixing of limits or boundaries. **2.** the limits or boundaries so fixed. **3.** a separation or differentiation: *a line of demarcation between two archaeological levels.* [Spanish *demarcación* a marking off of bounds, going back to *de-* completely (from Latin *dē* down) + *marcar* to mark (of Germanic origin).]

deme (dēm) *n.* one of the administrative subdivisions of ancient Attica. [Greek *dēmos* district, people.]

de·mean[1] (di mēn′) *v.t.* to lower the dignity or status of; degrade; debase: *to demean oneself by taking credit for another person's work.* [DE- and MEAN[2]; modeled on DEBASE.]

de·mean[2] (di mēn′) *v.t.* to behave, conduct, or comport (oneself): *The children demeaned themselves well at the reception.* [Middle English *demenen,* from Old French *demener* to conduct, going back to Latin *dē* down + *mināre* to drive (cattle).]

de·mean·or (di mē′nər) *also, British,* **de·mean·our.** *n.* the way one behaves and bears oneself; manner; deportment; conduct. [Middle English *demenure,* from *demenen* to conduct, from Old French *demener.* See DEMEAN[2].]

de·ment·ed (di men′tid) *adj.* having or seeming to have lost one's mental faculties; insane; mad; crazed. [Past participle of archaic *dement* to drive mad, from Late Latin *dēmentāre,* going back to Latin *dē* from + *mēns* mind.] —**de·ment′ed·ly,** *adv.*

de·men·tia (di men′shə) *n.* a disorder characterized by a loss of mental faculties, as memory, judgment, and abstract thinking, and by personality changes. [Latin *dēmentia* madness, going back to *dē* from + *mēns* mind.]

dementia prae·cox (prē′koks) schizophrenia. ➡ no longer used in psychiatry. [Modern Latin *dementia praecox* literally, premature insanity.]

de·mer·it (dē mer′it) *n.* **1.** a mark against a person for unsatisfactory work or behavior. **2.** a quality or act that deserves blame; fault. [Old French *demerite* misdeed, blame, going back to Latin *dē* down + *merēre* to deserve.]

de·mesne (di mān′, -mēn′) *n.* **1.** *Law.* the possession of land as one's own. **2.** a manor house and the adjoining untenanted land belonging to a feudal lord. **3.** the land of an estate. **4.** domain; realm. **5.** region; district; territory. [Old French *demeine* domain, belonging to a lord, from Latin *dominicus* relating to a master, from *dominus* master.]

De·me·ter (di mē′tər) *n.* in Greek mythology, the goddess of agriculture and of the fertility and fruits of the earth. Her Roman counterpart is Ceres.

demi- *prefix* **1.** half. **2.** less than usual; not complete; inferior: *demigod.* [French *demi* half, from Medieval Latin *dimidius,* from Latin *dīmidius.*]

dem·i·god (dem′ē god′) *n.* **1.a.** an inferior or lesser god. **b.** the offspring of a god and a mortal. **2.** a person who is regarded as having godlike qualities.

dem·i·god·dess (dem′ē god′is) *n.* a woman who is a demigod.

dem·i·john (dem′ē jon′) *n.* a narrow-necked bottle of glass or earthenware, usually enclosed in wicker and holding from one to ten gallons. [Modification of French *dame-jeanne* literally, Lady Jane (humorous name for a bottle). See DAME.]

demijohn

de·mil·i·ta·rize (dē mil′i tə rīz′) *v.t.,* -ized, -iz·ing. **1.** to remove or prohibit military installations, troops, or action in (an area or zone); declare neutral: *After the war the two nations agreed to demilitarize a strip of land along their border.* **2.** to remove military character from: *to demilitarize a government.* **3.** to remove from military control. —**de·mil′i·ta·ri·za′tion,** *n.*

demilitarized zone, a specified area in which it is prohibited by agreement of two or more nations to maintain military installations or troops or engage in military action.

dem·i·mon·daine (dem′ē mon dān′) *n.* a woman of the demimonde.

dem·i·monde (dem′ē mond′) *n.* **1.** a class of women of doubtful reputation and social standing because of social or sexual misconduct. **2.** demimondaine. [French *demi-monde* literally, half-world, from *demi-* (see DEMI-) + *monde* world (from Latin *mundus* world).]

de·mise (di mīz′) *n.* **1.** death: *The nation mourned the demise of the ex-president.* **2.** a cessation; end: *the demise of the feudal system.* **3.** *Law.* the transfer of an estate for life or for a limited number of years; lease. **4.** the transfer of sovereignty upon the death, abdication, or removal of a sovereign. —*v.t.,* -mised, -mis·ing. **1.** to transfer (an estate) for life or for a limited number of years; lease. **2.** to transfer (sovereignty) upon the death, abdication, or removal of a sovereign. [Old French *demise,* feminine past participle of *demettre* to dismiss, send away, from Latin *dīmittere.*]

dem·i·sem·i·qua·ver (dem′ē sem′ē kwā′vər) *n. Music.* thirty-second note.

dem·i·tasse (dem′ē tas′, -täs′) *n.* **1.** a small cup of black, usually strong, coffee. **2.** a small cup in which such coffee is served. [French *demi-tasse,* from *demi-* (see DEMI-) + *tasse* cup (from Arabic *tass* basin, from Persian *tast* cup).]

dem·o (dem′ō) *n., pl.* **dem·os.** *Informal.* **1.** demonstration *(defs. 5, 6).* **2.** something given out for demonstration or promotion, such as a phonograph record. [Short for DEMO(NSTRATION).]

de·mo·bi·lize (dē mō′bə līz′) *v.t., v.i.,* -lized, -liz·ing. **1.** to disband or dismiss (troops or an army); remove from military service: *The government demobilized many soldiers when the war ended.* **2.** to remove from a state of readiness for war; put on a peacetime basis: *The country demobilized its industries after the war.* —**de·mo′bi·li·za′tion,** *n.*

de·moc·ra·cy (di mok′rə sē) *n., pl.* -cies. **1.** government by the people, who rule either directly, as through town meetings and referendums, or indirectly, through elected representatives. **2.** a nation, state, or other political entity having such a government. **3.** political or social equality in spirit and practice. [Middle French *democratie* popular government, from Medieval Latin *democratia,* from Greek *dēmokratiā,* from *dēmos* people + *kratos* power, strength.]

dem·o·crat (dem′ə krat′) *n.* **1.** a person who believes in or advocates democracy as a principle of government. **2.** a person who believes in and practices political or social equality. **3. Democrat.** a member of the Democratic Party.

dem·o·crat·ic (dem′ə krat′ik) *adj.* **1.** of, relating to, or advocating democracy as a principle or form of government. **2.** relating to, characterized by, or exhibiting political or social equality. **3.** of or meant for all the people. **4. Democratic.** of, relating to, or characteristic of the Democratic Party. —**dem′o·crat′i·cal·ly,** *adv.*

Democratic Party, one of the two major political parties in the United States, evolving from the parties of Thomas Jefferson and Andrew Jackson. It adopted its present name about 1828.

Dem·o·crat·ic-Re·pub·li·can Party (dem′ə krat′ik ri pub′li-

kən) the U.S. political party opposed to the Federalist Party, founded in 1792 under the leadership of Thomas Jefferson. It was succeeded by the Democratic Party.

de·moc·ra·tize (di mok′rə tīz′) *v.t., v.i.,* -tized, -tiz·ing. to make or become democratic or more democratic. —**de·moc′ra·ti·za′tion,** *n.*

de·mod·u·late (dē moj′ə lāt′, -mod′yə-) *v.t.,* -lat·ed, -lat·ing. to separate the information-bearing signal from (a radio carrier wave); detect. —**de·mod′u·la′tion,** *n.* —**de·mod′u·la′tor,** *n.*

De·mo·gor·gon (dē′mə gôr′gən) *n.* a demon or devil, often associated with the mysterious and evil spirit of creation in ancient and medieval mythology.

dem·o·graph·ics (dem′ə graf′iks) *pl. n.* statistics and other information that describe the social characteristics of a given group of people, such as their age, sex, and income: *Many advertisers study demographics to help them identify potential customers.*

de·mog·ra·phy (di mog′rə fē) *n.* the statistical study of human populations, including their size, structure, distribution, and composition. [French *démographie,* from Greek *dēmos* people + French *-graphie* -graphy.] —**de·mog′ra·pher,** *n.* —**dem·o·graph·ic** (dē′mə graf′ik), *adj.* —**de′mo·graph′i·cal·ly,** *adv.*

dem·oi·selle (dem′wä zel′, dem′ə-) *n.* **1.** a young lady; damsel. **2.** a crane, *Anthropoides virgo,* of Asia, Europe, and northern Africa, having long white plumes on each side of the head behind the eyes. **3.** damselfly. [French *demoiselle* young lady, going back to Latin *domina* lady.]

demoiselle *(def. 2)*

de·mol·ish (di mol′ish) *v.t.* **1.** to tear down or apart; destroy the structure of: *to demolish an old apartment building.* **2.** to destroy or ruin completely: *New evidence demolished the lawyer's case.* [Old French *demoliss-,* a stem of *demolir,* from Latin *dēmōlīrī,* to tear down.] —**de·mol′ish·er,** *n.* —**de·mol′ish·ment,** *n.*

Synonyms Demolish, wreck, and raze can all mean to destroy by pulling down or breaking into pieces. **Demolish** connotes the complete destruction of something. *The attackers demolished the fort. An earthquake demolished the town.* **Wreck** also conveys destruction but with an emphasis on the broken remains: *The company wrecks old houses and sells the lumber and masonry.* **Raze** connotes leveling to the ground: *to raze a building to make way for a park.*

dem·o·li·tion (dem′ə lish′ən, dē′mə-) *n.* **1.** the act of demolishing or the state of being demolished; destruction. **2. demolitions.** explosives, esp. for military use. **3.** the business or trade of demolishing buildings or other structures: *to work in demolition.* —**dem·o·li′tion·ist,** *n.*

de·mon (dē′mən) *n.* **1.** an evil spirit; devil. **2.** an extremely wicked or cruel person. **3.** something regarded as a personification of evil or as an evil influence. **4.** a person who shows great skill or energy in some activity: *a demon on ice skates, a demon for work.* **5.** *also,* **daemon.** an attendant or guiding spirit; genius. **6.** *also,* **daemon.** in Greek mythology, a supernatural being lower in rank than a god. [Late Latin *daemōn* evil spirit, from Latin *daemōn* spirit, from Greek *daimōn* divinity, fate.]

de·mon·e·tize (dē mon′i tīz′, -mun′-) *v.t.,* -tized, -tiz·ing. **1.** to deprive (currency) of its standard value as money. **2.** to withdraw from use as money: *to demonetize silver.* —**de·mon′e·ti·za′tion,** *n.*

de·mo·ni·ac (di mō′nē ak′, dē′mə nī′ak) *adj.* **1.** of, like, or characteristic of a demon or evil spirit; devilish. **2.** caused by or as by a demon or evil spirit; wild; frantic. **3.** acting as if possessed by a demon or evil spirit. Also, **de·mo·ni·a·cal** (dē′mə nī′ə kəl). —*n.* a person supposedly possessed by a demon. —**de′mo·ni′a·cal·ly,** *adv.*

de·mon·ic (di mon′ik) *adj.* **1.** of, relating to, or characteristic of a demon. **2.** inspired as by a demon or guiding spirit.

de·mon·ism (dē′mə niz′əm) *n.* **1.** a belief in demons. **2.** demonolatry. —**de′mon·ist,** *n.*

de·mon·ol·a·try (dē′mə nol′ə trē) *n.* the worship of demons.

de·mon·ol·o·gy (dē′mə nol′ə jē) *n.* the study of demons or of beliefs about them.

de·mon·stra·ble (di mon′strə bəl, dem′ən-) *adj.* capable of being proved or made evident; possible to demonstrate. —**de·mon′stra·bil′i·ty, de·mon′stra·ble·ness,** *n.* —**de·mon′stra·bly,** *adv.*

dem·on·strate (dem′ən strāt′) *v.,* **-strat·ed, -strat·ing.** —*v.t.* **1.** to make known or evident: *Recent events demonstrate the need for caution.* **2.** to describe, explain, or exhibit by actual performance or by use of experiments or examples: *to demonstrate a chemical law in the laboratory.* **3.** to make a show of; express openly; manifest: *The crowd demonstrated its support of the candidate with loud cheers.* **4.** to show the uses or merits of (a product): *The salesclerk demonstrated the washing machine.* —*v.i.* to make or take part in a public demonstration; to show feelings about a particular issue or person: *to demonstrate in favor of cleaner air.* [Latin *dēmonstrātus,* past participle of *dēmonstrāre* to show forth clearly.]

dem·on·stra·tion (dem′ən strā′shən) *n.* **1.** the act or process of proving or making evident. **2.** something that serves as proof or evidence. **3.** an exhibition and explanation by actual performance or by the use of experiments or examples: *a demonstration of the law of gravity.* **4.** an open expression or show of feeling or emotion: *a demonstration of grief.* **5.** a gathering, meeting, or other public expression of feeling about a particular issue or person: *a demonstration against a proposed highway.* **6.** a display of the uses or merits of a product. **7.** the process of proving that from certain premises certain conclusions must follow.

de·mon·stra·tive (di mon′strə tiv) *adj.* **1.** given to or characterized by open display of feelings, esp. affectionate ones. **2.** serving to indicate or show clearly; explanatory; illustrative. **3.** having the power of proving; conclusive. **4.** *Grammar.* indicating and distinguishing the particular person or thing referred to. In the sentence *This is my book, this* is a demonstrative pronoun. In the phrase *that book, that* is a demonstrative adjective. —*n.* a demonstrative pronoun or adjective. —**de·mon′stra·tive·ly,** *adv.* —**de·mon′stra·tive·ness,** *n.*

dem·on·stra·tor (dem′ən strā′tər) *n.* **1.** a person who demonstrates, esp. someone who takes part in a demonstration of public feeling. **2.** something used for demonstration, as a sample product used in demonstrations to customers.

de·mor·al·ize (di môr′ə līz′, -mor′-) *v.t.,* **-ized, -iz·ing. 1.** to lower or destroy the morale of; deprive of courage, confidence, or hope; dishearten: *A series of defeats demoralized the team.* **2.** to corrupt the morals of. **3.** to throw into disorder. —**de·mor′al·iz·a′tion,** *n.* —**de·mor′al·iz′er,** *n.*

de·mote (di mōt′) *v.t.,* **-mot·ed, -mot·ing.** to reduce to a lower grade or rank: *to demote a soldier from corporal to private.* [DE- + (PRO)MOTE.] —**de·mo·tion** (di mō′shən) *n.*

de·mot·ic (di mot′ik) *adj.* **1.** of or relating to the common people; popular. **2.** of or relating to the simplified form of hieratic writing of ancient Egypt. —*n.* **Demotic.** the form of the modern Greek language based on colloquial use. [Greek *dēmotikos* relating to the people, popular, going back to *dēmos* people.]

de·mount (dē mount′) *v.t.* to remove from a mounting or setting, as a motor or gun. —**de·mount′a·ble,** *adj.*

de·mul·cent (di mul′sənt) *adj.* soothing. —*n.* a soothing substance, esp. a medicinal mucilage or oil used to relieve irritation caused by inflammation or abrasion. [Latin *dēmulcēns,* present participle of *dēmulcēre* to soothe.]

de·mur (di mûr′) *v.i.,* **-murred, -mur·ring. 1.** to raise objection; take exception; object: *I demurred at first, but then agreed to go.* **2.** to enter a legal demurrer. —*n.* **1.** an objection raised or exception taken. **2.** the act of demurring. Also, **demurral.** [Old French *demourer* to tarry, from Latin *dēmorārī.*]

de·mure (di myūr′) *adj.,* **-mur·er, -mur·est. 1.** quiet and modest; shy; reserved. **2.** affectedly modest; coy. [DE- + obsolete *mure* calm, from Old French *mēur* grave, mellow, from Latin *mātūrus* ripe.] —**de·mure′ly,** *adv.* —**de·mure′ness,** *n.*

de·mur·rage (di mûr′ij) *n.* **1.** the detention of a ship, railroad car, or other commercial conveyance due to the failure of the shipper to load or unload the cargo by a specified time. **2.** the payment owed or made to the carrier by the shipper for such a delay.

de·mur·ral (di mûr′əl) *n.* demur.

de·mur·rer (di mûr′ər) *n.* **1.** a pleading, now largely obsolete, in which the defendant in a civil lawsuit argues that even if the facts as stated by the complaint are true, they are insufficient to support a judgment for the plaintiff. **2.** an objection or exception; demur. **3.** a person who demurs.

den (den) *n.* **1.** a lair or secluded place inhabited by a wild animal: *a bear's den.* **2.** a retreat or secluded place, esp. one used as a hideout or secret headquarters by criminals. **3.** a private room, usually small and cozy, for relaxation or study. **4.** a small, squalid room or dwelling. **5.** a group of about eight cub scouts. —*v.i.,* **denned, den·ning.** to live in or as in a den. [Old English *denn* lair of a wild beast.]

Den., Denmark.

de·nar·i·us (di nâr′ē əs) *n., pl.* **-nar·i·i** (-nâr′ē ī′). **1.** a silver coin of ancient Rome. **2.** a gold coin of ancient Rome, worth twenty-five silver denarii. [Latin *dēnārius,* from *dēnārius* containing ten, from *dēnī* ten each; originally referring to a coin worth ten asses (see AS²). Doublet of DENIER², DINAR.]

de·na·tion·al·ize (dē nash′ə nə līz′) *v.t.,* **-ized, -iz·ing. 1.** to remove from national control or ownership, as an industry. **2.** to deprive of nationality; divest of national character or rights. —**de·na′tion·al·i·za′tion,** *n.*

de·nat·u·ral·ize (dē nach′ər ə līz′) *v.t.,* **-ized, -iz·ing. 1.** to deprive (something) of its original or true nature; make unnatural. **2.** to deprive of the status and rights of naturalization or citizenship. —**de·nat′u·ral·i·za′tion,** *n.*

de·na·tur·ant (dē nā′chər ənt) *n.* a substance used to denature another substance, as methyl alcohol added to ethyl alcohol to make it unfit for drinking.

de·na·ture (dē nā′chər) *v.t.,* **-tured, -tur·ing. 1.** to make (a substance, as alcohol) unfit for drinking or eating without destroying other useful properties. **2.** to change the nature of. **3.** to alter the structure of (a protein) so that the original properties are removed or greatly changed. —**de·na′tur·a′tion,** *n.*

denatured alcohol, ethyl alcohol made unfit for drinking by the addition of small amounts of foreign materials.

den·drite (den′drīt) *n.* **1.** a branching treelike marking found on certain stones or minerals. **2.** a stone or mineral having such markings. **3.** a crystallized treelike form, as of gold. **4.** a small branched fiber that extends from a neuron and conducts nerve impulses to the cell body.

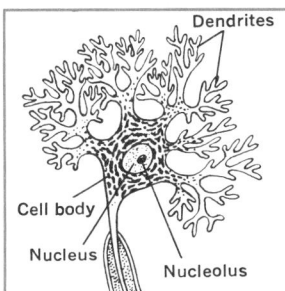

dendrite *(def. 4)*

[Greek *dendrītēs* relating to a tree, from *dendron* tree.] —**den·drit·ic** (den drit′ik), *adj.*

den·dro·chro·nol·o·gy (den′drō krə nol′ə jē) *n.* the science of dating past events by studying and comparing growth rings in samples of living and dead trees. —**den·dro·chron·o·log·i·cal** (den′drō kron′ə loj′i kəl), *adj.* —**den·dro·chron′o·log′i·cal·ly,** *adv.*

den·drol·o·gy (den drol′ə jē) *n.* the study of trees and shrubs. —**den·dro·log·ic** (den′drə loj′ik), **den′dro·log′i·cal,** *adj.* —**den·drol′o·gist,** *n.*

Den·eb (den′eb) *n.* a bluish white giant star, one of the brightest in the sky and the brightest in the constellation Cygnus.

den·gue (deng′gä, -gē) *n.* an acute, infectious tropical or subtropical disease, usually occurring in epidemics, caused by a virus transmitted by a mosquito, and characterized by headache, fever, skin rash, and severe pain in the joints and muscles. [Spanish *dengue* this disease, from Swahili *dinga* cramplike attack.]

de·ni·al (di nī′əl) *n.* **1.** the act of declaring something to be untrue; contradiction: *a defendant's denial of charges.* **2.** the act of refusing something asked for or desired: *a denial of a request for funds.* **3.** a refusal to acknowledge a connection with or responsibility for; disavowal: *the exiles' denial of their country.* **4.** a refusal to accept or believe in something, as a doctrine: *a denial of former beliefs.* **5.** self-denial. **6.** *Psychology.* a defense mechanism that consists of denying unpleasant or threatening facts or emotions.

de·ni·er¹ (di nī′ər) *n.* a person who denies. [DENY + -ER¹.]

den·ier² (*def. 1* den′yər, də nîr′; *def. 2* də nîr′) *n.* **1.** a unit of weight for expressing the fineness of silk, rayon, or nylon yarn, based on the standard of a yarn weighing 1 gram for each 9,000 meters. **2.** a former coin of France and western Europe, originally

a	at	e	end	o	hot	u	up	hw	white		about
ā	ape	ē	me	ō	old	ū	use	ng	song		taken
ä	far	i	it	ô	fork	ü	rule	th	thin	ə	pencil
âr	care	ī	ice	oi	oil	u̇	pull	th	this		lemon
				îr	pierce	ou	out	ûr	turn	zh	measure		circus

of silver and later of copper, varying in value. [Old French *denier* penny, from Latin *dēnārius* the Roman coin, containing ten, from *dēnī* ten each. Doublet of DENARIUS, DINAR.]

den·i·grate (den′i grāt′) *v.t.*, **-grat·ed, -grat·ing.** to make damaging statements about; blacken the reputation of; slander; defame: *The intense competition for the research grant led one scientist to denigrate his arch rival by accusing him of falsifying data.* [Latin *dēnigrātus*, past participle of *dēnigrāre* to blacken, defame.] **—den′i·gra′tion,** *n.* **—den′i·gra′tor,** *n.*

den·im (den′im) *n.* **1.** a heavy, twilled cotton fabric woven with a colored warp and white filling, used for such items as work clothes and sportswear. **2. denims.** overalls or trousers made of this fabric. [Short for French *(serge) de Nîmes* (serge) of Nîmes, a French city where the fabric was first made.]

de·ni·tri·fy (dē nī′trə fī′) *v.t.*, **-fied, -fy·ing. 1.** to remove nitrogen or its compounds from. **2.** to reduce (nitrates) to nitrites, ammonia, or nitrogen, as in soil by the action of certain microorganisms. **—de·ni′tri·fi·ca′tion,** *n.*

den·i·zen (den′ə zən) *n.* **1.a.** a person or animal that lives in a particular place; inhabitant; dweller: *Wolves are denizens of the forest.* **b.** a person who habitually spends time in a place: *the denizens of the local coffee shop.* **2.** *British.* a foreigner admitted to residence and certain rights in a country. **3.** anything that has become adapted to a new place or condition, as a plant or animal naturalized in an area to which it is not originally native. [Anglo-Norman *deinzein* literally, one living within, from *deinz* within, going back to Latin *dē* from + *intus* within.]

de·nom·i·nate (di nom′ə nāt′) *v.t.*, **-nat·ed -nat·ing.** to give a name to; name; designate. [Latin *dēnōminātus*, past participle of *dēnōmināre* to name.]

de·nom·i·nate number (di nom′ə nit, -nāt′) a number that specifies a concrete quantity by limiting a unit of measurement. In the expression *5 pounds, 5* is a denominate number.

de·nom·i·na·tion (di nom′ə nā′shən) *n.* **1.** a religious group or sect: *the Lutheran denomination.* **2.** the class of one kind of unit in a system of numbers, measures, or values: *The cashier gave the customer change in bills of the same denomination.* **3.** the name for a thing or class of things; designation. **4.** the act of denominating.

de·nom·i·na·tion·al (di nom′ə nā′shə nəl) *adj.* relating to or controlled by a religious denomination or sect; sectarian: *a denominational school.* **—de·nom′i·na′tion·al·ly,** *adv.*

de·nom·i·na·tion·al·ism (di nom′ə nā′shə nə liz′əm) *n.* **1.** strict adherence to a denomination or its principles; sectarianism. **2.** the tendency to form denominations or sects. **—de·nom′i·na′tion·al·ist,** *n.*

de·nom·i·na·tive (di nom′ə nā′tiv, -nə tiv) *adj.* **1.** giving or constituting a qualifying name; naming. **2.** derived from a noun or adjective. *To elbow* is a denominative verb formed from the noun *elbow.* —*n.* a word derived from a noun or adjective.

de·nom·i·na·tor (di nom′ə nā′tər) *n.* **1.** the number below or to the right of the line in a fraction, indicating the number of equal parts into which the whole is divided; divisor. In the fraction *1/2,* *2* is the denominator. ➡ distinguished from **numerator. 2.** a characteristic that is held in common; standard.

de·no·ta·tion (dē′nō tā′shən) *n.* **1.** the specific or literal meaning of a word or phrase, as distinct from what it suggests. ➡ distinguished from **connotation. 2.** the act of denoting or the state of being denoted. **3.** something that denotes; name; sign; indication.

de·no·ta·tive (dē′nō tā′tiv, di nō′tə-) *adj.* denoting or capable of denoting. **—de′no·ta′tive·ly,** *adv.*

de·note (di nōt′) *v.t.*, **-not·ed, -not·ing. 1.** to be an indication or sign of: *A frown often denotes displeasure.* **2.** to be a name or designation for; mean: *The word "dentist" denotes a doctor whose work is the care of teeth.* ➡ distinguished from **connote. 3.** to be a mark or symbol for: *The sign ° denotes degrees.* [Latin *dēnotāre* to indicate.]

de·noue·ment (dā′nü män′) *also,* **dé·noue·ment.** *n.* **1.** the final outcome, solution, or unraveling of a plot in a play, story, or other literary work. **2.** the point in the plot where this occurs. **3.** any final outcome or solution. [French *dénouement* an unraveling (esp. of a plot), from *denouer* to unravel, going back to Latin *dis-* apart + *nōdus* knot.]

de·nounce (di nouns′) *v.t.*, **-nounced, -nounc·ing. 1.** to attack or condemn publicly; censure openly: *The editorial denounced racial injustice.* **2.** to inform against; accuse: *They denounced the traitor to the authorities.* **3.** to give formal notice of the termination of (a treaty, armistice, or other agreement). [Old French *denoncier* to announce, declare, from Latin *dēnūntiāre.*] **—de·nounce′ment,** *n.* **—de·nounc′er,** *n.* **—For Synonyms,** see **accuse.**

de no·vo (dē nō′vō) *Latin.* from the beginning; anew.

dense (dens) *adj.*, **dens·er, dens·est. 1.** having its constituent parts closely packed together; thick; compact: *a dense forest, dense crowd.* **2.** slow to understand; thick-headed; dull. **3.** difficult to penetrate; intense; profound; extreme: *a dense fog, dense prose.* **4.** *Photography.* (of a developed negative) relatively opaque; having good contrast between light and dark areas. [Latin *dēnsus* thick.] **—dense′ly,** *adv.* **—dense′ness,** *n.* —For Synonyms, see **close.**

den·si·ty (den′si tē) *n., pl.* **-ties. 1.** the quality or condition of being closely packed together; thickness; compactness. **2.** *Physics.* the ratio of the mass of a substance to its volume: *Iron has a greater density than wood.* **3.** the quantity of something per unit, as of area: *That district has a very high population density.* **4.** stupidity. **5.** *Electricity.* **a.** the amount of electricity per unit area at a given point on a surface. **b.** current density. **6.** *Photography.* the degree of opaqueness of a developed negative.

dent (dent) *n.* **1.** a hollow or depression in a surface made by a blow or pressure: *a dent in an automobile fender.* **2.** effective headway; progress: *We worked all night, but barely made a dent in the work.* —*v.t.* to make a hollow or depression in. —*v.i.* to become dented. [Form of DINT.]

dent. 1. dental. **2.** dentist. **3.** dentistry.

den·tal (den′təl) *adj.* **1.** of, for, or relating to the teeth. **2.** of or relating to dentistry. **3.** *Phonetics.* of, designating, or made with the tip of the tongue against the back of the upper front teeth. —*n. Phonetics.* a dental consonant sound. [Modern Latin *dentālis,* from Latin *dēns* tooth.]

dental caries, caries.

dental floss, a strong thread, often waxed, used to clean between the teeth.

dental hygienist, a person trained and licensed to clean and examine teeth.

den·tate (den′tāt) *adj.* **1.** *Botany.* (of leaves) having toothlike projections along the edge. **2.** having teeth or toothlike projections; toothed; notched. [Latin *dentātus* toothed, from *dēns* tooth.] **—den′tate·ly,** *adv.* **—den·ta′tion,** *n.*

den·ti·frice (den′tə fris) *n.* a paste, powder, or liquid used for cleaning the teeth. [French *dentifrice,* from Latin *dentifricium* powder for cleaning teeth, from *dēns* tooth + *fricāre* to rub.]

den·tin (den′tin) *also,* **den·tine** (den′tin, den- tēn′). *n.* the hard, calcified material forming the major part of a tooth, covered by the enamel in the crown and the cementum in the root. For illustration, see **tooth.** [From Latin *dēns* tooth.]

dentate
leaf

den·tist (den′tist) *n.* a doctor who specializes in the health and care of the teeth and gums. [French *dentiste,* from *dent* tooth, from Latin *dēns* tooth.]

den·tist·ry (den′tis trē) *n.* **1.** the branch of medical science dealing with the health and care of the teeth and gums. **2.** the work done by a dentist.

den·ti·tion (den tish′ən) *n.* **1.** the process of teething. **2.** the kind, number, and arrangement of teeth characteristic of an animal. [Latin *dentītiō* teething, going back to *dēns* tooth.]

den·ture (den′chər) *n.* **1.** an artificial tooth or teeth, esp. a set of artificial teeth. **2.** a set of teeth. [French *denture* set of teeth, from *dent* tooth, from Latin *dēns.*]

de·nude (di nüd′, -nūd′) *v.t.*, **-nud·ed, -nud·ing. 1.** to strip or divest of all covering; make bare: *to denude land of trees.* **2.** *Geology.* to expose or uncover (rock) by the erosion of overlying matter. [Latin *dēnūdāre* to lay bare, uncover, going back to *dē* down + *nūdus* bare.] **—de·nu·da·tion** (dē′nü dā′shən, -nū-, den′yü-), *n.*

de·nun·ci·ate (di nun′sē āt′) *v.t.*, **-at·ed, -at·ing.** denounce.

de·nun·ci·a·tion (di nun′sē ā′shən) *n.* **1.** a public expression of disapproval; open condemnation. **2.** the act of informing against a person; accusation. **3.** a formal declaration that an agreement, as a treaty or armistice, is to be terminated. **4.** *Archaic.* a declaration of intended evil; threat. [Latin *dēnūntiātiō* declaration.] **—de·nun′ci·a·to′ry,** *adj.*

de·ny (di nī′) *v.t.*, **-nied, -ny·ing. 1.** to declare (something) to be untrue; contradict: *The defendant denied the allegations.* **2.** to refuse to believe or accept as being valid or true; reject: *to deny the reality of ghosts.* **3.** to refuse to give or grant: *to deny a request, to deny someone a passport.* **4.** to refuse to acknowledge; disavow: *to deny one's family.* [Old French *denoier* to oppose, reject, forbid, from Latin *dēnegāre* to reject, refuse.]

  ·to deny oneself. to practice self-denial; abstain from (something).

de·o·dar (dē′ə där′) *n.* **1.** a pyramid-shaped evergreen tree,

Cedrus deodara, of the pine family, found mostly in the Himalayas and California, bearing needlelike bluish green leaves and oval reddish brown cones. **2.** the fragrant, durable wood of this tree. [Hindi *dēwdār* this tree; literally, divine tree, going back to Sanskrit *dēvas* divine + *dāru* wood.]

de·o·dor·ant (dē ō′dər ənt) *n.* a substance that prevents or counteracts unpleasant odors, esp. a preparation used on the body to disguise or destroy perspiration odor. —*adj.* capable of preventing or counteracting unpleasant odors: *a deodorant soap, a deodorant spray.* [DE- + ODOR + -ANT.]

de·o·dor·ize (dē ō′də rīz′) *v.t.,* **-ized, -iz·ing.** to counteract or destroy the unpleasant odor of. —**de·o′dor·i·za′tion,** *n.* —**de·o′dor·iz′er,** *n.*

De·o vo·len·te (dē′ō vō len′tē) *Latin.* God willing.

de·ox·i·dize (dē ok′si dīz′) *v.t.,* **-dized, -diz·ing.** to remove oxygen from (a chemical compound), as by reducing from an oxidized state. —**de·ox′i·di·za′tion,** *n.* —**de·ox′i·diz′er,** *n.*

de·ox·y·gen·ate (dē ok′sə jə nāt′) *v.t.,* **-at·ed, -at·ing.** to remove oxygen from (a substance, esp. a liquid, as water or blood).

de·ox·y·ri·bo·nu·cle·ic acid (dē ok′si rī′bō nü klē′ik, -nū-) see DNA.

de·ox·y·ri·bose (dē ok′sē rī′bōs) *n.* a five-carbon sugar, derived from ribose, that helps form the sidepieces of a strand of DNA. For illustration, see **double helix.**

dep. 1. depart. **2.** department. **3.** departure. **4.** deponent. **5.** deposit. **6.** depot. **7.** deputy.

Dep., dependency.

de·part (di pärt′) *v.i.* **1.** to go away; leave: *The ship departs at noon.* **2.** to turn aside from something; deviate; diverge: *to depart from tradition, to depart from one's customary way of dressing.* **3.** to die. —*v.t.* to go away from; leave: *The plane departed Atlanta on time.* [Old French *departir* to divide, leave, going back to Latin *dis-* apart + *partīre* to divide.] —For Synonyms, see **diverge, go¹.**

de·part·ed (di pär′tid) *adj.* **1.** dead. **2.** past; gone: *departed glory.* —*n.* **the departed,** a person or persons who have died.

de·part·ment (di pärt′mənt) *n.* **1.** a separate part or division of an organization or government, established for a specific purpose: *a police department, the sales department of a company, the shoe department of a store.* **2.** a division of an educational institution devoted to a particular area of learning: *the physics department.* **3.** usually, **Department.** a major division of the executive branch of the U.S. government: *the Department of Agriculture.* **4.** an administrative district of government, esp. in France. **5.** *Informal.* a particular area of interest or proficiency: *Woodworking is not my department.* [French *département* administrative division, line¹, province, from *départir* to divide. See DEPART.] —**de·part·men·tal** (di pärt men′təl, dē′pärt-), *adj.* —**de·part·men′tal·ly,** *adv.*

de·part·men·tal·ize (di pärt men′tə līz′, dē′pärt-) *v.t., v.i.,* **-ized, -iz·ing.** to divide into departments. —**de·part·men′tal·i·za′tion,** *n.*

department store, a large retail store selling a variety of merchandise arranged in separate departments.

de·par·ture (di pär′chər) *n.* **1.** the act of departing or leaving. **2.** a turning aside, as from a standard or course of action; divergence: *a departure from custom.* **3.** a setting out, as on a course of action: *This bill marks a new departure in civil rights legislation.* **4.** *Archaic.* death.

de·pend (di pend′) *v.i.* **1.** to place confidence in; trust; rely (with *on* or *upon*): *You can depend on us to get the job done.* **2.** to look to for support or assistance (with *on* or *upon*): *Many students depend on relatives for support. Japan depends on other countries for oil.* **3.** to be influenced or determined by something else; be contingent (with *on* or *upon*): *Price depends on costs and demand. Whether I accept the job depends on the salary.* **4.** to hang down: *Icicles depended from the eaves.* [Old French *dependre* to hang from, rely, from Latin *dēpendēre* to hang from, be dependent on.]

de·pen·da·ble (di pen′də bəl) *adj.* capable of being depended on; reliable. —**de·pen′da·bil′i·ty,** *n.* —**de·pen′da·bly,** *adv.*

de·pen·dant (di pen′dənt) dependent.

de·pen·dence (di pen′dəns) *also,* **de·pen·dance.** *n.* **1.** the state of depending on another for support or assistance. **2.** the state of being influenced or determined by something else; contingency. **3.** subjection or subordination to someone or something. **4.** trust; reliance. **5.** a physical or psychological need for a drug not taken for medicinal purposes, resulting from prolonged use of the drug.

de·pen·den·cy (di pen′dən sē) *n., pl.* **-cies.** *also,* **de·pen·dan·cy. 1.** a country or territory that is not fully self-governing and does not form an integral part of the governing country. **2.** de-

pendence. **3.** something subordinate or dependent; subordinate part.

de·pen·dent (di pen′dənt) *also,* **dependant.** *adj.* **1.** looking to another for support or assistance. **2.** ruled by another; subordinate: *a dependent territory.* **3.** influenced or determined by something else; contingent. **4.** hanging down; pendent. —*n.* a person who depends on another for support or assistance. —**de·pen′dent·ly,** *adv.*

dependent clause, a clause that functions as a noun, adjective, or adverb within a sentence and cannot stand alone. In the sentence *After the guests had played tennis for an hour, they decided to go for a swim,* the clause *After the guests had played tennis for an hour* is a dependent clause. ➡ distinguished from **independent clause.** Also, **subordinate clause.**

dependent variable *Mathematics.* a variable whose values depend on the values of other variables. ➡ distinguished from **independent variable.**

de·per·son·al·ize (dē pûr′sə nə līz′) *v.t.,* **-ized, -iz·ing. 1.** to deprive of a sense of personal identity. **2.** to make impersonal. —**de·per′son·al·i·za′tion,** *n.*

de·pict (di pikt′) *v.t.* **1.** to represent by drawing, painting, or other artistic means; picture; portray. **2.** to represent in words; describe: *to depict a character in a novel.* [Latin *dēpictus,* past participle of *dēpingere.*] —**de·pic′tion,** *n.* —**de·pic′tor,** *n.* —For Synonyms, see **portray.**

dep·i·late (dep′ə lāt′) *v.t.,* **-lat·ed, -lat·ing.** to remove hair from. [Latin *dēpilātus,* past participle of *dēpilāre* to remove hair, going back to *dē* from + *pilus* hair.] —**dep′i·la′tion,** *n.*

de·pil·a·to·ry (di pil′ə tôr′ē) *n., pl.* **-ries.** an agent for removing hair, esp. a cosmetic preparation used to remove unwanted hair from the body. —*adj.* capable of removing hair.

de·plane (dē plān′) *v.i.,* **-planed, -plan·ing.** to get out of an airplane after landing.

de·plete (di plēt′) *v.t.,* **-plet·ed, -plet·ing. 1.** to reduce considerably, as in amount or substance: *War depleted the country's resources.* **2.** to use up completely; exhaust: *The campers' food supplies were depleted after three days.* [Latin *dēplētus,* past participle of *dēplēre* to empty out, exhaust.] —**de·ple′tion,** *n.*

Synonyms **Deplete, drain,** and **exhaust** mean to use up or draw off all or part of a substance. **Deplete** may be used of any reduction and suggests harm done: *Heavy use of air conditioners has depleted the electricity supply.* **Drain** connotes a gradual reduction, and suggests eventual emptiness: *Heavy expenses had drained the company's capital.* **Exhaust** implies using up completely so that nothing remains: *At the end of the marathon her strength was exhausted.*

de·plor·a·ble (di plôr′ə bəl) *adj.* **1.** to be strongly disapproved of: *deplorable behavior.* **2.** to be deeply regretted: *the deplorable decline of the star's singing ability.* **3.** wretched; miserable: *deplorable living conditions.* —**de·plor′a·ble·ness,** *n.* —**de·plor′a·bly,** *adv.*

de·plore (di plôr′) *v.t.,* **-plored, -plor·ing. 1.** to disapprove of strongly: *The minister deplored the use of violence to bring about social change.* **2.** to be very sorry about; regret deeply; lament: *to deplore the untimely death of a friend.* [Latin *dēplōrāre* to lament, weep bitterly.] —**de·plor′ing·ly,** *adv.*

de·ploy (di ploi′) *v.t.* **1.** to place in a desired position according to a plan; position strategically: *to deploy missiles, to deploy pieces on a chessboard.* **2.** to widen the front of (a military unit) by spreading out in battle formation. —*v.i.* to be come deployed. [French *déployer* to unfold, from Latin *displicāre* to unfold, scatter.] —**de·ploy′ment,** *n.*

de·po·lar·ize (dē pō′lə rīz′) *v.t.,* **-ized, -iz·ing.** to end or reduce the polarity or polarization of. —**de·po′lar·i·za′tion,** *n.* —**de·po′lar·iz′er,** *n.*

de·po·nent (di pō′nənt) *n.* **1.** *Law.* a person who gives written testimony under oath. **2.** in Greek and Latin grammar, a verb that is passive in form but active in meaning. —*adj.* denoting such a verb. [Medieval Latin *deponens,* present participle of *deponere* to testify, from Latin *dēpōnere* to put aside; in grammar having the sense of "putting aside the active voice."]

de·pop·u·late (dē pop′yə lāt′) *v.t.,* **-lat·ed, -lat·ing.** to reduce the population of, as by death or expulsion: *Heavy bombing depopulated the country.* —**de·pop′u·la′tion,** *n.* —**de·pop′u·la′tor,** *n.*

a	at	e	end	o	hot	u	up	hw	white		about
ā	ape	ē	me	ō	old	ū	use	ng	song	ə	taken
ä	far	i	it	ô	fork	ü	rule	th	thin		pencil
âr	care	ī	ice	oi	oil	ů	pull	th	this		lemon
		îr	pierce	ou	out	ûr	turn	zh	measure		circus

327

de·port (di pôrt′) *v.t.* **1.** to expel (an undesirable alien) from a country. **2.** to behave or conduct (oneself) in a specified way: *Please deport yourself courteously.* [Old French *deporter* to banish, behave, from Latin *dēportāre* to carry off.] —**de·port′a·ble,** *adj.* —For Synonyms, see **banish.**

de·por·ta·tion (dē′pôr tā′shən) *n.* the act or an instance of expelling an undesirable alien from a country.

de·por·tee (dē′pôr tē′, di-) *n.* a person who has been deported or sentenced to deportation.

de·port·ment (di pôrt′mənt) *n.* a manner of behaving or conducting oneself; bearing: *the deportment of a diplomat.*

de·pos·al (di pō′zəl) *n.* the act of deposing from office or the state of being deposed.

de·pose (di pōz′) *v.,* **-posed, -pos·ing.** —*v.t.* **1.** to remove from a throne or other high office: *The rebels deposed the king.* **2.** *Law.* to state in a deposition. —*v.i.* *Law.* to make a deposition; testify. [Old French *deposer* to put down, testify, going back to Latin *dē* from, away + Late Latin *pausāre* to place, from Latin *pausāre* to halt, rest, from *pausa.* See PAUSE.]

de·pos·it (di poz′it) *v.t.* **1.** to put (money or valuables) in a bank or other place for safekeeping: *to deposit fifty dollars in a savings account.* **2.** to set or lay down; place: *I deposited the packages on the table.* **3.** to leave as a layer; precipitate: *The river deposited silt at its mouth. The storm may deposit up to ten inches of snow.* **4.** to give as partial payment or security. **5.** to put in; insert: *The phone won't work unless you deposit money first.* —*n.* **1.** something put in a place for safekeeping, esp. money in a bank. **2.** something given as partial payment or security: *a deposit of $500 on a new car.* **3.** something that has settled: *a deposit of dust on the window sill.* **4.** a natural layer or accumulation, as of a mineral: *large deposits of iron ore.* **5.** depository *(def. 1).* **6.** the act of depositing. [Latin *dēpositus,* past participle of *dēpōnere* to put down, put aside, entrust.]

· **on deposit.** placed in a bank or other place for safekeeping.

de·pos·i·tar·y (di poz′i ter′ē) *n., pl.* **-tar·ies. 1.** a person or organization entrusted with something for safekeeping. **2.** depository *(def. 1).*

dep·o·si·tion (dep′ə zish′ən, dē′pə-) *n.* **1.** removal from a throne or other high office. **2.** a sworn, written statement given by a witness out of court, intended to be used as testimony in court. **3.** the act or process of laying down, esp. by a natural process. **4.** something deposited; deposit.

de·pos·i·tor (di poz′i tər) *n.* a person who makes a deposit, esp. one who deposits money in a bank.

de·pos·i·to·ry (di poz′i tôr′ē) *n., pl.* **-ries. 1.** a place where something is deposited for safekeeping. **2.** depositary *(def. 1).*

de·pot (*def. 1* dē′pō; *def. 2* dep′ō; *def. 3* dep′ō, dē′pō) *n.* **1.** a railroad station or bus terminal. **2.a.** a place where military matériel is stored or processed before distribution. **b.** a place where military personnel are assembled, trained, and classified. **3.** storehouse; warehouse. [French *dépôt* a deposit, warehouse, from Latin *dēpositum* a deposit, something put down.]

de·prave (di prāv′) *v.t.,* **-praved, -prav·ing.** to make morally bad; corrupt; pervert. [Latin *dēpravāre,* from *dē* down + *prāvus* wicked.]

de·praved (di prāvd′) *adj.* morally bad; corrupt; perverted: *a depraved criminal.* —**de·prav·ed·ly** (di prāvd′lē, -prā′vid-), *adv.* —**de·praved′ness,** *n.*

de·prav·i·ty (di prav′i tē) *n., pl.* **-ties. 1.** the state or quality of being depraved; corruption. **2.** a depraved act or practice.

dep·re·cate (dep′ri kāt′) *v.t.,* **-cat·ed, -cat·ing. 1.** to express disapproval of. **2.** to speak slightingly of; disparage; belittle. [Latin *dēprecātus,* past participle of *dēprecārī* to avert by prayer, pray for.] —**dep′re·ca′tor,** *n.* —**dep′re·ca′tor,** *n.*

dep·re·ca·to·ry (dep′ri kə tôr′ē) *adj.* **1.** expressing disapproval. **2.** apologetic. Also, **dep·re·ca·tive** (dep′ri kā′tiv). —**dep′re·ca′to·ri·ly,** *adv.*

de·pre·ci·a·ble (di prē′shē ə bəl, -prē′shə-) *adj.* capable of being depreciated, or lowered in price or value.

de·pre·ci·ate (di prē′shē āt′) *v.,* **-at·ed, -at·ing.** —*v.t.* **1.** to lower the price or market value of. **2.** to describe as of little worth; belittle; deprecate. —*v.i.* to fall in value or price. [Latin *dēpretiātus,* past participle of *dēpretiāre* to lower the price of, from *dē* down + *pretium* price.] —**de·pre′ci·at′ing·ly,** *adv.* —**de·pre′ci·a′tor,** *n.*

de·pre·ci·a·tion (di prē′shē ā′shən) *n.* **1.** a decrease in value, as a result of deterioration, age, or obsolescence: *the depreciation of a car over the years.* **2.a.** an allowance made for such a decrease, as in determining taxable value of property. **b.** the amount of such allowance that can be charged to a particular period, in computing taxable income. **3.** a decline in the purchasing power or exchange value of money. **4.** the act of depreciating.

de·pre·ci·a·to·ry (di prē′shē ə tôr′ē) *adj.* tending to speak slightingly or critically; disparaging. Also, **de·pre′ci·a′tive.**

dep·re·da·tion (dep′ri dā′shən) *n.* the act of laying waste; plundering; ravaging. [French *déprédation,* Late Latin *dēpraedātiō,* going back to Latin *dē* down + *praeda* booty.]

de·press (di pres′) *v.t.* **1.** to lower in spirits; make gloomy; sadden: *The death of our dog depressed us.* **2.** to lessen the force, vigor, or activity of; weaken: *The sedative depressed the patient's pulse rate.* **3.** to lower in price or value. **4.** to press or push down: *to depress the accelerator in an automobile.* [Latin *dēpressus,* past participle of *dēprimere* to press down.] —**de·press′ing,** *adj.* —**de·press′ing·ly,** *adv.*

de·pres·sant (di pres′ənt) *adj.* tending to reduce nervous, muscular, or other vital life activities. —*n.* **1.** a drug or other substance that reduces the activity of various body functions. Sedatives are depressants. **2.** anything that depresses.

de·pressed (di prest′) *adj.* **1.** low in spirits; dejected; sad. **2.** decreased in activity, force, value, or price. **3.** undergoing economic depression; having a high rate of unemployment and a low standard of living: *a depressed area.* **4.** pressed down: *a depressed key on a typewriter.* **5.** flattened down; broader than high.

de·pres·sion (di presh′ən) *n.* **1.** a sunken place or surface; hollow: *The potter made a depression in the clay.* **2.** lowness in spirit; sadness; dejection. **3.** *Psychiatry.* an abnormal emotional state characterized by severe feelings of sadness and dejection with no obvious cause or out of proportion to events causing them. **4.a.** a period marked by a severe reduction in business activity, a rise in unemployment, and falling wages and prices. **b. the Depression.** the international business depression lasting from 1929 to 1939. Also, **the Great Depression. 5.** a decrease in activity, force, value, or price. **6.** the act of pressing down. **7.** an area of low atmospheric pressure: *a tropical depression.*

de·pres·sive (di pres′iv) *adj.* **1.** relating to or characterized by mental depression. **2.** tending to cause depression.

de·pres·sor (di pres′ər) *n.* **1.** a person or thing that depresses. **2.** a medical instrument used to press down a part of the body: *a tongue depressor.* **3.a.** a muscle that draws down a part of the body. **b.** a nerve that acts to lower the heart rate and blood pressure when stimulated. Also *(def. 3b),* **depressor nerve.**

dep·ri·va·tion (dep′rə vā′shən) *n.* **1.** the act of depriving or the state of being deprived. **2.** loss; privation.

de·prive (di prīv′) *v.t.,* **-prived, -priv·ing. 1.** to take something away from; dispossess; divest (with *of*): *The proposed highway will deprive the children of their playground.* **2.** to keep from having or enjoying something; withhold from: *The bad weather this spring deprived farmers of a good harvest.* [Old French *depriver* to take from, going back to Latin *dē* down + *privare* to rob, bereave.]

de·pro·gram (dē prō′gram) *v.t.,* **-grammed** or **-gramed, -gram·ming** or **-gram·ing.** to try to free (a person) from the influence of certain ideas or beliefs, as of a religious cult or political group.

dept., department.

depth (depth) *n.* **1.** distance or extension downward, inward, or from front to back: *the depth of an elevator shaft, the depth of an incision, the depth of a theater stage.* **2.** the quality of being deep; deepness. **3.** intensity or strength: *The painting has great depth of color.* **4.** profundity or complexity of thought or feeling: *The movie was amusing, but it had no depth.* **5.** *usually,* **depths. a.** the most extreme or intense stage or state: *the depths of despair.* **b.** the deepest, innermost, or most remote part: *the depths of the jungle.* **c.** a deplorably low moral or intellectual state. **7.** lowness of pitch. [Middle English *depthe* deepness, going back to Old English *dēop* deep.]

depth charge, an explosive charge designed to go off underwater at a predetermined depth, used esp. against submarines. Also, **depth bomb.**

depth of field, the range of distances at which a camera lens set at a given aperture will produce a relatively sharp image of an object.

depth perception, the ability to judge the spatial relationship of objects that are different distances from the observer.

dep·u·ta·tion (dep′yə tā′shən) *n.* **1.** a person or persons authorized to represent or act for another; delegation. **2.** the act of deputing or the state of being deputed.

de·pute (di pūt′) *v.t.,* **-put·ed, -put·ing. 1.** to appoint as one's substitute, delegate, or agent. **2.** to transfer, as work or authority, to another. [Old French *deputer* to assign, from Late Latin *dēputāre* to allot, from Latin *dēputāre* to consider.]

dep·u·tize (dep′yə tīz′) *v.,* **-tized, -tiz·ing.** —*v.t.* to appoint as a deputy. —*v.i.* to act as deputy. —**dep′u·ti·za′tion,** *n.*

dep·u·ty (dep′yə tē) *n., pl.* **-ties. 1.** a person appointed or authorized to represent or act for another or others. **2.** an assistant with power to take charge in a superior's absence: *a sheriff's*

deputy. **3.** a member of the lower house of certain legislatures, as in France and Italy. —*adj.* acting as a deputy. [French *député* delegate, from *députer* to depute. See DEPUTE.]

der. **1.** derivation. **2.** derivative. **3.** derived.

de·rail (dē rāl′) *v.t.* to cause to run off the rails: *to derail a train.* —*v.i.* to run off the rails. —**de·rail′ment,** *n.*

de·rail·leur (di rā′lər) *n.* a device on a bicycle that shifts the drive chain from one sprocket to another to change gears. [French *dérailleur,* from *dérailler* to throw off track.]

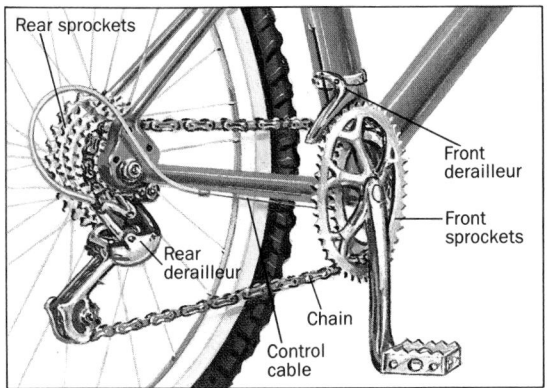

derailleur

de·range (di rānj′) *v.t.*, **-ranged, -rang·ing. 1.** to disturb the normal functioning of, as a machine. **2.** to disturb the order or arrangement of; disarrange. **3.** to disorder (someone's) mental functioning; make insane. [French *déranger* to disarray, going back to Old French *des-* (from Latin *dis-* apart) + *ranger* to rank (of Germanic origin).] —**de·range′ment,** *n.*

de·ranged (di rānjd′) *adj.* **1.** mentally disordered; insane. **2.** out of normal order; disarranged.

der·by (dûr′bē; *British* där′bē) *n., pl.* **-bies.** a hard, round man's hat with a narrow curled brim. Also, **bowler.**

Der·by (dûr′bē; *British* där′bē) *n., pl.* **-bies. 1.a.** an annual horse race held at Epsom Downs, near London, England, for three-year-old horses. **b.** Kentucky Derby. **2.** any similar horse race. **3. derby.** any large race or contest, esp. one open to all who wish to compete. [From Edward Stanley, 1752-1834, twelfth earl of *Derby,* who instituted the Epsom Derby in 1780.]

de·reg·u·late (dē reg′yə lāt′) *v.t.*, **-lat·ed, -lat·ing.** to free from government regulations or controls: *to deregulate the banking industry.*

der·e·lict (der′ə likt′) *n.* **1.** a degraded social outcast; vagrant; tramp. **2.** property abandoned by its owner or guardian, esp. a ship abandoned at sea. —*adj.* **1.** neglectful of one's duty; negligent; delinquent: *The sentry was derelict in failing to notice the approach of the enemy.* **2.** abandoned by the owner or guardian: *a derelict ship.* [Latin *dērelictus,* past participle of *dērelinquere* to abandon.]

der·e·lic·tion (der′ə lik′shən) *n.* **1.** neglect of one's duty; delinquency: *The guard's dereliction allowed the prisoners to escape.* **2.** the act of abandoning or the state of being abandoned; desertion.

de·ride (di rīd′) *v.t.*, **-rid·ed, -rid·ing.** to treat with contempt or scorn; mock; ridicule. [Latin *dērīdēre.*] —**de·rid′er,** *n.* —**de·rid′ing·ly,** *adv.* —For Synonyms, see **mock.**

de ri·gueur (də ri gûr′, də rē gœr′) *French.* required by etiquette, fashion, or custom; in good form; proper.

de·ri·sion (di rizh′ən) *n.* **1.** the act of treating with contempt, mockery, or ridicule. **2.** an object of such treatment. [Late Latin *dērīsiō* mockery, from Latin *dērīdēre* to mock.]

de·ri·sive (di rī′siv) *adj.* expressing or characterized by derision; mocking; ridiculing: *derisive laughter.* Also, **de·ri·so·ry** (də rī′-sə rē, -zə rē). —**de·ri′sive·ly,** *adv.* —**de·ri′sive·ness,** *n.*

deriv. **1.** derivation. **2.** derivative. **3.** derived.

der·i·va·tion (der′ə vā′shən) *n.* **1.** the act of deriving or the state of being derived. **2.** the source or origin from which something is derived: *a legend of Irish derivation, to trace the derivation of a custom.* **3.** something derived; derivative. **4.a.** the process of tracing the origin and development of a word. **b.** a statement of this; etymology. **5.** the formation of a new word from an existing

word, root, or stem, esp. by the addition of a prefix or suffix. The word *happiness* is formed by derivation from the adjective *happy* and the suffix *-ness.*

de·riv·a·tive (di riv′ə tiv) *adj.* obtained or characterized by derivation; not original: *a derivative theory, derivative words.* —*n.* **1.** something derived. **2.** a chemical substance obtained or regarded as being obtained from another specific substance by modification or by partial substitution of components. **3.** a word formed from another by derivation. **4.** *Mathematics.* the limit of the ratio of change in a function to the corresponding change in a variable in it, as the latter change approaches zero. —**de·riv′a·tive·ly,** *adv.*

de·rive (di rīv′) *v.*, **-rived, -riv·ing.** —*v.t.* **1.** to get or obtain from a source or origin (with *from*): *to derive pleasure from reading, a style of painting derived from primitive art.* **2.** to obtain by some process of reasoning; infer: *to derive a principle from various arguments.* **3.** to trace the origin of (something, as a word) from or to its source. **4.** to obtain (a chemical compound or substance) from another, as by substituting different elements or radicals. —*v.i.* to proceed from a source; originate: *The word "democracy" derives from Greek.* [Late Latin *dērīvāre* to flow, from Latin *dērīvāre* to draw off (a liquid), divert, from *dē* away + *rīvus* stream.] —**de·riv′a·ble,** *adj.* —**de·riv′er,** *n.*

der·ma (dûr′mə) *n.* **1.** dermis. **2.** skin; integument. [Modern Latin *derma,* from Greek *derma* skin.]

derm·a·bra·sion (dûr′mə brā′zhən) *n.* the surgical removal or reduction of acne scars or other blemishes by gentle abrasion of the skin.

der·mal (dûr′məl) *adj.* of or relating to the skin.

der·ma·ti·tis (dûr′mə tī′tis) *n.* inflammation of the skin.

der·ma·tol·o·gist (dûr′mə tol′ə jist) *n.* a physician specializing in dermatology.

der·ma·tol·o·gy (dûr′mə tol′ə jē) *n.* the branch of medical science dealing with the skin and its diseases.

der·mis (dûr′mis) *n.* the layer of skin beneath the epidermis, containing blood vessels, nerves, and other structures. Also, **co·rium.** For illustration, see **skin.** [Modern Latin *dermis,* from EPIDERMIS.]

der·o·gate (der′ə gāt′) *v.*, **-gat·ed, -gat·ing.** —*v.t.* to deny the importance or merit of; belittle: *The writer derogated the works of other authors.* —*v.i.* to take away; detract. [Latin *dērogātus,* past participle of *dērogāre.*] —**der′o·ga′tion,** *n.*

de·rog·a·to·ry (di rog′ə tôr′ē) *adj.* tending to lessen in importance or estimation; disparaging; belittling: *derogatory comments.* Also, **de·rog′a·tive.** —**de·rog′a·to′ri·ly,** *adv.*

der·rick (der′ik) *n.* **1.** a machine for lifting and moving heavy objects, usually stationary and consisting of a vertical support to which a slanted boom with hoisting tackle is attached. **2.** a framework over an oil well or other drill hole that supports the drilling machinery. [From earlier *Derrick* gallows, from surname of a seventeenth-century English hangman.]

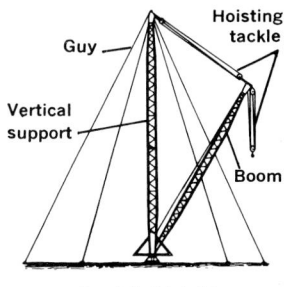

derrick *(def. 1)*

der·ri·ère (der′ē âr′) *also,* **der·ri·ere.** *n.* buttocks; rump; rear. [French *derrière,* going back to Latin *dē retrō* from back.]

der·ring-do (der′ing dü′) *n.* courageous behavior or feats; daring. [Middle English *dorryng don* daring to do. See DARE, DO[1].]

der·rin·ger (der′in jər) *n.* a small, short-barreled pistol of large caliber. [From Henry *Deringer,* the nineteenth-century American gunsmith who invented it.]

der·vish (dûr′vish) *n.* a member of any of various Muslim religious orders known for certain energetic forms of worship, as howling and whirling. [Turkish *dervīsh* literally, beggar, from Persian *dārvīsh* poor, a monk.]

de·sal·i·nate (dē sal′ə nāt′) *v.t.*, **-nat·ed, -nat·ing.** to remove salt from: *to desalinate seawater.* Also, **de·sal·in·ize** (dē sal′ə-nīz′).

a	at	e	end	o	hot	u	up	hw	white		about
ā	ape	ē	me	ō	old	ū	use	ng	song		taken
ä	far	i	it	ô	fork	ü	rule	th	thin	ə	pencil
âr	care	ī	ice	oi	oil	ù	pull	th	this		lemon
				ir	pierce	ou	out	ûr	turn	zh	measure	circus

de·sal·i·na·tion (dē sal′ə nā′shən) *n.* the act or process of removing salt from, esp. as applied to the distillation of seawater to make it useful for irrigation or drinking. Also, **de·sal·i·ni·za·tion** (dē sal′ə nə zā′shən).

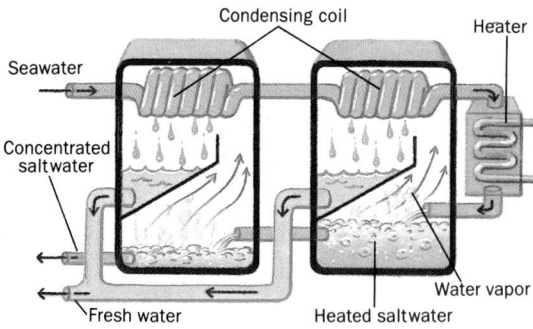

Condensing coil
Heater
Seawater
Concentrated saltwater
Fresh water
Heated saltwater
Water vapor

desalination of seawater

de·salt (dē sôlt′) *v.t.* desalinate.

des·cant (*n.,* des′kant; *v.,* des kant′, dis-) *n.* **1.** *Music.* **a.** an additional ornamental melody that is sung or played above another melody, usually by several soprano voices or instruments. **b.** the music containing these elements. **2.** a comment or discourse, esp. a lengthy one. —*v.i.* **1.** to comment at length; discourse; enlarge (with *on* or *upon*). **2.** *Music.* to sing or play a descant. [Dialectal Old French *descant* ornamental accompaniment in music, counterpoint, going back to Latin *dis-* apart + *cantus* song.]

de·scend (di send′) *v.i.* **1.** to move or pass from a higher place to a lower one; come or go downward: *We rode up in the elevator, but descended by the stairs.* **2.** to slope or extend downward: *a mountain path that descends to a lake.* **3.** to come down by inheritance: *an estate that descends through the eldest child.* **4.** to come down from an earlier source or ancestor; be derived, as by birth or transmission: *The family descends from the first French colonists.* **5.** to come in force or in overwhelming numbers; attack or visit suddenly (with *on* or *upon*): *The hounds descended on their prey. A group of friends descended on us over the weekend.* **6.** to pass from greater to less, or from higher to lower, in any scale or series. **7.** to pass from the general to the specific. **8.** to lower oneself; stoop. —*v.t.* to come or go downward on or along: *to descend a mountain trail.* [Old French *descendre* to go down, from Latin *descendere.*] —**de·scend′i·ble,** *adj.*

de·scen·dant (di sen′dənt) *n.* a person who is descended from a particular ancestor or group of ancestors; offspring: *a descendant of Polish immigrants.* —*adj.* also, **de·scen·dent.** **1.** coming or going downward. **2.** descending from an original source or ancestor.

de·scent (di sent′) *n.* **1.** movement or passage from a higher level to a lower one: *the descent of an elevator.* **2.** a downward slope or inclination: *a hill with a steep descent.* **3.** derivation, as by ancestry or transmission; birth: *Our family is of Russian descent.* **4.** a way or passage leading downward; means of descending. **5.** a fall to a lower state or condition; decline. **6.** a sudden attack or visit. **7.** hereditary succession to an estate or title. [Old French *descente* sudden fall, succession, from *descendre.* See DESCEND.]

de·scribe (di skrīb′) *v.t.,* **-scribed, -scrib·ing. 1.** to represent or give a picture of in words; tell or write about: *My essay describes my job last summer. Can you describe what you saw from the window?* **2.** to draw or trace the outline of: *to describe a circle with a compass.* **3.** to designate in a particular way; label: *I wouldn't describe myself as an art expert.* [Latin *dēscrībere* to write down, copy.] —**de·scrib′a·ble,** *adj.* —**de·scrib′er,** *n.*

de·scrip·tion (di skrip′shən) *n.* **1.** the act of setting forth or portraying in words; verbal or written representation. **2.** a statement or account that describes. **3.** kind; sort; variety: *birds of every description.* **4.** the act of tracing in outline.

de·scrip·tive (di skrip′tiv) *adj.* having the quality or function of describing; characterized by description: *a descriptive adjective.* —**de·scrip′tive·ly,** *adv.* —**de·scrip′tive·ness,** *n.*

de·scry (di skrī′) *v.t.,* **-scried, -scry·ing. 1.** to see from afar or through obscurity; catch sight of; espy: *to descry land in the distance.* **2.** to discover by observation; detect: *to descry a flaw in an opponent's argument.* [Old French *descrier* to proclaim, decry. See DECRY.]

des·e·crate (des′i krāt′) *v.t.,* **-crat·ed, -crat·ing.** to destroy the sanctity of; treat with irreverence; profane: *to desecrate a tomb.* [DE- + (CON)SECRATE.] —**des′e·crat′er;** *also,* **des′e·cra′tor,** *n.* —**des′e·cra′tion,** *n.*

de·seg·re·gate (dē seg′ri gāt′) *v.t., v.i.,* **-gat·ed, -gat·ing.** to eliminate racial segregation (in). —**de·seg′re·ga′tion,** *n.*

de·sen·si·tize (dē sen′si tīz′) *v.t.,* **-tized, -tiz·ing. 1.** to make less sensitive. **2.** to make (photographic film) less sensitive to light. **3.** to reduce or eliminate the sensitivity of (a person, organ, or tissue) to an allergen or other external stimulus. —**de·sen′si·ti·za′tion,** *n.* —**de·sen′si·tiz′er,** *n.*

des·ert[1] (dez′ərt) *n.* **1.a.** a dry, sandy, often hot region with little or no vegetation or animal life: *Many kinds of cactus grow in the American desert.* **b.** any expanse of land with little or no vegetation or animal life: *the polar deserts of Antarctica.* **2.** an unproductive area, period, or activity; wasteland: *a cultural desert.* —*adj.* **1.** relating to, inhabiting, or occurring in a desert: *desert plants.* **2.** not lived in or on; uninhabited; desolate: *a desert island.* [Middle English *desert,* from Old French *desert,* from Late Latin *dēsertum,* from Latin *dēsertus,* past participle of *dēserere* to desert, abandon, from *de-* from + *serere* to join.]

de·sert[2] (di zûrt′) *v.t.* **1.** to go away from (a person or thing that should not be left); abandon; forsake: *to desert one's wife and children.* **2.** to leave (a military force) without permission and with the intention of remaining away permanently. **3.** to fail (someone) when needed or expected: *My courage deserted me suddenly.* —*v.i.* **1.** to abandon one's duty, post, or cause. **2.** to abandon a military force with the intention of remaining away permanently. [French *déserter* to forsake, abandon, from Late Latin *dēsertāre,* from Latin *dēsertus,* past participle of *dēserere.* See DESERT[1].] —**de·sert′er,** *n.*

Synonyms *v.t.* **Desert**[2], **abandon,** and **forsake** mean to leave someone or something without intending to return. **Desert** connotes violating a responsibility or obligation: *to desert one's family, to desert a post one has sworn to defend.* **Abandon** suggests leaving behind something or someone that one no longer finds useful or desirable: *to abandon a farm, to abandon a plan of action.* **Forsake** suggests renouncing or spurning a person or thing one was attached to: *to forsake a friend, to forsake a political party.*

de·sert[3] (di zûrt′) *n. also,* **deserts.** something that is deserved; deserved reward or punishment: *to get one's just deserts.* [Middle English *desert,* from Old French *deserte,* from *deservir* to deserve, from Latin *deservire* to serve well, from *dē* from + *servire* to serve.]

de·sert·i·fi·ca·tion (di zûr′tə fi kā′shən) *n.* the process by which land is turned into desert, resulting from either climatic changes or human activities. [DESERT[1] + -FICATION.]

de·ser·tion (di zûr′shən) *n.* **1.** the act of deserting. **2.** the abandonment of one's spouse without consent or legal justification. **3.** the state of being deserted.

de·serve (di zûrv′) *v.,* **-served, -serv·ing.** —*v.t.* to have a right to; be worthy of; merit: *The author's first play deserved the criticism it received.* —*v.i.* to be worthy; merit. [Old French *deservir* to merit, from Latin *deservīre* to serve well.] —**de·serv′er,** *n.* —For Synonyms, see **merit.**

de·serv·ed·ly (di zûr′vid lē) *adv.* according to merit; justly; rightfully: *The rescuers were deservedly praised for their efforts.*

de·serv·ing (di zûr′ving) *adj.* **1.** that merits; worthy: *This plan is deserving of your attention.* **2.** worthy of or qualified to receive help, esp. financial aid: *The scholarship will be given to a deserving student.* —**de·serv′ing·ly,** *adv.*

des·ha·bille (dez′ə bēl′) dishabille.

des·ic·cant (des′i kənt) *n.* an agent or substance that has a drying effect, as calcium chloride. [Latin *desiccantis, desiccans,* genitive of present participle of *dēsiccāre* to dry up. See DESIC-CATE.]

des·ic·cate (des′i kāt′) *v.,* **-cat·ed, -cat·ing.** —*v.t.* **1.** to dry up completely. **2.** to preserve (food) by drying. —*v.i.* to become dry. [Latin *dēsiccātus,* past participle of *dēsiccāre* to dry up, going back to *dē* thoroughly + *siccus* dry.] —**des′ic·ca′tion,** *n.*

des·ic·ca·tor (des′i kā′tər) *n.* a device for drying foods.

de·sid·er·a·tum (di sid′ə rā′təm, -rä′təm) *n., pl.* **-ta** (-tə). something desired or required. [Latin *dēsīderātum* (something) longed for, from *dēsīderāre* to long for.]

de·sign (di zīn′) *n.* **1.** a preliminary plan, sketch, or outline made to serve as a guide or pattern: *an architect's design for a new house.* **2.** an arrangement or combination of parts, details, or colors so as to achieve a particular effect; pattern of an artistic work: *a geometrical design in a carpet.* **3.** the art or business of making designs: *a school of design.* **4.** an example of artistic work: *My design was exhibited in the annual show.* **5.** a plan, scheme, or project to be carried out. **6.** *also,* **designs.** a secret or sinister plot or scheme (usually with *upon, on,* or *against*): *The strangers had designs on the old couple's fortune.* **7.** the prear-

ranged purpose for something; aim; intention: *The design of the plot was to oust the dictator.* —*v.t.* **1.** to make a preliminary plan, sketch, or outline of; make a pattern for: *to design an advertisement, to design an automobile.* **2.** to plan and fashion with artistic skill; arrange parts, details, or colors of: *to design a dress.* **3.** to form in the mind; plan out; conceive; contrive: *The president designed a new foreign policy.* **4.** to have as an aim or purpose; intend: *The experiment is designed to test the new drug.* —*v.i.* **1.** to make plans, sketches, or outlines, esp. of an original, artistic nature. **2.** to originate and execute a plan or scheme. **3.** to work as a designer. [French *désigner* to indicate, denote, from Latin *dēsignāre* to mark out, denote.]
• **by design.** on purpose; intentionally; deliberately.

des·ig·nate (*v.,* dez′ig nāt′; *adj.,* dez′ig nit, -nāt′) *v.t.,* **-nat·ed, -nat·ing. 1.** to point out or indicate by means of a distinctive mark, sign, or name; specify; signify: *The limits of your property are designated by metal posts.* **2.** to call by a particular term or title; name; entitle. **3.** to select for a particular purpose or duty; appoint to an office: *She was designated to lead the expedition. The school board designated him chairman.* —*adj.* selected but not yet serving; appointed. ➡ usually used after a noun, often in combination: *The incumbent treasurer as well as the treasurer-designate was present.* [Latin *dēsignātus,* past participle of *dēsignāre* to mark out, denote.] —**des′ig·na′tor,** *n.*

designated driver, among a group of persons who travel in the same vehicle to a bar, social event, or the like, one who agrees not to consume alcohol so as to remain in proper condition to drive the group safely.

designated hitter, a baseball player who bats in place of the pitcher, but does not take a position in the field.

des·ig·na·tion (dez′ig nā′shən) *n.* **1.** the act of pointing out or indicating something: *designation of a boundary.* **2.** a distinguishing name, title, or mark. **3.** the act of designating for a particular purpose; appointment: *The designation of two ambassadors was announced.*

de·sign·ed·ly (di zī′nid lē) *adv.* by design; intentionally.

de·sign·er (di zī′nər) *n.* a person who creates designs or patterns for manufacture or construction: *a dress designer, a package designer.*

de·sign·ing (di zī′ning) *adj.* **1.** having motives other than those announced or apparent; scheming: *A designing person can't be trusted.* **2.** displaying planning or forethought. —*n.* the practice or art of making designs or patterns.

de·sir·a·ble (di zīr′ə bəl) *adj.* **1.** worth having or pursuing: *desirable goals.* **2.** possessing qualities worthy of desire; pleasing; beautiful. —**de·sir′a·bil′i·ty, de·sir′a·ble·ness,** *n.* —**de·sir′a·bly,** *adv.*

de·sire (di zīr′) *v.,* **-sired, -sir·ing.** —*v.t.* **1.** to have a strong wish for; long for; crave: *Both nations desired peace.* **2.** to express a wish for; request: *The caller desired information about vacationing in the mountains.* —*v.i.* to have or feel desire. —*n.* **1.** the state or condition of longing; wish: *the desire for wealth.* **2.** an expressed wish; request. **3.** a person or thing desired: *You will have your desire.* **4.** sexual longing; passion; lust. [Old French *desirer* to long for, from Latin *dēsīderāre.*]

de·sir·ous (di zīr′əs) *adj.* having desire; desiring: *desirous of fame.* —**de·sir′ous·ly,** *adv.*

de·sist (di zist′, -sist′) *v.i.* to cease some action; stop (usually with *from*): *The two factions desisted from fighting.* [Old French *desister,* from Latin *dēsistere* to stand aside, cease.] —For Synonyms, see **stop.**

desk (desk) *n.* **1.** an article of furniture having a flat or sloping surface and usually drawers or compartments, used esp. for reading or writing. **2.** a reading stand with a sloping top, used esp. to hold a book that is read in a church service. **3.** a booth or counter at which certain duties or services are performed, as the place in a hotel where guests register. **4.** a division or department of an organization or office: *the city desk of a newspaper.* **5.** a stand used to support sheet music. [Medieval Latin *desca* the article of furniture, table, from Italian *desco,* from Late Latin *discus* table, from Latin *discus* quoit, dish, from Greek *diskos* round plate, quoit. Doublet of DAIS, DISCUS, DISH, DISK.]

desk·top (desk′top′) *n.* the top or working surface of a desk. —*adj.* designating equipment that can fit on a desktop: *a desktop computer.*

desktop publishing, the use of a computer, esp. a microcomputer, for setting written copy and designing charts and other graphic materials to be printed in limited quantity.

des·mid (dez′mid) *n.* any of a large group of unicellular freshwater green algae whose cells are split into two identical halves connected in the middle. [Modern Latin *desmidium,* from Greek *desmos* a chain, from *dein* to bind.]

des·o·late (*adj.,* des′ə lit; *v.,* des′ə lāt′) *adj.* **1.** lacking inhabitants; deserted: *desolate ruins.* **2.** left alone; without companion-

ship; lonely: *I was desolate after my best friend moved away.* **3.** laid waste; devastated: *The forest was left desolate by the fire.* **4.** without joy or comfort; miserable; dreary: *January can be a desolate month.* —*v.t.,* **-lat·ed, -lat·ing. 1.** to lay waste; devastate: *The land was desolated by floods.* **2.** to deprive of inhabitants: *Plague desolated the town.* **3.** to make miserable, wretched, or forlorn: *We were desolated by the bad news.* [Latin *dēsōlātus,* past participle of *dēsōlāre* to abandon, going back to *dē* thoroughly + *sōlus* alone.] —**des′o·late·ly,** *adv.* —**des′o·late·ness,** *n.*

des·o·la·tion (des′ə lā′shən) *n.* **1.** the act of making desolate; devastation: *the desolation of life and land by war.* **2.** a ruined or deserted condition: *We found the old house in complete desolation.* **3.** a desolate place or region. **4.** a feeling of utter loneliness and sadness.

des·ox·y·ri·bo·nu·cle·ic acid (des ok′sē rī′bō nü klē′ik, -nū-) DNA.

de·spair (di spâr′) *n.* **1.** a complete loss of hope or expectation: *After declaring bankruptcy, the owner overcame feelings of despair and began rebuilding the business.* **2.** a person or thing that causes loss of hope. —*v.i.* to lose or give up hope; be without hope (usually with *of*): *They despaired of ever seeing their daughter again.* [Old French *desperer* to lose hope, from Latin *dēspērāre,* going back to *dē* away + *spēs* hope.]

de·spair·ing (di spâr′ing) *adj.* feeling or showing despair; hopeless: *a despairing lover, a despairing cry.* —**de·spair′ing·ly,** *adv.* —**de·spair′ing·ness,** *n.*

des·patch (di spach′) dispatch.

des·patch·er (di spach′ər) dispatcher.

des·per·a·do (des′pə rä′dō, -rā′dō) *n., pl.* **-does** or **-dos.** a bold, desperate, or reckless criminal. [Probably modification (influenced by Spanish ending -*ado*) of obsolete *despereate* wretch. See DESPERATE.]

des·per·ate (des′pər it, -prit) *adj.* **1.** reckless through hopelessness; ready to run any risk; rash; violent: *a desperate criminal.* **2.** done without regard to what happens afterward; irresponsibly or violently reckless: *desperate acts.* **3.** having or giving little or no hope of improvement or recovery; extremely bad; hopeless: *desperate circumstances, a desperate illness.* **4.** having an urgent desire or need: *desperate for attention.* **5.** deep; extreme: *desperate poverty.* [Latin *dēspērātus,* past participle of *dēspērāre* to lose hope. See DESPAIR.] —**des′per·ate·ly,** *adv.* —**des′per·ate·ness,** *n.*

des·per·a·tion (des′pə rā′shən) *n.* **1.** recklessness arising from loss of hope: *an act of desperation.* **2.** the state of being desperate: *I could see the desperation in their eyes.*

des·pi·ca·ble (des′pi kə bəl, di spik′ə-) *adj.* deserving scorn; contemptible; vile: *despicable cruelty.* [Late Latin *dēspicābilis* contemptible, from Latin *dēspicārī* to despise.] —**des′pi·ca·ble·ness,** *n.* —**des′pi·ca·bly,** *adv.*

de·spise (di spīz′) *v.t.,* **-spised, -spis·ing.** to regard as contemptible; look down on with hatred; scorn. [Old French *despis-,* a stem of *despire* to scorn, insult, from Latin *dēspicere,* from *dē* down + *spicere* to look.] —**de·spis′er,** *n.*

de·spite (di spīt′) *prep.* without regard to (some condition or fact); in spite of; notwithstanding: *I went to work despite my illness.* —*n.* **1.** *Archaic.* malice; spite. **2.** *Archaic.* contempt; scorn. [Old French *despit* spite, anger, from Latin *dēspectus* a looking down, contempt.]
• **in despite of.** notwithstanding; regardless of.

de·spite·ful (di spīt′fəl) *adj. Archaic.* malicious; spiteful.

de·spoil (di spoil′) *v.t.* to deprive of possessions or valuables by force; rob; pillage; plunder: *The marauders despoiled the countryside.* [Old French *despoillier* to strip, make bare, from Latin *dēspoliāre* to plunder.] —**de·spoil′ment,** *n.*

de·spo·li·a·tion (di spō′lē ā′shən) *n.* the act of despoiling or the state or occasion of being despoiled.

de·spond (di spond′) *v.i.* to lose heart or hope; be depressed. —*n.* despondency. [Latin *dēspondēre* to give up, lose.]

de·spon·den·cy (di spon′dēn sē) *n., pl.* **-cies.** loss of hope; depression of spirit; dejection. Also, **de·spon′dence.**

de·spon·dent (di spon′dənt) *adj.* having given up hope; discouraged; depressed; dejected: *She was despondent when her brother became ill.* —**de·spon′dent·ly,** *adv.*

des·pot (des′pət, -pot) *n.* **1.** a person who governs with unlimited authority; absolute ruler; autocrat. **2.** any person in authority

a	at	e	end	o	hot	u	up	hw	white	⎧	about
ā	ape	ē	me	ō	old	ū	use	ng	song	⎪	taken
ä	far	i	it	ô	fork	ü	rule	th	thin	⎨	pencil
âr	care	ī	ice	oi	oil	u̇	pull	th	this	⎪	lemon
		îr	pierce	ou	out	ûr	turn	zh	measure	⎩	circus

who acts cruelly or unjustly; tyrant; oppressor. [Old French *despot* chief lord, from Greek *despotēs* master, tyrant.]

des·pot·ic (des pot′ik, di spot′-) *adj.* of or like a despot or despotism; tyrannical; arbitrary. —**des·pot′i·cal·ly,** *adv.*

des·pot·ism (des′pə tiz′əm) *n.* **1.** the rule of a despot; exercise of absolute authority; autocracy. **2.** tyrannical rule; oppression. **3.** a government or state headed by a despot.

des·sert (di zûrt′) *n.* a course served at the end of a meal, usually a sweet food, as cake, pie, or ice cream. [French *dessert,* from *desservir* to clear a table, going back to Latin *dis-* away + *servīre* to serve.]

des·sert·spoon (di zûrt′spün′) *n.* a spoon intermediate in size between a teaspoon and a tablespoon.

des·ti·na·tion (des′tə nā′shən) *n.* **1.** the place to which a person is going or a thing is directed; intended end of a journey: *Our destination is Paris.* **2.** the end or purpose for which something is set apart.

des·tine (des′tin) *v.t.,* **-tined, -tin·ing. 1.** to intend or set apart for a particular purpose or use: *That land is destined for the new hospital.* **2.** to appoint or fix beforehand; preordain; predetermine: *The proposal was destined to be defeated.* *That athlete is destined for greatness.* **3.** to direct to a certain destination: *This ship is destined for America.* [Old French *destiner* to fix, determine, from Latin *dēstināre* to make firm, establish.]

des·ti·ny (des′tə nē) *n., pl.* **-nies. 1.** what happens or has happened to a person or thing; lot; fortune: *It was their destiny to become great writers.* **2.** a foreordained course of events: *They believed their discovery was destiny.* **3.** the power or agency thought to foreordain the course of events; fate: *No one knows what destiny will bring.* —For Synonyms, see **fate.**

des·ti·tute (des′ti tüt′, -tūt′) *adj.* **1.** lacking the necessities of life; in absolute want: *The villagers were left destitute by the flood.* **2.** entirely lacking; wanting; devoid (with *of*): *a plain destitute of trees, a story destitute of wit.* [Latin *dēstitūtus,* past participle of *dēstituere* to set down, abandon.]

des·ti·tu·tion (des′ti tü′shən, -tū′-) *n.* **1.** lack of the necessities of life; absolute want; dire poverty. **2.** deficiency; deprivation; lack.

de·stroy (di stroi′) *v.t.* **1.** to break into pieces or otherwise do away with the structure or value of; demolish; ruin; wreck: *The storm destroyed the house. Locusts destroyed the crops.* **2.** to put an end to; do away with: *to destroy an opportunity, to destroy a person's hopes.* **3.** to end the life of; kill: *The horse with the broken leg had to be destroyed. The frost destroyed many plants.* **4.** to counteract the effect of; detract from; make useless: *to destroy an argument, to destroy a person's influence.* —*v.i.* to bring about destruction. [Old French *destruire* to ruin, cause to decline, going back to Latin *dēstruere* to pull down.]

de·stroy·er (di stroi′ər) *n.* **1.** a person or thing that destroys. **2.** a small, fast, highly maneuverable warship, armed with guns, depth charges, torpedoes, and sometimes missiles, used to attack submarines.

destroyer escort, a warship similar to a destroyer but smaller, used to escort convoys.

destroying angel, death cup.

de·struct (di strukt′) *n.* the intentional destruction of a rocket or missile that fails to function properly after it has been launched. —*adj.* designed to destroy such a rocket or missile: *a destruct mechanism.* —*v.i.* to be destroyed automatically. —*v.t.* to destroy. [From DESTRUCTION.] —**de·struc′tor,** *n.*

de·struc·ti·ble (di struk′tə bəl) *adj.* capable of being destroyed. —**de·struc′ti·bil′i·ty,** *n.*

de·struc·tion (di struk′shən) *n.* **1.** the act or process of destroying: *The police charged them with the destruction of public property.* **2.** the fact or condition of being destroyed; ruin: *The hurricane left destruction in its wake.* **3.** a cause or means of destroying. [Latin *dēstructiō* a pulling down.]

Synonyms **Destruction, ruin,** and **devastation** denote damage so great that it renders a thing formless or useless. **Destruction** generally refers to any action that makes use or repair impossible: *the destruction of a crop by hailstorms, the destruction of a village by an earthquake.* **Ruin** implies a falling apart or tumbling down, usually through natural decay, but may not mean complete destruction: *The ruin of the statue through air pollution was not recognized until it was almost too late.* **Devastation** connotes a ravaging or laying waste that results in complete desolation: *the devastation of island communities by a hurricane.*

de·struc·tive (di struk′tiv) *adj.* **1.** causing or likely to cause destruction: *a destructive fire, a destructive insect, a destructive policy.* **2.** tending to overthrow, tear down, or discredit: *destructive criticism.* —**de·struc′tive·ly,** *adv.* —**de·struc′tive·ness,** *n.*

destructive distillation, a chemical process consisting of the

decomposition of an organic substance, as wood or coal, by heating it in a closed vessel, and the simultaneous collection of the volatile matter produced.

des·ue·tude (des′wi tüd′, -tūd) *n.* a condition of being no longer in use or in operation; obsolescence: *an ancient custom that has fallen into desuetude.* [Latin *dēsuētūdō.*]

des·ul·to·ry (des′əl tôr′ē) *adj.* **1.** shifting from one thing to another; not methodical; irregular; disconnected: *desultory movements, a desultory conversation.* **2.** occurring suddenly or by chance; random: *a desultory thought.* [Latin *dēsultōrius* relating to a leaper, fickle, from *dēsultor* leaper; originally referring to a performer in ancient Roman circuses who leaped from horse to horse.] —**des′ul·to′ri·ly,** *adv.* —**des′ul·to′ri·ness,** *n.*

de·tach (di tach′) *v.t.* **1.** to unfasten and separate; disconnect: *to detach three cars from a train, to detach the price tag from a gift.* **2.** to send away on a special mission: *A patrol boat was detached to search the harbor.* [French *détacher* to untie, from *dé-* (going back to Latin *dis-* apart) + *(at)tacher* to fasten. See ATTACH.] —**de·tach′a·bil′i·ty,** *n.* —**de·tach′a·ble,** *adj.* —**de·tach′a·bly,** *adv.*

de·tached (di tacht′) *adj.* **1.** not connected; unattached: *a detached house, a detached retina.* **2.** having or showing a lack of interest or emotional involvement; unconcerned: *a detached observer, a detached view of politics.*

de·tach·ment (di tach′mənt) *n.* **1.** the act of detaching or the state of being detached; separation. **2.** a group of military or naval units, esp. personnel, assigned to special duty: *A detachment of ten sailors remained behind to guard the prisoners.* **3.** the act of assigning or the state of being assigned to special duty. **4.** the act or an instance of standing apart; aloofness: *Your detachment from our mutual problems is resented by others in the group.* **5.** a lack of prejudice or bias; impartiality: *to examine an issue with detachment.*

de·tail (di tāl′, dē′tāl) *n.* **1.** a small or secondary part of a whole; item; particular: *We examined the details of the contract. We know few details of the life of Stone Age people.* **2.** the treatment of matters item by item; attention to particulars: *to have a pedantic fondness for detail.* **3.** a description or report of particulars; minute account: *to go into detail.* **4.** a small or secondary part of a work of art or architecture, as a painting, statue, or building, esp. when represented or considered separately. **5.** *Military.* **a.** a small group of people assigned to a particular service or duty: *A detail of soldiers patrolled the troubled area.* **b.** the act of selecting such a group. **c.** the particular duty assigned to such a group. —*v.t.* **1.** to relate or describe minutely; give particulars of: *He detailed the experiments leading up to the discovery.* **2.** to assign to or send on special duty: *The commander detailed troops to guard the frontiers.* [Old French *detail* piece cut off, from *detailler* to cut in pieces, going back to Latin *dē* thoroughly + *tālea* twig, cutting.]

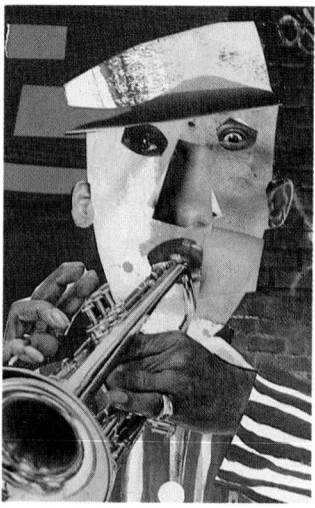

detail from a collage
by Romare Bearden
(see **collage**)

• **in detail.** part by part; minutely: *She described the day's events in detail.*

de·tailed (di tāld′, dē′tāld) *adj.* **1.** having many details: *a detailed description of an accident.* **2.** showing careful attention to detail: *The detective made a detailed examination of the room.*

de·tain (di tān′) *v.t.* **1.** to keep from proceeding; hold back; delay: *I was detained by a flat tire on my way home.* **2.** to keep in custody; confine: *to detain a person accused of a crime.* [Old French *detenir* to hold back, from Latin *dētinēre* to hold off, delay.] —**de·tain′er,** *n.* —**de·tain′ment,** *n.*

de·tect (di tekt′) *v.t.* **1.** to catch or uncover in the act of doing something; expose: *to detect someone stealing, to detect a thief.* **2.** to discover the presence, existence, or fact of: *We detected smoke. Do I detect a French accent in your speech?* **3.a.** demodu-

late. **b.** rectify. [Latin *dētectus,* past participle of *dētegere* to uncover.] —**de·tect′a·bil′i·ty;** *also,* **de·tect′i·bil′i·ty,** *n.* —**de·tect′a·ble;** *also,* **de·tect′i·ble,** *adj.*

de·tec·tion (di tek′shən) *n.* **1.** the act of detecting or the state of being detected; exposure or discovery: *the detection of a crime, the detection of a thief.* **2.a.** demodulation. **b.** rectification.

de·tec·tive (di tek′tiv) *n.* a person, usually a police officer, who makes investigations to obtain evidence and information, esp. for the solution of crime and the arrest of criminals. —*adj.* **1.** relating to detectives and their work: *a detective story.* **2.** used for the purpose of detection: *detective methods.*

de·tec·tor (di tek′tər) *n.* **1.** a person or thing that detects, esp. a device that indicates the presence of something, as smoke, radioactivity, electric current, or metal. **2.a.** demodulator. **b.** rectifier.

de·tent (di tent′) *n.* a mechanism, as a catch or pawl, that controls movement, as in the escapement of a clock. [French *détente* a loosening, easing, from *détendre* to relax, slacken, from *de-* from (going back to Latin *dis-* apart) + Old French *tendre.* See TEND[1].]

dé·tente (dā tänt′, -tänt′) *also,* **de·tente.** *n.* a relaxing or slackening of tension or strained relations, esp. a relaxation of political tension between two countries. [French *détente* a loosening, easing, from *détendre* to relax, slacken, going back to Latin *dis-* apart + *tendere* to stretch.]

de·ten·tion (di ten′shən) *n.* **1.** the act of detaining or keeping from proceeding. **2.** the state of being detained; delay. **3.** the act of keeping in custody; confinement, esp. as a temporary measure preceding trial. [Late Latin *dētentiō* a keeping back, from Latin *dētinēre* to hold off, delay.]

de·ter (di tûr′) *v.t.,* **-terred, -ter·ring.** to keep from acting or proceeding, esp. by arousing fear or doubt: *The huge waves deterred us from going swimming.* [Latin *dēterrēre* to frighten from.] —**de·ter′ment,** *n.*

de·ter·gen·cy (di tûr′jən sē) *n.* the ability to cleanse; cleansing power. [DETERG(ENT) + -ENCY.]

de·ter·gent (di tûr′jənt) *n.* any cleansing agent, esp. one made synthetically and resembling soap in its cleansing action but not in its chemical composition. —*adj.* cleansing; purging. [Latin *dētergēns,* present participle of *dētergēre* to wipe off.]

de·te·ri·o·rate (di tir′ē ə rāt′) *v.,* **-rat·ed, -rat·ing.** —*v.i.* to lessen in quality, character, or value; become worse; depreciate: *The car deteriorated with age.* —*v.t.* to make worse; impair. [Late Latin *dēteriōrātus,* past participle of *dēteriōrāre* to make worse, from Latin *dēterior* worse.] —**de·te′ri·o·ra′tion,** *n.* —**de·ter′i·o·ra′tive,** *adj.*

de·ter·mi·na·ble (di tûr′mə nə bəl) *adj.* **1.** capable of being determined. **2.** *Law.* liable to be terminated. —**de·ter′mi·na·bly,** *adv.*

de·ter·mi·nant (di tûr′mə nənt) *n.* **1.** something that determines; determining factor. **2.** *Mathematics.* a square array of numbers with a numerical value determined by a prescribed set of rules. Determinants are used esp. in solving algebraic problems in which variables having the same value occur simultaneously in two or more equations. —*adj.* determining. —For Synonyms, see **cause.**

de·ter·mi·nate (di tûr′mə nit) *adj.* **1.** having defined limits; fixed; definite: *a determinate quantity.* **2.** conclusive; settled; decided: *a determinate rule.* **3.** *Botany.* (of an inflorescence) having stems all of which end in flower buds, with the central flowers opening first, as in a cyme; cymose. —**de·ter′mi·nate·ly,** *adv.* —**de·ter′mi·nate·ness,** *n.*

de·ter·mi·na·tion (di tûr′mə nā′shən) *n.* **1.** the act of reaching a decision; deciding. **2.** the act of finding out something after consideration, observation, investigation, or calculation: *the determination that an ore bears uranium.* **3.** a decision or conclusion: *What was the judge's determination in the case?* **4.** fixed purpose; resoluteness: *a person of great determination in the face of obstacles.*

de·ter·mi·na·tive (di tûr′mə nā′tiv, -nə tiv) *adj.* serving or tending to determine. —*n.* something that serves or tends to determine. —**de·ter′mi·na·tive·ly,** *adv.* —**de·ter′mi·na′tive·ness,** *n.*

de·ter·mine (di tûr′min) *v.,* **-mined, -min·ing.** —*v.t.* **1.** to reach a definite, authoritative decision about: *The judge determined the sentence.* **2.** to find out after consideration, observation, investigation, or calculation; ascertain: *to determine the species of an animal, to determine the best method of solving a problem.* **3.** to make up one's mind about; decide upon: *The dramatist determined the title of the new play.* **4.** to be the cause or deciding factor of; regulate: *Seniority determines the chairmanship of a Congressional committee.* **5.** to give an aim, purpose, or direction to; direct; impel: *An impoverished boyhood determined him to become financially successful.* **6.** to fix or settle definitely or beforehand: *Genes determine one's hair color.* **7.** to fix or define the precise

position of. **8.** to fix the bounds of; limit: *Our budget will determine how much we can spend on a new car.* **9.** *Law.* to put an end to; conclude; terminate: *to determine an estate.* —*v.i.* **1.** to come to a decision; resolve. **2.** *Law.* to come to an end; cease to exist: *Under the terms of the will, the trust fund determined with the death of the last stated beneficiary.* [Old French *determiner* to conclude, from Latin *dētermināre* to limit, fix, going back to *dē* thoroughly + *terminus* boundary, end.] —For Synonyms, see **decide, fix.**

de·ter·mined (di tûr′mind) *adj.* having or showing determination or fixed purpose; resolute. —**de·ter′mined·ly,** *adv.* —**de·ter′mined·ness,** *n.*

de·ter·min·er (di tûr′mə nər) *n.* **1.** a person or thing that determines. **2.** a word belonging to a class of noun modifiers that includes articles, demonstratives, and possessive adjectives. Determiners always precede the noun they modify, occupying either the first position in a noun phrase or the second position after another determiner. *Our* in the phrase *our house* and *the* in the phrase *the blue car* are determiners.

de·ter·min·ism (di tûr′mə niz′əm) *n.* **1.** the doctrine that all human actions and historical events are fixed beforehand by a succession of causes over which human beings have no control. **2.** the doctrine that all events conform in a regular, orderly fashion to unchangeable laws of the universe. —**de·ter′min·ist,** *n.* —**de·ter′min·is′tic,** *adj.*

de·ter·rence (di tûr′əns, -ter′-) *n.* **1.** an act or means of deterring. **2.** the policy or method of deterring war by accumulating and threatening to use certain weapons against an enemy possessed of similar weapons: *nuclear deterrence.*

de·ter·rent (di tûr′ənt, -ter′-) *adj.* serving to deter; discouraging; restraining. —*n.* a person or thing that deters: *The article argues that capital punishment is a deterrent to crime.* —**de·ter′rent·ly,** *adv.*

de·test (di test′) *v.t.* to dislike intensely; hate; loathe; abominate. [Old French *detester,* from Latin *dētestārī* to curse while calling a god to witness, hate, going back to *dē* thoroughly + *testis* witness.] —**de·test′er,** *n.* —For Synonyms, see **hate.**

de·test·a·ble (di tes′tə bəl) *adj.* deserving to be detested; hateful; abominable. —**de·test′a·ble·ness,** *n.* —**de·test′a·bly,** *adv.*

de·tes·ta·tion (dē′tes tā′shən) *n.* **1.** intense hatred or dislike. **2.** a person or thing that is detested.

de·throne (dē thrōn′) *v.t.,* **-throned, -thron·ing. 1.** to remove from a throne; depose. **2.** to remove from any high position. —**de·throne′ment,** *n.* —**de·thron′er,** *n.*

det·o·nate (det′ə nāt′) *v.t., v.i.,* **-nat·ed, -nat·ing.** to explode or cause to explode suddenly and with a loud noise. [Latin *dētonātus,* past participle of *dētonāre* to thunder down.] —**det′o·na′tion,** *n.*

det·o·na·tor (det′ə nā′tər) *n.* **1.** a device used to detonate explosives. **2.** an explosive.

de·tour (dē′tur, di tur′) *n.* **1.** a road used temporarily when the main road cannot be traveled. **2.** a deviation from a direct course; indirect way. —*v.i., v.t.* to make or cause to make a detour. [French *détour* circuit, from *détourner* to turn away, going back to Latin *dis-* apart + *tornāre* to turn. See TURN.]

de·tox·i·fi·ca·tion (dē tok′sə fi kā′shən) *n.* **1.** medical treatment and counseling to help a person overcome addiction to drugs or alcohol. **2.** any of the processes by which the body changes toxins into less toxic substances.

de·tox·i·fy (dē tok′sə fī′) *v.t.,* **-fied, -fy·ing.** to remove a poison or its toxic effect from. [DE- TOXI(N) + -FY.]

de·tract (di trakt′) *v.i.* to lessen, esp. in value, quality, or reputation (with *from*); diminish: *That scratch detracts from the beauty of the table.* —*v.t.* to take (something) away; divert. [Latin *dētractus,* past participle of *dētrahere* to take away, disparage.] —**de·trac′tor,** *n.*

de·trac·tion (di trak′shən) *n.* **1.** the act of disparaging or belittling the reputation or worth of a person. **2.** a taking away; detracting.

de·trac·tive (di trak′tiv) *adj.* tending to detract; disparaging; belittling. —**de·trac′tive·ly,** *adv.*

de·train (dē trān′) *v.i., v.t.* to get off or take off a railroad train.

det·ri·ment (det′rə mənt) *n.* **1.** damage, injury, or harm: *to be able to pursue several hobbies without detriment to one's work.* **2.** something that causes damage, injury, or harm: *Your lack of political experience is a great detriment to your candidacy.* [Latin *dētrīmentum* damage; literally, a rubbing away.]

a	at	e	end	o	hot	u	up	hw	white		about
ā	ape	ē	me	ō	old	ū	use	ng	song	ə	taken
ä	far	i	it	ô	fork	ū	rule	th	thin		pencil
âr	care	ī	ice	oi	oil	u	pull	th	this		lemon
		îr	pierce	ou	out	ûr	turn	zh	measure		circus

detrimental / devil's advocate

det·ri·men·tal (det′rə men′təl) *adj.* causing damage, injury, or harm; injurious: *Poor eating habits are detrimental to health.* —**det′ri·men′tal·ly,** *adv.*

de·tri·tus (di trī′təs) *n.* **1.** fragments of rock, as gravel or sand, torn away from a larger mass by such forces as erosion or glacial ice. **2.** any accumulation of disintegrated material or debris. [Latin *dētrītus* a rubbing away.] —**de·tri′tal,** *adj.*

de trop (də tRŌ′) *French.* **1.** too much; too many. **2.** in the way; unwelcome.

Deu·ca·li·on and Pyr·rha (dü kā′lē ən) in Greek mythology, the husband and wife who were the only mortals to survive a great flood sent by Zeus and who became the ancestors of the renewed human race.

deuce[1] (düs, dūs) *n.* **1.** a playing card having two symbols of the suit it represents on its center. **2.a.** the face of a die having two spots. **b.** a throw of dice that totals two. **3.** *Tennis.* a tie score of forty points or more each in a game, or five games or more each in a set. **4.** *Informal.* two, esp. in games and sports. [Middle English *dewes, deus* two (in playing cards or throwing dice), from Old French *deus* two, from Latin *duōs,* accusative of *duo* two.]

deuce[2] (düs, dūs) *interj. Informal.* bad luck; the devil. ➡ used as a mild oath or exclamation: *What the deuce was that?* [Probably from Low German *duus* deuce[1], lowest throw in dice, going back to Latin *duo* two.]

deuc·ed (dü′sid, dū′-, düst, dūst) *adj. Informal.* devilish; confounded. —*adv.* devilishly. —**deuc′ed·ly,** *adv.*

de·us ex ma·chi·na (dē′əs eks mak′i nə, dā′əs) **1.** in classical drama, a god brought on stage to resolve difficulties in the plot. **2.** any person or thing that intervenes in an artificial or improbable way to resolve difficulties in a plot. [Latin *deus ex māchinā* literally, a god from a machine; because a god was brought on stage in classical drama by a mechanical contrivance.]

Deut., Deuteronomy.

deu·te·ri·um (dü tîr′ē əm, dū-) *n.* a stable isotope of hydrogen in which the atomic nucleus consists of one neutron and one proton, making the atomic weight about twice that of ordinary hydrogen. Symbols: D or H^2 Also, **heavy hydrogen.** For illustration, see **fusion.** [Modern Latin *deuterium,* from Greek *deuteros* second.]

deu·ter·on (dü′tə ron′, dū′-) *n.* a positively charged particle, the nucleus of a deuterium atom.

Deu·ter·on·o·my (dü′tə ron′ə me, dū′-) *n.* the fifth book of the Old Testament. The Mosaic law, first set forth in Exodus, is restated here. [Late Latin *Deuteronomium,* from Greek *Deuteronomion* literally, second or repeated law, from *deuteros* second + *nomos* law.]

deut·sche mark (doi′chə, doich) *also,* **Deutsche mark.** the monetary unit of Germany.

de·val·u·ate (dē val′ū āt′) *v.t.,* -**at·ed,** -**at·ing.** **1.** to lessen the value of. **2.** to lower the legal value of (a currency). —**de·val′u·a′tion,** *n.*

de·val·ue (dē val′ū) *v.t.,* -**val·ued,** -**val·u·ing.** devaluate.

dev·as·tate (dev′ə stāt′) *v.t.,* -**tat·ed,** -**tat·ing.** **1.** to lay waste; make desolate; ravage; destroy. **2.** to overwhelm, as with surprise; overpower. [Latin *dēvāstātus,* past participle of *dēvāstāre* to lay waste.] —**dev′as·tat′ing·ly,** *adv.* —**dev′as·ta′tor,** *n.*

dev·as·ta·tion (dev′ə stā′shən) *n.* the act of devastating or the state of being devastated; destruction; desolation. —For Synonyms, see **destruction.**

de·vel·op (di vel′əp) *v.t.* **1.** to bring into existence; make for the first time: *The drug company developed a new vaccine.* **2.** to come to have or show signs of: *The tank developed a leak. The child developed an interest in sports at an early age.* **3.** to cause to change or grow gradually: *to develop a character in a novel, to develop a business clientele.* **4.** to bring to a more advanced state; cause to grow, expand, or improve: *Only hard work will develop your skill as an artist. Many people read to develop their minds.* **5.** to put to use: *to develop natural resources.* **6.** to construct houses or other buildings on (land). **7.** to work out in detail; enlarge upon: *to develop an idea.* **8.** to make known; reveal; disclose: *The police investigation developed no new evidence.* **9.** to treat (photographic film or printing paper) with a chemical to make the latent image visible. —*v.i.* **1.** to come into existence; occur: *Renewed fighting developed along the border of the two countries.* **2.** to change or grow gradually; evolve: *The small river town developed into a great city.* **3.** to become known; be revealed: *Several new facts developed after the trial.* [French *développer* to unfold, probably going back to Latin *dis-* apart + blend of Medieval Latin *faluppa* wisp of straw, and Latin *volvere* to roll.] —**de·vel′op·a·ble,** *adj.*

de·vel·op·er (di vel′ə pər) *n.* **1.** a person or thing that develops. **2.** a chemical solution that makes the latent image visible on photographic film. **3.** a person or company that develops land for speculative purposes.

de·vel·op·ing (di vel′ə ping) *adj.* (of a country or geographical region) not yet having achieved a high level of economic or industrial development: *developing nations.*

de·vel·op·ment (di vel′əp mənt) *n.* **1.** the act or process of developing: *The development of this spacecraft took many years.* **2.** the state or condition of having been developed: *to improve one's muscular development.* **3.** an event or happening: *political developments.* **4.** a group of houses or other buildings, often of similar design and construction, usually constructed by one builder.

de·vel·op·men·tal (di vel′əp men′təl) *adj.* characterized by development; evolutionary. —**de·vel′op·men′tal·ly,** *adv.*

de·vi·ant (dē′vē ənt) *n.* a person who deviates, esp. a person whose behavior deviates from what is considered normal by a group or society. —*adj.* deviating from a standard or norm, esp. from accepted norms of social behavior: *deviant conduct, deviant tendencies.*

de·vi·ate (*v.,* dē′vē āt′; *n., adj.,* dē′vē it) *v.,* -**at·ed,** -**at·ing.** —*v.i.* to turn aside (from a course of action, standard, line of thought, or the like); diverge: *to deviate from the truth.* —*v.t.* to cause to turn aside. —*n.* a person who deviates; deviant. —*adj.* that deviates; deviant. [Late Latin *dēviātus,* past participle of *dēviāre* to go aside, from Latin *dē* away + *via* way.] —**de′vi·a′tor,** *n.* —For Synonyms (*v.i.*), see **diverge.**

de·vi·a·tion (dē′vē ā′shən) *n.* **1.** the act or an instance of deviating; divergence: *Getting up at five o'clock is a deviation from my usual routine.* **2.** the amount of divergence. **3.** *Statistics.* the difference between a number in a set and the mean value of the set.

de·vice (di vīs′) *n.* **1.** something made for a particular purpose; invention; mechanism. **2.** a plan or scheme, esp. one that is meant to trick: *By a subtle device, the burglar gained access to the vault.* **3.** an ornamental figure or design. **4.** a picture, design, or other emblem, usually symbolic and often accompanied by a motto, used as a heraldic bearing. **5.** motto; emblem. [Old French *devis, devise* invention, plan, emblem, division, from *deviser* to divide. See DEVISE.]

• **to leave (someone) to his (or her) own devices.** to permit (someone) to do as he or she wishes.

dev·il (dev′əl) *n.* **1.** the devil. also, the Devil. the supernatural figure thought to be the supreme ruler of hell, the spirit and principle of evil, the opponent of God, and the tempter and spiritual enemy of human beings, often represented as a creature having horns, a tail, and cloven feet; Lucifer; Satan. **2.** any subordinate evil spirit; demon. **3.** a wicked, cruel, or ill-natured person. **4.** a person of great cleverness, energy, impudence, or recklessness. **5.** a wretched or pitiful person: *The poor devil hasn't had a decent meal in weeks.* **6.** something difficult or trying: *We are in a devil of a spot.* **7.** something evil or undesirable. —*v.t.,* -**iled,** -**il·ing;** *also, British,* -**illed,** -**il·ling.** **1.** to tease or torment; bedevil. **2.** to prepare (food) by chopping fine and seasoning with hot condiments, as mustard or pepper: *to devil eggs.* —*interj.* **the devil.** used to lend emphasis or express disgust, anger, surprise, or vexation: *What the devil is this?* [Old English *dēofol* the devil, demon, wicked person, from Late Latin *diabolus* the devil, demon, from Greek *diabolos* the devil, slanderer, from *diaballein* to slander.]

• **between the devil and the deep blue sea.** between two equally unpleasant or dangerous alternatives; in a tight spot.

• **like the devil.** with great enthusiasm, vigor, or violence; to an extreme: *We ran like the devil to get help. The wind blew like the devil for two hours.*

• **the devil to pay.** trouble or difficulty ahead: *There will be the devil to pay if we don't finish on time.*

• **to give the devil his due.** to acknowledge someone's ability or success even though he or she is of bad character or is disliked.

• **to go to the devil.** to go to ruin; degenerate morally.

• **to let the devil take the hindmost.** to let the slowest, last, or least able person take care of himself or herself.

• **to raise the devil.** *Informal.* **a.** to cause a disturbance or make a protest. **b.** to have a noisy good time.

dev·il·fish (dev′əl fish′) *n., pl.* -**fish** or -**fish·es.** **1.** manta (*def. 1*). Also, **devil ray. 2.** any of several large cephalopods, esp. the octopus.

dev·il·ish (dev′ə lish, dev′lish) *adj.* **1.** relating to the devil or a devil; malicious; cruel. **2.** full of or showing mischief; mischievous. **3.** *Informal.* **a.** very difficult: *We had a devilish time fixing the car.* **b.** very great; extreme; excessive. —*adv. Informal.* extremely. —**dev′il·ish·ly,** *adv.* —**dev′il·ish·ness,** *n.*

dev·il-may-care (dev′əl mā kâr′) *adj.* carefree or reckless: *a devil-may-care attitude.*

dev·il·ment (dev′əl mənt) *n.* devilish activity; mischief.

dev·il·ry (dev′əl rē) *n., pl.* -**ries.** deviltry.

devil's advocate **1.** a person who supports an opposing cause or position for the sake of argument. **2.** in the Roman Catholic

334

Church, an official appointed to present the argument against a proposed beatification or canonization. [Translation of Medieval Latin *advocatus diaboli.*]

devil's darning needle, dragonfly.

devil's food cake, a rich, dark chocolate cake.

devil's paintbrush, a hawkweed, *Hieracium aurantiacum,* bearing clusters of orange-red flowers, commonly found growing as a weed. [Because the orange-red of its flowers resembles that of fire, with which hell and the devil are associated.]

dev·il·try (dev′əl trē′) *n., pl.* **-tries. 1.** diabolical action; wickedness or cruelty. **2.** mischievous behavior.

de·vi·ous (dē′vē əs) *adj.* **1.** departing from the direct way; winding; roundabout; wandering: *a devious route.* **2.** attempting to deceive; not straightforward, frank, or direct: *a devious explanation.* [Latin *dēvius* out of the way, from *dē* from + *via* way.] —**de′vi·ous·ly,** *adv.* —**de′vi·ous·ness,** *n.*

de·vise (di vīz′) *v.t.,* **-vised, -vis·ing. 1.** to think out; invent; plan; contrive: *to devise a secret code.* **2.** *Law.* to give (real property) by a will. —*n.* **1.** the willing of real property. **2.** a will or clause in a will disposing of real property. **3.** real property given by a will. [Old French *deviser* to divide, regulate, design, talk, going back to Latin *dīvidere* to divide.] —**de·vis′a·ble,** *adj.* —**de·vis′er,** *n.*

> **Synonyms** **Devise, contrive,** and **invent** mean to find a way to do, make, or solve something. **Devise** stresses mental effort and may imply experiment and observation over a period of time: *He devised a new way of teaching computer skills.* **Contrive** connotes ingenuity and cleverness in planning or designing. It may apply to useful or to dishonest ends: *The sailors rushed to contrive a substitute for their broken anchor. The burglar contrived a way to break into the cottage.* **Invent** emphasizes making something new through the exercise of imagination, study, or labor: *to invent a new method of manufacture, to invent a convincing plot for a mystery novel.*

de·vis·ee (di vī zē′, dev′ə zē′) *n. Law.* a person to whom real property is given by a will.

de·vi·sor (di vī′zər) *n. Law.* a person who gives real property by a will.

de·vi·tal·ize (dē vī′tə līz′) *v.t.,* **-ized, -iz·ing.** to deprive of vitality; weaken; exhaust. —**de·vi′tal·i·za′tion,** *n.*

de·void (di void′) *adj.* being entirely without; not possessing; lacking (with *of*): *devoid of reason, devoid of leadership.* [Originally past participle of obsolete *devoid* to empty out, from Old French *desvoidier,* going back to Latin *dis-* apart + *vacāre* to be empty.]

dev·o·lu·tion (dev′ə lü′shən) *n.* **1.** a passing down through successive stages. **2.** the passing from one person to another of a right, title, or property. **3.** the transfer of power, authority, or responsibility, as from one person to another or from a central government to local governmental bodies. **4.** the regression of an organism to a lower or less complex form; retrograde evolution; degeneration. [Medieval Latin *devolutio* passing of property to an heir, from Latin *dēvolvere* to roll down.] —**dev′o·lu′tion·ar′y,** *adj.*

de·volve (di volv′) *v.,* **-volved, -volv·ing.** —*v.t.* to transfer (work or responsibility) to another. —*v.i.* to be passed on; be transferred (with *on, upon,* or *to*): *The kingdom devolved upon the heir apparent.* [Latin *dēvolvere* to roll down.]

Dev·on (dev′ən) *n.* a small, hardy breed of cattle originally raised in Devon, England.

De·vo·ni·an (də vō′nē ən) *n.* the period of the Paleozoic era between the Mississippian and the Silurian periods, characterized by an abundance of fish and the advent of amphibians, insects, and forests. For table, see **geologic time.** —*adj.* **1.** of, relating to, or characteristic of this period. **2.** of or relating to Devon, England.

de·vote (di vōt′) *v.t.,* **-vot·ed, -vot·ing. 1.** to give or apply earnestly, as oneself or one's time, effort, or attention, to some person or purpose: *She devoted all her energies to her family. He devoted himself to study.* **2.** to set apart for a particular use or purpose; dedicate: *This area of the hospital is devoted to surgery.* [Latin *dēvōtus,* past participle of *dēvovēre* to commit by means of a vow.]

de·vot·ed (di vō′tid) *adj.* **1.** ardent; loyal; faithful: *a devoted friend.* **2.** dedicated to some purpose. —**de·vot′ed·ly,** *adv.* —**de·vot′ed·ness,** *n.*

dev·o·tee (dev′ə tē′) *n.* **1.** a person devoted to anything; enthusiast: *a devotee of boating.* **2.** a person ardently devoted to religion; zealot. —For Synonyms, see **enthusiast.**

de·vo·tion (di vō′shən) *n.* **1.** strong attachment to or affection for someone; loyalty; faithfulness. **2.** the act of devoting or the state of being devoted: *We appreciated your devotion of time and*

money *to the project.* **3.** religious piety; devoutness. **4. devotions.** religious worship; prayers.

de·vo·tion·al (di vō′shə nəl) *adj.* relating to religious devotion; used in worship. —**de·vo′tion·al·ly,** *adv.*

de·vour (di vour′) *v.t.* **1.** to eat up greedily or ravenously: *The hikers devoured their lunches.* **2.** to consume, waste, or destroy: *Fire devoured the old building.* **3.** to take in greedily or eagerly with the senses or the mind: *to devour a book.* **4.** to absorb or engross completely: *to be devoured by grief.* **5.** to swallow up; engulf. [Old French *devorer* to tear to pieces, to feed on prey, from Latin *dēvorāre* to gulp down, consume.] —**de·vour′er,** *n.* —**de·vour′ing·ly,** *adv.*

de·vout (di vout′) *adj.* **1.** devoted to worship and prayer; religious; pious: *a devout order of monks.* **2.** expressing devotion or piety: *devout prayer.* **3.** earnest; sincere: *You have my devout wishes for your safety.* [Old French *devot* devoted, from Latin *dēvōtus,* past participle of *dēvovēre* to give up.] —**de·vout′·ly,** *adv.* —**de·vout′ness,** *n.* —For Synonyms, see **pious.**

dew (dü, dū) *n.* **1.** moisture from the air that condenses in small drops upon cool surfaces during the night. **2.** any light moisture in small drops, as tears or perspiration. **3.** anything fresh, pure, or refreshing like dew: *the dew of youth.* —*v.t.* to moisten with or as with dew; bedew. [Old English *dēaw* moisture from the air that condenses upon cool surfaces.]

dew·ber·ry (dü′ber′ē, dū′-) *n., pl.* **-ries. 1.** the sweet, black edible berry of any of several trailing or climbing shrubs, genus *Rubus,* of the rose family, similar to the blackberry. **2.** the shrub bearing this berry.

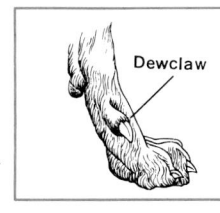

Dewclaw

dew·claw (dü′klô′, dū′-) *n.* **1.** a small, vestigial inner toe on the foot of certain dogs. **2.** the false hoof above the true hoof in deer, cattle, hogs, and other animals. —**dew′clawed′,** *adj.*

dewclaw
on a dog's foot

dew·drop (dü′drop′, dū′-) *n.* a drop of dew.

Dew·ey decimal system (dü′ē, dū′ē) a system used in libraries for classifying books and other publications according to subject matter. It uses the numbers 000 to 999 to designate major categories and decimal numbers to indicate special subdivisions to these fields. [From Melvil *Dewey,* 1851-1931, U.S. librarian who devised this system.]

dew·fall (dü′fôl′, dū′-) *n.* **1.** the formation of dew. **2.** the time of evening when dew begins to form.

dew·lap (dü′lap′, dū′-) *n.* **1.** a loose fold of skin under the throat of cattle and other animals. **2.** any similar part, as the wattle of a turkey or other fowl, or a pendulous fold of flesh on the human throat. —**dew′lapped′,** *adj.*

DEW line (dü, dū) a chain of radar stations across North America above the Arctic Circle, maintained to provide advance warning of the approach of hostile aircraft or missiles. [Short for *d(istant) e(arly) w(arning).*]

Dewlap

dew point, the temperature at which dew forms or vapor condenses into liquid.

dew·y (dü′ē, dū′ē) *adj.,* **dew·i·er, dew·i·est. 1.** moist with dew: *dewy grass, dewy eyes.* **2.** of dew: *dewy mists.* **3.** resembling or suggestive of dew; gentle; ephemeral; refreshing. —**dew′i·ly,** *adv.* —**dew′i·ness,** *n.*

dex·ter (dek′stər) *adj.* **1.** of or on the right-hand side. **2.** *Heraldry.* situated on the right side of an escutcheon or shield, and thus to the left of a viewer facing it. ➡ distinguished from **sinister.** [Latin *dexter* on the right side, skillful.]

dex·ter·i·ty (dek ster′i tē) *n.* **1.** skill in using the hands or body. **2.** mental skill; cleverness: *The diplomat handled the situation with dexterity.*

dex·ter·ous (dek′strəs, -stər əs) *also,* **dextrous.** *adj.* having or

a	at	e	end	o	hot	u	up	hw	white		about
ā	ape	ē	me	ō	old	ū	use	ng	song	ə	taken
ä	far	i	it	ô	fork	u	rule	th	thin		pencil
âr	care	ī	ice	oi	oil	u	pull	th	this		lemon
		îr	pierce	ou	out	ûr	turn	zh	measure		circus

showing physical or mental skill. [DEXTER + -OUS.] —**dex′ter·ous·ly,** *adv.* —**dex′ter·ous·ness,** *n.*

Synonyms **Dexterous** and **deft,** used of physical ability, mean skillful, especially in the use of one's hands. **Dexterous** connotes expertness in moving or using one's hands or body, and often suggests training: *a dexterous carpenter, a dexterous magician.* **Deft** suggests lightness, sureness, and grace in handling or execution, with few wasted movements: *to be deft in handling precision tools.*

dex·tral (dek′strəl) *adj.* **1.** on the right side. **2.** right-handed. ➡ distinguished from **sinistral.** —**dex·tral·i·ty** (dek stral′i tē), *n.* —**dex′tral·ly,** *adv.*

dex·trin (dek′strin) *also,* **dex·trine** (dek′strēn, -strin). *n.* a gummy substance obtained from the partial chemical breakdown of starch, used esp. as an adhesive. [French *dextrine,* from Latin *dexter* on the right side; because it turns the plane of polarization to the right.]

dextro- *combining form* toward the right: *dextrorotatory.*

dex·tro·ro·ta·to·ry (dek′strō rō′tə tôr′ē) *adj.* **1.** turning to the right or in a clockwise direction. **2.** *Physics, Chemistry.* turning the plane of polarization of light to the right, as a chemical solution, lens, or crystal: *dextrorotatory sugar.* Also, **dex·tro·ro·ta·ry** (dek′strō rō′tə rē). [DEXTRO- + ROTATORY.]

dex·trose (dek′strōs) *n.* a colorless, crystalline sugar found in many plants and in blood. Formula: $C_6H_{12}O_6$ Also, **corn sugar, grape sugar.**

dex·trous (dek′strəs) dexterous.

dey (dā) *n., pl.* **deys. 1.** any of various Turkish governors of Algiers from 1710 until the French conquest in 1830. **2.** any of various former rulers of Tunis or Tripoli. [French *dey,* from Turkish *dāī* maternal uncle (title formerly given to elderly people).]

dg *also,* **dg.** decigram; decigrams.

DH *Baseball.* designated hitter.

dhar·ma (dur′mə, där′-) *n.* **1.** in Hinduism and Buddhism, the order or law that underlies all existence and governs all beings and things. **2.** the conduct of a person who lives and acts in accordance with dharma; right living or conduct. [Sanskrit *dharma* custom, law, duty.]

dhole (dōl) *n., pl.* **dholes** or **dhole.** a wild dog, *Cuon alpinus,* native to India and other parts of Asia, that usually hunts in packs, preying on deer, pigs, goats, and other large animals. Length: 3½ feet (1.1 meters), including tail. [Of uncertain origin.]

dhow

dhow (dou) *n.* a lateen-rigged sailing ship used in coastal waters of Arabia and northern and eastern Africa. [Arabic *dāwa.*]

di-[1] *prefix* **1.** twice; double; twofold: *dicotyledon.* **2.** *Chemistry.* containing two atoms, groups, or radicals: *diatomic, disulfide.* [Greek *di-,* from *dis* twice.]

di-[2] form of **dis-**[1] before *b, d, l, m, n, r, s, v,* and sometimes before *g* and *j,* as in *direct, divert.*

di-[3] form of **dia-** before vowels, as in *diorama.*

dia- *prefix* **1.** through; across: *diagonal, dialogue.* **2.** apart; between: *diacritical.* [Greek *dia* through, apart.]

di·a·base (dī′ə bās′) *n.* a dark plutonic rock made up largely of labradorite feldspar and pyroxene. [French *diabase,* from Greek *diabasis* a crossing over, from *dia* through, across + *bainein* to go, come.] —**di′a·ba′sic,** *adj.*

di·a·be·tes (dī′ə bē′tis, -tēz) *n.* **1.** any of various abnormal conditions of the body characterized by an increase in the production of urine. **2.** a disorder of metabolism in which too little insulin is made or used in the body, resulting in excess sugar in the blood, damage to the blood vessels, and, sometimes, death. Also

(def. 2), **diabetes mellitus** (mə lī′təs). [Late Latin *diabētēs,* from Greek *diabētēs,* from *diabainein* to pass through; with reference to the excessive urination characteristic of the disease.]

di·a·bet·ic (dī′ə bet′ik) *adj.* of, relating to, or having diabetes. —*n.* a person having diabetes.

di·a·ble·rie (dē ä′blə rē) *n.* **1.** dealings with the devil; sorcery; witchcraft. **2.** deviltry; mischief. **3.** demonology. [French *diablerie* witchcraft, mischief, from *diable* devil, from Late Latin *diabolus* devil. See DEVIL.]

di·a·bol·i·cal (dī′ə bol′i kəl) *adj.* **1.** befitting the devil; very cruel or wicked; fiendish. **2.** relating to the devil or devils. Also, **di·a·bol′ic,** from *diabolos* devil. See DEVIL.] —**di·a·bol′i·cal·ly,** *adv.* —**di·a·bol′i·cal·ness,** *n.* [Late Latin *diabolicus* devilish, from Greek *diabolikos,* from *diabolos.* See DEVIL.] —**di·a·bol′i·cal·ly,** *adv.* —**di·a·bol′i·cal·ness,** *n.*

di·ab·o·lism (dī ab′ə liz′əm) *n.* **1.** dealings with the devil; sorcery; witchcraft. **2.** devilish action or behavior; deviltry. **3.** a belief in or worship of the devil or devils. **4.** the character or nature of a devil. —**di·ab′o·list,** *n.*

di·ac·o·nal (dī ak′ə nəl) *adj.* of or relating to a deacon. [Late Latin *diācōnālis,* from Latin *diācōnus* deacon. See DEACON.]

di·ac·o·nate (dī ak′ə nit, -nāt′) *n.* **1.** the rank or office of a deacon. **2.** a group of deacons.

di·a·crit·ic (dī′ə krit′ik) *n.* diacritical mark. —*adj.* diacritical. [Greek *diakritikos* able to distinguish, separative, from *diakrinein* to distinguish.]

di·a·crit·i·cal (dī′ə krit′i kəl) *adj.* **1.** serving to distinguish, as the sounds and values of letters. **2.** capable of distinguishing. —**di′a·crit′i·cal·ly,** *adv.*

diacritical mark, a mark or sign (as ¨, ^, ¯, ′, or ‚) placed over, under, or across a letter to indicate pronunciation or as part of the spelling.

Diacritical Marks			

Diacritical marks are used to supplement the alphabets of many languages or to indicate certain pronunciations. In English, diacritical marks are used primarily in dictionaries to show how to pronounce words and in the spelling of some words borrowed from other languages. Shown below are some of the more frequently encountered diacritical marks and how they are used.

NAME	SYMBOL	EXAMPLE	PURPOSE
acute	′	cliché (klē shā′)	Indicates the sound $\bar{a}$ or a syllable to be stressed.
cedilla	‚	façade (fe säd′)	Indicates the sound *s* preceding the vowels *a, o, u.*
circumflex	^	rôle (rōl)	Indicates the long $\bar{o}$ sound in words borrowed from French.
dieresis	¨	naïve (nä ēv′)	Indicates that a vowel is pronounced in a separate syllable.
grave	`	crèche (kresh)	Indicates the sound *e,* as in *bed.*
tilde	~	mañana (mä nyä′nä)	Indicates the sound *ny* in words borrowed from Spanish.

di·a·dem (dī′ə dem′) *n.* **1.** crown. **2.** a cloth headband, often set with jewels and precious metals, formerly worn as a crown by Oriental rulers. **3.** royal power, authority, or dignity. [Latin *diadēma* royal headdress, from Greek *diadēma* band, fillet, royal headdress, from *dia* around; literally, apart + *dein* to bind.]

di·aer·e·sis (dī er′ə sis) *n., pl.* **-ses** (-sēz′). dieresis.

di·ag·nose (dī′əg nōs′, -nōz′) *v.,* **-nosed, -nos·ing.** —*v.t.* to make a diagnosis of. —*v.i.* to make a diagnosis.

di·ag·no·sis (dī′əg nō′sis) *n., pl.* **-ses** (-sēz). **1.a.** the act or process of determining the nature of a disease or other harmful condition by careful examination and study of symptoms: *a thorough diagnosis of a patient's ailment.* **b.** a conclusion reached by such examination: *The doctor's diagnosis was that the child had measles.* **2.a.** an investigation and study of facts to determine the essential characteristics of something: *to make a complete diagnosis of a housing problem.* **b.** a conclusion reached by such investigation: *The diagnosis was that additional dwellings were urgently*

needed. **3.** *Biology.* a short technical description used in the taxonomic classification of an organism. [Modern Latin *diagnosis* from Greek *diagnōsis* a distinguishing.]

di·ag·nos·tic (dī′əg nos′tik) *adj.* relating to, helpful in, or used in diagnosis: *diagnostic procedures, diagnostic equipment.* —*n.* a computer program that tests hardware or software and alerts the user to any problems. —**di′ag·nos′ti·cal·ly,** *adv.*

di·ag·nos·ti·cian (dī′əg nos tish′ən) *n.* a person who makes diagnoses, esp. a specialist in medical diagnoses.

di·ag·o·nal (dī ag′ə nəl) *adj.* **1.** *Geometry.* **a.** connecting, as a straight line, two nonadjacent angles of a figure. **b.** connecting, as a plane, two nonadjacent edges of a solid figure. **2.** having an oblique direction; slanting: *The material has diagonal stripes.* **3.** having oblique lines, markings, or parts: *diagonal hatching, diagonal cloth.* —*n.* **1.** a diagonal straight line or plane. **2.** anything extending diagonally. **3.** fabric woven with diagonal lines. [Latin *diagōnālis* from one angle to another nonadjacent angle of a figure, from Greek *diagonios,* from *dia* through, across + *gōnia* angle[1], corner.] —**di·ag′o·nal·ly,** *adv.*

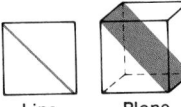

diagonals

di·a·gram (dī′ə gram′) *n.* **1.** a set of lines or a figure, plan, or sketch giving the outline or general scheme of something or showing the results of an action or process: *a diagram of a grasshopper's anatomy, a diagram of troop movements during a battle.* —*v.t.,* **-gramed** or **-grammed, -gram·ing** or **-gram·ming.** to represent by a diagram; make a diagram of. [Latin *diagramma* scale[3], gamut, from Greek *diagramma* figure marked out by lines, scale[3], list.] —For Synonyms *(n.),* see **map.**

di·a·gram·mat·ic (dī′ə grə mat′ik) *adj.* **1.** in the form of a diagram. **2.** in outline; sketchy. Also, **di′a·gram·mat′i·cal.** —**di′a·gram·mat′i·cal·ly,** *adv.*

dial (dī′əl, dīl) *n.* **1.** a graduated surface on which a measurement of something, as time, speed, or pressure, is indicated by a moving pointer or index. **2.** a movable disk, plate, or knob used to select or control an operation on a machine, as in tuning in to a radio station or television channel. **3.** a rotating disk or array of push buttons on a telephone, used to signal the number being called. **4.** sundial. —*v.,* **-aled, -al·ing;** *also, British,* **-alled, -al·ling.** —*v.t.* **1.** to tune in (a radio or television station or program). **2.** to call by means of a telephone dial: *to dial a wrong number.* **3.** to indicate or select by means of a dial: *to dial the combination of a safe.* —*v.i.* to operate or use a dial, as in telephoning. [Medieval Latin *dialis* relating to a day, daily, from Latin *diēs* day.]

dial. **1.** dialect. **2.** dialectal.

di·a·lect (dī′ə lekt′) *n.* **1.** a form of a language spoken in a particular area and differing from the standard form of the language in some of its grammar, pronunciation, vocabulary, and idioms: *the Scottish dialect of English, the Sicilian dialect of Italian.* **2.** one of a group of languages belonging to a family of languages: *French, Italian, Spanish, Portuguese, and Romanian are Romance dialects.* **3.** a vocabulary used by a particular group, as a profession or social class; jargon. **4.** a manner of expressing oneself; idiom. [Latin *dialectus* way of speaking, from Greek *dialektos* speech, language of a region.]

di·a·lec·tal (dī′ə lek′təl) *adj.* relating to or characteristic of dialect or a dialect. —**di′a·lec′tal·ly,** *adv.*

di·a·lec·tic (dī′ə lek′tik) *n.* **1.** *also,* **dialectics.** a method of arriving at conclusions by reasoning from commonly held but contradictory opinions. It is in the form of a dialogue. **2.** logical argumentation. **3.** a method of reasoning used by Georg Hegel and later by Karl Marx, based on a progression of thought through the clash of one idea (thesis) with its opposite (antithesis), which leads to the resolution of these ideas in a conclusion (synthesis). —*adj.* **1.** relating to or practicing dialectic: *dialectic method.* **2.** dialectal. [Latin *dialectica (ars)* logic, from Greek *dialektikē (technē)* (art) of discussion by question and answer.]

di·a·lec·ti·cal (dī′ə lek′ti kəl) *adj.* dialectic.

dialectical materialism, a philosophy formulated by Karl Marx and Friedrich Engels from Georg Hegel's dialectic, which views historical change as the result of conflict between economic groups.

di·a·lec·ti·cian (dī′ə lek tish′ən) *n.* **1.** a person who is skilled in dialectic; logician. **2.** a person who studies dialectics.

di·a·lec·tol·o·gy (dī′ə lek tol′ə jē) *n.* the study of dialects. —**di′a·lec·tol′o·gist,** *n.*

di·a·logue (dī′ə lôg′, -log′) *also,* **di·a·log.** *n.* **1.** a conversation between two or more persons. **2.** a literary work in the form of a conversation between two or more persons. **3.** conversation in a literary work or dramatic presentation: *a play with witty dialogue, a dialogue in the third act.* **4.** an exchange of ideas; discussion. —*v.t.,* **-logued, -logu·ing.** to express in the form of a dialogue. [Old French *dialoge* conversation between two people, from Latin *dialogus* conversation, from Greek *dialogos.*]

dial tone, a steady humming sound in a telephone, indicating to the user that a number may be dialed.

di·al·y·sis (dī al′ə sis) *n., pl.* **-ses** (-sēz′). **1.** a method of separating colloidal particles from the liquid of a crystalloid solution by using a semipermeable membrane through which the liquid, but not the particles, will diffuse. **2.** this method as used in medicine, employing a device that purifies the blood of patients whose kidneys have ceased functioning. [Latin *dialysis* from Greek *dialysis* separation, from *dialyein* to separate, from *dia-* apart + *lyein* to loosen.]

di·a·lyt·ic (dī′ə lit′ik) *adj.* relating to or characterized by dialysis.

di·a·lyze (dī′ə līz′) *v.t.,* **-lyzed, -lyz·ing.** to subject to dialysis.

diam., diameter.

di·a·mag·net·ism (dī′ə mag′ni tiz′əm) *n.* the property of some substances that causes them to be repelled by both poles of a magnet, a characteristic of superconductors. —**di′a·mag·net′ic** (dī′ə mag net′ik), *adj.* —**di′a·mag·net′i·cal·ly,** *adv.*

di·am·e·ter (dī am′i tər) *n.* **1.** a straight line passing through the center of a circle or sphere and bounded by the circumference or surface. **2.** the length of such a line; width or thickness of something: *the diameter of a pipe.* [Old French *diametre* diameter of a circle, from Latin *diametros,* from Greek *diametros* a diagonal, diameter of a circle, from *dia* through + *metron* measure.]

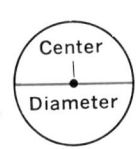

diameter

di·a·met·ri·cal (dī′ə met′ri kəl) *adj.* **1.** of or along a diameter: *The surveyor took a diametrical measurement of the tree.* **2.** directly opposite; completely contrary: *The two candidates have diametrical views on that issue.* Also, **di′a·met′ric.**

di·a·met·ri·cal·ly (dī′ə met′ri klē) *adv.* **1.** along a diameter; straight through: *The sphere was cut diametrically.* **2.** directly; completely: *While they were diametrically opposed on most issues, occasionally they could agree.*

di·a·mond (dī′mənd, dī′ə-) *n.* **1.** a mineral consisting of crystallized carbon, the hardest natural substance known. Transparent, nearly colorless forms have a very high index of refraction, which accounts for their exceptional brilliance when cut and polished as gems; opaque, imperfect forms are used for industrial purposes, as grinding and cutting. For illustration, see **semiprecious. 2.** a piece cut from this mineral, esp. when cut and polished for use as a gem. **3.** *Geometry.* a plane figure with four equal sides, forming two acute and two obtuse angles; rhombus; lozenge. **4.a.** a playing card with red diamondlike designs on it. **b. diamonds.** the suit of such cards. **5.** *Baseball.* **a.** infield. **b.** the entire field. —*adj.* **1.** resembling, made of, or set with a diamond or diamonds. **2.** of or being the sixtieth or seventy-fifth anniversary of an event: *a diamond wedding anniversary.* [Old French *diamant* the gem, lodestone, from Medieval Latin *diamas* the gem, adamant, modification of Latin *adamas,* from Greek *adamās.* See ADAMANT.]

·**diamond in the rough.** a person who has good qualities but lacks polish.

dia·mond·back (dī′mənd bak′, dī′ə-) *n.* **1.** a large rattlesnake, *Crotalus adamanteus,* having diamond-shaped markings on its back, found in the southeastern United States. Length: to 8 feet (2.4 meters). **2.** an edible freshwater turtle, *Malaclemys terrapin,* with diamond-shaped markings on its shell, found in Atlantic coastal waters from Massachusetts to northern Mexico. Length: 6-8 inches (15-20 centimeters). Also *(def. 2),* **diamondback terrapin.**

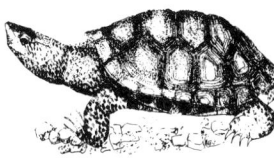

diamondback *(def. 2)*

Di·an·a (dī an′ə) *n.* in Roman mythology, the goddess of the moon, the woods, and the hunt, also worshiped as the protector of women. Her Greek counterpart is Artemis.

a	at	e	end	o	hot	u	up	hw	white		about
ā	ape	ē	end	ō	old	ū	use	ng	song		taken
ä	far	i	it	ô	fork	ü	rule	th	thin	ə	pencil
âr	care	ī	ice	oi	oil	u̇	pull	th	this		lemon
		îr	pierce	ou	out	ûr	turn	zh	measure		circus

di·a·pa·son (dī′ə pā′zən, -sən) *n.* **1.** either of two principal stops in a pipe organ that extend through the entire range of the organ. **Open diapason** gives full, majestic tones; **stopped diapason** gives flutelike tones. **2.** the entire range of a voice or instrument. **3.** a fixed standard of musical pitch. **4.** a tuning fork. **5.** a full, deep outpouring of harmonious sound. [Latin *diapāsōn* octave, from Greek *dia pāsōn (chordōn symphōniā)* (concord) through all (notes of the scale), octave.]

di·a·pause (dī′ə pôz′) *n.* a dormant period that interrupts development or slows activity in a living thing. [Greek *diapausis* pause, from *diapauein* to bring to an end, pause, from *dia* through, across + *pausis* a stopping.]

dia·per (dī′pər, dī′ə-) *n.* **1.** a baby's undergarment consisting of a soft, absorbent material, drawn up between the legs and fastened at the waist. **2.** a pattern made up of small, constantly repeated geometric figures. **3.** a white cotton or linen cloth woven with such a pattern. —*v.t.* **1.** to put a clean diaper on (a baby). **2.** to decorate with an overall, repeated pattern. [Old French *dia(s)pre* fine cloth, from Medieval Latin *diasprus* made of diaper cloth, from Middle Greek *diaspros* pure white.]

di·aph·a·nous (dī af′ə nəs) *adj.* sheer enough to be seen through or to let light through; translucent or transparent. [Greek *diaphanēs* transparent.] —**di·aph′a·nous·ly,** *adv.* —**di·aph′a·nous·ness,** *n.*

di·a·pho·re·sis (dī′ə fə rē′sis) *n.* profuse perspiration, especially when artificially induced. [Late Latin *diaphorēsis* a sweat, from Greek *diaphorēsis* perspiration.]

di·a·phragm (dī′ə fram′) *n.* **1.** a membrane of muscle and connective tissue between the chest cavity and the abdominal cavity, used in inhaling and exhaling. **2.** any membrane or partition that serves to separate. **3.** a disk used in the conversion of sound to electrical impulses or the reverse, as in a telephone or microphone. **4.** an adjustable mechanism for controlling the amount of light admitted through the lens of a camera, microscope, or similar optical equipment. **5.** a rubber contraceptive device worn over the cervix of the uterus during sexual intercourse. [Late Latin *diaphragma* midriff, from Greek *diaphragma* partition, midriff.]

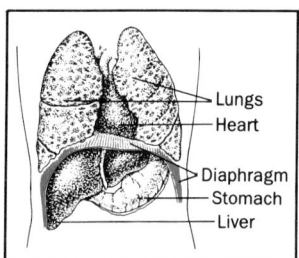

diaphragm *(def. 1)*

Labels: Lungs, Heart, Diaphragm, Stomach, Liver

di·a·phrag·mat·ic (dī′ə frag mat′ik) *adj.* relating to or like a diaphragm.

di·a·rist (dī′ə rist) *n.* a person who keeps a diary.

di·ar·rhe·a (dī′ə rē′ə) *also,* **di·ar·rhoe·a.** *n.* frequent and loose bowel movements caused by irritation or inflammation of the mucous membrane lining of the intestine. [Late Latin *diarrhoea,* from Greek *diarrhoia* literally, a flowing through.] —**di·ar·rhe′al, di′ar·rhe′ic,** *adj.*

di·a·ry (dī′ə rē) *n., pl.* -ries. **1.** a daily record of events, esp. of the writer's personal experiences and observations. **2.** a book for keeping such a record. [Latin *diārium* daily allowance, daily record, from *diēs* day.]

Di·as·po·ra (dī as′pər ə) *n.* **1.** the dispersion of the Jews among communities outside Palestine after their captivity in Babylon and after the capture of Jerusalem by the Romans in A.D. 70. **2.** all the Jews thus dispersed. **3.** *also,* **diaspora.** the scattering of any group of people outside their ancestral homeland. [Greek *diasporā* a scattering.]

di·a·stase (dī′ə stās′) *n.* amylase. —**di·a·stat·ic** (dī′ə stat′ik), *adj.* [French *diastase* enzyme, from Greek *diastasis* separation.]

di·as·to·le (dī as′tə lē′) *n.* the period of normal dilation or relaxation of the heart, alternating rhythmically with the period of contraction, or systole. [Greek *diastolē* dilation.]

di·a·stol·ic (dī′ə stol′ik) *adj.* relating to, involving, or taken during the diastole: *diastolic blood pressure.*

di·as·tro·phism (dī as′trə fiz′əm) *n. Geology.* the process that operates to reshape the earth's surface, raising mountains and plateaus and opening ocean basins, driven by forces that compress, stretch, or lift up the rocks of the earth's crust. [Greek *diastrophē* distortion, from *diastrephein* to turn, twist around, from *dia* aside + *strephein* to turn) + -ISM.] —**di·a·stroph·ic** (dī′ə strof′ik), *adj.*

di·a·ther·my (dī′ə thûr′mē) *n.* a method of treating muscular disorders and injuries by heating body tissues with high-frequency electric currents. [DIA- + Greek *thermē* heat.] —**di′a·ther′mic,** *adj.*

di·a·tom (dī′ə tom′) *n.* any of a large group of microscopic, one-celled, aquatic algae that have bivalve walls composed mostly of silica and are a source of food for most marine life. [Modern Latin *Diatoma,* from Greek *diatomos* cut in half.]

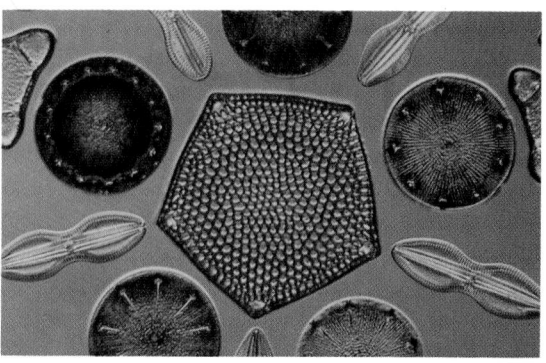

diatoms

di·a·to·ma·ceous (dī′ə tə mā′shəs) *adj.* relating to, consisting of, or containing diatoms or their fossil remains.

di·a·tom·ic (dī′ə tom′ik) *adj.* having two atoms in each molecule.

di·at·o·mite (dī at′ə mīt′) *n.* a light, soft, siliceous sedimentary rock consisting of fossilized diatoms, pulverized and used as an abrasive and organic insecticide, for filtration, and in polishes and insulation. Also, **diatomaceous earth.** [DIATOM + -ITE[1].]

di·a·ton·ic (dī′ə ton′ik) *adj. Music.* of or relating to a diatonic scale. ➡ distinguished from **chromatic.** [Late Latin *diatonicus,* from Greek *diatonikos,* going back to *dia* through + *tonos* tone.] —**di·a·ton′i·cal·ly,** *adv.*

diatonic scale, an eight-toned major or minor musical scale containing two half steps and five whole steps. ➡ distinguished from **chromatic scale.**

di·a·tribe (dī′ə trīb′) *n.* a bitter and violent criticism; invective. [Latin *diatriba* learned discussion, from Greek *diatribē* discussion; literally, a wearing away, as of time.]

di·az·e·pam (dī az′ə pam′) *n.* a drug used as a tranquilizer and muscle relaxant. Formula: $C_{16}H_{13}ClN_2O$ Trademark: **Valium.**

di·ba·sic (dī bā′sik) *adj.* **1.** (of an acid) containing two hydrogen atoms replaceable by two atoms or radicals of a base forming salts. **2.** containing two univalent atoms or radicals.

dib·ble (dib′əl) *n.* a pointed hand tool used to make holes in the ground for planting seeds, flower bulbs, or young plants. [Of uncertain origin.]

dib·buk (dib′ək) *n., pl.* **dib·buks** or **dib·buk·im** (di bü′kim). dybbuk.

dibs (dibz) *Informal. n.* a claim or rights: *Does anyone have dibs on that last muffin?* —*interj.* an exclamation asserting such a claim: *Dibs on the pie!* [Plural of **dib,** shortened for *dibstone* a jack used in a children's game, from *dib* (of unknown origin) + STONE.]

dice (dīs) *pl. n., sing.* **die. 1.** small cubes of wood, plastic, or other material, marked on each side with a different number of spots, the number varying from one to six, used in games of chance. **2.** a gambling game played with dice. —*v.,* **diced, dic·ing.** —*v.t.* **1.** to cut into small cubes: *to dice potatoes.* **2.** to decorate with a pattern of squares; checker. **3.** to lose by gambling with dice. —*v.i.* **1.** to play at dice. —**dic′er,** *n.*

•**no dice.** *Informal.* **a.** no. ➡ used in refusing a request. **b.** of no use: *The writer tried to get the book published, but it was no dice.*

dic·ey (dī′sē) *adj.,* **dic·i·er, dic·i·est.** *Informal.* involving risk or uncertainty; chancy: *An emergency landing of an airplane is always a dicey situation.*

di·chlo·ride (dī klôr′īd, -id) *n.* a chloride containing two atoms of chlorine. Also, **bichloride.**

di·chot·o·mize (dī kot′ə mīz′) *v.,* -mized, -miz·ing. —*v.t.* to divide into two parts. —*v.i.* to be divided into two parts. —**di·chot′o·mist,** *n.* —**di·chot′o·mi·za′tion,** *n.*

di·chot·o·mous (dī kot′ə məs) *adj.* **1.** divided or dividing into two parts or branches. **2.** relating to or involving dichotomy. —**di·chot′o·mous·ly,** *adv.*

di·chot·o·my (dī kot′ə mē) *n., pl.* -mies. **1.** a division into two

parts or classes, esp. ones that are very different from or opposed to one another. **2.** *Botany.* a branching by repeated divisions into two parts; bifurcation. [Greek *dichotomiā* a cutting in two.]

di·chro·ic (dī krō'ik) *adj.* **1.** exhibiting the property of dichroism. **2.** dichromatic. [Greek *dichroos* of two colors, from *di-* two + *chrōs* color, skin, complexion.]

di·chro·ism (dī'krō iz'əm) *n. Optics, Mineralogy.* the property that certain substances display of selectively absorbing light of different colors or light waves vibrating in certain planes, so that a mineral crystal may appear one color when viewed from one direction and another color when viewed from another.

di·chro·mate (dī krō'māt) *n.* a chromate containing two atoms of chromium. Also, **bichromate.**

di·chro·mat·ic (dī'krō mat'ik) *adj.* **1.** having or showing two colors. **2.** *Zoology.* exhibiting two color phases independent of those correlated with age, sex, or season, as certain species of insects, birds, and fish. —**di·chro·ma·tism** (dī krō'mə tiz'əm), *n.*

dick·cis·sel (dik sis'əl) *n.* a small finch, *Spiza americana,* found in the central United States, the male of which has a light brown body and a yellow breast with a black patch below the throat. Length: 6-7 inches (15-18 centimeters). [Imitative of its cry.]

dick·ens (dik'inz) *interj.* the devil; deuce. ➡ used as a mild oath or exclamation: *Where the dickens is my coat?*

Dick·en·si·an (di ken'zē ən) *adj.* of, relating to, or suggestive of the English novelist Charles Dickens or his writings.

dick·er (dik'ər) *v.i.* to trade by bargaining or haggling in a petty way: *to dicker over the price of a used car.* —*n.* petty bargaining or haggling. **2.** a petty bargain. [Possibly from earlier *dicker* set of ten pelts, going back to Latin *decuria* a set of ten, from *decem* ten; from the haggling of fur traders over hides or pelts.]

dick·ey (dik'ē) *n., pl.* -**eys.** *also,* **dicky. 1.** a turtleneck or other collar designed to fill in the neckline of a sweater, shirt, or dress. **2.** a false shirt front worn under a jacket. **3.** a child's bib or pinafore. **4.** a removable shirt collar. **5.** any small bird. Also, **dickey bird. 6.** a donkey. [From *Dick,* nickname for *Richard.*]

Dick test (dik) a test to determine whether a person is susceptible or immune to scarlet fever, made by injecting scarlet fever toxin into the skin. [From George F. *Dick,* 1881-1967, U.S. physician who devised it.]

dick·y (dik'ē) *n., pl.* **dick·ies.** dickey.

di·cli·nous (dī klī'nəs) *adj.* **1.** (of plants) having the stamens and pistils on separate flowers. **2.** (of flowers) unisexual. [DI-¹ + Greek *klīnē* bed + -OUS.]

di·cot·y·le·don (dī kot'ə lē'dən) *n.* a plant that has two cotyledons in the embryo. Dicotyledons constitute one of the two classes, Dicotyledones and Monocotyledones, of flowering plants. ➡ distinguished from **monocotyledon.** Also, **di·cot** (dī'kot). —**di·cot'y·le'don·ous,** *adj.*

dict. 1. dictator. **2.** dictionary.

dic·ta (dik'tə) a plural of **dictum.**

Dic·ta·phone (dik'tə fōn') *n. Trademark.* an instrument to record and reproduce speech, used esp. for the recording or dictating of business correspondence or the like. [Latin *dictāre* to dictate + Greek *phōnē* sound, voice.]

dic·tate (*v.,* dik'tāt, dik tāt'; *n.,* dik'tāt) *v.,* -**tat·ed,** -**tat·ing.** —*v.t.* **1.** to say or read aloud (something) to be recorded: *to dictate a letter to a secretary.* **2.** to order or give as a command forcefully with or as with authority: *The victorious nation dictated the conditions of peace.* —*v.i.* **1.** to say or read aloud something to be recorded: *The teacher dictated in French to the class.* **2.** to give orders; exercise authority. —*n.* **1.** an authoritative command: *the dictates of the law.* **2.** a guiding rule or principle: *the dictates of taste.* [Latin *dictātus,* past participle of *dictāre* to say often, dictate (for writing).]

dic·ta·tion (dik tā'shən) *n.* **1.** the act of dictating something to be recorded: *We listened carefully to the teacher's dictation.* **2.** something dictated or recorded: *Part of the French exam was a dictation.* **3.** the act of giving authoritative orders.

dic·ta·tor (dik'tā tər, dik tā'-) *n.* **1.** a ruler who exercises absolute authority, esp. one considered an oppressor or tyrant. **2.** a person who gives directions or rules authoritatively or by example; arbiter: *a dictator of fashion.* **3.** in ancient Rome, an absolute ruler appointed to serve temporarily in time of emergency. **4.** a person who dictates something to be recorded.

dic·ta·to·ri·al (dik'tə tôr'ē əl) *adj.* **1.** relating to or characteristic of a dictator: *dictatorial powers.* **2.** tending to give orders or be tyrannical; overbearing; dogmatic: *a dictatorial individual.* —**dic'ta·to'ri·al·ly,** *adv.*

dic·ta·tor·ship (dik tā'tər ship', dik'tā-) *n.* **1.** the office or tenure of a dictator. **2.** a state or government ruled by a dictator.

3. a form of government in which absolute authority is held by a dictator. **4.** any prescriptive authority: *literary dictatorship.*

dic·tion (dik'shən) *n.* **1.** the way in which ideas are expressed in words; choice and arrangement of words in speaking or writing: *The diction of poetry is often different from the language of common speech.* **2.** way of saying or pronouncing words; enunciation: *The actor has clear diction.* [Latin *dictiō* a saying, speech, going back to *dicere* to say.]

dic·tion·ar·y (dik'shə ner'ē) *n., pl.* -**ar·ies. 1.** a book containing words of a language arranged in an alphabetical listing, together with definitions, pronunciations, etymologies, and other information about their uses, forms, and functions. **2.** a book containing words of one language listed alphabetically, with their equivalent meanings in another language: *an Italian-English dictionary.* **3.** a book containing and defining words used in a special area of interest or knowledge, usually listed alphabetically: *a sports dictionary, a dictionary of cooking terms.* **4.** a book or series of books containing articles, arranged by title in alphabetical order, on a particular subject or group of related subjects: *The student consulted volume three of the "Dictionary of American History."* [Medieval Latin *dictionarium* literally, book of sayings or words, from Latin *dictiō* a saying.]

dic·tum (dik'təm) *n., pl.* -**ta** (-tə) or -**tums. 1.** a formal authoritative statement or opinion: *the dictum of a monarch.* **2.** obiter dictum. **3.** a popular saying; maxim: *My favorite dictum is "A penny saved is a penny earned."* [Latin *dictum* saying, something said, from *dicere* to say.]

did (did) a past tense of **do**¹.

di·dac·tic (dī dak'tik) *adj.* **1.** intended to instruct; informative: *a didactic treatise, a didactic lecture.* **2.** morally instructive: *Parables are didactic tales.* **3.** too inclined to instruct or moralize; pedantic: *a didactic writer.* Also, **di·dac'ti·cal.** [Greek *didaktikos* skilled in teaching, from *didaskein* to teach.] —**di·dac'ti·cal·ly,** *adv.* —**di·dac·ti·cism** (dī dak'tə siz'əm), *n.*

di·dac·tics (dī dak'tiks) *n.* the science or art of teaching.

did·dle (did'əl) *v.,* -**dled,** -**dling.** —*v.t. Informal.* **1.** to cheat; swindle. **2.** to spend (time) wastefully (usually with *away*): *We diddled away the day.* —*v.i.* **1.** to waste time (usually with *around*): *We diddled around all afternoon.* **2.** to tamper (usually with *with*): *Don't diddle with the radio.* [Possibly from Jeremy *Diddler,* a character who swindles in *Raising the Wind,* by James Kenney, 1780-1849, British playwright.]

did·n't (did'ənt) *contr.* did not.

di·do (dī'dō) *n., pl.* -**dos** or -**does.** *Informal.* a prank; antic. [Of uncertain origin.]

Di·do (dī'dō) *n.* in Roman legend, the founder and queen of Carthage. In the *Aeneid,* she falls in love with Aeneas and kills herself when he leaves Carthage.

didst (didst) *Archaic.* a second person singular past tense of **do**¹: *Thou didst.*

di·dym·i·um (dī dim'ē əm) *n.* a mixture of two rare-earth elements, neodymium and praseodymium, formerly thought to be an element.

die¹ (dī) *v.i.,* **died, dy·ing. 1.** to cease to live; suffer death; become dead: *Many civilians died in World War II.* **2.** to pass out of existence; come to an end: *The pony express died with the coming of the telegraph.* **3.** to lose force, strength, or active qualities; cease to flourish: *The wind suddenly died as the sailboat neared shore.* **4.** to stop functioning: *The engine died.* **5.** to end, pass, or fade away gradually: *The smile died on the listener's lips. The music died in the distance.* **6.** to suffer unbearably, as if dying: *We were dying of boredom in the isolated cabin.* **7.** *Informal.* to want very much; desire strongly: *I am dying for a hamburger. I am dying to see her again.* [Old Norse *deyja* to cease to live.]

•**to die away.** to decrease or end gradually: *The music of the marching band died away.*

•**to die down.** to come to an end or subside, usually gradually: *The talking in the theater died down as the curtain rose.*

•**to die hard.** to struggle against extinction; refuse to yield.

•**to die off.** to die one by one until all are gone: *The small herd died off during the drought.*

•**to die out. a.** to end gradually: *The fire died out during the night.* **b.** to pass out of existence: *The dinosaurs died out long before human beings appeared.*

a	at	e	end	o	hot	u	up	hw	white	(	about
ā	ape	ē	me	ō	old	ū	use	ng	song	{	taken
ä	far	i	it	ô	fork	ü	pull	th	thin	ə	pencil
âr	care	ī	ice	oi	oil	u̇	pull	th	this		lemon
		ir	pierce	ou	out	ûr	turn	zh	measure	(	circus

339

die² (dī) *n., pl. (def. 1)* **dice** or *(def. 2)* **dies. 1.** a small cube, usually one of a pair, marked with a different number of spots on each side, used in games of chance. **2.** any of various machines or devices with an attached cutter, plate, or stamp, used to impress, finish, trim, or give a particular shape to an object. [Middle English *de* one of a pair of dice, from Old French *de*, from Latin *datum* something given (as by chance), from *datum*, past participle of *dare* to give.]

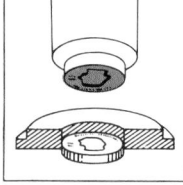

die² *(def. 2)*

• **the die is cast.** the decision is made and cannot be changed; the course of action has been decided.

dief·fen·bach·i·a (dē′fən bak′ē ə, -bä′kē ə) *n.* any of various tropical American plants, genus *Dieffenbachia,* having large, oblong leaves that are usually variegated, widely grown as houseplants.

die·hard (dī′härd′) *also,* **die·hard.** *adj.* resisting vigorously or obstinately to the very end: *a die-hard liberal.* —*n.* a person who refuses to change or modify his or her views.

diel·drin (dēl′drin) *n.* a long-lasting, highly toxic insecticide, made illegal for agricultural use. Formula: $C_{12}H_8OCl_6$.

di·e·lec·tric (dī′i lek′trik) *n.* a substance that does not conduct electricity. —*adj.* nonconducting.

di·en·ceph·a·lon (dī′en sef′ə lon′) *n.* the rear part of the vertebrate forebrain, located behind the cerebral hemispheres and including the thalamus and hypothalamus. [Modern Latin *diencephalon.* See DIA-, ENCEPHALON.] —**di·en·ce·phal·ic** (dī′en sə-fal′ik), *adj.*

di·er·e·sis (dī er′ə sis) *also,* **diaeresis.** *n., pl.* **-ses** (-sēz′). two dots (¨) placed over a vowel to show that it is pronounced in a separate syllable. [Late Latin *diaeresis* dividing of one syllable into two, from Greek *diairesis* division, separation.]

die·sel (dē′zəl, -səl) *also,* **Die·sel.** *n.* **1.** diesel engine. **2.** a vehicle powered by a diesel engine. —*adj.* of or for a diesel engine: *diesel fuel.*

diesel engine *also,* **Diesel engine.** an internal-combustion engine in which fuel oil, injected into the cylinder, is ignited by heat produced by compression of air in the cylinder, rather than by a spark plug. Also, **diesel motor.** [From Rudolf *Diesel,* 1858-1913, German automotive engineer who invented it.]

Di·es I·rae (dē′ās îr′ā) a medieval Latin hymn that describes the Day of Judgment, usually sung at masses for the dead. [Medieval Latin *diēs īrae* day of wrath, the first two words of this hymn.]

di·et¹ (dī′it) *n.* **1.** the food and drink usually eaten by a person or animal; customary daily fare: *My diet includes meat, vegetables, and fruit.* **2.** a regulated course of food and drink prescribed for reasons of health or weight control: *The doctor put him on a low-salt diet.* **3.** food considered as a nutrient or for its effects on the body: *Diet is an important factor in maintaining good health.* **4.** anything provided or consumed habitually: *a steady diet of books.* —*v.i.* to eat according to prescribed rules, esp. in order to lose weight: *She dieted for several weeks and lost 12 pounds.* [Middle English *diete,* from Old French *diete* daily fare, from Latin *diaeta* prescribed diet, from Greek *diaita* way of living, from *dia-* through + root of *iaita* fate.] —**di′et·er,** *n.*

di·et² (dī′it) *n.* **1.** a formal assembly: *A diet of church officials met to consider changes in the liturgy.* **2.** a legislative council or assembly, as the national legislature of Japan or the assembly of the estates of the Holy Roman Empire. [Medieval Latin *dieta* public assembly, appointed day, day's journey, from Latin *diēs* day.]

di·e·tar·y (dī′i ter′ē) *adj.* relating to diet: *Certain dietary rules must be observed for good health.* —*n., pl.* **-tar·ies.** a regulated allowance of food.

di·e·tet·ic (dī′i tet′ik) *adj.* **1.** relating to diet or to regulation of the use of food: *The doctor gave me all kinds of dietetic restrictions.* **2.** prepared for use in special diets: *Dietetic sweets are made without sugar.* —**di′e·tet′i·cal·ly,** *adv.*

di·e·tet·ics (dī′i tet′iks) *n.* the branch of the science of nutrition dealing with the nutritional needs of both healthy and sick persons, meal planning, and the preparation and serving of food. ➡ used as singular.

di·e·ti·tian (dī′i tish′ən) *also,* **di·e·ti·cian.** *n.* a person trained in dietetics, usually employed by an institution or other organization.

dif-, form of **dis-¹** before *f,* as in *diffuse.*

diff. 1. difference. **2.** different.

dif·fer (dif′ər) *v.i.* **1.** to not be the same in nature, form, or qualities; be unlike: *We differ in our interests. Wisdom differs from cunning.* **2.** to have a difference of opinion: *The candidate differs with the other members of the party on that issue.* [Old French

differer to be different, delay, from Latin *differre* to disperse, be different, delay. Doublet of DEFER¹.]

dif·fer·ence (dif′ər əns, dif′rəns) *n.* **1.** the state or quality of being unlike or different; dissimilarity: *Will the difference between the two colors cause a problem?* **2.** an instance of this dissimilarity: *We noticed a difference in their attitude.* **3.** a distinguishing characteristic: *The only difference between the two cars is the price.* **4.** the amount by which one quantity is greater or less than another; remainder left after subtracting one quantity from another: *The difference between six and five is one.* **5.a.** a failure to have the same opinion. **b.** a quarrel; dispute: *A difference arose between the neighbors over the height of the fence.* **c.** the cause of either of these.

• **to make a difference. a.** to have an effect on or change a situation: *Getting enough sleep will make a difference in how you feel and look.* **b.** to be important to; matter: *It makes a difference to me if you are angry.*

• **to split the difference. a.** to divide equally what is left over. **b.** to compromise by reaching a middle course: *We offered $75,000 for the house, but the owner wanted $95,000; so we split the difference and settled on $85,000.*

dif·fer·ent (dif′ər ənt, dif′rənt) *adj.* **1.** not similar or alike: *They have very different approaches to teaching. Your taste in movies is different from mine.* **2.** not the same; separate; distinct: *We went to different schools.* **3.** not like most others; not ordinary; unusual: *This book is quite different from others I've read.* ➡ usually used with *from* rather than *than* in all defs., but either is considered acceptable. [Old French *different,* from Latin *differens,* present participle of *differre* to delay.] —**dif′fer·ent·ly,** *adv.* —**dif′fer·ent·ness,** *n.*

Synonyms **Different, diverse, divergent,** and **disparate** mean not alike in some way. **Different** is the most general of these terms, used in any case where two or more things or aspects of them are not the same: *to have different ideas about something, cars painted different colors, two different kinds of parrot in one cage.* **Diverse** suggests marked distinctions and is often used where more than two things are being considered: *a diverse group of tourists, a diverse collection of paintings.* **Divergent** connotes a branching off in different directions, esp. of two things: *My friend's life and mine have taken divergent paths.* **Disparate** suggests a difference in kind or nature so great as to be incongruous or incompatible: *The two brothers are as disparate in nature as Dr. Jekyll and Mr. Hyde.*

dif·fer·en·ti·a (dif′ə ren′shē ə) *n., pl.* **-ti·ae** (-shē ē′). a distinguishing quality or characteristic, esp. one that distinguishes one species from all others of the same genus. [Latin *differentia* difference.]

dif·fer·en·tial (dif′ə ren′shəl) *adj.* **1.** relating to or exhibiting a difference or differences: *A differential diagnosis distinguishes between two similar diseases.* **2.** constituting a difference; distinguishing: *Each case presents differential features that make it unique.* **3.** depending on or showing a difference or distinction: *differential customs duties.* **4.** *Mathematics.* of or relating to differentiation or derivatives. **5.** *Mechanics.* relating to the difference of two or more motions, pressures, temperatures, or other measurable physical qualities. —*n.* **1.** a differential amount, factor, wage, or rate. **2.** *Mathematics.* an infinitesimal difference between consecutive values of a continuously varying quantity. **3.** a system of gears that enables the opposite driving wheels of a motor vehicle to rotate at different speeds when the vehicle rounds a curve. Also *(def. 3),* **differential gear.** —**dif′fer·en′tial·ly,** *adv.*

differential calculus, see **calculus.**

dif·fer·en·ti·ate (dif′ər en′shē āt′) *v.,* **-at·ed, -at·ing.** —*v.t.* **1.** to constitute the difference in; serve to distinguish between: *Coloring differentiates the sexes in many birds.* **2.** to perceive or express the differences in; distinguish between: *Not many people could differentiate this counterfeit bill from real money.* **3.** *Mathematics.* to find the derivative or differential of. —*v.i.* **1.** to become different or specialized: *Many millions of years ago, some reptilian scales apparently differentiated and became feathers.* **2.** to perceive or express a difference: *to differentiate between good and evil.* —**dif′fer·en′ti·a′tion,** *n.*

dif·fi·cult (dif′i kult′, -kəlt) *adj.* **1.** hard to do or perform; demanding effort; not easy: *Crossing the river in the little boat was a difficult task.* **2.** hard to understand or solve; perplexing: *a difficult problem, a difficult poem.* **3.** hard to deal with, please, persuade, or satisfy: *a difficult child, a difficult customer.* [From DIFFICULTY.] —For Synonyms, see **hard.**

dif·fi·cul·ty (dif′i kul′tē, -kəl tē) *n., pl.* **-ties. 1.** the fact or condition of being difficult: *a task of great difficulty, the difficulty of learning to drive a car.* **2.** something that is difficult to do or understand: *The hikers encountered many difficulties during the climb.* **3.** considerable effort; struggle: *I speak French with difficulty. They had no difficulty in getting the boat through the rapids.*

4. *usually,* **difficulties.** an embarrassing state of affairs, esp. financial trouble; dilemma. **5.** an angry dispute or disagreement; quarrel: *There was always some difficulty between them.* [Latin *difficultās* trouble, poverty, going back to *dis* apart + *facilis* easy.]

dif·fi·dence (dif′i dəns) *n.* a lack of confidence in oneself; shyness.

dif·fi·dent (dif′i dənt) *adj.* lacking confidence in oneself; shy. [Latin *diffīdēns,* present participle of *diffīdere* to distrust.] —**dif′-fi·dent·ly,** *adv.*

dif·fract (di frakt′) *v.t.* **1.** to bend or break up. **2.** to cause to undergo diffraction. [Latin *diffractus,* past participle of *diffringere* to break in pieces.]

dif·frac·tion (di frak′shən) *n.* **1.** the bending of the path of a ray of light as it passes through a narrow slit or is deflected around the edge of a solid or opaque object. The diffracted light wave spreads out to form a pattern of light and dark regions or the colored bands of the spectrum. **2.** a similar phenomenon in other waves, as sound, electricity, or X rays.

diffraction grating, any of several devices made by cutting very fine parallel slits or grooves in glass, metal, or plastic plates, used to produce a spectrum from rays of light by means of diffraction.

dif·fuse (*adj.,* di fūs′; *v.,* di fūz′) *adj.* **1.** widely spread out; not concentrated; dispersed: *diffuse light.* **2.** using many words; wordy; verbose: *a diffuse writer.* —*v.,* **-fused, -fus·ing.** —*v.t.* **1.** to spread widely; scatter in all directions; disperse: *to diffuse light, to diffuse one's talents, to diffuse knowledge.* **2.** to cause (gases or liquids) to intermingle by diffusion. —*v.i.* **1.** to be or become scattered or dispersed; spread out: *The scent from the roses diffused throughout the room.* **2.** to intermingle by diffusion: *Every gas diffuses at a certain rate.* [Latin *diffūsus,* past participle of *diffundere* to pour forth.] —**dif·fuse′ly,** *adv.* —**dif·fuse′-ness,** *n.* —**dif·fus′er,** *n.*

dif·fus·i·ble (di fū′zə bəl) *adj.* capable of being diffused.

dif·fu·sion (di fū′zhən) *n.* **1.** the act of diffusing or the state of being diffused; a spreading or scattering widely; dispersion. **2.** wordiness in speech or writing; verbosity. **3.** a gradual mixing together of the molecules of gases or of liquids due to the random movement of the molecules. **4.** the scattering of light when it passes through a material like frosted glass or fog or is reflected from a rough surface. —**dif·fu′sion·al,** *adj.*

dig (dig) *v.,* **dug** or (archaic) **digged, dig·ging.** —*v.t.* **1.** to break up or turn over and remove (earth), as with a shovel, the hands, or claws. **2.** to make or form by or as by digging; hollow out; excavate: *to dig a hole, to dig a tunnel.* **3.** to obtain or extract by digging: *to dig potatoes.* **4.** to discover or obtain by close search or investigation (often with *up* or *out*): *to dig up information; to dig out old records.* **5.** to poke; prod: *The rider dug the horse with the spurs.* **6.** *Slang.* **a.** to understand. **b.** to like, appreciate, or be in rapport with. —*v.i.* **1.** to break up, remove, or turn over the earth: *The dog dug in the yard for bones.* **2.** to make a way by or as by digging; make an excavation. —*n.* **1.** the act of digging. **2.** *Informal.* a thrust or poke: *a dig in the ribs.* **3.** *Informal.* a sarcastic remark; cutting statement; gibe. **4.** an archaeological site or excavation. **5. digs.** *Informal.* living quarters. [French *diguer* to make a dike, hollow out the ground, from *digue* dike, from Middle Dutch *dijc.*]

· **to dig in. a.** *Military.* to dig trenches or holes for defensive purposes. **b.** *Informal.* to begin to eat. **c.** *Informal.* to begin to work intensively: *With an exam coming up, I took my notes and dug in.* **d.** to refuse to give up an opinion or position; entrench oneself.

· **to dig into.** *Informal.* **a.** to examine thoroughly or carefully: *The lawyer dug into the old records for the missing deed.* **b.** to begin to eat hungrily: *Having skipped lunch, I really dug into dinner.*

di·gest (*v.,* dī jest′, di-; *n.,* dī′jest) *v.t.* **1.** to break down (food materials) by the process of digestion. **2.** to grasp and assimilate mentally: *It was difficult to digest all the information at once.* **3.** to condense and arrange systematically; summarize. **4.** *Chemistry.* to soften or decompose (a substance) with the aid of heat, moisture, or the like; dissolve. —*v.i.* **1.** to undergo digestion: *Protein digests slowly.* **2.** to digest food. —*n.* a systematically arranged collection or summary, esp. of literary, historical, legal, or scientific material; compilation: *to publish a digest of court decisions.* [Latin *dīgestus,* past participle of *dīgerere* to carry apart, dissolve.] —**di·gest′er,** *n.*

di·gest·i·ble (di jes′tə bəl, dī-) *adj.* capable of being digested; easily digested. —**di·gest′i·bil′i·ty,** *n.*

di·ges·tion (di jes′chən, dī-) *n.* **1.** the process by which food materials are broken down by physical and chemical action into simple compounds that can be assimilated by the body. **2.** the ability to digest food: *The patient's digestion is good.* **3.** mental assimilation; understanding.

di·ges·tive (di jes′tiv, dī-) *adj.* relating to, for, or aiding diges-

tion: *the digestive tract, a digestive medicine.* —*n.* a medicine or substance that aids digestion. —**di·ges′tive·ly,** *adv.*

digestive system, the system that breaks food down so that it can be used by the body. In mammals it includes the mouth and teeth, pharynx, esophagus, stomach, intestines, and various digestive enzymes and hormones.

dig·ger (dig′ər) *n.* **1.** a person who digs. **2.** a tool or machine for digging. **3. Digger.** a member of a tribe of North American Indians who dug roots for food.

digger wasp, any of a group of solitary wasps, family Sphecidae, that dig their nests in the ground.

dig·gings (dig′ingz) *pl. n.* **1.** a place where digging is done, as a mine. **2.** the materials dug out. **3.** *Informal.* living quarters.

dight (dīt) *v.t., v.i.,* **dight** or **dight·ed, dight·ing.** *Archaic.* **1.** to dress; adorn. **2.** to prepare; equip. [Old English *dihtan* to compose, arrange, from Latin *dictāre* to dictate.]

dig·it (dij′it) *n.* **1.** a finger or toe. **2.** any of the ten Arabic numerals from

human **digestive system**

0 through 9. Sometimes 0 is excluded. **3.** a former unit of measure, equal to the breadth of a finger, or about ¾ inch (2 centimeters). [Latin *digitus* finger, toe; with reference to counting with the fingers (and toes).]

dig·i·tal (dij′i təl) *adj.* **1.** relating to or resembling a digit or digits. **2.** having digits. **3.** having a numerical display, as an electronic calculator. **4.** representing data by means of the binary digits 0 and 1. **5.** of or relating to digital recording. —*n.* a key on a keyboard instrument played with the finger. —**dig′i·tal·ly,** *adv.*

digital audio tape, magnetic tape on which a digital recording has been made, or a cassette containing such tape.

digital computer, a computer that operates on data in the form of numerical digits, esp. the numbers 0 and 1. ➡ distinguished from **analog computer.**

dig·i·tal·is (dij′i tal′is, -tā′lis) *n.* **1.** a drug used for stimulating the heart, prepared from the dried leaves of the common foxglove. **2.** foxglove. [Modern Latin *digitalis,* from Latin *digitālis* relating to the finger, from *digitus* finger; from the fingerlike shape of the flower's corollas.]

digital recording 1. a method of sound recording in which audio signals are transformed into a series of binary digits and are recorded as bits on magnetic tape or a compact disc. **2.** a record, audio tape, or compact disc made by this system.

dig·i·tate (dij′i tāt′) *adj.* **1.** having fingers or toes. **2.** *Botany.* palmate. Also, **dig′i·tat′ed.** [Latin *digitātus* having fingers or toes, from *digitus* finger, toe.] —**dig′i·tate′ly,** *adv.* —**dig′i·ta′-tion,** *n.*

dig·i·ti·grade (dij′i ti grād′) *adj.* walking on the toes, as most four-footed mammals. ➡ distinguished from **plantigrade.** [French *digitigrade,* from Latin *digitus* finger, toe + *gradī* to walk.]

dig·i·tize (dij′i tīz′) *v.t.,* **-tized, -tiz·ing.** to convert (analog information, as data or an electronic signal) into digital form.

dig·ni·fied (dig′nə fīd′) *adj.* marked by or showing dignity of manner or style; noble; stately.

dig·ni·fy (dig′nə fī′) *v.t.,* **-fied, -fy·ing. 1.** to give dignity to; honor; ennoble: *The proceedings were dignified by the presence of the governor.* **2.** to give unmerited distinction or attention to, as by giving a high-sounding name: *to dignify violence by calling it a patriotic demonstration.* [Old French *dignifier* to make worthy,

a	at	e	end	o	hot	u	up	hw	white		about
ā	ape	ē	me	ō	old	ū	use	ng	song	ə	taken
ä	far	i	it	ô	fork	ü	rule	th	thin		pencil
âr	care	ī	ice	oi	oil	u̇	pull	th	this		lemon
		îr	pierce	ou	out	ûr	turn	zh	measure		circus

from Late Latin *dignificāre,* from Latin *dignus* worthy + *facere* to make.]

dig·ni·tar·y (dig′ni ter′ē) *n., pl.* **-tar·ies.** a person who has a high position or office, as in government or the church: *Several foreign dignitaries were entertained by the president.*

dig·ni·ty (dig′ni tē) *n., pl.* **-ties. 1.** nobility of character or manner; stateliness; serenity: *Even in great adversity, the family retained their dignity.* **2.** the state or quality of being worthy, honorable, esteemed, or excellent: *True dignity lies in who you are, not in what you possess.* **3.** a degree of excellence; relative importance or position; rank. **4.** a high office, rank, or title. [Old French *digneté* high rank, dignity, from Latin *dignitās* worth. See DAINTY.]

di·graph (dī′graf) *n.* two letters used to represent one sound, as *oa* in *boat* or *sh* in *ship.* [DI-[1] + Greek *graphē* writing.]

di·gress (di gres′, dī-) *v.i.* to deviate or depart from the main subject in speaking or writing. [Latin *dīgressus,* past participle of *dīgredī* to go apart, deviate.] —For Synonyms, see **diverge.**

di·gres·sion (di gresh′ən, dī-) *n.* **1.** the act of digressing. **2.** something that digresses: *The last chapter of the book was a long digression on the author's political opinions.*

di·gres·sive (di gres′iv, dī-) *adj.* tending to digress; marked by digression: *digressive essays.* —**di·gres′sive·ly,** *adv.* —**di·gres′sive·ness,** *n.*

di·he·dral (dī hē′drəl) *adj.* having two plane surfaces; formed by the intersection of two planes: *a dihedral angle.* —*n.* a dihedral angle. [DI-[1] + Greek *hedrā* base, seat.]

di·hy·brid (dī hī′brid) *adj.* having parents differing from one another in two genetically determined characters. —*n.* a dihybrid offspring. [DI-[1] + HYBRID.]

dik-dik (dik′dik′) *n.* any of a group of very small African antelopes, genus *Madoqua* or *Rhynchotragus.* Only the males possess horns, which are small and covered by tufts of hair in some species. Height: 12-16 inches (30-41 centimeters) at the shoulder. Weight: 5-10 pounds (2.3-4.5 kilograms).

dike (dīk) *also,* **dyke.** *n.* **1.** an embankment or dam intended to prevent flooding; levee. **2.** a ditch or watercourse. **3.** a bank of earth thrown up in digging a ditch. **4.** a low dividing wall of earth or stone. **5.** a raised causeway. **6.** a barrier; obstacle. **7.** *Geology.* a mass of igneous rock, often long and narrow, which was intruded while molten into a vertical fissure. —*v.t.,* **diked, dik·ing. 1.** to provide, protect, or surround with a dike or dikes. **2.** to drain with a ditch. [Old English *dīc* ditch.]

Di·lan·tin (dī lan′tin) *n. Trademark.* a drug used to reduce the number of seizures in epilepsy. Also, **dilantin sodium.** [Short for *di(pheny)l(hyd)ant(o)in.*]

di·lap·i·dat·ed (di lap′i dā′tid) *adj.* fallen into ruin or decay; broken down; neglected: *The houses were dilapidated beyond repair.* [From earlier *dilapidate* to fall into decay, from Latin *dīlapidātus,* past participle of *dīlapidāre* to throw away; literally, to scatter like stones, going back to *dis* apart + *lapis* stone.]

di·lap·i·da·tion (di lap′i dā′shən) *n.* **1.** a condition of ruin or decay: *The city official found several of the slum houses in complete dilapidation.* **2.** the process of falling into decay or ruin: *the dilapidation of ancient Greek temples.*

dil·a·ta·tion (dil′ə tā′shən, dī′lə-) *n.* **1.** dilation. **2.** *Medicine.* an abnormal expansion or stretching of an organ, body cavity, or the like. —**dil′a·ta′tion·al,** *adj.*

di·late (dī lāt′, di-) *v.,* **-lat·ed, -lat·ing.** —*v.t.* to make larger or wider; cause to expand. —*v.i.* **1.** to become larger or wider; expand: *At night the iris of the eye dilates to admit light.* **2.** to speak or write at length; enlarge (with *on* or *upon*): *The children dilated upon their day's adventures at camp.* [Old French *dilater* to enlarge, widen, from Latin *dīlātāre.*] —**di·lat′a·ble,** *adj.* —For Synonyms *(v.i.),* see **expand.**

di·la·tion (dī lā′shən, di-) *n.* **1.** the act of dilating or the state of being dilated. **2.** a dilated part.

di·la·tor (dī′lā tər, di lā′-) *n.* **1.** a person or thing that dilates. **2.** a muscle that dilates or expands a part of the body, as the muscle that widens the iris of the eye. **3.** an instrument for dilating wounds or canals or openings of the body.

dil·a·to·ry (dil′ə tôr′ē) *adj.* **1.** tending to delay; tardy; slow: *to be dilatory in paying one's bills.* **2.** tending to cause delay either to gain time or defer action: *a dilatory policy, dilatory tactics.* [Late Latin *dīlātōrius* delaying, from Latin *dīlātor* delayer.] —**dil′a·to′ri·ly,** *adv.* —**dil′a·to′ri·ness,** *n.*

di·lem·ma (di lem′ə) *n.* **1.** a situation requiring a difficult choice, usually between unpleasant or unsatisfactory alternatives: *the dilemma of enduring pain or having an operation.* **2.** any difficult or perplexing problem. [Late Latin *dilemma* double proposition, from Greek *dilēmma,* from *di-* (see DI-[1]) + *lēmma* assumption.]

dil·et·tante (dil′i tänt′, -tant′, -tän′tā, -tän′tē) *n., pl.* **-tantes** or **-tan·ti** (-tän′tē, -tan′-). **1.** a person who pursues an art or science

superficially or merely for amusement; dabbler. **2.** a lover of the fine arts. —*adj.* relating to or characteristic of a dilettante. [Italian *dilettante* lover of the arts, dabbler, from *dilettare* to delight, from Latin *dēlectāre.*]

dil·et·tant·ism (dil′i tänt′tiz əm, -tan′-) *n.* the quality or actions characteristic of a dilettante.

dil·i·gence[1] (dil′i jəns) *n.* serious, persistent attention to one's work or duty; constant effort; industry. [Old French *diligence* application, speed, from Latin *dīligentia* carefulness.]

dil·i·gence[2] (dil′i jəns) *n.* a public stagecoach formerly used in Europe, esp. in France. [Short for French *carrosse de diligence* literally, coach of speed. See DILIGENCE[1].]

dil·i·gent (dil′i jənt) *adj.* **1.** attentive and persistent in whatever is undertaken; industrious: *a diligent student.* **2.** showing or pursued with painstaking care and effort: *a diligent search.* [Old French *diligent* attentive, eager, from Latin *dīligēns* careful, attentive.] —**dil′i·gent·ly,** *adv.*

dill (dil) *n.* **1.** the dried, seedlike fruit and fresh or dried leaves of an annual Old World herb, *Anethum graveolens,* of the parsley family, chiefly used as a spice to flavor pickles and other foods. **2.** the plant itself, cultivated throughout the world, bearing light green, threadlike leaves and large clusters of small yellow flowers. [Old English *dile* the plant.]

dill pickle, a pickled cucumber flavored with dill.

dil·ly·dal·ly (dil′ē dal′ē) *v.i.,* **-lied, -ly·ing.** to waste time; loiter; trifle.

dil·u·ent (dil′ū ənt) *adj.* serving to dilute. —*n.* an agent that dilutes the strength or concentration of a substance, solution, or mixture. [Latin *diluentis, diluens,* genitive of present participle of *diluere* to wash away, dissolve.]

di·lute (di lüt′, dī-) *v.,* **-lut·ed, -lut·ing.** —*v.t.* **1.** to thin or weaken by the addition of a liquid: *to dilute concentrated fruit juice with water.* **2.** to weaken or reduce the strength, force, efficiency, or purity of by adding another element: *The addition of too many new features diluted the quality of the magazine.* —*v.i.* to become diluted. —*adj.* diluted; weak: *a dilute acid.* [Latin *dilūtus,* past participle of *diluere* to wash away, dissolve.] —**di·lut′er;** *also,* **di·lu′tor,** *n.*

di·lu·tion (di lü′shən, dī-) *n.* **1.** the act of diluting or the state of being diluted. **2.** something diluted.

di·lu·vi·al (di lü′vē əl, dī-) *adj.* **1.** relating to a flood or deluge. **2.** *Geology.* deposited by a glacier, flooding river, or the like. [Late Latin *dīluviālis* relating to a flood, from Latin *dīluvium* flood.]

dim (dim) *adj.,* **dim·mer, dim·mest. 1.** having or giving little light; not bright: *a dim corner of a basement, a dim light bulb.* **2.** lacking brilliance or luster; dull: *dim colors.* **3.** not easily or clearly seen or heard; indistinct; faint; obscure: *a dim sound, the dim outline of a figure in the distance.* **4.** not clear to the mind; vague; confused: *to have only a dim recollection of an accident.* **5.** not clearly understood; confused: *I have only a dim idea of what you're talking about.* **6.** not seeing or hearing clearly: *eyes dim with tears.* **7.** not understanding clearly: *to be dim about the importance of keeping records.* **8.** not favorable; discouraging: *a dim outlook for success.* —*v.,* **dimmed, dim·ming.** —*v.t.* to make dim: *The driver dimmed the car's headlights.* —*v.i.* to grow or become dim: *My memory of the event dimmed as the years passed.* —*n.* **dims.** headlights on low beam. [Old English *dimm* dark.] —**dim′ly,** *adv.* —**dim′ness,** *n.* —For Synonyms *(adj.),* see **dark, faint.**

dim. 1. diminuendo. **2.** diminutive.

dime (dīm) *n.* a coin of the United States equal to ten cents or one tenth of a dollar. [Old French *dime* tenth part, from Latin *decima (pars)* tenth (part), from *decem* ten.]

dime novel, a sensational or melodramatic novel having no literary merit, originally costing ten cents, popular in the late nineteenth and early twentieth centuries.

di·men·sion (di men′shən) *n.* **1.** any measurable extent, as length, breadth, thickness, or height. **2.** *Mathematics.* **a.** dimensions. the measurements in length, width, and often depth, of a specific geometrical shape: *The room's dimensions are 12 feet by 10 feet.* **b.** any of the three coordinates that define the position of a point in space. **3.** *usually,* **dimensions.** the limit to which something extends or has importance; degree of significance; magnitude: *The dimensions of this problem have not yet been fully realized by the public.* **4.** any of the various elements into which something may be broken; facet; aspect. [French *dimension* a measuring, from Latin *dīmēnsiō.*] —**di·men′sion·al,** *adj.* —**di·men′sion·al·ly,** *adv.*

dim·er·ous (dim′ər əs) *adj.* consisting of or divided into two parts, as a flower that has two members in each whorl. [Modern Latin *dimerus,* from Greek *di-* double + *meros* part.]

dime store, five-and-ten.

dim·e·ter (dim′i tər) *n.* a line of verse consisting of two metrical

feet. [Late Latin *dimeter* consisting of two metrical feet, from Greek *dimetros,* from *di-*[1] two + *metron* measure.]

dimin. 1. diminuendo. **2.** diminutive.

di·min·ish (di min′ish) *v.t.* to make smaller or less, as size, amount, degree, importance, or authority: *The new tax diminished the governor's popularity.* —*v.i.* to become smaller or less; decrease: *The campers' food supply diminished as the days wore on.* [Blend of obsolete *diminue* to lessen, reduce (going back to Latin *dēminuere*), and archaic *minish* to lessen, reduce (going back to Latin *minūtus* small).] —For Synonyms *(v.i.),* see **decrease.**

di·min·u·en·do (di min′ū en′dō) *Music. adj., adv.* with gradually decreasing loudness or force; decrescendo. —*n., pl.* **-dos. 1.** a gradual decrease in loudness or force; decrescendo. **2.** a passage played diminuendo. [Italian *diminuendo* diminishing, present participle of *diminuire* to lessen, reduce, from Latin *dēminuere.*]

dim·i·nu·tion (dim′ə nü′shən, -nū′-) *n.* the act of diminishing or the state of being diminished; reduction; decrease. [Old French *diminution* a lessening, from Latin *dēminūtiō* decrease.]

di·min·u·tive (di min′yə tiv) *adj.* **1.** small in size; little; tiny. **2.** *Grammar.* expressing smallness, familiarity, or affection, for example: *-let* in *droplet* is a diminutive suffix. —*n.* **1.** a small kind or variety of something. **2.** a word formed from another either by change in structure or by addition of a suffix, expressing smallness, familiarity, or affection. *Piglet* is a diminutive of *pig.* The nickname *Joe* is a diminutive of *Joseph.* [Old French *diminutif* expressing smallness, from Late Latin *dīminūtīvus, dēminūtīvus,* from Latin *dēminuere* to lessen.]

dim·i·ty (dim′i tē) *n., pl.* **-ties.** a sheer, crisp cotton fabric, usually woven with cords at intervals in a striped or checkered arrangement, used for such items as blouses, dresses, or curtains. [Italian *dimito* a coarse cotton cloth, from Medieval Latin *dimitum* cloth woven with two threads, from Greek *dimitos* of double thread.]

dim·mer (dim′ər) *n.* **1.** a device that dims an electric light or set of lights, as stage lights. **2.** a device that switches automobile headlights between high beam and low beam.

di·mor·phic (dī môr′fik) *adj.* dimorphous.

di·mor·phism (dī môr′fiz əm) *n.* the state or property of occurring in two distinct forms, as exhibited by certain minerals in their crystals, certain plants in their leaves, or certain birds in male and female plumage. [Greek *dimorphos* having two forms (from *di-* two + *morphē* form) + -ISM.]

di·mor·phous (dī môr′fəs) *adj.* having, showing, or characterized by dimorphism.

dim·out (dim′out′) *n.* a dimming or concealment of night lighting, esp. in a city to make it less visible from the air in case of an aerial attack.

dim·ple (dim′pəl) *n.* **1.** a small indentation of the flesh, esp. as formed in the cheek or chin in the act of smiling. **2.** a similar indentation on a surface. —*v.,* **-pled, -pling.** —*v.t.* to mark with dimples: *A smile dimpled her cheeks.* —*v.i.* to form dimples: *His face dimples when he smiles.* [Probably from an unrecorded Old English word.]

dim sum (dim′sum′) **1.** in Chinese cooking, steamed or fried dumplings stuffed with meat, fish, or vegetables. **2.** an assortment of these and other such delicacies served as a meal. [From the Cantonese phrase *dim sam* small heart or small center, used as the name of this food.]

din (din) *n.* a loud, continuous noise or clamor; rattle or clatter that goes on for some time: *the din of machines in a factory, the din of a New Year's Eve party.* —*v., dinned, din·ning.* —*v.t.* **1.** to bother or annoy repeatedly with a din: *The jet planes dinned the surrounding area day and night.* **2.** to say over and over again in a persistent or tiresome way: *to din complaints in someone's ear.* —*v.i.* to make a din. [Old English *dyne* noise.]

di·nar (di när′) *n.* **1.** the monetary unit of various countries, such as Algeria, Iraq, Tunisia, and Yugoslavia. **2.** an ancient gold coin used in Arab countries. [Arabic *dīnār* name of a gold coin, from Late Greek *dēnarion* denarius, from

dim sum

Latin *dēnārius* denarius, containing ten. Doublet of DENARIUS, DENIER[2].]

dine (dīn) *v.,* **dined, din·ing.** —*v.i.* **1.** to eat dinner: *to dine with friends.* **2.** to eat (with *on* or *upon*): *to dine on steak.* —*v.t.* to provide with dinner; give a dinner for: *to dine a prominent politician.* [Old French *disner* to have dinner, going back to Latin *dis-* away + *jējūnium* fast[2]; in the sense of "away from fasting" or "breaking a fast."]

din·er (dī′nər) *n.* **1.** a person who dines. **2.** dining car. **3.** a restaurant housed in a building designed to resemble a dining car.

di·nette (dī net′) *n.* an alcove or small room used for dining. [DINE + -ETTE.]

ding[1] (ding) *n.* a sound made by a bell, or any sound resembling it. —*v.t., v.i.* to make or cause to make a ringing sound. [Imitative.]

ding[2] (ding) *Informal. v.t.* **1.** to cause or make a nick in the surface of: *The rock dinged the windshield.* **2.** to hit forcefully: *The ball dinged me on the head.* —*n.* a cut or chip on the surface; nick: *The table top was full of dings.*

ding-a-ling (ding′ə ling′) *n. Slang.* an odd, silly, or foolish person; kook.

ding·bat (ding′bat′) *n.* **1.** *Slang.* a stupid or foolish person. **2.** dingus. [Of uncertain origin.]

ding-dong (ding′dông′, -dong′) *n.* **1.** the sound of repeated strokes made by a bell. **2.** any similar sound. —*adj. Informal.* closely contested: *a ding-dong battle.* [Imitative.]

din·ghy (ding′ē, ding′gē) *also,* **dingy.** *n., pl.* **-ghies.** any of various small open boats, propelled by oars, motor, or sail, and often used as tenders for larger boats. [Hindi *dīngī* small boat.]

din·gle (ding′gəl) *n.* a small, deep, wooded valley; dell. [Of uncertain origin.]

din·go (ding′gō) *n., pl.* **-goes.** a wolflike wild dog, *Canis dingo,* of Australia, having pointed, erect ears, reddish brown fur, and a long, bushy tail. Height: 2 feet (0.6 meter) at the shoulder. [Native Australian name.]

dingo

din·gus (ding′əs) *n. Informal.* a gadget or other thing whose name is unknown or forgotten; thingamabob. [Dutch *dinges.*]

din·gy[1] (din′jē) *adj.,* **-gi·er, -gi·est. 1.** not bright and fresh; discolored; dull: *The sheets looked dingy even after being washed.* **2.** having a drab, shabby appearance; dreary: *a dingy one-room apartment.* [Of uncertain origin.] —**din′gi·ly,** *adv.* —**din′gi·ness,** *n.*

din·gy[2] (ding′ē, ding′gē) *n., pl.* **-gies.** dinghy.

dining car, a railroad car in which meals are served.

dining room, a room in which meals are served and eaten, as in a home or hotel.

dink·ey (ding′kē) *also,* **dinky.** *n., pl.* **-eys.** a small locomotive used for shunting cars or hauling freight in a railroad yard.

dink·y[1] (ding′kē) *adj.,* **dink·i·er, dink·i·est.** *Informal.* of little value, size, or importance; small or insignificant.

din·ky[2] (ding′kē) *n., pl.* **-kies.** dinkey.

din·ner (din′ər) *n.* **1.** the principal meal of the day. **2.** a formal meal in honor of some person or occasion; banquet. [French *dîner,* noun use of infinitive *dîner* to dine, going back to Latin *dis-* (see DIS-[1]) + *jējūnium* fast[2].]

dinner jacket, a tuxedo jacket.

dinner theater, a restaurant in which plays or musical comedies are presented during or after dinner or luncheon.

din·ner·ware (din′ər wâr′) *n.* dishes, glasses, and tableware used for table service.

din·o·flag·el·late (din′ə flaj′ə lāt′) *n.* any of a large group of plankton found mostly in the ocean and having two whiplike flagella that help them move.

di·no·saur (dī′nə sôr′) *n.* a member of a large group of extinct four-limbed reptiles, order Saurischia or Ornithischia, of the Mesozoic era. Some species grew to 87 feet (27 meters) in length and weighed up to 50 tons (45 metric tons). [Modern Latin *Dinosauria,* from Greek *deinos* terrible + *sauros* lizard.]

a	at	e	end	o	hot	u	up	hw	white		about
ā	ape	ē	me	ō	old	ū	use	ng	song		taken
ä	far	i	it	ô	fork	ü	rule	th	thin	ə	pencil
âr	care	ī	ice	oi	oil	ù	pull	th	this		lemon
		îr	pierce	ou	out	ûr	turn	zh	measure		circus

D

di·no·sau·ri·an (dī′nə sôr′ē ən) *adj.* of, relating to, or like a dinosaur. —*n.* dinosaur.

dint (dint) *n.* **1.** exertion; force; power. ➡ now used chiefly in the phrase *by dint of: by dint of argument, by dint of effort.* **2.** dent. —*v.t.* **1.** to make a dent in. **2.** to impress or drive in with force. [Old English *dynt* blow[1].]

di·oc·e·san (dī os′ə sən) *adj.* of or relating to a diocese. —*n.* the bishop of a diocese.

di·o·cese (dī′ə sis, -sēz′, -sēs′) *n.*, *pl.* **-ces·es** (-sēz′, -sis′iz). an ecclesiastical district under a bishop's authority. [Old French *diocise* from Latin *dioecēsis* district, diocese, from Greek *dioikēsis* administration, diocese.]

di·ode (dī′ōd) *n.* a vacuum tube or semiconductor device with two terminals, used chiefly as a rectifier in electronic equipment. [DI-[1] + -ODE.]

di·oe·cious (dī ē′shəs) *adj.* having male and female reproductive organs, known as the stamen and pistil in flowering plants, on separate or different plants, as the holly tree. [Modern Latin *Dioecia* (from Greek *di-* double + *oikos* house) + -OUS.]

Di·o·me·des (dī′ə mē′dēz) *n.* in Greek legend, a king of Argos and one of the bravest of the Greek heroes in the Trojan War.

Di·o·nys·i·a (dī′ə nish′ē ə, -nis′ē ə) *pl. n.* ancient Greek festivals in honor of the god Dionysus, esp. those held in Athens. The origin of Greek drama is attributed to certain dramatic and ritualistic features of these festivals and to contests among poets and dramatists staged at them.

Di·o·nys·i·ac (dī′ə nis′ē ak′) *adj.* of or relating to Dionysus or the Dionysia.

Di·o·ny·sian (dī′ə nish′ən, -nis′ē ən) *adj.* **1.** Dionysiac. **2.** wildly uninhibited; frenzied; orgiastic.

Di·o·ny·sus (dī′ə nī′səs) *also,* **Di·o·ny·sos.** *n.* in Greek mythology, the son of Zeus and Semele, a mortal. As the god of fertility and wine, Dionysus was often worshiped with orgiastic rites. His Roman counterpart was Bacchus.

di·op·side (dī op′sīd) *n.* a white or green variety of the mineral pyroxene, usually found in limestone that has been metamorphosed by the heat of an igneous intrusion. [French *diopside,* from *di-* di-[3] + Greek *opsis* appearance, sight, from *ōps* eye; associated in meaning with Greek *diopsis* transparency, from *dia-* through + *opsis* sight.]

di·op·ter (dī op′tər) *n.* *Optics.* a unit of measure that expresses the power of a lens to refract light, equal to the reciprocal of the focal length in meters. [French *dioptre,* from Latin *dioptra* instrument for measuring the height of places or the sun's shadow, from Greek *dioptra.*] —**di·op′tric,** *adj.*

di·o·ram·a (dī′ə ram′ə, -rä′mə) *n.* **1.** a partly translucent picture, viewed through a small opening, in which various realistic effects are produced by means of lighting and other devices. **2.** an exhibit consisting of sculptured figures, stuffed animals, or other models, placed in a naturalistic setting against a curved, painted background, creating an illusion of depth and realism. [DI-[3] + Greek *horāma* sight.]

di·o·rite (dī′ə rīt′) *n.* a dark green or brown granular igneous rock consisting chiefly of feldspar and hornblende. [French *diorite,* from Greek *diorizein* to distinguish.]

Di·os·cu·ri (dī′əs kyûr′ī) *pl. n.* in classical mythology, Castor and Pollux. [Greek *Dioskouroi* literally, sons of Zeus, from *Dios,* genitive of *Zeus* Zeus + *kouroi,* plural of *kouros* boy, son.]

di·ox·ide (dī ok′sīd, -sid) *also,* **di·ox·id** (dī ok′sid). *n.* an oxide containing two atoms of oxygen per molecule.

di·ox·in (dī ok′sin) *n.* any of a group of highly toxic chlorinated hydrocarbons that occur as a persistent impurity in some herbicides and defoliants, as in Agent Orange. Some are known to cause fetal deformities. Formula: $C_{12}H_4Cl_4O_2$ [DI-[1] + *-ox-* oxygen + -IN[1].]

dip (dip) *v.,* **dipped** or **dipt, dip·ping.** —*v.t.* **1.** to put or let down into something for a moment: *to dip a pen into an inkwell, to dip oars into the water, to dip one's hand into a cookie jar.* **2.** to obtain or lift up and out by or as by scooping: *to dip water from a boat.* **3.** to lower and raise again quickly: *to dip a flag in a salute.* **4.** to immerse (sheep or other animals) in a disinfectant solution. **5.** to dye by immersing in a liquid. **6.** to make (a candle) by repeatedly plunging a wick into melted tallow or wax. **7.** to galvanize, plate, or coat by immersion in a prepared solution. —*v.i.* **1.** to plunge into and then emerge from water or other liquid, esp. quickly. **2.** to sink or go down: *The sun dipped below the horizon. Prices dipped on the stock market.* **3.** to incline or slope downward: *The land dips as it meets the sea.* **4.a.** to reach into, esp. to take something out (with *in* or *into*): *I dipped into my pocket for some change.* **b.** to make withdrawals from something in small amounts (with *in* or *into*): *We dipped into our savings for our new car.* **5.** to occupy oneself with briefly or superficially (with *into*): *The student dipped into the classics.* **6.** (of an airplane) to drop suddenly just before climbing. —*n.* **1.** the act of dipping,

esp. a brief immersion in water: *a dip in a pool.* **2.** a liquid preparation into which something is dipped, as for dyeing or disinfecting. **3.** a sudden drop or decline. **4.** a downward inclination or slope: *a dip in the road.* **5.** the amount or degree of such an inclination. **6.** a creamy mixture of foods intended to be scooped up on crackers or the like, often served as an hors d'oeuvre. **7.** a quantity of something taken out or up by dipping: *a dip of ice cream.* **8.** a hollow or depression in the land. **9.** a sudden rapid drop of an airplane, followed by a climb. **10.** a candle made by the repeated plunging of a wick into melted tallow or wax. **11.** *Geology.* the angle at which a stratum or similar formation is inclined from a horizontal plane. **12.** *Slang.* **a.** pickpocket. **b.** an eccentric or stupid person. [Old English *dyppan* to immerse.]

> **Synonyms** *v.t.* **Dip, immerse, plunge,** and **submerge** mean to insert into something, esp. into a liquid. **Dip** suggests a momentary insertion, either total or partial: *Dip the bread in the sauce before you eat it.* **Immerse** connotes complete covering: *Immerse the entire frame in the protective compound.* **Plunge** suggests a sudden, forceful, complete immersion: *The duck plunged its beak into the water.* **Submerge** connotes complete coverage for a period of time: *When the tide came in, the rock was completely submerged.*

di·pep·tide (dī pep′tīd) *n.* a peptide that consists of two molecules of amino acids. [DI-[1] + PEPTIDE.]

di·phase (dī′fāz′) *adj.* having, exhibiting, or characterized by two phases. Also, **di·pha′sic.** [DI-[1] + PHASE.]

diph·the·ri·a (dif thîr′ē ə, dip-) *n.* a contagious disease caused by a bacterium and characterized by fever, the formation of false membranes that may block the throat, and the production of a toxin that may affect the heart muscle. [Modern Latin *diphtheria,* from French *diphthérie,* from Greek *diphtherā* leather; from the formation of a leathery false membrane characterizing the disease.] —**diph·the′ri·al, diph·the′ri·an,** *adj.*

diph·the·rit·ic (dif′thə rit′ik, dip′-) *adj.* **1.** of, relating to, or resembling diphtheria or its symptoms. **2.** affected with or suffering from diphtheria. Also, **diph·ther·ic** (dif ther′ik, dip-).

diph·thong (dif′thông′, -thong′, dip′-) *n.* **1.** a blend of two vowel sounds in one syllable that is pronounced as one speech sound. The *ou* in *mouse* and *house* and the *oy* in *boy* and *soy* are diphthongs. **2.** digraph. **3.** ligature *(def. 4).* [French *diphthongue* two vowel sounds pronounced as one syllable, from Late Latin *diphthongus,* from Greek *diphthongos* having two sounds, from *dis* double + *phthongos* sound.] —**diph·thon·gal** (dif thông′gəl, -əl, -thong′-, dip-), *adj.*

diph·thong·ize (dif′thông gīz′, -īz′, -thong-, dip′-) *v.,* **-ized, -iz·ing.** —*v.t.* to make a diphthong of; pronounce as a diphthong. —*v.i.* to become a diphthong. —**diph′thong·i·za′tion,** *n.*

diplo- *also,* **dipl-** *combining form* double: *diploid.* [Greek *diplous* double.]

dip·lod·o·cus (dip lod′ə kəs) *n.,* *pl.* **-cus·es.** any sauropod dinosaur of the genus *Diplodocus,* having a very long neck and tail and living in western North America during Jurassic geologic time. [Modern Latin, from DIPLO- + Greek *dokos* beam.]

dip·loid (dip′loid) *adj.* **1.** double; twofold. **2.** having two complementary sets of chromosomes, as in an ordinary body cell. —*n.* a cell having two sets of chromosomes, twice the haploid number. [DIPL(O)- + -OID.] —**dip′loi·dy,** *n.*

di·plo·ma (di plō′mə) *n.,* *pl.* **-mas** or **-ma·ta** (-mə tə). **1.** a certificate granted by a school or college to a graduating student, indicating successful completion of a program or curriculum. **2.** any certificate conferring some privilege or honor. **3.** an official or state document; charter. [Latin *diplōma* document granting a privilege, passport, from Greek *diplōma* literally, something folded double (probably because it was originally folded double and sealed), from *diploun* to double.]

di·plo·ma·cy (di plō′mə sē) *n.,* *pl.* **-cies.** **1.** the art or practice of managing political relations between nations and conducting negotiations between governments. **2.** skill in dealing with other people; tact. [French *diplomatie* diplomatic service, from *diplomate* member of the diplomatic service, going back to Greek *diplōma.* See DIPLOMA.]

dip·lo·mat (dip′lə mat′) *n.* **1.** a person who is employed or skilled in international diplomacy, esp. an official who is assigned to a foreign country or to an international organization or conference as a representative of his or her government. **2.** any person who is skillful in dealing with others; tactful person. Also, **diplomatist.**

dip·lo·mat·ic (dip′lə mat′ik) *adj.* **1.** of, relating to, or connected with international diplomacy. **2.** possessing or exhibiting skill or tact in dealing with other people. Also, **dip′lo·mat′i·cal.** —**dip′lo·mat′i·cal·ly,** *adv.*

diplomatic corps, all of the foreign diplomats stationed in the capital of a country.

diplomatic immunity, the immunity of members of a diplomatic corps from taxes, duties, and legal proceedings while in a foreign country.

di·plo·ma·tist (di plō′mə tist) *n.* diplomat.

dip·lo·pod (dip′lə pod′) *n.* millipede.

dip needle, an instrument used to find the angle between the direction of the earth's magnetic force and the earth's horizontal surface.

di·pole (dī′pōl′) *n.* **1.** any object or system having two magnetic poles or two electrical charges that are opposite in sign but equal in magnitude. **2.** a radio or television antenna made of two horizontal rods set end-to-end. [DI-[1] + POLE[2].] —**di·po′lar,** *adj.*

dip·per (dip′ər) *n.* **1.** a person or thing that dips. **2.** a long-handled cup or vessel for scooping up liquids; ladle. **3. Dipper.** the Big Dipper or the Little Dipper. **4.** water ouzel.

dip·so·ma·ni·a (dip′sə mā′nē ə) *n.* an abnormal compulsion to drink alcoholic liquor, esp. in excessive amounts, as in alcoholism. [Modern Latin *dipsomania,* from Greek *dipsos* thirst + *maniā* madness.]

dip·so·ma·ni·ac (dip′sə mā′nē ak′) *n.* alcoholic. —**dip·so·ma·ni·a·cal** (dip′sō mə nī′ə kəl), *adj.*

dip·stick (dip′stik′) *n.* a graduated metal rod used for measuring the level of liquid in a container, esp. of oil in the crankcase of an automobile.

dipt (dipt) a past tense and past participle of **dip.**

dip·ter·ous (dip′tər əs) *adj.* **1.** of or belonging to an order, Diptera, of insects that have only one full pair of wings, including the gnat, mosquito, and housefly. The second pair of wings are small appendages. **2.** *Botany.* having only one pair of winglike parts, as certain seeds or stems. Also, **dip′ter·an.** [Greek *dipteros* having two wings.]

dip·tych (dip′tik) *n.* **1.** a double painting or carving consisting of two panels hinged together, esp. one depicting a religious subject and used as an altarpiece. **2.** an ancient writing tablet consisting of two hinged pieces of wood or ivory whose inner surfaces are waxed for writing on with a stylus. [Late Latin *diptycha* writing tablet with two leaves, from Greek *diptycha* pair of writing tablets, from *diptychos* folded, doubled.]

diptych

dire (dīr) *adj.,* **dir·er, dir·est.** **1.** causing great fear or suffering; dreadful; horrible: *a dire calamity, dire prophecies.* **2.** extremely urgent; desperate: *The victim was in dire need of medical attention.* [Latin *dīrus* dreadful.] —**dire′ly,** *adv.* —**dire′ness,** *n.*

di·rect (di rekt′, dī-) *v.t.* **1.** to regulate the course or affairs of; exercise authority over: *to direct traffic, to direct the affairs of state.* **2.** to give authoritative instructions to; command: *The general directed the troops to attack.* **3.** to tell or show (someone) the way: *Can you direct me to the nearest phone booth?* **4.** to cause to move in or follow a particular course or direction: *I directed my gaze to where the guide was pointing.* **5.** to intend (words) to be heard by a particular person or persons (with *to*): *Direct your remarks to the entire class.* **6.** to lead, guide, or supervise the production or performance of: *to direct a film.* **7.** to write the destination on: *to direct a letter.* —*v.i.* **1.** to give guidance or commands. **2.** to be a director, as of an orchestra, film, or play. —*adj.* **1.** proceeding in a straight line or by the shortest course; straight: *a direct route.* **2.** without an intervening or interceding person or thing; with nothing in between: *We made direct contact with the kidnappers.* **3.** characterized by or showing honesty and sincerity: *a direct manner, a direct reply.* **4.** in an unbroken line of descent: *a direct heir, a direct ancestor.* **5.** complete and total; absolute: *the direct antithesis.* **6.** in the exact words of the speaker or author: *a direct quotation.* **7.** of or by the action of the electorate without the intervention of representatives: *the direct election of senators.* —*adv.* directly. [Latin *dīrectus,* past participle of *dīrigere* to straighten, guide.] —**di·rect′ness,** *n.* —For Synonyms *(v.t.),* see **command, manage.**

direct address *Grammar.* when speaking to someone, the use of that person's name or of a word identifying the person, as in the sentences *Kim, come here* and *Professor, I enjoyed your lecture.*

direct current, an electric current in which the flow of electrons is in one direction only. ⇒ distinguished from **alternating current.**

direct discourse, a form of discourse in which a person's words are quoted exactly, as *I said, "I like cats."* ⇒ distinguished from **indirect discourse.**

di·rect·ed (di rek′tid, dī-) *adj. Mathematics.* (of a line) having positive or negative direction assigned, as a vector.

di·rec·tion (di rek′shən, dī-) *n.* **1.** the act of directing. **2.** guidance or control; management: *The recruits are under the direction of a sergeant.* **3.** a line or course along which something moves, faces, or lies: *I was walking in the direction of the park.* **4.** *also,* **directions.** instruction about how to proceed or act: *The farmer gave us directions to town. The directions on the package were to put the vegetables in boiling water.* **5.** a tendency or line of development: *efforts in the direction of reform.* **6.** a command to do something; order: *The soldiers waited for the officer's directions before attacking.* **7.** the supervision and organization of a play, film, or other presentation. **8.** *Music.* a word, phrase, or sign indicating how a particular note, chord, or passage is to be played. **9.** an address, as on a letter or package. [Latin *dīrēctiō* a making straight, directing.]

di·rec·tion·al (di rek′shə nəl, dī-) *adj.* **1.** of or relating to direction in space. **2.** *Electronics.* **a.** designed to determine the direction from which signals come. **b.** able to send or receive signals in one direction only. **3.** indicating direction: *directional signals on an automobile.*

direction finder, a radio receiving device that determines the direction of incoming radio signals, usually by means of a rotating antenna in the form of a loop or rectangle.

di·rec·tive (di rek′tiv, dī-) *n.* an order, regulation, or instruction, esp. one issued by a higher authority: *the officer received a directive from headquarters to attack.* —*adj.* serving to direct, guide, or prescribe.

di·rect·ly (di rekt′lē, dī-) *adv.* **1.** in a direct line or manner; straight: *The car came directly toward us.* **2.** without the intervention of another or others: *That person was directly responsible for the confusion.* **3.** without delay; at once: *to return directly.* **4.** completely and totally: *Your political views are directly opposed to mine.*

direct mail, printed matter, as advertisements or appeals for charitable donations, mailed directly to large numbers of potential customers or contributors. —**di·rect′-mail′,** *adj.*

direct object, a word or words designating the person or thing that receives the action expressed by a transitive verb. In *we saw them,* the direct object is *them.* ⇒ distinguished from **indirect object.**

di·rec·tor (di rek′tər, dī-) *n.* **1.** a person or thing that directs: *a camp director, a funeral director.* **2.** a person who supervises and guides the performers and technicians in the production of a play, film, television program, or other presentation. **3.** one of the members of the board chosen to govern the overall affairs of a company or institution. —**di·rec′tor·ship,** *n.*

di·rec·to·rate (di rek′tər it, dī-) *n.* **1.** the office or position of director. **2.** a body of directors.

di·rec·to·ri·al (di rek tôr′ē əl, dī′-) *adj.* **1.** of or relating to a director or directorate. **2.** serving to direct; directive.

di·rec·to·ry (di rek′tə rē, dī-) *n., pl.* **-ries. 1.** an alphabetical or classified list, as of the names, addresses, or occupations of a specific group of people: *a telephone directory.* **2.** *Computers.* a listing of all files stored in memory or on a disk. **3.** a board or tablet listing the locations of the occupants, offices, or departments in a building or store. **4.** a book or collection of rules, esp. one containing directions for religious worship. **5.** a body of directors; directorate. **6. Directory.** the executive branch of the revolutionary government in France from 1795 to 1799, consisting of five men selected by the French legislature. —*adj.* serving to direct or guide.

direct primary, an election in which those registered as members of a political party vote directly for the candidates of their party, rather than for delegates to a nominating convention.

di·rec·trix (di rek′triks, dī-) *n., pl.* **di·rec·trix·es** or **di·rec·tri·ces** (di rek′trə sēz′, dī-, dī′rek trī′sēz). *Geometry.* a fixed line that guides the motion of another line as it generates a surface or guides the motion of a point as it generates a curve. The circle forming the base of a cone is a directrix. For illustration, see **cone.**

direct tax, a tax levied directly on the persons who must pay it,

a	at	e	end	o	hot	u	up	hw	white		about
ā	ape	ē	me	ō	old	ū	use	ng	song		taken
ä	far	i	it	ô	fork	u̇	rule	th	thin	ə	pencil
âr	care	ī	ice	oi	oil	u̇	pull	th	this		lemon
		îr	pierce	ou	out	ûr	turn	zh	measure		circus

as an income or inheritance tax. ➡ distinguished from **indirect tax**.

dire·ful (dīr′fəl) *adj.* dire; dreadful; terrible. —**dire′ful·ly**, *adv.* —**dire′ful·ness**, *n.*

dire wolf, an extinct wolflike mammal, *Canis dirus,* found as a Pleistocene fossil in North America. It was stockier and somewhat larger than modern wolves. [From its Modern Latin species name. See DIRE.]

dirge (dûrj) *n.* a song or hymn of grief or mourning, esp. one performed at a funeral or memorial ceremony; lament. [Middle English *dirge,* from earlier *dirige,* from Latin *dirige* (singular imperative of *dirigere* to direct), the first word of the antiphon in the Latin version of the Roman Catholic Office for the Burial of the Dead.]

dir·ham (di ram′) *n.* the monetary unit of Morocco. [Arabic *dirham,* from Greek *drachmē.* See DRACHMA.]

dir·i·gi·ble (dir′i jə bəl, də rij′ə-) *n.* a motor-driven, rigid airship that can be steered. —*adj.* able to be directed, controlled, or steered. [Latin *dīrigere* to straighten, guide + -IBLE.]

dirk (dûrk) *n.* a dagger. —*v.t.* to stab with a dirk. [Of uncertain origin.]

dirn·dl (dûrn′dəl) *n.* **1.** a woman's dress with a fitted bodice and a full skirt gathered at the waist. **2.** a skirt of this style. Also *(def. 2),* **dirndl skirt.** [Short for German *Dirndlkleid* peasant costume for girls, from *Dirndl* young girl, diminutive of *Dirne* girl + *Kleid* dress.]

dirt (dûrt) *n.* **1.** any filthy, foul, or soiling substance: *Wash that dirt off your hands.* **2.** soil, esp. when loose: *I filled all the flowerpots with dirt.* **3.** something despised, mean, or worthless: *to treat someone like dirt.* **4.** moral indecency; corruption; immorality. **5.** obscene writing, pictures, or speech; pornography. **6.** *Informal.* gossip, esp. of a malicious nature. [Old Norse *drit* excrement.]
• **to do someone dirt.** *Slang.* to do something that harms another, esp. in a deliberately spiteful way.
• **to hit the dirt.** *Slang.* to drop down suddenly to the ground, as to avoid being hit.

dirt bike, a lightweight motorcycle specially designed for riding on dirt roads, trails, and the like.

dirt-cheap (dûrt′chēp′) *adj.* very low priced. —*adv.* at a very low price.

dirt farmer *Informal.* a farmer who works his or her own land, as distinguished from one who hires others to work the land.

dirt-poor (dûrt′pʉr′) *adj.* very poor: *The famous author was dirt-poor as a child.*

dirt·y (dûr′tē) *adj.,* **dirt·i·er, dirt·i·est. 1.** soiled with or as with dirt; not clean; filthy: *a dirty towel.* **2.** tending to soil or make unclean: *Digging the hole was a hard and dirty job.* **3.** worthy of being despised; contemptible; low: *a dirty trick.* **4.** given to or exhibiting moral indecency; obscene or corrupt: *dirty thoughts; a dirty joke.* **5.** not following or according to rules of fair play: *a dirty fighter.* **6.** *Informal.* showing annoyance or anger: *a dirty look.* **7.** (of colors) not clear or bright; impure. **8.** (of nuclear weapons) producing a large amount of radioactive fallout. **9.** (of weather) unsettled; stormy. —*v.t., v.i.,* **dirt·ied, dirt·y·ing.** to make or become dirty; soil. —**dirt′i·ly**, *adv.* —**dirt′i·ness**, *n.*

dirty pool *Slang.* unfair, dishonest, or underhanded actions or conduct.

dirty work *Informal.* **1.** a tiresome, unpleasant, or unrewarding job or part of a job. **2.** dishonest or unethical actions; foul play.

Dis (dis) *n.* **1.** in Roman mythology, the ruler of the underworld, identified with the Greek god Hades or Pluto. **2.** the land of the dead; underworld.

dis-[1] *prefix* **1.** opposite of; absence of; not: *disobedience, dishonesty.* **2.** undoing of; reverse of: *disconnect, disaffirm.* **3.** apart; away: *dismiss, disperse.* **4.** deprivation of; expulsion from: *dispossession, disbarment.* **5.** completely; thoroughly: *disannul.* [Latin *dis* apart, away, un-[2], exceedingly.]

dis-[2], form of **di-**[1] before *s,* as in *dissyllable.*

dis·a·bil·i·ty (dis′ə bil′i tē) *n., pl.* -**ties. 1.** a loss or lack of ability; disabled condition; incapacity: *My insurance covers disability arising from injury.* **2.** something that disables; handicap: *Lack of practical experience can be a serious disability in certain occupations.* **3.** a lack of legal ability to act; legal incapacity: *disability resulting from senility.*

dis·a·ble (dis ā′bəl) *v.t.,* -**bled, -bling. 1.** to deprive of ability or power; cripple; incapacitate. **2.** to make legally incapable. —**dis·a′ble·ment**, *n.*

dis·a·bled (dis ā′bəld) *adj.* **1.** having a disability; crippled. **2.** broken or temporarily out of order: *The disabled vehicle caused a traffic jam.* —*n.* **the disabled.** people with a disability or disabilities, considered as a group.

dis·a·buse (dis′ə būz′) *v.t., v.i.,* -**bused, -bus·ing.** to free from

false or mistaken ideas (often with *of*): *to disabuse people of their superstitions.*

di·sac·cha·ride (dī sak′ə rīd′) *n.* any of a group of carbohydrates, as sucrose, that yield two monosaccharides in hydrolysis. [DI-[1] + SACCHARIDE.]

dis·ac·cord (dis′ə kôrd′) *v.i.* to be out of accord or harmony; clash; disagree. —*n.* a lack of accord or harmony; disagreement.

dis·ad·van·tage (dis′ad van′tij, -əd-) *n.* **1.** something that interferes with or prevents success or achievement; drawback; handicap: *the disadvantage of a poor education.* **2.** the state or condition of being in an unfavorable or harmful situation; loss or injury: *It will be to your disadvantage if you give up now.* —*v.t.,* -**taged, -tag·ing.** to place in an unfavorable or harmful state or condition. [Old French *desavantage* unfavorable condition, from *des-* (from Latin *dis-* apart) + *avantage* advance. See ADVANTAGE.]

dis·ad·van·taged (dis′ad van′tijd, -əd-) *adj.* lacking a decent standard of living; underprivileged. —*n.* **the disadvantaged.** disadvantaged people, considered as a group.

dis·ad·van·ta·geous (dis ad′van tā′jəs, dis′ad-) *adj.* causing disadvantage; unfavorable or harmful; detrimental. —**dis·ad′van·ta′geous·ly**, *adv.* —**dis·ad′van·ta′geous·ness**, *n.*

dis·af·fect (dis′ə fekt′) *v.t.* to alienate the affection or loyalty of; estrange. —**dis′af·fec′tion**, *n.*

dis·af·fect·ed (dis′ə fek′tid) *adj.* unfriendly, disloyal, or discontented: *The disaffected workers failed to report to work.*

dis·af·fil·i·ate (dis′ə fil′ē āt′) *v.t., v.i.,* -**at·ed, -at·ing.** to sever affiliation (with). —**dis′af·fil′i·a′tion**, *n.*

dis·af·firm (dis′ə fûrm′) *v.t.* **1.** to deny or contradict (a prior statement). **2.** *Law.* **a.** to refuse to abide by (a settlement or agreement); repudiate. **b.** to reverse or set aside; annul. —**dis′af·firm′ance, dis·af·fir·ma·tion** (dis′af ər mā′shən), *n.*

dis·a·gree (dis′ə grē′) *v.i.,* -**greed, -gree·ing. 1.** to fail to share the same opinion; dissent: *I disagree with your first statement.* **2.** to quarrel; dispute; argue: *The brother and sister disagreed violently about the election.* **3.** to fail to agree or harmonize; differ; conflict: *Newspaper accounts of the robbery disagreed.* **4.** to cause physical discomfort or ill effects; be upsetting or unsuitable (with *with*): *Hot weather disagrees with me.*

dis·a·gree·a·ble (dis′ə grē′ə bəl) *adj.* **1.** not to one's taste or liking; unpleasant; offensive: *a disagreeable odor, a disagreeable task.* **2.** bad-tempered; quarrelsome: *a disagreeable person.* —**dis′a·gree′a·bil′i·ty, dis′a·gree′a·ble·ness**, *n.* —**dis′a·gree′a·bly**, *adv.*

dis·a·gree·ment (dis′ə grē′mənt) *n.* **1.** a failure to agree; difference; discrepancy: *There was an apparent disagreement between the two suspects' alibis.* **2.** a difference of opinion: *There was disagreement among the committee members.* **3.** a quarrel; dispute; argument.

> **Synonyms** **Disagreement, discord,** and **dissension** denote a lack of common ground among two or more parties. **Disagreement** is the most neutral of these terms, referring to any difference of opinion: *a disagreement over plans for the afternoon, disagreement on matters of taste.* **Discord** connotes a clash of opinions or ideas leading to rancor: *The discord among ethnic groups brought the country close to civil war.* **Dissension** suggests a break or disruption caused by strong disagreement: *Dissension in its ranks prevented the party from coming up with a strong candidate.*

dis·al·low (dis′ə lou′) *v.t.* **1.** to deny the truth or validity of: *to disallow a claim.* **2.** to refuse to allow; prohibit: *The town voted to disallow gambling.* —**dis′al·low′ance**, *n.*

dis·an·nul (dis′ə nul′) *v.t.,* -**nulled, -nul·ling.** to abolish completely; annul. —**dis′an·nul′ment**, *n.*

dis·ap·pear (dis′ə pîr′) *v.i.* **1.** to pass from sight; vanish: *The sun disappeared below the horizon.* **2.** to cease to exist or be known: *That species disappeared in the Ice Age.*

> **Synonyms** **Disappear** and **vanish** mean to become completely lost from sight. **Disappear** may connote either a temporary or a permanent disappearance: *The aircraft disappeared from the radar screen. By afternoon the clouds had disappeared.* **Vanish** suggests quickness and permanence, and often hints at mystery: *The star witness vanished into thin air. The pen I was using a moment ago has simply vanished.*

dis·ap·pear·ance (dis′ə pîr′əns) *n.* the act or fact of disappearing.

dis·ap·point (dis′ə point′) *v.t.* **1.** to fail to fulfill the hope, desire, or expectation of (someone). **2.** to prevent the realization or fulfillment of (something); thwart; frustrate: *to disappoint a person's hopes.* [Old French *desapointier* to frustrate, from *des-* (from Latin *dis-* apart) + *apoint(i)er* to arrange. See APPOINT.]

dis·ap·point·ment (dis′ə point′mənt) *n.* **1.** the act or fact of disappointing. **2.** the state or feeling of being disappointed: *The children couldn't hide their disappointment when the game was can-*

celed. **3.** a person or thing that disappoints: *The failed experiment was a major disappointment to the researchers.*

dis·ap·pro·ba·tion (dis′ap rə bā′shən) *n.* disapproval; censure.

dis·ap·prov·al (dis′ə prü′vəl) *n.* **1.** the act of disapproving. **2.** an unfavorable opinion or feeling; dislike; censure.

dis·ap·prove (dis′ə prüv′) *v.,* **-proved, -prov·ing.** —*v.t.* **1.** to have or express an unfavorable opinion of; regard with disfavor; censure; condemn: *to disapprove someone's rude behavior.* **2.** to refuse to approve or sanction; reject: *to disapprove a request.* —*v.i.* to have or express an unfavorable opinion (often with *of*): *We disapproved of the company's unethical business practices.* —**dis′ap·prov′ing·ly,** *adv.*

dis·arm (dis ärm′) *v.t.* **1.** to deprive of a weapon or weapons: *The sheriff disarmed the prisoner.* **2.** to overcome the hostility or suspicion of; win over: *The swindler's charming manner disarmed us.* **3.** to deprive of the means to attack or defend: *to disarm a defeated country.* **4.** to make harmless by removing a fuse or other detonating mechanism: *to disarm a bomb.* —*v.i.* **1.** to lay down arms: *The captured soldiers were forced to disarm.* **2.** to reduce, limit, or eliminate military weapons, equipment, or forces.

dis·ar·ma·ment (dis är′mə mənt) *n.* **1.** the act of disarming. **2.** the reduction, limitation, or elimination of military weapons, equipment, or forces of a country.

dis·arm·ing (dis är′ming) *adj.* tending to overcome hostility or suspicion; winning: *a disarming smile.* —**dis·arm′ing·ly,** *adv.*

dis·ar·range (dis′ə rānj′) *v.t.,* **-ranged, -rang·ing.** to disturb the arrangement of; create disorder in: *The children searched through the closet, disarranging everything.* —**dis′ar·range′ment,** *n.*

dis·ar·ray (dis′ə rā′) *n.* **1.** a condition of disorder; lack of orderly arrangement; confusion. **2.** a condition of disorder or incompleteness of dress. —*v.t.* **1.** to throw into disorder or confusion. **2.** to undress. —For Synonyms *(n.),* see **confusion.**

dis·as·sem·ble (dis′ə sem′bəl) *v.t.,* **-bled, -bling.** to take apart: *to disassemble an engine.*

dis·as·so·ci·ate (dis′ə sō′shē āt′, -sē-) *v.t.,* **-at·ed, -at·ing.** to cut off association, connection, or identification with; separate from; dissociate: *I disassociated myself from their company. The candidate disassociated herself from her party's stand on the issue.* —**dis′as·so′ci·a′tion,** *n.*

dis·as·ter (di zas′tər) *n.* any event causing much suffering, distress, or loss; sudden or great misfortune; calamity. [French *désastre,* going back to Latin *dis-* (see DIS-[1]) + *astrum* star, from Greek *astron;* from the astrological belief that when the stars are against one, great misfortune occurs.]

Synonyms Disaster, calamity, and **catastrophe** denote an occurrence with extremely bad consequences. **Disaster,** the broadest of the three terms, generally connotes widespread destruction, from natural or other causes: *The hurricane was the worst disaster to hit the city in a century. Careless driving led to the highway disaster.* **Calamity** refers more to the effect of such an occurrence on its victims: *The drought was a calamity for the peasants, who were threatened with starvation.* **Catastrophe** suggests a final misfortune: *The closing of the plant was a catastrophe from which the town could not recover.*

dis·as·trous (di zas′trəs) *adj.* causing or accompanied by disaster; calamitous: *a disastrous flood, a disastrous mistake.* —**dis·as′trous·ly,** *adv.*

dis·a·vow (dis′ə vou′) *v.t.* to deny knowledge of or responsibility for; refuse to acknowledge; repudiate: *to disavow a statement, to disavow a belief.*

dis·a·vow·al (dis′ə vou′əl) *n.* the act of disavowing; repudiation.

dis·band (dis band′) *v.t.* to break up the organization of; dissolve: *to disband a regiment.* —*v.i.* to cease to function as an organized body; disperse: *The club disbanded after three meetings.* —**dis·band′ment,** *n.*

dis·bar (dis bär′) *v.t.,* **-barred, -bar·ring.** to expel (a lawyer) from the legal profession; deprive of the right to practice law. —**dis·bar′ment,** *n.*

dis·be·lief (dis′bi lēf′) *n.* lack of belief; refusal to believe.

dis·be·lieve (dis′bi lēv′) *v.t., v.i.,* **-lieved, -liev·ing.** to fail to believe in (someone or something). —**dis′be·liev′er,** *n.*

dis·bur·den (dis bûr′dən) *v.t.* **1.** to rid of a burden or load: *to disburden a ship, to disburden an animal.* **2.** to relieve of something burdensome or oppressive: *to disburden one's conscience.* —*v.i.* to get rid of a burden or load.

dis·burse (dis bûrs′) *v.t.,* **-bursed, -burs·ing.** to pay out (funds); expend. [Old French *desbourser* to take money from a purse, pay, going back to Latin *dis-* apart + Late Latin *bursa* purse. See PURSE.] —**dis·burs′er,** *n.* —For Synonyms, see **spend.**

dis·burse·ment (dis bûrs′mənt) *n.* **1.** the act of disbursing. **2.** money disbursed; expenditure.

disc (disk) *n.* **1.** a phonograph record. **2.** disk. [Form of DISK.]

disc. 1. discount. **2.** discovered.

dis·cant (dis′kant, dis kant′) descant.

dis·card (*v.,* dis kärd′; *n.,* dis′kärd) *v.t.* **1.** to reject, or give up as useless, worthless, or unwanted; get rid of: *to discard an outdated theory.* **2.** *Card Games.* **a.** to throw away or put aside (an unwanted card or cards). **b.** to play (a card other than a trump or the suit led). —*v.i.* to discard a card or cards. —*n.* **1.** the act of discarding or the state of being discarded. **2.** a person or thing that is discarded. **3.** *Card Games.* a card or cards discarded. [DIS-[1] + CARD[1].]

disc brake, a brake operating by the retarding friction of two pads that press against either side of a rotating disc.

dis·cern (di sûrn′, -zûrn′) *v.t.* **1.** to recognize as different and distinct; separate or distinguish mentally: *to discern good from evil.* **2.** to detect or perceive by the senses or the mind: *I could barely discern the house in the fog. He discerned their plan immediately.* —*v.i.* to see a difference; distinguish: *to discern between truth and falsehood.* [Old French *discerner,* from Latin *discernere* to separate, distinguish.] —**dis·cern′er,** *n.*

Synonyms Discern, perceive, recognize, and **distinguish** mean to see something clearly. **Discern** connotes picking out one object, person, or impression from among many: *We discerned our friend among the crowd pouring out of the train.* **Perceive** frequently suggests getting at the real nature of something by using one's sight or other senses: *Because of their coloring, she perceived the mushrooms to be poisonous.* **Recognize** implies that the object is in some way already known: *I recognized you from your picture.* **Distinguish** is similar to *discern* in use, but stresses the act of separating the object from others: *The brightness of the planet allowed us to distinguish it from the stars around it.*

dis·cern·i·ble (di sûr′nə bəl, -zûr′) *adj.* capable of being discerned; perceptible: *There is no discernible difference between the two chairs.* —**dis·cern′i·bly,** *adv.*

dis·cern·ing (di sûr′ning, -zûr′-) *adj.* having or showing discernment; discriminating; perceptive: *a discerning judge of character, discerning taste in art.* —**dis·cern′ing·ly,** *adv.*

dis·cern·ment (di sûrn′mənt, -zûrn′-) *n.* **1.** the act of discerning. **2.** keenness of perception, judgment, or understanding; insight.

dis·charge (*v.,* dis chärj′; *n.,* dis′chärj, dis chärj′) *v.,* **-charged, -charg·ing.** —*v.t.* **1.a.** to release from service or office: *to discharge a soldier from the army.* **b.** to dismiss from employment; fire: *to discharge a worker.* **2.** to release from care or custody; set at liberty: *to discharge a prisoner, to discharge a patient.* **3.** to let go or clear out: *The boat discharged its passengers at the pier.* **4.** to remove the contents of; unload: *The longshoremen discharged the ship.* **5.** to fulfill the requirements of; carry out; execute: *to discharge an errand, to discharge a duty.* **6.a.** to propel a missile from or fire (a weapon): *to discharge a gun.* **b.** to cause (a missile) to be propelled. **7.** to send forth; emit: *The river discharged its water into the bay. The motor discharged fumes.* **8.** to give vent to or express: *to discharge pent-up emotion.* **9.** to relieve of responsibility, duty, or obligation: *to discharge a jury.* **10.** to pay off; settle: *to discharge a debt.* **11.** to rid of an electric charge; withdraw electricity from: *to discharge a battery.* **12.** *Law.* to annul or set aside (a court order). **13.** to remove (color or dye) from textiles, as by chemical bleaching. —*v.i.* **1.** to send forth contents: *The smaller pipes discharged into the main one.* **2.** to go off, as a firearm; fire. **3.** to get rid of or deliver a burden or load. **4.** to lose an electrical charge. —*n.* **1.** a dismissal from service, office, or employment. **2.** release from care or custody: *the discharge of a prisoner.* **3.** something that dismisses or releases, as a certificate discharging a person from military service. **4.** the act of discharging a weapon or missile. **5.** the act of carrying out; performance; execution: *to be faithful in the discharge of one's duties.* **6.** the act of flowing or letting out; emission; ejection: *the discharge of pus from a wound.* **7.** the rate or amount of outflow. **8.** something sent forth: *a watery discharge from sore eyes.* **9.** the act of relieving from responsibility, duty, or obligation. **10.** the act of paying off or settling: *the discharge of a debt.* **11.** the act of removing a charge or burden; unloading: *the discharge of cargo.* **12.** a transference of electricity between two charged bodies. **13.** *Law.* a dismissal or annulment, as of a court order. [Old

a	at	e	end	o	hot	u	up	hw	white		about
ā	ape	ē	me	ō	old	ū	use	ng	song		taken
ä	far	i	it	ô	fork	ü	rule	th	thin	ə	pencil
âr	care	ī	ice	oi	oil	u̇	pull	th	this		lemon
		îr	pierce	ou	out	ûr	turn	zh	measure		circus

French *descharger* to unload, from *des-*(from Latin *dis-* apart) + *charger* to load. See CHARGE.] —dis·charge′a·ble, *adj.* —discharg′er, *n.*

discharge tube, an electron tube containing a gas that is at low pressure and through which a current passes when sufficient voltage is applied.

dis·ci·ple (di sī′pəl) *n.* **1.** a follower or adherent of a particular teacher or doctrine: *Plato was a disciple of Socrates.* **2.** any of the early followers of Jesus, esp. one of the Apostles. **3. Disciple.** a member of the Disciples of Christ. [Old English *discipul,* from Latin *discipulus* pupil.] —dis·ci′ple·ship′, *n.*

Disciples of Christ, a Protestant denomination, organized in 1809, that rejects all creeds, holds that the Bible is the only basis for Christian faith and practice, and administers baptism by immersion.

dis·ci·plin·a·ble (dis′ə plin′ə bəl) *adj.* **1.** capable of being taught by discipline and training. **2.** subject to or deserving discipline.

dis·ci·pli·nar·i·an (dis′ə plə när′ē ən) *n.* a person who enforces or advocates strict discipline. —*adj.* disciplinary.

dis·ci·pli·nar·y (dis′ə plə ner′ē) *adj.* of, relating to, or used in discipline: *disciplinary measures.*

dis·ci·pline (dis′ə plin) *n.* **1.** training that develops, corrects, or perfects something, as the mind or moral character. **2.** orderly, obedient, or restrained conduct; self-control; self-restraint: *The students showed excellent discipline during the fire drill.* **3.** acceptance of or submission to authority and control; order: *Troop discipline in battle saved many lives.* **4.** punishment given to train or correct; chastisement: *The child's rude behavior required severe discipline.* **5.** a branch of instruction or knowledge; field of study: *Mathematics and physics are related disciplines.* **6.** a set or system of rules for conduct, as for a religion or religious order. —*v.t.* **1.** to train to be obedient; keep in order or under control: *to discipline troops.* **2.** to develop or train, as by instruction or exercise: *to discipline one's mind.* **3.** to punish; chastise. [Latin *disciplīna* instruction, knowledge.] —dis′ci·plin′er, *n.*

disc jockey *also,* **disk jockey.** an announcer or master of ceremonies on a radio program of recorded music.

dis·claim (dis klām′) *v.t.* **1.** to deny knowledge of, responsibility for, or connection with. **2.** to renounce a legal right or claim to: *to disclaim a share in an estate.* **3.** to reject or deny the claim or authority of. —*v.i.* to renounce a legal right or claim.

dis·claim·er (dis klā′mər) *n.* **1.** a disclaiming act, notice, or instrument. **2.** a person who disclaims.

dis·close (dis klōz′) *v.t.,* -closed, -clos·ing. **1.** to make known; reveal: *to disclose a secret, to disclose one's intentions.* **2.** to expose to view; lay bare; uncover: *The excavation disclosed the ruins of an ancient city.* —dis·clos′er, *n.* —For Synonyms, see reveal.

dis·clo·sure (dis klō′zhər) *n.* **1.** the act of disclosing. **2.** something disclosed.

dis·co (dis′kō) *n., pl.* -cos. **1.** a form of popular music for dancing, often using electronically synthesized sounds, and characterized by a strong bass beat. **2.** discothèque. —*adj.* of or relating to disco or a discothèque: *disco songs.* —*v.i.,* -coed, -co·ing. to dance to disco. [Short for DISCOTHÈQUE.]

dis·cog·ra·phy (dis kog′rə fē) *n., pl.* -phies. a list of phonograph records, esp. a comprehensive list of the recordings of a particular performer, composer, or type of music. [DISC + -GRAPHY.]

dis·coid (dis′koid) *adj.* **1.** having the form of a disk. **2.** (of some composite flowers) having only disk flowers, with no rays. —*n.* a disk or disklike object.

dis·col·or (dis kul′ər) *also, British,* dis·col·our. *v.t.* to change or spoil the color of; fade; stain. —*v.i.* to become discolored.

dis·col·or·a·tion (dis kul′ə rā′shən) *also, British,* dis·col·our·a·tion. **1.** the act of discoloring or the state of being discolored. **2.** a discolored spot or mark; stain. Also, dis′col′orment.

dis·com·bob·u·late (dis′kəm bob′yə lāt′) *v.t.,* -lat·ed, -lating. *Informal.* to confuse; upset. —dis′com·bob′u·la′tion, *n.*

dis·com·fit (dis kum′fit) *v.t.* **1.** to throw into confusion; disconcert; embarrass: *The reporter's pointed question discomfited the mayor.* **2.** to defeat the plans or expectations of; frustrate; thwart. **3.** *Archaic.* to defeat or overthrow in battle; rout. [Old French *desconfit,* past participle of *desconfire* to defeat, going back to Latin *dis-* apart + *conficere* to bring about, preserve.]

dis·com·fi·ture (dis kum′fi chər) *n.* the act of discomfiting or the state of being discomfited.

dis·com·fort (dis kum′fərt) *n.* **1.** lack of comfort; uneasiness, hardship, or pain: *the discomfort of sleeping on rocky ground.* **2.** something that causes discomfort; inconvenience or hardship. —*v.t.* to make uncomfortable or uneasy.

dis·com·mode (dis′kə mōd′) *v.t.,* -mod·ed, -mod·ing. to cause inconvenience to; disturb; trouble.

dis·com·pose (dis′kəm pōz′) *v.t.,* -posed, -pos·ing. **1.** to disturb the composure of; make uneasy: *The jeers of the crowd did not discompose the speaker.* **2.** to disturb the order of; disarrange.

dis·com·po·sure (dis′kəm pō′zhər) *n.* the state of being discomposed; agitation; disturbance.

dis·con·cert (dis′kən sûrt′) *v.t.* **1.** to disturb the self-possession or composure of; embarrass; confuse: *Their rude laughter disconcerted us.* **2.** to throw into disorder or confusion; frustrate, as a plan. —dis′con·cert′ed·ness, *n.* —dis′con·cert′ing, *adj.* —dis′con·cert′ing·ly, *adv.*

dis·con·nect (dis′kə nekt′) *v.t.* to sever or break the connection of or between: *to disconnect a locomotive from a train, to disconnect a television set before fixing it.* —dis′con·nec′tion, *n.*

dis·con·nect·ed (dis′kə nek′tid) *adj.* **1.** lacking order or logic; incoherent; disjointed: *a disconnected speech, disconnected thoughts.* **2.** physically or electronically separated or ended: *a disconnected telephone.* —dis′con·nect′ed·ly, *adv.* —dis′con·nect′ed·ness, *n.*

dis·con·so·late (dis kon′sə lit) *adj.* **1.** without cheer, hope, or comfort; dejected; inconsolable: *The children were disconsolate after their pet ran away.* **2.** causing or characterized by dejection or gloom; cheerless. [Medieval Latin *disconsolatus* comfortless, from Latin *dis-* apart + *consōlātus,* past participle of *consōlārī* to comfort.] —dis·con′so·late·ly, *adv.* —dis·con′so·lateness, dis·con′so·la′tion (dis′kon′sə lā′shən), *n.*

dis·con·tent (dis′kən tent′) *n.* lack of contentment; dissatisfaction with the way things are: *There was much discontent among the players after the team lost its first six games.* Also, dis′con·tent′ment. —*v.t.* to make discontented. —*adj.* discontented.

dis·con·tent·ed (dis′kən ten′tid) *adj.* dissatisfied with the way things are; uneasy in mind; not contented. —dis′con·tent′ed·ly, *adv.* —dis′con·tent′ed·ness, *n.*

dis·con·tin·u·ance (dis′kən tin′ū əns) *n.* **1.** discontinuation. **2.** an interruption or termination of a lawsuit by court order at the request of the plaintiff.

dis·con·tin·u·a·tion (dis′kən tin′ū ā′shən) *n.* the act of discontinuing or the state of being discontinued.

dis·con·tin·ue (dis′kən tin′ū) *v.,* -tin·ued, -tin·u·ing. —*v.t.* **1.** to break off or cease from; put an end to; stop: *We discontinued the project because of a lack of funds.* **2.** to cease to take, give, use, or receive: *We discontinued our subscription to the magazine.* **3.** to bring about discontinuance of (a lawsuit). —*v.i.* to come to an end; cease: *Publication of the paper discontinued.* —dis′con·tin′u·er, *n.*

dis·con·ti·nu·i·ty (dis′kon tə nü′i tē, -nū′-) *n., pl.* -ties. **1.** lack of continuity. **2.** a gap or break.

dis·con·tin·u·ous (dis′kən tin′ū əs) *adj.* not continuous; interrupted; intermittent. —dis′con·tin′u·ous·ly, *adv.* —dis′con·tin′u·ous·ness, *n.*

dis·cord (dis′kôrd) *n.* **1.** a lack of agreement, concord, or harmony; disagreement; dissension; conflict: *discord between nations, discord among the various factions of a political party.* **2.** a mingling or clashing of harsh or unpleasing sounds; din. **3.** *Music.* lack of harmony in notes sounded simultaneously; dissonance. ➡ opposed to **concord.** [Old French *descorde* a quarrel, from *descorder* to quarrel, from Latin *discordāre* to differ.] —For Synonyms, see disagreement.

dis·cor·dance (dis kôr′dəns) *n.* **1.** the state or fact of being discordant; disagreement. **2.** a discord of sounds; harsh or dissonant noise. Also, dis·cor′dan·cy.

dis·cor·dant (dis kôr′dənt) *adj.* **1.** not in agreement, concord, or harmony; disagreeing; dissenting; conflicting: *discordant opinions.* **2.** harsh, clashing, or disagreeable in sound; dissonant; inharmonious: *the discordant noises of the street traffic.* —dis·cor′dant·ly, *adv.*

dis·co·thèque (dis′kə tek′, -kō-) *n.* an establishment for dancing to recorded or sometimes live music, often having food and beverages available. Also, **disco.** [French *discothèque* record library, nightclub featuring music by records, from Greek *diskos* round disk, quoit + *thēkē* container.]

dis·count (*n.,* dis′kount; *v.,* dis′kount′, dis kount′) *n.* **1.** a deduction of a specified amount or percentage, as from a price or other amount charged or owed: *to sell a radio at a 25% discount.* **2.** the interest deducted beforehand in purchasing, selling, or lending money on a note, bill, or other negotiable paper. **3.** discount rate. **4.** the act of discounting. —*v.t.* **1.** to reduce the cost or value of; offer for sale at a reduced rate: *That store discounts all its merchandise.* **2.** to deduct (a specified amount or percentage) from the total amount otherwise charged or owed: *to discount 15% from the price of a car.* **3.** to take little or no account of; minimize; disregard: *We cannot discount the research that has already been done.* **4.** to make allowance for exaggeration or bias

in: *Discount most of the stories about that athlete's ability.* **5.** to lessen the effect or importance of by taking into account in advance. **6.** to purchase, sell, or lend money on (negotiable paper) after deducting a certain amount from its face value. —*v.i.* **1.** to lend money, deducting the interest in advance. **2.** to sell merchandise at a discount. [Old French *desconter, descompter* to relate, reckon off, going back to Latin *dis-* apart + *computāre* to count.] —**dis·count'a·ble,** *adj.* —**dis'count'er,** *n.*

dis·coun·te·nance (dis koun'tə nəns) *v.t.,* **-nanced, -nanc·ing. 1.** to look upon with disfavor or disapproval; discourage; frown on: *to discountenance a proposal.* **2.** to disconcert; abash; embarrass.

discount house, an establishment where merchandise is sold at a price lower than the usual or advertised retail price. Also, **discount store.**

discount rate, the rate of interest charged in advance for discounting notes, bills, and other negotiable paper.

dis·cour·age (dis kûr'ij, -kur'-) *v.t.,* **-aged, -ag·ing. 1.** to lessen the courage, hope, or confidence of; dishearten: *I won the race because my slow start did not discourage me.* **2.** to keep from doing something; dissuade or deter (with *from*): *Bad weather discouraged us from going on the picnic.* **3.** to try to prevent by expressing disapproval of; frown upon: *The principal discouraged unexcused absences.* **4.** to prevent, obstruct, or hinder, as by opposition or difficulty: *Strict laws were passed in an attempt to discourage the sale of illegal drugs.* [Middle French *descourager* to dishearten, going back to Latin *dis-* apart + *cor* heart.]

dis·cour·age·ment (dis kûr'ij mənt, -kur'-) *n.* **1.** the act of discouraging. **2.** the state or feeling of being discouraged: *The team was filled with discouragement by the defeat.* **3.** something that discourages: *Failure to pass an exam can be a discouragement.*

dis·course (*n.,* dis'kôrs; *v.,* dis kôrs') *n.* **1.** the communication of thought by speech; conversation; talk. **2.** a formal, extended, spoken or written treatment of a given subject, as a treatise, lecture, or sermon. —*v.i.,* **-coursed, -cours·ing. 1.** to speak or write formally and at length on a subject (with *on* or *upon*): *The police chief discoursed on the need for more community involvement in combating crime.* **2.** to participate in conversation; talk; confer. [Late Latin *discursus* conversation, from Latin *discursus* a running to and fro.] —**dis·cours'er,** *n.* —For Synonyms (*n.*), see **talk.**

dis·cour·te·ous (dis kûr'tē əs) *adj.* not courteous; rude; impolite. —**dis·cour'te·ous·ly,** *adv.* —**dis·cour'te·ous·ness,** *n.*

dis·cour·te·sy (dis kûr'tə sē) *n., pl.* **-sies. 1.** lack of courtesy; rudeness; impoliteness. **2.** a discourteous act.

dis·cov·er (dis kuv'ər) *v.t.* **1.** to come upon or gain sight or knowledge of (something previously unseen or unknown) for the first time: *Wilhelm Roentgen discovered X rays.* **2.** to learn of; come to know of: *I discovered the poetry of Emily Dickinson in an early age.* **3.** *Archaic.* to make known; reveal. [Old French *descovrir* to uncover, disclose, from Late Latin *discooperīre,* from Latin *dis-* apart + *cooperīre* to cover.] —**dis·cov'er·a·ble,** *adj.* —**dis·cov'er·er,** *n.*

dis·cov·er·y (dis kuv'ə rē) *n., pl.* **-er·ies. 1.** the act of discovering: *The discovery of the error was too late.* **2.** something discovered: *The dollar in my pocket was a pleasant discovery.*

dis·cred·it (dis kred'it) *v.t.* **1.** to cause to be doubted or disbelieved; destroy belief, confidence, or trust in: *New information discredited the old theory.* **2.** to damage the credit or reputation of; bring into disrepute; disgrace: *The unsportsmanlike play of the football team discredited the entire school.* **3.** to refuse to believe or give credit to; disbelieve: *I discredit all those rumors.* —*n.* **1.** lack or loss of credit, reputation, or esteem: *Their conduct brought discredit to the whole family.* **2.** lack or loss of belief, confidence, or trust; doubt: *The results of later experiments brought the original theory into discredit.* **3.** something that discredits: *That dishonest deal was a discredit to the entire firm.*

dis·cred·it·a·ble (dis kred'i tə bəl) *adj.* bringing discredit; injurious to reputation: *a discreditable attempt to deceive others.* —**dis·cred'it·a·bly,** *adv.*

dis·creet (di skrēt') *adj.* having or showing discernment and careful judgment in speech and action; prudent; circumspect. [Old French *discret,* from Medieval Latin *discretus* capable of distinguishing, from Latin *discrētus,* past participle of *discernere* to separate, distinguish.] —**dis·creet'ly,** *adv.* —**dis·creet'ness,** *n.*

dis·crep·an·cy (dis skrep'ən sē) *n., pl.* **-cies. 1.** lack of agreement or consistency; difference; contradiction; variance: *There was little discrepancy in the testimony of the two witnesses.* **2.** an instance of this: *to discover a discrepancy in a story.* Also, **dis·crep'ance.**

dis·crep·ant (di skrep'ənt) *adj.* lacking agreement or consistency; at variance; conflicting: *There were discrepant reports of the accident by the two witnesses.* [Latin *discrepāns,* present participle

of *discrepāre* to sound discordantly, be different.] —**dis·crep'ant·ly,** *adv.*

dis·crete (di skrēt') *adj.* **1.** detached from others; separate; distinct: *The word "heart" has several discrete meanings.* **2.** consisting of distinct or individual parts. [Latin *discrētus* past participle of *discernere* to separate, distinguish.] —**dis·crete'ly,** *adv.* —**dis·crete'ness,** *n.*

dis·cre·tion (di skresh'ən) *n.* **1.** the quality of being discreet; good judgment; caution; prudence. **2.** the freedom or power to act according to one's own judgment; independent choice or determination: *They left the matter to my discretion.*
• **at one's discretion.** according to one's own judgment.

dis·cre·tion·ar·y (di skresh'ə ner'ē) *adj.* left to or determined by one's own discretion; limited only by judgment: *The ambassador was invested with discretionary powers.*

dis·crim·i·nant (di skrim'ə nənt) *n. Mathematics.* an expression calculated from the coefficients of an algebraic equation that gives information about the solutions to that equation. [Latin *discrīminantis,* genitive of *discrīmināns,* present participle of *discrīmināre* to distinguish, separate.]

dis·crim·i·nate (*v.,* di skrim'ə nāt'; *adj.,* di skrim'ə nit) *v.,* **-nat·ed, -nat·ing.** —*v.i.* **1.** to show prejudice or partiality without a sound reason: *It is against the law to discriminate against people because of their race or religion.* **2.** to note or observe a difference; make a distinction; distinguish: *to discriminate between good and bad poetry.* —*v.t.* **1.** to perceive or note the difference in or between; distinguish: *to learn to discriminate good from evil.* **2.** to make or constitute a difference in or between; differentiate: *abilities that discriminate one person from another.* —*adj.* making or perceiving careful or exact distinctions; having or marked by discrimination. [Latin *discrīminātus,* past participle of *discrīmināre* to separate.] —**dis·crim'i·nate·ly,** *adv.* —**dis·crim'i·na'tor,** *n.*

dis·crim·i·nat·ing (di skrim'ə nā'ting) *adj.* **1.** perceiving and making distinctions with accuracy; discerning: *a discriminating judge of character.* **2.** attentive to small details; particular; fastidious: *to be discriminating in one's choice of clothes.* **3.** making or constituting a difference; differentiating. **4.** discriminatory. **5.** differential, as a tariff. —**dis·crim'i·nat'ing·ly,** *adv.*

dis·crim·i·na·tion (di skrim'ə nā'shən) *n.* **1.** the act of discriminating. **2.** prejudice or partiality in attitudes or actions: *The applicants were judged without discrimination as to race, color, or creed.* **3.** the power or ability to perceive distinctions or differences; discernment: *They showed taste and discrimination in furnishing their home.*

dis·crim·i·na·tive (di skrim'ə nā'tiv) *adj.* **1.** perceiving and making distinctions; discriminating. **2.** discriminatory. —**dis·crim'i·na'tive·ly,** *adv.*

dis·crim·i·na·to·ry (di skrim'ə nə tôr'ē) *adj.* **1.** characterized or marked by prejudice, esp. racial prejudice: *Discriminatory practices in hiring personnel are against the law.* **2.** discerning; discriminating. —**dis·crim'i·na·to'ri·ly,** *adv.*

dis·cur·sive (dis kûr'siv) *adj.* wandering from one subject to another; rambling; digressive: *a discursive lecture.* —**dis·cur'sive·ly,** *adv.* —**dis·cur'sive·ness,** *n.*

dis·cus (dis'kəs) *n.* **1.** a heavy circular plate, now usually made of wood with a smooth metal rim around its edges, hurled for distance in athletic contests. **2.** the act of hurling this plate in an athletic contest. [Latin *discus* quoit, dish, from Greek *diskos* round plate, quoit. Doublet of DAIS, DESK, DISH, DISK.]

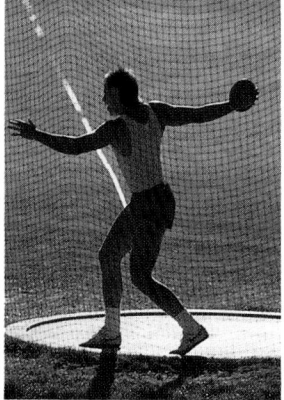

discus thrower

dis·cuss (di skus') *v.t.* to exchange or present ideas or opinions about; consider or examine in conversation or writing; talk or write about: *The council discussed plans for a new city hall. The next chapter dis-*

a	at	e	end	o	hot	u	up	hw	white		about
ā	ape	ē	me	ō	old	ū	use	ng	song		taken
ä	far	i	it	ô	fork	ü	rule	th	thin	ə	pencil
âr	care	ī	ice	oi	oil	u̇	pull	th	this		lemon
		îr	pierce	ou	out	ûr	turn	zh	measure		circus

cusses the Renaissance. [Late Latin *discussus,* past participle of *discutere* to discuss, investigate, from Latin *discutere* to shatter, disperse.]

dis·cus·sion (di skush′ən) *n.* **1.** the act of discussing: *Would you like to take part in our discussion?* **2.** an instance of discussing: *The book's discussion of the Middle Ages was thirty pages long.*

dis·dain (dis dān′) *n.* a feeling of contempt and aversion for something or someone regarded as unworthy or beneath one; scorn: *Don't treat your classmates with disdain.* —*v.t.* to consider unworthy or beneath oneself; look down on; scorn: *Despite their poverty, the old couple disdained charity.* [Old French *desdeignier* to scorn, going back to Latin *dis-* un-[2] + *dignārī* to think worthy.]

dis·dain·ful (dis dān′fəl) *adj.* feeling or showing disdain; scornful. —**dis·dain′ful·ly,** *adv.* —**dis·dain′ful·ness,** *n.*

dis·ease (di zēz′) *n.* **1.** a disturbance in the function or structure of an organ or group of organs in an organism, resulting from a specific cause or causes, as infection, characterized by particular symptoms, and producing particular effects; illness: *Arthritis is a chronic disease. Many antibiotic drugs are used to combat disease.* **2.** any disordered or harmful condition: *poverty, prejudice, and other diseases of society.* [Old French *desaise* sickness, discomfort, from *des-* (from Latin *dis-* apart) + *aise.* See EASE.]

dis·eased (di zēzd′) *adj.* affected with or suffering from disease: *a diseased tree.*

dis·em·bark (dis′em bärk′) *v.i.* to get off a ship or airplane: *We disembarked at New York.* —*v.t.* to put or let off a ship or airplane: *to disembark passengers at a port.* —**dis·em·bar·ka·tion** (dis em′bär kā′shən), *n.*

dis·em·bar·rass (dis′em bar′əs) *v.t.* to relieve or free from something that embarrasses, entangles, or encumbers.

dis·em·bod·y (dis′em bod′ē) *v.t.,* -**bod·ied,** -**bod·y·ing.** to separate or free, as a spirit, from the body or from physical existence. —**dis′em·bod′ied,** *adj.* —**dis′em·bod′i·ment,** *n.*

dis·em·bow·el (dis′em bou′əl) *v.t.,* -**eled,** -**el·ing;** *also, British,* -**elled,** -**el·ling.** to take out the bowels or entrails of; eviscerate. —**dis′em·bow′el·ment,** *n.*

dis·en·chant (dis′en chant′) *v.t.* to free from enchantment or strip of pleasant illusion; disillusion: *They had thought the area was scenic, but they were disenchanted.* —**dis′en·chant′er,** *n.* —**dis′en·chant′ment,** *n.*

dis·en·cum·ber (dis′en kum′bər) *v.t.* to relieve or free from something that burdens or troubles.

dis·en·fran·chise (dis′en fran′chīz) *v.t.,* -**chised,** -**chis·ing.** **1.** to deprive of the rights and privileges of citizenship, esp. of the right to vote. **2.** to deprive of a franchise, privilege, or right. Also, **disfranchise.** —**dis′en·fran′chise·ment,** *n.*

dis·en·gage (dis′en gāj′) *v.,* -**gaged,** -**gag·ing.** —*v.t.* **1.** to release or loosen from something that holds, connects, or entangles; detach; free: *Please disengage the arrow from the target.* **2.** to free, as from engagement, promise, or obligation: *We disengaged ourselves from the business deal as soon as we realized it was a fraud.* —*v.i.* to release, detach, or free oneself or itself: *The two wrestlers disengaged. The years disengaged.* —**dis′en·gage′ment,** *n.*

dis·en·tail (dis′en tāl′) *v.t. Law.* to free (an estate) from entail. —**dis′en·tail′ment,** *n.*

dis·en·tan·gle (dis′en tang′gəl) *v.,* -**tan·gled,** -**tan·gling.** —*v.t.* to free from tangles or confusion; extricate; untangle. —*v.i.* to become free from tangles or confusion. —**dis′en·tan′gle·ment,** *n.*

dis·en·throne (dis′en thrōn′) *v.t.,* -**throned,** -**thron·ing.** to dethrone; depose. —**dis′en·throne′ment,** *n.*

dis·en·twine (dis′en twīn′) *v.t., v.i.,* -**twined,** -**twin·ing.** to untwine; disentangle.

dis·e·qui·lib·ri·um (dis ē′kwə lib′rē əm) *n., pl.* -**ri·ums** or -**ri·a** (-rē ə). a lack or loss of equilibrium, as of physical or mental balance or economic stability. [DIS- + EQUILIBRIUM.]

dis·es·tab·lish (dis′e stab′lish) *v.t.* **1.** to deprive of fixed or established character or status. **2.** to withdraw exclusive state recognition or support from (a church). —**dis′es·tab′lish·ment,** *n.*

dis·es·teem (dis′e stēm′) *v.t.* to have a low opinion of or little regard for; hold in low esteem. —*n.* lack of esteem; disfavor: *That theory is held in disesteem by most scientists.*

dis·fa·vor (dis fā′vər) *n.* **1.** displeasure or lack of favor; dislike; disapproval: *The students looked with disfavor on the plan to shorten the spring vacation.* **2.** the state of being regarded unfavorably: *That political candidate is in disfavor with the party.* **3.** an unkind or detrimental act; disservice: *I did you a disfavor when I didn't back up your story.* —*v.t.* to regard or treat unfavorably; dislike; disapprove.

dis·fig·u·ra·tion (dis fig′yə rā′shən) *n.* disfigurement.

dis·fig·ure (dis fig′yər) *v.t.,* -**ured,** -**ur·ing.** to spoil or destroy the beauty or appearance of; deform; mar. —**dis·fig′ur·er,** *n.* —For Synonyms, see **deface.**

dis·fig·ure·ment (dis fig′yər mənt) *n.* **1.** the act of disfiguring or the state of being disfigured. **2.** something that disfigures; deformity; blemish. Also, **disfiguration.**

dis·fran·chise (dis fran′chīz) *v.t.,* -**chised,** -**chis·ing.** disenfranchise. —**dis·fran′chise·ment,** *n.*

dis·gorge (dis gôrj′) *v.t.,* -**gorged,** -**gorg·ing.** **1.** to throw up (something swallowed); vomit. **2.** to eject or pour (something) forth, esp. with force; discharge: *The volcano disgorged lava and smoke. The crowded train disgorged its passengers at the station.* **3.** to give up unwillingly. [Old French *desgorger* to vomit, going back to Latin *dis-* apart + Late Latin *gurges* throat, from Latin *gurges* whirlpool, abyss.] —**dis·gorge′ment,** *n.*

dis·grace (dis grās′) *n.* **1.** loss of honor, respect, or favor; shame; ignominy: *to bring disgrace to one's good name.* **2.** the state or condition of being dishonored or out of favor: *The senator resigned in disgrace.* **3.** a person or thing that brings about shame, dishonor, or reproach: *These slum conditions are a disgrace to the city.* —*v.t.,* -**graced,** -**grac·ing.** **1.** to bring shame, dishonor, or reproach to or upon: *to disgrace the family name.* **2.** to dismiss from favor or grace; treat with disfavor: *The monarch disgraced the disloyal courtier.* [French *disgrâce* misfortune, disfavor, going back to Latin *dis-* apart + *grātia* favor.]

dis·grace·ful (dis grās′fəl) *adj.* characterized by, deserving, or causing disgrace; shameful; disreputable: *disgraceful behavior.* —**dis·grace′ful·ly,** *adv.* —**dis·grace′ful·ness,** *n.*

dis·grun·tle (dis grun′təl) *v.t.,* -**tled,** -**tling.** to put in a bad humor; make dissatisfied, displeased, or cross: *Unnecessary delays always disgruntle me.* [DIS-[1] + earlier *gruntle* to grumble, from GRUNT.] —**dis·grun′tled,** *adj.* —**dis·grun′tle·ment,** *n.*

dis·guise (dis gīz′) *v.t.,* -**guised,** -**guis·ing.** **1.** to alter the appearance or dress of so as to make recognition difficult or impossible; conceal the identity of: *The children disguised themselves as ghosts on Halloween.* **2.** to conceal or obscure the existence or true nature or character of: *to disguise the taste of a medicine, to disguise sadness with a happy smile.* —*n.* **1.** something that disguises: *A mustache was part of his disguise. Her serene manner was only a disguise.* **2.** the act of disguising: *The spy was a master of disguise.* **3.** the state of being disguised: *a blessing in disguise.* [Old French *desguisier* to dress so as to be unrecognizable, from *des-* (from Latin *dis-* apart) + *guise* manner, fashion. See GUISE.] —**dis·guis′er,** *n.* —For Synonyms *(v.t.),* see **mask.**

dis·gust (dis gust′) *n.* a strong feeling of distaste or aversion aroused by something offensive; repugnance; loathing: *They were filled with disgust by such obvious lies.* —*v.t.* to arouse aversion, repugnance, or loathing in; sicken. [Middle French *desgouster* to loathe, going back to Latin *dis-* apart + *gustāre* to taste.]

Synonyms *n.* Disgust, aversion, abhorrence, and **repugnance** denote a feeling of dislike so strong as to cause a physical reaction. **Disgust** suggests that one's stomach turns at something: *The smell of rotting fish filled me with disgust.* **Aversion** suggests an impulse to turn away from something: *I have an aversion to people who try to sell me things on the telephone.* **Abhorrence** connotes a loathing so strong as to make the flesh crawl: *to have an abhorrence of spiders.* **Repugnance** suggests a desire to fight against the disliked object: *The school bully filled her with repugnance.*

dis·gust·ed (dis gus′tid) *adj.* filled with or showing disgust: *a disgusted look.* —**dis·gust′ed·ly,** *adv.*

dis·gust·ing (dis gus′ting) *adj.* causing disgust; repugnant; offensive. —**dis·gust′ing·ly,** *adv.*

dish (dish) *n.* **1.a.** a container, usually shallow and slightly concave, made of porcelain, earthenware, or other material, used chiefly for holding or serving food; plate. **b. dishes.** table utensils collectively, esp. those of porcelain, earthenware, or similar material: *We must clear the table and wash the dishes.* **2.** a serving of food on or in a dish; dishful: *a dish of cottage cheese.* **3.** food prepared in a particular way: *Spaghetti with a tomato sauce is my favorite dish.* **4.** a hollow or depression like that of a dish. **5.** something resembling a dish in shape or function. **6.** a radio, radar, or television antenna with a bowl-shaped reflector. —*v.t.* **1.** to put or serve in a dish (usually with *up* or *out*): *to dish up dinner.* **2.** to shape like a dish; make concave. **3.** *British. Slang.* to defeat, ruin, or cheat. **4.** *Informal.* to dispense or deal out; give (with *out*): *to dish out foreign aid to underdeveloped nations.* [Old English *disc* plate, from Latin *discus* quoit, dish, from Greek *diskos* round plate, quoit. Doublet of DAIS, DESK, DISCUS, DISK.]

·to dish it out. *Slang.* to abuse others physically or verbally.

dis·ha·bille (dis′ə bēl′) *also,* **deshabille.** *n.* **1.** the state of being carelessly or only partially dressed. **2.** *Archaic.* a garment worn in this state. [French *déshabillé* undress, from *déshabiller* to undress, from *dés-* (from Latin *dis-* un-[2]) + *habiller* to dress. See HABILIMENT.]

dis·har·mo·ny (dis här′mə nē) *n., pl.* -**nies.** lack of harmony or agreement; discord: *There was disharmony between the rival fac-*

tions of the political party. —**dis·har·mo·ni·ous** (dis'här mō'nē-əs), *adj.* —**dis'har·mo'ni·ous·ly,** *adv.*

dish·cloth (dish'klôth') *n., pl.* **-cloths** (-klôthz', -klôths'). a cloth for washing dishes. Also, **dishrag.**

dis·heart·en (dis här'tən) *v.t.* to cause to lose hope or courage; discourage; depress: *The bad news disheartened us.* —**dis·heart'-en·ing·ly,** *adv.*

di·shev·el (di shev'əl) *v.t.,* **-eled** or **-elled, -el·ing** or **-el·ling.** to disarrange or put in disorder, as hair or clothing. —**di·shev'-el·ment,** *n.*

di·shev·eled (di shev'əld) *also,* **di·shev·elled.** *adj.* not neat or in order; rumpled; tousled; untidy: *disheveled hair, a disheveled appearance.* [Old French *deschevele,* past participle of *descheveler* to disarrange the hair, going back to Latin *dis-* apart + *capillus* hair.]

dish·ful (dish'fùl') *n., pl.* **-fuls.** the amount that a dish can hold.

dis·hon·est (dis on'ist) *adj.* **1.** given to lying, stealing, or other untruthful or fraudulent acts; not honest. **2.** characterized by or showing a lack of honesty: *The salesperson used dishonest methods to sell the product.* —**dis·hon'est·ly,** *adv.*

dis·hon·es·ty (dis on'ə stē) *n., pl.* **-ties. 1.** lack of honesty or integrity. **2.** a dishonest act or statement.

dis·hon·or (dis on'ər) *also, British,* **dishonour.** *n.* **1.** lack or loss of honor or reputation; shame; disgrace: *to prefer death to dishonor.* **2.** a person or thing that causes or is the source of shame or disgrace. **3.** a refusal or failure to accept or pay (a check, note, or the like). —*v.t.* **1.** to deprive of honor; bring shame or discredit to; disgrace. **2.** to refuse or fail to accept or pay (a check, note, or the like) when due: *to dishonor a debt.* [Old French *deshonor* shame, going back to Latin *dis-* apart + *honor* reputation. See HONOR.]

dis·hon·or·a·ble (dis on'ər ə bəl) *adj.* **1.** characterized by or causing dishonor; shameful; disgraceful: *dishonorable conduct.* **2.** lacking honor; without honor: *a dishonorable person.* —**dis·hon'or·a·ble·ness,** *n.* —**dis·hon'or·a·bly,** *adv.*

dis·hon·our (dis on'ər) *British.* dishonor.

dish·pan (dish'pan') *n.* a pan in which to wash dishes.

dish·rag (dish'rag') *n.* dishcloth.

dish·tow·el (dish'tou'əl) *n.* a towel for drying dishes.

dish·wash·er (dish'wô'shər, -wosh'ər) *n.* **1.** a machine for washing dishes and cooking utensils. **2.** a person who washes dishes and cooking utensils, esp. a worker employed to do so in a restaurant or similar establishment.

dish·wat·er (dish'wô'tər, -wot'ər) *n.* water in which dishes and cooking utensils are or have been washed.

dis·il·lu·sion (dis'i lü'zhən) *v.t.* to free from or deprive of an illusion or false idea, esp. an idealistic false idea; disenchant: *The scandals in the city government disillusioned the mayor's admirers.* —*n.* disillusionment.

dis·il·lu·sion·ment (dis'i lü'zhən mənt) *n.* **1.** the act of disillusioning. **2.** the fact or state of being disillusioned.

dis·in·cli·na·tion (dis in'klə nā'shən) *n.* a slight distaste or aversion; unwillingness: *a disinclination to do hard work.*

dis·in·cline (dis'in klīn') *v.t.,* **-clined, -clin·ing.** to make unwilling or averse: *The low salary disinclined me to take the job.*

dis·in·fect (dis'in fekt') *v.t.* to destroy disease-causing microorganisms in: *to disinfect a hospital room.* —**dis'in·fec'tion,** *n.* —**dis'in·fec'tor,** *n.*

dis·in·fec·tant (dis'in fek'tənt) *n.* a substance used to destroy disease-causing microorganisms. —*adj.* serving to disinfect: *a disinfectant soap.*

dis·in·for·ma·tion (dis in'fər mā'shən, dis'in-) *n.* false or inaccurate information given to mislead or confuse: *The suspected spy was given disinformation.*

dis·in·gen·u·ous (dis'in jen'ū əs) *adj.* lacking frankness, candor, or sincerity; not straightforward. —**dis'in·gen'u·ous·ly,** *adv.* —**dis'in·gen'u·ous·ness,** *n.*

dis·in·her·it (dis'in her'it) *v.t.* to exclude (an heir) from an inheritance or the right to inherit. —**dis'in·her'it·ance,** *n.*

dis·in·te·grate (dis in'ti grāt') *v.,* **-grat·ed, -grat·ing.** —*v.i.* **1.** to break up into particles, fragments, or parts: *This type of rock disintegrates under pressure.* **2.** to deteriorate by or as if by breaking into constituent parts: *The empire disintegrated under the rule of that dynasty.* **3.** *Physics.* decay. —*v.t.* to cause to disintegrate. —**dis·in'te·gra'tor,** *n.* —For Synonyms *(v.i.),* see decay.

dis·in·te·gra·tion (dis in'ti grā'shən) *n.* **1.** the act or process of disintegrating or the state of being disintegrated. **2.** *Physics.* decay.

dis·in·ter (dis'in tûr') *v.t.,* **-terred, -ter·ring. 1.** to remove from a grave or tomb; dig up: *to disinter a body to perform an autopsy.* **2.** to bring to light; reveal: *The reporter disinterred previously unknown facts about the author's early life.* —**dis'in·ter'ment,** *n.*

dis·in·ter·est (dis in'trist, -tər ist) *n.* **1.** lack of interest; indifference. **2.** lack of self-interest or bias; impartiality.

dis·in·ter·est·ed (dis in'trə stid, -tə res'tid) *adj.* **1.** free from self-interest; not influenced by personal motives; impartial; unbiased: *disinterested advice, a disinterested decision.* **2.** lacking interest; indifferent. —**dis·in'ter·est·ed·ly,** *adv.* —**dis·in'ter·est·ed·ness,** *n.* —For Synonyms, see **indifferent.**

dis·join (dis join') *v.t.* to prevent or undo the joining of; separate. —*v.i.* to become separated, disunited, or detached.

dis·joint (dis joint') *v.t.* **1.** to take apart or separate at the joints; dismember: *to disjoint a turkey.* **2.** to put out of joint; dislocate: *I fell and disjointed my shoulder.* **3.** to disturb or destroy the order, connection, or coherence of: *Racial or religious strife disjoints the whole framework of society.* —*v.i.* **1.** to come apart at the joints; become out of joint. **2.** *Mathematics.* (of sets) having no elements in common. [Old French *desjoint,* past participle of *desjoindre* to disunite, from Latin *disjungere* to separate.]

dis·joint·ed (dis join'tid) *adj.* **1.** lacking order, coherence, or unity: *a rambling and disjointed letter.* **2.** taken apart or separated at or as if at the joints: *a disjointed fowl.* **3.** out of joint; dislocated: *a disjointed shoulder.* —**dis·joint'ed·ly,** *adv.* —**dis·joint'ed·ness,** *n.*

dis·junct (dis jungkt') *adj.* **1.** not joined; separated. **2.** *Zoology.* marked by separation of usually continuous parts, characteristic of certain insects that have deep constrictions between the head, thorax, and abdomen.

dis·junc·tion (dis jungk'shən) *n.* **1.** the act of disjoining or the state of being disjoined; separation. **2.** *Logic.* **a.** a disjunctive proposition. **b.** the relation existing between the terms of such a proposition.

dis·junc·tive (dis jungk'tiv) *adj.* **1.** causing or tending to separate or divide. **2.** *Grammar.* indicating choice, opposition, or contrast. In the phrase *poorer but wiser for their experience,* the word *but* is a disjunctive conjunction. **3.** *Logic.* involving a choice between alternatives. *It is day or it is night* is a disjunctive proposition. —*n.* **1.** *Grammar.* a disjunctive conjunction. **2.** *Logic.* a disjunctive proposition. —**dis·junc'tive·ly,** *adv.*

disk (disk) *also,* **disc.** *n.* **1.** a flat, circular platelike object. **2.** something resembling a disk in shape, as one of the circular, usually sharp-edged plates mounted on the shaft of a disk harrow. **3.** the circular, apparently flat shape of a heavenly body when viewed from earth: *the disk of Venus.* **4.** a rotary plate of plastic or metal coated with magnetic material on which computer data are recorded and stored; diskette. Also, **magnetic disk. 5.** the center of the flower head of certain composite plants, composed of small disk flowers. **6.** any flat, circular organ or structure, as the platelike growth of cartilage between adjacent vertebrae. **7.** *Archaic.* discus. —*v.t.* to work (land) with a disk harrow.

disk *(def. 5)*

[Latin *discus* quoit, dish, from Greek *diskos* round plate, quoit. Doublet of DAIS, DESK, DISCUS, DISH.]

disk drive, a device in a computer that allows a user to store data on or retrieve it from a hard disk, floppy disk, or the like.

disk·ette (dis ket') *n.* a magnetic disk that is enclosed in a protective envelope, used to store computer data; floppy disk.

disk flower, any one of the small tubular flowers that make up the flower head of certain composite plants, as the thistle. For illustration, see **composite.**

disk harrow, a harrow consisting of a series of sharp disks that are set on a rotating shaft, used in cultivating ground.

disk jockey, disc jockey.

disk operating system, an operating system required for use by computers with disk storage.

dis·like (dis līk') *n.* a feeling of disapproval, distaste, or aversion: *to have a strong dislike for cold weather.* —*v.t.,* **-liked,**

a	at	e	end	o	hot	u	up	hw	white		about
ā	ape	ē	me	ō	old	ū	use	ng	song		taken
ä	far	i	it	ô	fork	ü	rule	th	thin	ə	pencil
âr	care	ī	ice	oi	oil	ù	pull	th	this		lemon
		îr	pierce	ou	out	ûr	turn	zh	measure		circus

-lik·ing. to consider disagreeable; regard with aversion or disapproval: *Do you dislike doing housework?*

Synonyms *n.* **Dislike** and **distaste** denote a negative feeling or attitude toward someone or something. **Dislike** is the more general term: *a dislike of hot weather, a dislike for a co-worker.* **Distaste** connotes a more physical or more intense dislike: *I could not get over my distaste for raw onions. Their rowdy behavior evoked the distaste of their fellow passengers.*

dis·lo·cate (dis′lō kāt′, dis lō′kāt) *v.t.,* **-cat·ed, -cat·ing.** **1.** to upset the order of; throw into confusion; disrupt: *Their national economy was dislocated by war.* **2.** to put out of proper place or order; displace. **3.a.** to put (a bone) out of joint. **b.** to cause (any part of the body) to be in an abnormal position. —**dis′lo·ca′tion,** *n.*

dis·lodge (dis loj′) *v.t.,* **-lodged, -lodg·ing.** to move or force out of a place or position (with *from*): *The avalanche dislodged large rocks from the cliff. The hounds managed to dislodge the fox from its hiding place.* —**dis·lodg′ment;** also, **dis·lodge′ment,** *n.*

dis·loy·al (dis loi′əl) *adj.* going against one's allegiance; not loyal; unfaithful: *a disloyal friend, to be disloyal to one's country.* —**dis·loy′al·ly,** *adv.*

dis·loy·al·ty (dis loi′əl tē) *n., pl.* **-ties.** **1.** lack of loyalty; unfaithfulness; falseness. **2.** a disloyal act.

dis·mal (diz′məl) *adj.* **1.** marked by or causing gloom or depression; dreary; miserable; cheerless: *a damp and dismal winter day.* **2.** gloomy; depressed: *I was feeling dismal because I had failed the test.* **3.** disastrously bad; dreadful; terrible: *The project was a dismal failure.* [Middle English *dismal,* from Anglo-Norman *dis mal* evil days (referring to certain days considered unlucky during the Middle Ages), from Old French *dis mal,* from Medieval Latin *diēs malī,* from Latin *diēs* day + *malus* bad, evil.] —**dis′mal·ly,** *adv.* —**dis′mal·ness,** *n.*

dis·man·tle (dis man′təl) *v.t.,* **-tled, -tling.** **1.** to pull down or take apart; disassemble: *to dismantle a machine.* **2.** to strip of covering, furniture, or equipment: *Dismantle the room before you start painting.* [Middle French *desmanteller* to remove a cloak, raze, going back to Latin *dis-* apart + *matellum* napkin, cloak.] —**dis·man′tle·ment,** *n.*

dis·mast (dis mast′) *v.t.* to take or break off the masts of (a ship).

dis·may (dis mā′) *v.t.* **1.** to fill with fear or apprehension; make afraid; daunt: *The sight of the enemy forces dismayed the soldier.* **2.** to trouble or discourage greatly; depress; dishearten: *The audience's lack of interest dismayed the speaker.* —*n.* a feeling of alarm or uneasiness; frightened amazement: *We were filled with dismay when we heard the bad news.* [Middle English *dismayen* to dishearten, from an unrecorded Old French form which was partly of Latin and partly of Germanic origin.]

dis·mem·ber (dis mem′bər) *v.t.* **1.** to cut or tear off the limbs or members of; tear limb from limb. **2.** to divide into parts or sections; partition: *The conquering nations dismembered the defeated country.* —**dis·mem′ber·ment,** *n.*

dis·miss (dis mis′) *v.t.* **1.** to send away or give permission to leave: *The teacher dismissed the class.* **2.** to discharge, as from a position or job; fire: *to dismiss an employee for stealing.* **3.** to put aside from attention or serious consideration; reject: *to dismiss a story as a rumor.* **4.** to deal with or have done with, esp. quickly: *Before we dismiss this matter, we'll hear one more report.* **5.** to dispense with (an action or suit) without further hearing: *The judge dismissed the case because of lack of evidence.* [Modification (influenced by DIS-¹) of Latin *dīmissus,* past participle of *dīmittere* to send away.]

dis·miss·al (dis mis′əl) *n.* **1.** the act of dismissing or the state of being dismissed. **2.** a written or spoken order dismissing someone, as from a job.

dis·mis·sion (dis mish′ən) *n. Archaic.* dismissal.

dis·mount (dis mount′) *v.i.* to get off or down, as from a horse; alight: *The rider dismounted from the bicycle.* —*v.t.* **1.** to remove (something) from its setting, support, or mounting: *to dismount a cannon.* **2.** to knock off or bring down, as from a horse; unseat. **3.** to take apart; disassemble; dismantle: *to dismount a machine.* —*n.* an act or instance of dismounting.

dis·o·be·di·ence (dis′ə bē′dē əns) *n.* refusal or failure to obey, as an order.

dis·o·be·di·ent (dis′ə bē′dē ənt) *adj.* refusing or failing to obey; not obedient. —**dis′o·be′di·ent·ly,** *adv.*

dis·o·bey (dis′ə bā′) *v.t., v.i.* to refuse or fail to obey: *The soldier disobeyed the lieutenant's orders. That dog always disobeys.*

dis·o·blige (dis′ə blīj′) *v.t.,* **-bliged, -blig·ing.** **1.** to act contrary to the wishes or convenience of; fail to accommodate. **2.** to give offense to; slight; affront.

dis·or·der (dis ôr′dər) *n.* **1.** lack of order or regular arrangement; confusion: *The room was in disorder after the party.* **2.** a

breach of peace or public order, such as a riot; disturbance: *The police tried to quiet the disorders in the streets.* **3.** a disturbance of physical or mental health or functions; sickness; ailment: *a disorder of the digestive system.* —*v.t.* **1.** to disturb the order or regular arrangement of; throw into confusion; disarrange: *Noisy demonstrations disordered the political convention.* **2.** to disturb or upset the physical or mental health or functions of. —For Synonyms *(n.),* see **confusion.**

dis·or·dered (dis ôr′dərd) *adj.* **1.** in disorder; confused; disarranged. **2.** disturbed in physical or mental health or functions.

dis·or·der·ly (dis ôr′dər lē) *adj.* **1.** lacking order or regular arrangement; messy; untidy: *The papers lay in a disorderly pile.* **2.** causing a disturbance; uncontrolled; unruly: *a disorderly crowd.* **3.** violating public peace, order, or decency; guilty of disorderly conduct. —*adv.* in a disorderly manner. —**dis·or′der·li·ness,** *n.*

disorderly conduct, any behavior that is considered a petty violation of public peace, order, or decency.

dis·or·gan·ize (dis ôr′gə nīz′) *v.t.,* **-ized, -iz·ing.** to upset or destroy the organization, systematic arrangement, or order of; throw into confusion and disorder: *Heavy shelling by the enemy disorganized the army's retreat.* —**dis·or′gan·i·za′tion,** *n.*

dis·or·gan·ized (dis ôr′gə nīzd′) *adj.* lacking organization, systematic arrangement, or order: *a disorganized project, a novel with a badly disorganized plot.*

dis·o·ri·ent (dis ôr′i ent′) *v.t.* to disturb the sense of direction or position of; cause to lose one's bearings; mix up; confuse.

dis·o·ri·en·tate (dis ôr′ē en tāt′) *v.t.,* **-tated, -tat·ing.** disorient. —**dis·o′ri·en·ta′tion,** *n.*

dis·own (dis ōn′) *v.t.* to refuse to recognize as one's own; deny responsibility for or connection with; repudiate; reject: *The couple disowned their children and left their fortune to charity.*

dis·par·age (di spar′ij) *v.t.,* **-aged, -ag·ing.** **1.** to speak critically or slightingly of; belittle: *The candidate disparaged the incumbent's record in office.* **2.** to bring discredit upon; lower in esteem or reputation. [Old French *desparagier* originally, to cause to marry beneath one, from *des-* (from Latin *dis-* apart) + *parage* equality of rank (going back to Latin *pār* equal).]

Synonyms **Disparage** and **belittle** mean to say or suggest that something or someone is of little worth. **Disparage** suggests a less direct approach, as by faint praise or an unflattering comparison: *By emphasizing her son's accomplishments she seemed to be disparaging her daughter.* **Belittle** connotes a direct, contemptuous attempt to make someone or something appear insignificant: *The candidate belittled his opponent's ideas as immature.*

dis·par·age·ment (di spar′ij mənt) *n.* **1.** the act of disparaging. **2.** something that belittles or discredits.

dis·par·ag·ing (di spar′i jing) *adj.* that disparages; slighting; belittling: *disparaging remarks.* —**dis·par′ag·ing·ly,** *adv.*

dis·par·ate (dis par′it, dis′pər-) *adj.* essentially or distinctly different; unlike; dissimilar: *disparate points of view.* [Latin *disparātus,* past participle of *disparāre* to separate.] —**dis·par′ate·ly,** *adv.* —**dis·par′ate·ness,** *n.* —For Synonyms, see **different.**

dis·par·i·ty (di spar′i tē) *n., pl.* **-ties.** lack of agreement or similarity; inequality or difference: *There is a great disparity between the report and what actually happened.*

dis·part (dis pärt′) *v.t., v.i. Archaic.* to divide into parts; separate.

dis·pas·sion (dis pash′ən) *n.* freedom from prejudice or strong feeling; calm objectivity; impartiality: *to view a controversy with dispassion.*

dis·pas·sion·ate (dis pash′ə nit) *adj.* free from prejudice or strong feeling; unbiased; impartial: *an honest, dispassionate judge.* —**dis·pas′sion·ate·ly,** *adv.* —**dis·pas′sion·ate·ness,** *n.*

dis·patch (di spach′) *also,* **despatch.** *v.t.* **1.** to send off quickly to a specific destination or for a specific purpose: *to dispatch a messenger, to dispatch a telegram.* **2.** to finish or dispose of quickly or promptly: *to dispatch a business deal.* **3.** to put to death; kill. —*n.* **1.** the act of dispatching. **2.** prompt or quick action; quickness; speed: *The urgency of the situation called for great dispatch.* **3.** a written message sent off quickly or promptly, esp. an official government or military communication. **4.** a news story or report, as by a special reporter or from a news service: *The newspaper received a dispatch from its correspondent in London.* **5.** a putting to death; killing. [Spanish *despachar* to speed, send, from Old French *despeechier* to set free, going back to Latin *dis-* un-² + *pedica* shackle.] —For Synonyms *(v.t.),* see **send.**

dis·patch·er (di spach′ər) *also,* **despatcher.** *n.* **1.** a person who dispatches. **2.** a person who schedules and directs the arrivals and departures of trains, buses, taxicabs, and other means of transportation.

dis·pel (di spel′) *v.t.,* **-pelled, -pel·ling.** to drive away or cause

to disappear by or as by scattering; disperse: *The wind dispelled the smoke. Your reassuring words dispelled our doubts.* [Latin *dispellere*.]

dis·pen·sa·ble (di spen′sə bəl) *adj.* **1.** that can be dispensed with or done without; unessential; unimportant: *to eliminate dispensable items from a budget.* **2.** capable of being dispensed or administered: *dispensable funds, dispensable drugs.* **3.** subject to dispensation; pardonable, as an offense or sin. —**dis·pen′sa·bil′i·ty**, **dis·pen′sa·ble·ness**, *n.*

dis·pen·sa·ry (di spen′sə rē) *n., pl.* **-ries. 1.** a room in which medicines and medical supplies are dispensed: *a hospital dispensary.* **2.** a place where medicines and medical treatment are given without charge or for a small fee.

dis·pen·sa·tion (dis′pən sā′shən) *n.* **1.** the act of dispensing; giving out; distribution: *The dispensation of supplies in the disaster area was delayed.* **2.** something that is dispensed or distributed: *The victims of the disaster received a financial dispensation from the government.* **3.** a specific system of administration; management. **4.a.** an official exemption or release, as from an obligation or law, esp. exemption by ecclesiastical authority from a church law: *a papal dispensation.* **b.** an official document authorizing or containing such an exemption. **5.** *Theology.* **a.** a divine arrangement, provision, or ordering of events, as by providence or nature. **b.** a religious system believed to be divinely instituted: *Mosaic dispensation.* —**dis′pen·sa′tion·al**, *adj.*

dis·pen·sa·to·ry (di spen′sə tôr′ē) *n., pl.* **-ries. 1.** a book describing the composition, preparation, and use of medicines. **2.** *Archaic.* dispensary.

dis·pense (di spens′) *v.t.,* **-pensed**, **-pens·ing. 1.** to give or deal out in portions; distribute: *to dispense clothing to the needy, a machine that dispenses chewing gum.* **2.** to prepare and give out (medicine), esp. by prescription. **3.** to carry out or apply; administer: *to dispense justice.* **4.** to exempt or release, as from an obligation or law, esp. a church law. [Old French *dispenser* to distribute, from Latin *dispēnsāre* to weigh out, distribute, regulate, going back to *dis-* apart + *pendere* to weigh.]
 •**to dispense with. a.** to get along without; forgo: *You can dispense with a coat now that the weather is warm.* **b.** to do away with, as a requirement; make unnecessary: *The speaker dispensed with formalities and started the discussion.*

dis·pens·er (di spen′sər) *n.* **1.** a person or thing that dispenses. **2.** a container or mechanical device that dispenses something in convenient units or portions: *a soap dispenser.*

dis·per·sal (di spûr′səl) *n.* the act of dispersing or the state of being dispersed; dispersion: *the dispersal of a mob.*

dis·perse (di spûrs′) *v.,* **-persed**, **-pers·ing.** —*v.t.* **1.** to break up and send off in different directions; scatter: *The police dispersed the crowd.* **2.** to drive away or cause to vanish; dispel: *The winds dispersed the smoke.* **3.** to spread about or abroad; diffuse; disseminate: *to disperse information.* **4.** to separate (electromagnetic radiation) into component parts according to frequency or wavelength. A beam of white light is dispersed in passing through a prism. **5.** to scatter (colloidal particles) through a fluid medium. —*v.i.* to break up and go in different directions; scatter; dissipate: *The congregation dispersed when the service ended.* [Latin *dispersus*, past participle of *dispergere* to scatter.] —**dis·pers′i·ble**, *adj.* —For Synonyms (*v.t.*), see **scatter.**

dis·per·sion (di spûr′zhən, -shən) *n.* **1.** the act of dispersing or the state of being dispersed. **2.** the separation of electromagnetic radiation into its component parts according to frequency or wavelength. **3.** a colloidal system. **4.** *Statistics.* a measure of the variation in a set of data; scatter.

dis·per·sive (di spûr′siv) *adj.* dispersing or tending to disperse. —**dis·per′sive·ly**, *adv.* —**dis·per′sive·ness**, *n.*

dis·pir·it (di spir′it) *v.t.* to depress or lower the spirits of; discourage: *The failure of the experiments greatly dispirited the scientist.*

dis·pir·it·ed (di spir′ə tid) *adj.* depressed; dejected; discouraged: *The dispirited team could no longer stop their opponents from scoring.* —**dis·pir′it·ed·ly**, *adv.* —**dis·pir′it·ed·ness**, *n.*

dis·place (dis plās′) *v.t.,* **-placed**, **-plac·ing. 1.** to take the place of; replace; supplant: *Television displaced motion pictures as America's most popular form of entertainment.* **2.** to move or shift from the usual or proper place or position. **3.** to force (someone) to leave his or her home or country: *The apartment fire displaced five families.* **4.** to remove from a position or office: *to displace an officer of the government.* **5.** to occupy the space of (a certain weight or volume of fluid): *Large ships displace thousands of tons of water.*

displaced person, a person driven or taken from his or her own country or region, usually as a result of war.

dis·place·ment (dis plās′mənt) *n.* **1.** the act of displacing or the state of being displaced. **2.** the distance that something has moved from its original place or position. **3.** the weight of the

volume of fluid displaced by a body floating or immersed in it. The weight of the fluid displaced by a floating body equals the weight of the body itself. **4.** the volume the pistons of an engine displace during one cycle of operation. **5.a.** the distance that a geologic stratum has been displaced where cut by a fault. **b.** movement along a fault in rock, sediment, or the like. **6.** in psychology, the unconscious transference of an emotion or attitude to something other than the object that originally aroused it.

dis·play (di splā′) *v.t.* **1.** to expose to view; cause to be seen; exhibit; show or spread out: *to display a poster, to display a flag.* **2.** to manifest or make obvious, often unintentionally; reveal: *to display fear, to display one's ignorance.* **3.** to make a prominent or ostentatious show of; show off; flaunt: *The couple proudly displayed their wealth.* —*n.* **1.** the act of displaying; manifestation: *a display of anger, a display of courage.* **2.** something displayed or exhibited; arrangement or exhibition: *The floral display was tastefully arranged. The store had a display of gourmet cooking utensils.* **3.** an ostentatious show: *a vulgar display of wealth.* **4.a.** a device, esp. an electronic one, that presents information in visual form, as the monitor screen of a computer. **b.** the information itself. **5.** *Printing.* type or printing, as in headlines, designed for an eye-catching effect. [Old French *despleier* to unfold, show, from Medieval Latin *displicare* to unfold, from Latin *displicāre* to scatter.] —For Synonyms (*n.*), see **show.**

dis·please (dis plēz′) *v.,* **-pleased**, **-pleas·ing.** —*v.t.* to fail to please; cause annoyance to; offend; vex. —*v.i.* to cause displeasure or annoyance.

dis·pleas·ure (dis plezh′ər) *n.* **1.** the state or feeling of being displeased; annoyance; disapproval. **2.** *Archaic.* discomfort; uneasiness; pain. **3.** *Archaic.* offense; injury.

dis·port (di spôrt′) *v.t.* to amuse or divert (oneself): *The puppies disported themselves in the yard.* —*v.i.* to play; frolic. —*n. Archaic.* amusement; diversion; play. [Old French *(se)desporter* to amuse (oneself); literally, to carry (oneself) away, going back to Latin *dis-* apart + *portāre* to carry.]

dis·pos·a·ble (di spō′zə bəl) *adj.* **1.** capable of being disposed of, esp. designed to be discarded after being used: *disposable diapers.* **2.** free to be used; at hand; available: *disposable income, disposable property.*

dis·pos·al (di spō′zəl) *n.* **1.** the act of getting rid of something; throwing away: *the disposal of garbage.* **2.** the act of dealing with or settling (something): *the disposal of certain business matters.* **3.** a transferring of something to another, as by gift or sale: *the disposal of money in a will, the disposal of merchandise.* **4.** a particular ordering or position; arrangement: *the disposal of troops into three columns.* **5.** garbage disposal.
 •**at one's disposal.** available for use as one pleases: *The car will be at your disposal this week.*

dis·pose (di spōz′) *v.,* **-posed**, **-pos·ing.** —*v.t.* **1.** to give a tendency or inclination to; make receptive or willing: *Favoritism disposed you to decide the contest in their favor.* **2.** to make susceptible or subject: *Frailness disposed the child to frequent illness.* **3.** to place in a particular order or position; arrange: *The gardener disposed the seedlings in rows.* **4.** to control or direct; regulate: *to dispose the affairs of the empire.* —*v.i.* to determine or control the course of events; ordain. [Old French *disposer* to arrange, modification (influenced by Old French *poser* to place) of Latin *dispōnere* to arrange.] —**dis·pos′er**, *n.*
 •**to dispose of. a.** to get rid of; throw away: *to dispose of garbage.* **b.** to deal or finish up with; settle: *He quickly disposed of the matter.* **c.** to part with, as by gift or sale; transfer to another: *She disposed of her property in the country.* **d.** to consume (food or drink).

dis·posed (di spōzd′) *adj.* having a specified tendency or inclination: *That lazy student is not disposed to work hard.*

dis·po·si·tion (dis′pə zish′ən) *n.* **1.** a person's usual or general way of thinking, feeling, or acting; temperament; nature: *an irritable disposition, a pleasant disposition.* **2.a.** a habitual tendency, inclination, or willingness: *a disposition to accept the ideas of others too readily.* **b.** an organic tendency or inclination: *the disposition of water to freeze at low temperatures.* **3.** a placing in or being placed in a particular order; arrangement: *the orderly disposition of trees in an orchard.* **4.** regulation, management, or final settlement, as of legal affairs. **5.** a transferring of something

a	at	e	end	o	hot	u	up	hw	white		about
ā	ape	ē	me	ō	old	ū	use	ng	song		taken
ä	far	i	it	ô	fork	ü	rule	th	thin	ə	pencil
âr	care	ī	ice	oi	oil	u̇	pull	th	this		lemon
		îr	pierce	ou	out	ûr	turn	zh	measure		circus

to another, as by gift or sale: *the disposition of property after death.* **6.** the power or authority to deal with or settle; control.

Synonyms Disposition, temperament, character, and nature may all denote the combined qualities or traits that define an individual. **Disposition** connotes especially the habitual ways in which a person reacts to the world around him or her: *a happy-go-lucky disposition, an argumentative disposition.* **Temperament** connotes the mixture of physical and mental qualities that determine one's behavior: *He did not have the temperament to handle the pressures of political office.* **Character** suggests more central qualities, esp. moral ones: *She was too strong a character to be easily influenced. For so placid a man the outburst was out of character.* **Nature** connotes the essential, inherent qualities of something. Used of a person it suggests qualities one is born with: *the trusting nature of a child.*

dis·pos·sess (dis′pə zes′) *v.t.* **1.** to put out of occupancy or possession, esp. of real property, by legal action: *The landlord dispossessed the tenants for not paying rent.* **2.** to deprive of the possession of something: *The dictatorship dispossessed many citizens of their rights.* —**dis′pos·ses′sion,** *n.* —**dis′pos·ses′sor,** *n.*

dis·praise (dis prāz′) *v.t.,* **-praised, -prais·ing.** to express disapproval of; censure. —*n.* an act or instance of dispraising; censure. —**dis·prais′er,** *n.* —**dis·prais′ing·ly,** *adv.*

dis·prize (dis prīz′) *v.t.,* **-prized, -priz·ing.** *Archaic.* to hold in low esteem.

dis·proof (dis prüf′) *n.* **1.** the act of disproving; refutation. **2.** something that disproves, as evidence.

dis·pro·por·tion (dis′prə pôr′shən) *n.* **1.** lack of proportion or symmetry; disparity: *There is a disproportion between the price of that house and its true value.* **2.** an instance of this. —*v.t.* to make disproportionate.

dis·pro·por·tion·al (dis′prə pôr′shə nəl) *adj.* disproportionate. —**dis′pro·por′tion·al·ly,** *adv.*

dis·pro·por·tion·ate (dis′prə pôr′shə nit) *adj.* out of proportion, as in size, amount, or degree; lacking proportion: *The arms of the statue are disproportionate to its body.* —**dis′pro·por′tion·ate·ly,** *adv.* —**dis′pro·por′tion·ate·ness,** *n.*

dis·prove (dis prüv′) *v.t.,* **-proved, -prov·ing.** to prove to be false, incorrect, or invalid; refute: *The photograph disproves your claim that you have never met the defendant.* —**dis·prov′a·ble,** *adj.* —**dis·prov′al,** *n.*

dis·put·a·ble (di spū′tə bəl, dis′pyü-) *adj.* that can be disputed or called into question; arguable; debatable: *Whether or not the suspect is really guilty is disputable.* —**dis·put′a·bil′i·ty,** *n.* —**dis·put′a·bly,** *adv.*

dis·pu·tant (di spū′tənt, dis′pyü-) *n.* a person who takes part in a dispute or debate. —*adj.* engaged in dispute; disputing.

dis·pu·ta·tion (dis′pyü tā′shən) *n.* **1.** the act of disputing. **2.** a formal debate in which parties attack and defend a question or thesis, such as a philosophical or theological theory.

dis·pu·ta·tious (dis′pyü tā′shəs) *adj.* given to disputing; contentious; argumentative. Also, **dis·pu·ta·tive** (di spū′tə tiv). —**dis′pu·ta′tious·ly,** *adv.* —**dis′pu·ta′tious·ness,** *n.*

dis·pute (di spūt′) *v.,* **-put·ed, -put·ing.** —*v.t.* **1.** to discuss by giving opposing viewpoints; debate or quarrel about; argue: *The issue was disputed at the council meeting.* **2.** to deny or question the validity, accuracy, or existence of; express doubt or opposition to: *to dispute someone's authority, to dispute a claim.* **3.** to fight or compete for the possession of; strive or contend for: *The two countries disputed the strip of land on their common border.* **4.** to offer resistance against in any way; oppose. —*v.i.* to engage in argument, discussion, or debate: *The politicians disputed with each other on various issues.* —*n.* **1.** a difference of opinion; argument or debate: *The judge had to settle the dispute over the ownership of the house.* **2.** quarrel: *a bitter dispute between neighbors.* [Old French *desputer* to discuss, debate, quarrel, from Latin *disputāre* to examine, discuss.] —**dis·put′er,** *n.* —For Synonyms *(n.),* see **argument.**

dis·qual·i·fi·ca·tion (dis kwol′ə fi kā′shən) *n.* **1.** the act of disqualifying or the state of being disqualified. **2.** something that disqualifies.

dis·qual·i·fy (dis kwol′ə fī′) *v.t.,* **-fied, -fy·ing. 1.** to make unfit or unsuitable; disqualify: *Poor eyesight disqualifies many from pilot training.* **2.** to make or declare ineligible or unqualified: *Your age disqualifies you from voting.* **3.** to bar from competition or deprive of a victory or award because of an infraction of rules: *The officials disqualified the runner for leaving the racecourse.*

dis·qui·et (dis kwī′it) *v.t.* to make uneasy, anxious, or restless; disturb; alarm: *The violence of the storm disquieted us.* —*n.* lack of tranquillity; uneasiness; anxiety; unrest: *There was a feeling of disquiet among the ship's passengers as the storm approached.*

dis·qui·et·ing (dis kwī′i ting) *adj.* causing disquiet; disturbing. —**dis·qui′et·ing·ly,** *adv.*

dis·qui·e·tude (dis kwī′i tüd′, -tūd′) *n.* a state of uneasiness or unrest; anxiety.

dis·qui·si·tion (dis′kwə zish′ən) *n.* a formal treatise or discourse; dissertation. [Latin *disquīsītiō* a search into, inquiry.]

dis·re·gard (dis′ri gärd′) *v.t.* **1.** to pay no attention to: *The judge instructed the jury to disregard the witness's last statement.* **2.** to treat without due regard or respect; ignore: *We must not disregard their feelings in this matter.* —*n.* lack of attention or due regard; neglect: *Your actions show a disregard for the regulations.* —For Synonyms *(v.t.),* see **ignore.**

dis·rel·ish (dis rel′ish) *v.t.* to have a distaste for; dislike. —*n.* distaste; dislike.

dis·re·mem·ber (dis′ri mem′bər) *v.t., v.i. Informal.* forget.

dis·re·pair (dis′ri pâr′) *n.* the state of being in need of repairs; poor, run-down condition: *The old house had fallen into disrepair.*

dis·rep·u·ta·ble (dis rep′yə tə bəl) *adj.* **1.** not in good repute; not reputable, respectable, or decent: *a disreputable company.* **2.** not respectable in appearance; shabby: *a disreputable old jacket.* —**dis·rep′u·ta·ble·ness,** *n.* —**dis·rep′u·ta·bly,** *adv.*

dis·re·pute (dis′ri pūt′) *n.* lack or loss of reputation; ill repute; discredit; disfavor: *That scientific theory is now in disrepute.*

dis·re·spect (dis′ri spekt′) *n.* lack of respect, reverence, or courtesy: *to show disrespect for the rights of others.* —*v.t.* to have or show disrespect for.

dis·re·spect·ful (dis′ri spekt′fəl) *adj.* having or showing disrespect; rude; impolite. —**dis′re·spect′ful·ly,** *adv.* —**dis′re·spect′ful·ness,** *n.*

dis·robe (dis rōb′) *v.t., v.i.,* **-robed, -rob·ing.** to undress.

dis·rupt (dis rupt′) *v.t.* **1.a.** to throw into disorder; upset: *The fire alarm disrupted the class.* **b.** to interrupt or impede the normal continuation of; cause to break down: *The tornado disrupted telephone service throughout the area.* **2.** to break or burst apart; split; rupture. [Latin *disruptus,* past participle of *disrumpere* to break into pieces.] —**dis·rupt′er;** *also,* **dis·rupt′or,** *n.*

dis·rup·tion (dis rup′shən) *n.* **1.** the act of disrupting or the state of being disrupted. **2.** a break; interruption.

dis·rup·tive (dis rup′tiv) *adj.* causing, tending to cause, or caused by disruption: *a disruptive influence.* —**dis·rup′tive·ly,** *adv.* —**dis·rup′tive·ness,** *n.*

dis·sat·is·fac·tion (dis′sat is fak′shən, dis sat′-) *n.* **1.** a condition or feeling of being dissatisfied; discontent. **2.** something that dissatisfies.

dis·sat·is·fac·to·ry (dis′sat is fak′tə rē, dis sat′-) *adj.* not satisfying; causing discontent; unsatisfactory.

dis·sat·is·fied (dis sat′is fīd′) *adj.* **1.** not satisfied; displeased: *The dissatisfied workers struck for higher wages.* **2.** showing discontent or displeasure: *a dissatisfied look.*

dis·sat·is·fy (dis sat′is fī′) *v.t.,* **-fied, -fy·ing.** to fail to satisfy; cause discontent to; disappoint; displease: *The actor's performance dissatisfied the film's director.*

dis·sect (di sekt′, dī-) *v.t.* **1.** to cut apart or divide into parts, as for the purpose of study or scientific examination: *The biology student dissected a frog.* **2.** to examine carefully and critically; analyze in great detail: *The teacher dissected the poem and explained it to the class.* [Latin *dissectus,* past participle of *dissecāre* to cut asunder.] —**dis·sec′tor,** *n.*

dis·sect·ed (di sek′tid, dī-) *adj.* **1.** cut apart or divided into parts. **2.** (of certain leaves) divided into many fine segments or lobes.

dis·sec·tion (di sek′shən, dī-) *n.* **1.** the act of dissecting. **2.** something that has been dissected, such as an animal being studied. **3.** a detailed analysis or criticism.

dis·sem·ble (di sem′bəl) *v.,* **-bled, -bling.** —*v.t.* **1.** to disguise or conceal the real nature of (one's character, feelings, or intentions): *to dissemble one's excitement by acting bored.* **2.** to put on a false appearance of; pretend; feign: *The corrupt official dissembled honesty.* —*v.i.* to disguise or conceal one's true character, feelings, or intentions by false pretense; act hypocritically. [Modification (influenced by *resemble*) of obsolete *dissimule,* from Old French *dissimuler* to hide one's thoughts, deny, from Latin *dissimulāre* to disguise.] —**dis·sem′bler,** *n.*

dis·sem·i·nate (di sem′ə nāt′) *v.t.,* **-nat·ed, -nat·ing.** to scatter widely; spread abroad; diffuse: *to disseminate information.* [Latin *dissēminātus* past participle of *dissēmināre* to scatter seed.] —**dis·sem′i·na′tion,** *n.* —**dis·sem′i·na′tor,** *n.* —For Synonyms, see **spread.**

dis·sen·sion (di sen′shən) *n.* a difference of opinion or disagreement, often heated or angry; discord: *There was dissension among the president's foreign policy advisers.* —For Synonyms, see **disagreement.**

dis·sent (di sent′) *v.i.* **1.** to differ in opinion or feeling; withhold approval; disagree (often with *from*): *Many people dissented from the foreign policy of the government.* **2.** to refuse to conform to the rules, doctrines, or beliefs of an established church. —*n.* **1.** a

difference of opinion or feeling; disagreement: *A dictatorship does not permit dissent in political matters.* **2.** a refusal to conform to the rules, doctrines, or beliefs of an established church. [Latin *dissentīre* to disagree.]

dis·sent·er (di sen′tər) *n.* **1.** a person who dissents. **2.** *also,* **Dissenter.** a person who refuses to conform to the rules, doctrines, or beliefs of an established church, esp. the Church of England.

dis·sen·tient (di sen′shənt) *adj.* dissenting, esp. from the opinion of the majority. —*n.* a person who dissents; dissenter. —**dis·sen′tience,** *n.*

dis·sent·ing (di sen′ting) *adj.* expressing dissent: *a dissenting opinion.* —**dis·sent′ing·ly,** *adv.*

dis·sen·tious (di sen′shəs) *adj.* characterized by or inclined to dissension; quarrelsome.

dis·ser·ta·tion (dis′ər tā′shən) *n.* an extended formal treatise or discourse upon a given subject, esp. one written for a doctoral degree. [Latin *dissertātiō* discourse.]

dis·serv·ice (dis sûr′vis) *n.* an action that causes harm; ill turn; injury: *Those employees did their company a great disservice by their dishonest actions.*

dis·sev·er (di sev′ər) *v.t.* **1.** to sever; separate. **2.** to divide into parts. —*v.i.* to separate or part. —**dis·sev′er·ance, dis·sev′er·ment,** *n.*

dis·si·dence (dis′i dəns) *n.* dissent; disagreement.

dis·si·dent (dis′i dənt) *adj.* dissenting; disagreeing: *dissident views on an issue.* —*n.* a person who disagrees; dissenter. [Latin *dissidēns,* present participle of *dissidēre* to sit apart, disagree.]

dis·sim·i·lar (di sim′ə lər) *adj.* not similar or alike; different: *My cousin and I have dissimilar interests.* —**dis·sim′i·lar·ly,** *adv.*

dis·sim·i·lar·i·ty (di sim′ə lar′i tē) *n., pl.* **-ties. 1.** lack of similarity; difference. **2.** an instance of this; point of difference.

dis·si·mil·i·tude (dis′si mil′i tūd′, -tōōd′) *n.* dissimilarity; difference.

dis·sim·u·late (di sim′yə lāt′) *v.t., v.i.,* **-lat·ed, -lat·ing.** to disguise or conceal (as feelings or intentions) by pretense; dissemble. [Latin *dissimulātus,* past participle of *dissimulāre* to disguise, hide.] —**dis·sim′u·la′tion,** *n.* —**dis·sim′u·la′tive,** *adj.* —**dis·sim′u·la′tor,** *n.*

dis·si·pate (dis′ə pāt′) *v.,* **-pat·ed, -pat·ing.** —*v.t.* **1.** to disperse or drive away; scatter; dispel: *The wind dissipated the haze.* **2.** to expend wastefully or foolishly; squander: *In three years the heirs dissipated the family fortune.* —*v.i.* **1.** to become dispersed or scattered; be dispelled: *By noon the mist had dissipated.* **2.** to indulge in dissolute or extravagant pleasures, such as drinking and gambling, esp. so as to harm oneself. [Latin *dissipātus,* past participle of *dissipāre* to scatter, squander.]

dis·si·pat·ed (dis′ə pā′tid) *adj.* **1.** given to or characterized by indulgence in dissolute or extravagant pleasures; intemperate. **2.** wasted; squandered.

dis·si·pa·tion (dis′ə pā′shən) *n.* **1.** the act of dissipating or the state of being dissipated. **2.** excessive indulgence in dissolute or extravagant pleasures; intemperance.

dis·so·ci·ate (di sō′shē āt′, -sē-) *v.,* **-at·ed, -at·ing.** —*v.t.* **1.** to break the association or connection between; separate: *I dissociated myself from that club.* **2.** to subject to dissociation. —*v.i.* **1.** to no longer associate. **2.** to undergo dissociation. [Latin *dissociātus,* past participle of *dissociāre* to disunite.] —**dis·so′ci·a′tive,** *adj.*

dis·so·ci·a·tion (di sō′shē ā′shən, -sē-) *n.* **1.** the act of dissociating or the state of being dissociated. **2.** *Chemistry.* **a.** the decomposition of a substance into its constituent substances by some change in physical conditions, as heating. **b.** the decomposition of the molecules of an electrolyte into ions; ionization. **3.** *Psychology.* an unconscious defense mechanism in which an idea or feeling that is threatening to the personality is split off from the consciousness.

dis·sol·u·ble (di sol′yə bəl) *adj.* capable of being dissolved. —**dis·sol′u·bil′i·ty, dis·sol′u·ble·ness,** *n.*

dis·so·lute (dis′ə lüt′) *adj.* showing or characterized by lack of moral restraints; wanton; debauched: *dissolute youths, a dissolute life.* [Latin *dissolūtus* loose, part participle of *dissolvere* to loosen.] —**dis′so·lute′ly,** *adv.* —**dis′so·lute′ness,** *n.*

dis·so·lu·tion (dis′ə lü′shən) *n.* **1.** the act of dissolving or the state of being dissolved. **2.** separation into parts; disintegration. **3.** a breaking up; termination: *the dissolution of a partnership.* **4.** death.

dis·solve (di zolv′) *v.,* **-solved, -solv·ing.** —*v.t.* **1.a.** to cause to pass into solution with a liquid: *to dissolve sugar in water.* **b.** to cause to change from a solid or gas into liquid; liquefy; melt. **2.** to separate into parts; disintegrate. **3.** to put an end to; terminate: *to dissolve a partnership.* **4.** to cause to break up, disperse, or disappear. **5.** *Law.* to destroy the binding power, authority, or

force of; set aside; annul, as a marriage or injunction. —*v.i.* **1.a.** to pass into solution: *Salt dissolves in water.* **b.** to become liquid; melt. **2.** to dwindle or disappear gradually; fade away: *Our prospects for winning the election were dissolving rapidly.* **3.** to come to an end; terminate. **4.** to break up; disperse: *The fog dissolved.* **5.** to be overcome or emotionally moved: *to dissolve in tears.* **6.** (of a motion-picture or television image) to fade out while a succeeding image fades in. —*n.* in motion pictures or television, an act or instance of dissolving. [Latin *dissolvere* to loosen, separate, disunite.] —**dis·solv′a·ble,** *adj.* —**dis·solv′er,** *n.*

dis·so·nance (dis′ə nəns) *n.* **1.** a harsh, unpleasant, or inharmonious sound or combination of sounds. **2.** any lack of agreement or harmony; incongruity; disagreement. **3.** *Music.* inharmonious blending of tones that seem to be incomplete and require resolution. ➡ distinguished from **consonance.** Also, **dis′so·nan·cy.**

dis·so·nant (dis′ə nənt) *adj.* **1.** harsh or unpleasant in sound; inharmonious. **2.** lacking harmony or agreement; at variance; incongruous: *dissonant views on a subject.* **3.** *Music.* marked by or containing a dissonance. [Latin *dissonāns,* present participle of *dissonāre* to disagree in sound, differ.] —**dis′so·nant·ly,** *adv.*

dis·suade (di swād′) *v.t.,* **-suad·ed, -suad·ing.** to deter (someone) from an action or intention by persuasion or advice: *He dissuaded her from resigning her job.* [Latin *dissuādēre* to advise against.] —**dis·suad′er,** *n.*

dis·sua·sion (di swā′zhən) *n.* the act, fact, or process of dissuading.

dis·sua·sive (di swā′siv) *adj.* tending or intended to dissuade. —**dis·sua′sive·ly,** *adv.* —**dis·sua′sive·ness,** *n.*

dis·syl·la·ble (di sil′ə bəl, dis sil′-, dī′sil′-) *also,* **disyllable.** *n.* a word consisting of two syllables. [DI-[1] + SYLLABLE.] —**dis′syl·lab′ic,** *adj.*

dist. 1. distance. **2.** district.

dis·taff (dis′taf) *n.* **1.** a stick used for spinning, usually cleft at one end, on which wool, flax, cotton, or other fibers are held and from which they are drawn off and twisted into thread, either by hand or with a spinning wheel, onto a spindle. **2.** a woman's work, concerns, or domain. **3.** *Archaic.* women in general; the female sex. —*adj.* of, relating to, or characteristic of a woman; female. [Old English *distæf* stick for spinning.]

Distaff
Spindle
distaff

distaff side, the maternal branch or female side of a family. ➡ distinguished from **spear side.**

dis·tain (di stān′) *v.t. Archaic.* **1.** to discolor; stain; dye. **2.** to dishonor; disgrace; sully. [Old French *desteindre* to remove the color from, going back to Latin *dis-* apart + *tingere* to dye.]

dis·tal (dis′təl) *adj.* located away from the place or point of attachment or origin, such as a limb or a bone. ➡ distinguished from **proximal.** [DIST(ANT) + -AL[1].]

dis·tance (dis′təns) *n.* **1.** the extent of space between any two points or objects: *Astronomers can measure the distance of the moon from the earth. The distance from my house to school is two blocks.* **2.** a far-off point or place; remote region or position: *We saw a car in the distance.* **3.** the quality, state, or fact of being distant in space or time; remoteness. **4.** an extent of time or space: *There is a distance of four years between our two children. Our house is a considerable distance from here.* **5.** lack of friendliness or familiarity; coolness; aloofness. —*v.t.,* **-tanced, -tanc·ing. 1.** to leave far behind, as in a race; outdistance. **2.** to place or hold at a distance: *to distance oneself from a controversy.*

• **to keep one's distance.** to remain aloof or reserved.

dis·tant (dis′tənt) *adj.* **1.** far away or apart in space; not near: *Pluto is a distant planet. The farm is distant from the nearest town.* **2.** separated (from); removed (from): *The highway is eight miles distant from the house.* **3.** far away or off in time: *distant centuries, the distant past.* **4.** to, at, or from a distance: *a distant rumble of thunder.* **5.** far apart or remote, as in relationship, connection, or degree: *a distant cousin.* **6.** not friendly or familiar; cool in

a	at	e	end	o	hot	u	up	hw	white		about
ā	ape	ē	me	ō	old	ū	use	ng	song	ə	taken
ä	far	i	it	ô	fork	ū	rule	th	thin		pencil
âr	care	ī	ice	oi	oil	u̇	pull	th	this		lemon
		îr	pierce	ou	out	ûr	turn	zh	measure		circus

manner; aloof; reserved: *They've been very distant toward me since our argument.* [Latin *distāns*, present participle of *distāre* to stand apart.] —**dis′tant·ly,** *adv.*

dis·taste (dis tāst′) *n.* lack of taste, liking, or affinity for something; dislike; disinclination: *a distaste for spinach, to have a distaste for hard work.* —For Synonyms, see **dislike.**

dis·taste·ful (dis tāst′fəl) *adj.* causing dislike; unpleasant; disagreeable; offensive: *Arguing or shouting in public is distasteful behavior.* —**dis·taste′ful·ly,** *adv.* —**dis·taste′ful·ness,** *n.*

dis·tem·per¹ (dis tem′pər) *n.* **1.** a highly contagious viral disease of dogs and certain other mammals, characterized by fever, watery discharges from the nose and eyes, lack of appetite, and loss of strength. **2.** any of various other animal diseases with similar symptoms. **3.** *Archaic.* a mental or physical disorder or sickness; ailment. **4.** a disturbance or disorder, esp. of a political or civil nature. —*v.t. Archaic.* **1.** to upset or unbalance the functions of; throw out of order; disorder. **2.** to disturb; confuse; ruffle. [Middle English *distemperen,* from Old French *destemper* to upset, put out of order, disorder, from Medieval Latin *distemperāre,* from Latin *dis-* apart + *temperāre* to mix in proper proportion, regulate.]

dis·tem·per² (dis tem′pər) *n.* **1.** a painting medium prepared by mixing pigments with a glutinous medium, such as egg yolks or glue, and used primarily for scene painting or mural decoration. **2.** the art or method of painting with this medium. **3.** a painting done in this medium. —*v.t.* to paint in or with distemper. [Old French *distemprer* to soak, mix, going back to Latin *dis-* completely + *temperāre* to mix in proper proportion.]

dis·tem·per·a·ture (dis tem′pər ə chər, -prə chər) *n. Archaic.* a disordered condition, esp. of the mind or body.

dis·tend (di stend′) *v.t.* to enlarge by or as by pressure from within; stretch out; swell; expand: *Water pressure distended the weak spot in the hose.* —*v.i.* to become distended; swell. [Latin *distendere* to stretch out, swell out.] —For Synonyms, see **expand.**

dis·ten·si·ble (di sten′sə bəl) *adj.* capable of being distended. —**dis·ten′si·bil′i·ty,** *n.*

dis·ten·tion (di sten′shən) *also,* **dis·ten·sion.** *n.* the act of distending or the state of being distended.

dis·tich (dis′tik) *n.* two lines of verse, often rhymed, usually expressing a complete thought; couplet. [Latin *distichon,* from Greek *distichon.*]

dis·till (di stil′) *also, British,* **dis·til.** *v.,* -tilled, -till·ing. —*v.t.* **1.** to heat (a liquid or solid substance) until evaporation takes place and then condense the vapor given off, as for purification or concentration: *to distill water.* **2.** to extract, produce, or purify by distilling: *to distill whiskey, to distill alcohol from grain.* **3.** to obtain as if by distilling; extract the essence of: *to distill wisdom from experience, to distill a moral from a story.* **4.** to give forth or let fall in drops. —*v.i.* **1.** to undergo distillation. **2.** to fall or exude in drops; trickle. [Latin *dīstīllāre* to drip, going back to *dē* down + *stīlla* a drop; because during distillation cooled vapors fall as drops into a container.]

dis·til·late (dis′tə lit, -lāt′, di stil′it) *n.* **1.** a product obtained by distillation; liquid condensed from vapor during distillation. **2.** any concentration, essence, or abstraction.

dis·til·la·tion (dis′tə lā′shən) *n.* **1.** the act or process of separating the more volatile parts of a liquid or solid substance from those less volatile by heating until evaporation takes place and then condensing the vapor thus produced. **2.** distillate *(def. 1).* **3.** the act of distilling or the state of being distilled. **4.** an essential or concentrated quality of something; extract; essence.

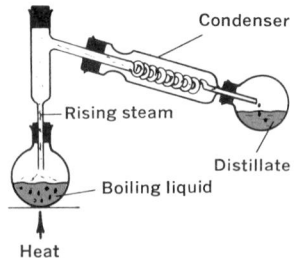

Condenser

Rising steam

Distillate

Boiling liquid

Heat

distillation

dis·tilled (di stild′) *adj.* obtained, produced, or purified by distilling.

dis·till·er (di stil′ər) *n.* **1.** a person or thing that distills. **2.** a person or corporation that makes distilled liquors, as rye, bourbon, or vodka.

dis·till·er·y (di stil′ə rē) *n., pl.* -er·ies. a place where distilling is performed, esp. an industrial plant where distilled liquors are made.

dis·tinct (dis stingkt′) *adj.* **1.** not identical; separate: *The twins had distinct personalities.* **2.** different in quality or kind: *The Spanish language is distinct from Japanese.* **3.** clearly seen, heard, or understood; clear; plain: *The sound of the drums was distinct even from a distance.* **4.** without question; definite; unmistakable:

a distinct improvement. [Latin *distinctus,* past participle of *distinguere* to separate.] —**dis·tinct′ly,** *adv.* —**dis·tinct′ness,** *n.*

dis·tinc·tion (di stingk′shən) *n.* **1.** the act of making or noting a difference: *to make a distinction between truth and fiction.* **2.** the condition or quality of being distinct; difference: *The distinction between the two arguments is not clear.* **3.** a distinguishing mark or characteristic: *That student has the distinction of being the fastest runner in the school.* **4.** a quality that merits special recognition; excellence: *acts of distinction, to write with distinction.* **5.** a mark or symbol of special recognition or honor.

dis·tinc·tive (dis stingk′tiv) *adj.* serving to distinguish or having a distinguishing quality; characteristic: *Roses have a distinctive scent.* —**dis·tinc′tive·ly,** *adv.* —**dis·tinc′tive·ness,** *n.*

dis·tin·gué (dēs′tang gā′, dis tang′gā) *adj.* having a distinguished appearance or manner. [French *distingué,* past participle of *distinguer* to separate, honor, from Latin *distinguere* to separate.]

dis·tin·guish (di sting′gwish) *v.t.* **1.** to recognize or indicate as different; differentiate: *to distinguish gold from brass.* **2.** to be a distinctive characteristic or quality of; characterize: *Brilliant red plumage distinguishes the male cardinal from the female.* **3.** to perceive clearly; discern: *We could see three people approaching but could not distinguish their faces.* **4.** to separate into categories; classify. **5.** to make prominent or worthy of special recognition. ➡ usually used in the reflexive in def. 5: *Those senators distinguished themselves as advocates for civil rights.* —*v.i.* to recognize or indicate a difference; differentiate (usually with *between* or *among*): *to distinguish between a genuine signature and a forgery.* [Latin *distinguere* to separate.] —**dis·tin′guish·a·ble,** *adj.* —**dis·tin′guish·a·bly,** *adv.* —For Synonyms, see **discern.**

dis·tin·guished (di sting′gwisht) *adj.* **1.** marked or characterized by excellence; noted; eminent: *a distinguished scientist.* **2.** having an air of distinction; distingué: *Their uniforms made them look very distinguished.* —For Synonyms, see **noted.**

dis·tort (di stôrt′) *v.t.* **1.** to twist or bend out of shape; change the natural or usual form of: *The curved mirror distorted my image.* **2.** to misrepresent, as statements, facts, or meaning: *The newspaper distorted my meaning by misquoting me.* [Latin *distortus,* past participle of *distorquēre* to twist.] —**dis·tort′er,** *n.*

dis·tor·tion (di stôr′shən) *n.* **1.** the act of distorting or the state of being distorted. **2.** anything that is distorted.

dis·tract (di strakt′) *v.t.* **1.** to cause the mind or attention of (someone) to be turned away; divert: *Noise distracted the writer from his work.* **2.** to disturb or confuse the mind of: *Worry about their missing daughter distracted the parents.* [Latin *distractus,* past participle of *distrahere* to pull apart, perplex.] —**dis·tract′ed·ly,** *adv.* —**dis·tract′ing·ly,** *adv.*

dis·trac·tion (di strak′shən) *n.* **1.** the act of turning away the mind or attention. **2.** something that draws away the mind or attention: *The noise from the construction site was a distraction.* **3.** something that diverts and relieves the mind; amusement: *Building model airplanes is a pleasant distraction for me.* **4.** a state of emotional or mental agitation or disturbance: *Your constant yelling nearly drove me to distraction.*

dis·trait (di strā′) *adj.* absent-minded; inattentive. [French *distrait,* past participle of *distraire* to distract, from Latin *distrahere* to pull apart, perplex.]

dis·traught (di strôt′) *adj.* **1.** mentally confused or bewildered; distracted: *The passengers were distraught with fear as the plane lost altitude.* **2.** crazed; mad. [Modification of obsolete *distract* distracted, from Latin *distractus,* past participle of *distrahere* to pull apart, perplex.]

dis·tress (di stres′) *n.* **1.** suffering of body or mind; anxiety; grief: *Losing my job caused me much distress.* **2.** a cause of pain or suffering: *His sister's illness was a great distress to him.* **3.** a dangerous condition marked by extreme or desperate need: *We received a radio message from a ship in distress.* —*v.t.* to cause pain, anxiety, grief, or suffering to; afflict: *The bad news from home distressed me.* [Old French *destrece* misfortune, anguish, going back to Latin *districtus,* past participle of *distringere* to draw asunder.] —**dis·tress′ing·ly,** *adv.*

dis·tressed (di strest′) *adj.* **1.a.** suffering mental pain or sorrow; troubled; anxious: *They became distressed when their grandparents did not answer the phone.* **b.** suffering physical or material hardship or trauma: *to send aid to a distressed area.* **2.** damaged or worn: *The store held a sale of distressed goods after the fire.* **3.** deliberately worn or marred so as to appear old or antique: *a table made of distressed walnut.*

dis·tress·ful (di stres′fəl) *adj.* **1.** causing or bringing distress; painful. **2.** feeling or expressing distress. —**dis·tress′ful·ly,** *adv.*

dis·trib·u·tar·y (dis trib′yə ter′ē) *n., pl.* -tar·ies. a branch of a

river that drains away from the river. A large river typically splits up into a complex network of distributaries in its delta. [From DISTRIBUTE, on the model of *tribute, tributary.*]

dis·trib·ute (di strib′ūt) *v.t.,* **-ut·ed, -ut·ing. 1.** to separate and give out, as in shares; deal out: *to distribute clothing to flood victims, to distribute pamphlets.* **2.** to scatter or spread out over an area or surface: *to distribute seed over plowed land.* **3.** to divide and arrange according to a classification or function: *The scientists distributed the plants they had found according to their species.* [Latin *distribūtus,* past participle of *distribuere* to divide.]

dis·tri·bu·tion (dis′trə bū′shən) *n.* **1.** the act of distributing or the state of being distributed. **2.** the manner in which something is distributed: *an even distribution of work.* **3.** something that is distributed. **4.** *Economics.* the allocation of goods and income of a society among the members of the society. **5.** the system or process of distributing produce or commodities to distributors or consumers. **6.** *Statistics.* an arrangement of data on the basis of some criterion, as frequency of occurrence. —**dis′tri·bu′tion·al,** *adj.*

dis·trib·u·tive (di strib′yə tiv) *adj.* **1.** of or relating to distribution. **2.** *Grammar.* referring to each member of a group considered individually. *Each* and *every* are distributive words. —*n.* a distributive word or expression. —**dis·trib′u·tive·ly,** *adv.*

distributive law *Algebra.* the law that states that the product of a compound expression and a factor, as $x(y + z)$, remains the same whether one takes the sum of the individual products $xy + xz$ or first takes the sum of y and z and then multiplies by x: $3(4 + 5) = 3 \times 4 + 3 \times 5 = 3 \times 9$.

dis·trib·u·tor (di strib′yə tər) *n.* **1.** a person or thing that distributes. **2.** a person or company that sells produce or commodities, usually of a particular type, to retailers or consumers. **3.** an electrical device that distributes current to the spark plugs of an internal-combustion engine so that they fire in proper sequence.

dis·trib·u·tor·ship (di strib′yə tər ship′) *n.* a franchise granted to a distributor.

dis·trict (dis′trikt) *n.* **1.** a territorial division of

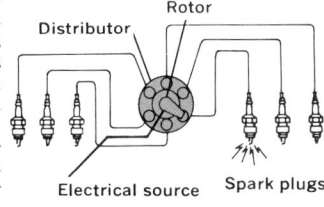

distributor

Labels: Rotor, Distributor, Electrical source, Spark plugs

a country, state, city, or other area, marked off for a special purpose: *a school district, an election district.* **2.** any region or locality having a particular characteristic: *the theater district of a city.* —*v.t.* to divide or organize into districts. [French *district,* from Medieval Latin *districtus* jurisdiction, from Latin *districtus,* past participle of *distringere* to stretch out, extend, from *dis-* apart + *stringere* to stretch.]

district attorney, a lawyer who serves as a prosecutor, esp. the chief prosecutor, for a judicial district, such as a county.

dis·trust (dis trust′) *v.t.* to have no trust or confidence in; be suspicious of; doubt. —*n.* lack of trust or confidence; suspicion; doubt.

dis·trust·ful (dis trust′fəl) *adj.* having or showing distrust; suspicious; doubtful: *to be distrustful of fast-talking salespeople.* —**dis·trust′ful·ly,** *adv.* —**dis·trust′ful·ness,** *n.*

dis·turb (di stûrb′) *v.t.* **1.** to agitate the mind of; make uneasy or anxious: *The news of the accident disturbed him.* **2.** to break in upon; interrupt; bother: *Don't disturb her while she's working.* **3.** to destroy or interfere with the peace or tranquillity of: *The noisy trucks disturbed the neighborhood.* **4.** to upset the order or arrangement of, as by moving out of position: *The child disturbed the flower arrangement.* **5.** to inconvenience. [Latin *disturbāre* to drive asunder, throw into confusion.] —**dis·turb′er,** *n.*

Synonyms Disturb, upset, agitate, and perturb mean to put into an unsettled or disordered state of mind. **Disturb** is the least specific of these terms. It suggests that normal functioning is hindered, but little more: *The news disturbed me, and I was unable to concentrate.* **Upset** implies that one's nerves are affected, and suggests distress: *The news upset me so much that I could not stop crying.* **Agitate** implies a stirring up to the point where physical action betrays inner turmoil: *She was visibly agitated by the prospect of speaking to a large audience.* **Perturb** connotes a deep or thorough disturbing: *He was so perturbed by the news that he grabbed his coat and ran out the door.*

dis·turb·ance (di stûr′bəns) *n.* **1.** the act of disturbing or the state of being disturbed. **2.** something that disturbs. **3.** a commotion or tumult, esp. a public disorder: *The police officer went to see*

what the disturbance was about. **4.** a state of mental agitation or uneasiness; anxiety.

dis·turbed (di stûrbd′) *adj.* showing symptoms of an emotional disorder; troubled; maladjusted.

di·sul·fide (dī sul′fīd) *n.* a chemical compound in which two atoms of sulfur are combined with another atom or radical. Also, **bisulfide.**

dis·un·ion (dis ūn′yən) *n.* **1.** a breaking apart; severance; separation. **2.** lack of agreement or unity; dissension; discord.

dis·u·nite (dis′ū nīt′) *v.,* **-nit·ed, -nit·ing.** —*v.t.* **1.** to break the union of; sever; separate. **2.** to cause dissension between; alienate. —*v.i.* to come apart; become separate.

dis·u·ni·ty (dis ū′ni tē) *n.* lack of unity; disunion; dissension.

dis·use (*n.,* dis ūs′; *v.,* dis ūz′) *n.* the condition or state of not being used or practiced: *The custom has fallen into disuse.* —*v.t.,* **-used, -us·ing.** to use no longer.

di·syl·la·ble (dī′sil′ə bəl, dī sil′-, di sil′-) dissyllable.

ditch (dich) *n.* a long, narrow excavation, usually used for drainage, irrigation, or protection; trench. —*v.t.* **1.** to land (a disabled aircraft) on water and abandon it. **2.a.** to cause (a car, wagon, or other vehicle) to go into a ditch. **b.** to derail (a train). **3.** to dig a ditch in or around. **4.** *Slang.* to get rid of; get away from: *The bank robbers ditched the stolen car.* —*v.i.* to land a disabled aircraft on water and abandon it. [Old English *dīc* dike.]

dith·er (dith′ər) *n.* a state of nervous excitement, agitation, or confusion: *I was in a dither when I heard that I had won the grand prize.* —*v.i.* to be in a dither. [Form of dialectal English *didder* to shake; probably imitative.]

dith·y·ramb (dith′ə ram′, -ramb′) *n.* **1.** in ancient Greece, a wild, boisterous choric hymn or chant sung in honor of Dionysus. **2.** any boisterous, enthusiastic, or emotional writing or speech. [Latin *dīthyrambus* the ancient Greek hymn, from Greek *dīthyrambos.*]

dith·y·ram·bic (dith′ə ram′bik) *adj.* **1.** of or like a dithyramb. **2.** wildly emotional or enthusiastic.

dit·sy (dit′sē) also, **dit·sey, dit·zy.** *adj.,* **-si·er, -si·est;** also, **-sey·er, -sey·est.** *Slang.* flighty and somewhat eccentric. [Of uncertain origin.]

dit·to (dit′ō) *n., pl.* **-tos. 1.** the same (as appeared or was mentioned before or above). ➡ often symbolized by ditto marks. **2.** ditto mark. **3.** a copy; duplicate. —*v.t.,* **-toed, -to·ing.** to duplicate or repeat: *to ditto the text of an agreement.* —*adv.* as before; likewise. —*interj.* the same; agreed. [Dialectal Italian *ditto* (thing) said, past participle of *dire* to say, from Latin *dīcere.*]

ditto mark, one of a pair of small marks (″) placed under something written or printed to indicate that it is to be repeated.

dit·ty (dit′ē) *n., pl.* **-ties.** a short, simple song. [Old French *ditie* kind of poem, from Latin *dictātum* (thing) dictated, from *dictāre* to say often, dictate.]

ditty bag, a small bag used by sailors to hold personal items, such as toiletries, needles, thread, and buttons. [Possibly from obsolete *dutty* coarse calico, probably from Hindi *dhōtī* loincloth.]

ditty box, a small box used like a ditty bag.

dit·zy (dit′sē) *adj.,* **-zi·er, -zi·est.** ditsy.

di·u·ret·ic (dī′ə ret′ik) *adj.* causing an increase in the amount of urine excreted by the kidneys. —*n.* a diuretic medicine. [Late Latin *diurēticus* that promotes urine, from Greek *diourētikos,* going back to *dia* through + *ouron* urine.]

di·ur·nal (dī ûr′nəl) *adj.* **1.** occurring or performed every day; daily: *the diurnal rotation of the earth.* **2.** of or occurring during the daytime: *diurnal noises.* **3.** more active during the day than at night: *a diurnal animal.* ➡ opposed to **nocturnal. 4.** (of a flower) opening during the day and closing at night. ➡ opposed to **nocturnal. 5.** lasting only one day. [Latin *diurnālis* daily, going back to *diēs* day. Doublet of JOURNAL.] —**di·ur′nal·ly,** *adv.*

div. 1. divided. **2.** dividend. **3.** division. **4.** divisor. **5.** divorced.

di·va (dē′və) *n., pl.* **-vas.** a famous female opera singer; prima donna. [Italian *diva,* from Latin *dīva* goddess; because of the exalted position of opera singers in Italy.]

di·va·gate (dī′və gāt′) *v.i.,* **-gat·ed, -gat·ing. 1.** to wander about; stray. **2.** to digress, as in speech. [Latin *dīvagātus,* past participle of *dīvagārī* to wander about.] —**di′va·ga′tion,** *n.*

di·va·lent (dī vā′lənt) *adj.* bivalent.

di·van (di van′, -vän′, dī′van) *n.* **1.** a long, low upholstered couch or sofa, usually having no back or arms. **2.a.** formerly, a court or council of state in Turkey and some other Middle Eastern

a	at	e	end	o	hot	u	up	hw	white		about
ā	ape	ē	me	ō	old	ū	use	ng	song	ə	taken
ä	far	i	it	ô	fork	ū	rule	th	thin		pencil
âr	care	ī	ice	oi	oil	ů	pull	th	this		lemon
		îr	pierce	ou	out	ûr	turn	zh	measure		circus

357

countries. **b.** a room where such a court or council convened. **3.** a smoking room. [Turkish *divan* council of state (that met in a chamber with a long couch along the walls), from Persian *dīvān* council of state, royal court.]

dive (dīv) *v.*, **dived** or **dove**, **dived**, **div·ing.** —*v.i.* **1.a.** to plunge headfirst into water. **b.** to go underwater: *The submarine dived when it spotted the enemy plane.* **2.** (of an airplane) to descend rapidly at a steep angle. **3.** to dash, leap, or drop suddenly and quickly, esp. headfirst downward: *to dive into a doorway, to dive under the covers.* **4.** to enter into or become deeply involved in something: *I dove into my studies.* **5.** to insert (the hand) quickly: *to dive into one's pockets.* —*v.t.* **1.** to send (an airplane) into a dive. **2.** to insert (the hand) into quickly: *The thief dived his hand into her purse.* —*n.* **1.a.** a headfirst plunge into water. **b.** a downward movement underwater: *The submarine made a dive for the bottom.* **2.** (of an airplane) a steep, rapid descent. **3.** any rapid or headlong dash, leap, or drop. **4.** *Informal.* a cheap, disreputable nightclub, tavern, or bar. [Old English *dȳfan* to immerse, dip.]

dive-bomb (dīv′bom′) *v.t., v.i.* to dive down on a target in a plane and release bombs at a low altitude.

dive bomber, a fighter plane equipped to carry one or more bombs that are usually released at the low point of a steep dive.

div·er (dī′vər) *n.* **1.** a person who dives into water, esp. one who takes part in diving competitions. **2.** a person whose job involves going underwater, as for pearls, exploration, or salvage work. **3.** any of various diving birds, such as the loon.

di·verge (di vûrj′, dī-) *v.*, **-verged**, **-verg·ing.** —*v.i.* **1.** to move or extend in different directions from a common point or from each other; draw apart; branch out: *The two roads ran side by side for several miles and then diverged.* **2.** to differ, as in character, form, or opinion: *Their dialects seem to diverge completely.* **3.** to turn aside or deviate, as from a course, line of thought, rule, or norm: *to diverge from the truth.* —*v.t.* to cause to diverge. [Modern Latin *dīvergere* to go in different directions, from Latin *dis-* apart + *vergere* to bend.]

Synonyms Diverge, depart, deviate, and digress mean to turn away or branch out from a course. **Diverge** is used of two branches that grow increasingly far apart: *They were very close in school, but as their careers diverged, they had less and less to say to each other.* **Depart** connotes leaving the main track: *tire tracks that depart from a highway, a speaker departing from a prepared text.* **Deviate** implies turning away from what is expected or normal: *Your findings deviate from those of every other study. Their behavior deviates from that of average teenagers.* **Digress** suggests a temporary detour: *to digress from a story one is telling.*

di·ver·gence (di vûr′jəns, dī-) *n.* **1.** the act of diverging or the state of being diverged. **2.** a difference, as of character, form, or opinion. **3.** a turning aside or deviation, as from a norm.

di·ver·gen·cy (di vûr′jən sē, dī-) *n., pl.* **-cies.** divergence.

di·ver·gent (di vûr′jənt, dī-) *adj.* **1.** moving or extending in different directions; diverging. **2.** differing, as in character, form, or opinion. **3.** deviating, as from a norm. —**di·ver′gent·ly,** *adv.* —For Synonyms, see **different.**

diverging lens, a lens that is thinner in the middle than at the edges, bending light waves away from its center. These lenses form virtual images rather than real images.

di·vers (dī′vərz) *adj.* various; several: *There are divers ways of doing the job.* [Old French *divers* differing, various, from Latin *dīversus.*]

di·verse (di vûrs′, dī-, dī′vûrs) *adj.* **1.** markedly different; unlike: *The two professors hold diverse opinions on the subject.* **2.** of different kinds; varied; diversified: *a person of diverse interests, a diverse collection of antiques.* [Form of DIVERS.] —**di·verse′ly,** *adv.* —**di·verse′-ness,** *n.* —For Synonyms, see **different.**

di·ver·si·fi·ca·tion (di vûr′sə fi kā′shən, dī-) *n.* the act of diversifying or the state of being diversified.

di·ver·si·fy (di vûr′sə fī′, dī-) *v.*, **-fied**, **-fy·ing.** —*v.t.* **1.** to make diverse; give variety to; vary: *The hotel diversified its menu with French and Italian foods.* **2.** to make or distribute (investments) among various types of securities. —*v.i.* to invest or deal in various lines or products. [Medieval Latin *dīversificare* to make unlike, from Latin *dīversus* different + *facere* to make.]

di·ver·sion (di vûr′zhən, dī-) *n.* **1.** the act of diverting or the state of being diverted: *the diversion of a stream.* **2.** a distraction of attention: *I created a diversion while my parents brought in my brother's surprise birthday present.* **3.** something that distracts the attention; amusement; entertainment; pastime: *Her favorite diver-*

sion is listening to classical music. **4.** an attack or action intended to draw the enemy away from the main point of operation. —For Synonyms, see **amusement.**

di·ver·sion·ar·y (di vûr′zhə ner′ē, dī-) *adj.* of or relating to a diversion, esp. serving to distract the enemy: *diversionary tactics.*

di·ver·si·ty (di vûr′si tē, dī-) *n., pl.* **-ties. 1.** the condition, quality, or instance of being diverse: *the diversity of a group of people.* **2.** variety; multiformity: *a diversity of opinion.*

di·vert (di vûrt′, dī-) *v.t.* **1.** to change the direction or course of; turn aside; deflect: *The police diverted traffic from the scene of the accident.* **2.** to distract the attention of. **3.** to amuse; entertain: *The children were diverted by the clown's antics.* [Middle French *divertir* to alter, avert, amuse, from Latin *dīvertere* to separate, turn in different ways.]

di·ver·tic·u·li·tis (dī′vər tik′yə lī′tis) *n.* an inflammation of a diverticulum, esp. as of the colon. [DIVERTICUL(UM) + -ITIS.]

di·ver·tic·u·lum (dī′vər tik′yə ləm) *n., pl.* **-la** (-lə). a pouch or sac opening out from a hollow organ, as the intestine. [Latin *dīverticulum* bypass, bypath.]

di·ver·ti·men·to (di vûr′tə men′tō) *n., pl.* **-ti** (-tē) or **-tos.** an instrumental musical composition, usually of a light character, consisting of several short movements. [Italian *divertimento* amusement, going back to French *divertir* to amuse. See DIVERT.]

di·ver·tisse·ment (di vûr′tis mənt; *French* dē ver tēs män′) *n.* **1.** a diversion; entertainment. **2.** a short ballet or other entertainment, usually performed during the course of a longer work, such as an opera or full-length ballet. **3.** divertimento. [French *divertissement,* from *divertir* to amuse. See DIVERT.]

di·vest (di vest′, dī-) *v.t.* **1.** to deprive or dispossess (someone), as of rights, authority, or possessions. **2.** to rid or free (oneself); renounce: *to divest oneself of all responsibility.* **3.** to strip, as of clothing. **4.** to sell off (an investment): *to divest one's holdings in the stock market.* [Medieval Latin *dīvestire* to undress, going back to Latin *dis-* apart + *vestīre* to clothe.]

di·vest·i·ture (di ves′ti chər, dī-) *n.* **1.** the sale of stock or other business holdings, as by an individual to avoid a conflict of interest or by an institution in an attempt to promote social change. **2.** the act of divesting or the state of being divested.

di·vide (di vīd′) *v.*, **-vid·ed**, **-vid·ing.** —*v.t.* **1.** to separate into parts or pieces; split up: *to divide an orange.* **2.** to separate into parts or pieces and distribute; share: *to divide profits among shareholders.* **3.** to make or cause to be separate or apart by or as by a boundary or partition: *The fence divides their land from ours.* **4.** to separate or arrange into groups or categories; classify: *The teacher divided the children in the class according to reading level.* **5.** to separate into opposing sides or opinions; cause dissension in or between; disunite: *The argument divided the friends.* **6.** *Mathematics.* **a.** to perform the operation of division on. **b.** to be an exact divisor of. —*v.i.* **1.** to become separated into parts; branch. **2.** to become separated into opposing sides or opinions; disagree: *The Senate divided on that issue.* **3.** to perform mathematical division. **4.** (of a parliament, esp. in Great Britain) to vote by separating into two groups. —*n.* a ridge or other land elevation separating two regions drained by different river systems; watershed. [Latin *dīvidere* to separate.]

di·vid·ed (di vī′did) *adj.* **1.** separated into parts or pieces. **2.** disunited, as by conflicting interests or opinions; disagreeing. **3.** shared; distributed: *a divided allegiance.* **4.** *Botany.* separated to the base or the midrib or deeply indented so as to form distinct segments, as certain leaves.

div·i·dend (div′i dend′, -dənd) *n.* **1.** a number or quantity that is to be divided by another. In dividing 15 by 3, the dividend is 15. **2.** the net earnings of a corporation for any given period of time, paid to the stockholders and representing their share of the profits of the business. **3.** a portion of such earnings given to each stockholder, usually in the form of money, according to the amount and kind of stock owned. **4.** a bonus or benefit: *Free use of the pool is one of the dividends of being a lifeguard.* [Latin *dīvidendum* thing to be divided, from *dīvidere* to separate.]

di·vid·er (di vī′dər) *n.* **1.** a person or thing that divides. **2.** **dividers.** an instrument for measuring and marking distances on a map or blueprint; compass.

div·i·na·tion (div′ə nā′shən) *n.* **1.** the art or practice of foretelling the future or discovering that which is hidden or unknown, as by occult means. **2.** the act of divining. **3.** something that is divined; prophecy.

di·vine (di vīn′) *adj.* **1.** of or relating to God or a god: *divine will.* **2.** given by or coming from God or a god: *divine forgiveness.* **3.** addressed or devoted to God or a god; sacred; religious: *divine worship.* **4.** having the nature or characteristics of God or a god; heavenly: *divine beauty.* **5.** supremely excellent or gifted: *a divine poet.* **6.** *Informal.* **a.** extremely pleasurable or delightful: *The party was divine.* **b.** very attractive; lovely: *a divine outfit.* —*v.*, **-vined**, **-vin·ing.** —*v.t.* **1.** to foretell or foresee (the future) or

diverging lenses

discover (something hidden or unknown), as by occult means. **2.** to conjecture or perceive by insight or intuition; guess. **3.** to discover by using a divining rod. —*v.i.* **1.** to practice divination; prophesy. **2.** to conjecture; guess. —*n.* **1.** a member of the clergy. **2.** theologian. [Latin *dīvīnus* relating to a deity, prophet, from *dīvus* godlike, god.] —**di·vine′ly,** *adv.* —**di·vine′ness,** *n.* —**di·vin′er,** *n.* —For Synonyms *(adj.)*, see **holy.**

divine right of kings, the doctrine that monarchs derive their authority from God and are accountable only to God.

diving bell, a large, watertight container open at the bottom and filled with compressed air, used for work under water.

diving board, a flexible board fastened at one end and extending over water, esp. over a swimming pool, upon which a diver jumps to gain momentum in executing a dive. Also, **springboard.**

diving suit, a suit with a helmet used for working under water. It is typically waterproof and is supplied with air through tubes from the surface or from portable tanks worn by the diver.

divining rod, a forked branch or stick that supposedly indicates underground water or minerals by bending downwards when held at the ends.

di·vin·i·ty (di vin′i tē) *n., pl.* **-ties. 1.** the state or quality of being God or a god. **2.** a godlike nature, esp. supreme excellence. **3.** a divine being; deity; god. **4.** theology. **5.** a soft, creamy candy made of sugar, egg whites, corn syrup, flavoring, and usually nuts. **6. the Divinity.** God.

di·vis·i·ble (di viz′ə bəl) *adj.* **1.** capable of being divided. **2.** capable of being divided without a remainder. —**di·vis′i·bil′i·ty,** *n.*

di·vi·sion (di vizh′ən) *n.* **1.** the act or process of dividing or the state of being divided. **2.** one of the parts into which something has been divided; section: *a division of a book, the marketing division of a company.* **3.** something that divides, such as a boundary, fence, or partition. **4.** lack of agreement; dissension; discord. **5.** an arithmetic operation that determines how many times one number is contained in another. **6.** in modern armies, a basic organizational unit composed of infantry, artillery, and armor, with supporting elements, forming part of a corps and constituting the smallest unit capable of independent sustained combat. **7.** *Botany.* **a.** the second largest unit of classification for plants, kingdom being the largest. **b.** a form of plant propagation in which parts of a plant divide into sections capable of reproducing roots and leaves. [Latin *dīvīsiō* separation.] —**di·vi′sion·al,** *adj.* —For Synonyms, see **section.**

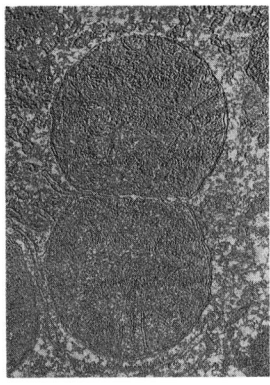

micrograph of the **division** of a cell

division of labor, the specialization of tasks in the process of making a product whereby the total operation is divided into a series of steps, each step being performed by a different worker or workers.

di·vi·sive (di vī′siv) *adj.* causing or tending to cause dissension or discord. —**di·vi′sive·ly,** *adv.* —**di·vi′sive·ness,** *n.*

di·vi·sor (di vī′zər) *n.* **1.** a number or quantity by which another is to be divided. **2.** a number that divides another without leaving a remainder.

di·vorce (di vôrs′) *n.* **1.** the legal dissolution of a marriage. **2.** any complete separation: *a divorce of word and deed.* Also, **di·vorce′ment.** —*v.,* **-vorced, -vorc·ing.** —*v.t.* **1.** to free oneself from (one's spouse) by divorce. **2.** to legally dissolve the marriage of: *The judge divorced the couple.* **3.** to separate; sever; disunite: *to divorce oneself from a controversy.* —*v.i.* to obtain a divorce. [Old French *divorce* dissolution of marriage, from Latin *dīvortium* separation, dissolution of marriage.]

di·vor·cé (di vôr sā′, -vôr′sā) *n.* a divorced man.

di·vor·cée (di vôr sē′, -sā′, -vôr′sē, -sā) *n.* a divorced woman.

div·ot (div′ət) *n.* a piece of turf torn up by a golf club in making a stroke.

di·vulge (di vulj′) *v.t.,* **-vulged, -vulg·ing.** to make known, as a secret; disclose. [Latin *dīvulgāre* to make common, going back to *dis-* apart + *vulgus* the common people.] —**di·vul′gence,** *n.* —**di·vul′ger,** *n.* —For Synonyms, see **reveal.**

div·vy (div′ē) *v.t.,* **-vied, -vy·ing.** *Informal.* to divide; allot; distribute (often used with *up*): *We divvied up the food left over*

after the party and each took some home. —*n.* share; allotment. [A form of DIVIDE.]

Dix·ie (dik′sē) *n.* the South, esp. the part of the South that was in the Confederate States of America. Also, **Dixieland.** [Possibly from the Mason-*Dixon* line dividing the North from the South prior to the American Civil War; possibly from French *dix* ten, printed on ten-dollar bills put out by a Louisiana bank before the Civil War.]

Dix·ie·crat (dik′sē krat′) *n.* a conservative Democrat from a Southern state who opposes the national policies of the Democratic Party, esp. one who left the party in 1948.

Dix·ie·land (dik′sē land′) **1.** a style of jazz originating in New Orleans, characterized by a fast, lively, two-beat rhythm and improvised solo performances. **2.** Dixie.

di·zen (dī′zən, diz′ən) *v.t. Archaic.* to dress in finery; deck out; bedizen. [Middle Low German *dise* bunch of flax on a distaff.]

diz·zy (diz′ē) *adj.,* **-zi·er, -zi·est. 1.** having the sensation of whirling, with a tendency to fall; giddy: *The children ran in a circle until they were dizzy.* **2.** thrown into a confused state or bewildered: *We were all dizzy from excitement the day before the wedding.* **3.** causing or tending to cause giddiness or confusion: *a dizzy pace, a dizzy height.* **4.** *Informal.* foolish; silly; inane. —*v.t.* to make giddy or confused: *The ride on the roller coaster dizzied us.* [Old English *dysig* foolish.] —**diz′zi·ly,** *adv.* —**diz′zi·ness,** *n.*

dl *also,* **dl.** deciliter; deciliters.

D. Lit., Doctor of Literature. Also, **D. Litt.**

dm *also,* **dm.** decimeter; decimeters.

DMZ, demilitarized zone.

DNA, a nucleic acid found in the chromosomes of all living cells, consisting of a coiled, ladderlike strand or double helix, made up of alternating units of sugar, in the form of deoxyribose, and phosphate connected by one of four nitrogen bases: adenine, cytosine, guanine, or thymine. It transmits all hereditary information from parent to child and determines the exact structure of all the protein produced by the cells. For illustration, see **double helix.** [Abbreviation of *d(eoxyribo)n(ucleic) a(cid).*]

do¹ (dü) *v.,* **did** or *(archaic second person sing.)* **didst, done, do·ing.** Present: *sing.,* first person, **do;** second, **do** or *(archaic)* **do·est** or **dost;** third, **does** or *(archaic)* **do·eth** or **doth;** *pl.,* **do.** —*v.t.* **1.** to perform or carry out, as an action: *He always does his duty. The nurses did everything they could to make the patient comfortable.* **2.** to produce, as by creative effort; make: *to do a sketch.* **3.** to bring to an end; complete; finish: *She interrupted him before his speech was done. We arrived after dinner was done.* **4.** to deal with or take care of; attend to. ➡ used as a substitute for a specific verb of action: *to do* (wash or set) *one's hair, to do* (launder) *the wash.* **5.** to work out; solve: *I can't do this algebra problem.* **6.** to bring about or be the cause of: *Who did the damage to the fence? A short vacation can do a lot of good.* **7.** to put forth; exert: *I'll do my utmost to help you.* **8.** to give or grant; render: *to do a favor, to do someone a good turn.* **9.** to work at, esp. as a vocation: *What are you planning to do for a living after you graduate?* **10.** to satisfy the needs of; serve; suffice: *The money will do us for a while.* **11.** to present or enact, as a play or reading: *The theater club did only comedies this season.* **12.** to cover (a distance); traverse: *She did 200 miles a day on her trip.* **13.** to travel at a speed of: *The car was doing 55 miles per hour.* **14.** *Informal.* to serve (time), as during a term in prison: *to do ten years for armed robbery.* **15.** *Informal.* to cheat; swindle: *They did us out of $1,000.* **16.** *Informal.* to visit or tour, esp. as a sightseer: *We did Spain in two weeks.* —*v.i.* **1.** to behave or conduct oneself: *Please do as you are told.* **2.** to be active or exert oneself; work; strive: *It's important to do as well as think.* **3.** to fare or manage; get along: *The patient is doing well.* **4.** to serve the purpose; be satisfactory; suffice: *Those clothes won't do for skiing.* **5.** to be fitting or proper: *It won't do for us to be late.* **6.** *Informal.* to happen; occur: *What's doing this weekend?* **7.** used as a substitute for a verb already used, to avoid repetition: *You speak French as well as I do.* —*auxiliary verb* **1.** used without specific meaning: **a.** to ask a question: *Do you need a new coat?* **b.** to form negative expressions: *I do not want any.* **c.** to form inverted expressions after some adverbs, as *rarely* or *little: little do they realize.* **2.** used to give emphasis: *Do be quiet! We do so enjoy seeing you.* [Old English *dōn* to make, cause, perform, carry out, act.]

a	at	e	end	o	hot	u	up	hw	white		about
ā	ape	ē	me	ō	old	ū	use	ng	song		taken
ä	far	i	it	ô	fork	ü	rule	th	thin	ə	pencil
âr	care	ī	ice	oi	oil	u̇	pull	th	this		lemon
				îr	pierce	ou	out	ûr	turn	zh	measure		circus

- **to do away with. a.** to kill; murder: *to do away with an enemy.* **b.** to put an end to; eliminate; abolish: *The law did away with slavery.*
- **to do by.** to act toward; treat: *The company does well by its employees.*
- **to do in.** *Informal.* **a.** to kill; murder. **b.** to tire or wear out; exhaust: *All that walking really did me in.*
- **to do over.** to redecorate.
- **to do up.** *Informal.* **a.** to tie or wrap up: *The salesclerk did up the package.* **b.** to put in order; arrange: *to do up one's hair.* **c.** to dress: *All the children were done up in their best clothes for the party.*
- **to make do.** to get along or manage: *We can make do without the extra money.*

do² (dō) *n. Music.* the first and last of the series of syllables used to name the eight tones of the diatonic scale. In the **fixed-do** method, do is always the note or tone C, while in **movable-do**, it is the keynote of any given diatonic scale. [Italian *do,* name of this note.]

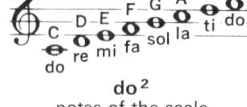

do² notes of the scale

do., ditto.
D.O.A., dead on arrival.
do·a·ble (dü′ə bəl) *adj.* capable of being done.
doat (dōt) dote.
dob·bin (dob′in) *n.* a horse, esp. a gentle, plodding one; workhorse. [Form of *Robin,* a familiar form of the masculine name *Robert.*]
Do·ber·man pin·scher (dō′bər mən pin′shər) a dog of a breed originally developed in Germany, having a long head, slender legs, and usually a sleek, black or brown coat with rust-colored markings, often used as a guard dog. Height: 27 inches (69 centimeters) at the shoulder. [German *Dobermann pinscher,* from the German dog breeder Ludwig *Dobermann,* 1834-94, + *pinscher* terrier, possibly from *Pinzgan,* area in northern Austria.]
dob·son·fly (dob′sən flī′) *n., pl.* **-flies.** a North American insect whose larva, the hellgrammite, is used as bait by anglers. [Of uncertain origin.]
doc (dok) *n. Informal.* doctor. [Short for DOCTOR.]
do·cent (dō′sənt) *n.* **1.** a lecturer or guide at a museum, esp. an art museum. **2.** a lecturer or teacher, esp. one who is not on the regular faculty, as in some American universities. [Latin *docēns,* present participle of *docēre* to teach.]
doc·ile (dos′əl) *adj.* easily managed, trained, or taught; tractable: *a docile pet, a docile child.* [Latin *docilis* teachable, from *docēre* to teach.] —**doc′ile·ly,** *adv.* —**do·cil·i·ty** (do sil′i tē), *n.*
dock¹ (dok) *n.* **1.** a structure built along the shore or out from the shore, typically secured by piles and serving as a landing place where boats and ships can be tied up and passengers and cargo loaded and discharged; wharf; pier. **2.** an area of water between two adjoining piers where boats and ships can be moored; slip. **3.** dry dock. —*v.t.* **1.** to bring (a boat or ship) to a dock. **2.** to bring together or couple (two or more orbiting objects, as spacecraft) in space. —*v.i.* **1.** to moor at or come into a dock: *We docked briefly in order to refuel.* **2.** (of orbiting objects) to come together or couple in space. [Middle Dutch *docke* pier.]

dock (*v., def. 2*)
docking in outer space

dock² (dok) *n.* **1.** the solid, fleshy part of an animal's tail. **2.** the stump of a tail left after clipping or cropping. —*v.t.* **1.** to cut the end off or shorten, as the tail of a horse or dog; clip; crop; bob. **2.** to deduct a part from; reduce: *to dock someone's wages.* **3.** to deduct from the wages of: *The company docked me a day's pay for being absent.* [Possibly from Old English *-docca,* as in *fingerdocca* finger muscle.]
dock³ (dok) *n.* the place in a criminal court where the defendant stands or sits during trial. [Flemish *dok* cage.]
dock⁴ (dok) *n.* any of various plants, genus *Rumex,* related to buckwheat, typically having large, wavy-edged leaves. [Old English *docce.*]
dock·age¹ (dok′ij) *n.* **1.** a charge made for using a dock. **2.** facilities for docking a boat or ship. **3.** the docking of boats or ships. [DOCK¹ + -AGE.]
dock·age² (dok′ij) *n.* the act of deducting, as from wages. [DOCK² + -AGE.]
dock·et (dok′it) *n.* **1.** a list of cases to be tried by a court of law. **2.** a list of legal judgments given in a specific court. **3.** a record or summary of the proceedings in a law court. **4.** a book containing such a record or summary. **5.** any list of matters to be acted upon; agenda. **6.** a label or tag attached to something, such as a package or document, listing its contents. —*v.t.* **1.** to enter in a docket. **2.** to put a label or tag on (something, such as a package or document). [Of uncertain origin.]
dock·yard (dok′yärd′) *n.* a place containing docks, workshops, and warehouses where boats and ships can be built, equipped, and repaired.
doc·tor (dok′tər) *n.* **1.** a person licensed to practice any of various branches of medicine, as pediatrics, neurosurgery, or psychiatry; physician or surgeon. **2.** a person licensed to practice any of several related sciences, as dentistry, osteopathy, or veterinary medicine. **3.** a person who holds the highest graduate degree conferred by a university, as in philosophy or divinity. **4.** *Archaic.* an eminently learned person. —*v.t.* **1.** to treat medicinally; apply remedies to. **2.** to tamper with; falsify: *to doctor evidence.* **3.** *Informal.* to modify or improve by special treatment (often with *up*): *to doctor up a sauce with spices.* —*v.i.* to practice medicine. [Latin *doctor* teacher.]
doc·tor·al (dok′tər əl) *adj.* of, relating to, or studying for a doctorate: *a doctoral thesis, a doctoral student.*
doc·tor·ate (dok′tər it) *n.* **1.** the highest graduate degree given by educational institutions, usually representing several years of advanced study and research. **2.** such a degree awarded as an honor.
doctor's degree, doctorate *(def. 1).*
doc·tri·naire (dok′trə nâr′) *n.* a person who stubbornly adheres to a theory without sufficient regard for practical considerations; impractical theorist; visionary. —*adj.* of or characteristic of a doctrinaire.
doc·tri·nal (dok′trə nəl) *adj.* of, relating to, or based on doctrine: *a doctrinal controversy.*
doc·trine (dok′trin) *n.* **1.** a particular position, principle, or body of principles that is taught or advocated, as by a religion or political party; tenet or tenets; dogma: *the doctrines of a religion.* **2.** something that is taught; teachings: *political doctrine.* [Old French *doctrine* teachings, from Latin *doctrīna* learning, teaching.]

Synonyms Doctrine and dogma may denote a body of principles held to be authoritative. **Doctrine** suggests that the principles are based on some form of proof or body of knowledge, and that they may be modified: *currently held scientific doctrine.* **Dogma** connotes acceptance on authority, no proof being considered necessary: *church dogma.*

doc·u·dra·ma (dok′yə drä′mə, -dram′ə) *n.* a television or motion-picture drama based on real events but containing some fictional elements. [DOCU(MENTARY) + DRAMA.]
doc·u·ment (*n.,* dok′yə mənt; *v.,* dok′yə ment′) *n.* something written or printed that furnishes evidence, support, proof, or information about a particular object or subject, such as a deed, record, or map. —*v.t.* **1.** to support or prove with facts, evidence, or examples: *to document research.* **2.** to provide with documents. [Old French *document,* lesson, written evidence, from Latin *documentum* lesson, proof, example.]
doc·u·men·ta·ry (dok′yə men′tə rē, -men′trē) *adj.* **1.** relating to, supported by, or consisting of documents: *documentary proof.* **2.** presenting factual material: *a documentary television program.* —*n., pl.* **-ries.** a documentary motion picture, television program, or radio program.
doc·u·men·ta·tion (dok′yə mən tā′shən, -men-) *n.* **1.** the preparation, furnishing, or citation of documents or documentary evidence: *I completed the documentation for my book.* **2.** documentary evidence or proof: *There was no documentation for the statement.* **3.** *Computers.* written instructions that describe the operation and use of hardware or software.

dod·der¹ (dod'ər) *v.i.* **1.** to move feebly and unsteadily; totter: *an old dog doddering down the street.* **2.** to tremble or shake, as from age. [Form of obsolete *dadder* to tremble; of uncertain origin.]

dod·der² (dod'ər) *n.* any of various leafless, twining, parasitic weeds, genus *Cuscuta,* related to the morning glory, that have no chlorophyll and absorb nourishment from the host plant by means of tiny suckers. [Possibly of Germanic origin.]

do·dec·a·gon (dō dek'ə gon') *n.* a plane figure having twelve sides and twelve angles. [Greek *dōdekagōnon,* from *dōdeka* twelve + *gōnia* angle.]

do·dec·a·he·dron (dō dek'ə hē'drən, dō'dek ə-) *n., pl.* **-drons** or **-dra** (-drə). a solid figure having twelve faces. [Greek *dōdekaedros* having twelve faces, from *dōdeka* twelve + *hedrā* seat, face.]

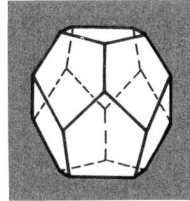
dodecahedron

dodge (doj) *v.,* **dodged, dodg·ing.** —*v.t.* **1.** to avoid by moving aside quickly or suddenly: *to dodge a blow.* **2.** to evade by strategy, deception, or cunning: *The senator dodged the reporter's question about campaign finances.* —*v.i.* **1.** to move quickly or suddenly: *The fleeing thief dodged in and out among the crowd.* **2.** to use evasive techniques. —*n.* **1.** the act of dodging. **2.** a trick used to cheat or deceive. **3.** a clever scheme, device, or plan. [Of uncertain origin.] —For Synonyms *(v.t.),* see **avoid.**

dodg·er (doj'ər) *n.* **1.** a person who dodges, esp. one who uses evasion or trickery: *a tax dodger.* **2.** a type of bread or cake made of cornmeal that is baked or fried, popular in the southern United States. **3.** a small handbill.

do·do (dō'dō) *n., pl.* **-dos** or **-does.** any of various extinct, flightless birds, genera *Raphus* and *Pezohaps,* once found on the Mascarene Islands of the Indian Ocean. Weight: 40-50 pounds (18-23 kilograms). [Portuguese *doudo* fool; because of its awkward appearance.]

doe (dō) *n.* an adult female animal, as of the deer, antelope, or rabbit. [Old English *dā* female deer.]

do·er (dü'ər) *n.* a person who does (something), esp. a person of action and vigor: *a doer of great deeds.*

does (duz) a third person singular present tense of **do¹.**

doe·skin (dō'skin') *n.* **1.** the skin of a female deer. **2.** the leather made from it. **3.** any of several slightly napped fabrics made of wool, cotton, or rayon, used for coats, suits, and sportswear.

does·n't (duz'ənt) *contr.* does not.

do·est (dü'ist) *Archaic.* a second person singular present tense of **do¹** used with **thou.**

do·eth (dü'ith) *Archaic.* a third person singular present tense of **do¹.**

doff (dof, dôf) *v.t.* **1.** to take off or remove (an article of clothing), esp. to lift (one's hat) in salutation. **2.** to rid oneself of; discard: *to doff old mannerisms.* [Contraction of *do off* to put off.]

dog (dôg) *n.* **1.** a domesticated carnivorous mammal, *Canis familiaris,* of which there are more than 200 distinct breeds, which vary greatly in appearance. **2.** any of various other animals of the dog family, Canidae, as the wolf, fox, coyote, and jackal. **3.** the male of any of these animals. **4.** any of various animals resembling or suggestive of a dog. **5.** a contemptible or undesirable person. **6.** any of various mechanical devices used to fasten, hold, or grip. **7.** andiron; firedog. **8.** *Informal.* person: *a sly dog, a lucky dog.* **9.** *Informal.* something considered ugly, undesirable, or inferior: *That rusty old car is a real dog.* **10.** **dogs.** *Slang.* feet. —*v.t.,* **dogged, dog·ging. 1.** to follow closely or pursue persistently; hound. **2.** to fasten or hold with any of various mechanical devices. [Old English *docga* a domesticated canine.]

  •**to go to the dogs.** *Informal.* to go to ruin; deteriorate.
  •**to put on the dog.** *Informal.* to make an ostentatious display; be pretentious.

dog·bane (dôg'bān') *n.* any of various plants, genus *Apocynum,* having clusters of small, white or pink bell-shaped flowers.

dog·ber·ry (dôg'ber'ē, -bə rē) *n., pl.* **-ries. 1.** the berrylike fruit of any of several plants, esp. the mountain ash. **2.** a tree or shrub bearing this fruit.

dog biscuit 1. a type of hard biscuit for dogs made of several ingredients, such as ground bones and scraps of meat. **2.** a hard biscuit used as army rations.

dog·cart (dôg'kärt') *n.* **1.** a light, open, one-horse carriage, usually two-wheeled, having two transverse seats set back to back and, originally, a space for dogs beneath the rear seat. **2.** a small cart drawn by one or more dogs.

dog·catch·er (dôg'kach'ər) *n.* a person employed or elected to pick up and impound stray, homeless, or unlicensed dogs.

dog days, the hot, sultry days of July and August. [Latin *diēs canīculārēs* days of the dog star; because the Romans believed that Sirius, called the Dog Star, which rose with the sun in July and August, increased the excessive heat of the season.]

doge (dōj) *n.* the chief magistrate in either of the former republics of Genoa and Venice. [Dialectal Italian *doge,* from Latin *dux* leader. Doublet of DUCE, DUKE.]

dog-ear (dôg'ir') *also,* **dog's-ear.** *n.* a turned-down corner of a page of a book or magazine. —*v.t.* to turn down the corner of (a page). —**dog'-eared',** *adj.*

dog-eat-dog (dôg'ēt'dôg') *adj.* marked or characterized by ruthless, unlimited competition: *a dog-eat-dog world.*

dog·face (dôg'fās') *n. Slang.* an infantryman in the U.S. Army in World War II.

dog·fight (dôg'fīt') *n.* **1.** a fight between or as between dogs; a rough, violent dispute, contest, or brawl. **2.** combat between fighter planes.

dog·fish (dôg'fish') *n., pl.* **-fish** or **-fish·es.** any of a group of relatively small sharks, found in warm and temperate seas, having long, slender, grayish green bodies, pointed snouts, and large asymmetrically forked tails.

dogfish

dog·ged (dô'gid) *adj.* not yielding; stubborn; persevering: *dogged courage.* [DOG + -ED².] —**dog'ged·ly,** *adv.* —**dog'ged·ness,** *n.*

dog·ger (dô'gər) *n.* a two-masted ship having a broad beam, used principally by fishermen in the North Sea. [Middle Dutch *dogger* fishing boat.]

dog·ger·el (dô'gər əl) *n.* poor or trivial poetry having little artistic merit in content or form. —*adj.* resembling or composed of such poetry. [Probably from DOG.]

dog·gy (dô'gē) *also,* **dog·gie.** *n., pl.* **-gies.** a dog, esp. a little dog. —*adj.,* **-gi·er, -gi·est.** of or like a dog.

doggy bag *also,* **doggie bag.** a bag or other container provided by a restaurant in which a person can carry home food left over from a meal eaten at the restaurant. [Because the contents supposedly were fed to a dog.]

dog·house (dôg'hous') *n., pl.* **-hous·es** (-hou'ziz). a small house or shelter for a dog.

  •**in the doghouse.** *Informal.* in disfavor.

do·gie (dō'gē) *also,* **dogy.** *n.* in the western United States, a stray or motherless calf on the range. [Said to be from *dough guts,* applied to an orphaned calf whose belly swells when fed on grass.]

dog·leg (dôg'leg') *n.* anything shaped like the bend in the hind leg of a dog, such as a fairway of a golf course or a part of a roadway or passage. —*adj.* bent in the shape of the hind leg of a dog: *a dogleg bend in a fence.* —*v.i.,* **-legged, -leg·ging.** to go in one direction and then angle off in another: *The road doglegs to the right just after the bridge.*

dog·ma (dôg'mə) *n., pl.* **-mas** or **-ma·ta** (-mə tə). **1.** a doctrine or system of doctrines formally propounded by a church or religious body and held to be authoritative. **2.** any principle, belief, or tenet, usually formally stated and viewed as authoritative: *a political dogma.* **3.** a system of such principles, beliefs, or tenets: *communist dogma.* **4.** an opinion asserted in an emphatic, positive manner, often without sufficient grounds. [Latin *dogma,* from Greek *dogma* opinion.] —For Synonyms, see **doctrine.**

dog·mat·ic (dôg mat'ik) *adj.* **1.** asserting or stating beliefs or opinions in a positive, authoritative, and often arrogant manner: *dogmatic writing, a dogmatic lecturer.* **2.** of or relating to dogma; doctrinal. Also, **dog·mat'i·cal.** —**dog·mat'i·cal·ly,** *adv.*

dog·ma·tism (dôg'mə tiz'əm) *n.* a positive, authoritative, often arrogant assertion of opinions or beliefs.

dog·ma·tist (dôg'mə tist) *n.* a person who expresses dogmas or who is dogmatic.

dog·ma·tize (dôg'mə tīz') *v.,* **-tized, -tiz·ing.** —*v.i.* to speak or write dogmatically. —*v.t.* to assert or state as a dogma.

do-good·er (dü'gud'ər) *n. Informal.* a person who is eager to do

a	at	e	end	o	hot	u	up	hw	white		about
ā	ape	ē	me	ō	old	ū	use	ng	song	ə	taken
ä	far	i	it	ô	fork	ü	rule	th	thin		pencil
âr	care	ī	ice	oi	oil	ů	pull	th	this		lemon
		îr	pierce	ou	out	ûr	turn	zh	measure		circus

things for others or to change things for the better. ➡ usually used derisively.

dog·pad·dle (dôg′pad′əl) *v.i.*, **-dled, -dling.** to swim using the dog paddle.

dog paddle *n.* a rudimentary stroke in swimming with the body in an almost upright position, the hands paddling at the surface, and the legs performing rough kicks.

dog rose, a shrub rose, *Rosa canina,* having single white or pink flowers.

dog's-ear (dôgz′îr′) dog-ear.

dog·sled (dôg′sled′) *n.* a sled that is drawn by one or more dogs. Also, **dog sledge.**

dog's life, a wretched or difficult life.

Dog Star, Sirius.

dog tag 1. a small metal disk or plate attached to the collar of a dog, indicating ownership. **2.** *Informal.* an oblong tag, usually worn on a chain around the neck, issued to a member of the armed forces for identification purposes.

dog-tired (dôg′tīrd′) *adj.* extremely tired.

dog·tooth violet (dôg′tüth′) *also,* **dog's-tooth violet. 1.** the drooping purple or reddish flower of a plant, *Erythronium dens-scanis,* of the lily family. Also, **adder's-tongue. 2.** the plant bearing this flower, having two mottled leaves and a bulbous stem. **3.** any of several related plants, as the common North American species *Erythronium americanum,* bearing yellow flowers.

dog·trot (dôg′trot′) *n.* a gentle, easy trot.

dog·watch (dôg′woch′) *n.* either of the two short watches on a ship, one from 4 to 6 P.M. and the other from 6 to 8 P.M.

dog·wood (dôg′wùd′) *n.* **1.** any of a group of hardy ornamental trees or shrubs, genus *Cornus,* bearing berrylike fruit and small greenish yellow flowers surrounded by showy pink or white bracts. **2.** the hard, heavy wood of this tree.

do·gy (dō′gē) *n., pl.* **-gies.** dogie.

doi·ly (doi′lē) *n., pl.* **-lies.** a small ornamental piece of linen, lace, or paper used as a decoration or to protect a surface upon which an object is placed. [Said to be from an eighteenth-century English cloth merchant named *Doily.*]

do·ing (dü′ing) *n.* **1.** an action for which one is responsible: *Your troubles are not my doing.* **2. doings.** activities, proceedings, or events: *social doings.*

doit (doit) *n.* **1.** formerly, a small Dutch copper coin. **2.** a trifling amount; bit. [Dutch *duit* this coin.]

do-it-your·self (dü′it yər self′) *adj. Informal.* designed for construction or use by a person without professional training or assistance: *a do-it-yourself bookcase kit.* —*n.* the practice of building, repairing, or doing something else without professional assistance. —**do′-it-your·self′er,** *n.*

Dol·by (dōl′bē) *n. Trademark.* a circuit in many tape recorders and other high-fidelity devices that reduces the amount of background noise heard when a recording is played back.

dol·ce (dōl′chä, dōl′-) *Music. adj.* sweet; soft. —*adv.* sweetly; softly. [Italian *dolce* sweet, from Latin *dulcis.*]

dol·ce far nien·te (dōl′chä fär nyen′tā) *Italian.* pleasant idleness.

dol·drums (dōl′drəmz, dol′-, dôl′-) *n.* **1.** a dull, listless, or depressed mood; low spirits. **2.** certain regions of the ocean along the equator, characterized by calms, very light or constantly shifting winds, low atmospheric pressure, and heavy precipitation. For illustration, see **wind**[1]. **3.** a state of inactivity or stagnation, as in business; slump. [Of uncertain origin.]

dole[1] (dōl) *n.* **1.** something distributed as charity, such as money, food, or clothing. **2.** anything distributed in limited or little amounts; small portion. **3.** the act of giving out or distributing something, esp. charitable gifts. **4.** relief paid by a government to the unemployed. **5.** *Archaic.* one's destiny or lot. —*v.t.,* **doled, dol·ing. 1.** to distribute as charity. **2.** to give or distribute in small quantities (often with *out*): *The counselor doled out snacks to the campers.* [Old English *dāl* portion.]

• **to go (or be) on the dole.** to receive relief payments from the government.

dole[2] (dōl) *n. Archaic.* mental distress; sorrow; grief. [Old French *doel,* going back to Latin *dolēre* to grieve.]

dole·ful (dōl′fəl) *adj.* full of or expressing grief or sorrow; sad: *a doleful cry, a doleful look.* —**dole′ful·ly,** *adv.* —**dole′ful·ness,** *n.*

dole·some (dōl′səm) *adj. Archaic.* doleful.

doll (dol) *n.* **1.** a child's toy made to resemble the human figure, esp. that of a baby. **2.** a pretty but shallow girl or woman. **3.** a pretty or delightful child. **4.** *Slang.* a pleasant or attractive person. —*v.t., v.i. Informal.* to dress or adorn smartly or ostentatiously (with *up*). [From *Doll,* pet name for *Dorothy* woman's name.]

dol·lar (dol′ər) *n.* **1.** the monetary unit of the United States, equal to 100 cents. **2.** the monetary unit of certain other countries, such as Canada, New Zealand, Australia, and various British dependencies and former dependencies, such as Brunei and Hong Kong. **3.** a piece of paper currency or silver or gold coin equivalent to one dollar. [Low German *daler* German silver coin, from German *T(h)aler,* abbreviation of *Joachimst(h)aler,* a coin so called because it was first coined in *Joachimsthal,* a Bohemian city, in the early sixteenth century.]

dollar diplomacy, a diplomatic policy of using the power of the government to promote the interests of businesses abroad.

dol·lop (dol′əp) *n.* **1.** a lump, blob, or portion: *a dollop of whipped cream.* **2.** a small amount: *It was a dull speech without even a dollop of humor.*

dol·ly (dol′ē) *n., pl.* **doll·ies. 1.** a child's word for doll. **2.** any of several frames with wheels, used for moving heavy loads. **3.** a wheeled platform on which a camera may be moved about a television or motion-picture set. —*v.,* **doll·ied, doll·y·ing.** —*v.t.* to move with a dolly. —*v.i.* to move a camera on a dolly.

dol·man (dōl′mən, dol′-) *n., pl.* **-mans. 1.** a woman's coat with dolman sleeves or capelike flaps instead of sleeves. **2.** a long outer robe worn by Turks. [French *dolman* jacket, through German and Magyar, from Turkish *dōlāmān* long robe.]

dolman sleeve, a sleeve that has a very wide armhole but is tapered to fit snugly around the wrist.

dol·men (dōl′mən, dol′-) *n.* a prehistoric structure consisting of a large, unhewn stone slab resting on two or more unhewn stones placed upright. Usually regarded as a tomb, it is typical of the Neolithic period in Europe. Also, **cromlech.** [French *dolmen,* probably from Cornish *tolmēn* hole of stone.]

dolmens at Stonehenge, England

do·lo·mite (dō′lə mīt′, dol′ə-) *n.* **1.** a mineral consisting of calcium magnesium carbonate, whose crystals are usually pink or white. Formula: $CaMg(CO_3)_2$ **2.** a rock consisting primarily of this mineral, usually associated with limestone. [From the eighteenth-century French geologist Déodat de *Dolomieu,* 1750-1801.] —**do·lo·mit·ic** (dō′lə mit′ik, dol′ə-), *adj.*

do·lor (dō′lər) *n.* emotional distress caused by loss, disappointment, or affliction; sorrow; grief. [Old French *dolour,* from Latin *dolor.*]

do·lor·ous (dō′lər əs, dol′ər-) *adj.* expressing or causing pain or sorrow: *a dolorous cry.* —**do′lor·ous·ly,** *adv.* —**do′lor·ous·ness,** *n.*

dol·phin (dol′fin, dôl′-) *n.* **1.** any of various mammals, family Delphinidae, related to the porpoise and the whale, found in all seas and in some freshwater rivers, having a curved dorsal fin, scaleless black, brown, or gray skin, two flippers that are modified front legs, and usually a beaklike snout. Length: 8-30 feet (2.4-9.1 meters). **2.** an edible, saltwater game fish, *Coryphaena hippurus,* found in warm waters, having long dorsal fins and a powerful, deeply forked tail. It is remarkable for its changes of color when taken from the water. Also *(def. 2),* **do·rado.** [Old French *daulphin* this mammal, going back to Latin *delphīnus,* from Greek *delphīs.*]

dolphin *(def. 1)*

dolt (dōlt) *n.* a dull, stupid person; blockhead. [Middle English *dult* blunt, from *dul* dull. See DULL.] —**dolt′ish,** *adj.* —**dolt′ish·ly,** *adv.* —**dolt′ish·ness,** *n.*

-dom *suffix* (used to form nouns) **1.** the office, rank, or domain

of: *earldom, kingdom.* **2.** the state or condition of being: *freedom, wisdom.* **3.** the totality of all those who are, as of a specified rank, condition, or state: *officialdom.* [Old English *-dōm* office, state, condition.]

dom. 1. domestic. **2.** dominion.

do·main (dō mān′) *n.* **1.** the territory controlled or governed by a sovereign or government; realm. **2.** a field or sphere, as of knowledge, action, or influence: *Financial decisions are not within my domain.* **3.** the land owned by one person or family; estate. **4.** *Mathematics.* the set of values that the independent variable in a relation or function may have. Also, **replacement set.** ➡ distinguished from **range. 5.** *Physics.* any of the numerous small areas in a ferromagnetic substance in which the atoms all share the same magnetic polarity. [French *domaine* estate, sphere, going back to Latin *dominius* relating to a master, from *dominus* master.]

dome (dōm) *n.* **1.** a hemispherical roof erected over a circular or many-sided base. **2.** something resembling this in shape: *the dome of a mountain.* **3.** *Archaic.* a stately, impressive structure or mansion. **4.** *Slang.* the head. —*v.,* **domed, dom·ing.** —*v.t.* **1.** to cover with or as with a dome. **2.** to shape or form like a dome. —*v.i.* to rise or swell into a shape resembling a dome. [French *dôme* vault, cupola, from Italian *duomo* cupola (a characteristic part of Italian cathedrals), cathedral, house (of God), from Latin *domus* house.]

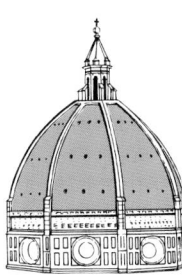

dome

Domes·day Book (dümz′dā′, dōmz′-) *also,* **Doomsday Book.** a document recording a detailed survey of landholdings in England in the eleventh century, ordered by William the Conqueror. [Middle English form of DOOMSDAY; because it was considered the final word on the data contained within it.]

do·mes·tic (də mes′tik) *adj.* **1.** of or relating to the home, household, or family: *domestic life, domestic problems.* **2.** devoted to or fond of things involving the home and family: *a domestic person.* **3.** living with or near human beings and cared for by them; domesticated; tame: *Cows and dogs are domestic animals.* **4.** of or made in one's own country or the country under consideration: *domestic trade policies, domestic wine.* —*n.* a household servant. [Latin *domesticus* relating to a household, from *domus* house.] —**do·mes′ti·cal·ly,** *adv.*

do·mes·ti·cate (də mes′ti kāt′) *v.t.,* **-cat·ed, -cat·ing. 1.a.** to develop (a strain of plants or animals) for a specific product or purpose useful to human beings and usually depending on human care. **b.** to adapt (an animal) to live with human beings; tame: *to domesticate a deer.* **2.** to make fond of or accustom to home, household affairs, and family life. —**do·mes′ti·ca′tion,** *n.*

do·mes·tic·i·ty (dō′mes tis′i tē) *n., pl.* **-ties. 1.** home and family life. **2.** devotion to the home and family. **3. domesticities.** household affairs.

domestic relations court, a court whose jurisdiction is limited to the resolution of matters arising within family relationships, as between spouses or parents and children. Also, **family court.**

domestic science, home economics.

dom·i·cile (dom′ə sīl′, -səl, dō′mə-) *also,* **dom·i·cil** (dom′ə səl, dō′mə-). *n.* **1.** a place of residence; home, house, or dwelling. **2.** an official or legal residence. —*v.t.,* **-ciled, -cil·ing.** to establish in a domicile. [Old French *domicile* house, from Latin *domicilium* dwelling.] —**dom·i·cil·i·ar·y** (dom′ə sil′ē er′ē, dō′mə-). —For Synonyms *(n.),* see **home.**

dom·i·nance (dom′ə nəns) *n.* the fact or state of being dominant. Also, **dom′i·nan·cy.**

dom·i·nant (dom′ə nənt) *adj.* **1.** exercising chief authority, influence, or control; commanding or prevailing, as over all others: *the dominant political party of the country, a dominant influence in one's life.* **2.** the most prominent or conspicuous: *The dominant color in the room was blue.* **3.** *Genetics.* **a.** relating to or designating one of a pair of alleles for a gene, when both are present in the same cell or organism, that masks the effect of the other allele: *The allele for tallness in sweet pea plants is dominant over the allele for shortness.* **b.** relating to or designating the trait or characteristic determined by such an allele. **4.** *Music.* of, based upon, or relating to the dominant. —*n.* **1.** *Genetics.* a dominant allele or characteristic. **2.** *Music.* the fifth tone of a diatonic scale. D is the dominant in the key of G. [Old French *dominant* ruling, predominating, from Latin *domināns,* present participle of *dominārī* to be master, rule.] —**dom′i·nant·ly,** *adv.*

dom·i·nate (dom′ə nāt′) *v.,* **-nat·ed, -nat·ing.** —*v.t.* **1.** to exercise control or rule over, as by will or strength; govern: *The Greeks once dominated a large portion of the Mediterranean. A person with a forceful personality can dominate other people.* **2.** to occupy a commanding or towering position over; loom over: *The skyscraper dominates the skyline.* **3.** to have an outstanding or preeminent place or position in; affect most prominently or conspicuously: *Fear dominated their lives during the war.* —*v.i.* **1.** to have or exercise control or preeminence: *Our basketball team dominated during the play-offs.* **2.** to occupy a commanding or towering position. [Latin *dominātus,* past participle of *dominārī* to control, rule.] —**dom′i·na′tor,** *n.*

dom·i·na·tion (dom′ə nā′shən) *n.* **1.** the act of dominating or the state of being dominated. **2.** the exercise of control or influence; rule; sway: *to be under someone's domination.*

dom·i·neer (dom′ə nîr′) *v.t., v.i.* to rule arrogantly or despotically; be overbearing; tyrannize; bully. [Dutch *domineren* to rule, from French *dominer,* from Latin *dominari* to be master, rule.]

dom·i·neer·ing (dom′ə nîr′ing) *adj.* tending to domineer; bossy; overbearing; tyrannical. —**dom′i·neer′ing·ly,** *adv.*

Do·min·i·can (də min′i kən) *adj.* **1.** of or relating to Saint Dominic or the religious order founded by him. **2.** of, relating to, or characteristic of the Dominican Republic or its people or culture. —*n.* **1.** a member of the Roman Catholic mendicant order of friars and nuns founded by Saint Dominic in 1215. **2.a.** a native or citizen of the Dominican Republic. **b.** a person of Dominican ancestry.

dom·i·nie (dom′ə nē, dō′mə-) *n.* **1.** *Scottish.* schoolmaster. **2.** *Informal.* a member of the clergy. [Latin *dominē,* vocative of *dominus* master; formerly a reverent greeting to members of the clergy.]

do·min·ion (də min′yən) *n.* **1.** sovereign or supreme authority; power or right to rule. **2.** a territory or country under the authority of a particular ruler or government. **3.** *also,* **Dominion.** formerly, any of several self-governing states belonging to the British Commonwealth, as Canada or Australia. [Old French *dominion* power, rule, going back to Latin *dominium* right of ownership, domain.]

Dominion Day, Canada Day.

dom·i·no[1] (dom′ə nō′) *n., pl.* **-noes** or **-nos. 1.** a small mask covering the upper part of the face, esp. the eyes. **2.** a loose cloak with a hood, usually worn with such a mask as a disguise at a masquerade. **3.** a person who wears a domino. [French *domino* priest's black hooded cloak, going back to Latin *dominus* master.]

dom·i·no[2] (dom′ə nō′) *n., pl.* **-noes. 1.** a small black tile divided into halves, each half either being blank or having from one to six white dots, used in playing certain games. **2. dominoes.** any of several games usually played with twenty-eight of these tiles. [From DOMINO[1]; because of the black backs of the pieces used in the game.]

domino theory 1. the theory or assumption that if one country came under communist control, neighboring countries would also become communist. **2.** a theory that one event can set off a series of similar events. [From DOMINO[2]; from the practice of lining up dominoes and knocking down the first one to cause a chain reaction.]

don[1] (don) *n.* **1. Don.** Sir. ➡ a Spanish title of respect for a man, usually used before the first name only: *Don Pedro.* **2.** a Spanish nobleman or gentleman. **3.** *Informal.* a head, fellow, or tutor of a college at Oxford or Cambridge University. **4.** *Archaic.* a distinguished or important person. [Spanish *don* mister, Spanish title, from Latin *domnus,* contraction of *dominus* master.]

don[2] (don) *v.t.,* **donned, don·ning.** to put on, as clothing: *We donned our costumes for the parade.* [Contraction of *do on.*]

do·ña (dōn′yə) *n.* **1. Doña.** Lady; Madam. ➡ a Spanish title of respect for a married woman, usually used before the first name only: *Doña Maria.* **2.** a Spanish noblewoman or lady. [Spanish

a	at	e	end	o	hot	u	up	hw	white		about
ā	ape	ē	me	ō	old	ū	use	ng	song		taken
ä	far	i	it	ô	fork	ü	rule	th	thin	ə	pencil
âr	care	ī	ice	oi	oil	u̇	pull	th	this		lemon
		îr	pierce	ou	out	ûr	turn	zh	measure		circus

363

doña, from Latin *domina* mistress, lady (feminine form of *dominus* master).]

do·nate (dō′nāt, dō nāt′) *v.t.,* **-nat·ed, -nat·ing.** to give, esp. to a fund or charitable cause; contribute. [From DONATION.]

Synonyms *v.t.* **Donate** and **contribute** both mean to give a gift for a specific purpose. **Donate** suggests a worthy cause: *The company donated a large sum of money to the school.* **Contribute** connotes adding something to a general giving effort: *They contributed $50 to a drive to help the homeless.*

do·na·tion (dō nā′shən) *n.* **1.** the act of giving; contributing: *We made our yearly donation of clothing to the poor.* **2.** a gift; contribution: *They gave a sizable donation to the college.* [French *donation* present, from Latin *dōnātiō* a presenting.]

done (dun) *v.* the past participle of **do**[1]. —*adj.* **1.** completed; finished; through. **2.** cooked sufficiently. **3.** socially acceptable: *Picking one's teeth at the dinner table isn't done.*
· **done for.** *Informal.* **a.** totally ruined or defeated: *We knew our team was done for when they failed to score that goal.* **b.** dead or dying.

do·nee (dō nē′) *n.* the recipient of a gift or donation.

dong[1] (dông, dong) *n.* a deep sound of or as of a bell. —*v.i.* to make such a sound.

dong[2] (dông, dong) *n., pl.* **dong.** the monetary unit of Vietnam.

don·jon (dun′jən, don′-) *also,* **dungeon.** *n.* the strongly fortified inner tower of a castle; keep. [Archaic form of DUNGEON.]

Don Juan (don wän′, hwän′) **1.** a legendary Spanish nobleman, famous as a seducer of women and as a reckless adventurer. **2.** any man who is a rake or seducer.

don·key (dong′kē, dung′-) *n., pl.* **-keys. 1.** a domestic animal, *Equus asinus asinus,* resembling a small horse but having longer ears and a shorter mane and often used as a beast of burden; domestic ass. Height: 4½ feet (1.4 meters) at the shoulder. **2.** a stupid or obstinate person. [Diminutive of DUN[2]; influenced in form by MONKEY.]

donkey engine, a small auxiliary engine, used as for pumping or hoisting.

don·na (don′ə, dō′nə) *n.* **1. Donna.** Lady; Madam. ➡ an Italian title of respect for a married woman, usually used before the first name only. **2.** an Italian noblewoman or lady. [Italian *donna,* from Latin *domina;* see DOÑA.]

don·nish (don′ish) *adj.* bookish or pedantic. —**don′nish·ly,** *adv.* —**don′nish·ness,** *n.*

don·ny·brook (don′ē brŏok′) *n.* a rough, noisy brawl; free-for-all. [From *Donnybrook* Fair, held regularly until 1855 at Donnybrook, Ireland, where such brawls were said to occur.]

donkey

do·nor (dō′nər) *n.* **1.** a person who donates. **2.** a person or animal used as a source of biological material, as blood or organs. [Anglo-Norman *donour* giver, Latin *dōnātor.*]

do·noth·ing (dü′nuth′ing) *adj.* not active, especially in regard to making changes or improvements: *a do-nothing city council.*

Don Qui·xo·te (don′ kē hō′tē, -tā, don kwik′sət) **1.** a tragicomic novel by the Spanish writer Miguel de Cervantes that satirizes chivalric romances. **2.** its hero, a chivalrous, idealistic, impractical old man who believes he is a knight and attempts to fight evil and injustice.

don't (dōnt) *contr.* **1.** do not: *Don't go.* **2.** does not; doesn't.

Usage The use of **don't** to mean "doesn't," although widespread in informal speech, is generally considered to be nonstandard English. It is unacceptable in formal speech or writing except where the aim is deliberately to show departure from standard usage, as in dialogue for characterization.

do·nut (dō′nut′, -nət) doughnut.

doo·dad (dü′dad′) *n. Informal.* **1.** a small, decorative object; bauble. **2.** doohickey.

doo·dle (dü′dəl) *v.t., v.i.,* **-dled, -dling.** to draw or scribble idly or aimlessly, as while talking. —*n.* a design or drawing produced by doodling. [Dialectal English *doodle* to waste time, from German *dudeln* literally, to play the bagpipes, from Polish *dudlic,* from *dudy* bagpipes, from Turkish *duduk* flute.] —**doo′dler,** *n.*

doo·dle·bug (dü′dəl bug′) *n.* **1.** the larva of the ant lion. **2.** *Informal.* a divining rod or similar device used to locate underground deposits. [DOODLE + BUG.]

doo·hick·ey (dü′hik′ē) *n., pl.* **-eys.** *Informal.* any gadget or small object. ➡ used as a substitute when the name of the gadget or object is forgotten or unknown.

doom (düm) *n.* **1.** something that cannot be escaped, esp.

something that brings pain, destruction, or death; fate; destiny. **2.** death, ruin, or destruction. **3.** a sentence or judgment, esp. an adverse judicial sentence. **4.** Judgment Day. —*v.t.* **1.** to pronounce judgment or sentence against; condemn. **2.** to destine, esp. to an adverse or terrible fate: *Without strong leadership, the program is doomed to fail.* [Old English *dōm* judgment, power.]

Dooms·day (dümz′dā′) *also,* **dooms·day.** *n.* **1.** Judgment Day. **2.** any day of final judgment. [Old English *dōmes dæg* Judgment Day.]

Doomsday Book, Domesday Book.

door (dôr) *n.* **1.** a movable structure, usually hinged, sliding, or rotating, that serves to open or close an entrance or opening, as into a building, vehicle, or cupboard. **2.** a doorway: *She's standing in the door.* **3.** a room or building to which a door belongs: *His house is four doors away.* **4.** any means of entrance or exit; access: *A college education helps to open the door to success in the business world.* [Old English *dor* gate.]
· **to lay (something) at someone's door.** to blame (something) on someone: *The failure of the advertising campaign was laid at our door.*
· **to show (someone) the door.** to ask or order (someone) to leave.

door·bell (dôr′bel′) *n.* a bell or buzzer activated by a button or other device at or near a door as a signal that someone is at the door and wishes to be admitted.

door·jamb (dôr′jam′) *n.* a vertical piece forming the side of a doorway.

door·keep·er (dôr′kē′pər) *n.* a person who guards an entrance.

door·knob (dôr′nob′) *n.* a rounded handle on a door, used to open or close it.

door·man (dôr′mən, -man′) *n., pl.* **-men** (-mən, -men′). an attendant at the door of a building, as a hotel, department store, or apartment house, who assists people entering and leaving, as by opening the door and hailing taxicabs.

door·mat (dôr′mat′) *n.* a mat placed before a doorway, used by people coming in for wiping their shoes.

door·nail (dôr′nāl′) *n.* a nail having a large head, used to strengthen or ornament doors.
· **dead as a doornail.** dead beyond question.

door·plate (dôr′plāt′) *n.* a plate, usually of metal, placed on or near a door, typically with the occupant's name and address.

door·post (dôr′pōst′) *n.* doorjamb.

door·sill (dôr′sil′) *n.* the sill of a door.

door·step (dôr′step′) *n.* a step or steps leading from an outside door to the ground.

door·stop (dôr′stop′) *n.* **1.** a device, as a wedge or spring, used to hold a door open or to prevent it from slamming shut. **2.** a device, usually with a rubber tip, projecting from a door or wall to prevent an opening door from hitting and damaging the wall.

door-to-door (dôr′tə dôr′) *adj.* making or involving a call at every residence in an area: *a door-to-door salesperson, a door-to-door survey.* —*adv.* with a call at every residence in an area: *to solicit magazine subscriptions door-to-door.*

door·way (dôr′wā′) *n.* **1.** an opening in a wall that is closed by a door. **2.** a means of access.

door·yard (dôr′yärd′) *n.* the yard around a house, esp. near the door.

doo·zy (dü′zē) *n., pl.* **-zies.** *Slang.* a remarkable thing or event, esp. because of its great size or effect. [Of uncertain origin.]

do·pa (dō′pə) *n.* an amino acid converted by an enzyme to dopamine in the bloodstream. Formula: $C_9H_{11}NO_4$ [*D(i-hydr)o(xy)p(henyl)* + A(MINE).]

do·pa·mine (dō′pə mēn′) *n.* a chemical substance found in the central nervous system that transmits nerve impulses. Dopamine helps control movement and emotions.

dop·ant (dō′pənt) *n.* a small amount of a chemical element, regarded as an impurity, that is added to a substance, esp. to a semiconductor, in order to improve conductivity or to alter some other characteristic. Arsenic and boron are common dopants. [DOPE + -ANT.]

dope (dōp) *n.* **1.** *Informal.* a stupid, dull-witted person. **2.** *Informal.* any narcotic, as heroin. **3.** *Slang.* secret or inside information. **4.** a clear varnish used to fasten a covering to an object, as tissue to a model airplane, and to strengthen and waterproof it. —*v.t.* **1.** *Slang.* to give dope to; drug. **2.** to treat with or apply dope to. [Dutch *doop* sauce, from *doopen* to dip, mix.] —**dop′er,** *n.*
· **to dope out.** *Slang.* to figure out or plan.

do·pey (dō′pē) *adj.,* **-pi·er, -pi·est.** *Informal.* **1.** mentally slow; stupid. **2.** dulled or sluggish from or as from a narcotic; in a stupor or daze. —**dop′i·ness,** *n.*

Dop·pler effect (dop′lər) *Physics.* an apparent or observed change in the frequency of a sound, light, or other wave as the distance between the wave source and the observer changes. The

frequency becomes higher as the source moves toward the observer and lower as the source moves away. [From Christian J. *Doppler*, 1803-53, Austrian physicist and mathematician who first investigated this phenomenon.]

do·ra·do (də rä′dō) *n., pl.* **-dos.** dolphin *(def. 2).*

Do·ri·an (dôr′ē ən) *adj.* of or relating to Doris, its inhabitants, or its culture. —*n.* a member of one of the four major Greek tribes of antiquity. The Dorians settled in the Peloponnesus, Crete, the Italian peninsula, and Sicily.

Dor·ic (dôr′ik, dŏr′-) *adj.* **1.** of or relating to the oldest, simplest, and most refined of the three orders of classical Greek architecture, characterized by columns having no base and unadorned capitals. **2.** Dorian. —*n.* one of the three principal dialects of ancient Greece.

Dor·king (dôr′king) *n.* any of a breed of domestic fowl having a large, heavy body and five toes on each foot instead of four. [From *Dorking,* an English market town.]

dorm (dôrm) *n. Informal.* dormitory. [Short for DORMITORY.]

dor·man·cy (dôr′mən sē) *n.* the state of being dormant.

dor·mant (dôr′mənt) *adj.*
1. characterized by a state of temporary inactivity; not operating: *a dormant volcano, dormant talents.* **2.** not awake; sleeping. **3.** (of animals and plants) characterized by a partial suspension of animation or vegetation: *Some plants and animals are dormant during the winter.* [Old French *dormant,* present participle of *dormir* to sleep, from Latin *dormīre.*]

dor·mer (dôr′mər) *n.* **1.** a vertical window projecting from a sloping roof. Also, **dormer window. 2.** a roofed projection containing such a window. [Old French *dormeor* room for sleeping, from Latin *dormītōrium.* Doublet of DORMITORY.]

dormer

dor·mi·to·ry (dôr′mi tôr′ē) *n., pl.* **-ries. 1.** a building having many bedrooms and providing sleeping and living accommodations, as for students at a college. **2.** a room containing a number of beds, as in a school. [Latin *dormītōrium* room for sleeping. Doublet of DORMER.]

dor·mouse (dôr′mous′) *n., pl.* **-mice** (-mīs′). any of various squirrellike rodents, suborder Myomorpha, native to Europe, Africa, and Asia, typically having brown or gray fur, and hibernating for up to six months of the year. Length: to 2 feet (0.6 meter), including tail. [Possibly from dialectal English *dorm* to sleep (from Old French *dormir,* from Latin *dormīre*) + MOUSE.]

dor·sal (dôr′səl) *adj.* of, on, or near the back: *a dorsal rib.* [Late Latin *dorsālis,* from Latin *dorsum* back.] —**dor′sal·ly,** *adv.*

dorsal fin, a vertical, median fin along the back of a fish or other aquatic animal. For illustration, see fin[1].

dormouse

do·ry[1] (dôr′ē) *n., pl.* **-ries.** a deep, flat-bottomed rowboat having high sides that slope upward and outward, often used for fishing. [Of uncertain origin.]

do·ry[2] (dôr′ē) *n., pl.* **-ries. 1.** John Dory. **2.** walleye *(def. 3).* [French *dorée* the John Dory; literally, gilded, going back to Latin *dēaurātus* gilded; because of its color.]

DOS, (dos) disk operating system.

dos·age (dō′sij) *n.* **1.** the amount of a medicine or other medical treatment in a single dose. **2.** the giving of such a dose.

dose (dōs) *n.* **1.** the amount of a medicine or other medical treatment prescribed to be given or taken at one time. **2.** the amount of ionizing radiation to which living tissue has been exposed or the amount that it has absorbed. **3.** an amount, esp. of something painful or unpleasant: *We gave the bullies a dose of their own medicine.* —*v.t.,* **dosed, dos·ing. 1.** to give medicine to: *The veterinarian dosed the cow with the medication.* **2.** to give (medicine) in doses. [French *dose* quantity, dose of medicine, from Late Latin *dosis,* from Greek *dosis* a giving.]

do·sim·e·ter (dō sim′i tər) *n.* a device to be carried or worn on the body, used to register the amount of ionizing radiation to which a person has been exposed.

dos·si·er (dos′ē ā′, dô′sē ā′) *n.* a collection of detailed documents or papers relating to some subject or person. [French *dossier* originally, package of papers labeled on the back, from *dos* back, from Latin *dorsum* back.]

dost (dust) *Archaic.* a second person singular present tense of do[1]. ➡ used with *thou.*

dot[1] (dot) *n.* **1.** a small, usually round, mark; speck or very small

spot: *I made a dot on the paper with my pencil. The ship was a dot on the horizon.* **2.** the shorter of the two sounds used in telegraphic codes, as in Morse code. ➡ distinguished from **dash. 3.** *Music.* **a.** a point placed after a note or rest that increases its time by one half. **b.** a point placed over or under a note indicating staccato. —*v.t.,* **dot·ted, dot·ting. 1.** to mark with a dot or dots. **2.** to be scattered over or about: *Houses dotted the landscape.* [Old English *dott* head of a boil.] —**dot′ter,** *n.*

· **on the dot.** as scheduled: *The train left at seven o'clock on the dot.*

dot[2] (dot) *n.* dowry *(def. 1).* [French *dot,* from Latin *dōs.*]

dot·age (dō′tij) *n.* **1.** the state of being feeble-minded, esp. because of old age; senility. **2.** foolish or excessive affection. [From DOTE.]

dot·ard (dō′tərd) *n.* a person whose mind is feeble, esp. from old age. [From DOTE.]

dote (dōt) *also,* **doat.** *v.i.,* **dot·ed, dot·ing. 1.** to lavish extreme or excessive affection (usually with *on*): *The grandparents doted on the child.* **2.** to be feeble-minded, esp. because of old age. [Middle English *doten* to be silly, possibly from Middle Low German *doten.*] —**dot′er,** *n.*

doth (duth) *Archaic.* a third person singular present tense of do[1].

dot·ing (dō′ting) *adj.* **1.** foolishly or excessively fond or indulgent: *doting parents.* **2.** feeble-minded; senile. —**dot′ing·ly,** *adv.*

dot matrix, a system of forming letters, numerals, and other symbols, employed by computer screens or certain printers, using a closely spaced pattern, or matrix, of dots.

dotted swiss, a light, often sheer, cotton fabric, having a pattern of small, raised dots.

dot·ter·el (dot′ər əl) *n.* a migratory plover, *Endromias morinellus,* native to northern Eurasia, having a short bill and black, white, and russet plumage. Length: 10 inches (25 centimeters). [From DOTE; possibly because of its supposed foolishness.]

dot·ty (dot′ē) *adj.,* **-ti·er, -ti·est.** *Informal.* crazy or eccentric.

Dou·ay Bible (dü′ā) an English translation from the Latin of the authorized Roman Catholic Vulgate Bible of Saint Jerome. Also, **Douay Version.** [From *Douai,* France, where this translation of the Old Testament was published in 1609-10.]

dou·ble (dub′əl) *adj.* **1.** twice as great, as many, or as much as the usual; multiplied by two: *a double blanket, double strength, double capacity.* **2.** having or forming two identical or similar parts; paired, coupled, or repeated: *a double dresser, a double line in front of the theater.* **3.** having a twofold relation, character, or application; combining two in one; dual or ambiguous: *a double role, a double meaning.* **4.** characterized by duplicity; deceitful; false: *The spy led a double life.* **5.** *Botany.* having more than one set of petals or sepals. —*adv.* **1.** in pairs or twos; doubly: *to see double, to ride a motorcycle double.* **2.** to twice the amount, extent, or degree; twofold. —*n.* **1.** something that is twice as much as the usual, as in size, amount, or value: *Ten is the double of five.* **2.** a person or thing that closely resembles or looks exactly like another; duplicate: *You are the double of your cousin.* **3.** an actor, singer, or other performer who can substitute for another, as in a motion picture, esp. in performing dangerous physical feats. **4.** *Baseball.* a hit that enables a player to reach second base safely without benefit of an error on the part of the opposing team. **5.** *Bridge.* **a.** a call indicating that the player feels a previous bidder cannot fulfill his or her bid, that doubles or increases the point value of the bid. **b.** strength in a hand sufficient to justify making such a call. **c.** a conventional call used as a signal to inform one's partner of the strength of one's hand and, frequently, as a request to the partner to bid his or her best suit. **6. doubles.** a game, as tennis, having two players on each side. —*v.,* **-bled, -bling.** —*v.t.* **1.** to make twice as great, as in size, amount, or degree; multiply by two: *to double a sum, to double one's weight.* **2.** to fold or bend, as to make two layers or thicknesses: *to double a bandage, to double a sheet of paper over.* **3.** to be or contain twice the quantity or number of: *The enemy's force doubles ours.* **4.** to turn, esp. sharply and suddenly, and trace the same or similar course (often with *back*): *to double in one's tracks, to double back across a field.* **5.** to clench (the fist) (often with *up*). **6.** (of a ship) to sail or go around, as a projecting piece of land: *to double Cape Horn.* **7.** *Baseball.* to advance (a base runner) by making a two-base hit. **8.** *Music.* to duplicate a note in a higher or lower octave. **9.** *Bridge.* to challenge (an opponent's bid) by calling a double.

a	at	e	end	o	hot	u	up	hw	white	⎧ about
ā	ape	ē	me	ō	old	ū	use	ng	song	⎪ taken
ä	far	i	it	ô	fork	ü	rule	th	thin	ə ⎨ pencil
âr	care	ī	ice	oi	oil	ů	pull	th	this	⎪ lemon
		îr	pierce	ou	out	ûr	turn	zh	measure	⎩ circus

—*v.i.* **1.** to become twice as great; be multiplied by two: *Food costs have doubled during this year.* **2.** to serve two purposes or perform in two capacities: *The coach doubles as captain of the team. This sofa doubles as a bed.* **3.** to bend or fold: *to double up with pain, to double over with laughter.* **4.** to serve as a double; be a substitute: *to double for the star in a play.* **5.** *Baseball.* to make a two-base hit. **6.** *Informal.* to go out on a double date: *We doubled with them last week.* [Old French *do(u)ble* twofold, from Latin *duplus.* Doublet of DUPLE.] —**dou′bler,** *n.*

• **on the double.** *Informal.* **a.** quickly: *Deliver the message and get back here on the double.* **b.** *Military.* in double time.

• **to double up.** *Informal.* to share accommodations with another.

double agent, a spy who works for two competing or hostile countries or organizations, usually having infiltrated the espionage service of one in order to spy on it for the other.

double bar *Music.* a double vertical line on the staff marking the end of a section, movement, or piece. For illustration, see **bar.**

dou·ble-bar·reled (dub′əl bar′əld) *adj.* **1.** having two barrels, as a firearm. **2.** having two possible meanings; ambiguous: *a double-barreled remark.* **3.** having two purposes.

double bass (bās) a musical instrument, largest and deepest-toned of the violin family, usually having four strings, and played in an upright position. For illustration, see **violin.** Also, **bass fiddle, bass viol, contrabass.**

double bassoon, contrabassoon.

double bed, a bed large enough for two adults, having a standard width of 54 inches (137 centimeters).

double bill, a program or performance offering two attractions, as two motion pictures or plays.

double bind **1.** a type of interaction between two people in which any action taken by one will seem wrong because of contradictory demands, signals, or expectations by the other. **2.** a situation requiring a difficult choice, as between unpleasant alternatives; dilemma.

dou·ble-blind (dub′əl blīnd′) *adj.* of, relating to, or designating an experimental procedure, as a test of the effects of a drug, in which neither the subjects nor the researchers know which subjects are receiving the actual item being tested.

double boiler, a cooking utensil consisting of a pair of nested pots, the upper one containing the food that is cooked gently by the heat generated from the boiling water in the lower pot.

double bond, a chemical bond in which two pairs of electrons are shared between two atoms, as in unsaturated organic compounds.

dou·ble-breast·ed (dub′əl bres′tid) *adj.* (of garments, as coats or jackets) overlapping enough to make two thicknesses across the breast and having two rows of buttons.

dou·ble-check (dub′əl chek′) *v.i., v.t.* to check again, esp. for accuracy; countercheck.

double check, the act or instance of double-checking; countercheck.

double chin, a fold of fatty flesh under the chin.

dou·ble-cross (dub′əl krôs′) *v.t.* *Informal.* to deceive or betray (someone) by failing to act as one has promised; be treacherous to. —**dou′ble-cross′er,** *n.*

double cross *Informal.* an act of betrayal; treachery.

double dagger, a reference mark (‡) used in printing to indicate a note or cross-reference.

dou·ble-date (dub′əl dāt′) *v.i.,* -**dat·ed,** -**dat·ing.** *Informal.* to go on a double date.

double date *Informal.* a social engagement involving two couples.

dou·ble-deal·er (dub′əl dē′lər) *n.* a person who acts in a deceitful, dishonest, or treacherous way.

dou·ble-deal·ing (dub′əl dē′ling) *n.* deceitful, dishonest, or treacherous behavior; duplicity. —*adj.* given to or characterized by such behavior.

dou·ble-deck·er (dub′əl dek′ər) *n.* **1.** a vehicle, as a bus, having two decks or levels. **2.** a sandwich consisting of three slices of bread and two layers of filling.

dou·ble-dig·it (dub′əl dij′it) *adj.* of or amounting to a number or percentage between 10 and 99: *double-digit inflation.*

double eagle, a gold coin of the United States, equal to twenty dollars, withdrawn from circulation in 1934.

dou·ble-edged (dub′əl ejd′) *adj.* **1.** having two cutting edges: *a double-edged sword.* **2.** acting or applicable both for and against: *a double-edged argument.*

dou·ble en·ten·dre (dub′əl än tän′drə, än tänd′; French dü-blän tän′dR) *n.* a word or expression having two meanings, one of which is usually indecent or indelicate. [Obsolete French *double entendre,* going back to Latin *duplus* twofold + *intendere* to apply oneself to.]

double entry, a self-balancing method of bookkeeping in which each transaction is recorded as both a debit and a credit.

double exposure **1.** the act of making two exposures on the same film or plate. **2.** a print made from a film or plate so exposed.

double-faced (dub′əl fāst′) *adj.* **1.** having two faces or aspects. **2.** (of a fabric) having the nap finished or patterned on both sides. **3.** two-faced; hypocritical.

double feature, a program showing two full-length motion pictures.

dou·ble-head·er (dub′əl hed′ər) *n.* **1.a.** two baseball games played on the same day, in close succession, by the same teams. **b.** two basketball games played on the same day, in close succession, by two different sets of teams. **2.** a train pulled by two locomotives.

double helix, the structure of a molecule of DNA, consisting of two strands of genetic material that wind around each other.

double jeopardy, the condition of being retried for the same offense for which one has already been tried and judged.

dou·ble-joint·ed (dub′əl join′tid) *adj.* having extremely flexible joints that permit movement of the body into unusual positions.

dou·ble-knit (dub′əl nit′) *n.* a fabric made from two layers of knitted material interwoven closely together.

double negative, the use in the same statement of two

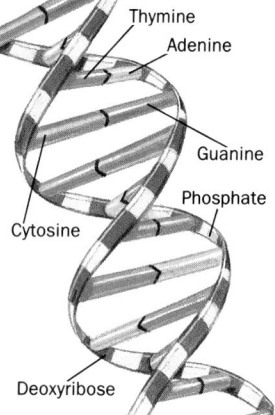

double helix of DNA

negative words or phrases, esp. to express one negative idea: *They could not any longer say nothing about the abuses they had witnessed.*

dou·ble-park (dub′əl pärk′) *v.t., v.i.* to park (a motor vehicle) next to one that is already legally parked parallel to the curb.

double play, a baseball play in which two base runners are put out.

double pneumonia, pneumonia affecting both lungs.

dou·ble-quick (dub′əl kwik′) *adj.* very quick; hurried; rapid: *They appeared in double-quick time.* —*n.* double time *(def. 1).* —*v.t., v.i.* to march or cause to march in double time.

dou·ble-reed (dub′əl rēd′) *Music. adj.* of or designating any of a group of wind instruments, as the oboe and the bassoon, having a reed with two tongues that vibrate together and produce sounds when wind is forced between them. —*n.* a double-reed instrument.

double refraction, birefringence.

double sharp *Music.* **1.** a symbol (✕ or ※) that, when placed before a note, indicates that the pitch must be raised two half tones. **2.** a note or tone so raised.

double standard, a standard that is applied more strictly to one group than to another, esp. a code of moral behavior permitting women less freedom than men.

double star **1.** two stars that appear as one when viewed with the naked eye. **2.** binary star.

dou·blet (dub′lit) *n.* **1.** a close-fitting waist-length jacket, with or without sleeves, worn esp. by men in western Europe from about 1400 to 1650. **2.** a pair of similar or equal things; couple. **3.** either of such a pair. **4.** one of two or more words in a language, derived from the same original word but differing in form and, usually, in meaning, as *clock* and *cloak.* [Old French *doublet* something folded, diminutive of *do(u)ble.* See DOUBLE.]

double take, a delayed reaction, as to a joke or surprising situation, characterized by initial blankness or acceptance and followed by a sudden understanding or recognition.

dou·ble-talk (dub′əl tôk′) *n.* **1.** deliberately deceptive or ambiguous talk. **2.** nonsensical speech made to appear or sound intelligible by mixing actual words with meaningless syllables.

dou·ble-think (dub′əl thingk′) *n.* thinking that ignores the conflict between opposite versions of a factual matter given at the same time, accepting both as true.

dou·ble-time (dub′əl tīm′) *v.i., v.t.,* -**timed,** -**tim·ing.** to move or cause to move in double time.

double time **1.** *Military.* a rapid marching rate of 180 three-foot steps per minute. **2.** a rate of pay that is twice one's normal pay rate.

dou·ble·tree (dub′əl trē′) *n.* a crossbar, as on a carriage, plow, or wagon, used in harnessing a pair of draft animals.

dou·bloon (du blün′) *n.* a gold coin formerly used in Spain and Spanish America. [Spanish *doblón*, from *doble* double, from Latin *duplus* twofold; because originally worth *double* the pistole.]

dou·bly (dub′lē) *adv.* in a twofold manner or degree; twice as.

doubt (dout) *v.t.* to be unconvinced or uncertain about; hesitate to believe or accept; distrust; question: *The police doubted the truth of the suspect's story. Do you doubt my word?* —*v.i.* to be wavering or undecided in opinion or belief; be unconvinced, uncertain, or distrustful: *Those who doubt will establish truths for themselves.* —*n.* **1.** a feeling of disbelief, uncertainty, or distrust: *to remove all doubt about a subject, to have doubts about someone's sincerity.* **2.** the state or condition of being uncertain or undecided about something: *We were in doubt about whether we would stay.* **3.** a condition or state of affairs giving rise to uncertainty: *The outcome of the elections was in doubt.* [Old French *doter* to fear, hesitate, from Late Latin *dubitāre* to fear, from Latin *dubitāre* to hesitate.] —**doubt′a·ble,** *adj.* —**doubt′er,** *n.* —**doubt′ing·ly,** *adv.*

• **no doubt.** **a.** without question; certainly. **b.** most likely; probably.

• **without doubt.** without question; certainly.

doubt·ful (dout′fəl) *adj.* **1.** having, showing, or experiencing doubt: *She had a doubtful look on her face. I'm doubtful about his prospects for success.* **2.** subject to or causing doubt; not clear or sure; ambiguous; uncertain: *The outcome of the war was doubtful. It's doubtful whether we'll go.* **3.** of questionable, suspect, or equivocal character: *a doubtful reputation.* —**doubt′ful·ly,** *adv.* —**doubt′ful·ness,** *n.*

Synonyms Doubtful and dubious may both mean open to doubt or uncertainty. Doubtful is more negative in connotation: *Long-range weather forecasts are of doubtful accuracy. It is doubtful that a relief ship can arrive in time.* Dubious is more suggestive of uncertainty: *The results of their research are of dubious value.*

doubting Thom·as (tom′əs) a person who is habitually doubtful and refuses to believe anything without proof; skeptic. [From the Apostle *Thomas,* who at first doubted the resurrection of Jesus (John 20:24-29).]

doubt·less (dout′lis) *adv.* **1.** without doubt; unquestionably; certainly. **2.** probably. Also, **doubt′less·ly.** —*adj.* free from doubt or uncertainty. —**doubt′less·ness,** *n.*

douche (düsh) *n.* **1.** a jet of water or other liquid directed into or onto a body part, organ, or cavity for cleansing or medicinal purposes. **2.** the application of such a jet. **3.** a device, as a spray or syringe, for making such an application. —*v.,* **douched, douch·ing.** —*v.t.* to apply a douche to. —*v.i.* to use a douche; take a douche. [French *douche* shower (bath), from Italian *doccia* canal, pipe, shower (bath), going back to Latin *ductiō* a leading, pipe.]

dough (dō) *n.* **1.** a soft, thick mass worked or kneaded from a mixture of flour or meal, liquid, and other ingredients for use in baking. **2.** any soft, thick, pasty mass. **3.** *Slang.* money. [Old English *dāg, dāh* flour paste for baking.]

dough·boy (dō′boi′) *n. Informal.* a soldier in the United States Army, esp. during World War I. [Possibly because the brass buttons on American Civil War infantry uniforms resembled the dumplings of those times known as *doughboys.*]

dough·nut (dō′nut′, -nət) *also,* **do·nut.** *n.* a small, usually ring-shaped cake made of dough, usually leavened and sweetened, cooked by frying in deep fat.

dough·ty (dou′tē) *adj.,* **-ti·er, -ti·est.** steadfast and courageous; valiant: *our doughty hero.* [Old English *dohtig.*] —**dough′ti·ly,** *adv.* —**dough′ti·ness,** *n.*

dough·y (dō′ē) *adj.,* **dough·i·er, dough·i·est.** of or like dough in consistency or appearance; pasty. —**dough′i·ness,** *n.*

Doug·las fir (dug′ləs) **1.** an evergreen timber tree, *Pseudotsuga menziesii,* of the pine family, found in western North America, having reddish brown ridged bark and bearing oval cones. It may grow to a height of 200 feet (61 meters) and is surpassed in size only by the sequoia of California. Also, **Douglas spruce.** **2.** the hard, strong wood of this tree, used chiefly in construction. [From the Scottish botanist David *Douglas,* 1798-1834.]

dour (dŭr, dour) *adj.* **1.** sullenly gloomy; grim; forbidding: *a dour look.* **2.** unyielding; obstinate. [Latin *dūrus* hard.] —**dour′ly,** *adv.* —**dour′ness,** *n.*

douse (dous) *v.t.,* **doused, dous·ing. 1.** to plunge into water or other liquid: *Douse the burning rag in a bucket of water.* **2.** to throw water or other liquid over; drench: *They doused me with the hose.* **3.** *Informal.* to put out; extinguish: *Douse the lights.* **4.** to lower (a sail) quickly and suddenly. [Of uncertain origin.]

dove¹ (duv) *n.* **1.a.** any small or medium-sized bird of the pigeon family, Columbidae, including the mourning dove and turtledove. **b.** a completely white bird of this family, often regarded as a symbol of peace or good fortune. **2.** an innocent, gentle, or loving person. **3. Dove.** the Holy Ghost. **4.** a person who advocates peaceful solutions to international conflicts. ➡ opposed to **hawk¹.** [Middle English *douve,* from Old Norse *dūfa* or possibly Old English *dufe.*] —**dov′ish,** *adj.*

dove² (dōv) a past tense of **dive.**

dove·cote (duv′kōt′) *also,* **dove·cot** (duv′kot′). *n.* a small house or boxlike shelter for doves or pigeons, usually having compartments and placed on a pole or other structure.

dove·key (duv′kē) *n., pl.* **-keys.** dovekie.

dove·kie (duv′kē) *also,* **dovekey.** *n.* a small auk, *Plautus alle,* native to the Arctic and North Atlantic regions.

dove·tail (duv′tāl′) *n.* **1.** a wedge-shaped tenon designed to interlock with a mortise of similar shape to form a joint. **2.** a joint formed by the interlocking of such tenons and mortises. —*v.t., v.i.* **1.** to fit together or join by means of dovetails. **2.** to fit together precisely, compactly, or harmoniously: *Our vacation plans dovetailed with theirs.*

dow·a·ger (dou′ə jər) *n.* **1.** a widow who holds property or a title derived from her deceased husband. ➡ often used as an additional title to differentiate her from the wife of her husband's heir: *a dowager queen, a dowager empress.* **2.** a dignified, elderly woman, esp. one of imposing appearance or social position. [Old French *douagere* widow who has received a dower, from *douage* a dower, from *douer* to endow, from Latin *dōtāre* from *dōs* dowry.]

dow·dy (dou′dē) *adj.,* **-di·er, -di·est.** lacking style or smartness in dress or appearance; not neat or fashionable; frumpish: *a dowdy dress.* —*n., pl.* **-dies. 1.** a dowdy woman. **2.** pandowdy. [Of uncertain origin.] —**dow′di·ly,** *adv.* —**dow′di·ness,** *n.*

dovetails

dow·el (dou′əl) *n.* a peg or pin fitting into corresponding holes in two adjacent pieces to hold them together. —*v.t.,* **-eled, -el·ing;** *also, British,* **-elled, -el·ling** to fasten or furnish with dowels. [Middle Low German *dövel* peg, plug.]

dow·er (dou′ər) *n.* **1.** the part of a deceased man's real property that is given by law to his widow. **2.** dowry *(def. 1).* **3.** a natural gift, talent, or endowment. —*v.t.* to provide with a dower. [Old French *doaire* widow's inheritance, from Medieval Latin *dotarium,* from Latin *dōtāre* to endow, from *dōs* dowry.]

down¹ (doun) *adv.* **1.a.** from a higher to a lower place, level, or position; in a descending direction; toward the ground: *I stepped down from the ladder. We looked down upon the valley.* **b.** in, on, or to a lower place, level, or position: *Please pull the shades down.* **2.** to or on the ground, floor, or bottom: *to knock someone down, to fall down, to beat a door down.* **3.** to, toward, or in a direction, position, or area considered geographically lower or distant, as to the south on a map: *We drove down from New York to Richmond. They're down at the seashore this week.* **4.** below the horizon or surface: *The sun's gone down. The ship went down during a storm.* **5.** to or at a lower or reduced amount, degree, or rate: *Please slow down the car. The price of milk has gone down. The temperature went down to zero.* **6.** from a higher to a lower rank or station; in, into, or toward a lower status or condition: *That person has gone down in my estimation since the scandal.* **7.** to or in a calmer, less active or intense state: *The crowd quieted down. Things finally settled down after the holidays.* **8.** in or into a low or depressed mental or emotional condition; dejected: *I feel down about moving.* **9.** fully; thoroughly: *to be loaded down with packages, to be weighted down with cares.* **10.** from an earlier time or individual: *That recipe has been passed down through my family for years.* **11.** at the time of purchase; as a down payment: *Pay thirty dollars down and the rest in installments.* **12.** in writing; on paper: *Write down this address. I took down their names.* **13.** all the way through and including: *The new rule applies to everyone in the company, from the president down to the secretaries.* **14.** to the point of submission, defeat, or inactivity; in or into subjection or control: *to vote down a proposal, to shout down the opposition.* **15.** so as to overtake or locate the source of; to the origin or actual position: *The hounds hunted down the fox. The reporter tracked down the story.* —*adj.* **1.** going or directed downward; descending: *a down staircase.* **2.** in a lower place, level, or position: *The curtain is down.* **3.** completed; done; gone: *Four days down, three to go before vacation.* **4.** sick; ill; ailing: *I was down with bronchi-*

a	at	e	end	o	hot	u	up	hw	white		about
ā	ape	ē	me	ō	old	ū	use	ng	song		taken
ä	far	i	it	ô	fork	ů	rule	th	thin	ə	pencil
âr	care	ī	ice	oi	oil	ů	pull	th	this		lemon
		îr	pierce	ou	out	ûr	turn	zh	measure		circus

tis. **5.** depressed; dejected. **6.** trailing an opponent by a specified number, as of points. **7.** (of a football) no longer in play. **8.** not functioning properly; out of order: *The computer system has been down since the thunderstorm struck.* —*prep.* **1.** in a descending direction along, through, or into: *to walk down a hill, to glance down a page.* **2.** along the course of: *to stroll down the street.* **3.** farther along: *three miles down the road.* **4.** during the course of: *down the years, down the ages.* —*v.t.* **1.** to cause to fall; bring, throw, knock, or put down: *He downed his opponent with three blows. The guns downed four bombers.* **2.** *Informal.* to swallow, esp. quickly; gulp: *She downed her milk and ran out to play.* **3.** *Informal.* to defeat, as in a game. —*n.* **1.** a downward movement; descent: *the ups and downs of the economic cycle.* **2.** a period of hardship, depression, or bad luck: *to have one's ups and downs.* **3.** *Football.* any of four successive plays during which a team must advance the ball at least ten yards in order to keep possession of it. [Middle English *doun,* from *adūne,* from Old English *adūne,* from *ofdūne* down from the hill, from *of-* off, from + *dune,* dative of *dūn* hill, akin to Low German *düne* sand hill.]
· **down and out. a.** completely bereft, as of money or friends; miserable. **b.** *Boxing.* knocked out.
· **down on.** *Informal.* angry at, annoyed with, or hostile to.
· **down with.** do away with; eliminate: *Down with tyranny!*
down² (doun) *n.* **1.** fine, soft feathers, as on young birds or under the exterior plumage of certain adult birds. **2.** any fine, soft hair or fuzz. [Old Norse *dūnn* soft plumage.]
down·beat (doun′bēt′) *n. Music.* **1.** a downward gesture made by a conductor to indicate the first accented beat in a measure. **2.** the first beat or the first accented beat in a measure. —*adj.* quiet or gloomy: *a downbeat mood.*
down·cast (doun′kast′) *adj.* **1.** low or dejected in spirit; sad; depressed: *The team was downcast after losing.* **2.** directed downward: *downcast eyes.*
down·draft (doun′draft′) *n.* a current of air or gas moving in a downward direction, as during a thunderstorm. [DOWN¹ + DRAFT.]
Down East *also,* **down East.** New England, esp. Maine.
down·er (dou′nər) *n. Informal.* **1.** a depressant or sedative, as a tranquilizer or barbiturate. **2.** a depressing person or thing. [DOWN¹ + -ER¹.]
down·fall (doun′fôl′) *n.* **1.** a descent to a lower position or standing; fall, as from power or prosperity; ruin: *the downfall of a government.* **2.** a person or thing causing this: *Excessive pride was the ruler's downfall.* **3.** a fall, as of rain or snow, esp. when sudden or heavy.
down·fall·en (doun′fô′lən) *adj.* fallen; ruined.
down·grade (doun′grād′) *n.* a downward or descending slope, as of a hill or road. —*v.t.,* **-grad·ed, -grad·ing. 1.** to lower in rank, position, or salary; demote. **2.** to minimize the importance or worth of; belittle. —*adj., adv.* downhill.
· **on the downgrade.** declining, as in strength or status; becoming worse; deteriorating.
down·heart·ed (doun′här′tid) *adj.* depressed or discouraged in spirit; sad; dejected. —**down′heart′ed·ly,** *adv.* —**down′heart′ed·ness,** *n.*
down·hill (*adv., adj.* doun′hil′; *n.* doun′hil′) *adv.* **1.** in a descending or downward direction; toward the bottom of a hill: *The car rolled downhill.* **2.** into or toward a lower or worse level or condition: *My health had been going downhill for months.* —*adj.* **1.** sloping or descending downward on or as on a hill: *a downhill slide.* **2.** of, relating to, or for skiing downhill: *downhill skis.* —*n.* a skiing race in which each participant skis down a steep course in as little time as possible.
down·home (doun′hōm′) *adj.* of, relating to, or having characteristics traditionally associated with rural areas or their inhabitants, esp. of the southern United States: *down-home cooking.*
Down·ing Street (dou′ning) **1.** a street in Westminster, London, site of several official residences and offices of the British government. The home and residence of the prime minister is at 10 Downing Street. **2.** the British prime minister or cabinet.
down·link (doun′lingk′) *n.* a transmission path for data or other signals from a satellite or spacecraft to an earth station. [DOWN¹ + LINK¹.]
down·load (doun′lōd′) *v.t.* **1.** to transfer (data) from a larger to a smaller computer. **2.** to transfer (data) from one computer to another by means of a modem or other telecommunications device.
down payment, a partial amount paid when purchasing something, with the balance to be paid later, often in installments.
down·play (doun′plā′) *v.t.* to treat as having little or no importance; understate the importance of; play down: *to downplay a serious error.*
down·pour (doun′pôr′) *n.* a heavy, drenching rainfall.
down·range (doun′rānj′) *adj., adv.* away from a launching site,

along the course toward the point designated as the target: *a downrange observer, a missile moving downrange.*
down·right (doun′rīt′) *adj.* **1.** thorough; absolute; utter: *downright nonsense, a downright lie.* **2.** frankly direct; straightforward; forthright: *a downright refusal.* —*adv.* thoroughly; utterly: *That's downright stupid!*
downs (dounz) *pl. n.* an open, rolling, grassy tract of upland, esp. in southern and southeastern England. [Old English *dūn* hill.]
down·scale (doun′skāl′) *adj.* of, relating to, or for people who are below a certain level of income or standard of living, esp. those at the lower end of the economic bracket. [Probably from *to scale down,* from SCALE³.]
down·shift (doun′shift′) *v.i.* to shift the transmission of a motor vehicle into a lower gear.
down·spout (doun′spout′) *n.* a vertical pipe that conveys rainwater from a roof or gutter to the ground or a drain.
down·stage (doun′stāj′) *adv.* at or toward the front of a stage. —*adj.* of or relating to the front of a stage. —*n.* the front half of a stage.
down·stairs (doun′stârz′) *adv.* **1.** down the stairs; toward the foot of a staircase. **2.** on or to a lower floor or level. —*adj.* situated on a lower or main floor: *a downstairs room.* —*n.* a lower or main floor or floors: *They rent the whole downstairs of the building.*
down·stream (doun′strēm′) *adv., adj.* with or in the direction of the current or flow of a stream.
down·swing (doun′swing′) *n.* **1.** a downward swing, as of a golf club. **2.** a downward trend, esp. in business.
Down syndrome (doun) *also,* **Down's syndrome.** a congenital condition caused by the presence of an extra chromosome, characterized by mental retardation and physical abnormalities, as a broad flat skull, protruding tongue, and eyes that appear slanted. Formerly, **mongolism.** [From John L. H. *Down,* 1828-96, British physician.]
down-to-earth (doun′tü ûrth′, -tə-) *adj.* realistic and unpretentious; practical; unaffected.
down·town (doun′toun′) *adv.* to, toward, or in the business center or geographically lower part of a town or city: *Let's go downtown this afternoon. They moved downtown.* —*adj.* of, relating to, or in the business center or geographically lower part of a town or city: *a downtown office, downtown traffic, the downtown branch of a bank.* —*n.* the central business district of a town or city.
down·trend (doun′trend′) *n.* a decline, as in business activity or economic growth.
down·trod·den (doun′trod′ən) *adj.* **1.** abused or subjugated, as by those in power; oppressed: *a downtrodden nation, the downtrodden serfs of the feudal period.* **2.** trampled underfoot: *downtrodden grass.* Also, **down′trod′.**
down·turn (doun′tûrn′) *n.* a decline, esp. in business activity.
down under *Informal.* Australia or New Zealand. —*adv.* in or to Australia or New Zealand.
down·ward (doun′wərd) *adv. also,* **down·wards. 1.** from a higher to a lower place, level, or condition. **2.** from an earlier time or individual. —*adj.* moving from a higher to a lower place, level, or condition.
down·wind (doun′wind′) *adj., adv.* located or moving in the same direction as that in which the wind is blowing.
down·y (dou′nē) *adj., adv.,* **down·i·er, down·i·est. 1.** of or covered with down. **2.** like down; soft; fluffy. —**down′i·ness,** *n.*
dow·ry (dour′ē) *n., pl.* **-ries.** **1.** the money or property that a woman brings to her husband at the time of their marriage. Also, **portion. 2.** a natural talent or endowment. [Form of DOWER.]
dowse (douz) *v.i.,* **dowsed, dows·ing.** to search for underground water or minerals with a divining rod. —**dows′er,** *n.*
dox·ol·o·gy (dok sol′ə jē) *n., pl.* **-gies.** a hymn or formula praising God. [Medieval Latin *doxologia* hymn of praise, from Greek *doxologiā* praise, going back to *doxa* glory + *logos* speaking.]
doy·en (doi en′, doi′ən) *n.* a person who has belonged to a group longest; senior member: *the doyen of American journalism.* [French *doyen* dean, from Old French *deien,* from Late Latin *decānus* chief of ten monks, leader of any ten people, from Latin *decem* ten.]
doy·enne (doi en′) *n.* a woman who has belonged to a group longest; female doyen. [French *doyenne,* feminine of *doyen.*]
doz., dozen; dozens.
doze (dōz) *v.,* **dozed, doz·ing.** —*v.i.* **1.** to sleep lightly, fitfully, or for a short while; be half asleep; nap: *She's dozing on the couch. He's dozing over his newspaper.* **2.** to fall into a light, brief sleep unintentionally (often with *off*): *I dozed off while reading.* —*v.t.* to spend or pass (time) in dozing: *You've dozed the afternoon away.* —*n.* a light, fitful, or brief sleep. [Probably of Scandinavian origin.] —**doz′er,** *n.*

doz·en (duz′ən) *n., pl.* **-en** or **-ens. 1.** a group of twelve: *three dozen eggs.* **2.** a large number: *dozens of things to see in town.* [Old French *dozaine,* from *do(u)ze* twelve, from Latin *duodecim.*]
doz·enth (duz′ənth) *adj.* twelfth.
DP, displaced person.
dpt. 1. department. **2.** deponent.
dr *also,* **dr.** dram; drams.
dr. 1. debtor. **2.** drawer.
Dr. 1. Doctor. **2.** Drive.
drab[1] (drab) *n.* **1.** a dull yellowish brown or gray color. **2.** a thick, strong woolen or cotton cloth of this color, often woven with a twill. —*adj.,* **drab·ber, drab·best. 1.** lacking brightness; dull; monotonous; cheerless: *a drab existence, a drab day.* **2.** having the color drab. [Form of obsolete *drap* cloth, from French *drap* cloth; with reference to the color of undyed cloth. See DRAPE.]
—**drab′ly,** *adv.* —**drab′ness,** *n.*
drab[2] (drab) *n.* **1.** a slovenly, untidy woman. **2.** a prostitute. [Of uncertain origin.]
drachm (dram) *n.* **1.** dram. **2.** drachma.
drach·ma (drak′mə) *n., pl.* **-mas** or **-mae** (-mē). **1.** the monetary unit of Greece. **2.** a silver coin of ancient Greece. **3.** a unit of weight of ancient Greece. **4.** any of several modern weights, esp. a dram. [Latin *drachma* coin or weight of ancient Greece, from Greek *drachmē* literally, handful. Doublet of DRAM.]
Dra·co (drā′kō) *n.* a constellation in the northern sky near the Little Dipper, conventionally depicted as a dragon. Also, **the Dragon.** [Latin *draco* dragon, from Greek *drakōn* dragon, snake; literally, the one who sees, from *derkesthai* to see.]
Dra·co·ni·an (drā kō′nē ən, dra-) *adj.* **1.** of or relating to the Athenian lawgiver Draco or his code of laws. **2.** *also,* **draconian.** very cruel or severe; harsh: *draconian rules.*
draft (draft) *also, British,* **draught.** *n.* **1.** a current of air in an enclosed space or area: *There is a draft in the room coming from the open window. The size of the chimney will affect the draft in the furnace.* **2.** a device for regulating the flow of air, as in a stove. **3.** a preliminary or rough version of something written: *a draft of a proposed law, the first draft of an essay.* **4.** a sketch, plan, or design of something to be made, as a building. **5.a.** the act or process of selecting an individual or individuals for some special purpose: *She accepted the party's draft and immediately outlined campaign plans.* **b.** the act or process of selecting persons, by an act of law, for compulsory military service. **6.** a group so selected. **7.** *Sports.* a system in professional leagues whereby each team is given exclusive rights to certain new players. **8.** a written order directing the payment of a specified amount of money, as from one person or bank to another. **9.** the act of drawing or pulling something, as a loaded wagon: *to use oxen for draft.* **10.a.** the act of drinking. **b.** the amount taken in one drink. **11.a.** the act of inhaling, as smoke or air. **b.** the quantity inhaled at one breath. **12.** a quantity or dose of liquid for drinking. **13.a.** the act of drawing in a fishnet. **b.** the amount of fish taken in a net at one time. **14.** *Nautical.* the depth of water required for a ship to float. —*v.t.* **1.** to make a preliminary plan, sketch, or version of: *He drafted his speech.* **2.** to select for some special purpose, esp. for compulsory military service. —*adj.* **1.** used for pulling loads: *a draft animal.* **2.** in a rough or preliminary form: *a draft plan.* **3.** drawn or ready to be drawn from a tap; not bottled: *draft beer.* [Possibly from Old Norse *drāttr* act of pulling.] —**draft′a·ble,** *adj.* —**draft′er,** *n.*
 •**on draft.** ready to be drawn from a tap: *ale on draft.*
draft board, an official board of civilians that selects qualified persons for compulsory service in the U.S. armed forces.
draft dodger, a person who avoids or attempts to avoid compulsory military service.
draft·ee (draf tē′) *n.* a person who is drafted for military service.
drafts·man (drafts′mən) *also, British,* **draughtsman.** *n., pl.* **-men** (-mən). a person who draws or designs plans for machinery, buildings, and other structures and facilities.
drafts·man·ship (drafts′mən ship′) *also, British,* **draughtsmanship.** the work or skill of a draftsman.
draft·y (draf′tē) *also, British,* **draughty.** *adj.,* **draft·i·er, draft·i·est.** exposed to or admitting drafts of air: *a drafty hallway.* —**draft′i·ly,** *adv.* —**draft′i·ness,** *n.*
drag (drag) *v.,* **dragged, drag·ging.** —*v.t.* **1.a.** to pull or draw heavily, slowly, or with great effort; haul: *She dragged the heavy suitcase along the ground.* **b.** to cause to move with difficulty or as if by force: *He went shopping for a new suit and dragged me along.* **2.** to search the bottom of, as with a net or hook; dredge: *to drag a pond for a sunken rowboat.* **3.** to harrow (land). **4.** to continue tediously or for a painfully long period of time; protract (often with *out*): *to drag out a story.* **5.** to introduce or bring in, as

something irrelevant or unnecessary (often with *in* or *up*): *Please don't drag up that silly old joke. Why drag them into the argument?* —*v.i.* **1.** to be drawn or hauled along; trail to or as to the ground: *The prisoner's chains dragged behind him.* **2.** to move heavily, slowly, or with great effort: *Her feet dragged as she walked along wearily.* **3.** to progress or pass slowly, tediously, or laboriously: *The days dragged on, one by one. The movie drags in the middle.* **4.** to search the bottom of a body of water, as with a net, hook, or dredge: *to drag for treasure.* **5.** to fall behind; lag. **6.** *Slang.* to puff or inhale, as on a cigarette. **7.** *Slang.* to take part in a drag race. —*n.* **1.** a person or thing that acts as a hindrance or obstacle: *A lack of business sense could be a drag on your career.* **2.** something that retards movement, as a brake on a wheel. **3.** frictional resistance that retards the movement of a body through a fluid, as an airplane through the air. **4.** something that is used in searching the bottom of a body of water, as a net, hook, or dredge. **5.** a slow, heavy, or difficult movement. **6.** something that is pulled or hauled along a surface. **7.** a strong sledlike platform that is dragged along the ground to move rocks or other heavy loads. **8.** a heavy harrow, usually homemade and consisting of planks fastened together. **9.** a large coach having seats inside and on top, usually designed to be drawn by four horses. **10.** *Slang.* a puff, as on a cigarette. **11.** *Slang.* a person or thing that is dull, boring, or vapid. **12.** *Slang.* street: *the main drag.* **13.** *Slang.* clothing of the opposite sex: *to dress in drag.* [Old Norse *draga* to draw.] —**drag′ger,** *n.*
 •**to drag one's feet.** *Informal.* to act with deliberate slowness; fail to act promptly.
drag·gle (drag′əl) *v.,* **-gled, -gling.** —*v.t.* to make wet or dirty, as by dragging through mud. —*v.i.* **1.** to become wet or dirty, as by being dragged through mud. **2.** to lag behind; straggle.
drag·net (drag′net′) *n.* **1.** a net, usually bag-shaped, to be towed over the bottom of a body of water for catching fish or the like. **2.** a system or operation for locating, gathering in, or catching something or someone, as a wanted criminal.
drag·o·man (drag′ə mən) *n., pl.* **-mans** or **-men** (-mən). in the Near East, an interpreter or guide for travelers. [Obsolete French *dragoman,* through Italian, Middle Greek, Arabic, and Aramaic, going back to Akkadian *targumānu* interpreter.]
drag·on (drag′ən) *n.* **1.** a mythical monster with a scaly reptile-like body and claws, often represented as having wings and breathing fire and smoke. **2.** a fierce, difficult person. **3.** a strict, watchful chaperon. **4. the Dragon.** Draco. [Old French *dragon* this mythical monster, from Latin *dracō* serpent, reptile monster, from Greek *drakōn.*]

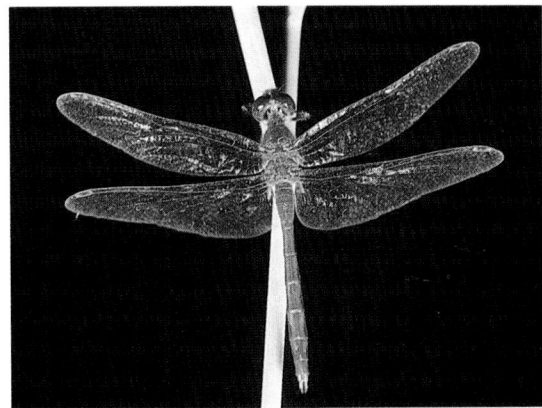

dragonfly

drag·on·fly (drag′ən flī′) *n., pl.* **-flies.** any of a large group of slender-bodied insects, suborder Anisoptera, found near fresh water and feeding on mosquitoes and other insects. They have broad heads, compound eyes, and two pairs of membranous, veined wings, which may grow to a spread of 7½ inches (19 centimeters). Also, **darning needle, devil's darning needle.**

a	at	e	end	o	hot	u	up	hw	white		about
ā	ape	ē	me	ō	old	ū	use	ng	song		taken
ä	far	i	it	ô	fork	ü	rule	th	thin	ə	pencil
âr	care	ī	ice	oi	oil	ů	pull	th	this		lemon
		îr	pierce	ou	out	ûr	turn	zh	measure		circus

dra·goon (drə gün′) *n.* **1.** any heavily armed member of a cavalry. **2.** formerly, a mounted infantryman armed with a musket. —*v.t.* **1.** to coerce or persecute by the use of dragoons or other troops. **2.** to force or pressure (*into* doing something): *They dragooned the senator into supporting the bill.* [French *dragon* cavalry soldier; earlier, soldier armed with a firearm called a *dragon* because it emitted fire. See DRAGON.]

drag race, a race on a short, straight course between automobiles beginning from a dead stop, the winner being the car that accelerates the fastest.

drain (drān) *v.t.* **1.** to draw water or other liquid from; empty or dry by drawing off liquid: *to drain a marsh, to drain a bathtub.* **2.** to draw off (a liquid) gradually or completely: *to drain water from a pool.* **3.a.** to use up slowly; exhaust gradually: *The war drained the nation's resources. The long hike drained my strength.* **b.** to exhaust physically or emotionally: *Opening night drained the cast.* **4.** to drink all the liquid from; empty by drinking: *to drain one's glass.* —*v.i.* **1.** to become dry or empty by the flowing off or away of liquid: *The dishes drained in the rack. The sink is draining.* **2.** to flow off or away gradually: *The water drained out of the hole in the pail.* **3.** to release or discharge waters: *The river drains into the sea. The pipe drains into the sewer.* —*n.* **1.** a channel, pipe, or similar device for drawing off water or other liquid: *The bathtub drain is clogged.* **2.** a slow or continuous outflow, withdrawal, or expenditure tending toward exhaustion: *The project was a drain on the institute's funds.* **3.** a material or device, as gauze or rubber tubing, used to remove fluid in a body cavity or wound. [Old English *drēahnian* to strain.] —**drain′er,** *n.* —For Synonyms *(v.t.),* see **deplete.**

 ·**down the drain.** lost, wasted, or worthless.

drain·age (drā′nij) *n.* **1.** the act or process of draining. **2.** a system of natural or artificial drains. **3.** something that is drained off. **4.** an area or region drained.

drainage basin, the area drained by a river and all its tributaries.

drain·pipe (drān′pīp′) *n.* a pipe for draining water or other liquid.

drake (drāk) *n.* a male duck. [Of uncertain origin.]

dram (dram) **1.** an apothecaries' weight equal to 60 grains, or ⅛ of an ounce (3.9 grams). **2.** an avoirdupois weight equal to 27.343 grains, or 1/16 of an ounce (1.8 grams). **3.** fluid dram. **4.** a small drink, esp. of alcoholic liquor. **5.** a small amount of anything. [Middle French *drame* one eighth of an ounce (4 milliliters), handful, going back to Latin *drachma* coin or weight of ancient Greece, from Greek *drachmē* literally, handful. Doublet of DRACHMA.]

dra·ma (drä′mə, dram′ə) *n.* **1.a.** a literary composition telling a story and written to be performed. **b.** such a composition dealing with a serious subject in a serious manner. **2.** the branch of literature comprising such compositions: *a student of drama, the classical drama.* **3.** the art or profession of writing, acting in, or producing plays. **4.** a situation or series of events having dramatic qualities: *The history of space exploration is an exciting drama.* **5.** a dramatic state, quality, or effect: *The witness's unexpected disclosure was filled with drama.* [Late Latin *drāma* play, from Greek *drāma* deed, play.]

Dram·a·mine (dram′ə mēn′) *n. Trademark.* an antihistamine used to treat allergies and to prevent motion sickness.

dra·mat·ic (drə mat′ik) *adj.* **1.** of, relating to, or characteristic of drama. **2.** appropriate to drama; exciting; vivid; striking: *a dramatic appeal for mercy, the dramatic events leading to the revolution.* —**dra·mat′i·cal·ly,** *adv.*

dramatic monologue, a lyric poem in which a single character reveals his or her personality by addressing a silent listener.

dra·mat·ics (drə mat′iks) *pl. n.* **1.** the art or activity of producing or performing plays: *a counselor in charge of dramatics.* **2.** exaggerated or theatrical behavior. ▶ used as singular in def. 1, as plural in def. 2.

dram·a·tis per·so·nae (dram′ə tis pər sō′nē, drä′mə-) **1.** the characters in a play. **2.** a list of these characters, often with the names of the actors who portray them. [Latin *drāmatis persōnae.*]

dram·a·tist (dram′ə tist, drä′mə-) *n.* a person who writes dramas.

dram·a·ti·za·tion (dram′ə tə zā′shən, drä′mə-) *n.* **1.** the act of dramatizing. **2.** something that is dramatized; dramatized version or representation.

dram·a·tize (dram′ə tīz′, drä′mə-) *v.t.,* **-tized, -tiz·ing. 1.** to put into the form of a play; adapt for dramatic performance: *to dramatize a novel.* **2.** to represent in an exaggerated or theatrical way; make seem exciting or spectacular: *Stop dramatizing your problems.* —**dram′a·tiz′er,** *n.*

dram·a·turge (dram′ə tûrj′, drä′mə-) *n.* a specialist in dramaturgy. Also, **dram′a·tur′gist.**

dram·a·tur·gy (dram′ə tûr′jē, drä′mə-) *n.* the art of writing, producing, or acting in plays. [Greek *drāmatourgiā* composition of plays.] —**dram′a·tur′gic;** *also,* **dram′a·tur′gi·cal,** *adj.* —**dram′a·tur′gi·cal·ly,** *adv.*

drank (drangk) a past tense of **drink.**

drape (drāp) *v.,* **draped, drap·ing.** —*v.t.* **1.** to cover or adorn gracefully with or as with cloth: *to drape a window, to drape a statue.* **2.** to place or arrange, as cloth or clothing, in loose, graceful folds. **3.** to arrange, spread, or let fall casually or carelessly: *He draped himself across the sofa. Don't drape your feet over the chair.* —*v.i.* to hang or fall in folds: *Silk drapes nicely.* —*n.* **1.** *usually,* **drapes.** cloth hung in folds, esp. when used as a window curtain; drapery: *She pulled the drapes back.* **2.** the way in which cloth hangs: *I like the drape of your jacket.* [French *draper* to cover with cloth, from *drap* cloth, from Late Latin *drappus;* probably of Celtic origin.]

drap·er (drā′pər) *n.* a dealer in cloth or dry goods.

dra·per·y (drā′pə rē) *n., pl.* **-per·ies. 1.** cloth hung or arranged in loose, graceful folds, esp. when used as a window curtain. **2.** the draping or arranging of cloth.

dras·tic (dras′tik) *adj.* having a forceful or severe effect; rigorous; extreme: *The closing of the mill was a drastic step.* [Greek *drastikos* active, effective.] —**dras′ti·cal·ly,** *adv.*

drat (drat) *interj. Informal.* darn². [Euphemism for *God rot.*]

drat·ted (drat′id) *adj. Informal.* damned; confounded.

draught (draft, dräft) *British.* **draft.**

draughts (drafts, dräfts) *n. British.* the game of checkers. ▶ used as singular.

draughts·man (drafts′mən, dräfts′-) *n., pl.* **-men** (-mən). *British.* draftsman.

draughts·man·ship (drafts′mən ship′, dräfts′-) *British.* draftsmanship.

draught·y (draf′tē, dräf′-) *adj.,* **draught·i·er, draught·i·est.** *British.* drafty. —**draught′i·ness,** *n.*

drave (drāv) *Archaic.* a past tense of **drive.**

Dra·vid·i·an (drə vid′ē ən) *n.* **1.** a family of languages spoken mainly in central and southern India and northern Sri Lanka. **2.** a member of a group of Dravidian-speaking peoples living primarily in this area. —*adj.* of or relating to these languages or these peoples.

draw (drô) *v.,* **drew, drawn, draw·ing.** —*v.t.* **1.a.** to cause to move in a particular direction or to a particular position by or as by pulling: *He drew me aside and told me the news. She drew her gloves on. I drew the covers over my head.* **b.** to cause to follow behind by exerting force or effort; drag; haul: *Three white stallions drew the chariot.* **2.** to remove or bring out, as by pulling from a receptacle; take out: *to draw a sword from a scabbard, to draw the cork from a bottle.* **3.** to produce a picture or likeness of with a pen, pencil, or the like; sketch: *to draw a cartoon.* **4.** to describe or represent in words: *The article drew a grim picture of conditions in the slums.* **5.** to cause (a liquid) to flow forth: *to draw water for a bath.* **6.** to stretch, extend, or pull tight: *The hunter drew the bowstring and fired.* **7.** to deduce or devise, as by reasoning; formulate: *Draw your own conclusions. The speaker drew a careful distinction between the two points of view.* **8.** to cause to come; bring; attract: *The concert drew a large audience. A flame draws moths. The teacher drew my attention to that fact.* **9.** to bring forth or result in; elicit; evoke: *Our planes drew enemy fire. The legislature's actions drew criticism from the governor.* **10.** to close; shut: *Please draw the drapes.* **11.** to take or get from a source; receive; derive: *I drew inspiration from that writer.* **12.** to write out or draft in proper form (often with *up*): *to draw up a will.* **13.** to obtain or select by or as by lot: *to draw the winning card, to draw a tough assignment.* **14.** to take in, as by inhaling or sucking: *The dust is drawn into the vacuum cleaner.* **15.** to take out (funds); withdraw: *to draw thirty dollars from a bank account.* **16.** to bring in; accumulate; produce: *Our investments are drawing interest.* **17.** to cause to pucker or shrink; wrinkle; contract: *Your forehead was drawn into a frown. Hot water draws wool.* **18.** to disembowel: *to draw a turkey.* **19.** to make (wire) by pulling through a series of dies. **20.** to extract the essence or strength of, as by steeping or infusing: *to draw tea.* **21.** *Card Games.* **a.** to take (a card or cards): *I drew a king and then a deuce.* **b.** to cause (a card or cards) to be played: *to cause an opponent's trump.* **22.** *Medicine.* to cause to soften, drain, or discharge, as by applying a poultice: *to draw an abscess.* **23.** (of a ship) to require (a certain depth of water) in order to float. —*v.i.* **1.** to create a likeness or picture with lines; sketch. **2.** to take out a weapon for action: *The police officer drew, aimed, and fired.* **3.** to apply or have recourse to; take (with *on, upon,* or *from*): *I'm going to draw on my savings account. Novelists often draw upon their own experiences for the plots of their*

books. We drew from our reserve of supplies. **4.** to approach; come; move: *We drew near the town. Night drew near.* **5.** to draw lots: *We drew for partners.* **6.** to have an attracting force or influence: *That director's films usually draw well.* **7.** to exert a pulling or sucking force: *to draw on one's straw.* **8.** to wrinkle or pucker; become contracted: *The child's eyebrows drew together in a frown.* **9.** to cause or allow a current of air to pass: *The chimney is not drawing well.* **10.** to tie, as in a game. **11.** in hunting, to track game by following its scent. —*n.* **1.** the act of drawing. **2.** the act of pulling out a gun: *The sheriff was quick on the draw.* **3.** something that is drawn, as a ticket in a lottery. **4.** a game or contest in which there is no winner; tie. **5.** something that draws or attracts; attracting force or influence: *That group is a big draw at the box office.* **6.** a gully or ravine into or through which water drains. **7.** the movable part or section of a drawbridge. [Old English *dragan* to drag, pull, go.]

• **to draw away.** to move ahead, as in a race.
• **to draw back.** to retreat: *The enemy troops drew back behind their lines.*
• **to draw oneself up.** to straighten up, as in anger or indignation.
• **to draw out. a.** to make longer; extend; prolong: *to draw out a story until it becomes boring.* **b.** to cause or persuade to talk freely: *to draw out a shy person.*
• **to draw up. a.** to come or bring to a halt; stop: *The car drew up at the tollbooth.* **b.** to arrange; align: *to draw up troops in battle order.*

draw·back (drô′bak′) *n.* an unpleasant or objectionable feature or characteristic; shortcoming; disadvantage: *The main drawback to that house is that it needs new wiring.*

draw·bar (drô′bär′) *n.* **1.** a bar across the back of a tractor to which implements are attached. **2.** coupler *(def. 3).*

draw·bridge (drô′brij′) *n.* a bridge that can be wholly or partly raised, lowered, or drawn aside so as to permit or prevent passage.

draw·ee (drô ē′) *n.* a person against whom an order to pay money is written and from whom payment is collected.

drawer *(def. 1* drôr; *def. 2* drô′ər) *n.* **1.** a boxlike receptacle that, when fitted into a piece of furniture, as a bureau, is drawn out to be opened and pushed in to be closed. **2.** a person who draws, esp. a person who writes an order to pay money.

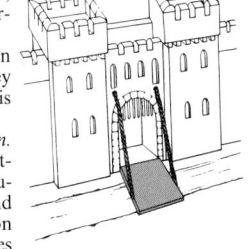

drawbridge

drawers (drôrz) *pl. n.* underpants.

draw·ing (drô′ing) *n.* **1.** a pictorial representation or visual pattern, as a sketch or design, usually made by the use of pencil, pen, crayon, or similar material. **2.** the art or technique of making such a representation or pattern: *Your drawing has improved.* **3.** the selection of the winning chance or chances in a lottery or raffle. **4.** the act of a person or thing that draws.

drawing board, a board on which paper or other material is placed or mounted for making drawings.
• **back to the drawing board.** back to a preliminary or planning stage.
• **on the drawing board.** in a preliminary or planning stage: *The new advertising campaign is still on the drawing board.*

drawing card, a person or thing, as a popular entertainer, that attracts much attention or a large audience.

drawing knife, drawknife.

drawing room 1. a room for receiving or entertaining guests, as a parlor or formal reception room. **2.** a private compartment in a sleeping car on a train. **3.** a formal reception, especially one that is held by royalty. [Short for *withdrawing room,* the room into which the ladies *withdrew* after dinner in earlier times.]

draw·knife (drô′nīf′) *n., pl.* **-knives** (-nīvz′). a tool consisting of a blade with a handle at each end, used for shaving or scraping a surface. Also, **drawing knife, drawshave.**

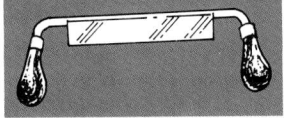

drawknife

drawl (drôl) *v.t., v.i.* to speak or pronounce slowly, esp. with a drawing out of the vowel sounds. —*n.* the act or manner of speech of a person who drawls. [Possibly from Dutch *dralen* to linger.] —**drawl′er,** *n.* —**drawl′ing·ly,** *adv.*

drawn (drôn) the past participle of **draw.**

drawn butter, melted butter, often thickened and seasoned, used as a sauce for food: *I looked forward to boiled lobster with drawn butter at my favorite seafood restaurant.*

drawn work, ornamental openwork that is made by drawing out threads from a fabric so as to form a pattern. The remaining threads are often formed into other patterns by needlework.

draw·shave (drô′shāv′) *n.* drawknife.

draw·string (drô′string′) *n.* a string, cord, or tape run through a hem, casing, or eyelets, as at the mouth of a bag, which, when pulled, draws together or closes an opening.

draw·tube (drô′tūb′, -tŭb′) *n.* a tube, as the one containing the eyepiece in a microscope or telescope, that slides up and down or in and out within another, larger tube.

dray (drā) *n.* a low, strong cart with detachable sides, used for carrying heavy loads. —*v.t.* to carry or transport by dray. [Old English *dræge* dragnet, from *dragan* to pull, drag.]

dray·age (drā′ij) *n.* **1.** the act of carrying or transporting by dray. **2.** the charge made for this.

dray·man (drā′mən) *n., pl.* **-men** (-mən). a person whose work is driving a dray.

dread (dred) *v.t.* **1.** to anticipate with fear or anxiety; fear greatly: *to dread flying.* **2.** to look forward to with misgiving or distaste: *I dread telling them the bad news.* **3.** *Archaic.* to be in awe of; venerate. —*n.* **1.** a fearful anticipation, as of impending evil or danger; great fear or uneasiness. **2.** a person or thing dreaded. **3.** *Archaic.* fearful reverence; awe. —*adj.* causing fear, terror, or awe: *a dread disease.* [Middle English *drēden* to fear greatly, short for Old English *ādrǣdan* to fear.] —For Synonyms *(n.),* see **fear.**

dread·ful (dred′fəl) *adj.* **1.** inspiring fear or awe; dire; terrible: *a dreadful omen.* **2.** very bad; awful: *a dreadful headache, a dreadful movie.* —**dread′ful·ly,** *adv.* —**dread′ful·ness,** *n.*

dread·nought (dred′nôt′) also, **dread·naught.** *n.* a battleship with heavy armor and high-powered guns. [From *Dreadnought,* a British battleship launched in 1906, the first of the modern type of battleship.]

dream (drēm) *n.* **1.** a series of thoughts, images, and sensations seen or experienced during sleep. **2.** a fanciful thought entertained while awake, esp. a wild or vain fancy; daydream: *I never thought I would win a free trip to Europe—not in my wildest dreams.* **3.** the mental state in which dreams occur. **4.** an object seen in a dream. **5.** a fervent hope or desire; cherished goal: *a dream of becoming a movie star.* **6.** something having great beauty or charm. —*v.,* **dreamed** or **dreamt, dream·ing.** —*v.i.* **1.** to have a dream or dreams: *I dreamt of you last night.* **2.** to have daydreams or fantasies: *He dreams too much in class. She dreams of going to medical school.* **3.** to think of as at all possible; have any conception of (usually with *of*): *I wouldn't dream of going without you.* —*v.t.* **1.** to see or imagine in a dream: *I dreamed I was a famous author.* **2.** to believe possible; suppose; imagine: *We never dreamed the play would be so long.* **3.** to spend (time) in reverie or dreaming (often with *away*): *to dream away the hours.* —*adj. Informal.* exactly as wished for or imagined; ideal: *That's my dream house.* [Old English *drēam* joy, noise, music; Modern English meaning influenced by Old Norse *draumr* vision.] —**dream′-less,** *adj.* —**dream′like′,** *adj.*
• **to dream up.** *Informal.* to create or devise in one's imagination; concoct: *to dream up an excuse.*

dream·boat (drēm′bōt′) *n. Slang.* a person or thing that is extremely attractive or desirable.

dream·er (drē′mər) *n.* **1.** a person who dreams. **2.** a person who seems to live in a world of dreams or fantasy; impractical or idle speculator.

dream·land (drēm′land′) *n.* **1.** a place where a person is said to be while sleeping; realm of dreams. **2.** a delightful or ideal place existing only in the imagination.

dreamt (dremt) a past tense and past participle of **dream.**

dream world, a world of illusion and fantasy.

dream·y (drē′mē) *adj.,* **dream·i·er, dream·i·est. 1.** like a dream; vague; indistinct: *a dreamy recollection.* **2.** given to dreaming or daydreaming: *a dreamy frame of mind.* **3.** pleasing to the senses; soothing; soft: *dreamy music.* **4.** of, relating to, or full

a	at	e	end	o	hot	u	up	hw	white		about
ā	ape	ē	me	ō	old	ū	use	ng	song	ə	taken
ä	far	i	it	ô	fork	ü	rule	th	thin		pencil
âr	care	ī	ice	oi	oil	u̇	pull	th	this		lemon
		îr	pierce	ou	out	ûr	turn	zh	measure		circus

of dreams. **5.** *Informal.* wonderful; ideal. —**dream′·ly,** *adv.*
—**dream′i·ness,** *n.*

drear (drîr) *adj. Archaic.* dreary.

drear·y (drîr′ē) *adj.,* **drear·i·er, drear·i·est. 1.** causing sadness or gloom; dismal; depressing: *a dreary room, dreary prospects for a job.* **2.** dull or uninteresting; monotonous: *Today was the dreariest day of the week.* [Old English *drēorig* sad.] —**drear′i·ly,** *adv.* —**drear′i·ness,** *n.*

dredge¹ (drej) *n.* **1.** an excavating apparatus for removing materials such as mud or sand from the bottom of a body of water. **2.** a dragnet for gathering oysters, crabs, and the like. —*v.,* **dredged, dredg·ing.** —*v.t.* **1.** to clear out, deepen, or enlarge with a dredge: *to dredge a harbor.* **2.** to gather or remove with or as with a dredge (often with *up*): *to dredge mud, to dredge up facts for an exposé.* —*v.i.* to use a dredge: *to dredge for oysters.* [Possibly going back to Old English *dragan* to pull, drag.]

dredge² (drej) *v.t.,* **dredged, dredg·ing.** to sprinkle or coat with a powdered substance, esp. flour or sugar. [From obsolete *dredge* sweetmeat, from Old English *dragge,* from Old French *dragie,* through Latin, from Greek *tragēmata,* plural of *tragēma* dessert, dried fruit, from *trōgein* to gnaw.]

dredg·er¹ (drej′ər) *n.* **1.** a person or thing that dredges. **2.** a barge used in dredging. [DREDGE¹ + -ER¹.]

dredg·er² (drej′ər) *n.* a container with a perforated lid, used for sprinkling powdered substances on food. [DREDGE² + -ER¹.]

dregs (dregz) *pl. n.* **1.** the sediment of liquids, esp. of beverages: *dregs of coffee, dregs of wine.* **2.** the most worthless or undesirable part: *the dregs of society.* [Probably from Old Norse *dreggjar* lees.]

drench (drench) *v.t.* **1.** to wet (someone or something) thoroughly; saturate; soak: *The sudden rainfall drenched the sightseers.* **2.** to force (an animal) to swallow a medicine. —*n.* **1.** the act of drenching. **2.** something that drenches. **3.** a dose of liquid medicine given orally, as with a syringe, to an animal. [Old English *drencan* to give to drink, drown.]

Dres·den (drez′dən) *n.* a fine porcelain decorated with elaborate, brightly colored designs, made near Dresden, Germany.

dress (dres) *v.,* **dressed** or **drest, dress·ing.** —*v.t.* **1.** to put clothes on; clothe: *The nurse dressed the baby.* **2.** to supply with clothing: *The costume designer dressed the entire cast.* **3.** to decorate, as by putting a display in; trim: *to dress a store window.* **4.** to clean or prepare for use or sale: *to dress a chicken, to dress leather.* **5.** to treat (a wound or sore) medicinally: *to dress a burn.* **6.** to comb and arrange (hair). **7.** to groom or curry (an animal): *to dress a horse.* **8.** to cultivate, prune, or fertilize. **9.** to make (wood or stone) smooth in preparation for a specific use. **10.** to get into proper alignment; adjust to a straight line: *to dress ranks.* —*v.i.* **1.** to put on clothes: *I dress quickly in the morning.* **2.** to select and wear clothes: *She dresses well.* **3.** to put on or wear formal clothes: *We are going to dress for the charity ball.* **4.** to come into proper alignment or form in a straight line, as troops. —*n.* **1.** a garment for a woman or girl, cut to appear as one piece and usually extending from the neck to the legs. **2.** clothing; apparel; attire: *soldiers in battle dress.* **3.** a style or choice of clothing; manner of wearing clothes: *conservative in one's dress.* **4.** external adornment, covering, or appearance: *trees in autumn dress.* —*adj.* **1.** of or for a dress: *dress material, a dress pattern.* **2.** worn or suitable for a formal or ceremonial occasion: *a dress suit, a dress uniform.* **3.** requiring formal dress: *a dress occasion.* [Old French *drecier* to arrange, set up, going back to Latin *dīrēctus* straight, just, past participle of *dīrigere* to straighten, guide.]

 · **to dress down.** *Informal.* to scold or reprimand severely.
 · **to dress ship.** to pay honor or respect by hoisting the flags of a ship, often by having a continuous line of flags flying from the bow to the stern.
 · **to dress up.** to put on formal wear or clothing more elaborate than that usually worn.

dres·sage (dre säzh′) *n.* the performance of elaborate gaits and unusual movements by a horse specially trained to respond to a rider's barely perceptible directions. [French *dressage,* from *dresser* to dress, arrange (from Old French *dresser*) + -*age* -age. See DRESS.]

dress circle, a section of seats in a theater that forms a ring around, and usually above, the orchestra section.

dress·er¹ (dres′ər) *n.* **1.** a person who dresses something: *a window dresser, a dresser of leather.* **2.** a person who assists another in dressing, as for the stage. **3.** a person who dresses in a particular way: *a fancy dresser, a good dresser.* **4.** any of several tools or machines for dressing or preparing materials, as leather or stone. [DRESS + -ER¹.]

dress·er² (dres′ər) *n.* **1.** a chest of drawers, often with a mirror; bureau. **2.** a sideboard or set of shelves for holding dishes and kitchen utensils. [Middle English *dressour,* from Old French *dreceor, dreceur* sideboard, from *drecier* to prepare, arrange.]

dress·ing (dres′ing) *n.* **1.** the act of a person or thing that dresses. **2.** a sauce, esp. for salads. **3.** a medication or bandage applied to a wound or sore. **4.** a mixture of bread or cracker crumbs and other ingredients, usually seasoned, used to stuff poultry, fish, or roasts; stuffing. **5.** manure or other fertilizing material.

dress·ing-down (dres′ing doun′) *n. Informal.* a severe scolding or reprimand.

dressing gown, a robe, esp. a long, loose one, usually worn before or while dressing or for lounging.

dressing room, a room for dressing, as backstage in a theater.

dressing station, a station set up near a combat area for giving medical attention to the wounded.

dressing table, a table, often with drawers, having a mirror to be used while grooming and dressing oneself. Also, **vanity.**

dress·mak·er (dres′mā′kər) *n.* a person whose work is making and altering dresses or other articles of clothing for women. —**dress′mak′ing,** *n.*

dress parade, a military or naval parade in dress uniform.

dress rehearsal, a full rehearsal in costume of a theatrical presentation or similar performance, esp. the final rehearsal in costume.

dress suit, a man's formal suit for evening wear.

dress·y (dres′ē) *adj.,* **dress·i·er, dress·i·est. 1.** suitable for formal occasions; elegant; elaborate: *a dressy blouse.* **2.** stylish; fashionable: *a dressy social affair.* —**dress′i·ly,** *adv.* —**dress′i·ness,** *n.*

drest (drest) a past tense and past participle of **dress.**

drew (drü) the past tense of **draw.**

drib·ble (drib′əl) *v.,* **-bled, -bling.** —*v.i.* **1.** to fall or flow in drops or small quantities; trickle: *Water dribbled out of the faucet.* **2.** to let saliva run from the mouth; drivel; drool. **3.** to come little by little or in small amounts (often with *in*): *Contributions dribbled in slowly.* **4.** in basketball, soccer, and some other games, to move a ball by a succession of bounces or kicks. —*v.t.* **1.** to let flow or fall in drops or small quantities: *The faucet is dribbling water.* **2.** to propel (a ball) by successive bounces or kicks. —*n.* **1.** a small quantity of a liquid falling in drops or flowing in a scanty stream. **2.** a small or insignificant quantity; fitful flow: *a dribble of funds.* **3.** the act of dribbling a ball. **4.** drizzling rain. [*Drib* (obsolete form of DRIP) + -LE.] —**drib′bler,** *n.*

drib·let (drib′lit) *also,* **drib·blet.** *n.* a small amount or part; bit.

dried (drīd) the past tense and past participle of **dry.**

dri·er (drī′ər) the comparative of **dry.** —*n.* **1.** *also,* **dryer.** a person or thing that dries. **2.** dryer *(defs. 1, 2).*

dri·est (drī′ist) the superlative of **dry.**

drift (drift) *v.i.* **1.** to be moved, driven, or borne along by or as by currents of water or air: *Columns of smoke drifted out of the chimney. We watched the leaves drift downstream. The two friends drifted apart over the years.* **2.** to move or seem to move aimlessly and without any particular goal or purpose: *The tramp drifted from town to town. Some people drift through life without ever settling down.* **3.** to accumulate in heaps by the force of wind or water: *The snow drifted against the garage.* —*v.t.* to cause to drift: *The wind drifted the sand.* —*n.* **1.** an act or instance of being driven along by or as by currents of water or air. **2.** the rate or direction of movement or drifting, esp. of a current of water. **3.** something driven along or heaped up by air or water currents: *Drifts of snow blocked the roads.* **4.** a general course of movement; tendency; trend: *The drift of the conversation switched from politics to religion.* **5.** a meaning or intent; purport: *I do not understand the drift of your remark.* **6.** a wide current of water, usually slow-moving, as in an ocean. **7.** material, as sand, gravel, or rocks, that has been moved from one place and deposited in another by a glacier or the melted water from a glacier. **8.** the deviation of a ship, aircraft, or missile from its course due to currents or crosswinds. **9.** a passage excavated horizontally or nearly horizontally in a mine, esp. one driven along the course of a vein or rock layer. [Partly from Old Norse *drift* snowdrift; partly from Middle Dutch *drift* herd, current.]

drift·age (drif′tij) *n.* **1.** the act of drifting. **2.** the amount of deviation caused by drifting. **3.** something that has drifted or been driven along or deposited by water or air currents.

drift·er (drif′tər) *n.* a person or thing that drifts, esp. one who moves aimlessly from one job or place to another.

drift·wood (drift′wůd′) *n.* wood drifting on or washed ashore by water.

drill¹ (dril) *n.* **1.a.** a tool with cutting edges or a pointed end used for boring holes in hard substances, usually by means of a rotary or hammering action. **b.** a machine operating such a tool. **2.** training or practice in military exercises, as marching or assembling a weapon. **3.** any strict, methodical training or instruction by repeated exercises and practice: *Our class got lots of drill in algebra.* **4.** an exercise used in such training: *a rifle drill, a spelling drill.* **5.** a sea snail, *Urosalpinx cinerea,* that bores through the shells of oysters and eats their flesh. Also *(def. 5),* **oyster drill.** —*v.t.* **1.** to pierce or bore a hole in (something) with or as with a drill: *The dentist drilled my tooth.* **2.** to make by boring: *I drilled three holes in the wall for the shelf brackets. They drilled two wells within one week.* **3.** to train or put through military exercises: *to drill recruits.* **4.** to train or instruct by repeated exercises and practice: *The teacher drilled the class in math all morning.* **5.** to impart or communi-

drill¹
electric hand drill

cate by constant repetition or strict training (with *into*): *Good manners were drilled into us from childhood.* —*v.i.* **1.** to bore or make a hole with or as with a drill: *to drill for oil.* **2.** to go through or perform drills: *The band drills for one hour every day.* [Dutch *dril,* from Middle Dutch *drillen* to bore, turn around, brandish.] —**drill′er,** *n.* —For Synonyms *(n.),* see **practice.**

drill² (dril) *n.* **1.** a machine for planting that makes a hole or furrow, drops the seed and sometimes fertilizer or other soil preparation, and then covers it with soil. **2.** a small furrow in which seeds are planted. **3.** a row of planted seeds. —*v.t.* **1.** to sow (seed) in rows. **2.** to sow or plant, as a field, in drills. [Possibly from archaic *drill* rill, small stream; related to German *Rille* furrow and *rillen* to groove.]

drill³ (dril) *n.* a closely woven, durable twilled cotton or linen fabric, used for such items as uniforms and work clothes. Also, **drilling.** [Short for *drilling,* modification of German *Drillich* canvas, ticking, going back to Latin *trilīx* having three threads, triply woven.]

drill⁴ (dril) *n.* a West African baboon, *Mandrillus leucophaeus,* related to, but less brightly colored and smaller than, the mandrill. [Probably of West African origin.]

drill·ing¹ (dril′ing) *n.* the act of a person or thing that drills.
drill·ing² (dril′ing) *n.* drill³.
drill·mas·ter (dril′mas′tər) *n.* **1.** a person who conducts military drills, esp. marching drills. **2.** an instructor who maintains strict discipline or who teaches by drilling.
drill press, a machine tool consisting of one or more drills mounted on an upright stand and having an adjustable horizontal table on which the material to be drilled is placed.
dri·ly (dri′lē) *adv.* dryly.

drink (dringk) *v.,* **drank** or *(archaic)* **drunk, drunk** or *(archaic)* **drunk·en** or *(archaic)* **drank, drink·ing.** —*v.t.* **1.** to take into the mouth and swallow (liquid): *We drink milk with our meals.* **2.** to take in or soak up (liquid or moisture); absorb: *The sponge drank up the water. The plants drank in the rain.* **3.** to swallow the contents of: *I quickly drank my cup of coffee.* **4.** to receive or absorb through the senses or the mind, esp. with eagerness and pleasure (with *in*): *They drank in the beauty of the woodland scene.* **5.a.** to give or join in (a toast): *The guests drank a toast to the couple's good fortune.* **b.** to honor or wish for with a toast: *I drink to your good health.* **6.** to bring to a specified state by drinking: *to drink a glass dry.* —*v.i.* **1.** to take liquid into the mouth and swallow it. **2.** to drink alcoholic liquor, esp. habitually or to excess. **3.** to make or join in a toast: *We drink to your continued success.* —*n.* **1.** a liquid for drinking; beverage: *Lemonade is my favorite summer drink.* **2.a.** a portion of liquid swallowed: *Would you like a drink of water?* **b.** a portion of alcoholic liquor. **3.** alcoholic liquor: *The restaurant serves food and drink.* **4.** the habitual or excessive use of alcoholic liquor. **5. the drink.** *Slang.* a body of water, esp. the ocean. [Old English *drincan* to imbibe.] —**drink′er,** *n.*
drink·a·ble (dring′kə bəl) *adj.* suitable or safe for drinking. —*n.* also, **drinkables.** something to drink; beverage.

drip (drip) *v.,* **dripped** or **dript, drip·ping.** —*v.i.* **1.** to fall in drops: *The rain came through the roof and dripped from the ceiling.* **2.** to have moisture or liquid falling off in drops: *The wet umbrella dripped all over the floor.* **3.** to be saturated or overflow: *This toast is dripping with butter.* —*v.t.* to let (something) fall in drops: *I accidentally dripped paint from the brush.* —*n.* **1.** a falling of liquid in drops. **2.** moisture or liquid falling in drops. **3.** the sound made by a liquid falling in drops. **4.** a projecting molding,

as on a cornice, for shedding rainwater. **5.** *Slang.* a dull or unattractive person. [Old English *dryppan* to let fall in drops.]
drip-dry (*adj.,* drip′drī′; *v.,* drip′drī′, -drī′) *adj.* of or designating a fabric or garment that dries quickly when hung dripping wet and requires little or no ironing. —*v.i.,* -**dried, -dry·ing.** to dry with few or no wrinkles when hung dripping wet: *a fabric that drip-dries quickly.*
drip·ping (drip′ing) *n.* **1.** the act or sound of a thing that drips: *The dripping of the leaky faucet kept me awake.* **2.** **drippings.** melted fat and juices that drip from meat, fowl, or fish while cooking. —*adv.* so as to drip; completely: *dripping wet.*
dripping pan, a pan placed under food while it is being cooked to catch and hold the drippings. Also, **drip pan.**
dript (dript) a past tense and past participle of **drip.**
drive (drīv) *v.,* **drove** or *(archaic)* **drave, driv·en, driv·ing.** —*v.t.* **1.** to propel or cause to move by or as by the application of physical force: *The waves drove the ship onto the rocks. The soldiers drove the enemy off.* **2.** to impel, goad, or force into some act or condition: *The noise from the construction site is enough to drive one mad. Oppression drove the people into open rebellion.* **3.** to put in motion and direct the movement of; steer: *to drive a car, to drive a team of horses.* **4.** to convey in a car or other vehicle: *Can you drive us to the party?* **5.** to cause to penetrate by force: *to drive a nail into wood.* **6.** to urge insistently to work or exertion, esp. excessively; overwork: *He's been driving himself lately and needs a vacation.* **7.** to carry on or bring about energetically and forcefully; execute vigorously: *She drives a hard bargain.* **8.a.** to cause to go rapidly, as by hitting or throwing with force: *The batter drove the ball over the fence.* **b.** *Golf.* to strike (the ball) forcefully, esp. from a tee. **9.** to set or keep in motion or operation; supply the motive or power for: *Steam drives the engine.* **10.** to form or produce by penetration: *They drove a tunnel through the mountain.* —*v.i.* **1.** to operate and steer a car or other vehicle: *Please don't drive so fast.* **2.** to go or be conveyed in a vehicle: *They drove through the park.* **3.** to go or be moved along swiftly before an impelling force; be impelled: *The ship drove before the gale.* **4.** to rush, dash, or move forcefully or violently: *The rain drove against the windshield of the car.* **5.** *Golf.* to strike the ball forcefully, esp. from a tee. —*n.* **1.** a trip in a car or other vehicle: *They took a drive in the country.* **2.** a driveway or a public road on which to drive: *The winding drive to the house was covered with gravel.* **3.a.** the act of driving, esp. a gathering together and impelling or urging forward, as of logs or animals: *a cattle drive.* **b.** the thing or things so driven: *a drive of logs floating down a river.* **4.** an organized group effort for some specific purpose; campaign: *a clothing drive, the club's annual membership drive.* **5.** forceful or dynamic energy or initiative; aggressiveness; vigor: *The committee's drive and enthusiasm helped make the project a success.* **6.** an impelling or motivating concern, interest, or longing: *a drive to succeed.* **7.** a vigorous or aggressive onward course or movement: *It seemed that nothing could stop their team's drive toward the goal line.* **8.** *Biology.* a strong, motivating urge or stimulus that incites an animal or person to action: *the hunger drive, the sex drive.* **9.** a large-scale military attack, usually consisting of a series of engagements sustained over a period of time. **10.a.** the act or instance of driving a ball, puck, or other object; forceful blow or stroke: *The batter hit a long drive to left field.* **b.** the manner in which a ball, puck, or other object is driven, or its flight when driven, as in golf. **11.** a part that transmits power to a machine or machine part. **12.** the manner in which power is applied to the wheels in a motor vehicle: *rear-wheel drive.* [Old English *drīfan* to force to move on, pursue, rush with violence.]
• **to drive at.** to attempt or intend to convey; suggest: *What were you driving at when you made that remark?*
• **to let drive.** to aim or release (a blow or missile).
drive-in (drīv′in′) *n.* **1.** an outdoor motion-picture theater where customers remain in their parked cars while viewing a movie projected on a large screen. **2.** any place of business, as a bank or restaurant, designed to serve customers while they remain in their cars. —*adj.* designed to give service to customers while they remain in their cars: *a drive-in restaurant, a drive-in bank.*
driv·el (driv′əl) *v.,* -**eled, -el·ing;** also, British, -**elled, -el·ling.** —*v.i.* **1.** to let saliva run from the mouth; dribble; slobber. **2.** to talk in a childish or foolish way; talk nonsense. —*v.t.* to utter childishly or foolishly: *to drivel absurdities.* —*n.* **1.** childish, foolish, or ridiculous talk; nonsense. **2.** saliva flowing from the

a	at	e	end	o	hot	u	up	hw	white		about
ā	ape	ē	me	ō	old	ū	use	ng	song		taken
ä	far	i	it	ô	fork	ü	rule	th	thin	ə	pencil
âr	care	ī	ice	oi	oil	u̇	pull	th	this		lemon
				îr	pierce	ou	out	ûr	turn	zh	measure		circus

D

mouth. [Old English *dreflian* to slobber.] —**driv′el·er**; *also, British*, **driv′el·ler**, *n.*

driv·en (driv′ən) *v.* the past participle of **drive**. —*adj.* **1.** piled up by the force of the wind: *driven snow.* **2.** motivated by a compulsive need or sense of urgency: *a driven person.*

driv·er (drī′vər) *n.* **1.** a person or thing that drives, esp. a person who drives a vehicle. **2.** a golf club with a wooden head, used to drive balls long distances from the tee; number one wood. **3.** any machine part that transmits motion or power.

driver ant, army ant.

driver's seat, a position of control, influence, or leadership.

drive shaft, a shaft that transmits power from a source to wheels or to other parts to be driven.

drive·way (drīv′wā′) *n.* a private road providing access to a house, garage, or other building.

driv·ing (drī′ving) *adj.* **1.** moving with force, intensity, or violence: *a driving rain.* **2.** extremely powerful or compelling; intensely energetic: *a driving desire to succeed, a driving guitar solo.* **3.** transmitting power or activating motion.

driving iron, a golf club with a metal head having very little loft; number one iron.

driving wheel, a wheel that transmits power or motion to some part of a machine.

driz·zle (driz′əl) *v.,* **-zled, -zling.** —*v.i.* to rain steadily in fine, mistlike drops. —*v.t.* to let fall in fine drops or a light stream: *to drizzle chocolate over cookies.* —*n.* a fine, misty rain. [Modification of Middle English *dresen* to fall, from Old English *drēosan.*] —**driz′zly,** *adj.*

drogue (drōg) *n.* **1.** a funnel-shaped device at the end of the fuel line of a tanker plane, used to aid the coupling of the fuel line to the plane being refueled. **2.** a parachute used to slow the descent of something, as a space capsule. Also, **drogue parachute. 3.** sea anchor. [Possibly a modification of DRAG.]

droll (drōl) *adj.* amusingly odd or quaint: *a droll fellow, droll antics.* [French *drôle* funny, odd, from Middle French *drolle* merry fellow, possibly from Middle Dutch *droll* funny little chap.] —**droll′ness,** *n.* —**drol′ly,** *adv.*

droll·er·y (drō′lə rē) *n., pl.* **-er·ies. 1.** the quality of being droll; quaint humor. **2.** something droll, as a whimsical drawing or story. **3.** the behavior or antics of a droll person; jesting: *a talent for drollery.*

drom·e·dar·y (drom′i der′ē, drum′-) *n., pl.* **-dar·ies.** a single-humped camel, *Camelus dromedarius,* native to Arabia and North Africa, valued for riding because of its relatively fast pace. Height: 6 feet (1.8 meters) at the shoulder. [Old French *dromedaire,* from Late Latin *dromedārius,* going back to Greek *dromas* running; because of its speed.]

dromedary

drone[1] (drōn) *n.* **1.** a male bee, esp. a honeybee, that develops from an unfertilized egg and does no work, its only function being to mate once with the queen bee, after which it dies. **2.** a person who lives on the labor of others; idler; loafer. **3.** a robot aircraft or ship controlled by radio signals, as certain pilotless reconnaissance planes. [Old English *drān* male bee.]

drone[2] (drōn) *v.,* **droned, dron·ing.** —*v.i.* **1.** to make a continuous, low, humming sound: *The planes droned overhead.* **2.** to talk in a dull, monotonous tone: *The speaker droned on.* —*v.t.* to say (something) in a dull, monotonous tone. —*n.* **1.** a dull, continuous buzzing or humming sound: *the drone of countless mosquitoes.* **2.** one of the bass pipes of a bagpipe that make a continuous, unvarying tone. [Possibly from DRONE[1]; possibly imitative of the sound made by a bee.]

drool (drül) *v.i.* **1.** to let saliva run from the mouth; drivel: *The baby drooled all over the bib.* **2.** to water at the mouth, as in anticipation of food: *The dog drooled as I opened the can of food.* **3.** *Informal.* to show great delight or pleasure; express great enthusiasm: *We drooled over the new car.* —*v.t.* to let run from the mouth. [From DRIVEL.]

droop (drüp) *v.i.* **1.** to hang or sink down or incline downward, as from weakness or exhaustion: *The dead flowers drooped over the side of the vase.* **2.** to become weak; lose energy or vigor; flag: *The losing team's spirits drooped.* **3.** to become dejected or depressed; lose spirit or courage. —*v.t.* to let hang or sink down; incline downward: *to droop one's head.* —*n.* the act or fact of drooping; drooping position or state. [Old Norse *drūpa* to hang the head, sink.] —**droop′ing·ly,** *adv.*

Synonyms *v.i.* Droop, wilt[1], and **sag** mean to hang or sink down or decline downwards. **Droop** suggests a loss of vigor or strength: *Their heads drooped in fatigue.* But it may connote merely a downward aspect: *The flag drooped in the still air.* **Wilt** connotes loss of freshness: *a vase filled with wilting flowers.* **Sag** suggests sinking through a loss of firmness: *an old sofa sagging on its broken springs, an old man with sagging muscles.*

droop·y (drü′pē) *adj.,* **droop·i·er, droop·i·est. 1.** drooping or tending to droop. **2.** gloomy; melancholy; forlorn: *a droopy face.* —**droop′i·ly,** *adv.* —**droop′i·ness,** *n.*

drop (drop) *v.,* **dropped** or **dropt, drop·ping.** —*v.i.* **1.** to fall in drops, as a liquid: *Beads of perspiration dropped from his brow.* **2.** to fall or descend, esp. rapidly or suddenly: *The wet dish dropped from my hand. The ground drops sharply as you go down the trail.* **3.** to fall down or sink, as from exhaustion or injury: *The runners dropped to their knees after the race.* **4.** to fall or decline in degree or amount; become less; diminish; decrease (often with *off*): *Her voice dropped to a whisper. Business dropped off during the summer.* **5.** to fall or move to a position that is lower, inferior, or further back: *He dropped behind the other runners.* **6.** to cease to appear or be seen; disappear; vanish: *They dropped from public notice after the trial.* **7.** to cease to be of concern; come to an end; lapse: *Let the matter drop.* **8.** to pay a casual or unexpected call; come or stop casually (with *in, over,* or *by*): *My cousins dropped in on us as they were passing through town.* **9.** to fall or pass into a particular state, condition, or activity: *The baby dropped off to sleep.* **10.** *Archaic.* to move along gently with a current of water or air. —*v.t.* **1.** to let fall by or as by releasing hold of: *She dropped her keys on the floor.* **2.** to cause to descend from one level to another; cause to sink, move, or hang down; lower: *If the skirt is too short, you can drop the hem. Conscious that he was being stared at, he dropped his eyes.* **3.** to let fall in small amounts: *The careless painter dropped paint all over the floor.* **4.** to stop pursuing, treating, or dealing with; cease to concern oneself with; abandon: *to drop a course in school, to drop a subject of discussion.* **5.** to write and send (a letter or note) in an offhand manner: *Drop me a line when you have time.* **6.** to utter or refer to in or as in a casual or incidental way: *I dropped a hint about what I'd like for my birthday.* **7.** to let out or leave; deposit (often with *off*): *Please drop me at the corner. I'll drop the book off at your house.* **8.** (of animals) to give birth to: *The mare dropped a foal.* **9.** to cause to fall, as by tackling, striking, or shooting; bring down: *The hunter dropped the deer with one shot.* **10.** to leave out; omit: *to drop a stitch in knitting, to drop a letter in pronouncing a word.* **11.** to break off an association or connection with; dismiss; discharge (often with *from*): *The firm dropped ten employees. They were dropped from the club.* **12.** to release (food, supplies, or personnel) by parachute from an aircraft. **13.** *Slang.* to lose: *We dropped $100 at the racetrack. The team dropped three games in a row.* —*n.* **1.** a small quantity of liquid shaped like a tiny sphere or pear: *a drop of water, a drop of blood.* **2.** a very small amount of liquid: *There wasn't a drop of milk left.* **3.** a very small amount of anything: *The tired hikers didn't have a drop of strength left.* **4.** something resembling a drop of liquid in shape or size, as an earring, pendant, or piece of candy. **5.** the act or instance of dropping; descent; fall: *We watched the drop of the parachutists from the plane.* **6.** a sudden decline or decrease: *a drop in prices, a drop in temperature.* **7. drops.** liquid medicine to be administered in drops: *The doctor put drops in my eyes to dilate the pupils.* **8.** the distance between a higher and a lower level; distance or depth to which anything drops: *There is a 15-foot drop from the second floor to the street.* **9.** something designed or arranged to fall or slide from above, or to be lowered, as a trap door. **10.** a slit or other opening, as in a mailbox, into which something is inserted or dropped. **11.** a curtain that can be raised and lowered, used as a backdrop for a presentation or part of a presentation. Also, **drop curtain. 12.** the dropping of food, supplies, or personnel by parachute; airdrop. [Old English *dropa* globule of liquid.]

• **a drop in the bucket.** an insignificant or tiny portion, as of what is needed: *The money that the charity ball raised was only a drop in the bucket.*

• **at the drop of a hat.** without any hesitation or inducement; immediately.

• **to drop off.** to fall asleep.

• **to drop out.** to stop being a member or participant; withdraw; quit.

• **to get** (or **have**) **the drop on.** *Informal.* **a.** to aim and be ready to shoot a gun at (a person) before the person can draw a gun. **b.** to get (or have) an advantage over.

drop cloth, a large sheet, as of cloth or plastic, used to protect furniture, floors, and the like against dripping or spilled paint.

drop cookie, a cookie made by dropping batter onto a cookie sheet for baking.

drop·forge (drop′fôrj′) *v.t.*, **-forged, -forg·ing.** to forge (hot metal) into shape with a device employing the force of a dropped weight, as a drop hammer.

drop hammer, a device for pounding metal into shape, having a heavy weight that is raised by machinery and then dropped on the metal to be shaped. Also, **drop press.**

drop-kick (drop′kik′) *v.t., v.i.* to give a drop kick to (a football). —**drop′-kick′er,** *n.*

drop kick, a kick given to a football just as it reaches the ground after being dropped by the kicker.

drop leaf, a hinged section, as of a table, that can be folded down when not in use. —**drop′-leaf′,** *adj.*

drop·let (drop′lit) *n.* a tiny drop.

drop·light (drop′līt′) *n.* a light fixture that can be suspended from a ceiling or other surface, often with a flexible, expandable cord.

drop·out (drop′out′) *also,* **drop-out.** *n.* **1.** a student who withdraws from school, esp. high school, before graduating. **2.** a person who drops out or withdraws, as from society.

drop·per (drop′ər) *n.* **1.** a person or thing that drops. **2.** a glass or plastic tube with a rubber bulb at one end and a small opening at the other end, used for measuring, transferring, or dispensing liquids in drops.

drop·ping (drop′ing) *n.* **1.** the act of a person or thing that drops. **2.** **droppings.** the dung of animals. **3.** *also,* **droppings.** something that drops or falls in drops.

drop press, drop hammer.

drop·si·cal (drop′si kəl) *adj.* of, relating to, or suffering from dropsy.

drop·sy (drop′sē) *n.* edema.

dropt (dropt) a past tense and past participle of **drop.**

drosh·ky (drosh′kē) *also,* **dros·ky** (dros′kē). *n., pl.* **-kies.** any of various light, open, four-wheeled carriages originating and formerly used in Russia. [Russian *drozhki,* diminutive of *drogi* wagon.]

dro·soph·i·la (drō sof′ə lə) *n., pl.* **-las** or **-lae** (-lē′). fruit fly *(def. 1).* [Modern Latin *drosophila,* from Greek *drosos* dew + *philos* loving.]

dross (drôs, dros) *n.* **1.** waste or impure matter that rises to the surface of molten metals. **2.** any worthless matter; refuse; waste. [Old English *drōs* dregs, dirt.]

drought (drout) *also,* **drouth** (drouth). *n.* **1.** a long period of dry weather; prolonged lack of normal or sufficient rainfall. **2.** a prolonged scarcity or shortage; dearth: *a period in history marked by a cultural drought.* [Old English *drūgath* dryness.] —**drought′y;** *also,* **drouth′y,** *adj.*

drove[1] (drōv) a past tense of **drive.**

drove[2] (drōv) *n.* **1.** a group of animals moving or driven along together: *a drove of cattle, a drove of sheep.* **2.** a group of human beings moving or acting together; crowd: *On a hot, muggy day people head for the beaches in droves.* —*v.t., v.i.,* **droved, drov·ing.** to drive (cattle or other animals). [Middle English *drove,* from Old English *drāf* herd, from *drīfan* to drive, force to move on.]

dro·ver (drō′vər) *n.* **1.** a person who takes a drove of cattle, sheep, or other animals to market. **2.** a sheep or cattle dealer.

drown (droun) *v.i.* to die by suffocation in water or other liquid. —*v.t.* **1.** to kill by suffocation in water or other liquid. **2.** to cover with or as with a flood; inundate; drench: *The dam broke and its waters drowned the entire valley. I drowned my pancakes in syrup.* **3.** to lessen or smother the sound of by greater loudness; muffle (often with *out*): *The music drowned out her words.* **4.** to get rid of or obliterate as if by immersion; submerge: *He tried to drown his sorrows by overworking.* [Possibly going back to Old English *druncnian* to become drunk, sink.]

drowse (drouz) *v.,* **drowsed, drows·ing.** —*v.i.* **1.** to be half asleep; doze: *I was drowsing during the lecture.* **2.** to be or grow inactive, dull, or sluggish. —*v.t.* to pass (time) drowsily or in drowsing (often with *away*): *to drowse away the morning.* —*n.* the act of drowsing or the state of being half asleep. [Possibly going back to Old English *drūsian* to sink, be sluggish.]

drow·sy (drou′zē) *adj.,* **-si·er, -si·est.** **1.** sleepy or inclined to sleep; half asleep: *I felt drowsy after that large dinner.* **2.** characterized by peaceful inactivity: *a drowsy little village.* **3.** inducing lethargy or sleepiness; lulling: *drowsy summer days.* —**drow′si·ly,** *adv.* —**drow′si·ness,** *n.*

drub (drub) *v.t.,* **drubbed, drub·bing.** **1.** to beat severely, as with a stick; cudgel; thrash. **2.** to defeat decisively; rout: *We drubbed the other team.* [Possibly from Arabic *darb* a beating with a stick.] —**drub′ber,** *n.*

drub·bing (drub′ing) *n.* **1.** a severe beating; thrashing. **2.** a decisive or humiliating defeat, as in an athletic contest.

drudge (druj) *n.* **1.** a person who works hard at wearying, tedious, or menial tasks. **2.** a person who works in a routine,

slavish, or unimaginative way. —*v.i.,* **drudged, drudg·ing.** to work hard at wearying, tedious, or menial tasks. [Of uncertain origin.]

drudg·er·y (druj′ə rē) *n., pl.* **-er·ies.** wearying, tedious, or menial labor.

drug (drug) *n.* **1.** any chemical agent that affects living cells, esp. one used to treat disease in human beings and animals. **2.** a substance to which a person may become addicted; narcotic. —*v.t.,* **drugged, drug·ging.** **1.** to administer drugs to, esp. narcotic drugs: *to drug a patient before an operation.* **2.** to add a drug or drugs to (food or drink), esp. narcotic or poisonous drugs. **3.** to affect or overcome, as if with a drug: *She was drugged by the music. He was drugged with sleep.* [Old French *drogue* medical ingredient, possibly from Dutch *droog* dry (with reference to dry ingredients).]

drug abuse, the use of a drug for other than medicinal purposes, usually a cause or result of drug addiction.

drug addict, a person who is addicted to narcotics.

drug·gist (drug′ist) *n.* **1.** a person licensed to fill prescriptions; pharmacist. **2.** a person who owns or operates a drugstore.

drug·store (drug′stôr′) *n.* a store where medicines, drugs, medical supplies, and miscellaneous merchandise are sold. Also, **pharmacy.**

dru·id (drü′id) *also,* **Dru·id.** *n.* a member of a pre-Christian religious order among the ancient Celts of Gaul and the British Isles. Druids functioned as religious leaders, teachers, judges, and poets. [Latin *Druidēs* priests of ancient Gaul; of Celtic origin.] —**dru·id′ic;** *also,* **dru·id′i·cal,** *adj.* —**dru′id·ism,** *n.*

drum (drum) *n.* **1.** a percussion instrument usually consisting of a hollow cylinder or frame with a membrane stretched tightly over one or both ends, played by beating on the membrane, as with sticks or the hands. **2.** the sound produced when a drum is beaten. **3.** any similar sound: *the drum of fingers on a table.* **4.** something resembling a drum in shape. **5.** a cylindrical metal container, as for oil. **6.** a metal cylinder around which something, as cable, is wound. **7.** eardrum. **8.** any of various saltwater and freshwater fish, family Sciaenidae, that make a drumming sound. Also, **drumfish.** —*v.,* **drummed, drum·ming.** —*v.i.* **1.** to beat or play a drum. **2.** to beat or tap rhythmically or repeatedly: *I drummed on the desk with my fingers.* **3.** to sound like a drum; pound; resound: *The noise drummed in our ears.* **4.** (of the partridge and other birds) to make a hollow, thumping sound by beating the wings. —*v.t.* to perform or play on or as on a drum. [Middle Dutch *tromme* the percussion instrument.]

· **to drum into.** to drive or force into by persistent or constant repetition.

· **to drum out of.** to expel or dismiss from in disgrace: *They drummed him out of the army.*

· **to drum up.** to obtain or create by vigorous effort: *She tried to drum up support for preserving the historic building by writing letters and making phone calls.*

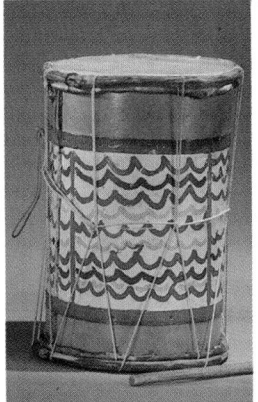

drums from the
Dominican Republic (left) and Korea (right)

a	at	e	end	o	hot	u	up	hw	white		about
ā	ape	ē	me	ō	old	ū	use	ng	song	ə	taken
ä	far	i	it	ô	fork	ü	rule	th	thin		pencil
âr	care	ī	ice	oi	oil	u̇	pull	th	this		lemon
		îr	pierce	ou	out	ûr	turn	zh	measure		circus

D

drum·beat (drum′bēt′) *n.* the sound of a stroke on a drum.

drum·fish (drum′fish′) *n.*, *pl.* **-fish** or **-fishes.** drum *(def. 8)*.

drum·head (drum′hed′) *n.* the skin or membrane stretched over the end or ends of a drum.

drumhead court-martial, a court-martial held during military operations to try offenses without delay. [From the former use of a *drumhead* as a table for the judges during such courts-martial.]

drum·lin (drum′lin) *n.* an oval hill formed from glacial deposits. [Irish Gaelic *druim* back, ridge + -LIN(G¹).]

drum major, a person who leads or directs a marching band or drum and bugle corps.

drum majorette, a girl or woman who twirls a baton while marching with a band or drum and bugle corps, as in a parade. Also, **majorette.**

drum·mer (drum′ər) *n.* **1.** a person or thing that drums. **2.** *Informal.* a traveling salesperson.

drum·stick (drum′stik′) *n.* **1.** a stick for beating a drum. **2.** the lower part of the leg of a fowl, esp. when cooked.

drunk (drungk) a past participle and past tense of **drink.** —*adj.* **1.** without normal control of one's faculties because of excessive drinking of alcoholic liquor; intoxicated; inebriated. **2.** powerfully affected; overwhelmed: *drunk with success, drunk with joy.* —*n.* *Informal.* **1.** a person who is drunk, esp. one who is habitually drunk. **2.** a drinking spree; binge.

drunk·ard (drung′kərd) *n.* a person who habitually drinks alcoholic liquor to excess; a person who is often drunk.

drunk·en (drung′kən) *v. Archaic.* a past participle of **drink.** —*adj.* **1.** drunk; intoxicated. **2.** habitually drunk. **3.** caused by or characteristic of the state of being drunk: *a drunken rage, a drunken stupor.* —**drunk′en·ly,** *adv.* —**drunk′en·ness,** *n.*

drunk·o·me·ter (drung kom′i tər) *n.* a device that chemically analyzes the breath to determine the alcohol content of a person's blood.

dru·pa·ceous (drü pā′shəs) *adj.* **1.** of or like a drupe. **2.** producing drupes.

drupe (drüp) *n.* a fleshy or fibrous fruit containing a hard pit or stone that encloses the seed. Cherries, peaches, almonds, and avocados are drupes. Also, **stone fruit.** [Latin *drup(p)a* overripe olive, from Greek *druppā,* from *drupepēs* ripened on the tree.]

drupe·let (drüp′lit) *n.* a small drupe, esp. one of the small drupes that form an aggregate fruit such as the raspberry or blackberry.

Dru·ry Lane (drur′ē) a street in London, England, noted for its theaters.

Druse (drüz) *also,* **Druze.** *n.* a member of a sect found chiefly in Syria and Lebanon that, although considered a branch of Islam, combines elements of Christianity, Judaism, and other religions. [Arabic *durūz,* plural of *darazī* a Druse, from *Ismail al-Darazī* Ismail the tailor, who founded the sect in the eleventh century.]

druth·ers (druth′ərz) *pl. n. Informal.* one's choice or preference: *If I had my druthers, I would leave right now.* [Plural of *druther,* contraction of *would rather.*]

dry (drī) *adj.,* **dri·er** or **dry·er, dri·est** or **dry·est. 1.** not wet or damp; free from moisture: *dry clothes, dry kindling.* **2.** exhausted of its supply of water or other liquid; empty of liquid contents: *The well has been dry for a month.* **3.** not under or in water: *They stepped from the boat onto dry land.* **4.** having or characterized by little or no rainfall: *It was the driest summer in years.* **5.** characterized by an absence or deficiency of normal moisture: *My skin becomes dry in the winter.* **6.** free from tears; not accompanied by tears: *dry eyes, a dry sob.* **7.** wanting water to drink; thirsty: *We were dry after the long climb.* **8.** without butter or other spreads: *dry toast.* **9.** not giving milk: *a dry cow.* **10.** marked by the absence of liquid discharge, as phlegm: *a dry cough.* **11.** witty in an ironic, matter-of-fact way: *dry humor, a dry remark.* **12.** not interesting; dull; boring: *a dry subject.* **13.** lacking embellishments; plain; bare: *a dry style of writing, dry facts.* **14.** lacking warmth, cordiality, or emotion; indifferent; cold: *a dry greeting.* **15.** consisting of substances that are not liquid; solid: *dry cereal, dry provisions.* **16.** free from sweetness or fruitiness: *a dry wine.* **17.** *Informal.* opposing or prohibiting the manufacture, sale, or use of alcoholic beverages: *a dry state, a dry law.* —*v.,* **dried, dry·ing.** —*v.t.* **1.** to make dry; remove moisture from (often with *off*): *He dried the dishes. She dried her hair.* **2.** to deprive wholly of moisture or stop the flow of; evaporate completely (with *up*): *The sun dried up the puddles.* —*v.i.* **1.** to become dry; lose moisture (often with *off* or *out*): *The clothes dried in the sun. This ink dries quickly.* **2.** to lose all moisture or cease to flow (with *up*): *The creek dried up last summer.* —*n., pl.* **drys.** *Informal.* prohibitionist. [Old English *drȳge* free from moisture, arid.]

　·**to dry up. a.** to cease to be productive: *After the third novel, the author's imagination seemed to dry up.* **b.** *Slang.* to stop talking.

dry·ad (drī′əd, -ad) *also,* **Dry·ad.** *n., pl.* **-ads** or **-a·des** (-ə dēz′). in Greek mythology, a nymph living in or guarding woods and trees. [Latin *dryas,* from Greek *dryas,* from *drȳs* tree.]

dry battery, a battery consisting of dry cells.

dry cell, a voltaic cell in which the electrolyte is in a form that does not spill, as a paste or jelly.

dry-clean (drī′klēn′) *v.t.* to subject to dry cleaning.

dry cleaner 1. a person or business that does dry cleaning. **2.** a substance used in dry cleaning.

dry cleaning 1. the act or process of cleaning garments or other articles of cloth with chemical solvents other than water. **2.** articles cleaned in this way.

dry-dock (drī′dok′) *v.t.* to put in a dry dock. —*v.i.* to go into a dry dock.

dry dock, any of various watertight structures in which a ship can be docked to allow for such work as repair, inspection, or cleaning of the hull.

ship in **dry dock**

dry·er (drī′ər) *also* (defs. 1, 2), **drier.** *n.* **1.** a device or appliance for drying: *a hair dryer, a clothes dryer.* **2.** a substance added to paints, varnishes, and other materials to make them dry more quickly. **3.** drier *(def. 1).*

dry·farm (drī′färm′) *v.t., v.i.* to practice dry farming (on land).

dry farming, the growing of crops on unirrigated land in semi-arid areas by using methods that conserve soil moisture, as contour plowing. —**dry farmer.**

dry fly, an artificial fly used in fishing that floats on the surface of the water.

dry goods, fabrics and related items, as thread, ribbon, or lace, as distinguished from other merchandise, as hardware or groceries.

dry ice, solid carbon dioxide, made by compressing and cooling the gas, which freezes at −110 degrees Fahrenheit. It is a widely used refrigerant because it changes from a solid back to a gas without melting. Trademark: **Dry Ice.**

dry·ly (drī′lē) *also,* **drily.** *adv.* in a dry manner.

dry measure, a system of units for measuring the volume of dry commodities, as grain, vegetables, or fruit. For Weights and Measures table, see **weight.**

dry·ness (drī′nis) *n.* the state or quality of being dry.

dry-nurse (drī′nûrs′) *v.t.,* **-nursed, -nurs·ing.** to be a dry nurse.

dry nurse, a nurse who takes care of a baby without suckling it. ➡ distinguished from **wet nurse.**

dry·o·pith·e·cine (drī′ō pith′ə sēn′) *n.* any of a group of extinct apes, genus *Dryopithecus* and related genera, living from 20 to 10 million years ago in Africa and Eurasia, thought to include the ancestors of modern apes and to be related to the stock that gave rise to modern humans. [Modern Latin *Dryopithecus,* from Greek *drȳs* tree + *pithēkos* ape.]

dry·point (drī′point′) *n.* **1.** the technique or process of engraving with a sharp needle on copperplate without the use of acid. **2.** the needle so used. **3.** a print or engraving made from a drypoint plate.

dry rot 1. the decay of seasoned timber so that it crumbles to a dry powder, caused by any of various fungi. **2.** any of various fungous diseases that attack fruits, vegetables, and other living plants, causing the infected part of the plant to become hard and dry. **3.** a fungus causing dry rot.

dry run 1. *Military.* a firing practice, bombing run, or other exercise carried out without the use of live ammunition. **2.** any practice session or trial run; rehearsal.

dry·shod (drī′shod′) *adj., adv.* having or keeping one's shoes or feet dry; without getting the feet wet.

dry·wall (drī′wôl′) *n.* plasterboard. [DRY + WALL.]

dry wash 1. laundry that has been washed and dried, but not ironed. **2.** wash *(def. 10).*

d.s. 1. daylight saving. **2.** *Commerce.* days after sight.

D.S. *also,* **d.s., d.S.** *Music.* repeat a passage or section from the sign 𝄋 or :S:. ➡ used as a direction to the performer. [Abbreviation of Italian *dal segno* from the sign.]

D.S. *also,* **D.Sc.** Doctor of Science.
DSC, Distinguished Service Cross.
DSM, Distinguished Service Medal.
DSO, Distinguished Service Order.
DST, daylight saving time.
d.t.'s (dē′tēz′) *Informal.* delirium tremens.
du·al (dü′əl, dū′-) *adj.* **1.** composed or consisting of two; two-fold; double: *dual controls, dual ownership.* **2.** designating or relating to two. **3.** *Grammar.* in some languages, as Sanskrit and ancient Greek, of or signifying two persons or things. [Latin *duālis* containing two, from *duo* two.] —**du′al·ly,** *adv.*
du·al·ism (dü′ə liz′əm, dū′-) *n.* **1.** the state of being dual; duality. **2.** the theory that all the phenomena of the universe can be explained in terms of two distinct essential factors, such as body and soul or good and evil. ➡ distinguished from **monism** and **pluralism.** —**du′al·ist,** *n.*
du·al·is·tic (dü′ə lis′tik, dū′-) *adj.* **1.** of or relating to dualism. **2.** characterized by duality; dual. —**du′al·is′ti·cal·ly,** *adv.*
du·al·i·ty (dü al′i tē, dū-) *n., pl.* **-ties.** the state or quality of being dual.
du·al-pur·pose (dü′əl pûr′pəs, dū′-) *adj.* having or designed for two functions or uses.
dub[1] (dub) *v.t.,* **dubbed, dub·bing. 1.** to confer knighthood upon by tapping on the shoulder with a sword; make, or designate as, a knight. **2.a.** to give a title or nickname to; name: *Her friends dubbed her "Freckles."* **b.** to speak of or refer to as: *They dubbed him a traitor.* **3.** to make smooth, as by cutting, rubbing, or beating: *to dub wood, to dub leather.* [Middle English *dubben,* from Old English *dubbian* literally, to strike.]
dub[2] (dub) *Slang. n.* a clumsy person. —*v.t., v.i.,* **dubbed, dub·bing.** to execute poorly; bungle: *to dub a golf shot.* [Of uncertain origin.]
dub[3] (dub) *v.t.,* **dubbed, dub·bing. 1.** to provide (a film or other recording) with a new soundtrack, esp. one in which the dialogue is in another language. **2.** to insert or substitute (music, dialogue, or other sounds) in the soundtrack of a film or other recording (often with *in*). [Short for DOUBLE.]
du·bi·e·ty (dü bī′i tē, dū-) *n., pl.* **-ties. 1.** the state or quality of being dubious. **2.** something doubtful or uncertain; matter of doubt.
du·bi·ous (dü′bē əs, dū′-) *adj.* **1.** feeling doubt or wavering in opinion; hesitant; skeptical: *I'm dubious about your chances for success.* **2.** viewed with or open to doubt or suspicion; questionable; suspect: *a dubious reputation.* **3.** causing doubt; not clear; ambiguous or equivocal: *a dubious reply that confuses the issue.* **4.** of uncertain or unpredictable outcome: *in dubious battle.* [Latin *dubiōsus* doubtful, from *dubium* doubt.] —**du′bi·ous·ly,** *adv.* —**du′bi·ous·ness,** *n.* —For Synonyms, see **doubtful.**
du·bi·ta·ble (dü′bi tə bəl, dū′-) *adj.* open to doubt; questionable; doubtful. [Latin *dubitābilis,* from *dubitāre* to be uncertain.]
du·cal (dü′kəl, dū′-) *adj.* of or relating to a duke or duchy. [French *ducal,* from *duc* duke, from Latin *dux* leader.]
duc·at (duk′ət) *n.* **1.** any of several gold or silver coins formerly used in certain European countries. **2.** *Slang.* a ticket, as for a sports event. [Italian *ducato* the coin, duchy, from Late Latin *ducātus* duchy, from Latin *dux* leader; with reference to the inscription with the word *ducatus* on ducats issued in Venice in the thirteenth century.]
du·ce (dü′chā) *n. Italian.* **1.** a leader. **2.** il Duce. the title assumed by Benito Mussolini as head of the Italian fascist state. [Italian *duce,* from Latin *dux* leader. Doublet of DOGE, DUKE.]
duch·ess (duch′is) *n.* **1.** the wife or widow of a duke. **2.** a woman holding in her own right a rank equal to a duke's, esp. the female sovereign of a duchy. [Old French *duchesse* wife of a duke, feminine of *duc* duke, from Latin *dux* leader.]
duch·y (duch′ē) *n., pl.* **duch·ies.** the territory under the rule of a duke or duchess; dukedom.
duck[1] (duk) *n.* **1.** any of various wild or domestic waterfowl, family Anatidae, having relatively short legs and neck, webbed feet, and usually a broad, flat bill. **2.** a female duck, as distinguished from a male, or drake. **3.** the flesh of a duck used as food. **4.** *Slang.* a person; fellow: *an odd duck.* **5.** *also,* **ducks.** *British. Slang.* a dear; darling; pet. ➡ used as singular. [Middle English *doke* the waterfowl, from Old English *duce* literally, ducker, diver.]
duck[2] (duk) *v.t.* **1.** to plunge or thrust under water quickly or suddenly: *We ducked our swimming instructor in the lake.* **2.** to

lower or bend (the head or body) suddenly and quickly: *I ducked my head to avoid being hit.* **3.** to avoid or evade: *to duck a blow, to duck a question.* —*v.i.* **1.** to lower the head or body suddenly; crouch, as to avoid being hit: *We all ducked when we heard the shots.* **2.** to move quickly; dart: *to duck in and out of a store.* —*n.* the act of ducking. [Middle English *douken* to plunge, dive.] —**duck′er,** *n.*
duck[3] (duk) *n.* **1.** any of various very durable cotton fabrics, similar to but lighter in weight than canvas, used for making small sails, tents, and clothing. **2. ducks.** trousers made of this. [Dutch *doek* linen cloth, canvas.]
duck[4] (duk) *n.* an amphibious military truck, used esp. during World War II. [Modification of its code name, *DUKW.*]
duck·bill (duk′bil′) *n.* platypus. Also, **duck-billed platypus.**
duck-billed (duk′bild′) *adj.* having a bill like that of a duck.
duck·ie (duk′ē) *adj.,* **duck·i·er, duck·i·est.** ducky[1].
ducking stool, a device for punishment formerly used in England and colonial America, consisting of a long plank with a chair at one end in which offenders were tied to be plunged into water.
duck·ling (duk′ling) *n.* a young duck.
duck·pin (duk′pin′) *n.* **1. duckpins.** a bowling game played with pins and a ball smaller than those used in tenpins. ➡ used as singular. **2.** a pin used in this game.
ducks and drakes, the game of skimming flat stones or other objects across the surface of water so as to make them skip several times.
   ·to make ducks and drakes of or **play (at) ducks and drakes with.** to handle recklessly; squander.
duck soup *Slang.* something easy to do or accomplish.
duck·weed (duk′wēd′) *n.* any of various very small green plants, genus *Lemna* or *Spirodela,* having no true stems and leaves, that float on still water, often forming a coating on the surface. They are the smallest and simplest of the flowering plants.
duck·y[1] (duk′ē) *also,* **duckie.** *adj.,* **duck·i·er, duck·i·est.** *Slang.* fine; delightful; excellent. [DUCK[1] + -Y[1].]
duck·y[2] (duk′ē) *n., pl.* **duck·ies.** *British. Slang.* a dear; darling; pet. [DUCK[1] + -Y[2].]
duct (dukt) *n.* **1.** a tube, pipe, or channel that conveys or conducts something, such as a liquid or gas. **2.** a tube or channel for carrying a body fluid, esp. a fluid secreted by a gland. **3.** a pipe or channel for carrying electric or telephone wires or cables. [Latin *ductus* a leading, conducting.] —**duct′less,** *adj.*
duc·tile (duk′təl) *adj.* **1.** able to be hammered out thin or drawn out into wire without breaking; malleable: *ductile metals.* **2.** easily molded or shaped; pliable; plastic: *Modeling clay is ductile.* **3.** easily controlled or influenced; compliant; tractable: *a ductile person.* [Latin *ductilis* easy to lead, from *dūcere* to lead.] —**duc·til·i·ty** (duk til′i tē), *n.* —For Synonyms, see **pliable.**
ductless gland, endocrine gland.
duct·work (dukt′wûrk′) *n.* a system of ducts used to carry liquids or gases. [DUCT + WORK.]
dud (dud) *n. Informal.* **1.** a bomb or shell that fails to explode. **2. duds.** clothing. **3.** a person or thing that is a failure. [Of uncertain origin.]
dude (düd, dūd) *n.* **1.** a man excessively concerned with his clothes, appearance, and manners. **2.** *Informal.* a city-bred person, esp. an Easterner visiting a ranch in the West. **3.** *Slang.* a fellow; guy. [Of uncertain origin.] —**dud′ish,** *adj.* —**dud′ish·ly,** *adv.*
dude ranch, a ranch operated as a resort for tourists, offering horseback riding, swimming, and other activities.
dudg·eon (duj′ən) *n.* a feeling of anger, resentment, or offense. ➡ now used chiefly in the phrase *in high dudgeon: After the argument, they stalked out of the room in high dudgeon.* [Of uncertain origin.]
due (dü, dū) *adj.* **1.** owed or owing as a debt; owed and expected to be paid; payable: *The rent will be due on the first of the month. The final payment is due.* **2.** owed or owing as by right or custom; expected to be given or rendered: *The lawyer addressed the judge with all due respect.* **3.** suited to or required by the purpose or object; appropriate; correct; proper: *The explosives were handled with due care.* **4.** as much as is necessary; adequate; sufficient: *due cause for alarm.* **5.** required or expected to arrive, be present, or be ready: *I am due at the theater in fifteen minutes. The train is due at 5:30.* —*n.* **1.** something that is due: *The boy gave his mother*

duck [1]

a	at	e	end	o	hot	u	up	hw	white	⎧	about
ā	ape	ē	me	ō	old	ū	use	ng	song	⎪	taken
ä	far	i	it	ô	fork	ü	rule	th	thin	ə	pencil
âr	care	ī	ice	oi	oil	u̇	pull	<u>th</u>	this	⎪	lemon
		îr	pierce	ou	out	ûr	turn	zh	measure	⎩	circus

the respect that was her due. **2. dues.** a fee or charge, esp. one paid to a group or organization for the rights of membership. —*adv.* in a direct line; straight; exactly: *We sailed due north.* [Old French *deu,* past participle of *devoir* to owe, from Latin *dēbēre.*] •**due to. a.** caused by: *The delay was due to heavy traffic.* **b.** because of: *The project was abandoned due to lack of support.*

Usage Because **due** is an adjective, it has traditionally been thought acceptable to use **due to** only as a predicate adjective, as in *The flood in the basement was due to a storm.* In the sentences *The basement was flooded due to a storm* or *Due to a storm, the basement was flooded,* purists would substitute *because of* or *owing to* for **due to.** However, the distinction is a fine one, and **due to** in the sense of "because of" is widely used and has gained acceptance, especially in informal speech and writing.

du·el (dū′əl, dū′-) *n.* **1.** a prearranged, formal combat between two people to settle an argument or decide a point of honor, fought in the presence of witnesses or seconds, usually with swords or firearms. **2.** any contest, struggle, or encounter between two contending parties: *a duel of wits.* —*v.t., v.i.,* **-eled, -el·ing;** *also,* **-elled, -el·ling.** to fight in a duel. [Medieval Latin *duellum* combat between two people, from Latin *duellum,* form of *bellum* war.] —**du′el·er, du′el·ist;** *also,* **du′el·ler, du′el·list,** *n.*

du·en·na (dū en′ə, dū-) *n.* **1.** an older woman who serves as the chaperon or escort of the young, unmarried women in a Spanish or Portuguese family. **2.** a governess; chaperon. [Spanish *dueña* chaperon, mistress, from Latin *domina* mistress, lady.]

due process of law, the regular administration of the law carried out according to established legal procedures and in such a way that the rights of the individual are protected. Also, **due process.**

du·et (dū et′, dū-) *n.* **1.** a musical composition for two voices or instruments. **2.** the two singers or musicians who perform a duet. [Italian *duetto,* diminutive of *due* two, from Latin *duo* two.]

duff[1] (duf) *n.* a thick flour pudding boiled or steamed in a cloth bag. [Form of DOUGH.]

duff[2] (duf) *n.* **1.** *Slang.* the buttocks: *Get off your duff and get to work.* **2.** a layer of partially decayed organic matter on the forest floor.

duf·fel (duf′əl) *also,* **duffle.** *n.* **1.** a coarse woolen cloth with a thick nap. **2.** equipment or supplies, esp. for camping. **3.** duffel bag. [Dutch *duffel* this cloth, from *Duffel,* town near Antwerp, Belgium, where it was first made.]

duffel bag *also,* **duffle bag.** a cylindrical bag, usually of canvas, used for carrying clothes, equipment, or other belongings.

duff·er (duf′ər) *n. Informal.* a clumsy, plodding, or incompetent person, esp. an unskilled golfer.

duf·fle (duf′əl) *n.* duffel.

dug[1] (dug) a past tense and past participle of **dig.**

dug[2] (dug) *n.* a nipple, teat, or udder. [Of uncertain origin.]

du·gong (dū′gông′, -gong′) *n.* a plant-eating aquatic mammal, *Dugong dugon,* related to the manatee, having a blunt snout, a short, flat tail, and a pair of front flippers, found in the warm coastal waters of the Indian and Pacific oceans; sea cow. Length: 7-9 feet (2.1-2.7 meters). [Malay *dūyōng.*]

dug·out (dug′out′) *n.* **1.** a rough shelter or dwelling formed by digging a hole in the ground or in a hillside or other slope, often covered or reinforced with sod, logs, or other material. **2.** *Baseball.* a long, three-sided, roofed structure in which players sit when not at bat or in the field. **3.** a canoe or boat that is made by hollowing out a large log.

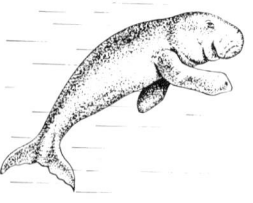

dugong

dui·ker (dī′kər) *n.* any of various small African antelopes, genera *Cephalophus* and *Sylvicapra,* varying from gray-tan to almost black, with some species striped. Both sexes usually have horns. Height: 22-36 inches (56-91 centimeters) at the shoulder. [Dutch *duiker* literally, diver, from *duiker* to dive; akin to DUCK[2].]

duke (dūk, dük) *n.* **1.** a British nobleman of the highest rank. **2.** a nobleman of certain other European countries having a similar rank. **3.** a prince who rules an independent duchy. **4. dukes.** *Slang.* fists: *Put up your dukes.* [Old French *duc* ruler of a duchy, lord, from Latin *dux* leader. Doublet of DOGE, DUCE.]

duke·dom (dūk′dəm, dük′-) *n.* **1.** duchy. **2.** the office, title, or rank of a duke.

dul·cet (dul′sit) *adj.* soothing or agreeable, esp. to the ear; sweet; pleasant: *the dulcet tones of a fine voice.* [Modification (influenced in spelling by Latin *dulcis* sweet) of Old French *doucet* sweet, diminutive of *doux,* from Latin *dulcis.*]

dul·ci·mer (dul′sə mər) *n.* **1.** a musical instrument shaped like a trapezoid and having metal strings, played by striking the strings with two leather-covered hammers. **2.** a musical instrument with three or more strings stretched over a long fingerboard attached to a sound box, played by plucking or strumming the string with a plectrum. [Old French *doulcemer,* form of *doulcemele,* probably going back to Latin *dulcis* sweet + Greek *melos* song; because of its sweet sound.]

dulcimer *(def. 1)*

dull (dul) *adj.* **1.** not sharp or pointed; blunt: *a dull blade, a pencil with a dull point.* **2.** not interesting; tedious; boring: *a dull speech, a dull subject.* **3.** lacking in intelligence or mental quickness; slow to learn or understand: *a dull student.* **4.** not keenly felt; not intense: *a dull ache.* **5.** lacking in perception, sensitivity, or responsiveness. **6.** not bright, clear, or vivid: *a dull red, a dull finish on the floor.* **7.** not distinct or ringing in sound; muffled: *a dull thud.* **8.** not active or brisk; sluggish: *Trading is dull on the stock exchange today.* **9.** not lively or cheerful; depressed; listless: *to be in a dull mood.* **10.** (of weather) cloudy or gloomy; overcast. —*v.t.* to make dull: *to dull a blade, to dull the appetite.* —*v.i.* to become dull: *The razor will dull if you use it to cut wood.* [Possibly from an unrecorded Old English word.] —**dull′ness;** *also,* **dul′ness,** *n.* —**dul′ly,** *adv.*

Synonyms *adj.* **Dull** and **blunt** may both mean lacking a sharp edge or point. **Dull** implies that overuse or disuse has reduced an object's normal sharpness: *This sickle is too dull to cut efficiently.* **Blunt,** used especially of pointed objects, may refer to one that is less sharp than others of its class, or to one not meant to be sharp at all: *This knife is too blunt to carve with. Use the blunt charcoal to shade your drawing.*

dull·ard (dul′ərd) *n.* a stupid or slow-witted person; dolt.

dulse (duls) *n.* any of various coarse, edible red seaweeds found on the northern coasts of North America, Asia, and Europe. [Irish Gaelic *duileasg.*]

du·ly (dū′lē, dü′-) *adv.* **1.** in a fitting or proper manner; suitably; rightfully: *They were duly sworn in.* **2.** to the extent or degree that is due; adequately; sufficiently: *These proposals should be duly considered.* **3.** at the proper time; when due; punctually: *rent duly paid.*

Du·ma (dū′mə) *n.* the elective legislative assembly that constituted the lower house of the Russian parliament, established in 1905 by Czar Nicholas II and permanently dissolved in early 1917. [Russian *duma* thought, council; of Germanic origin.]

dumb (dum) *adj.* **1.** lacking the power of speech; mute: *a person who is deaf and dumb.* **2.** temporarily speechless: *I was struck dumb when I heard the news.* **3.** refraining from speech; silent; taciturn: *The prisoner remained dumb, refusing to answer any questions.* **4.** not characterized or accompanied by speech or sound: *Pleasant answered with a short dumb nod* (Charles Dickens, 1865). **5.** *Informal.* slow-witted or stupid. [Old English *dumb* lacking the power of speech.] —**dumb′ly,** *adv.* —**dumb′ness,** *n.*

Dum·bar·ton Oaks (dum′bär tən) an estate in Washington, D.C., where conferences were held in 1944 to formulate plans for the organization of the United Nations.

dumb·bell (dum′bel′) *n.* **1.** a bar with heavy, usually metal disks or balls at either end, used for exercising. **2.** *Slang.* a stupid person.

dumb·found (dum found′, dum′found′) *also,* **dumfound.** *v.t.*

to strike dumb, as with amazement; astonish; confound: *Why were you dumbfounded to find out that you had passed the test?* [DUMB + (CON)FOUND.]

dumb show 1. gestures without speech; pantomime. 2. a part of a play presented in pantomime, performed esp. in early English drama.

dumb·wait·er (dum'wā'tər) *n.* 1. a small elevator used to convey dishes, food, rubbish, or other articles from one floor to another. 2. a movable serving table or stand.

dum·dum (dum'dum') *n.* a bullet with a soft nose, designed to expand on impact, causing a large wound. Also, **dumdum bullet.** [From *Dum Dum,* town near Calcutta, India, where it was formerly manufactured.]

dum·found (dum found', dum'found') dumbfound.

dum·my (dum'ē) *n., pl.* **-mies.** 1. a figure of the human body used to represent or serve as a real person: *department store dummies, a ventriloquist's dummy.* 2. an imitation object made to resemble the real thing, such as a false drawer. 3. a person who is unable to speak; mute. ➡ now considered offensive. 4. a person seeming to act independently or for his or her own interests but really controlled by another. 5. *Bridge.* **a.** the declarer's partner, whose cards are exposed on the table and played by the declarer. **b.** the cards so exposed. 6. a sample, as of a book or magazine, usually consisting of blank pages, arranged to show the size and appearance of the final version. 7. *Informal.* a stupid person; dolt. —*adj.* 1. not genuine; imitation; counterfeit; sham: *a dummy rifle.* 2. seeming to act independently but really serving or controlled by another: *a dummy organization.* 3. *Bridge.* played with a dummy. [DUMB + -Y¹.]

dump (dump) *v.t.* 1. to throw down or let fall in a heap or mass; fling down or drop heavily or suddenly: *They dumped the gravel in the driveway. She dumped her books on the bed.* 2. to unload or empty the contents of (a container), as by overturning: *He dumped out his briefcase on the table.* 3. to get rid of or throw away by or as by dumping; dispose of: *to dump the garbage, to dump an unpopular candidate.* 4. *Computers.* to transfer the contents of a file or memory storage unit) to a peripheral device, as a printer. 5. to put (goods) on the market in large quantities and at a low price, esp. on a foreign market at a price lower than that in the home country. —*v.i.* 1. to drop or fall suddenly or heavily. 2. to unload rubbish or refuse. —*n.* 1. a place where rubbish or refuse is deposited. 2. a pile or heap of rubbish or other discarded materials. 3. a place for temporary storage of military supplies: *an ammunition dump.* 4. *Slang.* a messy, shabby, or unattractive place: *The once luxurious hotel was a dump.* 5. *Computers.* the display or printing out of the entire contents of a file or memory storage unit. [Possibly imitative; possibly of Scandinavian origin.]

dump·cart (dump'kärt') *n.* a cart so constructed that its body can be tilted or its bottom opened to discharge its load.

dump·ling (dump'ling) *n.* 1. a ball of dough that is boiled or steamed and usually served with soup or stew. 2. a dessert made by enclosing fruit in a piece of dough and baking or steaming it. [Of uncertain origin.]

dumps (dumps) *pl. n.* a gloomy or depressed state of mind; low spirits. ➡ used chiefly in the phrase *down in the dumps.* [Probably from Dutch *domp* haze.]

dump·ster (dump'stər) *n.* a very large container on rollers for holding trash, designed to be raised and emptied into a garbage truck or set on the bed of a truck and hauled away. *Trademark:* Dumpster.

dump truck, a truck so constructed that its rear portion can be tilted to discharge its load through an open tailgate.

dump·y (dum'pē) *adj.,* **dump·i·er, dump·i·est.** short and stout; squat. —**dump'i·ly,** *adv.* —**dump'i·ness,** *n.*

dun¹ (dun) *v.t.,* **dunned, dun·ning.** 1. to make repeated and persistent demands upon (someone), esp. for the payment of a debt: *The department store kept dunning them until the old bill was paid.* 2. to annoy or harass continually. —*n.* 1. a repeated and insistent demand, esp. for payment of a debt. 2. a person who duns. [Of uncertain origin.]

dun² (dun) *n.* a dull, grayish brown color. —*adj.* having the color dun. [Middle English *dun,* from Old English *dun, dunn* dark, brownish black.]

dunce (duns) *n.* a person who is slow at learning; slow-witted or ignorant person. [From *Dunsman,* applied contemptuously to followers of the Scottish theologian John *Duns* Scotus, 1266?-1308, who were regarded as opponents of Renaissance humanism.]

dunce cap *also,* **dunce's cap.** a cone-shaped hat formerly placed on the head of a slow or lazy student in school as a punishment.

dun·der·head (dun'dər hed') *n.* a slow-witted, foolish, or stupid person; blockhead. [Possibly from Dutch *donder* thunder + HEAD; referring to the result of being struck by a thunderbolt.]

dunes

dune (dün, dūn) *n.* a mound, hill, or ridge of sand that is heaped up by the wind. [French *dune,* from Middle Dutch *dunen;* of Celtic origin.]

dune buggy, a small, lightweight motor vehicle with very large tires for driving on sand dunes and beaches. Also, **beach buggy.**

dung (dung) *n.* 1. animal excrement; manure. 2. something vile or foul. —*v.t.* to cover or fertilize with or as with dung. [Old English *dung* excrement.]

dun·ga·ree (dung'gə rē') *n.* 1. a denim fabric used for work clothes, sportswear, and sails. 2. **dungarees.** trousers or work clothes made of this fabric. [Hindi *dūngrī* coarse cotton cloth.]

dung beetle, any of a large group of beetles, family Scarabaeidae, that deposit their eggs in or feed on the dung of animals.

dun·geon (dun'jən) *n.* 1. a dark, close cell or prison, esp. one underground: *the dungeon of a castle.* 2. donjon. [Old French *donjon* donjon, going back to Late Latin *dominiō* tower, dominion, from Latin *dominus* master, lord.]

dung·hill (dung'hil') *n.* 1. a heap of dung. 2. something vile or foul.

dunk (dungk) *v.t.* 1. to dip (something to eat) into a liquid: *to dunk a roll in soup.* 2. to push or submerge (someone) underwater briefly; duck. 3. *Basketball.* to jump and thrust (the ball) down through the basket. —*n.* 1. an act or instance of dunking. 2. dunk shot. [German *tunken* to dip.] —**dunk'er,** *n.*

dunk shot *Basketball.* a shot made by jumping high enough to thrust the ball down through the basket.

dun·lin (dun'lin) *n., pl.* **-lins** or **-lin.** a reddish brown and white sandpiper, *Erolia alpina,* widely distributed throughout the Northern Hemisphere. [DUN² + -LIN(G¹).]

dun·nage (dun'ij) *n.* 1. any loose material packed around a cargo to protect it from damage during shipping. 2. personal belongings; baggage. [Of uncertain origin.]

du·o (dü'ō, dū'ō) *n., pl.* **du·os.** 1. a musical ensemble of two performers. 2. duet (*def. 1*). 3. two persons who perform together or who are commonly associated with one another; pair; couple. [Italian *duo* duet, two, from Latin *duo* two.]

dunk shot

du·o·dec·i·mal (dü'ə des'ə məl, dū'-) *adj.* relating to or based on twelfths or the number 12; proceeding by twelves: *duodecimal*

a	at	e	end	o	hot	u	up	hw	white	{	about
ā	ape	ē	me	ō	old	ū	use	ng	song		taken
ä	far	i	it	ô	fork	ü	rule	th	thin		pencil
âr	care	ī	ice	oi	oil	u̇	pull	th	this		lemon
				ir	pierce	ou	out	ûr	turn	zh	measure		circus

multiplication. —*n.* a number in a duodecimal system. [Latin *duodecimus* twelfth (from *duodecim* twelve) + -AL¹.]

du·o·dec·i·mal system, a system of numbers using a base of 12 rather than 10, which is used in the decimal system.

du·o·dec·i·mo (dü′ə des′ə mō′, dü′-) *n., pl.* -**mos. 1.** a page size of approximately 5 inches by 7½ inches (13 centimeters by 19 centimeters). **2.** a book or page of this size. —*adj.* being this size; consisting of pages of this size. Also, **twelvemo.** [Latin *duodecimō,* ablative of *duodecimus* twelfth, from *duodecim* twelve.]

du·o·de·nal (dü′ə dē′nəl, dü′-, dü od′ə-, dü-) *adj.* of or relating to the duodenum.

du·o·de·num (dü′ə dē′nəm, dü′-, dü od′ə-, dü-) *n., pl.* -**na** (-nə) or -**nums.** the first section of the small intestine, extending from the final portion of the stomach to the jejunum. [Medieval Latin *duodenum,* from Latin *duodēnī* twelve each, from *duodecim* twelve; because it is approximately the length of twelve finger widths.]

dup., duplicate.

dupe (düp, dūp) *n.* **1.** a person who is being deluded or tricked, or who unwittingly serves the ends of another. **2.** a person easily deceived or deluded. —*v.t.,* **duped, dup·ing.** to make a dupe of; deceive; delude: *The criminals duped the guard into helping them escape.* [French *dupe* deceived person; earlier, hoopoe (of uncertain origin); supposedly referring to the bird's stupidity.] —**dup′-er,** *n.*

dup·er·y (dü′pə rē, dü′-) *n., pl.* -**er·ies. 1.** the act or practice of duping. **2.** the state of being duped.

du·ple (dü′pəl, dü′-) *adj.* **1.** double; twofold. **2.** *Music.* having two, or a multiple of two, beats to the measure: *duple time, duple meter.* [Latin *duplus* twofold. Doublet of DOUBLE.]

du·plex (dü′pleks, dü′-) *adj.* having two parts; double; twofold. —*n.* a duplex house or duplex apartment. [Latin *duplex* twofold.]

duplex apartment, an apartment having rooms on two floors.

duplex house, a house having two separate single-family units.

du·pli·cate (*adj., n.,* dü′pli kit, dü′-; *v.,* dü′pli kāt′, dü′-) *adj.* **1.** exactly copied from an original: *to make a duplicate list.* **2.** exactly like or corresponding exactly to something else: *The costars wear duplicate costumes.* **3.** having or consisting of two corresponding or identical parts; double; twofold. **4.** designating a card game in which all players play the same series of hands, the winners being the partners with the best comparative score: *duplicate bridge.* —*n.* **1.** a copy exactly like an original; exact copy: *The secretary kept a duplicate of the letter.* **2.** something corresponding in every respect to something else; counterpart; double: *Your jacket's a duplicate of mine.* **3.** a duplicate game of cards, esp. bridge. —*v.t.,* -**cat·ed,** -**cat·ing. 1.** to copy exactly; reproduce: *to duplicate a letter.* **2.** to do again; repeat: *The tennis champion tried hard to duplicate past victories.* [Latin *duplicātus,* past participle of *duplicāre* to double.]

· **in duplicate.** in two identical copies: *Type this letter in duplicate.*

Synonyms *n.* **Duplicate, facsimile,** and **replica** denote a copy made to closely resemble the original. **Duplicate** connotes a copy so close as to be indistinguishable from the original: *We opened the door with a duplicate key.* **Facsimile** suggests a slightly less exact copy: *Could you give us at least a facsimile of the plan?* **Replica** connotes a reproduction that attempts to capture the spirit of the original, although it may differ in detail or scale: *The replica of the sailing ship included masts and rigging.*

du·pli·ca·tion (dü′pli kā′shən, dü′-) *n.* **1.** the act of duplicating or the state of being duplicated. **2.** a copy or counterpart; duplicate. —**du′pli·ca′tive,** *adj.*

du·pli·ca·tor (dü′pli kā′tər, dü′-) *n.* a machine for making duplicates, esp. of pages of written or typed material.

du·plic·i·ty (dü plis′i tē, dü-) *n., pl.* -**ties.** hypocritical deceit or treachery; dissimulation; double-dealing: *the duplicity of a spy.* [Late Latin *duplicitās* a being double, from Latin *duplex* twofold.] —**du·plic′i·tous,** *adj.*

du·ra (dü′ə, dyür′ə) *n.* dura mater.

du·ra·bil·i·ty (dür′ə bil′i tē, dyür′-) *n., pl.* -**ties.** the ability to resist wear, decay, change, or stress; quality of being durable.

du·ra·ble (dür′ə bəl, dyür′-) *adj.* **1.** able to resist wear or decay: *a durable floor, durable shoes.* **2.** able to resist change or stress; stable; enduring: *a durable friendship.* —*n.* **durables.** durable goods. [Old French *durable* lasting, from Latin *dūrābilis,* from *dūrāre* to last.] —**du′ra·ble·ness,** *n.* —**du′ra·bly,** *adv.*

durable goods, household appliances, automobiles, furniture, and other manufactured goods that usually last for several years.

du·ral·u·min (dü ral′yə min, dyü-) *n.* a strong, light alloy of aluminum that contains copper, manganese, and magnesium. *Trademark:* **Duralumin.** [German *Dural* (from *Düren,* German city where it was first made) + ALUMIN(UM).]

dura ma·ter (mā′tər) a tough, fibrous membrane that is the outermost of the three coverings of the brain and spinal

cord. Also, **dura.** [Medieval Latin *dura mater (cerebri)* hard mother (of the brain).]

du·ra·men (dü rā′mən, dyü-) *n.* heartwood.

du·rance (dür′əns, dyür′-) *n.* forced confinement or imprisonment. ➡ used chiefly in the phrase *in durance vile.* [Old French *durance* duration, from *durer* to last, from Latin *dūrāre.*]

du·ra·tion (dü rā′shən, dyü-) *n.* **1.** the length of time during which anything continues or exists: *for the duration of the war.* **2.** continuance in time: *a peace of short duration.* [Medieval Latin *duratio* hardness, perseverance, from Latin *dūrāre* to last, harden.]

dur·bar (dûr′bär′) *n.* **1.** the court of a native Indian ruler. **2.** formerly, a public audience or reception held in India by a native prince or by a British governor or viceroy. **3.** the hall or place where such a reception was held. [Hindi *darbār* court, from Persian *darbār,* from *dar* door + *bār* admission.]

du·ress (dü res′, dyü-, dûr′is, dyür′-) *n.* **1.** the condition of being compelled to do something by force or threat: *The prisoner signed the confession under duress.* **2.** unlawful confinement or imprisonment. [Old French *duresce* hardness, cruelty, from Latin *dūritia* hardness, severity.]

du·ri·an (dür′ē ən, dyür′-) *n.* **1.** the oval-shaped, edible fruit of a tree, *Durio zibethinus,* having a soft cream-colored pulp, a thorny rind, and an odor resembling that of Limburger cheese. **2.** the tropical tree bearing this fruit, native to the Malay region of Asia. [Malay *dūriān* the fruit, from *dūrī* thorn; referring to the fruit's thorny rind.]

dur·ing (dür′ing, dyür′-) *prep.* **1.** throughout the time or duration of: *I lived in the country during the summer.* **2.** at some point in the course of: *We arrived during the second act.* [Originally present participle of obsolete *dure* to last, from Old French *durer,* from Latin *dūrāre.*]

Du·roc (dür′ok, dyür′-) *n.* a hog of a hardy breed originally developed in New York and New Jersey, having a red coat and drooping ears, valued for its meat. Also, **Du·roc-Jer·sey** (dür′ok jûr′zē, dyür′-).

dur·ra (dür′ə) *n.* sorghum of a variety widely cultivated for its edible grain. [Arabic *dhurah* millet.]

durst (dûrst) *Archaic.* a past tense of **dare.**

du·rum (dür′əm, dyür′-) *n.* any plant belonging to a class of wheat, *Triticum turgidum,* having hard, amber-colored kernels from which a high-quality flour used primarily in making macaroni, spaghetti, and similar foods is produced. Also, **durum wheat.** [Modern Latin *durum,* from Latin *dūrus* hard.]

dusk (dusk) *n.* **1.** the time of day just before nightfall; darker part of twilight. **2.** shade or gloom; darkness: *in the dusk of the dense forest.* —*adj.* dark or gloomy; shadowy. —*v.t., v.i.* to make or become dark or gloomy. [Old English *dox* dark.]

dusk·y (dusk′kē) *adj.,* **dusk·i·er, dusk·i·est. 1.** dark in color: *The jacket was a dusky brown.* **2.** lacking light; shadowy; dim: *a dusky room.* —**dusk′i·ly,** *adv.* —**dusk′i·ness,** *n.*

dust (dust) *n.* **1.** fine, dry particles of earth or other matter, tiny enough to be easily suspended in or carried by air currents. **2.** earth, esp. as the burial place of the dead. **3.** what remains of something, such as a dead body, after decay or disintegration. **4.** a low, humble, or poor condition. —*v.t.* **1.** to free of dust, as by brushing or wiping: *to dust a table with a soft cloth.* **2.** to cover or sprinkle with or as if with dust: *to dust a pan with flour.* **3.** to strew or sprinkle in the form of dust: *to dust insecticide on plants.* —*v.i.* **1.** to remove dust, esp. from furniture. **2.** (of a bird) to bathe in dust. [Old English *dūst* powder, particles of earth.]

· **to bite the dust.** to die, esp. in battle.

· **to dust off.** to bring out, as from storage, and ready for use: *I should dust off my heavy coat now that fall is here.*

· **to shake the dust off one's feet.** to go away from a place with a feeling of anger or disdain.

· **to throw dust in someone's eyes.** to mislead (someone); deceive.

dust·bin (dust′bin′) *n. British.* a container for refuse or garbage; ashcan.

dust bowl *also,* **Dust Bowl.** an area of dry, dusty land having irregular rainfall and subject to frequent dust storms, esp. one that developed in the Great Plains of the United States in the 1930s.

dust devil, a small whirlwind that picks up dust and debris and carries them high into the air.

dust·er (dus′tər) *n.* **1.** someone or something that dusts. **2.** a cloth, brush, or other device for removing dust from objects. **3.** a loose-fitting, knee-length housecoat. **4.** a long, lightweight coat formerly worn in open automobiles to protect clothing from dust.

dust jacket, a removable paper cover for a book.

dust·man (dust′man′, -mən) *n., pl.* -**men** (-men′, -mən). *British.* a person whose work is collecting or removing refuse or garbage.

dust·pan (dust′pan′) *n.* a broad, short-handled shovellike utensil for collecting dust swept from a floor.

dust·proof (dust′prüf′) *adj.* keeping out dust; protecting from dust.

dust storm, a strong wind that carries clouds of dust and silt across dry plains or desert regions.

dust·y (dus′tē) *adj.*, **dust·i·er, dust·i·est. 1.** full of or covered with dust: *a dusty attic.* **2.** like dust; powdery: *a dusty snow.* **3.** of the color of dust; grayish: *dusty pink.* —**dust′i·ly,** *adj.* —**dust′i·ness,** *n.*

Dutch (duch) *adj.* **1.** of, relating to, or characteristic of the Netherlands or its people, language, or culture. **2.** *Archaic.* German. —*n.* **1. the Dutch. a.** the people of the Netherlands. **b.** *Archaic.* Germans or German speakers. **2.** the Germanic language of the Netherlands. [Middle Dutch *dutsch* Dutch (of the Netherlands), German.]

• **in Dutch.** *Informal.* in trouble or disfavor: *I'm in Dutch with my boss for showing up late.*

• **to go Dutch.** *Informal.* to have each person pay for himself or herself, as on a date.

Words from Dutch

Dutch is in the Germanic group of the Indo-European language family. Other languages in this group include English, German, Danish, Swedish, and Norwegian. Because of the maritime superiority of the Dutch Netherlands in the seventeenth century, many English words borrowed from Dutch are nautical terms. Below is a cross section of loanwords that have come into English from or through Dutch.

beleaguer	deck	pickle	splice
boom²	dope	pit²	splinter
boor	drill¹	quack²	split
boss¹	duffel	ravel	spook
brandy	easel	roster	spool
burgomaster	freebooter	Santa Claus	stoker
cam	furlough	school²	stoop²
cashier²	gin¹	scow	stove¹
catkin	hock³	scrod	trawl
clink¹	iceberg	skate¹	trigger
coleslaw	jibe¹	sketch	uproar
cookie	landscape	skipper¹	waffle
cruise	maelstrom	sled	wagon
cruller	monsoon	sleigh	yacht
dapper	morass	sloop	yawl

Dutch courage *Informal.* courage inspired or maintained by or as by intoxication.

Dutch door, a door divided horizontally so that the upper part can remain open while the bottom part is closed, or vice versa.

Dutch elm disease, a disease of elm trees that causes leaves and branches to wilt, eventually killing the tree, caused by a fungus and transmitted by certain beetles.

Dutch·man (duch′mən) *n., pl.* **-men** (-mən). **1.** a native or citizen of the Netherlands. **2.** a person of Dutch ancestry. **3.** *Archaic.* a German or German speaker.

Dutch·man's-breech·es (duch′mənz brich′iz) *n., pl.* **-breech·es. 1.** the drooping flower of a wild plant, *Dicentra cucullaria,* having white and yellow petals that form a sac resembling pantaloons. **2.** the plant bearing this flower, native to woodlands of eastern North America, having stalks and fernlike leaves that grow directly from underground tubers.

Dutch oven 1. a heavy metal or ceramic kettle with a tight-fitting cover, used chiefly for preparing meats and stews and sometimes for baking. **2.** a metal box having one side that opens, placed before a fire for cooking by reflected heat. **3.** a brick oven in which the walls are preheated for cooking.

Dutch treat *Informal.* a meal, entertainment, or outing at which each person pays for all of his or her own expenses by agreement.

Dutch uncle *Informal.* a person who criticizes or scolds another bluntly and severely, esp. in an authoritative or patronizing way.

du·te·ous (dü′tē əs, dū′-) *adj.* dutiful; obedient. —**du′te·ous·ly,** *adv.* —**du′te·ous·ness,** *n.*

du·ti·a·ble (dü′tē ə bəl, dū′-) *adj.* subject to the payment of customs duty or taxes: *a shipment of dutiable imports.*

du·ti·ful (dü′tə fəl, dū′-) *adj.* **1.** performing one's duty or duties; having a sense of duty; obedient; respectful: *a dutiful child, a dutiful citizen who always votes.* **2.** showing or resulting from a sense of duty: *The store manager displayed a dutiful interest in the customer's complaints.* —**du′ti·ful·ly,** *adv.* —**du′ti·ful·ness,** *n.*

du·ty (dü′tē, dū′-) *n., pl.* **-ties. 1.** something that a person is morally or legally bound to do; obligation: *It is the duty of parents to care for their children properly.* **2.** a commitment to or sense of such obligation: *I was motivated by duty, and not by any hope of reward, when I returned the lost wallet.* **3.** an act or action required by or involved in one's occupation or position: *One of the duties of a teacher is grading papers.* **4.** an obligatory or assigned task or service, esp. military service. **5.** a tax levied on imported or exported goods; tariff. **6.** obedient or respectful conduct due to a superior or elder. [Anglo-Norman *dueté* what is due or owing, from Old French *deu,* past participle of *devoir* to owe. See DUE.]

• **off duty.** finished with or not at one's work or assigned task.

• **on duty.** at or occupied with one's work or assigned task.

Synonyms **Duty** and **obligation** denote something that must be done. **Duty** implies a moral responsibility or a code of action or behavior that should be adhered to: *Serving on a jury is a civic duty.* **Obligation** connotes something specific one must do at a particular time or in particular circumstances: *Members have an obligation to keep the club tidy.* For other Synonyms, see **job.**

du·ty-free (dü′tē frē′, dū′-) *adj.* **1.** free of or exempt from customs duties: *duty-free cargo.* **2.** of, relating to, or selling goods exempt from customs duties: *a duty-free shop at an airport.* —*adv.* free of customs duties: *The goods were shipped duty-free.*

du·um·vir (dü um′vər, dū-) *n., pl.* **-virs** or **-vi·ri** (-və rī′). either of two magistrates in ancient Rome who jointly held the same office. [Latin *duumvir,* going back to *duo* two + *vir* man.]

du·um·vir·ate (dü um′vər it, dū-) *n.* **1.** any office held jointly by two people, as in ancient Rome. **2.** a coalition or partnership of two people, as in a governmental position.

du·ve·tyn (dü′vi tēn′) *n.* a soft, slightly napped fabric made of cotton, wool, or synthetic fibers, used esp. for women's suits and hats.

D.V., God willing. [Abbreviation of Latin *Deō volente.*]

dwarf (dwôrf) *n., pl.* **dwarfs** or **dwarves. 1.** a fully grown person of less than normal size, often having disproportionate limbs or features, usually due to a congenital or pathological process. **2.** a fully grown plant or animal of less than normal size for its species or kind. **3.** in folklore, a little man, often depicted as ugly and misshapen, having unusual or magical powers or skills. **4.** dwarf star. —*v.t.* **1.** to cause to seem small, as by contrast or comparison: *Most professional basketball players dwarf other people.* **2.** to prevent from growing to the normal size; hinder the natural development of; stunt: *to dwarf a tree by pruning it regularly.* —*adj.* of unusually small stature or size; diminutive. [Old English *dweorg* a being smaller than the normal size.]

dwarf·ish (dwôr′fish) *adj.* like a dwarf; unusually small; diminutive. —**dwarf′ish·ly,** *adv.* —**dwarf′ish·ness,** *n.*

dwarf·ism (dwôr′fiz əm) *n.* the condition of being a dwarf.

dwarf star, a star of average brightness that is average or below average in size and mass, as the sun. Also, **dwarf.**

dwarves (dwôrvz) a plural of **dwarf.**

dwell (dwel) *v.i.,* **dwelt** or **dwelled, dwell·ing. 1.** to live as a permanent resident; make one's home; reside: *to dwell in the suburbs, to dwell in a cottage by the sea.* **2.** to exist or be present: *a fond memory that always dwells in the heart.* **3.** to exist or continue in a condition or state: *to dwell in happiness.* [Partly from Old Norse *dvelja* to delay, tarry; partly from Old English *dwellan* to delay, remain.] —**dwell′er,** *n.*

• **to dwell on** (or **upon**). to linger over or emphasize in thought, speech, or writing: *The speaker dwelt at length upon the final point. Don't dwell too much on painful memories.*

dwell·ing (dwel′ing) *n.* a place of residence; house; abode. —For Synonyms, see **home.**

dwelt (dwelt) a past tense and past participle of **dwell.**

DWI, driving while intoxicated.

dwin·dle (dwin′dəl) *v.,* **-dled, -dling.** —*v.i.* to become gradually smaller or less; shrink; diminish: *After the parade was over, the*

a	at	e	end	o	hot	u	up	hw	white		about
ā	ape	ē	me	ō	old	ū	use	ng	song		taken
ä	far	i	it	ô	fork	ü	rule	th	thin	ə	pencil
âr	care	ī	ice	oi	oil	u̇	pull	th	this		lemon
		îr	pierce	ou	out	ûr	turn	zh	measure		circus

crowd began to dwindle. Hope of finding the lost campers dwindled as the week passed. —*v.t.* to make gradually smaller or less. [Diminutive of archaic *dwine* to waste away, from Old English *dwīnan.*] —For Synonyms, see **decrease**.

dwt., pennyweight.

DX *Radio.* **1.** distance. **2.** distant.

Dy, the symbol for dysprosium.

Dy·ak (dī′ak) *also,* **Dayak.** *n.* a member of any of several peoples native to the island of Borneo.

dyb·buk (dib′ək) *also,* **dibbuk.** *n., pl.* **dyb·buks** or **dyb·buk·im** (di bü′kim). in Jewish folklore, a demon or the soul of a dead person that enters the body of a living person and takes control. [Yiddish *dibek,* from Hebrew *dibuk* adhesion, sticking, from *davak* to adhere, stick.]

dye (dī) *n.* **1.** a pigment used to impart a particular color to cloth, hair, food, or other materials. It is either obtained from natural substances in plants, animals, and minerals or produced synthetically. **2.** a color or hue, esp. as produced by dyeing. —*v.,* **dyed, dye·ing.** —*v.t.* to impart a particular color to, esp. by soaking in a liquid dye. —*v.i.* to take on color in dyeing. [Old English *dēag* color, hue.] —**dy′er,** *n.*

• **of the deepest** (or **blackest**) **dye.** of the most pronounced or the worst sort: *a criminal of the deepest dye.*

dyed-in-the-wool (dīd′in tha wůl′) *adj.* **1.** dyed before being woven into fabric. **2.** thoroughgoing; absolute; complete: *a dyed-in-the-wool scoundrel.*

dye·ing (dī′ing) *v.* the present participle of **dye.** —*n.* the act, process, or trade of coloring cloth, hair, or other materials with dye.

dye·stuff (dī′stuf′) *n.* a substance used as a dye or as a source of a dye.

dye·wood (dī′wůd′) *n.* any wood, such as logwood, that yields a dyestuff.

dy·ing (dī′ing) *v.* the present participle of **die**[1]. —*adj.* **1.** approaching death; about to die: *the confession of a dying criminal.* **2.** of or associated with death or dying: *dying words.* **3.** drawing to a close; fading: *a dying flame, a dying institution.* —*n.* the act or process of ceasing to live, exist, or function.

dyke (dīk) *n.* —*v.t.,* **dyked, dyk·ing.** dike.

dy·nam·ic (dī nam′ik) *adj.* **1.** characterized by or full of energy and vigor; forceful: *a dynamic personality, a dynamic performance.* **2.** characterized by change or activity: *a dynamic economy.* **3.** of or relating to energy or force in motion. **4.** of or relating to dynamics. Also, **dy·nam′i·cal.** [French *dynamique* energetic, from Greek *dynamikos* powerful, from *dynamis* power.] —**dy·nam′i·cal·ly,** *adv.*

dy·nam·ics (dī nam′iks) *pl. n.* **1.** the branch of mechanics dealing with bodies in motion. It is often divided into kinetics and kinematics. ➡ used as singular. **2.** the motivating or governing forces operating in any field or activity, or the laws by which they act: *the dynamics of human behavior.* **3.** *Music.* gradations of loudness or softness.

dy·na·mism (dī′nə miz′əm) *n.* **1.** the state or quality of being dynamic; energy; vigor; forcefulness: *a dance group known for its dynamism.* **2.** any philosophical system, doctrine, or theory that explains the phenomena of the universe in terms of the action of some pervasive force or energy.

dy·na·mite (dī′nə mīt′) *n.* **1.** an explosive consisting of a porous, absorbent material saturated with nitroglycerin, usually packaged as cylindrical sticks. **2.** *Informal.* someone or something that has an exciting, powerful, or spectacular effect. —*v.t.,* **-mit·ed, -mit·ing.** to blow up or destroy with dynamite. —*adj. Slang.* exciting, powerful, or spectacular. [Greek *dynamis* power + -ITE[1].] —**dy′na·mit′er,** *n.*

dy·na·mo (dī′nə mō′) *n., pl.* **-mos. 1.** an electric generator or motor, esp. one that produces a direct current. **2.** an energetic, vigorous, forceful person. [Short for *dynamoelectric machine.* See DYNAMOELECTRIC, MACHINE.]

dy·na·mo·e·lec·tric (dī′nə mō i lek′trik) *adj.* relating to the conversion of mechanical energy into electric energy, or vice versa. Also, **dy′na·mo·e·lec′tri·cal.** [Greek *dynamis* power + ELECTRIC.]

dy·na·mom·e·ter (dī′nə mom′i tər) *n.* a device for measuring force or power. [Greek *dynamis* power + -METER.]

dy·na·mo·tor (dī′nə mō′tər) *n.* a machine that combines motor and generator action and is used to change the voltage of an electric current.

dy·nast (dī′nast, -nəst) *n.* a ruler, esp. a hereditary ruler. [Latin *dynastēs,* from Greek *dynastēs.*]

dy·nas·ty (dī′nəs tē) *n., pl.* **-ties. 1.** a succession of rulers of the same family or line of descent. **2.** any family or group that retains prominence or power for a considerable period of time: *a political dynasty.* **3.** the period of time during which a dynasty rules. [Late Latin *dynastīa* rule, kingship, from Greek *dynasteiā* power, domination.] —**dy·nas·tic** (dī nas′tik); *also,* **dy·nas′ti·cal,** *adj.* —**dy·nas′ti·cal·ly,** *adv.*

dyne (dīn) *n.* the basic unit of force in the centimeter-gram-second system of units. It is equal to the amount of force that must be applied to one gram to produce an acceleration of one centimeter per second per second. [French *dyne,* from Greek *dynamis* power.]

dys- *combining form* bad; defective; difficult: *dysfunction, dyspepsia.* [Greek *dys-* hard, bad, ill.]

dys·en·ter·y (dis′ən ter′ē) *n.* any of several intestinal disorders characterized by severe diarrhea, often with mucus and bloody discharges, pain, and cramps, caused by any of various organisms, such as bacteria, protozoa, or parasitic worms. [Latin *dysenteria,* from Greek *dysenteriā,* from *dys-* bad + *entera* intestines.] —**dys·en·ter′ic;** *also,* **dys′en·ter′i·cal,** *adj.*

dys·func·tion (dis fungk′shən) *n.* an abnormal or impaired functioning, as of an organ. —**dys·func′tion·al,** *adj.*

dys·gen·ic (dis jen′ik) *adj.* relating to or having a detrimental effect upon hereditary traits.

dys·lex·i·a (dis lek′sē ə) *n.* any of a number of disorders that impair the ability to read, write, or spell. A common form of dyslexia involves reversing words or letters, such as reading *was* for *saw* or *b* for *d.* [Modern Latin *dyslexia,* from Greek *dys-* bad + *lexis* speech.]

dys·lex·ic (dis lek′sik) *adj.* of, relating to, or having dyslexia. —*n.* a person who has dyslexia.

dys·pep·si·a (dis pep′sē ə, -shə) *n.* poor digestion; indigestion. ➡ opposed to **eupepsia.** [Latin *dyspepsia,* from Greek *dyspepsia.*]

dys·pep·tic (dis pep′tik) *adj.* **1.** of, relating to, or suffering from dyspepsia. **2.** gloomy or irritable; despondent. Also, **dys·pep′ti·cal.** —*n.* a person who suffers from dyspepsia. —**dys·pep′ti·cal·ly,** *adv.*

dys·pla·sia (dis plā′zhə, -zhē ə, -zē ə) *n.* abnormal development or growth of tissues or body parts. —**dys·plas·tic** (dis plas′tik), *adj.*

dysp·ne·a (disp nē′ə) *n.* difficulty in breathing; shortness of breath. [Latin *dispnoea,* from Greek *dyspnoia,* from *dys* (see DYS-) + *pnoē* breathing (from *pnein* to breathe).] —**dysp·ne′al, dysp·ne′ic,** *adj.*

dys·pro·si·um (dis prō′sē əm, -shē-) *n.* a rare-earth element that is more magnetic than any other substance known and is superconductive. Symbol: Dy For tables, see **element.** [Modern Latin *dysprosium,* from Greek *dysprositos* hard to get at; because it was originally isolated only with great difficulty.]

dys·tro·phy (dis′trə fē) *n., pl.* **-phies. 1.** a medical condition resulting from defective nutrition. **2.** defective or abnormal development of any part of the body, as in muscular dystrophy. [Modern Latin *dystrophia,* from Greek *dys-* (see DYS-) + *-trophia* nutrition, nourishment, growth, (from *trephein* to nourish).] —**dys·troph·ic** (dis trof′ik, -trō′fik), *adj.*

dz., dozen; dozens.

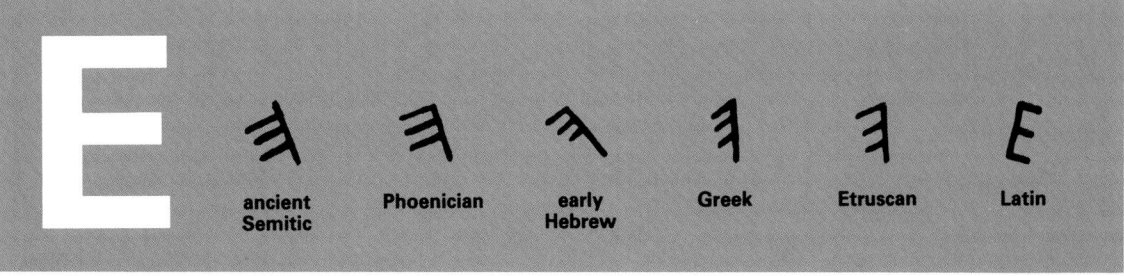

| ancient Semitic | Phoenician | early Hebrew | Greek | Etruscan | Latin |

E The earliest ancestor of our modern capital **E** was the letter *he*, which represented an *h* sound in the ancient Semitic alphabets. *He* was also used, with only slight changes in shape, in the Phoenician and early Hebrew alphabets. When the early Greeks borrowed *he*, they called it *epsilon* and used it for both the consonant sound *h* and the vowel sound *e*. Since the Greeks had another letter, *eta*, to represent the *h* sound, *epsilon* eventually came to be used only for the vowel sound *e*. *Epsilon* was adopted by the Etruscans, who later reversed it and gave it its modern shape. By the fourth century B.C., the Etruscan letter had come into the Latin alphabet. It was the ancestor of our modern capital **E**.

e, E (ē) *n., pl.* **e's, E's. 1.** the fifth letter of the English alphabet. **2.** the shape of this letter or something having this shape.
E (ē) *n., pl.* **E's. 1.** *Music.* **a.** the third note or tone of the diatonic scale of C major. For illustration, see **do²**. **b.** the scale or key that has this note or tone as its tonic. **2.** a grade or rating indicating inferior work that needs improvement in order to be acceptable: *an E in English.*
e- *prefix* form of **ex-¹** before consonants except *c, f, p, q, s,* and *t,* as in *evade* and *emit.*
e, the base of the natural system of logarithms. It has a numerical value exceeding 2.718.
E 1. *also,* **E.** east. **2.** *also,* **E.** eastern. **3.** *Physics.* energy. **4.** *also,* **E.** English. **5.** excellent.
ea., each.
each (ēch) *adj.* being one of two or more persons or things considered separately or individually: *Each player on the team has a different uniform number.* —*pron.* every individual person or thing, as of a group or number: *Each of my friends has a job this summer.* —*adv.* for each; apiece: *These cookies are a nickel each.* [Old English *ǣlc* every.] —For Usage Note, see **anybody.**
　• **each other.** each of two or more in reciprocal action or relation: *The two friends have known each other for twenty years.*
　➡ Although some people prefer to restrict **each other** to two persons or things and to use **one another** for three or more, they are commonly used interchangeably.

> **Synonyms** *adj.* **Each** and **every** indicate all of the individual members or parts of a group. **Each** emphasizes the individuality of the unit within the group: *Each of you is unique. Each student will make an original design.* **Every** stresses that the individual represents the group as a whole: *Every camper is responsible for keeping the paths clean. Every player had a part in the team's victory.*

ea·ger (ē'gər) *adj.* **1.** filled with keen desire and enthusiasm; impatiently anxious: *I was eager to start my vacation.* **2.** characterized by or showing keen desire or enthusiasm: *an eager look.* [Anglo-Norman *egre* keen, harsh, from Latin *ācer* sharp, ardent.] —**ea'ger·ly,** *adv.* —**ea'ger·ness,** *n.*

> **Synonyms** **Eager, anxious,** and **keen¹** mean filled with or driven by great desire. **Eager** is the most general of these terms. It suggests enthusiasm, sometimes accompanied by impatience: *to be eager for a game to start, to be eager to see old friends again.* **Anxious** implies uneasiness that what is longed for may not happen: *We were anxious to get the harvest in before the first frost.* **Keen** suggests sharpness or intensity of desire: *They were so keen on finishing the game that they missed supper completely.*

eager beaver *Informal.* a person who is overly zealous, diligent, or ambitious.
ea·gle (ē'gəl) *n.* **1.** any of various hawklike birds of prey, family Accipitridae, having keen eyesight, a sharply hooked bill, strong talons, and typically brown, gray, or black plumage with white markings. Wingspan: 6 feet (1.8 meters) or more. **2.a.** any of various representations of an eagle, often used as a symbol or emblem. **b.** a standard, seal, or other object bearing such a representation, such as the national seal of the United States. **3.** a golf score of two strokes less than par for any hole. **4.** a former gold coin of the United States, worth ten dollars. [Anglo-Norman *egle* the bird, from Latin *aquila.*]
ea·gle-eyed (ē'gəl īd') *adj.* able to perceive or discern clearly; keenly observant; sharp-sighted.
ea·glet (ē'glit) *n.* a young eagle.
ea·gre (ē'gər, ā'gər) *n.* tidal bore.
-ean, form of **-an,** as in *European, crustacean.*
ear¹ (îr) *n.* **1.** in vertebrates, the organ of hearing and balance. In humans and other mammals, the ear typically consists of three parts: the external ear, the middle ear, and the inner ear. **2.** in humans and other mammals, the outer, visible part of this organ: *The dog pricked up its ears at the noise.* **3.** the sense of hearing: *music pleasing to the ear.* **4.** the ability to appreciate, understand, or perceive differences in or refinements of something heard: *a good ear for music.* **5.** favorable or close attention: *to have someone's ear.* **6.** something resembling the outer, visible part of the ear in shape or position, such as the handle of a pitcher. [Old English *ēare* the organ of hearing.]
　• **to be all ears.** to be eagerly attentive.
　• **to bend someone's ear.** *Informal.* to talk to someone for a long time and become boring or annoying.
　• **to be up to one's** (or **the**) **ears.** to be deeply or thoroughly involved or immersed: *The lawyer was up to her ears in work.*
　• **to fall on deaf ears.** to receive no attention; be disregarded or unheeded: *Their complaints fell on deaf ears.*
　• **to go in one ear and out the other.** to be heard but not remembered or heeded; leave no impression: *The doctor's advice went in one ear and out the other.*

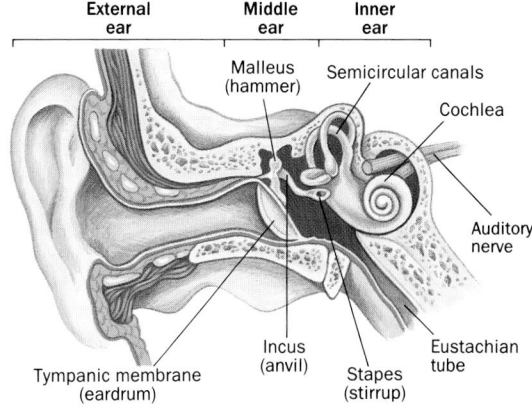

| External ear | Middle ear | Inner ear |

Malleus (hammer)
Semicircular canals
Cochlea
Auditory nerve
Tympanic membrane (eardrum)
Incus (anvil)
Stapes (stirrup)
Eustachian tube

human **ear**

a	at	e	end	o	hot	u	up	hw	white	⟨	about
ā	ape	ē	me	ō	old	ū	use	ng	song		taken
ä	far	i	it	ô	fork	ü	rule	th	thin	ə	pencil
âr	care	ī	ice	oi	oil	u̇	pull	th	this		lemon
		îr	pierce	ou	out	ûr	turn	zh	measure	⟨	circus

383

• **to keep** (or **have**) **an ear to the ground.** to pay attention to or keep well-informed about, esp. current trends or happenings.

• **to lend an** (or **one's**) **ear.** to pay attention; listen.

• **to play by ear.** to play (a musical instrument or piece) without the aid of written music: *Tom plays the piano by ear.*

• **to play it by ear.** *Informal.* to act without prior planning, according to the way a situation develops.

• **to turn a deaf ear.** to refuse to pay attention.

ear² (îr) *n.* the spike of cereal plants, esp. of corn, that contains the grains or seeds. —*v.i.* to form ears, as corn. [Old English *ēar* spike of grain.]

ear·ache (îr′āk′) *n.* a pain in the middle or inner ear.

ear·drum (îr′drum′) *n.* a thin membrane that separates the external ear from the middle ear and vibrates when sound waves strike it. Also, **tympanic membrane, tympanum.** For illustration, see **ear¹.**

eared seal, any of a group of seals, family Otariidae, including fur seals and sea lions, characterized by small, external ears and hind limbs that can be turned forward for locomotion.

ear·flap (îr′flap′) *n.* on a cap or hat, a part or parts that can be turned down to cover the ears, esp. to keep them warm. Also, **earlap.**

ear·ful (îr′fŭl′) *n., pl.* **-fuls.** *Informal.* **1.** surprising or especially interesting news or gossip. **2.** enough or too much of something heard. **3.** a scolding.

earl (ûrl) *n.* a British nobleman ranking below a marquis and above a viscount. The wife or widow of an earl is a countess. [Old English *eorl* warrior, nobleman.]

ear·lap (îr′lap′) *n.* earflap.

earl·dom (ûrl′dəm) *n.* **1.** the rank, title, or territory of an earl. **2.** earls collectively.

earless seal, any of a group of seals, family Phocidae, that lack external ears and have hind limbs that cannot be turned forward during locomotion. They are found throughout all oceans and in certain freshwater lakes.

ear·lobe (îr′lōb′) *n.* the lower fleshy part of the visible external ear.

ear·ly (ûr′lē) *adj.,* **-li·er, -li·est. 1.** relating to or occurring in the beginning of a period of time or of a course or series: *My family moved here in the early part of this century.* **2.** coming, occurring, or doing something before the customary or expected time: *an early marriage, an early riser.* **3.** belonging to a period far back in time: *early Greek sculpture.* **4.** occurring in the near future: *We would like to hold the meeting at an early date.* —*adv.* **1.** in or near the beginning of a period of time or of a course or series: *It's still too early in the election to predict who will be the winner.* **2.** before the customary or expected hour: *I arrived at work early.* **3.** far back in time; in remote times. [Old English *ǣrlīce* near the start of a time period, from *ǣr* before + *-līce* -ly¹.] —**ear′li·ness,** *n.*

• **early on.** in or near the beginning; at a beginning stage.

early bird *Informal.* a person who does something before others do, esp. one who rises or arrives early.

ear·mark (îr′märk′) *n.* **1.** a mark of identification, usually a cut, made on the ear of an animal to indicate ownership. **2.** any distinguishing or identifying mark or feature; characteristic; sign: *The book has all the earmarks of a bestseller.* —*v.t.* **1.** to make an earmark on (the ear of an animal). **2.** to mark with an identifying or characteristic sign. **3.** to set aside, as for a specific purpose; reserve: *The state earmarked too little money for conservation.*

ear·muffs (îr′mufs′) *pl. n.* a pair of ear coverings, usually connected by an adjustable band, to be worn for protection against the cold.

earn (ûrn) *v.t.* **1.** to receive or gain in return for work done or services rendered: *to earn money mowing lawns.* **2.** to acquire or get as a result of effort or merit; be worthy of; deserve: *The clerk really earned that promotion.* **3.** to produce as income; yield: *The bonds earn interest quarterly.* [Old English *earnian* to deserve, labor for.] —**earn′er,** *n.* —For Synonyms, see **merit.**

ear·nest¹ (ûr′nist) *adj.* **1.** sincere in purpose or feeling: *an earnest person, an earnest student.* **2.** showing or characterized by sincere feeling or conviction: *an earnest apology, an earnest plea.* **3.** of a serious or important nature: *an earnest matter.* [Old English *eornoste* serious.] —**ear′nest·ly,** *adv.* —**ear′nest·ness,** *n.*

• **in earnest.** with sincere intent: *Our offer of help was made in earnest.*

ear·nest² (ûr′nist) *n.* an act or object giving assurance or indication of something to come, as a deposit of money or a token or pledge. [Modification (influenced by EARNEST¹) of Middle English *ernes,* from Old French *erres,* from Latin *arrae,* plural of *arra, arrabo* earnest money, from Greek *arrhabōn,* from Hebrew *eravon,* from *arav* to pledge, guarantee.]

earnest money, partial payment of money as a token or pledge to bind a contract or secure a sale.

earn·ings (ûr′ningz) *pl. n.* money earned, esp. as wages or profits.

ear·phone (îr′fōn′) *n.* a listening device held at or worn over or in the ear, such as a radio or telephone receiver.

ear·plug (îr′plug′) *n.* a rubber or plastic plug inserted into the ear to keep out water or noise.

ear·ring (îr′ring′) *n.* an ornament attached to the earlobe.

ear·shot (îr′shot′) *n.* the distance within which a sound, esp. the human voice, can be heard.

ear·split·ting (îr′split′ing) *adj.* painfully loud; deafening: *an earsplitting crash.*

earth (ûrth) *n.* **1.** *also,* **Earth.** the planet on which humans live, the fifth largest planet of the solar system, and third in order of distance from the sun. **2.** the solid portion of this planet; land; the ground. **3.** soil; dirt. **4.** the inhabitants of the planet Earth collectively, esp. the human inhabitants. **5.a.** the abode of humans, often in contrast to heaven and hell. **b.** worldly pursuits and interests in contrast to spiritual concerns; human affairs: *Weary of earth and laden with my sin* (S. J. Stone, 1866). **6.** the hole or lair of a fox or other burrowing animal. **7.** any of several metallic oxides that are difficult to reduce, such as alumina. [Old English *eorthe* ground, world.]

• **down to earth.** simple and straightforward.

• **to come back** (or **down**) **to earth.** to return to or face reality.

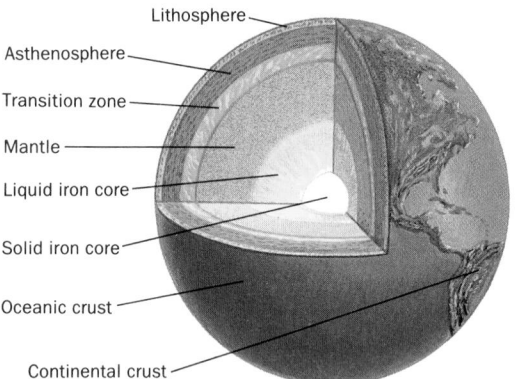

Lithosphere
Asthenosphere
Transition zone
Mantle
Liquid iron core
Solid iron core
Oceanic crust
Continental crust

layers of the **earth**

earth·born (ûrth′bôrn′) *also,* **earth-born.** *adj.* **1.** mortal; human: *earthborn cares.* **2.** of earthly origin; not divine.

earth·bound (ûrth′bound′) *also,* **earth-bound.** *adj.* **1.** headed for or going toward the earth: *The rocket ship was earthbound.* **2.** bound by earthly or materialistic ties or interests: *earthbound attitudes.*

earth·en (ûr′thən) *adj.* **1.** made of earth: *an earthen floor.* **2.** made of baked clay: *an earthen jug.*

earth·en·ware (ûr′thən wâr′) *n.* pottery made of a coarse and slightly porous grade of clay baked at a low temperature.

earth·light (ûrth′līt′) *n.* earthshine.

earth·ling (ûrth′ling) *n.* an inhabitant of the earth; human being.

earth·ly (ûrth′lē) *adj.,* **-li·er, -li·est. 1.** of or relating to the earth, esp. as opposed to heaven; worldly; secular: *earthly possessions.* **2.** possible; imaginable: *of no earthly use.* —**earth′li·ness,** *n.*

earth·mov·er (ûrth′mū′vər) *n.* a vehicle, such as a bulldozer or dump truck, used to move or carry excavated earth.

earth·nut (ûrth′nut′) *n.* the root, tuber, or underground pod of any of various plants, as the peanut. [Middle English *erthenote,* from Old English *eorthnutu.* See EARTH, NUT.]

earth·quake (ûrth′kwāk′) *n.* a shaking or movement in the earth, caused by the sudden shifting of rock along an existing fracture or fault or by volcanic or other disturbances.

earth science 1. any or all of the sciences, as geology, geography, oceanography, and geophysics, dealing with the origin and physical features of the earth. **2.** a course of study that surveys the basic facts of geology, meteorology, and astronomy, emphasizing the history of the earth's features rather than merely describing them.

earth·shak·ing (ûrth′shā′king) *adj.* influencing or challenging basic beliefs or attitudes; of fundamental or profound significance: *an earthshaking discovery.*

earth·shine (ûrth′shīn′) *n.* the faint illumination of the dark portion of the moon by sunlight reflected from the earth's surface.

earth station, a ground facility equipped to receive or transmit signals from or to satellites or spacecraft using a disk-shaped antenna.

earth·ward (ûrth′wərd) *adj.* moving toward the earth. —*adv.* also, **earth′wards.** toward the earth: *The plane plunged earthward.*

earth·work (ûrth′wûrk′) *n.* **1.** a fortification made of earth. **2.** the excavation and piling up of earth in engineering operations.

earth·worm (ûrth′wûrm′) *n.* any of several cylindrical, segmented worms, order Terricolae, found throughout the world, which live in the soil. Also, **angleworm.**

earth·y (ûr′thē) *adj.*, **earth·i·er, earth·i·est. 1.** containing, resembling, or characteristic of earth or soil: *an earthy smell, an earthy color.* **2.** natural and hearty; uninhibited: *earthy people.* **3.** unrefined; coarse; robust: *earthy humor.* —**earth′i·ness,** *n.*

ear trumpet, a trumpet-shaped instrument for collecting and concentrating sound waves when held to the ear, formerly used by the partially deaf.

ear·wax (îr′waks′) *n.* a waxy, yellowish substance produced by small glands that line the canal of the external ear. It serves to trap foreign bodies and protect the skin of the external canal from infection. Also, **cerumen.**

ear·wig (îr′wig′) *n.* any of a group of beetlelike insects, family Forficulidae, having a hard, slender body, threadlike antennae, and a pair of movable horny pincers at the end of the abdomen. [Old English *ēarwicga,* from *ēare* ear + *wicga* insect; from an earlier belief that it crawled into the ears of sleeping people.]

ease (ēz) *n.* **1.** freedom from pain, discomfort, toil, or worry: *a life of ease.* **2.** freedom from great effort or difficulty in doing something: *to swim with ease.* **3.** freedom from stiffness, formality, or constraint; naturalness; poise: *an ease of manner that showed self-confidence.* —*v.,* **eased, eas·ing.** —*v.t.* **1.** to free from pain, discomfort, or worry; make comfortable or relieve (often with *of): The good news eased my mind of worry. The nurse eased the patient's suffering.* **2.** to make less; lighten; alleviate: *Physical activity can often ease nervous tension.* **3.** to lessen the pressure, tension, or strain of (something); loosen: *to ease a tight waistband, to ease a rope.* **4.** to move or place (something) slowly and carefully: *to ease a bolt into place.* **5.** to make easier; facilitate: *to ease borrowing on credit.* —*v.i.* **1.** to lessen severity, tension, or pressure: *a warm bath and nap that eases.* **2.** to move slowly and carefully: *Latecomers at the theater eased into their seats.* [Old French *aise* comfort, opportunity, from Latin *adjacēns,* present participle of *adjacēre* to lie near.]

• **at ease. a.** free from stiffness and nervousness; relaxed: *The hosts' friendly manner helped their guests feel at ease.* **b.** *Military.* in a relaxed standing position with the feet apart and the hands behind the back. ➡ often used as a command.

• **to ease off.** to lessen, as in severity, tension, or pressure: *to ease off some of the responsibilities of a demanding job.*

• **to ease up on.** to reduce or relax the pressure on: *The coach eased up on the team after they won three games in a row.*

Synonyms *n.* **Ease** and **comfort** denote a state in which one is free from pain, stress, or exertion. **Ease** suggests that there is no work or obligation to interfere with one's relaxation: *to look forward to a life of ease after retirement.* **Comfort,** on the other hand, connotes the absence of strain or stress, and suggests enjoyment of good things: *The patient enjoyed the comfort of a warm, soft bed.*

ease·ful (ēz′fəl) *adj.* characterized by or giving ease; peaceful; restful. —**ease′ful·ly,** *adv.* —**ease′ful·ness,** *n.*

ea·sel (ē′zəl) *n.* an upright frame or tripod used chiefly to support an artist's canvas or a displayed item, as a poster. [Dutch *ezel* literally, little ass, from Latin *asinus* ass; because, like a beast of burden, it supports something.]

ease·ment (ēz′mənt) *n. Law.* **1.** a right or privilege to the limited use of land or a part of the land owned by another, such as a right of way for a driveway. **2.** the land affected by such a right or privilege: *The electric company is going to string transmission wires along the easement.*

eas·i·ly (ē′zə lē) *adv.* **1.** without difficulty, discomfort, or great effort; with ease. **2.** without a doubt; beyond question; certainly: *My friend is easily the best player on the team.* **3.** very likely: *It could easily take us more time than we expected.*

eas·i·ness (ē′zē nis) *n.* the quality or state of being easy.

east (ēst) *n.* **1.** the general direction of the sunrise in relation to an observer on earth. **2.** one of the four cardinal points of the compass, lying directly opposite west and 90 degrees right of north. **3.** also, **East.** any region situated toward this direction in relation to a specified point of reference. **4. the East.** Asia and the islands close to it. —*adj.* **1.** toward or in the east. **2.** coming

from the east: *an east wind.* —*adv.* toward the east. [Old English *ēast* in the direction of the sunrise.]

east·bound (ēst′bound′) *adj.* going eastward.

East·er (ēs′tər) *n.* **1.** the Christian feast commemorating Jesus' resurrection, celebrated on the Sunday after the first full moon following the vernal equinox. **2.** the Sunday on which this feast is celebrated. Also, (def. 2), **Easter Sunday.** [Old English *ēastre* this feast, from *Ēastre* the Teutonic goddess of the dawn whose rites were also celebrated in the spring.]

Easter egg, a decorated egg or an imitation of one, used as an Easter ornament or gift.

Easter lily, a lily, *Lilium longiflorum,* variety *eximium,* bearing large, white, trumpet-shaped flowers, often used at Easter for decoration.

east·er·ly (ēs′tər lē) *adj., adv.* **1.** toward the east: *to sail easterly.* **2.** from the east: *an easterly storm, easterly winds.* —*n., pl.* **-lies.** a wind blowing from the east.

east·ern (ēs′tərn) *adj.* **1.** toward, or in the east: *a room with an eastern exposure.* **2.** also, **Eastern.** of, relating to, or characteristic of the east or East: *an eastern accent.* **3. Eastern.** Oriental: *Eastern philosophy.* **4.** coming from the east.

Eastern Church 1. the Orthodox or Uniate Church. **2.** any of various independent Christian churches, such as the Coptic Church, deriving from the church of the Byzantine Empire.

east·ern·er (ēs′tər nər) *n.* **1.** a person who was born or lives in the east. **2.** *usually,* **Easterner.** a person who was born or lives in the eastern part of the United States.

Eastern Hemisphere, the half of the earth extending east of the Greenwich meridian, including Europe, Asia, Africa, and Australia.

east·ern·most (ēs′tərn mōst′) *adj.* farthest east.

Eastern Orthodox Church, Orthodox Church.

Eastern Standard Time, the local civil time of the 75th meridian west of Greenwich, England, used in much of the eastern United States and Canada. It is 5 hours earlier than Greenwich Time.

East·er·tide (ēs′tər tīd′) *n.* the ecclesiastical season extending from Easter to Trinity Sunday.

east-north·east (ēst′nôrth′ēst′; *Nautical* ēst′nôr′ēst′) *n.* a point on the compass halfway between east and northeast. —*adj., adv.* toward the east-northeast.

east-south·east (ēst′south′ēst′; *Nautical* ēst′sou′ēst′) *n.* a point on the compass halfway between east and southeast. —*adj., adv.* toward the east-southeast.

east·ward (ēst′wərd) *adv.* also, **east·wards.** toward the east: *to travel eastward.* —*adj.* toward or in the east. —*n.* an eastward direction, point, or part.

east·ward·ly (ēst′wərd lē) *adj., adv.* toward the east.

eas·y (ē′zē) *adj.*, **eas·i·er, eas·i·est. 1.** requiring little effort; not difficult: *an easy task, an easy test.* **2.** free from discomfort, trouble, or anxiety: *an easy mind.* **3.** not oppressive, demanding, or harsh; lenient: *easy terms of payment, an easy teacher.* **4.** providing or characterized by comfort; comfortable or restful: *an easy week in a hotel.* **5.** free from stiffness, formality, or awkwardness; relaxed: *an easy style of speaking.* **6.** readily influenced, persuaded, or taken advantage of; credulous: *an easy victim.* **7.** not readily agitated; even-tempered; easygoing: *an easy disposition.* **8.** not hurried or forced; gentle: *an easy pace.* **9.** not binding or tight: *an easy fit.* **10.** well-off; affluent: *in easy circumstances.* **11.a.** (of money) in abundance and available for loans, esp. at lower interest rates. **b.** (of a market) characterized by decreased demand and often lower prices. **c.** (of a commodity) in abundance and available, esp. at lower prices. —*adv. Informal.* easily. [Old French *aisie,* past participle of *aisier* to put at ease, from *aise* comfort. See EASE.]

• **to go easy on** (or **with**). *Informal.* **a.** to use in moderation; be sparing. **b.** to treat leniently or gently.

• **to take it easy.** *Informal.* **a.** to avoid too much effort or activity; relax. **b.** to stay calm.

Synonyms *adj.* **Easy** and **simple** mean without difficulty. **Easy** suggests that an undertaking requires little exertion, either physical or mental: *It's an easy walk from here to the beach. Writing the memo will be an easy job.* **Simple** connotes lack of complexity, and therefore ease in understanding or performing: *This model will be easy to build because the directions are simple.*

a	at	e	end	o	hot	u	up	hw	white		about
ā	ape	ē	me	ō	old	ū	use	ng	song		taken
ä	far	i	it	ô	fork	ü	rule	th	thin	ə	pencil
âr	care	ī	ice	oi	oil	u̇	pull	th	this		lemon
		îr	pierce	ou	out	ûr	turn	zh	measure		circus

E

easy chair, a comfortable chair, esp. a padded armchair.
eas·y·go·ing (ē′zē gō′ing) *adj.* **1.** inclined to be calm and unhurried; good-natured; relaxed. **2.** having an easy gait or step.
easy mark *Informal.* a person who is easily fooled or taken advantage of.
easy street, comfortable financial circumstances; well-to-do: *Since they inherited the money, they've been living on easy street.*
eat (ēt) *v.,* **ate, eat·en, eat·ing.** *—v.t.* **1.** to take in through the mouth and swallow, esp. to chew and swallow. **2.** to wear away gradually; waste; corrode (often with *away*): *Rust has eaten the surface of the metal.* **3.** to waste or consume by or as by eating (often with *away* or *up*): *Medical expenses ate our savings.* **4.** to make, as by gnawing or corroding: *The acid ate holes in the metal. The termites ate their way through the log.* **5.** *Slang.* to upset or annoy: *What's eating you?* *—v.i.* **1.** to take in and eat food; have a meal: *We eat at six o'clock. The starving dog ate ravenously.* **2.** to destroy something or wear it away gradually, as by gnawing or corroding (with *into* or *through*): *The mice ate into the cushions. Rust ate through the pipes.* *—pl. n.* **eats.** *Slang.* food. [Old English *etan* to consume food, devour, destroy.] **—eat′er,** *n.*
·to eat up. a. to use up or squander: *Taxes ate up their inheritance.* **b.** *Slang.* to take pleasure or delight in; accept eagerly: *She eats up praise.* **c.** *Slang.* to believe without question: *He eats up everything he reads in the newspaper.*
eat·a·ble (ē′tə bəl) *adj.* fit to be eaten; edible. *—n.* something fit to eat; food. ➡ usually used in the plural.
eat·er·y (ē′tə rē) *n., pl.* **-er·ies.** *Informal.* restaurant.
eat·ing (ē′ting) *n.* **1.** *Informal.* food with reference to the flavor or quality it displays when eaten: *This chicken is good eating.* **2.** the act of a person, animal, or thing that eats. *—adj.* good or fit to be eaten, esp. raw: *eating apples.*
eau de Co·logne (ō′ də kə lōn′) cologne. [French *eau de Cologne* literally, water of Cologne, a city in Germany.]
eau de vie (ō′ də vē′) *French.* brandy.
eaves (ēvz) *pl. n.* the lower edge of a sloping roof projecting beyond the sides of a building. [Old English *efes.*]

eaves·drop (ēvz′drop′) *v.i.,* **-dropped, -drop·ping.** to listen secretly to a private conversation. [Earlier *eavesdrip,* from Old English *efesdrypa* water that drips from the eaves; referring to standing under the eaves from which rainwater dripped in order to overhear a conversation in a house.] **—eaves′drop′per,** *n.*
ebb (eb) *n.* **1.** the receding of the tide from shore; flowing out of the tide. **2.** a point or condition of decline or decay: *The actor's career was at a low ebb.* *—v.i.* **1.** to flow out or recede, as the tide. **2.** to become less or weaker; decline; fail: *Hope of finding the lost child began to ebb.* [Old English *ebba* the receding of the tide.]
ebb tide 1. a falling or receding tide. ➡ opposed to **flood tide. 2.** the time or point of this.
EBCDIC (eb′sē dik′) an eight-bit computer code used to represent data, encoding 256 different letters, numerals, and other characters. [Short for *e(xtended) b(inary) c(oded) d(ecimal) i(nterchange) c(ode).*]
eb·on (eb′ən) *n., adj. Archaic.* ebony.
eb·on·ite (eb′ə nīt′) *n.* vulcanite. [EBON(Y) + -ITE[1].]
eb·on·y (eb′ə nē) *n., pl.* **-on·ies. 1.** the hard, heavy, deep black heartwood of any of several trees, genus *Diospyros,* used esp. for piano keys, knife handles, cabinets, and carvings. **2.** the tree yielding this wood, native to Africa, Sri Lanka, and the East Indies. *—adj.* **1.** made of ebony. **2.** like ebony, esp. in color; black. [Earlier *eban,* from Old French *eban, ebaine* the tree, from Latin *ebenos,* from Greek *ebenos;* of Egyptian origin.]
e·bul·lient (i bul′yənt) *adj.* **1.** overflowing or bubbling over with excitement or enthusiasm; exuberant: *The winner was ebullient.* **2.** boiling or bubbling up: *lava in an ebullient state.* [Latin *ēbulliēns,* present participle of *ēbullīre* to bubble or boil over.] **—e·bul′lience, e·bul′lien·cy,** *n.* **—e·bul′lient·ly,** *adv.*
eb·ul·li·tion (eb′ə lish′ən) *n.* **1.** the act or state of boiling or bubbling up. **2.** a sudden outburst or overflowing, as of emotions.
ec-, form of **ex-**[2] before consonants, as in *eclipse.*
EC, European Community.
é·car·té (ā′kär tā′) *n.* a card game for two people, played with a deck of thirty-two cards, consisting of sevens up through aces. [French *écarté,* past participle of *écarter* to discard, going back to Latin *ex* out of, away + *charta* paper; from the discarding of cards in the game. See CARD[1].]
ec·ce ho·mo (ech′ā hō′mō) *Latin.* **1.** "Behold the man," spoken in the Vulgate (John 19:5) by Pilate as he presented Jesus crowned with thorns. **2. Ecce Homo.** a representation of Jesus crowned with thorns.
ec·cen·tric (ek sen′trik, ik-) *adj.* **1.** deviating from established or conventional practices or conduct; peculiar; odd: *eccentric behavior, an eccentric family.* **2.a.** (of spheres and circles) not having the same center. **b.** not perfectly circular, as the orbit of a planet. **3.** not situated in the center, as an axis; having its axis set off center, as a wheel; off center. *—n.* **1.** a person who deviates from established or conventional practices or conduct. **2.** a disk set off center on a revolving shaft in order to change circular motion into reciprocating motion. [Middle English *eccentrik,* from Medieval Latin *eccentricus,* from Late Latin *eccentros* out of the center, from Greek *ekkentros,* from *ek-* out of, from + *kentron* center.] **—ec·cen′tri·cal·ly,** *adv.*

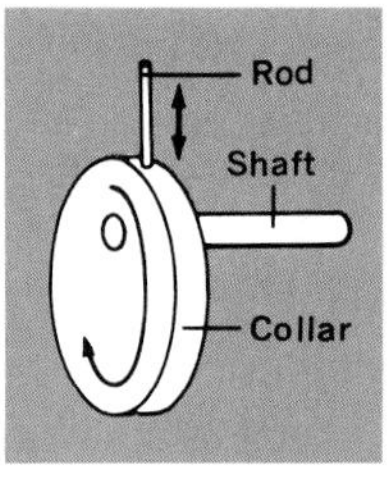

eccentric
(n., def. 2)

ec·cen·tric·i·ty (ek′sen tris′i tē) *n., pl.* **-ties. 1.** deviation from established or conventional practices or conduct; whimsical oddity. **2.** an act or characteristic that is unusual or odd; peculiarity. **3.** the state or quality of being eccentric: *the eccentricity of an axis.* **4.** the amount or degree by which something is eccentric.
eccl. *also,* **eccles.** ecclesiastic; ecclesiastical.
Eccl. *also,* **Eccles.** Ecclesiastes.
Ec·cle·si·as·tes (i klē′zē as′tēz) *n.* a book of the Old Testament, dealing with the frailties of human life, traditionally attributed to King Solomon. ➡ used as singular. [Greek *ekklēsiastēs* preacher, one who addresses an assembly, from *ekklēsiā* assembly, church.]
ec·cle·si·as·tic (i klē′zē as′tik) *n.* a member of the clergy or other person officially in the service of a church. *—adj.* ecclesiastical. [Late Latin *ecclēsiasticus* relating to the church, from Greek *ekklēsiastikos,* going back to *ekklēsiā* assembly, church.]
ec·cle·si·as·ti·cal (i klē′zē as′ti kəl) *adj.* of or relating to a church or clergy. **—ec·cle′si·as′ti·cal·ly,** *adv.*
Ec·cle·si·as·ti·cus (i klē′zē as′ti kəs) *n.* a book of the Old Testament, part of the Protestant Apocrypha and included in the canon of the Douay Bible. It is a collection of prayers and proverbs.
ec·dy·sis (ek′də sis) *n., pl.* **-ses** (-sēz′). the shedding of a shell or of the outer layer of skin to allow for growth, as in snakes, insects, and crustaceans; molting. [Modern Latin *ecdysis,* from Greek *ekdysis* a getting out, stripping, from *ekdyein* to strip off, from *ek-* out of + *dyein* to enter.]
ECG 1. electrocardiogram. **2.** electrocardiograph.
ech·e·lon (esh′ə lon′) *n.* **1.** a formation of military, naval, or air units in a steplike arrangement, with each successive unit behind and to one side of the preceding one. **2.a.** a subdivision of a military headquarters: *a rear echelon.* **b.** the part of a command to which a principal combat mission is assigned: *a support echelon.* **3.a.** a particular level of command, authority, or responsibility: *The clerical workers are in the lower echelons of the bureaucracy.* **b.** a group occupying such a level: *The higher echelon is in conference today.* *—v.t., v.i.* to move in or form into a steplike arrangement. [French *échelon* rung of a ladder, from *échelle* ladder, from Old French *eschelle,* going back to Latin *scāla.*]
e·chid·na (i kid′nə) *n.* any of various egg-laying, ant-eating mammals, genera *Tachyglossus* and *Zaglossus,* native to Australia, Tasmania, and New Guinea, having thick, grayish brown fur, yellow and black spines, a horny, toothless snout, and a long tongue. Length: 15-30 inches (38-76 centimeters). Also, **spiny anteater.** [Latin *echidna* viper, from Greek *echidna.*]

echidna

e·chi·no·derm (i kī′nə dûrm′, ek′ə nə-) *n.* any of a large, widespread group of invertebrate sea animals, as the starfish and sea urchin, phylum Echinodermata, having a limy, internal shell, spiny skin, and a radially symmetrical shape. [Modern Latin *Echinodermata,* from Greek *echīnos* hedgehog, sea urchin + *derma* skin.]
e·chi·noid (i kī′noid, ek′ə noid′) *n.* any of a group of

echinoderms, class Echinoidea, consisting of the sea urchins and sand dollars. [Greek *echīnos* sea urchin, hedgehog + -OID.]

e·chi·nus (i kī′nəs) *n., pl.* **-ni** (-nī). **1.** sea urchin. **2.** a convex molding below the abacus of a Doric capital, or a corresponding member in other capitals. [Latin *echinus* sea urchin, hedgehog, from Greek *echīnos.*]

ech·o (ek′ō) *n., pl.* **ech·oes. 1.a.** the repetition of a sound produced by the reflection of sound waves from an obstructing surface. **b.** the sound so produced. **2.** any repetition or close imitation, as of the ideas or opinions of another. **3.** a person who closely imitates another, as in speech, opinions, or dress. **4.** a radio wave or radar pulse reflected back to a transmitter or receiver. **5. Echo.** in Greek mythology, a nymph who pined away with love for Narcissus until only her voice remained. —*v.t.* **1.** to resound with or send back the sound of: *The cavern walls echoed our cries.* **2.** to repeat or closely imitate, as the ideas or opinions of another; repeat in imitation: *The revolutionaries echoed the thoughts of their leader.* **3.** to repeat or closely imitate the words, ideas, or actions of (another): *The young child echoed her older brother.* —*v.i.* **1.** to resound with or send back an echo; reverberate: *The corridor echoed with footsteps.* **2.** to be repeated by or as if by an echo: *Our laughter echoed through the house. Her words echoed in his ears.* [Middle English *ecco* (possibly through French *écho*), from Latin *ēchō*, from Greek *ēchō.*] —**ech′o·er,** *n.*

e·cho·ic (e kō′ik) *adj.* **1.** resembling an echo. **2.** formed in imitation of sounds; onomatopoeic.

ech·o·la·li·a (ek′ō lā′lē ə) *n. Psychiatry.* the meaningless and uncontrollable repetition of one person's words by another. [ECHO + Greek *laliā* chatter.]

ech·o·lo·ca·tion (ek′ō lō kā′shən) *n.* a method of determining the location of objects by sending out sound waves and interpreting the time and direction of their return. Bats and some fish use echolocation.

é·clair (ā klâr′) *n.* an oblong pastry shell filled with whipped cream or custard and usually topped with chocolate icing. [French *éclair* literally, lightning, from *éclairer* to illuminate, going back to Latin *ex* out + *clārus* clear.]

é·clat (ā klä′) *n.* **1.** dazzling or striking effect; conspicuous success; brilliance: *The guitarist performed with great éclat.* **2.** great applause or praise; acclaim: *The new play was received with éclat.* **3.** fame; renown. [French *éclat* burst, brightness, from *éclater* to burst out, shine; of Germanic origin.]

ec·lec·tic (e klek′tik, i klek′-) *adj.* **1.** selecting what seems best from various doctrines, systems, or sources: *an eclectic painter.* **2.** composed of elements selected from various sources: *an eclectic musical program.* —*n.* a person who uses an eclectic method or approach, as in science, art, or philosophy. [Greek *eklektikos* selecting, going back to *eklegein* to select.] —**ec·lec′ti·cal·ly,** *adv.*

ec·lec·ti·cism (e klek′tə siz′əm, i klek′-) *n.* **1.** the use or advocacy of an eclectic method. **2.** an eclectic method or system, as of philosophy.

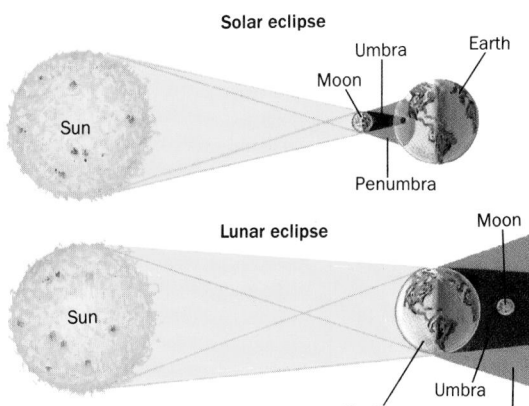

Solar eclipse

Earth
Umbra
Moon
Sun
Penumbra

Lunar eclipse

Moon
Sun
Umbra
Earth
Penumbra

eclipses

e·clipse (i klips′) *n.* **1.** an apparent partial or total darkening of one celestial body by its passage through the shadow of another. In a **solar eclipse** the moon passes between the sun and the earth, totally or partially blocking the sun's rays and darkening certain areas of the earth. In a **lunar eclipse** the earth moves between the sun and the moon, blocking the sun's rays and totally or partially

darkening the moon. **2.** any overshadowing or dimming, as of reputation or importance. —*v.t.,* **e·clipsed, e·clips·ing. 1.** to cause an eclipse of; darken. **2.** to overshadow or dim, esp. by comparison; outshine; surpass: *The star's performance eclipsed those of the other actors.* [Old French *eclipse* astronomical eclipse, from Latin *eclīpsis,* from Greek *ekleipsis* a leaving out, astronomical eclipse.]

e·clip·tic (i klip′tik) *n.* the path that the sun appears to follow annually in making a complete circuit of the celestial sphere. —*adj.* of or relating to eclipses or to the ecliptic. Also, **e·clip′ti·cal.** —**e·clip′ti·cal·ly,** *adv.*

ec·logue (ek′lôg, -log) *n.* a short pastoral poem, esp. in the form of dialogue between shepherds. [Latin *ecloga* short poem, from Greek *eklogē* selection.]

eco- *combining form* environment: *ecocide.* [Late Latin *oeco-,* from Greek *oiko,* from *oikos* house.]

ec·o·cide (ek′ə sīd′, ē′kə-) *n.* the destruction of the earth's environment, as by the overuse of natural resources, by pollution, or through nuclear warfare. [ECO- + -CIDE[1].]

ecol. 1. ecological. **2.** ecology.

é·cole (ā kôl′) *n. French.* school.

E. co·li (ē′ kō′lī) *n.* any of various strains of a coliform bacterium, *Escherichia coli,* occurring naturally in the intestines of humans and all vertebrates and widely used in genetic research. Its presence in water in large numbers indicates a health hazard. [Abbreviation of Modern Latin *E(scherichia) coli,* from T. *Escherich,* 1857-1911, German physician + Latin *coli* of the colon.]

e·col·o·gist (ē kol′ə jist) *n.* an expert in ecology.

e·col·o·gy (ē kol′ə jē) *n.* **1.a.** the relationship of living organisms to their environment and to each other: *the ecology of a region.* **b.** the branch of biology that deals with this. Also, **bionomics. 2.** *Sociology.* the study of the relationships of groups of people to their environment and to each other. [German *Ökologie* biological ecology, from Greek *oikos* house + *-logiā* -logy.] —**ec·o·log·ic** (ek′ə loj′ik, ē′kə-); *also,* **ec′o·log′i·cal,** *adj.* —**ec′o·log′i·cal·ly,** *adv.*

econ. 1. economic. **2.** economics. **3.** economy.

e·con·o·met·rics (ē kon′ə met′riks) *n.* the use of mathematical and statistical data to solve economic problems and to test and derive economic theories. ➡ used as singular. —**e·con′o·met′ric,** *adj.* —**e·con·o·me·tri·cian** (ē kon′ə mi trish′ən), *n.*

ec·o·nom·ic (ek′ə nom′ik, ē′kə-) *adj.* **1.** of or relating to the production, distribution, and consumption of wealth, goods, and services, as of a nation: *the economic policies of a country.* **2.** of or relating to the science of economics: *economic theory.* **3.** of or relating to money matters or concerns; financial: *We sold our second car for economic reasons.* **4.** economical.

ec·o·nom·i·cal (ek′ə nom′i kəl, ē′kə-) *adj.* **1.** not wasting money, goods, or other resources; frugal; thrifty: *an economical person, an economical car.* **2.** free from or avoiding waste or excess; efficient: *an economical use of time.* **3.** of or relating to economics; economic. —For Synonyms, see **thrifty.**

ec·o·nom·i·cal·ly (ek′ə nom′i klē, ē′kə-) *adv.* **1.** in a frugal manner; without waste. **2.** from an economic viewpoint.

ec·o·nom·ics (ek′ə nom′iks, ē′kə-) *n.* **1.** the science that deals with the production, distribution, and consumption of wealth, goods, and services, with the means of supplying the material needs of people, and with such related problems as capital, labor, and taxation. **2.** financial aspects or factors: *the economics of bridge construction.* ➡ used as singular in def. 1, as plural in def. 2.

e·con·o·mist (i kon′ə mist) *n.* a person trained or skilled in economics.

e·con·o·mize (i kon′ə mīz′) *v.,* **-mized, -miz·ing.** —*v.i.* to avoid waste or needless expense: *If we don't start economizing soon, we will have no money at all. We can economize on groceries this week.* —*v.t.* to use sparingly or to the best advantage: *to economize fuel, to economize one's time and effort.* —**e·con′o·miz′er,** *n.*

e·con·o·my (i kon′ə mē) *n., pl.* **-mies. 1.** the production, distribution, and consumption of wealth, goods, and services: *That nation's economy is growing rapidly.* **2.** a particular system on which these operate: *an agrarian economy.* **3.a.** the careful or frugal management of money or other material resources; thrift: *During a recession it is wise to practice economy.* **b.** an instance or means of economizing. **4.** an efficient and sparing use of something: *an economy of effort, an author who draws characters with an*

a	at	e	end	o	hot	u	up	hw	white	⎧	about
ā	ape	ē	me	ō	old	ū	use	ng	song		taken
ä	far	i	it	ô	fork	ü	rule	th	thin	ə	pencil
âr	care	ī	ice	oi	oil	u̇	pull	t͟h	this		lemon
				îr	pierce	ou	out	ûr	turn	zh	measure	⎩	circus

economy of detail. **5.** an orderly arrangement or regulation of parts or functions: *the economy of nature.* —*adj.* costing less than is usual or standard; money-saving: *an economy car.* [Latin *oeconomia* management of a household, from Greek *oikonomiā*, from *oikonomos* manager, administrator, from *oikos* house + *nemein* to manage, govern.]

ec·o·sphere (ek′ō sf îr′, ē′kō-) *n.* the parts of a planet or other celestial body habitable by living organisms, esp. the biosphere. [ECO- + SPHERE.]

ec·o·sys·tem (ek′ō sis′təm, ē′kō-) *n.* a group of living organisms and their environment, which function and are considered as an ecological unit. In a desert ecosystem, the plants and animals are highly adapted to conserve water.

ec·ru (ek′rü, ā′krü) *also,* **é·cru.** *n.* a pale yellowish brown color; light tan. —*adj.* having the color ecru. [French *écru* raw, unbleached, going back to Latin *ex* out of, utterly + *crūdus* raw.]

ec·sta·sy (ek′stə sē) *n., pl.* **-sies. 1.** a state of overwhelming joy or delight; rapture: *The children were in ecstasy at the thought of going to the circus.* **2.** the state of being completely absorbed by an emotion: *an ecstasy of fear.* **3.** a trance, esp. one thought to accompany mystic, prophetic, or poetic inspiration. [Old French *extasie* rapture, trance, from Late Latin *ecstasis* trance, from Greek *ekstasis* trance; literally, standing outside oneself.]

ec·stat·ic (ek stat′ik) *adj.* **1.** overwhelmed with joy or delight; enraptured. **2.** like, resulting from, or characterized by ecstasy. —*n.* a person who is subject to ecstasies or trances. —**ec·stat′i·cal·ly,** *adv.*

ECT, electroconvulsive therapy.

ecto- *combining form* outside; external; outer: *ectoderm, ectoplasm.* [Greek *ektos* outside.]

ec·to·derm (ek′tə dûrm′) *n.* the outermost of the three cell layers of the gastrula, from which develop the outer layer of skin, the nervous system, and the sense organs. [ECTO- + Greek *derma* skin.] —**ec′to·der′mal, ec′to·der′mic,** *adj.*

ec·to·morph (ek′tə môrf′) *n.* a person having a thin, bony body. ➡ distinguished from **endomorph** and **mesomorph.** [ECTO- + Greek *morphē* form, shape.] —**ec′to·mor′phic,** *adj.*

-ectomy *combining form* surgical removal of: *appendectomy.* [Latin *-ectomia* surgical removal, from Greek *ektemnein* to cut out, from *ex-* out + *temnein* to cut.]

ec·to·plasm (ek′tə plaz′əm) *n.* **1.** the outer layer of the cytoplasm of a cell. **2.** the supposed materialization of a spirit called forth by a medium. [ECTO- + -PLASM.]

ec·u·men·i·cal (ek′yə men′i kəl) *also,* **oecumenical.** *adj.* **1.** including the entire world; worldwide; universal. **2.** of, representing, or relating to all Christian churches: *an ecumenical council.* **3.** promoting worldwide Christian unity: *an ecumenical movement.* Also, **ec′u·men′ic.** [Late Latin *oecūmenicus* universal, from Greek *oikoumenikos,* from *oikoumenē* the inhabited world, going back to *oikos* house.] —**ec′u·men′i·cal·ism,** *n.* —**ec′u·men′i·cal·ly,** *adv.*

ec·u·me·nism (ek′yə mə niz′əm) *n.* **1.** a movement to promote worldwide Christian harmony and unity. **2.** a movement to promote better understanding among different religions. Also, **ec′u·men′i·cism.** —**ec′u·men′ist,** *n.*

ec·ze·ma (ek′sə mə, eg′zə-, eg zē′-) *n.* a skin disorder characterized by redness, itching, scaly patches, and, sometimes, tiny blisters that break and release a watery fluid. [Greek *ekzema,* from *ekzein* to boil over.]

-ed[1] *suffix* used to form the past tense of regular verbs: *I walked to work last week.* [Middle English *-ed,* from Old English *-de, -ede, -ode, -ade.*]

-ed[2] *suffix* **1.** used to form the past participle of regular verbs: *I have walked to work every day this month.* **2.** (used to form adjectives from nouns) **a.** characterized by or equipped with; having: *a blue-eyed baby, a fringed curtain.* **b.** having the characteristics of; like: *a bigoted neighbor, dogged pursuit.* **3.** used to form adjectives from adjectives ending in *-ate,* with the same general meaning: *bipinnated, dentated.* [Middle English *-ed,* from Old English *-ed, -od, -ad.*]

ed. *pl.* **eds. 1.** edited. **2.** edition. **3.** editor. **4.** education.

e·da·cious (i dā′shəs) *adj.* given to or characterized by voraciousness; devouring. [Latin *edāc-,* stem of *edāx* voracious + -OUS.] —**e·dac′i·ty** (i das′i tē), *n.*

E·dam (ē′dəm, ē′dam) *n.* a mild, solid, yellow cheese, usually round and flattened and enclosed in red paraffin. [From *Edam,* Dutch village where it was originally produced.]

Ed.B., Bachelor of Education.

Ed.D., Doctor of Education.

Ed·da (ed′ə) *n., pl.* **Ed·das.** either of two thirteenth-century collections of Icelandic literature. The **Poetic,** or **Elder, Edda** contains anonymous poems dealing primarily with Scandinavian mythology and heroic legends; the **Prose,** or **Younger, Edda** contains Scandinavian myths and heroic lore as well as commen-

taries on the techniques of ancient Icelandic court poetry. [Old Norse *edda,* possibly from *ōthr* spirit, poetry.] —**Ed·da·ic** (e dā′-ik), **Ed′dic,** *adj.*

ed·dy (ed′ē) *n., pl.* **-dies. 1.** a current, as of air or water, moving against the main current, esp. with a circular or whirling motion; small whirlwind or whirlpool. **2.** a movement or trend departing from a main movement or trend: *eddies of political thought.* —*v.i.,* **-died, -dy·ing.** to move in an eddy; move with a circular motion; whirl: *Smoke eddied from the chimney.* [Possibly from Old Norse *itha* whirlpool.]

e·del·weiss (ā′dəl vīs′) *n.* **1.** the starlike flower head of a plant, *Leontopodium alpinum,* of the composite family, having tiny yellow flowers surrounded by white, petallike leaves. **2.** the plant bearing this flower head, found on high mountains in Europe and Asia. [German *Edelweiss,* from *edel* noble + *weiss* white.]

e·de·ma (i dē′mə) *n., pl.* **-ma·ta** (-mə tə). an abnormal accumulation of clear, watery fluid in the tissues or cavities of the body, as in the sac that surrounds the heart. Formerly, **dropsy.** [Modern Latin *oedema,* from Greek *oidēma* swelling.]

E·den (ē′dən) *n.* **1.** Garden of Eden. **2.** any delightful region or place; paradise. **3.** a state of perfect or supreme happiness. [Late Latin *Eden,* from Hebrew *eden* Garden of Eden; literally, delight.]

e·den·tate (ē den′tāt) *n.* any of a group of mammals, order Edentata, having few or no teeth, including armadillos, sloths, and anteaters. —*adj.* **1.** of, relating to, or belonging to this order. **2.** toothless. [Latin *ēdentātus* toothless, going back to *ex* out of + *dēns* tooth.]

edge (ej) *n.* **1.** a line or place where an object or area begins or ends; extreme or outermost border: *the edge of a table, the water's edge.* **2.** the thin, sharp, cutting side of the blade of a cutting instrument, weapon, or tool. **3.** the line where surfaces of a solid meet. **4.** sharpness or intensity; keenness: *Eating the cracker took the edge off the child's appetite.* **5.** *Informal.* a favorable position; advantage: *to have a slight edge on one's opponent.* —*v.,* **edged, edg·ing.** —*v.t.* **1.** to furnish with a border: *The upholsterer edged the curtains with fringe.* **2.** to be or form a border for: *Tulips edged the walkway.* **3.** to advance or move slowly or gradually: *I edged the heavy crate across the floor.* **4.** to increase the cutting quality of; sharpen: *to edge a knife.* —*v.i.* to advance or move slowly, gradually, or sidewise: *to edge through a crowded room.* [Old English *ecg* cutting side of a blade, sword.]

• **on edge.** very tense, nervous, or impatient: *The athletes were on edge as they waited for the game to begin.*

• **to edge out.** to defeat by a narrow margin: *We edged out the other team for first place.*

> **Synonyms** *n.* **Edge, border,** and **rim** indicate an outer limit or end of something. **Edge** suggests sharpness or abruptness, as where two planes intersect or where a physical body ends: *the river's edge, the edge of a piece of paper.* **Border** connotes either the line separating one surface from another or the area near that line: *The borders of the sheet are hemmed. The country's border is closely guarded.* **Rim** connotes the curved edge of a circular or similar object: *the rim of a glass, the rim of a volcano.*

edge·wise (ej′wīz′) *adv.* **1.** with the edge forward. **2.** on, by, with, or toward the edge. Also, **edge·ways** (ej′wāz′).

• **to get a word in edgewise.** to succeed in saying something in a conversation dominated by a talkative person or persons.

edg·ing (ej′ing) *n.* something that forms or is attached along a border, as a fringe; trimming.

edg·y (ej′ē) *adj.,* **edg·i·er, edg·i·est. 1.** on edge; uneasy. **2.** having a sharp edge or edges. —**edg′i·ly,** *adv.* —**edg′i·ness,** *n.*

ed·i·ble (ed′ə bəl) *adj.* capable of being eaten; fit to eat; not poisonous. —*n.* something fit to eat; food. ➡ often used in the plural. [Late Latin *edibilis* eatable, from Latin *edere* to eat.] —**ed′i·bil′i·ty, ed′i·ble·ness,** *n.*

e·dict (ē′dikt) *n.* **1.** an official decree from a sovereign or other authority, publicly proclaimed and having the force of law. **2.** any authoritative command or prohibition. [Latin *ēdictum* proclamation.]

ed·i·fi·ca·tion (ed′ə fi kā′shən) *n.* the act of edifying or the state of being edified; intellectual or moral enlightenment or improvement: *to read the classics for one's own edification.*

ed·i·fice (ed′ə fis) *n.* a building or other structure, esp. one that is large and impressive. [Old French *edifice* building, from Latin *aedificium.*]

ed·i·fy (ed′ə fī′) *v.t.,* **-fied, -fy·ing.** to enlighten and improve, esp. morally or spiritually; instruct. [Old French *edifier* to build, from Latin *aedificāre.*] —**ed′i·fi′er,** *n.*

e·dile (ē′dīl) *n.* aedile.

ed·it (ed′it) *v.t.* **1.** to correct, revise, and otherwise prepare (a manuscript) for publication. **2.** to collect, arrange, and annotate (literary material) for publication. **3.** to review, cut, and arrange

for public presentation: *to edit a film, to edit a tape.* **4.** to direct the preparation and editorial policies of, as a newspaper or periodical. **5.** *Computers.* to change the format of or information in (a computer file). [From EDITOR.]

edit. **1.** edited. **2.** edition. **3.** editor.

e·di·tion (i dish′ən) *n.* **1.** a particular form in which a book or other literary work is published: *a two-volume edition, a pocket edition.* **2.a.** the total number of copies of a publication printed from the same plates or type. **b.** a single copy belonging to such a printing: *We have the Sunday edition of the newspaper delivered.* [Latin *ēditiō* a bringing forth, publishing.]

ed·i·tor (ed′i tər) *n.* **1.** a person who edits. **2.** a person in charge of the publication of a newspaper or magazine or one of its departments. [Latin *ēditor* one who brings forth or produces.]

ed·i·to·ri·al (ed′i tôr′ē əl) *n.* an article in a newspaper or magazine, or a statement on radio or television, expressing the opinion or viewpoint of the editor, publisher, or owner on a particular topic. —*adj.* of, relating to, or characteristic of an editor, editing, or an editorial: *an editorial staff, editorial duties, an editorial comment.* —**ed′i·to′ri·al·ly,** *adv.*

ed·i·to·ri·al·ist (ed′i tôr′ē ə list) *n.* a writer of editorials.

ed·i·to·ri·al·ize (ed′i tôr′ē ə līz′) *v.i.,* **-ized, -iz·ing. 1.** to express opinions in or as in an editorial. **2.** to insert or introduce editorial comments into a factual report. —**ed′i·to′ri·al·i·za′- tion,** *n.* —**ed′i·to′ri·al·iz′er,** *n.*

ed·i·tor·ship (ed′i tər ship′) *n.* the position, functions, or authority of an editor.

E·dom·ite (ē′də mīt′) *n.* a descendant of Esau; inhabitant of Edom.

EDP, electronic data processing.

EDT, Eastern Daylight Time.

ed·u·ca·ble (ej′ə kə bəl) *adj.* capable of being educated. Also, **ed·u·cat·a·ble** (ej′ə kā′tə bəl).

ed·u·cate (ej′ə kāt′) *v.t.,* **-cat·ed, -cat·ing. 1.** to develop knowledge, skills, ability, or character in, esp. by formal schooling or systematic instruction; teach. **2.** to provide with training for some particular purpose: *to be educated for the priesthood.* **3.** to develop and improve by teaching and training; cultivate: *to educate one's mind.* **4.** to provide schooling for; send to school: *The cost of educating children has risen enormously.* [Latin *ēducātus,* past participle of *ēducāre* to bring up, rear.] —For Synonyms, see **teach.**

ed·u·cat·ed (ej′ə kā′tid) *adj.* **1.** having an education, esp. one that is above the average. **2.** showing evidence of or developed by having been taught, trained, or instructed; cultivated: *educated speech.* **3.** based on some information or experience: *an educated guess.*

ed·u·ca·tion (ej′ə kā′shən) *n.* **1.** the act or process of educating; systematic instruction. **2.** knowledge, skill, or ability developed or obtained by such a process; learning. **3.a.** a course of scholastic instruction or formal schooling in an institution of learning: *a college education, a liberal arts education.* **b.** a program of instruction of a specified kind: *driver education.* **4.** a field of study dealing with the problems, methods, and theories of teaching and learning: *to get a degree in education.* [Latin *ēducātiō* a bringing up, rearing.]

ed·u·ca·tion·al (ej′ə kā′shə nəl) *adj.* **1.** of or relating to education: *educational methods.* **2.** giving or providing information or knowledge; instructive: *an educational television program.* —**ed′- u·ca′tion·al·ly,** *adv.*

educational television **1.** television programs containing educational or instructional material. **2.** public television.

ed·u·ca·tive (ej′ə kā′tiv) *adj.* **1.** tending to educate; educational. **2.** of or relating to education: *the educative process.*

ed·u·ca·tor (ej′ə kā′tər) *n.* **1.** a person whose profession it is to educate others; person trained in teaching. **2.** a specialist or authority in the field of education.

e·duce (i düs′, i düs′) *v.t.,* **e·duced, e·duc·ing. 1.** to bring out; draw forth; elicit. **2.** to infer from data; deduce. [Latin *ēdūcere* to bring out.] —**e·duc′i·ble,** *adj.*

Ed·ward·i·an (ed wär′dē ən, -wôr′-) *adj.* **1.** of or relating to King Edward VII of England or the period of his reign. **2.** of, relating to, characteristic of, or reminiscent of Edwardian England, in which styles were excessively ornate and manners and attitudes were overly genteel and pompous. —*n.* an English person who lived during the reign of Edward VII.

-ee *suffix* (used to form nouns from verbs) **1.** a person who is affected by or is the recipient of a specified action or process: *appointee, payee.* **2.** a person who performs a specified action or is in a specified condition: *escapee, standee.* [Anglo-Norman and Old French past participial ending *-e,* from Latin *-ātus.* See -ATE [1].]

E.E., Electrical Engineer.

EEC, European Economic Community.

EEG **1.** electroencephalogram. **2.** electroencephalograph.

eel (ēl) *n., pl.* **eels** or **eel. 1.** any of various scaleless, snakelike fish, order Anguilliformes, widely distributed in both salt and fresh water, having narrow fins that form a continuous line with the body. Length: to 10 feet (3 meters). **2.** any of various similar fish, such as the electric eel and lamprey. [Old English *ǣl* the fish of the order Anguilliformes.]

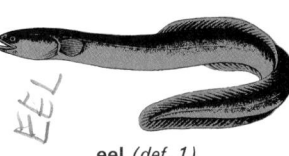

eel *(def. 1)*

eel·grass (ēl′gras′) *n.* either of two grasses that grow in shallow waters throughout the world, *Vallisneria americana,* found in fresh water and having short stems and grasslike leaves, and *Zostera marina,* found in salt water and having branching stems and long, ribbonlike leaves.

eel·pout (ēl′pout′) *n.* any of various eellike saltwater fish, family Zoarcidae, related to the blenny. [Old English *ǣlepūte.*]

eel·worm (ēl′wûrm′) *n.* any of numerous roundworms, some of which are parasitic on plants.

e'en (ēn) *adv. Archaic.* even.

e'er (âr) *adv. Archaic.* ever.

-eer *suffix* **1.** (used to form nouns) **a.** a person who makes or produces: *pamphleteer, sonneteer, profiteer.* **b.** a person who is concerned or has to do with: *auctioneer, engineer.* **2.** (used to form verbs) to be concerned or have to do with: *to electioneer.* [French *-ier,* from Latin *-ārius.* See -ARY [1].]

ee·rie (ir′ē) *also,* **ee·ry.** *adj.,* **-ri·er, -ri·est. 1.** strange and frightening, so as to arouse superstitious fear; weird; uncanny. **2.** nervously uneasy; fearful: *The old house gave us an eerie feeling.* [Old English *earg* timid.] —**ee′ri·ly,** *adv.* —**ee′ri·ness,** *n.*

ef-, form of **ex-** [1] before *f,* as in *efficient.*

ef·face (i fās′) *v.t.,* **-faced, -fac·ing. 1.** to make indistinct or destroy by or as by rubbing out; obliterate; erase: *The hieroglyphics on the tomb were effaced by wind and sand. I tried to efface the unhappy memory.* **2.** to make (oneself) inconspicuous: *After the public scandal, the city officials effaced themselves as best they could.* [French *effacer* to erase, going back to Latin *ex* out of, away + *faciēs* form, face.] —**ef·face′a·ble,** *adj.* —**ef·face′- ment,** *n.* —**ef·fac′er,** *n.* —For Synonyms, see **erase.**

ef·fect (i fekt′) *n.* **1.** something brought about by a cause or agent; result; consequence; outcome. **2.a.** the power or ability to bring about a result; efficacy: *The minor scandal proved to have no effect on the election.* **b.** the influence or impact that something has: *The bad news had a sobering effect on the party.* **3.** the state or fact of being operative or in force; operation: *to put a plan into effect.* **4.** an overall or distinctive impression produced on the mind or senses: *This painter achieves dramatic effects by the use of color.* **5.** something, as a technique, used to produce a distinctive impression or achieve a certain result: *I am in charge of lighting effects for the school play.* **6.** the general or basic meaning; intent (with *to*): *The governor's speech was to the effect that the state would preserve its wildlife.* **7.** **effects.** belongings; property; possessions: *personal effects, household effects.* —*v.t.* to bring about; produce as a result; cause; accomplish: *to effect a change in policy.* [Latin *effectus* accomplishment, performance.] —For Synonyms *(v.t.),* see **accomplish;** *(n.),* see **outcome.**

• **for effect.** in order to make an impression; for show.

• **in effect.** **a.** in actual fact; in reality. **b.** for all practical purposes; virtually: *There are, in effect, only two good players on that team.* **c.** in operation; functioning: *The curfew is now in effect.*

• **to take effect.** to have or begin to have results: *The pill should take effect in an hour.*

ef·fec·tive (i fek′tiv) *adj.* **1.** producing or capable of producing an intended or desired effect: *an effective method, an effective argument.* **2.** in effect; operative; active. **3.** producing a striking impression; impressive: *an effective speaker.* **4.** fit for action or duty: *Effective military forces numbered 10,000.* —**ef·fec′tive- ly,** *adv.* —**ef·fec′tive·ness,** *n.*

ef·fec·tor (i fek′tər) *n.* **1.** a muscle, gland, or cell capable of responding to a stimulus, esp. a nerve impulse. **2.** a nerve ending that sends an impulse to a muscle or gland. [Latin *effector* producer.]

a	at	e	end	o	hot	u	up	hw	white	⎧	about
ā	ape	ē	me	ō	old	ū	use	ng	song	⎪	taken
ä	far	i	it	ô	fork	ü	rule	th	thin	ə	pencil
âr	care	ī	ice	oi	oil	u̇	pull	th	this	⎪	lemon
		îr	pierce	ou	out	ûr	turn	zh	measure	⎩	circus

389

ef·fec·tu·al (i fek′chü əl) *adj.* **1.** effective *(def. 1).* **2.** legally valid or binding, as an agreement or document. —**ef·fec·tu·al·i·ty** (i fek′ chü al′i tē), **effec′tu·al·ness,** *n.*

ef·fec·tu·al·ly (i fek′chü ə lē) *adv.* in an effectual manner; with complete effect; thoroughly.

ef·fec·tu·ate (i fek′chü āt′) *v.t.,* **-at·ed, -at·ing.** to bring about or cause; accomplish; effect. [Medieval Latin *effectuatus,* past participle of *effectuare* to bring to pass, from Latin *effectus* accomplishment.] —**ef·fec′tu·a′tion,** *n.*

ef·fem·i·na·cy (i fem′ə nə sē) *n.* the state or quality of being effeminate.

ef·fem·i·nate (i fem′ə nit) *adj.* **1.** having more feminine qualities or traits than are suitable to or usual in a male; womanish; unmanly. **2.** characterized by softness, delicacy, and other qualities often associated with women. [Latin *effēminātus,* past participle of *effēmināre* to make womanish.] —**ef·fem′i·nate·ly,** *adv.* —**ef·fem′i·nate·ness,** *n.*

ef·fen·di (i fen′dē) *n., pl.* **-dis. 1.** sir; master. ➡ a Turkish title of respect. **2.** in Muslim countries, a man of property, education, or authority. [Turkish *efendi* master, sir, going back to Greek *authentēs* master.]

ef·fer·ent (ef′ər ənt) *adj.* carrying away from a central organ or point. Efferent nerves carry impulses from the central nervous system to the muscles and organs. ➡ opposed to **afferent.** [Latin *efferēns,* present participle of *efferre* to carry out.]

ef·fer·vesce (ef′ər ves′) *v.i.,* **-vesced, -vesc·ing. 1.a.** to give off bubbles of gas, as carbonated beverages do; bubble. **b.** (of a gas) to form or issue forth in bubbles. **2.** to show liveliness or exhilaration; be exuberant. [Latin *effervēscere* to boil over.]

ef·fer·ves·cence (ef′ər ves′əns) *n.* **1.** the act or process of bubbling up. **2.** liveliness; exuberance. Also, **ef′fer·ves′-cen·cy.**

ef·fer·ves·cent (ef′ər ves′ənt) *adj.* **1.** giving off bubbles of gas; bubbling. **2.** lively; exuberant. —**ef′fer·ves′cent·ly,** *adv.*

ef·fete (e fēt′, i fēt′) *adj.* having lost strength or vigor; worn-out; exhausted: *an effete and decadent civilization.* [Latin *effētus* exhausted (by bearing young), worn-out.] —**ef·fete′ness,** *n.*

ef·fi·ca·cious (ef′i kā′shəs) *adj.* producing or capable of producing the desired or intended effect; effective. —**ef′fi·ca′cious·ly,** *adv.* —**ef′fi·ca′cious·ness,** *n.*

ef·fi·ca·cy (ef′i kə sē) *n., pl.* **-cies.** the power to produce a desired or intended result; effectiveness. [Latin *efficācia* efficiency.]

ef·fi·cien·cy (i fish′ən sē) *n., pl.* **-cies. 1.** the quality of being efficient. **2.** the ratio of the useful work or energy output of an organism or machine to the energy supplied to it.

efficiency apartment, a small, usually one-room apartment having kitchen facilities and a bathroom.

efficiency expert, a person who devises more efficient and productive methods of using the material and human resources of a business or industrial plant. Also, **efficiency engineer.**

ef·fi·cient (i fish′ənt) *adj.* **1.** producing or capable of producing a desired effect with a minimum of effort or waste: *an efficient worker.* **2.** actually producing an effect; causative: *an efficient cause.* [Latin *efficiēns,* present participle of *efficere* to produce.] —**ef·fi′cient·ly,** *adv.*

ef·fi·gy (ef′i jē) *n., pl.* **-gies. 1.** a representation or likeness of a person, esp. a sculptured image. **2.** a crude representation of a disliked or hated person. [Latin *effigiēs* image.]

· **to burn** (or **hang**) **in effigy.** to burn or hang publicly a crude representation of someone as an expression of public contempt: *The angry citizens burned the governor in effigy.*

ef·flo·resce (ef′lə res′) *v.i.,* **-resced, -resc·ing. 1.** to blossom forth; bloom; flower. **2.** *Chemistry.* **a.** to change either wholly or partially from crystals to a powder by loss of water of crystallization when exposed to air. **b.** to become covered with a crust of particles resulting from evaporation or chemical change. [Latin *efflōrēscere* to blossom.]

ef·flo·res·cence (ef′lə res′əns) *n.* **1.** the act, state, or period of flowering. **2.** the result of growth and development; culmination. **3.** *Chemistry.* **a.** the act or process of efflorescing. **b.** a powder or deposit formed by this process. **4.** any eruption or rash on the skin.

ef·flo·res·cent (ef′lə res′ənt) *adj.* **1.** blossoming forth; blooming; flowering. **2.** *Chemistry.* **a.** changing from a crystalline to a powdery form. **b.** covered with a powdery crust.

ef·flu·ence (ef′lü əns) *n.* **1.** a flowing out or forth. **2.** something that flows out or forth; emanation.

ef·flu·ent (ef′lü ənt) *adj.* flowing out or forth. —*n.* **1.** something that flows out or forth. **2.** a stream flowing out of a larger stream, lake, or reservoir. **3.** sewage, esp. as released into the environment. [Latin *effluēns,* present participle of *effluere* to flow out.]

ef·flu·vi·um (i flü′vē əm) *n., pl.* **-vi·a** (-vē ə) or **-vi·ums.** a vapor or odor, esp. one that is noxious. [Latin *effluvium* a flowing out.]

ef·flux (ef′luks) *n.* **1.** a flowing out. **2.** something that flows out. [Latin *efflūxus,* past participle of *effluere* to flow out.]

ef·fort (ef′ərt) *n.* **1.** the use of the strength of the body or the power of the mind to do something: *Climbing the mountain took great effort.* **2.** a try, esp. a strong or serious try: *I make an effort to get to school on time.* **3.** a product or result of hard work; achievement: *This painting is the artist's latest effort.* [French *effort* endeavor, from Old French *esforcier* to force, make greater, going back to Latin *ex* out of, utterly + *fortis* strong.]

Synonyms Effort, exertion, and endeavor denote physical or mental energy put into some undertaking. **Effort** is most general. It may apply to a single act or to ongoing action: *Lifting the cartons didn't take much effort. Organizing the exhibition required a lot of time and effort.* **Exertion** implies straining to do something, usually something physical: *The exertion of climbing ten flights of stairs left some of the group exhausted.* **Endeavor** is similar to *effort,* but sometimes implies a stronger commitment: *The police were tireless in their endeavor to track down all possible suspects.*

ef·fort·less (ef′ərt lis) *adj.* showing or needing little or no effort; easy: *an effortless task, effortless grace.* —**ef′fort·less·ly,** *adv.* —**ef′fort·less·ness,** *n.*

ef·fron·ter·y (i frun′tə rē) *n., pl.* **-ter·ies.** shameless boldness or impudence; insolence. [French *effronterie,* going back to Late Latin *effrōns* shameless, barefaced, from Latin *ex* out of, away + *frōns* forehead.]

ef·ful·gence (i ful′jəns) *n.* great brightness or splendor; radiance.

ef·ful·gent (i ful′jənt) *adj.* shining brightly; radiant. [Latin *effulgēns,* present participle of *effulgēre* to shine forth.]

ef·fuse (i fūz′) *v.,* **-fused, -fus·ing.** —*v.t.* to pour out or forth. —*v.i.* **1.** to come forth; exude. **2.** (of a gas) to flow through a porous material or very small opening. [Latin *effūsus,* past participle of *effundere* to pour forth.]

ef·fu·sion (i fū′zhən) *n.* **1.** the act of effusing. **2.** something that is effused. **3.** an unrestrained outpouring or expression, as of feelings or ideas. **4.** *Medicine.* **a.** the escape of fluid from its natural vessel into body cavities or tissues. **b.** the fluid that so escapes.

ef·fu·sive (i fū′siv) *adj.* **1.** showing or expressing excessive feeling; overly demonstrative; gushing: *an effusive person, effusive thanks.* **2.** extrusive. —**ef·fu′sive·ly,** *adv.* —**ef·fu′sive·ness,** *n.*

eft (eft) *n.* a newt in its immature, land stage. [Old English *efeta.*]

eft·soon (eft sün′) *also,* **eft·soons.** *adv. Archaic.* **1.** soon afterward; forthwith. **2.** again. **3.** repeatedly; often. [Old English *eftsōna* again.]

e.g., for example. [Abbreviation of Latin *exemplī grātiā.*]

e·gad (i gad′) *interj.* by God. ➡ used as a mild oath.

e·gal·i·tar·i·an (i gal′i târ′ē ən) *also,* **equalitarian.** *adj.* of, relating to, or asserting belief in the equality of all people, esp. with respect to political, economic, and legal rights. —*n.* a person who believes in the equality of all people. [French *égalitaire* based on equality (from *égalité* equality, from Latin *aequālitās*) + -IAN.] —**e·gal′i·tar′i·an·ism,** *n.*

e·gest (ē jest′) *v.t.* to discharge or excrete, as from the body. [Latin *ēgestus,* past participle of *ēgerere* to carry out.] —**e·ges′-tion,** *n.* —**e·ges′tive,** *adj.*

egg¹ (eg) *n.* **1.** a reproductive body produced in the female sex organs of certain animals, such as birds, reptiles, and some mammals, usually rounded or oval and consisting of an ovum, nutrient substances, such as yolk or oil, and a protective membranous covering or shell. **2.a.** the hard-shelled egg produced by a bird, esp. by a hen or other domestic fowl, used as food. **b.** the contents of this: *Beat four eggs and then add milk.* **3.** a reproductive cell or gamete produced in the female sex organs of most animals; ovum. Also, **egg cell. 4.** something resembling or shaped like a hen's egg. **5.** *Slang.* a person; fellow: *a good egg.* —*v.t.* to cover (food) with beaten egg before cooking. [Old Norse *egg* bird's egg.]

· **to lay an egg.** *Slang.* to fail completely, esp. before an audience: *The comedian laid an egg at the club.*

· **to put** (or **have**) **all one's eggs in one basket.** to risk everything on a single chance or in a single effort.

· **to walk on eggs.** *Informal.* to behave in a cautious manner; act with caution.

· **with egg on one's face.** *Informal.* in an embarrassing condition or situation because of a foolish mistake.

egg² (eg) *v.t.* to incite or urge, as with taunts or dares; goad

(usually with *on*): *My friends egged me on to play the trick on you.* [Old Norse *eggja.*] —For Synonyms, see **urge.**

egg·beat·er (eg′bē′tər) *n.* **1.** a kitchen utensil, usually having rotary blades, for beating eggs, whipping cream, and mixing cooking ingredients. **2.** *Slang.* helicopter.

egg cell, egg¹ *(def. 3).*

egg cream, a cold drink made of milk and carbonated water, flavored with a syrup.

egg foo yung (eg′fü′yung′) a Chinese-American dish that is similar to an omelet and contains minced ingredients, such as pork or shrimp, with bean sprouts and onions. [EGG¹ + Cantonese *fuh yuhng* egg white.]

egg·head (eg′hed′) *n.* *Slang.* a person who is an intellectual; highbrow. ➡ often used derisively.

egg·nog (eg′nog′) *n.* a drink made of raw eggs beaten with milk or cream, sugar, and spices, and often containing an alcoholic beverage, as rum. [EGG¹ + earlier *nog* strong ale (of uncertain origin).]

egg·plant (eg′plant′) *n.* **1.** the oval-shaped fruit of a plant, *Solanum melongena,* variety *esculentum,* usually blackish purple, cooked and eaten as a vegetable. **2.** the bushy plant bearing this fruit, having purplish flowers.

egg roll, a thin, tubular piece of dough that is filled with a mixture of ingredients, such as minced vegetables, meat, and shrimp, and fried.

egg·shell (eg′shel′) *n.* **1.** the hard, brittle covering of a bird's egg. **2.** a pale yellow or ivory color. —*adj.* **1.** having the color eggshell. **2.** thin and fragile. **3.** (of paint) having little or no gloss; slightly glossy: *an eggshell enamel.*

egg tooth, a small horny growth on the snout of baby reptiles or the beak of baby birds, used to crack the eggshell during hatching.

e·gis (ē′jis) aegis.

eg·lan·tine (eg′lən tīn′, -tēn′) *n.* sweetbrier. [French *églantine,* from Old French *aiglent,* going back to Latin *acus* needle.]

eggplant

e·go (ē′gō, eg′ō) *n., pl.* **e·gos.** **1.** the self as a thinking, feeling, acting being, conscious of being distinct from its own thoughts and from the selves of others. **2.a.** confidence in oneself; self-image; self-esteem. **b.** *Informal.* conceit; egotism. **3.** *Psychoanalysis.* the conscious part of the psyche that is shaped by contact with the reality of the external world and adapts the primitive impulses of the id and the demands of the superego to the needs of society. [Latin *ego* I.]

e·go·cen·tric (ē′gō sen′trik, eg′ō-) *adj.* viewing everything in relation to oneself; excessively concerned with one's own activities and needs; self-centered. —*n.* an egocentric person. —**e·go·cen·tric·i·ty** (ē′gō sen tris′i tē, eg′ō-), *n.*

e·go·ism (ē′gō iz′əm, eg′ō-) *n.* **1.** arrogant conceit; egotism. **2.** excessive concern with one's own welfare and interests; selfishness.

e·go·ist (ē′gō ist, eg′ō-) *n.* **1.** an arrogantly conceited person; egotist. **2.** a selfish or self-centered person. —**e′go·is′tic;** *also,* **e′go·is′ti·cal,** *adj.* —**e′go·is′ti·cal·ly,** *adv.*

e·go·ma·ni·a (ē′gō mā′nē ə, eg′ō-) *n.* excessive or abnormal egotism. —**e′go·ma′ni·ac,** *n.* —**e·go·ma·ni·a·cal** (ē′gō mə nī′ə kəl, eg′ō-), *adj.*

e·go·tism (ē′gə tiz′əm, eg′ə-) *n.* **1.** an inflated sense of self-importance; conceit. **2.** a great tendency to talk or write about oneself, esp. in a bragging or boastful manner. **3.** selfishness; egoism.

e·go·tist (ē′gə tist, eg′ə-) *n.* **1.** a person characterized by egotism; conceited, boastful person. **2.** a selfish or self-centered person; egoist.

e·go·tis·tic (ē′gə tis′tik, eg′ə-) *adj.* **1.** relating to or characterized by egotism. **2.** inclined to think too highly of oneself; conceited. Also, **e′go·tis′ti·cal.** —**e′go·tis′ti·cal·ly,** *adv.*

ego trip *Informal.* something done mainly out of vanity or selfishness: *Did you run for class president because you wanted to serve the class, or was it just an ego trip?*

e·gre·gious (i grē′jəs) *adj.* **1.** conspicuously bad; glaring; outrageous; flagrant: *an egregious error.* **2.** *Archaic.* distinguished; remarkable. [Latin *ēgregius* excellent; literally, chosen from the herd, from *ex* out of + *grex* herd.] —**e·gre′gious·ly,** *adv.* —**e·gre′gious·ness,** *n.*

e·gress (ē′gres) *n.* **1.** the act of going out, as from a building; emergence. **2.** a place or means of going out; way out; exit. **3.** the right to go out: *to be granted egress.* [Latin *ēgressus* a going out.]

e·gret (ē′grit, eg′rit) *n.* **1.** any of various herons, order Ciconiiformes, having tufts of long, lacy feathers on the back, crown, and breast during the breeding season. **2.** the lacy feather of the egret. [French *aigrette,* from Provençal *aigreta* heron, from *aigron;* of Germanic origin.]

E·gyp·tian (i jip′shən) *adj.* of, relating to, or characteristic of Egypt or its people or culture. —*n.* **1.** a native, inhabitant, or citizen of ancient or modern Egypt. **2.** a person of Egyptian ancestry. **3.** the Hamitic language of the ancient Egyptians, from which Coptic descends.

Egyptian cotton, a fine, silky cotton with long fibers, grown chiefly in Egypt.

E·gyp·tol·o·gy (ē′jip tol′ə jē) *n.* the study of ancient Egypt. —**E′gyp·tol′o·gist,** *n.*

eh (ā) *interj.* an exclamation expressing surprise, doubt, or failure to hear what was said.

EHF, extremely high frequency.

ei·der (ī′dər) *n.* **1.** any of various sea ducks of the arctic and subarctic regions of the

egret

Pacific and North Atlantic oceans. The female of the common eider, *Somateria mollissima,* is the source of eiderdown. Also, **eider duck.** **2.** eiderdown. [Icelandic *æthr* the eider duck.]

ei·der·down (ī′dər doun′) *n.* **1.** small, soft feathers, or down, from the breast of the female common eider, used to stuff pillows and quilts. **2.** a quilt filled with eiderdown.

ei·det·ic (ī det′ik) *adj.* of or relating to visual images recalled in much detail and with great accuracy. [Greek *eidētikos* relating to images, from *eidos* form.] —**ei·det′i·cal·ly,** *adv.*

eight (āt) *n.* **1.** the cardinal number that is one more than seven. **2.** a symbol representing this number, such as 8 or VIII. **3.** something having this many units or members, such as a playing card. —*adj.* numbering one more than seven. [Old English *eahta.*]

eight ball *also,* **eight·ball** (āt′bôl′). **1.** a black ball bearing the number eight encircled with white. **2.** a pool game in which the eight ball must be pocketed last in order to win the game.

•**behind the eight ball.** *Slang.* in an unlucky, unfavorable, or risky position.

eight·een (ā′tēn′) *n.* **1.** the cardinal number that is eight more than ten. **2.** a symbol representing this number, such as 18 or XVIII. **3.** something having this many units or members. —*adj.* numbering eight more than ten. [Old English *eahtatȳne.*]

eight·eenth (ā′tēnth′) *adj.* **1.** (the ordinal of eighteen) next after the seventeenth. **2.** being one of eighteen equal parts. —*n.* **1.** something that is next after the seventeenth. **2.** one of eighteen equal parts; 1/18.

eight·fold (āt′fōld′) *adj.* **1.** eight times as great or numerous. **2.** having or consisting of eight parts. —*adv.* so as to be eight times greater or more numerous.

eighth (ātth, āth) *adj.* **1.** (the ordinal of eight) next after the seventh. **2.** being one of eight equal parts. —*n.* **1.** something that is next after the seventh. **2.** one of eight equal parts; 1/8. **3.** *Music.* octave *(defs. 1a, b, c).*

eighth note *Music.* a note having one eighth the time value of a whole note. For illustration, see **note.**

eight·i·eth (ā′tē ith) *adj.* **1.** (the ordinal of eighty) next after the seventy-ninth. **2.** being one of eighty equal parts. —*n.* **1.** something that is next after the seventy-ninth. **2.** one of eighty equal parts; 1/80.

eight·y (ā′tē) *n., pl.* **eight·ies. 1.** the cardinal number that is eight times ten. **2.** a symbol representing this number, such as 80 or LXXX. **3.** **eighties.** the number series from eighty to eighty-

a	at	e	end	o	hot	u	up	hw	white		about
ā	ape	ē	me	ō	old	ū	use	ng	song		taken
ä	far	i	it	ô	fork	ü	rule	th	thin	ə	pencil
âr	care	ī	ice	oi	oil	u̇	pull	th	this		lemon
		îr	pierce	ou	out	ûr	turn	zh	measure		circus

391

nine. ➡ used esp. in reference to the ninth decade of a century or of a person's life. —*adj.* being one more than seventy-nine. [Old English *eahtatig.*]

ein·stein·i·um (īn stī′nē əm) *n.* an artificially produced radioactive element, first discovered in the fallout of a hydrogen bomb explosion. Symbol: **Es** For tables, see **element.** [From Albert *Einstein,* 1879-1955, German-American physicist.]

Ein·stein's equation (īn′stīnz) mass-energy equation.

eis·tedd·fod (ī ste<u>th</u>′vod, ā ste<u>th</u>′-) *n., pl.* **-fods,** *Welsh* **eis·tedd·fod·au** (ī′ste<u>th</u> vod′ī, ā′ste<u>th</u>-). an annual festival in Wales celebrating Welsh culture with the reading of poetry and the playing and singing of traditional Welsh music. [Welsh *eisteddfod* literally, "session."]

ei·ther (ē′<u>th</u>ər, ī′<u>th</u>ər) *adj.* **1.** one or the other (of two): *I can write with either hand.* **2.** one and the other (of two); each: *to plant trees along either side of a road.* —*pron.* one or the other (of two): *Either is fine with me.* —*conj.* used with *or* to indicate the first of two or more possibilities: *Either go or don't go. You may come either tonight, tomorrow, or next week.* —*adv.* any more so; also: *She can't do it, and I can't either. That's mine; no, it isn't either.* [Old English *ǣgther* each of two.]

> **Usage** When two or more subjects are joined by **either . . . or,** the subject closest to the verb determines whether the verb is singular or plural: *Either checks or cash is acceptable.* If one of the subjects is plural, it may be preferable to place it closest to the verb, because a singular verb form may sound awkward in such constructions: *Either cash or checks are acceptable.*
>
> The use of the pronoun **either** to refer to more than two, as in *Either of the three applicants is qualified,* is generally considered unacceptable in formal speech and writing; *any* is preferred. As a conjunction, however, **either** can be used with three or more: *The houses were built of either wood, brick, or stone.* For another Usage Note, see **anybody.**

e·jac·u·late (i jak′yə lāt′) *v.,* **-lat·ed, -lat·ing.** —*v.t.* **1.** to utter suddenly and briefly; blurt out; exclaim. **2.** to eject or discharge suddenly, esp. semen by the male reproductive organs. —*v.i.* to eject or discharge a fluid. [Latin *ējaculātus,* past participle of *ējaculārī* to throw out.]

e·jac·u·la·tion (i jak′yə lā′shən) *n.* **1.** a sudden, brief emotional utterance; exclamation. **2.** the act or an instance of ejaculating, esp. the discharge of semen by the male reproductive organs; emission.

e·jac·u·la·to·ry (i jak′yə lə tôr′ē) *adj.* **1.** of or like an exclamatory utterance. **2.** of or adapted for sudden ejection: *an ejaculatory duct.*

e·ject (i jekt′) *v.t.* **1.** to throw out or discharge; emit: *The furnace ejected smoke.* **2.a.** to expel or drive out, esp. by force; cause to leave. **b.** to evict. [Latin *ējectus,* past participle of *ējicere* to throw out.]

e·jec·tion (i jek′shən) *n.* **1.** the act of ejecting or the state of being ejected. **2.** something ejected, as lava.

e·ject·ment (i jekt′mənt) *n.* **1.** dispossession; eviction. **2.** *Law.* an action to regain possession of real property.

e·jec·tor (i jek′tər) *n.* a person or thing that ejects.

eke[1] (ēk) *v.t.,* **eked, ek·ing.** to lengthen or enlarge; increase. [Old English *ēcan, īecan* to increase.]

  · **to eke out. a.** to barely manage to make (a living). **b.** to add to in order to make barely sufficient; supply what is lacking to: *to eke out a meal by adding rice to leftovers.* **c.** to make (something) last longer, as by practicing economy; prolong: *to eke out a limited water supply by rationing.*

eke[2] (ēk) *adv., conj. Archaic.* also; moreover. [Old English *ēac.*]

EKG 1. electrocardiogram. **2.** electrocardiograph.

e·kis·tics (ē kis′tiks) *n.* the scientific study of cities, towns, and other types of human settlements, how people relate to each other in them, and how the settlements relate to their surrounding environments. ➡ used as singular. [Greek *oikos* house + -ics.] —**e·kis′tic;** *also,* **e·kis′ti·cal,** *adj.* —**e′kis·ti′cian,** *n.*

el (el) *n.* **1.** ell[2]. **2.** *Informal* elevated railroad.

e·lab·o·rate (*adj.,* i lab′ər it; *v.,* i lab′ə rāt′) *adj.* **1.** worked out with great care or thoroughly; developed in intricate detail; complex: *an elaborate mathematical theory.* **2.** highly detailed or ornamented; ornate. —*v.,* **-rat·ed, -rat·ing.** —*v.i.* to give additional detail or fuller treatment; embellish (often with *on* or *upon*): *to elaborate upon a theme.* —*v.t.* **1.** to work out carefully or thoroughly; develop in greater detail: *to elaborate a blueprint for a new machine.* **2.** *Archaic* to make; fashion. [Latin *ēlabōrātus,* past participle of *ēlabōrāre* to labor greatly, work out.] —**e·lab′o·rate·ly,** *adv.* —**e·lab′o·rate·ness,** *n.* —**e·lab′o·ra′tive,** *adj.* —**e·lab′o·ra′tor,** *n.*

e·lab·o·ra·tion (i lab′ə rā′shən) *n.* **1.** the act of elaborating or the state of being elaborated. **2.** something that is added, as a detail.

E·laine (i lān′) *n. Arthurian Legend.* **1.** a beautiful maiden who died of unrequited love for Sir Lancelot. **2.** the mother of Sir Galahad.

é·lan (ā län′) *n.* spirited energy and style; dash. [French *élan,* from Middle French *s'eslancer* to rush, going back to Latin *ex* out of + *lancea* lance.]

e·land (ē′lənd) *n.* the largest living antelope, genus *Taurotragus,* native to southern Africa and having humped shoulders and long, twisted horns. Height: 5.5 feet (1.7 meters) at the shoulder. [Afrikaans *eland,* from Dutch *eland* elk, from obsolete German *elend,* from Lithuanian *elnis.*]

eland

e·lapse (i laps′) *v.i.,* **e·lapsed, e·laps·ing.** (of time) to slip by; pass away. [Latin *ēlapsus,* past participle of *ēlābī* to glide away.]

e·las·mo·branch (i las′mə brangk′, i laz′-) *n.* any of numerous cartilaginous fish, class Chondrichthyes, including the sharks, rays, and skates. [Modern Latin *Elasmobranchii* (plural), from Greek *elasmos* metal plate + *branchia* gills; because of the platelike structure of its gills.]

e·las·tic (i las′tik) *adj.* **1. a.** capable of returning to its original size or shape after being distorted: *A rubber band is elastic.* **b.** (of a gas) capable of indefinite expansion. **2.** capable of adapting to fit the circumstances; flexible; accommodating: *an elastic set of rules.* **3.** capable of recovering easily, as from emotional or physical distress; resilient; buoyant: *an elastic temperament.* **4.** marked by springiness; bouncy: *an elastic step.* —*n.* **1.** a fabric that is made stretchable by running rubber threads or strands through it. **2.** rubber band. [Modern Latin *elasticus,* from Greek *elastikos* propulsive, from *elaunein* to drive.] —**e·las′ti·cal·ly,** *adv.*

e·las·tic·i·ty (i las tis′i tē, ē′las-) *n.* the state or quality of being elastic.

e·las·ti·cized (i las′tə sīzd′) *adj.* made stretchable by interweaving with elastic threads or strands: *an elasticized waistband.*

e·las·tin (i las′tin) *n.* a fibrous protein, similar to collagen, that is the principal constituent of yellow connective tissue, present in the middle layer of artery walls and certain internal organs. [ELASTIC) + -IN[1].]

e·las·to·mer (i las′tə mər) *n.* any elastic, rubbery polymer, as natural or synthetic rubber. [ELAST(IC) + (POLY)MER.] —**e·las′to·mer′ic,** *adj.*

e·late (i lāt′) *v.t.,* **e·lat·ed, e·lat·ing.** to put in high spirits; make joyful; excite. [Latin *ēlātus* elevated.]

e·lat·ed (i lā′tid) *adj.* in high spirits; filled with joy; jubilant. —**e·lat′ed·ly,** *adv.* —**e·lat′ed·ness,** *n.*

el·a·ter (el′ə tər) *n.* **1.** click beetle. **2.** an elastic filament found in some plants, esp. liverworts, that functions to scatter ripe spores. [Modern Latin *elater,* from Greek *elatēr* driver, from *elaunein* to set in motion, beat out.]

e·la·tion (i lā′shən) *n.* a feeling of exultant joy; jubilation.

E layer, Heaviside layer.

el·bow (el′bō) *n.* **1.** the joint between the forearm and the upper arm, esp. the projecting outer part of this joint when the arm is bent. **2.** something having a bend like the elbow, as a curved pipe fitting. —*v.t.* **1.** to push with or as with the elbows; thrust aside or shove; jostle. **2.** to make or force (one's way) by or as by pushing with the elbows. —*v.i.* to proceed or advance by or as by pushing with the elbows: *to elbow through a crowd.* [Old English *el(n)boga* joint between the forearm and the upper arm.]

  · **to rub elbows with.** to associate with: *to rub elbows with rich and famous people.*

  · **up to one's (or the) elbows.** very busy; deeply immersed: *I'm up to my elbows in work.*

elbow grease *Informal.* energetic physical effort, applied to work.

el·bow·room (el′bō rüm′, -rùm′) *n.* ample room, as to move or work in.

eld (eld) *n. Archaic.* **1.** old age. **2.** old times; antiquity. [Old English *eldo* old age, from *eald* old.]

eld·er¹ (el′dər) *adj.* **1.** of earlier birth; older: *the elder sister.* **2.** of longer experience or higher rank: *an elder partner in a firm.* **3.** earlier; former. —*n.* **1.** a person who is older; senior. **2.** an older, influential member, as of a family or community. **3.** in the Mormon Church, a member of the higher priesthood. **4.** (in certain Protestant churches) **a.** an officer who often assists the minister. **b.** minister. **5.** an aged person. **6.** forefather; predecessor. [Old English *eldra* older, comparative of *eald* old.]

el·der² (el′dər) *n.* any of a group of shrubs and small trees, genus *Sambucus,* some of which bear edible red or purple-black berries. Also, **elderberry.** [Old English *ellærn.*]

el·der·ber·ry (el′dər ber′ē, -bə rē) *n., pl.* **-ries. 1.** the berry of the elder, used esp. for making wines, jellies, and pies. **2.** elder².

eld·er·ly (el′dər lē) *adj.* **1.** approaching old age; past middle age: *an elderly person.* **2.** of, relating to, or characteristic of a person approaching old age. —*n.* **the elderly.** people who are old. —For Synonyms, see **old.**

el·der·ship (el′dər ship′) *n.* **1.** the position or responsibilities of an elder in a church. **2.** a group or court of elders; presbytery.

elder statesman, a retired statesman who unofficially advises government leaders.

eld·est (el′dist) *adj.* first-born; oldest. [Old English *eldesta,* superlative of *eald* old.]

El Do·ra·do (el′də rä′dō) *pl.* **-dos.** *also,* **El·do·ra·do. 1.** a legendary South American city of great wealth sought by sixteenth-century explorers. **2.** any place of fabulous wealth. [Spanish *El Dorado* literally, the gilded; *el* the (from Latin *ille* that) + *dorado,* past participle of *dorar* to gild (going back to Latin *dē* from + *aurum* gold).]

elec. 1. electric. **2.** electrical. **3.** electricity.

e·lect (i lekt′) *v.t.* **1.** to choose (someone) by vote, as for an office or membership. **2.** to select (something) by preference; choose: *Jack elected biology as his major. Mary elected to go on the trip.* **3.** to select for salvation. ➡ used in the passive voice with God as the implied subject. —*v.i.* to make a selection; choose. —*adj.* **1.** elected but not yet formally installed in office. ➡ used in combination after a noun: *senator-elect.* **2.** chosen; select: *elect circles of society.* **3.** selected by God for salvation. —*n.* **the elect. 1.** people who are favored or preferred, esp. those belonging to a privileged group. **2.** people selected by God for salvation. [Latin *ēlectus,* past participle of *ēligere* to choose.]

e·lec·tion (i lek′shən) *n.* **1.** the act of electing or the state of being elected. **2.** the process of choosing a person or persons by vote, as for an office or position. **3.** selection by God for salvation.

e·lec·tion·eer (i lek′shə nîr′) *v.i.* to work or campaign for the election of a candidate or political party.

e·lec·tive (i lek′tiv) *adv.* **1.** of or relating to election. **2.** chosen or filled by vote: *an elective office.* **3.** having the power or right to choose by vote: *an elective body.* **4.** open to choice; not required; optional: *an elective course.* —*n.* an optional subject in a high school or college curriculum.

e·lec·tor (i lek′tər) *n.* **1.** a person who is qualified to vote in an election. **2.** a member of the U.S. electoral college. **3.** any of several German princes entitled to elect the emperor of the Holy Roman Empire.

e·lec·tor·al (i lek′tər əl) *adj.* of, relating to, or composed of an election or electors: *an electoral system, the electoral vote.*

electoral college, a body of representatives, chosen by popular vote, that formally elects the president and vice president of the United States. Each state has the same number of electors as it has members in Congress.

e·lec·tor·ate (i lek′tər it) *n.* **1.** all persons qualified to vote in an election. **2.a.** the territory of an elector of the Holy Roman Empire. **b.** the rank of office of an elector of the Holy Roman Empire.

E·lec·tra (i lek′trə) *n.* in Greek legend, the daughter of Agamemnon and Clytemnestra, who urged and helped her brother, Orestes, to kill their mother in revenge for the murder of their father.

e·lec·tric (i lek′trik) *adj.* **1.** of or relating to electricity. **2.** charged with or operated by electricity: *an electric shock.* **3.** resulting from or produced by electricity: *an electric shock.* **4.** producing or conveying electricity: *an electric generator, electric cables.* **5.** full of or causing tension or excitement; electrifying: *an electric moment.* —*n.* something that runs on electricity, as a train or car. [Modern Latin *electricus,* from Latin *ēlectrum* amber, from Greek *ēlektron;* because of amber's property of attracting other substances when rubbed.]

e·lec·tri·cal (i lek′tri kəl) *adj.* **1.** electric *(defs. 1-4).* **2.** dealing with electric phenomena: *electrical engineering.* —**e·lec′tri·cal·ly,** *adv.*

electrical storm, thunderstorm.

electrical transcription 1. a phonograph record or magnetic tape recording used to record programs for later broadcast. **2.** a broadcast from such a phonograph record or magnetic tape recording.

electric chair 1. a chair used for performing electrocution. **2.** execution by this means.

electric charge 1. a fundamental property of the subatomic particles of which matter is composed. An electron carries a negative electric charge; a proton carries a positive electric charge. **2.** the quantity of electricity, either positive or negative, contained on or in a body of matter. Electric charge is measured in coulombs.

electric eel, a long, eellike fish, *Electrophorus electricus,* native to rivers of the Amazon Basin in South America, capable of giving off strong electric shocks that ward off enemies and stun prey.

electric eye, a photoelectric cell upon which a beam of light is directed and which, when the beam is interrupted, causes a device to open a door, ring a bell, or perform a similar operation.

e·lec·tri·cian (i lek trish′ən, ē′lek-) *n.* a person who designs, installs, repairs, or maintains electric wiring or equipment.

e·lec·tric·i·ty (i lek tris′i tē, ē′lek-) *n.* **1.** energy carried by electrons or protons and capable of producing light, heat, and other effects. **2.** a flow of this energy; current. **3.** the branch of physics that deals with such energy, usually studied in conjunction with magnetism. **4.** a strong feeling of excitement.

electric motor, a motor that converts electric energy into mechanical energy.

electric ray, any of a group of rays, family Torpedinidae, with organs on each side of the head that give off electric discharges.

e·lec·tri·fi·ca·tion (i lek′trə fi kā′shən) *n.* the act of electrifying or the state of being electrified.

e·lec·tri·fy (i lek′trə fī′) *v.t.,* **-fied, -fy·ing. 1.** to charge with electricity: *to electrify a fence.* **2.** to equip for the use of electricity. **3.** to provide electric power to, as a community. **4.** to fill with great excitement; thrill.

electro- *combining form* of, relating to, or by means of electricity: *electromagnet, electrocute.* [Greek *ēlektron* amber. See ELECTRIC.]

e·lec·tro·car·di·o·gram (i lek′trō kär′dē ə gram′) *n.* a tracing made on a graph by an electrocardiograph.

e·lec·tro·car·di·o·graph (i lek′trō kär′dē ə graf′) *n.* an instrument that receives and records electrical impulses that originate in the muscle of the heart as it contracts and relaxes, used esp. to detect and diagnose heart disorders. —**e·lec′tro·car′di·o·graph′ic,** *adj.* —**e·lec·tro·car·di·og·ra·phy** (i lek′trō kär′dē·og′rə fē), *n.*

e·lec·tro·chem·i·cal (i lek′trō kem′i kəl) *adj.* of or relating to electrochemistry.

e·lec·tro·chem·is·try (i lek′trō kem′ə strē) *n.* the branch of chemistry that deals with the relationship between electricity and chemical changes or reactions.

e·lec·tro·con·vul·sive therapy (i lek′trō kən vul′siv) a method of treating certain mental disorders, esp. severe depression, in which an electric current is applied to the brain. Also, **electroshock, electroshock therapy.**

e·lec·tro·cute (i lek′trə kūt′) *v.t.,* **-cut·ed, -cut·ing. 1.** to execute (someone) in the electric chair. **2.** to kill by electricity. [ELECTRO- + (EXE)CUTE.] —**e·lec′tro·cu′tion,** *n.*

e·lec·trode (i lek′trōd) *n.* an electrical conductor, part of an electric circuit, through which electrons enter or leave a conducting medium, as air, other gases, or chemical solutions. [ELECTRO- + -ODE.]

e·lec·tro·de·pos·it (i lek′trō di poz′it) *v.t.* to deposit (a substance, esp. a metal) electrolytically, as in electroplating. —*n.* a substance deposited by electrolysis. [ELECTRO- + DEPOSIT.] —**e·lec·tro·dep·o·si·tion** (i lek′trō dep′ə zish′ən), *n.*

e·lec·tro·dy·nam·ic (i lek′trō dī nam′ik) *adj.* of or relating to electrodynamics.

e·lec·tro·dy·nam·ics (i lek′trō dī nam′iks) *n.* the branch of physics that deals with electric currents and forces produced by or related to electric currents. ➡ used as singular.

e·lec·tro·en·ceph·a·lo·gram (i lek′trō en sef′ə lə gram′) *n.* a tracing made on a graph by an electroencephalograph.

e·lec·tro·en·ceph·a·lo·graph (i lek′trō en sef′ə lə graf′) *n.* an instrument that detects and records electrical activity in the brain. —**e·lec′tro·en·ceph′a·lo·graph′ic,** *adj.* —**e·lec·tro·en·ceph·a·log·ra·phy** (i lek′trō en sef′ə log′rə fē), *n.*

E

a	at	e	end	o	hot	u	up	hw	white		about
ā	ape	ē	me	ō	old	ū	use	ng	song		taken
ä	far	i	it	ô	fork	ü	rule	th	thin	ə	pencil
âr	care	ī	ice	oi	oil	ů	pull	th	this		lemon
				ir	pierce	ou	out	ûr	turn	zh	measure		circus

e·lec·tro·ki·net·ics (i lek′trō ki net′iks) *n.* the branch of physics that deals with the study of electric charges in motion. ➡ used as singular. [ELECTRO- + KINETICS.] —**e·lec′tro·ki·net′ic**, *adj.*

e·lec·trol·y·sis (i lek trol′ə sis, ē′lek-) *n.* **1.** the chemical decomposition of a liquefied or dissolved substance into its components by passage of an electric current through the substance. Electrolysis is usually performed in an electrolytic cell. **2.** the permanent removal of unwanted body hair by destroying the root cells with an electrified needle. [ELECTRO- + Greek *lysis* a loosing.]

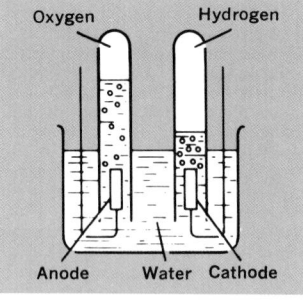

electrolysis of water

e·lec·tro·lyte (i lek′trə- līt′) *n.* **1.** any nonmetallic substance that will conduct an electric current, esp. a liquid solution. **2.** a chemical compound, usually an acid, base, or salt, that when liquefied or in solution will dissociate into ions and conduct an electric current. [ELECTRO- + Greek *lytos* that may be loosed or dissolved.]

e·lec·tro·lyt·ic (i lek′trə lit′ik) *adj.* **1.** of, relating to, or produced by electrolysis. **2.** of or relating to an electrolyte.

e·lec·tro·lyt·i·cal·ly (i lek′trə lit′i klē) *adv.* by means of electrolysis.

electrolytic cell, an apparatus consisting of an anode and a cathode that are immersed in an electrolyte and connected to a source of current, as a battery.

e·lec·tro·lyze (i lek′trə līz′) *v.t.,* **-lyzed, -lyz·ing.** to decompose by electrolysis. —**e·lec·tro·ly·za·tion** (i lek′trə lə zā′shən), *n.* —**e·lec′tro·lyz′er,** *n.*

e·lec·tro·mag·net (i lek′trō mag′nit) *n.* an iron core with insulated wire wound around it that becomes a magnet when electric current passes through the wire.

e·lec·tro·mag·net·ic (i lek′trō mag net′ik) *adj.* **1.** of or produced by an electromagnet. **2.** of or relating to electromagnetism.

electromagnetic radiation, energy in the form of electromagnetic waves.

electromagnetic spectrum, the entire range of frequencies of electromagnetic radiation, from long, low-frequency radio waves to short, high-frequency gamma rays.

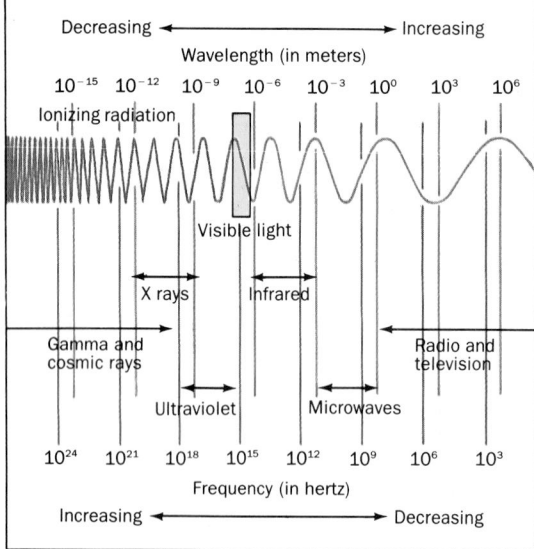

electromagnetic spectrum

electromagnetic wave, a wave of energy that consists of varying electric and magnetic fields and that travels through empty space at the speed of light (about 186,000 miles, or 300,000 km, per second). Radio waves, light rays, and X rays are electromagnetic waves.

e·lec·tro·mag·net·ism (i lek′trō mag′ni tiz′əm) *n.* **1.** the magnetism produced by a current of electricity. **2.** the branch of physics that studies the relation between magnetism and electricity.

elec·tro·me·chan·i·cal (i lek′trō mi kan′i kəl) *adj.* of or using electric energy to produce mechanical movement.

e·lec·tro·met·al·lur·gy (i lek′trō met′ə lûr′jē) *n.* the use of electricity in various processes of producing and refining metals.

e·lec·trom·e·ter (i lek trom′i tər, ē′lek-) *n.* an instrument for measuring differences in electrical potential. [ELECTRO- + -METER.]

e·lec·tro·mo·tive (i lek′trə mō′tiv) *adj.* **1.** producing a flow of electricity. **2.** of or relating to electromotive force.

electromotive force 1. the force that causes electric current to flow in a circuit. **2.** the amount of energy derived from an electric source.

electromotive series, the series of metallic chemical elements arranged in order of decreasing tendency to ionize in solution, beginning with potassium, the most electropositive metal, which ionizes by readily losing electrons, and ending with gold, the most electronegative, which ionizes by reluctantly gaining electrons.

e·lec·tron (i lek′tron) *n.* a subatomic particle that carries the smallest negative electric charge. For illustration, see **atom.** [Greek *ēlektron* amber. See ELECTRIC.]

e·lec·tro·neg·a·tive (i lek′trō neg′ə tiv) *adj.* **1.** having a negative electric charge. **2.** tending to move to the positive pole, or anode, in electrolysis. **3.** nonmetallic. —**e·lec′tro·neg′a·tiv′i·ty,** *n.*

electron gun, a device consisting of a series of electrodes at one end of a cathode-ray tube, such as a television picture tube, that emits and focuses a beam of electrons.

e·lec·tron·ic (i lek tron′ik, ē′lek-) *adj.* **1.** of or relating to electrons or electronics. **2.** produced or operating by the action of electrons, as in a radio or radar. —**e·lec′tron′i·cal·ly,** *adv.*

electronic banking, the use of computer systems to conduct banking transactions, as the transfer of funds between two accounts.

electronic bulletin board, a group of messages created and edited on a computer system and made accessible to subscribers at remote terminals by means of a telecommunications link.

electronic mail 1. a system of sending messages by means of computer terminals linked together. **2.** messages sent or received in this way.

electronic music, electronically generated and processed sounds that have been arranged into a finished musical composition and stored magnetically for future use.

e·lec·tron·ics (i lek tron′iks, ē′lek-) *n.* the scientific study and practical application of the motion of electrons and other charged particles in a vacuum and in gases, including such motion through empty spaces in the crystalline structure of semiconducting materials. ➡ used as singular.

electron microscope, a device that produces magnified images by means of a beam of electrons rather than a beam of light. It is much more powerful than an ordinary microscope.

electron tube, a sealed container in which electrons move through a vacuum or gas, used to produce, amplify, or regulate electrical signals. Also, **vacuum tube.**

electron volt, the amount of energy gained by an electron when it is accelerated through a potential difference of one volt.

e·lec·tro·pho·re·sis (i lek′trō fə rē′sis) *n.* the movement of charged colloidal particles in response to an electric field, a phenomenon that is the basis of a type of chromatography used in producing biochemical separations, as for determining the protein content of body fluids. —**e·lec·tro·pho·ret·ic** (i lek′trō fə ret′ik), *adj.*

e·lec·troph·o·rus (i lek trof′ər əs, ē′lek-) *n., pl.* **-troph·o·ri** (-trof′ə rī′). a device for generating charges of static electricity by means of induction. [ELECTRO- + Greek *-phoros* bearing.]

e·lec·tro·plate (i lek′trə plāt′) *v.t.,* **-plat·ed, -plat·ing.** to apply a metal coating to by means of electrolysis. —*n.* any article, esp. silverware, coated in this way. —**e·lec′tro·plat′er,** *n.*

e·lec·tro·pos·i·tive (i lek′trō poz′i tiv) *adj.* **1.** charged with positive electricity. **2.** tending to move to the negative pole, or cathode, in electrolysis. **3.** basic; metallic.

e·lec·tro·re·cep·tor (i lek′trō ri sep′tər) *n.* a sensory nerve ending specialized for the reception of electrical stimuli, as in certain fish that may be sensitive to the weak current emitted by their prey.

e·lec·tro·scope (i lek′trə skōp′) *n.* an instrument used to detect electric charges and determine whether they are positive or negative.

e·lec·tro·shock (i lek′trə shok′) *n.* **1.** shock[1] *(def. 2).* **2.** electroconvulsive therapy.

electroshock therapy, electroconvulsive therapy.

e·lec·tro·stat·ic (i lek′trə stat′ik) *adj.* of or relating to electricity at rest or static electric charges.

e·lec·tro·stat·ics (i lek′trə stat′iks) *n.* the branch of physics that studies static electricity. ➡ used as singular.

e·lec·tro·ther·a·py (i lek′trō ther′ə pē) *n.* the treatment of disease or injury using electricity, as in diathermy.

e·lec·tro·type (i lek′trə tīp′) *n.* **1.** a duplicate of a printing plate made by the electroplating process. **2.** a print made from such a plate. —*v.t., v.i.,* **-typed, -typ·ing.** to make such a plate or plates (of). —**e·lec′tro·typ′er,** *n.*

e·lec·tro·va·lence (i lek′trō vā′ləns) *n. Chemistry.* the number of electrons transferred from one atom to another in the creation of an electrovalent bond. —**e·lec·tro·va′lent,** *adj.*

e·lec·tro·va·lent bond (i lek′trō vā′lənt) a chemical bond between ions of opposite electric charge, formed by transfer of electrons. Also, **ionic bond.**

e·lec·trum (i lek′trəm) *n.* a natural pale yellow alloy of gold and silver, used in ancient times. [Latin *ēlectrum* amber, from Greek *ēlektron.*]

e·lec·tu·ar·y (i lek′chü er′ē) *n., pl.* **-ar·ies.** a medicinal paste made by mixing powdered drugs with syrup or honey and water. [Late Latin *ēlectuārium,* probably modification of Greek *ekleikton,* from *ekleichein* to lick up.]

el·ee·mos·y·nar·y (el′ə mos′ə ner′ē, el′ē ə-) *adj.* **1.** of or relating to charity or alms; charitable. **2.** provided or given as an act of charity; free: *an eleemosynary supply of clothing.* **3.** relying on or supported by charity: *eleemosynary travelers.* [Late Latin *eleēmosynārius* almoner, from Latin *eleēmosyna* alms, from Greek *eleēmosynē* pity.]

el·e·gance (el′i gəns) *n.* **1.** the state or quality of being elegant. **2.** something elegant.

el·e·gan·cy (el′i gən sē) *n., pl.* **-cies.** elegance.

el·e·gant (el′i gənt) *adj.* **1.** characterized by richness and good taste, as in dress or furnishings; luxurious. **2.** characterized by grace and refinement, as in manners, taste, or style; polished. **3.** characterized by simplicity and precision: *an elegant scientific analysis.* **4.** *Informal.* excellent; fine. [Latin *ēlegāns* tasteful, nice.] —**el′e·gant·ly,** *adv.* —For Synonyms, see **graceful.**

el·e·gi·ac (el′i jī′ak, i lē′jē ak′) *adj.* **1.** of, relating to, or suitable for an elegy. **2.** expressing sorrow or lamentation; mournful; plaintive. **3.** (of classical verse) composed of or written in two lines of dactylic hexameter, the second line of which has only one long or accented syllable in the third and sixth feet. —*n.* **1.** an elegiac verse. **2.** a poem composed of such verses.

el·e·gize (el′i jīz′) *v.,* **-gized, -giz·ing.** —*v.t.* to lament or commemorate in or as in an elegy. —*v.i.* to write an elegy.

el·e·gy (el′i jē) *n., pl.* **-gies. 1.** a mournful or melancholy poem or musical composition, esp. a lament for the dead. **2.** a poem composed of elegiacs. [Latin *elegīa* poetic lament, elegiac poem, from Greek *elegeiā.*] —**el′e·gist,** *n.*

elem. 1. element; elements. **2.** elementary.

el·e·ment (el′ə mənt) *n.* **1.** a substance that cannot be changed into a less complex substance or substances by ordinary chemical means, such as iron, carbon, oxygen, and hydrogen; substance consisting entirely of atoms having the same atomic number. See **tables of elements** on following page. **2.** a component or fundamental part of a whole: *The plan had all the elements of good design. There is an element of truth to the story.* **3.** a natural, suitable, or comfortable environment: *The theater is that singer's real element.* **4.** any of the four substances, earth, water, air, and fire, formerly regarded as composing all physical matter. **5.** any member of a given mathematical set. **6. elements.** the bread and wine used in Holy Communion. **7.** part of a military force: *Air elements preceded the ground forces.* **8. the elements.** atmospheric forces, such as rain, wind, or snow. [Latin *elementum* first principle, rudiment.] —For Synonyms, see **ingredient.**

element 104, rutherfordium.
element 105, hahnium.
element 106, unnilhexium.
element 107, unnilseptium.
element 108, unniloctium.
element 109, unnilennium.

el·e·men·tal (el′ə men′təl) *adj.* **1.** of or relating to all or any of the four elements, earth, water, air, and fire. **2.** of or like the forces of nature; natural; primitive; or unrestrained. **3.** relating to or being an indispensable or fundamental part; essential. **4.** elementary *(def. 1).* **5.** of or relating to chemical elements rather than compounds.

el·e·men·ta·ry (el′ə men′tə rē, -trē) *adj.* **1.** relating to or dealing with the rudimentary or fundamental parts or beginnings of something; basic: *elementary knowledge of a language, the elementary steps in a process.* **2.** of or relating to an elementary school: *the elementary grades.* **3.** composed of or being only one chemical element; not compounded: *Carbon is an elementary substance.* **4.** of or relating to the four elements; elemental: *the elementary forces of nature.* **5.** elemental *(def. 3).*

Synonyms **Elementary, fundamental,** and **basic** may refer to the first or early stages of some process. **Elementary** suggests an essential first step in such a process: *To understand algebra, it is necessary to master the elementary principles of mathematics.* **Fundamental** refers to a structure on which something can be built: *In the first week of football practice, the players worked to strengthen fundamental skills.* **Basic** is like **fundamental,** but more broadly suggests the lowest level or essential feature on which everything else rests: *the basic assumption on which a scientific theory is built, a resource basic to a region's economy.*

elementary particle, subatomic particle.

elementary school, a school that includes the first six or eight grades and sometimes a kindergarten. Also, **grade school, grammar school.**

el·e·phant (el′ə fənt) *n., pl.* **-phants** or **-phant.** any of various thick-skinned mammals, family Elephantidae, native to the tropical regions of the continents of Africa and Asia, having a massive head and body, a long, muscular trunk, a pair of ivory tusks, and large, fanlike ears. Height: 9 to 11 feet (2.7 to 3.4 meters) at the shoulder. [Old French *olifant, elefant* elephant, ivory, from Latin *elephantus,* from Greek *elephās,* possibly from Phoenician *āleph* ox.]

African elephant   Indian elephant

elephant bird, any of several extinct, flightless birds that were native to Madagascar. One species grew to a height of almost 9 feet (2.7 meters).

el·e·phan·ti·a·sis (el′ə fən tī′ə sis, -fan-) *n.* a permanent enlargement and thickening of the skin in parts of the body, esp. the lower extremities and the scrotum, caused by parasitic worms that block the flow of lymph. [Latin *elephantiāsis,* going back to Greek *elephās* elephant; because the diseased skin resembles that of an elephant. See ELEPHANT.]

el·e·phan·tine (el′ə fan′tin, -tīn, -tēn, el′ə fən tīn′, -tēn′) *adj.* **1.** like an elephant in size, strength, or movement; huge. **2.** of or relating to an elephant.

elephant seal, either of two species of large, earless seals, genus *Mirounga,* having a trunklike proboscis: *M. angustirostris,* found off the California coast, and *M. leonina,* of subantarctic waters. Length: 14-20 feet (4.3-6.1 meters). Weight: to 3½ tons (3.1 metric tons). Also, **sea elephant.** [Because its long proboscis resembles an elephant's trunk.]

el·e·phant's-ear (el′ə fənts îr′) *n.* any of various plants with large heart-shaped leaves, as the taro, begonia, or caladium.

El·eu·sin·i·an mysteries (el′yü sin′ē ən) one of the most important religious rites of ancient Greece, honoring Demeter and Persephone and celebrating the annual cycle of vegetative growth and decay in spring and fall.

el·e·vate (el′ə vāt′) *v.t.,* **-vat·ed, -vat·ing. 1.** to move to a higher level or position; raise; lift. **2.** to raise or improve the moral, intellectual, or cultural level of: *The inspiring speech elevated the audience.* **3.** to raise (a person) in rank or station: *I hope to be elevated to a managerial position in a year.* **4.** to raise the spirits of; cheer up; elate. **5.** to raise the pitch or volume of (the voice). [Latin *ēlevātus,* past participle of *ēlevāre* to raise, lift up.] —For Synonyms, see **raise.**

el·e·vat·ed (el′ə vā′tid) *adj.* **1.** lifted up; raised; high. **2.** characterized by dignity and refinement; noble: *an elevated style.* **3.** in high spirits; joyful; elated. **4.** higher than is usual or normal: *an elevated heart rate.*

elevated railroad, a railroad operating above the ground on an elevated structure, allowing traffic to pass freely underneath.

el·e·va·tion (el′ə vā′shən) *n.* **1.** the act of elevating or the state

E

a	at	e	end	o	hot	u	up	hw	white		about
ā	ape	ē	me	ō	old	ū	use	ng	song		taken
ä	far	i	it	ô	fork	ü	rule	th	thin	ə	pencil
âr	care	ī	ice	oi	oil	u̇	pull	th	this		lemon
		îr	pierce	ou	out	ûr	turn	zh	measure		circus

395

Elements

ELEMENT	SYMBOL	ATOMIC NUMBER	ATOMIC WEIGHT*	ELEMENT	SYMBOL	ATOMIC NUMBER	ATOMIC WEIGHT*	ELEMENT	SYMBOL	ATOMIC NUMBER	ATOMIC WEIGHT*
Actinium	Ac	89	227.028	Hafnium	Hf	72	178.49	Radium	Ra	88	226.025
Aluminum	Al	13	26.982	Hahnium**	Ha	105	(262)	Radon	Rn	86	(222)
Americium	Am	95	(243)	Helium	He	2	4.0026	Rhenium	Re	75	186.2
Antimony	Sb	51	121.75	Holmium	Ho	67	164.93	Rhodium	Rh	45	102.905
Argon	Ar	18	39.948	Hydrogen	H	1	1.00797	Rubidium	Rb	37	85.47
Arsenic	As	33	74.922	Indium	In	49	114.82	Ruthenium	Ru	44	101.07
Astatine	At	85	(210)	Iodine	I	53	126.904	Rutherfordium**	Rf	104	(261)
Barium	Ba	56	137.34	Iridium	Ir	77	192.2	Samarium	Sm	62	150.35
Berkelium	Bk	97	(247)	Iron	Fe	26	55.847 ±0.003	Scandium	Sc	21	44.956
Beryllium	Be	4	9.012					Selenium	Se	34	78.96
Bismuth	Bi	83	208.98	Krypton	Kr	36	83.80	Silicon	Si	14	28.086 ±0.001
Boron	B	5	10.811 ±0.003	Lanthanum	La	57	138.91	Silver	Ag	47	107.87 ±0.003
				Lawrencium	Lr	103	(260)				
Bromine	Br	35	79.909 ±0.002	Lead	Pb	82	207.19	Sodium	Na	11	22.99
				Lithium	Li	3	6.939	Strontium	Sr	38	87.62
Cadmium	Cd	48	112.4	Lutetium	Lu	71	174.97	Sulfur	S	16	32.06 ±0.003
Calcium	Ca	20	40.08	Magnesium	Mg	12	24.312				
Californium	Cf	98	(251)	Manganese	Mn	25	54.938	Tantalum	Ta	73	180.948
Carbon	C	6	12.011	Mendelevium	Md	101	(258)	Technetium	Tc	43	(98)
Cerium	Ce	58	140.12	Mercury	Hg	80	200.59	Tellurium	Te	52	127.6
Cesium	Cs	55	132.905	Molybdenum	Mo	42	95.94	Terbium	Tb	65	158.924
Chlorine	Cl	17	35.453 ±0.001	Neodymium	Nd	60	144.24	Thallium	Tl	81	204.37
				Neon	Ne	10	20.183	Thorium	Th	90	232.038
Chromium	Cr	24	51.996 ±0.001	Neptunium	Np	93	237.048	Thulium	Tm	69	168.934
				Nickel	Ni	28	58.71	Tin	Sn	50	118.69
Cobalt	Co	27	58.933	Niobium	Nb	41	92.906	Titanium	Ti	22	47.9
Copper	Cu	29	63.54	Nitrogen	N	7	14.0067	Tungsten	W	74	183.85
Curium	Cm	96	(247)	Nobelium	No	102	(259)	Unnilennium**	Une	109	(267)
Dysprosium	Dy	66	162.50	Osmium	Os	76	190.2	Unnilhexium**	Unh	106	(263)
Einsteinium	Es	99	(252)	Oxygen	O	8	15.9994	Unniloctium**	Uno	108	(265)
Erbium	Er	68	167.26	Palladium	Pd	46	106.4	Unnilseptium**	Uns	107	(262)
Europium	Eu	63	151.96	Phosphorus	P	15	30.974	Uranium	U	92	238.03
Fermium	Fm	100	(257)	Platinum	Pt	78	195.09	Vanadium	V	23	50.942
Fluorine	F	9	18.998	Plutonium	Pu	94	(244)	Xenon	Xe	54	131.3
Francium	Fr	87	(223)	Polonium	Po	84	(209)	Ytterbium	Yb	70	173.04
Gadolinium	Gd	64	157.25	Potassium	K	19	39.102	Yttrium	Y	39	88.905
Gallium	Ga	31	69.72	Praseodymium	Pr	59	140.907	Zinc	Zn	30	65.37
Germanium	Ge	32	72.59	Promethium	Pm	61	(145)	Zirconium	Zr	40	91.22
Gold	Au	79	196.967	Protactinium	Pa	91	231.036				

*Atomic weights are based on carbon 12. For radioactive elements, the mass number of the longest-lived isotope is given in parentheses.
**Tentative name.

Periodic Table of the Elements

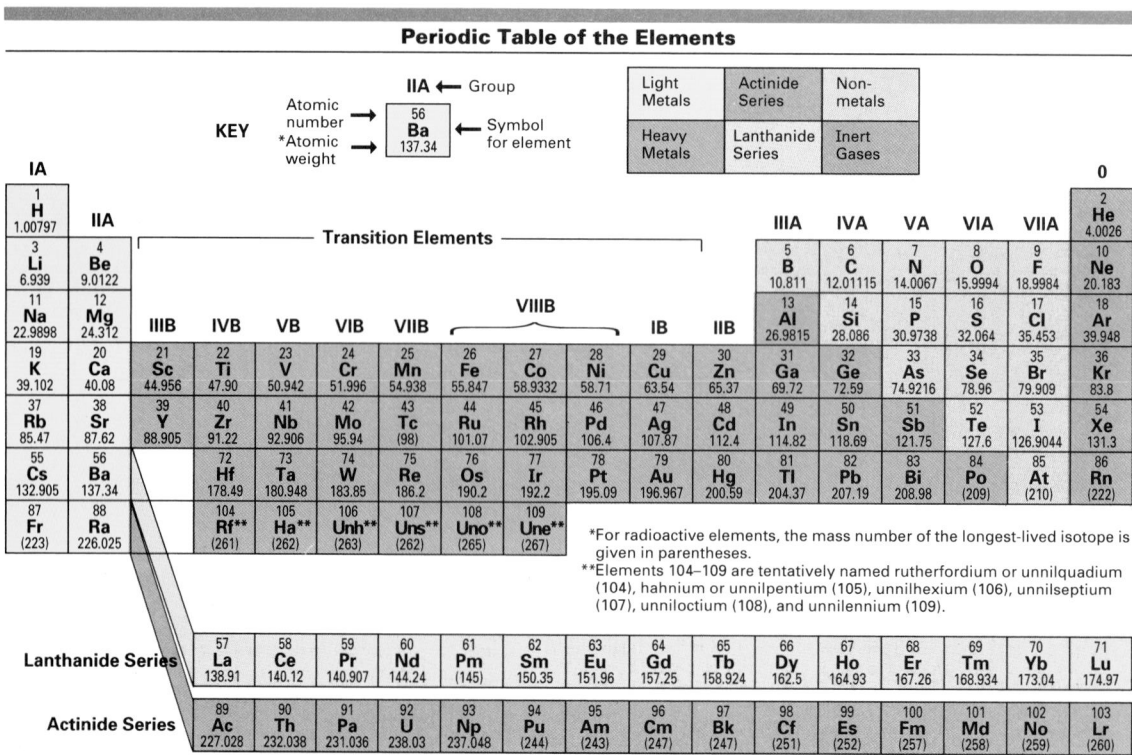

of being elevated. **2.** something that is elevated. **3.** the height above any given point, esp. above the earth's surface or above sea level; altitude: *The village is at an elevation of 10,000 feet.* **4.** loftiness; dignity; nobility. **5.** a scale drawing in a vertical plane of the front, rear, or side view of a building, machine, or other structure. —For Synonyms, see **height.**

el·e·va·tor (el′ə vā′tər) *n.* **1.** a movable platform or cage and its hoisting machinery, used for carrying people and things from one level to another, esp. between floors in a building. **2.** anything that raises or lifts up. **3.** a building for handling and storing grain or other crops. **4.** an airfoil on a horizontal stabilizer of an airplane.

e·lev·en (i lev′ən) *n.* **1.** the cardinal number that is one more than ten. **2.** a symbol representing this number, such as 11 or XI. **3.** something having this many units or members, such as a football team. —*adj.* numbering one more than ten. [Old English *endleofan* literally, one left (after ten).]

e·lev·enth (i lev′ənth) *adj.* **1.** (the ordinal of eleven) next after the tenth. **2.** being one of eleven equal parts. —*n.* **1.** something that is next after the tenth. **2.** one of eleven equal parts; 1/11.

eleventh hour, the last possible moment; just before it is too late.

elf (elf) *n., pl.* **elves. 1.** a small, often mischievous fairy or sprite having magical powers. **2.** a small or mischievous person. [Old English *ælf* the sprite.]

elf·in (el′fin) *adj.* of, characteristic of, or resembling an elf; impish; mischievous: *elfin laughter.* —*n.* elf.

elf·ish (el′fish) *also,* **elvish.** *adj.* elfin. —**elf′ish·ly,** *adv.* —**elf′ish·ness,** *n.*

elf·lock (elf′lok′) *n.* a lock of hair tangled as if by elves.

e·lic·it (i lis′it) *v.t.* to draw forth or bring out; evoke; educe: *to elicit a response to a question.* [Latin *ēlicitus,* past participle of *ēlicere* to draw out.] —**e·lic′i·ta′tion,** *n.*

e·lide (i līd′) *v.t.,* **e·lid·ed, e·lid·ing. 1.** to omit or slur over (a vowel or syllable) in pronunciation. **2.** to fail to include; omit. [Latin *ēlīdere* to strike out.]

e·li·gi·bil·i·ty (el′i jə bil′i tē) *n.* the state or quality of being eligible.

el·i·gi·ble (el′i jə bəl) *adj.* **1.** qualified or meeting the requirements for something: *eligible for retirement, eligible to vote.* **2.** desirable or suitable, esp. for marriage. —*n.* an eligible person. [French *éligible* qualified, from Late Latin *ēligibilis* to be preferred, from Latin *ēligere* to choose.] —**el′i·gi·bly,** *adv.*

e·lim·i·nate (i lim′ə nāt) *v.t.,* **-nat·ed, -nat·ing. 1.** to do away with or get rid of; remove: *to eliminate paragraphs from a lengthy article, to eliminate corruption and waste in government.* **2.** to leave out of consideration; disregard: *In our search for a house, we eliminated all those without a large backyard.* **3.** to expel (waste materials) from the body; excrete. **4.** to cause (an opponent or team) to be removed from competition by defeating. **5.** *Mathematics.* to remove (an unknown quantity) by combining two or more of the equations. [Latin *ēlīminātus,* past participle of *ēlīmināre* to expel, from *ex* out + *līmen* threshold.] —**e·lim′i·na·tive,** *adj.* —**e·lim′i·na′tor,** *n.*

e·lim·i·na·tion (i lim′ə nā′shən) *n.* the act or process of eliminating or the state of being eliminated.

e·li·sion (i lizh′ən) *n.* **1.** an act or instance of eliding. **2.** the omission or slurring over of a vowel or a syllable in pronouncing.

e·lite (i lēt′, ā lēt′) *also,* **é·lite.** *n.* **1.** the best or most distinguished or powerful members, as of a society or social group. ➤ used as singular or plural. **2.** a size of type for typewriters providing six lines to the vertical inch and twelve characters to the linear inch. [French *élite* select few, from *élire* to choose, going back to Latin *ēligere.*]

e·lit·ism (i lē′tiz əm, ā lē′-) *n.* **1.** rule or government by an elite. **2.** the act of supporting or advocating such rule or government. **3.** a feeling or sense of belonging to an elite. —**e·lit′ist,** *adj., n.*

e·lix·ir (i lik′sər) *n.* **1.** in medieval alchemy, a substance that was believed able to change base metals, such as iron and lead, into gold or to prolong life indefinitely. **2.** a sweetened alcoholic solution containing medicine. **3.** a universal remedy; cure-all; panacea. **4.** pure essence or essential principle. [Medieval Latin *elixir* the philosopher's stone, from Arabic *al-iksīr,* probably from *al* the + Greek *xērion* dry powder for wounds.]

E·liz·a·be·than (i liz′ə bē′thən, -beth′ən) *adj.* of, relating to, or characteristic of Queen Elizabeth I of England or her era. —*n.* an English person who lived during the reign of Elizabeth I, esp. a writer.

Elizabethan sonnet, Shakespearean sonnet.

elk (elk) *n., pl.* **elk** or **elks. 1.** a large deer, *Cervus canadensis,* of the mountain regions of western North America, having a predominantly fawn-colored coat. The male has antlers measuring more than 5 feet (1.5 meters) across. Height: 5 feet (1.5 meters) at the shoulder. Also, **wapiti. 2.** any of several varieties of large deer native to northern Europe and Asia, of the same species as, but larger than, the North American moose. [Old English *eolh* a large deer of northern Europe.]

ell¹ (el) *n.* **1.** the letter L, l. **2.a.** anything shaped like an L. **b.** an extension or wing built at right angles to the main part of a building. [Phonetic representation of letter *l.*]

ell² (el) *also,* **el.** *n.* formerly, a measure of length, chiefly used in measuring cloth, ranging from 27 inches (69 centimeters) in Holland to 45 inches (114 centimeters) in England. [Middle English *elle, elne,* from Old English *eln* length of the forearm.]

el·lipse (i lips′) *n.* a closed curve consisting of a set of points in a plane whose respective distances from two fixed points, or foci, add up to a fixed sum; conic section formed by the intersection of a cone by a plane not parallel to or intersecting the base. [Latin *ellīpsis,* from Greek *elleipsis* a falling short, defect, ellipse; because its plane forms with the base of the cone an angle falling short of, or less than, the angle formed by the intersecting plane making a parabola.]

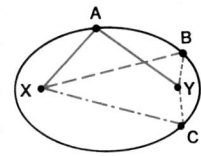

ellipse
AX + AY
= BX + BY
= CX + CY

el·lip·sis (i lip′sis) *n., pl.* **-ses** (-sēz). **1.** the omission of a word or words strictly required by grammatical rules to complete the construction of a sentence, but not necessary for comprehending its meaning. *They arrived sooner than expected* instead of *They arrived sooner than they had been expected to arrive* is an ellipsis. **2.** a mark or marks (. . . , ***, or —) used in writing or printing to indicate an omission, pause, change in thought, or other break. [Latin *ellīpsis* defect, ellipse. See ELLIPSE.]

el·lip·soid (i lip′soid) *n.* **1.** a solid whose plane sections are all ellipses or circles. **2.** the surface of such a solid. —*adj.* relating to or resembling an ellipsoid. —**el·lip·soi′dal,** *adj.*

el·lip·ti·cal (i lip′ti kəl) *adj.* **1.** of, relating to, or shaped like an ellipse. **2.** of, relating to, or characterized by ellipsis; having a word or words omitted. **3.** tending to be obscure or ambiguous: *an elliptical writing style.* Also, **el·lip′tic.** —**el·lip′ti·cal·ly,** *adv.*

elm (elm) *n.* **1.** any of a group of various tall, hardy trees, genus *Ulmus,* native to the Northern Hemisphere, often grown for ornament or shade. One of the best-known species is the **American elm,** *U. americana,* having a light gray bark and oval leaves with saw-toothed edges. **2.** the moderately hard, heavy wood of this tree. [Old English *elm* this tree.]

El Ni·ño (el nēn′yō) a warm current of water that forms during the months of December and January in the Pacific Ocean off the coast of Ecuador and every seven years or so extends southward to Peruvian waters, where it has disastrous effects on fishing and the weather. [From Spanish *el Niño* the (Christ) Child. This current appears around the time of Christmas.]

el·o·cu·tion (el′ə kū′shən) *n.* **1.** the art of public speaking or recitation, including delivery, pronunciation, tone, and gesture. **2.** a person's manner of speaking or reading in public. [Latin *ēlocūtiō* a speaking out, expression.] —**el′o·cu′tion·ar′y,** *adj.* —**el′o·cu′tion·ist,** *n.*

e·lo·de·a (i lō′dē ə) *n.* any of a small genus, *Elodea,* of submerged aquatic plants grown in aquariums and ponds. [Modern Latin *elodea,* from Greek *helōdēs,* from *helos* swamp.]

E·lo·him (e lō′him, el′ō hēm′) *n.* in the Old Testament, God.

e·lon·gate (i lông′gāt) *v.t., v.i.,* **-gat·ed, -gat·ing.** to increase in length; lengthen; stretch. —*adj.* **1.** lengthened; stretched. **2.** long and narrow; slender or tapering: *an elongate leaf, an elongate snout.* [Late Latin *ēlongātus,* past participle of *ēlongāre* to prolong, from Latin *ex* out + *longus* long.]

e·lon·ga·tion (i lông gā′shən, ē′lông-) *n.* **1.** the act of elongating or the state of being elongated. **2.** something that is elongated; extension; continuation.

e·lope (i lōp′) *v.i.,* **e·loped, e·lop·ing. 1.** to run away secretly with one's lover, esp. to get married. **2.** to run away; abscond. [Anglo-Norman *aloper,* possibly going back to Latin *ex* away + Middle Dutch *lōpen* to run.] —**e·lope′ment,** *n.* —**e·lop′er,** *n.*

a	at	e	end	o	hot	u	up	hw	white	⟨	about
ā	ape	ē	me	ō	old	ū	use	ng	song		taken
ä	far	i	it	ô	fork	u̇	rule	th	thin	ə	pencil
âr	care	ī	ice	oi	oil	u̇	pull	<u>th</u>	this		lemon
		îr	pierce	ou	out	ûr	turn	zh	measure	⟨	circus

el·o·quence (el′ə kwəns) *n.* **1.** expressive, effective, and stirring language, as in public speaking: *The speech was full of eloquence and wit.* **2.** the art of using such language. **3.** the power or quality of being expressive, effective, and stirring: *The eloquence of the plea aroused our sympathy.*

el·o·quent (el′ə kwənt) *adj.* **1.** possessing or characterized by eloquence: *an eloquent orator, an eloquent plea.* **2.** intensely or movingly expressive: *an eloquent look of pity.* [Old French *eloquent,* from Latin *ēloquēns,* present participle of *ēloquī* to speak out.] —**el′o·quent·ly,** *adv.*

else (els) *adj.* **1.** other than or different from that which has been mentioned or implied: *You remind me of someone else.* **2.** in addition to that which has been mentioned or implied; more; further: *If anyone else comes, we won't have enough chairs.* —*adv.* **1.** in another time or manner or at another place; instead or additionally: *Where else can we meet? How else can we help you?* **2.** under other circumstances; if not; otherwise: *Dress warmly, or else you'll catch cold.* [Old English *elles* otherwise.]

> **Usage** The adjective **else** is used chiefly after a pronoun in both meanings: *someone else, anyone else.* The possessive form of a pronoun followed by **else** is formed by adding an apostrophe and *s* to **else** rather than to the pronoun: *somebody else's,* not *somebody's else.*

else·where (els′hwâr′, -wâr′) *adv.* in, at, or to another place; somewhere or anywhere else: *This plant is not found elsewhere.*

e·lu·ci·date (i lü′si dāt′) *v.t.,* -**dat·ed,** -**dat·ing.** to make clear; explain: *The debater elucidated the point by giving a few examples.* [Late Latin *ēlūcidātus,* past participle of *ēlūcidāre* to enlighten, from Latin *ex* utterly + *lūcidus* bright.] —**e·lu′ci·da′tion,** *n.* —**e·lu′ci·da′tive,** *adj.* —**e·lu′ci·da′tor,** *n.* —For Synonyms, see **interpret.**

e·lude (i lüd′) *v.t.,* **e·lud·ed, e·lud·ing.** **1.** to avoid or get away from, as by dexterity or trickery; evade: *The bandit eluded the police.* **2.** to escape discovery, identification, remembrance, or comprehension by: *The answer to the riddle has eluded us.* [Latin *ēlūdere* to deceive, from *ex* out, away + *lūdere* to play.] —**e·lud′er,** *n.* —For Synonyms, see **avoid.**

e·lu·sion (i lü′zhən) *n.* the act of eluding; evasion. [Medieval Latin *elusio,* from Latin *ēlūdere* to deceive. See ELUDE.]

e·lu·sive (i lü′siv) *adj.* **1.** difficult to explain, define, or grasp: *an elusive idea.* **2.** difficult to catch, discover, or follow: *an elusive criminal.* Also, **e·lu·so·ry** (i lü′sə rē). —**e·lu′sive·ly,** *adv.* —**e·lu′sive·ness,** *n.*

e·lute (i lüt′) *v.t.,* **e·lut·ed, e·lut·ing.** to remove (an adsorbed substance) from an adsorbent by the action of a solvent; separate or extract by dissolving. [Latin *elutus,* past participle of *eluere* to wash out. See ELUTRIATE.] —**e·lu′tion,** *n.*

e·lu·tri·ate (i lü′trē āt′) *v.t.,* -**at·ed,** -**at·ing.** to separate and sort (the fine particles of a powder) by suspension in a current of air or water. [Latin *elutriatus,* past participle of *elutriare* to wash out, from *eluere,* from *e-* out + *luere* to wash, variant of *lavare.*] —**e·lu′tri·a′tion,** *n.* —**e·lu′tri·a′tor,** *n.*

e·lu·vial (i lü′vē əl) *adj.* of, relating to, or composed of eluvium.

e·lu·vi·um (i lü′vē əm) *n.* **1.** loose debris, as sand or gravel, formed by the decomposition of solid rock in place. **2.** fine sand or soil carried and deposited by the wind. [Modern Latin *eluvium,* from Latin *eluere* to wash out, wash clean, from *e-* out + *luere* to wash.]

el·ver (el′vər) *n.* a young eel. [Form of earlier *eelfare* brood of young eels, journey of young eels up a river, going back to Old English *æl* eel + *fær* journey.]

elves (elvz) the plural of **elf.**

elv·ish (el′vish) *adj.* elfin; elfish. —**elv′ish·ly,** *adv.*

E·ly·sian (i lizh′ən) *adj.* **1.** of, relating to, or like Elysium. **2.** blissful; happy.

E·ly·sium (i lizh′əm, i liz′ē əm) *n.* **1.** in Greek mythology, a happy land where heroes and virtuous people live after death. Also, **Elysian Fields. 2.** any place or condition of ideal or perfect happiness; paradise; heaven. [Latin *Elysium* the Elysian Fields, from Greek *Elysion (pedion)* Elysian (field).]

el·y·tron (el′i tron′) *also,* **el·y·trum** (el′i trəm). *n., pl.* -**tra** (-trə). one of the pair of hardened forewings forming a protective covering over the hind or flight wings in beetles and certain other insects. [Modern Latin *elytron,* from Greek *elytron* sheath.]

em (em) *n.* **1.** the letter M, m. **2.** *Printing.* a unit of measurement corresponding to the amount of line space occupied by a character that is as wide as the type size is high. A one-em dash in a ten-point font is ten points wide. [Originally referring to the amount of space occupied by the letter M in the various type fonts.]

'em (əm) *pron. Informal.* them.

em-¹ form of **en-¹** before *b, p,* and sometimes *m,* as in *embroider, embark.*

em-² form of **en-²** before *b, m, p, ph,* as in *embargo, emphasis.*

e·ma·ci·ate (i mā′shē āt′) *v.t.,* -**at·ed,** -**at·ing.** to cause to become abnormally thin; cause to lose much weight or flesh: *emaciated by a long illness.* [Latin *ēmaciātus,* past participle of *ēmaciāre* to make thin, going back to *ex* utterly + *maciēs* thinness.] —**e·ma′ci·a′tion,** *n.*

em·a·nate (em′ə nāt′) *v.,* -**nat·ed,** -**nat·ing.** —*v.i.* to come forth or originate from a source; issue: *Light emanates from the sun.* —*v.t.* to send forth; emit. [Latin *ēmānātus,* past participle of *ēmānāre* to flow out.] —**em′a·na′tive,** *adj.*

em·a·na·tion (em′ə nā′shən) *n.* **1.** the act of emanating. **2.** something that emanates. **3.** the gaseous product of certain disintegrating radioactive substances, consisting mainly of radon and its various radioisotopes. —**em′a·na′tion·al,** *adj.*

e·man·ci·pate (i man′sə pāt′) *v.t.,* -**pat·ed,** -**pat·ing.** to free from bondage, control, or restraint; liberate: *to emancipate a slave, to emancipate oneself from the limitations of conformity.* [Latin *ēmancipātus,* past participle of *ēmancipāre* to set free, going back to *ex* away + *manus* hand + *capere* to take. In ancient Roman custom, a father would take his son by the hand and then let go, symbolizing the son's release from paternal control.] —**e·man′ci·pa′tion,** *n.* —**e·man′ci·pa′tor,** *n.*

Emancipation Proclamation, a proclamation by President Abraham Lincoln on January 1, 1863, that freed all slaves in the territory still at war with the Union during the American Civil War.

e·mas·cu·late (*v.,* i mas′kyə lāt′; *adj.,* i mas′kyə lit, -lāt′) *v.t.* -**lat·ed,** -**lat·ing.** **1.** to deprive of virility or the ability to father offspring, esp. by removing the testicles; castrate. **2.** to deprive of strength, force, or vigor; weaken: *an earthy novel emasculated by censorship.* —*adj.* deprived of strength, vigor, or virility. [Latin *ēmasculātus,* past participle of *ēmasculāre* to castrate, from *ex* out of, away + *masculus* male.] —**e·mas′cu·la′tion,** *n.* —**e·mas′cu·la′tor,** *n.*

em·balm (em bäm′) *v.t.* **1.** to treat (a dead body) with certain antiseptics and preservatives to temporarily keep it from decaying. **2.** to preserve in fond memory. **3.** to give a fragrance to; perfume. [Old French *embaumer* to anoint with balm or balsam, going back to Latin *in* in, among + *balsamum* balsam. See BALM, BALSAM.] —**em·balm′er,** *n.* —**em·balm′ment,** *n.*

em·bank (em bangk′) *v.t.* to protect, enclose, or confine with an embankment, dike, or similar structure.

em·bank·ment (em bangk′mənt) *n.* **1.** a bank of earth, stones, or other materials, used esp. to support a roadbed or to hold back water. **2.** the act or process of embanking.

em·bar·ca·tion (em′bär kā′shən) *n.* embarkation.

em·bar·go (em bär′gō) *n., pl.* -**goes. 1.** an order by a government restraining or prohibiting merchant ships from entering or leaving its ports. **2.** a restriction imposed upon commerce by law, esp. upon the import, export, or sale of certain goods: *an embargo on the sale of arms to warring countries.* **3.** any restriction or prohibition. —*v.t.,* -**goed,** -**go·ing.** to put an embargo upon. [Spanish *embargo* arrest, seizure, going back to Latin *in* in + Late Latin *barra.* See BAR.]

em·bark (em bärk′) *v.i.* **1.** to go aboard a boat, aircraft, or other vehicle for a trip: *The passengers embarked at San Francisco.* **2.** to set out, as on a venture or course of action: *to embark upon a dangerous undertaking.* —*v.t.* to put or take on board a boat, aircraft, or other vehicle. [Old French *embarquer* to put on a boat, going back to Latin *in* in + Late Latin *barca* small boat.]

em·bar·ka·tion (em′bär kā′shən) *also,* **embarcation.** *n.* the act or process of embarking. Also, **em·bark·ment** (em bärk′mənt).

em·bar·rass (em bar′əs) *v.t.* **1.** to cause to feel self-conscious, uncomfortable, or ashamed: *My foolish mistake embarrassed me.* **2.** to burden with debt or financial difficulties. **3.** to hinder the movement of; impede. **4.** to make difficult or intricate; complicate. [French *embarrasser* to entangle, obstruct, trouble, through Spanish and Italian, going back to Latin *in* in + Late Latin *barra.* See BAR.]

em·bar·rass·ing (em bar′ə sing) *adj.* causing embarrassment: *an embarrassing situation.* —**em·bar′rass·ing·ly,** *adv.*

em·bar·rass·ment (em bar′əs mənt) *n.* **1.** the act of embarrassing or the state of being embarrassed. **2.** a person or thing that embarrasses.

em·bas·sy (em′bə sē) *n., pl.* -**sies. 1.** the official residence or headquarters of an ambassador in a foreign country. **2.** an ambassador and his or her staff: *The embassy gave a reception for the visiting dignitaries.* **3.** the position or functions of an ambassador.

4. a group of officials charged with a diplomatic assignment to a foreign country: *The president received an embassy from the Vatican.* **5.** any official or important mission or errand. [Old French *ambassee* mission, delegation, going back to Medieval Latin *ambactia* mission; of Celtic origin.]

em·bat·tle¹ (em bat′əl) *v.t.,* **-tled, -tling. 1.** to prepare or equip for battle; arrange in battle order. **2.** to prepare for any conflict or struggle; be ready to fight. [Old French *embatailllier* to prepare for battle, from *em-* in (from Latin *in*) + *bataille.* See BATTLE.]

em·bat·tle² (em bat′əl) *v.t.,* **-tled, -tling.** to furnish with battlements. [EM-¹ + Old French *bataillier* to furnish with battlements, from *batailles* battlements, plural of *bataille.* See BATTLE.]

em·bat·tled (em bat′əld) *adj.* **1.** armed and ready for battle: *The embattled troops awaited the attack of the enemy.* **2.** fortified against attack: *When their attack failed, the troops retreated to their embattled trenches.* **3.** involved in conflict or controversy: *an embattled politician.*

em·bay (em bā′) *v.t.* **1.** to put or force (a vessel) into a bay, as for shelter. **2.** to surround or enclose, as in a bay: *to be embayed in a maze.*

em·bay·ment (em bā′ment) *n.* **1.** a bay or something that resembles one. **2.** a process that results in the formation of a bay.

em·bed (em bed′) *also,* **imbed.** *v.,* **-bed·ded, -bed·ding.** —*v.t.* **1.** to set or enclose in a surrounding mass: *The workers embedded the posts in cement. The arrow was embedded in the tree.* **2.** to have as or make an essential or permanent part: *The event is embedded in my memory.* —*v.i.* to become embedded.

em·bel·lish (em bel′ish) *v.t.* **1.** to beautify with ornamentation; decorate; adorn: *The jeweler embellished the gold bracelet with pearls and rubies.* **2.** to make (a narrative) more interesting by adding details, usually of a fictitious nature; embroider. [Old French *embelliss-,* a stem of *embellir* to beautify, going back to Latin *in* + *bellus* handsome.] —**em·bel′lish·er,** *n.* —**em·bel′lish·ment,** *n.* —For Synonyms, see **decorate.**

em·ber (em′bər) *n.* **1.** a fragment, as of wood or coal, smoldering in the ashes of a fire. **2. embers.** the smoldering remains of a fire. [Old English *æmerge.*]

Ember days, three days of fasting and prayer observed quarterly by the Anglican Church, certain other Western churches, and, formerly, by the Roman Catholic Church. They occur on the Wednesday, Friday, and Saturday after the first Sunday in Lent, after Pentecost Sunday, after September 14, and after December 13. [Old English *ymbrendagas,* from *ymbryne* period, circuit; literally, a running around (with reference to seasonal fasting) + *dæg* day.]

em·bez·zle (em bez′əl) *v.t.,* **-zled, -zling.** to steal by fraud (something entrusted to one's care, esp. money or stocks and bonds): *The bank official embezzled funds.* [Anglo-Norman *enbeseiller* to do away with, destroy, from Old French *en-* in (from Latin *in*) + *besiler* to destroy, of uncertain origin).] —**em·bez′zle·ment,** *n.* —**em·bez′zler,** *n.*

em·bit·ter (em bit′ər) *v.t.* to make bitter or more bitter; cause to feel resentful: *The failure of the business embittered its owners.* —**em·bit′ter·ment,** *n.*

em·bla·zon (em blā′zən) *v.t.* **1.** to inscribe or decorate, esp. with one of the symbols or markings used in heraldry: *to emblazon a shield with a coat of arms.* **2.** to adorn or illuminate with bright colors. **3.** to honor or make known publicly; celebrate: *The warrior's deeds were emblazoned by poets.* —**em·bla′zon·ment,** *n.*

em·bla·zon·ry (em blā′zən rē) *n., pl.* **-ries. 1.** the act or art of emblazoning with heraldic devices. **2.** the symbols and markings used in heraldry, as a group. **3.** a brightly colored decoration or display.

em·blem (em′bləm) *n.* **1.** an object, or representation of it, which embodies or personifies something abstract; symbol: *The crown is an emblem of monarchy.* **2.** any object or symbolic design or figure used to identify or represent something: *The soldiers wore the emblem of their regiment.* [Latin *emblēma* raised ornament, from Greek *emblēma* embossed ornament.]

em·blem·at·ic (em′blə mat′ik) *adj.* of, relating to, or serving as an emblem; symbolic: *A gold medal is emblematic of first place in the Olympic games.* Also, **em′blem·at′i·cal.** —**em′blem·at′i·cal·ly,** *adv.*

em·bod·i·ment (em bod′ē mənt) *n.* **1.** the act of embodying or the state of being embodied. **2.** a person or thing that embodies something abstract: *Satan is the embodiment of evil.*

em·bod·y (em bod′ē) *v.t.,* **-bod·ied, -bod·y·ing. 1.** to give concrete or visible form to: *The idealistic mayor embodied the*

town's hopes. **2.** to collect into, or make part of, an organized whole; incorporate: *The report embodied the experiments of ten scientists.*

Synonyms Embody, incorporate, and embrace may all mean to take in something else. Embody suggests that the thing taken in is a whole in itself: *The story embodies the ancient myth of the birth of the sun.* Incorporate implies that the thing taken in is absorbed and assimilated: *All their suggestions were incorporated in the final report.* Embrace suggests inclusiveness, and sometimes acceptance, of what is taken in: *The party embraced members of widely differing backgrounds.*

em·bold·en (em bōl′dən) *v.t.* to make bold or bolder; hearten; encourage.

em·bo·lism (em′bə liz′əm) *n.* the obstruction of a blood vessel by a mass of material carried in the blood, as a blood clot or a fat globule. [Late Latin *embolismus* insertion, from Late Greek *embolismos* intercalation, from Greek *emballein* to throw in.]

em·bo·lus (em′bə ləs) *n., pl.* **-li** (-lī′). abnormal or undissolved matter, as a blood clot or fat globule, carried in the blood and causing an embolism. [Latin *embolus* piston of a pump, from Greek *embolos* stopper.]

em·bos·om (em būz′əm, -bü′zəm) *v.t.* **1.** to take to one's heart or bosom; embrace; cherish. **2.** to surround protectively; shelter: *a house embosomed in the woods.*

em·boss (em bôs′, -bos′) *v.t.* **1.** to decorate or cover with a design that is raised above the surface: *My stationery was embossed with my initials.* **2.** to cause (a design) to be raised above a surface. [Old French *embosser* to swell in protuberances, from *en-* in (from Latin *in*) + *bosse, boce* protuberance. See BOSS².] —**em·boss′er,** *n.* —**em·boss′ment,** *n.*

em·bou·chure (äm′bə shùr′, äm′bə shùr′) *n.* **1.** the mouth of a river. **2.** an opening out of a river valley into a plain. **3.a.** the mouthpiece of a wind instrument. **b.** the position and adjustment of the lips and tongue in playing a wind instrument. [French *embouchure* mouth, mouthpiece, opening, going back to Latin *in* in + *bucca* cheek, mouth.]

em·bow·er (em bou′ər) *v.t.* to cover or shelter in or as in a bower.

em·brace (em brās′) *v.,* **-braced, -brac·ing.** —*v.t.* **1.** to clasp or hold in the arms, esp. as a sign of love or affection; hug. **2.** to take up or adopt: *to embrace medicine as a career.* **3.** to avail oneself of; take willingly: *I eagerly embraced the opportunity to travel to Europe.* **4.** to have as a part; include; contain: *Botany embraces the study of all plant life.* **5.** to form a circle around; encircle; surround; enclose. —*v.i.* to hug one another: *The young lovers embraced.* —*n.* the act of clasping or holding in the arms; hug. [Old French *embracer* to hug, seize, going back to Latin *in* in + *brachium* arm (from Greek *brachiōn* arm).] —**em·brace′a·ble,** *adj.* —**em·brace′ment,** *n.* —**em·brac′er,** *n.* —For Synonyms (*v.t.*), see **adopt, embody.**

em·bra·sure (em brā′zhər) *n.* **1.** an opening in a wall or parapet through which a gun may be fired. The sides usually spread outward to permit the gun to be swung from side to side. For illustration, see **battlement. 2.** an opening in a wall, as for a window, having the sides slanted so that the inside outline is larger than the outside. [French *embrasure* opening of a window, recess, from *embraser* to widen; of uncertain origin.]

em·bro·cate (em′brō kāt′) *v.t.,* **-cat·ed, -cat·ing.** to moisten and rub (a part of the body) with liniment or lotion. [Medieval Latin *embrocatus,* past participle of *embrocare* to moisten, from Late Latin *embrocha* lotion, from Greek *embrochē.*]

em·bro·ca·tion (em′brō kā′shən) *n.* **1.** the act of embrocating. **2.** a liniment or lotion used in embrocating.

em·broi·der (em broi′dər) *v.t.* **1.** to decorate (fabric or other material) with a design in needlework. **2.** to make (a design) on fabric or other material in needlework. **3.** to make (a narrative) more interesting by exaggerating or by adding fictitious details; embellish. —*v.i.* **1.** to do embroidery. **2.** to add interesting fictitious details; exaggerate. [EM-¹ + archaic *broider* to ornament with needlework (from French *broder;* of Germanic origin).] —**em·broi′der·er,** *n.*

em·broi·der·y (em broi′də rē, -drē) *n., pl.* **-der·ies. 1.** the act or art of decorating fabric or other material with raised designs done in needlework. **2.** an embroidered design or work. **3.** interesting fictitious details; exaggeration.

a	at	e	end	o	hot	u	up	hw	white	(	about
ā	ape	ē	me	ō	old	ū	use	ng	song		taken
ä	far	i	it	ô	fork	ü	rule	th	thin	ə	pencil
âr	care	ī	ice	oi	oil	u̇	pull	th	this		lemon
				îr	pierce	ou	out	ûr	turn	zh	measure	(	circus

em·broil (em broil′) *v.t.* **1.** to involve in conflict or strife: *They tried to embroil me in their quarrel.* **2.** to throw into confusion or disorder: *The transit strike embroiled the entire city.* [French *embrouiller* to confuse, from *en-* in (from Latin *in*) + *brouiller* to confuse (of uncertain origin).] —**em·broil′ment,** *n.*

em·bry·o (em′brē ō′) *n., pl.* **-bry·os. 1.** an animal in the early stages of its development after fertilization and before hatching or birth. The human embryo is called a fetus after the first six to eight weeks of development. **2.** an undeveloped plant within a seed. **3.** the early or undeveloped stage or form of anything: *the embryo of an idea.* —*adj.* embryonic. [Modern Latin *embryo* fetus, from Greek *embryon.*]

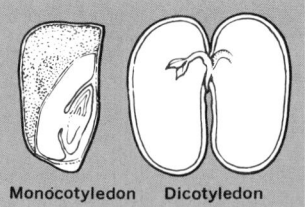

Monócotyledon   Dicotyledon

embryos of seeds

em·bry·ol·o·gist (em′brē ol′ə jist) *n.* a specialist in embryology.

em·bry·ol·o·gy (em′brē ol′ə jē) *n.* the branch of biology dealing with the formation and development of embryos. —**em·bry·o·log·ic** (em′brē ə loj′ik); *also,* **em′bry·o·log′i·cal,** *adj.*

em·bry·on·ic (em′brē on′ik) *adj.* **1.** of, relating to, or of the nature of an embryo: *embryonic development.* **2.** in an early or undeveloped stage or form: *an embryonic idea.*

embryo sac, the female gametophyte of flowering plants, situated in the ovule and containing one egg cell or nucleus from which the embryo plant develops after fertilization.

em·cee (em′sē′) *Informal. n.* master of ceremonies. —*v.t., v.i.,* **-ceed, -cee·ing.** to act as master of ceremonies (of). [Short for *m(aster of) c(eremonies).*]

e·meer (ə mîr′) emir.

e·mend (i mend′) *v.t.* to remove errors from or make changes in the text of (a written work, such as a book or document). [Latin *ēmendāre* to correct, from *ex* out of, without + *menda* fault.] —**e·mend′a·ble,** *adj.*

e·men·date (ē′mən dāt′, em′ən-) *v.t.* **-dat·ed, -dat·ing.** emend.

e·men·da·tion (ē′mən dā′shən, em′ən-) *n.* **1.** the act of emending. **2.** an alteration or correction in the text of a written work.

em·er·ald (em′ər əld, em′rəld) *n.* **1.** a bright green variety of the mineral beryl, prized as a gem. For illustration, see **semiprecious. 2.** a bright green color. —*adj.* **1.** containing an emerald or emeralds. **2.** having the color emerald. [Old French *esmeraude* the gem, from Latin *smaragdus,* from Greek *smaragdos;* probably of Semitic origin.]

Emerald Isle, Ireland.

e·merge (i mûrj′) *v.i.* **e·merged, e·merg·ing. 1.** to come forth from or as from something that envelops: *The whale emerged from the ocean depths. Ten people emerged from the elevator.* **2.** to come into being or notice: *New evidence emerged from the investigation.* **3.** to rise or come out, as from a difficult situation or inferior condition: *to emerge from an accident unharmed.* [Latin *ēmergere* to rise up, come forth, from *ex* out of + *mergere* to dip.]

e·mer·gence (i mûr′jəns) *n.* the act or process of emerging.

e·mer·gen·cy (i mûr′jən sē) *n., pl.* **-cies.** a situation or occurrence, esp. an unexpected or sudden one, demanding immediate action: *In case of emergency, call the police.* —*adj.* used in an emergency: *an emergency brake, an emergency exit, an emergency room in a hospital.*

Synonyms Emergency and crisis both denote a situation in which immediate action may be required. An **emergency** is generally something that occurs suddenly and without warning: *After the earthquake, which left thousands homeless, many countries sent supplies to cope with the emergency.* In a **crisis,** the course of future events may be in the balance: *If the economic crisis is not resolved, the government may fall.*

e·mer·gent (i mûr′jənt) *adj.* **1.** coming into view, notice, or being; emerging. **2.** recently created or independent: *an emergent nation.*

e·mer·i·tus (i mer′i təs) *adj.* retired from active service, usually because of age, but retaining rank and title: *a professor emeritus.* —*n., pl.* **-ti** (-tī′, -tē′). a person who is emeritus. [Latin *ēmeritus,* past participle of *ēmerēri* to earn by service.]

e·mer·sion (i mûr′zhən, -shən) *n.* the act or process of emerging. [From Latin *ēmersus,* past participle of *ēmergere.* See EMERGE.]

em·er·y (em′ə rē, em′rē) *n.* a hard black or brown mixture of granular corundum and, usually, magnetite or hematite, used chiefly as an abrasive. [French *émeri,* from Italian *smeriglio,* going back to Greek *smyris* emery powder.]

emery board, a small, flat piece of thin wood or cardboard coated with powdered emery, used esp. in filing the fingernails.

e·met·ic (i met′ik) *n.* a medicine that induces vomiting. —*adj.* inducing vomiting: *an emetic drug.* [Latin *emeticus* causing vomiting, from Greek *emetikos* inclined to vomit, from *emetos* vomiting.]

e.m.f. *also,* **E.M.F.** electromotive force.

-emia *also,* **-aemia.** *combining form* an abnormal condition or disease of the blood: *leukemia, septicemia.* [Modern Latin *-emia,* from Greek *-aimia,* from *haima* blood.]

em·i·grant (em′i grənt) *n.* a person who emigrates. —*adj.* moving from one place or country to settle in another.

em·i·grate (em′i grāt′) *v.i.* **-grat·ed, -grat·ing.** to move from one place or country to settle in another: *Albert Einstein emigrated from Germany to the United States.* [Latin *ēmigrātus,* past participle of *ēmigrāre* to move away from.]

em·i·gra·tion (em′i grā′shən) *n.* **1.** the act or process of emigrating: *The population of that country has decreased because of emigration.* **2.** emigrants collectively.

é·mi·gré (em′i grā′, em′i grā′) *also,* **em·i·gré.** *n.* emigrant, esp. one who has fled for political reasons. [French *émigré,* from *émigrer* to emigrate, from Latin *ēmigrāre* to move away from, from *ex* away, out of + *migrāre* to migrate.]

em·i·nence (em′ə nəns) *n.* **1.** a position above others, as in rank, power, or achievement; prominence; superiority: *The scientist attained a position of eminence in her field.* **2.** a person who has attained eminence. **3.** an elevation of the earth's surface, as a hill. **4. Eminence.** a title or form of address for a cardinal of the Roman Catholic Church. ➡ usually preceded by *Your* or *His.*

em·i·nent (em′ə nənt) *adj.* **1.** above others, as in rank, power, or achievement; distinguished; prominent: *an eminent writer.* **2.** displaying or characterized by eminence; conspicuous; noteworthy: *an eminent achievement, eminent bravery.* **3.** towering above the surroundings; high; lofty. **4.** projecting outward; prominent. [Latin *ēminēns,* present participle of *ēminēre* to stand out.] —**em′i·nent·ly,** *adv.* —For Synonyms, see **noted.**

eminent domain, the power or right of the government to take privately owned land for public use or for the public welfare, compensation being given to the owner.

e·mir (ə mîr′) *also,* **emeer.** *n.* **1.** a chief, prince, or military leader in certain Arab or Muslim countries. **2.** a title of honor for a descendant of Muhammad. **3.** formerly, any of certain high Turkish officials. [Arabic *amīr* commander.]

e·mir·ate (em′ər it, ə mîr′-) *n.* **1.** the office, rank, or authority of an emir. **2.** the territory ruled by an emir. **3.** in the United Arab Emirates, a territory ruled by a sheik.

em·is·sar·y (em′ə ser′ē) *n., pl.* **-sar·ies.** an agent, as of a government, on an official or secret mission. [Latin *ēmissārius* scout, spy.]

e·mis·sion (i mish′ən) *n.* **1.** the act or process of emitting. **2.** something that is emitted. [Latin *ēmissiō* a sending out.]

e·mis·sive (i mis′iv) *adj.* **1.** able or tending to emit; emitting. **2.** relating to emission.

e·mit (i mit′) *v.t.* **e·mit·ted, e·mit·ting. 1.** to send forth or out; give off; discharge: *Fireflies emit light but not heat. Boiling water emits steam.* **2.** to say aloud; utter: *The child did not emit a sound.* **3.** to put into circulation, as paper money. [Latin *ēmittere* to send out.] —**e·mit′ter,** *n.*

Em·man·u·el (i man′ū əl) Immanuel.

Em·my (em′ē) *n., pl.* **-mys** or **-mies.** one of the gold-plated statuettes presented annually for outstanding achievement in television.

e·mol·lient (i mol′yənt) *adj.* soothing or softening, esp. to the skin. —*n.* a medicine or preparation that softens and soothes: *Lanolin is an emollient for the skin.* [Latin *ēmolliēns,* present participle of *ēmollīre* to soften.]

e·mol·u·ment (i mol′yə mənt) *n.* profit or compensation arising from an occupation, service, or position; wages. [Latin *ēmolumentum,* going back to *ex* out + *molere* to grind.]

e·mote (i mōt′) *v.i.* **e·mot·ed, e·mot·ing.** *Informal.* to show or express emotion, esp. in an exaggerated manner, in or as in acting. [From EMOTION.]

e·mo·tion (i mō′shən) *n.* **1.** a mental state in which a feeling, often intense, as love, hate, or sorrow, is experienced, often accompanied by a physical change or manifestation, as blushing, laughing, or crying. **2.** any of various feelings thus experienced, as love, hate, happiness, or sorrow. [French *émotion,* from *émouvoir* to move, stir up, going back to Latin *ēmovēre* to move out, stir up.]

e·mo·tion·al (i mō'shə nəl) *adj.* **1.** of, relating to, or characterized by emotion: *an emotional farewell, an emotional outburst.* **2.** subject to or easily affected by emotion: *an emotional person, an emotional temperament.* **3.** appealing to or arousing emotion: *The lawyer made an emotional plea to the jury.* —**e·mo'tion·al·ly,** *adv.*

e·mo·tion·al·ism (i mō'shə nə liz'əm) *n.* **1.** a tendency to show or be affected by emotion too easily. **2.** an appeal to the emotions: *The speech was full of emotionalism.* **3.** an unwarranted display of emotion.

e·mo·tive (i mō'tiv) *adj.* **1.** expressing, arousing, or appealing to emotion. **2.** of or relating to emotion. —**e·mo'tive·ly,** *adv.*

em·pa·na·da (em'pə nä'də) *n.* a turnover with a savory or sweet filling, as of ground meat, vegetables, or fruit. [Spanish *empanada* this food; literally, breaded, from *empanar* to bread, going back to Latin *en-* in and *panis* bread.]

em·pan·el (em pan'əl) *v.t.,* **-eled, -el·ing;** *also, British,* **-elled, -el·ling.** impanel.

em·pa·thet·ic (em'pə thet'ik) *adj.* of, relating to, or characterized by empathy. Also, **em·path·ic** (em path'ik).

em·pa·thize (em'pə thīz') *v.i.,* **-thized, -thiz·ing.** to experience or feel empathy: *The novelist was able to empathize with the farm workers.*

em·pa·thy (em'pə thē) *n.* a sharing through imagination of another's feelings or state of mind without actually going through the same experiences. [Greek *empatheia* passion, going back to *en* in + *pathos* feeling.] —For Synonyms, see **sympathy.**

em·pen·nage (em'pə näzh', äm'-, em pen'ij, em'pə nij) *n.* the assembly that makes up the tail of an aircraft, typically consisting of the stabilizers, rudder, fin, and elevators. [French *empennage,* from Old French *empenner* to feather an arrow (from *em-* in + *penne* quill; see PEN¹) + *-age* -AGE.]

em·per·or (em'pər ər) *n.* the male ruler of an empire. [Old French *empereor,* from Latin *imperātor* emperor, ruler, general, commander.]

em·pha·sis (em'fə sis) *n., pl.* **-ses** (-sēz'). **1.** special importance or significance attached to something: *Too little emphasis was placed on the safety regulations.* **2.** something given special importance or significance: *Faith was the emphasis of the sermon.* **3.** a vocal accent given to a particular syllable, word, or phrase. [Latin *emphasis* rhetorical stress, from Greek *emphasis* appearance, significance.]

> **Synonyms** Emphasis, stress, and accent denote special treatment used to make something stand out. **Emphasis** is the most general of these words, connoting any effort to draw attention to something: *In commenting on the essays, the teacher put a lot of emphasis on originality. Too little emphasis was placed on driver education.* **Stress** connotes applying weight or pressure, and may suggest urgency: *The company's stress on high production made it impossible to focus on the quality of the product.* **Accent** connotes making something stand out through contrast, as by using different colors or tones: *The painting was done in blacks and grays, with a splash of red for accent.*

em·pha·size (em'fə sīz') *v.t.,* **-sized, -siz·ing.** to give emphasis to; stress: *My speech emphasized the need for conservation of wildlife.*

em·phat·ic (em fat'ik) *adj.* **1.** spoken or done with emphasis; strongly expressive: *an emphatic denial.* **2.** forceful and committed; insistent: *The senator was emphatic about opposing the proposed tax.* **3.** striking, significant, or decisive: *The jury's verdict was an emphatic vindication of the defendant.* [Greek *emphatikos* expressive, from *emphainein* to exhibit, indicate.] —**em·phat'i·cal·ly,** *adv.*

em·phy·se·ma (em'fə sē'mə) *n.* a chronic disease that impairs breathing, characterized by enlargement of the air sacs in the lungs. [Modern Latin *emphysema,* from Greek *emphȳsēma* inflation.]

em·pire (em'pīr) *n.* **1.** a union of countries or territories ruled or controlled by the government of one country. **2.** a country or union of countries or territories ruled by an emperor or empress. **3.** absolute power, authority, or control; dominion. **4.** a large territory or enterprise under the domination of an individual or group of individuals: *a real estate empire.* [Old French *empire* state ruled by an emperor, dominion, from Latin *imperium* dominion, command.]

Em·pire (*def. 1* em'pīr; *defs. 2, 3, also,* om pîr') *adj.* **1.** of or relating to the French Empire (1804-15) of Napoleon Bonaparte. **2.** of or designating a style of furniture of this period, characterized by heavy, massive rectangular forms, classical and Egyptian motifs, and ornamentation with gilded bronze. **3.a.** of or desig-

nating a style of women's fashion of this period, characterized by a high waistline, a décolleté bodice, short, puffed sleeves, and a long, loosely fitted straight skirt. **b.** *also,* **empire.** (of a dress) having a high waistline.

em·pir·ic (em pir'ik) *n.* a person who relies entirely on observation and practical experience as a source of knowledge. —*adj.* empirical. [Latin *empīricus* doctor who relies on experience only, from Greek *empeirikos* experienced, going back to *en* in + *peira* experiment.]

em·pir·i·cal (em pir'i kəl) *adj.* **1.** based on or derived from experience, experiment, or observation: *empirical proof.* **2.** relying on practical experience, without regard for, or benefit of, scientific principles or practice, esp. in medicine. —**em·pir'i·cal·ly,** *adv.*

empirical formula, see **formula** *(def. 3).*

em·pir·i·cism (em pir'ə siz'əm) *n.* **1.** a method or practice based on experience, experiment, or observation. **2.** a philosophical theory that all knowledge is derived from experience as perceived through the senses. —**em·pir'i·cist,** *n.*

em·place (em plās') *v.t.,* **-placed, -plac·ing.** to put or place in position.

em·place·ment (em plās'mənt) *n.* **1.** a prepared position for heavy guns. **2.** a setting or putting into position; placement.

em·ploy (em ploi') *v.t.* **1.** to engage the services of (someone) for wages, salary, or other compensation; hire: *The store employed extra workers during the big sale.* **2.** to provide jobs for: *Industry employs thousands of people.* **3.** to make use of, esp. as a means or instrument: *to employ radar for tracking airplanes.* **4.** to take up, as time, energy, or attention; occupy: *My studies employ much of my time.* **5.** to take up or devote the time, energy, or attention of: *I employ myself with gardening on weekends.* —*n.* the state of being employed; service: *The agent was in the employ of a foreign country.* [Old French *employer* to use, from Late Latin *implicāre,* from Latin *implicāre* to infold, involve. Doublet of IMPLICATE, IMPLY.] —**em·ploy'a·ble,** *adj.*

> **Synonyms** *v.t.* Employ and hire mean to use the services of someone, for compensation. Although the difference in use of these words is slight, **employ** suggests more regularity of work, hours, and pay: *to employ an accountant, to employ two new teachers in the French department.* **Hire,** the more common word, tends to suggest less steady work: *to hire workers for a construction project.* For other Synonyms *(v.t.),* see **use.**

em·ploy·ee (em ploi'ē, em'ploi ē') *also,* **em·ploy·e.** *n.* a person who is employed by another person or a business for wages, salary, or other compensation. [French *employé,* noun use of past participle of *employer* to use, give employment to. See EMPLOY.]

em·ploy·er (em ploi'ər) *n.* a person or thing that employs, esp. a person or business that employs one or more persons for wages, salary, or other compensation.

em·ploy·ment (em ploi'mənt) *n.* **1.** an act or instance of employing or the state of being employed. **2.** the work in which a person engages or is employed; job; occupation. **3.** the number or percentage of people employed: *Employment in the state increased last month.*

em·po·ri·um (em pôr'ē əm) *n., pl.* **-po·ri·ums** or **-po·ri·a** (-pôr'ē ə). **1.** a large store selling a wide variety of merchandise. **2.** a principal center of commerce or trade. [Latin *emporium* trading place, from Greek *emporion,* from *emporos* merchant.]

em·pow·er (em pou'ər) *also,* **impower.** *v.t.* **1.** to give power or authority to; authorize: *The ambassador was empowered to sign the treaty.* **2.** to give ability or capacity to; enable; permit: *Technological advances have empowered us to explore space.*

em·press (em'pris) *n.* **1.** the wife or widow of an emperor. **2.** the female ruler of an empire.

emp·ty (emp'tē) *adj.,* **-ti·er, -ti·est. 1.** having nothing in it; containing nothing, esp. without the usual or appropriate contents: *an empty glass, an empty warehouse.* **2.** without a person or persons in it; vacant, deserted, or unoccupied: *an empty house, an empty town, an empty chair.* **3.** lacking force, effect, substance, or value; meaningless; hollow: *an empty promise, empty dreams.* **4.** lacking or showing a lack of intelligence or mental activity: *an empty head, an empty stare.* **5.** *Informal.* hungry. —*v.,* **-tied, -ty·ing.** —*v.t.* **1.** to make empty; remove the contents of: *to*

a	at	e	end	o	hot	u	up	hw	white		about
ā	ape	ē	me	ō	old	ū	use	ng	song		taken
ä	far	i	it	ô	fork	ü	rule	th	thin	ə	pencil
âr	care	ī	ice	oi	oil	u̇	pull	th	this		lemon
				îr	pierce	ou	out	ûr	turn	zh	measure		circus

E

empty a wastebasket. **2.** to transfer the contents of (a container): *to empty a glass into the sink.* **3.** to take out, pour off, or otherwise remove (the contents of something): *to empty the water out of a tub.* —*v.i.* **1.** to become empty: *The theater emptied when the movie ended.* **2.** to pour or flow out; discharge: *That river empties into the sea. The crowd emptied into the street.* —*n., pl.* **-ties.** *Informal.* something that is empty, as a container or bottle. [Old English *æmtig* containing nothing, vacant, idle.] —**emp′ti·ly,** *adv.* —**emp′ti·ness,** *n.*

  • **empty of.** not having; devoid of; lacking: *The streets are empty of traffic at night.*

emp·ty-hand·ed (emp′tē han′did) *adj.* **1.** having nothing in the hands; bringing or carrying nothing away. **2.** having gained or acquired nothing: *The negotiators left the meeting empty-handed.*

emp·ty-head·ed (emp′tē hed′id) *adj.* foolish or brainless; stupid.

empty set *Mathematics.* a set that has no members; null set. The set of even numbers between 8 and 10 is an empty set.

em·py·re·al (em pir′ē əl, em′pī rē′əl) *adj.* of or relating to the empyrean; celestial.

em·py·re·an (em pir′ē ən, em′pī rē′ən) *n.* **1.** in ancient and medieval astronomy, the highest heaven, believed to be the region of pure fire or light. **2.** the visible heavens; firmament; sky. —*adj.* empyreal. [Late Latin *empyreus* fiery (from Greek *empyrios,* from *en* in + *pyr* fire) + -AN.]

e·mu (ē′mū) *n.* a flightless bird, *Dromiceius novaehollandiae,* native to Australia, resembling, but smaller than, an ostrich. It can run at speeds up to 40 miles (64 kilometers) per hour. Height: 5-6 feet (1.5-1.8 meters). [Portuguese *ema* crane, ostrich; possibly from a native word from the Moluccas.]

em·u·late (em′yə lāt′) *v.t.,* **-lat·ed, -lat·ing. 1.** to try to equal or surpass, esp. by imitating: *The younger players emulated the team's star player.* **2.** to rival or vie with successfully. [Latin *aemulātus,* past participle of *aemulārī* to try to equal.] —**em′u·la′tive,** *adj.* —**em′u·la′tor,** *n.*

emu

em·u·la·tion (em′yə lā′shən) *n.* the effort or desire to equal or surpass.

em·u·lous (em′yə ləs) *adj.* **1.** eager to equal or surpass; competitive. **2.** of, of the nature of, or arising from emulation: *an emulous act.* [Latin *aemulus* striving to equal.] —**em′u·lous·ly,** *adv.* —**em′u·lous·ness,** *n.*

e·mul·si·fy (i mul′sə fī′) *v.t., v.i.,* **-fied, -fy·ing.** to make into or form an emulsion. —**e·mul′si·fi·ca′tion,** *n.* —**e·mul′si·fi′er,** *n.*

e·mul·sion (i mul′shən) *n.* **1.** a mixture consisting of very small droplets of one liquid suspended, rather than dissolved, in another liquid. **2.** a milky medicinal preparation in which droplets of one liquid, as fat or oil, are suspended in another liquid by means of a substance that keeps them from separating. **3.** a light-sensitive coating on photographic film, plates, or paper, such as a suspension of silver bromide in gelatin. [Modern Latin *emulsio,* from Latin *ēmulgēre* to milk out, drain.] —**e·mul′sive,** *adj.*

e·mul·soid (i mul′soid) *n. Chemistry.* a sol in which the colloid and the medium in which the colloid is dispersed are liquid. [EMULS(ION) + -OID.]

en (en) *n.* **1.** the letter N, n. **2.** *Printing.* a unit of measure equal to half the width of an em.

en-[1] *prefix* **1.** (used to form verbs from nouns) **a.** to put in, into, or on: *enthrone, enchain.* **b.** to cover or surround with: *encircle, enshroud.* **c.** to get or put into or onto: *entrain.* **2.** (used to form verbs from adjectives and nouns) to cause to be or resemble; make: *enfeeble, enslave.* **3.** used as an intensifier to form verbs from other verbs: *enliven, enwrap.* ➡ The addition of *en-* often does not alter the meaning of the verb to which it is prefixed. [Middle English *en-,* from Old French *en-* in, into, on, from Latin *in-,* from *in,* from Old Latin *en.*]

en-[2] *prefix* in, into, or on: *energy, enthusiasm.* [Greek *en* in.]

-en[1] *suffix* **1.** (used to form verbs from adjectives) to cause to be or become: *sharpen, madden, harden.* **2.** (used to form verbs from nouns) to cause or come to have: *heighten, strengthen, lengthen.* [Old English *-nian.*]

-en[2] *suffix* (used to form adjectives from nouns) made of or resembling: *silken, wooden, golden.* [Old English *-en* made of.]

-en[3] *suffix* used in the past participles of many strong verbs: *risen, written, sworn.* [Old English *-en.*]

-en[4] *suffix* used in the plural of a few nouns: *children, brethren, oxen.* [Old English *-an.*]

en·a·ble (e nā′bəl, i nā′-) *v.t.,* **-bled, -bling.** to give adequate power, means, ability, or opportunity to; make able: *Tutoring enabled the student to pass the test. The club bylaws enable the president to veto certain proposals.*

en·act (e nakt′, i nakt′) *v.t.* **1.** to make into a law, as a bill. **2.** to act out on or as on stage; perform. —**en·act′a·ble,** *adj.* —**en·ac′tor,** *n.*

en·act·ment (e nakt′mənt, i nakt′-) *n.* **1.** the act of enacting or the state of being enacted. **2.** something that is enacted, as a law.

e·nam·el (i nam′əl) *n.* **1.** a glasslike substance, usually opaque, fused to metal, pottery, and other surfaces, used for ornamentation or protection. Enamel is usually made from quartz, feldspar, clay, soda, and borax. **2.** a paint, varnish, or other substance that dries to form a hard, glossy coating or surface. **3.** any hard, glossy coating or surface. **4.** a hard, glossy substance composed chiefly of calcium and phosphorus, covering the crown of a tooth. **5.** something made of or coated with enamel. For illustration, see **tooth.** —*v.t.,* **-eled, -el·ing;** *also, British,* **-elled, -el·ling. 1.** to cover or inlay with enamel. **2.** to form a hard, glossy surface on. [Anglo-Norman *enameler* to decorate with enamel, adorn, from *en* on (from Latin *in*) + *amail* the glasslike substance (of Germanic origin).] —**e·nam′el·er;** *also, British,* **e·nam′el·ler,** *n.*

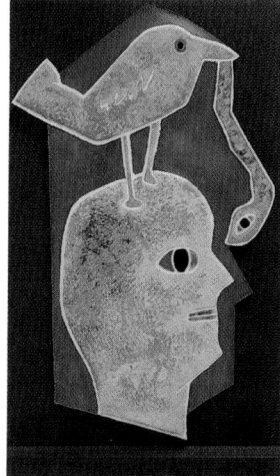

enamel on copper

e·nam·el·ware (i nam′əl wâr′) *n.* metal objects coated with enamel, esp. kitchenware or dinnerware.

en·am·or (i nam′ər, i nam′-) *also, British,* **en·am·our.** *v.t.* to fill with love, desire, or delight; captivate or charm. ➡ usually used in the passive with *of: He was enamored of the actress.* [Old French *enamourer,* going back to Latin *in* in + *amor* love.]

en bloc (en blok′, än) as a whole; all together; in a mass. [French *en bloc,* from *en* in (from Latin *in*) + *bloc* lump. See BLOCK.]

en·camp (en kamp′) *v.i.* to make or live in a camp: *They encamped in the valley.* —*v.t.* to place in a camp: *to encamp soldiers near the river.*

en·camp·ment (en kamp′mənt) *n.* **1.** the location or quarters occupied in encamping; camp. **2.** the people occupying such a place. **3.** the act of encamping or the state of being encamped.

en·cap·su·late (en kap′sə lāt′, -syu̇-) *v.t.,* **-lat·ed, -lat·ing. 1.** to put in or as if in a capsule or sheath. **2.** to put into a brief form; condense; summarize: *The writer encapsulates events of the last century in the second chapter.* Also, **encapsule.** [EN-[1] + CAPSULE + -ATE[1].] —**en·cap′su·la′tion,** *n.*

en·cap·sule (en kap′səl, -sūl) *v.t.,* **-suled, -sul·ing.** encapsulate. [EN-[1] + CAPSULE.]

en·case (en kās′) *also,* **incase.** *v.t.,* **-cased, -cas·ing.** to enclose in or as if in a case. —**en·case′ment,** *n.*

en·caus·tic (en kôs′tik) *n.* a method of painting or decorating in which dry pigments are mixed with melted beeswax and applied to a surface, usually with heated instruments so that the colored wax melts into the surface. —*adj.* of, relating to, or produced by a process of burning into a surface. [Latin *encausticus* done in the encaustic manner, from Greek *enkaustikos* of burning in, from *enkaiein* to burn in.]

-ence *suffix* (used to form nouns from adjectives ending in *-ent*) the action, quality, state, or condition of being: *violence, existence, independence, absence.* [Latin *-entia,* often through French *-ence.*]

en·ceinte (en sänt′; *French* än sant′) *adj. French.* pregnant. [French *enceinte,* possibly going back to Latin *inciēns.*]

en·ce·phal·ic (en′sə fal′ik) *adj.* **1.** of or relating to the vertebrate brain. **2.** situated within the cranial cavity.

en·ceph·a·li·tis (en sef′ə lī′tis) *n.* inflammation of the brain. [Modern Latin *encephalitis,* from Greek *enkephalos* brain + -ITIS.] —**en·ceph′a·lit′ic,** *adj.*

en·ceph·a·lo·gram (en sef′ə lə gram′) *n.* an X ray of the brain taken after the cerebrospinal fluid has been replaced with a gas or other contrasting material.

en·ceph·a·lon (en sef′ə lon′) *n., pl.* -la (-lə). *Anatomy.* the brain. [Modern Latin *encephalon,* from Greek *enkephalos,* from *en* in + *kephalē* head.]

en·chain (en chān′) *v.t.* **1.** to bind with or as if with chains; fetter: *to be enchained by a fear of open spaces.* **2.** to attract and hold, as the attention or emotions; captivate. —**en·chain′ment,** *n.*

en·chant (en chant′) *v.t.* **1.** to cast a spell on; bewitch: *Circe enchanted Odysseus's companions.* **2.** to charm or delight greatly: *The children's performance enchanted the audience.* [Old French *enchanter,* from Latin *incantāre* to chant a magic formula, bewitch, from *in* against + *cantāre* to chant, sing; with reference to the Roman belief in the magical effectiveness of chanted or sung words.] —**en·chant′er,** *n.*

en·chant·ing (en chan′ting) *adj.* very charming or delightful. —**en·chant′ing·ly,** *adv.*

en·chant·ment (en chant′mənt) *n.* **1.** the act of enchanting or the state of being enchanted. **2.** something that enchants.

en·chan·tress (en chan′tris) *n.* **1.** a woman who casts spells; witch; sorceress. **2.** an alluring, charming, or fascinating woman.

en·chase (en chās′) *v.t.,* -chased, -chas·ing. **1.** to encase or mount in a setting: *to enchase a jewel.* **2.** to ornament (a surface), as with engraved, embossed, or inlaid work. **3.** to engrave or carve (a design) on a surface: *a family crest enchased on silver.* [French *enchâsser* to enshrine, set (jewels), going back to Latin *in* in + *capsa* box, chest.]

en·chi·la·da (en′chə lä′də) *n.* a tortilla with a filling, usually of meat or cheese, served in a spicy tomato or chili sauce. [Spanish *enchilada,* from *enchilar* to season with chili, from *en-* in (from Latin *in)* + *chile* red pepper. See CHILI.]

en·cir·cle (en sûr′kəl) *v.t.,* -cled, -cling. **1.** to form a circle around; surround: *The soldiers encircled the enemy camp.* **2.** to move in a circle around; make a circuit of: *Many artificial satellites encircle the earth today.* —**en·cir′cle·ment,** *n.*

en·clave (en′klāv, än′-) *n.* **1.** a country or part of a country completely or largely surrounded by the territory of another country. San Marino and Lesotho are enclaves. **2.** a distinct district or group within and usually somewhat isolated from a larger unit: *a Chinese enclave in an American city, an enclave of scholars in a university.* [French *enclave* piece of enclosed land, from *enclaver* to enclose, going back to Latin *in* in + *clāvis* key.]

en·clit·ic (en klit′ik) *adj.* (of a word or particle) having no stress of its own, and as a result pronounced as part of the word preceding it. —*n.* an enclitic word or particle. [Late Latin *encliticus,* from Greek *enklitikos,* from *enklinein* to lean on.]

en·close (en klōz′) *also,* **inclose.** *v.t.,* -closed, -clos·ing. **1.** to close in on all sides with or as with a wall or fence; surround. **2.** to include with a letter, parcel, or the like: *The store enclosed an itemized bill with my purchases.* **3.** to contain or include: *The letter enclosed a check.* [Old French *enclos,* past participle of *enclore* to shut in, going back to Latin *inclūdere.]*

en·clo·sure (en klō′zhər) *also,* **inclosure.** *n.* **1.** the act of enclosing or the state of being enclosed. **2.** an enclosed space, such as a corral. **3.** something that has been included with a letter, parcel, or the like, such as money or a bill. **4.** something that encloses, as a fence or wall.

en·code (en kōd′) *v.t.,* -cod·ed, -cod·ing. to convert (a message or information) into code. —**en·cod′er,** *n.*

en·co·mi·ast (en kō′mē ast′) *n.* a person who speaks or writes an encomium; eulogist. [Greek *enkōmiastēs,* going back to *enkōmion* eulogy.]

en·co·mi·um (en kō′mē əm) *n., pl.* -mi·ums or -mi·a (-mē ə). a formal expression of praise; eulogy. [Latin *encōmium,* from Greek *enkōmion,* going back to *en* in + *kōmos* revelry.] —For Synonyms, see eulogy.

en·com·pass (en kum′pəs, -kom′-) *v.t.* **1.** to form a circle around; encircle; surround: *A wide moat encompassed the castle.* **2.** to contain or include: *The biography encompasses every aspect of the governor's career.* —**en·com′pass·ment,** *n.*

en·core (äng′kôr, än′-) *interj.* once more; again. ➡ used by an audience to call for a performer or performers to perform again. —*n.* **1.** a call by the audience for the repetition of part of a performance, as of a dance or song, or for the performance of an additional piece. **2.** something that is performed in response to such a call: *The pianist played three encores.* —*v.t.,* -cored, -cor·ing. to call for an encore of or from. [French *encore* still, again, from Latin *(in) hanc hōram* (to) this hour.]

en·coun·ter (en koun′tər) *v.t.* **1.** to meet unexpectedly or casually; come upon. **2.** to meet in conflict; confront in battle: *We encountered enemy troops and routed them.* **3.** to be faced with, as opposition or difficulties; experience: *They encountered little resistance to the plan.* —*n.* **1.** an unexpected or casual meeting. **2.** a meeting of enemies in conflict; skirmish; engagement. [Old French *encontrer* to meet, going back to Latin *in* in + *contrā* against.]

encounter group, a group of people who gather to discuss and act out problems of daily living in order to develop self-awareness and a sensitivity to the needs of others.

en·cour·age (en kûr′ij, -kur′-) *v.t.,* -aged, -ag·ing. **1.** to inspire with courage, hope, or confidence; hearten: *The good news encouraged us.* **2.** to spur or stimulate, as by showing approval or giving help: *The teacher encouraged us to ask questions.* **3.** to give support to; foster; promote: *Public apathy encourages corruption in government.* [Old French *encoragier* to hearten, from *en-* in (from Latin *in)* + *corage* feelings. See COURAGE.]

en·cour·age·ment (en kûr′ij mənt, -kur′-) *n.* **1.** the act of encouraging or the state of being encouraged. **2.** something that encourages.

en·cour·ag·ing (en kûr′i jing, -kur′-) *adj.* giving or tending to give courage, hope, or confidence: *encouraging news, an encouraging smile.* —**en·cour′ag·ing·ly,** *adv.*

en·croach (en krōch′) *v.i.* **1.** to intrude gradually on the property or rights of another; trespass (with *on* or *upon*): *They felt their neighbors had encroached on their privacy.* **2.** to go beyond usual or natural limits; make gradual inroads (with *on* or *upon*): *The winds caused the desert sand to encroach on the oasis.* [Old French *encrochier* to seize upon, from *en-* in (from Latin *in)* + *croc* hook (of Scandinavian origin).] —For Synonyms, see **intrude.**

en·croach·ment (en krōch′mənt) *n.* **1.** the act of encroaching. **2.** something that is gained by encroaching.

en·crust (en krust′) *also,* **incrust.** *v.t.* **1.** to cover with or as with a crust or hard coating: *Dried mud encrusted our shoes.* **2.** to ornament lavishly, as with jewels or precious metal: *The sword handle was encrusted with diamonds and gold.* —*v.i.* to form a crust. [Latin *incrustāre* to cover with a crust.]

en·crus·ta·tion (en′krus tā′shən) *also,* **incrustation.** *n.* **1.** the act of encrusting or the state of being encrusted. **2.** a crust or hard coating. **3.** an elaborate ornamental covering or coating: *an encrustation of gold, pearls, and jewels.*

en·cryp·tion (en krip′shən) *n.* the act of putting information or a signal into a coded form, or a method for doing this.

en·cum·ber (en kum′bər) *v.t.* **1.** to hinder the motion or action of, as with a burden: *Bulky packages encumbered the holiday shoppers.* **2.** to weigh down or burden, as with debts, duties, or obligations. **3.** to obstruct, as with obstacles or unnecessary additions; block: *Discarded furniture encumbered the hallway.* [Old French *encombrer* to block up, obstruct, going back to Latin *in* in + Late Latin *cumbrus* barrier (of uncertain origin).] —For Synonyms, see **hinder¹.**

en·cum·brance (en kum′brəns) *n.* **1.** something that encumbers; hindrance; burden. **2.** a claim attached to real or personal property, as a lien or mortgage.

-ency *suffix* (used to form nouns from adjectives ending in *-ent*) the act, fact, quality, or state of being: *dependency, fluency, emergency.* [Latin *-entia.]*

ency., encyclopedia. Also, **encyc., encycl.**

en·cyc·li·cal (en sī′kli kəl, -sik′li-) *n.* a formal letter written by a pope, addressed to bishops, and usually relating to doctrinal, moral, or disciplinary matters. —*adj.* (of a letter) intended for general circulation; to be read by many or all. [Late Latin *encyclicus,* going back to Greek *en* in + *kyklos* circle.]

en·cy·clo·pe·di·a (en sī′klə pē′dē ə) *also,* **en·cy·clo·pae·di·a.** *n.* a comprehensive reference work in one or more volumes, presenting information on all branches of knowledge or on a specific field, usually in articles arranged alphabetically. [Medieval Latin *encyclopaedia* course of general education, going back to Greek *enkyklios paideia* general education, from *enkyklios* circular, general + *paideia* instruction, from *pais* child.]

en·cy·clo·pe·dic (en sī′klə pē′dik) *also,* **en·cy·clo·pae·dic.** *adj.* **1.** of or relating to an encyclopedia. **2.** covering a broad

a	at	e	end	o	hot	u	up	hw	white		about
ā	ape	ē	me	ō	old	ū	use	ng	song		taken
ä	far	i	it	ô	fork	ü	rule	th	thin	ə	pencil
âr	care	ī	ice	oi	oil	u̇	pull	th̲	this		lemon
		îr	pierce	ou	out	ûr	turn	zh	measure		circus

E

range of subjects or information; extensive; comprehensive: *an encyclopedic knowledge of history.* —en·cy'clo·pe'di·cal·ly, *adv.*

en·cy·clo·pe·dist (en sī'klə pē'dist) *also,* **en·cy·clo·pae·dist.** *n.* a compiler of or writer for an encyclopedia.

en·cyst (en sist') *v.t., v.i.* to enclose or become enclosed in a cyst or sac. —**en·cyst'ment,** *n.*

end (end) *n.* **1.** the point of termination or beginning of something that has greater length than width: *the end of a street, the end of a rope, the end of a line.* **2.** the extreme or outermost part of anything that is extended into or occupies space; boundary; limit: *the end of town, the ends of the earth.* **3.** the point at which continuity or duration of something is terminated; conclusion: *the end of a year, the end of a controversy.* **4.** a final part: *The end of the book was better than the beginning.* **5.** the intended result of an action; purpose; goal: *The end does not always justify the means.* **6.** the reason for which something exists: *This author believes the end of society should be the common good of the people.* **7.a.** the termination of existence; death or destruction: *He came to a sudden and violent end.* **b.** the cause or manner of this: *Hard work will be the end of her.* **8.** an outcome or consequence; result. **9.** a remnant or fragment. **10.** *Football.* **a.** a player whose position is at the left or right end of the line. **b.** the position played by this player. —*v.t.* **1.** to bring to an end; conclude; finish: *to end a meeting, to end a war.* **2.** to be or form the end of. —*v.i.* **1.** to come to an end: *The play ended at ten o'clock.* **2.** to attain or reach a final state, condition, or objective (often with *up*): *They will end up in jail someday.* [Old English *ende* extremity, conclusion, final limit.]

• **at loose ends.** in an unsettled, undecided, or confused condition: *They were at loose ends once school was out for the summer.*
• **end to end.** with the ends touching or meeting: *The workers laid the rails end to end.*
• **in the end.** finally or ultimately: *They argued violently, but in the end they remained friends.*
• **no end.** *Informal.* **a.** a vast amount: *We had no end of fun at the party.* **b.** very much: *The good news pleased us no end.*
• **on end. a.** in an upright position: *to stand a ladder on end.* **b.** without a stop or interruption: *The fire burned for days on end.*
• **to make (both) ends meet.** to have enough money to cover expenses; spend no more than one has or earns: *I work after school to help my family make ends meet.*
• **to put an end to.** to stop or eliminate: *Please put an end to this squabbling.*

Synonyms *v.t.* **End, conclude, finish, terminate,** and **close** mean to bring to a stop or to a final point. **End** is the most general of these words: *to end a recital, to end a friendship, to end an unsuccessful rescue attempt.* **Conclude** is more formal and often implies ending at a certain point intentionally: *to conclude a speech with a line of poetry.* **Finish** suggests completing a task before stopping: *They finished cleaning the house just before the guests arrived.* **Terminate,** which is somewhat formal, suggests stopping something completely and often before originally planned: *We decided to terminate our vacation early.* **Close** suggests resolving an open question or unfinished issue: *The committee closed its investigation, satisfied that there had been no wrongdoing.* For other Synonyms (*n.*), see **objective.**

en·dan·ger (en dān'jər) *v.t.* to expose to danger; imperil: *The mine explosion endangered the miners.* —**en·dan'ger·ment,** *n.*

en·dan·gered (en dān'jərd) *adj.* (of a plant or animal) in danger of becoming extinct: *The whooping crane is an endangered species.*

en·dear (en dîr') *v.t.* to make dear or beloved: *The puppy quickly endeared itself to the children.* —**en·dear'ing·ly,** *adv.*

en·dear·ment (en dîr'mənt) *n.* **1.** the act of endearing or the state of being endeared. **2.** an action or utterance expressive of love or affection: *The lovers whispered endearments to each other.*

en·deav·or (en dev'ər) *also, British,* **en·deav·our.** *v.i.* to make an effort to do or accomplish something; strive; try: *The senator endeavored to gain support for the bill.* —*n.* a serious or strenuous attempt to accomplish or achieve something; effort. [Middle English *endeveren* literally, to exert oneself in duty, from EN-[1] + *dever* duty (from Middle French *devoir* duty, from *devoir* to owe, from Latin *dēbēre*).] —For Synonyms (*n.*), see **effort;** (*v.t.*), see **try.**

en·dem·ic (en dem'ik) *adj.* prevalent in or restricted or peculiar to a particular people or locality: *endemic diseases, endemic plants.* —*n.* an endemic disease. [Greek *endēmos* native (from *en* in + *dēmos* people) + -IC.]

end·ing (en'ding) *n.* **1.** a final part; conclusion: *The story has a sad ending.* **2.** one or more letters or syllables added to a word or word stem, esp. to indicate an inflection.

en·dive (en'dīv, än'dēv) *n.* **1.** the creamy white or curly green leaves of a plant, *Cichorium endivia,* of the composite family, usually eaten raw in salads. **2.** the lettucelike plant that bears these leaves, related to chicory. Also, **escarole.** [Old French *endive* chicory, through Medieval Latin and Middle Greek, going back to Latin *intibus* chicory, endive; possibly of Semitic origin.]

end·less (end'lis) *adj.* **1.** having or seeming to have no limit or end; infinite; boundless: *endless space.* **2.** going on or seeming to go on forever; eternal: *the endless orbit of the moon around the earth; an endless wait.* **3.** perpetually recurring; constant; incessant: *endless repetition, endless interruptions.* **4.** having the ends joined so as to form a circle or loop; continuous: *an endless chain.* —**end'less·ly,** *adv.* —**end'less·ness,** *n.* —For Synonyms, see **eternal.**

end man, a person at either end of a row of performers in a minstrel show who carries on a comic dialogue with the interlocutor.

end·most (end'mōst') *adj.* at or nearest to the end; farthest.

endo- *combining form* within; inside; inner: *endoderm, endogamy.* [Greek *endon.*]

en·do·blast (en'də blast') *n.* endoderm.

en·do·car·di·tis (en'dō kär dī'tis) *n.* inflammation of the endocardium.

en·do·car·di·um (en'dō kär'dē əm) *n.* a thin membrane lining the cavities of the heart. [Modern Latin *endocardium,* from ENDO- + Greek *kardiā* heart.] —**en'do·car'di·al,** *adj.*

en·do·carp (en'də kärp') *n.* the inner layer of a fruit or ripened ovary of certain plants, forming a covering for the cavity containing the seed, as the shell of a cherry or peach stone. [ENDO- + Greek *karpos* fruit.]

en·do·crine (en'də krin, -krīn', -krēn') *adj.* **1.** producing internal secretions that pass directly into the bloodstream or lymph. **2.** of or relating to an endocrine gland or its secretion. —*n.* **1.** endocrine gland. **2.** the secretion of an endocrine gland; hormone. ➤ distinguished from **exocrine.** [ENDO- + Greek *krīnein* to separate.]

endocrine gland, any of various ductless glands, as the thyroid and pituitary, that secrete hormones directly into the bloodstream or lymph.

endocrine system, the system composed of all the endocrine glands, including the pituitary, adrenals, ovaries, testes, and thyroid, some of which regulate metabolic activity and others sexual development.

en·do·cri·nol·o·gy (en'də kri nol'ə jē, -krī-) *n.* the branch of medicine dealing with the endocrine glands and their secretions. —**en'do·cri·nol'o·gist,** *n.*

en·do·derm (en'də dûrm') *n.* the innermost of the three primary germ layers of animal embryos, which later develops into the lining of most of the digestive and respiratory systems and into certain internal organs, as the liver and pancreas. Also, **endoblast.** [ENDO- + Greek *derma* skin.] —**en'do·der'mal, en'do·der'mic,** *adj.*

en·do·der·mis (en'də dûr'mis) *n.* the inner layer of the cortex, surrounding the vascular tissue, found in many roots and in some stems and leaves. [Modern Latin *endodermis,* from ENDO- + DERMIS.]

en·dog·a·my (en dog'ə mē) *n.* marriage within one's own class, group, or tribe in accordance with custom or law. ➤ distinguished from **exogamy.** [ENDO- + -GAMY.] —**en·do·gam·ic** (en'dō gam'ik), **en·dog'a·mous,** *adj.*

en·dog·e·nous (en doj'ə nəs) *adj. Biology, Geology.* growing from within; originating internally. ➤ distinguished from **exogenous.** [ENDO- + -GEN + -OUS.]

en·do·lymph (en'də limf') *n.* the fluid contained in the inner ear.

en·do·me·tri·um (en'də mē'trē əm) *n., pl.* **-tri·a** (-trē ə). the mucous membrane that forms the inner lining of the uterus, which becomes engorged during the month, the excess being shed during menstruation. [ENDO- + Greek *mētra* uterus.] —**en'do·me'tri·al,** *adj.*

en·do·morph (en'də môrf') *n.* a person having a round, fleshy body. ➤ distinguished from **ectomorph** and **mesomorph.** [ENDO- + *morphē* form, shape.] —**en'do·mor'phic,** *adj.*

en·do·plasm (en'də plaz'əm) *n.* the granular inner portion of the cytoplasm of a cell, containing the nucleus, esp. in an ameba. [ENDO- + -PLASM.] —**en'do·plas'mic,** *adj.*

endive leaves and root

endoplasmic reticulum *Biology.* a ribbonlike network of membranes in the cytoplasm of eukaryotic cells, its function specific to the location of the cell. For illustration, see **cell.**

en·dor·phin (en dôr′fin) *n.* any of a group of neurotransmitter peptides in the brain and pituitary gland that are chemically similar to opiates and that alter the body's perception of pain. [Greek *endon* within + MORPHINE.]

en·dorse (en dôrs′) *also,* **indorse.** *v.t.,* **-dorsed, -dors·ing.** **1.** to write one's signature, with or without qualifying comments, on the back of (a check, draft, note, or similar document) as evidence of its legal transfer or validity. **2.** to give support or approval to; sanction: *The unions endorsed the mayor's candidacy for reelection.* [Modification of Middle English *endossen* to write on the back of, from Old French *endosser* literally, to put on the back, going back to Latin *in* in, on + *dorsum* back.] —**en·dors′er,** *n.* —For Synonyms, see **approve.**

en·dor·see (en dôr sē′, en′dôr-) *also,* **indorsee.** *n.* a person to whom a check, draft, note, or similar document is legally transferred by endorsement.

en·dorse·ment (en dôrs′mənt) *also,* **indorsement.** *n.* **1.** the act of endorsing. **2.** writing, as a signature or comments, placed on the back of a check, draft, note, or similar document as evidence of its legal transfer or validity. **3.** approval or support; sanction: *The chef gave an endorsement to the new frozen food.* **4.** an amendment or addition to a contract, record, or legislative bill, esp. an alteration in the coverage provided by an insurance policy; rider.

en·do·scope (en′də skōp′) *n.* any of several medical instruments used to look inside hollow organs and tubes of the body.

en·do·skel·e·ton (en′dō skel′i tən) *n.* an internal skeleton that provides support for the body of certain animals, as all vertebrates. ➡ distinguished from **exoskeleton.** —**en′do·skel′e·tal,** *adj.*

en·do·sperm (en′də spûrm′) *n.* tissue containing food material, surrounding and providing nourishment for the embryo in the seeds of many plants.

en·do·spore (en′də spôr′) *n.* **1.** an asexual spore of certain bacteria, highly resistant to heat and dehydration. **2.** the inner wall of a spore or of a grain of pollen. [ENDO- + SPORE.] —**en′do·spor′ous,** *adj.*

en·do·the·li·um (en′dō thē′lē əm) *n.* the thin layer of epithelial tissue lining the heart, blood vessels, and lymph vessels. [Modern Latin *endothelium,* from *endo-* inner, within + *epithelium.* See EPITHELIUM.] —**en′do·the′li·al,** *adj.*

en·do·ther·mic (en′dō thûr′mik) *adj.* relating to a chemical reaction or other process that is accompanied by the absorption of heat. ➡ opposed to **exothermic.** Also, **en′do·ther′mal.** [ENDO- + THERMIC.]

en·do·tox·in (en′dō tok′sin) *n.* a toxin produced by certain bacteria that is released only after the bacteria are destroyed. [ENDO- + TOXIN.] —**en′do·tox′ic,** *adj.*

en·dow (en dou′) *v.t.* **1.** to give money or property to as a source of permanent income: *Several wealthy families endowed the addition to the library.* **2.** to provide or equip with an ability, talent, or quality (usually with *with*): *a dancer endowed with natural grace.* **3.** to regard as having a particular quality or characteristic. [Anglo-Norman *endouer* to provide with a dower, from *en-* in (from Latin *in*) + *douer* to give a dowry (from Latin *dōtāre*).]

en·dow·ment (en dou′mənt) *n.* **1.** money or property given to provide a permanent income, as for a church or college. **2.** a natural talent, ability, or quality. **3.** the act of endowing.

end·point (end′point′) *n.* the point in space where a line segment ends, or a point that marks the end of a ray.

end product 1. the final result of a process; outcome. **2.** a stable, nonradioactive isotope that is the last member of a radioactive series.

end run 1. *Football.* a play in which the ball carrier attempts to run around the defensive end. **2.** an attempt to get around a problem or difficulty by using evasive tactics rather than dealing with it directly.

end table, a small table placed at the end of a sofa or beside a chair.

en·due (en dü′, -dū′) *also,* **indue.** *v.t.,* **-dued, -du·ing.** to provide or equip with an ability, talent, or quality; endow (with *with*). [Old French *enduire* to lead on, put on, introduce, from Latin *indūcere* to lead into; influenced in spelling and meaning by ENDOW and by Latin *induere* to put on.]

en·dur·a·ble (en dür′ə bəl, -dyür′-) *adj.* capable of being endured; bearable. —**en·dur′a·bly,** *adv.*

en·dur·ance (en dür′əns, -dyür′-) *n.* **1.** the act, fact, or power of bearing up under or continuing despite hardships or difficulties,

as pain, stress, or fatigue: *A long-distance runner must have endurance.* **2.** the fact, quality, or power of lasting; continued existence: *the endurance of a custom, the endurance of a machine.*

Endurance and **stamina**[1] denote the ability to withstand hardship or stress. **Endurance** suggests toughness, either mental or physical, that makes it possible to withstand fatigue and to continue on to the end of something: *the endurance required to cross the Atlantic in a small boat.* **Stamina** is used chiefly of physical hardiness: *Running a marathon requires great stamina.*

en·dure (en dür′, -dyür′) *v.,* **-dured, -dur·ing.** —*v.t.* **1.** to undergo, as pain, fatigue, stress, or other hardship, without impairment or yielding; stand; bear: *She endured the strenuous hike through the forest without complaint.* **2.** to put up with; tolerate: *I can't endure his rudeness.* —*v.i.* **1.** to continue to be; last. **2.** to suffer without yielding; hold out. [Old French *endurer* to make hard or strong, from Latin *indūrāre* to harden.] —For Synonyms *(v.t.),* see **bear**[1]; *(v.i.),* see **continue.**

en·dur·ing (en dür′ing, -dyür′-) *adj.* lasting; permanent. —**en·dur′ing·ly,** *adv.*

end·ways (end′wāz′) *adv.* **1.** with the end forward or upward. **2.** on end; upright. **3.** lengthwise. **4.** end to end. Also, **end·wise** (end′wīz′).

En·dym·i·on (en dim′ē ən) *n.* in Greek legend, a handsome shepherd loved by Selene, the moon goddess.

end zone, the area at either end of a football field between the goal line and the line marking the final boundary of the field.

-ene *suffix* designating certain hydrocarbons, esp. those of the alkene, or olefin, series: *ethylene.*

ENE, east-northeast.

en·e·ma (en′ə mə) *n.* **1.** an injection of liquid into the rectum for purgative or diagnostic purposes. **2.** the liquid thus injected or for such an injection. [Greek *enema* injection.]

en·e·my (en′ə mē) *n., pl.* **-mies. 1.** a person or group that bears hatred for, or wishes or tries to cause harm to, another. **2.a.** a hostile nation or military force. **b.** a person or thing, such as a ship, belonging to such a nation or force. **3.** a person or group that is hostile to or actively working against something, such as a cause, condition, or idea: *The judge was an enemy of corruption.* **4.** something dangerous or injurious: *Disease is an enemy of all living things.* —*adj.* of or relating to a hostile nation or military force. [Old French *enemi* foe, one who bears hatred for another, from Latin *inimīcus* unfriendly, from *in-* not + *amīcus* friend.]

Enemy and **foe** denote a person who hates or wishes to harm another or others. **Enemy** is more general and more common: *The two clans have been enemies for centuries. The king's enemies were plotting to overthrow him.* **Foe** is more rhetorical, sometimes has an archaic quality, and suggests active hostility: *They met their foes on the field of battle.*

en·er·get·ic (en′ər jet′ik) *adj.* having, exerting, or showing energy; vigorous; forceful. —**en′er·get′i·cal·ly,** *adv.*

en·er·gize (en′ər jīz′) *v.,* **-gized, -giz·ing.** —*v.t.* to give energy, force, or strength to. —*v.i.* to exert energy; be active. —**en′er·giz′er,** *n.*

en·er·gy (en′ər jē) *n., pl.* **-gies. 1.** a capacity for, or tendency toward, action: *The child had more energy than her parents.* **2.** *also,* **energies.** power forcefully or actively exerted: *It took a lot of energy to move the furniture. I put all my energies into helping him.* **3.** vigor or force of expression or action: *a speech marked by honesty and energy, a person of great energy.* **4.** *Physics.* the capacity for doing work; potential or kinetic energy. Energy takes various forms, such as radiant energy, electrical energy, chemical energy, and mechanical energy. **5.** a source or supply of power for doing work or making electricity. [Late Latin *energīa* efficiency, from Greek *energeia* action, efficiency.]

energy level *Physics.* a fixed amount of energy that an atom, molecule, nucleus, or subatomic particle can have. For an electron in orbit within an atom, this amount depends on the distance of the electron from the nucleus.

en·er·vate (en′ər vāt′) *v.t.,* **-vat·ed, -vat·ing.** to lessen the strength or vitality of; weaken; debilitate: *Recurring attacks enervated the patient.* [Latin *ēnervātus,* past participle of *ēnervāre* to weaken, from *ex* away, out of + *nervus* nerve, sinew.] —**en′er·va′tion,** *n.* —**en′er·va′tor,** *n.*

a	at	e	end	o	hot	u	up	hw	white		about
ā	ape	ē	me	ō	old	ū	use	ng	song		taken
ä	far	i	it	ô	fork	ü	rule	th	thin	ə	pencil
âr	care	ī	ice	oi	oil	ù	pull	th	this		lemon
				îr	pierce	ou	out	ûr	turn	zh	measure		circus

E

en·fa·mille (äN fä mē′yə) *French.* **1.** within one's family; at home. **2.** informally: *to dine en famille.* [French *en famille* in or with family.]

en·fant ter·ri·ble (äN fäN te Rē′blə) *n., pl.* **en·fants ter·ri·bles** (äN fäN te Rē′blə). *French.* a person, esp. a young one, whose remarks or conduct cause embarrassment to others. [French *enfant terrible* incorrigible child, going back to Latin *infāns* child, baby + *terribilis* frightful, dreadful.]

en·fee·ble (en fē′bəl) *v.t.,* **-bled, -bling.** to make feeble; weaken. —**en·fee′ble·ment,** *n.*

en·fi·lade (en′fə lād′) *n.* **1.** gunfire directed from either flank along the length of a line of troops, an enemy position, or other objective. **2.** a position vulnerable to such fire. —*v.t.,* **-lad·ed, -lad·ing.** to fire or be in a position to fire along the length of, as a line of troops or an enemy position. [French *enfilade* suite of rooms, string of phrases, raking gunfire, from *enfiler* to thread, going back to Latin *in* in + *fīlum* thread.]

en·fold (en fōld′) *also,* **infold.** *v.t.* **1.** to wrap in or as if in folds; envelop: *to enfold fragile glasses in newspaper.* **2.** to embrace; clasp: *to enfold a child in one's arms.* —**en·fold′ment,** *n.*

en·force (en fôrs′) *v.t.,* **-forced, -forc·ing.** **1.** to ensure the observance of (a law or rule); force obedience to. **2.** to compel or impose by physical or moral force: *They enforced payment by threats of legal action.* **3.** to give force to; strengthen: *The lawyers enforced their case with new evidence.* [Old French *enforcier* to strengthen, going back to Latin *in* in + *fortis* strong.] —**en·force′a·ble,** *adj.* —**en·forc′er,** *n.*

en·force·ment (en fôrs′mənt) *n.* the act or process of enforcing.

en·fran·chise (en fran′chīz) *v.t.,* **-chised, -chis·ing.** **1.** to grant a franchise to, esp. the right to vote. **2.** to set free, as from slavery; liberate. —**en·fran′chise·ment,** *n.*

eng. 1. engine; engineer; engineering. **2.** engraved; engraver; engraving.

Eng. 1. England. **2.** English.

en·gage (en gāj′) *v.,* **-gaged, -gag·ing.** —*v.t.* **1.** to hire or employ (a person) or secure (services, aid, or the like): *to engage two new employees, to engage the professional skills of a surgeon.* **2.** to secure the use of, as lodgings; reserve: *to engage a hotel room.* **3.** to attract and hold (one's attention, interest, or the like); engross; involve: *Our plight engaged his concern.* **4.** to keep busy; occupy: *Legal research engages much of her time.* **5.** to bind or pledge (oneself): *We engage ourselves to fulfill certain obligations.* **6.** to pledge to marry; affiance; betroth. ➡ now used only in the passive: *They were engaged in January and married in June.* **7.** to meet in combat with; encounter and fight: *The Union soldiers engaged the Confederate soldiers at Gettysburg.* **8.** *Mechanics.* to interlock with; mesh: *to engage gears.* —*v.i.* **1.** to occupy or involve oneself; take part (with *in*): *Everyone engaged in the search. The committee engaged in a serious study of the problem.* **2.** to pledge oneself; promise; guarantee: *They engaged to accept the financial responsibility for the project.* **3.** to enter into combat: *The troops engaged with the enemy.* **4.** *Mechanics.* to interlock; mesh: *The gears engaged.* [Old French *engager* to pawn[1], pledge, from *en-* in (from Latin *in*) + *gage* pledge (of Germanic origin).]

en·gaged (en gājd′) *adj.* **1.** occupied or busy: *All the phone lines are engaged. The manager is engaged at the moment.* **2.** formally committed to be married; betrothed: *The couple are engaged. A friend of mine just became engaged.* **3.** involved in combat: *armies engaged on a plain.* **4.** committed to a business relationship, esp. under contract: *This cab is engaged. The company is engaged to build three new houses.* **5.** of gears or similar machinery, interlocked or in position to function together: *Is the mowing apparatus engaged?* **6.** emotionally or intellectually involved, as in a political cause. **7.** *Architecture.* partially attached to or embedded in a wall or other surface: *engaged columns.*

en·gage·ment (en gāj′mənt) *n.* **1.** the act of engaging or the state of being engaged. **2.** something that engages or binds, as a pledge, agreement, or obligation. **3.** a promise to marry; betrothal. **4.** a meeting or a promise to meet with someone at a certain time; appointment: *I have an engagement for dinner this evening.* **5.** employment or period of employment: *The singer signed a contract for a two-week engagement.* **6.** a meeting of hostile forces; battle; conflict. —For Synonyms, see **appointment.**

en·gag·ing (en gā′jing) *adj.* pleasingly attractive; winning; charming: *an engaging smile.* —**en·gag′ing·ly,** *adv.* —**en·gag′ing·ness,** *n.*

en·gen·der (en jen′dər) *v.t.* to develop, bring into being, or give rise to; cause or produce: *The talks engendered several proposals. Your attitude has engendered much ill will.* [Old French *engendrer,* from Latin *ingenerāre* to produce.]

en·gine (en′jin) *n.* **1.** a machine that converts energy into mechanical work. **2.** a railroad locomotive. **3.** any mechanical contrivance; instrument; device: *Cannons are engines of war.* **4.** a fire engine. **5.** any driving force or source of energy: *the thermonuclear engine of the sun.* [Old French *engin* skill, invention, from Latin *ingenium.*]

en·gi·neer (en′jə nîr′) *n.* **1.** a person skilled in or practicing any branch of engineering: *an electrical engineer, an aeronautical engineer.* **2.** a person who drives or manages an engine, esp. a locomotive. **3.** a member of the branch of a military force that performs engineering work. **4.** a skillful or shrewd manager or leader: *The general was the chief engineer of the victory.* —*v.t.* **1.** to plan, construct, or superintend as an engineer: *to engineer the building of a bridge.* **2.** to manage or lead skillfully or shrewdly: *The politician engineered a successful campaign.*

en·gi·neer·ing (en′jə nîr′ing) *n.* **1.** the science or profession that puts matter and energy to use for human purposes by the practical application of scientific knowledge. **2.** the use of advances in scientific research to achieve practical ends, as in genetics. **3.** skillful or shrewd managing or maneuvering.

engine house, a building that houses an engine or engines.

en·gine·ry (en′jin rē) *n.* engines collectively.

Eng·land·er (ing′glən dər) *n.* Englishman or Englishwoman.

Eng·lish (ing′glish) *adj.* **1.** of, relating to, or characteristic of England or its people or culture. **2.** of, relating to, or expressed in the English language. —*n.* **1. the English.** the people of England collectively. **2.** a language of the Germanic branch of the Indo-European family, spoken in the United Kingdom, the United States, Canada, Australia, and New Zealand and in varying degrees in other parts of the world. The English language is divided into three major periods: Old English, Middle English, and Modern English. **3.** the English language as spoken in a particular place, at a particular time, or by a particular person or group: *Canadian English, Elizabethan English, to speak broken English.* **4.** an English translation or equivalent: *"Francis" is English for the French name "François."* **5.** the English language or its literature as a course of study. **6.** *also,* **english.** a spinning motion given to a ball by striking it off-center or by throwing or bowling it with a twist of the wrist. —*v.t.* **1.** to translate into English. **2.** to adopt (a foreign word) into English; anglicize. [Old English *Englisc* relating to the Angles, from *Engle* the Angles.]

English daisy, a daisy, *Bellis perennis,* bearing white or pink flowers and growing wild in western Europe.

English horn, a double-reed woodwind instrument of the oboe family, having a pitch one fifth lower than the oboe.

English ivy, a woody, evergreen climbing vine, *Hedera helix,* or any of its cultivars, widely grown as a decorative covering for walls and in gardens.

Eng·lish·man (ing′glish mən) *n., pl.* **-men** (-mən). **1.** a native or citizen of England. **2.** a person of English ancestry.

English muffin, a round, flat, unsweetened muffin, usually eaten toasted.

English setter, a medium-sized setter of a breed first developed in England, having a wavy coat that is usually white with dark markings. Height: 2 feet (0.6 meter) at the shoulder.

English sonnet, Shakespearean sonnet.

English sparrow, house sparrow.

English system, the system of measurement in which the foot is the fundamental unit of length, the pound is the fundamental unit of weight or mass, and the second is the fundamental unit of time. The system has been officially replaced in Great Britain by the metric system, but it is still used in the United States.

English walnut 1. the oily, sweet, edible nut of a tree, *Juglans regia,* of the walnut family, enclosed in a hard, tan, ridged shell. **2.** the tree that produces this nut.

Eng·lish·wom·an (ing′glish wŭm′ən) *n., pl.* **-wom·en** (-wim′ən). **1.** a woman who is a native or citizen of England. **2.** a woman who is of English ancestry.

en·gorge (en gôrj′) *v.t., v.i.,* **-gorged, -gorg·ing.** **1.** to fill or congest with blood, as a blood vessel or organ. **2.** to swallow greedily; gorge. —**en·gorge′ment,** *n.*

engr. 1. engineer; engineering. **2.** engraved; engraver; engraving.

en·graft (en graft′) *also,* **ingraft.** *v.t.* **1.** to graft (a shoot from one tree or plant) into or onto another. **2.** to add permanently into or onto; set firmly; implant.

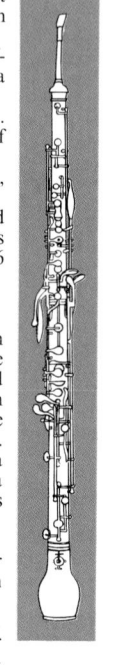

English horn

en·grave (en grāv′) *v.t.*, **-graved, -grav·ing. 1.** to cut or carve letters, figures, or the like into or onto: *to engrave a tombstone.* **2.** to cut or carve (letters, figures, or the like) into or onto an object or surface: *A jeweler engraved my initials on my ring.* **3.** to cut or carve (letters, figures, or the like) into a metal plate, stone, wood, or other material for printing. **4.** to print (something) from a metal plate or other material that has been engraved: *to engrave an invitation.* **5.** to impress deeply; fix indelibly: *The coach's words were engraved in our minds.* [EN-¹ + GRAVE³.] —**en·grav′er,** *n.*

en·grav·ing (en grā′ving) *n.* **1.** the act, art, or process of creating a design, inscription, or picture by cutting lines into a metal plate, stone, wood, or other material. Engravings may be done directly on a finished product, as on jewelry or on the base of a statue, or on a plate from which prints are made, as on some stationery. **2.** a design, inscription, or picture engraved on a surface. **3.** an engraved printing plate. **4.** a printed impression made from such a plate.

en·gross (en grōs′) *v.t.* **1.** to engage or occupy all the attention of; absorb: *The scientist was engrossed in research. The audience was completely engrossed by the musician's performance.* **2.** to write or copy out in large letters or in a formal manner, as a document. **3.** to buy up large quantities or all of (something, as a commodity) in order to control prices. [Partly from French *en gros* in the lump, wholesale; partly from Anglo-Norman *engrosser* to write in large letters; both going back to Latin *in* in + Late Latin *grossus* thick.] —**en·gross′ment,** *n.*

en·gross·ing (en grō′sing) *adj.* occupying one's full attention; absorbing. —For Synonyms, see **interesting.**

en·gulf (en gulf′) *also,* **ingulf.** *v.t.* to swallow up, as in a gulf or abyss; overwhelm completely: *The avalanche engulfed the small cabin. Civil war engulfed the country.*

en·hance (en hans′) *v.t.,* **-hanced, -hanc·ing.** to make greater or heighten, as in beauty, quality, or value; augment; intensify: *The seasonings enhanced the flavor of the stew.* [Anglo-Norman *enhauncer* to promote, modification of Old French *enhaucier* to raise, going back to Latin *in*- in, on + *altus* high.] —**en·hance′ment,** *n.*

en·har·mon·ic (en′här mon′ik) *adj. Music.* of or relating to notes, as A sharp and B flat, that have different notations but nearly or exactly the same tone when played on instruments using the tempered scale.

e·nig·ma (i nig′mə) *n.* **1.** a cryptic or ambiguous statement; riddle. **2.** a baffling or perplexing person or thing; mystery: *The ultimate origin of the universe remains an enigma. The couple was a total enigma to all but their closest friends.* [Latin *aenigma* riddle, from Greek *ainigma.*] —For Synonyms, see **mystery.**

en·ig·mat·ic (en′ig mat′ik, ē′nig-) *adj.* of or like an enigma; mysterious; puzzling. Also, **en′ig·mat′i·cal.** —**en′ig·mat′i·cal·ly,** *adv.* —For Synonyms, see **vague.**

en·join (en join′) *v.t.* **1.** *Law.* to order (a person or group) to do or to refrain from doing some act, as by an injunction: *The union was enjoined from striking for a period of thirty days.* **2.** to order or direct (a course of action, condition, or the like) on or upon; impose: *The doctor enjoined the patient to stay in bed.* [Old French *enjoindre* to direct, from Latin *injungere* to join to, charge.] —**en·join′ment,** *n.*

en·joy (en joi′) *v.t.* **1.** to experience joy, pleasure, or satisfaction in: *to enjoy a party.* **2.** to have the use or benefit of: *to enjoy good health.* [Old French *enjoier* to give joy to, from *en* in (from Latin *in*) + *joie* joy (going back to Latin *gaudium*).]

•**to enjoy oneself.** to have a nice time: *Did you enjoy yourself at the party?*

en·joy·a·ble (en joi′ə bəl) *adj.* giving or capable of giving enjoyment. —**en·joy′a·ble·ness,** *n.* —**en·joy′a·bly,** *adv.*

en·joy·ment (en joi′mənt) *n.* **1.** the act or state of enjoying. **2.** something that gives joy, pleasure, or satisfaction: *This work is enjoyment for me.* **3.** joy, pleasure, or satisfaction.

en·keph·a·lin (en kef′ə lin) *n.* either of two peptides occurring naturally in the brain that act as neurotransmitters in reducing pain and play a role in a wide range of neural and metabolic processes.

en·kin·dle (en kin′dəl) *v.t.,* **-dled, -dling. 1.** to set on fire; kindle. **2.** to stir up; arouse; excite.

en·lace (en lās′) *v.t.,* **-laced, -lac·ing. 1.** to bind with or as with laces; encircle; enfold. **2.** to intertwine; entangle. [Old French *enlacer* to entangle, going back to Latin *in* in + *laqueāre* to ensnare.]

en·large (en lärj′) *v.,* **-larged, -larg·ing.** —*v.t.* **1.** to increase the size or amount of; make larger: *to enlarge a house, to enlarge one's investment in a company by purchasing more shares.* **2.** to make (a photographic print) larger than the original negative. —*v.i.* to become larger. [Old French *enlarg(i)er* to increase, make larger, going back to Latin *in*- in + *largus* abundant.] —For Synonyms *(v.t.),* see **increase.**

•**to enlarge on** (or **upon**). to speak or write at greater length or in more detail concerning: *Can you enlarge upon your idea at our next meeting?*

en·large·ment (en lärj′mənt) *n.* **1.** the act of enlarging or the state of being enlarged. **2.** something added so as to enlarge; addition. **3.** an enlarged form of something else, esp. a photographic print larger than its original negative.

en·larg·er (en lär′jər) *n.* an apparatus for making photographic prints larger than the original negatives.

en·light·en (en lī′tən) *v.t.* to give or reveal knowledge, wisdom, or spiritual insight to; deliver from prejudice, ignorance, or superstition. —**en·light′en·er,** *n.*

en·light·en·ment (en lī′tən mənt) *n.* **1.** the act of enlightening or the state of being enlightened. **2. the Enlightenment.** a European philosophical movement of the eighteenth century, characterized by rationalism, skepticism about traditional doctrines, and the empirical method in science.

en·list (en list′) *v.i.* **1.** to join a branch of the armed forces, esp. voluntarily. **2.** to join in some cause or enterprise; give support or aid (with *in*). —*v.t.* **1.** to engage (someone) for military service; induct. **2.** to persuade to join in some cause or enterprise; secure the support or services of: *I enlisted my friends to help me move.* **3.** to gain (the help or support of another).

en·list·ed (en lis′tid) *adj.* of, relating to, or serving in a military or naval force in a rank below that of a commissioned or warrant officer: *enlisted men and women.*

en·list·ment (en list′mənt) *n.* **1.** the act of enlisting or the state of being enlisted. **2.** the period of time for which a person enlists.

en·liv·en (en lī′vən) *v.t.* to make lively, active, sprightly, or cheerful; animate: *The writer's witty comments enlivened the discussion.*

en masse (än mas′, en) in a group; all together; as a whole: *The club's officers resigned en masse.* [French *en masse,* going back to Latin *in* in + *massa* lump, mass). See MASS.]

en·mesh (en mesh′) *v.t.* to catch or entangle in or as in a net: *A struggle for power enmeshed the two political factions.*

en·mi·ty (en′mi tē) *n., pl.* **-ties.** a bitter, hostile feeling or attitude, as that between enemies; ill will; hostility; animosity. [Old French *enemistie,* going back to Latin *inimīcus* unfriendly. See ENEMY.] —For Synonyms, see **antagonism.**

en·no·ble (en nō′bəl) *v.t.,* **-bled, -bling. 1.** to elevate in nature, quality, or reputation: *This philosopher believes that suffering ennobles a person.* **2.** to confer a title of nobility on. —**en·no′ble·ment,** *n.* —**en·no′bler,** *n.*

en·nui (än wē′) *n.* a feeling of listlessness and discontent resulting from inactivity or lack of interest; boredom. [French *ennui,* going back to Latin *in odiō* literally, in hatred.]

e·nor·mi·ty (i nôr′mi tē) *n., pl.* **-ties. 1.** extreme wickedness; outrageousness; heinousness: *the enormity of a crime.* **2.** something wicked or outrageous; heinous crime; atrocity. **3.** enormous size, scope, or extent.

e·nor·mous (i nôr′məs) *adj.* **1.** much greater than the usual size, amount, degree, or the like. **2.** *Archaic.* extremely wicked; atrocious; monstrous. [Latin *ēnormis* huge, irregular, from *ex* out of + *norma* carpenter's square, rule.] —**e·nor′mous·ly,** *adv.* —**e·nor′mous·ness,** *n.* —For Synonyms, see **huge.**

e·nough (i nuf′) *adj.* as much or as many as needed or desired: *enough room, enough money, enough players for a baseball game.* —*pron.* a quantity or number that satisfies a need or desire: *There is enough here to feed the whole family.* ➡ used as singular or plural. —*adv.* **1.** in a quantity or to a degree that satisfies a need or desire: *I think the steak is cooked enough. Are you well enough to travel?* **2.** quite; very: *The path up the mountain is steep enough.* **3.** tolerably; fairly: *The children behaved well enough.* —*interj.* that's enough; stop. [Old English *genōg* sufficient, abundant.]

Synonyms *adj.* **Enough, sufficient, adequate,** and **ample** mean meeting the requirements of a given situation. **Enough** connotes simply that whatever is needed is present, but not in excess: *We have enough fuel to reach port.* **Sufficient** is similar, but may be more approximate: *The autumn rains were sufficient to produce a good harvest.* **Adequate,** like *sufficient,* is

a	at	e	end	o	hot	u	up	hw	white		about
ā	ape	ē	me	ō	old	ū	use	ng	song	ə	taken
ä	far	i	it	ô	fork	ü	rule	th	thin		pencil
âr	care	ī	ice	oi	oil	ů	pull	<u>th</u>	this		lemon
				îr	pierce	ou	out	ûr	turn	zh	measure		circus

inexact, but it may imply meeting a requirement comfortably: *adequate food supplies for two weeks' hiking.* **Ample** more clearly connotes meeting a requirement by a comfortable margin: *The money we earn is ample for our needs.*

e·now (i nou′) *adj., adv. Archaic.* enough.

en pas·sant (äN pa säN′) *French.* **1.** by the way; in passing; incidentally. **2.** in chess, a method of capturing a pawn that, in making its first move of two squares, passes over a square controlled by an opposing pawn. The opposing pawn has the right to capture it by advancing immediately to the square that was passed.

en·quire (en kwīr′) *v.i., v.t.,* **-quired, -quir·ing.** inquire.

en·quir·y (en kwīr′ē, en′kwə rē) *n., pl.* **-quir·ies.** an inquiry.

en·rage (en rāj′) *v.t.,* **-raged, -rag·ing.** to put into a rage; arouse great anger in. [Old French *enrager* to rave, rage, going back to Latin *in* in + *rabiēs* madness, rage.]

en·rapt (en rapt′) *adj.* filled with intense delight; charmed; enraptured.

en·rap·ture (en rap′chər) *v.t.,* **-tured, -tur·ing.** to bring into a state of rapture; delight intensely: *The spectacle of the circus enraptured the children.*

en·rich (en rich′) *v.t.* **1.** to make rich or richer: *Revenue from taxes enriched the national treasury.* **2.** to improve, as by adding desirable elements or ingredients: *This fish stock will enrich the chowder.* **3.** to increase the nutritive value of (a food) by the addition of vitamins and minerals in processing. **4.** to make (soil) more fertile. [Old French *enrichir* to make wealthy, adorn, from *en* in (from Latin *in*) + *riche* rich, powerful (of Germanic origin).]

en·rich·ment (en rich′mənt) *n.* **1.** the act of enriching or the state of being enriched. **2.** something that enriches.

en·roll (en rōl′) *also,* **en·rol.** *v.,* **-rolled, -roll·ing.** —*v.t.* **1.** to put or record (a name) in a list; register. **2.** to accept as or make a member: *The club enrolled three people last week.* —*v.i.* **1.** to have or put one's name on a list. **2.** to become a member; join: *to enroll in a history course.* [Old French *enroller* to register, from *en* in (from Latin *in*) + *rolle* roll (from Medieval Latin *rotulus* roll of paper, going back to Latin *rota* wheel).]

en·roll·ment (en rōl′mənt) *also,* **en·rol·ment.** *n.* **1.** the act or process of enrolling or the state of being enrolled. **2.** the number enrolled: *The enrollment in this school is 1,317 students.* **3.** a list of those enrolled: *The new student wasn't on the enrollment.*

en route (än rüt′, en) on the way: *They will stop en route.* [French *en route,* from *en* (see EN-¹) + *route* road, way. See ROUTE.]

Ens., Ensign.

en·sconce (en skons′) *v.t.,* **-sconced, -sconc·ing.** **1.** to settle or lodge (oneself) comfortably and securely: *She ensconced herself in a chair by the fireplace.* **2.** to hide or shelter: *He must discover where this Stewart hath ensconced himself* (Sir Walter Scott, 1828). [EN-¹ + earlier *sconce* fortification, from Dutch *schans* bulwark.]

en·sem·ble (än säm′bəl) *n.* **1.** all the parts of something considered as a whole; total effect: *The furniture made a charming ensemble.* **2.** a harmonious set of clothes designed as a whole: *The ensemble consisted of a dress, shoes, a hat, and a coat.* **3.** a group of singers, musicians, actors, or the like who perform together. **4.** a united performance of an entire group of singers, musicians, or the like. [French *ensemble* together, going back to Latin *in* in + *simul* at the same time.]

en·shrine (en shrīn′) *v.t.,* **-shrined, -shrin·ing.** **1.** to enclose in or as in a shrine. **2.** to hold sacred; cherish: *Her words were enshrined in his memory.* —**en·shrine′ment,** *n.*

en·shroud (en shroud′) *v.t.* to shroud; conceal: *Darkness enshrouded the house.*

en·sign (en′sən; *defs. 1, 3, 4, also* en′sīn) *n.* **1.** a flag or banner, esp. a national or a naval standard. **2.** in the U.S. Navy or Coast Guard, the lowest-ranking commissioned officer, ranking below a lieutenant junior grade. **3.** formerly, a British army officer who acted as a standardbearer. **4.** a badge or emblem of rank, office, or authority. [Old French *enseigne* sign, standard, from Latin *insignia,* plural of *insigne* mark, badge, standard. Doublet of INSIGNIA.]

en·si·lage (en′sə lij) *n.* **1.** the process of preserving green, moist fodder for cattle by packing it into an airtight silo or pit. **2.** silage. [French *ensilage* putting grain in a silo, from *ensiler* to preserve grain in a silo, from Spanish *ensilar* to preserve grain in a pit, from *en* in (from Latin *in*) + *silo* pit. See SILO.]

en·sile (en sīl′) *v.t.,* **-siled, -sil·ing.** to store and preserve (green fodder) in an airtight silo or pit.

en·slave (en slāv′) *v.t.,* **-slaved, -slav·ing.** to make a slave of; reduce to or as if to slavery. —**en·slave′ment,** *n.* —**en·slav′-er,** *n.*

en·snare (en snâr′) *also,* **insnare.** *v.t.,* **-snared, -snar·ing.** to catch or entangle in or as in a snare; entrap. —**en·snare′ment,** *n.*

en·snarl (en snärl′) *v.t.* to catch in or as in a snare; ensnare: *to ensnarl a political opponent in an argument over technicalities.* [EN-¹ + SNARL².]

en·sue (en sü′) *v.i.,* **-sued, -su·ing.** **1.** to come or happen afterward; arise subsequently; follow: *The first chapters were better than those that ensued.* **2.** to occur as a consequence; result: *The two groups met, and a brief argument ensued.* [Old French *ensu-,* a stem of *ensuivre* to follow, going back to Latin *insequī.*] —For Synonyms, see **follow.**

en·sure (en shūr′) *v.t.,* **-sured, -sur·ing.** **1.** to make sure or certain: *to ensure the success of a venture.* **2.** to make the getting of certain; secure or guarantee: *A letter from your teacher will ensure you access to the library's rare books.* **3.** to make safe or secure; protect: *Vaccinations ensure one against diseases.* [Anglo-Norman *enseurer,* modification of Old French *as(s)eurer* to make sure, assure. See ASSURE.]

-ent *suffix* **1.** (used to form adjectives) being or acting in a particular state or manner: *independent, persistent.* **2.** (used to form nouns) a person or thing that performs a particular action: *president, superintendent.* [French *-ent,* from Latin *-ēns* (stem *-ent-*) present participial ending.]

en·tab·la·ture (en tab′lə chər) *n.* a horizontal member used in the classical orders of architecture, supported on columns and composed of the architrave, frieze, and cornice. [Middle French *entablature,* going back to Latin *in* on + *tabula* board, tablet.]

en·tail (en tāl′) *v.t.* **1.** to impose or require as a consequence; involve: *The project entailed the purchase of expensive equipment.* **2.** to limit the inheritance of (property) to a specified line or class of heirs so that it cannot be inherited by anyone else. —*n.* **1.** the act of entailing or the state of being entailed. **2.** property that is entailed, as an estate. **3.** a rule that specifies who inherits an estate or succeeds to an office: *The entail indicated that the estate was to go to male heirs only.* [EN-¹ + Old French *taille* cutting, tax (from *taillier* to cut, limit, tax, from Late Latin *tāliāre* to cut, from Latin *tālea* rod, cutting).]

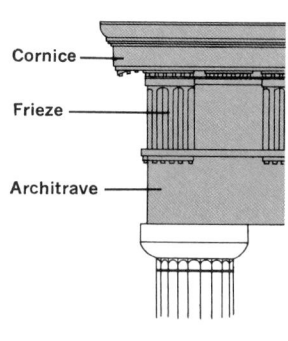

Cornice

Frieze

Architrave

entablature

en·tan·gle (en tang′gəl) *v.t.,* **-gled, -gling.** **1.** to catch in or as in a tangle or net; ensnare: *The seaweed entangled the fishing line.* **2.** to involve, as in difficulties: *An innocent bystander became entangled in the argument.* **3.** to cause to become knotted or tangled; snarl: *to entangle yarn.* **4.** to confuse or complicate: *Their reasoning was hopelessly entangled.*

en·tan·gle·ment (en tang′gəl mənt) *n.* **1.** the act of entangling or the state of being entangled. **2.** something that entangles.

en·tente (än tänt′; *French* äN täNt′) *n., pl.* **-tentes** (-tänts′; *French* -täNt′) **1.** a broad understanding or agreement between two or more countries, esp. on common diplomatic policies. An entente is less specific and binding than a formal alliance. **2.** the countries having such an understanding or agreement. [French *entente* understanding, from *entendre* to hear, understand, from Latin *intendere* to stretch out, apply oneself to.]

entente cor·diale (kôr dyäl′) **1.** a friendly, informal collaboration or agreement, esp. between countries. **2. Entente Cordiale.** a friendly diplomatic relationship, short of a formal alliance, established before World War I between Great Britain and France against Germany.

en·ter (en′tər) *v.t.* **1.a.** to go or come into: *She entered the room. A sudden thought entered his mind.* **b.** to pass into or through, esp. with force; penetrate; pierce: *The bullet entered the arm above the elbow.* **2.** to become a member or participant in; join: *to enter a university, to enter a campaign, to enter a contest.* **3.a.** to cause to be admitted or accepted; enroll (someone or something): *She entered her dog in the competition.* **b.** to set down in writing; make a record of; register: *to enter one's name in a book.* **4.** to take the initial steps in; begin; start: *The organism entered a new phase in its development.* **5.** to place formally before a court of law or on record: *to enter a plea of not guilty.* **6.** to put into a computer system: *to enter new data in a computer file.* **7.** to register or make a report of (a ship or its cargo) at customs. —*v.i.* **1.** to go or come

in: *The actor entered when he heard his cue.* **2.** to pierce; penetrate: *The bullet entered above the shoulder.* [Old French *entrer* to go into, begin, from Latin *intrāre* to go into.]

• **to enter into. a.** to begin to take part in or engage in: *The wealthy executive entered into politics as a hobby.* **b.** to take an active part in and contribute to: *She entered into the discussion enthusiastically.* **c.** to form a part of; be an element in: *Many factors entered into his decision not to go.* **d.** to consider or discuss; treat: *The report failed to enter into the city's financial problems.*

• **to enter on** (or **upon**). **a.** to set out on: *The travelers entered on the voyage in winter.* **b.** to make a start in: *The young dentist entered upon independent practice with some anxiety.*

en·ter-, form of **entero-** before vowels, as in *enteritis.*

en·ter·ic (en ter′ik) *adj.* intestinal. [Greek *enterikos,* from *entera* intestines.]

en·ter·i·tis (en′tə rī′tis) *n.* inflammation of the lining of the intestines, characterized by diarrhea and sometimes cramps, nausea, and vomiting. [Greek *entera* intestines + -ITIS.]

entero- *combining form* intestine: *enterokinase.* [Greek *enteron* intestine.]

en·ter·o·ki·nase (en′tə rō kī′nās) *n.* an enzyme secreted by the small intestine that converts the inactive precursor of trypsin into trypsin.

en·ter·on (en′tə ron′) *n.* the alimentary canal; intestine. [Modern Latin *enteron,* from Greek *enteron* intestine.]

en·ter·prise (en′tər prīz′) *n.* **1.** a project or undertaking, esp. one of a difficult, dangerous, or important nature. **2.** readiness to take part in such projects or undertakings; energy and initiative: *If you want your boss to notice you, you should show more enterprise.* **3.** a business undertaking, organization, or firm. [Old French *entreprise* undertaking, from *entreprendre* to undertake, going back to Latin *inter* among + *prehendere* to take, seize.] —For Synonyms, see **project.**

en·ter·pris·ing (en′tər prī′zing) *adj.* showing energy and initiative; venturesome.

en·ter·tain (en′tər tān′) *v.t.* **1.** to hold the attention of so as to divert, interest, or amuse: *The clown entertained the children.* **2.** to have or receive as a guest; give hospitality to: *Every summer they entertain the neighbors at an outdoor party.* **3.** to have or hold in the mind, as an idea; take into consideration: *The wronged prospector entertained thoughts of revenge.* —*v.i.* to have or receive guests: *a family that entertains often.* [French *entretenir* to maintain, amuse, provide for, going back to Latin *inter* among + *tenēre* to hold.]

en·ter·tain·er (en′tər tā′nər) *n.* a person who entertains, esp. a professional in one of the performing arts.

en·ter·tain·ing (en′tər tā′ning) *adj.* serving to entertain; engaging; diverting; amusing. —**en′ter·tain′ing·ly,** *adv.*

en·ter·tain·ment (en′tər tān′mənt) *n.* **1.** the act of entertaining or the state of being entertained. **2.** intellectual and emotional enjoyment that results from being entertained: *Tonight, for your entertainment, we present a famous magician.* **3.** something that entertains, esp. a performance. **4.** the performing arts as a whole: *the world of entertainment.* **5.** reception and treatment of guests; hospitality. —For Synonyms, see **amusement.**

en·thal·py (en′thal pē, en thal′-) *n.* in thermodynamics, a measure of the amount of heat contained by a given mass of substance. [Greek *enthalpein* to warm in, from *en-* in + *thalpein* to heat.]

en·thrall (en thrôl′) *also,* **en·thral, in·thrall, in·thrall.** *v.t.,* -thralled, -thrall·ing. **1.** to hold spellbound; captivate; charm: *The magnificent acting enthralled the audience.* **2.** to make a slave of; enslave. —**en·thrall′ment;** *also,* **en·thral′ment,** *n.*

en·throne (en thrōn′) *also,* **inthrone.** *v.t.,* -throned, -thron·ing. **1.** to invest ceremonially with authority, rank, or office, as a sovereign or bishop: *to enthrone a king.* **2.** to put highest of all; exalt; revere. **3.** to place on or as on a throne: *The great-grandmother was enthroned at the head of the table.* —**en·throne′ment,** *n.*

en·thuse (en thüz′) *Informal. v.,* -thused, -thus·ing. —*v.i.* to show enthusiasm. —*v.t.* to make enthusiastic. [From ENTHUSIASM.]

Although **enthuse** has been recorded in use as early as 1827, it has failed to gain wide acceptance. Most people strongly object to its use, especially in formal speech or writing.

en·thu·si·asm (en thü′zē az′əm) *n.* **1.** eager or fervent interest; ardor; zeal: *He showed great enthusiasm for the ingenious plan.* **2.** something that arouses such interest: *Golfing is one of her enthusiasms.* [Greek *enthousiasmos* divine inspiration, going back to *entheos* inspired by a god, possessed, from *en* in + *theos* god.]

en·thu·si·ast (en thü′zē ast′) *n.* a person who is filled with enthusiasm; ardent supporter or follower: *a sports enthusiast.*

Enthusiast, zealot, fanatic, fan², and **devotee** denote one who is filled with intense feeling for, or is thoroughly preoccupied with, some cause, subject, or person. **Enthusiast** connotes fervent interest in something, sometimes to the exclusion of more practical matters: *a skiing enthusiast who spent every weekend on the slopes.* **Zealot** implies devotion to and action for a cause, sometimes going to extremes: *the fervor of religious zealots.* **Fanatic** connotes undeviating determination to follow a course, often to the point of irrationality: *Some fanatics stayed up all night to see the eclipse, even though the sky was completely overcast.* **Fan,** a popular shortening of *fanatic,* is used chiefly of avid followers of sports or of some forms of entertainment: *Baseball fans were glued to their television sets throughout the World Series.* **Devotee** connotes one who is faithful to something or someone, from a religion to a mere pastime: *a devotee of a guru, a devotee of crossword puzzles.*

en·thu·si·as·tic (en thü′zē as′tik) *adj.* full of or characterized by enthusiasm; ardent; zealous. —**en·thu′si·as′ti·cal·ly,** *adv.*

en·tice (en tīs′) *v.t.,* -ticed, -tic·ing. to attract or lure by offering pleasure or reward; tempt: *They enticed the general into joining the conspiracy.* [Old French *enticier* to excite, going back to *in* on + *tītiō* firebrand.] —**en·tic′er,** *n.* —**en·tic′ing·ly,** *adv.*

en·tice·ment (en tīs′mənt) *n.* **1.** the act of enticing or the state of being enticed. **2.** something that entices.

en·tire (en tīr′) *adj.* **1.** having or including all the parts or elements; total; complete; whole: *The entire faculty was present. I donated the entire sum to charity.* **2.** not broken or impaired; in one piece; intact. **3.** *Botany.* (of leaves) having smooth edges and not divided. [Old French *entier* upright, genuine, from Latin *integer* whole. Doublet of INTEGER.] —**en·tire′ness,** *n.* —For Synonyms, see **complete.**

en·tire·ly (en tīr′lē) *adv.* **1.** without exception or reservation; wholly; completely: *I agree with you entirely.* **2.** to the exclusion of all else or others; solely; exclusively: *The responsibility for making the decision is entirely mine.*

en·tire·ty (en tīr′tē) *n., pl.* -ties. **1.** the state of being whole or complete; totality: *The opera was too long to be performed in its entirety.* **2.** something that is entire; whole: *He spent the entirety of his life pursuing success.*

en·ti·tle (en tī′təl) *also,* **intitle.** *v.t.,* -tled, -tling. **1.** to give the title of; call; designate: *John Bunyan wrote a book entitled "Pilgrim's Progress."* **2.** to give a title, claim, or right to something; qualify; authorize: *Her high score entitled her to the prize. What entitles you to criticize them?* [Old French *entiteler* to mention, relate, from Late Latin *intitulāre* to give a name to, from Latin *in* in + *titulus* title, label.]

en·ti·ty (en′ti tē) *n., pl.* -ties. **1.** something with real and distinct existence, whether objectively or in the mind; an actual thing. **2.** being; existence: *A thought has no entity independent of the person who thinks it.* [Medieval Latin *entitas* existence, real substance, from Late Latin *ēns* a thing, from Latin *esse* to be.]

en·tomb (en tüm′) *also,* **intomb.** *v.t.* **1.** to place in a tomb; bury. **2.** to serve as a tomb for: *The snow from the avalanche entombed the climber.* —**en·tomb′ment,** *n.*

entomo- *combining form* insect or insects; of insects: *entomology.* Also (before a vowel), **entom-.** [French *entomo-,* from Greek *entoma(zōa)* notched (animals), insects, from *entomos* cut, notched, from *en-* in + *temnein* to cut.]

en·to·mo·log·i·cal (en′tə mə loj′i kəl) *adj.* of or relating to entomology. Also, **en′to·mo·log′ic.**

en·to·mol·o·gy (en′tə mol′ə jē) *n.* the branch of zoology dealing with insects. [Greek *entomon* insect + -LOGY.] —**en′to·mol′o·gist,** *n.*

en·tou·rage (än′tů räzh′) *n.* a group of attendants, followers, or companions, esp. one accompanying a person of rank or importance; retinue. [French *entourage* circle of attendants, from *entourer* to surround, from *en-* in (from Latin *in*) + *tour* turn, circuit. See TOUR.]

en·tr'acte (än trakt′) *n.* **1.** an interval between two parts of a theatrical performance. **2.** entertainment provided during this interval. [French *entracte* interval between the acts, from *entre* between (Latin *inter*) + *acte* action, act. See ACT.]

en·trails (en′trālz, -trəlz) *pl. n.* **1.a.** the inner organs of the trunk of a human being or animal; guts, viscera. **b.** the intestines;

a	at	e	end	o	hot	u	up	hw	white		about
ā	ape	ē	me	ō	old	ū	use	ng	song		taken
ä	far	i	it	ô	fork	ü	rule	th	thin	ə	pencil
âr	care	ī	ice	oi	oil	ů	pull	th	this		lemon
				îr	pierce	ou	out	ûr	turn	zh	measure		circus

E

bowels. **2.** the inner parts or mechanism of anything; innards. [Old French *entrailles* intestines, going back to Latin *interānea*, from *inter* within.]

en·train¹ (en trān') *v.i., v.t.* to go or put aboard a train. —**en·train'ment,** *n.*

en·train² (en trān') *v.t.* to suspend and transport (fine droplets) in a moving stream of vapor, as during distillation. [French *entraîner*, from *en-* away (from Latin *inde* thence, from there) + *traîner* to drag (from Old French *traîner*). See TRAIN.] —**en·train'ment,** *n.*

en·trance¹ (en'trəns) *n.* **1.** an act or instance of entering: *Everyone rose at the judge's entrance. The campaign marked the candidate's entrance into politics.* **2.** a place or means for entering: *an entrance to a building.* **3.** the right or power of entering; admittance: *Students were given free entrance to the basketball game.* [Old French *entrance* a going in, passage for entering, beginning, from *entrans*, present participle of *entrer* to go into, begin. See ENTER.]

en·trance² (en trans') *v.t.*, **-tranced, -tranc·ing. 1.** to put into a trance. **2.** to fill with joy, delight, or wonder; charm; enchant: *The musician's performance entranced the audience.* [EN-¹ + TRANCE.] —**en·trance'ment,** *n.* —**en·tranc'ing·ly,** *adv.*

en·trance·way (en'trəns wā') *n.* entryway.

en·trant (en'trənt) *n.* **1.** a person or animal that enters or is entered in a contest; contestant; competitor. **2.** a person who enters, esp. a new member of a profession or association. [French *entrant*, present participle of *entrer* to go into. See ENTER.]

en·trap (en trap') *v.t.*, **-trapped, -trap·ping. 1.** to catch in or as in a trap. **2.** to involve in difficulty or danger by trickery or deception; entangle; ensnare. **3.** to use illegal enticement to lure (a person) into committing a crime that he or she might not otherwise have committed. [Old French *entraper* to pester, catch, from *en-* in (from Latin *in*) + *trape* trap (of Germanic origin).]

en·trap·ment (en trap'mənt) *n.* **1.** the act of entrapping, esp. illegal actions by a police officer that lure a person into committing a crime that he or she might not otherwise have committed. **2.** the state of being entrapped.

en·treat (en trēt') *also*, intreat. *v.t.* to ask earnestly; beseech; implore. —*v.i.* to make an earnest appeal; plead. [Old French *entraiter* to treat of, treat, going back to Latin *in* in + *tractāre* to handle.] —For Synonyms, see **beg.**

en·treat·y (en trē'tē) *n., pl.* **-treat·ies.** an earnest request; supplication; plea.

en·tre·chat (än'trə shä', än'trə shä') *n., pl.* **-chats** (-shäz', -shäz'). in ballet, a leap during which a dancer crosses his or her feet a number of times, sometimes beating them together. [French *entrechat*, from earlier *entrechasse*, from Italian *(capriola) intrecciata* literally, intertwined (caper).]

en·tree (än'trā) *also*, en·trée. *n.* **1.a.** a main dish or course at a meal. **b.** food served between courses at a meal, esp. between the fish and meat courses. **2.** the freedom, right, or privilege to enter; access; admission. **3.** a means of doing this: *Their wealth was their entree into the society parties.* [French *entrée* entrance, first course, from *entrer* to go into. See ENTER.]

en·trench (en trench') *also*, intrench. *v.t.* **1.** to place in a trench; surround or fortify with trenches. **2.** to establish firmly or securely: *The practice became entrenched in tradition and law.* —*v.i.* **1.** to dig or occupy a trench or trenches. **2.** to encroach or trespass (with *on* or *upon*): *My job has begun to entrench on my free time.*

en·trench·ment (en trench'mənt) *also*, intrenchment. *n.* **1.** the act of entrenching or the state of being entrenched. **2.** a fortification consisting of a trench or trenches, usually with a bank of earth along the side facing the enemy.

en·tre nous (än trə nü') *French.* between ourselves; confidentially.

en·tre·pot (än'trə pō', än'trə pō') *n., pl.* **-pots** (-pōz', -pōz') a warehouse or commercial center, esp. one from which goods are distributed. [French *entrepot*, from *entre* inter + *(de)pot* depot.]

en·tre·pre·neur (än'trə prə nûr', -nûr') *n.* a person who organizes, controls, and assumes the risks of a business or other financial enterprise. [French *entrepreneur* contractor, from *entreprendre* to undertake, going back to Latin *inter* among + *prehendere* to take.]

en·tro·py (en'trə pē) *n.* **1.** in a thermodynamic system, a measure of the amount of heat energy unavailable for performing mechanical work. **2.** in cosmological theory, the hypothetical tendency for all matter in the universe to approach a uniform temperature. **3.** a measure of disorder within a system or a tendency toward disorder. [German *entropie*, from Greek *entropē* a turning toward, as if from German *energie* energy + Greek *tropē* a turning.]

en·trust (en trust') *also*, intrust. *v.t.* **1.** to put something in the trust of; invest or charge with a trust or responsibility: *I entrusted*

a friend with the care of my cat during my absence. **2.** to commit the care or safety of; assign responsibility for: *The chemist entrusted the completion of the work to an assistant.*

en·try (en'trē) *n., pl.* **-tries. 1.** the act, right, or instance of entering. **2.** a place for entering; entrance. **3.a.** the act of entering or recording something in a book, diary, file, list, or the like. **b.** information or an item recorded or entered in a book, diary, file, list, or other record: *daily entries in a ship's log.* **4.a.** a word, term, phrase, affix, symbol, abbreviation, or the like, defined or identified in a dictionary, usually set off by boldface type. **b.** such an item together with its definitions or other accompanying information. **5.** a person or thing entered in a contest, race, or other competition: *All entries must be twenty-five words or less.* **6.** the act of submitting imported goods for inspection at customs for the purpose of estimating the duty to be paid on them. **7.** the act of claiming possession of real property by entering or setting foot on it. [Old French *entree* act of entering, place for entering, admittance to a place, beginning, from *entrer* to go into, being. See ENTER.]

en·try-lev·el (en'trē lev'əl) *adj.* of, relating to, or constituting a job at a level low enough to enable a new employee to fill it while acquiring skill and experience: *high school graduates looking for entry-level positions.*

en·try·way (en'trē wā') *n.* an opening, hall, or small chamber through which a room or structure is entered. Also, **entrance-way.**

en·twine (en twīn') *v.t., v.i.*, **-twined, -twin·ing.** to twine together; twist or twine around.

en·twist (en twist') *v.i., v.t.* to twist together or around.

e·nu·mer·ate (i nü'mə rāt', i nū'-) *v.t.*, **-at·ed, -at·ing. 1.** to name one by one; list: *I enumerated my reasons for resigning.* **2.** to ascertain the number of; count. [Latin *ēnumerātus*, past participle of *ēnumerāre* to reckon up, from *ex* out, utterly + *numerus* number.] —**e·nu'mer·a·tive,** *adj.* —**e·nu'mer·a'tor,** *n.*

e·nu·mer·a·tion (i nü'mə rā'shən, i nū'-) *n.* **1.** the act of enumerating. **2.** a list or catalog.

e·nun·ci·ate (i nun'sē āt') *v.*, **-at·ed, -at·ing,** —*v.t.* **1.** to utter (words or speech sounds), esp. in a particular manner; articulate: *It is often difficult to understand someone who does not enunciate words clearly.* **2.** to state definitely, as a theory or principle. **3.** to announce; proclaim: *The newly elected legislators enunciated their opposition to the proposed law.* —*v.i.* to utter words or speech sounds, esp. in a particular manner. [Latin *ēnūntiātus*, past participle of *ēnūntiāre* to declare, disclose, going back to *ex* out, utterly + *nūntius* messenger.] —**e·nun'ci·a'tor,** *n.*

e·nun·ci·a·tion (i nun'sē ā'shən) *n.* **1.** an act or way of pronouncing; pronunciation. **2.** a statement or declaration. —For Synonyms, see **pronunciation.**

en·u·re·sis (en'yə rē'sis) *n., pl.* **-ses** (-sēz). inability to control urination, esp. bed-wetting. [Modern Latin *enuresis,* from Greek *enourein* to urinate in.] —**en·u·ret·ic** (en'yə ret'ik), *adj.*

env., environment.

en·vel·op (en vel'əp) *v.t.* **1.** to wrap or cover completely: *to envelop a baby in a blanket.* **2.** to hide from view; conceal: *Clouds enveloped the mountain peak.* **3.** to surround or encircle: *to envelop an enemy force.* [Old French *enveloper* to enfold, probably going back to Latin *in* in + a blend of Medieval Latin *faluppa* wisp of straw, and Latin *volvere* to roll.]

en·ve·lope (en'və lōp', än'-) *n.* **1.** a flat, usually paper, wrapper or container, used esp. for mailing letters. **2.** something that envelops; covering; wrapper. **3.a.** the outer covering of a balloon or airship, usually made of fabric. **b.** a bag containing the gas in a balloon or airship. [French *enveloppe* covering, envelope of a letter, from *envelopper* to wrap up, cover. See ENVELOP.]

en·vel·op·ment (en vel'əp mənt) *n.* **1.** the act of enveloping or the state of being enveloped. **2.** something that envelops; wrapping; covering.

en·ven·om (en ven'əm) *v.t., v.i.* **1.** to fill with venom; make poisonous. **2.** to fill with hate or vindictiveness; embitter: *thoughts envenomed by betrayal.* [Old French *envenimer* to poison, contaminate, going back to Latin *in* in + *venēnum* poison.]

en·vi·a·ble (en'vē ə bəl) *adj.* capable of arousing envy; highly desirable. —**en'vi·a·ble·ness,** *n.* —**en'vi·a·bly,** *adv.*

en·vi·ous (en'vē əs) *adj.* characterized by envy; feeling or showing envy. [Old French *envieus* covetous, greedy, exciting envy, from Latin *invidiōsus* full of envy.] —**en'vi·ous·ly,** *adv.* —**en'vi·ous·ness,** *n.*

Synonyms **Envious** and **jealous** mean feeling resentment at another's good fortune or superiority. **Envious** connotes a gnawing discontent because of another's attributes or success: *He was envious of his brother's athletic ability.* **Jealous** suggests a feeling of rivalry with another person because of something that person possesses: *She was jealous because her friend got a promotion before she did.*

410

en·vi·ron (en vī′rən, -vī′ərn) *v.t.* to encircle or envelop; surround: *Clear air and grassy plains environ the city.* [Old French *environner* to surround, from *environ* around, from *en-* in (from Latin *in*) + *virer* to turn round, veer. See VEER.]

en·vi·ron·ment (en vī′rən mənt, -vī′ərn-) *n.* **1.** all of the surrounding, external factors that actually or potentially affect the development and functioning of a living thing. In the societal environment, these factors include language, laws, and customs; in the natural environment, they include climate, air, water, vegetation, and soil. **2.** the conditions, circumstances, or objects that surround a person, place, or thing; situation or surroundings: *The environment at work has become more pleasant under our new boss.* **3. the environment.** the surroundings or conditions in which all inhabitants of the earth live; the air, land, and water: *to pollute the environment.*

en·vi·ron·men·tal (en vī′rən men′təl, -vī′ərn-) *adj.* **1.** of or relating to environment or the environment. **2.** of or relating to environmentalists or environmentalism: *environmental organizations.* —**en·vi′ron·men′tal·ly,** *adv.*

en·vi·ron·men·tal·ist (en vī′rən men′tə list, -vī′ərn-) *n.* **1.** a person who is concerned about or working to improve the quality of the environment, esp. with respect to the pollution of the earth's air, land, and water and the depletion of the earth's natural resources. **2.** an expert on the environment and environmental problems. —**en·vi′ron·men′tal·ism,** *n.*

en·vi·rons (en vī′rənz, -vī′ərnz, en′vər ənz) *pl. n.* **1.** the surrounding districts, as of a town or city; outskirts. **2.** surroundings; environment. **3.** the area or space that surrounds or is nearby; vicinity.

en·vis·age (en viz′ij) *v.t.,* **-aged, -ag·ing. 1.** to form a mental picture of; visualize, esp. as a possibility for the future: *She envisaged a thriving town in what was then desert.* **2.** to regard or consider (someone or something) in a certain way; conceive of: *He envisages himself as a hero.* [French *envisager* to face, consider, from *en-* in (from Latin *in*) + *visage* face. See VISAGE.]

en·vi·sion (en vizh′ən) *v.t.* to form a conception of; imagine.

en·voy¹ (en′voi, än′-) *n.* **1.a.** a diplomat ranking next below an ambassador. **b.** any diplomat. **2.** anyone sent as messenger or representative of another. [French *envoyé* person sent, from *envoyer* to send, going back to Latin *in viam* on the way.]

en·voy² (en′voi, än′-) *also,* **en·voi.** *n.* the concluding stanza of a verse or prose work, usually written as a dedication or summary. Also, l'envoy, l'envoi. [Old French *envoi* a sending, conclusion, from *envoyer* to send. See ENVOY¹.]

en·vy (en′vē) *n., pl.* **-vies. 1.** a feeling of resentment, jealousy, or desire brought on by another's abilities, possessions, or good fortune. **2.** the object of this feeling: *His new bike made him the envy of every child in the neighborhood.* —*v.t.,* **-vied, -vy·ing. 1.** to feel envy toward (someone); regard with envy. **2.** to feel envy because of: *I envy her good marks.* [Old French *envie* jealousy, grudge, from Latin *invidia* jealousy, from *invidēre* to look maliciously at.] —**en′vi·er,** *n.* —**en′vy·ing·ly,** *adv.*

en·womb (en wüm′) *v.t.* to enclose in or as if in a womb.

en·wrap (en rap′) *v.t.,* **-wrapped, -wrap·ping.** to enfold or envelop (with *in* or *with*).

en·wreathe (en rēth′) *v.t.,* **-wreathed, -wreath·ing.** to encircle or envelop with or as if with a wreath; wreathe.

en·zy·mat·ic (en′zī mat′ik) *adj.* of, relating to, or catalyzed by an enzyme. —**en′zy·mat′i·cal·ly,** *adv.*

en·zyme (en′zīm) *n.* any of the complex proteins produced by living organisms that act as catalysts in regulating biological processes such as digestion, metabolism, and blood clotting. [German *Enzym,* from Middle Greek *enzýmos* leavened, from Greek *en* in + *zýmē* leaven.]

E·o·cene (ē′ə sēn′) *n.* the second geologic epoch of the Tertiary period of the Cenozoic era, when such animals as the horse, the elephant, and the camel first appeared. For table, see **geologic time.** —*adj.* of or relating to this epoch. [Greek *ēōs* dawn + *kainos* new.]

e·o·hip·pus (e′ō hip′əs) *n.* an early ancestor of the horse, genus *Hyracotherium,* found as a fossil in Eocene deposits in North America and Europe. Height: 10-12 inches (25-30 centimeters) at the shoulder. [Modern Latin *Eohippus,* from Greek *ēōs* dawn + *hippos* horse.]

e·o·li·an (ē ō′lē ən) **1.** of or produced by wind. Dune sand and loess are eolian deposits. **2.** Eolian. Aeolian².

E·ol·ic (ē ol′ik) Aeolian².

e·o·lith (ē′ə lith′) *n.* a primitive stone implement, either naturally shaped or chipped, believed to have been used as a tool by human beings at the dawn of the Stone Age. [Greek *ēōs* dawn + *lithos* stone.] —**e′o·lith′ic,** *adj.*

e·on (ē′ən, ē′on) *also,* **aeon.** *n.* **1.** a very long, indefinite period of time; thousands of years. **2.** the largest division of geologic time, longer than an era: *the Phanerozoic eon.* [Latin *aeōn* age, from Greek *aiōn.*]

E·os (ē′əs) *n.* in Greek mythology, the goddess of the dawn. Her Roman counterpart is Aurora. [Latin *Ēōs,* from Greek *Ēōs,* from *ēōs* dawn.]

e·o·sin (ē′ə sin) *also,* **e·o·sine** (ē′ə sin, -sēn′). *n.* **1.** a reddish coloring matter, obtained from coal tar, used as a dye or stain. **2.** any of several related dyes obtained from coal tar. [Greek *ēōs* dawn + -IN¹; from the rosy color of the dye.]

ep-, form of **epi-** before vowels and *h,* as in *eponym, ephemeral.*

EPA, Environmental Protection Agency.

ep·au·let (ep′ə let′ -lət, ep′ə let′) *also,* **ep·au·lette.** *n.* an ornamental device designed to be worn on the shoulder of a uniform, as by a military officer, sometimes indicating rank. [French *épaulette,* diminutive of *épaule* shoulder, going back to Late Latin *spatula,* from Latin *spatula* blade. See SPATULA.]

e·pee (ā pā′) *also,* **é·pée.** *n.* **1.** a long, thin fencing sword with no cutting edge, less flexible than a foil. **2.** the art or sport of fencing with an epee. [French *épée* this sword, from Latin *spatha* broadsword. See SPATULA.]

Eph., Ephesians.

e·phah (ē′fə) *n.* an ancient Hebrew dry measure, a little more than a bushel. [Middle English *ephi,* from Late Latin *ephi,* from Hebrew *efa;* probably of Egyptian origin.]

e·phed·rine (i fed′rin, ef′ə drēn′, -drin) *n.* a crystalline, alkaloid drug used esp. to treat asthma, hay fever, and bronchitis. Formula: $C_{10}H_{15}NO$ [Modern Latin *Ephedra* (genus name) (from Latin *ephedra* horsetail plant, from Greek *ephedrā*) + -INE²; because the drug was first derived from plants of the genus *Ephedra.*]

e·phem·er·a (i fem′ər ə) *pl. n.* **1.** printed items that are designed to be useful for a short period of time but are considered valuable by collectors, such as postcards, advertisements, posters, and tickets. **2.** persons or things that live for a very short time.

e·phem·er·al (i fem′ər əl) *adj.* **1.** lasting for a very short time; short-lived; fleeting. **2.** *Biology.* having a very brief life cycle; short-lived. —*n.* something that is ephemeral, such as a plant whose complete life cycle lasts just a few days. [Greek *ephēmeros* lasting for a day (from *epi* for + *hēmerā* day) + -AL¹.] —For Synonyms, see **momentary.**

e·phem·er·id (i fem′ər id) *n.* mayfly.

e·phem·er·is (i fem′ər is) *n., pl.* **eph·e·mer·i·des** (ef′ə mer′i-dēz′). a table or collection of tables showing the predicted positions of celestial bodies, esp. the sun, moon, or planets, during a specified period of time. [Latin *ephēmeris* diary, from Greek *ephēmeris* diary, calendar, from *ephēmeros* lasting for a day.]

e·phem·er·on (i fem′ə ron′) *n., pl.* **-er·a** (-ər ə) or **-er·ons.** a person or thing that lives for a very short time.

E·phe·sians (i fē′zhənz) *n.* a book of the New Testament, consisting of an Epistle written by the Apostle Paul to the Christians in Ephesus. ➡ used as singular.

eph·od (ef′od, ē′fod) *n.* among the ancient Hebrews, an apronlike vestment worn by priests in performing sacred duties and by judges. [Middle English *ephod,* from Late Latin *ephod,* from Hebrew *efod,* from *afad* to put on, don.]

eph·or (ef′ôr, -ər) *n., pl.* **-ors** or **-o·ri** (-ə rī′). one of the five chief magistrates elected annually in ancient Sparta to advise the kings. [Latin *ephorus,* from Greek *ephoros,* from *ephorān* to oversee.]

E·phra·im (ē′frē əm, ē′frəm) *n.* the kingdom of Israel.

epi- *prefix* on; upon; near; among: *epidermis, epigram.* [Greek *epi* upon, at, after, to, besides.]

ep·ic (ep′ik) *n.* **1.** a long narrative poem, written in an elevated style, celebrating the adventures and achievements of one or more heroic figures of legend, history, or religion. The *Odyssey,* the *Aeneid,* and *Beowulf* are epics. **2.** any written work or play having similar characteristics. **3.** a story or series of events worthy of being told in this manner: *the epic of the exploration of America.* —*adj. also,* **ep′i·cal. 1.** of or relating to an epic. **2.** like an epic in subject or scope: *an epic novel.* **3.** suitable for an epic in nature, subject, or scope; heroic: *the epic events of westward expansion in the United States.* **4.** very long or of unusually large size or wide scope: *an epic voyage around the globe.* [Latin *epicus* epic poem, from Greek *epikos,* from *epos* word, song, story.] —**ep′i·cal·ly,** *adv.*

a	at	e	end	o	hot	u	up	hw	white		about
ā	ape	ē	me	ō	old	ū	use	ng	song		taken
ä	far	i	it	ô	fork	ü	rule	th	thin	ə	pencil
âr	care	ī	ice	oi	oil	u̇	pull	th	this		lemon
		îr	pierce	ou	out	ûr	turn	zh	measure		circus

411

ep·i·ca·lyx (ep′i kā′liks, -kal′iks) *n., pl.* **-ca·lyx·es** or **-ca·ly·ces** (-kā′lə sēz′, -kal′ə-). *Botany.* an involucre resembling a calyx.

ep·i·can·thus (ep′i kan′thəs) *n.* a downward fold of skin from the upper eyelid that covers the inner corner of the human eye. It is a normal feature of many Asian peoples. Also, **epicanthic fold.** [EPI- + Modern Latin *canthus* corner at either side of the eye, from Greek *kanthos.*] —**ep′i·can′thic,** *adj.*

ep·i·car·di·um (ep′i kär′dē əm) *n., pl.* **-di·a** (-dē ə). the layer of the pericardium in direct contact with the heart. [Modern Latin *epicardium,* from EPI- + Greek *kardia* heart.] —**ep′i·car′di·al,** *adj.*

ep·i·carp (ep′i kärp′) *n.* exocarp. [EPI- + Greek *karpos* fruit.]

ep·i·cen·ter (ep′i sen′tər) *n.* the point on the earth's surface directly above the focus of an earthquake.

ep·i·cot·yl (ep′i kot′əl) *n.* the part of the stem of a plant embryo or seedling above the cotyledon.

ep·i·cure (ep′i kyûr′) *n.* a person who cultivates a refined taste for and enjoys good food and drink. [From *Epicurus,* 342?-270? B.C., a Greek philosopher who thought that pleasure, as found in the virtues of honesty, justice, and friendship, was the highest goal of a human being.]

ep·i·cu·re·an (ep′i kyū rē′ən, -kyûr′ē ən) *adj.* **1.** given to luxurious tastes or habits, esp. in eating and drinking; of or like an epicure. **2.** fit for an epicure: *an epicurean meal.* **3. Epicurean.** of, relating to, or characteristic of Epicurus or his philosophy. —*n.* **1.** epicure. **2. Epicurean.** a follower of or believer in Epicurus or his philosophy.

Ep·i·cu·re·an·ism (ep′i kyū rē′ə niz′əm, -kyûr′ē ə-) *n.* **1.** the philosophy founded by the Greek philosopher Epicurus, which holds that pleasure, sought by the wise person in the lasting virtues of honesty, justice, and friendship, is the highest goal of life. **2.** *also,* **epicureanism.** belief in or the practice of this philosophy.

ep·i·cy·cle (ep′ə sī′kəl) *n.* a small circle, the center of which moves around the circumference of a larger circle. —**ep·i·cy·clic** (ep′ə sī′klik, -sik′lik), *adj.*

ep·i·cy·cloid (ep′ə sī′kloid) *n.* a curve generated by a point on a circle rolling on the outside circumference of another circle.

ep·i·dem·ic (ep′i dem′ik) *n.* **1.** the rapid spread or sudden, widespread appearance of a disease in a locality or large area. **2.** a disease thus prevalent: *The epidemic was diagnosed as a virulent form of influenza.* **3.** the rapid spread or sudden, widespread appearance of anything, as an idea, fad, or fashion: *an epidemic of burglaries.* —*adj.* spreading among and simultaneously affecting many people; widespread: *an epidemic disease.* Also, **ep′i·dem′i·cal.** [French *épidémique* widespread, from *épidémie* prevalence of a disease, from Medieval Latin, going back to Greek *epidēmios* among the people.] —**ep′i·dem′i·cal·ly,** *adv.*

ep·i·de·mi·ol·o·gy (ep′i dē′mē ol′ə jē) *n.* the branch of medicine that deals with epidemic diseases. —**ep·i·de·mi·o·log·ic** (ep′i dē′mē ə loj′ik); *also,* **ep′i de′mi·o·log′i·cal,** *adj.* —**ep′i·de′mi·o·log′i·cal·ly,** *adv.* —**ep′i·de′mi·ol′o·gist,** *n.*

ep·i·der·mal (ep′i dûr′məl) *adj.* of or relating to the epidermis.

ep·i·der·mis (ep′i dûr′mis) *n.* **1.** the protective outer layer of the skin of vertebrates, lacking blood vessels and nerves. For illustration, see **skin. 2.** a protective outer layer of various invertebrates. **3.** a skinlike outer layer of cells of seed plants and ferns; cuticle. [Late Latin *epidermis* the surface skin, from Greek *epidermis.*]

ep·i·dote (ep′i dōt′) *n.* a hydrous silicate mineral of variable composition, in which calcium and aluminum are the principal metallic elements, found as green crystals in metamorphic rocks. [French *épidote,* from Greek *epididonai* to give besides, increase (because of the enlarged base of some of the crystal forms), from *epi-* besides + *didonai* to give.]

ep·i·gen·e·sis (ep′i jen′ə-sis) *n.* the development of an embryo by stages, progressively forming new parts, rather than being perfectly formed from the beginning. [Modern Latin *epigenesis.* See EPI-, GENESIS.] —**ep·i·ge·net·ic** (ep′i jə net′ik), *adj.*

e·pig·e·nous (i pij′ə nəs) *adj.* *Botany.* growing on the surface, esp. the upper surface, as fungi on a leaf.

ep·i·glot·tis (ep′i glot′is) *n.* a thin triangular flap of cartilage that covers the glottis during swallowing, preventing foreign matter from

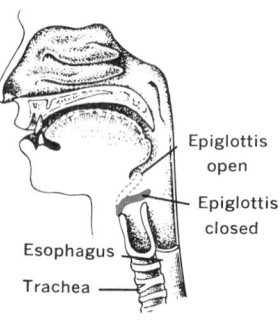

Epiglottis open

Epiglottis closed

Esophagus

Trachea

epiglottis

entering the lungs through the trachea. [Greek *epiglōttis,* from *epi* near + *glōtta* tongue.] —**ep′i·glot′tal,** *adj.*

ep·i·gram (ep′i gram′) *n.* **1.** a concise, pointed statement expressing a thought in a witty manner, for example: *There is only one thing in the world worse than being talked about, and that is not being talked about* (Oscar Wilde, 1871). **2.** a short poem leading to a witty or satirical turn at the end. [Latin *epigramma* short poem, inscription, from Greek *epigramma.*]

ep·i·gram·mat·ic (ep′i gra mat′ik) *adj.* **1.** of, relating to, or using epigrams. **2.** like or suitable to an epigram; witty, pointed, and concise. Also, **ep′i·gram·mat′i·cal.** —**ep′i·gram·mat′i·cal·ly,** *adv.*

ep·i·gram·ma·tist (ep′i gram′ə tist) *n.* a person who composes epigrams.

ep·i·gram·ma·tize (ep′i gram′ə tīz′) *v.,* **-tized, -tiz·ing.** —*v.i.* **1.** to compose an epigram or epigrams; speak or write epigrammatically. —*v.t.* **1.** to express in the form of an epigram. **2.** to make the subject of an epigram.

ep·i·graph (ep′i graf′) *n.* **1.** *Archaeology.* an inscription, as on a building, tomb, or monument. **2.** a quotation at the beginning of a book or a chapter, suggesting the theme of its contents. [Greek *epigraphē* inscription, from *epigraphein* to write on, from *epi-* on + *graphein* to write.]

e·pig·ra·phy (i pig′rə fē) *n.* **1.** inscriptions collectively. **2.** the study that deals with the deciphering and interpretation of inscriptions, esp. ancient ones. —**e·pig′ra·pher, e·pig′ra·phist,** *n.*

e·pig·y·nous (i pij′ə nəs) *adj. Botany.* with stamens, petals, and sepals appearing to originate at or near the top of the ovary. [EPI- + *gynē* woman + -OUS.]

ep·i·lep·sy (ep′ə lep′sē) *n.* any of a group of brain disorders in which an uncontrolled electrical discharge from the nerve cells in the cerebral cortex causes loss of consciousness and convulsions or less severe symptoms such as twitching. [Late Latin *epilepsia,* from Greek *epilēpsiā,* from *epilambanein* to seize.]

ep·i·lep·tic (ep′ə lep′tik) *adj.* of, relating to, or having epilepsy. —*n.* a person who has epilepsy.

ep·i·logue (ep′ə lôg′, -log′) *also,* **ep·i·log.** *n.* **1.** a passage or section added to the end of a novel, poem, or other written work as an explanation, summary, or conclusion. **2.** a speech or short poem addressed to the audience by one of the actors at the end of a play. [Old French *epilogue* peroration of a speech, from Latin *epilogus,* from Greek *epilogos* peroration, concluding part of a play.]

ep·i·neph·rine (ep′ə nef′rin, -rēn) *also,* **ep·i·neph·rin** (ep′ə-nef′rin). *n.* adrenaline.

e·piph·a·ny (i pif′ə nē) *n., pl.* **-nies. 1.** a manifestation or appearance, esp. of a divine or supernatural being. **2. Epiphany.** a Christian holy day commemorating the manifestation of Christ on earth, observed on January 6. In the Western Church it commemorates the visit of the Three Wise Men to the infant Jesus. In the Eastern Church it usually commemorates the baptism of Jesus. **3.** a moment of sudden insight into the essential meaning or nature of something. [Old French *epiphanie* the Epiphany, from Late Latin *epiphania,* from Greek *epiphania* manifestation.]

e·piph·y·sis (i pif′ə sis) *n., pl.* **-ses** (-sēz′). **1.** the end portion of a long bone, as in one of the limbs, separated by cartilage from the main shaft while the bone is growing. **2.** pineal body. [Modern Latin *epiphysis,* from Greek *epiphysis* a growth upon, excrescence, going back to *epi-* upon + *phyein* to grow.] —**ep·i·phys·e·al;** *also,* **ep·i·phys·i·al** (ep′ə fiz′ē əl), *adj.*

ep·i·phyte (ep′ə fīt′) *n.* any of various plants, usually having aerial roots, that grow on other plants for support but are not parasites. Spanish

epiphyte

moss and certain orchids are epiphytes. Also, **air plant.** [EPI- + Greek *phyton* plant.] —**ep′i·phyt′ic,** *adj.*

Epis. 1. Episcopal. **2.** Episcopalian. **3.** Epistle.

e·pis·co·pa·cy (i pis′kə pə sē) *n., pl.* **-cies. 1.** a system of church government by bishops. **2.** episcopate.

e·pis·co·pal (i pis′kə pəl) *adj.* **1.** of or relating to bishops.

2. governed by bishops. **3. Episcopal.** of or relating to the Church of England or the Episcopal Church. [Late Latin *episcopālis* relating to a bishop, from *episcopus* bishop, overseer, from Greek *episkopos*.] —**e·pis′co·pal·ly,** *adv.*

Episcopal Church, a church in the United States that agrees with the Church of England in doctrine, beliefs, and most practices. Also, **Protestant Episcopal Church.**

E·pis·co·pa·lian (i pis′kə pāl′yən, -pā′lē ən) *n.* a member of an Episcopal church. —*adj.* Episcopal.

e·pis·co·pate (i pis′kə pit, -pāt′) *n.* **1.** the position, rank, or term of office of a bishop. **2.** the district under the authority of a bishop; diocese. **3.** bishops collectively. Also, **episcopacy.**

ep·i·sode (ep′ə sōd′) *n.* **1.** an incident or event that stands out in any series of events. **2.** an incidental narrative or digression separate from the main plot or subject of a literary work. **3.** an installment of a dramatic or literary work that is presented in serial form: *an episode of a soap opera.* **4.** a digressive, secondary passage or section in a musical composition or movement. [Greek *epeisodion* addition, from *epoisodios* coming in besides, going back to *epi* besides + *eis* into + *hodos* way.] —For Synonyms, see **event.**

ep·i·sod·ic (ep′ə sod′ik) *adj.* **1.** of the nature of an episode; incidental. **2.** divided into separate parts that are often not closely related. Also, **ep′i·sod′i·cal.**

e·pis·te·mol·o·gy (i pis′tə mol′ə jē) *n.* a branch of philosophy that analyzes the origin, nature, methods, and validity of human knowledge. [Greek *epistemē* knowledge + -LOGY.] —**e·pis′te·mol′o·gist,** *n.*

e·pis·tle (i pis′əl) *n.* **1.** a letter, esp. a long, formal one giving advice or instruction. ➡ now usually used humorously. **2. Epistle. a.** any one of the letters written by an Apostle and contained in the New Testament. **b.** a selection from one of these, read as part of a Christian liturgical service. [Old French *epistle* letter, from Latin *epistola*, from Greek *epistolē* letter, message.]

e·pis·to·lar·y (i pis′tə ler′ē) *adj.* **1.** written in the form of letters; consisting of letters: *an epistolary novel.* **2.** carried on by or contained in letters: *an epistolary romance.* **3.** of or relating to letters: *an epistolary style.*

ep·i·style (ep′ə stīl′) *n.* architrave. [Latin *epistȳlium,* from Greek *epistȳlion.*]

ep·i·taph (ep′i taf′) *n.* **1.** a brief statement inscribed on a tombstone or other monument in memory of a dead person. **2.** a brief eulogy, written as if it were to be inscribed on a tombstone. [Latin *epitaphium* funeral oration, from Greek *epitaphion,* from *epi* on + *taphos* tomb.]

ep·i·tha·la·mi·on (ep′ə thə lā′mē ən) *n., pl.* -mi·a (-mē ə). epithalamium.

ep·i·tha·la·mi·um (ep′ə thə lā′mē əm) *n., pl.* -mi·ums or -mi·a (-mē ə). a poem or song in honor of a newly married person or couple. [Latin *epithalamium,* from Greek *epithalamion,* from *epi* at + *thalamos* bridal chamber.]

ep·i·the·li·al (ep′ə thē′lē əl) *adj.* of or relating to the epithelium.

ep·i·the·li·oid (ep′ə thē′lē oid′) *adj.* resembling epithelium.

ep·i·the·li·um (ep′ə thē′lē əm) *n., pl.* -li·ums or -li·a (-lē ə). a sheet of body tissue, consisting of one or more layers of cells, that covers the entire surface of the body and lines the body cavities and tubes. [Modern Latin *epithelium,* from Greek *epi* on + *thēlē* nipple.]

 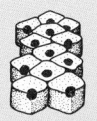 

Squamous cells   Cuboidal cells   Columnar cells

epithelium

ep·i·thet (ep′ə thet′) *n.* **1.** a descriptive word or phrase used with or in place of a name: *Homer's epithet for his hero Odysseus is "great-hearted."* **2.** an insulting or abusive word or phrase, esp. one used in place of a person's name. [Latin *epitheton,* from Greek *epithēton* something added.] —**ep′i·thet′ic;** *also,* **ep′i·thet′i·cal,** *adj.*

e·pit·o·me (i pit′ə mē) *n.* **1.** a person or thing that has or represents all of the qualities or characteristics of something: *That house is the epitome of extravagant taste.* **2.** a condensed account or summary, esp. of a literary work; abridgment. [Latin *epitomē* abridgment, from Greek *epitomē.*]

e·pit·o·mize (i pit′ə mīz′) *v.t.,* -mized, -miz·ing. **1.** to be the epitome of: *That painting epitomizes the use of colors to convey mood.* **2.** to make a short summary of (a written work).

ep·i·zo·ot·ic (ep′ə zō ot′ik) *adj.* (of diseases) temporarily prevalent in an animal population. —*n.* an epizootic disease.

e plu·ri·bus u·num (ē′plŭr′ə bəs ū′nəm) *Latin.* out of many, one. ➡ the motto on the official seal of the United States.

ep·och (ep′ək; *British* ē′pok) *n.* **1.** the starting point of a new and important period of time: *The discovery of the New World marked an epoch in exploration.* **2.** such a period of time distinguished by some particular characteristic, development, or course of events: *an epoch of social and political change.* **3.** a division of geologic time, smaller than a period. [Late Latin *epocha* measure of time, fixed point in time from which years are numbered, from Greek *epochē* pause, fixed point in time.] —For Synonyms, see **period.**

ep·och·al (ep′ə kəl) *adj.* of, relating to, or marking an epoch.

ep·och·mak·ing (ep′ək mā′king) *adj.* introducing something new and important; beginning an epoch.

ep·ode (ep′ōd) *n.* **1.** a lyric poem in which a shorter verse follows a longer one. **2.** that part of a lyric ode that comes after the strophe and antistrophe. [Latin *epōdos* such a poem, from Greek *epōidos* this part of an ode.]

ep·o·nym (ep′ə nim) *n.* a person, either real or legendary, from whose name something, such as a country, a people, a place, or a period of time, derives, or supposedly derives, its name: *Amerigo Vespucci is the eponym of America. The Roman goddess Juno became the eponym for the month of June.* [Greek *epōnymos* given as a name, from *epi* on + *onyma* (dialectal form) name, word.]

Eponyms

Many real or fictitious people have had their names used as the basis for English words. Below is a selection of eponymous terms from various fields such as science, history, mythology, and the arts. Following the derived term is the name from which it came.

ampere
from *André Marie Ampère*
(French physicist)

boycott
from *Charles Boycott*
(ostracized by Irish farmers for his harsh actions against them)

braille
from *Louis Braille*
(French developer of this system of writing and printing for the blind)

calliope
from *Calliope*
(in Greek mythology, the muse of eloquence and poetry)

cardigan
from *Earl of Cardigan*
(English army officer who popularized this type of sweater)

cereal
from *Ceres*
(in Roman mythology, the goddess of grain and agriculture)

curie
from *Marie Curie*
(Polish-French chemist and physicist, the first person to win two Nobel Prizes)

Elizabethan
from *Elizabeth I*
(Queen of England, 1558-1603)

flora
from *Flora*
(in Roman mythology, goddess of flowers)

gerrymander
from *Elbridge Gerry*
(U.S. politician and governor under whom an election district was rearranged in the shape of a salamander)

iris
from *Iris*
(in Greek mythology, goddess of the rainbow)

leotard
from *Jules Léotard*
(French aerialist who popularized this garment)

melba toast
from *Nelly Melba*
(Australian opera singer)

saxophone
from *Antoine Joseph Sax*
(Belgian inventor of this instrument)

Victorian
from *Victoria*
(Queen of England, 1837-1901)

volcano
from *Vulcan*
(in Roman mythology, god of fire)

watt
from *James Watt*
(Scottish inventor)

---

a	at	e	end	o	hot	u	up	hw	white		about
ā	ape	ē	me	ō	old	ū	use	ng	song		taken
ä	far	i	it	ô	fork	ü	rule	th	thin	ə	pencil
âr	care	ī	ice	oi	oil	ů	pull	th	this		lemon
		îr	pierce	ou	out	ûr	turn	zh	measure		circus

ep·on·y·mous (e pon′ə məs) *adj.* giving one's name to something like a country, a people, a place, or an era.

ep·ox·y (e pok′sē) *n., pl.* **-ox·ies.** *Chemistry.* a resin compound formed by polymerization, characterized by powerful adhesion and durability, used esp. in glues and coatings. Also, **epoxy resin.** —*v.t.* **-ox·ied, -ox·y·ing.** to bond with epoxy. [EP- + OXY(GEN).]

ep·si·lon (ep′sə lon′, -lən) *n.* the fifth letter of the Greek alphabet (E, ε). [Greek *e psīlon* literally, simple *e*.]

Ep·som salts (ep′səm) *also,* **Epsom salt.** hydrated magnesium sulfate, a bitter, crystalline compound that is used esp. as a laxative and in baths for sore muscles or minor infections. Formula: $MgSO_4 \cdot 7H_2O$ [From *Epsom*, England, where the salt was first obtained from the water of a mineral spring.]

eq. 1. equal. 2. equation. 3. equator. 4. equivalent.

eq·ua·bil·i·ty (ek′wə bil′i tē, ē′kwə-) *n.* an equable condition or quality.

eq·ua·ble (ek′wə bəl, ē′kwə-) *adj.* 1. not easily disturbed; tranquil: *an equable state of mind.* 2. not changing; unvarying; steady: *an equable temperature.* 3. free from inequalities; equal and uniform: *to establish a more equable system of taxation.* [Latin *aequābilis* uniform, from *aequāre* to make equal.] —**eq′ua·ble·ness,** *n.* —**eq′ua·bly,** *adv.*

e·qual (ē′kwəl) *adj.* 1. the same in some measure, as in amount, number, rank, magnitude, or the like: *One tablespoon of the liquid soap is equal in cleansing power to one half cup of the powder.* 2. having the same rights, privileges, and responsibilities: *to be equal under the law.* 3. evenly matched or balanced; even: *Their chances to win are equal.* 4. *Mathematics.* (of sets) having exactly the same elements. —*n.* a person or thing that is equal. —*v.t.,* **e·qualed, e·qual·ing;** *also, British,* **e·qualled, e·qual·ling.** 1. to be equal to: *Two plus two equals four.* 2. to make or do something equal to: *No one has equaled that doctor's service to the community.* [Latin *aequālis* even, like, from *aequus* just, even.]

· **equal to.** adequately fit or qualified for; having the strength or ability necessary for: *The young teacher was not equal to the task of controlling and teaching a large class.*

e·qual-ar·e·a (ē′kwəl âr′ē ə) *adj.* relating to, designating, or using a cartographic projection on which areas are proportionally equal to the land or sea areas that they represent but forms are distorted: *an equal-area map.*

e·qual·i·tar·i·an (i kwol′i târ′ē ən) *adj.* egalitarian.

e·qual·i·ty (i kwol′i tē) *n., pl.* **-i·ties.** the state or quality of being equal, esp. the state of having the same rights, privileges, and responsibilities.

e·qual·ize (ē′kwə līz′) *v.t.,* **-ized, -iz·ing.** 1. to make uniform: *to equalize water pressure along the length of a dam.* 2. to make equal: *Giving runners handicaps according to their demonstrated abilities equalizes the chances of everyone in a race.* —**e′qual·i·za′tion,** *n.* —**e′qua·li′zer,** *n.*

e·qual·ly (ē′kwə lē) *adv.* 1. in an equal manner: *to treat everyone equally.* 2. to an equal degree: *The two performers are equally talented.*

equal opportunity employer, an employer who agrees not to practice discrimination in employment because of race, color, sex, religion, national origin, age, or handicap.

equal sign, a mathematical symbol (=) used to show that two quantities or expressions are equal, as in $1 + 6 = 7$.

e·qua·nim·i·ty (ē′kwə nim′i tē, ek′wə-) *n.* evenness of mind or temper; calmness: *The candidate accepted defeat with equanimity.* [Latin *aequanimitās* evenness of mind, going back to *aequus* even + *animus* mind.]

e·quate (i kwāt′) *v.t.,* **e·quat·ed, e·quat·ing.** 1. to regard, treat, or represent as equal or comparable: *to equate good manners with real concern for others.* 2. to regard or represent as usually, or always, related: *Some people equate wealth and happiness.* 3. *Mathematics.* to state the equality of; put in the form of an equation. 4. to reduce to an average for comparison or to obtain a result. [Latin *aequātus,* past participle of *aequāre* to make equal.]

e·qua·tion (i kwā′zhən, -shən) *n.* 1. *Mathematics.* a statement that one quantity or expression is equal to another, esp. such a statement using the equal sign (=). 2. *Chemistry.* a representation of a chemical reaction. Symbols for the original substances appear to the left and those for the resulting substances to the right of the symbol (=) or (→). $FeS + 2HCl \rightarrow FeCl_2 + H_2S$ is an equation indicating that ferrous sulfide and hydrochloric acid react to produce ferrous chloride and hydrogen sulfide. 3. the act of equating or the state of being equated. —**e·qua′tion·al,** *adj.*

e·qua·tor (i kwā′tər) *n.* 1. an imaginary line encircling the earth halfway between the North and South poles. Degrees of latitude

are measured from it. 2. a similar line on any celestial body. 3. celestial equator. [Medieval Latin *aequātor* equalizer, short for *aequātor diei et noctis* equalizer of day and night (day and night being of equal length when the sun is over the equator), from Latin *aequāre* to make equal.]

e·qua·to·ri·al (ē′kwə tôr′ē əl, ek′wə-) *adj.* 1. of, at, near, or relating to an equator, esp. the earth's equator: *an equatorial country.* 2. characteristic of the earth's equator or the regions near it: *equatorial heat.*

equatorial plate, a plane perpendicular to the spindle, along which the aggregated mass of replicating chromosomes lines up during the metaphase stage of meiosis or mitosis. Also, **equatorial plane.**

eq·uer·ry (ek′wə rē) *n., pl.* **-ries.** 1. an officer of a royal or noble household charged with the care of its horses. 2. a personal attendant to any of the members of the British royal family. [French *ècurie* stable, from Old French *escuerie* office of a squire, stable, from *escuier* squire, shield bearer, going back to Latin *scūtum* shield; influenced in form by Latin *equus* horse.]

e·ques·tri·an (i kwes′trē ən) *adj.* 1. of or relating to horsemen or horsewomen, horsemanship, or horseback riding. 2.a. mounted on horseback: *an equestrian performer.* b. (esp. of a statue or portrait) representing a person on horseback: *an equestrian statue.* —*n.* a rider, esp. a performer on horseback in a circus or other show. [Latin *equester* relating to a horseman (from *eques* horseman, knight, from *equus* horse) + -AN.]

e·ques·tri·enne (i kwes′trē en′) *n.* a female equestrian.

equi- *combining form* 1. equal: *equilibrium, equivalence.* 2. equally: *equiangular, equidistant.* [Latin *aequus* even, just, like, equal.]

e·qui·an·gu·lar (ē′kwē ang′gyə lər, ek′wē-) *adj.* *Geometry.* having all angles equal. Regular polygons are equiangular.

e·qui·dis·tant (ē′kwi dis′tənt, ek′wi-) *adj.* equally distant. —**e′qui·dis′tant·ly,** *adv.*

e·qui·lat·er·al (ē′kwə lat′ər əl, ek′wə-) *adj.* having all sides equal. —*n.* a geometrical figure having all sides equal. [Late Latin *aequilaterālis* having all sides equal, from Latin *aequus* even, equal + *later-,* stem of *latus* side.]

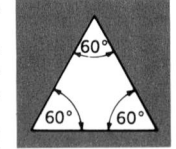

equilateral triangle

e·quil·i·brant (i kwil′ə brənt) *n.* *Physics.* a force equal but opposite in direction to a given force and able to balance that force, creating a state of equilibrium.

e·quil·i·brate (i kwil′ə brāt′, ē′kwə lī′brāt) *v.,* **-brat·ed, -brat·ing.** —*v.t.* 1. to bring into or keep in a state of equilibrium; counterbalance. 2. to be in equilibrium with. —*v.i.* to be in a state of equilibrium; balance. [Late Latin *aequilībrātus,* past participle of *aequilībrāre* to balance, going back to Latin *aequus* even, equal + *lībra* balance.] —**e·quil′i·bra′tion,** *n.*

e·qui·lib·ri·um (ē′kwə lib′rē əm, ek′wə-) *n.* 1. a state or condition in which forces acting on or within a body or system exactly balance each other: *A cone resting on its base will remain in equilibrium unless additional force is applied to it.* 2. a state of balance between powers or factors of any kind: *equilibrium in the international political community.* 3. mental and emotional balance: *I usually maintain my equilibrium under stress.* 4. *Chemistry.* the state of balance that is reached when a chemical reaction and its reverse proceed simultaneously at the same rate. A pair of reactants in such a reaction combine to form a new pair and those, in turn, combine to form the original pair. [Latin *aequilībrium* level position, from *aequus* even, equal, + *lībra* balance.]

e·quine (ē′kwīn, ek′wīn) *adj.* of, relating to, or like a horse. —*n.* a horse. [Latin *equīnus* relating to horses, from *equus* horse.]

e·qui·noc·tial (ē′kwə nok′shəl, ek′wə-) *adj.* 1. of or relating to an equinox. 2. occurring at or near the time of an equinox: *an equinoctial storm.* 3. equatorial. —*n.* a storm occurring at or near the time of an equinox.

equinoctial line, celestial equator. Also, **equinoctial circle.**

e·qui·nox (ē′kwə noks′, ek′wə-) *n.* 1. the time at which day and night are equal all over the earth. Twice a year the sun crosses the celestial equator, northward about March 21, vernal equinox, and southward about September 23, autumnal equinox. For illustration, see **solstice.** 2. either of the two points where the sun crosses the celestial equator. Also *(def. 2),* **equinoctial point.** [Old French *equinoxe,* from Medieval Latin *equinoxium,* modification of Latin *aequinoctium* time of equal days and nights, from *aequus* even, equal + *nox* night.]

e·quip (i kwip′) *v.t.,* **e·quipped, e·quip·ping.** to provide or outfit with whatever is necessary for an event or undertaking: *to*

equip a boat for a long cruise. [French *équiper* to fit out, from Old Norse *skipa* to man a ship, arrange, from *skip* ship.] —For Synonyms, see **furnish.**

eq·ui·page (ek′wə pij) *n.* **1.** equipment, as for an army or camp; gear. **2.** a carriage, esp. when fully outfitted, with horses, driver, and attendants.

e·quip·ment (i kwip′mənt) *n.* **1.** anything that is necessary or provided for equipping someone or something; supplies; gear. **2.** the act of equipping or the state of being equipped.

e·qui·poise (ē′kwə poiz′, ek′wə-) *n.* **1.** a state of balance or equilibrium. **2.** a weight or force that balances another; counterpoise.

e·qui·po·ten·tial (ē′kwə pə ten′shəl, ek′wə-) *adj. Physics.* having the same or uniform electrical potential.

eq·ui·se·tum (ek′wə sē′təm) *n., pl.* **-tums** or **-ta** (-tə). any of a group of flowerless plants, genus *Equisetum,* including the horsetail, having hollow, jointed stems with conelike, spore-producing structures at the top. [Modern Latin *Equisetum,* from Latin *equisaetum* horsetail plant, from *equus* horse + *saeta* bristle.]

eq·ui·ta·ble (ek′wi tə bəl) *adj.* **1.** characterized by equity; fair; just: *an equitable settlement of a financial dispute.* **2.** *Law.* relating to, valid in, or existing in equity, as distinguished from common law or civil law. —**eq′ui·ta·ble·ness,** *n.* —**eq′ui·ta·bly,** *adv.*

eq·ui·ta·tion (ek′wi tā′shən) *n.* the art of riding horses; horsemanship. [Latin *equitātiō* riding, going back to *equus* horse.]

eq·ui·tes (ek′wi tēz′) *pl. n.* (in ancient Rome) members of the privileged class, originally the cavalry and later the merchants and civil servants. [Latin *equitēs,* plural of *eques* horseman, knight, from *equus* horse.]

eq·ui·ty (ek′wi tē) *n., pl.* **-ties. 1.** the quality of being impartial, fair, and just. **2.** something that is fair and just. **3.** *Law.* **a.** justice by ethical judgment and fairness rather than from established principles of law. **b.** a set of principles dealing with matters for which there are no adequate or fair remedies under the common law or the civil law. Equity was originally separate from the law, but it has come to be considered a branch of the law. **c.** a claim or right recognized by a court of equity. **4.** the money value of a property in excess of any debts owed on it. [Old French *equite* rectitude, integrity, from Latin *aequitās* equality, fairness, from *aequus* even, just, equal.]

e·quiv·a·lence (i kwiv′ə ləns) *n.* the state or property of being equivalent.

e·quiv·a·lent (i kwiv′ə lənt) *adj.* **1.** equal, as in value, measure, force, effect, or meaning; corresponding: *A quarter is equivalent to five nickels.* **2.** virtually the same; parallel, as in function or effect: *That state's department of commerce is equivalent to our bureau of economic development.* **3.** *Geometry.* equal in area or volume, but not alike in shape. **4.** *Mathematics.* **a.** having the same solution set: *equivalent equations.* **b.** (of sets) having the same number of members. —*n.* something that is equivalent. [Late Latin *aequivalēns,* present participle of *aequivalēre* to have equal power, from Latin *aequus* even, just, equal + *valēre* to be worth.] —**e·quiv′a·lent·ly,** *adv.* —For Synonyms *(adj.),* see **same.**

equivalent weight, in a chemical reaction, the weight or mass of an element or compound that will combine with or replace one gram atom of hydrogen, regarded as a measure of the combining power of the substance.

e·quiv·o·cal (i kwiv′ə kəl) *adj.* **1.** capable of being interpreted in more than one way; having two or more meanings; ambiguous: *an equivocal answer.* **2.** undecided or uncertain; doubtful: *The evidence the police accumulated was of equivocal value.* **3.** of a suspicious nature; suspect; questionable: *equivocal behavior.* [Late Latin *aequivocus* ambiguous, of equal voice (from Latin *aequus* even, equal + *vocāre* to call) + -AL[1].] —**e·quiv′o·cal·ly,** *adv.*

e·quiv·o·cate (i kwiv′ə kāt′) *v.i.,* **-cat·ed, -cat·ing.** to express oneself in terms having more than one possible meaning, esp. to use ambiguous language in order to mislead or avoid committing oneself: *The politician has equivocated on the issue for many years.* [Late Latin *aequivocātus,* past participle of *aequivocare* to call by the same name, from *aequivocus* ambiguous. See EQUIVOCAL.] —**e·quiv′o·ca′tor,** *n.*

e·quiv·o·ca·tion (i kwiv′ə kā′shən) *n.* **1.** the act of equivocating. **2.** an equivocal statement.

Er, the symbol for erbium.

-er[1] *suffix* **1.** (used to form nouns from verbs) a person or thing that carries out the action of the verb: *driver, grater.* **2.** (used to form nouns) **a.** a person who is a native or inhabitant of: *northerner, New Yorker.* **b.** a person who makes or is professionally concerned with: *clothier, biographer.* **c.** a person or thing that is characterized by: *three-decker, foreigner.* [Middle English *-er,*

-ere (from Old English *-ere*) and Old French *-ier* (from Latin *-arius*), all denoting an agent or agency.]

-er[2] *suffix* (used to form nouns) a person or thing that is connected with: *officer.* [Old French *-er, -ier,* from Latin *-ārius, -ārium.*]

-er[3] *suffix* **1.** used to form the comparative degree of adjectives: *colder.* **2.** used to form the comparative degree of adverbs: *sooner.* [Old English *-ra* (masculine), *-re* (feminine, neuter), *-or.*]

-er[4] *suffix* (used to form verbs) repeatedly: *linger, pucker.* [Old English *-rian.*]

e·ra (îr′ə, er′ə) *n.* **1.** a period of time characterized by certain events, conditions, ideas, persons, or things: *Elizabeth Barrett Browning and Alfred Tennyson were two famous poets of the Victorian era.* **2.** an extended period of time beginning with a particular event: *The modern era in European history is thought to have begun with the Italian Renaissance.* **3.** an event or date from which the beginning of a new period of time in the history of something is reckoned. **4.** one of the principal divisions of geological time, including two or more periods. [Late Latin *aera* number, epoch (from which time is calculated), from Latin *aera* counters (for calculating), plural of *aes* brass.] —For Synonyms, see **period.**

e·rad·i·ca·ble (i rad′i kə bəl) *adj.* that can be eradicated.

e·rad·i·cate (i rad′i kāt′) *v.t.,* **-cat·ed, -cat·ing.** to remove or destroy completely; eliminate: *to eradicate weeds, to eradicate a disease.* [Latin *ērādīcātus,* past participle of *ērādīcāre* to root out, from *ex* out + *rādix* root.] —**e·rad′i·ca′tor,** *n.*

e·rad·i·ca·tion (i rad′i kā′shən) *n.* the act of eradicating or the state of being eradicated.

e·rase (i rās′) *v.,* **e·rased, e·ras·ing.** —*v.t.* **1.** to rub, scrape, or scratch out; wipe off: *I erased the notes written in the margin.* **2.** to remove marks, writing, or recorded information from: *Please erase the blackboard.* **3.** to remove or destroy completely as if by rubbing or blotting out: *Time had dulled but not erased their memories of the war.* **4.** *Slang.* to kill. —*v.i.* **1.** to be capable of being erased: *Make light pencil lines so that they will erase easily.* **2.** to remove marks, writing, or recorded information: *The tape recorder erases if it is operated in reverse.* [Latin *ērāsus,* past participle of *ērādere* to scrape off, scratch out; with reference to the ancient Roman practice of scratching out words written on a wax tablet by scraping off the wax.] —**e·ras′a·ble,** *adj.*

| **Synonyms** | **Erase, delete,** and **efface** mean to remove something written or recorded. **Erase** connotes rubbing out or removing something so that its impression disappears: *to erase writing on a blackboard, to erase sounds from recording tape, to erase something from one's memory.* **Delete** connotes crossing out or marking some written material for omission: *The editor deleted several sentences from the introduction.* **Efface** suggests complete or effective removal through wear and tear or abrasive action: *Years of harsh weather had effaced the inscription over the doorway.* |

e·ras·er (i rā′sər) *n.* a device for erasing, esp. a rubber device for removing marks made with a pencil or ink.

e·ra·sure (i rā′shər, -zhər) *n.* **1.** the act of erasing or the state of being erased. **2.** something that has been erased, such as a word, letter, or mark. **3.** a place or mark left where something has disappeared or been erased.

Er·a·to (er′ə tō′) *n.* in Greek mythology, the Muse of lyric poetry, esp. love poetry.

er·bi·um (ûr′bē əm) *n.* a soft, silver-gray metallic element of the rare-earth group, used to color glass. Symbol: **Er** For tables, see **element.** [Modern Latin *erbium,* from *(Ytt)erb(y),* Swedish village where it was first found + *-ium* suffix used to form names of elements.]

ere (âr) *Archaic. prep.* before (in time). —*conj.* **1.** before. **2.** sooner than; rather than [Old English *ær* soon, before.]

Er·e·bus (er′ə bəs) *n. Greek Mythology.* **1.** the gloomy region of the underworld through which the dead passed on their way to Hades. **2.** the personification of darkness.

E·rech·the·um (i rek′thē əm) *n.* a white marble temple on the Acropolis of Athens, noted as an outstanding example of Ionic architecture.

e·rect (i rekt′) *adj.* in a vertical or upright position or posture; raised: *The dog was trained to stand with its ears erect.* —*v.t.* **1.a.** to build; construct: *A construction company is going to erect*

E

a	at	e	end	o	hot	u	up	hw	white		about
ā	ape	ē	me	ō	old	ū	use	ng	song		taken
ä	far	i	it	ô	fork	ü	rule	th	thin	ə	pencil
âr	care	ī	ice	oi	oil	ů	pull	th	this		lemon
		îr	pierce	ou	out	ûr	turn	zh	measure		circus

an apartment house on that lot. **b.** to raise or put in a vertical or upright position: *It takes only a few moments to erect the tent.* **2.** to create or set up: *to erect barriers against foreign investors.* **3.** to put together; assemble. **4.** *Geometry.* to construct on a given line: *Erect a perpendicular at this point.* **5.** *Optics.* to restore (an inverted image) to an upright position. **6.** *Archaic.* to establish; found: *to erect a kingdom, to erect a new university.* [Latin *ērēctus,* past participle of *ērigere* to set up.] —e·rect′ly, *adv.* —e·rect′ness, *n.*

e·rec·tile (i rek′təl, -tīl) *adj.* **1.** capable of being raised to an erect position or posture: *erectile feathers on a bird.* **2.** *Physiology.* (of tissue) capable of becoming distended and rigid. —e·rec·til·i·ty (i rek til′i tē), *n.*

e·rec·tion (i rek′shən) *n.* **1.** the act of erecting or the state of being erected. **2.** something that is erected, as a building or other structure. **3.** *Physiology.* a state in which soft body tissue becomes rigid and erect as a result of an influx of blood.

e·rec·tor (i rek′tər) *n.* a person or thing that erects.

ere·long (âr lông′) *adv. Archaic.* before long; soon.

er·e·mite (er′ə mīt′) *n.* a hermit, esp. a religious recluse. [Late Latin *erēmīta,* from Greek *erēmītēs* literally, dweller in a desert, from *erēmiā* desert. Doublet of HERMIT.]

e·rep·sin (i rep′sin) *n.* a mixture of enzymes secreted by the small intestine that helps break down proteins into amino acids. [German *erepsin,* from Latin *ereptus,* past participle of *eripere* to grab away (from *e-* out + *rapere* to grab) + German *pepsin* pepsin.]

ere·while (âr hwīl′, -wīl′) *adv. Archaic.* some time ago.

erg (ûrg) *n.* a unit of work or energy in the centimeter-gram-second system of units. One erg is the work done by a force of one dyne acting through a distance of one centimeter. [Greek *ergon* work.]

er·go (ûr′gō) *adv., conj. Latin.* therefore.

er·go·nom·ics (ûr′gə nom′iks) *n.* the science of designing objects in such a way that human beings can use them more efficiently and comfortably: *The knowledge of ergonomics made it possible to design a chair that helped reduce back pain.* ➡ used as singular. [From Greek *ergon* work and *(ec)onomic(s).*]

er·gos·ter·ol (ûr gos′tə rôl′, -rōl′) *n.* a steroid alcohol produced in ergot, yeast, molds, and other fungi that is converted to vitamin D when irradiated with ultraviolet light. Formula: $C_{28}H_{44}O$

er·got (ûr′gət, -got) *n.* **1.** a disease of rye and other cereal grains caused by a poisonous fungus, *Claviceps purpurea,* in which the grains are replaced by a hard, blackish growth. **2.** this fungus growth itself, used to prepare several drugs useful in medicine. [French *ergot* cock's spur; of uncertain origin; because of the resemblance of the fungus to a cock's spur.]

er·got·ism (ûr′gə tiz′əm) *n. Medicine.* ergot poisoning, caused by the eating of infected grain or by misuse of drugs prepared from ergot.

Er·in (er′in, îr′-) *n.* Ireland. [Old Irish *Ērinn,* dative of *Ēriu* Ireland.]

E·rin·y·es (i rin′ē ēz′) *pl. n., sing.* **E·rin·ys** (i rin′is, i rī′nis) in Greek mythology, the Furies.

E·ris (îr′is, er′-) *n.* in Greek mythology, the goddess of strife and discord.

erl·king (ûrl′king′) *n.* in German and Scandinavian folklore, an evil spirit who roams the forests, bringing harm to people, esp. children. [German *Erlkönig.*]

er·mine (ûr′min) *n., pl.* **-mines** or **-mine.** **1.** a carnivorous weasel, *Mustela erminea,* of northern regions of North America, Europe, and Asia, having a long, slender body, short legs, a thick, muscular neck, black-tipped tail, and brown coat, which usually changes to white in winter. Length: 7-15 inches (18-38 centimeters), including tail. **2.** the white winter fur of this animal used esp. for women's coats, trimming, and the ornamentation of royal or judges' formal robes in some European countries. The black fur of the tail is sometimes inserted at regular intervals on the white for decorative effect. **3.** the rank, office, or functions of a judge. [Old French *ermine,* probably from Medieval Latin *Armenius (mus)* Armenian (mouse), going back to Greek *Armeniā* Armenia.]

ermine

erne (ûrn) *also,* **ern.** *n.* sea eagle. [Old English *earn* eagle.]

e·rode (i rōd′) *v.,* **e·rod·ed, e·rod·ing.** —*v.t.* **1.** to wear or wash away gradually, as by rubbing or friction: *The heavy rains eroded the topsoil on the hills.* **2.** to eat into or eat away; corrode: *Salt water collected in the bottom of the boat and eroded the metal parts.* **3.** to form (a channel or type of landform) by a gradual eating or wearing away: *Glaciers eroded a valley in the side of the mountain.* **4.** to destroy or cause to disappear gradually: *Rising inflation has eroded our buying power.* —*v.i.* to become eroded. [Latin *ērōdere* to gnaw away.]

e·rog·e·nous (i roj′ə nəs) *adj.* of, relating to, or originating from those areas of the body particularly sensitive to sexual stimulation: *an erogenous zone.* Also, **erotogenic.** [Greek *erōs* love + -GEN + -OUS.]

E·ros (îr′os, er′-) *n.* in Greek mythology, the god of love and the son of Aphrodite. His Roman counterpart is Cupid. [Latin *Erōs,* from Greek *Erōs,* from *erōs* love.]

e·ro·sion (i rō′zhən) *n.* **1.** the gradual wearing or washing away of the soil and rock of the earth's surface by glaciers, running water, waves, or wind: *Soil conservation is intended to curb erosion.* **2.** the act of eroding or the state of being eroded. [French *érosion,* from Latin *ērōsiō* a gnawing away.] —e·ro′sion·al, *adj.*

e·ro·sive (i rō′siv) *adj.* causing erosion; eroding.

e·rot·ic (i rot′ik) *adj.* **1.** of, relating to, or concerned with sexual love or desire. **2.** arousing or designed to arouse sexual desire. **3.** strongly influenced by sexual desire. [Greek *erōtikos* relating to love, from *erōs* love.] —e·rot′i·cal·ly, *adv.*

e·rot·i·cism (i rot′ə siz′əm) *n.* **1.** an erotic tendency or character. **2.** a preoccupation with sex.

e·ro·to·gen·ic (i rō′tə jen′ik) *adj.* erogenous. [From Greek *erōto-,* stem of *erōs* love + -GEN + -IC.]

err (ûr, er) *v.i.* **1.** to do something wrong; make a mistake; be in error: *I erred in making my decision before I knew all the facts.* **2.** to do something that is morally wrong; sin. [Old French *errer* to make a mistake, wander, from Latin *errāre* to wander.]

er·rand (er′ənd) *n.* **1.** a short trip to do something, often for someone else. **2.** what someone is sent to do; the purpose or object of a trip. [Old English *ǣrende* message, mission.]

er·rant (er′ənt) *adj.* **1.** traveling or roaming in search of adventure; wandering; roving: *the errant knights of legend.* **2.** straying from the proper place or correct behavior; erring: *an errant child, errant conduct.* **3.** having no fixed course; erratic: *an errant breeze.* [Partly from Old French *errant,* present participle of *errer* to travel, going back to Latin *iter* journey; partly from Old French *errant,* present participle of *errer* to make a mistake. See ERR.]

er·rant·ry (er′ən trē) *n., pl.* **-ries.** the conduct or way of life of a knight-errant.

er·ra·ta (i rä′tə, i rā′-, i rat′ə, e-) the plural of **erratum.**

er·rat·ic (i rat′ik) *adj.* **1.** having no fixed course; acting or moving irregularly or unpredictably: *the erratic path of a storm.* **2.** deviating from the conventional or usual standard; inconsistent; eccentric: *erratic behavior.* —*n. Geology.* a boulder or rock at a distance from its original site, moved from its place of origin, esp. by glacial action. [Latin *errāticus* wandering, from *errāre* to wander.] —er·rat′i·cal·ly, *adv.*

er·ra·tum (i rä′təm, i rā′-, i rat′əm, e-) *n., pl.* **-ta.** an error, esp. an error in a book that has already been printed, listed with a correction and bound or inserted into the book. [Latin *errātum* error, from *errāre* to wander.]

er·ro·ne·ous (i rō′nē əs) *adj.* marked by or containing error; mistaken; incorrect: *an erroneous conclusion.* [Latin *errōneus* wandering.] —er·ro′ne·ous·ly, *adv.* —er·ro′ne·ous·ness, *n.* —For Synonyms, see **wrong.**

er·ror (er′ər) *n.* **1.** something incorrectly done, believed, or stated; something that deviates from what is accurate, proper, or true; mistake. **2.** the state or condition of being mistaken or incorrect (usually preceded by *in*): *They are in error if they think that I will give up that easily.* **3.** *Baseball.* a fielding misplay that allows a base runner to reach a base safely or a batter to remain at bat when, if the play had been made properly, the runner or batter would have been put out. **4.** *Mathematics.* the difference between an observed or estimated value and the actual value: *How large was the error in our calculations?* **5.** an act or instance of deviation from an accepted moral code; wrongdoing; sin; transgression. [Old French *errour* distress, mistake, from Latin *error* mistake, wandering.] —For Synonyms, see **mistake.**

error message, a sentence or code number appearing on a computer screen or on a printout that indicates an error in the program or data.

er·satz (er′zäts, -sats) *adj.* serving as a substitute, esp. an inferior one; artificial; synthetic: *ersatz leather.* —*n.* substitute. [German *Ersatz* replacement, from *ersetzen* to replace.]

Erse (ûrs) *n.* **1.** Scots Gaelic. **2.** Irish Gaelic. —*adj.* of or relating to either of these languages or the Celtic people of Scotland and Ireland. [Scottish form of IRISH.]

erst (ûrst) *adv. Archaic.* formerly; long ago. [Old English ǣrst soonest, first, superlative of ǣr soon, before.]

erst·while (ûrst′hwīl′, -wīl′) *adj.* former. —*adv. Archaic.* formerly.

e·ruct (i rukt′) *v.i., v.t.* belch. [Latin ēructāre to belch forth.]

e·ruc·tate (i ruk′tāt) *v.i., v.t.,* **-tat·ed, -tat·ing.** eruct. —**e·ruc·ta′tion,** *n.*

er·u·dite (er′yu̇ dīt′, er′u̇-) *adj.* having or showing extensive knowledge; scholarly; learned. [Latin ērudītus learned, skilled, going back to ex out of, from, away + rudis rough.] —**er′u·dite′ly,** *adv.* —**er′u·dite′ness,** *n.*

er·u·di·tion (er′yu̇ dish′ən, er′u̇-) *n.* extensive knowledge acquired esp. from reading in the humanities; scholarship; learning.

e·rupt (i rupt′) *v.i.* **1.** to eject something suddenly and violently: *The geyser erupts every few hours.* **2.** to burst or be thrown forth: *Enough lava erupted from the volcano to bury the entire village.* **3.** to break out suddenly and violently: *A fight erupted during the game between the opposing teams.* **4.** to break out, as in a rash: *Many teenagers erupt with acne.* **5.** (of teeth) to break through the gums. —*v.t.* to throw forth (something, as steam or lava) suddenly and violently. [Latin ēruptus, past participle of ērumpere to break or burst forth.]

e·rup·tion (i rup′shən) *n.* **1.** the act of erupting. **2.** a violent bursting forth, as of lava from a volcano. **3.a.** a breaking out in a rash. **b.** a superficial inflammation of the skin; rash. **4.** a sudden bursting forth; outbreak: *an eruption of laughter.*

e·rup·tive (i rup′tiv) *adj.* **1.** bursting forth; tending to erupt: *an eruptive geyser.* **2.** causing or accompanied by a rash, as certain diseases. **3.** of or relating to volcanic eruptions; formed by a volcano.

-ery *suffix* (used to form nouns) **1.** a place of business or place where something is made, stored, or sold: *bakery, brewery.* **2.** a place for: *nunnery.* **3.** the art, practice, or profession of: *thievery, cookery, archery.* **4.** the state of: *slavery.* **5.** the characteristics, practices, or principles of: *knavery, trickery.* **6.** a collection or group of: *greenery, crockery.* [Old French -erie, from -er, -ier (see -ER [2]) + ie (see -Y [3]).]

er·y·sip·e·las (er′ə sip′ə ləs, îr′ə-) *n.* an acute infectious skin disease characterized by a deep red inflammation of the skin, caused by a streptococcus. [Greek erysipelas erysipelas; literally, red skin.]

e·ryth·ro·cyte (i rith′rə sīt′) *n.* red blood cell.

e·ryth·ro·my·cin (i rith′rə mī′sin) *n.* an antibiotic drug used to treat certain bacterial infections in patients allergic to penicillin or to treat infections that are penicillin-resistant. [Greek erythros red + mykēs fungus + -IN [1].]

Es, the symbol for einsteinium.

es·ca·drille (es′kə dril′) *n.* a small unit or squadron of airplanes or warships. [French escadrille small squadron, flotilla, from Spanish escuadrilla, diminutive of escuadra squadron, squad, going back to Latin ex out + quadra square; because the men in a squadron at one time were formed in a square.]

es·ca·lade (es′kə lād′) *n.* the act of scaling the walls of a fortified place, esp. by ladders. [French escalade scaling (a wall), from Italian scalata scaling, going back to Latin scālae (plural) ladder, staircase.]

es·ca·late (es′kə lāt′) *v.t., v.i.,* **-lat·ed, -lat·ing.** to increase or enlarge by stages, as in size, scope, intensity, or cost: *to escalate a conflict.* [From ESCALATOR.] —**es′ca·la′tion,** *n.*

es·ca·la·tor (es′kə lā′tər) *n.* a moving stairway consisting of a series of steps attached to a continuous chain, used to transport passengers from one floor or level to another. [Probably blend of ESCAL(ADE) and (ELEV)ATOR.]

escalator clause, a provision in the financial terms of a labor contract allowing for increases or decreases, as in wages, under specified conditions, usually in proportion to the cost of living.

es·cal·lop (e skol′əp, e skal′-) *n., v.t.* scallop.

es·ca·pade (es′kə pād′) *n.* an action or behavior that flouts convention or that breaks rules; wild, reckless adventure. [French escapade prank; originally, escape, from Italian scappata escape, going back to Late Latin ex cappa out of one's cape. See ESCAPE.]

es·cape (e skāp′) *v.,* **-caped, -cap·ing.** —*v.i.* **1.** to get away or free, as from restraint or confinement; gain or regain liberty: *The bird escaped from the cage.* **2.** to evade or avoid capture, punishment, or any present or imminent danger: *The guards chased the bank robbers, but they escaped in the crowd.* **3.** to leak or flow out from a container or enclosure, esp. gradually: *Gas escaped from the pipe.* —*v.t.* **1.** to get away or free from; elude: *We escaped the traffic by taking a side street.* **2.** to avoid or remain free from (something threatening, harmful, or unpleasant): *The driver of the car narrowly escaped death.* **3.** to fail to be noticed or recollected by; slip by or away from: *Their name escapes me at the moment.* **4.** to be uttered inadvertently or involuntarily by: *A sigh escaped my lips.* —*n.* **1.** the act of escaping: *The refugees' escape was by way of the sea.* **2.** the fact or state of having escaped. **3.** a means of escaping: *A rope ladder served as an escape from the burning house.* **4.** a way of temporarily avoiding or forgetting problems, worries, or the like: *Reading detective stories is my escape.* **5.** a gradual or sudden outflow or leakage, as of gas or water. [Dialectal Old French escaper to get away, keep clear of, going back to Late Latin ex cappa out of one's cape; with reference to escaping by slipping out of one's cape when seized.]

escape artist, a person who is adept at escaping from handcuffs, ropes, locked rooms, and other forms of confinement, esp. someone who does this for the entertainment of others.

escape clause, a clause permitting one or both parties to a contract to abstain from performing some or all of the contract's requirements under specified circumstances.

es·cap·ee (e skā pē′, es′kā-) *n.* a person who has escaped, esp. from a prison or other place of confinement.

escape mechanism *Psychiatry.* a means of avoiding unpleasant facts or the responsibilities of real life, as by daydreaming; defense mechanism.

es·cape·ment (e skāp′mənt) *n.* **1.** a device in a timepiece consisting of a toothed wheel and a pawl. The back-and-forth movement of the pawl allows one tooth of the wheel to escape at each swing, thus controlling the regular movement of a system of gears that moves the hands. **2.** a mechanism that regulates the movement of a typewriter carriage during use.

escape velocity, the minimum speed a body must attain to pass out of a gravitational field. Escape velocity from earth is about 7 miles per second.

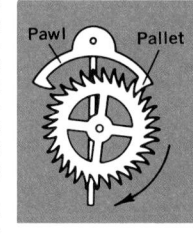

escapement

es·cap·ism (e skā′piz əm) *n.* a tendency to escape the dull routine and responsibilities of daily life by constantly engaging the mind in vicarious activities, esp. of the imagination, such as fantasy or passive entertainment. —**es·cap′ist,** *adj., n.*

es·car·got (es′kär gō′) *n.* a snail, esp. an edible one. [French.]

es·ca·role (es′kə rōl′) *n.* a kind of endive, used esp. in salads. [French escarole endive, going back to Late Latin escariola, from Latin ēsca food.]

es·carp (e skärp′) *n.* escarpment; scarp.

es·carp·ment (e skärp′mənt) *n.* **1.** a steep slope or cliff formed by erosion or faulting. **2.** a fortification consisting of a steep slope. [French escarpment, from escarp scarp, from Italian scarpa. See SCARP.]

-esce *suffix* (used to form verbs) to begin to be; become: *fluoresce.* [Latin -ēscere.]

-escence *suffix* (used to form nouns) the state of becoming: *fluorescence.* [Latin -ēscentia, from -ēscēns, often through French -escence. See -ESCENT.]

-escent *suffix* (used to form adjectives) beginning to be; becoming: *fluorescent.* [Latin -ēscent-, stem of -ēscēns, present participial ending of verbs in ēscere to begin to, often through French -escent.]

es·cha·tol·o·gy (es′kə tol′ə jē) *n.* the branch of theology dealing with doctrines concerning the last things, as death, judgment, and the final destiny of the soul. [Greek eschatos last, extreme + -LOGY.]

es·cheat (es chēt′) *n.* **1.** the reversion of property to the state or, in feudal law, to the lord of a manor, when there are no persons legally qualified to inherit it. **2.** property that has so reverted. —*v.i.* to revert by escheat. —*v.t.* to cause (property) to revert by escheat. [Old French eschete what falls to one, inheritance, from escheoir to fall to one's share, fall out, going back to Latin ex out + cadere to fall.] —**es·cheat′a·ble,** *adj.*

es·chew (es chū′) *v.t.* to abstain or keep away from; avoid;

a	at	e	end	o	hot	u	up	hw	white		about
ā	ape	ē	me	ō	old	ū	use	ng	song		taken
ä	far	i	it	ô	fork	u̇	rule	th	thin	ə	pencil
âr	care	ī	ice	oi	oil	u̇	pull	th	this		lemon
		îr	pierce	ou	out	ûr	turn	zh	measure		circus

E

shun: *to eschew wickedness.* [Old French *eschiver* to shun; of Germanic origin.] —**es·chew′a·ble,** *adj.*

Es·co·ri·al (e skôr′ē əl) *also,* **Escurial.** *n.* a huge granite structure built in the sixteenth century near Madrid, including a monastery, palace, church, and royal crypt.

es·cort (*n.,* es′kôrt; *v.,* e skôrt′, es′kôrt) *n.* **1.** a person or persons who accompany another as a courtesy, honor, or protection: *The visiting monarch had an escort of armed guards.* **2.** a man or boy who accompanies a woman or girl to a party, dance, or the like. **3.** one or more ships or airplanes accompanying or protecting another: *a fighter escort, an escort of destroyers.* **4.** the act of accompanying as a courtesy, honor, or protection. —*v.t.* to accompany as a courtesy, honor, or protection; act as an escort to. [French *escorte* guide, from Italian *scorta,* from *scorgere* to guide, going back to Latin *ex* out + *corrigere* to set right.]

es·cri·toire (es′kri twär′) *n.* a writing desk or table. [Early French *escritoire,* from Late Latin *scriptōrium* place for writing, from Latin *scrībere* to write.]

es·crow (es′krō, e skrō′) *n. Law.* a document, such as a deed or bond, or money or other property deposited with a third party to be returned only upon fulfillment of certain conditions. [Old French *escroe* scroll, shred; of Germanic origin.]

· **in escrow.** held by a third party pending the fulfillment of certain conditions: *The tenants put the rent in escrow until the lawsuit against the landlord was settled.*

es·cu·do (e skü′dō) *n., pl.* **-dos. 1.** the monetary unit of Portugal. **2.** formerly, any of several gold or silver coins of Spain, Portugal, or their colonies. [Spanish and Portuguese *escudo* coin, shield, from Latin *scūtum* shield.]

es·cu·lent (es′kyə lənt) *adj.* suitable for food; edible. —*n.* something fit for food, esp. an edible plant: *Mallow and chicory are wild esculents.* [Latin *ēsculentus* eatable, good to eat, from *ēsca* food.]

Es·cu·ri·al (e skyùr′ē əl) Escorial.

es·cutch·eon (e skuch′ən) *also,* **scutcheon.** *n.* a shield or shield-shaped surface carrying armorial bearings. It is the central figure in the coat of arms and is often shown separately, as on stationery, jewelry, or other personal or family possessions. [Dialectal Old French *escuchon* shield, coat of arms, going back to Latin *scūtum* shield.]

· **a blot on one's escutcheon.** a stain on one's reputation; something dishonorable or disgraceful.

escutcheon

Esd., Esdras.

Es·dras (ez′drəs) *n.* **1.** either of two canonical books in the Douay Bible, I Esdras corresponding to the book of Ezra in other versions and II Esdras, considered a continuation of the history in I Esdras, corresponding to the book of Nehemiah. **2.** either of two apocryphal books of the Protestant (I Esdras and II Esdras) or Catholic (III Esdras and IV Esdras) Old Testament.

-ese *suffix* **1.** (used to form nouns) **a.** a person who was born in, is a citizen of, or has ancestors from: *Burmese.* **b.** the language of: *Japanese.* **c.** a style or diction characteristic of a particular area, person, or group: *journalese.* **2.** (used to form adjectives) of, relating to, or originating in: *Chinese.* [Old French *-eis,* from Latin *-ēnsis* belonging to, originating in.]

ESE, east-southeast.

es·ker (es′kər) *n.* a low, sinuous ridge formed of sand and gravel deposited by water from a melting glacier. [Irish *eiscir* ridge.]

Es·ki·mo (es′kə mō′) *n., pl.* **-mo** or **-mos. 1.** one of a Mongoloid race of formerly nomadic hunters living in Alaska, northern Canada, Greenland, and northeastern Siberia. **2.** any of the languages spoken by these people. —*adj.* of, relating to, or characteristic of the Eskimo, their language, or their culture. Also, **Inuit.** —**Es′ki·mo′an,** *adj.*

Usage The term **Eskimo** is considered derogatory by many Inuit, who prefer to use **Inuit** to describe all Eskimo peoples. The use of **Inuit** is increasing, particularly in Canada, where it is the official governmental term. However, **Eskimo** continues to be widely used, especially in historical and cultural references.

Eskimo dog, a dog of a sturdy breed native to Greenland and northern Canada, having a thick, shaggy coat, broad chest, and curved bushy tail, used by the Eskimo to draw heavy sleds. Height: 2 feet (0.6 meter) at the shoulder. The name is often also applied to the Alaskan malamute, Siberian husky, and Samoyed.

e·soph·a·gus (i sof′ə gəs, e sof′-) *n., pl.* **-gi** (-jī′). *also,* **oe·sophagus.** a muscular passageway or canal in humans and animals, through which food passes from the pharynx to the stomach;

gullet. [Modern Latin *oesophagus,* from Greek *oisophagos* literally, carrier of food.] —**e·soph·a·ge·al** (i sof′ə jē′əl, e sof′-), *adj.*

es·o·ter·ic (es′ə ter′ik) *adj.* **1.** understood by or intended for a small and select group of people, as secret rites or doctrines; of or for a chosen few. **2.** difficult to understand; abstruse; recondite: *an esoteric discussion on philosophy.* **3.** kept secret; private; confidential: *esoteric aims, esoteric pleasures.* [Greek *esōterikos* inner, going back to *esō* within.] —**es′o·ter′i·cal·ly,** *adv.*

esp., especially.

ESP, extrasensory perception.

es·pa·drille (es′pə dril′) *n.* a casual shoe usually having a canvas upper part and a flexible sole made of rope. [French *espadrille,* going back to Latin *spartum* a tough grass (from which these shoes were originally woven). See ESPARTO.]

es·pal·ier (e spal′yər, -yā) *n.* **1.** a method of pruning and training trees and shrubs to grow flat against a framework or wall. **2.** a tree or shrub trained to grow this way. **3.** a framework or other surface upon which plants are thus trained. —*v.t.* to train or provide (a plant) with an espalier. [French *espalier* framework or wall on which plants are trained, row of plants so trained, from Italian *spalliera,* from *spalla* shoulder (suggesting a support), from Late Latin *spatula,* from Latin *spatula* blade. See SPATULA.]

espalier

es·par·to (e spär′tō) *n.* any of several species of tough grass, esp. *Stipa tenacissima* and *Lygeum spartum,* native to the Mediterranean region, used to make paper, cord, and baskets. Also, **esparto grass.** [Spanish *esparto,* from Latin *spartum,* from Greek *sparton* rope, esparto.]

es·pe·cial (e spesh′əl) *adj.* out of the ordinary; special; particular; extraordinary: *The smallest kitten was an especial favorite of the children.* [Old French *especial* special, from Latin *speciālis* particular, special, from *speciēs* a particular kind, sight, appearance.]

es·pe·cial·ly (e spesh′ə lē, e spesh′lē) *adv.* particularly; principally: *The sea is rough here, especially in the winter. I came by especially to see you.*

Synonyms **Especially** and **particularly** mean above all or most importantly. **Especially** connotes standing apart from other things considered: *I love fruit, especially apricots and peaches.* **Particularly** suggests an emphasis on the individual characteristics that differentiate something: *A dictionary is particularly useful for students.*

Es·pe·ran·to (es′pə rän′tō, -ran′-) *n.* an artificial language for international use, having simplified grammar and vocabulary based on the major European languages. [From Dr. *Esperanto,* the pen name of its originator, Dr. L. L. Zamenhof, 1859-1917, the name meaning, in Esperanto, one who is hoping.]

es·pi·al (e spī′əl) *n.* **1.** the act of watching or spying. **2.** the act of catching sight of; notice; discovery.

es·pi·o·nage (es′pē ə näzh′, -nij) *n.* the practice of spying, esp. the use of spies by one government to discover the military or political secrets of other countries or by one firm to discover the business or manufacturing secrets of another. [French *espionnage* spying, from *espion* spy, from Old French *espier* to spy; of Germanic origin.]

es·pla·nade (es′plə näd′, -näd′) *n.* an open, level space, esp. along a shore, used for public walking or as a roadway; promenade. [French *esplanade,* from *esplaner* to level, from Latin *explānāre* to flatten, explain.]

es·pous·al (e spou′zəl) *n.* **1.** the act of espousing; adoption; advocacy: *the espousal of a political doctrine.* **2.** *also,* **espousals.** a ceremony of betrothal or marriage.

es·pouse (e spouz′) *v.t.,* **-poused, -pous·ing. 1.** to take up or adopt, as a cause; advocate; embrace. **2.** to marry; wed. **3.** to promise or give in marriage. [Old French *espouser* to marry, from Latin *spōnsāre* to betroth, marry.]

es·pres·so (e spres′ō) *n.* a strong coffee, usually made by forcing steam upward through finely ground darkly roasted coffee

beans. [Italian *(caffè) espresso* literally, pressed out (coffee), from *esprimere* to press out, express, from Latin *exprimere.* See EX-PRESS.]

es·prit (e sprē′) *n.* a lively wit; spirit; vivacity. [French *esprit* soul, mind, from Latin *spīritus* breath, soul, mind. Doublet of SPIRIT, SPRITE.]

es·prit de corps (e sprē′də kôr′) a feeling of unity and mutual regard existing in a group and among its members who are all working together toward some common goal. [French *esprit de corps* literally, spirit of a body (of people). See ESPRIT, CORPS.]

es·py (e spī′) *v.t.* **-pied, -py·ing.** to catch sight of (something hidden or at a distance); discern; see. [Old French *espier* to watch, spy upon; of Germanic origin.]

Esq., Esquire.

-esque *suffix* (used to form adjectives) **1.** in or like the style of: *Romanesque.* **2.** resembling; like: *picturesque.* [French *-esque,* from Italian *-esco;* of Germanic origin.]

es·quire (es′kwīr, e skwīr′) *n.* **1.** a young aspirant to knight-hood who attended a medieval knight; squire. **2.** a man belonging to the English gentry, ranking immediately below a knight. **3.** *Archaic.* English landholder; country gentleman; squire. **4. Esquire.** a title of respect or courtesy used in writing, esp. in addressing letters. ➡ in Britain, placed after a man's last name and a comma. In the United States, placed after the name of a lawyer of either sex. In both cases it is usually abbreviated as *Esq.* [Old French *escuier* squire, shield bearer, from Late Latin *scūtārius* shield bearer, from Latin *scūtum* shield.]

ess (es) *n.* **1.** the letter S. **2.** something shaped like an S.

-ess *suffix* used to form feminine nouns: *actress, lioness.* [Old French *-esse,* from Late Latin *-issa,* from Greek *-issa.*]

es·say (*n.,* es′ā, def. 2, also e sā′; *v.,* e sā′) *n.* **1.** a short literary composition, often informal and personal in tone and expressing the author's opinions, theories, and analysis of a particular sub-ject. **2.** an effort or attempt to do something; endeavor. —*v.t.* to try; attempt. [Old French *essai* trial, going back to Late Latin *exagium* a weighing, from Latin *exigere* to weigh, examine.] —**es·say′er,** *n.*

es·say·ist (es′ā ist) *n.* a writer of essays.

es·sence (es′əns) *n.* **1.** that which gives a thing its nature; necessary and fundamental part; distinctive feature: *The essence of poetry is invention* (Samuel Johnson, 1779-81). **2.a.** a substance containing the basic ingredients or characteristic properties of a thing in concentrated form; extract. **b.** such a concentrate or extract, as vanilla flavoring, in a solution of alcohol. **3.** a perfume. [French *essence* being, nature, perfume, from Latin *essentia* being or essence of a thing, from *esse* to be.] —For Synonyms, see **heart.**

Es·sene (es′ēn, e sēn′) *n.* a member of a Jewish monastic community in Palestine from approximately 100 B.C. to A.D. 100. —**Es·se′ni·an,** *adj.*

es·sen·tial (i sen′shəl) *adj.* **1.** necessary for the existence or continuance of something; indispensable: *It is essential that we arrive early for the surprise party.* **2.** forming or being the basis for something; fundamental; intrinsic. **3.** necessary for health and growth and that cannot be made by the body but must be ingested in food: *an essential amino acid.* **4.** of, like, or consisting of an essence or extract. —*n.* a necessary or fundamental element or quality; indispensable part: *to outline the essentials of a plan.* [Late Latin *essentiālis* relating to being, from Latin *essentia* being. See ESSENCE.] —**es·sen·ti·al·i·ty** (i sen′shē al′i tē), **es·sen′tial-ness,** *n.* —**es·sen′tial·ly,** *adv.* —For Synonyms *(adj.),* see **necessary.**

essential oil, any of various volatile oils that give a plant its characteristic flavor or fragrance. They are extracted from plant tissues and used to make perfumes and flavorings.

-est[1] *suffix* **1.** used to form the superlative degree of adjectives: *coldest.* **2.** used to form the superlative degree of adverbs: *soon-est.* [Old English *-est, -ost.*]

-est[2] *suffix* used to form the archaic second person singular of verbs: *doest.* [Old English *-est, -ast.*]

est. 1. established. **2.** estate. **3.** estimated. **4.** estuary.

EST, Eastern Standard Time.

es·tab·lish (e stab′lish) *v.t.* **1.** to set up permanently; found: *to establish a new political party, to establish a university.* **2.** to settle securely or permanently, as in a place, position, or occupation: *I established myself in the clothing business.* **3.** to introduce and secure permanent acceptance for; gain recognition of: *to establish a hypothesis, to establish one's reputation.* **4.** to put beyond dis-pute; show convincingly; prove: *to establish a motive, to establish a claim.* **5.** to cause to happen; bring about: *The new government was eager to establish good relations with neighboring countries.*

6. to make (a church), by law or decree, the official religion of a nation, financially supported by the government. [Old French *establiss-,* a stem of *establir* to found, install, decide, from Latin *stabilīre* to make firm.] —**es·tab′lish·er,** *n.*

established church, a church recognized as the official religion of a nation and financially supported by the government.

es·tab·lish·ment (e stab′lish mənt) *n.* **1.** the act of establishing or the state of being established. **2.** something established, such as a household, business, or institution: *Stores and restaurants are private establishments. The police and fire departments are public establishments.* **3. the Establishment. a.** a group of people or institutions that, directly or indirectly, have dominant influence in a nation or society. **b.** an established church, esp. the Church of England.

es·tate (e stāt′) *n.* **1.** a large piece of land, esp. with a large house, owned by one person; landed property. **2.a.** property or possessions, esp. everything owned by a person at his or her death or on becoming bankrupt. **b.** the type or extent of interest a person has in property, esp. land: *A tenant's estate is much more limited than an owner's.* **c.** any form of ownership of land. **3.** a condition or stage of life; status; rank. **4.** one of the classes into which the people of a nation are divided with regard to social and political rights and powers. In late medieval and early modern Europe, the **three estates** were the clergy, the nobility, and the common people. [Old French *estat* possession, state, from Latin *status* position, condition.]

Es·tates-Gen·er·al (e stāts′jen′ər əl) *n.* the States-General in France.

es·teem (e stēm′) *v.t.* **1.** to consider good or important; regard favorably; value highly: *to esteem someone's opinion.* **2.** to judge to be; consider; regard: *They esteemed themselves lucky to escape with minor injuries.* —*n.* **1.** a favorable opinion; high regard; respect: *Their acts of charity won them much esteem in the commu-nity.* **2.** *Archaic.* an opinion; judgment; consideration. [Old French *estimer* to determine the value of, from Latin *aestimāre* to value.]

es·ter (es′tər) *n.* an organic compound formed by the reaction of an alcohol with an acid, occurring naturally as animal or vege-table fat, oil, and wax. [German *Ester,* abbreviation of *Essigäther* acetic ether, going back to Latin *acētum* vinegar + *aethēr.* See ETHER.]

es·ter·ase (es′tə rās′) *n.* any of a group of enzymes that break down esters into acids and alcohols. [ESTER + -ASE.]

es·ter·i·fy (e ster′ə fī′) *v.t., v.i.* **-fied, -fy·ing.** to transform or become transformed into an ester. —**es·ter′i·fi·ca′tion,** *n.*

Es·ther (es′tər) *n.* a book of the Old Testament that tells the story of a Jewish queen of Persia who saved her people from being slaughtered.

es·thete (es′thēt) aesthete.

es·thet·ic (es thet′ik) *adj.* aesthetic. —**es·thet′i·cal·ly,** *adv.*

es·thet·i·cism (es thet′ə siz′əm) aestheticism.

es·thet·ics (es thet′iks) aesthetics.

es·ti·ma·ble (es′tə mə bəl) *adj.* **1.** worthy of favorable opinion; deserving high regard or respect: *The senator has an estimable reputation for honesty.* **2.** capable of being estimated or valued; calculable. —**es′ti·ma·bly,** *adv.*

es·ti·mate (*n.,* es′tə mit, -māt′; *v.,* es′tə māt′) *n.* **1.** a judgment or opinion, as of the value, quality, extent, or size of something: *an estimate of the height of a mountain, an estimate of the age of an antique.* **2.** a written statement made by a person or business assigned to or seeking to be assigned to do a job, which states the probable or approximate cost, duration, and other details of the work. —*v.t.* **-mat·ed, -mat·ing. 1.** to make a rough judgment or calculation of (the value, quality, extent, or other property of something); form an approximation of: *We estimated the cost of repairing the tractor.* **2.** to form an opinion about; judge: *What do you estimate your chances are of winning the election?* [Latin *aes-timātus,* past participle of *aestimāre* to value.] —**es′ti·ma·tor,** *n.*

Synonyms *v.t.* Estimate, evaluate, and rate[1] mean to judge the value or worth of something. **Estimate** connotes a judgment that is tentative, rough, and not final: *to estimate the price an object may bring at auction, to estimate the contribution of each member of the team.* **Evaluate** suggests a more precise judgment than *estimate: to evaluate a collection of*

a	at	e	end	o	hot	u	up	hw	white	(	about
ā	ape	ē	me	ō	old	ū	use	ng	song		taken
ä	far	i	it	ô	fork	ü	rule	th	thin	ə ⟨	pencil
âr	care	ī	ice	oi	oil	u	pull	th	this		lemon
		îr	pierce	ou	out	ûr	turn	zh	measure	(	circus

Greek vases, to evaluate a body of scientific work. **Rate** connotes placing on a scale of value: *to rate the chances of the top three players of winning the tournament.* For other Synonyms *(v.t.),* see **calculate.**

es·ti·ma·tion (es′tə mā′shən) *n.* **1.** a judgment or opinion: *The project was a feasible one in their estimation.* **2.** the act of estimating. **3.** a favorable opinion; esteem; regard: *a leader held in the highest estimation by everyone.*

es·ti·val (es′tə vəl, e stī′-) *also,* **aestival.** *adj.* of or relating to summer. [Latin *aestīvālis* relating to summer, going back to *aestās* summer.]

es·ti·vate (es′tə vāt′) *also,* **aestivate.** *v.i.,* **-vat·ed, -vat·ing.** to spend the summer in a torpid state, as some snakes, fish, and certain other animals do. ➡ distinguished from **hibernate.** [Latin *aestīvātus,* past participle of *aestīvāre* to spend the summer.]

Es·to·ni·an (e stō′nē ən) *adj.* of, relating to, or characteristic of Estonia or its people, language, or culture. —*n.* **1.** a native or inhabitant of Estonia. **2.** a language of the Finno-Ugric subfamily of the Ural-Altaic family, spoken predominantly in Estonia.

es·top (e stop′) *v.t.,* **-topped, -top·ping. 1.** *Law.* to bar or impede by estoppel. **2.** *Archaic.* to stop up; obstruct. [Old French *estoper* to stop, going back to Latin *stuppa* tow[2]; with reference to stopping up something with tow; hence, impeding. See STOP.]

es·top·pel (e stop′əl) *n. Law.* the prevention of a party from asserting or denying a fact or claim when the assertion or denial is inconsistent with that party's previous statements or acts.

es·tra·di·ol (es′trə dī′ôl) *n.* a potent female sex hormone produced in the ovary that functions to prepare the uterus for pregnancy. Natural and synthetic forms of estradiol are used in oral contraceptives, to treat certain cancers, and as an estrogen replacement in menopause. Formula: $C_{18}H_{24}O_2$

es·trange (e strānj′) *v.t.,* **-tranged, -trang·ing. 1.** to turn (someone) from kindness or affection to indifference or hostility; alienate the friendliness of. **2.** to keep apart or stay away; dissociate: *to estrange oneself from a group.* [Old French *estrangier* to alienate, from Late Latin *extrāneāre* to treat as a stranger, from *extrāneus* strange, foreign.] **—es·trange′ment,** *n.*

es·tray (e strā′) *n.* something that has strayed, esp. a stray domestic animal whose owner is unknown.

es·tro·gen (es′trə jən) *n.* any of a group of hormones, secreted primarily by the ovaries or female sex glands, that cause the body to produce the secondary female sex characteristics and that function with progesterone to control menstruation, to prepare the uterus for pregnancy, and to help the body maintain pregnancy. Synthetic estrogen is used in birth-control pills and in treating certain cancers. [ESTRUS + -GEN.] **—es′tro·gen′ic,** *adj.*

es·trous (es′trəs) *adj.* relating to or involving estrus.

estrous cycle, a series of changes in the sexual organs and behavior of female mammals that is associated with the estrus and that prepares them for mating and bearing young.

es·trus (es′trəs) *n.* the period during which a female mammal is able to mate and conceive; heat. [Modern Latin *estrus,* from Latin *oestrus* frenzy, enthusiasm; literally, gadfly (referring to the behavioral changes that take place during this period), from Greek *oistros.*]

es·tu·a·rine (es′chü ə rīn′) *adj.* of, relating to, deposited by, or formed in an estuary. [ESTUARY + -INE[1].]

es·tu·ar·y (es′chü er′ē) *n., pl.* **-ar·ies. 1.** the mouth or lower course of a river where the current meets the sea and is affected by the tides. **2.** an arm or inlet of the sea. [Latin *aestuārium* marsh, inlet, from *aestus* heat, tide.]

-et *suffix* used to form the diminutive of nouns: *islet.* ➡ The diminutive meaning has lost its force in most words. [Old French *-et;* of uncertain origin.]

e·ta (ā′tə, ē′tə) *n.* the seventh letter of the Greek alphabet (H, η).

é·ta·gère (ā′tə zhâr′) *n.* a piece of furniture having open shelves for the display of small objects. [French *étagère,* going back to Old French *estage* floor, station, stage.]

et al. (et al′, äl′, ôl′) **1.** and others. [Latin *et aliī.*] **2.** and elsewhere. [Latin *et alibī.*]

eta meson, a subatomic particle of the meson group.

etc., et cetera.

et cet·er·a (et set′ər ə, set′rə) and so forth; and the rest; and others. [Latin *et cētera* (neuter plural) and the rest.]

et·cet·er·as (et set′ər əz, -set′rəz) *pl. n.* miscellaneous other things; odds and ends.

etch (ech) *v.t.* **1.** to engrave by means of a corrosive, esp. to engrave a printing plate with acid. **2.** to sketch or delineate by this method. —*v.i.* to make plates or designs by this method. [Dutch *etsen,* from German *ätzen* to eat into, corrode, etch.] **—etch′er,** *n.*

etch·ing (ech′ing) *n.* **1.** the art or process of engraving in which lines are scratched with a needle on a wax-coated plate, usually of metal, and acid or another corrosive is used to bite the design into the exposed surface. **2.** an etched figure, design, or plate. **3.** the impression or print from an etched plate.

e·ter·nal (i tûr′nəl) *adj.* **1.** without beginning or end; existing throughout all time; lasting forever. **2.** forever the same; never changing; immutable: *eternal laws of nature.* **3.** seeming to last or continue forever; perpetual; incessant: *We complained about the eternal noise of construction next door.* —*n.* **the Eternal.** God. [Late Latin *aeternālis* everlasting, from Latin *aeternus.*] **—e·ter′-nal·ly,** *adv.*

Synonyms *adj.* **Eternal, everlasting,** and **endless** may all mean having infinite duration. **Eternal** connotes the absence of either an end or a beginning and is used chiefly in religious contexts: *the eternal deity, eternal truths.* **Everlasting** does not imply the absence of a beginning, but it, too, is used chiefly in religious contexts: *everlasting grace.* It may also be applied to human concerns that last, or seem to last, forever: *everlasting fame, to our everlasting sorrow.* **Endless** simply implies continuation forever or for as long as can be imagined: *the endless movement of the tides.* It is often used in hyperbole: *an endless recital of complaints.*

eternal flame, a fire that is kept burning continuously for symbolic or memorial purposes.

e·ter·ni·ty (i tûr′ni tē) *n., pl.* **-ties. 1.** time without beginning or end; all time; infinite time. **2.** the state or quality of being eternal; timelessness. **3.** all future time, esp. the infinite time or condition after death. **4.** a seemingly endless length of time; extremely long or indefinite duration: *I waited an eternity in the dentist's office.* [Old French *eternité* time without beginning or end, from Latin *aeternitās* duration, immortality.]

e·ter·nize (i tûr′nīz) *v.t.,* **-nized, -niz·ing. 1.** to prolong the existence or duration of infinitely or indefinitely. **2.** to perpetuate the fame or memory of; immortalize. Also, **e·ter′nal·ize.** **—e·ter′ni·za′tion,** *n.*

-eth *suffix* used to form the archaic third person singular of verbs: *doeth.* [Old English *-eth, -th.*]

eth·ane (eth′ān) *n.* a colorless, odorless, flammable gas present in natural gas and also obtained from petroleum refining and coal distillation. Formula: C_2H_6 [ETHER + -ANE.]

eth·a·nol (eth′ə nôl) *n.* alcohol *(def. 1).*

e·ther (ē′thər) *n.* **1.a.** a colorless, volatile, flammable liquid with a strong, sweetish odor, used as a solvent and, formerly, as an anesthetic. Formula: $C_4H_{10}O$ **b.** any of a group of organic compounds in whose molecules two carbon atoms are separated by an oxygen atom. **2.** *also,* **aether. a.** the upper regions of the atmosphere or the space beyond; heavens. **b.** *Physics.* a hypothetical medium once assumed to fill all space and to transmit light and other forms of radiation. [Latin *aethēr* upper air, from Greek *aithēr.*]

e·the·re·al (i thîr′ē əl) *also,* **aethereal.** *adj.* **1.** very light and delicate; exquisite; spiritual: *ethereal music.* **2.** of or relating to heaven or the heavens; celestial. **3.** of or relating to the upper regions of the atmosphere, or the space beyond: *The ethereal aurora lit the vast snows.* **4.** of or relating to the ether formerly believed to fill space. **—e·the′re·al·ly,** *adv.*

e·the·re·al·ize (i thîr′ē ə līz′) *v.t.,* **-ized, -iz·ing.** to make ethereal. **—e·the′re·al·i·za′tion,** *n.*

e·ther·i·fy (i ther′ə fī′, ē′thər-) *v.t.,* **-fied, -fy·ing.** *Chemistry.* to convert into an ether.

e·ther·ize (ē′thə rīz′) *v.t.,* **-ized, -iz·ing. 1.** *Medicine.* to subject to the influence of ether; anesthetize with ether. **2.** etherify. **—e′ther·i·za′tion,** *n.*

eth·ic (eth′ik) *n.* a code of ethics; moral system.

eth·i·cal (eth′i kəl) *adj.* **1.** of or relating to standards of morality; pertaining to a science or system of ethics. **2.** in accordance with accepted standards of conduct, esp. the standards or code of a profession: *It is not ethical for a lawyer to communicate directly with a client's opponent in a lawsuit, rather than with the opponent's lawyer.* [Latin *ēthicus* moral (from Greek *ēthikos,* from *ēthos* custom, character) + -AL[1].] **—eth′i·cal·ly,** *adv.* **—eth′i·cal·ness,** *n.* —For Synonyms, see **moral.**

Ethical Culture, a movement founded in New York in 1876 whose members stress the inviolability of human personality and the relation of individual to individual as the essential human problem.

eth·ics (eth′iks) *n.* **1.** a branch of philosophy that deals with the pursuit of the good, the meaning and justification of moral codes, and the criteria for evaluating right and wrong. **2.** standards of conduct or code of behavior, as of a profession: *ethics of the legal profession.* ➡ used as singular in def. 1, as plural in def. 2.

E·thi·op (ē′thē op′) *adj., n. Archaic.* Ethiopian.

E·thi·o·pi·an (ē′thē ō′pē ən) *adj.* **1.** of or relating to Ethiopia, its people, or their culture. **2.** *Archaic.* Negro. —*n.* a native or citizen of Ethiopia, or a person of Ethiopian ancestry.

E·thi·op·ic (ē′thē op′ik, -ō′pik) *n.* the ancient Semitic language of Ethiopia, still used in the Christian church of that country. Also, **Geez.** —*adj.* of, in, or relating to this language or church.

eth·moid (eth′moid) *n.* a spongy bone of the skull that forms the walls and the septum of the nasal cavity and contains openings through which the olfactory nerve passes. Also, **ethmoid bone.** —*adj.* of or relating to the ethmoid bone. Also, **eth·moi′dal.** [Greek *ēthmoeidēs* like a sieve, perforated, from *ēthmos* sieve + *eidos* form.]

eth·nic (eth′nik) *adj.* of or relating to a group of people having distinctive characteristics in common, such as language, culture, history, race, or national origin. Also, **eth′ni·cal.** —*n.* a member of an ethnic group. [Latin *ethnicus* pagan, from Greek *ethnikos* national, foreign, from *ethnos* race, nation.]

eth·nic·i·ty (eth nis′i tē) *n.* ethnic classification, quality, or character.

ethno- *combining form* race, nation, or people: *ethnology.* [Greek *ethnos.*]

eth·no·cen·tric (eth′nō sen′trik) *adj.* relating to or characterized by ethnocentrism. —**eth′no·cen′tri·cal·ly,** *adv.*

eth·no·cen·trism (eth′nō sen′triz əm) *n.* the belief that a person's own culture or race is more advanced or better developed than others.

eth·no·graph·ic (eth′nə graf′ik) *adj.* of or relating to ethnography. Also, **eth′no·graph′i·cal.** —**eth′no·graph′i·cal·ly,** *adv.*

eth·nog·ra·phy (eth nog′rə fē) *n.* a branch of anthropology dealing with description of individual cultures.

eth·no·log·i·cal (eth′nə loj′i kəl) *adj.* of or relating to ethnology. Also, **eth′no·log′ic.** —**eth′no·log′i·cal·ly,** *adv.*

eth·nol·o·gy (eth nol′ə jē) *n.* a branch of anthropology dealing with cultures, esp. of living peoples, and specifically with the comparative study of human culture as a whole. [ETHNO- + -LOGY.] —**eth·nol′o·gist,** *n.*

e·thol·o·gy (ē thol′ə jē) *n.* the study of the individual and group behavior of animals in their natural environment. [Greek *ēthologiā* the depiction of character, from *ēthos* custom, character + -*logiā.* See -LOGY.] —**e·tho·log·i·cal** (ē′thə loj′i kəl) *adj.* —**e·thol′o·gist,** *n.*

e·thos (ē′thos, ē′thōs) *n.* the distinctive character, features, or beliefs of a people, culture, or group. [Greek *ēthos* custom, character.]

eth·yl (eth′əl) *n.* **1.** a univalent organic radical present in many compounds, as ether and ethyl alcohol. Formula: C_2H_5 **2.a.** a poisonous lead compound added to gasoline to reduce knocking. Formula: $Pb(C_2H_5)_4$ **b.** gasoline or other motor fuel containing this. [ETH(ER) + -YL.]

ethyl alcohol, alcohol *(def. 1).*

eth·yl·ene (eth′ə lēn′) *n.* a colorless, flammable gas of the alkene, or olefin, series, used esp. in making organic compounds, such as polyethylene, and for coloring and ripening certain fruits. Formula: C_2H_4 [ETHYL + -ENE.]

ethylene glycol, a clear, colorless alcohol, used as an antifreeze. Formula: $C_2H_6O_2$ Also, **glycol.**

e·ti·o·late (ē′tē ə lāt′) *v.t.,* -**lat·ed,** -**lat·ing.** to cause (a green plant) to bleach by excluding sunlight. [French *étioler* to make pale (probably from *éteule* stalk[1], going back to Latin *stipula*) + -ATE[1].] —**e′ti·o·la′tion,** *n.*

e·ti·ol·o·gy (ē′tē ol′ə jē) *n., pl.* -**gies. 1.** an analysis of the origins and causes of something. **2.** a scientific or philosophical discipline that deals with origins or causes. **3.** the study or theory of the causes of disease. [Late Latin *aetiologia* a bringing of proofs, from Greek *aitiologiā* giving the cause of something.] —**e·ti·o·log·ic** (ē′tē ə loj′ik); *also,* **e′ti·o·log′i·cal,** *adj.* —**e′ti·ol′o·gist,** *n.*

et·i·quette (et′i kit, -ket′) *n.* **1.** forms of proper or polite behavior in society; good manners; decorum. **2.** rules governing proper or formal conduct in a specific area, as a profession or official ceremony: *Protocol is the etiquette of diplomacy.* [French *étiquette* label, ticket, ceremonial, from Old French *estiquier* to attach, from Dutch *stikken* to stitch; with reference to an earlier custom of "attaching" a "ticket" with the rules of the day in army posts or courts.]

E·ton College (ē′tən) an English preparatory school for boys, located at Eton, a town near London.

E·to·ni·an (ē tō′nē ən) *adj.* of or relating to Eton College, England. —*n.* a person educated at Eton College, England.

Eton jacket, a short, black jacket having broad lapels and reaching only to the waist, as that worn by students at Eton College, England.

E·tru·ri·an (i trŏŏr′ē ən) *adj., n.* Etruscan.

E·trus·can (i trus′kən) *adj.* of or relating to Etruria or its people, language, or culture. —*n.* **1.** a native or inhabitant of Etruria. **2.** the extinct language of Etruria.

et seq., and the following; and what follows. [Latin *et sequēns* and following.]

-ette *suffix* **1.** used to form the diminutive of nouns: *kitchenette.* **2.** used to form feminine nouns: *suffragette.* **3.** (used to form nouns) substitute for or imitation of: *leatherette.* [French *-ette,* feminine of *-et.* See -ET.]

é·tude (ā′tüd, ā′tūd, ā tüd′, ā tūd′) *n.* a musical composition for a solo instrument designed to develop the performer's technical ability. [French *étude* study, from Latin *studium* zeal, application.]

et·y·mo·log·i·cal (et′ə mə loj′i kəl) *adj.* of or relating to etymology. —**et′y·mo·log′i·cal·ly,** *adv.*

et·y·mol·o·gist (et′ə mol′ə jist) *n.* a specialist in etymology.

et·y·mol·o·gy (et′ə mol′ə jē) *n., pl.* -**gies. 1.** the history of a word, tracing it from its origin to its present form, including the changes in spelling and meaning that have taken place. **2.** the study of the history of words. [Latin *etymologia* analysis of the origins of words, from Greek *etymologia,* from *etymos* true + -*logia.* See -LOGY.]

Eu, the symbol for europium.

eu- *prefix* good or well: *euphemism.* [Greek *eū* well, *eus* good.]

eu·ca·lyp·tus (ū′kə lip′təs) *n., pl.* -**tus·es** or -**ti** (-tī). any of a genus of evergreen trees or shrubs, *Eucalyptus,* that belong to the myrtle family, are found in Australia, and are widely cultivated in warm climates for their hard, durable wood, resins, and oils and for use as ornamentals. [Modern Latin *Eucalyptus* literally, well-covered, from Greek *eū* well + *kalyptos* covered; with reference to the covering of its buds.]

eu·car·y·ote (ū kar′ē ōt′) *n.* eukaryote. —**eu·car·y·ot·ic** (ū kar′ē ot′ik), *adj.*

Eu·cha·rist (ū′kə rist) *n.* Holy Communion. [Latin *eucharistia* thanksgiving, the Lord's Supper, from Greek *eucharistiā,* going back to *eū* well + *charis* grace, favor.] —**Eu′cha·ris′tic,** *adj.*

eu·chre (ū′kər) *n.* a card game for two to seven players, using a deck of fifty-two cards or a variable number of the highest cards in the deck depending on the number of players. —*v.t.,* **eu·chred, eu·chring. 1.** to prevent (the maker of trumps) from winning three tricks. **2.** *Informal.* to defeat (someone), as by trickery; outwit. [Of uncertain origin.]

Eu·clid·e·an (ū klid′ē ən) *also,* **Eu·clid·i·an.** *adj.* of or relating to the ancient Greek mathematician Euclid or to a system of geometry based on his axioms.

eu·gen·ic (ū jen′ik) *adj.* **1.** relating to the improvement of the human race according to the principles of eugenics. **2.** of or concerning eugenics. [Greek *eugenēs* wellborn (from *eū* well + *genos* race, kind) + -IC.] —**eu·gen′i·cal·ly,** *adv.*

eu·gen·i·cist (ū jen′ə sist) *n.* a specialist in or advocate of eugenics. Also, **eu·gen′ist.**

eu·gen·ics (ū jen′iks) *n.* a science that deals with the improvement of the human race by controlling hereditary factors, as by careful selection of parents. ➡ used as singular.

eu·ge·o·syn·cline (ū jē′ō sing′klīn, -sin′klīn) *n. Geology.* a geosyncline in which beds of volcanic material alternate with sedimentary strata. [EU- + GEOSYNCLINE.] —**eu·ge′o·syn·cli′nal,** *adj.*

eu·gle·na (ū glē′nə) *n.* any of a large genus, *Euglena,* of unicellular freshwater protists containing chlorophyll and having a single emergent flagellum, sometimes classified as algae. [Modern Latin *euglena,* from Greek *eū-* (see EU-) + *glēnē* pupil of the eye.]

eu·kar·y·ote (ū kar′ē ōt′) *also,* **eucaryote.** *n.* any organism made up of one or more cells having a membrane-bound nucleus and membrane-bound organelles. All forms of life except for the bacteria and the blue-green algae are eukaryotes. ➡ distinguished from **prokaryote.** —**eu·kar·y·ot·ic** (ū kar′ē ot′ik), *adj.*

eu·lo·gist (ū′lə jist) *n.* a person who eulogizes.

eu·lo·gis·tic (ū′lə jis′tik) *adj.* of or relating to eulogy; praising. Also, **eu′lo·gis′ti·cal.** —**eu′lo·gis′ti·cal·ly,** *adv.*

a	at	e	end	o	hot	u	up	hw	white		about
ā	ape	ē	me	ō	old	ū	use	ng	song		taken
ä	far	i	it	ô	fork	ü	rule	th	thin	ə	pencil
âr	care	ī	ice	oi	oil	u̇	pull	th	this		lemon
		îr	pierce	ou	out	ûr	turn	zh	measure		circus

E

eu·lo·gi·um (ū lō′jē əm) *n., pl.* -gi·a (-jē ə) or -gi·ums. eulogy.

eu·lo·gize (ū′lə jīz′) *v.t.,* -gized, -giz·ing. to praise highly in speech or writing; deliver a eulogy about. —**eu′lo·giz′er,** *n.*

eu·lo·gy (ū′lə jē) *n., pl.* -gies. **1.** a speech or writing in praise of someone, esp. in honor of a deceased person. **2.** strong praise or commendation. [Greek *eulogiā* praise, from *eū* well + *legein* to speak.]

> **Synonyms** Eulogy, encomium, panegyric, and tribute denote praise expressed in speech or writing. A **eulogy** is a formal speech or piece of writing, usually lauding the virtues of someone who has recently died: *This poem is a eulogy for a lifelong friend.* An **encomium** is a warm expression of praise for an unusual achievement: *When the astronauts returned to earth, they drew many encomiums for their performance.* A **panegyric** is a high-flown, rhetorical expression of acclaim: *The speaker's description of the candidate was a panegyric that few listeners found convincing.* **Tribute** is the most general of these terms, connoting any more or less formal expression of praise: *a tribute to bravery in action, a tribute to a special guest.*

Eu·men·i·des (ū men′i dēz′) *pl. n.* **1.** in Greek mythology, the Furies. **2.** a Greek play by Aeschylus. ➡ used as plural in def. 1, as singular in def. 2. [Latin *Eumenides,* going back to Greek *eumenēs* favorable, kindly, from *eū* well + *menos* temper, mind, intent; a euphemistic epithet to propitiate the Furies.]

eu·nuch (ū′nək) *n.* **1.** a castrated man. **2.** a castrated man in the service of an Oriental ruler as a court official or supervisor of a harem. [Latin *eunūchus* castrated man, from Greek *eunouchos,* from *eunē* bed + *echein* to hold, keep; with reference to the employment of eunuchs in the Orient to guard the bedchambers of women.]

eu·pep·sia (ū pep′shə, -sē ə) *n.* good digestion. ➡ opposed to **dyspepsia.** [Modern Latin *eupepsia,* from Greek *eupepsiā* good digestion, going back to *eū* well + *peptein* to digest.] —**eu·pep·tic** (ū pep′tik), *adj.*

eu·phe·mism (ū′fə miz′əm) *n.* **1.** the substitution of a mild or indirect word or phrase for a blunter or harsher one. **2.** a word or phrase used in this way. In the sentence *We put the dog to sleep, put to sleep* is a euphemism for *kill.* [Greek *euphēmismos* use of auspicious words, going back to *eū* well + *phēmē* saying, speech.] —**eu′phe·mist,** *n.*

> **Usage** A **euphemism** is a mild, vague, or polite word or phrase used in place of one that is more precise and blunt. **Euphemisms** are often used to refer to concepts that many people find frightening or disturbing, such as aging and death. They are also used to spare people's feelings and to disguise hard or unpleasant truths. *Passed away, passed on,* or *departed,* for example, often replace the more direct word *died,* and *put to sleep* is an expression used for euthanasia in animals. People over sixty-five are described as *senior citizens,* rather than as *aging* or *elderly.* And a politician may use *recession* in preference to the more drastic *depression* or *revenue enhancement* when what is meant is *new taxes.* One characteristic of a **euphemism** is that in time it may tend to lose its euphemistic quality and take on the connotation of the stronger term it stands for, thus eventually becoming unacceptable itself. The words *primitive* or *backward,* once used by advanced nations to describe less advanced nations, were rejected as sounding arrogant and patronizing and replaced by the milder term *underdeveloped.* This, in turn, has given way to the more positive-sounding *developing* or *emerging* nations.

eu·phe·mis·tic (ū′fə mis′tik) *adj.* **1.** of or using euphemisms. **2.** serving as a euphemism. —**eu′phe·mis′ti·cal·ly,** *adv.*

eu·phon·ic (ū fon′ik) *adj.* **1.** of or relating to euphony. **2.** pleasant-sounding; euphonious. Also, **eu·phon′i·cal.** —**eu·phon′i·cal·ly,** *adv.*

eu·pho·ni·ous (ū fō′nē əs) *adj.* pleasant and agreeable in sound; pleasant to hear. —**eu·pho′ni·ous·ly,** *adv.* —**eu·pho′ni·ous·ness,** *n.*

eu·pho·ni·um (ū fō′nē əm) *n.* a brass musical instrument, used esp. in military and marching bands, usually having four valves and producing tones resembling, but higher and mellower than, a tuba's. Some euphoniums have two bells. [Modern Latin *euphonium,* from Greek *euphōnos* sweet-voiced.]

eu·pho·ny (ū′fə nē) *n., pl.* -nies. **1.** the quality of having a pleasant sound; pleasing effect of sounds

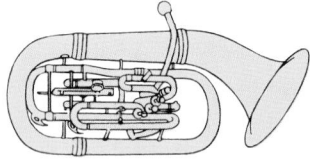

euphonium

free from harshness. **2.** *Phonetics.* the tendency for sounds to change to make pronunciation easier. [French *euphonie* an agreeable sound, from Greek *euphōniā* sweetness of voice.]

eu·phor·bi·a (ū fôr′bē ə) *n.* any plant of the genus *Euphorbia,* as poinsettia, with milky juice and often spiny stems. [Latin *euphorbea;* said to be named after *Euphorbus,* an ancient Greek physician.]

eu·pho·ri·a (ū fôr′ē ə) *n.* **1.** a feeling of well-being and happiness. **2.** *Psychology.* an exaggerated sense of well-being and happiness. [Modern Latin *euphoria,* from Greek *euphoriā* well-being, going back to *eū* well + *pherein* to bear.] —**eu·pho′ric,** *adj.*

eu·pho·tic (ū fō′tik) *adj.* of or constituting the upper layers of a body of water into which sufficient light penetrates to allow photosynthetic organisms to live. [Eu- + Greek *phōt-,* stem of *phōs* light + -ic.]

Eu·phros·y·ne (ū fros′ə nē) *n.* in Greek mythology, one of the three Graces.

eu·phu·ism (ū′fū iz′əm) *n.* **1.** an elaborate and affected literary style fashionable in England at the end of the sixteenth and beginning of the seventeenth centuries, characterized by antitheses, similes, mythological and historical allusions, consonance, and alliteration. **2.** any similar, affected style of writing; artificial or exaggerated elegance of language; bombast. [From the affected style of two romances by the English writer John Lyly, 1554?-1606, in which *Euphues* was the principal character; from Greek *euphuēs* excellent.] —**eu′phu·is′tic,** *adj.* —**eu′phu·is′ti·cal·ly,** *adv.*

Eur. 1. Europe. **2.** European.

Eur·a·sian (yů rā′zhən, -shən) *adj.* **1.** of or relating to Eurasia. **2.** of mixed European and Asian descent. —*n.* a person who is of mixed European and Asian descent.

eu·re·ka (yů rē′kə) *interj.* used as an exclamation of triumph upon discovering something or solving a problem. [Greek *heurēka* I have found (it); the supposed exclamation of the Greek physicist Archimedes, 287?-212 B.C., upon discovering the test for the purity of gold.]

Eu·ro-dol·lars (yůr′ō dol′ərz) *pl. n.* U.S. dollars deposited in foreign banks, mainly in Europe, and lent to other banks or commercial borrowers, serving as a medium of international finance and world trade.

Eu·ro·pa (yů rō′pə) *n.* in Greek mythology, a Phoenician princess abducted by Zeus in the disguise of a white bull. [Latin *Eurōpa,* from Greek *Eurōpē;* probably of Semitic origin and originally having the sense of "land of the setting sun."]

Eu·ro·pe·an (yůr′ə pē′ən) *adj.* of, relating to, or characteristic of Europe or its population. —*n.* **1.** a person who was born in Europe or is a citizen of a European country. **2.** a person of European ancestry.

European Community, an organization of European countries, having as its purpose the furthering of economic and political integration, which was formed in 1967 through the merging of three units: the European Economic Community, or Common Market, the European Atomic Energy Community, and the European Coal and Steel Community. Also, **Communities.**

European Economic Community, an economic association formed in 1958 by France, West Germany, Italy, Belgium, the Netherlands, and Luxembourg to abolish barriers to free trade among members by allowing goods, workers, capital, and services to move freely across national boundaries. Denmark, Great Britain, Greece, Ireland, Portugal, and Spain are now also members. Also, **Common Market.**

Eu·ro·pe·an·ize (yůr′ə pē′ə nīz′) *v.t.,* -ized, -iz·ing. to make European, as in appearance or culture.

European plan, a system of hotel operation in which the charge for rooms is separate from the charge for meals. ➡ distinguished from **American plan.**

European Recovery Program, Marshall Plan.

eu·ro·pi·um (yů rō′pē əm) *n.* a soft, grayish metallic element of the rare-earth group, used esp. in nuclear reactors and in color television tubes. Symbol: Eu For tables, see **element.** [Modern Latin *europium,* from *Europa* Europe + -ium suffix used to form names of elements.]

Eu·ryd·i·ce (yů rid′ə sē) *n.* in Greek mythology, the wife of Orpheus, killed by the bite of a snake. Hades agreed to release her from the underworld, but Orpheus, who had promised not to look at her until they were back in the upper world, looked back and thus lost her.

eu·ryp·ter·id (yů rip′tə rid) *n.* any of an extinct group of large, streamlined, aquatic arthropods, subclass Eurypterida, related to horseshoe crabs and living from Ordovician to Permian geologic time. Length: to 6 feet (2 meters). [Modern Latin *Eurypterida* name of the subclass, from Greek *eurys* broad + *pteron* feather, wing; referring to their broad swimming appendages.]

Eu·sta·chi·an tube (ū stā′kē ən, -shən) a canal or passage extending from the pharynx to the middle ear. It equalizes the air pressure on the inside of the eardrum with the atmospheric pressure on the outside. For illustration, see **ear¹**. [From the Italian anatomist Bartolommeo *Eustachio,* 1524-74, who described it.]

eu·stat·ic (ū stat′ik) *adj. Geology.* of or characterized by changes in sea level that occur throughout the world, as those that accompany the onset or the end of an ice age.

eu·tec·tic (ū tek′tik) *adj. Chemistry. Metallurgy.* having the lowest possible melting point, as an alloy or mixture of two or more substances that melts at a lower temperature than any other mixture of those substances. —*n.* a eutectic mixture or alloy. [Greek *eutēktos* easily fused (from *eū* well + *tēkein* to melt) + -IC.]

Eu·ter·pe (ū tûr′pē) *n.* in Greek mythology, the Muse of music and lyric poetry. [Latin *Euterpe,* from Greek *Euterpē,* from *eū* well + *terpein* to please.]

eu·tha·na·sia (ū′thə nā′zhə) *n.* the painless killing of a person or domestic animal suffering from an agonizing and incurable disease, esp. during the terminal stage. [Greek *euthanasiā* easy death, from *eū* well + *thanatos* death.]

eu·than·a·tize (ū than′ə līz′) *v.t.,* **-tized, -tiz·ing.** euthanize.

eu·tha·nize (ū′thə nīz′) *v.t.* **-nized, -niz·ing.** to kill in a painless way; subject to euthanasia. Also, **euthanatize.**

eu·troph·ic (ū trof′ik, ū trō′fik) *adj.* (of a body of water) in a condition that results from the process of eutrophication. [EU- + Greek *trophikos* relating to food, from *trophē* food, from *trephein* to feed.]

eu·troph·i·ca·tion (ū trof′i kā′shən) *n.* a process by which a body of water is abundantly supplied with nutrients, either naturally or because of pollutants, resulting in an overgrowth of algae, subsequent deoxygenation of the water, and death of fish and higher plants.

eV, electron volt.

EVA, extravehicular activity.

e·vac·u·ate (i vak′ū āt′) *v.,* **-at·ed, -at·ing.** —*v.t.* **1.a.** to leave or vacate for safety or protection: *The troops evacuated their position. The audience evacuated the theater.* **b.** to remove all the air from; create a vacuum in: *to evacuate a container.* **c.** to discharge waste matter from: *to evacuate the bladder.* **2.a.** to cause to leave or vacate for safety or protection: *Firefighters evacuated the tenants from the burning building.* **b.** to remove entirely: *to evacuate air from a container.* **c.** to discharge (waste matter); void: *to evacuate urine from the bladder.* —*v.i.* to leave or withdraw for safety or protection: *The townspeople were ordered to evacuate because of the bombing.* [Latin *ēvacuātus,* past participle of *ēvacuāre* to empty out, from *ex* out + *vacuus* empty.] —**e·vac′u·a′tor,** *n.*

e·vac·u·a·tion (i vak′ū ā′shən) *n.* **1.** the act of evacuating or the state of being evacuated. **2.a.** the expulsion of waste matter from the body, esp. from the bladder or bowels. **b.** the waste matter so discharged; feces.

e·vac·u·ee (i vak′ū ē′, i vak′ū ē′) *n.* a person removed from an area of danger or disaster: *The evacuees from the flooded area were housed in the school.*

e·vade (i vād′) *v.,* **e·vad·ed, e·vad·ing.** —*v.t.* **1.** to avoid, as by trickery or cunning; elude: *He evaded his pursuers.* **2.** to escape or avoid the responsibility of: *to evade taxes.* **3.** to avoid answering: *to evade a question.* **4.** to remain hidden from; baffle: *The key to the code evaded all her efforts.* —*v.i.* to avoid honesty or directness; be evasive. [Latin *ēvādere* to escape.] —**e·vad′er,** *n.* —For Synonyms, see **avoid.**

e·val·u·ate (i val′ū āt′) *v.t.,* **-at·ed, -at·ing.** **1.** to establish the value or the amount of; appraise: *to evaluate a stamp collection.* **2.** to determine the meaning or importance of; assess: *The diplomat was asked to evaluate the peace negotiations. The scientists are still evaluating their data.* **3.** to compute the numerical value of. [From EVALUATION.] —For Synonyms, see **estimate.**

e·val·u·a·tion (i val′ū ā′shən) *n.* **1.** the act or process of evaluating. **2.** the result of evaluating; appraisal; judgment. [French *évaluation* estimate, from *évaluer* to estimate, going back to Latin *ex* out + *valēre* to be worth.]

ev·a·nesce (ev′ə nes′) *v.i.,* **-nesced, -nesc·ing.** to fade away gradually like smoke or vapor; dissipate; vanish. [Latin *ēvānēscere* to vanish.]

ev·a·nes·cence (ev′ə nes′əns) *n.* **1.** a gradual dissipation; fading away: *the evanescence of a rainbow.* **2.** the tendency to fade away or become indistinct; quality of being insubstantial.

ev·a·nes·cent (ev′ə nes′ənt) *adj.* tending to fade away or pass away; impermanent; insubstantial. —For Synonyms, see **momentary.**

e·van·gel (i van′jəl) *n.* **1.** the good news of the redemption of the world through Christ. **2.** any good tidings. **3.** evangelist. **4. Evangel.** any one of the four Gospels. [Old French *evangile* gospel, from Church Latin *evangelium,* from Greek *euangelion* good news, gospel, going back to *eū* well + *angellein* to announce.]

e·van·gel·i·cal (ē′van jel′i kəl, ev′ən-) *adj.* **1.** of, in, or according to the four Gospels or the New Testament. **2.** of or relating to the Protestant churches, such as the Methodist and Baptist, that teach that salvation is achieved through a personal conversion to religious faith in Jesus and that the Bible, esp. the New Testament, is the sole religious authority. **3.** evangelistic. Also, **e′van·gel′ic.** —*n.* a person who is a member of an evangelical church. —**e′van·gel′i·cal·ly,** *adv.*

e·van·gel·i·cal·ism (ē′van jel′i kə liz′əm, ev′ən-) *n.* **1.** the doctrines or principles of an evangelical church. **2.** advocacy or support of such doctrines.

e·van·gel·ism (i van′jə liz′əm) *n.* **1.** zealous preaching or promulgation of the Gospel, as by traveling preachers; work of evangelists. **2.** evangelicalism.

e·van·gel·ist (i van′jə list) *n.* **1.** a preacher of the Gospel, esp. one who travels from place to place holding religious meetings. **2. Evangelist.** one of the four authors of the Gospels; Matthew, Mark, Luke, or John.

e·van·gel·is·tic (i van′jə lis′tik) *adj.* **1.** of or relating to the Evangelists. **2.** of or relating to evangelists or evangelism.

e·van·gel·ize (i van′jə līz′) *v.,* **-ized, -iz·ing.** —*v.t.* **1.** to preach the Gospel to. **2.** to convert to Christianity. —*v.i.* to do the work of an evangelist. —**e·van′gel·i·za′tion,** *n.*

e·vap·o·rate (i vap′ə rāt′) *v.,* **-rat·ed, -rat·ing.** —*v.i.* **1.** to be changed from a liquid or solid into a gas; become gaseous. **2.** to give off moisture: *Let the mixture simmer until it has evaporated to half its volume.* **3.** to fade away or disappear; be dissipated: *Their fears evaporated when the lost child reappeared.* —*v.t.* **1.** to cause (a liquid or solid) to change into a gaseous state; convert into a vapor: *The sun soon evaporated the morning dew.* **2.** to drive off or remove moisture from, as by heating: *If you evaporate seawater, a residue of salt will remain.* [Latin *ēvapōrātus,* past participle of *ēvapōrāre* to disperse in vapor, from *ex* out + *vapor* exhalation, steam.] —**e·vap·o·ra·tive** (i vap′ə rā′tiv, -ər ə tiv), *adj.*

evaporated milk, unsweetened canned milk, which is thickened by evaporating some of the water from whole milk.

e·vap·o·ra·tion (i vap′ə rā′shən) *n.* **1.** the change from a liquid or solid state into vapor; vaporization. **2.** the extraction or removal of moisture or liquid: *Powdered milk is produced by complete evaporation of whole milk.*

e·vap·o·ra·tor (i vap′ə rā′tər) *n.* an apparatus for evaporating.

e·vap·o·rite (i vap′ə rīt′) *n. Geology.* any of various kinds of sedimentary deposit, as rock salt, gypsum, or anhydrite, that form from evaporation of stagnant salt water in a hot, dry environment. [EVAPOR(ATE) + -ITE¹.]

e·va·sion (i vā′zhən) *n.* **1.** an act of evading something, as a duty or a question; avoidance, as by cleverness or deceit: *to be charged with income tax evasion.* **2.** a means of evading something: *Changing the subject in response to a question is an evasion.* [Late Latin *ēvāsiō* a going out, escape, from Latin *ēvādere* to escape.]

e·va·sive (i vā′siv, -ziv) *adj.* tending to evade; characterized by evasion; elusive: *evasive answers, an evasive person.* —**e·va′sive·ly,** *adv.* —**e·va′sive·ness,** *n.*

eve (ēv) *n.* **1.** the evening or day preceding a holiday or other important day. **2.** the period just before: *the eve of an election.* **3.** evening. [Form of EVEN².]

e·ven¹ (ē′vən) *adj.* **1.** without slope or hills; completely flat; level: *an even piece of ground, even countryside.* **2.** having no roughness, indentations, or other irregularities; smooth: *an even surface, an even hemline.* **3.** at the same level; of uniform height: *The two mountain peaks looked even in the distance.* **4.** in or extending along the same plane; parallel: *They moved the desk to make it even with the others. The soil was even with the top of the pot.* **5.** of uniform quality throughout; equally distributed: *an even coat of paint.* **6.** free from variations or sudden changes; regular; constant: *an even rhythm, even spacing.* **7.** not easily excited; calm; tranquil: *an even disposition.* **8.** fully revenged, as for a wrong. **9.** equitable; fair: *an even bargain, an even hand in meting out justice.* **10.** being approximately equal or the same:

a	at	e	end	o	hot	u	up	hw	white		about
ā	ape	ē	me	ō	old	ū	use	ng	song		taken
ä	far	i	it	ô	fork	ü	rule	th	thin	ə	pencil
âr	care	ī	ice	oi	oil	u̇	pull	th	this		lemon
		îr	pierce	ou	out	ûr	turn	zh	measure		circus

E

Our chances of winning or losing the game are even. **11.** identical or equal, as in quantity, measure, or size: *an even score.* **12.** without fractional parts; exact: *an even hundred yards.* **13.** having nothing owed to one or owing nothing; balanced: *Pay me back the quarter, and we'll be even.* **14.** exactly divisible by two. ➡ opposed to **odd. 15.** denoted by or having such numbers: *the even pages of a book.* —*adv.* **1.** at the very same moment; while; just: *They came ashore even as the sun was setting.* **2.** in the very same way; exactly; precisely; quite: *It occurred even as I'd thought it would.* **3.** as a matter of fact; really; actually; indeed: *to be happy, even joyous.* **4.** though it may seem improbable or unlikely: *They were generous even to strangers.* **5.** all the way; fully: *They were friends even to death.* **6.** in comparison; still; yet: *Today's weather is even better than yesterday's.* —*v.t.* to make smooth, level, or equal: *to even a road surface, to even an account.* —*v.i.* to become smooth, level, or equal (often with *out*). [Old English *efen* level, equal.] —**e′ven·er,** *n.* —**e′ven·ly,** *adv.* —**e′ven·ness,** *n.* —For Synonyms *(adj.),* see **regular.**
- **even if.** for all that; although.
- **to break even.** *Informal.* to have one's gains equal one's losses.
- **to get even. a.** to obtain revenge upon; retaliate: *I promise that I'll get even for that remark.* **b.** to settle or balance one's accounts.

e·ven² (ē′vən) *n. Archaic.* evening. [Middle English *even,* from Old English *ǣfen,* from *ǣfnung* close of day.]

e·ven·hand·ed (ē′vən han′did) *adj.* characterized by fairness; unbiased; just: *an evenhanded decision.* —**e′ven·hand′ed·ly,** *adv.* —**e′ven·hand′ed·ness,** *n.*

eve·ning (ēv′ning) *n.* **1.** late afternoon and early nighttime; period from twilight to bedtime. **2.** the last part or closing period, as of a life. —*adj.* of, relating to, or occurring in the evening: *evening classes, the evening meal.* [Old English *ǣfnung* close of day.]

evening dress, formal clothing, designed to be worn in the evening. Also, **evening clothes.**

evening gown, a woman's evening dress, usually floor-length.

evening primrose, any of various plants, genus *Oenothera,* widely distributed in North America and Europe, esp. *O. biennis,* the common evening prim-rose, having narrow, lance-shaped leaves and spikes of yellow flowers that open at night and are closed during the day.

evening star, the first planet, most often Venus or, rarely, Mercury, to appear after sunset in the western sky.

e·ven·song (ē′vən sông′) *n.* **1.** (in the Anglican Church) a prayer service said or sung at evening. **2.** (in the Roman Catholic Church) vespers. **3.** *Archaic.* evening. [Old English *ǣfensang* vespers, from *ǣfen* evening + *sang* song.]

e·vent (i vent′) *n.* **1.** anything that happens, esp. an incident or occurrence of some importance: *The signing of the Declaration of Independence was an important historical event.* **2.** any of the

evening primrose

contests in a program or series of sports: *The mile run was the third event in the track meet.* **3.** *Archaic.* the outcome of anything; result or conclusion. [Latin *ēventus* occurrence, result.]
- **at all events.** in any case; whatever happens.
- **in any event.** in any case; whatever happens.
- **in the event of.** if (something specified) should occur; in case of: *In the event of rain, the game will be played tomorrow.*
- **in the event that.** if it should happen that: *In the event that I'm late, you should start without me.*

Event, episode, incident, and occurrence denote something that happens. An **event** is something relatively noteworthy: *The signing of the peace treaty was a historic event.* An **episode** generally refers to a single or discrete element in a series of events: *another exciting episode in a dramatic journey.* An **incident** is often more isolated or less important than an *episode: The argument was a minor incident*

that did not affect our friendship. **Occurrence** is the most general of these terms, connoting something that happens without reference to its importance: *Traffic jams are daily occurrences on the main highways leading into the city.*

e·ven-tem·pered (ē′vən tem′pərd) *adj.* not easily disturbed, excited, or angered; calm.

e·vent·ful (i vent′fəl) *adj.* **1.** marked by important or striking occurrences: *an eventful year.* **2.** having important issues or results; momentous: *an eventful meeting.*

e·ven·tide (ē′vən tīd′) *n. Archaic.* evening.

e·ven·tu·al (i ven′chü əl) *adj.* **1.** happening at some indefinite time in the future; bound to occur: *The eventual death of the dictator will bring chaos.* **2.** resulting from preceding events; final; ultimate: *The eventual outcome of the project will depend on how much money is raised.*

e·ven·tu·al·i·ty (i ven′chü al′i tē) *n., pl.* **-ties.** possible event, occurrence, or condition; contingency; possibility.

e·ven·tu·al·ly (i ven′chü ə lē) *adv.* in the end; ultimately; finally.

e·ven·tu·ate (i ven′chü āt′) *v.i.,* **-at·ed, -at·ing. 1.** to turn out finally; culminate; result (often with *in*): *The border incidents eventuated in war.* **2.** to come about; result as a consequence: *They feared that an economic crisis would eventuate when the currency was devalued.*

ev·er (ev′ər) *adv.* **1.** at any time: *Did you ever get to see that movie?* **2.** at all times; always: *to be ever willing to help a friend.* **3.** throughout all the time: *They lived happily ever after.* **4.** in any possible way: *How can we ever repay you?* [Old English *ǣfre* always.]
- **ever and again** (or **anon**). now and then; occasionally.
- **ever so.** *Informal.* very; exceedingly; extremely: *The salesperson was ever so helpful.*
- **for ever.** forever; eternally.
- **for ever and a day.** forever; eternally; always.
- **for ever and ever.** forever; eternally.

In informal speech and writing, **ever** is used to intensify a question or exclamation: *What ever do you mean by that remark? Was it ever hot at the beach today!*

ev·er·glade (ev′ər glād′) *n.* a large tract of low marshland partly covered with tall grass.

ev·er·green (ev′ər grēn′) *adj.* (of plants, trees, and shrubs) having green foliage throughout the year. ➡ distinguished from **deciduous.** —*n.* **1.** an evergreen plant, tree, or shrub. **2. evergreens.** evergreen twigs or branches used for decoration, as at Christmas.

ev·er·last·ing (ev′ər las′ting) *adj.* **1.** existing, continuing, or lasting forever; having infinite duration. **2.** existing, continuing, or lasting indefinitely; perpetual: *everlasting joy.* **3.** seeming to go on without an end; interminable; tiresome: *They told tedious, everlasting stories of their vacation.* —*n.* **1.** all time; past and future; eternity. **2. the Everlasting.** God. —**ev′er·last′ing·ly,** *adv.* —For Synonyms *(adj.),* see **eternal.**

ev·er·more (ev′ər môr′) *adv.* for and at all times; forever; eternally.
- **for evermore.** forever.

e·ver·sion (i vûr′zhən, -shən) *n. Medicine.* the act of everting or the state of being everted: *eversion of the eyelid.* [Old French *eversion* an upsetting, overthrow, from Latin *ēversiō* a turning out, overthrowing.]

e·vert (i vûrt′) *v.t. Medicine.* to turn (something, esp. a part of the body) outward or inside out. [Latin *ēvertere* to turn out.]

eve·ry (ev′rē) *adj.* **1.** each (of the persons or things that make up a group or whole) without excepting any: *Every student in the class was in the room.* **2.** all possible; the utmost: *I have every confidence in your ability.* **3.** at a regular interval of: *Take a pill every four hours.* [Old English *ǣfre* always + *ǣlc* each.] —For Synonyms, see **each.**
- **every bit.** in every respect; entirely; quite: *You are every bit as smart as they are.*
- **every now and then** (or **again**). from time to time; occasionally.
- **every once in a while.** from time to time; occasionally.
- **every other.** each alternate; each second: *They took turns driving to school every other week.*
- **every so often.** from time to time; occasionally.
- **every which way.** *Informal.* in all directions; in total disorder.

eve·ry·bod·y (ev′rē bod′ē, -bud′ē) *pron.* every person. —For Usage Note, see **anybody.**

eve·ry·day (ev′rē dā′) *adj.* **1.** of or relating to every day; daily: *everyday chores.* **2.** suitable for ordinary days: *everyday clothes.* **3.** not unusual; commonplace; ordinary; usual: *an everyday occurrence.*

eve·ry·one (ev′rē wun′, -wən) *pron.* every person; everybody: *Everyone agreed that it was a good movie.*

Usage The pronoun **everyone** should not be used in place of the adjective and pronoun *every one,* as in *The judge gave a prize to every one of the contestants. The judge gave a prize to everyone.* If **everybody** cannot be substituted in the sentence, *every one* should be used. For another Usage Note, see **anybody.**

eve·ry·place (ev′rē plās′) *n.* in all places; everywhere.

eve·ry·thing (ev′rē thing′) *pron.* **1.** all things; all: *We bought everything we needed for the trip.* **2.** most important, highly valued, or very much wanted: *Their grandchildren were everything to them.*

eve·ry·where (ev′rē hwâr′, -wâr′) *adv.* in or to every place; in all places: *They traveled everywhere in England.*

e·vict (i vikt′) *v.t.* to expel (a tenant) from land or a building, esp. by legal process; dispossess: *The landlord evicted the tenant for nonpayment of rent.* [Latin *ēvictus,* past participle of *ēvincere* to overcome, conquer.] —**e·vic′tion,** *n.*

ev·i·dence (ev′i dəns) *n.* **1.** something that serves to prove or disprove a belief or conclusion; proof: *The scientists produced much research as evidence for their theory.* **2.** something that is legally presented to a court, such as a document or the testimony of a witness, for the purpose of proving or disproving an issue in question. **3.** an indication or sign: *Their silence was evidence of their anger.* —*v.t.,* **-denced, -denc·ing.** to give proof of; show clearly; demonstrate: *Lines of people waiting to buy tickets evidenced the play's success.* [Old French *evidence* clearness, from Latin *ēvidentia.*]

 • **in evidence.** plainly seen; noticeably present: *The effects of the war were very much in evidence.*

Synonyms *n.* **Evidence, testimony,** and **proof** are legal terms that are often used in general contexts. They all denote grounds cited to uphold a statement or to demonstrate the truth of something. **Evidence** broadly connotes anything brought forward to prove or contradict something: *The overgrown garden and broken windows are evidence that the owners have abandoned the property.* **Testimony** suggests the act of giving evidence under oath: *The gardener's testimony provided the defendant with an alibi.* **Proof** connotes evidence so conclusive as to eliminate doubt: *These footprints are proof that someone broke into the house.*

ev·i·dent (ev′i dənt) *adj.* easily seen or understood; clear; apparent: *It was evident that no one understood the lecturer.* [Latin *ēvidēns.*] —**ev′i·dent·ly,** *adv.*

ev·i·den·tial (ev′i den′shəl) *adj.* **1.** based or relying on evidence. **2.** of, having the nature of, or furnishing evidence. —**ev′i·den′tial·ly,** *adv.*

e·vil (ē′vəl) *adj.* **1.** morally bad or wrong; wicked; sinful: *evil thoughts.* **2.** causing trouble or injury; harmful; pernicious: *an evil custom, evil laws.* **3.** characterized by or threatening misfortune or suffering; disastrous; unlucky: *an evil omen, evil times.* **4.** resulting from bad character or conduct: *an evil reputation.* —*n.* **1.** that which is morally bad; sin; wickedness: *The sermon was about good and evil.* **2.** something that causes misfortune, suffering, or injury: *War is a great evil.* [Old English *yfel* bad.] —**e′vil·ly,** *adv.* —**e′vil·ness,** *n.* —For Synonyms *(adj.),* see **bad¹.**

e·vil·do·er (ē′vəl dü′ər) *n.* a person who does evil. —**e′vil·do′ing,** *n.*

evil eye, an eye or glance superstitiously believed to have the power to inflict harm or misfortune.

e·vil-mind·ed (ē′vəl mīn′did) *adj.* having evil thoughts; malicious; malignant. —**e′vil-mind′ed·ly,** *adv.* —**e′vil-mind′ed·ness,** *n.*

Evil One, Satan.

e·vince (i vins′) *v.t.,* **e·vinced, e·vinc·ing. 1.** to be evidence of; reveal clearly: *Their questions evinced their ignorance of the subject.* **2.** to exhibit (a quality, feeling, or condition): *to evince a total lack of consideration for one's friends.* [Latin *ēvincere* to overcome, conquer.] —**e·vin′ci·ble,** *adj.* —**e·vin′cive,** *adj.*

e·vis·cer·ate (i vis′ə rāt′) *v.t.,* **-at·ed, -at·ing. 1.** to remove the internal organs, esp. the intestines, from; disembowel. **2.** to deprive of an essential part: *The bill was eviscerated before being passed by the legislature.* [Latin *ēviscerātus,* past participle of *ēviscerāre* to disembowel, from *ex* out + *viscera* internal organs.] —**e·vis′cer·a′tion,** *n.*

ev·o·ca·tion (ē′vō kā′shən, ev′ə-) *n.* the act or an instance of evoking.

e·voc·a·tive (i vok′ə tiv) *adj.* tending to evoke. —**e·voc′a·tive·ly,** *adv.*

e·voke (i vōk′) *v.t.,* **e·voked, e·vok·ing.** to call forth or bring out; elicit: *The reporter's question evoked an angry response. The song evoked happy memories.* [Latin *ēvocāre.*]

ev·o·lu·tion (ev′ə lü′shən) *n.* **1.** a gradual process of development, growth, or change through a series of stages: *the evolution of music, the evolution of socialism.* **2.** the result of this process. **3.** *Biology.* **a.** the theory that all living plants and animals arose from one simple form of life and gradually developed into widely different and more complicated forms through natural processes of change over millions of generations. **b.** the continuous adaptation of a species to its environment, resulting from changes in the gene pool from generation to generation, caused esp. by mutation and natural selection. **4.** a movement, esp. one that is part of a series: *the evolutions of a dancer, the evolutions of a machine.* **5.** a releasing or giving off, as of gas, heat, or sound; emission. **6.** *Mathematics.* the process of extracting the root of a number. ➡ opposed to **involution** in def. 6. [Latin *ēvolūtiō* unrolling of a scroll, opening of a book.]

ev·o·lu·tion·ar·y (ev′ə lü′shə ner′ē) *adj.* **1.** of, relating to, or resulting from gradual development, growth, or change. **2.** of, relating to, or in accordance with the biological theory of evolution.

ev·o·lu·tion·ist (ev′ə lü′shə nist) *n.* a believer in or adherent of evolution, esp. biological evolution. —**ev′o·lu′tion·ism,** *n.*

e·volve (i volv′) *v.,* **e·volved, e·volv·ing.** —*v.t.* **1.** to develop gradually; work out: *to evolve a theory.* **2.** to release or give off, as a gas; emit. —*v.i.* **1.** to undergo gradual development, growth, or change. **2.** *Biology.* to develop by a process of change to a more highly organized condition; undergo evolution. [Latin *ēvolvere* to unroll.] —**e·volve′ment,** *n.*

ewe (ū) *n.* an adult female sheep. [Old English *ēowu.*]

ew·er (ū′ər) *n.* a wide-mouthed pitcher, used esp. for holding or pouring water. [Anglo-Norman *ewer,* form of Old French *aiguier,* going back to Latin *aquārius* relating to water, from *aqua* water.]

ex (eks) *prep.* **1.** *Commerce.* free of charges until removed from (a specified place or thing): *ex warehouse, ex dock.* **2.** *Finance.* exclusive of; without: *an ex dividend stock.* —*n., pl.* **exes.** *Informal.* a divorced person's former spouse. [Latin *ex* out of, without.]

ex-¹ *prefix* **1.** out of or from: *excursion, exit, export.* **2.** thoroughly; completely: *exhilarate, exasperate.* **3.** former; previous. ➡ followed by a hyphen: *ex-minister, ex-president.* [Latin *ex* out, out of, away, from, utterly, without.]

ex-² *also,* **ec-.** *prefix* from; forth; out: *exorcise, exodus.* [Greek *ex* out of.]

ex-³ form of **exo-** before vowels, as in *exegesis.*

ex. 1. examined. **2.** example. **3.** exchange. **4.** execute.

Ex., Exodus.

ex·ac·er·bate (eg zas′ər bāt′, ig-, ek sas′-) *v.t.,* **-bat·ed, -bat·ing. 1.** to make more intense or severe; aggravate, as pain, disease, or anger. **2.** to irritate, provoke, or exasperate (a person). [Latin *exacerbātus,* past participle of *exacerbāre* to irritate, aggravate, from *ex* utterly + *acerbus* harsh, bitter.] —**ex·ac′er·ba′tion,** *n.*

ex·act (eg zakt′, ig-) *adj.* **1.** strictly accurate; precise; correct: *exact time, exact measurements.* **2.** being what is needed or required: *I gave the clerk a check for the exact amount.* **3.** duplicating in every detail; corresponding perfectly: *an exact copy.* **4.** characterized by or using strict accuracy: *an exact thinker.* —*v.t.* **1.** to demand and get by or as by force or authority: *to exact payment of a debt, to exact obedience.* **2.** to call for; require: *The problem exacted hours of concentration.* [Latin *exāctus,* past participle of *exigere* to drive out, demand, measure.] —**ex·act′ness,** *n.* —For Synonyms *(adj.),* see **correct.**

ex·act·ing (eg zak′ting, ig-) *adj.* **1.** rigorously demanding; strict; severe: *an exacting tutor.* **2.** requiring great skill, accuracy, care, or attention: *an exacting task.* —**ex·act′ing·ly,** *adv.*

ex·ac·tion (eg zak′shən, ig-) *n.* **1.** the act of exacting. **2.** something that is exacted, such as taxes, duties, or tribute.

ewer

a	at	e	end	o	hot	u	up	hw	white		about
ā	ape	ē	me	ō	old	ū	use	ng	song		taken
ä	far	i	it	ô	fork	ü	rule	th	thin	ə	pencil
âr	care	ī	ice	oi	oil	ů	pull	th	this		lemon
		îr	pierce	ou	out	ûr	turn	zh	measure		circus

ex·act·i·tude (eg zak′ti tüd′, -tūd′, ig-) *n.* the quality of being exact; accuracy; precision.

ex·act·ly (eg zakt′lē, ig-) *adj.* **1.** in an exact manner; accurately; precisely: *Please follow my instructions exactly.* **2.** in every way; just; quite: *It happened exactly as you described it.*

exact science, a science, such as mathematics or physics, that theoretically allows exact analysis and prediction.

ex·ag·ger·ate (eg zaj′ə rāt′, ig-) *v.,* **-at·ed, -at·ing.** —*v.t.* **1.** to represent (something) as greater than it is; overstate: *to exaggerate the seriousness of a problem, to exaggerate a person's faults.* **2.** to make more noticeable or more important than usual; overemphasize: *The makeup exaggerates the color of your eyes.* —*v.i.* to represent a thing as greater than it is; overstate: *I exaggerated when describing the fish I had caught.* [Latin *exaggerātus,* past participle of *exaggerāre* to heap up, magnify, going back to *ex* out + *agger* heap.] —**ex·ag′ger·a′tor,** *n.*

ex·ag·ger·a·tion (eg zaj′ə rā′shən, ig-) *n.* **1.** the act of exaggerating or the state of being exaggerated. **2.** an instance of exaggerating; overstatement.

ex·alt (eg zôlt′, ig-) *v.t.* **1.** to praise; glorify; extol: *to exalt honesty above all other virtues.* **2.** to elevate, as in rank, character, or esteem. [Latin *exaltāre* to raise, from *ex* out + *altus* high.]

ex·al·ta·tion (eg′zôl tā′shən, ek′sôl-) *n.* **1.** the act of exalting or the state of being exalted. **2.** a feeling of great exhilaration; rapture; elation.

ex·alt·ed (eg zôl′tid) *adj.* **1.** high, as in rank, position, or character: *an exalted member of the medical profession.* **2.** noble, lofty, elevated, or sublime: *exalted prose.*

ex·am (eg zam′, ig-) *n. Informal.* examination.

ex·am·i·na·tion (eg zam′ə nā′shən, ig-) *n.* **1.** the act or process of examining or the state of being examined. **2.** a test, esp. of knowledge, skill, or qualifications. **3.** a medical checking and testing of the body or a part of it, as by a dentist or physician. **4.** an interrogation of a witness in a court of law for the purpose of eliciting any knowledge that the witness may have of the matter before the court.

ex·am·ine (eg zam′in, ig-) *v.t.,* **-ined, -in·ing. 1.** to look at closely and carefully; investigate; inspect; scrutinize: *to examine the merchandise before buying it.* **2.** to test, esp. in order to determine the knowledge, skill, or qualifications of: *to examine applicants for a job.* **3.** to subject (a person or body part) to medical checking and testing. **4.** to subject (a witness) to an examination in a court of law. [Old French *examiner* to question, test, from Latin *exāmināre* to weigh, test, from *exāmen* a weighing.] —**ex·am′in·er,** *n.*

> **Synonyms** **Examine, inspect,** and **scrutinize** mean to observe something carefully. **Examine** is applied broadly to informal as well as formal observations: *They examined the magazines in the waiting room. The doctor examined the patient for signs of arthritis.* **Inspect,** although it can be used generally, is often applied to a formal or technical process: *Workers inspect the product at several stages of manufacture.* **Scrutinize** stresses close attention to detail: *The immigration officer scrutinized my passport.*

ex·am·i·nee (eg zam′ə nē′, ig-) *n.* a person who is being examined or is a candidate for an examination.

ex·am·ple (eg zam′pəl, ig-) *n.* **1.** a particular thing that belongs to a group of things and represents what the others are like; sample; illustration: *The instructor gave us several examples of the artist's work.* **2.** a person or thing that is worthy of imitation; model: *That student's study habits are a good example for others to follow.* **3.** a problem or exercise used to illustrate a rule, method, or process, as in arithmetic. **4.** an instance or object, as of punishment, used to serve as a warning or deterrent to others: *The judge made an example of the criminal by imposing a harsh sentence.* [Old French *essample, example* illustration, pattern, from Latin *exemplum* sample, pattern.]

· **for example.** by way of illustration.

· **to set an example.** to act so as to inspire imitation; serve as a model for others.

· **without example.** without equal or precedent.

> **Synonyms** **Example, specimen,** and **sample** denote something that displays at least some of the qualities of a larger body, group, or system from which it is drawn. An **example** is something held up as typical: *examples of a composer's early pieces, examples of how leaves change color in the fall.* A **specimen** is a unit separated from a whole for purposes of examination: *a urine specimen, a handwriting specimen.* A **sample** is some part or piece of a larger body from which characteristics of the larger body may be inferred: *The people interviewed were chosen as a representative sample of the population.*

ex·as·per·ate (eg zas′pə rāt′, ig-) *v.t.,* **-at·ed, -at·ing.** to irritate greatly; provoke to anger; infuriate: *Your constant interruptions exasperate me.* [Latin *exasperātus,* past participle of *exasperāre* to make rough, provoke, going back to *ex* utterly + *asper* rough.] —**ex·as′per·at′ing·ly,** *adv.*

ex·as·per·a·tion (eg zas′pə rā′shən, ig-) *n.* the act of exasperating or the state of being exasperated.

Exc., Excellency.

Ex·cal·i·bur (eks kal′ə bər) *n.* in Arthurian legend, the sword of King Arthur. [Old French *Escalibor,* from Medieval Latin *Caliburnus,* possibly from Irish *Caladbolg* literally, hard belly, name of a sword famous in Irish folklore.]

ex ca·the·dra (eks′kə thē′drə, kath′i-) from the seat of authority. ➡ used esp. in referring to pronouncements from the pope. [Latin *ex cathedrā* literally, from the chair.]

ex·ca·vate (eks′kə vāt′) *v.t.,* **-vat·ed, -vat·ing. 1.** to remove by digging: *to excavate earth.* **2.** to uncover by digging; unearth: *to excavate an ancient burial site.* **3.** to make by hollowing out; dig: *to excavate a tunnel.* **4.** to make a hole in; hollow out: *The workers excavated the mountainside for a tunnel.* [Latin *excavātus,* past participle of *excavāre* to hollow out, from *ex* out + *cavus* hollow.]

ex·ca·va·tion (eks′kə vā′shən) *n.* **1.** the act or process of excavating. **2.** a hole made by excavating: *A new building will go up at the site of that excavation.* **3.** something uncovered by excavating, such as ruins.

an **excavation** in Saudi Arabia

ex·ca·va·tor (eks′kə vā′tər) *n.* a person or thing that excavates, esp. a machine used for digging, such as a power shovel.

ex·ceed (ek sēd′, ik-) *v.t.* **1.** to go beyond the limits of: *to exceed one's authority.* **2.a.** to go beyond in quantity, degree, or rate: *to exceed the speed limit.* **b.** to be greater than or superior to; surpass; excel: *Your knowledge of history exceeds mine.* [Old French *exceder,* from Latin *excēdere* to go beyond, surpass.] —For Synonyms, see **excel.**

ex·ceed·ing (ek sē′ding, ik-) *adj.* unusually great; surpassing. —*adv. Archaic.* exceedingly.

ex·ceed·ing·ly (ek sē′ding lē, ik-) *adv.* to a great degree; very; unusually.

ex·cel (ek sel′, ik-) *v.,* **-celled, -cel·ling.** —*v.t.* to be better or greater than, as in ability or quality; surpass; outdo. —*v.i.* to be superior to others; surpass others: *to excel in music and art.* [Latin *excellere.*]

> **Synonyms** *v.t.* **Excel, exceed, surpass,** and **outdo** mean to do better or more than someone or something else. **Excel** connotes greater accomplishment or performance: *to excel someone in debating.* **Exceed** connotes going beyond a limit: *to exceed the speed limit, to exceed a quota.* **Surpass** implies the existence of a criterion of some kind: *to surpass expectations.* **Outdo** is a general term for going beyond the expected and may imply competition or emulation: *Out of a desire to outdo their neighbors, they spent a fortune renovating their house.*

ex·cel·lence (ek′sə ləns) *n.* **1.** the fact or condition of excelling; superiority, as in quality, ability, or worth. **2.** a way or area in which a person or thing excels. **3. Excellence.** excellency *(def. 2).*

ex·cel·len·cy (ek′sə lən sē) *n., pl.* **-cies. 1.** excellence *(defs. 1, 2).* **2. Excellency.** a title of honor used in referring to or addressing certain dignitaries, such as governors or ambassadors. ➡ often preceded by *His, Her,* or *Your.*

ex·cel·lent (ek′sə lənt) *adj.* remarkably good; superior; exceptional. [Latin *excellēns,* present participle of *excellere* to surpass.] —**ex′cel·lent·ly,** *adv.*

ex·cel·si·or (ek sel'sē ər, ik-) *n.* fine shavings, as of wood or paper, used as a packing material or for stuffing.

ex·cept (ek sept', ik-) *prep.* with the exception of; not including; but; excluding: *All the boys went home except Jack.* —*conj.* **1.** only; but: *I would go with you, except that I have to work that day.* **2.** *Archaic.* unless. —*v.t.* to leave out; omit; exclude: *Certain people were excepted from the invitation.* —*v.i.* to object (often with *to*): *to except to a statement.* [Latin *exceptus,* past participle of *excipere* to take out.]
   · **except for.** were it not for; but for.

ex·cept·ing (ek sep'ting, ik-) *prep.* except. —*conj. Archaic.* unless.

ex·cep·tion (ek sep'shən, ik-) *n.* **1.** the act of excepting or the state of being excepted. **2.** a person or thing that differs or is excluded, as from a general class or rule. **3.** an objection; complaint. **4.** a formal objection to a ruling of a court during the course of a trial.
   · **to take exception to. a.** to raise an objection to; protest: *to take exception to an unfair rule.* **b.** to feel resentful or displeased about: *to take exception to an insulting remark about one's work.*

ex·cep·tion·a·ble (ek sep'shə nə bəl, ik-) *adj.* liable to objection. —**ex·cep'tion·a·bly,** *adv.*

ex·cep·tion·al (ek sep'shə nəl, ik-) *adj.* out of the ordinary; unusual; extraordinary: *exceptional talent, an exceptional student.* —**ex·cep'tion·al·ly,** *adv.* —For Synonyms, see **extraordinary.**

ex·cerpt (*n.,* ek'sûrpt; *v.,* ek sûrpt', ik-) *n.* a passage or scene selected from a larger work; extract: *excerpts from a poem, excerpts from a film.* —*v.t.* to take out a passage or scene from; extract; quote: *to excerpt a novel.* [Latin *excerptum* extract, from *excerpere* to select.]

ex·cess (ek'ses, ek ses', ik-) *n.* **1.** an amount greater than needed or desired; more than enough; superfluity: *an excess of money.* **2.** the amount or degree by which one thing exceeds another: *We spent an excess of ten dollars over our budget.* **3.** an action or behavior that goes beyond what is usual, proper, just, or necessary. **4.** a lack of moderation, as in eating or drinking; intemperance. —*adj.* being more than what is usual or required; extra: *excess baggage, excess detail.* [Old French *exces* superfluity, from Latin *excessus* departure, deviation.]
   · **in excess of.** greater or more than: *Our bank balance is in excess of $5,000.*
   · **to excess.** too much: *to eat to excess.*

ex·ces·sive (ek ses'iv, ik-) *adj.* beyond what is necessary, usual, just, or proper; immoderate: *excessive noise, excessive force.* —**ex·ces'sive·ly,** *adv.* —**ex·ces'sive·ness,** *n.*

> **Synonyms** **Excessive, immoderate, inordinate,** and **intemperate** mean going beyond what is proper or normal. **Excessive** suggests an amount or quantity greater than what is required or acceptable: *excessive noise, excessive summer rain.* **Immoderate** connotes failing to adhere to a reasonable standard: *The opposition reacted to the speech with immoderate displays of laughter.* **Inordinate** suggests a lack of judgment or regulation: *His inordinate haste was responsible for the accident.* **Intemperate** suggests a loss of control: *Her intemperate eating and drinking may have contributed to the deterioration of her health.*

ex·cess-prof·its tax (ek'ses prof'its) a tax on business profits above a certain average defined as normal for a specified period of years, usually applied in time of war or high defense spending.

ex·change (eks chānj', iks-) *v.,* **-changed, -chang·ing.** —*v.t.* **1.** to give and receive (similar things); reciprocate; interchange: *to exchange gifts, to exchange marriage vows, to exchange ambassadors.* **2.** to part with in return for something regarded as equivalent; trade: *to exchange dollars for francs.* **3.** to give up for something in return: *to exchange a life of ease for one of hard labor.* **4.** to return (a purchase) for something else: *to exchange a blouse for another of a smaller size.* —*v.i.* **1.** to make a trade; replace one thing for another. **2.** to be received as an equivalent: *For many years the British pound exchanged for about five U.S. dollars.* —*n.* **1.** the act of giving or receiving similar things; mutual transfer: *an exchange of prisoners of war.* **2.** the act of giving one thing in return for something regarded as equivalent: *the exchange of a purchase for credit.* **3.** the substitution of one thing or state for another. **4.** something given or received in return for something else. **5.** a place where things, as commodities or securities, are bought, sold, or traded: *a jewelry exchange.* **6.** a central office, station, or system where groups of telephone lines are connected, providing communication in a town or part of a large city. **7.a.** a system of settling financial accounts by using negotiable instruments, as bills of exchange or drafts, instead of money. **b.** bill of exchange. **8.** the conversion or transfer of money of one country into its equivalent in money of another country. **9.** exchange rate. **10. exchanges.** negotiable instruments, as checks or drafts, presented for collection through a clearinghouse. [Old French *eschangier* to give and receive reciprocally, barter, going back to Late Latin *ex* out + *cambiāre* to barter, change (probably of Celtic origin).]

ex·change·a·ble (eks chān'jə bəl, iks-) *adj.* capable of being exchanged. —**ex·change'a·bil'i·ty,** *n.*

exchange rate, the rate at which the money of one country can be exchanged for that of another; price of one currency in terms of another currency.

exchange student, a high school or university student from one country who attends school in another country as part of a special program organized by an international agency, the participating countries, or the participating schools.

ex·cheq·uer (eks chek'ər, iks-, eks'chek-) *n.* **1.** a royal or national treasury. **2.** any treasury, as of an organization. **3. Exchequer. a.** the department of the British government that manages the national finances, including the collection and spending of the public revenue. **b.** the contents of the Exchequer. [Old French *eschequier* chessboard, counting table (so called because the English king's accounts were once reckoned with counters on a checkered cloth resembling a chessboard), from *eschec* a check (at chess). See CHECK.]

ex·ci·mer (ek'sə mər) *n.* a chemical compound formed by the union of molecules in an excited state. When such molecules disassociate, they lase, emitting coherent pulses of ultraviolet radiation. [EXCI(TED DI)MER(IC MOLECULE).]

ex·cise[1] (ek'sīz, -sīs) *n.* an indirect tax levied on the manufacture, sale, or use of certain commodities within a country, such as liquor, tobacco, or gasoline. Also, **excise tax.** [Modification (influenced by EXCISE[2]) of earlier *acise,* from Middle Dutch *accijs,* from *asijs,* from Old French *aceis* tax, from Latin *ad* to + *cēnsus* register of citizens, tax, property.]

ex·cise[2] (ek sīz', ik-) *v.t.,* **-cised, -cis·ing.** to remove by or as by cutting: *to excise a tumor, to excise a paragraph from an essay.* [Latin *excīsus,* past participle of *excīdere* to cut out, from *ex-* out + *caedere* to cut.] —**ex·ci·sion** (ek sizh'ən, ik-), *n.*

ex·cise·man (ek'sīz mən) *n., pl.* **-men** (-mən). an official of the British government who collects excises and enforces the laws relating to them.

ex·cit·a·ble (ek sī'tə bəl, ik-) *adj.* **1.** easily excited. **2.** (of an organ or organism) capable of reacting to a stimulus. —**ex·cit'a·bil'i·ty, ex·cit'a·ble·ness,** *n.* —**ex·cit'a·bly,** *adv.*

ex·ci·ta·tion (ek'sī tā'shən) *n.* **1.** the act of exciting or the state of being excited. **2.** the production of a magnetic field by electricity, as in an electric generator. **3.** the effect of a stimulus on an organ or organism.

ex·cite (ek sīt', ik-) *v.t.,* **-cit·ed, -cit·ing. 1.** to stimulate the mind or emotions of: *The idea of a picnic excited the children. The inflammatory speech excited the mob.* **2.** to call forth; evoke: *to excite fear, to excite a person's curiosity.* **3.a.** to move to action; put in motion: *The loud noise excited the dogs.* **b.** to increase the activity of (an organ or organism); stimulate. **4.** to raise (an atom, molecule, or other particle) to a higher energy level. **5.** to produce a magnetic field in: *to excite an electric generator.* [Latin *excitāre* to call out, rouse, stir up.]

ex·cit·ed (ek sī'tid, ik-) *adj.* **1.** moved to action or activity; stirred up; aroused; agitated. **2.** (of an atom, molecule, or other particle) at a higher energy level than previously. —**ex·cit'ed·ly,** *adv.*

ex·cite·ment (ek sīt'mənt, ik-) *n.* **1.** the act of exciting or the state of being excited. **2.** something that excites.

ex·cit·er (ek sī'tər, ik-) *also,* **ex·ci·tor.** *n.* **1.** a person or thing that excites. **2.** an electric generator or battery that supplies current to produce a magnetic field in an electric motor or generator.

ex·cit·ing (ek sī'ting, ik-) *adj.* causing excitement; stirring; thrilling. —**ex·cit'ing·ly,** *adv.*

ex·ci·ton (ek sī'ton) *n.* a quantum of electrical excitation that transmits energy but not charge. In a semiconductor, an exciton results from the pairing of an electron and a hole. [Possibly from EXCIT(ATION) + -ON or EXCIT(ED) + -ON.]

a	at	e	end	o	hot	u	up	hw	white		about
ā	ape	ē	me	ō	old	ū	use	ng	song		taken
ä	far	i	it	ô	fork	ü	rule	th	thin	ə	pencil
âr	care	ī	ice	oi	oil	u̇	pull	th	this		lemon
		îr	pierce	ou	out	ûr	turn	zh	measure		circus

427

ex·claim (ek sklām′, ik-) *v.t., v.i.* to speak or cry out suddenly or vehemently, as in anger or surprise. [Latin *exclāmāre.*] —**ex·claim′er**, *n.*

ex·cla·ma·tion (ek′sklə mā′shən) *n.* **1.** the act of exclaiming. **2.** something that is exclaimed; sudden or vehement utterance.

exclamation point, a punctuation mark (!) used after a word, phrase, or sentence to indicate an exclamation, as of surprise or anger. Also, **exclamation mark.**

ex·clam·a·to·ry (ek sklam′ə tôr′ē, ik-) *adj.* using, containing, or expressing exclamation.

ex·clude (ek sklüd′, ik-) *v.t.,* **-clud·ed, -clud·ing. 1.** to prevent from entering; shut or keep out: *All those under twenty years of age were excluded from the club.* **2.** to not consider or include; leave out; omit: *The author excluded certain passages from the original book in the new edition.* **3.** to put out; expel; eject. [Latin *exclūdere* to shut out.]

ex·clu·sion (ek sklü′zhən, ik-) *n.* the act of excluding or the state of being excluded. [Latin *exclūsiō* a shutting out.]

ex·clu·sive (ek sklü′siv, ik-) *adj.* **1.** belonging to a single individual or group; not divided or shared: *exclusive rights, exclusive ownership.* **2.** open to or admitting only a certain select group, esp. as with regard to social standing or wealth: *an exclusive club.* **3.** given to or appearing in only one source: *an exclusive news item, an exclusive interview.* **4.** catering to a wealthy, famous, or socially prominent clientele: *an exclusive restaurant, an exclusive dress shop.* **5.** excluding another or others: *mutually exclusive concepts.* **6.** not divided or distracted; entire: *The matter will be given our exclusive attention.* **7.** leaving out; excluding (with *of*): *The price is fifty dollars, exclusive of the sales tax.* —**ex·clu′sive·ly,** *adv.* —**ex·clu′sive·ness,** *n.*

ex·clu·siv·i·ty (ek′sklü siv′i tē) *n.* **1.** the quality of being exclusive, esp. of being available to only one or a few: *Exclusivity in dress design is important in the world of fashion.* **2.** exclusive rights, as of use or reproduction: *Publishers usually have exclusivity over the books they sell.*

ex·com·mu·ni·cate (*v.,* eks′kə mū′ni kāt′; *n.,* eks′kə mū′ni kit) *v.t.,* **-cat·ed, -cat·ing.** to expel from membership in a church by ecclesiastical authority; deny (a person) the right to participate in the services of or receive the benefits of a church. —*n.* a person who has been excommunicated. [Church Latin *excommūnicātus,* past participle of *excommūnicāre* to expel from membership in a church, going back to Latin *ex* out of + *commūnis* general.]

ex·com·mu·ni·ca·tion (eks′kə mū′ni kā′shən) *n.* **1.** the act of excommunicating or the state of being excommunicated. **2.** an ecclesiastical pronouncement by which a person is excommunicated.

ex·co·ri·ate (ek skôr′ē āt′, ik-) *v.t.,* **-at·ed, -at·ing. 1.** to strip off or abrade the skin of. **2.** to reprove scathingly; censure; berate: *The judge excoriated the murderer during sentencing.* [Latin *excoriātus,* past participle of *excoriāre* to strip of its skin, from *ex* from + *corium* skin.] —**ex·co′ri·a′tion,** *n.*

ex·cre·ment (ek′skrə mənt) *n.* waste matter discharged from the body, esp. from the bowels; feces. [Latin *excrēmentum* refuse.] —**ex′cre·men′tal,** *adj.*

ex·cres·cence (ek skres′əns, ik-) *n.* **1.** any abnormal or disfiguring outgrowth or addition, as a wart or mole. **2.** a normal outgrowth, as hair or fingernails.

ex·cres·cent (ek skres′ənt, ik-) *adj.* forming an abnormal or superfluous outgrowth or addition. [Latin *excrēscēns,* past participle of *excrēscere* to grow out.]

ex·cre·ta (ek skrē′tə, ik-) *pl. n.* waste matter discharged from the body, such as sweat or urine. [Latin *excrēta* literally, things sifted out, neuter plural of *excrētus.* See EXCRETE.] —**ex·cre′tal,** *adj.*

ex·crete (ek skrēt′, ik-) *v.t.,* **-cret·ed, -cret·ing.** to discharge (waste matter) from the body; separate (waste products) from the blood or tissues: *The kidneys excrete the waste products of metabolism.* [Latin *excrētus,* past participle of *excernere* to sift out.]

ex·cre·tion (ek skrē′shən, ik-) *n.* **1.** the act of excreting. **2.** matter excreted, such as sweat or urine.

ex·cre·to·ry (ek′skri tôr′ē) *adj.* of, relating to, or for excretion: *an excretory duct.* Also, **ex·cre·tive** (ek skrē′tiv).

ex·cru·ci·ate (ek skrü′shē āt′, ik-) *v.t.,* **-at·ed, -at·ing. 1.** to cause severe pain to; torture. **2.** to subject to mental distress; torment. [Latin *excruciātus,* past participle of *excruciāre* to torture, going back to *ex* utterly + *crux* cross.] —**ex·cru′ci·a′tion,** *n.*

ex·cru·ci·at·ing (ek skrü′shē ā′ting, ik-) *adj.* causing extreme pain or suffering; agonizing; torturous. —**ex·cru′ci·at′ing·ly,** *adv.*

ex·cul·pate (ek′skul pāt′, ek skul′pāt, ik-) *v.t.,* **-pat·ed, -pat-**

ing. to declare free from blame or guilt; exonerate. [Ex-[1] + Latin *culpātus,* past participle of *culpāre* to blame.] —**ex′cul·pa′-tion,** *n.*

ex·cur·rent (ek skûr′ənt, -skur′-) *adj.* **1.** *Botany.* **a.** having a prolonged axis, forming an undivided main stem or trunk, as many conifers. **b.** projecting or extending beyond an apex or margin, as the midrib in certain leaves. **2.** *Zoology.* characterized by a current that flows outward, as certain channels in sponges. [Latin *excurrens,* present participle of *excurrere* to run out, project, from *ex* out + *currere* to run.]

ex·cur·sion (ek skûr′zhən, -shən, ik-) *n.* **1.** a short trip made esp. for pleasure or a special purpose: *The class went on an excursion to the museum.* **2.** a round trip on a train, ship, or other public conveyance, offered at reduced rates: *We took the weekend excursion to the seashore.* **3.** a group of people taking such a trip. [Latin *excursiō* a running out.]

ex·cur·sion·ist (ek skûr′zhə nist, -shə-, ik-) *n.* a person who goes on an excursion.

ex·cur·sive (ek skûr′siv, ik-) *adj.* tending to wander off a subject; rambling; digressive. —**ex·cur′sive·ly,** *adv.* —**ex·cur′sive·ness,** *n.*

ex·cus·a·ble (ek skū′zə bəl, ik-) *adj.* capable of being forgiven; pardonable: *an excusable error.* —**ex·cus′a·bly,** *adv.*

ex·cuse (*v.,* ek skūz′, ik-; *n.,* ek skūs′, ik-) *v.t.,* **-cused, -cus·ing. 1.** to grant pardon or forgiveness to: *Please excuse me for inconveniencing you.* **2.** to release or exempt, as from duty, obligation, or attendance: *The judge excused the jury. I was excused from class to go to the doctor.* **3.** to accept as understandable or regard with indulgence; disregard; overlook: *Knowing how upset she was, we excused her rudeness.* **4.** to serve as a reason or explanation for; justify: *Ignorance does not excuse disobedience of the law.* —*n.* **1.a.** a reason given in explanation: *Their excuse for missing the meeting was that they were exhausted.* **b.** a reasonable or acceptable explanation; justification: *Oversleeping is no excuse for being late.* **2.** something that offers an explanation: *a written excuse.* **3.** the act of excusing. **4.** *Informal.* an example; sample; specimen (with *for*): *That's a poor excuse for a sailboat.* [Old French *excuser* to cancel, exclude, seek to free from, from Latin *excūsāre* to free from blame, from *ex* from + *causa* lawsuit, cause.] —**ex·cus′er,** *n.*

·to excuse oneself. a. to make an apology for oneself: *I excused myself for being late.* **b.** to ask to be released, as from attendance or duty.

Synonyms *v.t.* **Excuse, pardon, forgive,** and **condone** mean to overlook an offense or not to exact punishment or redress. **Excuse** mainly applies to minor misdeeds like social errors: *to excuse someone for keeping you waiting.* **Pardon** connotes freeing from punishment, often for a relatively serious offense: *to pardon a criminal, to pardon sins.* **Forgive** is less formal than *pardon,* suggesting personal willingness to overlook something: *to forgive a friend's rudeness.* **Condone** connotes tolerating or failing to protest an infraction or violation: *By not speaking up, you are condoning their selfish behavior.*

exec. 1. executive. **2.** executor.

ex·e·cra·ble (ek′si krə bəl) *adj.* **1.** deserving of disgust or hatred; abominable; detestable. **2.** of inferior quality; very bad. —**ex′e·cra·ble·ness,** *n.* —**ex′e·cra·bly,** *adv.*

ex·e·crate (ek′si krāt′) *v.,* **-crat·ed, -crat·ing.** —*v.t.* **1.** to call down evil upon; curse. **2.** to condemn scathingly. **3.** to have disgust or hatred for; abhor; loathe. —*v.i.* to utter curses; swear. [Latin *ex(s)ecrātus,* past participle of *ex(s)ecrārī* to curse.]

ex·e·cra·tion (ek′si krā′shən) *n.* **1.** the act of cursing or condemning. **2.** an expression of abomination; curse. **3.** utter hatred; abhorrence; loathing. **4.** a person or thing that is execrated.

ex·e·cute (ek′si kūt′) *v.t.,* **-cut·ed, -cut·ing. 1.** to carry out; fulfill: *to execute a command, to execute a plan.* **2.** to put into effect, as a law; administer; enforce. **3.** to put to death in accordance with a legal sentence. **4.** to produce, esp. in accordance with a plan or design: *to execute a sculpture.* **5.** to perform or play, as a piece of music: *The pianist executed the sonata with feeling.* **6.** to carry out or make valid, as a will, deed, or contract, by doing whatever is legally required. [Old French *executer* to carry out, kill, from *executeur* one who carries out, from Late Latin *ex-(s)ecūtor,* from Latin *ex(s)equī* to follow up, pursue.] —For Synonyms, see **perform.**

ex·e·cu·tion (ek′si kū′shən) *n.* **1.** a carrying out or putting into effect: *the execution of a plan.* **2.** the carrying out of a death sentence. **3.** performance or production, as of a work of art or piece of music. **4.** a method or technique used in producing or performing something, such as a work of art or piece of music. **5.** a carrying out or making valid by doing whatever is legally

required. **6.** a court document directing that a judgment be put into effect.

ex·e·cu·tion·er (ek′si kū′shə nər) *n.* a person who carries out a legally imposed death sentence.

ex·ec·u·tive (eg zek′yə tiv, ig-) *adj.* **1.** of, relating to, or suitable for the management of affairs, as in business or industry: *executive talents, an executive position.* **2.** concerned with the administration and enforcement of laws or the affairs of government: *the executive branch of government.* —*n.* **1.** a person who directs or manages affairs, as of a corporation: *a meeting of a company's senior executives.* **2.a.** the branch of government responsible for enforcing the laws and managing the affairs of a state or nation. **b.** a person or persons constituting this branch of government.

Executive Mansion 1. White House *(def. 1).* **2.** the official residence of the governor of a state.

executive officer, an officer who is second in command of a military or naval unit.

executive session, a meeting of a legislative body or its leaders, esp. one that is closed to the public.

ex·ec·u·tor (eg zek′yə tər, ig-; *def. 2, also* ek′si kū′tər) *n.* **1.** a person named in a will to carry out its provisions. **2.** a person who carries out something or puts something into effect. [Old French *executeur* one who carries out. See EXECUTE.]

ex·ec·u·trix (eg zek′yə triks′, ig-) *n., pl.* **ex·ec·u·tri·ces** (eg-zek′yə trī′sēz, ig-) or **ex·ec·u·trix·es.** a woman named in a will to carry out its provisions.

ex·e·ge·sis (ek′si jē′sis) *n., pl.* **-ses** (-sēz) a critical analysis or interpretation of a word, sentence, or passage, esp. of the Bible. [Greek *exēgēsis* interpretation.]

ex·e·get·ic (ek′si jet′ik) *adj.* of or relating to exegesis; expository; explanatory. Also, **ex′e·get′i·cal.**

ex·em·plar (eg zem′plər, -plär, ig-) *n.* **1.** a person or thing that is worthy of imitation; model; archetype. **2.** a typical example or instance. [Old French *exemplaire* sample, pattern, going back to Latin *exemplum.*]

ex·em·pla·ry (eg zem′plə rē, ig-, eg′zəm pler′ē) *adj.* **1.** serving as a model; worthy of imitation; commendable: *exemplary conduct.* **2.** serving as a warning: *exemplary punishment.* **3.** serving as a typical example or instance; illustrative. [Late Latin *exemplāris* that serves as a pattern, from Latin *exemplum* sample, pattern.]

ex·em·pli·fi·ca·tion (eg zem′plə fi kā′shən, ig-) *n.* **1.** the act of exemplifying. **2.** something that exemplifies; illustration; example.

ex·em·pli·fy (eg zem′plə fī′, ig-) *v.t.,* **-fied, -fy·ing.** to serve as an example of; show by example. [Medieval Latin *exemplificāre* to copy out, from Latin *exemplum* pattern, sample + *facere* to make.]

ex·em·pli gra·ti·a (eg zem′plī grā′shē ə, ig-) *Latin.* for (the sake of) example; for instance.

ex·empt (eg zempt′, ig-) *v.t.* to free from a duty or obligation to which others are subject; excuse: *The teacher exempted the absent students from the test.* —*adj.* not subject to something, as a duty or obligation; excused: *Much church property is exempt from real estate taxes.* [Latin *exemptus,* past participle of *eximere* to take out, free.]

ex·emp·tion (eg zemp′shən, ig-) *n.* **1.** the act of exempting or the state or privilege of being exempted. **2.a.** a deduction from taxable income allowed for oneself and for each of one's dependents. **b.** oneself or one of one's dependents, used as a basis for such a deduction: *to list three exemptions.*

Synonyms **Exemption** and **immunity** denote freedom from some obligation or burden, esp. a legal one. An **exemption** frees one from a duty or burden imposed on others in a similar situation: *an exemption from local taxes, an exemption from military service.* **Immunity** is broader, implying membership in a class or group that is protected or privileged: *the immunity of the elderly from performing jury duty, the immunity from prosecution conferred on certain witnesses.*

ex·er·cise (ek′sər sīz′) *n.* **1.** physical activity performed for the training or improvement of the body: *Walking is good exercise.* **2.** an activity or lesson designed or performed for practice, improvement, or development: *a piano exercise, exercises in mathematics.* **3.** active use or performance: *the exercise of patience, the exercise of power.* **4.** usually, **exercises.** a ceremony, program, or proceedings: *The graduation exercises consisted of speeches and the presentation of awards.* —*v.,* **-cised, -cis·ing.** —*v.t.* **1.** to train or improve by means of exercise: *to exercise the body, to exercise a horse.* **2.** to make active use of; employ: *to exercise one's strength, to exercise one's constitutional rights.* **3.** to perform or fulfill, as functions or duties: *to exercise the duties of governor.* **4.** to bring to bear; exert: *to exercise influence.* **5.a.** to occupy the

attention of. **b.** to make uneasy; worry; trouble: *We were very exercised about our mounting debts.* —*v.i.* to perform exercises: *The athlete exercises in the gymnasium three times a week.* [Old French *exercice* training, practice, from Latin *exercitium* physical exercise.] —**ex′er·cis′a·ble,** *adj.* —For Synonyms *(n.),* see **practice.**

ex·er·cis·er (ek′sər sī′zər) *n.* **1.** a person who exercises. **2.** an apparatus used for exercising the body.

ex·ert (eg zûrt′, ig-) *v.t.* to employ actively or put forth: *to exert power, to exert one's influence.* [Latin *ex(s)ertus,* past participle of *ex(s)erere* to stretch or thrust out.]

·**to exert oneself.** to put forth great effort; try hard.

ex·er·tion (eg zûr′shən, ig-) *n.* **1.** vigorous use of energy; strenuous effort: *Climbing a mountain involves great physical exertion.* **2.** the act or process of putting forth or into action: *The problem demanded the exertion of considerable thought.* —For Synonyms, see **effort.**

ex·e·unt (ek′sē ənt) *Latin.* they go out. ▶ used as a stage direction to indicate that the two or more actors specified are to leave the stage.

ex·fo·li·ate (eks fō′lē āt′) *v.t., v.i.,* **-at·ed, -at·ing. 1.** to remove or shed in layers, flakes, or scales, as skin or bark. **2.** *Geology.* to cast off or come off in scales or sheets, as weathered rock. —**ex·fo′li·a′tion,** *n.* —**ex·fo′li·a′tive,** *adj.*

ex·ha·la·tion (eks′hə lā′shən, ek′sə-) *n.* **1.** the act or process of exhaling. **2.** something exhaled, as air or an odor.

ex·hale (eks hāl′, ek sāl′) *v.,* **-haled, -hal·ing.** —*v.t.* **1.** to expel (air) from the lungs. **2.** to give off or release, as vapor or an odor: *The stranger thoughtlessly exhaled smoke in my face.* **3.** to draw off in the form of vapor; evaporate. —*v.i.* **1.** to expel air from the lungs: *We inhale and exhale in breathing.* **2.** to be given off or rise as vapor. [Latin *exhālāre* to breathe out.]

ex·haust (eg zôst′, ig-) *v.t.* **1.** to make extremely weak or tired; deprive of strength or energy: *Working in the garden all day exhausted me.* **2.** to consume entirely: *to exhaust one's resources, to exhaust one's patience.* **3.** to empty completely by removing the contents of; drain: *to exhaust a reservoir.* **4.** to study, develop, or treat thoroughly: *to exhaust a subject.* **5.** to draw out, as air or other gases, from or as from a container. **6.** to withdraw air or other gases from a scientific apparatus to produce a partial vacuum within the apparatus. —*v.i.* to escape or be emitted, as gases or steam. —*n.* **1.** an escape or discharge, as of used steam or gases from an engine cylinder. **2.** waste products, as steam or gases, that escape or are discharged. **3.** the means or passage, such as a pipe or manifold, by which such waste products escape or are discharged. **4.** air or other gases withdrawn from a room by a fan. [Latin *exhaustus,* past participle of *exhaurīre* to draw out.] —**ex·haust′ed·ly,** *adv.* —**ex·haust′i·bil′i·ty,** *n.* —**ex·haust′i·ble,** *adj.* —For Synonyms *(v.t.),* see **deplete.**

ex·haus·tion (eg zôs′chən, ig-) *n.* **1.** the act or process of exhausting or the state of being exhausted. **2.** a lack of strength or energy; extreme fatigue.

ex·haus·tive (eg zôs′tiv, ig-) *adj.* overlooking or omitting nothing; thorough; comprehensive: *an exhaustive survey, an exhaustive study.* —**ex·haus′tive·ly,** *adv.* —**ex·haus′tive·ness,** *n.*

ex·haust·less (eg zôst′lis, ig-) *adj.* incapable of being exhausted; inexhaustible. —**ex·haust′less·ly,** *adv.* —**ex·haust′less·ness,** *n.*

ex·hib·it (eg zib′it, ig-) *v.t.* **1.** to put on public display; show publicly: *to exhibit paintings.* **2.** to make evident; reveal: *to exhibit a talent, to exhibit bravery, to exhibit emotion.* **3.** to submit (something) to a court or judicial officer as evidence. —*v.i.* to put something on public display; give an exhibition: *Two new artists are exhibiting at the gallery.* —*n.* **1.** a public display; show: *an exhibit of sculpture.* **2.** an object or collection of objects displayed publicly. **3.** a document or object submitted to a court or judicial officer as evidence. [Latin *exhibitus,* past participle of *exhibēre* to hold forth, display.] —For Synonyms *(n.),* see **show.**

ex·hib·it·er (eg zib′i tər, ig-) *n.* exhibitor.

ex·hi·bi·tion (ek′sə bish′ən) *n.* **1.** the act of exhibiting: *an exhibition of bravery.* **2.** a public display or presentation: *a skiing exhibition, an automobile exhibition.* —For Synonyms, see **show.**

ex·hi·bi·tion·ism (ek′sə bish′ə niz′əm) *n.* **1.** the act or practice of attracting attention to oneself intentionally. **2.** a compulsive tendency to expose the sex organs publicly for sexual pleasure or excitement.

a	at	e	end	o	hot	u	up	hw	white		about
ā	ape	ē	me	ō	old	ū	use	ng	song		taken
ä	far	i	it	ô	fork	th	thin	ə	pencil
âr	care	ī	ice	oi	oil	u̇	pull	th	this		lemon
		îr	pierce	ou	out	ûr	turn	zh	measure		circus

429

ex·hi·bi·tion·ist (ek′sə bish′ə nist) *n.* a person who engages in exhibitionism. —**ex′hi·bi′tion·is′tic,** *adj.*

ex·hib·i·tor (eg zib′i tər, ig-) *also,* **exhibiter.** *n.* a person or organization that exhibits or presents an exhibition.

ex·hil·a·rate (eg zil′ə rāt′, ig-) *v.t.,* **-rat·ed, -rat·ing.** to make cheerful, lively, or excited; enliven; invigorate. [Latin *exhilarātus,* past participle of *exhilarāre* to gladden, going back to *ex* utterly + Greek *hilaros* gay.] —**ex·hil′a·rat′ing·ly,** *adv.* —**ex·hil′a·ra′tive,** *adj.*

ex·hil·a·ra·tion (eg zil′ə rā′shən, ig-) *n.* **1.** an exhilarated feeling or condition. **2.** the act of exhilarating.

ex·hort (eg zôrt′, ig-) *v.t.* to try to persuade by appeal, argument, or warning; urge strongly: *The first mate exhorted the crew to mutiny.* —*v.i.* to give advice or warning. [Latin *exhortārī* to encourage, stimulate.] —**ex·hort′er,** *n.* —For Synonyms, see **urge.**

ex·hor·ta·tion (eg′zôr tā′shən, ek′sôr-) *n.* **1.** the act of exhorting. **2.** something that exhorts or is intended to exhort, as a sermon or appeal.

ex·hor·ta·tive (eg zôr′tə tiv, ig-) *adj.* serving or intended to exhort. Also, **ex·hor′ta·to′ry.**

ex·hu·ma·tion (eks′hū mā′shən, eg′zū-) *n.* the act of exhuming: *the exhumation of a corpse.*

ex·hume (eks hūm′, eg zūm′, -zūm′, ig-) *v.t.,* **-humed, -hum·ing. 1.** to remove (something buried, esp. a corpse) from the earth; dig up. **2.** to bring to light; disclose; reveal: *to exhume hidden facts, to exhume an ancient theory.* [Medieval Latin *exhumāre* to unearth, from Latin *ex* out of + *humus* ground.]

ex·i·gen·cy (ek′si jən sē) *n., pl.* **-cies. 1.** a situation or occurrence requiring prompt action or attention; emergency. **2.** a pressing demand or necessity; urgent need. ➡ usually used in the plural: *Many families were divided by the exigencies of war.* Also, **ex′i·gence.**

ex·i·gent (ek′si jənt) *adj.* **1.** requiring prompt action or attention; urgent; pressing. **2.** unusually or unreasonably demanding; exacting. [Latin *exigēns,* present participle of *exigere* to drive out, demand.] —**ex′i·gent·ly,** *adv.*

ex·ig·u·ous (eg zig′ū əs, ig-, ek sig′-, ik-) *adj.* scanty; diminutive; meager. [Latin *exiguus.*] —**ex·i·gu·i·ty** (ek′si gū′i tē), **ex·ig′u·ous·ness,** *n.* —**ex·ig′u·ous·ly,** *adv.*

ex·ile (eg′zīl, ek′sīl) *v.t.,* **-iled, -il·ing.** to expel (a person) from his or her country or home by law or decree: *The controversial writer was exiled for political reasons.* —*n.* **1.** expulsion or voluntary absence from one's country or home; state of being exiled: *Exile was the fate of many citizens after the revolution. The writer lived in exile for many years.* **2.** a person who is expelled from or voluntarily leaves his or her country or home; expatriate. **3. the Exile.** the captivity of the Jews in Babylon during the sixth century B.C. [Old French *exil* banishment, from Latin *ex(s)ilium.*] —For Synonyms *(v.t.),* see **banish.**

ex·ist (eg zist′, ig-) *v.i.* **1.** to have reality; be real: *I do not believe that ghosts exist.* **2.** to continue to have being or life: *The prisoners could not exist on bread and water. Democracy could no longer exist under those conditions.* **3.** to be present or found; occur: *Outside of zoos, koalas exist only in Australia.* [Latin *ex(s)istere* to come forth, be.]

ex·ist·ence (eg zis′təns, ig-) *n.* **1.** the state or fact of existing. **2.** a condition or mode of existing; living; life: *a meager existence.* **3.** all that exists.

ex·ist·ent (eg zis′tənt, ig-) *adj.* **1.** now existing; present; extant: *the existent economic situation.* **2.** having existence; living: *The dodo is no longer existent.*

ex·is·ten·tial (eg′zis ten′shəl, ek′sis-) *adj.* **1.** of or relating to existentialism. **2.** of or involving the question of one's life or one's choices and their value and meaning. **3.** of or relating to existence: *Primitive peoples grappled daily with the existential problems of finding food and shelter.*

ex·is·ten·tial·ism (eg′zis ten′shə liz′əm, ek′sis-) *n.* the philosophical view that stresses concreteness and individuality in existing things and human experience. Religious proponents stress the individual's personal discovery of God, while the nonreligious emphasize the individual's self-determination through personal decisions and actions in an otherwise meaningless universe. —**ex′is·ten′tial·ist,** *adj., n.*

ex·it (eg′zit, ek′sit) *n.* **1.** a way out; egress: *We left by the rear exit.* **2.** the act of leaving; departure. **3.** the departure of a performer from the stage. —*v.i.* **1.** to go out; leave; depart: *They exited from the back door.* **2.** *Latin.* he or she goes out. ➡ used as a stage direction to indicate that the actor specified is to leave the stage. —*v.t.* to go away from; leave: *to exit a room.* [Partly from Latin *exitus* a going out; partly from Latin *exit* (he) goes out.]

exit poll, a poll of voters taken when they leave a voting place, esp. one taken by a news reporter.

ex li·bris (eks lī′bris, lē′-) **1.** from the library (of). ➡ used before the owner's name as an inscription in or on a book. **2.** bookplate. [Latin *ex librīs* from the books (of).]

exo- combining form outside; external: *exoskeleton.* [Greek *exō,* from *ex* out of.]

ex·o·bi·ol·o·gist (ek′sō bī ol′ə jist) *n.* an expert in exobiology.

ex·o·bi·ol·o·gy (ek′sō bī ol′ə jē) *n.* the branch of biology that deals with the effects of extraterrestrial environments on living organisms and with the search for extraterrestrial life.

ex·o·carp (ek′sə kärp′) *n.* epicarp. [Exo- + Greek *karpos* fruit.]

ex·o·crine (ek′sə krin, -krīn′) *adj.* **1.** producing external secretions, as sweat or saliva, discharged to an epithelial surface. **2.** of or relating to an exocrine gland or its secretion. —*n.* exocrine gland. ➡ distinguished from **endocrine.** [Exo- + Greek *krīnein* to separate.]

exocrine gland, a gland, such as a sweat gland, that produces external secretions that are discharged through a duct to an epithelial surface.

Exod., Exodus.

ex·o·dus (ek′sə dəs) *n.* **1.** a departure, esp. of a mass of people: *an exodus from the cities to the suburbs.* **2. the Exodus.** the departure of the Israelites from Egypt under the leadership of Moses. **3. Exodus.** the second book of the Old Testament, containing an account of this departure. [Latin *exodus* second book of the Old Testament, from Greek *exodos* a going out.]

ex of·fi·ci·o (eks′ ə fish′ē ō′) by virtue of or because of one's office or position: *A ship's captain may ex officio perform marriages on the high seas.* [Latin *ex* out of + *officiō,* ablative of *officium* office, duty.]

ex·og·a·my (ek sog′ə mē) *n.* marriage outside one's own tribe, class, or group in accordance with custom or law. ➡ distinguished from **endogamy.** [Exo- + -GAMY.] —**ex·og′a·mous,** *adj.*

ex·og·e·nous (ek soj′ə nəs) *adj. Biology, Geology.* having an external origin; due to external causes. ➡ distinguished from **endogenous.** [Exo- + -GEN + -OUS.]

ex·on·er·ate (eg zon′ə rāt′, ig-) *v.t.,* **-at·ed, -at·ing.** to free from blame or guilt; prove or declare innocent; exculpate: *The accused was fully exonerated by the new evidence.* [Latin *exonerātus,* past participle of *exonerāre* to free from a burden, from *ex* from + *onus* burden.] —**ex·on′er·a′tion,** *n.* —**ex·on′er·a′tive,** *adj.* —For Synonyms, see **absolve.**

ex·or·bi·tance (eg zôr′bi təns, ig-) *n.* a going beyond what is proper, reasonable, or usual, as in price or demand. Also, **ex·or′bi·tan·cy.**

ex·or·bi·tant (eg zôr′bi tənt, ig-) *adj.* going beyond what is proper, reasonable, or usual; excessive: *exorbitant prices, exorbitant demands.* [Late Latin *exorbitāns,* present participle of *exorbitāre* to go out of the track, from *ex* out of + *orbita* track.] —**ex·or′bi·tant·ly,** *adv.*

ex·or·cise (ek′sôr sīz′, -sər-) *also,* **exorcize.** *v.t.,* **-cised, -cis·ing. 1.** to drive out (an evil spirit), as by prayers or incantations. **2.** to free (a person or place) from an evil spirit. [Late Latin *exorcizāre,* from Greek *exorkizein* to bind by oath, conjure.] —**ex′or·cis′er,** *n.*

ex·or·cism (ek′sôr siz′əm, -sər-) *n.* **1.** the act or fact of exorcising. **2.** a ritual used in exorcising. —**ex′or·cist,** *n.*

ex·or·cize (ek′sôr sīz′, -sər-) *v.t.,* **-cized, -ciz·ing.** exorcise.

ex·or·di·um (eg zôr′dē əm, ig-, ek sôr′-, ik-) *n., pl.* **-di·ums** or **-di·a** (-dē ə). a beginning or introductory part, as of a speech or dissertation. [Latin *exōrdium.*] —**ex·or′di·al,** *adj.*

ex·o·skel·e·ton (ek′sō skel′i tən) *n.* a protective external skeleton, such as that of crustaceans, insects, or lobsters. ➡ distinguished from **endoskeleton.** [Exo- + SKELETON.]

ex·o·sphere (ek′sō sf îr′) *n.* the outermost layer of the earth's atmosphere, which begins at an altitude of about 400 miles (650 kilometers) and gradually merges with interplanetary space. For illustration, see **atmosphere.** [Exo- + (ATMO)SPHERE.] —**ex·o·spher·ic** (ek′sō sfer′ik), *adj.*

ex·o·ter·ic (ek′sō ter′ik) *adj.* **1.** capable of being understood by or suitable for the general public; not esoteric. **2.** not intended for or restricted to a select group, as of disciples. **3.** well-known; popular. [Greek *exōterikos* external, going back to *exō* outside.]

ex·o·ther·mic (ek′sō thûr′mik) *adj.* relating to a chemical reaction or other process that is accompanied by the liberation of heat. ➡ opposed to **endothermic.** Also, **ex′o·ther′mal.**

ex·ot·ic (eg zot′ik, ig-) *adj.* **1.** of foreign origin or character; not native: *exotic flowers, exotic birds.* **2.** strangely beautiful or fascinating; strikingly unusual. —*n.* something exotic, such as a plant. [Latin *exōticus* foreign, from Greek *exōtikos,* from *exō* outside.] —**ex·ot′i·cal·ly,** *adv.*

ex·ot·i·ca (eg zot′i kə) *pl. n.* things that are strikingly unusual;

exotic things: *rare shells and other exotica.* [Latin *exotica*, feminine of *exoticus* foreign.]

ex·ot·i·cism (eg zot′ə siz′əm) *n.* **1.** the quality or condition of being exotic: *the exoticism of life in a foreign land.* **2.** something exotic: *The English language adopts many exoticisms from other languages.* **3.** a tendency to adopt things that are exotic.

exp. 1. expenses. **2.** export. **3.** exported. **4.** express.

ex·pand (ek spand′, ik-) *v.t.* **1.** to make larger, as in size, extent, or scope; enlarge: *to expand one's chest, to expand one's group of friends, to expand one's interests.* **2.** to stretch or spread (something) out; unfold: *The bird expanded its wings.* **3.** to develop or express (something) in fuller form or greater detail: *to expand an idea.* **4.** to develop a number, algebraic expression, or function to its completed or fullest form according to given rules. $(a + b)^3$ expanded is $a^3 + 3a^2b + 3ab^2 + b^3$. —*v.i.* **1.** to increase, as in size, extent, or volume: *Metal expands when heated. The baseball league expanded by adding four new teams.* **2.** to stretch or spread out; unfold. [Latin *expandere* to spread out. Doublet of SPAWN.] —**ex·pand′a·ble**, *adj.*

· **to expand on** (or **upon**). to discuss in greater detail: *The teacher expanded on the causes of the American Revolution.*

Synonyms *v.i.* **Expand, swell, distend,** and **dilate** mean to increase in volume or any dimension. **Expand** suggests a spread in any direction, from any cause: *a town that expands into the countryside, socks that expand to fit the foot.* **Swell** suggests expansion beyond normal or established limits: *My hand swelled as a result of the injury. The crowd swelled beyond the edges of the square.* **Distend** connotes pressure from within that stretches something abnormally and perhaps painfully: *His nostrils distended with indignation. Her stomach distended as a result of the illness.* **Dilate** simply connotes stretching to become wider: *The pupils of the eyes dilate in the dark.* For other Synonyms *(v.t.),* see **increase.**

ex·panse (ek spans′, ik-) *n.* a wide, unbroken stretch or area, as of land or water: *a vast expanse of desert.* [Latin *expānsum*, noun use of neuter past participle of *expandere* to spread out.]

ex·pan·si·ble (ek span′sə bəl, ik-) *adj.* capable of being expanded. —**ex·pan′si·bil′i·ty,** *n.*

ex·pan·sile (ek span′səl, ik-) *adj.* of, relating to, capable of, or causing expansion.

ex·pan·sion (ek span′shən, ik-) *n.* **1.** the act of expanding or the state of being expanded. **2.** an amount or degree of enlargement or increase: *The bird's wing expansion is six feet.* **3.** an expanded part or form. **4.** a number, algebraic expression, or function in its expanded form. The expansion of $(x + y)^2$ is $x^2 + 2xy + y^2$; the expansion of 125 is $(1 \times 10 \times 10) + (2 \times 10) + (5 \times 1)$. [Late Latin *expānsiō* a spreading out, from Latin *expandere* to spread out.] —**ex·pan′sion·ar′y,** *adj.*

ex·pan·sion·ism (ek span′shə niz′əm, ik-) *n.* the policy of expanding a nation's territory, esp. at the expense of other nations. —**ex·pan′sion·ist,** *n.* —**ex·pan′sion·is′tic,** *adj.*

ex·pan·sive (ek span′siv, ik-) *adj.* **1.** capable of expanding or tending to expand. **2.** extending widely; broad; extensive. **3.** having or showing a generous and outgoing nature; demonstrative; open: *an expansive host, an expansive manner.* **4.** *Psychiatry.* characterized by inappropriate or exaggerated euphoria and delusions of power or importance. —**ex·pan′sive·ly,** *adv.* —**ex·pan′sive·ness,** *n.*

ex par·te (eks pär′tē) on, from, or in the interest of one side only. [Latin *ex* from + *parte*, ablative of *pars* part, side.]

ex·pa·ti·ate (ek spā′shē āt′, ik-) *v.i.,* -at·ed, -at·ing. to write or speak at length or in detail; elaborate (with *on* or *upon*): *The explorer expatiated for hours on life in the Arctic.* [Latin *ex-(s)patiātus*, past participle of *ex(s)patiārī* to go out of the way, digress.] —**ex·pa′ti·a′tion,** *n.* —**ex·pa′ti·a′tor,** *n.*

ex·pa·tri·ate (*v.,* eks pā′trē āt′; *adj., n.,* eks pā′trē it, -āt′) *v.t.,* -at·ed, -at·ing. **1.** to expel (a person) from his or her native country. **2.** to voluntarily withdraw (oneself) from one's native country: *Many American writers expatriated themselves to Europe after World War I.* —*n.* a person who is expatriated; exile. —*adj.* living in a foreign country; expatriated. [Medieval Latin *expatriātus*, past participle of *expatriāre* to banish, from Latin *ex* out of + *patria* native land.] —**ex·pa′tri·a′tion,** *n.*

ex·pect (ek spekt′, ik-) *v.t.* **1.** to look forward to the occurrence or coming of; regard as certain or probable; anticipate: *The club officers had expected a larger group at the meeting.* **2.** to look for as just, proper, necessary, or due; require: *to expect an explanation, to expect a reward.* **3.** *Informal.* to consider as likely; think; suppose: *I rather expect he doesn't intend to come.* [Latin *ex-(s)pectāre* to look for, hope.]

· **to be expecting.** *Informal.* to be awaiting the birth of one's child.

Synonyms **Expect, anticipate,** and **await** mean to look forward to something. **Expect** indicates a degree of certainty that something will happen: *We expect to get an answer in this afternoon's mail.* **Anticipate** suggests knowing or sensing what lies ahead: *I anticipate difficulty getting them to change their minds.* **Await** suggests waiting for and perhaps the preparing for an event: *We eagerly awaited her return from overseas. They awaited the birth of their first child.*

ex·pect·an·cy (ek spek′tən sē, ik-) *n., pl.* -cies. **1.** the state or quality of expecting; expectation. **2.** something that is expected, esp. on the basis of statistical probability. Also, **ex·pect′ance.**

ex·pect·ant (ek spek′tənt, ik-) *adj.* **1.** having or exhibiting expectation: *an expectant look, an expectant heir, an expectant attitude.* **2.** waiting in expectation: *to be expectant of a promotion.* **3.** awaiting the birth of one's child: *an expectant mother.* —**ex·pect′ant·ly,** *adv.*

ex·pec·ta·tion (eks′pek tā′shən) *n.* **1.** the act of expecting or the state or condition of expecting. **2.** the mental attitude of a person who expects; anticipation. **3.** a reason or ground for expecting; prospect or hope, as of future good or success. ➡ usually used in the plural: *to have great expectations.* **4.** something that is expected. **5.** the degree of probability that something will occur: *There is little expectation that we will win the game.* **6.** the state of being expected: *a sum of money in expectation.*

ex·pec·to·rant (ek spek′tər ənt, ik-) *adj.* aiding or promoting the discharge of phlegm or mucus from the respiratory tract. —*n.* a medicine that promotes and aids expectoration.

ex·pec·to·rate (ek spek′tə rāt′, ik-) *v.,* -rat·ed, -rat·ing. —*v.i.* **1.** to discharge phlegm, mucus, or other congestive matter from the respiratory tract by coughing up and spitting. **2.** to spit. —*v.t.* to discharge from the respiratory tract by coughing up and spitting. [Latin *expectorātus*, past participle of *expectorāre* to drive from the breast, from *ex* out of + *pectus* breast.] —**ex·pec′to·ra′tion,** *n.*

ex·pe·di·en·cy (ek spē′dē ən sē, ik-) *n., pl.* -cies. **1.** the state or quality of being expedient. **2.** concern for what is conducive to immediate results or personal advantage or gain rather than for what is right or just. **3.** something that is expedient. Also, **ex·pe′di·ence.**

ex·pe·di·ent (ek spē′dē ənt, ik-) *adj.* **1.** conducive to or promoting immediate results or personal advantage or gain; based on self-interest rather than consideration for what is right or just. **2.** suitable or desirable for a given situation or purpose; appropriate. —*n.* a means employed to bring about a desired result; means to an end. [Latin *expediēns*, present participle of *expedīre* to free the feet, extricate, make ready, from *ex* out + *pēs* foot.] —**ex·pe′di·ent·ly,** *adv.*

ex·pe·dite (ek′spi dīt′) *v.t.,* -dit·ed, -dit·ing. **1.** to speed up the process or progress of; facilitate: *to expedite the shipment of a carton of fruit.* **2.** to do quickly and efficiently: *to expedite a task.* [Latin *expedītus*, past participle of *expedīre*. See EXPEDIENT.]

ex·pe·dit·er (ek′spi dī′tər) *also,* **expeditor.** *n.* a person who expedites, esp. a person who is responsible for expediting the flow of materials so that a production schedule will be maintained.

ex·pe·di·tion (ek′spi dish′ən) *n.* **1.** a journey, excursion, or voyage made for a specific purpose, such as exploration: *an expedition to the North Pole.* **2.** a body of persons or things, such as ships or equipment, involved in such a journey. **3.** prompt and efficient action: *to perform one's work with expedition.*

ex·pe·di·tion·ar·y (ek′spi dish′ə ner′ē) *adj.* of, relating to, or composing an expedition: *an expeditionary force.*

ex·pe·di·tious (ek′spi dish′əs) *adj.* prompt and efficient: *Use the most expeditious means possible to finish this job.* —**ex′pe·di′-tious·ly,** *adv.* —**ex′pe·di′tious·ness,** *n.*

ex·pe·di·tor (ek′spi dī′tər) expediter.

ex·pel (ek spel′, ik-) *v.t.,* -pelled, -pel·ling. **1.** to drive out or discharge by force; force out: *to expel water from a hose.* **2.** to compel to leave; oust: *to expel a student from school.* [Latin *expellere* to drive out.]

ex·pend (ek spend′, ik-) *v.t.* **1.** to pay out; spend. **2.** to use up; consume: *to expend one's energy.* [Latin *expendere* to weigh out, pay. Doublet of SPEND.] —For Synonyms, see **spend.**

ex·pend·a·ble (ek spen′də bəl, ik-) *adj.* **1.** capable of being expended. **2.** that may be sacrificed, often in order to gain a greater advantage, as troops or equipment in battle. **3.** consumed in normal use and not subject to inventory, as ammunition. —*n.*

a	at	e	end	o	hot	u	up	hw	white		about
ā	ape	ē	me	ō	old	ū	use	ng	song		taken
ä	far	i	it	ô	fork	u̇	rule	th	thin	ə	pencil
âr	care	ī	ice	oi	oil	u̇	pull	th	this		lemon
		îr	pierce	ou	out	ûr	turn	zh	measure		circus

431

a person or thing considered expendable. —**ex·pend′a·bil′i·ty,** *n.*

ex·pend·i·ture (ek spen′di chər, ik-) *n.* **1.** the act of expending. **2.** something that is expended, as money, time, or effort.

ex·pense (ek spens′, ik-) *n.* **1.** the spending of money; expenditure: *The project involved great expense.* **2.** an object or cause of spending money: *The rent on my apartment is my biggest monthly expense.* **3.** money spent in order to buy or do something; cost: *We cannot afford the expense of a new car.* **4.** loss, injury, or sacrifice: *The war was won at great expense.* **5. expenses. a.** costs or charges incurred in the undertaking of some business, action, or activity: *traveling expenses.* **b.** money paid in reimbursement of these costs. [Late Latin *expēnsa* outlay, money to defray costs, from Latin *expendere* to weigh out, pay; with reference to a former practice of determining the amount of payment required by weighing in a scale.]
   • **at the expense of. a.** with the loss, injury, or sacrifice of: *to devote too much time to sports at the expense of one's studies.* **b.** so as to be paid for by: *My business trip was at the expense of the company.*

expense account 1. an arrangement between a company and an employee whereby the company pays for all charges incurred in the performance of the employee's duties, such as travel, hotel, and food costs. **2.** a record of such expenses.

ex·pen·sive (ek spen′siv, ik-) *adj.* involving great expense; costly. —**ex·pen′sive·ly,** *adv.* —**ex·pen′sive·ness,** *n.*

ex·pe·ri·ence (ek spîr′ē əns, ik-) *n.* **1.** a particular event or events that one has seen, done, or participated in: *frightening war experiences.* **2.** all of the events that have happened to an individual or to a group, community, or people in general: *the human experience.* **3.** the actual participation in, contact with, or seeing of such an event or events: *the experience of being hungry.* **4.** knowledge, skill, or understanding acquired in this way, usually over a period of time: *The job requires three years' experience as an accountant. She doesn't have any business experience.* —*v.t.,* **-enced, -enc·ing.** to have happen to one; encounter and feel; undergo: *to experience love.* [Old French *experience* testing, acquired knowledge, from Latin *experientia* proof, trial.]

Synonyms *v.t.* **Experience** and **feel** may mean to encounter and come to know. **Experience** may connote nothing more than this: *I experienced snow for the first time when I came north to school.* Or, it may suggest that one has been permanently changed: *We experienced great hardship in those wartime years.* **Feel** connotes being emotionally touched by something: *to feel sorrow, to feel the joy of friendship.*

ex·pe·ri·enced (ek spîr′ē ənst, ik-) *adj.* made skillful, knowledgeable, or wise through experience: *an experienced politician, an experienced carpenter.*

ex·pe·ri·en·tial (ek spîr′ē en′shəl, ik-) *adj.* relating to or derived from experience; empirical: *experiential knowledge.*

ex·per·i·ment (*v.,* ek sper′ə ment′, ik-; *n.,* ek sper′ə mənt, ik-) *n.* **1.** an action or procedure designed to discover, test, or illustrate something, such as a hypothesis or principle: *Benjamin Franklin's experiments showed that lightning is an electrical discharge.* **2.** the conduct of such procedures; experimentation: *to demonstrate the validity of a theory by experiment.* —*v.i.* to make an experiment or experiments: *A good cook experiments with different ingredients.* [Latin *experimentum* proof, test.] —**ex·per′i·ment′er,** *n.*

ex·per·i·men·tal (ek sper′ə men′təl, ik-) *adj.* **1.** relating to, derived from, or based on experiments: *experimental evidence.* **2.** used for experimentation: *an experimental drug.* **3.** of the nature of an experiment; tentative. **4.** derived from or based on experience; empirical. —**ex·per′i·men′tal·ly,** *adv.*

ex·per·i·men·ta·tion (ek sper′ə mən tā′shən, ik-) *n.* the act or process of experimenting.

ex·pert (ek′spûrt; *adj.,* also ek spûrt′, ik-) *n.* a person having special skill or knowledge in something; specialist; authority: *an expert in mathematics, an expert on foreign affairs.* —*adj.* **1.** highly skilled or knowledgeable: *an expert skier.* **2.** characteristic of or from an expert; authoritative: *expert advice.* [Old French *expert* able, knowing, clever, from Latin *expertus,* past participle of *experīrī* to try, test, prove.] —**ex·pert′ly,** *adv.* —**ex·pert′ness,** *n.*

Synonyms *adj.* **Expert, adept, skilled,** and **proficient** mean having great competence or superior ability derived from training. **Expert** implies the accumulation of both knowledge and practice: *It takes training and experience to become an expert in computer programming.* **Adept** suggests aptitude combined with practice: *He quickly became adept at weaving.* **Skilled,** like **expert,** suggests having gained mastery of something, but is generally applied to more concrete things: *She*

is a skilled carpenter. **Proficient** stresses the result of ability combined with practice, ease, and excellence: *He is a proficient pianist who has been playing since early childhood.*

ex·per·tise (ek′spər tēz′) *n.* expert knowledge or skill. [Middle French *expertise,* from *expert* skillful. See EXPERT.]

expert system, a computer program that follows steps or decision-making procedures used by experts in a specific field of study, such as those in medical diagnosis or engineering design and analysis.

ex·pi·a·ble (ek′spē ə bəl) *adj.* capable of being expiated.

ex·pi·ate (ek′spē āt′) *v.t.,* **-at·ed, -at·ing.** to make amends for; atone for: *to expiate one's sins.* [Latin *expiātus,* past participle of *expiāre* to atone for, going back to *ex* utterly + *pius* devout.]

ex·pi·a·tion (ek′spē ā′shən) *n.* **1.** the act of expiating. **2.** something that expiates; means of atonement.

ex·pi·a·to·ry (ek′spē ə tôr′ē) *adj.* serving to or intended to expiate.

ex·pi·ra·tion (ek′spə rā′shən) *n.* **1.** a closing or ending; termination; close: *The expiration of a contract.* **2.** the act of breathing out air; exhalation.

ex·pir·a·to·ry (ek spîr′ə tôr′ē, ik-) *adj.* relating to or used in the expiration of air from the lungs.

ex·pire (ek spîr′, ik-) *v.,* **-pired, -pir·ing.** —*v.i.* **1.** to come to an end; terminate: *The lease expires on May 1. My magazine subscription expires with the March issue.* **2.** to expel air from the lungs; exhale. **3.** to die. —*v.t.* to expel (air) from the lungs. [Latin *ex(s)pīrāre* to breathe out, die.]

ex·pi·ry (ek spîr′ē, ik-, ek′spə rē) *n., pl.* **-ries.** expiration; termination.

ex·plain (ek splān′, ik-) *v.t.* **1.** to make clear or understandable: *The pilot explained that the plane's departure would be delayed by the storm.* **2.** to reveal the meaning of; interpret: *to explain a prophecy.* **3.** to give the reason or reasons for; account for: *Can you explain your absence from the meeting?* —*v.i.* to give an explanation. [Latin *explānāre* to flatten, make plain.] —**ex·plain′a·ble,** *adj.* —For Synonyms *(v.t.),* see **interpret.**
   • **to explain away. a.** to do away with by reasoning or offering an explanation: *to explain away a child's fear of the dark.* **b.** to give reasons so as to justify or minimize the importance of: *to explain away a friend's faults.*
   • **to explain oneself.** to offer an explanation for what one has done or said.

ex·pla·na·tion (ek′splə nā′shən) *n.* **1.** the act or process of explaining: *a teacher's explanation of a problem.* **2.** something that explains: *Is there any explanation for their strange behavior?* **3.** an interpretation given in explaining something; meaning.

ex·plan·a·to·ry (ek splan′ə tôr′ē, ik-) *adj.* serving or tending to explain: *explanatory notes.*

ex·plant (ek splant′) *v.t.* to remove (living tissue) from an organism for culture in an artificial medium. —*n.* tissue that has been explanted. [EX-¹ + PLANT.] —**ex·plan·ta·tion** (ek′splan-tā′shən), *n.*

ex·ple·tive (ek′spli tiv) *n.* **1.** a word, syllable, or phrase added to fill out a sentence or to complete the rhythmical pattern in a line of verse but contributing nothing to the content. In the sentence *There are six birds on the roof,* the word *there* is an expletive. **2.** an exclamation or oath. —*adj.* added to fill out a sentence or to complete the rhythm in a line of verse. Also *(adj.),* **ex·ple·to·ry** (eks′plə tôr′ē). [Late Latin *explētīvus* serving to fill out, from Latin *explēre* to fill out.]

ex·plic·a·ble (ek splik′ə bəl, ik-, ek′spli kə-) *adj.* capable of being explained. [Latin *explicābilis,* from *explicāre* to explain.]

ex·pli·cate (ek′spli kāt′) *v.t.,* **-cat·ed, -cat·ing. 1.** to explain clearly and in detail: *to explicate a difficult passage in a book.* **2.** to develop, as a principle or proposition. [Latin *explicātus,* past participle of *explicāre* to unfold, explain.]

ex·pli·ca·tion (ek′spli kā′shən) *n.* **1.** the act or process of explicating. **2.** an explanation, as of a passage in a text; interpretation. **3.** a detailed account or description.

ex·plic·a·tive (ek′spli kā′tiv, ek splik′ə-, ik-) *adj.* serving to explicate; explanatory. Also, **ex·pli·ca·to·ry** (ek′spli kə tôr′ē, ek splik′ə-, ik-).

ex·plic·it (ek splis′it, ik-) *adj.* clear and definite; leaving nothing unexplained: *explicit instructions.* [Latin *explicitus,* form of *explicātus,* past participle of *explicāre* to unfold, explain.] —**ex·plic′it·ly,** *adv.* —**ex·plic′it·ness,** *n.* —For Synonyms, see **precise.**

ex·plode (ek splōd′, ik-) *v.,* **-plod·ed, -plod·ing.** —*v.i.* **1.** to burst suddenly and violently with a loud noise: *The bottle exploded in the fire.* **2.** to expand suddenly and violently because of chemical reactions or nuclear fission or fusion, giving off light, heat, and noise: *The nitroglycerin exploded on impact.* **3.** to break forth violently or noisily: *to explode with rage.* **4.** to increase rapidly: *The country's population has exploded in the last few*

years. —*v.t.* **1.** to cause (something) to burst suddenly and violently with a loud noise. **2.** to cause to expand suddenly and violently by chemical reaction or nuclear fission or fusion, giving off light, heat, and noise. **3.** to bring into disrepute; refute: *to explode a theory.* [Latin *explōdere* to drive off the stage by clapping, from *ex* away + *plaudere* to clap the hands.]

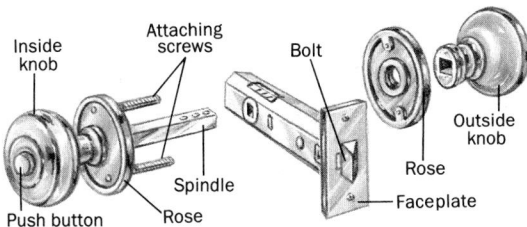

exploded view of a lock for a door

exploded view, a graphic representation of the individual parts of a mechanism separately but in correct relationship to one another.

ex·ploit (*n.,* ek′sploit, ek sploit′, ik-; *v.,* ek sploit′, ik-) *n.* a notable, heroic deed; feat: *military exploits.* —*v.t.* **1.** to use unjustly or unfairly for selfish profit or advantage: *to exploit laborers, to exploit a friendship.* **2.** to make practical use of; use or develop profitably: *to exploit natural resources.* [Old French *esploit* achievement, deed, from Latin *explicitum* something unfolded or settled, from *explicāre* to unfold, explain.] —**ex·ploit′a·ble,** *adj.* —**ex·ploit′er,** *n.*

ex·ploi·ta·tion (ek′sploi tā′shən) *n.* the act of exploiting, esp. for selfish profit or advantage.

ex·ploi·ta·tive (ek sploi′tə tiv, ik-) *adj.* relating to or tending to use exploitation: *the exploitative policies of a colonial power.* Also, **ex·ploi·tive** (ek sploi′tiv, ik-).

ex·plo·ra·tion (ek′splə rā′shən) *n.* the act or an instance of exploring, esp. for the purpose of discovering previously unknown regions or investigating unfamiliar ones.

ex·plor·a·to·ry (ek splôr′ə tôr′ē, ik-) *adj.* of, relating to, or for exploration: *an exploratory voyage, exploratory surgery.* Also, **ex·plor′a·tive.**

ex·plore (ek splôr′, ik-) *v.,* **-plored, -plor·ing.** —*v.t.* **1.** to travel over or in (previously unfamiliar or unknown regions) in order to discover or investigate: *to explore the surface of the moon.* **2.** to examine or look through or into closely; scrutinize: *The historian explored the causes of the revolution.* **3.** to examine closely (an organ, wound, or diseased part) in order to make a diagnosis, as by probing or experimental surgery. —*v.i.* to make an exploration. [Latin *explōrāre* to search out; originally, to cry out (in the sense of drawing forth game at a hunt by cries).]

ex·plor·er (ek splôr′ər, ik-) *n.* a person or thing that explores.

ex·plo·sion (ek splō′zhən, ik-) *n.* **1.** the act of bursting or expanding suddenly and violently: *an atomic explosion.* **2.** a loud noise caused by exploding: *The explosion of the dynamite was deafening.* **3.** a sudden, violent outburst of emotion: *an explosion of rage.* **4.** a large, rapid increase: *a population explosion.* [Latin *explōsiō* a driving off by clapping.]

ex·plo·sive (ek splō′siv, ik-) *adj.* **1.** of, relating to, or of the nature of an explosion: *an explosive laugh.* **2.** tending or liable to explode or cause an explosion: *explosive chemicals, an explosive situation.* **3.** *Phonetics.* plosive. —*n.* **1.** a substance that can explode. **2.** *Phonetics.* plosive. —**ex·plo′sive·ly,** *adv.* —**ex·plo′sive·ness,** *n.*

ex·po (ek′spō) *n., pl.* **-pos.** *Informal.* exposition *(def. 1).* [Short for EXPO(SITION).]

ex·po·nent (ek spō′nənt, ik-; *def. 3, also* ek′spō nənt) *n.* **1.** a person who explains or interprets something: *a leading exponent of the theory of evolution.* **2.** a person or thing that represents or advocates something, as an idea, principle, or cause: *an exponent of nonviolence.* **3.** a numeral or symbol placed at the upper right side of another numeral or symbol to indicate the power to which the latter is to be raised or how many times it is to be taken as a factor. In 4^3 the exponent is 3, indicating $4 \times 4 \times 4$; in A^2 the exponent is 2, indicating $A \times A$; in 5^x the exponent is x, indicating 5 multiplied by itself x times. [Latin *expōnēns,* present participle of *expōnere* to set forth, explain.]

ex·po·nen·tial (ek′spō nen′shəl) *adj.* of or relating to mathematical exponents, esp. those involving unknown or variable quantities as exponents. —**ex′po·nen′tial·ly,** *adv.*

ex·po·nen·ti·a·tion (ek′spō nen′shē ā′shən) *n.* the process of raising a number to any power.

ex·port (*v.,* ek spôrt′, ik-, ek′spôrt′; *n.,* ek′spôrt′) *v.t.* to carry or send (commodities) to other countries for sale or trade: *Colombia exports coffee to the United States.* —*n.* **1.** something exported: *The leading export of Australia is wool.* **2.** the act or process of exporting: *The government prohibited the export of certain raw materials during the war.* [Latin *exportāre* to carry out or away.] —**ex·port′er,** *n.*

ex·por·ta·tion (ek′spôr tā′shən) *n.* **1.** the act of exporting. **2.** something exported.

ex·pose (ek spōz′, ik-) *v.t.,* **-posed, -pos·ing. 1.** to place in contact with or leave open to the action or influence of (something): *to expose a metal to corrosives and extreme temperatures, to expose a child to the measles, to expose a student to good literature.* **2.** to leave (oneself) open, as to danger, ridicule, or criticism: *Police officers expose themselves to danger every day.* **3.** to make known; disclose: *to expose a conspiracy, to expose a crime.* **4.** to reveal the actions, character, or identity of; unmask: *to expose a spy.* **5.** to show openly or publicly; cause to be seen; display: *Bikinis expose much of the body.* **6.** to abandon in an open and unprotected place so as to cause death. **7.** to submit (a photographic film or plate) to the action of light. [Old French *exposer* to lay out, place in view, make known, modification (influenced by French *poser* to place, put) of Latin *expōnere* to set forth, exhibit, explain.] —**ex·pos′er,** *n.*

ex·po·sé (ek′spō zā′) *n.* **1.** a public disclosure of something secret or discreditable, as a scandal or crime. **2.** a book or article making such a disclosure. [French *exposé* statement, account, from *exposer* to set forth, explain, show. See EXPOSE.]

ex·posed (ek spōzd′, ik-) *adj.* **1.** open to view; unconcealed: *The living room has exposed beams.* **2.** without protection; unsheltered.

ex·po·si·tion (ek′spə zish′ən) *n.* **1.** an extensive or elaborate public show or display, as of industrial products; collection of exhibitions. Also, **expo. 2.** the act or process of setting forth or explaining facts or ideas. **3.** a detailed statement or explanation of facts or ideas, esp. in writing. **4.** the initial section in certain musical forms, esp. the sonata and fugue, in which the theme or themes of the movement or composition are introduced. [Latin *expositiō* a setting forth, a showing.] —**ex′po·si′tion·al,** *adj.*

ex·pos·i·tor (ek spoz′i tər, ik-) *n.* a person who expounds or explains something. [Late Latin *expositor,* from Latin *expōnere* to set out, explain.]

ex·pos·i·to·ry (ek spoz′i tôr′ē, ik-) *adj.* of, relating to, of the nature of, or containing exposition; explanatory: *an expository text.*

ex post fac·to (eks′ pōst′ fak′tō) made or done afterward but having a retroactive effect: *An ex post facto law applies to actions that took place prior to the enactment of the law.* [Late Latin *ex post facto* from what is done afterwards, from Latin *ex* from + *post* after + *factum,* neuter past participle of *facere* to do.]

ex·pos·tu·late (ek spəs′chə lāt′, ik-) *v.i.,* **-lat·ed, -lat·ing.** to reason earnestly with a person against something; remonstrate: *The senator expostulated with a colleague concerning the advisability of passing the bill.* [Latin *expostulātus,* past participle of *expostulāre* to demand urgently.] —**ex·pos′tu·la′tor,** *n.* —**ex·pos′tu·la′tive, ex·pos·tu·la·to·ry** (ek spos′chə lə tôr′ē) *adj.*

ex·pos·tu·la·tion (ek spos′chə lā′shən, ik-) *n.* the act of expostulating.

ex·po·sure (ek spō′zhər, ik-) *n.* **1.** the act of exposing or the state of being exposed. **2.** a lack of protection from the elements resulting in harm to the body, esp. serious harm: *One of the stranded climbers died of exposure.* **3.** a position in relation to sunlight, wind, or points of the compass: *a room with a southern exposure.* **4.a.** the act of subjecting a photographic film or plate to actinic light. **b.** the length of time light falls on a photographic film or plate, at a certain lens opening, controlled by the lens aperture and shutter speed of the camera. **c.** a section of film for one photograph. [EXPOSE + -URE.]

exposure meter, light meter.

ex·pound (ek spound′, ik-) *v.t.* **1.** to set forth in detail: *to expound a theory.* **2.** to clarify the meaning of; explain; interpret. —*v.i.* to explain a point of view (usually with *on*). [Old French *espondre* to explain, from Latin *expōnere* to set forth, explain.] —**ex·pound′er,** *n.* —For Synonyms *(v.t.),* see **interpret.**

ex·press (ek spres′, ik-) *v.t.* **1.** to put into words; verbalize: *to express one's opinions.* **2.** to give an outward indication of; make known or convey; manifest: *The artist's work expresses feelings of*

a	at	e	end	o	hot	u	up	hw	white		about
ā	ape	ē	me	ō	old	ū	use	ng	song		taken
ä	far	i	it	ô	fork	th	rule	th	thin	ə	pencil
âr	care	ī	ice	oi	oil	u̇	pull	th	this		lemon
		ir	pierce	ou	out	ûr	turn	zh	measure		circus

alienation. **3.** to represent, as by a figure, symbol, or formula; indicate: *The sign ÷ expresses division.* **4.** to send by a means of rapid transportation or delivery: *to express a package.* **5.** to press out; squeeze out: *to express juice from oranges.* —*adj.* **1.** particular or sole; special: *He came here for the express purpose of seeing her.* **2.** clear and unmistakable; unambiguous: *to give express orders.* **3.** of or relating to a system of rapid transportation or delivery: *an express company, an express shipment.* **4.** quick, direct, and making few or no intermediate stops: *an express train.* **5.** designed for rapid and direct traveling: *an express highway.* —*adv.* by a system of rapid transportation or delivery: *to send a package express.* —*n.* **1.** a system for the rapid and direct transportation or delivery of goods or money. **2.** a company engaged in such transportation or delivery. **3.** goods or money transported by such a system. **4.** a means of conveyance, as a train, bus, or elevator, that is quick and direct and makes few stops. [Latin *expressus,* past participle of *exprimere* to press out, represent, describe, from *ex-* out + *premere* to press.] —**ex·press′i·ble,** *adj.*

· **to express oneself. a.** to put one's thoughts and opinions into words: *The teenager expresses herself very eloquently.* **b.** to communicate one's thoughts or feelings through artistic or creative activity: *The artist paints to express himself.*

ex·press·age (ek spres′ij, ik-) *n.* **1.** the transportation of goods by express. **2.** the charge for such transportation.

ex·pres·sion (ek spresh′ən, ik-) *n.* **1.** the act of expressing or communicating something in words. **2.** an outward indication or means of conveying: *Crying is an expression of grief. All of his novels were an expression of his rebellion against society.* **3.** a particular look, action, or vocal intonation indicating something, such as a thought or feeling: *Her face wore an expression of disapproval.* **4.** a quality or manner of communicating feeling or meaning: *The speaker's voice lacked expression.* **5.** a particular word or phrase: *"Look before you leap" is a familiar expression.* **6.** a symbol or combination of symbols used to indicate a mathematical quantity or operation.

ex·pres·sion·ism (ek spresh′ə niz′əm, ik-) *n.* a movement in the arts originating in Europe about the time of World War I, characterized by the artist's concern with the expression of personal ideas and feelings about the subject, rather than with the realistic representation of it. —**ex·pres′sion·ist,** *n., adj.* —**ex·pres′sion·is′tic,** *adj.*

expressionism
a painting by Ernst Ludwig Kirchner

ex·pres·sion·less (ek spresh′ən lis, ik-) *adj.* revealing little or no feeling: *an expressionless face.*

ex·pres·sive (ek spres′iv, ik-) *adj.* **1.** serving to indicate; expressing (with *of*): *a manner expressive of anger.* **2.** full of or conveying much feeling or meaning: *an expressive tone, an expressive look.* **3.** of, relating to, or concerned with expression. —**ex·pres′sive·ly,** *adv.* —**ex·pres′sive·ness,** *n.*

ex·press·ly (ek spres′lē, ik-) *adv.* **1.** particularly or solely; specially: *We went to Europe expressly to visit old churches.* **2.** in clear and unmistakable terms; plainly: *The children were expressly warned against feeding the bears.*

ex·press·man (ek spres′mən, ik-) *n., pl.* **-men** (-mən). a person who is employed by an express company, esp. a person who picks up or delivers parcels and other articles.

ex·press·way (ek spres′wā′, ik-) *n.* a wide, usually divided highway with limited points of access or exit, designed for rapid and direct travel.

ex·pro·pri·ate (eks prō′prē āt′) *v.t.,* **-at·ed, -at·ing. 1.** to take (private property) from a person or business, esp. for public use by right of eminent domain. **2.** to deprive (a person) of ownership or possession. [Medieval Latin *expropriātus,* past participle of *expropriāre* to deprive of property, from Latin *ex* out of + *proprium* property.] —**ex·pro′pri·a′tion,** *n.* —**ex·pro′pri·a′tor,** *n.*

ex·pul·sion (ek spul′shən, ik-) *n.* the act of expelling or the state of being expelled. [Latin *expulsiō* a driving out.]

ex·pul·sive (ek spul′siv) *adj.* serving or tending to expel.

ex·punge (ek spunj′, ik-) *v.t.,* **-punged, -pung·ing. 1.** to delete or erase (something written): *to expunge passages from a manuscript.* **2.** to wipe out or destroy; obliterate. [Latin *expungere* to erase.] —**ex·pung′er,** *n.*

ex·pur·gate (ek′spər gāt′) *v.t.,* **-gat·ed, -gat·ing.** to remove obscene or otherwise objectionable passages or words from: *to expurgate a book.* [Latin *expurgātus,* past participle of *expurgāre* to purge out, cleanse.] —**ex′pur·ga′tion,** *n.* —**ex′pur·ga′tor,** *n.*

ex·qui·site (ek′skwi zit, ek skwiz′it, ik-) *adj.* **1.** marked by rare and delicate beauty, charm, or perfection: *an exquisite face.* **2.** marked by excellence, as in design, execution, or craftsmanship: *a vase of exquisite workmanship.* **3.** intensely sharp; keen; acute: *exquisite pain, exquisite delight.* **4.** extremely refined or elegant: *exquisite taste.* **5.** keenly sensitive or discriminating: *an exquisite palate.* [Latin *exquīsītus* choice, past participle of *exquīrere* to search out.] —**ex′qui·site·ly,** *adv.* —**ex′qui·site·ness,** *n.*

ex·tant (ek′stənt, ek stant′, ik-) *adj.* not lost, destroyed, or extinct; still existing: *The only extant copy of the book is in a private collection.* [Latin *ex(s)tāns,* present participle of *ex(s)tāre* to exist, stand out.]

ex·tem·po·ral (ek stem′pər əl, ik-) *adj. Archaic.* extemporaneous.

ex·tem·po·ra·ne·ous (ek stem′pə rā′nē əs, ik-) *adj.* **1.** spoken, performed, or composed with little or no preparation; impromptu: *The winner of the award made a few extemporaneous remarks.* **2.** prepared or thought out in advance but not read or memorized: *an extemporaneous political address.* **3.** skilled at or given to speaking with little or no preparation: *The master of ceremonies was a good extemporaneous speaker.* **4.** made for the occasion; improvised: *extemporaneous recipes, an extemporaneous brunch.* [Late Latin *extemporāneus* extempore, from Latin *ex tempore* at the moment. See EXTEMPORE.] —**ex·tem′po·ra′ne·ous·ly,** *adv.* —**ex·tem′po·ra′ne·ous·ness,** *n.*

ex·tem·po·rar·y (ek stem′pə rer′ē, ik-) *adj.* extemporaneous. —**ex·tem′po·rar′i·ly,** *adv.*

ex·tem·po·re (ek stem′pə rē, ik-) *adv.* with little or no preparation; offhand; extemporaneously: *The mayor spoke extempore.* —*adj.* extemporaneous; impromptu. [Latin *ex tempore* at the moment; literally, from the time.]

ex·tem·po·rize (ek stem′pə rīz′, ik-) *v.t., v.i.,* **-rized, -riz·ing.** to speak, make, perform, or compose (something) extempore; improvise. —**ex·tem′po·ri·za′tion,** *n.*

ex·tend (ek stend′, ik-) *v.t.* **1.** to lengthen in a specified direction or for a given distance: *The builders extended the road for three more miles.* **2.** to open or spread out to full length: *to extend a folding ladder.* **3.** to straighten or stretch out (a part of the body) to its fullest length: *The dancer extended her leg.* **4.** to increase the duration of; prolong or continue: *We extended our visit.* **5.** to offer or give: *We extended our sympathy to the family. The store extended credit privileges to us.* **6.** to hold out; put forth: *He extended his hand in friendship.* **7.** to enlarge or widen, as in bulk or area; expand: *The ancient Romans extended their empire into Asia.* **8.** to broaden, as in scope, range, or meaning; make more comprehensive: *We extended the definition so as to include that usage.* —*v.i.* **1.** to continue or be continued for a specified distance or time; stretch out: *The driveway extends from the house to the highway. The meeting extended late into the night.* **2.** to cover an area; reach: *That company's distribution network extends from California to the Midwest.* [Latin *extendere* to stretch out.]

ex·tend·ed (ek sten′did, ik-) *adj.* **1.** prolonged or continued: *an extended vacation, an extended conversation.* **2.** enlarged or broadened, as in area, scope, or range; extensive: *an extended empire.* **3.** opened or stretched out.

extended family, a family that includes parents, children, and other near relatives, such as grandparents, usually all living in the same household.

ex·tend·er (ek sten′dər, ik-) *n.* something that extends, esp. a substance or ingredient added to another to increase its bulk.

ex·tend·i·ble (ek sten′də bəl, ik-) *also,* **ex·tend·a·ble.** *adj.* extensible. —**ex·tend′i·bil′i·ty;** *also,* **ex·tend′a·bil′i·ty,** *n.*

ex·ten·si·ble (ek sten′sə bəl, ik-) *adj.* capable of being extended. —**ex·ten′si·bil′i·ty,** *n.*

ex·ten·sile (ek sten′səl, ik-) *adj.* **1.** *Biology.* capable of being stuck out or protruded: *an extensile tongue.* **2.** extensible.

ex·ten·sion (ek sten′shən, ik-) *n.* **1.** the act of extending or the state of being extended. **2.** something that prolongs, lengthens, or enlarges: *I was given a three-month extension for filing my tax return. We added a two-room extension to the house.* **3.** the act of straightening or stretching out a part of the body, esp. a limb. ➡ opposed to **flexion. 4.** an additional telephone connected to the same line as the principal one. **5.** *Physics.* the property that enables a body to occupy space. [Late Latin *extēnsiō* a stretching out, from Latin *extendere* to stretch out.]

extension cord, an electric cord fitted with a plug at one end and a receptacle at the other, used as an addition to the power cord of an appliance or other electric device.

ex·ten·sive (ek sten′siv, ik-) *adj.* **1.** covering or extending over a large area; great in extent; vast: *an extensive estate.* **2.** broad, as in scope, effect, or range; comprehensive or far-reaching: *extensive influence, extensive research.* **3.** large in amount, degree, or number: *My grandmother has extensive real estate holdings.* —**ex·ten′sive·ly,** *adv.* —**ex·ten′sive·ness,** *n.*

ex·ten·sor (ek sten′sər, -sôr, ik-) *n.* any muscle that straightens or stretches out a part of the body, esp. a limb. ➡ opposed to **flexor.** [Late Latin *extēnsor* one who stretches, from Latin *extendere* to stretch out.]

ex·tent (ek stent′, ik-) *n.* **1.** the space, amount, degree, or limit to which something extends or is extended: *the extent of a survey, the extent of someone's duties.* **2.** an extended area or space: *an extent of uninhabited country.* [Anglo-Norman *extente, estente* area in space, noun use of feminine past participle of Old French *estendre* to stretch out, from Latin *extendere.*]

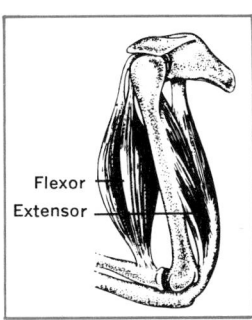
Flexor
Extensor

extensor in the arm

ex·ten·u·ate (ek sten′ū āt′, ik-) *v.t.,* **-at·ed, -at·ing.** to lessen the seriousness of (something), as a fault or offense, by serving as or giving an excuse for it: *The boy's youth does not extenuate his crime.* [Latin *extenuātus,* past participle of *extenuāre* to make thin, lessen, from *ex* out + *tenuis* thin.] —**ex·ten′u·a′tion,** *n.*

ex·ten·u·at·ing (ek sten′ū ā′ting, ik-) *adj.* tending to extenuate something, esp. a crime: *extenuating circumstances.*

ex·te·ri·or (ek stîr′ē ər, ik-) *n.* **1.** an external surface or part; outside: *the exterior of a building.* **2.** an outward appearance or demeanor: *to have a calm exterior.* —*adj.* **1.** of, relating to, on, or for the outside; outer; external: *an exterior surface, exterior paint.* **2.** coming or acting from without: *exterior help, exterior causes.* [Latin *exterior* outer, outward, comparative of *exterus* outward, external.]

> **Synonyms** *adj.* **Exterior, outside, external,** and **outer** may all mean situated on the surface or beyond the limit of something. **Exterior** is used of things on a surface: *exterior paint.* **Outside** connotes anything at or beyond a boundary: *the building's outside lighting.* **External** suggests comparison with or separation from what is within: *External appearances may be deceiving.* **Outer** suggests comparative distance from a center or from inner parts: *the outer courtyard, the outer districts of a city.*

exterior angle 1. any of the four angles formed outside two lines that are cut by a third line. For illustration, see **alternate angles. 2.** an angle formed between a side of a polygon and the extension of an adjacent side.

ex·ter·mi·nate (ek stûr′mə nāt′, ik-) *v.t.,* **-nat·ed, -nat·ing.** to destroy (a living thing or things); wipe out; annihilate: *to exterminate household pests.* [Late Latin *exterminātus,* past participle of *extermināre* to destroy, from Latin *exermināre* to banish; literally, to drive beyond the boundaries, from *ex* out of + *terminus* boundary.]

ex·ter·mi·na·tion (ek stûr′mə nā′shən, ik-) *n.* total destruction; annihilation.

ex·ter·mi·na·tor (ek stûr′mə nā′tər, ik-) *n.* a person or thing that exterminates, esp. a person whose business is exterminating cockroaches, termites, rats, and other vermin.

ex·ter·nal (ek stûr′nəl, ik-) *adj.* **1.** of, relating to, or situated on the outside; outer: *an external covering.* **2.** originating or acting from without: *an external force, external causes.* **3.** relating to outward appearance; superficial: *external beauty.* **4.** of or relat-

ing to foreign countries; not confined within a single country: *external affairs.* **5.** on or to be used on the outside of the body: *Rubbing alcohol is for external use only.* **6.** existing outside the mind or independently of perception; objective. —*n.* **externals.** outward form, appearance, feature, or circumstance; superficial aspects: *You put too much weight on externals in judging others.* [Latin *externus* outward + -AL[1].] —**ex·ter′nal·ly,** *adv.* —For Synonyms *(adj.),* see **exterior.**

ex·ter·nal-com·bus·tion engine (ek stûr′nəl kəm bus′chən; ik-) a heat engine, as a steam engine, that runs on energy derived from fuel that is burned outside the engine cylinder.

external ear, the outer, visible part of the ear and the passage leading to the eardrum. For illustration, see **ear**[1].

ex·ter·nal·i·ty (ek′stər nal′i tē) *n., pl.* **-ties. 1.** the quality or state of being external. **2.** an external thing or aspect.

ex·ter·nal·ize (ek stûr′nə līz′, ik-) *v.t.,* **-ized, -iz·ing. 1.** to give external existence to; make external. **2.** to attribute to external causes or factors: *to externalize one's problems.* —**ex·ter′nal·i·za′tion,** *n.*

external respiration, the exchange of oxygen and carbon dioxide across respiratory surfaces, as gills or lungs, in multicellular organisms; breathing. ➡ distinguished from **internal respiration.**

ex·ter·o·cep·tor (ek′stər ə sep′tər) *n.* an organ in or near the skin or a mucous membrane responding to stimuli from outside the body, such as pressure or temperature. [Latin *exterus* on the outside, external + (RE)CEPTOR.]

ex·ter·ri·to·ri·al (eks′ter i tôr′ē əl) *adj.* extraterritorial. —**ex·ter′ri·to′ri·al′i·ty,** *n.* —**ex′ter·ri·to′ri·al·ly,** *adv.*

ex·tinct (ek stingkt′, ik-) *adj.* **1.** no longer in existence: *an extinct species.* **2.** no longer active; extinguished: *an extinct volcano.* [Latin *ex(s)tinctus,* past participle of *ex(s)tinguere* to quench, kill.]

ex·tinc·tion (ek stingk′shən, ik-) *n.* **1.** the state or condition of being or becoming extinct: *Efforts have been made to prevent the extinction of the buffalo.* **2.** the act of extinguishing or the state of being extinguished.

ex·tin·guish (ek sting′gwish, ik-) *v.t.* **1.** to put out; quench: *to extinguish a fire.* **2.** to put an end to; destroy: *to extinguish hope.* **3.** to obscure, as by some superior quality; eclipse: *The scientist's discovery extinguished the achievements of her colleague.* [Latin *ex(s)tinguere* to quench, kill + *-ish* (as in PERISH).] —**ex·tin′guish·a·ble,** *adj.*

ex·tin·guish·er (ek sting′gwi shər, ik-) *n.* **1.** a person or thing that extinguishes. **2.** fire extinguisher.

ex·tir·pate (ek′stər pāt′, ek stûr′pāt, ik-) *v.t.,* **-pat·ed, -pat·ing. 1.** to remove or destroy completely; eradicate: *The church strove to extirpate heresy.* **2.** to tear up by the roots; uproot. [Latin *ex(s)tirpātus,* past participle of *ex(s)tirpāre* to pluck out by the stem, from *ex* out + *stirps* stem.] —**ex′tir·pa′tion,** *n.*

ex·tol (ek stōl′, ik-) *also,* **ex·toll.** *v.t.,* **-tolled, -tol·ling.** to praise highly; laud: *She extolled her brother's virtues.* [Latin *extollere* to raise up.] —For Synonyms, see **praise.**

ex·tort (ek stôrt′, ik-) *v.t.* to obtain (something) by threats, force, abuse of authority, or other type of oppression: *to extort money, to extort a confession.* [Latin *extortus,* past participle of *extorquēre* to twist out.] —**ex·tort′er,** *n.* —**ex·tor′tive,** *n.*

ex·tor·tion (ek stôr′shən, ik-) *n.* **1.** the obtaining of money or another valuable thing by threats, force, abuse of authority, or other type of oppression. **2.** something that has been extorted.

ex·tor·tion·ate (ek stôr′shə nit, ik-) *adj.* **1.** grossly excessive; exorbitant: *an extortionate price.* **2.** characterized by extortion. —**ex·tor′tion·ate·ly,** *adv.*

ex·tor·tion·ist (ek stôr′shə nist, ik-) *n.* a person who is guilty of or practices extortion. Also, **ex·tor′tion·er.**

ex·tra (ek′strə) *adj.* more than what is usual, expected, or needed: *extra work, extra books, extra pay.* —*n.* **1.** something in addition to what is usual, expected, or needed: *an automobile with power brakes, air conditioning, and other extras.* **2.** an additional charge or expense: *The dinner cost eight dollars without the tax and other extras.* **3.** a special edition of a newspaper, issued at a time other than that of a regular edition, to carry the account of an extraordinary news event. **4.** a person employed to play a minor, usually nonspeaking, part, esp. in a crowd scene, in a motion picture or other production. —*adv.* unusually; extraordinarily: *an extra large size, extra dry wine.* [Probably short for EXTRAORDINARY.]

a	at	e	end	o	hot	u	up	hw	white	⟨	about
ā	ape	ē	me	ō	old	ū	use	ng	song		taken
ä	far	i	it	ô	fork	ü	rule	th	thin	ə	pencil
âr	care	ī	ice	oi	oil	u̇	pull	th	this		lemon
				îr	pierce	ou	out	ûr	turn	zh	measure	⟨	circus

adj. **Extra** and **additional** mean beyond a normal or required amount. **Extra** more often refers to a specific number or quantity: *They bought five extra cups to allow for breakage.* It may also suggest superfluousness: *We won't need the extra blankets because it's a warm night.* **Additional** implies something attached or added on: *This doll comes with an additional set of clothes.*

extra- *prefix* outside; beyond; besides: *extraordinary, extracurricular.* [Latin *extrā.*]

ex·tra·cel·lu·lar (ek′strə sel′yə lər) *adj. Biology.* located or occurring outside the cell membrane. ➡ distinguished from **intracellular.** [EXTRA- + CELLULAR.]

ex·tract (*v.*, ek strakt′, ik–; *n.*, ek′strakt) *v.t.* **1.** to draw or pull out by effort or force: *to extract a tooth.* **2.** to obtain (a substance) by a chemical or mechanical process, as by pressing, cooking, or distilling: *to extract oil from safflowers, to extract wine from grapes.* **3.** to obtain by force, threats, or similar oppression; extort: *to extract information.* **4.** to derive (something, as pleasure or happiness) from a particular source: *She extracted great satisfaction from winning the award.* **5.** to take out or select, as a passage from a book. **6.** to deduce, as a principle or doctrine; infer. **7.** *Mathematics.* to find or calculate (the root of a number). —*n.* **1.** something that is extracted, esp. a passage from a book. **2.** a concentrated preparation containing the essence of a substance: *vanilla extract.* [Latin *extractus,* past participle of *extrahere* to draw out.] —**ex·tract′a·ble;** also **ex·tract′i·ble,** *adj.*

ex·trac·tion (ek strak′shən, ik–) *n.* **1.** the act of extracting or the state of being extracted. **2.** descent; lineage: *He is of Swedish extraction.* **3.** something that is extracted.

ex·trac·tive (ek strak′tiv, ik–) *adj.* **1.** tending or serving to extract. **2.** capable of being extracted. **3.** relating to or the nature of, or produced by extraction. —*n.* something that is extracted.

ex·trac·tor (ek strak′tər, ik–) *n.* **1.** a person or thing that extracts, such as a device for extracting teeth. **2.** the part of a firearm that withdraws the spent cartridge from the chamber.

ex·tra·cur·ric·u·lar (ek′strə kə rik′yə lər) *adj.* not part of the regular academic program or course of study: *Working on the school paper is an extracurricular activity.*

ex·tra·dit·a·ble (ek′strə dī′tə bəl) *adj.* subject to or deserving extradition: *an extraditable crime.*

ex·tra·dite (ek′strə dīt′) *v.t.,* **-dit·ed, -dit·ing. 1.** to transfer custody of (an accused individual or fugitive) to the legal jurisdiction of another nation or state, for trial or punishment there. **2.** to obtain the extradition of (an accused individual or fugitive) from another state or nation. [From EXTRADITION.]

ex·tra·di·tion (ek′strə dish′ən) *n.* the surrender of an accused individual or fugitive by one state or nation to the legal jurisdiction of another. [French *extradition,* from Latin *ex* out + *trāditiō* a delivering up, surrender.]

ex·tra·dos (ek′strə dos′, -dōs′, ek strā′dos, -dōs) *n.* an exterior curve or surface of an arch or vault. For illustration, see **arch[1].** [French *extrados,* from Latin *extrā* outside + French *dos* back (from Latin *dorsum*).]

ex·tra·ga·lac·tic (ek′strə gə lak′tik) *adj.* beyond or originating beyond the Milky Way. [EXTRA- + GALACTIC.]

ex·tra·mar·i·tal (ek′strə mar′i təl) *adj.* relating to sexual relations outside of marriage.

ex·tra·mu·ral (ek′strə myūr′əl) *adj.* involving participants from more than one school or organization. [EXTRA- + Latin *mūrālis* relating to a wall, from *mūrus* wall.]

ex·tra·ne·ous (ek strā′nē əs, ik–) *adj.* **1.a.** having no relevance; not pertinent; irrelevant: *That statement is extraneous to this discussion.* **b.** not belonging or essential: *extraneous ornamentation.* **2.** of external origin; not belonging; foreign: *extraneous matter.* [Latin *extrāneus* external, foreign. Doublet of STRANGE.]

ex·tra·or·di·naire (eks trä ôr dē neR′) *adj. French.* very remarkable; exceptional. ➡ used after the noun: *a chef extraordinaire.* [French *extra-* extra- + *ordinaire* regular, ordinary.]

ex·traor·di·nar·y (ek strôr′də ner′ē, ik–, ek′strə ôr′-) *adj.* **1.** beyond or above the usual or ordinary; very unusual or remarkable; exceptional: *extraordinary strength, extraordinary intelligence.* **2.** additional to the regular staff; specially appointed or employed. ➡ usually used after the noun: *an envoy extraordinary.* [Latin *extrāōrdinārius* out of the usual order, from *extrā* ōrdinem outside the (usual) order.] —**ex·traor′di·nar′i·ly,** *adv.* —**ex·traor′di·nar′i·ness,** *n.*

Extraordinary, exceptional, and **unusual** are often used to mean so uncommon as to be noteworthy. In this sense, **extraordinary** implies a sense of wonder: *What an extraordinary building that is!* **Exceptional** connotes falling outside a rule or norm: *This building is exceptional in its efficient use of solar energy.* **Unusual** is a more neutral term than the other two: *There are several unusual buildings in this part of town.*

ex·trap·o·late (ek strap′ə lāt′, ik–) *v.t., v.i.,* **-lat·ed, -lat·ing. 1.** *Mathematics.* to estimate (the value of a quantity or function that lies outside the range of known values) on the basis of values already determined. **2.** to make conjectures about (something unknown) on the basis of something known: *to extrapolate the results of an election from early returns.* [EXTRA + (INTER)POLATE.] —**ex·trap′o·la′tion,** *n.*

ex·tra·sen·so·ry (ek′strə sen′sə rē) *adj.* beyond the range of normal sense perception.

extrasensory perception, the ability to perceive external objects, thoughts, or events without the aid of the senses.

ex·tra·ter·res·tri·al (ek′strə tə res′trē əl) *adj.* originating in or inhabiting regions outside the earth and its atmosphere. —*n.* an extraterrestrial being.

ex·tra·ter·ri·to·ri·al (ek′strə ter′i tôr′ē əl) *adj.* **1.** outside the jurisdiction of the country in which it is situated: *extraterritorial property, extraterritorial rights.* **2.** outside the territory of a country: *extraterritorial waters.* Also, **exterritorial.** —**ex′tra·ter′ri·to′ri·al·ly,** *adv.*

ex·tra·ter·ri·to·ri·al·i·ty (ek′strə ter′i tôr′ē al′i tē) *n.* **1.** immunity from the force of local law, as accorded foreign diplomats and their residences. **2.** the operation of a country's laws outside its own territory, as over its citizens living in other countries.

ex·trav·a·gance (ek strav′ə gəns, ik–) *n.* **1.** lavish or wasteful spending of money. **2.** extreme or unreasonable excess, as in speech or behavior. **3.** an instance of excess or wastefulness: *With my present income, the purchase of a car would be an extravagance.*

ex·trav·a·gant (ek strav′ə gənt, ik–) *adj.* **1.** lavish or wasteful in the spending of money: *an extravagant person.* **2.** characterized by a disregard for reasonable limits in the spending of money: *an extravagant purchase, extravagant tastes, extravagant living.* **3.** beyond reasonable limits; unrestrained: *extravagant demands.* **4.** unreasonably high; exorbitant: *extravagant prices.* [Medieval Latin *extrāvagāns,* present participle of *extrāvagārī* to wander outside (bounds), from Latin *extrā* beyond + *vagārī* to wander.] —**ex·trav′a·gant·ly,** *adv.* —For Synonyms, see **wasteful.**

ex·trav·a·gan·za (ek strav′ə gan′zə, ik–) *n.* a lavish, elaborate show or theatrical production; spectacle. [Italian *(e)stravaganza* oddness, eccentricity, going back to Medieval Latin *extrāvagāns.* See EXTRAVAGANT.]

ex·trav·a·sate (ek strav′ə sāt′, ik–) *v.,* **-sat·ed, -sat·ing.** —*v.t.* to force out or to cause to escape from its proper channel, as blood from a blood vessel. —*v.i.* to escape or flow from the proper vessel or channel into surrounding tissue, as lymph or blood. [EXTRA- + VAS + -ATE[1].] —**ex′trav′a·sa′tion,** *n.*

ex·tra·ve·hic·u·lar activity (ek′strə vē hik′yə lər) any of various maneuvers or experiments performed or occurring outside a vehicle in outer space.

ex·tra·ver·sion (ek′strə vûr′zhen, -shən) *n.* extroversion.

ex·tra·vert (ek′strə vûrt′) extrovert.

ex·treme (ek strēm′, ik–) *adj.,* **-trem·er, -trem·est. 1.** of the highest or greatest degree; exceedingly great or severe: *extreme pain, extreme pleasure, extreme danger.* **2.** going beyond what is usual or considered as moderate or reasonable: *extreme fashions, extreme views, extreme measures.* **3.** at the outermost limit; farthest: *The house is at the extreme end of the street.* —*n.* **1.** the greatest or highest degree: *Starvation is the extreme of hunger.* **2.** something extreme, as an action, condition, or measure. **3.** outermost limit; farthest point: *Red is at one extreme of the visible spectrum.* **4.** extremes. complete opposites: *Joy and grief are extremes.* **5.** *Mathematics.* the first or fourth term of a proportion. In the proportion *a:b::c:d, a* and *d* are the extremes. ➡ distinguished from **mean[3].** [Old French *extreme* outermost, ultimate, from Latin *extrēmus* outermost, superlative of *exterus* outward.] —**ex·treme′ness,** *n.*

• **to go to extremes.** to use extreme measures; do something drastic.

ex·treme·ly (ek strēm′lē, ik–) *adv.* very; exceedingly: *extremely tired, an extremely difficult problem.*

extremely high frequency, a radio frequency between 30,000 and 300,000 megahertz.

extreme unction, see **anointing of the sick.**

ex·trem·ism (ek strē′miz′əm, ik–) *n.* a tendency to be extreme, esp. in politics.

ex·trem·ist (ek strē′mist, ik–) *n.* a person who advocates extreme measures or holds extreme views, esp. in politics. —*adj.* of or relating to extremism or extremists.

ex·trem·i·ty (ek strem′i tē, ik–) *n., pl.* **-ties. 1.** the farthest or outermost part or point; very end. **2.** a limb of the body. **3.** extremities. the hands and feet. **4.** the greatest or highest degree: *the extremity of pain.* **5.** an extreme measure or action. **6.** an extreme condition, as of need or danger: *In their extremity, they sought help anywhere they could find it.*

ex·tri·ca·ble (ek′stri kə bəl) *adj.* capable of being extricated.

ex·tri·cate (ek′stri kāt′) *v.t.*, **-cat·ed, -cat·ing.** to set free or remove, as from entanglement or difficulty: *We extricated the fish from the net. The family extricated itself from debt.* [Latin *extrīcātus,* past participle of *extrīcāre* to disentangle, from *ex* out of + *trīcae* trifles, perplexities.] **—ex′tri·ca′tion,** *n.*

ex·trin·sic (ek strin′sik, -zik, ik-) *adj.* **1.** not inherent in, or essential to, the nature of a thing; extraneous: *That statement is extrinsic to the discussion.* **2.** coming or acting from without; external: *an extrinsic force.* [Late Latin *extrīnsecus* outer, from Latin *extrīnsecus* from without.] **—ex·trin′si·cal·ly,** *adv.*

ex·trorse (ek strôrs′, ek′strôrs) *adj. Botany.* facing or directed outward, as anthers that open away from the center of the flower. ➡ opposed to **introrse.** [French *extrorse,* from Late Latin *extrorsus,* from Latin *extra* outside + *vorsus* turned, variant of *versus,* past participle of *vertere* to turn.]

ex·tro·ver·sion (ek′strə vûr′zhən, -shən) *also,* **extraversion.** *n.* a preoccupation with things outside oneself rather than with one's own inner experiences. ➡ opposed to **introversion.** [*Extro-,* form of EXTRA- + Late Latin *versiō* a turning (from Latin *vertere* to turn).]

ex·tro·vert (ek′strə vûrt′) *also,* **extravert.** *n.* **1.** a person whose attention is largely directed outside himself or herself. **2.** an active, outgoing person. ➡ opposed to **introvert.** [*Extro-,* form of EXTRA- + Latin *vertere* to turn.] **—ex′tro·vert′ed,** *adj.*

ex·trude (ek strüd′, ik-) *v.,* **-trud·ed, -trud·ing.** —*v.t.* **1.** to force or push out, as by squeezing. **2.** to shape (plastic or metal) by forcing through a die or mold. —*v.i.* to stick out; protrude. [Latin *extrūdere* to thrust out.]

ex·tru·sion (ek strü′zhən, ik-) *n.* **1.** the act or process of extruding. **2.** a thing that has been extruded. [From EXTRUDE, on the model of *intrusion* and *intrude.*]

ex·tru·sive (ek strü′siv, ik-) *adj.* **1.** tending to extrude. **2.** having been extruded onto the earth's surface: *Solidified lava is extrusive rock.*

ex·u·ber·ance (eg zü′bər əns, ig-) *n.* the state or quality of being exuberant. Also, **ex·u′ber·an·cy.**

ex·u·ber·ant (eg zü′bər ənt, ig-) *adj.* **1.** overflowing with high spirits, enthusiasm, or vigor; elated: *The fans were exuberant when their team won the championship.* **2.** given or produced in great abundance; lavish; effusive: *exuberant praise.* **3.** producing abundantly; prolific; fertile: *an exuberant imagination.* [Latin *exūberāns,* present participle of *exūberāre* to grow luxuriantly, be abundant, going back to *ex* utterly + *ūber* fertile.] **—ex·u′ber·ant·ly,** *adv.*

ex·u·date (eks′yŭ dāt′, ek′sə-, eg′zə-) *n.* **1.** something that is exuded, such as sweat or sap. **2.** exuded biological material, esp. matter with a high content of protein and cells discharged into areas of inflammation.

ex·u·da·tion (eks′yŭ dā′shən, ek′sə dā′-, eg′zə-) *n.* **1.** the act of exuding. **2.** exudate.

ex·ude (eg zŭd′, ig-, ek süd′, ik-) *v.,* **-ud·ed, -ud·ing.** —*v.t.* **1.** to discharge (a substance) gradually, as through pores; ooze forth. **2.** to give forth: *to exude warmth, to exude charm.* —*v.i.* to come out gradually; ooze out: *Sap exuded from the pine tree.* [Latin *ex(s)ūdāre* to sweat out.]

ex·ult (eg zult′, ig-) *v.i.* to rejoice greatly; be joyful: *to exult in triumph.* [Latin *ex(s)ultāre,* from *ex* out + *salīre* to leap.] **—ex·ult′ing·ly,** *adv.*

ex·ult·ant (eg zul′tənt, ig-) *adj.* triumphantly joyful; jubilant; elated. **—ex·ult′ant·ly,** *adv.*

ex·ul·ta·tion (eg′zul tā′shən, ek′sul-) *n.* triumphant joy; jubilation; elation.

ex·urb (ek′sûrb, eg′zûrb) *n.* a residential area between the suburbs of a city and the country. [EX-[1] + (SUB)URB.] **—ex·ur′ban,** *adj.*

ex·ur·ban·ite (ek sûr′bə nīt′, eg zûr′-) *n.* a person who lives in an exurb.

ex·ur·bi·a (ek sûr′bē ə, eg zûr-′) *n.* exurbs collectively.

ex·u·vi·ate (eg zü′vē āt′, ek sü′-) *v.t., v.i.,* **-vi·at·ed, -vi·at·ing.** to shed or cast off; molt. [Latin *exuvial* castoff coverings of animals (from *exuere* to strip off) + -ATE[1].]

-ey *suffix* form of -Y[1], as in *gooey.*

ey·as (ī′əs) *n.* a nestling hawk. [Earlier *nyas,* from Old French *niais* nestling, going back to Latin *nīdus* nest. The phrase *a nyas* came to be divided incorrectly as *an eyas.* For a similar development, see ADDER.]

eye (ī) *n.* **1.a.** an organ of vision. **b.** the organ of sight in vertebrate animals, typically one of a pair of spherical bodies set within a socket in the skull. **2.** the iris of this organ, esp. with respect to its color: *She has blue eyes.* **3.** the area surrounding this organ, including the eyelids: *a swollen eye.* **4.** this organ with respect to its capacity for seeing: *My eyes are not as good as they used to be.* **5.** a heedful glance; look: *We cast an envious eye on the shiny new car.* **6.** an attentive or close watch: *Please keep an eye*

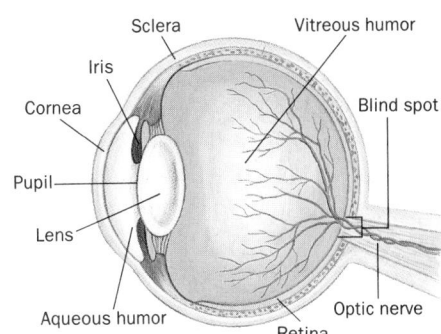

human **eye**

out for trouble. The police are keeping an eye on them. **7.** the ability to discriminate, perceive, or judge with the eyes: *to have an eye for beauty.* **8.** *usually,* **eyes.** a point of view; opinion; judgment: *In the eyes of his fellow citizens, he was an honest man.* **9.** something resembling the eye in shape, position, or function, as the bud of a potato or the hole at the end of a needle through which the thread passes. **10.** the small, cloudless center of a hurricane, having very light winds and low pressure. **11.** the center or focus, as of light, power, or influence: *Athens, the eye of Greece* (John Milton, 1671). —*v.t.,* **eyed, ey′ing** or **eye·ing.** to look at; watch carefully. [Old English *ēage* organ of sight, eye of a needle.]

· **all eyes.** closely attentive.

· **an eye for an eye.** punishment or retribution similar or equivalent to the injury or damage suffered.

· **in the public eye.** noticed by the public; widely known: *Her outspoken remarks to reporters kept her in the public eye.*

· **to catch (someone's) eye.** to attract (someone's) attention.

· **to give (someone) the eye.** *Slang.* to look at (someone) with desire, invitation, or admiration.

· **to make eyes at.** to look at flirtatiously or amorously.

· **to see eye to eye.** to agree completely.

· **to set (or lay) eyes on.** to perceive with the eyes; see.

· **to shut one's eyes to.** to refuse to see or think about; ignore.

· **with an eye to.** in anticipation of; for the purpose of: *to buy land with an eye to building a house.*

eye·ball (ī′bôl′) *n.* the ball-shaped portion of the eye, enclosed by the eyelids and the eye socket.

eye·brow (ī′brou′) *n.* **1.** the bony ridge projecting over the eye. **2.** the fringe of hair growing on this.

eye·catch·er (ī′kach′ər) *n.* a person or thing that attracts one's close attention: *My friend's shiny new car is quite an eyecatcher.*

eye·catch·ing (ī′kach′ing) *adj.* attracting one's close attention; very appealing; striking: *an eyecatching advertisement.* [From the phrase *to catch (one's) eye.*]

eye contact, the act or fact of looking into the eyes of another.

eye·cup (ī′kup′) *n.* a small cup with a rim shaped to fit closely over the eye, used in washing the eyes or applying medicine to them.

eye doctor 1. ophthalmologist. **2.** optometrist.

eye·drop·per (ī′drop′ər) *n.* a dropper for administering eye medicine.

eye·ful (ī′fŭl′) *n., pl.* **-fuls. 1.** an amount of something thrown, blown, or squirted into the eye: *an eyeful of dust.* **2.** a full or satisfying look. **3.** *Informal.* a person who is very attractive.

eye·glass (ī′glas′) *n.* **1.** a glass lens, as a monocle, used to aid or correct poor vision. **2.** **eyeglasses.** a pair of glass lenses mounted in frames, used to aid or correct poor vision. **3.** eyepiece. **4.** eyecup.

eye hole 1. eye socket. **2.** peephole. **3.** a round opening for a hook or lace to go through; eyelet.

eye·lash (ī′lash′) *n.* **1.** one of the stiff hairs growing on the edge of the eyelid. **2.** *also,* **eyelashes.** a fringe of these hairs that helps to keep foreign matter out of the eyes.

eye·less (ī′lis) *n.* without eyes; blind.

a	at	e	end	o	hot	u	up	hw	white		about
ā	ape	ē	me	ō	old	ū	use	ng	song		taken
ä	far	i	it	ô	fork	ü	rule	th	thin	ə	pencil
âr	care	ī	ice	oi	oil	u̇	pull	t͟h	this		lemon
				îr	pierce	ou	out	ûr	turn	zh	measure		circus

437

eye·let (ī′lit) *n.* **1.** a small hole in a material, such as leather or cloth, for the passage of a cord or lace: *Shoelaces are passed through eyelets.* **2.** a metal or plastic ring lining such a hole to reinforce it. **3.** a small hole edged with stitches, used to make a pattern or edging in embroidery. **4.** any of various fabrics, esp. cotton, decorated with this pattern. [Old French *oeillet* little eye, small hole, diminutive of *oeil* eye, from Latin *oculus;* Modern English spelling influenced by EYE.]

eye·lid (ī′lid′) *n.* a movable, protective fold of skin that serves to open and shut the eyes.

eye·lin·er (ī′lī′nər) *n.* a cosmetic used to outline the eyes to emphasize their shape.

eye-o·pen·er (ī′ō′pə nər) *n. Informal.* **1.** something surprising or enlightening, as a piece of news or an experience. **2.** a drink of alcoholic liquor taken after awakening.

eye·piece (ī′pēs′) *n.* the lens or combination of lenses nearest to the eye of the user in an optical instrument, esp. a telescope or microscope.

eye shadow, a tinted cosmetic cream, powder, or liquid applied to the eyelids.

eye·shot (ī′shot′) *n.* range of vision: *There was nothing moving within eyeshot.*

eye·sight (ī′sīt′) *n.* **1.** the power or faculty of seeing; sight: *A hawk has keen eyesight.* **2.** range of vision; view.

eye socket, the bony cavity in which the eyeball is located; orbit.

eye·sore (ī′sôr′) *n.* something ugly or unpleasant to look at: *That old shack is an eyesore.*

eye·spot (ī′spot′) *n.* a sensory structure present in many lower animals, such as protozoa, flatworms, and certain echinoderms. It is believed to be used for distinguishing between light and dark.

eye·stalk (ī′stôk′) *n.* a jointed, movable stalk upon which the eye is borne in certain crustaceans, such as lobsters, crayfish, and shrimp.

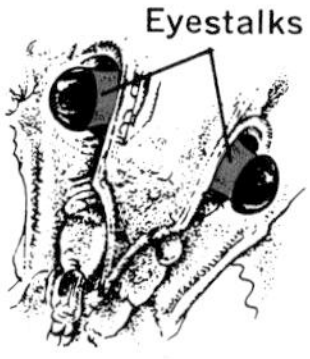

eye·strain (ī′strān′) *n.* a tired or irritated condition of the eyes caused by defects in vision that are uncorrected, use of the eyes under poor conditions, or excessive use, such as the extended watching of motion pictures.

eye·tooth (ī′tüth′) *n., pl.* **-teeth** (-tēth′). either one of the two canine teeth in the upper jaw between the incisors and the bicuspids.

Eyestalks

eyestalks on a crayfish

eye·wash (ī′wôsh′, ī′wosh′) *n.* **1.** a liquid solution used to clean or bathe the eyes. **2.** *Slang.* nonsense; hogwash.

eye·wit·ness (ī′wit′nis) *n.* a person who has actually seen something happen and can testify concerning it.

ey·rie (âr′ē, îr′ē, ir′ē) *also,* **ey·ry.** *n., pl.* **-ries.** aerie.

Ezek., Ezekiel.

E·ze·ki·el (i zē′kē əl) *also,* **E·ze·chi·el.** *n.* a book of the Old Testament, containing the writings and prophecies of the Hebrew prophet Ezekiel.

Ez·ra (ez′rə) *n.* a book of the Old Testament, attributed to the Hebrew prophet Ezra. Also, **Esdras.**

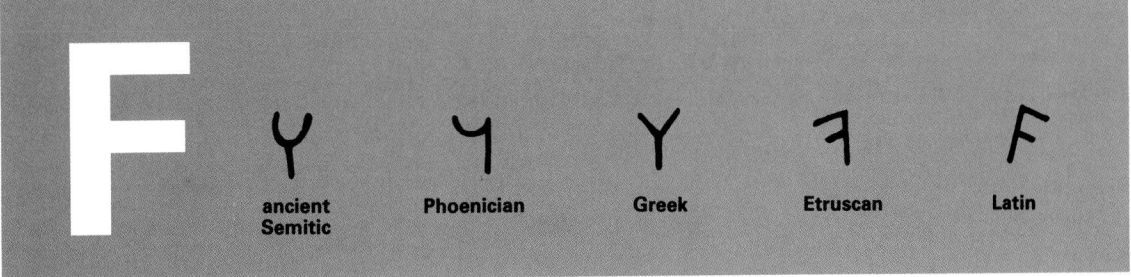

| ancient Semitic | Phoenician | Greek | Etruscan | Latin |

F Although the *f* sound, as in *fish*, was not represented in early alphabets, the shape of the English letter **F**, like **V** and **Y**, has its origins in the ancient Semitic letter *waw*, which depicted a hook and stood for the sound of *w* in *water*. When the Phoenicians borrowed *waw*, they used it to represent both the consonant sound *w* and the vowel sound *ü*, as heard in the English word *rude*. The Greeks adopted *waw* and called it *upsilon*, writing it as the capital letter **Y** is written today and using it only to represent the *ü* sound. The *w* sound was represented by the Greek letter *digamma*, which looked something like a modern capital letter **F**. The Etruscans borrowed *digamma*, which they wrote facing in either direction, and used it to stand for the *f* sound. The Etruscan form of *digamma* was adopted by the Romans to represent the *f* sound in the Latin alphabet. The shape of our modern capital **F** closely resembles the letter the Romans used about 2,400 years ago.

---

f, F (ef) *n., pl.* **f's, F's. 1.** the sixth letter of the English alphabet. **2.** the shape of this letter or something having this shape.
F (ef) *n., pl.* **F's. 1.** *Music.* **a.** the fourth note or tone of the diatonic scale of C major. For illustration, see **do²**. **b.** the scale or key that has this note or tone as its tonic. **2.** a grade or rating indicating failure: *an F in a course.*
F, the symbol for fluorine.
f. 1. farthing. **2.** female. **3.** feminine. **4.** forte. **5.** franc; francs. **6.** *Mathematics.* function.
F 1. Fahrenheit. **2.** *Photography.* **a.** f-number. **b.** focal length.
F. 1. February. **2.** French. **3.** Friday.
fa (fä) *n. Music.* the fourth of the series of syllables used to name the eight tones of the diatonic scale. For illustration, see **do²**. [See GAMUT.]
FAA, Federal Aviation Administration.
Fa·bi·an (fā'bē ən) *adj.* **1.** characterized by prolonged harassment of an opponent, while avoiding direct conflict: *The general's Fabian tactics helped to conserve ammunition.* **2.** of or relating to the Fabian Society. —*n.* a member of the Fabian Society. [Latin *Fabiānus,* relating to the Roman general *Fabius* Maximus, who helped to win the Second Punic War by avoiding a direct conflict with Hannibal, the Carthaginian general.]
Fabian Society, an English socialist organization founded in 1884, advocating the gradual introduction of socialism through legislation.
fa·ble (fā'bəl) *n.* **1.** a short story meant to teach a moral, esp. one using animals or inanimate objects as characters. **2.** a traditional story about supernatural beings or heroic figures; legend; myth. **3.** an untrue story or account; falsehood; fabrication. —*v.t.,* **-bled, -bling.** to tell or write about as if true: *The house is fabled to have been inhabited by ghosts.* [Old French *fable* story, tale, from Latin *fābula.*] —For Synonyms, see **legend.**
fa·bled (fā'bəld) *adj.* **1.** described or told about in fables; mythical; legendary: *a fabled hero.* **2.** not real; fictitious; invented. **3.** famous.
fab·li·au (fab'lē ō') *n., pl.* **-aux** (-ōz'). a short, metrical tale about an incident of ordinary life, usually treated in a comic or bawdy way, popular in France and England in the twelfth and thirteenth centuries. [French *fabliau,* going back to Old French *fable.* See FABLE.]
fab·ric (fab'rik) *n.* **1.** woven, knitted, or otherwise fabricated material, usually made from natural or synthetic fibers; cloth. **2.** the texture of such a material: *cloth with a rough fabric.* **3.** a system of connected or related parts; framework; structure: *Inflation is weakening the fabric of our economy.* [French *fabrique*

factory, a making, from Latin *fabrica* workshop. Doublet of FORGE¹.]
fab·ri·cate (fab'ri kāt') *v.t.,* **-cat·ed, -cat·ing. 1.** to make up; invent: *to fabricate an excuse.* **2.** to manufacture, construct, or process, esp. by assembling or creating standardized parts: *to fabricate a boat.* [Latin *fabricātus,* past participle of *fabricārī* to build, from *fabrica* workshop.] —**fab'ri·ca'tor,** *n.*
fab·ri·ca·tion (fab'ri kā'shən) *n.* **1.** the process of manufacturing or constructing. **2.** something fabricated, esp. a false statement.
fab·u·list (fab'yə list) *n.* **1.** an inventor or writer of fables. **2.** a liar.
fab·u·lous (fab'yə ləs) *adj.* **1.** so great or extreme as to seem unreal; incredible; amazing: *They spend fabulous sums of money on clothes.* **2.** *Informal.* exceptionally good; wonderful: *I had a fabulous time at the party.* **3.** of or like a fable; imaginary; legendary: *We read about a winged dragon and other fabulous monsters.* [Latin *fābulōsus,* from *fābula* story, tale.] —**fab'u·lous·ly,** *adv.* —**fab'u·lous·ness,** *n.*
fa·cade (fə säd') *also,* **fa·çade.** *n.* **1.** the front of a building. **2.** a false front or outward appearance; illusion; pretense: *Behind a facade of prosperity, the company was going bankrupt.* [French *façade* front of a building, going back to Latin *facies* face.]
face (fās) *n.* **1.** the front of the head. **2.a.** a specific look or expression; countenance: *to put on a happy face.* **b.** a specific attitude, esp. one assumed in public: *to put on a brave face about one's illness.* **3.** a distorted or peculiar expression; grimace: *to make faces in the mirror.* **4.** *Informal.* the quality of being bold or impudent; effrontery: *She had the face to insult him in public.* **5.** dignity, self-respect, or prestige: *to lose face, to save face.* **6.** the front, principal, or outward surface of something: *the face of a cliff, on the face of the earth.* **7.** the surface or side of something that is marked, finished, or otherwise prepared for use: *the face of a clock, the face of a fabric.* **8.** an outward appearance: *to put a new face on an old issue.* **9.** facial cosmetics: *to take off one's face before going to bed.* **10.** *Geometry.* one of the surfaces or sides of a solid: *A cube has six faces.* **11.** the excavated surface of a mineral deposit, as in a coal mine. **12.** *Economics.* face value. **13.** *Printing.* **a.** the surface of a piece of type, which carries the letter or character to be printed. **b.** the style or design of this surface. —*v.,* **faced, fac·ing.** —*v.t.* **1.a.** to have or turn the face toward: *The model faced the camera.* **b.** to front on: *The house faces the park.* **2.** to turn the face of: *Face the plant toward the light.* **3.** to meet in competition; confront: *The candidate faced strong opposition.* **4.a.** to be sure or likely to experience: *to face many obstacles to a goal.* **b.** to be confronted with or by: *to face a new situation, to face criticism.* **c.** to be a matter of concern for: *What problems are facing you?* **5.** to realize and admit; accept: *to face the facts.* **6.** to cover or line the surface of: *to face the collar of a coat with fur, to face a building with brick.* **7.** to smooth or dress the surface of: *to face stone.* **8.** to turn the face of (a playing card) upward. —*v.i.* **1.** to be turned or placed with the face in a particular direction: *The house faced west.* **2.** to turn in a particular direction: *She faced left.* [Old French *face* visage, going back to Latin *faciēs* form, visage.] —**fac'er,** *n.*
•**face to face.** facing each other: *The two men stood face to face.*
•**face to face with.** in or into the presence of or confrontation with: *She was nervous about coming face to face with her critics.*
•**in the face of. a.** when near or confronted with: *He ran in the*

---

a	at	e	end	o	hot	u	up	hw	white		about
ā	ape	ē	me	ō	old	ū	use	ng	song		taken
ä	far	i	it	ô	fork	ü	rule	th	thin	ə	pencil
âr	care	ī	ice	oi	oil	u̇	pull	th	this		lemon
		ir	pierce	ou	out	ûr	turn	zh	measure		circus

F

439

face of danger. **b.** in defiance or disregard of; notwithstanding; despite: *They married in the face of strong opposition from their families.*

• **on the face of it.** judging from outward appearances; seemingly: *On the face of it her complaint doesn't seem justified.*

• **to face down.** to cause to retreat or feel uneasy by speaking or acting confidently: *to face down one's opponent in debate.*

• **to face off. a.** *Hockey.* to start or resume play with a face-off. **b.** to confront or compete: *The teams faced off in the last game of the season. The senator will face off against her opponent in a debate tonight.*

• **to face up to. a.** to confront boldly; resist courageously: *to face up to a bully.* **b.** to admit and accept: *to face up to one's mistakes.*

• **to fly in the face of.** to act in defiance of or in direct opposition to: *a change that flies in the face of tradition.*

• **to put a good** (or **bold** or **brave**) **face on.** to interpret or present in a favorable or optimistic light: *The coach tried to put a good face on the tie by pointing out how strong the other team was.*

• **to show one's face.** to make an appearance: *I was embarrassed to show my face at school after failing the class.*

• **to someone's face.** directly and boldly in someone's presence: *Would you criticize him to his face?*

face card, a jack, queen, king, or, sometimes, ace in a deck of cards.

face·less (fās′lis) *adj.* **1.** lacking a face: *worn and faceless coins.* **2.** having no identity or individuality: *a faceless bureaucracy, a faceless crowd.*

face·lift (fās′lift′) *also,* **face-lift.** *n.* **1.** cosmetic plastic surgery to tighten sagging or wrinkled skin of the face. **2.** any procedure that renovates or modernizes, esp. in a superficial way: *The old city hall is getting new windows as part of its facelift.* Also, **face lifting.**

face-off (fās′ôf′, -of′) *n.* **1.** the act or an instance of starting or resuming play in hockey by having the referee drop the puck between the sticks of two opposing players. **2.** an act or instance of confronting.

face·plate (fās′plāt′) *n.* **1.** a disk that holds work for rotation in a lathe or other machine. **2.** a plate that covers or protects the front of an object.

face powder, cosmetic powder applied to the face to dull the shine, conceal blemishes, or otherwise improve its appearance.

face-sav·ing (fās′sā′ving) *adj.* serving or intended to maintain one's dignity or reputation: *a face-saving excuse.* —*n.* the act of preserving or attempting to preserve one's dignity or reputation: *After my terrible social gaffe, I'm going to have to do some face-saving.*

fac·et (fas′it) *n.* **1.** any of the small, polished plane surfaces of a cut gem. **2.** any of various sides or aspects: *the many facets of a problem, the many facets of one's personality.* **3.** a fillet between the flutings of a column. **4.** any of the segments of the external surface of the compound eye of an insect or crustacean. —*v.t.,* **-et·ed, -et·ing;** *also, British,* **-et·ted, -et·ting.** to cut facets on. [French *facette* little face, small surface, diminutive of *face* face, visage. See FACE.]

gem with nine **facets** showing

fa·ce·tious (fə sē′shəs) *adj.* characterized by flippant humor; not appropriately serious; frivolously amusing: *a facetious writer, a facetious comment.* [French *facétieux,* from *facétie* jest, from Latin *facétia.*] —**fa·ce′tious·ly,** *adv.* —**fa·ce′tious·ness,** *n.*

face-to-face (fās′tə fās′) *adj.* involving close, personal contact; carried on personally between individuals: *a face-to-face discussion.*

face value 1. the value appearing on currency, stamps, and financial instruments: *a gold coin with a face value of two dollars.* **2.** the apparent value: *to accept promises at face value.*

fa·cial (fā′shəl) *adj.* of, for, or relating to the face. —*n.* a massage or other treatment to beautify the face. —**fa′cial·ly,** *adv.*

fa·cies (fā′shē ēz′, -shēz) *n., pl.* **-cies. 1.** general appearance, as of a species of plant. **2.** *Geology.* an attribute of a stratum of rock, as appearance or composition, that reflects the origin of the rock and distinguishes it from adjacent strata. **3.** *Medicine.* a characteristic expression on a patient's face that indicates a specific disease or symptom, such as the pinched, anxious look that accompanies abdominal disease. [Latin *facies* face, appearance, from *facere* to do.]

fac·ile (fas′əl) *adj.* **1.** acting or working with skill and ease; fluent; dexterous: *the facile mind of a genius.* **2.** requiring little effort; easily accomplished or done: *a facile task assigned to a new employee.* **3.** characterized by shallowness or insincerity; too easy:

a facile smile, a facile suggestion. **4.** having a mild disposition; easygoing; mild-tempered. **5.** *Archaic.* easily moved or persuaded; yielding. [Latin *facilis* easy, from *facere* to do.] —**fac′ile·ly,** *adv.* —**fac′ile·ness,** *n.*

fa·cil·i·tate (fə sil′i tāt′) *v.t.,* **-tat·ed, -tat·ing.** to make easier; assist in the success, completion, or operation of: *Zip Codes facilitate mail service.* —**fa·cil′i·ta′tion,** *n.* —**fa·cil′i·ta′tive,** *adj.* —**fa·cil′i·ta′tor,** *n.*

fa·cil·i·ty (fə sil′i tē) *n., pl.* **-ties. 1.** ease of doing or accomplishing; freedom from difficulty or impediment: *Interstate highways have increased the facility of long-distance travel.* **2.** skill or ability; aptitude; dexterity; fluency: *a facility for language, a facility with tools.* **3.** *often,* **facilities.** something, such as a building or piece of equipment, that provides a convenience or serves a particular purpose: *a cabin with cooking facilities, inadequate hospital facilities in rural areas.* **4.** *Archaic.* a tendency to be easily moved or persuaded.

fac·ing (fā′sing) *n.* **1.a.** a fitted piece of fabric sewn inside or outside along an edge of a garment to reinforce or trim it. **b.** the fabric used for this purpose. **2.** a covering in front for ornamentation, protection, or other purposes: *a house with marble facing.* **3. facings.** the cuffs, collar, and trimmings of certain military coats.

fac·sim·i·le (fak sim′ə lē) *n.* **1.** an exact copy or reproduction: *a facsimile of the Constitution.* **2.a.** the high-speed transmission of pictures and printed material by telephone or radio, as in Wirephoto systems. **b.** something, as a photograph or a letter, transmitted by facsimile. Also *(def. 2),* **fax.** [Latin *fac simile* make like, from *fac* make, imperative of *facere* to make + *simile,* neuter of *similis* like.] —For Synonyms, see **duplicate.**

• **in facsimile.** as an exact copy: *This inscription is produced in facsimile.*

fact (fakt) *n.* **1.** something known to be true or real; something that exists or has actually occurred: *Restrict your story to the facts.* **2.** something said to be true or real; something that has supposedly occurred: *The writer's facts are far from trustworthy.* **3.** the quality or state of being actual; reality; truth: *to distinguish fact from fiction.* **4.** something done, esp. a criminal or evil act: *to feel remorse after the fact.* [Latin *factum* deed, act, from *facere* to do. Doublet of FEAT.]

• **as a matter of fact.** actually; really.

• **in fact.** with respect to what is actual or real; actually; really.

• **in point of fact.** actually; really.

fac·tion (fak′shən) *n.* **1.** a group of people within a larger group or organization who share a goal or point of view, esp. such a group acting to promote its own ends. **2.** strife or dissension within an organization. [French *faction* factious party, from Latin *factiō* a doing, party. Doublet of FASHION.]

fac·tion·al (fak′shə nəl) *adj.* of, characteristic of, or producing a faction or factions; partisan: *factional quarrels, factional issues.* —**fac′tion·al·ly,** *adv.*

fac·tion·al·ism (fak′shə nə liz′əm) *n.* the quality or condition of being divided into factions or of tending toward such division: *The political party was split by factionalism.*

fac·tious (fak′shəs) *adj.* **1.** inclined to produce faction; causing dissension: *a factious issue, the factious effect of ambition.* **2.** of, relating to, or characterized by faction: *factious disputes.* [Latin *factiōsus* seditious, from *factiō* a doing, party.] —**fac′tious·ly,** *adv.* —**fac′tious·ness,** *n.*

fac·ti·tious (fak tish′əs) *adj.* lacking naturalness, reality, or spontaneity; not conforming to actual conditions; artificial: *The biased report gave a factitious view of the problem.* [Latin *factīcius,* from *facere* to do, make.] —**fac·ti′tious·ly,** *adv.* —**fac·ti′tious·ness,** *n.*

fac·tor (fak′tər) *n.* **1.** one of several elements that bring about a result or contribute to the formation of a thing or circumstance: *The higher rent was the main factor in their decision to move.* **2.** any of the numbers or algebraic expressions that, when multiplied together, form a product. The factors of $14xy$ are 2, 7, x, and y. **3.** a financial agent or business organization that purchases the accounts receivable of a company, assuming the full risk of and responsibility for their collection. **4.** gene. **5.** a person who transacts business for another; commission merchant. —*v.t.* to break up (a mathematical product) into factors. [Latin *factor* doer, maker, from *facere* to do, make.]

• **to factor in.** to include or take account of: *to factor in property taxes when calculating the cost of a house.*

• **to factor (something) into.** to include or take account of (something) in: *to factor price increases into an estimate.*

fac·tor·age (fak′tər ij) *n.* **1.** the commission charged by a factor or agent. **2.** the business of such an agent; buying and selling on commission.

fac·to·ri·al (fak tôr′ē əl) *n.* the product of an integer and all

lower positive integers. The factorial of 3, written as 3!, is $3 \times 2 \times 1 = 6$.

fac·tor·ize (fak′tə rīz′) *v.t.,* **-ized, -iz·ing.** to factor. —**fac′·tor·i·za′tion,** *n.*

fac·to·ry (fak′tə rē) *n., pl.* **-ries.** a building or group of buildings where goods are manufactured. [Partly from Medieval Latin *factoria* agency; partly from Late Latin *factōrium* oil mill; literally, place where things are made, both from Latin *factor* doer, maker. See FACTOR.]

factory outlet, outlet (*def.* 4).

fac·to·tum (fak tō′təm) *n.* a person employed to do all kinds of work, particularly odd jobs. [Medieval Latin *factotum,* from Latin *fac* do (imperative of *facere* to do) + *tōtum* the whole.]

fac·tu·al (fak′chü əl) *adj.* **1.** of or relating to facts: *factual accuracy.* **2.** consisting of or based on facts: *a factual account.* —**fac′tu·al′i·ty,** *n.* —**fac′tu·al·ly,** *adv.*

fac·u·la (fak′yə lə) *n., pl.* **-lae** (-lē′). a luminous eruption of hot gases near the sunspots on the surface of the sun. [Latin *facula* small torch, diminutive of *fax* torch.]

fac·ul·ty (fak′əl tē) *n., pl.* **-ties. 1.** one of the natural powers of the mind or body: *the faculty of speech, in full possession of one's faculties.* **2.** a special skill or aptitude; gift; talent: *a faculty for putting people at their ease.* **3.** the teachers and administrators of an educational institution, esp. the teaching staff. **4.** a department of learning in an educational institution: *the faculty of nursing.* [Old French *faculte* ability, from Latin *facultās* ability, power.]

fad (fad) *n.* a popular practice, interest, or fashion followed enthusiastically for a short time. [Of uncertain origin.] —**fad′dist,** *n.*

fad·dish (fad′ish) *adj.* **1.** of or characteristic of a fad: *faddish clothes.* **2.** given to following fads: *a faddish crowd.* —**fad′dish·ly,** *adv.* —**fad′dish·ness,** *n.*

fade (fād) *v.,* **fad·ed, fad·ing.** —*v.i.* **1.** to lose color, brightness, or distinctness: *fabrics that won't fade in the wash.* **2.** to lose freshness, vigor, or strength; wither: *The roses faded after three days.* **3.** to disappear gradually; die down: *The sound of the footsteps faded away.* **4.** *Football.* (of an offensive back) to move back from the line of scrimmage, usually in order to throw a forward pass. —*v.t.* **1.** to cause to fade: *Sunlight faded my curtains.* **2.** *Slang.* to cover the bet of (the roller) in dice. —*n.* **1.** a gradual shift from one image to another in a television or film production. **2.** fade-out. [Old French *fader* to make faint or insipid, from *fade* tasteless, weak, going back to a blend of Latin *vapidus* tasteless, insipid + *fatuus* foolish.]

  • **to fade in.** to become or make gradually clearer or louder, as an image or sound.

  • **to fade out.** to become or make gradually less clear, loud, or perceptible.

fade-in (fād′in′) *n.* in motion pictures, radio, television, or recording, the gradual appearance of an image or sound.

fade-out (fād′out′) *n.* **1.** in motion pictures, radio, television, or recording, the gradual disappearance of an image or sound. **2.** any gradual disappearance. Also, **fade.**

fae·cal (fē′kəl) fecal.

fae·ces (fē′sēz) feces.

faer·ie (fâr′ē, fā′ə rē) *also,* **faer·y.** *n., pl.* **faer·ies.** *Archaic.* **1.** fairyland. **2.** fairy. —*adj.* fairy.

Faf·nir (fäv′nir, fäf′-) *n.* in Norse legend, a giant who took the form of a dragon and guarded a treasure until he was killed by Sigurd.

fag[1] (fag) *v.,* **fagged, fag·ging.** —*v.t.* to tire by hard work; exhaust (often with *out*): *After the race, I was completely fagged out.* —*v.i.* **1.** to work hard; toil. **2.** *British. Informal.* to do menial work for an older boy, as in certain English public schools. —*n.* **1.** *British. Informal.* a boy who does menial work for an older boy, as in certain English public schools. **2.** hard, menial work; drudgery. [Of uncertain origin.]

fag[2] (fag) *n. Slang.* cigarette. [From FAG END; originally referring to the last part of a cigarette.]

fag end. 1. a frayed or unfinished end, as of a piece of cloth or rope. **2.** the last and worst part of anything; remnant.

fag·ot (fag′ət) *also,* **fag·got.** *n.* **1.** a bundle of sticks, twigs, or branches, used esp. for fuel. **2.** a bundle of iron or steel pieces to be welded, esp. into bars. —*v.t.* **1.** to make into a fagot; bind together. **2.** to ornament with fagoting. [Old French *fagot* bundle of sticks, probably going back to Greek *phakelos* bundle.]

fag·ot·ing (fag′ə ting) *also,* **fag·got·ing.** *n.* **1.** an ornamental effect in textiles made by drawing a number of parallel threads out of the fabric and tying the cross threads together in the middle. **2.** a decorative openwork stitch used to connect two edges.

Fahr., Fahrenheit.

Fahrenheit, Celsius, and Kelvin temperature scales

Fahr·en·heit (far′ən hīt′) *adj.* of, according to, or designating the temperature scale on which the freezing point of water is at 32 degrees and the boiling point is at 212 degrees under standard atmospheric pressure. [From Gabriel Daniel *Fahrenheit,* 1686-1736, German physicist who devised this scale.]

fa·ience (fī äns′, fā-) *also,* **fa·ïence.** *n.* a variety of earthenware, usually highly decorated and having an opaque glaze. [French *faïence,* from *Faenza,* Italian town where it supposedly was first made.]

fail (fāl) *v.i.* **1.** to be unsuccessful in achieving something attempted, desired, or expected: *The plan failed when it was tested.* **2.** to be deficient or negligent, as in one's duties or obligations: *to fail in one's responsibilities to someone else.* **3.** to be unsuccessful in passing an examination, assignment, or course of study. **4.** to become weaker, as in health or strength: *The elderly woman's eyesight failed.* **5.** to stop working; die out: *The lights failed during the storm.* **6.** to be insufficient; fall short; run out: *The water supply failed.* **7.** to become insolvent; go bankrupt. —*v.t.* **1.** to neglect or not act in such a way as: *He failed to make his point.* **2.** to prove of no use or assistance; disappoint: *His friends failed him in his hour of need.* **3.** to be absent in or depart from; abandon; desert: *Her courage failed her.* **4.a.** to receive a grade of failure in (an examination, assignment, or course). **b.** to give a grade of failure to (a student). [Old French *faillir* to be wanting, going back to Latin *fallere* to deceive, disappoint.]

  • **without fail.** despite whatever happens; definitely; certainly.

fail·ing (fā′ling) *n.* **1.** a negative quality; shortcoming; fault: *My chief failing is a lack of discipline.* **2.** an act, instance, or process of failing; failure. —*prep.* in the absence of; without: *Failing a reply, we will cancel your subscription.* —For Synonyms (*n.*), see **fault.**

faille (fīl, fāl) *n.* a ribbed fabric, usually made with silk or rayon yarn, used for clothing. [French *faille;* of uncertain origin.]

fail-safe (fāl′sāf′) *adj.* **1.** of, relating to, or designating a system that prevents the dropping of bombs or the firing of missiles without confirmation from a specified authority. **2.** designed to continue operating despite mechanical or electrical failure; safe from failure. **3.** guaranteed not to fail; foolproof: *a fail-safe method for losing weight.*

fail·ure (fāl′yər) *n.* **1.** a lack of success in achieving something attempted, desired, or expected: *Failure to win their first game discouraged the team.* **2.** a person or thing that is unsuccessful. **3.** an omission or neglect (of something required): *failure to comply with the law.* **4.a.** the act or an instance of failing to pass an examination or subject. **b.** a grade or mark indicating this. **5.** an instance or the process of becoming weaker or losing, as health or strength. **6.** the act or an instance of ceasing to function; dying out: *a power failure, kidney failure.* **7.** the state or an instance of falling short; insufficiency: *a crop failure.* **8.** the act or an instance of becoming insolvent; bankruptcy.

fain (fān) *Archaic. adv.* with pleasure; gladly. —*adj.* **1.** glad; inclined. **2.** willing, but not eager. **3.** eager; desirous. [Old English *fægen* glad.]

faint (fānt) *adj.* **1.** hardly perceptible; dim; indistinct: *faint colors, a faint cry.* **2.** without enthusiasm or strength; feeble; halfhearted: *faint praise, a faint attempt.* **3.** weak and dizzy; likely to faint: *We were faint with hunger.* **4.** without courage; cow-

a	at	e	end	o	hot	u	up	hw	white		about
ā	ape	ē	me	ō	old	ū	use	ng	song		taken
ä	far	i	it	ô	fork	ü	rule	th	thin	ə	pencil
âr	care	ī	ice	oi	oil	u̇	pull	th	this		lemon
		îr	pierce	ou	out	ûr	turn	zh	measure		circus

ardly. ➡ used only in the phrase *a faint heart.* —*n.* a brief loss of consciousness because of a temporary decrease in the amount of blood that flows to the brain. —*v.i.* **1.** to lose consciousness briefly; swoon. **2.** *Archaic.* to lose courage; weaken. [Old French *feint* weak, cowardly, past participle of *feindre* to simulate, dissemble. See FEIGN.] —**faint′er,** *n.* —**faint′ly,** *adv.* —**faint′ness,** *n.*

Synonyms *adj.* **Faint, dim,** and **indistinct** may all mean lacking clarity or definition. **Faint** connotes a lack of strength: *Listening closely, we could make out a faint radio signal.* **Dim,** though close in meaning to *faint,* often suggests a lack of light or vividness: *In the dim light of evening, I could barely make out the figure under the trees.* **Indistinct** connotes a lack of distinguishing characteristics: *The mountain formed an indistinct mass against the dark sky.*

faint·heart·ed (fānt′här′tid) *adj.* lacking courage; timid. —**faint′heart′ed·ly,** *adv.* —**faint′heart′ed·ness,** *n.*

fair¹ (fâr) *adj.* **1.** free from bias or prejudice; impartial; just: *a fair decision.* **2.** according to accepted rules or standards; legitimate: *a fair play in a game.* **3.** average or a little better than average; moderate: *He has a fair chance of winning.* **4.a.** light in color or blond: *a fair complexion, fair hair.* **b.** having a light complexion or blond hair: *People who are fair usually sunburn easily.* **5.** not cloudy; clear; bright; sunny: *fair weather, fair skies.* **6.** pleasing in appearance; attractive; beautiful: *The prince sought the fairest woman in the land.* **7.** *Baseball.* **a.** (of a batted ball) ruled to be in play because of its position in relation to the foul lines. **b.** within the foul lines: *fair territory.* —*adv.* **1.** in a fair manner; according to rule. **2.** directly; straight; squarely. —*n. Archaic.* a woman, esp. a beloved or beautiful one. [Old English *fæger* beautiful, pleasing.] —**fair′ness,** *n.* —For Synonyms (*adj.*), see **just**¹.
• **fair and square.** *Informal.* **a.** honest; just. **b.** honestly; justly.
• **to bid fair.** to seem likely or favorable.

fair² (fâr) *n.* **1.** an exhibition, as of livestock and agricultural products or of cultural and industrial displays of different nations, often with shows, competitions, or other entertainment. **2.** an exhibition and sale of articles for a charitable cause; bazaar: *a church fair.* **3.** a gathering of people to exhibit and sell goods: *a book fair.* [Middle English *feire,* from Old French *feire* market, from Medieval Latin *feria* market, holiday, from Latin *fēriae* holidays, festivals, from Old Latin *fesiae;* from the ancient custom of holding fairs on religious holidays.]

fair ball, in baseball, a batted ball that, because of its position in relation to the foul lines, is ruled to be in play.

fair catch *Football.* a catch of a punt made by a player who signals that the ball will not be advanced and who therefore may not be touched by any member of the kicking team.

fair copy, a neat and exact copy of a document after final correction.

Fair Deal, the domestic program of President Harry S Truman after his election in 1948.

fair game **1.** animals, birds, or fish that can be lawfully hunted. **2.** any person or thing considered fit for pursuit, attack, or acquisition: *The administration's tax reforms were considered fair game by its political foes.*

fair·ground (fâr′ground′) *n.* an outdoor place where fairs are held. Also, **fair′grounds′.**

fair-haired (fâr′hârd′) *adj.* having light-colored hair.
• **fair-haired boy.** a person who is a favorite or is considered especially promising: *the boss's fair-haired boy.*

fair·ing (fâr′ing) *n.* an auxiliary part fitted to an airplane or other machine to produce a smooth outline that reduces drag.

fair·ish (fâr′ish) *adj.* moderately good, well, or large.

fair·lead (fâr′lēd′) *n.* any of various devices used at sea to guide lines and prevent them from chafing, esp. a strip of wood or metal with holes in it used to guide the running rigging of a sailing craft. Also, **fair′lead′er.**

fair·ly (fâr′lē) *adv.* **1.** in a fair manner; impartially; justly: *We were not treated fairly.* **2.** to a fair degree; somewhat; moderately: *a fairly large fortune.* **3.** in actual fact; actually; completely: *The audience fairly roared its approval.*

fair-mind·ed (fâr′mīn′did) *adj.* without prejudice or bias; impartial; just. —**fair′-mind′ed·ly,** *adv.* —**fair′-mind′ed·ness,** *n.*

fair sex, women as a group.

fair·spo·ken (fâr′spō′kən) *adj.* speaking or spoken smoothly and courteously; civil.

fair trade, trade under an agreement that forbids a retailer to sell certain products for less than a minimum price specified by the manufacturer or distributor. —**fair′-trade′,** *adj.*

fair·way (fâr′wā′) *n.* **1.** *Golf.* the area of short grass between the tee and putting green of a hole. **2.** a navigable channel or course through a river, harbor, or bay.

fair-weath·er (fâr′weth′ər) *adj.* **1.** not reliable or helpful in time of distress or need: *a fair-weather friend.* **2.** occurring in or suitable only in good weather: *a fair-weather voyage, a fair-weather outfit.*

fair·y (fâr′ē) *n., pl.* **fair·ies.** an imaginary, usually very small being in human form, supposed to possess magic powers. —*adj.* **1.** of or relating to fairies. **2.** resembling a fairy. **3.** having the magic powers of or of the nature of a fairy. [Old French *faerie* enchantment, from *fae* the imaginary being, from Late Latin *fāta* the imaginary being, goddess of fate, from Latin *fāta* (plural) the Fates.]

fair·y·land (fâr′ē land′) *n.* **1.** the imaginary land of the fairies. **2.** any enchanting, beautiful place.

fairy ring, a ring of mushrooms growing in the ground, supposedly formed by fairies dancing at night.

fairy shrimp, any of a group of small, delicately colored crustaceans, order Anostraca, using gill-bearing legs for swimming on the back, and usually appearing irregularly in small temporary pools. Length: to 1 inch (3 centimeters). [Because it is small.]

fairy tale **1.** a story, usually for children, about imaginary beings or magical events. **2.** an unbelievable or highly imaginative story, esp. one designed to delude. Also, **fairy story.**

fait ac·com·pli (fāt′ə kom plē′; *French* fet ä kôn plē′) *pl.* **faits ac·com·plis** (fāt′ə kom plēz′, fāts′; *French* fez ä kôn plē′). something done that no longer can be changed or reversed. [French *fait accompli* literally, accomplished fact, going back to Latin *factum* deed + *ad* to + *complēre* to fulfill.]

faith (fāth) *n.* **1.** a belief not based on proof: *to have faith in an untested theory.* **2.** confidence, reliance, or trust: *to have faith in one's doctor.* **3.** belief in God or the doctrines of a religion. **4.** a system of religious belief: *the Lutheran faith.* **5.** anything believed strongly. **6.** loyalty; fidelity. [Old French *feit* trust, belief, from Latin *fidēs.*] —For Synonyms, see **belief.**
• **in bad faith.** with dishonest intentions; insincerely.
• **in faith.** truly; indeed.
• **in good faith.** with good intentions; honestly.
• **on faith.** without any evidence: *to accept a statement on faith.*
• **to break faith.** **a.** to be disloyal to one's principles or beliefs. **b.** to break a promise.
• **to keep faith.** **a.** to adhere to one's principles or beliefs. **b.** to keep a promise.

faith cure, faith healing.

faith·ful (fāth′fəl) *adj.* **1.** steadfast in loyalty and devotion; trustworthy: *a faithful companion.* **2.** steadfast in keeping one's word or doing one's duty: *a faithful worker.* **3.** conforming to the truth or the original; accurate; exact: *a faithful translation.* —*n.* **the faithful. a.** the followers or adherents of a religion. **b.** the loyal adherents of any cause or group. —**faith′ful·ly,** *adv.* —**faith′ful·ness,** *n.*

Synonyms *adj.* **Faithful, loyal,** and **steadfast** mean firmly devoted to something, as a person or cause. **Faithful** suggests a devotion growing out of a sense of honor or based on a firm commitment: *to be faithful to one's beliefs, to be faithful to one's promise.* **Loyal** implies an ongoing devotion to a person or cause: *loyal to friends, loyal to one's school.* **Steadfast** stresses the unwavering quality of one's commitment: *steadfast support for the college football team.*

faith healing **1.** a method of trying to cure disease by prayer and religious faith. **2.** a cure supposedly achieved by this method. Also, **faith cure.** —**faith healer.**

faith·less (fāth′lis) *adj.* **1.** lacking trustworthiness or loyalty: *a faithless companion.* **2.** without faith or belief, esp. religious belief. —**faith′less·ly,** *adv.* —**faith′less·ness,** *n.*

fake¹ (fāk) *n.* **1.** a person or thing that is not genuine; fraud; sham: *The chair that we thought was an antique is a fake.* **2.** *Sports.* an action intended to mislead an opponent, such as a feigned throw to one player prior to the real throw to another. —*v.,* **faked, fak·ing.** —*v.t.* **1.** to pretend to have or experience; feign: *to fake illness.* **2.** to make (something) seem genuine; counterfeit: *The records were faked to show an improvement in sales that didn't exist.* **3.** to do or make a version or imitation of; improvise: *I don't know the dance step, but I can fake it.* **4.** *Sports.* to perform (an action) as a fake: *to fake a throw to the catcher in order to prevent a run.* —*v.i.* to practice faking. —*adj.* lacking genuineness; false; sham; counterfeit: *a fake fireplace.* [Of uncertain origin.] —**fak′er,** *n.*
• **to fake (someone) out.** *Informal.* to deceive (someone).

fake² (fāk) *n.* one of the turns or loops of a coiled rope or cable. —*v.t.,* **faked, fak·ing.** to coil (a rope or cable). [Of uncertain origin.]

fak·er·y (fā′kə rē) *n., pl.* **-er·ies. 1.** the act of faking. **2.** something that is faked: *The supposedly ancient statue proved to be a modern fakery.*

fa·kir (fə kîr′, fā′kər) *n.* **1.** a member of a Muslim sect who lives by begging. **2.** a Hindu ascetic. [Arabic *faqīr* poor.]

Fa·lange (fā′lanj, fə lanj′; *Spanish* fä län′hä) *n.* a fascist party in Spain, founded in 1933, the official party of the government under Francisco Franco. [Spanish *Falange*, from *falange* phalanx, from Latin *phalanx* (stem *phalang-*). See PHALANX.] —**Fa·lan·gist** (fə lan′jist), *n.*

fal·cate (fal′kāt) *adj. Anatomy, Astronomy.* shaped like a sickle; curved; hooked: *a falcate ligament, a falcate moon.* [Latin *falcātus*, from *falx* sickle.]

fal·chion (fôl′chən, -shən) *n.* **1.** a sword with a broad, curved blade, used in the Middle Ages. **2.** *Archaic.* any sword. [Old French *fauchon* curved short sword, going back to Latin *falx* sickle.]

fal·con (fôl′kən, fal′-, fô′kən) *n.* **1.** any of various hawklike birds of prey, family Falconidae, having short, hooked bills, pointed wings, and gray or brown plumage, usually with buff or white markings, esp. those of the genus **Falco**, such as the peregrine falcon. Length: 6-25 inches (15-64 centimeters). **2.** the female of any of various hawks trained for falconry. [Old French *faucon*, from Late Latin *falcō*, from Latin *falx* sickle; because of its hooked claws.]

fal·con·er (fôl′kə nər, fal′-, fô′kə-) *n.* **1.** a person who hunts with falcons. **2.** a breeder or trainer of falcons.

fal·con·ry (fôl′kən rē, fal′-, fô′kən-) *n.* **1.** the sport of hunting with falcons; hawking. **2.** the art of training falcons to hunt birds and small game.

fal·de·ral (fal′də ral′) *also,* **fal·de·rol** (fal′də rol′). *n.* folderol.

fall (fôl) *v.,* **fell, fall·en, fall·ing.** —*v.i.* **1.** to come down from a higher place by the force of gravity; drop: *The radio fell off the shelf. Snow fell during the night. The curtain fell after the first act.* **2.** to come down suddenly or involuntarily from an erect position: *to fall on one's knees before a king, to fall on an icy sidewalk.* **3.** to become lower or less, as in quantity, quality, intensity, or degree: *Her voice fell to a whisper. Production fell sharply. The president's popularity is falling.* **4.** to come into contact with something; reach a stopping place; strike; land: *The spear fell wide of its intended victim.* **5.** to take place; happen; occur: *Easter falls late this year.* **6.** to come as if by descending: *Night fell upon the town. Silence fell as he entered the room.* **7.** to pass into a specified mental or physical condition; become: *to fall ill, to fall in love.* **8.** to be defeated, captured, or conquered: *The city fell after a long siege.* **9.** to lose power: *The dictatorship fell in a military coup. The government fell as a result of the scandal.* **10.** to decline in estimation, rank, or dignity: *He fell into disgrace.* **11.** to be wounded or killed, as in battle. **12.** to come down in pieces or ruins; collapse: *Several buildings fell during the earthquake.* **13.** to yield to temptation; sin: *In the Bible, Adam and Eve fell when they ate the apple.* **14.** to be classified or divided: *His argument falls into three parts.* **15.** to show sadness or disappointment: *Her face fell.* **16.** to hang down: *The dress fell in gentle folds. The ringlets fell around her shoulders.* **17.** to come by chance or lot: *It fell to him to tell his brother the bad news.* **18.** to slope or extend downward: *Their property falls gently toward the brook.* **19.** to pass by inheritance or right: *The estate falls to the eldest child.* **20.** to come at a specified place; be positioned: *The accent falls on the last syllable. The perpendicular falls on the midpoint of the line.* **21.** to be cast down: *Her eyes fell.* **22.** to be uttered: *The words fell from his lips.* **23.** to be directed: *His glance fell on the old clock.* —*v.t.* to fell or cut down (a tree or trees). —*n.* **1.** the act of coming down from a higher place by the force of gravity: *the fall of a meteor.* **2.** an amount that comes down: *a six-inch fall of rain.* **3.** the distance through which anything falls: *It's a short fall from the window to the ground.* **4.** a sudden or involuntary drop from an erect position: *to take a fall on the ice.* **5.** defeat, capture, or destruction: *the fall of Troy.* **6.** a loss of power or influence; overthrow: *the fall of the Roman Empire.* **7.** a decline in estimation, rank, or dignity: *a fall from favor.* **8.** the act of yielding to temptation; moral ruin; sin. **9.** a reduction or decrease, as in value, quality, or quantity: *a fall in prices.* **10.** a hanging down: *the fall of her hair about her shoulders.* **11.** a downward slope or direction. **12.** *also,* **Fall.** autumn. **13.** *usually,* **falls.** a waterfall; cascade. ➡ used as singular or plural. **14.** a woman's hairpiece, usually worn with the natural hair to add length or fullness. **15.** *Wrestling.* **a.** the act of throwing one's opponent to the mat and holding both shoulders there for a specified number of seconds. **b.** a match or division of a match. **16.** *Nautical.* an apparatus used for hoisting, esp. that part, such as a rope, that is actually pulled on to raise the object. **17. the Fall (of Man).** *Theology.* the disobedience to God shown by

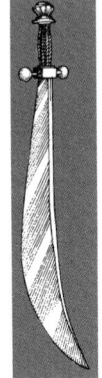

falchion

Adam and Eve in eating the forbidden fruit, resulting in their loss of innocence and in humanity's inheritance of original sin. —*adj.* of, relating to, or suitable for the autumn: *fall clothing.* [Old English *feallan* to drop.]

• **to fall (all) over oneself.** to act too eagerly or enthusiastically: *The guests fell all over themselves admiring the house.*

• **to fall apart. a.** to break into pieces; disintegrate. **b.** to stop existing or functioning; dissolve: *The coalition fell apart over economic policy.* **c.** to suffer a mental breakdown.

• **to fall away. a.** to withdraw friendship, support, or allegiance; desert. **b.** to become thin or emaciated. **c.** to decline gradually; fade; perish. **d.** *Nautical.* to be blown, or drift, clear of something.

• **to fall back.** to retreat; withdraw.

• **to fall back on. a.** to have recourse to; rely on. **b.** to retreat to: *The troops fell back on their defenses.*

• **to fall behind.** to fail to keep up: *to fall behind in one's work.*

• **to fall down on.** *Informal.* to fail in: *to fall down on the job.*

• **to fall for.** *Informal.* **a.** to fall in love with. **b.** to be deceived or tricked by.

• **to fall in. a.** to take one's proper place in a military formation. **b.** to cave in.

• **to fall in with. a.** to meet and join company with: *The runaway fell in with thieves.* **b.** to agree or comply with; be agreeable or favorable to: *They fell in with our plans.*

• **to fall off. a.** to become less; diminish; drop: *The demand for the product fell off.* **b.** *Nautical.* to veer to leeward.

• **to fall on** (or **upon**). **a.** to attack vigorously; assault. **b.** to come upon; discover; find.

• **to fall out. a.** to leave one's proper place in a military formation. **b.** to happen; occur.

• **to fall through.** to come to nothing; fail: *Their plans fell through.*

• **to fall to. a.** to set about; begin: *She fell to work.* **b.** to begin to attack. **c.** to start eating. **d.** to move or come into place; shut.

• **to fall under. a.** to be classified as; be included in: *a case that falls under the jurisdiction of a lower court.* **b.** to be or come under the operation or influence of; be subjected to: *to fall under a spell.*

• **to ride for a fall.** to endanger one's position; put oneself in jeopardy.

fal·la·cious (fə lā′shəs) *adj.* **1.** based on or containing a fallacy; logically unsound: *a fallacious conclusion.* **2.** characterized by or resulting from a misconception; deceptive; misleading; delusive: *a fallacious peace, fallacious hopes.* —**fal·la′cious·ly,** *adv.* —**fal·la′cious·ness,** *n.*

fal·la·cy (fal′ə sē) *n., pl.* **-cies. 1.** a false or mistaken belief; misconception: *the ancient fallacy that the planets revolve around the earth.* **2.** false or illogical reasoning; unsound argument. **3.** the quality or fact of being unsound or deceptive: *the fallacy of an argument.* [Latin *fallācia* deceit.]

fal·lal (fal lal′) *n.* a piece of finery; trifling ornament.

fall·en (fô′lən) *v.* the past participle of **fall.** —*adj.* **1.** having come down from a higher place; dropped: *fallen snow.* **2.** degraded or disgraced: *a fallen idol.* **3.** captured, overthrown, or defeated: *a fallen castle.* **4.** having died, esp. in battle: *a fallen hero.* **5.** on the ground; prostrate.

fall guy *Slang.* a person who is made a victim or is left to take the blame for another's crime or mistake; scapegoat.

fal·li·ble (fal′ə bəl) *adj.* **1.** capable of being deceived or mistaken; liable to err: *a fallible judge.* **2.** liable to be erroneous; inaccurate: *a fallible judgment.* [Medieval Latin *fallibilis* deceitful, prone to slip, from Latin *fallere* to deceive.] —**fal′li·bil′i·ty,** *n.* —**fal′li·bly,** *adv.*

fall·ing-out (fô′ling out′) *n., pl.* **fall·ings-out** or **fall·ing-outs.** a quarrel or bad feelings between people who had been on good terms: *The children were pals again soon after their falling-out.*

falling sickness *Archaic.* epilepsy.

falling star, meteor.

fall line 1. the boundary between an upland and a lowland, or the edge of a plateau, often marked by waterfalls and rapids. **2. Fall Line.** the boundary east of the Appalachian Mountains between the Atlantic coastal plain and the Piedmont region.

fal·lo·pi·an tube (fə lō′pē ən) *also,* **Fal·lo·pi·an tube.** either of the pair of slender tubes in the female of higher mammals

a	at	e	end	o	hot	u	up	hw	white		about
ā	ape	ē	me	ō	old	ū	use	ng	song	ə	taken
ä	far	i	it	ô	fork	ü	rule	th	thin		pencil
âr	care	ī	ice	oi	oil	u̇	pull	th	this		lemon
		îr	pierce	ou	out	ûr	turn	zh	measure		circus

F

through which eggs pass from the ovaries to the uterus; oviduct. [From Gabriello *Fallopio,* 1523-62, Italian anatomist who first described these tubes.]

fall·out (fôl′out′) *n.* **1.** particles that fall to earth from the atmosphere, such as radioactive dust from a nuclear explosion or ash from a volcanic eruption or forest fire. **2.** an effect or result, esp. an incidental or unexpected one: *the fallout from a political scandal.*

fal·low[1] (fal′ō) *adj.* **1.** (of land) tilled or untilled and left unseeded for one or more growing seasons. **2.** left uncultivated or inactive: *a fallow talent.* —*n.* **1.** fallow land. **2.** the act of tilling land and leaving it unseeded for one or more growing seasons to improve fertility. —*v.t.* to make (land) fallow. [Old English *fealh* arable land.] —**fal′low·ness,** *n.*

fal·low[2] (fal′ō) *n.* a pale yellowish brown color. —*adj.* having the color fallow. [Old English *fealu.*]

fallow deer, a small European deer, *Dama dama,* usually having a yellowish coat with white spots. Height: 3 feet (0.9 meter) at the shoulder.

false (fôls) *adj.,* **fals·er, fals·est. 1.** not true; incorrect; erroneous: *a false conclusion, a false accusation.* **2.** not genuine or natural; artificial: *false eyelashes, false modesty.* **3.** tending to mislead; deceptive: *false advertising.* **4.** showing disloyalty; unfaithful: *a false friend.* **5.** showing dishonesty; untruthful: *a false witness.* **6.** substituting for a similar structure for the purpose of decoration, protection, or temporary support: *a false pocket, a false front on an old building.* **7.** based on mistaken ideas or impressions: *false pride, a false sense of confidence.* **8.** *Music.* inaccurate or not true in pitch: *a false note.* [Latin *falsus* deceptive, spurious, past participle of *fallere* to deceive.] —**false′ly,** *adv.* —**false′ness,** *n.* —For Synonyms *(adj.),* see **wrong.**

fallow deer

· **to play (someone) false.** to deceive or cheat (someone).

false alarm 1. a fire alarm mistakenly or deliberately sounded when no real fire or danger exists. **2.** a mistaken, misleading, or otherwise groundless warning or indication of something.

false arrest, the illegal arrest of a person.

false bottom 1. a horizontal partition, as in a suitcase or drawer, that looks like the bottom but conceals a lower, secret compartment. **2.** the base of a glass, bottle, or other container that is raised or narrowed to make the capacity of the container look greater than it really is.

false face, mask.

false-heart·ed (fôls′här′tid) *adj.* pretending faithfulness and loyalty; deceitful: *a false-hearted friend.* —**false′-heart′ed·ly,** *adv.* —**false′-heart′ed·ness,** *n.*

false·hood (fôls′hů̇d′) *n.* **1.** a false statement; lie: *to tell falsehoods about one's past.* **2.** the quality of being false; absence of truth: *to distinguish between falsehood and truthfulness.* **3.** something that is false, such as a theory or idea: *the falsehood that the earth is flat.* **4.** the act or practice of telling lies; lying.

false imprisonment, the illegal imprisonment or detention of a person.

false pretenses, intentional misrepresentation of fact in order to defraud, esp. of money or property.

false ribs, ribs not attached to the breastbone, such as the five lower pairs of ribs in a human being.

false start 1. an unsuccessful or inadequate beginning: *to solve a problem after a false start.* **2.** *Sports.* a premature beginning of a race, forcing a new beginning.

false step 1. a stumble. **2.** an unwise action; blunder.

false teeth, a complete or partial set of artificial teeth used in place of real teeth that have been extracted or are missing.

fal·set·to (fôl set′ō) *n., pl.* **-tos. 1.** an unnaturally or artificially high-pitched voice, esp. one used by a male singer. **2.** a singer using such a voice. —*adj.* of or having the quality of a falsetto: *falsetto notes.* —*adv.* in falsetto. [Italian *falsetto* falsetto voice, diminutive of *falso* untrue, counterfeit, from Latin *falsus,* past participle of *fallere* to deceive.]

fal·si·fy (fôl′sə fī′) *v.,* **-fied, -fy·ing.** —*v.t.* **1.** to change with the intent to deceive; make false: *to falsify the date of one's birth, to falsify an accident report.* **2.** to give a false account of; misrepresent: *This book falsifies the events of the Spanish Civil War.* **3.** to prove to be false; disprove: *No man can falsify any material fact*

here stated (Thomas Jefferson, 1805). —*v.i.* to tell falsehoods; lie. [Late Latin *falsificāre* to make false, from Latin *falsus* (see FALSE) + *facere* to make.] —**fal′si·fi·ca′tion,** *n.* —**fal′si·fi′er,** *n.*

fal·si·ty (fôl′si tē) *n., pl.* **-ties. 1.** the quality or condition of being false; untruthfulness. **2.** something that is false; falsehood.

Fal·staff, Sir John (fôl′staf) the fat, boastful, swaggering old knight, given to drinking, jesting, and good-natured lying, in Shakespeare's *Henry IV* and *The Merry Wives of Windsor.*

Fal·staff·i·an (fôl staf′ē ən) *adj.* of, characteristic of, or like Sir John Falstaff: *Falstaffian bragging.*

falt·boat (fält′bōt′) *n.* foldboat. [Partial translation of German *Faltboot,* from *falten* fold[1] + *boot* boat.]

fal·ter (fôl′tər) *v.i.* **1.** to act with hesitation or uncertainty; waver: *Our hopes will not falter in adversity.* **2.** to speak with hesitation; stammer: *The witness faltered in describing the accident.* **3.** to move unsteadily; stumble; totter. **4.** to lose power, effectiveness, or the like; become weaker: *When the factory closed, the local economy faltered.* —*v.t.* to utter haltingly or brokenly: *to falter an excuse.* [Of uncertain origin.] —**fal′ter·er,** *n.* —**fal′ter·ing·ly,** *adv.* —For Synonyms, see **hesitate.**

fame (fām) *n.* a widespread reputation, esp. for great achievement: *The singer's fame spread quickly.* —*v.t.,* **famed, fam·ing.** *Archaic.* to make famous. [Old French *fame* reputation, rumor, from Latin *fāma.*]

famed (fāmd) *adj.* well-known; famous.

fa·mil·i·al (fə mil′yəl, -mil′ē əl) *adj.* **1.** of, relating to, or characteristic of a family. **2.** inherited by or common to the members of a family: *a familial disease, a familial trait.*

fa·mil·iar (fə mil′yər) *adj.* **1.** commonly seen, heard, or experienced; well-known: *She was whistling a familiar tune. Smog is a familiar occurrence in many cities.* **2.** well-acquainted; aware of or knowing the facts or details about something or someone (with *with*): *He is familiar with the book.* **3.** characteristic of or resembling the relationships within a family; close; intimate: *to be on familiar terms with one's neighbors.* **4.** free of formality or reserve; friendly; unconstrained: *an easy and familiar manner.* **5.** too friendly or intimate; presumptuous; forward. **6.** (of animals) domesticated. —*n.* **1.** a close friend or associate. **2.a.** in folklore, a spirit or demon, usually in the form of an animal, that is supposed to attend a person. **b.** such an animal. **3.** a domestic servant in the household of a Roman Catholic bishop or the pope. [Old French *familier* closely acquainted, from Latin *familiāris* relating to a household, from *familia* household.] —**fa·mil′iar·ly,** *adv.* —For Synonyms, see **common, intimate**[1].

fa·mil·i·ar·i·ty (fə mil′ē ar′i tē) *n., pl.* **-ties. 1.** close acquaintance: *familiarity with a subject.* **2.** an absence of formality; friendliness or intimacy: *to be on terms of familiarity.* **3.** undue intimacy; forwardness. **4.** an action or remark suitable only for an intimate acquaintance: *to resent the familiarities of a stranger.*

fa·mil·iar·ize (fə mil′yə rīz′) *v.t.,* **-ized, -iz·ing. 1.** to make (oneself or someone else) accustomed or well acquainted (with *with*): *to familiarize oneself with the duties of a new job.* **2.** to make (something) well known: *Advertising familiarized the new soft drink.* —**fa·mil′iar·i·za′tion,** *n.*

fam·i·ly (fam′ə lē, fam′lē) *n., pl.* **-lies. 1.** a social unit based on a parent or parents and their children. **2.** the group of children born to or adopted by the same parent or parents: *The couple wanted a large family.* **3.** one's spouse and children: *I'm taking my family to the beach.* **4.** a group of people connected by blood or marriage; relatives. **5.** a group of people descended from a common ancestor; house, line, or clan. **6.** a group of people who live together. **7.** a group of things related by common or similar characteristics: *a family of musical instruments.* **8.** *Biology.* in taxonomic classification, a group of related living things forming a category ranking below an order and above a genus. Zebras, asses, and horses belong to the horse family. **9.** *Linguistics.* a group of related languages descended from a common parent language. The English language belongs to the Indo-European family. —*adj.* of, relating to, or suitable for a family: *a family gathering.* [Latin *familia* household, from *famulus* servant.]

family circle 1. the members of a family considered as an intimate group. **2.** a section in the upper balcony of a theater or opera house containing inexpensive seats.

family court, domestic relations court.

family man 1. a man with a wife and child or children. **2.** a man who is devoted to his family.

family name, a last name; surname.

family planning, planning used to determine the number and spacing of the birth of children in a family by use of birth control.

family room, a room that is used for casual relaxation in a home, as for playing games and watching television.

family therapy, a form of psychotherapy that seeks to improve relationships within a family. Family therapy concentrates on

problems that affect the family as a whole, rather than on those that affect only a single individual.

family tree **1.** a chart or diagram showing the ancestry, relationships, and descent of the members of a family. **2.** the ancestors and descendants in a family collectively.

fam·ine (fam′in) *n.* **1.** an extreme and widespread scarcity of food. **2.** an extreme scarcity of anything; dearth: *a rice famine.* **3.** *Archaic.* starvation. [French *famine,* going back to Latin *famēs* hunger.]

fam·ish (fam′ish) *v.i., v.t. Archaic.* to be or make intensely hungry; starve. [Modification of Middle English *famen,* shortened from Old French *afamer,* going back to Latin *ad* to + *famēs* hunger.]

fam·ished (fam′isht) *adj.* intensely hungry; starving: *We were famished after not eating all day.*

fa·mous (fā′məs) *adj.* having fame or celebrity; well-known; renowned: *a famous author.* [Old French *fameus* renowned for good or ill, from Latin *fāmōsus* renowned, from *fāma* rumor, reputation.]

Synonyms Famous, renowned, celebrated, and illustrious mean widely known and of good reputation. **Famous** suggests being well known at a particular time or place: *a writer famous in eighteenth-century France, one of the most famous artists in Japan today.* **Renowned** suggests a wider recognition than *famous: renowned throughout all Europe in that period.* **Celebrated** emphasizes widespread public acclaim and attention: *The celebrated singer's life story was featured in all the popular magazines.* **Illustrious** stresses the glory and prestige that may attach to a figure: *The illustrious visitor brought honor and world attention to our town.*

fa·mous·ly (fā′məs lē) *adv.* **1.** remarkably well; splendidly: *We got along famously.* **2.** with renown.

fan¹ (fan) *n.* **1.** a device that is waved by hand to produce a current of air, esp. a collapsible object of various materials, such as paper, ivory, or feathers, which, when opened, is shaped like a sector of a circle. **2.** anything resembling an open fan, as the tail of a peacock. **3.** a mechanical device having several blades that are attached to a central hub and rotated by a motor, used for producing a current of air to cool, heat, or ventilate. **4.** a winnowing machine. —*v.,* **fanned, fan·ning.** —*v.t.* **1.** to move (air) with or as with a fan: *The bird's wings fanned the air.* **2.** to direct a current of air upon or toward, with or as with a fan: *to fan a fire.* **3.** to blow gently or refreshingly upon: *The cool breeze fanned my hot face.* **4.** to sweep or drive away with or as with a fan: *to fan smoke from one's face.* **5.** to stir up; excite; stimulate: *The touchdown fanned the crowd's enthusiasm.* **6.** to spread out (something) like a fan: *to fan a deck of cards.* **7.** to winnow. **8.** *Baseball.* to cause (a batter) to strike out. —*v.i.* **1.** to spread out like a fan (often with *out*): *The campers fanned out to search for firewood.* **2.** *Baseball.* to strike out. [Middle English *fanne,* from Old English *fann* winnowing implement, from Latin *vannus* basket for winnowing grain.]

fan² (fan) *n. Informal.* an enthusiastic devotee or admirer, as of a sport or performer. [Short for FANATIC.] —For Synonyms, see **enthusiast.**

fa·nat·ic (fə nat′ik) *n.* a person whose devotion to a cause or belief is unreasonably strong or enthusiastic: *a religious fanatic, to be a fanatic about punctuality.* —*adj.* fanatical. [Latin *fānāticus* inspired by a divinity, frenzied, from *fānum* temple.] —For Synonyms (*n.*), see **enthusiast.**

fa·nat·i·cal (fə nat′i kəl) *adj.* unreasonably or excessively enthusiastic or zealous: *fanatical opposition to change, a fanatical patriot.* —**fa·nat′i·cal·ly,** *adv.*

fa·nat·i·cism (fə nat′ə siz′əm) *n.* excessive or unreasonable enthusiasm or zeal.

fan belt, a rubber belt behind the radiator of an engine, as of an automobile, driven by the crankshaft to turn a fan that draws air through the radiator.

fan·cied (fan′sēd) *adj.* produced by fancy; imagined; imaginary: *their real and fancied accomplishments.*

fan·ci·er (fan′sē ər) *n.* a person who has a special liking for or interest in something: *a bird fancier.*

fan·ci·ful (fan′sə fəl) *adj.* **1.** produced or suggested by fancy; imaginary; unreal: *a fanciful story.* **2.** showing fancy: *a fanciful costume.* **3.** influenced by fancy; imaginative; whimsical: *a fanciful mind.* —**fan′ci·ful·ly,** *adv.* —**fan′ci·ful·ness,** *n.*

fan·cy (fan′sē) *n., pl.* -**cies.** **1.** imagination, esp. of a capricious or whimsical nature: *The unicorn is a product of fancy.* **2.** something that is imagined by the fancy; mental image: *a pleasing fancy.* **3.** an idea or opinion based on few or no facts; notion; supposition: *a mere fancy.* **4.** a capricious preference or inclination; fondness; liking: *to have a sudden fancy to visit the zoo, to take a fancy to someone.* —*adj.,* -**ci·er,** -**ci·est.** **1.** made or designed to please the fancy; highly decorated; ornamental; elabo-

rate: *fancy embroidery on a shirt.* **2.** of highest quality; superior; choice: *fancy fruits and vegetables.* **3.** *Informal.* extravagant (in cost or price): *How can you afford to give such a fancy party?* **4.** dealing in fancy goods; geared to extravagant or elegant taste. **5.** displaying or requiring great skill or grace: *a fancy restaurant.* **5.** displaying or requiring great skill or grace: *a fancy footwork.* **6.** (of animals) bred for excellence of specific qualities. —*v.t.,* -**cied, -cy·ing. 1.** to picture mentally; imagine: *to fancy oneself a hero.* **2.** to have a fondness for; like: *Which dessert do you fancy?* **3.** to believe without proof or certainty; suppose; presume: *I fancy that they will arrive soon.* [Contraction of FANTASY.] —**fan′ci·ly,** *adv.* —**fan′ci·ness,** *n.* —For Synonyms (*n.*), see **caprice, imagination.**

fancy dress, a masquerade costume. —**fan′cy-dress′,** *adj.*

fan·cy-free (fan′sē frē′) *adj.* **1.** free to marry or fall in love. **2.** carefree.

fan·cy·work (fan′sē wûrk′) *n.* ornamental needlework, such as embroidery or tatting.

fan·dan·go (fan dang′gō) *n., pl.* -**gos. 1.** a lively dance of Spanish origin performed in three-quarter time, usually with castanets. **2.** music for such a dance. [Spanish *fandango;* of uncertain origin.]

fane (fān) *n. Archaic.* a temple or church. [Latin *fānum* temple.]

fan·fare (fan′fâr′) *n.* **1.** a short tune sounded by bugles, trumpets, or other brass instruments, esp. for military and ceremonial occasions. **2.** ostentatious noise, excitement, fuss, or activity, as in celebration or promotion of something: *The museum opening was surrounded with fanfare.* [French *fanfare* flourish of trumpets; probably imitative.]

Fangs

fang (fang) *n.* **1.** a long, pointed tooth, as of a carnivore, with which an animal slashes or holds its prey. **2.** one of the two sharp, slender, hollow or grooved teeth with which a poisonous snake injects venom. **3.** any pointed, tapered projection. [Old English *fang* a seizing, from Old Norse *fang* capture.]

fanged (fangd) *adj.* having fangs.

fan·jet (fan′jet′) *n.* a type of aircraft equipped with turbofan engines.

fan·light (fan′līt′) *n.* a semicircular window over a door or larger window, esp. one with sash bars radiating like an open fan.

fan mail, letters of admiration received by a performer, author, or other celebrity.

fan·tail (fan′tāl′) *n.* **1.** a tail, end, or other part resembling an open fan. **2.** a domestic pigeon having a fan-shaped tail. **3.** an overhanging projection from the stern of a ship.

fanlight

fan·tan (fan′tan′) *n.* **1.** a card game in which two to eight players, using a deck of fifty-two cards, discard cards in a certain sequence. The winner is the first player to play all of his or her cards. **2.** a Chinese gambling game in which the players bet on the number of beans or counters that will remain after an uncounted pile of them has been counted off by fours. [Chinese (Mandarin) *fan t'an* the Chinese game; literally, repeated division.]

fan·ta·si·a (fan tā′zhə, -zhē ə, fan′tə zē′ə) *n.* **1.** a fanciful musical composition not conforming to a strict style or form. **2.** a medley of familiar tunes or themes embellished with interludes and flourishes. Also, **fantasy.** [Italian *fantasia* imagination, fantasia, from Latin *phantasia* fancy, idea, from Greek *phantasiā* imagination, perception, appearance. Doublet of FANTASY.]

fan·ta·size (fan′tə sīz′) *v.i., v.t.,* -**sized, -siz·ing.** to create fanciful mental images (of); daydream (about).

fan·tas·tic (fan tas′tik) *adj.* **1.** strikingly unusual or strange; bizarre; grotesque: *Driftwood sometimes takes fantastic shapes.* **2.** existing in the mind only; imaginary; irrational: *the fantastic fears of young children.* **3.** wildly or extremely fanciful; capricious: *a fantastic scheme for becoming famous in a year.* **4.** *Informal.* particularly good; splendid: *a fantastic view from a mountaintop.* **5.** hard to believe; remarkable; amazing: *to consume a fantastic*

a	at	e	end	o	hot	u	up	hw	white		about
ā	ape	ē	me	ō	old	ū	use	ng	song	ə	taken
ä	far	i	it	ô	fork	ü	rule	th	thin		pencil
âr	care	ī	ice	oi	oil	u̇	pull	th	this		lemon
		îr	pierce	ou	out	ûr	turn	zh	measure		circus

amount of food. Also, **fan·tas'ti·cal.** [Medieval Latin *fantasticus* disordered, strange, imaginary, from Late Latin *phantasticus* imaginary, from Greek *phantastikos* able to produce the appearance of something, from *phantazein* to make visible.] —**fan·tas'ti·cal·ly,** *adv.* —For Synonyms *(adj.)*, see **grotesque.**

fan·ta·sy (fan'tə sē, -zē) *also,* **phantasy.** *n., pl.* **-sies. 1.** unrestrained imagination or fancy. **2.** an unreal or grotesque mental image: *fantasies brought on by fever.* **3.a.** a fanciful or imaginative creation or invention. **b.** literature of a highly fanciful nature, esp. that dealing with supernatural creatures or events. **4.** *Psychology.* **a.** a daydream or train of fanciful mental images, usually in the form of a wish fulfillment, through which a person escapes from reality. **b.** the capacity for or process of creating such images. **5.** a caprice; whim. **6.** fantasia. [Old French *fantasie* imagination, fancy, from Latin *phantasia* fancy, idea, from Greek *phantasiā* imagination, perception, appearance. Doublet of FANTASIA.] —For Synonyms, see **imagination.**

far (fär) *adv.,* **far·ther** or **fur·ther, far·thest** or **fur·thest. 1.** at or to a great distance in space: *to travel far from home.* **2.** at or to an advanced or remote point in time, degree, or extent: *The party continued far into the night. That painting is far from finished.* **3.** to or at a specific distance, point in time, or degree: *Practical jokes often go too far.* **4.** to a great degree; very much: *Your eyesight is far better than mine.* —*adj.* **1.** distant or remote in time or space: *the far future, the far north.* **2.** more distant; farther: *the far side of the moon.* **3.** extending over a long distance or time: *a far journey.* **4.** characterized by extreme political views; extremist: *the far right, the far left.* —*n.* a distant place or region: *The stranger had come from far.* [Old English *feor(r)* at a distance, remote, beyond.]

- **as far as.** to the distance, degree, or extent that: *Read as far as you can in ten minutes.*
- **by far.** to a great degree; very much: *She is by far the tallest.*
- **far and away.** without a doubt; very much: *He is far and away the best actor for the part.*
- **far and wide** (or **near**). **a.** to, from, or in all areas, including distant ones; everywhere: *We've looked far and wide for a house we'd like.* **b.** all areas; everywhere: *The fans came from far and wide to greet their idol.*
- **far be it from me.** I do not have the desire or courage: *Far be it from me to criticize such an expert.*
- **how far.** to what distance, extent, or degree.
- **so far. a.** up to now. **b.** up to a certain point or extent: *You can go just so far in being candid.*
- **so far as.** to the degree or extent that.
- **so far so good.** up to now everything has been satisfactory.
- **to go far. a.** to achieve success; accomplish much: *With her musical talent she should go far.* **b.** to last a long time; cover a considerable extent: *The cookies didn't go far among those hungry boys.* **c.** to have a positive effect; help: *The testimony went far in clarifying the sequence of events.*

far·ad (far'əd, -ad) *n.* a unit of capacitance. An object that stores one coulomb of charge when raised to a potential of one volt has a capacitance of one farad. [From Michael *Faraday,* 1791-1867, English physicist and chemist.]

far·a·day (far'ə dē', -dā') *n.* in electrolysis, the quantity of electricity necessary to deposit or dissolve one gram equivalent of a substance. It is equivalent to 96,500 coulombs. [From Michael *Faraday,* 1791-1867, English physicist and chemist.]

far·a·dize (far'ə dīz') *v.t.,* **-dized, -diz·ing.** to stimulate or treat (a nerve or muscle) by means of induced electricity. —**far'a·di·za'tion,** *n.* —**far'a·diz'er,** *n.*

far·a·way (far'ə wā') *adj.* **1.** at a great distance; remote: *faraway places.* **2.** creating the impression that attention is focused elsewhere; dreamy; pensive: *a faraway look in one's eyes.* Also, **far-off.**

farce (färs) *n.* **1.a.** a humorous play in which the situation and characters are greatly exaggerated. **b.** the broad humor used in such a play. **2.** a hollow pretense; mockery; absurdity: *The meeting turned out to be a farce.* —*v.t.,* **farced, farc·ing.** to fill out (a speech, play, or composition) with wit or humor. [French *farce* stuffing, humorous play, going back to Latin *farcīre* to stuff; originally used to denote comic interludes "stuffed" between the acts of medieval religious plays.]

far·ceur (fär sûr') *n.* **1.** a person who writes or acts in a farce. **2.** a person who makes jokes; joker; wag. [French *farceur* writer or actor of farce, from *farce* stuffing, humorous play. See FARCE.]

far·ci·cal (fär'si kəl) *adj.* of, relating to, or characteristic of a farce; absurd; ludicrous. —**far·ci·cal·i·ty** (fär'si kal'i tē), **far'ci·cal·ness,** *n.* —**far'ci·cal·ly,** *adv.*

far cry, a great distance; long way: *The official story on the accident was a far cry from the truth.*

far·cy (fär'sē) *n.* a disease of horses that affects the skin and lymph glands. It is a form of glanders. [French *farcin,* from Late Latin *farcīminum,* from Latin *farcīre* to stuff; because the diseased animal is "stuffed" with pustules.]

far·del (fär'dəl) *n. Archaic.* bundle; burden. [Old French *fardel,* going back to Arabic *farda* package, load for a camel.]

fare (fâr) *n.* **1.** the cost of a ride on a bus, airplane, or other conveyance. **2.** a passenger who pays a fare: *The bus stopped to pick up two fares.* **3.** food and drink: *The prison fare was very simple.* —*v.i.,* **fared, far·ing. 1.** to be in a specified state, esp. with regard to good or bad fortune; get along: *to fare well at school.* **2.** to turn out; result; happen: *Things fared badly with us on our trip.* **3.** to eat and drink; dine. **4.** *Archaic.* to go; travel. [Old English *faran* to go, travel, get along, happen.] —**far'er,** *n.*

fare-thee-well (fâr'ŧ͟hē wel') *n.* **1.** the highest or utmost degree; maximum extent. **2.** a state of perfection. ➡ used esp. in the phrase *to a fare-thee-well.* Also, **fare-you-well** (fâr'ū wel').

fare·well (fâr'wel') *interj.* good-bye and good luck. —*n.* **1.** a parting word; good-bye: *They said their farewells and left.* **2.** the act of parting; departure; leave-taking: *a farewell delayed by illness.* —*adj.* of or relating to a farewell; last: *a farewell luncheon, a farewell speech.*

far-fetched (fär'fecht') *adj.* not natural or reasonable; forced; strained: *a far-fetched comparison.*

far-flung (fär'flung') *adj.* extending over a great distance or area; widespread: *a far-flung empire.*

fa·ri·na (fə rē'nə) *n.* **1.** flour or meal made from cereal grains, nuts, or starchy roots, used as a breakfast cereal or in puddings. **2.** starch. [Latin *farīna* meal[2], ground corn.]

far·i·na·ceous (far'ə nā'shəs) *adj.* **1.** of, relating to, or containing flour or meal. **2.** containing starch; starchy. **3.** having a mealy texture.

far·kle·ber·ry (fär'kəl ber'ē) *n., pl.* **-ries.** a spreading shrub or small tree, *Vaccinium arboreum,* found in the southern United States, bearing small, smooth, inedible black berries. [Of uncertain origin.]

farm (färm) *n.* **1.** an area of land used to raise crops, livestock, or poultry. **2.** a tract of water used for the cultivation of fish or other forms of aquatic life: *a catfish farm.* **3.** farm team. —*v.t.* **1.** to cultivate (land). **2.** to let out the labor or services of (a person) for hire (often with *out*): *to farm out convicts for highway construction.* **3.** to contract for the maintenance and care of (a person or institution) for a fixed amount (often with *out*): *to farm out orphans to foster parents.* **4.** *Archaic.* to pay a fixed amount in order to collect proceeds or profits of (a tax or business) and keep what is collected. **5.** *Archaic.* to let or lease (land or the authority to collect taxes) to another in return for a fixed amount (usually with *out*). —*v.i.* to engage in agricultural farming. [Old French *ferme* rural property, lease, from Medieval Latin *firma* fixed payment, from Latin *firmāre* to strengthen, fix; a farm was originally a tax or rent based on property and later came to mean the property itself.]

- **to farm out. a.** to assign (a baseball player) to a minor-league team. **b.** to arrange to have (work) done by someone not directly associated with a main organization; subcontract.

farm club, farm team.

farm·er (fär'mər) *n.* **1.** a person who engages in agricultural farming. **2.** a person who contracts to perform certain duties or services at a fixed price, such as caring for children or paupers: *a farmer of infants* (Charles Dickens, 1838). **3.** *Archaic.* a person who contracts to pay a fixed sum for the privilege of collecting taxes and keeping what is collected.

farmers' market, a market to which farmers can bring vegetables, fruits, and other farm products for sale directly to consumers.

farm·hand (färm'hand') *n.* a person who works on a farm, esp. a hired laborer.

farm·house (färm'hous') *n., pl.* **-hous·es** (-hou'ziz). a house on a farm, esp. one in which the owner or manager lives.

farm·ing (fär'ming) *n.* **1.** the cultivation of crops, livestock, or poultry; agriculture. **2.** *Archaic.* the practice of leasing the authority to collect taxes.

farm·land (färm'land') *n.* land that is farmed or is suitable for farming.

farm·stead (färm'sted') *n.* a farm and its buildings.

farm team, a minor-league baseball team owned by or associated with a major-league club and used to train its recruits. Also, **farm, farm club.**

farm·yard (färm'yärd') *n.* a yard enclosed by or surrounding farm buildings.

far·o (fâr'ō) *n.* a card game using a deck of fifty-two cards, in which any number of players bet against the house as to the order in which cards will be drawn from the dealing box. [Modification of PHARAOH; because a Pharaoh was once depicted on one of the cards.]

far-off (fär'ôf', -of') *adj.* faraway.

far-out (fär'out') *adj. Slang.* outside or beyond what is usual or conventional; avant-garde; extreme: *far-out taste in music.*

far·ra·go (fə rä'gō, -rā'gō) *n., pl.* **-goes.** a confused mixture; hodgepodge; medley: *The editorial was a farrago of exaggerations and half-truths.* [Latin *farrāgō* medley, mixed fodder.]

far·reach·ing (fär'rē'ching) *adj.* having wide influence, effect, or range: *far-reaching changes.*

far·ri·er (fär'ē ər) *n.* a blacksmith who shoes horses. [Old French *ferrier,* from Latin *ferrārius,* from *ferrum* iron.]

far·row (far'ō) *n.* a litter of pigs. —*v.i., v.t.* to give birth to (pigs). [Old English *fearh* young pig.]

far·see·ing (fär'sē'ing) *adj.* **1.** able to see distant objects. **2.** having or showing foresight and careful planning; farsighted: *a farseeing executive, a farseeing program to improve public education.*

Far·si (fär'sē) *n.* Persian *(def. 2).*

far·sight·ed (fär'sī'tid) *adj.* **1.** able to see distant objects more clearly than those nearby; hyperopic. ➡ opposed to **nearsighted.** **2.** having or showing foresight and careful planning; prudent: *a farsighted leader, a farsighted plan.* —**far'sight'ed·ly,** *adv.* —**far'sight'ed·ness,** *n.*

far·ther (fär'thər) *adv.* a comparative of **far.** **1.** at or to a more distant or remote point in space: *The raft drifted farther and farther from the dock.* **2.** to a greater degree or extent; more completely: *to proceed farther in carrying out a plan.* —*adj.* more distant or remote: *They live on the farther side of the city.* [Middle English *ferther,* form of FURTHER and used as a comparative of FAR.]

far·ther·most (fär'thər mōst') *adj.* most distant or remote; farthest.

far·thest (fär'thist) *adv.* a superlative of **far.** **1.** at or to the most distant or remote point in space: *She lives farthest from the school.* **2.** to the greatest degree or extent; most completely: *He went farthest in his support.* —*adj.* most distant or remote: *the farthest hill.* [Form of FURTHEST and used as a superlative of FAR.]

far·thing (fär'thing) *n.* **1.** a former British monetary unit and coin equal to one fourth of a penny. **2.** something of little or no value; the smallest amount. [Old English *fēorthung* the coin; literally, a little fourth, from *fēortha* fourth.]

far·thin·gale (fär'thing gāl') *n.* a framework for expanding a woman's skirt, worn in the sixteenth and seventeenth centuries. [Modification of Middle French *verdugalle,* from Spanish *verdugado* (referring to the rods of which it was made), from *verdugo* rod, shoot of a tree, going back to Latin *viridis* green.]

fas·ces (fas'ēz) *n.* a bundle of rods containing an ax with a projecting blade and bound with a red cord, carried before a magistrate in ancient Rome as a symbol of authority. ➡ used as singular or plural. [Latin *fascēs,* plural of *fascis* bundle.]

fas·ci·a (fash'ē ə) *n., pl.* **fas·ci·ae** (fash'ē ē'). **1.** a band, sash, or fillet. **2.** a subcutaneous sheet of fibrous tissue that holds muscles and various organs of the body in place. [Latin *fascia* band, fillet.] —**fas'ci·al,** *adj.*

fas·ci·cle (fas'i kəl) *n.* **1.** a small bundle. **2.** a division of a book published in installments. **3.** a close cluster, as of flowers, leaves, or fruits. [Latin *fasciculus* small bundle, bunch, diminutive of *fascis* bundle.] —**fas·cic·u·lar** (fə sik'yə lər, fa-), **fas·cic·u·late** (fə sik'yə lit, fa-), *adj.* —**fas·cic'u·late·ly,** *adv.*

fas·ci·nate (fas'ə nāt') *v.t.* **-nat·ed, -nat·ing.** **1.** to attract and hold the close interest of by some compelling quality or charm; captivate: *The magician's tricks fascinated the audience.* **2.** to hold motionless or paralyze, as by inspiring terror or awe: *The snake fascinated its prey.* [Latin *fascinātus,* past participle of *fascināre* to enchant.] —**fas'ci·na'tor,** *n.*

fas·ci·nat·ing (fas'ə nā'ting) *adj.* intensely interesting; captivating; irresistible: *a thriller with a fascinating plot.* —**fas'ci·nat·ing·ly,** *adv.*

fas·ci·na·tion (fas'ə nā'shən) *n.* **1.** the act of fascinating or the state of being fascinated. **2.** strong attraction; charm; enchantment: *The room's fascination was in its decor.*

fas·cine (fa sēn', fə-) *n.* a bundle of sticks bound at short intervals, used for fortification, as in filling ditches and lining trenches. [French *fascine,* going back to Latin *fascis* bundle.]

fas·cism (fash'iz əm) *n.* **1.** Fascism. a nationalist movement that controlled Italy from 1922 to 1943 under the dictatorship of Benito Mussolini. Fascism established rigid economic controls and attempted to organize most phases of Italian life. **2.** any similar movement, such as German Naziism or the Falange in Spain, that advocates a nationalist dictatorship, private ownership of property but state control of the economy, militarism, suppres-

sion of opposing political movements, and sometimes racism. **3.** *also,* Fascism. the doctrines or methods of such movements. [Italian *Fascismo* Italian fascism, from *fascio* bundle, political group, from Latin *fascis* bundle; with reference to the *fasces* of ancient Rome. See FASCES.]

fas·cist (fash'ist) *n.* **1.** Fascist. a member of the ruling political party in Italy under the dictatorship of Benito Mussolini. **2.** a member of any similar political party. **3.** a person who advocates or supports fascism. —*adj. also,* Fascist. of, relating to, or supporting fascism or fascists.

fash·ion (fash'ən) *n.* **1.** a prevailing custom or style, as in dress, home furnishings, speech, or behavior; current practice: *the latest fashion in raincoats.* **2.** the condition of conforming to a prevailing custom or style: *The old hat was once again in fashion.* **3.** items, esp. clothing, of a particular style: *the spring fashions now in the stores.* **4.** manner; way: *to act in a carefree fashion.* **5.** fashionable people collectively. —*v.t.* **1.** to give form to; shape; mold: *to fashion a boot out of leather, to fashion a child's character.* **2.** *Archaic.* to adapt; accommodate; fit. [Old French *façon* appearance, form, from Latin *factiō* a doing, party. Doublet of FACTION.] —**fash'ion·er,** *n.*

•**after** (or **in**) **a fashion.** to some extent but not too well or completely: *The young children washed the car after a fashion.*

> **Synonyms** *n.* **Fashion, vogue,** and **style** may all denote a contemporary way of doing things, esp. dressing. **Fashion** connotes widespread popularity and general acceptance at a particular time and suggests the importance of being up to date: *After World War II long skirts came back into fashion. The fashion at the beach this year seems to be bright pink.* **Vogue** emphasizes the latest trends adopted by those who set fashion: *Hats with large brims appear to be the vogue this season.* **Style** is a broader term suggesting a mode of dress or manner of conducting oneself that is distinctive or elegant: *the style of tasteful urbanites, a classic way of dressing that never goes out of style.*

fash·ion·a·ble (fash'ə nə bəl) *adj.* **1.** conforming to current styles or practices; in fashion; stylish: *a fashionable hair style.* **2.** of, relating to, or frequented by people of fashion: *a fashionable resort.* —**fash'ion·a·ble·ness,** *n.* —**fash'ion·a·bly,** *adv.*

fashion plate **1.** a person who dresses in the latest style. **2.** an illustration showing new or current fashions in dress.

fast¹ (fast) *adj.* **1.** acting or moving with speed; quick; rapid: *a fast train, a fast thinker.* **2.** accomplished in relatively little time; performed rapidly: *a fast game, to make a fast retreat.* **3.** (of a clock or watch) showing a time later than the true time. **4.** suitable for or promoting rapid movement: *a fast racetrack.* **5.** characterized by the reckless pursuit of pleasure; dissipated: *fast living, a fast crowd.* **6.** firmly attached; secure; tight: *a fast knot, a fast grip on a child's arm.* **7.** loyal; steadfast; faithful: *fast friends.* **8.** (of colors) not easily faded. **9.** resistant to. ➡ used in combination, as in *acid-fast.* **10.** *Photography.* allowing for a short exposure time: *fast film.* —*adv.* **1.** in a firm manner; securely; tightly: *The tent was held fast by stakes.* **2.** soundly; deeply: *fast asleep.* **3.** with speed; quickly; rapidly: *to move fast.* **4.** so as to show a time later than the true time: *My watch is running fast.* **5.** in a wild, dissipated manner; recklessly: *to live fast.* **6.** *Archaic.* close; near: *fast by.* [Old English *fæst* firm, fixed.] —For Synonyms *(adj.),* see **quick.**

•**to play fast and loose. a.** to act recklessly or irresponsibly: *to play fast and loose with someone else's money.* **b.** to act dishonestly or deceitfully: *to play fast and loose with the evidence to prove a point.*

fast² (fast) *v.i.* to eat little or no food or only certain kinds of food, esp. as a religious observance. —*n.* **1.** the act of fasting. **2.** a day or period of fasting. [Old English *faesten* a fast, fasting, from Old English *faestan* to abstain from food; literally, to hold firm, from *faest* firm, fixed.]

fast·back (fast'bak') *n.* an automobile with a roof that slopes down to the rear in an unbroken curve.

fast break *Sports.* a sudden rush, as down a court or rink, by the team that has gained control of the ball or puck, in an effort to score before the opposing team can establish a defense.

fast day, a day on which fasting is observed, esp. as a religious observance.

fas·ten (fas'ən) *v.t.* **1.** to attach firmly to something else; join: *to fasten a corsage to a dress.* **2.** to make fast; close tightly; secure: *to fasten a seat belt.* **3.** to direct steadily or fix (one's eyes or mind).

fasces

a	at	e	end	o	hot	u	up	hw	white	⎧	about
ā	ape	ē	me	ō	old	ū	use	ng	song	⎪	taken
ä	far	i	it	ô	fork	ü	rule	th	thin	ə	pencil
âr	care	ī	ice	oi	oil	u̇	pull	th	this	⎨	lemon
		îr	pierce	ou	out	ûr	turn	zh	measure	⎩	circus

447

—*v.i.* **1.** to become attached or firmly joined: *This snap won't fasten.* **2.** to take a firm hold; concentrate (with *on*): *to fasten on a plan.* [Old English *fæstnian* to make firm, secure.] —**fas′ten·er,** *n.*

fas·ten·ing (fas′ə ning) *n.* **1.** something that fastens, such as a hook, bolt, or button. **2.** the act of making fast.

fast-food (fast′füd′) *adj.* of or serving fast foods: *a fast-food restaurant.*

fast food, food that is cooked in large quantities by standardized methods and then served quickly in restaurants, to be eaten there or taken out.

fas·tid·i·ous (fas tid′ē əs) *adj.* **1.** difficult to please or satisfy; exacting or particular, esp. in matters of taste: *The fastidious customer examined each sweater closely.* **2.** extremely or excessively dainty or refined; easily or too easily disgusted: *The avant-garde play shocked the fastidious audience.* **3.** showing or caused by extreme or excessive particularity or refinement: *a fastidious concern about cleanliness, a fastidious rejection of an informal invitation.* [Latin *fastīdiōsus* full of disgust, disdainful, from *fastīdium* loathing.] —**fas·tid′i·ous·ly,** *adv.* —**fas·tid′i·ous·ness,** *n.*

fast·ness (fast′nis) *n.* **1.** the quality or state of being securely fixed. **2.** the quality of acting or moving with speed; swiftness; rapidity. **3.** a secure place; stronghold: *They retreated to an impenetrable fastness.*

fat (fat) *n.* **1.** any of a group of oily or greasy substances, white or yellow in color, found esp. in deposits in certain tissues of animals and some plants, for which they serve as reserve sources of energy. Fats constitute one of the three major food compounds, together with carbohydrates and proteins. **2.** animal tissue consisting mainly of such a substance; adipose tissue. **3.** a fat or oil used in cooking: *bacon fat, to fry potatoes in deep fat.* **4.** the condition of having excess adipose tissue; obesity; corpulence. **5.** the best or richest part. **6.** nonessential persons or things: *to trim the fat from a corporation.* **7.** *Chemistry.* any of a class of organic compounds, such as olein, formed by the reaction of fatty acids and glycerol. —*adj.,* **fat·ter, fat·test. 1.a.** having excess flesh or fat; obese. **b.** having abundant flesh; well-fed; plump: *a fat turkey.* **2.** containing much fat, oil, or grease; fatty: *fat beef, fat gravy.* **3.** containing much; full; abundant: *a fat wallet, a fat letter.* **4.** thick or big: *a fat paperback.* **5.** profitable; lucrative: *That fat job pays well.* **6.** gross; stupid. —*v.i., v.t.,* **fat·ted, fat·ting.** to fatten. [Old English *fætt* plump, obese, fatty.] —**fat′ly,** *adv.* —**fat′ness,** *n.*

· **the fat is in the fire. a.** something has been started that cannot be stopped. **b.** something has been done to make matters worse.

· **to chew the fat.** to talk or chat, usually at leisure.

fa·tal (fā′təl) *adj.* **1.** causing death; lethal: *a fatal heart attack.* **2.** causing destruction or harm; disastrous: *a fatal mistake.* **3.** extremely important or decisive; fateful: *the fatal hour.* **4.** influencing or controlling human fate: *fatal powers.* [Latin *fātālis* destined, deadly, from *fātum* oracle, destiny.] —For Synonyms, see **deadly.**

fa·tal·ism (fā′tə liz′əm) *n.* **1.** the belief that all events and conditions are determined by fate and cannot be altered by human beings. **2.** acceptance of all events and conditions as inevitable; submission to fate. —**fa′tal·ist,** *n.* —**fa′tal·is′tic,** *adj.* —**fa′tal·is′ti·cal·ly,** *adv.*

fa·tal·i·ty (fā tal′i tē, fə-) *n., pl.* **-ties. 1.** a death resulting from a disaster: *highway fatalities.* **2.** the power to cause death; deadly effect: *Penicillin has reduced the fatality of many diseases.* **3.** the quality or condition of being determined or influenced by fate. **4.** a predetermined liability to disaster or danger. **5.** fate or destiny.

fa·tal·ly (fā′tə lē) *adv.* **1.** so as to cause death or disaster; mortally: *to be fatally ill.* **2.** as determined by fate; inevitably.

fatal sisters, Fates.

fa·ta mor·ga·na (fä′tə môr gä′nə) a mirage, esp. the one seen in the Strait of Messina between the Italian mainland and Sicily. [Italian *fata Morgana* MORGAN LE FAY; because her magic power was once believed to cause mirages.]

fat·back (fat′bak′) *n.* a fatty strip from the back of a hog, usually salted and dried.

fat body, any of various masses of fatty tissue found in certain mature larval insects, serving as a food reserve.

fat cat *Slang.* **1.** a wealthy person, esp. one expected to make substantial contributions to a political party or campaign. **2.** a person who receives special privileges.

fate (fāt) *n.* **1.** a power that is believed to determine events before they happen and over which human beings have no control. **2.** something believed to be caused by fate; inescapable lot or fortune: *It was their fate to die young.* **3.** final state; outcome: *to be awaiting the fate of an appeal to a higher court.* **4.** death or destruction; doom. —*v.t.,* **fat·ed, fat·ing.** to determine before-hand; destine. ➡ now used only in the passive: *The team was fated to win.* [Latin *fātum* oracle, destiny; literally, what is spoken, from *fārī* to speak.]

Synonyms *n.* **Fate, destiny,** and **lot** may all denote something which befalls one in life and which may be ascribed to some power or design. **Fate,** which derives from a Roman religious concept, suggests the working of a supernatural force or law: *It is our fate to live only so long.* **Destiny** stresses that what happens has been predetermined. It lacks the negative connotations of *fate: I believe it is my destiny to become a great artist.* **Lot** connotes a share drawn by chance: *It was their lot to live their lives in poverty.* **Lot** one confides.

fat·ed (fā′tid) *adj.* **1.** determined by fate; destined. **2.** destined to disaster; doomed.

fate·ful (fāt′fəl) *adj.* **1.** determining what will happen; decisive; momentous: *a fateful battle.* **2.** showing or telling what will happen; prophetic: *a fateful prediction.* **3.** controlled or influenced by fate. **4.** causing death or disaster; deadly. —**fate′ful·ly,** *adv.* —**fate′ful·ness,** *n.*

Fates (fāts) *pl. n.* in classical mythology, Clotho, Lachesis, and Atropos, the three goddesses who controlled human life and destiny. Also, **fatal sisters.**

fat·head (fat′hed′) *n. Slang.* a stupid person; fool; blockhead. —**fat′head′ed,** *adj.*

fa·ther (fä′thər) *n.* **1.** a male parent. **2.a.** a man who acts or is regarded as a male parent; guardian or provider. **b.** an adoptive father or stepfather. **c.** a father-in-law. **3.** a man who originates, invents, or founds something: *Gutenberg is thought of as the father of printing.* **4.** also, **Father.** a title of respect used with or without a name to address a priest or another clergyman. **5. Father. a.** God. **b.** the first person of the Trinity. **6.** a male ancestor; forefather. **7.** one of the leaders or elders, as of a city or assembly. ➡ usually used in the plural: *the city fathers.* **8.** a senator in ancient Rome. —*v.t.* **1.** to be the father of. **2.** to act as a father toward: *to father an orphan.* **3.** to originate, invent, or establish: *The revolutionaries fathered a new form of government.* [Old English *fæder* male parent, forefather, God.]

father confessor 1. a priest who hears confession. **2.** a man in whom one confides.

fa·ther·hood (fä′thər hud′) *n.* the state of being a father.

fa·ther-in-law (fä′thər in lô′) *n., pl.* **fa·thers-in-law.** the father of one's husband or wife.

fa·ther·land (fä′thər land′) *n.* the country in which a person or his or her ancestors were born.

fa·ther·less (fä′thər lis) *adj.* **1.** having no living father. **2.** having no known father.

fa·ther·ly (fä′thər lē) *adj.* **1.** of, relating to, or characteristic of a father: *fatherly advice.* **2.** like a father in behavior or attitude: *a fatherly uncle.* —**fa′ther·li·ness,** *n.*

Father's Day, a day set aside in honor of fathers, observed annually on the third Sunday in June.

Fathers of the Church, the leaders of the early Christian Church whose writings on Church doctrines and teachings are considered authoritative. Also, **Church Fathers.**

fath·om (fath′əm) *n., pl.* **-oms** or **-om.** a unit of measure equal to 6 feet (1.8 meters), used esp. in nautical measurements, as of the depth of water. —*v.t.* **1.** to determine the depth of (water); sound. **2.** to understand fully: *I could not fathom the strange remark.* [Old English *fæthm* length of the outstretched arms, grasp.] —**fath′om·a·ble,** *adj.*

Fa·thom·e·ter (fa thom′i tər) *n. Trademark.* a sonic depth finder.

fath·om·less (fath′əm lis) *adj.* **1.** of immeasurable depth. **2.** difficult or impossible to understand; incomprehensible.

fa·tigue (fə tēg′) *n.* **1.** loss of strength resulting from physical or mental exertion; weariness; exhaustion. **2.** a cause of such weariness; toil; exertion: *the fatigues of an election campaign.* **3.** the weakening of a material, esp. metal, caused by continued use or excessive strain. **4.** the condition of decreased response or functioning that occurs when a muscle has been repeatedly contracted without rest. **5.** manual or general labor performed by military personnel, such as cleaning the grounds or doing other maintenance work. Also, **fatigue duty. 6. fatigues.** a heavy-duty, two-piece uniform worn by military personnel in the field or during fatigue. Also, **fatigue clothes.** —*v.,* **-tigued, -ti·guing.** —*v.t.* **1.** to cause weariness in; tire out. **2.** to weaken (metal or another material) by continued use or excessive strain. —*v.i.* to become weary. [French *fatigue* weariness, from Old French *fatiguer* to weary, from Latin *fatigāre*.]

fatigue clothes, fatigue *(def. 6).*

fatigue duty, fatigue *(def. 5).*

fat·ling (fat′ling) *n.* a young animal fattened for slaughter.

fat-sol·u·ble (fat′sol′yə bəl) *adj.* capable of being dissolved in fats or oils or in solvents of them.

fat·ten (fat′ən) *v.t.* **1.** to make fat or plump; fill out. **2.** to enrich or make more substantial. —*v.i.* to grow or become fat. —**fat′·ten·er,** *n.*

fat·ty (fat′ē) *adj.,* **-ti·er, -ti·est. 1.** made of or containing fat, esp. in large amounts. **2.** resembling fat; greasy. —**fat′ti·ness,** *n.*

fatty acid, any of several hydrocarbon compounds, such as stearic acid, consisting of a long chain of carbon atoms with an acid group, —COOH, at one end. Fatty acids combine with glycerol to form fat.

fa·tu·i·ty (fə tü′i tē, -tū′-) *n., pl.* **-ties. 1.** smug stupidity or foolishness. **2.** something fatuous, as an action or statement. [Latin *fatuitās* foolishness.]

fat·u·ous (fach′ü əs) *adj.* smugly stupid or foolish; inane: *a fatuous person, a fatuous remark.* [Latin *fatuus* foolish.] —**fat′u·ous·ly,** *adv.* —**fat′u·ous·ness,** *n.*

fau·bourg (fō′bŏŏr, -bŏŏrg) *n.* **1.** a suburb. **2.** a district within a city. [French *faubourg* suburb, modification (influenced by French *faux* false), because a suburb was not regarded as a true city) of Old French *forsbourc* literally, what is outside the town, going back to Latin *forīs* outside + Late Latin *burgus* fortress; of Germanic origin.]

fau·ces (fô′sēz) *n.* the cavity at the back of the mouth, opening into the pharynx. ➡ used as singular or plural. [Latin *faucēs.*]

fau·cet (fô′sit) *n.* a device with a valve that regulates the flow of liquid from a pipe or container. [French *fausset* spigot, possibly from *fausser* to damage, falsify, going back to Latin *falsus* false, deceptive.]

faugh (fô) *interj.* an expression of disgust. [Imitative.]

fault (fôlt) *n.* **1.** something that impairs character, appearance, or structure; flaw: *The roof collapsed because of a fault in its construction. A bad temper is a serious fault.* **2.** responsibility for a mistake or wrongdoing: *That error in subtraction is my fault.* **3.** a mistake; error: *The faults in the manuscript have been corrected.* **4.** *Geology.* a break in the earth's crust along which rock masses have been displaced with respect to one another. Sudden movement of such masses generates earthquakes. **5.a.** a failure to serve the ball into the correct area of the court or in a correct manner in tennis, squash, and similar games. **b.** a ball served in this manner. **6.** *Hunting.* loss of the scent by the dogs. —*v.t.* **1.** to find an error in: *to fault an argument.* **2.** to blame or criticize: *to fault the mayor for corruption.* **3.** *Geology.* to cause or produce a fault in. —*v.i.* **1.** *Geology.* to develop a fault. **2.** (in tennis, squash, and similar games) to fail to serve the ball correctly. **3.** *Archaic.* to commit an error; blunder. [Old French *faute* default, lack, gap, going back to Latin *fallere* to deceive.]

• **at fault. a.** open to or deserving blame; wrong: *The driver was not at fault in the accident.* **b.** at a loss; puzzled. **c.** (of hunting dogs) off or unable to find the scent.

• **to a fault.** to an extreme or excessive degree: *to be generous to a fault.*

• **to find fault (with).** to look for and point out faults (in); complain (about); criticize: *You are always finding fault. They seem to find fault with everything.*

fault *(def. 4)*

Synonyms *n.* **Fault, failing,** and **weakness** denote a flaw, or shortcoming, in a person's character. **Fault** connotes an identifiable element in a person's makeup that may or may not be serious: *Impatience is a common fault in people who like to get things over and done with.* **Failing** is more suggestive of a minor character flaw: *My friend's chief failing is an inability to be on time.* **Weakness** suggests that one is not as forceful in some way as one could be: *Your weakness is that you are too timid to speak up for yourself.*

fault·find·er (fôlt′fīn′dər) *n.* a person who looks for and points out faults; one who criticizes excessively.

fault·find·ing (fôlt′fīn′ding) *n.* the act or habit of criticizing or pointing out faults. —*adj.* tending to point out faults; critical.

fault·less (fôlt′lis) *adj.* without a fault; perfect. —**fault′less·ly,** *adv.* —**fault′less·ness,** *n.*

fault·y (fôl′tē) *adj.,* **fault·i·er, fault·i·est.** having faults or defects. —**fault′i·ly,** *adv.* —**fault′i·ness,** *n.*

faun (fôn) *n.* in Roman mythology, a minor god of the woods and fields, having the body of a man and the ears, horns, tail, and sometimes hind legs of a goat. It is identified with the satyr of Greek mythology. [Latin *Faunus.*]

fau·na (fô′nə) *n., pl.* **-nas** or **-nae** (-nē). the animals characteristic of a particular place, time, or environment: *the fauna of the African plains.* ➡ distinguished from **flora.** [Modern Latin

fauna, from Late Latin *Fauna* rural goddess in Roman mythology.] —**fau′nal,** *adj.*

Faust (foust) *n.* in German legend, a magician and philosopher who sold his soul to the devil in return for knowledge and power.

fauv·ism (fō′viz əm) *also,* **Fauv·ism.** *n.* a French art movement in the early 1900s that emphasized bold colors and freely distorted forms. [French *fauvisme,* from *(les) fauves* (the) wild animals (from a critic's reference to the painters' bold style); of Germanic origin.] —**fauv′ist;** *also,* **Fauv′ist,** *n.*

fauvism
a painting by André Derain

faux pas (fō′pä′) *pl.* **faux pas** (fō′päz′, pä′). an embarrassing mistake; blunder, esp. a social one: *Forgetting my host's name was a faux pas.* [French *faux pas* literally, false step, going back to Latin *falsus* deceptive + *passus* step.]

fa·va bean (fä′və) broad bean.

fa·vor (fā′vər) *also, British,* **favour.** *n.* **1.** an act of kindness or goodwill: *You could do me a favor by lending me a dollar.* **2.** friendly regard; approval; liking: *The boss looked with favor on the hard-working employee.* **3.** special or excessive consideration or kindness; partiality: *Judges must not show favor to either side in a case.* **4.** the state of being liked, highly regarded, or approved: *a politician in favor with the people.* **5.** something given, such as a souvenir at a party; gift. **6.** *Archaic.* a letter, esp. a business letter. —*v.t.* **1.** to show favor to; oblige: *Please favor us with a reply.* **2.** to approve of; like: *to favor long hair rather than short.* **3.** to show special consideration for; be partial to: *to favor one child over another, a law that favors rural areas.* **4.** to be in support of; endorse; advocate: *to favor tax reform.* **5.** to prove advantageous to; make easy; assist: *Crowded conditions favor the spread of disease.* **6.** to treat with gentleness; spare: *to favor a sprained ankle.* **7.** to resemble in facial features; look like: *The older boy favors his mother's side of the family.* [Old French *favor* kindness, partiality, support, from Latin *favor* goodwill, partiality.]

• **in favor of. a.** in support of; advocating: *The students were in favor of longer vacations.* **b.** to the advantage of: *The jury decided in favor of the defendant.* **c.** (of a check, money order, or the like) payable to.

• **in one's favor.** to (one's) advantage or interest: *The score was 35 to 13 in our favor.*

• **to find favor (with).** to be regarded with approval (by); become accepted (by): *a plan that found favor with the mayor.*

fa·vor·a·ble (fā′vər ə bəl, fāv′rə-) *also, British,* **favourable.** *adj.* **1.** expressing approval; complimentary: *The movie received a favorable review.* **2.** in one's favor; advantageous: *favorable conditions for sailing, to create a favorable impression.* **3.** granting something desired or requested; affirmative: *a favorable reply.*

a	at	e	end	o	hot	u	up	hw	white		about
ā	ape	ē	me	ō	old	ū	use	ng	song	ə	taken
ä	far	i	it	ô	fork	ü	rule	th	thin		pencil
âr	care	ī	ice	oi	oil	u̇	pull	th	this		lemon
		îr	pierce	ou	out	ûr	turn	zh	measure		circus

F

4. indicating a good chance of achieving a desired end or outcome; promising: *a favorable sign for improvement in the economy.* —**fa′vor·a·ble·ness,** *n.* —**fa′vor·a·bly,** *adv.*

Synonyms Favorable, auspicious, and propitious mean suggesting that something will come out well. **Favorable** suggests that everything necessary for a good outcome is present: *With the economy booming, this seems a favorable moment to approach potential investors.* **Auspicious** connotes that signs of eventual success are visible: *Drawing the inside position on the starting line was an auspicious beginning for the racer.* **Propitious** is similar to *auspicious,* but suggests more strongly favoring forces: *The morning breeze, blowing out to sea, made it seem a propitious time for us to set sail.*

fa·vored (fā′vərd) *also, British,* **favoured.** *adj.* **1.** regarded or treated with favor or partiality: *a favored child.* **2.** endowed with special advantages or superior qualities: *a favored country with abundant natural resources and a stable government.* **3.** having a certain kind of appearance or features. ➡ used in combination, as in *ill-favored, well-favored.*

fa·vor·ite (fā′vər it, fāv′rit) *also, British,* **favourite.** *adj.* regarded with special liking or favor; preferred, esp. over all others: *What is your favorite baseball team?* —*n.* **1.** a person or thing that is preferred or liked best: *Mystery stories are my favorites.* **2.** a person who is treated with partiality by a superior: *The boss's favorite got a large raise.* **3.** in a contest, the competitor considered most likely to win: *That horse is the favorite in the next race.* [Obsolete French *favorit* favored, from Italian *favorito,* past participle of *favorire* to favor, going back to Latin *favor* goodwill.]

favorite son, a political leader nominated as a presidential candidate by the delegates of his state at a national nominating convention, now usually only as an honor.

fa·vor·it·ism (fā′vər i tiz′əm, fāv′ri-) *also, British,* **favouritism.** *n.* **1.** a show of special favor toward one or more persons to the neglect of others; partiality. **2.** the state of being a favorite.

fa·vour (fā′vər) *British.* favor.

fa·vour·a·ble (fā′vər ə bəl, fāv′rə-) *adj. British.* favorable. —**fa′vour·a·ble·ness,** *n.* —**fa′vour·a·bly,** *adv.*

fa·voured (fā′vərd) *British.* favored.

fa·vour·ite (fā′vər it, fāv′rit) *British.* favorite.

fa·vour·it·ism (fā′vər i tiz′əm, fāv′ri-) *British.* favoritism.

fawn[1] (fôn) *n.* **1.** a deer less than one year old. **2.** a light yellowish brown color. —*adj.* having the color fawn. [Middle English *fawn,* from Old French *faon, feon* young animal, young deer, going back to Latin *fētus* offspring.]

fawn[2] (fôn) *v.i.* **1.** to seek favor by acting in a servile manner; be obsequious: *People fawned on the politician.* **2.** (of dogs) to show affection, as by wagging the tail. [Middle English *faunen* to show fondness as a dog does, to show fondness servilely, from Old English *fagnian* to rejoice, from *fagen,* variant of *faegan* glad.] —**fawn′er,** *n.* —**fawn′ing·ly,** *adv.*

fax (faks) *n., pl.* **fax·es. 1.** facsimile *(def. 2).* **2.** an image or document transmitted by fax. —*v.t.* to transmit by fax.

fay[1] (fā) *n.* a fairy.

fay[2] (fā) *n. Archaic.* faith.

faze (fāz) *v.t.,* **fazed, faz·ing.** to disrupt the composure of; disconcert: *The accident didn't faze the bus driver.* [Form of obsolete *feeze* to drive away, worry, from Old French *fēsian* to drive away.]

FBI, Federal Bureau of Investigation, an agency of the U.S. Department of Justice that investigates violations of federal law and subversive activities against the United States.

FCC, Federal Communications Commission, an agency of the U.S. government that regulates wire, radio, and television communications media.

F clef, bass clef.

FDA, Food and Drug Administration.

FDIC, Federal Deposit Insurance Corporation.

Fe, the symbol for iron. [Latin *ferrum.*]

fe·al·ty (fē′əl tē) *n., pl.* **-ties. 1.** the loyalty and duty owed by a vassal or feudal tenant to his lord. **2.** *Archaic.* faithfulness; loyalty. [Old French *fealté* fidelity, from Latin *fidēlitās* faithfulness. See FIDELITY.]

fear (fir) *n.* **1.** a strong feeling caused by the awareness or threat of danger, pain, or evil; dread: *to tremble with fear during a violent thunderstorm.* **2.** the state of feeling fear: *to live in fear.* **3.** a feeling of concern or anxiety: *the fear that one has forgotten something.* **4.** a cause for fear or alarm; danger: *There was some fear that the plane could crash.* **5.** awe or reverence, esp. toward God. —*v.t.* **1.** to be afraid of; dread: *Many children fear the dark.* **2.** to anticipate with concern or anxiety: *I fear that we will be late.* **3.** to feel awe or reverence for: *to fear God.* —*v.i.* to feel fear; be afraid. [Old English *fǣr* danger, panic.]

• **for fear of.** in order to avoid or prevent: *We left early for fear of missing the last train home.*

• **to fear for.** to be concerned about: *to fear for one's safety.*

Synonyms *n.* Fear, fright, and dread denote a state of emotional agitation experienced when facing or sensing danger. **Fear** is a general term for apprehension that may be accompanied by a loss of courage, and that may be temporary or permanent: *fear of the dark, to feel fear when walking on an empty street, to have fear of failing.* **Fright** connotes a sudden attack of fear: *to be overcome by fright when a strange dog jumps at you.* **Dread** suggests intense fear, or foreboding, particularly in the face of an unknown or undefined event: *We were filled with dread as we approached, wondering what awaited us in the dark, empty house.*

fear·ful (fir′fəl) *adj.* **1.** feeling fear; afraid; apprehensive: *a child fearful of a barking dog.* **2.** causing fear; dreadful; frightening: *a fearful blizzard.* **3.** showing fear; produced by fear: *a fearful look.* **4.** *Informal.* very bad; appalling; offensive: *fearful manners.* —**fear′ful·ly,** *adv.* —**fear′ful·ness,** *n.*

fear·less (fir′lis) *adj.* showing or feeling no fear; intrepid; brave: *a fearless action, a fearless soldier.* —**fear′less·ly,** *adv.* —**fear′less·ness,** *n.*

fear·some (fir′səm) *adj.* **1.** causing fear; frightening. **2.** feeling fear; frightened; apprehensive. —**fear′some·ly,** *adv.* —**fear′some·ness,** *n.*

fea·sance (fē′zəns) *n. Law.* performance, as of a duty or condition.

fea·si·ble (fē′zə bəl) *adj.* **1.** capable of being done or carried out; practicable: *a feasible design for a bridge.* **2.** capable of being used successfully; suitable: *a feasible site for a dam.* **3.** capable of being believed; likely; probable: *a feasible explanation for being absent.* [Old French *faisible* capable of being done, from *fais-,* a stem of *faire* to do, make, from Latin *facere.*] —**fea′si·bil′i·ty, fea′si·ble·ness,** *n.* —**fea′si·bly,** *adv.*

feast (fēst) *n.* **1.** an elaborate and lavish meal, esp. one prepared for many guests on a special occasion: *a wedding feast.* **2.** a religious celebration or festival: *the feast of the Annunciation.* **3.** something that provides great pleasure; treat: *The snowcapped mountains were a feast for our eyes.* —*v.t.* to provide a feast for; entertain lavishly. —*v.i.* to have or partake of a feast; eat lavishly. [Old French *feste* festival, going back to Latin *fēsta* festivals.] —**feast′er,** *n.*

• **to feast one's eyes on.** to enjoy the sight of: *Feast your eyes on this beautiful painting.*

Synonyms *n.* Feast and banquet denote an elaborate meal on a special occasion, usually for a large number of people. **Feast** connotes celebration and ample food and drink: *a wedding feast, to invite friends for a holiday feast.* **Banquet** may be used similarly but also stresses the formality of the occasion: *a banquet for the retiring president, complete with speakers and toasts.*

Feast of Tabernacles, Sukkoth.

Feast of Weeks, Shavuoth.

feat (fēt) *n.* a noteworthy act or deed, esp. one displaying exceptional skill, strength, or courage: *Climbing that mountain was quite a feat.* [Old French *fait* deed, exploit, from Latin *factum,* thing done, deed, from *facere* to do. Doublet of FACT.]

feath·er (feth′ər) *n.* **1.** one of the outgrowths from a bird's skin, consisting of a horny, hollow shaft with soft, flexible barbs on either side. **2.** something resembling a feather in appearance or lightness, as a fringe of hair on the leg of a dog or a feather-shaped flaw in a precious stone. **3.** pieces of feather or featherlike parts attached to the base of an arrow to guide its flight. **4.** kind, character, or species: *The neighborhood was inhabited by artists of every feather.* **5.** *Archaic.* attire; dress: *I saw him in full clerical feather* (William Makepeace Thackeray, 1855). —*v.t.* **1.** to cover, line, or adorn with or as with feathers. **2.** to supply with a feather or feathers: *to feather an arrow.* **3.** to turn (the blade of an oar) parallel to the water's surface after a stroke, keeping it in that position until the beginning of the next stroke. **4.** to change the blade angle of (an airplane propeller blade) in order to decrease wind resistance. —*v.i.* **1.** to grow feathers. **2.** to move, grow, or expand like feathers: *The ivy feathered over the edge of the brick wall.* [Old English *fether* plume.]

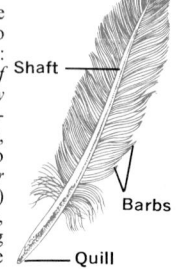
Shaft

Barbs

Quill

feather

• **birds of a feather.** people or things of the same kind: *She argued that Nazis and Communists were birds of a feather.*

F

• **feather in one's cap.** an accomplishment to be proud of: *Winning the lead role was a feather in the young actor's cap.*

• **in fine** (or **good,** or **high**) **feather.** in good condition or form, esp. in health or spirits: *The comic was in fine feather and kept us laughing for hours.*

• **to feather one's nest.** to enrich oneself, esp. by taking advantage of a position of trust: *The corrupt officials feathered their nests with bribes.*

feather bed 1. a soft, warm quilt or mattress filled with feathers. **2.** a bed with such a quilt or mattress.

feath·er·bed·ding (feth′ər bed′ing) *n.* the requiring of an employer to hire or continue to employ more people than are necessary to do the work, esp. as practiced by some labor unions to preserve jobs.

feath·er·brain (feth′ər brān′) *n.* a flighty, weak-minded person. —**feath′er·brained′,** *adj.*

feath·ered (feth′ərd) *adj.* having or covered with feathers.

feath·er·edge (feth′ər ej′) *n.* a very thin, often fragile edge, as of a tapered board. —*v.t.,* **-edged, -edg·ing.** to give a featheredge to. —**feath′er·edged′,** *adj.*

feather star, crinoid.

feath·er·stitch (feth′ər stich′) *n.* an embroidery stitch that resembles a feather or small branches on a stem. —*v.i., v.t.* to embroider with this stitch.

feath·er·weight (feth′ər wāt′) *n.* **1.** a boxer competing in the weight class of up to 126 pounds (57 kilograms), or a competitor, as a wrestler, in a similar class. **2.** a person or thing that is small or very light. **3.** a person or thing that is insignificant: *a political featherweight.* —*adj.* **1.** relating to featherweights. **2.** of little importance; trivial.

feath·er·y (feth′ə rē) *adj.* **1.** covered with or having feathers. **2.** resembling a feather; soft and lightweight; insubstantial: *a feathery soufflé, feathery wool.*

fea·ture (fē′chər) *n.* **1.** a distinctive or prominent part or characteristic: *Fountains are a common feature of city parks.* **2.a.** a part of the face, such as the eyes, mouth, or chin. **b. features.** the form or appearance of the face: *This photo doesn't do justice to your features.* **3.** a full-length motion picture, esp. one shown as a main attraction. **4.** anything presented as a main or special attraction, such as an item specially priced for sale or a particular act in a variety show. **5.a.** a newspaper or magazine column, cartoon, or the like, usually appearing regularly in a prominent place. **b.** feature story. —*v.,* **-tured, -tur·ing.** —*v.t.* **1.** to give a prominent place to: *The concert features a guitarist.* **2.** to have as a feature: *The house features central air conditioning and parquet floors.* —*v.i.* to play an important part: *Local issues featured prominently in the campaign.* [Old French *feture* fashion, form, from Latin *factūra* formation, a making.] —**fea′ture·less,** *adj.*

fea·tured (fē′chərd) *adj.* **1.** presented as a special attraction: *a featured guest on a panel.* **2.** having a specified kind of facial features. ➡ used in combination, as in *a fine-featured model.*

feature story, a newspaper or magazine article that is not an account of a news event but focuses on a particular aspect of such an event or on a person, trend, or other topic, often in a relaxed or distinctive style.

Feb., February.

feb·ri·fuge (feb′rə fūj′) *adj.* reducing or removing fever: *a febrifuge drug.* —*n.* a febrifuge medicine or agent. [French *fébrifuge,* from Latin *febris* fever + *fugāre* to drive away.]

fe·brile (fē′brəl, feb′rəl) *adj.* **1.** of, relating to, or causing fever: *a febrile infection.* **2.** affected with fever; feverish. [Medieval Latin *febrilis* relating to fever, from Latin *febris* fever.] —**fe·bril·i·ty** (fi bril′i tē), *n.*

Feb·ru·ar·y (feb′rü er′ē, feb′ū-) *n., pl.* **-ar·ies.** the second month of the year, containing twenty-eight days in regular years and twenty-nine days in leap years. [Latin *Februārius,* from *februarius (mens)* (month) of purification, from *februm* means of purification.]

fe·cal (fē′kəl) *also,* **faecal.** *adj.* of or relating to feces.

fe·ces (fē′sēz) *also,* **faeces.** *pl. n.* waste matter discharged from the bowels; excrement. [Latin *faecēs,* plural of *faex* dregs.]

feck·less (fek′lis) *adj.* **1.** having or showing a lack of strength or force; ineffective; weak; feeble: *a feckless leader, a feckless effort.* **2.** having or showing a lack of proper care or concern; irresponsible; careless: *a feckless youth, a feckless attitude.* [Scottish *feckless* ineffective, feeble, from *feck* (short for EFFECT) + -LESS.] —**feck′less·ly,** *adv.* —**feck′less·ness,** *n.*

fe·cund (fē′kənd, fek′ənd) *adj.* producing abundantly; fertile; fruitful; productive: *fecund earth, a fecund mind, a fecund era in art.* [Latin *fēcundus.*] —For Synonyms, see **fertile.**

fe·cun·date (fek′ən dāt′, fē′kən-) *v.t.,* **-dat·ed, -dat·ing. 1.** to cause the fertilization of; fertilize; impregnate. **2.** to make fertile, fruitful, or productive. —**fe·cun·da·tion** (fē′kən dā′shən, fek′ən-), *n.*

fe·cun·di·ty (fi kun′di tē) *n.* the quality or power of being fecund; fertility; fruitfulness; productiveness.

fed¹ (fed) *v.* the past tense and past participle of **feed.**

• **fed up.** *Informal.* disgusted, annoyed, or bored: *After waiting for an hour, we got fed up and left.*

fed² (fed) *n. Informal.* **1.** *also,* **Fed.** an officer or agent of the U.S. federal government. **2. the Fed.** the Federal Reserve Board or Federal Reserve System. [Short for FEDERAL.]

fe·da·yeen (fe dä yēn′) *pl. n., sing.* **-yee** (-yē′). Palestinian Arab guerrillas, operating esp. against Israel.

fed·er·al (fed′ər əl, fed′rəl) *adj.* **1.** of, relating to, or formed by an agreement among states or other groups establishing a central governing body to control matters of common concern, with each of the states or groups maintaining control over its own internal affairs. **2.** of, relating to, or designating a central government formed in this way. **3.** *also,* **Federal.** of, relating to, or designating the central government of the United States as distinguished from the governments of the individual states. **4. Federal.** of, relating to, or supporting the Union during the American Civil War. **5. Federal.** of or relating to the Federalist Party. —*n.* **Federal.** a person who supported the Union during the American Civil War, esp. a Union soldier. [Latin *foeder-,* stem of *foedus* league, treaty + -AL¹.] —**fed′er·al·ly,** *adv.*

fed·er·al·ism (fed′ər ə liz′əm, fed′rə-) *n.* **1.a.** a principle or system of federal government. **b.** belief in or support of such a system of government. **2. Federalism.** the principles of the Federalist Party.

fed·er·al·ist (fed′ər ə list, fed′rə-) *n.* **1.** a person who advocates a federal system of government. **2. Federalist.** a member or supporter of the Federalist Party. —*adj.* **1.** of, relating to, or supporting federalism. **2. Federalist.** of, relating to, or supporting the Federalist Party. Also, **fed′er·a·lis′tic.**

Federalist Party, a political party in the United States, active from 1788 to at least 1824, that supported the adoption of the Constitution and advocated a strong central government. Its principal leader was Alexander Hamilton. Also, **Federal Party.**

fed·er·al·ize (fed′ər ə līz′, fed′rə-) *v.t.,* **-ized, -iz·ing. 1.** to unite in a federal union. **2.** to place under the control of a federal government. —**fed′er·al·i·za′tion,** *n.*

Federal Party, Federalist Party.

Federal Reserve Bank, any of the twelve district banks belonging to the Federal Reserve System.

Federal Reserve Board, the board that directs the Federal Reserve System, composed of seven members appointed by the president of the United States and confirmed by the Senate.

Federal Reserve System, the central banking system of the United States, controlled by the federal government through the Federal Reserve Board and operated through a system of twelve Federal Reserve Banks that are privately owned by commercial banks and that regulate the member banks in their respective districts. It is intended to stabilize the economy by regulating the flow of currency and credit.

fed·er·ate (*v.,* fed′ə rāt′; *adj.,* fed′ər it) *v.t., v.i.,* **-at·ed, -at·ing.** to unite in a federal union: *The thirteen colonies federated to form one nation.* —*adj.* united in a federation or alliance. [Latin *foederātus,* past participle of *foederāre* to establish by treaty, from *foedus* treaty.] —**fed′er·a′tor,** *n.*

fed·er·a·tion (fed′ə rā′shən) *n.* **1.** the act of forming a federal union by agreement between states, nations, or other groups: *The federation of the first Swiss cantons occurred in the Middle Ages.* **2.** a union so formed, esp. as a form of government: *a federation of neutral nations to promote peace, a federation of labor unions.*

fed·er·a·tive (fed′ə rā′tiv, fed′ər ə-) *adj.* of or relating to a federation or the formation of a federation. —**fed′er·a′tive·ly,** *adv.*

fe·do·ra (fi dôr′ə) *n.* a soft felt hat with a curved brim and a lengthwise crease in the crown. [Supposedly from *Fédora,* a play by Victorien Sardou, 1831-1908, French dramatist.]

fee (fē) *n.* **1.** a charge or payment for a service or privilege: *an initiation fee, a registration fee.* **2.** a gratuity; tip: *a waiter's fee.*

a	at	e	end	o	hot	u	up	hw	white	⟨	about
ā	ape	ē	me	ō	old	ū	use	ng	song		taken
ä	far	i	it	ô	fork	ü	rule	th	thin	ə	pencil
âr	care	ī	ice	oi	oil	ů	pull	th	this		lemon
		îr	pierce	ou	out	ûr	turn	zh	measure	⟨	circus

451

3. an estate in land held from a feudal lord; fief. **4.** *Law.* an estate in land, esp. fee simple or fee tail. [Anglo-Norman *fee* fief; of Germanic origin.]

fee·ble (fē′bəl) *adj.*, **-bler, -blest. 1.** lacking physical strength; weak; infirm: *a feeble patient, a feeble body.* **2.** lacking force, durability, or effectiveness; inadequate: *a feeble cry, a feeble objection.* **3.** lacking intelligence or moral judgment: *a feeble mind.* [Anglo-Norman *feble* lacking strength, from Latin *flēbilis* lamentable, from *flēre* to weep.] **—fee′ble·ness,** *n.* **—fee′bly,** *adv.*

fee·ble-mind·ed (fē′bəl mīn′did) *adj.* **1.** having less than normal intelligence; mentally deficient. **2.** showing a lack of intelligence; foolish; absurd: *a feeble-minded plan.* **3.** *Archaic.* indecisive; irresolute. **—fee′ble-mind′ed·ly,** *adv.* **—fee′ble-mind′ed·ness,** *n.*

feed (fēd) *v.,* **fed, feed·ing.** **—***v.t.* **1.** to give food or nourishment to; provide with food: *to feed an infant.* **2.** to provide as food or nourishment: *to feed grain to cattle.* **3.** to yield or serve as food or nourishment for: *Three acres of wheat will feed many people.* **4.a.** to supply with something that is used for growth or maintaining existence: *Melting mountain snow feeds the river each spring.* **b.** to supply material to be used or consumed by: *He used newspaper to feed the fire. She fed the computer new data.* **5.** to supply (material to be used or consumed): *to feed data into a computer, to feed fuel into an engine.* **6.** to give satisfaction to; gratify: *to feed one's ego, to feed someone's vanity.* **7.** *Sports.* **a.** to deliver (the ball or puck) to a teammate who is in a more favorable position. **b.** to deliver the ball or puck to (such a teammate). **8.** to provide (cues or lines), as to an actor or comedian. **—***v.i.* (esp. of animals) to eat. **—***n.* **1.a.** food for animals; fodder. **b.** the amount of such food given at one time. **2.a.** the act or process of supplying material, as to a machine: *to slow the feed of paper to the printing press.* **b.** material so supplied or used. **c.** a mechanical part that supplies such material. **3.** *Informal.* a meal; food. [Old English *fēdan* to give food to, nourish.]

· **to feed on** (or **upon**). **a.** to consume, as food or nourishment: *Vultures feed on dead animals.* **b.** to receive support or satisfaction from: *to feed on hope.*

feed·back (fēd′bak′) *n.* **1.** *Electronics.* **a.** the return of a portion of the output of a machine, system, or process to the input, esp. in order to correct, control, or modify the output. **b.** acoustic feedback. **2.** *Biology.* the process by which living organisms regulate or correct their own voluntary and involuntary activities. When a person reaches to catch a ball, the feedback of information to the brain about the relative position of the hand and the ball enables the brain to guide the hand correctly. **3.** response or reaction to something, esp. when given as a means of influencing it, such as helpful criticism: *The trainees received daily feedback from the boss on their performance.*

feed·bag (fēd′bag′) *n.* a bag that holds feed for a horse, fastened in place below the animal's mouth by straps wrapped around the head or muzzle.

feed·er (fē′dər) *n.* **1.** a person or thing that supplies food or that feeds material to a machine. **2.** anything that supplies or leads into a main line, such as a tributary of a river, a branch of a railroad, or a side road leading into a highway. **3.** a conductor that supplies electrical energy to some point in an electrical distribution system.

feel (fēl) *v.,* **felt, feel·ing.** **—***v.t.* **1.** to perceive or examine by touching or handling; touch: *The doctor felt the arm for broken bones.* **2.** to be aware of through the sense of touch: *to feel the cold, to feel the rain on one's face, to feel the difference between two fabrics.* **3.** to be conscious of or affected by (an emotion): *to feel hope for the future.* **4.** to be aware of through an emotional or intellectual perception: *She could feel the hostility in the room.* **5.** to be emotionally affected by: *He felt the loss deeply.* **6.** to hold as an opinion; believe: *They felt that the law was unfair.* **7.** to experience the impact of; suffer under: *to feel the full force of an attack.* **8.** to find (one's way) by or as by touching; grope: *He felt his way up the dark stairs. She had to feel her way for a while in her new job.* **—***v.i.* **1.** to be aware of being: *to feel uncertain, to feel fine.* **2.** to produce the sensation or feeling of being; seem: *The water feels warm. Today feels like spring.* **3.** to search or explore by touch; grope: *The doctor felt for broken bones.* **4.** to have sympathy or compassion: *to feel for a sick child.* **5.** to have or be capable of the sense of touch. **—***n.* **1.** a quality of an object perceived by touch: *the cold feel of snow.* **2.** perception of this quality by the sense of touch: *Most children enjoy the feel of grass under their bare feet.* **3.** the sense of touch. **4.** a general sensation or feeling: *to like the feel of a beach at sunset.* **5.** an innate ability, appreciation, or understanding: *to have a feel for music.* [Old English *fēlan* to touch, perceive.] **—For Synonyms** *(v.t.),* see **experience.**

· **to feel like.** *Informal.* to have an interest in or desire for: *He's exhausted and doesn't feel like helping out.*

· **to feel (like) oneself.** to seem to be in one's usual good health or mood: *I've got a cold and don't feel like myself today.*

· **to feel out.** to try to discover the attitudes of (someone) or the nature of (a situation) in a cautious and indirect way: *She felt out her boss about a raise by asking about the company's prospects.*

· **to feel up to.** to feel capable of or ready for: *The swimmer does not feel up to racing today.*

feel·er (fē′lər) *n.* **1.** an organ of touch, such as the antenna of an insect or the tentacle of an octopus. **2.** an act, remark, or plan used to try to determine the feelings of a person or group: *The warring nations sent out peace feelers to each other.*

feel·ing (fē′ling) *n.* **1.** the capacity to feel by touching; sense of touch: *She rubbed her numb foot to restore the feeling.* **2.** a physical sensation: *a feeling of dampness, a feeling of hunger.* **3.** an emotion, as joy, fear, or anger. **4.** the state of being aware or conscious; impression; perception: *a feeling of security.* **5. feelings.** the emotionally sensitive part of a person's character or nature; susceptibilities: *The criticism hurt his feelings.* **6.a.** a capacity for emotion, esp. sympathy or compassion: *a person of deep feeling.* **b.** sympathy or compassion; tender emotion: *to have great feeling for the afflicted.* **7.** something believed or held as an opinion; sentiment: *It is my feeling that the bill should be passed.* **8.** something suspected; suspicion: *I have a feeling that something is wrong.* **9.** a quality perceived by the emotions or intellect; atmosphere: *The big empty room had a cold feeling.* **10.** an emotional quality or impression conveyed by a work of art or an artistic performance: *a soloist who performs with great feeling.* **11.** appreciation and sensitivity: *to have a feeling for abstract art.* **—***adj.* **1.** affected by emotion; sensitive. **2.** expressing emotion. **—feel′ing·ly,** *adv.*

fee simple *pl.* **fees simple.** *Law.* an estate in land whose owner has an unconditional right to sell it, give it away, or will it.

feet (fēt) *n.* the plural of **foot.**

· **on one's feet.** **a.** in a standing position: *The dentist was on her feet all day.* **b.** in a stable or secure position: *The new job put him back on his feet financially.* **c.** in a restored state of health: *to be back on one's feet after a long illness.*

· **to have one's feet on the ground.** to be sensible or practical.

· **to sit at someone's feet.** to be a follower or admirer of.

· **to stand on one's own (two) feet.** to be independent or self-supporting: *After I finished school, my family helped me financially until I could stand on my own two feet.*

· **to sweep (someone) off his** (or **her**) **feet.** to create sudden, overwhelming love or enthusiasm in: *The speaker's stirring words swept the audience off their feet.*

fee tail *pl.* **fees tail.** *Law.* an estate in land that cannot be sold or given away and inheritance of which is limited to a particular class of heirs.

feign (fān) *v.t.* **1.** to put on a false appearance of; pretend; simulate: *to feign sickness, to feign joy.* **2.** to invent, as a story or excuse, and assert as true; fabricate. **—***v.i.* to make believe; pretend. [Old French *feign-,* a stem of *feindre* to simulate, dissemble, from Latin *fingere* to form, make.] **—feign′er,** *n.* **—For Synonyms** *(v.t.),* see **pretend.**

feint (fānt) *n.* **1.** a deceptive blow or movement, esp. one used in boxing, fencing, or warfare to divert attention from the real point of attack. **2.** a false appearance or show; pretense: *to make a feint of listening to someone.* **—***v.i.* to make a deceptive blow or movement. **—***v.t.* **1.** to deceive with a feint; divert. **2.** to create a false appearance of; feign: *to feint an attack.* [French *feinte* pretense, dissimulation, from *feindre* to simulate. See FEIGN.]

feist·y (fī′stē) *adj.,* **feist·i·er, feist·i·est.** *Informal.* **1.** full of courage or energy; spirited; frisky. **2.** easily excited; touchy; quick-tempered: *a feisty terrier eager for a fight.* [From dialectal *feist* a small, irascible hound + -Y¹.]

feld·spar (feld′spär′) *also,* **felspar.** *n.* any of a group of aluminum silicate minerals containing sodium, potassium, or calcium, used commercially in the manufacture of glass. [Modification of German *Feldspat* literally, field spar; influenced in form by SPAR³.]

fe·lic·i·tate (fi lis′i tāt′) *v.t.,* **-tat·ed, -tat·ing.** to wish happiness to; congratulate. [Late Latin *fēlīcitātus,* past participle of *fēlīcitāre* to make happy, from Latin *fēlīcitās* happiness.]

fe·lic·i·ta·tion (fi lis′i tā′shən) *n.* an expression of pleasure over another's happiness or good fortune; congratulation. ➡ usually used in the plural.

fe·lic·i·tous (fi lis′i təs) *adj.* **1.** well-chosen; appropriate; apt: *a felicitous reply.* **2.** adept at appropriate and effective expression:

a felicitous speaker. **3.** marked by happiness or good feeling: *a felicitous occasion.* —**fe·lic′i·tous·ly,** *adv.* —**fe·lic′i·tous·ness,** *n.*

fe·lic·i·ty (fi lis′i tē) *n., pl.* **-ties. 1.** great happiness; bliss. **2.** a source of happiness; blessing. **3.** skill at appropriate or graceful expression: *to write with felicity.* **4.** an instance of such skill; an appropriate or graceful expression. [Old French *felicite* happiness, from Latin *fēlicitās.*]

fe·line (fē′līn) *adj.* **1.** of or relating to cats or the cat family. **2.** resembling or suggesting a cat, as in stealthiness or grace: *feline movements.* —*n.* an animal belonging to the cat family, such as a lion, tiger, or domestic cat. [Latin *fēlīnus* relating to a cat, from *fēlis* cat.]

fell[1] (fel) the past tense of **fall.**

fell[2] (fel) *v.t.* **1.** to strike and knock down; cause to fall: *The hunter felled a deer. The blow felled the tiring boxer.* **2.** to cut down (a tree or trees). **3.** in sewing, to finish (a seam) by joining the edges, turning them under, and stitching them to the fabric. —*n.* **1.** the timber cut down in one season. **2.** a felled seam. [Old English *fellan* to cause to fall, cut down.] —**fell′er,** *n.*

fell[3] (fel) *adj.* **1.** characterized by cruelty or savagery; dreadful: *a fell deed.* **2.** intensely painful or destructive; deadly: *a fell poison.* [Middle English *fel,* from Old French *fel* cruel, fierce, from Medieval Latin *fello* villain; of uncertain origin.]

fell[4] (fel) *n.* the skin or hide of an animal; pelt. [Middle English *fel,* from Old English *fel, fell.*]

fell[5] (fel) *n. British.* a tract of high wasteland; moor; down. [Old Norse *fjall* mountain, hill.]

fel·lah (fel′ə) *n., pl.* **fel·lahs** or **fel·la·hin** or **fel·la·heen** (fel′ə-hēn′). a peasant or laborer in Arabic-speaking countries. [Arabic *fellāh.*]

fel·loe (fel′ō) felly.

fel·low (fel′ō) *n.* **1.** a man or boy: *What a clever fellow he is.* **2.** a person in general; anyone: *Give a fellow a chance!* **3.** a person with whom one associates; companion; comrade: *His fellows helped the injured player off the field.* **4.** *Informal.* a man or boy with whom one has a romantic relationship; beau; suitor; boyfriend. **5.** a member of a learned society. **6.** a graduate student who holds a fellowship at a university or college. **7.** one of a pair, as of shoes or gloves; mate; match. **8.** a person who is equal to another in rank, character, or ability; peer: *That mathematician has no fellow in her field.* **9.** *Archaic.* a contemptible or disreputable person. —*adj.* belonging to the same class or group; joined by a common interest, activity, or condition: *fellow workers, fellow Americans.* [Old English *fēolaga* partner, from Old Norse *fēlagi,* from *fē* cattle, money + *lag* a laying down.]

fellow feeling 1. sympathy. **2.** a feeling of common interest: *to tutor other students out of fellow feeling.*

fel·low·ship (fel′ō ship′) *n.* **1.** the condition or quality of friendly relations; companionship; camaraderie: *the warm fellowship between schoolmates.* **2.** the condition of sharing of beliefs, experiences, or other matters of common interest; mutual participation. **3.** a group of people joined by common interests, beliefs, or goals. **4.** a position or sum of money granted to a graduate student to enable him or her to continue studying.

fellow traveler, a nonmember who supports or sympathizes with the program of a group or political party, esp. the Communist Party.

fel·ly (fel′ē) *also,* **felloe.** *n., pl.* **-lies.** the rim or a section of the rim of a wheel, into which the outer ends of the spokes are inserted. [Old English *felg.*]

fel·on[1] (fel′ən) *n.* a person who has committed a felony. —*adj. Archaic.* wicked; cruel; malicious. [Old French *felon* villain, from Medieval Latin *fello*; of uncertain origin.]

fel·on[2] (fel′ən) *n.* a deep and painful infection in a finger or toe, usually near the nail. Also, **whitlow.** [Of uncertain origin.]

fe·lo·ni·ous (fə lō′nē əs) *adj.* **1.** of, relating to, or classified as a felony: *a felonious assault.* **2.** *Archaic.* malicious; villainous: *a felonious deed.* —**fe·lo′ni·ous·ly,** *adv.* —**fe·lo′ni·ous·ness,** *n.*

fel·o·ny (fel′ə nē) *n., pl.* **-nies.** any of several crimes, such as murder, rape, or burglary, designated by statute to be more serious than a misdemeanor and usually punishable by a more severe sentence, such as death or imprisonment for more than one year.

fel·site (fel′sīt) *n.* a light-colored, very finely grained volcanic rock composed chiefly of quartz and feldspar. [FELS(PAR) + -ITE[1].]

fel·spar (fel′spär′) feldspar.

felt[1] (felt) the past tense and past participle of **feel.**

felt[2] (felt) *n.* **1.** a nonwoven fabric made by subjecting layers of fibers, usually of wool, hair, or fur, to heat, moisture, and pres-

sure, which causes them to shrink and become firmly interlocked. **2.** any similar fabric. —*adj.* of, made of, or relating to felt. —*v.t.* **1.** to make into felt. **2.** to cover with felt. [Old English *felt* felt cloth.]

felt·ing (fel′ting) *n.* **1.** felt cloth; felt. **2.** the process by which felt is made.

felt-tip pen (felt′tip′) a pen holding ink that flows through a tip made of felt. Also, **felt-tip.**

fe·luc·ca (fə luk′ə) *n.* a long, narrow ship with oars or lateen sails, or both, used esp. along the Mediterranean coast. [Italian *feluca,* from Arabic *fulk* ship.]

fem. 1. female. **2.** feminine.

fe·male (fē′māl) *adj.* **1.** of or relating to the sex that bears young or produces eggs. **2.** feminine *(def. 1).* **3.** of or relating to a plant that bears pistillate flowers. **4.** (of an object or device) having a hollowed part into which a corresponding part fits, as an electric socket. —*n.* a female person, animal, or plant. [Old French *femelle* being of the female sex, from Latin *fēmella* young woman, diminutive of *fēmina* woman; Modern English spelling influenced by MALE.]

fem·i·nine (fem′ə nin) *adj.* **1.** of, characteristic of, or relating to women: *feminine taste, feminine interests.* **2.** having characteristics traditionally regarded as womanly, such as gentleness and delicateness. **3.** (of a man) effeminate; womanish. **4.** female *(def. 1).* **5.** *Grammar.* of the gender that includes words applying to females or to things originally regarded as female. —*n. Grammar.* **1.** the feminine gender. **2.** a word or other element belonging to the feminine gender. [Latin *fēminīnus* of the feminine gender, from *fēmina* woman.]

feminine rhyme, a rhyme involving two words that end in an unaccented syllable, as *after* and *laughter* or *nourishing* and *flourishing.*

fem·i·nin·i·ty (fem′ə nin′i tē) *n.* **1.** the quality or state of being feminine. **2.** effeminacy; womanishness. **3.** *Archaic.* women collectively.

fem·i·nism (fem′ə niz′əm) *n.* **1.** the principle that women are entitled to the same social, economic, and political rights as men. **2.** the movement to obtain such rights for women. —**fem′i·nis′tic,** *adj.*

fem·i·nist (fem′ə nist) *n.* a person who believes in or supports feminism. —*adj.* of, relating to, characteristic of, or supporting feminism.

femme fa·tale (fem′ fə tal′, -täl′) *pl.* **femmes fa·tales** (fem′ fə-talz′, -tälz′). a seductively attractive woman, esp. one who leads her lovers into danger or ruin. [French *femme fatale,* going back to Latin *fēmina* woman + *fātālis* deadly. See FATAL.]

fem·o·ral (fem′ər əl) *adj.* of, relating to, or near the femur or thigh. [Latin *femor-,* stem of *femur* thigh + -AL[1].]

femto- *combining form* one quadrillionth (10^{-15}) part of. [Danish *femten* fifteen.]

fe·mur (fē′mər) *n., pl.* **fe·murs** or **fem·o·ra** (fem′ər ə). the long bone of the upper leg, extending from the pelvis to the knee. Also, **thighbone.** For illustration, see **skeleton.** [Latin *femur* thigh.]

fen[1] (fen) *n.* a marshy lowland; swamp; bog. [Old English *fenn* marsh, mud.]

fen[2] (fun) *n., pl.* **fen.** a unit of currency of China, equal to $1/100$ of a yuan. [Chinese (Mandarin) *fen.*]

fence (fens) *n.* **1.** a structure, often made of wire mesh or wood, used to bound, enclose, or protect an area; barrier: *a fence around a construction site.* **2.a.** a person who receives and sells stolen goods. **b.** a place where such goods are received and sold. —*v.,* **fenced, fenc·ing.** —*v.t.* **1.** to surround or separate with a fence or other structure (often with *in, off,* or *out*): *to fence a garden, to fence in cattle, to fence off an area.* **2.** to sell (stolen property) to a fence. **3.** *Archaic.* to defend against; ward off. —*v.i.* **1.** to engage in the sport of fencing. **2.** to avoid answering a question directly; parry with words. **3.** to deal in stolen goods. [Short for DEFENCE.]

•**on the fence.** undecided about something; not committed to any side.

•**to mend one's fences.** to make amends in order to restore one's position or friendly relations.

fenc·er (fen′sər) *n.* **1.** a person who engages in fencing with a foil, epee, or similar weapon. **2.** a person who makes or repairs fences.

a at	e end	o hot	u up	hw white	⎧ about
ā ape	ē me	ō old	ū use	ng song	taken
ä far	i it	ô fork	ü rule	th thin	ə pencil
âr care	ī ice	oi oil	u̇ pull	th this	lemon
	îr pierce	ou out	ûr turn	zh measure	⎩ circus

fencing

fenc·ing (fen′sing) *n.* **1.** the art, act, sport, or practice of using a foil, epee, or similar weapon in attack and defense. **2.** the parrying of words or arguments, esp. to avoid answering directly. **3.** material used in making fences. **4.** a fence or fences.

fend (fend) *v.i.* to offer resistance; parry. —*v.t.* to ward off or keep away; repel (often with *off*): *to fend off an angry mob.* [Short for DEFEND.]
· **to fend for oneself.** to provide or shift for oneself: *The children can fend for themselves while you're gone.*

fend·er (fen′dər) *n.* **1.** one of the metal guards projecting over the wheels of an automobile, bicycle, or other vehicle to protect against splashed water or mud; mudguard. **2.** a metal frame or screen placed in front of a fireplace to protect against escaping coals or sparks. **3.** a metal frame projecting from the front of a locomotive or streetcar, used to push obstacles from the tracks; cowcatcher. **4.** any of various cushioning devices, such as cork-filled pads or braids of rope, used on the side of a ship to prevent damage from chafing or impact when docking or lying alongside another vessel. [FEND + -ER¹.]

fend·er-bend·er (fen′dər ben′dər) *also,* **fender bender.** *n. Informal.* an automobile collision involving only minor damage.

fe·nes·tra (fə nes′trə) *n., pl.* **-trae** (-trē) a small, windowlike opening, as the oval aperture in the wall of bone between the middle ear and inner ear. [Modern Latin *fenestra,* from Latin *fenestra* window, probably of Etruscan origin.] —**fe·nes′tral,** *adj.*

fen·es·tra·tion (fen′ə strā′shən) *n.* the arrangement of windows and doors in a building. [Latin *fenestrātus,* past participle of *fenestrāre* to furnish with windows (going back to *fenestra* window) + -ION.]

Fe·ni·an (fē′nē ən, fēn′yən) *n.* **1.** a member of an Irish secret society organized in New York in 1858 to promote Irish independence from Great Britain. **2.** in Irish legend, a member of an ancient band of warriors, the subject of a cycle of tales. —*adj.* of or relating to the Fenians. [Blend of Old Irish *Fēne,* the ancient inhabitants of Ireland, and Old Irish *Fiann,* a group of Irish heroes in the period of Finn, a legendary king of Ireland.]

fen·nec (fen′ik) *n.* a small, fawn-colored fox, *Fennecus zerda,* of desert regions of northern Africa, having very long, broad ears. Length: 24 inches (61 centimeters), including tail. [Arabic *fanak.*]

fen·nel (fen′əl) *n.* **1.** the aromatic seeds of a plant, *Foeniculum vulgare,* of the parsley family, which taste like licorice and are used as a flavoring in certain foods and liqueurs. **2.** the plant itself, widely cultivated for its edible seeds, leaves, and bulb, bearing bright green feathery leaves and clusters of yellow flowers. [Old English *finul, fenol* the plant, going back to Latin *fēniculum,* diminutive of *fēnum* hay.]

fen·ny (fen′ē) *adj.* **1.** having the characteristics of a fen; swampy. **2.** of or found in a fen.

fen·u·greek (fen′yù grēk′, fen′ù-) *n.* an Old World herb, *Trigonella foenum-graecum,* of the pea family, having white flowers and aromatic seeds that are used medicinally and in cooking. [Middle English *fenugrek,* from Old French *fenugrec,* from Latin *faenum graecum* literally, Greek hay.]

feoff (fēf) *n.* fief.

fe·ral (fîr′əl) *adj.* **1.** not domesticated; wild; untamed. **2.** relating to or characteristic of a wild beast; brutal; savage. [Latin *fera* wild beast + -AL¹.]

fer-de-lance (fer′də lans′, -läns′) *n.* an extremely poisonous tropical American snake, *Bothrops atrox,* related to the rattlesnake. [French *fer de lance* literally, spearhead (with reference to

its shape), iron of a spear, going back to Latin *ferrum* iron + *dē* from + *lancea* spear.]

fer·ment (*v.,* fər ment′; *n.,* fûr′ment) *v.i.* **1.** to undergo chemical fermentation. **2.** to be excited or agitated; seethe: *The thought fermented in my mind.* —*v.t.* **1.** to cause chemical fermentation in. **2.** to cause excitement in; agitate; stir up; foment: *Poverty helped to ferment the revolution.* —*n.* **1.** a substance or agent causing chemical fermentation, such as the enzymes secreted by yeast or certain bacteria. **2.** a state of excitement, agitation, or unrest: *political ferment.* [Latin *fermentum* leaven, from *fervēre* to boil; with reference to the bubbles formed in moistened dough causing it to rise, resembling the bubbles in boiling liquids.]

fer·men·ta·tion (fûr′men tā′shən) *n.* **1.** a chemical reaction or series of chemical reactions in carbohydrates that is caused by enzymes, resulting in the formation of bubbles of gas. Fermentation causes milk to turn sour and the juice of grapes to turn into wine. **2.** the process of undergoing this reaction. **3.** excitement; agitation; unrest.

fer·mi·on (fûr′mē on′) *n.* any of a class of subatomic particles whose spin equals half of an odd integer, as ½ or ³⁄₂, including protons, neutrons, and electrons. [From Enrico *Fermi,* 1901-54, Italian-American nuclear physicist.]

fer·mi·um (fûr′mē əm) *n.* a radioactive element produced artificially by bombarding plutonium or uranium with neutrons. It was first discovered in the debris of nuclear explosions. Symbol: **Fm** For tables, see **element.** [From Enrico *Fermi,* 1901-54, Italian-American nuclear physicist.]

fern (fûrn) *n.* **1.** any of a large group of plants that constitute a major division, Filicophyta, of the plant kingdom. Ferns lack flowers, usually bear large feathery leaves, and generally reproduce in alternating sporophyte and gametophyte generations. **2.** the large, feathery leaves of certain of these plants, widely used in flower arrangements. [Old English *fern.*]

fern·er·y (fûr′nə rē) *n., pl.* **-er·ies.** **1.** a place in which ferns are grown, such as a case or stand. **2.** a collection of growing ferns.

fern·y (fûr′nē) *adj.,* **fern·i·er, fern·i·est.** **1.** of or like ferns, as in shape: *ferny frost on the windowpane.* **2.** abounding or overgrown with ferns.

fe·ro·cious (fə rō′shəs) *adj.* **1.** wildly fierce; savage: *ferocious beasts.* **2.** *Informal.* very intense: *a ferocious headache.* [Latin *ferōc-,* stem of *ferōx* wild, fierce + -OUS.] —**fe·ro′cious·ly,** *adv.* —**fe·ro′cious·ness,** *n.* —For Synonyms, see **fierce.**

fe·roc·i·ty (fə ros′i tē) *n., pl.* **-ties.** the state or quality of being ferocious; fierceness. [Latin *ferōcitās.*]

-ferous *suffix* containing; producing; bearing: *coniferous, carboniferous.* [Latin *-fer* bearing, producing (from *ferre* to bear) + -OUS.]

fer·re·dox·in (fer′ə dok′sin) *n.* any of a group of iron-bearing proteins, found in the chloroplasts of plants, that serve as electron carriers in photosynthesis, nitrogen fixation, or related biochemical reactions.

fer·ret (fer′it) *n.* any of various weasellike mammals, genus *Mustela,* of Europe, Asia, and North America, usually having yellowish white fur and pink eyes, esp. a domesticated variety, *M. putorius furo,* used by hunters to flush game from burrows. Length: to 2 feet (0.6 meter), including tail. —*v.t.* **1.** to hunt (game) with ferrets. **2.** to drive out of hiding, as in hunting with ferrets: *to ferret rabbits from their burrows.* **3.** to search out; bring to light (with *out*): *to ferret out the facts.* —*v.i.* **1.** to hunt with ferrets: *to ferret for rabbits.* **2.** to search: *The collector ferreted through old books for rare editions.* [Old French *furet* the animal, going back to Latin *fūr* thief.]

ferret

fer·ric (fer′ik) *adj.* of or containing iron, esp. in the higher oxidation state. [Latin *ferrum* iron + -IC.]

ferric oxide, a dark red compound of iron in its higher oxidation state and oxygen, used esp. in pigments and in recording tapes. Formula: Fe_2O_3

Fer·ris wheel (fer′is) a large, upright, revolving wheel with seats hung at regular intervals within its rim, used as an amusement ride. [From G. W. G. *Ferris,* 1859-96, American engineer who invented it.]

ferro- *combining form* relating to, containing, or derived from iron: *ferromanganese.* [Latin *ferrum* iron.]

fer·ro·al·loy (fer′ō al′oi, -ə loi′) *n.* any of various alloys of iron and another element, such as tungsten, manganese, chromium, or vanadium, used in making hard steel. [FERRO- + ALLOY.]

fer·ro·con·crete (fer'ō kon'krēt, -kon krēt') *n.* reinforced concrete.

fer·ro·mag·net·ic (fer'ō mag net'ik) *adj.* of or relating to a substance, such as iron or steel, that is able to become highly magnetic. —**fer·ro·mag·ne·tism** (fer'ō mag'ni tiz'əm), *n.*

fer·ro·man·ga·nese (fer'ō mang'gə nēs', -nēz') *n.* a ferroalloy containing manganese and varying amounts of carbon, used in making hard steel.

fer·rous (fer'əs) *adj.* of or containing iron, esp. in the lower oxidation state: *ferrous oxide.* [Latin *ferrum* iron + -OUS.]

fer·ru·gi·nous (fə rü'jə nəs) *adj.* **1.** like or containing iron. **2.** rust-colored; reddish brown. [Latin *ferrūginus* rusty, from *ferrūgō* rust, from *ferrum* iron.]

fer·rule (fer'əl, -ül) *also,* **ferule.** *n.* a metal ring or cap put around the end of a shaft, as of a cane, tool handle, stem of a pipe, or umbrella, to give added strength or protect against splitting. [Modification (influenced by Latin *ferrum* iron) of earlier *verrel,* from Old French *virole,* from Latin *viriola* little bracelet, diminutive of *viriae* bracelets.]

fer·ry (fer'ē) *n., pl.* -**ries. 1.** a boat or other craft used to convey people, vehicles, and goods over a designated route, esp. across a river or other narrow body of water. **2.** a place of embarkation at either end of such a route: *They waited at the ferry for the boat to return.* **3.** a service that conveys people, vehicles, and goods across a river or other body of water by boat: *The ferry has closed for the winter.* **4.** a system for delivery of aircraft by flying them to their destination. —*v.,* -**ried,** -**ry·ing.** —*v.t.* **1.** to convey across a narrow body of water by a boat or other craft: *They ferried the storm victims to the mainland.* **2.** to cross (a body of water) in a ferryboat: *to ferry the Mississippi.* **3.** to deliver (aircraft) by the ferry system. —*v.i.* to cross a body of water in a ferryboat. [Old English *ferian* to carry, convey.]

fer·ry·boat (fer'ē bōt') *n.* a boat used as a ferry.

fer·ry·man (fer'ē mən) *n., pl.* -**men** (-mən). a person who owns, operates, or works on a ferry.

fer·tile (fûr'təl) *adj.* **1.** producing or capable of producing crops or vegetation abundantly: *fertile soil.* **2.** able to produce young, eggs, seeds, pollen, or the like; capable of reproducing. **3.** capable of developing into a new individual; fertilized: *a fertile egg.* **4.** producing offspring abundantly; prolific. **5.** causing or aiding productiveness: *fertile rain.* **6.** mentally productive; inventive: *a fertile imagination.* [Latin *fertilis* fruitful, from *ferre* to bear[1].] —**fer'tile·ly,** *adv.* —**fer'tile·ness,** *n.*

> **Synonyms** **Fertile, fruitful,** and **fecund** may all refer to the ability to bear offspring or fruit. **Fertile** connotes the innate ability to reproduce: *a fertile cow.* It may also suggest producing in abundance: *That is a particularly fertile field, which produces bumper crops.* **Fruitful** suggests abundant production, esp. by plants: *fruitful vineyards.* **Fecund,** a more formal term, also suggests prolific yield, but is used more of animals: *a fecund sow with many offspring.*

fer·til·i·ty (fər til'i tē) *n.* **1.** the state or quality of being fertile; fecundity; productiveness. **2.** the number of offspring produced by a population; birthrate.

fer·til·i·za·tion (fûr'tl ə zā'shən) *n.* **1.** the act or an instance of fertilizing or the state of being fertilized. **2.** *Biology.* the uniting of a sperm cell with an egg cell to form a cell that will develop into a new individual.

fer·til·ize (fûr'tə līz') *v.t.,* -**lized,** -**liz·ing. 1.** to make fertile; render productive: *Rain fertilizes the soil.* **2.** to spread fertilizer, such as manure or nitrates, on (land). **3.** *Biology.* to make (an egg cell) capable of reproducing a new individual by uniting a sperm cell with it. —**fer'ti·liz'a·ble,** *adj.*

fer·til·iz·er (fûr'tə lī'zər) *n.* **1.** any of a wide variety of substances added to soil to promote the growth and yield of plants by ensuring that the proper kinds and amounts of nutritional elements, such as nitrogen, potassium, and phosphorus, are present. **2.** a person or thing that fertilizes.

fer·ule[1] (fer'əl, -ül) *n.* a flat stick, such as a ruler, to punish schoolchildren by striking them, esp. on the hand. —*v.t.,* -**uled,** -**ul·ing.** to punish with a ferule. [Late Latin *ferula* rod.]

fer·ule[2] (fer'əl, -ül) ferrule.

fer·ven·cy (fûr'vən sē) *n.* great warmth or intensity of feeling; ardency, devotion, or zeal.

fer·vent (fûr'vənt) *adj.* **1.** having or showing great warmth or intensity of feeling; ardent: *fervent prayers, fervent support of a political movement.* **2.** intensely hot; burning; glowing: *fervent rays.* [Latin *fervēns,* present participle of *fervēre* to boil, glow.] —**fer'vent·ly,** *adv.* —For Synonyms, see **passionate.**

fer·vid (fûr'vid) *adj.* **1.** extremely fervent; intense; impassioned: *Fervid devotion to a cause sometimes leads to rash acts.* **2.** intensely

hot; burning: *fervid heat.* [Latin *fervidus* burning, vehement.] —**fer'vid·ly,** *adv.* —**fer'vid·ness,** *n.*

fer·vor (fûr'vər) *also, British,* **fer·vour.** *n.* **1.** great warmth or intensity of feeling; ardor: *moral fervor, patriotic fervor.* **2.** intense heat. [Old French *fervor* ardor, from Latin *fervor* raging heat.]

fes·cue (fes'kū) *n.* **1.** any of a large group of grasses, genus *Festuca,* having long narrow leaves and often growing in dense tufts, found in temperate and cooler regions throughout the world. Most species are used for pasture, although some are cultivated as lawn grasses. **2.** a small stick or straw formerly used to point out the letters in teaching children to read. [Old French *festu* straw, stalk[1], going back to Latin *festūca.*]

fess (fes) *also,* **fesse.** *n.* a wide horizontal band forming the middle third of a heraldic shield. [Old French *fesse, faisse* band[2], strip[2], from Latin *fascia* band[2].]

fes·tal (fes'təl) *adj.* relating to or befitting a feast or holiday; joyous; convivial; festive. [Latin *fēstum* feast, holiday + -AL[1].] —**fes'tal·ly,** *adv.*

fes·ter (fes'tər) *v.i.* **1.** to form pus. **2.** to become increasingly stronger, as a feeling of resentment or irritation: *Rebellion festered in the provinces.* **3.** to putrefy; rot. —*v.t.* to cause pus to form in. —*n.* a small sore that forms pus. [Old French *festre* ulcer, from Latin *fistula* tube, ulcer.]

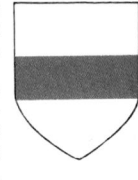

fess

fes·ti·val (fes'tə vəl) *n.* **1.** a particular feast, holiday, or celebration, marked by special observances and recurring periodically, esp. annually: *a harvest festival, the festival of Pentecost.* **2.** a period or program of activities and cultural events such as performances and exhibitions: *a Shakespeare festival, a jazz festival.* **3.** any gay merrymaking; conviviality: *Holidays are a time of festival and mirth.* —*adj.* relating to or befitting a festival; festive: *a festival mood.* [Old French *festival* relating to a festival or holiday, going back to Latin *fēstum* feast, holiday.]

Festival of Lights, Hanukkah.

fes·tive (fes'tiv) *adj.* relating to or suitable for a festival; festal; gay: *a festive New Year's celebration, festive costumes.*

fes·tiv·i·ty (fes tiv'i tē) *n., pl.* -**ties. 1.** the rejoicing and gaiety typical of a celebration or other joyous occasion. **2.** **festivities.** festive activities; merrymaking: *Costume balls and street processions are part of the Mardi Gras festivities in New Orleans.* **3.** festival.

fes·toon (fes tün') *n.* **1.** an ornamental string or chain of flowers, leaves, ribbons, or other decorative elements suspended in a curve between two points. **2.** a carved, molded, or painted ornament resembling this. —*v.t.* **1.** to decorate with festoons: *The walls were festooned with crepe paper and flowers.* **2.** to arrange in festoons. **3.** to connect by festoons. [French *feston* garland, from Italian *festone* garland, festal ornament, going back to Latin *fēstum* feast, holiday; with reference to the use of garlands in celebrating holidays.]

fet·a (fet'ə) *n.* a semisoft, white cheese made from sheep's or goat's milk and preserved in brine.

fe·tal (fē'təl) *also,* **foetal.** *adj.* of, relating to, or having the character of a fetus.

fetch (fech) *v.t.* **1.** to go after and bring back; come and take back; get: *to fetch a chair from another room.* **2.** to cause to come; succeed in bringing; draw forth; elicit: *to fetch an answer.* **3.** to be sold for; bring, as a price: *The car should fetch at least $2,000.* **4.a.** to draw or take in (a breath). **b.** to give forth with or as with effort, as a groan or sigh; heave. **5.** *Informal.* to attract; allure; interest. **6.** *Informal.* to give a (blow); strike: *She fetched him a blow on the head.* **7.** *Informal.* to arrive at, as by sailing against the wind or tide. —*v.i.* **1.** to go after or get something and bring it back. **2.** *Hunting.* (of dogs) to retrieve game. **3.** *Nautical.* (of ships) **a.** to move to a point or place. **b.** to swing around; veer: *The boat fetched into the wind.* —*n.* **1.** the act or an instance of fetching. **2.** a trick; dodge; artifice. [Old English *feccan* to bring, go and get.]

•**to fetch and carry.** to perform menial tasks or services.

•**to fetch up.** *Informal.* to come to or arrive at a particular point and stop: *The travelers fetched up at the inn.*

a	at	e	end	o	hot	u	up	hw	white		about
ā	ape	ē	me	ō	old	ū	use	ng	song		taken
ä	far	i	it	ô	fork	ü	rule	th	thin	ə	pencil
âr	care	ī	ice	oi	oil	u̇	pull	th	this		lemon
		îr	pierce	ou	out	ûr	turn	zh	measure		circus

F

fetch·ing (fech′ing) adj. Informal. attractive; alluring. —**fetch′ing·ly,** adv.

fete (fāt, fet) also, **fête.** n. a festival, esp. an elaborate celebration held outdoors. —v.t., **fet·ed, fet·ing.** to entertain at or honor with a fete: The ambassador was feted by all the local dignitaries. [French fête holiday, festival, from Old French feste festival. See FEAST.]

fet·id (fet′id, fē′tid) also, **foetid.** adj. having an offensive smell; stinking: a fetid swamp. [Latin fētidus stinking.] —**fet′id·ly,** adv. —**fet′id·ness,** n.

fet·ish (fet′ish, fē′tish) also, **fet·ich.** n. 1. an object believed to have magical or supernatural powers. 2. anything to which excessive devotion, concern, or reverence is given: to make a fetish of frugality. 3. Psychology. something that is an object of fetishism. [French fétiche object having magic power, from Portuguese feitiço amulet used as a charm, sorcery, from Latin factīcius artificial, made by art.]

fet·ish·ism (fet′i shiz′əm, fē′ti-) also, **fet·ich·ism.** n. 1. belief in or devotion to fetishes. 2. blind devotion to or excessive concern with something. 3. Psychology. a. an abnormal feeling of sexual excitement aroused by an inanimate object or by a part of the body not normally considered erotic, such as the foot. b. practices associated with this excitement. —**fet′ish·ist;** also, **fet′ich·ist,** n. —**fet′ish·is′tic;** also, **fet′ich·is′tic,** adj.

fet·lock (fet′lok′) n. 1. a tuft of hair on the back part of the leg of a horse or similar animal, just above the hoof. 2. the part of the leg where this tuft grows. [Probably of Germanic origin.]

fe·tor (fē′tər) n. a strong, offensive smell; stench. [Latin fētor.]

fet·ter (fet′ər) n. 1. a chain or shackle put on the feet to restrain movement. 2. **fetters.** anything that confines or restrains: Artists have always rebelled against the fetters of convention. —v.t. 1. to bind with fetters; shackle. 2. to confine; restrain: An educated person should not be fettered by prejudice. [Old English feter chain for the feet.]

fet·tle (fet′əl) n. a condition or state of the body and mind: You seem to be in fine fettle. [Middle English fetlen to gird up, from Old English fetel belt, girdle.]

fet·tuc·ci·ne (fet′ə chē′nē) also, **fet·tu·ci·ni.** pl. n. pasta in the form of long, narrow strips. ➡ used as singular or plural. [Italian fettuccine literally, little ribbons, from fetta slice, ribbon.]

fe·tus (fē′təs) also, **foetus.** n., pl. -tus·es. an animal embryo in its later stages of development, esp. a human embryo from the beginning of the third month of pregnancy until birth. [Latin fētus offspring.]

feud¹ (fūd) n. 1. a state of bitter mutual hostility between families, tribes, or clans, usually lasting for generations and marked by violent clashes. 2. bitter and lasting strife or hostility between individuals or groups: a feud between two scholars. —v.i. to carry on a feud: The two tribes have been feuding for decades. [Middle English fede, from Old French faide lasting hostility, related to Old High German fahida quarrel, hatred.]

feud² (fūd) n. land held by feudal tenure; fief. [Medieval Latin feudum; of Germanic origin.]

feu·dal (fū′dəl) adj. 1. relating to or characteristic of feudalism: feudal law. 2. of or relating to a fief: feudal rights. [Medieval Latin feudalis relating to a fief, from feudum fief. See FEUD².] —**feu′dal·ly,** adv.

feu·dal·ism (fū′də liz′əm) n. 1. a system of political and social organization prevalent in western Europe during the Middle Ages, based upon the relation between a lord who provided land and protection and a vassal who in return pledged military and certain other services to the lord. 2. any similar political system. —**feu′dal·is′tic,** adj.

feu·dal·i·ty (fū dal′i tē) n., pl. -ties. 1. the state or quality of being feudal. 2. feudalism. 3. a feudal holding; fief.

feudal system, feudalism (def. 1).

feu·da·to·ry (fū′də tôr′ē) adj. 1. under feudal allegiance to a lord: a feudatory noble. 2. (of land) held by feudal tenure. —n., pl. -ries. 1. a person holding land by feudal tenure; vassal. 2. land held by feudal tenure; fief.

feud·ist¹ (fū′dist) n. a person who engages in a feud. [FEUD¹ + -IST.]

feud·ist² (fū′dist) n. a writer or authority on feudal law. [FEUD² + -IST.]

fe·ver (fē′vər) n. 1. a body temperature higher than normal. 2. any of various diseases marked by higher than normal body temperature. 3.a. a state of intense emotion, as of excitement, anxiety, or restlessness: The children were in a fever of anticipation for the holidays. b. a strong but temporary enthusiasm for a person or thing; craze. —v.t. to affect with or as with fever. [Old English fēfor abnormally high body temperature, from Latin febris.] —**fe′vered,** adj.

fever blister, cold sore.

fe·ver·few (fē′vər fū′) n. a bushy plant, Chrysanthemum parthenium, of the composite family, native to Europe, having daisy-like flower heads and deeply lobed leaves with a strong, acrid odor. [Old English feferfuge, from Latin febrifugia a plant that was said to alleviate fever, from febris fever + fugāre to drive away.]

fe·ver·ish (fē′vər ish) adj. 1. having fever, esp. a slight degree of fever: a feverish patient. 2. indicating or characteristic of fever: feverish symptoms. 3. tending to cause fever. 4. excited, agitated, or restless, as if from fever: feverish joy, feverish activity in preparation for a party. Also, **fe′ver·ous.** —**fe′ver·ish·ly,** adv. —**fe′ver·ish·ness,** n.

fever pitch, a state of great excitement; excited activity; commotion: to work at fever pitch.

fe·ver·root (fē′vər rūt′, -rút′) n. any of several coarse plants, genus Triosteum, of the honeysuckle family, found in northern temperate regions, having white, yellow, or purple flowers.

fever sore, cold sore.

few (fū) adj. not many: Few people attended. —pron. not many persons or things. ➡ used as plural: Few of the houses were new. Many were invited, but few actually came. —n. 1. a small number. ➡ used as plural: I sold only a few of the papers. 2. a limited or select group of people; minority: The new tax law benefits the lucky few at the expense of the many. [Old English fēawe, fēa not many.] —**few′ness,** n.

• **quite a few.** Informal. a considerable number; a good many.

fey (fā) adj. 1. having an unworldly attitude or manner; strange. 2. seemingly under a spell; apparently enchanted or possessed. [Old English fǣge doomed to die.]

fez (fez) n., pl. **fez·zes.** a brimless felt cap, usually red, having a conical shape and a flat crown and ornamented with a tassel, worn esp. by men in the Middle East. [French fez, from Turkish fez, from Fez, where it was chiefly manufactured.]

ff, fortissimo.

ff. 1. and the following (pages, lines, sections, or the like). 2. folios.

FHA, Federal Housing Administration.

fi·an·cé (fē′än sā′, fē än′sā) n. a man to whom a woman is engaged to be married. [French fiancé, originally past participle of fiancer to betroth, going back to Latin fīdus trusty, faithful.]

fi·an·cée (fē′än sā′, fē än′sā) n. a woman to whom a man is engaged to be married. [French fiancée, feminine of fiancé. See FIANCÉ.]

fi·as·co (fē as′kō) n., pl. -coes or -cos. a complete or humiliating failure. [Italian fiasco bottle, utter failure, from (far) fiasco (to make) a bottle, fail (sense development not explained), possibly from Late Latin flascō wine bottle; of Germanic origin.]

fi·at (fē′ät, fī′ət, -at) n. 1. an authoritative order or decree. 2. authorization; sanction. [Latin fiat let it be done, from fierī to be done, become.]

fiat money, paper currency made legal tender by the decree of a government, but not based on or convertible into gold or silver.

fib (fib) n. a lie about something unimportant; trivial lie. —v.i., **fibbed, fib·bing.** to tell a fib. [Possibly from obsolete fible-fable nonsense; repetition with vowel change of FABLE.] —**fib′ber,** n.

fi·ber (fī′bər) also, British, **fibre.** n. 1. any fine, threadlike part of a substance; filament: asbestos fiber, cotton fiber, nerve fiber. 2.a. a substance composed of threadlike parts or filaments: rope made of hemp fiber. b. the filaments collectively. 3. the composition or structure of a filamentous substance; texture: cloth of coarse fiber. 4. the fine, indigestible material in fruit, vegetables, and grains that cleanses the digestive tract by stimulating peristalsis. 5. essential character, nature, or strength: a person of great moral fiber, the fiber of an argument. [French fibre thread, filament, from Latin fibra.]

fi·ber·board (fī′bər bôrd′) n. a material made from processed cellulose fiber, particularly wood fiber, pressed into sheets and used for panels, partitions, or the like.

fi·ber·glass (fī′bər glas′) also, **fi·ber·glas.** n. a durable nonflammable material made of fine threads of glass, used for insulation, textiles, boat bodies, and many other purposes. Trademark: **Fiberglas.** Also, **spun glass.**

Hock

Shank

Fetlock

Fetlock joint

Pastern

Hoof

fetlock and other parts of a horse's leg

glass fibers used in **fiber optics**

fiber optics 1. the technology of transmitting information by means of very thin, transparent fibers of glass or plastic. Modern telecommunications rely increasingly on transmission lines of such fibers because they can carry more information than conventional copper lines, and the signals require less amplification. **2.** the fibers themselves. ➡ used as singular. **—fi′ber-op′tic,** *adj.*

Fi·bo·nac·ci sequence (fē′bə nä′chē) an infinite series of numbers in which each number is the sum of the two numbers that precede it: 0, 1, 1, 2, 3, 5, 8, 13, 21, ... Also, **Fibonacci numbers.** [From Leonardo *Fibonacci,* thirteenth-century Italian mathematician.]

fi·bre (fī′bər) *British.* fiber.

fi·bril (fī′brəl, fib′rəl) *n.* **1.** a small or slender fiber. **2.** root hair. [Modern Latin *fibrilla,* diminutive of Latin *fibra* thread, filament.] **—fi′bril·lar,** *adj.*

fi·bril·la·tion (fī′brə lā′shən, fib′rə-) *n.* rapid, irregular contractions of the heart muscle that disrupt normal functioning of the heart.

fi·brin (fī′brin) *n.* a fibrous, insoluble protein formed during the clotting of blood. [Latin *fibra* thread, filament + -IN[1].] **—fi′brin·ous,** *adj.*

fi·brin·o·gen (fī brin′ə jen) *n.* a soluble protein in the blood plasma from which fibrin is formed. [FIBRIN + -GEN.]

fi·bro·blast (fī′brə blast′) *n.* a large, flat, star-shaped cell that secretes the fibers that form connective tissue. [Latin *fibra* thread, filament + Greek *blastos* germ, embryo.] **—fi′bro·blas′tic,** *adj.*

fi·broid (fī′broid) *adj.* made up of or resembling fibers or fibrous tissue. **—n.** a benign tumor made up of fibrous tissue.

fi·bro·sis (fī brō′sis) *n.* an abnormal increase in the amount of fibrous tissue in an organ, part, or tissue. [Latin *fibra* thread, filament + -OSIS.]

fi·brous (fī′brəs) *adj.* made up of, having, or resembling fibers.

fi·bro·vas·cu·lar (fī′brō vas′kyə lər) *adj.* composed of fibers and ducts that convey a fluid, such as sap: *the fibrovascular tissue of wood.*

fib·u·la (fib′yə lə) *n., pl.* **-lae** (-lē′) or **-las. 1.** the outer and more slender of the two bones of the human lower leg, extending from the knee to the ankle. **2.** a similar bone in the hind leg of an animal. **3.** in ancient Greece and Rome, a brooch or pin used to fasten garments. [Latin *fībula* clasp, buckle, brooch.] **—fib′u·lar,** *adj.*

-fic *suffix* (used to form adjectives) making; causing: *pacific, terrific.* [Latin *-ficus,* from *facere* to do, make.]

-fication *suffix* (used to form nouns) a making or causing: *falsification, purification.* [French *-fication,* from Latin *-ficātiō,* going back to *facere* to make, do.]

fiche (fēsh) *n.* microfiche. [Short for MICROFICHE.]

fich·u (fish′ü) *n.* a triangular scarf or kerchief of lightweight material, such as lace, formerly worn by women to cover the shoulders. [French *fichu,* from *ficher* to fix, fasten, going back to Latin *fīgere.*]

fick·le (fik′əl) *adj.* not constant or dependable; changeable; capricious: *a fickle sweetheart, fickle winds.* [Old English *ficol* deceitful, false.] **—fick′le·ness,** *n.*

fic·tion (fik′shən) *n.* **1.** narrative literature, esp. prose works such as novels and short stories, dealing with partly or completely imaginary characters and events. **2.** something feigned, invented, or imagined, such as a story, explanation, or statement: *to distinguish fact from fiction.* **3.** the act of feigning or imagining; false conclusion: *It was fiction to assume that others were plotting against you.* **4.** *Law.* something assumed as fact that in reality may

not be fact, as for argument's sake. [Latin *fictiō* a feigning, forming.]

fic·tion·al (fik′shə nəl) *adj.* relating to or having the nature of fiction. **—fic′tion·al·ly,** *adv.*

fic·tion·al·ize (fik′shə nə līz′) *v.t.,* **-ized, -iz·ing.** to make into fiction; give a fictional account of. **—fic′tion·al·i·za′tion,** *n.*

fic·ti·tious (fik tish′əs) *adj.* **1.** made up in the imagination; not corresponding to fact; invented: *fictitious claims.* **2.** assumed for deception; not genuine; false: *a fictitious identity.* **3.** fictional: *Sherlock Holmes is a fictitious character.* [Latin *fictīcius* feigned, artificial.] **—fic·ti′tious·ly,** *adv.* **—fic·ti′tious·ness,** *n.*

fid (fid) *n.* **1.** a square bar of wood or metal for supporting a topmast. **2.** a conical pin of hard wood used to open the strands of rope in splicing. [Of uncertain origin.]

-fid *suffix* (used to form adjectives) split; cleft; lobed: *bifid.* [Latin *-fidus* divided, split, from *findere* to cleave, split.]

fid·dle (fid′əl) *n. Informal.* a violin or other instrument of the violin family. **—v., -dled, -dling. —v.i. 1.** *Informal.* to play a fiddle. **2.** to make aimless or nervous movements, as with the fingers or hands; fidget: *She fiddled nervously with her pencil.* **3.** to act idly or frivolously; trifle: *He fiddled over his work and did not finish on time.* **—v.t. 1.** *Informal.* to play (a tune) on a fiddle. **2.** to waste in an idle or frivolous way (with *away*): *to fiddle away the afternoon.* [Old English *fithele* the instrument, probably from Medieval Latin *vitula,* possibly from Latin *vitulārī* to be joyful.]

• **fit as a fiddle.** in excellent health or physical condition.

• **to fiddle around.** to pass time in an idle manner: *We fiddled around all day.*

• **to fiddle with.** to manipulate in order to adjust or make work properly: *If you fiddle with the dial, the radio reception will improve.*

• **to play second fiddle.** to take a minor or subordinate position.

fid·dle-de-dee (fid′əl dē dē′) *n., interj. Informal.* nonsense.

fid·dle-fad·dle (fid′əl fad′əl) *n., interj. Informal.* nonsense.

fid·dle·head (fid′əl hed′) *n.* the young, unfolding frond of certain ferns, often eaten as a vegetable. [Because its coiled tip resembles the scroll of a violin head.]

fid·dler (fid′lər) *n.* **1.** a person who fiddles. **2.** fiddler crab.

fiddler crab, a member of a widespread group of burrowing crabs, genus *Uca,* the male of which has one claw much larger than the other. Shell width: about 1 inch (2.5 centimeters).

fid·dle·stick (fid′əl stik′) *n.* **1.** a violin bow. **2.** something insignificant or absurd.

fid·dle·sticks (fid′əl stiks′) *interj. Informal.* nonsense.

fi·del·i·ty (fi del′i tē, fī-) *n., pl.* **-ties. 1.** observance of or faithfulness to duties, obligations, or vows; steadfast loyalty. **2.** adherence to factual truth: *The novel was written with strict fidelity to historical facts.* **3.** accuracy of reproduction: *The translation was made with complete fidelity to the original.* **4.** the degree of accuracy with which electronic devices, such as radios or recorders, reproduce original sound. [Latin *fidēlitās* faithfulness, from *fides* faith.]

fiddler crab

fidg·et (fij′it) *v.i.* to make restless movements; be nervous or uneasy: *The audience fidgeted in their seats.* **—v.t.** to cause to fidget; make restless or uneasy. **—n. 1.** a person who fidgets. **2. the fidgets.** a state of being restless or of making nervous movements: *I had the fidgets all morning waiting for my interview.* [From dialectal English *fidge* to move restlessly; probably of Scandinavian origin.]

fidg·et·y (fij′i tē) *adj.* inclined to make restless movements; uneasy.

fi·du·ci·ar·y (fi dü′shē er′ē, -dü′-) *adj.* **1.a.** of, relating to, or designating the management of money or property by one person on behalf of another, as in a trust fund: *a fiduciary guardian, a fiduciary relationship.* **b.** of, relating to, or designating a relationship in which one person, such as a lawyer, is obligated to pursue

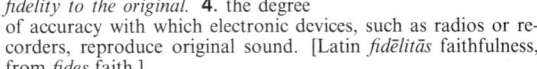

a	at	e	end	o	hot	u	up	hw	white		about
ā	ape	ē	me	ō	old	ū	use	ng	song	ə	taken
ä	far	i	it	ô	fork	ü	rule	th	thin		pencil
âr	care	ī	ice	oi	oil	u̇	pull	th	this		lemon
		îr	pierce	ou	out	ûr	turn	zh	measure		circus

F

457

the interests of another, such as a client. **2.** held in trust: *a fiduciary estate.* **3.** depending upon public confidence for value or currency, as fiat money. —*n., pl.* **-ar·ies.** a person assuming fiduciary obligations; trustee. [Latin *f ĭdūciārius* relating to a thing held in trust, from *f ĭdūcia* trust.]

fie (fī) *interj.* for shame. ➡ now usually used humorously as a mild or pretended reproach: *Fie on you!* [Old French *fi,* possibly from Latin *f ī* an expression of disgust at a bad smell.]

fief (fēf) *n.* **1.** land held by a vassal; estate held in feudal tenure. **2.** the office and rights of a vassal holding land in feudal tenure. Also, **fee, feoff.** [Old French *fief* estate held in feudal tenure; of Germanic origin.]

field (fēld) *n.* **1.** a piece of land, usually covered with low vegetation and having few or no trees or structures. **2.** a piece of cleared land, usually bounded, devoted to or suitable for cultivation or pasture: *a wheat field.* **3.** a region or area containing and yielding some natural resource: *an oil field.* **4.** a broad, level expanse: *a field of snow.* **5.a.** battlefield. **b.** battle: *The field was won after four hours of fighting.* **6.a.** an area or region of active military operations: *Early in the spring, the army took to the field.* **b.** an area of operations away from a fixed headquarters: *The general established command in the field.* **7.** *Sports.* **a.** an enclosed piece of ground, or one with defined boundaries, on which games are played or events are held: *a baseball field, a football field.* **b.** a portion or division of such an area, usually surrounded by or adjacent to a track, where such contests as the pole vault, long jump, discus, and shot put are held. **c.** all those who participate in a particular event or contest: *I placed tenth in a field of fifty in last week's race.* **d.** the entire body of participants in a contest, esp. a race, except the one or ones specified: *The winning runner finished five yards ahead of the field.* **e.** in baseball, the defensive role: *Having scored three runs, the team took to the field with renewed confidence.* **8.** a surface on which something is shown: *The artist painted white figures against a field of black.* **9.a.** a particular area or sphere of activity, knowledge, or interest: *to be an expert in one's field, the field of medicine.* **b.** a sphere of practical activity, as in research or business, away from the laboratory or home office: *The professor spent the summer in the field, excavating the prehistoric village.* **10.** *Physics.* an area or space within which a given effect or property, such as electricity, magnetism, or gravity, may be measured at every point. Also, **force field.** **11.** *Optics.* the space or range within which objects are visible through the eyepiece of a stationary optical instrument. Also, **field of view.** **12.** *Mathematics.* any set, as the set of all real numbers, for which multiplication and addition are defined between any two members of the set, the result of which is a member of the set: *a number field.* **13.** *Computers.* a group of related characters treated as a data unit, the most basic unit of information storage. —*v.t.* **1.** to successfully catch, stop, or pick up (a ball in play) in baseball, cricket, and other games. **2.** to put or send (a team or player) into a game or a position in the field. —*v.i.* to act as a fielder, as in baseball or cricket. —*adj.* **1.** relating to, growing in, or having fields as a natural habitat: *field flowers.* **2.** of, made, used, or suitable for use in a field or fields: *a field tent.* **3.** *Sports.* played in or held on the field rather than the track: *field events.* [Old English *feld* open land, pasture.]

• **to keep the field.** to continue activity, as in a military campaign or in a game.

• **to play the field. a.** to be unlimited in one's activity within a range of interests. **b.** *Informal.* to date several or many people rather than one person exclusively.

• **to take the field.** to begin or renew activity, as in a game.

field artillery 1. mobile artillery for use by an army in the field. **2. Field Artillery.** a former branch of the U.S. Army in charge of such weapons.

field corn, any of several varieties of corn used primarily for feeding livestock and for grinding into grain.

field day 1. a day set aside for athletic contests, games, and races. **2.** a day or time of unusual opportunity, as for fun: *The children had a field day while their parents were away.*

field·er (fēl′dər) *n.* **1.** *Baseball.* any of the players in the field, esp. an outfielder, attempting to put out the side at bat. **2.** any player with such defensive duties in softball, cricket, or similar ball games.

fielder's choice *Baseball.* a play in which a fielder chooses to try to put out a base runner rather than the batter. A batter who reaches first base safely as a result of this is not credited with a hit.

field·fare (fēld′fâr′) *n.* a thrush, *Turdus pilaris,* native to Europe and Asia, having a gray head, nape, and tail, brown back, black and rust breast, and white belly. Length: 10 inches (25

centimeters). [Old English *feldefare* literally, field-traveler, from *feld* open land + *faran* to travel.]

field glasses, compact, portable binoculars, used esp. outdoors. Also, **field glass.**

field goal 1. *Football.* a play in which the ball is place-kicked or drop-kicked from scrimmage over the crossbar and between the posts of the opponent's goal. It scores three points. **2.** *Basketball.* a goal made while the ball is in play. It scores two or three points depending on how far the player shooting the ball is from the basket.

field guide, a book used to identify plants, animals, rocks, or other things found in nature: *a field guide to mushrooms.*

field gun, a mobile artillery piece for field use. Also, **fieldpiece.**

field hockey, a game played on a grassy field by two teams of eleven players each, in which wooden sticks with curved ends are used to hit a ball along the ground, the object being to drive the ball into the opponent's goal.

field hospital, a temporary hospital for emergency treatment close to a combat or disaster area.

field house 1. a building used for indoor athletic events, such as track and field or basketball. **2.** a building near an athletic field, having dressing rooms, showers, and the like for the athletes, and facilities for storing sports equipment.

field magnet, a magnet used to produce and maintain a magnetic field, esp. in an electric motor or generator.

field marshal, an officer of highest rank in the armies of some nations, such as Great Britain.

field mouse, any of various mice or voles living in fields or meadows.

field officer, a colonel, lieutenant colonel, or major.

field of fire, the area that a weapon or a group of weapons can cover effectively with fire from a given position.

field of force, field *(def. 10).*

field of view, field *(def. 11).*

field pea, a variety of pea, *Pisum sativum arvense,* grown esp. as animal feed.

field·piece (fēld′pēs′) *n.* field gun.

field·stone (fēld′stōn′) *n.* undressed stone, esp. when used as construction material.

field-test (fēld′test′) *v.t.* to subject (something) to a field test: *These new binoculars seem good, but I want to field-test them in the mountains this weekend.*

field test, a test of the performance, durability, or effectiveness of something under normal conditions of use rather than under controlled conditions, as in a laboratory.

field trial 1. a competition in which sporting dogs are judged on the basis of their performance in the field, under natural hunting conditions. **2.** field test.

field trip, a trip away from the classroom for direct observation and study, as to a museum or to examine plants or animals in their natural environment.

field·work (fēld′wûrk′) *n.* **1.** a temporary work or fortification erected by troops operating in the field. **2.** observation, investigation, and study done in the field, as by botanists, geologists, sociologists, or other scientists. —**field′work′er,** *n.*

fiend (fēnd) *n.* **1.a.** an evil spirit; devil; demon. **b. the Fiend.** the devil; Satan. **2.** an extremely wicked or cruel person. **3.** *Informal.* **a.** a person who is much involved with or highly skilled in a particular field, interest, or activity: *a chess fiend.* **b.** a person who is addicted to a practice or habit, esp. an injurious one: *a dope fiend.* [Old English *fēond* enemy, devil.]

fiend·ish (fēn′dish) *adj.* **1.** extremely wicked or cruel; diabolic. **2.** very difficult or unpleasant: *a fiendish task.* —**fiend′ish·ly,** *adv.* —**fiend′ish·ness,** *n.*

fierce (fîrs) *adj.,* **fierc·er, fierc·est. 1.** violent or cruel in nature or behavior; savage; ferocious: *a fierce bear, a fierce enemy.* **2.** violent in force or activity; raging: *a fierce storm, fierce fighting.* **3.** characterized by intense emotions; vehement; ardent: *a fierce controversy.* **4.** *Informal.* very bad; disagreeable: *a fierce headache.* [Old French *f(i)ers* wild, savage, from Latin *ferus.*] —**fierce′ly,** *adv.* —**fierce′ness,** *n.*

Synonyms Fierce, ferocious, and savage may all mean threatening or acting with wild fury. **Fierce** connotes an appearance that causes terror or suggests that no pity can be expected: *Fierce warriors attacked the fort from all sides. Fierce panthers pawed at the bars of their cages.* **Ferocious** is a stronger word than *fierce,* and implies violence and cruelty in action: *The ferocious beast, mad from hunger, was poised to pounce on its prey and tear it apart.* **Savage** is similar to *ferocious,* but when used of humans it connotes a lack of restraint or pity: *A savage mob mauled the victim.*

fier·y (fīr'ē, fī'ə rē) *adj.,* **fier·i·er, fier·i·est.** **1.** containing or composed of fire; aflame; flaming: *a fiery furnace.* **2.** hot as fire; burning: *the fiery heat of the sun.* **3.** suggestive of fire; flashing; glowing: *a fiery red, a fiery sunset, fiery eyes.* **4.a.** like fire in character or quality; ardent; passionate: *a fiery speech.* **b.** easily excited; fierce: *a fiery temper.* **5.** causing a burning sensation: *fiery food.* **6.** easily set on fire; flammable. **7.** inflamed, as a sore. —**fier'i·ly,** *adv.* —**fier'i·ness,** *n.*

fi·es·ta (fē es'tə) *n.* **1.** a religious festival, esp. a saint's day as celebrated in Spain or Latin America. **2.** any festive celebration; holiday. [Spanish *fiesta* feast, festival, going back to Latin *fēsta* festivals.]

fife (fīf) *n.* a shrill-toned musical instrument of the flute family, often used with drums in marching bands. —*v.t., v.i.,* **fifed, fif·ing.** to play on a fife. [German *Pfeife* this instrument, pipe, going back to Latin *pīpāre* to chirp.] —**fif'er,** *n.*

fife and drum parade

fif·teen (fif'tēn') *n.* **1.** the cardinal number that is five more than ten. **2.** a symbol representing this number, such as 15 or XV. **3.** something having this many units or members. —*adj.* numbering five more than ten. [Old English *fīftyne.*]

fif·teenth (fif'tēnth') *adj.* **1.** (the ordinal of fifteen) next after the fourteenth. **2.** being one of fifteen equal parts. —*n.* **1.** something that is next after the fourteenth. **2.** one of fifteen equal parts; 1/15.

fifth (fifth) *adj.* **1.** (the ordinal of five) next after the fourth. **2.** being one of five equal parts. —*n.* **1.** something that is next after the fourth. **2.** one of five equal parts; 1/5. **3.** one fifth of a gallon (0.8 liter), used as a measure of liquor. **4.** *Music.* **a.** a tone, esp. the dominant, five diatonic degrees from a given tone. **b.** an interval of five degrees between two tones of the diatonic scale. **c.** a harmonic combination of two tones separated by this interval. —*adv.* in the fifth place.
 · **to take the Fifth.** to invoke one's rights under the Fifth Amendment, thereby refusing to testify against oneself.

Fifth Amendment, an amendment to the United States Constitution, ratified in 1791 and part of the Bill of Rights. It includes the provision that a defendant or witness in a criminal case or other proceeding shall not be compelled to give self-incriminating testimony.

fifth column, a group of persons within a country who sympathize with and secretly aid its enemies. [From a statement by a rebel general during the Spanish Civil War, who said that he was marching on Madrid with four columns and had a *fifth column* of sympathizers within the city.] —**fifth columnist,** *n.*

fifth·ly (fifth'lē) *adv.* in the fifth place.

fifth wheel *Informal.* an unnecessary or superfluous person or thing.

fif·ti·eth (fif'tē ith) *adj.* **1.** (the ordinal of fifty) next after the forty-ninth. **2.** being one of fifty equal parts. —*n.* **1.** something that is next after the forty-ninth. **2.** one of fifty equal parts; 1/50.

fif·ty (fif'tē) *n., pl.* **-ties. 1.** the cardinal number that is five times ten. **2.** a symbol representing this number, such as 50 or L. **3.** something having this many units or members. **4. fifties.** the number series from fifty to fifty-nine. ➡ used esp. in reference to the sixth decade of a century or of a person's life. —*adj.* numbering five times ten. [Old English *fīftig.*]

fif·ty-fif·ty (fif'tē fif'tē) *adj. Informal.* **1.** divided equally; equal: *a fifty-fifty division of the profits.* **2.** as likely to turn out one way as another; even: *The mission has a fifty-fifty chance of success.* —*adv.* equally: *to share fifty-fifty.*

fig[1] (fig) *n.* **1.** the small, sweet, edible fruit of a tree, *Ficus carica,* of the mulberry family, consisting of a fleshy sac containing many tiny seedlike structures. **2.** the shrub or small tree bearing this fruit, grown mainly in the Mediterranean region and California. **3.** the merest trifle; least bit: *I don't care a fig for your opinion.* [Old French *figue* the fruit, through Provençal, going back to Latin *fīcus* the fruit, the tree.]

fig[2] (fig) *n. Informal.* **1.** dress; array: *in full fig.* **2.** physical condition; form: *in good fig.* [Of uncertain origin.]

fig. 1. figurative; figuratively. **2.** figure; figures.

fig·eat·er (fig'ē'tər) *n.* a large, destructive green and red beetle, *Cotinis nitida,* found in the southern United States, that feeds on ripe fruit. Also, **June bug.**

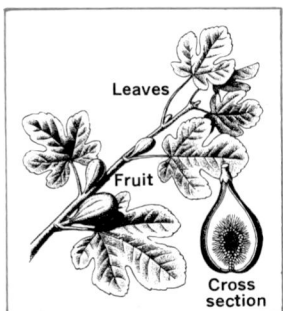

fig[1]

fight (fīt) *n.* **1.** a physical struggle between two opposing individuals or groups; battle; conflict: *a fight between two gangs.* **2.** a contest between two boxers; boxing match. **3.** a heated dispute; quarrel: *They had a fight over whose turn it was.* **4.** any struggle, esp. one to gain some objective or goal: *a fight for control of a government.* **5.** the power or inclination to carry on a struggle; pugnacity: *The team had no fight left.* —*v.,* **fought** (fôt), **fighting.** —*v.t.* **1.** to engage in physical struggle or combat with: *The soldiers fought the enemy and won.* **2.** to oppose in a boxing match: *The champion fought three opponents last year.* **3.** to struggle against or contend with in any manner: *I fought my desire to cry. The ship fought the storm.* **4.** to carry on or wage (a battle, contest, or struggle): *The armies fought the battle on an open plain. The lawyer fought the case well.* **5.** to gain or make (one's way) by struggle: *We fought our way through the crowd.* **6.** to cause to fight; manage the fighting of: *to fight a light heavyweight against a heavyweight.* —*v.i.* **1.** to take part in a physical struggle or combat; try to subdue or overcome an opponent: *The two armies fought for days.* **2.** to contend or struggle, as to gain an end; strive energetically: *to fight for equal rights.* [Old English *feohtan* to contend, struggle.]
 · **to fight it out.** to fight until a decisive result is attained.
 · **to fight off. a.** to repel by fighting: *The garrison fought off the attackers.* **b.** to struggle to get rid of or avoid: *to fight off a cold.*
 · **to fight shy of.** to avoid or evade confrontation with: *to fight shy of an issue.*

Synonyms *n.* **Fight, struggle, combat,** and **conflict** may all denote a physical contest, usually between two individuals or groups. **Fight** connotes an open, often brief contest between two parties, usually individuals: *They had a fight after school, which was broken up by their friends.* **Struggle** implies a vigorous, prolonged fight at close quarters: *The struggle between the two continued, as each tried to wrestle the other to the ground.* **Combat** is a more limited term usually applied to a formal, individual contest: *hand-to-hand combat between two chosen heroes.* **Conflict** is a broader term, suggesting continued hostility: *The hostility between the two tribes frequently erupted into armed conflict.*

fight·er (fī'tər) *n.* **1.** a person or animal that fights. **2.** a professional boxer. **3.** a fast, maneuverable airplane designed for use against enemy airplanes or ground forces, usually having a crew of one or two.

fighter bomber, an airplane that can perform the functions of both a fighter and a bomber.

fighting chance *Informal.* a possibility of success contingent on a determined struggle: *It won't be easy, but now at least we have a fighting chance.*

fig·ment (fig'mənt) *n.* something imagined or made up; fiction: *a figment of the imagination.* [Latin *figmentum* a fiction, something made.]

fig·ur·a·tion (fig'yə rā'shən) *n.* **1.** the act of shaping figures or

a	at	e	end	o	hot	u	up	hw	white	⎧	about
ā	ape	ē	me	ō	old	ū	use	ng	song		taken
ä	far	i	it	ô	fork	ü	rule	th	thin	ə ⎨	pencil
âr	care	ī	ice	oi	oil	u̇	pull	th	this		lemon
		îr	pierce	ou	out	ûr	turn	zh	measure	⎩	circus

marking with figures. **2.** a figure; configuration; shape. **3.** a figurative representation.

fig·u·ra·tive (fig′yər ə tiv) *adj.* **1.** characteristic of, using, or based on a figure of speech; not literal; metaphorical. *To throw caution to the wind* is a figurative expression. **2.** containing or using figures of speech; flowery: *figurative poetry.* **3.** representing by a symbol, figure, or likeness; emblematic: *a ceremony figurative of patriotism.* **4.** pictorial or plastic in representation: *figurative sculpture.* —**fig′ur·a·tive·ly,** *adv.* —**fig′ur·a·tive·ness,** *n.*

Usage Writers use figurative language, such as images, similes, and metaphors, to appeal directly to our emotions and senses, to evoke memories, and to conjure up associations. Such language engages the reader much more deeply than factual statements. For example, *fog-colored* describes an elephant's skin more vividly than *gray,* and *The night has a thousand eyes* is much more descriptive than *The sky is full of stars.* When used by a good writer, figurative language is not a mere embellishment added on for effect, but an integral part of the text, arising naturally from setting, characters, or action. Figurative language is the language of poetry and fiction, but by no means exclusively so. It can enliven almost any kind of prose, from biography to travel, from reporting to how-to.

fig·ure (fig′yər) *n.* **1.** a symbol representing a number, such as 0, 1, 2, 3, 4, 5. **2. figures.** the use of such symbols in calculating; arithmetic: *to be good at figures.* **3.** an amount or value as expressed in figures; price; sum: *The figure asked for the house was too high.* **4.** the visible external form or appearance of anything; shape; outline: *We saw the figure of a man silhouetted in the window.* **5.** the human body or form, or its appearance, esp. as matching an ideal: *a slender figure, a fine figure of a youth.* **6.** a person as he or she appears or looks to others: *to cut a comical figure, to be a figure of despair.* **7.** a person, esp. one of importance or distinction; character: *a well-known figure, a figure famous in local history.* **8.** a person or thing that represents or symbolizes another person or thing, or a principle: *a figure of evil, a figure of strength.* **9.** a representation or likeness, esp. of the human form: *The figure of a goddess appears on the coin.* **10.** a pictorial diagram; illustration; drawing: *The book contains many figures of automobile engines.* **11.** a design; pattern: *The cloth had bold figures woven into it.* **12.** *Geometry.* a bounded surface or space; series of lines, solids, or surfaces having a definite shape: *The circle is a plane figure. The sphere is a solid figure.* **13.** a set or series of movements, as in dancing or skating. **14.** figure of speech. **15.** *Music.* a series of notes or chords forming a short, distinct phrase or theme; subject; motif. —*v.,* -**ured, -ur·ing.** —*v.t.* **1.** to solve or find out by using numbers; calculate; compute: *Let's figure the total cost of the trip if we drive.* **2.** to represent or depict in any way, as in a picture or diagram: *The sculptor figured the bird in clay.* **3.** to ornament or cover with a design or pattern: **4.** *Informal.* **a.** to think; believe: *How many people do you figure will come to the party?* **b.** to reach a conclusion about; decide: *They figured he was the best person for the job.* **5.** to have a mental picture of; imagine. **6.** *Music.* to mark (the bass) with figures to indicate accompanying chords or intended harmony. —*v.i.* to be conspicuous or prominent; take part: *The ambassador figured in the conspiracy.* [Old French *figure* form, shape, face, from Latin *figūra* thing made, form.] —**fig′ur·er,** *n.* —For Synonyms *(n.),* see **shape.**

• **to figure on.** *Informal.* **a.** to depend on; rely on: *They figured on me to complete my part of the job.* **b.** to include in plans; take into consideration: *We didn't figure on rain when we planned the picnic.* **c.** to plan on: *They figured on going if the weather was nice.*

• **to figure out. a.** to solve by using figures; compute: *to figure out the answer to an arithmetic problem.* **b.** to arrive at the explanation or solution of; understand: *I figured out who the murderer was before the end of the book.*

fig·ured (fig′yərd) *adj.* **1.** decorated with figures or designs: *figured wallpaper.* **2.** represented by a figure, diagram, or picture: *The bird is figured in stone.* **3.** *Music.* (of the bass part) having the accompanying chords indicated by figures.

figure eight, a traced line resembling the numeral 8, as formed in flying, skating, or embroidery.

fig·ure·head (fig′yər hed′) *n.* **1.** a person having nominal authority but no real power or responsibility. **2.** a carved, ornamental figure on the bow of a ship.

figure of speech, a form of expression in which words are intentionally used out of their literal sense or in fanciful or incongruous combinations so as to produce a vivid, fresh, or poetic effect. Simile, metaphor, and personification are figures of speech.

Figures of Speech

Although figures of speech are often thought of primarily as features of formal literary language, they are also an important part of everyday conversation. Shown below are examples of some common figures of speech and their use in both literary and colloquial contexts.

simile (comparison of objects or ideas, using the words *like* or *as*)
LITERARY: My heart is like a singing bird.
—*Christina Georgina Rossetti*
COLLOQUIAL: happy as a clam, strong as a horse

metaphor (comparison of one object or idea with another to suggest similarity)
LITERARY: Eden is that old-fashioned House
We dwell in every day . . . —*Emily Dickinson*
COLLOQUIAL: My parents are night owls.

personification (attributing human characteristics or reactions to inanimate objects or abstractions)
LITERARY: The thirsty earth soaks up the rain . . .
—*Abraham Cowley*
COLLOQUIAL: a user-friendly computer, a hostile environment

apostrophe (addressing an object, abstract quality, or imaginary person as if present and capable of understanding)
LITERARY: Quick, sunrise, come! —*Langston Hughes*
COLLOQUIAL: Come on, fish, bite!

hyperbole (extreme exaggeration)
LITERARY: Will all great Neptune's oceans wash this blood / Clean from my hand?
—*William Shakespeare*
COLLOQUIAL: That movie has been on TV a million times. We were dying of hunger by dinner time.

oxymoron (combining of contradictory or incongruous terms)
LITERARY: Blind mouths! That scarce themselves know how to hold A sheep-hook . . . —*John Milton*
COLLOQUIAL: friendly enemies, pretty ugly, terribly good, deafening silence

---

figure skating, the sport or pastime of skating, usually on ice, in which the skater executes various patterns and movements somewhat resembling those of modern dance or ballet. —**figure skater.**

fig·ur·ine (fig′yə rēn′) *n.* a small carved or molded figure; statuette. [French *figurine,* from Italian *figurina,* diminutive of *figura* shape, form, image, from Latin *figūra* thing made, form.]

fig·wort (fig′wûrt′) *n.* **1.** any of a large group of strong-smelling, weedy plants, genus *Scrophularia,* found growing in damp places throughout the Northern Hemisphere, bearing oval, toothed leaves and loose clusters of small, tubular, greenish yellow or purple flowers. **2.** any plant of the same family, such as the snapdragon or foxglove.

Fi·ji·an (fē′jē ən, fi jē′-) *adj.* of, relating to, or characteristic of Fiji or its people, language, or culture. —*n.* **1.** a language of the Melanesian group of the Austronesian family, spoken predominantly on the Fiji Islands. **2.** a native or citizen of Fiji.

fil·a·ment (fil′ə mənt) *n.* **1.** a very fine thread or threadlike structure; fiber: *a filament of a spider's web, filaments of lint.* **2.** a wire in a light bulb, usually of tungsten, that gives off light when an electric current passes through it. For illustration, see **incandescent lamp. 3.** a wire in a vacuum tube that emits electrons when heated by the passage of an electric current and that often acts as a cathode. **4.** the stalklike part of a stamen that supports the anther in some flowers. For illustration, see **flower.** [Modern Latin *filamentum,* going back to Latin *fīlum* thread.] —**fil′a·men′tous,** *adj.*

5 6 6
3 3 4
Written

Played

figured bass

fi·lar·i·a (fi lâr′ē ə) *n., pl.* **-lar·i·ae** (-lâr′ē ē′). any of various threadlike roundworms, phylum Nematoda, that live as parasites in the blood and tissues of human beings and other vertebrate animals. The larvae of filariae are usually transmitted by mosquitoes and other insects. [Modern Latin *Filaria,* from Latin *fīlum* thread.] —**fi·lar′i·al,** *adj.*

fil·a·ri·a·sis (fil′ə rī′ə sis) *n.* any of various tropical diseases, such as elephantiasis, caused by the presence of filariae in the body, esp. in the lymph vessels.

fil·bert (fil′bərt) *n.* **1.** the thick-shelled, edible nut of either of two European shrubs, *Corylus maxima* or *C. avellana.* Also, **hazelnut.** **2.** the shrub producing this nut, widely cultivated in southern Europe and the northwestern United States. [From dialectal French *noix de filbert* literally, nut of (Saint) Philibert; because this nut becomes ripe around Saint Philibert's day (August 22).]

filch (filch) *v.t.* to steal (things, esp. of small value); pilfer. [Of uncertain origin.] —**filch′er,** *n.* —For Synonyms, see **steal.**

file¹ (fīl) *n.* **1.** any device, as a folder or cabinet, in which papers, cards, records, or documents are arranged in order for easy reference. **2.** a collection of items thus arranged. **3.** *Computers.* a collection of data stored as a unit on a disk or in memory. **4.a.** a line of persons, animals, or things placed one behind another. **b.** a line or row of soldiers standing one behind another. ➡ distinguished from **rank. 5.** any row of squares on a chessboard running from one player toward the other, each named for the piece at its head: *king's bishop's file.* ➡ distinguished from **rank.** For illustration, see **chessboard.** —*v.,* **filed, fil·ing.** —*v.t.* **1.** to keep (papers or similar items) arranged in order. **2.** to place in a file: *I filed the cards in alphabetical order.* **3.** to submit legally or officially; enter on a record: *to file an accident report, to file one's income tax return.* **4.** to send in (a news story) to a newspaper office. —*v.i.* **1.** to march or move in a file: *The soldiers filed out of the barracks.* **2.** to make application: *to file for a hunting permit, to file for divorce.* **3.** to register as a candidate for a political office. [Middle English *filen,* from Middle French *filer* to string documents on a wire, from Old French *filer* to spin thread, from Late Latin *filare* to spin, from Latin *filum* thread.] —**fil′er,** *n.*

• **on file.** arranged in order and kept for reference; in a file.

file² (fīl) *n.* a steel tool having one or more closely ridged surfaces used to smooth, form, or wear away metal, wood, or another material or the nails of one's fingers. —*v.t.,* **filed, filing.** to cut, smooth, or grind down with a file. [Old English *fēol* the tool.] —**fil′er,** *n.*

file clerk, an office worker employed to keep files and records in order.

file·fish (fīl′fish′) *n., pl.* **-fish** or **-fish·es.** any of several tropical saltwater fish, family Balistidae, having scales set closely together in fine ridges and one or more sharp dorsal spines.

fi·let (fi lā′, fil′ā) *n.* **1.** a net or lace with a square mesh. **2.** fillet *(def. 3).* —*v.t.,* **fi·leted** (fi lād′, fil′ād), **fi·let·ing** (fi lā′ing, fil′ā ing). fillet *(def. 2).* [French *filet* fishnet, from Old French *filé* what has been spun, yarn, from Old Provençal *filat* literally, made of threads, from *fil* thread, from Latin *fīlum.*]

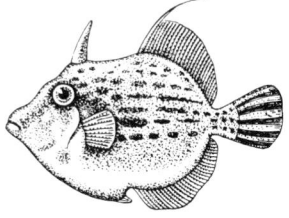
filefish

fi·let mi·gnon (fi lā′ min-yon′) *pl.* **fi·lets mi·gnons** (fi lā′min yonz′). a small, thick steak from the tip of the tenderloin, noted for its tenderness. [French *filet mignon* dainty filet.]

fil·i·al (fil′ē əl) *adj.* **1.** relating to or befitting a son or daughter: *filial obedience.* **2.** *Genetics.* relating to or designating a generation following the parental generation. [Late Latin *fīliālis* befitting a son, from Latin *fīlius* son.] —**fil′i·al·ly,** *adv.*

fil·i·bus·ter (fil′ə bus′tər) *n.* **1.a.** a method of delaying or stopping action on a legislative issue by the use of lengthy speeches, prolonged debate, or other obstructive tactics. **b.** a member of a legislature, esp. the U.S. Senate, who obstructs the passage of a bill by such measures. Also *(def. 1b),* **fil′i·bus′ter·er. 2.** an adventurer who engages in unlawful warfare against a foreign country, esp. a U.S. adventurer involved in an armed expedition into a Latin American country during the nineteenth century. —*v.i.* **1.** to obstruct legislative action by use of filibuster, as by prolonged speeches. **2.** to engage in unlawful warfare against a foreign country. —*v.t.* to obstruct the passage of (a bill)

by filibuster. [Spanish *filibustero* buccaneer, from French *filibustier* buccaneer, robber, from Dutch *vrijbuiter,* going back to *vrij* free + *buit* booty. Doublet of FREEBOOTER.]

fil·i·gree (fil′i grē′) *n.* **1.** delicate, lacelike ornamental work of intertwined gold or silver wire. **2.** anything ornate, delicate, or fanciful, such as a pattern or design: *The sun shining through the leaves made a green and gold filigree.* —*adj.* resembling, made of, or ornamented with filigree: *filigree earrings.* —*v.t.,* **-greed, -gree·ing.** to adorn with or shape in filigree. [Modification of earlier *filigrane* filigree work, from French *filigrane,* from Italian *filigrana,* going back to Latin *fīlum* thread + *grānum* seed; because metal threads are used.]

fil·ings (fī′lingz) *pl. n.* particles removed by a file.

Fil·i·pi·no (fil′ə pē′nō) *n., pl.* **-nos.** a native or citizen of the Philippines. —*adj.* Philippine.

fill (fil) *v.t.* **1.** to supply with as much as can be held or contained; make full, as a container or space: *to fill a bucket with water.* **2.** to occupy the whole capacity or extent of: *The crowd filled the auditorium.* **3.** to spread over or throughout; pervade; permeate: *Smoke filled the room. Angry shouts filled the air.* **4.** to sate with or as with food; feed: *She filled her stomach.* **5.** to be enough to meet, as a need, demand, or requirement; fulfill; satisfy: *His contribution fills the need for additional funds.* **6.** to supply or make up whatever is required or asked for: *to fill a grocery order, to fill a prescription.* **7.a.** to stop up or close by putting something in; plug: *to fill a hole in a wall with putty.* **b.** to put a filling in (a tooth). **8.** to hold or occupy, as a position or office; discharge the duties of: *to fill the office of treasurer.* **9.** to place or appoint a person for: *to fill a vacancy on the Supreme Court.* **10.** *Nautical.* to distend (a sail) by pressure of the wind. **11.** to build up, as low ground or an embankment, by adding stone and earth. —*v.i.* to become full: *The room filled with smoke.* —*n.* **1.** a quantity sufficient to fill; enough to satiate a desire or need; full supply: *to eat one's fill.* **2.** something used to fill: *Stone and gravel were used as fill for the hole.* [Old English *fyllan* to make full.]

• **to fill in. a.** to fill entirely with something: *to fill in a hole with dirt.* **b.** to complete by inserting something: *to fill in a questionnaire.* **c.** to insert to make something complete: *Fill in your name on the application form.* **d.** to act as a substitute: *I filled in for the goalkeeper.*

• **to fill out. a.** to complete by inserting something: *to fill out an application.* **b.** to become larger, fuller, or more rounded: *You will fill out as you grow older.*

• **to fill someone in on.** to supply someone with additional or the latest information about: *We filled our new members in on our plans.*

• **to fill the bill.** to fulfill or satisfactorily supply the requirements of.

• **to fill up. a.** to make completely full: *Fill up the gas tank, please.* **b.** to become completely full: *The rain barrel filled up quickly.*

• **to have one's fill.** to have enough or too much.

fill·er (fil′ər) *n.* **1.** a person or thing that fills. **2.a.** material used to fill a gap, to even the grain of wood, to stiffen fabric, or to increase the bulk of something. **b.** an item, esp. a brief paragraph, used to fill space in a newspaper or magazine. **c.** a sheaf of paper for a loose-leaf notebook.

fil·lér (fē′lâr, fil′âr) *n., pl.* **-lér.** a unit of currency of Hungary, equal to ¹/₁₀₀ of a forint. [Hungarian *fillér.*]

fil·let (fil′it; *n. def. 3, v. def. 2,* fi lā′, fil′ā) *n.* **1.** a narrow band or ribbon for binding or adorning the hair. **2.** a narrow band or strip of any material. **3.** *also,* **filet.** a lean, boneless piece or slice of fish or meat. —*v.t.* **1.** to bind or adorn with a fillet. **2.** *also,* **filet.** to cut (fish or meat) into fillets. [Old French *filet* little thread, diminutive of *fil* thread, from Latin *fīlum.*]

fill-in (fil′in′) *n.* a person or thing filling a gap or vacancy.

fill·ing (fil′ing) *n.* **1.** anything used to fill something: *pie filling.* **2.** a substance, such as amalgam or cement, put into a cavity in a tooth. **3.** threads running from side to side across the warp threads in a woven fabric; woof. **4.** the act of filling.

filling station, gas station.

fil·lip (fil′ip) *n.* **1.a.** the snap of a finger that has been pressed down by the thumb and suddenly released. **b.** a sharp tap given by such a means. **2.** something that serves to arouse, excite, or

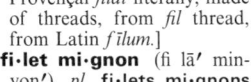

a	at	e	end	o	hot	u	up	hw	white	(	about
ā	ape	ē	me	ō	old	ū	use	ng	song		taken
ä	far	i	it	ô	fork	ü	rule	th	thin	ə	pencil
âr	care	ī	ice	oi	oil	u̇	pull	<u>th</u>	this		lemon
				ir	pierce	ou	out	ûr	turn	zh	measure	(	circus

enliven; stimulus: *That news was a fillip to my spirits.* —*v.t.* **1.** to tap or strike with a fillip. **2.** to project or drive by or as by a fillip. **3.** to rouse; stimulate. —*v.i.* to make a fillip. [Probably imitative.]

fil·ly (fil′ē) *n., pl.* **-lies.** a young female horse. [Old Norse *fylja.*]

film (film) *n.* **1.** a thin layer, sheet, covering, or membrane: *The windows were covered by a film of dirt.* **2.** a thin, flexible roll or strip of material, usually of cellulose acetate coated with a light-sensitive emulsion, used in making photographs. **3.a.** such a roll or strip containing pictures to be projected on a screen: *The film was rewound for the next showing.* **b.** motion picture: *We saw a good film.* **4.** **films. a.** motion pictures collectively: *She was a star in films twenty years ago.* **b.** the motion-picture industry. **5.** a thin veil or haze that blurs: *a film of tears.* —*v.t.* **1.** to cover or obscure by a thin layer or haze. **2.a.** to photograph with a motion-picture camera: *He filmed the football game.* **b.** to make a motion picture of: *to film a popular novel.* —*v.i.* **1.** to become covered or obscured by a thin layer or haze. **2.a.** to be suitable for filming: *Some plays do not film well.* **b.** to make a motion picture: *They were filming in the neighborhood yesterday.* [Old English *filmen* membrane.]

film·ic (fil′mik) *adj.* of or relating to motion pictures.

film·strip (film′strip′) *n.* a length of film containing pictures that are projected one at a time on a screen, often used as a teaching aid.

film·y (fil′mē) *adj.,* **film·i·er, film·i·est. 1.** composed of or resembling a thin layer; gauzy: *filmy material.* **2.** covered with or as with a thin layer; hazy: *filmy vision.* —**film′i·ness,** *n.*

fil·ter (fil′tər) *n.* **1.** a device for straining solids or impurities from a liquid or gas. **2.** porous material used in such a device, such as sand, charcoal, or paper. **3.** a device that allows certain electrical frequencies to pass and restricts others. **4.** a transparent disk, often colored, that allows light of certain frequencies to pass and blocks other frequencies, used on still and motion-picture cameras: *a lens filter.* —*v.t.* **1.** to pass (liquid or gas) through a filter; strain: *The water was filtered through charcoal.* **2.** to act as a filter for. **3.** to separate or remove (impurities, solid particles, or other matter) by or as by a filter: *The traces of metal were filtered from the solution.* —*v.i.* to pass through or as through a filter: *Sunlight filtered through the leaves.* [Medieval Latin *filtrum* strainer made of felt; of Germanic origin.]

fil·ter·a·ble (fil′tər ə bəl) *also,* **filtrable.** *adj.* **1.** capable of being filtered. **2.** capable of passing through a filter that stops bacteria: *a filterable virus.* —**fil′ter·a·bil′i·ty,** *adv.*

filter bed, a pond or tank having a false bottom covered with sand or gravel, serving to filter water or sewage.

filter paper *n.* porous paper used to strain suspended solids from liquids.

filth (filth) *n.* **1.** something that is foul or putrid; offensive dirt or refuse: *Industrial filth pollutes the air and water.* **2.** a foul condition: *living in filth.* **3.** moral defilement or corruption; obscenity. **4.** obscene language. [Old English *fӯlth* putrid matter, rottenness.]

filth·y (fil′thē) *adj.,* **filth·i·er, filth·i·est. 1.** of the nature of or containing filth; dirty; foul: *filthy streets.* **2.** morally foul; obscene. **3.** highly unpleasant or objectionable; contemptible: *That was a filthy accusation.* —**filth′i·ly,** *adv.* —**filth′i·ness,** *n.*

fil·tra·ble (fil′trə bəl) filterable.

fil·trate (fil′trāt) *n.* a liquid that has been separated by filtration. —*v.t.,* **-trat·ed, -trat·ing.** filter.

fil·tra·tion (fil trā′shən) *n.* the act of filtering or the state of being filtered.

fin[1] (fin) *n.* **1.** one of the movable structures extending from the body of a fish, supported by bone or cartilage, and enabling the fish to swim and to guide and balance itself in the water. **2.** a similar structure of other aquatic animals, such as whales and some porpoises. **3.** anything resembling a fin in shape or function. **4.** a vertical surface attached longitudinally to an aircraft or rocket to provide stability. **5.** a fin-shaped appendage on the hull of a submarine or boat. —*v.,* **finned, fin·ning.** —*v.t.* to cut the fins from (a fish). —*v.i.* to move the fins violently, as a whale when dying. [Old English *finn* the movable structure of a fish.]

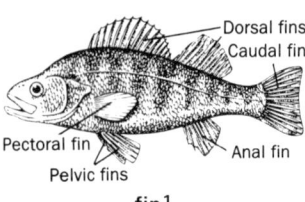

Dorsal fins
Caudal fin
Pectoral fin
Anal fin
Pelvic fins

fin[1]

fin[2] (fin) *n. Slang.* a five-dollar bill. [Yiddish *finf* five, going back to Old High German *finf.*]

fi·na·gle (fi nā′gəl) *v.,* **-gled, -gling.** —*v.t. Informal.* **1.** to get or manage (something) by trickery or deceit; wangle: *We finagled free tickets to the game.* **2.** to cheat or trick (someone): *The swindler finagled them out of their money.* —*v.i.* to use trickery or deceit; cheat. [Of uncertain origin.] —**fi·na′gler,** *n.*

fi·nal (fī′nəl) *adj.* **1.** relating to or coming at the end; last; ultimate: *the final chapter of a book, the final revision of a manuscript.* **2.** allowing no further action, discussion, or change; deciding; conclusive: *a final decision, the final word on a subject.* **3.** relating to or constituting an end or purpose: *a final cause.* —*n.* **1.** something that is last or terminal. **2.** *also,* **finals. a.** the last examination of a school or college course: *a history final, to study for the math finals.* **b.** the last and decisive game, match, or trial in a series of athletic contests: *Our team reached the finals of the basketball tournament.* [Late Latin *fīnālis* relating to the end, concluding, from Latin *fīnis* end.] —For Synonyms *(adj.),* see **last**[1].

fi·na·le (fi nä′lē) *n.* **1.** the last part or conclusion of any performance or course of action. **2.** the concluding part of a piece of music or of a performance, such as a play or opera. [Italian *finale* end, close, from Late Latin *fīnālis* concluding. See FINAL.]

fi·nal·ist (fī′nə list) *n.* a person or team that takes part in the final match or event of a series of games or contests.

fi·nal·i·ty (fī nal′i tē, fi-) *n., pl.* **-ties. 1.** the state or quality of being final, settled, or complete; conclusiveness; decisiveness: *The finality of the decision was not to be doubted.* **2.** something final, as a final act or utterance.

fi·nal·ize (fī′nə līz′) *v.t.,* **-ized, -iz·ing.** to put into final or finished form; bring to completion: *We must finalize our plans.* —**fi′nal·i·za′tion,** *n.*

fi·nal·ly (fī′nə lē) *adv.* **1.** at the end; in conclusion; ultimately: *We finally reached our destination.* **2.** so as to finish or resolve; completely; irrevocably; decisively: *We must deal with this problem finally.*

fi·nance (fi nans′, fī-, fī′nans) *n.* **1.** the theory and management of monetary affairs of individuals, businesses, or governments, including such matters as credit, banking, and investment. **2.** **finances.** the monetary affairs or resources of a government, organization, or individual; budgetary balance; funds; revenue; income. —*v.t.,* **-nanced, -nanc·ing. 1.** to raise or provide money for: *to finance a new car, to finance a child's education.* **2.** to give money or credit to: *The bank financed us in our new business.* [Old French *finance* end, payment, wealth, from *finer* to end, pay, settle, going back to Latin *fīnīre* to end.]

finance company, a business, other than a bank, that makes loans to customers, usually for a short period of time.

fi·nan·cial (fi nan′shəl, fī-) *adj.* relating to finance or financiers: *financial skills, a financial crisis.* —**fi·nan′cial·ly,** *adv.*

fin·an·cier (fin′ən sîr′, fī′nan-) *n.* **1.** a person engaged in financial operations on a large scale. **2.** a person skilled in financial matters, such as a banker. [French *financier,* from *finance* ready money, money resources. See FINANCE.]

fin·back (fin′bak′) *n.* **1.** any of a group of large, streamlined baleen whales, family Balaenopteridae, with furrows or pleats along the throat and chest and a small pointed dorsal fin, and including the humpback and blue whales. **2.** any of a group of whalebone, or baleen, whales, genus *Balaenoptera,* esp. the **common finback,** *B. physalus,* dark above and light below, found in all oceans. Length: 60-80 feet (18.3-24.3 meters). Also, **rorqual, fin whale.**

finch (finch) *n.* any of a large group of songbirds, family Fringillidae, such as the sparrow, bunting, canary, and cardinal, that typically have a cone-shaped bill and stout body and feed on seeds. Length: 4-11 inches (10-28 centimeters). [Old English *finc.*]

finch

find (fīnd) *v.,* **found, find·ing.** —*v.t.* **1.** to come upon accidentally; meet with by chance; happen on: *I found a wallet on the sidewalk.* **2.** to get or learn by calculation; obtain (the solution to a problem): *to find the sum of several numbers.* **3.** to discover or obtain by or as by search or effort: *to find a place to live, to find a cure for a disease, to find the right person for a job.* **4.** to discover, learn, or become aware of through experience, investigation, or observation: *I found I couldn't study past midnight. They found that the fire had been set deliberately.* **5.** to recover (something lost): *We found the missing book under the couch.* **6.** to gain or recover the use of: *He finally found his voice and replied to her*

shocking accusation. **7.** to have as a sensation; experience; feel: *I find great satisfaction in doing crossword puzzles.* **8.** to get or obtain by arrangement or management: *I haven't found time to read that book.* **9.** to arrive at; reach: *Water finds its level. The arrow found its target.* **10.** to determine and declare: *The jury found the defendant guilty.* **11.** to feel or think to be; consider; regard: *to find the climate too humid, to find something very amusing.* **12.** to provide; supply; furnish: *to find room for a guest.* *—v.i.* to arrive at a decision after judicial inquiry: *The jury found for the plaintiff.* *—n.* **1.** the act or an instance of finding: *The archaeologist's summer dig resulted in a startling find.* **2.** something that is found, esp. something of value: *We made a find at the antique auction.* [Old English *findan* to come upon, attain.]
 • **to find oneself. a.** to discover one's abilities or talents and the best manner or way to employ them: *After changing jobs many times, he finally found himself.* **b.** to perceive oneself to be (in some specified place or mental or physical condition): *I found myself in a dilemma.*
 • **to find out. a.** to learn; discover: *She found out that prices were much higher in the city.* **b.** to detect or discover the identity or true character of (a person or thing): *The investigator found them out before they could commit another crime.*
find·er (fīn′dər) *n.* **1.** a person or thing that finds. **2.** viewfinder. **3.** a small telescope attached to a larger one to help sight the objects to be viewed.
fin de siè·cle (faN də sye′klə) *French.* the end of the century, esp. as used of the last years of the nineteenth century, thought of as being a period of artistic and social sophistication, innovation, and decadence.
find·ing (fīn′ding) *n.* **1.** the act of a person who finds; discovery. **2.** something that is found: *a remarkable finding.* **3.** *also,* **findings.** the result or conclusions of a judicial or other inquiry: *The committee announced its findings.* **4. findings.** tools and incidental materials used by certain artisans: *a goldsmith's findings.*
fine[1] (fīn) *adj.,* **fin·er, fin·est. 1.** of superior grade or quality; very good; excellent: *a fine piece of work, fine linens.* **2.** very satisfactory; enjoyable: *We had a fine time.* **3.** highly accomplished; of superior ability; skilled: *a fine musician.* **4.** characterized by or displaying elegance or refinement; polished: *fine manners.* **5.** delicate, as in structure, texture, or workmanship: *fine facial features, fine embroidery.* **6.** capable of delicate discrimination; highly perceptive: *to have a fine eye for color.* **7.** involving close discrimination; subtle; refined: *to clarify the fine points in an argument.* **8.a.** extremely thin; slender: *a fine thread.* **b.** extremely small: *fine script.* **9.** consisting or composed of minute particles; not coarse: *fine sand.* **10.** sharp; keen: *the fine edge of a razor.* **11.** overly decorated; showy; ornate: *fine flourishes in speaking.* **12.** healthy; well: *We are fine.* **13.** free from clouds or rain; clear; bright: *fine weather.* **14.** free from impurities or foreign matter; clear; pure: *fine gold.* **15.** containing a stated proportion of pure metal, such as gold or silver. Commercial silver is usually 999 fine, containing 999 parts of silver in 1,000 parts of the metal. *—adv.* **1.** *Informal.* very well; excellently: *I'm doing fine in school.* **2.** finely: *The tailor cut the material pretty fine.* [Old French *fin* perfect, exact, going back to Latin *fīnis* end, limit.]
fine[2] (fīn) *n.* a sum of money exacted as penalty for an offense: *There is a fine of fifty dollars for littering.* *—v.t.,* **fined, fin·ing.** to subject to or punish by a fine: *to fine a motorist for speeding.* [Old French *fin* end, settlement, from Medieval Latin *finis* final payment, from Latin *fīnis* end, limit.]
 • **in fine. a.** in conclusion; finally. **b.** in a few words; so as to be brief.
fi·ne[3] (fē′nā) *n. Music.* the end. ➡ a direction marking the end of a repeated section or movement. [Italian *fine* end, limit, from Latin *fīnis.*]
fine arts 1. those arts considered as being concerned mainly with the creation of beauty, including painting, drawing, and sculpture, and sometimes architecture, literature, music, drama, and dance. **2.** objects created mainly for beauty: *an auction of fine arts.* **3. fine art.** something requiring skill or ability: *Gourmet cooking is a fine art.*
fine-drawn (fīn′drôn′) *adj.* drawn out to extreme fineness or subtlety: *fine-drawn wire, a fine-drawn argument.*
fine-grained (fīn′grānd′) *adj.* having a fine, close grain.
fine·ly (fīn′lē) *adv.* **1.** in a fine manner; excellently. **2.** in small pieces: *The carrots should be finely chopped.*
fine·ness (fīn′nis) *n.* **1.** the state or quality of being fine. **2.** the proportion of pure gold or silver in an alloy, usually stated in parts per thousand.
fine print, the part of a contract or other document that is

difficult to read because it is printed in very small type and usually contains material written in language that is difficult to understand.
fin·er·y (fī′nə rē) *n., pl.* **-er·ies.** fine or showy dress or ornaments; elaborate adornment. [FINE[1] + -ERY.]
fine-spun (fīn′spun′) *adj.* **1.** spun or drawn out to extreme fineness or delicacy. **2.** excessively subtle or refined.
fi·nesse (fi nes′) *n.* **1.** refinement or subtlety of execution, skill, or discernment: *The pianist displayed great finesse and virtuosity.* **2.** smooth or artful handling of a delicate situation; craft; cunning: *The mediator showed great finesse in settling the labor dispute.* **3.** *Bridge.* an attempt to take a trick by playing the lower of two cards not in sequence, in the hope that the intervening card is in the hand of an opponent who has already played. *—v.,* **-nessed, -ness·ing.** *—v.i.* **1.** to use finesse. **2.** *Bridge.* to make a finesse. *—v.t.* **1.** to bring about or change by finesse. **2.** *Bridge.* to make a finesse with (a card). [Old French *finesse* delicacy, fineness, from *fin.* See FINE[1].]
fine-tune (fīn′tün′, -tūn′) *v.t.,* **-tuned, -tun·ing.** to make fine adjustments in to achieve optimum performance or results: *to fine-tune an engine, to fine-tune a speech.*
fin·ger (fing′gər) *n.* **1.** one of the five separate parts of the end of the hand, esp. the four excluding the thumb; digit. **2.** a part of a glove that is made to receive or cover one of these. **3.** anything resembling a finger in shape or use. **4.a.** a unit of measure equal to the breadth of a finger, approximately ¾ inch (2 centimeters). **b.** the length of a finger, approximately 4½ inches (11 centimeters). *—v.t.* **1.** to touch, feel, or handle with the fingers; toy with: *I fingered the silk gently.* **2.** *Music.* **a.** to play (a musical instrument) with the fingers. **b.** to mark (musical notes or a piece of music) with figures indicating a specific fingering to be used. **3.** *Slang.* **a.** to point out or identify (someone) as the victim of an impending crime: *The thief fingered the bank messenger.* **b.** to identify or inform on to the police or other authorities: *The witness fingered the suspect in the lineup.* *—v.i.* **1.** to touch, feel, or handle something with the fingers. **2.** *Music.* **a.** to use the fingers in a certain way in playing a musical instrument. **b.** (of musical instruments) to be arranged for playing with the fingers. [Old English *finger* one of the end parts of the hand.]
 • **to burn one's fingers.** to bring suffering or loss upon oneself by meddling or interfering.
 • **to have a finger in the pie. a.** to take part in something; have a share in doing something. **b.** to meddle; interfere.
 • **to put one's finger on.** to indicate or point out precisely or correctly: *to put one's finger on the cause of a problem.*
 • **to put the finger on.** *Slang.* **a.** to inform on, as to the police; betray. **b.** to indicate or point out, as a victim to be killed.
 • **to twist around one's little finger.** to be able to handle or control completely or with ease; make subservient.
fin·ger·board (fing′gər bôrd′) *n.* a strip of wood on the neck of a violin, guitar, or similar instrument, against which strings are pressed by the fingers. For illustration, see violin.
finger bowl, a small bowl containing water for rinsing the fingers during or after a meal.
fin·ger·ing (fing′gər ing) *n.* **1.** the act of touching or handling with the fingers. **2.a.** the action, method, or technique of using the fingers in playing a musical instrument. **b.** numerals or other notations on a piece of music indicating which fingers are to be used in playing its notes. **c.** the pattern in which the fingers are used in performing a piece of music: *The fingering in this piece is very difficult.*
fin·ger·ling (fing′gər ling) *n.* **1.** a young or small fish, esp. a salmon or trout no longer than a finger. **2.** something very small.
fin·ger·nail (fing′gər nāl′) *n.* **1.** the horny substance that develops from the skin and forms a hard plate on the upper surface of the end of a finger. **2.** the hard plate itself.
finger painting 1. the technique or process of painting by spreading paint on dampened paper with the fingers or palms. **2.** a painting made in this way.
finger post, a sign or guidepost in the shape of a hand with a pointing finger, indicating direction.
fin·ger·print (fing′gər print′) *n.* an impression of the markings on the inner surface of the tip of a finger or thumb, esp. such an impression made with ink and used for purposes of identification. *—v.t.* to take fingerprints of.

a	at	e	end	o	hot	u	up	hw	white	ə	about
ā	ape	ē	me	ō	old	ū	use	ng	song		taken
ä	far	i	it	ô	fork	ü	rule	th	thin		pencil
âr	care	ī	ice	oi	oil	u̇	pull	th	this		lemon
		î	pierce	ou	out	ûr	turn	zh	measure		circus

463

fin·ger·tip (fing′gər tip′) *n.* the last joint of a finger, esp. its very end.
   • **to have at one's fingertips.** to have immediate access to or knowledge of: *I don't have that information at my fingertips.*
fin·i·al (fin′ē əl) *n.* **1.** a terminal ornament at the tip or end of a spire, post, or other architectural member. **2.** a similar ornament on a chair, bed, or other piece of furniture. [Form of FINAL.]
fin·i·cal (fin′i kəl) *adj.* finicky. [FINE¹ + -ICAL.] —**fin′i·cal·ly,** *adv.*
fin·ick·ing (fin′i king) *adj.* finicky.
fin·ick·y (fin′i kē) *adj.* excessively fastidious, exacting, or precise; fussy: *a finicky eater.* —**fin′ick·i·ness,** *n.*
fi·nis (fin′is, fī′nis) *n.* end; conclusion. [Latin *finis.*]
fin·ish (fin′ish) *v.t.* **1.** to bring to an end; stop; end: *to finish speaking.* **2.** to come to the end of: *I didn't finish the test before the time was up. I want to finish

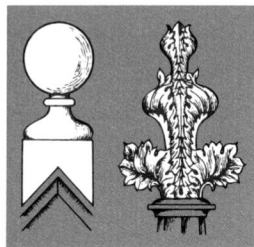

finials

reading today's paper.* **3.** to use up or consume completely: *to finish one ream of paper, to finish the peanut butter.* **4.** to complete and perfect in detail; put final and perfecting touches on: *to finish a statue.* **5.** to treat and give a certain surface, quality, or effect to, as cloth or wood: *We used clear varnish to finish the cabinet.* **6.** *Informal.* to defeat, destroy, or kill: *The scandal finished the mayor's political career.* —*v.i.* **1.** to reach or come to an end: *The game did not finish until after five o'clock.* **2.** to come to the end of a job, task, or other undertaking: *The painters finished ahead of schedule. Our horse finished in last place.* —*n.* **1.** the last stage of anything; conclusion; end: *the finish of a race, a fight to the finish.* **2.** something that ends, perfects, or completes: *The glorious sunset was an appropriate finish to the day.* **3.** the condition or quality of being finished; perfection; completion. **4.** polish or perfection, as in education or social manners. **5.** the manner in which a surface is finally treated; effect produced by the finishing process: *a rough finish.* [Old French *finiss-,* a stem of *finir* to end, from Latin *finire.*] —**fin′ish·er,** *n.* —For Synonyms *(v.t.),* see **end.**
   • **to finish off. a.** to bring to completion; end: *to finish off a school year with a party.* **b.** to cause the defeat, death, or destruction of: *We finished off our opponents with two quick goals.*
   • **to finish up.** to complete; end: *Please finish up what you are doing as soon as possible.*
   • **to finish with. a.** to bring to completion; end: *I finished with the first draft this morning.* **b.** to sever relations with; cease to have anything to do with.
fin·ished (fin′isht) *adj.* **1.** brought to an end; concluded: *The project is finished.* **2.** completed in all details: *a finished product.* **3.** perfected; polished: *The ballet is a finished work.* **4.** highly skilled or accomplished: *a finished dancer.*
finishing school, a private school, emphasizing social and cultural attainments, that prepares young women for entrance into society.
finish line, the line that marks the end of a course or race.
fi·nite (fī′nīt) *adj.* **1.a.** having a beginning and an end; having limits or bounds: *Her essay described the universe as infinite and our galaxy as finite.* **b.** subject to human or natural limitations or conditions: *finite existence.* **2.** *Mathematics.* **a.** able to be equaled or completed by counting. **b.** neither infinite nor infinitesimal. **c.** of or relating to a set containing a limited number of elements. **3.** *Grammar.* (of a verb or verb phrase) limited by person, number, tense, and mood; capable of serving as a predicate. In the sentence *He attends college, attends* is a finite verb. —*n.* something that is finite. [Latin *finitus,* past participle of *finire* to end.] —**fi′nite·ly,** *adv.* —**fi′nite·ness,** *n.*
fin·i·tude (fin′i tüd′, -tūd′, fī′nə-) *n.* the quality or condition of being finite.
fink (fingk) *n. Slang.* **1.a.** strikebreaker. **b.** a person who spies on workers for an employer. **2.** informer. **3.** an obnoxious or contemptible person.
Finn (fin) *n.* **1.** a native or citizen of Finland. **2.** a person of Finnish ancestry. **3.** a person whose native language is Finnish or a Finnic language.
fin·nan had·die (fin′ən had′ē) smoked haddock. Also, **finnan haddock.** [Modification of earlier *Findhorn haddock,* from *Findhorn,* fishing town in Scotland, + HADDOCK.]
finned (find) *adj.* having fins.

Finn·ic (fin′ik) *adj.* **1.** Finnish. **2.** of, relating to, or designating a branch of the Finno-Ugric subfamily of the Ural-Altaic family of languages, including Finnish, Lapp, and Estonian. —*n.* the Finnic branch of Finno-Ugric.
Finn·ish (fin′ish) *adj.* of, relating to, or characteristic of Finland or its people, language, or culture. —*n.* a language spoken predominantly in Finland, a member of the Finno-Ugric subfamily of the Ural-Altaic family of languages.
Fin·no-U·gric (fin′ō ü′grik, -ū′grik) *n.* a subfamily of the Ural-Altaic family of languages, including Finnish, Estonian, and Hungarian.
fin·ny (fin′ē) *adj.* **1.** having fins. **2.** resembling a fin. **3.** relating to or abounding in fish: *the finny deep.*
fin whale, finback.
fiord (fyôrd) fjord.
fir (fûr) *n.* **1.** any of a group of pyramid-shaped evergreen trees, genus *Abies,* of the pine family, widely distributed in temperate and cooler climates, bearing cones that grow erect on the branches. **2.** any of certain other trees of the pine family. [Old English *furh.*]
fire (fīr) *n.* **1.** the flame, heat, and light given off in combustion. **2.a.** a mass of burning material, such as wood, coal, or other fuel: *He added another log to the fire.* **b.** some material arranged to be burned: *She lit the fire with one match.* **3.** an instance of destructive burning: *a forest fire.* **4.** something resembling or suggestive of fire because of its glow, luminosity, heat, or brilliance: *the fire of a sunset, the fire of a diamond.* **5.** intense emotional feeling or spirit; fervor; passion: *eyes full of fire, words of fire.* **6.** liveliness of imagination; capacity for ardor or zeal; animation: *the fire of youth.* **7.** fever or inflammation of the body or a part of the body: *the fire of disease.* **8.** a severe trial; overwhelming trouble: *the fire of affliction.* **9.** the discharge of firearms; shooting: *the crackle of rifle fire.* **10.** a rapid or intense series of verbal outbursts: *a fire of questions.* —*v.,* **fired, fir·ing.** —*v.t.* **1.** to supply with fuel; tend the fire of: *to fire a furnace.* **2.** to make burn; ignite: *to fire a heap of dead leaves.* **3.** to expose to the action of fire; process by the use of heat; bake: *to fire pottery.* **4.** to cause to shine or glow as if on fire: *The setting sun fires the western sky.* **5.** to cause to explode, esp. by application of fire: *to fire gunpowder.* **6.** to discharge, as a gun or bullet: *to fire a shotgun.* **7.** to arouse the feelings or passions of; inflame; excite: *to fire someone's anger.* **8.** to animate; inspire: *to fire a child's imagination.* **9.** *Informal.* to direct or hurl forcibly or suddenly: *to fire a puck toward the goal, to fire questions at a witness.* **10.** *Informal.* to dismiss from a position; discharge: *The firm fired seven employees.* —*v.i.* **1.** to discharge artillery or firearms; shoot: *The enemy fired on the town.* **2.** to go off, as a gun: *The gun fired accidentally.* **3.** to become inflamed, angered, or excited: *I fired at their accusations.* **4.** to show a certain result or reaction after being fired in a kiln: *The glaze fired poorly and cracked.* **5.** to begin burning; ignite. [Old English *fȳr* flame, burning material.] —**fir′er,** *n.*
   • **between two fires.** under physical or verbal attack from both sides.
   • **on fire. a.** burning; ignited. **b.** inflamed or overwhelmed with intense emotional feeling; eager; zealous; passionate.
   • **to catch fire.** to begin to burn; become ignited.
   • **to fire away.** *Informal.* to begin or start, esp. with energy or rapidity.
   • **to fire up. a.** to start a fire, as in an engine, furnace, or boiler. **b.** to become or cause to become irritated, angry, or excited.
   • **to go through fire and water.** to experience or endure great danger, hardships, or trials.
   • **to hang fire. a.** to fail or be slow to discharge: *The cannon hung fire.* **b.** to be slow in acting; hesitate: *The legislature hung fire on the tax question.* **c.** to be delayed: *The deal hung fire for several weeks.*
   • **to lay a fire.** to arrange material so that it may be burned.
   • **to open fire. a.** to begin to shoot: *They opened fire on the enemy.* **b.** to begin; commence.
   • **to play with fire.** to do or meddle with something dangerous or risky.
   • **to set fire to.** to cause to burn; ignite.
   • **to set on fire. a.** to cause to burn; ignite. **b.** to arouse an intense emotional feeling or spirit in; inflame; excite.
   • **to set the world on fire.** to achieve great success or fame; become renowned.
   • **to strike fire. a.** to produce a spark, as by friction. **b.** to evoke a response.
   • **to take fire. a.** to become ignited; begin to burn. **b.** to become aroused, excited, or zealous.

·under fire. a. exposed to the enemy's shooting or attack. **b.** exposed to verbal assault; subjected to criticism or censure.

fire alarm 1. a signal calling attention to a fire. **2.** an apparatus for giving such a signal.

fire ant, any of various ants, genus *Solenopsis,* whose sting feels like a burn, esp. a species originally from South America that is a major pest in the southeastern United States. [From the burning sensation caused by its bite.]

fire·arm (fīr′ärm′) *n.* a weapon from which shot is discharged by means of gases created by the rapid burning of an explosive charge, esp. such a weapon normally carried and fired by one person, as a rifle, pistol, or shotgun.

fire·ball (fīr′bôl′) *n.* **1.** something resembling a ball of fire, such as the sun or a globular burst of lightning. **2.** a brilliant meteor; shooting star. **3.** the luminous sphere of hot gases that forms after the detonation of a nuclear weapon. **4.** *Informal.* a dynamic, energetic person or thing.

fire·boat (fīr′bōt′) *n.* a boat equipped with apparatus for fighting fires.

fire·bomb (fīr′bom′) *n.* a bomb or missile designed to cause a fire. —*v.t.* to attack with a firebomb or firebombs. —**fire′-bomb′er,** *n.*

fire·box (fīr′boks′) *n.* **1.** a chamber in which fuel is burned, as in a furnace, boiler, or locomotive. **2.** a box with a device for sounding a fire alarm.

fire·brand (fīr′brand′) *n.* **1.** a piece of burning wood. **2.** a person who stirs up unrest or dissension; agitator.

fire·break (fīr′brāk′) *n.* a strip of land plowed or cleared to check the spread of a fire.

fire·brick (fīr′brik′) *n.* brick that can stand great heat, used to line furnaces and fireplaces.

fire·bug (fīr′bug′) *n. Informal.* a person who purposely sets destructive fires; incendiary; pyromaniac.

fire clay, a clay that can resist high temperatures, used for making such things as crucibles or firebricks.

fire company, a company of people established to put out fires.

fire·crack·er (fīr′krak′ər) *n.* a paper cylinder containing an explosive and an attached fuse, discharged as a noisemaker.

fire·damp (fīr′damp′) *n.* a gas that forms in coal mines, composed primarily of methane. It is dangerously explosive when mixed with certain proportions of air.

fire department 1. a municipal department organized and equipped to prevent and put out fires. **2.** the members of this department collectively.

fire·dog (fīr′dôg′) *n.* andiron.

fire drill, a practice drill, esp. in a school or aboard ship, involving the procedures to be followed in case of fire.

fire-eat·er (fīr′ē′tər) *n.* **1.** a performer who pretends to eat fire. **2.** a hotheaded person always ready to fight or quarrel.

fire engine, a truck designed to carry equipment with which to fight fire, esp. one that has a pumping apparatus to spray water or chemicals on the fire. Also, **fire truck.**

fire escape 1. a metal stairway attached to the outside of a building for use as a means of escape in case of fire. **2.** any device for similar use, such as a ladder.

fire extinguisher, an apparatus used to put out fires by spraying chemicals on them.

fire·fight·er (fīr′fī′tər) *n.* a person who is employed, as by a city, or who volunteers, to extinguish and prevent fires; member of a fire department.

fire·fight·ing (fīr′fī′ting) *n.* the work of a firefighter. —*adj.* of, relating to, or used in the work of a firefighter: *firefighting equipment.*

fire·fly (fīr′flī′) *n., pl.* **-flies.** any of a number of soft-bodied beetles, family Lampyridae, widely distributed throughout the world, that have specialized abdominal organs that give off flashes of phosphorescent light as a mating signal. Also, **lightning bug.**

firefly

fire·house (fīr′hous′) *n., pl.* **-hous·es** (-hou′ziz). a building housing a fire company and its equipment. Also, **fire station.**

fire hydrant, hydrant.

fire insurance, insurance covering property damage or loss by fire.

fire·less (fīr′lis) *adj.* without fire.

fireless cooker, an insulated container that retains heat long enough to allow food to cook or be kept warm without further heating of the container.

fire·light (fīr′līt′) *n.* the light from a fire, esp. an open fire.

fire·lock (fīr′lok′) *n. Archaic.* any of various types of gunlocks, such as the flintlock, in which sparks were produced to ignite the priming.

fire·man (fīr′mən) *n., pl.* **-men** (-mən). **1.** firefighter. **2.** a person who tends the fire in a furnace or steam engine, esp. on a locomotive; stoker. **3.** an enlisted person in the navy who tends engineering machinery aboard a ship.

fire·place (fīr′plās′) *n.* an open structure or recess in which a fire is built, esp. such a recess opening into a room at the base of a chimney.

fire·plug (fīr′plug′) *n.* a hydrant for supplying water in case of fire.

fire pot 1. that part of a stove or furnace in which the fire is made. **2.** crucible.

fire·pow·er (fīr′pou′ər) *n. Military.* **1.** the amount of fire that can be delivered by any particular weapon, unit, or weapon system. **2.** the ability to deliver such fire.

fire·proof (fīr′prūf′) *adj.* resistant to fire; comparatively incombustible. —*v.t.* to make resistant to fire.

fire sale, a special sale of goods damaged by fire.

fire screen, a metal screen placed in front of a fireplace to prevent sparks from entering the room.

fire ship, a ship loaded with combustibles and explosives and directed so that it will explode when it reaches an enemy target or position, such as a ship or bridge.

fire·side (fīr′sīd′) *n.* **1.** the space around a fireplace; hearth. **2.** the home or home life. —*adj.* **1.** of, in, or near the hearth or home. **2.** suitable to the hearth or home; informal or intimate.

fire station, firehouse.

fire tower, a watchtower, usually overlooking a forest, where a lookout is posted to watch for and report fires.

fire·trap (fīr′trap′) *n.* a building that is highly flammable or lacks adequate means of escape in case of fire.

fire truck, fire engine.

fire wall 1. a wall of fire-resistant material designed to prevent the spread of fire from one room or compartment to another. **2.** a fireproof plate behind the engine of an automobile or aircraft.

fire·ward·en (fīr′wôr′dən) *n.* an official charged with the prevention and extinguishing of fires, esp. forest fires.

fire·wa·ter (fīr′wô′tər, -wot′ər) *n. Informal.* hard liquor, esp. whiskey. [Probably translation of Ojibwa *ishkodewaaboo* literally, burning water (whiskey, rum, brandy), from *ishkoden* fire + *aaboo* liquid, water.]

fire·weed (fīr′wēd′) *n.* a weedy plant, *Epilobium angustifolium,* of the evening primrose family, found throughout Eurasia and North America, bearing narrow, lance-shaped leaves and striking clusters of purple-pink, red, or white flowers. It often appears in areas cleared by fires.

fire·wood (fīr′wŭd′) *n.* wood for fuel.

fire·works (fīr′wûrks′) *pl. n.* **1.** combustible or explosive devices ignited to produce a brilliant display of light or loud noises. **2.** a show or display in which such devices are exploded. **3.** *Informal.* any loud or dramatic controversy or clash: *The scandal caused political fireworks.*

fir·ing (fīr′ing) *n.* **1.** the act or process of subjecting to fire or intense heat, as in baking and glazing pottery. **2.** the discharge of firearms. **3.** fuel, as firewood or coal.

firing line 1. a line from which shooting is done, as in battle or on a firing range. **2.** the foremost position in any action or activity.

firing pin, the part of a firearm that strikes the primer to explode the charge.

firing squad 1. a detachment assigned to execute a person condemned to death by shooting. **2.** a detachment of troops assigned to fire a volley of shots as a tribute at a military funeral.

fir·kin (fûr′kin) *n.* **1.** a British measure of capacity equal to one fourth of a barrel. **2.** a wooden cask or tub used for holding food, such as butter or fish.

firm¹ (fûrm) *adj.* **1.** relatively solid or compact in structure or texture; unyielding to pressure: *The frozen ground is firm.* **2.** securely fixed; not easily moved; stable: *a firm foundation.* **3.** unalterably fixed or settled; immutable: *a firm belief, firm convictions, a firm deal.* **4.** steadfast and unwavering; resolute: *a firm friendship, firm supporters.* **5.** having or indicating determination or

a	at	e	end	o	hot	u	up	hw	white		about
ā	ape	ē	me	ō	old	ū	use	ng	song		taken
ä	far	i	it	ô	fork	ü	rule	th	thin	ə	pencil
âr	care	ī	ice	oi	oil	u̇	pull	th	this		lemon
		î	pierce	ou	out	ûr	turn	zh	measure		circus

F

solidity; steady: *a firm voice, to write with a firm hand.* **6.** not fluctuating widely; steady, as prices. —*adv.* in a firm manner: *The stock market held firm. The workers stood firm in their demands.* —*v.t., v.i.* to make or become firm (often with *up*): *Exercise will firm your muscles. The dessert firmed in the mold.* [Old French *ferme* strong, from Latin *firmus* steadfast, strong.] —**firm′ly,** *adv.* —**firm′ness,** *n.*

Synonyms *adj.* **Firm¹, hard,** and **solid** may all mean resisting distortion or pressure. **Firm** connotes an ability to absorb some pressure by giving way slightly and temporarily: *The court surface is firm but not hard, so that a player who falls will not be injured.* **Hard** is used to describe an unyielding surface that will not give way at all: *a hard cover to protect delicate instruments.* **Solid** connotes compactness and denseness that allow something to resist change: *This wall is too solid to be knocked down easily.*

firm² (fûrm) *n.* **1.** a company or partnership of two or more persons for carrying on a business; business establishment: *to join a law firm.* **2.** the name or title under which a company carries on business. [Italian *firma* name of a business partnership, signature, from *firmare* to confirm in writing, sign, from Late Latin *firmāre* to confirm by signature, from Latin *firmāre* to strengthen, from *firmos* steadfast, strong.]

fir·ma·ment (fûr′mə mənt) *n.* the expanse of the heavens; sky. [Latin *firmāmentum* support, extent of the sky.]

fir·man (fûr′mən, fər män′) *n., pl.* **-mans.** an edict or decree issued by a Middle Eastern sovereign. [Persian *fermān* order.]

firm·ware (fûrm′wâr′) *n.* computer programs or data stored permanently in ROM.

firn (fîrn) *n.* névé. [German *firn* of last year, old.]

first (fûrst) *adj.* **1.** (the ordinal of one) preceding all others in an order or series. **2.** preceding all others in time; earliest: *George Washington was the first president of the United States.* **3.** foremost in importance, estimation, dignity, or excellence; superior; highest; best: *to be first among writers of one's era.* **4.** *Music.* (of a performer or instrument) playing or singing the instrumental or vocal part of highest pitch or principal melodic importance: *first violin, first tenor.* **5.** denoting or being the lowest forward gear of a mechanical transmission, as in an automobile. —*adv.* **1.** before all other persons or things, as in order, rank, or importance: *She was chosen first.* **2.** before any other action, time, or event: *First, apologize to him.* **3.** for the first time: *I first heard of it yesterday.* **4.** in preference to something else; rather; sooner: *I would starve first.* —*n.* **1.** a person or thing that is first, as in rank, importance, order, time, or place: *That engine was the first of its type.* **2.** the first day of a month: *Bills are received on the first.* **3.** the time at which something begins or began: *From the first, our group was part of the project.* **4.** the winning place, as in a race or contest: *First went to the American team.* **5.** the lowest forward gear, as of an automobile. **6.** first base. **7. firsts.** commercial articles of the highest quality or finest grade. [Old English *fyrst* earliest, foremost.]
· **first and last.** more than everything else: *to be first and last a patriot.*
· **first thing.** before anything else: *I'll take care of it first thing tomorrow.*

first aid, emergency treatment given to an ill or injured person before full medical care can be obtained. —**first′-aid′,** *adj.*

First Amendment, an amendment to the United States Constitution, ratified in 1791 and part of the Bill of Rights. It prohibits Congress from passing laws that would establish any religion as official or that would infringe on freedom of religion, speech, or the press, or on the right of citizens to assemble to petition the government.

first base *Baseball.* **1.** the base that a batter must reach first on the way around the bases. **2.** the position of a player stationed in the area near this base.
· **to get to first base.** *Slang.* to make initial progress toward some goal: *Our sales representative never got to first base with that client.*

first-born (fûrst′bôrn′) *adj.* born first; eldest. —*n.* a first-born child.

first cause 1. a cause not stemming from any other, or that cannot be analyzed as owing to any other; ultimate cause or origin. **2. First Cause.** *Theology.* God.

first-class (fûrst′klas′) *adj.* **1.** of the highest rank or best quality: *a first-class performance.* **2.** designating a class of mail consisting primarily of letters, parcels, and other written or sealed matter meeting certain governmental limits, as on size or weight,

and carrying the highest regular postage rate. **3.** designating the best-equipped or most luxurious accommodations on a train, ship, or airplane. —*adv.* by first-class mail or conveyance: *We sent the package first-class.*

first class 1. first-class travel accommodations. **2.** first-class mail.

First Day, Sunday. ➠ used by the Society of Friends.

first-de·gree burn (fûrst′di grē′) a burn of the outer layer of the skin; burn that causes redness.

first fruits 1. the earliest produce of the season. **2.** the first profits, products, or results of anything.

first·hand (fûrst′hand′) *adj.* direct from the original source or producer: *firsthand knowledge of an event.* —*adv.* from the original source: *to learn of something firsthand.*

first lady 1. the wife of the president of the United States or of a state governor, or of the leader of a foreign country. **2.** a leading or outstanding woman in a particular field or profession: *the first lady of the theater.*

first lieutenant, an officer in the U.S. Army, Air Force, or Marine Corps ranking above a second lieutenant and below a captain.

first·ling (fûrst′ling) *n.* **1.** the first of its class or kind. **2.** the first product or result of something. **3.** the first offspring of an animal.

first·ly (fûrst′lē) *adv.* in the first place; first.

first night, the night of a first performance, as of a play or opera.

first-night·er (fûrst′nī′tər) *n.* a person who regularly attends opening performances, as of plays or operas.

first person, the form of a pronoun or verb that indicates the speaker, such as the pronoun *I,* or a group in which the speaker is included, as *we.*

first quarter, the half moon that follows a new moon.

first-rate (fûrst′rāt′) *adj.* **1.** of the highest class, quality, or importance: *a first-rate military power.* **2.** *Informal.* excellent; very good: *a first-rate tennis player.* —*adv.* *Informal.* excellently.

first sergeant, a senior noncommissioned officer of a company or similar military unit.

first string, the players that comprise the regular or starting lineup of an athletic team, as distinguished from substitutes. —**first′-string′,** *adj.*

first water 1. the highest degree of quality in a diamond or other gem. **2.** the highest degree, grade, or quality: *a scoundrel of the first water.*

firth (fûrth) *n.* **1.** a long, narrow arm of the sea. **2.** the lower part of an estuary. Also, **frith.** [Old Norse *fjörthr.*]

fisc (fisk) *n.* *Archaic.* a royal or state treasury; exchequer. [Latin *fiscus* purse, treasury; originally, a basket used to hold money.]

fis·cal (fis′kəl) *adj.* **1.** relating to the treasury, finances, or revenues of a government: *fiscal policy.* **2.** relating to money matters; financial. —*n.* a public prosecutor in some countries. [Late Latin *fiscālis* relating to the treasury, from Latin *fiscus* treasury. See FISC.] —**fis′cal·ly,** *adv.*

fiscal year, any twelve-month period used as a basis for settling financial accounts in a business or government. The fiscal year of the U.S. government begins July 1.

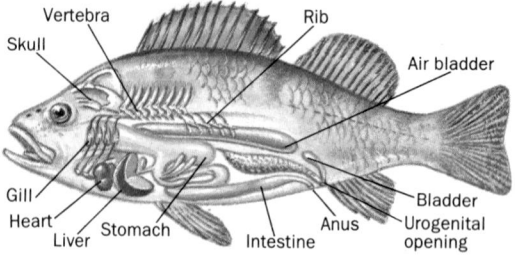

internal view of a **fish**

fish (fish) *n., pl.* **fish** or **fish·es.** ➠ The plural form **fishes** is used esp. when referring to more than one kind or species of fish. **1.** a cold-blooded aquatic vertebrate having gills for respiration, fins for mobility, and, usually, a scaly external covering for protection. Fish, which outnumber all other backboned animals, comprise three classes of the subphylum Vertebrata. **2.** any of various other animals that inhabit the water, such as a porpoise, starfish, or cuttlefish. **3.** the flesh of fish used as food. **4.** *Informal.* a person thought to have the characteristics of a fish, such as lack of

emotion or intelligence. **5.** a flat strip, as of iron or wood, fastened alongside a beam or mast to strengthen it. —*v.t.* **1.** to catch or try to catch fish in: *to fish a stream.* **2.** to catch or try to catch (fish): *to fish eels.* **3.** to search for, as by groping; find and bring to the surface (often with *up* or *out*): *She fished the keys out of her purse.* —*v.i.* **1.** to catch or try to catch fish: *They fished all day.* **2.** to get or try to get by cunning or artifice: *He fished for an invitation to the party.* **3.** to look; search: *I fished in my pocket for a nickel.* [Old English *fisc* animal that lives in water.]

 · **like a fish out of water.** ill at ease, as if out of one's customary or familiar environment.
 · **other fish to fry.** other more important things to attend to.
 · **to fish in troubled waters.** to take advantage of a disturbance or troubled situation to achieve one's ends.
 · **to fish or cut bait.** to go ahead with a task, project, or the like or give it up; act immediately or quit.
 · **to fish out.** to deplete the supply of fish in.

fish and chips, fish fillets and potatoes, cut into short, broad strips and deep fried.

fish ball, fish cake.

fish·bowl (fish′bōl′) *n.* **1.** a glass bowl serving as an aquarium for small fish. **2.** an area of activity completely exposed to public view or scrutiny.

fish cake, a fried patty or ball made of chopped fish, usually cod, and mashed potato. Also, **fish ball.**

fish·er (fish′ər) *n.* **1.** fisherman. **2.** any animal that catches fish for food. **3.** a carnivorous North American mammal, *Martes pennanti,* of the marten family, having a long body, short legs, and a pointed face. Length: 40 inches (102 centimeters), including tail. **4.** the dark brown fur of this animal.

fish·er·man (fish′ər mən) *n., pl.* **-men** (-mən). **1.** a person who fishes as an occupation or for sport. **2.** a boat used in commercial fishing.

fish·er·y (fish′ə rē) *n., pl.* **-er·ies. 1.** the occupation or industry of catching fish or taking other products from seas, lakes, or rivers. **2.** a place for catching fish or other sea products; fishing ground. **3.** fish hatchery.

fish-eye lens (fish′ī′) an extremely wide-angle lens for taking photographs that cover a field of view of up to 180 degrees, producing a circular image with increasing distortion toward the outside edge.

fish farm, a place where fish are raised, usually in large pools, to be sold as food.

fish glue, a glue derived from bones and waste parts of fish, used in paints and sizes.

fish hatchery, an establishment for the hatching and growing of fish under controlled conditions.

fish hawk, osprey.

fish·hook (fish′hŭk′) *n.* a hook, usually barbed, for catching fish.

fish·ing (fish′ing) *n.* **1.** the occupation or sport of catching fish. **2.** a place to catch fish.

fishing pole, fishing rod. Also, **fish pole.**

fishing rod, a long pole, usually made of wood, metal, or fiberglass, with a line, hook, and usually a reel attached to it, used to catch fish.

fishing tackle, equipment used for fishing, such as rods, lines, hooks, and nets.

fish ladder, an arrangement of successive ascending pools of water by which fish can pass around a dam or waterfall in swimming upstream.

fish·line (fish′līn′) *n.* a line, usually with a hook attached, used for fishing.

fish meal, ground, dried fish, used chiefly as a fertilizer or animal feed.

fish·mon·ger (fish′mung′gər, -mong′-) *n.* a merchant who deals in fish.

fish·net (fish′net′) *n.* **1.** a net for catching fish. **2.** meshed fabric resembling the netting used for catching fish.

fish·plate (fish′plāt′) *n.* a plate for fastening two rails or beams end to end, as on a railroad track.

fish·pond (fish′pond′) *n.* a pond containing fish, esp. a pond stocked with edible fish for sport or food.

fish stick, an oblong, flattened fish fillet breaded and fried.

fish story *Informal.* an exaggerated or improbable story. [From the belief that people who fish habitually exaggerate in describing the size of fish.]

fish·tail (fish′tāl′) *adj.* resembling a fish's tail in shape or action. —*v.i.* to move forward with the rear end swinging from side to side in the manner of a fish's tail: *The car fishtailed as it sped around the sharp curve.*

fish·wife (fish′wīf′) *n., pl.* **-wives** (-wīvz′). **1.** a woman who sells fish. **2.** a coarse, abusive woman.

fish·y (fish′ē) *adj.,* **fish·i·er, fish·i·est. 1.** resembling a fish, as in odor or taste. **2.** consisting of fish. **3.** abounding in fish. **4.** *Informal.* not likely to be true; improbable; unlikely: *a fishy story.* **5.** *Informal.* of questionable character; suspicious: *fishy business.* **6.** vacant of expression; dull: *a fishy stare.* —**fish′i·ly,** *adv.* —**fish′i·ness,** *n.*

fis·sile (fis′əl) *adj.* **1.** capable of being split or divided. **2.** fissionable. **3.** tending to split. [Latin *fissilis* that may be split, from *findere* to split.]

fis·sion (fish′ən) *n.* **1.** the act of splitting or breaking apart. **2.** *Physics.* the splitting of a heavy atomic nucleus into two lighter ones, occurring when the nucleus is bombarded by and absorbs a neutron. When fission is initiated in a nuclear reactor, a chain reaction results, releasing energy that can be utilized as an efficient power source. **3.** *Biology.* a method of asexual reproduction in which the parent cell divides to form two or more new individuals. Many single-celled plants and animals reproduce by means of fission. —*v.i., v.t.* to undergo or cause to undergo fission. [Latin *fissiō* a cleaving.] —**fis′sion·a·ble,** *adj.*

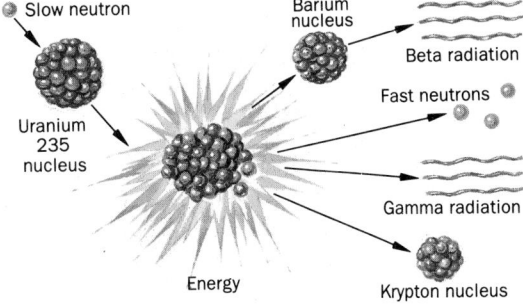

fission of uranium 235

fis·sion·a·ble (fish′ə nə bəl) *adj.* (of an element or isotope) capable of undergoing nuclear fission. Uranium, plutonium, and thorium are fissionable materials.

fission bomb, atomic bomb.

fis·sure (fish′ər) *n.* **1.** a long, narrow opening; cleft or crack: *a fissure in a rock.* **2.** the act of splitting apart or the state of being split; cleavage. —*v.t., v.i.,* **-sured, -sur·ing.** to split or be split apart; cleave. [Latin *fissūra* a cleft.]

fist (fist) *n.* **1.** a hand clenched with fingers doubled into the palm. **2.** *Informal.* **a.** grasp; grip; clutch. **b.** hand. **c.** handwriting. **3.** *Printing.* index *(def. 7).* [Old English *fȳst* clenched hand.]

fist·ful (fist′fŭl′) *n., pl.* **-fuls.** handful.

fist·ic (fis′tik) *adj. Informal.* of or relating to boxing or fighting with the fists; pugilistic.

fist·i·cuffs (fis′ti kufs′) *pl. n.* **1.** a fight with the fists, esp. bare fists. **2.** the art of boxing.

fis·tu·la (fis′chə lə) *n., pl.* **-las** or **-lae** (-lē′). a tubelike passage that connects body cavities or organs that are normally not connected, either congenital or resulting from the improper healing of a wound or abscess. [Latin *fistula* tube, ulcer.]

fis·tu·lous (fis′chə ləs) *adj.* **1.** of, relating to, or resembling a fistula. **2.** hollow and cylindrical, like a pipe or reed; tubelike. **3.** having or consisting of tubelike parts. Also, **fis′tu·lar.**

fit[1] (fit) *adj.,* **fit·ter, fit·test. 1.** adapted to or qualified for an end, object, or purpose; appropriate; suited: *This dress style is fit for a long, slender figure.* **2.** becoming; right; proper: *It was a fit occasion to announce their engagement.* **3.** possessing the necessary qualifications; competent: *Either candidate is fit to lead the government.* **4.** being in a proper state; ready; prepared: *The fruit will be fit to eat in three days.* **5.** in good physical or mental condition; healthy: *I'm exercising to stay fit.* —*v.,* **fit·ted, fit·ting.** —*v.t.* **1.** to be suitable or proper for; be adapted to; befit: *Let the punishment fit the crime.* **2.** to be of the proper or correct

a	at	e	end	o	hot	u	up	hw	white	⎧	about
ā	ape	ē	me	ō	old	ū	use	ng	song		taken
ä	far	i	it	ô	fork	ü	rule	th	thin	ə ⎨	pencil
âr	care	ī	ice	oi	oil	u̇	pull	th	this		lemon
		îr	pierce	ou	out	ûr	turn	zh	measure	⎩	circus

size or shape for: *The coat fits you well.* **3.** to make fit or suitable; alter; adjust: *to fit a coat to the occasion.* **4.** to make ready; prepare or qualify: *The management course will fit you for your new position.* **5.** to supply with what is necessary or suitable; equip (often with *out* or *up*): *The society fitted out the members of the expedition with supplies.* **6.** to adjust, join, or insert precisely: *to fit the pieces of a jigsaw puzzle together.* **7.** to make or arrange to conform or correspond to something else: *We will fit our plans to yours.* **8.** to measure for something: *The tailor fitted me for a new suit.* —*v.i.* **1.** to be suitable, proper, or becoming. **2.** to be of the proper size or shape: *The coat fits perfectly.* **3.** to be in harmony or accord; be adapted (with *in* or *into*): *That painting does not fit in with the others in the room.* —*n.* **1.** the manner in which something fits: *a loose fit.* **2.** anything that fits or is fitted: *The dress is a perfect fit.* [Middle English *fitten,* possibly from Old Norse *fitja* to knit.] —**fit′ly,** *adv.* —**fit′ness,** *n.*

Synonyms *adj.* **Fit¹, suitable,** and **appropriate** mean right for a purpose or circumstance. **Fit** generally connotes having the required attributes or qualities: *a meal fit for royalty, a tool fit for the job.* **Suitable** and **appropriate** are often interchangeable, although *suitable* more often connotes something that is practical for a particular purpose while *appropriate* is more likely to be used of something that is correct for a particular occasion: *a sturdy pair of shoes suitable for walking in the country, a dressy outfit appropriate for a formal wedding.*

fit² (fit) *n.* **1.a.** an acute, sudden attack of illness, esp. a chronic one: *a fit of the gout.* **b.** a sudden attack or seizure, esp. when resulting in unconsciousness: *a fainting fit.* **2.** a sudden, quickly passing outburst of emotion or feeling: *a fit of anger, a fit of laughter.* **3.** an impulsive and irregular effort or activity: *In a fit of meticulousness, we cleaned the whole house.* [Old English *fitt* conflict.]
 • **by** (or **in**) **fits and starts.** in a spasmodic or irregular manner.
 • **to have** (or **throw**) **a fit.** *Informal.* to show extreme anger; become upset.

fitch (fich) *n.* **1.** polecat. **2.** its buff-gray, black-tipped fur, used to make coats and jackets. [Middle Dutch *vitsche* polecat.]

fit·ful (fit′fəl) *adj.* irregular or intermittent, as in occurrence or behavior; spasmodic. [FIT² + -FUL.] —**fit′ful·ly,** *adv.* —**fit′-ful·ness,** *n.*

fit·ter (fit′ər) *n.* **1.** a person who fits or alters garments. **2.a.** a person who adjusts or assembles parts or machinery. **b.** a person who supplies, installs, and fixes fittings and fixtures of any kind. **3.** a person who furnishes all necessary equipment and supplies for an undertaking, esp. an expedition; outfitter.

fit·ting (fit′ing) *adj.* suitable, as for an occasion; proper; appropriate: *fitting praise, a fitting conclusion.* —*n.* **1.** the act of a person who fits. **2.** the trying on of an article of clothing so that it can be marked for adjustments. **3.** an accessory part or attachment used to adjust something: *a pipe fitting.* **4. fittings.** furnishings, fixtures, or decorations, as for a house or automobile. —**fit′ting·ly,** *adv.* —**fit′ting·ness,** *n.* —For Synonyms *(adj.)*, see **proper.**

five (fīv) *n.* **1.** the cardinal number that is one more than four. **2.** a symbol representing this number, such as 5 or V. **3.** something having this many units or members, such as a basketball team or a playing card. —*adj.* numbering one more than four. [Old English *fīf.*]

five-and-ten (fīv′ən ten′) *n.* a store offering a wide variety of inexpensive merchandise. Also, **dime store, five-and-dime, five-and-ten-cent store.** [Because such stores originally sold many articles costing five or ten cents.]

five·fold (fīv′fōld′) *adj.* **1.** five times as great or numerous. **2.** having or consisting of five parts. —*adv.* so as to be five times greater or more numerous.

Five Nations, Iroquois.

fives (fīvz) *n.* an English game similar to handball.

five-year plan (fīv′yîr′) any of several programs for national economic development, esp. in a socialist country, intended to be completed within a five-year period.

fix (fiks) *v.,* **fixed** or **fixt, fix·ing.** —*v.t.* **1.** to mend; repair: *to fix a broken chair.* **2.** to prepare (food or a meal): *to fix dinner.* **3.** to make firm, stable, or secure; fasten tightly: *to fix a stake in the ground.* **4.** to establish firmly in the mind. **5.** to place permanently; set: *to fix a bracket to a wall.* **6.** to settle or arrange definitely; set: *to fix a price, to fix a wedding date.* **7.** to determine or specify with certainty; establish as fact: *to fix the details of an event.* **8.** to direct or hold, as the eyes or attention, steadily: *He fixed his gaze on her.* **9.** to attract and hold fast; arrest: *to fix the attention of an audience.* **10.** to make rigid or motionless. **11.** to

place, assign, or impose upon: *to fix blame, to fix a responsibility.* **12.** to treat so as to make permanent or lasting: *to fix colors in a fabric.* **13.** to cause (insoluble gaseous nitrogen) to combine with other substances into a soluble compound. **14.** *Photography.* to treat (a photograph) with a chemical solution to prevent fading. **15.** *Informal.* to put in order; get ready (often with *up*): *We fixed up the room for our guest.* **16.** *Informal.* to prearrange or influence the result of (a contest) to one's advantage, as by a bribe: *to fix a race, to fix a basketball game.* **17.** *Informal.* to get revenge upon; get even with; punish: *I'll fix you yet!* **18.** to spay or castrate: *to fix a cat.* —*v.i.* **1.** to become firm, stable, secure, or permanent: *The stain fixes if you wash it in hot water.* **2.** *Informal.* to get ready; prepare: *We're fixing to leave.* —*n.* **1.** *Informal.* a position from which it is difficult to escape; difficulty; predicament: *I got myself into a fix by accepting two dates for the same dance.* **2.** *Informal.* prearrangement of the result or outcome of a contest, such as an athletic event, by illegal means. **3.** *Slang.* a dosage of a narcotic. **4.** the position of a ship or aircraft, as determined by observations or from radio signals: *The SOS helped rescue crews get a fix on the disabled freighter.* [Latin *fīxus,* past participle of *fīgere* to fasten.] —**fix′a·ble,** *adj.*
 • **to fix on** (or **upon**). to decide on; choose; select: *We fixed on a plan after much discussion.*
 • **to fix up.** *Informal.* **a.** to mend; repair: *to fix up a broken chair.* **b.** to provide what is needed for; accommodate: *We fixed them up for the evening at our house.*

Synonyms *v.t.* **Fix, set,** and **determine** mean to make firm and definite. **Fix** suggests establishing something that is not to be changed: *to fix a price below which the product will not be sold.* **Set** similarly denotes establishing something, but implies less permanence: *to set a date for a meeting.* **Determine** emphasizes the process of taking account of relevant factors before settling something: *to determine the time for a meeting after checking the schedules of the key participants.* For other Synonyms *(v.t.),* see **mend.**

fix·ate (fik′sāt) *v.,* **-at·ed, -at·ing.** —*v.i.* **1.** to become fixed, as one's gaze or attention. **2.** to develop an obsessive preoccupation or attachment: *to fixate on one small problem.* —*v.t.* **1.** to focus one's gaze or attention on (something): *I gazed at everything, fixating no special object.* **2.** to make fixed so that a habit is established. [From FIXATION.]

fix·a·tion (fik sā′shən) *n.* **1.** the act of fixing or the state of being fixed. **2.** a treatment to prevent dyes or colors from fading, as in film. **3.** nitrogen fixation. **4.** an obsessive preoccupation or attachment to a person, thing, or idea.

fix·a·tive (fik′sə tiv) *n.* something that serves to fix, make permanent, or promote fixation, esp. a substance sprayed on a charcoal or crayon drawing to preserve it. —*adj.* serving to fix or make permanent.

fixed (fikst) *adj.* **1.** made firm in position; securely placed or fastened; not movable; stationary: *fixed seats.* **2.** steadily intent or directed; rigid; set: *a fixed stare.* **3.** not fluctuating; settled; unalterable: *a fixed rate of interest.* **4.** definite; resolute: *a fixed purpose.* **5.** *Chemistry.* **a.** not volatile. **b.** incorporated into a stable compound. **6.** *Informal.* prearranged privately or dishonestly as to outcome or decision: *a fixed race.* **8.** *Informal.* provided with something, esp. money: *They are very well fixed.* —**fix·ed·ly** (fik′sid lē), *adv.* —**fix′ed·ness,** *n.*

fixed-point (fikst′point′) *adj.* of, relating to, or designating a representation of real numbers in which each number has a fixed number of digits before the decimal point, a fixed number of digits after the decimal point, and a plus or minus sign.

fixed star, a star that is so far from the earth that it appears to remain in the same position in relation to other stars.

fix·er (fik′sər) *n.* **1.** a person or thing that fixes. **2.** a person who prearranges or influences the result of something, as a contest or race, by bribery or other means. **3.** *Photography.* a chemical substance, as sodium thiosulfate, used in developing photographs to promote fixation; fixative. [FIX + -ER¹.]

fix·ings (fik′singz) *pl. n. Informal.* accessories; trimmings; garnishes: *a turkey dinner with all the fixings.*

fix·i·ty (fik′si tē) *n., pl.* **-ties. 1.** the state or quality of being fixed; stability; permanence. **2.** something that is fixed into position.

fixt (fikst) a past tense and past participle of **fix.**

fix·ture (fiks′chər) *n.* **1.** anything fixed or securely fastened into position, esp. a permanently attached part or accessory of a house: *bathroom fixtures.* **2.** a person or thing permanently established or regarded as fixed in a particular place or job. [Modification (influenced by *mixture*) of obsolete *fixure* fixed condition, from Late Latin *fīxūra* a fastening, from Latin *fīgere* to fasten.]

fizz (fiz) *v.i.* to make a hissing or sputtering sound. —*n.* **1.** a hissing or sputtering sound. **2.** an effervescent beverage, such as champagne or soda water. **3.** a mixed drink made with liquor, soda water, and flavorings: *a gin fizz.* [Imitative.]

fiz·zle (fiz′əl) *v.i.,* **-zled, -zling. 1.** to make a hissing or sputtering sound: *The wet wood fizzled in the fireplace.* **2.** *Informal.* to fail or end feebly, esp. after a good start (often with *out*): *All our plans fizzled out.* —*n.* **1.** a hissing or sputtering sound. **2.** *Informal.* an abortive effort; failure. [FIZZ + -LE.]

fizz·y (fiz′ē) *adj.,* **fizz·i·er, fizz·i·est.** fizzing; effervescent.

fjord in Norway

fjord (fyôrd) *also,* **fiord.** *n.* a deep narrow inlet of the sea between high steep banks or cliffs, esp. one along the coast of Norway. [Norwegian *fjord,* from Old Norse *fjörthr.*]

Fl, fluorine.

fl. 1. floor. **2.** florin. **3.** flourished. ➡ used before a date or dates when a person was at a peak of activity, creativity, or success or is generally accepted as having been alive. **4.** fluid.

FL, the postal abbreviation for Florida.

Fla., Florida.

flab (flab) *n. Informal.* **1.** something that is soft and lacks firmness, esp. sagging, excessive flesh: *Without exercise, muscles can turn to flab.* **2.** an excessive amount of anything: *to cut the flab out of city spending.* [From FLABBY.]

flab·ber·gast (flab′ər gast′) *v.t. Informal.* to surprise greatly; astonish; confound. [Possibly blend of FLABBY and AGHAST.]

flab·by (flab′ē) *adj.,* **-bi·er, -bi·est. 1.** lacking firmness; soft; flaccid: *flabby skin.* **2.** lacking substance or force; weak: *flabby logic.* [Form of earlier *flappy,* from FLAP + -Y¹.] —**flab′bi·ly,** *adv.* —**flab′bi·ness,** *n.*

flac·cid (flak′sid, flas′id) *adj.* lacking firmness or elasticity; limp; weak: *flaccid muscles.* [Latin *flaccidus* flabby.] —**flac·cid′i·ty,** *n.*

flack (flak) flak.

fla·con (flak′ən, flȧ kôn′) *n.* a small bottle or flask with a stopper. [French *flacon* bottle, vial, from Old French *flascon* bottle. See FLAGON.]

flag¹ (flag) *n.* **1.** a piece of cloth or bunting of varying size and colors with symbolic emblems or devices, used to represent something, such as a country or organization, or as a signaling device. **2.** something suggesting a flag, such as the bushy tail of a dog or deer. **3. flags. a.** feathers on the second joint of a bird's wing. **b.** long feathers on the lower parts of certain birds' legs. —*v.t.,* **flagged, flag·ging. 1.** to put a flag or flags over or on; decorate or adorn with flags. **2.** to stop or signal with or as with a flag: *to flag a taxicab.* **3.** to communicate (information) by signaling with a flag or flags: *to flag a message.* **4.** to decoy (game) by waving a flag or similar object to attract attention. [Middle English *flagge,* possibly from Old Norse *flogra* to flutter.]

 •**to flag down.** to signal (something or someone) to stop by using a flag or by a waving motion: *to flag down a train.*

flag² (flag) *n.* **1.** any of various irises having sword-shaped leaves and blue, yellow, purple, or white flowers. **2.** the flower of

any of these plants. **3.** sweet flag. [Middle English *flagge* reed, rush; of uncertain origin.]

flag³ (flag) *v.i.,* **flagged, flag·ging. 1.** to run low in interest or activity; grow weak or tired; lose vigor: *The child's interest flagged.* **2.** to hang down; become limp; droop: *When the wind died down, the sails flagged.* [Probably from Old Norse *flogra* to flutter.]

flag⁴ (flag) *n.* flagstone. —*v.t.,* **flagged, flag·ging.** to pave with flagstones. [Middle English *flagge* flagstone, block of peat, from Old Norse *flaga* slab of stone.]

Flag Day, the anniversary of the day in 1777 when the Stars and Stripes was adopted as the official flag of the United States. It is observed on June 14.

flag·el·lant (flaj′ə lənt, flə jel′ənt) *n.* a person who whips, esp. one who whips himself or herself, or is whipped, for religious reasons or for sexual excitement. —*adj.* flagellating. [Latin *flagellāns,* present participle of *flagellāre.* See FLAGELLATE.]

flag·el·late (*adj.,* flaj′ə lit, -lāt′; *v.,* flaj′ə lāt′) *adj.* **1.** having a flagellum or flagella. **2.** shaped like a flagellum. Also, **flag′ellat′ed.** —*v.t.,* **-lat·ed, -lat·ing.** to whip; scourge. —*n.* any of a class of protozoans that use a flagellum to move and to obtain food. The euglena is a flagellate. [Latin *flagellātus,* past participle of *flagellāre* to scourge, going back to *flagrum* whip.] —**flag′ella′tion,** *n.*

fla·gel·lum (flə jel′əm) *n., pl.* **-gel·la** (-jel′ə) or **-gel·lums. 1.** a long, whiplike projection that serves as an organ of locomotion in certain cells, bacteria, and protozoa. **2.** whip. [Latin *flagellum* whip, diminutive of *flagrum.*]

flag·eo·let (flaj′ə let′) *n.* a wind instrument of the flute family, similar to the recorder, having six finger holes, four on the top and two on the underside. [French *flageolet* pipe, flute, diminutive of Old French *flageol* flute, through Provençal, going back to Latin *flāre* to blow.]

flag·ging¹ (flag′ing) *adj.* weakening; tiring; drooping: *flagging spirits.* [FLAG³ + -ING².]

flag·ging² (flag′ing) *n.* **1.** flagstones. **2.** a pavement of flagstones. **3.** the act of paving with flagstones. [FLAG⁴ + -ING¹.]

fla·gi·tious (flə jish′əs) *adj.* **1.** guilty of atrocious acts or extreme wickedness: *a flagitious ruler.* **2.** extremely wicked or atrocious; heinous: *flagitious crimes.* [Latin *flāgitiōsus* shameful, from *flāgitium* shameful act.] —**fla·gi′tious·ly,** *adv.* —**fla·gi′tious·ness,** *n.*

flagellum
of a
protozoan

flag·man (flag′mən) *n., pl.* **-men** (-mən). **1.** a person who carries a flag. **2.** a person who signals with a flag or lantern, esp. at a railroad crossing.

flag officer, a naval officer above the rank of captain, entitled to display a flag indicating rank.

flag of truce, a white flag used to signal a desire for a conference with the enemy or for a cessation of hostilities.

flag·on (flag′ən) *n.* **1.** a large vessel for liquids, having a handle, a spout, and usually a cover. **2.** a large bottle used to hold alcoholic beverages, as wine or ale. **3.** the contents of a flagon. [Old French *flascon* bottle, from Late Latin *flascō;* possibly of Germanic origin.]

flag·pole (flag′pōl′) *n.* a pole on which a flag is raised and displayed. Also, **flagstaff.**

flag rank, any naval rank above captain, including commodore, rear admiral, vice admiral, and admiral.

fla·grant (flā′grənt) *adj.* so obviously bad as to shock; glaring; notorious; scandalous: *flagrant violations of the law, a flagrant display of cowardice.* [Latin *flagrāns,* present participle of *flagrāre* to burn.] —**fla′gran·cy,** *n.* —**fla′grant·ly,** *adv.*

Synonyms Flagrant, glaring, and gross mean openly or conspicuously bad. **Flagrant** is used of misdeeds that one cannot fail to notice and may imply a deliberate offender: *Climbing over that wall is a flagrant breach of regulations.* **Glaring** is used of errors rather than misdeeds, which may be unintentional but are quite obvious: *Leaving out the title page was a glaring mistake.* **Gross** suggests an act or fault so far from

a	at	e	end	o	hot	u	up	hw	white		about
ā	ape	ē	me	ō	old	ū	use	ng	song		taken
ä	far	i	it	ô	fork	ü	rule	th	thin	ə	pencil
âr	care	ī	ice	oi	oil	ů	pull	<u>th</u>	this		lemon
		îr	pierce	ou	out	ûr	turn	zh	measure		circus

F

469

normal that it seems to offend nature or taste: *Holding political prisoners without trial is generally held to be a gross violation of human rights.*

flag·ship (flag'ship') *n.* a ship carrying the commanding officer of a fleet.

flag·staff (flag'staf') *n.* flagpole.

flag station, a railroad station at which trains stop only when given a signal. Also, **flag stop.**

flag·stone (flag'stōn') *n.* a large, flat stone, used for paving.

flag·wav·ing (flag'wā'ving) *n.* an emotional, usually excessive, appeal to patriotic or chauvinist sentiments. —**flag'-wav'er,** *n.*

flail (flāl) *n.* an instrument for threshing grain by hand, consisting of a wooden staff at the end of which a stouter, shorter pole is hung so as to swing freely. —*v.t.* **1.** to strike with or as with a flail; thresh. **2.** to wave or swing, esp. violently or swiftly: *I flailed my arms at the bees swarming around me.* —*v.i.* to toss or thrash about. [Old French *flaiel* scourge, from Latin *flagellum* whip. See FLAGELLUM.]

flair (flâr) *n.* **1.** a distinctive quality of stylishness or elegance: *The room had been decorated with flair.* **2.** a natural talent or aptitude: *to have a flair for acting.* [French *flair* sense of smell, discernment, from *flairer* to smell, going back to Latin *frāgrāre* to smell sweet.]

flak (flak) *also,* **flack.** *n.* **1.** antiaircraft fire. **2.** fragments from exploding shells fired at enemy aircraft. **3.** *Slang.* criticism or abuse: *The senator had not expected the proposal to meet with so much flak.* [Abbreviation of German *Fl(ieger)a(bwehr)k(anone)* antiaircraft gun; literally, gun warding off aviators.]

flake (flāk) *n.* **1.** a small, thin particle of light substance: *soap flakes.* **2.** a thin, scalelike piece or layer split or peeled from the surface of something; chip: *paint flakes.* **3.** *Slang.* an eccentric or unconventional person; oddball. —*v.,* **flaked, flak·ing.** —*v.t.* **1.** to chip or peel off in flakes: *to flake paint from a wall.* **2.** to form into flakes: *You can use a fork to flake the tuna.* **3.** to spot or cover with or as with flakes: *hair flaked with silver.* —*v.i.* **1.** to peel off in flakes: *The plaster cracked and flaked.* **2.** to become spotted with or as with flakes. [Probably of Scandinavian origin.] —**flake'like',** *adj.*

flak·y (flā'kē) *adj.,* **flak·i·er, flak·i·est. 1.** resembling or consisting of flakes: *a flaky mineral.* **2.** separating easily into flakes: *a flaky pie crust.* **3.** *Slang.* eccentric; odd. —**flak'i·ly,** *adv.* —**flak'i·ness,** *n.*

flam·beau (flam'bō) *n., pl.* **-beaux** (-bōz) or **-beaus. 1.** a flaming torch. **2.** a large, decorated candlestick. [French *flambeau* torch, from Old French *flamble* flame, going back to Latin *flamma.*]

flam·boy·ant (flam boi'ənt) *adj.* **1.** extravagantly ornate; overly decorated; showy; florid: *a flamboyant writing style, flamboyant fashions.* **2.** full of rich color; brilliant; resplendent: *a flamboyant sunset.* **3.** designating a style of architecture, as French Gothic of the fifteenth and sixteenth centuries, characterized by florid decoration and wavy, flamelike tracery in windows and openwork. [French *flamboyant,* present participle of *flamboyer* to flame, blaze, going back to Latin *flamma* blaze, flame.] —**flam·boy'ance, flam·boy'an·cy,** *n.* —**flam·boy'ant·ly,** *adv.* —For Synonyms, see **ornate.**

flame (flām) *n.* **1.** one of the tongues of light emitted from a fire: *Flames shot out of the burning house.* **2.** ignited gas or vapor that gives off light and heat: *Lower the flame under the frying pan.* **3.** the condition or state of visible combustion; blaze: *The house was in flames.* **4.** something resembling or suggesting a flame: *The sun was a flame on the horizon.* **5.** a bright or glowing light; flamelike color or appearance; brilliance: *the flame of a jewel.* **6.** strong emotional feeling; passion; ardor: *the flame of love.* **7.** *Informal.* sweetheart. —*v.,* **flamed, flam·ing.** —*v.i.* **1.** to burn with flames; burst into flame; blaze: *The fire flamed intensely.* **2.** to light up or glow as if with flames; grow hot or red: *The child's face flamed with embarrassment.* **3.** to emit or display a flamelike color or appearance; shine like flame; glow brilliantly: *The autumn trees flamed with color.* **4.** to become aroused or excited; break out with violence or passion: *They flamed with rage at the very thought of such injustice.* —*v.t.* to subject to the action of fire or flame. [Old French *flam(m)e* blaze, tongue of light emitted from a fire, from Latin *flamma.*] —**flame'like',** *adj.* —**flam'er,** *n.*
·to flame up. to burst out in or as in flames.

flame cell, a specialized cup-shaped cell in flatworms and certain other invertebrates that functions to regulate water balance. It bears a tuft of cilia that aid in excretion of excess tissue fluid. [Because the tuft of cilia resembles a flickering flame.]

flamenco dancer

fla·men·co (flə meng'kō) *n., pl.* **-cos. 1.** a type of vigorous dance associated with the Andalusian Gypsies of Spain, characterized by slow twisting arm and hand movements, stamping of the feet, clapping of the hands, and the use of castanets. **2.** the music for this dance.

flame·out (flām'out') *n.* a sudden cessation of functioning in a jet engine.

flame·throw·er (flām'thrō'ər) *n.* a weapon or instrument that projects a stream of burning fuel.

flam·ing (flā'ming) *adj.* **1.** in flames; blazing; fiery. **2.** very bright; brilliant: *flaming orange.* **3.** characterized by strong emotion; ardent; passionate; vehement: *a flaming speech.* —**flam'ing·ly,** *adv.*

fla·min·go (flə ming'gō) *n., pl.* **-gos** or **-goes.** any of various wading birds, genus *Phoenicopterus,* of tropical and subtropical regions, having long, thin legs and neck, a down-curved beak, webbed feet, and plumage that ranges from pinkish white to deep crimson. Height: to 5 feet (1.5 meters). [Portuguese *flamingo,* going back to Latin *flamma* flame; because of its color.]

Fla·min·i·an Way (flə min'ē ən) one of the principal ancient Roman roads in central Italy, leading north from Rome to the Adriatic.

flam·ma·ble (flam'ə bəl) *adj.* capable of being set on fire easily; combustible. —*n.* something flammable. —**flam'ma·bil'i·ty,** *n.*

flange (flanj) *n.* a projecting rim or collar on an object, designed to keep it in place, as on railroad wheels, to attach it to another object, as on pipes, or for various other purposes. —*v.t.,* **flanged, flang·ing.** to provide with a flange. [Probably form of obsolete *flanch* projection, from Old French *flanche,* form of *flanc* side, flank. See FLANK.]

flank (flangk) *n.* **1.** the part between the ribs and the hip on either side of an animal or human being. **2.** a cut of meat, esp. beef, from this part of an animal. **3.** the outer side of the human thigh. **4.** *Military.* the right or left side of a unit, formation, position, or fortification. **5.** the side or lateral part of something: *the flanks of a building.* —*v.t.* **1.** to be located at the side of: *Two statues flanked the entrance of the library.* **2.a.** to defend or guard the flank of. **b.** to attack the flank of. **c.** to move around the flank of. —*v.i.* to be located at the side of something; be in a flanking position (with *on* or *upon*). [Old French *flanc* side; of Germanic origin.]

flank·er (flang'kər) *n.* **1.** a person or thing that flanks. **2.** a member of a body of soldiers protecting the flank of an army. **3.** a projecting extension at either side of a fortification. **4.** an offensive back in football who lines up in a flanking position.

flan·nel (flan'əl) *n.* **1.** a soft cotton fabric, napped on one or both sides, used for such items as nightgowns, infants' wear, and shirts. **2.** a soft woolen fabric having a slightly napped surface. **3. flannels. a.** clothes made of flannel. **b.** warm woolen underwear. **4.** flannelette. [Earlier *flannen,* from Welsh *gwlanen* woolen article, from *gwlân* wool.]

flan·nel·ette (flan'ə let') *also,* **flan·nel·et.** *n.* a soft, light, cotton fabric with a nap.

flap (flap) *v.*, **flapped, flap·ping.** —*v.t.* **1.** to move up and down, esp. with a muffled, slapping sound: *The birds flapped their wings.* **2.** to cause to move in a swaying or rippling manner, esp. with noise: *The wind flapped the shutters.* **3.** to strike with something broad and flat; slap. —*v.i.* **1.** to move the wings or arms up and down, esp. with a muffled, slapping sound. **2.** to sway or wave loosely, esp. with noise: *The curtains flapped in the breeze.* —*n.* **1.a.** a flapping motion. **b.** the muffled, slapping sound produced by flapping. **2.** the part of an envelope folded down in closing or sealing it. **3.** a blow given with something broad and flat; slap. **4.** a piece of material attached at one edge only so that it may move as though hinged, esp. one covering the opening of a pocket. **5.** a hinged section, usually on the trailing edge of an airplane wing, that is used to increase lift during a takeoff or a landing. **6.** *Slang.* a dispute, commotion, or scandal. [Probably imitative.]

flap·jack (flap′jak′) *n.* pancake.

flap·per (flap′ər) *n.* **1.** a person or thing that flaps. **2.** a young bird not yet able to fly. **3.** *Informal.* a young woman in the 1920s who was unconventional in dress and behavior.

flare (flâr) *v.*, **flared, flar·ing.** —*v.i.* **1.** to burn with a very bright light, esp. for only a short time: *The torch flared in the darkness.* **2.** to burst suddenly into a blaze (often with *up*): *The campfire flared up in the gust of wind.* **3.** to break out in sudden or violent emotion or activity (often with *up*): *Tempers flared. Rebellion flared up in the outlying provinces. The fever flared up again during the night.* **4.** to open or spread outward: *The skirt flares from the waist.* —*v.t.* **1.** to cause to flare. **2.** to signal with flares. —*n.* **1.** a bright or glaring light, usually lasting only a short time. **2.a.** a fire or blaze of light used for signaling or illumination. **b.** a device producing such a light. **3.** a sudden outburst, as of emotion or activity: *a flare of resentment.* **4.a.** a widening or spreading outward. **b.** the thing or part that spreads out: *the flare of a dress.* [Possibly blend of FLAME + GLARE.]

flare-up (flâr′up′) *n.* **1.** a sudden outburst of flame or light. **2.** *Informal.* a sudden outburst, as of emotion or activity: *a flare-up of violence at a political rally.*

flar·ing (flâr′ing) *adj.* **1.** blazing brightly or unsteadily. **2.** showy; gaudy. **3.** widening or spreading gradually outward. —**flar′ing·ly,** *adv.*

flash (flash) *n.* **1.** a sudden, brief burst, as of light or flame: *a flash of lightning.* **2.** a very brief period of time; instant; moment: *The police were there in a flash.* **3.** a sudden outburst or brief display, as of thought or understanding: *a flash of merriment, a flash of inspiration.* **4.** a brief bulletin or report of very recent or urgent news. **5.** an ostentatious or vulgar display; showiness. **6.** flashlight. **7.a.** a burst of artificial light used for taking photographs. **b.** a device that produces such a burst of light, as a flashbulb or flashgun. —*v.i.* **1.** to burst forth in sudden, brief light or fire: *Lightning flashed in the sky.* **2.** to reflect or burst forth with light in sudden brilliance; shine; gleam: *The swords flashed in the sun. Her eyes flashed with anger.* **3.** to burst suddenly into view or perception: *An idea flashed into his mind.* **4.** to come or move suddenly or quickly: *The car flashed by.* —*v.t.* **1.** to cause to flash: *He flashed the light in her eyes.* **2.** to emit or send forth in a sudden flash or flashes: *The flagship flashed a signal to the fleet.* **3.** to communicate by flashes, as by telegraph or radio: *The news was flashed all over the country.* **4.** *Informal.* to make an ostentatious display of; show off: *He flashed a roll of fifty-dollar bills.* **5.** to show suddenly and briefly: *The detective flashed her badge.* —*adj.* **1.** happening or done very quickly; lasting for a short time: *a flash fire.* **2.** flashy; showy; ostentatious. [Probably imitative.] —**flash′er,** *n.*

• **flash in the pan.** a person or thing that at first seems promising or successful but is ultimately a failure.

flash·back (flash′bak′) *n.* **1.** a break in the normal time sequence of a motion picture, radio script, novel, or play, during which a scene or episode describing earlier events is inserted. **2.** a scene or episode thus inserted. **3.** *Psychiatry.* the recurrence of a drug-induced hallucination long after the drug was taken: *an LSD flashback.*

flash·bulb (flash′bulb′) *n.* an incandescent light bulb filled with metal foil that gives off a single bright flash when ignited, used for taking photographs. Also, **photoflash.**

flash burn, a burn caused by exposure to intense thermal radiation, esp. from an atomic explosion.

flash·card (flash′kärd′) *n.* any of a set of cards bearing information, as words or numbers, on either or both sides, used in classroom drills or in private study, as of mathematics or a foreign language.

flash·cube (flash′kūb′) *n.* a camera accessory consisting of a plastic cube containing four flashbulbs that can be ignited in sequence by tripping the shutter mechanism of the camera.

flash flood, a sudden, violent flood caused by heavy rainfall.

flash·gun (flash′gun′) *n.* a battery-powered camera attachment or accessory that holds and ignites a flashbulb.

flash·ing (flash′ing) *n.* sheet metal or other protective material used as weatherproof covering over joints and angles, as of a roof where it meets the edges of walls or chimneys.

flash lamp, an electric lamp that produces a brief, very bright light, used in taking photographs.

flash·light (flash′līt′) *n.* **1.** a portable electric lamp powered by batteries. **2.** a bright, flashing light used for signaling, as from a lighthouse. **3.** a burst of artificial light used for taking photographs.

flash point, the lowest temperature at which the vapor of a combustible substance will ignite.

flash·y (flash′ē) *adj.*, **flash·i·er, flash·i·est.** **1.** momentarily brilliant; sparkling; flashing. **2.** that draws the attention; showy; gaudy: *a flashy car.* —**flash′i·ly,** *adv.* —**flash′i·ness,** *n.*

flask (flask) *n.* **1.** any of various bottle-shaped containers, usually made of glass or metal, esp. a small, broad, flattened container, as for liquor, made to be carried in the pocket. **2.** a rounded glass container with a long neck used in laboratory work, esp. for heating liquids. **3.** a box or frame for holding a sand mold in a foundry. [Partly from Middle French *flasque* container for gunpowder; partly from Italian *fiasco* bottle; both from Late Latin *flasca, flascō* (wine) bottle; possibly of Germanic origin.]

flat¹ (flat) *adj.*, **flat·ter, flat·test.** **1.** extended horizontally with little or no slope or inclination: *A flat roof has poor drainage.* **2.** relatively smooth or even; level: *The plasterer made the surface of the wall flat.* **3.** lying or stretched at full length; spread out: *to be flat on one's back.* **4.** placed or having an entire length or surface in contact with something: *Stand with your back flat against the wall.* **5.** having little depth or thickness; shallow: *a flat sheet of metal.* **6.** having relatively little curvature or projection: *The rock has a flat face.* **7.** plain; positive; absolute; downright: *a flat denial, a flat refusal.* **8.** not changing; fixed; uniform: *a flat rate.* **9.** lacking in interest, vigor, or animation; lifeless; dull; monotonous: *a flat performance.* **10.a.** having little or no flavor; stale; tasteless; insipid: *flat food.* **b.** having little or no sparkle or effervescence: *a flat soft drink.* **11.** not clear or sharp in sound; lacking resonance: *a flat voice.* **12.a.** having little or no feeling of depth: *The painting was very flat.* **b.** not shiny or glossy: *flat paint.* **c.** uniform in color or shading: *a flat tint.* **d.** without emphasizing contour or shadows: *flat lighting.* **13.** containing little or no air; deflated: *a flat tire.* **14.** *Informal.* lacking or short of money. **15.** *Music.* **a.** below the true, regular, or intended pitch. **b.** one half step or half note lower than natural pitch. **c.** having a flat in the signature. **16.** (of the letter *a*) having the sound of the vowel in *can* or *sat.* —*n.* **1.** a flat part or surface: *the flat of a sword, the flat of the hand.* **2.** a piece or expanse of level ground. **3.** a tract of low-lying marshy land; swamp. **4.** *also,* **flats.** level, partially submerged ground near a river; shoal. **5.** something that is flat. **6.** a shallow box or container in which seedlings are grown. **7.** flatcar. **8.** a piece of theatrical scenery, consisting of a frame, usually of wood, with a fabric, as canvas, stretched over it. **9.** flats. women's shoes having low heels. **10.** a deflated tire. **11.** *Music.* **a.** a tone or note lowered one half step or half note below its natural pitch. **b.** a character (♭) that indicates such a tone or note. —*adv.* **1.** in a flat manner; flatly: *The cat lay flat on the ground. The ladder was placed flat against the wall.* **2.** exactly; precisely: *to run a mile in four minutes flat.* **3.** *Music.* below the true pitch: *to sing flat.* —*v.*, **flat·ted, flat·ting.** —*v.t.* **1.** to make flat. **2.** *Music.* to sing or play flat. —*v.i.* to become flat. [Old Norse *flatr* level.] —**flat′ly,** *adv.* —**flat′ness,** *n.* —For Synonyms *(adj.)*, see **level.**

• **to fall flat.** to fail completely; prove uninteresting or ineffective: *My joke fell flat.*

• **flat out.** *Informal.* **a.** at full speed or force: *to drive flat out.* **b.** in an honest, direct manner; frankly; openly: *They flat out refused to help.*

flat² (flat) *n.* an apartment or suite of rooms on one floor of a building. [Old English *flet* floor, dwelling.]

flat·bed (flat′bed′) *n.* a truck or trailer with a body shaped like a shallow box or a platform without top or sides.

flat·boat (flat′bōt′) *n.* a large boat with a flat bottom and square ends, used for transport on rivers or canals.

a	at	e	end	o	hot	u	up	hw	white		about
ā	ape	ē	me	ō	old	ū	use	ng	song		taken
ä	far	i	it	ô	fork	ü	rule	th	thin	ə	pencil
âr	care	ī	ice	oi	oil	u̇	pull	th	this		lemon
		îr	pierce	ou	out	ûr	turn	zh	measure		circus

F

flat·car (flat′kär′) *n.* a railroad car consisting of a platform without sides or roof, used for transporting freight.

flat·fish (flat′fish′) *n., pl.* **-fish** or **-fish·es.** any of a group of food fishes, order Pleuronectiformes, that have flattened bodies. In the adult, both eyes are on the pigmented side of the body, which is always turned toward the surface of the water. Halibut, flounder, and sole are flatfishes.

flat·foot (flat′fŏt′; *for def. 1, also* flat′fŏt′) *n., pl. (def. 1)* **-feet** (-fēt′) or *(def. 2)* **-foots.** **1.a.** a condition in which the arch of the foot is abnormally low and most or all of the sole touches the ground. **b.** a foot with an abnormally low arch. **2.** *Slang.* a police officer, esp. one who walks a beat.

flat·foot·ed (flat′fŏt′id) *adj.* **1.** having flat feet. **2.** *Informal.* without hesitation; direct; resolute: *a flatfooted refusal.* **3.** *Informal.* off one's guard; not ready; unprepared: *to be caught flatfooted.* —**flat′foot′ed·ly,** *adv.* —**flat′foot′ed·ness,** *n.*

flat·i·ron (flat′ī′ərn) *n.* a heavy iron for pressing clothes, esp. one that must be heated in an oven or fireplace before it can be used.

flat·land (flat′land′) *n.* land that is almost or completely flat, with no hills or valleys.

flat-out (flat′out′) *adj.* **1.** out-and-out; thoroughgoing; utter; complete: *flat-out contempt, a flat-out lie.* **2.** working or moving with the greatest speed, strength, or energy: *a flat-out effort to meet a deadline.*

flat·ten (flat′ən) *v.t.* **1.** to make flat or flatter. **2.** to make prostrate; knock down: *A single punch flattened the boxer.* —*v.i.* **1.** to become flat or flatter. **2.** to fall or lie prostrate. —**flat′ten·er,** *n.*

· **to flatten out.** to spread out.

flat·ter (flat′ər) *v.t.* **1.** to praise excessively or insincerely. **2.** to try to please or gain the favor of by praising excessively. **3.** to cause to be pleased; compliment: *She was flattered by the invitation.* **4.** to represent or portray favorably, esp. to show as more attractive than is actually the case: *The painting flatters him.* —*v.i.* to flatter someone or something; use flattery. [Old French *flater* to soothe, caress; of Germanic origin.] —**flat′ter·er,** *n.* —**flat′ter·ing·ly,** *adv.*

· **to flatter oneself.** to have the satisfaction of feeling; delude oneself (with *that*): *Don't flatter yourself that we're talking about you.*

flat·ter·y (flat′ə rē) *n., pl.* **-ter·ies.** **1.** the act of flattering; excessive or insincere praise. **2.** a flattering remark or speech.

flat·tish (flat′ish) *adj.* somewhat flat.

flat·top (flat′top′) *n. Informal.* **1.** aircraft carrier. **2.** a hair style in which the hair is cut short and flat across the top of the head.

flat·u·lent (flach′ə lənt) *adj.* **1.** having gas or air in the stomach or intestines. **2.** producing gas in the stomach or intestines. **3.** empty and boastful; vain; pretentious: *flatulent speech.* [French *flatulent* windy, going back to Latin *flātus* blowing.] —**flat′u·lence,** *n.* —**flat′u·lent·ly,** *adv.*

fla·tus (flā′təs) *n.* gastrointestinal gas. [Latin *flatus,* from *flare* to blow.]

flat·ware (flat′wâr′) *n.* **1.** table utensils, as knives, forks, and spoons. **2.** dishes, bowls, and other tableware that are more or less flat, as plates, platters, or saucers. ➡ distinguished from **hollowware** in def. 2.

flat·wise (flat′wīz′) *adj.* in a flat position; with the flat side in contact; not edgewise. Also, **flat·ways** (flat′wāz′).

flat·worm (flat′wûrm′) *n.* any of a large group of soft, flat-bodied worms, phylum Platyhelminthes, that exhibit bilateral symmetry, including planarians, parasitic flukes, and tapeworms. For illustration, see **worm.**

flaunt (flônt, flänt) *v.i.* **1.** to show off in order to impress others; make a gaudy display. **2.** to wave or flutter freely or conspicuously: *banners flaunting.* —*v.t.* to show or display ostentatiously or impudently: *to flaunt one's achievements.* —*n.* the act of flaunting. [Of uncertain origin.] —**flaunt′ing·ly,** *adv.*

flau·tist (flô′tist, flou′-) flutist.

fla·vin (flā′vin) *n.* any of a class of yellow biochemical compounds that are derived from a complex ketone and are coenzymes of flavoproteins, as riboflavin.

fla·vo·pro·tein (flā′vō prō′tēn, -tē in) *n.* any of a group of yellow enzymes active in cellular oxidation that contain a protein molecule linked to riboflavin.

fla·vor (flā′vər) *also, British,* **flavour.** *n.* **1.** a particular or characteristic taste: *Adding pepper to the stew will give it a spicy flavor.* **2.** a substance having such a taste: *You can choose from ten different flavors at the ice-cream parlor.* **3.** a characteristic, distinctive, or predominant quality; aura: *The village has a quaint flavor.* **4.** flavoring. **5.** *Archaic.* odor; aroma: *the flavor of the rose.* —*v.t.* to give flavor to: *to flavor apples for a pie with cinnamon.* [Old French *flaur* odor, going back to Latin *flāre* to blow.] —**fla′vor·less,** *adj.*

fla·vor·ful (flā′vər fəl) *adj.* full of flavor; tasty. Also, **fla·vor·some** (flā′vər səm), **fla′vor·y.**

fla·vor·ing (flā′vər ing) *n.* something, as an extract, added to food or drink to give or heighten flavor: *The baker added lemon flavoring to the cookies.*

fla·vour (flā′vər) *British.* flavor.

flaw[1] (flô) *n.* **1.** something that detracts from or mars completeness, soundness, or perfection: *a flaw in a person's character, a flaw in a plan.* **2.** a broken, faulty, or weak spot, as a crack: *The glass has a flaw.* —*v.t., v.i.* to make or become defective. [Possibly from Old Norse *flaga* slab of stone.] —For Synonyms *(n.),* see **blemish.**

flaw[2] (flô) *n.* a sudden gust of wind, often accompanied by rain or snow; squall. [Possibly from Middle Dutch *vlāghe* stroke[1], storm.]

flaw·less (flô′lis) *adj.* having no flaw; perfect: *a flawless emerald, a flawless complexion, to give a flawless performance.* —**flaw′less·ly,** *adv.* —**flaw′less·ness,** *n.* —For Synonyms, see **perfect.**

flax (flaks) *n.* **1.** a fiber that is obtained from the stem of a plant, *Linum usitatissimum,* and processed to be spun into the thread used to make linen and such products as rope and rugs. **2.** the plant itself, cultivated throughout the world, having small, lance-shaped leaves and clusters of blue, white, or pink flowers. **3.** any of certain plants resembling flax. [Old English *fleax* the plant.]

flax·en (flak′sən) *adj.* **1.** relating to, resembling, or made of flax: *flaxen thread.* **2.** having a pale yellow color like that of flax fiber or straw: *flaxen hair.*

flax·seed (flaks′sēd′, flak′-) *n.* the seed of flax, valued chiefly as a source of linseed oil; linseed.

flay (flā) *v.t.* **1.** to strip off the skin or outer covering of, as by lashing. **2.** to criticize or scold severely or harshly. [Old English *flēan* to skin.] —**flay′er,** *n.*

flea (flē) *n.* **1.** any of a large group of small, wingless, parasitic insects, order Siphonaptera, that feed on the blood of warm-blooded animals. They have strong legs for leaping and sharp mouthparts for piercing the skin and sucking blood, and may transmit certain diseases, such as bubonic plague. Length: to 1/8 inch (0.3 centimeter). **2.** water flea. **3.** any of several beetles that leap like fleas. Also *(def. 3),* **flea beetle.** [Old English *flēa* the wingless, parasitic insect.]

· **a flea in one's ear.** an irritating hint or sharp, stinging rebuke or rebuff.

flea

flea·bane (flē′bān′) *n.* any of a large group of plants, genus *Erigeron,* of the composite family, that were believed to repel or destroy fleas.

flea-bit·ten (flē′bit′ən) *adj.* **1.** bitten by or infested with fleas: *a flea-bitten dog.* **2.** *Informal.* in poor condition; run-down; decrepit.

flea collar, a collar for dogs, cats, or other pets containing a chemical that repels or kills fleas.

flea market, an outdoor market that sells cheap or used goods.

fleck (flek) *n.* **1.** a small patch or streak; spot, as of light or color: *flecks of sunlight on the water, black marble with flecks of white in it.* **2.** a small particle; flake; speck: *flecks of dust.* —*v.t.* to mark with flecks; spot; speckle. [Probably from Old Norse *flekkr* spot.]

flec·tion (flek′shən) *n.* **1.** the act of bending or the state of being bent. **2.** a bent part; bend. **3.** *Anatomy.* flexion *(def. 1).* [Form of FLEXION.]

fled (fled) the past tense and past participle of **flee.**

fledge (flej) *v.,* **fledged, fledg·ing.** —*v.t.* **1.** to furnish (an arrow) with feathers. **2.** to rear (a young bird) until capable of flight. —*v.i.* (of a young bird) to grow the feathers needed for flight; acquire full plumage (often with *out*). [Old English *-flycge* (found in *unflycge* without feathers, unfledged).]

fledg·ling (flej′ling) *also,* **fledge·ling.** *n.* **1.** a young bird just fledged. **2.** a young or inexperienced person.

flee (flē) *v.,* **fled, flee·ing.** —*v.i.* **1.** to run away, as from danger or pursuers; take flight: *The robbers fled down the alley. The deer fled when it saw us.* **2.** to move or pass away swiftly: *Color fled from the sky. Their troubles fled when they read the report.* —*v.t.* to run away or try to escape from: *citizens forced to flee the besieged city.* [Old English *flēon* to run away from, avoid.] —**fle′er,** *n.*

fleece (flēs) *n.* **1.** a coat of wool covering a sheep or similar animal. **2.** a quantity of wool sheared from a sheep or similar

animal at any one time. **3.** something resembling fleece: *a fleece of snow.* **4.** a fabric with a thick nap or pile resembling the wool of sheep, used for such purposes as lining coats or gloves. —*v.t.*, **fleeced, fleec·ing. 1.** to shear the fleece from. **2.** to deprive of money or property by deception; cheat; swindle. [Old English *flēos* coat of wool of a sheep or similar animal.] —**fleec′er,** *n.*

fleec·y (flē′sē) *adj.,* **fleec·i·er, fleec·i·est. 1.** made of or covered with fleece. **2.** resembling fleece: *fleecy clouds in a clear blue sky.* —**fleec′i·ly,** *adv.* —**fleec′i·ness,** *n.*

fleer (flir) *v.i.* to laugh or grin sneeringly. —*v.t.* to mock; deride. —*n.* a sneering look or laugh. [Probably of Scandinavian origin.]

fleet¹ (flēt) *n.* **1.** a group of warships organized under one command. **2.** a group, as of boats or of vehicles, organized into or regarded as a unit or operated by a single company: *a fleet of taxis, a fleet of barges, the fleet of a steamship company.* [Old English *flēot* ship, from *flēotan* to float.]

fleet² (flēt) *adj.* swift; fast: *fleet of foot.* —*v.i.* to move or pass swiftly. [Middle English *flēten* to flow, glide, from Old English *flēotan* to float, swim, akin to German *fliessen* to flow.] —**fleet′-ly,** *adv.* —**fleet′ness,** *n.*

fleet admiral, an officer of the highest rank in the U.S. Navy.

fleet·ing (flē′ting) *adj.* lasting a short time; passing quickly; transitory; brief: *a fleeting glimpse, a fleeting moment.* —**fleet′-ing·ly,** *adv.* —**fleet′ing·ness,** *n.*

Flem·ing (flem′ing) *n.* **1.** a Belgian whose native language is Flemish. **2.** one of the people of historic Flanders.

Flem·ish (flem′ish) *adj.* of, relating to, or characteristic of Flanders or its people, language, or culture. —*n.* **1. the Flem-ish.** the people historically inhabiting Flanders and those who have descended from them. **2.** a Germanic language of the Indo-European family resembling Dutch and spoken chiefly in northern Belgium and northwestern France.

flesh (flesh) *n.* **1.** the part of the body of a human being or animal that covers the bones, consisting mainly of muscle and fat, esp. the muscular tissue of this part. **2.** the surface of the human body; skin. **3.** the parts of an animal used as food; meat, esp. as distinguished from fish or fowl. **4.** the soft, pulpy portion of fruits or vegetables, as distinguished from the core, seeds, or skin. **5.** the body of a person, as opposed to the soul or spirit: *The spirit indeed is willing, but the flesh is weak* (Matthew 25:41). **6.** the sensual or physical nature of a person, as distinguished from the moral or spiritual nature: *to satisfy the desires of the flesh.* **7.** human beings collectively; humanity. **8.** a light pinkish or yellowish tan color. —*v.t.* **1.** to remove the adhering flesh from (a skin or hide). **2.** to add substance to; fill out (with *out*): *to flesh out a story by adding details.* —*v.i.* to put on flesh; become fleshy (with *out*): *The baby has fleshed out.* [Old English *flæsc* part of the body covering the bones, meat.]

· **flesh and blood. a.** offspring, immediate family, or other blood relatives. **b.** the human body.

· **in the flesh.** physically present before one's eyes; in person.

flesh-col·ored (flesh′kul′ərd) *adj.* having a light pinkish or yellowish tan color.

flesh fly, any of several flies, family Sarcophagidae, that deposit their eggs or larvae in the wounds, waste, or decaying flesh of animals.

flesh·ly (flesh′lē) *adj.,* **-li·er, -li·est. 1.** sensual; carnal. **2.** of or relating to the flesh or body; bodily; physical. —**flesh′li·ness,** *n.*

flesh·pot (flesh′pot′) *n.* **1.** a place offering unrestrained or luxurious pleasure or entertainment. **2. fleshpots.** material or sensual luxuries; physical comforts.

flesh wound, a superficial wound that does not extend beyond the flesh or affect a bone or vital organ.

flesh·y (flesh′ē) *adj.,* **flesh·i·er, flesh·i·est. 1.** having much flesh; plump; fat. **2.** of or like flesh. **3.** firm and pulpy: *a fleshy fruit, fleshy leaves.* —**flesh′i·ness,** *n.*

fletch (flech) *v.t.* to at-tach feathers to (an arrow).

fleur-de-lis (flûr′də lē′, -lēs′, flûr′-) *n., pl.* **fleurs-de-lis** (flûr′də-lēz′, flûr′-). **1.** a heraldic design or device repre-senting a lily or iris. **2.** the distinctive armorial bearing of the former royal family of France. **3.** iris *(defs. 2, 3).* [French *fleur de lis* lily flower; *fleur* flower (from Latin *flōs*) + *de* of (from Latin *dē* from) + *lis* lily (from Latin *līlium*).]

fleurs-de-lis

flew (flü) a past tense of **fly².**

flews (flüz) *pl. n.* the loose, hanging parts of the upper lip of a dog, esp. a hound.

flex (fleks) *v.t.* **1.** to bend: *to flex one's arm, to flex a bow.* **2.** to tighten or contract: *to flex one's muscles.* —*v.i.* to tighten or contract a muscle or muscles. [Latin *flexus,* past participle of *flectere* to bend.]

flex·i·ble (flek′sə bəl) *adj.* **1.** able to bend without breaking; not stiff or rigid; easily bent. **2.** able to adjust easily to change; adaptable: *a flexible schedule, flexible rules.* [Latin *flexibilis* pli-ant, from *flexus,* past participle of *flectere* to bend.] —**flex′i·bil′-i·ty, flex′i·ble·ness,** *n.* —**flex′i·bly,** *adv.*

flex·ion (flek′shən) *n.* **1.** *Anatomy.* the act of bending a limb or contracting a flexor muscle. ➡ opposed to **extension. 2.** flec-tion. [Latin *flexiō* a bending.]

flex·or (flek′sər) *n.* any muscle that bends a part of the body, esp. a limb. ➡ opposed to **extensor.** For illustration, see **extensor.** [Modern Latin *flexor,* from Latin *flexus.* See FLEX.]

flex·time (fleks′tīm′) *n.* a system that permits employees to choose, within limits, the times at which they start and finish work. Also, **flexitime.**

flex·ure (flek′shər) *n.* **1.** the act of bending or the state of being bent. **2.** a bent part; bend; curve. [Latin *flexūra* a bending.]

flib·ber·ti·gib·bet (flib′ər tē jib′it) *n.* a frivolous or flighty person. [Of uncertain origin.]

flick¹ (flik) *n.* **1.** a light, quick, snapping movement or stroke: *with a flick of the wrist, a flick with a whip.* **2.** a sound made by such a movement or stroke. **3.** a fleck, splotch, or daub. —*v.t.* **1.** to strike or remove (something) with a light, quick, snapping movement or stroke, as of the hand: *to flick a horse's rump, to flick crumbs from one's lap.* **2.** to cause to move or snap with a light, quick movement: *to flick a towel at someone.* [Probably imita-tive.]

flick² (flik) *also,* **flicks.** *n. Slang.* a motion picture. [From FLICKER¹.]

flick·er¹ (flik′ər) *v.i.* **1.** to shine or burn with an unsteady or wavering light: *The match flickered in the draft.* **2.** to move back and forth with a quick, fluttering movement; quiver; tremble: *Shadows flickered on the wall.* —*v.t.* to cause to flicker. —*n.* **1.** an unsteady or wavering light. **2.** a slight indication or stirring; brief appearance: *a flicker of hope, a flicker of fear.* **3.** a quick fluttering or quivering movement: *the flicker of an eyelid.* [Middle English *flikeren,* from Old English *flicorian* to flutter, hover, akin to *flacor* flying.]

flick·er² (flik′ər) *n.* any of various woodpeckers, genus *Co-laptes,* native to areas from Alaska to southern Chile, having a curved, slender bill and brightly marked plumage. Length: 12 inches (30 centimeters). [Possibly from FLICK¹ + -ER¹.]

flied (flīd) a past tense and past participle of **fly²** *(v.i., def. 8).*

fli·er (flī′ər) *also,* **flyer.** *n.* **1.** a person or thing that flies, esp. an aviator. **2.** a person or thing that moves swiftly, as an express train. **3.** *Informal.* a small handbill or leaflet, as one used in advertising. **4.** a risky financial invest-ment or speculation, as on the stock market.

flies (flīz) *n.* the plural of **fly¹** and **fly².** —*v.* the third person singular present tense of **fly².**

flight¹ (flīt) *n.* **1.** the act, manner, or power of flying: *The scientist admired the graceful flight of the butterfly. Flight is natural to birds.* **2.** the distance or course traveled by a flying object, as an airplane or bird. **3.** a group flying or passing through the air together: *a flight of swallows, a flight of arrows.* **4.** a trip made by

flicker²

or in an aircraft. **5.** an aircraft making a scheduled trip. **6.** the basic tactical unit of an air force, consisting of from two to five aircraft. **7.** swift movement or passage: *the flight of time.* **8.** a departure from or soaring above or beyond the ordinary: *a flight of fancy.* **9.** a continuous series of stairs or steps between adjacent floors or landings. [Middle English *fliht,* from Old English *flyht,* from *flēogan* to fly.]

flight² (flīt) *n.* the act of fleeing. [Middle English *fluht, fliht,* from Old English *flyht,* from *fleon* to flee.]

· **to put to flight.** to cause to flee; rout.

· **to take (to) flight.** to retreat or flee.

a	at	e	end	o	hot	u	up	hw	white	⎧	about
ā	ape	ē	me	ō	old	ū	use	ng	song		taken
ä	far	i	it	ô	fork	ü	rule	th	thin	ə	pencil
âr	care	ī	ice	oi	oil	u̇	pull	th	this		lemon
		îr	pierce	ou	out	ûr	turn	zh	measure	⎩	circus

F

flight attendant, a person employed to provide service to passengers on an airplane.

flight bag, a small bag of cloth, plastic, or other material, used for carrying clothes and personal effects on board an airplane.

flight control, the control from the ground of aircraft takeoffs and landings, esp. by radio.

flight deck, the upper deck of an aircraft carrier, on which aircraft take off and land.

flight deck of the USS *Enterprise*

flight feather, one of the strong, stiff feathers that form the major portion of the wing and tail of a bird and are essential to flight.

flight·less (flīt′lis) *adj.* (of birds) incapable of flying, as an ostrich.

flight path, the path or trajectory of an object in flight, as an airplane, spacecraft, or meteoroid.

flight recorder, an electronic device that records information about an aircraft in operation, such as instrument readings or conversations in the cockpit, and that can be retrieved and analyzed after an accident to help determine the cause. Also, **black box.**

flight·y (flī′tē) *adj.,* **flight·i·er, flight·i·est.** guided by whim or impulse rather than by reason or mature judgment; irresponsible; capricious. —**flight′i·ly,** *adv.* —**flight′i·ness,** *n.*

flim·flam (flim′flam′) *Informal. n.* **1.** trickery or deception. **2.** foolish talk; rubbish; nonsense. —*v.t.,* **-flammed, -flamming.** to trick or deceive; swindle; cheat. [Probably of Scandinavian origin.]

flim·sy (flim′zē) *adj.,* **-si·er, -si·est. 1.** lacking strength, solidity, or substance; thin; frail: *The blouse was made of a flimsy material. The platform is too flimsy to support our weight.* **2.** lacking validity or effectiveness; not convincing or adequate; weak: *a flimsy excuse.* —*n., pl.* **-sies.** a sheet of thin paper used to make multiple copies, as in newspaper work. [Of uncertain origin.] —**flim′si·ly,** *adv.* —**flim′si·ness,** *n.*

flinch (flinch) *v.i.* to draw back or away, as from something painful, dangerous, or unpleasant; shrink; wince: *to flinch at loud noises, to flinch at the thought of going to the dentist.* —*n.* an act or instance of flinching. [Old French *flenchir* to bend, turn aside; probably of Germanic origin.] —**flinch′er,** *n.*

fling (fling) *v.,* **flung, fling·ing.** —*v.t.* **1.** to throw, esp. with force or violence; hurl: *They flung stones into the pond. The horse flung the rider to the ground.* **2.** to send or put suddenly or violently, as if by throwing; thrust: *to fling someone into prison, to fling one's hands up in disgust.* **3.** to enter into vigorously or completely: *They flung themselves into the campaign.* —*v.i.* to move suddenly or violently; rush headlong. —*n.* **1.** the act of flinging. **2.** a period of freely indulging oneself, as in pleasures or adventure: *to have a fling before settling down.* **3.** a lively or spirited dance, esp. the Highland fling. [Probably of Scandinavian origin.] —**fling′er,** *n.*

  ·**to have** (or **take**) **a fling at.** to have a try at; make an attempt at.

flint (flint) *n.* **1.** a hard, fine-grained variety of quartz, usually dull gray in color, that produces sparks when struck against steel. **2.** a piece of this, esp. as used for kindling a fire or spark. **3.** a piece of this used to produce sparks in cigarette lighters. [Old English *flint* rock.]

flint glass, glass containing lead, used esp. in making lenses.

flint·lock (flint′lok′) *n.* **1.** a gunlock in which a flint was struck against steel to produce sparks and ignite the gunpowder in the pan. **2.** a firearm with such a gunlock.

flint·y (flin′tē) *adj.,* **flint·i·er, flint·i·est. 1.** consisting of, containing, or resembling flint. **2.** hard; unyielding; cruel: *a flinty heart, a flinty look.* —**flint′i·ly,** *adj.* —**flint′i·ness,** *n.*

flip¹ (flip) *v.,* **flipped, flip·ping.** —*v.t.* **1.** to toss with a quick, jerking movement so as to cause to turn over in the air: *to flip a coin.* **2.a.** to turn over, esp. with a quick, jerking movement: *to flip the pages of a book.* **b.** to move with a quick, jerking movement: *to flip a switch.* —*v.i.* **1.** to move or turn with a jerk: *The turtle flipped onto its back.* **2.** to turn, glance at, or proceed quickly; leaf (with *through*): *to flip through the pages of a book.* **3.** *Slang.* to react violently or excitedly (often with *over* or *out*). —*n.* a quick turning or jerking movement. —*adj.,* **flip·per, flip·pest.** *Informal.* impertinent; saucy; flippant: *a flip remark.* [Probably imitative.]

  ·**to flip one's lid** (or **wig** or **top**). *Slang.* to react angrily, violently, or excitedly; lose self-control.

flip² (flip) *n.* a sweetened drink containing an alcoholic beverage, spices, eggs, and sometimes milk. [Probably from FLIP¹; because the drink is prepared by flipping the ingredients.]

flip-flop (flip′flop′) *also,* **flip·flop.** *n.* **1.** *Informal.* a change to the opposite, as in opinion, policy, or loyalty. **2.** an electronic switch that completes either of two circuits depending on preset conditions. **3.** a loose rubber sandal held on the foot by a thong. **4.** the sound made by something flapping. —*v.i.,* **-flopped, -flop·ping.** *Informal.* to change to the opposite, as in opinion; reverse: *The senator flip-flopped on the proposed bill.*

flip·pant (flip′ənt) *adj.* lacking proper respect or seriousness: *a flippant answer, a flippant attitude.* [FLIP¹ + -ANT.] —**flip′pan·cy,** *n.* —**flip′pant·ly,** *adv.*

flip·per (flip′ər) *n.* **1.** a broad, flat limb, as of a seal, dolphin, penguin, or turtle, adapted for swimming. **2.** one of a pair of broad, paddle-shaped shoes, usually of rubber, worn as an aid in swimming, skin diving, and other water sports; fin. **3.** a person or thing that flips.

flip side *Informal.* **1.** the reverse, usually less popular, side of a phonograph record. **2.** the other or opposite side or aspect; reverse: *The mayor's new safety program seemed effective, but the flip side was its high cost.*

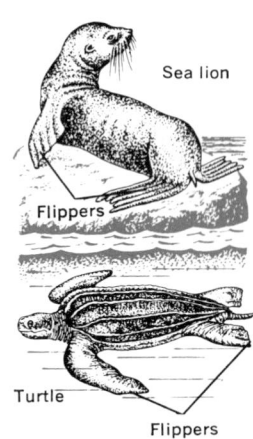

Sea lion

Flippers

Turtle

Flippers

flipper

flirt (flûrt) *v.i.* **1.** to act romantically or affectionately in an enticing, coy, or playful manner; be coquettish. **2.** to approach or handle carelessly, casually, or lightly; trifle or toy with: *to flirt with danger, to flirt with an idea.* **3.** to move quickly or jerkily; flick. —*v.t.* to move or toss with a quick, jerking movement: *The squirrel flirted its tail.* —*n.* **1.** a person who flirts or is coquettish. **2.** a quick movement: *With a flirt of its tail, the deer ran away.* [Of uncertain origin.] —**flirt′y,** *adj.*

flir·ta·tion (flûr tā′shən) *n.* **1.** an act or instance of flirting. **2.** a brief or casual romance.

flir·ta·tious (flûr tā′shəs) *adj.* **1.** inclined to flirt or be coquettish. **2.** characteristic of a flirt: *flirtatious behavior.* —**flir·ta′tious·ly,** *adv.* —**flir·ta′tious·ness,** *n.*

flit (flit) *v.i.,* **flit·ted, flit·ting. 1.** to move or fly lightly and swiftly; dart: *Butterflies flitted among the flowers.* **2.** to pass lightly and swiftly: *The days flit by. Thoughts flitted through my mind.* —*n.* the act of flitting. [Possibly from Old Norse *flytja* to carry.]

flitch (flich) *n.* a side of a hog salted and cured. [Old English *flicce.*]

flit·ter (flit′ər) *n., v.* flutter. [FLIT + -ER⁴.]

fliv·ver (fliv′ər) *n. Slang.* an old, cheap, or dilapidated automobile. [Of uncertain origin.]

float (flōt) *v.i.* **1.** to rest on or at the surface of or be suspended in a liquid: *This bar of soap won't float. I like to float on my back. Bits of cork floated in the glass of wine.* **2.** to move or be carried along gently on or at the surface of liquid: *The toy sailboat floated across the lake. Our raft floated downstream.* **3.** to remain sus-

pended or be carried along in the air or some other gas: *The clouds floated across the sky. Leaves floated down from the trees.* **4.** to hover or move as if suspended or carried along in this manner: *Rumors were floating all about town. Strains of music floated across the lawn.* **5.** to move effortlessly or gracefully, as if buoyed up: *She floated down the stairs.* **6.** to move about aimlessly or in a random or unsettled way; drift: *He floated from job to job.* —*v.t.* **1.** to cause to float: *to float a raft, to float lumber down a river.* **2.** to offer for sale, as stocks or bonds; put on the market: *to float an issue of stock.* **3.** to obtain or negotiate: *to float a loan.* **4.** to flood or irrigate. —*n.* **1.** an object that floats or helps something else to float in a liquid, as a raft anchored near a shore for use by swimmers. **2.** a tableau or exhibit carried on a vehicle or wheeled platform in parades or pageants. **3.** a drink consisting of ice cream floating in a beverage, as soda. **4.** a piece of cork or other material, used to support the end of a fishing line and indicate by its bobbing movement the presence of a fish. **5.** an air-filled sac that serves to keep certain animals afloat, as in the Portuguese man-of-war. **6.** a hollow metal ball or other device that floats on the surface of a body of liquid and is attached to a valve that regulates the level, supply, or outflow of the liquid, as in a carburetor, tank of a toilet, or boiler. [Old English *flotian* to rest on the surface of a liquid.] —**float′a·ble,** *adj.* —For Synonyms *(v.i.),* see **fly**[2].

float·er (flō′tər) *n.* **1.** a person or thing that floats. **2.** a person who votes illegally, esp. for pay, in several voting districts. **3.** a person who changes residences or jobs often. **4.** an insurance policy that covers movable property, as jewelry, wherever it is when lost or damaged.

float·ing (flō′ting) *adj.* **1.** that floats. **2.** not appropriated to any fixed, permanent investment; available for use: *floating capital.* **3.** *Medicine.* displaced, esp. downward, from the usual position: *a floating kidney.*

floating island, a dessert made of boiled custard and meringue, whipped cream, or other topping floating on the surface.

float·ing-point (flō′ting point′) *adj.* of, relating to, or designating a representation of real numbers in which each number has a decimal point, a fixed number of digits after the decimal point, a power of ten or two with a fixed number of digits in the exponent, and a plus or minus sign.

floating rib, a rib attached to the backbone but not to the breastbone. In human beings, the bottom two pairs of ribs are floating ribs.

floc·cu·late (flok′yə lāt′) *v.i., v.t.,* -**lat·ed,** -**lat·ing.** to form or cause to form clumps or fluffy masses, as a chemical precipitate. [Modern Latin *flocculus* small clump, as of wool, from Latin *floccus* + -ATE[1].] —**floc′cu·la′tion,** *n.*

floc·cu·lent (flok′yə lənt) *adj.* **1.** resembling, containing, or covered with tufts of wool or any soft, fluffy substance. **2.** *Chemistry.* consisting of soft, wooly masses, as some precipitates. [Latin *floccus* tuft of wool + -*ulentus* full of.] —**floc′cu·lence,** *n.*

flock[1] (flok) *n.* **1.** a group of animals of one kind gathered or herded together: *a flock of goats, a flock of geese, a shepherd and his flock.* **2.** a large number or group: *a flock of reporters.* **3.** the members of a church; congregation, esp. in relation to its pastor. —*v.i.* to move or gather in crowds: *People flocked to the beaches during the heat wave.* [Old English *flocc* band[1], company.]

flock[2] (flok) *n.* **1.** a tuft, as of wool or hair. **2.** waste wool, cotton, or other fabric, cut up and used to stuff such items as mattresses and cushions. **3.** finely powdered wool or other fiber applied to a surface, as wallpaper, as a decorative or protective coating. —*v.t.* to cover or fill with flock. [Old French *floc* tuft of wool, from Latin *floccus.*]

floe (flō) *n.* **1.** a field or sheet of floating ice. **2.** a detached floating portion of such a field or sheet. Also, **ice floe.** [Norwegian *flo* layer, from Old Norse *flō.*]

flog (flog, flôg) *v.t.,* **flogged, flog·ging.** to beat or whip severely, esp. as punishment. [Possibly modification of Latin *flagellāre* to whip.] —**flog′ger,** *n.*

flood (flud) *n.* **1.** a great flow, rise, or overflowing of water, esp. over ordinarily dry land; deluge. **2.** a great outpouring or abundance; overwhelming quantity: *a flood of tears, a flood of words.* **3.** flood tide. **4.** *also,* **the Flood.** in the Old Testament, the great deluge that occurred in the time of Noah. **5.** *Informal.* floodlight. —*v.t.* **1.** to cover or cause to be covered with a flood; inundate: *The valley was flooded when the dam broke. A heavy rain flooded the town.* **2.** to fill or overwhelm, as with a flood: *Light flooded the stage. The box office was flooded with requests for tickets.* **3.** to supply excessively: *to flood an engine with gasoline.* —*v.i.* **1.** to rise in a flood; overflow. **2.** to become filled with or submerged under a flood: *Our cellar floods after a heavy rain.* **3.** to flow, pour

out, or stream in or as in a flood. [Old English *flōd* flood tide, deluge, body of flowing water.]

flood control, an attempt to prevent or reduce the occurrence of floods, as by the use of dams, artificial channels, or soil conservation.

flood·gate (flud′gāt′) *n.* **1.** a gate in a waterway designed to control the flow of water. Also, **water gate. 2.** something that controls or restrains a flow or outburst.

flood·light (flud′līt′) *n.* **1.** a lamp that provides a broad beam of bright light. **2.** the broad beam of light projected by such a lamp. —*v.t.,* -**light·ed** or -**lit** (-lit′), -**light·ing.** to illuminate with a floodlight.

flood·plain (flud′plān′) *n.* a plain formed by sedimentary deposits, adjacent to and subject to flooding by a river.

flood tide, a rising or incoming tide. ➡ opposed to **ebb tide.**

flood·wa·ter (flud′wô′tər, -wot′ər) *n.* water flooding normally dry land.

floor (flôr) *n.* **1.** the lower enclosing surface of a room, building, or similar structure. **2.** any surface resembling a floor in position or function; bottom surface: *the ocean floor, the forest floor, the floor of a cave.* **3.** a platform or level structure or area used for a specific purpose: *a threshing floor.* **4.** a level or story of a building. **5.** a part of a room or building, as in a legislative house or stock exchange, where members sit, speak, and conduct business: *The bill was debated at length on the floor of the Senate.* **6.** the members of an assembly; audience: *The speaker asked for questions from the floor.* **7.** in parliamentary procedure, the right or privilege to speak to the assembly: *The chair gave me the floor.* **8.** a lower limit or minimum, as of an amount charged or paid: *The economic council demanded that the government fix a wage floor.* —*v.t.* **1.** to cover or furnish with a floor: *to floor a house, to floor a porch.* **2.** to knock unconscious or knock down, as to the floor: *A single punch floored the boxer.* **3.** to depress (the accelerator of a motor vehicle) all the way to the floor. **4.** *Informal.* to bewilder or surprise completely; flabbergast; dumbfound: *I was floored by the news.* [Old English *flōr* bottom of a room or house.]

Synonyms	*n.* **Floor** and **story**[2] denote one of the levels of a building. **Floor** is used chiefly when speaking of the interior, and connotes the unit comprising all the space between floor and ceiling: *Our office is on the third floor.* **Story** is used in speaking of a building from the outside, chiefly as a measure: *That's a thirty-story building.*

floor·board (flôr′bôrd′) *n.* **1.** one of the boards in a floor. **2.** the floor of an automobile.

floor·ing (flôr′ing) *n.* **1.** material for making floors. **2.** a floor or floors.

floor lamp, a tall lamp that stands on the floor.

floor leader, a member of a legislative assembly who is chosen to assist the majority or minority leader in managing his or her party's forces and legislative strategy for a certain period of time or during deliberations on a specific bill.

floor plan, a scale drawing or plan of the sections or spaces of a room, floor, or building, drawn as if seen from above.

floor show, entertainment consisting of singing, dancing, or comic acts, as presented on the dance floor of a nightclub.

floor·walk·er (flôr′wô′kər) *n.* a person employed in a department store or other large store to supervise sales and services.

floo·zy (flü′zē) *also,* **floo·zie.** *n., pl.* -**zies.** *Slang.* a disreputable or promiscuous woman. [Of uncertain origin.]

flop (flop) *v.,* **flopped, flop·ping.** —*v.i.* **1.** to drop or fall loosely, clumsily, or heavily: *to flop into a chair, to flop into bed.* **2.** to move, swing, or flap about loosely or clumsily: *The spaniel's ears flopped about its face.* **3.** *Informal.* to be completely unsuccessful; fail totally: *The play flopped.* —*v.t.* **1.** to throw or drop heavily: *I flopped my books onto the table.* —*n.* **1.** the act of flopping: *The skater took a flop on the ice.* **2.** the sound of flopping; thud: *The toddler fell down with a flop.* **3.** *Informal.* a total failure. [Form of FLAP.] —**flop′per,** *n.*

flop·house (flop′hous′) *n., pl.* -**hous·es** (-hou′ziz). a cheap, shabby rooming house or hotel, esp. one having many beds to a room.

flop·py (flop′ē) *adj.,* -**pi·er,** -**pi·est.** that flops or tends to flop: *a large straw hat with a floppy brim.* —*n., pl.* -**pies.** floppy disk. —**flop′pi·ly,** *adv.* —**flop′pi·ness,** *n.*

a	at	e	end	o	hot	u	up	hw	white		about
ā	ape	ē	me	ō	old	ū	use	ng	song		taken
ä	far	i	it	ô	fork	ü	rule	th	thin	ə	pencil
âr	care	ī	ice	oi	oil	u̇	pull	th	this		lemon
		îr	pierce	ou	out	ûr	turn	zh	measure		circus

floppy disk *Computers.* a flexible plastic disk coated with a magnetic substance and housed inside a protective envelope. It is used to store digitized data and programs. Also, **diskette.**

flo·ra (flôr′ə) *n., pl.* **flo·ras** or **flo·rae** (flôr′ē). the plants or plant life characteristic of a particular place, time, or environment. ➡ distinguished from **fauna.** [Latin *Flora.* See FLORA.]

Flo·ra (flôr′ə) *n.* in Roman mythology, the goddess of flowers. [Latin *Flōra,* from *flōr-,* stem of *flōs* flower.]

flo·ral (flôr′əl) *adj.* of, relating to, or like flowers: *a floral arrangement, a perfume with a floral fragrance.* —**flo′ral·ly,** *adv.*

floral envelope *Botany.* perianth.

Flor·en·tine (flôr′ən tēn′, flor′-) *adj.* **1.** of, relating to, or characteristic of Florence or its people or culture. **2.** *also,* **florentine.** relating to or having a dull, brushed finish engraved with finely traced lines: *florentine gold.* **3.** (of food) prepared or served with spinach. —*n.* a native or inhabitant of Florence.

flo·res·cence (flô res′əns, flə-) *n.* the act, state, or period of blooming or blossoming. [Modern Latin *florescentia,* from Latin *flōrēscere* to begin to blossom.] —**flo·res′cent,** *adj.*

flo·ret (flôr′it) *n.* **1.** a small flower. **2.** *Botany.* one of the small flowers that make up the flower head of a composite plant, as the dandelion, or of a plant of certain other kinds, as the clover. [Old French *florete,* diminutive of *flor* flower, from Latin *flōs.*]

flo·ri·cul·ture (flôr′i kul′chər) *n.* the cultivation of flowers or ornamental flowering plants. [Latin *flōr-,* stem of *flōs* flower + CULTURE.] —**flo′ri·cul′tur·al,** *adj.* —**flo′ri·cul′tur·ist,** *n.*

flor·id (flôr′id, flor′-) *adj.* **1.** flushed with redness; ruddy: *a florid complexion.* **2.** excessively elaborate; ornate; flowery: *The author has a florid style of writing.* [Latin *flōridus* full of flowers, from *flōs* flower.] —**flo·rid·i·ty** (flə rid′i tē), **flor′id·ness,** *n.* —**flor′id·ly,** *adv.* —For Synonyms, see **ornate.**

flor·in (flôr′in, flor′-) *n.* **1.** a former coin of the United Kingdom equal to two shillings. **2.** guilder. **3.** formerly, a gold coin issued at Florence in 1252. **4.** formerly, any of various other gold or silver coins issued in European countries since 1252. [Old French *florin* coin of Florence, from Italian *fiorino,* from *fiore* flower, from Latin *flōs;* because the Florentine coin was decorated with the emblem of Florence, the lily.]

flo·rist (flôr′ist, flor′-) *n.* a person who raises or sells flowers and ornamental plants. [Latin *flōr-,* stem of *flōs* flower + -IST.]

flo·ris·tic (flô ris′tik) *adj.* of or relating to flowers or floristics.

flo·ris·tics (flô ris′tiks) *n.* the branch of botany concerned with identifying and listing all the plant species in a particular area. ➡ used as singular. [FLORIST + -ICS.]

floss (flôs, flos) *n.* **1.** short silk fibers or waste. **2.** a soft, loosely twisted silk thread made from such fibers, used for embroidery. **3.** soft, silky fibers or fluff found in cotton, corn, milkweed, and other plants. **4.** dental floss. —*v.t.* to clean (teeth) with dental floss. —*v.i.* to clean the teeth with dental floss. [French *floche* flossy, shaggy, possibly going back to Latin *flūxus* weak, frail.]

floss·y (flô′sē, flos′ē) *adj.,* **floss·i·er, floss·i·est.** of, relating to, or like floss.

flo·ta·tion (flō tā′shən) *n.* **1.** the act or state of floating. **2.** a method of separating a mineral in an ore from waste materials or from other minerals by using a chemical solution that makes the ore particles water resistant and causes them to float. [FLOAT + -ATION.]

flo·til·la (flō til′ə) *n.* **1.** a fleet of small vessels. **2.** a small fleet. **3.** in the U.S. Navy, a group of small ships, as destroyers, usually consisting of two or more squadrons. [Spanish *flotilla* small fleet¹, diminutive of *flota* fleet¹, from Old French *flote,* from Old Norse *floti* fleet¹, raft.]

flot·sam (flot′səm) *n.* **1.** the wreckage of a ship or its cargo, found floating on the sea. ➡ distinguished from **jetsam.** **2.** flotsam and jetsam *(defs. 2, 3).* [Anglo-Norman *floteson* floating wreckage, from Old French *floter* to float; of Germanic origin.]

flotsam and jetsam 1. the wreckage of a ship or its cargo floating on the water or washed ashore. **2.** worthless or miscellaneous things; trifles; odds and ends. **3.** unemployed drifters or vagrants; transients.

flounce¹ (flouns) *v.i.,* **flounced, flounc·ing. 1.** to go or move with abrupt, agitated, or impatient movements of the body, as in anger or petulance: *The child flounced out of the room in anger.* **2.** to move in an exaggerated manner, as if to attract attention: *The twins flounced about the room in their new outfits.* —*n.* an act or instance of flouncing; abrupt or impatient movement: *to sit down with a flounce.* [Possibly of Scandinavian origin.]

flounce² (flouns) *n.* a wide strip of cloth, gathered along one edge and attached as a trimming, as on a dress or a sofa. —*v.t.,* **flounced, flouncing.** to trim or furnish with a flounce or flounces. [Earlier *frounce* wrinkle, fold, from Middle English *frounce,* from Old French *fronce,* from *froncir* to wrinkle, fold; of Germanic origin.] —**flounc′y,** *adj.*

floun·der¹ (floun′dər) *v.i.* **1.** to move with stumbling or plunging motions; struggle awkwardly or clumsily: *The boat floundered in the surf. The explorers floundered about in the swamp.* **2.** to speak, act, or move in a stumbling, awkward, or confused manner: *to flounder through a speech.* —*n.* the act or movement of floundering. [Earlier *flunder,* possibly blend of FOUNDER¹ and BLUNDER.]

floun·der² (floun′dər) *n., pl.* **-der** or **-ders.** a flatfish of either of two families, Bothidae and Pleuronectidae, valued as both a food and a game fish. Length: 1½ feet (46 centimeters). [Middle English *flounder;* of Scandinavian origin.]

flour (flour, flou′ər) *n.* **1.** a soft, powdery substance obtained by grinding and sifting grain, esp. wheat, used chiefly as a basic ingredient in baked goods and other foods. **2.** any soft, powdery substance. —*v.t.* to cover or sprinkle with flour. [Form of FLOWER in the sense of "finest part"]

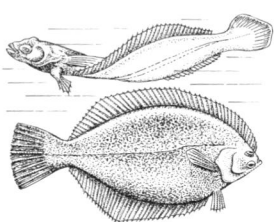

flounder²

flour·ish (flûr′ish) *v.i.* **1.** to grow or develop vigorously or prosperously; thrive: *Their business is flourishing.* **2.** to reach or be at the peak of development, achievement, or influence: *a civilization that flourished thousands of years ago.* —*v.t.* **1.** to wave about with bold or sweeping gestures; brandish: *to flourish a sword.* **2.** to display ostentatiously; flaunt. —*n.* **1.** a brandishing: *He bowed with a flourish of his hat.* **2.** an ostentatious or dramatic display or gesture: *She entered the room with a flourish.* **3.** a decorative stroke or embellishment in writing. **4.** an elaborate, ornamental passage or series of notes, as a trill or fanfare, added to a musical work. [Old French *floriss-,* a stem of *florir* to flower, bloom, going back to Latin *flōrēre* to flower, bloom.] —**flour′ish·er,** *n.* —**flour′ish·ing·ly,** *adv.* —For Synonyms *(v.i.),* see **prosper.**

flour·y (flour′ē, flou′ə rē) *adj.* **1.** of, relating to, or resembling flour. **2.** covered with or as with flour.

flout (flout) *v.t.* to treat with disdain or contempt; scoff at; defy: *to flout the authorities, to flout tradition.* —*n.* a disdainful or contemptuous remark or act. [Middle English *flouten* to play the flute, from Old French *flauter,* from *flaute, fleute.* See FLUTE.] —**flout′er,** *n.* —**flout′ing·ly,** *adv.*

flow (flō) *v.i.* **1.** to move or pass along steadily and smoothly, as in a continuous stream: *The river flows northward. Electricity flowed through the wire.* **2.** to move along steadily, smoothly, or readily, as in a stream: *Money from investments flowed in. Conversation at the party flowed freely.* **3.** to issue or proceed, as from a source: *The crowd flowed out of the stadium. Orders for supplies flow from the manager's office.* **4.** to appear to move with harmonious, continuous motion; have smooth continuity: *The lines in the painting flowed together.* **5.** to be full or plentiful; overflow: *My heart was flowing with happiness.* **6.** to hang, fall, or ripple loosely: *The skirt flows from the waist.* **7.** to come in or advance; rise, as the tide: *The waters ebb and flow.* **8.** to menstruate. —*n.* **1.** the act or manner of flowing: *to stop the flow of blood, to move in a steady flow.* **2.** menstrual discharge. **3.** any continuous, uninterrupted movement; outpouring; stream: *the flow of traffic.* **4.** something that flows. **5.** an amount that flows in a given time. **6.** the coming in or rising of the tide. **7.** a movement of energy: *heat flow in the earth's crust.* [Old English *flōwan* to move in a stream.]

flow·chart, (flō′chärt′) *also,* **flow chart.** *n.* a schematic diagram showing a sequence of operations, as for a computer program or industrial process.

flow·er (flou′ər) *n.* **1.** the part of a flowering plant composed of the reproductive organs and their surrounding, usually brightly colored petals; blossom; bloom. **2.** a plant cultivated for the beauty of its blossoms. **3.** the state or time of blossoming: *an orchard in flower.* **4.** the finest or choicest part or example: *the flower of a country's youth, the flower of chivalry.* **5.** the finest or most flourishing period: *in the flower of youth, the days when knighthood was in flower.* **6.** a decorative feature or embellishment, esp. a figure of speech. **7. flowers.** *Chemistry.* a substance in the form of a fine powder, produced by condensation or sublimation: *flowers of zinc.* ➡ used as singular in def. 7. —*v.i.* **1.** to produce flowers; bloom: *Cherry trees flower in the early spring.*

2. to be at or reach fullest development or growth: *The author's writing ability flowered early.* —*v.t.* to decorate or cover with flowers or a floral design. [Old French *flo(u)r* blossom, finest part, from Latin *flōr-*, stem of *flōs* blossom.] —**flow′er·less,** *adj.* —**flow′er·like′,** *adj.*

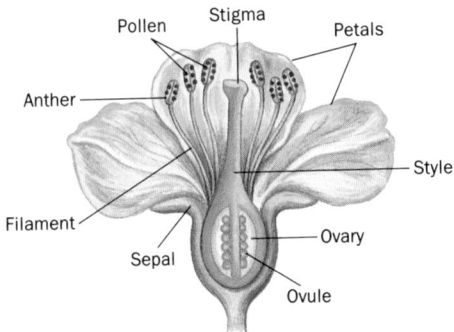

parts of a **flower**

flow·ered (flou′ərd) *adj.* **1.** having or covered with flowers: *a flowered hillside.* **2.** having or decorated with a floral design: *a flowered blouse.*

flow·er·et (flou′ər it) *n.* a small flower; floret.

flower girl, a young girl who carries flowers and precedes the bride in a wedding procession.

flower head *Botany.* an inflorescence consisting of a dense cluster of tiny flowers.

flowering plant, any of a large group of plants, division Anthophyta, including trees and shrubs, whose seeds are borne enclosed in an ovary. They constitute the largest division of the plant kingdom, including more than half of all known species. Also, **angiosperm.**

flow·er·pot (flou′ər pot′) *n.* a pot, often clay, in which to grow plants.

flow·er·y (flou′ə rē) *adj.,* **-er·i·er, -er·i·est. 1.** covered with or resembling flowers. **2.** using or containing elaborate, elegant, or highly embellished language; florid. **3.** having or decorated with a floral design. —**flow′er·i·ly,** *adv.* —**flow′er·i·ness,** *n.*

flown (flōn) a past participle of **fly**[2].

fl oz *also,* **fl. oz.** fluid ounce.

flu (flü) *n.* **1.** *Informal.* influenza. **2.** a variety of influenza named for the area in which it originated, as Asian flu, or for the animal that transmits it, as swine flu. **3.** a viral infection, esp. a respiratory or intestinal one.

flub (flub) *Informal. v.t.,* **flubbed, flub·bing.** to do in an awkward, unskillful manner; bungle: *I flubbed my lines in the second act.* —*n.* a bungling error; blunder. [Of uncertain origin.]

fluc·tu·ate (fluk′chü āt′) *v.i.* **-at·ed, -at·ing. 1.** to change, vary, or move up and down continually or irregularly; be wavering, unsteady, or unstable: *The stock market fluctuates daily.* **2.** to move in or as in waves. [Latin *flūctuātus,* past participle of *flūctuāre* to waver, from *flūctus* wave.] —**fluc′tu·a′tion,** *n.*

flue (flü) *n.* **1.** a passage, as in a chimney, for conveying smoke, hot air, or waste gas. **2.a.** flue pipe. **b.** the air passage in such a pipe. [Of uncertain origin.]

flu·en·cy (flü′ən sē) *n.* the quality or condition of being fluent; ease or smoothness, as in speech or writing.

flu·ent (flü′ənt) *adj.* **1.** spoken or written smoothly and effortlessly: *fluent poetry, fluent English.* **2.** capable of speaking or writing smoothly and effortlessly: *a fluent speaker, to be fluent in Spanish.* **3.** characterized by smoothness and grace: *fluent motion.* [Latin *fluēns,* present participle of *fluere* to flow.] —**flu′ent·ly,** *adv.*

flue pipe, an organ pipe whose tone is produced by a current of air striking the mouth, or opening, of the pipe.

fluff (fluf) *n.* **1.** a soft, light, downy material: *The kitten looked like a ball of fluff.* **2.** a soft, downy mass: *Fluffs of hair lay on the barber's floor.* **3.** something that is inconsequential or trivial. **4.** an error or blunder, esp. one made by a performer in the delivery of his or her lines. —*v.t.* **1.** to shake, pat, or puff out into a soft, downy mass; make fluffy: *The nurse fluffed up my pillows. The bird fluffed its feathers. She fluffed her hair out with her fingers.* **2.** to make an error or blunder in: *The actor fluffed his lines.* [Probably modification of obsolete *flue* downy material, from Flemish *vluwe,* from French *velu* shaggy, going back to Latin *villus* shaggy hair.]

fluff·y (fluf′ē) *adj.,* **fluff·i·er, fluff·i·est.** consisting of, covered with, or resembling fluff: *a fluffy sweater, to beat egg whites until fluffy.* —**fluff′i·ly,** *adv.* —**fluff′i·ness,** *n.*

flu·id (flü′id) *n.* **1.** a substance, as a liquid or gas, that is capable of flowing, has no definite shape, and adapts itself to the shape of any container that confines it. **2.** any liquid: *The doctor told me to stay in bed and drink plenty of fluids.* —*adj.* **1.** capable of flowing; not solid; liquid or gaseous. **2.** of, relating to, or consisting of fluids: *a fluid diet.* **3.** changing readily; not fixed, firm, or stable: *a fluid political situation.* **4.** characterized by smoothness and grace, as in movement or style. [Latin *fluidus* flowing, liquid.] —**flu·id′i·ty, flu′id·ness,** *n.* —**flu′id·ly,** *adv.*

fluid dram, a liquid measure of capacity equal to $1/8$ of a fluid ounce (3.7 milliliters).

flu·id·ic (flü id′ik) *adj.* relating to or like a fluid.

flu·id·ics (flü id′iks) *n.* a science concerned with the study and application of the properties of flowing gases and liquids, esp. as they can be used to replace mechanical and electronic devices in performing various functions, as amplification. ➡ used as singular.

fluid mechanics, the branch of physics that deals with fluids in motion and at rest, including aerodynamics, hydrodynamics, and hydrostatics.

fluid ounce, a liquid measure of capacity equal to $1/16$ of a pint (29.6 milliliters).

fluke[1] (flük) *n.* **1.** either of the two flat, triangular pieces on an anchor designed to catch in the bottom of a body of water. For illustration, see **anchor. 2.** a barb or barbed head, as of an arrow, harpoon, or spear. **3.** either of the lobes, or horizontal fins, of a whale's tail. [Possibly from FLUKE[3]; because of the similarity of shape.]

fluke[2] (flük) *n.* an unexpected or accidental stroke or turn, esp. of good luck; chance happening. [Of uncertain origin.]

fluke[3] (flük) *n.* **1.** any of various flatfish, esp. some flounder. **2.** any of a group of parasitic flatworms, class Trematoda, that infest many kinds of animals, including snails, fish, birds, and mammals. Also *(def. 2),* **trematode.** [Old English *flōc* flatfish.]

fluk·y (flü′kē) *adj.,* **fluk·i·er, fluk·i·est. 1.** unexpected or accidental, as a stroke of good luck. **2.** uncertain; changeable: *a fluky breeze.* —**fluk′i·ness,** *n.*

flume (flüm) *n.* **1.** a deep, narrow passage or ravine through which a stream runs. **2.** an artificial chute or trough, esp. an inclined one, that carries water, as for conveying logs or furnishing water power. [Old French *flum* river, from Latin *flūmen.*]

flum·mer·y (flum′ə rē) *n., pl.* **-mer·ies. 1.** any of various sweet, puddinglike dishes. **2.** empty flattery; utter nonsense. [Welsh *llymru* jellied and boiled sour oatmeal.]

flum·mox (flum′əks) *v.t. Informal.* to throw into confusion; bewilder; perplex. [Of uncertain origin.]

flung (flung) the past tense and past participle of **fling.**

flunk (flungk) *Informal. v.t.* **1.** to fail to pass; fail: *to flunk an exam, to flunk a course.* **2.** to give a failing grade or mark to: *The teacher flunked five students.* —*v.i.* to fail, as in an examination: *I flunked because I didn't study.* —*n.* a failure, as in an examination or course. [Possibly blend of FLINCH and FUNK.]

  •**to flunk out.** to be dismissed, as from a school, because of failing grades.

flunk·ey (flung′kē) *n., pl.* **-eys.** flunky.

flunk·y (flung′kē) *n., pl.* **flunk·ies. 1.** a person who fawningly serves and tries to please another; servile follower or hanger-on. **2.** a footman or other male servant, esp. one who wears livery. **3.** a person who performs menial tasks; lackey. [Possibly modification of earlier *flanker* person stationed at another's *flank* or side. See FLANK.]

flu·or (flü′ər, -ôr, flür) *n.* fluorite. [Latin *fluor* a flowing; referring to its use as a flux in smelting.]

fluo·resce (flü res′, flô-) *v.i.,* **-resced, -resc·ing.** to produce or show fluorescence. [From FLUORESCENCE.]

fluo·res·ce·in (flü res′ē in, flô-) *n.* a reddish powder that dissolves in alkaline solutions to produce a fluorescent green dye, used in medical tests and in tracing the movements of ground water. Formula: $C_{20}H_{12}O_5$ [FLUORESCE + -IN[1].]

fluo·res·cence (flü res′əns, flô-) *n.* **1.** the emission of visible light from a substance that is absorbing radiant energy, such as X rays or ultraviolet rays. Fluorescence continues only as long as the substance is exposed to the source of energy. ➡ distinguished from **phosphorescence. 2.** light so emitted. [FLUOR(SPAR) +

a	at	e	end	o	hot	u	up	hw	white		about
ā	ape	ē	me	ō	old	ū	use	ng	song		taken
ä	far	i	it	ô	fork	ü	rule	th	thin	ə	pencil
âr	care	ī	ice	oi	oil	u̇	pull	th̲	this		lemon
		îr	pierce	ou	out	ûr	turn	zh	measure		circus

477

-ESCENCE; because this phenomenon was first observed in the mineral *fluorspar,* in 1852.]

fluo·res·cent (flù res'ənt, flô-) *adj.* **1.** producing, resulting from, or showing fluorescence. **2.** extremely bright or vivid, as if glowing: *a fluorescent nylon jacket.*

fluorescent lamp, an electric lamp that produces ultraviolet light and converts it into a cooler form of visible light than that given off by an incandescent lamp.

fluor·i·date (flùr'i dāt', flôr'-) *v.t.,* -dat·ed, -dat·ing. to add a fluoride to (drinking water), esp. to reduce tooth decay. Also, **fluorinate.** —**fluor'i·da'tion,** *n.*

fluo·ride (flùr'īd, flôr'-) *n.* a compound consisting of fluorine and another element or radical. [FLUOR + -IDE. See FLUORINE.]

fluor·i·nate (flùr'ə nāt', flôr'-) *v.t.,* -nat·ed, -nat·ing. **1.** to treat or combine with fluorine. **2.** fluoridate. —**fluor'i·na'tion,** *n.*

fluo·rine (flùr'ēn, flôr'-) *n.* the most reactive nonmetallic element, a greenish yellow gas that is poisonous and very corrosive. Symbol: **F** For tables, see **element.** [French *fluorine,* from Latin *fluor* a flow, from *fluere* to flow; because minerals containing fluorine were used as a flux during refining.]

fluo·rite (flùr'īt, flôr'-) *n.* a transparent to translucent mineral that consists of calcium fluoride and occurs in a variety of colors, used esp. as a flux to help melt iron ore in steel production. Formula: CaF_2 Also, **fluor, fluorspar.** [FLUOR + -ITE¹.]

fluor·o·car·bon (flùr'ō kär'bən, flôr'-) *n.* any of a group of organic compounds containing both carbon and fluorine, such as Freon, having great chemical stability and resistance to heat, widely used as refrigerants, lubricants, and insulators. Fluorocarbons are no longer used as propellants in aerosol cans because they are destructive of the ozone layer of the atmosphere.

fluor·o·scope (flùr'ə skōp', flôr'-) *n.* an instrument used to examine internal structures or parts, as of the body. It consists of an X-ray machine and a fluorescent screen that registers patterns of light and shadow made by variations in the resistance that different materials offer to the passage of X rays. —*v.t.,* -scoped, -scop·ing. to examine with a fluoroscope. [FLUOR(ESCENCE) + -SCOPE.] —**fluor·o·scop·ic** (flùr'ə skop'ik, flôr'-), *adj.* —**fluor'o·scop'i·cal·ly,** *adv.*

fluor·os·co·py (flù ros'kə pē, flô-) *n.* an examination conducted by means of a fluoroscope. —**fluor·os'co·pist,** *n.*

flu·or·spar (flü'ər spär', -ôr-) *n.* fluorite. [FLUOR + SPAR³.]

flur·ry (flûr'ē) *n., pl.* -ries. **1.** a sudden or nervous movement, commotion, or agitation; stir: *a flurry of activity, a flurry of excitement.* **2.** a light, scattered snowfall, accompanied by gusts of wind. **3.** a brief, sudden gust: *a flurry of wind.* **4.** a sudden, brief outburst of heavy trading on a stock or commodity exchange. —*v.,* -ried, -ry·ing. —*v.t.* to agitate or confuse; fluster. —*v.i.* to move in an agitated or nervous manner: *The performers flurried about backstage.* [Obsolete *flurr* to scatter, whir (of imitative origin) + -Y³.]

flush¹ (flush) *v.i.* **1.** to glow or become suffused with a reddish color: *Your face flushed with embarrassment.* **2.** to become red in the face, as from emotion; blush: *I flushed when I realized my mistake.* **3.** to flow or rush suddenly or copiously: *Water flushed through the pipes.* **4.** to become cleaned or emptied through a sudden, rapid rush or flow, as of water. —*v.t.* **1.** to cause to redden: *The child was flushed with fever.* **2.** to clean, empty, or wash with a sudden, rapid rush or flow, as of water: *to flush out a drain.* **3.** to stir up or fill, as with pride, elation, or excitement: *to be flushed with success.* —*n.* **1.** a reddish color or glow. **2.** a rush or surge of elation, excitement, or other emotion. **3.** a flowing vigor or freshness: *the first flush of spring.* **4.** a rapid, sudden rush or flow, as of water. **5.** a brief, sudden feeling of being hot. [Of uncertain origin.]

flush² (flush) *adj.* **1.** having immediate contact; directly abutting or adjacent; touching: *The table was flush against the wall.* **2.** even or level, as with a surface; forming one plane; being in exact alignment: *The top of the wall is flush with the roof.* **3.** well or abundantly supplied, esp. with money: *I'm feeling particularly flush because it's payday.* **4.** abundant or plentiful, as money. **5.** prosperous: *flush times.* —*adv.* **1.** in immediate or direct contact: *We set the bureau flush against the wall.* **2.** in an even or level manner, so as to form one plane or be in exact alignment: *They placed the second picture flush with the first.* **3.** directly; squarely: *to hit someone flush on the chin.* [Middle English *flusshen;* of uncertain origin.]

flush³ (flush) *v.t.* to drive from cover or from a hiding place, as birds: *The hunter flushed the quail from the bushes. The police flushed out the fugitive.* —*v.i.* to start up or flee from cover. [Middle English *flusshen* rush, spring.]

flush⁴ (flush) *n.* in card games, a hand or set of cards all of one suit. A **royal flush** consists of the five highest cards of a particular suit; a **straight flush** consists of any five consecutive cards of a

particular suit. [Middle French *flus,* from Latin *fluxus* a flow, flux, from *fluere* to flow.]

flus·ter (flus'tər) *v.t.* to cause to be embarrassed or at a loss; agitate and confuse. —*n.* a state of agitated confusion. [Probably of Scandinavian origin.]

flute (flüt) *n.* **1.** a reedless musical instrument of the woodwind family, consisting of a hollow cylinder with finger holes or keys along its length, played through a mouthpiece near one end, and producing a high-pitched tone. **2.a.** a shallow, rounded groove on the shaft of a column. **b.** any similar groove, esp. a decorative one, as on silverware or in a ruffle or pie crust. —*v.,* **flut·ed, flut·ing.** —*v.i.* **1.** to play on a flute. **2.** to produce a sound like that of a flute. —*v.t.* **1.** to utter with a sound like that of a flute. **2.** to make flutes in: *to flute the edges of a pie crust.* [Old French *flaute, fleute* this musical instrument; possibly of imitative origin.]

flut·ed (flü'tid) *adj.* decorated with flutes: *a fluted column.*

flut·ing (flü'ting) *n.* **1.** ornamentation or decoration with flutes or grooves. **2.** a groove or a series of grooves; flutes or grooves collectively. **3.** the act of making such flutes or grooves.

flut·ist (flü'tist) *also,* **flautist.** *n.* a person who plays the flute.

flut·ter (flut'ər) *v.i.* **1.** to wave or flap quickly and irregularly: *The flag fluttered in the breeze.* **2.** to fly, hover, or flap the wings lightly, gracefully, and with quick, irregular movements: *Butterflies fluttered among the flowers.* **3.** to fall or move with light, irregular motion: *Leaves fluttered to the ground.* **4.** to move about lightly, quickly, or in a nervous, excited manner. **5.** to beat quickly and irregularly, as the heart. —*v.t.* to cause to flutter: *to flutter one's eyelashes.* Also, **flitter.** —*n.* **1.** a quick, irregular movement: *the flutter of a bird's wings.* **2.** a state of nervous confusion or excitement: *to be in a flutter.* **3.** *Medicine.* an abnormally rapid pulsation, as of the heart or diaphragm. **4.** a variation in the pitch of recorded sound. [Old English *flotorian* to float about, flap the wings.] —**flut'ter·er,** *n.*

flutter kick, a kick in swimming in which the legs are moved alternately up and down with the feet pointed out.

flu·vi·al (flü'vē əl) *adj.* relating to, found in, or produced by a river, as a delta: *fluvial deposits.* [Latin *fluviālis,* from *fluvius* river.]

flux (fluks) *n.* **1.** constant change or movement: *Our vacation plans are currently in a state of flux.* **2.** a flowing or flow. **3.** a flowing in of the tide. **4.** *Metallurgy.* **a.** a substance, as lime, that promotes the fusion of metals or minerals, used chiefly in metal refining. **b.** a substance, as rosin, used in soldering to promote the flowing of the solder. **5.** *Physics.* **a.** the rate of flow of fluids, particles, or energy, such as light or other radiant energy, through a given area. **b.** magnetic flux. **6.** *Medicine.* an abnormal, excessive discharge of liquid matter from the body. —*v.t.* to treat, as metal, with a flux. [Latin *flūxus* a flowing.]

flux·ion (fluk'shən) *n.* the act of flowing; flow or flux.

fly¹ (flī) *n., pl.* **flies. 1.** any of a large group of insects, order Diptera, including houseflies, mosquitoes, and gnats, that have sucking mouthparts and one pair of transparent wings. **2.** any of various other flying insects. **3.** a fishhook decorated, as with feathers or other material, so as to resemble an insect. [Old English *flēoge* winged insect.]

• **fly in the ointment.** something that detracts from or spoils the value, usefulness, or enjoyment of something else.

fly¹ *(def. 3)*
fishing flies

fly² (flī) *v.* *(v.i. defs. 1-7, v.t.)* **flew, flown, fly·ing** or *(v.i. def.- 8)* **flied, fly·ing.** —*v.i.* **1.** to move through the air by using wings, as a bird does. **2.** to operate, move, or travel in an aircraft or spacecraft: *The pilot flew to Chicago. They flew to Los Angeles last night.* **3.** to pass, move, or be propelled through the air by the wind or other force: *Bullets flew in all directions. The ocean spray flew into our faces.* **4.** to wave or flutter in the air: *A flag flew from the ship's mast.* **5.** to move or pass swiftly; speed: *We flew up the stairs when we heard the child crying. The summer flew by.* **6.** to change rapidly and suddenly from one state, condition, or position to another; pass abruptly into a particular state: *The door flew open. The clay pigeon flew apart when the pellets struck it. The spoiled child flew into a rage.* **7.** to run away; flee. **8.** *Baseball.* to hit a fly ball: *The batter flied to left field.* —*v.t.* **1.** to cause to move through or float in the air: *to fly a kite. The ship flew the flag of its country.* **2.** to operate (an aircraft or spacecraft): *My cousin flew a bomber during the war.* **3.** to traverse or pass over, as in an aircraft: *They flew the Atlantic Ocean in five hours.* **4.** to take part in or perform (something) in an aircraft or spacecraft: *The pilot had flown fifteen missions.* **5.** to carry or transport by air: *They flew supplies to the city.* **6.** to flee from; avoid; shun. —*n., pl.* **flies. 1.** an opening in the front of a pair of trousers, usually having a zipper, buttons, or other fastening, concealed by a flap of material. **2.** a flap at the entrance of a tent. **3.** a piece of canvas pitched in front of or over a tent to provide extra protection. **4.a.** the length of a flag from its supported edge to the outer edge. **b.** the outer edge of a flag. **5.** flyleaf. **6.** fly ball. **7.** flywheel. **8.** *British.* a light carriage used for public transportation, as a hackney or hansom. **9.** **flies.** *Theater.* the space above and behind the proscenium of a stage. [Old English *flēogan* to move with wings through the air, flee.] —**fly'a·bil'i·ty,** *n.* —**fly'a·ble,** *adj.*

• **on the fly.** while still in flight; before touching the ground: *to catch a ball on the fly.*
• **to fly at** (or **into**). to attack or lash out at suddenly and violently.
• **to fly in the face** (or **teeth**) **of.** to defy openly or brazenly: *to fly in the face of the law.*
• **to let fly.** to discharge or hurl with force or violence: *to let fly a stone, to let fly an oath.*

Synonyms *v.i.* **Fly², soar, sail, glide,** and **float** may all mean to move through the air on or as if on wings. **Fly** is the general term, which usually suggests rapid movement: *Some birds fly south in the winter. How fast do they fly?* **Soar** connotes easy-seeming upward movement and height above the ground, as seen in the flight of hawks: *The new jet soared into the stratosphere.* **Sail** is similar to *soar,* but is also used of flight parallel to the ground, and suggests the filling of the wings, like a boat's sails, with air: *The eagle sailed across the mouth of the canyon.* **Glide** connotes riding on air currents without moving one's wings or employing other power: *To save fuel, the pilot turned off the motor and glided.* **Float** connotes moving easily but slowly, almost to the point of standing still: *Buzzards floated overhead, as if motionless.*

fly agaric, a very poisonous mushroom, *Amanita muscaria,* with a glossy, bright red or orange cap and white spots.

fly ash, a sooty substance consisting of fine, solid particles of noncombustible ash carried out of a furnace flue with the waste gases produced during combustion of solid fuel.

fly·a·way (flī'ə wā') *adj.* tending to muss or become disarranged; loosely streaming: *flyaway hair.*

fly ball *Baseball.* A ball hit high into the air. Also, **fly.**

fly·blown (flī'blōn') *adj.* **1.** covered or tainted with the eggs or larvae of flies. **2.** tainted; impure; corrupt.

fly·by (flī'bī') *n., pl.* **-bys.** the flight of a spacecraft close to a celestial body, esp. to collect scientific data.

fly-by-night (flī'bī nīt') *adj.* not established or operating on a sound or permanent basis; not to be trusted, esp. in financial matters: *a fly-by-night scheme, a fly-by-night business.* —*n.* a person or thing that is fly-by-night, esp. someone who cheats creditors by departing secretly.

fly casting, the sport of casting a fishing line using artificial flies and a longer, more flexible rod than used when fishing with bait. Also, **fly fishing.**

fly·catch·er (flī'kach'ər) *n.* any insect-eating bird of either of two large families, the **tyrant flycatchers,** family Tyrannidae, of North and South America, and the **Old World flycatchers,** family Muscicapidae, of the Eastern Hemisphere. Length: 3½-16 inches (9-41 centimeters).

fly·er (flī'ər) flier.

flying boat, a seaplane having a fuselage shaped like the hull of a boat, enabling it to float on water.

flying buttress, an arched masonry support between a pier or other structure and the wall of a building that helps support the weight of the roof, used esp. in Gothic architecture.

flying colors, complete and triumphant success: *I passed the exam with flying colors.* [From the custom of displaying or raising the colors, that is, one's flag, to indicate victory.]

flying fish, any of a group of saltwater fish, family Exocoetidae, that are found in warm waters and have one to two pairs of winglike, pectoral fins that enable them to leap into the air and glide for some distance. They are valued as both food and game fish. Length: to 1½ feet (50 centimeters).

flying fox, any of various large tropical fruit bats, family Pteropodidae, having a foxlike face and, often, gray or black fur with yellow markings on the shoulders. It is the largest of all bats. Wingspan: to 5 feet (1.5 meters).

flying gurnard, a tropical marine fish, family Dactylopteridae, having a large pectoral fin that enables it to glide in the air for several yards.

flying
buttress

flying jib, a small, triangular sail set out beyond the jib on an extension of the jib boom.

flying machine, an airplane or other aircraft that is heavier than air.

flying saucer, any of various UFOs allegedly having a saucerlike or disklike shape and presumed to be from outer space.

flying squirrel, any of various squirrellike rodents, family Sciuridae, of the forests of Europe, Asia, and North America, having winglike membranes between the front and hind legs that enable them to make long, gliding leaps through the air. Length: to 3 feet (0.9 meter).

flying start 1. the start of a race in which the contestants are already moving when they cross the starting line. **2.** any swift, promising, or vigorous start or beginning: *The tremendous reception launched the fundraising campaign with a flying start.*

fly·leaf (flī'lēf') *n., pl.* **-leaves** (-lēvz'). a blank sheet of paper at the beginning or end of a book or other bound printed matter. Also, **fly.**

fly·o·ver (flī'ō'vər) *n.* a low-altitude flight over a specific area

flying squirrel

by one or more aircraft, often as part of a display or exhibition.

fly·pa·per (flī'pā'pər) *n.* paper covered with a sticky or poisonous substance, placed so as to catch or kill flies.

fly·speck (flī'spek') *n.* **1.** a tiny spot of excrement left by a fly. **2.** any very small or hardly noticeable spot.

fly swatter, a device for swatting or killing flies or other insects, usually a square sheet of wire or plastic mesh attached to a long handle.

fly·trap (flī'trap') *n.* **1.** any of various plants that trap insects, as the Venus's-flytrap or the pitcher plant. **2.** any device for catching flies.

fly·way (flī'wā') *n.* a particular air route along which migratory birds regularly travel.

fly·weight (flī'wāt') *n.* a boxer competing in the lowest weight class of up to 112 pounds (51 kilograms), or a competitor, as a wrestler, in a similar class.

fly·wheel (flī'hwēl', -wēl') *n.* a heavy wheel driven by an engine shaft, serving to regulate and make more uniform the speed of an engine.

Fm, the symbol for fermium.

fm. **1.** fathom. **2.** from.

FM 1. a method of radio broadcasting by which a signal is transmitted over radio carrier waves by altering the frequency of the waves. **2.** a broadcasting system using this method. **3.** of, relating

a	at	e	end	o	hot	u	up	hw	white		(about
ā	ape	ē	me	ō	old	ū	use	ng	song		{ taken
ä	far	i	it	ô	fork	ü	rule	th	thin	ə	pencil
âr	care	ī	ice	oi	oil	u̇	pull	th	this		lemon
				îr	pierce	ou	out	ûr	turn	zh	measure	(circus

F

to, or using an FM broadcasting system: *an FM radio, an FM station.* ➡ distinguished from **AM**. [Abbreviation of *f(requency) m(odulation).*]

f-num·ber (ef′num′bər) *n.* a number obtained by dividing the focal length of a lens by its diameter. A camera lens whose focal length is 50 mm and diameter is 28 mm has an f-number of 1.8, written f/1.8 or f1.8. [Abbreviation of *f(ocal length)* + NUMBER.]

foal (fōl) *n.* a young offspring of a horse, donkey, zebra, or other member of the horse family, esp. one under one year of age. —*v.i., v.t.* to give birth to (a foal). [Old English *fola.*]

foam (fōm) *n.* **1.** a frothy mass of bubbles, as that formed on the surface of a liquid by violent agitation or by fermentation: *the foam formed by breaking waves, the foam on top of a milk shake.* **2.** a similar frothy mass, as of saliva or sweat: *After the race, the horse's flanks were covered with foam.* **3.** the thick, frothy mass that results when a liquid under pressure is released from its container, as certain shaving creams. **4.** a similar substance used in firefighting to smother flames. —*v.i.* **1.** to form or produce foam: *The water foamed and bubbled when the soap flakes were added.* **2.** to flow or gush in a foam: *The soda foamed over the top of the glass.* [Old English *fām* froth, spume.]
  ·**to foam at the mouth.** *Informal.* to be extremely or uncontrollably angry; be enraged or furious.

foam rubber, a spongy synthetic rubber, chiefly used in mattresses and as upholstery and insulation.

foam·y (fō′mē) *adj.,* **foam·i·er, foam·i·est.** covered with, consisting of, or resembling foam. —**foam′i·ly,** *adv.* —**foam′i·ness,** *n.*

fob¹ (fob) *n.* **1.** a short chain or ribbon attached to a watch and often worn hanging from a watch pocket. **2.** an ornament worn at the end of such a chain or ribbon. **3.** a watch pocket, as in the front of a vest or just below the waistband in trousers. [Probably of Germanic origin.]

fob² (fob) *v.t.,* **fobbed, fob·bing.** *Archaic.* to trick; cheat. [Middle English *fobben* to deceive, possibly from German *foppen* to jeer at, fool.]
  ·**to fob off. a.** to dispose of (something worthless) by trickery or deception; palm off. **b.** to put (someone) off by trickery or deception.

f.o.b. *also,* **F.O.B.** free on board.

fo·cal (fō′kəl) *adj.* of, at, or relating to a focus. —**fo′cal·ly,** *adv.*

fo·cal·ize (fō′kə līz′) *v.t., v.i.,* **-ized, -iz·ing.** to **1.** to bring to a focus or into focus. **2.** *Medicine.* localize. —**fo′cal·i·za′tion,** *n.*

focal length, the distance from the center of a lens or mirror to the focus. Also, **focal distance, focus.**

fo′c's'le (fōk′səl) *n.* forecastle.

fo·cus (fō′kəs) *n., pl.* **-cus·es** or **-ci** (-sī). **1.a.** the point at which converging rays, esp. light rays, meet, after being refracted by a lens or reflected by a mirror. Also, **real focus. b.** the point from which diverging rays, esp. light rays, appear to originate, after having undergone such refraction or reflection. Also, **virtual focus. 2.** focal length. **3.a.** the adjustment, as of a lens or the eye, necessary to produce a clear image: *My binoculars aren't in focus.* **b.** the position, as of an object viewed or photographed, necessary to produce a clear image: *The background isn't*

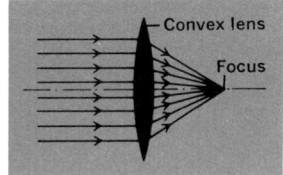

focus *(def. 1a)*

in focus in this picture. **4.** the condition of being distinct, comprehensible, or clearly defined: *The reporter's explanation brought the meaning of the events into focus for us.* **5.** a central point or center, as of activity, interest, or importance: *The speaker was the focus of attention.* **6.** *Geometry.* a fixed point or one of two fixed points used in determining an ellipse, parabola, or hyperbola. **7.** *Pathology.* the chief center at which a disease develops or is localized or from which it spreads. **8.** the center or underground point of origin of an earthquake, located directly below the epicenter. —*v.,* **-cused, -cus·ing;** *also, British,* **-cussed, -cus·sing.** —*v.t.* **1.** to bring to a focus or into focus: *I focused the binoculars on the distant ship. Unless the object is properly focused, the photograph will be blurred.* **2.** to fix firmly; concentrate: *Focus your attention on the speaker.* —*v.i.* **1.** to become focused. **2.** to focus the eye, a camera lens, or the like: *Hold that pose while I focus.* [Latin *focus hearth;* because the hearth was once the center of the home.]

fod·der (fod′ər) *n.* food for livestock, obtained by cutting and drying any of various grasses, as alfalfa or the stalks and leaves of corn; feed. —*v.t.* to feed with fodder. [Old English *fōdor* food for cattle.]

foe (fō) *n.* **1.** a person who is an enemy. **2.** a person who opposes or rivals another, as in a game or contest; adversary: *They've been political foes for years.* **3.** a person or thing that is opposed to or acts to the detriment of (something): *a foe of religion, a foe to all measures of reform.* [Old English *fāh* hostile, *gefā* adversary.] —For Synonyms, see **enemy.**

foehn (fān; *German* fœn) *also,* **föhn.** a warm, dry wind that blows down the side of a mountain, esp. in Europe. [German *Föhn,* going back to Latin *favōnius* the west wind.]

foe·tal (fē′təl) fetal.

foe·tid (fē′tid) fetid.

foe·tus (fē′təs) fetus.

fog (fôg, fog) *n.* **1.** a suspension of very small water droplets in the air, at or close to the earth's surface. **2.** any hazy or smoggy condition of the atmosphere, as one caused by smoke or dust. **3.** a state of mental confusion or bewilderment; daze: *I was really in a fog after the exam.* **4.** a hazy blur on developed photographic film caused by chemical action or by stray light or other radiation. —*v.,* **fogged, fog·ging.** —*v.t.* **1.** to cover, envelop, or obscure with or as with fog. **2.** to produce a hazy blur on (photographic film). **3.** to confuse; bewilder. —*v.i.* **1.** to become covered, enveloped, or obscured with or as with fog. **2.** (of photographic film) to become clouded with a hazy blur. [Probably of Scandinavian origin.]

fog bank, a dense, low-lying mass of fog, esp. over a body of water.

fog·bound (fôg′bound′, fog′-) *adj.* shut in, surrounded, or immobilized by fog: *The plane was fogbound at the airport.*

fo·gey (fō′gē) *n., pl.* **-geys.** fogy.

fog·gy (fô′gē, fog′ē) *adj.,* **-gi·er, -gi·est. 1.** full of or obscured by fog: *a foggy day.* **2.** confused or unclear; vague; cloudy: *foggy thinking.* —**fog′gi·ly,** *adv.* —**fog′gi·ness,** *n.*

fog·horn (fôg′hôrn′, fog′-) *n.* a horn or similar device for sounding warning signals, as to boats, when visibility is reduced by fog.

fo·gy (fō′gē) *also,* **fogey.** *n., pl.* **-gies.** an old-fashioned or very conservative person. [Of uncertain origin.]

föhn (fān; *German* fœn) foehn.

foi·ble (foi′bəl) *n.* a minor weakness or failing of character; flaw; shortcoming. [French *foible,* form of *faible* weak, from Latin *flēbilis* mournful.]

foil¹ (foil) *v.t.* to interfere with or prevent from being successful; frustrate; thwart: *The rain foiled our plans for a picnic at the beach.* [Middle English *foilen* to trample on, from Old French *fouler* to trample on, hurt, prepare woolen cloth, from Latin *fullo* person who prepares woolen cloth.] —For Synonyms, see **frustrate.**

foil² (foil) *n.* **1.** metal hammered or rolled into a very thin, flexible sheet. **2.** a person or thing that, by comparison or contrast, serves to set off or enhance the qualities of another: *A black sweater is a good foil for blond hair.* **3.** a leaf-shaped space or arc, as in the tracery of Gothic architecture. **4.** a thin piece of bright metal placed under a gem to add brilliancy or color. [Old French *foil* leaf, from Latin *folium* leaf.]

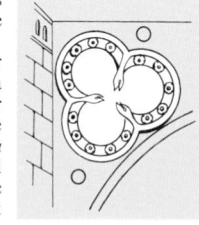

foil² *(def. 3)*

foil³ (foil) *n.* a long, flexible, four-sided fencing sword that tapers from the hilt to the point, which is blunted or padded to prevent injury. [Probably from FOIL¹.]

foist (foist) *v.t.* to pass off or offer wrongfully as genuine or valuable; impose slyly or deceitfully; palm off. [Probably from dialectal Dutch *vuisten* to take in the fist, from *vuist* fist.]

fold¹ (fōld) *v.t.* **1.** to bring one part of (something) over another, as by bending; bend or double over on itself: *Fold the paper in half. Fold the towels and put them away.* **2.** to close, collapse, or make more compact by bending or laying parts together (often with *up*): *Fold the chairs and lean them against the wall.* **3.** to bring together and interlock or intertwine: *She folded her hands in her lap. He folded his arms over his chest.* **4.** to bring (the wings) close to the body. **5.** to enfold in or as in the arms; embrace; clasp: *I folded the crying child into my arms.* **6.** to cover or wrap; enclose: *Fold all the dishes in newspaper before packing them.* **7.** *Cooking.* to add or blend (an ingredient) into a mixture by repeatedly turning one

part over another gently (often with *into*): *Fold the beaten eggs into the sauce.* —*v.i.* **1.** to become folded; be capable of being folded: *Paper folds more easily than cardboard.* **2.** *Informal.* to end or close due to financial failure: *The business folded. The show folded within a month.* —*n.* **1.** a part that is folded; layer; pleat: *The dress hung in graceful folds. The child was hidden in the folds of the drapes.* **2.** a hollow or space produced by folding: *She cuddled the child in the fold of her arms until he stopped crying.* **3.** a mark or crease produced by folding: *Cut the paper along the fold.* **4.** *Geology.* a bend in a layer of rock, esp. of the sort caused by forces that deform the earth's crust. [Old English *fealdan* to wrap, double together, bend.] —**fold′a·ble,** *adj.*

fold² (fōld) *n.* **1.** a pen or other enclosure for livestock, esp. sheep. **2.** sheep or other animals kept together in such a pen. **3.** a flock of sheep. **4.** a group, as the congregation of a church or a political party, under the guidance of a leader or sharing common beliefs, aims, or values. —*v.t.* to confine (sheep or other livestock) in a fold. [Old English *falod* pen².]

-fold *suffix* **1.** (a specified number of) times as much or as great: *a hundredfold increase.* **2.** having (a specified number of) parts: *a threefold disaster, a twofold problem.* [Old English *-feald.*]

fold·a·way (fōld′ə wā′) *adj.* designed to be folded and put out of the way when not in use: *a foldaway bed.*

fold·boat (fōld′bōt) *n.* a light, collapsible boat, similar to a kayak, made of rubberized fabric stretched over a framework. Also, **faltboat.** [Translation of German *faltboot.* See FALTBOAT.]

fold·er (fōl′dər) *n.* **1.** a holder or container for loose papers, usually a folded sheet of light cardboard. **2.** a sheet of printed material, as a circular, timetable, or map, folded rather than stitched or bound into a number of pagelike sections. **3.** a person or thing that folds.

fol·de·rol (fol′də rol′) *also,* **falderal, falderol.** *n.* **1.** mere nonsense. **2.** a trivial ornament; trifle.

folding door, a door having two or more hinged sections that open by folding back.

fold·out (fōld′out′) *n.* a larger than normal page in a book or magazine that is folded so it will not project beyond the other pages. [FOLD¹ + OUT.]

fo·li·a (fō′lē ə) a plural of **folium.**

fo·li·a·ceous (fō′lē ā′shəs) *adj.* **1.** of, relating to, or resembling the leaf of a plant. **2.** consisting of thin, leaflike plates or layers, as certain rocks. Also *(def. 2),* **foliate.** [Latin *foliāceus* leafy, from *folium* leaf.]

fo·li·age (fō′lē ij) *n.* **1.** the growth of leaves on a tree or other plant. **2.** leaves collectively. **3.** a representation of leaves, flowers, and branches, as in architectural ornamentation. [Modification (influenced by Latin *folium* leaf) of Middle French *feuillage* leafage, from *feuille* leaf, from Latin *folia* leaves, plural of *folium.*]

fo·li·ate (*adj.,* fō′lē it, -lē āt′; *v.,* fō′lē āt′) *adj.* **1.** having leaves; leafy. **2.** foliaceous *(def. 2).* —*v.,* **-at·ed, -at·ing.** —*v.i.* **1.** to put forth leaves, as a tree. **2.** to split into thin, leaflike plates or layers. —*v.t.* to decorate with foliage or with leaf-shaped ornaments. [Latin *foliātus* leafy, from *folium* leaf.]

fo·li·a·tion (fō′lē ā′shən) *n.* **1.** the act of putting forth leaves or the state of being in leaf. **2.** the arrangement of leaves in a bud. **3.** decoration with foliage or with leaf-shaped ornaments. **4.** a foliate texture, as in a rock.

fo·lic acid (fō′lik) a crystalline vitamin of the vitamin B complex group, a deficiency of which causes certain forms of anemia. [Latin *folium* leaf + -IC + ACID; because found in green leaves.]

fo·li·o (fō′lē ō′) *n., pl.* **-li·os. 1.** a sheet of paper folded once to form two leaves, or four pages, as of a book or manuscript. **2.** a book or manuscript, usually more than 11 inches (28 centimeters) in height, made up of sheets folded in this way. **3.** a page number, as of a book. **4.** a leaf, as of a book, numbered only on the front side. —*adj.* of or having the size or form of a folio. [Latin *foliō,* ablative of *folium* leaf (of a tree, of paper).]

fo·li·um (fō′lē əm) *n., pl.* **-li·ums** or **-li·a** (-lē ə). a thin layer or stratum, as of a rock. [Latin *folium* leaf.]

folk (fōk) *n., pl.* **folk** or **folks. 1.** *also,* **folks.** people: *city folk, old folks.* **2.** **folks.** *Informal.* one's family or relatives, esp. one's parents: *I'm going home to see my folks tomorrow.* **3.** a nation or race; people. —*adj.* of the common people; originating or widespread among the common people: *a folk custom.* [Old English *folc* a people, nation, crowd.]

folk dance 1. a dance originating among the common people of a region or country and handed down from generation to generation. **2.** the music for such a dance.

folk etymology 1. a change in the form of a word or phrase due to an incorrectly assumed etymology, for example, **humble pie** for the earlier form "umble pie." **2.** an incorrectly assumed etymology, for example, **sirloin,** which was once thought to have come into the language when an English king knighted a loin of beef.

folk·lore (fōk′lôr′) *n.* **1.** the tales, beliefs, customs, or other traditions of a people, handed down from generation to generation orally or by performance, rather than in writing. **2.** the study of such material. —**folk′lor′ic, folk′lor·is′tic,** *adj.* —**folk′lor′ist,** *n.*

folk medicine, the treatment of disease using traditional procedures and remedies, esp. the therapeutic use of plants and other natural products.

folk music 1. the traditional music, usually of anonymous origin, of the common people of a region or country, reflecting their customs, characteristics, and occupations. **2.** music written in imitation of the style and character of traditional folk music.

folk rock, a form of popular music combining elements of folk music and rock 'n' roll.

folk singer, a singer who specializes in the performance of folk songs.

folk song 1. a traditional song, usually originating among the common people and handed down orally from generation to generation, often having a simple tune and appearing in various versions. **2.** a song written in imitation of the style and character of a traditional folk song.

folk·sy (fōk′sē) *adj.,* **-si·er, -si·est.** *Informal.* unaffected and neighborly; friendly and unpretentious. —**folk′si·ly,** *adv.* —**folk′si·ness,** *n.*

folk·tale (fōk′tāl′) *n.* a prose narrative, as a tale or legend, that is part of the folklore of a people and is sometimes handed down in writing as well as orally, often appearing in several different versions. Also, **folk story.**

folk·way (fōk′wā′) *n.* a customary way of acting common to a people or group.

fol·li·cle (fol′i kəl) *n.* **1.** a small cavity, sac, or gland in the body. Hair grows from follicles. **2.** a dry fruit that splits open along one seam when it is ripe and releases its seeds, as a milkweed pod. [Latin *folliculus* little bag, diminutive of *follis* bellows, bag.]

fol·li·cle-stim·u·lat·ing hormone (fol′i kəl stim′yə lā′ting) a hormone secreted by the pituitary gland that stimulates the development of Graafian follicles within the ovaries of females and the development of sperm in males.

fol·low (fol′ō) *v.t.* **1.** to go, proceed, or come after; move behind in the same direction: *The dog followed me obediently. We followed them in our car.* **2.** to come or occur after in sequence, order, or time; succeed: *Spring follows winter. The riot followed a night of disorder.* **3.** to proceed along or hold to the course of; go along: *Follow the river to the fork.* **4.** to conform to, comply with, or act in accordance with; obey: *to follow orders, to follow the directions on a package.* **5.** to watch or observe closely or steadily: *to follow a tennis match.* **6.** to be actively interested in or attentive about; keep abreast of: *Have you been following this serial on television? We closely followed the progress of the local basketball team.* **7.** to grasp the continuity or logic of; keep up with and understand: *I don't follow your reasoning.* **8.** to use or take as a model; imitate: *Follow their example.* **9.** to employ oneself in; make a living from: *to follow medicine as a profession.* **10.** to accept as a guide or leader; support or advocate the opinions or cause of. **11.** to come after or take place as a consequence or result; result from: *Disaster followed the flood.* **12.** to try to overtake, capture, or keep under surveillance; pursue; chase: *The detective followed the suspect for three days.* —*v.i.* **1.** to proceed, come, or occur after. **2.** to come as a logical consequence: *Your statement doesn't follow from the original premise.* [Old English *folgian* to go or come after.]

· **to follow out.** to carry out or comply with fully: *to follow out a promise.*

· **to follow through. a.** to proceed with or pursue to an end or conclusion; complete: *to follow through an assignment.* **b.** to

a	at	e	end	o	hot	u	up	hw	white		about
ā	ape	ē	me	ō	old	ū	use	ng	song		taken
ä	far	i	it	ô	fork	ü	rule	th	thin	ə	pencil
âr	care	ī	ice	oi	oil	u̇	pull	th	this		lemon
		îr	pierce	ou	out	ûr	turn	zh	measure		circus

continue the motion of a stroke after hitting the ball, as in tennis or golf.

• **to follow up. a.** to pursue to a conclusion or check thoroughly (with *on*): *The reporter followed up on the story.* **b.** to reinforce or increase the effect of by further action: *The enemy followed up one devastating attack with another.*

Synonyms *v.i.* **Follow, ensue,** and **succeed** mean to come after something. **Follow** is the general term: *I have three classes, and then lunch follows. B follows A in the alphabet.* **Ensue** is used of something that follows logically or inevitably: *It wasn't surprising that a flood ensued after all that rain.* **Succeed** emphasizes an order or sequence: *If the president leaves office, the vice president succeeds.*

fol·low·er (fol′ō ər) *n.* **1.** a person who follows another, or the opinions or cause of another, as a supporter, disciple, or admirer; adherent. **2.** a person or thing that follows. **3.** a part of a machine that receives motion from or follows the motion of another part. **4.** servant; attendant.

fol·low·ing (fol′ō ing) *adj.* **1.** coming after or next in sequence, order, or time: *the following morning.* **2.** about to be mentioned, related, or set forth: *I did it for the following reasons.* —*n.* **1.** a body of followers: *an author who has a large following.* **2. the following. a.** those about to be mentioned, related, or set forth: *The following are the alternatives we discussed.* **b.** that which comes after or next in sequence, order, or time.

fol·low-through (fol′ō thrü′) *n.* **1.a.** the act or manner of continuing the motion of a stroke after hitting the ball, as in tennis or golf. **b.** the part of the stroke itself after the ball has been hit. **2.** the act of proceeding to an end or conclusion.

fol·low-up (fol′lō up′) *n.* **1.** the act of following up. **2.** something used or done to make an original action or thing effective, such as a letter sent as a reminder of an obligation or a medical examination of a patient after surgery. —*adj.* of or relating to an act or instance of following up: *a follow-up visit, follow-up care.*

fol·ly (fol′ē) *n., pl.* -lies. **1.** the quality or state of being foolish; lack of good sense or understanding; foolishness. **2.** something foolish; foolish act, idea, or practice. **3.** a foolish and costly undertaking, as a ruinous investment or purchase. [Old French *folie* madness, foolishness, from *fol* fool, from Latin *follis* bellows, bag, windbag.]

Fol·som (fōl′səm) *adj.* of or relating to a prehistoric people believed to have lived on the North American continent about 10,000 years ago, noted esp. for their use of stone spearheads with a long groove on each side. [From *Folsom*, New Mexico, where such spearheads were found.]

Fo·mal·haut (fō′məl hôt′, -mə lō′) *n.* a white star, one of the brightest in the sky and the brightest in the constellation Piscis Austrinus. [Arabic *fum 'l-haut* literally, mouth of the fish.]

fo·ment (fō ment′) *v.t.* **1.** to promote or incite; instigate: *to foment rebellion, to foment trouble.* **2.** to apply heat and moisture to (a part of the body) to reduce pain or inflammation. [Late Latin *fōmentāre* to restore with poultices, foster, from Latin *fōmentum* poultice.] —**fo·ment′er,** *n.*

fo·men·ta·tion (fō′men tā′shən) *n.* **1.** incitement, as to rebellion or unrest; instigation. **2.a.** the application of heat and moisture to a part of the body to reduce pain or inflammation. **b.** a hot, moist application so applied; poultice.

fond (fond) *adj.* **1.** having strong liking or affection for (with *of*): *fond of chocolates, fond of animals.* **2.** characterized by or showing affection or care; affectionate; tender; loving: *a fond embrace.* **3.** excessively loving or weakly indulgent; doting: *a fond grandparent.* **4.** entertained with great affection; deeply felt; cherished: *a fond wish, fond dreams of glory.* **5.** *Archaic.* foolish. [Of uncertain origin.] —**fond′ly,** *adv.* —**fond′ness,** *n.*

fon·dant (fon′dənt) *n.* a smooth, creamy confection, made of sugar, used as a filling or icing or eaten as candy. [French *fondant* sweetmeat, from *fondre* to melt, from Latin *fundere;* because it melts readily when eaten.]

fon·dle (fon′dəl) *v.t.,* -dled, -dling. to stroke or touch lovingly or tenderly; caress. [Obsolete *fond* to be fond of, caress (from FOND) + -LE.] —**fond′ler,** *n.*

fon·due (fon dü′) *n.* **1.** a dish containing melted cheese, seasonings, wine, and often brandy, served as a dip for cubes of bread. **2.** a dish consisting of hot oil into which chunks of meat, esp. beef, are dipped and cooked quickly, usually served with a variety of sauces. **3.** a dish made of melted cheese, eggs, butter, milk, and seasonings and usually baked. [French *fondue* dish of melted cheese and eggs, from *fondre* to melt, from Latin *fundere* to melt, cast (metal), pour out.]

font¹ (font) *n.* **1.** a receptacle, often of stone, used to hold the water for baptism. **2.** a receptacle for holy water; stoup. **3.** source; origin: *the font of life, a font of wisdom.* [Middle English *font,* from Old English *font,* from Latin *font-,* stem of *fōns* spring, fountain.]

font² (font) *n. Printing.* a complete assortment of printing type of one size and style. [French *fonte* a casting (of metals), from *fondre* to melt, cast, from Latin *fundere* to melt, cast (metal), pour out.]

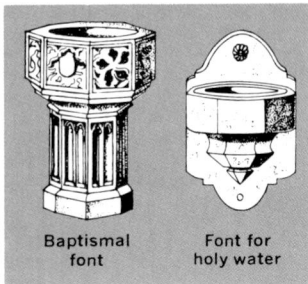

Baptismal font Font for holy water

fonts¹

fon·ta·nel (fon′tə nel′) *also,* **fon·ta·nelle.** *n.* any of the soft, membrane-covered spots between the bones of the skull in fetuses and infants, which later close as the bones grow together. [Modification (influenced by French *fontanelle*) of Middle English *fontinel* hollow, pit (of the body), from Old French *fontanele,* diminutive of *fontaine* spring.]

food (füd) *n.* **1.** anything eaten or otherwise assimilated by an organism to sustain life, provide energy, and promote the growth and repair of tissues; nourishment. **2.** nourishment that is solid rather than liquid or eaten rather than drunk: *food and drink.* **3.** a particular kind of food: *snack foods.* **4.** something that aids, sustains, or stimulates an activity: *The book was food for thought.* [Old English *fōda* nourishment.]

food chain, a sequence of the organisms of an ecological community, in which each member of the sequence feeds upon the member below it.

food poisoning, a gastrointestinal disorder caused by eating foods that are naturally toxic or that have been contaminated by chemicals or by harmful bacteria or their toxins, usually characterized by nausea, vomiting, and severe abdominal cramps.

food processor, an electric appliance consisting of a container in which rapidly rotating blades chop, slice, mince, or otherwise process food. Also, **processor.**

food stamp, a coupon issued by the federal government that can be used by eligible persons to buy food.

food·stuff (füd′stuf′) *n.* a substance suitable for or used as food.

food vacuole, a vacuole in the cytoplasm of certain protozoans, formed around food particles and functioning in the digestion and elimination of such particles.

food web, a network of interrelated food chains in an ecological community.

fool (fül) *n.* **1.** a person who lacks judgment or good sense; unwise or silly person. **2.** a clown formerly kept by royalty or the nobility to provide entertainment for the household; jester. **3.** a person who has been tricked, taken advantage of, or made to appear foolish; dupe: *The swindler made a fool of me.* —*v.t.* to make a fool of; deceive; trick: *Your disguise didn't fool anyone. We shouldn't have been fooled by their ridiculous stories.* —*v.i.* **1.** to act like a fool; be silly: *Stop fooling and get to work.* **2.** to act or speak in a jesting or playful manner; tease; joke: *Don't be offended; I was only fooling.* —*adj. Informal.* foolish; silly: *a fool notion.* [Old French *fol* madman, foolish person, from Latin *follis* bellows, bag, windbag.]

• **to be nobody's fool.** to be wise or shrewd.

• **to fool around.** to spend time idly or aimlessly: *The team was fooling around and not really practicing.*

• **to fool away.** to spend (time or money) wastefully or unwisely; fritter: *to fool away a whole afternoon.*

• **to fool with.** to play or meddle with aimlessly or thoughtlessly: *Do not fool with that machine.*

fool·er·y (fü′lə rē) *n., pl.* -er·ies. foolish action or behavior.

fool·har·dy (fül′här′dē) *adj.,* -di·er, -di·est. bold or daring in a foolish or unthinking way; rash; reckless: *a foolhardy teenager, a foolhardy thing to do.* —**fool′har′di·ly,** *adv.* —**fool′har′di·ness,** *n.*

fool·ish (fü′lish) *adj.* **1.** marked by or showing a lack of understanding or good sense; unwise; silly: *a foolish move.* **2.** like or relating to a fool; ridiculous; absurd: *You look foolish in that outfit.* **3.** embarrassed; abashed: *I felt foolish when I gave the wrong answer.* —**fool′ish·ly,** *adv.* —**fool′ish·ness,** *n.*

fool·proof (fül′prüf′) *adj.* so simple or safe as to make error, misuse, or failure impossible: *a foolproof recipe.*

fools·cap (fülz′kap′) *n.* **1.** writing paper varying in size from about 12 by 15 inches to 13½ by 17 inches (30 by 38 centimeters to 34 by 43 centimeters). **2.** fool's cap. [Because the writing paper once had a FOOL'S CAP as a watermark.]

fool's cap *also,* **fools cap, foolscap. 1.** a jester's cap or hood, usually having several drooping peaks from which bells are hung. **2.** dunce cap.

fool's errand, a profitless or pointless undertaking.

fool's gold, pyrite or chalcopyrite.

fool's paradise, a state of deceptive or illusory happiness based on false hopes or beliefs.

foot (fŭt) *n., pl.* **feet. 1.** in certain vertebrates, the terminal part of the leg, on which the body stands. **2.** in invertebrate animals and plants, any structure or organ used by the organism for locomotion or for attaching itself to surfaces or objects. **3.** this part of the human body considered as the organ or source of movement or motion: *They drove, but we came on foot. After paddling to shore, they proceeded by foot.* **4.** something resembling a foot in shape, position, or function, as the part of a sewing machine that holds the cloth in place. **5.** the part that covers or encloses the foot: *the foot of a stocking, the foot of a boot.* **6.** the lowest or supporting part: *the foot of a mountain, the foot of a ladder, the foot of a vase.* **7.** the part far from or opposite the head: *the foot of a bed.* **8.** a measure of length equal to 12 inches (30 centimeters). **9.** a basic unit of rhythm in poetry, consisting of a group of stressed and unstressed syllables. The line *The time/you won/your town/the race* has four feet. **10.** unmounted soldiers; infantry. —*v.t.* **1.** to make or renew the foot of; furnish with a foot: *to foot a sock.* **2.** *Informal.* to pay, as a bill. **3.** to walk, run, or dance on or over. **4.** to add up (a column of figures). [Old English *fōt* terminal part of the leg, measure of length equal to 12 inches (30 centimeters).]

• **to foot it.** *Informal.* to walk, run, or dance.
• **to put one's best foot forward. a.** to try to appear at one's best, esp. in order to make a good impression. **b.** to do one's best.
• **to put one's foot down.** to take a firm position; act decisively.
• **to put one's foot in it** (or **in one's mouth**). *Informal.* to make an embarrassing mistake.
• **to start** (or **get**) **off on the right foot.** to begin in a good manner.
• **to start** (or **get**) **off on the wrong foot.** to begin in a poor manner.

foot·age (fŭt′ij) *n.* a length or amount, as of lumber or motion-picture film, measured in feet.

foot-and-mouth disease (fŭt′ən mouth′) a highly contagious virus disease of cattle, pigs, and other cloven-hoofed animals, causing blisters in the mouth and around the udder and hooves. Infected animals are often quarantined and destroyed because the disease spreads so rapidly. Also, **hoof-and-mouth disease.**

foot·ball (fŭt′bôl′) *n.* **1.a.** a game played between two teams, officially of eleven players each, on a field 100 yards (91.4 meters) long and 53 yards (48.5 meters) wide with goals at each end, in which points are made by getting a ball across the opponent's goal line. **b.** the elliptical ball used in this game, usually leather-covered and having an inflatable rubber bladder inside. **2.** *British.* **a.** any of several games that involve kicking a ball, as rugby or soccer. **b.** the ball used in such a game. **3.** a person or thing tossed about or passed back and forth like a football, as from one group to another: *The issue soon became a political football.*

foot·board (fŭt′bôrd′) *n.* **1.** an upright board at the foot of a bedstead. **2.** a board or small platform used to support or rest the feet.

foot brake, a brake operated by pressure of the foot, as in an automobile.

foot·bridge (fŭt′brij′) *n.* a bridge for pedestrians only.

foot·can·dle (fŭt′kan′dəl) *also,* **foot·can·dle.** *n.* a unit for measuring illumination, equal to the light produced by an international candle at a distance of one foot.

foot·ed (fŭt′id) *adj.* **1.** having a foot or feet: *a footed goblet.* **2.** having a specified kind or number of feet. ➡ used in combination in def. 2, as in *flatfooted, a four-footed animal.*

foot·fall (fŭt′fôl′) *n.* a footstep or its sound.

foot·gear (fŭt′gîr′) *n.* footwear.

foot·hill (fŭt′hil′) *n.* a low hill at the foot of a mountain or mountain range.

foot·hold (fŭt′hōld′) *n.* **1.** a place where one may stand or tread securely; hold or support for the feet, as in climbing. **2.** a secure position, esp. a firm base for further progress or advancement: *Once it gained a foothold, the disease spread rapidly.*

foot·ing (fŭt′ing) *n.* **1.** a secure or firm placing of the feet: *to lose one's footing.* **2.** a hold or support for the feet: *The icy ledge provided no footing.* **3.** an established or secure position or foundation: *to put an enterprise on a sound footing.* **4.** position with regard to each other; relationship: *We're on a friendly footing.* **5.** the total obtained by adding a column of figures; sum.

foot·less (fŭt′lis) *adj.* **1.** lacking a foot or feet. **2.** having no basis; insubstantial: *a footless accusation.* **3.** *Informal.* awkward; inept. —**foot′less·ly,** *adv.* —**foot′less·ness,** *n.*

foot·lights (fŭt′līts′) *pl. n.* **1.** lights in one or more rows along the front of a stage, either recessed in the stage floor or resting on it. **2. the footlights.** acting as a profession; the stage.

foot·lock·er (fŭt′lok′ər) *n.* a small trunk for the belongings of a soldier or camper and often kept at the foot of his or her bed.

foot·loose (fŭt′lūs′) *adj.* free to travel about or live as one pleases; free from attachments or responsibilities.

foot·man (fŭt′mən) *n., pl.* **-men** (-mən). a male servant in livery who assists a butler with various duties, as serving, cleaning, answering the door, or attending an automobile or carriage. [FOOT + MAN; because he originally accompanied his master's carriage on foot.]

foot·mark (fŭt′märk′) *n.* footprint.

foot·note (fŭt′nōt′) *n.* **1.** an explanatory note, comment, or reference, usually below the text on a page and indicated in the body of the text by a number or symbol referring to it. **2.** a subordinate addition to a major statement or event: *The essay viewed all subsequent research as only a footnote to Einstein's work.* —*v.t.,* **-not·ed, -not·ing.** to furnish with or add a footnote to footnotes to.

foot·pace (fŭt′pās′) *n. Archaic.* a slow or walking pace.

foot·pad (fŭt′pad′) *n. Archaic.* a highwayman who goes on foot.

foot·path (fŭt′path′) *n., pl.* **-paths** (-pathz′, -paths′). a path for pedestrians.

foot·pound (fŭt′pound′) *n.* a unit of work or energy in the foot-pound-second system of units. One foot-pound is equal to the amount of energy required to raise one pound through a vertical distance of one foot.

foot-pound-sec·ond (fŭt′pound′sek′ənd) *adj.* of, relating to, or being a system of measurement in which the foot is the unit of length, the pound is the unit of mass, and the second is the unit of time.

foot·print (fŭt′print′) *n.* a mark or impression made by a foot: *footprints in the sand, dirty footprints all over the kitchen floor.*

foot·race (fŭt′rās′) *n.* a race run on foot.

foot·rest (fŭt′rest′) *n.* something, as a small stool or platform, on which the feet may be rested or propped.

foot soldier, a soldier trained or equipped to fight on foot; infantryman.

foot·sore (fŭt′sôr′) *adj.* having sore or tired feet, as from much walking.

foot·step (fŭt′step′) *n.* **1.** a step or tread of the foot: *a baby's first awkward footsteps.* **2.** the sound made by this: *I heard your footsteps in the hall.* **3.** the distance covered in a step: *The shop is just a footstep away.* **4.** footprint. **5.** a step by which to ascend or descend, as on a carriage.
• **to follow in someone's footsteps.** to imitate or succeed someone.

foot·stool (fŭt′stül′) *n.* a low stool on which to place the feet when sitting.

foot·way (fŭt′wā′) *n.* footpath.

foot·wear (fŭt′wâr′) *n.* coverings to be worn on the feet, as shoes or slippers.

foot·work (fŭt′wûrk′) *n.* **1.** the use or management of the feet, as in boxing or dancing. **2.** adroit or skillful management; maneuvering.

fop (fop) *n.* a man or boy who is overly concerned about or affected in his manner and appearance; dandy. [Possibly from Dutch *foppen* to fool, dupe, from German *foppen* to fool, jeer at.]

fop·per·y (fop′ə rē) *n., pl.* **-per·ies. 1.** the behavior, clothing, or manner of a fop. **2.** something foppish.

fop·pish (fop′ish) *adj.* like or characteristic of a fop. —**fop′-pish·ly,** *adv.* —**fop′pish·ness,** *n.*

for (fôr; *unstressed* fər) *prep.* **1.** to the length, extent, or duration

a	at	e	end	o	hot	u	up	hw	white		about
ā	ape	ē	me	ō	old	ū	use	ng	song		taken
ä	far	i	it	ô	fork	ü	rule	th	thin	ə	pencil
âr	care	ī	ice	oi	oil	u̇	pull	th	this		lemon
		îr	pierce	ou	out	ûr	turn	zh	measure		circus

F

of: *We agreed for the moment. Our guests stayed for an hour. They hiked for 5 miles. You can see for miles from the roof.* **2.** used with or adapted to; suited or appropriate to: *a closet for linens, a dress for the occasion, a movie for children, a time and a place for everything.* **3.** as a result of; by reason of; because of: *to jump for joy, a city known for its beauty.* **4.** in defense, support, or approval of; in favor or on the side of: *to vote for a measure, to demonstrate for civil rights, to stand up for one's rights.* **5.** to or in the amount of: *a check for fifty dollars.* **6.** at the cost or price of: *I bought the book for five dollars. We sold our car for $400.* **7.** in exchange as the equivalent of or in requital or payment of: *to swap pelts for supplies, five points for each correct answer.* **8.** in order to find, keep, or obtain: *to work for a living, to compete for a prize, to sue for damages, to look for a job.* **9.** meant to be received by or belong to; sent or given to: *Any mail for me? There's a package for you. I bought presents for everybody.* **10.** as a substitute of; in place of; instead of: *to use a cardboard box for a table.* **11.** focused upon or directed toward: *to have a craving for chocolate.* **12.** appreciative of or discerning about; sensitive or responsive to: *an eye for color, an ear for music.* **13.** in the interest or behalf of; as representative of: *The lawyers acted for their client. I spoke for the group. Say hello to your parents for me.* **14.** in honor of: *The child was named for her grandmother. A banquet was given for him.* **15.** with respect or regard to; concerning: *We were pressed for time. So much for that topic.* **16.** considering the nature or usual characteristics of, in spite of being: *It's very cool for August. You are tall for your age.* **17.** dependent upon or assigned to; up to: *It's for you to decide. It's not for me to say.* **18.** in spite or regardless of; despite: *For all I know, she could have left. For all his fancy manners, he's still a boor.* **19.** in order to reach or go toward: *He set out for London. She just left for school.* **20.** with the aim, object, or purpose of; with a view to: *I'm saving for my college education. The house was insulated for warmth.* **21.** in order to be, become, or do: *to run for president, to volunteer for a task.* **22.** to serve as; as: *We had cereal for breakfast. I'll have salad for my first course.* **23.** in proportion to: *For every rainy day there were four sunny ones.* **24.** as being: *I know it for a fact. The story was mistaken for fact.* **25.** to take care of or accommodate: *There's enough meat left for three people. There's room for you in the back of the car.* **26.** corresponding or equivalent to: *an English word for every French word in a translation.* **27.** necessary in order to obtain admission to: *Did you get tickets for the play?* **28.** because of the effect on: *Exercise can be good for your health.* **29.** at or during (a specified time or occasion): *I made an appointment for one o'clock.* —*conj.* seeing that; inasmuch as; because: *Let's go, for it is late.* [Old English *for* on account of, instead of, because of.]

for- *prefix* **1.** away; off: *forget.* **2.** extremely; completely: *forlorn.* [Old English *for-.*]

for., foreign.

for·age (fôr′ij, for′-) *n.* **1.** food for livestock, esp. when obtained by grazing, consisting of leaves and stalks, as of grasses and legumes. **2.** a search for food or provisions. —*v.,* **-aged, -aging.** —*v.i.* **1.** to hunt or search about for food or provisions: *The birds foraged in the snow. The troops foraged near the village.* **2.** to make a search; rummage. —*v.t.* **1.** to obtain by hunting or searching about: *to forage mushrooms for a meal.* **2.** to obtain food or provisions from: *The refugees foraged the countryside.* **3.** to supply, as horses, with food or provisions. **4.** *Archaic.* to plunder; loot. [Old French *fourage* pillage, from *forre* fodder; of Germanic origin.] —**for′ag·er,** *n.*

for·am (fôr′əm) *n.* foraminifer. [Short for FORAMINIFER.]

fo·ra·men (fə rā′mən) *n., pl.* **-ram·i·na** (-ram′ə nə). a natural opening in a bone or membrane. [Latin *forāmen* opening.]

foramen magnum, the large opening in the skull through which the spinal cord passes to become the medulla oblongata.

for·a·min·i·fer (fôr′ə min′ə fər, for′-) *n.* any of a large group of chiefly saltwater protozoans, order Foraminifera, having perforated calcareous or silicate shells that, when accumulated and buried, form chalk and limestone deposits. [Latin *forāmen* opening, hole + *ferre* to bear[1].] —**fo·ram·i·nif·er·al** (fə ram′ə nif′-ər əl), **fo·ram′i·nif′er·ous,** *adj.*

for·as·much as (fôr′əz much′az) in view of the fact that; because; since.

for·ay (fôr′ā, for′ā) *n.* an attack or raid, as for plunder or spoils. —*v.t., v.i.* to raid; plunder. [Middle English *forraien* to raid, from *forrier* forager, from Old French *forrier,* from *forrer* to forage, from *forre* fodder. See FORAGE.]

forb (fôrb) *n.* any herbaceous plant that is not a grass or grasslike. [Greek *forbē* fodder, from *pherbein* to feed, graze.]

for·bad (fər bad′, fôr-) a past tense of **forbid.**

for·bade (fər bad′, -bād′, fôr-) a past tense of **forbid.**

for·bear[1] (fôr bâr′) *v.,* **-bore, -borne, -bear·ing.** —*v.i.* **1.** to keep oneself from doing something; abstain or refrain: *to forbear from quarreling.* **2.** to control oneself or be patient, as when provoked: *When friends are exasperating, try to forbear, if you can.* —*v.t.* to keep oneself from (doing something); abstain or refrain from: *to forbear laughing.* [Old English *forberan.*] —**for·bear′er,** *n.* —**for·bear′ing·ly,** *adv.*

for·bear[2] (fôr′bâr′) forebear.

for·bear·ance (fôr bâr′əns) *n.* **1.** the act of forbearing: *forbearance from sin.* **2.** self-control or patience: *She showed great forbearance during his long illness.*

for·bid (fər bid′, fôr-) *v.t.,* **-bade** or **-bad, -bid·den** or (*archaic*) **-bid, -bid·ding.** **1.a.** to command (someone) not to do something; refuse to allow: *I forbid you to go out.* **b.** to prohibit (something); ban: *to forbid smoking in public areas.* **2.** to command to keep away from; bar or exclude from: *I forbid you the car.* **3.** to stand in the way of or make impossible; hinder; prevent: *The snowstorm forbids air travel.* [Old English *forbēodan* to prohibit, restrain.]

Synonyms **Forbid** and **prohibit** mean to order that something not to be done. **Forbid** connotes the expectation of obedience: *I forbid you to tell anyone about what happened.* **Prohibit** implies a legal or official order: *The law prohibits smoking in this area. The occupying forces prohibited residents from walking on certain streets.*

for·bid·den (fər bid′ən, fôr-) *adj.* not permitted; prohibited: *Gambling is forbidden.*

Forbidden City, a walled area in the center of Beijing, China, enclosing the palaces and grounds of the former Chinese emperors. It was closed to the public for many centuries.

forbidden fruit 1. in the Old Testament, the fruit of the tree of knowledge, forbidden to Adam and Eve. **2.** something desired but forbidden, as unlawful pleasure.

for·bid·ding (fər bid′ing, fôr-) *adj.* appearing to be threatening, hostile, or dangerous; grim; ominous: *a forbidding manner, forbidding cliffs.* —**for·bid′ding·ly,** *adv.*

for·bore (fôr bôr′) the past tense of **forbear**[1].

for·borne (fôr bôrn′) the past participle of **forbear**[1].

force (fôrs) *n.* **1.a.** power or energy; strength: *great force of character.* **b.** impetus or intensity of effect: *The leaves broke the force of the cat's fall.* **2.a.** strength, constraint, or power exerted upon an object: *They used force to open the door.* **b.** the use of such power; physical coercion: *They dragged him off by force.* **3.** power to convince, influence, or control; efficacious power: *the force of an argument, the force of circumstances.* **4.** something that exerts such power; agency of movement or change: *the forces of nature, the forces contributing to the decline of feudalism.* **5. forces. a.** armed forces. **b.** the individuals comprising or belonging to the armed forces: *Our forces suffered severe casualties.* **6.** a group of people organized or available for some purpose or activity: *the police force, a sales force.* **7.** *Law.* binding effect; validity: *the force of a contract.* **8.** *Physics.* something that causes bodies to move or change their motion: *gravitational force.* —*v.t.,* **forced, forc·ing. 1.** to make (someone) do something, as by threats or physical violence; constrain: *Your question forced me to solve the problem. The city council forced the mayor to resign.* **2.** to bring or cause to come into a particular state or condition; drive: *Various conditions forced prices down last summer.* **3.** to get or obtain by or as by force; extort; wrest: *They forced a confession out of the suspect.* **4.** to bring forth or produce by or as by effort: *She forced a smile.* **5.** to propel or cause to move, as against resistance: *to force enemy troops back, to force a pill into a dog's mouth.* **6.** to cause to open or give way by using force; break open: *to force a lock.* **7.** to press or impose on by or as by force: *to force one's attentions on a person.* **8.** to make or effect by force: *to force a passage through a mountain, to force one's way through a crowd.* **9.** to overpower or capture by force: *They forced the enemy's stronghold.* **10.** to urge or exert to the utmost; strain, as the voice. **11.** to hasten the growth or development of (plants) by artificial means. **12.** *Card Games.* **a.** to compel (an opponent) to trump if he or she wishes to take a trick. **b.** to cause a player to play (a certain card). **c.** to compel (a player) to play so as to show the strength of his or her hand. **13.** *Baseball.* **a.** to cause (a base runner) to be put out by making a hit that compels the runner to move to the next base. **b.** to cause (a base runner on third base) to score a run by walking the batter when the bases are loaded (often with *in*). **c.** to allow (a run) to be scored in this way. [Old French *force* strength, might, going back to Latin *fortis* strong.] —**force′a·ble,** *adj.* —**force′less,** *adj.* —**forc′er,** *n.*

Synonyms *v.t.* **Force, compel, oblige,** and **constrain** mean to cause someone to act in a certain way. **Force** is the general term, connoting the exercise or effect of any sort of power: *They forced the enemy to abandon the fort. Bad weather forced us to cancel the tournament.* **Compel** implies pushing into an unavoidable course of action: *to compel a defeated enemy to surrender without condition.* **Oblige** suggests the operation of

some social or moral pressure: *Visitors are obliged to remove their hats when entering the temple.* **Constrain** suggests the narrowing of choices until only one option is left: *We felt constrained to explain our plan in great detail in order to enlist the committee's support.*

forced (fôrst) *adj.* **1.** imposed or compelled by force; compulsory: *forced labor.* **2.** brought forth or produced by or as by effort; affected; strained: *forced gaiety.* **3.** done as the result of or in an emergency: *The plane made a forced landing.* —**forc·ed·ly** (fôr′sid lē), *adv.*

forced march, an unusually long march undertaken and performed under pressure.

force-feed (fôrs′fēd′) *v.t.,* **-fed** (-fed′), **-feed·ing.** **1.** to force to eat or take nourishment, as by means of a tube inserted down the throat: *to force-feed a sick animal.* **2.** to force to assimilate or accept, as propaganda.

force field *Physics.* field *(def. 10).*

force·ful (fôrs′fəl) *adj.* full of or having much force; powerful; vigorous; effective: *a forceful personality, a forceful argument.* —**force′ful·ly,** *adv.* —**force′ful·ness,** *n.*

force·meat (fôrs′mēt′) *n.* finely chopped, seasoned meat that is served separately or used for stuffing. [Obsolete *force,* form of obsolete *farce* to stuff (from Old French *farsir,* from Latin *farcīre*) + MEAT.]

for·ceps (fôr′səps, -seps) *n., pl.* **-ceps.** a pincerlike or tonglike instrument used for holding or manipulating objects, esp. in surgery. [Latin *forceps* pincers, from *formus* hot + *capere* to hold; because it was sometimes used to hold hot things.]

force pump, a pump that delivers liquid under pressure by the action of a one-piece piston that forces the liquid through a pipe.

for·ci·ble (fôr′sə bəl) *adj.* **1.** effected by or involving the use of force or violence: *a forcible entry.* **2.** characterized by or having force; powerful; effective. —**for′ci·ble·ness,** *n.* —**for′ci·bly,** *adv.*

ford (fôrd) *n.* a shallow place where a river, stream, or other body of water may be crossed, as by wading. —*v.t.* to cross (a body of water) at a shallow place, as by wading. [Old English *ford* the shallow place.] —**ford′a·ble,** *adj.*

fore[1] (fôr) *adj.* at or toward the front; forward: *the fore part of a ship.* —*n. Nautical.* the foremast or bow of a boat or ship. —*adv. Nautical.* at or toward the bow of a boat or ship. [Old English *fore* for, before.]

• **to the fore.** in or into a prominent position: *to come to the fore as a candidate for mayor.*

fore[2] (fôr) *interj.* in golf, a warning cry to persons ahead who may be in danger of being hit by a ball. [Probably short for BEFORE.]

fore- *prefix* **1.** situated at or near the front; in front: *foremast, forelock.* **2.** before in time or order; prior; beforehand: *forenamed, foretell.* [Old English *fore-* before.]

fore-and-aft (fôr′ən aft′) *adj.* leading or lying in the direction of a ship's length; from bow to stern: *a fore-and-aft sail.*

fore and aft 1. from the bow to the stern of a ship; lengthwise. **2.** in, at, or toward both the bow and the stern of a ship.

fore-and-aft-rigged (fôr′ən aft′rigd′) *adj.* fitted with fore-and-aft sails.

fore·arm[1] (fôr′ärm′) *n.* the part of the arm between the elbow and wrist. [FORE- + ARM[1].]

fore·arm[2] (fôr ärm′) *v.t.* to prepare or arm beforehand. [FORE- + ARM[2].]

fore·bear (fôr′bâr′) *also,* **forbear.** *n.* an ancestor; forefather. [FORE- + BE + -ER[1].]

fore·bode (fôr bōd′) *v.t.,* **-bod·ed, -bod·ing.** **1.** to be a warning or indication of; predict; portend: *omens that forebode disaster.* **2.** to have a premonition of (an approaching misfortune or evil). —**fore·bod′er,** *n.*

fore·bod·ing (fôr bō′ding) *n.* a feeling that something evil is going to happen; premonition, inner certainty, or dread of an approaching misfortune: *The news filled me with foreboding.* —**fore·bod′ing·ly,** *adv.*

fore·brain (fôr′brān′) *n.* the part of the brain that includes the cerebrum, the thalamus, and the hypothalamus.

fore·cast (fôr′kast′) *v.t.,* **-cast** or **-cast·ed, -cast·ing.** **1.** to predict, esp. on the basis of observation or analysis of information and data: *to forecast the weather, to forecast election results.* **2.** to be an advance indication of; foreshadow: *events that forecast an outbreak of war.* —*n.* a prediction, esp. one made on the basis of observation or analysis of information and data: *a weather forecast.* —**fore′cast·er,** *n.* —For Synonyms *(v.t.),* see **predict.**

fore·cas·tle (fōk′səl, fôr′kas′əl) *n.* **1.** the part of a ship's upper deck forward of the foremast. **2.** the forward section of a merchant ship, in which the sailors' quarters are located. Also, **fo·c's·le.** [FORE- + CASTLE. A ship's forward section was formerly equipped for sea warfare with a battlement resembling that of a *castle.*]

fore·close (fôr klōz′) *v.,* **-closed, -clos·ing.** —*v.t.* **1.** to subject (a person, mortgage, or lien) to the process of foreclosure. **2.** to exclude; prevent: *to foreclose all discussion.* —*v.i.* to foreclose a mortgage or lien. [Old French *forclos,* past participle of *forclore* to exclude, going back to Latin *forīs* outside + *claudere* to shut.]

fore·clo·sure (fôr klō′zhər) *n.* a legal proceeding in which a person who has subjected his or her property to a mortgage or lien is deprived of the right to redeem it because the conditions of the mortgage or lien have not been met.

fore·court (fôr′kôrt′) *n.* **1.** a court or enclosed space in front of a building. **2.** the part of a tennis court that is nearest the net.

fore·deck (fôr′dek′) *n.* the forward part of a ship's main deck.

fore·doom (fôr düm′) *v.t.* to doom or condemn in advance.

fore·fa·ther (fôr′fä′thər) *n.* **1.** ancestor. **2.** a predecessor from whom national or traditional descent is claimed: *Our forefathers framed the Constitution of the United States.*

fore·fend (fôr fend′) forfend.

fore·fin·ger (fôr′fing′gər) *n.* index finger.

fore·foot (fôr′fůt′) *n., pl.* **-feet. 1.** one of the front feet of a four-legged animal. **2.** the forward part of a ship's keel where it meets the stem.

fore·front (fôr′frunt′) *n.* a place or part in front; most advanced position; vanguard: *the forefront of a reform movement.*

fore·gath·er (fôr gath′ər) forgather.

fore·go[1] (fôr gō′) *v.t., v.i.,* **-went, -gone, -go·ing.** forgo.

fore·go[2] (fôr gō′) *v.t., v.i.,* **-went, -gone, -go·ing.** to go before; precede. [Old English *foregān.*]

fore·go·ing (fôr′gō′ing) *adj.* going before; preceding: *the foregoing example, in the foregoing quotation.*

fore·gone (fôr′gôn′, -gon′) *adj.* that has gone before or gone by; previous; past: *in a foregone era.*

foregone conclusion, an inevitable or foreseen outcome or result.

fore·ground (fôr′ground′) *n.* **1.** the part of a picture or scene perceived as nearest to the spectator's eye. ➡ opposed to **background.** **2.** the most conspicuous or prominent position; forefront.

fore·gut (fôr′gut′) *n.* **1.** the top portion of the embryonic digestive tract in vertebrates, developing into the mouth, pharynx, esophagus, and stomach. **2.** the anterior part of an arthropod's digestive system, as in insects and crustaceans. [FORE- + GUT.]

fore·hand (fôr′hand′) *adj.* performed or made with the arm extended outward from the body and the palm of the hand toward

Outlet

Piston

Water

Valve

Valve

force pump

fore-and-aft-rigged ship

a	at	e	end	o	hot	u	up	hw	white		about
ā	ape	ē	me	ō	old	ū	use	ng	song		taken
ä	far	i	it	ô	fork	ü	rule	th	thin	ə	pencil
âr	care	ī	ice	oi	oil	ů	pull	th	this		lemon
		îr	pierce	ou	out	ûr	turn	zh	measure		circus

F

the front: *a forehand stroke.* Also, **fore′hand′ed.** —*n.* a fore-hand stroke, as in tennis. ➤ distinguished from **backhand.**

fore·head (fôr′id, -hed′, for′-) *n.* the part of the face above the eyes. [Old English *forhēafod.*]

for·eign (fôr′ən, for′-) *adj.* **1.** belonging to, derived from, or characteristic of another country; not native: *a foreign accent, foreign currency, on foreign soil.* **2.** outside one's own country: *foreign lands.* **3.** related to or dealing with other countries: *foreign trade, foreign policy.* **4.** not typical or characteristic of the person or thing mentioned (often with *to*): *Aggressiveness is foreign to my friend's disposition.* **5.** not within a person's experience or knowledge; strange; unfamiliar: *a concept foreign to my way of thinking.* **6.** having little or no relation; not pertinent; irrelevant: *foreign to our purpose.* **7.** not normally occurring in or belonging to the place where found: *a foreign body in the eye, foreign matter in the bloodstream.* [Old French *forain* alien, strange, going back to Latin *forās* outside.] —**for′eign·ness,** *n.*

foreign affairs, the dealings or diplomatic relations of a country with other countries.

foreign aid, assistance given by one country to another, esp. to one that is less developed in order to help it develop its economy and military forces and to strengthen the ties between the two countries.

for·eign-born (fôr′ən bôrn′, for′-) *adj.* born in a foreign country.

for·eign·er (fôr′ə nər, for′-) *n.* a person born in another country; citizen or native of another country.

foreign exchange 1. the transaction of financial affairs and settling of accounts or debts by persons, businesses, or governments of one country with those of another. **2.** bills of exchange drawn in one country and made payable in another.

for·eign·ism (fôr′ə niz′əm, for′-) *n.* something peculiar to or characteristic of a foreign people or language, as a word, idiom, or custom.

foreign legion 1. a military unit composed chiefly of foreign volunteers serving in a national army. **2.** *also,* **Foreign Legion.** such a unit in the French army, traditionally assigned to military operations and service outside of France.

foreign minister, in certain countries, the minister of a governmental cabinet who conducts and supervises foreign affairs.

foreign office, in certain countries, the department of a government that handles foreign affairs.

foreign policy, the official political positions and actions of a country in its relations with other countries.

fore·judge (fôr juj′) *v.t.,* **-judged, -judg·ing.** prejudge.

fore·know (fôr nō′) *v.t.,* **-knew, -known, -know·ing.** to know beforehand.

fore·knowl·edge (fôr′nol′ij, fôr nol′-) *n.* knowledge of something before it exists or occurs.

fore·la·dy (fôr′lā′dē) *n., pl.* **-dies.** forewoman.

fore·land (fôr′land′) *n.* a promontory or area of high land jutting into the sea.

fore·leg (fôr′leg′) *n.* **1.** one of the front legs of a four-legged animal. **2.** one of the front legs of any of various insects.

fore·limb (fôr′lim′) *n.* a front limb, as a foreleg, wing, fin, or arm.

fore·lock (fôr′lok′) *n.* a lock or tuft of hair growing just above the forehead.

fore·man (fôr′mən) *n., pl.* **-men** (-mən). **1.** a worker who supervises a body of workers or oversees a particular operation or section of a plant. **2.** a person who chairs and speaks for a jury.

fore·mast (fôr′mast′, -məst) *n.* the mast nearest the bow of a ship, or the lower section of such.

fore·most (fôr′mōst′, -məst) *adj.* **1.** first in position, rank, or importance: *the foremost dramatist of the nineteenth century.* —*adv.* before any other or anything else, as in position or rank; in the first place: *to be first and foremost a scholar.* [Old English *formest,* superlative of *forma* first, in turn a superlative of FORE¹; Modern English spelling influenced by FORE¹ and by association with MOST.]

fore·name (fôr′nām′) *n.* a first or given name.

fore·named (fôr′nāmd′) *adj.* previously named or mentioned.

fore·noon (fôr′nün′) *n.* the period between sunrise and noon; morning. —*adj.* of, relating to, or occurring in the forenoon.

fo·ren·sic (fə ren′sik) *adj.* **1.** relating to, appropriate for, or used in courts of law or public discussion and debate. **2.** adapted or suited to argumentation; argumentative; rhetorical. Also, **fo·ren′si·cal.** —*n.* **forensics.** the art or study of formal argumentation or debate. ➤ used as singular or plural. [Latin *forēnsis* relating to the forum (from *forum* public place, marketplace) + -IC.] —**fo·ren′si·cal·ly,** *adv.*

forensic medicine, the application of the medical sciences to the purposes of the law, as the use of pathology to determine the cause of a death.

fore·or·dain (fôr′ôr dān′) *v.t.* to ordain or appoint beforehand; predestine; preordain. —**fore′or·dain′ment, fore′or·di·na′tion,** *n.*

fore·part (fôr′pärt′) *also,* **fore part.** *n.* the first, front, or early part.

fore·paw (fôr′pô′) *n.* a paw of a foreleg; front paw.

fore·quar·ter (fôr′kwôr′tər) *n.* **1.** the front half of a side of beef or other meat, including the leg, shoulder, and adjacent parts. **2. forequarters.** the forelegs, shoulders, and adjacent parts of an animal.

fore·reach (fôr rēch′) *v.i. Nautical.* to catch up with or move ahead of a ship (with *on* or *upon*).

fore·run (fôr run′) *v.t.,* **-ran** (-ran′), **-run, -run·ning.** *Archaic.* **1.** to be a sign or prediction of; foreshadow. **2.** to go before; precede.

fore·run·ner (fôr′run′ər) *n.* **1.** a person or thing that precedes another, as in a line of descent or development; predecessor; ancestor: *The bicycle was the forerunner of the motorcycle.* **2.** a sign of something to come; omen. **3.** a person or thing that announces in advance the approach of something or someone; herald.

fore·said (fôr′sed′) *adj.* aforesaid.

fore·sail (fôr′sāl′, -səl) *n.* **1.** the lowest sail, fastened to the foreyard, on the foremast of a square-rigged ship. **2.** the principal sail on the foremast of a schooner.

fore·see (fôr sē′) *v.t.,* **-saw** (-sô′), **-seen, -see·ing.** to know or see beforehand: *It was easy to foresee the difficulties we would encounter in climbing the mountain.* [Old English *foreseon.*] —**fore·see′a·ble,** *adj.* —**fore·se′er,** *n.*

fore·shad·ow (fôr shad′ō) *v.t.* to show or indicate beforehand; presage: *The surrender of the city foreshadowed the fate of the country at large.*

fore·shad·ow·ing (fôr shad′ō ing) *n.* an indication or warning of something to come; sign of a future event; omen; presage.

fore·shank (fôr′shangk′) *n.* in cattle, the upper foreleg.

fore·sheet (fôr′shēt′) *n.* **1.** a rope attached to one of the clews of a foresail for the purpose of adjusting the angle of the sail. **2. foresheets.** forward spaces, not occupied by thwarts, in an open boat.

fore·shore (fôr′shôr′) *n.* that part of the shore between the high-water mark and low-water mark, uncovered at low tide.

fore·short·en (fôr shôr′tən) *v.t.* in drawing or painting, to shorten or reduce parts of (an object) in order to create an illusion of perspective, depth, and distance. —**fore·short′ened,** *adj.* —**fore·short′en·ing,** *n.*

fore·show (fôr shō′) *v.t.,* **-showed, -shown, -show·ing.** foreshadow.

fore·sight (fôr′sīt′) *n.* **1.** care, provision, or thought for the future; prudence. **2.** the act or ability of foreseeing what is likely to happen.

fore·sight·ed (fôr′sī′tid, fôr sī′-) *adj.* having or showing foresight. —**fore′sight′ed·ly,** *adv.* —**fore′sight′ed·ness,** *n.*

fore·skin (fôr′skin′) *n.* a fold of skin that covers the end of the penis; prepuce. It is removed in circumcision.

for·est (fôr′ist, for′-) *n.* **1.** an area of land, usually an extensive area, covered with a dense growth of trees and underbrush. **2.** the trees themselves: *to cut down a forest.* —*v.t.* to plant or cover with trees; make into a forest. [Old French *forest* woodland, from Late Latin *forestis* open or unfenced wood, from Latin *forīs* outside.] —**for′est·ed,** *adj.*

fore·stage (fôr′stāj′) *n.* the part of a stage in front of the curtain in a theater; apron.

fore·stall (fôr stôl′) *v.t.* **1.** to hinder, prevent, or get ahead of by taking action in advance: *Tax reforms forestalled an economic crisis.* **2.** to interfere with sales at (a market), as by buying up goods not yet on the market in order to sell at a higher price. [Middle English *forestallen* to obstruct, going back to Old English *foresteall* interception.] —**fore·stall′er,** *n.* —**fore·stall′ment,** *n.*

for·est·a·tion (fôr′ə stā′shən, for′-) *n.* the planting or care of forests.

fore·stay (fôr′stā′) *n.* a rope or cable that runs from the top of a ship's foremast to the bow and helps support the foremast.

for·est·ed (fôr′ə stid, for′-) *adj.* covered with forest; wooded.

for·est·er (fôr′ə stər, for′-) *n.* a person who practices or has been trained in forestry.

forest ranger, an officer supervising the care of a forest, esp. a public forest. Also, **ranger.**

for·est·ry (fôr′ə strē, for′-) *n.* the science that deals with the

care and management of forests, including their protection, the harvesting and cultivation of trees, and the planting of new timber crops.

fore·taste (*n.*, fôr′tāst′; *v.*, fôr tāst′) *n.* a brief experience, taste, or sample of something to come. —*v.t.*, **-tast·ed, -tast·ing.** to have a foretaste of.

fore·tell (fôr tel′) *v.t.*, **-told, -tell·ing. 1.** to tell of beforehand; give a prophecy of. **2.** to show or indicate beforehand; be an omen of; foreshadow. —**fore·tell′er,** *n.*

Synonyms **Foretell** and **prophesy** mean to predict some future event. **Foretell** suggests having some kind of special knowledge, although its source may be unspecified: *The astrologer foretold the deaths of the king and queen.* **Prophesy** more clearly suggests access to occult or supernatural sources: *The priests prophesied the end of the empire.*

fore·thought (fôr′thôt′) *n.* **1.** a thinking or consideration of something beforehand; advance planning. **2.** thoughtful consideration for the future; foresight.

fore·to·ken (*v.*, fôr tō′kən; *n.*, fôr′tō′kən) *v.t.* to indicate beforehand; foreshadow. —*n.* a sign or indication of something to come; omen. [Old English *foretācn* omen, sign.]

fore·told (fôr tōld′) the past tense and past participle of **foretell.**

fore·top (fôr′top′, -təp) *n.* a platform at the top of the foremast.

fore-top·gal·lant (fôr′top gal′ənt, fôr′tə-) *adj.* of, relating to, or designating the mast, sails, yards, and other parts immediately above the fore-topmast.

fore-top·mast (fôr top′mast′, -məst) *n.* the section of mast next above the foremast.

fore-top·sail (fôr top′sāl′, -səl) *n.* a sail set on the fore-topmast.

for·ev·er (fôr ev′ər, fə rev′-, fô-) *adv.* **1.** to the end of time; without ever ending; eternally. **2.** without letting up; incessantly; constantly: *They are forever complaining about something.*

for·ev·er·more (fôr ev′ər môr′, fə rev′-, fô-) *adv.* forever.

fore·warn (fôr wôrn′) *v.t.* to warn in advance.

fore·went (fôr went′) the past tense of **forego**[1] and **forego**[2].

fore·wing (fôr′wing′) *n.* either of the two front wings of a four-winged insect.

fore·wom·an (fôr′wùm′ən) *n.*, *pl.* **-wom·en** (-wim′ən). **1.** a woman who supervises a body of workers or oversees a particular operation or section of a plant. **2.** a woman who chairs and speaks for a jury. Also, **forelady.**

fore·word (fôr′wûrd′, -wərd) *n.* an introductory statement in a book or other literary work, usually written by someone other than the author. —For Synonyms, see **introduction.**

fore·yard (fôr′yärd′) *n.* the lowest yard on the foremast of a square-rigged ship.

for·feit (fôr′fit) *v.t.* to lose or lose the right to as a penalty for some offense, error, or omission: *The team forfeited the game when they failed to show up.* —*n.* **1.** something that is lost as a penalty for some offense, error, or omission. **2.** the act of forfeiting. —*adj.* forfeited or liable to be forfeited. [Old French *forfait* crime, fine[2], from *forfaire* to transgress; literally, to act beyond (the law), going back to Latin *forīs* outside + *facere* to do.]

for·fei·ture (fôr′fi chər) *n.* **1.** the act of forfeiting. **2.** something that is forfeited.

for·fend (fôr fend′) *also,* **forefend.** *v.t.* **1.** to ward off; prevent. **2.** to defend or protect. **3.** *Archaic.* forbid.

for·gat (fər gat′) *Archaic.* a past tense of **forget.**

for·gath·er (fôr gath′ər) *also,* **foregather.** *v.i.* to meet or gather together; assemble.

for·gave (fər gāv′) the past tense of **forgive.**

forge[1] (fôrj) *n.* **1.** a furnace or hearth in which metal is heated and softened so that it can be worked into shape, as by hammering. **2.** a workshop in which metals are heated in such an apparatus and then worked into shape; smithy. —*v.*, **forged, forging. 1.** to heat (metal) in a forge and then work into shape. **2.** to make or form; fashion: *to forge an agreement.* **3.** to copy, sign, or alter for purposes of deception or fraud; counterfeit; falsify: *to forge a signature, to forge a passport.* —*v.i.* **1.** to commit forgery. **2.** to work at a forge. [Middle English *forge,* from Old French *forge,* from Latin *fabrica* workshop, from *faber* worker, artisan.] —**forg′er,** *n.*

forge[2] (fôrj) *v.i.*, **forged, forging. 1.** to move forward slowly but steadily, as if with difficulty: *The ferry forged through the choppy bay. We forged ahead on the project.* **2.** to advance or progress with increased speed or efficiency: *The runner forged into the lead during the final lap of the race.* [Of uncertain origin.]

for·ger·y (fôr′jə rē) *n.*, *pl.* **-ger·ies. 1.** the crime of copying, falsifying, or altering written or printed matter, or an original

work of art, for the purpose of fraud. **2.** something that is forged; fraudulent imitation: *The painting I purchased was a forgery.*

for·get (fər get′) *v.*, **-got** or *(archaic)* **-gat, -got·ten** or **-got, -get·ting.** —*v.t.* **1.** to be unable to recall: *I have forgotten your telephone number.* **2.** to omit or neglect unintentionally; overlook: *to forget to pay a bill.* **3.** to fail to take through carelessness or thoughtlessness; leave behind inadvertently: *I forgot my keys.* **4.** to put out of mind deliberately; cease to think of: *Try to forget what happened.* **5.** to neglect willfully and intentionally; slight; disregard: *Don't forget your friends when you become rich and famous!* —*v.i.* to cease or neglect to think (often with *about*): *I forgot about the food cooking on the stove.* [Old English *forgitan* to lose memory of, neglect.] —**for·get′ta·ble,** *adj.* —**for·get′ter,** *n.*

·**to forget oneself.** to act improperly or in an unbecoming manner; lose self-control.

for·get·ful (fər get′fəl) *adj.* **1.** likely to forget; having a poor memory. **2.** failing to think of or do something; neglectful; careless: *forgetful of one's duty.* **3.** causing to forget; causing oblivion: *forgetful sleep.* —**for·get′ful·ly,** *adv.* —**for·get′ful·ness,** *n.*

for·get-me-not (fər get′mē not′) *n.* **1.** a small blue, pink, or white five-petaled flower of any of a group of plants, genus *Myosotis,* growing singly or in clusters. **2.** the small perennial plant that bears these flowers, widely cultivated in gardens.

forg·ing (fôr′jing) *n.* **1.** the act of a person or thing that forges. **2.** a forged piece of metal.

for·give (fər giv′) *v.*, **-gave, -giv·en, -giv·ing. 1.** to cease to blame or feel resentment against (someone): *I forgive you for losing my book.* **2.** to cease to feel resentment or demand a penalty for (something); grant pardon for: *to forgive an insult.* **3.** to require no payment of (a debt); cancel; remit. —*v.i.* to grant pardon: *to forgive easily.* [Old English *forgifan* to give, remit.] —**for·giv′a·ble,** *adj.* —**for·giv′er,** *n.* —For Synonyms, see **excuse.**

forget-me-not

for·give·ness (fər giv′nis) *n.* **1.** the act of forgiving or the state of being forgiven. **2.** a disposition or willingness to forgive.

for·giv·ing (fər giv′ing) *adj.* having or showing forgiveness: *a forgiving nature, a forgiving glance.* —**for·giv′ing·ly,** *adv.* —**for·giv′ing·ness,** *n.*

for·go (fôr gō′) *also,* **forego.** *v.t.*, **-went, -gone, -go·ing.** to abstain or refrain from; give up; do without: *Let's forgo the usual formalities and start the meeting.* [Old English *forgān* to pass over, neglect.] —**for·go′er,** *n.*

for·got (fər got′) the past tense and a past participle of **forget.**

for·got·ten (fər got′ən) a past participle of **forget.**

fo·rint (fôr′int) *n.* the monetary unit of Hungary. [Magyar *forint,* from Italian *fiorino* coin of Florence. See FLORIN.]

fork (fôrk) *n.* **1.** any of various-sized utensils having a handle at one end and two or more prongs at the other, used esp. for lifting or handling food. **2.** something resembling a fork in shape, as any of various agricultural tools used for such purposes as digging or lifting. **3.a.** a branching or dividing into branches, as of a road or river. **b.** the point at which such a branching occurs. **c.** any one of these branches or divisions: *Take the left fork of the road.* —*v.t.* **1.** to lift, spear, or pitch with or as with a fork: *We forked the hay into the wagon.* **2.** to make or put into the shape of a fork. —*v.i.* to divide into branches: *The road forks further ahead.* [Old English *forca* pronged instrument, from Latin *furca* two-pronged fork, fork-shaped stake.] —**fork′like′,** *adj.*

·**to fork over** (or **out** or **up**). *Informal.* to give up or pay: *We forked out five dollars per ticket.*

forked (fôrkt, fôr′kid) *adj.* shaped like a fork; divided into forks: *a forked road, a forked tongue.*

fork·ful (fôrk′fùl′) *n.*, *pl.* **-fuls.** as much as a fork will hold.

a	at	e	end	o	hot	u	up	hw	white		about
ā	ape	ē	me	ō	old	ū	use	ng	song		taken
ä	far	i	it	ô	fork	ü	rule	th	thin	ə	pencil
âr	care	ī	ice	oi	oil	ù	pull	th	this		lemon
		îr	pierce	ou	out	ûr	turn	zh	measure		circus

fork·lift (fôrk′lift′) *n.* a motor-driven vehicle with a mechanical lifting device on the front to which steel prongs are attached. The prongs can be inserted under heavy loads to move them from one place to another.

for·lorn (fôr lôrn′) *adj.* **1.** dejected; hopeless; wretched. **2.** feeling or showing extreme unhappiness; feeling or being lost and alone; abandoned; forsaken; deserted. **3.** deprived or bereft (with *of*). [Old English *forloren,* past participle of *forlēosan* to lose.] —**for·lorn′ly,** *adv.* —**for·lorn′ness,** *n.*

forlorn hope 1. an undertaking that is almost certain to fail; vain hope. **2.** a group of people chosen to perform some perilous or desperate undertaking. [Modification of Dutch *verloren hoop* literally, lost company or troop.]

form (fôrm) *n.* **1.** the outline or external contour of something, not including its substance or color; shape: *three benches in the form of a triangle.* **2.** a body or figure: *A large form loomed ahead of us in the darkness.* **3.** external appearance: *the many myths in which Zeus assumed the form of an animal.* **4.** the particular state, structure, or character in which something appears or exists: *water in the form of ice.* **5.** a particular kind; type; variety: *Democracy is a form of government.* **6.** a manner or style of arranging and organizing parts, esp. in an orderly or effective way, as in a literary or musical composition: *These papers will be graded on form as well as content.* **7.** an orderly or systematic arrangement or progression; organization: *Your ideas are fuzzy and lack form.* **8.** a way of doing something, esp. with regard to established standards of technique: *Practice will improve your form in diving.* **9.** fitness of mind or body, as for performance; condition: *an athlete who is in top form.* **10.** a document having blank spaces for insertion of required information: *an order form.* **11.** a prescribed or set order of words or wording; formula. **12.** something, such as a frame or mold, that holds, supports, or gives or determines shape: *a dressmaker's form, to pour concrete into a form.* **13.** behavior or conduct judged in relation to etiquette or the established customs of society: *It was bad form to ask them personal questions.* **14.** customary or established practice or ritual; ceremony; formality: *diplomatic forms, to shake hands as a matter of form.* **15.** a grade or level in a British secondary school or in some U.S. private schools: *the fifth form.* **16.** *British.* a long, backless seat or bench. **17.** *Grammar.* any of the ways in which a word may appear as a result of inflection or modification in spelling or pronunciation. *People is a plural form of person; was is a form of the verb to be; disc and disk are variant forms.* **18.** linguistic form. **19.** *Printing.* a body of type or other material properly arranged and locked in a frame for printing or electrotyping. —*v.t.* **1.** to give shape or form to; fashion: *to form patties out of meat.* **2.** to make or produce: *He tried to form a sentence without a verb.* **3.** to make up or constitute: *Students formed the bulk of the crowd.* **4.** to construct in the mind; conceive; devise: *to form a plan, to form an opinion.* **5.** to combine into; organize; establish: *The workers formed a union.* **6.** to develop; acquire: *to form a habit.* **7.** to shape or mold, as by discipline or instruction: *Her mind was formed by study of the classics.* **8.** to place or arrange in order. **9.** *Grammar.* to construct or produce (a word) by adding, subtracting, or changing elements. —*v.i.* **1.** to take shape: *Clouds formed in the sky.* **2.** to come into existence; be produced: *Mold formed on the stale bread. Ice won't form on the lake until the temperature is lower.* [Old French *forme* shape, figure, from Latin *forma.*] —For Synonyms *(n.),* see **shape.**
 · **to form into.** to take the form of: *Below 32 degrees Fahrenheit, water forms into ice.*

-form *suffix* (used to form adjectives) **1.** having the form of: *cruciform.* **2.** having (a specified number of) forms: *multiform, uniform.* [Latin *-formis,* from Latin *forma* shape, figure, pattern.]

for·mal (fôr′məl) *adj.* **1.** characterized by or given to observance, esp. strict observance, of the requirements of form, convention, or etiquette: *You needn't be so formal with me.* **2.** marked by or requiring ceremony or elaborate detail or dress: *a formal wedding, a formal banquet.* **3.** appropriate for or worn at elaborate or state occasions: *formal dress.* **4.** being a matter of form only; perfunctory; nominal: *The president is the formal head of state.* **5.** of or relating to form or structure, as distinguished from content: *the formal elements of a poem.* **6.** done or made so as to be binding and valid; official: *a formal contract, a formal agreement.* **7.** received in school; academic: *formal education.* **8.** (of language) relating to or characterized by grammar, syntax, and pronunciation that conforms to traditional standards of correctness and avoids the use of colloquial, informal, or contracted forms. **9.** having a regular, symmetrical, or orderly pattern or arrangement: *formal gardens.* —*n.* something formal, as a dance or evening gown. [Latin *formālis* relating to a form, having a set form, from *forma* shape, figure, pattern.] —**for′mal·ly,** *adv.* —For Usage Note, see **informal.**

form·al·de·hyde (fôr mal′də hīd′) *n.* a colorless, poisonous gas with a sharp, suffocating odor, used esp. in solution as a disinfectant and preservative, and in the manufacture of synthetic resins. Formula: CH_2O [FORM(IC ACID) + ALDEHYDE.]

for·ma·lin (fôr′mə lin) *n.* a solution of 40% formaldehyde in water, used as a disinfectant and preservative.

for·mal·ism (fôr′mə liz′əm) *n.* the strict observance of or adherence to prescribed or traditional forms, as in art or religion. —**for′mal·ist,** *n.* —**for′mal·is′tic,** *adj.*

for·mal·i·ty (fôr mal′i tē) *n., pl.* **-ties. 1.** the state or quality of being formal: *the formality of a wedding ceremony.* **2.** observance of or attention to the requirements of form, convention, or etiquette: *She treated all of us with great formality.* **3.** an established, proper, or customary act, practice, or procedure: *The will was executed with all the due legal formalities.* **4.** something that is a matter of form only; requirement or outward observance of convention or etiquette: *He was already assured of the job, and his interview was a mere formality.*

for·mal·ize (fôr′mə līz′) *v.t.,* **-ized, -iz·ing. 1.** to make formal. **2.** to give a definite or official form to: *to formalize an agreement.* —**for′mal·i·za′tion,** *n.* —**for′mal·iz′er,** *n.*

for·mat (fôr′mat) *n.* **1.** the arrangement or general makeup of a book, magazine, or other publication, including size, shape, and type size. **2.** general organization or style, as of a television program: *the format of a quiz show.* —*v.t.,* **-mat·ted, -mat·ting. 1.** to arrange in a format. **2.** *Computers.* to prepare (a disk) to accept data or text. [French *format* format (of a book), from German *Format* size (of a book), form, shape, from Latin *formātus* formed, past participle of *formāre* to form, shape.]

for·ma·tion (fôr mā′shən) *n.* **1.** the act or process of forming: *the formation of good habits.* **2.** something that is formed: *The cloud formation covered the sun.* **3.** the manner in which something is formed or arranged; disposition of parts; arrangement: *The troops lined up in parade formation.* **4.** *Geology.* masses of rock or deposits of minerals that have the same characteristics or origin.

form·a·tive (fôr′mə tiv) *adj.* **1.** giving or capable of giving form; helping to develop, shape, or mold: *a formative influence.* **2.** of or relating to growth, formation, or development: *the formative years of childhood.* **3.** *Grammar.* of, relating to, or characteristic of a grammatical element, as an affix, that, when added to words, changes their meanings or functions, or acts as a means of word formation. —*n.* a formative element, as an affix.

for·mer¹ (fôr′mər) *adj.* **1.** being first (of two) mentioned or understood. ➡ opposed to **latter.** For Usage Note, see **latter. 2.** belonging to, being of, or occurring in the past; previous; earlier: *our former governor, in former times.* [Middle English *formere,* from *forme* first, from Old English *forma.* See FOREMOST.]

form·er² (fôr′mər) *n.* a person or thing that forms. [FORM + -ER¹.]

for·mer·ly (fôr′mər lē) *adv.* in time past; once; previously.

form-fit·ting (fôrm′fit′ing) *adj.* (of clothing) conforming closely to the shape of the body: *a formfitting sweater, formfitting ski pants.*

for·mic (fôr′mik) *adj.* **1.** of or relating to ants. **2.** relating to or derived from formic acid.

For·mi·ca (fôr mī′kə) *n. Trademark.* a laminated plastic covering resistant to water, heat, and most chemicals, used esp. for kitchen and bathroom surfaces. [FOR + MICA; because when first introduced, it was used in place of the mineral *mica.*]

formic acid, a colorless, pungent liquid that is irritating to the skin, found esp. in ants and spiders and in some plants, and also produced synthetically, used in dyeing. Formula: CH_2O_2 [Latin *formīca* ant + ACID; because it was originally obtained from the fluid that the red ant secretes when it bites, which causes pain.]

for·mi·da·ble (fôr′mi də bəl) *adj.* **1.** causing fear, dread, or awe, as by reason of strength, size, or power: *a formidable enemy.* **2.** difficult to deal with, perform, or overcome: *a formidable task.* **3.** arousing admiration or wonder; strikingly impressive: *a formidable accomplishment.* [Latin *formīdābilis* terrible, from *formīdāre* to dread.] —**for′mi·da·bil′i·ty,** *n.* —**for′mi·da·bly,** *adv.*

form·less (fôrm′lis) *adj.* lacking a definite or regular shape; shapeless. —**form′less·ly,** *adv.* —**form′less·ness,** *n.*

form letter, one of a number of duplicate copies of a letter written in such a way that it may be sent to various individuals or groups.

for·mu·la (fôr′myə lə) *n., pl.* **-las** or **-lae** (-lē′). **1.** a prescribed or conventional form or method for doing something; fixed rule: *There is no formula for making friends.* **2.** a set or prescribed order of words or wording, as used in conventional expressions or cere-

monial, legal, or similar proceedings: *"Yours truly" is a formula for closing a letter.* **3.** a representation, using symbols and numbers, of the composition of a chemical compound. An **empirical formula** gives the proportion of the constituents, as H_2O; a **structural formula** gives, in addition, the approximate arrangement of the atoms in a molecule, as H—O—H. **4.** a conventionally used rule or principle stated as an equation in algebraic form. The formula $A = \pi r^2$ states that the area of a circle equals the product of pi and the radius squared. **5.** a list of ingredients and directions for making something: *a formula for mixing paints.* **6.** something made from this, esp. a mixture of milk or a milk substitute, water, and a sugar, used to feed infants. **7.** a formal statement of religious faith or doctrine. [Latin *formula* small pattern, method, diminutive of *forma* shape, plan, pattern.]

for·mu·la·ic (fôr′myə lā′ik) *adj.* based on, consisting of, or made according to a formula or formulas: *The defendant's answers were confined to rather formulaic responses.*

for·mu·lar·y (fôr′myə ler′ē) *n., pl.* **-lar·ies. 1.** a collection or system of formulas. **2.** a set order of words or wording; formula. **3.** a book containing a list of pharmaceutical substances and formulas for medicinal preparations. —*adj.* relating to or resembling a formula.

for·mu·late (fôr′myə lāt′) *v.t.,* **-lat·ed, -lat·ing. 1.** to put or state in precise and systematic form: *to formulate one's ideas.* **2.** to work out in detail; devise or develop: *The general formulated a plan of attack.* **3.** to reduce to or express in a formula. —**for′mu·la′tion,** *n.* —**for′mu·la′tor,** *n.*

for·ni·cate (fôr′ni kāt′) *v.i.,* **-cat·ed, -cat·ing.** to commit fornication. [Late Latin *fornicātus,* past participle of *fornicārī* to commit fornication, from Latin *fornix* arch, brothel; with reference to the location of ancient Roman brothels under an arch or in a cave.] —**for′ni·ca′tor,** *n.*

for·ni·ca·tion (fôr′ni kā′shən) *n.* voluntary sexual intercourse between two persons of the opposite sex who are unmarried or who are not married to each other.

for·nix (fôr′niks) *n., pl.* **-ni·ces** (-nə sēz′). *Anatomy.* any of various arched surfaces or structures, as the top of the pharynx. [Modern Latin *fornix,* from Latin *fornix* arch.]

for·sake (fôr sāk′) *v.t.,* **-sook** (-sŏk′), **-sak·en, -sak·ing. 1.** to give up completely, as an idea or belief. **2.** to leave completely; desert: *to forsake one's friends.* [Old English *forsacan* to give up.] —**for·sak′er,** *n.* —For Synonyms, see **desert**[2].

for·sooth (fôr sŏŏth′) *adv. Archaic.* in truth; indeed. [Old English *forsōth.*]

for·swear (fôr swâr′) *v.,* **-swore, -sworn, -swear·ing.** —*v.t.* **1.** to give up on oath; swear to give up; abjure: *to forswear smoking.* **2.** to deny emphatically or on oath: *to forswear a debt.* —*v.i.* to swear falsely. [Old English *forswerian* to swear falsely.] • **to forswear oneself.** to perjure oneself.

for·sworn (fôr swôrn′) *adj.* perjured.

for·syth·i·a (fôr sith′ē ə) *n.* any of a group of shrubs, genus *Forsythia,* widely cultivated as ornamentals, bearing bell-shaped, yellow flowers that grow in clusters along the stems and usually appear before the leaves do. [From William *Forsyth,* 1737-1804, an English botanist who introduced it from China.]

fort (fôrt) *n.* **1.** a fortified structure or enclosure that can be defended against an enemy; fortification. **2.** a permanent military post. [Old French *fort* stronghold, from *fort* strong, from Latin *fortis.*] • **to hold the fort.** *Informal.* to keep in operation; carry on.

fort
Fort McHenry, Maryland

forte[1] (fôrt) *n.* something in which one excels; strong point: *Mathematics is my forte.* [French *fort* strength, from *fort* strong, from Latin *fortis.*]

for·te[2] (fôr′tā) *Music. adj.* loud and forceful. —*adv.* loudly and forcefully. —*n.* a forte note, chord, or passage. [Italian *forte* strong, loud, from Latin *fortis* strong.]

forth (fôrth) *adv.* **1.** forward in time, place, or order; onward: *from this day forth.* **2.** out into view or consideration, as from concealment, obscurity, or latency: *The tree put forth new leaves. New arguments were brought forth by the prosecution.* [Old English *forth* forward, onward.] —For Synonyms, see **forward.** • **and so forth.** and the rest; and others; et cetera.

forth·com·ing (fôrth′kum′ing) *adj.* **1.** about to appear or occur; approaching in time: *the forthcoming election.* **2.** available or ready when required or expected: *Relief will be forthcoming for those left homeless by the flood.* —*n.* a coming forth; approach or appearance.

forth·right (fôrth′rīt′) *adj.* **1.** going straight to the point; straightforward; frank: *forthright criticism.* **2.** proceeding in a straight line or course; direct: *a forthright line of attack.* —*adv.* **1.** in a direct or straightforward course or manner. **2.** without delay; immediately. —**forth′right′ly,** *adv.* —**forth′right′ness,** *n.*

forth·with (fôrth with′, -with′) *adv.* without delay; at once; immediately: *The doctor came forthwith.*

for·ti·eth (fôr′tē ith) *adj.* **1.** (the ordinal of forty) next after the thirty-ninth. **2.** being one of forty equal parts. —*n.* **1.** something that is next after the thirty-ninth. **2.** one of forty equal parts; $1/40$.

for·ti·fi·ca·tion (fôr′tə fi kā′shən) *n.* **1.** the act, art, or science of fortifying. **2.** something that fortifies, such as a wall or ditch. **3.** a fortified military work or place of defense.

for·ti·fy (fôr′tə fī′) *v.,* **-fied, -fy·ing.** —*v.t.* **1.** to provide or protect with a wall, ditch, or other defensive work; strengthen against attack: *The Great Wall fortified China against barbarian invasions.* **2.** to strengthen structurally: *They fortified the dam against the flood.* **3.** to give physical strength or endurance to: *Good eating habits help to fortify the body against disease.* **4.** to give support to; confirm; corroborate: *Each of the lawyer's arguments was fortified by facts.* **5.** to give mental or moral strength to: *The soldiers' spirits were fortified by their captain's fearlessness.* **6.** to strengthen with alcohol: *to fortify wine.* **7.** to enrich (food), as with vitamins and minerals: *to fortify bread.* —*v.i.* to erect defensive works. [Old French *fortifier* to strengthen, going back to Latin *fortis* strong + *facere* to make.]

for·tis·si·mo (fôr tis′ə mō′) *Music. adj.* very loud. —*adv.* very loudly. —*n., pl.* **-mos** or **-mi** (-mē′). a fortissimo note, chord, or passage. [Italian *fortissimo,* superlative of *forte* loud, strong. See FORTE[2].]

for·ti·tude (fôr′ti tūd′, -tūd′) *n.* courage or strength of mind in the face of pain, danger, or adversity. [Latin *fortitūdō.*]

fort·night (fôrt′nīt′) *n.* two weeks. [Old English *fēowertīene niht* fourteen nights.]

fort·night·ly (fôrt′nīt′lē) *adv.* once every two weeks. —*adj.* occurring, issued, or appearing every two weeks. —*n., pl.* **-lies.** something published every two weeks, such as a magazine.

FORTRAN (fôr′tran) *n.* a computer coding system using modified mathematical notation for solving scientific problems. [Short for *for(mula) tran(slation).*]

for·tress (fôr′tris) *n.* **1.** a fortified place; stronghold; fort. **2.** any place or thing providing protection or security. —*v.t.* to furnish or protect with or as with a fortress. [Old French *forteresse* strong place, going back to Latin *fortis* strong.]

for·tu·i·tous (fôr tū′i təs, -tū′-) *adj.* **1.** happening by chance; accidental; casual: *a fortuitous encounter.* **2.** causing or bringing a favorable result; fortunate; lucky: *fortuitous circumstances.* [Latin *fortuītus* casual, accidental, going back to *fors* chance.] —**for·tu′i·tous·ly,** *adv.* —**for·tu′i·tous·ness,** *n.*

> **Usage** The use of **fortuitous** to mean "fortunate" is considered unacceptable by many people and often causes confusion in sentences such as *I got the job through a fortuitous meeting with an old friend,* where it is not clear whether "fortunate" or the original meaning, "chance or accidental," is intended.

F

a	at	e	end	o	hot	u	up	hw	white		about
ā	ape	ē	me	ō	old	ū	use	ng	song		taken
ä	far	i	it	ô	fork	ü	rule	th	thin	ə	pencil
âr	care	ī	ice	oi	oil	ů	pull	th	this		lemon
		îr	pierce	ou	out	ûr	turn	zh	measure		circus

for·tu·i·ty (fôr tü′i tē, -tū′-) *n., pl.* **-ties. 1.** the quality of being fortuitous. **2.** an accidental occurrence; chance.

for·tu·nate (fôr′chə nit) *adj.* **1.** having good fortune; lucky. **2.** bringing good fortune; favorable: *fortunate circumstances.* [Latin *fortūnātus,* past participle of *fortūnāre* to make prosperous, to prosper, from *fortūna* chance, luck.] —**for′tu·nate·ly,** *adv.*

for·tune (fôr′chən) *n.* **1.** something that happens or is going to happen to a person, whether good or bad: *to claim to tell fortunes by looking into a crystal ball.* **2.** luck, esp. when good: *It was our good fortune to meet you when we did.* **3.** *also,* **Fortune.** a force, often personified, that controls the future; destiny; fate. **4.** great wealth; riches: *a fortune in stocks and bonds.* [Old French *fortune* chance, from Latin *fortūna* fate, chance, luck.] —For Synonyms, see **luck.**

fortune cookie, a thin, folded cookie containing a piece of paper with a prediction or other message.

fortune hunter, a person who seeks to gain wealth, esp. through marriage.

for·tune·tell·er (fôr′chən tel′ər) *n.* someone who professes to foretell future events in a person's life. —**for′tune·tell′ing,** *n.,* *adj.*

for·ty (fôr′tē) *n., pl.* **-ties. 1.** the cardinal number that is four times ten. **2.** a symbol representing this number, such as 40 or XL. **3.** something having this many units or members. **4. forties.** the number series from forty through forty-nine. ➡ used esp. in reference to the fifth decade of a century or of a person's life. —*adj.* numbering four times ten. [Old English *fēowertig.*]

for·ty-nin·er (fôr′tē nī′nər) *n.* a person who went to California seeking gold in the gold rush of 1849.

forty winks *Informal.* a short nap.

fo·rum (fôr′əm) *n.* **1.** the public square or marketplace of an ancient Roman city, where public assemblies met, and where most legal and political activities took place. **2. the Forum.** the political, commercial, social, and religious center of ancient Rome. **3.** an assembly, meeting, or other medium for discussion of issues or questions of public interest. **4.** a court of law; tribunal. [Latin *forum* marketplace, public place.]

for·ward (fôr′wərd) *adv.* **1.** *also,* **forwards.** toward what is ahead or in front; onward: *Step forward to accept your trophy.* **2.** toward the future: *from this day forward.* **3.** into view or consideration; forth: *to bring forward an opinion.* **4.** at the front; in front: *The ship's boiler room was forward of the steward's cabin.* —*adj.* **1.** situated in, at, near, or toward the front: *the forward cabins of a ship.* **2.** moving or directed toward a point in front: *a forward movement.* **3.** toward the future: *a forward look.* **4.** well-advanced or progressive, as in thinking. **5.** offensively bold; impertinent; presumptuous: *forward children, a forward question.* —*v.t.* **1.** to send onward or ahead, esp. to a new address: *They forwarded my mail to my new address.* **2.** to help along; promote; advance: *to forward one's interests, to forward a cause.* —*n.* a player whose position is at or near the front line in certain games, such as basketball or hockey. [Old English *foreweard* onward.]

Synonyms *adv.* **Forward, onward,** and **forth** mean moving toward what is ahead. **Forward** generally connotes progress in relation to things being passed or left behind: *to take three steps forward and one back, to move forward on a project.* **Onward** more clearly suggests the goal toward which there is movement and may imply stops along the way: *After exploring the first island, they sailed onward toward their destination. The space probe moved onward through the solar system.* **Forth** adds the suggestion of movement outward or away from something: *The expedition set forth from the city.*

for·ward·er (fôr′wər dər) *n.* a person or thing that forwards, esp. a person or company acting as an agent in receiving or delivering goods for reshipment to the proper destination.

for·ward·ly (fôr′wərd lē) *adv.* in a forward manner; impertinently; presumptuously; boldly.

for·ward·ness (fôr′wərd nis) *n.* **1.** the condition or quality of being forward; impertinence; presumptuousness; boldness. **2.** the condition of being well-advanced or progressive: *The forwardness of that senator's policies is in keeping with the times.* **3.** the state of being ready or eager.

forward pass, the passing of a football from behind the line of scrimmage toward the opponent's goal.

for·went (fôr went′) the past tense of **forgo.**

fos·sa (fos′ə) *n., pl.* **fos·sae** (fos′ē). a shallow depression, pit, or cavity, as in a bone. [Latin *fossa* ditch.]

fosse (fos) *also,* **foss.** *n.* a ditch or moat, esp. one in a fortification. [Old French *fosse* pit, from Latin *fossa* ditch.]

fos·sil (fos′əl) *n.* **1.** the remains or traces of an animal or plant of ancient geological times, preserved in rock in the earth's crust. **2.** *Informal.* a person or thing that is outmoded or antiquated. —*adj.* **1.** relating to, of the nature of, or forming a fossil. **2.** belonging to the past; outmoded; antiquated. [Latin *fossilis* dug up, from *fossus,* past participle of *fodere* to dig.]

fossil fuel, any fuel formed in the earth from the fossilized remains of prehistoric life. Fossil fuels include coal, petroleum, and natural gas.

fos·sil·if·er·ous (fos′ə lif′-ər əs) *adj.* containing fossils.

fos·sil·ize (fos′ə līz′) *v.,* **-ized, -iz·ing.** —*v.t.* **1.** to change into a fossil; petrify. **2.** to make antiquated, rigid, or out of date. —*v.i.* to become a fossil. —**fos′sil·i·za′tion,** *n.*

fos·so·ri·al (fo sôr′ē əl) *adj.* digging or adapted for burrowing: *fossorial feet.* [Late

fossil of a reptile

Latin *fossorius,* from *fossor* digger, from *fossus,* past participle of *fodere* to dig + -AL¹.]

fos·ter (fôs′tər) *v.t.* **1.** to promote the growth or development of: *The teacher fostered our interest in science.* **2.** to bring up (a child); rear. **3.** to cling to, as a feeling; cherish: *to foster a feeling of pride.* —*adj.* **1.** providing shelter, food, and supervision temporarily for one or more persons who are not related by birth or adoption. Such care is often arranged and paid for by a social service agency: *foster care, foster parents, a foster home.* **2.** being a member of a family to which one is not related by birth or adoption and receiving or sharing the parental care afforded by that relationship: *a foster child.* [Old English *fōstrian* to nourish, feed.] —**fos′ter·er,** *n.*

fos·ter·age (fôs′tər ij) *n.* **1.** the rearing of a foster child. **2.** the condition of being a foster child. **3.** the act of promoting the growth or development of something.

fos·ter·ling (fôs′tər ling) *n.* a foster child.

Fou·cault pendulum (fü kō′) a pendulum consisting of a heavy weight attached to a long wire in such a way that the weight can swing freely in any direction, used to demonstrate the earth's rotation. [From Jean *Foucault,* 1819-68, French physicist.]

foul (foul) *adj.* **1.** extremely offensive to the senses, esp. to the sense of smell: *a foul odor.* **2.** containing dirt or other offensive matter: *foul air, foul water.* **3.** extremely soiled; filthy: *foul clothing.* **4.** obscene, abusive, or profane: *foul language.* **5.** cloudy, rainy, or stormy; inclement: *foul weather.* **6.** (of food) rotten or spoiled. **7.** morally offensive; vile; abominable: *a foul deed.* **8.** treacherous; dishonest. **9.** entangled or obstructed; jammed: *a foul anchor.* **10.** (of a ship) having the bottom covered or encumbered with foreign matter, as seaweed or barnacles. **11.** *Sports.* contrary to or violating the rules; unfair. **12.** *Baseball.* **a.** (of a batted ball) ruled to be out of play because of its position in relation to the foul lines. **b.** outside the foul lines: *foul territory.* **13.** *Printing.* having corrections or changes indicated on it: *foul copy.* —*n.* **1.** *Sports.* an infraction of the rules. **2.** foul ball. —*v.t.* **1.** to make dirty; soil or pollute: *They fouled the water by throwing in garbage.* **2.** to entangle or obstruct; jam: *I fouled my fishing line.* **3.** to clog or choke (something) with foreign matter: *Dirt fouled the carburetor.* **4.** to dishonor; disgrace: *The scandal fouled the premier's reputation.* **5.** to cover or encumber (a ship's bottom) with foreign matter, as seaweed or barnacles. **6.** *Sports.* to commit a foul against (an opponent). **7.** *Baseball.* to hit (a ball) into foul territory. —*v.i.* **1.** to be or become dirty. **2.** to become entangled or obstructed; jam: *The rope fouled on the anchor.* **3.** to be or become clogged or choked. **4.** *Sports.* to commit a violation of the rules. **5.** *Baseball.* to hit a ball into foul territory. —*adv.* afoul: *to run foul of the law.* [Old English *fūl* dirty, rotten, stinking, abominable, abusive.] —**foul′-ly,** *adv.*

·to foul out. a. *Baseball.* to be retired by hitting a foul ball that is caught before it touches the ground. **b.** *Basketball.* to be put out of the game for having committed a particular number of fouls.

·to foul up. *Informal*. **a.** to mix up or mess up; throw into disorder or confusion: *The flat tire fouled up our schedule*. **b.** to make a mistake.

fou·lard (fü lärd′) *n*. **1.** a soft, lightweight fabric made of silk, rayon, cotton, or similar fibers, usually having a small printed motif, used esp. for neckties, scarves, and dresses. **2.** a scarf or necktie made of this fabric. [French *foulard;* of uncertain origin.]

foul ball, in baseball, a batted ball that, because of its position in relation to the foul lines, is ruled to be out of play.

foul line 1. *Baseball.* either of the lines that extend from home plate through first or third base to the limits of the playing field. **2.** *Basketball.* free throw line. **3.** *Bowling.* the line across the alley that the bowler may not touch or cross when bowling the ball.

foul·mouthed (foul′mouthd′, -mouth′) *adj*. using or tending to use obscene, abusive, or profane language.

foul·ness (foul′nis) *n*. **1.** the state or quality of being foul. **2.** foul matter; filth. **3.** moral impurity; sinfulness.

foul play, unfair or treacherous action, esp. when violent.

foul shot, free throw.

foul tip, a pitched baseball that the batter barely deflects off his or her bat into foul territory.

foul-up (foul′up′) *n. Informal*. **1.** a state of confusion or difficulty; complete mix-up or mess. **2.** a mechanical problem: *a foul-up in a car's engine*.

found¹ (found) *v*. the past tense and past participle of **find**.

found² (found) *v.t.* **1.** to bring into being; set up or establish: *to found a college, to found a political party*. **2.** to rest or rely on for support; base; ground: *a house founded on rock, an argument founded on fact*. [Middle English *founden,* from Old French *fonder* to establish, from Latin *fundāre* to lay the foundation of, establish, from *fundus* bottom, base.]

found³ (found) *v.t.* **1.** to melt and pour (metal) into a mold. **2.** to form or make by pouring molten metal into a mold; cast. [Middle English *founden,* from Old French *fondre* to melt, cast (metal), from Latin *fundere* to pour, melt, cast (metal).]

foun·da·tion (foun dā′shən) *n*. **1.** the act of founding or the state of being founded; establishment. **2.** something on which anything is based or supported; basis: *the foundations of society*. **3.** the supporting portion or base of a wall or building, usually of masonry, constructed partly or wholly below the surface of the ground. **4.** an endowed institution or organization, esp. one that grants money to support worthwhile causes, such as scientific, artistic, or scholarly work. **5.** the fund endowed for such an institution or organization; endowment. **6.** foundation garment. **7.** a cosmetic cream or liquid used as a base for makeup. —For Synonyms, see **base¹**.

foundation garment, any of various undergarments, as a girdle, corset, or brassiere, designed to give shape and support to the body.

foun·der¹ (foun′dər) *v.i.* **1.** to fill with water and sink, as a boat. **2.** to fall down or give way: *Several buildings foundered in the earthquake*. **3.** to fail completely: *The business foundered*. **4.** to stumble and become lame or otherwise disabled: *The horse foundered on the rocky path*. —*v.t.* to cause to founder. [Old French *fondrer* to sink, from *fond* bottom, from Latin *fundus*.]

foun·der² (foun′dər) *n*. a person who founds or establishes something: *the founders of a colony*. [FOUND² + -ER¹.]

foun·der³ (foun′dər) *n*. a person who founds or casts metal. [FOUND³ + -ER¹.]

Founding Father 1. any of the colonial statesmen of the period of the American Revolution, especially those who helped to write the Constitution of the United States. **2. founding father.** a person who originates or establishes something, such as an institution or movement; founder.

found·ling (found′ling) *n*. a deserted infant of unknown parents. [Middle English *fundling,* from *funden,* past participle of *finden* to find + -LING¹. See FIND.]

found·ry (foun′drē) *n., pl.* **-ries. 1.** a place where metal is melted and cast. **2.** the act or process of founding metal. [French *fonderie,* from *fondre* to melt, cast (metal). See FOUND³.]

fount (fount) *n*. **1.** source: *That book is a fount of information*. **2.** a fountain or spring. [From FOUNTAIN.]

foun·tain (foun′tən) *n*. **1.** a stream of water made to rise or spout upward artificially, as to provide water for drinking or to serve as an ornament. **2.** a structure designed for such a stream to rise and fall into. **3.** a spring of water issuing from the earth. **4.** the source or origin of anything: *The coach is a fountain of information about baseball*. **5.** soda fountain. **6.** a reservoir or compartment for holding a supply of ink, oil, or other liquid. [Old French *fontaine* spring, from Late Latin *fontāna,* from Latin *fōns*.]

foun·tain·head (foun′tən hed′) *n*. **1.** a spring from which a stream flows; source of a stream. Also, **wellspring**. **2.** the primary source or origin of anything.

Fountain of Youth, a legendary spring whose waters were said to have the power to restore youth and health.

fountain pen, a pen having a reservoir or replaceable cartridge that automatically feeds a steady supply of ink to the writing point.

four (fôr) *n*. **1.** the cardinal number that is one more than three. **2.** a symbol representing this number, such as 4 or IV. **3.** something having this many units or members, such as a playing card. —*adj*. numbering one more than three. [Old English *fēower*.]

·on all fours a. on all four feet: *The cat landed on all fours*. **b.** on hands and knees: *We were on all fours looking for the lost contact lens*.

four-di·men·sion·al (fôr′di men′shə nəl) *adj*. relating to or having four dimensions.

four-eyed fish (fôr′īd′) any of a group of fish, genus *Anableps,* of tropical America, having horizontally divided eyes able to see above and below the water's surface simultaneously.

four-flush·er (fôr′flush′ər) *n. Slang*. a person who bluffs or fakes. [From an expression used in poker, meaning a player who pretends to have a five-card flush when having only four cards of a suit.]

four·fold (fôr′fōld′) *adj*. **1.** four times as great or as numerous. **2.** having or consisting of four parts. —*adv*. so as to be four times greater or more numerous.

four-foot·ed (fôr′fut′id) *adj*. having four feet.

Four Freedoms, the human rights set forth as essential to a free society by President Franklin D. Roosevelt in a message to Congress on January 6, 1941. They are freedom of speech, freedom of worship, freedom from want, and freedom from fear.

four-hand·ed (fôr′han′did) *adj*. **1.** for or played by four players: *a four-handed card game*. **2.** in music, intended for two performers, as a piano duet. **3.** having four feet resembling hands in shape or function.

Four-H clubs (fôr′āch′) *also*, **4-H clubs**. an educational and recreational organization for youth, sponsored by the U.S Department of Agriculture, designed to provide training in the fields of agriculture and home economics. [Because it is the purpose of these clubs to improve their members' Heads, Hearts, Hands, and Health.]

four hundred, the most exclusive social set of a particular city or area. ➡ preceded by *the: a banker whose family belongs to the four hundred*. [Probably from the claim in 1889 by the American lawyer and society leader Ward McAllister, 1827-95, that only 400 people were accepted in the best social circles of New York City.]

four-in-hand (fôr′in hand′) *n*. **1.** a necktie tied in a slipknot with the ends hanging down vertically. **2.** a team of four horses driven by one person. **3.** a vehicle drawn by such a team.

four-leaf clover (fôr′lēf′) a clover with four leaflets, considered to bring good luck to the person who finds it.

four-let·ter word (fôr′let′ər) any of several short words regarded as obscene or objectionable.

four-o'clock (fôr′ə klok′) *n*. any of a large group of plants, genus *Mirabilis,* found chiefly in tropical America, esp. *M. jalapa,* having red, white, yellow, or striped trumpet-shaped flowers that open in the late afternoon and close in the morning.

four-post·er (fôr′pōs′tər) *n*. a bedstead with four tall corner posts designed to support a canopy or curtains.

four·score (fôr′skôr′) *adj., n*. four times twenty; eighty.

four·some (fôr′səm) *n*. a group of four persons or things, such as four people playing golf together. —*adj*. relating to, consisting of, or designed for a group of four.

four·square (fôr′skwâr′) *adj*. **1.** having a square shape; square. **2.** going straight to the point; frank; forthright. **3.** not giving way; unyielding; firm. —*adv*. **1.** without yielding; firmly. **2.** in a forthright manner; frankly.

four·teen (fôr′tēn′) *n*. **1.** the cardinal number that is four more than ten. **2.** a symbol representing this number, such as 14 or XIV. **3.** something having this many units or members. —*adj*. numbering four more than ten. [Old English *fēowertēne*.]

Fourteen Points, a statement of the peace aims of the United States and its allies made by President Woodrow Wilson on January 8, 1918.

four·teenth (fôr′tēnth′) *adj*. **1.** (the ordinal of fourteen) next

a	at	e	end	o	hot	u	up	hw	white	⟨	about
ā	ape	ē	me	ō	old	ū	use	ng	song		taken
ä	far	i	it	ô	fork	ü	rule	th	thin	ə	pencil
âr	care	ī	ice	oi	oil	u̇	pull	th	this		lemon
		îr	pierce	ou	out	ûr	turn	zh	measure	⟨	circus

491

after the thirteenth. **2.** being one of fourteen equal parts. —*n.* **1.** something that is next after the thirteenth. **2.** one of fourteen equal parts; $1/14$.

Fourteenth Amendment, an amendment to the United States Constitution, ratified in 1868, that, among other things, prohibits the states from infringing on basic civil rights or from violating the standards of due process of law and equal protection under the law.

fourth (fôrth) *adj.* **1.** (the ordinal of four) next after the third. **2.** being one of four equal parts. —*n.* **1.** something that is next after the third. **2.** one of four equal parts; $1/4$. **3.** *Music.* **a.** a tone, esp. the subdominant, four diatonic degrees from a given tone. **b.** an interval of four degrees between two tones of the diatonic scale. **c.** a harmonic combination of two tones separated by this interval. **4.** the fourth forward gear, as of an automobile. **5.** **the Fourth.** Independence Day. —*adv.* in the fourth place.

Fourth Amendment, an amendment to the United States Constitution, ratified in 1791 and part of the Bill of Rights. It guarantees the individual protection against search or seizure of his or her self, home, or effects unless a warrant has been issued, on the basis of probable cause, clearly describing what is to be searched or seized.

fourth-class (fôrth′klas′) *adj.* designating mail matter consisting of merchandise and sent for the lowest rate. Also, **parcel post.** —*adv.* by fourth-class mail.

fourth dimension, a dimension in addition to the three spatial dimensions of length, width, and depth. In the theory of relativity, time is regarded as the fourth dimension.

fourth estate, journalists or journalism; the press.

fourth·ly (fôrth′lē) *adv.* in the fourth place.

Fourth of July, Independence Day.

Fourth World *also,* **fourth world.** the poorest and most underdeveloped nations of the world that have no exploitable natural resources, found in Africa, Asia, and Latin America.

four-wheel (fôr′hwēl′, -wēl′) *adj.* **1.** *also,* **four-wheeled.** having four wheels. **2.** acting on or controlled by four wheels: *four-wheel drive.* —**four′-wheel′er,** *n.*

fo·ve·a (fō′vē ə) *n., pl.* **-ve·ae** (-vē ē′). a small pit or depression in the surface of a structure or organ, esp. the eye. [Latin *fovea* small pit.] —**fo′ve·al,** *adj.*

fovea cen·tra·lis (sen trā′lis) a small pit at the back of the retina, where vision is most acute.

fowl (foul) *n., pl.* **fowl** or **fowls. 1.** a domestic hen or rooster; chicken. **2.** any of various domestic or wild birds raised or hunted for meat, such as the turkey, duck, pheasant, or grouse. **3.** the flesh of such a bird used as food. **4.** any bird. —*v.i.* to hunt or catch wild birds. [Old English *fugol* bird.] —**fowl′er,** *n.*

fowl·ing (fou′ling) *n.* the hunting of wild birds for sport.

fowling piece, a light gun for shooting wild birds.

fox (foks) *n.* **1.** any of various wild, carnivorous mammals of the genus *Vulpes* and related genera, belonging to the dog family, but smaller than a wolf, and having a pointed muzzle, large erect ears, a bushy tail, and a thick coat. Height: 12-16 inches (30-41 centimeters) at the shoulder. **2.** the fur of a fox. **3.** a sly, crafty person. —*v.t.* **1.** *Informal.* to trick or deceive; outwit: *The escaped prisoner foxed the police by taking another route.* **2.** to cause to become discolored with yellowish brown stains, as the pages of an old book. [Old English *fox* this animal, crafty person.]

fox

Fox (foks) *n., pl.* **Fox** or **Foxes. 1.** a member of a North American Indian tribe formerly living in the Great Lakes region, now living in Iowa. **2.** the Algonquian language spoken by this tribe.

fox·fire (foks′fīr′) *n.* **1.** an eerie bioluminescence exhibited by decaying wood, caused by certain fungi. **2.** any of the fungi that cause this effect.

fox·glove (foks′gluv′) *n.* any plant, genus *Digitalis,* of the figwort family, widely cultivated and bearing white, yellow, or purple thimble-shaped flowers on long spikes. The **common,** or **purple, foxglove,** *D. purpurea,* is grown as a garden flower and for its leaves, which yield the drug digitalis. [Old English *foxes glōfa* literally, fox's glove.]

fox·hole (foks′hōl′) *n.* a hole dug in the ground by soldiers as shelter from enemy fire.

fox·hound (foks′hound′) *n.* any of various breeds of swift hound, usually having a tan, black, and white coat, raised esp. to hunt foxes. Height: to 25 inches (64 centimeters) at the shoulder.

fox hunting, a sport in which the participants, on horseback, follow hounds that trail a fox.

fox·tail (foks′tāl′) *n.* **1.** the tail of a fox. **2.** any of various weedy grasses, esp. genus *Alopecurus,* bearing soft, brushlike flower spikes that resemble the tails of foxes.

fox terrier, a dog of a breed originally used to drive foxes from their burrows, having a long head, short tail, and a smooth-haired or wirehaired white coat with tan or black and tan markings. Height: 15 inches (38 centimeters) at the shoulder.

fox-trot (foks′trot′) *v.i.,* **-trot·ted, -trot·ting.** to dance the fox trot.

fox trot 1. a dance performed in $2/4$ or $4/4$ time, combining slow steps and short, quick ones. **2.** the music for this dance.

fox·y (fok′sē) *adj.,* **fox·i·er, fox·i·est. 1.** like a fox; sly; crafty. **2.** discolored with yellowish brown stains: *The old print was foxy.* **3.** *Slang.* good-looking, appealing. —**fox′i·ly,** *adv.* —**fox′i·ness,** *n.*

foy·er (foi′ər, foi′ā) *n.* **1.** the lobby of a theater, hotel, or other public building. **2.** an entrance hall in a house or apartment. [French *foyer* hearth, home, lobby of a theater, going back to Latin *focus* hearth. Formerly, theaters often had hearths in their lobbies.]

fps, foot-pound-second.

Fr, the symbol for francium.

fr. 1. fragment. **2.** franc; francs. **3.** from.

Fr. 1. Father. **2.** France. **3.** French. **4.** Friar. **5.** Friday.

Fra (frä) *n.* Brother. ➡ used as the title of a monk or friar. [Italian *fra,* short for *frate,* from Latin *frāter.*]

fra·cas (frā′kəs) *n.* a noisy disturbance, quarrel, or fight; brawl. [French *fracas,* from *fracasser* to shatter, from Italian *fracassare,* possibly going back to a blend of Latin *frangere* to break and *quassāre* to shake.]

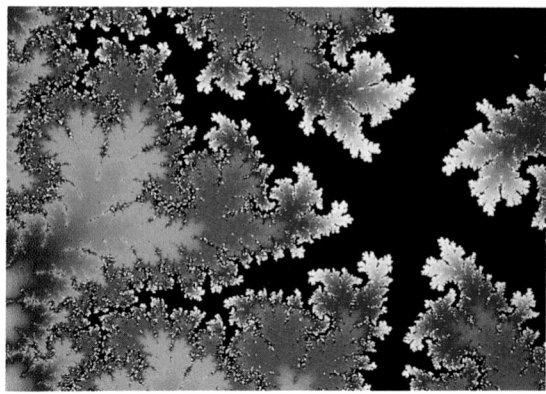

fractal

frac·tal (frak′təl) *n. Mathematics.* a structure of fragmented shape characterized by intricate patterns that repeat themselves on ever smaller scales, so that an enlargement of any small part of the structure has a shape identical to that of the whole. [Latin *frāctus,* past participle of *frangere* to break + -AL [1].]

frac·tion (frak′shən) *n.* **1.a.** one or more of the equal portions of a whole quantity. **b.** a mathematical expression representing part of some whole quantity or the ratio of two quantities, shown in the form of a numerator over a denominator, for example: $-a/b$, $2/3$, $1/\sqrt{2}$, and $(x^2 - 2y)/(x^2 - y^2)$. **2.** a small portion or disconnected part; fragment: *Only a fraction of the crowd left before the game was over.* **3.** a component of a liquid mixture separated by crystallization or distillation: *Gasoline and kerosene are fractions of crude oil.* [Church Latin *frāctiō* a breaking, from Latin *frāctus,* past participle of *frangere* to break.]

frac·tion·al (frak′shə nəl) *adj.* **1.** of, relating to, or constituting a fraction or fractions. **2.** small or unimportant; insignificant: *You've made only fractional improvements in your work.* **3.** *Chemistry.* separating into fractions: *fractional distillation.* —**frac′tion·al·ly,** *adv.*

frac·tion·ate (frak′shə nāt′) *v.t.,* **-at·ed, -at·ing. 1.** to separate into parts or fragments; divide into fractions. **2.** to separate into chemical fractions, as by distillation. [FRACTION + -ATE [1].] —**frac′tion·a′tion,** *n.* —**frac′tion·a′tor,** *n.*

frac·tious (frak′shəs) *adj.* **1.** difficult to control; unruly; rebellious: *a fractious youth.* **2.** tending to be quarrelsome; bad-tempered; irritable; cranky: *a fractious temperament.* —**frac′tious·ly,** *adv.* —**frac′tious·ness,** *n.*

frac·ture (frak′chər) v., **-tured, -tur·ing.** —v.t. to cause to come apart or crack: *to fracture a bone.* —v.i. to come apart or crack: *Brittle bones fracture easily.* —n. **1.** the act of fracturing or the state of being fractured. **2.** a break or crack, esp. in a bone. **3.** the characteristic appearance or texture of the freshly broken surface of a mineral. [Latin *frāctūra* a breach, cleft.]

frae (frā) prep. Scottish. from.

frag·ile (fraj′əl, -īl) adj. easily broken, damaged, or destroyed; delicate. [Latin *fragilis.* Doublet of FRAIL.] —**frag′ile·ly,** adv. —**fra·gil·i·ty** (frə jil′i tē), n. —For Synonyms, see **delicate.**

frag·ment (n., frag′mənt; v., frag′ment, frag ment′) n. **1.** a part broken off; small detached portion: *fragments of broken pottery.* **2.** an incomplete or isolated bit: *fragments of news.* **3.** a part of something left incomplete or unfinished: *Schubert's Unfinished Symphony is a fragment.* —v.t., v.i. to break into fragments. [Latin *fragmentum* a piece.] —**frag·ment·ed** (frag′men tid, fragmen′-), adj.

frag·men·tal (frag men′təl) adj. **1.** fragmentary. **2.** Geology. clastic. —**frag·men′tal·ly,** adv.

frag·men·tar·y (frag′mən ter′ē, frag men′tə rē) adj. composed of fragments; broken; incomplete: *fragmentary remains, fragmentary knowledge.* Also, **fragmental.** —**frag′men·tar′i·ly,** adv. —**frag′men·tar′i·ness,** n.

frag·men·ta·tion (frag′mən tā′shən) n. **1.** the act or process of breaking into fragments. **2.** the scattering of the fragments of a bomb, shell, or grenade. —adj. capable of scattering fragments upon explosion: *a fragmentation grenade.*

fragmentation bomb, an aerial bomb that scatters the fragments of its casing over a wide area when it explodes.

fra·grance (frā′grəns) n. **1.** a sweet or pleasing smell. **2.** the state or quality of being fragrant. **3.** perfume.

fra·grant (frā′grənt) adj. having a sweet or pleasing smell. [Latin *fragrāns,* present participle of *fragrāre* to smell sweet.] —**fra′grant·ly,** adv.

frail (frāl) adj. **1.** lacking in strength; weak: *The child was too frail to take part in active sports.* **2.** easily broken, damaged, or destroyed; delicate; fragile. **3.** morally weak; easily tempted. [Old French *fraile* weak, brittle, from Latin *fragilis* easily broken. Doublet of FRAGILE.] —**frail′ness,** n. —For Synonyms, see **delicate.**

frail·ty (frāl′tē) n., pl. **-ties. 1.** the state or quality of being frail; weakness. **2.** a fault or failing arising from moral weakness: *Gambling can be a costly frailty.*

frame (frām) n. **1.** a structure into which something is set, used for support or protection: *a window frame, a picture frame.* **2.** a structure composed or constructed of parts fitted and joined together, serving as an underlying support; skeleton; framework: *the metal frame of a bed.* **3.** a body, esp. the human body, with reference to its physical structure; build: *to have a thin frame.* **4.** a general or established form, arrangement, or system: *the frame of the Constitution.* **5.** one of the individual pictures on a length of motion-picture film. **6.** the total television picture transmitted by one scan of the electronic beam. **7. frames.** the parts of a pair of eyeglasses, connected by hinges, that hold the lenses and enable the glasses to be worn. **8.** a machine built on, within, or in the shape of a frame: *a spinning frame.* **9.** one of the ten divisions of a game of bowling; one turn at bowling. **10.** Informal. an inning in a baseball game. **11.** Slang. frame-up. —v.t., **framed, fram·ing. 1.** to enclose or set in or as in a frame: *to frame a painting, a house framed by a background of trees.* **2.** to form or construct mentally; conceive: *to frame an idea.* **3.** to give expression to or utter: *to frame a reply.* **4.** to shape or adapt, as to a purpose: *That law was framed to protect freedom of speech.* **5.** to draw up; devise: *to frame a plan of action.* **6.** Informal. **a.** to cause (an innocent person) to appear guilty by using false evidence. **b.** to arrange or contrive (a false accusation). **7.** to prearrange the outcome of (a contest or competition). [Old English *framian* to be profitable, avail.] —**fram′er,** n.

frame house, a house constructed on a wooden framework, usually covered with boards or shingles.

frame of mind, mental or emotional state; mood: *Losing my job put me in a low frame of mind.*

frame of reference, a set or system, as of facts or ideas, that serves to define or direct a person's thinking.

frame-up (frām′up′) n. Informal. a conspiracy or scheme to make an innocent person appear guilty through the use of false evidence.

frame·work (frām′wûrk′) n. **1.** a structure, usually rigid, serving to support, enclose, or give shape to something: *the framework of a building.* **2.** the basic structure or arrangement of the parts of something: *the framework of a novel, the framework of society.*

franc (frangk) n. the monetary unit of France, Belgium, Switzerland, Luxembourg, and several African countries. [Old French *franc,* short for Medieval Latin *Francorum rex* king of the Franks,

inscribed on some fourteenth-century French gold coins. See FRANK[1].]

fran·chise (fran′chīz) n. **1.** the right to vote; suffrage. **2.** the right or authorization to have or do something, given to an individual or group, esp. by a government or company: *a franchise to sell food at a state park.* **3.a.** the geographical area for which such a right or authorization is granted. **b.** a store or other business granted such a right or authorization. —v.t., **-chised, -chis·ing.** to give a franchise to. [Old French *franchise* freedom, from *franc* free. See FRANK.]

fran·chi·see (fran′chī zē′) n. a person or business to whom a franchise is granted.

fran·chis·er (fran′chī zər) also, **fran·chi·sor.** n. a person or company that grants a franchise.

Fran·cis·can (fran sis′kən) adj. **1.** of or relating to Saint Francis of Assisi. **2.** belonging to a religious order of the Roman Catholic Church founded by Saint Francis in the thirteenth century, now divided into three independent branches. —n. a member of this order.

fran·ci·um (fran′sē əm) n. a rare, radioactive, metallic element. Symbol: **Fr** For tables, see **element.** [Modern Latin *francium,* from *France* + Latin *-ium* suffix used to form names of elements; named by the French chemist Marguerite Perey, 1909-75.]

Franco- combining form French: *Franco-American.*

Fran·co·phile (frang′kə fīl′) also, **Fran·co·phil** (frang′kə fil′). n. a person who is extremely fond of France, its people, traditions, manners, or customs. —adj. extremely fond of France or the French.

fran·gi·ble (fran′jə bəl) adj. easily broken; fragile. [Old French *frangible,* going back to Latin *frangere* to break.] —**fran′gi·bil′i·ty,** n.

fran·gi·pan·i (fran′ji pan′ē, frän′ji pä′nē) n. **1.** any of several tropical American shrubs or trees, genus *Plumeria,* related to dogbane, having large, showy, fragrant flowers, esp. *P. rubra.* **2.** a perfume extracted from these flowers. [Italian *frangipani,* from Marquis Muzio *Frangipani,* a sixteenth-century Italian nobleman, said to have invented the perfume.]

Fran·glais (fräng glā′; French frän gle′) n. French spoken or written with many words borrowed from English, for example: *la weekend.* [French *franglais,* blend of *français* French + *anglais* English.]

frank[1] (frangk) adj. **1.** open or honest in expressing one's thoughts and feelings; outspoken; candid. **2.** clearly manifest; undisguised; open: *There was frank hostility between the two enemies.* —v.t. **1.** to mark (a letter, package, or other mail), as with a signature, for delivery without charge. **2.** to send (mail) without charge by marking in this way. —n. **1.a.** the right or privilege to send mail without charge: *Members of Congress are given the frank.* **b.** a mark indicating this right or privilege. **2.** a letter, package, or other mail sent without charge. [Old French *franc* free, pure, from Medieval Latin *francus* a Frank, free; of Germanic origin. The Franks were associated with freedom because, as rulers of Gaul, they alone had freedom there.] —**frank′ly,** adv. —**frank′ness,** n.

Synonyms adj. **Frank**[1], candid, blunt, and outspoken mean expressing what one believes to be true. **Frank,** the most general term, connotes freedom and openness: *Please be frank with us about your financial situation.* **Candid** more clearly implies refusing to hide some truth: *My candid opinion is that your finances are in very bad shape.* **Blunt** implies that no effort is made to spare feelings: *To be blunt, if you don't cut back on expenses, you are heading toward bankruptcy.* **Outspoken** connotes saying what one is thinking, even if not asked: *an outspoken critic, who has often embarrassed the mayor by statements made in public.*

frank[2] (frangk) n. Informal. frankfurter.

Frank (frangk) n. a member of a Germanic people living along the Rhine River in the third century A.D. In the late fifth and early sixth centuries, the Franks expanded into Gaul, giving their name to present-day France. [Old English *Franca;* of Germanic origin; said to be from the Franks' national weapon, in Old English *franca* javelin.]

Frank·en·stein (frang′kən stīn′) n. **1.** the medical student in Mary Wollstonecraft Shelley's novel *Frankenstein,* who creates a monster that eventually destroys him. **2.** the monster created by him. **3.** anything that threatens or destroys its creator.

a	at	e	end	o	hot	u	up	hw	white	⟨	about
ā	ape	ē	me	ō	old	ū	use	ng	song		taken
ä	far	i	it	ô	fork	ü	rule	th	thin	ə	pencil
âr	care	ī	ice	oi	oil	u	pull	th	this		lemon
		îr	pierce	ou	out	ûr	turn	zh	measure	⟨	circus

493

Usage Although **Frankenstein** originally referred to a fictional medical student who created a monster that destroyed him, over time the meaning of the word was extended to the monster itself and then to anything that threatens or destroys its creator. Some people consider it more precise to reserve the word for the original meaning and to use a phrase such as *Frankenstein's monster* or *a Frankenstein monster* for the other definitions.

frank·furt (frangk′fərt) *also,* **frank·fort.** *n.* frankfurter.

frank·furt·er (frangk′fər tər) *also,* **frank·fort·er.** *n.* **1.** a reddish variety of smoked and seasoned sausage made of beef, beef mixed with pork, or poultry and shaped in cylindrical pieces. **2.** such a sausage served hot in a long, soft roll, often with mustard, relish, or sauerkraut. Also, **hot dog.** [German *Frankfurter* of Frankfurt.]

frank·in·cense (frang′kin sens′) *n.* a fragrant resin obtained from various Asian and African trees, genus *Boswellia,* esp. *B. carteri.* It is used for embalming, as an incense, and in the manufacture of perfumes and face powders. [Old French *franc encens* pure incense, from Medieval Latin *francus* free + Late Latin *incensum* incense. See FRANK [1], INCENSE [1].]

Frank·ish (frang′kish) *adj.* of or relating to the Franks. —*n.* the extinct language of the Franks, belonging to the western branch of the Germanic languages.

frank·lin (frangk′lin) *n.* in England in the fourteenth and fifteenth centuries, a landowner of free but not noble birth, ranking next below the gentry. [Middle English *frankeleyn, fraunkeleyn,* from Norman French *fraunclein,* from *fraunc* free + *-lein* -ling [1] (modeled on Old French *chamberlenc* chamberlain).]

Frank·lin stove (frangk′lin) a cast-iron wood-burning stove resembling an open fireplace, used for heating a room. [From the American scientist and statesman Benjamin *Franklin,* 1706-90, its inventor.]

fran·tic (fran′tik) *adj.* marked by extreme or uncontrollable emotion, as of worry, grief, fear, or rage; wildly excited; frenzied. [Old French *frenetique* seized with frenzy, from Latin *phrenēticus* mad, from Greek *phrenētikos,* from *phrenītis* delirium, from *phrēn* mind.] —**fran′ti·cal·ly;** *also,* **fran′tic·ly,** *adv.* —**fran′tic·ness,** *n.*

frap·pé (*adj., n., defs. 1, 2* fra pā′; *n., def. 3* frap) *adj.* iced; chilled. —*n.* **1.** a sweetened fruit juice mixture partially frozen to a mushy consistency. **2.** a liqueur or other beverage poured over shaved ice. **3. frappe.** a sweet dish or beverage made with ice cream, such as a milk shake. [French *frappé* struck, iced, past participle of *frapper* to strike, ice; probably imitative.]

fra·ter·nal (frə tûr′nəl) *adj.* **1.** of, relating to, or like a brother; brotherly. **2.** of or relating to a fraternal order. **3.** (of twins) developed from two separate fertilized eggs and thus having different hereditary characteristics. ➡ distinguished from **identical.** [Medieval Latin *fraternalis* brotherly, from Latin *frāternus,* from *frāter* brother.] —**fra·ter′nal·ism,** *n.* —**fra·ter′nal·ly,** *adv.*

fraternal order, an association, usually of men, organized for their mutual benefit or attainment of a common goal. Also, **fraternal association, fraternal society.**

fra·ter·ni·ty (frə tûr′ni tē) *n., pl.* **-ties. 1.** a society of students, usually male, often having chapters in various institutions, organized esp. for social purposes and usually designated by a Greek letter name. **2.** the state or quality of being brotherly; brotherhood. **3.** a group of people sharing the same interests or profession, or having other common ties: *the medical fraternity.* **4.** fraternal order. [Old French *fraternite* brotherhood, from Latin *frāternitās,* going back to *frāter* brother.]

frat·er·nize (frat′ər nīz′) *v.i.,* **-nized, -niz·ing. 1.** to associate closely with someone in a friendly or brotherly way. **2.** to associate in a friendly or intimate way with the citizens of an enemy or conquered country. —**frat′er·ni·za′tion,** *n.* —**frat′er·niz′er,** *n.*

frat·ri·cide [1] (frat′rə sīd′) *n.* the act of killing one's brother or sister. [Latin *frātricīdium,* from *frāter* brother + *-cīdium.* See -CIDE [1].] —**frat′ri·cid′al,** *adj.*

frat·ri·cide [2] (frat′rə sīd′) *n.* a person who kills his or her brother or sister. [Latin *frātricīda,* from *frāter* brother + *-cīda.* See -CIDE [2].]

Frau (frou) *n., pl. German* **Frau·en** (frou′ən) or **Fraus.** a married woman; wife. ➡ the German title of respect and form of polite address for a married woman, equivalent to *Mrs.* or *Madam.* [German *Frau.*]

fraud (frôd) *n.* **1.** deceit or trickery, esp. deliberate deception practiced to cheat another of rights or property: *to be found guilty of fraud.* **2.** an act or instance of such deceit or trickery. **3.** a person who deceives; phony; imposter. **4.** something that is intended to deceive; sham. [Old French *fraude* guile, from Latin *fraus* guile, deceit.]

fraud·u·lent (frô′jə lənt) *adj.* **1.** given to or using fraud; deceitful; dishonest: *a fraudulent merchant.* **2.** proceeding from, achieved by, or characterized by fraud: *a fraudulent deal.* [Latin *fraudulentus* deceitful, from *fraus* deceit.] —**fraud′u·lence, fraud′u·len·cy,** *n.* —**fraud′u·lent·ly,** *adv.*

fraught (frôt) *adj.* filled or accompanied (with *with*): *fraught with grief, a mission fraught with danger.* [Past participle of obsolete *fraught* to load (a ship), from *fraught* cargo, load, from Middle Dutch *vracht.*]

Fräu·lein (froi′līn) *n., pl. German* **-lein** or **-leins.** an unmarried woman; young lady. ➡ the German title of respect and form of polite address for an unmarried woman, equivalent to *Miss.* [German *Fräulein.*]

fray [1] (frā) *n.* a noisy quarrel, fight, or disturbance; brawl. [Form of AFFRAY.]

fray [2] (frā) *v.t.* **1.** to cause (something, as cloth or rope) to separate into loose threads, esp. along the edges; ravel. **2.** to wear the surface of, as by rubbing. **3.** to strain or irritate, as the nerves. —*v.i.* to become frayed; ravel. [Middle English *fraien,* from Old French *freier* to rub, from Latin *fricāre,* from *frictiō* a rubbing.]

fraz·zle (fraz′əl) *v.t., v.i.,* **-zled, -zling. 1.** to wear to shreds; fray. **2.** to tire out mentally or physically; exhaust. —*n. Informal.* the state of being frazzled. [Possibly blend of FRAY [2] and obsolete *fasel* to ravel.]

freak (frēk) *n.* **1.** an abnormally developed person, animal, or plant; monstrosity. **2.** anything odd, unusual, or unexplainable. **3.** a sudden whim; caprice. **4.** *Slang.* a person greatly or excessively devoted to or fascinated by something: *an exercise freak.* —*adj.* abnormal, unusual, or bizarre: *a freak accident.* [Of uncertain origin.]

• **to freak out.** to become extremely excited and irrational, esp. while under the influence of a hallucinogenic drug.

freak·ish (frē′kish) *adj.* **1.** relating to or characteristic of a freak; abnormal. **2.** odd, unusual, or unexplainable: *a freakish turn of events.* **3.** whimsical; capricious. Also, **freak′y.** —**freak′ish·ly,** *adv.* —**freak′ish·ness,** *n.*

freak·out (frēk′out′) *also,* **freak-out.** *n. Slang.* **1.a.** an act or instance of becoming extremely excited and often somewhat irrational. **b.** such an experience or behavior while under the influence of a hallucinogenic drug. **2.** a person who acts in an excited and irrational way, esp. while under the influence of a hallucinogenic drug.

freck·le (frek′əl) *n.* a small yellowish or brownish spot on the skin due to accumulation of pigment, often caused by exposure to the sun. —*v.t., v.i.,* **-led, -ling.** to mark or become marked with freckles. [Old Norse *freknur* the small spots on the skin.]

freck·led (frek′əld) *adj.* marked with or full of freckles. Also, **freck′ly.**

free (frē) *adj.,* **fre·er, fre·est. 1.** having personal liberty or rights; independent in thought or action; not under another's control. **2.a.** having or existing under a government that allows civil, political, or religious liberty: *a free country, a free society.* **b.** not subject to foreign domination or control; autonomous. **3.** not held, imprisoned, or confined, as by a court or legal charges; acquitted: *The prisoner was now free.* **4.** released from or unhindered by a specified thing or condition, such as obligation, pain, or discomfort (with *from* or *of*): *free from care, free of family ties.* **5.** lacking or without a specified thing or condition (with *from* or *of*): *The administration was free from corruption.* **6.** allowed or permitted (to do something): *You are free to come and go as you choose.* **7.** given or provided without cost or payment; gratis: *We received a free ticket to the show.* **8.** not busy; available: *I'll be free at two o'clock for the conference.* **9.** not motivated, controlled, or determined by anything other than one's own limitations or nature: *a free choice.* **10.** open and unreserved in expressing one's thoughts, feelings, or opinions; frank; outspoken: *to be very free in discussing one's personal problems.* **11.** characterized by a willingness to give or share; generous; liberal: *a free spender.* **12.** unimpeded or unrestrained, as in movement; unhampered: *free access to a place.* **13.** not adhering strictly to generally accepted rules or methods or to an original source; not literal: *a free translation.* **14.** not attached, bound, or fastened; loose: *the free end of a rope.* **15.** coming or appearing in profusion; heavy: *a free flow of blood.* **16.** easy and graceful; smooth: *a bold, free stroke.* **17.** unrestrained by decency or propriety. **18.** made, done, or given willingly or voluntarily. **19.** clear of obstruction or impediment; open. **20.** exempt from or not subject to something, as regulations or taxes. **21.** *Chemistry.* not part of a compound; uncombined; native: *free oxygen, free copper.* —*adv.* **1.** without cost or payment: *to be admitted to a concert free.* **2.** in a free manner; easily: *The children ran free across the meadow.* **3.** into an unconfined or unrestrained condition; loose: *The horse broke free.* —*v.t.,* **freed, free·ing. 1.** to release, as from burden, constraint, or obligation: *She freed herself of worry. They freed the*

prisoners. *The inheritance freed him from debt.* **2.** to clear or disentangle (a person or thing) from some obstruction or hindrance: *They freed the traffic lane by removing the stalled car.* [Old English *frēo, frī* having liberty.] —**free′ly,** *adv.* —**free′ness,** *n.*

· **to make free with.** to use, treat, or act toward (a person or thing) with an undue amount of liberty or familiarity: *They made free with their parents' money.*

· **to set free.** to liberate, as from confinement, restraint, or obligation; release: *The new government set the prisoners free.*

free agent, a professional athlete who is not under contract to play for a particular team and is free to negotiate an agreement with any team.

free and easy, unrestrained by formality or conventionality; unceremonious; natural: *a free and easy manner.*

free association, a psychoanalytical procedure in which a patient says whatever comes to mind without restriction or embarrassment. The thoughts and feelings thus expressed disclose the content of the patient's unconscious mind.

free·bie (frē′bē) *also,* **free·bee.** *n. Slang.* something obtained or received free of charge. [A form of FREE + -IE.]

free·board (frē′bôrd′) *n.* the part of the side of a ship that is out of the water.

free·boot·er (frē′bū′tər) *n.* a person who plunders; pirate. [Dutch *vrijbuiter* robber, going back to *vrij* free + *buit* booty. Doublet of FILIBUSTER.] —**free′boot′ing,** *n.*

free·born (frē′bôrn′) *adj.* **1.** not in slavery or servitude; born free. **2.** of or relating to those born free.

free city, a city having an autonomous government and constituting an independent state, as certain medieval cities.

free coinage, a system under which a government is legally required to mint coins for private persons from specified bullion, as gold or silver, with or without a fixed charge.

freed·man (frēd′mən) *n., pl.* **-men** (-mən). a person who has been legally freed from slavery.

free·dom (frē′dəm) *n.* **1.** political independence, as of a people or nation. **2.** a setting free, as from slavery, confinement, or imprisonment. **3.** independence of thought, choice, or action; personal liberty. **4.** the ability to move or act without interference, coercion, or restraint: *You have the freedom to do as you please.* **5.** the absence of or release from a specified condition or thing: *freedom from fear.* **6.** the possession of a particular privilege, right, or immunity: *The government has the freedom to levy taxes.* **7.** frankness or familiarity in manner or speech; informality. **8.** unrestricted access or use: *We gave our guests the freedom of our home.* **9.** ease of movement or action; facility. **10.** the state or condition of being free. [Old English *frēodōm* liberty.]

> **Synonyms** **Freedom** and **liberty** denote an absence of outside control over one's thoughts, beliefs or actions. **Freedom** suggests something more basic and general than *liberty: to live in freedom, to enjoy religious freedom.* **Liberty** tends to be used of the power to make choices or to act in particular ways: *to have the liberty to live where one wants, to exercise religious liberties.*

freedom of the seas, the principle that all ocean areas, other than territorial waters, are open to any ship without interference.

freed·wom·an (frēd′wŭm′ən) *n., pl.* **wom·en** (-wim′ən). a woman who has been legally freed from slavery.

free energy *Physics.* that portion of the energy of a system that is available to do work.

free enterprise, an economic system based on private ownership and operation of the means of production with a minimum of government control. Also, **private enterprise.**

free fall **1.** the state or condition of falling unrestrained after jumping from an aircraft and before opening the parachute: *The skydiver was in free fall.* **2.** the period of time that elapses before the opening of the parachute. **3.** the state or condition of a body, as a space vehicle, when it is subject only to gravitational and inertial forces, and is not guided, under thrust, or slowed down by a parachute or other braking device.

free-fall·ing (frē′fô′ling) *adj.* characterized by free fall: *a free-falling missile.*

free flight, the free and unhampered motion of a body along a trajectory, subject only to gravitational and inertial forces.

free-for-all (frē′fər ôl′) *n.* **1.** a disorderly or noisy fight or quarrel. **2.** a contest, game, or other activity in which anyone may take part.

free-form (frē′fôrm′) *adj.* characterized by a shape or design not adhering to any regular or rigid pattern: *free-form sculpture, free-form furniture.*

free gold, formerly, gold or gold certificates held by the U.S. Treasury in excess of the amount needed to back gold certificates or meet other Federal Reserve requirements.

free·hand (frē′hand′) *adj.* drawn or sketched by hand without using measurements or instruments, as rulers: *a freehand diagram.*

—*adv.* by hand without measurements or instruments: *to draw freehand.*

free hand, unrestricted liberty or action: *Give me a free hand and I will get the job done.*

free·hand·ed (frē′han′did) *adj.* liberal in giving; openhanded; generous.

free·hold (frē′hōld′) *n.* **1.** a piece of land held for life with the right to transfer it to one's heirs. **2.** the holding of land in this way. —**free′hold·er,** *n.*

free·lance (frē′lans′) *also,* **free·lance.** *adj.* relating to or working as a free lance. —*v.i.* **-lanced, -lanc·ing.** to work as a free lance.

free lance *also,* **free·lance** (frē′lans′). **1.** a writer, artist, or other professional whose services are not sold exclusively to, or committed under contract to, any single buyer. **2.** a person who works for or supports a variety of causes without being fully or exclusively committed to any organization. **3.** a mercenary in the Middle Ages, esp. one of rank, who would fight for anyone who paid the price.

free-lanc·er (frē′lan′sər) *also,* **free·lanc·er.** *n.* free lance.

free list, a list of goods not subject to tariff duties.

free-liv·ing (frē′liv′ing) *adj.* **1.** existing independently of other organisms; neither parasitic nor symbiotic. **2.** indulging freely in physical pleasures.

free·load (frē′lōd′) *v.i. Informal.* to act as a freeloader. —**free′load′ing,** *n.*

free·load·er (frē′lō′dər) *n. Informal.* a person who makes a practice of living at the expense of others.

free love, the doctrine or practice of free choice in sexual relations, without legal marriage or other restraints.

free·man (frē′mən) *n., pl.* **-men** (-mən). **1.** a person who is free from bondage of any kind. **2.** a person who has full civil and political rights.

free market, any market in which buying and selling is not regulated by government or other control and in which prices for an item or commodity are set by supply and demand. —**free′-mar′ket,** *adj.*

Free·ma·son (frē′mā′sən) *n.* a member of a secret international fraternal and service society that grew out of the medieval stonemasons' organizations. Also, **Mason.**

Free·ma·son·ry (frē′mā′sən rē) *n.* **1.** the principles, practices, and doctrines of the Freemasons. **2.** Freemasons collectively. Also *(defs. 1, 2),* **Masonry. 3. freemasonry.** instinctive sympathy and understanding among people with common interests and experiences.

free on board, a commercial term signifying that the seller of goods pays for transportation, and bears the risk of damage up to a specified point where the goods are placed aboard a ship, train, or other carrier. ➡ The abbreviation **f.o.b.** is most commonly used: *goods to be f.o.b. Los Angeles.*

free port **1.** a port or zone where customs duties are not charged on foreign goods to be shipped elsewhere rather than imported. **2.** a port open to all traders on equal terms.

free press, the publishing of books, magazines, and newspapers without government control or censorship.

free radical *Chemistry.* a highly reactive atom or group of atoms with one or more unpaired electrons, formed during the course of chemical and biochemical reactions, as in photolysis.

free·sia (frē′zhə, -zē ə, -zhē ə) *n.* a South African plant, genus *Freesia,* of the iris family, having fragrant funnel-shaped white, yellow, or dark red flowers and narrow sword-shaped leaves. [Modern Latin *Freesia,* from Friedrich H. T. *Freese,* 1795-1876, a German doctor.]

free silver, free coinage of silver, esp. at a fixed ratio to gold coined at the same time.

free soil, a U.S. territory in which slavery was prohibited before the American Civil War.

Free Soil Party, a U.S. political party formed in 1848 to oppose the extension of slavery into the western territories and the admission of new Slave States to the Union. It also urged the granting of free land in the territories to small homesteaders.

free-spo·ken (frē′spō′kən) *adj.* given to speaking frankly or without reserve; outspoken.

free·stand·ing (frē′stan′ding) *adj.* standing alone or independently on its own foundation apart from any supporting framework: *a freestanding sculpture.*

a	at	e	end	o	hot	u	up	hw	white	⟨	about
ā	ape	ē	me	ō	old	ū	use	ng	song		taken
ä	far	i	it	ô	fork	ü	rule	th	thin	ə	pencil
âr	care	ī	ice	oi	oil	u̇	pull	th	this		lemon
		îr	pierce	ou	out	ûr	turn	zh	measure	⟨	circus

495

Free State 1. a U.S. state in which slavery was prohibited before the American Civil War. **2.** Irish Free State.

free·stone (frē′stōn′) *adj.* having a pit that is easily separated from the pulp: *a freestone peach, a freestone plum.* ➡ distinguished from **clingstone.** —*n.* **1.** any fine-grained stone, as limestone or sandstone, that can be cut easily in any direction without splitting. **2.** a freestone fruit, as a peach.

free·style (frē′stīl′) *adj.* in swimming, using or allowing any stroke the swimmer chooses. —*n.* a freestyle race or event: *We participated in the 200-meter freestyle.* —**free′styl′er,** *n.*

free·think·er (frē′thing′kər) *n.* a person who forms opinions by relying on reason rather than authority or tradition, esp. in matters of religion. —**free′think′ing,** *adj., n.*

free thought, thought or belief, esp. in religious matters, formed by relying on reason, rather than authority or tradition.

free throw *Basketball.* the privilege granted to a player to take an unhindered shot from the free throw line because of a foul made by a member of the opposing team. Also, **foul shot.**

free throw line *Basketball.* a line 15 feet (4.6 meters) from the front of the backboard, behind which a player stands while shooting a free throw. Also, **foul line.**

free trade 1. international commerce free from governmental restrictions, such as import and export duties. **2.** the practice, policy, or system of such commerce.

free-trad·er (frē′trā′dər) *n.* a person who advocates or engages in free trade.

free verse, poetry marked by the lack of a regular metrical pattern or rhyme scheme.

free·way (frē′wā′) *n.* a multiple-lane highway, usually divided, with limited points of access or exit, designed for rapid and direct traveling.

free·wheel·ing (frē′hwē′ling, -wē′-) *adj. Informal.* **1.** acting in a free, independent, or casual manner: *a freewheeling news commentator.* **2.** not bound by rules or restraints: *a freewheeling discussion.*

free·will (frē′wil′) *adj.* given or done freely or of one's own accord; voluntary: *a freewill offering.*

free will 1. the power of determining one's own actions; free choice; voluntary decision: *I did it of my own free will.* **2.** the doctrine that human beings' ability to choose between alternatives is not completely determined by divine will or external circumstances, and that people are therefore responsible for their actions.

freeze (frēz) *v.,* **froze, fro·zen, freez·ing.** —*v.i.* **1.** to change from a liquid to a solid form or state. When water freezes, it is called ice. **2.** to become covered, obstructed, or clogged with ice: *The water pipes froze. The lake froze last night.* **3.** to be or become extremely cold: *We froze while waiting for the bus during the snowstorm.* **4.** to become hard or rigid because of cold: *The wet clothes froze on the clothesline.* **5.** to adhere or become fixed because of cold: *The wipers froze to the windshield.* **6.** to become motionless or unable to move because of an intense, sudden surge of emotion, such as fear or shock: *I froze when I saw the bear.* **7.** to become motionless or fixed: *The smile froze on her face when she saw him.* **8.** to be at or near the temperature at which water becomes ice: *It is freezing tonight.* **9.** to be destroyed or damaged by frost or extreme cold: *The orange crop froze this winter.* **10.** to become formal, unfriendly, or aloof (often with *up*): *The child froze up around strangers.* —*v.t.* **1.** to cause (a liquid) to change to a solid state or form; cause to become ice. **2.** to cover, obstruct, or clog (something) with ice: *The cold weather froze the lake.* **3.** to cause to adhere or become fixed by the action of cold or frost. **4.** to make very cold; chill: *The cold wind froze me to the bone.* **5.** to preserve (food) by rapid reduction of its temperature: *to freeze a steak.* **6.** to damage or kill by exposure to extreme cold or frost. **7.** to make (a part of the body) insensitive, as to pain, by subjecting to extreme cold; anesthetize. **8.** to cause to become or remain motionless or stiff through a sudden surge of emotion, as fear or shock. **9.** to fix (a person or thing) at a definite level or amount: *The government froze food prices.* **10.** to prevent collection, use, or liquidation of (funds or other assets) by governmental decree. **11.** to prohibit further production, sale, or use of (a raw material): *to freeze gold.* **12.** *Sports.* to attempt to retain possession of (a ball or puck) so that the opponent will not have an opportunity to score, as in the closing minutes of play. —*n.* **1.** the act of freezing or the state of being frozen. **2.** a period of weather characterized by temperatures below the freezing point of water. **3.** *Sports.* an act or instance of freezing a ball or puck. [Old English *frēosan* to turn to ice.]
 • **to freeze out.** *Informal.* to drive or force out, as by unfriendliness or severe competition.

freeze-dry (frēz′drī′) *v.t.,* **-dried, -dry·ing.** to dry (something), as food or serum, while frozen in a high vacuum, esp. for preservation.

freeze-frame (frēz′frām′) *also,* **freeze frame.** *n.* a single motion-picture frame that is repeated to give the illusion of a still photograph. [FREEZE + FRAME.]

freez·er (frē′zər) *n.* **1.** a refrigerator or compartment that freezes food rapidly and preserves it for long periods of time. **2.** an apparatus for freezing ice cream.

freezer burn, a condition or appearance of frozen food caused by improper packaging or temperature control, or too long a period of storage. Freezer burn produces a loss of color, flavor, and nutritional value.

freezing point, the temperature at which a liquid freezes. The freezing point of water at the standard atmospheric pressure of 14.7 pounds per square inch is 32 degrees Fahrenheit, or 0 degrees Celsius.

freight (frāt) *n.* **1.** the transportation of goods by means of land, air, or water. It is usually less expensive and slower than express. **2.** goods transported by such means; cargo. **3.** the charge for the transportation of goods by such means. **4.** freight train. —*v.t.* **1.** to load with goods for transportation. **2.** to send as or transport by freight. [Middle Dutch *vrecht,* form of *vracht* cargo, load.]

| **Synonyms** | *n.* **Freight** and **cargo** denote goods in transit. **Freight** connotes merchandise or other goods carried over a long distance: *Trains carry freight from coast to coast.* **Cargo** is restricted to freight carried by a ship or aircraft: *Our furniture is part of the cargo being unloaded from this vessel.* |

freight·age (frā′tij) *n.* **1.** the transportation of goods. **2.** the charge for the transportation of goods. **3.** goods transported; freight; cargo.

freight car, a railroad car for carrying freight.

freight·er (frā′tər) *n.* **1.** a ship used primarily for transporting cargo. **2.a.** a person who receives and transports freight. **b.** a person who sends freight. **3.** a person who loads cargo.

freight train, a railroad train composed of freight cars.

French (french) *adj.* of, relating to, or characteristic of France or its people, language, or culture. —*n.* **1. the French.** the people of France collectively. **2.** one of the Romance languages, spoken as the native language of France. It is also spoken in parts of Belgium, Switzerland, Canada, and former French colonies. [Old English *frencisc* relating to France, from *franca.* See FRANK[1].]

Words from French

French, like all Romance languages, is descended from Latin and belongs to the Indo-European language family. Because of the close political, military, and social relationships between France and England beginning with the Norman French conquest of England in 1066, thousands of French words have been incorporated into English. The loanwords shown below have come into English from or through French.

accolade	chic	grill
allemande	chiffon	intrigue
amateur	chowder	jalousie
aperitif	clarinet	jardiniere
aplomb	cliché	laissez faire
appliqué	clique	lingerie
apropos	coiffure	malaise
arabesque	collage	mannequin
argot	concert	mayonnaise
baccarat	connoisseur	menu
ballet	corsage	morgue
barrage	cotillion	motif
bassoon	cravat	mousse
bayonet	crèche	naive
bijou	crepe	parfait
bisque	critique	penchant
blasé	croissant	protégé
boudoir	crouton	quiche
bouffant	cuisine	rapport
bouillon	daub	reconnaissance
bourgeoisie	debris	revue
boutique	demitasse	risqué
bracelet	denouement	roulette
brioche	détente	sabotage
buccaneer	dossier	sauté
cadet	encore	souvenir
café	espionage	svelte
casserole	filet	tableau
chagrin	genre	tart[2]
chateau	gourmet	troupe

French and Indian War, a war in North America between the French and their Indian allies and the English from 1754 to 1763, as a result of which France was forced to give up all its Canadian territory to England.

French chalk, a fine-grained white talc used for marking lines on cloth or removing grease.

French Community, a political association established in 1958, consisting of France, its overseas departments and territories, and several independent countries in Africa that formerly were French colonies.

French cuff, the cuff of a sleeve that is folded back and fastened with a cuff link.

French curve, a drafting instrument made of a sheet of clear plastic, the edges of which have been cut into various scroll-like curves, used to draw curved lines.

French doors, a pair of doors, usually with glass panes, hinged at opposite sides of a doorway and opening in the middle.

French dressing, salad dressing made of oil, vinegar, and spices.

french-fry (french′frī′) *also,* **French-fry.** *v.t.,* **-fried, -fry·ing.** to fry in deep fat until brown and crisp, as potato strips or onion rings.

french fry, *also,* **French fry.** a thin strip of potato fried in deep fat until brown and crisp.

French horn, a valved brass instrument consisting of a long, coiled tube ending in a flared bell, and producing a rich, mellow tone.

French leave, an informal, secret, or hurried departure. [From the eighteenth-century French custom of leaving a social affair without saying good-bye to the host or hostess.]

French·man (french′mən) *n., pl.* **-men** (-mən). **1.** a native or citizen of France. **2.** a person of French ancestry.

French pastry, a rich pastry, usually elaborately shaped and fancily decorated, often filled with custard, preserved fruit, or whipped cream.

French Revolution, a revolution in France from 1789 to 1799 that overthrew the monarchy and aristocracy and gave rise to the First French Republic. It ended with the election of Napoleon I as First Consul in 1799.

French seam, a strong, smooth seam sewed on both sides of a fabric, so that no raw edges are exposed.

French toast, bread dipped in a mixture of egg and milk and then fried.

French windows, a pair of doorlike windows hinged at opposite sides and opening in the middle.

French·wom·an (french′wûm′ən) *n., pl.* **-wom·en** (-wim′ən). **1.** a woman who is a native or citizen of France. **2.** a woman who is of French ancestry.

fre·net·ic (frə net′ik) *also,* **phrenetic.** *adj.* characterized by frenzy; frenzied; frantic. Also, **fre·net′i·cal·ly,** *adv.* [Form of PHRE-NETIC.]

fre·num (frē′nəm) *n., pl.* **-nums** or **-na** (-nə). a band or fold of membrane that supports or restrains an organ or part, as the fold under the tongue. [Latin *frēnum* bridle.]

fren·zied (fren′zēd) *adj.* marked by frenzy; frantic.

fren·zy (fren′zē) *n., pl.* **-zies.** a state of intense or delirious emotion, as of excitement or agitation. —*v.t.,* **-zied, -zy·ing.** to drive to frenzy; make frantic. [Old French *frenesie* delirium, from Latin *phrenēsis,* going back to Greek *phrēn* mind.]

Fre·on (frē′on) *n. Trademark.* any of various liquid or gaseous fluorocarbons or chlorofluorocarbons used as refrigerants and aerosol propellants and in fire extinguishers. [F(LUORINE) + RE(FRIGERANT) + *-on,* on the model of *neon.*]

fre·quen·cy (frē′kwən sē) *n., pl.* **-cies.** **1.** the state or fact of being frequent; repeated occurrence. **2.** the number of times an action or occurrence is repeated within a given period; rate of recurrence. **3.** *Physics.* the number of cycles per second of an alternating current, electromagnetic radiation, or sound. **4.** *Statistics.* the ratio of the number of times an event occurs to the total number of possible occurrences. [Latin *frequentia* crowd.]

frequency distribution, an arrangement of statistical data, as in a table or graph, in which the values of a variable are grouped by classes and the frequency of the classes is displayed.

frequency modulation, see FM.

fre·quent (*adj.,* frē′kwənt; *v.,* fri kwent′, frē′kwənt) *adj.* **1.** happening often, esp. at short intervals; occurring again and again: *There is frequent rainfall on that island.* **2.** appearing or coming often; regular; habitual: *a frequent visitor.* —*v.t.* to go to often; be at or in regularly: *to frequent the theater.* [Latin *frequēns* repeated, crowded.] —**fre·quent′er,** *n.* —**fre′quent·ly,** *adv.*

fresco by Diego Rivera
showing how a fresco is made

fres·co (fres′kō) *n., pl.* **-coes** or **-cos.** **1.** the art or method of painting on a surface of plaster, esp. while it is still wet, using pigments mixed with water. **2.** a picture or design painted in this manner. —*v.t.,* **-coed, -co·ing.** to paint using this method. [Italian *a fresco* on fresh (plaster), from *fresco* fresh; of Germanic origin; because it is painted on plaster that is still fresh.]

fresh (fresh) *adj.* **1.** newly applied, made, arrived, obtained, or received: *a fresh coat of paint, fresh fingerprints, fresh coffee, a fresh wound.* **2.** not known, seen, worn, or used before; new: *a fresh shirt, a fresh approach to an old problem.* **3.** most recent; latest: *They received fresh information from the battlefront.* **4.** additional or different; further; another: *a fresh start.* **5.** not spoiled, stale, musty, or wilted: *fresh bread, fresh flowers.* **6.** (of food) not canned, frozen, or preserved, as by salting or pickling: *fresh vegetables.* **7.** not faded; vivid: *Your words remained fresh in my mind.* **8.** looking or appearing healthy or youthful: *a fresh complexion.* **9.** cool and invigorating: *a fresh breeze, fresh air.* **10.** (of water) not salty. **11.** not fatigued; vigorous; energetic: *to feel fresh after a rest.* **12.** (of wind) having considerable force; brisk. **13.** not experienced or trained: *fresh recruits.* **14.** *Informal.* showing impudence and disrespect; sassy. —*adv.* just recently; newly: *fresh picked vegetables.* [Partly from Old English *fersc* unsalted; partly from Old French *freis* (feminine, *fresche*) new, cool, brisk; of Germanic origin.] —**fresh′ly,** *adv.* —**fresh′ness,** *n.*

·**to be fresh out of.** *Informal.* to have recently sold or exhausted the supply of.

fresh·en (fresh′ən) *v.t., v.i.* to make or become fresh.

·**to freshen up.** to make fresh, as by cleaning, washing, or changing clothes: *We freshened up before going to the party. We freshened up the room for our guests.*

fresh·et (fresh′it) *n.* **1.** a sudden rise or overflow of a stream, caused by heavy rains or melted snow. **2.** a stream of fresh water flowing into the sea.

fresh·man (fresh′mən) *n., pl.* **-men** (-mən). **1.** a student in the first year of high school or college. **2.** a person who is in the first year of any enterprise or activity. **3.** a beginner; novice.

fresh·wa·ter (fresh′wô′tər, -wot′ər) *adj.* of, relating to, or living in fresh water: *a freshwater fish.*

fret[1] (fret) *v.,* **fret·ted, fret·ting.** —*v.i.* **1.** to be irritated or worried: *Don't fret about such a minor incident.* **2.** to become corroded or worn away, as by friction. **3.** to become rough or agitated, as water. —*v.t.* **1.** to irritate or worry. **2.** to wear away or corrode, as by friction: *The acid fretted the metal.* **3.** to make or form by wearing away or corroding. **4.** to roughen or agitate, as water: *The breeze fretted the surface of the water.* —*n.* **1.** agitation or uneasiness of mind; vexation. **2.** the act of wearing away or corroding. [Old English *fretan* to eat up, consume.]

a	at	e	end	o	hot	u	up	hw	white	(	about
ā	ape	ē	me	ō	old	ū	use	ng	song		taken
ä	far	i	it	ô	fork	ü	rule	th	thin	ə	pencil
âr	care	ī	ice	oi	oil	u̇	pull	th	this		lemon
		îr	pierce	ou	out	ûr	turn	zh	measure	(	circus

fret² (fret) *n.* **1.** an ornamental pattern, usually consisting of horizontal and vertical straight lines, symmetrically arranged within a band or border. **2.** any ornamental work consisting of such a pattern, often perforated or in relief. —*v.t.,* **fret·ted, fret·ting.** to decorate with a fret. [Middle English *fret,* probably a blend of Old French *frete* interlaced work and Old English *frætwa* ornament; both of uncertain origin.]

fret³ (fret) *n.* one of a series of bars or ridges, as of wood or metal, across the fingerboard of instruments of the guitar family, used for regulating the fingering to produce the desired tones. [Of uncertain origin.]

fret·ful (fret′fəl) *adj.* inclined to fret; irritable; peevish. —**fret′ful·ly,** *adv.* —**fret′ful·ness,** *n.*

fret saw, compass saw.

fret·work (fret′wûrk′) *n.* **1.** ornamental openwork, usually consisting of frets or interlaced patterns. **2.** any pattern, as of light and shade, resembling such openwork.

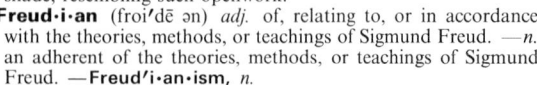

fret²

Freud·i·an (froi′dē ən) *adj.* of, relating to, or in accordance with the theories, methods, or teachings of Sigmund Freud. —*n.* an adherent of the theories, methods, or teachings of Sigmund Freud. —**Freud′i·an·ism,** *n.*

Freudian slip, a misstatement or other slip of the tongue believed, in Freudian theory, to reveal a person's inner thoughts or subconscious feelings.

Frey (frā) *n.* in Norse mythology, the god of sun and rain, fertility, love, and marriage.

Frey·a (frā′ə) *n.* in Norse mythology, the goddess of love and beauty, and sister of Frey.

Fri., Friday.

fri·a·ble (frī′ə bəl) *adj.* easily crumbled or pulverized: *friable rock.* [Latin *friābilis,* from *friāre* to crumble.] —**fri′a·bil′i·ty, fri′a·ble·ness,** *n.*

fri·ar (frī′ər) *n.* a man who is a member of any of various monastic orders of the Roman Catholic Church, esp. the Franciscans, Dominicans, Carmelites, and Augustinians. [Old French *frere* brother, friar, from Latin *frāter* brother.]

fri·ar·y (frī′ə rē) *n., pl.* **-ar·ies. 1.** a building or group of buildings where friars live. **2.** a brotherhood of friars.

fric·as·see (frik′ə sē′) *n.* a dish consisting of meat, esp. chicken, that is cut up, stewed, and served in a sauce made with its own gravy. —*v.t.,* **-seed, -see·ing.** to make (meat) into a fricassee. [French *fricassée* this dish, from *fricasser* to fry; of uncertain origin.]

fric·a·tive (frik′ə tiv) *adj.* (of a speech sound) articulated by forcing the breath through a narrow opening formed by placing the tongue or lips against the palate or teeth. —*n.* a fricative consonant, as *f, v,* or *th.* [Modern Latin *fricativus,* from Latin *fricātus,* past participle of *fricāre* to rub.]

fric·tion (frik′shən) *n.* **1.** the rubbing of one object against another. **2.** *Physics.* the force that resists motion between two surfaces that are in contact with one another. **3.** anger or ill will caused by conflict or disagreement: *There is great friction between the two countries.* [Latin *frictiō* a rubbing, from *fricare* to rub.]

fric·tion·al (frik′shə nəl) *adj.* of, relating to, or produced by friction. —**fric′tion·al·ly,** *adv.*

friction tape, cloth tape treated with an adhesive and moisture-resistant substance, used esp. in electrical work to protect and insulate electric conductors.

Fri·day (frī′dē, -dā) *n.* the sixth day of the week. [Old English *Frīgedæg* Frig's day, from *Frīge,* genitive of *Frīg* Frigg + *dæg* day.]

fridge (frij) *n. Informal.* refrigerator.

fried (frīd) the past tense and past participle of **fry¹.**

friend (frend) *n.* **1.** a person who is known intimately and regarded with affection by another; person one knows well and likes. **2.** an associate or acquaintance. **3.** a person who belongs to the same nation or group as oneself; ally: *Are you friend or foe?* **4.** a patron or supporter: *a friend of the museum.* **5. Friend.** a member of the Society of Friends. Also *(def. 5),* **Quaker.** [Old English *frēond* intimate acquaintance, lover.]
 • **to be friends with.** to be a friend of.
 • **to make friends with.** to become a friend of.

friend at court, an influential person who has the ability and the disposition to further the interests of another.

friend·less (frend′lis) *adj.* having no friends. —**friend′less·ness,** *n.*

friend·ly (frend′lē) *adj.,* **-li·er, -li·est. 1.** of, relating to, or characteristic of a friend: *friendly advice, a friendly letter.* **2.** showing friendship, kindness, or warmth of feeling: *a friendly person, a friendly pat on the back.* **3.** favorably disposed; not hostile: *friendly relations between two nations.* **4.** helpful or favorable: *a friendly breeze.* —*adv.* in a friendly manner. —**friend′li·ness,** *n.*

friendly fire *Military.* artillery, aerial bombardment, or other fire by one's own forces, esp. when causing damage to or casualties among one's own forces.

friend·ship (frend′ship′) *n.* **1.** the state or fact of being friends. **2.** mutual liking or attachment between friends. **3.** friendly feeling or disposition; friendliness: *We offered the new neighbors our friendship.*

fri·er (frī′ər) *n.* fryer.

frieze¹ (frēz) *n.* **1.** a horizontal band, often decorated with sculpture or other ornamentation, between the cornice and architrave of a building. For illustration, see **entablature. 2.** any decorative horizontal band, as around the top of a wall or building. [French *frise,* possibly from Medieval Latin *frisium, phrygium* embroidery, going back to Latin *Phrygium (opus)* Phrygian (work); possibly because the decorations on a frieze often recalled elaborate embroidery, for which the Phrygians were noted.]

frieze² (frēz) *n.* a heavy woolen fabric with a coarse, rough nap on one side. [French *frise,* from Old French *drap de frise* literally, cloth of Friesland.]

frig·ate (frig′it) *n.* **1.** a three-masted, square-rigged sailing warship carrying one row of guns broadside, in use from the seventeenth to nineteenth centuries. **2.** a warship smaller than a cruiser but larger than a destroyer, used for escort and patrol duties. [French *frégate,* from Italian *fregata;* of uncertain origin.]

frigate bird, any of various tropical seabirds, genus *Fregata,* having long, pointed wings, predominantly black plumage, and a thin, hooked bill. The male has an inflatable orange throat pouch that becomes bright red during the breeding season. The frigate bird feeds chiefly on small fish caught on the surface of the sea or stolen from other birds in flight. Wingspan: to 8 feet (2.4 meters). Also, **man-o'-war bird.**

frigate bird

Frigg (frig) *n.* in Norse mythology, the wife of Odin and queen of the gods and goddesses of the sky. Also, **Frig·ga** (frig′ə).

fright (frīt) *n.* **1.** a sudden, violent alarm or fear. **2.** *Informal.* a person or thing that is grotesque, shocking, or ridiculous in appearance: *I was a fright after three months of camping in the mountains.* [Old English *fyrhto* terror, fear.] —For Synonyms *(n.),* see **fear.**

fright·en (frī′tən) *v.t.* **1.** to make suddenly alarmed or afraid; scare: *The explosion frightened me.* **2.** to drive or compel by scaring: *The dog frightened away the squirrels.* —*v.i.* to become suddenly alarmed or afraid: *Wild deer frighten easily.* [From FRIGHT.]

fright·ened (frī′tənd) *adj.* filled with fright; afraid. —For Synonyms, see **afraid.**

fright·en·ing (frī′tə ning) *adj.* causing alarm or fear; terrifying: *a frightening experience.* —**fright′en·ing·ly,** *adv.*

fright·ful (frīt′fəl) *adj.* **1.** causing fright; terrifying: *a frightful enemy.* **2.** disgusting, shocking, or revolting: *a frightful spectacle of poverty and disease.* **3.** *Informal.* most distressing or unpleasant: *a frightful headache, to make a frightful racket.* **4.** *Informal.* to a great degree or extent; extreme: *to be in a frightful rush.* —**fright′ful·ly,** *adv.* —**fright′ful·ness,** *n.*

frig·id (frij′id) *adj.* **1.** intensely cold. **2.** lacking warmth of feeling or enthusiasm; unfriendly or indifferent: *a frigid reception.* [Latin *frīgidus* cold.] —**fri·gid′i·ty, frig′id·ness,** *n.* —**frig′id·ly,** *adv.*

Frigid Zone, either of two extremely cold climatic regions, one lying north of the Arctic Circle and the other south of the Antarctic Circle. For illustration, see **zone.**

fri·jol (frē′hōl′, frē hōl′) *also,* **fri·jo·le** (frē hō′lē). *n., pl.* **fri-**

joles (frē′hōlz′, frē hō′lēz, -lās). any of various beans used for food, esp. in the southwestern United States, Mexico, and Central and South American countries. [Spanish *frijol* kidney bean, going back to Greek *phasēlos* kind of bean.]

frill (fril) *n.* **1.** an ornamental trimming consisting of a strip of material, as lace, gathered and attached along one edge and left free along the other; ruffle. **2.** *also,* **frills.** anything showy or unnecessary, as an affectation of dress or manner: *dinner with no frills.* **3.** a ruff of feathers or hair around the necks of some birds, dogs, or other animals. [Of uncertain origin.] —**frill′y,** *adj.*

fringe (frinj) *n.* **1.** a border or trimming consisting of hanging threads, cords, tassels, or the like. **2.** anything resembling or suggestive of such a border or trimming: *A fringe of bushes lined the driveway.* **3.** an outer edge; border; margin: *the fringes of a city.* **4.** a part, as of a group or political party, considered to be marginal or extreme: *a member of the radical fringe of a movement.* —*v.t.,* **fringed, fring·ing. 1.** to furnish with or as with a fringe. **2.** to serve as a fringe for. —*adj.* along the outer edge; marginal: *a fringe area.* [Old French *frenge* border of hanging threads, going back to Latin *fimbriae* (plural) threads, border.]

fringe benefit, a benefit received by an employee in addition to wages or salary, as pensions, health insurance, or paid vacations.

frip·per·y (frip′ə rē) *n., pl.* **-per·ies. 1.** cheap, showy clothes or ornaments. **2.** showiness or affectation, as in speech or manner. [French *friperie* rubbish, old clothes, going back to Old French *frepe* rag.]

Fris·bee (friz′bē) *n. Trademark.* a plastic disk that is thrown back and forth through the air between players.

Fri·sian (frizh′ən, frē′zhən) *adj.* of, relating to, or characteristic of Friesland or its people, language, or culture. —*n.* **1.** a native or inhabitant of Friesland. **2.** a person of Frisian ancestry. **3.** the language belonging to the Germanic branch of the Indo-European family of languages, spoken predominantly in Friesland.

frisk (frisk) *v.i.* to leap, skip, or move about playfully; gambol; frolic. —*v.t. Informal.* to search (someone), esp. for concealed weapons, by running the hand quickly over the pockets and clothing. [From obsolete *frisk* lively, from Middle French *frisque;* of Germanic origin.]

frisk·y (fris′kē) *adj.,* **frisk·i·er, frisk·i·est.** tending to frolic; playful; lively. —**frisk′i·ly,** *adv.* —**frisk′i·ness,** *n.*

frith (frith) *n.* firth.

frit·il·lar·y (frit′ə ler′ē) *n., pl.* **-lar·ies. 1.** any of a group of hardy plants, genus *Fritillaria,* of the lily family, found throughout northern temperate regions, bearing drooping, bell-shaped flowers often checkered with dark green or purple markings. **2.** any of a group of butterflies, genus *Argynnis* and related genera, having multicolored spots. [Modern Latin *Fritillaria,* from Latin *fritillus* dice box; because of the markings on the petals.]

frit·ter¹ (frit′ər) *v.t.* to waste or squander little by little (often with *away*): *to fritter away time doing nothing.* [Possibly modification of obsolete *fitter* to break into fragments (of uncertain origin) or possibly from Old French *fraiture* a breaking, from Latin *fractura.*] —**frit′ter·er,** *n.*

frit·ter² (frit′ər) *n.* a small cake made of sautéed or fried batter, often containing fruit, vegetables, meat, or fish: *an apple fritter, a corn fritter.* [Middle English *friture,* from Old French *friture* a frying, going back to Latin *frīctus,* past participle of *frīgere* to roast, fry.]

fritz (frits) *n. Informal.* **on the fritz.** in a condition of being broken or in disrepair; out of order. [Of uncertain origin.]

fri·vol·i·ty (fri vol′i tē) *n., pl.* **-ties. 1.** the quality or condition of being frivolous. **2.** a frivolous act or thing.

friv·o·lous (friv′ə ləs) *adj.* **1.** given to trifling or levity; not serious; silly. **2.** of little value or importance; trivial; petty: *frivolous matters.* [Latin *frīvolus.*] —**friv′o·lous·ly,** *adv.* —**friv′o·lous·ness,** *n.*

frizz (friz) *also,* **friz.** *v.t., v.i.,* **frizzed, friz·zing.** to form into small, tight curls. —*n., pl.* **friz·zes. 1.** something frizzed, esp. hair. **2.** the condition of being frizzed. [French *friser* to curl, possibly from *fris-,* a stem of *frire* to fry, from Latin *frīgere* to fry; with reference to the curled appearance of fried meat.]

friz·zle¹ (friz′əl) *v.t., v.i.,* **-zled, -zling.** to form into small, tight curls; frizz. —*n.* something frizzled, esp. hair. [FRIZZ + -LE; probably akin to Frisian *frislen* to braid (the hair).]

friz·zle² (friz′əl) *v.t., v.i.,* **-zled, -zling. 1.** to fry or cook with a sizzling noise. **2.** to fry until crisp. [Probably from *fry¹.*]

friz·zly (friz′lē) *adj.,* **-zli·er, -zli·est.** having small, tight curls; frizzy.

friz·zy (friz′ē) *adj.,* **-zi·er, -zi·est.** having small, tight curls. —**friz′zi·ly,** *adv.* —**friz′zi·ness,** *n.*

fro (frō) *adv.* **to and fro.** in different directions; back and forth. [Middle English *frō, frā,* from Old Norse *frā* from.]

frock (frok) *n.* **1.** a woman's or girl's dress. **2.** a long, loose robe, esp. one worn by monks and friars. **3.** a loose outer garment; smock. —*v.t.* **1.** to invest with the powers of the ministry or priesthood. **2.** to clothe in a frock. [Old French *froc* hood; of Germanic origin.]

frock coat, a man's coat reaching to the knees, usually double-breasted and fitted at the waist, popular in the late nineteenth century.

frog¹ (frôg, frog) *n.* **1.** any of a wide-spread group of web-footed, tailless amphibians, order Anura, found mostly near fresh water and having strong hind legs adapted for leaping. **2.** a triangular horny pad on the sole of a horse's foot. **3.** a device permitting the wheels of a railroad car to pass over a junction at intersecting tracks without difficulty. [Old English *frogga* the amphibian.]

frog¹

• **frog in the** (or **one's**) **throat.** a slight irritation of the throat causing hoarseness or difficulty in speaking.

frog² (frôg, frog) *n.* an ornamental fastening for clothing, usually made of braid that forms a loop on one side and a button on the other.

frog kick, a kick in swimming in which the legs are drawn toward the body, knees out and heels together, then pressed out and to the rear.

frog²

frog·man (frôg′man′, frog′-) *n., pl.* **-men** (-men′). a swimmer specially equipped and trained for underwater reconnaissance and demolition, esp. for military purposes.

frol·ic (frol′ik) *v.i.,* **-icked, -ick·ing.** to move about or play with spirit or playfulness; make merry. —*n.* **1.** joyful or spirited activity; romp. **2.** the quality or state of being cheerful; merriment; gaiety. [Dutch *vrolijk* merry, gay, from Middle Dutch *vro* glad.]

frol·ic·some (frol′ik səm) *adj.* joyful and spirited; merry: *a frolicsome colt.*

from (from, frum; *unstressed* frəm) *prep.* **1.** starting at; beginning with: *We flew from New York to Chicago. We waited from six o'clock to ten.* **2.** with a particular person, place, or thing as the source, origin, or instrument: *a letter from my cousin, light from the sun.* **3.** out of: *I took the money from my pocket.* **4.** out of the control, custody, or possession of: *The rabbit escaped from the trap.* **5.** out of the whole of: *to subtract two from five.* **6.** at a distance from; out of contact with: *They live about ten miles from my house.* **7.** by reason of; because of: *to shiver from the cold.* **8.** as being another or different than: *Can you tell one twin from the other?* **9.** beyond the reach, realm, or possibility of: *My lack of experience prevented me from getting the job I wanted.* [Old English *from, fram* away, apart, starting at.]

frond (frond) *n.* **1.** the leaf of a fern or palm. **2.** a leaflike part of certain other plants, as a seaweed or lichen. [Latin *frond-,* stem of *frōns* leafy branch, foliage.] —**frond′ed,** *adj.*

front (frunt) *n.* **1.** the part which faces, or is regarded as facing, forward; forepart: *the front of the body, the front of a dress.* **2.** the first or foremost part: *The introduction is always in the front of the book.* **3.** a place or position directly ahead or before: *a school with a flagpole in the front.* **4.** the part or side that is normally used: *Sign the check on the front.* **5.** the side of a building or similar structure containing the main entrance. **6.a.** a person's attitude or bearing when confronted with anything, esp. of a dangerous or problematic nature: *to put on a bold front.* **b.** cool assurance; impudence; effrontery. **7.a.** a broad movement uniting various groups for the achievement of a common goal, esp. of a political or economic nature: *the labor front.* **b.** an area or field of activity or interest: *good news on the economic front.* **8.** land facing or lying along a street, river, or the like; frontage. **9.a.** the line or area of combat between two enemy forces: *a nation forced to fight a war on two fronts.* **b.** the foremost part of a military position:

a	at	e	end	o	hot	u	up	hw	white		about
ā	ape	ē	me	ō	old	ū	use	ng	song		taken
ä	far	i	it	ô	fork	ü	rule	th	thin	ə	pencil
âr	care	ī	ice	oi	oil	u̇	pull	th	this		lemon
		î	pierce	ou	out	ûr	turn	zh	measure		circus

The supplies were sent to the front. **10.** an apparently respectable person or thing used to disguise secret objectives or activities, as of an illegal organization: *The drugstore was a front for the gang's gambling activities.* **11.** a prestigious person who serves as an official leader or spokesperson of an organization but usually lacks real authority within it. **12.** an outward, usually assumed or feigned appearance, as of wealth or importance. **13.** the boundary between two air masses of different origin and properties: *a warm front, a cold front.* —*adj.* **1.** situated at, on, or near the front: *the front door of a house, the front page of a newspaper.* **2.** of, relating to, or directed toward the front: *a front view of the house.* **3.** *Phonetics.* (of vowels) pronounced by raising the tongue so that the highest point is toward the front of the mouth. The *a* in *bay* is a front vowel. —*v.t.* **1.** to face toward: *The cottage fronts the lake.* **2.** to furnish with a front: *They fronted the building with brick.* **3.** to serve as a front for. **4.** to meet face to face, as in defiance or opposition: *to front an enemy.* —*v.i.* **1.** to have the front toward; face: *The house fronts on the street.* **2.** to serve as a front (with *for*): *a business that fronts for organized crime, a celebrity who fronts for a charity.* [Latin *frōns* forehead, forepart of something.]
  • **in front of. a.** in a place or position before or ahead of. **b.** in the presence of: *Let's not talk about the party in front of them.*
  • **up front.** *Informal.* **a.** in the beginning; initially: *a project that requires a big investment up front.* **b.** frank or honest: *to be up front about one's problems.*

front·age (frun'tij) *n.* **1.** the front of a building or lot. **2.** the lineal extent of this. **3.** the direction toward which the front of something faces. **4.** land facing or abutting on a street, body of water, or the like: *ocean frontage.* **5.** land between the front of a building and another boundary, as a road or body of water.

fron·tal (frun'təl) *adj.* **1.** of, relating to, or situated at the front. **2.** of or relating to the forehead or frontal bone. —*n. also,* **frontal bone.** the bone of the front of the skull, forming the forehead. For illustration, see **parietal.** [Modern Latin *frontalis*, from Latin *frōns* forehead, forepart of something.] —**fron'tal·ly,** *adv.*

frontal lobe, the foremost part of each half of the cerebrum in humans, behind the forehead, concerned with such functions as reasoning and speech.

fron·tier (frun tîr') *n.* **1.** the settled region of a country lying along the border of unsettled or undeveloped territory. **2.** that part of a country lying along the border of another country; border. **3.** *also,* **frontiers.** any new or unexplored area of a field, as science or philosophy: *the frontiers of medicine.* —*adj.* of, relating to, or situated on the frontier: *a frontier town.* [Old French *frontiere* border of a country, from *front* forehead, front, from Latin *frōns.*]

fron·tiers·man (frun tîrz'mən) *n., pl.* **-men** (-mən). a person who lives on the frontier.

fron·tis·piece (frun'tis pēs', fron'-) *n.* an illustration facing the title page of a book or division of a book. [French *frontispice* title page, from Late Latin *frontispicium* façade; literally, front view, from Latin *frōns* forehead, forepart + *specere* to look.]

front·let (frunt'lit) *n.* **1.** a band or ornament worn on the forehead, esp. a decorative headband of the medieval period. **2.** the forehead of an animal or bird, esp. when distinctively marked.

front man **1.** a person who serves as a spokesperson for an organization, group, or activity. **2.** a person who serves to conceal an illegal activity or secret operation. **3.** a performer who leads a musical group.

front office, the main office or executive body of a business or other organization.

front-page (frunt'pāj') *adj.* printed on, or important enough to be printed on, the front page of a newspaper.

front-run·ner (frunt'run'ər) *n.* the leading contestant in any competition: *the frontrunner in the race for mayor.*

frost (frôst) *n.* **1.** a deposit of minute ice crystals formed by the freezing of dew or water vapor on the surface of an exposed object or on the ground. **2.** the state or temperature of the atmosphere below the freezing point of water; severe cold. **3.** the act of freezing. **4.** coldness of manner, feeling, or action. —*v.t.* **1.** to cover with frost. **2.** to damage or destroy by frost. **3.** to produce a dull, frostlike surface on, as glass. **4.** to cover with frosting: *to frost a cake.* **5.** to bleach (strands of hair). —*v.i.* to become frosted. [Old English *forst, frost* extreme cold, frozen vapor.]

frost·bite (frôst'bīt') *n.* a frozen or partially frozen condition of some part of the body as a result of excessive exposure to extreme

cold. —*v.t.,* **-bit, -bit·ten.** to affect, injure, or destroy by freezing.

frost·bit·ten (frôst'bit'ən) *adj.* affected or injured by frostbite.

frost·ed (frôs'tid) *adj.* **1.** covered with frost: *frosted blades of grass.* **2.** covered with frosting; iced: *a frosted cake.* **3.** having a dull surface like frost: *frosted glass.*

frost heave, an upheaval of the ground resulting from the formation of ice beneath the ground's surface when moist soil freezes.

frost·ing (frôs'ting) *n.* **1.** a mixture of sugar, a liquid, butter, flavoring, and sometimes egg whites, used to cover baked goods; icing. **2.** a dull, frostlike finish, as produced on glass or metal.

frost·y (frôs'tē) *adj.,* **frost·i·er, frost·i·est. 1.** producing frost: *frosty weather.* **2.** containing or covered with frost: *frosty windows.* **3.** marked by coldness of manner or feeling: *a frosty reception.* **4.** resembling frost; hoary. —**frost'i·ly,** *adv.* —**frost'i·ness,** *n.*

froth (frôth) *n.* **1.** a mass of bubbles formed in or on a liquid through agitation or fermentation; foam. **2.** any foamy matter or excretion, as from disease or exertion: *The tired horse had froth at its mouth.* **3.** something light, trivial, or worthless, as ideas or conversation. —*v.i.* to emit or form froth; foam: *The rabid dog frothed at the mouth.* —*v.t.* **1.** to cause to foam. **2.** to cover with froth. [Old Norse *frotha* foam, spray.]

froth·y (frô'thē) *adj.,* **froth·i·er, froth·i·est. 1.** consisting of, covered with, or full of froth; foamy. **2.** light, trivial, or worthless: *a frothy speech.* —**froth'i·ly,** *adv.* —**froth'i·ness,** *n.*

frou·frou (frü'frü') *n.* **1.** a swishing or rustling, as of silk. **2.** *Informal.* affected elegance or excessive ornamentation, as of a woman's dress. [French *frou-frou* rustling; imitative.]

fro·ward (frō'wərd) *adj.* not easily managed; stubborn or disobedient: *a froward child, froward behavior.* [FRO + -WARD.] —**fro'ward·ly,** *adv.* —**fro'ward·ness,** *n.*

frown (froun) *n.* **1.** a contraction of the brow, as in displeasure or concentration. **2.** any expression of displeasure or disapproval. —*v.i.* **1.** to contract the brow, as in displeasure or concentration. **2.** to look with displeasure or disapproval (with *on* or *upon*): *My parents frowned on my staying out late.* —*v.t.* to express (displeasure or disapproval) by contracting the brow: *to frown defiance.* [Old French *fro(i)gnier* to look sternly, scowl; of Celtic origin.] —**frown'ing·ly,** *adv.*

Synonyms *v.i.* **Frown, scowl,** and **glower** mean to assume a facial expression in which the brow is contracted. **Frown** is the general term for such an expression, which may connote disapproval, anger, puzzlement, or concentration: *to frown at noise in a library, to frown in frustration at a complicated repair job.* **Scowl** suggests a fixed, more intense expression of discontent or anger: *to scowl while cleaning up a mess, to scowl at a heckler in the audience.* **Glower** is similar to *scowl,* but more strongly suggests anger or disapproval directed at someone: *to glower at people who break into a movie line.*

frows·y (frou'zē) *adj.,* **frows·i·er, frows·i·est.** frowzy.

frowz·y (frou'zē) *adj.,* **frowz·i·er, frowz·i·est. 1.** having a slovenly appearance; unkempt. **2.** having an unpleasant smell; musty. [Of uncertain origin.] —**frowz'i·ly,** *adv.* —**frowz'i·ness,** *n.*

froze (frōz) the past tense of **freeze.**

fro·zen (frō'zən) *v.* the past participle of **freeze.** —*adj.* **1.** converted into ice; congealed by cold. **2.** covered, obstructed, or clogged with ice: *a frozen water pipe, a frozen lake.* **3.** unable to move: *frozen with fear.* **4.** (of food) preserved by freezing quickly. **5.** damaged or destroyed by frost or extreme cold. **6.** extremely cold; frigid: *a frozen climate.* **7.** maintained or set at a definite level or amount: *frozen wages.* **8.** cold and unfeeling: *a frozen stare.* —**fro'zen·ly,** *adv.*

FRS, Federal Reserve System.

frt., freight.

fruc·tif·er·ous (fruk tif'ər əs, frŭk-) *adj.* fruit-bearing.

fruc·ti·fy (fruk'tə fī', frŭk'-) *v.,* **-fied, -fy·ing.** —*v.t.* to make fruitful or productive: *minerals that fructify the soil, books that fructify our minds.* —*v.i.* to bear fruit. [Old French *fructifier* to bear fruit, from Late Latin *frūctificāre,* from Latin *frūctus* fruit + *facere* to make.] —**fruc'ti·fi·ca'tion,** *n.*

fruc·tose (fruk'tōs, frŭk'-) *n.* a simple sugar occurring naturally in fruits and honey. Formula: $C_6H_{12}O_6$ Also, **fruit sugar, levulose.** [Latin *frūctus* fruit + -OSE[2].]

fru·gal (frü'gəl) *adj.* **1.** avoiding waste; economical; saving: *a frugal person.* **2.** of little cost or amount; meager; spare: *a frugal meal.* [Latin *frūgālis* temperate, thrifty; literally, relating to fruit, going back to *frūx* fruit.] —**fru·gal·i·ty** (frü gal'i tē), *n.* —**fru'gal·ly,** *adv.* —For Synonyms, see **thrifty.**

fruit (frūt) *n., pl.* **fruit** or **fruits. 1.** any edible plant product. **2.** the ripened ovary of a plant. **3.** any useful plant product. **4.** the effect, result, or product of an action: *the fruit of hard work.* —*v.i., v.t.* to bear or cause to bear fruit. [Old French *fruit* edible product of a plant, advantageous result, from Latin *frūctus* produce of the earth, result, enjoyment.]

fruit·age (frū′tij) *n.* **1.** the state or process of producing fruit. **2.** fruit collectively. **3.** the result, effect, or product of an action.

fruit bat, any of a group of tropical and subtropical Old World fruit-eating or flower-eating bats, family Pteropodidae, as the flying foxes. Wingspan: 10-60 inches (25 centimeters-1.5 meters).

fruit·cake (frūt′kāk′) *n.* a rich cake containing preserved or dried fruits, nuts, and spices, and sometimes wine or brandy.

fruit cup, a mixture of cut fruits, usually served in a cup or glass as an appetizer or dessert. Also, **fruit cocktail.**

fruit·er (frū′tər) *n.* **1.** a ship that carries fruit. **2.** a tree or plant that produces fruit. **3.** a fruit dealer or grower. Also, **fruit′er·er.**

fruit fly 1. a small fly, *Drosophila melanogaster,* whose larvae feed chiefly on decaying fruit. It is valuable in genetic studies because of the extraordinarily large chromosomes of the larvae and its short life span. Also, **drosophila. 2.** any of various other flies, family Trypetidae, whose larvae feed on fruit, leaves, and roots.

fruit·ful (frūt′fəl) *adj.* **1.** producing results; profitable: *a fruitful discussion.* **2.** bearing fruit or offspring in abundance; prolific: *a fruitful tree.* **3.** promoting growth or productivity: *fruitful soil.* —**fruit′ful·ly,** *adv.* —**fruit′ful·ness,** *n.* —For Synonyms, see **fertile.**

fruiting body, a plant structure that produces or bears spores, as in fungi.

fru·i·tion (frū ish′ən) *n.* **1.** the realization or accomplishment of one's efforts or desires; fulfillment: *After many years of experimentation, the scientist brought her theories to fruition.* **2.** the bearing of fruit. [Old French *fruition* enjoying, from Late Latin *fruitiō* enjoyment, from Latin *fruī* to enjoy.]

fruit·less (frūt′lis) *adj.* **1.** producing no effect or result; useless: *a fruitless effort.* **2.** bearing no fruit or offspring; barren: *a fruitless tree, a fruitless marriage.* —**fruit′less·ly,** *adv.* —**fruit′less·ness,** *n.* —For Synonyms, see **vain.**

fruit sugar, fructose.

fruit tree, a tree bearing edible fruit.

fruit·y (frū′tē) *adj.,* **fruit·i·er, fruit·i·est.** of, relating to, or suggestive of fruit, as in taste or smell.

frump (frump) *n.* **1.** a dowdy, often ill-tempered woman. **2.** a person who is staid and old-fashioned.

frump·ish (frum′pish) *adj.* **1.** dowdy or outdated in dress. **2.** staid and old-fashioned in manner. **3.** ill-tempered; cross.

frump·y (frum′pē) *adj.,* **frump·i·er, frump·i·est.** frumpish.

frus·trate (frus′trāt) *v.t.,* **-trat·ed, -trat·ing. 1.** to keep (someone) from doing or achieving something; disappoint or thwart: *He was frustrated by not being able to find a job.* **2.** to prevent something from being attained or fulfilled; defeat: *to frustrate a plan.* [Latin *frūstrātus,* past participle of *frūstrārī* to disappoint, render vain, from *frūstra* in vain.]

Synonyms Frustrate, foil[1], and **thwart** mean to interfere with and defeat some effort. Although they are very close in meaning, **frustrate** is the most general of these terms: *The rainy weather frustrated my desire to spend the day gardening. The opposing team's superb defense frustrated all our attempts to score.* **Foil** more clearly suggests deliberately bringing something to naught: *The alarm system went off, foiling the robbers' attempt to escape with the money.* **Thwart** suggests standing in the way or blocking the path of something or someone: *The city's plan to build a new stadium was thwarted by the lack of agreement on a site.*

frus·tra·tion (frus trā′shən) *n.* **1.** the act of frustrating or the state of being frustrated. **2.** something that frustrates.

frus·tum (frus′təm) *n., pl.* **-tums** or **-ta** (-tə). **1.** a section of a cone or pyramid between the base and a plane parallel to the base and cutting through the solid. **2.** a part of any solid between two parallel planes cutting through it. [Latin *frustum* piece.]

fry[1] (frī) *v.t., v.i.,* **fried, fry·ing.** to cook or be cooked in hot fat or oil in a pan or on a griddle, usually over direct heat. —*n., pl.* **fries.** a social gathering, usually outdoors, at which food is fried and eaten: *a fish fry.* [Middle English *frieen,* from Old French *frire* to cook in a frying pan with fat, from Latin *frīgere* to roast, fry.]

fry[2] (frī) *n., pl.* **fry. 1.** newly hatched fish. **2.** a

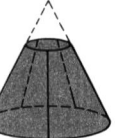

frustum

small adult fish, esp. when living in a large group. **3.** the young of certain animals, as the frog. [Probably a blend of Old Norse *frjo* offspring and Anglo-Norman *frie* spawn, from Old French *freier* to rub, spawn, from Latin *fricāre* to rub.]

fry·er (frī′ər) *n.* **1.** a young chicken suitable for frying. **2.** a deep pan for frying food. **3.** a person or thing that fries. Also, **frier.**

frying pan, a shallow pan with a handle, used for frying food. •**out of the frying pan into the fire.** from one difficult or dangerous situation to another that is worse.

FSH, follicle-stimulating hormone.

f stop, any of the various diaphragm settings, corresponding to f-numbers, of the adjustable aperture of a camera lens.

ft *also,* **ft.** foot; feet.

ft. 1. fort. **2.** fortification.

FTC, Federal Trade Commission.

fuch·sia (fū′shə) *n.* **1.** any shrub or small tree, genus *Fuchsia,* of the evening primrose family, native mostly to tropical America, bearing pink, white, red, or purple clusters of funnel-shaped, usually drooping flowers. **2.** a bright purplish pink color. [Modern Latin *Fuchsia,* from Leonhard *Fuchs,* 1501-66, a German botanist.]

fuch·sin (fūk′sin, fūk′-) *also,* **fuch·sine** (fūk′sin, -sēn, fūk′-). *n.* a synthetic, dark green, powdery or crystalline mixture containing anilines, used as a red dye.

fu·cus (fū′kəs) *n.* any of several large, brown seaweeds, genus *Fucus,* having branching fronds often bearing air bladders, commonly found attached to rocks along the shore. [Modern Latin *fucus,* from Latin *fucus* rock lichen or the red or purple paint obtained from it, from Greek *phykos;* possibly of Semitic origin.]

fud·dle (fud′əl) *v.t.,* **-dled, -dling.** to stupefy or confuse with or as with liquor; befuddle. —*n.* the state of being fuddled: *to be in a fuddle.* [Of uncertain origin.]

fud·dy-dud·dy (fud′ē dud′ē) *n., pl.* **-dud·dies.** *Informal.* **1.** a person who is old-fashioned. **2.** a person who is overly critical or fussy about trifles.

fudge (fuj) *n.* **1.** a soft candy made of sugar, milk, butter, flavoring, and sometimes nuts. **2.** empty talk; nonsense; foolishness. —*interj.* used to express disappointment, annoyance, or disbelief. —*v.,* **fudged, fudg·ing.** —*v.t.* **1.** to avoid giving a direct response to, as a question, or committing oneself on, as an issue. **2.** to make seem genuine; fake: *to fudge the data.* —*v.i.* **1.** to avoid giving a direct response or committing oneself. **2.** to act dishonestly; cheat. [Of uncertain origin.]

Fueh·rer (fyūr′ər) Führer.

fu·el (fū′əl) *n.* **1.** combustible matter, as coal, wood, or oil, burned as a source of heat and power. **2.** fissionable material used as a source of energy in a nuclear reactor. **3.** anything that sustains or intensifies an emotion: *Their rudeness added fuel to my anger.* —*v.,* **-eled, -el·ing;** *also, British,* **-elled, -el·ling.** —*v.t.* to supply with fuel. —*v.i.* to take in fuel. [Old French *fouaille* fagots, anything used for heating, from Late Latin *focālia,* plural of *focāle,* from Latin *focus* hearth.]

fuel cell, a device that produces electricity by a direct chemical reaction between a fuel and an oxidizer.

fuel element, a rod, plate, or other form into which nuclear fuel is fabricated for use in a nuclear reactor.

fuel injection 1. the spraying of liquid fuel directly into the combustion chamber of an internal-combustion engine. **2.** a system that serves this function, taking the place of a carburetor in some motor vehicle engines.

fuel oil, a petroleum product burned as fuel, as for heating a building.

fu·gi·tive (fū′ji tiv) *n.* a person who flees or has fled, as from danger, pursuit, or intolerable circumstances: *a fugitive from tyranny.* —*adj.* **1.** fleeing or having fled, as from danger or pursuit. **2.** not fixed or durable; not lasting; fleeting: *fugitive thoughts.* **3.** dealing with subjects of passing interest; occasional: *fugitive essays.* [Old French *fugitif* fleeing, from Latin *fugitīvus,* from *fugere* to flee.]

Fugitive Slave Laws, laws passed by Congress before the American Civil War that made it illegal to aid a runaway slave or prevent his or her being returned.

fugue (fūg) *n.* a polyphonic musical composition, based on one

a	at	e	end	o	hot	u	up	hw	white	⟨	about
ā	ape	ē	me	ō	old	ū	use	ng	song		taken
ä	far	i	it	ô	fork	ü	rule	th	thin	ə	pencil
âr	care	ī	ice	oi	oil	u̇	pull	th	this		lemon
		îr	pierce	ou	out	ûr	turn	zh	measure	⟨	circus

501

or more short themes or subjects taken up in turn by different voices or instruments and developed according to the rules of counterpoint. [French *fugue* flight, fugue, from Italian *fuga*, from Latin *fuga* flight; possibly because the notes seem to be in flight.]

Füh·rer (fyŏŏr′ər; *German* fY′RƏR) *also,* **Fuehrer.** *n. German.* **1.** a leader. **2. der Führer.** the title assumed by Adolf Hitler as head of Nazi Germany.

-ful *suffix* **1.** full of or characterized by: *graceful, peaceful.* **2.** tending or able to: *forgetful, helpful.* **3.** having the qualities of: *manful.* **4.** the number or amount that fills or will fill: *spoonful, glassful.* [Old English *-ful,* suffix representing *full* filled, complete.]

ful·crum (fŭl′krəm, fŭl′-) *n., pl.* **-crums** or **-cra** (-krə). a support or point of support upon which a lever rests, or about which it rotates when in use. [Latin *fulcrum* bedpost, from *fulcīre* to support.]

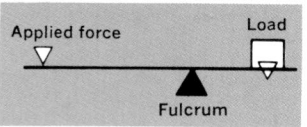

fulcrum

ful·fill (fŭl fĭl′) *also,* **ful·fil.** *v.t.,* **-filled, -fill·ing. 1.** to carry out or bring to completion, as a promise, hope, or prophecy; cause to happen. **2.** to answer the conditions or requirements of: *to fulfill a need.* **3.** to bring to an end (a period of time or a task); finish. **4.** to execute or perform (a duty or request). [Old English *fullfyllan* to accomplish; literally, to fill full.]

 · **to fulfill oneself.** to realize completely one's potential or ambition.

ful·fill·ment (fŭl fĭl′mənt) *also,* **ful·fil·ment.** *n.* **1.** the act of being fulfilled. **2.** something that fulfills.

full¹ (fŭl) *adj.* **1.** containing as much or as many as possible; with no empty space: *a full glass of water.* **2.** containing a large number or quantity: *a house full of people.* **3.** having an abundant or ample supply: *The book was full of adventure.* **4.** complete, as in extent, quantity, or number; entire: *a full dozen, a full share.* **5.a.** of or having reached the maximum, as of size, quantity, amount, or intensity: *full speed, full strength.* **b.** not restricted or qualified in any way; absolute; total: *a full break in relations, a full stop.* **6.** having had enough food or drink to satisfy: *I am full.* **7.** having a rounded outline; well filled out; plump: *full lips, a full face.* **8.** completely absorbed or occupied, as in thought: *to be full of concern for the future.* **9.** filled with emotion: *a full heart.* **10.** having ample resonance and volume: *a full tone, a full voice.* **11.** (of garments) having loose, wide folds or an abundance of cloth: *a full skirt.* **12.** having the same mother and father: *They are full brothers.* **13.** having reached the most complete status or highest rank or position: *a full colonel, a full member of a club, a full professor at a university.* **14.** *Informal.* having had all that one can endure: *I am full of that person's nonsense.* —*adv.* **1.** in a direct manner; straight: *He looked her full in the face.* **2.** to the greatest degree or extent; completely; entirely: *to fill a bag full.* **3.** very; exceedingly: *You know full well that I am right.* [Old English *full* filled, complete, entire.]

 · **in full. a.** to or for the entire amount: *She paid the bill in full.* **b.** without shortening or cutting: *The newspaper printed the document in full.*

 · **to the full.** to the utmost extent; completely; entirely: *My grandparents enjoy life to the full.*

full² (fŭl) *v.t.* to finish (woolen fabric) by subjecting it to moisture, heat, friction, and pressure, causing it to shrink and giving it a smooth, tight finish. [From FULLER.]

full·back (fŭl′bak′) *n. Football.* **1.** a player on the offensive team who usually lines up farthest behind the front line. **2.** the position played by this player.

full blast, with full power or resources; at maximum capacity, power, or speed: *a factory operating at full blast, a stereo playing full blast.*

full-blood·ed (fŭl′blŭd′ĭd) *adj.* **1.** of unmixed race, breed, or ancestry. **2.** full of energy and vigor; vigorous; virile; hearty.

full-blown (fŭl′blōn′) *adj.* **1.** (of flowers) in full bloom: *a full-blown rose.* **2.** fully developed or matured: *a full-blown infection.*

full-bod·ied (fŭl′bŏd′ēd) *adj.* having a rich flavor and aroma: *a full-bodied wine.*

full dress, formal attire, as worn for ceremonial occasions.

full·er (fŭl′ər) *n.* a person who fulls fabric. [Old English *fullere,* from Latin *fullō.*]

fuller's earth, a fine, claylike earth, used as an adsorptive agent, as to remove grease from wool or to decolorize oil.

full-fash·ioned (fŭl′fash′ənd) *adj.* knitted to conform to the shape of the body, as hosiery.

full-fledged (fŭl′flejd′) *adj.* **1.** having full rank or status: *a full-fledged citizen.* **2.** completely developed or mature. **3.** (of a bird) having full plumage.

full gainer, a dive in which the diver starts in the forward position and then does a full backward somersault, entering the water feet first.

full-grown (fŭl′grōn′) *adj.* having attained full size or maturity; fully grown.

full house, a poker hand made up of three cards of one kind and two of another, as three aces and two fours.

full-length (fŭl′lengkth′, -length′, -lenth′) *adj.* **1.** showing or covering the whole length of an object or figure: *a full-length mirror, a full-length gown.* **2.** being of the original or standard length; unabridged: *a full-length novel.*

full moon 1. the moon when the whole of its face is illuminated, as seen from the earth. **2.** the time of month when this occurs. For illustration, see **moon.**

full·ness (fŭl′nĭs) *also,* **fulness.** *n.* the state or quality of being full.

fullness of time, a sufficient length of time.

full-rigged (fŭl′rĭgd′) *adj.* (of a ship) having complete rigging for three or more masts and a full set of sails.

full-scale (fŭl′skāl′) *adj.* **1.** of the same size as the original; of actual size: *a full-scale drawing.* **2.** undertaken to the fullest extent possible or with the fullest use of resources: *a full-scale war.*

full-serv·ice (fŭl′sûr′vĭs) *adj.* providing a variety of services: *a full-service bank, a full-service gas station.*

full swing, the height of activity: *The party was in full swing.*

full-time (fŭl′tīm′) *adj.* for or during the normal or usual hours of working time: *a full-time employee, a full-time schedule.* —*adv.* on a full-time basis: *to work full-time as a typist.*

ful·ly (fŭl′ē) *adv.* **1.** to the fullest extent or degree; completely; entirely: *to be fully aware of something.* **2.** at least; not less than: *You are fully two hours late.*

ful·mi·nate (fŭl′mə nāt′, fŭl′-) *v.,* **-nat·ed, -nat·ing.** —*v.i.* **1.** to make loud and violent threats or denunciations; inveigh (often with *against*): *The speaker fulminated against war.* **2.** to explode with sudden violence. —*v.t.* **1.** to threaten or denounce vehemently. **2.** to cause (something) to explode with sudden violence. —*n.* any of several explosive salts of cyanic acid used as detonators, such as fulminate of mercury; cyanate. [Latin *fulminātus,* past participle of *fulmināre* to thunder, lightning.]

ful·mi·na·tion (fŭl′mə nā′shən, fŭl′-) *n.* **1.** the act of fulminating. **2.** a violent denunciation or censure. **3.** a loud, violent explosion.

ful·ness (fŭl′nĭs) fullness.

ful·some (fŭl′səm) *adj.* **1.** offensive to good taste, esp. because of excess or insincerity: *I was embarrassed by their fulsome praise.* **2.** full or abundant. [FULL¹ + -SOME¹; possibly influenced in meaning by Middle English *ful* foul.] —**ful′some·ly,** *adv.* —**ful′some·ness,** *n.*

Usage Fulsome is often misused, especially in the phrase *fulsome praise.* In its earliest sense, it meant "full" or "abundant," but it has since acquired an additional meaning that refers to excess, insincerity, or other negative qualities. For this reason, it is best to avoid using it in its original sense in order to avoid misunderstanding.

fu·ma·role (fū′mə rōl′) *n.* a small volcanic vent that emits hot gases and vapor. [Italian *fumaruolo,* from Late Latin *fumariolum* smoke hole, diminutive of Late Latin *fumarium* chimney.] —**fu·ma·rol·ic** (fū′mə rol′ik), *adj.*

fum·ble (fum′bəl) *v.,* **-bled, -bling.** —*v.i.* **1.** to search or grope clumsily: *He fumbled under the seat for his hat.* **2.** to make an awkward attempt: *I fumbled at opening the lock.* **3.** to handle or finger something clumsily or aimlessly: *She fumbled nervously with her necklace.* **4.** in sports, to catch and lose hold of a ball. —*v.t.* **1.** to handle or deal with awkwardly; botch: *You fumbled your chances.* **2.** in sports, to catch and lose hold of (a ball). —*n.* **1.** the act of fumbling. **2.** a ball that is fumbled. [Dutch *fommelen* to grope.] —**fum′bler,** *n.* —**fum′bling·ly,** *adv.*

fume (fūm) *n.* **1.** *also,* **fumes.** smoke, gas, vapor, or other exhalation, esp. when irritating or offensive. **2.** *also,* **fumes.** a strongly penetrating odor: *fumes from the city dump.* **3.** a state of irritation or rage. —*v.,* **fumed, fuming.** —*v.i.* **1.** to give off fumes. **2.** to rise or pass off in fumes. **3.** to be filled with or show anger or irritation: *I fumed as I waited in the traffic jam.* —*v.t.* to expose to or treat with fumes. [Old French *fum* smoke, from Latin *fūmus.*]

fumed (fūmd) *adj.* darkened or colored by exposure to ammonia fumes, as oak wood.

fu·mi·gant (fū′mi gənt) *n.* a substance used in fumigating. [Latin *fumigant-*, present participial stem of *fūmigāre* to smoke. See FUMIGATE.]

fu·mi·gate (fū′mi gāt′) *v.t.*, **-gat·ed, -gat·ing.** to expose to fumes, as smoke, esp. for disinfection. [Latin *fūmigātus*, past participle of *fūmigāre*, from *fūmus* smoke + *agere* to do, drive.] **—fu′mi·ga′tion**, *n.* **—fu′mi·ga′tor**, *n.*

fun (fun) *n.* **1.** amusement or enjoyment; diversion; recreation: *We got great fun out of the circus.* **2.** playfulness or gaiety: *He is full of fun.* **3.** a source of amusement or pleasure: *She is great fun to be with.* *—adj.* providing amusement or enjoyment. [Probably from obsolete *fun* to hoax; of uncertain origin.]
 • **for** (or **in**) **fun.** not seriously; in jest; playfully.
 • **like fun.** *Slang.* by no means; not at all.
 • **to make fun of** (or **to poke fun at**). to laugh at; ridicule.

fu·nam·bu·list (fū nam′byə list) *n.* a tightrope walker. [Latin *fūnambulus* ropedancer (from *fūnis* rope + *ambulāre* to walk) + -IST.]

func·tion (fungk′shən) *n.* **1.** a natural or characteristic action or use of anything; purpose: *The function of the kidneys is to excrete wastes from the body.* **2.** a special duty or action required of a person, as in an occupation or role: *What is your function on the committee?* **3.** a formal social gathering or official ceremony. **4.** *Mathematics.* **a.** a quantity whose value is dependent on that of another quantity. **b.** a relationship between two sets in which at least one element of the second set is assigned to one element of the first set. *—v.i.* **1.** to perform a job or operation effectively or properly; operate; work: *The motor functions best when it is kept well lubricated.* **2.** to perform the role of something else; serve: *The cellar functioned as a shelter during the storm.* [Latin *functiō* performance.] **—func′tion·less**, *adj.*

func·tion·al (fungk′shə nəl) *adj.* **1.** of or relating to a function or functions: *The system has functional problems.* **2.** designed for or serving a particular purpose; having a function: *Is this part functional or merely decorative?* **3.** capable of functioning: *The system will be functional immediately after installation.* **4.** designed or adapted so that use is easy: *Our new kitchen is very functional.* **5.** *Medicine.* affecting the functioning of an organ but not its structure: *functional impotence.* ➡ distinguished from **organic**. **—func′tion·al·ly**, *adv.*

functional group, a group of atoms that determines the characteristic reactions of a class of chemical compounds, as the hydroxyl group in alcohols.

functional illiterate, a person who does not meet a minimum standard of literacy or is unable to read and write well enough to do certain tasks necessary for coping with a complex society.

func·tion·al·ism (fungk′shə nə liz′əm) *n.* the doctrine or practice of adapting the form, structure, or material of an object or building to its practical use or function. **—func′tion·al·ist**, *n.*

func·tion·ar·y (fungk′shə ner′ē) *n., pl.* **-ar·ies.** a person who serves in a specific function, esp. a public official.

function word, a word used to express a grammatical relationship in a sentence or phrase, as a conjunction, preposition, or auxiliary verb. In the sentence *I do enjoy swimming, do* is a function word.

fund (fund) *n.* **1.** a sum of money set aside for a specific purpose: *a fund for a political campaign.* **2.** an available supply, as of information or knowledge. **3. funds.** money that is readily available, as in a bank account: *What funds do you have to finance this venture?* *—v.t.* **1.** to provide money for payment of the interest or principal on (a debt). **2.** to provide a fund for: *to fund an organization.* [Blend of French *fond* bottom, basis, and French *fonds* capital, property, both from Latin *fundus* bottom, piece of land.]

fun·da·men·tal (fun′də men′təl) *adj.* **1.** relating to or serving as a foundation; basic; essential: *Rules are fundamental to any game.* **2.** most important; principal: *Food and shelter are fundamental needs.* **3.** *Music.* of or relating to the lowest tone or root of a chord. *—n.* **1.** anything that forms or serves as the basis of a system, principle, rule, or law; essential part. **2.** *Music.* the lowest tone or root of a chord. Also, **fundamental note, fundamental tone. 3.** *Physics.* the component of a wave that has the lowest frequency. [Middle English *fundamental*, from Medieval Latin *fundāmentālis* of the foundation, from Late Latin *fundāmentālis*, from Latin *fundāmentum* foundation, from *fundus* bottom.] **—fun′da·men′tal·ly**, *adv.* **—**For Synonyms, see **elementary.**

fun·da·men·tal·ism (fun′də men′tə liz′əm) *n.* **1.** a movement in U.S. Protestantism based upon a literal interpretation of the Bible. **2.** the beliefs associated with this movement. **—fun′da·men′tal·ist**, *n., adj.*

fundamental particle, subatomic particle.

fund·rais·ing (fund′rā′zing) *n.* the act of raising money to support an organization or activity, such as a charity or political campaign. **—fund′rais·er**, *n.*

fu·ner·al (fū′nər əl) *n.* **1.** the burial or cremation of the body of a dead person, together with religious services or other observances. **2.** a procession accompanying the body of a dead person to the place of burial or cremation. *—adj.* relating to or suitable for a funeral: *a funeral oration.* [Medieval Latin *funeralia* funeral rites, going back to Latin *fūnus* burial, death.]

funeral home, a business establishment with rooms for preparing the dead for burial or cremation and often a chapel for funeral services. Also, **funeral parlor.**

fu·ner·ar·y (fū′nə rer′ē) *adj.* of, relating to, or intended for a funeral.

fu·ne·re·al (fū nîr′ē əl) *adj.* **1.** of, relating to, or suitable for a funeral. **2.** sad; gloomy; dismal: *a funereal atmosphere.* [Latin *fūnereus*, from *fūnus* burial, death.] **—fu·ne′re·al·ly**, *adv.*

fun·gal (fung′gəl) *adj.* of, relating to, or caused by fungus: *a fungal disease.* Also, **fungous.** [FUNGI- + AL.]

fun·gi (fun′jī, fung′gī) a plural of **fungus.**

fungi- *also*, **fung-.** *combining form* fungus: *fungicide.*

fun·gi·cide (fun′jə sīd′) *n.* any substance used in destroying fungi or inhibiting their growth. [FUNGI- + -CIDE[2].] **—fun′gi·cid′al**, *adj.*

fun·go (fung′gō) *n., pl.* **-goes.** *Baseball.* in fielding practice, a high fly ball that a player throws into the air and hits before it falls to the ground. [Of uncertain origin.]

fun·goid (fung′goid) *adj.* resembling or characteristic of fungi.

fun·gous (fung′gəs) *adj.* fungal. [Latin *fungōsus* spongy, from *fungus*. See FUNGUS.]

fun·gus (fung′gəs) *n., pl.* **-gi** or **-gus·es. 1.** any of a kingdom of living things that lack chlorophyll, vascular tissue, and mobility, live as parasites or saprophytes, and reproduce sexually or asexually. A fungus usually consists of a network of filaments to which are attached reproductive bodies that in some instances, as the mushroom, are the most conspicuous part. **2.** something that springs up or spreads rapidly like a mushroom. **3.** *Medicine.* **a.** a fungal infection. **b.** a diseased, spongy growth on the body. *—adj.* fungal. [Latin *fungus* mushroom, fungous excrescence on the skin, possibly from Greek *sphongos, spongos* sponge.]

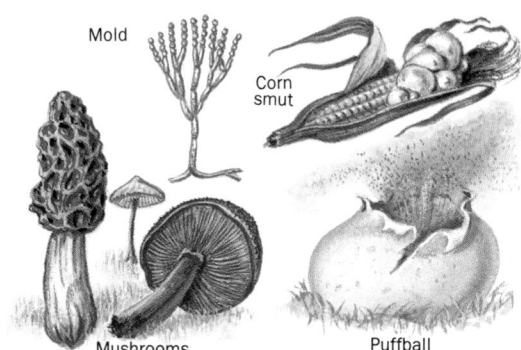

Mold

Corn smut

Mushrooms

Puffball

types of **fungi**

fu·nic·u·lar (fū nik′yə lər) *n.* a railway system in which two cars attached to both ends of a cable along a steep slope move alternately up and down the slope by counterbalancing and pulling each other. Also, **funicular railway.** *—adj.* of or relating to such a system. [Latin *fūniculus* small rope, diminutive of *fūnis* rope + -AR[1].]

funk (fungk) *Informal. n.* **1.** a state of cowardly fear or panic.

a	at	e	end	o	hot	u	up	hw	white		about
ā	ape	ē	me	ō	old	ū	use	ng	song		taken
ä	far	i	it	ô	fork	ü	rule	th	thin	ə	pencil
âr	care	ī	ice	oi	oil	u̇	pull	th	this		lemon
		î	pierce	ou	out	ûr	turn	zh	measure		circus

503

2. a person who cowers with fear; coward. **3.** a state of depression or moodiness. —*v.t.* **1.** to be afraid of. **2.** to shrink from or try to evade (something) through fear. —*v.i.* to shrink from or try to evade something through fear. [Possibly from Flemish *fonck* fear.]

funk·y¹ (fung′kē) *adj.,* **funk·i·er, funk·i·est.** *Informal.* in a state of funk; fearful; panicky. [Probably from Low German origin.]

funk·y² (fung′kē) *adj.,* **funk·i·er, funk·i·est. 1.** having the deeply felt, emotional quality of the blues: *funky music.* **2.** *Slang.* unconventional, offbeat, or odd: *funky clothes.* [Of uncertain origin.] —**funk′i·ness,** *n.*

fun·nel (fun′əl) *n.* **1.** a utensil with a tube at one end and a wide, cone-shaped mouth at the other, used to facilitate pouring a substance into a container with a small opening. **2.** a cylindrical chimney or smokestack, as on a steamship or locomotive. **3.** something shaped like a funnel. —*v.,* **-neled, -nel·ing;** *also, British,* **-nelled, -nel·ling.** —*v.t.* to cause (something) to pass through or as through a funnel. —*v.i.* to pass through or as through a funnel: *The water funneled down the drainpipe.* [Provençal *fonilh* this utensil, from Late Latin *fundibulum,* short for Latin *infundibulum,* going back to *in* in + *fundere* to pour.]

fun·nies (fun′ēz) *pl. n.* **1.** comic strips. **2.** the section of a newspaper containing them.

fun·ny (fun′ē) *adj.,* **-ni·er, -ni·est. 1.** causing laughter or amusement; comical: *a funny joke.* **2.** *Informal.* not usual; strange or suspicious; odd: *The stranger was behaving in a funny way.* **3.** *Informal.* involving deceit or fraud: *The criminals printed and tried to circulate funny money.* [FUN + -Y¹.] —**fun′ni·ly,** *adv.* —**fun′ni·ness,** *n.* —For Synonyms, see **humorous.**

funny bone, the part of the elbow where the ulnar nerve passes very close to the skin. When it is struck, a sharp, tingling sensation is felt.

funny papers, funnies *(def. 2).*

fur (fûr) *n.* **1.** the soft, thick, hairy coat of the skin of certain animals. **2.a.** a piece of animal skin with such a coat, prepared for use in garments, rugs, and other items. **b.** such skins collectively. **3.** an article of apparel, as a coat, made of such skin. **4.** a coating of furlike foul matter, as on the tongue in illness. —*v.t.,* **furred, fur·ring. 1.** to cover, trim, or line with fur. **2.** to apply furring to (a wall or floor) in order to make a level surface or create air spaces. [Old French *forrer* to encase, sheathe, from *forre* sheath, case; of Germanic origin.] —**fur′less,** *adj.* —**fur′like′,** *adj.*

fur·be·low (fûr′bə lō′) *n.* **1.** a frill, ruffle, or similar ornamentation, esp. on women's clothing. **2.** *also,* **furbelows.** any showy or superfluous ornamentation. —*v.t.* to furnish or ornament with furbelows. [Modification of dialectal French *farbella* flounce; of uncertain origin.]

fur·bish (fûr′bish) *v.t.* **1.** to make bright by rubbing; polish; burnish: *We furbished the old armor.* **2.** to restore to a fresh or usable condition; renovate (often with *up*): *to furbish up the storefronts in an old part of town.* [Old French *forbiss-,* a stem of *forbir* to polish; of Germanic origin.] —**fur′bish·er,** *n.* —**fur′bishment,** *n.*

fur·fur·al (fûr′fə ral′, -fyə-) *n.* a colorless, liquid organic chemical with an almondlike odor, used esp. in the production of certain plastics and nylon, and as an industrial solvent. Formula: $C_5H_4O_2$

Fu·ries (fyūr′ēz) *n.* in classical mythology, three hideous female spirits who punished wrongdoers. Also, **Erinyes, Eumenides.**

fu·ri·ous (fyūr′ē əs) *adj.* **1.** extremely angry; enraged: *I was furious that they left without me.* **2.** extremely violent or intense: *a furious thunderstorm.* **3.** very great, as in intensity or speed: *They raced down the highway at a furious speed.* [Old French *furieux* given over to rage or madness, from Latin *furiōsus* full of rage, from *furia* rage, madness.] —**fu′ri·ous·ly,** *adv.* —**fu′ri·ous·ness,** *n.*

furl (fûrl) *v.t.* to roll up and secure, as to a staff or mast: *to furl a flag.* —*v.i.* to become furled. —*n.* **1.** the act of furling or the state of being furled. **2.** a rolled-up section, as of a flag. [Old French *ferl(i)er* to tie tightly, from *fer(m)* tight (from Latin *firmus* strong) + *lier* to bind (from Latin *ligāre*).]

fur·long (fûr′lông) *n.* a measure of distance equal to ⅛ of a mile (0.2 kilometer) or 220 yards (201 meters). [Old English *furlang* literally, length of a furrow, from *furh* furrow + *lang* long, tall; because in early times in England the length of a furrow was used as a unit of measure.]

fur·lough (fûr′lō) *n.* **1.** an official leave of absence from duty, esp. in the armed services. **2.** a document authorizing such a leave of absence. —*v.t.* **1.** to grant a furlough to. **2.** to dismiss from work, esp. temporarily. [Dutch *verlof* leave².]

furn. 1. furnished. **2.** furniture.

fur·nace (fûr′nis) *n.* **1.** a structure or apparatus containing an enclosed chamber for the production of intense heat, as for heating buildings, melting metals, or generating steam power: *a blast furnace producing pure molten iron.* **2.** any extremely hot place. [Old French *fornais* large oven, from Latin *fornāx* oven.]

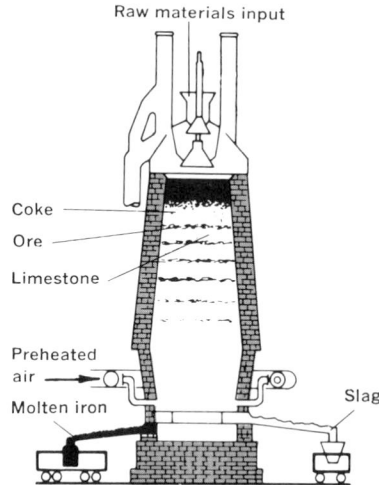

blast **furnace**

fur·nish (fûr′nish) *v.t.* **1.** to equip with furniture, fixtures, appliances, or the like: *The newlyweds furnished their home.* **2.** to provide with whatever is necessary or needed; supply: *The supply sergeant furnished the soldiers with uniforms and gear. The book furnished us with facts.* [Old French *forniss-,* a stem of *fornir* to supply; of Germanic origin.] —**fur′nish·er,** *n.*

Synonyms Furnish, equip, supply¹, and **provide** mean to make available whatever is needed. **Furnish** connotes fitting out with essentials for a particular purpose: *to furnish an expedition with tents, to furnish a room for use as an office.* **Equip** implies providing materials that will improve functioning or increase efficiency: *to equip a boat with the newest type of radar.* **Supply** suggests making available on a regular basis: *to supply local high school teams with athletic clothing.* **Provide** suggests that the materials or services in question will be ready and available when needed: *We can provide the hospitals with electricity if an emergency arises.*

fur·nish·ings (fûr′ni shingz) *pl. n.* **1.** furniture, fixtures, or appliances, as for a house or office. **2.** articles of clothing and accessories.

fur·ni·ture (fûr′ni chər) *n.* **1.** movable articles, as tables, chairs, or beds, used to prepare a room for occupancy or use. **2.** any necessary equipment, as for a ship or factory. [French *fourniture* furnishing, supplying, from *fournir* to supply, provide; of Germanic origin.]

fu·ror (fyūr′ôr) *also,* **fu·rore.** *n.* **1.** a great outburst of enthusiasm or excitement; commotion. **2.** frenzy; rage. [Latin *furor* rage, madness.]

furred (fûrd) *adj.* **1.** having or wearing fur. **2.** made, trimmed, or lined with fur. **3.** coated with furlike foul matter, as the tongue.

fur·ri·er (fûr′ē ər) *n.* a person who deals in or works with furs.

fur·ri·er·y (fûr′ē ə rē) *n., pl.* **-er·ies. 1.** furs collectively. **2.** the business or work of a furrier.

fur·ring (fûr′ing) *n.* **1.** fur trimming or lining. **2.** thin strips of wood or metal fastened, as to walls or floors, to make a level surface or to provide air spaces.

fur·row (fûr′ō, fur′ō) *n.* **1.** a long, narrow groove or channel made in the ground by a plow. **2.** anything resembling this, as a rut or wrinkle: *furrows in one's brow, furrows in a dirt road.* —*v.t.* **1.** to make a furrow or furrows in, as with a plow. **2.** to make deep wrinkles in. —*v.i.* to become furrowed or wrinkled. [Old English *furh* channel made by a plow.]

fur·ry (fûr′ē) *adj.,* **-ri·er, -ri·est. 1.** made of or resembling fur. **2.** covered with or wearing fur. **3.** furred *(def. 3).* —**fur′ri·ness,** *n.*

fur seal, any of several eared seals, genera *Callorhinus* and *Arctocephalus,* having soft, dense underfur.

fur·ther (fûr′thər) *adj.* a comparative of **far**. **1.** being an added amount; additional; more: *without further delay.* **2.** more distant or remote in time, space, or degree; farther: *on the further side.* —*adv.* a comparative of **far**. **1.** at or to a more distant or remote point in time or space: *to move further away.* **2.** to a greater degree or extent; more: *to inquire further into a problem.* **3.** in addition; moreover. —*v.t.* to help forward; promote: *to further the cause of peace.* [Old English *furthra* before, and *furthor* to a more advanced point, more (comparative of *forth* forwards, hence).]

Usage Traditionally, **farther** has been used more commonly than **further** in referring to physical distance: *I cannot walk any farther.* **Further** rather than **farther** has been more common in the sense of "additional" or "more": *There will be no further discussion of the matter.* Recently, however, the use of **further** in both senses has grown more frequent.

fur·ther·ance (fûr′thər əns) *n.* the act of furthering; advancement; promotion: *the furtherance of a project.*

fur·ther·more (fûr′thər môr′) *adv.* in addition; moreover; besides.

fur·ther·most (fûr′thər mōst′) *adj.* furthest.

fur·thest (fûr′thist) *adv.* a superlative of **far**. **1.** at or to the most distant or remote point in time or space. **2.** to the greatest degree or extent; most. —*adj.* (a superlative of **far**) most distant or remote in time, space, or degree. [Superlative of FORTH, formed as a result of taking FURTHER as the comparative of *forth*.]

fur·tive (fûr′tiv) *adj.* **1.** done by stealth; secret; surreptitious: *a furtive glance.* **2.** shifty; sly: *furtive eyes.* [Latin *fūrtīvus* stolen, secret, going back to *fūr* thief.] —**fur′tive·ly,** *adv.* —**fur′tive·ness,** *n.*

fu·run·cle (fyŭr′ung kəl) *n.* boil². [Latin *fūrunculus* petty thief, boil, diminutive of *fūr* thief.]

fu·ry (fyŭr′ē) *n., pl.* **-ries. 1.** extreme, uncontrollable anger. **2.** a fit of such anger. **3.** great force; violence; fierceness: *the fury of a storm.* **4.** a person of fierce or uncontrollable temper. **5. Fury.** one of the Furies. [Old French *furie* madness, rage, from Latin *furia*.]

· **like fury.** *Informal.* violently or very rapidly; furiously: *The tornado roared into town like fury. We rushed like fury to rescue the horses from the burning barn.*

furze (fûrz) *n.* any of a group of spiny shrubs, genus *Ulex*, of the pea family, found in Europe, Asia, and parts of North America, bearing yellow flowers and usually small, scalelike leaves. Also, **gorse, whin.** [Old English *fyrs*.]

fuse¹ (fūz) *n.* **1.** *also,* **fuze.** a safety device, consisting of a strip of metal encased in a container, that is inserted in an electric circuit. The strip will melt and break the circuit if the current becomes excessive. **2.** *also,* **fuze.** a length of cord or tubing filled or saturated with combustible material, used to ignite an explosive charge. **3.** fuze. [Italian *fuso* spindle, shaft, from Latin *fūsus* spindle.]

· **to blow a fuse.** *Informal.* to become extremely angry.

fuse² (fūz) *v.t., v.i.,* **fused, fus·ing. 1.** to liquefy, esp. by heating; melt. **2.** to blend or unite by or as by melting together. [Latin *fūsus,* past participle of *fundere* to melt, cast (metal), pour out.]

fu·see (fū zē′) *also,* **fuzee.** *n.* **1.** a friction match with a large head that will burn in a wind. **2.** a red or green flare used as a railroad signal. [Old French *fusee* spindleful, going back to Latin *fūsus* spindle.]

fu·se·lage (fū′sə läzh′, -lij, -zə-) *n.* the main body of an airplane, accommodating the passengers, cargo, and crew. [French *fuselage,* from *fuselé* spindle-shaped, from *fuseau* spindle, going back to Latin *fūsus.*]

fu·sel oil (fū′zəl, -səl) a colorless, poisonous oily liquid consisting largely of amyl alcohol, produced as a by-product of grain fermentation. [German *Fusel* bad liquor + OIL.]

fu·si·bil·i·ty (fū′zə bil′i tē) *n.* **1.** the quality of being fusible. **2.** the degree of this quality.

fu·si·ble (fū′zə bəl) *adj.* capable of being fused or melted.

fu·si·form (fū′zə fôrm′) *adj.* tapering from the middle toward each end; spindle-shaped. [Latin *fūsus* spindle + -FORM.]

fu·sil (fū′zəl) *n.* a light flintlock musket. [French *fusil* musket; earlier, steel for a tinderbox, going back to Latin *focus* hearth.]

fu·sil·ier (fū′zə lir′) *also,* **fu·sil·eer.** *n.* **1.** a soldier of any of several regiments of the British army. **2.** formerly, a soldier armed with a fusil. [French *fusilier* soldier armed with a musket, from *fusil* musket. See FUSIL.]

fu·sil·lade (fū′sə läd′, -läd′, -zə-) *n.* **1.** a simultaneous or continuous discharge of firearms. **2.** anything resembling this: *a fusillade of rain, a fusillade of criticism.* —*v.t.,* **-lad·ed, -lad·ing.** to attack or shoot down by a fusillade. [French *fusillade* discharge of firearms, from *fusiller* to shoot, from *fusil* musket. See FUSIL.]

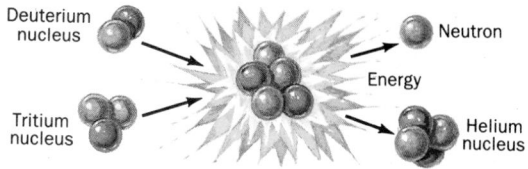

fusion of hydrogen isotopes

fu·sion (fū′zhən) *n.* **1.** the act or process of fusing; melting together: *the fusion of metals.* **2.** the state or condition of being fused: *metals in fusion.* **3.** a union or blending together of different things, as a coalition of political parties. **4.** something that is formed by fusing; fused mass. **5.** a popular music that combines two or more styles, esp. a combination of jazz and another style. **6.** *Physics.* the combining of two light nuclei to form a heavier nucleus. It occurs naturally in the sun, where it continually releases vast amounts of energy, and artificially in the explosion of a hydrogen bomb. [Latin *fūsiō* a pouring out, melting.]

fusion bomb, hydrogen bomb.

fuss (fus) *n.* **1.** an unnecessary or excessive display, as of excitement, attention, or activity: *They spoiled their children by making a fuss over them. There was a great fuss in the convention hall when the president appeared.* **2.** a slight quarrel or dispute; spat: *The children had a fuss over the game's rules.* **3.** a protest or objection: *There will be a fuss if the train is late again.* —*v.i.* **1.** to make an unnecessary or excessive display, as of excitement, attention, or activity: *The cook fussed over dinner.* **2.** to have a slight quarrel or dispute: *The children fussed over which television program to watch.* **3.** *Informal.* to complain or fret: *The baby fussed to be picked up.* **4.** *Informal.* to scold: *Don't fuss at me.* [Possibly imitative.] —**fuss′er,** *n.*

fuss·budg·et (fus′buj′it) *n.* *Informal.* a person who fusses; fussy person.

fuss·y (fus′ē) *adj.,* **fuss·i·er, fuss·i·est. 1.** hard to please; finicky: *She is very fussy about what she eats.* **2.** requiring much attention to details: *a fussy matter.* **3.** elaborately made or trimmed: *a fussy dress.* **4.** given to fussing: *a fussy baby.* —**fuss′i·ly,** *adv.* —**fuss′i·ness,** *n.*

fus·tian (fus′chən) *n.* **1.** any of various heavy cotton fabrics with a thick nap resembling corduroy or moleskin. **2.** a coarse, heavy fabric made of cotton and linen, or a similar fabric made of wool, used for clothing in Europe during the Middle Ages. **3.** pompous, pretentious writing or speech; bombast. —*adj.* **1.** made of fustian. **2.** pompous; bombastic. [Old French *fustaine* coarse cotton cloth, from Medieval Latin *fustaneum,* possibly from Arabic *fūstat* Fostat, a suburb of Cairo, where this type of cloth was first made.]

fus·tic (fus′tik) *n.* **1.** a yellow, brown, or green dye made from the wood of a tree, *Chlorophora tinctoria.* **2.** the yellowish wood that yields this dye. **3.** the tree itself, native to the West Indies and South and Central America. [Spanish *fustoc* this wood, from Arabic *fustuq* pistachio tree, from Greek *pistakē,* from Persian *pistā* pistachio nut.]

fust·y (fus′tē) *adj.,* **fust·i·er, fust·i·est. 1.** having a stale smell; musty; moldy. **2.** old-fashioned in appearance or behavior; not up-to-date. [Old French *fuste* odor of a cask, from *fust* tree trunk, cask, from Latin *fūstis* stick, staff.] —**fust′i·ly,** *adv.* —**fust′i·ness,** *n.*

fu·tile (fū′təl, -tīl) *adj.* **1.** having no chance for success; useless or hopeless; ineffective; vain: *The party factions made futile efforts at reaching an agreement.* **2.** of little importance; trifling; frivolous. [Latin *fūtilis* that pours out easily, worthless.] —**fu′tile·ly,** *adv.* —For Synonyms, see **vain.**

fu·til·i·ty (fū til′i tē) *n., pl.* **-ties. 1.** the quality of being futile. **2.** something that is futile.

a	at	e	end	o	hot	u	up	hw	white		about
ā	ape	ē	me	ō	old	ū	use	ng	song		taken
ä	far	i	it	ô	fork	ü	rule	th	thin	ə	pencil
âr	care	ī	ice	oi	oil	ū	pull	th	this		lemon
				îr	pierce	ou	out	ûr	turn	zh	measure		circus

fu·ton (fü'ton) *n.* a Japanese bed quilt or mattress, traditionally placed on the floor for sleeping. It can also be used on a wooden frame. [Japanese *futon.*]

fut·tock (fut'ək) *n.* one of the curved timbers that forms a compound rib in the frame of a wooden ship. [Of uncertain origin.]

fu·ture (fū'chər) *adj.* **1.** that is to be or happen in time to come: *a future occurrence.* **2.** *Grammar.* indicating or expressing time to come: *a future tense.* —*n.* **1.** time that is to come: *In the future, please call if you're going to be late.* **2.** something that will be or happen in time to come: *No one can predict the future.* **3.** an opportunity of success or prosperity in time to come: *There is a good future in that business.* **4. futures.** commodities bought and sold for future receipt or delivery. [Old French *futur* what is to come, from Latin *fūtūrus* about to be, future participle of *esse* to be.]

future life, the existence of the soul after death.

future perfect 1. a verb tense expressing an action or state of being that is completed before a specified time in the future. In the sentence *By six o'clock they will have finished the work,* the phrase *will have finished* is in the future perfect tense. **2.** a verb in this tense.

future tense 1. a verb tense expressing future action. In the sentence *We will see you on Saturday,* the phrase *will see* is in the future tense. **2.** a verb in this tense.

fu·tur·ism (fū'chə riz'əm) *also,* **Fu·tur·ism.** *n.* a movement in art and literature originating in Italy early in the twentieth century and marked by a rejection of traditional forms in order to express the intensity and dynamic energy of the modern, mechanical age. —**fu'tur·ist;** *also* **Fu'tur·ist,** *n., adj.*

fu·tur·is·tic (fū'chə ris'tik) *adj.* of or relating to the future or futurism. —**fu'tur·is'ti·cal·ly,** *adv.*

fu·tu·ri·ty (fū tūr'i tē, -tyùr'-, -chùr'-) *n., pl.* **-ties. 1.** the future. **2.** the state or quality of being future. **3.** a future event or prospect.

fuze (fūz) *n.* **1.** *also,* **fuse.** a device for detonating a bomb or torpedo. **2.** fuse[1] *(defs. 1, 2).*

fu·zee (fū zē') fusee.

fuzz[1] (fuz) *n.* fine, loose particles, hair, or fibers: *peach fuzz.* —*v.t., v.i.* to make or become fuzzy. [From FUZZY.]

fuzz[2] (fuz) *n.* *Slang.* **1.** the police. **2.** a police officer. [Of uncertain origin.]

fuzz·bust·er (fuz'bus'tər) *n.* *Slang.* an electronic device used in an automobile to detect the use of radar by police measuring the speed of vehicles. [FUZZ[2] + BUST[2] + -ER[1].]

fuzz·y (fuz'ē) *adj.,* **fuzz·i·er, fuzz·i·est. 1.** having or covered with fuzz. **2.** resembling fuzz. **3.** not clear; indistinct; blurred: *fuzzy recollections, fuzzy thinking.* [Possibly from Low German *fussig* loose, spongy.] —**fuzz'i·ly,** *adv.* —**fuzz'i·ness,** *n.*

-fy *suffix* **1.** to cause to be or become; make: *nullify, pacify.* **2.** to become: *solidify.* **3.** to make similar to: *countrify.* [French *-fier,* from Latin *-ficāre,* going back to *facere* to do, make.]

fyl·fot (fil'fot) *n.* swastika. [Possibly modification of *fill foot;* with reference to *filling* the *foot,* or lower part, of a painted window with a design. See FILL, FOOT.]

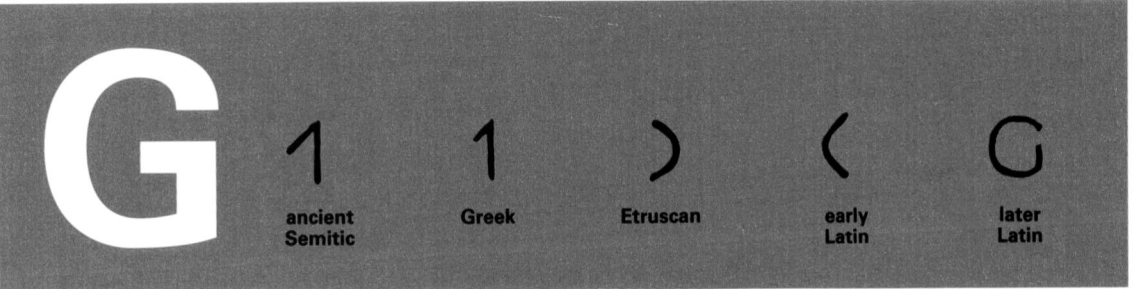

ancient Semitic	Greek	Etruscan	early Latin	later Latin

G The modern letter **G** has its roots in the earliest alphabets. The oldest form of **G** was *gimel*, the third letter of the ancient Semitic alphabets. In the ninth century B.C., *gimel* was adopted by the Greeks, who called it *gamma*. Both *gimel* and *gamma* represented a hard *g* sound, as in the English word *game*. The Etruscans borrowed *gamma* and, because they made no distinction between a hard *g* and a *k*, used it to represent both sounds, as did the early Romans. Later, the Latin letter **C** came to represent only the *k* sound, and a new letter was formed, by adding a short line to the **C**, to represent the hard *g* sound. This letter was the predecessor of our modern capital **G**, which is almost identical to it in shape. As Old French words entered the English language, the letter **G** also came to represent the soft *g* sound, as in the word *gentle*.

g, G (jē) *n., pl.* **g's, G's. 1.** the seventh letter of the English alphabet. **2.** the shape of this letter or something having this shape.

G (jē) *n., pl.* **G's. 1.** *Music.* **a.** the fifth note or tone of the diatonic scale of C major. For illustration, see **do²**. **b.** the scale or key that has this note or tone as its tonic. **2.** a unit of measurement of the force exerted on a body undergoing acceleration. One G is equal to the acceleration of gravity at sea level, approximately 32.2 feet (9.7 meters) per second. **3.** *Slang.* one thousand dollars: *We bought the car for four G's.*

g 1. *also,* **g.** gram; grams. **2.** gravity.

g. 1. gauge. **2.** guinea.

G 1. German. **2.** good. **3.** specific gravity.

G. 1. German. **2.** Gulf.

Ga, the symbol for gallium.

Ga., Georgia.

GA 1. the postal abbreviation for Georgia. **2.** *also,* **G.A.** General Assembly.

gab (gab) *Informal. v.i.,* **gabbed, gab·bing.** to talk idly or excessively; chatter. —*n.* idle or excessive talk; chatter. [Probably imitative.] —**gab′ber,** *n.*
•**gift of gab,** the ability to speak fluently or glibly.

GABA (gab′ə) *n.* an amino acid that acts as an inhibitory neurotransmitter, preventing the transmission of impulses between nerve cells. [Short for *g(amma-)a(mino)b(utyric) a(cid)*.]

gab·ar·dine (gab′ər dēn′) *n.* **1.a.** a durable, closely woven fabric, having diagonal ribs on its surface, used for such items as sportswear, coats, and suits. **b.** a garment made of this fabric. **2.** gaberdine *(def. 1).* [Form of GABERDINE.]

gab·ble (gab′əl) *v.,* **-bled, -bling.** —*v.i.* to talk rapidly, foolishly, or incoherently; jabber. —*v.t.* to utter (something) rapidly or incoherently. —*n.* rapid, foolish, or incoherent talk. [GAB + -LE.] —**gab′bler,** *n.*

gab·bro (gab′rō) *n., pl.* **-bros.** a dark, basic, plutonic rock composed of labradorite feldspar and augite. [Italian *gabbro,* from Latin *glaber* bare, smooth, bald.] —**gab·bro·ic** (ga brō′ik), *adj.*

gab·by (gab′ē) *adj.,* **-bi·er, -bi·est.** *Informal.* very talkative; loquacious.

gab·er·dine (gab′ər dēn′) *n.* **1.** a loose cloak or smock, esp. one worn by men in the Middle Ages. **2.** gabardine *(def. 1).* [Spanish *gabardina* coarse frock (probably once worn by pilgrims), probably going back to Middle High German *wallevart* pilgrimage, from Old High German *wallōn* to wander + *vart* journey.]

ga·bi·on (gā′bē ən) *n.* **1.** a wicker cylinder filled with earth and stones, formerly used in military fortifications. **2.** a cylinder, usually of metal, filled with stones, used in constructing foundations, as for dams, jetties, and bridges. [French *gabion* the wicker cylinder, from Italian *gabbione* large cage, going back to Latin *cavea* cage, den.]

ga·ble (gā′bəl) *n.* **1.** the outside section of wall surface, usually triangular, between the sides of a sloped roof, extending from the level of the eaves to the ridgepole. **2.** an end wall of a gable section. **3.** any architectural feature having the form of a gable, as over a door or window. [Old French *gable* pediment of a house, from Old Norse *gafl* end of a ridged roof with the triangular piece of wall sheltered by it.]

ga·bled (gā′bəld) *adj.* having or built with a gable or gables.

gable roof, a ridged roof that forms a gable at either one or both ends.

Ga·bri·el (gā′brē əl) *n.* in Jewish, Christian, and Islamic Scriptures and tradition, an archangel appointed by God as his divine messenger.

gable roof

gad¹ (gad) *v.i.,* **gad·ded, gad·ding.** to move about restlessly or aimlessly, as in search of fun or excitement; roam: *The tourists gadded about Paris.* [Possibly from obsolete *gadling* companion, from Old English *gædeling*.] —**gad′der,** *n.*

gad² (gad) *n.* a goad, esp. for driving cattle. [Old Norse *gaddr* goad.]

Gad (gad) *also,* **gad.** *interj.* God. ➡ used as a mild oath.

gad·a·bout (gad′ə bout′) *n. Informal.* a person who moves about restlessly or aimlessly, esp. in search of fun or excitement.

gad·fly (gad′flī′) *n., pl.* **-flies. 1.** any of various large blood-sucking flies, esp. those of the family Tabanidae, such as the horsefly, that bite animals, esp. horses and cattle. **2.** a person who persistently annoys, irritates, or stirs up others: *a political gadfly.* [GAD² + FLY¹.]

gadg·et (gaj′it) *n. Informal.* a small mechanical or electronic device or contrivance. [Of uncertain origin.]

gadg·et·ry (gaj′i trē) *n.* **1.** small mechanical or electronic devices; gadgets: *radio gadgetry.* **2.** the invention, construction, or use of gadgets: *Gadgetry is an outgrowth of technology.*

gad·o·lin·ite (gad′ə lə nīt′) *n.* a dark brown or black silicate mineral made up of iron and several rare-earth elements, including gadolinium.

gad·o·lin·i·um (gad′ə lin′ē əm) *n.* a magnetic metallic element, one of the rare-earth elements. Symbol: **Gd** For tables, see **element.** [Modern Latin *gadolinium,* from earlier *gadolinia,* from Johan Gadolin, 1760-1852, Finnish chemist.]

gad·wall (gad′wôl′) *n., pl.* **-walls** or **-wall.** a North American freshwater duck, *Anas strepera,* the male of which is mostly gray with a white belly and the female mottled brown. Average length: 20 inches (51 centimeters).

gae (gā) a past tense of **gie.**

Gae·a (jē′ə) *also,* **Gaia.** *n.* in Greek mythology, the earth goddess who was the mother and wife of Uranus and mother of the Cyclopes and Titans.

Gael (gāl) *n.* **1.** Highlander *(def. 2a).* **2.** a Celt of Scotland, Ireland, or the Isle of Man. [Scottish Gaelic *Gàidheal*.]

a	at	e	end	o	hot	u	up	hw	white		about
ā	ape	ē	me	ō	old	ū	use	ng	song		taken
ä	far	i	it	ô	fork	ü	rule	th	thin	ə	pencil
âr	care	ī	ice	oi	oil	u̇	pull	th	this		lemon
				îr	pierce	ou	out	ûr	turn	zh	measure		circus

G

Gael·ic (gā′lik) *adj.* of or relating to the Gaels or their languages. —*n.* any of the Celtic languages of the Gaels, esp. those traditionally spoken in Ireland or Scotland.

Words from Irish and Scottish Gaelic

Irish Gaelic and Scottish Gaelic are Gaelic languages that belong to the Celtic language group of the Indo-European language family. These Gaelic languages should not be confused with Irish, the dialect of English spoken in Ireland, or Scottish, the dialect of English spoken in Scotland. Below is a selection of words that have entered English from or through Irish Gaelic or Scottish Gaelic.

balbriggan	colleen	leprechaun	shamrock
banshee	donnybrook	loch	shillelagh
blarney	drumlin	pibroch	slogan
bog	dulse	pillion	smithereens
brogan	galore	plaid	Tory
brogue²	gillie	ptarmigan	trousers
claymore	glen	raid	whiskey

---

gaff (gaf) *n.* **1.a.** a large, sharp hook at the end of a pole, used to help pull large fish out of the water. **b.** a pole equipped with such a hook. **2.** a sharp metal spur fastened to the leg of a gamecock. **3.** a spar for extending the upper edge of a fore-and-aft sail. —*v.t.* to hook or land (a fish) with a gaff. [French *gaffe* a fishing gaff, from Provençal *gaf* boat hook.]
•**to stand the gaff.** *Slang.* to bear up well, as under hardship, ridicule, or punishment.

gaffe (gaf) *n.* a social blunder; faux pas. [French *gaffe* a fishing gaff, blunder. See GAFF.]

gaf·fer (gaf′ər) *n.* **1.** an old man. **2.** an electrician who is responsible for the lighting of the set of a motion-picture or television production. [Modification of GODFATHER.]

gag (gag) *n.* **1.** something stuffed into or put over the mouth to prevent a person from talking or crying out. **2.** any restraint or suppression of freedom of speech. **3.** *Informal.* **a.** an amusing act or remark; joke. **b.** a prank or practical joke. —*v.t.*, **gagged, gag·ging.** —*v.t.* **1.a.** to prevent from speaking or crying out by means of a gag: *The kidnappers gagged and bound their victims.* **b.** to put a gag into or over (the mouth) to prevent from speaking or crying out. **2.** to restrain or suppress freedom of speech; silence: *The government gagged the revolutionary newspaper.* **3.** to cause to choke or retch. —*v.i.* to heave with nausea; choke or retch. [Imitative.] —**gag′ger,** *n.*

gage¹ (gāj) *n.* **1.** something given as security that an obligation or promise will be fulfilled; pledge. **2.** something, as a glove thrown on the ground by a knight, used to issue a challenge to fight. **3.** any challenge. —*v.t.*, **gaged, gag·ing.** *Archaic.* to offer as a pledge or security; stake; wager. [Old French *gage* pledge; of Germanic origin.]

gage² (gāj) *n.* gauge. —*v.t.*, **gaged, gag·ing.** gauge. [Form of GAUGE.] —**gag′er,** *n.*

gag·gle (gag′əl) *n.* **1.** a flock of geese. **2.** a group; cluster: *A gaggle of photographers waited for the rock stars to arrive.* [Middle English *gagyl* a flock, from *gagelen* to cackle.]

gag·man (gag′man′) *n., pl.* **-men** (-men′). **1.** a person who writes jokes or makes up comic routines for entertainers. **2.** a comedian who uses jokes or comic routines.

Gai·a (jē′ə) Gaea.

gai·e·ty (gā′i tē) *also,* **gayety.** *n., pl.* **-ties. 1.** the quality or state of being gay; cheerfulness. **2.** merrymaking; festivity: *the gaieties of the city during the holiday season.* **3.** brightness or showiness, as of dress; finery. [Old French *gaiete* mirth, from *gai* merry. See GAY.]

gai·ly (gā′lē) *also,* **gayly.** *adv.* in a gay manner.

gain (gān) *v.t.* **1.** to obtain, as by effort or striving; get; secure: *to gain the advantage in an argument, to gain time by stalling.* **2.** to get or develop as an increase, addition, advantage, or profit: *to gain momentum, to gain weight, to gain strength.* **3.** (of a timepiece) to run fast by (a specified amount): *My watch gains three minutes each day.* **4.** to win over to one's side, esp. by persuasion (often with *over*): *to gain new allies.* **5.** to obtain in competition or combat; win: *They gained the battle but lost many soldiers.* **6.** to attract: *I couldn't gain the attention of our waiter.* **7.** to get to; arrive at; reach: *The ship gained the port before the storm struck.* —*v.i.* **1.** to improve, progress, or advance; make progress: *The patient appears to be gaining.* **2.** to acquire advantage or wealth; profit: *The corrupt mayor hoped to gain by the scheme.* **3.** to advance nearer, as to an opponent in a race; come closer (often with *on* or *upon*): *The black horse is gaining on the brown one.* **4.** to increase in weight; become heavier. —*n.* **1.** something that

is gained, as an increase, addition, advantage, or profit: *The recovering patient had a ten-pound gain in weight. Our gain was their loss.* **2. gains.** something that is acquired, such as profits, earnings, or winnings. **3.** the act of gaining; acquisition. **4.** the acquisition of wealth: *the love of gain.* **5.** *Electronics.* a measure of increase in signal strength, expressed as the ratio of output to input. [Old French *gaigner* win; of Germanic origin.]

Synonyms	*v.t.* **Gain, acquire, secure,** and **obtain** mean to get something. **Gain** generally connotes getting something advantageous or valuable: *to gain a friend, to gain access to important information.* **Acquire** may connote sustained effort, or simply serve as a more formal word for *buy: to acquire a good reputation, to acquire a piece of property.* **Secure** more strongly implies making sure one has possession: *to secure a crucial document, to secure a commitment from a buyer.* **Obtain** implies seeking out, perhaps with effort: *After going to several auto supply stores, I finally obtained the part I needed for my car.*

gain·er (gā′nər) *n.* **1.** a person or thing that gains. **2.** a dive in which the diver leaves the board in the forward position and then spins backward toward the diving board.

gain·ful (gān′fəl) *adj.* bringing or producing gain; profitable; lucrative: *gainful employment.* —**gain′ful·ly,** *adv.* —**gain′ful·ness,** *n.*

gain·ly (gān′lē) *adj.,* **-li·er, -li·est.** having grace of movement or form; graceful, shapely, or comely: *the gainly stride of a thoroughbred.* [Middle English *geinli,* from *gein* suitable, from Old Norse *gegn* straight, suitable.]

gain·say (gān′sā′) *v.t.,* **-said** (-sād′, -sed′), **-say·ing. 1.** to deny, contradict, or dispute. **2.** to speak or act against; oppose. [Obsolete *gain-* against (from Old Norse *gegn*) + SAY.] —**gain′say′er,** *n.*

gainst (genst; *British* gānst) *also,* **'gainst.** *prep. Archaic.* against.

gait (gāt) *n.* **1.** a particular manner of moving on foot: *The child walked with a slow and easy gait.* **2.** one of the particular ways in which a horse steps or runs, as a trot or canter. [Old Norse *gata* way, path.]

gait·ed (gā′tid) *adj.* **1.** having a particular gait. ➡ used in combination, as in *slow-gaited horses.* **2.** trained when to use a gait or gaits: *a gaited horse.*

gai·ter (gā′tər) *n.* **1.** a covering for the top of a shoe, the ankle, and sometimes the lower leg, similar to a puttee or spats, and made of cloth or leather. **2.** a shoe with elastic inserts on the sides. **3.** an overshoe with a cloth top. [French *guêtre*; probably of Germanic origin.]

gal (gal) *n. Informal.* a girl or woman. [A form of GIRL.]

gal *also,* **gal.** gallon; gallons.

Gal., Galatians.

ga·la (gā′lə, gal′ə) *adj.* of, relating to, or suitable for a festive occasion; festive: *Their anniversary was marked with a gala celebration.* —*n.* a festive occasion or celebration, esp. one with special entertainment. [Italian *gala* festivity, finery, from Spanish *gala* court dress, from Arabic *khil'a* robe presented as an honor by an Oriental ruler.]

ga·lac·tic (gə lak′tik) *adj.* of or relating to a galaxy or galaxies, esp. the Milky Way. [Greek *galaktikos* milky, from *gala* milk.]

ga·lac·tose (gə lak′tōs, -tōz) *n.* a white sugar obtained from lactose. Formula: $C_6H_{12}O_6$ [Greek *galakt-,* stem of *gala* milk + -OSE².]

ga·la·go (gə lā′gō, -lä′-) *n.* bush baby.

Gal·a·had (gal′ə had′) **1. Sir Galahad.** in Arthurian legend, the son of Lancelot and Elaine, the purest and most virtuous knight of the Round Table. According to one account, he was the only knight to find the Holy Grail. **2.** any man of great purity and nobility.

gal·an·tine (gal′ən tēn′) *n.* a dish made with meat, esp. white meat, or fish that is boned, stuffed, and poached, and then chilled and served with its own jelly. [French *galantine,* from Old French *galantine* sauce for fish, going back to Latin *gelātus* frozen, past participle of *gelāre* to freeze.]

Gal·a·te·a (gal′ə tē′ə) *n.* in Greek legend, a statue of a maiden carved by Pygmalion, who then fell in love with it. Aphrodite brought the statue to life in response to Pygmalion's prayers.

Ga·la·tians (gə lā′shənz) *n.* a book of the New Testament, consisting of an Epistle written by the Apostle Paul to the Christians of Galatia. ➡ used as singular.

gal·a·vant (gal′ə vant′) gallivant.

ga·lax (gā′laks) *n.* an evergreen plant, genus *Galax,* native to the southeastern United States, having shiny leaves and small, white flowers, often grown as a ground cover or for use in floral decorations. [Modern Latin *galax,* probably from Greek *galaktos,* genitive of *gala* milk; because of its white flowers.]

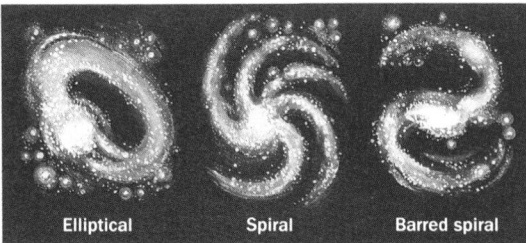

three types of **galaxies**

gal·ax·y (gal′ək sē) *n., pl.* **-ax·ies.** **1.** any of the vast groupings of stars and other celestial bodies, dust, and gases scattered throughout the universe. **2.** *also,* **Galaxy.** Milky Way. **3.** a brilliant or splendid group: *The opening of the show was attended by a galaxy of celebrities.* [Old French *galaxie* the Milky Way, from Latin *galaxiās,* from Greek *galaxiās (kyklos)* milky white (circuit), Milky Way, from *gala* milk.]

gale¹ (gāl) *n.* **1.** a very strong wind, esp. one having a velocity of from 32 to 63 miles (51 to 101 kilometers) per hour. **2.** a noisy outburst, as of laughter. [Of uncertain origin.]

gale² (gāl) *n.* sweet gale. [Old English *gagel.*]

ga·le·na (gə lē′nə) *n.* a gray metallic mineral consisting of lead sulfide, a major ore of lead. It is found in association with other minerals, esp. silver and zinc. Formula: PbS Also, **ga·le·nite** (gə lē′nīt). [Latin *galēna* lead ore.]

Gal·i·le·an (gal′ə lē′ən) *adj.* of, relating to, or characteristic of Galilee or its people. —*n.* **1.** a native or inhabitant of Galilee. **2.** **the Galilean.** Jesus.

gall¹ (gôl) *n.* **1.** bile *(def. 1).* **2.** something bitter or unpleasant: *the gall of disappointment.* **3.** bitterness of feeling; rancor. **4.** *Informal.* impudence; nerve; effrontery: *They had the gall to insult their grandparents.* [From Middle English *galle,* from Old English *gealla* bile, probably from Latin *galla* gallnut.]

gall² (gôl) *v.t.* **1.** to make sore by rubbing or chafing. **2.** to annoy or irritate greatly; vex: *It galled her to hear him insult her friend.* —*v.i.* to become sore or chafed. —*n.* **1.** a sore spot on the skin caused by rubbing or chafing. **2.** a cause, instance, or state of great annoyance or irritation. [Old English *gealla* sore spot on skin, probably from Latin *galla* gallnut.]

gall³ (gôl) *n.* an abnormal growth or swelling on a plant, usually caused by insects, fungi, or other plant parasites. [Old French *galle,* from Latin *galla* gallnut.]

gal·lant (*adj., defs. 1, 3, 4* gal′ənt; *adj., def. 2, n.,* gə lant′, -länt′, gal′ənt) *adj.* **1.** brave or noble in spirit or conduct; heroic: *a gallant soldier, a gallant knight.* **2.** characterized by politeness and attentiveness to women; courtly. **3.** grand; imposing; stately: *Our royal, good, and gallant ship* (Shakespeare, *The Tempest*). **4.** gay or showy, as in dress. —*n.* **1.** a chivalrous, brave, or noble man. **2.** a fashionable or dashing young man. **3.** a man who is particularly polite and attentive to women. **4.** a suitor or lover. [Old French *galant* brave, gay, present participle of *galer* to make merry, rejoice, from *gale* mirth, pleasure; of Germanic origin.]

gal·lant·ry (gal′ən trē) *n., pl.* **-ries.** **1.** bravery or nobility of spirit or conduct; heroism: *The soldier received a medal for gallantry in combat.* **2.** courtly politeness and attentiveness to women. **3.** a courtly action or speech: *to exchange a few gallantries with the lady* (Charles Dickens, 1838).

gall·blad·der (gôl′blad′ər) *also,* **gall bladder.** *n.* a small, muscular sac that is attached to the liver and in which bile is stored and concentrated.

gal·le·ass (gal′ē as′) *n.* a large, three-masted galley propelled by both oars and sails, used chiefly as a war vessel in the Mediterranean in the fifteenth to seventeenth centuries. [Old French *galeace,* from Italian *galeazza* large galley, from Italian *galea* galley, from Medieval Latin *galea.* See GALLEY.]

galleon

gal·le·on (gal′ē ən, gal′yən) *n.* a large, square-rigged, usually four-masted sailing ship with a square stern and usually three or four decks, used for both commerce and warfare, esp. by Spain, in the fifteenth to seventeenth centuries. [Spanish *galeón,* from Medieval Latin *galea.* See GALLEY.]

gal·ler·y (gal′ə rē, gal′rē) *n., pl.* **-ler·ies.** **1.** a narrow platform or passage, usually roofed and open on one side, projecting from the interior or exterior wall of a building; balcony. **2.a.** a room or building where works of art are exhibited or sold. **b.** a business or institution that exhibits or sells works of art. **c.** a collection of works of art for exhibition. **3.** a platform or floor projecting from the rear interior wall or side of a building, providing additional seating capacity, esp. the highest of a series of such floors in a theater, usually containing the cheapest seats. **4.a.** the part of the audience occupying the highest gallery of a theater. **b.** the part of the general public regarded as unrefined or uninformed. **5.** any group of spectators or listeners: *The gallery applauded when the golfer made a difficult putt.* **6.** a long, narrow room or passage; hall; corridor. **7.** a covered walk or porch, wholly or partially open on one side, the roof of which is supported by pillars; portico. **8.** a room or other wholly or partially enclosed area used for a particular activity, such as target shooting or photography. **9.** an underground passage, as in a mine or an animal's burrow. [Old French *galerie* long room, from Medieval Latin *galeria* long portico; of uncertain origin.]

• **to play to the gallery.** to do something or act in a manner designed, often crudely or obviously, to appeal to the general public, esp. that part of it regarded as unsophisticated or uninformed.

gal·ley (gal′ē) *n., pl.* **-leys.** **1.** a long, low ship of ancient and medieval times, propelled chiefly by a row or rows of oars on either side, and sometimes also by sails. **2.** the kitchen of a ship or airplane. **3.** *Printing.* **a.** galley proof. **b.** a long, shallow tray for holding type that has been set. [Old French *galie* large ship, from Medieval Latin *galea* large, fast ship, from Middle Greek *galaia*; of uncertain origin.]

galley proof *Printing.* a proof made from type set by the printer before it is composed into pages, used esp. for making corrections in the printed matter, originally printed from type set in a galley. Also, **galley.**

galley slave **1.** a slave or convict condemned to row in a galley. **2.** a person who does wearying, tedious, or menial work; drudge.

gall·fly (gôl′flī′) *n., pl.* **-flies.** any of various insects whose eggs, when deposited in plant tissue, cause galls to be formed.

Gal·lic (gal′ik) *adj.* of, relating to, or characteristic of Gaul or France or their people. [Latin *Gallicus* relating to the Gauls, from *Gallus* a Gaul.]

gal·lic acid (gal′ik) an organic compound obtained from galls on certain plants or produced synthetically, used esp. in making ink and dyes. Formula: $C_7H_6O_5 \cdot H_2O$

Gal·li·cism (gal′ə siz′əm) *also,* **gal·li·cism.** *n.* an idiom, form of expression, custom, trait, or the like peculiar to the French people or language.

gal·li·gas·kins (gal′i gas′kinz) *pl. n.* **1.** loose trousers, esp. loose breeches or hose worn in the sixteenth and seventeenth centuries. **2.** leggings. [Earlier *garragascoyne,* from Old French *garguesque,* form of *greguesque* type of hose or breeches associated with Venice, Grecian, from Italian *grechesca,* short for *alla grechesca* in the Grecian manner, from *greco* Greek, from Latin *Graecus;* influenced in form by *galley* and *Gascony* because associated with sailors' hose and Gascony respectively. See GREEK.]

gal·li·na·ceous (gal′ə nā′shəs) *adj.* of or relating to an order, Galliformes, of typically terrestrial birds, such as pheasants, grouse, partridges, and all domestic fowl. [Latin *gallīnāceus* relating to poultry, from *gallīna* hen, from *gallus* cock¹.]

gall·ing (gô′ling) *adj.* extremely annoying; irritating; exasperating: *a galling defeat.*

gal·li·nule (gal′ə nūl′, -nül′) *n.* any of several long-toed wading birds of the rail family, of temperate and tropical regions, having a small head, slender body, and typically green, blue, or black plumage, such as the **common gallinule,** or **moorhen,** *Gallinula chloropus.* Length: 12-14 inches (30-36 centimeters). [Latin *gallīnula* chicken, diminutive of *gallīna* hen, from *gallus* cock¹.]

gal·li·pot (gal′ə pot′) *n.* a small, glazed earthenware jar, used esp. by druggists for ointments and other medicines. [GALLEY + POT; possibly because this type of pottery was once transported in galleys.]

gal·li·um (gal′ē əm) *n.* a rare, bluish white metallic element, found in aluminum ore and zinc ore, having a very low melting point (30 degrees Celsius), used as a substitute for mercury in high-temperature thermometers. Symbol: **Ga** For tables, see **element.** [Modern Latin *gallium,* from Latin *gallus* cock¹, a transla-

a	at	e	end	o	hot	u	up	hw	white		about
ā	ape	ē	me	ō	old	ū	use	ng	song	ə	taken
ä	far	i	it	ô	fork	ü	rule	th	thin		pencil
âr	care	ī	ice	oi	oil	u̇	pull	th	this		lemon
				ir	pierce	ou	out	ûr	turn	zh	measure		circus

tion of part of the name of its discoverer, *Lecoq* de Boisbaudran, 1838-1912, French chemist.]

gal·li·um ar·se·nide (är′sə nīd′, -nid) a widely used semiconductor combining gallium and arsenic. Formula: GaAs

gal·li·vant (gal′ə vant′) *also,* **galavant.** *v.i.* to wander about or travel in search of fun or excitement; gad. [Possibly modification of GALLANT.]

gall·nut (gôl′nut′) *n.* a nutlike gall, esp. on oaks.

gal·lon (gal′ən) *n.* a liquid measure of capacity, in the United States equal to 4 quarts, 231 cubic inches, or 128 fluid ounces (3.8 liters). The British imperial gallon is equal to 277.42 cubic inches or 160 fluid ounces (4.8 liters). [Old French *galon, jalon,* probably from Medieval Latin *galeta* jug, liquid measure; of uncertain origin.]

gal·lon·age (gal′ə nij) *n.* an amount expressed in gallons.

gal·loon (gə lün′) *n.* a narrow band of braid, lace, or other trimming, often made with metallic thread. [French *galon,* from *galonner* to adorn with lace; of uncertain origin.]

gal·loot (gə lüt′) galoot.

gal·lop (gal′əp) *n.* **1.** the fastest gait of a horse or other four-footed animal, in which all four feet are off the ground at the same time during each leaping stride. **2.** a ride or run at a gallop: *They took one gallop around the field before going back to the barn.* **3.** any rapid pace or action. —*v.i.* **1.** to ride or move at a gallop: *The zebra galloped away from the lion.* **2.** to go or act very fast; hurry; race: *The children galloped home from school.* —*v.t.* **1.** to cause to gallop: *The trainer galloped the horse around the track.* [Old French *galoper* to go at a gallop; of Germanic origin.] —**gal′lop·er,** *n.*

gal·lows (gal′ōz) *n., pl.* **-lows** or **-lows·es. 1.** a framework, usually consisting of upright beams supporting a crossbar from which criminals are hanged. Also, **gallows tree. 2.** the punishment of death by hanging: *to be sentenced to the gallows.* [Old English *gealga.*]

gallows humor, humor that makes fun of a serious, painful, or catastrophic situation.

gallows tree, gallows *(def. 1).*

gall·stone (gôl′stōn′) *n.* a small, hard mass that sometimes forms in the gallbladder or its ducts. When a gallstone blocks the flow of bile through a duct, it produces severe pain.

gall wasp, any of a group of small hymenopterous insects, family Cynipidae, the larvae of which produce galls in oaks and roses.

ga·loot (gə lüt′) *also,* **galloot.** *n. Slang.* a rough or awkward person. [Of uncertain origin.]

gal·op (gal′əp) *n.* **1.** a lively dance in two-four time. **2.** a piece of music composed for or in the rhythm characteristic of this dance. [French *galop,* from *galoper* to dance a galop, run very fast; of Germanic origin.]

ga·lore (gə lôr′) *adj.* in large or plentiful amounts. ➡ appears after the noun or nouns it modifies: *The table was covered with food and drink galore.* [Irish *go leōr* sufficiently; literally, to sufficiency.]

ga·losh (gə losh′) *n.* a rubber overshoe reaching above the ankle, usually worn in wet or snowy weather. [Old French *galoche* wooden shoe (worn over silk shoes by the nobles in medieval France), probably from Late Latin *gallicula* Gallic shoe, from Latin *gallica (solea)* Gallic (sandal).]

gals *also,* **gals.** gallons.

gal·van·ic (gal van′ik) *adj.* **1.** of or relating to direct electric current, esp. such produced by chemical action; voltaic. **2.** relating to or having the characteristics of a reaction to an electric shock; startling; convulsive. —**gal·van′i·cal·ly,** *adv.*

gal·va·nism (gal′və niz′əm) *n.* **1.** direct current electricity produced by chemical action. **2.** *Medicine.* the therapeutic application of a direct electric current to the human body. [French *galvanisme* such electricity, from Italian *galvanismo,* from Luigi *Galvani,* 1737-98, Italian physician and physicist who experimented with electricity and animals.]

gal·va·nize (gal′və nīz′) *v.t.,* **-nized, -niz·ing. 1.** to cover (metal, esp. iron or steel) with a protective coating of zinc. **2.** to rouse suddenly into action; startle; excite: *The unexpected news galvanized them into action.* **3.** to stimulate by the application of electric current. —**gal′va·ni·za′tion,** *n.*

gal·va·nom·e·ter (gal′və nom′i tər) *n.* an instrument for detecting and measuring a small electric current and determining the direction of its flow. [GALVANIC + -METER.] —**gal·va·no·met·ric** (gal′və nō met′rik, -və nə-), *adj.* —**gal′va·nom′e·try,** *n.*

gam·bit (gam′bit) *n.* **1.** in chess, an opening move in which a pawn or other piece is risked or sacrificed to gain some advantage. **2.** any opening move or maneuver designed to gain an advantage.

[French *gambit* chess opening, from Spanish *gambito,* from Italian *gambetto* a tripping up, from *gamba* leg. See GAMBOL.]

gam·ble (gam′bəl) *v.,* **-bled, -bling.** —*v.i.* **1.** to play games of chance for stakes, esp. money. **2.** to risk something of value with the hope of making a gain; wager. **3.** to take a risk: *The hikers gambled when they decided to carry less water.* —*v.t.* **1.** to bet or wager (something of value): *She gambled her paycheck on the horse race.* **2.** to lose or squander by gambling (usually with *away*): *He gambled away his fortune.* —*n.* any risky or uncertain undertaking: *Investing in the stock was a bad gamble. Driving in the snow was a gamble we had to take.* [Probably modification of Middle English *gamenen* to play at games, from Old English *gamenian* to play, sport.] —**gam′bler,** *n.*

gam·boge (gam bōj′, -büzh′) *n.* a gum resin obtained from any of various tropical trees, genus *Garcinia,* used as a yellow pigment and in veterinary medicine as a cathartic. [Modern Latin *gambogium,* from *Cambodia,* where the resin is found.]

gam·bol (gam′bəl) *v.i.,* **-boled, -bol·ing;** *also, British,* **-bolled, -bol·ling.** to run, skip, or leap about in play; frolic: *The children loved to gambol in the woods.* —*n.* a running, skipping, or leaping about in play; frolic. [Earlier *gambad(e), gambold,* from French *gambade* leap, spring, from Italian *gambata* kick, from *gamba* leg, from Late Latin *gamba* hoof, leg, going back to Greek *kampē* bend, joint.]

gam·brel (gam′brəl) *n.* **1.** the hock of a horse or similar animal. **2.** gambrel roof. [Dialectal Old French *gamberel* crooked stick, from *gambe* leg, from Late Latin *gamba* hoof, leg. See GAMBOL.]

gambrel roof, a ridged roof having two slopes on each side, the lower slope being steeper than the upper.

gambrel roof

game¹ (gām) *n.* **1.** a form of playing; diversion; pastime; amusement: *Hopscotch is a children's game. What we took seriously was only a game to them.* **2.** a form of mental or physical competitive play, governed by specific rules, and testing the skill, endurance, or luck of the participants: *the game of baseball, the game of bridge.* **3.a.** a single match between two opposing players or teams: *Our school won the football game.* **b.** one of several divisions in a fixed series or number of contests: *The tennis player won the first game of the set.* **4.** the score at any given point in a competition: *In the third inning the game was two to two.* **5.** the number of points required for winning a game: *In squash, game is fifteen.* **6.** the materials or equipment used in playing certain games: *They bought several toys and games for their children.* **7.** a particular manner of playing or degree of ability shown in a competition: *Her tennis game is excellent.* **8.** *Informal.* any proceeding, vocation, activity, or undertaking, esp. one involving some risk: *the game of diplomacy.* **9.** a plan, scheme, or trick designed to gain an end: *They spoiled his little game by exposing him as an impostor.* **10.** wild animals, birds, or fish hunted or caught for sport or for food: *zebra, antelope, and other game.* **11.** the flesh of such animals used for food. **12.** something that is hunted or pursued; quarry; prey: *The hounds got nearer to their game.* —*adj.,* **gam·er, gam·est. 1.** having a fighting spirit; plucky and resolute: *a game fighter.* **2.** *Informal.* having enough spirit or will; ready: *Are you game for a swim in the cold water?* **3.** of, relating to, or hunted or fished for as game: *a game preserve.* —*v.i.,* **gamed, gam·ing.** to play games of chance for money or other stakes; gamble. [Old English *gamen* sport, amusement.]

• **the game is up.** the plan, scheme, or the like has failed or will fail.

• **to make game of.** to make fun of; ridicule; tease.

• **to play games.** to act so as to deceive, manipulate, or trifle with another or others: *After he gave several evasive answers, she felt he was playing games with her.*

• **to play the game.** *Informal.* to act in accordance with the rules, expected behavior, custom, or propriety.

game² (gām) *adj.* lame or injured: *a game leg.* [Of uncertain origin.]

game·cock (gām′kok′) *n.* a rooster bred and trained for cockfighting.

game fish, a fish that puts up a fight when hooked, providing sport for the person fishing.

game fowl 1. a fowl of any of several breeds trained for cockfighting. **2.** any fowl that is hunted as game.

game·keep·er (gām′kē′pər) *n.* a person employed to breed, protect, and care for game, esp. on private lands.

game laws, laws to protect and conserve game by limiting the size and number that may be killed or caught and by restricting hunting and fishing seasons.

game·ly (gām′lē) *adv.* in a plucky manner; courageously.

game·ness (gām′nis) *n.* the condition of being plucky and resolute; fighting spirit.

game plan 1. *Sports.* the strategy devised for or used in winning a particular game or match. **2.** any plan, scheme, or other strategy for gaining an end: *The candidate's election game plan called for placing ads on radio and television.*

game show, a television or radio program featuring a game in which contestants compete for prizes.

games·man·ship (gāmz′mən ship′) *n.* **1.** the art or practice of winning a game by using strategies that are of questionable sportsmanship but not strictly illegal. **2.** the art of using ethically questionable strategies to gain one's ends.

game·some (gām′səm) *adj.* full of or ready for fun; playful; frolicsome. —**game′some·ly,** *adv.* —**game′some·ness,** *n.*

game·ster (gām′stər) *n.* a person who gambles; gambler.

gam·ete (gam′ēt, gə mēt′) *n. Biology.* either of two mature reproductive cells, the sperm or the ovum, capable of uniting to form a zygote; germ cell. [Modern Latin *gameta,* from Greek *gametē* wife, and *gametēs* husband.]

game theory, a branch of applied mathematics dealing with situations of conflict involving a choice of strategies, as in warfare or economics. It seeks to determine the strategy that best maximizes gain and minimizes loss.

ga·met·ic (gə met′ik) *adj.* of, relating to, or derived from a gamete or gametes. [GAMETE + -IC.]

ga·me·to·cyte (gə mē′tə sīt′) *n. Biology.* a cell that produces gametes. [GAMETE + Greek *kytos* hollow vessel.]

ga·me·to·gen·e·sis (gə mē′tə jen′ə sis) *n. Biology.* the production of gametes. [GAMETE + GENESIS.] —**ga·me′to·gen′ic,** *adj.*

ga·me·to·phyte (gə mē′tə fīt′) *n. Botany.* a plant or a generation in the life cycle of a plant that produces sex cells, or gametes.
➡ distinguished from **sporophyte.** [GAMETE + -PHYTE.]

game warden, a public official who enforces the hunting and fishing laws in a given district.

gam·in (gam′in) *n.* **1.** a neglected or homeless child left to roam about the streets; urchin. **2.** gamine *(def. 2).* [French *gamin* boy, urchin; of uncertain origin.]

gam·ine (gam′ēn, -in) *n.* **1.** a neglected or homeless girl left to roam about the streets. **2.** a small or slight, charmingly pert and spirited girl. [French *gamine* girl of the streets; of uncertain origin.]

gam·ing (gā′ming) *n.* the act or practice of playing games of chance for money or other stakes; gambling.

gam·ma (gam′ə) *n.* the third letter of the Greek alphabet (Γ, γ), corresponding to the English letter *G, g.*

gamma globulin, any of a group of proteins in blood plasma. Most gamma globulins are antibodies that protect the body against a recurrence of certain diseases, as measles or polio. An injection of gamma globulins can be used for immunization against such diseases.

gamma ray, electromagnetic radiation similar to the X ray but of shorter wavelength and greater penetrating power, given off by nuclei of radioactive atoms. It is used for such purposes as detection of internal defects in metal casting and welded structures.

gam·mer (gam′ər) *n.* an old woman. [Probably modification of GODMOTHER or GRANDMOTHER.]

gam·mon (gam′ən) *n.* **1.** a smoked or cured ham. **2.** the lower end of a side of bacon. [Dialectal Old French *gambon* ham, from *gambe* leg. See GAMBREL, GAMBOL.]

gam·o·pet·al·ous (gam′ə pet′ə ləs) *adj. Botany.* (of a flower) having the petals wholly or partially united, as the morning glory. Also, **sympetalous.** [Greek *gamos* marriage + PETAL + -OUS.]

gam·o·sep·al·ous (gam′ə sep′ə ləs) *adj. Botany.* (of a flower) having the sepals wholly or partially united. [Greek *gamos* marriage + SEPAL + -OUS.]

-gamous *combining form* marrying or uniting sexually: *exogamous, bigamous.* [Greek *gamos* marriage + -OUS.]

gam·ut (gam′ət) *n.* **1.** the entire range, scope, or extent of anything: *the gamut of emotions from ecstasy to despair.* **2.** the entire series of recognized notes or tones in modern music. **3.** the major diatonic scale. [From Medieval Latin *gamma,* the note below *a* in the musical scale of Guido d'Arezzo, 991?-1050?, + *ut* (now called DO²), another old name for the first note of the scale. The names of the notes of the scale apparently came from syllables in a Latin hymn, *ut* queant laxis *re*sonare fibris, *Mi*ra gestorum *fa*muli tuorum, *Sol*ve polluti *la*bi reatum, Sancte *Io*hannes.]

gam·y (gā′mē) *adj.,* **gam·i·er, gam·i·est. 1.** having the taste or smell of game, esp. game that has been kept uncooked until

slightly spoiled. **2.** having a fighting spirit; plucky and resolute. —**gam′i·ly,** *adv.* —**gam′i·ness,** *n.*

-gamy *combining form* marriage or sexual union: *monogamy, polygamy.* [Greek *-gamia,* from *gamos* marriage.]

gan (gan) a past tense and past participle of **gin⁴.**

gan·der (gan′dər) *n.* **1.** an adult male goose. **2.** *Slang.* a look, esp. a longish one: *Take a gander at this new car.* [Old English *gandra* male goose.]

gang¹ (gang) *n.* **1.** a group of people organized or associated together for illegal or disreputable purposes: *The bank was held up by a gang of robbers.* **2.** a group of laborers working together under one foreman; crew. **3.** a group of people who are friends and who associate together regularly: *Our gang went to the party after the football game.* **4.** a group of youths, esp. from one neighborhood, who band together and typically engage in acts of juvenile delinquency. **5.** any group or band: *A gang of reporters gathered around the mayor.* **6.** a set of tools or machines designed to work together. —*v.t.* **1.** to arrange in or as in a gang: *The captain ganged the sailors together. Several illustrations were ganged to be printed at one time.* **2.** to attack as a group. —*v.i. Informal.* to form or act as a gang (often with *up*): *The townspeople ganged together to clean up the dump.* [Old Norse *gangr* a going.]
·**to gang up on.** *Informal.* to attack or oppose together: *The wolves ganged up on the weakened buck.*

gang² (gang) *v.i. Scottish.* to go or walk. [Old English *gangan.*]

gan·gling (gang′gling) *adj.* awkwardly tall and thin; gangly; lank. [Possibly a modification of Scottish *gangrel* a wandering beggar, from Middle English *gangrel;* of Germanic origin.]

gan·gli·on (gang′glē ən) *n., pl.* **-gli·a** (-glē ə) or **-gli·ons. 1.** a group of nerve cell bodies outside the brain or spinal cord. **2.** a center of force, activity, or energy: *That scene is the chief ganglion of the tale* (Robert Louis Stevenson, 1882). [Greek *ganglion* tumor on a tendon.] —**gan′gli·on′ic,** *adj.*

gan·gly (gang′glē) *adj.,* **-gli·er, -gli·est.** awkwardly tall and thin; gangling. [Modification of GANGLING.]

gang·plank (gang′plangk′) *n.* a movable bridge between a ship and a wharf, used for boarding or leaving the ship. Also, **gangway.**

gang plow, a set of plows or plowshares that are designed to operate together.

gan·grene (gang′grēn, gang grēn′) *n.* the death and decay of body tissue caused when the blood supply is cut off or as a result of certain bacterial infections. —*v.,* **-grened, -gren·ing.** —*v.t.* to cause gangrene in. —*v.i.* to become affected with gangrene. [Latin *gangraena* cancerous ulcer, from Greek *gangraina.*] —**gan·gre·nous** (gang′grə nəs), *adj.*

gang·ster (gang′stər) *n.* a member of a gang of criminals.

gangue (gang) *n.* worthless rock that contains an ore deposit and that must be mined along with the ore and then separated from the ore minerals. [French *gangue,* from German *gang* vein of a metal, passage.]

gang·way (*n.,* gang′wā′; *interj.,* gang′wā′) *n.* **1.** a passageway. **2.** *Nautical.* **a.** a passageway on either side of the upper deck of a ship. **b.** an opening in the side of a ship for boarding passengers or loading freight. **c.** gangplank. —*interj.* get out of the way; make room.

gan·net (gan′it) *n.* any of various web-footed seabirds, genus *Morus,* of coastal islands and waters of most temperate regions, having a long, pointed bill and predominantly white plumage and capable of prolonged flight. Length: to 40 inches (102 centimeters). [Old English *ganot.*]

gan·oid (gan′oid) *adj.* of or relating to a large group, Ganoidei, of primitive, bony fishes, including sturgeon and gar, many of which have hard scales of bone overlaid with an enamellike substance. —*n.* a ganoid fish. [French *ganoïde* ganoid fish, from Greek *ganos* brightness.]

gant·let¹ (gônt′lit, gant′-) gauntlet¹.

gant·let² (gônt′lit, gant′-) gauntlet².

gan·try (gan′trē) *n., pl.* **-tries. 1.** a framework consisting of a horizontal bridge fixed to upright supports, which may be stationary or mounted on wheels. Gantries are used to support traveling cranes, winches, and railroad signals. **2.** a scaffold mounted on tracks for mobility and used to assemble and service a large rocket on its launching pad. [Possibly modification of Old French *gan-*

G

a	at	e	end	o	hot	u	up	hw	white		about
ā	ape	ē	me	ō	old	ū	use	ng	song		taken
ä	far	i	it	ô	fork	ü	rule	th	thin	ə	pencil
âr	care	ī	ice	oi	oil	u̇	pull	th	this		lemon
		ir	pierce	ou	out	ûr	turn	zh	measure		circus

tier, chantier wooden frame for barrels, from Latin *canthērius* rafter, trellis, ass, possibly from Greek *kanthēlios* pack ass.]

gantry crane, a crane mounted on a gantry.

Gan·y·mede (gan′ə mēd′) *n.* in Greek mythology, a beautiful youth who was a favorite of Zeus and cupbearer to the Olympian gods.

gaol (jāl) *British. n., v.t.* jail. —**gaol′er,** *n.*

gap (gap) *n.* **1.** a break, crack, or opening, as in a wall. **2.** a deep ravine or pass through a mountain ridge. **3.a.** an unfilled part or empty space, as between teeth. **b.** spark gap. **4.** a break in continuity; hiatus: *There were gaps of a week or more in the diary.* **5.** a wide difference or divergence, as of opinion, character, or ideas: *There is a large gap between their political philosophies.* —*v.,* **gapped, gap·ping.** —*v.i.* to form a gap or opening. —*v.t.* to make a gap or opening in. [Old Norse *gap* chasm.]

gape (gāp, gap) *v.i.* **gaped, gap·ing. 1.** to stare with or as if with the mouth open, as in wonder or surprise (often with *at*): *The children gaped at the acrobats' performance.* **2.** to open the mouth wide, as when yawning. **3.** to open or be opened wide, so as to form or have a gap or hole: *The earth split and gaped during the earthquake.* —*n.* **1.** the act or an instance of gaping: *a child's wide-eyed gape, a deep gape in the cave floor.* **2. the gapes. a.** a fit of yawning. **b.** a disease of birds and poultry, caused by a parasitic worm, the gapeworm, that infests the trachea, producing gasping and choking. ➡ used as singular in def. 2b. [Old Norse *gapa* to open the mouth.] —**gap′er,** *n.* —**gap′ing·ly,** *adv.*

gape·worm (gāp′wûrm, gap′-) *n.* a nematode worm, *Syngamus trachea,* that causes the gapes in birds.

gar (gär) *n., pl.* **gars** or **gar.** any of a group of predatory fish, order Semionotiformes, usually found in shallow, weedy waters of eastern North and Central America, having elongated jaws and a long, narrow body covered with bony scales. Length: to 12 feet (3.7 meters). Also, **garfish, garpike.** [Old English *gār* spear; probably because of its shape.]

GAR also, **G.A.R.** Grand Army of the Republic.

ga·rage (gə räzh′, -räj′; *British* gar′ij) *n.* **1.** a building or part of a building where motor vehicles are kept, repaired, or serviced. **2.** a business establishment that repairs or services motor vehicles. —*v.t.,* **-raged, -rag·ing.** to put or keep in a garage. [French *garage* place for storage, storing away, from Middle French *garer* to take care, protect; of Germanic origin.]

garage sale, a sale of used or unwanted personal or household items, usually held in the seller's garage or yard. Also, **yard sale.**

Gar·and rifle (gar′ənd) a .30 caliber, gas-operated, automatic or semiautomatic rifle used by U.S. ground troops in World War II. [From American inventor John C. *Garand,* 1888-1974, who was its designer.]

garb (gärb) *n.* **1.** clothing or attire, esp. a particular or distinctive form of dress: *military garb.* **2.** outward appearance, form, or covering: *the principal's customary garb of strictness.* —*v.t.* to clothe; dress: *The parents had garbed the child in a stylish outfit.* [Middle French *garbe* grace, good fashion, from Italian *garbo* grace; of Germanic origin.]

gar·bage (gär′bij) *n.* **1.** waste material, esp. animal or vegetable matter that has been thrown away, such as food scraps from a kitchen. **2.** anything worthless or offensive: *The book you're reading is garbage.* [Of uncertain origin.]

garbage disposal, a machine that is attached to a sink and disposes of garbage by grinding it up to be carried away with the wastewater.

gar·ban·zo (gär bän′zō) *n., pl.* **-zos.** chickpea.

gar·ble (gär′bəl) *v.t.,* **-bled, -bling. 1.** to confuse or mix up unintentionally: *He garbled the telephone message.* **2.** to make unfair selections from (facts or a text) in order to give a false impression or distort: *The debater garbled her opponent's argument to make it seem illogical.* —*n.* the act or an instance of garbling: *The message was such a garble that no one could understand it.* [Italian *garbellare* to sift, from Arabic *gharbala,* going back to Latin *crībrum* sieve.] —**gar′bler,** *n.*

gar·çon (gȧʀ sôɴ′) *n., pl.* **-çons** (-sôɴ′). *French.* **1.** a waiter. ➡ usually used as a form of address. **2.** a boy or young man. **3.** a male servant.

gar·den (gär′dən) *n.* **1.** a plot of ground where flowers, vegetables, herbs, or other small plants are cultivated. **2.** a fertile, well-cultivated area or region. Also, **garden spot. 3.** also, **gardens.** a park or other piece of ground used by the public for recreation or amusement. —*adj.* **1.** of, relating to, or grown in a garden: *garden vegetables.* **2.** common; ordinary: *an unexciting performance by an actor of the garden variety.* —*v.i.* to cultivate or work in a garden. —*v.t.* to cultivate as a garden: *We garden*

the lot behind our house. [Dialectal Old French *gardin* plot of ground with plants; of Germanic origin.]

garden apartment 1. a ground-floor apartment with an adjoining garden. **2.** an apartment building having landscaped grounds and only two or three stories of units.

gar·den·er (gärd′nər) *n.* a person who cultivates or tends a garden, lawn, or other grounds professionally or as a hobby: *an avid weekend gardener.*

gar·de·nia (gär dēn′yə, -dē′nē ə) *n.* **1.** a fragrant yellow or white flower of any of a group of shrubs and small trees, genus *Gardenia,* having waxy, dish-shaped petals, as the evergreen cape jasmine, *G. jasminoides,* often grown commercially for corsages. **2.** the shrub or tree bearing this flower, having shiny oval leaves, widely cultivated in many parts of the world. [Modern Latin *Gardenia,* from Alexander *Garden,* 1730-91, Scottish naturalist.]

Garden of Eden, in the Bible, the original home of Adam and Eve. Also, **Eden.**

garden spot, garden *(n.,* def. 2).

gar·den-va·ri·e·ty (gär′dən və rī′i tē) *adj.* regularly seen or experienced; not unusual or exotic; ordinary: *The unknown bird that caused so much excitement turned out to be a garden-variety sparrow.*

Gar·eth (gar′ith) *n.* in Arthurian legend, a knight of the Round Table, brother of Sir Gawain, and nephew of King Arthur.

gar·fish (gär′fish′) *n., pl.* **-fish** or **-fish·es.** gar.

gar·gan·tu·an (gär gan′chü ən) *also,* **Gar·gan·tu·an.** *adj.* of enormous size; gigantic; huge: *a gargantuan redwood tree.* [*Gargantua* giant in *Gargantua and Pantagruel,* by the French satirist François Rabelais, 1494-1553, + -AN.]

gar·get (gär′git) *n.* an inflammation of the udder in cows, ewes, and other domestic mammals. [Old French *gargate* throat, gullet; of imitative origin.]

gar·gle (gär′gəl) *v.,* **-gled, -gling.** —*v.i.* to wash or rinse the mouth or upper portion of the throat with a liquid kept in motion by an exhalation of the breath. —*v.t.* **1.** to use (a liquid) for gargling: *to gargle salt water.* **2.** to wash or rinse (the throat or mouth) by gargling. —*n.* a liquid used for gargling. [French *gargouiller* to gurgle, from Old French *gargouille* throat; of imitative origin.]

gar·goyle (gär′goil) *n.* **1.** a waterspout in the form of a grotesque human or animal figure, projecting from the gutter of a building to throw off rainwater. **2.** a decorative figure on a building resembling this. [Old French *gargouille* throat, waterspout; of imitative origin.]

gar·ish (gâr′ish, gar′-) *adj.* excessively or tastelessly bright or ornate; glaring, gaudy, or flashy. [Of uncertain origin.] —**gar′ish·ly,** *adv.* —**gar′ish·ness,** *n.*

gar·land (gär′lənd) *n.* a wreath or rope of flowers, leaves, vines, or other materials. —*v.t.* to decorate with or form into a garland or garlands. [Old French *garlande* the wreath; of uncertain origin.]

gar·lic (gär′lik) *n.* **1.** the strong-tasting bulb of a plant, *Allium sativum,* of the amaryllis family, used as an herb. The bulb is composed of separate sections called cloves. **2.** the plant itself, widely cultivated in most parts of the world,

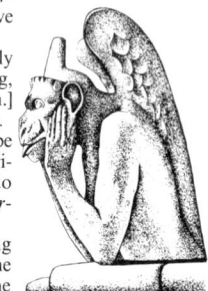

gargoyle *(def. 2)*

having long, flat, ridged leaves and bearing clusters of small pink or purple flowers. [Old English *gārlēac* the plant, from *gār* spear + *lēac* leek; with reference to the shape of its leaves.]

gar·lick·y (gär′li kē) *adj.* containing or tasting or smelling of garlic.

gar·ment (gär′mənt) *n.* **1.** an article of clothing. **2.** an outer covering or appearance: *to put these forms into the garment of words* (George Macdonald, 1866). —*v.t.* to dress with or as if with a garment; clothe. [Old French *garnement* robe, equipment, from *garnir* to protect, adorn. See GARNISH.]

garment bag, a long bag, usually of plastic, cloth, or leather, fitted with or over a hanger, used for storing clothes or for holding or protecting them during travel.

gar·ner (gär′nər) *v.t.* **1.** to earn, accumulate, or collect: *to garner praise for a heroic effort, to garner large profits from a business venture.* **2.** to gather and store in or as if in a granary: *to garner grain during a harvest.* —*n.* **1.** a place for storing grain; granary. **2.** a store of anything: *a great garner of knowledge.* [Old French *gernier* granary, from Latin *grānārium.*]

gar·net (gär′nit) *n.* **1.** any of a group of hard, vitreous, silicate minerals with a glassy to resinous luster and a transparent to

translucent appearance. Garnet occurs in various colors, the deep red variety being the most commonly used as a gem. **2.** a deep red color. *—adj.* having a deep red color. [Old French *grenat* the precious stone, going back to Latin *grānātum* pomegranate; stone probably so called because of its similarity in color and shape to the seeds of the pomegranate.]

garnet

gar·nish (gär′nish) *v.t.* **1.** to decorate or trim: *The monarch's robes were garnished with gems and fur.* **2.** to decorate (food) with something that enhances its appearance or flavor: *The fish was garnished with lemon slices.* **3.** garnishee. *—n.* **1.** something placed on or around served food to enhance its appearance or flavor: *to serve steak with a garnish of parsley.* **2.** a decoration or trimming. [Old French *garniss-*, a stem of *garnir* to protect, equip, adorn; of Germanic origin.] **—gar′nish·er,** *n.*

gar·nish·ee (gär′ni shē′) *v.t.,* **-nish·eed, -nish·ee·ing. 1.** to attach (a debtor's money or property in the possession or control of another person) by legal authority for payment of a debt. **2.** to warn (a person in control or possession of a defendant's money or property) to hold that money or property pending settlement of the suit. *—n.* a person served with a garnishment.

gar·nish·ment (gär′nish mənt) *n.* **1.** a decoration or trimming. **2.** a legal proceeding by which a person who has won a money judgment, as against a debtor, compels a third person who is in possession of funds or property of the defendant to hold it and pay part of it over to satisfy the judgment: *The defendant's paycheck was subject to garnishment.* **3.** a warning or summons to a person to appear in court in an action in which he or she is not a party.

gar·ni·ture (gär′ni chər) *n.* something that garnishes; decoration; trimming. [French *garniture,* from *garnir* to provide, adorn; of Germanic origin.]

ga·rotte (gə rot′, -rōt′) *n., v.t.,* **-rot·ted, -rot·ting.** garrote. **—ga·rot′ter,** *n.*

gar·pike (gär′pīk′) *n., pl.* **-pikes** or **-pike.** gar.

gar·ret (gar′it) *n.* the floor or a room directly below the roof of a house; attic. [Old French *garite* watchtower, place of refuge, from *garir* to defend; of Germanic origin.]

gar·ri·son (gar′ə sən) *n.* **1.** a military post. **2.** the soldiers stationed in a town or post. *—v.t.* **1.** to station soldiers in (a town or post): *to garrison a village to protect it from attack.* **2.** to station (soldiers) in a garrison: *The army garrisoned a battalion in the captured town.* [Old French *garison* defense, provision, from *garir* to defend; of Germanic origin.]

gar·rote (gə rot′, -rōt′) *also,* **garotte.** *n.* **1.** a method of execution by strangulation with a cord or an iron collar tightened by a screw. **2.** the cord or collar used in this method of execution. **3.** a strangling, esp. with the intent of robbing. **4.** any device used for or designed for use in strangling. *—v.t.,* **-rot·ed, -rot·ing. 1.** to execute with a garrote. **2.** to strangle, esp. with the intent of robbing. [Spanish *garrote* cudgel to twist cord, method of execution by strangling; possibly of Celtic origin.] **—gar·rot′er,** *n.*

gar·ru·li·ty (gə rü′li tē) *n.* the quality of being garrulous; talkativeness.

gar·ru·lous (gar′ə ləs, gar′yə-) *adj.* given to too much talking, esp. about unimportant matters; talkative. [Latin *garrulus,* from *garrīre* to chatter.] **—gar′ru·lous·ly,** *adv.* **—gar′ru·lous·ness,** *n.* —For Synonyms, see **talkative.**

gar·ter (gär′tər) *n.* **1.** a band or strap, usually elastic, worn to hold up a stocking or sock. **2.** Garter. **a.** see **Order of the Garter. b.** the badge of this order. **c.** membership in this order. *—v.t.* to fasten or support with a garter. [Dialectal Old French *gartier* band to support hose, from *garet* bend of the knee; probably of Celtic origin.]

garter snake, any of a group of harmless, brownish or greenish snakes, genus *Thamnophis,* found in North and Central America, typically having yellow stripes along the body. Length: to 2 feet (0.6 meter).

gas (gas) *n., pl.* **gas·es. 1.** a form of matter characterized by the unconstrained movement of the atoms and molecules. It has no definite shape or volume and expands to fill its container. ➡ distinguished from **solid** and **liquid. 2.** any substance, as an element or compound, or mixture of substances in such a form. **3.** any combustible gas or gaseous mixture used for heating or lighting, such as natural gas. **4.** any gas or gaseous mixture used as an anesthetic, as nitrous oxide. **5.** a chemical substance, as mustard

gas or tear gas, that is intentionally dispersed in the air to irritate, stun, or kill. **6.** gasoline. **7.** the presence of gas in the stomach or intestines; flatulence. **8.** *Slang.* anyone or anything extraordinary, exciting, or satisfying: *The fireworks show was a gas.* **9.** *Slang.* empty or boastful talk: *Don't give us a lot of gas about how important you are. —v.,* **gassed, gas·sing.** *—v.t.* **1.** to irritate, stun, or kill with gas, as in chemical warfare. **2.** to supply with gas or gasoline (often with *up*): *to gas up a car before a long drive.* **3.** to treat with gas: *to gas lime with chlorine. —v.i.* **1.** to give off gas. **2.** *Slang.* to talk idly or boastfully. *—adj.* **1.** of or for gas or gasoline: *a gas tank.* **2.** using or powered by gas or gasoline: *a gas grill.* [Dutch *gas* this form of matter (that is not liquid or solid), adaptation of Greek *chaos* empty space, chaos, by J. B. van Helmont, 1577-1644, Belgian chemist.]

• **to step on the gas. a.** to press or step down on the accelerator of a vehicle. **b.** to go faster; hurry: *We'll have to step on the gas if we want to finish this project by the deadline.*

gas burner, the part of a gas fixture at which the gas is burned, esp. one that distributes the flame.

gas chamber, a sealed room in which one or more persons are executed by poisonous gas.

gas chromatography, a technique for separating or chemically analyzing a volatile mixture by vaporizing it, mixing the vapor with a gas, and passing this through a tube containing material that selectively adsorbs the vapor.

Gas·con (gas′kən) *n.* **1.** a native or inhabitant of Gascony. **2.** the dialect of the French language spoken in Gascony. **3.** gas·con. a boastful person; braggart. *—adj.* **1.** of, relating to, or characteristic of Gascony or its people, dialect, or culture. **2.** gas·con. boastful. [French *Gascon,* going back to Latin *Vasco* Basque.]

gas·con·ade (gas′kə nād′) *n.* boastful or blustering talk. *—v.i.,* **-ad·ed, -ad·ing.** to boast or bluster. [French *gasconnade* boasting, from *gascon* (see GASCON); because the Gascons were noted for bragging.]

gas engine, an internal-combustion engine that uses natural gas or gases derived from petroleum instead of gasoline.

gas·e·ous (gas′ē əs, gash′əs) *adj.* of, relating to, of the nature of, or in the form of gas.

gas fitter, a person who assembles, installs, and repairs gas pipes and fixtures.

gas-guz·zler (gas′guz′lər) *also,* **gas guzzler.** *n. Informal.* an automobile that uses an excessive amount of fuel. **—gas′-guz′-zling,** *adj.*

gash (gash) *n.* a long, deep cut or wound: *The doctor closed the gash with ten stitches. —v.t.* to make a gash in: *The horse gashed its leg on a spike.* [Earlier *garsh,* from Old French *garser* to scarify, incise, possibly going back to Late Latin *charaxāre* to scratch, engrave, from Greek *charassein.*]

gas·i·fy (gas′ə fī′) *v.t., v.i.,* **-fied, -fy·ing.** to make into or become a gas. **—gas′i·fi·ca′tion,** *n.*

gas jet 1. the part of a gas fixture at which the gas is burned; burner or nozzle. **2.** a flame of gas issuing from this.

gas·ket (gas′kit) *n.* **1.** a ring, disk, or other piece of packing used to keep a joint or closure, as in a pipe or piston, from leaking. **2.** *Nautical.* a cord or rope used to secure furled sails to the yard or boom. [French *garcette* little girl, thin rope, diminutive of *garce* wench, feminine of Old French *gars* boy; possibly of Germanic origin.]

gas·light (gas′līt′) *n.* **1.** light produced by the burning of illuminating gas. **2.** a gas burner or gas jet.

gas main, a large underground pipe that carries gas to branch pipes.

gas mantle, a tube, made by impregnating fabric with oxides of cerium and thorium, that glows brightly when a hot gas flame is directed through it.

gas mask, a mask worn over the mouth, nose, and eyes, designed to filter contaminated air to make it suitable for breathing.

gas·o·hol (gas′ə hôl′) *n.* a fuel used in motor vehicles, made from gasoline and alcohol.

gas·o·line (gas′ə lēn′, gas′ə lēn′) *also,* **gas·o·lene.** *n.* a highly flammable and volatile fuel consisting of a mixture of hydrocarbons, used chiefly in internal-combustion engines. It is obtained by cracking or distilling petroleum, by polymerization, or by condensing natural gas. [GAS + *-ol* (suffix from Latin *oleum* oil) + -INE[2].]

G

a	at	e	end	o	hot	u	up	hw	white		about
ā	ape	ē	me	ō	old	ū	use	ng	song		taken
ä	far	i	it	ô	fork	ü	rule	th	thin	ə	pencil
âr	care	ī	ice	oi	oil	u̇	pull	th	this		lemon
		îr	pierce	ou	out	ûr	turn	zh	measure		circus

gasoline engine, an internal-combustion engine that uses gasoline as fuel.

gas·om·e·ter (gas om′i tər) *n.* an apparatus for holding and measuring gas. [French *gazomètre,* from *gaz* gas, from Dutch *gas* (see GAS) + *mètre* (see -METER).]

gasp (gasp) *v.i.* to draw in the breath suddenly, sharply, or with difficulty, as in fear, surprise, or exhaustion. —*v.t.* to utter while gasping: *The excited child gasped the news to us.* —*n.* the act or an instance of gasping. [Old Norse *geispa* to yawn.] —**gasp′ing·ly,** *adv.*

•**at the last gasp. a.** at the point of death; about to die: *The murderer confessed at the last gasp.* **b.** at the end or last moment.

gas station, an establishment that sells gasoline, oil, and other items necessary to keep motor vehicles operating, often having repair facilities as well. Also, **filling station, service station.**

gas·sy (gas′ē) *adj.,* **-si·er, -si·est. 1.a.** full of or containing gas. **b.** having, producing, or bothered by gas in the stomach or intestines; flatulent. **2.** resembling or of the nature of gas. —**gas′si·ness,** *n.*

gas·tric (gas′trik) *adj.* of, relating to, or near the stomach. [Greek *gastr-,* stem of *gastēr* stomach + -IC.]

gastric juice, a digestive fluid secreted by glands in the stomach lining, containing hydrochloric acid and certain enzymes, such as pepsin and rennin.

gastric ulcer, an ulcer on the wall of the stomach.

gas·trin (gas′trin) *n.* a hormone that stimulates the flow of gastric juice.

gas·tri·tis (gas trī′tis) *n.* inflammation of the mucous membrane lining the stomach, characterized by nausea and cramplike pain. [Modern Latin *gastritis,* from Greek *gastēr* stomach + -ITIS.]

gas·troc·ne·mi·us (gas′trok nē′mē əs, gas′trə-) *n., pl.* **-mi·i** (-mē ī′). a muscle of the lower hind leg in vertebrates. It forms the bulge of the calf in humans, attaching to the femur above and the heel bone below. [Modern Latin *gastrocnemius,* from Greek *gastroknēmia,* calf of the leg.]

gas·tro·en·ter·ol·o·gy (gas′trō en′tə rol′ə jē) *n.* the branch of medicine that deals with diseases or abnormalities of the stomach and intestines. —**gas′tro·en′ter·ol′o·gist,** *n.*

gas·tro·in·tes·ti·nal (gas′trō in tes′tə nəl) *adj.* of or relating to the stomach and the intestines, considered collectively.

gas·tro·nom·ic (gas′trə nom′ik) *adj.* of or relating to gastronomy. Also, **gas′tro·nom′i·cal.** —**gas′tro·nom′i·cal·ly,** *adv.*

gas·tron·o·my (gas tron′ə mē) *n.* the art or science of good eating or of appreciating fine food. [French *gastronomie,* going back to Greek *gastēr* stomach + *nomos* law.]

gas·tro·pod (gas′trə pod′) *n.* any of a widespread group of one-shelled mollusks, class Gastropoda, including the snail, slug, and whelk, that move by means of a muscular foot on the ventral surface of the body. Most gastropods have a single-chambered, usually spiral, shell. —*adj.* of or relating to gastropods. [Formed from Greek *gastēr* stomach + *pod-,* stem of *pous* foot.]

gas·tro·vas·cu·lar (gas′trō vas′kyə lər) *adj.* relating to or having both digestive and circulatory functions: *a gastrovascular disorder, a gastrovascular cavity.* [Greek *gastr-,* stem of *gastēr* stomach + VASCULAR.]

gas·tru·la (gas′trə lə) *n., pl.* **-las** or **-lae** (-lē′). the stage of embryonic development following the blastula, in which the ectoderm, mesoderm, and endoderm are formed. [Modern Latin *gastrula,* diminutive of Greek *gastēr* stomach.] —**gas′tru·lar,** *adj.*

gas·tru·late (gas′trə lāt′) *v.i.,* **-lat·ed, -lat·ing.** to form a gastrula. —**gas′tru·la′tion,** *n.*

gas turbine, a turbine that uses the gaseous products of combustion for motive power.

gas well, a well that produces natural gas.

gat[1] (gat) *Archaic.* a past tense of **get.**

gat[2] (gat) *n. Slang.* a pistol. [Short for GATLING GUN.]

gate (gāt) *n.* **1.** a movable barrier, usually swinging on hinges, used to close off a passage, as in a wall or fence. **2.** an opening in a wall or fence, used for entering or leaving, esp. such an opening equipped with a movable barrier; gateway. **3.** a structure, usually defensive, monumental, or decorative, built on either side and sometimes across the top of such an opening: *The archers fired from their position on the castle gate.* **4.a.** any means of entering or leaving, such as those used for boarding trains at railroad stations or airplanes at airports. **b.** gateway *(def. 2).* **5.** any movable barrier used for restricting passage, such as that of a railroad crossing. **6.** a device to control the flow of a fluid, esp. water, as through a pipe, dam, or lock. **7.** *Electronics.* a circuit with multiple inputs but only one output, used as a switch in computers. **8.a.** the number of people who pay to see a sports event, play, or other contest or performance. **b.** the total amount of money received from these people: *The race drew in a gate of $2,000.* [Old English *geat* barrier, door, opening.]

•**to get the gate.** *Slang.* to be dismissed, rejected, or sent away.

•**to give (someone) the gate.** *Slang.* to dismiss, reject, or send away: *The coach gave the runner the gate for missing practice.*

gate-crash·er (gāt′krash′ər) *n. Informal.* a person who gains admittance to a party or other private gathering without having been invited, or to a performance or game without having a ticket.

gate·house (gāt′hous′) *n., pl.* **-hous·es** (-hou′ziz). a house or other structure built next to or over a gate, used esp. as the gatekeeper's quarters.

gate·keep·er (gāt′kē′pər) *n.* a person in charge of a gate.

gate·post (gāt′pōst′) *n.* a post on which a gate is hinged or to which a gate is fastened when closed.

gate·way (gāt′wā′) *n.* **1.** an opening in a wall or fence that may be closed with a gate, used for entering or leaving. **2.** a means of entering some place or achieving something: *the gateway to the West, the gateway to happiness.* Also *(def. 2),* **gate.**

gath·er (gath′ər) *v.t.* **1.** to bring together in one place or group: *The general gathered the army and marched forward.* **2.** to bring together gradually from various places or sources; accumulate: *The bird gathered twigs for its nest. She gathered a large collection of manuscripts over the years.* **3.** to take or collect by selecting from among various things; cull: *The teacher gathered the best of our essays for the school magazine.* **4.** to pick and harvest, as fruit or crops: *The farmer gathered the corn in August.* **5.** to increase little by little; gain gradually: *The ball gathered speed as it rolled down the hill.* **6.** to learn or realize by observation or reasoning; deduce; infer: *I gather it was he who called. She gathered from the evidence that they were guilty.* **7.** to prepare or collect (oneself or something, such as one's energies) for an effort: *He gathered his strength for the fight.* **8.** to take and hold; enfold: *I gathered the child in my arms.* **9.** to wrap or draw closer, as a garment: *She gathered the shawl about her shoulders to keep out the wind.* **10.** to draw (cloth) into pleats, folds, or puckers along a line of stitching; shirr: *The drapes were gathered at the top.* **11.** to wrinkle (one's brow): *He gathered his brow in a frown.* —*v.i.* **1.** to come together or assemble: *Students gathered in the auditorium.* **2.** to increase or collect gradually; grow or accumulate: *Sweat gathered on my brow. The hurricane gathered in strength over tropical waters.* **3.** to form pus and come to a head, as a boil or sore. —*n.* a pleat, fold, or pucker made by gathering cloth. [Old English *gaderian* to bring together, come together, collect, from *geador* together.] —**gath′er·er,** *n.*

•**to gather up. a.** to pick up and assemble: *The child gathered up the toys and put them away.* **b.** to draw or bring closer together; make smaller or more compact: *to gather up a rope and put it in a box.*

| **Synonyms** | *v.t.* **Gather, assemble,** and **collect** mean to |

bring together to form a group. **Gather** is the broadest of these terms, implying nothing about the use or arrangement of what is brought together: *to gather twigs in the woods.* **Assemble** connotes more purpose, and suggests similarity in the persons or objects brought together: *to assemble a group of students.* **Collect** suggests a systematic and gradual accumulation based on some principle or purpose: *to collect postage stamps, to collect antique toys.*

gath·er·ing (gath′ər ing) *n.* **1.** the act of a person or thing that gathers. **2.** something that is gathered. **3.** a meeting, assembly, or crowd. **4.** a series of gathers in a garment or fabric. **5.** a boil; abscess. —For Synonyms, see **meeting.**

Gat·ling gun (gat′ling) the earliest effective machine gun, consisting of from six to ten barrels mounted in a circle on a frame, the whole assembly being rotated by a hand crank. [From Richard J. *Gatling,* 1818-1903, its American inventor.]

gauche (gōsh) *adj.* lacking social grace; awkward, boorish, or tactless. [French *gauche* left, awkward, from *gauchir* to turn aside, warp; of Germanic origin.] —**gauche′ly,** *adv.* —**gauche′ness,** *n.*

gau·che·rie (gō′shə rē′) *n.* **1.** the quality of being gauche. **2.** a gauche act or statement. [French *gaucherie* awkwardness, from *gauche* left, awkward. See GAUCHE.]

gau·cho (gou′chō) *n., pl.* **-chos.** a cowboy of the pampas of South America, esp. one of mixed Spanish and Indian descent. [Spanish *gaucho* herdsman, horseman, rustic, possibly from Quechua *wáhcha* poor person.]

Gatling gun

gaud (gôd) *n.* a cheap, tasteless, or showy ornament or trinket. [Old French *gaudir* to rejoice, going back to Latin *gaudēre.*]

gaud·y (gô′dē) *adj.,* **gaud·i·er, gaud·i·est.** tastelessly bright or ornate; cheap and showy in appearance; garish: *This stretch of town is full of neon and gaudy storefronts.* —**gaud′i·ly,** *adv.* —**gaud′i·ness,** *n.*

gauge (gāj) *also,* **gage.** *n.* **1.** a standard measure or scale of measurements. **2.** an instrument or device used for measuring or indicating measurements: *a gasoline gauge.* **3.** a means of estimating or judging; standard; criterion: *His performance on the test is a gauge of his ability.* **4.** the distance between two rails on a railroad. The standard U.S. gauge is 56.5 inches (144 centimeters). **5.** the diameter of the bore of a gun, esp. a shotgun. **6.** the thickness or diameter, as of a sheet of metal or a wire. —*v.t.,* **gauged, gaug·ing. 1.** to determine accurately the dimensions, amount, force, or capacity of, esp. with a gauge; measure: *to gauge the depth of a well, to gauge the speed of the wind.* **2.** to estimate or judge; appraise: *The jeweler gauged the worth of the gem. It was difficult to gauge what her family's reaction would be.* **3.** to make conform to a standard or measurement. [Dialectal Old French *gauge* gauging rod; possibly of Germanic origin.] —**gauge′a·ble,** *adj.* —**gaug′er,** *n.* —For Synonyms (*n.*), see **standard.**

Gaul (gôl) *n.* **1.** a Celtic inhabitant of ancient Gaul. **2.** a Frenchman or Frenchwoman. [French *Gaule* the country of the Gauls, from Latin *Gallia,* from *Gallus* native of Gaul, Gallic.]

Gaull·ist (gō′list, gô′-) *n.* in French politics, a supporter or follower of Charles de Gaulle or of parties or policies held to represent continued adherence to his thinking.

gaunt (gônt) *adj.* **1.** extremely thin and hollow-eyed, as from hunger or illness; haggard. **2.** desolate, bare, and gloomy; grim; bleak: *a gaunt stretch of desert.* [Possibly of Scandinavian origin.] —**gaunt′ly,** *adv.* —**gaunt′ness,** *n.*

gaunt·let[1] (gônt′lit) *also,* **gantlet.** *n.* **1.** a heavy glove, usually made of leather covered with armor plate or mail, used in medieval times to protect the hand. **2.a.** a glove having a long, flaring cuff extending above the wrist. **b.** the cuff of such a glove. [Middle English *gauntlet,* from Old French *gantelet* armored glove, mitten, diminutive of *gant* glove; of Germanic origin.]

• **to take up the gauntlet.** to accept a challenge or undertake to defend someone or something.

• **to throw** (or **fling**) **down the gauntlet.** to challenge, as to combat.

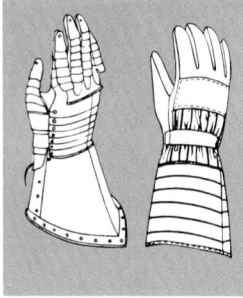

gauntlet[1]

gaunt·let[2] (gônt′lit) *also,* **gantlet.** *n.* **1.** a form of punishment in which the offender is forced to run between two rows of people who strike out with clubs, whips, or other weapons. **2.** a series or siege of difficulties or troubles. [Modification (influenced by GAUNTLET[1]) of earlier *gantlope,* from Swedish *gatlopp* the military punishment; literally, a running down a lane, from *gata* lane + *lopp* running.]

• **to run the gauntlet. a.** to undergo the punishment of the gauntlet. **b.** to be besieged by difficulties, opposition, or criticism.

gaur (gour, gou′ər) *n., pl.* **gaur** or **gaurs.** a large wild ox, *Bos (Bibos) gaurus,* native to India and Southeast Asia. Weight: to 1 ton (0.9 metric ton). [Hindi *gaur,* from Sanskrit *gaura.*]

gauss (gous) *n., pl.* **gauss** or **gauss·es.** the centimeter-gram-second unit of magnetic induction.

gauze (gôz) *n.* **1.** a very thin, lightweight cloth woven from any of various fibers, used for such items as bandages, surgical dressings, and curtains. **2.** a similar mesh woven of metal or plastic. **3.** a thin haze, mist, or fog. [French *gaze* light, transparent, thin cloth; supposedly because it first came from *Gaza.*]

gauz·y (gô′zē) *adj.,* **gauz·i·er, gauz·i·est.** resembling gauze; thin; transparent: *The gauzy curtain let sunlight in but also provided some privacy.* —**gauz′i·ness,** *n.*

gave (gāv) the past tense of **give.**

gav·el (gav′əl) *n.* a small mallet used by the person presiding at a trial, meeting, or other gathering to call for attention or order. [Of uncertain origin.]

ga·vi·al (gā′vē əl) *n.* a large freshwater reptile, family Gavialidae, related to and resembling crocodiles and alligators, found along rivers in India and Pakistan. Length: to 21 feet (6.4 meters). Also, **gharial.** [French *gavial,* modification of Hindi *ghariyāl* crocodile.]

gavial

ga·votte (gə vot′) *n.* **1.** a dance of French origin, resembling the minuet, but much faster and livelier. **2.** the music for such a dance. [French *gavotte* the dance, from Provençal *gavato,* from *Gavot* native of the Alps; supposedly originally a dance of this people.]

Ga·wain (gä′win, gô′-, gə wān′) *n.* in Arthurian legend, a knight of the Round Table, brother of Sir Gareth, and nephew of King Arthur.

gawk (gôk) *v.i.* to stare stupidly; gape: *The crowd gawked at the wreckage.* —*n.* a clumsy, foolish, or stupid person. [Possibly modification of obsolete *gaw,* from Old Norse *gā* to heed.]

gawk·y (gô′kē) *adj.,* **gawk·i·er, gawk·i·est.** awkward; clumsy. —**gawk′i·ly,** *adv.* —**gawk′i·ness,** *n.*

gay (gā) *adj.,* **gay·er, gay·est. 1.** full of joy and fun; merry; happy. **2.** brightly colored or showy: *a gay dress.* **3.** given to or full of lightheartedness or pleasure: *They lead a gay life, free from responsibility and worry.* **4.** of, relating to, or for homosexuals or homosexuality. —*n.* a homosexual person, esp. a homosexual man. [Old French *gai* merry; possibly of Germanic origin.] —**gay′ness,** *n.*

gay·e·ty (gā′i tē) gaiety.

gay·ly (gā′lē) gaily.

gaz. 1. gazette. **2.** gazetteer.

gaze (gāz) *v.i.,* **gazed, gaz·ing.** to look long and steadily or fixedly, as in admiration or wonder or with rapt attention. —*n.* a long, steady or fixed look. [Possibly of Scandinavian origin.] —**gaz′er,** *n.*

ga·ze·bo (gə zē′bō, -zä′-) *n., pl.* **-bos** or **-boes.** a small, open-air or screened-in structure, usually affording a view of the surrounding area, used as a retreat or resting spot. [Humorous coinage, modeled on Latin *videbo* I shall see.]

gaze·hound (gāz′hound′) *n. Archaic.* any dog that hunts by sight rather than scent, as a greyhound.

ga·zelle (gə zel′) *n., pl.* **-zelles** or **-zelle.** any of various graceful antelopes, genus *Gazella,* native to hot, dry regions of northern Africa and southern Asia, having a fawn-colored coat with black and white markings, curving, ridged horns, and large, lustrous eyes. They can run as fast as 60 miles (97 kilometers) per hour. Height: 2-3 feet (0.6-0.9 meter) at the shoulder. [French *gazelle,* from Arabic *ghazāl.*]

ga·zette (gə zet′) *n.* **1.** a newspaper or similar periodical. **2.** an official publication, as of a government or institution, esp. any of several journals containing public notices published by the British government. —*v.t.,* **-zet·ted, -zet·ting.** *British.* to publish, list, or announce in a gazette. [French *gazette* newspaper, from Italian *gazzetta* originally, coin of little worth (because in sixteenth-century Venice it cost a *gazzetta* (coin) to read a government newspaper), probably diminutive from Latin *gaza* wealth, from Greek *gaza,* from Persian *ganj* treasure.]

gaz·et·teer (gaz′ə tîr′) *n.* a dictionary or list of geographical names. [French *gazetier* writer for a gazette, geographical dictionary, from *gazette* newspaper. See GAZETTE.]

gaz·pa·cho (gə spä′chō) *n., pl.* **-chos.** a cold soup made of chopped raw tomatoes and other vegetables, often combined with olive oil, vinegar, and spices. [Spanish *gazpacho.*]

G.B., Great Britain.

GCD, greatest common divisor.

G clef, treble clef.

Gd, the symbol for gadolinium.

Ge, the symbol for germanium.

gear (gîr) *n.* **1.** a device, esp. a wheel, with projections or teeth spaced evenly on its perimeter, designed to mesh with corresponding projections on another such device. **2.** *also,* **gears.** a mechanical assembly of such devices, used for transmitting or chang-

a	at	e	end	o	hot	u	up	hw	white		about
ā	ape	ē	me	ō	old	ū	use	ng	song		taken
ä	far	i	it	ô	fork	ü	rule	th	thin	ə	pencil
âr	care	ī	ice	oi	oil	u̇	pull	th	this		lemon
		îr	pierce	ou	out	ûr	turn	zh	measure		circus

G

ing motion. **3.** a certain arrangement of the gears in such an assembly, as in an automobile transmission: *second gear, low gear.* **4.** a mechanism or part of a mechanism within a machine, performing a specific function: *steering gear.* **5.** any equipment used for a specific purpose: *Their fishing gear consisted of rods, reels, and hooks, but not lures.* **6.** personal belongings or clothing. —*v.t.* **1.a.** to furnish or equip with gears. **b.** to connect by gears: *to gear the wheels to the engine.* **c.** to put in gear. **2.** to adapt, change, or regulate (something) in order to conform to or suit something else: *to gear a political campaign to capture the middle-class vote.* —*v.i.* to come into or be in gear; mesh: *The teeth of the wheels gear into each other.* [Old Norse *gervi* equipment, apparel.]
- **in gear. a.** connected or engaged, as one gear with another or with a motor. **b.** in proper working order; ready for use.
- **out of gear. a.** not connected or engaged, as one gear with another or with a motor. **b.** not in proper condition for use or operation; out of order.
- **to gear up.** to prepare for a future event or circumstances or for future use: *The manufacturer is gearing up to deal with expected foreign competition.*
- **to shift gears. a.** to shift from one arrangement of gears to another, as when accelerating in an automobile. **b.** to suddenly change one's method, manner, attitude, or the like: *The strikers shifted gears and voted to accept the contract they had rejected.*

gear·box (gîr′boks′) *n.* a transmission, as of an automobile or other vehicle.

gear·ing (gîr′ing) *n.* an apparatus for the transmission of motion or power; a system of gears.

gear·shift (gîr′shift′) *n.* a device for engaging or disengaging any of several sets of gears in a transmission system.

gear train, a system of more than one set of gears working in conjunction with one another.

gear·wheel (gîr′hwēl′, -wēl′) *n.* cogwheel.

geck·o (gek′ō) *n., pl.* **geck·os** or **geck·oes.** any of a widespread group of tropical lizards, family Gekkonidae, having pads on the bottom of the toes covered with minute hooks that enable them to walk on walls and ceilings. [Malay *gēkoq;* from the sound of its cry.]

gee[1] (jē) *interj.* **1.** to the right. **2.** go faster. ➡ used to direct horses and other draft animals in both defs. —*v.t., v.i.,* **geed, gee·ing.** to turn to the right. [Of uncertain origin.]

gee[2] (jē) *interj.* used to express enthusiasm, surprise, awe, or disappointment.

geese (gēs) a plural of **goose.**

Ge·ez (gē ez′, gā-) *n.* Ethiopic.

ge·fil·te fish (gə fil′tə) a ball or cake of chopped fish mixed with onion, egg, and matzoh meal or bread crumbs and cooked, usually in fish broth. [Yiddish *gefilte fisch* literally, filled fish.]

Ge·hen·na (gə hen′ə) *n.* **1.** in the New Testament, hell. **2.** a place of torment and suffering. [Church Latin *gehenna* hell, from Greek *geenna,* from Hebrew *gey hinom* literally, valley of Hinnom (a valley near Jerusalem, where children were sacrificed to the god Moloch).]

Gei·ger counter (gī′gər) an electronic device used to detect and measure the intensity of ionizing radiation. [From Hans *Geiger,* 1882-1945, German physicist, one of its inventors.]

gei·sha (gā′shə, gē′-) *n., pl.* **-sha** or **-shas.** a Japanese girl or woman who has been trained to provide entertainment for men, as by singing, dancing, and making amusing conversation. [Japanese *gēisha* artiste, from *gei* art + *sha* person.]

gel (jel) *n.* a jellylike, solid substance, formed by a colloidal dispersion of a solid in a liquid. —*v.t., v.i.,* **gelled, gel·ling.** to form into a gel: *Pudding gels when cooled.* [From GELATIN.]

gel·ate (jel′āt) *v.i.,* **-at·ed, -at·ing.** gel. [GEL + -ATE[1].] —**ge·la′tion,** *n.*

gel·a·tin (jel′ə tən) *also,* **gel·a·tine** (jel′ə tən, -tēn′). *n.* **1.** a colorless, tasteless protein substance obtained from skin, bones, and other animal tissues. It is soluble in hot water and is used in jellies, desserts, and other foods and in the manufacture of drugs and photographic film. **2.** a preparation or product made primarily with or resembling gelatin. [French *gélatine* the protein substance from animal tissues, from Italian *gelatina* jelly, gelatinous substance, from *gelata* jelly, frost, going back to Latin *gelātus,* past participle of *gelāre* to freeze.]

ge·lat·i·nous (jə lat′ə nəs) *adj.* **1.** of the nature of or resembling gelatin. **2.** of, consisting of, or containing gelatin. —**ge·lat′i·nous·ly,** *adv.* —**ge·lat′i·nous·ness,** *n.*

ge·la·to (jə lä′tō) *n.* a type of Italian ice cream with an especially smooth and creamy texture. [Italian *gelato* something frozen, ice cream, from *gelare* to freeze, going back to Latin *gelu* icy coldness, frost.]

geld (geld) *v.t.,* **geld·ed** or **gelt, geld·ing.** to castrate (a horse or similar animal). [Old Norse *gelda.*]

geld·ing (gel′ding) *n.* a gelded animal, esp. a gelded horse.

gel·id (jel′id) *adj.* very cold; icy. [Latin *gelidus* cold, from *gelū* frost.]

gelt (gelt) a past tense and past participle of **geld.**

gem (jem) *n.* **1.** a cut and polished precious or, sometimes, semiprecious stone; jewel. **2.** someone or something that is considered perfect, extremely beautiful, or precious: *This novel is a gem.* **3.** a kind of muffin. —*v.t.,* **gemmed, gem·ming.** to set or adorn with or as if with gems: *Tiny blossoms gemmed the branches of the tree.* [Old French *gemme* jewel, from Latin *gemma* bud, jewel.]

Ge·ma·ra (gə mär′ə, -môr′ə) *n.* a commentary on and supplement to the Mishnah, which together with it forms the Talmud. [Hebrew-Aramaic *gemara,* from Aramaic *gemara* literally, studying, learning, from the root of the verb *gamar* to finish.]

gem·i·nate (*v.,* jem′ə nāt′; *adj.,* jem′ə nit, -nāt′) *v.t., v.i.,* **-nat·ed, -nat·ing.** to make or become double; form into identical pairs. —*adj.* formed or combined in a pair or pairs; coupled. [Latin *geminātus,* past participle of *gemināre* to double, from *geminus* twin, double.] —**gem′i·na′tion,** *n.*

Gem·i·ni (jem′ə nī′) *n.* **1.** a constellation in the northern sky containing the bright stars Castor and Pollux, conventionally depicted as the mythological brothers for whom these stars are named. **2.** the third sign of the zodiac. [Latin *geminī* twins, plural of *geminus* twin, double.]

gem·ma (jem′ə) *n., pl.* **gem·mae** (jem′ē). *Biology.* a bud or, in some plants, budlike structure that becomes detached and develops into a new individual. [Latin *gemma* bud, jewel.]

gem·mate (jem′āt) *v.i.,* **-mat·ed, -mat·ing.** to form or reproduce by gemmae. —*adj.* having or reproducing by gemmae. [Latin *gemmātus,* past participle of *gemmāre* to bud, from *gemma* bud, jewel.] —**gem·ma′tion,** *n.*

gem·mip·a·rous (je mip′ər əs) *adj. Botany.* forming or reproducing by gemmae. [GEMMA + Latin *-parus,* from *parere* to bring forth, produce.]

gem·mule (jem′ūl) *n.* **1.** an internal bud composed of several cells inside a heavy coat of organic material, formed by freshwater sponges as a method of reproduction. **2.** a gemma. [Latin *gemmula* little bud, diminutive of *gemma* bud.]

gem·ol·o·gy (je mol′ə jē) *n.* the science or study of gemstones and gems. [GEM + -LOGY.] —**gem·o·log·i·cal** (jem′ə loj′i kəl), *adj.* —**gem·ol′o·gist,** *n.*

gems·bok (gemz′bok′) *n., pl.* **-boks** or **-bok.** a swift southern African antelope, *Oryx gazella,* having very long, straight horns, a long, tufted tail, and a sandy gray coat with striking dark markings on the side and brown and white markings on the face. Height: 46 inches (117 centimeters) at the shoulder. [Afrikaans *gemsbok* male chamois, from German *Gemsbock,* from *Gemse* chamois (from Late Latin *camox*) + *Bock* male, buck[1]. See CHAMOIS.]

gem·stone (jem′stōn′) *n.* a mineral or petrified material that can be used in jewelry when cut and polished.

-gen *suffix* (used to form nouns) **1.** something that produces: *oxygen, estrogen.* **2.** something that is produced: *antigen.* [Greek *-genēs* born, produced, often through French *-gène.*]

gen. 1. gender. **2.** general. **3.** genitive. **4.** genus.

Gen. 1. General. **2.** Genesis.

gen·darme (zhän′därm) *n., pl.* **-darmes** (-därmz). **1.** an armed police officer in France and French-speaking parts of certain other European countries. **2.** *Informal.* any police officer. [French *gendarme,* from *gens d'armes* men at arms, going back to Latin *gēns* nation, people + *dē* from + *arma* weapons.]

gen·der (jen′dər) *n.* **1.** a grammatical classification of words, used primarily in Indo-European and Semitic languages, which distinguishes chiefly between masculine and feminine, but which in some languages also includes the classifications neuter, animate, and inanimate. **2.** any one of such classes. **3.** the quality or condition of being of the male or female sex; sex: *Discrimination based on a person's gender is illegal.* [Old French *gendre* kind, sort, from Latin *genus.*]

gene (jēn) *n.* one of the units located on a chromosome that determine the characteristics an organism inherits from its parent or parents. Genes are made up largely of DNA. [German *gen,* from Greek *genos* descent, race.]

ge·ne·al·o·gist (jē′nē ol′ə jist, -al′-, jen′ē-) *n.* a person who traces or studies genealogies.

ge·ne·al·o·gy (jē′nē ol′ə jē, -al′-, jen′ē-) *n., pl.* **-gies. 1.** the study of the descent of persons or families from an ancestor or ancestors. **2.** an account or chart of such a descent for a particular

person or family: *This genealogy goes back to the American Revolution.* **3.** direct descent from an ancestor or progenitor; pedigree; lineage. [Late Latin *genealogia* account of a descent, from Greek *genealogiā* tracing a descent, going back to *geneā* race, breed + *-logia* (see -LOGY).] —**ge·ne·a·log·i·cal** (jē′nē ə loj′i kəl, jen′ē-), *adj.* —**ge′ne·a·log′i·cal·ly,** *adv.*

gene pool, the total stock of all the genes of all the individuals in a species or population of organisms.

gen·er·a (jen′ər ə) a plural of **genus.**

gen·er·al (jen′ər əl) *adj.* **1.** concerned with or affecting all or the whole: *to work for the general good.* **2.** common to or occurring among many or most; widespread; prevalent: *a word in general use, general unrest.* **3.** not limited in scope or application: *a general principle.* **4.** not concerned with details or specifics: *to get a general idea of someone's job, to speak in a general way.* **5.** not restricted to one class, type, or group: *general merchandise.* **6.** concerned with or skilled in all branches, as of business or learning; not specialized. **7.** of superior rank; highest; chief. —*n.* **1.** the commander of a large army; military officer of the highest rank: *Julius Caesar was a famous Roman general.* **2.a.** in the U.S. Army and Air Force, an officer ranking below general of the army or general of the air force above lieutenant general. **b.** in the U.S. Marine Corps, an officer of the highest rank. **c.** any officer ranking above a colonel; general officer. **3.** the head of any of a number of religious orders: *the general of the Dominicans.* **4.** something that describes or embraces all or the whole; general idea, condition, fact, or the like. [Old French *general* universal, Latin *generālis* relating to a species, relating to all, from *genus* kind, sort.]

• **in general. a.** for the most part; commonly. **b.** without regard to specifics or details. **c.** considering all persons or things mentioned.

Synonyms *adj.* **General** and **common** mean characteristic of or affecting a group or whole. **General** stresses extensiveness and broad applicability: *a general characteristic of human beings, the general rule governing magnetic fields.* **Common** stresses what is typical or shared: *Losing one's sense of direction at night is a common experience. Freedom is the common heritage of Americans.*

General Assembly 1. the highest deliberative assembly of the United Nations, in which every member nation has an equal vote. **2.** the legislative body in certain states of the United States.

General Court, the bicameral legislative body of Massachusetts or New Hampshire.

general delivery 1. the department of the post office that handles mail picked up by addressees at a post office window. **2.** the mail sent through this department.

general election, an election in which the voters usually make their final choice among the candidates for public office, esp. such an election held nationwide or statewide.

gen·er·al·is·si·mo (jen′ər ə lis′ə mō′) *n., pl.* **-mos.** in certain countries, the commander in chief of all the military forces of the country, or of several armies in the field. [Italian *generalissimo,* superlative of *generale* a general, from *generale* universal, from Latin *generālis.* See GENERAL.]

gen·er·al·ist (jen′ər ə list) *n.* a person whose interest or expertise covers a wide range of fields or activities rather than being specialized.

gen·er·al·i·ty (jen′ə ral′i tē) *n., pl.* **-ties. 1.** an undetailed or unspecific statement, phrase, or idea, esp. one that is too broad or vague to be meaningful: *to speak in generalities.* **2.** the greater part or number; main body; majority: *The generality of a person's problems are often minor.* **3.** the quality or condition of being general.

gen·er·al·i·za·tion (jen′ər ə lə zā′shən) *n.* **1.** the act or process of generalizing. **2.** something that results from such an act or process, as a general statement.

gen·er·al·ize (jen′ər ə līz′) *v.,* **-ized, -iz·ing.** —*v.i.* **1.** to treat a subject without going into details or specifics; use generalities. **2.** to infer a general rule or principle from particular facts or instances. —*v.t.* **1.** to give a more general form to; state in general terms. **2.** to formulate (a general rule or principle) from particular facts or instances. **3.** to form a general conclusion or principle from. **4.** to promote the wide use or knowledge of; popularize. —**gen′er·al·iz′a·ble,** *adj.* —**gen′er·al·iz′er,** *n.*

gen·er·al·ly (jen′ər ə lē) *adv.* **1.** in most cases; usually; as a rule: *We generally walk home.* **2.** for the most part; commonly: *a generally accepted theory.* **3.** without regard to specific details: *Generally speaking, the book was good.*

general officer, in the U.S. Army, Air Force, or Marine Corps, any officer holding a rank above that of a colonel.

general of the air force, in the U.S. Air Force, an officer of the highest rank.

general of the army, in the U.S. Army, an officer of the highest rank.

general paresis, a disease of the brain caused by syphilis, characterized by progressive loss of physical and mental faculties. Also, **paresis.**

general practitioner, a physician whose practice is not limited to a specific branch of medicine.

gen·er·al-pur·pose (jen′ər əl pûr′pəs) *adj.* suitable for more than one use: *a general-purpose cleanser.*

gen·er·al·ship (jen′ər əl ship′) *n.* **1.** the military skill of a general. **2.** skill in management of any sort; leadership. **3.** the rank, office, or term of office of a general.

general staff 1. in the U.S. Army and Marine Corps, a group of officers in the headquarters of a large unit, such as a division, who assist the commander in planning, coordinating, and supervising operations. **2.** a similar group in any of various other militaries.

general store, a store, usually located in a rural or small community, that carries a large variety of items but is not divided into departments.

general strike, a strike that involves all the workers in an industry or in an entire area or country.

gen·er·ate (jen′ə rāt′) *v.t.,* **-at·ed, -at·ing. 1.** to produce or cause to be; bring into existence: *to generate electricity in an atomic power plant, to generate interest in a new film by advertising.* **2.** to produce (offspring); beget. **3.** *Mathematics.* to trace out a line, surface, plane figure, or solid by moving a point, line, or plane: *A line moved around a circle, remaining always parallel to itself, generates a cylinder.* [Latin *generātus,* past participle of *generāre* to produce.]

gen·er·a·tion (jen′ə rā′shən) *n.* **1.a.** a group of individuals born at about the same time: *the younger generation.* **b.** such a group thought of as characterized by or having common attitudes, experiences, or the like: *the television generation.* **2.** one step or degree in the line of natural descent, as of people, animals, or plants. Grandparents, parents, and children are three generations. **3.** the period of time between the birth of one generation and the next, usually about thirty years for human beings. **4.** the act or process of causing to be or bringing into existence; production: *the generation of new jobs in an expanding economy.* **5.** the act or process of producing offspring; procreation. **6.** *Mathematics.* the formation of a line, surface, plane figure, or solid by the motion of a point, line, or plane. **7.** a group of devices produced within a certain time period and reflecting the technology of that period: *the next generation of computers, a first-generation weapons system.* [Latin *generātiō* a generating.] —**gen′er·a′tion·al,** *adj.*

generation gap, the difference in values, attitudes, and outlook between one generation and the next, esp. between parents and adolescents.

gen·er·a·tive (jen′ər ə tiv, -ə rā′-) *adj.* **1.** of or relating to production of offspring. **2.** having the ability or power to produce or bring into existence.

generative grammar, a set of rules for generating all possible grammatical phrases and sentences in a language.

gen·er·a·tor (jen′ə rā′tər) *n.* **1.** a device that converts mechanical energy into electrical energy. **2.** an apparatus for the production of gas or steam. **3.** a person or thing that generates. [Latin *generātor* producer.]

gen·er·a·trix (jen′ə rā′triks) *n., pl.* **gen·er·a·tri·ces** (jen′ər ə-trī′sēz). *Mathematics.* a point, line, or plane that generates a line, plane figure, or solid. [Latin *generātrix* she that produces.]

ge·ner·ic (jə ner′ik) *adj.* **1.** of, relating to, or applied to a whole kind, class, or group; general: *"Fruit" is a generic term for apples, oranges, and the like.* **2.** of, relating to, or characteristic of a genus of plants or animals. **3.** not under trademark registration: *generic drugs, generic canned goods.* —*n.* a product, such as a drug, that is not sold under a trade name. [Latin *gener-,* stem of *genus* kind, sort + -IC.] —**ge·ner′i·cal·ly,** *adv.*

gen·er·os·i·ty (jen′ə ros′i tē) *n., pl.* **-ties. 1.** the quality of being unselfish; willingness to give or share freely. **2.** the quality of being noble-minded and free from pettiness; magnanimity; graciousness. **3.** a generous act.

gen·er·ous (jen′ər əs) *adj.* **1.** characterized by or showing a

G

a	at	o	hot	u	up	hw	white	(	about
ā	ape	ē	me	ō	old	ū	use	ng	song		taken
ä	far	i	it	ô	fork	ü	rule	th	thin	ə	pencil
âr	care	ī	ice	oi	oil	u̇	pull	th	this		lemon
		îr	pierce	ou	out	ûr	turn	zh	measure	(	circus

willingness to give or share freely; unselfish: *a generous gift, a generous donor.* **2.** noble-minded and gracious; free from pettiness; magnanimous: *a generous nature.* **3.** large or plentiful; abundant: *a generous helping.* **4.** fertile: *generous soil.* **5.** (of wine) rich and strong in flavor. [Latin *generōsus* of noble birth, noble, from *genus* sort, kind, race.] —**gen′er·ous·ly,** *adv.*

gen·e·sis (jen′ə sis) *n., pl.* **-ses** (-sēz′). the coming into being of anything; origin; creation. [Latin *genesis* birth, creation, from Greek *genesis* origin, creation.]

Gen·e·sis (jen′ə sis) *n.* the first book of the Old Testament, giving an account of the origin of the world.

gene-splic·ing (jēn′splī′sing) *n.* any of various methods for joining a fragment of DNA from one organism to the genetic material of another organism to produce recombinant DNA.

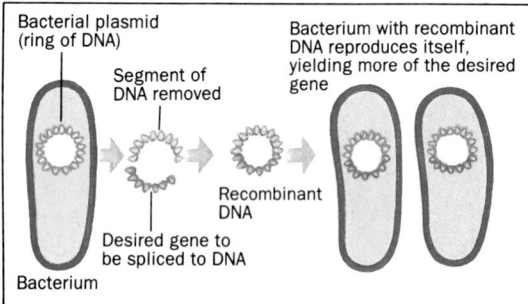

gene-splicing

gen·et (jen′it, jə net′) *n.* any of a group of African carnivorous mammals, genus *Genetta,* in the same family as civets and mongooses, usually gray-yellow with black blotches and a ringed tail. The **common genet,** *G. genetta,* is also found in southwestern Europe. Length: to 5 feet (1.5 meters), including tail. [Middle English *genet,* from Old French *genette,* from Spanish *gineta,* from Arabic *jarnayt.*]

ge·net·ic (jə net′ik) *adj.* **1.** of or relating to genetics. **2.** of, relating to, or produced by a gene or genes. **3.** of or relating to the origin and development of anything. Also, **ge·net′i·cal.** [From GENESIS, on the model of *antithesis, antithetic.*] —**ge·net′i·cal·ly,** *adv.*

genetic code, the biochemical information on a sequence of DNA that directs the synthesis of a particular kind of protein molecule, thereby enabling inherited characteristics to be handed down from one generation to another.

genetic engineering, the altering of the genetic material of a cell or an organism by means of techniques such as gene-splicing. Genetic engineering can be used to develop vaccines and create new and useful organisms, such as bacteria that produce human insulin. For illustration, see **gene-splicing.**

ge·net·i·cist (jə net′ə sist) *n.* an expert in genetics.

ge·net·ics (jə net′iks) *n.* the branch of biology that deals with the principles of heredity and the inherited similarities and differences found in organisms. ➡ used as singular.

Ge·ne·va Convention (jə nē′və) an international agreement regulating the wartime treatment of sick and wounded soldiers and prisoners of war. It was first adopted in 1864 at Geneva, Switzerland, and was supplemented by three later agreements.

gen·ial (jēn′yəl, jē′nē əl) *adj.* **1.** pleasant and cheerful; friendly; cordial: *a genial host.* **2.** favorable to life or growth; pleasantly warm and comfortable: *a genial climate.* [Latin *geniālis* pleasant, from Latin *genius* guardian spirit, spirit of social enjoyment.] —**gen′ial·ly,** *adv.* —**gen′ial·ness,** *n.*

ge·ni·al·i·ty (jē′nē al′i tē) *n.* the quality or condition of being genial.

gen·ic (jen′ik) *adj.* of, relating to, consisting of, or produced by a gene or genes; genetic. [GENE + -IC.]

-genic *combining form* (used to form adjectives) **1.** relating to production or generation: *carcinogenic.* **2.** suitable to: *photogenic.*

ge·nie (jē′nē) *n., pl.* **-nies** or **-ni·i. 1.** a spirit who will fulfill wishes and follow commands. **2.** jinni. [French *génie* (from Latin *genius* guardian spirit), used to translate Arabic *jinnī* spirit.]

ge·ni·i (jē′nē ī′) **1.** the plural of **genius** *(defs. 6, 7, 9).* **2.** a plural of **genie.**

gen·i·tal (jen′i təl) *adj.* of or relating to the sex organs or reproduction. [Latin *genitālis.*]

gen·i·ta·li·a (jen′i tā′lē ə, -tāl′yə) *pl. n.* genitals.

gen·i·tals (jen′i təlz) *pl. n.* the reproductive organs, esp. the external sex organs.

gen·i·ti·val (jen′i tī′vəl) *adj.* of, in, or belonging to the genitive case.

gen·i·tive (jen′i tiv) *n.* **1.** the grammatical case in Latin, Greek, and certain other Indo-European languages that indicates possession, source or origin, or the object of certain prepositions, corresponding to the possessive case in English. **2.** a word or construction in this case. —*adj.* of, relating to, belonging to, or designating this case. [Latin *(casus) genitīvus* genitive (case); literally, relating to origin.]

gen·i·to·u·ri·nar·y (jen′i tō yûr′ə ner′ē) *adj.* of or relating to the genital and urinary organs.

gen·ius (jēn′yəs) *n., pl.* *(defs. 2-5, 8)* **gen·ius·es** or *(defs. 6, 7, 9)* **ge·ni·i. 1.** extraordinary mental power, esp. as shown by creative or inventive achievement in science or the arts: *Marie and Pierre Curie were persons of genius.* **2.a.** a person who has such power: *Beethoven was a genius.* **b.** a person having a very high intelligence quotient. **3.** great aptitude or talent for a particular thing: *She has a genius for drawing.* **4.** a person who has such an aptitude: *a genius at diplomatic negotiations.* **5.** a distinctive character or spirit, as of a nation, age, group, or institution: *the genius of classical Greece.* **6.** a guardian spirit, as of a person or place. **7.** either of two warring spirits, one good and one evil, assumed to be fighting for control over one's fate. **8.** a person who exerts a powerful influence over another: *an evil genius.* **9.** a supernatural being; spirit; jinni. [Latin *genius* guardian spirit, talent, inclination.]

gen·o·cide (jen′ə sīd′) *n.* the deliberate and methodical annihilation of a national or racial group. [Greek *genos* race + -CIDE[1].] —**gen′o·cid′al,** *adj.*

ge·nome (jē′nōm) *n.* one set of all the genes on all the chromosomes, as contained in each cell of an individual. [German *genom,* from *gen* gene + -om from *chromosom* chromosome.] —**ge·no·mic** (ji nō′mik, -nom′ik), *adj.*

gen·o·type (jen′ə tīp′, jē′nə-) *n.* **1.** the genetic makeup of an organism with respect to a single trait or its entire set of traits. ➡ opposed to **phenotype. 2.** a group or class of organisms having the same genetic makeup. [Greek *genos* origin, race, kind + TYPE.]

gen·re (zhän′rə; *French* zhän′Rə) *n., pl.* **-res** (-rəz; *French* -Rə). **1.** a kind; type; sort. **2.** a particular class or style of work in literature or art: *the genre of the short story.* **3.a.** genre painting *(def. 1).* **b.** genre paintings as a group. —*adj.* of or relating to a genre or genre painting: *The western is a genre film.* [French *genre* kind, style, from Latin *genus* kind, sort.]

genre painting 1. a style of painting that shows scenes and events from everyday life. **2.** a painting in this style.

gens (jenz) *n., pl.* **gen·tes** (jen′tēz). **1.** in ancient Rome, a group of families descended from a common male ancestor and united by a common name and by certain religious, social, and political functions. **2.** a group of individuals related through a common ancestor in the male line and sharing the same surname; tribe; clan. [Latin *gēns.*]

gent (jent) *n. Informal.* gentleman *(defs. 1-3).*

gen·teel (jen tēl′) *adj.* **1.** polite in manner or behavior; well-bred or refined: *a genteel person.* **2.** of, relating to, or suitable for those who are well-bred or refined: *genteel manners.* **3.** refined or polite to the point of excessiveness or affectation. [Old French *gentil* nobly born, from Latin *gentīlis* of the same clan, from *gēns* clan. Doublet of GENTILE, GENTLE, JAUNTY.] —**gen·teel′ly,** *adv.* —**gen·teel′ness,** *n.*

gen·tian (jen′shən) *n.* any of a large group of plants, genus *Gentiana,* found in temperate and mountainous regions, bearing tubular, often blue, flowers. [Latin *gentiāna,* said to be from *Gentius,* an ancient king of Illyria who supposedly discovered its medicinal use.]

gentian violet, a dark green, powdery or crystalline substance that forms a purple solution, used esp. as an antiseptic and as a biological stain.

gen·tile (jen′tīl) *also,* **Gen·tile.** *n.* **1.** a person who is not a Jew, esp. a Christian as distinguished from a Jew. **2.** among Mormons, a person who is not a Mormon. **3.** a heathen; pagan. —*adj.* **1.** of, relating to, or designating any people who are not Jewish. **2.** among Mormons, of, relating to, or designating any people who are not Mormon. **3.** heathen; pagan. [Late Latin *gentīlis* heathen, foreign, from Latin *gentīlis* of the same clan, from *gēns* clan. Doublet of GENTEEL, GENTLE, JAUNTY.]

gen·til·i·ty (jen til′i tē) *n.* **1.** refinement or good manners characteristic of a person who is well-bred. **2.** the condition of belonging to the upper class. **3.** the upper class collectively. **4.** excessive or affected politeness or refinement.

gen·tle (jen′təl) *adj.,* **-tler, -tlest. 1.** mild and kindly in manner, nature, or tone: *to be gentle when speaking to a young child.*

2. not severe, rough, or loud; soft; moderate: *the gentle tapping of the rain.* **3.** easily handled; docile; tame: *a gentle horse.* **4.** not extreme or abrupt; moderate or gradual: *gentle heat, a gentle slope.* **5.** of good family or birth; wellborn. **6.** characteristic of or like one of good family; respectable; polite; refined. **7.** *Archaic.* chivalrous; noble: *a gentle knight.* —*v.t.,* **-tled, -tling.** to treat in a way that calms, soothes, or mollifies. [Old French *gentil* nobly born, noble, from Latin *gentīlis* of the same clan, from *gēns* clan. Doublet of GENTEEL, GENTILE, JAUNTY.] —**gen'tle·ness,** *n.* —**gen'tly,** *adv.*

gen·tle·folk (jen'təl fōk') *also,* **gen·tle·folks.** *pl. n.* people of good family and breeding.

gen·tle·man (jen'təl mən) *n., pl.* **-men** (-mən). **1.** a man who is honorable, courteous, and considerate. **2.** a man of good family and high social standing. **3.** any man. ➡ used also in the plural as a polite form of address. **4.** a man's personal servant; valet. **5.** in English history, a man ranking above a yeoman but below a nobleman.

gen·tle·man-farm·er (jen'təl mən fär'mər) *n., pl.* **gen·tle-men-far·mers** (jen'təl mən fär'mərz). a man of wealth who owns a farm but does not depend on it for income.

gen·tle·man·ly (jen'təl mən lē) *adj.* having the character, behavior, or appearance of a gentleman; courteous; well-bred. —**gen'tle·man·li·ness,** *n.*

gentleman's agreement *also,* **gentlemen's agreement.** an unwritten agreement guaranteed only by the honor of the parties involved, and not legally binding.

gen·tle·wom·an (jen'təl wùm'ən) *n., pl.* **-wom·en** (-wim'ən). **1.** a woman of good family and high social standing. **2.** a well-mannered, refined woman; lady. **3.** formerly, a woman attending a lady of rank.

gen·tri·fi·ca·tion (jen'trə fi kā'shən) *n.* the conversion of a run-down urban area, especially a poor or working-class neighborhood, into one that is more expensive or exclusive, resulting in an increase in property values and displacement of the original residents and businesses. [GENTRI(FY) + -FICATION.]

gen·tri·fy (jen'trə fī') *v.t.,* **-fied, -fy·ing.** to change (a neighborhood, block, or the like) by gentrification. [GENTR(Y) + -FY.]

gen·try (jen'trē) *n.* **1.** people of good family or high social standing. **2.** the landowning class in England ranking below the nobility and above the yeomanry. **3.** the people of any particular area, class, or group: *the sporting gentry.* [Earlier *gentrise,* from Old French *genterise* rank, nobility, going back to *gentil* nobly born, noble. See GENTLE.]

gen·u·flect (jen'yù flekt') *v.i.* to bend the knee while standing or touch the knee to the ground, as in worship or respect. [Late Latin *genuflectere,* from Latin *genū* knee + *flectere* to bend.]

gen·u·flec·tion (jen'yù flek'shən) *n.* the act of genuflecting.

gen·u·ine (jen'ū in) *adj.* **1.** actually being what it seems or is claimed to be; real; true: *genuine pearls, a genuine antique.* **2.** actually proceeding from its reputed source or author: *The painting is a genuine Rembrandt.* **3.** free from affectation or hypocrisy; sincere: *a genuine expression of sympathy, a genuine effort to help.* [Latin *genuīnus* native, innate, natural.] —**gen'u·ine·ly,** *adv.* —**gen'u·ine·ness,** *n.*

> **Synonyms** **Genuine** and **authentic** indicate that something is just what it is said to be. **Genuine** suggests that something can be traced to its source or origins to prove what it is: *We have papers that show that this desk is a genuine antique.* By extension, *genuine* is frequently used of feelings that are sincere and real: *genuine enthusiasm, genuine sympathy.* **Authentic** implies that there are facts that can be checked to show something is what it purports to be: *Handwriting experts have examined this signature and found it to be authentic.*

ge·nus (jē'nəs) *n., pl.* **gen·er·a** or **ge·nus·es.** **1.** the category in the classification of organisms ranking next below the family and next above the species. The scientific designation of an organism or group of related organisms consists of the genus, which is capitalized, followed by the species, which is not capitalized, as *Canis latrans,* the coyote, or *Taraxacum officinale,* the common dandelion. **2.** *Logic.* a class of individuals or things divided into subordinate groups or species. **3.** a kind; sort; class. [Latin *genus* kind, sort.]

geo- *combining form* earth; of the earth: *geology, geography.* [Greek *gē* earth.]

Geo., George.

ge·o·cen·tric (jē'ō sen'trik) *adj.* **1.** as measured or viewed from the earth's center. **2.** based on the idea that the earth is the center of the universe: *a geocentric astronomic system.* Also, **ge'o·cen'tri·cal.** —**ge'o·cen'tri·cal·ly,** *adv.*

ge·o·chem·is·try (jē'ō kem'ə strē) *n.* the branch of earth science dealing with the chemical composition of the earth's crust and the chemical changes occurring there. —**ge'o·chem'i·cal,** *adj.* —**ge'o·chem'ist,** *n.*

ge·o·chro·nol·o·gy (jē'ō krə nol'ə jē) *n.* the study of time in the context of the geologic history of the earth, considering events in the millions and billions of years. —**ge'o·chron·o·log·i·cal** (jē'ō kron'ə loj'i kəl); *also,* **ge'o·chron'o·log'ic,** *adj.*

ge·ode (jē'ōd) *n.* **1.** a round stone having a cavity lined with crystals. **2.a.** the cavity itself. **b.** any formation similar to this. [French *géode,* from Latin *geōdēs* precious stone, from Greek *geoidēs* earthlike, from *gē* earth + *-eidos* -OID.]

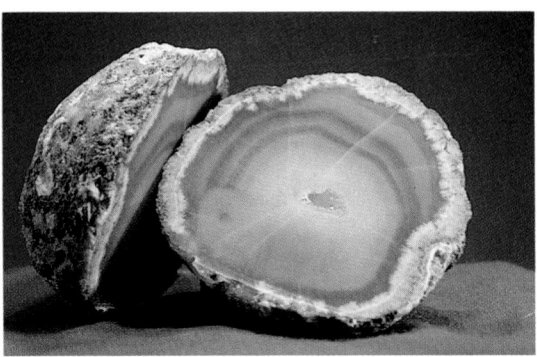

geode

ge·o·des·ic (jē'ə des'ik, -dē'sik) *n.* the shortest line segment that joins two points lying on a surface, esp. a curved surface. Also, **geodesic line.** —*adj.* **1.** of or relating to geodesy. **2.** of or relating to geodesic lines.

geodesic dome, a light, strong dome, usually constructed of struts that divide its surface into triangular or polygonal planes.

geodesic line, geodesic *(n.).*

ge·od·e·sy (jē od'ə sē) *n.* the branch of earth science concerned with determining the shape and dimensions of the earth and with the mapping of large areas of its surface. It employs the methods of surveying and of astronomical and gravitational measurement and observation. [Greek *geōdaisiā* division of the earth, from *gē* earth + *daiesthai* to divide.] —**ge·od'e·sist,** *n.*

ge·o·det·ic (jē'ə det'ik) *adj.* **1.** of, relating to, or produced through the use of geodesy: *a geodetic survey.* **2.** geodesic. —**ge'o·det'i·cal·ly,** *adv.*

geog. 1. geographer. **2.** geographical. **3.** geography.

ge·og·ra·pher (jē og'rə fər) *n.* an expert in geography.

ge·o·graph·i·cal (jē'ə graf'i kəl) *adj.* **1.** of or relating to geography. **2.** of, relating to, or constituting the surface features, climate, population, and the like of a place or region: *a geographical inventory of the countryside.* Also, **ge'o·graph'ic.** —**ge'o·graph'i·cal·ly,** *adv.*

geographical mile, nautical mile.

ge·og·ra·phy (jē og'rə fē) *n., pl.* **-phies. 1.** the study of the characteristics of particular places on the surface of the earth, and of all the physical and cultural factors affecting these characteristics. Geography includes the study of the earth's natural surface, its climate, the distribution of plant, animal, and human life, and the effects of human activity on an area. **2.** the surface or topographic features of a place or region: *the geography of Siberia.* **3.** a book about geography or the geography of a given area. [Latin *geōgraphia* description of the earth's surface, from Greek *geōgraphiā* writing about the earth, from *gē* earth + *graphein* to write.]

geol. 1. geological. **2.** geologist. **3.** geology.

ge·o·log·ic (jē'ə loj'ik) *adj.* **1.** of or relating to geology. **2.** of or relating to the structure and composition of the earth: *An earthquake is a geologic disturbance.* Also, **ge'o·log'i·cal.** —**ge'o·log'i·cal·ly,** *adv.*

geologic time, in historical geology, the span of time that extends from when the earth first formed, several billion years ago, to the present. See table of geologic time on following page.

ge·ol·o·gist (jē ol'ə jist) *n.* an expert in or student of geology.

ge·ol·o·gy (jē ol'ə jē) *n., pl.* **-gies. 1.** the science that deals with the earth's structure, composition, and history, including the changes that have taken place on the earth's surface and the pro-

G

a	at	e	end	o	hot	u	up	hw	white	⌠	about
ā	ape	ē	me	ō	old	ū	use	ng	song		taken
ä	far	i	it	ô	fork	ū	rule	th	thin	ə	pencil
âr	care	ī	ice	oi	oil	ù	pull	th	this		lemon
		îr	pierce	ou	out	ûr	turn	zh	measure	⌡	circus

Standard Geologic Time Scale

Years Ago	Time Units			Events and Characteristics*
10 thousand	CENOZOIC ERA	QUATERNARY PERIOD	Recent or Holocene epoch	Temperate climate melts ice sheets. Civilization spreads and flourishes.
2 million			Pleistocene epoch	The Ice Age. Ice sheets advance and retreat many times in North America and Europe. Ancestors of present-day humans appear.
11 million		TERTIARY PERIOD	Pliocene epoch	Many of the world's mountain ranges are uplifted. *Throughout the Cenozoic the landmasses drift toward their Holocene positions. Separation of Australia from Antarctica and of North America from Northern Europe is completed.*
25 million			Miocene epoch	Tremendous volcanic activity. Spread of grasses and grazing animals. Sea lions, walruses, and modern whales appear.
40 million			Oligocene epoch	Monkeys and apes appear. Spread of tropical, then hardwood, forests.
58 million			Eocene epoch	Early horses, rhinoceroses, and camels appear. *India collides with Asia,* and the Himalayas begin to form.
70 million			Paleocene epoch	Beginning of Age of Mammals as first placental mammals appear. Flowering plants are dominant.
135 million	MESOZOIC ERA		Cretaceous period	Profound environmental changes accompany the building of mountains and retreat of seas. Dinosaurs and many other species become extinct. Rocky Mountains form. *South Atlantic Ocean opens as South America completes separation from Africa.*
190 million			Jurassic period	Height of Age of Reptiles, particularly dinosaurs. First known birds and flowering plants. Much of Europe and Asia submerged. *North America drifts away from Africa and Europe. Africa and South America begin to separate.*
230 million			Triassic period	Dinosaurs and mammals appear. *Much volcanic activity as Pangaea begins to split into two great landmasses, Laurasia and Gondwana.*
280 million	PALEOZOIC ERA		Permian period	Mammal-like reptiles, cycads, and conifers appear. Many marine species become extinct because of environmental changes. *All continents are gathered into a single great landmass called Pangaea (all lands).*
305 million		CARBONIFEROUS PERIOD	Pennsylvanian period	Land mostly low-lying and covered with lush, coal-forming vegetation in swamps. Extensive limestone deposits formed. In the Pennsylvanian, or Upper Carboniferous, reptiles appear, and amphibians and insects are abundant.
345 million			Mississippian period	
395 million			Devonian period	Amphibians, first-known insects and spiders, and forests (tree ferns) appear. Urals and Appalachians begin to form.
430 million			Silurian period	Land plants (club mosses) appear. Mountain-building in western Europe and northern Siberia at end of period.
500 million			Ordovician period	Corals, sponges, shellfish, and first vertebrates (fish) appear. Beginning of mountain formation in New England near end of period.
570 million			Cambrian period	Animals develop hard shells and skeletons that remain as fossils. All invertebrate phyla appear. Land areas covered by sea during most of the period.
	PRECAMBRIAN ERA			Since Precambrian rocks are often strongly metamorphosed and buried by younger rocks, little is known of the long history of this era. Fossil algae have been found on all continents, but otherwise fossilized organisms are rare.
4.5 billion	THE ORIGIN OF THE EARTH			

*Italicized statements describe movements of the continents about the surface of the earth, called continental drift. The dates and the sequence shown for these movements are tentative.

520

cesses by which such changes have occurred. **2.** the structure and composition of the earth in a given area. **3.** a book about geology or the geology of a given area. [Modern Latin *geologia,* from Greek *gē* earth + *-logiā* (see -LOGY).]

geom. 1. geometric. **2.** geometrician. **3.** geometry.

ge·o·mag·net·ic (jē′ō mag net′ik) *adj.* of or relating to the magnetic properties of the earth. —**ge′o·mag′ne·tism,** *n.*

ge·om·e·ter (jē om′i tər) *n.* geometrician. [Latin *geōmetrēs,* from Greek *geōmetrēs* one who measures land.]

ge·o·met·ric (jē′ə met′rik) *adj.* **1.** of or relating to geometry. **2.** consisting of or decorated with straight lines, angles, circles, triangles, or similar forms. Also, **ge′o·met′ri·cal.** —**ge′o·met′ri·cal·ly,** *adv.*

ge·om·e·tri·cian (jē om′i trish′ən, jē′ə mi-) *n.* an expert in or student of geometry.

geometric mean *Mathematics.* the *n*th root of the product of *n* numbers. The geometric mean of 3, 6, and 12 is the cube root of 216, or 6.

geometric progression *Mathematics.* a series in which each number other than the first is the product of the preceding number and a constant factor. $1\frac{1}{2}$, 3, 6, 12, and 24 is a geometric progression, as is $\frac{1}{3}$, $\frac{1}{9}$, $\frac{1}{27}$. ➡ distinguished from **arithmetic progression.**

ge·om·e·trid (jē om′i trid) *n.* any of a large group of moths, family Geometridae, whose larvae are inchworms. At rest, their wings spread out flat, exposing similar patterns on fore- and hind wings. [Modern Latin *Geometridae,* from Latin *geōmetrēs* geometer. See GEOMETER.]

ge·om·e·try (jē om′i trē) *n., pl.* **-tries. 1.** the branch of mathematics that deals with the properties, measurements, and relations of points, lines, angles, plane figures, and solids. **2.** a particular system of geometry. **3.** shape or design: *the geometry of a building.* [Old French *geometrie* this branch of mathematics, from Latin *geōmetria,* from Greek *geōmetriā,* from *gē* earth + *-metriā* measurement.]

ge·o·mor·phol·o·gy (jē′ō môr fol′ə jē) *n.* the branch of earth science that deals with the physical features of the surface of the earth and the geological processes that formed them. —**ge·o·mor·pho·log·i·cal** (jē′ō môr′fə loj′i kəl), *adj.* —**ge′o·mor·phol′o·gist,** *n.*

ge·o·phone (jē′ə fōn′) *n.* an electronic instrument placed on or in the ground in order to detect seismic vibrations. [GEO- + PHONE², as in TELEPHONE (from Greek *phōnē* sound).]

ge·o·phys·ics (jē′ō fiz′iks) *n.* the branch of earth science dealing with the physical nature, motions, atmosphere, and hydrosphere of the earth. It includes seismology, oceanography, meteorology, and geodesy. ➡ used as singular. —**ge′o·phys′i·cal,** *adj.* —**ge′o·phys′i·cist,** *n.*

ge·o·pol·i·tics (jē′ō pol′i tiks) *n.* **1.** the study of the effects of geography, population, economics, and other factors on politics. **2.** the influence of geography and related factors on politics: *The geopolitics of the region has prevented a settlement of the war.* **3.** any political doctrine, as in Nazi Germany, asserting the right of aggressive expansion for geographic reasons. ➡ used as singular in all defs. —**ge·o·po·lit·i·cal** (jē′ō pə lit′i kəl), *adj.* —**ge′o·po·lit′i·cal·ly,** *adv.* —**ge′o·pol′i·ti′cian,** *n.*

geor·gette (jôr jet′) *n.* a sheer, lightweight silk fabric having a pebbly, crepelike surface, used for such items as dresses and blouses. Also, **georgette crepe.** [From Madame *Georgette* de la Plante, famous nineteenth-century French dressmaker.]

Geor·gian (jôr′jən) *adj.* **1.** of or relating to the reigns of the first four kings of England named George, who ruled from 1714 to 1830. **2.** of, relating to, or designating the style of architecture, art, or decoration of this period. **3.** of, relating to, or characteristic of the U.S. state of Georgia. **4.** of, relating to, or characteristic of the country of Georgia or its people, language, or culture. —*n.* **1.** a native or inhabitant of the U.S. state of Georgia. **2.a.** a native or citizen of the country of Georgia, a former republic of the Soviet Union. **b.** the language of the country of Georgia. **3.** a person living in England during the Georgian period.

ge·o·sci·ence (jē′ō sī′əns) *n.* earth science.

ge·o·syn·chro·nous (jē′ō sing′krə nəs) *adj.* (of a satellite in earth orbit) completing one rotation of the earth in the time that it takes the earth to rotate once. A geosynchronous satellite appears to remain stationary over a fixed point on the earth's equator.

ge·o·syn·cline (jē′ō sing′klīn, -sin′klīn) *n.* an elongate ocean basin where the earth's crust is sinking under the weight of an influx of sediment. The Gulf of Mexico is a modern geosyncline, with the Mississippi River providing much of the sediment.

ge·o·tax·is (jē′ō tak′sis) *n.* the involuntary movement of an organism in response to the force of gravity. —**ge′o·tac·tic** (jē′ō tak′tik), *adj.* —**ge′o·tac′ti·cal·ly,** *adv.*

ge·o·ther·mal (jē′ō thûr′məl) *adj.* **1.** of or relating to the heat

of the earth's interior. **2.** of or relating to the use of this heat to produce power or to heat buildings: *a geothermal system.* Also, **ge′o·ther′mic.**

ge·ot·ro·pism (jē ot′rə piz′əm) *n. Botany.* the movement or growth of a plant in response to the force of gravity. **Positive geotropism** is a tendency to move or grow toward the earth's gravitational pull, as roots do. **Negative geotropism** is a tendency to move or grow away from the earth's gravitational pull, as a stem does. [GEO- + Greek *tropē* turning + -ISM.] —**ge·o·trop·ic** (jē′ə trop′ik, -trō′pik), *adj.* —**ge′o·trop′i·cal·ly,** *adv.*

ger., gerund.

Ger. 1. German. **2.** Germany.

ge·ra·ni·um (jə rā′nē əm) *n.* **1.** any of a group of plants, genus *Pelargonium,* widely cultivated for their showy clusters of red, pink, or white flowers. **2.** any of various other plants of the geranium family, having lobed leaves and small, usually white or purple flowers. **3.** the flower of any of these plants. [Latin *geranium* cranesbill, from Greek *geranion,* from *geranos* crane; because its seed pod is shaped like a crane's bill.]

ger·bil (jûr′bil) *also,* **ger·bille.** *n.* any of various burrowing rodents, genus *Gerbillus,* native to desert regions of southern Africa and Asia, having a slender, tufted tail and a short, soft coat that is usually gray, brown, or reddish. Length: to 9 inches (23 centimeters), including tail. [French *gerbille,* from Modern Latin *gerbillus,* diminutive of *gerboa, jerboa.* See JERBOA.]

ger·fal·con (jûr′fôl′kən, -fal′-, -fô′-) *n.* gyrfalcon.

ger·i·at·rics (jer′ē at′riks) *n.* **1.** the branch of medicine that deals with the physiology, diseases, and hygiene of old age and aging. **2.** gerontology. ➡ used as singular. [Greek *gēras* old age + *iātros* physician + -ICS.] —**ger′i·at′ric,** *adj.* —**ger·i·a·tri·cian** (jer′ē ə trish′ən), **ger′i·at′rist,** *n.*

germ (jûrm) *n.* **1.** any microorganism, esp. one that causes disease. **2.** a rudimentary stage in the development of an organism. **3.** a rudimentary form of anything; initial stage: *the germ of a plan.* [French *germe* rudimentary stage of an organism or a thing, from Latin *germen* offshoot, embryo.]

ger·man (jûr′mən) *adj.* **1.** having the same parents. **2.** having the same grandparents. ➡ used in combination after a noun: *brother-german, cousin-german.* [Old French *germain* having the same parents, from Latin *germānus.*]

Ger·man (jûr′mən) *adj.* of, relating to, or characteristic of Germany or its people, language, or culture. —*n.* **1.** a native or

G

a	at	e	end	o	hot	u	up	hw	white		about
ā	ape	ē	me	ō	old	ū	use	ng	song		taken
ä	far	i	it	ô	fork	ū	rule	th	thin	ə	pencil
âr	care	ī	ice	oi	oil	u̇	pull	th	this		lemon
		îr	pierce	ou	out	ûr	turn	zh	measure		circus

citizen of Germany. **2.** a person of German ancestry. **3.** the Germanic language spoken predominantly in Germany, Austria, and parts of Switzerland. It includes the subdivisions High German and Low German. [Latin *Germānus* of the Germans, a German; possibly of Celtic origin.]

ger·man·der (jər man′dər) *n.* any of a group of plants, genus *Teucrium,* of the mint family, bearing bluish, white, or purple flowers. [Old French *germandree,* through Latin, going back to Greek *chamaidrȳs* literally, tree on the ground.]

ger·mane (jər mān′) *adj.* directly or closely related; pertinent; relevant: *The speaker's comments were in no way germane to the issue.* [Form of GERMAN.] —For Synonyms, see **pertinent.**

Ger·man·ic (jər man′ik) *n.* a branch of the Indo-European language family that includes English, German, Dutch, and Flemish in its western division, Norwegian, Swedish, Danish, and Icelandic in its northern division, and the extinct Gothic language in its eastern division. —*adj.* **1.** of or relating to this family of languages. **2.** German. **3.** Teutonic.

Ger·man·ism (jûr′mə niz′əm) *n.* **1.** a word, phrase, or usage originating in Germany or peculiar to the German language. **2.** a custom or belief characteristic of or peculiar to Germany and its people. **3.** devotion to or support of Germany and its institutions.

ger·ma·ni·um (jər mā′nē əm) *n.* a grayish white metalloid element, widely used in the manufacture of semiconductor devices, such as transistors. Symbol: Ge For tables, see **element.** [Modern Latin *germanium,* from Latin *Germānia* Germany, the homeland of its discoverer, Clemens Winkler, 1838-1904.]

Ger·man·ize (jûr′mə nīz′) *v.,* **-ized, -iz·ing.** —*v.t.* **1.** to cause to conform to or acquire German traits, institutions, or beliefs: *Three years of living in Berlin had completely Germanized my friend.* **2.** *Archaic.* to translate into German. —*v.i.* to conform to or acquire German traits, institutions, or beliefs. —**Ger′man·i·za′tion,** *n.*

German measles, rubella.

German shepherd, an intelligent, wolflike dog of a breed developed in Germany, having a thick coat of black, brown, or gray fur, often trained to be a watchdog, guard dog, or Seeing Eye dog. Height: 25 inches (64 centimeters) at the shoulder. Also, **police dog, Alsatian.**

German silver, nickel silver.

germ cell, a male or female reproductive cell; sperm or egg; gamete. ➡ distinguished from **somatic cell.**

ger·mi·cid·al (jûr′mə sī′dəl) *adj.* capable of killing germs: *a germicidal liquid.*

ger·mi·cide (jûr′mə sīd′) *n.* an agent that kills germs, esp. those causing disease. [GERM + -CIDE².]

ger·mi·nal (jûr′mə nəl) *adj.* **1.** of, relating to, or characteristic of germs or germ cells. **2.** in a very early stage of development: *a germinal idea.*

ger·mi·nant (jûr′mə nənt) *adj.* that germinates; sprouting.

ger·mi·nate (jûr′mə nāt′) *v.,* **-nat·ed, -nat·ing.** —*v.i.* to begin growing or developing, as from a seed; sprout. —*v.t.* to cause to sprout: *Warmth and moisture germinate seeds.* [Latin *germinātus,* past participle of *germināre* to sprout, bud, from *germen* a sprout, bud.] —**ger′mi·na′tion,** *n.* —**ger′mi·na′tive,** *adj.* —**ger′mi·na′tor,** *n.*

germ layer, any of the three principal layers of embryonic cells from which the various tissues and bodily systems develop. These layers are the ectoderm, mesoderm, and endoderm.

germ plasm, the substance in germ cells that contains the chromosomes.

germ theory, the theory that infectious and contagious diseases are caused and transmitted by the activity of microorganisms.

germ warfare, biological warfare.

ger·on·tol·o·gy (jer′ən tol′ə jē) *n.* the scientific study of the processes and problems of aging. —**ger·on·to·log·i·cal** (jə-ron′tə loj′i kəl), *adj.* —**ger′on·tol′o·gist,** *n.*

ger·ry·man·der (jer′ē man′dər, ger′-) *n.* **1.** the arrangement of voting districts in a state or other political unit to give one political party an unfair advantage. **2.** a district arranged in this way. —*v.t.* **1.** to subject (a state or other political unit) to a gerrymander. **2.** to manipulate unfairly in order to gain an advantage. [Elbridge *Gerry,* 1744-1814, U.S. political leader + (SALA)-MANDER; from the salamanderlike shape of a Massachusetts election district rearranged in 1812 during Gerry's governorship of the state.]

ger·und (jer′ənd) *n.* a verb form ending in *-ing* that functions as a noun. In the sentence *Swimming is good exercise,* the word *swimming* is a gerund. [Late Latin *gerundium* verb form that functions as a noun, going back to Latin *gerendum* that which is to be done, gerund of *gerere* to do.] —**ge·run·di·al** (jə run′dē əl), *adj.*

ge·run·dive (jə run′div) *n.* a verbal adjective in Latin that is similar to a gerund in form, used primarily to express necessity or

obligation. [Late Latin *gerundīvus (modus)* gerund (mood), from *gerundium.* See GERUND.]

Ge·ry·on (jîr′ē ən, ger′-) *n.* in Greek mythology, a three-bodied, winged giant killed by Hercules, who then stole his cattle.

ges·so (jes′ō) *n.* **1.** a mixture of plaster of Paris and glue or other materials used as a ground in painting or gilding or in the making of bas-reliefs and plaster casts and molds. **2.** a prepared surface or ground for painting made of such a mixture. [Italian *gesso* chalk, plaster, from Latin *gypsum* chalk. See GYPSUM.]

gest (jest) *also,* **geste.** *n. Archaic.* **1.** a notable deed or exploit. **2.** a tale of achievement or adventure, esp. one in verse; romance. [Old French *geste* deed, exploit, from Latin *gesta* deeds.]

ge·stalt (gə shtält′, -shtôlt′) *also,* **Ge·stalt.** *n., pl.* **-stalts** or **-stal·ten** (-shtäl′tən, -shtôl′-). *Psychology.* a unified pattern of experience whose properties cannot be derived from the parts of the whole or from their relationships. [German *Gestalt* form, shape, aspect.]

Gestalt psychology, a school of psychology based on the belief that experience is a unified pattern and is more than the sum of its smaller, independent events. It emphasizes that an event cannot be analyzed in isolation because of its interaction with other events and their relation to the whole.

Ge·sta·po (gə stä′pō) *n.* the secret police force of Nazi Germany. [Abbreviation of German *Ge(heime) Sta(ats)po(lizei)* secret state police.]

ges·tate (jes′tāt) *v.,* **-tat·ed, -tat·ing.** —*v.t.* **1.** to carry (developing young) in the uterus. **2.** to form and develop (an idea or plan) in the mind. —*v.i.* to carry developing young in the uterus: *Dogs gestate for approximately sixty days.* [From GESTATION.]

ges·ta·tion (jes tā′shən) *n.* **1.** the period from conception to birth during which unborn young are carried in the uterus; pregnancy. **2.** development or conception in the mind, as of a project, plan, or idea. [Latin *gestātiō* a carrying.] —**ges·ta′tion·al,** *adj.*

ges·tic·u·late (jes tik′yə lāt′) *v.,* **-lat·ed, -lat·ing.** —*v.i.* to make or use gestures to express a thought or feeling or for emphasis. —*v.t.* to indicate or express by gestures. [Latin *gesticulātus,* past participle of *gesticulārī* to make gestures.] —**ges·tic′u·la′tive,** *adj.* —**ges·tic′u·la′tor,** *n.*

ges·tic·u·la·tion (jes tik′yə lā′shən) *n.* **1.** an expressive or emphatic gesture. **2.** the act of gesticulating.

ges·ture (jes′chər) *n.* **1.** a movement of the head, body, or limbs, used to express a thought or feeling or to emphasize what is said. **2.** something said or done for effect or as a symbol: *to shake hands as a gesture of friendship.* —*v.,* **-tured, -tur·ing.** —*v.i.* to make or use gestures: *The police officer gestured for us to proceed.* —*v.t.* to express by a gesture or gestures. [Medieval Latin *gestura* bearing, behavior, from Latin *gestus,* past participle of *gerere* to perform.] —**ges′tur·al,** *adj.* —**ges′tur·er,** *n.*

Ge·sund·heit (gə zunt′hīt′) *interj. German.* used to wish good health to someone who has just sneezed.

get (get) *v.,* **got** or *(archaic)* **gat, got** or **got·ten, get·ting.** —*v.t.* **1.** to obtain possession of; receive; acquire: *to get a new hat, to get a good price for a car.* **2.** to achieve; earn; gain: *The team got three touchdowns.* **3.** to go for and return with; fetch: *Please get me a glass of water.* **4.** to lay hold of; seize; capture: *My friend and I got the heavy sofa by the legs and lifted it. The police got the escaped prisoner.* **5.** to cause to do or become: *to get a picture to hang straight, to get a bill passed by Congress.* **6.** to cause (something) to move: *to get a stalled car off the road.* **7.** to become ill with; suffer from; catch: *to get the measles.* **8.** to obtain as a result of calculation or experiment: *If you add three and seven, you get ten.* **9.** to establish communication with; reach: *Please get the doctor on the phone.* **10.** to prevail upon; induce; persuade: *She got her brother to walk the dog.* **11.** to learn through study; master; memorize: *The student got the grammar lesson without difficulty.* **12.** to receive as punishment: *The criminal got six years.* **13.** to make ready; prepare: *Relax while I get lunch.* **14.** to arrive in time for or go aboard: *to get the ten o'clock train.* **15.** to manage or be permitted: *We got to take a trip last August. At the ranch I got to ride a horse.* **16.** (of animals) to beget. **17.** *Informal.* to understand; comprehend: *I get the idea.* **18.** *Informal.* to cause an emotional response, such as annoyance or excitement, in: *Her arrogance always gets me.* **19.** *Informal.* to puzzle; baffle. **20.** *Slang.* to hit: *The ball got him in the eye.* **21.** *Slang.* to overcome, destroy, or kill. —*v.i.* **1.** to come to or reach a certain place or position: *to get to shore safely, to get to work on time.* **2.** to move, come, or go: *to get into an elevator, to get down from a ladder, to get nowhere in trying to reach a decision.* **3.** to be in or come to be in a specified condition; be or become: *to get lost, to get ready to leave, to get caught in the rain.* **4.** to gain or acquire wealth: *Getting and spending, we lay waste our powers* (William Wordsworth, 1806). **5.** *Informal.* to go away immediately; be off. —*n.* **1.** the return of a shot thought to be out of reach in tennis,

handball, and similar games. **2.** the offspring of an animal. [Old Norse *geta* to obtain, beget, learn.] —**get′ter,** *n.*

• **has got** or **have got.** *Informal.* **a.** to possess; have: *She's got blond hair.* **b.** to be obliged or have need: *You've got to say the password to enter. I've got to ace this test in order to pass the course.*

• **to get about.** to get around *(defs. a-c).*

• **to get across. a.** to make intelligible or understandable: *to use visual aids to get across a lesson.* **b.** to be intelligible or understandable: *The explanation got across to the group.*

• **to get after.** *Informal.* **a.** to follow in order to catch; pursue: *Get after that dog; it has my left shoe.* **b.** to urge on; spur; incite: *I got after my friend to enter the contest.* **c.** to scold; nag: *My parents would get after me if I failed to clean my room.*

• **to get along. a.** to manage to make do: *The young couple get along on their combined salaries.* **b.** to be compatible; agree: *The children got along together.* **c.** to go away; move on: *The police told the crowd to get along.* **d.** to advance; progress: *My grandparents are getting along in years.*

• **to get around. a.** to move or go from place to place. **b.** to be circulated; become known: *The rumor got around quickly.* **c.** to be active socially: *He gets around a lot for a newcomer.* **d.** to influence, persuade, or outwit: *The little girl used her charm to get around her father.* **e.** to avoid, evade, or circumvent: *to get around a rule.*

• **to get around to.** to do after a delay.

• **to get at. a.** to arrive at; reach: *to move the couch to get at an electrical outlet.* **b.** to find out; ascertain: *to get at the truth.* **c.** to apply oneself to: *to get at one's work.* **d.** to attempt to express; mean or suggest: *I don't see what you're getting at.* **e.** to tamper with or influence underhandedly; bribe: *The defendant's lawyer tried to get at a juror.*

• **to get away. a.** to leave; depart. **b.** to escape. **c.** to start, as in a horse race.

• **to get away with.** *Informal.* to do (something) without being noticed, caught, or punished: *to get away with a crime.*

• **to get back. a.** to return to a former condition or place: *to get back from a trip.* **b.** to recover: *to get back one's strength.*

• **to get back at.** *Slang.* to take revenge on.

• **to get by.** *Informal.* **a.** to pass without notice: *to get by sentries in the dark.* **b.** to barely manage; survive: *to get by on a salary of $150 a week.*

• **to get down. a.** to move to a lower position: *to get down from a platform, to get a book down from a shelf.* **b.** to depress or discourage: *The bad news really got me down.* **c.** to swallow, esp. with difficulty: *a medicine that is hard to get down.* **d.** to record in writing; write down.

• **to get down to.** to start to consider or take action on: *to get down to work.*

• **to get in. a.** to go in; enter: *They got in through the hole in the fence.* **b.** to come in; arrive: *The train got in at noon.* **c.** to insert, as in conversation: *to get in a word or two.* **d.** to become or cause to become friendly, involved, or associated: *to get in with the wrong crowd.*

• **to get it.** *Informal.* **a.** to receive a scolding or punishment. **b.** to understand.

• **to get it** (or **one's act**) **together.** *Slang.* to organize one's life or one's affairs in an orderly or systematic manner.

• **to get off. a.** to move down from or out of. **b.** to start; depart: *to get off on time.* **c.** to be released or escape, as from punishment. **d.** to help to gain the release or reduce the punishment of: *The lawyer got his client off with merely a fine.* **e.** to write and send: *to get off a telegram.* **f.** to take off; remove: *Get your coat off.* **g.** *Informal.* to utter or deliver, esp. a joke. **h.** *Slang.* to have the audacity (to do something): *Where does he get off saying that?* **i.** to be excused from work: *to get off early the day before a holiday.*

• **to get on. a.** to move up on or into: *to get on a horse.* **b.** to get along.

• **to get out. a.** to go away; depart. **b.** to escape, as from danger, difficulty, or obligation. **c.** to take out. **d.** to become known; leak out: *No one could discover how the secret got out.* **e.** to publish; issue: *to get out a daily newspaper.* **f.** to say with difficulty: *The patient got out a weak hello.*

• **to get out of. a.** to depart from; leave: *to get out of bed.* **b.** to avoid or escape from: *to get out of shoveling the snow.* **c.** to help to remove or escape from: *She got her friend out of difficulty.* **d.** to obtain from: *They finally got the information out of him.* **e.** to go beyond: *to get out of sight, to get out of earshot.*

• **to get over. a.** to recover from: *to get over a cold.* **b.** to overcome; surmount. **c.** *Informal.* to make understandable.

• **to get there.** to achieve a goal; succeed.

• **to get through. a.** to complete; finish: *to get through dinner quickly.* **b.** to manage to survive: *to get through the day after a sleepless night.*

• **to get through to. a.** to make or become clear or convincing to. **b.** to establish communication with; reach.

• **to get to. a.** to reach; contact. **b.** *Informal.* to produce a strong emotion, such as anger, joy, or melancholy, in: *Those old tunes really get to me.*

• **to get together. a.** to come together, esp. informally; meet; assemble. **b.** to bring together; gather; collect: *to get together pictures for an album.* **c.** to come to or reach an agreement, esp. after discussion or negotiation.

• **to get up. a.** to rise from bed or sleep. **b.** to bring oneself to a sitting or standing position. **c.** to mount; climb; ascend. **d.** to bring into existence; arrange; organize: *to get up an excursion to a museum.* **e.** to work up; develop; arouse: *to get up the courage to do something.* **f.** to dress in a certain style, esp. an unusual one: *to get oneself up as a clown.*

get·a·way (get′ə wā′) *n. Informal.* **1.** the act or an instance of escaping: *The thief made a fast getaway.* **2.** the act or an instance of starting in a race.

get-to·geth·er (get′tə geth′ər) *n. Informal.* an informal meeting, gathering, or party.

get-up (get′up′) *n. Informal.* **1.** a style of dress, esp. an unusual one; outfit. **2.** the style or way in which something is made or arranged, as of a book; arrangement.

get-up-and-go (get′up′ən gō′) *n. Informal.* drive; vigor; energy.

GeV, giga-electron volt.

gew·gaw (gū′gô′, gü′-) *n.* a gaudy, worthless plaything or ornament; showy trifle; bauble. —*adj.* showy but without value; gaudy. [Of uncertain origin.]

gey·ser (gī′zər) *n.* a natural hot spring from which steam and hot water burst into the air after being heated underground by surrounding masses of hot rock. [Icelandic *Geysir* a noted hot spring in Iceland; literally, gusher, from *geysa* to gush.]

gey·ser·ite (gī′zə rīt′) *n.* a variety of opaline silica deposited around the edges of geysers and hot springs.

G-force (jē′fôrs′) *n.* the force exerted on a body by gravity or by reaction to acceleration or deceleration, as when an aircraft or rocket changes speed or direction. [G(RAVITY) + FORCE.]

geyser

gha·ri·al (gur′ē əl) *n.* gavial. [Hindi *ghariyāl* crocodile.]

ghast·ly (gast′lē) *adj.,* -li·er, -li·est. **1.** causing fear, horror, or dread; horrible; dreadful: *the ghastly sights of war.* **2.** deathly pale; ghost-like: *a ghastly look.* **3.** *Informal.* extremely bad or unpleasant: *a ghastly mistake.* —*adv.* in a ghastly manner; dreadfully. [Old English *gāstlīc* spiritual, ghostly, from *gāst* spirit, ghost + *-lic* (see -LY²).] —**ghast′li·ness,** *n.*

ghat (gôt) *also, ghaut.* *n.* **1.** in India, a passage or stairway leading to a river or river landing. **2.** in India, a mountain pass. [Hindi *ghāt* landing place, from Sanskrit *ghattah.*]

ghee (gē) *n.* in India, a clarified, semiliquid butter made by boiling and straining the milk of cows and buffaloes. [Hindi *ghī,* from Sanskrit *ghrta.*]

gher·kin (gûr′kin) *n.* **1.** a small, prickly, many-seeded cucumber, *Cucumis anguria,* pickled and eaten usually as a relish. **2.** a slender trailing vine of the gourd family bearing this cucumber. **3.** a small, immature common cucumber used for pickling. [Dutch *gurken,* plural of *gurk* cucumber, through Low German and Polish, from Middle Greek *agouros,* from Persian *angārah.*]

ghet·to (get′ō) *n., pl.* -tos or -toes. **1.** a section of some European cities where Jews were formerly required to live. **2.** a section of a city, esp. a slum area, in which members of a minority

a	at	e	end	o	hot	u	up	hw	white		about
ā	ape	ē	me	ō	old	ū	use	ng	song		taken
ä	far	i	it	ô	fork	ü	rule	th	thin	ə	pencil
âr	care	ī	ice	oi	oil	u̇	pull	th	this		lemon
		îr	pierce	ou	out	ûr	turn	zh	measure		circus

523

group live because of social discrimination or poverty. [Italian *ghets, gets* literally, foundry, from *gettare* to pour, going back to Latin *jactare* to throw, fling; so called from *Ghèto* a part of Venice, Italy, set aside for Jews in 1516 and where there had previously been a foundry.]

ghost (gōst) *n.* **1.** the spirit of a dead person, thought of as making its presence known to the living in a visible form or in some other way; specter. **2.** a shadowy outline or semblance of something: *a ghost of a smile.* **3.** the slightest bit; trace: *a ghost of a chance.* **4.** an image on a television screen that is a fainter duplicate of the desired image, resulting from the reflection of the television signals from tall buildings or other surfaces. **5.** a haunting memory of something: *to be troubled by the ghost of an early failure.* **6. Ghost.** Holy Ghost. **7.** a spelling game for two or more players whose object is to avoid completing a word of four or more letters. **8.** *Informal.* ghostwriter. —*v.t., v.i. Informal.* to ghostwrite. [Old English *gāst* spirit, soul.]

• **to give up the ghost.** to die.

Synonyms *n.* **Ghost, specter, apparition,** and **spirit** may all denote a manifestation of a person who is dead, either in visible form or in some other way. **Ghost** is the most general term for the soul or spirit of someone who has died: *The ghosts of their ancestors are said to haunt the castle graveyard.* **Specter** suggests something that terrorizes the one who sees it: *The specter of the victim arose before the killers when they returned to the scene of the crime.* **Apparition** connotes something that appears quickly or faintly: *An apparition appeared on the stairs, then vanished in an instant.* **Spirit,** in this use, suggests more strongly that the dead person is present in what is seen or felt: *I could sense the spirits of my grandparents on the porch where they used to sit.*

ghost dance, a religious dance practiced by certain North American Indian tribes in the late nineteenth century, intended to establish communication with the dead and to bring about a return to former conditions.

ghost·ly (gōst′lē) *adj.,* **-li·er, -li·est. 1.** relating to, characteristic of, or suggestive of a ghost; spectral: *The scarecrow took on a ghostly shape in the dim light.* **2.** *Archaic.* of or relating to the spirit or soul; spiritual. —**ghost′li·ness,** *n.*

ghost town, a town that has been deserted, esp. a mining town in the western United States abandoned after nearby mines closed.

ghost·write (gōst′rīt′) *v.,* **-wrote** (-rōt′), **-writ·ten** (-rit′ən), **-writ·ing.** —*v.i.* to be or work as a ghostwriter. —*v.t.* to write (something) as a ghostwriter: *An assistant ghostwrites all the senator's speeches.*

ghost·writ·er (gōst′rī′tər) *also,* **ghost-writ·er.** *n.* a person who writes a speech, article, book, or other work for another person who gets the credit for the work.

ghoul (gül) *n.* **1.** in Muslim legend, a horrible demon believed to rob graves and feed on human corpses. **2.** anyone who robs graves. **3.** a person who enjoys revolting acts or horrible things. [Arabic *ghūl* the demon.] —**ghoul′ish,** *adj.* —**ghoul′ish·ly,** *adv.* —**ghoul′ish·ness,** *n.*

GHQ, General Headquarters.

GHz, gigahertz.

GI (jē′ī′) *n., pl.* **GI's** or **GIs.** *Informal.* an enlisted person in any of the branches of the U.S. military service, esp. the army. —*adj.* **1.** of, relating to, or characteristic of GI's: *a GI haircut.* **2.** issued by the U.S. government for use by the armed forces: *GI boots.* **3.** *Informal.* conforming strictly to military regulations. —*v.t.,* **GI′ing.** *Informal.* to clean thoroughly, as in preparation for inspection: *to GI a barracks.* [Originally abbreviation of *g(alvanized) i(ron);* written by U.S. Army clerks listing items, such as trash cans, made of this metal; later, during World War II, misunderstood to stand for *g(overnment) i(ssue)* or *g(eneral) i(ssue);* thereafter used in a broader sense.]

GI, gastrointestinal.

gi·ant (jī′ənt) *n.* **1.** in folklore, legend, and myth, a huge and powerful creature having human form. **2.** a person or thing that is extraordinary in strength, importance, size, or ability: *Isaac Newton was an intellectual giant. That company is a giant in the field of electronics.* **3.** in Greek mythology, one of a race of huge beings who fought against and were defeated by the Olympian gods. —*adj.* like a giant in strength or size; extremely large or strong: *a giant telescope.* [Old French *geant* huge person, legendary huge creature, going back to Latin *gigās* one of the huge mythical beings, from Greek *gigas.*]

gi·ant·ism (jī′ən tiz′əm) *n.* gigantism.

giant panda, panda *(def. 1).*

giant star, a bright, comparatively large star.

giaour (jour, jou′ər) *n.* among Muslims, a person who does not believe in Islam, esp. a Christian. [Turkish *giaur* infidel, from Persian *gaur,* form of *gābr* fire worshiper.]

gib[1] (gib) *n.* a piece of metal or other material, often wedge-shaped, used to hold parts of a machine in place. —*v.t.,* **gibbed, gib·bing.** to hold in place with a gib. [Of uncertain origin.]

gib[2] (gib) *n.* a male cat, esp. one that has been castrated. [Contraction of the proper name *Gilbert* used for a cat.]

Gib., Gibraltar.

gib·ber (jib′ər, gib′-) *v.t., v.i.* to speak rapidly and unintelligibly; jabber. —*n.* gibberish. [Imitative.]

gib·be·rel·lic acid (jib′ə rel′ik) a gibberellin, first obtained from a fungus of the genus *Gibberella,* that regulates the rate of growth and size of plants and fungi. [GIBBERELL(IN) + -IC.]

gib·ber·el·lin (jib′ə rel′in) *n.* any of a group of hormones, including gibberellic acid, that regulate growth in fungi and plants and are used commercially to germinate seeds and to promote the growth and yields of certain fruits and flowers. [Modern Latin *Gibberella* (from Latin *gibber* hump on the back) + -IN[1].]

gib·ber·ish (jib′ər ish, gib′-) *n.* **1.** rapid, unintelligible chatter. **2.** meaningless or obscure spoken or written language; nonsense.

gib·bet (jib′it) *n.* **1.** gallows. **2.** an upright post with a projecting arm from which the bodies of executed criminals were suspended. —*v.t.,* **-bet·ed, -bet·ing. 1.** to hang (a corpse) on a gibbet. **2.** to put to death by hanging. **3.** to expose to public scorn or ridicule. [Old French *gibet* staff, gallows, diminutive of *gibe* staff, club; possibly of Germanic origin.]

gib·bon (gib′ən) *n.* any of various small tree-dwelling anthropoid apes, genera *Hylobates* and *Symphalangus,* of southeastern Asia and the East Indies, having long, slender limbs and a predominantly black, brown, or pale gray coat. Height: 3 feet (0.9 meter). [French *gibbon;* supposedly from a language of India.]

gib·bos·i·ty (gi bos′i tē) *n., pl.* **-ties. 1.** the state or quality of being gibbous. **2.** a hump or protuberance, esp. a curvature of the spine.

gib·bous (gib′əs) *adj.* **1.** of or relating to that phase of the moon or a planet in which it appears more than half full but less than full. For illustration, see **moon. 2.** curved out; rounded; convex; humped. [Latin *gibbōsus* humpbacked, crooked, from *gibbus* hump.] —**gib′bous·ly,** *adv.* —**gib′bous·ness,** *n.*

gibbon

gibe (jīb) *also,* **jibe.** *n.* a derisive remark; jeer; taunt. —*v.,* **gibed, gib·ing.** —*v.i.* to utter gibes; jeer. —*v.t.* to utter gibes at. [Possibly from Old French *giber* to handle roughly; of uncertain origin.] —**gib′er,** *n.*

GI Bill of Rights, federal legislation providing disability compensation, medical care, educational assistance, and other benefits for veterans of the U.S. armed forces. Also, **GI Bill.**

gib·let (jib′lit) *n.* usually, **giblets.** any of the edible visceral parts of a fowl, such as the heart, liver, or gizzard. [Old French *gibelet* stewed game, possibly going back to *gibier* hunting, game; of Germanic origin.]

gid·dy (gid′ē) *adj.,* **-di·er, -di·est. 1.** having a reeling or swimming sensation in one's head; dizzy. **2.** causing or tending to cause dizziness. **3.** lacking seriousness; frivolous; flighty; lightheaded. [Old English *gidig, gydig* foolish, mad.] —**gid′di·ly,** *adv.* —**gid′di·ness,** *n.*

gid·dy·ap (gid′ē ap′, gid yap′) *interj.* used as a command to make a horse start or go faster. Also, **gid·dap** (gi dap′).

gie (gē) *v.t., v.i.,* **gied** or **gae, gi·en** (gē′ən, gēn), **gie·ing.** *Scottish.* to give.

gift (gift) *n.* **1.** something given; present; donation: *a graduation gift.* **2.** a natural ability or endowment; talent: *a gift for writing.* **3.** the act, power, or right of giving. [Old Norse *gipt* present.]

• **to look a gift horse in the mouth.** to find fault with something given.

gift·ed (gif′tid) *adj.* having natural ability; talented: *a gifted artist.*

gift-wrap (gift′rap′) *v.t.,* **-wrapped, -wrap·ping.** to wrap (something) as a gift in ornamental paper, with ribbons or stickers.

gig[1] (gig) *n.* **1.** a light, open, two-wheeled carriage drawn by a single horse. **2.** a long, light ship's boat propelled by oars, sails, or a motor. [Probably of Scandinavian origin.]

gig² (gig) *n.* **1.** a fishing spear. **2.** a device made of hooks fastened back to back, used to catch fish by their bodies. —*v.t., v.i.,* **gigged, gig·ging.** to catch or spear (fish) with a gig. [Short for earlier *fishgig* harpoon, form of *fisgig,* from Spanish *fisga,* from *fisgar* to thrust into, fasten, going back to Latin *fīgere.*]

gig³ (gig) *Slang. n.* a job performing music, esp. jazz or rock, for a limited time. —*v.i.,* **gigged, gig·ging.** to work as a musician. [Of unknown origin.]

giga- *combining form* multiplied by a billion; 1 billion (of a specified unit): *gigahertz.* [Greek *gigās* giant.]

gi·ga·e·lec·tron volt (jig′ə i lek′tron, gig′ə-) a unit of energy equal to 1 billion electron volts.

gi·ga·hertz (jig′ə hûrts′, gig′ə-) *n.* a unit for measuring the frequency of vibrations and waves, equal to 1 billion hertz. [GIGA- + HERTZ.]

gi·gan·tic (jī gan′tik) *adj.* of, characteristic of, or suited to a giant, esp. in size; huge; enormous. [Latin *gigant-,* stem of *gigās* giant + -IC. See GIANT.] —**gi·gan′ti·cal·ly,** *adv.*

gi·gan·tism (jī gan′tiz əm, jī′gan tiz′-) *n.* abnormal size or stature of the body, or abnormal growth of certain parts of the body, a condition usually caused by improper functioning of the pituitary gland. Also, **giantism.**

gi·ga·volt (jig′ə vōlt′, gig′-) *n.* a unit of electromotive force equal to 1 billion volts. [GIGA- + VOLT.]

gig·gle (gig′əl) *v.i.,* **-gled, -gling.** to laugh in a silly, high-pitched, or nervous way. —*n.* silly, high-pitched, or nervous laughter. [Imitative.] —**gig′gler,** *n.*

gig·gly (gig′lē) *adj.,* **-gli·er, -gli·est.** inclined to giggle.

gig·o·lo (jig′ə lō′) *n., pl.* **-los. 1.** a man kept as a lover and supported by a woman. **2.** a man paid as an escort or dancing partner for a woman. [French *gigolo,* from *gigue* leg; of Germanic origin.]

gig·ot (jig′ət) *n.* **1.** a leg-of-mutton sleeve. **2.** a leg of lamb, mutton, or veal for cooking. [French *gigot* leg of mutton, diminutive of Old French *gigue* leg, fiddle (in the Middle Ages shaped like a leg of mutton); of Germanic origin.]

Gi·la monster (hē′lə) a large, sluggish, poisonous lizard, *Heloderma suspectum,* native to desert regions of northern Mexico and the southwestern United States. It has a black or brown scaly body with orange or yellow blotches. Length: 2 feet (0.6 meter), including tail. [From the *Gila* River in Arizona, near which this lizard is found.]

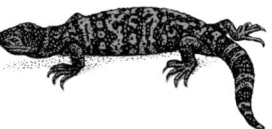

Gila monster

gild¹ (gild) *v.t.,* **gild·ed** or **gilt, gild·ing. 1.** to coat with or as with a thin layer of gold. **2.** to adorn, esp. with a golden light or color; brighten. **3.** to make (something) seem better or more attractive than it is. [Middle English *gilden,* from Old English *gyldan* to cover with a thin layer of gold; of Germanic origin.] —**gild′er,** *n.*

  • **to gild the lily.** to add needless decoration to something that is beautiful in its own right.

gild² (gild) guild.

gil·der (gil′dər) guilder.

gild·ing (gil′ding) *n.* **1.** the art or process of covering surfaces with a thin layer of gold or similar material. **2.** a thin layer of gold or similar material used in this process. **3.** a deceptively attractive covering or appearance.

Gil·ga·mesh (gil′gə mesh′) *n.* in Babylonian and Sumerian legend, a king who is the hero of a long epic poem.

gill¹ (gil) *n.* **1.** the respiratory organ of fish and most other aquatic animals, consisting of a thin layer of tissue well supplied with blood, capable of absorbing oxygen from water and releasing carbon dioxide from the blood. **2.** one of the thin, bladelike structures radially arranged on the underside of the cap of a mushroom. Also *(def. 2),* **lamella.** For illustration, see **mushroom. 3. gills.** *Informal.* the flesh around a person's chin or under the jaws. **4.** *also,* **gills.** the wattles of a fowl. [Of Scandinavian origin.]

  • **green around the gills.** *Informal.* sickly or nervous in appearance: *The new recruit looked a bit green around the gills and would find basic training especially grueling.*

gill² (jil) *n.* a liquid measure equal to ¼ of a pint (118.3 milliliters). [Middle English *gille,* from Old French *gille* wine measure, from Late Latin *gillō* water pot; possibly of Semitic origin.]

gil·lie (gil′ē) *also,* **gil·ly.** *n., pl.* **-lies. 1.** an attendant of a hunter or fisherman in the Scottish Highlands. **2.** a male servant, esp. of a Highland chief. [Scottish Gaelic *gille* lad, servant.]

gil·ly·flow·er (jil′ē flou′ər) *also,* **gil·li·flow·er.** *n.* any of various flowers having a spicy, clovelike fragrance, such as *Mathiola incana,* the most common variety. [Old French *gilofre, girofle* clove, from Medieval Latin *caryophyllum,* from Greek *karyophyllon;* the Modern English spelling is due to an incorrect association with *flower.*]

gilt¹ (gilt) *v.* a past tense and past participle of **gild¹.** —*adj.* covered with gold or a golden color; gilded: *The baroque cabinet had intricate scrollwork, marble inlay, and gilt fittings.* —*n.* gold or similar material used in gilding.

gilt² (gilt) *n.* an immature female pig. [Middle English *gilte,* from Old Norse *gyltr.*]

gilt-edged (gilt′ejd′) *adj.* **1.** having gilded edges: *a gilt-edged book.* **2.** of the highest quality, value, or rating: *gilt-edged bonds and other securities.*

gim·bals (jim′bəlz, gim′-) *pl. n.* a device consisting of two rings, one inside another, with the axes perpendicular to one another and pivoted so that each one can rotate freely about its own axis, used to support something, such as a gyroscope or ship's compass, that must move freely or remain level despite the motion of the machine in which it is enclosed. [Earlier *gimmal,* from Old French *gemel* a twin, from Latin *gemellus.*]

gim·crack (jim′krak′) *n.* a showy object of little use and value; trifle; bauble. —*adj.* showy but of little use and value. [Of uncertain origin.]

gim·let (gim′lit) *n.* a small pointed screw tool with a cross handle, used for boring holes. [Middle French *guimbelet,* probably from Middle Dutch *wimmelkijn.*]

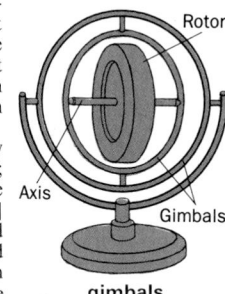

gimbals

gim·let-eyed (gim′lit īd′) *adj.* having eyes that are sharp and piercing.

gim·mick (gim′ik) *n. Slang.* **1.** a clever feature, device, or idea, esp. one used to attract attention: *a new car with many expensive gimmicks, a publicity gimmick.* **2.** a hidden condition or feature; catch. **3.** a small device or gadget, esp. one that is hidden or is used to deceive: *The roulette wheel had a gimmick that controlled its spin.* [Of uncertain origin.] —**gim′mick·y,** *adj.*

gimp¹ (gimp) *n.* a narrow strip of fabric, sometimes stiffened with wire, used for trimming borders of garments, curtains, or furniture. [Dutch *gimp;* of uncertain origin.]

gimp² (gimp) *Slang. n.* **1.** a person who limps. **2.** a limp; hobble. —*v.i.* to limp; hobble. [Of uncertain origin.] —**gim′py,** *adj.*

gin¹ (jin) *n.* **1.** a strong aromatic alcoholic liquor, distilled from grains and flavored with juniper berries. **2.** a similar liquor flavored with other substances, such as angelica root or licorice. [Short for earlier *geneva,* from obsolete Dutch *genever* juniper, from Old French *genevre,* going back to Latin *jūniperus.*]

gin² (jin) *n.* **1.** a machine for separating cotton fibers from the seed. Also, **cotton gin. 2.** a trap or snare, as for game. —*v.t.* **ginned, gin·ning. 1.** to separate (cotton fibers) from seeds with a gin. **2.** to trap or snare (game). [Middle English *gin,* shortened from Old French *engin* machine, skill, from Latin *ingenium* skill, invention.] —**gin′ner,** *n.*

gin³ (jin) *n.* gin rummy.

gin⁴ (gin) *v.t., v.i.,* **gan** or **gun, gin·ning.** *Archaic.* to begin.

gin·ger (jin′jər) *n.* **1.** any of a group of plants, genus *Zingiber,* growing in warm areas, cultivated for their aromatic rhizomes. **2.** the pungent, aromatic spice ground from these rhizomes, used in cooking and in medicine. **3.** the rhizome itself, often candied or preserved in syrup. **4.** *Informal.* high spirits; liveliness; pep. **5.** a dull tawny or reddish brown color. —*adj.* having the color ginger. [Old English *gingifer* ginger plant, ginger root, through Latin and Greek, going back to Sanskrit *çṛṅgavēram* ginger plant, from *çṛngam* horn + *vera* body; because the root is shaped like a horn.]

ginger ale, a carbonated soft drink flavored with ginger.

ginger beer, a carbonated soft drink made with yeast and flavored with ginger.

G

a	at	e	end	o	hot	u	up	hw	white	⎧	about
ā	ape	ē	me	ō	old	ū	use	ng	song	⎪	taken
ä	far	i	it	ô	fork	ü	rule	th	thin	ə	pencil
âr	care	ī	ice	oi	oil	u̇	pull	t͟h	this	⎪	lemon
				îr	pierce	ou	out	ûr	turn	zh	measure	⎩	circus

gin·ger·bread (jin′jər bred′) *n.* **1.** a dark, sweet cake or cookie flavored with ginger and molasses. **2.** showy, often gaudy, ornamentation, as on furniture or buildings. —*adj.* showy or gaudy.

gin·ger·ly (jin′jər lē) *adv.* with extreme caution; carefully; timidly: *to walk gingerly on thin ice.* —*adj.* extremely cautious or wary: *gingerly steps.* —**gin′ger·li·ness,** *n.*

gin·ger·snap (jin′jər snap′) *n.* a thin, crisp cookie flavored with ginger and molasses.

gin·ger·y (jin′jə rē) *adj.* **1.** having the pungent and spicy flavor of ginger; like ginger. **2.** having the dull tawny or reddish brown color of ginger. **3.** lively, snappy, or outspoken, as a comment.

ging·ham (ging′əm) *n.* a strong, medium-weight dyed cotton fabric, usually woven in checks, stripes, or plaids. [French *guingan,* from Malay *ginggang* striped, striped cotton.]

gin·gi·vi·tis (jin′jə vī′təs) *n.* inflammation of the gums. [Latin *gingīva* gum + -ITIS.]

gink·go (ging′kō) *also,* **ging·ko.** *n., pl.* **-goes** or **-koes.** a large tree with fan-shaped leaves, *Ginkgo biloba,* native to China. The female form is noted for its foul-smelling yellow, plumlike seeds. Male ginkgoes are popular as ornamental or shade trees. [Japanese *ginkyō,* from Chinese *ginkyō,* from *gin* silver + *kyō* apricot.]

gin rummy (jin) a variation of the card game rummy, in which two or more players form matched sets of cards until one of the players has matched all the cards in his or her hand or has ten points or less of unmatched cards. [GIN¹ + RUMMY²; *gin* was probably suggested by *rum* since rum is the first syllable of RUMMY² and since both are alcoholic beverages.]

gin·seng (jin′seng) *n.* **1.** either of two low plants, genus *Panax,* cultivated in North America and Asia, having a thick branched root and bearing toothed leaves, each consisting of three to seven leaflets, and small, pale green flowers. **2.** the root of these plants, used in medicine by the Chinese. [Chinese (Mandarin) *jen shen* man image; referring to the shape of the root, which resembles the Chinese character for man.]

Gip·sy (jip′sē) *n., pl.* **-sies.** Gypsy.

gipsy moth, gypsy moth.

gi·raffe (jə raf′) *n.* a cud-chewing African mammal, genus *Giraffa,* the tallest living animal, having a very long neck, long slender legs, two or four small bony horns, and a coat with brown patches outlined with white. Height: to 19 feet (5.8 meters). [French *girafe,* from Arabic *zarāfah.*]

gird¹ (gûrd) *v.t.,* **girt** or **gird·ed, gird·ing. 1.** to surround or fasten with a cord or belt; gird: *to gird one's waist with a gold chain.* **2.** to encircle as if with a belt; hem in. **3.** to prepare (oneself) for action: *They were girding themselves for the long and arduous journey ahead.* **4.** to invest, equip, or endow, as with power. [Old English *gyrdan* to surround, encircle.]

gird² (gûrd) *v.t., v.i.* to jeer; gibe; scoff (at). —*n.* Archaic. a biting remark; gibe. [Of uncertain origin.]

gird·er (gûr′dər) *n.* a large horizontal beam, usually made of steel, used to support joists and other beams, as for a floor or the framework of a bridge or building. [GIRD¹ + -ER¹.]

gir·dle (gûr′dəl) *n.* **1.** a flexible undergarment worn to support or shape the waist, abdomen, or hips; corset. **2.** a belt or band worn around the waist. **3.** anything that encircles in the manner of a belt. **4.** a complete ring around the trunk or branch of a tree cut through the bark, preventing the flow of sap and nutrients above that point and causing the tree to die. **5.** a bony arch supporting a limb or limbs: *the pelvic girdle.* **6.** the outer rim of a cut gem. —*v.t.,* **-dled, -dling. 1.** to encircle with a belt or girdle. **2.** to encircle as if with a belt; surround: *High walls girdled the castle.* **3.** to cut a girdle through the bark of (a tree). [Old English *gyrdel* belt worn around the waist.] —**gir′dler,** *n.*

girl (gûrl) *n.* **1.** a female child. **2.** a young, unmarried woman. **3.** a female servant or employee. **4.** Informal. a female sweetheart. **5.** Informal. a woman of any age, single or married. [Of uncertain origin.]

girl Friday, a female employee, esp. in an office, with a wide variety of duties. [Patterned after MAN FRIDAY.]

girl·friend (gûrl′frend′) *n.* Informal. a female friend, esp. a sweetheart.

girl guide, a member of the Girl Guides.

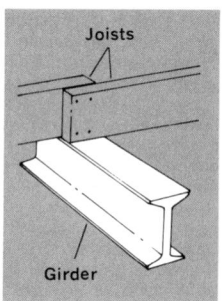

girder

Girl Guides, a worldwide organization for young girls, founded in England to develop character and physical fitness and to encourage helpfulness to others. The Girl Guides are similar to the Girl Scouts in the United States.

girl·hood (gûrl′hud′) *n.* **1.** the time or state of being a girl. **2.** girls collectively.

girl·ish (gûr′lish) *adj.* **1.** of or relating to girls or girlhood. **2.** suitable for a girl or girls. —**girl′ish·ly,** *adv.* —**girl′ish·ness,** *n.*

girl scout, a member of the Girl Scouts.

Girl Scouts, a worldwide organization for young girls, founded in the United States to develop character and physical fitness and encourage community service.

Gi·ron·dist (jə ron′dist) *n.* a member of a political party that advocated moderate republican principles during the French Revolution, from 1791 to 1793. —*adj.* of or relating to this party.

girt¹ (gûrt) a past tense and past participle of **gird¹.**

girt² (gûrt) *v.t.* **1.** to encircle; gird. **2.** to measure the girth of. —*v.i.* to measure in girth. [Form of GIRD¹.]

girth (gûrth) *n.* **1.** the distance around something; circumference: *the girth of a pillar, the girth of a person's waist.* **2.** a strap or band, usually of leather or webbing, that is passed under the belly of a horse or other animal to keep a saddle or pack in place. **3.** a band or girdle. —*v.t.* **1.** to surround; encircle; gird. **2.** to fasten or fit with a girth. —*v.i.* to measure in girth. [Old Norse *gjörth* girdle, hoop.]

gis·mo (giz′mō) *n., pl.* **-mos.** gizmo.

gist (jist) *n.* the main idea; central point: *the gist of a speech.* [Old French *gist* it lies, from *gesir* to lie², *gesir en* to depend on, from Latin *jacēre* to lie².]

git·tern (git′ərn) *n.* a medieval musical instrument similar to a guitar, having wire strings. [Old French *guiterne* cithern, guitar, from Latin *cithara.* See CITHARA.]

give (giv) *v.,* **gave, giv·en, giv·ing.** —*v.t.* **1.** to hand over as a present: *to give a sweater as a birthday gift.* **2.** to place in the custody or care of another; entrust: *to give a package to a messenger.* **3.** to transfer ownership of in exchange for something else, esp. to sell for payment: *The dealer gave the car to the buyer for $6,000.* **4.** to hand over: *Give the letter to me.* **5.** to confer as an honor: *to give an award to the best student in the class.* **6.** to allow to have or do; grant; accord: *to give permission.* **7.** to communicate to; transmit: *Give her my regards.* **8.** to make an assignment of: *The manager gave the job to John.* **9.** to administer: *to give medicine to a baby.* **10.** to make available for use; provide; supply: *to give food to the hungry, to give evidence in court.* **11.** to be a source or cause of; produce: *That lamp gives good light.* **12.** to put forth or present; offer: *to give an alibi.* **13.** to issue forth in words, sound, or motion: *to give a shout, to give the signal to start.* **14.** to perform, esp. in front of an audience: *to give a piano recital.* **15.** to arrange and carry out, esp. for entertainment: *to give a Halloween party.* **16.** to sacrifice; surrender: *to give one's life in war.* **17.** to concede; yield: *to give ground to the enemy, to give a point in an argument.* **18.** to set apart for a special purpose; devote: *to give an afternoon to shopping for clothes.* —*v.i.* **1.** to make a gift; contribute: *to give to charity.* **2.** to move or break under pressure: *The dam gave and the town was flooded.* **3.** to make concessions: *The two countries reached an agreement after each had given a little.* **4.** to stop functioning; break down: *The runner's knees gave after the race.* **5.** to have elastic qualities; be resilient. —*n.* **1.** the quality of being elastic. **2.** the tendency to yield to force or pressure. [Of Scandinavian origin.] —**giv′er,** *n.*

• **to give and take,** to make mutual concessions; compromise. **b.** to talk in a good-natured way.

• **to give away. a.** to give as a gift; donate. **b.** to present (the bride) to the bridegroom in a marriage ceremony. **c.** to reveal; expose: *The boy gave away his hiding place when he sneezed.*

• **to give back,** to return; restore.

• **to give forth,** to emit; issue: *The dog gave forth a howl.*

• **to give in. a.** to end opposition; yield: *Father gave in and let me drive the car.* **b.** to hand in; deliver; submit: *The teacher asked the students to give in their homework.*

• **to give it to.** Informal. to punish or scold: *Ann's mother gave it to her for being late.*

• **to give off.** to put forth; emit: *The flowers gave off a sweet fragrance.*

• **to give out. a.** to make public; announce. **b.** to become exhausted, broken down, or used up: *The swimmer gave out after ten laps. The old car finally gave out.*

• **to give over. a.** to relinquish; surrender. **b.** to set aside; devote: *The guidance counselor gave over afternoons for interviews with students.*

• **to give rise to.** to produce; cause.

·to give up. a. to relinquish; surrender; yield: *to give up a town to the enemy.* **b.** to stop; cease: *to give up eating between meals.* **c.** to acknowledge that one has failed and stop trying. **d.** to abandon as hopeless or useless: *to give up the search for a lost dog.* **e.** to devote completely or sacrifice: *to give up one's life for a cause.*

> **Synonyms** *v.t.* **Give, present**[2], and **confer** mean to deliver into the possession of another. **Give** is the general term: *to give a gift, to give money to a fund.* **Present** connotes a formal act of giving: *After the tournament I presented the prizes to the winners.* **Confer** connotes giving from a position of authority, or as an honor: *to confer a title on someone, to confer an award upon a longtime worker.*

give-and-take (giv′ən tāk′) *n.* **1.** mutual yielding or concession; compromise. **2.** good-natured exchange of ideas; repartee; banter.

give·a·way (giv′ə wā′) *n. Informal.* **1.** an unintentional revelation, as of a secret; exposure. **2.** something given away or sold at a very low price, as to promote sales. **3.** a radio or television program on which prizes are given away to contestants.

giv·en (giv′ən) *v.* the past participle of **give.** —*adj.* **1.** presented; bestowed. **2.** inclined; disposed; prone: *given to spreading gossip.* **3.** stated; specified: *to do something on a given day.* **4.** granted or assigned as a basis of calculating or reasoning: *Given $a = b$ and $b = c$, then $a = c$.* **5.** executed, dated, and delivered, as an official document. —*n.* something that is, is accepted as, or has been known to be true.

given name, the name given to a person at birth or baptism; first name. ➡ distinguished from **surname.**

giz·mo (giz′mō) *also,* **gismo.** *n., pl.* **-mos.** *Slang.* a gadget or object, esp. one whose name is not known or remembered.

giz·zard (giz′ərd) *n.* **1.** the second and muscular part of the stomach of a bird, in which partially digested food from the first part of the stomach is finely ground. For illustration, see **bird. 2.** the first stomach of an insect. **3.** *Slang.* the human stomach. [Old French *giser* second stomach of a bird, going back to Latin *gigeria* (plural) cooked entrails of poultry.]

Gk., Greek.

gla·brous (glā′brəs) *adj. Zoology, Botany.* free of hair, down, or fuzz. [Latin *glaber* without hair, smooth + -OUS.]

gla·cé (gla sā′) *adj.* **1.** covered with icing or sugar; glazed. **2.** frozen; iced. **3.** having a smooth, shiny surface; glossy: *glacé silk.* [French *glacé* iced, glazed, past participle of *glacer* to ice, glaze, from Latin *glaciāre* to turn into ice.]

gla·cial (glā′shəl) *adj.* **1.** of, relating to, or produced by ice or glaciers. **2.** of or relating to a period of time when glaciers covered large areas of the earth, esp. the Pleistocene. **3.** extremely cold; icy: *The mountain pool felt glacial.* **4.** coldly indifferent; unfriendly: *a glacial manner.* **5.** *Chemistry.* tending to assume a crystalline structure: *glacial acetic acid.* [Latin *glaciālis* icy, from *glaciēs* ice.] —**gla′cial·ly,** *adv.*

glacial epoch, ice age *(def. 2).*

gla·ci·ate (glā′shē āt′, -sē-) *v.t.,* **-at·ed, -at·ing. 1.** to cover with ice. **2.** to subject to or change by glacial action: *glaciated river valleys that were widened and deepened.* [Latin *glaciātus,* past participle of *glaciāre* to turn into ice.] —**gla′ci·a′tion,** *n.*

glacier

gla·cier (glā′shər) *n.* a large mass of ice moving slowly over some land surface or down a valley, formed over long periods from the accumulation of snow in areas where the amount of snow that falls exceeds the amount that melts. [French *glacier,* from *glace* ice, going back to Latin *glaciēs.*]

gla·ci·ol·o·gy (glā′shē ol′ə jē, -sē-) *n.* the branch of geology concerned with the study of glaciers. —**gla·ci·o·log·i·cal** (glā′shē ə loj′i kəl, -sē-), *adj.* —**gla·ci·ol′o·gist,** *n.*

gla·cis (glā′sis, glas′is) *n., pl.* **-cis** or **-cis·es. 1.** a gently sloping surface; incline. **2.** a sloping surface in front of a fortification, exposing attackers to defensive fire. [French *glacis,* from Old French *glacier* to slip, slide, from Latin *glaciāre* to turn into ice.]

glad[1] (glad) *adj.,* **glad·der, glad·dest. 1.** feeling or expressing joy, pleasure, or satisfaction, esp. about a particular condition or event; happy. **2.** causing joy or pleasure; pleasing: *glad tidings.* **3.** very willing: *I will be glad to go with you.* [Old English *glæd* bright, cheerful.] —**glad′ly,** *adv.* —**glad′ness,** *n.*

> **Synonyms** **Glad**[1], **happy, delighted,** and **joyful** mean experiencing feelings of pleasure ranging from satisfaction to elation. **Glad** connotes pleasure or satisfaction taken from some event or circumstance: *I was glad the weather had improved. I'm very glad I met you.* **Happy** may have the same connotations as *glad,* but may also be used to suggest a feeling of pleasure unrelated to specific causes: *I felt happy all day.* **Delighted** connotes a quick, lively emotion brought on by some cause: *The delighted new owner drove away in the car.* **Joyful** suggests high, jubilant emotion, usually attributable to a particular cause: *a joyful winner, a joyful new parent.*

glad[2] (glad) *n. Informal.* gladiolus.

glad·den (glad′ən) *v.t.* to make glad.

glade (glād) *n.* an open space in a forest. [Of uncertain origin.]

glad·i·a·tor (glad′ē ā′tər) *n.* **1.** a slave, captive, or paid professional who engaged in public combat in the arenas of ancient Rome. **2.** a person who engages in physical or verbal combat. [Latin *gladiātor* swordsman, from *gladius* sword; probably of Celtic origin.] —**glad·i·a·to·ri·al** (glad′ē ə tôr′ē əl), *adj.*

glad·i·o·lus (glad′ē ō′ləs) *n., pl.* **-li** (-lī) or **-lus·es. 1.** the funnel-shaped, showy flower of any of a large group of plants, genus *Gladiolus,* growing in long clusters along one side of the stem. **2.** the leafy plant of the iris family bearing this flower, having stiff, sword-shaped leaves that grow from a corm. It is native to the Mediterranean region and Africa. Also, **glad·i·o·la** (glad′ē ō′lə). [Latin *gladiolus* little sword, diminutive of *gladius* sword; referring to the plant's sword-shaped leaves.]

glad·some (glad′səm) *adj.* **1.** causing joy or pleasure. **2.** glad. —**glad′some·ly,** *adv.* —**glad′some·ness,** *n.*

Glad·stone bag (glad′stōn′, -stən) a lightweight, hinged suitcase that opens flat into two compartments. Also, **Gladstone.** [From William Ewart *Gladstone,* 1809-98, British statesman.]

glam·or·ize (glam′ə rīz′) *v.t.,* **-ized, -iz·ing.** to make glamorous. —**glam′or·i·za′tion,** *n.* —**glam′or·iz′er,** *n.*

glam·or·ous (glam′ər əs) *also,* **glam·our·ous.** *adj.* full of glamour; fascinatingly attractive; alluring. —**glam′or·ous·ly,** *adv.* —**glam′or·ous·ness,** *n.*

glam·our (glam′ər) *also,* **glam·or.** *n.* **1.** elusive or alluring beauty or charm attached to a person or object; fascinating attraction. **2.** *Archaic.* a magic spell; magic. [Modification of GRAMMAR; because of the earlier association of learning with magic.]

glance (glans) *n.* **1.** a brief or hurried look; glimpse. **2.** a flash or gleam of light; glint. **3.** a swift, oblique impact and deflection. —*v.,* **glanced, glanc·ing.** —*v.i.* **1.** to take a brief or hurried look: *We glanced in the store windows as we walked by.* **2.** to be deflected and move off at an oblique angle: *The bullet glanced off the rock.* **3.** to make an incidental or passing allusion, as in speaking or writing. **4.** to gleam or flash with light; glint: *The sequins on the singer's dress glanced under the spotlights.* —*v.t.* to cause (something) to strike a surface so that it is deflected at an oblique angle. [Modification of obsolete *glace* to glide, slip, from Old French *glacier* to slip, slide, from Latin *glaciāre* to turn into ice.]

gland (gland) *n.* **1.** any cell, tissue, or organ that produces and discharges one or more substances that are utilized by or discharged from the body. Important glands include the thyroid and pituitary glands and the pancreas. **2.** a secreting structure in certain plants, such as a hair or small prominence, usually located on the surfaces of stems, leaves, or flowers. [French *glande* organ of secretion, going back to Latin *glandula* gland of the throat, diminutive of *glāns* acorn.]

G

a	at	e	end	o	hot	u	up	hw	white	about
ā	ape	ē	me	ō	old	ū	use	ng	song	taken
ä	far	i	it	ô	fork	ü	rule	th	thin	ə pencil
âr	care	ī	ice	oi	oil	u̇	pull	th	this	lemon
		îr	pierce	ou	out	ûr	turn	zh	measure	circus

glan·ders (glan′dərz) *n.* a highly contagious, usually fatal, bacterial disease of horses, mules, and related animals that can affect the respiratory system and skin. It is communicable to human beings and certain other animals. [Old French *glandres,* plural of *glandre* glandular swelling, from Latin *glandula.* See GLAND.]

glan·du·lar (glan′jə lər) *adj.* **1.** of, relating to, or affecting a gland: *a glandular disease.* **2.** consisting of or containing a gland or glands: *a glandular mass of tissue.* Also, **glan′du·lous.**

glandular fever, infectious mononucleosis.

glans (glanz) *n., pl.* **glan·des** (glan′dēz). the erectile, acorn-shaped structure that forms the end of the penis or of the clitoris. [Latin *glans* literally, acorn.]

glare (glâr) *n.* **1.** a strong, usually unpleasant light, as from sunlight reflected on a shiny surface. **2.** a piercing, hostile look or stare. **3.** a too showy appearance; gaudiness. —*v.,* **glared, glar·ing.** —*v.i.* **1.** to shine with a strong, harsh brilliance. **2.** to stare piercingly and with hostility. **3.** to be too showy or conspicuous. —*v.t.* to express with a glare: *to glare defiance at an accuser.* [Middle Low German *glaren* to gleam.]

glar·ing (glâr′ing) *adj.* **1.** giving off or reflecting a harsh light; unpleasantly bright. **2.** extremely conspicuous; flagrant: *a glaring mistake.* **3.** staring piercingly and with hostility. —**glar′ing·ly,** *adv.* —For Synonyms, see **flagrant.**

glar·y (glâr′ē) *adj.,* **glar·i·er, glar·i·est.** unpleasantly bright; glaring.

glas·nost (glas′nōst, gläz′nəst) *n.* in the Soviet Union, the policy of open discussion of public problems and issues, initiated in the mid-1980s by Mikhail Gorbachev. [Russian *glasnost'* openness, being public.]

glass (glas) *n.* **1.** a hard, brittle, usually transparent material made by melting a mixture of sand, soda ash, and lime. The characteristic that distinguishes glass from other materials is that it cools from the liquid state to a hardened state without developing a crystalline structure, thus retaining the amorphous molecular structure characteristic of liquids. **2.** any substance, artificial or natural, that has similar properties or composition: *glass of phosphorus, glass of lead.* **3.** an open container, esp. of glass, usually without a handle, used chiefly for drinking. **4.a.** glassful: *I'd like half a glass of water.* **b.** a drink: *I gave him a glass of milk.* **5.** something partially or entirely made of glass, such as a window or a mirror. **6.** glassware. **7. glasses. a.** eyeglasses. **b.** binoculars. —*adj.* **1.** made of glass: *a glass bottle.* **2.** fitted with or covered with glass: *a glass door.* —*v.t.* **1.** to enclose or protect with glass (with *in*): *They glassed in the open porch.* **2.** *Archaic.* to reflect, as a mirror. [Old English *glæs* the hard, brittle substance.]

glass·blow·er (glas′blō′ər) *n.* a person who engages in glassblowing.

glass·blow·ing (glas′blō′ing) *n.* the art or process of shaping a mass of molten glass into various shapes or objects by blowing a controlled stream of air through a tube into the mass.

glass·ful (glas′fûl′) *n., pl.* **-fuls.** the quantity that can be contained in a drinking glass.

glass·house (glas′hous′) *n., pl.* **-hous·es** (-hou′ziz). *British.* greenhouse.

glass·ine (gla sēn′) *n.* a thin, glazed, translucent paper, used esp. for book jackets, envelopes, and envelope windows.

glass snake, any of several legless, snakelike lizards, genus *Ophisaurus,* found in the United States, Europe, and Asia. When it is struck, its fragile tail readily breaks into several wiggling pieces that can distract an enemy while the lizard escapes. Length: 1-3½ feet (0.3-1.1 meters).

glass·ware (glas′wâr′) *n.* objects of glass fashioned by hand or produced by machine, esp. drinking glasses.

glass wool, fibers of spun glass having a woollike appearance, used esp. for insulation and filtration.

glass·wort (glas′wûrt′) *n.* any of a small group of low-growing wild plants, genus *Salicornia,* of the goosefoot family, that grows in saltwater marshes and bears fleshy, jointed stems and small scalelike leaves. Also, **samphire.** [Because formerly used in the manufacture of glass.]

glass·y (glas′ē) *adj.,* **glass·i·er, glass·i·est. 1.** resembling or having properties of glass; smooth and shiny: *the glassy surface of a lake on a windless day.* **2.** fixed, expressionless, or lifeless: *a glassy stare.* **3.** having a fixed, unintelligent, or expressionless look: *glassy eyes.* —**glass′i·ly,** *adv.* —**glass′i·ness,** *n.*

glass·y-eyed (glas′ē īd′) *adj.* having a fixed, lifeless expression in one's eyes.

Glas·we·gian (glas wē′jən, -jē ən) *adj.* of or relating to Glasgow. —*n.* a native or inhabitant of Glasgow.

Glau·ber's salt (glou′bərz) hydrated sodium sulfate, which is used as a mild laxative and in textile dyeing and printing. Formula:

$Na_2SO_4 \cdot 10H_2O$ [From Johann R. *Glauber,* 1604-68, German chemist who first made it.]

glau·co·ma (glô kō′mə, glou-) *n.* a serious eye disease characterized by increased pressure in and gradual hardening of the eyeball. It may lead to damage of the retina and gradual loss of sight. [Latin *glaucōma* cataract of the eye, from Greek *glaukōma,* from *glaukos* gray.]

glau·cous (glô′kəs) *adj.* **1.** having a bluish green color. **2.** (of plants or plant parts) covered with a whitish powder, as plums or grapes. [Latin *glaucus* bluish green, grayish, gleaming, from Greek *glaukos.*]

glaze (glāz) *v.,* **glazed, glaz·ing.** —*v.t.* **1.** to overlay or cover with a smooth, glossy coating: *The cook glazed the doughnuts with sugar. After the freezing rain, ice glazed the street.* **2.** to furnish or fit with glass: *to glaze store windows.* **3.** to cover (pottery) with a mixture of silica, feldspar or clay, and a flux, such as borax or lead, to produce a glossy or matte coating after firing in a kiln. —*v.i.* to become glassy or glazed: *The patient's eyes glazed with pain.* —*n.* **1.** a smooth, glossy covering or coating: *a glaze on a porcelain vase.* **2.** any substance used to produce such a coating. [Middle English *glasen* to fit with glass, make a glassy coating, from *glas* glass, from Old English *glæs.*] —**glaz′er,** *n.*

gla·zier (glā′zhər) *n.* a person who installs glass panes, as in windows.

glaz·ing (glā′zing) *n.* **1.** the act or business of a glazier. **2.** glass used for this. **3.** a smooth, glossy surface; glaze. **4.** the process or art of applying a glaze.

gleam (glēm) *n.* **1.** a flash or beam of bright light. **2.** reflected brightness, as from a polished surface: *the gleam of a new car.* **3.** subdued or transient light; glow: *the distant gleam of a candle.* **4.** a faint or fleeting appearance or sign: *a gleam of humor, a gleam of understanding.* —*v.i.* **1.** to shine with subdued, transient, or reflected light: *A light gleamed in the fog. The polished floor gleamed.* **2.** to be manifested faintly or fleetingly: *Hope gleamed for an instant.* [Old English *glǣm* brightness, splendor.]

glean (glēn) *v.t., v.i.* **1.** to collect slowly and with great effort: *to glean information.* **2.** to gather (grain or other remains of a crop) left on a field after reaping. [Old French *glener* to gather grain left after reaping, from Late Latin *glennāre;* of Celtic origin.] —**glean′a·ble,** *adj.* —**glean′er,** *n.*

glean·ings (glē′ningz) *pl. n.* things acquired by gleaning.

glebe (glēb) *n. British.* a portion of land assigned to a clergyman and considered as part of his income during his tenure of office. [Latin *glēba* soil¹, clod.]

glee (glē) *n.* **1.** a high degree of pleasure; joy; delight. **2.** an unaccompanied song for three or more male voices, popular in the eighteenth century. [Old English *glēo* joy, mirth, music.]

glee club, a group organized for singing choral music.

glee·ful (glē′fəl) *adj.* full of glee; merry; joyous. —**glee′ful·ly,** *adv.* —**glee′ful·ness,** *n.*

glee·man (glē′mən) *n., pl.* **-men** (-mən). a medieval minstrel.

glee·some (glē′səm) *adj. Archaic.* gleeful.

glen (glen) *n.* a small, narrow, usually secluded valley. [Scottish Gaelic *gleann.*]

glen·gar·ry (glen gar′ē) *n., pl.* **-ries.** a Scottish cap made of wool, having straight sides and a crease lengthwise across the crown, often with short ribbons at the back. [From *Glengarry,* a valley in Scotland.]

glib (glib) *adj.,* **glib·ber, glib·best. 1.** speaking or spoken smoothly and easily but with little thought or sincerity: *a glib speaker, a glib compliment.* **2.** relaxed or informal; offhand: *a glib manner.* [Probably modification of Dutch *glibberig* slippery.] —**glib′ly,** *adv.* —**glib′ness,** *n.*

glengarry

glide (glīd) *v.i.,* **glid·ed, glid·ing. 1.** to move smoothly, continuously, and effortlessly: *The skater glided over the ice.* **2.** to pass gradually and imperceptibly, as time. **3.** *Aeronautics.* to maintain flight or descend slowly without the use of a motor or engine. —*n.* **1.** the act of moving smoothly and effortlessly. **2.** *Aeronautics.* the act of gliding. **3.** *Music.* slur. **4.** *Phonetics.* **a.** a transitional sound produced when the voice shifts from the articulation of one sound to that of another sound. **b.** semivowel. [Old English *glīdan* to slide, slip.] —For Synonyms *(v.i.),* see **fly**².

glid·er (glī′dər) *n.* **1.** an aircraft constructed of lightweight materials and designed to fly without the aid of an engine, relying on rising air currents to remain aloft. **2.** a person or thing that glides. **3.** a piece of furniture resembling a couch, usually used outdoors, suspended from a frame that permits a backward and forward movement.

glim·mer (glim′ər) *n.* **1.** a dim, wavering light. **2.** a faint hint or sign; inkling: *a glimmer of hope.* —*v.i.* **1.** to shine with a dim, wavering light; flicker. **2.** to appear faintly. [Probably of Scandinavian origin.]

glim·mer·ing (glim′ər ing) *n.* glimmer.

glimpse (glimps) *n.* **1.** a brief view; passing glance: *I caught a glimpse of the driver's face as the car sped by.* **2.** a faint or hasty view or appearance: *The short story gave only a glimpse of the writer's true ability.* —*v.,* **glimpsed, glimps·ing.** —*v.t.* to catch a brief view of; see momentarily. —*v.i.* to look quickly; glance (with *at*). [Probably of Germanic origin.]

glint (glint) *n.* **1.** a bright, quick flash; gleam. **2.** sparkle or luster, as of metal. —*v.i.* **1.** to shine; gleam. **2.** to move quickly; dart: *Rays of light glinted off the lake's surface.* [Possibly from dialectal Swedish *glinta* to slip, gleam.]

glis·sade (gli säd′, -sād′) *n.* **1.** the act of gliding over snow or ice, as in skiing. **2.** a gliding or sliding dance step, esp. in ballet. [French *glissade* a sliding, from *glisser* to slide, a blend of Old French *glier* to glide (of Germanic origin) and Old French *glacier* to slide. See GLACIS.]

glis·san·do (gli sän′dō) *Music. n., pl.* **-di** (-dē). **1.** a gliding effect performed in various ways, as by rapidly running one finger over the white keys of a piano or sliding one finger across the strings of a harp. **2.** a passage of music having such a gliding effect. —*adj.* of or performed with a gliding effect. [Possibly modification (using Italian present participle ending -*ando*) of French *glissade* a sliding. See GLISSADE.]

glis·ten (glis′ən) *v.i.* to shine or sparkle with or as with reflected light: *The snow glistened in the sun.* —*n.* reflected brightness; gleam; sparkle. [Old English *glisnian* to glitter.]

glitch (glich) *n. Slang.* a minor breakdown, mishap, or malfunction, esp. in a mechanism or a computer program. [Probably from German *glitschen* to slip, slide.]

glit·ter (glit′ər) *v.i.* **1.** to shine with scattered light; sparkle: *The jewels glittered.* **2.** to be superficially attractive or showy. —*n.* **1.** sparkling brightness or light; brilliance: *the glitter of crystal.* **2.** showiness or splendor: *the glitter of New York City's theater district.* **3.** small bits of sparkling material, used for ornamentation. [Old Norse *glitra* to sparkle.] —**glit′ter·y,** *adj.*

glitz (glits) *n. Slang.* flashy display; showiness: *The remodeled restaurant was all glitz, with its mirrored walls and shiny chrome fixtures.* [Probably from German *glitzern* to glitter.]

glitz·y (glit′sē) *adj.,* **glitz·i·er, glitz·i·est.** *Slang.* given to or characterized by flashy display and glitter; showy: *a glitzy hotel lobby, glitzy tastes.*

gloam·ing (glō′ming) *n.* twilight; dusk. [Old English *glōmung.*]

gloat (glōt) *v.i.* **1.** to observe or think with great satisfaction and often malicious delight (often with *over*): *to gloat over a rival's misfortune.* **2.** to express such satisfaction or delight. [Old Norse *glotta* to smile scornfully.] —**gloat′er,** *n.* —**gloat′ing·ly,** *adv.*

glob (glob) *n.* a rounded mass, lump, or drop: *a glob of paint.* [Possibly blend of GLOBE and BLOB.]

glob·al (glō′bəl) *adj.* **1.** of or relating to the entire world; worldwide: *global warfare.* **2.** shaped like a globe; spherical. **3.** *Computers.* (of an operation) performed throughout an entire file: *a global deletion.* —**glob′al·ly,** *adv.*

glo·bate (glō′bāt) *adj.* shaped like a globe; globular.

globe (glōb) *n.* **1. the globe.** the earth; world. **2.** a sphere on which a map of the earth or of the heavens appears. **3.** a solid spherical body; sphere. **4.** anything spherical or spherelike, such as a glass covering for a light bulb. [Latin *globus* ball.]

globe·fish (glōb′fish′) *n., pl.* **-fish** or **-fish·es.** any of various spiny-finned fish, family Tetraodontidae, of tropical seas, that can inflate their bodies into a globular form with air or water. Also, **puffer.**

globe·flow·er (glōb′flou′ər) *n.* any of several plants, genus *Trollius,* of the crowfoot family, bearing globe-shaped, usually yellow flowers.

globe·trot·ter (glōb′trot′ər) *n.* a person who travels extensively, esp. for social reasons or as a sightseer. —**globe′trot′ting,** *n., adj.*

glo·bose (glō′bōs, glō bōs′) *adj.* having the shape of a globe; globular. [Latin *globōsus* round as a ball, from *globus* ball.]

glob·u·lar (glob′yə lər) *adj.* **1.** having the shape of a globe; spherical. **2.** composed of globules.

glob·ule (glob′ūl) *n.* a small ball or drop: *a globule of oil.* [Latin *globulus* little ball, diminutive of *globus* ball.]

glob·u·lin (glob′yə lin) *n.* any of a group of proteins found in many kinds of plant and animal cells, insoluble in water but readily soluble in dilute salt solutions. Globulins occur in seeds, milk, egg yolks, muscle cells, and blood plasma. [GLOBULE + -IN[1].]

glock·en·spiel (glok′ən spēl′, -shpēl′) *n.* a musical percussion instrument consisting of a series of metal bars mounted in a frame, played by striking with two small hammers. [German *Glockenspiel* chimes, from *Glocke* bell + *Spiel* play.]

glom·er·ate (glom′ər it, -ə rāt′) *adj.* having the form of a compact rounded mass; clustered. [Latin *glomerātus,* past participle of *glomerāre* to form into a ball or heap, from *glomus* ball.]

glom·er·ule (glom′ə rūl′) *n.* a dense flower cluster, esp. a cyme. [Modern Latin *glomerulus.* See GLOMERULUS.]

glo·mer·u·lus (glō mer′yə ləs, -ə ləs) *n., pl.* **-li** (-lī′). any clustered structure of blood vessels or nerves, esp. the minute capillary cluster in the nephron of a kidney through which blood plasma is filtered during the formation of urine. [Modern Latin *glomerulus,* diminutive of Latin *glomus* ball, round knot.] —**glo·mer′u·lar,** *adj.*

glockenspiel

gloom (glüm) *n.* **1.** a depressing or sullen atmosphere. **2.** a state or feeling of dejection or sadness: *We were filled with gloom over the loss of our cat.* **3.** complete or partial darkness; dimness: *The car's headlights pierced the gloom.* —*v.i.* **1.** to be or look sullen, depressed, or displeased. **2.** to be or become dark or dismal. [Middle English *gloumen* to look sullen; of uncertain origin.]

gloom·y (glü′mē) *adj.,* **gloom·i·er, gloom·i·est. 1.** characterized by or causing gloom; sad or depressing: *There was a gloomy atmosphere in the losing candidate's headquarters.* **2.** low in spirits; melancholy; depressed; dejected: *The team looked gloomy after losing the game.* **3.** having little or no light; dark; dim. —**gloom′i·ly,** *adv.* —**gloom′i·ness,** *n.* —For Synonyms, see **dark.**

glop (glop) *n.* **1.** any sloppy, mushy, or gluey substance. **2.** trite or overly sentimental statements or emotions. [Of uncertain origin.] —**glop′py,** *adj.*

Glo·ri·a (glôr′ē ə) *n.* **1.a.** any of several hymns of praise to God, beginning with the Latin word *Gloria,* as the Gloria in Excelsis Deo or the Gloria Patri. **b.** the second part of the ordinary of the Mass, the Gloria in Excelsis Deo, sung or said between the Kyrie eleison and the Credo. **c.** a musical setting for any of these. **2. gloria. a.** a halo or nimbus, esp. in art. **b.** a closely woven, lightweight fabric made of nylon, rayon, acetate, or various other materials, used chiefly for umbrellas. [Latin *glōria* honor, praise, fame.]

Glo·ri·a in Ex·cel·sis De·o (glôr′ē ə in ek sel′sis dā′ō) a hymn of praise beginning with the words *Glory to God in the highest.*

Glo·ri·a Pa·tri (glôr′ē ə pä′trē) a hymn of praise beginning with the words *Glory be to the Father.*

glo·ri·fi·ca·tion (glôr′ə fi kā′shən) *n.* **1.** the act of glorifying or the state of being glorified. **2.** a transformation of something into a more magnificent form.

glo·ri·fy (glôr′ə fī′) *v.t.,* **-fied, -fy·ing. 1.** to exalt with praise; honor: *The Romans glorified Julius Caesar.* **2.** to make glorious; procure glory for: *Great artists glorified the Italian Renaissance with their work.* **3.** to cause to appear or seem more glorious or splendid than it actually is: *The author glorified the life of the peasants.* [Old French *glorifier* to honor greatly, from Church Latin *glōrificāre* to make glorious, from Latin *glōria* praise, fame + *facere* to make.] —**glo′ri·fi′er,** *n.*

glo·ri·ous (glôr′ē əs) *adj.* **1.** exceedingly beautiful or splendid; magnificent: *a glorious day, a glorious sunset.* **2.** possessing or deserving glory; famous; renowned: *a glorious career.* **3.** conferring glory: *a glorious deed.* **4.** *Informal.* extremely enjoyable or delightful: *We had a glorious time.* [Old French *glorios* blessed, famous, splendid, from Latin *glōriōsus* famous, full of glory, from *glōria.* See GLORY.] —**glo′ri·ous·ly,** *adv.* —**glo′ri·ous·ness,** *n.*

glo·ry (glôr′ē) *n., pl.* **-ries. 1.** exalted praise, honor, or distinction; fame; renown: *The Nobel prize winner finally received all the glory due her for her work.* **2.** a person or thing that brings such praise, honor, distinction, or renown; source of pride: *The glory of the tropical island was its climate. The teacher was a glory to the*

G

a	at	e	end	o	hot	u	up	hw	white		about
ā	ape	ē	me	ō	old	ū	use	ng	song	ə	taken
ä	far	i	it	ô	fork	u̇	rule	th	thin		pencil
âr	care	ī	ice	oi	oil	u̇	pull	th	this		lemon
		îr	pierce	ou	out	ûr	turn	zh	measure		circus

profession. **3.** resplendent beauty; magnificence: *The sun shone in all its glory.* **4.** the state or condition of greatest magnificence or prosperity: *That city was in its glory during the years just before the war.* **5.** the highest degree of self-satisfaction or pleasure: *The politician was in his glory in front of the television cameras.* **6.** praise and honor offered in adoration: *Give glory to God.* **7.** the bliss of heaven. **8.** a halo or nimbus. —*v.i.,* **-ried, -ry·ing.** to rejoice proudly; exult (with *in*): *They gloried in the election victory.* [Old French *glorie, gloire* great renown, from Latin *glōria* honor, praise, fame.]

gloss¹ (glôs) *n.* **1.** a superficial shine, as of satin or a polished surface; luster. **2.** a deceptive appearance; semblance: *After their gloss of politeness wore off, their selfishness and rudeness became apparent.* —*v.t.* **1.** to put a superficial shine or luster on. **2.** to minimize or attempt to hide (often with *over*): *to gloss over the faults of a friend.* [Of Scandinavian origin.] —For Synonyms *(n.),* see **luster.**

gloss² (glôs) *n.* **1.** an explanation or interpretation, as of a text; commentary. **2.** glossary. **3.** a notation or translation placed between the lines or in the margin of a text, esp. of an ancient or medieval manuscript. —*v.t.* to provide a gloss for, as a word or text; explain or comment on. [Middle English *glose,* from Old French or Medieval Latin *glosa,* from Latin *glōssa* word needing explanation, from Greek *glōssa* tongue, language.] —**gloss'er,** *n.*

glos·sa·ry (glos'ə rē) *n., pl.* **-ries.** an alphabetized list of difficult or foreign words or technical terms found in a text or a particular subject area, each with an accompanying definition. [Latin *glōssārium,* from *glōssa* word needing explanation. See GLOSS².] —**glos·sar'i·al,** *adj.* —**glos'sar·ist,** *n.*

glos·so·la·li·a (glô'sə lā'lē ə, glos'ə-) *n.* **1.** incomprehensible speech associated with religious ecstasy; speaking in tongues. **2.** imaginary, unintelligible language associated with the insane. [Modern Latin *glossolalia,* going back to Greek *glōssa* language + *lalein* to talk.]

gloss·y (glô'sē) *adj.,* **gloss·i·er, gloss·i·est. 1.** having a shiny surface; lustrous. **2.** having a false air or appearance of sophistication: *We were not taken in by the glossy advertisement promoting the product.* —*n., pl.* **gloss·ies. 1.** a photograph printed on smooth, glossy paper. **2.** *Informal.* a magazine printed on smooth, glossy paper; slick. —**gloss'i·ly,** *adv.* —**gloss'i·ness,** *n.*

glot·tal (glot'əl) *adj.* **1.** of or relating to the glottis. **2.** *Phonetics.* articulated in the glottis, as *h* in English.

glottal stop, a speech sound produced by closing the glottis and then suddenly releasing the breath with a slight gulping sound.

glot·tis (glot'is) *n.* a narrow opening in the larynx between the vocal cords. [Greek *glōttis* mouth of the windpipe, from *glōtta* tongue.]

glove (gluv) *n.* **1.** a covering for the hand made of fabric or leather, with a separate section for each finger. **2.a.** any of several coverings for the hand used in various sports, such as baseball, hockey, or golf. **b.** a boxing glove. —*v.t.,* **gloved, glov·ing. 1.** to cover or provide with gloves. **2.** to catch (a ball) with a glove. [Old English *glōf* covering for the hand.]

• **to fit like a glove.** to fit or suit perfectly.

• **to handle with kid gloves.** to treat gently and tactfully.

glove box, an enclosed, transparent compartment with openings to which gloves are attached, permitting a person to reach inside and handle the contents without risking injury or contamination.

glove compartment, a small storage space in the dashboard of an automobile.

glow (glō) *n.* **1.** a shine from or as from a heated substance; incandescence: *the glow of a candle.* **2.** richness and warmth of color: *The child's face had the glow of good health.* **3.** a warm, ardent feeling or appearance: *a glow of pleasure.* —*v.i.* **1.** to shine from or as from intense heat: *The candle glowed. The face of the clock glowed in the dark.* **2.** to be bright and warm in color: *Her cheeks glowed after her hike.* **3.** to show or be filled with warm, ardent emotion: *His eyes glowed with pleasure.* [Old English *glōwan* to shine, to glow with heat.]

glow·er (glou'ər) *v.i.* to look at angrily or threateningly; scowl: *The customer glowered at the rude salesclerk.* —*n.* an angry or threatening stare. [Possibly of Scandinavian origin.] —**glow'er·ing·ly,** *adv.* —For Synonyms *(v.i.),* see **frown.**

glow·ing (glō'ing) *adj.* **1.** emitting light and intense heat: *glowing coals.* **2.** enthusiastic and favorable: *glowing praise, to describe something in glowing terms.* **3.** having the facial coloring caused by excitement or health; radiant. **4.** rich and warm; vivid: *a glowing red.* —**glow'ing·ly,** *adv.*

glow·worm (glō'wûrm') *n.* any of various female beetles or their larvae that give off light, such as the larva of the firefly.

glox·in·i·a (glok sin'ē ə) *n.* a low-growing tropical plant, *Sinningia speciosa,* native to the rain forests of Brazil, often cultivated for its large, velvety leaves and showy, tubular or bell-shaped flowers. [Modern Latin *Gloxinia,* from Benjamin P. *Gloxin,* an eighteenth-century German botanist.]

glu·ca·gon (glü'kə gon) *n.* a hormone secreted by the pancreas that raises the level of sugar in the bloodstream.

glu·cose (glü'kōs) *n.* **1.** a simple sugar occurring in plants and in the blood of humans and animals that is an important source of energy for the body. Formula: $C_6H_{12}O_6$ **2.** a thick, yellowish syrup made from starch, used in foods, in intravenous feedings, in the curing of tobacco, and in the tanning industry. [Greek *glykys* sweet + -OSE².]

glu·co·side (glü'kə sīd') *n.* a glycoside that yields the sugar glucose when it is decomposed, as in hydrolysis. [GLUCOS(E) + -IDE.] —**glu·co·sid·ic** (glü'kə sid'ik), *adj.*

glue (glü) *n.* **1.** an adhesive consisting of impure gelatin derived from various animal proteins, widely used in the manufacture of furniture, paints, and plywood. **2.** any sticky substance used as an adhesive. —*v.t.,* **glued, glu·ing.** to stick together or fasten with or as with glue. [Old French *glu* sticky substance, from Late Latin *glūs,* from Latin *glūten.*]

glu·ey (glü'ē) *adj.,* **glu·i·er, glu·i·est. 1.** resembling glue; viscous. **2.** full of or smeared with glue: *a gluey surface.*

glum (glum) *adj.,* **glum·mer, glum·mest.** characterized by sullenness or gloom; gloomy; morose: *a glum mood, a glum look.* [From Middle English *glomen, gloumen* to look sullen. See GLOOM.] —**glum'ly,** *adv.* —**glum'ness,** *n.*

glume (glüm) *n.* a small bract in grasses and similar plants, esp. either of two dry bracts at the base of a spikelet of grass. [Modern Latin *gluma,* from Latin *gluma* husk, from *glubere* to peel, flay.]

glu·on (glü'on) *n.* a hypothetical subatomic particle that has no mass or charge but transmits the strong force between quarks, uniting them to form mesons and baryons. [GLUE + -ON.]

glut (glut) *v.t.,* **glut·ted, glut·ting. 1.** to satisfy completely or to excess: *We glutted ourselves at dinner.* **2.** to supply (a market) with goods to excess; oversupply. —*n.* **1.** an excess of something, esp. a commodity. **2.** a great quantity. [Old French *gloutir* to gulp down, from Latin *gluttīre.*]

glu·ta·mate (glü'tə māt') *n.* a salt or ester of glutamic acid, as monosodium glutamate. [GLUTAM(IC ACID) + -ATE².]

glu·tam·ic acid (glü tam'ik) a nonessential amino acid present in wheat, beets, and a large number of plant and animal proteins, used to make monosodium glutamate. Formula: $C_5H_9NO_4$

glu·ta·mine (glü'tə mēn', -min) *n.* a nonessential amino acid widely distributed in the protein of plants and animals that yields glutamic acid and ammonia when decomposed in hydrolysis. Formula: $C_5H_{10}N_2O_3$

glu·te·al (glü'tē əl, glü tē'əl) *adj.* of or relating to the buttocks or muscles of the buttocks.

glu·ten (glü'tən) *n.* a tough, sticky protein substance obtained from grains, esp. wheat and rye, used to make bread dough rise. [Latin *glūten* glue.] —**glu'te·nous,** *adj.*

glu·te·us (glü'tē əs) *n., pl.* **-te·i** (-tē ī'). any of the three large muscles that form each buttock and function to move the thigh. [Modern Latin *gluteus,* from Greek *gloutos* buttock.]

glu·ti·nous (glü'tə nəs) *adj.* like glue; sticky. —**glu'ti·nous·ly,** *adv.*

glut·ton¹ (glut'ən) *n.* **1.** a person who eats to excess. **2.** a person who has an excessive fondness or capacity for something: *a glutton for work, a glutton for punishment.* [Old French *glouton* greedy eater, from Latin *gluttō.*]

glut·ton² (glut'ən) *n.* wolverine. [Translation of German *Vielfrass* wolverine, glutton¹ (from *viel* much + *fressen* to devour).]

glut·ton·ous (glut'ə nəs) *adj.* given to excessive eating; greedy; voracious. —**glut'ton·ous·ly,** *adv.* —**glut'ton·ous·ness,** *n.*

glut·ton·y (glut'ə nē) *n., pl.* **-ton·ies.** excess in eating; greediness.

glyc·er·al·de·hyde (glis'ə ral'də hīd') *n.* a sweet compound, produced by the oxidation of glycerin, that forms as an intermediate in the metabolic breakdown of complex carbohydrates into monosaccharides. Formula: $C_3H_6O_3$ [GLYCER(IN) + ALDEHYDE.]

glyc·er·ide (glis'ə rīd') *n.* an ester of glycerin formed by linking hydroxyl groups and fatty acids. [GLYCER(IN) + -IDE.]

glyc·er·in (glis'ər in) *also,* **glyc·er·ine** (glis'ər in, -ə rēn'). *n.* a colorless, syrupy, sweet liquid obtained from fats or produced synthetically, used esp. in making nitroglycerin, medicines, soaps, and certain plastics. Formula: $C_3H_5(OH)_3$ [French *glycérine,* from Greek *glykeros* sweet.]

glyc·er·ol (glis'ə rôl') *n.* glycerin.

gly·cine (glī′sēn, glī sēn′) *n.* a sweet, nonessential amino acid present in plants and animal products, used in the treatment of muscular dystrophy and other muscle diseases. Formula: $C_2H_5NO_2$

gly·co·gen (glī′kə jən) *n.* a white, starchlike carbohydrate that is one of the forms in which sugar is stored in the body of animals and, when needed, is converted into simple sugar glucose. [Greek *glykys* sweet + -GEN.]

gly·col (glī′kôl) *n.* ethylene glycol.

gly·col·y·sis (glī kol′ə sis) *n.* the catabolic process by which a carbohydrate, as glucose, is broken down into pyruvic or lactic acid and energy is released in the form of ATP. —**gly·co·lyt·ic** (glī′kə lit′ik), *adj.*

gly·co·pro·tein (glī′kō prō′tēn, -tē in) *n.* any of a group of compounds in which a protein is linked to a carbohydrate. [Greek *glykys* sweet + PROTEIN.]

gly·co·side (glī′kə sīd′) *n.* any of a group of compounds that yield a sugar when decomposed in hydrolysis. [French *glycose* glucose (modification of *glucose,* influenced by Greek *glykys* sweet) + -*ide* -IDE.] —**gly·co·sid·ic** (glī′kə sid′ik), *adj.*

glyph (glif) *n.* **1.** a hieroglyphic or pictograph. **2.** *Architecture.* a vertical channel or groove, as in a Doric frieze. [Greek *glyphē* carving, from *glyphein* to hollow out, carve.] —**glyph′ic,** *adj.*

gm *also,* **gm.** gram; grams.

G-man (jē′man′) *n., pl.* **-men** (-men′). *Informal.* an agent of the Federal Bureau of Investigation. [Short for *g(overnment) man.*]

GMAT, Graduate Management Admission Test.

Gmc., Germanic.

gnarl (närl) *n.* a twisted knot or lump, as on a tree. —*v.t.* to make twisted, knotted, or deformed. [From GNARLED.] —**gnarl′y,** *adj.*

gnarled (närld) *adj.* **1.** having many rough, twisted knots, as a tree trunk or branches. **2.** (of the hands) rough and slightly deformed, with prominent knuckles. [Probably modification of earlier *knurled* knotted, from KNURL.]

gnash (nash) *v.t.* **1.** to strike, grate, or grind (the teeth) together, as in anger or pain. **2.** to bite by grinding the teeth. [Probably of Scandinavian origin.]

gnat (nat) *n.* **1.** any of various small mosquitolike insects, order Diptera, having sharp, piercing mouthparts. Some suck blood; others feed on plants. **2.** *British.* mosquito. [Old English *gnætt* small fly with two wings.]

gnath·ic (nath′ik) *adj.* of or relating to the jaw. [Greek *gnáth-(os)* jaw + -IC.]

gnaw (nô) *v.,* **gnawed, gnawed** or **gnawn, gnaw·ing.** —*v.t.* **1.** to bite or chew on (something) persistently, so as to wear away: *The dog gnawed the bone.* **2.** to make by gnawing: *The rat gnawed a hole through the box.* **3.** to cause constant discomfort, pain, or trouble to. —*v.i.* **1.** to bite repeatedly: *The lion gnawed on the bars of the cage.* **2.** to torment or trouble (with *on, at,* or *into*): *Guilt can gnaw at one's conscience.* [Old English *gnagan* to bite repeatedly.]

gnaw·ing (nô′ing) *n.* a dull, constant sensation of pain or discomfort, as from hunger.

gneiss (nīs) *n.* a metamorphic rock that is composed of layers of light-colored feldspar and quartz that alternate with darker layers of other minerals. [German *Gneis,* possibly from Middle High German *gneiste* spark; because it sparkles.] —**gneiss′ic,** *adj.*

gnome¹ (nōm) *n.* in folklore, a dwarf who inhabits a mountain grotto or a mine in the earth. [French *gnome,* from Modern Latin *gnomus,* said to be from Greek *gnōmē* intelligence (supposedly because gnomes had knowledge of the riches of the earth).]

gnome² (nōm, nō′mē) *n.* a short, pithy saying; maxim; aphorism. [Greek *gnōmē* maxim, intelligence.]

gno·mic (nō′mik, nom′ik) *adj.* **1.** containing or consisting of gnomes; aphoristic. **2.** of or designating a writer of maxims. [Greek *gnōmikos* relating to maxims, didactic, from *gnōmē* maxim.]

gno·mon (nō′mon) *n.* a triangular piece on a sundial, the projecting end of which shows the time of day by casting a shadow on the face of the dial. [Latin *gnōmōn,* from Greek *gnōmōn* one that knows, interpreter, gnomon.]

Gnos·tic (nos′tik) *n.* an adherent of Gnosticism. —*adj.* of or relating to Gnosticism or Gnostics. [Greek *gnōstikos* relating to knowing, going back to *gignōskein* to know; because the Gnostics claimed to have a superior knowledge of spiritual matters.]

Gnos·ti·cism (nos′tə siz′əm) *n.* an ancient religious movement whose members believed that people are completely material and therefore doomed, but that God sent Christ to the few who possess a divine spark and thus can be saved.

GNP, gross national product.

gnu (nü, nū) *n., pl.* **gnus** or **gnu.** any of several swift African antelope, genera *Connochaetes* and *Gorgon,* having an oxlike head, short horns that curve sharply upward, and horselike legs, body, and tail. Height: to 4½ feet (1.4 meters) at the shoulder. Also, **wildebeest.** [Modification of Khoikhoi *nqu.*]

gnu

go¹ (gō) *v.,* **went, gone, go·ing.** —*v.i.* **1.** to move or travel: *The car is going too fast.* **2.** to move away; depart; leave: *I have to go now.* **3.a.** to advance or move in a specified direction: *to go right, to go downstairs.* **b.** to move or proceed with a specified goal or purpose: *He went to dress for the theater. I went to the cafeteria for lunch.* **4.** to be in or maintain action or movement; operate: *The machines go day and night.* **5.** to be given or awarded: *The estate went to the children when the millionaire died.* **6.** to be, appear, or continue in a particular state or condition: *to go unrewarded, to go in rags, to go naked.* **7.** to enter or pass into a particular state or condition: *to go insane, to go to sleep, to go into hiding, to go into mourning.* **8.** to be contributed or put: *Months of research went into the term paper.* **9.** to be appropriated, spent, or applied: *Most of the money went for food.* **10.** to proceed or be guided: *to go by the rules.* **11.** to extend, reach, or lead: *Our land goes as far as the eye can see. The stairs go to the basement.* **12.** to pass away; cease to exist: *The pain has gone.* **13.** die: *The accident victim was gone before the ambulance arrived.* **14.** to be given up, discarded, removed, or abolished: *That ugly wallpaper must go.* **15.** to be compatible or suitable; harmonize: *The shoes go with the handbag.* **16.** to pass; elapse: *When you are busy, time goes quickly.* **17.** to put or subject oneself: *She'd go to any expense for her children. He went to a lot of trouble for us.* **18.** to have recourse; resort; appeal: *We may have to go to court to settle the matter.* **19.** to be consumed: *The food went quickly because we were hungry.* **20.** to pass from person to person; circulate: *The flu went through the family. News of the plane crash went around like wildfire.* **21.** to be sold: *The sofa went for $50 at the auction.* **22.** to result in a specified manner; turn out: *The election went against him. Her speech went well.* **23.** to be known: *She went by the name of Smith.* **24.** to fail, break down, or give way: *The old man's eyesight started to go.* **25.** to hold up or out; endure; last: *The boxer couldn't go two more rounds.* **26.** to be expressed or phrased; have a particular form or arrangement: *How does the poem go?* **27.** to serve or help: *Your conduct just goes to show that you are basically lazy.* **28.** to have a usual or proper place; belong: *These sheets go in the linen closet.* **29.** to be able to be accommodated or contained; fit: *Will the books go in that box?* **30.** to be capable of being divided: *Four goes into two five times.* **31.** to follow or continue a course of action: *How far will you go before you get hurt?* **32.** to emit or make a certain sound. **33.** to be compared with or ranked among others of its kind: *This is luxurious, as hotels go.* **34.** to work or function properly or as intended. **35.** to be authoritative: *Whatever she says goes.* **36.** to be acceptable or permitted: *Anything goes in this school.* —*v.t.* **1.** to move, travel, or proceed along: *Are you going my way?* **2.** *Informal.* to bet or bid: *to go a dollar on the first race.* **3.** to share or participate in the manner of or to the extent of: *to go halves, to go partners.* **4.** to furnish (bail) with *for): He went bail for his friend.* **5.** *Informal.* to say. ➡ used in reporting dialogue: *I go, "What's your name?" and he goes, "None of your business."* —*n., pl.* **goes. 1.** the act of going: *the come and go of the tide.* **2.** *Informal.* spirit; energy; vigor: *She was full of go.* **3.** *Informal.* try; attempt: *to have a go at something.* **4.** *Informal.* success: *to make a go of a business.* —*adj. Informal.* functioning correctly; ready to proceed: *All systems are go for the launch of the space shuttle.* [Old English *gān* to move along, proceed, be in a particular condition.]

·**from the word "go."** from the very beginning.

·**no go.** *Informal.* not to be done; useless; hopeless: *The rocket launching was no go because of the weather.*

·**on the go.** *Informal.* constantly active or in motion: *to be on the go all day.*

a	at	e	end	o	hot	u	up	hw	white		about
ā	ape	ē	me	ō	old	ū	use	ng	song		taken
ä	far	i	it	ô	fork	ü	rule	th	thin	ə	pencil
âr	care	ī	ice	oi	oil	u̇	pull	th	this		lemon
		îr	pierce	ou	out	ûr	turn	zh	measure		circus

G

• **to go. a.** left; remaining: *We have six days to go before the holidays.* **b.** *Informal.* prepared and packaged to be taken out: *One hamburger to go.*

• **to go about. a.** to be occupied with or busy at: *to go about one's business.* **b.** to set about; begin: *How does one go about getting the information?* **c.** *Nautical.* to change from one tack to another; change direction.

• **to go after. a.** to chase: *The puppy went after the ball.* **b.** to go to purchase: *I'll go after the hamburgers and sodas.* **c.** to seek: *to go after more sales for the company.*

• **to go against.** to be contrary to or antagonize; oppose: *Betting on horses goes against my principles.*

• **to go along. a.** to agree; cooperate (often with *with*): *We'll go along with whatever you decide.*

• **to go around.** to be sufficient to provide or give a portion to all: *Will there be enough cake to go around?*

• **to go at. a.** to undertake or work at: *They went at the job with vigor.* **b.** to attack: *to go at someone with a knife.*

• **to go back on.** *Informal.* **a.** to fail to keep or fulfill; break: *to go back on one's word.* **b.** to be unfaithful or disloyal to; betray: *to go back on one's friends.*

• **to go beyond.** to exceed; surpass.

• **to go by.** to pass unnoticed or be disregarded: *We'll let the error go by this time.*

• **to go down. a.** to be recorded or remembered: *He'll go down in history.* **b.** to suffer defeat; lose: *to go down without a fight.* **c.** to be swallowed: *The pill went down smoothly.*

• **to go for.** *Informal.* **a.** to try to secure or obtain: *The contestant went for the money instead of the car.* **b.** to favor or support: *The state went for the Democrats.* **c.** to be strongly attracted by or interested in: *My friend really goes for you.* **d.** to attack: *The dog went for the thief.*

• **to go hard with.** to cause or result in hardship, trouble, or suffering for.

• **to go in for.** *Informal.* to like or engage in.

• **to go into. a.** to examine or discuss: *We can't go into all the causes of the war at this time.* **b.** to enter or take up, as a profession or study: *She went into medicine.*

• **to go in with.** to form an alliance or partnership with; join: *He went in with his friend on the deal.*

• **to go it alone.** to do something without help.

• **to go off. a.** to explode or be discharged: *The gun went off accidentally.* **b.** to ring: *My alarm went off at 6 A.M.* **c.** *Informal.* to take place; happen; occur: *Everything went off as expected.* **d.** to be sent: *The proofs went off to the printer.*

• **to go on. a.** to continue: *He went on working as he talked. The party went on until midnight.* **b.** to take place; happen; occur: *What's going on? You won't believe what went on last night.* **c.** to approach; near: *It's going on two years since we last saw her.* **d.** to proceed: *He said he had visited thirty countries, and went on to list them.* **e.** *Informal.* to chatter or rant: *She is always going on about her problems.* **f.** to admit of being put on: *These shoes won't go on.*

• **to go (someone) one better.** to outdo; surpass: *That was a funny story, but I can go you one better.*

• **to go out. a.** to have a date or dates: *My friend has been going out with the same person for a year.* **b.** to become obsolete or out-of-date: *Those shoes went out about ten years ago.* **c.** to attend a social function or functions. **d.** to be moved, esp. by love or sympathy: *My heart went out to him.* **e.** to strike: *The workers went out for better pay.* **f.** to be a candidate; try: *She went out for the basketball team.* **g.** to play the first nine holes of an eighteen-hole golf course. **h.** *Card Games.* to get rid of the last card in one's hand in one round or for the entire game.

• **to go over. a.** to examine carefully: *The accountant went over the books.* **b.** to read, rehearse, or review: *She went over her notes before the exam. The actor went over his lines many times.* **c.** to do again: *Go over the floor with a mop.* **d.** to be successful: *The party went over very well.*

• **to go through. a.** to perform thoroughly or in detail: *We went through the scene three times during rehearsal.* **b.** to undergo; experience: *She went through one hardship after another.* **c.** to search or examine thoroughly: *The thief went through all the drawers.* **d.** to spend, use up, or wear out: *He went through the inheritance in six months. Our family goes through a gallon of milk every day.* **e.** to be accepted or approved: *My application went through, and I was hired.*

• **to go through with.** to carry out to the finish; complete: *Are you prepared to go through with the project?*

• **to go together,** to harmonize; match: *The blouse and the skirt go together.*

• **to go under. a.** to be overwhelmed or defeated. **b.** to sink: *The ship went under with 1,000 passengers.* **c.** to fail: *The business went under because of poor management.* **d.** to yield to the influence of a drug or hypnosis; become drugged or hypnotized.

• **to go up.** to be raised or constructed: *Barricades went up along the street.*

• **to go without saying.** to be taken for granted; be obvious.

• **to let go. a.** to release or set free: *He let the bird go. She let go the child's hand.* **b.** to allow to pass by without taking action or notice: *I'll let their rudeness go for the time being.* **c.** to fail to maintain in working order or good condition: *The lazy manager let the business go.*

• **to let oneself go. a.** to allow oneself to be uninhibited. **b.** to fail to maintain one's appearance or health.

Synonyms *v.i.* **Go¹, leave¹,** and **depart** mean to move from a place. **Go** is the general term: *It's time to go to class. Are you going out of town this weekend?* **Leave** suggests a less casual going and may also carry the idea of separation: *Why are you leaving so soon? Next year I'm leaving this town for good.* **Depart** is similar to *leave,* but more formal and generally connotes leaving for a trip: *The train departs at six o'clock. We depart for Europe tomorrow.*

go² (gō) *n.* a Japanese game for two players played with stone-like black and white counters on a board divided into squares. [Japanese *go.*]

go·a (gō′ə) *n.* a black-tailed gazelle, *Procapra picticaudata,* of Tibet, the male of which has horns that curve backward. Height: 25 inches (64 centimeters) at the shoulder. [Tibetan *dgoba.*]

goad (gōd) *n.* **1.** a sharp-pointed stick used for driving cattle or oxen. **2.** anything that drives or urges; stimulus. —*v.t.* to urge or prod with or as if with a goad. [Old English *gād* pointed stick used for driving cattle.] —For Synonyms *(v.t.),* see **urge.**

go·a·head (gō′ə hed′) *n. Informal.* a permission, signal, or order to proceed: *The teacher gave us the go-ahead for the class picnic.*

goal (gōl) *n.* **1.** an object to which effort is directed; aim. **2.** the terminal point of a race or journey. **3.** an area or object into, or through which, players in certain games try to get a ball or puck in order to score. **4.** the act of getting a ball or puck into, or through, such an area or object. **5.** the point or points made by such an act. **6.** the position of goalkeeper: *to play goal for a hockey team.* [Middle English *gōl* boundary, limit; of uncertain origin.] —For Synonyms, see **objective.**

goal·keep·er (gōl′kē′pər) *n.* a player who defends the goal in certain games, such as ice hockey, field hockey, lacrosse, and soccer. Also, **goal·ie** (gō′lē), **goaltender.**

goal line, either of two lines marking the goals in a game.

goal·post (gōl′pōst′) *n.* either of two structures consisting of a pair of posts supporting a crossbar, situated on either the end line or the goal line, as in football.

goal·tend·er (gōl′ten′dər) *n.* goalkeeper.

go·a·round (gō′ə round′) *n.* **1.** the act or an instance of going around: *The airplane made a go-around of the airport before landing.* **2.** a meeting or session, esp. one filled with conflict or argument. **3.** runaround. Also *(defs. 2, 3),* **go-round.**

goat (gōt) *n., pl.* **goats** or **goat. 1.** any of various wild or domesticated cloven-hoofed, cud-chewing mammals, family Bovidae, esp. genus *Capra,* having hollow horns and frequently a beardlike tuft of hair under the chin. Height: 30-35 inches (76-89 centimeters) at the shoulder. **2.** a lecherous man. **3.** *Informal.* **a.** a person who is made to take the blame or punishment for others; scapegoat. **b.** a person who is the butt of a joke. [Old English *gāt* the female of this animal.] —**goat′like′,** *adj.*

• **to get someone's goat.** *Informal.* to cause to become angry, annoyed, or irritated.

goat·ee (gō tē′) *n.* a small pointed beard on the chin. [From GOAT; because it resembles a goat's beard.]

goat·herd (gōt′hûrd′) *n.* a person who tends goats.

goat·skin (gōt′skin′) *n.* **1.** the skin of a goat. **2.** leather made from it. **3.** a container made from this leather, used esp. for wine.

goat·suck·er (gōt′suk′ər) *n.* nightjar.

gob¹ (gob) *n. Informal.* **1.** a mass or lump. **2.** gobs. a large quantity; a lot: *gobs of money.* [Old French *gobe* lump, mouthful, from *gober* to swallow; possibly of Celtic origin.]

gob² (gob) *n. Slang.* a sailor in the U.S. Navy. [Of uncertain origin.]

gob·bet (gob′it) *n. Archaic.* a piece or fragment, esp. of raw flesh or meat. [Old French *gobet* piece, bit, diminutive of *gobe* lump. See GOB¹.]

gob·ble¹ (gob′əl) *v.,* **-bled, -bling.** —*v.t.* **1.** to eat (food) hastily and greedily. **2.** *Informal.* to seize eagerly or greedily (often with *up*): *The corporation gobbled up many competing small com-*

panies. —*v.i.* to eat hastily and greedily. [GOB¹ + -LE or Middle English *gobben* to drink greedily.]

gob·ble² (gob'əl) *v.i.,* **-bled, -bling.** to make the throaty sound characteristic of a male turkey. —*n.* such a sound. [Imitative.]

gob·ble·dy·gook (gob'əl dē gůk') *also,* **gob·ble·de·gook.** *n.* *Informal.* speech or writing that is wordy, involved, and not easily understood. [Possibly based on GOBBLE².]

gob·bler (gob'lər) *n.* a male turkey.

Gob·e·lin (gob'ə lin; *French* gô blaɴ') *n.* a fine, handwoven tapestry, esp. of the late seventeenth and eighteenth centuries. [From *Gobelin,* family of French dyers who founded a factory for making tapestries in Paris in the fifteenth century.]

go·be·tween (gō'bi twēn') *n.* a person who goes back and forth between persons or groups to make arrangements, conduct business, or settle disputes.

gob·let (gob'lit) *n.* **1.** a drinking vessel, usually of glass, with a base and stem. **2.** *Archaic.* a bowl-shaped drinking vessel without handles. [Old French *gobelet* cup, diminutive of *gobel* large drinking bowl; possibly of Celtic origin.]

gob·lin (gob'lin) *n.* an ugly, mischievous sprite or elf, esp. one that is evil and malicious. [Old French *gobelin,* from Medieval Latin *gobelinus,* possibly going back to Greek *kobālos* evil spirit.]

go·by (gō'bē) *n., pl.* **-bies** or **-by.** any of a group of colorful saltwater fish, family Gobiidae, found in temperate and tropical coastal waters and usually having pelvic fins that join to form a ventral sucker by which it attaches itself to the bottom. One species, *Mistichthys luzohensis,* is the smallest living vertebrate. Length: ½-4 inches (1-10 centimeters). [Latin *gobius* gudgeon, from Greek *kōbios.*]

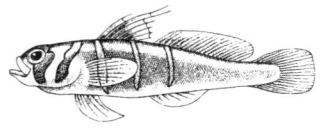

goby

go-by (gō'bī') *n.* *Informal.* a passing by without notice, esp. when done intentionally: *to give someone the go-by.*

go·cart (gō'kärt') *n.* **1.** a small wagon for young children to ride in or pull. **2.** a small, light framework mounted on rollers, used to support a baby learning to walk. **3.** a light carriage. **4.** handcart. **5.** go-kart.

God (god) *n.* **1.** in monotheistic religions, the eternal, almighty being who is the creator, sustainer, and ruler of the universe; Supreme Being. **2. god. a.** any of various beings, as in Greek and Roman mythology and certain primitive religions, regarded as immortal, as personifying or controlling a specific aspect or element of nature, or as having special powers over the lives and affairs of humans. **b.** a male god. **c.** an image of a god that is an object of worship; idol. **d.** a person or thing that is made an object of worship, devotion, or admiration. [Old English *god.*]

god·child (god'chīld') *n., pl.* **-chil·dren** (-chil'drən). a person for whom another person is sponsor, as at baptism.

god·daugh·ter (god'dô'tər) *n.* a female godchild.

god·dess (god'is) *n.* **1.** a female god. **2.** an extraordinarily beautiful woman.

god·fa·ther (god'fä'thər) *n.* a man who sponsors a child, as at baptism. —*v.t.* to act as a godfather to.

god·for·sak·en (god'fər sā'kən) *adj.* **1.** remote or desolate. **2.** wretched; miserable.

God·head (god'hed') *n.* **1.** the Deity; God. **2.** *also,* **godhead.** divine nature; divinity.

god·hood (god'hůd') *n.* the state or quality of being divine; divinity.

god·less (god'lis) *adj.* **1.** not believing in a god or God. **2.** wicked. —**god'less·ness,** *n.*

god·like (god'līk') *adj.* befitting or like a god or God.

god·ly (god'lē) *adj.,* **-li·er, -li·est. 1.** devoutly observant of the laws of God; pious. **2.** *Archaic.* godlike. —**god'li·ness,** *n.*

god·moth·er (god'muth'ər) *n.* a woman who sponsors a child, as at baptism. —*v.t.* to act as a godmother to.

god·par·ent (god'pâr'ənt) *n.* a godfather or godmother.

God's acre, a cemetery, esp. in a churchyard.

god·send (god'send') *n.* something that is needed or desired and arrives or occurs unexpectedly, as if sent by God: *The inheritance was a godsend to the poor family.*

god·son (god'sun') *n.* a male godchild.

God·speed (god'spēd') *n.* good luck; success: *to wish someone Godspeed.*

god·wit (god'wit) *n.* any of various wading birds, genus *Limosa,* that breed in the Arctic tundra and usually winter south of the equator. They have a slender body, long slender legs, and a long, narrow, slightly upturned bill. Length: 14-20 inches (36-51 centimeters). [Of uncertain origin.]

go·fer (gō'fər) *also,* **go-fer, gopher.** *n.* *Slang.* an employee whose duties include running errands for a work crew or office staff. [From the phrase *go for* to fetch.]

Gog and Magog (gog) in the New Testament, the two nations that, led by Satan, will war with the kingdom of God at Armageddon.

go·get·ter (gō'get'ər, -get'-) *n.* *Informal.* an energetic, aggressive, and enterprising person.

gog·gle (gog'əl) *n.* **goggles.** large, close-fitting spectacles used to protect the eyes, as from sparks, dust, or wind. Skiers, motorcyclists, and welders often wear goggles. —*v.,* **-gled, -gling.** —*v.i.* **1.** to roll one's eyes or stare with bulging eyes. **2.** (of eyes) to roll or bulge: *The frog's hideous eyes goggling out of his head* (William Makepeace Thackeray, 1855). —*v.t.* to roll (one's eyes). —*adj.* (of eyes) rolling, bulging, or staring. [Of uncertain origin.]

gog·gle-eyed (gog'əl īd') *adj.* having rolling, bulging, or staring eyes.

Goi·del·ic (goi del'ik) *n.* a branch of the Celtic group of the Indo-European family of languages, which includes Irish Gaelic, Scottish Gaelic, and Manx. [Old Irish *Gōidel* a Gael + -IC.]

go·ing (gō'ing) *n.* **1.** the act of moving away or departing: *Their going was unexpected.* **2.** the condition of a surface or the environment, as for walking, driving, or flying: *The going was muddy because of heavy rain.* **3.** *Informal.* a condition that affects action or progress: *It was tough going during exams.* —*adj.* **1.** in action or movement; operating; functioning: *The machine is going.* **2.** doing or conducting business successfully: *The store is now a going concern.* **3.** current; prevalent: *the going price for a used car.* **4.** *Informal.* in existence: *the funniest joke going.*

go·ing-o·ver (gō'ing ō'vər) *n.* *Informal.* **1.** a careful, intensive search, check, or examination: *The police gave the room a goingover.* **2.** a severe scolding or beating.

goings on, actions, behavior, or incidents, esp. when disapproved of: *The police investigated the strange goings on at the old house.*

goi·ter (goi'tər) *also,* **goi·tre.** *n.* an enlargement of the thyroid gland causing a swelling in the neck. It is often caused by improper functioning of the thyroid or a deficiency of iodine in the diet. Also, **struma.** [French *goître,* from Old French *goitron* throat, going back to Latin *guttur.*] —**goi·trous** (goi'trəs), *adj.*

go-kart (gō'kärt') *also,* **go·cart.** *n.* a small vehicle consisting of a bare frame on four wheels and a low-powered gasoline engine, used esp. for recreation and for racing.

gold cup from Iran (c.1100 B.C.)

G

gold (gōld) *n.* **1.** a heavy, soft, lustrous, yellow metallic element that is extremely ductile, malleable, and resistant to corrosion, used esp. as a standard for currency, in jewelry, and in electronic devices. Symbol: **Au** For tables, see **element. 2.** coins made of this metal, collectively. **3.** wealth; riches. **4.** a bright yellow color. **5.** anything resembling or compared to gold, as in value, beauty, or luster: *a heart of gold.* —*adj.* **1.** relating to, containing, or made of gold: *a gold bracelet, a gold tooth.* **2.** having the color gold; bright yellow. [Old English *gold* this metal, coin made of this metal; wealth.]

gold·beat·ing (gōld'bē'ting) *n.* the act or process of beating gold into very thin sheets to make gold leaf. —**gold'beat'er,** *n.*

gold·brick (gōld'brik') *Slang.* *v.i.* to get out of or avoid work or duty, esp. by pretending to be ill. —*n.* a person, esp. in the armed forces, who shirks work or duty. Also, **gold'brick'er.**

a	at	e	end	o	hot	u	up	hw	white		about
ā	ape	ē	me	ō	old	ū	use	ng	song		taken
ä	far	i	it	ô	fork	ü	rule	th	thin	ə	pencil
âr	care	ī	ice	oi	oil	ů	pull	th	this		lemon
		îr	pierce	ou	out	ûr	turn	zh	measure		circus

gold certificate, a certificate issued by the U.S. government, formerly circulated as money, stating that a certain amount of gold has been deposited in the Treasury for redemption on demand. Only Federal Reserve Banks now hold gold certificates.

gold digger *Slang.* a woman who uses feminine charm to get money and gifts from men.

gold dust, gold in very small particles or as a fine powder.

gold·en (gōl′dən) *adj.* **1.** made of or containing gold. **2.** having the color or luster of gold: *the golden sun.* **3.** excellent or very valuable: *a golden opportunity.* **4.** very happy and prosperous; flourishing: *the golden days of youth.* **5.** of or marking the fiftieth year or event in a series: *My parents recently celebrated their golden wedding anniversary.*

Golden Age 1. in classical mythology, the first or early period in human history, supposed to be a time of peace, innocence, and plenty. **2. golden age.** a period during which the highest level of prosperity, achievement, or progress is reached: *the golden age of Greece, the golden age of exploration.*

golden algae, any of a large division, Chrysophyta, of mostly flagellated unicellular algae, including diatoms and yellow-green algae, in which the chlorophyll is masked by a carotenoid pigment. Also, **golden brown algae.**

golden calf 1. in the Old Testament, the golden statue of a calf that the Israelites persuaded Aaron to make for them to worship. **2.** wealth or material possessions regarded as being of supreme value.

golden eagle, an eagle, *Aquila chrysaëtos,* widely distributed throughout the Northern Hemisphere and having dark brown feathers with golden tints on the head and back of the neck. Length: 33 inches (84 centimeters).

gold·en·eye (gōl′dən ī′) *n., pl.* **-eyes** or **-eye.** a diving duck, genus *Bucephala,* found in woods and forests in most parts of the Northern Hemisphere and having bright yellow eyes. The male is black and white, and the female is brown and white. Length: 17-23 inches (43-58 centimeters).

Golden Fleece, in Greek legend, a sheepskin from a golden ram, kept in a grove guarded by a dragon. It was stolen by Jason and the Argonauts.

golden glow, a tall plant, *Rudbeckia laciniata,* of the composite family, found in North America and bearing showy double flower heads consisting of yellowish or greenish disk flowers surrounded by yellow, petallike rays.

golden mean, a course or way that avoids extremes and pursues moderation.

golden retriever, any of a breed of medium-sized hunting dogs with hanging ears and dense, golden fur that is feathered on the legs, neck, and tail.

gold·en·rod (gōl′dən rod′) *n.* any of a large group of plants, genus *Solidago,* of the composite family, found in north temperate regions of the world and widely distributed as a weed in eastern North America. They bear many small yellow flower heads in spikes on tall, branching stalks.

golden rule, the rule of conduct, set forth by Jesus in the Sermon on the Mount, that one should treat others as one wishes to be treated.

gold·en·seal (gōl′dən sēl′) *n.* a low, perennial North American herb, *Hydrastis canadensis,* related to the buttercup, having large, round leaves and a thick, yellow root, formerly used in medicines and as a dye.

gold-filled (gōld′fild′) *adj.* made of or containing a base metal covered with a layer of gold.

gold·finch (gōld′finch′) *n.* **1.** a European songbird, *Carduelis carduelis,* having yellow markings on its wings. **2.** any of several American finches, genus *Spinus,* esp. the **American** or **common goldfinch,** *Spinus tristis,* the male of which has bright yellow and black summer plumage. [Old English *goldfinc* the European songbird.]

gold·fish (gōld′fish′) *n., pl.* **-fish** or **-fish·es.** a freshwater fish, *Carassius auratus,* of the carp family, native to southeastern Asia, and ranging in color from gold to black. Many domestic varieties are raised in home aquariums and outdoor ponds.

goldfinch *(def. 2)*

gold leaf, gold beaten into extremely thin sheets, used in gilding.

gold mine 1. a mine from which ore yielding gold is obtained. **2.** any source of great wealth or profit: *Their business turned out to be a gold mine. This book is a gold mine of information.*

gold rush, the sudden rush of people to an area where gold has been discovered, as to California in 1849 and to the Klondike in 1897.

gold·smith (gōld′smith′) *n.* a person who fashions or deals in objects made from gold, such as jewelry. [Old English *goldsmith.*]

gold standard, a monetary system that defines the basic currency unit of a country in terms of a specific amount of gold.

go·lem (gō′lem, -ləm) *n.* in Jewish legend, an artificial being made in the shape of a human being and given life by incantation. [Yiddish *goylem,* from Hebrew *golem* formless mass.]

golf (golf, gôlf) *n.* a game played on a golf course with a small, hard ball and a set of golf clubs, the object being to sink the ball in a succession of holes with as few strokes as possible. —*v.i.* to play this game. [Of uncertain origin.] —**golf′er,** *n.*

golf club 1. any of various clubs with long thin shafts and wooden or iron heads, used to hit the ball in golf. **2.** a private club that maintains such facilities as a golf course and clubhouse.

golf course, an area of land laid out in nine or eighteen holes, each having obstacles or traps, and comprising a tee, fairway, and green. Also, **golf links.**

Gol·gi apparatus (gôl′jē) an organelle found in eukaryotic cells, consisting of flat, membrane-enclosed, stacked sacs surrounded by vesicles. It functions to assemble and distribute complex molecules, such as proteins, from simple ones, such as amino acids. Also, **Golgi body.** [From Camillo *Golgi,* 1844-1926, Italian physician and histologist who first observed it.]

gol·li·wog (gol′ē wog′) *also,* **gol·li·wogg.** *n.* **1.** a grotesque black doll. **2.** a grotesque person. [From *Golliwogg,* name of a doll in a series of children's books, possibly patterned after POLLIWOG.]

gol·ly (gol′ē) *interj. Informal.* a word used to express surprise or wonder.

go·nad (gō′nad, gon′ad) *n.* a sex organ in which reproductive cells develop and in which sex hormones are produced in vertebrates. The ovaries are the female gonads, and the testes are the male gonads. [Modern Latin *gonad-,* stem of *gonas* gonad, from Greek *gonos* a seed, generation.] —**go·nad′al,** *adj.*

go·nad·o·tro·pin (gō nad′ə trō′pin) *also,* **go·nad·o·tro·phin** (gō nad′ə trō′fin). *n.* any of several hormones formed in the pituitary gland that stimulate the development and functioning of the gonads. —**go·nad·o·trop·ic** (gō nad′ə trop′ik, -trō′pik); *also,* **go·nad·o·troph·ic** (gō nad′ə trof′ik, -trō′fik), *adj.*

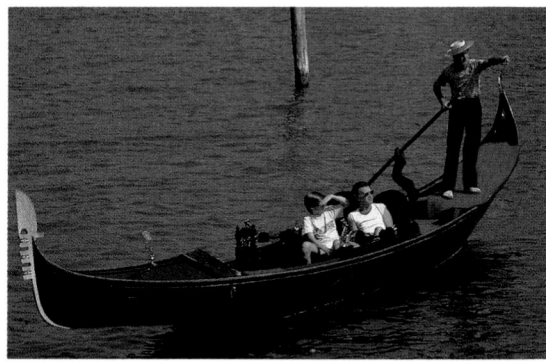

Venetian **gondola**

gon·do·la (gon′də lə) *n.* **1.** a long, narrow, flat-bottomed boat with high peaks at the ends, propelled at the stern by one person with an oar or pole, used on the canals of Venice. **2.** gondola car. **3.** a small car that runs along and is suspended from an overhead cable, used esp. as a ski lift. **4.** a car that hangs from a dirigible or balloon. [Italian *gondola* Venetian boat, diminutive of *gonda,* possibly going back to Greek *kondy* drinking vessel; with reference to a gondola's shape.]

gondola car, a railroad freight car with low sides and no top, used for hauling bulk commodities, such as coal.

gon·do·lier (gon′də lîr′) *n.* a person who rows or poles a gondola.

gone (gôn, gon) *v.* the past participle of **go**[1]. —*adj.* **1.** moved away; left; departed: *She is gone for the summer.* **2.** used up or spent: *The supplies are all gone.* **3.** dead. **4.** beyond hope or recovery; lost; ruined: *But don't talk so, as if it were a gone case* (Harriet Beecher Stowe, 1852). **5.** characterized by weakness or faintness: *He had a sad, gone look on his face.*

  •**to be far gone.** to be much advanced or deeply involved: *The epidemic was too far gone to be stopped.*

  •**to be gone on.** *Informal.* to be in love with: *My younger brother is really gone on the girl next door.*

gon·er (gô′nər, gon′ər) *n. Informal.* a person or thing that is dying, ruined, lost, or beyond help or recovery.

gon·fa·lon (gon′fə lən) *n.* a banner or flag hung vertically from a crossbar rather than a pole, often composed of, or ending in, several streamers, esp. such a banner or flag used by various medieval Italian republics. [Italian *gonfalone;* of Germanic origin.]

gong (gông, gong) *n.* **1.** an Oriental musical instrument consisting of a metal disk, usually with an upturned rim, that makes a loud, resonant tone when struck. For illustration, see **percussion instrument. 2.** a saucer-shaped bell sounded by a mechanical hammer. [Malay *gōng* the musical instrument.]

go·nid·i·um (gō nid′ē əm) *n., pl.* **-nid·i·a** (-nid′ē ə). **1.** an asexual reproductive cell in algae, as a zoospore. **2.** any of the algal cells in a lichen. [Modern Latin *gonidium,* diminutive of Greek *gonos* seed, generation.] **—go·nid′i·al,** *adj.*

gon·o·coc·cus (gon′ə kok′əs) *n., pl.* **-coc·ci** (-kok′sī). the bacterium that causes gonorrhea. **—gon′o·coc′cal, gon·o·coc·cic** (gon′ə kok′sik), *adj.*

gon·or·rhe·a (gon′ə rē′ə) *also,* **gon·or·rhoe·a.** *n.* a contagious sexually transmitted disease that causes inflammation of the genital and urinary organs. It can usually be cured with penicillin, but may lead to serious complications if left untreated. [Late Latin *gonorrhoea,* from Greek *gonorrhoia,* from *gonos* seed + *rhoiā* flow; because mistakenly thought to be a discharge of semen.]

goo (gü) *n. Informal.* any sticky substance, such as glue. [Possibly modification of GLUE.]

goo·ber (gü′bər) *n. Informal.* a peanut. Also, **goober pea.** [Bantu *nguba.*]

good (gud) *adj.,* **bet·ter, best. 1.** above average; commendable: *good food, a good movie.* **2.** characterized by, possessing, or exhibiting moral excellence; virtuous: *a good person, good deeds.* **3.** agreeable; pleasant: *good news, a good frame of mind.* **4.** kind or generous: *He was always good to me.* **5.** competent or skillful: *a good dancer, to be good at figures.* **6.** honorable: *He was a member in good standing. She has a good reputation among her colleagues.* **7.** safe or correct; reliable: *good advice, a good risk.* **8.** satisfactory or suitable to a specific purpose: *It's a good day for sailing.* **9.** genuine or valid: *He had a good excuse for his tardiness.* **10.** satisfyingly full or adequate: *a good night's sleep.* **11.** beneficial; advantageous: *Milk is good for children.* **12.** representative; typical: *a good example of Greek architecture.* **13.** having the necessary or desired requirements; qualified: *to be good for the job.* **14.** sound; unimpaired: *good eyesight.* **15.** fairly great, as in amount or extent; more than a little; considerable: *a good deal of trouble.* **16.** well-behaved; obedient: *She was always good as a child.* **17.** best or most formal: *We used our good china and crystal.* **18.** thorough: *a good scolding.* **19.** favorable; approving: *She had a good opinion of him.* **20.** entire; complete: *The town is a good day's trip from here.* **21.** pleasing to the eye; attractive: *a good figure.* **22.** loyal or devout: *a good Democrat, a good Catholic.* **23.** fresh; unspoiled: *Is the meat still good?* **24.** right; proper: *She speaks good English.* —*n.* **1.** benefit; advantage: *It's for your own good.* **2.** what is morally excellent, honorable, or correct: *There is much good in him.* **3. the good.** good people: *The minister said that the good will receive eternal happiness.* —*adv. Informal.* well. [Old English *gōd* satisfactory, excellent, kind, pleasant, thorough, full.]

 • **as good as.** almost; practically: *Although the buyer hasn't actually given me a check, my car is as good as sold.*
 • **for good.** finally; permanently: *The college is closing for good because of declining enrollment.*
 • **good and.** *Informal.* completely or extremely; thoroughly: *Their insults made me good and mad.*
 • **good for. a.** able to survive or remain valid or functioning: *My car is good for another 2,000 miles.* **b.** able or willing to pay or give: *My mother is always good for $20.* **c.** worth: *The coupon is good for five dollars of merchandise.*
 • **no good.** worthless or useless.
 • **to be in good with.** to have the approval, confidence, or friendship of: *to be in good with a teacher.*
 • **to get in good with.** to obtain the approval, confidence, or friendship of.
 • **to make good. a.** to fulfill: *to make good a promise.* **b.** to make up for; repay or replace: *to make good a mistake by an apology, to make good on a debt.* **c.** to be successful: *After years of minor parts, the actor finally made good with a starring role on Broadway.* **d.** to carry out successfully; accomplish: *The army made good its retreat.* **e.** to prove; substantiate: *to make good a claim.*
 • **to the good.** as a profit or advantage: *The club ended the fiscal year $800 to the good.*

Good Book, Bible.

good-bye (gud′bī′) *also,* **good·by, good-by.** *interj.* farewell. —*n., pl.* **-byes, -bys.** farewell: *After the necessary good-byes, we left on our trip.* [Contraction of *God be with you* (or *ye*).]

good cheer 1. a feeling of joy or optimism; high spirits: *to be of good cheer.* **2.** good food or drink: *Have some good cheer.* **3.** feasting and merrymaking; revelry.

good day, a salutation of greeting or farewell used in the daytime.

good evening, a salutation of greeting or farewell used in the evening.

good-for-noth·ing (gud′fər nuth′ing, -nuth′-) *adj.* useless or worthless. —*n.* a person who is idle, worthless, or useless.

Good Friday, Friday of Holy Week, commemorating the crucifixion of Jesus.

good-heart·ed (gud′här′tid) *adj.* kind or generous. **—good′-heart′ed·ly,** *adv.* **—good′-heart′ed·ness,** *n.*

good-hu·mored (gud′hū′mərd, -ū′mərd) *adj.* having or showing a cheerful or pleasant mood or feeling. **—good′-hu′mored·ly,** *adv.* **—good′-hu′mored·ness,** *n.*

good·ish (gud′ish) *adj.* fairly good or large: *a goodish amount.*

good-look·ing (gud′luk′ing) *adj.* pleasing or attractive in appearance.

good·ly (gud′lē) *adj.,* **-li·er, -li·est. 1.** considerable, as in amount or degree: *Her trip cost her a goodly sum of money.* **2.a.** of good quality: *The land which sent forth such goodly stores* (Edward A. Freeman, 1871). **b.** having a pleasing or attractive appearance; good-looking. [Old English *gōdlīc* good-looking.] **—good′li·ness,** *n.*

good·man (gud′mən) *n., pl.* **-men** (-mən). *Archaic.* **1.** the master or male head of a household. **2.** a man below the rank of gentleman; mister.

good morning, a salutation of greeting or farewell in the morning.

good-na·tured (gud′nā′chərd) *adj.* having or showing a pleasant or kindly disposition; agreeable. **—good′-na′tured·ly,** *adv.* **—good′-na′tured·ness,** *n.*

Good Neighbor Policy, a U.S. policy toward Latin America urging political and economic cooperation and a system of mutual defense, established by President Franklin D. Roosevelt in 1933.

good·ness (gud′nis) *n.* **1.** the state or quality of being good. **2.** moral excellence; virtue. **3.** kindness, benevolence, or generosity: *He did it out of the goodness of his heart.* **4.** the best or most valuable part of something. **5.** God. ➡ used as a euphemism: *Goodness knows.* —*interj.* used to express surprise or vexation. [Old English *gōdnes* virtue, kindness.]

goods (gudz) *pl. n.* **1.** things for sale; merchandise; wares: *sporting goods.* **2.** movable personal property; belongings: *They lost all their worldly goods in the flood.* **3.** fabric; material; cloth. [Plural of GOOD.]

 • **to deliver the goods.** *Slang.* to do or produce what is promised or needed.
 • **to get the goods on.** *Slang.* to get proof of guilt or wrongdoing by.
 • **to have the goods on.** *Slang.* to have proof of guilt or wrongdoing by.

Good Samaritan 1. in the New Testament, a traveler who aided a fellow traveler who had been beaten and robbed. **2.** a person who is compassionate and helpful toward others.

Good Shepherd, Jesus.

good-sized (gud′sīzd′) *adj.* fairly big or large.

good speed, Godspeed.

good-tem·pered (gud′tem′pərd) *adj.* not easily angered or irritated.

G

a	at	e	end	o	hot	u	up	hw	white		about
ā	ape	ē	me	ō	old	ū	use	ng	song		taken
ä	far	i	it	ô	fork	ü	rule	th	thin	ə	pencil
âr	care	ī	ice	oi	oil	u̇	pull	th	this		lemon
				îr	pierce	ou	out	ûr	turn	zh	measure		circus

good·wife (gŏŏd′wīf′) *n., pl.* -**wives** (-wīvz′). *Archaic.* **1.** the mistress of a household. **2.** a woman below the rank of lady. [GOOD + WIFE]

good·will (gŏŏd′wil′) *also,* **good will.** *n.* **1.** kindness or benevolence: *a feeling of goodwill toward others.* **2.** cheerful consent; willingness: *She accepted the task with goodwill.* **3.** an intangible asset of a business, resulting from the good relations it has established with the public.

good·y[1] (gŏŏd′ē) *n., pl.* **good·ies.** *Informal.* **1.** something very tasty and sweet, such as candy or a cookie. **2.** a choice or special thing: *There are some goodies in this record collection.* —*interj.* great or wonderful. [GOOD + -Y[2].]

good·y[2] (gŏŏd′ē) *n., pl.* **good·ies.** *Archaic.* a married woman of humble station. ➡ used as a title or term of address. [Short for GOODWIFE.]

good·y-good·y (gŏŏd′ē gŏŏd′ē) *adj.* affectedly or self-righteously pious. —*n., pl.* -**good·ies.** a goody-goody person.

goo·ey (gü′ē) *adj.,* **goo·i·er, goo·i·est.** *Informal.* soft and sticky. [GOO + -EY.]

goof (gŭf) *Informal. n.* **1.** a stupid or clumsy mistake; blunder. **2.** a stupid, silly, or blundering person. **3.** a prank or joke. —*v.i.* to make a stupid or clumsy mistake; blunder. —*v.t.* to make a mess of; botch (often with *up*): *I really goofed up that assignment.* [Possibly form of obsolete *goff* fool, from French *goffe* awkward, stupid, from Italian *goffo;* of uncertain origin.]
  ·**to goof off** (or **around**). to waste time or avoid work or duty: *We spent most of the day goofing off.*

goof-off (gŭf′ôf′, -of′) *n. Slang.* a person who wastes time or avoids work or duty; shirker.

goof-up (gŭf′up′) *n.* **1.** a person who makes a mess of things; bungler. **2.** an error resulting from confusion or bungling; mess or muddle: *The incorrect statements were caused by a goof-up in the store's billing department.*

goof·y (gü′fē) *adj.,* **goof·i·er, goof·i·est.** *Slang.* stupid, silly, or ridiculous. —**goof′i·ness,** *n.*

goo·gol (gü′gôl, -gəl) *n.* the numeral 1 followed by 100 zeros, written as 10^{100}. [Coined by the American mathematician Edward Kasner, 1878-1955.]

goo·gol·plex (gü′gôl pleks′, -gəl-) *n.* the numeral 1 followed by a googol of zeros, written as $10^{10^{100}}$. [GOOGOL + (DU)PLEX.]

goon (gün) *n. Slang.* **1.** a hoodlum or thug, esp. one hired as a strikebreaker or to intimidate workers. **2.** a stupid, rough, or clumsy person. [Partly from dialectal English *gooney* booby (of uncertain origin); partly from Alice the *Goon,* subhuman character in the American comic strip "Thimble Theatre" by E. C. Segar, 1894-1938.]

goo·ney (gü′nē) *n.* albatross. Also, **gooney bird.**

goose (güs) *n., pl. (defs. 1-4)* **geese** or *(def. 5)* **goos·es. 1.** any of various wild or domesticated web-footed water birds, family Anatidae, found throughout most of the world, resembling, but larger than, a duck and usually having a longer neck. Wild geese are usually a combination of gray, brown, black, and white, while domesticated geese are often gray or white. **2.** a female goose. ➡ distinguished from **gander. 3.** the flesh of a goose used as food. **4.** a foolish, silly person. **5.** a tailor's smoothing iron with a handle shaped like a goose's neck. [Old English *gōs* this bird.]
  ·**to cook one's goose.** *Informal.* to ruin one's chances.

goose·ber·ry (güs′ber′ē, -bə rē, güz′-) *n., pl.* -**ries. 1.** the tart edible berry of any of a group of thorny shrubs, genus *Ribes,* widely cultivated in many parts of Europe and North America. **2.** the thorny shrub bearing this berry. [Possibly GOOSE + BERRY.]

goose egg *Slang.* **1.** zero or a score of zero. **2.** a large lump or swelling caused by a blow, esp. on the head.

goose flesh, a temporary, rough condition of the skin caused by the contraction of tiny muscles near the surface, usually resulting from cold or fear. Also, **goose bumps, goose pimples.**

goose·foot (güs′fŏŏt′) *n., pl.* -**foots.** any of a genus of weedy plants, *Chenopodium,* found throughout the world, bearing coarse, often broad leaves and clusters of small greenish flowers, and usually having a strong, unpleasant odor. Also, **pigweed.** —*adj.* designating a family, Chenopodiaceae, of mostly weedy plants of wide distribution, including the beet and several ornamental plants.

goose·neck (güs′nek′) *n.* something long and curved like a goose's neck, such as an S-shaped pipe or a flexible support for a desk lamp.

goose pimples, goose flesh.

goose-step (güs′step′) *v.i.* -**stepped, -step·ping.** to march in a goose step.

goose step, a marching step in which the legs are held straight and kicked high with the knees unbent.

GOP *also,* **G.O.P.** Grand Old Party.

go·pher (gō′fər) *n.* **1.** any of various burrowing rodents, family Geomyidae, found throughout North and Central America, having large cheek pouches. Length: 5-17 inches (13-43 centimeters). Also, **pocket gopher. 2.** ground squirrel. **3.** gofer. [Possibly from French *gaufre* honeycomb; of Germanic origin; because it honeycombs the earth as it burrows.]

gopher

Gor·di·an knot (gôr′dē ən) in Greek legend, an intricate knot that could be untied only by the person who should rule Asia. Alexander the Great, instead of trying to untie it, cut through it with his sword. [From *Gordius,* legendary king of Phrygia, who first tied the knot.]
  ·**to cut the Gordian knot.** to find and use quick or bold means to solve a problem or difficulty.

Gor·don setter (gôr′dən) a medium-sized setter of a breed that originated in Scotland, having a black-and-tan coat. [From the fourth duke of *Gordon,* who first popularized the breed in the nineteenth century.]

gore[1] (gôr) *n.* **1.** blood that has been shed, esp. when thick or clotted. **2.** bloody violence: *a movie full of gore.* [Old English *gor* dung, dirt.]

gore[2] (gôr) *v.t.,* **gored, gor·ing.** to pierce with or as with a horn or tusk: *The bull gored the matador.* [Middle English *goren,* from *gore* spear, from Old English *gār.*]

gore[3] (gôr) *n.* a triangular or tapered piece of fabric, used esp. in making umbrellas or certain skirts or sails to provide fullness. —*v.t.,* **gored, gor·ing.** to insert or furnish with a gore or gores: *to gore a skirt.* [Old English *gāra* triangular piece of land.]

gorge (gôrj) *n.* **1.** a deep, narrow opening or passage between steep and rocky sides of walls or mountains. **2.a.** a mass that stops up or clogs a passage: *an ice gorge.* **b.** a mass that fills one's stomach. **3.** *Archaic.* throat; gullet. —*v.,* **gorged, gorg·ing.** —*v.t.* **1.** to stuff with food: *He gorged himself at dinner.* **2.** to swallow or devour greedily: *She gorged her food.* —*v.i.* to stuff oneself with food: *We gorged on cheese and crackers.* [Old French *gorge* throat, probably going back to Latin *gurges* abyss.] —**gorg′er,** *n.*
  ·**to make someone's gorge rise.** to provoke anger or disgust.

gor·geous (gôr′jəs) *adj.* **1.** dazzling or magnificent, as in beauty or brilliance; resplendent: *a gorgeous sunset.* **2.** *Informal.* very beautiful or attractive: *a gorgeous woman.* **3.** *Informal.* very pleasant; delightful: *It's been a gorgeous party.* [Old French *gorgias* fine, elegant; of uncertain origin.] —**gor′geous·ly,** *adv.* —**gor′geous·ness,** *n.*

gor·get (gôr′jit) *n.* **1.** a piece of armor used to protect the throat. For illustration, see **armor. 2.** a covering for the neck worn by women during the Middle Ages to fill in the neckline of a dress. [Old French *gorgete* little throat, diminutive of *gorge* throat. See GORGE.]

Gor·gon (gôr′gən) *n.* **1.** in Greek legend, any one of three sisters who had snakes for hair and whose appearance was so horrible that anyone who looked at them was turned to stone. **2. gorgon.** a very ugly, hideous, or repellent woman. [Latin *Gorgō,* from Greek *Gorgō,* from *gorgos* fearful.]

Gor·gon·zo·la (gôr′gən zō′lə) *n.* a sharp Italian cheese veined with bluish mold. [From *Gorgonzola,* small town in northern Italy where this cheese is made.]

go·ril·la (gə ril′ə) *n.* **1.** an herbivorous ape, *Gorilla gorilla,* of equatorial Africa, having a massive body, short legs, long arms, and a gray or black coat. It is the largest and most powerful anthropoid ape. Height: to 6 feet (1.8 meters). **2.** *Informal.* a muscular, ugly, or brutal man. **3.** *Slang.* hoodlum; thug. [Greek *gorillai,* the name of a tribe of supposedly hairy women, from the West African name of this tribe, according to the third-century B.C. Carthaginian navigator Hanno.]

gor·mand (gôr′mənd, gôr mänd′) gourmand.

gor·mand·ize (gôr′mən dīz′) *v.i.,* -**ized, -iz·ing.** to eat like a glutton; gorge. [From obsolete *gormandize* gluttony, from Old French *gourmandise,* from *gourmand* glutton; of uncertain origin.] —**gor′mand·iz′er,** *n.*

go-round (gō′round′) go-around *(defs. 2, 3).*

gorp (gôrp) *n.* a high-energy snack consisting of a mixture of foods such as nuts, seeds, dried fruit, or chocolate.

gorse (gôrs) *n.* furze. [Old English *gorst.*]

gor·y (gôr′ē) *adj.,* **gor·i·er, gor·i·est. 1.** covered with gore; bloody. **2.** characterized by bloodshed or carnage: *a gory clash of two armies.* **3.** resembling or suggesting gore; disgusting; horrible: *Please spare us the gory details of the murder.* —**gor′i·ly,** *adv.* —**gor′i·ness,** *n.*

gosh (gosh) *interj.* used to express pleasure or surprise. [Euphemism for GOD.]

gos·hawk (gos′hôk′) *n.* a powerful, short-winged hawk, *Accipi-*

ter gentilis, of northern North America and Eurasia, formerly used in falconry. Length: to 26 inches (66 centimeters). [Old English *gōshafoc,* from *gōs* goose + *hafoc* hawk.]

Go·shen (gō′shən) *n.* a land of plenty. [From *Goshen,* in the Old Testament, a fertile region in Egypt inhabited by the Israelites.]

gos·ling (goz′ling) *n.* a young goose.

gos·pel (gos′pəl) *n.* **1.** the teachings of Jesus and the Apostles. **2.** Gospel. **a.** any one of the first four books of the New Testament, attributed to Matthew, Mark, Luke, and John. **b.** an excerpt from one of these books read as part of a religious service. **3.** something accepted or regarded as absolutely true. **4.** a doctrine or precept regarded as being of major importance and serving as a guide for action: *The insurgents preached the gospel of revolution.* **5.** gospel music. —*adj.* of, relating to, or according to the gospel; evangelical: *gospel preaching, gospel studies.* [Old English *gōdspel* teachings of Jesus and the Apostles, the Gospel, from *gōd* good + *spel* tidings.]

gospel music, a kind of religious vocal music developed by Southern blacks that combines the rhythms and intensity of spirituals with the melodies and harmonies of folk music. Also, **gospel.**

gos·sa·mer (gos′ə mər) *n.* **1.** a fine filmy cobweb, seen esp. in autumn floating in the air or suspended from bushes or grass. **2.** any light or filmy substance. **3.** a light, delicate, gauzelike fabric. —*adj.* of or like gossamer; light, filmy, or delicate. [Middle English *gossomer* fine film of cobwebs; literally, goose summer; probably because it is most common in early November, the time of Saint Martin's summer, which was also the season for eating geese in England. See GOOSE, SUMMER.]

gos·sip (gos′ip) *n.* **1.** idle talk or rumors, often malicious, esp. about the personal affairs of other people. **2.** a person who is given to repeating gossip. **3.** *Archaic.* **a.** a friend, esp. a woman. **b.** godparent. —*v.i.,* **-siped, -sip·ing.** to repeat gossip: *to gossip about one's neighbors.* [Old English *godsibb* godparent, from *god* God + *sibb* relative; from the association of a godparent with a friend, who in turn was associated with a person of idle talk.] —**gos′sip·er,** *n.*

gos·sip·y (gos′ə pē) *adj.* **1.** inclined to or fond of gossip. **2.** full of gossip: *a gossipy news item.*

got (got) a past tense and past participle of **get.**

Goth (goth) *n.* a member of a powerful Germanic people who invaded the Roman Empire in the third, fourth, and fifth centuries A.D., including the Visigoths, who captured Rome itself, and the Ostrogoths. [Late Latin *Gothī* (plural); of Gothic origin.]

Goth·am (goth′əm, gō′thəm) *n.* New York City. ➡ a nickname used chiefly in journalism. [From *Gotham,* a village in England, noted in legend for the foolishness of its inhabitants.]

Gothic windows

Goth·ic (goth′ik) *adj.* **1.** of or relating to a style of architecture developed in Europe between the twelfth and sixteenth centuries, characterized esp. by tall structures, pointed arches, rib vaulting, and flying buttresses. **2.** of or relating to the Goths, their language, or their culture. **3.** *also,* **gothic. a.** of, relating to, or characteristic of a literary genre emphasizing elements of the grotesque, horrible, violent, and mysterious. **b.** of, relating to, or characteristic of the Middle Ages; medieval. **c.** uncivilized; barbarous. —*n.* **1.a.** a typeface characterized by straight, unornamented lines without serifs. **b.** black letter. **2.** an extinct Germanic language of the Indo-European family, formerly spoken by various peoples such as the Visigoths. [Late Latin *Gothicus* relating to the Goths, from *Gothī* Goths. See GOTH.]

got·ten (got′ən) a past participle of **get.**

gouache (gwäsh, gü äsh′) *n.* **1.** a method of painting with watercolors in which the pigments are mixed with zinc white and gum to produce an opaque effect similar to that of oils. **2.** a painting done by this method. **3.** a pigment used in this method. [French *gouache,* from Italian *guazzo* puddle, going back to Latin *aqua* water.]

Gou·da (gou′də, gü′-) a Dutch cheese resembling Edam cheese in texture and flavor. [From *Gouda,* Dutch city where it originated.]

gouge (gouj) *n.* **1.** a tool similar to a chisel but having a concave blade, used for cutting rounded grooves or holes in wood. **2.** a groove or hole made by or as by a gouge. **3.** *Informal.* the act of cheating or defrauding. —*v.t.,* **gouged, goug·ing. 1.** to cut or scoop out with or as with a gouge. **2.** to dig, tear, or poke (with *out*): *to gouge out an eye.* **3.** *Informal.* to cheat or defraud. [French *gouge* hollow chisel, from Late Latin *gubia;* possibly of Celtic origin.]

gou·lash (gü′läsh) *n.* a stew made of beef or veal and vegetables, usually seasoned with paprika. [Magyar *gulyás (hús)* herdsman's (meat).]

gou·ra·mi (gu̇ rä′mē) *n., pl.* **-mies** or **-mi.** any of various small to large tropical, freshwater fish, family Anabantidae, esp. a large food fish, *Osphronemus goramy,* of Southeast Asia. [Malay *gurami.*]

gourd (gôrd, gu̇rd) *n.* **1.** the hard-shelled fruit of any of a group of trailing or climbing vines of the gourd family, Cucurbitaceae, usually brightly colored, esp. the calabash gourd. **2.** the vine bearing this fruit, growing in most tropical and temperate regions of the world. **3.** the dried shell of a gourd, used esp. as a drinking vessel or dipper. **4.** any of various other plants of the gourd family, as the watermelon, cucumber, squash, and pumpkin. [Old French *gourde,* going back to Latin *cucurbita.*]

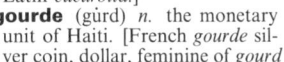

gourds

gourde (gu̇rd) *n.* the monetary unit of Haiti. [French *gourde* silver coin, dollar, feminine of *gourd* dull, heavy (suggesting a heavy coin), from Latin *gurdus* dull.]

gour·mand (gu̇r′mənd, gu̇r mänd′) *also,* **gormand.** *n.* a person who is fond of fine food and drink. [French *gourmand* glutton; of uncertain origin.]

gour·met (gu̇r mā′) *n.* a connoisseur of fine food and drink. [French *gourmet;* earlier, wine merchant's assistant; of uncertain origin; influenced in meaning by GOURMAND.]

gout (gout) *n.* **1.** any of a group of metabolic diseases characterized by an increase in uric acid in the blood, which is deposited as crystals in the joints, esp. the big toe, causing painful swelling. **2.** a drop or clot, esp. of blood. [Old French *goute,* from Latin *gutta* drop; because it was associated in medieval times with drops of humors or fluids in the body that affected the joints. See HUMOR.]

gout·y (gou′tē) *adj.,* **gout·i·er, gout·i·est. 1.** of, relating to, or of the nature of gout. **2.** resulting from or causing gout. **3.** affected with or subject to gout. **4.** swollen, as with gout. —**gout′i·ly,** *adv.* —**gout′i·ness,** *n.*

gov. *also,* **Gov. 1.** government. **2.** governor.

gov·ern (guv′ərn) *v.t.* **1.** to rule, control, or direct by authority. **2.** to direct or influence; guide: *Concern for our children governed our actions.* **3.** to serve as or constitute a rule or law for: *Does the statute govern this case?* **4.** to hold in check; restrain; curb: *Please try to govern your temper.* **5.** *Grammar.* to require the use of (a particular case, mood, or other form): *Transitive verbs govern the objective case.* —*v.i.* to exercise or have control, authority, or influence; rule. [Old French *governor* to rule, steer (a ship), from Latin *gubernāre,* from Greek *kybernān.*] —**gov′ern·a·ble,** *adj.* —For Synonyms *(v.i.),* see **rule.**

gov·ern·ance (guv′ər nəns) *n.* the exercise of control or authority; rule.

gov·ern·ess (guv′ər nis) *n.* a woman employed to teach and train children in a private household.

a	at	e	end	o	hot	u	up	hw	white	⎧	about
ā	ape	ē	me	ō	old	ū	use	ng	song	⎪	taken
ä	far	i	it	ô	fork	ü	rule	th	thin	ə ⎨	pencil
âr	care	ī	ice	oi	oil	u̇	pull	th	this	⎪	lemon
		îr	pierce	ou	out	ûr	turn	zh	measure	⎩	circus

gov·ern·ment (guv'ərn mənt, -ər mənt) *n.* **1.** an organization or body through which control or administration, as of a city or state, is exercised. **2.** a system or established form of ruling by which a given political unit is governed: *parliamentary government, democratic government.* **3.** the exercise of control or authority, as over the affairs of a state, city, or other political unit; rule. **4.** a body of elected officials holding power. **5.** the act of holding in check; regulation. —**gov'ern·men'tal,** *adj.* —**gov'ern·men'tal·ly,** *adv.*

government issue, supplied or issued by the government, as a uniform.

gov·er·nor (guv'ər nər) *n.* **1.** the chief executive of a state or commonwealth of the United States. **2.** an official appointed to govern, as over a province, colony, or territory. **3.** a person who manages or directs a social organization or financial institution: *the board of governors of a club, a governor of a bank.* **4.** an automatic device for regulating the speed of an engine by controlling the rate at which fuel or steam is used. [Old French *gouverneur* ruler, pilot, from Latin *gubernātor.*]

governor general *pl.* **governors general** or **governor generals. 1.** a governor who has authority over subordinate or deputy governors. **2.** in the Commonwealth of Nations, the official representative of the Crown.

gov·er·nor·ship (guv'ər nər ship') *n.* the functions, position, or term of office of a governor.

govt. *also,* **Govt.** government.

gown (goun) *n.* **1.** a woman's dress, esp. a formal dress. **2.** a long, loose outer garment worn to signify the wearer's office, profession, or status; robe: *a judge's gown.* **3.** a long, loose garment, as a nightgown or dressing gown. **4.** the faculty and students of a college or university: *town and gown.* —*v.t.* to dress in a gown. [Old French *goune* long coat, from Late Latin *gunna* fur, fur garment; of uncertain origin.]

GP *also,* **G.P.** general practitioner.

gph, gallons per hour.

gr *also,* **gr. 1.** grain; grains. **2.** gram; grams.

gr. 1. grade. **2.** grammar. **3.** gross. **4.** group.

Gr. 1. Grecian. **2.** Greece. **3.** Greek.

Graaf·i·an follicle (grä'fē ən, graf'ē-) one of many small, round sacs in the ovary of a mammal in which ova are developed. [From Regnier de *Graaf,* 1641-73, Dutch anatomist.]

grab (grab) *v.,* **grabbed, grab·bing.** —*v.t.* **1.** to grasp or snatch suddenly or forcibly: *The child grabbed the toy and ran.* **2.** to obtain forcibly, unscrupulously, or illegally: *The conquerors grabbed the land from the natives.* **3.** *Slang.* to have a strong influence on; affect greatly: *Their story really grabbed my attention.* —*v.i.* to make a grasping or snatching motion (often with *at* or *for*): *The monkey grabbed at the vine.* —*n.* **1.** the act of grabbing. **2.** a forcible, unscrupulous, or illegal seizure or acquisition, as of land or power. **3.** any of various mechanical devices used to grip or clutch something that is to be lifted. [Middle Dutch *grabben* to grasp.] —**grab'ber,** *n.* —**grab'by,** *adj.*

•**up for grabs.** *Informal.* open or available to any taker or successful competitor: *The job is up for grabs.*

grab bag 1. a bag filled with wrapped articles, from which a person draws one without knowing what it is. **2.** any miscellaneous collection of things: *The book was a grab bag of jokes, gossip, and serious criticism.*

grace (grās) *n.* **1.** harmony or beauty of form, movement, or expression: *The ballerina danced with grace.* **2.** a short prayer or blessing before or after a meal. **3.** a sense of propriety; good manners or consideration: *He had the grace to leave after behaving so rudely.* **4.** freely given goodwill, beneficence, or mercy: *The government existed by the grace of the people.* **5.** *Theology.* **a.** unmerited and freely bestowed divine assistance, favor, and love, esp. in saving one from eternal damnation. **b.** the divine influence that inspires virtue in a person. **c.** divine influence or intervention: *By the grace of God the children were rescued.* **6.** any attractive or charming quality or feature: *Speaking French and playing the piano are social graces.* **7.** grace period. **8.** *Music.* an embellishment or ornament consisting of an additional note or notes not essential to the melody or harmony, esp. a grace note or appoggiatura. **9. Grace.** worship; eminence. ➡ a title or form of address for royalty, nobility, or clergy: *Your Grace.* **10. Graces.** in Greek mythology, three young and beautiful goddesses, Aglaia, Thalia, and Euphrosyne, who personified loveliness and charm. —*v.t.,* **graced, grac·ing. 1.** to add grace or beauty to; adorn: *A lovely park graced the town.* **2.** to favor or honor (something): *You graced the party with your presence.* **3.** *Music.* to add grace notes or other embellishments to. [Old French *grace* favor, thanks, pardon, charm, from Latin *grātia* favor, thanks, charm.]

•**in the bad graces of.** disliked or disapproved by; in disfavor with.

•**in the good graces of.** liked or approved by; in favor with.

•**to fall from grace.** *Informal.* to lose the favor or approval of another or others.

•**with bad grace.** with obvious reluctance: *The apology was made with bad grace.*

•**with good grace.** willingly; gladly; sincerely.

grace·ful (grās'fəl) *adj.* characterized by harmony or beauty of form, movement, or expression: *a graceful dancer, graceful prose.* —**grace'ful·ly,** *adv.* —**grace'ful·ness,** *n.*

Synonyms **Graceful** and **elegant** mean exhibiting harmony or beauty in appearance and behavior. **Graceful** connotes qualities that create an impression of ease and naturalness: *the graceful movements of a child, the graceful way they danced together.* **Elegant** often connotes qualities likely to have been acquired through training and to be reinforced by a degree of wealth: *the elegant presence of a monarch, the elegant crowd at the theater opening.*

grace·less (grās'lis) *adj.* **1.** lacking beauty or harmony of form, movement, or expression. **2.** lacking a sense of propriety; inconsiderate. —**grace'less·ly,** *adv.* —**grace'less·ness,** *n.*

grace note *Music.* an ornamental note having no inherent time value, added to embellish the melody.

grace period, an extension or allowance of time after an official due date: *If the tuition is paid within the five-day grace period, no fine is assessed.*

gra·cious (grā'shəs) *adj.* **1.** having or showing kindness and courtesy: *a gracious host, a gracious speech.* **2.** prosperous, leisurely, and comfortable: *gracious living.* **3.** merciful; compassionate. —*interj.* used to express surprise. [Old French *gracieux* charming, pleasant, from Latin *grātiōsus* popular, obliging, from *grātia* favor.] —**gra'cious·ly,** *adv.* —**gra'cious·ness,** *n.*

grack·le (grak'əl) *n.* **1.** any of several North American blackbirds, family Icteridae, having a long, wedge-shaped tail and iridescent black plumage. Length: 1-1½ feet (30-46 centimeters). **2.** any of several Asian starlings, family Sturnidae, as the myna. [Latin *grāculus* jackdaw.]

grad (grad) *n. Informal.* graduate: *The old grads came back for their fifth reunion.*

grad. 1. graduate. **2.** graduated.

gra·date (grā'dāt) *v.t., v.i.,* **-dat·ed, -dat·ing.** to pass or cause to pass through a series of imperceptible stages or degrees, as from one color to another. [From GRADATION.]

gra·da·tion (grā dā'shən) *n.* **1.** gradual progression or change by a series of steps, stages, or degrees, as of size or intensity. **2.** a step, stage, or degree in such a series. **3.** the act or process of arranging in steps, stages, or degrees. **4.** planation. [Latin *gradātiō* series of steps, from *gradus* step.] —**gra·da'tion·al,** *adj.*

grade (grād) *n.* **1.** a step or degree in a scale, as of quality, merit, or value: *an inferior grade of ore.* **2.** a stage in an orderly process or progression. **3.a.** any one of the divisions, representing one year's work, that together make up the elementary and secondary curriculum. **b.** the pupils in any of these divisions: *The play was presented by the third grade.* **4.** a number or letter indicating the level, merit, or quality of a student's work or conduct; mark: *He received a failing grade on the term paper. She got a grade of seventy-nine on the test.* **5.a.** a slope, as of a road or railroad track. **b.** the amount or degree of slope: *There was a 10% grade in the road.* **6.** a class or group of people or things that are the same or equal, as in quality, rank, or value. **7.** a military rank or rating: *the grade of sergeant.* **8.** (of food) classification according to certain standards, as of quality or size. **9.** an animal that is the result of crossbreeding a pureblooded animal with one of another breed or of mixed stock; hybrid. **10. the grades.** elementary school. —*v.,* **grad·ed, grad·ing.** —*v.t.* **1.** to arrange or classify by grades; sort. **2.** to give or assign a mark to: *to grade term papers.* **3.** to make (ground) more level; reduce the slope of. **4.** to improve (livestock) by crossbreeding a purebred animal with one of another breed or of mixed stock (often with *up*). —*v.i.* **1.** to be of a particular grade. **2.** to pass through a series of imperceptible stages or degrees; change gradually: *The colors graded from dark red to bright pink.* [Latin *gradus* step, degree.]

•**at grade.** at the same level or degree of slope.

•**to make the grade.** *Informal.* to be successful in reaching or attaining a desired goal or objective.

•**up to grade.** conforming to established standards.

grade crossing, a place where a railroad track crosses a road or another railroad track at the same level.

grad·er (grā'dər) *n.* **1.** a person or thing that grades. **2.** a pupil in a specified grade in school: *a twelfth grader.*

grade school, elementary school.

gra·di·ent (grā'dē ənt) *n.* **1.** the amount or degree of slope, as of

a road or railroad track; grade. **2.** a sloping surface, as of a road or railroad track. **3.** *Physics.* the rate at which a variable quantity, as temperature or pressure, changes in a certain direction. —*adj.* rising or descending gradually by regular degrees of inclination. [Latin *gradiēns,* present participle of *gradī* to walk, go.]

grad·u·al (graj′ü əl) *adj.* **1.** moving, changing, or happening slowly or by degrees: *a gradual change in the weather.* **2.** rising or descending with a slight degree of inclination; not steep or abrupt: *gradual steps.* —*n. Christianity.* **1.** an antiphon sung between the Epistle and the Gospel in the Mass. **2.** a book containing the words and music of the parts of the Mass sung by the choir. [Medieval Latin *gradualis* in steps, by degrees, from Latin *gradus* step, degree.] —**grad′u·al·ly,** *adv.* —**grad′u·al·ness,** *n.*

grad·u·al·ism (graj′ü ə liz′əm) *n.* the policy of approaching a goal, esp. a political or social goal, by slow stages. —**grad′u·al·ist,** *n.* —**grad′u·al·is′tic,** *adj.*

grad·u·ate (*v.,* graj′ü āt′; *n., adj.,* graj′ü it) *v.,* **-at·ed, -at·ing.** —*v.i.* **1.** to receive an academic diploma or degree signifying the completion of a course of study. **2.** to change gradually; pass by degrees: *My mood graduated from mild irritation to anger.* —*v.t.* **1.** to grant an academic diploma or degree to (someone) in recognition of the completion of a course of study: *The university graduated a class of 500.* **2.** to arrange or place in a series of steps, stages, or degrees. **3.** to mark with or divide into degrees, units, or similar divisions: *to graduate a thermometer.* **4.** *Informal.* to be a graduate of: *I graduated high school last year.* —*n.* a person who has been granted an academic diploma or degree upon completion of a course of study. —*adj.* **1.** engaged in postgraduate work or studies: *a graduate student.* **2.** of, relating to, or for graduates; postgraduate: *graduate courses.* [Medieval Latin *graduatus,* past participle of *graduari* to take a degree, from Latin *gradus* step, degree.]

graduate school, a school, usually part of a university, offering academic degrees beyond the baccalaureate.

grad·u·a·tion (graj′ü ā′shən) *n.* **1.** the act of graduating or the state of being graduated. **2.** the ceremony of conferring diplomas or degrees, as at a school or university; commencement. **3.** a mark or series of marks, as on a cylinder or beaker, indicating degrees or quantity.

Grae·co·Ro·man (grek′ō rō′mən, grē′kō-) Greco-Roman.

graf·fi·ti (grə fē′tē) *pl. n., sing.* **-to** (-tō). drawings or inscriptions on a wall, sidewalk, rock, or other surface. ➡ used as singular or plural. [Italian *graffito* drawing or writing on a wall, diminutive of *graffio* scratch, going back to Latin *graphium* stylus (used to scratch writing on wax), from Greek *grapheion.*]

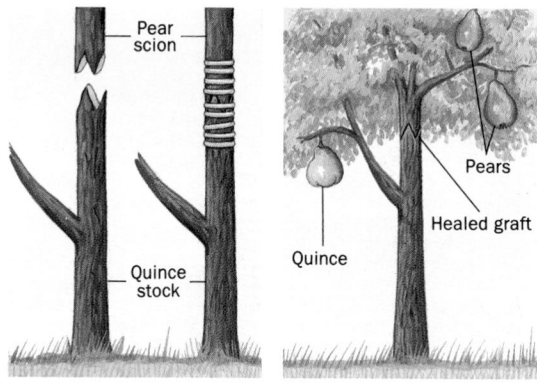

graft¹

graft¹ (graft) *v.t.* **1.** to insert (a scion from one plant, esp. a tree) into a cut in another plant or the same plant so as to cause to grow together. **2.** to propagate (a new plant) by grafting. **3.** to transplant (tissue) from one part of the body to another or from one person to another. **4.** to unite or incorporate as by grafting. —*v.i.* **1.** to insert a scion from one plant into another or the same plant. **2.** to be or become grafted. —*n.* **1.** a scion, as a bud or stem part, that has been grafted. **2.** the place where a scion has been inserted. **3.** a plant propagated by grafting. **4.** tissue surgically transplanted from one part of the body to another or from one person to another. **5.** the act or process of grafting. [Earlier *graff,* from Middle English *graffe,* from Old French *grafe* stylus, young shoot, from Latin *graphium* stylus, from Greek *grapheion,* from *graphein* to write; because a shoot used in grafting resembles a stylus.] —**graft′er,** *n.*

graft² (graft) *n.* **1.** the act or practice of gaining profit or advantages by dishonest or unethical means, esp. through one's political influence or position. **2.** something that is acquired by such means. —*v.i.* to practice graft. —*v.t.* to obtain by graft. [Possibly from GRAFT¹.] —**graft′er,** *n.*

gra·ham (grā′əm) *adj.* made from or consisting of unsifted whole-wheat flour: *graham crackers.* [From Sylvester *Graham,* 1794-1851, American dietary reformer.]

Grail (grāl) *n.* Holy Grail. [Old French *graal,* from Medieval Latin *gradalis* dish; of uncertain origin.]

grain (grān) *n.* **1.a.** the edible seed or seedlike fruit of various cereal grasses, as rye, wheat, or corn. **b.** such seeds collectively: *to thresh grain.* **c.** plants that produce such seeds. **2.** a tiny, hard particle: *a grain of sand.* **3.a.** the arrangement or direction of fibers or layers of different composition, density, or color, as in wood or stone. **b.** markings or patterns resulting from this. **4.** the smallest unit of weight in the avoirdupois, apothecaries', and troy measurement systems, equal to 64.8 milligrams. **5.** the texture of a substance, as compared with others of its type: *The salt used on city streets to melt snow is of coarser grain than table salt.* **6.** the smallest possible quantity; tiny bit: *There is a grain of truth in that statement.* **7.** character or temperament: *Inefficiency goes against my boss's grain.* **8.** the markings or texture formed on the outer side of a piece of leather by the cavities that remain after the hair has been removed. **9.** threads or fibers that run parallel with the selvage in a piece of fabric. —*v.t.* **1.** to produce an imitation grain upon, as by painting or stamping: *to grain plastic to look like leather.* **2.** to make (something) form into grains or granules: *to grain a block of salt.* **3.** to remove the hair from (leather) so as to bring out the grain. [Old French *grain* seedlike fruit of cereals, small quantity, ground piece of a substance, from Latin *grānum* seed.] —**grain′er,** *n.*

grain alcohol, alcohol *(def. 1).*

grain elevator, a building, usually tall and with conveyor belts, for the storage of grain.

grain·y (grā′nē) *adj.,* **grain·i·er, grain·i·est. 1.** of or resembling grains; granular. **2.** having a grain, as wood. **3.** (of a photograph) appearing to have a grain. —**grain′i·ness,** *n.*

gram (gram) *also, British,* **gramme.** *n.* the fundamental unit of mass in the metric system, equal to ¹⁄₂₈ of an ounce or ¹⁄₁,₀₀₀ of a kilogram. [French *gramme,* from Greek *gramma* a small weight.]

-gram¹ *combining form* something written or drawn: *telegram, diagram.* [Greek *gramma* something written, letter of the alphabet, from *graphein* to write.]

-gram² *combining form* of a gram; grams: *centigram, kilogram.* [From GRAM.]

gram. 1. grammar. **2.** grammarian. **3.** grammatical.

gra·ma (grä′mə, gram′ə) *also,* **gramma.** *n.* any of various American grasses, genus *Bouteloua,* esp. those grown for pasture in the southwestern United States. [Mexican Spanish *grama,* from Spanish *grama,* from Latin *gramen* grass.]

gram atom, the quantity of a chemical element having a weight in grams numerically equal to the atomic weight of the element. One gram atom of aluminum, which has an atomic weight of 27, weighs 27 grams. Also, **gram-atomic weight.**

gra·mer·cy (grə mûr′sē) *interj. Archaic.* **1.** many thanks. **2.** used to express surprise. [Old French *grand merci.* See GRAND, MERCY.]

gram·i·ci·din (gram′ə sī′dən) *n.* any of several antibiotic substances produced by the growth of a soil bacterium, *Bacillus brevis,* used to treat localized gram-positive bacterial infections of the skin and eyes. [GRAM(-POSITIVE) + -CID(E)² + -IN¹.]

gram·ma (gram′ə) grama.

gram·mar (gram′ər) *n.* **1.a.** the structures and forms of a language, and the rules governing the use of these structures and forms, considered as a whole. **b.** the systematic study of these structures and forms. **2.** a book dealing with such forms and structures: *a French grammar.* **3.** speech or writing judged according to its conformity to established usage: *The language student's pronunciation and grammar were very good.* **4.** the fundamental principles or rules of an art, science, or field of knowledge: *the grammar of clothing design.* [Old French *gramaire* science of the rules of language, book of such rules, from Latin *grammatica* science of the rules of language, philology, from Greek *grammatikē.*]

G

a	at	e	end	o	hot	u	up	hw	white		about
ā	ape	ē	me	ō	old	ū	use	ng	song		taken
ä	far	i	it	ô	fork	ü	rule	th	thin	ə	pencil
âr	care	ī	ice	oi	oil	u̇	pull	th	this		lemon
				îr	pierce	ou	out	ûr	turn	zh	measure		circus

gram·mar·i·an (grə mâr'ē ən) *n.* a student of or expert in grammar.

grammar school 1. elementary school. **2.** a secondary school, esp. in England, that prepares students for professional life or for university.

gram·mat·i·cal (grə mat'i kəl) *adj.* **1.** of or relating to grammar. **2.** conforming to the established rules of grammar: *That sentence was not grammatical.* —**gram·mat'i·cal·ly,** *adv.* —**gram·mat'i·cal·ness,** *n.*

gramme (gram) gram.

gram molecule, mole[4]. Also, **gram-mo·lec·u·lar weight** (gram'mə lek'yə lər).

Gram·my (gram'ē) *n., pl.* **-mys** or **-mies.** any of a number of awards given annually by the recording industry for outstanding achievement in many categories of recording.

gram-neg·a·tive (gram'neg'ə tiv) *adj.* of or relating to bacteria that do not retain the violet color when stained using Gram's method.

gram·o·phone (gram'ə fōn') *n.* phonograph. [From *Gramophone,* trademark for an early phonograph, by inversion of *phonogram* phonographic cylinder, from Greek *phōnē* sound + -GRAM[1].]

gram-pos·i·tive (gram'poz'i tiv) *adj.* of or relating to bacteria stained using Gram's method that retain the violet color stain.

gram·pus (gram'pəs) *n., pl.* **-pus·es. 1.** a dolphin, *Gramphidelphis griseus,* found in all seas except those in polar regions. **2.** killer whale. [Modification (influenced by GRAND) of Middle English *graspeys,* from Old French *graspeis, craspois* whale, seal[1]; literally, fat fish, going back to Latin *crassus piscis* fat fish.]

Gram's method (gramz), a technique for classifying bacteria by staining them with solutions of gentian violet and iodine and exposing them to alcohol. The violet stain is retained by gram-positive bacteria and lost by gram-negative bacteria. [From H. C. J. *Gram,* 1853–1938, Danish bacteriologist who developed it.]

gra·na (grā'nə) the plural of **granum.**

gran·a·dil·la (gran'ə dil'ə) *n.* **1.** any of several tropical passion-flowers grown for their fruit, esp. *Passiflora quadrangularis.* **2.** the edible fruit of these plants, used as a dessert and in flavoring beverages; passion fruit. [Spanish *granadilla,* diminutive of *granada* pomegranate, from Latin *Malum granatum* literally, grainy apple.]

gra·na·ry (grā'nə rē, gran'ə rē) *n., pl.* **-ries. 1.** a storehouse for threshed grain. **2.** a region that produces much grain. [Latin *grānārium,* from *grānum* grain, seed.]

grand (grand) *adj.* **1.** imposing or impressive, as in magnitude, scope, or magnificence: *a grand palace.* **2.** noble or dignified, as in character or manner. **3.a.** most important; main; principal: *The party was held in the grand ballroom.* **b.** chief or highest in rank among those of similar rank: *the grand marshal.* **4.** including everything; complete; comprehensive: *The grand total was 2,164.* **5.** lofty and dignified in subject, treatment, or expression: *the grand style of an epic poem.* **6.** admired or respected because of age, position, or experience: *a grand figure among the leaders of the profession.* **7.** *Informal.* very good or excellent: *We had a grand time at the party.* —*n.* **1.** grand piano. **2.** *Slang.* a thousand dollars: *The thieves stole ten grand from the safe.* [French *grand* great, tall, lofty, from Latin *grandis.*] —**grand'ly,** *adv.* —**grand'ness,** *n.*

> **Synonyms** *adj.* **Grand, stately,** and **majestic** may mean impressive in size, manner, or appearance. **Grand** emphasizes magnitude combined with splendor: *The palace was grand, its enormous rooms magnificently furnished.* **Stately** emphasizes the dignity of something large and well-proportioned: *the cathedral's stately dome.* **Majestic** connotes impressiveness because of a commanding or lofty appearance: *a majestic battleship, a majestic view of the mountains.*

gran·dam (gran'dəm, -dam') *also,* **gran·dame** (gran'dām', -dəm). *n. Archaic.* **1.** grandmother. **2.** an old woman. [Anglo-Norman *graund dame* grandmother, going back to Latin *grandis* great + *domina* lady, mistress.]

grand·aunt (grand'ant', -änt') *n.* great-aunt.

grand·child (grand'chīld') *n., pl.* **-chil·dren** (chil'drən). a child of one's son or daughter.

Grand Cou·lee (kü'lē) a large dam on the Columbia River, in east-central Washington.

grand·dad (gran'dad') *n. Informal.* grandfather.

grand·dad·dy (gran'dad'ē) *n., pl.* **-dies.** *Informal.* **1.** grandfather. **2.** something that is the earliest or foremost of its kind: *The powerful grizzly is the granddaddy of all bears.*

grand·daugh·ter (gran'dô'tər) *n.* a daughter of one's son or daughter.

grand duchess 1. the wife or widow of a grand duke. **2.** in certain European countries, a woman holding in her own right the sovereignty of a grand duchy. **3.** in czarist Russia, a princess of the royal family.

grand duchy, the territory or country under the rule of a grand duke or grand duchess.

grand duke 1. in certain European countries, the sovereign of a grand duchy, ranking next below a king. **2.** in czarist Russia, a prince of the royal family.

gran·dee (gran dē') *n.* **1.** a Spanish or Portuguese nobleman of the highest rank. **2.** any person of high rank or great importance. [Spanish *grande* nobleman of the highest rank, from *grande* great, from Latin *grandis.*]

gran·deur (gran'jər, -jūr') *n.* the state or quality of being majestic or imposing; magnificence; splendor. [French *grandeur,* from *grand* great, from Latin *grandis.*]

grand·fa·ther (grand'fä'thər, gran'-) *n.* **1.** the father of one's father or mother. **2.** a forefather; ancestor.

grandfather clause 1. a provision of a law that allows a person or persons who previously had some right or privilege to be exempt from a new law curtailing that right or privilege. **2.** a clause formerly in the constitutions of some Southern states that restricted the right to vote, esp. among blacks, by imposing literacy and other qualifications but exempting anyone whose ancestors had been entitled to vote before the American Civil War.

grandfather clock *also,* **grandfather's clock.** a clock having a pendulum and enclosed in a tall, usually wooden, cabinet that stands on the floor.

grand·fa·ther·ly (grand'fä'thər lē, gran'-) *adj.* **1.** of a grandfather. **2.** like or characteristic of a grandfather; kindly; benevolent: *He gave her a grandfatherly pat on the head.*

gran·dil·o·quence (gran dil'ə kwəns) *n.* the quality of being grandiloquent.

gran·dil·o·quent (gran dil'ə kwənt) *adj.* using or characterized by a lofty, pompous, or pretentious style in speech or writing. [Latin *grandiloquus* speaking loftily (from *grandis* great + *loquī* to speak) + -ENT.] —**gran·dil'o·quent·ly,** *adv.*

gran·di·ose (gran'dē ōs') *adj.* **1.** imposing or impressive, esp. because of size; magnificent. **2.** pompous or pretentious: *a poem written in a grandiose style.* [French *grandiose* majestic, imposing, from Italian *grandioso,* from *grande,* great, from Latin *grandis.*] —**gran·di·ose'ly,** *adv.* —**gran·di·os·i·ty** (gran'dē os'i tē), *n.*

grand jury, a jury summoned to hear accusations in criminal cases and to bring indictments if there is enough evidence for a trial. ➡ distinguished from **petit jury.**

Grand Lama, Dalai Lama.

grand larceny, larceny in which the goods stolen equal or exceed a specified statutory value. ➡ distinguished from **petty larceny.**

grand·ma (grand'mä', gran'-, grand'-, gram'ə) *n. Informal.* grandmother. Also, **grand·ma·ma, grand·mam·ma** (grand'mə mä', -mä'mə).

grand mal (gran' mal') the most severe form of epilepsy, characterized by sudden loss of consciousness and convulsions. [French *grand mal* literally, great sickness, going back to Latin *grandis* great + *malus* bad.]

grand·moth·er (grand'muth'ər, gran'-) *n.* **1.** the mother of one's father or mother. **2.** a female ancestor.

grand·moth·er·ly (grand'muth'ər lē, gran'-) *adj.* **1.** of a grandmother. **2.** like or characteristic of a grandmother; kindly; benevolent.

grand·neph·ew (grand'nef'ū, gran'-) *n.* a son of one's nephew or niece. Also, **great-nephew.**

grand·niece (grand'nēs', gran'-) *n.* a daughter of one's nephew or niece. Also, **great-niece.**

grand opera, the form of opera in which the entire text is sung. It usually has a serious theme.

grand·pa (grand'pä', gran'-, gram'-, gram'pə) *n. Informal.* grandfather. Also, **grand·pa·pa** (grand'pə pä', -pä'pə).

grand·par·ent (grand'pâr'ənt) *n.* a grandfather or grandmother.

grand piano, a large piano having horizontally arranged strings in a harp-shaped case. ➡ distinguished from **upright piano.**

grand prix (grän prē'; *French* GRAN PRĒ') *pl.* **grand prix** or **grands prix** or **grand prixes** (grän prēz'; *French* GRAN PRĒZ'). **1.** *usually,* **Grand Prix.** any of a series of international automobile races held over courses that may include sections of road or highway, for cars with specified engine sizes. **2.** the grand or first prize in a major, esp. international, competition: *The film won the grand prix at this year's festival.* [French *grand prix* great prize.]

grand·sire (grand'sīr') *n. Archaic.* **1.** grandfather. **2.** a male ancestor; forefather. **3.** an old man.

grand slam **1.** *Bridge.* the winning of all thirteen tricks in a round of play. **2.** *Baseball.* a home run with the bases loaded. **3.** in certain sports, winning of all of a specified number of tournaments, usually four.

grand·son (grand′sun′, gran′-) *n.* a son of one's son or daughter.

grand·stand (grand′stand′) *n.* **1.** a main seating area accommodating spectators, as at an outdoor sports event or parade. **2.** the spectators seated in such an area: *The entire grandstand cheered when our team won.* —*v.i. Informal.* to perform an action or conduct oneself in an unnecessarily showy or flamboyant manner in order to impress those watching.

grandstand play, any action, esp. in sports, performed in an unnecessarily showy or flamboyant manner in order to impress those watching.

grand tour, formerly, an extended tour of the principal cities and places of interest in continental Europe, considered to be part of the education of young men and women of wealthy families.

grand·un·cle (grand′ung′kəl) *n.* great-uncle.

grange (grānj) *n.* **1.** *British.* a farm and the buildings on it. **2. Grange. a.** a fraternal organization, founded in 1867, to promote the interests and welfare of farm families and rural communities in the United States. **b.** a lodge or local branch of this organization. [Old French *grange* barn, farm, going back to Latin *grānum* seed, grain.]

grang·er (grān′jər) *n.* **1.** farmer. **2. Granger.** a member of a Grange.

gran·ite (gran′it) *n.* a hard, durable igneous rock composed of feldspar and quartz with specks of darker minerals, often used for buildings and monuments. [Italian *granito* literally, speckled, grained, going back to *grano* grain, from Latin *grānum;* because it has a grained appearance.] —**gra·nit·ic** (grə nit′ik), *adj.*

gran·ite·ware (gran′it wâr′) *n.* **1.** a kind of ironware covered with gray, stonelike enamel, used for plates, cups, and other household items. **2.** a type of fine, hard pottery.

gran·ny (gran′ē) *also,* **gran·nie.** *n., pl.* **-nies.** *Informal.* **1.** grandmother. **2.** an old woman. **3.** a fussy, meddling person.

granny knot, a knot like a square knot but with the ends crossing in the wrong way, causing it to jam easily.

gra·no·la (grə nō′lə) *n.* a mixture of rolled oats, dried fruit, nuts, and honey or brown sugar, used esp. as a breakfast cereal or snack. [From *Granola,* trademark for this food, from Latin *grānum* grain.]

granny knot

grant (grant) *v.t.* **1.** to agree to let have (what is asked for): *We granted them permission to cut trees on our property.* **2.** to admit to be true, as for the sake of argument; concede: *I'll grant that you may be right, but I want proof.* **3.** to bestow, as property, a right, or a privilege, esp. by a formal act: *The Crown granted a charter to the colonists.* **4.** to transfer (real property), esp. by deed. —*n.* **1.** the act of granting. **2.** something that is granted, as a right or privilege. **3.** the transferal of real property, esp. by deed. **4.** one of certain tracts of land in New Hampshire, Vermont, or Maine, originally granted by the state to an individual, group of individuals, or an institution. [Old French *granter,* form of *creanter* to guarantee, promise, going back to Latin *crēdere* to trust, believe.] —**grant′a·ble,** *adj.* —**grant′er,** *n.*

• **to take for granted. a.** to assume to be true. **b.** to accept, possess, or regard without due thought, consideration, or acknowledgment: *Don't take this opportunity for granted.*

Synonyms *v.t.* **Grant** and **concede** mean to acknowledge or accept as true. **Grant** simply connotes accepting another's argument or point of view: *Even if we grant that your theory is convincing, we still need the data to prove it.* **Concede** suggests giving ground reluctantly: *Your evidence is so compelling that I'll have to concede that point.*

grant·ee (gran tē′) *n.* a person to whom a grant is made.

gran·tor (gran′tər, gran tôr′) *n.* a person who makes a grant.

gran·u·lar (gran′yə lər) *adj.* **1.** consisting of, containing, or resembling grains or granules. **2.** having a granulated surface. —**gran·u·lar·i·ty** (gran′yə lar′i tē), *n.* —**gran′u·lar·ly,** *adv.*

gran·u·late (gran′yə lāt′) *v.,* **-lat·ed, -lat·ing.** —*v.t.* **1.** to form into grains or granules. **2.** to roughen the surface; raise in granules. —*v.i. Medicine.* to become roughened on the surface; develop granulations. —**gran′u·la·tive,** *adj.* —**gran′u·la·tor,** *n.*

gran·u·la·tion (gran′yə lā′shən) *n.* **1.** the act or process of granulating or the state of being granulated. **2.** *Medicine.* **a.** a roughened surface, as of a wound or ulcer that is healing. **b.** a granule on such a surface.

gran·ule (gran′ūl) *n.* a minute particle; grain. [Late Latin *grānulum,* diminutive of *grānum* grain, seed.]

gran·u·lo·cyte (gran′yə lə sīt′) *n.* any of various mature white blood cells having a granular cytoplasm. —**gran′u·lo·cyt′ic,** *adj.*

gran·u·lose (gran′yə lōs′) *adj.* granular.

gra·num (grā′nəm) *n., pl.* **-na** (-nə). one of the very small, chlorophyll-containing granules in chloroplasts. [Latin *granum* seed, kernel.]

grape (grāp) *n.* **1.** the smooth, thin-skinned edible fruit of any of a group of climbing woody vines, genus *Vitis,* usually growing in large clusters, and usually green or purple in color. Grapes are used to make wine and raisins or are eaten raw. **2.** the vine bearing this fruit, grown in temperate regions throughout the world and having large clusters of small greenish flowers; grapevine. **3.** a dark purple or reddish purple color. **4.** grapeshot. —*adj.* having the color grape. [Old French *grape* bunch of grapes; originally, hook (with reference to plucking clusters of grapes by a hook); of Germanic origin.]

grape·fruit (grāp′frūt′) *n., pl.* **-fruit** or **-fruits. 1.** the large, round, edible citrus fruit of an evergreen tree, *Citrus paradisi,* having a thick skin that ranges in color from pale yellow to reddish brown and a tart, pink or white, juicy pulp. **2.** the tree that bears this fruit, cultivated in warm regions of the world, esp. in the United States. [Because this *fruit* grows in clusters like *grapes.*]

grape hyacinth 1. the spikelike cluster of small blue or white bell-shaped flowers of any of a group of plants, genus *Muscari,* of the lily family. **2.** the plant bearing this flower cluster, widely cultivated, and having long narrow leaves.

grape·shot (grāp′shot′) *n.* a cluster of small iron balls formerly used as a charge for cannon.

grape sugar, dextrose.

grape·vine (grāp′vīn′) *n.* **1.** a vine bearing grapes. **2.** *Informal.* a secret or informal means of spreading information, esp. from person to person.

graph (graf) *n.* **1.** a diagram representing the changes of and the relationship between two or more elements by means of various forms of notation, such as a series of dots, lines, bars, or wedge-shaped sections. **2.** *Mathematics.* the locus of a function or equation plotted on coordinate axes. —*v.t.* to express or represent by a graph: *to graph a business's weekly profits to make inventory adjustments.* [Short for *graphic formula.* See GRAPHIC, FORMULA.]

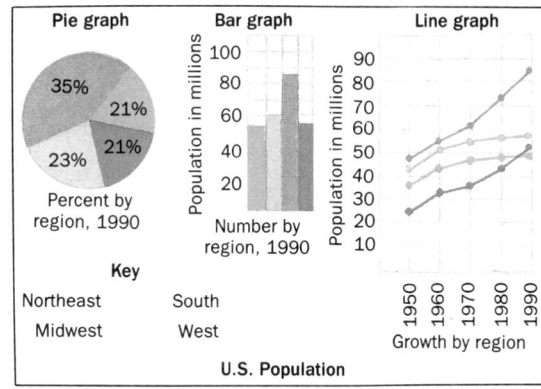

three types of **graphs**

-graph *combining form* **1.** a machine or other apparatus that writes or records: *telegraph, seismograph.* **2.** something that is written or recorded: *autograph.* [Greek *-graphos* written, writing, writer (from *graphein* to write), often through French *-graphe* and Latin *-graphus.*]

graph·ic (graf′ik) *adj.* **1.** vividly descriptive; lifelike: *The book gave a graphic description of the battle.* **2.** of, relating to, or represented by a graph: *a graphic representation of rising business*

a	at	e	end	o	hot	u	up	hw	white		about
ā	ape	ē	me	ō	old	ū	use	ng	song		taken
ä	far	i	it	ô	fork	ü	rule	th	thin	ə	pencil
âr	care	ī	ice	oi	oil	u̇	pull	th	this		lemon
				îr	pierce	ou	out	ûr	turn	zh	measure		circus

G

profits. **3.** of or relating to graphics or the graphic arts. **4.** of, relating to, or expressed by writing: *Letters are graphic symbols.* Also, **graph′i·cal.** [Latin *graphicus* relating to painting or drawing, from Greek *graphikos,* from *graphein* to write, draw.] —**graph′i·cal·ly,** *adv.*

Synonyms *adj.* **Graphic** and **vivid** mean capable of leaving a clear image in the mind. **Graphic,** whether used of the visual arts or of words, connotes a picturelike clarity: *a graphic depiction of autumn foliage, a graphic account of the battle.* **Vivid** connotes a lifelike quality that is sensed immediately: *The description of the town was so vivid that I felt as if I had been there.*

graphic arts 1. those forms of representation in which impressions are made from blocks, plates, and the like, as in etching or lithography. **2.** all forms of visual artistic representation on a flat surface, as drawing, painting, and photography.

graph·ics (graf′iks) *pl. n.* **1.** pictorial material such as drawings or photographs, as used in books, newspapers, or other printed matter. **2.** graphic arts *(def. 1).* **3.** computer graphics. **4.** the making of drawings according to mathematical rules, as for use in architecture or engineering.

graph·ite (graf′īt) *n.* a soft, black mineral, a crystalline form of carbon, commonly used as a lubricant when mixed with oil and as lead for pencils when mixed with clay. Also, **plumbago.** [German *Graphit,* from Greek *graphein* to write; because used for pencils.] —**gra·phit·ic** (gra fit′ik), *adj.*

graph·ol·o·gy (gra fol′ə jē) *n.* the study of handwriting, esp. when used to try to analyze a person's character or personality traits.

graph paper, paper ruled in small squares on which to draw graphs, diagrams, or charts.

-graphy *combining form* **1.** a process or form of writing, describing, or recording: *photography, biography.* **2.** a descriptive science: *oceanography.* [Greek *-graphiā* description of (from *graphein* to write), often through French *-graphie* and Latin *-graphia.*]

grap·nel (grap′nəl) *n.* **1.** grappling iron. **2.** a small anchor with three to six flukes at the end of the shank. [Diminutive of Old French *grapin* hook, from *grape;* of Germanic origin.]

grap·ple (grap′əl) *v.,* **-pled, -pling.** —*v.t.* to seize or hold with or as with a grappling iron. —*v.i.* **1.** to contend or attempt to deal (usually with *with*): *to grapple with a problem.* **2.a.** to struggle in hand-to-hand combat; wrestle: *to grapple with an assailant.* **b.** to seize another or each other in a close grip, as in wrestling. **3.** to use a grappling iron. —*n.* **1.** an act or instance of grappling. **2.** grappling iron. [Middle French *grappil* grappling iron, from Old French *grape* hook. See GRAPNEL.] —**grap′pler,** *n.*

grapnel (def. 2)

grappling iron, any of various devices having one or more hooks or clamps, used esp. for grasping or holding something.

grap·to·lite (grap′tə līt′) *n.* any of an extinct group of colonial animals, class Graptolithina, whose fossil skeletons, made of a horny material and consisting of rows of cups or tubes, are found in marine limestone of Paleozoic age. Some colonies floated near the ocean surface, while others were attached to the sea floor. [Greek *graptós* painted, marked with letters (from *gráphein,* to write) + -LITE.]

grasp (grasp) *v.t.* **1.** to take hold of firmly with or as with the hand: *to grasp a baseball bat.* **2.** to take in with the mind; understand; comprehend: *It's a hard concept to grasp.* **3.** to take possession of eagerly or greedily. —*v.i.* **1.** to make the motion of grasping; try to seize (with *at* or *for*): *to grasp at a life preserver.* **2.** to accept eagerly (with *at*): *to grasp at an opportunity.* —*n.* **1.** an act or instance of grasping. **2.** the power or ability to obtain: *Happiness was within his grasp.* **3.** comprehension; understanding: *She had a good grasp of algebra.* **4.** firm control; possession: *The patriots freed the country from the grasp of the enemy.* [Possibly from an unrecorded Old English word.] —**grasp′a·ble,** *adj.* —**grasp′er,** *n.* —For Synonyms *(v.t.),* see **take.**

grasp·ing (gras′ping) *adj.* **1.** full of or characterized by greed; avaricious. **2.** that grasps. —**grasp′ing·ly,** *adv.* —**grasp′ing·ness,** *n.* —For Synonyms, see **greedy.**

grass (gras) *n.* **1.** any of a large group of plants, family Poaceae or, in some classification systems, Gramineae, having fibrous roots, jointed, usually hollow, stems, narrow leaves, and often bearing spikelets of small flowers. Wheat, rye, oats, corn, sugarcane, rice, and bamboo are grasses. **2.** any of a number of such

plants covering lawns, pastures, or fields, as **Kentucky blue grass,** *Poa pratensis,* or **creeping bent grass,** *Agrostis stolonifera,* which are grown for lawns and golf courses. **3.** land on which grass grows, as a lawn or pasture. **4.** *Slang.* marijuana. —*v.t.* to cover with grass or turf. [Old English *græs* herbage.] —**grass′like′,** *adj.*

• **to let the grass grow under one's feet.** to waste time or miss chances or opportunities.

grass·hop·per (gras′hop′ər) *n.* any of a widespread group of chirping, winged insects, order Orthoptera, having long, powerful hind legs used for jumping. Length: about 1 1/4 inches (3.2 centimeters).

grass·land (gras′land′) *n.* **1.** land on which grass grows, used for pasturage. **2.** land or territory where grass is the predominant type of vegetation.

grass-roots (gras′rüts′, -ruts′) *adj.* of, relating to, or coming from the common people, esp. in rural areas: *The candidate had grass-roots support.*

grass roots, the common people, esp. from rural areas, considered as the originators of political feelings or cultural forms.

grass snake, any of various harmless green or brown snakes of North America, as the garter snake, commonly seen in the grass or garden.

grass widow, a woman who is divorced, separated, or living apart from her husband.

grass widower, a man who is divorced, separated, or living apart from his wife.

grass·y (gras′ē) *adj.,* **grass·i·er, grass·i·est. 1.** covered with or abounding in grass. **2.** consisting of or containing grass. **3.** resembling grass, esp. in color. —**grass′i·ness,** *n.*

grate¹ (grāt) *n.* **1.** a framework of parallel or crossed bars set in or over an opening, as in a window, door, or drain; grating. **2.** a framework or basket of iron bars to hold burning fuel, as in a fireplace or furnace. **3.** fireplace. **4.** a screen used in mining to sift and grade crushed ore. —*v.t.,* **grat·ed, grat·ing.** to fit or furnish with a grate or grating. [Middle English *grate,* from Medieval Latin *grata* grating¹, hurdle, from Latin *crātis* hurdle, wicker frame.]

grate² (grāt) *v.,* **grat·ed, grat·ing.** —*v.t.* **1.** to reduce to small particles or shreds by rubbing against a rough or sharply indented surface: *to grate cheese.* **2.** to rub together so as to produce a harsh, scraping sound; grind: *to grate one's teeth.* —*v.i.* **1.** to have an annoying or irritating effect: *The noise from the street grates on my nerves.* **2.** to produce a harsh, scraping sound by rubbing: *The old gate grated on its rusty hinges.* [Middle English *graten,* from Old French *grater* to scratch, scrape; of Germanic origin.]

grate·ful (grāt′fəl) *adj.* **1.** feeling or expressing proper acknowledgment for kindness or benefits received; appreciative: *grateful for someone's help, a grateful look.* **2.** received with pleasure; pleasing; welcome; agreeable: *a grateful shower of rain.* [Obsolete *grate* agreeable (from Latin *grātus* pleasing) + -FUL.] —**grate′ful·ly,** *adv.* —**grate′ful·ness,** *n.*

Synonyms **Grateful, thankful,** and **appreciative** mean feeling or expressing gratitude. **Grateful** connotes the feeling of gratitude to someone for a favor or kindness: *I was grateful for their concern during my illness.* **Thankful** may connote the outward expression of that gratitude: *I'm thankful to you for your concern.* But it may also connote a general awareness of one's good fortune: *I was thankful for my narrow escape.* **Appreciative** suggests an understanding of the importance of a favor or kindness: *I was especially appreciative of their financial help when a huge bill came for the repairs.*

grat·er (grā′tər) *n.* **1.** a kitchen utensil having a rough surface of sharp raised edges above each of a number of perforations, used to grate vegetables, cheese, spices, and other foods. **2.** a person or thing that grates.

grat·i·fi·ca·tion (grat′ə fi kā′shən) *n.* **1.** the act of gratifying or the state of being gratified. **2.** a source or cause of pleasure or satisfaction.

grat·i·fy (grat′ə fī′) *v.t.,* **-fied, -fy·ing. 1.** to give pleasure or satisfaction to; please: *The news that they were well gratified us.* **2.** to satisfy, indulge, or humor, as a feeling, need, or desire: *My indulgent grandparents gratified my every whim.* [Latin *grātificārī* to please, do a favor to, going back to *grātus* pleasing + *facere* to make, do.] —**grat′i·fi′er,** *n.* —For Synonyms, see **please.**

grat·i·fy·ing (grat′ə fī′ing) *adj.* able or tending to gratify; pleasing or satisfying. —**grat′i·fy′ing·ly,** *adv.*

grat·ing¹ (grā′ting) *n.* **1.** a framework of parallel or crossed bars set in or over an opening, as a window or sewer, serving as

a cover, guard, or screen. **2.** diffraction grating. [GRATE¹ + -ING¹.]

grat·ing² (grā'ting) *adj.* **1.** producing or characterized by a harsh or irritating sound: *a grating hinge, a grating cough.* **2.** causing annoyance; irritating: *a grating habit.* [GRATE² + -ING².]

grat·is (grat'is, grā'tis) *adv.* without charge, cost, or payment; free: *The batteries come gratis with the clock.* —*adj.* given or provided without charge, cost, or payment. [Latin *grātis,* going back to *grātia* favor.]

grat·i·tude (grat'i tüd', -tūd') *n.* the quality or condition of being grateful, as for a kindness or favor. [Late Latin *grātitūdō,* from Latin *grātus* pleasing, thankful.]

gra·tu·i·tous (grə tü'i təs, -tū'-) *adj.* **1.** given or provided without obligation of payment or return; free. **2.** without good reason or cause; unjustifiable; unwarranted: *a gratuitous insult.* [Latin *grātuītus* done without pay, free.] —**gra·tu'i·tous·ly,** *adv.* —**gra·tu'i·tous·ness,** *n.*

gra·tu·i·ty (grə tü'i tē, -tū'-) *n., pl.* **-ties.** a gift, esp. of money, given freely in return for services rendered; tip: *I gave a gratuity to the concierge.* [Medieval Latin *gratuitas* free gift, from Latin *grātuītus* done without pay.]

gra·va·men (grə vā'mən) *n., pl.* **-va·mens** or **-vam·i·na** (-vam'ə nə). *Law.* **1.** grievance. **2.** the most significant part or gist of a complaint, lawsuit, or part of a lawsuit. [Medieval Latin *gravamen* grievance, going back to Latin *gravis* heavy.]

grave¹ (grāv) *n.* **1.** a place dug in the earth for the burial of a body. **2.** any place of burial: *The ship sank to a watery grave.* **3.** *also,* **the grave.** death. [Old English *græf* place of burial.]
 • **to have one foot in the grave.** to be near death, as from old age or illness.
 • **to turn (over) in one's grave.** to be supposedly distressed or displeased after one's death by the actions of the living.

grave² (grāv; *adj., def. 4, n., also* gräv) *adj.* **grav·er, grav·est.** **1.** of great importance; weighty: *grave decisions.* **2.** of a threatening nature; dangerous; critical: *a grave illness.* **3.** earnest and dignified; sober; sedate: *a grave, humorless speaker.* **4.** of, relating to, or marked with a grave accent. **5.** (of colors) somber. —*n.* grave accent. [French *grave,* from Latin *gravis* heavy, important.] —**grave'ly,** *adv.* —**grave'ness,** *n.* —For Synonyms *(adj.),* see **serious.**

grave³ (grāv) *v.t.,* **graved, graved** or **grav·en, grav·ing.** **1.** to form or shape by carving; sculpt. **2.** to engrave on a hard substance; incise. **3.** to impress deeply; fix firmly, as in the memory. [Old English *grafan* to dig, engrave.]

grave accent (grāv, gräv) a diacritical mark (`) placed over a vowel to indicate correct pronunciation, as in French *père,* to distinguish between two words identically spelled, as in French *a* and *à,* to indicate that a final syllable is pronounced, as in English *learnèd,* or to indicate that a final syllable is stressed, as in Italian *città.*

grave·dig·ger (grāv'dig'ər) *n.* a person whose work is digging graves.

grav·el (grav'əl) *n.* a loose mixture of pebbles and small rock fragments, often mixed with sand, used esp. for roads and walks. —*v.t.,* **-eled, -el·ing;** *also, British,* **-elled, -el·ling** **1.** to cover or lay with gravel. **2.** *Informal.* to irritate; annoy. [Old French *gravele* small stones or pebbles mixed with sand, diminutive of *grave* sandbank, of Celtic origin.]

grav·el·ly (grav'ə lē) *adj.* **1.** consisting of, containing, or like gravel. **2.** (of voices) harsh; grating.

grav·en (grā'vən) a past participle of **grave³.**

graven image, idol.

grav·er (grā'vər) *n.* **1.** burin. **2.** an engraver, sculptor, or stonecutter.

grave·stone (grāv'stōn') *n.* a stone marking a grave.

grave·yard (grāv'yärd') *n.* cemetery.

graveyard shift *Informal.* a work shift usually beginning at midnight.

grav·id (grav'id) *adj.* pregnant *(def. 1).* [Latin *gravidus,* from *gravis* heavy.] —**gra·vid·i·ty** (gra vid'i tē), *n.*

gra·vim·e·ter (gra vim'i tər) *n.* **1.** an instrument for measuring specific gravity. **2.** an instrument for measuring variations in the earth's gravitational field. [French *gravimètre,* from Latin *gravis* heavy + French *mètre* meter.]

grav·i·tate (grav'i tāt') *v.i.,* **-tat·ed, -tat·ing. 1.** to move or tend to move as a result of the force of gravity. **2.** to move or be attracted as a result of a natural tendency or strong influence (with *to* or *toward*): *The two new students in the class gravitated toward each other.* **3.** to sink or fall: *The sediment in the liquid gravitated to the bottom of the jar.* [Modern

Latin *gavitatus,* past participle of *gravitare,* from Latin *gravitās* weight.]

grav·i·ta·tion (grav'i tā'shən) *n.* **1.** the force of mutual attraction that exists between any two bodies in the universe. It is directly proportional to the product of the masses of the two bodies and inversely proportional to the square of the distance between them. **2.** the act or process of gravitating. **3.** movement toward or attraction to a person or thing as the result of a natural tendency or strong influence. —**grav'i·ta'tion·al,** *adj.* —**grav'i·ta'tion·al·ly,** *adv.*

gravitational wave, a hypothetical wave of energy, predicted by the general theory of relativity, that travels at the speed of light and exerts gravitational force on anything in its path. Also, **gravity wave.**

grav·i·ton (grav'i ton') *n.* a hypothetical elementary particle, having no mass or electric charge, representing a quantum of gravitational energy. [From GRAVITY + ION.]

grav·i·ty (grav'i tē) *n., pl.* **-ties. 1.a.** the gravitational force that the earth exerts on bodies at or near its surface. The pull of gravity on a body is called the weight of the body. **b.** the acceleration caused by this force. **2.** gravitation. **3.** weight; heaviness: *a body's center of gravity.* **4.** serious or critical nature: *We were not aware of the gravity of the problem.* **5.** dignity of manner or character; solemnity; seriousness. **6.** lowness of pitch, as of musical tones. [Latin *gravitās* weight, dignity, importance.]

gravity wave, gravitational wave.

gra·vure (grə vyūr', grāv'yər) *n.* photogravure. [French *gravure* engraving, print, from *graver* to engrave, imprint; of Germanic origin.]

gra·vy (grā'vē) *n., pl.* **-vies. 1.** the juice that exudes from meat during and after cooking. **2.** a thickened sauce made by blending this juice with other ingredients, as flour and seasonings. **3.** *Slang.* money or profit acquired or obtained easily or unexpectedly: *We should get $500 for the car, and anything more is gravy.* [Middle English *grave* spiced sauce, as for meats, possibly a misreading of Old French *grane* literally, grained (since gravies may be seasoned with grains of spices), from Latin *grānātus* having many grains, from *grānum* grain, seed.]

gravy boat, a boat-shaped dish, usually having a pouring spout on one end and a handle on the other, used for serving gravy or sauce.

gravy train *Slang.* a job, position, or situation from which a person receives money or other gain with little or no work: *the governor's friends were all on the gravy train.*

gray (grā) *also,* **grey.** *n.* an achromatic color produced by blending black and white. —*adj.* **1.** having the color gray. **2.** lacking sunlight; dark, gloomy, or dismal: *a gray day.* **3.** grayheaded. **4.** (of a knitted or woven fabric) not yet dyed, bleached, or otherwise processed. —*v.t., v.i.* to make or become gray. [Old English *græg* color produced by blending black and white.] —**gray'ly,** *adv.* —**gray'ness,** *n.*

gray·beard (grā'bîrd') *n.* an old man.

Gray Friar, a Franciscan friar.

gray·head·ed (grā'hed'id) *adj.* **1.** having gray hair. **2.** old.

gray·ish (grā'ish) *adj.* somewhat gray.

gray·lag (grā'lag') *n.* a wild, gray goose, *Anser anser,* found in Europe, considered to be the ancestor of the domestic goose. Length: 30-35 inches (76-89 centimeters). [GRAY + LAG; because it migrates later than other migratory geese.]

gray·ling (grā'ling) *n.* **1.** any of several troutlike, silver-blue or purple fish, genus *Thymallus,* found in cold, running streams, having a large dorsal fin, and valued as both a food and a game fish. Length: 12-16 inches (30-41 centimeters). **2.** any of several grayish or brownish butterflies, family Nymphalidae, esp. *Eumenis semele,* common in Europe.

gray market, the purchasing and selling of legally imported goods at lower prices, esp. those with lower manufacturing standards or without warranty.

gray matter 1. grayish tissue in the brain and spinal cord containing the bodies and dendrites of nerve cells. ➡ distinguished from **white matter. 2.** *Informal.* intelligence; brains: *I think my classmate is a little short on gray matter.*

gray squirrel, a squirrel, genus *Sciurus,* found in both urban and rural areas of the United States, having gray fur. There are two

a	at	e	end	o	hot	u	up	hw	white	(	about
ā	ape	ē	me	ō	old	ū	use	ng	song		taken
ä	far	i	it	ô	fork	ü	rule	th	thin	ə	pencil
âr	care	ī	ice	oi	oil	ù	pull	th	this		lemon
		îr	pierce	ou	out	ûr	turn	zh	measure	(	circus

G

species, the **eastern gray squirrel**, *S. caroliensis,* and the **western gray squirrel**, *S. griseus.* Length: 15-28 inches (38-71 centimeters).

gray whale, a slaty black, white-spotted baleen whale, *Eschrichtius glaucus,* of the North Pacific. Length: 35-50 feet (10.7-15.2 meters).

gray wolf, a large wolf, *Canis lupus,* having a pointed muzzle, bushy tail, and usually gray fur, once widely distributed across North America, Europe, and Asia. Length: to over 4 feet (1.2 meters), excluding the tail. Also, **timber wolf.**

graze[1] (grāz) *v.,* **grazed, graz·ing.** —*v.i.* to feed on growing grass and other herbage: *Cattle and sheep grazed in the meadow.* —*v.t.* **1.** to put (livestock) to feed on growing grass and other herbage: *The farmer grazed the herd in the north pasture.* **2.** to feed on (growing grass and other herbage). **3.** to tend (livestock) while they graze. [Middle English *grasen,* from Old English *grasian* to feed on herbage, from *græs* grass.]

graze[2] (grāz) *v.,* **grazed, graz·ing.** —*v.t.* **1.** to scrape the skin from slightly in passing; abrade: *The bullet grazed the victim's arm.* **2.** to touch or rub against lightly in passing. —*v.i.* to move so as to touch, rub, or scrape something lightly in passing. —*n.* **1.** an act or instance of grazing. **2.** a scratch, scrape, or superficial wound caused by grazing; abrasion. [Possibly from GRAZE[1].]

gra·zier (grā′zhər) *n. British.* a person who grazes cattle, esp. for market.

graz·ing (grā′zing) *n.* pasture land; pasturage.

Gr. Br. Also, **Gr. Brit.** Great Britain.

grease (*n.,* grēs; *v.,* grēs, grēz) *n.* **1.** soft animal fat, esp. when it has been melted or rendered: *bear grease, bacon grease.* **2.** a thick, oily substance, used esp. as a lubricant. **3.** shorn wool that has not been cleaned. —*v.t.,* **greased, greas·ing. 1.** to smear or lubricate with grease. **2.** to cause to operate more easily, freely, or smoothly; facilitate: *to grease the wheels of progress.* [Old French *graisse* animal fat, going back to Latin *crassus* thick, fat.] —**greas′er,** *n.*

·**to grease (someone's) palm** (or **hand**). to bribe or tip.

grease cup, a lubricating device, as in certain machines, consisting of a cup that feeds grease to the bearing or other part to which it is attached.

grease monkey *Informal.* a mechanic, esp. one who works on automobiles or airplanes.

grease paint, thick makeup having a heavy oil or wax base, used esp. by performers.

grease·wood (grēs′wud′) *n.* **1.** a spiny shrub, *Sarcobatus vermiculatus,* of the goosefoot family, abundant in dry, alkaline regions of the western plains of North America, having a hard, yellow wood, used esp. as fuel. **2.** any of several related plants, as the creosote bush. [GREASE + WOOD; possibly because the wood contains some oil and burns easily.]

greas·y (grē′sē, -zē) *adj.,* **greas·i·er, greas·i·est. 1.** smeared or soiled with grease. **2.** containing excessive grease or fat: *greasy food.* **3.** resembling grease, as in consistency or appearance; slippery. **4.** *Informal.* disagreeably unctuous: *The sales representative had a greasy manner.* —**greas′i·ly,** *adv.* —**greas′i·ness,** *n.*

great (grāt) *adj.* **1.** extraordinary in ability or achievement; eminent: *a great writer, a great baseball player.* **2.** of more than ordinary importance, distinction, or effect: *a great occasion, a great honor, a great achievement.* **3.** very large, as in size, number, or extent: *a great expanse of land, a great crowd.* **4.a** more than usual; extreme: *great poverty.* **b.** to a degree far beyond normal: *a great believer in the power of faith.* **5.** of long duration: *a great while.* **6.** exhibiting nobility or loftiness, as of character or purpose: *a great soul.* **7.** largest or most important among others of its kind: *the great hall of a castle.* **8.** belonging to the generation one more remote than the relative specified. ➡ used in combination, often with itself: *great-great-grandparents.* **9.** *Informal.* very good; exceptional: *We had a great vacation.* —*adv. Informal.* very well: *You're doing great.* —*n.* a person or thing that is extraordinary or outstanding: *That painter is one of the greats of the nineteenth century.* [Old English *grēat* large, thick, massive.] —**great′ness,** *n.* —For Synonyms *(adj.),* see **big.**

great ape, any anthropoid ape, as a gorilla, chimpanzee, or orangutan.

great-aunt (grāt′ant′, -änt′) *n.* an aunt of one's father or mother. Also, **grandaunt.**

great circle 1. any circle on a sphere formed by a plane intersecting the surface of the sphere and passing through the center of the sphere. **2.** an arc of a great circle on the earth's surface representing the shortest distance between any two points: *The navigator plotted a great circle course.*

great·coat (grāt′kōt′) *n.* a heavy overcoat.

Great Dane, a dog of a breed noted for its size and strength, having a square muzzle and a smooth, short-haired coat. Height: 32 inches (81 centimeters) at the shoulder.

Great Dane

Great Divide 1. the elevation of land in North America formed by the Rocky Mountains; Continental Divide. **2.** the borderline between life and death: *to cross the Great Divide.*

great·er (grā′tər) *adj.* designating a city and its suburbs: *the greater Dallas area.* ➡ capitalized when used with the name of the city alone: *Greater Chicago.*

greatest common divisor, the largest integer that divides exactly into a pair or a group of integers. Also, **greatest common factor, highest common factor.**

great-grand·child (grāt′gran′chīld′) *n., pl.* **-chil·dren** (-chil′drən). a child of one's grandchild.

great-grand·daugh·ter (grāt′gran′dô′tər) *n.* a daughter of one's grandchild.

great-grand·fa·ther (grāt′grand′fä′thər, -gran′-) *n.* the father of one's grandmother or grandfather.

great-grand·moth·er (grāt′grand′muth′ər, -gran′-) *n.* the mother of one's grandmother or grandfather.

great-grand·par·ent (grāt′grand′pâr′ənt, -gran′-) *n.* the mother or father of one's grandmother or grandfather.

great-grand·son (grāt′grand′sun′, -gran′-) *n.* a son of one's grandchild.

great·heart·ed (grāt′här′tid) *adj.* **1.** having a generous and forgiving nature; magnanimous. **2.** brave; courageous. —**great′heart′ed·ly,** *adv.* —**great′heart′ed·ness,** *n.*

great horned owl, a brown horned owl, *Bubo virginianus,* which is found throughout North and South America. Height: 2 feet (0.6 meter).

great·ly (grāt′lē) *adv.* **1.** in or to a great degree; very much: *I would greatly appreciate your help.* **2.** in a great manner; nobly; magnanimously.

Great Mogul, the title of the ruler of the Mogul empire.

great-neph·ew (grāt′nef′ū) *n.* a son of one's nephew or niece. Also, **grandnephew.**

great-niece (grāt′nēs′) *n.* a daughter of one's nephew or niece. Also, **grandniece.**

Great Pyramid, the tomb of Cheops at Giza, Egypt, the largest structure erected in ancient times, and the greatest of the Pyramids.

Great Russian, Russian *(n., defs. 1a, 2, 3).*

great seal, the principal seal of a government, placed on documents as proof of their official approval.

Great Spirit, the chief god in the religion of certain North American Indian tribes.

great-un·cle (grāt′ung′kəl) *n.* an uncle of one's father or mother. Also, **granduncle.**

Great Wall of China, a defensive wall extending about 1,500 miles (2,414 kilometers) along the boundary between north and northwest China and Mongolia. It was originally built in the third century B.C. as a defense against Huns and other invaders from Mongolia. Also, **Great Wall, Chinese Wall.**

Great War, World War I.

great white shark, a large shark found in tropical and warm seas. It is gray or brown above and white below and can grow to a length of 20 feet (6.1 meters).

greave (grēv) *n.* a piece of armor for the leg below the knee. For illustration, see **armor.** [Old French *greve* shin, armor for the leg; of uncertain origin.]

grebe (grēb) *n.* any of various water birds, family Podicipedidae, having soft, lustrous plumage that in winter is typically gray or black above and white below, legs set far back on the body, and lobed toes rather than webbed feet. Length: 9-24 inches (23-61 centimeters). [French *grèbe;* of uncertain origin.]

Gre·cian (grē′shən) *adj.* Greek. —*n.* Greek *(defs. 1, 2).*

Gre·co-Ro·man (grek′ō rō′mən, grē′kō-) *also,* **Graeco-Roman.** *adj.* of or characteristic of ancient Greece and Rome: *Greco-Roman art.*

greed (grēd) *n.* an excessive, usually selfish, desire to have or acquire something, esp. wealth. [From GREEDY.]

greed·y (grē'dē) *adj.,* **greed·i·er, greed·i·est. 1.** excessively eager to have or acquire something; wanting more than one's share. **2.** wanting to eat or drink too much or too quickly; gluttonous. [Old English *grǣdig.*] —**greed'i·ly,** *adv.* —**greed'i·ness,** *n.*

> **Synonyms** Greedy, grasping, and avaricious mean keenly desiring to possess something, esp. wealth. **Greedy** connotes a lack of moderation and a continuing desire to acquire something: *Greedy for power, the general plotted to overthrow the government.* **Grasping** adds the suggestion of aggressiveness: *a grasping need to accumulate land.* **Avaricious** implies obsessiveness in the drive to acquire and also suggests stinginess: *They spent a lifetime accumulating money, but were too avaricious to spend it, even on themselves.*

Greek (grēk) *adj.* of, relating to, or characteristic of ancient or modern Greece or its people, language, or culture. —*n.* **1.** a native or citizen of ancient or modern Greece. **2.** a person of Greek ancestry. **3.** the Indo-European language spoken predominantly in Greece and surrounding areas in varying forms since prehistoric times. For alphabet table, see **alphabet. 4.** *Informal.* any language or subject matter that cannot be understood: *It's all Greek to me.* [Old English *Grēcas* (plural) natives of Greece, from Latin *Graecī,* plural of *Graecus* native of Greece, Grecian, from Greek *Graikos* native of Greece.]

Words from Greek

Greek is one of the largest contributors of root words to the English language. Many of the loanwords that have come into English from or through Greek include words in such areas as science, medicine, philosophy, language, literature, and government. Below are a few of these.

alphabet	democracy	harmony	philosophy
anatomy	devil	hero	phrase
angel	diagnosis	idea	physics
architect	dialect	idol	planet
arctic	diet[1]	logic	poliomyelitis
arithmetic	drama	magnet	politic
arthritis	echo	marathon	pragmatic
astronomy	eclipse	mathematics	psychiatry
athlete	ecstasy	monopoly	pygmy
atom	enzyme	music	rhetoric
barbaric	epic	mystery	sarcasm
biography	ethical	myth	school[1]
camera	euphemism	nectar	skeptic
card[1]	galaxy	ode	sympathy
ceramic	geography	organic	synonym
chaos	geometry	osmosis	syntax
crisis	grammar	panic	theology
cynic	gymnasium	pathology	zodiac

Greek cross, a cross having four arms of equal length.

Greek fire, an incendiary material that burned in water, used as a weapon in ancient and medieval warfare. It was first used by the Byzantine Greeks.

Greek Orthodox Church 1. Orthodox Church. **2.** the established church of Greece, a self-governing member of the Orthodox Church. Also *(def. 2),* **Greek Church.**

green (grēn) *n.* **1.** the color between yellow and blue in the spectrum; color of most growing grass and leaves in summer. **2.** something that imparts this color, as a dye or paint. **3.** a grassy, usually level, piece of land used for a particular purpose: *a village green.* **4.** *Golf.* the area around a cup, having very thick, closely cut grass. Also, **putting green. 5. greens. a.** the green leaves or stems of certain plants, as turnips, lettuce, spinach, or dandelions, used for food: *salad greens mixed with dressing.* **b.** freshly cut leaves or branches used for decoration: *The mantelpiece was decorated with greens for the holiday.* **6. the Green.** the national color of the Irish Republic. —*adj.* **1.** having the color green. **2.** covered with growing plants, grass, or green foliage; verdant: *green pastures.* **3.** not fully grown or mature; not ripe: *green tomatoes.* **4.** consisting of edible green leaves or other plant parts: *a tossed green salad.* **5.a.** having little or no training or experience; immature, as in judgment: *a green recruit.* **b.** easily fooled; gullible; naive. **6.** having a pale, sickly color, as from illness or fear: *Their faces were green when they came off the roller coaster.* **7.** not dried, cured, or otherwise ready for use: *green lumber.*

8. full of vitality; lively: *green youth.* —*v.i.* to become green: *The land greened with the coming of spring.* —*v.t.* to make green: *The sunshine greened the vines on the slope.* [Old English *grēne* of the color green, verdant.] —**green'ness,** *n.*

• **to be green with envy.** to be sick with jealousy; be extremely envious.

green algae, any of a large division, Chlorophyta, of unicellular, colonial, and multicellular algae colored bright green and growing mostly in fresh water but also on snow or moist rocks, soil, or wood.

green·back (grēn'bak') *n.* **1.** paper currency not backed by gold or silver, first issued by the U.S. government in 1862 to finance the Union effort in the Civil War and slowly retired until 1879, when those still in circulation were made convertible into gold. **2.** any piece of U.S. paper currency. [GREEN + BACK[1]; because the back is usually printed in green ink.]

Greenback Party, a U.S. political party organized by farm leaders in 1874 and active through the 1880s. It favored the continued issuing of greenbacks not redeemable for gold or silver as the only U.S. paper currency. —**Green'back·er,** *n.*

green bean, string bean.

green·belt (grēn'belt') *n.* a strip or zone of land that adjoins or surrounds a community and is left undeveloped or is used for recreational areas, parks, or similar public facilities.

green·bri·er (grēn'brī'ər) *n.* any of a large group of vines, genus *Smilax,* of the lily family, bearing clusters of white, yellow, or green flowers and usually having prickly stems. Also, **catbrier, smilax.**

green card, an official identity card issued to a foreign citizen who has the right to live and work in the United States.

green corn, young tender ears of corn, used esp. for roasting.

green·er·y (grē'nə rē) *n., pl.* **-er·ies.** green plants or foliage; verdure.

green-eyed (grēn'īd') *adj.* **1.** having green eyes. **2.** jealous.

green·finch (grēn'finch') *n.* any of several finches, genus *Chloris,* esp. *C. chloris,* of Europe and western Asia, the male of which is olive-green with yellow and black markings.

green·gage (grēn'gāj') *n.* a variety of sweet plum, *Prunus insititia italica,* having a greenish yellow skin and flesh. [From the English botanist Sir William *Gage,* who brought it to England from France about 1725.]

green·gro·cer (grēn'grō'sər) *n. British.* a merchant who sells fresh vegetables and fruit. —**green'gro'cer·y,** *n.*

green·horn (grēn'hôrn') *n. Informal.* **1.** an inexperienced person; novice. **2.** a person easily fooled or imposed upon. [GREEN + HORN; in reference to the immature, or green, horns of oxen not fully grown.]

green·house (grēn'hous') *n., pl.* **-hous·es** (-hou'ziz). a structure having the roof and sides of glass or transparent plastic that traps the heat of the sun and in which plants can be cultivated throughout the year.

greenhouse effect, the process in which heat from the sun is trapped in the earth's atmosphere by carbon dioxide and other gases, such as methane, resulting in higher temperatures and a warming of the surface of the earth. Industrial pollution, esp. the burning of fossil fuels, is a major source of some of these gases.

green·ing (grē'ning) *n.* any of several apples having a greenish yellow skin when ripe and a tart flavor, used esp. for cooking.

green·ish (grē'nish) *adj.* somewhat green.

green light 1. a green traffic signal indicating permission to proceed. **2.** *Informal.* authorization or permission to proceed with a particular project or activity: *We got the green light to go on the camping trip.*

green manure 1. a crop, as clover or alfalfa, that is plowed under while still green to enrich the soil. **2.** manure that has not yet decayed.

green onion, scallion *(def. 1).*

green pepper, an unripe sweet pepper.

green plant, any plant containing chlorophyll.

green·room (grēn'rüm', -rûm') *n.* a lounge in a theater for the use of the performers.

green·sick·ness (grēn'sik'nis) chlorosis *(def. 2).*

G

a	at	e	end	o	hot	u	up	hw	white	⌠	about
ā	ape	ē	me	ō	old	ū	use	ng	song	⎨	taken
ä	far	i	it	ô	fork	ü	rule	th	thin	ə	pencil
âr	care	ī	ice	oi	oil	u̇	pull	th	this	⎬	lemon
		îr	pierce	ou	out	ûr	turn	zh	measure	⌡	circus

green soap, a soft soap made chiefly from potassium hydroxide and vegetable oils, used esp. in treating skin disorders.

green·stick fracture (grēn′stik′) *Medicine.* a partial fracture in which only one side of a bone is broken.

green·sward (grēn′swôrd′) *n.* green grass; grassy ground.

green tea, tea made from leaves that have been steamed to prevent fermentation.

green thumb, a special talent for making plants grow.

green turtle, a large sea turtle, *Chelonia mydas,* found in warm waters throughout the world, having a green shell, and used for food, esp. in soup. Length: to 4 feet (1.2 meters).

Green·wich Time (grin′ij, -ich, gren′-) the time at the prime meridian in Greenwich, England, used as the standard time by which the time zones of the world are established.

green·wood (grēn′wŏŏd′) *n.* a forest when green, as in the summer.

greet (grēt) *v.t.* **1.** to speak to or welcome in a friendly or polite way, as upon meeting: *We greeted our guests at the door.* **2.** to meet or receive in a specified way: *The pianist was greeted with applause.* **3.** to present itself to: *The morning sun greeted us as we came out on deck.* [Old English *grētan* to approach, address.] —**greet′er,** *n.*

greet·ing (grē′ting) *n.* **1.** the act or words of a person who greets another or others. **2. greetings.** friendly wishes or a cordial message, esp. from someone absent: *My friends sent greetings on my birthday.* —*interj.* **greetings.** hello.

greeting card, card[1] *(def. 4).*

gre·gar·i·ous (gri gâr′ē əs) *adj.* **1.** enjoying and seeking the company of others; sociable; outgoing. **2.** living in flocks, herds, or similar groups, as sheep. **3.** of or relating to flocks or herds. [Latin *gregārius* relating to a flock[1], from *grex* flock[1].] —**gre·gar′i·ous·ly,** *adv.* —**gre·gar′i·ous·ness,** *n.*

Gre·go·ri·an (gri gôr′ē ən) *adj.* of, relating to, or introduced by one of several popes named Gregory, esp. Pope Gregory I or Pope Gregory XIII.

Gregorian calendar, the calendar now in use in most countries of the world. Introduced as a reform of the Julian calendar by Pope Gregory XIII in 1582, it provides for an ordinary year of 365 days and a leap year of 366 days.

Gregorian chant, a form of plainsong used in the liturgy of the Roman Catholic and certain other churches. [From Pope *Gregory* I, 540?-604, who collected and edited the great body of church songs.]

grem·lin (grem′lin) *n.* a small, mischievous spirit blamed for sudden or unaccountable mishaps, esp. in the operation of airplanes. [Of uncertain origin.]

gre·nade (gri nād′) *n.* a small explosive missile that can be thrown by hand or launched from a rifle with a grenade launcher. [French *grenade* small bomb, pomegranate, going back to Latin *grānātus* having many grains, from *grānum* grain, seed; because a grenade resembles a pomegranate both in shape and in its "grains" of gunpowder.]

grenade launcher, a device attached to the muzzle or barrel of a rifle, used to fire grenades.

gren·a·dier (gren′ə dîr′) *n.* **1.** a member of a special regiment of infantry in the British Army attached to the royal household. Also, **Grenadier Guard. 2.** formerly, a soldier who threw hand grenades. [French *grenadier,* soldier who throws grenades, pomegranate tree, from *grenade* small bomb, pomegranate. See GRENADE.]

gren·a·dine (gren′ə dēn′, gren′ə dēn′) *n.* **1.** a syrup made from fruit, esp. pomegranates, used as a flavoring. **2.** a thin, openwork fabric, woven from any of various fibers, used esp. for women's dresses. [French *grenadine* rough-grained silk, syrup made from the juice of the pomegranate, from *grenade* pomegranate. See GRENADE.]

Gresh·am's law (gresh′əmz) a theory in economics that of two kinds of money having the same face value, such as paper money and coins of some precious metal, the more intrinsically valuable (coins) will be saved and the cheaper (paper money) will be spent, so that the so-called bad money will tend to drive the good out of circulation. [From the English financier Sir Thomas *Gresham,* 1519-79.]

grew (grü) the past tense of **grow.**

grew·some (grü′səm) gruesome.

grey (grā) gray.

grey·hound (grā′hound′) *n.* one of a breed of slender swift dogs, having a smooth blue-gray, black, white, brown, or red short-haired coat, raised esp. for racing or hunting. Height: 26 inches (66 centimeters) at the shoulder. [Old English *grīghund* the dog.]

grid (grid) *n.* **1.** an arrangement of parallel or intersecting bars or wires with openings between them; grating: *The heat came through grids in the floor.* **2.** something resembling or arranged in a manner similar to this: *The city was crisscrossed by a grid of railroad tracks.* **3.** a pattern of intersecting parallel lines used to form a system of coordinates, as on a map or chart. **4.** a metal plate that forms an electrode in a storage battery. **5.** an electrode in a vacuum tube, used to control the flow of electrons. **6.** an interconnected system of electric generating stations and electric transmission and distribution devices that serves a large area. [Short for GRIDIRON.]

grid·dle (grid′əl) *n.* a heavy, flat metal pan or surface, used for cooking. —*v.t.,* **-dled, -dling.** to cook on a griddle. [Anglo-Norman *gridil* grate[1], going back to Latin *crāticula* small gridiron.]

grid·dle·cake (grid′əl kāk′) *n.* pancake.

grid·i·ron (grid′ī′ərn) *n.* **1.** football field. **2.** grill *(def. 1).* [Middle English *gredire* griddle, form of *gredil,* from Anglo-Norman *gridil* grate[1]; Modern English spelling influenced by association with IRON. See GRIDDLE.]

grid·lock (grid′lok′) *n.* **1.** a condition in which all the vehicles in a grid of intersecting streets come to a stop because the streets are blocked by traffic. **2.** any condition in which motion or activity is impeded: *a telephone gridlock during the holidays.*

grief (grēf) *n.* **1.** intense emotional suffering caused by trouble, remorse, or loss; mental anguish; deep sorrow. **2.** a cause of such suffering or sorrow: *The loss of the dog was the greatest grief the child had known.* [Old French *grief* sorrow, from *grever.* See GRIEVE.]

·to come to grief. to meet with disaster; fail.

grief-strick·en (grēf′strik′ən) *adj.* overcome by grief; deeply anguished.

griev·ance (grē′vəns) *n.* **1.a.** a real or imagined wrong that causes anger, resentment, or distress: *The employees drew up a list of grievances to give to the boss.* **b.** a complaint arising from such a wrong: *We must respond to this grievance quickly.* **2.** resentment or anger caused by such a wrong: *to harbor a grievance for a long time.*

grievance committee, a committee formed by a labor union or by labor and management jointly to try to settle grievances.

grieve (grēv) *v.,* **grieved, griev·ing.** —*v.i.* to feel grief; mourn. —*v.t.* to cause to feel grief; deeply sadden; distress. [Old French *grever* to burden, from Latin *gravāre.*]

griev·ous (grē′vəs) *adj.* **1.** causing grief or anguish: *a grievous loss, a grievous injury.* **2.** of a very serious nature; grave; outrageous: *a grievous crime, a grievous complaint.* **3.** expressing or full of grief; sorrowful; mournful: *a grievous wail of pain.* —**griev′ous·ly,** *adv.* —**griev′ous·ness,** *n.*

grif·fin (grif′ən) *also,* **grif·fon, gryph·on.** *n.* a mythical creature that is usually depicted with the head, wings, and talons of an eagle and the body and legs of a lion. [Old French *griffon,* going back to Latin *grȳphus,* form of *grȳps,* from Greek *grȳps,* possibly from *grȳpos* curved; because of its hooked beak.]

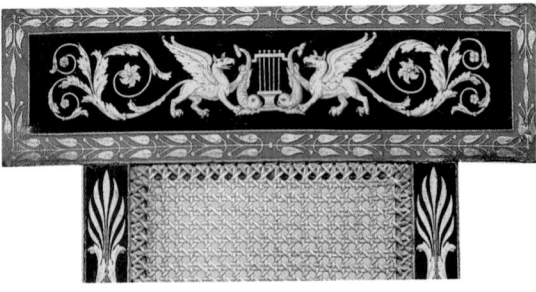

griffins painted on the back of a 19th-century American chair

grill (gril) *n.* **1.a.** a cooking utensil consisting of a framework of parallel metal bars or wires on which food is placed to be cooked over an open fire. **b.** a heavy, flat metal cooking surface. **2.** a food, esp. a dish of meat, that has been cooked on such a utensil or surface. **3.** grillroom. —*v.t.* **1.** to broil on or as on a grill: *to grill a cheese sandwich, to grill hamburgers.* **2.** to question or cross-examine closely and relentlessly: *The police grilled the suspect.* [French *gril* gridiron, going back to Latin *crāticula* small gridiron.]

grille (gril) *n.* a grating, often of ornamental metalwork, used to cover or enclose a space or as a screen or gate. [French *grille* grill, grating[1], going back to Latin *crātīcula* small gridiron.]

grill·room (gril′rüm′, -rüm′) *n.* a restaurant or dining room, as in a hotel, that features grilled foods.

grill·work (gril′wûrk′) *n.* a grille or a pattern of grilles: *the grillwork of an automobile.*

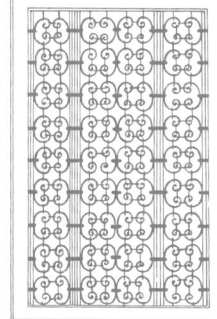

grille

grilse (grils) *n., pl.* **grilse.** a young salmon on its first return from the sea to fresh water, esp. a male. [Of uncertain origin.]

grim (grim) *adj.,* **grim·mer, grim·mest. 1.** having a stern, forbidding, or formidable quality or appearance: *a cold, grim smile.* **2.** that will not yield easily; resolute; uncompromising: *grim determination.* **3.** without mercy; fierce; merciless: *horns locked in grim battle.* **4.** having a ghastly, repellent, or sinister nature; horrifying: *a grim story.* [Old English *grim* fierce, cruel.] —**grim′ly,** *adv.* —**grim′ness,** *n.*

gri·mace (grim′is, gri mās′) *n.* a wry or otherwise contorted facial expression, esp. one indicating pain or displeasure. —*v.i.,* -maced, -mac·ing. to contort the face in such a manner. [French *grimace,* possibly from Spanish *grimazo* contortion; of Germanic origin.]

gri·mal·kin (gri mal′kən, -môl′-) *n.* **1.** a cat, esp. an old female cat. **2.** a bad-tempered, spiteful old woman. [GRAY + *Malkin,* diminutive of *Maud,* feminine proper name.]

grime (grīm) *n.* dirt, esp. sooty dirt, covering or rubbed into a surface: *The windows were black with grime.* —*v.t.,* **grimed, grim·ing.** to cover with grime; soil: *The walls were grimed from the smoke and grease in the air.* [Flemish *grijm* soot, from Middle Dutch *grīme.*]

grim·y (grī′mē) *adj.,* **grim·i·er, grim·i·est.** full of or covered with grime; filthy: *a grimy napkin, a grimy face.* —**grim′i·ness,** *n.*

grin (grin) *v.,* **grinned, grin·ning.** —*v.i.* **1.** to smile broadly. **2.** to draw back the lips and show the teeth, as in scorn or anger: *The villain grinned maliciously.* —*v.t.* to express by smiling broadly: *to grin one's pleasure at an idea.* —*n.* a facial expression made by grinning, esp. a broad smile. [Old English *grennian* to show the teeth, as in pain or anger.] —**grin′ner,** *n.*

grind (grīnd) *v.,* **ground, grind·ing.** —*v.t.* **1.** to crush or chop into small particles or powder; mill; pulverize: *to grind corn into meal.* **2.** to wear down, smooth, or sharpen by abrasion: *to grind the blade of a knife.* **3.** to produce by crushing: *to grind pepper from peppercorns.* **4.** to rub together, press down, or move in a harsh or noisy manner: *to grind one's teeth.* **5.** to operate by turning a crank: *to grind a coffee mill.* **6.** to oppress harshly: *The laborers were mercilessly ground down by their overseers.* **7.** to impart or implant by constant effort or repetition (with *into*): *Showing respect for my elders is something that has been ground into me from early childhood.* —*v.i.* **1.** to perform the operation of crushing, sharpening, or smoothing. **2.** to become ground; undergo grinding. **3.** to rub together, press down, or move in a harsh or noisy manner; grate. **4.** *Informal.* to work or study hard or for a long time: *to grind away for an exam.* —*n.* **1.** the size of the particles of a material that has been crushed: *different grinds of coffee, a coarse grind of pepper.* **2.** the act of grinding. **3.** hard, tedious work or study: *the grind of working a 12-hour day.* **4.** a harsh, gnashing sound, as that caused by two surfaces rubbing against one another: *the annoying grind of machinery.* **5.** *Informal.* a person who is thought to spend too much time and effort at studies or work. [Old English *grindan* to reduce to small particles, make a grating noise.]

• **to grind out.** to produce mechanically, without imagination or special effort: *That writer grinds out one book after another.*

grind·er (grīn′dər) *n.* **1.** a person or thing that grinds, esp. a machine that grinds: *a spice grinder.* **2.** one of the back teeth; molar.

grind·stone (grīnd′stōn′) *n.* a stone disk that can be revolved on an axle to sharpen or smooth something, as a knife blade.

• **to keep** (or **have** or **put**) **one's nose to the grindstone.** to work steadily or very diligently at one's job.

grin·go (gring′gō) *n., pl.* **-gos.** in Latin America, a foreigner, esp. someone who is American or English. ➡ used disparagingly. [Spanish *gringo* gibberish, foreigner, probably modification of *griego* Greek, from Latin *Graecus* native of Greece. See GREEK.]

grip (grip) *n.* **1.** a firm hold; tight grasp: *I tried to get a good grip on the dog's leash.* **2.** the strength of such a hold; ability to hold firmly: *His grip on the rope weakened as he tired.* **3.a.** the manner of holding or taking hold of something, esp. a sword or piece of sports equipment, as a golf club or tennis racket. **b.** a special manner of shaking or clasping hands, esp. one used by members of a secret or fraternal organization. **4.** firm control; mastery; power: *to get a grip on one's emotions, a country in the grip of a dictator.* **5.** mental grasp; knowledge or understanding: *She is just beginning to get a grip on the subject.* **6.** that part of an object, esp. certain pieces of sports equipment, by which it is supposed to be held: *The golf clubs had black leather grips.* **7.** a mechanical device or part that holds something firmly. **8.** a suitcase, usually a small one. —*v.,* **gripped, grip·ping.** —*v.t.* **1.** to take hold of firmly and tightly with or as with the hand: *to grip a baseball bat.* **2.** to attract and keep the interest of: *The movie gripped the audience.* —*v.i.* to take and hold firmly. [Partly from Old English *gripe* grasp; partly from Old English *gripa* handful.] —**grip′per,** *n.*

• **to come to grips with.** to face and deal with in a firm, decisive manner.

gripe (grīp) *v.,* **griped, grip·ing.** —*v.i.* **1.** *Informal.* to complain; grumble. **2.** to have a sharp, intermittent intestinal pain. —*v.t.* **1.** *Informal.* to be annoying to; irritate. **2.** to cause to have a sharp, intermittent intestinal pain. —*n.* **1.** *Informal.* a complaint. **2.** a sharp, intermittent intestinal pain. [Old English *grīpan* to seize.]

grippe (grip) *n.* influenza. [French *grippe,* from *gripper* to seize; of Germanic origin.]

gris·ly (griz′lē) *adj.,* **-li·er, -li·est.** causing one to feel horror, revulsion, or fear; gruesome: *a grisly sight.* [Old English *grislīc* horrible.] —**gris′li·ness,** *n.*

grist (grist) *n. Archaic.* grain to be ground. [Old English *grīst* act of grinding.]

• **grist for one's** (or **the**) **mill.** anything that can be used to one's profit.

gris·tle (gris′əl) *n.* cartilage or cartilaginous tissue, esp. in meat. [Old English *gristle.*]

gris·tly (gris′lē) *adj.,* **-tli·er, -tli·est.** consisting of, containing, or resembling gristle. —**gris′tli·ness,** *n.*

grist·mill (grist′mil′) *n.* a mill for grinding grain.

grit (grit) *n.* **1.** very small, hard granules, as of sand or stone. **2.** strength of mind and spirit; courage: *It took grit to stick out the storm in that boat.* **3.** a coarse-grained sandstone. —*v.,* **grit·ted, grit·ting.** —*v.t.* to grind or tightly clamp together (the teeth), as in determination or anger: *I gritted my teeth as I entered the dentist's office.* —*v.i.* to make a grinding or gnashing sound. [Old English *grēot* dust, sand, gravel.]

grits (grits) *pl. n.* **1.** coarsely ground hominy, used as a cereal and in bread and puddings. Also, **hominy grits. 2.** coarsely ground, hulled grain. [Old English *gryttan,* plural of *grytt* bran, chaff[1].]

grit·ty (grit′ē) *adj.,* **-ti·er, -ti·est. 1.** of, containing, or resembling grit: *a gritty substance.* **2.** covered or soiled with or as with grit: *gritty hands.* **3.** having or showing strength of mind and spirit; courageous. —**grit′ti·ness,** *n.*

griz·zled (griz′əld) *adj.* **1.** gray or mixed with gray: *a grizzled beard.* **2.** gray-haired. [From earlier *grizzle* gray, from Old French *grisel,* diminutive of *gris;* of Germanic origin.]

griz·zly (griz′lē) *n., pl.* **-zlies.** grizzly bear. —*adj.,* **-zli·er, -zli·est.** grayish; grizzled.

grizzly bear, a long-clawed bear, *Ursus horribilis,* of western North America, having a massive head and body and usually brown or gray fur. Height: to 8 feet (2.4 meters) when standing erect.

groan (grōn) *n.* a deep mournful sound, as one uttered in grief, pain, or mock disapproval. —*v.i.* **1.** to utter such a sound: *He groaned when she tried to move his broken arm.* **2.** to make a sound resembling this: *The roof*

grizzly bear

G

creaked and groaned under the weight of the snow. **3.** to be over-burdened, oppressed, or strained: *shelves groaning with books, a people groaning under a tyrant.* —*v.t.* to express or utter with a groan: *The fans groaned their disappointment when their team lost.* [Old English *grānian* to lament, murmur.] —**groan′er,** *n.*

groat (grōt) *n.* **1.** an English silver coin worth four pence, issued from the thirteenth through the seventeenth centuries. **2.** a very small sum or amount. [Middle Dutch *groot* thick (coin).]

groats (grōts) *pl. n.* hulled grain, esp. oats or wheat, usually coarsely ground. [Old English *grotan* (plural).]

gro·cer (grō′sər) *n.* a person who owns or manages a grocery. [Old French *grossier* wholesale dealer, from Medieval Latin *grossarius,* from Late Latin *grossus* great, large, because he sold in great quantities or by the gross.]

gro·cer·y (grō′sə rē) *n., pl.* **-cer·ies. 1.** a store that sells food and household supplies. **2. groceries.** goods, esp. food, sold by such a store.

grog (grog) *n.* **1.** a drink made by diluting a strong alcoholic liquor, as rum, with water. **2.** any alcoholic beverage. [From "Old *Grog,*" nickname of English Admiral Edward Vernon, 1684-1757, because he wore a grogram cloak. He instituted the dilution of rum with water in the British Navy in 1740.]

grog·gy (grog′ē) *adj.,* **-gi·er, -gi·est.** not fully alert or awake; in a dazed or unsteady condition: *to be groggy from lack of sleep.* [GROG + -Y[1].] —**grog′gi·ly,** *adv.* —**grog′gi·ness,** *n.*

grog·ram (grog′rəm) *n.* a coarse, loosely woven fabric made of silk, mohair, wool, or combinations of these, formerly used for such items as cloaks and coats. [French *gros grain* coarse grain; because of its coarse texture. See GROSS, GRAIN.]

grog·shop (grog′shop′) *n. British.* saloon.

groin (groin) *n.* **1.** the fold or hollow on either side of the front of the body where the thigh joins the trunk. **2.** *Architecture.* a curved edge formed by the intersection of two vaults. —*v.t. Architecture.* to furnish or build with groins. [Possibly from Old English *grynde* abyss; probably originally, depression.]

grom·met (grom′it) *n.* **1.** a ring, as of metal or plastic, that reinforces a hole in material, as leather or cloth. **2.** *Nautical.* a ring of rope or metal used for various purposes, as to hold oars in place or to fasten the edges of sails to spars. [Obsolete French *gromette* curb of a bridle, from *gourmer* to curb; of uncertain origin.]

grom·well (grom′wəl) *n.* any of several plants, genus *Lithospermum,* found on all continents except Australia, bearing yellow, orange, or white flowers and having smooth white seeds resembling stones. [Old French *gromil,* possibly from *gres* sandstone (of Germanic origin) + *mil* (see MILLET).]

groom (grüm, grùm) *n.* **1.** bridegroom. **2.** a worker who washes, curries, and otherwise takes care of animals, esp. horses. **3.** one of several officers of the English royal household. **4.** *Archaic.* manservant. —*v.t.* **1.** to wash, curry, and otherwise take care of (an animal, esp. a horse). **2.** to make neat, tidy, and attractive in appearance: *She groomed herself carefully before the interview. He groomed his lawn and garden meticulously.* **3.** to train or prepare (someone) for some purpose, as political office: *to groom one's successor.* [Of uncertain origin.]

grooms·man (grümz′mən, grùmz′-) *n., pl.* **-men** (-mən). a male attendant of the bridegroom at a wedding.

groove (grüv) *n.* **1.** a long, narrow channel or depression cut in a surface, as in a phonograph record. **2.** a narrow, limited manner of doing things; routine; rut: *After a brief period of excitement, we fell back into the old groove again.* —*v.t.,* **grooved, groov·ing.** to make a groove or grooves in: *The cabinetmaker grooved the board to fit the other tightly.* [Middle Dutch *groeve* channel, furrow.]

· **in the groove.** *Slang.* functioning or performing smoothly and expertly; in good form.

groov·y (grü′vē) *adj.,* **groov·i·er, groov·i·est.** *Slang.* very pleasing, enjoyable, or commendable; great: *a groovy person, groovy music.*

grope (grōp) *v.,* **groped, grop·ing.** —*v.i.* **1.** to feel about with or as with the hands: *He groped for the door handle in the dark hall.* **2.** to search blindly and uncertainly; try desperately to think of: *I groped for a solution to the problem.* —*v.t.* to find (one's way) by groping: *She groped her way in the dark.* —*n.* an act or instance of groping. [Old English *grāpian* to seize, touch.] —**grop′er,** *n.* —**grop′ing·ly,** *adv.*

gros·beak (grōs′bēk′) *n.* any of various birds of the finch or weaverbird families, having a stout, cone-shaped bill, as the **rose-breasted grosbeak,** *Pheucticus ludovicianus,* and the **evening grosbeak,** *Hesperiphona vespertina.* [French *grosbec,* from *gros* great, thick + *bec* beak. See GROSS, BEAK.]

gro·schen (grō′shən) *n., pl.* **-schen. 1.** a unit of currency of Austria, equal to 1/100 of a schilling. **2.** a former silver coin of Germany. [German *groschen,* from dialectal *grosch, grosche,* from Czech *groš,* from Medieval Latin *(denārius) grossus* thick (denarius), from Late Latin *grossus* thick.]

gros·grain (grō′grān′) *n.* a closely woven, ribbed fabric, often of silk or rayon, used chiefly for ribbons. [French *gros grain* coarse grain. See GROGRAM.]

gross (grōs) *adj.* **1.** with nothing deducted; total; entire: *On gross earnings of $5,000, my net income was only $2,000.* **2.** extremely obvious; glaring; flagrant: *a gross mistake, a gross injustice.* **3.** not refined; coarse; vulgar: *gross behavior, a gross joke.* **4.** excessively or repulsively fat. **5.** *Archaic.* thick; heavy; dense. —*n.* **1.** a total amount, as of income, before deductions: *My gross for the year was $50,000.* **2.a.** a unit of quantitative measure equivalent to 12 dozen. **b.** a group or quantity of 12 dozen items. —*v.t.* to earn a total of before deductions: *The company grossed $1 million.* [Old French *gros* great, thick, coarse, from Late Latin *grossus.*] —**gross′ly,** *adv.* —**gross′ness,** *n.* —For Synonyms *(adj.),* see **coarse, flagrant.**

· **by the gross. a.** in large quantities; in bulk. **b.** wholesale.

· **in the gross. a.** as a whole. **b.** wholesale.

· **to gross out.** *Slang.* to disgust or offend thoroughly.

gross national product, the total value of all the goods and services produced by a country during a certain period of time, before any deductions or allowances are made.

grosz (grôsh) *n., pl.* **gro·szy** (grô′shē). a unit of currency of Poland, equal to 1/100 of a zloty.

gro·tesque (grō tesk′) *adj.* **1.** distorted, deformed, or otherwise unnatural or ugly in shape, appearance, or character: *The grotesque figures in the painting scared the child.* **2.** amusingly or fantastically absurd; ludicrous; incongruous: *a grotesque situation, to wear a hat at a grotesque angle.* **3.** of or relating to art characterized by a fantastic combination of human and animal forms with foliage, scrolls, and other ornamental patterns. —*n.* ornamentation having characteristics of the grotesque style of art. [French *grotesque* strange painting, from Italian *(pittura) grottesca* strange (painting), from *grotta* cave; because of the strange nature of paintings found in certain old grottoes in Italy. See GROTTO.] —**gro·tesque′ly,** *adv.* —**gro·tesque′ness,** *n.*

Synonyms *adj.* **Grotesque, bizarre,** and **fantastic** may all mean unnatural in form, appearance, or character. **Grotesque** suggests distortion or an absurd combination of incongruous elements: *The portrait was grotesque, with twisted features and elongated limbs.* **Bizarre** suggests something that is strikingly odd, sometimes as the result of a clash of opposing elements: *The building is a bizarre combination of classical and modern architectural styles.* **Fantastic** more generally implies the presence of exaggeration or the indulgence of one's imagination: *The artist's conception of the city was fantastic to the point of being unrecognizable.*

gro·tes·quer·ie (grō tes′kə rē) *also,* **gro·tes·quer·y.** *n.* **1.** something that is grotesque. **2.** a grotesque character or style.

grot·to (grot′ō) *n., pl.* **-toes** or **-tos. 1.** a cave. **2.** an excavation or structure made to resemble a cave, as one designed as a shrine or retreat. [Italian *grotta* cave, going back to Latin *crypta,* from Greek *kryptē* vault. Doublet of CRYPT.]

grouch (grouch) *n.* **1.** a person who is very irritable, sulky, or ill-tempered. **2.** a complaint. **3.** a sulky or grumbling mood. —*v.i.* to grumble or sulk. [Form of obsolete *grutch* to complain, from Old French *grouch(i)er* to murmur; of Germanic origin.]

grouch·y (grou′chē) *adj.,* **grouch·i·er, grouch·i·est.** in a bad mood, either habitually or momentarily; irritable; sulky. —**grouch′i·ly,** *adv.* —**grouch′i·ness,** *n.*

ground[1] (ground) *n.* **1.a.** the solid surface of the earth: *The ground was covered with snow. After months at sea, we were happy to feel the ground beneath our feet.* **b.** the material, as soil, sand, or clay, at or near the earth's surface: *The ground is too sterile here to support plant life.* **2. grounds.** the land surrounding or attached to a house or other building or group of buildings: *The college grounds were beautifully planted.* **3.** *also,* **grounds.** an area or piece of land, esp. one designated for a particular use: *parade ground, picnic grounds.* **4.** *also,* **grounds.** that on which something is established or rests; basis; foundation: *grounds for suspicion, a friendship that is on shaky ground.* **5.** a subject area or material, as for discussion, study, or work: *The end of the book touches on unfamiliar ground.* **6.** something that serves as the underlying surface or background: *The wallpaper is printed with a red floral design on a green ground.* **7. grounds.** particles that

settle at the bottom of a liquid or are left over in the container that held it; dregs: *Throw out the coffee grounds.* **8.a.** a connection between an electric circuit or device, as a television, and the earth, established through a conductor. **b.** the electric conductor itself. —*adj.* **1.** of, on, at, or near the surface of the earth: *at ground level.* **2.** operating, living, or growing on or near the surface of the earth. —*v.t.* **1.** to place, set, or force onto the ground; bring to or cause to touch the ground: *to ground an opponent with a blow to the jaw.* **2.** to provide a firm foundation or basis for; establish, as on some fact or circumstance; base: *Ground your argument on facts. Their fears were grounded in superstition.* **3.** to instruct in the basic principles or elements of a subject: *The teacher grounded them thoroughly in mathematics.* **4.** to forbid (a person or aircraft) to fly; confine to the ground. **5.** to connect an electric circuit or device, as a radio, with the earth by means of a wire or other conductor. **6.** to cause (a boat or ship) to run aground: *The captain grounded the ship on the shoal.* **7.** to furnish with or place on an underlying surface or background. **8.** *Baseball.* to hit (a ball) along the ground: *to ground the ball to second base.* —*v.i.* **1.** to fall to or strike the ground: *The kite grounded because the wind stopped.* **2.** (of a boat or ship) to run aground. **3.** *Baseball.* to hit a ground ball: *The first batter grounded to the shortstop.* [Old English *grund* bottom, foundation, earth, land.]

• **from the ground up.** from the beginning or most elementary to the end or most complex; completely; thoroughly.

• **on one's own (or home) ground. a.** in a familiar place or situation. **b.** dealing with a subject that one is well versed in.

• **to break ground.** to begin some undertaking, esp. the construction of a building: *They broke ground for the new school last spring.*

• **to cover ground. a.** to go or move over a certain distance or area. **b.** to make progress in work, a project, or the like: *We covered a lot of ground at the meeting.*

• **to cut the ground from under (someone's) feet.** to render someone's defense or argument invalid.

• **to gain ground. a.** to make progress: *They gained ground in their effort to end the strike.* **b.** to become more popular or widespread: *Their candidate had gained ground since the primary election.*

• **to give ground.** to withdraw from or as from attack; retreat; yield.

• **to ground out.** *Baseball.* to hit a ground ball that puts one out at first base.

• **to hold (or stand) one's ground.** to maintain one's position; not retreat, yield, or withdraw.

• **to lose ground. a.** to move farther away from one's goal; go backward: *to lose ground in the negotiations.* **b.** to decline in popularity; become less widespread: *The television program was rapidly losing ground in the ratings.*

• **to run into the ground. a.** to overdo or overwork (something) to the point where it is useless; wear out: *to run a discussion into the ground, to run a car into the ground.* **b.** to disprove or criticize severely: *to run someone's argument into the ground.*

• **to shift one's ground.** to change one's position or opinion.

ground² (ground) the past tense and past participle of **grind.**

ground ball *Baseball.* a batted ball that strikes the ground in the infield and then rolls or moves along in low bounces. Also, **grounder.**

ground·break·ing (ground'brā'king) *n.* the act of breaking ground for new construction. —*adj.* **1.** of or relating to the beginning of new construction: *a groundbreaking ceremony for a school.* **2.** opening new possibilities or establishing a basis for further development: *groundbreaking work in genetics, a groundbreaking theory.* —**ground'break'er,** *n.*

ground control, the personnel and equipment on the ground at an airport or spaceport, responsible for monitoring and guiding the operation of aircraft or spacecraft.

ground cover 1. low-growing plants, such as ivy, that provide dense cover for an area of ground, esp. one that is difficult to plant, as a slope. **2.** any plant used for that purpose: *Pachysandra is a good ground cover.*

ground crew, the personnel responsible for the servicing and maintenance of aircraft.

ground-ef·fect machine (ground'i fekt') hovercraft.

ground·er (groun'dər) *n.* ground ball.

ground floor, the floor in a building that is level or nearly level with the ground.

• **to be (or get) in on the ground floor.** to be involved in some activity, as a business deal or project, from or soon after its beginning.

ground glass, glass that has had its surface roughened so that it will diffuse light and not be transparent.

ground hemlock, a low-growing yew, *Taxus canadensis,* found

in North America, sometimes grown as a hedge because it can be easily trimmed into various shapes.

ground·hog (ground'hôg', -hog') *n.* woodchuck.

Groundhog Day, the day when the groundhog, according to popular belief, emerges from hibernation, observed on February 2. If it sees its shadow, it returns underground for another six weeks of winter.

ground ivy, a creeping plant, *Glechoma hederacea,* of the mint family, found in North America, Europe, and Asia, bearing round or kidney-shaped leaves and light blue, tube-shaped flowers.

ground·less (ground'lis) *adj.* having no real cause or reason: *a groundless fear.* —**ground'less·ly,** *adv.* —**ground'less·ness,** *n.* —For Synonyms, see **unfounded.**

ground·ling (ground'ling) *n.* **1.** an animal or plant that lives or grows close to the ground. **2.** a spectator who stood in the pit of the theater in Elizabethan times. **3.** a person of unrefined or uncritical taste, esp. with regard to literature and the theater.

ground loop, a sharp, uncontrolled turn made by an airplane while taxiing, taking off, or landing.

ground·mass (ground'mas') *n. Geology.* the material in which the crystals of a porphyry are embedded.

ground·nut (ground'nut') *n.* **1.** any of several plants of the pea family having edible tubers, roots, or underground seed pods, esp. the peanut. **2.** the edible tuber, root, or seed of such a plant.

ground pine 1. any of several club mosses, esp. *Lycopodium obscurum* or *L. complanatum.* **2.** a creeping European herb, *Ajuga chamaepitys,* having a pinelike odor.

ground plan 1. the plan of any floor of a building. **2.** a first or fundamental plan of any kind.

ground rule, a basic principle or statement of procedure that governs a particular situation or activity: *to set up ground rules for the class debate.*

ground·sel (ground'səl) *n.* any of a large group of plants, including trees and shrubs, genus *Senecio,* of the composite family, many of which bear showy, yellow flower heads. [Old English *grundeswelge,* earlier *gundaeswelg(i)ae,* probably from *gund* pus + *swelgan* to swallow; probably because it was used to reduce abscesses.]

ground·sill (ground'sil') *n.* the lowest horizontal timber in a wooden framework, as of a building.

ground sloth, any of various extinct edentate mammals, related to the living tree sloths, inhabiting South and North America until about 6,000 years ago. Length: to 20 feet (6.1 meters).

groundsel

ground·speed (ground'spēd') *n.* the speed of an aircraft relative to the ground. ➡ distinguished from **air speed.**

ground squirrel 1. any of various rodents of North America, Eurasia, and Africa that live in burrows in the ground, usually having gray or light brown fur, often with striped or spotted markings. Length: 8-21 inches (20-53 centimeters), including tail. Also, **gopher. 2.** a chipmunk or prairie dog.

ground state, the most stable state of an atom or other particle, in which its energy level is lowest.

ground swell 1. broad, deep waves or a rolling sea, caused by an often distant storm. Also, **swell. 2.** a rising wave or surge, as of emotion: *There was a ground swell of public opinion against the proposed new tax.*

ground water, water that has flowed or seeped beneath the surface of the earth and saturated the soil and other porous material below. It is the source of water for wells and underground springs.

ground wave, a radio wave that travels along the surface of the earth, rather than being reflected by the air or clouds. ➡ distinguished from **sky wave.**

G

a	at	e	end	o	hot	u	up	hw	white		about
ā	ape	ē	me	ō	old	ū	use	ng	song		taken
ä	far	i	it	ô	fork	ü	rule	th	thin	ə	pencil
âr	care	ī	ice	oi	oil	u̇	pull	th	this		lemon
		îr	pierce	ou	out	ûr	turn	zh	measure		circus

ground wire, a wire connecting an electric circuit or device to the earth or to some other conducting body.

ground·work (ground′wûrk′) *n.* the preliminary work or material on which something is built or based; foundation: *I completed the groundwork for my thesis a year ago.*

ground zero, the point on the surface of land or water that is at or directly above or below the center of the explosion of a nuclear weapon.

group (grüp) *n.* **1.** a number of persons or things that form or are regarded as forming a unit. **2.** a number of persons or things classed together because of similarities: *an ethnic group.* **3.** an administrative and tactical military unit consisting of two or more battalions or squadrons. **4.** *Chemistry.* **a.** a number of chemical elements having similar properties and arranged in a vertical column on the periodic table. ➡ distinguished from **period** *(def. 15).* **b.** a configuration of atoms attached to different molecules, giving similar properties to a family of compounds. The amino group symbol is NH_2. **5.** *Mathematics.* a set of mathematical elements that may be combined by addition or multiplication, provided that certain conditions are satisfied: *a finite group, group theory.* —*v.t.* to arrange or place in a group: *The counselor grouped the younger children together.* —*v.i.* to form or belong to a group: *The campers grouped around the fire.* [French *groupe* assemblage, unit, cluster, from Italian *groppo* assemblage; earlier, knot; of Germanic origin.] —For Synonyms *(n.),* see **company.**

group·er (grü′pər) *n., pl.* **-ers** or **-er.** any of a number of spiny-rayed saltwater fish, family Serranidae, including many food fish found in warm waters. They have huge mouths and sharp teeth, and may weigh as much as 1,000 pounds (454 kilograms). [Portuguese *garoupa;* probably of native South American origin.]

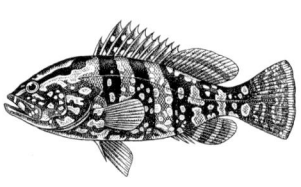

grouper

group·ie (grü′pē) *n. Slang.* **1.** a fan of rock music who follows a particular performer or group around on tours. **2.** a fan or follower of any celebrity or activity.

group·ing (grü′ping) *n.* **1.** the act of placing in a group. **2.** a set of things arranged in a group: *There was an attractive grouping of prints on one wall.*

group insurance, life, health, or travel insurance issued at a discount to members of an organization, employees of a company, or some other group.

group practice, a group of doctors practicing their individual specialties in association with each other, usually sharing offices and often having the same secretarial and nursing help.

group therapy, a form of psychotherapy in which a group of patients, usually under the supervision of a therapist, attempt to understand and deal with their emotional problems, esp. through open discussion.

grouse[1] (grous) *n., pl.* **grouse** or **grous·es.** any of a group of fowllike game birds, family Tetraonidae, including the ruffed grouse, prairie chicken, capercaillie, and sage grouse, having brown, black, or gray feathers, often with white markings, and feathered legs. Length: 1-3 feet (0.3-0.9 meter). [Of uncertain origin.]

grouse[2] (grous) *Informal. v.i.,* **groused, grous·ing.** to grumble; complain. —*n.* complaint. [Of uncertain origin.] —**grous′-er,** *n.*

grout (grout) *n.* **1.** a thin mortar used to fill cracks and crevices, as between stones, bricks, or tiles. **2.** a finishing coat of plaster for walls and ceilings. —*v.t.* to fill up or finish with grout. [Old English *grūt* coarse meal.] —**grout′er,** *n.*

grove (grōv) *n.* **1.** a small forested area or group of trees without underbrush. **2.** a group of fruit trees, esp. citrus trees: *an orange grove.* [Old English *grāf* group of trees.]

grov·el (gruv′əl, grov′-) *v.i.,* **-eled, -el·ing;** *also, British,* **-elled, -el·ling. 1.** to act in a cringing or servile manner, as through fear or the desire to please or flatter; abase oneself: *The slave groveled in hopes of securing the master's favor.* **2.** to lie or crawl face downward, as in fear or humility: *The subjects groveled before their monarch.* **3.** to take great pleasure in that which is base or contemptible. [From obsolete *groveling* prone, from obsolete *gruf* on the face, from Old Norse *ā grūfu.*] —**grov′el·er;** *also, British,* **grov′el·ler,** *n.*

grow (grō) *v.,* **grew, grown, grow·ing.** —*v.i.* **1.** to become larger or older by a natural process of development: *I grew 2 inches this year.* **2.** to become greater, as in size, amount, or degree; expand; increase: *My savings account began to grow rapidly.* **3.** to be produced and develop; thrive; flourish: *Orchids grow wild in the jungles of South America.* **4.** to come into existence; arise. **5.** to come to be by degrees: *The days seem to grow longer.* **6.** to become fixed to or united by or as by a natural growth process: *The graft grew to the skin. The two trees intertwined and grew together.* —*v.t.* **1.** to cause to grow; raise; cultivate: *The farmer grows tomatoes.* **2.** to allow to grow: *to grow a mustache.* **3.** to cover with a growth: *The lawn was grown with weeds.* [Old English *grōwan* to increase, spring up, sprout.]

·to grow on. to become increasingly acceptable, attractive, or pleasurable to: *Her unusual sense of humor grew on me.*

·to grow out of. a. to outgrow. **b.** to develop or arise from: *Arguments often grow out of misunderstandings.*

·to grow up. a. to advance to or reach maturity or full growth: *He wanted to be a firefighter when he grew up.* **b.** to come into existence; develop: *Antagonism had grown up between them.*

grow·er (grō′ər) *n.* **1.** a person who grows something: *the largest wheat grower in the state.* **2.** a plant that grows in a certain way: *a rapid grower.*

growing pains 1. pains in the limbs during childhood and youth, thought to be caused by growing. **2.** emotional problems encountered by adolescents during the process of maturing. **3.** difficulties arising in the early development of something new, as a project or a new business.

growing season, the period suitable for growth and reproduction of a plant in a particular climate.

growl (groul) *v.i.* **1.** to make a deep, harsh, guttural sound, in anger or as a threat: *The bear growled at us.* **2.** to speak or make an angry sound or sounds like this. —*v.t.* to express by growling: *to growl a reply.* —*n.* **1.** a deep, harsh, rumbling sound made by an angry animal. **2.** any sound or utterance resembling this. [Probably imitative.] —**growl′er,** *n.*

grown (grōn) *v.* the past participle of **grow.** —*adj.* having attained one's full growth or maturity; adult: *That is no way for a grown person to behave.*

grown-up (*adj.,* grōn′up′; *n.,* grōn′up′) *adj.* **1.** adult: *We tried to act grown-up when visiting the museum.* **2.** characteristic of or suitable for adults: *grown-up clothes.* —*n.* adult: *The grown-ups watched as the children swam in the pool.*

growth (grōth) *n.* **1.** the process of growing toward full size or maturity; development: *the growth of a child, the growth of a plant.* **2.** an increase as in size, importance, or power: *the growth of industry, a rapid growth in popularity.* **3.** something that grows or has grown: *The gardener cleared a month's growth of weeds from the garden.* **4.** a mass of new tissue that results from an abnormal increase in cells and serves no useful function for the body; tumor; neoplasm.

growth factor, any of various genetic, hormonal, or nutritional factors, as vitamins and minerals, that are essential to normal growth.

growth hormone 1. a hormone secreted by the pituitary gland that regulates or stimulates growth. **2.** any of various plant substances, as an auxin, that stimulate growth.

growth ring, the increment in wood produced in the trunk, limbs, or roots of a tree or shrub during any one growing season. An annual ring may be made up of more than one growth ring.

grub (grub) *n.* **1.** a thick-bodied, soft, wormlike larva of an insect, esp. of a beetle. **2.** *Informal.* food. **3.** *Informal.* an unkempt, sloppy person. —*v.,* **grubbed, grub·bing.** —*v.i.* **1.** to dig in the ground; root: *Trained pigs are used to grub for truffles.* **2.** to work very hard, esp. doing menial or dreary work; drudge: *to grub for a meager existence.* —*v.t.* **1.** to dig up by the roots; uproot: *to grub out mushrooms in the lawn.* **2.** to clear (ground) of plants, roots, and stumps. **3.** *Slang.* to borrow without intending to return or repay: *That person is notorious for grubbing money.* [Possibly from an unrecorded Old English word.] —**grub′ber,** *n.*

grub·by (grub′ē) *adj.,* **-bi·er, -bi·est. 1.** covered with grime or dirt; filthy: *Please wash your grubby hands.* **2.** infested with grubs. **3.** deserving of contempt; mean; despicable: *a grubby lie.* —**grub′bi·ly,** *adv.* —**grub′bi·ness,** *n.*

grub·stake (grub′stāk′) *n.* **1.** money or supplies advanced to a prospector in return for a share of future profits. **2.** money or assistance advanced for any project. —*v.t.,* **-staked, -stak·ing.** to supply with a grubstake.

Grub Street, needy, inferior writers; literary hacks collectively. [From *Grub Street* (now Milton Street), London, where a number of poor and inferior writers once lived.]

grudge (gruj) *n.* a strong feeling of ill will, anger, or resentment. —*v.t.,* **grudged, grudg·ing. 1.** to give or allow unwillingly: *to*

grudge *a beggar a few coins.* **2.** to be envious of (someone) for their enjoyment or possession of something; begrudge: *to grudge someone his or her good fortune.* [Old French *groucier, grouch(i)er* to grumble, murmur; of Germanic origin.] —**grudg′ing·ly,** *adv.*

gru·el (grü′əl) *n.* a thin porridge made by boiling meal, esp. oatmeal, in water or milk. [Old French *gruel,* diminutive of *gru* oatmeal; of Germanic origin.]

gru·el·ing (grü′ə ling, grü′ling) *also,* **gru·el·ling.** *adj.* very difficult or punishing; exhausting: *The marathon is a grueling race.*

grue·some (grü′səm) *also,* **grewsome.** *adj.* inspiring horror, revulsion, or fear; frightful; repulsive. [Dialectal English *grue* to feel horror (probably of Scandinavian origin) + -SOME[1].] —**grue′some·ly,** *adv.* —**grue′some·ness,** *n.*

gruff (gruf) *adj.* **1.** (of the voice) deep and rough. **2.** abrupt, stern, or rude; brusque: *a person with a gruff manner but a kind heart.* [Dutch *grof* coarse, heavy, blunt.] —**gruff′ly,** *adv.* —**gruff′ness,** *n.*

grum·ble (grum′bəl) *v.,* **-bled, -bling.** —*v.i.* **1.** to mutter in discontent; complain in a grouchy or sullen manner. **2.** to make a rumbling sound, as thunder. —*v.t.* to express by grumbling. —*n.* **1.** a mutter of discontent or complaint. **2.** rumble. [French *grommeler* to complain, from Old French *gromer* to growl, mutter, from Middle Dutch *grommen* to growl.] —**grum′bler,** *n.*

grump (grump) *n.* **1.** an ill-tempered, complaining person. **2.** *usually,* **grumps.** a fit of bad humor. —*v.i.* to sulk or complain. [Possibly imitative.]

grump·y (grum′pē) *adj.,* **grump·i·er, grump·i·est.** in an irritable or gloomy mood; surly; ill-tempered: *Lack of sleep made me grumpy.* [From obsolete *grump* sulkiness (probably imitative) + -Y[1].] —**grump′i·ly,** *adv.* —**grump′i·ness,** *n.*

Grun·dy, Mrs. (grun′dē) a person who has narrow-minded and prudish views regarding personal conduct, manners, and morals. [From *Mrs. Grundy,* a character referred to in the play *Speed the Plough* by the English playwright Thomas Morton, 1764?-1838, in which the question "What will Mrs. Grundy say?" is constantly asked.] —**Grun′dy·ism,** *n.*

grun·gy (grun′jē) *adj.,* **-gi·er, -gi·est.** *Slang.* dirty, run-down, or shabby: *a grungy hotel, grungy clothes.* [Of uncertain origin.]

grun·ion (grun′yən) *n.* a saltwater food fish, *Leuresthes tenuis,* found in the coastal waters of southern and Lower California, noted for spawning on the beach at high tide before it is carried back out to sea by the waves. Length: 5-7 inches (13-18 centimeters). [Probably from Spanish *gruñón* grunter, from *gruñir* to grunt, from Latin *grunnīre.*]

grunt (grunt) *n.* **1.** a short, deep, hoarse sound, as that made by a hog. **2.** any of a group of tropical saltwater fish, family Pomadasyidae, that make a similar sound by rubbing their teeth together. —*v.i.* **1.** to make the short, deep, hoarse sound of a hog. **2.** to make a similar sound, as in effort or discontent. —*v.t.* to utter or express with a grunt: *to grunt a surly reply.* [Old English *grunnettan* to utter a sound like that of a hog.] —**grunt′er,** *n.*

Gru·yère (grü yâr′, gri-) *n.* a variety of firm, light yellow cheese that is made from whole milk and resembles Swiss cheese in flavor. [From *Gruyère,* Swiss district where this cheese was first made.]

gryph·on (grif′ən) griffin.

G-suit (jē′süt′) *n.* a suit designed to counteract the physiological effects of rapid acceleration or deceleration, worn by a pilot or astronaut. [GRAVITY + SUIT.]

gt., great.

Gt. Br. *also,* **Gt. Brit.** Great Britain.

GU, the postal abbreviation for Guam.

guai·a·cum (gwī′ə kəm) **1.** lignum vitae. **2.** the oil or oily resin obtained from this tree, used in varnishes, as an antioxidant in food, and as a source of blue dye. [Modern Latin *guaiacum,* from Spanish *guayaco,* from Taino *guayacan.*]

gua·na·co (gwä nä′kō) *n., pl.* **-cos.** a hoofed mammal, *Lama guanicoe,* of the Andes Mountains, thought to be the ancestor of the domesticated llama and alpaca. Height: 3½ feet (1.1 meters) at the shoulder. [Spanish *guanaco,* from Quechua *huanacu* wild sheep.]

guanaco

gua·nine (gwä′nēn) *n.* a purine base that is an essential constituent of DNA and RNA. Formula: $C_5H_5N_5O$ For illustration, see **double helix.**

gua·no (gwä′nō) *n., pl.* **-nos. 1.** waste matter of seabirds, widely used as fertilizer, found in large deposits on islands off the coast

of Peru. **2.** any similar fertilizer, such as the excrement of bats. [Spanish *guano* manure of seabirds, from Quechua *huanu* dung.]

gua·ra·ni (gwär′ə nē′) *n., pl.* **-ni** or **-nis.** the monetary unit of Paraguay. [Spanish *guaraní,* from the *Guaraní* people.]

Gua·ra·ni (gwär′ə nē′) *n., pl.* **-ni** or **-nis. 1.** a member of any of several South American Indian tribes formerly living in what are now Paraguay and parts of Bolivia and Brazil. **2.** one of the descendants of these Indians and the early Spanish settlers, now constituting more than half the population of Paraguay. **3.** their language, belonging to the Tupi-Guarani language family.

guar·an·tee (gar′ən tē′) *n.* **1.** a binding assurance given by a seller to a buyer to repair, replace, or refund the purchase price of the seller's product if it is not what it is claimed to be or if it proves defective within a given period of time; warranty. **2.** anything that assures a certain outcome or condition: *Beauty is no guarantee of popularity.* **3.** a person who receives a guaranty. **4.** guarantor. —*v.t.,* **-teed, -tee·ing. 1.a.** to give assurance of the quality of; give a guarantee for: *The manufacturer guaranteed the toaster for one year.* **b.** to agree to be responsible for the debts or obligations of another; make a guaranty. **2.** to make a certainty: *The band that we hired will guarantee the success of the dance.* **3.** to state or otherwise affirm (something); promise: *I guarantee that we will finish the job tomorrow.* **4.** to give security to; ensure: *The policy would guarantee them against fire and theft.* [Modification of GUARANTY.]

guar·an·tor (gar′ən tôr′, -tər) *n.* a person who makes or gives a guarantee.

guar·an·ty (gar′ən tē′) *n., pl.* **-ties. 1.** an agreement or promise to be responsible for the debts or obligations of another person in case of that person's default. **2.** something given or taken as security for a debt or obligation. **3.** guarantee; warranty. **4.** guarantor. —*v.t.,* **-tied, -ty·ing.** guarantee. [Anglo-Norman *guarantie* warranty, from Old French *garantir* to warrant, from *garant* warrant, protection; of Germanic origin.]

guard (gärd) *v.t.* **1.** to watch over or tend carefully so as to keep safe from harm; defend; protect: *Secret Service agents guarded the president.* **2.** to maintain close supervision or surveillance over, as to prevent escape or to control activity: *Police guarded the prisoners.* **3.** to prevent or regulate entrance or exit through: *Two soldiers guarded the gate of the fort.* **4.** to keep in check; control: *to guard one's feelings.* **5.** in certain sports, to attempt to prevent (an opponent) from scoring. **6.** to provide a cover or other protective device for: *Using this lotion will guard your skin against the sun.* —*v.i.* to take precautions (with *against*): *to guard against illness.* —*n.* **1.** a person or group that guards: *a museum guard, a guard made up of ten soldiers.* **2.** any cover, attachment, or other device that protects against loss, injury, or damage. **3.** careful or restraining watch or supervision: *A sentry kept guard at the door.* **4.** something that guards or protects; defense; safeguard: *Brushing your teeth after each meal is a good guard against tooth decay.* **5.** *Football.* **a.** one of two players positioned at the right and the left of the center. **b.** the position played by such a player. **6.** *Basketball.* **a.** one of two primarily defensive players positioned toward the rear of the court. **b.** the position played by such a player. **7.** a posture of defense or readiness, as in boxing or fencing. **8. guards.** any of several units of soldiers in the British army attached to the royal household. [Old French *garder* to keep, watch over, protect; of Germanic origin.] —**guard′er,** *n.* —For Synonyms *(v.t.),* see **defend.**

•**off (one's) guard.** unprepared, as for danger, difficulties, or attack; not alert: *They were caught off guard by the enemy.*

•**on (one's) guard.** prepared or watchful, as for danger, difficulties, or attack; vigilant; alert.

•**to stand guard. a.** to serve as a sentry. **b.** to keep a protective watch: *The bear stood guard over its injured cub.*

guard cell *Botany.* one of a pair of bean-shaped cells, scattered throughout the epidermis of a leaf, whose responses to heat, light, and water control the amount of transpiration and respiration that takes place through the stoma.

guard·ed (gär′did) *adj.* **1.** characterized by or showing caution; careful; prudent: *a guarded reply to a provocative question.* **2.** closely watched, defended, or restrained. —**guard′ed·ly,** *adv.*

guard hair, a long, coarse outer hair serving to protect the soft inner fur in certain animals, such as dogs.

a	at	e	end	o	hot	u	up	hw	white		about
ā	ape	ē	me	ō	old	ū	use	ng	song	ə	taken
ä	far	i	it	ô	fork	ü	rule	th	thin		pencil
âr	care	ī	ice	oi	oil	u̇	pull	th	this		lemon
		îr	pierce	ou	out	ûr	turn	zh	measure		circus

G

guard·house (gärd'hous') *n., pl.* **-hous·es** (-hou'ziz). **1.** a building used as a temporary jail for military personnel who have been convicted of minor offenses or are awaiting court-martial. **2.** a building used to house military personnel on guard duty.

guard·i·an (gär'dē ən) *n.* **1.** a person who guards or watches over; protector. **2.** a person who is legally entrusted with the care of the person, property, or rights of a minor or other individual who is considered incapable of managing his or her own affairs. —*adj.* acting as protection; protecting: *a guardian angel.* [Anglo-Norman *gardein* warden, keeper, from Old French *garder.* See GUARD.] —**guard'i·an·ship'**, *n.*

guard·rail (gärd'rāl') *n.* a railing for support or protection, as on a staircase or a highway.

guard·room (gärd'rüm', -rùm') *n.* a room used to accommodate military personnel on guard duty.

guards·man (gärdz'mən) *n., pl.* **-men** (-mən). **1.** a person who serves as a guard. **2.** a soldier in the National Guard. **3.** a soldier in a guards regiment of the British army.

Guar·ner·i·us (gwär nâr'ē əs) *n., pl.* **-us·es.** a violin made by a member of the Guarneri family.

gua·va (gwä'və) *n.* **1.** the round or pear-shaped berrylike fruit of any of a group of trees or shrubs, genus *Psidium,* of the myrtle family, having a sweet, firm flesh that may be white, yellow, or deep pink, used for making jellies and other sweets. **2.** the tree or shrub bearing this fruit, grown in tropical America, having large oval leaves and white flowers. The most widely cultivated species is the **common guava,** *P. guajava,* having a scaly bark and hairy twigs. [Spanish *guayaba* the fruit; of South American Indian origin.]

gua·yu·le (gwä ū'lē) *n.* a low-growing shrub, *Parthenium argentatum,* of the composite family, found in desert areas, chiefly in Mexico and Texas, bearing narrow, silvery leaves and small, white, daisylike flower heads, and having tissues that yield granules of natural rubber. [Spanish *guayule,* from Nahuatl *cuauhuli* literally, tree gum, from *cuahuitl* tree + *uli* gum.]

gu·ber·na·to·ri·al (gü'bər nə tôr'ē əl, gū'-) *adj.* of or relating to a governor or the office of governor. [Latin *gubernātor* ruler, pilot + -IAL.]

gudg·eon (guj'ən) *n.* **1.** a freshwater fish of Europe, easily caught and often used for bait. **2.** any of various similar fish, as the minnow. [Old French *goujon* this freshwater fish, from Latin *gōbiō,* form of *gōbius* (see GOBY).]

Gud·run (gùd'rün) *n.* in Norse legend, the wife of the hero Sigurd.

guer·don (gûr'dən) *Archaic. n.* a reward or recompense. —*v.t.* to give a reward to. [Old French *guerdon* a reward, modification (influenced by Latin *dōnum* gift) of Old High German *widarlōn.*]

Guern·sey (gûrn'zē) *n., pl.* **-seys. 1.** any of a breed of dairy cattle originally developed on Guernsey in the Channel Islands, typically having a reddish or fawn coat with white markings. Weight: to 1,700 pounds (771 kilograms). **2. guernsey.** a close-fitting knitted woolen shirt worn by sailors.

guer·ril·la (gə ril'ə) *also,* **gue·ril·la.** *n.* a person who fights as a member of an armed band, usually not a part of a regular military unit, that combats the enemy with such acts as sabotage, ambushes, and sudden raids. —*adj.* of, relating to, or by guerrillas: *guerrilla warfare.* [Spanish *guerrilla* skirmish, diminutive of *guerra* war, from Old High German *werra* discord.]

guess (ges) *v.t.* **1.** to form an opinion or estimate of (something) from incomplete or uncertain knowledge or evidence: *Without a clock I could only guess what time it was.* **2.** to judge (something) correctly by doing this: *to guess the answer to a teacher's question.* **3.** to be of the opinion that; think; believe; suppose: *I guess they forgot about the meeting.* —*v.i.* **1.** to make a guess (often with *at*): *We guessed at the height of the building.* **2.** to judge something correctly by guessing. —*n.* an opinion, estimate, or conclusion formed by guessing. [Probably of Scandinavian origin.] —**guess'a·ble,** *adj.* —**guess'er,** *n.*

> **Synonyms** *v.t.* **Guess, conjecture,** and **surmise** mean to form an opinion or estimate on less than conclusive evidence. **Guess** is the most general of these terms, embracing anything from having fairly adequate evidence to having almost none: *I knew most of the facts and could guess the rest. I had no time to prepare for the test, so I had to guess at many of the answers.* **Conjecture** connotes a plausible choice made from some evidence: *We were able to conjecture what happened from the clues we found in the building.* **Surmise** suggests the operation of mere intuition: *I surmised that you had lost interest, though you didn't come out and say so.*

guess·ti·mate (*n.,* ges'tə mit, -māt'; *v.,* ges'tə māt') *also,* **guesstimate.** *Informal. n.* an estimate based on or involving a guess; surmise. —*v.,* **-mat·ed, -mat·ing.** —*v.t.* to estimate by guessing: *to guesstimate the cost of repairs.* —*v.i.* to make an estimate by guessing. [Blend of GUESS + ESTIMATE.]

guess·work (ges'wûrk') *n.* the process or result of guessing: *to arrive at an answer by guesswork.*

guest (gest) *n.* **1.** a person who is received and entertained by another, as for a party, meal, or visit. **2.** a person who pays for accommodations, food, or other services, as at a hotel, boarding house, or restaurant. **3.** an organism that shares the food supply or dwelling of another; commensal organism. **4.** a person who is invited to perform or participate in a program: *a guest on a television show.* —*v.i.* to be a guest. —*adj.* **1.** of, relating to, or for a guest or guests: *a guest bedroom.* **2.** appearing or performing as a guest: *a guest speaker.* [Old Norse *gestr* visitor, stranger.]

gues·ti·mate (*n.,* ges'tə mit, -māt'; *v.,* ges'tə māt') *Informal. n.* guesstimate. —*v.,* **-mat·ed, -mat·ing.** guesstimate.

guest room, a room used esp. for the accommodation of overnight guests.

guest-star (gest'stär') *v.i.* **-starred, -star·ring.** to appear or perform as a guest star: *to guest-star on a TV show.*

guff (guf) *n. Slang.* empty talk; nonsense. [Probably imitative.]

guf·faw (gu fô', gə-) *n.* a loud, boisterous burst of laughter. —*v.i.* to laugh loudly and boisterously. [Imitative.]

guid·ance (gīd'əns) *n.* **1.** the act or process of guiding; leadership; direction: *to write a term paper under a teacher's guidance.* **2.** something that guides. **3.** counseling and advice dealing with educational and career plans and personal problems, esp. that given to students by school services. **4.** the process by which a missile can be guided while in flight.

guide (gīd) *n.* **1.** a person who guides, esp. someone who is employed to lead or conduct tours, hunting expeditions, or the like. **2.** a person or thing that directs conduct or a course of action: *Let your conscience be your guide.* **3.** guidebook. **4.** a book explaining or outlining the basic elements of some subject: *a guide to medieval literature.* **5.** a part of a machine serving to steady or direct motion. A power saw has a guide to keep wood in position as it is being sawed. **6.** a member of a military formation who sets the pace and direction of a march. **7.** guidepost. —*v.,* **guid·ed, guid·ing.** —*v.t.* **1.** to show the way to; lead; conduct: *I guided the tour group through the museum.* **2.** to direct the course or motion of: *The driver guided the truck around the curves in the road.* **3.** to lead or direct, as the actions, affairs, or motives of; regulate: *Let common sense guide you.* —*v.i.* to act as a guide. [Old French *guider* to lead, modification of earlier *gvier;* of Germanic origin.] —**guid'er,** *n.*

guide·book (gīd'bùk') *n.* a book of directions and information for travelers and tourists.

guided missile, a missile that is guided during its flight by external means, as transmitted electronic signals, or by internal means, as a heat-seeking device.

guide dog, a dog specially trained to act as a guide for a blind person. Also, **Seeing Eye dog.**

guide·line (gīd'līn') *n.* a principle or procedure to be followed in determining some course of action: *The city council laid down guidelines for establishing new programs to help the homeless.*

guide·post (gīd'pōst') *n.* a post at a roadside or intersection bearing a sign containing directions for travelers.

guide word, one of the two or more words appearing at the top of a page in a dictionary or other alphabetical reference book, used to indicate the first and last entries on the page.

gui·don (gī'don) *n.* **1.** a flag, streamer, or pennant representing a military unit. **2.** a soldier who carries a guidon. [French *guidon* banner, from Italian *guidone,* from *guida* guide, from *guidare* to lead; of Germanic origin.]

guild (gild) *also,* **gild.** *n.* **1.** in the Middle Ages, a group of merchants or artisans in one trade or craft, organized to uphold standards and to protect the interests of members. **2.** any association of persons with similar interests or aims: *an actors' guild.* [Old Norse *gildi* payment, fraternity.]

guil·der (gil'dər) *also,* **gilder.** *n.* **1.** the monetary unit of the Netherlands. **2.** any of several gold or silver coins formerly used in the Netherlands, Germany, and Austria. Also, **gulden.** [Modification of Dutch *gulden.* See GULDEN.]

guild·hall (gild'hôl') *n.* a hall in which a guild meets.

guilds·man (gildz'mən) *n., pl.* **-men** (-mən). a member of a guild.

guile (gīl) *n.* skill in deception; cunning; deceit; slyness. [Old French *guile;* of Germanic origin.] —For Synonyms, see **deceit.**

guile·ful (gīl'fəl) *adj.* full of guile; deceitful; cunning. —**guile'ful·ly,** *adv.* —**guile'ful·ness,** *n.*

guile·less (gīl'lis) *adj.* without guile; sincere; candid. —**guile'less·ly,** *adv.* —**guile'less·ness,** *n.*

guil·le·mot (gil'ə mot') *n.* any of several web-footed birds, genera *Uria* and *Cepphus,* of the auk family, inhabiting the northern regions of the Atlantic and Pacific oceans, having a narrow, pointed bill and black or black-and-white plumage. [French *guillemot* diminutive of *Guillaume* William.]

guil·lo·tine (*n.,* gil′ə tēn′, gē′ə-; *v.,* gil′ə tēn′, gē′ə-) *n.* a machine consisting of a heavily weighted knife that falls between two grooved posts, used for beheading people. It was adopted as the legal means of execution in France during the French Revolution. —*v.t.,* **-tined, -tin·ing.** to behead by the guillotine. [French *guillotine* this machine, from Joseph I. *Guillotin,* 1738-1814, French physician who advocated its use instead of crueler methods of capital punishment. Popular belief notwithstanding, he did not invent it.]

guilt (gilt) *n.* **1.** the state or fact of having done wrong, esp. of having committed a crime: *The new evidence proved the defendant's guilt.* **2.** a wrongful action; guilty behavior; wrongdoing. **3.** a feeling of remorse or shame for real or imagined wrongdoing. [Old English *gylt* crime, offense.]

guilt·less (gilt′lis) *adj.* **1.** free from guilt; innocent. **2.** having no knowledge or experience of something. —**guilt′less·ly,** *adv.* —**guilt′less·ness,** *n.*

guilt·y (gil′tē) *adj.,* **guilt·i·er, guilt·i·est. 1.** having committed an offense; deserving of blame or punishment: *We are all guilty of losing our temper sometimes.* **2.** convicted of a crime: *The prisoner was guilty of arson.* **3.** experiencing, involving, or showing guilt or a sense of guilt: *a guilty look, a guilty conscience.* [Old English *gyltig* criminal.] —**guilt′i·ly,** *adv.* —**guilt′i·ness,** *n.*

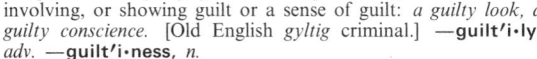

guimpe (gimp, gamp) *n.* a short blouse designed to be worn under certain dresses, as jumpers. [French *guimpe* wimple, veil; of Germanic origin.]

guin·ea (gin′ē) *n.* **1.** a former English gold coin last minted in 1813 and fixed in value in 1717 at twenty-one shillings. **2.** in England, the sum of money equal to twenty-one shillings. **3.** guinea fowl.

guinea fowl, any of various pheasantlike fowl, family Numididae, native to Africa, having dark gray feathers speckled with white, widely domesticated and raised for its flesh, esp. the common species, *Numida meleagris.* Length: 17-30 inches (43-76 centimeters).

guinea hen 1. a female guinea fowl. **2.** guinea fowl.

guinea pig 1. a rabbitlike rodent, genus *Cavia,* having a large head, small rounded ears, a stout body, and a long or short coat that may be solid or variegated, used for biological and medical research and kept as a pet. Length: 11 inches (28 centimeters). **2.** any person or thing used in experimentation.

guinea fowl

Guin·e·vere (gwin′ə vîr′) *n.* in Arthurian legend, the wife of King Arthur and mistress of Lancelot.

guise (gīz) *n.* **1.** an external appearance or aspect; semblance: *The mayor proposed an old approach to the problem of unemployment in a new guise.* **2.** an assumed or false appearance; pretense: *They exploited us under the guise of friendship.* **3.** style or manner of dress; garb. [Old French *guise* way, manner; of Germanic origin.]

gui·tar (gi tär′) *n.* a musical instrument having a somewhat violinlike body, a long, fretted neck, and strings, usually six, that are plucked or strummed with the fingers or a plectrum. [French *guitare,* from Spanish *guitarra,* from Arabic *qītāra* stringed instrument like a guitar, from Greek *kitharā* type of lyre. Doublet of CITHARA, ZITHER.]

gui·tar·ist (gi tär′ist) *n.* a person who plays the guitar, esp. professionally.

Gu·ja·ra·ti (gùj′ə rä′tē) *n.* an Indo-Iranian language of the Indo-European family, spoken in India.

gu·lag (gü′läg) *also,* **Gu·lag.** *n.* a forced labor camp, esp. in the former Soviet Union, used to confine persons considered politically dangerous by the government. [Russian *Gulág,* short for *Glávnoe upravlénie ispravítel no-trudouy̆kh lageréǐ* Main Directorate of Corrective Labor Camps.]

gulch (gulch) *n.* a deep, narrow ravine with steep sides, esp. one marking the course of a stream or torrent. [Possibly from dialectal English *gulch* to swallow; of imitative origin.]

gul·den (gùl′dən) *n., pl.* **-dens** or **-den.** guilder. [Dutch *gulden,* short for *gulden florijn* golden florin.]

gules (gūlz) *n. Heraldry.* the color red. In representations without color, it is indicated by parallel vertical lines. [Old French *gueules* red; originally, scarfs of red fur for the neck, plural of *gueule* throat, from Latin *gula.*]

gulf (gulf) *n.* **1.** a body of water forming an indentation in the shoreline of an ocean or sea, usually larger and deeper than a bay. **2.** a deep hollow in the earth; chasm. **3.** any wide separation or interval; gap: *There is a great gulf between the rich and the poor in that country.* **4.** something that engulfs or swallows up, esp. a whirlpool. [Old French *golfe* bay[1], whirlpool, from Italian *golfo,* going back to Greek *kolpos* bosom, hollow, bay[1].]

Gulf Stream, a warm ocean current flowing northeast across the North Atlantic Ocean from the Gulf of Mexico along the eastern coast of North America to the northern coast of Europe.

gulf·weed (gulf′wēd′) *n.* any of a group of tropical marine seaweeds, genus *Sargassum,* found floating in large masses in the Gulf Stream and the Sargasso Sea, consisting of branches of leaflike blades having small berrylike sacs filled with air that keep it afloat.

gull[1] (gul) *n.* any of several graceful, long-winged birds, family Laridae, found on most seacoasts and near other large bodies of water, having webbed feet, a thick, slightly hooked beak, and typically gray and white plumage with black wing tips. Length: 8-30 inches (20-76 centimeters). Also, **sea gull.** [Middle English *gull,* from Celtic *gull,* as in Cornish *guilan* or Welsh *gwylan.*]

gull[2] (gul) *v.t.* to deceive or cheat; dupe: *Swindlers gulled us into giving them money.* —*n.* a person who is easily deceived or cheated; dupe. [Middle English *gulle* stupid fellow; literally, unfledged bird.]

Gul·lah (gul′ə) *n.* **1.** a member or recent descendant of a group of American blacks living along the coast of South Carolina and Georgia and on the Sea Islands. **2.** the dialect of these people, consisting of mixed African and English elements.

gul·let (gul′it) *n.* **1.** a tube or passage through which food passes from the mouth to the stomach; esophagus. **2.** throat. [Old French *goulet* neck of a bottle or vase, water passage, diminutive of *gole* throat, from Latin *gula.*]

gul·li·ble (gul′ə bəl) *adj.* easily deceived, cheated, or duped; credulous. [GULL[2] + -IBLE.] —**gul′li·bil′i·ty,** *n.* —**gul′li·bly,** *adv.*

gul·ly (gul′ē) *n., pl.* **-lies.** a ditch or channel cut in the earth by running water; small ravine. —*v.t.,* **-lied, -ly·ing.** to make a gully in. [Modification of GULLET.]

gulp (gulp) *v.t.* **1.** to swallow hastily, greedily, or in large amounts (often with *down*): *to gulp down a sandwich.* **2.** to choke back or stifle as if by swallowing (often with *down*): *to gulp down one's anger.* —*v.i.* to draw in or swallow air, as in surprise or fear. —*n.* **1.** the act of gulping. **2.** an amount swallowed at one time; mouthful: *a gulp of milk.* [Middle Dutch *gulpen* to guzzle; imitative.] —**gulp′er,** *n.*

gum[1] (gum) *n.* **1.** a thick, sticky juice, secreted by various plants and trees, that dissolves or softens in cold water and hardens when exposed to air or heat. **2.** any similar plant or tree secretion, as resin. **3.** a preparation made from such substances, used in manufacturing textiles, adhesives, dyes, and paints. **4.** chewing gum. **5.** mucilage, glue, or similar adhesive: *There is no gum on the back of this stamp.* **6.** gum tree. —*v.,* **gummed, gum·ming.** —*v.t.* to coat, stiffen, or glue with gum or a gummy substance: *The machine gummed the back of the stamps.* —*v.i.* **1.** to secrete or form gum. **2.** to become coated, clogged, stiffened, or glued with gum or a gummy substance. [Middle English *gomme,* from Old French *gomme* sticky secretion from certain trees, from Late Latin *gummi, cummi,* from Greek *kommi,* from Egyptian *gmyt.*]

·to gum up. *Slang.* **a.** to ruin or spoil (something); mess up: *You really gummed things up when you didn't show up on time.* **b.** to make inoperable, as by clogging with a gummy substance: *Grease gummed up the motor.*

gum[2] (gum) *also,* **gums.** *n.* the tough fibrous tissue covered by a mucous membrane surrounding the necks of the teeth. [Old English *gōma* palate.]

gum ammoniac, ammoniac.

gum arabic, a gum obtained from any of several trees, genus *Acacia,* esp. *A. senegal,* used chiefly in the manufacture of candies, adhesives, inks, textiles, and medicines. Also, **acacia.**

G

a	at	e	end	o	hot	u	up	hw	white		about
ā	ape	ē	me	ō	old	ū	use	ng	song		taken
ä	far	i	it	ô	fork	ü	rule	th	thin	ə	pencil
âr	care	ī	ice	oi	oil	ù	pull	th	this		lemon
		îr	pierce	ou	out	ûr	turn	zh	measure		circus

gum·bo (gum′bō) *n., pl.* **-bos. 1.** okra. **2.** a highly seasoned soup thickened with okra pods and usually containing other vegetables and meat or fish. **3.** a clayey soil found in parts of the southern and western United States that becomes very sticky when wet. [Of Bantu origin.]

gum·boil (gum′boil′) *n.* a small abscess on the gum.

gum·drop (gum′drop′) *n.* a small, jellylike piece of candy made of gum arabic or gelatin, sweetened, variously flavored and colored, and usually coated with sugar.

gum·my (gum′ē) *adj.,* **-mi·er, -mi·est. 1.** of, containing, or resembling gum; sticky. **2.** covered or clogged with gum or a similar substance. **3.** secreting gum or a similar substance. —**gum′mi·ness,** *n.*

gump·tion (gump′shən) *n. Informal.* courage and energy; initiative; resourcefulness: *It took a lot of gumption to take on that much responsibility.* [Of uncertain origin.]

gum resin, a mixture of gum and resin, usually obtained by cutting the outer covering of certain plants.

gum·shoe (gum′shü′) *Slang. n.* detective. —*v.i.,* **-shoed, -shoe·ing.** to go around quietly and stealthily; sneak.

gum tragacanth, tragacanth.

gum tree, any of various gum-producing trees, such as the sapodilla, tupelo, sour gum, sweet gum, and including several trees of the genus *Eucalyptus.*

gum·wood (gum′wùd′) *n.* the wood of a gum tree, esp. a eucalyptus, used for construction, flooring, and inexpensive furniture.

gun (gun) *n.* **1.** any of various weapons, as a pistol, rifle, or cannon, consisting of a metal tube through which a projectile is shot in a flat trajectory by the force of an explosive. **2.** a similar device that discharges a projectile: *a dart gun.* **3.** any device resembling a gun in form or use: *They painted the wall with a spray gun.* **4.** the firing of a gun as a signal or salute: *The gun started the race.* **5.** a person skilled in the use of guns: *a hired gun, the fastest gun in the West.* —*v.,* **gunned, gun·ning.** —*v.t.*

Australian **gum tree**

1. *Informal.* to shoot (a person or animal) with a gun (often with *down*). **2.** *Slang.* to open the throttle of so as to increase the speed: *The driver gunned the engine.* —*v.i.* to shoot or hunt with a gun. [Short for Old Norse *Gunnhildr,* feminine proper name (from *gunnr* war + *hildr* battle); applied to a type of weapon.]

· **to give it the gun.** to cause to start or speed up, esp. a motor vehicle.

· **to go great guns.** to work or proceed with great skill, speed, and efficiency.

· **to gun for. a.** *Informal.* to look for in order to harm or kill. **b.** *Slang.* to try to obtain; seek: *to gun for a promotion.*

· **to spike (someone's) guns.** to ruin or foil someone's plans; defeat.

· **to stick to one's guns.** to be firm despite opposition; refuse to retreat or yield.

· **under the gun.** in a difficult, trying, or demanding situation or position: *We were under the gun to draw up the plans in a week.*

gun·boat (gun′bōt′) *n.* a small, armed ship used for patrolling rivers and coastal waters.

gun·cot·ton (gun′kot′ən) *n.* a highly explosive form of nitrocellulose made by treating cotton with a mixture of concentrated nitric and sulfuric acids.

gun·fight (gun′fīt′) *n.* a fight between people using guns. —**gun′fight′er,** *n.*

gun·fire (gun′fīr′) *n.* the shooting of a gun or guns.

gung ho (gung′hō′) *Informal.* very enthusiastic; eager: *They were gung ho about the party.* [Probably from Chinese (Mandarin) *kung ho* work together.]

gunk (gungk) *n. Informal.* an unpleasantly dirty substance that is usually sticky or greasy. —**gunk′y,** *adj.*

gun·lock (gun′lok′) *n.* the part of the mechanism in certain guns by which the charge is exploded.

gun·man (gun′mən) *n., pl.* **-men** (-mən). a person armed with a gun, esp. a criminal.

gun·met·al (gun′met′əl) *n.* **1.** any of various metallic alloys with a grayish color used for making such items as chains, buckles,

and other trinkets. **2.** a kind of bronze formerly used for making guns. **3.** a dark gray color with a bluish tinge. —*adj.* **1.** of or like gunmetal. **2.** having the color gunmetal.

Gun·nar (gùn′är, -ər) *n.* in Norse legend, the brother of Gudrun and husband of Brynhild.

gun·nel¹ (gun′əl) *n.* gunwale. [Form of GUNWALE.]

gun·nel² (gun′əl) *n.* a slender fish, *Pholis gunnellus,* of the blenny family, found in the North Atlantic. Length: to 12 inches (30 centimeters). [Of uncertain origin.]

gun·ner (gun′ər) *n.* **1.** a member of the armed forces who operates or helps to operate a firearm. **2.** a naval warrant officer in charge of ordnance. **3.** a person who hunts with a gun.

gun·ner·y (gun′ə rē) *n.* **1.** the use and firing of guns. **2.** guns collectively.

gun·ny (gun′ē) *n., pl.* **-nies.** a strong, coarse fabric made of jute or hemp, used esp. for making sacks or bags. [Hindi *gōnī* sack, from Sanskrit *gōnī.*]

gun·ny·sack (gun′ē sak′) *n.* a sack or bag made of gunny. Also, **gunny bag.**

gun·point (gun′point′) *n.* the end of a gun barrel.

· **at gunpoint.** under threat of being shot: *to be held up at gunpoint.*

gun·pow·der (gun′pou′dər) *n.* an explosive consisting of charcoal, sulfur, and potassium nitrate, used esp. in bullets, artillery shells, fireworks, and blasting.

gun room **1.** a room where guns are kept or displayed. **2.** a junior officers' quarters on a British warship.

gun·run·ning (gun′run′ing) *n.* the smuggling of firearms and ammunition into a country. —**gun′run′ner,** *n.*

gun·shot (gun′shot′) *n.* **1.** a bullet or other shot fired from a gun. **2.** the distance within which a gun will shoot accurately; range of a gun. **3.** the firing of a gun: *We could hear gunshots in the distance.* —*adj.* of or caused by a gunshot: *a gunshot wound.*

gun·shy (gun′shī′) *adj.* **1.** easily frightened by the firing of a gun. **2.** overly cautious or suspicious because of a prior bad experience: *After the accident, we were gun-shy about boats.*

gun·smith (gun′smith′) *n.* a person who makes or repairs firearms.

gun·stock (gun′stok′) *n.* a wooden support or handle to which the barrel of a gun is attached.

Gun·ther (gùn′tər) *n.* in the medieval German epic poem *Nibelungenlied,* the king of Burgundy and husband of Brunhild.

gun·wale (gun′əl) *also,* **gunnel.** *n.* the upper edge of the side of a ship or boat: *grabbing the gunwales to steady oneself in a boat.* [GUN + WALE because it once supported a ship's guns.]

gup·py (gup′ē) *n., pl.* **-pies.** a small, slender fish, *Lebistes reticulatus,* native to the fresh waters of Trinidad and northern South America, the male of which is brightly colored. This hardy fish is sold commercially for use in home aquariums. Length: to 2 inches (5 centimeters). [From R. J. L. *Guppy,* died 1916, British clergyman and naturalist in Trinidad, who first gave specimens to the British Museum.]

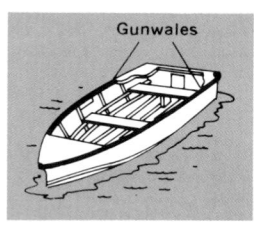
Gunwales

gur·gle (gûr′gəl) *v.,* **-gled, -gling.** —*v.i.* **1.** to flow irregularly with a bubbling sound: *The stream gurgled around the rocks.* **2.** to make a bubbling sound: *The baby cooed and gurgled with delight.* —*v.t.* to utter with a gurgling sound. —*n.* the act or sound of gurgling. [Probably imitative.]

Gur·kha (gûr′kə, gùr′-) *n.* a member of a Hindu people living in Nepal, famous as soldiers.

gur·nard (gûr′nərd) *n., pl.* **-nards** or **-nard. 1.** any of various tropical saltwater fish, family Triglidae, having an armored head and large pectoral fins with rays that move separately like fingers for crawling on the sea bottom. **2.** flying gurnard. [Old French *gornard* literally, grunter, from *gronir* to grunt, going back to Latin *grunnīre;* because it grunts when removed from water.]

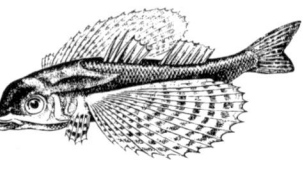
gurnard

gur·ney (gûr′nē) *n., pl.* **-neys.** a bedlike structure or stretcher on four wheels, used to carry the sick, injured, or dead. [Of uncertain origin.]

gu·ru (gŏŏ′rŏŏ, gŏŏ rŏŏ′) *n.* **1.** a holy man and religious and spiritual teacher, esp. in the Hindu religion. **2.** *Informal.* a respected leader or teacher. [Hindi *gurū* teacher, priest, from Sanskrit *guru* weighty, venerable.]

gush (gush) *v.i.* **1.** to flow or rush out suddenly and abundantly: *Water gushed from the broken pipe.* **2.** to emit a sudden, abundant flow of something (with *with*): *The cut gushed with blood.* **3.** *Informal.* to be overly or insincerely enthusiastic or emotional in speech or writing: *The young poet gushed with sentimentality.* —*v.t.* to emit in a sudden and abundant flow. —*n.* **1.** a sudden rush or outflow: *a gush of water.* **2.** something that gushes forth. **3.** *Informal.* a display of extravagant and insincere emotion or enthusiasm. [Probably imitative.]

gush·er (gush′ər) *n.* **1.** an oil well from which oil flows abundantly without being pumped. **2.** a person who gushes.

gush·y (gush′ē) *adj.*, **gush·i·er, gush·i·est.** overly emotional or enthusiastic; effusive. —**gush′i·ness,** *n.*

gus·set (gus′it) *n.* **1.** a triangular piece of material inserted into a garment or other article to reinforce or expand some part. **2.** a triangular metal brace or bracket used to reinforce a corner or angle of a structure. [Old French *gousset* piece of armor or cloth inserted under the armhole, diminutive of *gousse* husk of a bean; of uncertain origin; because it supposedly resembled a bean husk.]

gus·sy (gus′ē) *v.t., v.i.,* **-sied, -sy·ing.** *Slang.* to dress or decorate in a showy, overdone way (usually with *up*): *We gussied up the church for the wedding. They gussied up for the big party.* [Of uncertain origin.]

gust (gust) *n.* **1.** a sudden, strong rush of wind or air. **2.** any sudden burst or outflow, as of rain, fire, or sound. **3.** an outburst of emotion, as anger or enthusiasm. —*v.i.* to blow in gusts: *The wind gusted at 50 miles per hour.* [Old Norse *gustr* blast.]

gus·ta·to·ry (gus′tə tôr′ē) *adj.* of or relating to the sense of taste or the act of tasting. [Latin *gustātus,* past participle of *gustāre* to taste + -ORY.]

gus·to (gus′tō) *n.* great enthusiasm or enjoyment: *We ate with gusto after returning from our hike.* [Italian *gusto* taste, liking, from Latin *gustus* taste.]

gust·y (gus′tē) *adj.*, **gust·i·er, gust·i·est.** characterized by or coming in gusts; windy; blustery: *the gusty weather of March.* —**gust′i·ly,** *adv.* —**gust′i·ness,** *n.*

gut (gut) *n.* **1.** the digestive tract or any part of it, esp. the stomach or intestine. **2. guts. a.** *Informal.* courage; pluck; spirit; fortitude: *It took guts to play when you were injured.* **b.** entrails; bowels. **3.** catgut. **4.** a narrow passage or channel, such as a strait or gorge. —*v.t.,* **gut·ted, gut·ting. 1.** to remove the entrails of; disembowel; eviscerate: *to gut fish.* **2.** to destroy the inside of: *Fire gutted the house.* —*adj. Informal.* **1.** felt deeply or instinctively; visceral; spontaneous: *a gut feeling, a gut reaction.* **2.** basic or vital; fundamental: *gut issues in a political campaign.* [Old English *guttas* (plural) bowels, entrails.]

gut·less (gut′lis) *adj. Informal.* **1.** having no courage or pluck: *a gutless coward.* **2.** having no vitality; lifeless or useless: *a gutless project or program.*

gut·sy (gut′sē) *adj.*, **-si·er, -si·est.** *Informal.* having or characterized by courage, boldness, or vitality.

gut·ta-per·cha (gut′ə pûr′chə) *n.* a pliable, pale gray material obtained from the latex of several evergreen trees found in Malaya and the East Indies, esp. *Palaquium gutta.* It is used esp. in electrical insulation, in dentistry, and as waterproofing. [Malay *getah* gum, balsam + *percha* tree from which it comes.]

gut·ter (gut′ər) *n.* **1.** a narrow channel, ditch, or low area along the side of a street or road to carry off surface water. **2.** a trough fixed under or along the eaves of a roof to carry off rainwater. **3.** any channel or groove, as at the side of a bowling alley. **4.** a place or way of life characterized by poverty, filth, squalor, and immorality. **5.** the inner margins of two facing pages where the pages of a book, magazine, or other bound publication are joined together. —*v.t.* to form gutters in or furnish with gutters. —*v.i.* **1.** to flow in streams. **2.** (of a candle) to melt rapidly so that the wax or tallow runs down the sides in channels. [Old French *goutiere* channel, from *goute* drop, from Latin *gutta.*]

gut·ter·snipe (gut′ər snīp′) *n. Informal.* **1.** a poor, neglected child who spends much time in the streets. **2.** a person who has the manners or morals characteristic of the gutter.

gut·tur·al (gut′ər əl) *adj.* **1.** of or relating to the throat. **2.** having a harsh, rasping quality, as a sound produced in the throat: *a fierce, guttural growl.* **3.** *Phonetics.* pronounced with the back of the tongue raised toward the soft palate. The *g* in *go* is a guttural sound. —*n.* a guttural sound. [Modern Latin *gutturalis,* from *guttur* throat.] —**gut′tur·al·ly,** *adv.*

gut·ty (gut′ē) *adj.,* **-ti·er, -ti·est.** *Slang.* gutsy.

guy[1] (gī) *n.* a rope, chain, wire, or rod used to steady or secure something. —*v.t.,* **guyed, guy·ing.** to steady or secure with a guy. [Middle English *gie,* from Old French *guie* guide, from *guier* to guide, from *guider;* of Gothic origin.]

guy[2] (gī) *Informal. n.* **1.** a man; fellow. **2. guys.** *Informal.* persons of either sex: *We haven't seen you guys in a long time.* —*v.t.,* **guyed, guy·ing.** to make fun of; tease. [From *Guy Fawkes,* 1570-1606, leader of a conspiracy to blow up the British Parliament in 1605.]

guz·zle (guz′əl) *v.t., v.i.,* **-zled, -zling.** to drink (something) greedily or excessively. [Of uncertain origin.] —**guz′zler,** *n.*

gym (jim) *n.* **1.** gymnasium. **2.** a course in physical education in a school or college.

gym·kha·na (jim kä′nə) *n.* **1.** a meet consisting of various sports contests, esp. equestrian events. **2.** a sports car event over a planned course in which driving skill, rather than speed, is tested. [Modification (influenced by GYMNASIUM) of Hindi *gend-khāna* ball house, racket court: *khāna* house, from Persian *khāna.*]

gym·na·si·um (jim nā′zē əm) *n., pl.* **-si·ums** or **-si·a** (-zē ə). **1.** a room or building provided with equipment for physical exercise or training and for indoor sports. **2. Gymnasium.** a secondary school in various European countries, emphasizing classical studies, esp. Greek and Latin. [Latin *gymnasium* athletic school, school, from Greek *gymnasion,* going back to *gymnos* naked; because ancient Greek athletes exercised naked.]

gym·nast (jim′nast, -nəst) *n.* a person skilled in gymnastics. [Greek *gymnastēs* trainer of athletes.]

gym·nas·tic (jim nas′tik) *adj.* of or relating to gymnastics. —**gym·nas′ti·cal·ly,** *adv.*

gym·nas·tics (jim nas′tiks) *pl. n.* **1.** physical exercises, with or without apparatus, designed to develop strength, agility, coordination, and balance. **2.** the art, practice, or sport of such exercises. ➡ used as singular in def. 2.

gym·no·sperm (jim′nə spûrm′) *n.* any of a large group of plants whose seeds are not enclosed in ovaries and are generally borne in cones. Gymnosperms are usually characterized by thin needlelike leaves, as in pines, yews, spruces, and junipers. [Modern Latin *Gymnospermae,* from Greek *gymnospermos,* from *gymnos* naked + *sperma* seed.] —**gym′no·sper′mous,** *adj.*

gy·ne·col·o·gist (gī′ni kol′ə jist, jin′i-) *n.* a doctor who specializes in gynecology.

gy·ne·col·o·gy (gī′ni kol′ə jē, jin′i-) *n.* a branch of medicine dealing with the functions and disorders of the female reproductive system. [Greek *gynaik-,* stem of *gynē* woman + -LOGY.] —**gyn′e·co·log′ic;** *also,* **gyn′e·co·log′i·cal,** *adj.*

gy·noe·ci·um (jə nē′sē əm, gī-) *n., pl.* **-ci·a** (-sē ə). the pistil or pistils of a flower considered as a unit. [Modern Latin *gynoecium,* modification (influenced by Greek *oikion* house) of *gynaeceum,* going back to Greek *gynaikeion* women's apartment, from *gynē* woman.]

-gynous *combining form* (used to form adjectives) **1.** of females or wives: *polygynous.* **2.** of or having female reproductive organs or characteristics: *androgynous.* **3.** of or having pistils: *hypogynous.* [Modern Latin *-gynus,* from Greek *-gynos,* from *gynē* woman.]

gyp (jip) *Informal. v.t., v.i.,* **gypped, gyp·ping.** to cheat, swindle, or defraud. —*n.* **1.** an act or instance of cheating; fraud; swindle. **2.** a person who cheats; swindler. [Probably short for GYPSY.]

gyp·soph·i·la (jip sof′ə lə) *n.* any of a group of plants, genus *Gypsophila,* found mostly in northern temperate regions of the world, bearing clusters of small white or pink flowers on branching stalks with few leaves. Baby's breath is one of the most familiar species. [Modern Latin *Gypsophila,* going back to Greek *gypsos* chalk, gypsum + *philos* loving, dear.]

gyp·sum (jip′səm) *n.* a hydrated calcium sulfate mineral, used esp. in cements, in the production of plaster of Paris, and as a fertilizer. Alabaster is a type of gypsum. Formula: $CaSO_4 \cdot 2H_2O$ [Latin *gypsum* chalk, plaster, from Greek *gypsos* chalk; of Semitic origin.]

Gyp·sy (jip′sē) *also,* **Gipsy.** *n., pl.* **-sies. 1.** *also,* **gypsy.** a member of a migratory Caucasian people having dark skin and

a	at	e	end	o	hot	u	up	hw	white		about
ā	ape	ē	me	ō	old	ū	use	ng	song		taken
ä	far	i	it	ô	fork	ü	rule	th	thin	ə	pencil
âr	care	ī	ice	oi	oil	u̇	pull	th	this		lemon
				îr	pierce	ou	out	ûr	turn	zh	measure		circus

G

black hair, who left northwestern India over 1,000 years ago and appeared in Europe around the fourteenth century. They now live mainly in Europe and the United States. **2.** Romany *(def. 2).* **3. gypsy.** a person who resembles or leads the life of a Gypsy. [Modification of *Egyptian;* from the mistaken belief that Gypsies came from Egypt.]

gypsy moth *also,* **gipsy moth.** an insect pest, *Porthetria dispar,* native to Europe and Japan, now found in the northeastern United States, whose larvae attack the leaves of trees. The female is unable to fly.

gy·rate (jī′rāt, jī rāt′) *v.i.,* **-rat·ed, -rat·ing.** to move in a circle or spiral, esp. around an axis or fixed point; whirl; rotate: *The dancing couple gyrated around the room.* [Latin *gȳrātus,* past participle of *gȳrāre* to turn around, from *gȳrus* circle, from Greek *gȳros.*] **—gyra′tor,** *n.*

gy·ra·tion (jī rā′shən) *n.* the act of gyrating; circular or spiral motion.

gy·ra·to·ry (jī′rə tôr′ē) *adj.* moving in a circle or spiral; revolving; whirling.

gyre (jīr) *n.* **1.** a circular or spiral motion, course, or form. **2.** any of several circular ocean currents centered in subtropical regions. [Latin *gyrus* circle, ring, from Greek *gyros.*]

gyr·fal·con (jûr′fal′kən, -fôl′-, -fô′-) *also,* **gerfalcon.** *n.* a falcon, *Falco rusticolus,* living mainly in the Arctic. It is the largest of the falcons. Length: 2 feet (0.6 meter). [Old French *gerfaucon;* of Germanic origin.]

gy·ro[1] (jī′rō) *n., pl.* **-ros. 1.** gyrocompass. **2.** gyroscope. [Short for GYROCOMPASS, from Greek *gyros* round, rounded + COMPASS.]

gy·ro[2] (jîr′ō, jī′rō, zhîr′ō) *n., pl.* **-ros. 1.** lamb or beef roasted on a vertical spit. **2.** a sandwich made of this, usually with toma-

toes, onion, and sauce, served in pita bread. [From the Modern Greek word *gyros* a turning, used as the name of this food. The meat is roasted on a turning spit.]

gyro- *combining form* **1.** gyrating; rotating: *gyroscope.* **2.** incorporating a gyroscope: *gyrocompass.* [Greek *gȳros* circle.]

gy·ro·com·pass (jī′rō kum′pəs, -kom′-) *n.* a compass using a rapidly spinning gyroscope to indicate the north. It indicates true north rather than magnetic north.

gy·ro·scope (jī′rə skōp′) *n.* a wheel mounted so that the axis on which it spins can point in any direction. When the wheel is spinning, the axis sets itself in a fixed direction and resists changes from that direction. Gyroscopes are used as stabilizers, compasses, and automatic pilots. **—gy·ro·scop·ic** (jī′rə skop′ik), *adj.*

gyroscope

gy·ro·sta·bi·liz·er (jī′rō-stā′bə lī′zər) *n.* a gyroscopic device designed to stabilize a ship by counteracting the rolling motion of the ship.

gyve (jīv) *n.* a fetter or shackle, esp. for the leg. **—***v.t.,* **gyved, gyv·ing.** to bind with or as with fetters; shackle. [Of uncertain origin.]

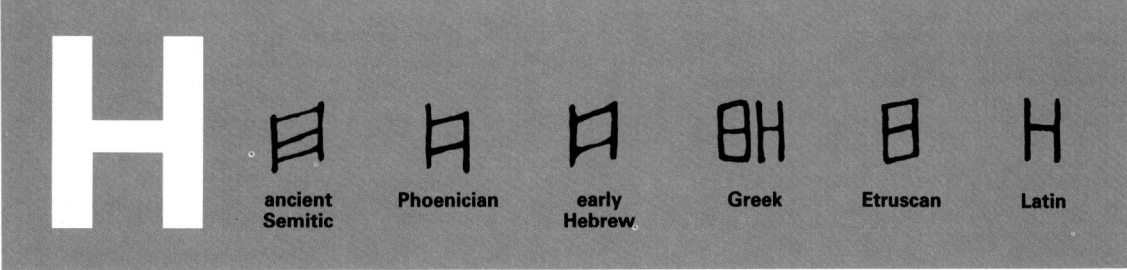

H The earliest form of the letter **H** was probably the letter *cheth*, or *het*, in the ancient Semitic, Phoenician, and early Hebrew alphabets. *Cheth*, which may have meant "fence," represented an *h* sound made at the back of the throat. When the ancient Greeks borrowed *cheth*, in the ninth century B.C., they called it *eta*. The early form of *eta* looked something like a square capital letter **B**. Later, the Greeks eliminated the upper and lower crossbars, giving it the modern form of two vertical lines connected by a short bar. When the Etruscans adopted *eta*, they went back to its earlier form. Unlike most Latin letters, which were derived from the Etruscan alphabet, the Latin letter **H** came directly from the later form of the Greek *eta*, and thus the shape of our modern capital **H** goes back about 2,400 years.

---

h, H (āch) *n., pl.* **h's, H's. 1.** the eighth letter of the English alphabet. **2.** the shape of this letter or something having this shape.

H¹, the symbol for hydrogen.

H², a symbol for deuterium.

H³, a symbol for tritium.

h *also,* **h. 1.** hectare; hectares. **2.** hour; hours.

H 1. *Physics.* **a.** henry. **b.** the intensity of a magnetic field. **2.** hour; hours.

H. 1. harbor. **2.** hard. **3.** hardness. **4.** height. **5.** high. **6.** *Baseball.* hit; hits. **7.** *Music.* horn. **8.** hour; hours. **9.** hundred. **10.** husband.

ha (hä) *interj.* **1.** *also,* **hah.** used to express a sudden feeling, as of surprise, joy, triumph, or scorn. **2.** used repetitively to express laughter.

ha, hectare; hectares.

Hab., Habakkuk.

Ha·bak·kuk (hə bak′ək, hab′ə kuk′) *n.* a book of the Old Testament, containing the prophecies of the Hebrew prophet Habakkuk. Also, in the Douay Bible, **Ha·bac·uc.**

ha·be·as cor·pus (hā′bē əs kôr′pəs) a writ or order commanding that a prisoner be brought before a court or judge to determine if he or she is being imprisoned or detained lawfully. [Medieval Latin *habeas corpus* you shall have the body (the opening words of this writ).]

hab·er·dash·er (hab′ər dash′ər) *n.* **1.** a person who sells men's furnishings, such as neckties, shirts, and gloves. **2.** *British.* a person who sells notions, such as buttons, thread, and ribbons. [Possibly from Anglo-Norman *hapertas* fabric, cloth; of uncertain origin.]

hab·er·dash·er·y (hab′ər dash′ə rē) *n., pl.* **-er·ies. 1.** the merchandise sold by a haberdasher. **2.** a haberdasher's shop.

hab·er·geon (hab′ər jən) *n.* **1.** *also,* **haubergeon.** a sleeveless jacket or short coat of mail or scale armor. **2.** hauberk. [Old French *haubergeon,* diminutive of *hauberc.* See HAUBERK.]

ha·bil·i·ment (hə bil′ə mənt) *n.* **1.** garb or attire for a particular occupation or occasion. **2.** clothing; dress. ➡ usually used in the plural in both definitions. [French *habillement* clothing, from Old French *(h)abiller* to dress; originally, to get ready, prepare a log of wood, from *a* to (from Latin *ad*) + *bille* tree trunk, large branch (of Celtic origin).]

hab·it (hab′it) *n.* **1.** an action that has become nearly automatic through deliberate or unconscious repetition: *Biting one's nails is a bad habit.* **2.** a tendency to act in a customary way: *They have a habit of always being late.* **3.** an addiction: *a drug habit.* **4.** a type of dress characteristic of a particular profession, rank, religious order, or activity: *a nun's habit.* **5.** a customary pattern of behavior: *eating habits of animals, good study habits.* **6.** the

characteristic form or manner of growth of an animal or plant: *Ivy has a climbing habit.* —*v.t.* to dress or clothe (oneself): *The jockeys habited themselves in blue and gold.* [Old French *habit* practice, dress, from Latin *habitus* condition, dress.]

Synonyms **Habit, custom,** and **practice** denote a way of doing something that has become fixed or usual over a period of time. **Habit** connotes something a person does without thinking about it: *I have a habit of opening my mouth when I concentrate on something.* **Custom** may refer to patterns of behavior established by a person or a group: *Their art and architecture reveal a lot about the customs of the Aztec people. It is our custom to begin each dinner with a toast.* **Practice** suggests an action that has been made habitual by conscious choice: *They made a practice of arriving early to get the best seats.*

hab·it·a·ble (hab′i tə bəl) *adj.* suitable for living in; inhabitable. —**hab′it·a·bil′i·ty, hab′it·a·ble·ness,** *n.* —**hab′it·a·bly,** *adv.*

hab·i·tant (hab′i tənt; *def. 2, also French* ä bē täN′) *n.* **1.** inhabitant. **2.** *also,* **ha·bi·tan.** a farmer of French descent who has settled in Canada or Louisiana. [French *habitant* inhabitant, from *habiter* to dwell, from Latin *habitāre.*]

hab·i·tat (hab′i tat′) *n.* **1.** an area or region in which an animal or plant naturally lives or grows, such as salt water or the desert. **2.** a place where a person or thing is most frequently found. **3.** a dwelling place; habitation. [Latin *habitat* it dwells.]

hab·i·ta·tion (hab′i tā′shən) *n.* **1.** a dwelling place; living quarters. **2.** the act of inhabiting; occupancy: *The cabin is not fit for human habitation.* **3.** settlement or colony: *the habitations of pioneers.* [Latin *habitātiō.*]

hab·it-form·ing (hab′it fôr′ming) *adj.* causing or tending to cause a habit or addiction, esp. a physical addiction: *habit-forming drugs.*

ha·bit·u·al (hə bich′ü əl) *adj.* **1.** done by habit; resulting from habit: *habitual optimism.* **2.** being or acting in a certain way by habit: *a habitual latecomer.* **3.** commonly occurring or used; usual: *a habitual diet.* —**ha·bit′u·al·ly,** *adv.* —**ha·bit′u·al·ness,** *n.*

ha·bit·u·ate (hə bich′ü āt′) *v.t.,* **-at·ed, -at·ing.** to familiarize through habit; accustom: *Living near the highway habituated them to noise.* [Late Latin *habituātus,* past participle of *habituāre* to bring into a condition, from Latin *habitus* condition.] —**ha·bit′u·a′tion,** *n.* —For Synonyms, see **accustom.**

hab·i·tude (hab′i tüd′, -tūd′) *n.* **1.** a disposition to act in a customary way. **2.** a habitual action; custom. [French *habitude* custom, from Latin *habitūdō* condition.]

ha·bit·u·é (hə bich′ü ā′) *n.* a person who frequents (a specified place): *a habitué of auctions.* [French *habitué,* from *habituer* to accustom, from Late Latin *habituāre.* See HABITUATE.]

ha·chure (ha shúr′) *n.* one of a series of short, closely spaced lines used as shading and to represent surfaces, such as mountains or hills, in relief, esp. on maps. —*v.t.,* **-chured, -chur·ing.** to mark with or show by hachures. [French *hachure,* from Old French *hacher* to chop (from *hache* ax).]

ha·ci·en·da (hä′sē en′də, ä′sē-) *n.* **1.** a landed estate, country house, ranch, or plantation. **2.** in the southwestern United States and Spanish America, a low, sprawling ranch house with wide porches. [Spanish *hacienda* landed estate, domestic work, going back to Latin *facienda* things to be done, from *facere* to do.]

hack¹ (hak) *v.t.* **1.** to cut or chop irregularly with heavy blows,

a	at	e	end	o	hot	u	up	hw	white		about
ā	ape	ē	me	ō	old	ū	use	ng	song		taken
ä	far	i	it	ô	fork	ü	rule	th	thin	ə	pencil
âr	care	ī	ice	oi	oil	u̇	pull	th	this		lemon
		îr	pierce	ou	out	ûr	turn	zh	measure		circus

H

557

as with a hatchet or cleaver. **2.** to clear or break up (land), as with a hoe. **3.** to cut ruthlessly, as if by hacking: *to hack a story, to hack a budgetary program.* **4.** *Slang.* to cope with successfully: *I couldn't hack running in such a long race.* —*v.i.* **1.** to make uneven or crude cuts or chops; deal cutting blows; chop: *The gardener hacked at the vines.* **2.** to emit short, harsh, repeated coughs. —*n.* **1.** a rough gash, cut, or notch made by or as by a heavy blow. **2.** a sharp tool or implement used for hacking, as a pick, hatchet, or cleaver. **3.** a short, harsh, repeated cough. [Old English *-haccian* to cut.]

• **to hack around.** *Slang.* to be idle; waste time; fool around.

hack² (hak) *n.* **1.** a person who renounces a talent, training, independence, or integrity and works solely for money or other reward; hireling. **2.** a person hired to write banal or pedestrian material; literary drudge. **3.** a carriage for hire; hackney. **4.** an old, worn-out horse. **5.** *Informal.* **a.** a taxicab. **b.** a taxicab driver. **6.** *British.* **a.** a horse kept for hire or for general work. **b.** a horse for riding. —*v.i.* **1.** *Informal.* to drive a taxicab. **2.** *British.* to ride on horseback on a road at an ordinary pace. —*adj.* **1.** of or relating to someone hired as a hack; working as or done by a hack: *a hack writer, a hack job.* **2.** trite; hackneyed; typical of a hack: *hack writing.* [Short for HACKNEY.]

hack·a·more (hak′ə môr′) *n.* a kind of halter consisting of a coil of rope or rawhide that can be tightened around the nose of a horse, used to break horses. [Spanish *jáquima,* going back to Arabic *shakīmah* bridle bit, curb.]

hack·ber·ry (hak′ber′ē, -bə rē) *n., pl.* **-ries. 1.** any of a large group of shrubs and trees, genus *Celtis,* of the elm family, found throughout the Northern Hemisphere, having gray bark and tiny flowers. **2.** the cherrylike fruit of this tree. [Form of *hagberry;* of Scandinavian origin.]

hack·er (hak′ər) *n.* **1.** a person or thing that hacks. **2.** a person who devotes much time to using computers, esp. someone who is skillful in gaining access to other computer systems without proper authorization.

hack·ie (hak′ē) *n. Slang.* a taxicab driver.

hack·le¹ (hak′əl) *n.* **1. a.** any of the long, slender feathers on the neck of certain birds, esp. the domestic rooster. **b.** neck plumage, as of the domestic rooster. **2.** an artificial fishing fly made with such feathers, often without wings. Also, **hackle fly. 3. hackles.** the hairs along the neck and back of an animal, esp. a dog, that stand up when it is angry or frightened. **4.** a board set with metal teeth, used to comb and clean flax, hemp, or jute. Also *(def. 4),* **hatchel.** —*v.t.,* **-led, -ling. 1.** to equip (a fishing fly) with a hackle. **2.** to comb (flax, hemp, or jute) with a hackle. Also *(def. 2),* **hatchel.** [Possibly from an unrecorded Old English word.] —**hack′ler,** *n.*

• **to get one's hackles up.** to be ready for an argument or fight.

hack·le² (hak′əl) *v.t.,* **-led, -ling.** to cut or chop roughly; hack. [HACK¹ + -LE.]

hack·man (hak′mən) *n., pl.* **-men** (-mən). **1.** a driver of a hack. **2.** *Slang.* a taxicab driver.

hack·ma·tack (hak′mə tak′) *n.* tamarack. [Of Algonquian origin.]

hack·ney (hak′nē) *n., pl.* **-neys. 1.** a horse used for ordinary riding or driving. **2.** a carriage for hire. **3.** *Archaic.* a person who is hired to do menial work; drudge. —*adj.* **1.** let out, employed, or done for hire. **2.** hackneyed. —*v.t.* to make trite or banal by overuse. [Middle English *hakene, hakenei* hackney horse, from *Hakeney, Hackney,* an English town (now a borough of London) once famous for its horses.]

hack·neyed (hak′nēd) *adj.* made dull or ordinary by being used too frequently; trite; banal. *As busy as a bee* is a hackneyed phrase. [HACKNEY + -ED²; because a hackney horse was often worn out from being overused.]

hack·saw (hak′sô′) *n.* a saw having a narrow, fine-toothed blade held firm in a frame, used esp. for cutting metal.

had (had; *unstressed* həd, əd) the past tense and past participle of **have.** ➡ often used to express necessity or preference: *You had better do your homework before dinner.*

ha·dal (hā′dəl) *adj.* of or relating to the greatest ocean depths, below 20,000 feet (6,096 meters), or the few creatures inhabiting these depths. [French *hadal,* from *Hadès,* Hades + *-al* -al¹.]

hacksaw

had·dock (had′ək) *n., pl.* **-dock** or **-docks.** a commercially valuable food fish, *Melanogrammus aeglefinus,* of the cod family, widely distributed in North Atlantic coastal waters, having five fins, a barbel, and a black line running along each side of the body from the gills to the tail. Weight: usually 2-4 pounds (0.9-1.8 kilograms).

Ha·des (hā′dēz) *n.* **1.** *Greek Mythology.* **a.** the place where the spirits of the dead dwell; underworld. **b.** the god who ruled the underworld; Pluto. **2.** hades. hell. [Greek *Haidēs* the lower world.]

hadj (haj) *also,* **hajj.** *n.* a pilgrimage to Mecca that each Muslim is required to make at least once during his or her life. [Arabic *hajj* pilgrimage.]

hadj·i (haj′ē) *also,* **hajji.** *n.* a Muslim who has made the required pilgrimage to Mecca. ➡ used as a title of respect. [Arabic *hājjī* pilgrim, from *hajj.* See HADJ.]

had·n't (had′ənt) *contr.* had not.

had·ron (had′ron) *n.* any of a class of subatomic particles, including mesons and baryons, that are subject to the interaction known as the strong force.

hadst (hadst) *Archaic.* a second person singular past tense of **have.** ➡ used with **thou.**

ha·fiz (hā′fiz) *n.* a Muslim who has memorized the Koran. ➡ used as a title of respect. [Arabic *hāfiz.*]

haf·ni·um (haf′nē əm) *n.* a gray metallic element resembling zirconium in physical and chemical properties. Symbol: **Hf** For tables, see **element.** [Modern Latin *hafnium,* from Latin *Hafnia* Copenhagen, where it was discovered.]

haft (haft) *n.* the handle of a knife, sword, or other tool or weapon; hilt. —*v.t.* to furnish with or set in a haft. [Old English *hæft* a handle.]

hag (hag) *n.* **1.** an ugly, repulsive, often vicious old woman. **2.** witch. **3.** hagfish. [Short for Old English *hægtesse* witch.] —**hag′gish,** *adj.* —**hag′gish·ly,** *adv.* —**hag′gish·ness,** *n.*

Hag., Haggai.

Ha·gen (hä′gən) *n.* in the medieval German epic poem *Nibelungenlied,* the king's henchman who murders the hero Siegfried and steals the Nibelungs' treasure.

hag·fish (hag′fish′) *n., pl.* **-fish** or **-fish·es.** any of a group of eellike saltwater cyclostome fish, family Myxinidae, having a round, sucking mouth surrounded by tentacles and a tongue with comblike teeth. Some attach themselves by mouth to other fish, bore into their bodies, and feed on their organs. Length: usually under 2½ feet (0.8 meter). Also, **hag.**

Hag·ga·dah (hə gä′də) *also,* **Hag·ga·da.** *n., pl.* **-ga·doth** or **-ga·dot** (-gä′dōt, -gä dōt′). **1.** a book of services for the celebration of the Jewish festival of Passover, including prayers, the story of the Exodus, legends, and songs. **2.** a nonlegal part of rabbinical literature, including explanations, legends, and parables. ➡ distinguished from **Halakah** in def. 2. [Hebrew *hagada,* from *higid* to tell, from the root *ngd* to oppose.] —**hag·gad·ic** (hə gad′ik, -gä′dik), *adj.* —**hag·ga′dist,** *n.*

Hag·ga·i (hag′ē ī′, hag′ī) *n.* a book of the Old Testament, containing the prophecies of the Hebrew prophet Haggai. Also, in the Douay Bible, **Aggeus.**

hag·gard (hag′ərd) *adj.* having a worn look, as from fatigue, anxiety, hunger, or other suffering; gaunt. [Old French *hagard* wild, wild hawk; of Germanic origin.] —**hag′gard·ly,** *adv.* —**hag′gard·ness,** *n.*

hag·gis (hag′is) *n.* a Scottish dish consisting of the heart, lungs, and liver of a sheep or calf, combined with suet, onions, oatmeal, and seasonings and boiled in the stomach of the animal. [Possibly from dialectal English *hag* to chop, hew; of Scandinavian origin.]

hag·gle (hag′əl) *v.,* **-gled, -gling.** —*v.i.* to bargain in a petty way, esp. about price or terms of an agreement; dicker: *to haggle with the grocer about prices.* —*v.t.* to cut roughly; mangle; hack. —*n.* an act or instance of haggling. [From dialectal English *hag* to chop, hew (of Scandinavian origin) + -LE.] —**hag′gler,** *n.*

Hag·i·og·ra·pha (hag′ē og′rə fə, hā′jē-) *n.* the last of the three divisions of the Jewish Scriptures, following the Law of Moses and the Prophets, comprising Psalms, Proverbs, Job, Song of Solomon, Ruth, Lamentations, Ecclesiastes, Esther, Daniel, Ezra, Nehemiah, and Chronicles I and II. ➡ used as singular or plural. [Late Latin *Hagiographa,* from Late Greek *Hagiographa* sacred writings, from Greek *hagios* holy + *graphein* to write.]

hag·i·og·ra·phy (hag′ē og′rə fē, hā′jē-) *n., pl.* **-phies. 1.** the writing about the lives and legends of saints. **2.** a book on this subject. [Greek *hagios* holy + -GRAPHY.]

hag·i·ol·o·gy (hag′ē ol′ə jē, hā′jē-) *n., pl.* **-gies. 1.** literature dealing with the lives and legends of saints. **2.** a work or collection on this subject. **3.** a list of the saints. [Greek *hagios* holy + -LOGY.]

hag·rid·den (hag′rid′ən) *adj.* tormented as if by a witch; harassed.

hah (hä) ha.

ha-ha (hä′hä′) *interj.* used to express amusement or scorn.

hahn·i·um (hä′nē əm) *n.* a proposed name for the artificially

produced radioactive element with atomic number 105. Proposed symbol: **Ha** Also, **element 105, nielsbohrium, unnilpentium.** For tables, see **element.**

Hai·da (hī′də) *n., pl.* **-da** or **-das.** **1.** a member of a North American Indian tribe living along the coast of British Columbia. **2.** the language of this tribe.

Haida wooden raven rattle

hai·ku (hī′kü) *n., pl.* **-ku.** **1.** a Japanese verse form in three lines containing seventeen syllables, five in the first line, seven in the second, and five in the third. **2.** a poem written in this form, usually on a subject from nature. [Japanese *haiku.*]

hail¹ (hāl) *v.t.* **1.** to greet by calling or shouting: *I hailed them across the street.* **2.** to attract the attention of through motions or calls: *Let's hail a taxi.* **3.** to acknowledge with acclaim; salute: *Many people hailed the astronauts.* —*v.i.* to call out in order to greet or to attract attention, as to a passing ship. —*n.* **1.** a greeting. **2.** a motion or call intended to attract attention. **3.** the act of hailing. —*interj.* ➡ used as an expression of acclaim, greeting, or salutation: *Hail to the victor!* [Middle English *hailen* to greet, from *hail, heil,* from Old Norse *heill* well, sound, whole.] —**hail′er,** *n.*
- **to hail from.** to have come from (a particular place, such as a birthplace or point of departure).
- **within hail.** close enough to hear a call or greeting; within earshot.

hail² (hāl) *n.* **1.** the small, usually round pieces of layered ice that fall in a shower, esp. during thunderstorms. **2.** a heavy shower of anything: *They escaped in a hail of bullets.* —*v.i.* to pour down hail (often with *it*): *It hailed for an hour.* —*v.t.* to pour down or shower something heavily (often with *on* or *upon*): *Our grandparents hailed presents on us.* [Middle English *haile,* from Old English *hægel, hagol.*]

hail-fel·low (*adj.,* hāl′fel′ō; *n.,* hāl′fel′ō) *adj.* cordial or friendly, esp. in a superficial manner. —*n. also,* **hail fellow.** a congenial companion; comrade. Also, **hail fellow well met.** [From earlier greeting *hail, fellow.*]

Hail Mary, a Roman Catholic prayer to the Virgin Mary. Also, **Ave Maria.**

hail·stone (hāl′stōn′) *n.* a pellet of hail.

hail·storm (hāl′stôrm′) *n.* a storm in which hail falls.

hair (hâr) *n.* **1.** a fine, threadlike outgrowth of the skin of mammals. **2.** such growths collectively, as on human heads or animal bodies. **3.** a similar growth on insect bodies. **4.** a fine, threadlike outgrowth of the outer layer of plants. **5.** an extremely small amount or distance; least degree: *to miss a bull's-eye by a hair.* —*adj.* **1.** of or containing hair: *a hair mattress.* **2.** for the hair: *a hair dryer.* [Old English *hær* fine, threadlike outgrowth of the skin of mammals.] —**hair′less,** *adj.* —**hair′like′,** *adj.*
- **hair of the dog (that bit one).** *Informal.* a drink of an alcoholic beverage believed to relieve a hangover.
- **not turn a hair.** to give no indication of disturbance or embarrassment; remain calm.
- **to a hair.** with utmost exactness; precisely.
- **to get in someone's hair.** *Informal.* to annoy (someone); pester.

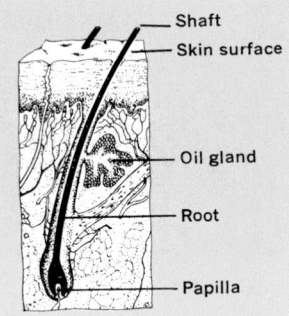

- Shaft
- Skin surface
- Oil gland
- Root
- Papilla

root of a **hair**

- **to let one's hair down.** to relax completely; be informal.
- **to make someone's hair stand on end.** to frighten or terrify (someone).
- **to split hairs.** to make petty or overly subtle distinctions.
- **to tear one's hair (out).** to feel utterly exasperated.

hair·breadth (hâr′bredth′, -bretth′) *also,* **hairsbreadth, hair's-breadth.** *adj.* very narrow or close: *a hairbreadth escape.* —*n.* hairsbreadth.

hair·brush (hâr′brush′) *n.* a brush used for grooming the hair.

hair cell, any of various cells with delicate, hairlike processes, esp. one of the sensory cells in the inner ear.

hair·cloth (hâr′klôth′) *n.* a stiff, coarse cloth made of horsehair or camel's hair, used chiefly as an interlining or stiffening material.

hair·cut (hâr′kut′) *n.* the act of cutting the hair or the style in which it is cut.

hair·do (hâr′dü′) *n., pl.* **-dos.** the style in which the hair, esp. of a woman, is arranged; coiffure.

hair·dress·er (hâr′dres′ər) *n.* a person whose job is to style, cut, and arrange hair, esp. women's hair.

hair·line (hâr′līn′) *n.* **1.** the outline of hair on the head, esp. around the forehead. **2.** a very thin or fine line, as in printing. —*adj.* very thin or fine: *a hairline crack in a china bowl.*

hair net, a net worn on the head to keep the hair in place.

hair·piece (hâr′pēs′) *n.* a quantity of artificial or natural hair made into a removable wig, toupee, switch, or fall and worn to cover baldness or as part of a hair style.

hair·pin (hâr′pin′) *n.* a small, two-pronged U-shaped pin usually made of wire, shell, or plastic, used to keep hair or a hairpiece in place. —*adj.* shaped like a hairpin: *a hairpin curve in the road.*

hair·rais·ing (hâr′rā′zing) *adj. Informal.* causing great fear; terrifying.

hairs·breadth (hârz′bredth′, -bretth′) *also,* **hair's-breadth** or **hairbreadth.** *n.* an extremely small space or distance: *to lose by a hairsbreadth.* —*adj.* hairbreadth.

hair seal, any of various seals that have coarse protective fur and lack an undercoat of softer fur.

hair shirt, a rough shirt made of horsehair, worn next to the skin as penance or self-punishment.

hair·split·ting (hâr′split′ing) *n.* the act of making distinctions that are too subtle; pettiness. —*adj.* characterized by overly subtle distinctions or pettiness. —**hair′split′ter,** *n.*

hair spray, a liquid cosmetic that is sprayed on the hair to hold it in place.

hair·spring (hâr′spring′) *n.* a fine coiled spring in a watch or clock that regulates the movement of the balance wheel.

hair-trig·ger (hâr′trig′ər) *adj.* reacting at once to the slightest stimulus: *a hair-trigger temper.*

hair trigger, a trigger that can discharge a firearm with very slight pressure.

hair·y (hâr′ē) *adj.,* **hair·i·er, hair·i·est.** **1.** covered with hair; having much hair; hirsute. **2.** of or resembling hair: *a hairy sweater.* **3.** *Slang.* hair-raising; frightening: *Racing cars can be a hairy experience.* —**hair′i·ness,** *n.*

Hai·tian (hā′shən, -tē ən) *adj.* of or relating to Haiti or its people, dialect, or culture. —*n.* **1.** a native or citizen of Haiti. **2.** a person of Haitian ancestry. **3.** Haitian Creole.

Haitian Creole, the language of the Haitians, a dialect of French. Also, **Creole, Haitian.**

hajj (haj) hadj.

haj·ji (haj′ē) hadji.

hake (hāk) *n., pl.* **hake** or **hakes.** any of several valuable food fish of the cod family, Gadidae, found in cold and temperate seas. Weight: up to 8 pounds (3.6 kilograms). [Possibly from Old Norse *haki* hook; because of the shape of its lower jaw.]

ha·kim¹ (hä kēm′) *also,* **ha·keem.** *n.* in Muslim countries, a learned man, esp. a physician. [Arabic *hakīm.*]

ha·kim² (hä′kim) *n.* in Muslim countries, a ruler, judge, or governor. [Arabic *hākim.*]

Ha·la·kah (hä lä′κнə, hä′lə κнä′) *also,* **Ha·la·chah.** *n.* in Judaism, the civil and ritual law of rabbinical literature. ➡ distinguished from **Haggadah** (*def.* 2.). [Hebrew *halacha* rule, law, way (to conduct oneself), from *halach* to go.]

ha·la·tion (hā lā′shən) *n.* a blur or halo of light around bright objects or areas on a photographic negative or print, as is common around street lights in photographs taken at night. [HAL(O) + -ATION.]

a	at	e	end	o	hot	u	up	hw	white		about
ā	ape	ē	me	ō	old	ū	use	ng	song		taken
ä	far	i	it	ô	fork	ü	rule	th	thin	ə	pencil
âr	care	ī	ice	oi	oil	u̇	pull	th	this		lemon
				ir	pierce	ou	out	ûr	turn	zh	measure		circus

hal·berd (hal′bərd) *also*, **hal·bert** (hal′bərt). *n.* a poleax with a long spear and hook-shaped blade, used as a weapon, esp. in fifteenth- and sixteenth-century Europe. [French *hallebarde*, from Middle High German *helmbarde* literally, ax with a long handle, from *helm* handle + *barde* ax.]

hal·berd·ier (hal′bər dîr′) *n.* a soldier or guard armed with a halberd.

hal·cy·on (hal′sē ən) *adj.* peaceful and happy; undisturbed: *to yearn for the halcyon days of youth.* —*n.* a legendary bird, identified with the kingfisher, that supposedly had the power of calming the sea at the winter solstice to protect its floating nest during the period of incubation. [Middle English *alcioun*, from Latin *alcyon* kingfisher, from Greek *(h)alkyōn.*]

hale[1] (hāl) *adj.*, **hal·er**, **hal·est**. in good physical condition; healthy; robust. ➧ used chiefly in the phrase **hale and hearty.** [Old English *hāl.*]

hale[2] (hāl) *v.t.*, **haled**, **hal·ing**. **1.** to compel (someone) to go: *to hale a thief into court.* **2.** to drag or pull, esp. by force. [Old French *haler* to pull, of Germanic origin.]

halberd

half (haf) *n.*, *pl.* **halves**. **1.** either of two equal parts into which anything is or may be divided: *A pint is half of a quart.* **2.** either of two approximately equal parts: *to be awake half the night.* **3.** *Sports.* **a.** either of two time periods into which certain games are divided. **b.** half time. **c.** one of the two divisions of an inning in baseball. **d.** halfback. **5.** *Informal.* half dollar. —*adj.* **1.** being one of two equal parts; forming a half: *a half gallon of milk.* **2.** being or amounting to approximately one half. **3.** lacking in some part; incomplete; partial: *half answers.* ➧ often used in combination, as in *half-breed* or *half-moon.* —*adv.* **1.** to exactly or approximately half of the full amount, degree, or capacity: *The theater was half empty.* **2.** to a great extent; nearly: *The house was half hidden by the trees.* **3.** not completely; partially: *half understood, half believed.* ➧ often used in combination, as in *half-baked.* [Old English *h(e)alf* side, either of two equal parts.]
· **by half.** by a great deal; considerably.
· **in half.** into two equal or approximately equal parts.
· **not half bad.** rather good.
· **one's better half.** *Informal.* a person's husband or wife; spouse.

half-and-half (haf′ən haf′) *n.* **1.** a mixture that is half one thing and half another, esp. a liquid composed of half milk and half cream. **2.** *British.* a mixture of two malt beverages, esp. one composed of half bitter ale and half mild ale. —*adj.* that is half one thing and half another. —*adv.* in two equal parts.

half·back (haf′bak′) *n.* **1.** in football, either of two players whose positions are behind the line of scrimmage and who are used primarily as ball carriers. **2.** the position played by either of these players. **3.** in some other sports, such as soccer, a player who is positioned behind the forward line and in front of the back line.

half-baked (haf′bākt′) *adj.* **1.** not completely cooked; underdone. **2.** *Informal.* badly planned; incomplete; inadequate: *a half-baked plan.* **3.** *Informal.* lacking experience or common sense; stupid: *half-baked technicians.*

half-blood (haf′blud′) *n.* **1.** a person who is related to another through one parent only. **2.** half-breed.

half blood, the relationship between persons who have only one parent in common.

half-blood·ed (haf′blud′id) *adj.* **1.** born of parents of different races. **2.** being related to another through one parent only.

half boot, a boot reaching about halfway between the ankle and the knee.

half-breed (haf′brēd′) *n.* a person whose parents are of different races, esp. an offspring of a Caucasian and an American Indian. —*adj.* half-blooded; hybrid. ➧ considered offensive in both defs.

half brother, a brother related through one parent only.

half-caste (haf′kast′) *n.* **1.** anyone of mixed race; half-breed. **2.** an offspring of one European and one Asian parent; Eurasian. ➧ considered offensive in both defs.

half cock, the position in which the hammer of a gun is raised halfway, causing the trigger to be locked.

half-cocked (haf′kokt′) *adj.* **1.** (of a gun) having the hammer at the position of half cock. **2.** lacking adequate forethought or planning; rash: *a half-cocked scheme for getting rich.*
· **to go off half-cocked** (or **at half cock**). **a.** (of a gun) to fire prematurely. **b.** *Informal.* to act or speak too hastily or without adequate forethought.

half crown, formerly, a British coin equal to two and one half shillings.

half dollar, a coin of the United States equal to fifty cents.

half eagle, a former gold coin of the United States equal to five dollars.

half gainer, a dive in which the diver starts in the forward position and then does a half backward somersault, entering the water headfirst.

half·heart·ed (haf′här′tid) *adj.* lacking interest or enthusiasm; indifferent; perfunctory: *a halfhearted attempt.* —**half′heart′ed·ly,** *adv.* —**half′heart′ed·ness,** *n.*

half hitch, a knot made by passing the end of a rope around the rope, then through the loop thus formed, and finally drawing the end tight.

half-hour (haf′our′) *n.* **1.** a half of an hour; thirty minutes. **2.** a point thirty minutes past a given hour: *The bus runs on the half-hour.* —*adj.* of, lasting for, or occurring at a half-hour: *a half-hour ride.* —**half′-hour′ly,** *adv., adj.*

half-life (haf′līf′) *n.* the time required by any given quantity of a radioactive isotope to decay to half that quantity.

half-line (haf′līn′) *n.* the part of an infinitely long line extending in one direction from a point on the line.

half hitch

half-mast (haf′mast′) *n.* a position of a flag about halfway down from the top of a mast, staff, or pole, used esp. as a sign of mourning or as a distress signal. Also, **half-staff.**

half-moon (haf′mün′) *n.* **1.** the moon when only half of its disk appears illuminated. **2.** anything in the shape of a half-moon.

half nelson, a wrestling hold made from behind by hooking one arm under the opponent's corresponding arm and pressing the hand across the back of the neck.

half note, a musical note having one half the time value of a whole note. For illustration, see **note.**

half·pen·ny (hā′pə nē, hāp′nē) *n.*, *pl.* **half·pence** (hā′pəns) or **half·pennies.** a former coin of Great Britain equal to half a penny. —*adj.* **1.** having the value of a halfpenny. **2.** having very little value; insignificant.

half pint 1. a unit of measure that is half a pint, equal to 8 fluid ounces or 1 cup (0.24 liter). **2.** *Slang.* a very small person.

half-plane (haf′plān′) *n.* the part of a plane extending in one direction from a line in the plane.

half sister, a sister related through one parent only.

half-slip (haf′slip′) *n.* a slip that extends from the waist down.

half-sole (haf′sōl′) *v.t.*, **-soled, -sol·ing.** to repair (a shoe or boot) by putting on a new half sole.

half sole, the part of the sole of a shoe or boot extending from the arch to the toe.

half sovereign, a former gold coin of Great Britain equal to ten shillings.

half-staff (haf′staf′) *n.* half-mast.

half step 1. *Music.* the difference in pitch between any two adjacent keys on a keyboard instrument. Also, **half tone, semitone. 2.** a military marching step 15 inches (38 centimeters) in length.

half-tim·bered (haf′tim′bərd) *adj.* (of a building) constructed of a framework of timbers, the spaces between which are filled with masonry or plaster: *a half-timbered house.*

half-timbered buildings

half time, the intermission period between two halves of a sporting event, as football or basketball.

half·tone (haf′tōn′) n. **1.** a picture consisting of dots that vary in size in proportion to the gradations of tones of the subject, with the small dots representing the light tones and the large dots representing the dark tones. **2.** the photoengraving process by which such a picture is made, used esp. for reproducing photographs and other pictures with tones, as in books. **3.** any intermediate tone between a high light and a deep shadow in art or photography.

half tone, half step *(def. 1)*.

half-track (haf′trak′) *also,* **half·track.** n. an armored military vehicle having wheels in front and caterpillar tracks in the rear.

half-truth (haf′trüth′) n. a statement that contains only part of the truth, esp. one that is intended to deceive: *to spread half-truths and false rumors about an opponent.*

half·way (haf′wā′) adv. **1.** at or to the midway point; half the distance: *to climb halfway up a mountain.* **2.** not complete; partially: *The movie is halfway over.* —adj. **1.** midway between two points: *The racers reached the halfway mark.* **2.** incomplete or inadequate; partial: *Halfway measures will not solve the problem.* **·to meet halfway.** to agree to make concessions to; compromise with: *The union met management halfway on the request for raises.*

halfway house 1. an inn or other place to stop and rest in the middle of a journey. **2.** a residence in which persons formerly in a mental hospital, prison, or other institution live for a time in preparation for reentering society.

half-wit (haf′wit′) n. **1.** a feeble-minded person. **2.** a foolish, idiotic, or stupid person. —**half′-wit′ted,** adj.

hal·i·but (hal′ə bət, hol′-) n., pl. **-but** or **-buts. 1.** either of two large flatfishes, genus *Hippoglossus,* found in northern waters of the Atlantic and Pacific oceans and highly valued as a source of food and vitamin oil. Weight: Atlantic halibut—up to 700 pounds (318 kilograms). Pacific halibut—female, up to 500 pounds (227 kilograms); male, up to 50 pounds (23 kilograms). **2.** any of several related flatfishes. [Middle English *hāly* HOLY + *butte* flatfish; because it was eaten on holy days.]

hal·ide (hal′īd, -id, hā′līd, -lid) n. a binary compound of a halogen with an element or radical, such as sodium chloride. [Greek *hals* salt + -IDE.]

hal·i·dom (hal′i dəm) *also,* **hal·i·dome** (hal′i dōm′). n. *Archaic.* **1.** a holy place; sanctuary. **2.** anything regarded as holy; sacred relic. [Old English *hāligdōm,* from *hālig* holy + -*dōm* state, condition.]

hal·ite (hal′īt, hā′līt) n. a soft, white crystalline mineral, sodium chloride, common salt; rock salt. Formula: NaCl [Greek *hals* salt + -ITE².]

hal·i·to·sis (hal′i tō′sis) n. a condition in which the breath has an unpleasant or offensive odor. [Latin *hālitus* breath + -OSIS.]

hall (hôl) n. **1.** a passageway through a building; corridor. **2.** a passageway or room at the entrance to a building; vestibule or lobby. **3.** a room or building in which public meetings, entertainment, or lectures are held: *a concert hall.* **4.** a room or building in a school, college, or university set aside for a particular purpose: *a residence hall, a dining hall.* **5.** a building housing public offices. **6.** *British.* a manor house on the estate of a noble. **7.** the main room of a medieval castle. [Old English *heall* large roofed place.]

hal·le·lu·jah (hal′ə lü′yə) *also,* **hal·le·lu·iah, al·le·lu·ia.** interj. **1.** praise ye the Lord. ➡ used in songs of praise or thanksgiving. **2.** used to express relief, joy, praise, or the like. —n. a hymn or other musical composition based on the word *hallelujah.* [Late Latin *alleluja,* from Greek *hallēlouia,* from Hebrew *halelu* praise + *ya* God.]

Hal·ley's comet (hal′ēz) a comet that can be seen from the earth approximately every seventy-six years. It was last seen in 1986. [From Edmund *Halley,* 1656-1742, English astronomer who discovered this comet's cycle.]

hal·liard (hal′yərd) halyard.

hall·mark (hôl′märk′) n. **1.** an official symbol stamped on gold and silver items to guarantee their high quality or purity. **2.** any mark that indicates high quality or purity. **3.** a distinguishing quality or characteristic: *Suspense is a hallmark of a good mys-*

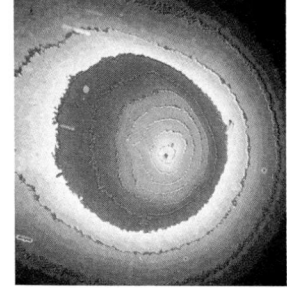
head of **Halley's comet**
(color-enhanced)

tery. —v.t. to stamp with a hallmark. [From the *mark* indicating quality or purity that was stamped on gold or silver articles in the Goldsmiths' *Hall* in London, the center of the guild of goldsmiths in charge of certification.]

hall of fame 1. a room or building containing tablets, busts, or other commemorative items honoring eminent people: *a sports hall of fame.* **2. Hall of Fame.** a national shrine in New York City commemorating famous Americans. **3.** a group of people in a particular profession or field, as a sport, who have been named as being especially outstanding.

hal·loo (hə lü′) *also,* **hal·loa** (hə lō′), **hol·lo.** interj. used to attract attention or to urge on hounds in fox hunting. —n., pl. **-loos.** a call or cry of *halloo.* —v.i., v.t., **-looed, -loo·ing. 1.** to call or shout to attract the attention of (someone). **2.** to urge on (hounds) with cries of *halloo.* **3.** to shout. [Possibly from Old French *halloer* to follow with shouts; imitative.]

hal·low (hal′ō) v.t. **1.** to make or select as holy; sanctify; consecrate: *to hallow ground for a burial.* **2.** to regard or honor as sacred or holy; venerate. [Old English *hālgian.*]

hal·lowed (hal′ōd; *also, in liturgical use,* hal′ō id) adj. **1.** made holy; sanctified; consecrated. **2.** regarded as sacred or holy; venerated. —**hal′lowed·ness,** n.

Hal·low·een (hal′ə wēn′, hol′-) *also,* **Hal·low·e'en.** n. the eve of All Saints' Day, now celebrated esp. by children in costumes and masks. It falls on October 31. [Short for *all hallow even* eve of All Saints' Day, from ALL + *hallow* saint (from Old English *hālga* holy person, from *halig* holy) + EVEN².]

Hal·low·mas (hal′ō məs, -mas′) n. All Saints' Day.

hal·lu·ci·nate (hə lü′sə nāt′) v. **-nat·ed, -nat·ing.** —v.i. to have hallucinations. —v.t. to experience (something not present) as real.

hal·lu·ci·na·tion (hə lü′sə nā′shən) n. **1.** a false sensory perception in which a person experiences as real something that is not present. **2.** something that is falsely perceived: *The voices the patient heard were actually hallucinations.* [Latin *hallūcinātiō* wandering of the mind, possibly going back to Greek *halȳein* to be distraught, wander.]

hal·lu·ci·na·to·ry (hə lü′sə nə tôr′ē) adj. of, relating to, or causing hallucinations; hallucinogenic.

hal·lu·cin·o·gen (hə lü′sə nə jen′, hal′yə sin′ə-) n. any of several drugs that cause hallucinations, such as mescaline or LSD. [HALLUCIN(ATION) + -GEN.]

hal·lu·cin·o·gen·ic (hə lü′sə nə jen′ik) adj. of, relating to, or causing hallucinations: *a hallucinogenic drug.*

hall·way (hôl′wā′) n. **1.** a passageway through a building; corridor; hall. **2.** an entrance hall; foyer.

ha·lo (hā′lō) n., pl. **-los** or **-loes. 1.** in artistic representation, a ring or disk of light surrounding the head of a deity, saint, or other sacred figure; nimbus. **2.** a circle of light that appears to surround the sun, moon, or other celestial body, caused by the reflection and refraction of light by ice crystals in the earth's upper atmosphere. **3.** an aura of glory or splendor surrounding a person or thing held in high esteem or reverence. —v.t. to surround or invest with a halo. [Latin *halōs* circle of light appearing to surround the sun or moon, from Greek *halōs* threshing floor (around which the oxen moved in a circular path), disk of the sun or moon.]

hal·o·gen (hal′ə jən) n. any of five very reactive nonmetallic elements, fluorine, chlorine, bromine, iodine, or astatine, that combine readily with metals to form salts. [Greek *hals* salt + -GEN.]

hal·o·gen·ate (hal′ə jə nāt′) v.t., **-at·ed, -at·ing.** *Chemistry.* to introduce a halogen molecule into (the molecular structure of a compound), as in chlorination or fluorination. [HALOGEN + -ATE¹.] —**hal′o·gen·a′tion,** n.

hal·on (hal′on) n. any of a group of halogenated hydrocarbons, derived from methane or ethane, used in fire extinguishers, esp. those for electrical fires, and suspected of damaging the atmosphere's ozone layer.

hal·o·phyte (hal′ə fīt′) n. a plant adapted to live in salty soils, as in salt marshes or mud flats. —**hal·o·phyt·ic** (hal′ə fit′ik), adj.

halt¹ (hôlt) n. a temporary discontinuation of movement; stop. —v.t., v.i. to stop or cause to stop. —interj. stop. ➡ used esp. as a military command. [German *halt,* from the phrase *halt machen,* from *halt* (imperative of *halten* to stop) + *machen* to make.] **·to call a halt to.** to bring to a stop.

halt² (hôlt) v.i. **1.** to proceed imperfectly or faultily, as in speech,

a	at	e	end	o	hot	u	up	hw	white		about
ā	ape	ē	me	ō	old	ū	use	ng	song		taken
ä	far	i	it	ô	fork	ü	rule	th	thin	ə	pencil
âr	care	ī	ice	oi	oil	u̇	pull	th	this		lemon
		î	pierce	ou	out	ûr	turn	zh	measure		circus

or meter in verse; falter: *The child's voice halted in apprehension.* **2.** to be indecisive; hesitate between alternate choices; vacillate. **3.** *Archaic.* to be lame; limp. —*adj. Archaic.* unable to walk without limping; lame. —*n. Archaic.* lameness; limp. [Old English *healt* lame.]

hal·ter (hôl′tər) *n.* **1.** a rope or strap used for leading or tying an animal, usually designed to fit around the animal's nose and over or behind its ears. **2.** a garment resembling a blouse, worn by women and girls, usually fastening behind the neck and across the lower back, leaving the arms and back bare. **3.** a rope used for hanging someone; noose. **4.** death by hanging. —*v.t.* **1.** to put a halter on or secure with a halter: *to halter a horse.* **2.** to hang (someone). [Old English *hælfter* rope with a noose for leading a horse.]

halt·ing (hôl′ting) *adj.* **1.** hesitating or indecisive: *the halting policy of a weak government.* **2.** imperfect; faulty: *a halting line of verse.* **3.** lame; limping: *a halting gait.* —**halt′ing·ly,** *adv.*

hal·vah (häl vä′, häl′vä) *n.* a sweet, mealy confection consisting esp. of ground sesame seeds and honey. [Yiddish *khalva,* going back to Arabic *halwa, halāwe.*]

halve (hav) *v.t.,* **halved, halv·ing. 1.** to divide into two equal parts: *to halve an apple.* **2.** to share equally: *We halved our food during the hike.* **3.** to reduce to half: *For only two people, halve the recipe.* **4.** to play (a hole) in golf in the same number of strokes as one's opponent. [Middle English *halven,* from HALF.]

halves (havz) *n.* the plural of **half.**
• **by halves. a.** incompletely; imperfectly. **b.** in a halfhearted manner; halfheartedly.
• **to go halves.** to share equally; divide in half.

hal·yard (hal′yərd) *also,* **halliard.** *n. Nautical.* a rope or tackle used for hoisting or lowering something, such as a sail, yard, or flag. [Modification (influenced by YARD²) of Middle English *halier,* from *halen* to HALE², pull.]

ham (ham) *n.* **1.** the meat from the hind leg or shoulder of a hog, usually cured and smoked. **2.** the hind leg of an animal, esp. a hog. **3. hams.** the back part of the thighs and the buttocks. **4.** the back or bend of the knee. **5.** *Informal.* an actor who overacts or who performs in a showy way. **6.** *Informal.* an amateur radio operator. —*v.i., v.t.,* **hammed, ham·ming.** *Informal.* (of an actor) to act in an exaggerated way; overact. [Old English *hamm* bend of the knee.]

ham·a·dry·ad (ham′ə drī′əd, -ad) *n.* in Greek and Roman mythology, a wood nymph who inhabited or took the shape of a tree. [Latin *Hamādryades* (plural), from Greek *Hamādryades,* from *hama* together with + *drȳs* tree; because the life of each nymph was connected with that of her tree.]

ham·burg·er (ham′bûr′gər, -bər-) *n.* **1.** ground beef. **2.** a round, flat patty of such meat, broiled or fried. **3.** a sandwich consisting of such a patty in a round bun. Also, **burg·er, ham′-burg′.** [Short for *Hamburger steak,* from *Hamburg,* Germany.]

hame (hām) *n.* either of two curved wood or metal pieces, located on either side of a draft animal's collar, to which the traces and other straps are fastened. [Middle Dutch *hame* yoke for the neck.]

Ham·ite (ham′īt) *n.* **1.** a descendant of Ham. **2.** one of a group of people in northern and eastern Africa, most of whom speak a Hamitic language, such as the Berbers.

Ham·it·ic (ha mit′ik, hə-) *n.* a group of languages belonging to the Semito-Hamitic language family. These languages, including Berber, Somali, ancient Egyptian, and Coptic, are spoken predominantly in northern and eastern Africa. —*adj.* of or relating to Ham, the Hamites, or their languages.

ham·let (ham′lit) *n.* a cluster of houses in the country; small rural village. [Old French *hamelet,* diminutive of *hamel* village, diminutive of *ham;* of Germanic origin.]

Ham·let (ham′lit) *n.* the central character in William Shakespeare's play *Hamlet,* a prince of Denmark who seeks to avenge his father's murder.

ham·mer (ham′ər) *n.* **1.** a tool with a solid head, usually of metal, set crosswise on a handle, usually used for driving nails and beating or shaping metal. **2.** anything resembling such a tool in shape or function, as the lever that strikes a bell in a clock. **3.** the part of a gun that strikes the firing pin, causing the gun to go off; cock. **4.** any of the padded mallets in a piano which, when activated by the depression of a key, strike the strings. **5.** *Anatomy.* malleus. **6.** a metal sphere attached to a wire, thrown for distance in track and field contests. **7.** a small mallet used by an auctioneer to indicate that an item has been sold. —*v.t.* **1.** to strike repeatedly with, or as with, a hammer; drive; pound: *to hammer nails into a wall.* **2.** to pound into shape or form with a hammer: *to hammer a bowl out of metal.* **3.** to fasten with a hammer, as by nailing: *to hammer a picture hook.* **4.** to force by constant repetition, as of words, ideas, or actions: *It's no use trying to hammer sense into a fool.* —*v.i.* to strike blows repeatedly with, or as with,

a hammer; pound: *The carpenter hammered all day.* [Old English *hamor* tool with a head and a handle.] —**ham′mer·er,** *n.*
• **hammer and tongs.** with great energy and force; vigorously; violently.
• **to come** (or **go**) **under the hammer.** to be for sale or sold at auction.
• **to hammer away (at). a.** to work industriously or persistently on: *I hammered away at the chemistry problem for an hour.* **b.** to repeat for emphasis or to make something understood: *The mayor hammered away at the city's need for federal aid.*
• **to hammer out. a.** to pound into shape or form with a hammer: *to hammer out a tray.* **b.** to flatten or remove with, or as with, a hammer: *to hammer out a dent.* **c.** to work out with great care and effort, esp. in collaboration with another person: *It took many meetings to hammer out a settlement.* **d.** to bring about by pounding: *to hammer out a tune on a xylophone.*

hammer and sickle, a Communist emblem, consisting of a crossed sickle and hammer and symbolizing the alliance of workers and peasants.

ham·mer·head (ham′ər hed′) *n.* **1.** a shark, genus *Sphyrna,* whose head extends on each side in a broad, flat lobe, resembling a double-headed hammer. Length: to 15 feet (4.6 meters). **2.** the head of a hammer.

ham·mer·lock (ham′ər-lok′) *n.* a wrestling hold in which an opponent's arm is twisted and held in a right-angle position behind his back.

hammerhead

ham·mer·toe (ham′ər-tō′) *n.* a deformed, downward-bent toe, usually the second, in which the two distal joints are permanently flexed. [Because the deformed toe looks like a claw hammer.]

ham·mock (ham′ək) *n.* a swinging bed made from a long piece of canvas, leather, or netting hung between two vertical supports, such as trees or poles. [Spanish *hamaca;* of Carib origin.]

ham·per¹ (ham′pər) *v.t.* to obstruct the action or progress of; impede: *Stalled cars hampered snow-removal efforts.* [Middle English *hamperen* to surround, enclose, harass.]

ham·per² (ham′pər) *n.* a large basket or other receptacle, usually with a cover: *a picnic hamper, a hamper for laundry.* [Earlier *hanaper,* from Middle English *haniper,* from Old French *hanapier* basket for cups, from *hanap* cup; of Germanic origin.]

ham·ster (ham′stər) *n.* any of various burrowing, mouselike rodents, family Cricetidae, found in Europe, Asia, and Africa, having a stout body, stumpy tail, and large cheek pouches. Length: 7 inches (18 centimeters). [German *Hamster.*]

ham·string (ham′string′) *n.* **1.** a tendon at the back of the human knee. **2.** the great tendon at the back of the hock of a quadruped. —*v.t.,* **-strung** (-strung′), **-string·ing. 1.** to cripple or disable (a person or animal) by cutting the hamstring. **2.** to destroy the power or efficiency of; make ineffective: *The project was hamstrung by a lack of funds.*

hand (hand) *n.* **1.** the end of the forelimb in human beings, consisting of the wrist, five fingers including an opposable thumb, and the metacarpus, the area between the wrist and the fingers. It is used esp. for holding and grasping. **2.** the end of a limb in animals that corresponds in function to the human hand, such as that of an ape. **3.** anything resembling a hand in shape or function, as the pointers on a clock. **4.** *usually,* **hands.** personal possession, custody, control, or authority: *The child is in good hands. The letter fell into the wrong hands. You should never take the law into your own hands.* **5.** participation or influence in something; share; role: *Each of them had a hand in the matter.* **6.** direction in relation to the position of the hand; side: *at my left hand.* **7.** a worker employed in manual labor; laborer: *the hands on a farm.* **8.** a person who produces a particular kind of work: *The book was translated by several hands.* **9.** a member of a group or crew: *All hands on deck.* **10.** skill in working with one's hands; workmanship; performance: *the hand of a master.* **11.** a manner of doing

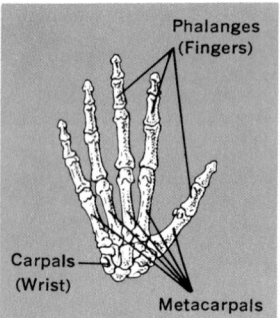

Phalanges (Fingers)

Carpals (Wrist)

Metacarpals

bones of the **hand**

something: *a deft hand at juggling.* **12.** a person in reference to his or her skill at doing something: *to be an old hand at diving.* **13.** the act of helping; aid; assistance: *Give me a hand moving the piano.* **14.** a round of applause; clapping: *The audience gave the singer a big hand.* **15.a.** a single round of a card game. **b.** the cards held by a player during a round. **c.** any of the players. **16.** handwriting style; penmanship: *an illegible hand.* **17.** a person's signature. **18.** a promise or pledge, as of marriage or to seal an agreement. **19.** a unit of measure equal to 4 inches (10.2 centimeters), or the approximate breadth of the hand, used in expressing the height of a horse. —*v.t.* **1.** to give or pass with the hand; transmit: *I handed the book to the librarian.* **2.** to lead or assist with the hand. —*adj.* **1.** of, relating to, or for the hand or hands: *hand lotion.* **2.** performed or operated by hand: *a hand tool.* **3.** suited to be held in or worn on the hand: *a hand mirror.* [Old English *hand* end of the arm from wrist to fingers, possession, custody, authority, direction.]
- **at hand. a.** accessible or ready for use. **b.** near in time; close.
- **at the hand** (or **hands**) **of.** by the action of: *to suffer at the hands of the enemy.*
- **by hand.** with the hands, as opposed to mechanical means: *to wash clothes by hand.*
- **from hand to hand.** from one person to another.
- **from hand to mouth.** using everything for one's immediate needs without considering the future: *to live from hand to mouth.*
- **hand and foot. a.** with both hands and feet restricted: *bound hand and foot.* **b.** totally; diligently: *to wait on someone hand and foot.*
- **hand in** (or **and**) **glove.** in close association and cooperation; intimately: *to work hand in glove.*
- **hand in hand. a.** holding each other's hand. **b.** in close cooperation; together: *Good study habits and good grades usually go hand in hand.*
- **hand over fist.** rapidly and in great quantity: *to make money hand over fist.*
- **hands down.** with great ease; effortlessly: *to win hands down.*
- **hands off.** do not interfere or touch; keep away. ➡ used as a command.
- **hands up.** hold your hands over your gun. ➡ used as a command, esp. by someone pointing a gun.
- **in hand. a.** in one's possession. **b.** under one's control: *The police had the crowd well in hand.* **c.** in the process of being carried out: *to concentrate on the matter in hand.*
- **off one's hands.** out of one's control or responsibility.
- **on hand. a.** readily available for use: *to have cash on hand.* **b.** present: *There was a large crowd on hand to greet the president.*
- **on one's hands.** in one's possession or control.
- **on the one hand.** from one side or viewpoint.
- **on the other hand.** from another side or viewpoint, esp. the opposite one.
- **out of hand. a.** out of control: *Things got out of hand and a fight broke out.* **b.** without delay or hesitation; immediately: *to act out of hand.* **c.** ended; finished.
- **the upper hand.** superior position; advantage.
- **to change hands.** to pass from one person or group to another.
- **to eat out of one's hand.** to be completely devoted to or controlled by someone.
- **to force someone's hand.** to compel someone to act before he or she had intended to act.
- **to hand. a.** within reach; accessible. **b.** in or into one's possession: *to bring land to hand.*
- **to hand down. a.** to pass along in succession, as to one's heirs. **b.** to make and announce (a decision): *The Supreme Court handed down a decision.*
- **to hand in.** to give, as to someone in authority; deliver: *to hand in one's resignation.*
- **to hand on.** to pass along in succession; hand down.
- **to hand out.** to give out to people; distribute.
- **to hand over.** to yield or give up to another.
- **to have one's hands full.** to be occupied with as much as or more than one can do: *I have my hands full with five children. The police had their hands full in the riot-torn city.*
- **to join hands. a.** to become business partners or associates. **b.** to get married.
- **to keep one's hand in.** to maintain one's interest or skill in; to remain proficient in.
- **to lay one's hands on. a.** to get possession of; seize. **b.** to injure or harm; attack. **c.** to touch in blessing or consecration, as in the rites of confirmation.
- **to tie one's hands.** to hinder one's efforts; prevent one from acting.

- **to try one's hand at.** to make an attempt at doing (something).
- **to turn** (or **put**) **one's hand to.** to begin to work at; undertake: *They turned their hand to running a family store.*
- **to wash one's hands of.** to refuse to associate with or be responsible for any longer.
- **with a heavy hand. a.** in an insensitive, clumsy manner: *The news program covered the incident with a heavy hand.* **b.** in an oppressive manner; overbearingly: *The tyrant ruled the country with a heavy hand.*
- **with a high hand.** in an arbitrary, arrogant manner.

hand·bag (hand′bag′) *n.* **1.** a bag or case used to carry small personal articles, such as cosmetics, keys, and money; pocketbook. **2.** a small traveling suitcase.

hand·ball (hand′bôl′) *n.* **1.** a game in which the players, normally two or four, alternately hit a small rubber ball against a wall with the hand, which is usually gloved. **2.** the small rubber ball used in this game.

hand·bar·row (hand′bar′ō) *n.* a flat, rectangular frame having handles at each end for lifting and carrying loads.

hand·bill (hand′bil′) *n.* a written or printed announcement or advertisement, intended to be distributed by hand.

hand·book (hand′bŭk′) *n.* **1.** a concise book of information or instructions on a particular subject; manual: *a photography handbook.* **2.** a travel guidebook.

hand brake, a brake operated by pressure of the hand, as on a bicycle.

hand·breadth (hand′bredth′, -bretth′) *also,* **hand's-breadth.** *n.* a unit of linear measurement, based on the width of the hand, varying from 2½ to 4 inches (6 to 10 centimeters).

hand·car (hand′kär′) *n.* a small, light, open railroad car propelled by means of a hand pump, used for carrying workers to inspect or maintain tracks.

hand·cart (hand′kärt′) *n.* a small cart pushed or drawn by hand; pushcart.

hand·craft (*n.* hand′kraft′; *v.* hand′kraft′) *n.* handicraft. —*v.t.* to make by hand. —**hand′craft′ed,** *adj.*

hand·cuff (hand′kuf′) *n.* either of a pair of metal rings joined by a short chain, designed to be locked around the wrist of a person to be restrained, such as a prisoner. —*v.t.* **1.** to restrain by enclosing the wrists in handcuffs; manacle: *to handcuff a prisoner.* **2.** to impede the action or progress of: *Indecision handcuffed the city council.*

hand·ed (han′did) *adj.* **1.** of, characterized by, performed with, or designed to be used by a (specified) hand: *a left-handed pitch, left-handed scissors.* **2.** of, characterized by, or performed with (a specified number of) hands or people: *a four-handed piano duet, a game of three-handed bridge.* ➡ used in combination in both defs.

hand·ful (hand′fŭl′) *n., pl.* **-fuls. 1.** the amount that the hand can hold at one time. **2.** a small number or quantity. *a handful of people.* **3.** *Informal.* a person or thing that is as much as one can handle: *My little cousin is a handful to take care of.*

hand grenade, a small bomb designed to be thrown by hand.

hand·gun (hand′gun′) *n.* a firearm that can be held and fired with one hand; pistol; revolver.

hand·hold (hand′hōld′) *n.* **1.** a firm hold with the hand or hands. **2.** something that can be held for support.

hand·i·cap (han′dē kap′) *n.* **1.** a race, contest, or game in which opponents of unequal ability are given certain advantages or disadvantages in an attempt to equalize the competition. **2.** the advantage or disadvantage given in such a contest. **3.** anything that places a person at a disadvantage and hampers achievement, esp. a physical disability: *Being short can be a handicap in playing basketball.* —*v.t.,* **-capped, -cap·ping. 1.** to place at a disadvantage; hamper: *Poor eyesight handicaps me in my work.* **2.** (in a contest) to give one or more handicaps to: *to handicap an opponent.* **3.** to try to predict the winners of (races or other contests). [From *hand in cap;* possibly alluding to a way of drawing lots.] —**hand′i·cap′per,** *n.*

hand·i·capped (han′dē kapt′) *adj.* having a handicap; disabled: *a handicapped person.* —*n.* **the handicapped.** handicapped persons considered as a group.

hand·i·craft (han′dē kraft′) *n.* **1.** a trade, occupation, or art in which great skill with the hands is required, as in working with mosaics or leather. **2.** skill in working with the hands; manual expertise. **3.** an object made or work done by a skilled hand.

a	at	e	end	o	hot	u	up	hw	white		about
ā	ape	ē	me	ō	old	ū	use	ng	song		taken
ä	far	i	it	ô	fork	ü	rule	th	thin	ə	pencil
âr	care	ī	ice	oi	oil	ù	pull	th	this		lemon
				îr	pierce	ou	out	ûr	turn	zh	measure		circus

[Modification (influenced by HANDIWORK) of obsolete *handcraft* manual skill, from Old English *handcræft.*] —**hand′i·craft′er,** *n.*

hand·i·work (han′dē wûrk′) *n.* **1.** work done by hand. **2.** the product of one's work or action. [Old English *handgeweorc.*]

hand·ker·chief (hang′kər chif, -chēf′) *n.* **1.** a soft piece of cloth, usually square, used esp. to wipe the nose or brow or worn as an accessory. **2.** kerchief *(def. 1).* [HAND + KERCHIEF.]

han·dle (han′dəl) *n.* **1.** the part of an object that is made to be grasped by the hand: *to carry a suitcase by the handle.* **2.** something that is like, or can be used like, a handle. **3.** *Slang.* an individual's name. —*v.,* -dled, -dling. —*v.t.* **1.** to touch or hold with the hand or hands: *Please do not handle the glassware.* **2.** to work at with the hands: *to handle clay skillfully.* **3.** to represent, manage, control, or train: *Which lawyer will handle your case?* **4.** to act on or toward; deal or cope with: *to handle a problem, to handle a customer politely.* **5.** to have business dealings in; specialize or trade in: *That company handles exports.* —*v.i.* to act or respond to being handled: *Your new car handles nicely.* [Old English *handlian* to touch with the hands, deal with, from HAND.]
· **to fly off the handle.** to become very angry suddenly.
· **to get a handle on.** to understand something in an attempt to control or manage it: *to get a handle on a situation.*

Synonyms *v.t.* **Handle** and **manipulate** mean to manage or use with skill. Both words originally referred to skill with one's hands. **Handle** is the more general term: *to handle a bicycle easily, to handle a tricky situation.* **Manipulate** more clearly suggests technical skill, and often adroitness: *to manipulate a set of controls, a speaker who manipulates the emotions of an audience.*

han·dle·bar (han′dəl bär′) *also,* **han·dle·bars.** *n.* the usually curved steering bar connected with the front wheel of a bicycle, motorcycle, or similar vehicle, having right and left ends extending toward the rider, often with a grip for the rider to hold.

handlebar mustache, a thick mustache extending in a prominent curve to either side.

han·dler (hand′lər) *n.* **1.** a person or thing that handles anything. **2.** a person who helps to train a boxer or is the boxer's second during a boxing match. **3.** a person who trains or shows a dog or other animal.

hand·made (hand′mād′) *adj.* made by hand rather than by machine.

hand·maid (hand′mād′) *n.* a female servant or personal attendant. Also, **hand′maid′en.**

hand-me-down (hand′mē doun′) *n.* something, esp. a piece of clothing, that has been owned or used by one person and then given to another person for additional use. —*adj.* previously used; secondhand: *hand-me-down toys.*

hand·off (hand′ôf′, -of′) *n.* in football, an act or instance of handing the ball to another player after the ball has been put in play.

hand organ, a portable musical instrument combining features of a pipe organ and a music box, played by means of a hand crank. Also, **barrel organ.**

hand·out (hand′out′) *n.* **1.** food, clothing, or money given out to a beggar. **2.** a prepared news story or statement released to the press for free publicity. **3.** anything handed out without charge, such as a pamphlet or leaflet.

hand·pick (hand′pik′) *v.t.* **1.** to collect or pick by hand. **2.** to select personally and with care: *to handpick a successor.* —**hand′picked′,** *adj.*

hand·rail (hand′rāl′) *n.* a railing designed to be grasped by the hand, used esp. as a guard on stairs or at the edge of a balcony.

hand·saw (hand′sô′) *n.* a saw operated by hand.

hand's-breadth (handz′bredth′, -bretth′) handbreadth.

hand·sel (han′sal) *also,* **hansel.** *n.* **1.** a gift given as a token of good luck at the beginning of something new, as a new year. **2.** a first experience of anything, considered as a sample of what is to come. **3.** a first installment, given as a promise of further payment. —*v.t.,* -seled *or* -selled, -sel·ing *or* -sel·ling. **1.** to give a handsel to. **2.** to inaugurate with ceremony. **3.** to do or experience for the first time. [Old Norse *handsal* concluding a bargain by shaking hands, promise; literally, hand sale.]

hand·set (hand′set′) *n.* a part of a telephone containing the receiver and transmitter at opposite ends of a handle.

hand·shake (hand′shāk′) *n.* the act of clasping and shaking a person's hand as a sign of greeting, friendliness, or agreement: *They concluded the deal with a handshake.*

hands-off (handz′ôf′, -of′) *adj.* of or characterized by noninterference or noninterventionism: *a hands-off foreign policy.*

hand·some (han′səm) *adj.,* -som·er, -som·est. **1.** having a pleasing, often masculine or dignified appearance; good-looking: *a handsome actor, a handsome desk.* **2.** considerable in size or quantity; relatively large: *to be paid a handsome fee.* **3.** character-

ized by generosity; gracious. [Middle English *handsom* easy to handle, from HAND + -SOME[1].] —**hand′some·ly,** *adv.* —**hand′some·ness,** *n.* —For Synonyms, see **beautiful.**

hands-on (handz′ôn′, -on′) *adj.* involving or characterized by direct, personal experience or participation: *hands-on training.*

hand·spike (hand′spīk′) *Nautical. n.* a bar used as a lever.

hand·spring (hand′spring′) *n.* a kind of somersault in which a person springs onto one or both hands and then returns to a standing position.

hand·stand (hand′stand′) *n.* the act of balancing the body on the hands with the legs extended upward.

hand-to-hand (hand′tə hand′) *adj.* in direct contact; at close quarters: *hand-to-hand combat.*

hand-to-mouth (hand′tə mouth′) *adj.* concerned only with one's immediate needs, esp. because of lack of money: *a hand-to-mouth existence.*

hand·work (hand′wûrk′) *n.* work done by hand; handiwork.

hand·wo·ven (hand′wō′vən) *adj.* woven on a loom worked by hand: *handwoven cotton fabric.*

hand·writ·ing (hand′rī′ting) *n.* **1.** writing done by hand, as distinguished from typewriting or printing. **2.** a style of writing; penmanship: *Your handwriting is hard to read.*

hand·writ·ten (hand′rit′ən) *adj.* written by hand.

hand·y (han′dē) *adj.,* hand·i·er, hand·i·est. **1.** within reach; at hand; accessible: *That's a handy place for the telephone.* **2.** able to use the hands skillfully; dexterous: *to be handy at woodworking.* **3.** convenient to handle or use: *a handy carrying case.* —**hand′i·ly,** *adv.* —**hand′i·ness,** *n.*

hand·y·man (han′dē man′) *n., pl.* -men (-men′). a person who is skilled in or works at various small jobs.

hang (hang) *v.,* hung *or (v.t. def. 3, v.i. def. 3),* hanged, hang·ing. —*v.t.* **1.** to fasten or attach (an object) from above only, without any support from below; suspend: *to hang wet towels on a clothesline.* **2.** to attach (an object), as with a hinge, to allow for free movement at the point of attachment: *to hang a garden gate.* **3.** to kill by suspending by the neck, as from a gallows. **4.** to turn downward; droop: *to hang one's head in grief.* **5.a.** to attach or suspend for decoration or display: *to hang wallpaper, to hang drapes, to hang a picture.* **b.** to furnish, cover, or decorate with anything that is attached or suspended: *to hang a room with tapestries.* **6.** (of a juror) to prevent (a jury) from reaching a verdict by withholding one's vote; deadlock. **7.** to fasten or attach in a well-balanced position: *to hang a scythe to a handle.* —*v.i.* **1.** to be attached to or suspended from something above without any support from below; dangle: *A light fixture hung from the ceiling.* **2.** to be fastened in a way that allows for free movement at the point of attachment: *A door hangs on its hinges.* **3.** to die by hanging. **4.** to cling, esp. for support; hold fast: *They hung onto the capsized boat.* **5.** to be dependent: *The defendant's fate hung on the jury's decision.* **6.** to be in a suspenseful or undecided state; vacillate; waver: *The patient hung between life and death for two days.* **7.** to bend forward or downward; droop: *The tree hangs over the lake.* **8.** to be suspended, usually without motion, above something; hover: *Polluted air hangs over the city.* **9.** to be imminent; threaten: *The prospect of war hung over the country.* **10.** to be completely attentive; listen intently (with *on* or *upon*): *The audience hung on the poet's words.* **11.** to fit the figure with ease: *That dress hangs nicely.* **12.** to be on display, esp. in a gallery or museum: *My art teacher's paintings hang in many museums.* —*n.* **1.** the way in which something hangs or falls: *the hang of a dress.* **2.** a particular way of doing something; knack: *to get the hang of riding a bicycle.* **3.** general meaning; gist: *to get the hang of a conversation.* [Partly from Old English *hōn* (past tense *heng*) to suspend; partly from Old English *hangian* to be suspended; partly from Old Norse *hanga* to suspend.]
· **hang it.** *Slang.* I give up. ➡ used to express annoyance, anger, or frustration.
· **to be hung up. a.** to be hampered or detained by (someone or something); be temporarily handicapped: *We were hung up on a problem we couldn't solve. The plan for a new school was hung up by lack of funds.* **b.** *Slang.* to be overly fond of or obsessed by: *He is hung up on his girlfriend. She is hung up on sports.*
· **to hang around** (or **about**). *Informal.* **a.** to linger or loiter: *My friends used to hang around the parking lot after school.* **b.** to spend much time: *I hang around with my best friend.*
· **to hang back.** to be reluctant to begin, continue, or move on; hesitate.
· **to hang fire. a.** to fail or be slow to discharge: *The cannon hung fire.* **b.** to be slow in acting; hesitate: *The legislature hung fire on the tax question.* **c.** to be delayed: *The deal hung fire for several weeks.*
· **to hang in** or **to hang in there.** *Slang.* to be strong and determined; persevere: *Don't let petty criticism bother you; just hang in there.*

• **to hang loose.** *Slang.* to become or remain calm and relaxed: *Hang loose and don't worry about the test.*

• **to hang on. a.** to continue firmly and steadily; persevere: *Don't give up; hang on until graduation.* **b.** to continue to exist; persist: *My cold hung on for two weeks.* **c.** *Informal.* to wait, esp. during a telephone call: *Hang on while I turn down the radio.*

• **to hang one on.** *Slang.* **a.** to strike with the fist. **b.** to get very drunk.

• **to hang out. a.** to lean out of: *The dog hung out the car window.* **b.** *Slang.* to be at a place often: *We used to hang out at the corner drugstore.* **c.** *Slang.* to spend much time; hang around: *My friend and I hung out together.*

• **to hang together. a.** to keep together; be united: *Those who were opposed to the plan hung together.* **b.** to be related in a logical or understandable way: *ideas that don't hang together.*

• **to hang tough.** *Slang.* to be strong and firm; be unyielding.

• **to hang up. a.** to suspend from a hanger or peg: *Don't forget to hang up your coat.* **b.** to end a telephone conversation by replacing the receiver in its cradle. **c.** to hinder the progress of; delay: *The heavy snowfall hung up mail delivery for several days.* **d.** *Informal.* to cause a psychological problem; create a hang-up.

han·gar (hang′ər, -gər) *n.* **1.** a building or other structure for sheltering and servicing aircraft. **2.** shed. [French *hangar* shed; of uncertain origin.]

hang·dog (hang′dôg′) *adj.* having an ashamed, defeated, or cringing manner or appearance: *a hangdog look.*

hang·er (hang′ər) *n.* **1.** a frame or device on which something is hung, esp. one that fits under the shoulders of a garment. **2.** a loop or ring for hanging something, as at the back of the neck of a coat. **3.** a person who hangs something: *a wallpaper hanger.*

hang·er-on (hang′ər ôn′, -on′) *n., pl.* **hang·ers-on.** a person who spends much time with another person or a group, esp. for personal gain, favors, or prestige.

hang glider 1. a diamond-shaped sail beneath which a person hangs face down in a harness, used for hang gliding. **2.** a person who engages in hang gliding.

hang glider

hang gliding, the sport of gliding and soaring in the air with a hang glider, launched from a cliff or hill.

hang·ing (hang′ing) *n.* **1.** an execution in which a person is hanged, as from a gallows. **2.** *also,* **hangings.** a drape or other fabric that hangs as a decoration from a wall or window. —*adj.* **1.** attached to something above without any support from below; dangling: *a hanging lamp.* **2.** leaning over; overhanging: *a hanging balcony.* **3.** placed on a steep slope: *hanging gardens.* **4.** deserving or punishable by hanging: *a hanging offense.*

hang·man (hang′mən) *n., pl.* **-men** (-mən). a person who performs hangings; executioner.

hang·nail (hang′nāl′) *n.* a piece of skin partially torn away and hanging loose at the side or base of a fingernail. [Modification (influenced by HANG) of earlier *agnail,* from Old English *angnægl,* from *ang-* (only in compounds) painful + *nægl* nail.]

hang·out (hang′out′) *n. Informal.* a place in which a person or group spends much time.

hang·o·ver (hang′ō′vər) *n.* **1.** an unpleasant aftereffect, as nausea or a headache, from drinking too much alcoholic liquor. **2.** something remaining from a past time or condition, such as a family custom.

hang-up (hang′up′) *n. Informal.* **1.** a psychological problem that handicaps a person; mental block. **2.** anything that hampers progress; problem or difficulty.

hank (hangk) *n.* **1.** a loop or coil, as of hair. **2.** a skein, esp. one of yarn containing a specific number of yards. A hank of cotton or silk yarn contains 840 yards (768 meters); a hank of worsted yarn contains 560 yards (512 meters). [Of Scandinavian origin.]

han·ker (hang′kər) *v.i., v.t.* to desire strongly; yearn or crave (with *after, for,* or an infinitive). [Probably from Flemish *hankeren* to long for.]

han·ker·ing (hang′kər ing) *n.* a strong desire; yearning; craving.

han·kie (hang′kē) *also,* **han·ky.** *n., pl.* **-kies.** *Informal.* handkerchief. [Short for HAN(D)K(ERCHIEF) + -Y².]

han·ky-pan·ky (hang′kē pang′kē) *n. Slang.* deceitful activity or behavior; trickery. [Rhyming modification of HOCUS-POCUS; possibly influenced by *hand* or *handkerchief* with reference to their use in jugglery.]

Han·o·ve·ri·an (han′ō vîr′ē ən) *adj.* **1.** of, relating to, or characteristic of Hanover. **2.** of or relating to the English royal family of Hanover. —*n.* **1.** a person who was born in or is a citizen of Hanover. **2.** a member or supporter of the English royal family of Hanover.

hanse (hans) *n.* **1.** a medieval guild or association of merchants. **2.** a payment made to this guild, such as a membership fee. **3. Hanse.** Hanseatic League. [Old French *hanse* guild of merchants, from Middle Low German *hanse,* from Old High German *hansa* troop of soldiers.]

Han·se·at·ic (han′sē at′ik) *adj.* of or relating to the Hanseatic League or the cities that formed it.

Hanseatic League, an association of cities in northern Germany established in 1241 to promote mutual defense and mutual free trade.

han·sel (han′səl) handsel.

Han·sen's disease (han′sənz) leprosy. [From Gerhard A. H. *Hansen,* 1841-1912, Norwegian physician who discovered the bacterium causing the disease.]

han·som (han′səm) *n.* a two-wheeled horse-drawn carriage with the driver's seat elevated behind the cab. Also, **hansom cab.** [From Joseph A. *Hansom,* 1803-82, English architect who designed such cabs.]

Ha·nuk·kah (hä′nə kə; *Hebrew* кнä nü kä′) *also,* **Chanukah.** *n.* a Jewish holiday, celebrated for eight days, commemorating the rededication of the Temple of Jerusalem after the victory of Judas Maccabeus over the king of Syria in 165 B.C. It is celebrated by lighting candles on eight successive nights. [Yiddish *khanike,* from Hebrew *chanuka* literally, dedication, from the root *hnx* to dedicate.]

hap (hap) *Archaic. n.* **1.** chance; luck; lot. **2.** something that happens; occurrence. —*v.i.,* **happed, hap·ping.** to occur by chance; happen. [Old Norse *happ* chance, good luck.]

hap·haz·ard (hap haz′ərd) *adj.* characterized by a lack of order, direction, or planning; random; aimless: *books arranged in a haphazard manner.* —**hap·haz′ard·ly,** *adv.* —**hap·haz′ard·ness,** *n.* —For Synonyms, see **random.**

hap·less (hap′lis) *adj.* unlucky; unfortunate. —**hap′less·ly,** *adv.* —**hap′less·ness,** *n.*

hap·loid (hap′loid) *adj.* **1.** single. **2.** having a single set of unpaired chromosomes. —*n.* a cell, as an ovum or sperm, having only one set of chromosomes, half the diploid number present in other living cells. [Greek *haploeidēs* single, from *haplous* single, simple + *-oeidēs* -OID.]

hap·ly (hap′lē) *adv. Archaic.* by chance; perhaps.

hap·pen (hap′ən) *v.i.* **1.** to take place; occur: *The accident happened last week.* **2.** to be or occur by chance; take place without planning or apparent reason: *Your birthday happens to be the same day as mine.* **3.** to have the occasion or luck; chance: *I happened to be there at the right time.* **4.** to come or go by chance (with *along* or *by*): *I happened along just after the accident.* [Middle English *happenen* to befall, from *happen,* from *hap* chance. See HAP.]

• **to happen on** (or **upon**). to meet or find accidentally: *The scientist happened upon the discovery.*

• **to happen to. a.** to be done to; befall: *Something happened to the phone, and it doesn't work.* **b.** to be the fate of; become of: *What ever happened to your cousin?*

| **Synonyms** | **Happen** and **occur** mean to take place. **Happen** is the more common of these terms: *Did anything interesting happen while I was gone?* **Occur** is very close to *happen,* but is slightly more formal: *The accident occurred at a busy intersection.* |

hap·pen·ing (hap′ə ning) *n.* **1.** something that happens; event; occurrence. **2.** a meeting, event, or performance considered inter-

a	at	e	end	o	hot	u	up	hw	white	⎧	about
ā	ape	ē	me	ō	old	ū	use	ng	song		taken
ä	far	i	it	ô	fork	ü	rule	th	thin	ə	pencil
âr	care	ī	ice	oi	oil	u	pull	th	this		lemon
			î	pierce	ou	out	ûr	turn	zh	measure	⎩	circus

esting, important, or entertaining: *The film festival was quite a happening.*

hap·pen·stance (hap′ən stans′) *n.* an occurrence that happens by chance; accident. —*adj.* of or relating to something that occurs by chance; accidental. [HAPPEN + (CIRCUM)STANCE.]

hap·pi·ly (hap′ə lē) *adv.* **1.** with pleasure, joy, or contentment: *They lived happily on their farm.* **2.** by good luck; luckily; fortunately: *Happily, no one was hurt.* **3.** aptly; appropriately.

hap·pi·ness (hap′ē nis) *n.* **1.** the quality or state of being joyous, glad, or contented. **2.** good fortune; luck. **3.** the quality of being appropriate or suitable; aptness.

hap·py (hap′ē) *adj.,* **-pi·er, -pi·est. 1.** having, showing, or providing pleasure, joy, or contentment: *a happy home, a happy occasion.* **2.** lucky; fortunate: *a happy discovery.* **3.** particularly well-suited; apt; felicitous: *a happy choice of words.* [HAP + Y¹.] —For Synonyms, see **glad¹.**

hap·py-go-luck·y (hap′ē gō luk′ē) *adj.* free from worry; carefree.

har·a-kir·i (har′ə kîr′ē) *also,* **hari-kari.** *n.* suicide by cutting open the abdomen with a knife. It is a form of ritual suicide in Japan, committed to redeem honor or express grief. Also, **seppuku.** [Japanese *hara-kiri* suicide by disembowelment, from *hara* belly + *kiri* to cut.]

ha·rangue (hə rang′) *n.* a long noisy speech, often pompous or didactic, delivered in a vehement manner; tirade. —*v.,* **-rangued, -rangu·ing.** —*v.t.* to address with a harangue. —*v.i.* to deliver a harangue. [Middle French *harangue* oration, from Medieval Latin *harenga* meeting, speech made at a meeting; of Germanic origin.] —**ha·rangu′er,** *n.*

har·ass (har′əs, hə ras′) *v.t.* **1.** to bother or annoy repeatedly; torment: *The visiting team complained that they had been harassed by the crowd.* **2.** to trouble (an enemy) by repeated raids or attacks. [French *harasser,* from Old French *harer* to set a dog on, from *hare* a cry used to do this; of Germanic origin.] —**har′ass·ment,** *n.*

har·bin·ger (här′bin jər) *n.* **1.** a person or thing that goes before to announce or indicate the arrival of someone or something; herald. **2.** a person, thing, or event that foreshadows what is to come; omen: *a harbinger of impending evil.* —*v.t.* to act as a harbinger of; foretell. [Old French *herbergere* provider of lodging, from *herbergier* to provide lodging for, from *herberge* lodging; of Germanic origin; supposedly so called because this person went ahead of an army or important individual to secure lodging.]

har·bor (här′bər) *also, British,* **harbour.** *n.* **1.** a protected place on the coastline of a sea, lake, or river, used as a shelter for ships and boats. **2.** any place of shelter. —*v.t.* **1.** to give shelter or protection to; conceal: *to harbor a criminal.* **2.** to keep or foster in the mind: *to harbor a grudge.* —*v.i.* to take shelter in a harbor. [Old English *hereborg* lodgings, quarters, from *here* army + *beorg* protection.] —**har′bor·er,** *n.*

Synonyms *n.* Harbor and **port¹** denote a place where ships may dock safely. A **harbor** is any such place, natural or artificial: *We found a small harbor behind a point on the island, where we sheltered from the storm.* A **port** is almost always designed both to harbor vessels and to supply them with facilities for loading and unloading cargo and passengers: *Many immigrants have entered the United States through the port of Boston.*

har·bor·age (här′bər ij) *also, British,* **har·bour·age.** *n.* **1.** a shelter for ships and boats. **2.** any shelter; lodging.

harbor master, an officer in charge of enforcing the regulations of a harbor.

har·bour (här′bər) *British.* harbor.

hard (härd) *adj.* **1.** not readily pierced, dented, scratched, or crushed; resistant to pressure; firm to the touch: *the hard surface of a concrete floor.* **2.** full of strength; not flabby or weak: *hard muscles.* **3.** needing much physical or mental effort to do or make: *a hard task, a hard decision.* **4.** not easy to make clear, deal with, or solve: *a hard problem.* **5.** needing much patience, care, and understanding: *to be hard to get along with.* **6.** causing or involving something unpleasant, as sorrow, pain, or discomfort; severe; oppressive: *a hard life.* **7.** without sympathy or sensitivity; lacking feeling; stern; strict: *a hard heart.* **8.** showing or carried on with much energy, vigor, or industry: *a hard day's work.* **9.** exacting or rigorous in terms: *a hard bargain.* **10.** having or done with great force or strength: *a hard blow.* **11.** not easily explained away; undeniable; actual: *cold, hard facts.* **12.** unpleasantly severe or harsh to the sight or hearing: *a hard face, a hard voice.* **13.** firmly formed; tight: *a hard knot.* **14.** containing much alcohol: *hard liquor.* **15.** (of water) containing calcium and magnesium salts that interfere with the sudsing and cleansing action of

soap. **16.** (of currency) easily converted into gold or other currencies; worth full face value in purchasing power. **17.** high and firm; stable: *hard prices, a hard market.* **18.** *Phonetics.* **a.** (of *c* and *g*) pronounced with the sound of *k* in *cat* and *g* in *good.* **b.** (of consonants) pronounced without vibration of the vocal cords; voiceless. —*adv.* **1.** with effort or energy: *to work hard.* **2.** with force or strength: *It rained hard.* **3.** with difficulty: *to breathe hard.* **4.** so as to be or become solid or firm: *The ground was frozen hard.* **5.** with a deep emotional reaction, as of grief or bitterness: *to take tragic news hard.* **6.** in a firm, tight manner: *The child held hard to her mother's hand.* **7.** with resistance or reluctance: *to die hard.* **8.** in close proximity; near: *The dogs were hard upon the fox.* **9.** *Nautical.* to the extreme limit; to the fullest extent: *hard alee.* [Old English *heard* solid, unfeeling, severe.] —**hard′ness,** *n.*

· **hard and fast.** that cannot be changed or put aside; fixed; strict: *a hard and fast rule.*

· **hard of hearing.** partially deaf.

· **hard up.** *Informal.* **a.** without any money; broke. **b.** in need of (something): *hard up for a job.*

· **to be hard on.** to treat roughly or harshly: *The children are hard on shoes. The sergeant was hard on the new recruits.*

· **to be hard put.** to have much difficulty or trouble: *I was hard put to find an excuse for my lateness.*

Synonyms *adj.* Hard, difficult, arduous, and laborious mean requiring effort to accomplish. **Hard** is the general term for anything calling for physical or mental exertion: *a hard job, a hard day's traveling.* **Difficult** implies the need for skill to accomplish something complicated or involved: *a difficult climb through brush, a difficult aria to sing.* **Arduous** implies that great effort or persistence is required: *an arduous climb up a mountain.* **Laborious** also suggests extended effort, but also implies work, which may be detailed or repetitious: *the laborious task of cataloging a large collection of books.* For other Synonyms *(adj.),* see **firm¹.**

hard·back (härd′bak′) *adj., n.* hard-cover.

hard·ball (härd′bôl′) *n.* the game of baseball, as opposed to softball. —*adj. Informal.* tough, aggressive, even ruthless: *hardball tactics in politics.*

· **to play hardball.** *Informal.* to use tough, aggressive, even ruthless methods: *to play hardball in business to eliminate competition.*

hard-bit·ten (härd′bit′ən) *adj.* not easily moved by the emotions; unyielding; tough.

hard-boiled (härd′boild′) *adj.* **1.** (of eggs) boiled until yolk and white are hard. **2.** *Informal.* not sympathetic or sensitive; tough; callous.

hard·bound (härd′bound′) *adj.* of, relating to, or designating a book bound in a stiff material that is usually covered with cloth or leather: *a hardbound copy of a book.*

hard cash *Informal.* **1.** ready cash. **2.** coin as distinguished from paper money.

hard cider, apple cider that has fermented.

hard coal, anthracite.

hard copy, printed information from a computer file, as opposed to information displayed on a monitor or stored on disk.

hard-core (härd′kôr′) *adj.* **1.** relating to, belonging to, or making up a hard core: *the hard-core workers in a political campaign.* **2.** not likely to yield to change or to persuasion to change: *hard-core poverty, hard-core conservatism.* **3.** (of pornography) graphically depictive or descriptive.

hard core, the most dedicated or extreme members at the center of a group or movement; those persons who resist change: *the hard core of a political party.*

hard-cov·er (härd′kuv′ər) *adj.* of, relating to, or designating a book bound in a stiff material that is usually covered with cloth or leather. —*n.* a hard-cover book. Also, **hardback.**

hard disk, a permanently installed microcomputer storage device that uses a rigid disk with many times the storage capacity of a floppy disk.

hard·en (här′dən) *v.i.* **1.** to become solid and firm to the touch: *The clay hardened in the sun.* **2.** to become capable of great mental or physical endurance: *The recruits hardened during basic training.* **3.** to become insensitive or cruel. **4.** to become rigid, unyielding, or strengthened. **5.** (of prices) to become stable or to rise. —*v.t.* **1.** to make solid and firm to the touch. **2.** to make unfeeling or callous: *to harden one's heart to the suffering of others.* **3.** to make tough or hardy: *Rigorous training hardened the athletes.* **4.** to strengthen or make rigid or unyielding.

hard goods, items that can be used for a long time, as furniture or appliances.

hard·hack (härd′hak′) *n.* a hardy shrub, *Spiraea tomentosa,* of the rose family, found in eastern North America, bearing narrow clusters of small pink, purple, or white flowers. Also, **steeple-bush.**

hard hat *also,* **hard·hat** (härd′hat′). **1.** a protective hat made of a hard material, worn esp. by construction workers. **2.** *Informal.* a construction worker.

hard·head·ed (härd′hed′id) *adj.* **1.** not easily tricked or moved by the emotions; practical; shrewd. **2.** not yielding to change or persuasion; stubborn; obstinate: *to be hardheaded and not admit a mistake.* —**hard′head′ed·ly,** *adv.* —**hard′head′ed·ness,** *n.*

hard·heart·ed (härd′här′tid) *adj.* without sympathy or sensitivity; lacking pity; cruel; unfeeling. —**hard′heart′ed·ly,** *adv.* —**hard′heart′ed·ness,** *n.*

hard·hit·ting (härd′hit′ing) *adj. Informal.* forceful; bold; aggressive: *a hard-hitting investigation of a scandal.*

har·di·hood (här′dē hòòd) *n.* boldness, daring, and firmness of character: *The hardihood of the settlers was put to the test during their first winter.*

har·di·ness (här′dē nis) *n.* **1.** the state of being hardy; physical endurance; strength. **2.** boldness; daring.

hard labor, compulsory labor imposed on imprisoned criminals as part of the punishment for certain crimes.

hard landing, the landing of a spacecraft at so high a speed that the vehicle or its payload is damaged or destroyed.

hard line, a firmly held opinion or point of view: *to take a hard line regarding the need to reduce taxes.* —**hard′-line′,** *adj.* —**hard′-lin′er,** *n.*

hard·ly (härd′lē) *adv.* **1.** only just; barely: *We could hardly see in the dim light.* **2.** not quite; not: *You're hardly the type to do such a thing.* **3.** probably not; not likely. **4.** with difficulty or effort: *a hardly fought battle.* **5.** in a hard or severe way: *to treat hardly.*

hard-nosed (härd′nōzd′) *adj. Informal.* fixed in purpose or opinion; tough and unyielding: *a hard-nosed disciplinarian.* —**hard′-nose′,** *n.*

hard palate, a bony structure in the front of the roof of the mouth that separates the mouth from the nasal cavity.

hard·pan (härd′pan′) *n.* **1.** a layer of hard, impenetrable earth underneath soft soil. **2.** hard, unbroken ground. **3.** a firm foundation of anything.

hard rock, a form of rock music characterized by highly amplified sound and a powerful beat.

hard rubber, an inelastic rubber, as vulcanite, made by adding as much as 30% sulfur during vulcanizing, used for electrical parts, combs, and tool handles.

hard sauce, an uncooked, creamy mixture of butter, sugar, and flavoring, used as a topping for certain dishes, as plum pudding.

hard·scrab·ble (härd′skrab′əl) *adj.* providing little from much labor or other effort: *hardscrabble subsistence farming.*

hard sell, an aggressive and usually highly insistent method of selling or advertising. ➡ distinguished from **soft sell.**

hard-shell (härd′shel′) *also,* **hard-shelled** (härd′sheld′). *adj.* **1.** (of certain shellfish) having a hard shell. **2.** rigid and uncompromising.

hard·ship (härd′ship′) *n.* a cause or condition of difficulty, pain, or suffering, such as poverty or illness: *The lack of rain caused the farmers great hardship.*

hard·tack (härd′tak′) *n.* unleavened bread, shaped into a hard, dry biscuit, traditionally eaten by sailors. Also, **pilot biscuit, sea biscuit, ship biscuit.**

hard·top (härd′top′) *n.* an automobile having the general design of a convertible, but with a nonfolding, rigid top.

hard·ware (härd′wâr′) *n.* **1.** metal articles or parts, as tools, nails and screws, fittings, or cutlery. **2.** the physical equipment of a computer, as distinguished from theory, programs, or data. **3.** weapons, esp. heavy equipment.

hard wheat, a hardy type of wheat having hard grains and a high gluten content, used in making pasta, semolina, and similar products.

hard·wood (härd′wòòd′) *n.* **1.** any of a large group of trees having broad leaves that are shed every year, as the oak, beech, or maple. **2.** the wood of such trees, usually denser, heavier, and harder than softwood, used to make such items as furniture, flooring, and athletic equipment. **3.** any hard, compact, heavy wood.

har·dy (här′dē) *adj.,* **-di·er, -di·est. 1.** able to endure hardship or harsh physical conditions; strong; robust. **2.** (of plants) able to endure extreme conditions, such as cold and wind, without protection. **3.** filled with confidence; bold; daring; audacious. [Old French *hardi* bold, stout; originally past participle of *hardir* to make bold; of Germanic origin.]

hare (hâr) *n., pl.* **hares** or **hare.** any of various rodentlike mammals, family Leporidae, related to and usually larger than the rabbit, having very long ears, hind legs and feet, a short tail, white, brown, or gray fur, and a divided upper lip. Length: to 25 inches (64 centimeters). [Old English *hara.*]

hare·bell (hâr′bel′) *n.* a plant having a slender stem with bright blue, bell-shaped flowers, *Campanula rotundifolia,* of the bellflower family, found in Europe, Asia, and North America; bluebell.

hare·brained (hâr′brānd′) *adj.* showing or having a lack of common sense or careful thought; foolish; flighty; reckless.

hare

hare·lip (hâr′lip′) *n.* a birth defect consisting of a vertical split in the lip that often impairs speech. —**hare′lipped′,** *adj.*

har·em (hâr′əm) *n.* **1.** the part of a Muslim house where the women live. **2.** the women of a Muslim household. [Arabic *harīm* literally, forbidden, prohibited, from *harama* to forbid, prohibit; because men are forbidden to enter.]

har·i·cot (har′i kō′) *n.* the unripe pod or ripe seeds of any of several beans, as the string bean or kidney bean. [French *haricot* kidney bean, from Nahuatl *ayacotl* bean.]

har·i·kar·i (har′ē kar′ē) hara-kiri.

hark (härk) *v.i.* to listen. ➡ used chiefly in the imperative. [Middle English *herkien,* probably from an unrecorded Old English word.]

· **to hark back.** to return to some previous point of reference; go back; revert: *a custom that harks back to the last century.*

hark·en (här′kən) hearken.

har·le·quin (här′lə kwin, -kin) *n.* **1.** Harlequin. a stock character in sixteenth-century Italian commedia dell'arte, later adapted to English pantomime, traditionally appearing in a skin-tight costume of brightly colored diamond pattern and carrying a small wooden sword. **2.** buffoon. —*adj.* having a brightly colored pattern; parti-colored. [Obsolete French *harlequin,* from earlier *Herlequin* legendary leader of a demon host, possibly going back to Old English *Herla cyning* King Herla (who was probably originally identical with Woden); modern meaning from Italian *arlecchino* buffoon, from obsolete French *harlequin,* which an Italian troupe of actors in France used for the name of the buffoon in their plays.]

harlequin bug, a small, colorful bug, *Murgantia histrionica,* having bright red, orange, and yellow markings, found in North and Central America, destructive to cabbage, turnips, and related plants. Also, **calicoback.**

har·lot (har′lət) *n.* a prostitute or woman of loose or immoral behavior. [Old French *harlot* rascal, vagabond; of uncertain origin.]

har·lot·ry (här′lə trē) *n.* the state or quality of being a harlot or the behavior of a harlot.

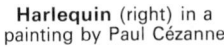

Harlequin (right) in a painting by Paul Cézanne

harm (härm) *n.* **1.** the cause of damage, pain, or loss; injury; hurt: *bodily harm.* **2.** moral injury or offense; evil; wrong: *They saw no harm in lying to their friends.* —*v.t.* to do damage to; hurt: *The leader said that they wouldn't harm the hostages.* [Old English *hearm* injury, evil.] —For Synonyms *(v.t.),* see **injure.**

harm·ful (härm′fəl) *adj.* causing or able to cause harm; injurious; damaging: *Stress can be harmful to your health.* —**harm′ful·ly,** *adv.* —**harm′ful·ness,** *n.*

a	at	e	end	o	hot	u	up	hw	white		about
ā	ape	ē	me	ō	old	ū	use	ng	song		taken
ä	far	i	it	ô	fork	ü	rule	th	thin	ə	pencil
âr	care	ī	ice	oi	oil	ù	pull	th	this		lemon
			ir	pierce	ou	out	ûr	turn	zh	measure	circus

H

harm·less (härm′lis) *adj.* not capable of causing harm; not injurious or damaging: *a harmless snake, a harmless prank.* —**harm′less·ly,** *adv.* —**harm′less·ness,** *n.*

har·mon·ic (här mon′ik) *adj.* **1.** of, relating to, or characterized by musical harmony. **2.** of or relating to a higher tone or tones produced along with the main tone or tones when a musical note is played. —*n.* **1.** *Music.* overtone. **2.** *Physics.* the component of a wave whose frequency is a simple multiple of the frequency of the fundamental. The frequency of a second harmonic is twice that of a fundamental. [Latin *harmonicus* relating to harmony, from Greek *harmonikos* skilled in music, harmonious, from *harmoniā* joining, concord. See HARMONY.] —**harmon′i·cal·ly,** *adv.*

harmonica

har·mon·i·ca (här mon′i-kə) *n.* a musical wind instrument consisting of a series of metallic reeds mounted in a slotted panel, played by inhaling and exhaling through the slots. Also, **mouth organ.** [Latin *harmonica,* feminine of *harmonicus.* See HARMONIC.]

harmonic motion *Physics.* the motion of an object vibrating about a fixed point, as a pendulum does.

har·mon·ics (här mon′iks) *pl. n.* **1.** the science of musical sounds. ➡ used as singular. **2.** secondary sounds or overtones produced along with the main tone when a musical note is played.

har·mo·ni·ous (här mō′nē əs) *adj.* **1.** characterized by agreement in feelings, thoughts, or actions; in accord: *a harmonious relationship.* **2.** having elements that combine agreeably or pleasingly: *a harmonious mixture of colors.* **3.** agreeable or pleasing to the ear; sweet-sounding. —**har·mo′ni·ous·ly,** *adv.*

har·mo·ni·um (här mō′nē əm) *n.* a keyboard musical instrument whose tones are produced by currents of air vibrating small metal reeds. Also, **melodeon, reed organ.** [French *harmonium,* from Latin *harmonia.* See HARMONY.]

har·mo·nize (här′mə nīz′) *v.,* -**nized, -niz·ing.** —*v.i.* **1.** to arrange, sing, or play in harmony. **2.** to be in agreement; combine agreeably or pleasingly: *The color scheme in the hall harmonizes with the one in the dining room.* —*v.t.* **1.** to bring into agreement; make harmonious. **2.** to add notes to (a melody) so as to form chords; add harmony to. —**har′mo·niz′er,** *n.*

har·mo·ny (här′mə nē) *n., pl.* -**nies. 1.a.** a combination of simultaneously sounded musical notes so as to form chords. **b.** the chordal structure of a musical work, as distinguished from its melody and rhythm. **c.** the science or study of the structure, relations, and combination of chords. **2.** any sweet or pleasant sound. **3.** an agreement of feeling, thoughts, or actions; good relations: *to live in harmony.* **4.** an agreeable or pleasing arrangement among the various elements of a whole: *a harmony of colors.* **5.** a collation of parallel passages from different authors or sources, esp. the four Gospels, showing their points of agreement and disagreement. [Latin *harmonia* agreement of sounds, concord, from Greek *harmoniā,* from *harmos* joint.]

har·ness (här′nis) *n.* **1.** the gear of a draft animal, which includes a combination of straps and bands by which the animal is attached to the load it is pulling, and the bridle by which the animal is controlled and guided. **2.** any combination of straps and bands resembling this: *a dog's harness, the harness of a parachute.* **3.** *Archaic.* the armor for a knight, soldier, or horse. —*v.t.* **1.** to put a harness on. **2.** to control and make use of: *to harness water power to generate electricity.* **3.** *Archaic.* to put armor on. [Old French *harneis* armor, equipment; possibly of Scandinavian origin.]

·**in harness.** in or at one's routine work.

harness racing, a sport in which horses pull two-wheeled sulkies in trotting or pacing races.

harp (härp) *n.* a musical instrument consisting of a series of strings of varying length set in an upright, triangular frame with a curved top, played by plucking the strings with the fingers. —*v.i.* to play a harp. [Old English *hearpe* this musical instrument.]

·**to harp on.** to refer to continually and annoyingly: *You're always harping on how much work you have to do.*

harp·ist (här′pist) *n.* a person who plays the harp.

har·poon (här pün′) *n.* a barbed spearlike missile with a rope attached, used to kill or capture whales and other sea animals. —*v.t.*

harp

to strike, catch, or kill with a harpoon. [Probably from Dutch *harpoen* a harpoon, from Old French *harpon* clamp, clasp, from *harper* to seize; probably of Scandinavian origin.] —**har·poon′-er,** *n.*

harp·si·chord (härp′si kôrd′) *n.* a stringed musical instrument with a keyboard, widely used esp. in the sixteenth through eighteenth centuries. It resembles a grand piano, but has the wire strings plucked by leather or quill points, and produces a guitar-like tone. [Obsolete French *harpechorde,* from *harpe* harp (of Germanic origin) + *chorde* string (from Latin *chorda* string of a musical instrument). See CHORD².]

Har·py (här′pē) *n., pl.* -**pies. 1.** in Greek mythology, one of several foul-smelling, ugly monsters having an old woman's head and the body, wings, and claws of a bird. **2. harpy.** a person who is extremely greedy and who preys upon other people. [Latin *harpyia,* from Greek *harpȳiai* (plural) Harpies of mythology; literally, snatchers.]

har·que·bus (här′kwə bəs) *also,* **arquebus.** *n.* an early portable firearm, used in the fifteenth and sixteenth centuries, later replaced by the musket. [French *arquebuse,* from Middle Dutch *hakebusse* literally, hook gun, from *hake* hook + *busse* gun (going back to Latin *buxus;* see BOX¹); referring to the hook that was cast on the gun.]

har·ri·dan (har′i dən) *n.* a mean, shrewish woman. [Supposedly modification of French *haridelle* worn-out horse; of uncertain origin.]

har·ri·er¹ (har′ē ər) *n.* **1.** a hunting dog of a breed developed in England, resembling the English foxhound, originally raised for hunting hares. Height: 20 inches (51 centimeters) at the shoulder. **2.** a runner in a cross-country race. [HARE + -IER.]

har·ri·er² (har′ē ər) *n.* **1.** a person or thing that harries. **2.** any of various hawks, genus *Circus,* whose plumage is gray or brown above and white below, that prey on rodents, frogs, and other small animals. Wingspan: 4 feet (1.2 meters). [HARRY + -ER¹.]

har·row (har′ō) *n.* a heavy frame with upright disks or teeth, drawn by a tractor to break up and level plowed land. —*v.t.* **1.** to draw a harrow over (land). **2.** to cause (someone) much mental pain, fright, or distress. —**har′row·er,** *n.*

Har·row (har′ō) *n.* one of England's oldest and best-known boys' preparatory schools, founded in 1571. It is located in Harrow-on-the-Hill, a borough of London.

har·row·ing (har′ō ing) *adj.* causing extreme anxiety or distress; very disturbing: *Driving through the snowstorm was a harrowing experience.*

har·ry (har′ē) *v.t.,* -**ried, -ry·ing. 1.** to trouble constantly; torment; vex: *The attorney harried the witness with difficult questions.* **2.** to rob or pillage, as in a raid or attack. [Old English *her-gian* to make raids, lay waste, from *here* army.]

harsh (härsh) *adj.* **1.** rough or unpleasant to any of the physical senses: *a harsh sound.* **2.** extremely cruel or difficult; severe: *harsh treatment, a harsh winter.* [Probably of Scandinavian origin.] —**harsh′ly,** *adv.* —**harsh′ness,** *n.*

hart (härt) *n., pl.* **harts** or **hart.** a stag, esp. a male red deer, usually after its fifth year. ➡ distinguished from **hind².** [Old English *heorot.*]

har·te·beest (här′tə bēst′, härt′bēst′) *n., pl.* -**beests** or -**beest.** a reddish brown African

hartebeest

antelope, genus *Alcelaphus,* having a long, narrow head and ringed, U-shaped horns that bend backward at the tips. Height: 4 feet (1.2 meters) at the shoulder. [Obsolete Afrikaans *hartebeest,* from Dutch *hert* hart + *beest* beast (from Old French *beste* BEAST.]

harts·horn (härts′hôrn′) *n.* smelling salts. [So called because formerly obtained chiefly from a hart's horns.]

har·um-scar·um (hâr′əm skâr′əm) *adj.* reckless or rash. —*adv.* in a reckless or rash manner: *They raced harum-scarum down the block.* [Possibly from obsolete *hare* to frighten (of uncertain origin) + SCARE.]

ha·rus·pex (hə rus′peks, har′əs peks′) *n., pl.* **ha·rus·pi·ces** (hə rus′pə sēz′). a member of a group of priests in ancient Etruria or Rome who divined the will of the gods by observing the entrails of sacrificed animals, patterns of lightning, and the flight of birds. [Latin *haruspex* literally, inspector of entrails.]

Har·vard (här′vərd) *n.* a private accredited university in Cambridge, Massachusetts, the oldest college in the United States.

har·vest (här′vist) *n.* **1.** the act of gathering a crop when it is ripe. **2.** the crop that is gathered; season's yield of a crop: *a large harvest of beets.* **3.** the time of year when ripened crops are gathered. **4.** the product or result of any action, effort, or labor: *a harvest of goodwill.* —*v.t.* **1.** to gather as a crop: *to harvest corn.* **2.** to gather the crop from: *to harvest wheat fields.* **3.** to reap or get as a result or product of: *to harvest the benefits of a long, productive life.* —*v.i.* to gather a crop. [Old English *hærfest* autumn, the season for gathering crops.]

har·vest·er (här′və stər) *n.* **1.** any of various machines for harvesting field crops. **2.** a person who harvests.

harvest home 1. the last harvest of the year; the close of harvesting. **2.** an old English festival celebrating the close of harvesting. **3.** a song sung at this festival.

har·vest·man (här′vist mən) *n., pl.* **-men** (-mən). **1.** daddylonglegs. **2.** a person who harvests.

harvest moon, the full moon occurring nearest the autumnal equinox.

has (haz) the third person singular present tense of **have.**

has-been (haz′bin′) *n. Informal.* a person or thing that is no longer popular, powerful, or effective: *That movie star is now a has-been.*

hash[1] (hash) *n.* **1.** a mixture of cooked meat and potatoes and often onions or other vegetables, esp. one that is chopped fine and either browned, fried, or baked. **2.** a confusing mess; jumble; muddle. —*v.t.* **1.** to chop into small pieces: *to hash potatoes.* **2.** to consider or discuss carefully; review (often with *out* or *over*): *to hash out differences, to hash over a decision.* [Old French *hacher* to hack, from *hache* ax; of Germanic origin.]
• **to make a hash of.** *Informal.* to make a mess of; bungle.
• **to settle one's hash.** *Informal.* to treat (someone) harshly; subdue.

hash[2] (hash) *n. Slang.* hashish.

hash browns, boiled potatoes that are chopped into small pieces and fried in fat until brown.

hash·ish (hash′ēsh, -ish, ha shēsh′) *also,* **hash·eesh** (hash′ēsh, ha shēsh′). *n.* the dried flowering top parts of a hemp plant, *Cannabis sativa,* smoked or chewed as a narcotic. [Arabic *hashīsh.*]

hash mark 1. *Slang.* service stripe. **2.** either of two rows of short lines that run the length of a football field and mark each yard.

Has·id (has′id) *n., pl.* **Ha·sid·im** (has′i dim, hä sē′dim). a follower of Hasidism. Also, **Chassid.** [Hebrew *hāsīdh* pious.] —**Ha·sid·ic** (hə sid′ik), *adj.*

Has·i·dism (has′i diz′əm) *n.* a Jewish sect and movement that stresses mysticism, strict ritual observance, and intense religious feeling, usually centered on a venerated spiritual leader or leaders. Also, **Chassidism.** [Yiddish *khosed* follower of this movement (from Hebrew *chasid* pious, from *chesed* loving kindness) + -ISM.]

has·n't (haz′ənt) *contr.* has not.

hasp (hasp) *n.* any of several clasps or fastenings, esp. a hinged metal clasp that fits over a staple and is fastened by a pin or padlock, used to keep a door, window, or box closed. [Old French *hæpse.*]

has·sle (has′əl) *Informal. n.* **1.** a heated argument; squabble. **2.** something troublesome; bother; irritation: *Getting home in the rainstorm was a hassle.* —*v.,* **-sled, -sling.** —*v.i.* to squabble; fight. —*v.t.* to bother or irritate. [Possibly blend of HAGGLE and TUSSLE.]

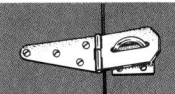
hasp

has·sock (has′ək) *n.* **1.** a low, cushioned stool or other piece of furniture used for resting the feet, sitting, or kneeling on. **2.** a tuft of coarse grass. [Old English *hassuc* coarse grass. The stool was formerly made of coarse grass.]

hast (hast) *Archaic.* a second person singular present tense of **have.** ➡ used with *thou.*

has·tate (has′tāt) *adj. Botany.* (of leaves) shaped like the head of a spear but with lobes near the stem turned outward. [Latin *hastātus* armed with a spear, from *hasta* spear.]

haste (hāst) *n.* **1.** swiftness of motion or action; hurry; speed: *They departed in great haste in order to make the train.* **2.** rash or careless hurry: *In our haste we forgot the keys.* —*v.t., v.i.,* **hasted, hast·ing.** *Archaic.* hasten. [Middle English *haste,* from Old French *haste* speed; of Frankish origin.] —For Synonyms (*n.*), see **hurry.**
• **to make haste.** to move quickly; hurry.

has·ten (hā′sən) *v.t.* to cause to move or act quickly; speed up:

Outrage at the government's corruption hastened its downfall. —*v.i.* to move or act quickly; hurry.

hast·y (hās′tē) *adj.,* **hast·i·er, hast·i·est. 1.** swift in motion or action; hurried; quick: *a hasty meal.* **2.** characterized by careless hurry; rash: *to be hasty in drawing conclusions.* **3.** showing anger or easily made angry; impatient: *My hasty remarks were later regretted.* —**hast′i·ly,** *adv.* —**hast′i·ness,** *n.*

hasty pudding 1. a mush made of flour or oatmeal boiled with water or milk. **2.** a mush made of cornmeal.

hat (hat) *n.* any of various coverings for the head, usually having a brim and crown. —*v.t.,* **hat·ted, hat·ting.** to furnish or cover with a hat. [Old English *hæt.*]
• **to pass the hat.** to take up a collection; ask for contributions.
• **to take off one's hat to.** to praise or congratulate.
• **to talk through one's hat.** to speak ignorantly; talk nonsense.
• **to toss one's hat into the ring.** to enter into a competition, esp. as a candidate for office.
• **under one's hat.** as a secret; in confidence.

hat·band (hat′band′) *n.* a cloth band around the crown of a hat, just above the brim.

hat·box (hat′boks′) *n.* a box or piece of luggage for a hat.

hatch[1] (hach) *v.t.* **1.** to cause young to be brought forth from (the egg): *to hatch eggs in an incubator.* **2.** to bring forth (young) from the egg: *The hen hatched the chickens yesterday.* **3.** to devise or bring forth, as a plan or plot; scheme. —*v.i.* **1.** to come forth from the egg by pecking through their shells. **2.** (of eggs) to produce young: *All the eggs hatched today.* —*n.* **1.** the act of hatching. **2.** a brood of young that have just been hatched. [Middle English *hacchen* to incubate, akin to Old English *hagan* genitals.] —**hatch′er,** *n.*

hatch[2] (hach) *n.* **1.a.** an opening in a ship's deck for access to lower decks or to the ship's hold. **b.** a similar opening in the floor or roof of a building. Also, **hatchway. 2.** a cover or trap door for such openings. **3.** the lower half of a door or gate with two movable parts. [Old English *hæc* small door, gate.]
• **down the hatch.** *Informal.* drink up or eat up.

hatch[3] (hach) *v.t.* to mark with fine parallel or crossed lines, as for shading in drawing and engraving; hachure. —*n.* one of these lines. [Old French *hacher* to hack. See HASH.]

hatch·back (hach′bak′) *n.* an automobile with a sloping back section and rear window that lifts open to give access to a storage area. [HATCH[2] + BACK[2].]

hatch·el (hach′əl) *n.* hackle[1] (def. 4). —*v.t.* hackle[1] (def. 2). [Form of HACKLE[1].]

hatch·er·y (hach′ə rē) *n., pl.* **-er·ies.** a place where eggs are hatched, esp. those of fish or poultry.

hatch·et (hach′it) *n.* **1.** a small, short-handled ax designed to be used with one hand. **2.** tomahawk. [Old French *hachette,* diminutive of *hache* ax; of Germanic origin.]
• **to bury the hatchet.** to stop fighting; make peace.

hatch·et-faced (hach′it fāst′) *adj.* having a narrow face with sharp features.

hatchet man *Informal.* **1.** a person who attacks or criticizes the beliefs, writings, or political allegiance of another in a vicious manner. **2.** a person hired to make such an attack or to carry out unpleasant duties, as dismissing employees.

hatch·ing (hach′ing) *n.* hachure. [HATCH[3] + -ING[1].]

hatch·ment (hach′mənt) *n.* a square tablet set diagonally bearing the coat of arms of a deceased person. [Earlier *achement, atcheament,* form of ACHIEVEMENT.]

hatch·way (hach′wā′) *n.* hatch[2] (def. 1).

hate (hāt) *v.,* **hat·ed, hat·ing.** —*v.t.* **1.** to have an intense dislike for; have strong feelings against: *I hate cruelty toward animals.* **2.** to think of as unpleasant or distasteful; be unwilling: *I hate to sew.* —*v.i.* to feel intense dislike. —*n.* **1.** an intense dislike or animosity; hatred. **2.** a person or thing that is hated. [Old English *hatian* to detest.] —**hat′er,** *n.*

Synonyms *v.t.* **Hate, detest, abhor,** and **loathe** mean to have a strong dislike for or aversion to. **Hate** is the most general term, and the negative emotions it expresses may vary in intensity: *I hate getting up in the morning. The two rivals hated each other from the start.* **Detest** suggests a dislike that may be stronger than *hate* and may also imply disdain: *I detest artificial sweeteners.* **Abhor** connotes aversion to the point of repugnance: *I abhor cockroaches.* **Loathe** suggests total revulsion: *Don't you loathe this hot, humid weather?*

H

a	at	e	end	o	hot	u	up	hw	white		about
ā	ape	ē	me	ō	old	ū	use	ng	song		taken
ä	far	i	it	ô	fork	ü	rule	th	thin	ə	pencil
âr	care	ī	ice	oi	oil	u̇	pull	t͟h	this		lemon
		îr	pierce	ou	out	ûr	turn	zh	measure		circus

hate·ful (hāt′fəl) *adj.* **1.** deserving or arousing hatred; detestable: *a hateful crime.* **2.** feeling or showing hate; full of hate: *a hateful remark, a hateful stare.* **3.** nasty, rude, or unpleasant: *a hateful person, a hateful job.* —**hate′ful·ly,** *adv.* —**hate′fulness,** *n.* —For Synonyms, see **offensive.**

hath (hath) *Archaic.* a third person singular present tense of **have.**

hat·pin (hat′pin′) *n.* a long, sometimes decorative, pin for fastening a hat to one's hair.

hat·rack (hat′rak′) *n.* a rack or pole with hooks used to hold hats or other garments.

ha·tred (hā′trid) *n.* a strong feeling of intense dislike or animosity. [Middle English *hatereden,* going back to Old English *hete* intense dislike + *rǣden* condition.]

hat·ter (hat′ər) *n.* a person who makes, sells, or repairs hats.

hat trick *Ice Hockey.* the scoring of three goals in one game by the same player.

hau·ber·geon (hô′bər jən) habergeon *(def. 1).*

hau·berk (hô′bûrk′) *n.* a long coat of chain mail or scale armor worn in medieval Europe. [Old French *hauberc;* of Germanic origin.]

haugh·ty (hô′tē) *adj.* **-ti·er, -ti·est.** having or showing excessive pride in oneself and great disdain for others. [From obsolete *haught* (from Old French *haut* high, from Latin *altus*) + -Y¹.] —**haugh′ti·ly,** *adv.* —**haugh′ti·ness,** *n.* —For Synonyms, see **proud.**

haul (hôl) *v.t.* **1.** to pull or draw with force; drag; tug: *We hauled the cart up the hill.* **2.** to transport, as in a truck or car: *Railroads haul freight.* **3.** *Nautical.* to change the course of (a vessel), esp. to sail closer to the wind. —*v.i.* **1.** to pull; tug. **2.** (of the wind) to change direction; shift: *The wind hauled to the south.* **3.** *Nautical.* to change course, esp. to sail closer to the wind. —*n.* **1.** a forceful pull or tug. **2.** something that is obtained or taken, as by catching or winning: *a big haul of fish.* **3.** a distance over which a load is hauled: *From here to the warehouse is a long haul.* **4.** a quantity or load hauled. [Form of HALE².] —**haul′er,** *n.*

•**to haul off. a.** to draw back the arm to deliver a blow. **b.** *Nautical.* to change course or move away from an object.

•**to haul up. a.** to force to appear, as before a court or judge. **b.** to come to a stop.

haul·age (hô′lij) *n.* **1.** the act or process of hauling. **2.** the force used in hauling. **3.** a fee charged for hauling.

haulm (hôm) *n.* **1.** the stalks or stems of plants, as beans, peas, or potatoes, esp. after a crop is gathered. **2.** a single plant stalk or stem. [Middle English *halm,* from Old English *healm, halm* straw.]

haunch (hônch) *n.* **1.** the part of the body including the hip, buttock, and upper thigh in humans and four-footed animals. **2.** the leg and loin of an animal, as a deer or sheep, used for food. [Old French *hanche* hip; of Germanic origin.]

haunt (hônt) *v.t.* **1.** (of ghosts or spirits) to visit or inhabit: *A ghost haunts that house.* **2.** to appear to or come to the mind of persistently: *Memories of the shipwreck still haunt the old sailor.* **3.** to visit often; frequent: *to haunt antique shops.* —*n.* **1.** a place often visited; hangout: *The barn was our haunt during rainy days.* **2.** *Informal.* ghost. [Old French *hanter* to frequent; of Germanic origin.]

haunt·ed (hôn′tid) *adj.* **1.** visited or inhabited by ghosts: *a haunted house.* **2.** very disturbed or troubled: *a haunted look in someone's eyes.*

haunt·ing (hôn′ting) *adj.* appearing or coming to the mind persistently; hard to forget: *a haunting melody.* —**haunt′ing·ly,** *adv.*

haus·to·ri·um (hô stôr′ē əm) *n., pl.* **haus·to·ri·a** (hô stôr′ē ə). an organ that a parasitic plant, as a fungus, uses to obtain nutrients from its host. [Modern Latin *haustorium,* from Latin *haustus,* past participle of *haurire* to drink, draw water.]

haut·boy (hō′boi′, ō′boi′) *n.* oboe. [French *hautbois,* from *haut* high (from Latin *altus*) + *bois* wood (from Late Latin *boscus*). See BUSH.]

haute (ōt) *adj.* elevated or developed to a high degree of refinement; fashionable or influential. [French *haute,* from Latin *altus.*]

haute couture 1. very fashionable, expensive clothing for women, created by influential designers who often set trends. **2.** the fashion houses or designers who create such clothing.

haute cuisine 1. the preparation of elaborate or fine food by skilled chefs; gourmet cooking. **2.** the food so prepared; gourmet food.

hau·teur (hō tûr′) *n.* a haughty or arrogant manner; arrogance: *With much hauteur, the guard told us to leave.* [French *hauteur,* from *haut* high, from Latin *altus.*]

Ha·van·a (hə van′ə) *n.* a cigar made in Cuba or from Cuban tobacco.

Ha·va·su·pai (hä′və sü′pī) *n., pl.* **-su·pai** or **-su·pais.** a member of a North American Indian tribe living in the area of the Grand Canyon.

have (hav; *unstressed* həv, əv) *v.,* **had** or *(archaic second person sing.)* **hadst, hav·ing.** Present: *sing.,* first person, **have;** second, **have** or *(archaic)* **hast;** third, **has** or *(archaic)* **hath;** *pl.* **have.** —*v.t.* **1.** to hold in one's hand or bear on one's person: *to have a scarf around one's neck.* **2.** to own or be in possession of: *They have a house in the country. I have brown eyes.* **3.** to be related to or connected with: *I have five cousins.* **4.** to contain or be characterized by: *The year has twelve months.* **5.** to hold or keep in the mind: *Do you have any doubts?* **6.** to show or use: *One must have patience when training dogs.* **7.** to cause to or cause to be: *Please have the matter taken care of.* **8.** to engage in; carry on or out: *to have a discussion.* **9.** to experience; undergo: *We had a good time.* **10.** to be affected with; suffer from: *I had the mumps when I was ten years old.* **11.a.** to be obliged to do or deal with: *I have a lot of errands this afternoon.* **b.** to be obligated: *I have to go to the grocery store.* ➡ used with an infinitive. **12.** to make arrangements for: *The senator had a dinner party for the ambassador.* **13.** to give birth to. **14.** to eat or drink: *We always have cereal for breakfast.* **15.** to invite or entertain as a guest: *We had the Smiths over for dinner last week.* **16.** to receive, take, or obtain: *Used cars can be had for as little as $500.* **17.** to permit or tolerate: *I won't have you talk to me like that.* **18.** to maintain or assert: *Rumor has it that they eloped.* **19.** to possess knowledge of or understand: *The new student has some Spanish but little French.* **20.** *Informal.* to cheat or deceive: *You've been had.* **21.** *Informal.* to hold at a disadvantage: *The boxer has his opponent now.*—*auxiliary verb.* used with past participles to form the perfect tenses, expressing completed action: *We have done the work. We had done the work. We shall have done the work.* —*n.* a person or country that has much property, wealth, or resources. ➡ usually used in the plural: *the haves and the have-nots.* [Old English *habban* to hold, possess.]

•**to have done.** to get through; stop: *Let's pay all the bills now and have done with them.*

•**to have had it. a.** to be filled with disgust; endure all that one is able: *I've had it with people calling at supper time trying to sell something.* **b.** to come to an end; be finished: *That fad has had it.*

•**to have it in for.** *Informal.* to have or hold a grudge against.

•**to have it out.** to settle a matter once and for all.

•**to have on.** to be wearing: *That's a fine suit you have on.*

•**to have to do with. a.** to be of concern to; be the business of: *What does this matter have to do with you?* **b.** to associate with as a friend, companion, or partner.

have·lock (hav′lok′) *n.* a white cloth covering for a military cap, having a flap that hangs over the back of the neck. [From Sir Henry *Havelock,* nineteenth-century British general in India.]

ha·ven (hā′vən) *n.* **1.** a sheltered harbor; port. **2.** a place of safety or shelter; refuge: *The quiet park was a welcome haven from the noise of the city.* —*v.t.* to shelter in or as in a haven. [Old English *hæfen* harbor, from Old Norse *höfn.*]

have-not (hav′not′) *n.* a person or country having little or no property, wealth, or resources. ➡ usually used in the plural.

have·n't (hav′ənt) *contr.* have not.

hav·er·sack (hav′ər sak′) *n.* a bag, usually worn over the shoulder or suspended at one's side by a strap, used to carry food and other provisions, as by a soldier or hiker. [French *havresac* knapsack, from German *Habersack* oat sack.]

Ha·ver·sian canal (hə vûr′zhən) any of the tiny canals that pass longitudinally through the compact bone and contain blood vessels and nerves. [From Clopton *Havers,* 1650?-1702, English anatomist.]

hav·oc (hav′ək) *n.* general destruction; devastation; ruin: *The flood caused havoc in the town.* [Anglo-Norman *havok,* form of Old French *havot* plunder; possibly of Germanic origin.]

•**to cry havoc.** to give the signal for pillage and destruction.

•**to play havoc with.** to cause great destruction to; devastate: *The hurricane played havoc with the boats in the marina.*

haw¹ (hô) *n.* **1.** the fruit of any hawthorn. **2.** hawthorn. **3.** a shrub, *Viburnum rudum,* having white or yellow flowers and blue-black fruit. [Old English *haga* hedge, hawthorn.]

haw² (hô) *v.i.* to hesitate in speaking; grope for words. ➡ usually used in the phrase *to hem and haw.* —*n.* a stammering sound made by a speaker when hesitating between words. [Imitative.]

haw³ (hô) *interj.* to the left. ➡ used to direct horses and other draft animals. —*v.t., v.i.* to turn to the left. [Of uncertain origin.]

Ha·wai·i-A·leu·tian Standard Time (hə wī′ē ə lü′shən) the local time used in Hawaii and the western Aleutian Islands. It is 10 hours earlier than Greenwich Time.

Ha·wai·ian (hə wī′ən) *adj.* of, relating to, or characteristic of Hawaii or its people, language, or culture. —*n.* **1.** a native or inhabitant of Hawaii. **2.** a language belonging to the Polynesian branch of the Austronesian family of languages, spoken predominantly in Hawaii.

Words from Hawaiian and Other Polynesian Languages

Hawaiian is in the Polynesian branch of the Austronesian language family, together with such languages as Samoan, Maori, and Tahitian. In the selection of words below, which have entered English from or through Hawaiian and other Polynesian languages, the first two columns of words are from Hawaiian, the last two from other Polynesian languages.

aloha	lei	kauri	tapa
hula	luau	kea	taro
Kanaka	mahimahi	kiwi	tattoo
lanai	poi	moa	tuatara
lehua	ukulele	taboo	

---

hawk[1] (hôk) *n.* **1.** any of various birds of prey, genera *Accipiter* and *Buteo,* having a sharp, hooked beak, strong talons, and short, rounded wings. Length: to 2 feet (0.6 meter). **2.** any of various other birds of prey, as the eagle, buzzard, and kite. **3.** a person who preys on others; swindler. **4.** a person who advocates or supports the use of aggressive military force to resolve international conflicts. ➡ opposed to **dove**[1]. —*v.i.* to hunt game with trained hawks; engage in falconry. —*v.t.* to hunt (prey) as a hawk does. [Old English *hafoc* bird of prey used in falconry.] —**hawk′like′,** *adj.*

hawk[2] (hôk) *v.t.* to offer (goods) for sale by calling out in public: *to hawk goods in a marketplace.* [From HAWKER[2].]

hawk[3] (hôk) *v.i.* to clear the throat noisily by coughing. —*v.t.* to bring up (phlegm) by coughing. [Imitative.]

hawk·er[1] (hô′kər) *n.* falconer. [Old English *hafocere,* from *hafoc* hawk[1] + *-ere* -ER[1].]

hawk·er[2] (hô′kər) *n.* a person who hawks goods. [Middle Low German *hoker* huckster, from *hoken* to peddle + *-er* -ER[1].]

hawk-eyed (hôk′īd′) *adj.* very observant or having keen vision.

hawk·ing (hô′king) *n.* falconry.

hawk·ish (hô′kish) *adj.* **1.** like a hawk, as in appearance. **2.** advocating aggressive military force in international affairs.

hawk moth, any of a group of large, stout-bodied moths, family Sphingidae, noted for their strong, rapid flight.

hawks·bill (hôks′bil′) *also,* **hawk's-bill.** *n.* a saltwater turtle, *Eretmochelys imbricata,* found in warm waters, whose brown and yellow, shieldlike shell is the major commercial source of tortoise shell. Length: 2-3 feet (0.6-0.9 meter). Weight: to 160 pounds (73 kilograms). Also, **hawksbill turtle.**

hawk·weed (hôk′wēd′) *n.* any of a large group of plants, genus *Hieracium,* of the composite family, found growing as a weed in Europe and North and South America, bearing yellow or orange daisylike flower heads and usually having hairy leaves and stems.

hawse (hôz) *n.* **1.** that part of a ship's bow where the hawseholes are located. **2.** hawsehole. **3.** the space from the hawsehole in the bow of a moored ship to the point where the anchor cable enters the water. [Old Norse *hāls* neck, ship's bow.]

hawse·hole (hôz′hōl′) *n.* a hole on either side of the bow of a ship through which the anchor cable or hawser is passed.

haw·ser (hô′zər) *n.* a heavy rope, cable, or chain, used esp. for mooring or towing ships. [Anglo-Norman *hauceor,* from Old French *haucier, halcier* to hoist, going back to Latin *altus* high.]

haw·thorn (hô′thôrn′) *n.* any of a group of thorny shrubs or trees, genus *Crataegus,* of the rose family, found esp. in eastern North America and bearing red, yellow, or black fruits that are used to make jelly. Also, **haw.** [Old English *hagathorn,* from *haga* hedge + *thorn* thorn.]

Hawsehole

Hawser

hawse

hay (hā) *n.* **1.** any of various plants, as grass, alfalfa, or clover, cut and dried for use as feed for livestock. **2.** *Slang.* a small amount of money: *The salary is $50,000 a year and that's not hay.* —*v.i.* to mow, dry, and store hay. —*v.t.* **1.** to feed with hay. **2.** to cut the hay in: *to hay a field.* [Old English *hēg* grass cut and dried for fodder.]

• **to hit the hay.** *Slang.* to go to bed.

• **to make hay while the sun shines.** to profit from, or take full advantage of, an opportunity.

hay·cock (hā′kok′) *n.* a small, cone-shaped pile of hay.

hay fever, an allergy caused by breathing pollen in the air, characterized by inflammation of the nasal passages, itching of the eyes, and sneezing.

hay·field (hā′fēld′) *n.* a field where grass, alfalfa, clover, or other plants are grown or cut for hay.

hay·fork (hā′fôrk′) *n.* **1.** pitchfork. **2.** a mechanical device for moving or loading hay.

hay·loft (hā′lôft′) *n.* a loft in a stable or barn for storing hay.

hay·mak·er (hā′mā′kər) *n.* **1.** a person or machine that cuts hay and spreads it out to dry. **2.** *Slang.* a powerful punch that results in, or is intended to result in, the person hit being knocked unconscious.

hay·mow (hā′mou′) *n.* **1.** hayloft. **2.** a pile of hay stored in a barn.

hay·rack (hā′rak′) *n.* **1.** a rack or frame for holding hay on which livestock may feed. **2.a.** a framework mounted on a wagon to increase its capacity for holding hay or other bulky material. **b.** a wagon equipped with such a framework.

hay·rick (hā′rik′) *n.* haystack.

hay·ride (hā′rīd′) *n.* a pleasure ride in a wagon partly filled with hay, taken by a group as an outing.

hay·seed (hā′sēd′) *n.* **1.** the seed of any of various grasses. **2.** the clinging bits of straw, chaff, and seed that fall from hay during processing. **3.** *Slang.* a person from the country; country bumpkin; hick.

hay·stack (hā′stak′) *n.* a pile of hay, usually cone-shaped, stored outdoors. Also, **hayrick.**

hay·wire (hā′wīr′) *n.* wire used for baling hay. —*adj. Informal.* **1.** out of order; broken down. **2.** crazy or upset.

haz·ard (haz′ərd) *n.* **1.** exposure to danger, harm, or loss; risk; peril. **2.** a potential source of danger or harm: *Icy roads are a hazard to motorists.* **3.** a fortuitous event; accident: *On what hazards turns our fate* (Edward Bulwer-Lytton, 1843). **4.** any obstruction, as sand, water, or a bunker, on a golf course. **5.** a dice game from which craps developed. —*v.t.* **1.** to dare to put forth; venture: *I'll hazard a guess.* **2.** to expose to danger, harm, or loss; risk. [Middle English *hazard,* from Old French *hasard* dice game, risk, accident, from Spanish *azar* accident, bad throw at dice, from Arabic *yasara* he played at dice.] —For Synonyms *(n.),* see **danger.**

haz·ard·ous (haz′ər dəs) *adj.* involving danger, harm, or loss; risky: *a hazardous climb up a mountain.* —**haz′ard·ous·ly,** *adv.* —**haz′ard·ous·ness,** *n.*

hazardous waste, any waste material or industrial by-products that may endanger health or pollute the environment if not managed or disposed of properly.

haze[1] (hāz) *n.* **1.** a fine suspension of mist, smoke, dust, or other particles in the air: *An early morning haze limited visibility on the highway.* **2.** vagueness of mind or mental confusion. [From HAZY.]

haze[2] (hāz) *v.t.,* **hazed, haz·ing.** to harass, humiliate, and play pranks on, often with some physical abuse, esp. as part of initiation in certain colleges, fraternities, or sororities. [Possibly from Old French *haser* to vex, annoy.] —**haz′er,** *n.*

ha·zel (hā′zəl) *n.* **1.** any of a group of shrubs or trees, genus *Corylus,* grown in North America and Europe, having oval, tooth-edged leaves and clusters of small flowers. **2.** hazelnut. **3.** a reddish brown or yellowish brown color, like that of the hazelnut. —*adj.* **1.** of or relating to the hazel. **2.** having the color hazel; reddish or yellowish brown in color. [Old English *hæsel* hazel tree.]

ha·zel·nut (hā′zəl nut′) *n.* the light brown, round or oval, edible nut of a hazel. Also, **filbert.**

ha·zy (hā′zē) *adj.,* **-zi·er, -zi·est. 1.** characterized or obscured by haze: *a hazy day, a hazy view.* **2.** lacking intellectual clarity; vague: *My knowledge of the subject is hazy.* [Of uncertain origin.] —**ha′zi·ly,** *adv.* —**ha′zi·ness,** *n.*

Hb, hemoglobin.

H-bomb (āch′bom′) *n.* hydrogen bomb.

H.C., House of Commons.

hcf *also,* **h.c.f.** highest common factor. See **greatest common divisor.**

hd. 1. hand. **2.** head.

HDL, a blood lipoprotein responsible for transporting cholesterol from the tissues to the liver for excretion, and associated with a

---

a	at	e	end	o	hot	u	up	hw	white		about
ā	ape	ē	me	ō	old	ū	use	ng	song		taken
ä	far	i	it	ô	fork	ü	rule	th	thin	ə	pencil
âr	care	ī	ice	oi	oil	u̇	pull	th	this		lemon
		îr	pierce	ou	out	ûr	turn	zh	measure		circus

H

571

lower risk of atherosclerotic heart disease. [Abbreviation of *h(igh-)d(ensity) l(ipoprotein).*]

hdqrs., headquarters.

he (hē; *unstressed* ē) *pron., sing.* nominative, **he;** possessive, **his;** objective, **him;** *pl.* nominative, **they;** possessive, **their, theirs;** objective, **them. 1.** a male person or animal, or an object personified as male, that has been previously mentioned. **2.** a person; anyone: *He who hesitates is lost.* —*n., pl.* **hes.** a male person or animal. [Old English *hē,* masculine pronoun of the third person singular.]

He, the symbol for helium.

H.E. 1. His Eminence. **2.** His Excellency.

head (hed) *n., pl.* **heads** or *(def. 14)* **head. 1.** the anterior or upper part of the body of a vertebrate animal, containing the brain, organs of sight, hearing, taste, and smell, and part of the organs of vocalization or, in humans, speech. **2.** a corresponding part of any animal or organism. **3.** the top part of anything: *the head of the stairs, the head of a page.* **4.a.** the foremost part or end of anything; front: *the head of a line.* **b.** either end of something, as a barrel. **5.** the part associated with, or regarded as forming, the top end: *Who should sit at the head of the table?* **6.a.** a part of a tool, weapon, or machine that cuts, strikes, or engraves: *the head of a hammer.* **b.** a part resembling a head in position or shape: *the head of a pin.* **7.** a person to whom others are subordinate; chief; leader: *The shaman was the head of the tribe.* **8.** the head regarded as the center of intelligence, memory, or imagination: *You have a good head on your shoulders.* **9.** mental ability; aptitude: *to have a good head for figures.* **10.** a dominant rank or position; command: *The lawyer was placed at the head of the crime commission.* **11.** the most honorable or prominent position or place: *Mary graduated at the head of her class.* **12.** self-control; poise: *John always loses his head when discussing politics.* **13.** the decisive or final point; crisis or conclusion: *The demonstrations brought matters to a head.* **14.** a single person or animal, esp. when considered as one of a number: *The cowhands rounded up fifty head of cattle after the stampede.* **15. heads.** the obverse of a coin. ➡ opposed to **tails;** used as singular. **16.** a representation of the head, as on a frieze. **17.** foam or froth on the surface of certain liquids, esp. beer. **18.** a compact cluster of leaves, as of cabbage or lettuce, or of leafstalks, flowers, or any other plant part, usually growing from the top of a main stem. **19.** the source, as of a river or stream. **20.** a tip or point, as of a boil or abscess, where pus has accumulated and is at the point of breaking through the skin. **21.** pressure, as of a fluid: *a head of steam.* **22.** a body of water kept at a height, as to supply power. **23.** *Botany.* flower head. **24.** a projecting, usually high, point of a coast; headland. **25.** a tightly stretched membrane covering the end or ends of a percussion instrument, as a drum or tambourine. **26.a.** heading. **b.** the topic of a section of a speech or written work. **27.** headway. **28.** *Nautical.* **a.** the forward part of a ship; bow. **b.** the upper corner or top of a sail. **c.** toilet. **29.** a device, as on a tape recorder or the disk drive of a computer, that magnetically records, reads, or erases electronic signals, as on a tape or disk. **30.** headmaster. **31.** *Slang.* a person who frequently uses a drug, as LSD or marijuana. —*adj.* **1.** first or most important; principal; chief: *head lifeguard, head dog of a dog team.* **2.** situated at the top or front: *head part of a list.* **3.** coming from in front. **4.** of or relating to the head: *a head covering.* —*v.t.* **1.** to be or go at the top or front of: *The professors headed the procession. Your name heads the list.* **2.** to be the chief or leader of; be in charge of; direct: *to head a project.* **3.** to turn or direct the course of: *The captain headed the ship northward.* **4.** to go around the head of, as a stream. **5.** to cut off the head of: *to head fish.* **6.** to fit or furnish with a head or heading. **7.** *Soccer.* to hit (the ball) with the head. —*v.i.* **1.** to move in a certain direction or toward a certain point: *We headed for the mountains for our vacation.* **2.** (of streams) to originate; rise. **3.** to come to or form a head. [Old English *hēafod* part of the body containing the brain and sense organs, highest point, chief, source.]

• **head and shoulders above.** greatly superior to.
• **head over heels. a.** in a somersault: *The child tumbled head over heels down the hill.* **b.** completely; thoroughly: *They were head over heels in love with each other.*
• **on** (or **upon) one's head.** as one's responsibility.
• **one's head off.** *Informal.* too much; excessively: *We laughed our heads off.*
• **out of** (or **off) one's head.** *Informal.* crazy; insane.
• **over one's head. a.** beyond one's power or ability to comprehend. **b.** beyond one's power to handle or manage.
• **to give someone his** (or **her) head.** to let someone do as he (or she) pleases.
• **to go over (someone's) head.** to bypass (someone) and go to a higher authority: *We went over the manager's head and complained to the vice president.*

• **to go to one's head. a.** to make one dizzy or intoxicated. **b.** to make one conceited.
• **to hang one's head.** to lower or hide one's face, as when embarrassed.
• **to head off.** to get in front of and turn back or aside; intercept.
• **to keep one's head.** to remain calm; not get excited.
• **to keep one's head above water.** to manage to avoid disaster, loss, or failure.
• **to lose one's head.** to lose self-control; become excited.
• **to make head or tail of.** to understand: *I wasn't able to make head or tail of the book.*
• **to put heads together.** to consult together; confer.
• **to take it into one's head.** to conceive the idea, notion, or intention.
• **to turn one's head.** to make one overly confident or conceited.

head·ache (hed′āk′) *n.* **1.** a pain in the head. **2.** *Informal.* a source or cause of annoyance, trouble, or worry.

head·band (hed′band′) *n.* **1.** a narrow band, usually of cloth, worn around the head to hold the hair in place or as an ornament. **2.** in bookbinding, a narrow strip of cloth attached to the top or both top and bottom of the spine of a book for strength or decoration.

head·board (hed′bôrd′) *n.* a board that forms the head of a bedstead.

head·cheese (hed′chēz′) *n.* a food made from the boiled meat of the head and feet of a hog or calf, finely chopped, seasoned, and chilled to form a jellylike mass.

head cold, a cold having nasal congestion as its main symptom.

head·dress (hed′dres′) *n.* **1.** a covering or decoration for the head. **2.** a style in which the hair is arranged; coiffure.

head·ed (hed′id) *adj.* **1.** having a head or heading. **2.** grown or formed into a head, as cabbage. **3.** having a specified kind of head or number of heads. ➡ used in combination: *clear-headed, a three-headed monster.*

head·er (hed′ər) *n.* **1.a.** a person or thing that removes heads, esp. a machine that removes the heads from grain. **b.** a person or thing that puts on or makes heads, as for rivets or nails. **2.** a brick or stone laid in a wall with its short end toward the face of the wall. **3.a.** in a floor or roof, a beam framed between two joists or rafters and supporting the ends of the tail beams. **b.** in a wall, a beam framed between two studs

Indonesian **headdress**

and supporting the short studs above it, as over a door or window.
• **to take a header.** to fall or plunge headfirst.

head·first (hed′fûrst′) *adv.* **1.** with the head going in front. Also, **head′fore′most′. 2.** without due consideration; rashly; impetuously.

head gate 1. an upstream gate of a canal or river lock. **2.** a floodgate of a race, sluice, or other channel for the control of water.

head·gear (hed′gîr′) *n.* a covering for the head, esp. one worn for protection: *Football players wear special headgear.*

head·hunt·er (hed′hun′tər) *n.* **1.** a person who practices headhunting. **2.** *Slang.* a person or agency that recruits personnel, esp. executive personnel, for a company or corporation.

head·hunt·ing (hed′hun′ting) *n.* **1.** a custom of cutting off the head of an enemy and preserving it as a trophy. **2.** *Slang.* the recruiting of personnel, esp. executive personnel, for a company or corporation.

head·ing (hed′ing) *n.* **1.a.** the part of a written work that describes or sets apart a section of the text. **b.** a division or section of a subject of discourse; topic. **2.** a part serving as or forming the top or front. **3.** a direction or course, as of a ship or aircraft, as indicated on the compass.

head·land (hed′lənd) *n.* a point of land, usually high, projecting out into the water; cape; promontory.

head·less (hed′lis) *adj.* **1.** having no head; beheaded. **2.** having no leader or chief. **3.** foolish or stupid; brainless: *a headless mistake.*

head·light (hed′līt′) *n.* a bright light mounted at the front of an automobile, motorcycle, or other vehicle.

head·line (hed′līn′) *n.* one or more lines of type at the top of an article, as in a newspaper, summarizing or highlighting the contents and printed in larger type than the body of the article. —*v.t.,* -**lined, -lining. 1.** to provide with a headline, as a newspaper article. **2.** to be the main attraction of (a theatrical presentation): *A magic act headlined the show.*

head·lin·er (hed′lī′nər) *n.* a person or thing that is the main attraction of a theatrical presentation.

head·lock (hed′lok′) *n.* a wrestling hold in which the arm or arms encircle the opponent's head.

head·long (hed′lông′) *adv.* **1.** headfirst *(def. 1).* **2.** without giving much thought; recklessly; impetuously. **3.** with unrestrained speed or force. —*adj.* **1.** made or moving with the head foremost: *a headlong dive.* **2.** moving with great speed or force. **3.** rash; impetuous. [Modification of Middle English *hedling* headfirst, precipitate, from *hed* HEAD + -LING².]

head·man (hed′man′, -mən) *n., pl.* -**men** (-men′, -mən). chief; leader.

head·mas·ter (hed′mas′tər) *n.* a man who is principal or head of a school, esp. a private elementary or secondary school. —**head′mas′ter·ship′,** *n.*

head·mis·tress (hed′mis′tris) *n.* a woman who is principal or head of a school, esp. a private elementary or secondary school.

head·most (hed′mōst′) *adj.* most advanced; foremost.

head of state, the highest ranking official in a national government, as a president or monarch.

head-on (hed′ôn′, -on′) *adj., adv.* with the head or front end foremost: *a head-on collision, to collide head-on.*

head·phone (hed′fōn′) *n.* **1.** a receiver or small speaker, as for a radio or telephone, held against or worn over the ear. **2. headphones.** a pair of such speakers designed for use with stereo components.

head·piece (hed′pēs′) *n.* **1.** a covering for the head, as a hat, cap, or helmet. **2.** headset. **3.** *Printing.* a decorative design, usually at the beginning of a book or chapter or at the top of a page. **4.** the mind or intellect.

head·pin (hed′pin′) *n.* the front pin of the triangle of pins in bowling; kingpin.

head·quar·ter (hed′kwôr′tər) *Informal. v.t.* to provide with headquarters: *The company is headquartered overseas.* —*v.i.* to establish headquarters: *The rescue workers headquartered in the school.*

head·quar·ters (hed′kwôr′tərz) *n.* **1.** the center of operations from which a commanding officer, chief, or other leader, as of an army or police force, issues orders. **2.** any center of operations, as of a business or other organization; main control center. **3.** the entire staff of a center of operations. ➡ used as singular or plural in all defs.

head·rest (hed′rest′) *n.* a support for the head.

head·room (hed′rüm′, -rùm′) *n.* clear space overhead; room above the head; headway: *a small car with very little headroom.*

head·sail (hed′sāl′, -səl) *n.* any sail set forward of the foremast, as a jib.

head·set (hed′set′) *n.* a pair of headphones, often with a transmitter, or mouthpiece, attached.

head·ship (hed′ship′) *n.* the position or office of a person in charge.

head·shrink·er (hed′shring′kər) *n. Slang.* a psychiatrist.

heads·man (hedz′mən) *n., pl.* -**men** (-mən). a person who beheads condemned criminals; public executioner.

head·stall (hed′stôl′) *n.* the part of a bridle or halter that fits around the head of an animal.

head·stand (hed′stand′) *n.* the balancing of the body on the head in an upside-down vertical position, usually assisted by the hands.

head start 1. the advantage of starting a race ahead of others. **2.** a similar advantage in any competition.

head·stock (head′stok′) *n.* the part of a machine that supports a revolving or working part or parts, as the part supporting the spindle of a lathe.

head·stone (hed′stōn′) *n.* **1.** a stone, usually with an inscription, set at the head of a grave; tombstone. **2.** the principal stone in a structure, as a cornerstone or keystone.

head·strong (hed′strông′) *adj.* **1.** determined to have one's own way or do as one pleases; willful. **2.** characterized by or proceeding from obstinate willfulness: *headstrong decisions.*

Headstrong and **willful** suggest being unyielding or ungovernable by temperament or nature. **Headstrong** stresses unreasonable insistence on having one's own way, even to the point of foolhardiness: *They were headstrong in their determination to continue the climb, even though the slopes were icy and dangerous.* **Willful** may be used the same way, but may also suggest a more deliberate and stubborn adherence to something: *Their willful refusal to follow instructions antagonized the rest of the group.*

head-to-head (hed′tə hed′) *adj.* **1.** very close in score; almost even in finishing. **2.** in direct confrontation or opposition.

head tone, a tone produced in the higher registers of a vocal range, bringing the cavities of the head and nose into sympathetic vibration. Also, **head voice.**

head·wait·er (hed′wā′tər) *n.* a man who supervises the dining room staff of a restaurant and sometimes takes reservations and seats guests.

head·wait·ress (hed′wā′tris) *n.* a woman who supervises the dining room staff of a restaurant and sometimes takes reservations and seats guests.

head·wa·ters (hed′wô′tərz, -wot′ərz) *pl. n.* the small streams at the source of a river that unite to form the main channel.

head·way (hed′wā′) *n.* **1.** forward motion or progress: *The ship made little headway in the storm.* **2.** clear space overhead, as under a bridge. **3.** the interval of time or distance between two trains, ships, or other vehicles traveling over the same route.

head·wind (hed′wind′) *n.* a wind blowing from the direction in which something, as a ship, is moving.

head·word (hed′wûrd′) *n.* a word used as a title or subtitle to introduce or set apart an article or section of a written work, as a paragraph or an entry in a dictionary or encyclopedia.

head·work (hed′wûrk′) *n.* mental labor or effort; thought.

head·y (hed′ē) *adj.,* **head·i·er, head·i·est. 1.** tending to make one dizzy or giddy; intoxicating: *a heady wine.* **2.** headstrong; willful. —**head′i·ly,** *adv.* —**head′i·ness,** *n.*

heal (hēl) *v.i.* **1.** to close, as a wound, or knit, as a broken bone: *The wound healed without leaving a scar.* **2.** to become whole or sound; get well: *The injured patient healed quickly.* —*v.t.* **1.** to restore to health or soundness; cure: *The doctor healed the sick child.* **2.** to effect the cure or remedy of, as a wound. **3.** to remedy, repair, or remove: *Nothing could heal the rift between the estranged friends.* **4.** to free from an evil or distressing state or condition; purify; cleanse: *Heal me with your pardon* (Alfred, Lord Tennyson, 1847). [Old English *hælan* to make whole, cure, repair.] —**heal′er,** *n.* —For Synonyms, see **cure.**

health (helth) *n.* **1.** soundness of body and mind; freedom from defect or disease. **2.** the condition of body or mind: *The doctor said the patient was in very good health.* **3.** a toast drunk in a person's honor expressing a wish for his or her well-being: *We drank a health to them before their ship sailed.* [Old English *hælth* soundness of body or mind.]

health·care (helth′kâr′) *also,* **health care.** *n.* **1.** the healing and care of the sick or injured. **2.** any of the procedures used in doing this.

health-care (helth′kâr′) *adj.* of, relating to, or concerned with healthcare: *a health-care facility.*

health club, a club with facilities and equipment for physical exercise and indoor sports.

health food, any food thought to be especially good for one's health, esp. food without preservatives or other chemical additives, or food grown without the use of chemical fertilizers or pesticides.

health·ful (helth′fəl) *adj.* **1.** promoting or conducive to health; wholesome: *a healthful diet.* **2.** healthy *(def. 1).* —**health′ful·ly,** *adv.* —**health′ful·ness,** *n.*

health maintenance organization, a medical organization that provides medical care and hospitalization to its members.

health·y (hel′thē) *adj.,* **health·i·er, health·i·est. 1.** having good health; well: *a healthy child.* **2.** characteristic of or showing good health or sound condition: *a healthy appearance, a healthy outlook on life.* **3.** conducive to health; healthful. **4.** *Informal.* considerable or great in amount, size, or intensity: *There was healthy trading on the stock exchange. The trainer kept a healthy distance from the tiger.* —**health′i·ly,** *adv.* —**health′i·ness,** *n.*

Strictly speaking, **healthful** should be used to mean "promoting or conducive to health" and **healthy** should be used to mean "having good health." However, it is generally considered acceptable to use **healthy** for both senses: *a healthy diet, a healthy person.*

heap (hēp) *n.* **1.** a collection of things randomly piled together; mass: *a heap of clothes on the floor.* **2.** *also,* **heaps.** *Informal.* a large number or quantity; lot: *We saw heaps of people that we knew.* —*v.t.* **1.** to make into a heap; pile. **2.** to fill (something)

H

a	at	e	end	o	hot	u	up	hw	white		about
ā	ape	ē	me	ō	old	ū	use	ng	song		taken
ä	far	i	it	ô	fork	ü	rule	th	thin	ə	pencil
âr	care	ī	ice	oi	oil	ù	pull	th	this		lemon
		îr	pierce	ou	out	ûr	turn	zh	measure		circus

full or more than full: *I heaped my dish with mashed potatoes.* **3.** to cast or bestow in large amounts: *to heap compliments on an actor.* [Old English *hēap* pile of things, crowd.]

heap·ing (hē′ping) *adj.* filled above the normal capacity: *The recipe called for a heaping teaspoon of flour.*

hear (hîr) *v.,* **heard** (hûrd), **hear·ing.** —*v.t.* **1.** to perceive or be able to perceive (sound) by means of the ear. **2.** to pay attention to; listen to: *We heard both sides of the argument before we made a decision.* **3.** to be informed of; become aware of: *We heard the news on the radio.* **4.** to give a formal, official, or legal hearing to: *The judge heard the testimony of all the witnesses.* **5.** to listen to with compliance; accede to; grant: *Our prayers were heard.* **6.** to attend and listen to as part of an audience: *I heard most of the concert last night at the auditorium.* —*v.i.* **1.** to perceive or be able to perceive sound by means of the ear. **2.** to receive information; be told; learn: *Have you heard about the situation?* —*interj.* **hear, hear.** well done or well spoken. [Old English *hēran* to perceive sound, listen.] —**hear′er,** *n.*

· **to hear of.** to allow, consider, or agree to. ➡ used with a negative: *They would not hear of our leaving so early.*

· **to hear out.** to listen to until the end: *Please hear me out before you decide.*

· **to hear tell.** *Informal.* to learn: *I hear tell you're getting married.*

hear·ing (hîr′ing) *n.* **1.** the faculty or sense by which sound is perceived; ability to hear: *to have acute hearing.* **2.** the act or process of perceiving sound: *Hearing your voice brought back happy memories.* **3.** the opportunity to be heard; audience: *We were granted a hearing to air our grievances.* **4.a.** an investigation or trial before a judge or a government agency invested with judicial power. **b.** an investigation by a legislative committee to gather information. **5.** the distance within which sound may be heard; earshot: *The child was told to play within hearing of the house.*

hearing aid, a small electronic device that amplifies sound, worn to compensate for poor hearing.

heark·en (här′kən) *also,* **harken.** *v.i.* to pay close attention; listen carefully.

hear·say (hîr′sā′) *n.* information received from others rather than by personal knowledge; gossip; rumor.

hearsay evidence, any statement made out of court that is offered by a witness at a trial to prove a matter at issue. It is usually not admissible as evidence.

hearse (hûrs) *n.* a vehicle for conveying a dead person from one place to another before or after a funeral service. [Old French *herse* harrow, frame holding candles, as at a funeral, going back to Latin *hirpex* harrow, from Samnite *hirpus* wolf; with reference to the resemblance of the teeth of a wolf to the teeth of a harrow.]

heart (härt) *n.* **1.** the hollow, muscular organ that pumps the blood through the body of a vertebrate by means of rhythmic contractions and dilations. It has four chambers in mammals and birds and three in reptiles and amphibians. **2.** a similar organ in invertebrate creatures. **3.** the region of the body containing the heart; bosom. **4.** one's innermost feelings or thoughts: *I knew in my heart that we would never meet again.* **5.** the heart considered as the center of the emotions, esp. of love and affection: *to speak from the heart.* ➡ opposed to **mind** (def. 2). **6.** love and affection: *The puppy won our hearts.* **7.** disposition; nature: *a kind heart.* **8.** a capacity for kindness or compassion for others: *Have a heart!* **9.** mental state; mood: *a heavy heart.* **10.** firmness of will; spirit; courage: *to lose heart.* **11.** passion and enthusiasm; ardor: *You must have put your heart into your work.* **12.** a person, esp. one who is admired or loved: *a dear heart.* **13.** the center or innermost part of anything: *in the heart of the city, hearts of celery.* **14.** the main, vital, or most essential part: *Let's get to the heart of the matter.* **15.** anything shaped like the heart: *They cut out paper hearts.* **16.** a playing card bearing one or more red, heart-shaped figures ♥. **17. hearts. a.** the suit of such playing cards. **b.** a card game played with a fifty-two-card deck in which the players try to get either none or all of the cards of this suit. [Middle English *herte,* from Old English *heorte.*]

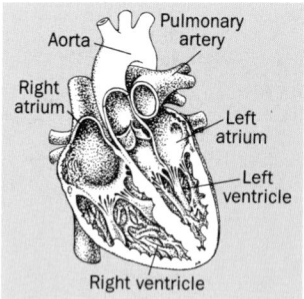

Aorta
Right atrium
Pulmonary artery
Left atrium
Left ventricle
Right ventricle

human **heart**

· **after one's own heart.** corresponding or conforming perfectly to one's own ideas, tastes, or desires.

· **by heart.** from memory: *to know a poem by heart.*

· **from (the bottom of) one's heart.** with deepest feeling; sincerely.

· **heart and soul.** with all of one's affection and energy; completely; wholly: *to love someone heart and soul.*

· **in one's heart of hearts.** in the deepest and most intimate part of one's feelings or nature: *In my heart of hearts, I knew you were right.*

· **to break one's heart.** to cause one to feel great sorrow, disappointment, or grief: *The sad story broke my heart.*

· **to eat one's heart out. a.** to feel great sorrow, grief, or remorse. **b.** to pine away.

· **to have a change of heart.** to change one's feelings, attitude, or opinion.

· **to have one's heart in one's mouth.** to be terrified or very excited.

· **to have one's heart in the right place.** to have good intentions; mean well.

· **to lose one's heart to.** to fall in love with.

· **to set one's heart on.** to desire strongly; long for.

· **to take to heart. a.** to consider seriously or carefully: *I took the advice to heart.* **b.** to be deeply affected or worried by.

· **to wear one's heart on one's sleeve.** to behave in a manner that plainly exposes one's feelings.

· **with all one's heart. a.** with great sincerity or earnestness. **b.** very willingly; gladly.

> **Synonyms** **Heart, core,** and **essence** denote the central or vital part of something. **Heart** connotes that part in which force or life is thought to reside: *the heart of a community, the heart of a plan to revitalize a neighborhood.* **Core** connotes the center around which something is seen as being formed: *the core of an empire, the core of one's personality.* **Essence** suggests the intrinsic and indispensable properties that make something what it is: *Simplicity is the essence of good taste.*

heart·ache (härt′āk′) *n.* emotional anguish; sorrow; grief.

heart attack, a sudden, serious disruption in the function of the heart, usually resulting from blockage of an artery supplying blood to the heart.

heart·beat (härt′bēt′) *n.* a pulsation of the heart, consisting of one complete contraction and dilation.

heart block, a partial or complete interruption of the transmission of impulses that regulate the heartbeat, resulting in uncoordinated contractions of the atria and ventricles and a reduced flow of blood.

heart·break (härt′brāk′) *n.* overwhelming sorrow or grief. —**heart′break′er,** *n.* —**heart′break′ing,** *adj.* —**heart′break′ing·ly,** *adv.*

heart·bro·ken (härt′brō′kən) *adj.* overwhelmed with sorrow or grief. —**heart′bro′ken·ly,** *adv.*

heart·burn (härt′bûrn′) *n.* a burning sensation under the breastbone, produced by stomach acid rising into the esophagus.

heart disease, any abnormal organic condition of the heart or of the heart and circulatory system.

heart·ed (här′tid) *adj.* having or marked by a (specified kind of) disposition. ➡ used in combination, as in *lighthearted, goodhearted.*

heart·en (här′tən) *v.t.* to give heart to; encourage; cheer: *The story of their success heartened us.*

heart failure, a condition in which the heart can no longer pump enough blood to and from the body tissues to satisfy their metabolic needs.

heart·felt (härt′felt′) *adj.* deeply and earnestly felt; sincere; genuine: *heartfelt congratulations.*

hearth (härth) *n.* **1.** the floor of a fireplace, often extending out into the room. **2.** the family circle; home; fireside. **3.** the lowest part of a blast furnace. [Old English *heorth.*]

hearth·stone (härth′stōn′) *n.* **1.** the stone forming a hearth. **2.** the family circle; home; fireside.

heart·i·ly (här′tə lē) *adv.* **1.** with genuine sincerity or cordiality; earnestly: *They welcomed us heartily.* **2.** with enthusiasm or zeal; eagerly; vigorously: *to laugh heartily.* **3.** with a good appetite: *After the day's labors, they ate heartily.* **4.** with no reservations; completely; thoroughly; exceedingly: *We heartily support your plan.*

heart·land (härt′land′) *n.* a geographic area whose control is considered vital to a nation for strategic and economic reasons.

heart·less (härt′lis) *adj.* **1.** without kindness or compassion; unfeeling; cruel. **2.** without courage or enthusiasm; spiritless. —**heart′less·ly,** *adv.* —**heart′less·ness,** *n.*

heart murmur, an abnormal sound, as a rumbling or blowing, produced in the heart in addition to the normal rhythmic beating.

heart·rend·ing (härt′ren′ding) *adj.* causing much sorrow or anguish.

hearts·ease (härts′ēz′) *also,* **heart's-ease.** *n.* **1.** peace of mind; tranquillity. **2.** a pansy of the variety *hortensis,* cultivated as a garden flower.

heart·sick (härt′sik′) *adj.* deeply depressed or unhappy; despondent. —**heart′sick′ness,** *n.*

heart·sore (härt′sôr′) *adj.* heartsick.

heart-strick·en (härt′strik′ən) *adj.* deeply affected by grief, fear, or dismay. Also, **heart′struck′.**

heart·strings (härt′stringz′) *pl. n.* strongest or deepest feelings or affections: *The sad story touched their heartstrings.*

heart·throb (härt′throb′) *n.* **1.** a beat of the heart; heartbeat. **2.** *Informal.* a pleasant emotion. **3.** *Informal.* a sweetheart.

heart-to-heart (härt′tə härt′) *adj.* frank; sincere; candid: *a heart-to-heart talk.* —*n. Informal.* a frank conversation.

heart·warm·ing (härt′-wôr′ming) *adj.* causing or characterized by warm, tender, and pleasant feelings: *a heartwarming reunion of childhood friends.*

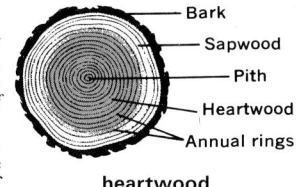

— Bark
— Sapwood
— Pith
— Heartwood
— Annual rings

heartwood

heart·wood (härt′wùd′) *n.* the central portion of the wood of a tree, composed of nonliving cells and usually harder and darker than the surrounding sapwood. Also, **duramen.**

heart·worm (härt′wûrm′) *n.* a parasitic roundworm, *Dirofilaria immitis,* infesting the bloodstream and heart of dogs and transmitted by mosquitoes.

heart·y (här′tē) *adj.,* **heart·i·er, heart·i·est. 1.** full of affection, warmth, or kindness; cordial; friendly: *a hearty welcome.* **2.** full of vigor or enthusiasm; unrestrained: *a hearty laugh.* **3.** of sound health; strong and well. **4.** satisfying to the appetite; full; nourishing: *a hearty meal.* **5.** requiring or using abundant nourishment: *a hearty appetite.* —*n., pl.* **heart·ies.** a bold, good fellow or comrade, esp. a sailor. [HEART + -Y[1].] —**heart′i·ness,** *n.*

heat (hēt) *n.* **1.** the state or quality of being hot. **2.** the degree of hotness; temperature. **3.** great warmth; high temperature: *The heat in the room is stifling.* **4.** the sensation or perception of hotness or warmth: *He felt the heat of the fire on his face.* **5.** warmth provided, as for a house, by any of various heating mechanisms: *She turned on the heat as soon as she got home.* **6.** hot weather or climate: *It's very difficult to work in this heat.* **7.** the most intense or violent stage; point of greatest activity: *in the heat of the battle.* **8.** intensity of feeling, esp. of anger or excitement. **9.** an indication of high temperature, as by the color of a body or object. **10.** *Physics.* a form of energy represented by the random motion of molecules, atoms, or smaller particles of a body. It is transferred from body to body by contact, by convection, or by infrared radiation. **11.** the period during which female animals are able to conceive; estrus: *a cat in heat.* **12.a.** a single trial or effort in a contest, as a race, used to determine the contestants who will compete in the final. **b.** a single division of a harness race. **13.a.** a single heating operation, as of iron, in a furnace. **b.** a material so heated. **14.** *Informal.* great pressure: *The heat was on to get the road paved before winter.* **15.** spicy, sharp flavor. **16.** *Slang.* the police. —*v.t., v.i.* **1.** to make or become hot or warm. **2.** to make or become excited. [Old English *hǣtu* great warmth, warmth of feeling.]

  ·**to heat up.** to grow livelier, stronger, or more excited.

heat barrier, thermal barrier.

heat·ed (hē′tid) *adj.* very angry or excited: *a heated argument.* —**heat′ed·ly,** *adv.* —**heat′ed·ness,** *n.*

heat engine, a mechanism that changes heat energy into mechanical energy, as a steam engine or internal-combustion engine.

heat·er (hē′tər) *n.* **1.** an apparatus that produces or gives heat or warmth. **2.** *Slang.* a pistol.

heat exchanger, in a heating or cooling system, a device that transfers heat from one fluid or gas to another, as in a condenser or furnace. For illustration, see **solar.**

heat exhaustion, a condition in which the body loses excessive amounts of fluids due to long exposure to high temperatures. It is characterized by low blood pressure, low body temperature, clammy skin, and faintness or unconsciousness. Also, **heat prostration.**

heath (hēth) *n.* **1.a.** an open wasteland overgrown with heather or low bushes; moor. **b.** a shrub or shrubs growing upon such land. **2.** any of a large group of plants of the genus *Erica,* or of

the family Ericaceae, including ornamentals, such as the rhododendron, azalea, and heather, and plants cultivated for their fruit, such as the cranberry and blueberry. [Old English *hǣth* open wasteland, plants growing on it.]

hea·then (hē′thən) *n., pl.* **-thens** or **-then. 1.** a person who does not believe in the God of the Bible; a person who is not a Christian, Jew, or Muslim. **2.** any irreligious, uncivilized, or uncultured person. —*adj.* **1.** of or relating to heathens; pagan. **2.** irreligious, uncivilized, or uncultured. [Old English *hǣthen* pagan; originally, dweller on a heath, from *hǣth* open wasteland; referring to the first converts to Christianity, who were city dwellers, while the inhabitants of remote rural areas were then pagan.] —**hea′then·ism,** *n.* —**hea′then·ness,** *n.* —For Synonyms *(n.),* see **pagan.**

hea·then·dom (hē′thən dəm) *n.* **1.** heathen practices or beliefs; paganism. **2.** heathen countries or people.

hea·then·ish (hē′thə nish) *adj.* **1.** of or relating to heathens. **2.** characteristic of heathens; barbarous. —**hea′then·ish·ly,** *adv.*

heath·er (heth′ər) *n.* **1.** the small, usually purple or pink bell-shaped flower of a shrub, *Calluna vulgaris,* of the heath family, growing in dense clusters. **2.** the low, evergreen shrub bearing this flower, having small, scalelike leaves. It grows wild and is particularly abundant in Scotland. [Of uncertain origin.]

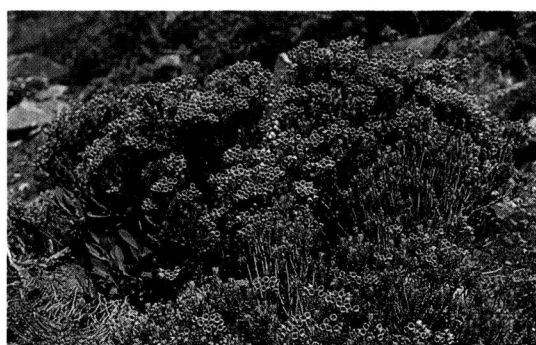

mountain **heather**

heath·er·y (heth′ə rē) *adj.* **1.** of or resembling heather. **2.** covered with heather.

heating pad, a pad fitted with electrical wires that heat up, applied to a part of the body to relieve pain or other ailment.

heat lightning, flashes of lightning occurring too far away for the thunder to be heard, seen near the horizon, esp. on summer evenings.

heat prostration, heat exhaustion.

heat pump, a device that heats a building by transferring heat from one location to another by means of a pressurized refrigerant. The heat used may be extracted from the ground, a pond of water, or some other outside source.

heat rash, an acute inflammation of the sweat glands, characterized by small, white or red skin eruptions and usually accompanied by intense itching and a prickling or tingling sensation. Also, **prickly heat.**

heat shield, a covering on a spacecraft designed to protect it against the intense heat caused by the friction of reentry into the earth's atmosphere.

heat·stroke (hēt′strōk′) *n.* an illness caused by exposure to high temperatures, characterized by high fever, rapid pulse, and weakness or unconsciousness.

heat wave, a period of extremely hot weather.

heave (hēv) *v.,* **heaved** or *(nautical)* **hove, heav·ing.** —*v.t.* **1.** to lift or raise with force or effort: *We heaved bales of hay onto the truck.* **2.** to throw, esp. with great effort: *We heaved rocks into a ravine as we cleared the land.* **3.** to utter or emit with much effort or pain: *to heave a sigh of relief.* **4.** to cause to rise or swell. **5.** *Nautical.* **a.** to raise or haul up, as an anchor. **b.** to pull, raise, or haul with or as if with a rope or cable. —*v.i.* **1.** to rise and fall

H

a	at	e	end	o	hot	u	up	hw	white	⎧	about
ā	ape	ē	me	ō	old	ū	use	ng	song		taken
ä	far	i	it	ô	fork	ü	rule	th	thin	ə	pencil
âr	care	ī	ice	oi	oil	ù	pull	th	this		lemon
		îr	pierce	ou	out	ûr	turn	zh	measure	⎩	circus

continuously in a rhythmic manner: *The ship heaved with the waves.* **2.** to rise and swell; bulge: *The runner's chest heaved with every breath.* **3.** to retch; vomit. **4.** *Nautical.* **a.** to pull, haul, or push with force or effort, as on a capstan or rope. **b.** (of a ship) to move or proceed in some direction. —*n.* **1.** the act or effort of heaving. **2. heaves.** a chronic, respiratory disease of horses. ➡ used as singular. —*interj.* **heave ho.** pull or push hard together. [Old English *hebban* to lift.] —**heav′er,** *n.*
· **to heave in** (or **into**) **sight.** to come into view over the horizon, as a ship.
· **to heave to.** to bring (a ship) to a standstill; make (a ship) lie to.

heav·en (hev′ən) *n.* **1.** *also,* **Heav·en.** in Christian theology, the abode of God, the angels, and those who are saved. **2. Heaven.** God. **3.** *also,* **heavens.** the space above and around the earth; firmament; sky. **4.** a happy, pleasing, or beautiful place. **5.** a state of bliss or supreme happiness. [Old English *heofon.*]
· **to move heaven and earth.** to do all that one possibly can.

heav·en·ly (hev′ən lē) *adj.* **1.** of, belonging to, or in heaven; divine; holy. **2.** of, relating to, or in the sky: *The sun and moon are heavenly bodies.* **3.** fit for or characteristic of heaven; happy, pleasing, or beautiful. —**heav′en·li·ness,** *n.*

heav·en·ward (hev′ən wərd) *adv.* toward heaven. Also, **heav·en·wards.** —*adj.* directed toward heaven.

heav·i·er-than-air (hev′ē ər thən âr′) *adj.* having a weight that is greater than that of air, as an airplane.

heavier-than-air craft, an aircraft that flies because of aerodynamic forces acting on its wings, tail, or rotor.

heav·i·ly (hev′ə lē) *adv.* **1.** with great weight or burden: *The moving van was heavily loaded with furniture.* **2.** in a dense manner; thickly: *a heavily populated area.* **3.** slowly, clumsily, or laboriously: *to walk heavily.* **4.** to a great or excessive degree: *The poor peasants were heavily taxed. It snowed heavily last night.*

heav·i·ness (hev′ē nis) *n.* the state or quality of being heavy.

Heav·i·side layer (hev′ē sīd′) the highly ionized second layer of the ionosphere, 60 to 75 miles (97 to 121 kilometers) above the earth's surface. Certain radio waves can be transmitted by repeated bouncing between the earth and this layer. Also, **Kennelly-Heaviside layer.** [From Oliver *Heaviside,* 1850-1925, English physicist.]

heav·y (hev′ē) *adj.,* **heav·i·er, heav·i·est. 1.** hard to lift or move; of great weight: *The furniture was very heavy.* **2.** having more than the usual weight: *heavy paper, heavy wool.* **3.** of an unusually large amount, size, volume, or quantity: *a heavy rainfall, heavy traffic, heavy casualties.* **4.** having much weight in proportion to size; of great specific gravity: *a heavy metal.* **5.** of great force, intensity, momentum, or impact: *a heavy blow.* **6.** acting or indulging on a large scale or to an excessive degree: *a heavy investor, a heavy drinker.* **7.** hard to bear or endure; oppressive; severe: *The judge imposed a heavy sentence on the defendant.* **8.** hard to do, accomplish, or deal with: *heavy labors, heavy debts.* **9.** causing sorrow; sad; grievous: *heavy news.* **10.** expressing or feeling grief; sorrowful; despondent: *a heavy heart.* **11.** of great importance; serious: *a heavy responsibility.* **12.** profound or intense: *heavy music, heavy thoughts.* **13.** not lively or interesting; ponderous; dull: *a heavy style of writing.* **14.** weighted down; laden; burdened: *trees heavy with fruit.* **15.** broad, thick, or coarse: *to draw a heavy line.* **16.** strong or lingering: *a heavy odor.* **17.** considerable or pronounced: *a heavy accent.* **18.** acting or moving slowly, clumsily, or with difficulty: *a heavy gait.* **19.** overcast; gloomy. **20.** loud and deep; resounding. **21.** not having leavened or risen properly, as bread. **22.** (of food) not easily digestible. **23.** hindering passage or progress: *heavy underbrush.* **24.** in a theatrical presentation, designating a role that is tragic, serious, or villainous. **25.** pregnant: *heavy with child.* **26.** (of an isotope) having a greater atomic weight than other isotopes of the same element. **27.** *Military.* **a.** of large size; massive: *heavy guns.* **b.** heavily armed or equipped: *heavy cavalry.* **28.** designating any industry that uses massive equipment to produce or process materials, such as oil or steel, that are basic to other industries. **29.** *Slang.* profound; important. —*n., pl.* **heav·ies. 1.** a tragic, serious, or villainous role in a theatrical presentation. **2.** an actor portraying such a role. —*adv.* heavily. [Old English *hefig* of great weight, important, oppressive, grievous.]
· **to hang heavy.** to pass slowly and tediously, as time.

Synonyms *adj.* **Heavy, weighty,** and **ponderous** mean having great weight. **Heavy** is used of anything greater in weight than its size would suggest, or than other things of the same type: *This chair is heavy! The truck carried a heavy load.* **Weighty** connotes actual, rather than relative, weight: *The bridge was supported by ten weighty girders.* **Ponderous** connotes weight and bulk that make something unwieldy: *It took four people to move the ponderous machine.*

heav·y-du·ty (hev′ē dü′tē, -dū′-) *adj.* designed, made, or constructed for sturdiness and durability: *The work clothes were made of heavy-duty material.*

heav·y-hand·ed (hev′ē han′did) *adj.* **1.** without grace or delicacy; clumsy; awkward. **2.** oppressive; cruel: *heavy-handed tyranny.* —**heav′y-hand′ed·ly,** *adv.* —**heav′y-hand′ed·ness,** *n.*

heav·y-heart·ed (hev′ē här′tid) *adj.* full of or showing sadness; melancholy; depressed. —**heav′y-heart′ed·ly,** *adv.* —**heav′y-heart′ed·ness,** *n.*

heavy hydrogen, deuterium.

heavy metal 1. a type of rock music with a heavy beat and highly amplified instruments, esp. electric guitars. **2.** any metal with a moderate to high atomic number, esp. one toxic to plant life, as lead, copper, or zinc.

heav·y-set (hev′ē set′) *adj.* having a solid, sturdy, and compact build.

heavy water, water whose molecules consist of atoms of deuterium and oxygen. It is used as a moderator in nuclear reactors. Formula: D_2O

heav·y·weight (hev′ē wāt′) *n.* **1.** a person or animal of much more than average weight. **2.** a boxer competing in the highest weight class of over 175 pounds (79 kilograms), or a competitor, as a wrestler, in a similar class. **3.** *Informal.* an influential, important, or intelligent person.

Heb., Hebrew; Hebrews.

heb·dom·a·dal (heb dom′ə dəl) *adj.* weekly. Also, **heb·dom·a·dar·y** (heb dom′ə der′ē). [Late Latin *hebdomadālis,* from Latin *hebdomas* seven, a week, from Greek *hebdomas.*] —**heb·dom′a·dal·ly,** *adv.*

He·be (hē′bē) *n.* in Greek mythology, the goddess of youth, cupbearer to the gods until replaced by Ganymede. [Latin *Hēbē,* from Greek *Hēbē,* from *hēbē* youth.]

He·bra·ic (hi brā′ik) *adj.* of, relating to, or characteristic of the Hebrews or their language or culture. [Late Latin *Hebrāicus,* from Greek *Hebraikos,* from *Hebraios* Jew, Jewish. See HEBREW.] —**He·bra′i·ca·ly,** *adv.*

He·bra·ism (hē′brā iz′əm, -brē-) *n.* **1.** a word or idiom peculiar to Hebrew. **2.** Hebrew character, thought, or practice.

He·bra·ist (hē′brā ist, -brē-) *n.* **1.** an expert in or a student of the Hebrew language, literature, and culture. **2.** an adherent of Hebrew thought, traditions, ethics, or religion.

He·bra·is·tic (hē′brā is′tik, -brē-) *adj.* of, relating to, or characteristic of Hebraism or Hebraists.

He·brew (hē′brü) *n.* **1.** a member of one of the Jewish tribes of ancient times. **2.** the language originally spoken by the ancient Jews, belonging to the Semitic group of the Semito-Hamitic family of languages. It is the religious language of Judaism. A modern form of Hebrew is the official language of Israel. For alphabet table, see **alphabet.** —*adj.* Hebraic. [Old French *hebreu,* from Late Latin *Hebraeus* Jew, Jewish, from Greek *Hebraios,* from Aramaic *ivray,* from Hebrew *ivri,* possibly literally meaning person from across (the Euphrates River); presumably because in the Bible Abraham, the first Hebrew, was from the farther side of the Euphrates.]

Words from Hebrew

Hebrew, the language of the Old Testament and the Jewish religion, is a Northern Semitic language. It is unrelated to Yiddish, a Germanic language that has borrowed many words from Hebrew. Modern Hebrew, an adaptation of ancient Hebrew, is the official language of Israel. Below are some of the loanwords that have entered English from or through Hebrew.

amen	hosanna	matzoh	schwa
bat mitzvah	jubilee	menorah	Seder
behemoth	Hanukkah	Messiah	seraph
bethel	Israel	mezuzah	shalom
brouhaha	kibbutz	rabbi	shekel
cabala	Knesset	Sabbath	shibboleth
cherub	kosher	sabra	shofar
dybbuk	leviathan	sack[1]	Torah
hallelujah	manna	Satan	yeshiva

Hebrew calendar, the calendar that begins with the assumed date of the Creation, 3761 B.C., and varies in the number of days per year from 353 to 385. It is used for dating Jewish religious observances and is the official calendar of Israel. Also, **Jewish calendar.**

He·brews (hē′brūz) *n.* a book of the New Testament, the Epistle to the Hebrews. ➡ used as singular.

Hec·a·te (hek′ə tē, hek′it) *n.* in Greek mythology, the goddess who had power over the moon, the earth, and the realm of the dead, and was also associated with sorcery.

hec·a·tomb (hek′ə tōm′, -tüm′) *n.* **1.** any great slaughter or sacrifice. **2.** in ancient Greece and Rome, a public sacrifice of 100 oxen or other animals at one time. [Latin *hecatombē,* from Greek *hekatombē,* from *hekaton* hundred + *bous* ox.]

heck·le (hek′əl) *v.t.,* **-led, -ling.** to harass and annoy (a speaker) with questions, taunts, and gibes. [Form of HACKLE[1]; referring to the teasing of flax with a comb.] —**heck′ler,** *n.*

hect-, form of **hecto-** before vowels, as in *hectare.*

hec·tare (hek′târ) *n.* a metric measure of area equal to 10,000 square meters. [French *hectare* literally, 100 ares, from Greek *hekaton* hundred + French *are.* See ARE[2].]

hec·tic (hek′tik) *adj.* **1.** characterized by great excitement, agitation, haste, and activity: *a hectic day.* **2.** *Medicine.* relating to or having a daily recurrent fever, as in tuberculosis or septicemia. **3.** feverish. [Late Latin *hectica (febris)* continuous (fever), from Greek *hektikos (pyretos)* continuous or consumptive (fever), from *hexis* condition of the body.] —**hec′ti·cal·ly,** *adv.* —**hec′tic·ness,** *n.*

hecto- *combining form* hundred: *hectometer.* [French *hecto-,* from Greek *hekaton.*]

hec·to·gram (hek′tə gram′) *also, British,* **hec·to·gramme.** *n.* a metric measure of weight equal to 100 grams.

hec·to·graph (hek′tə graf′) *n.* a duplicating machine in which the ink impression from an original copy is transferred onto a gelatin-coated surface from which other copies may be made. —*v.t.* to make copies of with a hectograph. —**hec′to·graph′ic,** *adj.* —**hec′to·graph′i·cal·ly,** *adv.*

hec·to·li·ter (hek′tə lē′tər) *also, British,* **hec·to·li·tre.** *n.* a metric measure of capacity equal to 100 liters.

hec·to·me·ter (hek′tə mē′tər) *also, British,* **hec·to·me·tre.** *n.* a metric measure of length equal to 100 meters.

hec·tor (hek′tər) *v.t., v.i.* to threaten or bully. —*n.* a brawling, swaggering fellow; bully. [From HECTOR.]

Hec·tor (hek′tər) *n.* in Greek legend, the eldest son of King Priam of Troy, killed by Achilles. [Latin *Hector,* from Greek *Hektōr,* from *hektōr* holding fast.]

Hec·u·ba (hek′yə bə) *n.* in Greek legend, the wife of King Priam of Troy and mother of Hector, Paris, Troilus, and Cassandra.

he'd (hēd; *unstressed* ēd) *contr.* **1.** he had. **2.** he would.

hedge (hej) *n.* **1.** a row of shrubs or small trees planted close together, forming a fence or barrier. **2.** any barrier or boundary. **3.** an act or means of protecting oneself against loss or risk. —*v.,* **hedged, hedg·ing.** —*v.t.* **1.** to surround, enclose, or separate with a hedge. **2.** to protect oneself from losing money on (a bet or investment) by making another bet or investment that would compensate for any possible loss on the first. **3.** to surround as with a barrier so as to hinder or obstruct free movement. —*v.i.* **1.** to avoid giving a direct answer or committing oneself: *to hedge on a question.* **2.** to protect oneself from losing money on a bet or investment by making another bet or investment that would compensate for any possible loss on the first. [Old English *hecg* row of bushes planted as a boundary.] —**hedg′er,** *n.*

hedge·hog (hej′hôg′, -hog′) *n.* **1.** any of various insect-eating mammals, family Erinaceidae, having a pointed snout and a thick mass of sharp, hard spines. When frightened or attacked, it rolls up into a tight ball with only its spines exposed. Length: 1 foot (0.3 meter). **2.** porcupine.

hedgehog

hedge·hop (hej′hop′) *v.i.,* **-hopped, -hop·ping.** to fly close to the ground, rising over obstacles as they occur. —**hedge′hop′per,** *n.*

hedge·row (hej′rō′) *n.* a row of shrubs or small trees planted close together, forming a fence or barrier; hedge.

he·don·ism (hē′də niz′əm) *n.* **1.** the theory that pleasure is the highest good. **2.** the pursuit of pleasure as a way of life. [Greek *hēdonē* pleasure + -ISM.]

he·don·ist (hē′də nist) *n.* a person who advocates or practices hedonism. —**he·don·is′tic,** *adj.* —**he·don·is′ti·cal·ly,** *adv.*

hee·bie-jee·bies (hē′bē jē′bēz) *pl. n. Informal.* a fit of nervousness; jitters. [Coined by the American comic-strip cartoonist Billy De Beck, 1890-1942.]

heed (hēd) *v.t.* to pay careful attention to; mind. —*v.i.* to pay careful attention; listen. —*n.* careful attention; notice: *The children paid no heed to our warnings.* [Old English *hēdan* to take notice.] —**heed′er,** *n.*

heed·ful (hēd′fəl) *adj.* giving or taking heed; attentive; mindful. —**heed′ful·ly,** *adv.* —**heed′ful·ness,** *n.*

heed·less (hēd′lis) *adj.* not attentive; unmindful. —**heed′less·ly,** *adv.* —**heed′less·ness,** *n.*

hee·haw (hē′hô′) *n.* **1.** the braying sound made by a donkey. **2.** a loud, rude laugh. —*v.i.* **1.** to bray. **2.** to laugh in a loud, rude manner. [Imitative.]

heel[1] (hēl) *n.* **1.** the rounded, projecting rear part of the human foot, below the ankle. **2.** a corresponding part of the hind leg of an animal. **3.** the fleshy, rounded part of the palm of the hand, near the wrist. **4.** the part of a stocking, shoe, or other piece of footwear that covers the heel. **5.** the thick, built-up part of a shoe or boot that is under or raises the heel: *Certain shoe styles have low heels.* **6.** anything resembling the human heel in shape, function, or position. **7.** *Informal.* a low or hateful person. —*v.t.* **1.** to furnish with a heel or heels: *to heel a shoe.* **2.** to follow (something or someone) closely. —*v.i.* to follow closely: *to teach a dog to heel.* [Old English *hēla* rear part of the human foot.] —**heel′less,** *adj.*

• **down at the heel** (or **heels**). poor or shabby.
• **on** (or **upon**) **the heels of.** close behind or immediately after.
• **to kick up one's heels.** to enjoy oneself; have fun.
• **to take to one's heels.** to run away; flee.

heel[2] (hēl) *v.t., v.i.* to lean or cause to lean to one side, as a ship or boat. —*n.* the act of heeling; list. [Modification of obsolete *heeld, hield* to lean, from Old English *hildan.*]

heel·er (hē′lər) *n.* **1.** a person who heels shoes. **2.** ward heeler.

heel·tap (hēl′tap′) *n.* **1.** the lift of a shoe. **2.** a small amount of liquor left in a glass after drinking.

heft (heft) *Informal. v.t.* **1.** to test the weight of by lifting. **2.** to lift up; heave: *The movers hefted the sofa onto the truck.* —*n.* **1.** weight; heaviness. **2.** the greater part; bulk. [From HEAVE.]

heft·y (hef′tē) *adj.,* **heft·i·er, heft·i·est.** *Informal.* **1.** big and strong; muscular. **2.** heavy; weighty. [HEFT + -Y[1].] —**heft′i·ly,** *adv.* —**heft′i·ness,** *n.*

he·gem·o·ny (hi jem′ə nē, hej′ə mō′-) *n., pl.* **-nies.** leadership or domination, esp. of one state over other independent states, as in a political union or geographic area. [Greek *hēgemoniā.*]

He·gi·ra (hi jīr′ə, hej′ər ə) *also,* **Hejira.** *n.* **1.** the flight of the Prophet Muhammad from Mecca to Medina in A.D. 622, marking the establishment of Islam. **2. hegira.** a sudden departure or flight, esp. from a dangerous or oppressive situation; exodus. [Arabic *hijrah* flight[2].]

heif·er (hef′ər) *n.* a young cow that has not borne a calf. [Old English *hēahfore.*]

heigh (hī, hā) *interj. Archaic.* used to attract attention, give encouragement, or express surprise or pleasure.

heigh-ho (hī′hō′, hā′-) *interj. Archaic.* used to express surprise, happiness, sadness, or weariness.

height (hīt) *n.* **1.** the distance or measurement from bottom to top: *The height of the statue is 11 feet.* **2.** the state or condition of being relatively tall or high: *Height is an advantage in playing basketball.* **3.** the distance above a given level, as the sea or horizon. **4.** *also,* **heights.** a high point or place: *The climbers scaled the heights.* **5.** greatest degree; culmination: *the height of fashion.* **6.** the highest point or part of something; summit. [Old English *hēahthu.*]

Synonyms Height, altitude, and elevation denote distance above some level. **Height** is the distance from the ground or floor to the top of something: *The building reaches a height of 250 feet.* **Altitude** applies to the vertical elevation of an object above a given level, esp. above the surface of the earth: *The balloon hovered over the city at an altitude of 500 feet.* **Elevation** is the measurement from sea level up to some point on the earth's surface: *The city is at an elevation of 750 feet.*

height·en (hī′tən) *v.t.* **1.** to make high or higher; increase the height of. **2.** to increase (something), as in amount, degree, or intensity. —*v.i.* **1.** to become high or higher. **2.** to increase, as in amount, degree, or intensity. —**height′en·er,** *n.*

Heim·lich maneuver (hīm′lik) a first-aid procedure for saving

a	at	e	end	o	hot	u	up	hw	white		about
ā	ape	ē	me	ō	old	ū	use	ng	song	ə	taken
ä	far	i	it	ô	fork	ü	rule	th	thin		pencil
âr	care	ī	ice	oi	oil	u̇	pull	th	this		lemon
		îr	pierce	ou	out	ûr	turn	zh	measure		circus

a person from choking on an object, such as a piece of food, trapped in the windpipe by the application of sudden upward pressure on the abdomen just below the rib cage. [From the American surgeon Henry J. *Heimlich,* born 1920, who devised the procedure.]

hei·nous (hā′nəs) *adj.* extremely wicked; atrocious; odious: *heinous crimes.* [Old French *haïneus,* from *haïne* hate, from *haïr* to hate; of Germanic origin.] —**hei′nous·ly,** *adv.* —**hei′nous·ness,** *n.*

heir (âr) *n.* **1.** a person who inherits or is entitled to inherit money, property, or a title after the death of the former owner. **2.** a person who inherits anything, as a tradition or trait. [Old French *(h)eir,* from Latin *hērēs.*] —**heir′ship,** *n.*

heir apparent *pl.* **heirs apparent.** a person who will become heir to a throne, title, or inheritance when an owner or ancestor dies.

heir·ess (âr′is) *n.* a woman who inherits or is entitled to inherit money, property, or the like.

heir·loom (âr′lüm′) *n.* a personal possession handed down, as in a family, from generation to generation. [HEIR + LOOM¹.]

heir presumptive *pl.* **heirs presumptive.** a person who will become heir to a throne, title, or inheritance if an heir more closely related to the ancestor is not born.

heist (hīst) *n. Slang.* an act or instance of stealing; larceny; robbery. —*v.t.* to rob or steal: *to heist a bank, to heist a million dollars.* [A form of HOIST.]

He·ji·ra (hi jī′rə, hej′ər ə) Hegira.

Hel (hel) *n.* **1.** in Teutonic mythology, the daughter of Loki and goddess of the underworld. **2.** the region of the underworld that she ruled, where those who died of sickness or old age, and not in battle, were sent.

held (held) a past tense and past participle of **hold¹.**

Helen of Troy in Greek legend, the very beautiful wife of King Menelaus. When she was carried off by Paris, the Greeks, in revenge, waged war against Troy.

hel·i·cal (hel′i kəl) *adj.* of, relating to, or having the form of a helix; spiral. —**hel′i·cal·ly,** *adv.*

hel·i·ces (hel′ə sēz′) a plural of **helix.**

hel·i·coid (hel′i koid) *n. Geometry.* a surface having the form of a coil or screw. —*adj.* arranged in or having the form of a flattened spring or spiral, as the shell of a snail. Also *(adj.),* **hel′i·coi′dal.** [Greek *helikoeidēs,* from *helix* spiral + *eidos* form, shape.]

hel·i·con (hel′i kon′, -kən) *n.* a very large tuba, carried over the shoulder, used esp. in marching bands.

hel·i·cop·ter (hel′i kop′tər, hē′lə-) *n.* an aircraft supported in the air by one or more power-driven rotors that rotate horizontally above the craft. —*v.i., v.t.* to fly or transport in a helicopter. [French *héicoptère,* from Greek *heliko-,* stem of *helix* spiral + *pteron* wing.]

helio- *combining form* of or relating to the sun: *heliocentric.* [Greek *hēlios* sun.]

he·li·o·cen·tric (hē′lē ō sen′trik) *adj.* **1.** of or relating to the modern or Copernican astronomic system, in which the earth and other planets move about the sun. **2.** having or regarding the sun as the center. ➡ opposed to **geocentric** in both defs. [HELIO- + CENTRIC.]

he·li·o·graph (hē′lē ə graf′) *n.* an instrument for signaling by means of mirrors that reflect light from the sun. The signal may be interrupted by a shutter to form a code, such as a telegraphic code. —*v.t.* to communicate or signal by means of a heliograph.

He·li·os (hē′lē os′) *n.* in Greek mythology, the god of the sun and father of Phaëthon. His Roman counterpart is Sol. [Greek *Hēlios,* from *hēlios* sun.]

he·li·o·stat (hē′lē ə stat′) *n.* an instrument consisting of a mirror that turns automatically at about half the speed of the rotation of the earth and reflects sunlight in a fixed direction, as through the fixed tube of a solar telescope.

he·li·o·ther·a·py (hē′lē ō ther′ə pē) *n.* the treatment of disease by means of sunlight.

he·li·o·trope (hē′lē ə trōp′, hēl′yə-) *n.* **1.** any of a group of plants and shrubs, genus *Heliotropium,* growing wild in warm regions of the world, bearing clusters of fragrant, tube-shaped, blue, pink, white, or purple flowers. **2.** a reddish purple color. **3.** bloodstone. —*adj.* having the color heliotrope. [Latin *hēliotropium* one of these plants, bloodstone, from Greek *hēliotropion,* from *hēlios* sun + *tropos* turning; referring to the turning of the plant toward the sun.]

he·li·ot·ro·pism (hē′lē ot′rə piz′əm) *n.* a type of phototropism that causes plants and certain other organisms to orient themselves with respect to sunlight. **Positive heliotropism** is a turning or moving toward the light. **Negative heliotropism** is a turning

positive **heliotropism**

or moving away from the light. [HELIO + Greek *tropos* turning + -ISM.] —**he·li·o·trop·ic** (hē′lē ə trop′ik, -trō′pik) *adj.*

hel·i·port (hel′ə pôrt′, hē′lə-) *n.* a place, as on the top of a building, for helicopters to take off and land.

he·li·um (hē′lē əm) *n.* an inert, extremely light, gaseous element with no color or odor, used esp. to give buoyancy to lighter-than-air craft and to dilute oxygen and other gases. Symbol: **He** For tables, see **element.** [Modern Latin *helium,* from Greek *hēlios* sun; referring to the initial discovery of helium in the spectrum of the sun.]

he·lix (hē′liks) *n., pl.* **he·lix·es** or **hel·i·ces.** **1.** anything spiral in shape. **2.** a three-dimensional curve lying along the surface of a cylinder or cone at a fixed angle. **3.** a curved fold of skin and cartilage forming the rim of the outer ear. **4.** a small, ornamental volute, as on a Corinthian or Ionic capital. [Latin *helix* spiral, from Greek *helix* spiral, anything twisted.]

hell (hel) *n.* **1.** *also,* **Hell.** in Christian theology, the abode of Satan and the fallen angels, where the wicked will be punished after death. **2.** in various religions, the abode of the dead; Hades. **3.** any place or condition of great evil, torment, or misery: *The prison was a hell on earth.* [Old English *hell.*]

he'll (hēl) *contr.* **1.** he will. **2.** he shall.

hell·bend·er (hel′ben′dər) *n.* a large, aquatic salamander, *Cryptobranchus alleganiensis,* having a flat body and a wide head, found in the south-central and eastern United States. Length: to 2 feet (0.6 meter).

hell-bent (hel′bent′) *adj. Informal.* stubbornly or recklessly determined to do or achieve something (with *on* or *for*).

hell·cat (hel′kat′) *n.* **1.** an evil, bad-tempered, or wrathful woman. **2.** witch.

Hel·le (hel′ē) *n.* in Greek legend, a young girl who, while fleeing on the ram with the Golden Fleece, fell into the Hellespont and drowned.

hel·le·bore (hel′ə bôr′) *n.* **1.** any of a group of thick-rooted poisonous plants, genus *Helleborus,* often cultivated for their large attractive flowers that grow at the ends of long stalks. **2.** any of various plants of the genus *Veratrum,* esp. *V. viride,* a tall poisonous plant. [Latin *(h)elleborus* the plant *(def. 1),* from Greek *helleboros.*]

Hel·lene (hel′ēn) *n.* Greek. [Greek *Hellēn* mythical ancestor of the Greeks.]

Hel·len·ic (he len′ik) *adj.* of or relating to Greece, esp. ancient Greece, its language, history, or culture before the time of Alexander the Great. —*n.* a subfamily of the Indo-European language family, to which Greek and its dialects, both ancient and modern, belong.

Hel·len·ism (hel′ə niz′əm) *n.* **1.** the culture of the ancient Greeks. **2.** in ancient times, the adoption or imitation of Greek culture: *the Hellenism of the Romans.* **3.** a word or idiom peculiar to the Greek language.

Hel·len·ist (hel′ə nist) *n.* **1.** a person who in ancient times adopted or imitated the culture of the Greeks. **2.** an expert in the study of ancient Greek language, literature, or culture.

Hel·len·is·tic (hel′ə nis′tik) *adj.* **1.** of or relating to the period in Greek or Near Eastern history after the death of Alexander the Great in 323 B.C. until the first century B.C. **2.** of, relating to, or having the characteristics of a style in the arts developed during the Hellenistic age. **3.** of or relating to Hellenists. —**Hel′le·nis′ti·cal·ly,** *adv.*

Hel·le·nize (hel′ə nīz′) *v.t., v.i.,* **-nized, -niz·ing.** to make or become Greek, as in customs, form, or character. —**Hel′le·ni·za′tion,** *n.*

hell·fire (hel′fīr′) *n.* the fire of, or punishment in, hell: *a sermon full of threats of hellfire and damnation.*

hell·gram·mite (hel′grə mīt′) *n.* the larva of the dobsonfly. [Of uncertain origin.]

hel·lion (hel′yən) *n.* a very devilish, rowdy, or troublesome person.

hell·ish (hel′ish) *adj.* **1.** of, like, relating to, or fit for hell; diabolical. **2.** *Informal.* very difficult or unpleasant. —**hell′ish·ly,** *adv.* —**hell′ish·ness,** *n.*

hel·lo (he lō′, hə-) *also,* **hullo.** *interj.* used to express greeting, attract attention, or indicate surprise. —*n., pl.* **-los.** the utterance of this interjection. —*v.i., v.t.,* **-loed, -lo·ing.** to say, call, or shout this, as to someone.

helm[1] (helm) *n.* **1.** the tiller, wheel, or entire steering apparatus of a ship. **2.** a position of control or authority; head: *to be at the helm of a company.* [Old English *helma* tiller[1].]

helm[2] (helm) *Archaic. n.* helmet. —*v.t.* to cover or furnish with a helmet. [Old English *helm* helmet.]

hel·met (hel′mit) *n.* any of various protective coverings for the head, as those worn by soldiers or participants in various sports. [Old French *helmet,* diminutive of *helme;* of Germanic origin.]

hel·minth (hel′minth) *n.* a parasitic worm, esp. one that invades the intestines. [Greek *helminth-,* stem of *helmins.*] —**hel·min′thic,** *adj.*

helms·man (helmz′mən) *n., pl.* **-men** (-mən). a person at the helm of a ship. Also, **steersman.**

hel·ot (hel′ət) *n.* **1.** *also,* **Helot.** one of a class of serfs in ancient Sparta. **2.** any serf. [Latin *Hēlōtes,* from Greek *Heilōtes,* plural of *Heilōs;* possibly from *Helos,* a town in Laconia whose inhabitants were enslaved by the Spartans.]

hel·ot·ism (hel′ə tiz′əm) *n.* **1.** the system of serfdom in ancient Sparta. **2.** any similar system. **3.** the condition of being a serf.

hel·ot·ry (hel′ə trē) *n.* **1.** helots as a class. **2.** helotism.

help (help) *v.,* **helped** or *(archaic)* **holp, helped** or *(archaic)* **hol·pen, help·ing.** —*v.t.* **1.** to provide with support, as in the performance of a task; be of service to: *He helped his sister paint the room.* ➡ also used elliptically with a preposition or adverb: *She helped the old man up the stairs.* **2.** to enable (someone or something) to accomplish a goal or achieve a desired effect: *The coach's advice helped the team to win.* **3.** to provide with sustenance or relief, as in time of need or distress; succor: *The Red Cross helped the flood victims.* **4.** to promote or contribute to; further: *The new medication helped the patient's recovery.* **5.** to be useful or profitable to; be of advantage to: *It might help you if you read the book.* **6.** to improve or remedy: *Nothing really helped my sinus condition.* **7.** to prevent; stop: *I can't help her rudeness.* **8.** to refrain from; avoid: *I couldn't help smiling when I heard the story.* **9.** to wait on or serve (often with *to*): *The clerk helped us. The hostess helped him to the dessert.* —*v.i.* to provide support, as in the performance of a task; be of service. —*n.* **1.** the act of providing support, service, or sustenance. **2.** a source of support, service, or sustenance. **3.** a person or group of persons hired to work for another or others. **4.** a means of improving, remedying, or preventing. [Old English *helpan* to aid, succor, benefit.]

· **cannot help but.** cannot but.

· **so help me (God).** used as an oath of affirmation.

· **to help oneself to.** a. to take for oneself: *Please help yourselves to dessert.* b. to take or appropriate, esp. without permission: *The thieves helped themselves to all the jewels.*

· **to help out.** to provide support, aid, or service: *I helped out when they got behind schedule.*

| **Synonyms** | *v.t.* **Help, aid,** and **assist** mean to provide whatever is needed to accomplish something, or to |

make it easier to accomplish. **Help** is the most common term, and suggests supporting a particular end or responding to a need: *They helped us get our car out of the mud. I helped them with their chores so we could leave for the game more quickly.* **Aid** more strongly suggests responding to distress or difficulty: *Community organizations raised money to aid the flood victims.* **Assist** often connotes working with another in a secondary or subordinate role: *I assisted the accountant in getting the records together.*

help·er (hel′pər) *n.* a person or thing that provides support, as in the performance of a task.

help·ful (help′fəl) *adj.* giving or providing support or service; useful. —**help′ful·ly,** *adv.* —**help′ful·ness,** *n.*

help·ing (hel′ping) *n.* an individual portion of food.

helping verb, auxiliary verb.

help·less (help′lis) *adj.* **1.** unable to take care of oneself; dependent: *to be made helpless by an accident.* **2.** without power or strength: *We were helpless to do anything in that situation.* **3.** without a source of relief, support, or sustenance: *The family*

was left destitute and helpless. **4.** expressing confusion or bewilderment: *With a helpless look, the bystander shrugged and walked away.* —**help′less·ly,** *adv.* —**help′less·ness,** *n.*

help·mate (help′māt′) *n.* a companion and helper, esp. a spouse. Also, **help·meet** (help′mēt′).

hel·ter-skel·ter (hel′tər skel′tər) *adv.* in a hurried, confused, and disorderly manner: *The papers were thrown helter-skelter on the table.* —*adj.* hurried, confused, and disorderly: *a helter-skelter sort of person.* —*n.* hurried, confused, and disorderly activity. [Possibly rhyming expression based on obsolete *skelt* to hasten; of uncertain origin.]

helve (helv) *n.* a handle, as of an ax, hatchet, or hammer. [Old English *hielfe.*]

hem[1] (hem) *n.* **1.a.** that part of a garment or piece of cloth made by turning the unfinished edge back and fastening it down, usually by sewing: *She ripped the hem of her coat.* **b.** the edge formed by this: *The hem is uneven.* **2.** hemline *(def. 1).* —*v.t.,* **hemmed, hem·ming.** to turn back the unfinished edge of (a garment or piece of cloth) and fasten it down, usually by sewing. [Middle English *hem,* from Old English *hem, hemm* border of a piece of cloth, akin to Middle Low German *ham* fenced or walled off piece of land.]

· **to hem in** (or **about** or **around**). to be on all sides of; surround; enclose: *The valley was hemmed in by steep cliffs.*

hem[2] (hem) *n., interj.* a sound resembling the clearing of the throat, made to attract attention or to express hesitation, doubt, or embarrassment. —*v.i.,* **hemmed, hem·ming. 1.** to make this sound. **2.** to hesitate in speaking. [Imitative.]

· **to hem and haw.** to hesitate in speaking, esp. in order to avoid making a clear or definite statement.

hem-, form of **hemo-** used before a vowel, as in *hemagglutination.*

he·mag·glu·ti·na·tion (hē′mə glü′tə nā′shən, hem′ə-) *n.* the clumping together of red blood cells, caused by specific antibodies or certain viruses. [HEM- + AGGLUTINATION.]

he-man (hē′man′) *n., pl.* **-men** (-men′). *Informal.* a strong, virile man.

hemat-, form of **hemato-** used before a vowel, as in *hematoma.*

hem·a·tite (hē′mə tīt′, hem′ə-) *n.* a common mineral consisting mainly of ferric oxide and ranging in color from reddish brown to black. It is the principal ore of iron. Formula: Fe_2O_3 [Latin *haematītēs* bloodstone, from Greek *haimatītēs* bloodlike, from *haima* blood.]

hemato- *combining form* blood: *hematology.* [Greek *haimatos,* genitive of *haima* blood.]

he·ma·tol·o·gy (hē′mə tol′ə jē, hem′ə-) *n.* the branch of medicine that deals with blood and blood-forming tissues, including the diagnosis and treatment of blood diseases. [HEMATO- + -LOGY.] —**he·ma·to·log·ic** (hē′mə tə loj′ik, hem′ə-); *also,* **he′ma·to·log′i·cal,** *adj.* —**he′ma·tol′o·gist,** *n.*

he·ma·to·ma (hē′mə tō′mə, hem′ə-) *n., pl.* **-mas** or **-ma·ta** (-mə tə). an accumulation of clotted or fluid blood in body tissues following a break in a blood vessel, as due to injury or disease.

heme (hēm) *n.* the nonprotein, iron-containing component in hemoglobin that binds with oxygen and gives blood its red color. [From *hematin* the hydroxide of heme.]

hemi- *prefix* half: *hemisphere.* [Greek *hēmi-.*]

hem·i·chor·date (hem′i kôr′dāt) *n.* any of a group of wormlike marine animals, phylum Hemichordata, having a vestigial notochord and pharynx with gill slits. [HEMI- + CHORDATE.]

hem·i·mor·phite (hem′i môr′fīt) *n.* a lustrous, transparent to translucent mineral consisting of zinc silicate. It is an important ore of zinc. Formula: $Zn_4Si_2O_7(OH)_2H_2O$ Also, **calamine.** [HEMI- + Greek *morphē* form, shape + -ITE[1].]

he·mip·ter·an (hi mip′tər ən) *n.* bug *(def. 1).* —*adj.* hemipterous. [Modern Latin *Hemiptera* (from HEMI- + Greek *pteron* wing) + -AN.]

he·mip·ter·ous (hi mip′tər əs) *adj.* of or belonging to an order, Hemiptera, of insects that have beaklike sucking mouthparts and forewings that are leathery near the body and membranous near the tip. [Modern Latin *Hemiptera* (from HEMI- + Greek *pteron* wing) + -OUS.]

hem·i·sphere (hem′i sfīr′) *n.* **1.** one half of the earth, as divided by the equator or the prime meridian. The equator divides the earth into the Northern and Southern hemispheres; the prime meridian divides it into the Eastern and Western hemispheres. **2.** one half of a sphere formed by a plane passing through the center of the sphere. **3.** either of the lateral halves of the cerebrum.

a	at	e	end	o	hot	u	up	hw	white	⟨	about
ā	ape	ē	me	ō	old	ū	use	ng	song		taken
ä	far	i	it	ô	fork	ü	rule	th	thin	ə	pencil
âr	care	ī	ice	oi	oil	u̇	pull	th	this		lemon
		îr	pierce	ou	out	ûr	turn	zh	measure	⟨	circus

H

[Latin *hēmisphaerium* a half globe, from Greek *hēmisphairion,* from *hēmi-* half + *sphaira* ball, sphere.] —**hem·i·spher·ic** (hem′i sfer′ik), **hem′i·spher′i·cal,** *adj.*

hem·i·stich (hem′i stik′) *n.* **1.** half of a line of verse, esp. as divided by a caesura. **2.** a line of verse that is incomplete or has less than the usual length. [Latin *hēmistichium* a half verse, from Greek *hēmistichion,* from *hēmi-* half + *stichos* row, verse.]

hem·line (hem′līn′) *n.* the length of a garment as measured from the ground: *a slip with a 21-inch hemline.* **2.** hem[1] *(def. 1b).*

hem·lock (hem′lok′) *n.* **1.a.** any of a group of tall evergreen trees, genus *Tsuga,* of the pine family, found in North America and Asia, having a pyramidal shape, reddish bark, and flat, blunt needles. One of the best-known species in the United States is the eastern hemlock, *T. canadensis,* whose bark yields tannin. **b.** the soft, coarse-grained wood of this tree. **2.a.** a poisonous plant, *Conium maculatum,* of the parsley family, found in Europe, Asia, and the Americas, having speckled, hollow stems with many branches, finely divided leaves, and clusters of white flowers. **b.** the poison prepared from this plant. [Old English *hemlic* the poisonous plant.]

hemo- *combining form* blood: *hemoglobin.* [Greek *haima* blood.]

he·mo·glo·bin (hē′mə glō′bin, hem′ə-) *n.* the iron-bearing protein matter contained in red blood cells that carries oxygen from the lungs to the body tissues and carbon dioxide from the body tissues to the lungs. [Earlier *haematoglobulin,* from Greek *haimat-,* stem of *haima* blood + Latin *globulus,* diminutive of *globus* ball + -IN[1].]

he·mol·y·sis (hi mol′ə sis) *n.* the destruction of red blood cells, accompanied by release of hemoglobin into the surrounding fluid. [HEMO- + Greek *lysis* a releasing, dissolution (from *lyein* to dissolve).] —**he·mo·lyt·ic** (hē′mə lit′ik, hem′ə-), *adj.*

he·mo·phil·i·a (hē′mə fil′ē ə, -fēl′yə, hem′ə-) *n.* a hereditary, sex-linked disease, usually only appearing in males, that prevents blood from clotting normally, so that a small injury may result in profuse internal or external bleeding. [Modern Latin *haemophilia,* from Greek *haima* blood + *philiā* fondness for, tendency to.]

he·mo·phil·i·ac (hē′mə fil′ē ak′, -fē′lē ak′, hem′ə-) *n.* a person who has hemophilia.

hem·or·rhage (hem′ər ij, hem′rij) *n.* a discharge of blood, esp. one that is severe. —*v.i.,* **-rhaged, -rhag·ing.** to bleed profusely or uncontrollably. [French *hémorrhagie,* from Latin *haemorrhagia* severe bleeding, from Greek *haimorrhagiā,* from *haima* blood + *rhēgnȳnai* to burst.] —**hem·or·rhag·ic** (hem′ə raj′ik), *adj.*

hem·or·rhoids (hem′ə roidz′, hem′roidz) *pl. n.* enlarged veins on or within the lower part of the rectum. Also, **piles.** [Latin *haemorrhoidae,* from Greek *haimorrhoides,* plural of *haimorrhois* liable to discharge blood, from *haima* blood + *rhein* to flow.] —**hem′or·rhoid′al,** *adj.*

he·mo·stat (hē′mə stat′, hem′ə-) *n.* any agent or device that arrests the flow of blood, as a clamp used on blood vessels in surgery.

he·mo·stat·ic (hē′mə stat′ik, hem′ə-) *adj.* acting to check the flow of blood. —*n.* a drug that checks bleeding by shortening the clotting time of blood.

hemp (hemp) *n.* **1.** a strong, durable fiber used chiefly to make rope and twine, obtained from the stem of a tall plant, *Cannabis sativa.* **2.** the plant from which this fiber and the drugs marijuana and hashish are obtained, cultivated in Asia, Europe, and the United States, having a hollow, thin stem and large leaves. Also, **marijuana. 3.** any of the drugs obtained from this plant. [Old English *henep* this plant.]

hemp·en (hem′pən) *adj.* made of or like hemp.

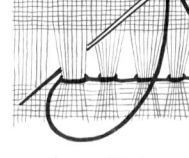

hemstitch

hem·stitch (hem′stich′) *v.t.* to stitch across an area of cloth from which cross threads have been removed, gathering several of the remaining threads at a time into small bundles. —*n.* **1.** ornamental needlework that has been hemstitched, often used to decorate borders and hems. Also, **hem′stitch′ing. 2.** a single stitch made by hemstitching.

hen (hen) *n.* **1.** the mature female of the domestic fowl. **2.** the female of other birds, esp. of gallinaceous birds. **3.** the female of the lobster and various fish. [Old English *henn* female domestic fowl.]

hen·bane (hen′bān′) *n.* any of a small group of poisonous, foul-smelling plants, genus *Hyoscyamus,* of the nightshade family, found in Mediterranean regions and in eastern North America, bearing hairy leaves and clusters of funnel-shaped yellow flowers marked with purple veins. [HEN + BANE; because of its poisonous effect on fowl.]

hence (hens) *adv.* **1.** as a consequence or result of this fact or circumstance; therefore: *It is winter now, hence the days will be shorter.* **2.a.** from this time: *We plan to meet three weeks hence.* **b.** *Archaic.* from this time onward; henceforth. **3.** away from this place; from here: *not more than three miles hence.* [Middle English *hennes* away, from this place or time, going back to Old English *heonan.*]

hence·forth (hens′fôrth′, -fôrth′) *adv.* from this time on; from now on. Also, **hence′for′ward.**

hench·man (hench′mən) *n., pl.* **-men** (-mən). **1.** a willing partner in crime or misdeed: *The burglar was helped by two henchmen.* **2.** a trusted follower. **3.** a person who supports a political figure for his or her own personal gain. [Middle English *hensman* groom, squire, from Old English *hengest* horse + MAN.]

hen·e·quen (hen′ə kin) *also,* **hen·e·quin.** *n.* **1.** a strong fiber obtained from a Mexican agave, *Agave fourcroydis.* **2.** the plant itself. [Spanish *henequén;* probably of Taino origin.]

hen·house (hen′hous′) *n., pl.* **-hous·es** (-hou′ziz). a house, coop, or shelter for poultry. Also, **hen·coop** (hen′kūp′).

hen·na (hen′ə) *n.* **1.** an orange dye obtained from the dried leaves of a shrub, *Lawsonia inermis,* used for centuries in Asia and Africa to color various items as hair, fingernails, and fabrics, and used today chiefly in commercial hair rinses. **2.** the tall, slender shrub from whose leaves this dye is obtained. **3.** a reddish brown or copper color. —*v.t.,* **-naed, -na·ing.** to color or tint with henna. —*adj.* having the color henna. [Arabic *hinnā'* the shrub.]

hen·ner·y (hen′ə rē) *n., pl.* **-ner·ies.** a place where poultry is kept or raised.

hen party *Informal.* a party or gathering for women only.

hen·peck (hen′pek′) *v.t.* to domineer over (one's husband) by persistent nagging. —**hen′pecked′,** *adj.*

hen·ry (hen′rē) *n., pl.* **-rys** or **-ries.** *Physics.* the meter-kilogram-second unit of electromagnetic inductance in an electric circuit. One henry is the amount of inductance that produces an electromotive force of one volt when the current changes at the rate of one ampere per second. [From Joseph *Henry,* 1797-1878, U.S. physicist.]

hep (hep) *adj. Slang.* hip[3].

hep·a·rin (hep′ə rin) *n.* a compound present in the liver, lungs, and other tissues that prevents blood from clotting, used medically in the treatment of thrombosis. [Greek *hepar* liver + -IN[1].]

he·pat·ic (hi pat′ik) *adj.* **1.** of, relating to, or resembling the liver. **2.** acting on or affecting the liver. **3.** liver-colored. [Latin *hēpaticus,* from Greek *hēpatikos,* from *hēpar* liver.]

he·pat·i·ca (hi pat′i kə) *n.* any of a group of low-growing plants, genus *Hepatica,* of the crowfoot family, found in northern temperate regions of the world, bearing three- to five-lobed leaves and small purple, pink, blue, or white flowers. Also, **liverleaf.** [Medieval Latin *hepatica,* from feminine of Latin *hēpaticus* relating to the liver; because the shape of the leaf resembles that of the liver. See HEPATIC.]

hep·a·ti·tis (hep′ə tī′tis) *n.* an inflammation of the liver, usually caused by a virus, resulting in fever, weakness, and often jaundice. [Modern Latin *hepatitis,* from Greek *hēpar* liver + -ITIS.]

hep·cat (hep′kat′) *n. Slang.* a jazz musician or enthusiast, esp. of the 1930s or 1940s.

He·phaes·tus (hi fes′təs) *n.* in Greek mythology, the ugly and lame god of fire, who was a skilled blacksmith and workman for the other gods. His Roman counterpart is Vulcan.

Hep·ple·white (hep′əl hwīt′, -wīt′) *adj.* of or belonging to a style of furniture noted for subtle and gracefully proportioned curves, extensive use of satinwood, and much painted decoration: *a Hepplewhite chair.* —*n.* a piece of furniture in this style. [From George *Hepplewhite,* eighteenth-century English cabinetmaker, who designed this style of furniture.]

hept-, form of hepta- before vowels, as in *heptarchy.*

hepta- *combining form* seven: *heptagon.* [Greek *hepta.*]

hep·ta·gon (hep′tə gon′) *n.* a polygon with seven sides and seven angles. [Greek *heptagōnos* having seven angles, from *hepta* seven + *gōniā* angle.] —**hep·tag·o·nal** (hep-tag′ə nəl), *adj.*

hep·tam·e·ter (hep tam′i tər) *n.* a line of verse consisting of seven metrical feet, for example: *The ships/ that sailed/ across/ the sea/ have reached/ the dis/tant shore.* [HEPTA- + -METER.]

hep·tane (hep′tān) *n.* any of nine liquid hydrocarbons of the alkane, or paraffin, series, derived from petroleum and used as solvents or to test octane ratings. Formula: C_7H_{16} [HEPT- + -ANE.]

hep·tar·chy (hep′tär kē) *n., pl.* **-chies. 1.** government by seven rulers. **2.** *also,* **Heptarchy.** a group of seven kingdoms or states, each under its own ruler, esp. the seven principal kingdoms of England in the seventh and eighth centuries. [HEPT- + Greek *-archiā* rule.]

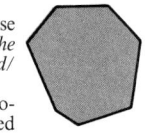

irregular **heptagon**

her (hûr; *unstressed* hər, ər) *pron.* the objective case of **she**: *He called her and offered her a ride.* —*adj.* (the possessive form of **she**) of, relating to, or belonging to her: *her fears, her piano, her accomplishments.* [Old English *hire.*] —For Usage Note, see **me.**

her. **1.** heraldic. **2.** heraldry.

He·ra (hîr′ə) *n.* in Greek mythology, the goddess of marriage and the protector of married women, who was the sister and wife of Zeus. Her Roman counterpart is Juno.

Her·a·cles (her′ə klēz′) *also,* **Her·a·kles.** *n.* Hercules.

her·ald (her′əld) *v.t.* to proclaim, indicate, or announce; usher in: *Trumpets heralded the hero's arrival.* —*n.* **1.** formerly, an officer who carried messages between princes or sovereign powers, announced royal or state proclamations, and arranged and supervised various state ceremonies and functions. **2.** a person who proclaims or announces; messenger. **3.** a person or thing that announces or indicates the approach of someone or something; harbinger: *The robin is a herald of spring.* **4.** an official in charge of heraldry who grants, records, and regulates the use of coats of arms, traces genealogies, and has the authority to settle certain questions of precedence and protocol. [Old French *herau(l)t* the royal officer; of Germanic origin.]

he·ral·dic (he ral′dik) *adj.* of or relating to heraldry or heralds.

her·ald·ry (her′əl drē) *n., pl.* **-ries.** **1.** the study and craft of describing and representing coats of arms, granting rights to bear certain coats of arms, tracing genealogies, and settling certain questions of precedence. **2.a.** a heraldic device or collection of such devices. **b.** a coat of arms; armorial bearings. **3.** heraldic ceremony or pomp.

herb (ûrb, hûrb) *n.* **1.a.** any plant or plant part valued for its flavor or odor or for making medicines. **b.** the leaves, stems, seeds, roots, or other plant parts themselves, often chopped and dried. **2.** any flowering plant that does not form a persistent, woody stem but instead dies down at the end of each growing season. [Old French *(h)erbe* grass, green vegetation used to feed animals, from Latin *herba* grass, green crops.] —**herb′y,** *adj.*

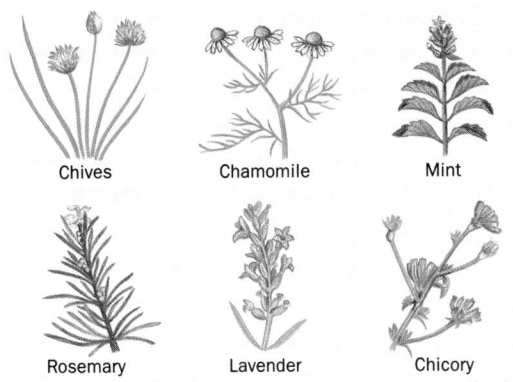

Chives Chamomile Mint
Rosemary Lavender Chicory

common **herbs**

her·ba·ceous (hûr bā′shəs, ûr-) *adj.* **1.** of, relating to, or of the nature of plants that do not develop a persistent, woody stem. **2.** having the texture and color of an ordinary leaf: *flowers with herbaceous petals.* [Latin *herbāceus* grassy, herblike, from *herba.* See HERB.]

herb·age (ûr′bij, hûr′-) *n.* **1.** soft-stemmed plants collectively, esp. when suitable for grazing. **2.** the green leaves and stems of herbaceous plants.

herb·al (hûr′bəl, ûr′-) *adj.* of, relating to, or made of herbs. —*n.* a book or treatise on herbs or plants, esp. one concerned with the medicinal properties of herbs or plants.

herb·al·ist (hûr′bə list, ûr′-) *n.* **1.** a dealer in herbs, esp. medicinal herbs. **2.** an expert in the study of herbs or plants.

her·bar·i·um (hûr bâr′ē əm, ûr-) *n., pl.* **-bar·i·ums** or **-bar·i·a** (-bâr′ē ə). **1.** a systematically arranged collection of dried plants. **2.** a room or building in which such a collection is kept. [Late Latin *herbārium* such a collection, from *herba.* See HERB.]

her·bi·cide (hûr′bi sīd′, ûr′-) *n.* any of a group of organic or inorganic chemical compounds used to kill plants. [HERB + -CIDE².] —**her′bi·ci′dal,** *adj.*

her·bi·vore (hûr′bə vôr′, ûr′-) *n.* an animal, esp. a mammal, that feeds chiefly on plants, as a cow or a kangaroo. [Modern Latin *Herbivora,* from *herbivorus.* See HERBIVOROUS.]

her·biv·o·rous (hûr biv′ər əs, ûr-) *adj.* feeding chiefly on grass or other plants. [Modern Latin *herbivorus* grass-eating, from Latin *herba* grass + *vorāre* to devour.]

her·cu·le·an (hûr′kyə lē′ən, hər kū′lē-) *adj.* **1.** requiring great strength or effort: *Clearing the land was a herculean task.* **2.** *also,* **Herculean.** like Hercules, esp. in strength or courage. **3.** **Herculean.** of or relating to Hercules: *the twelve Herculean labors.*

Her·cu·les (hûr′kyə lēz′) *n.* **1.** in classical legend, the son of Zeus and Alcmene, a hero celebrated for his exceptional strength and bravery. Also, **Heracles, Herakles. 2.** a constellation in the northern sky. [Latin *Herculēs* this hero, from Greek *Hēraklēs* literally, glory of Hera, from HERA + *kleos* glory.]

herd¹ (hûrd) *n.* **1.** a number of animals, esp. large mammals, as cattle, sheep, reindeer, or elephants, feeding, traveling, or being kept together. **2.** a large number of people; crowd: *a herd of job seekers.* **3. the herd.** the common people; masses; rabble. —*v.t.* **1.** to group (persons or animals) in or as in a herd: *They herded the cattle and drove them to market.* **2.** to lead or drive in or as in a herd: *The guide herded the tourists into the bus.* —*v.i.* to group or join together in or as in a herd. [Old English *heord* number of animals kept together, flock.]

herd² (hûrd) *n.* herdsman. —*v.t.* to take care of; tend: *to herd goats in the mountains.* [Middle English *herde* herdsman, shepherd, from Old English *hirde, hierde* shepherd; guardian.] —**herd′er,** *n.*

• **to ride herd on.** to keep close watch or control over: *to ride herd on new recruits.*

herds·man (hûrdz′mən) *n., pl.* **-men** (-mən). a person who owns, tends, or drives a herd. Also, **herd′er.**

here (hîr) *adv.* **1.** at or in this place: *I like it here.* ➡ also used to indicate or emphasize a specific person or thing being referred to: *this person here.* **2.** to or toward this place: *Bring the book here.* **3.** at this point, as in time, action, or thought: *Here the story ends. I suggest that we stop here and read the rest tomorrow.* **4.** now to be presented; as follows: *Here are my replies to your questions.* **5.** in the present life: *Both here and hence pursue me lasting strife . . .* (Shakespeare, *Hamlet*). —*n.* **1.** this place: *How can I get to your house from here?* **2.** this life: *the here and now.* —*interj.* used as an exclamation, as in answering a roll call, calling an animal, or attracting attention. [Old English *hēr* in this place, in this life, at this point, now.]

• **here and there.** in, to, or at various places: *The balloons were hung here and there.*
• **here goes.** here I go.
• **neither here nor there.** not pertinent or important.

here·a·bout (hîr′ə bout′) *also,* **here·a·bouts.** *adv.* about or near this place; in this vicinity.

here·af·ter (hîr′af′tər) *adv.* **1.** from now on; after this: *When you see them hereafter, be polite.* **2.** after the present life. —*n.* **the hereafter.** life after the present life; future life.

here·at (hîr at′) *adv.* when this took place; at this time.

here·by (hîr′bī′) *adv.* by virtue of this: *I hereby resign.*

he·red·i·ta·ble (hə red′i tə bəl) *adj.* heritable. —**he·red′i·ta·bil′i·ty,** *n.* —**he·red′i·ta·bly,** *adv.*

he·red·i·tar·y (hə red′i ter′ē) *adj.* **1.** transmitted or transmissible genetically from an animal, plant, or other living thing to its offspring. **2.** derived from a custom, belief, or prejudice held by ancestors or predecessors; inherited: *a hereditary custom.* **3.** of or relating to inheritance or heredity. **4.** *Law.* **a.** transmitted or transmissible from an ancestor to an heir according to rules of descent. **b.** holding title or possession by inheritance. [Latin *hērēditārius* relating to an inheritance, from *hērēditās* inheritance.] —**he·red′i·tar′i·ly** (hə red′i ter′ə lē, -red′i ter′-), *adv.* —**he·red′i·tar′i·ness,** *n.*

he·red·i·ty (hə red′i tē) *n., pl.* **-ties.** **1.** the process by which characteristics are transmitted genetically from an animal, plant, or other living thing to its offspring. **2.** all the characteristics so transmitted. [Latin *hērēditās* inheritance.]

Here·ford (hûr′fərd, her′ə-) *n.* any of a breed of beef cattle having a thick, curly, red coat, white face, and white body markings. Weight: to 2,200 pounds (998 kilograms). [From *Herefordshire,* English county where the breed was developed.]

here·in (hîr′in′) *adv.* in this place, matter, or circumstance; in this.

here·in·af·ter (hîr′in af′tər) *adv.* afterward in this document, statement, or narrative.

here·in·be·fore (hîr′in bi fôr′) *adv.* in a preceding part of this document, statement, or narrative.

a	at	e	end	o	hot	u	up	hw	white		about
ā	ape	ē	me	ō	old	ū	use	ng	song		taken
ä	far	i	it	ô	fork	ü	rule	th	thin	ə	pencil
âr	care	ī	ice	oi	oil	ù	pull	th	this		lemon
		îr	pierce	ou	out	ûr	turn	zh	measure		circus

H

here·in·to (hîr′in′tü) *adv.* into this place, matter, or circumstance; into this.

here·of (hîr′uv′, -ov′) *adv.* of or concerning this.

here·on (hîr′ôn′, -on′) *adv.* hereupon.

here's (hîrz) *contr.* here is.

her·e·sy (her′ə sē) *n., pl.* **-sies.** **1.a.** a religious belief or doctrine that is at variance with accepted church doctrine. **b.** any belief or doctrine at variance with accepted or established doctrine. **2.** the maintaining of such a belief or doctrine. [Old French *heresie* heretical religious belief or doctrine, going back to Latin *haeresis* sect, heretical religious doctrine, from Greek *hairesis* sect, choice.]

her·e·tic (her′ə tik) *n.* **1.** a person who maintains a religious belief or doctrine at variance with accepted church doctrine. **2.** a person who maintains any belief or doctrine at variance with accepted or established doctrine. [Old French *heretique* person holding heretical religious views, from Church Latin *haereticus,* from Greek *hairetikos* able to choose.]

he·ret·i·cal (hə ret′i kəl) *adj.* of, relating to, or characterized by heresy: *heretical beliefs, heretical movement.* **—he·ret′i·cal·ly,** *adv.*

here·to (hîr′tü′) *adv.* to this matter, subject, point, or place.

here·to·fore (hîr′tə fôr′) *adv.* before now; until this time.

here·un·der (hîr′un′dər) *adv.* **1.** under this. **2.** according to the authority of this.

here·un·to (hîr′un tü′) *adv.* to this matter, subject, point, or place; hereto.

here·up·on (hîr′ə pôn′, -pon′) *adv.* immediately following this.

here·with (hîr′with′, -with′) *adv.* **1.** along or together with this. **2.** by means of this; hereby.

her·it·a·ble (her′i tə bəl) *adj.* that can be inherited. Also, **hereditable.** **—her·it·a·bil′i·ty,** *n.*

her·it·age (her′i tij) *n.* **1.** something that is handed down from previous generations or from the past; tradition. **2.** the totality of property that has been or may be inherited by someone, including possessions or land. **3.** something that comes from the circumstances of birth; lot: *To earn bread by the sweat of the brow is the common heritage of the sons of Adam* (F. D. Maurice, 1874). [Old French *heritage* inheritance, from *heriter* to inherit, from Late Latin *hērēditāre,* from Latin *hērēs* heir.] **—For Synonyms, see** **tradition.**

her·maph·ro·dite (hûr maf′rə dīt′) *n.* **1.** an animal of a species that normally has both male and female reproductive organs in the same individual. Many species of worms are hermaphrodites. **2.** any individual born with reproductive organs of both sexes. **3.** hermaphrodite brig. **—adj.** hermaphroditic. [Latin *hermaphrodītus* person having the attributes of both sexes, from Greek *hermaphrodītos,* from *Hermaphrodītos* son of *Hermes* and *Aphrodite,* who, according to legend, became united in one body with a nymph.]

hermaphrodite brig, a two-masted ship with the foremast square-rigged and the mainmast fore-and-aft-rigged.

her·maph·ro·dit·ic (hûr maf′rə dit′ik) *adj.* of, relating to, or characteristic of a hermaphrodite. **—her·maph′ro·dit′i·cal·ly,** *adv.*

Her·mes (hûr′mēz) *n.* in Greek mythology, the god of science and invention, who was the swift messenger of the gods, usually pictured with winged sandals and a helmet. His Roman counterpart is Mercury.

her·met·ic (hûr met′ik) *adj.* **1.** made airtight, as by fusion: *a hermetic seal.* **2.** impervious to outward influence; sealed off. Also, **her·met′i·cal.** [Medieval Latin *hermeticus* relating to alchemy, relating to Hermes, from Greek *Hermēs* the god Hermes, who supposedly discovered the secrets of alchemy.] **—her·met′i·cal·ly,** *adv.*

Her·mi·o·ne (hûr mī′ə nē) *n.* in Greek legend, the daughter of Menelaus and Helen of Troy.

her·mit (hûr′mit) *n.* a person who lives a solitary, ascetic life, often from religious motives and in a place far removed from society; recluse. [Old French *(h)ermite,* from Late Latin *(h)e-rēmīta,* from Greek *erēmītēs* literally, dweller in a desert, from *erēmiā* desert. Doublet of EREMITE.] **—her·mit′ic,** *adj.* **—her′-mit·like′,** *adj.*

her·mit·age (hûr′mi tij) *n.* **1.** the habitation of a hermit. **2.** any solitary or secluded dwelling place.

hermit crab, any of a widespread group of soft-bodied, mostly ocean-dwelling crabs that occupy the empty shells of snails, whelks, and similar animals for protection. Length: to 18 inches (46 centimeters).

hermit thrush, a North American

Snail shell

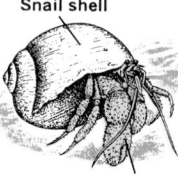

Hermit crab

thrush, *Hylocichla guttata,* having a brown body, white-and-brown spotted breast, and reddish tail, noted for its melodious song. Length: to 7½ inches (19 centimeters).

her·ni·a (hûr′nē ə) *n., pl.* **-ni·as** or **-ni·ae** (-nē ē′). **1.** a condition in which a part of an organ bulges out through the wall of its body cavity; rupture. **2.** the part bulging out. [Latin *hernia.*] **—her′-ni·al,** *adj.*

he·ro (hîr′ō) *n., pl.* **-roes. 1.** a person who is admired and looked up to for valor, achievements, and noble qualities. **2.** a person who performs a particularly courageous act, esp. an act that rescues or protects a person or animal. **3.** the principal male character in a story, play, or poem. **4.** in mythology and legend, a man, often descended from a god, having great strength and courage and the ability to perform superhuman feats. **5.** a sandwich consisting of a small loaf of bread filled with meat, cheese, and vegetables. [Latin *hērōs* man descended from a god, illustrious man, from Greek *hērōs.*]

He·ro (hîr′ō) *n.* in Greek legend, a priestess of Aphrodite whose lover, Leander, swam the Hellespont every night to visit her. One night he was drowned, and in her sorrow, Hero killed herself.

he·ro·ic (hi rō′ik) *adj.* **1.** of or appropriate to a hero; individually daring and courageous: *heroic deeds.* **2.** relating to or describing the deeds of heroes from myth and legend: *a heroic poem.* **3.** on a grand scale; large or impressive. **4.** involving boldness, courage, and risk, often as a last resort: *The doctors took heroic measures to save the victim's life.* Also, **he·ro′i·cal. —n. heroics. a.** melodramatic or extravagant language or actions. **b.** heroic verse. **—he·ro′i·cal·ly,** *adv.*

heroic couplet, two successive, rhyming lines of verse written in iambic pentameter, for example: *Let such teach others who themselves excel / And censure freely who have written well* (Alexander Pope, 1711).

heroic verse, any of several verse forms, adapted to the treatment of heroic or exalted themes. In English, German, and Italian it is iambic pentameter; in French, the Alexandrine; and in Greek and Latin, dactylic hexameter.

her·o·in (her′ō in) *n.* a white, crystalline, narcotic drug made from morphine. It is addictive and, if taken in overdose, may be fatal. [German *Heroin.*]

her·o·ine (her′ō in) *n.* **1.** a woman or girl admired for her valor, achievements, or noble qualities. **2.** a woman or girl who performs a difficult or courageous act, esp. an act that saves or protects a person or animal. **3.** the principal female character in a story, play, or poem. [Latin *hērōïne* woman descended from a god, illustrious woman, from Greek *hērōïnē,* feminine of *hērōs* person descended from a god, illustrious man.]

her·o·ism (her′ō iz′əm) *n.* **1.** the qualities of a hero; courage; fortitude. **2.** courageous conduct that saves or protects a person or animal.

her·on (her′ən) *n.* any of various wading birds, family Ardeidae, of temperate and tropical regions, having a long, slender neck, a long, pointed bill, and long, thin legs. Length: 1-6 feet (0.3-1.8 meters). [Old French *hairon;* of Germanic origin.]

her·on·ry (her′ən rē) *n., pl.* **-ries.** a place where herons congregate during the breeding season.

hero worship, immoderate or intense admiration or reverence for a hero or one who is thought of as a hero: *a teenager's hero worship of a movie star.*

her·pes sim·plex (hûr′pēz sim′pleks) a virus disease of the skin or mucous membranes, characterized by the formation and spreading of blisters. Cold sores are an example of herpes simplex. Also, **herpes.** [Modern Latin *herpes simplex,* from Latin *herpes* skin eruption that creeps and spreads, from Greek *herpēs* shingles, from *herpein* to creep + Latin *simplex* simple.]

herpes zos·ter (zos′tər) shingles. [Modern Latin *herpes zoster,* from Greek *herpēs* shingles + *zōstēr* belt; because the disease most commonly affects the area around the waist.]

her·pe·tol·o·gy (hûr′pi tol′ə jē) *n.* the branch of zoology that deals with reptiles and amphibians. [Greek *herpeton* reptile, from *herpein* to creep + -LOGY.] **—her′pe·tol′o·gist,** *n.*

Herr (heR) *n., pl.* **Her·ren** (heR′ən) or **Herrn** (heRn). a man; gentleman. ➡ the German title of respect and form of polite address for a man, equivalent to *Mr.* or *Sir.* [German.]

her·ring (her′ing) *n., pl.* **-ring** or **-rings.** any of a widespread group of bony, saltwater food fish, family Clupeidae, esp. the **Atlantic herring,** *Clupea harengus,* which grows to 12 inches (30 centimeters) in length. [Old English *hæring.*]

her·ring·bone (her′ing bōn′) *n.* a pattern of short lines slanting back from either side of a longer line, forming a series of arrow-

head designs resembling the spine of a herring. —*adj.* having or making this pattern.

herring gull, a common sea gull, *Larus argentatus,* with gray and white plumage and black-tipped wings, found throughout the Northern Hemisphere. Average length: 22 inches (56 centimeters).

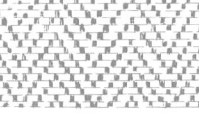

herringbone

hers (hûrz) *pron.* **1.** of, relating to, or belonging to her: *The blue sweater is hers.* ➤ used with *of* after a noun or pronoun: *a friend of hers, some of hers.* **2.** the one or ones that relate or belong to her: *His room was neat; hers was messy.* ➤ **Hers** is the absolute form of the possessive adjective **her,** used when no noun follows. It is used as singular or plural depending on the noun to which it refers.

her·self (hûr self′) *pron.* **1.** the emphatic form of **she** or **her:** *She herself was opposed to the idea.* **2.** the reflexive form of **her:** *She blamed herself.* **3.** her normal, average, or true self: *She has not been herself lately.*

hertz (hûrts) *n., pl.* **hertz.** the meter-kilogram-second unit for measuring the frequency of vibrations and waves, equal to one cycle per second.

Hertz·i·an wave (hûrt′sē ən) an electromagnetic wave, as a radio wave, produced by the acceleration or oscillation of an electric charge. [From Heinrich *Hertz,* 1857-94, German physicist who was the first to broadcast radio waves.]

he's (hēz; *unstressed* ēz) *contr.* **1.** he is. **2.** he has.

hes·i·tan·cy (hez′i tən sē) *n., pl.* **-cies.** the quality or condition of being hesitant. Also, **hes′i·tance.**

hes·i·tant (hez′i tənt) *adj.* lacking certainty or willingness; doubtful or reluctant. —**hes′i·tant·ly,** *adv.*

hes·i·tate (hez′i tāt′) *v.i.,* **-tat·ed, -tat·ing. 1.** to wait or stop a moment; pause briefly: *The visitor hesitated and then rang the doorbell again.* **2.** to be afraid, reluctant, or unwilling (with *to*): *I hesitate to tell you the real truth.* **3.** to delay action because of fear, uncertainty, or doubt: *If you hesitate too long, you will miss this opportunity.* **4.** to falter in speech; stammer. [Latin *haesitātus,* past participle of *haesitāre* to stick fast, be undecided, from *haerēre* to stick.] —**hes′i·tat′er;** *also,* **hes′i·ta′tor,** *n.* —**hes′i·tat′ing·ly,** *adv.*

> **Synonyms** Hesitate, waver, vacillate, and falter mean to show indecision or irresolution. **Hesitate** connotes pausing in uncertainty before making up one's mind: *When they asked me which painting I preferred, I hesitated.* **Waver** connotes fluctuating between choices or holding back even after a decision seems to have been made, and suggests weakness: *The battle plan had been drawn up, but the commander wavered before issuing the order to attack.* **Vacillate** connotes prolonged hesitation while shifting back and forth in resolution: *While the management vacillated about how best to improve efficiency, the company went deeper and deeper into debt.* **Falter** suggests wavering in a way that shows nervousness, fear, or lack of purpose: *The exhausted fighter faltered as the next round was about to begin.*

hes·i·ta·tion (hez′i tā′shən) *n.* **1.** a delay due to reluctance or indecision: *The actor accepted the part without hesitation.* **2.** an act or instance of stopping; pause: *In this dance, there is a slight hesitation after each step.*

Hes·pe·ri·an (hes pir′ē ən) *adj.* **1.** of or relating to the west; western. **2.** of or relating to the Hesperides. [Latin *hesperius* western (from Greek *hesperios,* from *hesperos*) + -AN. See *Hesperus.*]

Hes·per·i·des (hes per′i dēz′) *n. Greek Mythology.* **1.** the daughters of Atlas who guarded the golden apples given to Hera when she married Zeus. **2.** the garden at the western edge of the world where Hera's golden apples were grown and kept. ➤ used as plural in def. 1, as singular in def. 2.

Hes·per·us (hes′pər əs) *n.* the evening star, esp. Venus. Also, **Hes·per** (hes′pər). [Latin *Hesperus,* from Greek *Hesperos* evening star, relating to the evening, western.]

Hes·sian (hesh′ən) *n.* **1.** a native or inhabitant of Hesse. **2.** a mercenary from Hesse who fought for the British during the American Revolution. **3.** any mercenary. —*adj.* of or relating to Hesse or its people.

Hessian boots, high, tasseled boots, popular in England during the nineteenth century.

Hessian fly, a small, black, two-winged insect, *Phytophaga destructor,* found in nearly all cereal-growing areas of the United States, whose larvae live and feed on wheat and other cultivated grains. [From the *Hessian* mercenaries of the American Revolution, who supposedly brought the insect to America in their straw bedding.]

hest (hest) *n. Archaic.* behest; command. [Old English *hǣs.*]

Hes·ti·a (hes′tē ə) *n.* in Greek mythology, the goddess of the

hearth and a daughter of Cronus and Rhea. Her Roman counterpart is Vesta.

he·tae·ra (hi tîr′ə) *n., pl.* **-tae·rae** (-tîr′ē). in ancient Greece, a female companion, esp. one who was well educated and associated with men of wealth and rank. [Greek *hetairā,* feminine of *hetairos* companion.]

he·tai·ra (hi tîr′ə) *n., pl.* **-tai·rai** (-tī′rī). hetaera.

hetero- *combining form* not the same; other: *heterodox.* ➤ opposed to **homo-.** [Greek *heteros* other.]

het·er·o·cyst (het′ər ə sist) *n.* a large, colorless cell occurring at intervals along the filaments of certain cyanobacteria, thought to be involved in nitrogen fixation. [HETERO- + CYST.]

het·er·o·dox (het′ər ə doks′) *adj.* **1.** diverging from accepted beliefs or doctrines; unorthodox. **2.** holding opinions at variance with accepted beliefs or doctrines. [Greek *heterodoxos* differing in opinion, from *heteros* other + *doxā* opinion.]

het·er·o·dox·y (het′ər ə dok′sē) *n., pl.* **-dox·ies. 1.** the state or quality of being heterodox. **2.** a heterodox belief or doctrine.

het·er·o·dyne (het′ər ə dīn′) *adj.* of or relating to the process of combining an incoming radio wave with a wave that has been generated in the receiver and has a slightly different frequency. Two new frequencies, representing the sum of and difference between the original two frequencies, are produced. [HETERO- + DYNE.]

het·er·oe·cious (het′ə rē′shəs) *adj. Biology.* passing through different stages of a life cycle in or on different species of hosts, as certain parasitic insects and fungi. [HETERO- + Greek *oikia* house + -OUS.] —**het′er·oe′cism,** *n.*

het·er·o·gam·ete (het′ər ə gam′ēt, -gə mēt′) *n.* a mature reproductive cell that is different in size, structure, or activity from the one with which it unites during fertilization. The relatively large ovum and much smaller, motile sperm of vertebrates are heterogametes. ➤ opposed to **isogamete.** [HETERO- + GAMETE.] —**het·er·o·ga·met·ic** (het′ə rō gə met′ik), *adj.*

het·er·og·a·my (het′ə rog′ə mē) *n.* **1.** sexual reproduction by the fusion of heterogametes. ➤ opposed to **isogamy. 2.** an alternation of generations in which two different sorts of reproduction, each involving gametes, alternate. [HETERO- + -GAMY.] —**het·er·og′a·mous,** *adj.*

het·er·o·ge·ne·i·ty (het′ər ō jə nē′i tē) *n., pl.* **-ties.** the state or quality of being heterogeneous; dissimilarity.

het·er·o·ge·ne·ous (het′ər ə jē′nē əs, -jēn′yəs) *adj.* **1.** having dissimilar or unrelated parts or elements; not homogeneous: *a heterogeneous nation.* **2.** differing in kind or nature; dissimilar: *a collection of heterogeneous writings, a heterogeneous group of people.* [Medieval Latin *heterogeneus,* going back to Greek *heteros* other + *genos* race, kind.] —**het′er·o·ge′ne·ous·ly,** *adv.* —**het′er·o·ge′ne·ous·ness,** *n.*

het·er·o·mor·phic (het′ər ə môr′fik) *adj. Biology.* exhibiting different forms, as among insects that undergo metamorphosis. [HETERO- + Greek *morphē* shape, form + -IC.] Also, **het′er·o·mor′phous.**

het·er·o·nym (het′ər ə nim′) *n.* a word with the same spelling as another, but having a different pronunciation and meaning. *Bow,* the front of a ship, and *bow,* the weapon, are heteronyms. [Greek *heterōnymos* with different designation, from *heteros* other + (dialectal form) *onyma* name, word.]

het·er·o·sex·u·al (het′ər ə sek′shü əl) *adj.* of, relating to, or characterized by heterosexuality. —*n.* a person who manifests or practices heterosexuality.

het·er·o·sex·u·al·i·ty (het′ər ə sek′shü al′i tē) *n.* **1.** sexual attraction toward members of the opposite sex. **2.** sexual relations with a member of the opposite sex. ➤ opposed to **homosexuality** in both defs.

het·er·o·sis (het′ə rō′sis) *n. Genetics.* a condition, resulting from hybridization, in which the offspring are stronger, larger, or more vigorous than the parents. Also, **hybrid vigor.** [HETERO- + -OSIS.] —**het′er·ot′ic,** *adj.*

het·er·o·troph (het′ər ə trof′) *n.* an organism, as an animal or fungus, that obtains its food from organic materials, lacking the ability to synthesize carbohydrates and proteins from inorganic matter, as plants do. ➤ distinguished from **autotroph.** —**het′er·o·troph′ic,** *adj.* —**het′er·o·troph′i·cal·ly,** *adv.*

het·er·o·zy·gote (het′ər ə zī′gōt) *n.* a heterozygous organism.

het·er·o·zy·gous (het′ər ə zī′gəs) *adj.* of or relating to an organism in which two different alleles control a particular hereditary trait.

a	at	e	end	o	hot	u	up	hw	white		about
ā	ape	ē	me	ō	old	ū	use	ng	song	ə	taken
ä	far	i	it	ô	fork	ü	rule	th	thin		pencil
âr	care	ī	ice	oi	oil	u̇	pull	th	this		lemon
				îr	pierce	ou	out	ûr	turn	zh	measure			circus

het·man (het′mən) *n., pl.* **-mans** (-mən). a Cossack chieftain elected by his community. Also, **ataman.** [Polish *hetman* captain, from German *Hauptmann,* from *Haupt* chief + *Mann* man.]

heu·ris·tic (hyü ris′tik) *adj.* **1.** helping or guiding to discover or learn. **2.** designating an educational approach that encourages a student to learn by making his or her own investigations and discoveries. [Modern Latin *heuristicus,* from Greek *heuriskein* to discover.] —**heu·ris′ti·cal·ly,** *adv.*

hew (hū) *v.,* **hewed, hewed** or **hewn, hew·ing.** —*v.t.* **1.** to make or shape with cutting blows, as from an ax: *Indians had hewed steps into the side of the mountain.* **2.** to strike or cut, as with an ax or sword; chop; hack: *We hewed the dead branches off the tree.* —*v.i.* **1.** to inflict cutting blows. **2.** to conform or adhere (with *to*): *to hew to official doctrine.* [Old English *hēawan* to cut, strike.] —**hew′er,** *n.*

hewn (hūn) a past participle of **hew.**

hex (heks) *v.t.* to put an evil spell on; bewitch. —*n.* **1.** an evil spell. **2.** witch. [German *Hexe* witch.]

hexa- also, **hex-.** *combining form* six. [Greek *hex.*]

hex·a·dec·i·mal (hek′sə des′ə məl) *adj.* of or relating to a system of numbers that has a base of 16. Hexadecimal numbers are often used in computer programs.

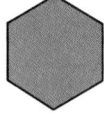
regular **hexagon**

hex·a·gon (hek′sə gon′) *n.* a plane figure with six sides and six angles. [Latin *hexagōnum,* from Greek *hexagōnos* having six angles, from *hex* six + *gōniā* angle, corner.]

hex·ag·o·nal (hek sag′ə nəl) *adj.* **1.** of, relating to, or having the shape of a hexagon. **2.** (of a solid figure) having a hexagon as a base or cross section. —**hex·ag′o·nal·ly,** *adv.*

hex·a·gram (hek′sə gram′) *n.* a six-pointed star formed of two intersecting equilateral triangles.

hex·a·he·dron (hek′sə hē′drən) *n., pl.* **-drons** or **-dra** (-drə). a polyhedron with six faces. A regular hexahedron is a cube. For illustration, see **cube.** [Greek *hexaedron,* going back to *hex* six + *hedrā* seat, base.] —**hex′a·he′dral,** *adj.*

hexagram

hex·am·e·ter (hek sam′i tər) *n.* a line of verse consisting of six metrical feet, esp. one consisting of five dactyls and a spondee or trochee, for example: *Ghosts′ of the/ fear′some O′/ Fla′hertys/ ride′ through the/ val′leys of/ Eng′land.* [Latin *hexameter,* from Greek *hexametros* (verse) having six measures, from *hex* six + *metron* measure.]

hex·ane (hek′sān) *n.* any of five liquid hydrocarbons of the alkane, or paraffin, series that are major constituents of petroleum and benzine. Formula: C_6H_{14}. [HEX(A)- + -ANE.]

hex·a·pod (hek′sə pod′) *n.* a true, six-legged insect. —*adj.* having six feet. [Greek *hexapod-,* stem of *hexapous,* from *hex* six + *pous* foot.]

hex·ose (hek′sōs) *n.* any monosaccharide, as glucose or fructose, that contains six carbon atoms in each molecule. Formula: $C_6H_{12}O_6$ [HEX(A)- + -OSE^2.]

hey (hā) *interj.* used to attract attention or to express a sudden feeling, as of surprise, pleasure, or annoyance.

hey·day (hā′dā′) *n.* a period of greatest strength, popularity, or prosperity. [Possibly from Middle English *hey day* literally, high day.]

Hf, the symbol for hafnium.

hf. 1. half. **2.** high frequency.

HF, high frequency.

Hg, the symbol for mercury. [Latin *hydrargyrus,* going back to Greek *hydōr* water + *argyros* silver.]

hg also, **hg.** hectogram; hectograms.

HG, High German.

H.H. 1. His (or Her) Highness. **2.** His Holiness.

hhd also, **hhd.** hogshead.

H-hour (āch′our′) *n.* zero hour. [H abbreviation for hour + HOUR.]

hi (hī) *interj. Informal.* hello.

HI, the postal abbreviation for Hawaii.

H.I., Hawaiian Islands.

hi·a·tus (hī ā′təs) *n., pl.* **-tus·es** or **-tus. 1.** a break, interruption, or empty space, as in time or the continuity of something: *After a brief hiatus, the argument flared up again. There was a long hiatus in the old letter because of a missing page.* **2.** a slight pause in sound between two successive vowels that are separately pronounced in consecutive syllables or words, as between the *o*'s in *cooperate.* [Latin *hiātus* gap.] —For Synonyms, see **interruption.**

Hi·a·wath·a (hī′ə woth′ə, hē′-) *n.* an Indian brave who is the hero of a poem by the American poet Henry Wadsworth Longfellow, based on a hero of Chippewa mythology.

hi·ba·chi (hi bä′chē) *n.* a portable metal cooking utensil, consisting of a grill covering a deep container in which charcoal is placed. [Japanese *hibachi,* from *hi* fire + *bachi* bowl.]

hi·ber·nal (hī bûr′nəl) *adj.* of or relating to winter; wintry: *a hibernal landscape.*

hi·ber·nate (hī′bər nāt′) *v.i.,* **-nat·ed, -nat·ing. 1.** to spend the winter in a dormant or inactive state, as do many mammals, most reptiles and amphibians, a few fish and birds, and certain insects. ➡ distinguished from **estivate. 2.** to be inactive or secluded for any period of time. [Latin *hibernātus,* past participle of *hibernāre* to pass the winter, from *hibernus* wintry.] —**hi′ber·na′tion,** *n.*

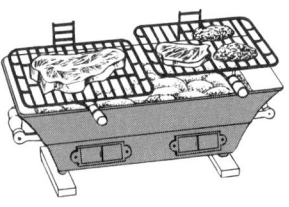
hibachi

Hi·ber·ni·a (hī bûr′nē ə) *n.* Ireland. ➡ used primarily in literature. —**Hi·ber′ni·an,** *n., adj.*

hi·bis·cus (hī bis′kəs, hə-) *n., pl.* **-cus·es.** any of a large group of herbs, shrubs, or trees, genus *Hibiscus,* found in tropical and temperate regions, bearing large, bell-shaped flowers of various colors. [Latin *hibiscus;* possibly of Celtic origin.]

hic·cup (hik′up) also, **hic·cough** (hik′up). *n.* **1.** a spasm of involuntary inhaling that is stopped suddenly by closure of the vocal cords, producing a characteristic sound that resembles a catch in the voice. **2. hiccups.** the condition of being affected by such spasms: *Having the hiccups can be frustrating.* —*v.i.,* **-cupped, -cup·ping. 1.** to have hiccups. **2.** to make a similar sound. [Imitative.]

hic ja·cet (hik jā′set) **1.** *Latin.* here lies. **2.** epitaph.

hick (hik) *Informal. n.* a person who is awkward or unsophisticated, esp. one from a rural area. —*adj.* of or characteristic of a hick or hicks. [From *Hick,* an earlier nickname for Richard.]

hick·o·ry (hik′ə rē, hik′rē) *n., pl.* **-ries. 1.** any of a group of tall trees, genus *Carya,* of the walnut family, found in North America, having gray bark, leaflets with saw-toothed edges, and hard edible nuts. **2.** the hard, strong wood of this tree, used esp. for tool handles. **3.** the round or oblong edible nut of this tree. Also *(def. 3),* **hickory nut.** [Short for *pohickery,* from Algonquian *pawcohiccora* food made of crushed hickory nuts.]

hid (hid) the past tense and a past participle of **hide**[1].

hi·dal·go (hi dal′gō) *n., pl.* **-gos.** a Spanish nobleman of the lower rank of the nobility. [Spanish *hidalgo,* earlier *hijo de algo* literally, son with something (i.e., some property), going back to Latin *filius* son + *dē* from, of + *aliquid* something.]

hid·den (hid′ən) *v.* a past participle of **hide**[1]. —*adj.* not easily seen, found, or known; concealed; secret; obscure.

hide[1] (hīd) *v.,* **hid, hid·den** or **hid, hid·ing.** —*v.t.* **1.** to put or keep out of sight: *to hide Christmas presents.* **2.** to keep from the knowledge of others; keep secret: *Sometimes it is difficult to hide your feelings.* **3.** to obstruct the view of; prevent from being seen: *The heavy snowfall hid the tracks of the fugitive.* —*v.i.* to keep oneself out of sight; conceal oneself: *The rabbit hid in the high grass.* [Old English *hȳdan.*] —**hid′er,** *n.*

| **Synonyms** | *v.t.* **Hide**[1] and **conceal** mean to put or keep something out of sight. **Hide,** the more common term, is general: *A tall hedge hid the building from view. I hid the birthday presents where no one would find them.* **Conceal** may be used similarly, but it is more formal and usually suggests the idea of covering up: *to conceal the facts, to conceal a weapon.* |

hide[2] (hīd) *n.* **1.** the skin of an animal, esp. one of the larger animals, either raw or tanned. **2.** *Informal.* human skin. —*v.t.,* **hid·ed, hid·ing.** *Informal.* to give a severe beating to; thrash. [Middle English *hide,* from Old English *hid, hȳd* skin.]
· **neither hide nor hair.** absolutely nothing: *The police have found neither hide nor hair of the robbers.*

hide-and-seek (hīd′ən sēk′) *n.* a children's game in which one of the players has to find all of the others, who have hidden themselves. Also, **hide′-and-go-seek′.**

hide·a·way (hīd′ə wā′) *n.* a secret or secluded place where a person may go to hide or be alone.

hide·bound (hīd′bound′) *adj.* **1.** stubbornly narrow-minded. **2.** (of an animal) having the skin adhering closely to the bones and muscles, often as a result of undernourishment.

hid·e·ous (hid′ē əs) *adj.* very ugly; repulsive; ghastly; detestable: *a hideous creature, hideous crimes.* [Old French *hideus,* from *hide* terror; of uncertain origin.] —**hid′e·ous·ly,** *adv.* —**hid′e·ous·ness,** *n.*

hide·out (hīd′out′) *n.* a place where a person can hide, esp. from the police or other authorities.

hid·ing¹ (hī′ding) *n.* **1.** the state or a place of concealment: *The outlaw went into hiding.* **2.** the act of concealing. [Middle English *huydinge.*]

hid·ing² (hī′ding) *n. Informal.* a severe beating or thrashing. [Earlier *hide* to beat, flog, from HIDE².]

hie (hī) *v.i., v.t.,* **hied, hie·ing** or **hy·ing.** *Archaic.* to take oneself quickly; hasten: *Hie thee hence!* [Old English *hīgian.*]

hi·er·arch (hī′ə rärk′) *n.* **1.** a person who holds a high position in any hierarchy. **2.** a religious leader holding an important office, esp. a high priest. —**hi′er·arch′al,** *adj.*

hi·er·ar·chi·cal (hī′ə rär′ki kəl) *adj.* of, relating to, or consisting of a hierarchy. Also, **hi′er·ar′chic.**

hi·er·ar·chy (hī′ə rär′kē) *n., pl.* **-chies. 1.** an organization of persons or things by rank, with each rank subordinate to the one above it: *a governmental hierarchy.* **2.** a body of clergy organized in this manner. **3.** church government by such a body of clergy. [Medieval Latin *hierarchia* rule of a priest, from Greek *hierarchia,* going back to *hieros* sacred + *archein* to rule.]

hi·er·at·ic (hī′ə rat′ik) *adj.* **1.** of, relating to, or used by priests; sacerdotal. **2.** of or relating to an abridged form of hieroglyphics used by ancient Egyptian priests for keeping records. Also, **hi′er·at′i·cal.** [Latin *hierāticus* relating to sacred uses, from Greek *hierātikos* relating to a priest, going back to *hieros* sacred.] —**hi′er·at′i·cal·ly,** *adv.*

hi·er·o·glyph (hī′ər ə glif′, hīr′ə-) *n.* hieroglyphic.

hi·er·o·glyph·ic (hī′ər ə glif′ik, hīr′ə-) *n.* **1.a.** a picture or symbol representing an object, word, syllable, or sound, used in writing systems by certain ancient peoples, esp. the Egyptians. **b.** any figure or symbol that has an obscure or hidden meaning. **2. hieroglyphics. a.** a system of writing that uses hieroglyphics. **b.** any writing that is difficult to read. —*adj.* **1.** of, relating to, or resembling hieroglyphics. **2.** written in hieroglyphics. **3.** difficult to read. Also, **hi′er·o·glyph′i·cal.** [French *hiéroglyphique,* from Late Latin *hieroglyphicus,* from Greek *hieroglyphikos,* from *hieros* sacred + *glyphē* carving, from *glyphein* to carve.] —**hi′er·o·glyph′i·cal·ly,** *adv.*

hi·er·o·phant (hī′ər ə fant′, hīr′ə-, hī er′ə-) *n.* **1.** in ancient Greece, a priest who presided at sacred mysteries. **2.** a person who interprets sacred or hidden knowledge. [Late Latin *hierophantēs* teacher of religious rites, from Greek *hierophantēs,* from *hieros* sacred + *phainein* to show.]

Egyptian **hieroglyphics,** dated 1250 B.C.

hi-fi (hī′fī′) *n.* **1.** high fidelity. **2.** a phonograph or other apparatus that reproduces sound, esp. music, with high fidelity. —*adj.* of or relating to high fidelity or hi-fis.

hig·gle (hig′əl) *v.i.,* **-gled, -gling.** haggle. [Form of HAGGLE.]

hig·gle·dy-pig·gle·dy (hig′əl dē pig′əl dē) *adv.* in jumbled confusion. —*adj.* jumbled; confused. [Rhyming expression probably based on PIG and suggested by the way pigs huddle together.]

high (hī) *adj.* **1.** extending upward a great or unusual distance; tall: *The walls were strong and high.* **2.** being or elevated above the ground or some other surface: *The bridge is high above the water.* **3.** having a specified elevation: *The building is forty stories high.* **4.** reaching to or performed from a height: *The horse made a high jump over the fence.* **5.** great or above normal, as in force, strength, degree, or value: *The rain stopped, but the high winds continued.* **6.** above or more important than others, as in rank or position: *a high city official.* **7.** of a noble or lofty nature: *high ideals.* **8.** above the usual or desired amount or price: *Interest rates are high.* **9.** luxurious; extravagant: *living in high style.* **10.** having advanced to or nearing its peak or most complete stage, extent, or degree: *high summer.* **11.** produced or characterized by relatively rapid vibrations; above the middle range in pitch: *a high note.* **12.** of serious consequence; grave: *a high crime against the state.* **13.** very happy; joyful: *in high spirits.* **14.** full of pride; haughty; pretentious: *a high and mighty air.* **15.** (of meat, esp. wild game) slightly decomposed: *high venison.* **16.** *Informal.* feeling the effect of a liquor or drug; intoxicated. **17.** Pho-

netics. pronounced with the back of the tongue raised toward the roof of the mouth. The *e* in *me* is a high vowel. —*adv.* **1.** at or to a high position, point, or degree: *The climbers camped high on the mountain. Prices have risen too high.* **2.** in an extravagant manner: *to live high.* —*n.* **1.** a high level, place, or position: *The temperature reached a new high.* **2.** an arrangement of gears that produces maximum speed. **3.** *Slang.* a state of intoxication caused by or as by liquor or drugs. [Old English *hēah* tall, lofty, sublime.]

· **high and dry. a.** completely out of the water: *a ship stranded high and dry on the rocks.* **b.** without aid or assistance; abandoned; alone: *My so-called friend left me high and dry when I needed money.*

· **high and low.** in every place; everywhere: *We looked high and low for the missing book.*

· **on high. a.** in or at a high place; above: *The flag waved on high.* **b.** in heaven.

Synonyms *adj.* **High, tall,** and **lofty** may all mean at or rising to a height greater than the average. **High** is the general term: *high clouds, a high plateau.* **Tall** is used of things extending upward from ground level: *a tall teenager, a tall building.* **Lofty** is used to suggest imposing height: *a lofty tower, lofty mountain peaks.*

high·ball (hī′bôl′) *n.* a drink consisting of an alcoholic beverage, such as rye or Scotch, mixed with water, ginger ale, soda, or other liquid and served with ice in a tall glass.

high beam, a beam of a vehicle's headlight aimed to illuminate objects in the distance.

high blood pressure, blood pressure in the arteries that is consistently higher than normal. It often has no apparent cause, but is sometimes a symptom of disease in another part of the body. Also, **hypertension.**

high·born (hī′bôrn′) *adj.* of noble birth.

high·boy (hī′boi′) *n.* a tall chest of drawers supported on legs.

high·bred (hī′bred′) *adj.* **1.** of superior breed or stock. **2.** showing good breeding; well-mannered; refined.

high·brow (hī′brou′) *Informal. n.* a person who has or appears to have cultivated tastes or interests. —*adj.* of, relating to, or suitable for a highbrow: *highbrow music.*

high·chair (hī′chār′) *n.* a chair for an infant or young child to use when being fed, having high legs and a tray extended across the arms.

High Church, a group in the Anglican Church that emphasizes church authority, the liturgy, and the sacraments. —**High′-Church′,** *adj.* —**High′-Church′man,** *n.*

high-col·ored (hī′kul′ərd) *adj.* **1.** having a strong or deep color; brilliant; vivid. **2.** florid; red.

high comedy, comedy dealing with polite society and relying on witty dialogue and sophisticated characterization.

high commissioner 1. the chief of a group of persons appointed to administer some policy or govern an occupied territory. **2.** the chief delegate of one country to another in the Commonwealth of Nations.

high-den·si·ty lipoprotein (hī′den′si tē) see **HDL.**

higher education, college or university education.

high·er·up (hī′ər up′) *n. Informal.* a person occupying a superior rank or position.

highest common factor, greatest common divisor.

high explosive, any of a class of explosives, such as TNT, in which combustion occurs so rapidly as to be virtually instantaneous, used in shells and bombs.

high-fa·lu·tin (hī′fə lü′tən) *also,* **high-fa·lu·ting** (hī′fə lü′ting). *adj. Informal.* pompous or pretentious, as in speech or manner. [HIGH + *falutin,* possibly a modification of *fluting,* present participle of FLUTE.]

high fidelity, the reproduction by electronic equipment, such as a phonograph or tape deck, of the full range of audible frequencies of a recorded or broadcast signal, so that the original sound is almost exactly duplicated. Also, **hi-fi.** —**high′-fi·del′i·ty,** *adj.*

high-fli·er (hī′flī′ər) *also,* **high-fly·er.** *n.* **1.** a person or thing that flies high. **2.** a person who is extravagant or pretentious, as in ideas, ambitions, or tastes.

high-flown (hī′flōn′) *adj.* pretentious or extravagant, as in ambitions, ideas, or language.

high frequency, a radio frequency between 3 and 30 megahertz. —**high′-fre′quen·cy,** *adj.*

High German, the literary and official form of the German

a	at	e	end	o	hot	u	up	hw	white		about
ā	ape	ē	me	ō	old	ū	use	ng	song		taken
ä	far	i	it	ô	fork	ü	rule	th	thin	ə	pencil
âr	care	ī	ice	oi	oil	u̇	pull	tẖ	this		lemon
		îr	pierce	ou	out	ûr	turn	zh	measure		circus

language. [Translation of German *Hochdeutsch;* because originally used mainly in the southern regions of Germany near the Alps. Compare LOW GERMAN.]

high-grade (hī′grād′) *adj.* of superior quality.

high-hand-ed (hī′han′did) *adj.* acting or done in a haughty way, without consideration for others; arbitrary; overbearing. —**high′-hand′ed-ly,** *adv.* —**high′-hand′ed-ness,** *n.*

high-hat (hī′hat′) *Informal. v.t.,* **-hat-ted, -hat-ting.** to treat snobbishly; snub. —*adj.* **1.** stylish; elegant. **2.** snobbish.

high hat, top hat.

High Holidays, the two most sacred Jewish holidays, Rosh Hashanah and Yom Kippur. Also, **High Holy Days.**

high-jack (hī′jak′) *v.t.* hijack. —**high′jack′er,** *n.*

high jinks (jingks) boisterous, good-natured pranks or fun. [HIGH + *jinks* frolic; of uncertain origin.]

high jump 1. a field event in which the contestant jumps, usually from a running start, over a crossbar set between two uprights. **2.** such a jump. —**high jumper.**

high-land (hī′lənd) *n. also,* **highlands.** a portion of land rising above the surrounding land and having hills or mountains. —*adj.* **1.** of, relating to, or characteristic of such a region or portion of land. **2. Highland.** of or relating to the Scottish Highlands.

high-land-er (hī′lən dər) *n.* **1.** a person living in a highland. **2. Highlander. a.** a member of the Gaelic people who inhabit the Scottish Highlands. **b.** a soldier of a regiment recruited from the Scottish Highlands.

Highland fling, a lively Scottish folk dance that originated in the Scottish Highlands.

dancing the **Highland fling**

high-lev-el language (hī′lev′əl) a computer language that uses common words and statements or symbols to represent commands and to identify memory locations and requires translation, as by a compiler.

high-light (hī′līt′) *n.* **1.** a point or area in a painting or picture that is represented as brightly lighted. **2.** the most important, interesting, or memorable part of something: *The lighting of the Christmas tree was the highlight of the evening.* —*v.t.,* **-light-ed, -light-ing. 1.** to give a highlight or highlights to. **2.** to give emphasis or prominence to.

high-light-er (hī′līt′ər) *n.* **1.** a pen with a broad felt tip and bright ink, used to mark passages in a text for emphasis without obscuring the text. **2.** a cosmetic used to emphasize the eyes, the cheeks, or another part of the face.

high-ly (hī′lē) *adv.* **1.** in or to a high degree; very much: *a highly motivated student.* **2.** with much approval or praise; very favorably: *The critics think highly of the author's work.* **3.** at a high price: *The consultant is being highly paid for advice.*

High Mass, a Mass celebrated with the use of a choir, music, and incense, in which the celebrant is assisted by a deacon and subdeacon. ➡ distinguished from **Low Mass.**

high-mind-ed (hī′mīn′did) *adj.* **1.** having or characterized by noble ideals or feelings. **2.** *Archaic.* proud; arrogant. —**high′-mind′ed-ly,** *adv.* —**high′-mind′ed-ness,** *n.*

high-ness (hī′nis) *n.* **1.** the state or quality of being high; loftiness. **2. Highness.** used in speaking or referring to a member of a royal family, preceded by *His, Her,* or *Your.*

high noon 1. exactly twelve o'clock in the daytime. **2.** the highest

point or pinnacle, as of creativity or achievement; acme: *the high noon of a ballplayer's career.* **3.** a crisis situation.

high-oc-tane (hī′ok′tān) *adj.* (of gasoline) having a relatively high octane number and thus not liable to cause engine knock. Also, **high-test.**

high-pitched (hī′picht′) *adj.* **1.** having a high pitch: *a high-pitched voice.* **2.** (of a roof) having a steep slope.

high-pow-ered (hī′pou′ərd) *also,* **high-pow-er.** *adj.* high in power, energy, or force: *a high-powered automobile, high-powered salespeople.*

high-pres-sure (hī′presh′ər) *adj.* **1.** having, using, or able to withstand pressure higher than normal. **2.** having high barometric pressure. **3.** *Informal.* using forceful and bold methods of persuasion: *a high-pressure sales approach.* —*v.t.,* **-sured, -suring.** to use aggressive methods of persuasion on.

high-priced (hī′prīst′) *adj.* very expensive; costly.

high priest 1. a chief priest. **2.** in the Old Testament, the head of the ancient Jewish priesthood, who presided over the Temple worship. **3.** a leader, as of a cult or movement.

high relief, sculpture in which the figures project from the background by half their thickness or more. Also, **alto relievo.**

high-rise (hī′rīz′) *n.* a building having many stories. —*adj.* having many stories: *a high-rise building.*

high-road (hī′rōd′) *n.* **1.** a main road; highway. **2.** a direct and easy course.

high school, a school attended after elementary school, usually comprising grades nine through twelve. ➡ often used instead of **senior high school** and distinguished from **junior high school.**

high seas, those portions of seas and oceans that are not within the territorial limits of any country.

high-sound-ing (hī′soun′ding) *adj.* having an important, imposing, or pretentious sound: *a high-sounding title.*

high-spir-it-ed (hī′spir′i tid) *adj.* having a proud, courageous, or fiery spirit.

high-strung (hī′strung′) *adj.* extremely tense or nervous; excitable.

hight (hīt) *adj. Archaic.* named; called: *a lady hight Elinore.* [Old English *heht,* past tense of *hātan* to call.]

high-tail (hī′tāl′) *v.i. Informal.* to leave or go quickly; hurry. ➡ often used with *it,* as in *to hightail it home.*

high-tech (hī′tek′) *adj.* **1.** relating to, characteristic of, or decorated in the style of high tech. **2.** of or relating to high technology.

high tech, a style of interior decoration for homes and offices that uses utilitarian, unadorned equipment and materials, such as those found in factories and warehouses.

high technology, any technology that involves highly advanced, specialized, or sophisticated scientific procedures or equipment, such as those used in electronics, computer design, or genetic engineering. —**high′-tech-nol′o-gy,** *adj.*

high-ten-sion (hī′ten′shən) *adj.* having or using high voltage: *a high-tension wire.*

high-test (hī′test′) *adj.* high-octane.

high tide 1. the tide at its highest level. **2.** the time when this level is reached. **3.** a culminating point.

high time 1. later than the proper time but not too late: *It's high time you start thinking about your future.* **2.** *Informal.* a rollicking good time.

high-toned (hī′tōnd′) *adj.* **1.** having or showing a high quality or character; dignified: *a high-toned speech about responsibility and morality.* **2.** *Informal.* high in social status; fashionable or stylish: *a high-toned neighborhood.*

high treason, treason, esp. against a monarch.

high water 1. a body of water that has reached its highest level, as during a flood. **2.** high tide.

high-wa-ter mark (hī′wô′tər, -wot′ər) **1.** a mark indicating the highest level reached by a body of water. **2.** the highest point of anything, as of a career.

high-way (hī′wā′) *n.* **1.** a public road, esp. one that is extensive and a major route of travel. **2.** any main route or direct course, esp. one to a specific objective: *Wealth is not always the highway to happiness.*

high-way-man (hī′wā′mən) *n., pl.* **-men** (-mən). a robber who holds up travelers on a public road.

high wire, a tightly stretched wire placed high above the ground, on which acrobats perform.

H.I.H., His (or Her) Imperial Highness.

hi-jack (hī′jak′) *also,* **highjack.** *v.t.* **1.** to seize or take (a vehicle in transit) by force: *Terrorists hijacked the airplane.* **2.** to steal (cargo) from a vehicle in transit: *The thieves hijacked a load of tires from a truck.* [Possibly from the supposed use by robbers of the phrase *High, Jack* when ordering victims to raise their hands.] —**hi′jack′er,** *n.*

hike (hīk) *v.*, **hiked, hik·ing.** —*v.i.* to walk a long distance, esp. for pleasure or exercise. —*v.t.* **1.** to raise, esp. with a sharp movement (with *up*): *to hike up one's trousers.* **2.** to increase sharply, as prices: *The ferry company hiked the fare.* —*n.* **1.** a long walk or march. **2.** an increase: *a hike in rent.* [Possibly dialectal form of HITCH.] —**hik′er,** *n.*

hi·la (hī′lə) the plural of **hilum.**

hi·lar·i·ous (hi lâr′ē əs, -lar′-, hī-) *adj.* **1.** causing great merriment or laughter; extremely funny: *hilarious stories.* **2.** merry, lively, and noisy; boisterous: *a hilarious party.* —**hi·lar′i·ous·ly,** *adv.* —**hi·lar′i·ous·ness,** *n.*

hi·lar·i·ty (hi lâr′i tē, -lar′-, hī-) *n.* **1.** great merriment or laughter; boisterous gaiety: *The hilarity at the party downstairs kept us up half the night.* **2.** extremely humorous quality or aspect; funniness: *The hilarity of their predicament escaped them.* [French *hilarité* mirth, from Latin *hilaritās,* going back to Greek *hilaros* gay.]

hill (hil) *n.* **1.** a portion of the earth's surface that is usually rounded and elevated above the surrounding land but is not as high as a mountain. **2.** a small heap or mound, such as one made by ants or a mole. **3.** a slope, as in a road or on a piece of land: *Stay in gear if you park on a hill.* **4.a.** a small mound or pile of earth in which seed is planted or plants are cultivated. **b.** the plants growing in such a mound. —*v.t.* to form in a small heap or mound. [Old English *hyll* small mountain.]
  • **over the hill.** *Informal.* no longer strong, active, or effective; past one's prime.

hill·bil·ly (hil′bil′ē) *n., pl.* **-lies.** *Informal.* a person who lives in or comes from the backwoods or mountain country, esp. from such an area in the southern United States. ➡ sometimes considered offensive. —*adj.* of or relating to hillbillies or to their culture: *hillbilly music.* [HILL + BILLY.]

hill·ock (hil′ək) *n.* a small hill or mound.

hill·side (hil′sīd′) *n.* the side or slope of a hill.

hill·top (hil′top′) *n.* the top of a hill.

hill·y (hil′ē) *adj.*, **hill·i·er, hill·i·est. 1.** having many hills: *hilly countryside.* **2.** like a hill; steep: *a hilly street.* —**hill′i·ness,** *n.*

hilt (hilt) *n.* the handle of a sword, dagger, or similar weapon. [Old English *hilt.*]
  • **to the hilt.** thoroughly; completely: *The house is mortgaged to the hilt.*

hi·lum (hī′ləm) *n., pl.* **-la** (-lə). **1.** *Botany.* a mark or scar formed on a seed at the point where it was attached to a pod, cone, or the like. **2.** *Anatomy.* a small depression in the surface of an organ that marks the place where a blood vessel or nerve enters or leaves. [Latin *hīlum* trifle.] —**hi′lar,** *adj.*

him (him; *unstressed* im) *pron.* the objective case of **he:** *She saw him last night at the theater.* —For Usage Note, see **me.**

H.I.M., His (or Her) Imperial Majesty.

him·self (him self′) *pron.* **1.** the emphatic form of **he** or **him:** *The president himself was unable to solve the problem.* **2.** the reflexive form of **him:** *He talks to himself when he is trying to figure out a complex problem.* **3.** his usual or normal state or condition: *He just hasn't been himself since his wife died.* **4.** used in absolute constructions: *Having experienced a similar tragedy himself, he could understand her grief.*

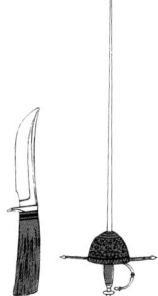

hilts

hind[1] (hīnd) *adj.*, **hind·er, hind·most** or **hind·er·most.** situated at the back; rear: *The dog injured one of its hind legs.* [Middle English *hinde,* from *hindan* from behind, from the rear.]

hind[2] (hīnd) *n., pl.* **hinds** or **hind.** a doe, esp. a female red deer in and after its third year. ➡ distinguished from **hart.** [Old English *hind.*]

hind[3] (hīnd) *n. Archaic.* **1.** a farm worker. **2.** a peasant. [Old English *hīne* (plural) household servants.]

hind·brain (hīnd′brān′) *n.* the part of the brain that includes the pons, cerebellum, and medulla oblongata.

hin·der[1] (hin′dər) *v.t.* to make difficult or delay the movement or progress of; hold back: *The storm hindered the search for the missing child.* [Old English *hindrian.*]

Synonyms Hinder[1], **impede, obstruct,** and **encumber** mean to slow or stop a movement or action. **Hinder** connotes holding back or getting in the way of anything or anyone, and may suggest an annoying delay: *Heavy snow hindered construction work.* **Impede,** which is very close to *hinder,* originally meant to fetter the feet. It connotes holding back or slowing something, perhaps temporarily: *The bandage was so tight that it impeded the circulation of the blood.* **Obstruct** connotes getting in the way of progress to the point of stopping it completely: *The filibuster by two senators succeeded in obstructing*

the legislation. **Encumber** connotes hampering progress by weighing down: *Outdated regulations encumbered their efforts to introduce new methods of teaching.*

hin·der[2] (hīn′dər) *adj.* at the back or rear. [Old English *hinder* behind.]

hind·er·most (hīn′dər mōst′) *adj.* hindmost.

hind·gut (hīnd′gut′) *n.* **1.** the posterior portion of the embryonic digestive tract in vertebrates, developing into the bladder and large intestine. **2.** the posterior part of an arthropod's digestive system, as in insects and crustaceans. [HIND[1] + GUT.]

Hin·di (hin′dē) *n.* **1.** an Indic language of the Indo-Iranian subfamily of the Indo-European family of languages, spoken predominantly in northern India. **2.** the official language of India, derived from Hindustani. [Hindustani *Hindī* relating to India, Indian, from Persian *Hind* India. See HINDU.]

hind·most (hīnd′mōst′) *adj.* farthest back; nearest the rear.

hind·quar·ter (hīnd′kwôr′tər) *n.* **1.** the back half of a side of beef or other meat, including the leg, loin, and adjacent parts. **2. hindquarters.** the hind legs, loins, and adjacent parts of an animal.

hin·drance (hin′drəns) *n.* **1.** a person or thing that hinders; obstacle. **2.** the act of hindering.

hind·sight (hīnd′sīt′) *n.* the understanding of an event after it is over, esp. of what should have been done.

Hin·du (hin′dü) *n.* **1.** a person who adheres to the teachings, beliefs, or practices of Hinduism. **2.** a member of one of the peoples of India that speak an Indo-European language. —*adj.* of, relating to, or characteristic of Hindus or Hinduism. [Persian *Hindū* native of India, from *Hind* India, from Sanskrit *Sindhu* Indus River, region of the Indus River.]

Hin·du-Ar·a·bic numerals (hin′dü ar′ə bik) Arabic numerals.

Hin·du·ism (hin′dü iz′əm) *n.* the principal religious, philosophical, and social system of India. Its goal is salvation through communion with the Supreme Being, or Brahman, who appears in the form of the three major gods: Brahma, the creator; Vishnu, the sustainer; and Shiva, the destroyer.

Hin·du·sta·ni (hin′dü stä′nē, -stan′ē) *adj.* of, relating to, or characteristic of India or its people, languages, or culture. —*n.* a language, including elements of Hindi and Urdu, that is spoken throughout most of India. [Hindustani *Hindustānī* relating to Hindustan, from Persian *Hindūstān* India; literally, country of the Hindus, from *Hindū* native of India + *stān* country. See HINDU.]

hinge (hinj) *n.* **1.** a mechanical device usually consisting of two metal plates attached to one another by a pin, forming a movable joint on which something, such as a door, can swing, turn, or otherwise move. **2.** a joint

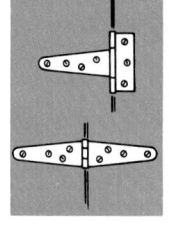

hinges

a	at	e	end	o	hot	u	up	hw	white		about
ā	ape	ē	me	ō	old	ū	use	ng	song		taken
ä	far	i	it	ô	fork	ü	rule	th	thin	ə	pencil
âr	care	ī	ice	oi	oil	ù	pull	<u>th</u>	this		lemon
		îr	pierce	ou	out	ûr	turn	zh	measure		circus

H

whose motion is limited to one plane forward or backward, as the elbow or knee joint. **3.** a rectangular piece of translucent paper gummed on one side, used to mount a stamp in an album. **4.** something on which another thing turns or depends; basic or central principle; critical point. —*v.*, **hinged, hing·ing.** —*v.t.* to furnish with or attach by a hinge or hinges. —*v.i.* **1.** to hang or turn on a hinge. **2.** to depend upon: *The fate of the prisoner hinges upon the jury's decision.* [Middle English *heng* mechanism on which a door is hung, going back to Old English *hangian* to be suspended.]

hinge joint, a joint between bones where movement is in only one plane, as the knee or elbow.

hin·ny (hin′ē) *n., pl.* **-nies.** the hybrid offspring of a male horse and a female donkey. ➡ distinguished from **mule**[1]. [Latin *hinnus,* from Greek *innos* small mule.]

hint (hint) *n.* **1.** a slight sign, indication, or suggestion: *There was a hint of spring in the morning air. We needed one more hint before we could find the treasure.* **2.** a small amount: *a hint of curry in a sauce.* —*v.t.* to give a slight sign or indication of; make a subtle reference to: *My friend hinted that she knew about the party.* —*v.i.* to make a subtle reference to or suggestion of (with *at*): *What is he hinting at?* [Possibly a form of obsolete *hent* act of seizing, going back to Old English *hentan* to seize.] —**hint′er,** *n.*

> **Synonyms** *v.t.* **Hint, intimate**[2], and **insinuate** mean to suggest subtly or indirectly. **Hint** implies the use of veiled suggestion and stresses a lack of candor: *The manager hinted the job might be open, but did not offer it to me directly.* **Intimate** connotes a very slight hint: *Their letter intimated that they would like to visit us, but they never came out and said so.* **Insinuate** connotes sly or artful hinting that conveys an unpleasant message: *to insinuate by one's manner that someone is not welcome.*

hin·ter·land (hin′tər land′) *n.* **1.** a region or district lying inland from the coast. **2.** a region that is remote from urban centers; back country. [German *Hinterland* back country, from *hinter* behind + *Land* land.]

hip[1] (hip) *n.* **1.** the projecting part of each side of the human body where the top of the thighbone joins the side of the pelvis. **2.** the corresponding part of the body of an animal. **3.** the joint between the thighbone and the pelvic bone. Also, **hip joint. 4.** an inclined, projecting ridgelike angle formed by the meeting of adjacent sloping sides of a roof. ➡ distinguished from **valley** in def. 4. [Old English *hype* the haunch.]

hip[2] (hip) *n.* a ripe fruit of a rosebush. [Old English *hēope.*]

hip[3] (hip) *adj.*, **hip·per, hip·pest.** *Slang.* familiar with or informed about what is happening or what is new. [Of uncertain origin.]

hip·bone (hip′bōn′) *n.* either of two large, irregularly shaped bones consisting of the ilium, ischium, and pubis and forming the two sides of the pelvic cavity.

hip joint, hip[1] *(def. 3).*

hipped (hipt) *adj.* **1.** characterized by or having a particular kind of hip. ➡ used in combination, as *narrow-hipped.* **2.** *Architecture.* having a hip or hips, as a roof. [HIP[1] + -ED[2].]

hip·pie (hip′ē) *n.* a usually young person of the 1960s and early 1970s who turned away from many of the values and practices of conventional middle-class society, as by wearing long hair and unusual clothing and experiencing psychedelic drugs, mystical religious beliefs, and communal living. [From HIP[3].]

hip·po (hip′ō) *n., pl.* **-pos.** *Informal.* hippopotamus.

Hip·po·crat·ic oath (hip′ə krat′ik) a vow taken by most beginning physicians that sets forth an ethical code for medical practice, the original version of which is attributed to the ancient Greek physician Hippocrates.

Hip·po·crene (hip′ə krēn′, hip′ə krē′nē) *n.* in Greek mythology, a spring on Mount Helicon, sacred to the Muses, whose waters were regarded as a source of poetic inspiration. [Latin *Hippocrēnē,* from Greek *Hippokrēnē,* from *hippos* horse + *krēnē* fountain. According to myth, the spring was produced by a stroke of Pegasus' hoof.]

hip·po·drome (hip′ə drōm′) *n.* **1.** in ancient Greece and Rome, an outdoor arena for horse races and chariot races. **2.** an arena or similar structure for circuses, horse shows, or other spectacles. [Latin *hippodromos* racecourse, going back to Greek *hippos* horse + *dromos* course.]

Hip·pol·y·ta (hi pol′i tə) *also,* **Hip·pol·y·te** (hi pol′i tē). *n.* in Greek mythology, the queen of the Amazons and mother of Hippolytus. Hercules' ninth labor was to bring back her girdle.

Hip·pol·y·tus (hi pol′i təs) *n.* in Greek mythology, the son of Hippolyta and the Greek hero Theseus. Falsely accused by his

stepmother, Phaedra, of raping her, he was cursed by his father and consequently suffered a violent death.

Hip·pom·e·nes (hi pom′ə-nēz′) *n.* in Greek mythology, a youth who defeated Atalanta in a race and thereby won her in marriage.

hippopotamus

hip·po·pot·a·mus (hip′ə-pot′ə məs) *n., pl.* **-mus·es** or **-mi** (-mī′). a plant-eating mammal, *Hippopotamus amphibius,* native to parts of central and southern Africa, living in and near rivers and lakes and having a massive, thick-skinned, hairless body, short legs, and the largest mouth of any land animal. Weight: to 4 tons (3.6 metric tons). Length: to 14 feet (4.3 meters). [Latin *hippopotamus,* going back to Greek *hippos* horse + *potamos* river.]

hip roof, a roof having sloping ends and sides.

hir·cine (hûr′sīn, -sin) *adj.* **1.** of, relating to, or resembling a goat, esp. in odor. **2.** lustful. [Latin *hircīnus* relating to a goat, from *hircus* male goat.]

hire (hīr) *v.t.,* **hired, hir·ing. 1.** to engage the services of (a person) for pay: *The school hired two new science teachers.* **2.** to pay for the use of (a thing): *They hired a car for the trip.* **3.** to give the use of (a thing) or

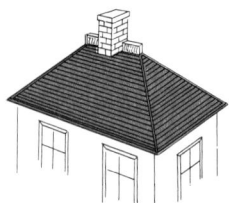

hip roof

the services of (a person) in return for payment: *We hired out our boat for the summer.* —*n.* **1.** payment for the use of an object, services rendered, or labor performed. **2.** the act of hiring. [Old English *hȳr* wages, payment for the use of something.] —For Synonyms *(v.t.),* see **employ, lease.**

· **for** (or **on**) **hire.** available for use or work in return for payment.

· **to hire out.** to give one's work or services in return for payment: *My cousin hires out as a house painter during the summer.*

hire·ling (hīr′ling) *n.* a person who works only for the sake of money, esp. a person who can be hired to do something unpleasant or dishonest. —*adj.* of or like a hireling; mercenary.

hir·sute (hûr′süt) *adj.* hairy. [Latin *hirsūtus* bristly.] —**hir′-sute·ness,** *n.*

his (hiz; *unstressed* iz) *pron.* **1.** of, relating to, or belonging to him: *That book is his.* ➡ used with *of* after a noun or pronoun: *That's a jacket of his.* **2.** the one or ones that relate or belong to him: *We went together with my sisters and his.* ➡ used as singular or plural depending on the noun to which it refers. —*adj.* (the possessive form of **he**) of, relating to, or belonging to him: *his dog.* [Old English *his,* genitive of *hē.* See HE.]

His·pa·ni·a (hi spā′nē ə, -spän′yə) *n. Archaic.* Spain. [Latin *Hispānia.*]

His·pan·ic (hi span′ik) *adj.* **1.** of or relating to Spain or Latin America or their people, language, or culture. **2.** of or relating to Hispanics. —*n.* a person of Spanish or Latin-American descent living in the United States.

Hispanic American, a person of Spanish or Latin-American descent living in the United States. —**His·pan·ic-A·mer·i·can** (hi span′ik ə mer′i kən), *adj.*

hiss (his) *v.i.* **1.** to make a sound similar to a prolonged *s*: *Startled snakes hiss.* **2.** to make such a sound to show disapproval or great dislike: *The angry crowd hissed when the politician spoke.* —*v.t.* **1.** to show disapproval of by hissing: *The fans hissed the umpire.* **2.** to force into silence or drive away by hissing. **3.** to say or express by hissing: *to hiss an angry reply.* —*n.* a sound similar to a prolonged *s.* [Imitative.]

hist (hist) *interj.* used to call attention or obtain silence.

hist. 1. histology. **2.** historian. **3.** historical. **4.** history.

his·ta·mine (his′tə mēn′, -min) *n.* a chemical compound, released by the body in allergic reactions, that lowers the blood pressure, stimulates secretion of gastric juice, and causes body tissues to swell. It is an amine derived from histidine. Formula: $C_5H_9N_3$ [Greek *histos* web, tissue + English *amine* (from AM(MONIA) + -INE[2].] —**his′ta·min′ic,** *adj.*

his·ti·dine (his′ti dēn′, -din) *n.* an amino acid essential for satisfactory growth in infants, obtainable by hydrolysis of most proteins and converted to histamine by elimination of a molecule of carbon dioxide. Formula: $C_6H_9N_3O_2$

his·to·gram (his′tə gram′) *n. Statistics.* a representation of a frequency distribution as a bar graph in which the width of each

adjoining bar proportionally represents a class interval and the height the frequency of that class interval. [Histo(ry) + -gram[1].]

his·tol·o·gy (hi stol′ə jē) n. **1.** the science that deals with the microscopic study of plant and animal tissues. **2.** the tissue structure of a plant or animal organism, in whole or in part. [Greek *histos* web, tissue + -logy.] —**his·to·log·i·cal** (his′tə loj′i kəl), *adj.* —**his·tol′o·gist**, *n.*

his·to·ri·an (hi stôr′ē ən, -stor′-) n. **1.** a person who writes a history or about history. **2.** a person who is an authority on history.

his·tor·ic (hi stôr′ik, -stor′-) *adj.* **1.** famous or noteworthy in history: *a historic site.* **2.** historical *(defs. 1, 2).* **3.** worthy of note or remembrance: *This is a historic moment.*

his·tor·i·cal (hi stôr′i kəl, -stor′-) *adj.* **1.** of, relating to, or involving history: *historical events, the historical method.* **2.** based on the facts, events, or persons of history rather than on fiction or legend: *a historical novel.* **3.** historic *(defs. 1, 3).* [Latin *historicus* relating to history (from Greek *historikos*, from *historiā* history) + -al.] —**his·tor′i·cal·ly**, *adv.* —**his·tor′i·cal·ness**, *n.*

historical present, the present tense used in relating past events.

his·to·ri·og·ra·pher (hi stôr′ē og′rə fər) n. a historian, esp. one who serves officially: *historiographer to a queen.* [Late Latin *historiographus* writer of history, from Greek *historiographos*, from *historiā* history + *graphein* to write.]

his·to·ri·og·ra·phy (hi stôr′ē og′rə fē) n. **1.** the writing or recording of history. **2.** historical writings collectively, as of a particular school. **3.** the science or study of the writing of history; principles of historical study.

his·to·ry (his′tə rē, his′trē) n., pl. -ries. **1.** a story or record of what has happened in the past. **2.** all past events in general. **3.** the branch of knowledge or study dealing with past events. **4.** a noteworthy past: *There is a long history behind that building.* **5.** something that is, or is considered to be, no longer important or of current concern: *That troubled period of his life is history now, and is best forgotten.* **6.** a drama representing historical events. [Latin *historia* narrative of past events, from Greek *historiā* inquiry, information, account, historical narrative. Doublet of story[1].]

his·tri·on·ic (his′trē on′ik) *adj.* **1.** insincere or exaggerated in character or manner; overemotional or theatrical: *a histrionic display of feelings.* **2.** of or relating to actors or acting. [Late Latin *histriōnicus* relating to an actor, from Latin *histriō* actor; possibly of Etruscan origin.]

his·tri·on·ics (his′trē on′iks) n. **1.** overemotional or theatrical behavior. **2.** a dramatic representation; acting; dramatics. ➡ used as plural in def. 1, as singular in def. 2.

hit (hit) v., **hit**, **hit·ting.** —v.t. **1.** to give a physical blow to; strike: *The batter hit the ball over the fence.* **2.** to come against forcibly; meet with a physical impact: *The car hit the tree.* **3.** to cause (something) to make forceful contact with: *She hit her head against the shelf.* **4.** to strike, as with a bullet or other projectile: *He was an expert at darts and could hit the bull's-eye.* **5.** to come to; reach: *She hit the high note perfectly.* **6.** to have a painful or harmful effect on: *The lack of job opportunities hit the town hard that winter.* **7.** to arrive or appear in, on, or at: *The news hit the front page this morning.* **8.** to become suddenly discovered or realized by: *The truth hit me at the last moment.* **9.** *Informal.* to attack or otherwise assail: *The guerrillas hit the camp at midnight. The audience hit the speaker with a huge number of questions.* **10.** *Informal.* to start traveling on: *The commuters hit the road at six o'clock every morning.* **11.** *Informal.* to appeal to or agree with; suit: *The proposed building site did not hit the company president as the best one.* **12.** *Informal.* to ask for money: *to hit someone for a loan.* **13.** *Baseball.* to make (a specified base hit): *to hit a home run.* **14.** *Slang.* to murder. —v.i. **1.** to give a blow; strike: *The heavyweight champion hits hard.* **2.** to come into forcible contact; collide: *The cars hit with a loud crash.* **3.** to arrive or appear: *The tornado hit without warning.* **4.** to discover or arrive at, esp. by accident (with *on* or *upon*): *We hit upon the solution to the problem.* —n. **1.** a blow or strike on something aimed at: *The missile made a direct hit.* **2.** a person or thing that is successful: *He was a hit with his roommate's sister. The song was a big hit.* **3.** base hit. **4.** *Slang.* a murder by a hired killer. [Old Norse *hitta* to meet with, light upon.] —**hit′ter**, *n.*
• **hit it off**, to like or get along well with one another: *We really hit it off from the day we met.*

hit-and-run (hit′ən run′) *adj.* **1.** of or relating to an accident in which a driver hits someone or something and then drives away without stopping or reporting the accident. **2.** *Baseball.* of or relating to a play in which a batter must attempt to hit the ball to protect a base runner who has started for the next base.

hitch (hich) v.t. **1.** to attach, as with a hook, rope, or strap, esp. temporarily; fasten; tie: *to hitch a trailer to a car.* **2.** to harness; yoke: *The farmer hitched the mule to the plow.* **3.** to raise or lift with a jerk: *I hitched the box up to my shoulder. He hitched up his suspenders.* **4.** *Informal.* to marry. ➡ usually used in the passive: *They're getting hitched tomorrow.* **5.** *Informal.* to obtain by hitch-hiking: *to hitch a ride to the station.* —v.i. **1.** to become fastened or caught: *Look at the burrs that have hitched onto my sweater.* **2.** *Informal.* to hitchhike: *We hitched all the way to Boston.* —n. **1.** a device used for connecting two things together; fastening; catch: *The hitch between the boat and the dock was slipping.* **2.** something that causes an unforeseen delay; obstacle; catch: *A hitch in the proceedings gave her time to review her notes.* **3.** an abrupt movement or pull; jerk: *to give one's trousers a hitch.* **4.** a hobble; limp; lameness: *a hitch in one's gait.* **5.** any of various knots used for temporary fastenings. **6.** *Informal.* a period spent in military service: *My cousin served a three-year hitch in the navy.* [Of uncertain origin.]

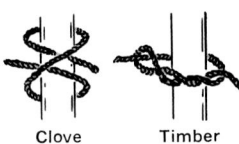

Clove   Timber

hitch *(n., def. 5)*

hitch·hike (hich′hīk′) v.i., -hiked, -hik·ing. to travel by getting free rides from passing motorists. —**hitch′hik′er**, *n.*

hitching post, a railing or pole to which animals, esp. horses, may be tied.

hith·er (hith′ər) *adv.* to or toward this place. —*adj.* on or toward this side; nearer. [Old English *hider* to this place.]

hith·er·most (hith′ər mōst′) *adj.* nearest.

hith·er·to (hith′ər tü′) *adv.* up to this time; until now.

hith·er·ward (hith′ər wərd) *also*, **hith·er·wards.** hither.

Hit·ler·ism (hit′lə riz′əm) n. the policies and practices of the German dictator Adolf Hitler and the Nazi Party.

hit man *Slang.* a person, esp. a member of an underworld organization, who is hired or assigned to kill someone.

hit-or-miss (hit′ər mis′) *adj.* done without or lacking care or planning; haphazard: *a hit-or-miss approach.*

Hit·tite (hit′īt) n. **1.** a member of a people whose civilization dominated Asia Minor and part of Syria between 2000 and 1200 B.C. **2.** the ancient language of the Hittites, belonging to the Indo-European family of languages. —*adj.* of or relating to the Hittites or their language. [Hebrew *Chiti* (from Hittite *Hatti* the Hittite people) + -ite[1].]

HIV, any of several retroviruses, at least one of which causes AIDS by invading the body's immune system and destroying certain cells that help fight disease. [Short for *h(uman) i(mmunodeficiency) v(irus)*.]

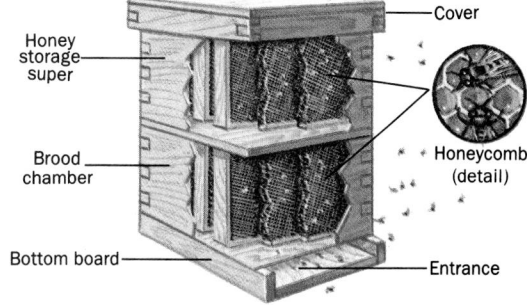

Honey storage super

Cover

Brood chamber

Honeycomb (detail)

Bottom board

Entrance

hive *(def. 1b)*

hive (hīv) n. **1.a.** any nest built by a colony of bees, esp. honeybees. **b.** any structure designed for honeybees to build a nest in. **2.** the colony of bees inhabiting a hive. **3.** a place swarming with busy or active people. **4.** a swarming, bustling crowd. —v., **hived**, **hiv·ing.** —v.t. **1.** to put (bees) into a hive. **2.** to store in or as in a hive for future use. —v.i. **1.** to enter a hive. **2.** to live in or as in a hive. [Old English *hȳf* beehive.]

a	at	e	end	o	hot	u	up	hw	white		about
ā	ape	ē	me	ō	old	ū	use	ng	song		taken
ä	far	i	it	ô	fork	ü	rule	th	thin	ə {	pencil
âr	care	ī	ice	oi	oil	u̇	pull	th	this		lemon
		îr	pierce	ou	out	ûr	turn	zh	measure		circus

hives (hīvz) *pl. n.* an allergic skin condition characterized by itching and burning and raised white welts surrounded by red areas. ➡ used as singular or plural. [Of uncertain origin.]

H.J., hic jacet.

hl *also*, **hl.** hectoliter; hectoliters.

HLA, any of a genetically determined complex of antigens present on the surface of human body cells, used for determining the compatibility of tissues for grafting or transplanting and susceptibility to certain diseases, as arthritis. [Abbreviation of *h(uman) l(eukocyte) a(ntigen)*.]

h'm (hm) *interj.* used to express hesitation, doubt, or meditation.

hm *also*, **hm.** hectometer; hectometers.

H.M., His (or Her) Majesty.

HMO, health maintenance organization.

H.M.S. 1. His (or Her) Majesty's Service. **2.** His (or Her) Majesty's Ship.

ho (hō) *interj.* **1.** used to express pleasure, surprise, or doubt. **2.** used to attract attention or call attention to: *Land ho!*

Ho, the symbol for holmium.

hoa·gy (hō′gē) *also*, **hoa·gie.** *n.* hero *(def. 5).* [Of uncertain origin.]

hoar (hôr) *adj.* hoary. —*n.* hoarfrost. [Old English *hār* gray, gray-haired, old.]

hoard (hôrd) *v.t.* to accumulate and store or hide away (money, food, or the like), esp. for future use. —*v.i.* to accumulate and store or hide away money, food, or the like, esp. for future use. —*n.* an accumulation of items stored up and often hidden, esp. for future use. [Old English *hord* accumulated stock, treasure.] —**hoard′er,** *n.*

hoard·ing[1] (hôr′ding) *n.* **1.** the act of one who hoards. **2.** *also*, **hoardings.** something that is hoarded. [HOARD + -ING[1].]

hoard·ing[2] (hôr′ding) *n. British.* **1.** a temporary board fence around a building under construction or repair. **2.** a billboard. [Obsolete *hoard* fence (probably from Old French *hourd* scaffold; of Germanic origin) + -ING[1].]

hoar·frost (hôr′frôst′) *n.* frost, esp. when it forms a white coating on a surface. Also, **hoar.**

hoar·hound (hôr′hound′) *n.* horehound.

hoarse (hôrs) *adj.*, **hoars·er, hoars·est. 1.** sounding deep and harsh or grating: *a hoarse voice.* **2.** having a harsh or grating voice: *to be hoarse after singing for an hour.* [Old English *hās.*] —**hoarse′ly,** *adv.* —**hoarse′ness,** *n.*

hoar·y (hôr′ē) *adj.*, **hoar·i·er, hoar·i·est. 1.** white or gray with or as with age: *the hoary beard of an old man, leaves hoary with frost.* **2.** old; ancient. —**hoar′i·ness,** *n.*

hoax (hōks) *n.* a trick or deception, meant either as a practical joke or as a fraud. —*v.t.* to trick or deceive by a hoax. [Modification of HOCUS.] —**hoax′er,** *n.*

hob[1] (hob) *n.* a projection or shelf at the back or side of the interior of a fireplace, used for keeping things warm. [Of uncertain origin.]

hob[2] (hob) *n.* a hobgoblin; elf. [Middle English *hobbe,* from *Hobbe,* an earlier nickname for *Robert* or *Robin.*]

· **to play** (or **raise**) **hob with.** *Informal.* to be a cause of trouble, mischief, or confusion to: *Her slowness played hob with our plan to leave early.*

hob·ble (hob′əl) *v.*, **-bled, -bling.** —*v.i.* to move or walk awkwardly with or as if with a limp: *The injured athlete had to hobble around in a cast for a month.* —*v.t.* **1.** to hold together the front legs or hind legs of (a horse or other animal) with a very short rope, strap, or similar material, esp. to prevent it from moving far. **2.** to impede the action or progress of: *Lack of time hobbled the project.* **3.** to cause to limp or move unsteadily. —*n.* **1.** a rope, strap, or other device used to hobble an animal. **2.** an awkward or faltering walk; limp. **3.** *Archaic.* an awkward or difficult situation. [Probably of Low German origin.]

hob·ble·de·hoy (hob′əl dē hoi′) *n.* an adolescent boy, esp. one who is awkward or gawky. [Of uncertain origin.]

hobble skirt, a woman's skirt, popular around the end of World War I, that was very narrow below the knees, making it necessary for the wearer to take small steps when walking.

hob·by (hob′ē) *n., pl.* **-bies.** an activity or interest that is undertaken for pleasure or relaxation in one's spare time. [Middle English *hobyn* small horse, form of the name *Robin* or *Robert;* the pursuit of a *hobby* being likened to a child's playing with a toy horse.]

hob·by·horse (hob′ē hôrs′) *n.* **1.** a toy horse, usually consisting of a horse's head attached to a pole that a child can straddle and pretend to ride. **2.** rocking horse. [HOBBY + HORSE.]

hob·by·ist (hob′ē ist) *n.* a person who follows a hobby.

hob·gob·lin (hob′gob′lin) *n.* **1.a.** a mischievous goblin or elf. **b.** a frightful apparition. **2.** anything, usually imaginary, that arouses fear or unreasonable concern: *A foolish consistency is the*

hobgoblin of little minds (Ralph Waldo Emerson, 1841). [HOB[2] + GOBLIN.]

hob·nail (hob′nāl′) *n.* a nail with a large head used to protect the soles of heavy boots or shoes. [Archaic *hob* peg + NAIL.]

hob·nob (hob′nob′) *v.i.* **-nobbed, -nob·bing.** to be on close or familiar terms; be friendly (with *with*): *Their family hobnobs with the wealthiest people.* [Earlier *hob or nob* give or take, have or have not, hit or miss; with reference to the custom of alternating in treating to drinks, going back to Old English *habban* to have + *nabban* not to have.]

ho·bo (hō′bō) *n., pl.* **-boes** or **-bos.** a tramp. [Possibly from *hoe-boy* migrant farm worker.]

Hob·son's choice (hob′sənz) a choice of taking whatever is offered or nothing at all. [From Thomas *Hobson,* seventeenth-century English owner of a livery stable, who forced customers to rent either the horse nearest the stable door or none.]

hock[1] (hok) *n.* a joint in the hind leg, as of a horse or cow, that is above the fetlock joint and corresponds to the ankle in humans. For illustration, see **fetlock.** [Old English *hōh* heel.]

hock[2] (hok) *n.* any white Rhine wine. [Short for obsolete *hockamore,* modification of German *Hochheimer* (wine) of *Hochheim,* German village from which the wine comes.]

hock[3] (hok) *Informal. v.t.* to pawn. [Dutch *hok* pen for animals, prison.]

· **in hock. a.** in the possession of a pawnbroker. **b.** in debt: *to be in hock for over a thousand dollars.*

hock·ey (hok′ē) *n.* **1.** a game played on ice by two teams of six players each, in which the object is to hit a puck into the opponent's goal. Also, **ice hockey. 2.** field hockey. [Possibly from Old French *hoquet* bent stick, diminutive of *hoc* hook; of Germanic origin.]

hockey stick, a long stick with a flat curved blade used to hit the puck in ice hockey or the ball in field hockey.

ho·cus (hō′kəs) *v.t.,* **-cused, -cus·ing;** *also, British,* **-cussed, -cus·sing.** to play a trick on; hoax. [Short for HOCUS-POCUS.]

ho·cus-po·cus (hō′kəs pō′kəs) *n.* **1.** meaningless words used as a magical-sounding formula in conjuring or performing tricks. **2.** sleight of hand or any other magic trick. **3.** any bit of trickery or nonsense; deception. [Coined to imitate Latin.]

hod (hod) *n.* **1.** a long-handled tool with an open-ended container consisting of two sides meeting in a V and a third side blocking one end, used for carrying bricks, mortar, and similar materials on the shoulder, esp. to supply workers at a building site. **2.** coal scuttle. [Middle Dutch *hodde* basket.]

hod carrier, a worker who carries materials, such as bricks or mortar, in a hod to other workers.

hodge·podge (hoj′poj′) *also,* **hotchpotch.** *n.* a jumbled mixture; conglomeration. [Modification of earlier *hotchpot,* from Old French *hochepot,* from *hocher* to shake (of Germanic origin) + *pot* pot (of Germanic origin).]

Hodg·kin's disease (hoj′kinz) a cancerous disease characterized by progressive enlargement of the lymph glands. [From Thomas *Hodgkin,* 1798-1866, English physician who discovered it.]

hoe (hō) *n.* **1.** a tool with a wide, thin blade set at an angle to a long handle, used esp. for weeding and loosening soil. **2.** any of various similar tools used for weeding or loosening soil or for mixing mortar, plaster, and the like. —*v.i., v.t.,* **hoed, hoe·ing.** to dig or cultivate with a hoe. [Old French *houe* this tool; of Germanic origin.] —**ho′er,** *n.*

hoe·cake (hō′kāk′) *n.* a coarse bread made of cornmeal, water, and salt, shaped into a flat, thin cake, originally baked on a hoe over a fire.

hoe·down (hō′doun′) *n.* **1.** a square dance, esp. a lively or noisy one. **2.** a party or dance where people square-dance. [HOE + DOWN[1].]

hog (hôg, hog) *n.* **1.** a domestic pig, esp. one weighing over 120 pounds (54 kilograms) and raised for its meat. **2.** wild boar. **3.** *Informal.* a gluttonous, greedy, or filthy person. —*v.t.,* **hogged, hog·ging.** *Informal.* to take more than one's share of: *The truck hogged the road so that we couldn't pass.* [Old English *hogg* a swine.]

· **to go hog wild.** *Informal.* to act without control or inhibitions.

· **to go whole hog.** *Informal.* to act or indulge without restraint or limits: *My friend went whole hog and bought a car with all the extras.*

· **to live** (or **eat**) **high on the hog.** *Informal.* to live (or eat) very well: *Our neighbors won the lottery, and they've been living high on the hog ever since.*

ho·gan (hō′gän, -gan) *n.* a dwelling of the Navaho Indians, usually made of timber and branches covered with earth.

hog·back (hôg′bak′, hog′-) *n. Geology.* a sharply crested ridge with abruptly sloping sides, typically formed by exposure of steeply inclined strata.

hog cholera, a highly contagious, often fatal viral disease of swine, characterized by fever, diarrhea, and emaciation and usually accompanied by a secondary salmonella infection.

hog·gish (hôg′gish, hog′ish) *adj.* gluttonous, greedy, or filthy like a hog. —**hog′gish·ly,** *adv.* —**hog′gish·ness,** *n.*

hog·nose snake (hôg′nōz′, hog′-) any of several thick-nosed, harmless North American snakes, family Colubridae, that flatten their bodies and hiss ferociously when disturbed.

hogs·head (hôgz′hed′, hogz′-) *n.* **1.** a large cask or barrel, esp. one that can contain from 63 to 140 gallons (238 to 530 liters). **2.** a liquid measure, esp. one equal to 63 gallons (238 liters).

hog-tie (hôg′tī, hog′-) *v.t.,* **-tied, -ty·ing. 1.** to tie up by binding the four feet together: *to hog-tie a calf before branding it.* **2.** to restrict the action of; restrain; hamper; hinder: *a new social program hog-tied by lack of funds.*

hog·wash (hôg′wôsh′, hog′wosh′) *n.* **1.** worthless or nonsensical talk or writing. **2.** refuse fed to hogs; swill.

ho-hum (hō′hum′, -hum′) *interj.* a sound made to show one is bored or indifferent. —*adj. Slang.* **1.** lacking interest; routine; boring: *to have a ho-hum job.* **2.** not caring; indifferent; bored: *a ho-hum reaction.* [Imitative.]

hoi·den (hoi′dən) hoyden.

hoi pol·loi (hoi′ pə loi′) the common people; the masses. ➡ usually used contemptuously. [Greek *hoi polloi* the many.]

> **Usage** Hoi polloi means "the masses." Since *the* is part of the definition, it is redundant to say *the hoi polloi,* which would be the same as saying *the the masses.* However, it is widely used and is generally considered acceptable.

hoist (hoist) *v.t.* to lift or pull up, esp. by means of some mechanical device: *The sailors hoisted the cargo on board.* —*n.* **1.** an apparatus, such as a block and tackle or elevator, for hoisting. **2.** the act of hoisting. [Earlier *hoise, hysse,* probably from Middle Dutch *hischen, hyssen* to raise up.]

hoi·ty-toi·ty (hoi′tē toi′tē) *adj.* **1.** snobbish or pompous; haughty: *a hoity-toity manner.* **2.** giddy; flighty. —*n.* giddy or flighty behavior. [Rhyming expression based on obsolete *hoit* to romp; of uncertain origin.]

ho·key-po·key (hō′kē pō′kē) *n.* mild deception or trickery; funny business. [Modification of HOCUS-POCUS.]

ho·kum (hō′kəm) *n. Informal.* meaningless or false talk or ideas; nonsense; bunk. [Possibly blend of HOCUS-POCUS and BUNKUM.]

hold¹ (hōld) *v.,* **held, held** or *(archaic)* **hold·en, hold·ing.** —*v.t.* **1.** to take and keep in the hands or arms; clasp; grip: *The mother held the squirming child on her lap. He held the packages while I unlocked the door.* **2.** to keep up; support; bear: *Will the chair hold my weight?* **3.a.** to keep in a particular position; maintain: *The photographer asked me to hold the pose. Hold your arms over your head.* **b.** to keep in a particular state or condition; have control or influence over: *to hold an audience's attention.* **4.** to keep under control; keep back; check: *The troops held their fire. The little boy held his breath.* **5.** to prevent the movement or escape of; detain: *The deputy held the prisoner at gunpoint. The dam held back the river.* **6.** to set aside or reserve: *to hold theater tickets at the box office.* **7.** to be able to contain: *The bus can hold twenty-five people. A sponge holds water.* **8.** to keep or have in or as in the mind; harbor: *to hold an opinion, to hold a grudge.* **9.** to keep forcibly against an enemy; defend: *The troops held the territory.* **10.** to have and retain as one's own; possess; occupy: *to hold a high position in government.* **11.** to carry on; engage in: *to hold a conversation, to hold a celebration.* **12.** to cause to come about; call; convene: *to hold a meeting.* **13.** to believe or judge to be; think; assert; consider: *The scientist held that the drug was dangerous.* **14.** *Law.* **a.** to decree: *The jury held the defendant not guilty.* **b.** to decide (a question of law): *The court held that the statute did not apply to the facts.* **c.** to possess or have title to: *to hold property.* **15.** *Music.* to sustain (a musical note): *The singer held high C for fifteen seconds.* —*v.i.* **1.** to remain fast or unbroken; not yield: *The anchor held even in the rough seas.* **2.** to keep one's clasp or grip: *The old woman held tightly to the railing as she came down the steps.* **3.** to remain faithful or attached; adhere: *to hold to one's beliefs, to hold to a purpose.* **4.** to remain valid; be in force; apply: *My decision still holds.* **5.** to remain or continue in a state, position, or condition: *The humidity held all day.* —*n.* **1.a.** the act of holding; grasp; grip: *to have a tight hold on a rope.* **b.** a way of gripping with the hands or arms: *a wrestling hold.* **2.** controlling force; strong influence: *The dictator kept a tight hold on the country. Some ideas exert an unshakable hold on people's imagination.* **3.** something that can be grasped, as for support: *The diver found a hold in the coral reef.* **4.** an order to put aside or delay (something): *Put a hold on the delivery until the balance is paid.* **5.** a halt made in the countdown for a rocket or missile launch to allow correction of a problem or problems. **6.** a prison cell: *the hold of a castle.* **7.** *Music.* a sign or symbol indicating a pause. **8.** *Archaic.* a fortified place; stronghold. [Old English *h(e)aldan*

to detain, keep, support, defend.] —For Synonyms *(v.t.),* see **contain.**

• **to hold back. a.** to keep back; restrain: *I tried to hold the dog back.* **b.** to stop or hesitate in one's actions; refrain: *She held back from asking the favor of him.* **c.** to keep in or as in one's possession; retain: *Do not hold back the truth.*

• **to hold down. a.** to keep under subjection or control; repress: *The police officers held down the unruly crowd.* **b.** to have and work at: *His frequent illnesses made it difficult for him to hold down a job.*

• **to hold forth. a.** to talk at great length; lecture; harangue: *The candidate was holding forth on the incumbent's mistakes.* **b.** to offer; propose: *The advertisement holds forth the promise of a superior product.*

• **to hold in. a.** to keep in check; curb; restrain: *The rider held in the horse with the reins.* **b.** to control or hide (one's feelings or impulses): *to hold in the urge to cry.*

• **to hold off. a.** to keep away or at a distance: *The troops held off the enemy.* **b.** to refrain temporarily from action; delay: *The committee held off giving a decision until hearing more evidence.*

• **to hold on.** *Informal.* **a.** to maintain one's hold or grasp on something: *Hold on so you don't fall off the swing.* **b.** to continue; persist: *The custom held on for two generations.* **c.** to stop; wait. ➡ usually used in the imperative: *Hold on; don't get so excited!*

• **to hold one's own.** to maintain one's condition, advantage, or position; stand one's ground: *The gymnast held her own in the last event and finished in first place.*

• **to hold out. a.** to last; endure: *The food supplies held out for a week.* **b.** to maintain or continue resistance: *The soldiers in the besieged fort held out for two weeks.* **c.** to extend; offer; present: *to hold out a promise of new jobs.* **d.** *Informal.* to keep back or delay (something expected or due): *The employer held out the workers' pay as punishment for striking.*

• **to hold over. a.** to keep for future action or consideration; postpone: *The bill was held over for the next session.* **b.** to remain in office or in possession beyond the regular term. **c.** to have or use as an advantage, control, or threat.

• **to hold up. a.** *Informal.* to rob: *The thieves held up the store.* **b.** to bring or point attention to: *to hold up as an example.* **c.** to maintain a state or position; last; endure: *The prisoner held up under the questioning.* **d.** to stop; delay: *The filibuster held up action on the bill.*

• **to hold water.** to be sound, believable, or consistent; stand up: *Will your argument hold water?*

• **to hold with.** to approve of.

hold² (hōld) *n.* the space below the deck of a ship where cargo is stowed. [Modification (influenced by HOLD¹) of HOLE or of Middle Dutch *hol* hole, ship's hold.]

hold·back (hōld′bak′) *n.* something that holds back; check; restraint.

hold·en (hōl′dən) *Archaic.* a past participle of **hold¹.**

hold·er (hōl′dər) *n.* **1.** a person who holds something, esp. an owner or possessor, as of property or a title. **2.** an object that holds or aids in holding something: *a napkin holder.* **3.** a person who is the legal possessor of a bill, note, or check and is entitled to receive payment on it.

hold·fast (hōld′fast′) *n.* **1.** a device that secures or holds something in place, as a clamp, catch, or hook. **2.** *Botany.* any of various structures functioning in plants, esp. rootless algae, for attachment to a surface. **3.** *Zoology.* any of various hooks, suckers, or other organs functioning in parasitic or sessile animals for attachment, as to a host or to the sea floor. [HOLD¹ + FAST¹.]

hold·ing (hōl′ding) *n.* **1.** a piece of rented land. **2.** *also,* **holdings.** legally held property, esp. stocks or bonds. **3.** *Sports.* an act or instance of illegally hindering the movement of an opposing player.

holding company, a company that exists for the primary purpose of holding ownership of other companies, usually by owning portions of stock. A holding company is generally not involved in the other companies' day-to-day operations.

holding pattern 1. a path flown by an aircraft as it waits for permission to land. **2.** any period or condition during which there is no change or progress; static situation.

hold·out (hōld′out′) *n. Informal.* **1.** a person or group that continues to resist some change, rule, or condition: *We took a vote, and there were two holdouts.* **2.** the act of refusing to accept

a	at	e	end	o	hot	u	up	hw	white		about
ā	ape	ē	me	ō	old	ū	use	ng	song		taken
ä	far	i	it	ô	fork	ü	rule	th	thin	ə	pencil
âr	care	ī	ice	oi	oil	u̇	pull	th	this		lemon
				îr	pierce	ou	out	ûr	turn	zh	measure		circus

or of resisting some rule, change, or condition: *Some strikers took part in a holdout and would not accept the new contract.*

hold·o·ver (hōld′ō′vər) *n.* **1.** something postponed for future action: *The bill is a holdover from the last session of Congress.* **2.** a person or thing that remains: *The movie is a holdover from last week.*

hold·up (hōld′up′) *n.* **1.** the act of, or an attempt at, armed robbery. **2.** a stoppage or delay: *There was a traffic holdup because of the accident.*

hole (hōl) *n.* **1.** a hollow place or cavity in a solid body or surface; pit: *The workers dug a hole in the ground for the foundation. The apples were riddled with holes made by insects.* **2.** an opening in or through something; perforation: *The bullet made a hole in the window.* **3.** any small, dingy, squalid place: *My first apartment was a real hole.* **4.** a prison cell; dungeon. **5.** a flaw; defect; fault: *There were many holes in the suspect's alibi.* **6.** a pond or deep, calm place in a river, stream, or pond: *a swimming hole, a fishing hole.* **7.** *Informal.* an awkward or embarrassing position; predicament: *Your poor judgment got you into one hole after another.* **8.** *Golf.* **a.** a small, round cavity with a cup into which the ball is hit. **b.** the area between a tee and this hole, including the fairway and the putting green. **9.** *Physics.* a spot vacated by an electron in the crystal structure of a semiconductor, acting as a carrier of a positive charge. —*v.,* **holed, hol·ing.** —*v.t.* **1.** to make a hole or holes in: *to hole the earth along the road for telephone posts.* **2.** to hit or drive into a hole: *The golfer holed the ball on the third stroke.* **3.** to make by or as by digging or boring: *to hole a tunnel through a mountain.* —*v.i.* to make a hole or holes: *The miners holed through from one shaft to another.* [Old English *hol* hollow place.]

  •**hole in one.** *Golf.* a single drive from a tee that goes into the cup.

  •**in the hole.** in debt.

  •**to burn a hole in one's pocket.** (of money) to create a strong desire to spend it.

  •**to hole out.** to hit a golf ball into a hole.

  •**to hole up. a.** to hibernate in or as in a hole: *The bear holed up for the winter.* **b.** to seclude or hide oneself: *The townspeople holed up until the enemy soldiers had left the area.*

  •**to make a hole in.** to consume a considerable part of: *Paying the unexpected bills made a considerable hole in our savings.*

Synonyms **Hole, cavity,** and **hollow** denote an empty space in a body or surface. **Hole** is the general term and means an unfilled space in a solid body, which connects with the surface: *a hole in the side of a barn, a hole in one's stocking.* **Cavity** connotes an unfilled space that may or may not connect with the surface: *a cavity inside a mountain, a cavity in a tooth.* **Hollow** often connotes a space entirely enclosed within an object, although it is also used to describe some unfilled spaces, such as depressions or concavities: *a hollow inside a gold ball, a hollow in the side of a hill, a hollow in a tree.*

hol·i·day (hol′i dā′) *n.* **1.** a day when work is stopped by custom or law, in order to commemorate a special event. **2.** any day free from work. **3.** a vacation. ➡ often used in the plural: *to go home for the holidays.* **4.** a holy day. —*adj.* relating or suited to a holiday; gay; festive. [Old English *hāligdæg* holy day.]

ho·li·er-than-thou (hō′lē ər then thou′) *adj.* showing a feeling of superiority or self-righteousness: *a holier-than-thou attitude.*

ho·li·ness (hō′lē nis) *n.* **1.** the quality or state of being holy. **2. Holiness.** used as a form of address in speaking or referring to the pope and some patriarchs of the Orthodox Church, preceded by *His* or *Your.* [Old English *hāligness* quality of being holy.]

ho·lis·tic (hō lis′tik) *adj.* emphasizing understanding of the whole person and the interaction of physical, mental, and social factors that affect a person's health: *holistic medicine.* [Greek *holos* whole + -IST + -IC.]

hol·land (hol′ənd) *n.* a linen or cotton fabric, sometimes given a glazed finish, used for such items as window shades and upholstery. [From *Holland,* where it was first made.]

hol·lan·daise sauce (hol′ən dāz′) a rich, creamy sauce made from egg yolks, butter, lemon juice, and seasoning. [French *sauce hollandaise* Dutch sauce; *hollandaise,* feminine of *hollandais* Dutch, from *Hollande* the Netherlands, from Dutch *Holland,* former county of the Netherlands. See SAUCE.]

Hol·lands (hol′əndz) *n.* a very dry gin, originally made in Holland, in which the flavoring agent, juniper, is ground up directly with the malt. Also, **Hollands gin.**

hol·ler (hol′ər) *v.t., v.i. Informal.* to shout. —*n.* a shout.

hol·lo (hol′ō, hə lō′) halloo.

hol·loa (hol′ō, hə lō′) halloo.

hol·low (hol′ō) *adj.* **1.** having a hole or cavity within; not solid: *a hollow pipe, a hollow tree trunk.* **2.** having a depression or groove in the surface; concave; scooped out: *a hollow place in the road.* **3.** set deeply within; sunken, as the cheeks or eyes. **4.** deep and

muffled in tone, as though reverberating in an empty space: *Our footsteps made a hollow sound in the cave.* **5.** devoid of worth, sincerity, or substance; false; deceitful: *hollow oaths.* **6.** empty or lacking, as emotion: *The news left me with a hollow feeling.* —*n.* **1.** a cavity, depression, or concavity in any surface; empty space; hole. **2.** a feeling of emptiness or void. **3.** a valley or basin. —*v.t.* **1.** to make hollow (with *out*): *The cook hollowed out the tomatoes before stuffing them.* **2.** to form by making hollow (with *out*): *to hollow out a tunnel in a hillside.* [Old English *holh* hole, cave.] —**hol′low·ly,** *adv.* —**hol′low·ness,** *n.* —For Synonyms (n.), see **hole.**

  •**to beat all hollow.** to defeat or surpass completely.

hol·low-eyed (hol′ō īd′) *adj.* having deep-set eyes, often encircled by dark rings due to illness or fatigue.

hol·low·ware (hol′ō wâr′) *n.* dishes, bowls, and other tableware that have depth, made of metal, earthenware, or the like. ➡ distinguished from **flatware.**

hol·ly (hol′ē) *n., pl.* **-lies. 1.** any of a group of trees or woody shrubs, genus *Ilex,* bearing greenish white flowers, the females of which have bright red, black, or yellow fruit. The best-known species is the evergreen English holly, *I. aquifolium,* bearing glossy spiny-toothed leaves and bright red berries. **2.** the shiny leaves and berries of any of several of these trees or shrubs, widely used as Christmas decorations. [Old English *hole(g)n* shrub of the genus *Ilex.*]

hol·ly·hock (hol′ē hok′) *n.* any of several plants of the genus *Alcea,* esp. *A. rosea,* having wrinkled leaves and a hairy stem and bearing spikelike stalks of large, showy white, pink, purple, or yellow flowers. [Middle English *holihoc* marsh mallow, from *holi* holy + *hoc* mallow (from Old English *hoc*). See HOLY.]

Hol·ly·wood (hol′ē wùd′) *n.* the U.S. motion-picture and television industries or their characteristic image: *to achieve success in Hollywood.* [From *Hollywood,* California, center of the American motion-picture industry.]

Hollywood bed, a single bed with or without a headboard, usually supported by four short legs.

holm (hōm) *n.* holm oak.

hol·mi·um (hōl′mē əm) *n.* a lustrous metallic element, nearly as heavy as copper, one of the rare-earth elements. Symbol: **Ho** For tables, see **element.** [Modern Latin *holmium,* from earlier *holmia,* from *Holmia* Stockholm; because its second discoverer, Per Teodor Cleve, 1840-1905, was born there.]

hollyhock

holm oak, an ornamental evergreen tree, *Quercus ilex,* grown in warm regions of the world, having broad, leathery leaves. Also, **holm, ilex.** [*Holm* (going back to Old English *holegn* holly) + OAK.]

hol·o·caust (hol′ə kôst′, hō′lə-) *n.* **1.** great or complete destruction, esp. by fire. **2.** a sacrifice that is entirely consumed by fire. **3. the Holocaust.** the systematic persecution and murder of millions of European Jews by the Nazis during World War II. [Middle English *holocaust,* from Old French *holocauste,* from Late Latin *holocaustum* whole burnt offering or sacrifice, from Greek *holokauston,* from *holos* whole + *kauston* burnt.]

Hol·o·cene (hol′ə sēn′, hō′lə-) *Geology. adj.* recent *(def. 3).* —*n.* recent. [Greek *holos* whole + *kainos* recent.]

ho·lo·gram (hol′ə gram′, hō′lə-) *n.* a piece of photographic film on which are recorded the interference patterns made by two beams of laser light, one beam having been reflected by an object or scene. When properly illuminated, the hologram produces a realistic three-dimensional image of the object or scene. [Greek *holos* whole + -GRAM[1].]

hol·o·graph (hol′ə graf′, hō′lə-) *adj.* written entirely in the handwriting of the person who signed it: *a holograph document.* —*n.* any document written in this way. [Late Latin *holographus,* going back to Greek *holos* whole + *graphein* to write.]

ho·log·ra·phy (hə log′rə fē) *n.* the process in which laser beams are used to make holograms. [Greek *holos* whole + -GRAPHY.] —**ho·lo·graph·ic** (hō′lə graf′ik, hol′ə-), *adj.*

hol·o·thu·ri·an (hol′ə thůr′ē ən) *n.* sea cucumber. [Latin *holothuria,* from Greek *holothouria,* plural of *holothourion* kind of water polyp.]

holp (hōlp) *Archaic.* a past tense of **help.**

hol·pen (hōl′pən) *Archaic.* a past participle of **help.**

Hol·stein (hōl′stīn, -stēn′) *n.* one of a breed of black-and-white dairy cattle that produce large amounts of milk. They are the largest of all dairy breeds, the bull weighing at least 2,200 pounds (998 kilograms). Also, **Hol·stein-Frie·sian** (hōl′stīn′ frē′zhən, -stēn′).

hol·ster (hōl′stər) *n.* a case, usually of leather, for a pistol, rifle,

or similar weapon, attached to a belt at the waist or shoulder or to a rider's saddle. [Dutch *holster.*] —**hol′stered,** *adj.*

ho·ly (hō′lē) *adj.,* **-li·er, -li·est. 1.** belonging to, dedicated to, or coming from a deity; sacred. **2.** having a sacred quality by religious use or authority; consecrated: *holy bread.* **3.** spiritually pure; free from sin; pious; saintly. **4.** worthy of or inspiring reverence. [Old English *hālig* sacred, pure, saintly.]

Synonyms Holy, **sacred,** or **divine** are religious terms that may all mean worthy of worship or veneration. **Holy** is used of things either believed to have innate sanctity or to have been consecrated to the service of a god: *holy scriptures, a holy place.* **Sacred,** often opposed to profane, is similar to and often interchangeable with *holy,* but it most often describes a sanctity derived from the act of consecration: *the sacred ground of a temple, sacred relics.* **Divine,** used of abstract concepts, connotes something coming from or having the characteristics of a god: *divine guidance, divine will.*

Holy Alliance, an agreement uniting European monarchs in 1815, the object of which was to perpetuate existing dynasties and suppress revolutionary movements.

holy city, a city considered sacred by the followers of a particular religion, as Jerusalem is by Jews, Christians, and Muslims.

Holy Communion 1. a church service in which bread and wine are consecrated and distributed to members of the congregation in commemoration of the Last Supper. **2.** the bread and wine, or elements, used in this service, esp. when received as a sacrament.

holy day, a day set apart for religious observance.

Holy Father, used as a title in speaking to or referring to the pope.

Holy Ghost, the third person of the Trinity. Also, **Holy Spirit.**

Holy Grail, in medieval legend, the sacred chalice considered to be either the cup used by Jesus at the Last Supper or the vessel that caught the blood of Jesus at the Crucifixion. King Arthur's Knights of the Round Table searched for the Holy Grail.

Holy Land, Palestine.

holy of holies 1. the innermost chamber of the Temple in ancient Jerusalem, concealed from public view by a veil. It housed the Ark of the Covenant and could be entered only by the high priest on the Day of Atonement. **2.** any place or thing of special sacredness.

holy orders 1. the rite or sacrament of ordination. **2.** the rank of an ordained Christian minister or priest, esp. in a church with an official hierarchy. **3.** the higher grades of the ministry, as in the Roman Catholic, Anglican, or Orthodox Church.

Holy Roman Empire, an empire in western and central Europe that was founded by Charlemagne in 800 and lapsed into anarchy late in the ninth century. It was revived by Otto I of Germany in 962 and lasted until 1806.

Holy Rood 1. the cross on which Jesus was crucified. **2. holy rood.** a crucifix, esp. one above an ornamented screen at a church altar.

Holy Saturday, Saturday of Holy Week, the day before Easter Sunday.

Holy Scripture, the Bible *(def. 1).*

Holy See, the office, authority, or jurisdiction of the pope. Also, **Apostolic See.**

Holy Spirit, Holy Ghost.

ho·ly·stone (hō′lē stōn′) *n.* a flat piece of soft sandstone used for scouring the wooden decks of ships. —*v.t.,* **-stoned, -ston·ing.** to scrub with a holystone. [HOLY + STONE; supposedly because its users kneel while working.]

Holy Synod, the administrative council of a self-governing Orthodox Church.

Holy Thursday 1. Maundy Thursday. **2.** in the Anglican Church, Ascension Day.

holy water, water blessed by a priest, used in religious services and devotional acts, as in baptizing or blessing.

Holy Week, the week before Easter, beginning with Palm Sunday.

Holy Writ, the Bible *(def. 1).*

hom·age (hom′ij, om′-) *n.* **1.** honor, respect, or reverent regard: *The university paid homage to the professor at commencement.* **2.** the formal acknowledgment of allegiance and obligation by a feudal vassal to his lord. **3.** an act done or payment made to indicate such acknowledgment. [Old French *homage* duty owed by a vassal to his lord, from *hom* man, vassal, from Latin *homō* man.]

hom·bre (ōm′brā, -brē) *n.* *Informal.* man; fellow. [Spanish *hombre,* from Latin *homō.*]

hom·burg (hom′bûrg′) *also,* **Hom·burg.** *n.* a felt hat with a brim turned up slightly at the sides and a crown dented lengthwise. [From *Homburg,* Germany, where it was first made.]

home (hōm) *n.* **1.** the place in which one lives; domicile; residence: *I'll be at home if you need me.* **2.** the home regarded as

representing a family unit; household: *a happy home, a broken home.* **3.** a country, region, town, or locality where one was born or reared or where one lives: *New York has been my home for five years now.* **4.** the place or region where something originated, developed, or is commonly or natively found: *Australia is the home of the koala bear.* **5.** a place where one feels one belongs or where one finds refuge or satisfaction: *The popular teacher found a home in the school and taught there for many years.* **6.** an institution or establishment for the shelter and care of certain people: *a foundling home, a home for the aged.* **7.** a place from which activities are initiated or coordinated; base of operations; headquarters: *The pilot turned the plane around and headed for home.* **8.** a goal or place of safety in certain sports and games. **9.** *Baseball.* home plate. —*adv.* **1.** at, to, or toward home: *to walk someone home.* **2.a.** to the place or mark aimed at; so as to penetrate effectively: *The dart hit home.* **b.** so as to reach or affect intimately and completely; to the very heart: *Her criticism hit home. The examples he used drove his argument home.* —*v.,* **homed, hom·ing.** —*v.i.* **1.** to go or return home: *The pigeon homed from a distance of 100 miles.* **2.** to proceed or be directed toward a particular point or target, as by means of radio waves or by heat radiation emanating from the point or target (often with *in* or *on*). —*v.t.* to cause, as an aircraft or guided missile, to proceed toward a particular point or target, esp. toward a target emitting heat radiation. [Old English *hām* dwelling house.] —**home′like′,** *adj.*

• **at home. a.** at one's ease; comfortable: *I always felt at home at my friend's house.* **b.** ready to receive guests. **c.** thoroughly familiar with; knowledgeable; proficient: *to be at home in the fine arts.*

Synonyms *n.* Home, **house, residence, dwelling, domicile,** and **abode** all denote a place where a person or persons live. **Home** is the common term, which often suggests warmth, comfort, and protection: *I miss my home.* **House** refers only to the building itself: *My house is on the corner.* **Residence** is a more formal term, which may imply wealth. It may also be used to indicate where one lives for legal purposes: *a substantial four-story residence, to have a residence in the city.* **Dwelling** is a somewhat quaint term, which usually describes a simple or even lowly structure. It is also used to distinguish a home from a business address: *We came upon a humble dwelling under the trees. How many dwellings are there on this block?* **Domicile,** like *residence,* is used in legal contexts: *List your domicile on the form.* **Abode,** like *dwelling,* is used poetically: *the abode of an obscure forest dweller.*

home base 1. home plate. **2.** a headquarters or base of operations, as for an organization or company. **3.** a goal or place of safety in certain sports and games.

home·bod·y (hōm′bod′ē) *n., pl.* **-bod·ies.** a person who prefers to stay at home or whose interests center on the home.

home·bred (hōm′bred′) *adj.* bred or raised at home; native; domestic.

home brew *also,* **home-brew.** any alcoholic beverage or liquor made at home.

home care, medical care provided at the patient's home, esp. for the elderly or those with long-term illnesses. —**home′-care′,** *adj.*

home·com·ing (hōm′kum′ing) *n.* **1.** a return to one's home. **2.** an annual celebration in many colleges and universities, marked by the return of alumni.

home economics, the science, art, and study of managing a household, including such subjects as nutrition, budgeting, and child care.

home fries, boiled potatoes sliced and fried in butter or shortening. Also, **home-fried potatoes.**

home front, the civilian population of a country at war.

home·grown (hōm′grōn′) *adj.* grown, produced, or developed locally or at home.

home·land (hōm′land′) *n.* **1.** a person's native or adopted land. **2.** a region or country considered as the ancestral land of a particular ethnic group.

home·less (hōm′lis) *adj.* having no home. —*n.* **the homeless.** homeless persons considered as a group.

home·ly (hōm′lē) *adj.,* **-li·er, -li·est. 1.** having plain features; not good-looking. **2.** of a familiar or everyday nature; unpretentious; simple: *homely truths, homely virtues.* —**home′li·ness,** *n.*

home·made (hōm′mād′) *adj.* **1.** made at home: *homemade*

a	at	e	end	o	hot	u	up	hw	white		about
ā	ape	ē	me	ō	old	ū	use	ng	song		taken
ä	far	i	it	ô	fork	ü	rule	th	thin	ə	pencil
âr	care	ī	ice	oi	oil	u̇	pull	th	this		lemon
		îr	pierce	ou	out	ûr	turn	zh	measure		circus

soup. **2.** crudely or simply done; not professionally made: *a dress that looks homemade.*

home·mak·er (hōm′mā′kər) *n.* a person who manages a household.

ho·me·op·a·thy (hō′mē op′ə thē) *n.* a method of treating disease with small amounts of drugs that, if given in larger doses to a healthy person, would produce symptoms similar to those of the disease. ➡ opposed to **allopathy.** [Modern Latin *homoeopathia,* from Greek *homoios* like + *-patheia* -PATHY.] —**ho·me·o·path** (hō′mē ə path′), **ho′me·op′a·thist,** *n.* —**ho′me·o·path′ic,** *adj.*

ho·me·o·sta·sis (hō′mē ə stā′sis) *n.* the tendency of the body of an organism to maintain internal equilibrium by means of coordinated physiological responses to changes in the external environment. Such responses include changes in body temperature, blood pressure, and heartbeat. This equilibrium is essential for the normal functioning of the body. [Modern Latin, from Greek *homoios* like + *stasis* a standing still.]

ho·me·o·stat·ic (hō′mē ə stat′ik) *adj.* of or relating to homeostasis.

home·own·er (hōm′ō′nər) *n.* a person who owns a home. —**home′own′er·ship,** *n.*

home plate, a flat, five-sided white rubber slab, beside which a baseball player stands to hit the pitched ball and which must be touched after rounding the bases to score a run. Also, **home base.**

hom·er (hō′mər) *n. Informal.* home run.

Ho·mer·ic (hō mer′ik) *adj.* **1.** of, relating to, or characteristic of the Greek poet Homer, his poetry, or the period of Greek history about which he wrote. **2.** enormous in scale and extent; epic.

Homeric laughter, loud, hearty laughter. [From *Homer,* Greek poet of the eighth century B.C.]

home·room (hōm′rüm′, -rûm′) *n.* a class to which students report at the beginning of each school day, at which time attendance is checked and school announcements made before the start of regular classes.

home rule, a system under which one political unit within a larger one, such as a city within a state, is granted power to manage its own affairs.

home run 1. a hit made by a baseball player that enables him or her to immediately round the bases and score a run. **2.** a score made in this way.

home·school (hōm′skül′, -skül′) *also,* **home-school.** *v.i., v.t.* to teach one's child or children at home instead of enrolling them in a public or private school. —**home′school′er,** *n.*

home·sick (hōm′sik′) *adj.* depressed or ill because one is away from one's home or family; longing for home. —**home′sick′ness,** *n.*

home·spun (hōm′spun′) *adj.* **1.** spun or made at home: *homespun cloth.* **2.** simple and plain in character; unsophisticated: *homespun jokes.* —*n.* **1.** a fabric woven of yarn spun at home or by hand. **2.** any of various coarse, strong fabrics woven to resemble this.

home·stead (hōm′sted′) *n.* **1.** any house together with adjacent buildings and the land they are on. **2.** a parcel of 160 acres of public land granted to a settler under the Homestead Act of 1862. —*v.t.* to settle on and claim (land). —*v.i.* to settle and claim a homestead.

Homestead Act, a law passed by the U.S. Congress in 1862 to distribute public land to settlers for farming.

home·stead·er (hōm′sted′ər) *n.* **1.** a person who has a homestead. **2.** a person granted land under the Homestead Act.

homestead law, a law exempting a homestead from attachment or sale for debt.

home·stretch (hōm′strech′) *n.* **1.** the straight part of a racetrack between the last turn and the finish line. **2.** the last part of any trip or endeavor.

home·town (hōm′toun′) *n.* the town or city where a person was born, was raised, or has lived a long time.

home·ward (hōm′wərd) *adv. also,* **home·wards.** toward home: *to be traveling homeward after a long journey.* —*adj.* directed or going toward home: *the homeward leg of a voyage.*

home·work (hōm′wûrk′) *n.* **1.** a school lesson to be studied or prepared outside the classroom, usually at home. **2.** any work, esp. preparatory study, that must be done at home or on one's own time, rather than during regular working hours.

home·y (hō′mē) *adj.,* **hom·i·er, hom·i·est.** *Informal.* having homelike qualities; informal and friendly; cozy; comfortable.

hom·i·cid·al (hom′ə sī′dəl, hō′mə-) *adj.* **1.** of or relating to homicide. **2.** tending to or leading to homicide; murderous: *a homicidal maniac, a homicidal rage.*

hom·i·cide[1] (hom′ə sīd′, hō′mə-) *n.* the killing of one human being by another. [Old French *homicide,* from Latin *homicīdium,* from *homō* man + *-cīdium.* See -CIDE[1].]

hom·i·cide[2] (hom′ə sīd′, hō′mə-) *n.* a person who kills another. [Old French *homicide,* from Latin *homicīda,* from *homō* man + *-cīda.* See -CIDE[2].]

hom·i·let·ic (hom′ə let′ik) *adj.* **1.** of, relating to, or characteristic of a homily or homilies. **2.** of or relating to homiletics. [Greek *homīlētikos* sociable, conversable, going back to *homīlein* to associate with.]

hom·i·let·ics (hom′ə let′iks) *pl. n.* the branch of theology dealing with the art of writing and preaching sermons. ➡ used as singular.

hom·i·ly (hom′ə lē) *n., pl.* **-lies. 1.** a sermon, esp. one based on some portion of the Bible. **2.** a solemn and usually long discourse, esp. on the subject of morals. [Late Latin *homīlia* sermon, from Greek *homīlia* instruction, sermon.]

homing pigeon, a pigeon trained to fly home, often used to carry messages. Also, **carrier pigeon.**

hom·i·nid (hom′ə nid) *n.* any of a family of primates, Hominidae, of which the only surviving species is the human being. —*adj.* of or relating to a hominid or hominids: *hominid fossils.*

hom·i·noid (hom′ə noid′) *n.* any of a group of higher primates, superfamily Hominoidea, comprising extinct and living apes, ancestral humans, and living humans. —*adj.* of or relating to a hominoid or hominoids. [Modern Latin *Hominoid(ea),* from Latin *homo* human being + -OID.]

hom·i·ny (hom′ə nē) *n.* kernels of white corn that have been dried and hulled, and sometimes coarsely ground or crushed, prepared for eating by being mixed with water and boiled. [Possibly of Algonquian origin.]

hominy grits, grits *(def. 1).*

Ho·mo (hō′mō) *n., pl.* **hom·i·nes** (hom′ə nēz′). any of a group of extinct and living humans, genus *Homo,* including the present species, *H. sapiens,* as well as Java man, *H. erectus.* [Latin *homo* human being.]

homo- *combining form* same. ➡ opposed to **hetero-.** [Greek *homos.*]

ho·mog·e·nate (hə moj′ə nāt′, -nit) *n.* a substance that has been homogenized, esp. for study or analysis. [HOMOGEN(IZE) + -ATE[3].]

ho·mo·ge·ne·i·ty (hō′mə jə nē′i tē, hom′ə-) *n.* the state or quality of being homogeneous.

ho·mo·ge·ne·ous (hō′mə jē′nē əs, -jēn′yəs, hom′ə-) *adj.* **1.** of the same kind; similar or identical: *two homogeneous parts.* **2.** having similar or identical components or character throughout: *a homogeneous mass.* [Medieval Latin *homogeneus* of the same kind, from Greek *homogenēs,* from *homos* same + *genos* kind, race.] —**ho′mo·ge′ne·ous·ly,** *adv.* —**ho′mo·ge′ne·ous·ness,** *n.*

ho·mog·e·nize (hə moj′ə nīz′) *v.t.,* **-nized, -niz·ing. 1.** to make homogeneous. **2.** to reduce the particles of one or more insoluble substances, as of the fat in milk, to such a small size that they will form a stable emulsion with one another.

homogenized milk, milk that has been homogenized so that the fat will not separate and rise to the top.

hom·o·graph (hom′ə graf′, hō′mə-) *n.* a word with the same spelling as another, but of different origin, meaning, and, sometimes, pronunciation. *Bow* meaning "to bend forward at the waist" and *bow* meaning "a weapon for shooting arrows" are homographs. [HOMO- + -GRAPH.]

ho·moi·o·ther·my (hō moi′ə thûr′mē) *n. Zoology.* the maintenance of a steady body temperature by means of metabolic processes, as in birds and mammals, regardless of environmental conditions; warm-bloodedness. [Greek *homos* same + *thermē* heat.] —**ho·moi′o·ther′mal, ho·moi′o·ther′mic,** *adj.*

hom·o·log (hom′ə lôg′, -log′) homologue.

ho·mol·o·gous (hə mol′ə gəs, hō-) *adj.* **1.** corresponding, as in position, proportion, function, or structure. **2.** *Biology.* corresponding in structure and evolutionary origin, but not necessarily serving the same function. The human arm, the wing of a bird, and the foreleg of a horse are homologous. ➡ distinguished from **analogous. 3.** *Chemistry.* of or relating to a series of compounds that contain the same group

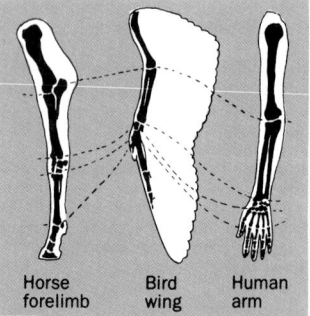

Horse forelimb | Bird wing | Human arm

homologous structures

but exhibit regular differences in formula. [Greek *homologos* agreeing.]

hom·o·logue (hom′ə lôg′, -log′) *also,* **homolog.** *n.* something that is homologous, such as an organ, part, or chemical compound.

ho·mol·o·gy (hə mol′ə jē, hō-) *n., pl.* **-gies. 1.** the state or quality of being homologous. **2.** *Biology.* a homologous similarity of organs or parts. **3.** *Chemistry.* the relationship between compounds in a homologous series. [Greek *homologiā* agreement.]

hom·o·nym (hom′ə nim′) *n.* **1.** homophone *(def. 1).* **2.** a word that has the same pronunciation and spelling as another, but is different in meaning and origin. *Chase* meaning "to pursue" and *chase* meaning "to ornament metal" are homonyms. [Latin *homōnymum* the same word employed to indicate different things, going back to Greek *homōnymos* having the same name.]

hom·o·phone (hom′ə fōn′, hō′mə-) *n.* **1.** a word that has the same pronunciation as another, but is different in spelling, origin, and meaning. *Air* and *heir* are homophones. **2.** a letter or group of letters having the same sound as another. The letters *ks* and *x* are homophones. [HOMO- + Greek *phōnē* sound.]

hom·o·phon·ic (hom′ə fon′ik, hō′mə-) *adj.* **1.** of or having the same sound. **2.** *Music.* having one predominant melodic line, with the other parts or voices providing harmony. ➡ opposed to **polyphonic.**

ho·moph·o·nous (hə mof′ə nəs) *adj.* homophonic.

ho·moph·o·ny (hə mof′ə nē) *n.* **1.** the state or quality of being homophonic. **2.** homophonic music.

ho·mop·te·ran (hō mop′tər ən) *n.* any of a group of insects, order Homoptera, having sucking, beaklike mouthparts and two pairs of uniformly membranous wings, including cicadas, leafhoppers, aphids, and scale insects. —*adj.* homopterous. [Modern Latin *Homoptera,* from HOMO- + Greek *pteron* wing + -AN.]

ho·mop·ter·ous (hə mop′tər əs, hō-) *adj.* of or belonging to the homopterans. [Modern Latin *Homoptera,* from HOMO- + Greek *pteron* wing + -OUS.]

Ho·mo sa·pi·ens (hō′mō sā′pē ənz) the human being regarded as the only surviving species of the genus *Homo,* including all existing races. ➡ italicized when used as a Modern Latin taxonomic classification but often used without italics in general contexts, esp. as a facetious or scientific-sounding synonym for *people* or *person.* [Modern Latin *homo* human being + *sapiens* wise, intelligent.]

ho·mo·sex·u·al (hō′mə sek′shü əl, -mō-) *adj.* of, relating to, or characterized by homosexuality. —*n.* a person who manifests or practices homosexuality.

ho·mo·sex·u·al·i·ty (hō′mə sek′shü al′i tē, -mō-) *n.* **1.** sexual attraction toward members of one's own sex. **2.** sexual relations with a member of one's own sex. ➡ opposed to **heterosexuality.**

ho·mo·zy·gote (hō′mə zī′gōt) *n.* an organism that is homozygous for one or more hereditary traits and that will, therefore, produce identical gametes for that trait. [HOMO- + ZYGOTE.]

ho·mo·zy·gous (hō′mə zī′gəs) *adj.* having two like forms of a gene for a particular hereditary trait.

ho·mun·cu·lus (hō mung′kyə ləs) *n., pl.* **-li** (-lī′). **1.** a little person; manikin. **2.** in occult tradition, a tiny human being that could be developed artificially by an alchemist. [Latin *homunculus,* diminutive of *homō,* man.]

Hon. 1. Honorable. **2.** Honorary.

hon·cho (hon′chō) *Slang. n., pl.* **-chos.** a person who is in charge of or is very important in an organization, department, or division. —*v.t.,* **-choed, -cho·ing.** to take charge of; organize or lead: *to honcho a project.* [Japanese *hanchō* squad leader, from *han* squad, group, + *chō* chief.]

hone (hōn) *n.* a whetstone with a fine grain, used to sharpen the cutting edges of tools, such as razors or scissors. —*v.t.,* **honed, hon·ing.** to sharpen on or as on a hone. [Old English *hān* a stone.]

hon·est (on′ist) *adj.* **1.** truthful, fair, and trustworthy, as in character, principles, or actions: *an honest person, an honest effort.* **2.** earned or gotten fairly or legitimately; obtained without deceit: *to make an honest living.* **3.** without guile; sincere; frank; open: *to have an honest face, to express an honest opinion.* **4.** being what it seems or is claimed to be; genuine; pure: *an honest measure.* **5.** *Archaic.* chaste; virtuous. [Old French *honeste* good, virtuous, from Latin *honestus* honorable.] —**hon′est·ly,** *adv.* —**hon′est·ness,** *n.*

hon·es·ty (on′ə stē) *n.* **1.** the state or quality of being honest; integrity: *The honesty of your action is not in question.* **2.** truthfulness; sincerity: *We could not, in all honesty, agree to their terms.* **3.** *Archaic.* chastity.

Honesty, integrity, and **probity** denote uprightness in character and conduct. **Honesty** connotes truthfulness and straightforwardness, esp. in dealing with others: *Because of their honesty in business dealings, they were well respected in the community.* **Integrity** connotes soundness of moral principles: *Integrity demands being honest with oneself.* **Probity** connotes honesty or integrity that can be proved by one's behavior: *Over a long career the judge earned a reputation for probity.*

hon·ey (hun′ē) *n., pl.* **-eys. 1.** a thick, sweet liquid, made by bees from the nectar they collect from flowers, used for food and as a sweetening agent. **2.** a sweet quality; sweetness. **3.** sweet one; darling; dear. ➡ used as a term of endearment. **4.** *Informal.* something thought to be exceptionally good or exemplary: *a honey of a boat.* —*adj.* of or like honey; sweet. —*v.t.,* **hon·eyed** or **hon·ied, hon·ey·ing. 1.** to sweeten with or as with honey. **2.** to talk to in a sweet or flattering manner. [Old English *hunig* the sweet liquid made by bees.]

honey bear, kinkajou.

hon·ey·bee (hun′ē bē′) *n.* any bee that makes and stores honey, esp. *Apis mellifera,* the common bee that is widely domesticated.

hon·ey·comb (hun′ē kōm′) *n.* **1.** a wax structure formed by bees, consisting of six-sided cells arranged back to back, that hangs vertically in the hive, used for storing honey, pollen, eggs, and larvae. **2.** anything resembling this in appearance or structure. —*adj.* resembling a honeycomb: *Termites chew wood in a honeycomb pattern.* —*v.t.* **1.** to make full of holes or cavities like a honeycomb: *Secret passages honeycombed the castle.* **2.** to penetrate or pervade: *an alibi honeycombed with inconsistencies.* [Old English *hunigcamb* wax structure formed by bees, from *hunig* honey + *camb* comb.]

hon·ey·dew (hun′ē dü′, -dū′) *n.* **1.** honeydew melon. **2.** a sweet substance secreted by aphids and certain other plant-sucking insects. It forms a part of the diet of certain kinds of ants. **3.** a sweet substance exuded by the leaves of certain plants in hot weather.

honeydew melon, a muskmelon having a smooth creamy yellow rind and sweet, light green or white flesh.

hon·eyed (hun′ēd) *adj.* **1.** sweetened with or full of honey. **2.** sweet as honey, as speech designed to flatter: *Your honeyed words fooled no one.*

honey locust, any of a group of tall, usually thorny trees, genus *Gleditsia,* of the pea family, found in Asia, Africa, and North and South America, often having very durable wood and bearing long, divided leaves, clusters of small, greenish flowers, and large, flat pods.

hon·ey·moon (hun′ē mün′) *n.* **1.** a vacation taken by a newly married couple, usually right after the wedding. **2.** the very beginning of married life, esp. the first month. **3.** an initial blissful period in any relationship: *The honeymoon is over between Congress and the president.* —*v.i.* to go or be on a honeymoon. [HONEY + MOON; said to be from an early Scandinavian custom of having a newly married couple drink wine containing honey for the first *moon* (i.e., month) of their marriage.] —**hon′ey·moon′er,** *n.*

hon·ey·suck·le (hun′ē suk′əl) *n.* **1.** any of a group of erect or climbing shrubs, genus *Lonicera,* found throughout the Northern Hemisphere, often bearing fragrant, tubular or bell-shaped flowers. A sweet nectar can usually be obtained from the base of the flower. **2.** any of various similar plants. [Going back to Old English *hunig* honey + *sūcan* to suck; because one can *suck honey,* i.e., sweet nectar, from the flower.]

hon·ied (hun′ēd) *v.* a past tense and past participle of **honey.** —*adj.* honeyed.

honk (hôngk, hongk) *n.* **1.** the cry of a goose. **2.** any similar sound, esp. that of the horn of an automobile. —*v.i.* to utter or make such a sound. —*v.t.* to cause (something) to make such a sound: *Stop honking the horn!* [Imitative.] —**honk′er,** *n.*

honk·y-tonk (hông′kē tôngk′, hong′kē tongk′) *Slang. n.* a cheap, disreputable nightclub or bar. —*adj.* of, relating to, or designating a kind of ragtime music typically played on a tinny-sounding piano.

hon·or (on′ər) *also, British,* **honour.** *n.* **1.** a sense of what is right or moral; integrity: *A person of honor would not behave in a cowardly way.* **2.** good name or reputation; position of being respected or esteemed: *The nation's honor was at stake.* **3.a.** a source or cause of respect, esteem, or pride: *It was a great honor*

a	at	e	end	o	hot	u	up	hw	white	⌠	about
ā	ape	ē	me	ō	old	ū	use	ng	song		taken
ä	far	i	it	ô	fork	ü	rule	th	thin	ə	pencil
âr	care	ī	ice	oi	oil	u̇	pull	th	this		lemon
				îr	pierce	ou	out	ûr	turn	zh	measure	⌡	circus

H

to receive the award. **b.** privilege: *We request the honor of your presence. I have the honor to introduce Mr. Jones.* **4.** glory; renown; fame: *They shared in the honor.* **5.** exalted rank or position; dignity; distinction: *The queen bestowed the honor of knighthood upon the great scientist.* **6. Honor.** used as a form of address in speaking or referring to certain officials, such as a judge or mayor, preceded by *His, Her,* or *Your.* **7. honors.** something done or conferred as a token of respect, esteem, or distinction: *The hero was buried with full military honors.* **8. honors.** special recognition conferred on a student by an educational institution for outstanding academic achievement: *The valedictorian was graduated with highest honors.* **9.** chastity or purity in a woman. **10. honors.** the five highest trump cards or the four aces in no-trump. —*v.t.* **1.** to regard with great respect or esteem: *Honor thy father and thy mother* (Exodus 20:12). **2.** to treat with courtesy or deference: *to honor the flag by saluting it.* **3.** to confer honor or dignity upon; favor; dignify. **4.** to accept as valid for payment or credit: *The bank honored the check. The store would not honor my credit card.* **5.** in square dancing, to curtsy or bow to: *Honor your partner.* [Old French *honor* glory, esteem, chastity, virtue, from Latin *honor* office, dignity, reputation, esteem.]
  • **in honor of.** as an expression of respect, esteem, or affection for; in celebration or recognition of: *The new college dormitory was named in honor of the school's chief benefactor.*
  • **on** (or **upon**) **one's honor.** pledging one's word as to the truth of a statement or the fulfilling of a promise: *On my honor I will faithfully execute the duties of the office of mayor.*
  • **to do honor to. a.** to treat with great respect and esteem: *to do honor to a visiting dignitary.* **b.** to be a credit to: *to do honor to one's family name.*
  • **to do the honors.** to perform certain social courtesies: *The host did the honors and carved the roast.*

hon·or·a·ble (on′ər ə bəl) *also, British,* **honourable.** *adj.* **1.** characterized by or consistent with principles of morality and integrity; upright: *honorable intentions.* **2.** bringing honor; creditable: *an honorable achievement.* **3.** worthy of honor and respect: *an honorable profession.* **4.** having high rank or eminence; noble; illustrious: *to come from an honorable family.* **5.** performed or accompanied with tokens of honor or respect: *The soldier received an honorable discharge at the end of the war.* **6. Honorable.** used as a form of address in speaking of or referring to certain government officials, such as members of Congress and cabinet officers, or certain members of the nobility. —**hon′or·a·ble·ness;** *also, British,* **hon′our·a·ble·ness,** *n.* —**hon′or·a·bly;** *also, British,* **hon′our·a·bly,** *adv.*

hon·o·rar·i·um (on′ə rär′ē əm) *n., pl.* **-rar·i·ums** or **-rar·i·a** (-rär′ē ə). a fee for services rendered, esp. by a professional person: *The visiting lecturer received an honorarium of $300.* [Latin *honōrārium* gift made for admission to a post of honor, fee, going back to *honor* office, dignity, reputation.]

hon·or·ar·y (on′ə rer′ē) *adj.* **1.** given as an honor without the usual duties, requirements, or salary: *an honorary degree.* **2.** holding a title or position given as an honor: *honorary chairperson of a fund drive.* **3.** given or made as a token of honor: *Honorary arches were erected to the monarch.* **4.** depending on one's honor for fulfillment; not legally binding: *an honorary obligation.* [Latin *honōrārius* relating to honor, from *honor* office, dignity, reputation.]

hon·or·ee (on′ə rē′) *n.* a person who receives an honor.

honor guard, a special group of soldiers, police officers, or firefighters having certain ceremonial functions, such as protecting a visiting dignitary or escorting the coffin of a notable person at a public funeral.

hon·or·if·ic (on′ə rif′ik) *adj.* conferring honor or respect: *an honorific title.* [Latin *honōrificus* honorable, going back to *honor* office, dignity, reputation + *facere* to make, do.]

honor roll 1. a list of students who have achieved high grades. **2.** a list of local citizens who have served in the armed forces, usually displayed in a public place.

honors of war, courtesies shown to a defeated enemy, such as permission to retain weapons and flags.

honor system, a system in which the individual is trusted to obey rules and carry out responsibilities without direct supervision, used esp. in schools, colleges, and correctional institutions.

hon·our (on′ər) *British.* honor.

hon·our·a·ble (on′ər ə bəl) *British.* honorable.

hooch (hüch) *n. Slang.* an alcoholic beverage, esp. cheap or illegal liquor. [Short for *hoochinoo* a liquor made by the *Hoochinoo,* an Alaskan Indian tribe.]

hood[1] (hůd) *n.* **1.** a covering for the head and back of the neck, often attached to the neckline of a coat, jacket, or other garment.

2. anything resembling a hood in form or use, such as the loose skin on the neck of a cobra or the collapsible top of a convertible car. **3.** a movable covering over the engine of an automobile. **4.** an ornamental fold of cloth worn over the back of an academic gown. The color and cut of the hood indicate the degree held by the wearer. **5.** a covering that is used in falconry to prevent the hawk from seeing when it is not pursuing game. —*v.t.* to cover or furnish with or as with a hood: *to hood a falcon, heavy eyelids that appear to hood the eyes.* [Old English *hōd* covering for the head and neck.]

hood[2] (hůd) *n. Slang.* hoodlum. [Short for HOODLUM.]

-hood *suffix* **1.** the state, quality, condition, or time of being: *childhood, likelihood.* **2.** an entire group, class, or body of: *priesthood, brotherhood.* [Old English *hād* condition, quality.]

hood·ed (hůd′id) *adj.* **1.** having, wearing, or covered with a hood. **2.** shaped like a hood.

hood·lum (hüd′ləm, hůd′-) *n. Informal.* **1.** a ruffian or rowdy, esp. a teenage member of a street gang. **2.** a gangster; thug. [Of uncertain origin.]

hood[1] *(def. 4)*

hoo·doo (hü′dü′) *n., pl.* **-doos. 1.** voodoo. **2.** *Informal.* a person or thing that brings bad luck. **3.** *Informal.* bad luck. —*v.t.* **-dooed, -doo·ing.** *Informal.* to bring bad luck to. [Form of VOODOO.]

hood·wink (hůd′wingk′) *v.t.* **1.** to trick or deceive. **2.** *Archaic.* to blindfold. [HOOD + WINK.]

hoof (hůf, hüf) *n., pl.* **hooves** or **hoofs. 1.** a hard, horny covering on the feet of certain mammals, such as horses, cattle, pigs, or deer. **2.** the entire foot of such an animal. **3.** a human foot. ➡ used humorously. —*v.t., v.i.* **1.** *Informal.* to walk. **2.** *Slang.* to dance. [Old English *hōf* this horny covering.]
  • **on the hoof.** (of cattle and other livestock) not butchered; alive.

hoof-and-mouth disease (hůf′ ən-mouth′, hüf′-) foot-and-mouth disease.

hoof·beat (hůf′bēt′, hüf′-) *n.* the sound made by a hoofed animal when it walks, trots, or runs.

Single-toe Cloven
hoof   hoof

hoofed (hůft, hüft) *adj.* having hooves.

hoof·er (hůf′ər, hü′fər) *n. Slang.* a professional dancer, esp. a tap dancer.

hook (hůk) *n.* **1.** a bent piece of metal, wood, or other firm material, having one or more free ends adapted for catching, suspending, fastening, or holding something: *a meat hook, a coat hook.* **2.** a fishhook. **3.** something resembling a hook in shape or use. **4.** a sharp bend or angle in the length or course of something, as in a river. **5.** a curved, projecting point or spit of land. **6.** *Baseball.* curve. **7.** *Golf.* a stroke in which the ball curves in the direction opposite to that in which the player is facing. **8.** *Boxing.* a short, swinging blow made with the arm bent. **9.** *Music.* a line on the stem of certain musical notes, indicating the duration of the note. —*v.t.* **1.** to attach, fasten, or secure with or as with a hook or hooks: *The sailor hooked the line to the side of the boat. The seamstress hooked the train onto the gown.* **2.** to catch or take hold of with a hook: *The fisherman hooked three trout in the stream.* **3.** to make into the shape of a hook; bend; crook: *The girl hooked her arm over the back of the chair.* **4.** to catch or win by artifice; entrap: *The competing ad agencies were determined to hook the big client. The swindlers tried to hook their victim with a scheme to get rich quick.* **5.** to make, as a rug or mat, by pulling yarn or strips of cloth through a piece of fabric with a hook. **6.** *Baseball.* to pitch or throw (a ball) so that it curves. **7.** *Golf.* to drive (a ball) so that it curves in the direction opposite to that in which the player is facing. **8.** *Boxing.* to strike with a hook. **9.** *Informal.* to steal; pilfer: *Someone hooked five dollars from my wallet.* —*v.i.* **1.** to have the form of a hook; curve: *The river hooks at Smithtown.* **2.** to be attached, fastened, or secured with or as with a hook or hooks: *The jacket hooks in the front on a diagonal.* [Old English *hōc* bent piece of metal, fishhook, type of agricultural implement.]
  • **by hook or by crook.** by any means fair or foul; in any way possible: *The dishonest politician was determined to win the election by hook or by crook.*
  • **hook, line, and sinker.** completely; entirely: *The youths fell for the swindler's story hook, line, and sinker.*

• **off the hook.** *Informal.* **a.** free from a difficult situation, unpleasant duty, or blame. **b.** (of a telephone receiver) not on the cradle: *People who tried to call us got a busy signal because our phone was off the hook.*

• **on one's own hook.** *Informal.* by oneself; independently: *I got the job on my own hook without any help.*

• **on the hook.** (of a telephone receiver) on the cradle.

• **to hook up.** to assemble a mechanical or electrical device and connect it to a source of power: *The electrician hooked up the doorbell.*

• **to hook up with.** *Informal.* to become connected or joined with: *The American army hooked up with the French for the march to Paris.*

hook·ah (hŭk′ə) *also,* **hook·a.** *n.* a tobacco pipe of Oriental origin, having a long, flexible tube attached to a vessel of water through which the smoke is drawn and cooled. [Urdu *huqqah,* from Arabic *huqqah* box, water vessel of a hookah.]

hook and eye, a clothing fastener consisting of a metallic or plastic hook and a loop or bar to which the hook may be attached.

hooked (hŭkt) *adj.* **1.** curved or bent like a hook. **2.** having a hook or hooks. **3.** *Informal.* fascinated by or devoted to some practice or thing: *hooked on sports.* **4.** *Informal.* addicted to narcotics.

hooked rug, a rug made by looping yarn or strips of cloth through a piece of fabric, such as canvas or burlap.

hook·er (hŭk′ər) *n.* **1.** a small, one-masted fishing boat. **2.** any ship that is old, poorly designed, or hard to maneuver. [Dutch *hoeker* fishing boat, dogger, from *hoek* hook, fishhook.]

hook·up (hŭk′ŭp′) *n.* **1.** an arrangement and connection of electric or electronic parts or circuits, esp. a temporary connection, such as a network of television stations connected for a particular event: *a nationwide television hookup for election returns.* **2.** any arrangement or connection of separate or related parts.

hook·worm (hŭk′wûrm′) *n.* **1.** any of several small, threadlike, parasitic worms, phylum Nematoda, that may infest the intestines of humans and other mammals. **2.** a disease caused by hookworms, characterized by abdominal pain, diarrhea, fatigue, and sometimes anemia. Also *(def. 2),* **hookworm disease.** [HOOK + WORM; with reference to the small, hooked, toothlike structures around its mouth with which it attaches itself to the intestinal walls of the host.]

hook·y (hŭk′ē) *n. Informal.* **to play hooky.** to stay out of school without permission or a good excuse; be truant. [Possibly from dialectal English *hook* to make off.]

hoo·li·gan (hü′li gən) *n. Informal.* a ruffian or hoodlum, esp. a member of a street gang. [Supposedly from an Irish surname applied to certain rowdies in late nineteenth-century London.] —**hoo′li·gan·ism,** *n.*

hoop (hüp, hŭp) *n.* **1.** a circular band or ring, as of wood or metal, esp. for holding together the staves of a barrel. **2.** a child's toy consisting of a large circular band of wood, metal, or plastic that can be rolled along the ground or spun around the body. **3.** a circular band of flexible metal, whalebone, or similar support for a hoop skirt. **4.** *Basketball.* the circular band of metal supporting the net. **5.** a croquet wicket. —*v.t.* to bind or fasten with a hoop or hoops. [Old English *hōp* round band, as of wood or metal.]

hoop·la (hüp′lä, hŭp′-) *n. Informal.* boisterous activity or excitement; great noise and fuss. [French *houp-là* interjection used to rouse someone; of uncertain origin.]

hoo·poe (hü′pü) *n.* a brightly colored bird, *Upupa epops,* of Europe, Asia, and Africa, having a long, slender bill, a fanlike, erectile crest, and usually pinkish brown plumage with black and white markings. Length: 1 foot (0.3 meter). [Earlier *hoop,* from French *huppe,* from Latin *upupa;* imitative of the bird's call.]

hoop skirt **1.** a framework of hoops connected by tapes, formerly worn as a petticoat to make a woman's skirt stand out from her body. **2.** a skirt worn with such a framework.

hoo·ray (hü rā′) hurrah.

hoose·gow (hüs′gou′) *also,* **hoosgow.** *n. Slang.* jail. [Spanish *juzgado* court of justice, from *juzgar* to judge, from Latin *jūdicāre.*]

Hoo·sier (hü′zhər) *n. Informal.* a native or resident of Indiana. [Of uncertain origin.]

hoot (hüt) *n.* **1.** the cry of an owl. **2.** a cry or shout of derision or disapproval. **3.** *Informal.* a very small or insignificant amount; the least bit: *advice not worth a hoot.* —*v.i.* **1.** to utter the cry of an owl. **2.** to

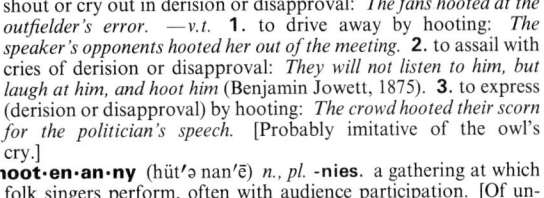

hoopoe

shout or cry out in derision or disapproval: *The fans hooted at the outfielder's error.* —*v.t.* **1.** to drive away by hooting: *The speaker's opponents hooted her out of the meeting.* **2.** to assail with cries of derision or disapproval: *They will not listen to him, but laugh at him, and hoot him* (Benjamin Jowett, 1875). **3.** to express (derision or disapproval) by hooting: *The crowd hooted their scorn for the politician's speech.* [Probably imitative of the owl's cry.]

hoot·en·an·ny (hüt′ə nan′ē) *n., pl.* **-nies.** a gathering at which folk singers perform, often with audience participation. [Of uncertain origin.]

hooves (hüvz, hŭvz) a plural of **hoof.**

hop¹ (hop) *v.,* **hopped, hop·ping.** —*v.i.* **1.** to make a short leap or series of leaps on one foot: *to hop up and down to keep warm.* **2.** to move in short leaps on both or all feet at once: *The frog hopped along the shore of the pond.* **3.** to move quickly: *Russell hopped up and offered the lady his chair.* **4.** *Informal.* to make a short, quick trip: *Let's hop over to see your friends this weekend.* —*v.t.* **1.** to jump over: *to hop a fence.* **2.** *Informal.* to board and ride in (a vehicle), esp. without paying: *The hobo hopped a freight to Houston.* —*n.* **1.** the act or an instance of hopping. **2.** *Informal.* a short, quick trip, esp. in an airplane: *It's a short hop from Paris to London.* **3.** *Informal.* a dance or dancing party. **4.** *Informal.* a bounce or rebound: *The ball took a bad hop and the shortstop missed it.* [Middle English *hoppen,* from Old English *hoppian* to leap, dance.]

• **to hop to it.** to move or begin to act quickly.

• **to hop up.** *Informal.* to increase the power of: *The teenager hopped up the engine of the old car.*

hop² (hop) *n.* **1. hops.** the conelike, greenish yellow inflorescence of any of a group of plants, genus *Humulus,* of the hemp family, containing bitter-tasting oils and used in the brewing of beer and other malt beverages. **2.** the long-stemmed climbing plant bearing this fruit, having hairy leaves with saw-toothed edges. —*v.t.,* **hopped, hop·ping.** to flavor or treat with hops. [Middle Dutch *hoppe* this plant.]

hope (hōp) *v.,* **hoped, hop·ing.** —*v.t.* **1.** to desire with expectation of fulfillment: *Susan hoped her book review would be published.* **2.** to have as a wish, belief, or desire: *We hope you will enjoy your vacation.* —*v.i.* **1.** to have expectation or desire: *to hope for support from one's friends.* **2.** *Archaic.* to trust; rely. —*n.* **1.** desire accompanied by expectation of fulfillment: *Hope springs eternal in the human breast* (Alexander Pope, 1732). **2.** something hoped for: *The senator staked his career on the hope of winning reelection.* **3.** a person or thing on which hopes are centered: *The younger generation is the hope of the nation.* **4.** *Archaic.* trust; reliance. [Old English *hopa* expectation, trust.]

• **to hope against hope.** to hope for something when there is little chance of receiving it.

hope chest, a chest or box in which a young woman keeps linens, clothing, and similar articles in anticipation of marriage.

hope·ful (hōp′fəl) *adj.* **1.** full of or showing hope. **2.** inspiring hope; promising fulfillment: *a hopeful sign.* —*n.* a person who aspires to success or who is considered likely to succeed: *a presidential hopeful.* —**hope′ful·ness,** *n.*

hope·ful·ly (hōp′fə lē) *adv.* **1.** in a hopeful manner: *She looked up hopefully when her name was called.* **2.** it is to be hoped (that): *Hopefully he will remember to send in the application.*

Usage The use of **hopefully** to mean "it is to be hoped (that)," as in *Hopefully the weather will improve in time for the picnic,* has become so common that it is now accepted as standard by some authorities. However, many people object to this usage, maintaining that **hopefully** should be used only to mean "in a hopeful way."

hope·less (hōp′lis) *adj.* **1.** having or feeling no hope: *a mood of hopeless depression.* **2.** inspiring no hope: *a hopeless case.* —**hope′less·ly,** *adv.* —**hope′less·ness,** *n.*

hop hornbeam, any of a small group of Eurasian and North American trees, genus *Ostrya,* bearing fruits that resemble hops.

Ho·pi (hō′pē) *n., pl.* **-pi** or **-pis.** **1.** a member of a tribe of Pueblo Indians living in northeastern Arizona. **2.** the language of the Hopi. [Hopi *hópi* peaceful.]

hop·lite (hop′līt′) *n.* a heavily armed foot soldier of ancient Greece. [Greek *hoplītēs,* from *hoplon* weapon.]

H

a	at	e	end	o	hot	u	up	hw	white		about
ā	ape	ē	me	ō	old	ū	use	ng	song		taken
ä	far	i	it	ô	fork	ü	rule	th	thin	ə	pencil
âr	care	ī	ice	oi	oil	u	pull	th	this		lemon
		îr	pierce	ou	out	ûr	turn	zh	measure		circus

hop·per (hop′ər) *n.* **1.** a person or thing that hops. **2.** any of various jumping or hopping insects. **3.** a container, usually having a wider top than bottom, used to hold something temporarily, as coal or gain, and to feed it into another container or part.

hop·scotch (hop′skoch′) *n.* a children's game played on numbered squares drawn on the pavement or ground. The players hop into the squares in sequence and try to retrieve a stone or other object that has been tossed into one of the squares. [HOP¹ + the now rare term *scotch* line, incision; of uncertain origin.]

hor. **1.** horizon. **2.** horizontal.

ho·ra (hôr′ə) *also,* **ho·rah.** *n.* a traditional Israeli or Romanian folk dance performed by dancers moving in a circle.

Ho·rae (hôr′ē, hôr′ī) *pl. n.* in Greek mythology, the Hours.

Ho·ra·tian (hə rā′shən) *adj.* of, relating to, or characteristic of Horace or his poetry.

Input

Hopper

Output

hopper

horde (hôrd) *n.* **1.** a large group; swarm; multitude: *A horde of people poured out of the stadium when the game ended.* **2.** a nomadic tribe or clan of Mongols. **3.** any nomadic tribe or clan. [French *horde* pack, band, through German and Polish, from Turkish *ordū* camp.]

hore·hound (hôr′hound′) *also,* **hoarhound.** *n.* **1.** a bitter, aromatic plant, *Marrubium vulgare,* of the mint family, having whitish, woolly leaves and stems and clusters of small, white flowers. **2.** a bitter extract obtained from the leaves of this plant. **3.** a candy or cough medicine flavored with this extract. [Old English *hārhūne* this plant.]

ho·ri·zon (hə rī′zən) *n.* **1.** the line where the sky and the earth or sea appear to meet: *Two ships were barely visible on the horizon.* **2.** *usually,* **horizons.** the limit or range of knowledge, perception, interest, or experience: *Meeting new people widened the young person's horizons.* **3.** *Geology.* a distinct layer of soil or rock that can be traced from one locale to another. [Old French *horizon* line of apparent meeting of the sky and the earth or sea, from Late Latin *horizōn,* from Greek *horizōn (kuklos)* bounding (circle), going back to *horos* limit.]

hor·i·zon·tal (hôr′ə zon′təl, hor′-) *adj.* **1.** parallel to the horizon; level. ➡ opposed to **vertical. 2.** contained, measured, or operating in a plane parallel to the horizon: *horizontal distance.* **3.** of, relating to, or near the horizon. —*n.* something horizontal, such as a line, plane, direction, or member. —**hor′i·zon′tal·ly,** *adv.* —**hor′i·zon′tal·ness,** *n.*

hor·mo·nal (hôr mō′nəl) *adj.* of, relating to, or caused by a hormone or hormones: *a hormonal imbalance in the body.*

hor·mone (hôr′mōn) *n.* **1.** any of numerous chemical substances, such as insulin and testosterone, that are formed in and by the endocrine glands and that enter the bloodstream directly and affect the activity of other organs. Hormones regulate body growth, control sexual activity and development, and maintain the body's chemical balance. **2.** a similar substance in plants, such as gibberellin. [Greek *hormōn,* present participle of *hormān,* to set in motion, urge on, from *hormē* impulse, assault.]

horn (hôrn) *n.* **1.** a hard, permanent, unbranched projection, usually occurring in pairs, growing on the upper part of the head of various hoofed mammals, including cattle, sheep, antelope, and rhinoceroses. **2.** one of the antlers of a deer. **3.** a projection that resembles a horn on the head of various other animals, such as the tuft of feathers on a horned owl. **4.a.** the hard material of which a horn is composed. **b.** any similar natural or synthetic substance. **5.** a vessel or other container formed from or shaped like a horn. **6.** *Music.* **a.** any of various brass instruments usually consisting of a coiled metal tube that gradually widens into a flaring bell, esp. the French horn. **b.** *Informal.* any wind instrument, esp. a trumpet. **c.** any wind instrument resembling or originally made from the horn of an animal. **7.** a device used to sound a warning signal: *The bus driver honked the horn at the children in the street.* **8.** something shaped like a horn, such as a cape or peninsula. **9.** either of the pointed extremities of a crescent. [Old English *horn* hard growth on the head of some animals, container made of a horn, type of wind instrument.] —**horn′less,** *adj.* —**horn′like′,** *adj.*

• **on the horns of a dilemma.** having to choose between two equally unpleasant alternatives.

• **to blow one's own horn.** to praise oneself; brag.

• **to draw** (or **pull**) **in one's horns. a.** to restrain oneself: *to draw in one's horns when angry to avoid a rash act.* **b.** to withdraw; retract: *In the panel discussion, the columnist was challenged, and forced to pull in his horns.*

• **to horn in.** *Slang.* to enter without being invited; butt in: *She horned in on our conversation.*

• **to lock horns.** *Informal.* to get into a heated discussion or argument.

horn·beam (hôrn′bēm′) *n.* any of various deciduous trees, genus *Carpinus,* of the birch family, having smooth, gray bark and strong, heavy wood used in making tools.

horn·bill (hôrn′bil′) *n.* any of various songless birds, family Bucerotidae, native to tropical and subtropical forests of Africa, Asia, and the East Indies, usually having a large, colorful bill surmounted by a horny growth. Length: 15-60 inches (38-152 centimeters), including tail.

horn·blende (hôrn′blend′) *n. Mineralogy.* a dark, shiny variety of amphibole occurring in both igneous and metamorphic rocks. [German *Hornblende.*]

horn·book (hôrn′bûk′) *n.* **1.** a primer consisting of a page with the alphabet and a prayer or numerals on it, covered with a sheet of transparent horn and fastened in a frame with a handle, formerly used in teaching children to read. **2.** a beginning treatise.

horned (hôrnd) *adj.* having a horn, horns, or hornlike projections.

hornbill

horned lizard, horned toad.

horned owl, any of various owls having hornlike ear tufts, esp. the great horned owl.

horned pout, the bullhead, esp. a brown species, *Ictalurus nebulosus,* of the eastern United States.

horned toad, any of a group of insect-eating lizards, genus *Phrynosoma,* common in dry areas of the western United States, having spiny horns on the head and fringed scales along the sides of the body. Length: to 4½ inches (11 centimeters). Also, **horn toad, horned lizard.**

hor·net (hôr′nit) *n.* any of various large wasps, family Vespidae, that live in colonies and are often reddish brown or black with dull markings. The female can inflict a painful sting. Length: ½-1 inch (1-2.5 centimeters). [Old English *hyrnet.*]

hornet's nest *also,* **hornets' nest.** a situation involving great controversy or trouble: *The reporter stirred up a hornet's nest by uncovering a political scandal.*

horn·fels (hôrn′felz) *n.* a dark metamorphic rock that forms when shale is baked by the heat of an intrusion of igneous rock. [German *hornfels* literally, horn rock, from *horn* horn + *fels* rock.]

horn of plenty, cornucopia.

horn·pipe (hôrn′pīp′) *n.* **1.** a lively British folk dance, usually performed solo. **2.** music for such a dance. **3.** an obsolete musical wind instrument having the bell and mouthpiece made of horn.

horn·y (hôr′nē) *adj.,* **horn·i·er, horn·i·est. 1.** made of horn or of something resembling it. **2.** having horns or hornlike growths. **3.** hard like horn; calloused: *horny and rough feet.*

hor·o·loge (hôr′ə lōj′) *n.* a timepiece, such as a clock, watch, sundial, or hourglass. [Old French *hor(o)loge* clock, from Latin *hōrologium* sundial, water clock, from Greek *hōrologion,* going back to *hōrā* season, hour + *-logos* telling.]

ho·rol·o·ger (hō rol′ə jər, hə-) *n.* a person skilled in horology; clock maker.

ho·rol·o·gy (hō rol′ə jē, hə-) *n.* **1.** the science of measuring time. **2.** the art of making, regulating, or testing timepieces. —**hor·o·log·ic** (hôr′ə loj′ik), **hor′o·log′i·cal,** *adj.* —**ho·rol′o·gist,** *n.*

hor·o·scope (hôr′ə skōp′, hor′-) *n.* **1.** a prediction about one's personal fate, often with advice, esp. for a particular day. It is based on an interpretation of the positions of the planets at a given time. **2.** the appearance of the heavens with reference to the positions of the planets at any particular moment, esp. at the time of a person's birth. **3.** a diagram of the twelve signs of the zodiac. [French *horoscope* nativity, from Latin *hōroscopus,* from Greek *hōroskopos,* from *hōrā* hour + *skopos* watcher.]

hor·ren·dous (hō ren′dəs, hə-) *adj.* causing horror or dread; frightful. [Latin *horrēndus.*] —**hor·ren′dous·ly,** *adv.*

hor·ri·ble (hôr′ə bəl, hor′-) *adj.* **1.** arousing or tending to arouse horror; terrible; dreadful. **2.** *Informal.* extremely unpleasant, disagreeable, shocking, or ugly: *That was a horrible thing to*

say. The weather is horrible today. [Old French *horrible,* from Latin *horribilis,* from *horrēre* to bristle, tremble.] —**hor′ri·ble·ness,** *n.* —**hor′ri·bly,** *adv.*

hor·rid (hôr′id, hor′-) *adj.* **1.** causing aversion or horror; dreadful; abominable. **2.** *Informal.* extremely unpleasant; disagreeable or offensive: *What a horrid person!* [Latin *horridus* bristly, frightful.] —**hor′rid·ly,** *adv.* —**hor′rid·ness,** *n.*

hor·rif·ic (hô rif′ik, hə-) *adj.* causing horror; horrifying; horrible.

hor·ri·fy (hôr′ə fī′, hor′-) *v.t.,* **-fied, -fy·ing. 1.** to cause to feel horror. **2.** *Informal.* to shock greatly and unpleasantly: *The cost of a new car horrified us.* [Latin *horrificāre* to cause terror.]

hor·ror (hôr′ər, hor′-) *n.* **1.** an intense and painful feeling of fear and dread; terror. **2.** great dislike; loathing: *a horror of snakes.* **3.** the quality of causing horror: *the horror of war.* **4.** a person or thing that causes horror. **5.** *Informal.* something that is extremely disagreeable, shocking, or ugly: *That blue dress is a horror.* [Latin *horror* terror.]

hors de com·bat (ôr də kôN bä′) *French.* out of the fight; disabled.

hors d′oeuvre (ôr dûrv′) *pl.* **hors d′oeuvres** or **hors d′oeuvre** (ôr dûrvz′). a hot or cold appetizer, such as olives, celery, or cheese, served before the main courses of a meal. [French *hors d′œuvre* literally, outside of work, going back to Latin *forīs* out of doors + *dē* from, of + *opera* work; originally referring to an outbuilding not included in the central architectural plan and later applied to a course separate from the main part of a meal.]

horse (hôrs) *n., pl.* **hors·es** or **horse. 1.** a four-legged, hoofed mammal, *Equus caballus,* having a long, flowing mane and tail, domesticated since prehistoric times, used as a beast of burden and a draft animal, and for riding. Height: to 6 feet (1.8 meters) at the shoulder. **2.** a full-grown male horse; stallion or gelding. **3.** any of various animals of the horse family, Equidae, such as the zebra or donkey. **4.** a gymnastic apparatus consisting of a leather-covered block mounted on legs, used for vaulting and other exercises. **5.** a frame or structure, usually having four legs, used for holding or supporting something. **6.** *Military.* mounted troops; cavalry. ➡ used as plural. **7.** *Informal.* horsepower. ➡ usually used in the plural: *This engine has fifty horses.* **8.** *Slang.* heroin. —*v.t.,* **horsed, hors·ing.** to furnish with a horse or horses: *to horse a cavalry regiment.* —*adj.* **1.** of or relating to a horse or horses. **2.** mounted on horses: *horse soldiers.* [Old English *hors* the animal.]

  • **a horse of a different** (or **another**) **color.** something completely different.
  • **from the horse′s mouth.** from the original or most reliable source: *The information came straight from the horse′s mouth.*
  • **to be** (or **get**) **on one′s high horse.** to have or assume a haughty or pretentious attitude or manner.
  • **to hold one′s horses.** to be patient or restrain oneself.
  • **to horse.** get on your horse; mount. ➡ used as a command, esp. to cavalry troops.
  • **to horse around.** to engage in horseplay.

horse-and-bug·gy (hôrs′ən bug′ē) *adj.* **1.** of or in the time before the automobile was used, when horses and carriages were a common form of transportation: *an outfit from horse-and-buggy times.* **2.** keeping to old ways or constituting old ideas and styles; out-of-date: *horse-and-buggy notions about behavior.*

horse·back (hôrs′bak′) *n.* the back of a horse. —*adv.* on the back of a horse: *to ride horseback.*

horse·car (hôrs′kär′) *n.* **1.** a streetcar drawn by horses. **2.** a railroad car for transporting horses.

horse chestnut 1. a large ornamental tree, *Aesculus hippocastanum,* widely grown in Europe and the United States, bearing pyramid-shaped clusters of white flowers and inedible nuts. **2.** the nut itself, containing one or two large, shiny brown, poisonous seeds.

horse·flesh (hôrs′flesh′) *n.* **1.** horses collectively, esp. for riding, driving, or racing: *The trainer is a good judge of horseflesh.* **2.** the flesh of a horse, esp. as used for food.

horse·fly (hôrs′flī′) *n., pl.* **-flies. 1.** any of a large group of bloodsucking flies, family Tabanidae, having a stout, hairy, usually black or brown body. The female attacks various mammals, including humans, and inflicts a painful bite. **2.** any of various other insects, as the botfly, that attack horses and cattle.

Horse Guards, a body of cavalry, esp. the cavalry brigade forming the household guard of the British sovereign.

horse·hair (hôrs′hâr′) *n.* **1.** the hair of a horse, esp. from the mane or tail. **2.** a stiff fabric made with this hair, usually in combination with other fibers, used esp. for upholstery and outer garments. —*adj.* made of, covered, or stuffed with horsehair.

horse·hide (hôrs′hīd′) *n.* **1.** the hide of a horse. **2.** leather made from this hide.

horse latitudes, two belts of high atmospheric pressure and predominantly calm, dry weather, extending over the oceans at about 30 degrees north and south of the equator. For illustration, see **wind**[1].

horse·laugh (hôrs′laf′) *n.* a loud, coarse, or boisterous laugh.

horse·less carriage (hôrs′lis) an automobile.

horse·man (hôrs′mən) *n., pl.* **-men** (-mən). **1.** a person who rides on horseback. **2.** a person skilled in riding or handling horses.

horse·man·ship (hôrs′mən ship′) *n.* the art of riding or handling horses; equestrian skill.

horse pistol, a large pistol formerly carried by horsemen.

horse·play (hôrs′plā′) *n.* rough, boisterous play or fun.

horse·pow·er (hôrs′pou′ər) *n.* a foot-pound-second unit for measuring power or rate of work, as of an engine, equal to 550 foot-pounds per second or 746 watts.

horse·rad·ish (hôrs′rad′ish) *n.* **1.** the sharp-tasting white root of a plant, *Armoracia rusticana,* of the mustard family. **2.** the plant itself, widely cultivated in southeastern Europe and North America. **3.** a condiment made from the grated root of this plant.

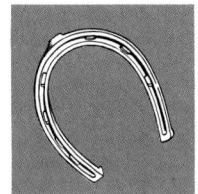

horseshoe

horse sense *Informal.* plain, practical common sense.

horse·shoe (hôrs′shü′, hôrsh′-) *n.* **1.** any of several types of U-shaped metal pieces curved to fit the shape of a horse′s hoof, attached by means of nails driven into the hard, horny, outer shell of the hoof. **2.** something shaped like a horseshoe. **3. horseshoes.** a game for two or more players in which the object is to pitch a U-shaped piece so that it encircles a stake, normally placed 40 feet (12.2 meters) away from the pitcher, or lands closer to the stake than the opponent′s piece. ➡ used as singular. —*v.t.,* **-shoed, -shoe·ing.** to provide with horseshoes. —**horse′sho′er,** *n.*

horseshoe crab, a saltwater invertebrate of any of four families, order Xiphosura, having a hard, horseshoe-shaped shell and a stiff, spinelike tail. Length: to 20 inches (51 centimeters), including tail. Also, **king crab.**

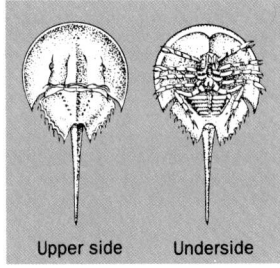

Upper side   Underside

horseshoe crab

horse·tail (hôrs′tāl′) *n.* **1.** any of a small group of flowerless plants, genus *Equisetum,* having hollow, jointed stems and scalelike leaves. Also, **mare′s-tail. 2.** the tail of a horse, esp. one formerly used in Turkey as a military standard indicating the rank of pasha.

horse-trade (hôrs′trād′) *v.i.,* **-trad·ed, -trad·ing.** *Informal.* to arrange a shrewd deal; trade or bargain shrewdly.

horse trade 1. a trade involving horses. **2.** *Informal.* a deal or transaction arranged by shrewd bargaining. —**horse trader.**

horse·whip (hôrs′hwip′, -wip′) *n.* a whip used for driving or controlling a horse or horses. —*v.t.,* **-whipped, -whip·ping.** to beat with or as if with a horsewhip.

horse·wom·an (hôrs′wùm′ən) *n., pl.* **-wom·en** (-wim′ən). **1.** a woman who rides on horseback. **2.** a woman skilled in riding or handling horses.

hors·ey (hôr′sē) *adj.,* **hors·i·er, hors·i·est.** horsy.

horst (hôrst) *n.* *Geology.* a block of the earth′s crust that has been uplifted between two faults. [German *Horst* thicket.]

hors·y (hôr′sē) *also,* **horsey.** *adj.,* **hors·i·er, hors·i·est. 1.** relating to, characteristic of, or suggestive of a horse or horses: *a horsy smell.* **2.a.** interested in or fond of horses or sports involving horses: *They don′t ride, but they hang out with a horsy crowd.* **b.** like or characteristic of horsemen or horsewomen. **3.** *Slang.* large and awkward in appearance or manner. —**hors′i·ly,** *adv.* —**hors′i·ness,** *n.*

hor·ta·tive (hôr′tə tiv) *adj.* hortatory. —**hor′ta·tive·ly,** *adv.*

hor·ta·to·ry (hôr′tə tôr′ē) *adj.* of, relating to, or giving exhortation; serving to urge or encourage. [Late Latin *hortātōrius,* from Latin *hortārī* to encourage.]

a	at	e	end	o	hot	u	up	hw	white		about
ā	ape	ē	me	ō	old	ū	use	ng	song		taken
ä	far	i	it	ô	fork	ü	rule	th	thin	ə	pencil
âr	care	ī	ice	oi	oil	ù	pull	th	this		lemon
				ou	out	ûr	turn	zh	measure		circus
			ir	pierce							

H

hor·ti·cul·ture (hôr′ti kul′chər) *n.* **1.** the art and science of growing flowers, fruits, vegetables, and ornamental plants. **2.** the cultivation of a garden. [Latin *hortus* garden + *cultūra* cultivating.] —**hor′ti·cul′tur·al,** *adj.* —**hor′ti·cul′tur·al·ly,** *adv.* —**hor′ti·cul′tur·ist,** *n.*

Ho·rus (hôr′əs) *n.* a sun god of ancient Egypt, represented as having the head of a falcon.

Hos., Hosea.

ho·san·na (hō zan′ə) *interj.* praise to God. —*n.* **1.** a cry of hosanna. **2.** any cry or shout of adoration, acclamation, or praise. [Late Latin *hōsanna,* from Greek *hōsanna,* from Hebrew *hoshia na* save now, we pray.]

hose (hōz) *n., pl.* **hose** or *(def. 1)* **hos·es** or *(defs. 2, 3, archaic)* **hos·en. 1.** a flexible tube of rubber, canvas, or other material, used for conveying water or other liquids to a desired point. **2.** a stocking or sock. ➡ usually used in the plural. **3.** close-fitting trousers resembling tights, formerly worn by men. —*v.t.,* **hosed, hos·ing.** to spray, wash, or water with a hose. [Old English *hosa* garment for the leg.]

Ho·se·a (hō zē′ə, -zā′ə) *n.* a book of the Old Testament, attributed to the Hebrew prophet Hosea.

hos·en (hō′zən) *Archaic.* a plural of **hose** *(defs. 2, 3).*

ho·sier (hō′zhər) *n.* a person who manufactures or sells hosiery or similar goods.

ho·sier·y (hō′zhə rē) *n.* **1.** stockings and socks. **2.** the business of a hosier.

hos·pice (hos′pis) *n.* **1.** a place of lodging for travelers or pilgrims, esp. one maintained by a religious order. **2.** an organization or facility that provides medical care and emotional support to people who are terminally ill and their families. [French *hospice,* from Latin *hospitium* lodging, hospitality, from *hospes* guest, host[1].]

hos·pi·ta·ble (hos′pi tə bəl, hos pit′ə-) *adj.* **1.** offering a friendly and generous welcome to guests or strangers: *The townspeople were very hospitable.* **2.** characterized by or affording welcome and generosity toward guests: *a hospitable resort.* **3.** favoring or supporting growth, development, or the like: *a hospitable environment for tropical plants.* **4.** receptive or open in mind or disposition: *The committee members were hospitable to my plan.* [Modern Latin *hospitabilis,* going back to Latin *hospitārī* to be a guest.] —**hos′pi·ta·bly,** *adv.*

hos·pi·tal (hos′pi təl) *n.* **1.** an institution providing medical, surgical, or psychiatric treatment for the sick or injured. **2.** a place providing medical care for animals. **3.** a repair shop for specified small items: *a watch hospital, a doll hospital.* [Old French *hospital* place to receive persons in need, from Medieval Latin *hospitale* place to receive guests, going back to *hospes* guest, host[1]. Doublet of HOSTEL, HOTEL.]

hos·pi·tal·i·ty (hos′pi tal′i tē) *n., pl.* -**ties. 1.** the act, practice, or quality of being hospitable. **2.** an instance of this. [Old French *hospitalite,* from Latin *hospitālitās.*]

hos·pi·tal·i·za·tion (hos′pi tə lə zā′shən) *n.* **1.a.** the act of hospitalizing or the state of being hospitalized. **b.** the period of time during which a person is hospitalized. **2.** a form of insurance providing partial or total payment of a patient's hospital expenses. Also *(def. 2),* **hospitalization insurance.**

hos·pi·tal·ize (hos′pi tə līz′) *v.t.,* -**ized,** -**iz·ing.** to admit to or put in a hospital as a patient: *The skier was hospitalized with a broken leg.*

host[1] (hōst) *n.* **1.** a person who receives or entertains others, usually as guests in the home. **2.** a person, place, institution, or the like that provides facilities and services for a convention, sports event, or the like: *Los Angeles has twice been host for the Olympics.* **3.** a person acting as master of ceremonies or moderator on a radio or television program. **4.** the proprietor or keeper of an inn or hotel. **5.** a living plant or animal in or upon which a parasite lives and obtains nourishment. —*v.t.* to be or serve as host for: *to host a party, to host a game show.* [Middle English *hoste,* from Old French *hoste* innkeeper, guest, one who entertains a guest, from Latin *hospes* guest, one who entertains a guest.]

host[2] (hōst) *n.* **1.** a large number; multitude: *A host of sailboats approached the harbor at dusk.* **2.** an army. [Middle English *host,* from Old French *host* army, assembly, from Medieval Latin *hostis,* from Latin *hostis* enemy, stranger.]

Synonyms Host[2], multitude, legion, and myriad denote a very large number of persons or things. **Host** connotes concentration in great numbers or in striking array: *a host of troubles, a host of stars in the night sky.* **Multitude** is used more generally of great number: *a multitude of possibilities, a multitude assembled in the park for the concert.* **Legion** suggests numbers too large to count, but it is often used facetiously: *You have a legion of admirers.* **Myriad** also connotes incalculable numbers, but tends to suggest small, even minuscule things: *a myriad of tiny insects.*

host[3] (hōst) *also,* **Host.** *n.* the bread or a wafer of unleavened bread used for Holy Communion in the Roman Catholic Church and certain other churches. [Middle English *hoste,* from Old French *(h)oiste,* from Medieval Latin *hostia* consecrated host, from Latin *hostia* sacrificial offering.]

hos·ta (hos′tə) *n.* plantain lily. [Modern Latin *hosta,* from Nicolaus Thomas *Host,* 1761-1834, Austrian physician.]

hos·tage (hos′tij) *n.* a person held, given, or abducted to ensure or force the fulfillment of certain promises or conditions: *Two people were held as hostages by the terrorists.* [Old French *(h)ostage* surety, pawn, going back to Latin *obses;* probably influenced in form by Latin *hospes* guest, host[1].]

• **to hold** (or **take**) **hostage.** to hold or take as a hostage: *The bank robbers took a teller hostage to ensure their escape.*

hos·tel (hos′təl) *n.* a lodging place, esp. a supervised lodging place for young people. [Old French *hostel* inn, from Medieval Latin *hospitale* place to receive guests, going back to Latin *hospes* guest, host[1]. Doublet of HOSPITAL, HOTEL.]

hos·tel·ry (hos′təl rē) *n., pl.* -**ries.** an inn or hotel.

host·ess (hōs′tis) *n.* **1.** a woman who receives or entertains others, usually as guests in her own home. **2.** a woman employed, as by a restaurant or nightclub, to greet and assist patrons. **3.** stewardess. **4.** a woman who is the proprietor or keeper of an inn or hotel. —*v.t.* to be or serve as hostess for.

hos·tile (hos′təl, -tīl) *adj.* **1.** feeling or showing hatred, dislike, or antagonism: *The speaker was shouted down by the hostile crowd.* **2.** of or belonging to an enemy: *The battalion encountered hostile forces.* **3.** unfavorable for growth, development, or the like; not hospitable: *The hostile desert environment does not support much life.* —*n.* a hostile person or thing. [Latin *hostīlis* relating to an enemy, from *hostis* enemy.]

hos·til·i·ty (ho stil′i tē) *n., pl.* -**ties. 1.** the state of being hostile; hostile attitude or feeling; antagonism. **2.** a hostile act. **3.** hostilities. acts of war; warfare; war: *The hostilities ended when the truce was signed.* **4.** resistance or opposition, as to a plan or idea: *The proposed highway through the woodlands met with hostility from environmentalists.* —For Synonyms, see antagonism.

hos·tler (hos′lər, os′lər) *also,* **ostler.** *n.* a person who takes care of horses at an inn or stable. [Old French *hostelier* innkeeper, from *hostel* inn. See HOSTEL.]

hot (hot) *adj.,* **hot·ter, hot·test. 1.** having or communicating much heat; having a high temperature: *to make a crease with a hot iron.* **2.** having a relatively high temperature; very warm: *It was surprisingly hot for an autumn day.* **3.** having, showing, or feeling the sensation of an abnormally high body temperature: *The child is hot with fever. The ointment made my skin hot. The runner was hot and tired after the race.* **4.** having or producing an effect of heat or burning, as in the mouth or on the skin: *Mexican food can be very hot.* **5.** having or carrying an electric current or charge, esp. one of high voltage: *a hot wire.* **6.** radioactive, esp. to a high or lethal degree. **7.** showing or characterized by intensity of feeling, excitability, or anger: *to exchange hot words over a controversial issue, to try to control a hot temper.* **8.** highly controversial: *a hot topic of debate.* **9.** intensely active; violent; raging: *a hot battle.* **10.** in constant use or action: *During the crisis, the telephones were kept hot between the two governments.* **11.** following very closely; close behind: *The police were hot on the heels of the fugitive.* **12.** in certain games, close to the object or answer sought: *She told us we were getting hot when we nearly guessed the secret.* **13.** in hunting, strong or fresh, as a scent or trail. **14.** *Informal.* dangerous; unsafe: *The political activists fled when conditions in their own country became too hot.* **15.** *Informal.* **a.** new; fresh: *The book is hot off the press.* **b.** very popular or very successful commercially: *a hot new toy.* **16.** *Music. Informal.* of or relating to jazz characterized by heavily accented beat, fast tempo, and much improvisation. **17.** *Informal.* very eager or enthusiastic; ardent: *to be hot for all the new styles.* **18.** *Informal.* unusually lucky or showing unusual skill: *While the baseball player was hot, his batting average rose thirty points.* **19.** *Slang.* filled with activity; lively; exciting: *to have a hot time at a party.* **20.** *Slang.* **a.** recently stolen or illegally procured: *The thief tried to sell the hot jewelry.* **b.** wanted by the police. **21.** *Slang.* sexually excited or exciting. —*adv.* in a hot manner. [Old English *hāt* having much heat, excitable, violent.] —**hot′ly,** *adv.* —**hot′ness,** *n.*

• **hot under the collar.** *Informal.* extremely agitated; very angry.

• **to make it hot for.** *Informal.* to make a situation very difficult or uncomfortable for.

hot air *Slang.* empty, boastful, or pretentious talk or writing.

hot·bed (hot′bed′) *n.* **1.** a garden frame used for growing plants, in which the soil is heated by decaying manure or by electricity, steam, or hot water pipes. **2.** an environment fostering rapid growth or development, esp. of something disliked or bad: *The investigation of the department exposed a hotbed of corruption.*

hot-blood·ed (hot′blud′id) *adj.* very excitable; passionate; impulsive; rash. —**hot′-blood′ed·ness,** *n.*

hot·box (hot′boks′) *n.* (on a railroad car) an overheated bearing on a shaft or axle.

hot cake, a pancake; griddlecake.
 · **to go** (or **sell**) **like hot cakes.** *Informal.* to be sold quickly and in great quantity.

hotch·potch (hoch′poch′) hodgepodge.

hot cross bun, a sweet bun marked with a cross made of icing and sometimes containing small bits of dried fruit, such as raisins, traditionally eaten during Lent.

hot-dog (hot′dôg′) *also,* **hot·dog.** *Slang. v.i.* **-dogged, -dog-ging.** **1.** to perform stunts, as on skis or a surfboard. **2.** to display a skill in a showy, exhibitionist manner, esp. in sports; show off. —**hot′-dog′ger,** *n.*

hot dog *Informal.* **1.** a frankfurter, esp. one cooked and served on a roll. **2.** *Slang.* a person who performs stunts, as on skis or a surfboard. **3.** *Slang.* a person who shows off, esp. in sports.

ho·tel (hō tel′) *n.* a commercial establishment that provides lodging and often food, entertainment, and other services for the public, esp. for travelers. [French *hôtel* large house, inn, from Old French *hostel* inn, from Medieval Latin *hospitale* place to receive guests, going back to Latin *hospes* guest, host¹. Doublet of HOSPI-TAL, HOSTEL.]

hot flash, the sensation of a sudden rush of heat over the body, as experienced by some women during menopause.

hot·foot (hot′fut′) *Informal. n., pl.* **-foots.** a practical joke in which a match is secretly inserted between the sole and upper portion of the victim's shoe and then lit. —*v.i. Informal.* to go in great haste; hurry (usually with *it*): *We hotfooted it downtown after school.* —*adv. Informal.* in great haste.

hot·head (hot′hed′) *n.* a hotheaded person.

hot·head·ed (hot′hed′id) *adj.* **1.** easily angered; quick-tempered. **2.** impetuous; rash. —**hot′head′ed·ly,** *adv.* —**hot′-head′ed·ness,** *n.*

hot·house (hot′hous′) *n., pl.* **-hous·es** (-hou′ziz). a heated building, usually made mainly of glass, where plants are grown; greenhouse. —*adj.* grown in a hothouse: *hothouse flowers.*

hot line *also,* **hot·line** (hot′līn′) **1.** a direct telephone or other communications link kept ready for use in a crisis or emergency, as by the heads of two governments. **2.** a telephone service established to provide callers with immediate and confidential counseling or assistance for a particular problem: *a drug abuse hot line, a hot line for runaways.*

hot pepper, the pungent, podlike edible fruit of any of several pepper plants, genus *Capsicum.*

hot plate **1.** an electrical or gas device usually consisting of one or two burners, used for cooking or heating food. **2.** an apparatus that can be heated and is used to keep food warm.

hot potato *Informal.* something that no one wants to deal with because it is controversial or complicated: *The proposed tax increase was a Congressional hot potato.*

hot·press (hot′pres′) *v.t.* to produce a glossy surface on (paper or fabric) by applying heat and mechanical pressure. —*n.* a machine for hotpressing.

hot rod *Slang.* an automobile, esp. an older model, rebuilt or modified for high speeds. —**hot rodder.**

hot seat **1.** *Slang.* electric chair. **2.** *Informal.* an uncomfortable or unpleasant position or situation.

hot·shot (hot′shot′) *n. Slang.* a person who is aggressively or flamboyantly successful at something, often showing conceit about it.

hot spot **1.** *Informal.* a place where trouble or violence is occurring or is likely to occur; dangerous locality: *There were hot spots of rebel activity throughout the countryside.* **2.** *Slang.* a popular nightclub or café attended regularly by celebrities. **3.** an area or region in which either radiation or geothermal heat is at an abnormally high level.

hot spring, a natural spring emitting water above 98 degrees Fahrenheit (37 degrees Celsius).

hot·spur (hot′spûr′) *n.* an impetuous or rash person; hothead.

hot-tem·pered (hot′tem′pərd) *adj.* easily angered; hotheaded; short-tempered.

Hot·ten·tot (hot′ən tot′) *n., pl.* **-tot** or **-tots.** Khoikhoi. [Dutch *Hottentot* member of this southern African people, stutterer; said to be an imitative word suggested by the speech of these Africans, which sounded like stuttering to the Dutch.]

hot toddy, toddy *(def. 1).*

hot tub, a large tub, usually made of wood and installed outdoors, that is filled with hot water and used for bathing or relaxation, often by several people socially.

hot war, a conflict involving actual fighting; open warfare.
 ➡ distinguished from **cold war** *(def. 2).*

hot water *Informal.* a state of difficulty; trouble: *a mischievous child who always gets into hot water.*

hot-wire (hot′wīr′) *v.t.,* **-wired, -wir·ing.** *Slang.* to start the motor of (a car, boat, or the like) by short-circuiting the ignition switch.

hou·dah (hou′də) howdah.

hound (hound) *n.* **1.** any of various dogs that are bred and trained to hunt by scent, such as the beagle, bloodhound, and foxhound, or by sight, such as the deerhound and Irish wolfhound. **2.** any dog. **3.** a mean, contemptible person. **4.** *Informal.* a person who avidly enjoys something, such as a specific pastime or food; devotee; enthusiast: *an autograph hound.* —*v.t.* **1.** to pursue relentlessly. **2.** *Informal.* to urge persistently; nag; pester: *My parents hounded me about cleaning my room.* [Old English *hund* dog, detestable person.]
 · **to follow** (or **ride to**) **the hounds.** to participate in a fox hunt.

hound's-tooth (houndz′tüth′) *n.* a broken-check pattern used in weaving fabrics. Also, **hound's-tooth check.**

hour (our) *n.* **1.** a unit of time equal to 1/24 of a day; sixty minutes. **2.** one of the points on a timepiece indicating such a unit of time or the time indicated by such a point: *The bus to the city leaves on the hour.* **3.a.** a definite time of day as indicated by a timepiece, esp. a timepiece marked with only twelve hours: *At what hour should we leave? They met at the appointed hour.* **b. hours.** a definite time of day as indicated by a timepiece that shows twenty-four hours, expressed as a four-digit number: *The attack began at 0100 hours.* **4.** a particular or fixed time for some activity: *The family always gathered at the dinner hour.* **5.** an indefinite, usually short period of time: *the hour of death.* **6. hours. a.** a fixed time devoted to one's work or other regular pursuits: *The doctor had office hours four days a week. Do you work long hours?* **b.** a habitual time for retiring and rising: *She keeps late hours and gets very little sleep.* **7.** the present time or current situation: *The astronaut was a national hero and the man of the hour.* **8.a.** the amount of distance that can be traveled in an hour: *We were an hour away from home.* **b.** the amount of work that can be done in an hour: *We were an hour from finishing the job.* **9.** *Astronomy.* a measure of longitude equal to 1/24 of a great circle, or 15 degrees. **10. hours. a.** canonical hours. **b.** the prayers or services recited at the canonical hours. **11.a.** a single period of classroom instruction, usually less than sixty minutes: *The daily schedule is divided into eight hours.* **b.** in colleges and universities, a unit of academic credit, one of which is usually given for each hour of instruction per week. [Old French *(h)ore* 1/24 of a day, time, period, from Latin *hōra* certain space of time, time, season, from Greek *hōra.*]
 · **after hours.** after the normal hours for business or school; after closing time: *The offices are cleaned after hours.*
 · **the wee** (or **small**) **hours.** the early morning hours after midnight: *They didn't get home from the party until the wee hours.*

hour·glass (our′glas′) *n.* a device for measuring time, consisting of a glass vessel with a narrow passage in the middle, through which a quantity of sand or mercury runs from the upper to the lower part in exactly one hour.

hour hand, the short hand on a clock or watch, indicating the hour.

hou·ri (hûr′ē, hour′ē) *n.* in Islam, one of the eternally young and beautiful women given as a companion to those who attain paradise. [French *houri,* from Persian *hūrī,* from Arabic *hūrīyah* black-eyed (woman).]

hour·ly (our′lē) *adj.* **1.** done, occurring, or counted every hour: *hourly airplane departures.* **2.** done in the course of or computed on the basis of an hour: *hourly production, hourly wages.* **3.** paid wages on the basis of hours worked: *hourly employees.* **4.** frequent; continual: *The parents made hourly appeals for news of their lost child.* —*adv.* **1.** every hour: *The nurse looked in on the patient hourly.* **2.** frequently; continually.

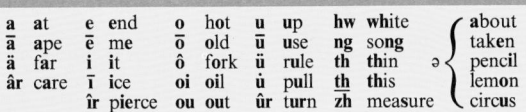

hourglass

Hours (ourz) *pl. n.* in Greek mythology, the goddesses of time and seasons, the daughters of the earth and the sky. Also, **Horae.**

house (*n.,* hous; *v.,* houz) *n., pl.* **hous·es** (hou′ziz). **1.** a building or part of a building in which people live, esp. one in which a

a	at	e	end	o	hot	u	up	hw	white	⎧	about
ā	ape	ē	me	ō	old	ū	use	ng	song		taken
ä	far	i	it	ô	fork	ü	rule	th	thin	ə	pencil
âr	care	ī	ice	oi	oil	u̇	pull	th	this		lemon
		îr	pierce	ou	out	ûr	turn	zh	measure	⎩	circus

family dwells; place of residence: *Come to my house for dinner.*
2. the people, esp. a family, inhabiting a house; household: *The whole house was ill with the mumps. The house was in an uproar.*
3.a. a building in which people live together as a social group or unit: *a fraternity house.* **b.** the people living in such a building. **c.** *Informal.* a club or organization, as a fraternity or sorority: *What house did you pledge?* **4.** anything serving as protection or habitation for an animal: *The snail carries its house on its back.*
5. a building or other structure in which animals or objects are kept: *We visited the monkey house at the zoo.* **6.** a structure or area used for a purpose other than human occupation: *a drug house, a carriage house.* **7.** a place of worship, as a church or temple. **8.a.** a place of entertainment, esp. a theater: *The house was filled for the premiere.* **b.** the audience in such a place: *The house gave her a standing ovation.* **9.** also, **House.** **a.** a legislative or deliberative body: *Did the bill pass in the House?* **b.** the building or chamber in which such a body meets. **10.** also, **House.** a family, esp. of royal or noble blood, including ancestors, descendants, and kindred: *The British sovereign is a member of the House of Windsor.* **11.** a business firm or establishment: *a banking and investment house.* **12.** in gambling, the person who acts as banker in a game, or the gambling establishment itself: *to bet against the house.* **13.** one of the twelve signs of the zodiac into which the heavens are divided in astrology. —*v.,* **housed, housing.** —*v.t.* **1.** to put or receive into a house; provide with a house; shelter; lodge: *They were housed in the old mansion. The colonial structure housed a family of five.* **2.** to store or keep in a house or building: *The art collection was housed in the museum.* **3.** to place in a secure or protected position in or as if in a house. —*v.i.* to take shelter; reside; dwell. [Old English *hūs* building for human habitation, family, animal habitation.] —For Synonyms *(n.),* see **home.**

• **on the house.** at the expense of the owner; without charge: *Our meal at the restaurant was on the house.*
• **to bring down the house.** *Informal.* to receive enthusiastic, prolonged applause from an audience.
• **to clean house. a.** to clean a house or put it in order. **b.** to get rid of or put an end to a person, element, or situation that is unnecessary or undesirable.
• **to keep house.** to manage and take care of a house and its household.
• **to put** (or **set**) **one's house in order.** to straighten out one's own affairs.

house arrest, confinement after arrest to one's own home or quarters rather than in a prison.

house·boat (hous′bōt′) *n.* a boat or barge with a superstructure that is fitted out as a dwelling.

house·bound (hous′bound′) *adj.* confined to one's home or quarters, as by an illness, handicap, or severe weather.

house·break (hous′brāk′) *v.t.,* **-broke** (-brōk′), **-bro·ken, -break·ing.** to make (a pet) housebroken.

house·break·ing (hous′brā′king) *n.* the act of breaking into and entering a residence with intent to steal or commit some other crime. —**house′break′er,** *n.*

house·bro·ken (hous′brō′kən) *adj.* (of a household pet) trained to excrete outdoors or in a specific place.

house call 1. a visit by a doctor, nurse, therapist, or the like to the home of a person who is sick or handicapped in order to care for that person. **2.** a service call made to a home to repair some appliance or device.

house·clean·ing (hous′klē′ning) *n.* **1.** the act or process of cleaning a house, including its furniture and other furnishings. **2.** the act or process of getting rid of undesirable conditions or unnecessary procedures or personnel: *The new police chief immediately began a housecleaning of the department.*

house·coat (hous′kōt′) *n.* a robe or dresslike garment worn at home.

house·dress (hous′dres′) *n.* a dress, usually of a light-weight fabric, to be worn while doing housework.

house·fly (hous′flī′) *n., pl.* **-flies.** the common fly, *Musca domestica,* that lives in and around houses and other domiciles in most parts of the world, feeding on food and refuse and carrying a variety of disease-producing organisms.

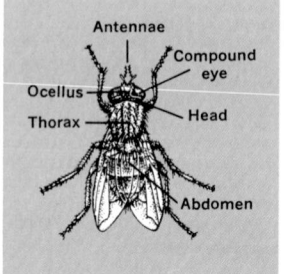

housefly

house·hold (hous′hōld′) *n.* **1.** all the inhabitants of a house;

family and servants. **2.** a home and its affairs. —*adj.* **1.** of or relating to a household; domestic: *household chores.* **2.** intended for use in a home: *household appliances.* **3.** familiar; common: *Successful advertising made the product a household name.*

Household Cavalry, the cavalry troops that are part of the personal guard of the British sovereign.

house·hold·er (hous′hōl′dər) *n.* **1.** a person who owns or occupies a house. **2.** the head of a family.

household word, a widely familiar word, name, or phrase: *The astronaut's name became a household word.*

house·keep·er (hous′kē′pər) *n.* **1.** a person who manages the affairs of a household or does housework, esp. one paid for doing this. **2.** a person hired to direct the people who do the cleaning, as in a hotel or hospital.

house·keep·ing (hous′kē′ping) *n.* the maintenance of a household and the managing of its affairs.

house·leek (hous′lēk′) *n.* any of a number of plants, genus *Sempervivum,* esp. *S. tectorum,* native to Europe and bearing thick leaves, usually in rosettes, and hairy, erect, pink flowers.

house·lights (hous′līts′) *pl. n.* lights that illuminate the seating area of a theater, concert hall, or the like.

house·maid (hous′mād′) *n.* a woman employed to do housework.

housemaid's knee, a chronic inflammation in the front of the kneecap, usually caused by kneeling.

house·man (hous′man′, -mən) *n., pl.* **-men** (-men′, -mən). a man who does general work and housekeeping, as in a house, hotel, or rest home.

house·moth·er (hous′muth′ər) *n.* a woman who supervises a group of people, esp. young people, living together, as in a dormitory.

House of Burgesses, the popularly elected lower house of the legislature in colonial Virginia or Maryland.

house of cards, anything that is unstable or flimsy and can be easily knocked down or destroyed.

House of Commons, the lower, elective house of either the British or the Canadian Parliament. Also, **Commons.**

house of correction, a place for the confinement and rehabilitation of persons convicted of minor offenses.

House of Delegates, the lower branch of the legislature in Maryland, Virginia, or West Virginia.

House of Lords, the upper, nonelective house of the British Parliament, composed of the nobility and high-ranking Anglican clergy.

House of Representatives 1. the lower elective house of the U.S. Congress and of many state legislatures, in which representation is based on population. **2.** a similar legislative body, as in the Australian parliament.

house organ, a magazine or newspaper published by a business for its employees or clients.

house party, an occasion involving the entertainment of guests, usually for several days, esp. in a home or at a fraternity or sorority house.

house physician, a resident physician, as of a hotel or hospital.

house·plant (hous′plant′) *n.* a plant grown indoors.

house·sit (hous′sit′) *v.i.,* **-sat** (-sat′), **-sit·ting.** to live in and take care of a house or apartment while the owner or tenant is away. [HOUSE + (BABY)-SIT.] —**house′-sit′ter,** *n.*

house sparrow, a hardy sparrow, *Passer domesticus,* found in rural and urban areas throughout warm and temperate regions of the world, having dull gray-and-brown plumage with black-and-white markings. Length: 6 inches (15 centimeters). Also, **English sparrow.**

house·top (hous′top′) *n.* the roof or top of a house.
• **from the housetops.** loudly and publicly: *The victory was proclaimed from the housetops.*

house·wares (hous′wârz′) *pl. n.* articles sold for use in the house, esp. in the kitchen and bathroom, such as pots and pans, wastebaskets, laundry hampers, and small appliances.

house·warm·ing (hous′wôr′ming) *n.* a party given when people move into a house or other residence.

house·wife (hous′wīf′; *def. 2, usually* huz′if) *n., pl.* **-wives** (-wīvz′; *def. 2, also* -ivz). **1.** a married woman who manages a home and its affairs. **2.** a small case for needles, pins, thread, and similar items.

house·wife·ly (hous′wīf′lē) *adj.* of, relating to, or characteristic of a housewife or her duties. —**house′wife′li·ness,** *n.*

house·wif·er·y (hous′wī′fə rē, -wīf′rē) *n.* the work or duties of a housewife; housekeeping.

house·work (hous′wûrk′) *n.* work done in housekeeping, such as washing, ironing, cleaning, and cooking.

hous·ing¹ (hou′zing) *n.* **1.** houses collectively: *Housing for the middle class in the city was insufficient.* **2.** the act of sheltering or providing houses, as for a group of people. **3.** any shelter or

covering. **4.** a frame, plate, or casing that supports, secures, or contains a machine or part of a machine. [HOUSE + -ING¹.]

hous·ing² (hou′zing) *n.* an ornamental covering for a horse. [Middle English *housinge* buildings, property, shelter, from *housen* to house, from Old English *hūs* house.]

hove (hōv) a past tense and past participle of **heave.**

hov·el (huv′əl, hov′-) *n.* **1.** a small, wretched house or shack; hut. **2.** an open shed, as for sheltering cattle or tools. [Of uncertain origin.]

hov·er (huv′ər, hov′-) *v.i.* **1.** to remain in the air over or around a particular spot: *The helicopter hovered above the wreck and dropped supplies to the survivors.* **2.** to linger or remain nearby: *The nurse hovered over the sick child. The thought hovered in my mind.* **3.** to continue in an indeterminate or irresolute state: *to hover between tears and laughter.* —*n.* the act of hovering. [Middle English *hoveren* to remain in the air, tarry; of uncertain origin.] —**hov′er·er,** *n.*

hov·er·craft (huv′ər kraft′) *n.* a vehicle that can hover or travel over land or water on a thin cushion of high-pressure air created beneath the craft by means of fans or rotors. Also, **air-cushion vehicle, ground-effect machine.** Trademark: **Hovercraft.**

how (hou) *adv.* **1.** in what manner or way; by what means: *How do you plan to get there?* **2.** to what degree, amount, or extent: *How hot is it outside? How do you like this dress?* **3.** in what state or condition: *How's the weather today? How are you?* **4.** for what reason or purpose; why: *How did you happen to be there?* **5.** with what meaning; to what effect: *How did you interpret this last remark?* **6.** by what name: *How is she known?* **7.** *Informal.* what: *How's that?* —*n.* a manner or method of doing; means: *Have you considered the whys and hows of this plan?* —*conj.* **1.** the way or manner in which: *The tour guide told us how to get there.* **2.** of the way or manner in which: *Be careful how you drive.* **3.** in whatever way or manner: *You can do the job how you like.* **4.** *Informal.* that: *She mentioned how she was due for a raise.* [Old English *hū* in what way, to what extent.]

· **and how.** *Informal.* that's absolutely true. ➡ used to emphasize agreement with a previous statement.
· **how about.** would you like or consider; what do you think of: *How about joining us? How about a glass of water?*
· **how come.** *Informal.* how does it happen that: *How come they aren't here?*
· **how much. a.** what quantity, amount, or price: *How much will it cost to repair this damage?* **b.** what portion: *How much of the earth is covered with water?* **c.** what quantity or amount of: *How much milk do we have left?*

how·be·it (hou bē′it) *adv.* however it may be; nevertheless. ➡ used in literature.

how·dah (hou′də) *also,* **houdah.** *n.* a seat, usually equipped with a railing and canopy, used for riding on the back of an elephant or camel. [Hindustani *haudah,* from Arabic *haudaj.*]

how·dy (hou′dē) *interj., n., pl.* **-dies.** *Informal.* hello. [Short for *How do you do?*]

how·e'er (hou âr′) however.

how·ev·er (hou ev′ər) *conj.* nevertheless; yet; notwithstanding: *It was a good guess; however, it was wrong.* —*adv.* **1.** in whatever way; by whatever means: *You may do the work however you like.* **2.** to whatever degree or extent: *However far our dog wandered, it always returned home by dusk.*

how·itz·er (hou′it sər) *n.* a cannon of medium length used to fire shells at high angles of elevation. [Dutch *houwitser,* from German *Haubitze,* from Czech *houfnice* catapult.]

howl (houl) *v.i.* **1.** to utter a loud, wailing cry, as that of a dog or wolf. **2.** to utter a similar loud cry, as from pain, rage, grief, scorn, or amusement. **3.** to make a similar sound: *The wind howled during the storm.* **4.** to laugh or yell loudly or scornfully: *The audience howled at the joke.* —*v.t.* **1.** to utter or express with howling: *to howl one's scorn.* **2.** to force or drive by or as by howling: *The audience howled the actor off the stage.* —*n.* **1.** a loud, wailing cry, as that of a dog or wolf. **2.** any similar sound, esp. a shout or cry of pain, rage, grief, scorn, or amusement. **3.** a loud cry or yell: *Howls of laughter greeted the ridiculous suggestion.* **4.** *Informal.* something extremely funny: *The new comedy is really a howl.* [Probably imitative.]

how·ler (hou′lər) *n.* **1.** a person, animal, or thing that howls. **2.** *Informal.* a ridiculous or glaring blunder.

howler monkey, any of a group of large Central and South American monkeys, genus *Alouatta,* characterized by loud, howling cries. Length: 2-3 feet (0.6-0.9 meter), with an equally long tail.

howl·ing (hou′ling) *adj.* **1.** uttering or making howls or a similar sound, or characterized by howling: *a howling wind.* **2.** dismal, gloomy, or depressing: *They were lost deep in the howling wilds of the jungle.* **3.** *Slang.* very great: *a howling success.*

how·so·ev·er (hou′sō ev′ər) *adv.* **1.** in whatever way; by whatever means. **2.** to whatever degree or extent.

how-to (hou′tü′) *adj. Informal.* providing basic instructions or advice on how to make or do something: *a how-to book on car repair.*

hoy·den (hoi′dən) *also,* **hoiden.** *n.* a boisterous, ill-mannered, or saucy girl, esp. a tomboy. [Middle Dutch *heiden* heathen, rustic.] —**hoy′den·ish,** *adj.*

Hoyle (hoil) *n.* **according to Hoyle.** according to the rules; fairly or correctly. [From Edmond *Hoyle,* 1672-1769, English lawyer and author of books on games.]

hp *also,* **hp., HP** horsepower.

HQ *also,* **hq** headquarters.

hr *also,* **hr.** *pl.* **hrs** hour.

H.R., House of Representatives.

H.R.H., His (or Her) Royal Highness.

H.S. *also,* **HS** High School.

ht *also,* **ht.** height.

hub (hub) *n.* **1.** the central part of a wheel into which the axle is inserted. **2.** a central point of interest, importance, or activity: *The seaport was the hub of commerce in the region.* [Form of HOB¹.] —**hub′like′,** *adj.*

hub·bub (hub′ub) *n.* **1.** a loud, confused noise, as of many voices or sounds. **2.** noisy confusion, excitement, or agitation; uproar: *The scandal created quite a hubbub.* [Probably of Irish origin.]

hub·by (hub′ē) *n., pl.* **-bies.** *Informal.* husband.

hub·cap (hub′kap′) *n.* a removable metal disk covering the hub of a wheel, esp. of an automobile.

hu·bris (hū′bris, hü′-) *n.* insolence or arrogance resulting from excessive pride or passion. [Greek *hubris* insolence, outrage.]

hub

huck·a·back (huk′ə bak′) *n.* an absorbent linen or cotton fabric woven with a rough, uneven surface and used for towels. [Of uncertain origin.]

huck·le·ber·ry (huk′əl ber′ē) *n., pl.* **-ries. 1.** the small, shiny blue or black berry of any of a group of shrubs, genus *Gaylussacia,* of the heath family, resembling the blueberry but darker in color and having ten hard seeds, used esp. to make pie fillings and preserves. **2.** the low shrub bearing this fruit, found growing wild in North and South America and bearing drooping clusters of tiny white, pink, or red flowers. [Probably modification of dialectal *hurtleberry,* a form of WHORTLEBERRY.]

huck·ster (huk′stər) *n.* **1.** a peddler or hawker of small articles, esp. fruits and vegetables. **2.** a person who does business in a mean, petty, or unscrupulous way. **3.** *Informal.* a person in the advertising business. —*v.t.* **1.** to sell or peddle. **2.** to sell or advertise in an unscrupulous, misleading way. [Possibly from Middle Dutch *hoekster,* feminine of *hoeker* hawker¹.]

HUD, (Department of) Housing and Urban Development.

hud·dle (hud′əl) *v.,* **-dled, -dling.** —*v.i.* **1.** to crowd or nestle, as from cold or fear: *The children huddled together under the umbrella.* **2.** to draw oneself together; hunch: *The cold wind made me huddle inside my coat.* **3.** *Football.* to gather behind the line of scrimmage before a play in order to plan the play or receive instructions or signals. **4.** *Informal.* to meet privately in order to consult or discuss; confer: *The judges huddled before they announced the winner.* —*v.t.* **1.** to drive or crowd together closely. **2.** to draw (oneself) together; hunch (often with *up*). —*n.* **1.** a group of persons or things crowded or clustered together; jumble: *In thirty years the huddle of houses grew into a city.* **2.** *Football.* a gathering of players behind the line of scrimmage before a play in order to plan the play or receive instructions or signals. **3.** *Informal.* a small, private meeting or conference: *The politician's advisers went into a huddle to discuss strategy.* [Of uncertain origin.]

Hud·son seal (hud′sən) muskrat fur that has been dyed and plucked to look like seal.

hue¹ (hū) *n.* **1.** the property of a color that determines its

howdah

a	at	e	end	o	hot	u	up	hw	white		about
ā	ape	ē	me	ō	old	ū	use	ng	song		taken
ä	far	i	it	ô	fork	ü	rule	th	thin	ə	pencil
âr	care	ī	ice	oi	oil	u̇	pull	th	this		lemon
		î	pierce	ou	out	ûr	turn	zh	measure		circus

603

position in the spectrum. **2.** color *(def. 2)*. **3.** appearance, form, or type: *Organizations of every hue have their headquarters here.* [Middle English *hewe,* from Old English *hīw, hēow* shape, form, kind.]

Synonyms **Hue¹, tint,** and **shade** mean varieties of a color. **Hue** is sometimes used interchangeably with *color,* but is also applied to the modification of a particular color: *Both fabrics were red, but one had a more pinkish hue.* **Tint** suggests a delicate gradation of color or a degree of lightness: *The pale blue tint of the curtains gave the room a light and airy look.* **Shade** usually indicates a color's degree of darkness and suggests subtle variations: *The decorator asked for a softer shade of gray on the walls.*

hue² (hū) *n.* **hue and cry.** a clamor or public stir, as of alarm or opposition: *The newspaper raised a great hue and cry when the scandal was disclosed.* [Middle English *hu,* from Old French *heu* the sound of a trumpet, outcry; imitative.]

huff (huf) *n.* a sudden, temporary feeling of anger, irritation, or indignation: *He walked off in a huff when she insulted him.* —*v.t.* to make angry; offend. —*v.i.* to puff; blow: *I huffed and puffed and blew out the birthday candles.* [Imitative.]

huff·y (huf′ē) *adj.,* **huff·i·er, huff·i·est. 1.** easily offended or angered; touchy. **2.** offended or angered; sulking. —**huff′i·ly,** *adv.* —**huff′i·ness,** *n.*

hug (hug) *v.t.,* **hugged, hug·ging. 1.a.** to clasp the arms around and hold close, esp. in affection; embrace closely. **b.** to grasp and squeeze tightly with the arms, as a bear does. **2.** to keep close to: *The bicycle rider hugged the curb.* **3.** to cling firmly to; cherish. —*n.* **1.** a strong clasp with the arms, esp. as a sign of affection; embrace. **2.** a tight clasp or squeeze with the arms, as in wrestling. [Probably of Scandinavian origin.] —**hug′ger,** *n.*

huge (hūj) *adj.,* **hug·er, hug·est.** of great size, extent, or degree; extremely large. [Short for Old French *ahuge;* of uncertain origin.] —**huge′ly,** *adv.* —**huge′ness,** *n.*

Synonyms **Huge, enormous, vast,** and **immense** mean extremely large. **Huge** is used particularly when speaking of an object's bulk or visible size: *a huge boulder, a huge truck.* **Enormous** stresses dimensions that go well beyond normal bounds: *All the pumpkins are big, but that one is enormous.* **Vast** generally refers to great horizontal extent: *a vast plain, a vast ocean.* **Immense** suggests size that cannot be measured: *An immense galaxy called the Milky Way.*

hug·ger-mug·ger (hug′ər mug′ər) *n.* a state of confusion; disorder. —*adj.* confused; disorderly. —*adv.* in a confused or disorderly way. [Of uncertain origin.]

Hu·gue·not (hū′gə not′) *n.* a French Calvinist, esp. one of the sixteenth or seventeenth century. [French *huguenot,* going back to German (Swiss dialect) *Eidgenoss* confederate.]

huh (hu) *interj.* used to express surprise, contempt, doubt, or lack of understanding.

hu·la (hū′lə) *n.* a traditional Hawaiian dance in which highly stylized gestures of the dancers' arms and hands are used to relate a story. Also, **hu′la-hu′la.** [Of Hawaiian origin.]

hulk (hulk) *n.* **1.a.** the body of an old, wrecked, or dismantled ship. **b.** the shell of something that has been abandoned, wrecked, or gutted: *Only the hulk of the building remained after the explosion.* **2.** a ship used for a prison, storehouse, or similar purpose other than sailing. **3.** a large, clumsy person or thing. —*v.i.* to loom or rise bulkily. [Old English *hulc* light ship, possibly from Medieval Latin *holcas* merchantman, from Greek *holkas.*]

hulk·ing (hul′king) *adj.* massive and clumsy.

hull (hul) *n.* **1.a.** the outer covering of a seed, as of a nut or grain of rice. **b.** the small leaves at the base of the stem of certain fruits, such as strawberries or raspberries. **2.** any outer covering: *Their prejudices were encased within a hull of ignorance.* **3.** the frame or body of a ship, exclusive of the masts, sails, yards, and rigging. **4.a.** the part of the body of a seaplane that rests on the water. **b.** the frame of a rigid dirigible. —*v.t.* **1.** to remove the hull of. **2.** to strike or pierce the hull of (a ship), as with a shell or torpedo. [Old English *hulu* the outer covering of a seed or fruit.] —**hull′er,** *n.*

hul·la·ba·loo (hul′ə bə lü′) *n., pl.* **-loos.** great noise, excitement, or confusion; disturbance; uproar.

hul·lo (hə lō′) *interj., n., v. Informal.* hello.

hum (hum) *v.,* **hummed, hum·ming.** —*v.i.* **1.** to make a low, continuous murmuring sound: *Bumblebees hummed in the garden. The refrigerator motor hummed.* **2.** to sing with closed lips, without saying words. **3.** to give forth a confused or indistinct buzzing sound: *The train station's waiting room hummed with voices.* **4.** *Informal.* to be in a condition of busy activity: *Things were really humming at the newspaper office on election night.* —*v.t.* **1.** to sing (something, as a tune) with closed lips, without saying words. **2.** to bring or put into a specified condition by humming: *to hum*

an infant to sleep. —*n.* **1.** a low, continuous murmuring sound. **2.** a singing with closed lips, without saying words: *The hum of the chorus contrasted with the soprano's high tones.* **3.** a low vocal sound uttered with closed lips, used to express an attitude, as of hesitation, disagreement, surprise, or approval: *There arose a little hum of approbation from all present* (Anthony Trollope, 1877). —*interj.* used to express an attitude, as of hesitation, disagreement, surprise, or approval. [Imitative.]

hu·man (hū′mən, ū′mən) *adj.* **1.** of or relating to human beings or humanity: *human evolution, the human condition.* **2.** having or showing the nature, attributes, or good or bad qualities characteristic of human beings: *the milk of human kindness, human frailty, a pet that seems almost human.* **3.a.** having the form of a human being: *You are a human adding machine.* **b.** consisting of human beings: *The police formed a human wall around the building. There are no signs of human life on other planets.* —*n.* human being. [Latin *hūmānus* relating to man, kind, refined.] —**hu′man·ness,** *n.*

human being, an erect primate, *Homo sapiens,* distinguished from other animals by extraordinary development of the brain and by the ability to alter the environment to an unprecedented degree, esp. through the use of technology, language, and social organization.

hu·mane (hū mān′, ū mān′) *adj.* **1.** having or showing sympathy and compassion for other human beings or animals; kind; merciful; benevolent. **2.** (of certain branches of learning and literature) tending to refine or civilize: *an honorary degree in humane letters.* [Form of HUMAN.] —**hu·mane′ly,** *adv.* —**hu·mane′ness,** *n.*

hu·man·ism (hū′mə niz′əm, ū′mə-) *n.* **1.** any system of thought or action concerned primarily with human interests, needs, values, and ideals, rather than with superhuman beings and questions of theology. **2.** *also,* **Humanism.** the study of classical Greek and Roman culture by European scholars in the Renaissance, and the secular intellectual revival that arose out of this study.

hu·man·ist (hū′mə nist, ū′mə-) *n.* **1.** a follower or student of any philosophy concerned primarily with human interests, needs, values, and ideals. **2.a.** a student of the humanities, esp. a classical scholar. **b.** *also,* **Humanist.** a Renaissance scholar involved in the study of classical culture and the secular intellectual revival fostered by this study.

hu·man·i·tar·i·an (hū man′i târ′ē ən, ū man′-) *adj.* concerned with or promoting the general welfare of humanity: *the humanitarian goals of social reformers.* —*n.* a person who devotes himself or herself to the welfare of humanity; philanthropist.

hu·man·i·tar·i·an·ism (hū man′i târ′ē ə niz′əm, ū man′-) *n.* humane or humanitarian principles or actions; philanthropy.

hu·man·i·ty (hū man′i tē, ū man′-) *n., pl.* **-ties. 1.** human beings collectively; the human race: *Disease is the scourge of humanity.* **2.** the condition or quality of being human; human character or nature: *The ability to reason is central to our humanity.* **3.** the quality of being humane; kindness; benevolence: *The cruel dictator had no humanity.* **4. the humanities. a.** the branch of learning concerned with human culture, including languages, literature, philosophy, and art. **b.** the branch of learning concerned with classical Latin and Greek languages and literature. [Old French *humanite* human nature, kindness, from Latin *hūmānitās.*]

hu·man·ize (hū′mə nīz′, ū′mə-) *v.,* **-ized, -iz·ing.** —*v.t.* **1.** to give or attribute a human character to; make human. **2.** to cause to be kind, merciful, or benevolent; make humane. —*v.i.* to become humane. —**hu′man·i·za′tion,** *n.* —**hu′man·iz′er,** *n.*

hu·man·kind (hū′mən kīnd′, -kīnd′, ū′mən-) *n.* the human race; humanity.

hu·man·ly (hū′mən lē, ū′mən-) *adv.* **1.** within human ability or power; by human means: *It isn't humanly possible to run that far in a minute.* **2.** in accordance with human nature; in a human manner: *humanly fallible.* **3.** according to human knowledge or experience: *under circumstances never humanly matched* (James Glentworth Butler, 1883-84).

human nature, essential characteristics and qualities belonging to all human beings.

hu·man·oid (hū′mə noid′, ū′mə-) *adj.* having the appearance of human form or character; looking or behaving like a human. —*n.* a humanoid being: *The cover of the science fiction magazine pictured humanoids from other galaxies.*

human rights, the fundamental rights and claims of people, esp. as individuals, the violation of which, as by a government, is rarely justifiable, such as the rights to food and shelter, freedom from torture, and freedom of speech.

hum·ble (hum′bəl) *adj.,* **-bler, -blest. 1.** having or showing a low estimate of one's own importance or worth; not proud. **2.** low in position, station, or condition; not pretentious: *a peasant's*

humble abode. **3.** courteous or respectful: *to offer one's humble opinion.* —*v.t.,* **-bled, -bling. 1.** to make humble in spirit; humiliate. **2.** to make lower in position, station, or condition. [Old French *humble* meek, modest, from Latin *humilis* low, base, from *humus* ground.] —**hum′ble·ness,** *n.* —**hum′bler,** *n.* —**hum′bly,** *adv.*

Synonyms *adj.* **Humble** and **modest** mean lacking in pride or assertiveness. **Humble** may also connote a low estimate of oneself. In some uses it suggests exaggeration: *The new students felt humble in the presence of the great professor. Welcome to our humble abode!* **Modest** implies not low self-esteem but a refusal to boast or make more of oneself than seems appropriate: *Modest people tend to make light of their accomplishments.*

hum·ble·bee (hum′bəl bē′) *n.* bumblebee. [Middle English *humbylbee,* possibly from Middle English *humblen* to buzz (imitative) + BEE.]

humble pie *Archaic.* a pie made of the entrails of a deer or other animal. [From the earlier form *umble pie,* from *umbles* entrails, form of *numbles,* from Old French *nombles,* going back to Latin *lumbulus,* diminutive of *lumbus* loin; spelling due to association with *humble* because *umble pie* was usually eaten by the servants while the master ate venison.]

  • **to eat humble pie.** to submit to humiliation, esp. to be forced to admit to and apologize for a mistake in a groveling manner.

hum·bug (hum′bug′) *n.* **1.** foolish or empty talk; nonsense. **2.** something intended to deceive or trick; hoax; sham. **3.** a person who tries to deceive or trick others; impostor; fraud. —*v.t.,* **-bugged, -bug·ging.** to deceive or trick with false pretense; delude; cheat. —*interj.* nonsense. [Of uncertain origin.] —**hum′bug′ger·y,** *n.*

hum·ding·er (hum′ding′ər) *n. Informal.* an unusual, remarkable, or excellent thing or person. [Possibly from HUM + DING[1]; suggesting an object *humming* through the air and *dinging* as it hits its mark.]

hum·drum (hum′drum′) *adj.* lacking variety or excitement; monotonous; tedious; dull: *a humdrum existence.* —*n.* a humdrum routine, talk, or the like: *the humdrum of everyday life.* [Rhyming compound formed from HUM.]

hu·mec·tant (hū mek′tənt, ū mek′-) *n.* a moisture-absorbing substance, such as glycerin, used as an additive to prevent the drying out of foods, inks, cosmetics, and tobacco. [Latin *humectantis,* genitive of *humectans,* variant of *umectans,* present participle of *umectare* to moisten, from *umectus* moist, from *umere* to be moist.]

hu·mer·al (hū′mər əl) *adj.* **1.** of, relating to, or near the humerus. **2.** of, relating to, or near the shoulder or shoulders.

hu·mer·us (hū′mər əs) *n., pl.* **-mer·i** (-mə·rī′). the long bone in the upper arm or forelimb, extending from the shoulder to the elbow. [Latin *(h)umerus* shoulder.]

hu·mic (hū′mik, ū′mik) *adj.* of, relating to, or produced from humus: *a humic acid.* [HUM(US) + -IC.]

hu·mid (hū′mid, ū′mid) *adj.* containing or characterized by the presence of much water vapor; damp: *a hot and humid summer day.* [Latin *(h)ūmidus.*] —**hu′mid·ly,** *adv.*

hu·mid·i·fy (hū mid′ə fī, ū mid′-) *v.t.,* **-fied, -fy·ing.** to make more humid or moist, as the air in a room. —**hu·mid′i·fi·ca′tion,** *n.* —**hu·mid′i·fi′er,** *n.*

hu·mid·i·ty (hū mid′i tē, ū mid′-) *n.* **1.** moistness or dampness, esp. of the atmosphere. **2.** *Meteorology.* the ratio, expressed as a percentage, of the amount of water vapor present in the air to the maximum amount the air could hold at the same temperature.

hu·mi·dor (hū′mi dôr′, ū′mə-) *n.* a container or storage room for cigars or other tobacco products, containing a device that keeps the air and tobacco moist.

hu·mil·i·ate (hū mil′ē āt′, ū mil′-) *v.t.,* **-at·ed, -at·ing.** to lower the pride or dignity of; cause to seem foolish or worthless; mortify. [Late Latin *humiliātus,* past participle of *humiliāre* from Latin *humilis.* See HUMBLE.] —**hu·mil′i·at′ing·ly,** *adv.*

hu·mil·i·a·tion (hū mil′ē ā′shən, ū mil′-) *n.* **1.** a feeling of shame and extreme embarrassment; mortification. **2.** the act of humiliating or the state of being humiliated.

hu·mil·i·ty (hū mil′i tē, ū mil′-) *n.* the quality of being humble;

Humerus

Radius

Ulna

humerus

lack of pride or arrogance. [Old French *humilite,* from Latin *humilitās* lowness, baseness.]

hum·ming·bird (hum′ing bûrd′) *n.* any of numerous small, brightly colored, New World birds, family Trochilidae, having a slender, pointed bill that it uses to sip nectar and narrow wings that beat very rapidly when it flies. Capable of flying sideways as well as backwards, hummingbirds range from 2½ to 8½ inches (6 to 22 centimeters) in length. The **bee hummingbird,** *Calypte helenae,* is the smallest of all living birds. [From the *humming* sound made by its rapidly moving wings.]

hummingbird

hum·mock (hum′ək) *n.* **1.** a low mound of earth or rock; knoll; hillock. **2.** a tract of wooded land rising above a plain or swamp. **3.** a bump or ridge on an ice field. [Of uncertain origin.] —**hum′mock·y,** *adj.*

hum·mus (hum′əs) *n.* a dip or spread made of puréed chickpeas, garlic, and ground sesame seeds.

hu·mon·gous (hū mong′gəs, ū mong′-) *adj. Slang.* extremely large; enormous; gigantic; huge. [Probably a blend of HUGE, MONSTROUS, and TREMENDOUS.]

hu·mor (hū′mər, ū′mər) *also, British,* **humour.** *n.* **1.** that quality of something that makes it amusing or funny; comicality: *There often is humor in the most difficult situations.* **2.** the ability to perceive, appreciate, or express what is amusing or funny: *a dour person devoid of humor.* **3.** speech, writing, or action that is amusing or funny: *The movie never rose above the level of slapstick humor.* **4.** a temporary state of mind; mood: *The prospect of a vacation put us in a good humor.* **5.** a sudden, unpredictable, or capricious inclination; fancy; whim. **6.** *Physiology.* any fluid substance of the body, such as blood, bile, lymph, aqueous humor, or vitreous humor. **7.** in ancient and medieval physiology, any of the four body fluids believed to determine, according to their relative proportions in the system, a person's health and temperament. —*v.t.* to comply with the moods, wishes, or whims of (someone); indulge: *Please humor me and look through the house again for my missing keys.* [Middle English *humor,* from Old French *humor* fluid influencing bodily health, temperament, from Latin *(h)ūmor* moisture, fluid. Formerly there were thought to be four humors in the human body: yellow bile or choler (Latin *bīlis* and Greek *chólē*), blood (Latin *sanguis*), phlegm (Greek *phlegma*), and black bile or melancholy (Greek *melas* black + *chólē* bile). If the humors were evenly mixed, the health was good. If any one humor predominated, a person might be *bilious* or *choleric, sanguine, phlegmatic,* or *melancholy.*]

  • **out of humor.** in a bad mood; irritable; cross.

Synonyms *v.t.* **Humor, indulge,** and **pamper** mean to yield to someone's wishes or caprices. **Humor** connotes going along with someone's moods, sometimes in order to avoid unpleasantness: *I didn't agree with their views, but I humored them out of politeness.* **Indulge** connotes an undue giving in to someone's desires: *If you keep on indulging the children, they'll always expect to get anything they want.* **Pamper** connotes gratifying a person's tastes or wishes to a point of softening or spoiling that person: *They pampered me so much that I never had to lift a finger.*

hu·mor·al (hū′mər əl, ū′mər-) *n.* of or relating to the humors, or fluid substances, of the body. [Modern Latin *humoralis,* from Latin *(h)ūmor* moisture, fluid. See HUMOR.]

hu·mor·esque (hū′mə resk′, ū′mə-) *n.* a musical composition written in a light, spirited, or whimsical style; capriccio. [German *Humoreske.*]

hu·mor·ist (hū′mər ist, ū′mər-) *n.* **1.** a professional writer or performer of humorous material: *Mark Twain was one of America's greatest humorists.* **2.** a person with a good sense of humor.

hu·mor·less (hū′mər lis, ū′mər-) *adj.* without a sense of humor or humorous qualities. —**hu′mor·less·ly,** *adv.* —**hu′mor·less·ness,** *n.*

hu·mor·ous (hū′mər əs, ū′mər-) *adj.* characterized by or full of humor; funny; comical: *a humorous writer, a humorous situation.* —**hu′mor·ous·ly,** *adv.* —**hu′mor·ous·ness,** *n.*

a	at	e	end	o	hot	u	up	hw	white		about
ā	ape	ē	me	ō	old	ū	use	ng	song		taken
ä	far	i	it	ô	fork	ü	rule	th	thin	ə	pencil
âr	care	ī	ice	oi	oil	ů	pull	th	this		lemon
		îr	pierce	ou	out	ûr	turn	zh	measure		circus

H

Humorous, funny, amusing, and **comical** mean appealing to the sense of humor. **Humorous** is a broad term that can be applied equally well to something funny enough to cause laughter and to something that amuses in a deeper or more subtle way: *Both plays were humorous, but while one used witty dialogue, the other relied on satire for effect.* **Funny** applies to anything that causes enjoyment or laughter: *a funny joke.* **Amusing** suggests something entertaining or diverting that is more likely to provoke a smile than a laugh: *a book filled with amusing anecdotes, an amusing person who is always good company.* **Comical** is generally used of something that causes laughter: *The first skit was really comical.*

hu·mour (hū′mər) *British.* humor.

hump (hump) *n.* **1.** a rounded protuberance, esp. on the back, as that which occurs as a normal feature in camels and bison or as a deformity resulting from curvature of the spine in humans. **2.** a hillock; knoll; hummock. —*v.t.* to bend or arch (something, as the back) so as to form a hump; hunch. —*v.i. Slang.* to exert oneself. [Possibly of Low German origin.]
• **over the hump.** past the critical, most difficult, or time-consuming part.

hump·back (hump′bak′) *n.* **1.** a back having a hump. **2.** hunchback *(def. 1).* **3.** a black-and-white whale, *Megaptera novaeangliae,* having a humplike dorsal fin and long flippers. Length: 40 feet (12.2 meters). —**hump′backed′,** *adj.*

humph (humpf) *interj.* used to express contempt, dissatisfaction, disbelief, or the like.

hump·y (hum′pē) *adj.,* **hump·i·er, hump·i·est.** **1.** having or full of humps. **2.** like a hump.

hu·mus (hū′məs, ū′məs) *n.* the decomposed organic matter in soil, brown or black in color, derived from plant and animal remains. Humus is a major source of the nutrients that plants need for growth. [Latin *humus* ground, earth, soil.]

Hun (hun) *n.* **1.** a member of a nomadic Asian people who invaded Europe in the fourth and fifth centuries A.D. and helped to destroy the Roman Empire. They were led in the middle of the fourth century by Attila. **2.** *also,* **hun.** a barbarous, willfully destructive person. ➡ used esp. as a derogatory epithet for a German during World War I. [Old English (plural) *Hūne* members of this Asian people, from Late Latin *Hūnī;* of Turkic origin.]

hunch (hunch) *v.t.* to draw up, raise, or bend: *The cold air made him hunch his shoulders.* —*v.i.* to assume a bent, stooped, or crouched posture: *She had to hunch over the paper to read the small print.* —*n.* **1.** *Informal.* an intuitive guess or feeling: *I have a hunch it's going to rain.* **2.** a rounded protuberance; hump. [Of uncertain origin.]

hunch·back (hunch′bak′) *n.* **1.** a person who has a hump on the back that results from curvature of the spine. **2.** a back having a hump; humpback. —**hunch′backed′,** *adj.*

hun·dred (hun′drid) *n., pl.* **-dreds** or **-dred.** **1.** the cardinal number that is ten times ten. **2.** a symbol representing this number, such as 100 or C. **3. hundreds.** a number between 100 and 999, as of people or money: *Hundreds were injured in the earthquake.* **4.** a large number; lot: *There are hundreds of ways to prepare chicken.* **5.a.** formerly, a subdivision of an English county. **b.** a similar subdivision in the early United States, still existing in Delaware. —*adj.* numbering ten times ten. [Old English *hundred* ten times ten.]

Hundred Days, the period from March 20 to June 28, 1815, during which Napoleon I restored his rule over France. It began with his escape from exile on the island of Elba and ended with his defeat at Waterloo.

hun·dred·fold (hun′drid fōld′) *adj.* **1.** one hundred times as great or as numerous. **2.** having or consisting of one hundred parts. —*adv.* so as to be one hundred times greater or more numerous.

hun·dredth (hun′dridth, -dritth) *adj.* **1.** (the ordinal of hundred) next after the ninety-ninth. **2.** being one of a hundred equal parts. —*n.* **1.** something that is next after the ninety-ninth. **2.** one of a hundred equal parts; $1/100$.

hun·dred·weight (hun′drid wāt′) *n., pl.* **-weight** or **-weights.** a unit of weight, equal to 100 pounds avoirdupois (45.4 kilograms) in the United States or 112 pounds (50.8 kilograms) in England.

Hundred Years' War, the intermittent struggle between England and France from 1337 to 1453, during which England lost all its French possessions except Calais.

hung (hung) *v.* a past tense and past participle of **hang.**
• **hung over.** *Informal.* feeling ill as a result of drinking alcohol; suffering from a hangover.
• **hung up.** *Informal.* **a.** delayed or detained temporarily: *to get*

hung up in a meeting. **b.** baffled, disturbed, or obsessed, as by a problem or with a situation or person (often with *on* or *over*): *Don't get hung up on how much everything costs.*

Hun·gar·i·an (hung gâr′ē ən) *adj.* of, relating to, or characteristic of Hungary or its people, language, or culture. —*n.* **1.** a citizen of Hungary or a member or close descendant of the people historically inhabiting Hungary. **2.** a language spoken predominantly in Hungary, belonging to the Ural-Altaic family of languages. Also *(def. 2),* **Magyar.**

hun·ger (hung′gər) *n.* **1.** discomfort, pain, or weakness caused by a lack of food: *to ache with hunger, a people afflicted with hunger.* **2.** a desire or craving for food: *The sandwich temporarily satisfied my hunger.* **3.** any strong desire or craving: *a hunger for success.* —*v.i.* **1.** to have or feel a need or desire for food. **2.** to have a strong desire or craving (often with *for* or *after*): *to hunger for attention, to hunger after financial success.* [Old English *hungor* state caused by lack of food, famine.]

hunger strike, a refusal to eat, as by a prisoner or political activist, in order to protest something or attain certain demands.

hung jury, a jury so divided in opinion that it is unlikely it could ever agree on a verdict and is therefore dismissed by the judge.

hun·gry (hung′grē) *adj.,* **-gri·er, -gri·est.** **1.** desiring or needing food. **2.** caused by or characteristic of a lack of or desire for food: *The stray dog had a hungry look.* **3.** having a strong desire or craving; eager; longing: *hungry for companionship.* **4.** not fertile; barren; poor: *hungry soil.* [Old English *hungrig* feeling hunger.] —**hun′gri·ly,** *adv.* —**hun′gri·ness,** *n.*

hunk (hungk) *n.* **1.** *Informal.* a large lump or piece; chunk: *The keeper fed the lion a hunk of meat.* **2.** *Slang.* a physically attractive man, esp. one with a muscular body. [Flemish *hunke.*]

hun·ker (hung′kər) *v.i.* to squat or crouch close to the ground (often with *down*): *The child hunkered down and hid behind the bush.* —*n.* **hunkers.** haunches. [Possibly of Scandinavian origin.]

hun·ky-do·ry (hung′kē dôr′ē) *adj. Slang.* quite satisfactory; all right; fine. [Of uncertain origin.]

hunt (hunt) *v.t.* **1.** to pursue (game) for the purpose of killing or catching: *to hunt deer, to hunt lions.* **2.** to attempt to obtain or find; search for: *to hunt strawberries.* **3.** to scour (a region) in pursuit of game: *Indians hunted the prairie for buffalo.* **4.** to search (a place) carefully and thoroughly: *to hunt the woods for a fugitive.* **5.** to pursue or drive with force, violence, or hostility: *The outcasts had been hunted out of society.* **6.** to use or direct (horses or dogs) in pursuing game. —*v.i.* **1.** to pursue game for the purpose of killing or catching. **2.** to look for; seek (often with *after* or *for*): *to hunt for buried treasure.* **3.** to search thoroughly or carefully: *to hunt through a house for one's keys.* —*n.* **1.** the act or an instance of pursuing game: *They were mounted and ready for the hunt.* **2.** a group of persons engaged in or associated for the purpose of hunting game together. **3.** the act or an instance of seeking something; search: *A hunt was conducted for the missing child.* [Old English *huntian* to pursue game.]
• **to hunt down. a.** to pursue until captured or killed. **b.** to search for until found: *to hunt down every piece of evidence relating to a crime.*
• **to hunt up. a.** to search for carefully: *to hunt up all the information on a subject.* **b.** to find by searching: *to hunt up an old friend.*

v.t. **Hunt, pursue,** and **chase¹** may all mean to go after for the purpose of catching or overtaking. **Hunt** connotes searching for something, as game or prey, for the purpose of killing or capturing it: *to hunt deer.* **Pursue** also connotes following a quarry for a purpose, but not necessarily to kill or capture it: *to pursue wild horses to photograph them, to pursue a fleeing criminal.* **Chase** suggests close and immediate pursuit: *The pig broke through the fence and we chased it across the field.*

hunt·er (hun′tər) *n.* **1.** a person who pursues game. **2.** a person who searches for something. **3.** a horse or dog used in hunting.

hunt·ing (hun′ting) *n.* the act or sport of chasing game for the purpose of killing or catching. —*adj.* designed for or used in hunting: *hunting boots.*

hunting horn, a horn on which signals are blown during a hunt.

hunting knife, a large, sharp knife for killing, skinning, or cutting up game.

Hun·ting·ton's chorea (hun′ting tənz) an inherited disorder of the central nervous system, usually appearing in early middle age and resulting in progressive involuntary muscular spasms and mental deterioration and, eventually, death. Also, **Huntington's disease.** [From George *Huntington,* 1851-1916, U.S. physician who first described it.]

hunt·ress (hun′tris) *n.* a woman who hunts.

hunts·man (hunts′mən) *n., pl.* **-men** (-mən). **1.** a person who pursues game; hunter. **2.** a person who manages a hunt, esp. a fox hunt.

hur·dle (hûr′dəl) *n.* **1.** an obstacle over which a runner or horse must leap in certain races. **2. hurdles.** either of two track events, **high hurdles** or **low hurdles,** in which the contestants must leap over hurdles while running, the winner being the person who crosses the finish line first. ➡ used as singular. **3.** an obstacle, difficulty, or problem that must be overcome: *Getting an education was the biggest hurdle before me.* **4.** a movable frame made of sticks or narrow boards, used as a temporary fence or pen. —*v.t.,* **-dled, -dling. 1.** to jump over (a hurdle or similar obstacle) in a race. **2.** to overcome or surmount (something, as an obstacle, difficulty, or problem). [Old English *hyrdel* movable frame of sticks used as a fence.] —**hur′dler,** *n.*

hurdle *(n., def. 1)*

hur·dy-gur·dy (hûr′dē gûr′dē) *n., pl.* **-dies. 1.** any of various mechanized musical instruments, as a barrel organ, played by turning a handle or crank. **2.** an obsolete stringed musical instrument shaped somewhat like a guitar, played by turning a hand crank that causes a revolving wheel to make the strings vibrate. [Probably imitative.]

hurl (hûrl) *v.t.* **1.** to throw with violence or force; fling. **2.** to utter or emit with vehemence: *The senator's opponent hurled insults and accusations at her.* —*v.i. Baseball.* to pitch: *He began his career hurling for the local team.* —*n.* the act or an instance of throwing forcefully or violently. [Probably imitative.] —**hurl′er,** *n.* —For Synonyms *(v.t.),* see **throw.**

hurl·y-burl·y (hûr′lē bûr′lē) *n.* noisy confusion and disorder; commotion; uproar. [Earlier *hurling and burling,* rhyming phrase based on obsolete *hurling* commotion, from HURL.]

Hu·ron (hyūr′ən) *n., pl.* **-ron** or **-rons. 1.** a member of a tribe of North American Indians formerly living east of Lake Huron, now living in Oklahoma and Quebec. **2.** the language of the Huron, belonging to the Iroquoian family of languages. [French *huron* boor, disheveled person, from *hure* disheveled head of hair; of uncertain origin; applied by the French in about 1600 to the Huron Indians because of the way they wore their hair.]

hur·rah (hə rä′, -rô′) *also,* **hoo·ray, hur·ray** (hə rā′). *interj.* used to express joy, triumph, praise, or encouragement. —*n.* **1.** a shout of joy, triumph, praise, or encouragement. **2.** noisy excitement or commotion. —*v.i.* to shout *hurrah;* cheer. —*v.t.* to shout *hurrah* for; cheer. [Possibly from German *hurra* cry of cheer; imitative.]

hur·ri·cane (hûr′i kān′, hûr′-) *n.* **1.** a storm with violent winds of more than 75 miles (121 kilometers) per hour revolving around a calm center and accompanied by heavy rain, high tides, and flooding in coastal regions. **2.** something resembling a hurricane in force or speed; violent outburst or commotion: *a hurricane of emotion.* [Spanish *huracán* violent storm, from Carib *hurakan* name of an evil spirit.]

hurricane deck, a upper deck on a passenger ship, esp. on an American riverboat.

hurricane lamp, an oil lamp or candle protected by a glass chimney.

hur·ried (hûr′ēd, hûr′-) *adj.* **1.** urged or made to act, move, or go faster than is easy or natural: *I have felt hurried since moving to the city.* **2.** done, performed, or carried on quickly or too quickly: *a hurried glance, a hurried letter full of typographical errors.* —**hur′ried·ly,** *adv.* —**hur′ried·ness,** *n.*

hur·ry (hûr′ē, hur′ē) *v.,* **-ried, -ry·ing.** —*v.i.* to move or act with evident or apparent speed; go faster than is easy or natural: *If you don't hurry, you'll miss the train.* —*v.t.* **1.** to cause or urge to act, move, or go with greater speed: *We hurried the children along.* **2.** to cause or urge to act, move, or go too quickly; rush: *The judge would not be hurried into making a decision.* **3.** to hasten the preparation, progress, or completion of: *The cook hurried the meal.* —*n., pl.* **-ries. 1.** the act of hurrying: *I forgot the package in my hurry to leave.* **2.** the state or condition of desiring or needing to act, move, or go with greater speed: *We have to leave now because we're in a hurry.* [Probably imitative.] —**hur′ri·er,** *n.*

Synonyms *n.* **Hurry** and **haste** denote unusual quickness in getting something done. **Hurry** suggests the effort is accompanied by emotional agitation: *In my hurry to get to the hospital, I forgot to lock the door behind me.* **Haste** suggests urgency and speed, but not necessarily agitation: *I left home in haste so I would get to work on time.*

hur·ry-scur·ry (hûr′ē skûr′ē, hûr′ē skur′ē) *also,* **hur·ry-skur·ry.** *n., pl.* **-ries.** a condition of haste, bustle, and confusion. —*adv.* in haste and confusion. —*adj.* hurried and confused. —*v.i.,* **-ried, -ry·ing.** to act in or proceed with haste and confusion. [Rhyming compound based on HURRY.]

hurt (hûrt) *v.,* **hurt, hurt·ing.** —*v.t.* **1.** to cause physical pain or injury to. **2.** to do harm to; be detrimental to; damage: *The scandal hurt the mayor's chance for reelection.* **3.** to cause mental pain or suffering to; injure the feelings of: *The insult hurt her deeply.* **4.** to cause offense or irritation to: *His cruel joke hurt his sister's feelings.* —*v.i.* **1.** to be or feel painful: *His knee hurts.* **2.** to cause or inflict pain or injury: *The doctor said that the injection wouldn't hurt much.* —*n.* **1.** any physical pain or injury. **2.** mental pain or suffering. **3.** damage; harm. —*adj.* **1.** injured physically: *a hurt leg.* **2.** feeling, affected by, or showing mental pain, suffering, or insult: *a hurt soul, a hurt look.* **3.** damaged: *The library is selling hurt books for a dollar each.* [Old French *hurter* to strike; of Germanic origin.] —**hurt′er,** *n.* —For Synonyms *(v.t.),* see **injure.**

• **to be hurting for.** *Informal.* to be suffering from a lack of: *I've been hurting for money since I lost my job.*

hurt·ful (hûrt′fəl) *adj.* causing hurt; painful; injurious. —**hurt′ful·ly,** *adv.* —**hurt′ful·ness,** *n.*

hur·tle (hûr′təl) *v.,* **-tled, -tling.** —*v.i.* **1.** to collide or strike, esp. violently or noisily: *The racing car hurtled against the metal fence.* **2.** to move rapidly, esp. with much force or noise: *The hubcap hurtled down the street.* —*v.t.* to throw or fling violently; hurl. [HURT + -LE.]

hus·band (huz′bənd) *n.* the man in a married couple; married man. —*v.t.* to manage carefully and frugally; use, spend, or apply economically: *to husband one's time and energy.* [Old English *hūsbonda* master of a house, from Old Norse *hūsbōndi.*]

hus·band·man (huz′bənd mən) *n., pl.* **-men** (-mən). *Archaic.* farmer.

hus·band·ry (huz′bən drē) *n.* **1.** the cultivation of the soil or the breeding and raising of livestock; agriculture; farming. **2.** careful or frugal management; thrift; economy.

hush (hush) *n.* a silence or stillness, esp. after noise or commotion has ceased: *A hush fell over the audience.* —*v.t.* **1.** to quiet or silence: *The teacher hushed the noisy children.* **2.** to calm; soothe; lull: *He hushed her fears.* **3.** to keep knowledge or discussion of (something) from spreading; impose silence concerning (usually with *up*): *The mayor tried to hush up the scandal.* —*v.i.* to become quiet or silent. —*interj.* be quiet; be calm. [From archaic *husht* (interjection) be quiet; imitative.]

hush money, money paid to keep someone from telling something that he or she knows.

husk (husk) *n.* **1.** the dry outer covering of certain seeds or fruits, as of an ear of corn. **2.** the outer shell or covering of something, esp. when useless or worthless. —*v.t.* to remove the husk of: *to husk corn.* [Middle Dutch *huusken* little house, little cover, diminutive of *huus* house, cover.] —**husk′er,** *n.*

husk·ing bee (hus′king) a festive social event in which neighbors and friends gather to help a farmer husk corn. Also, **husk·ing.**

husk·y¹ (hus′kē) *adj.,* **husk·i·er, husk·i·est. 1.** big and

a	at	e	end	o	hot	u	up	hw	white	⟨	about
ā	ape	ē	me	ō	old	ū	use	ng	song		taken
ä	far	i	it	ô	fork	ü	rule	th	thin	ə	pencil
âr	care	ī	ice	oi	oil	u̇	pull	th	this		lemon
				îr	pierce	ou	out	ûr	turn	zh	measure	⟨	circus

strong: *a husky child.* **2.** hoarse and deep in tone, as a voice. **3.** having, full of, or like husks. —*n., pl.* **husk·ies.** *Informal.* a big, strong person. [HUSK + -Y¹ (with reference to the toughness or dryness of husks).] —**husk′i·ly,** *adv.* —**husk′i·ness,** *n.*

husk·y² (hus′kē) *also,* **Husk·y.** *n., pl.* **husk·ies.** Siberian husky. [Probably a modification of ESKIMO.]

hus·sar (hə zär′) *n.* a member of a light cavalry regiment in any of several European armies. [Hungarian *huszár* light cavalry horseman, earlier, pirate, going back to Late Latin *cursārius* pirate, from *cursus* plunder, from Latin *cursus* course. Doublet of CORSAIR.]

Huss·ite (hus′īt) *n.* a follower of the Bohemian religious reformer John Huss or his doctrines. —*adj.* of or relating to John Huss or his doctrines or followers.

hus·sy (huz′ē, hus′ē) *n., pl.* **-sies. 1.** a woman of improper behavior or low character. **2.** an impertinent, forward, or mischievous girl; minx. [Modification of Middle English *hūswif* housewife, from *hūs* house + *wīf* wife.]

hus·tings (hus′tingz) *n.* **1.** formerly, a temporary platform from which candidates for the British Parliament were nominated and from which they made speeches. **2.** any place where political speeches are made and campaigning is carried on. ➡ usually used as singular in both defs. [Old English *hūsting* council, from Old Norse *husthing,* from *hūs* house + *thing* assembly.]
　·**on the hustings. a.** in the political election campaign. **b.** involved in political campaigning: *The candidate was out on the hustings.*

hus·tle (hus′əl) *v.,* **-tled, -tling.** —*v.i.* **1.** to move or work quickly or energetically: *She had to hustle to finish the job on time.* **2.** *Slang.* to make money by clever, deceitful, or unscrupulous means. —*v.t.* **1.** to hasten along quickly or hurriedly: *The nurse hustled patients in and out of the office.* **2.** to push or force roughly or hurriedly: *The police hustled the strikers away from the factory gate.* **3.** *Informal.* **a.** to obtain (something), esp. by begging: *to hustle a meal.* **b.** to sell (something) illegally or unethically: *to hustle cheap watches.* **c.** to obtain something from (someone) by deceit, trickery, or begging: *They hustled him for five dollars and a free meal.* —*n.* **1.** the act or practice of hustling. **2.** *Informal.* energy and enthusiasm; drive: *A good shortstop has to have lots of hustle.* [Dutch *hutselen* to shake.]

hus·tler (hus′lər) *n. Informal.* **1.** a person who works hard or energetically. **2.** a person who earns a living by scheming, begging, or cheating.

hut (hut) *n.* **1.** a small, one-story dwelling or shelter, esp. of rough or primitive construction. **2.** a large, temporary structure, often made of metal, used by the military to house personnel and equipment. [French *hutte* cottage, probably from Old High German *hutta.*]

hutch (huch) *n.* **1.** a covered pen or box for keeping rabbits or other small animals. **2.** a cupboard with open shelves on top. **3.** a chest or bin used for storing things. [Old French *huche* bin, from Medieval Latin *hutica* chest; of uncertain origin.]

huz·zah (hə zä′) *also,* **huz·za.** *Archaic.* hurrah. [Possibly imitative.]

hwy., highway.

hy·a·cinth (hī′ə sinth′) *n.* **1.** the fragrant, funnel-shaped flower of any of a group of plants, genus *Hyacinthus,* of the lily family, growing in spikelike clusters. **2.** the plant bearing this flower, native to the Mediterranean region and southern Africa. One of the best-known species is *H. orientalis,* widely cultivated as a garden and house plant. **3.** a reddish orange zircon used in jewelry. Also *(def. 3),* **jacinth.** [Latin *hyacinthus* iris, larkspur, blue precious stone, from Greek *hyakinthos* bluebell, larkspur, blue precious stone; named after the youth *Hyacinthus* because, according to Greek mythology, it sprang from his blood after he was killed by Apollo. Doublet of JACINTH.] —**hy·a·cin·thine** (hī′ə sin′thin, -thīn), *adj.*

Hy·a·cin·thus (hī′ə sin′thəs) *n.* in Greek mythology, a handsome youth, killed accidentally by a discus thrown by Apollo.

Hy·a·des (hī′ə dēz′) *pl. n.* **1.** a V-shaped group of stars near the Pleiades in the constellation Taurus, thought by ancient astronomers to indicate the approach of rain when they rose with the sun. **2.** in Greek mythology, five nymphs who were daughters of the god Atlas and who raised the infant Dionysus. As a reward they were placed among the stars by Zeus.

hy·ae·na (hī ē′nə) hyena.

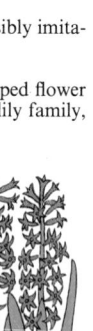

hyacinth

hy·a·lin (hī′ə lin) *also,* **hyaline.** *n.* any of several clear, glossy substances resembling chitin that are normally present in translucent cartilage and are also produced by degeneration of certain diseased tissues.

hy·a·line (hī′ə lin, -līn′) *adj.* resembling glass; glassy; transparent or translucent, as certain types of cartilage or membrane. —*n.* **1.** hyalin. **2.** a glassy or transparent substance or surface: *Meadows . . . fluttered with the pearly hyaline of dew* (Richard D. Blackmore, 1876). [Late Latin *hyalinus* of glass, from Greek *hyalinos,* from *hyalos* glass.]

hy·a·lite (hī′ə līt′) *n.* a colorless, often transparent opal that resembles glass. [Greek *hyalos* glass + -ITE¹.]

hy·a·loid (hī′ə loid′) *adj.* hyaline.

hy·brid (hī′brid) *n.* **1.** the offspring of two animals or plants of different varieties, lines, breeds, or species that combines differing qualities of the parents. **2.** anything derived from different sources or made up of unlike elements. —*adj.* of, relating to, or of the nature of a hybrid: *a hybrid flower.* [Latin *hybrida* mongrel.]

hy·brid·ism (hī′bri diz′əm) *n.* **1.** the condition, quality, or fact of being hybrid. Also, **hy·brid·i·ty. 2.** the production of hybrids; crossbreeding.

hy·brid·ize (hī′bri dīz′) *v.,* **-ized, -iz·ing.** —*v.t.* **1.** to cause to crossbreed and produce hybrids. **2.** to cause the production of (a hybrid or hybrids). —*v.i.* to produce a hybrid or hybrids. —**hy′·brid·i·za′tion,** *n.* —**hy′brid·iz′er,** *n.*

hy·brid·o·ma (hī′bri dō′mə) *n.* a cell culture prepared in the laboratory by fusing cancer cells and lymphocytes in order to take advantage of the desired qualities of both. The hybrid cell thus produced multiplies quickly, like the cancer cells, yielding larger quantities of the antibodies produced by the lymphocytes.

hybrid vigor, heterosis.

hyd. 1. hydraulics. **2.** hydrostatics.

hy·da·tid (hī′də tid) *n.* a watery cyst containing the larvae of certain tapeworms, found in the body tissue of infected animals. —*adj.* relating to or like such a cyst. [Greek *hydatidos,* genitive of *hydatis* watery vesicle, from *hydōr* water.]

Hyde, Mr. (hīd) see Jekyll and Hyde.

hydr-, form of hydro- before vowels, as in *hydrate.*

hy·dra (hī′drə) *n., pl.* **-dras** *or* **-drae** (-drē). **1. Hydra.** in classical mythology, a deadly, snakelike monster with nine heads and the power to grow two more whenever one was cut off. It was slain by Hercules. **2.** any persistent evil that is difficult to overcome because it tends to reappear: *the hydra of government corruption.* **3.** a small freshwater polyp related to the jellyfish, class Hydrozoa, having a tubelike body with a single mouth, or open end, surrounded by thin tentacles that bear clusters of poison-filled stinging cells. If a hydra is cut into pieces, each piece will develop into a complete, new organism. **4. Hydra.** a large constellation in the southern sky, conventionally depicted as a serpent. It is the largest of the constellations. [Latin *Hydra* the monster, from Greek *Hydrā.*]

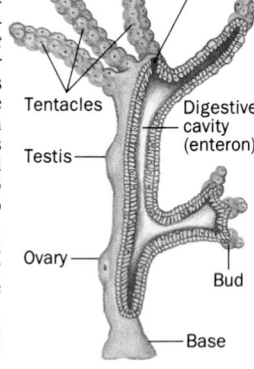

Mouth
Tentacles
Testis
Ovary
Digestive cavity (enteron)
Bud
Base

hydra

hy·dran·gea (hī drān′jə) *n.* **1.** the large, showy flower of any of a group of shrubs or vines, genus *Hydrangea,* growing in clusters of usually white, pink, or blue blossoms. **2.** the shrub or vine bearing this flower. [Modern Latin *hydrangea,* from Greek *hydōr* water + *angeion* vessel; with reference to the shape of the seed vessel.]

hy·drant (hī′drənt) *n.* a street fixture for drawing water directly from a main, consisting of an upright pipe with spouts to which hoses may be attached. Also, **fire hydrant.** [HYDRO- + -ANT.]

hy·drate (hī′drāt) *n.* any crystalline substance formed by the union of a chemical compound with molecules of water in a definite ratio. Copper sulfate, $CuSO_4 \cdot 5H_2O$, is a hydrate. —*v.t.,* **-drat·ed, -drat·ing.** to combine (a chemical compound) with water to form a hydrate; cause to form a hydrate. [HYDRO- + -ATE².] —**hy·dra′tion,** *n.*

hy·drau·lic (hī drô′lik) *adj.* **1.** operated by water or some other liquid: *a hydraulic jack, hydraulic brakes.* **2.** of or relating to the forces exerted by liquids in motion and at rest or to the science of hydraulics. **3.** hardening under water: *hydraulic cement.* [Latin

hydraulicus relating to an ancient pipe organ that used water pressure, going back to Greek *hydōr* water + *aulos* pipe.] —**hy·drau′li·cal·ly**, *adv.*

hydraulic ram, a pump that uses the energy of downward flowing water to raise water to a higher level.

hy·drau·lics (hī drô′liks) *n.* the branch of fluid mechanics dealing with the study of liquids in motion and at rest and their use to perform work. ➡ used as singular.

hy·dra·zine (hī′drə zēn′) *n.* a colorless, poisonous liquid having an odor like ammonia, a compound of nitrogen and hydrogen, used esp. as a rocket fuel. Formula: N_2H_4 [HYDR(O)- + French *az(ote)* nitrogen + -INE[2].]

hy·dride (hī′drīd, -drid) *also,* **hy·drid** (hī′drid). *n.* a compound composed of hydrogen and a more electropositive element or radical.

hydro- *combining form* **1.** of or relating to water: *hydrodynamics, hydroplane.* **2.** *Chemistry.* combined with or composed of hydrogen: *hydrocarbon, hydrofluoric acid.* [Greek *hydōr* water.]

hy·dro·car·bon (hī′drə kär′bən, hī′drə kär′-) *n.* any of a large group of organic compounds composed solely of the chemical elements hydrogen and carbon. Ethane, C_2H_6, and propane, C_3H_8, are hydrocarbons.

hy·dro·ceph·a·lus (hī′drə sef′ə ləs) *n.* a condition characterized by an excessive accumulation of fluid in the cranium, forcing the cranial bones apart and causing enlargement of the head. Also, **hy·dro·ceph·a·ly** (hī′drə sef′ə lē). —**hy·dro·ce·phal·ic** (hī′drō sə fal′ik), *adj.*

hy·dro·chlo·ric acid (hī′drə klôr′ik) a poisonous, highly corrosive solution of hydrogen chloride, HCl, in water, fumes of which cause severe irritation of the eyes and nose.

hy·dro·chlo·ride (hī′drə klôr′īd) *n.* a salt formed from the reaction of hydrochloric acid with an organic base. [HYDRO- + CHLORIDE.]

hy·dro·cor·ti·sone (hī′drə kôr′tə sōn′, -zōn′) *n.* a hormone produced by the adrenal glands that plays a key role in the body's synthesis and storage of glucose. It is used primarily in treating rheumatoid arthritis and various allergic and inflammatory conditions.

hy·dro·cy·an·ic acid (hī′drō sī an′ik) a weak, colorless acid that is a deadly poison. A solution of a compound of hydrogen, carbon, and nitrogen, HCN, in water, it is used esp. to make plastics and pesticides. Also, **prussic acid.**

hy·dro·dy·nam·ic (hī′drō dī nam′ik) *adj.* of or relating to the forces exerted by fluids in motion or to the science of hydrodynamics. —**hy′dro·dy·nam′i·cal·ly**, *adv.*

hy·dro·dy·nam·ics (hī′drō dī nam′iks) *n.* the branch of fluid mechanics that deals with the forces exerted by liquids in motion. ➡ used as singular.

hy·dro·e·lec·tric (hī′drō i lek′trik) *adj.* **1.** of or relating to electricity generated by water power. **2.** generating electricity using the energy of moving water: *a hydroelectric dam.* —**hy′dro·e·lec·tric′i·ty**, *n.*

hy·dro·fluor·ic acid (hī′drə flûr′ik, -flôr′ik) a colorless, active, poisonous solution of hydrogen fluoride, HF, in water, used esp. to frost and etch glass.

hy·dro·foil (hī′drə foil′) *n.* **1.** a bladelike or winglike structure under a motor-powered boat that raises the hull out of the water, facilitating high speeds. The hydrofoil is shaped so that pressure on its upper surface decreases when it moves through the water, resulting in an upward lift. **2.** a boat fitted with hydrofoils.

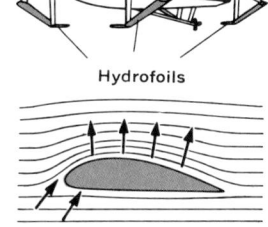
Hydrofoils

hy·dro·gen (hī′drə jən) *n.* a colorless, odorless, highly flammable gas that is the lightest and simplest of all chemical elements and the most abundant element in the universe. Symbol: **H** For tables, see **element.** [French *hydrogène,* going back to Greek *hydōr* water + *gennān* to produce; because water is produced when hydrogen is burned.] —**hy·drog·e·nous** (hī droj′ə nəs), *adj.*

hy·dro·gen·ate (hī′drə jə nāt′, hī droj′ə-) *v.t.,* **-at·ed, -at·ing.** to combine or treat with hydrogen: *Oils are hydrogenated to produce margarine.* —**hy′dro·gen·a′tion,** *n.*

hydrogen bomb, a bomb whose explosive energy is derived from the fusion of hydrogen atoms to form helium atoms. Its destructive force is much greater than that of an atomic bomb. Also, **H-bomb.**

hydrogen bond, an intermolecular attraction caused by electrostatic forces between covalently bonded hydrogen atoms and the electronegative atom, as oxygen, nitrogen, or fluorine, of another molecule. A water molecule, itself held together by covalent bonds, is loosely bound to other water molecules by hydrogen bonds.

hydrogen ion, an atom of hydrogen that has lost its electron and gained a positive charge; proton. The concentration of these ions determines the acidity of a solution, as measured by pH.

hydrogen peroxide, a colorless, unstable liquid that is an active oxidizing agent, diluted for use as a bleach and antiseptic. In concentrated form it is highly explosive. Formula: H_2O_2

hydrogen sulfide, a flammable, poisonous gas, having a characteristic rotten-egg odor, formed by decomposition of organic matter. Formula: H_2S

hy·drog·ra·phy (hī drog′rə fē) *n.* the scientific measurement, charting, and description of the features of oceans, lakes, rivers, and other surface waters, esp. to determine their use for navigation. —**hy·dro·graph·ic** (hī′drə graf′ik), *adj.*

hy·droid (hī′droid) *n.* any of various hydrozoans having the polyp form as the dominant stage in the life cycle and typically living in delicate branching colonies. —*adj.* of or relating to hydroids. [HYDRA + -OID.]

hydrologic cycle, the continuous exchange of water between the land and the sea, via the atmosphere. Water evaporated from seas and lakes forms clouds, which precipitate rain and snow. Precipitation that falls on land is carried by rivers to the sea, where it evaporates again to form clouds, and the process is repeated. Also, **water cycle.**

hy·drol·o·gy (hī drol′ə jē) *n.* the branch of earth science that deals with the world's water, solid as well as liquid, both on and beneath the earth's surface, studying its properties, circulation, and distribution. [HYDRO- + -LOGY.] —**hy·dro·log·ic** (hī′drə loj′ik); *also,* **hy′dro·log′i·cal,** *adj.* —**hy·drol′o·gist,** *n.*

hy·drol·y·sis (hī drol′ə sis) *n., pl.* **-ses** (-sēz′). a chemical reaction in which one of the reactants is water. Starch undergoes hydrolysis to form glucose. [HYDRO- + Greek *lysis* a loosing, dissolution.] —**hy·dro·lyt·ic** (hī′drə lit′ik), *adj.*

hy·dro·lyze (hī′drə līz′) *v.i., v.t.,* **-lyzed, -lyz·ing.** to undergo or cause to undergo hydrolysis.

hy·drom·e·ter (hī drom′i tər) *n.* an instrument that measures the specific gravity of a liquid, used to determine the strength, concentration, or acidity of the liquid, such as the acid in a storage battery or the antifreeze in a radiator.

hy·dro·met·ric (hī′drə met′rik) *adj.* of or relating to hydrometry or a hydrometer. —**hy′dro·met′ri·cal.**

hy·drom·e·try (hī drom′i trē) *n.* the determination of specific gravity by means of a hydrometer.

hy·dro·ni·um (hī drō′nē əm) *n.* a hydrogen ion united with a water molecule, the state in which such ions are found when in solution in water. Formula: H_3O^+ Also, **hydronium ion.**

hy·drop·a·thy (hī drop′ə thē) *n.* hydrotherapy. —**hy·dro·path·ic** (hī′drə path′ik), *adj.*

hy·dro·phil·ic (hī′drə fil′ik) *adj.* readily dissolving in or absorbing water; having an affinity for water.

hy·dro·pho·bi·a (hī′drə fō′bē ə) *n.* **1.** rabies. **2.** an abnormal fear of water. [Latin *hydrophobia,* from Greek *hydrophobiā,* from *hydōr* water + *-phobiā* fear of; with reference to the contractions of the mouth and throat caused by rabies, which are intensified by drinking and, eventually, by the mere sight of liquid.] —**hy′dro·pho′bic,** *adj.*

hy·dro·phone (hī′drə fōn′) *n.* an instrument designed to receive sound waves traveling through water, used as a listening device in various types of sonar. [HYDRO- + Greek *phōnē* sound.]

hy·dro·phyte (hī′drə fīt′) *n.* any plant growing in water or very wet soil. Water lilies are hydrophytes. —**hy·dro·phyt·ic** (hī′drə fit′ik), *adj.*

hy·dro·plane (hī′drə plān′) *n.* **1.** a motorboat whose hull is designed to skim over the surface of the water rather than push through it, used esp. in racing. **2.** seaplane. —*v.i.* **1.** to skim the surface of the water. **2.** to travel in a hydroplane. **3.** (of a tire or vehicle) to skim along with loss of control on the water covering a surface, as on a wet road or runway, instead of riding on the surface itself.

a	at	e	end	o	hot	u	up	hw	white		about
ā	ape	ē	me	ō	old	ū	use	ng	song		taken
ä	far	i	it	ô	fork	ü	rule	th	thin	ə	pencil
âr	care	ī	ice	oi	oil	u̇	pull	th	this		lemon
		îr	pierce	ou	out	ûr	turn	zh	measure		circus

hydroponics
hydroponically grown lettuce

hy·dro·pon·ics (hī'drə pon'iks) *n.* the science or practice of cultivating plants in a liquid nutrient solution rather than in soil. ➡ used as singular. [HYDRO- + Greek *ponos* work + -ICS.] —**hy'dro·pon'ic,** *adj.* —**hy'dro·pon'i·cal·ly,** *adv.*

hy·dro·pow·er (hī'drə pou'ər) *n.* hydroelectric power. [HYDRO- + POWER.]

hy·dro·qui·none (hī'drō kwi nōn', -kwin'ōn) *n.* a white, soluble, crystalline compound, used in photographic developers and in medicine. Formula: $C_6H_4(OH)_2$

hy·dro·sphere (hī'drə sfir') *n.* **1.** all the water on the surface of the earth. **2.** all the water on the surface of and moisture in the atmosphere surrounding the earth. [HYDRO- + SPHERE.]

hy·dro·stat·ic (hī'drə stat'ik) *adj.* of or relating to the forces exerted by liquids at rest or to the science of hydrostatics.

hy·dro·stat·ics (hī'drə stat'iks) *n.* the branch of fluid mechanics that deals with the forces exerted by liquids at rest. ➡ used as singular.

hy·dro·ther·a·py (hī'drō ther'ə pē) *n.* the medical treatment of disease, illness, or injury by immersion of all or part of the body in water. Also, **hy·drop·a·thy,** **hy·dro·ther·a·peu·tics** (hī'drō ther'ə pū'tiks).

hy·dro·ther·mal (hī'drə thûr'məl) *adj. Geology.* of, relating to, or produced by the action of hot, subterranean solutions, esp. in the formation of ore deposits. [HYDRO- + THERMAL.]

hy·drot·ro·pism (hī drot'rə piz'əm) *n.* the tendency of a plant or part of a plant, as a root, to grow toward moisture. —**hy·dro·trop·ic** (hī'drə trop'ik, -trō'pik), *adj.*

hy·drous (hī'drəs) *adj.* (of a chemical compound) containing water, esp. water of hydration. [HYDRO- + -OUS.]

hy·drox·ide (hī drok'sīd, -sid) *n.* any chemical compound containing one or more hydroxyl radicals.

hy·drox·yl (hī drok'səl) *n.* an ion or chemical group consisting of one atom of oxygen and one of hydrogen and having a valence of −1. Formula: —OH [HYDR(OGEN) + OX(YGEN) + -YL.]

hy·dro·zo·an (hī'drə zō'ən) *n.* any of various marine and freshwater coelenterates constituting the class Hydrozoa and generally existing in two unlike forms, that of a free-swimming jellyfish or that of a stationary polyp, such as a hydra, which may live in a colony. For illustration, see **hydra.** —*adj.* of or relating to hydrozoans. [Modern Latin *Hydrozoa* class of coelenterates, from HYDRA + Greek *zōion* animal.]

hy·e·na (hī ē'nə) *also,* **hyaena.** *n.* any of various wolflike, carnivorous mammals, family Hyaenidae, of Africa and Asia, having a large head, extremely strong jaws, and front legs longer than the back ones. They feed chiefly on carrion by day, but hunt live prey at night. Height: to 3 feet (0.9 meter) at the shoulder. [Latin *hyaena,* from Greek *hyaina.*]

Hy·ge·ia (hī jē'ə) *n.* in Greek mythology, goddess of health. [Greek *Hygeiā* or *Hygieia,* from *hygieia* health.]

hy·giene (hī'jēn) *n.* **1.** practices or conditions conducive to good health. **2.** the science that deals with maintenance of good health and the prevention of disease. [French *hygiène,* from Greek *hygieinon,* neuter of *hygieinos* healthful.]

hy·gi·en·ic (hī'jē en'ik, hī jen'-) *adj.* **1.** sanitary. **2.** of or relating to health or hygiene.

hy·gien·ist (hī jē'nist, hī'jē en'ist) *n.* **1.** a person who is trained or expert in the principles of hygiene. **2.** dental hygienist.

hygro- *combining form* moisture; humidity: *hygroscope.* [Greek *hygros* wet.]

hy·grom·e·ter (hī grom'i tər) *n.* an instrument for determining the humidity of the atmosphere. —**hy·gro·met·ric** (hī'grə met'rik), *adj.*

hy·gro·scope (hī'grə skōp') *n.* an instrument for recording variations in the humidity of the atmosphere.

hy·gro·scop·ic (hī'grə skop'ik) *adj.* readily attracting or absorbing moisture from the atmosphere.

hy·ing (hī'ing) a present participle of **hie.**

hy·la (hī'lə) *n.* any of a genus, *Hyla,* of tree frogs. [Modern Latin *Hyla,* from Greek *hȳlē* wood, forest.]

hy·men (hī'mən) *n.* a fold of mucous membrane partially covering the external vaginal opening in a virgin. Also, **maidenhead.** [Greek *hymēn* membrane.] —**hy·men·al,** *adj.*

Hy·men (hī'mən) *n.* in Greek mythology, the god of marriage.

hy·me·ne·al (hī'mə nē'əl) *adj.* of or relating to a wedding or marriage. —*n. Archaic.* a wedding song or poem.

hy·me·nop·ter·an (hī'mə nop'tər ən) *n.* any of a group of insects, order Hymenoptera, characteristically having four membranous wings (when winged) and chewing and sucking mouthparts. Many species live in social colonies, including wasps, bees, and ants. —*adj.* hymenopterous. [Modern Latin *Hymenoptera,* from Greek *hymenopteros* membrane-winged, from *hymēn* membrane + *pteron* wing + -AN.]

hy·me·nop·ter·ous (hī'mə nop'tər əs) *adj.* of, relating to, or belonging to the hymenopterans. [Greek *hymenopteros* membrane-winged, from *hymēn* membrane + *pteron* wing.]

hymn (him) *n.* **1.** a song of praise or thanksgiving to God or a god. **2.** any song or ode of praise or joy. —*v.t.* to worship or praise in a hymn. —*v.i.* to sing hymns. [Latin *hymnus* song of praise, from Greek *hymnos.*]

hym·nal (him'nəl) *n.* a book or collection of hymns for use in a religious service. Also, **hymn·book** (him'bůk').

hym·no·dy (him'nə dē) *n., pl.* **-dies. 1.** hymns collectively, as of a particular period, nation, or church. **2.** the singing or composing of hymns. [Greek *hymnōidiā* singing of hymns.]

hym·nol·o·gy (him nol'ə jē) *n.* **1.** the study of hymns. **2.** hymnody *(def. 1).* **3.** the composing of hymns. —**hym·no·log·ic** (him'nə loj'ik); *also,* **hym'no·log'i·cal,** *adj.* —**hym·nol'o·gist,** *n.*

hy·oid (hī'oid) *n.* a bone or series of bones at the base of the tongue in vertebrates. In a human being, it is a single, small, horseshoe-shaped bone. Also, **hyoid bone.** —*adj.* of or relating to the hyoid. [French *hyoïde,* from Greek *hyoeidēs* shaped like the Greek letter ʋ (upsilon), from ʋ upsilon + *eidos* shape.]

hy·o·scine (hī'ə sēn') *n.* scopolamine.

hyp. 1. hypotenuse. **2.** hypothesis.

hype (hīp) *Slang. n.* advertising or publicity with exaggerated, often misleading claims: *There was a lot of hype surrounding the introduction of the new computer.* —*v.t.,* **hyped, hyp·ing.** to advertise or publicize with exaggerated, often misleading claims. [Probably a shortened form of HYPERBOLE.]

hy·per (hī'pər) *adj. Slang.* **1.** easily or excessively agitated or excited. **2.** hyperactive.

hyper- *prefix* over; above; excessive; excessively: *hypercritical, hypertension.* [Greek *hyper* above, over, beyond.]

hy·per·a·cid·i·ty (hī'pər ə sid'i tē) *n.* excessive acidity, esp. of the gastric juice. —**hy·per·ac·id** (hī'pər as'id), *adj.*

hy·per·ac·tive (hī'pər ak'tiv) *adj.* overly or abnormally active: *a hyperactive child, a hyperactive gland.* —**hy·per·ac·tiv·i·ty** (hī'pər ak tiv'i tē), *n.*

hy·per·bar·ic (hī'pər bar'ik) *adj.* of, relating to, producing, or using pressures greater than normal atmospheric pressure, as in administering oxygen: *a hyperbaric chamber.* [HYPER- + *baric* relating to atmospheric weight or pressure, from Greek *barys* weighty.]

hy·per·bo·la (hī pûr'bə lə) *n.* an open curve with two branches consisting of a set of points in a plane whose distances from two fixed points, or foci, differ by a constant value; a conic section formed by the intersection of a plane with the surface of a double cone. [Modern Latin *hyperbola,* from Greek *hyperbolē* literally, a throwing beyond, excess.]

hy·per·bo·le (hī pûr'bə lē) *n.* a figure of speech consisting of an extreme exaggeration not meant to be taken literally, for example: *We shopped in a million stores today.* [Latin *hyperbole,* from Greek *hyperbolē* a throwing beyond.]

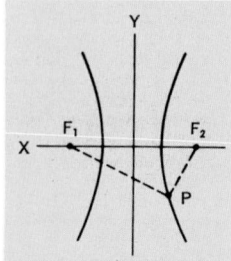

P = any point on hyperbola
F_1, F_2 = foci
$PF_1 - PF_2$ = a constant

hyperbola

hy·per·bol·ic (hī′pər bol′ik) *adj.* **1.** of, relating to, or using hyperbole; exaggerated or exaggerating. **2.** of, relating to, or having the form of a hyperbola. Also, **hy′per·bol′i·cal.** —**hy′per·bol′i·cal·ly,** *adv.*

hy·per·bo·lize (hī′pûr′bə līz′) *v.t., v.i.,* **-lized, -liz·ing.** to express with or use hyperbole; exaggerate.

Hy·per·bo·re·an (hī′pər bôr′ē ən) *n.* in Greek legend, a member of a people who lived happily and virtuously in a land of perpetual spring beyond the north wind. —*adj.* **1.** of or relating to the Hyperboreans. **2. hyperborean.** of, relating to, or like the far north; arctic or frigid. [Late Latin *hyperboreānus* relating to the Hyperboreans, northern, going back to Greek *hyper* beyond + *boreās* north wind.]

hy·per·crit·i·cal (hī′pər krit′i kəl) *adj.* excessively critical. —**hy′per·crit′i·cal·ly,** *adv.*

hy·per·e·mi·a (hī′pə rē′mē ə) *n.* an excessive amount of blood in any part of the body, resulting from dilated blood vessels or blocked drainage. [HYPER- + -EMIA.] —**hy′per·e′mic,** *adj.*

hy·per·gly·ce·mi·a (hī′pər glī sē′mē ə) *n.* an abnormally high amount of the sugar glucose in the blood. [HYPER- + Greek *glykys* sweet + *haima* blood.] —**hy′per·gly·ce′mic,** *adj.*

hy·per·gol·ic (hī′pər gô′lik, -gol′ik) *adj.* (of two chemical compounds) igniting spontaneously when mixed together, as a rocket fuel and oxidizer do. [HYP(ER-) + Greek *(erg)on* work + Latin *ol(eum)* oil + -IC.]

Hy·pe·ri·on (hī pîr′ē ən) *n.* **1.** in Greek mythology, one of the thirteen Titans, a son of Uranus and Gaea. **2.** *Astronomy.* a moon of Saturn.

hy·per·me·tro·pi·a (hī′pər mi trō′pē ə) *n.* hyperopia. —**hy·per·me·trop·ic** (hī′pər mi trop′ik, -trō′pik), *adj.*

hy·per·on (hī′pə ron′) *n.* a subatomic particle whose mass is greater than that of a neutron.

hy·per·o·pi·a (hī′pə rō′pē ə) *n.* the condition of being able to see distant objects more clearly than those nearby; farsightedness. ➡ opposed to **myopia.** Also, **hypermetropia.** [Modern Latin *hyperopia,* from Greek *hyper* beyond + *ōps* eye.] —**hy·per·op·ic** (hī′pə rop′ik), *adj.*

hy·per·pla·si·a (hī′pər plā′zhə, -zhē ə, -zē ə) *n.* an increase in the size of an organ or tissue due to an abnormal increase in the number of cells. —**hy·per·plas·tic** (hī′pər plas′tik), *adj.*

hy·per·sen·si·tive (hī′pər sen′si tiv) *adj.* excessively or abnormally sensitive: *hypersensitive skin, to be hypersensitive to criticism.* —**hy′per·sen′si·tive·ness, hy′per·sen′si·tiv′i·ty,** *n.*

hy·per·son·ic (hī′pər son′ik) *adj.* of or relating to the speed of an object moving at Mach 5 or greater, relative to the surrounding medium. [HYPER- + SONIC.]

hy·per·ten·sion (hī′pər ten′shən) *n.* **1.** *Medicine.* **a.** high blood pressure. **b.** a diseased condition characterized by high blood pressure. **2.** a condition of excessive tenseness or edginess.

hy·per·ten·sive (hī′pər ten′siv) *adj.* characterized by, relating to, or causing hypertension. —*n.* a person who has hypertension. [HYPER- + TENSIVE.]

hy·per·thy·roid·ism (hī′pər thī′roi diz′əm) *n.* hyperactivity of the thyroid gland, resulting in an excess of thyroid hormone in the blood, enlargement of the gland, bulging eyes, emaciation, and a rapid pulse.

hy·per·ton·ic (hī′pər ton′ik) *adj.* **1.** (of muscle tissue) having abnormally high tension or tone. **2.** (of a solution) having a higher osmotic pressure than another solution. ➡ opposed to **hypotonic.** [HYPER- + TONIC.] —**hy·per·to·nic·i·ty** (hī′pər·tō nis′i tē), *n.*

hy·per·tro·phy (hī pûr′trə fē) *n., pl.* **-phies.** abnormal or excessive growth, esp. of a body part or organ. —*v.i., v.t.,* **-phied, -phy·ing.** to grow or cause to grow abnormally large. [HYPER- + Greek *trophē* food.] —**hy·per·troph′ic,** *adj.*

hy·per·ven·ti·late (hī′pər ven′tə lāt′) *v.i.,* **-lat·ed, -lat·ing.** to breathe too rapidly or deeply, as under emotional stress, causing a drop in the level of carbon dioxide in the blood and consequent dizziness or fainting. —**hy′per·ven′ti·la′tion,** *n.*

hy·phae (hī′fē) *pl. n., sing.* **hy·pha** (hī′fə). the thin, threadlike fibers that form the mycelium of a fungus. —**hy′phal,** *adj.*

hy·phen (hī′fən) *n.* a punctuation mark (-) used to connect two or more elements or words to form a compound word, or to join the syllables of a word that have been separated, as at the end of a line. —*v.t.* hyphenate. [Late Latin *hyphen* unification of two words, from Greek *hyphen* together, all in one (word), from *hypo* under + *hen,* neuter of *heis* one.]

hy·phen·ate (hī′fə nāt′) *v.t.,* **-at·ed, -at·ing.** to separate, connect, or write with a hyphen. —**hy′phen·a′tion,** *n.*

Hyp·nos (hip′nos) *n.* in Greek mythology, the god of sleep. His Roman counterpart is Somnus.

hyp·no·sis (hip nō′sis) *n., pl.* **-ses** (-sēz). **1.** a trance resembling sleep, induced by deep relaxation and concentration and characterized by extreme responsiveness to suggestion. **2.** hypnotism *(def. 1).* [Modern Latin *hypnosis,* from Greek *hypnos* sleep + -OSIS.]

hyp·no·ther·a·py (hip′nō ther′ə pē) *n.* the treatment of disease, a physical symptom, or an unwanted habit by means of hypnotism.

hyp·not·ic (hip not′ik) *adj.* **1.** of or relating to hypnosis or hypnotism: *a hypnotic trance, hypnotic suggestion.* **2.** tending to produce sleep or a trancelike state: *The speaker had a droning, hypnotic voice. The long stretch of straight highway had a hypnotic effect on the truck driver.* **3.** easily hypnotized. —*n.* **1.** a drug or other agent that produces sleep; soporific. **2.** a person who is or can easily be hypnotized. [Late Latin *hypnōticus* putting to sleep, from Greek *hypnōtikos,* going back to *hypnos* sleep.] —**hyp·not′i·cal·ly,** *adv.*

hyp·no·tism (hip′nə tiz′əm) *n.* **1.** the science, practice, or act of inducing hypnosis. **2.** hypnosis *(def. 1).*

hyp·no·tist (hip′nə tist) *n.* a person who induces hypnosis.

hyp·no·tize (hip′nə tīz′) *v.t.,* **-tized, -tiz·ing. 1.** to induce hypnosis in. **2.** to entrance; enthrall; mesmerize: *We were hypnotized by the acrobats' performance.* —**hyp′no·tiz′a·ble,** *adj.* —**hyp′no·ti·za′tion,** *n.* —**hyp′no·tiz′er,** *n.*

hy·po[1] (hī′pō) *n.* sodium thiosulfate. [Short for HYPOSULFITE.]

hy·po[2] (hī′pō) *n., pl.* **-pos.** *Informal.* a hypodermic syringe or injection. [Short for HYPODERMIC.]

hypo- *prefix* **1.** under; beneath; below: *hypodermic.* **2.** less than normal; deficient in; lacking: *hypoxia.* [Greek *hypo* under, below.]

hy·po·chlo·rite (hī′pə klôr′īt) *n.* a salt or ester of hypochlorous acid. [HYPO- + CHLORITE[2].]

hy·po·chlo·rous acid (hī′pə klôr′əs) a weak, unstable acid that exists only in water solution, formed when chlorine is dissolved in water, used esp. as a disinfectant. Formula: HOCl

hy·po·chon·dri·a (hī′pə kon′drē ə) *n.* a neurotic disorder characterized by obsessive preoccupation with personal health, imagined diseases and symptoms, and extreme depression. Also, **hy·po·chon·dri·a·sis** (hī′pō kən drī′ə sis). [Late Latin *hypochondria* (plural) abdomen, from Greek *hypochondria,* from *hypo* under + *chondros* cartilage of the breastbone; with reference to the early belief that the abdomen was the seat of depression.]

hy·po·chon·dri·ac (hī′pə kon′drē ak′) *n.* a person who is subject to hypochondria. —*adj.* of, relating to, or suffering from hypochondria. Also *(adj.),* **hy·po·chon·dri·a·cal** (hī′pə kən-drī′ə kəl). —**hy′po·chon·dri′a·cal·ly,** *adv.*

hy·po·cot·yl (hī′pə kot′əl) *n.* the part of the stem below the cotyledons in the embryo or seedling stage of a plant. [HYPO- + COTYL(EDON).]

hy·poc·ri·sy (hi pok′rə sē) *n., pl.* **-sies. 1.** the act or practice of presenting one's character, feelings, or beliefs as being other than they really are, esp. the feigning of virtue or piety. **2.** an act or example of hypocrisy. [Old French *hypocrisie* pretending, from Late Latin *hypocrisis* acting (in a play), pretending, from Greek *hypokrisis.*]

hyp·o·crite (hip′ə krit′) *n.* a person who is given to or practices hypocrisy. [Old French *hypocrite* pretender, from Late Latin *hypocrita,* from Greek *hypokritēs* actor, pretender.] —**hyp′o·crit′i·cal,** *adj.* —**hyp′o·crit′i·cal·ly,** *adv.*

hy·po·der·mic (hī′pə dûr′mik) *adj.* **1.** lying beneath the skin. **2.** made to be injected under the skin. —*n.* **1.** a hypodermic syringe. **2.** an injection given under the skin, as with a hypodermic syringe. Also *(n., def. 2),* hypodermic injection. [HYPO- + Greek *derma* skin + -IC.] —**hy′po·der′mi·cal·ly,** *adv.*

hypodermic needle, a fine, hollow steel needle that, when fitted to a syringe, is used to administer medication under the skin or into a muscle.

hy·po·der·mis (hī′pə dûr′mis) *n.* **1.** *Botany.* one or more layers of cells lying immediately beneath the epidermis of the leaves and other parts of a plant, serving for support or water storage. **2.** *Zoology.* a layer of cells that secretes the chitinous cuticle of arthropods and certain other invertebrates. [Modern Latin *hypo-*

Cotyledons

Hypocotyl

Roots

hypocotyl

a	at	e	end	o	hot	u	up	hw	white		about
ā	ape	ē	me	ō	old	ū	use	ng	song		taken
ä	far	i	it	ô	fork	ü	rule	th	thin	ə	pencil
âr	care	ī	ice	oi	oil	u̇	pull	t͟h	this		lemon
				ou	out	ûr	turn	zh	measure		circus
		îr	pierce								

dermis, from Greek *hypo* under + *derma* skin.] —**hy′po·der′-mal,** *adj.*

hy·po·gas·tri·um (hī′pə gas′trē əm) *n., pl.* **-tri·a** (-trē ə). the lower middle region of the abdomen. [Modern Latin *hypogastrium,* from Greek *hypogastrion* the lower belly.] —**hy′po·gas′-tric,** *adj.*

hy·po·glos·sal (hī′pə glos′əl) *adj.* **1.** located under the tongue. **2.** of, relating to, or constituting either of the final pair of cranial nerves, which control the muscles of the tongue. —*n.* a hypoglossal nerve. [HYPO- + Modern Latin *glossa* tongue of an animal (going back to Greek *glōssa*) + -AL[1].]

hy·po·gly·ce·mi·a (hī′pō glī sē′mē ə) *n.* an abnormally low amount of the sugar glucose in the blood. It most commonly occurs when a person with diabetes takes too much insulin. [HYPO- + Greek *glykys* sweet + *haima* blood.] —**hy′po·gly-ce′mic,** *adj.*

hy·pog·y·nous (hī poj′ə nəs) *adj.* having sepals, petals, and stamens attached to the receptacle, below but not attached to the pistil, as in a tulip.

hy·po·phos·phate (hī′pə fos′fāt) *n.* a salt or ester of hypophosphoric acid. [HYPO- + PHOSPHATE.]

hy·po·phos·phite (hī′pə fos′fīt) *n.* a salt of hypophosphorous acid. [HYPO- + PHOSPHITE.]

hy·po·phos·phor·ic acid (hī′pə fos fôr′ik) a crystalline solid produced by slowly oxidizing phosphorus in humid air. Formula: $H_4P_2O_6$ [HYPO- + PHOSPHORIC.]

hy·po·phos·phor·ous acid (hī′pə fos′fər əs) a monobasic acid that is an effective reducing agent. Formula: H_3PO_2 [HYPO- + PHOSPHOROUS.]

hy·poph·y·sis (hī pof′ə sis) *n., pl.* **-ses** (-sēz′). pituitary gland. [Greek *hypophysis* attachment underneath; with reference to its position below the brain.] —**hy·poph·y·se·al** (hī pof′ə sē′əl), *adj.*

hy·po·sul·fite (hī′pə sul′fīt) *n.* **1.** a salt of hyposulfurous acid. **2.** sodium thiosulfate.

hy·po·sul·fur·ous acid (hī′pə sul′fər əs) an unstable acid, known only in solution, whose salts are strong reducing agents. Formula: $H_2S_2O_4$ [HYPO- + SULFUROUS.]

hy·po·ten·sion (hī′pə ten′shən) *n.* **1.** low blood pressure. **2.** a condition in which the blood pressure is abnormally low, as following severe blood or fluid loss. [HYPO- + TENSION.] —**hy′po-ten′sive,** *adj.*

hy·pot·e·nuse (hī pot′ə nüs′, -nūs′) *also,* **hypothenuse.** *n.* the side of a right triangle opposite the right angle. [Latin *hypotēnusa,* from Greek *hypoteinousa (grammē)* literally, (a) subtending (line), from *hypoteinein* to stretch under.]

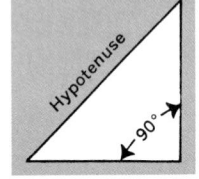

hy·po·thal·a·mus (hī′pə thal′ə məs) *n., pl.* **-mi** (-mī′). an area of the brain lying below the thalamus that controls the autonomic nervous system. —**hy-po·tha·lam·ic** (hī′pō thə lam′ik), *adj.*

hy·poth·e·cate (hī poth′i kāt′) *v.t.,* **-cat·ed, -cat·ing.** to pledge (property, as a ship or its cargo) as security for a loan or debt without transferring ownership; mortgage. [Medieval Latin *hypothecatus,* past participle of *hypothecare* to pledge, from Late Latin *hypothēca* a pledge, mortgage, from Greek *hypothēkē*.] —**hy·poth′e·ca′tion,** *n.*

hy·poth·e·nuse (hī poth′ə nüs′, -nūs′) hypotenuse.

hy·po·ther·mi·a (hī′pə thûr′mē ə) *n.* an abnormally low body temperature, caused by prolonged exposure to the cold.

hy·poth·e·sis (hī poth′ə sis) *n., pl.* **-ses** (-sēz′). **1.** an unproved, tentative explanation or supposition that is based on known facts and can be used as a basis for further experimentation or investiga-

tion; theory. **2.** a proposition, assumption, or principle put forth as a basis for reasoning or argument. [Greek *hypothesis* a placing under, foundation, supposition.]

hy·poth·e·size (hī poth′ə sīz′) *v.,* **-sized, -siz·ing.** —*v.t.* to suggest or assume as a hypothesis. —*v.i.* to make a hypothesis.

hy·po·thet·i·cal (hī′pə thet′i kəl) *adj.* of the nature of, involving, or based on a hypothesis; theoretical: *a hypothetical example.* Also, **hy′po·thet′ic.** [Greek *hypothetikos* supposed, relating to a hypothesis + -AL[1].] —**hy′po·thet′i·cal·ly,** *adv.*

hy·po·thy·roid·ism (hī′pə thī′roi diz′əm) *n.* a deficiency in thyroid function resulting in insufficient thyroid hormone in the blood, slowed metabolism, and, when present and untreated from birth, cretinism.

hy·po·ton·ic (hī′pə ton′ik) *adj.* **1.** (of muscle tissue) having abnormally low tension or tone. **2.** (of a solution) having a lower osmotic pressure than another solution. ➡ opposed to **hypertonic.** [HYPO- + TONIC.] —**hy·po·to·nic·i·ty** (hī′pō tō nis′i tē), *n.*

hy·pox·e·mi·a (hī′pok sē′mē ə) *n.* hypoxia. —**hy′pox·e′mic,** *adj.*

hy·pox·i·a (hī pok′sē ə) *n.* a condition resulting from a reduction in the oxygen supply to the tissues, characterized by dizziness, rapid pulse, and impairment of the senses. Also, **hypoxemia.** [Modern Latin *hypoxia,* from HYPO- + OX(YGEN).] —**hy·pox′ic,** *adj.*

hy·rax (hī′raks) *n., pl.* **-rax·es** or **-ra·ces** (-rə sēz′). any of various rabbitlike mammals, family Procaviidae, of Africa and the Middle East, having hooflike claws, sharp canine teeth, and a coarse black, brownish gray, or tan coat. Length: 20 inches (51 centimeters). [Greek *hyrax* mouselike shrew.]

hys·sop (his′əp) *n.* **1.** a stiff, shrublike plant, *Hyssopus officinalis,* of the mint family, having leaves with a pungent odor that are used in the Middle East for flavoring food and for medicinal purposes. **2.** in the Old Testament, a plant whose twigs were used for sprinkling water in purification ceremonies. [Old English *(h)ysope,* from Latin *hyssōpus* an aromatic plant, from Greek *hyssōpos,* from Hebrew *ezov* literally, moss.]

hys·ter·ec·to·my (his′tə rek′tə mē) *n., pl.* **-mies.** the total or partial removal of the uterus by surgery. [Greek *hystera* uterus, womb + -ECTOMY.]

hys·ter·e·sis (his′tə rē′sis) *n. Physics.* the lag that a body exhibits in responding to changes in external forces, such as variations in stress or in the intensity of a magnetic field.

hys·te·ri·a (hi ster′ē ə, -stir′-) *n.* **1.** excessive, uncontrollable terror, panic, or other strong emotion; frenzy: *The end of the war was greeted with joyous hysteria.* **2.** any of several psychiatric disorders, usually characterized by physical symptoms, such as paralysis or amnesia, that have no physical discernible cause. [Modern Latin *hysteria,* going back to Greek *hysterā* womb; because it was formerly thought that hysteria occurred more frequently in women than in men.]

hys·ter·ic (hi ster′ik) *n.* a person who is subject to hysteria. —*adj.* hysterical.

hys·ter·i·cal (hi ster′i kəl) *adj.* **1.** resembling or caused by hysteria; uncontrollably emotional; frenzied: *hysterical outbursts, hysterical sobbing.* **2.** of, characteristic of, or occurring as a symptom of hysteria: *hysterical blindness.* **3.** suffering from or prone to hysteria. **4.** *Informal.* extremely funny. [Latin *hystericus* subject to uncontrollable feelings (from Greek *hysterikos* relating to the womb, from *hysterā* womb) + -AL[1]. See HYSTERIA.] —**hys·ter′i-cal·ly,** *adv.*

hys·ter·ics (hi ster′iks) *pl. n.* a fit of uncontrollable emotion, esp. of alternate laughing and crying. ➡ sometimes used as singular.

Hz, hertz.

| ancient Semitic | early Greek | later Greek | Etruscan | Latin |

The earliest form of the letter **I** was found in the ancient Semitic alphabets and called *yod*, meaning "hand." When the early Greeks adopted *yod*, they simplified it, called it *iota*, and used it to represent the sound of the short vowel *i*. By about the fifth century B.C., the Greeks had further simplified *iota* to a single vertical line. The Etruscans and later the Romans used this same form of *iota*. In Latin, this letter sometimes represented the vowel *i* and sometimes the consonant *j*. Our modern capital letter **I** is often written with a short horizontal stroke at the top and bottom of the vertical line. The dot over the lower case letter *i* was added about 1,000 years ago in order to distinguish *i* from the letters *m* and *n* in words such as the Latin *minimus*. At that time *m* and *n* were made up of strokes that resembled the lower case *i*, so that a word containing a combination of these letters was very hard to read.

i, I (ī) *n., pl.* **i's, I's. 1.** the ninth letter of the English alphabet. **2.** the shape of this letter or something having this shape.

I (ī) *pron., sing.* nominative, **I**; possessive, **my, mine**; objective, **me**; *pl.* nominative, **we**; possessive, **our, ours**; objective, **us.** the person who is speaking or writing. —*n.* a person; ego. [Old English *ic* the pronoun.]

I (ī) *also,* **i** *n., pl.* **I's.** the Roman numeral for 1.

I, the symbol for iodine.

i., intransitive.

I. 1. Island; Islands. **2.** Isle; Isles.

Ia., Iowa.

IA, the postal abbreviation for Iowa.

I·a·go (ē ä′gō) *n.* the villain in Shakespeare's *Othello.*

-ial, form of **-al**[1] after some stressed syllables, as in *celestial.*

i·amb (ī′amb) *n.* a metrical foot consisting of two syllables, the first unstressed and the second stressed (in English verse) or the first long and the second short (in classical Greek and Latin verse), for example, *That fought/ with us/ upon/ Saint Cris/pin's day.* [Latin *iambus,* from Greek *iambos.*]

i·am·bic (ī am′bik) *adj.* of, relating to, or consisting of iambs. —*n.* **1.** iamb. **2.** *usually,* **iambics.** poetry written in iambs.

-ian, form of **-an,** as in *Australian, simian.*

-iatrics *combining form* medical treatment of: *pediatrics, geriatrics.* [Greek *iātrikos* of medicine or doctors, from *iātros* physician, from *iasthai* to cure, heal.]

i·a·tro·gen·ic (ī at′rə jen′ik) *adj.* (of an ailment or disorder) caused by medical treatment, as by prescribed drugs or surgery.

-iatry *combining form* medical treatment: *psychiatry.* [Modern Latin *-iatria,* from Greek *iātreiā* healing.]

ib., ibidem.

I·be·ri·an (ī bir′ē ən) *adj.* **1.** of, relating to, or characteristic of Iberia in Europe or its people, language, or culture. **2.** of or denoting members of an ancient race that inhabited Iberia in Europe. **3.** of or relating to ancient Iberia in Asia or its inhabitants. —*n.* **1.** a native or inhabitant of Iberia in Europe. **2.** an almost completely unknown language formerly spoken in Iberia in Europe. **3.** a native or inhabitant of ancient Iberia in Asia.

i·bex (ī′beks) *n., pl.* **i·bex** or **i·bex·es.** a mountain-dwelling wild goat, *Capra ibex,* native to Europe, Asia, and northern Africa, having ridged, curving horns that in the male may grow to as much as 5 feet (1.5 meters) in length. Height: to 40 inches (102 centimeters) at the shoulder. [Latin *ibex* chamois.]

ibid., ibidem.

i·bi·dem (ib′i dəm, i bī′dem) *adv.* in the work previously mentioned or cited. ➡ used mainly in footnotes in the abbreviated form **ibid.** [Latin *ibidem* in the same place.]

-ibility, form of **-ability,** as in *sensibility, flexibility.*

i·bis (ī′bis) *n., pl.* **i·bis·es** or **i·bis.** a long-legged wading bird of any of several species, family Threskiornithidae, related to the stork and heron, having a long, downward curving bill, esp. the **sacred ibis,** *Threskiornis aethiopica,* which was worshiped by the ancient Egyptians. Height: 3½ feet (1.1 meters). [Latin *ibis,* from Greek *ībis;* of Egyptian origin.]

-ible, form of **-able,** as in *convertible.*

i·bu·pro·fen (ī′bū prō′fən) *n.* a drug used to reduce inflammation and pain, esp. in the treatment of arthritis. Formula: $C_{13}H_{18}O_2$ [Contraction, rearrangement, and respelling of *isobutyl phenyl propionic acid,* the drug's chemical name.]

scarlet **ibis**

-ic *suffix* **1.** (used to form adjectives from nouns) **a.** of or relating to: *psychiatric, Celtic.* **b.** having the qualities of; being or like: *athletic, angelic.* **c.** made of or containing: *alcoholic, granitic.* **d.** characterized by: *cyclic.* **e.** produced or caused by: *seismic.* ➡ Many words ending in *-ic* have more than one of the above meanings. **2.** *Chemistry.* **a.** of a higher oxidation state than a related compound or ion whose name ends in *-ous.* The oxidation state of copper is +2 in *cupric* oxide and +1 in *cuprous* oxide. **b.** designating the most commonly used of a group of related ternary acids. Nitric acid is more commonly used than nitrous acid. [Latin *-icus* or Greek *-ikos,* often through French *-ique.*]

IC, integrated circuit.

-ical *suffix* **1.** (used to form adjectives from nouns) **a.** of, relating to, characterized by, or caused by: *pontifical, farcical.* **b.** characterized by in a special way: *economical, philosophical.* **2.** (used to form adjectives from nouns ending in *-ic*) of, relating to, or characterized by: *logical, musical.* [Latin *-icālis,* sometimes through French *-ical(e).*]

Ic·a·rus (ik′ər əs) *n.* in Greek mythology, a youth who escaped from Crete on wings made by his father, Daedalus. As he flew too near the sun, the wax holding the wings melted, and he fell into the sea.

ICBM, a ballistic missile with a range of over 3,000 miles (4,827 kilometers). [Abbreviation of *i(nter)c(ontinental) b(allistic) m(issile).*]

ICC, Interstate Commerce Commission.

ice (īs) *n.* **1.** the solid state of water, normally produced at or below 32 degrees Fahrenheit (0 degrees Celsius). **2.a.** pieces or a layer of this: *Do you have ice in your glass? There was ice on the windshield.* **b.** a frozen surface, esp. of a body of water, as a lake: *We cut a hole in the ice to fish.* **3.** something that resembles ice in appearance or consistency. **4.** a frozen dessert made of sweetened water and fruit flavoring or fruit juice. **5.** *Slang.* a diamond or diamonds. —*v.,* **iced, ic·ing.** —*v.i.* to become covered or blocked with ice (often with *up* or *over*): *The lake iced over. The lock iced up.* —*v.t.* **1.** to cause ice to form on; cover with ice.

a	at	e	end	o	hot	u	up	hw	white		about
ā	ape	ē	me	ō	old	ū	use	ng	song		taken
ä	far	i	it	ô	fork	ü	rule	th	thin	ə	pencil
âr	care	ī	ice	oi	oil	u̇	pull	th	this		lemon
				îr	pierce	ou	out	ûr	turn	zh	measure		circus

613

2. to chill or keep cold, esp. with ice: *The bartender iced the champagne.* **3.** to cover or decorate with icing; frost. **4.** to convert into ice. [Old English *īs* frozen water.]
  • **on ice.** *Informal.* **a.** in reserve, as for future consideration: *We'll keep the matter on ice until the next meeting.* **b.** out of communication with others; incommunicado: *The police kept the suspect on ice for several days.* **c.** certain to be won or gained; clinched: *We have the game on ice.*
  • **on thin ice.** in a risky or precarious situation.
  • **to cut no ice.** *Informal.* to have little effect or influence: *Your excuse cuts no ice with me.*

ice age 1. any prehistoric period when glaciers and ice sheets covered much of the surface of the earth. **2. Ice Age.** Pleistocene.

ice bag, a waterproof bag for holding ice, used to apply cold to parts of the body, esp. to alleviate pain or lessen swelling.

ice·berg (īs′bûrg′) *n.* a large mass of floating ice that has broken off from a glacier or polar icecap. [Probably from Dutch *ijsberg* literally, ice mountain.]
  • **tip of the iceberg.** a small part of something very large or extensive, esp. something bad: *The scandal was shocking enough in itself, but it proved to be only the tip of the iceberg.*

iceberg lettuce, any of various kinds of lettuce having round, tight heads of crisp, light green leaves.

ice-boat (īs′bōt′) *n.* **1.** a boatlike, often triangular, frame equipped with runners and usually sails for sailing on ice. **2.** icebreaker.

ice·bound (īs′bound′) *adj.* **1.** obstructed and made inaccessible by ice: *an icebound coast.* **2.** held fast or surrounded by ice: *an icebound ship.*

ice·box (īs′boks′) *n.* **1.** a box or chest cooled by blocks of ice, used for storing food and drinks. **2.** *Informal.* refrigerator.

ice·break·er (īs′brā′kər) *n.* a ship with a strong prow, used in harbors, rivers, and other waterways to break a navigable channel through ice.

ice·cap (īs′kap′) *n.* a dome-shaped glacier covering a large land area: *the Greenland icecap.*

ice-cold (īs′kōld′) *adj.* very cold: *I would like a glass of ice-cold milk.*

ice cream, a frozen dessert made chiefly of milk or cream, sweeteners, and flavoring.

ice cube, a small, often cube-shaped piece of ice, formed in a metal or plastic tray in a refrigerator or freezer, or made in an ice machine.

iced (īst) *adj.* **1.** chilled or kept cold, esp. with ice: *iced tea, iced melon.* **2.** covered or coated with ice: *an iced airplane wing.* **3.** covered or decorated with icing: *an iced cupcake.*

ice field, a large expanse of floating ice, found esp. in polar regions.

ice floe, floe.

ice hockey, hockey *(def. 1).*

ice·house (īs′hous′) *n., pl.* **-hous·es** (-hou′ziz). a building for storing ice.

Ice·lan·dic (īs lan′dik) *adj.* of, relating to, or characteristic of Iceland or its people, language, or culture. —*n.* a language spoken predominantly in Iceland, belonging to the Germanic branch of the Indo-European language family.

Ice·land moss (īs′lənd) an edible lichen, *Cetraria islandica,* found in the Arctic and in mountainous regions of the Northern Hemisphere, growing in a tangled mass of thin, spiny-edged branches.

ice·man (īs′man′) *n., pl.* **-men** (-men′). a person whose job or business is selling or delivering ice.

ice pack 1. an ice bag or folded cloth filled with ice and applied to parts of the body, esp. to alleviate pain or lessen swelling. **2.** pack ice.

ice pick, a pointed tool used to break or chip ice.

ice sheet, a thick layer of ice covering an extensive area, esp. of land, for a long period of time.

ice shelf, a very thick sheet of glacial ice that extends from land out into the sea, as along the coast of Antarctica or Greenland.

ice-skate (īs′skāt′) *v.i.,* **-skat·ed, -skat·ing.** to skate on ice.

ice skate 1. a bootlike shoe with a runner, usually of metal, attached, used for skating on ice. **2.** a runner with straps and clamps, designed to be attached to a boot or shoe, used for skating on ice.

ice skating, skating on ice. —**ice skater.**

ice water 1. water that is chilled with ice or is as cold as ice. **2.** water from melted ice.

ich·neu·mon (ik nü′mən, -nū′-) *n.* **1.** a mongoose, *Herpestes ichneumon,* native to Africa, having a gray body and brownish black feet, considered sacred by the ancient Egyptians. Length: 40 inches (102 centimeters), including tail. **2.** ichneumon fly. [Latin *ichneumōn,* from Greek *ichneumōn* literally, tracker. The mon-

goose was believed to hunt out crocodile eggs; the ichneumon fly, to hunt spiders.]

ichneumon fly, any of a group of stingless, wasplike insects, family Ichneumonidae, found throughout the world, whose larvae are parasites on many destructive crop pests.

i·chor[1] (ī′kôr, ī′kər) *n.* the ethereal fluid supposed by the Greeks to flow in the veins of the gods. [Greek *īchōr.*]

i·chor[2] (ī′kôr, ī′kər) *n.* a thin watery discharge from an ulcer or wound. [Late Latin *ichor* bloody matter, from Greek *īchōr* blood of the gods, watery fluid.] —**i·chor·ous** (ī′kər əs), *adj.*

ich·thy·ol·o·gy (ik′thē ol′ə jē) *n.* the branch of zoology that deals with fish. [Greek *ichthȳs* fish + -LOGY.] —**ich·thy·o·log·ic** (ik′thē ə loj′ik); *also,* **ich′thy·o·log′i·cal,** *adj.* —**ich′thy·ol′o·gist,** *n.*

ich·thy·o·saur (ik′thē ə sôr′) *n.* any of an extinct group of porpoiselike marine reptiles, order Ichthyosauria, of the Mesozoic, having a large head with a thin, elongated snout, and four paddlelike flippers. Length: from 4 to 40 feet (1 to 12 meters). [Modern Latin *Ichthyosaurus,* from Greek *ichthȳs* fish + *sauros* lizard.]

ich·thy·o·sau·rus (ik′thē ə-sôr′əs) *n.* ichthyosaur.

ichthyosaur

i·ci·cle (ī′si kəl) *n.* a tapered, hanging piece of ice formed by the freezing of dripping water. [Middle English *isikel,* from Old English *īs* ice + *gicel* icicle.]

i·ci·ly (ī′sə lē) *adv.* in a cold, unfriendly manner.

i·ci·ness (ī′sē nis) *n.* the state or quality of being icy.

ic·ing (ī′sing) *n.* a mixture of sugar, butter, flavoring, a liquid, and sometimes egg whites, used to cover or decorate a cake or other baked goods; frosting.

ick·y (ik′ē) *adj.,* **ick·i·er, ick·i·est.** *Informal.* **1.** sticky or messy, often in an unpleasant way. **2.** annoying, disagreeable, or offensive: *to suffer from an icky cold.* **3.** overly sentimental; unsophisticated: *icky poetry.* [Probably baby talk for STICKY.] —**ick′i·ness,** *n.*

i·con (ī′kon) *n.* **1.** *also,* **ikon.** a painted representation of a holy person, as Jesus, the Virgin Mary, or a saint. Icons are held in reverence by Christians in the Eastern churches. **2.** *Computers.* a symbol or picture used in an operating system that represents commands by the display of graphics, rather than by words or numbers. [Latin *īcōn* image, from Greek *eikōn.*]

i·con·o·clasm (ī kon′ə klaz′əm) *n.* the beliefs or behavior of an iconoclast.

i·con·o·clast (ī kon′ə klast′) *n.* **1.** a person who attacks traditional or cherished ideas, beliefs, or institutions as being false or harmful. **2.** a person who destroys icons and is opposed to their religious use. [Modern Latin *iconoclastes,* going back to Greek *eikōn* image + *-klastēs* breaker.] —**i·con′o·clas′tic,** *adj.* —**i·con′o·clas′ti·cal·ly,** *adv.*

i·co·sa·he·dron (ī′kō sə hē′drən) *n., pl.* **-drons** or **-dra** (-drə). *Geometry.* a polyhedron with twenty faces. [Greek *eikosaedron,* from *eikosi* twenty + *hedrā* base[1], seat.]

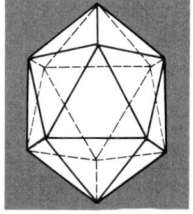
icosahedron

-ics *suffix* (used to form nouns) **1.** an art, science, or field of study: *physics, graphics.* **2.** procedures, practices, or activities: *gymnastics.* [Plural of -IC, imitating Greek *-ika,* neuter plural of *-ikos,* as in *(ta) ethika* (the) ethics.]

ic·tus (ik′təs) *n., pl.* **-tus·es** or **-tus.** rhythmical or metrical stress. [Latin *ictus* blow, stroke.]

i·cy (ī′sē) *adj.,* **i·ci·er, i·ci·est. 1.** made of, containing, or covered with ice: *icy pavement, icy regions, icy mounds.* **2.** very cold: *icy winds, icy hands.* **3.** without warmth of feeling; coldly indifferent: *an icy stare.*

id (id) *n. Psychoanalysis.* one of the divisions of the psyche that resides in the unconscious and is the source of the psychic energy based on primitive instincts and drives. [Latin *id* it, translation of German *es* it.]

I'd (īd) *contr.* **1.** I had. **2.** I would. **3.** I should.

ID (ī′dē′) *n., pl.* **ID's.** a card or document that identifies its bearer, such as a driver's license or birth certificate. Also, **ID card.**

-id[1] *suffix* (used to form nouns) **1.** in mythology, children of: *Nereid.* **2.** *Astronomy.* a meteor that seems to originate or radiate from a specified constellation: *Leonid.* [Greek *-id-,* stem of *-is* (feminine) offspring of, often through Latin *-id-,* stem of *-is.*]

-id² *suffix* (used to form nouns) member of a specified family or class: *hominid.* [Modern Latin *-idae* and *-ida,* masculine and neuter plural, respectively, of *-ides,* from Greek *-idēs,* (masculine) offspring of.]

-id³ *suffix* (used to form adjectives) having a particular quality, state, or condition: *fluid, morbid, torrid, solid.* [Latin *-idus,* often through French *-ide.*]

id., idem.

ID 1. the postal abbreviation for Idaho. **2.** identification.

Ida., Idaho.

-ide *suffix Chemistry.* **1.** a salt comprising only two elements: *sodium chloride, potassium sulfide.* **2.** a compound related to or derived from another: *actinide.* [From (OX)IDE.]

i·dea (ī dē′ə) *n.* **1.** something formulated by the mind; thought: *You have good ideas, but have difficulty expressing them.* **2.** a mental image: *The retired sailor's idea of life at sea grew dim after a few years.* **3.** an abstract form or essence; general concept: *the idea of war, the idea of the good.* **4.** a firmly established opinion or belief; conviction: *My ancestors had strong ideas about religion.* **5.** a vague feeling; inkling: *John had an idea that he had met the woman somewhere before.* **6.** a plan of action; intention: *Talking with her uncle gave Juana the idea of becoming an artist.* **7.** the aim or purpose of something: *The idea of the game is to put the ball into the net.* [Latin *idea* archetype, model, from Greek *idéā* look, form, model, notion.]

Synonyms Idea, thought, concept, and notion denote a product, expressed or not, of conscious mental activity. **Idea** connotes some degree of seriousness: *The architect had many fresh ideas about the design of the new stadium.* **Thought** suggests a product of reasoning rather than of imagination: *I arranged my thoughts before getting up to speak.* **Concept** connotes an idea that results from knowledge or experience: *Visiting Florida allows one to form a concept of what the tropics are like.* **Notion** suggests a less solidly grounded concept: *Your notion of country life is far different from the reality.*

i·de·al (ī dē′əl) *n.* **1.** a concept or standard of perfection or excellence: *the ideal of beauty.* **2.** a person or thing that is the embodiment of such a concept or standard, esp. one to be admired and imitated: *Florence Nightingale is the ideal of many a young nurse.* **3.** the best or most satisfactory situation; eventual aim or goal: *The ideal would be to have a round-the-clock trauma center in each district.* —*adj.* **1.** meeting or embodying standards of perfection or excellence; much better than currently exists: *an ideal society.* **2.** most desirable or suitable: *These boots are ideal for a wet, slushy day. He is the ideal person for the job.* **3.** existing only as or in a concept; not concrete: *an ideal economy.* [Late Latin *ideālis* relating to an archetype or model, from Latin *idea.* See IDEA.] —For Synonyms *(adj.),* see **perfect.**

ideal gas *Physics.* a gas that obeys laws such as Boyle's and Avogadro's without any deviation.

i·de·al·ism (ī dē′ə liz′əm) *n.* **1.** action or thought in accordance with standards of perfection or excellence, rather than in accordance with what currently exists: *the idealism of those who would eliminate hunger and poverty.* **2.** in art and literature, the imaginative treatment of subject matter, usually expressing an ethical or aesthetic standard of perfection rather than the accidental details of nature. ➡ opposed to **realism. 3.** the philosophical theory that reality is essentially mental or spiritual rather than material. **Objective idealism** maintains that reality consists essentially of ideal forms, such as beauty and justice, that exist outside of and independent of anyone's mind. **Subjective idealism** maintains that nothing is real but the perceptions and ideas that exist in one's mind.

i·de·al·ist (ī dē′ə list) *n.* **1.** a person who thinks or acts in accordance with ideals. **2.** a person who thinks that things are better than they are; dreamer. **3.** a person who adheres to or expresses idealism in art, literature, or philosophy. —*adj.* idealistic: *idealist philosophy.*

i·de·al·is·tic (ī′dē ə lis′tik) *adj.* **1.** motivated by standards of perfection or excellence. **2.** tending to ignore practical limitations; unrealistic. **3.** tending to think or assume that things are better than they are. **4.** of, relating to, or characterized by idealism in art, literature, or philosophy. —**i′de·al·is′ti·cal·ly,** *adv.*

i·de·al·i·za·tion (ī dē′ə lə zā′shən) *n.* **1.** the act of idealizing or the state of being idealized. **2.** something that is the result of idealizing.

i·de·al·ize (ī dē′ə līz′) *v.t.,* **-ized, -iz·ing. 1.** to portray or represent as ethically or aesthetically perfect, as in art: *portraits that idealize their subjects.* **2.** to remember or think of (something) as better than it was or is: *Some people idealize their childhood.* —**i·de′al·iz′er,** *n.*

i·de·al·ly (ī dē′ə lē) *adv.* **1.** in the best possible manner; perfectly or very well: *a personality ideally suited to a doctor.* **2.** in accord-

ance with a standard or concept; under the best conditions: *Ideally, each child should receive three shots of the vaccine.*

i·de·a·tion (ī′dē ā′shən) *n.* the process of forming ideas.

i·dem (ī′dem, id′em) *pron., adj. Latin.* the same; ditto. ➡ used, esp. in footnotes, to refer to something previously mentioned.

i·den·ti·cal (ī den′ti kəl) *adj.* **1.** one and the same; the very same: *We saw the identical car somewhere else an hour later.* **2.** exactly alike: *identical uniforms, identical statements.* **3.** (of values or amounts) numerically the same; equal. **4.** (of twins) developing from a single fertilized egg cell, and thus having the same sex and genotype. ➡ distinguished from **fraternal.** [Medieval Latin *identicus* the same (from Late Latin *identitās* sameness) + -AL¹. See IDENTITY.] —**i·den′ti·cal·ly,** *adv.* —**i·den′ti·cal·ness,** *n.* —For Synonyms, see **same.**

i·den·ti·fi·ca·tion (ī den′tə fi kā′shən) *n.* **1.** the act or process of identifying or the state of being identified. **2.** something used to give evidence of or to establish one's identity: *Can you show some identification?*

i·den·ti·fy (ī den′tə fī′) *v.,* **-fied, -fy·ing.** —*v.t.* **1.** to establish that (someone or something) is a particular person or thing: *I identified the book as mine by showing my name written in the front. How many species of birds can you identify?* **2.** to be a means of proving who or what a person or thing is: *This mark identifies the book as yours.* **3.** to regard or treat as identical; assume to be one and the same: *The Roman goddess Venus is identified with the Greek goddess Aphrodite.* **4.** to associate closely (with *with*): *to identify money with success.* —*v.i.* to become as one with another or others (with *with*): *I identified with the protagonist of the novel.* —**i·den′ti·fi′a·ble,** *adj.* —**i·den′ti·fi′er,** *n.*

i·den·ti·ty (ī den′ti tē) *n., pl.* **-ties. 1.** one's sense of being distinguishable from other persons; individuality: *to suffer a loss of identity.* **2.** the state of being a certain person or thing; being who or what one or it is: *The traveler's passport established his identity.* **3.** the state or condition of being identical: *She and I have an identity of interests.* **4.** *Mathematics.* a statement of equality that is true for all values of a variable. The equation $3x + 2x = 5x$ is true for all values of x and is therefore an identity. [Late Latin *identitās* sameness, from Latin *idem* the same.]

identity crisis, a state of confusion and anxiety in which a person is unsure of his or her place in society, occurring esp. in a self-conscious stage of personality development or adjustment, as during adolescence.

identity element *Mathematics.* an element in a set that, when added to or multiplied by any other element, yields that element. For addition, 0 is the identity element; for multiplication, 1 is the identity element.

id·e·o·graph (id′ē ə graf′, ī′dē-) *n.* a written symbol, such as a character in Chinese, that stands for an object or idea rather than for a word or sound. Also, **id·e·o·gram** (id′ē ə gram′, ī′dē-). [Greek *idéā* form, kind, idea + -GRAPH; literally, idea writing.] —**id′e·o·graph′ic;** *also,* **id′e·o·graph′i·cal,** *adj.*

i·de·o·log·i·cal (ī′dē ə loj′i kəl, id′ē-) *adj.* **1.** due to or based on ideologies or an ideology: *ideological differences.* **2.** of or relating to ideologies or an ideology: *ideological studies.* Also, **i′de·o·log′ic.** —**i′de·o·log′i·cal·ly,** *adv.*

i·de·o·logue (ī′dē ə lôg′, -log′) *n.* **1.** a person whose ideas or attitudes about some subject adhere to a particular ideology: *a communist ideologue.* **2.** a person with firmly fixed ideas, often of an impractical nature. [French *idéologue,* from *idéologie* ideology.]

i·de·ol·o·gy (ī′dē ol′ə jē, id′ē-) *n., pl.* **-gies. 1.** the total complex of beliefs, attitudes, and concepts that directs and channels the thinking of members of a group, as of a political party or social class. **2.** an individual's beliefs and ideas: *My cousin's ideology is so different from mine that we can't agree on anything.* [Greek *idéā* idea, form, kind + -LOGY.]

ides (īdz) *pl. n.* in the ancient Roman calendar, the fifteenth day of March, May, July, or October and the thirteenth day of the other months. ➡ used as singular or plural. [French *ides,* from Latin *īdūs;* possibly of Etruscan origin.]

id est (id est′) *Latin.* that is (to say).

id·i·o·cy (id′ē ə sē) *n., pl.* **-cies. 1.** the condition of being an idiot. **2.** excessive silliness or stupidity. **3.** an excessively silly or stupid thought, statement, or action.

id·i·om (id′ē əm) *n.* **1.** any expression peculiar to a language whose meaning cannot be construed simply from the meanings of the words composing it. *To pull one's leg* is an idiom. **2.** a lan-

a	at	e	end	o	hot	u	up	hw	white	⌠	about
ā	ape	ē	me	ō	old	ū	use	ng	song		taken
ä	far	i	it	ô	fork	ü	rule	th	thin	ə	pencil
âr	care	ī	ice	oi	oil	u̇	pull	th	this		lemon
		îr	pierce	ou	out	ûr	turn	zh	measure	⌡	circus

guage or dialect peculiar to a people or to a specific region: *the colorful cockney idiom.* **3.** the characteristic way in which words are used in a particular language. **4.** a characteristic style or form of expression, esp. in the arts: *Jazz is a distinctly American idiom.* [Late Latin *idiōma* peculiarity in language, from Greek *idiōma,* going back to *idios* one's own.]

Usage Idioms are metaphorical phrases that cannot be understood simply by knowing the meaning of each individual word. Every language has its own special **idioms,** which native speakers instinctively comprehend as they learn their language. Such phrases as *to go out on a limb, to be beside oneself,* and *to come to grips with* are **idioms** that native speakers of American English may hear and immediately incorporate into their own vocabulary. **Idioms** develop from a variety of sources, including sayings, mythology, the Bible, literature, and technical and other specialized language. Many **idioms** have historical roots and, often, a phrase that is now metaphorical was originally used in a literal sense. *To know the ropes,* for example, which now means to know how something is done, was at one time a nautical expression meaning to know how to work the ropes controlling the sails of a ship. Another **idiom,** *between Scylla and Charybdis,* which means to be trapped between two dangerous alternatives, comes from the Greek myth in which sailors navigating the Strait of Messina had to confront one of two monsters, Scylla and Charybdis, who guarded the strait. Scylla is, in fact, a whirlpool on one side of the narrow strait and Charybdis a huge rock on the other. The modern phrase *between a rock and a hard place* expresses the same idea of being caught between two undesirable alternatives.

id·i·o·mat·ic (id′ē ə mat′ik) *adj.* **1.** having the nature of an idiom or idioms: *an idiomatic expression.* **2.** characterized by the use of idioms: *idiomatic speech.* **3.** peculiar to or characteristic of a particular language. —**id′i·o·mat′i·cal·ly,** *adv.*

id·i·o·syn·cra·sy (id′ē ə sing′krə sē) *n., pl.* **-sies.** an unusual or distinguishing characteristic of an individual, such as a habit or mannerism; peculiarity; eccentricity. [Greek *idiosynkrāsiā* peculiar temperament, from *idios* one's own + *syn* with + *krāsis* mixture.] —**id·i·o·syn·crat·ic** (id′ē ə sin krat′ik, -sing-), *adj.* —**id′i·o·syn·crat′i·cal·ly,** *adv.*

id·i·ot (id′ē ət) *n.* **1.** a very silly or stupid person; fool. **2.** a person who is mentally retarded, having a mental age of up to four years. ➡ now considered obsolete. [Middle English *idiote,* from Old French *idiote,* from Latin *idiōta* ignorant person, from Greek *idiōtēs* private person (as opposed to one holding public office), uneducated person, from *idios* one's own, private.]

id·i·ot·ic (id′ē ot′ik) *adj.* of, relating to, or characteristic of an idiot; very foolish. —**id′i·ot′i·cal·ly,** *adv.*

id·i·ot sa·vant (id′ē ət sa vänt′, sə-, sav′ənt) *pl.* **id·i·ot sa·vants** or **id·i·ots sa·vants.** a person who is mentally retarded but who has a remarkable skill or aptitude, such as for playing complex music or for making involved mathematical calculations very quickly. [French *idiot savant* literally, learned idiot. See IDIOT, SAVANT.]

i·dle (ī′dəl) *adj.,* **i·dler, i·dlest. 1.a.** not engaged in work or activity; unemployed; inactive: *an idle worker.* **b.** not in use: *an idle typewriter.* **2.** unwilling to work or exert oneself; lazy. **3.** having little worth, usefulness, or significance; frivolous: *an idle pastime, idle chatter.* **4.** without any basis in fact; groundless: *idle gossip.* **5.** leading to no result; ineffective; futile: *idle threats.* —*v.,* **i·dled, i·dling.** —*v.i.* **1.** to spend time doing nothing; be inactive: *He idled around the house all morning.* **2.** to move sluggishly or aimlessly: *She idled along the sidewalk.* **3.** (of machines) to run slowly, out of gear, or without transmitting power: *The car idled in the driveway.* —*v.t.* **1.** to spend or waste (time) doing nothing (often with *away*): *We idled away our entire vacation.* **2.** to cause (someone or something) to be inactive: *The strike idled the crew for days.* [Old English *īdel* empty, useless, inactive.] —**i′dle·ness,** *n.* —**i′dly,** *adv.*

i·dler (īd′lər) *n.* **1.** a person who is lazy or inactive. **2.** a wheel or gear located between two other wheels or gears that transmits motion from one to the other without altering their direction or speed. Also *(def. 2),* **idle wheel.**

i·dol (ī′dəl) *n.* **1.** a representation of a god, used as an object of worship. **2.** in the Old Testament, a false god, esp. of a heathen people. **3.** a person who is the object of great or excessive admiration or devotion: *The athlete was the idol of many fans.* [Latin *īdōlum* image, form, from Greek *eidōlon.*]

i·dol·a·ter (ī dol′ə tər) *n.* **1.** a person who worships an idol or idols. **2.** a person who idolizes another: *The famous singer was surrounded by idolaters.*

i·dol·a·trous (ī dol′ə trəs) *adj.* **1.** of, relating to, or characteristic of idolatry. **2.** given to worshiping an idol or idols: *an idolatrous people.* **3.** given to great or excessive admiration or devotion. —**i·dol′a·trous·ly,** *adv.* —**i·dol′a·trous·ness,** *n.*

i·dol·a·try (ī dol′ə trē) *n., pl.* **-tries. 1.** the worship of idols. **2.** great or excessive admiration or devotion. [Old French *idolatrie* worship of idols, through Latin, going back to Greek *eidōlo-latreiā,* from *eidōlon* image + *latreiā* worship.]

i·dol·ize (ī′də līz′) *v.t.,* **-ized, -iz·ing. 1.** to look upon with great or excessive admiration or devotion. **2.** to worship as an idol. —**i′dol·i·za′tion,** *n.*

I·dom·e·neus (ī dom′ə nūs′, -nūs′) *n.* in Greek legend, a king of Crete and leader of the Cretans in the Trojan War.

i·dyll (ī′dəl) *also,* **i·dyl.** *n.* **1.** a short descriptive pastoral poem or work of prose in which the characters are usually shepherds and the setting is simple, rustic, and peaceful. **2.** a situation or scene suitable for such a work: *Their valley is an idyll.* **3.** a long descriptive or narrative poem. [Latin *īdyllium* pastoral poem, from Greek *eidyllion* little picture, pastoral poem, diminutive of *eidos* form, picture.]

i·dyl·lic (ī dil′ik) *adj.* **1.** of, relating to, or having the nature of an idyll. **2.** having natural, simple, or poetic charm: *Their home has an idyllic setting.* —**i·dyl′li·cal·ly,** *adv.*

-ie *suffix* (used to form nouns) **1.** little or dear: *lassie.* ➡ also used with proper nouns as an expression of affection or intimacy, as in *Joanie.* **2.** of a certain kind or quality: *sweetie, meanie.* [Form of -Y².]

i.e., that is. [Abbreviation of Latin *id est.*]

-ier *suffix* (used to form nouns) a person who is concerned or has to do with (that which is indicated by the stem): *cashier, financier.* [French *-ier,* from Latin *-ārius.* See -ARY¹.]

if (if) *conj.* **1.a.** in case that; supposing that: *If I make a mistake, I'll admit it. If he is sick, will he still come?* **b.** granting that: *Even if she stays, I can't. If you didn't see the incident, who did?* **2.** on condition that: *I will sing, if you will accompany me.* **3.** whether: *I don't know if they will be there.* **4.** even though; although: *It was a nice, if humid, day.* **5.** used in exclamatory clauses to express wish, surprise, or annoyance: *If we had only known. Well, if it isn't my old friend!* —*n.* **1.** a restriction or condition: *The plan has too many ifs.* **2.** a supposition or possibility. [Old English *gif* supposing that, whether, though.]

• **if not.** perhaps; possibly: *It was a good, if not excellent, play.*

if·fy (if′ē) *adj.,* **-fi·er, -fi·est.** *Informal.* not certain or definite; questionable: *The outcome of the election is still iffy.* [IF + -Y¹.]

ig·loo (ig′lü) *n., pl.* **-loos.** a dome-shaped hut used by Eskimos, usually built of blocks of hardened snow. [Eskimo *igdlu* house.]

ig·ne·ous (ig′nē əs) *adj.* **1.** *Geology.* produced by conditions involving great heat or volcanic action, as rocks formed from molten material within the earth. **2.** of, relating to, resembling, or characteristic of fire. [Latin *igneus* of fire, from *ignis* fire.]

ig·nis fat·u·us (ig′nis fach′ü əs) *pl.* **ig·nes fat·u·i** (ig′nēz-fach′ü ī′). will-o'-the-wisp. [Modern Latin *ignis fatuus* literally, foolish fire; referring to the unpredictability of its movement.]

ig·nite (ig nīt′) *v.,* **-nit·ed, -nit·ing.** —*v.t.* **1.** to burn or set on fire; kindle. **2.** to make intensely excited or agitated: *to ignite a mob with fiery words.* —*v.i.* to begin to burn; catch on fire. [Latin *ignītus,* past participle of *ignīre* to set on fire, from *ignis* fire.] —**ig·nit′a·ble,** *adj.* —**ig·nit′er,** *n.* —For Synonyms *(v.t.),* see light¹.

ig·ni·tion (ig nish′ən) *n.* **1.** the act of igniting or the state of being ignited. **2.** a device or system for igniting the fuel and air mixture within the cylinders of an internal-combustion engine.

ig·no·ble (ig nō′bəl) *adj.* **1.** without honor or worth; mean; base: *an ignoble motive.* **2.** of low birth or common origin. [Latin *īgnōbilis* unknown, undistinguished, from *in-* not + Old Latin *gnōbilis* famous, of noble birth.] —**ig·no′ble·ness,** *n.* —**ig·no′bly,** *adv.*

ig·no·min·i·ous (ig′nə min′ē əs) *adj.* **1.** marked by or involving dishonor or disgrace; shameful: *ignominious punishment, an ignominious defeat.* **2.** deserving of shame or contempt; despicable. [Latin *īgnōminiōsus* disgraceful, from *īgnōminia.* See IGNO-MINY.] —**ig·no·min′i·ous·ly,** *adv.*

ig·no·min·y (ig′nə min′ē) *n., pl.* **-min·ies. 1.** a state or condition of disgrace; dishonor; infamy. **2.** something that causes or deserves disgrace or dishonor. [Latin *īgnōminia* disgrace, dishonor, from *in-* not + *nōmen* name, reputation.]

ig·no·ra·mus (ig′nə rā′məs, -ram′əs) *n., pl.* **-mus·es.** a thoroughly ignorant person. [From *Ignoramus,* a satirical play by George Ruggle, 1575-1622, from Latin *īgnōrāmus* we do not know.]

ig·no·rance (ig′nər əns) *n.* the state or quality of being ignorant.

ig·no·rant (ig′nər ənt) *adj.* **1.** lacking in knowledge or education. **2.** uninformed or unaware (of something): *ignorant of the details.* **3.** resulting from or showing lack of knowledge or education: *an ignorant statement.* [Latin *īgnōrāns,* present participle of *īgnōrāre* not to know.] —**ig′no·rant·ly,** *adv.*

ig·nore (ig nôr′) *v.t.,* **-nored, -nor·ing.** to refuse to take notice

of or recognize; disregard intentionally. [Latin *ignōrāre* not to know.] —**ig·nor′er,** *n.*

Ig·o·rot (ig′ə rōt′) *n., pl.* **-rot** or **-rots**. **1.a.** any of several tribes of the Philippines, living in the mountainous area of north-central Luzon. **b.** a member of one of these tribes. **2.** their language, a member of the Austronesian family of languages. [Spanish *igorrote;* probably of Tagalog origin.]

i·gua·na (i gwä′nə) *n.* **1.** a large, greenish brown, black-banded lizard, *Iguana iguana,* found from Mexico to northern South America, usually living in trees and having a large fold of skin suspended from its throat and a ridge of enlarged scales down the center of the back.

iguana

Length: to 6 feet (2 meters). **2.** any of various other lizards, family Iguanidae, as the chuckwalla, *Sauromalus obesus,* of the United States and Mexico. [Spanish *iguana,* from Carib *iwana.*]

IHS, a monogram and symbol representing the name of Jesus. [Late Latin *IHS,* representing Greek IHΣ, short for Greek IHΣOYΣ Jesus (in Greek capital letters).]

i·kon (ī′kon) *n.* icon *(def. 1).*

il-¹, form of **in-¹** before *l,* as in *illegitimate.*

il-², form of **in-²** before *l,* as in *illuminate.*

IL, the postal abbreviation for Illinois.

-ile *also,* **-il.** *suffix* used to form adjectives expressing relationship, similarity, capability, suitability, or liability: *contractile, motile.* [Latin *-ilis, -īlis,* often through French *-il, -ile.*]

il·e·ac (il′ē ak′) *adj.* of or relating to the ileum.

il·e·i·tis (il′ē ī′tis) *n.* inflammation of the ileum.

il·e·um (il′ē əm) *n., pl.* **il·e·a** (il′ē ə). the last section of the small intestine, extending from the jejunum to the large intestine. [Modern Latin *ileum,* from Latin *īleum* groin, flank.]

i·lex (ī′leks) *n.* **1.** holly. **2.** holm oak.

il·i·ac (il′ē ak′) *adj.* of, relating to, or near the ilium.

Il·i·ad (il′ē əd) *n.* an ancient Greek epic poem describing some of the events of the Trojan War, believed to have been composed by Homer.

il·i·um (il′ē əm) *n., pl.* **il·i·a** (il′ē ə). the broad upper portion of the hipbone forming the prominence of the hip. [Modern Latin *ilium,* from Latin *īlium* groin, flank.] For illustration, see **pelvis.**

ilk (ilk) *n.* kind; sort; class: *you and others of your ilk.* [Old English *ilca* same.]

ill (il) *adj.,* **worse, worst. 1.** not healthy or well; sick. **2.** less or poorer than hoped for; unsatisfactory: *ill health, ill fortune.* **3.** hostile, cruel, or unfriendly: *ill treatment, ill feeling.* **4.** causing or caused by harm, destruction, or evil; adverse: *The war had many ill consequences.* *—adv.* **1.** in a hostile, cruel, or unfriendly manner; badly: *to speak ill of someone.* **2.** imperfectly; poorly: *Such an opinionated statement ill becomes a judge.* **3.** scarcely; hardly: *We can ill afford the time wasted.* *—n.* **1.** something causing trouble, evil, or misfortune: *war, pestilence, and other ills.* **2.** a sickness or ailment: *Arthritis is a common ill.* [Old Norse *illr* bad.]

• **ill at ease.** nervous and uncomfortable: *The shy child was ill at ease with strangers.*

I'll (īl) *contr.* **1.** I will. **2.** I shall.

ill. 1. illustrated. **2.** illustration.

Ill., Illinois.

ill-ad·vised (il′əd vīzd′) *adj.* acting or done without sound advice or sufficient consideration; unwise. —**ill-ad·vis·ed·ly** (il′əd vī′zid le), *adv.*

ill-bred (il′bred′) *adj.* badly brought up or trained; unmannerly; rude.

ill-con·sid·ered (il′kən sid′ərd) *adj.* done without proper consideration or forethought; unwise.

ill-de·fined (il′di fīnd′) *adj.* poorly defined or outlined; unclear: *ill-defined areas of responsibility.*

ill-dis·posed (il′dis pōzd′) *adj.* **1.** having a hostile attitude; unfriendly: *They are ill-disposed toward us.* **2.** not disposed to-

ward something; reluctant: *The dictator was ill-disposed to holding a free election.*

il·le·gal (i lē′gəl) *adj.* **1.** not legal; unlawful. **2.** not authorized by official rules, as in sports. —**il·le′gal·ly,** *adv.*

il·le·gal·i·ty (il′ē gal′i tē) *n., pl.* **-ties. 1.** the state or quality of being illegal; unlawfulness. **2.** an illegal act.

il·leg·i·ble (i lej′ə bəl) *adj.* difficult or impossible to read; not legible: *The tiny handwriting on the envelope was illegible.* —**il·leg′i·bil′i·ty, il·leg′i·ble·ness,** *n.* —**il·leg′i·bly,** *adv.*

il·le·git·i·ma·cy (il′i jit′ə mə sē) *n., pl.* **-cies.** the state or quality of being illegitimate.

il·le·git·i·mate (il′i jit′ə mit) *adj.* **1.** having no authority; not authorized; not lawful: *an illegitimate ruler.* **2.** born of parents who are not married to each other. **3.** contrary to logic or to good usage; improper; incorrect: *an illegitimate conclusion, an illegitimate construction in writing.* —**il′le·git′i·mate·ly,** *adv.*

ill-fat·ed (il′fā′tid) *adj.* **1.** having a bad fate; doomed from the start: *The ill-fated play closed after the second performance.* **2.** characterized by or causing misfortune; unlucky: *an ill-fated day.*

ill-fa·vored (il′fā′vərd) *adj.* **1.** unpleasant in appearance; ugly. **2.** offensive; disagreeable; objectionable.

ill-found·ed (il′foun′did) *adj.* having a weak or invalid basis; not supported by facts or logical reasoning.

ill-got·ten (il′got′ən) *adj.* acquired by evil or dishonest means: *ill-gotten gains.*

ill-hu·mored (il′hū′mərd, -ū′mərd) *adj.* having or showing a bad temperament or humor; irritable; cross.

il·lib·er·al (i lib′ər əl, i lib′rəl) *adj.* **1.** narrow in outlook or attitude; bigoted; intolerant. **2.** not generous in giving; stingy. —**il·lib′er·al′i·ty,** *n.* —**il·lib′er·al·ly,** *adv.*

il·lic·it (i lis′it) *adj.* forbidden by law; not allowed. —**il·lic′it·ly,** *adv.* —**il·lic′it·ness,** *n.*

il·lim·it·a·ble (i lim′i tə bəl) *adj.* incapable of being limited or bounded; limitless. —**il·lim′it·a·bil′i·ty, il·lim′it·a·ble·ness,** *n.* —**il·lim′it·a·bly,** *adv.*

Il·li·nois (il′ə noi′, -noiz′) *n., pl.* **-nois.** a member of a confederation of North American Indians of the Algonquian language family, formerly living in northern Illinois, southern Wisconsin, and parts of Iowa and Missouri, now living in northeast Oklahoma. [French *Illinois;* of Algonquian origin.]

il·liq·uid (i lik′wid) *adj.* **1.** of or relating to financial assets not easily converted to cash. **2.** of or relating to a debt or claim not recorded in a document. [IL-¹ + LIQUID.]

il·lit·er·a·cy (i lit′ər ə sē) *n., pl.* **-cies. 1.** an inability to read or write. **2.** a lack of education or culture. **3.** an error indicative of such an inability to read.

il·lit·er·ate (i lit′ər it) *adj.* **1.** unable to read or write. **2.** lacking or indicating a lack of education or culture. *—n.* a person who is illiterate. —**il·lit′er·ate·ly,** *adv.* —**il·lit′er·ate·ness,** *n.*

ill-man·nered (il′man′ərd) *adj.* having bad manners; rude.

ill-na·tured (il′nā′chərd) *adj.* having or showing a disagreeable or surly disposition. —**ill′-na′tured·ly,** *adv.*

ill·ness (il′nis) *n.* **1.** a condition or period of being ill: *During my illness, I stayed indoors.* **2.** something one is ill with; disease: *Children are susceptible to various illnesses.*

il·log·i·cal (i loj′i kəl) *adj.* **1.** devoid of or contrary to logic: *an illogical conclusion.* **2.** showing a lack of good sense or reasoning: *illogical behavior.* —**il·log′i·cal′i·ty** (i loj′i kal′i tē), **il·log′i·cal·ness,** *n.* —**il·log′i·cal·ly,** *adv.*

ill-spent (il′spent′) *adj.* spent or passed unwisely; wasted: *ill-spent earnings, an ill-spent afternoon.*

ill-starred (il′stärd′) *adj.* ill-fated or unlucky as if under the influence of an evil star.

ill-suit·ed (il′sū′tid) *adj.* not fit or well adapted; inappropriate: *behavior ill-suited to an occasion.*

ill-tem·pered (il′tem′pərd) *adj.* having or showing a bad temper; grouchy; cross.

ill-timed (il′tīmd′) *adj.* coming at the wrong time; badly timed.

ill-treat (il′trēt′) *v.t.* to treat badly or cruelly; maltreat. —**ill′-treat′ment,** *n.*

il·lume (i lūm′) *v.t.,* **-lumed, -lum·ing.** *Archaic.* illuminate.

il·lu·mi·nant (i lū′mi nənt) *n.* something that gives light.

il·lu·mi·nate (i lū′mə nāt′) *v.t.,* **-nat·ed, -nat·ing. 1.** to give light to; light up: *The full moon illuminated the sky.* **2.** to decorate with lights: *to illuminate a fountain at night.* **3.** to make clear; elucidate; clarify: *lectures that illuminate history.* **4.** to give

a	at	e	end	o	hot	u	up	hw	white		about
ā	ape	ē	me	ō	old	ū	use	ng	song		taken
ä	far	i	it	ô	fork	ü	rule	th	thin	ə	pencil
âr	care	ī	ice	oi	oil	u̇	pull	th	this		lemon
		îr	pierce	ou	out	ûr	turn	zh	measure		circus

knowledge to; enlighten; inform: *We were greatly illuminated by the discussion.* **5.** to decorate (a scroll, manuscript, or page) with ornamental designs and miniature figures in gold, silver, and brilliant colors, as was done esp. in medieval times. [Latin *illūminātus*, past participle of *illūmināre* to make light, from *in* in + *lūmen* light.]

il·lu·mi·nat·ing (i lü′mə nā′ting) *adj.* **1.** giving knowledge; enlightening; instructive. **2.** giving light.

il·lu·mi·na·tion (i lü′mə nā′shən) *n.* **1.** the act of illuminating or the state of being illuminated. **2.** an amount or supply of light: *This lamp gives poor illumination.* **3.** decoration with lights. **4.** the decoration of a scroll, manuscript, or page of a book with gold or colored designs and figures, as in medieval times. **5.** intellectual or spiritual enlightenment. **6.** the amount of light falling on a square unit of surface area, measured in lumens.

illumination *(def. 4)*

il·lu·mi·na·tive (i lü′mə nā′tiv) *adj.* illuminating.

il·lu·mi·na·tor (i lü′mə nā′tər) *n.* **1.** something that illuminates; source of light. **2.** any of several devices for projecting, concentrating, or reflecting light. **3.** an artisan who illuminates a scroll, manuscript, or page.

il·lu·mine (i lü′min) *v.t.,* **-mined, -min·ing.** illuminate. [Latin *illūmināre* to make light. See ILLUMINATE.]

illus. 1. illustrated. **2.** illustrator.

ill-use (*v.,* il′ūz′; *n.,* il′ūs′) *v.t.,* **-used, -us·ing.** to treat badly, cruelly, or unfairly; abuse. —*n.* bad, cruel, or unfair treatment. Also (*n.*), **ill-us·age** (il′ūs′ij, -zij).

il·lu·sion (i lü′zhən) *n.* **1.a.** a false or misleading belief or idea; misconception. **b.** a general impression that does not correspond to actual fact: *The spire gives the illusion that the church is taller than it is.* **2.** a sensory perception that causes a false or distorted impression: *an optical illusion.* **3.** a very fine silk net used over wedding gowns and for such items as veils; tulle. [Latin *illūsiō* mocking, deception.] —**il·lu′sion·ar′y,** *adj.*

il·lu·sion·ist (i lü′zhə nist) *n.* an entertainer who produces illusions; magician.

il·lu·sive (i lü′siv) *adj.* deceptive or unreal; illusory. —**il·lu′sive·ly,** *adv.* —**il·lu′sive·ness,** *n.*

il·lu·so·ry (i lü′sə rē) *adj.* of the nature of or causing an illusion; deceptive or unreal.

illust. 1. illustrated. **2.** illustration.

il·lus·trate (il′ə strāt′, i lus′trāt) *v.t.,* **-trat·ed, -trat·ing. 1.** to make clear or explain, as by the use of examples or comparisons. **2.** to provide with pictures, diagrams, or other visual representations that serve to explain or decorate: *An artist was hired to illustrate the book.* **3.** to be or serve as an example, explanation, or instance of: *These early stories illustrate the writer's preoccupation with death.* [Latin *illūstrātus,* past participle of *illūstrāre* to light up.]

il·lus·tra·tion (il′ə strā′shən) *n.* **1.** something, as an example or comparison, used to clarify or explain. **2.** a picture, diagram, drawing, or other visual representation used to explain or decorate written or printed matter. **3.** the act or art of illustrating.

il·lus·tra·tive (i lus′trə tiv, il′ə strā′-) *adj.* used or serving to illustrate. —**il·lus′tra·tive·ly,** *adv.*

il·lus·tra·tor (il′ə strā′tər) *n.* **1.** an artist who makes or creates illustrations, as for books or magazines. **2.** a person or thing that illustrates.

il·lus·tri·ous (i lus′trē əs) *adj.* **1.** known for greatness or excellence; distinguished or renowned; eminent: *an illustrious edu-*

cator. **2.** conferring greatness, distinction, or glory: *illustrious acts.* [Latin *illūstris* bright, famous + -OUS.] —**il·lus′tri·ous·ly,** *adv.* —**il·lus′tri·ous·ness,** *n.* —For Synonyms, see **famous.**

ill will, hostile feeling; enmity.

il·men·ite (il′mə nīt′) *n.* a lustrous, black oxide mineral mined as an ore of titanium. Formula: $FeTiO_3$ [German *ilmenit,* from the *Ilmen* Mountains of the southern Urals, where it was first identified, + *-it* -ite[1].]

I'm (īm) *contr.* I am.

im-[1], form of **in-[1]** before *b, m, p,* as in *immoral.*

im-[2], form of **in-[2]** before *b, m, p,* as in *imbibe.*

im·age (im′ij) *n.* **1.** a representation or likeness of a person, animal, or thing: *The ancient coin bore an image of the emperor.* **2.** a picture or idea held in the mind of something that is not actually present to the senses: *I had formed an image of the house before I saw it.* **3.** a person or thing that closely resembles another; counterpart: *You are the image of your father.* **4.** a typical example; picture: *She is the image of good health.* **5.** a description or figure of speech, esp. a metaphor or simile. **6.** the impression created by a person, group, or organization, as by actions or advertising: *The company is promoting its new image.* **7.** *Optics.* **a.** a representation of an object produced when light rays from the object are focused on a surface, as by a lens or mirror. Also, **real image. b.** a representation of an object as seen through a lens or in a mirror, which cannot be focused and viewed on a screen. Also, **virtual image. 8.** a chemical change that occurs in the emulsion on a photographic plate when a real image is focused on the plate. The image is invisible until the film is developed. Also *(def. 8),* **latent image.** —*v.t.,* **-aged, -ag·ing. 1.** to make or form an image of. **2.** to form a mental image of; imagine. **3.** to give back an image of; reflect. **4.** to give a vivid description of in speech or writing. [Old French *image* statue, representation of a divinity, from Latin *imāgō* statue, likeness.]

im·age·ry (im′ij rē) *n., pl.* **-ries. 1.** mental images collectively, as formed by memory or imagination. **2.a.** the use of descriptions or figures of speech in writing or speech. **b.** such descriptions or figures collectively.

i·mag·i·na·ble (i maj′ə nə bəl) *adj.* capable of being imagined. —**i·mag′i·na·bly,** *adv.*

i·mag·i·nar·y (i maj′ə ner′ē) *adj.* **1.** existing only in the imagination; unreal. **2.** of or relating to imaginary numbers.

imaginary number 1. a complex number of the form $a + bi$, in which i is the square root of negative one $(\sqrt{-1})$, a and b are real numbers, and b is not equal to zero. **2.** any number or expression incorporating the square root of a negative number, as $4 + \sqrt{-9}$.

i·mag·i·na·tion (i maj′ə nā′shən) *n.* **1.** the power or process of forming mental images of what is not actually present to the senses: *I'll have to use my imagination to think how the furniture should be arranged.* **2.** the mental ability to create original images or ideas of things never experienced or to reconstruct or combine past experiences to form new images or ideas: *Think of the imagination it took to create that painting!* **3.** the mental ability to understand or respond intelligently to new ideas, esp. to the original ideas of others.

> **Synonyms** Imagination, fancy, and fantasy denote the faculty or process of forming or projecting mental images. Imagination is the most general term, connoting the capacity of the mind to create or call up images of things not present to the senses: *the use of imagination in painting or poetry, to see something in one's imagination.* Fancy suggests images unrelated to reality or in unlikely conjunction: *Fairies are creatures of fancy. Many modern paintings are products of fancy, and are not meant to be realistic.* Fantasy connotes images even less related to reality: *I escaped from my humdrum existence by conjuring up a fantasy world for myself.*

i·mag·i·na·tive (i maj′ə nə tiv) *adj.* **1.** having or exhibiting creative ability or a good or active imagination: *an imaginative child.* **2.** produced or characterized by creativity or imagination: *an imaginative story.* —**i·mag′i·na·tive·ly,** *adv.* —**i·mag′i·na·tive·ness,** *n.*

i·mag·ine (i maj′in) *v.,* **-ined, -in·ing.** —*v.t.* **1.** to picture in the mind; form a mental image of: *Can you imagine me with blond hair?* **2.** to have as an opinion; suppose; guess: *I don't imagine that they will come if it rains.* —*v.i.* **1.** to have as a picture in the mind; think. **2.** to use the imagination. [Old French *imaginer* to fancy, conceive, from Latin *imāginārī* to fancy.]

im·ag·ing (im′ij ing) *n.* **1.** the use of a remote-control machine or instrument to obtain pictures of distant objects, as of the earth from a satellite in space. **2.** the use of specialized radiographic techniques and instruments, as in a CAT scan or MRI, to view the internal organs of the human body. [IMAGE + -ING[1].]

im·ag·ism (im′ə jiz′əm) *n.* a movement in poetry in the early twentieth century that emphasized the use of free verse, colloquial

language, a wide range of subjects, and precise, concrete images. —im'ag·ist, *n., adj.*

i·ma·go (i mā'gō) *n., pl.* **i·ma·goes** or **i·mag·i·nes** (i maj'ə-nēz'). an insect in the adult, sexually mature stage following metamorphosis. [Latin *imāgō* likeness.]

i·mam (i mäm') *n.* **1.** the leader of prayer in a Muslim mosque. **2.** *also,* **Imam.** any of various Muslim leaders having both temporal and religious authority, esp. one claiming descent from Muhammad. [Arabic *imām.*]

im·bal·ance (im bal'əns) *n.* a lack of balance.

im·be·cile (im'bə səl) *n.* **1.** a stupid or foolish person. **2.** a person who is mentally retarded, having a mental age of up to eight years. ➡ now considered obsolete. —*adj.* imbecilic. [French *imbécile* weak, from Latin *imbēcillus* literally, without support, from *in-* not + *bacillus* little staff.]

im·be·cil·ic (im'bə sil'ik) *adj.* stupid or foolish: *imbecilic behavior.*

im·be·cil·i·ty (im'bə sil'i tē) *n., pl.* **-ties. 1.** the condition of being an imbecile. **2.** stupidity or foolishness. **3.** an imbecilic thought, statement, or act.

im·bed (im bed') embed.

im·bibe (im bīb') *v.,* **-bibed, -bib·ing.** —*v.t.* **1.** to take into the mouth and swallow (liquid); drink. **2.** to take in as if by drinking; absorb. **3.** to take in and keep mentally: *to imbibe knowledge.* —*v.i.* to drink something, esp. liquor. [Latin *imbibere* to drink in.] —im·bib'er, *n.*

im·bri·cate (*adj.,* im'bri kit, -kāt'; *v.,* im'bri kāt') *adj.* **1.** arranged in a regular, overlapping pattern, as fish scales or shingles. **2.** decorated with a regular pattern of overlapping edges. —*v.t., v.i.,* **-cat·ed, -cat·ing.** to overlap in a regular pattern. [Latin *imbricātus,* past participle of *imbricāre* to cover with tiles, from *imbrex* roof tile.]

im·bri·ca·tion (im'bri kā'shən) *n.* **1.** an overlapping of the edges. **2.** decoration consisting of a regular pattern of overlapping edges.

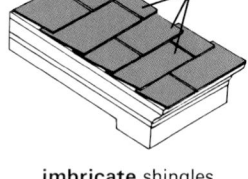

Shingles

imbricate shingles

im·bro·glio (im brōl'yō) *n., pl.* **-glios. 1.a.** a complicated dispute or disagreement: *to get into an imbroglio over property boundaries.* **b.** a confused or complicated state of affairs. **2.** a confused heap. [Italian *imbroglio* trouble, intrigue, from *imbrogliare* to confuse; of uncertain origin.]

im·brue (im brü') *v.t.,* **-brued, -bru·ing.** to stain or soak, esp. with blood. [Old French *embruer* to moisten, possibly going back to Latin *in* in + *bibere* to drink.]

im·bue (im bū') *v.t.,* **-bued, -bu·ing. 1.** to pervade, permeate, or inspire, as with emotions, ideals, or opinions: *to be imbued with the spirit of justice.* **2.** to fill completely, as with color; saturate. [Latin *imbuere* to moisten, stain, accustom.]

im·i·ta·ble (im'i tə bəl) *adj.* capable of being imitated.

im·i·tate (im'i tāt') *v.t.,* **-tat·ed, -tat·ing. 1.** to follow or try to follow the example of: *to imitate an older brother or sister.* **2.** to reproduce the behavior or mannerisms of: *The comedian imitated many famous people.* **3.** to make a duplicate of: *That diagram is difficult to imitate.* **4.** to have the appearance of; look like; resemble: *The floors are painted to imitate marble.* [Latin *imitārī,* past participle of *imitārī* to copy.] —im'i·ta'tor, *n.*

Synonyms Imitate, copy, mimic, and ape mean to follow or reproduce something, as an action, very closely. Imitate means to emulate the essentials of a model faithfully, even though the details may not be exact: *to imitate a painter's style.* Copy, on the other hand, connotes reproducing in detail in order to resemble the original in every way: *She spent her days painting in the museum, trying to copy great masterpieces.* Mimic connotes reproducing or simulating actions or behavior so as to produce a comic or ironic effect: *The children mimicked the teacher behind his back.* Ape connotes imitating in such a way that either the original or the imitator seems ridiculous: *to ape someone's mannerisms to get a laugh, to mindlessly ape the gestures of someone admired.*

im·i·ta·tion (im'i tā'shən) *n.* **1.** the act of imitating. **2.** a result or product of imitating. **3.** a reproduction, esp. one that is inferior in quality: *That is not an authentic Ming vase, but merely an imitation.* —*adj.* made to counterfeit something genuine or superior; not genuine: *imitation mink.*

im·i·ta·tive (im'i tā'tiv) *adj.* **1.** imitating or tending to imitate: *Children are very imitative of their elders.* **2.** characterized by or showing imitation: *Portrait painting is an imitative art. The word "chirp" is imitative of the sound made by a bird.* **3.** not genuine: *imitative jewelry.* **4.** onomatopoeic. —im'i·ta'tive·ly, *adv.* —im'i·ta'tive·ness, *n.*

im·mac·u·late (i mak'yə lit) *adj.* **1.** free from dust, grime, or clutter; extremely clean or neat: *Their house is always immaculate.* **2.** free from spot or stain; unblemished: *an immaculate complexion.* **3.** free from fault; flawless: *an immaculate performance of a play.* **4.** free from sin; undefiled; pure. [Latin *immaculātus* unstained, going back to *in-* not + *macula* spot.] —im·mac'u·late·ly, *adv.* —im·mac'u·late·ness, *n.*

Immaculate Conception, the Roman Catholic dogma that the Virgin Mary was conceived free from original sin.

im·ma·nent (im'ə nənt) *adj.* existing or remaining within; indwelling: *the idea that deity is immanent in the universe.* [Late Latin *immanēns,* present participle of *immanēre* to dwell within, from Latin *in* in + *manēre* to remain.] —im'ma·nence, im'ma·nen·cy, *n.* —im'ma·nent·ly, *adv.*

Im·man·u·el (i man'ū əl) *also,* **Emmanuel.** *n.* in Judaism and Christianity, the Messiah. [Hebrew *imanu el* God is with us, from *imanu* with us + *el* God.]

im·ma·te·ri·al (im'ə tîr'ē əl) *adj.* **1.** of little or no significance or value; unimportant: *It is wholly immaterial to me what you decide.* **2.** not consisting of matter; incorporeal. **3.** *Law.* not material to the issue at hand. —im'ma·te'ri·al·ly, *adv.* —im'ma·te'ri·al·ness, *n.*

im·ma·ture (im'ə chûr', -tûr', -tyùr') *adj.* **1.** not having reached full growth or development; not mature. **2.** foolish, puerile, or infantile: *immature behavior.* —im'ma·ture'ly, *adv.* —im'ma·ture'ness, im'ma·tu'ri·ty, *n.*

im·meas·ur·a·ble (i mezh'ər ə bəl) *adj.* not capable of being measured; boundless. —im·meas'ur·a·bil'i·ty, im·meas'ur·a·ble·ness, *n.* —im·meas'ur·a·bly, *adv.*

im·me·di·a·cy (i mē'dē ə sē) *n.* the state or quality of being immediate.

im·me·di·ate (i mē'dē it) *adj.* **1.** occurring or accomplished without delay; instant: *We received an immediate reaction to our proposal. The commander ordered an immediate withdrawal of the troops.* **2.** of, relating to, or involving the present time: *We must take care of our immediate needs.* **3.** close in time or space; near: *the immediate neighborhood, the immediate future.* **4.** nearest in line or relationship: *one's immediate family, a worker's immediate superior.* **5.** acting or existing without any intervening agency; directly related: *The evidence had no immediate bearing on the case.* [Late Latin *immediātus* next, going back to Latin *in-* not + *medius* middle.] —im·me'di·ate·ness, *n.*

im·me·di·ate·ly (i mē'dē it lē) *adv.* **1.** without delay; at once; instantly: *She recognized him immediately.* **2.** without intervening time or space: *We spoke to them immediately after the meeting.* **3.** without anything coming in between; directly: *The airplane was immediately overhead.*

im·med·i·ca·ble (i med'i kə bəl) *adj.* incurable.

im·me·mo·ri·al (im'ə môr'ē əl) *adj.* extending back beyond memory or record; very ancient. —im'me·mo'ri·al·ly, *adv.*

im·mense (i mens') *adj.* of great size, extent, or degree; huge; vast. [Latin *immēnsus* literally, not measured.] —im·mense'ly, *adv.* —im·mense'ness, *n.* —For Synonyms, see **huge.**

im·men·si·ty (i men'si tē) *n., pl.* **-ties.** the state or quality of being immense; hugeness; vastness.

im·merge (i mûrj') *v.t.,* **-merged, -merg·ing.** immerse. [Latin *immergere* to plunge into.]

im·merse (i mûrs') *v.t.,* **-mersed, -mers·ing. 1.** to plunge or dip into water or other liquid, so as to cover completely. **2.** to baptize by immersion. **3.** to involve deeply; absorb: *They immersed themselves in their work.* [Latin *immersus,* past participle of *immergere* to plunge into.] —im·mers'i·ble, *adj.* —For Synonyms, see **dip.**

im·mer·sion (i mûr'zhən, -shən) *n.* **1.** the act of immersing or the state of being immersed. **2.** a method of baptism in which part or all of the body is submerged in water.

im·mi·grant (im'i grənt) *n.* a person who immigrates. —*adj.* **1.** of or relating to an immigrant or immigrants. **2.** coming into a country or region of which one is not a native in order to make a permanent residence there.

im·mi·grate (im'i grāt') *v.,* **-grat·ed, -grat·ing.** —*v.i.* to come into a country or region of which one is not a native in order to make a permanent residence there. —*v.t.* to bring in as immigrants. [Latin *immigrātus,* past participle of *immigrāre* to go into.]

im·mi·gra·tion (im'i grā'shən) *n.* **1.** the act of immigrating. **2.** a group of immigrants.

a	at	e	end	o	hot	u	up	hw	white	(	about
ā	ape	ē	me	ō	old	ū	use	ng	song	{	taken
ä	far	i	it	ô	fork	ü	rule	th	thin		pencil
âr	care	ī	ice	oi	oil	ù	pull	th	this		lemon
		îr	pierce	ou	out	ûr	turn	zh	measure	(	circus

im·mi·nence (im′ə nəns) *n.* the state or quality of being imminent. Also, **im′mi·nen·cy.**

im·mi·nent (im′ə nənt) *adj.* about to happen; impending; threatening. [Latin *imminēns,* present participle of *imminēre* to hang over, threaten.] —**im′mi·nent·ly,** *adv.*

im·mis·ci·ble (i mis′ə bəl) *adj.* not capable of being mixed. —**im·mis′ci·bil′i·ty,** *n.*

im·mo·bile (i mō′bəl, -bēl) *adj.* **1.** incapable of moving or of being moved; fixed. **2.** not moving; motionless: *to stand immobile.* —**im′mo·bil′i·ty,** *n.*

im·mo·bi·lize (i mō′bə līz′) *v.t.,* **-lized, -liz·ing.** to make immobile; fix in place. —**im·mo′bi·li·za′tion,** *n.*

im·mod·er·ate (i mod′ər it) *adj.* exceeding usual or proper limits; not moderate: *immoderate demands.* —**im·mod′er·ate·ly,** *adv.* —**im·mod′er·ate·ness, im·mod·er·a·tion** (i mod′ə rā′shən), *n.* —For Synonyms, see **excessive.**

im·mod·est (i mod′ist) *adj.* **1.** lacking or indicating a lack of shame, esp. about one's body. **2.** tending to praise oneself too much or take too much credit; boastful. **3.** not proper or decent: *immodest dress.* —**im·mod′est·ly,** *adv.* —**im·mod′es·ty,** *n.*

im·mo·late (im′ə lāt′) *v.t.,* **-lat·ed, -lat·ing. 1.** to offer in sacrifice, esp. to kill as a sacrificial victim. **2.** to destroy, esp. by burning: *The bombing immolated the city.* [Latin *immolātus,* past participle of *immolāre* to sacrifice; literally, to sprinkle meal on a sacrificial victim, from *in* in, on + *mola* meal.] —**im′mo·la′tion,** *n.* —**im′mo·la′tor,** *n.*

im·mor·al (i môr′əl, i mor′-) *adj.* **1.** not conforming to what is generally considered to be good or right; not moral; wicked: *an immoral person, an immoral action.* **2.** violating standards of decency; lewd: *an immoral show.* —**im·mor′al·ly,** *adv.*

Immoral, amoral, and **unmoral** mean not moral. They are used differently, however, and are often confused. **Immoral** connotes consciously opposing or overstepping ethical bounds and restraints: *Everyone knows that stealing is immoral.* **Amoral** may connote being indifferent to or unaffected by moral standards: *I think it is amoral to ignore poverty in our society. The laws of science are by their nature amoral.* **Unmoral,** a rarer term, usually connotes a complete lack of morality or understanding of morality: *Animals are unmoral.* It may, however, be used to suggest something closer to *amoral: their unmoral disregard of the community's well-being.*

im·mor·al·ist (i môr′ə list, i mor′-) *n.* an advocate of immorality.

im·mo·ral·i·ty (im′ə ral′i tē) *n., pl.* **-ties. 1.** immoral character or quality. **2.** an immoral act.

im·mor·tal (i môr′təl) *adj.* **1.** not subject to death; undying or living on after death. **2.** remembered or celebrated through all subsequent time: *Shakespeare's immortal works.* **3.** lasting through all time; existing forever; eternal. **4.** of or relating to immortality or immortal beings. —*n.* **1.** an immortal being, as a god in Greek mythology. **2.** a person remembered or celebrated through all subsequent time. [Latin *immortālis* deathless, everlasting, going back to *in-* not + *mors* death.] —**im·mor′tal·ly,** *adv.*

im·mor·tal·i·ty (im′ôr tal′i tē) *n.* **1.** the supposed power of living on after death; not being subject to death. **2.** the fact of being remembered or celebrated through all subsequent time. **3.** existence through all time; fact of being eternal.

im·mor·tal·ize (i môr′tə līz′) *v.t.,* **-ized, -iz·ing.** to make remembered or celebrated through all subsequent time.

im·mor·telle (im′ôr tel′) *n.* an everlasting plant or flower. [French *immortelle,* from Latin *immortālis* deathless. See IMMORTAL.]

im·mov·a·ble (i mü′və bəl) *adj.* **1.** incapable of moving or being moved; fixed firmly in place; stationary. **2.** not easily altered or shaken; steadfast; unyielding: *to be immovable in one's opinions.* **3.** not easily stirred or affected by emotion: *an immovable audience.* —*n.* **immovables.** *Law.* property that cannot be moved from place to place, as land; real property. —**im·mov′a·bil′i·ty, im·mov′a·ble·ness,** *n.* —**im·mov′a·bly,** *adv.*

im·mune (i mūn′) *adj.* **1.** protected from a disease or infection, as by inoculation. **2.** of or relating to the production of antibodies, usually in reaction to a particular antigen: *an immune response to a virus.* **3.** not susceptible or responsive; as to something disagreeable or harmful: *immune to threats.* **4.** exempt, as from laws. [Latin *immūnis* exempt.]

immune system, a network of cells and tissues that protects the body from disease by destroying microbes, toxins, and other foreign substances. Lymphocytes, a major component of this network, produce antibodies that render antigens harmless.

im·mu·ni·ty (i mū′ni tē) *n., pl.* **-ties. 1.** resistance to a specific disease or infection because of the presence of antibodies. **2.** freedom or protection from anything disagreeable or harmful: *immunity from attack.* **3.** freedom from prosecution or civil lawsuits, or exemption, as from taxes, granted to an individual or group or retained by the government: *Foreign diplomats are often granted immunity from some of the laws of a country. The witness testified after being granted immunity from prosecution in the case.* [Latin *immūnitās exemption.*] —For Synonyms, see **exemption.**

im·mu·nize (im′yə nīz′) *v.t.,* **-nized, -niz·ing.** to make immune, as by inoculation against a disease. —**im′mu·ni·za′tion,** *n.*

im·mu·no·as·say (im′yə nō as′ā, i mū′-) *n.* a method for measuring and analyzing the levels of various antibodies in the body, used to determine the presence of disease-causing organisms, drugs, or tumors.

im·mu·no·de·fi·cien·cy (im′yə nō di fish′ən sē, i mū′-) *n., pl.* **-cies.** an inability to produce sufficient antibodies or properly activated T cells to fight infection. —**im′mu·no·de·fi′cient,** *adj.*

im·mu·no·glob·u·lin (im′yə nō glob′yə lin, i mū′-) *n.* any globulin that can act as an antibody, found in plasma, urine, spinal fluid, and other tissues.

im·mu·nol·o·gy (im′yə nol′ə jē) *n.* the branch of medical science dealing with the immune system and immunity from disease. —**im′mu·no·log′ic;** *also,* **im′mu·no·log′i·cal,** *adj.* —**im′mu·nol′o·gist,** *n.*

im·mure (i myùr′) *v.t.,* **-mured, -mur·ing.** to enclose within or as within walls, as in a prison. [Medieval Latin *immurare* to put within four walls, from Latin *in* in + *mūrus* wall.] —**im·mure′ment,** *n.*

im·mu·ta·ble (i mū′tə bəl) *adj.* not capable of changing or being changed; unchanging: *an immutable law of nature.* —**im·mu′ta·bil′i·ty, im·mu′ta·ble·ness,** *n.* —**im·mu′ta·bly,** *adv.*

imp (imp) *n.* **1.** a young or small demon; mischievous spirit. **2.** a mischievous child. [Old English *impa* young shoot, graft, going back to Late Latin *impotus* a graft, from Greek *emphytos* engrafted. In English this word once meant young shoot or offspring of a family and later came to mean mischievous child or young demon.]

imp. 1. imperative. **2.** imperfect. **3.** import. **4.** important. **5.** imported. **6.** importer. **7.** imprimatur.

im·pact (im′pakt) *n.* **1.a.** the impetus or force of one object striking against another: *The car hit the wall with great impact.* **b.** the action of one object striking against another: *The glass shattered upon impact. At the time of impact, I had my seat belt on.* **2.** a forcible impression or influence; strong effect: *Computerization has had a great impact on business.* —*v.t.* **1.** to pack closely together. **2.** to hit with force: *The asteroid may impact the earth.* **3.** to have a strong influence on; affect greatly: *Rainy weather impacted our harvest this year.* —*v.i.* to have an impact; affect greatly (with *on*): *The economic slowdown will impact on our sales.* [Latin *impactus,* past participle of *impingere* to strike against.]

im·pact·ed (im pak′tid) *adj.* **1.** (of a tooth) wedged between the jawbone and another tooth so that it cannot erupt. **2.** closely packed together or wedged in.

im·pair (im pâr′) *v.t.* to lessen the quality, strength, or value of; damage; weaken: *The accident impaired the worker's vision. Short-sightedness impaired the negotiations.* [Old French *empeier,* going back to Latin *in* in + *pējor* worse.] —**im·pair′er,** *n.*

im·pair·ment (im pâr′mənt) *n.* the act of impairing or the state of being impaired.

im·pa·la (im pal′ə, -pä′lə) *n.* a slender antelope, *Aepyceros melampus,* native to eastern and southern Africa, having a reddish or golden brown coat, the male of which has curving black horns. It is noted for its speed and grace and can cover as much as 35 feet (11 meters) in one leap. Height: 3 feet (0.9 meter) at the shoulder. [Of Zulu origin.]

impala

im·pale (im pāl′) *v.t.,* **-paled, -pal·ing. 1.** to fix on a stake or other pointed object by piercing. **2.** to torture or put to death in this way. [Medieval Latin *impalare,* going back to Latin *in* in, on + *pālus* stake.] —**im·pale′ment,** *n.*

im·pal·pa·ble (im pal′pə bəl) *adj.* **1.** incapable of being perceived by the sense of touch: *Moonlight is impalpable.* **2.** not readily grasped by the mind; incomprehensible: *impalpable distinctions.* —**im·pal′pa·bil′i·ty,** *n.* —**im·pal′pa·bly,** *adv.*

im·pan·el (im pan′əl) *also,* **empanel** *v.t.,* **-eled, -el·ing;** *also, British,* **-elled, -el·ling. 1.** to place (someone) on a panel or list, as for jury duty. **2.** to select (a jury) from such a list. —**im·pan′el·ment,** *n.*

im·part (im pärt′) *v.t.* **1.** to make known; disclose; tell: *to impart information.* **2.** to provide or bestow: *The judge's presence imparted a sense of dignity to the committee.* [Latin *impartīre* to share with, going back to *in* in + *pars* portion, share.] —For Synonyms, see **communicate.**

im·par·tial (im pär′shəl) *adj.* not favoring one more than another; without prejudice; unbiased. —**im·par′tial·ly,** *adv.* —For Synonyms, see **just**[1].

im·par·ti·al·i·ty (im pär′shē al′i tē) *n.* freedom from bias; fairness.

im·pass·a·ble (im pas′ə bəl) *adj.* that cannot be passed or traveled over, across, or through: *an impassable road.* —**im·pass′a·bil′i·ty, im·pass′a·ble·ness,** *n.* —**im·pass′a·bly,** *adv.*

im·passe (im′pas′, im pas′) *n.* **1.** a position or situation from which proceeding or advancing is impossible; deadlock: *The jury reached an impasse in its deliberations.* **2.** a road or passage open only at one end; dead end. [French *impasse,* from *in-* not (from Latin *in-*) + *passer* to go across. See PASS.]

im·pas·si·ble (im pas′ə bəl) *adj.* **1.** incapable of suffering or pain. **2.** not subject to injury or harm; invulnerable. **3.** impassive. [Church Latin *impassibilis* incapable of suffering, going back to Latin *in-* not + *passus,* past participle of *patī* to suffer.] —**im·pas′si·bly,** *adv.*

im·pas·sioned (im pash′ənd) *adj.* filled with or characterized by passion or strong feeling; fiery; ardent: *an impassioned speech.*

im·pas·sive (im pas′iv) *adj.* not feeling or showing emotion; apathetic; unmoved. —**im·pas′sive·ly,** *adv.* —**im·pas′sive·ness, im·pas′siv′i·ty,** *n.*

im·pas·to (im pas′tō) *n., pl.* **-tos. 1.** the style or technique of painting by laying on paint thickly. **2.** the application of a thick layer of paint. **3.** the paint laid on in this manner, often with a palette knife. —*v.t.,* **-toed, -to·ing.** to paint with this technique. [Italian *impasto,* from *impastare* to cover with a paste, from *in-*[2] (from Latin *in* in, into) + *pasta* paste. See PASTA.]

im·pa·tience (im pā′shəns) *n.* **1.** the inability to tolerate or endure irritation, delay, or opposition; lack of patience. **2.** restless eagerness, as for change or activity.

im·pa·tiens (im pā′shənz) *n., pl.* **-tiens.** any of numerous plants, genus *Impatiens,* of the balsam family, that have fleshy stems and flowers bearing five petals, grown in gardens or as houseplants for their colorful flowers.

impatiens

im·pa·tient (im pā′shənt) *adj.* **1.** unable to tolerate or endure irritation, delay, or opposition. **2.** showing lack of patience: *an impatient expression.* **3.** restlessly eager: *The children were impatient for the weekend to come.* **4.** intolerant (with *of*): *My teacher is impatient of bad manners.* —**im·pa′tient·ly,** *adv.*

im·peach (im pēch′) *v.t.* **1.** to bring formal charges of crime or misconduct in office against (a public official) before a tribunal authorized to try the charges. **2.** to question, challenge, or cast doubt on: *The attorney impeached the credibility of the witness.* **3.** to show that (a witness) is not credible. [Old French *empe(s)cher* to hinder, from Late Latin *impedicāre* to entangle, from Latin *in* in, on + *pedica* fetter.]

> **Usage** **Impeach** is often mistakenly used to refer to the action of trying, convicting, and removing a public official from office for crime or misconduct, but the word actually refers only to the action of bringing a formal accusation. For example, President Andrew Johnson was impeached by the House of Representatives and tried by the Senate, but he was found not guilty and remained in office.

im·peach·a·ble (im pē′chə bəl) *adj.* **1.** liable to be impeached. **2.** making liable to impeachment: *an impeachable offense.* —**im·peach′a·bil′i·ty,** *n.*

im·peach·ment (im pēch′mənt) *n.* **1.** the act of impeaching or the state of being impeached. **2.a.** the arraignment of a public official before a competent tribunal. **b.** in the United States, the presentation of formal charges against a federal official by the House of Representatives, after which a trial is held before the Senate. **c.** the act or instance of showing that a witness at a trial is untruthful or not credible.

im·pearl (im pûrl′) *v.t.* **1.** to form into pearllike drops. **2.** to make pearly. **3.** to adorn with pearls or pearllike drops.

im·pec·ca·ble (im pek′ə bəl) *adj.* **1.** free from error or defect; faultless; flawless: *impeccable taste, impeccable judgment.* **2.** incapable of sinning or doing wrong; unerring. [Latin *impeccābilis,* from *in-* not + *peccāre* to sin.] —**im·pec′ca·bil′i·ty,** *n.* —**im·pec′ca·bly,** *adv.*

im·pe·cu·ni·ous (im′pi kū′nē əs) *adj.* having little or no money; poor; penniless. [IN-[1] + Latin *pecūniōsus* rich, from *pecūnia* money, from *pecu* cattle (wealth in early times being computed in terms of the number of cattle owned).] —**im′pe·cu′ni·ous·ly,** *adv.* —**im′pe·cu′ni·ous·ness,** *n.*

im·ped·ance (im pē′dəns) *n.* the opposition that an electric circuit offers to the flow of alternating current, measured in ohms.

im·pede (im pēd′) *v.t.,* **-ped·ed, -ped·ing.** to interfere with or stop the progress or action of; hinder; obstruct. [Latin *impedīre* to shackle, hamper, from *in-* not + *ped-,* stem of *pēs* foot.] —**im·ped′er,** *n.* —For Synonyms, see **hinder**[1].

im·ped·i·ment (im ped′ə mənt) *n.* **1.** something that impedes; obstruction; obstacle. **2.** a physical defect, esp. of speech. [Latin *impedīmentum* hindrance, from *impedīre.* See IMPEDE.] —For Synonyms, see **obstacle.**

im·ped·i·men·ta (im ped′e men′tə) *pl. n.* things that impede, esp. the baggage, equipment, or supplies of an army. [Latin *impedīmenta* baggage, plural of *impedīmentum* hindrance. See IMPEDIMENT.]

im·pel (im pel′) *v.t.,* **-pelled, -pel·ling. 1.** to force or urge some action: *War impelled them to leave the country.* **2.** to propel or cause to move forward: *The boat was impelled by a strong wind.* [Latin *impellere* to drive on or against.]

im·pel·ler (im pel′ər) *n.* **1.** a person or thing that impels. **2.** a rotor, as of a pump or blower, for transmitting motion.

im·pend (im pend′) *v.i.* **1.** to be about to occur; threaten: *A storm impended.* **2.** to be suspended; hang (with *over*): *The cliffs seem to impend over the road.* [Latin *impendēre.*]

im·pend·ent (im pen′dənt) *adj.* impending.

im·pend·ing (im pen′ding) *adj.* about to occur; threatening: *an impending crisis.*

im·pen·e·tra·ble (im pen′i trə bəl) *adj.* **1.** not able to be pierced, entered, or passed through: *an impenetrable forest.* **2.** not open or receptive, as to influences or ideas. **3.** incapable of being comprehended; inscrutable: *an impenetrable mystery.* —**im·pen′e·tra·bil′i·ty, im·pen′e·tra·ble·ness,** *n.* —**im·pen′e·tra·bly,** *adv.*

im·pen·i·tent (im pen′i tənt) *adj.* not penitent; obdurate. —**im·pen′i·tence,** *n.* —**im·pen′i·tent·ly,** *adv.*

imper., imperative.

im·per·a·tive (im per′ə tiv) *adj.* **1.** not to be avoided or evaded; absolutely necessary; urgent: *It is imperative that we leave at once.* **2.** of the nature of or expressing a command; commanding; authoritative: *an imperative tone of voice.* **3.** of, relating to, or designating the grammatical mood used to express commands, requests, or exhortations. —*n.* **1.** something that is imperative, as a command or obligation. **2.a.** the imperative mood. **b.** a verb or verb form in this mood. [Late Latin *imperātīvus* relating to a command, from Latin *imperātum* command.] —**im·per′a·tive·ly,** *adv.* —**im·per′a·tive·ness,** *n.* —For Synonyms *(adj.),* see **urgent.**

im·pe·ra·tor (im′pə rā′tər, -rä′-) *n.* **1.a.** a Roman emperor. ➠ often used as a title. **b.** a victorious Roman general. ➠ conferred as an honorary title. **2.** any emperor. [Latin *imperātor,* from *imperāre* to command.]

im·per·cep·ti·ble (im′pər sep′tə bəl) *adj.* **1.** too slight, gradual, delicate, or subtle to be easily perceived: *imperceptible changes.* **2.** not perceptible by the mind or senses. —**im′per·cep′ti·bil′i·ty,** *n.* —**im′per·cep′ti·bly,** *adv.*

im·per·cep·tive (im′pər sep′tiv) *adj.* not having the power or

a	at	e	end	o	hot	u	up	hw	white		about
ā	ape	ē	me	ō	old	ū	use	ng	song		taken
ä	far	i	it	ô	fork	u̇	rule	th	thin	ə	pencil
âr	care	ī	ice	oi	oil	u̇	pull	<u>th</u>	this		lemon
				îr	pierce	ou	out	ûr	turn	zh	measure		circus

faculty of perception; not perceptive. —**im′per·cep′tive·ly**, *adv.* —**im′per·cep′tive·ness**, *n.*

imperf., imperfect.

im·per·fect (im pûr′fikt) *adj.* **1.** having a fault or flaw; not perfect; faulty: *an imperfect diamond.* **2.** not fully developed, formed, or done; incomplete: *I have an imperfect understanding of Spanish.* **3.** of, relating to, or designating the verbal tense that expresses action, usually in the past, that is continuous or not completed. **4.** *Botany.* diclinous; unisexual. —*n.* the imperfect tense, expressed in English by the use of progressive verb forms, for example, *was reading.* —**im′per·fect·ly**, *adv.* —**im·per′fect·ness**, *n.*

im·per·fec·tion (im′pər fek′shən) *n.* **1.** the state or quality of being imperfect. **2.** something that detracts from or impairs completeness, soundness, or perfection; fault; flaw: *There was an imperfection in the cloth.*

im·per·fo·rate (im pûr′fər it, -fə rāt′) *adj.* **1.** having no holes or openings; not perforated. **2.** (of stamps) not separated by rows of perforations. —*n.* an imperforate stamp.

im·pe·ri·al (im pîr′ē əl) *adj.* **1.** of or relating to an empire or to the rule of an emperor or empress. **2.** of or relating to a country's military, political, or economic power or influence over other countries or tributaries. **3.** of, relating to, or having the rank of emperor or empress. **4.a.** having great dignity; majestic; magnificent. **b.** overbearing; imperious: *a haughty and imperial manner.* **5.** of imposing size or superior quality. **6.** conforming to the official British standard of weights and measures: *an imperial bushel.* —*n.* a small, pointed beard growing on the chin. [Late Latin *imperiālis* relating to an empire, from *imperium* rule, empire.] —**im·pe′ri·al·ly**, *adv.* —For Synonyms, see **royal.**

imperial gallon, a British gallon, equal to 1⅕ U.S. gallons (4.54 liters).

im·pe·ri·al·ism (im pîr′ē ə liz′əm) *n.* **1.** the policy of extending a country's power or influence over other countries by military, political, or economic means. **2.** an imperial system of government; rule of an emperor or empress.

im·pe·ri·al·ist (im pîr′ē ə list) *n.* **1.** a person who favors or supports imperialism. **2.** a person who engages in imperialism. —*adj.* of, relating to, or favoring imperialism. —**im·pe′ri·al·is′tic**, *adj.* —**im·pe′ri·al·is′ti·cal·ly**, *adv.*

im·per·il (im per′əl) *v.t.* **-iled, -il·ing;** *also, British,* **-illed, -il·ling.** to expose to danger; put in peril.

im·pe·ri·ous (im pîr′ē əs) *adj.* **1.** like or characteristic of an emperor or dictator; domineering; overbearing. **2.** not to be avoided; imperative; urgent: *an imperious necessity.* [Latin *imperiōsus* powerful, tyrannical, from *imperium* rule, empire.] —**im·pe′ri·ous·ly**, *adv.* —**im·pe′ri·ous·ness**, *n.*

im·per·ish·a·ble (im per′i shə bəl) *adj.* not subject to destruction or decay; not perishable; enduring. —**im·per′ish·a·bil′i·ty, im·per′ish·a·ble·ness**, *n.* —**im·per′ish·a·bly**, *adv.*

im·pe·ri·um (im pîr′ē əm) *n., pl.* **-pe·ri·a** (-pîr′ē ə). **1.** supreme power or authority. **2.** the right to command, esp. the right to use the force of the state to enforce the law. [Latin *imperium* rule, empire.]

im·per·ma·nent (im pûr′mə nənt) *adj.* subject to change; not permanent; transient. —**im·per′ma·nence, im·per′ma·nen·cy**, *n.* —**im·per′ma·nent·ly**, *adv.*

im·per·me·a·ble (im pûr′mē ə bəl) *adj.* not capable of being permeated; impenetrable. —**im·per′me·a·bil′i·ty**, *n.* —**im·per′me·a·bly**, *adv.*

im·per·mis·si·ble (im′pər mis′ə bəl) *adj.* not permissible. —**im′per·mis′si·bil′i·ty**, *n.* —**im′per·mis′si·bly**, *adv.*

im·per·son·al (im pûr′sə nəl) *adj.* **1.** not concerned with or referring to a particular person or persons; not personal: *impersonal comments.* **2.** not existing or thought of as existing as a person: *an impersonal deity.* **3.a.** lacking feeling or emotion; unfeeling: *an impersonal manner.* **b.** lacking warmth; cold and inhospitable: *an impersonal waiting room.* **4.** *Grammar.* **a.** (of a verb) denoting an action by an unspecified subject, used in the third person singular, as *rained* in *It rained for several days.* **b.** (of a pronoun) referring to an indefinite subject. —**im·per·son·al·i·ty** (im pûr′sə nal′i tē), *n.* —**im·per′son·al·ly**, *adv.*

im·per·son·al·ize (im pûr′sə nə līz′) *v.t.* **-ized, -iz·ing.** to make impersonal.

im·per·son·ate (im pûr′sə nāt′) *v.t.* **-at·ed, -at·ing. 1.** to take on or reproduce the appearance, behavior, or mannerisms of: *The comedian impersonates famous politicians.* **2.** to act the part of (a character) in a play. [IM-² + Latin *persōna* mask + -ATE¹ (suggesting the putting on of a mask, with reference to the use of masks in the ancient Greek or Roman theater).] —**im·per′son·a′tion**, *n.* —**im·per′son·a′tor**, *n.*

im·per·ti·nence (im pûr′tə nəns) *n.* **1.** offensive boldness or rudeness; insolence. **2.** an impertinent act or remark. **3.** lack of pertinence; inappropriateness. Also, **im·per′ti·nen·cy.**

im·per·ti·nent (im pûr′tə nənt) *adj.* **1.** offensively bold or rude; insolent. **2.** not pertinent; inappropriate. —**im·per′ti·nent·ly**, *adv.*

im·per·turb·a·ble (im′pər tûr′bə bəl) *adj.* not able to be excited or disturbed; calm. —**im′per·turb′a·bil′i·ty**, *n.* —**im′per·turb′a·bly**, *adv.*

im·per·vi·ous (im pûr′vē əs) *adj.* **1.** not easily affected, influenced, or disturbed; unreceptive: *impervious to criticism.* **2.** incapable of being passed through or penetrated; impenetrable: *impervious to water.* —**im·per′vi·ous·ly**, *adv.* —**im·per′vi·ous·ness**, *n.*

im·pe·ti·go (im′pi tī′gō) *n.* a contagious skin disease, usually caused by bacterial infection, characterized by small blisters that break open and release pus. [Latin *impetīgō*, from *impetere* to attack.]

im·pet·u·os·i·ty (im pech′ü os′i tē) *n., pl.* **-ties. 1.** the state or quality of being impetuous. **2.** an impetuous act.

im·pet·u·ous (im pech′ü əs) *adj.* **1.** tending to rush headlong into things; impulsive and energetic: *an impetuous person.* **2.** made or done impulsively and suddenly; rash: *an impetuous choice.* **3.** moving with great force or violence; rapid; furious: *impetuous winds.* [Late Latin *impetuōsus* violent, from Latin *impetus* attack.] —**im·pet′u·ous·ly**, *adv.* —**im·pet′u·ous·ness**, *n.*

im·pe·tus (im′pi təs) *n.* **1.a.** the momentum of a moving body. **b.** the force that puts a body in motion. **2.** the force, strength, or energy that leads to action; incentive or stimulus: *The exposure of widespread graft among officials gave impetus to demands for reform.* [Latin *impetus* attack.]

im·pi·e·ty (im pī′i tē) *n., pl.* **-ties. 1.** lack of reverence for the gods or a god. **2.** lack of dutifulness or respect toward those deserving of respect. **3.** an impious act.

im·pinge (im pinj′) *v.i.* **-pinged, -ping·ing. 1.** to intrude on the rights or property of another; encroach; infringe: *to impinge upon another's domain.* **2.** to strike or dash; hit (with *on, upon,* or *against*): *The light from the projector impinged on the screen.* **3.** to have an effect; impact: *The new research impinged on several scientific theories.* [Latin *impingere* to strike against.] —**im·pinge′ment**, *n.*

im·pi·ous (im′pē əs, -pī′əs) *adj.* lacking in reverence for gods or a god; irreligious. **2.** undutiful or disrespectful. —**im′pi·ous·ly**, *adv.* —**im′pi·ous·ness**, *n.*

imp·ish (im′pish) *adj.* of or like an imp; mischievous: *an impish grin.* —**imp′ish·ly**, *adv.* —**imp′ish·ness**, *n.*

im·plac·a·ble (im plak′ə bəl, -plā′kə-) *adj.* not able to be placated or appeased: *implacable anger.* —**im·plac′a·bil′i·ty**, *n.* —**im·pla′ca·bly**, *adv.*

im·plant (*v.,* im plant′; *n.,* im′plant′) *v.t.* **1.** to fix firmly and deeply; instill: *Parents implant their values in their children.* **2.** to set firmly in the ground; root; embed: *We implanted the tree in a permanent location.* **3.** to insert (an object or material) in the body by surgery. —*n.* an object or material, as tissue, an artificial device, or a drug pellet, surgically inserted in the body.

im·plan·ta·tion (im′plan tā′shən) *n.* **1.** the act of implanting or the state of being implanted. **2.** something implanted.

im·plau·si·ble (im plô′zə bəl) *adj.* not believable as being likely: *an implausible explanation.* —**im·plau′si·bil′i·ty**, *n.* —**im·plau′si·bly**, *adv.*

im·ple·ment (*n.,* im′plə mənt; *v.,* im′plə ment′) *n.* **1.** something used in performing a task; tool; instrument. **2.** a person who serves as a tool or agent. —*v.t.* **1.** to put into effect; make actual; carry out: *to implement a decision of the court, to implement a proposal.* **2.** to provide with implements. [Late Latin *implēmentum* a filling up, instrument, from Latin *implēre* to fill, fulfill.] —**im′ple·men·ta′tion**, *n.*

im·pli·cate (im′pli kāt′) *v.t.* **-cat·ed, -cat·ing. 1.** to claim or show to be involved, as in a crime or conspiracy: *The suspect implicated two others in the crime.* **2.** to connect closely with something; involve; include (often with *in*): *Researchers believe a new virus is implicated in the spread of the disease.* **3.** *Archaic.* to imply. **4.** *Archaic.* to fold or twist together; entangle; intertwine. [Latin *implicātus*, past participle of *implicāre* to infold, involve. Doublet of EMPLOY, IMPLY.]

im·pli·ca·tion (im′pli kā′shən) *n.* **1.a.** something that is logically implied; requirement or consequence: *a decision with many implications for the future.* **b.** something that is hinted or suggested, but not directly expressed: *Did you gather the implications of the speaker's remark?* **2.** the act of implicating or the state of being implicated, as in a crime. **3.** the act of implying or the state of being implied.

im·plic·it (im plis′it) *adj.* **1.** suggested or understood, though not directly expressed: *Disapproval was implicit in their reaction.* **2.** without reservation or doubt; unquestioning; absolute: *implicit faith, implicit confidence.* **3.** contained in the nature of something

or someone, though not apparent; latent; potential: *implicit ability.* [Latin *implicitus,* the later past participle of *implicāre* to infold, involve.] —im·plic'it·ly, *adv.* —im·plic'it·ness, *n.*

im·plied (im plīd') *adj.* involved, suggested, or required without being directly expressed: *implied criticism.*

im·pli·ed·ly (im plī'id lē) *adv.* by implication.

im·plode (im plōd') *v.,* -plod·ed, -plod·ing. —*v.i.* to explode inward. —*v.t.* to cause to explode inward.

im·plore (im plôr') *v.t.,* -plored, -plor·ing. 1. to call upon in supplication; ask earnestly; beseech: *They implored the entire community to become involved in the project.* 2. to beg or pray for earnestly: *to implore pardon.* [Latin *implōrāre* to invoke with tears, beseech.] —im·plor'er, *n.* —im·plor'ing·ly, *adv.* —For Synonyms, see **beg.**

im·plo·sion (im plō'zhən) *n.* explosion inward.

im·ply (im plī') *v.t.,* -plied, -ply·ing. 1. to indicate or suggest without direct statement: *Are you implying that I caused the trouble?* 2. to involve as a necessary part, condition, or consequence; require the truth of: *"They have left" implies "they have been here."* [Middle French *emplier* to infold, involve, from Latin *implicāre.* Doublet of EMPLOY, IMPLICATE.]

im·po·lite (im'pə līt') *adj.* not having or exhibiting good manners; not courteous; rude. [Latin *impolītus* rough, unpolished.] —im'po·lite'ly, *adv.* —im'po·lite'ness, *n.*

im·pol·i·tic (im pol'i tik) *adj.* not conforming to or showing good judgment; not politic; inexpedient.

im·pon·der·a·ble (im pon'dər ə bəl) *adj.* not capable of being weighed or evaluated with certainty. —*n.* an imponderable thing or factor: *There are too many imponderables for a hasty decision.* —im·pon'der·a·bil'i·ty, im·pon'der·a·ble·ness, *n.* —im·pon'der·a·bly, *adv.*

im·port (*v.,* im pôrt'; *n.,* im'pôrt') *v.t.* 1.a. to bring in (goods) from a foreign country for commercial purposes. b. to bring in or introduce from an external or foreign source: *to import ideas.* 2. to have as a meaning; mean: *Do those words import trouble?* —*v.i.* to be of importance; matter. —*n.* 1. something that is imported for commercial purposes. 2. the act of importing goods; importation. 3. meaning; significance: *the import of a statement.* 4. consequence; importance: *That is a matter of great import.* [Latin *importāre* to carry in.] —im·port'a·bil'i·ty, *n.* —im·port'a·ble, *adj.* —im·port'er, *n.*

im·por·tance (im pôr'təns) *n.* 1. the state or quality of being important. 2. special authority, social position, or influence.

im·por·tant (im pôr'tənt) *adj.* 1. having special value, relevance, or meaning: *Your friendship is very important to me.* 2. having special authority, social position, or influence: *They are important members of the community.* 3. having or giving the impression of a false or exaggerated sense of importance: *All the clerks in the boutique had an important air about them.* [French *important* of consequence, from Medieval Latin *importans,* present participle of *importare* to be of weight or force, from Latin *importāre* to carry in.] —im·por'tant·ly, *adv.*

im·por·ta·tion (im'pôr tā'shən) *n.* 1. the act of importing. 2. something that is imported.

im·por·tu·nate (im pôr'chə nit) *adj.* annoyingly or stubbornly persistent; insistent: *an importunate shopkeeper, an importunate demand.* —im·por'tu·nate·ly, *adv.* —im·por'tu·nate·ness, *n.*

im·por·tune (im'pôr tün', -tūn', im pôr'chən) *v.t.,* -tuned, -tun·ing. to trouble with persistent requests or demands. —*adj.* importunate. [Medieval Latin *importunari* to be troublesome, from Latin *importūnus* difficult of access, unsuitable; literally, lacking a harbor, from *in-* not + *portus* harbor.] —im'por·tune'ly, *adv.* —im'por·tun'er, *n.*

im·por·tu·ni·ty (im'pôr tü'ni tē, -tū'-) *n., pl.* -ties. 1. the act of importuning. 2. the state of being importunate. 3. importunities. persistent requests or demands.

im·pose (im pōz') *v.,* -posed, -pos·ing. —*v.t.* 1. to establish or apply by legal means as an obligation: *to impose taxes, to impose a penalty.* 2. to inflict or enforce by or as by authority: *to impose one's will on others.* 3. to force (oneself or one's presence) upon another or others: *They imposed themselves on us for a month.* 4. to pass off (something false or worthless) as genuine or valuable. 5. to arrange (type or plates) for printing so that the printed sheets will be in proper order when folded. —*v.i.* 1. to force oneself or one's presence upon another or others; intrude: *Are you sure I'm not imposing?* 2. to take advantage of (with *on* or *upon*): *I wouldn't impose on our friendship by asking you to lend me money.* [French *imposer* to put on, inflict; a modification (influenced by French *poser* to place, put) of Latin *impōnere* to place on, deceive.] —im·pos'er, *n.*

im·pos·ing (im pō'zing) *adj.* marked by great size or dignity; exciting awe or admiration; impressive. —im·pos'ing·ly, *adv.*

im·po·si·tion (im'pə zish'ən) *n.* 1. the act of imposing.

2. something that is imposed. 3. a request or demand that takes advantage of someone's goodwill. 4. the act or process of arranging type or plates for printing so that the printed sheets will be in proper order when they are folded.

im·pos·si·bil·i·ty (im pos'ə bil'i tē, im'pos-) *n., pl.* -ties. 1. the state or quality of being impossible. 2. something impossible.

im·pos·si·ble (im pos'ə bəl) *adj.* 1.a. not capable of coming into being or occurring; not possible: *It is impossible for humans to live forever.* b. not capable of being realized or accomplished; not feasible; impracticable: *That is an impossible scheme.* 2. not likely to occur; not probable: *Winning the sweepstakes is an impossible dream.* 3. not capable of being endured; extremely objectionable; intolerable: *an impossible person to work with, an impossible situation.* 4. not acceptable as truth; inconceivable: *an impossible story.* —im·pos'si·bly, *adv.*

im·post[1] (im'pōst') *n.* a duty, esp. on imported goods. [Medieval Latin *impostus,* from Latin *impositus,* past participle of *im·pōnere* to place on.]

im·post[2] (im'pōst') *n.* the uppermost part of a pillar, wall, or column, usually serving as a support for an arch. [Italian *imposta* upper part of a column, from *imporre* to place on, from Latin *impōnere.*]

impost[2]

im·pos·tor (im pos'tər) *n.* a person who deceives, esp. by assuming the name or character of another. [Late Latin *impostor,* from Latin *impōnere* to place on, deceive.]

im·pos·ture (im pos'chər) *n.* a deception; a fraudulent impersonation. [Late Latin *impostūra,* from Latin *impōnere* to place on, deceive.]

im·po·tence (im'pə təns) *n.* the quality or condition of being impotent. Also, **im'po·ten·cy.**

im·po·tent (im'pə tənt) *adj.* 1. lacking force or effectiveness; helpless. 2. physically weak. 3. (of males) incapable of having or maintaining an erection of the penis. [Latin *impotēns* powerless.] —im'po·tent·ly, *adv.*

im·pound (im pound') *v.t.* 1. to shut up in a pound: *to impound a stray dog.* 2. to seize and put in the custody of a court of law. 3. to collect (water), as in a reservoir. —im·pound'er, *n.* —im·pound'ment, *n.*

im·pov·er·ish (im pov'ər ish, -pov'rish) *v.t.* 1. to reduce to poverty; make very poor. 2. to deprive of strength, richness, or resources: *to impoverish the mind, to impoverish land.* [Old French *empoveriss-,* a stem of *empoverir* to make poor, going back to Latin *in* in + *pauper* poor.] —im·pov'er·ish·ment, *n.*

im·pov·er·ished (im pov'ə risht, -pov'risht) *adj.* 1. reduced to poverty; very poor: *an impoverished artist.* 2. reduced in strength, richness, or resources: *barren and impoverished soil.*

im·pow·er (im pou'ər) empower.

im·prac·ti·ca·ble (im prak'ti kə bəl) *adj.* 1. incapable of being accomplished, carried out, or put into practice: *an economically impracticable plan.* 2. incapable of being used; unserviceable: *an impracticable mechanism.* —im·prac'ti·ca·bil'i·ty, im·prac'ti·ca·ble·ness, *n.* —im·prac'ti·ca·bly, *adv.*

im·prac·ti·cal (im prak'ti kəl) *adj.* lacking good sense or usefulness; not practical. —im·prac'ti·cal·ly, *adv.*

im·prac·ti·cal·i·ty (im prak'ti kal'i tē) *n., pl.* -ties. 1. the state or quality of being impractical. 2. something impractical.

im·pre·cate (im'pri kāt') *v.t.,* -cat·ed, -cat·ing. to invoke or call down (evil or harm). [Latin *imprecātus,* past participle of *imprecārī* to call down on.] —im'pre·ca'tor, *n.* —im·pre·ca·to·ry (im'pri kə tôr'ē), *adj.*

im·pre·ca·tion (im'pri kā'shən) *n.* 1. the act of imprecating. 2. a curse.

im·pre·cise (im'prə sīs') *adj.* not precise; inexact. —im'pre·cise'ly, *adv.* —im·pre·ci·sion (im'prə sizh'ən), *n.*

im·preg·na·ble (im preg'nə bəl) *adj.* 1. incapable of being taken by force; able to resist attack: *an impregnable fortress.* 2. incapable of being moved, shaken, or overcome; firm: *an impregnable argument, impregnable virtue.* [Old French *imprenable* untakable, from *im-* not (from Latin *in-*) + *prenable.* See PREGNABLE.] —im·preg'na·bil'i·ty, *n.* —im·preg'na·bly, *adv.*

im·preg·nate (im preg'nāt) *v.t.,* -nat·ed, -nat·ing. 1. to make

a	at	e	end	o	hot	u	up	hw	white		about
ā	ape	ē	me	ō	old	ū	use	ng	song	ə	taken
ä	far	i	it	ô	fork	ů	rule	th	thin		pencil
âr	care	ī	ice	oi	oil	ů	pull	th	this		lemon
				îr	pierce	ou	out	ûr	turn	zh	measure		circus

pregnant; cause to conceive. **2.** to fertilize, as an ovum. **3.** to cause to be saturated, as with a liquid; permeate. **4.** to imbue or fill, as with ideas or feelings. —*adj.* impregnated. [Late Latin *impraegnātus,* past participle of *impraegnāre* to make pregnant, from Latin *in* in + *praegnāns* with child.] —**im·preg′na·tor,** *n.*

im·preg·na·tion (im′preg nā′shən) *n.* **1.** the act of impregnating or the state of being impregnated. **2.** something with which anything is impregnated.

im·pre·sa·ri·o (im′prə sär′ē ō′, -sâr′-) *n., pl.* **-sa·ri·os.** an organizer or manager of live entertainment events, esp. ballets, operas, or concerts. [Italian *impresario* manager, from *impresa* undertaking, going back to Latin *in* in, on + *prehendere* to take.]

im·pre·scrip·ti·ble (im′pri skrip′tə bəl) *adj.* that cannot legally be withdrawn or revoked; not subject to invalidation: *imprescriptible rights.* —**im′pre·scrip′ti·bil′i·ty,** *n.* —**im′pre·scrip′ti·bly,** *adv.*

im·press[1] (*v.,* im pres′; *n.,* im′pres′) *v.t.,* **-pressed** or *(archaic)* **-prest, -press·ing. 1.** to influence or produce a strong effect on the mind or feelings of: *The speaker's sincerity impressed us.* **2.** to strike in a specified manner: *She impressed me as being very rude.* **3.** to fix firmly in the mind or memory: *He impressed his belief in the cause on others.* **4.** to form or make a mark or design on: *to impress wax.* **5.** to form or make by pressing or stamping: *to impress figures on coins.* **6.** to apply with pressure: *to impress a seal into wax.* —*n.* **1.** the act of forming or making a mark or design on something by pressing or stamping. **2.** a mark or design made in this way. [Middle English *impressen,* from Latin *impressus,* past participle of *imprimere* to press into, imprint, from *in-* in, into + *premere* to press.] —**im·press′er,** *n.*

im·press[2] (im pres′) *v.t.* **-pressed** or *(archaic)* **-prest, -press·ing. 1.** to compel to enter military service, esp. the navy. **2.** to seize (property) for public use. [IM-[2] + PRESS[2].]

im·press·i·ble (im pres′ə bəl) *adj.* impressionable. —**im·press′i·bil′i·ty,** *n.*

im·pres·sion (im presh′ən) *n.* **1.** an effect or influence produced on the mind, senses, or feelings: *The experience left a lasting impression on me.* **2.** a generalized feeling or judgment about someone or something: *My first impression of him proved to be correct.* **3.** a notion or belief: *We were under the impression that they were sisters.* **4.** a mark or design produced by pressing or stamping: *We made impressions of our hands in the wet concrete.* **5.** an imitation of the behavior or mannerisms of a person or thing: *The child gave an impression of a monkey.* **6.** the act or process of impressing. **7.a.** the process of pressing plates or type onto a surface, esp. paper; printing. **b.** a printed copy. **c.** the total number of copies of a book or publication printed at one time. **8.** a mold or imprint of a tooth or the teeth and surrounding tissues, made in plaster, wax, or plastic.

im·pres·sion·a·ble (im presh′ə nə bəl, -presh′nə-) *adj.* easily impressed or influenced; very receptive to impressions. —**im·pres′sion·a·bil′i·ty,** *n.* —**im·pres′sion·a·bly,** *adv.*

impressionism
a painting of Monet by Pierre Auguste Renoir

im·pres·sion·ism (im presh′ə niz′əm) *also,* **Im·pres·sion·ism.** *n.* **1.** a method or school of painting developed in France in the nineteenth century by such painters as Claude Monet and Pierre Auguste Renoir, characterized by a careful study of nature

and the direct observation of the effects of light and color on a subject at a given moment. **2.** a method and style of musical composition of the late nineteenth and early twentieth centuries, typified by the works of Claude Debussy and Maurice Ravel, in which mood, atmosphere, and emotions are subtly evoked by characteristic harmonies and tonal progressions.

im·pres·sion·is·tic (im presh′ə nis′tik) *adj.* impressionist. —**im·pres′sion·is′ti·cal·ly,** *adv.*

im·pres·sion·ist (im presh′ə nist) *also,* **Im·pres·sion·ist.** *n.* a person who practices impressionism, esp. in painting. —*adj.* of, relating to, or characteristic of impressionism, esp. in painting.

im·pres·sive (im pres′iv) *adj.* producing or tending to make a strong impression; exciting attention, emotion, or admiration: *an impressive feat of strength, an impressive victory.* —**im·pres′sive·ly,** *adv.* —**im·pres′sive·ness,** *n.*

im·press·ment (im pres′mənt) *n.* **1.** the act of impressing persons into military service, esp. the navy. **2.** the act of seizing property for public use.

im·prest (im prest′) *Archaic.* a past tense and past participle of **impress**[1] and **impress**[2].

im·pri·ma·tur (im′pri mä′tər, -mā′-) *n.* **1.** an official license authorizing or approving the printing and publication of a book or article, esp. such a license granted by prelates of the Roman Catholic Church. **2.** any authorization or sanction; approval. [Modern Latin *imprimatur* let it be printed, from Latin *imprimere* to press into, imprint.]

im·print (*n.,* im′print′; *v.,* im print′) *n.* **1.** a mark or depression produced by pressing or stamping: *My head left an imprint on the pillow.* **2.** an effect or mark: *Years of struggle left their imprint on the artist.* **3.a.** a publisher's name, the place and date of publication, and sometimes a trademark, usually printed on the title page of a book. **b.** a printer's name and address on any printed matter. —*v.t.* **1.** to make or produce (a mark or design) by pressing or stamping. **2.** to mark, or produce a mark or design on, by pressing or stamping; print. **3.** to fix firmly in the mind or memory.

im·pris·on (im priz′ən) *v.t.* **1.** to put or keep in prison. **2.** to confine or restrain in any way: *The town was imprisoned by the heavy snow.* —**im·pris′on·ment,** *n.*

im·prob·a·bil·i·ty (im prob′ə bil′i tē, im′prob ə-) *n., pl.* **-ties. 1.** the quality of being improbable; unlikelihood. **2.** something improbable.

im·prob·a·ble (im prob′ə bəl) *adj.* not probable; unlikely. —**im·prob′a·ble·ness,** *n.* —**im·prob′a·bly,** *adv.*

im·promp·tu (im promp′tü, -tū) *adj.* made or done on the spur of the moment; without preparation; offhand: *The president gave an impromptu press conference.* —*n.* anything made or done on the spur of the moment. —*adv.* without preparation. [French *impromptu* unprepared, from Latin *in prōmptū* in readiness.]

im·prop·er (im prop′ər) *adj.* **1.** not in accordance with fact, truth, or established usage; erroneous: *That is an improper usage of the word.* **2.** not in accordance with accepted standards of propriety or good taste; indecorous: *improper behavior.* **3.** not suitable for the purpose or the circumstances; inappropriate: *improper dress for a formal occasion.* —**im·prop′er·ly,** *adv.*

improper fraction, a fraction whose numerator is greater than, or equal to, the denominator, such as $8/5$ or $6/6$.

im·pro·pri·e·ty (im′prə prī′i tē) *n., pl.* **-ties. 1.** the quality of being improper. **2.** improper action or behavior. **3.** the improper usage of a word or of language.

im·prove (im prüv′) *v.,* **-proved, -prov·ing.** —*v.t.* **1.** to raise to a higher or more desirable quality or condition; increase, as in value or excellence; make better: *to improve one's tennis, to improve one's mind by reading.* **2.** to increase the value of (land or property), as by cultivation or the erection of buildings. —*v.i.* to become better: *My French improved after a summer in Paris.* [Anglo-Norman *emprower* to benefit, turn to profit, from Old French *em-* in (from Latin *in*) + *prou* a benefit, profit (going back to Latin *prōdesse* to be of advantage).] —**im·prov′a·bil′i·ty,** *n.* —**im·prov′a·ble,** *adj.* —**im·prov′er,** *n.*

· **to improve on** (or **upon**). to do or make something better or more perfect than: *It is difficult to improve on nature. They improved on my plan.*

im·prove·ment (im prüv′mənt) *n.* **1.** the act of improving or the state of being improved. **2.** a change or addition that improves something, as in quality or value. **3.** a person or thing that is better or more perfect than another: *The group's new treasurer is an improvement over the past one.*

im·prov·i·dence (im prov′i dəns) *n.* the quality of being improvident; lack of foresight or thrift.

im·prov·i·dent (im prov′i dənt) *adj.* not cautious in providing for future needs; lacking foresight. —**im·prov′i·dent·ly,** *adv.*

im·prov·i·sa·tion (im prov′ə zā′shən, im′prə və-) *n.* **1.** the act or art of improvising. **2.** something that is improvised. —**im·prov′i·sa′tion·al,** *adj.*

im·pro·vi·sa·to·ry (im prov′ə zə tôr′ē, im′prə vī′zə-) *adj.* of, relating to, or characteristic of an improviser or improvisation.

im·pro·vise (im′prə vīz′) *v.,* **-vised, -vis·ing.** —*v.t.* **1.** to produce without preparation, esp. to make up and perform extemporaneously: *to improvise a monologue.* **2.** to devise or construct from whatever resources are on hand: *to improvise a bookcase out of crates.* —*v.i.* to do or make anything on the spur of the moment. [Italian *improvvisare* to produce without preparation, going back to Latin *imprōvīsus* unforeseen.] —**im′pro·vis′er;** *also,* **im′pro·vi′sor.**

im·pru·dence (im prü′dəns) *n.* **1.** the quality of being imprudent. **2.** imprudent action or behavior.

im·pru·dent (im prü′dənt) *adj.* lacking or showing a lack of prudence or discretion; rash; unwise. [Latin *imprūdēns* not foreseeing.] —**im·pru′dent·ly,** *adv.*

im·pu·dence (im′pyə dəns) *n.* **1.** the quality of being impudent; sauciness; insolence. **2.** impudent speech or behavior.

im·pu·dent (im′pyə dənt) *adj.* offensively forward; saucy; insolent. [Latin *impudēns* shameless.] —**im′pu·dent·ly,** *adv.*

im·pugn (im pūn′) *v.t.* **1.** to suggest there is something bad about; question the rightness of: *to impugn a benefactor's motives, to impugn the courts and laws.* **2.** *Archaic.* to challenge or attack; fight against; assail. [Latin *impūgnāre* to fight against.] —**im·pugn′a·ble,** *adj.* —**im·pugn′er,** *n.*

im·pulse (im′puls) *n.* **1.** a force that impels one to act without planning or reflection: *A sudden impulse led me to give away my favorite sweater.* **2.** a force that causes immediate motion; thrust; push: *The impulse of falling water turns the waterwheel.* **3.** motion caused immediately upon the application of force. **4.** a brief surge or pulsation of power or energy, as of a radio signal. **5.** a signal produced and carried by nerve cells to or from the central nervous system. [Latin *impulsus* a pushing against, incitement.]

im·pul·sion (im pul′shən) *n.* **1.** the act of impelling. **2.** onward motion resulting from such an act. **3.** an impulse to act: *We felt an impulsion to help them.*

im·pul·sive (im pul′siv) *adj.* **1.** inclined to act on impulse. **2.** resulting from impulse: *You will regret your impulsive decision.* **3.** having the power of producing motion. —**im·pul′sive·ly,** *adv.* —**im·pul′sive·ness,** *n.*

im·pu·ni·ty (im pū′ni tē) *n.* freedom from punishment, penalty, injury, or loss. [Latin *impūnitās* freedom from punishment, going back to *in-* not + *poena* punishment (from Greek *poinē*).]

im·pure (im pyůr′) *adj.* **1.** not pure; contaminated; dirty; unclean: *impure water.* **2.** containing something foreign or extraneous: *an impure iron ore.* **3.** not morally pure; unchaste. [Latin *impūrus* unclean.] —**im·pure′ly,** *adv.*

im·pu·ri·ty (im pyůr′i tē) *n., pl.* **-ties. 1.** the quality or state of being impure. **2.** an impure thing or substance.

im·pu·ta·tion (im′pyə tā′shən) *n.* **1.** the act of imputing. **2.** something that is imputed or charged.

im·pute (im pūt′) *v.t.,* **-put·ed, -put·ing.** to charge or attribute (something, esp. something bad) to someone or something: *to impute cowardice to a deserter, to impute defeat to lack of practice.* [Latin *imputāre* to reckon, charge.] —**im·put′a·ble,** *adj.* —**im·put′a·bly,** *adv.* —For Synonyms, see **attribute.**

in (in) *prep.* **1.** bounded, confined, or enclosed by: *in the closet, in a cage.* **2.** with the location of; among or in the midst of: *a camping trip in the mountains, a home in San Juan.* **3.** through or into: *You can go in the door on your left.* **4.** during the act of; while; when: *In clearing the table, I dropped a knife.* **5.** during: *in the winter.* **6.** before the end of: *Repayment is due in sixty days.* **7.** made of; consisting of: *a statue in bronze, music in triple time.* **8.** by means of; with; using: *to paint in oils.* **9.** clothed with; wearing: *two children in snowsuits.* **10.** out of; among: *One in every four children examined had bad teeth.* **11.** affected by or having: *to live in fear of one's life, to be in love.* **12.** within the power, range, or scope of: *in my hearing, to have it in one to be a doctor.* **13.** with the purpose or result of; for: *to strike in self-defense, to say in conclusion.* **14.** engaged at: *in training, in business.* **15.** with the shape of; so as to form: *arranged in rows, to run in circles.* **16.** with respect to; as regards: *The two writers differ in style.* **17.** according to: *in my opinion.* —*adv.* **1.** to or toward a point or place inside: *to come in out of the cold.* **2.** at a specific place, esp. one's home or office: *I stayed in because I was so tired.* **3.** into a position of power: *The election put the Democrats in.* **4.** into some substance so as to form a part of it: *Mix the butter in.* **5.** so as to agree with: *to join in with a plan.* —*adj.* **1.a.** having power or control: *the in group.* **b.** pertaining to or understandable by only a select group: *an in joke.* **2.** leading or going in: *the in door.* **3.** *Informal.* fashionable or popular: *an in restaurant.* —*n.* **1.** a person in office or in power. ➡ opposed to **out;** usually used in the plural. **2.** a means of access or influence: *to have an in with the boss.* [Old English *in* within, into, on, among.]
 • **ins and outs. a.** turns and twists, as of a road. **b.** details;

intricacies; complexities: *to know the ins and outs of legal procedures.*
 • **in that.** in consequence or view of; because; since.
 • **to be in for.** to be due or destined to do, have, or receive: *to be in for a hard time, to be in for a scolding.*
 • **to be in with.** to be on friendly or intimate terms with.
 • **to have it in for.** to harbor bad feeling toward; hold a grudge against.

In, the symbol for indium.

in-[1] *prefix* without; not: *inanimate, inequality.* [Middle English *in-,* from Latin *in-* not, sometimes through French *in-* or *en-.*]

in-[2] *prefix* **1.** in; into: *inquire, invade.* **2.** strongly; fully: *inundate.* [Middle English *in-,* from Latin *in* in, into, within, on, toward, against, often through French *in-* or *en-.*]

in-[3] *prefix* **1.** within; into: *insight, indwelling.* [Old English *in* within the limits of something.]

-in[1], form of **-ine**[2], as in *lanolin, pectin.*

-in[2] *combining form* used with verbs to form compound nouns describing a gathering of people for a particular purpose, esp. as a form of protest: *sit-in, teach-in.* [From IN.]

in. also, in inch; inches.

IN, the postal abbreviation for Indiana.

in·a·bil·i·ty (in′ə bil′i tē) *n.* the quality or condition of being unable; lack of power, means, or ability.

in ab·sen·tia (in′ ab sen′shə, -shē ə) *Latin.* during or despite one's absence.

in·ac·ces·si·bil·i·ty (in′ak ses′ə bil′i tē) *n.* the state or quality of being inaccessible.

in·ac·ces·si·ble (in′ak ses′ə bəl) *adj.* difficult or impossible to reach or approach; not accessible. —**in′ac·ces′si·bly,** *adv.*

in·ac·cu·ra·cy (in ak′yər ə sē) *n., pl.* **-cies. 1.** the quality or condition of being inaccurate. **2.** something wrong; error; mistake.

in·ac·cu·rate (in ak′yər it) *adj.* not accurate; incorrect. —**in·ac′cu·rate·ly,** *adv.*

in·ac·tion (in ak′shən) *n.* absence of action or motion; inertness; passivity.

in·ac·ti·vate (in ak′tə vāt′) *v.t.,* **-vat·ed, -vat·ing. 1.** to render inactive, as a bomb or a catalyst; deactivate. **2.** *Biology.* to destroy the activity of, as a serum or bacteria. [IN-[1] + ACTIVATE.] —**in·ac′ti·va′tion,** *n.*

in·ac·tive (in ak′tiv) *adj.* **1.** not active; passive; inert. **2.** not on active military duty. —**in·ac′tive·ly,** *adv.*

in·ac·tiv·i·ty (in′ak tiv′i tē) *n.* lack of activity; idleness.

in·ad·e·qua·cy (in ad′i kwə sē) *n., pl.* **-cies. 1.** the state or quality of being inadequate. **2.** something inadequate; insufficiency.

in·ad·e·quate (in ad′i kwit) *adj.* less than required; not adequate or sufficient: *an inadequate water supply, an inadequate excuse.* —**in·ad′e·quate·ly,** *adv.* —**in·ad′e·quate·ness,** *n.*

in·ad·mis·si·ble (in′ad mis′ə bəl) *adj.* not to be admitted, considered, or allowed; not admissible: *inadmissible evidence.* —**in′ad·mis′si·bil′i·ty,** *n.* —**in′ad·mis′si·bly,** *adv.*

in·ad·ver·tence (in′əd vûr′təns) *n.* **1.** the quality of being inadvertent. **2.** a result of being inadvertent, as a mistake.

in·ad·ver·ten·cy (in′əd vûr′tən sē) *n., pl.* **-cies.** inadvertence.

in·ad·ver·tent (in′əd vûr′tənt) *adj.* not sought or intended; unconscious or accidental: *an inadvertent oversight, an inadvertent discovery.* —**in′ad·ver′tent·ly,** *adv.*

in·ad·vis·a·ble (in′əd vī′zə bəl) *adj.* apt to be detrimental; not advisable; unwise. —**in′ad·vis′a·bil′i·ty,** *n.* —**in′ad·vis′a·bly,** *adv.*

in·al·ien·a·ble (in āl′yə nə bəl, -ā′lē ə-) *adj.* that cannot be given up, taken away, or transferred. —**in·al′ien·a·bil′i·ty,** *n.* —**in·al′ien·a·bly,** *adv.*

in·am·o·ra·ta (in am′ə rä′tə) *n., pl.* **-tas.** a woman with whom one is in love. [Italian *innamorata,* from *innamorare* to inspire with love, going back to Latin *in* in + *amor* love.]

in·ane (i nān′) *adj.* **1.** empty of meaning, sense, or significance; silly and senseless: *a speech full of inane remarks.* **2.** empty; void. [Latin *inānis* empty.] —**in·ane′ly,** *adv.* —**in·ane′ness,** *n.*

in·an·i·mate (in an′ə mit) *adj.* **1.** not moving, growing, or feeling; not having the functions of life; not alive: *Rocks are inanimate objects.* **2.** lacking spirit; dull: *an inanimate expression, inanimate conversation.* —**in·an′i·mate·ly,** *adv.* —**in·an′i·mate·ness,** *n.*

a	at	e	end	o	hot	u	up	hw	white		about
ā	ape	ē	me	ō	old	ū	use	ng	song		taken
ä	far	i	it	ô	fork	ů	rule	th	thin		pencil
âr	care	ī	ice	oi	oil	ů	pull	th	this		lemon
		îr	pierce	ou	out	ûr	turn	zh	measure		circus

625

in·a·ni·tion (in′ə nish′ən) *n.* **1.** lack, esp. of intellectual or spiritual vitality; lethargy. **2.** exhaustion because of lack of food or water. [Late Latin *inānītiō* emptiness, from Latin *inānīre* to empty.]

in·an·i·ty (i nan′i tē) *n., pl.* **-ties. 1.** the quality or state of being inane. **2.** something inane, as a remark or act.

in·ap·pli·ca·ble (in ap′li kə bəl, -ə plik′ə bəl) *adj.* not relevant or suitable; not applicable: *The rule is inapplicable in this case.* —in·ap′pli·ca·bil′i·ty, *n.*

in·ap·po·site (in ap′ə zit) *adj.* not to the point; out of place: *inapposite remarks.* —in·ap′po·site·ly, *adv.*

in·ap·pre·cia·ble (in′ə prē′shə bəl) *adj.* too small to be given attention; slight; unimportant: *an inappreciable variation in style from one opera to the next.* —in′ap·pre′cia·bly, *adv.*

in·ap·pro·pri·ate (in′ə prō′prē it) *adj.* not appropriate; unsuitable: *It was inappropriate to laugh at such a solemn moment.* —in′ap·pro′pri·ate·ly, *adv.* —in′ap·pro′pri·ate·ness, *n.*

in·apt (in apt′) *adj.* not suitable; inappropriate: *an inapt comparison.* —in·apt′ly, *adv.* —in·apt′ness, *n.*

in·ap·ti·tude (in ap′ti tūd′, -tūd′) *n.* lack of aptitude or skill.

in·ar·tic·u·late (in′är tik′yə lit) *adj.* **1.** not clearly expressed or pronounced, as speech or speech sounds; not having distinct, meaningful units: *The patient's speech was inarticulate because of the bandage around his mouth.* **2.** not able to express oneself in a clear or meaningful way. **3.** not fully expressed; not made definite and clear: *inarticulate anger.* **4.** not capable of speech or expression, esp. because of anger or other strong emotion. **5.** *Zoology.* **a.** not jointed. **b.** (of the shells of certain bivalves) held together by muscles rather than by a hinge: *an inarticulate brachiopod.* [Late Latin *inarticulātus* indistinct, from Latin *in-* not + *articulātus,* past participle of *articulāre.* See ARTICULATE.] —in′ar·tic′u·late·ly, *adv.* —in′ar·tic′u·late·ness, *n.*

in·ar·tis·tic (in′är tis′tik) *adj.* not artistic; lacking taste. —in′ar·tis′ti·cal·ly, *adv.*

in·as·much as (in′əz much′) *conj.* **1.** in view of the fact that; since: *Inasmuch as you are here, you might as well stay for dinner.* **2.** to the degree that; insofar as.

in·at·ten·tion (in′ə ten′shən) *n.* lack of attention.

in·at·ten·tive (in′ə ten′tiv) *adj.* not attentive; neglectful: *to be inattentive to details.* —in′at·ten′tive·ly, *adv.* —in′at·ten′tive·ness, *n.*

in·au·di·ble (in ô′də bəl) *adj.* that cannot be heard. —in·au′di·bly, *adv.*

in·au·gu·ral (in ô′gyər əl, -gər-) *adj.* **1.** of, relating to, or for an inauguration: *an inaugural ball.* **2.** marking or being the first of a series: *the inaugural running of a race.* —*n.* an address by a person being inaugurated, esp. one by a president of the United States. [French *inaugural* relating to inauguration, from *inaugurer* to establish, usher in, from Latin *inaugurāre.* See INAUGURATE.]

in·au·gu·rate (in ô′gyə rāt′, -gə-) *v.t.,* **-rat·ed, -rat·ing. 1.** to install (an official, as a president or governor) in office with a formal ceremony. **2.** to initiate, esp. with formalities; usher in: *to inaugurate a new policy.* **3.** to begin public use of or access to (something) with a formal opening ceremony: *to inaugurate a bridge.* [Latin *inaugurātus,* past participle of *inaugurāre* to seek guidance from omens (before undertaking an enterprise), consecrate, install.] —in·au′gu·ra′tor, *n.*

in·au·gu·ra·tion (in ô′gyə rā′shən, -gə-) *n.* **1.** a formal ceremony installing a person in office. **2.** an act or instance of initiating: *the inauguration of telephone service.* **3.** a ceremony formally opening something for public use or access.

in·aus·pi·cious (in′ô spish′əs) *adj.* not favorable for success; not especially notable or fortunate: *an inauspicious beginning.* —in′aus·pi′cious·ly, *adv.* —in′aus·pi′cious·ness, *n.*

in·be·tween (in′bi twēn′) *adj.* characterized by neither of two opposed or contrasting conditions: *to take an in-between position, neither for nor against a proposal.*

in·board (in′bôrd′) *adj.* **1.** inside the hull of a ship: *an inboard engine.* **2.** on an aircraft, closer or closest to the fuselage: *the right inboard engine.* —*adv.* inside the hull or within the sides of a ship: *to stow cargo inboard.*

in·born (in′bôrn′) *adj.* born or seemingly in a person; natural: *inborn optimism.*

in·bound (in′bound′) *adj.* inward bound: *an inbound train.*

in·bred (in′bred′) *adj.* **1.** resulting from inbreeding. **2.** inborn or deeply ingrained: *inbred curiosity, an inbred distrust of strangers.*

in·breed (in′brēd′) *v.t., v.i.,* **-bred, -breed·ing. 1.** to breed with closely related stock or individuals: *to inbreed a strain of cows.* **2.** to make or become closed in, narrow, or self-perpetuating.

in·breed·ing (in′brē′ding) *n.* **1.** breeding among closely related stock or individuals, resulting in certain traits becoming more marked. **2.** the practice of remaining closed in, narrow, or self-perpetuating, as in personnel or outlook: *The inbreeding of the general's staff kept out any new ideas.*

inc. 1. included. **2.** including. **3.** inclusive. **4.** incorporated. **5.** increase.

In·ca (ing′kə) *n.* **1.** a member of a group of Quechua-speaking Indians whose large empire extended from the northern border of Ecuador south into central Chile. The Incas had a highly developed civilization until they were conquered by the Spanish in the sixteenth century. **2.** a ruler or member of the nobility of this people. [Spanish *inca* king, prince, noble, from the Quechua *inca.*] —In′can, *adj., n.*

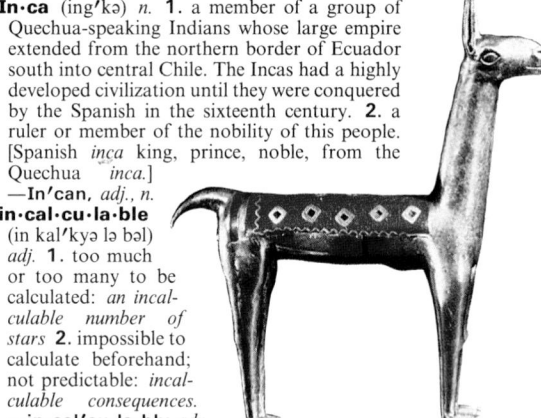

Inca silver llama

in·cal·cu·la·ble (in kal′kyə lə bəl) *adj.* **1.** too much or too many to be calculated: *an incalculable number of stars* **2.** impossible to calculate beforehand; not predictable: *incalculable consequences.* —in·cal′cu·la·bly, *adv.*

in·can·desce (in′kən des′) *v.i., v.t.,* **-desced, -desc·ing.** to become or cause to become incandescent; glow or cause to glow with heat. [Latin *incandēscere.* See INCANDESCENT.]

in·can·des·cence (in′kən des′əns) *n.* the condition of being or becoming incandescent.

in·can·des·cent (in′kən des′ənt) *adj.* **1.** glowing with heat. **2.** brightly shining; brilliant; sparkling: *incandescent wit.* **3.** giving off light by incandescence: *an incandescent fixture, incandescent lighting.* [Latin *incandēscent-,* stem of *incandēscens,* present participle of *incandēscere* to become hot, glow, from *in-* in, into + *candēscere* to begin to glow, from *candēre* to glow.]

incandescent lamp, a lamp in which light is produced by passing an electric current through a thin, high-resistance wire or filament, causing it to glow.

in·can·ta·tion (in′kan tā′shən) *n.* **1.** a formula of words spoken or chanted in casting a spell or performing or producing other magic. **2.** the use of such a formula. [Late Latin *incantātiō* enchantment, from Latin *incantāre.* See ENCHANT.]

in·ca·pa·ble (in kā′pə bəl) *adj.* lacking ability, training, or qualification; not capable; incompetent: *an incapable employee.* [Late Latin *incapābilis* unable to grasp, from Latin *in-* not + *capābilis* able to hold.] —in·ca′pa·bil′i·ty, in·ca′pa·ble·ness, *n.* —in·ca′pa·bly, *adv.* ·incapable of. **a.** without the capacity or ability for; prevented from: *incapable of walking.* **b.** not open or susceptible to; not allowing or admitting: *incapable of explanation.* **c.** legally disqualified for.

in·ca·pac·i·tate (in′kə pas′i tāt′) *v.t.,* **-tat·ed, -tat·ing. 1.** to deprive of power or ability, esp. of power to do physical activity or labor; lay up: *A broken ankle incapacitated the gymnast.* **2.** *Law.* to deny legal power to; disqualify. —in′ca·pac′i·ta′tion, *n.*

in·ca·pac·i·ty (in′kə pas′i tē) *n., pl.* **-ties. 1.** lack of power or ability. **2.** lack of legal ability to act.

in·car·cer·ate (in kär′sə rāt′) *v.t.,* **-at·ed, -at·ing.** to put in prison. [Medieval Latin *incarcerātus,* past participle of *incarcerāre* to imprison, going back to Latin *in* in + *carcer* prison.] —in·car′cer·a′tion, *n.*

in·car·na·dine (in kär′nə dīn′, -din, -dēn′) *n.* **1.** a crimson color. **2.** a pale red or pink color. —*adj.* having the color incarnadine. —*v.t.,* **-dined, -din·ing.** to make incarnadine. [French *incarnadin* flesh-colored, from dialectal Italian *incarnadino,* going back to Latin *in* in + *carō* (stem *carn-*) flesh.]

in·car·nate (*adj.,* in kär′nit, -nāt; *v.,* in kär′nāt) *adj.* **1.** being a real or true example of; in pure form; personified: *to think of*

oneself as wisdom incarnate. **2.** given a body, esp. human form. —v.t., **-nat·ed, -nat·ing. 1.** to embody, esp. in human form: *The Roman god Mars incarnated war.* **2.** to be a real or true example of; typify. [Late Latin *incarnātus*, past participle of *incarnāre* to make flesh, from Latin *in* in + *carō* flesh.]

in·car·na·tion (in′kär nā′shən) n. **1.** the assumption of bodily form, esp. human form, by a supernatural being. **2.** a person or thing that embodies, personifies, or typifies: *The lighthouse keeper was the incarnation of loneliness.* **3.** the act or process of embodying, personifying, or typifying. **4. the Incarnation.** in Christian belief, the assumption of human flesh and nature by the Son of God in the historical person of Jesus.

in·case (in kās′) v.t., **-cased, -cas·ing.** encase.

in·cau·tion (in kô′shən) n. lack of caution; carelessness; heedlessness; rashness.

in·cau·tious (in kô′shəs) adj. not cautious; heedless. —**in·cau′tious·ly,** adv.

in·cen·di·a·rism (in sen′dē ə riz′əm) n. the activity or behavior of an incendiary.

in·cen·di·ar·y (in sen′dē er′ē) adj. **1.** causing or designed to cause a fire: *incendiary grenades.* **2.** tending to excite or inflame; inflammatory: *incendiary publications.* **3.** of or relating to arson. —n., pl. **-ar·ies. 1.** arsonist. **2.** a person who stirs up trouble; inflammatory agitator. **3.** a bomb, shell, grenade, or other device designed to cause a fire. [Latin *incendiārius* causing a fire, from *incendium* fire.]

in·cense[1] (in′sens′) n. **1.** any of several substances, as gums or spices, burned to produce a fragrant aroma. **2.** the odor or smoke that is emitted from such a substance. **3.** any pleasant aroma: *the incense of a meadow.* [Middle English *encens,* from Old French *encens,* from Late Latin *incēnsum,* from Latin *incēnsus,* past participle of *incendere* to set on fire, from *in-* in, into + *candēre* to glow.]

in·cense[2] (in sens′) v.t., **-censed, -cens·ing.** to make (someone) very angry or indignant; enrage: *It incensed me when I realized that they were lying.* [Middle English *encensen,* from Old French *incenser* to set on fire, enrage, from Latin *incēnsus;* see INCENSE[1].]

in·cen·ter (in′sen′tər) n. the center of a circle inscribed in a triangle or in a regular polygon. [IN-[3] + CENTER.]

in·cen·tive (in sen′tiv) n. something that urges to action; stimulus: *The possibility of a raise was offered as an incentive to work harder.* [Latin *incentīvus* setting the tune, inciting, from *incinere* to sound.]

> **Synonyms** **Incentive, inducement,** and **stimulus** may all denote an external force or cause that leads a person to act in a certain way. **Incentive** is frequently used to describe something that motivates competitive effort: *The company used bonuses as an incentive to get workers to increase production.* An **inducement** more clearly leads or entices: *I held out a bone as an inducement to get the dog to come in.* A **stimulus** generally describes something that quickens the momentum or invigorates the mind: *The breakthrough on a possible vaccine was a stimulus for further research.*

in·cep·tion (in sep′shən) n. the point of beginning or being begun; commencement: *The television program was popular from its inception.* [Latin *inceptiō.*]

in·cep·tive (in sep′tiv) adj. **1.** beginning; initial. **2.** (of verbs or tenses) expressing the beginning of action. —n. an inceptive verb or tense.

in·cer·ti·tude (in sûr′ti tüd′, -tūd′) n. **1.** the condition of not being sure or certain; doubt. **2.** instability or insecurity: *the incertitude of one's situation.* [French *incertitude,* going back to Latin *in-* not + Late Latin *certitūdō.* See CERTITUDE.]

in·ces·sant (in ses′ənt) adj. continuing without interruption; unceasing: *the incessant buzz of mosquitoes.* [Late Latin *incessāns* unceasing, going back to Latin *in-* not + *cessāre* to stop.] —**in·ces′sant·ly,** adv.

in·cest (in′sest′) n. a sexual relationship between two persons who are closely related and cannot legally marry, as a parent and child or a brother and sister. [Latin *incestum,* from *incestus* unchaste.]

in·ces·tu·ous (in ses′chü əs) adj. **1.** involving incest. **2.** guilty of incest. **3.** resembling incest in involving or constituting a too close relationship or association. —**in·ces′tu·ous·ly,** adv. —**in·ces′tu·ous·ness,** n.

inch (inch) n. **1.** a linear measure, equal to 1/12 of a foot, or 2.54 centimeters. **2.** the smallest distance, amount, or degree: *They wouldn't budge an inch to help us.* —v.i. to move very slowly, as if an inch at a time: *The snake inched through the grass.* —v.t. to move (someone or something) very slowly. [Old English *ynce* 1/12 of a foot, from Latin *uncia* a twelfth part. Doublet of OUNCE[1].]

• **every inch.** in every way; totally: *to look every inch a sailor.*

• **inch by inch.** little by little.

• **within an inch of.** very close to: *The driver came within an inch of having an accident.*

in·cho·ate (in kō′it) adj. **1.** in an initial or early stage; not yet fully developed or formed. **2.** not well formed or organized; disorderly; chaotic. [Latin *inchoātus,* past participle of *incho(h)āre* to begin; originally, to harness, from *in* in + *cohum* strap tying the plow beam and the yoke together.]

in·cho·a·tive (in kō′ə tiv) *Grammar.* n. inceptive. —adj. inceptive *(def. 2).*

inch·worm (inch′wûrm′) n. any of a group of caterpillars, family Geometridae, that move by drawing the rear of the body up toward the front, forming a loop, and then stretching the front end forward. Also, **measuring worm, spanworm.**

inchworm

in·ci·dence (in′si dəns) n. **1.** the rate, frequency, or range of an occurrence: *Our town has a low incidence of crime.* **2.** the act or fact of falling on, affecting, or happening; occurrence. **3.** *Physics.* **a.** the falling of something, as radiation or an object, on a surface. **b.** angle of incidence.

in·ci·dent (in′si dənt) n. **1.** something that takes place; occurrence or action: *a funny incident.* **2.** a distinct event or piece of action, as in a novel, play, or poem; episode. **3.** an occurrence, seemingly of little importance, that may lead to serious consequences: *The war began with a series of border incidents.* —adj. **1.** naturally connected with; belonging to as a part (with *to*): *the responsibilities incident to a job.* **2.** falling on or striking an object or surface: *Photographers use a meter to measure incident light.* [Latin *incidēns,* present participle of *incidere* to happen.] —For Synonyms, see event.

in·ci·den·tal (in′si den′təl) adj. **1.a.** belonging to as a minor part or a relatively unimportant condition (with *to*): *problems incidental to maintaining a lawn.* **b.** of minor, but usually related, importance: *walking the dog and other incidental tasks.* **2.** not belonging with or pertaining to anything else; thrown in; random: *an incidental remark.* **3.** happening without being expected: *an incidental meeting of friends on the street.* —n. often, **incidentals.** something that is incidental or unimportant: *Just bring the necessary supplies, and we will buy the incidentals on the way.*

in·ci·den·tal·ly (in′si dent′lē, -den′tə lē) adv. **1.** in an incidental manner. **2.** apart from the main topic, but related; by the way: *Incidentally, have you heard about my new job?*

in·cin·er·ate (in sin′ə rāt′) v.t., **-at·ed, -at·ing.** to burn (something) in or as in an incinerator. [Medieval Latin *incinerātus,* past participle of *incinerāre* to reduce to ashes, from *in* in + *cinis* ashes.] —**in·cin′er·a′tion,** n.

in·cin·er·a·tor (in sin′ə rā′tər) n. a piece of equipment, as a furnace, used to dispose of garbage or other waste material by burning it to ashes.

in·cip·i·ence (in sip′ē əns) n. the fact or condition of being incipient.

in·cip·i·ent (in sip′ē ənt) adj. **1.** in an early stage; just beginning to appear: *an incipient disease.* **2.** characterized by the onset or first appearance of something: *the incipient stage of a disease.* [Latin *incipiēns,* present participle of *incipere* to begin.]

in·cise (in sīz′) v.t., **-cised, -cis·ing. 1.** to cut into. **2.** to make (marks or designs) by cutting; carve; engrave: *to incise glass.* [French *inciser* to cut into, from Latin *incīsus,* past participle of *incīdere.*]

in·ci·sion (in sizh′ən) n. **1.** the act or result of incising. **2.** a precise cut, esp. one made with a surgeon's scalpel.

in·ci·sive (in sī′siv) adj. characterized by or exhibiting a sharp, penetrating quality; keen; acute: *an incisive mind, an incisive comment.* [Medieval Latin *incisivus* cutting in, from Latin *incīsus,* past participle of *incīdere* to cut into.] —**in·ci′sive·ly,** adv. —**in·ci′sive·ness,** n.

in·ci·sor (in sī′zər) n. any of the front teeth of the upper or lower jaw having sharp flattened edges used for cutting food rather than grinding it. [Modern Latin *incisor* literally, cutter, from Latin *incīsus.* See INCISE.]

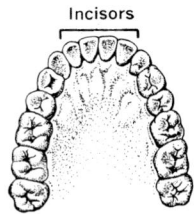

Incisors

a	at	e	end	o	hot	u	up	hw	white		about
ā	ape	ē	me	ō	old	ū	use	ng	song		taken
ä	far	i	it	ô	fork	ü	rule	th	thin	ə	pencil
âr	care	ī	ice	oi	oil	u̇	pull	th	this		lemon
		îr	pierce	ou	out	ûr	turn	zh	measure		circus

in·cite (in sīt′) *v.t.*, **-cit·ed, -cit·ing. 1.** to move or urge; rouse: *to incite someone to action.* **2.** to cause by urging or arousing; do something to bring about: *to incite a riot.* [Latin *incitāre.*] —**in·ci·ta·tion** (in′sī tā′shən), *n.* —**in·cit′er,** *n.*

> **Synonyms** Incite, instigate, and provoke may all mean to spur or urge on to action. **Incite** suggests causing agitation or disturbance: *to incite a mob to attack.* **Instigate** connotes starting someone on a questionable or nefarious course: *It was the defendant who instigated the others to plan the robbery.* **Provoke** connotes goading or rousing someone into an emotional, often angry reaction: *The mayor's controversial statements provoked jeers from the audience.*

in·cite·ment (in sīt′mənt) *n.* **1.** the act of inciting. **2.** incentive.

in·ci·vil·i·ty (in′sə vil′i tē) *n., pl.* **-ties. 1.** lack of politeness and courtesy. **2.** an impolite, discourteous act.

incl. 1. inclosure. **2.** including. **3.** inclusive.

in·clem·ent (in klem′ənt) *adj.* **1.** (of climate or weather) harsh, cold, or stormy; unfavorable. **2.** not having or showing leniency or compassion; harsh; unmerciful: *an inclement ruler.* [Latin *inclēmēns* harsh, from *in-* not + *clēmēns* mild, merciful.] —**in·clem′en·cy,** *n.* —**in·clem′ent·ly,** *adv.*

in·cli·na·tion (in′klə nā′shən) *n.* **1.** a natural tendency; bent: *an inclination to thinness.* **2.** a feeling or disposition that is more favorable to one thing or person than to another; preference; liking: *an inclination to go swimming rather than to stay at home.* **3.** tendency toward or movement in the direction of some quality or condition: *Prices have an inclination to go up.* **4.** the act, fact, or state of being or going at an angle or of bending or leaning: *The inclination of the hillside made it hard to stand.* **5.** an inclined surface; slope; incline. **6.** the angle formed between two lines or planes, or between a line and its projection on a plane. [Latin *inclīnātiō* leaning, bending.]

in·cline (*v.,* in klīn′; *n.,* in′klīn, in klīn′) *v.,* **-clined, -clin·ing.** —*v.i.* **1.** to be or go at an angle; slope; slant: *The road inclines upward.* **2.** to bend the body or head; lean: *The sailor inclined forward on the rail.* **3.** to have an inclination or preference; be favorable (with *toward* or *to*): *My cousin inclines toward becoming a mechanic.* **4.** to tend toward or move in the direction of some quality or condition; have a tendency. —*v.t.* **1.** to cause to bend, lean, slope, or slant: *Incline your head this way.* **2.** to give (someone) an inclination; cause (someone) to be favorable: *The teenagers' artistic interests inclined them toward careers in design.* —*n.* a plane or surface that is set or situated at an angle: *The wagon rolled down the incline.* [Old French *incliner* to bend, bow¹, from Latin *inclīnāre.*] —For Synonyms *(v.i.),* see **slant.**

in·clined (in klīnd′) *adj.* **1.** having an inclination or tendency: *I am inclined to agree.* **2.** sloping or leaning.

inclined plane, any plane surface, as a ramp, set at an angle to a horizontal surface. An inclined plane is a simple machine that is used to make mechanical work easier.

in·cli·nom·e·ter (in′klə nom′i tər) *n.* **1.** an instrument for measuring the inclination or slope of anything. **2.** an instrument for determining the angle with the horizontal made by an aircraft or ship. [INCLINE + -METER.]

in·close (in klōz′) *v.t.*, **-closed, -clos·ing.** enclose.

in·clo·sure (in klō′zhər) enclosure.

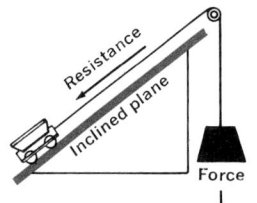

inclined plane

in·clude (in klüd′) *v.t.*, **-clud·ed, -clud·ing. 1.** to have as a part of the whole; contain: *The book includes an appendix.* **2.** to cause to be a part; put in: *to include the whole class on a field trip.* **3.** to involve or imply: *Their religion includes opposition to violence.* [Latin *inclūdere* to shut in.] —**in·clud′a·ble;** *also,* **in·clud′i·ble,** *adj.*

in·clu·sion (in klü′zhən) *n.* **1.** the act of including or the state of being included. **2.** something included. [Latin *inclūsiō* a shutting up.]

in·clu·sive (in klü′siv) *adj.* **1.** including the stated limits and everything in between: *five days, Monday to Friday inclusive.* **2.** including everything relevant; comprehensive: *an inclusive list of schools in an area.* —**in·clu′sive·ly,** *adv.* —**in·clu′sive·ness,** *n.*

   • **inclusive of.** taking into account; including: *We added up the cost of the trip, inclusive of food and entertainment.*

in·cog·ni·to (in′kog nē′tō, in kog′ni tō′) *adj., adv.* having one's identity concealed so as to be unknown; in disguise. —*n., pl.* **-tos. 1.** something that makes a person incognito; disguise. **2.** a person who is incognito. [Italian *incognito* unknown, from Latin *incog-*

nitus unknown, from *in-* not + *cognitus,* past participle of *cognoscere* to know, recognize.]

in·co·her·ence (in′kō hîr′əns, -her′-) *n.* the state or quality of being incoherent. Also, **in′co·her′en·cy.**

in·co·her·ent (in′kō hîr′ənt, -her′-) *adj.* **1.** characterized by confused, disjointed speech or thought; not understandable: *The patient was incoherent when brought to the hospital.* **2.** lacking cohesiveness, organization, or logical connection; confused; disconnected: *an incoherent argument.* —**in′co·her′ent·ly,** *adv.*

in·com·bus·ti·ble (in′kəm bus′tə bəl) *adj.* that cannot burn. —*n.* an incombustible substance. —**in′com·bus′ti·bil′i·ty,** *n.*

in·come (in′kum′) *n.* **1.** money or other compensation received as payment for services, labor, property, or investments, esp. in a certain period of time. **2.** the amount of such payment, as to a particular person: *The rent from the cottage yields a low income.*

income tax, a tax levied on personal and corporate incomes, usually graduated and with certain legally permitted deductions.

in·com·ing (in′kum′ing) *adj.* coming in: *the incoming tide, incoming telephone calls, the incoming senior class.*

in·com·men·su·ra·ble (in′kə men′sər ə bəl, -shər-) *adj.* **1.** having no common basis for comparison; not measurable by the same standards, values, or units. **2.** not in proportion; incommensurate. **3.** (of two or more numbers or quantities) having no common divisor. —**in′com·men′su·ra·bil′i·ty,** *n.* —**in′com·men′su·ra·bly,** *adv.*

in·com·men·su·rate (in′kə men′sər it, -shər-) *adj.* **1.** not corresponding or proportionate; not of equal size: *an increase in housing incommensurate with the growth of population.* **2.** having no common basis for comparison; not measurable. —**in′com·men′su·rate·ly,** *adv.*

in·com·mode (in′kə mōd′) *v.t.*, **-mod·ed, -mod·ing.** to inconvenience or make uncomfortable: *The lack of heat and hot water incommoded us.* [Latin *incommodāre.*]

in·com·mo·di·ous (in′kə mō′dē əs) *adj.* inconvenient or uncomfortable, esp. because too small: *The single room was incommodious for three travelers.*

in·com·mu·ni·ca·ble (in′kə mū′ni kə bəl) *adj.* that cannot be told or communicated. —**in′com·mu′ni·ca·bil′i·ty,** *n.*

in·com·mu·ni·ca·do (in′kə mū′ni kä′dō) *adj., adv.* without the right or means of communicating with others: *The prisoner was held incommunicado.* [Spanish *incomunicado,* from *incomunicar* to deprive of communication, going back to Latin *in-* not + *commūnicāre* to impart, share.]

in·com·pa·ra·ble (in kom′pər ə bəl, -kom′prə-) *adj.* **1.** having no equal; matchless: *That opera singer has an incomparable voice.* **2.** that cannot be compared; without a basis for comparison: *two incomparable social systems.* —**in·com′pa·ra·ble·ness,** *n.* —**in·com′pa·ra·bly,** *adv.*

in·com·pat·i·bil·i·ty (in′kəm pat′ə bil′i tē) *n., pl.* **-ties. 1.** the quality or condition of being incompatible. **2.** something that is itself or that makes another thing incompatible.

in·com·pat·i·ble (in′kəm pat′ə bəl) *adj.* not capable of existing or functioning together in harmony; not consistent or congenial: *incompatible roommates.* —**in′com·pat′i·bly,** *adv.*

in·com·pe·tence (in kom′pi təns) *n.* the state or fact of being incompetent or an incompetent. Also, **in·com′pe·ten·cy.**

in·com·pe·tent (in kom′pi tənt) *adj.* **1.** not having or showing sufficient ability; not capable or adequate: *an incompetent typist, an incompetent repair job.* **2.** not legally qualified: *A child is incompetent to sign a contract.* —*n.* **1.** a person who lacks sufficient ability. **2.** a person who is legally incapable of acting for himself or herself, because of insanity, severe illness, or age. —**in·com′pe·tent·ly,** *adv.*

in·com·plete (in′kəm plēt′) *adj.* not complete. [Late Latin *incomplētus,* going back to Latin *in-* not + *complēre* to finish.] —**in′com·plete′ly,** *adv.* —**in′com·plete′ness,** *n.*

incomplete dominance, a hereditary pattern in which neither of the alleles of a gene is completely dominant or completely recessive, so that the traits of each are blended in the offspring. For example, pink flowers result in the offspring of red-flowered and white-flowered four-o'clock plants because their genes for flower color are incompletely dominant.

in·com·pre·hen·si·ble (in′kom pri hen′sə bəl, in kom′-) *adj.* that cannot be comprehended or understood. —**in′com·pre·hen′si·bil′i·ty,** *n.* —**in′com·pre·hen′si·bly,** *adv.*

in·com·pre·hen·sion (in′kom pri hen′shən, in kom′-) *n.* the fact or condition of not comprehending or understanding.

in·con·ceiv·a·ble (in′kən sē′və bəl) *adj.* that cannot be conceived, imagined, or thought of. —**in′con·ceiv·a·bil′i·ty,** *n.* —**in′con·ceiv′a·bly,** *adv.*

in·con·clu·sive (in′kən klü′siv) *adj.* not leading to a conclusion or result: *The preliminary reports were inconclusive.* —**in′con·clu′sive·ly,** *adv.* —**in′con·clu′sive·ness,** *n.*

in·con·gru·ent (in kong′grü ənt, -kən grü′-) *adj.* not congruent. —**in·con′gru·ence,** *n.* —**in′con′gru·ent·ly,** *adv.*

in·con·gru·i·ty (in′kən grü′i tē) *n., pl.* **-ties. 1.** the quality or condition of being incongruous or incongruent. **2.** something that is incongruous.

in·con·gru·ous (in kong′grü əs) *adj.* **1.** not harmoniously related or joined; discordant: *Among the modern chairs and bookshelves, the antique washstand looked incongruous.* **2.** not appropriate, as for an occasion or situation; unfitting; inappropriate: *an incongruous remark.* [Latin *incongruus* inconsistent.]

in·con·se·quence (in kon′si kwens′, -kwəns) *n.* the condition or quality of being inconsequential.

in·con·se·quent (in kon′si kwent′, -kwənt) *adj.* **1.** not following from anything; illogical; unrelated. **2.** not leading to anything; inconsequential. —**in·con′se·quent·ly,** *adv.*

in·con·se·quen·tial (in′kon si kwen′chəl, in kon′-) *adj.* **1.** not leading to anything important; trivial. **2.** not following from anything; inconsequent. —**in′con·se·quen′tial·ly,** *adv.*

in·con·sid·er·a·ble (in′kən sid′ər ə bəl) *adj.* small or not worth considering: *inconsiderable amounts of rain.* —**in′con·sid′er·a·ble·ness,** *n.* —**in′con·sid′er·a·bly,** *adv.*

in·con·sid·er·ate (in′kən sid′ər it) *adj.* having or showing insufficient regard for others and their feelings: *It was inconsiderate of you to hang up in the middle of our conversation.* [Latin *incōnsīderātus.*] —**in′con·sid′er·ate·ly,** *adv.* —**in′con·sid′er·ate·ness,** *n.*

in·con·sist·en·cy (in′kən sis′tən sē) *n., pl.* **-cies. 1.** the quality or condition of being inconsistent. **2.** something that is inconsistent.

in·con·sist·ent (in′kən sis′tənt) *adj.* **1.** not in agreement; contradictory: *Their practice of praising peace while waging war is inconsistent.* **2.** not keeping to the same thoughts or course of action; lacking constancy or dependability; erratic: *inconsistent behavior.* —**in′con·sist′ent·ly,** *adv.*

in·con·sol·a·ble (in′kən sō′lə bəl) *adj.* that cannot be consoled; grief-stricken. —**in′con·sol′a·bly,** *adv.*

in·con·so·nant (in kon′sə nənt) *adj.* not in agreement or harmony. —**in′con·so·nant·ly,** *adv.*

in·con·spic·u·ous (in′kən spik′ū əs) *adj.* likely to escape notice; not obvious or easily seen. —**in′con·spic′u·ous·ly,** *adv.* —**in′con·spic′u·ous·ness,** *n.*

in·con·stan·cy (in kon′stən sē) *n.* the state or quality of being inconstant.

in·con·stant (in kon′stənt) *adj.* **1.** not faithful or steadfast; fickle. **2.** likely to change; variable: *The lamp gave off a flickering and inconstant light.*

in·con·test·a·ble (in′kən tes′tə bəl) *adj.* that cannot be disputed or challenged: *incontestable evidence.* —**in′con·test′a·bly,** *adv.*

in·con·ti·nence (in kon′tə nəns) *n.* the condition of being incontinent.

in·con·ti·nent (in kon′tə nənt) *adj.* **1.** lacking self-restraint or moderation, esp. with regard to sexual desires. **2.** not able to control urination or defecation. [Latin *incontinēns* immoderate.]

in·con·tro·vert·i·ble (in′kon trə vûr′tə bəl, in kon′-) *adj.* that cannot be argued against or debated; certain: *incontrovertible proof.* —**in′con·tro·vert′i·bly,** *adv.*

in·con·ven·ience (in′kən vēn′yəns) *n.* **1.** the quality or state of being inconvenient: *The inconvenience of their out-of-the-way location discouraged business.* **2.** an inconvenient situation or thing: *Not having a telephone was an inconvenience.* **3.** lack of ease or comfort; difficulty or bother: *The delay caused great inconvenience to the passengers.* —*v.t.,* **-ienced, -ienc·ing.** to cause (someone) to have difficulty or to go out of his or her way: *We hope this delay will not inconvenience you.*

in·con·ven·ient (in′kən vēn′yənt) *adj.* not easy to do, use, or reach; not favorable for one's needs or purposes; troublesome: *an inconvenient place to meet.* [Latin *inconveniēns* unsuitable.]

in·con·vert·i·ble (in′kən vûr′tə bəl) *adj.* that cannot be converted, as from paper money into coins. —**in′con·vert′i·bil′i·ty,** *n.*

in·cor·po·rate (in kôr′pə rāt′) *v.t.* **1.a.** to include (something) as a part; embody: *The proposed law incorporates many changes.* **b.** to add (something) as a part to (with *in* or *into*): *We incorporated your suggestions into the proposal.* **2.** to form into a corporation: *to incorporate a business.* **3.** to combine or unite into one uniform body. —*v.i.* to become or form a corporation. [Late Latin *incorporātus,* past participle of *incorporāre* to embody, going back to Latin *in* in + *corpus* body.] —For Synonyms *(v.t.),* see **embody.**

in·cor·po·rat·ed (in kôr′pə rā′tid) *adj.* **1.** formed into or constituting a corporation. **2.** added to or combined into one body; made into a part of.

in·cor·po·ra·tion (in kôr′pə rā′shən) *n.* the act of incorporating or the state of being incorporated.

in·cor·po·ra·tor (in kôr′pə rā′tər) *n.* **1.** a person who incorporates. **2.** one of the organizers of a corporation, named in the incorporating charter.

in·cor·po·re·al (in′kôr pôr′ē əl) *adj.* not consisting of matter; not having body or a body; spiritual. —**in′cor·po′re·al·ly,** *adv.*

in·cor·rect (in′kə rekt′) *adj.* **1.** not agreeing with fact or truth; not accurate: *an incorrect answer.* **2.** not conforming to an acknowledged or approved standard; not proper: *an incorrect mode of dress for the office.* —**in′cor·rect′ly,** *adv.* —**in′cor·rect′ness,** *n.*

in·cor·ri·gi·ble (in kôr′i jə bəl, -kor′-) *adj.* **1.** bad beyond or almost beyond all correction or reform: *an incorrigible criminal.* **2.** that cannot be corrected or amended: *an incorrigible habit.* —*n.* a person who is incorrigible. —**in·cor′ri·gi·bil′i·ty,** *n.* —**in·cor′ri·gi·bly,** *adv.*

in·cor·rupt·i·ble (in′kə rup′tə bəl) *adj.* **1.** that cannot be corrupted; morally strong: *an incorruptible public official.* **2.** that does not decay or become rotten: *an incorruptible substance.* —**in′cor·rupt′i·bil′i·ty,** *n.* —**in′cor·rupt′i·bly,** *adv.*

in·crease (*v.,* in krēs′; *n.,* in′krēs′) *v.,* **-creased, -creas·ing.** —*v.t.* to make greater in any respect, as in number, size, intensity, or extent: *to increase enrollment, to increase farm holdings, to increase community involvement.* —*v.i.* **1.** to become greater in any respect. **2.** to grow in numbers by having offspring; multiply; propagate. —*n.* **1.** the act, process, or instance of increasing. **2.** the amount by which something is increased: *I received a salary increase of ten dollars per week.* [Anglo-Norman *encress-,* a stem of *encrestre* to grow, augment, from Latin *incrēscere* to grow in or upon.]

•**on the increase.** increasing.

Synonyms *v.t.* **Increase, enlarge, augment,** and **expand** mean to make greater in some respect. **Increase,** the most general term, connotes adding to something or making it grow gradually or by increments: *to increase one's savings, to increase the volume of a radio, to increase one's knowledge.* **Enlarge** stresses the idea of making something grow in some particular dimension: *to enlarge a garden, to enlarge one's circle of friends.* **Augment** implies adding something to what is already in existence: *to augment a collection of coins.* **Expand** is much like *enlarge,* but more clearly suggests widening or stretching: *to expand one's horizons, to expand a playing field.*

in·creas·ing·ly (in krē′sing lē) *adv.* to a greater and greater extent; more and more.

in·cred·i·ble (in kred′ə bəl) *adj.* **1.** impossible to believe: *an incredible story.* **2.** seemingly impossible: *an incredible feat of daring.* [Latin *incrēdibilis* that cannot be believed.] —**in·cred′i·bil′i·ty,** *n.* —**in·cred′i·bly,** *adv.*

in·cre·du·li·ty (in′krə dü′li tē, -dū′-) *n.* unreadiness or unwillingness to believe; doubt.

in·cred·u·lous (in krej′ə ləs) *adj.* **1.** not able or not willing to believe something; skeptical; unbelieving: *When the discovery was first announced, many scholars were incredulous.* **2.** indicating or showing disbelief: *an incredulous gasp.* [Latin *incrēdulus.*] —**in·cred′u·lous·ly,** *adv.*

in·cre·ment (ing′krə mənt, in′-) *n.* **1.** something that is added on to what is already there; increase. **2.** the amount of such an increase, esp. when part of a series: *Current sales show an increment of $2,000 over last year. The weights were arranged in 5-pound increments.* **3.** *Mathematics.* a quantity added to the value of a variable, usually a very small quantity. [Latin *incrēmentum* increase.]

in·crim·i·nate (in krim′ə nāt′) *v.t.,* **-nat·ed, -nat·ing. 1.** to charge with a crime or fault. **2.** to imply or show the guilt of: *Having run away seemed to incriminate the suspect.* [Late Latin *incrīminātus,* past participle of *incrīmināre* to accuse, from Latin *in* against + *crīmen* charge.] —**in·crim′i·na′tion,** *n.*

in·crim·i·na·to·ry (in krim′ə nə tôr′ē) *adj.* tending to incriminate.

in·crust (in krust′) encrust.

in·crus·ta·tion (in′krus tā′shən) encrustation.

in·cu·bate (ing′kyə bāt′, in′-) *v.t.,* **-bat·ed, -bat·ing. 1.** to sit on and keep (eggs) warm for hatching. **2.** to hatch artificially using heat: *to incubate eggs in an incubator.* **3.** to form or develop gradually: *to incubate an idea.* [Latin *incubātus,* past participle of *incubāre* to lie on.]

a	at	e	end	o	hot	u	up	hw	white	ə	about
ā	ape	ē	me	ō	old	ū	use	ng	song		taken
ä	far	i	it	ô	fork	ü	rule	th	thin		pencil
âr	care	ī	ice	oi	oil	ú	pull	th	this		lemon
		îr	pierce	ou	out	ûr	turn	zh	measure		circus

629

in·cu·ba·tion (ing′kyə bā′shən, in′-) *n.* **1.** the process of incubating or the state of being incubated. **2.** the length of the development stage of a disease from the time of infection until the first appearance of symptoms. Also *(def. 2),* **incubation period.**

in·cu·ba·tor (ing′kyə bā′tər, in′-) *n.* a boxlike apparatus or room with a controlled environment, used to keep premature or sick babies until they are stronger or well, to hatch eggs, or to grow organisms. [Latin *incubātor* one who lies in or on something.]

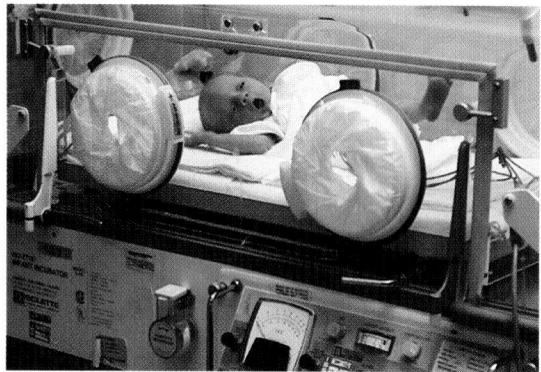

incubator

in·cu·bus (ing′kyə bəs, in′-) *n., pl.* **-bi** (-bī′) or **-bus·es. 1.** an evil spirit or demon supposed to descend on sleeping people, esp. one who seeks sexual intercourse with sleeping women. **2.** any oppressive burden that is like a nightmare. **3.** nightmare. [Late Latin *incubus* nightmare; literally, that which lies on one, from Latin *incubāre* to lie on.]

in·cu·des (ing kū′dēz) the plural of **incus.**

in·cul·cate (in kul′kāt, in′kul kāt′) *v.t.,* **-cat·ed, -cat·ing.** to produce or encourage (an attitude or belief) by persistent teaching or indoctrination; implant in the mind or memory: *to inculcate a love of reading in children.* [Latin *inculcātus,* past participle of *inculcāre* to impress on, tread in with the heel, going back to *in* in + *calx* heel.] —**in′cul·ca′tion,** *n.* —**in·cul′ca·tor,** *n.*

in·cul·pate (in kul′pāt, in′kul pāt′) *v.t.,* **-pat·ed, -pat·ing.** to incriminate. [Late Latin *inculpātus,* past participle of *inculpāre* to blame, going back to Latin *in* on + *culpa* blame.] —**in′cul·pa′tion,** *n.*

in·cum·ben·cy (in kum′bən sē) *n., pl.* **-cies. 1.** the holding of an office and performance of its duties. **2.** the term of office of an incumbent. **3.** the condition or quality of being incumbent.

in·cum·bent (in kum′bənt) *adj.* **1.** existing or imposed as a duty or obligation; obligatory (with *on* or *upon*): *It is incumbent upon a witness to tell the truth.* **2.** holding an office: *an incumbent president.* **3.** lying, leaning, or resting upon something. —*n.* a person who holds an office. [Latin *incumbēns,* present participle of *incumbere* to lie or lean on.]

in·cu·nab·u·la (in′kyə nab′yə lə) *pl. n., sing.* **-lum** (-ləm). **1.** books produced during the early development of printing from movable type, esp. during the fifteenth century. **2.** the earliest stages or first traces in the development of anything. [Latin *incūnābula* cradle, infancy, origin.]

in·cur (in kûr′) *v.t.,* **-curred, -cur·ring.** to bring (something) on oneself by one's own actions: *to incur an expense, to incur someone's anger.* [Latin *incurrere* to run into.]

in·cur·a·ble (in kyūr′ə bəl) *adj.* that cannot be cured, healed, corrected, or remedied: *an incurable disease.* —*n.* a person who has a disease that cannot be cured or healed. —**in·cur′a·bil′i·ty,** *n.* —**in·cur′a·bly,** *adv.*

in·cu·ri·ous (in kyūr′ē əs) *adj.* **1.** not eager to know or learn; not curious. **2.** *Archaic.* not arousing attention; lacking interest. [Latin *incūriōsus* indifferent.] —**in·cu·ri·os′i·ty** (in kyūr′ē os′i-tē), **in·cu′ri·ous·ness,** *n.* —**in·cu′ri·ous·ly,** *adv.*

in·cur·sion (in kûr′zhən) *n.* **1.** the act or process of spreading, intruding, or running in; inroad: *an incursion of disease.* **2.** a sudden attack; raid; invasion. [Latin *incursiō* attack.] —For Synonyms, see **invasion.**

in·cur·sive (in kûr′siv) *adj.* making incursions.

in·curve (in kûrv′) *v.t.,* **-curved, -curv·ing.** to bend so as to curve inward. —*n.* an inward curve. [Latin *incurvāre* to bend inward, from *in* in + *curvāre* to curve.]

in·cus (ing′kəs) *n., pl.* **in·cu·des.** one of the three small bones of the middle ear. For illustration, see **ear¹.** Also, **anvil.** [Latin *incūs* anvil.]

ind. 1. independent. **2.** indicative. **3.** industrial.

Ind. 1. India. **2.** Indian. **3.** Indiana.

in·debt·ed (in det′id) *adj.* **1.** owing gratitude or recognition to; in the debt of (with *to*): *All later playwrights are indebted to Shakespeare.* **2.** owing money; in debt.

in·debt·ed·ness (in det′id nis) *n.* **1.** the state of being indebted. **2.** an amount or the total amount owed.

in·de·cen·cy (in dē′sən sē) *n., pl.* **-cies. 1.** the quality or condition of being indecent. **2.** something that is indecent.

in·de·cent (in dē′sənt) *adj.* **1.** offensive to social standards; not modest or moral; obscene: *indecent language.* **2.** not in accordance with standards of good taste; improper: *an indecent delay in returning a visit.* —**in·de′cent·ly,** *adv.*

in·de·ci·pher·a·ble (in′di sī′fər ə bəl) *adj.* that cannot be deciphered.

in·de·ci·sion (in′di sizh′ən) *n.* the inability to decide or to make up one's mind.

in·de·ci·sive (in′di sī′siv) *adj.* **1.** not coming to a decision; characterized by indecision; hesitating: *an indecisive leader.* **2.** not leading to a decision; inconclusive: *an indecisive contest.* —**in′de·ci′sive·ly,** *adv.* —**in′de·ci′sive·ness,** *n.*

in·de·clin·a·ble (in′di klī′nə bəl) *adj. Grammar.* having no inflections; that cannot be declined.

in·dec·o·rous (in dek′ər əs, in′di kôr′-) *adj.* not in conformity with the approved standards of good taste; improper: *indecorous behavior.* [Latin *indecōrus* unsuitable.] —**in·dec′o·rous·ly,** *adv.* —**in·dec′o·rous·ness,** *n.*

in·de·co·rum (in′di kôr′əm) *n.* lack of decorum; impropriety. [Latin *indecōrum,* neuter of *indecōrus.* See INDECOROUS.]

in·deed (in dēd′) *adv.* in actual fact; truly. ➡ used for emphasis or in questions to seek confirmation: *I am indeed grateful to you. Are you indeed their cousin?* —*interj.* used to express surprise, disbelief, or contempt: *Pigs with wings? Indeed!*

indef., indefinite.

in·de·fat·i·ga·ble (in′di fat′i gə bəl) *adj.* that does not become tired or exhausted; tireless: *an indefatigable worker.* [Latin *in-dēfatīgābilis,* going back to *in-* not + *dē* extremely + *fatīgāre* to weary.] —**in′de·fat′i·ga·bil′i·ty,** *n.* —**in′de·fat′i·ga·bly,** *adv.*

in·de·fea·si·ble (in′di fē′zə bəl) *adj.* that cannot be set aside, annulled, or forfeited. —**in′de·fea′si·bly,** *adv.*

in·de·fen·si·ble (in′di fen′sə bəl) *adj.* **1.** that cannot be defended against attack: *The platoon's position became indefensible.* **2.** that cannot be proved, justified, or excused: *an indefensible argument.* —**in′de·fen′si·bly,** *adv.*

in·de·fin·a·ble (in′di fī′nə bəl) *adj.* that cannot be defined. —**in′de·fin′a·bly,** *adv.*

in·def·i·nite (in def′ə nit) *adj.* **1.** not clearly defined; not exact: *My plans for the summer are still indefinite.* **2.** having no limits or no precise limits; unmeasured: *a line of indefinite length.* **3.** *Grammar.* not limiting or specifying precisely. *Some, any,* and *others* are indefinite pronouns. [Latin *indēfinītus.*] —**in·def′i·nite·ly,** *adv.* —**in·def′i·nite·ness,** *n.*

indefinite article, the article *a* or *an,* which classifies the noun it modifies as single but unspecified. ➡ distinguished from **definite article.**

in·de·his·cent (in′di his′ənt) *adj. Botany.* not opening at maturity to release its seeds; not dehiscent. —**in′de·his′cence,** *n.*

in·del·i·ble (in del′ə bəl) *adj.* **1.** that cannot be removed, washed out, or obliterated: *indelible markings, indelible memories.* **2.** that makes indelible writing or marks: *an indelible pen.* [Latin *indēlēbilis* imperishable.] —**in·del′i·bil′i·ty,** *n.* —**in·del′i·bly,** *adv.*

in·del·i·ca·cy (in del′i kə sē) *n., pl.* **-cies. 1.** the quality of being indelicate. **2.** something that is indelicate.

in·del·i·cate (in del′i kit) *adj.* **1.** not tactful or considerate; coarse; crude: *indelicate behavior.* **2.** not in accord with what is becoming, proper, or modest; offensive: *indelicate language.* —**in·del′i·cate·ly,** *adv.* —**in·del′i·cate·ness,** *n.*

in·dem·ni·fi·ca·tion (in dem′nə fi kā′shən) *n.* **1.** the act of indemnifying or the state of being indemnified. **2.** something that is given to indemnify; indemnity.

in·dem·ni·fy (in dem′nə fī′) *v.t.,* **-fied, -fy·ing. 1.** to compensate (someone) for damage, loss, or expense incurred: *The airline indemnified the passenger for the loss of a suitcase.* **2.** to protect against future damage, loss, or expense; insure. [Latin *indemnis* unhurt (from *in-* not + *damnum* harm) + -FY.] —**in·dem′ni·fi′er,** *n.*

in·dem·ni·ty (in dem′ni tē) *n., pl.* **-ties. 1.** compensation given for loss, damage, or expenses incurred. **2.** protection against future damage, loss, or expense; insurance. **3.** legal protection

against liabilities or penalties for one's actions. [Late Latin *indemnitās* security from loss or harm, from *indemnis*. See INDEMNIFY.]

in·dent¹ (*v.,* in dent′; *n.,* in′dent′, in dent′) *v.t.* **1.** to start (a line of writing, typing, or printing) farther in than the other lines, as at the beginning of a paragraph. **2.** to cut or make toothlike notches on the edge or border of. **3.** *Archaic.* to make identical cuts or tears in (copies of an agreement or contract) that can be matched for identification. —*n.* indentation. [Middle English *endenten,* from Old French *endenter* to notch (a document), from Medieval Latin *indentāre* to furnish with teeth, notch, from Latin *in* in + *dent-,* stem of *dēns* tooth.]

in·dent² (in dent′) *v.t.* to make a dent or an impression in. [IN-² + DENT.]

in·den·ta·tion (in′den tā′shən) *n.* **1.** the act of indenting or the state of being indented. **2.** a part set or pushed back from the rest; dent or recess: *a series of indentations where the hailstones hit the car roof.*

in·den·tion (in den′shən) *n.* **1.** the starting of a line of writing, typing, or printing farther in than the other lines: *to begin each new paragraph with an indention.* **2.** the empty or blank space left by this. **3.** a dent or recess.

in·den·ture (in den′chər) *n.* **1.** a contract by which a person, such as an apprentice, is bound to serve another person for a stated period of time. **2.** a document stating the terms under which a security, usually a bond, is issued. —*v.t.,* -tured, -tur·ing. to bind (a person or persons) by such a contract: *to be indentured as a servant.* [Middle English *endenture,* from Medieval Latin *indentūra* document in duplicate that has been indented or provided with notched matching edges to prevent fraud, from *indentāre* to notch. See INDENT¹. The indentured person kept a copy of the agreement to prove when the period of service was over.]

in·de·pend·ence (in′di pen′dəns) *n.* **1.** the state or quality of being independent: *The American colonies fought to win independence from England.* **2.** *Archaic.* independency *(def. 1).*

Independence Day, a holiday observed on July 4, commemorating the adoption of the Declaration of Independence on July 4, 1776. Also, **Fourth of July.**

in·de·pend·en·cy (in′di pen′dən sē) *n., pl.* -cies. *Archaic.* **1.** enough money to live on without working; competence. **2.** independence.

in·de·pend·ent (in′di pen′dənt) *adj.* **1.** not influenced, guided, or controlled by others: *an independent mind, an independent person.* **2.** not subject to external political control or rule; politically autonomous: *an independent country.* **3.** not depending or contingent on something else (often with *of*): *The seasons change, independent of anyone's wishes.* **4.** not connected with, derived from, or part of anything larger, such as a chain or system: *an independent grocery store, an independent record company.* **5.** not affiliated with or regularly supporting any political party: *an independent voter.* **6.** providing enough for someone to live on without working: *an independent income.* **7.** not relying on anyone for what is necessary or desirable: *a financially independent person.* —*n.* a person or thing that is independent, esp. someone who is not affiliated with any political party. —in′de·pend′ent·ly, *adv.*

independent clause, a clause within a compound or complex sentence that can stand alone as a complete sentence. In the sentence *After we had played tennis for an hour, we decided to go for a swim,* the clause *we decided to go for a swim* is an independent clause. ➡ distinguished from **dependent clause.** Also, **main clause.**

independent counsel, a lawyer appointed by a panel of judges from the Federal Appeals Court to investigate and prosecute alleged misconduct of government officials. Also, **special prosecutor.**

independent variable *Mathematics.* a variable to which values are assigned without regard to other variables. ➡ distinguished from **dependent variable.**

in-depth (in′depth′) *adj.* penetrating and comprehensive: *an in-depth study of the crisis in the cities.*

in·de·scrib·a·ble (in′di skrī′bə bəl) *adj.* that cannot be described in words; beyond description: *a sunset of indescribable beauty.* —in′de·scrib′a·bly, *adv.*

in·de·struc·ti·ble (in′di struk′tə bəl) *adj.* that cannot be destroyed; durable; hardy. —in′de·struc′ti·bil′i·ty, in′de·struc′ti·ble·ness, *n.* —in′de·struc′ti·bly, *adv.*

in·de·ter·mi·na·ble (in′di tûr′mə nə bəl) *adj.* that cannot be defined, decided, or determined with certainty: *a specimen of indeterminable genus, a person of indeterminable age.* —in′de·ter′mi·na·bly, *adv.*

in·de·ter·mi·na·cy (in′di tûr′mə nə sē) *n.* the state or quality of being indeterminate.

in·de·ter·mi·nate (in′di tûr′mə nit) *adj.* **1.** without defined limits; indefinite or vague: *phrases of indeterminate meaning, an*

indeterminate length of time. **2.** *Botany.* (of an inflorescence) having flowers arranged on short stalks arising from the main stem, as in a raceme. —in′de·ter′mi·nate·ly, *adv.* —in′de·ter′mi·nate·ness, *n.*

in·dex (in′deks) *n., pl.* -dex·es or -di·ces. **1.a.** an alphabetical list that comes at the end of a book, indicating where in the book reference to a person or subject can be found. **b.** any similar list, as on the front page of a newspaper, in the last volume of an encyclopedia, or in regularly issued separate volumes, that refers the user to the place where something can be found. **2.** a pointer or indicator, as on a scale or a compass. **3.** something that shows or indicates; indication; sign: *Their work is an index of their ability.* **4.** the relation of size, function, or capacity of one thing to that of another, expressed in terms of a ratio or formula. **5.** index number: *the consumer price index.* **6.** Index. Index Librorum Prohibitorum. **7.** *Printing.* a symbol or character (such as ☞) used to direct the reader's attention to a particular note or paragraph. **8.** *Mathematics.* **a.** exponent. **b.** the number in a radical expressing the root. In ∛256, the index is 3. —*v.t.* **1.** to make an index of or for: *to index periodicals, to index a book.* **2.** to enter in an index: *to index a word.* **3.** to adjust, as wages or interest rates, according to changes in the cost of living: *to index wages to offset inflation.* [Latin *index* forefinger, indicator, indication.]

index card, a rectangular card used to record information, usually filed alphabetically in a box or drawer.

index finger, the finger next to the thumb; forefinger.

index fossil, a fossil useful in geochronological research, as in establishing the age of a rock stratum.

In·dex Li·bro·rum Pro·hib·i·to·rum (in′deks lī brôr′əm prō-hib′i tôr′əm) a list, now abolished, of books that the Roman Catholic Church forbade its members to read without special permission. [Modern Latin *Index Librorum Prohibitorum* literally, list of forbidden books.]

index number *Statistics.* a number that measures relative change, as of stock market prices or the cost of living, sometimes expressed as a percentage of an arbitrary base.

index of refraction *Physics.* a number expressing the ratio of the velocity of light in a vacuum to its velocity in a given substance, used to characterize the substance. Also, **refractive index.**

In·di·a ink (in′dē ə) **1.** ink made from a special black pigment, used for both writing and drawing. **2.** the pigment used to make this ink, consisting of carbon black and gum often formed into sticks, that came originally from China and Japan but was thought by the British to come from India.

In·di·an (in′dē ən) *adj.* **1.** of or relating to American Indians. **2.** of, relating to, or characteristic of India or its people or culture. —*n.* **1.** American Indian *(def. 1).* **2.** any one of the languages of the American Indians. **3.** a person who was born in or is a citizen of India. **4.** a person of Indian ancestry. [Late Latin *Indianus,* from Latin *India* India; Columbus thought the land he had discovered was India.]

Indian club, a bottle-shaped club used in arm exercises.

Indian corn, corn¹ *(defs. 1, 2).*

Indian file, single file.

Indian giver *Informal.* a person who wants back or takes back a gift. ➡ may be considered offensive.

Indian meal, cornmeal.

Indian paintbrush, any of several plants, genus *Castilleja,* of the figwort family, having greenish flowers and brightly colored bracts.

Indian pipe, a waxy, white, leafless saprophytic plant, *Monotropa uniflora,* shaped like a smoker's pipe, that bears a single white or pink flower and is found chiefly in dark, damp woodlands of North America and Asia.

Indian pudding, a sweet pudding made mainly of cornmeal, molasses, and milk.

Indian summer, a period of warm, mild weather occurring in autumn, usually after the first frost.

Indian Territory, a former region in what is now Oklahoma, where the Cherokee, Creek, Seminole, Chickasaw, and Choctaw Indians of the Southeast were sent in the nineteenth century.

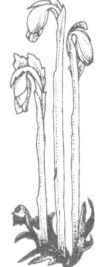

Indian pipe

Indian tobacco, a plant, *Lobelia inflata,* native to eastern North America, bearing spikelike clusters of light blue flowers.

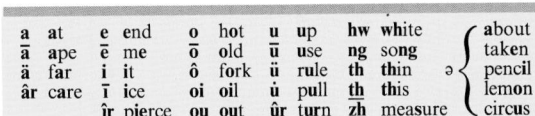

a	at	e	end	o	hot	u	up	hw	white		about
ā	ape	ē	me	ō	old	ū	use	ng	song		taken
ä	far	i	it	ô	fork	ü	rule	th	thin	ə	pencil
âr	care	ī	ice	oi	oil	u̇	pull	th	this		lemon
		îr	pierce	ou	out	ûr	turn	zh	measure		circus

I

Indian turnip, jack-in-the-pulpit.

Indian wrestling, any of several types of physical contests in which one opponent tries to force the other into a position of submission, esp. a contest in which one person grips the hand of the other while both are resting their corresponding elbows on a table, the object being to force the other's forearm sideways onto the table.

India paper **1.** a thin, strong, opaque paper, used chiefly for Bibles. **2.** a thin, absorbent paper made from vegetable fiber, used in taking proofs from engraved plates. It originally came from China and Japan.

India rubber *also,* **india rubber.** rubber[1] *(def. 1).*

In·dic (in′dik) *n.* a subdivision of the Indo-Iranian branch of the Indo-European language family, which includes Bengali, Hindi, Hindustani, Urdu, and other related languages. —*adj.* **1.** of or relating to this group of languages. **2.** of, relating to, or characteristic of India or its people or culture; Indian.

indic., indicative.

in·di·cate (in′di kāt′) *v.t.,* **-cat·ed, -cat·ing. 1.** to be a sign of; show: *A high fever indicates the presence of infection.* **2.** to direct attention to; point out: *The guide indicated the best trail for us to take.* **3.a.** to express briefly or generally; suggest: *My friends indicated that they might go to camp this summer.* **b.** to state, describe, or make known: *Indicate your preferences on these cards.* **4.** to require or point to (a specific course of treatment): *The patient's condition indicated the need for immediate surgery.* [Latin *indicātus,* past participle of *indicāre* to point out, show.]

in·di·ca·tion (in′di kā′shən) *n.* **1.** the act of indicating. **2.** something that indicates; sign: *The study found many indications that the economy was in a recession.* **3.** something that is indicated: *All indications are that we are in for a hard winter.*

in·dic·a·tive (in dik′ə tiv) *adj.* **1.** that points out, shows, or suggests (often with *of*): *a gift indicative of our high regard.* **2.** *Grammar.* of or relating to the mood of a verb that expresses a relation of objective fact between the subject and the predicate. In the sentences *The water is hot* and *Did you buy something?* the verbs *is* and *buy* are in the indicative mood. —*n. Grammar.* the indicative mood or a verb in this mood. —**in·dic′a·tive·ly,** *adv.*

in·di·ca·tor (in′di kā′tər) *n.* **1.** a person or thing that indicates. **2.** any of various instruments that show the position of, measure, or record something, as an instrument on an airplane that indicates air speed. **3.** the pointer on the dial of such an instrument. **4.** a substance, such as litmus, that indicates chemical conditions or changes, esp. by changing color. **5.** *Economics.* **a.** any of various indexes and facts and figures concerning interest rates, wholesale and retail prices, value of the national currency abroad, unemployment, industrial productivity, foreign trade, and the like, used as a means of showing present economic conditions and predicting future economic tendencies or trends. **b.** any of various indexes and averages that show the level of buying and selling taking place on a stock, bond, or commodity market.

in·di·ces (in′də sēz′) a plural of **index.**

in·dict (in dīt′) *v.t.* **1.** (of a grand jury) to accuse formally of an act or omission that is punishable by law; return an indictment against. **2.** to accuse of an offense, as if on legal authority; criticize harshly: *The press indicted the candidate for lack of concern with housing problems.* [Modification (influenced by Medieval Latin *indictāre* to accuse) of INDITE.] —**in·dict′er;** *also,* **in·dict′or,** *n.*

in·dict·a·ble (in dī′tə bəl) *adj.* **1.** making a person liable to be indicted: *an indictable offense.* **2.** liable to be indicted: *All three suspects are indictable.*

in·dict·ment (in dīt′mənt) *n.* **1.** a legal accusation returned by a grand jury, charging the commission or omission of some act that is punishable by law. **2.** any accusation or criticism.

in·dif·fer·ence (in dif′ər əns, -dif′rəns) *n.* **1.** a lack of feeling, concern, or care. **2.** lack of importance: *What they think is a matter of indifference to me.*

in·dif·fer·ent (in dif′ər ənt, -dif′rənt) *adj.* **1.** having or showing a lack of feeling, concern or care: *to be indifferent to other people's troubles.* **2.** not particularly good; routine and average: *an indifferent performance.* **3.** making no important difference one way or the other; not significant: *an indifferent result.* **4.** not interested one way or another; not partial to one more than another. [Latin *indifferēns* making no difference.] —**in·dif′fer·ent·ly,** *adv.*

Synonyms Indifferent, uninterested, disinterested, and unconcerned mean not feeling or showing interest or involvement in something. **Indifferent** means having or showing a lack of feeling, concern, or care: *to be indifferent about going or staying, to seem indifferent to someone's suffering.* **Uninterested** suggests a complete lack of response: *They seemed uninterested in anything we suggested.* **Disinterested,** on the other hand, connotes a freedom from self-interest in considering something: *Since you are disinterested, you are the best person to decide who should be chosen to head the project.* **Unconcerned** connotes a lack of feeling when there should be some: *Why are you so unconcerned about passing the exam?*

in·di·gence (in′di jəns) *n.* the fact or condition of being poor; poverty.

in·dig·e·nous (in dij′ə nəs) *adj.* originating in a particular place; not brought in from outside; native: *Kangaroos are indigenous to Australia.* [Latin *indigena* native + -OUS.] —**in·dig′e·nous·ly,** *adv.* —For Synonyms *(adj.),* see **native.**

in·di·gent (in′di jənt) *adj.* not having enough to live on; poor; needy. [Latin *indigēns,* present participle of *indigēre* to need.]

in·di·gest·i·ble (in′di jes′tə bəl, -dī-) *adj.* that cannot be digested or that is difficult to digest. —**in′di·gest′i·bil·i·ty,** *n.*

in·di·ges·tion (in′di jes′chən, -dī-) *n.* a condition characterized by gas, heartburn, belching, and other symptoms that show a disturbance of the normal process of digesting food. Also, **dyspepsia.**

in·dig·nant (in dig′nənt) *adj.* filled with or expressing indignation. [Latin *indignāns,* present participle of *indignārī* to be angry at.] —**in·dig′nant·ly,** *adv.*

in·dig·na·tion (in′dig nā′shən) *n.* anger aroused by something mean, unjust, or unworthy. [Latin *indignātiō.*] —For Synonyms, see **anger.**

in·dig·ni·ty (in dig′ni tē) *n., pl.* **-ties.** an act or circumstance that humiliates, insults, or injures. [Latin *indignitās.*]

in·di·go (in′di gō′) *n., pl.* **-gos** or **-goes. 1.** a very dark blue dye obtained from various plants or made synthetically from aniline. **2.** any of the plants from which this dye is obtained, esp. those belonging to the genus *Indigofera,* found in the warmer parts of the world. **3.** a deep violet-blue color. —*adj.* having the color indigo. [Spanish *índigo* the plant and the dye, from Latin *indicum* the dye, from Greek *indikon (pharmakon)* Indian (dye), going back to Persian *Hind* India. See HINDU.]

indigo bunting, a North American finch, *Passerina cyanea,* the male of which has deep blue summer plumage that, in winter, turns brown, the year-round color of the female's plumage. Length: 5½ inches (14 centimeters). Also, **indigo bird.**

indigo bunting

in·di·rect (in′di rekt′, -dī-) *adj.* **1.** not in a straight line; roundabout: *an indirect route.* **2.** having or depending on something intervening; not immediate: *an indirect result.* **3.** not straightforward and open; devious: *The witness gave only an indirect answer.* —**in′di·rect′ly,** *adv.* —**in′di·rect′ness,** *n.*

indirect discourse, a form of discourse in which a person's words or thoughts are repeated without exact quotation, for example: *He said that she didn't like dresses.* ➡ distinguished from **direct discourse.**

in·di·rec·tion (in′di rek′shən, -dī-) *n.* **1.** a roundabout action or procedure. **2.** lack of straightforwardness and openness. **3.** something that lacks straightforwardness and openness. **4.** the absence of guidance and control.

indirect lighting, illumination by light reflected from a ceiling, wall, or other surface.

indirect object, a word designating the person or thing indirectly affected by an action, with the stated or understood accompaniment of a preposition. In *She gave him a book, him* is the indirect object. ➡ distinguished from **direct object.**

indirect tax, a tax, such as a customs duty or excise tax, that is paid indirectly by the consumer because it is included in the price of the goods. ➡ distinguished from **direct tax.**

in·dis·cern·i·ble (in′di sûr′nə bəl, -zûr′-) *adj.* that cannot be

detected, perceived, or recognized as distinct: *The spotted fawn was indiscernible among the trees.*

in·dis·creet (in′di skrēt′) *adj.* lacking discernment, prudence, tact, or careful judgment; not discreet: *Don't be indiscreet in discussing your personal affairs.* —**in′dis·creet′ly,** *adv.* —**in′dis·creet′ness,** *n.*

in·dis·crete (in′di skrēt′) *adj.* not made up of distinct parts. [Latin *indiscretus* unseparated, from *in-* not + *discretus* separated (from *discernere* to separate, from *dis-* apart + *cernere* to separate).]

in·dis·cre·tion (in′di skresh′ən) *n.* **1.** the quality of being indiscreet. **2.** something that is indiscreet.

in·dis·crim·i·nate (in di skrim′ə nit) *adj.* **1.** not noting differences or making careful distinctions: *An indiscriminate television fan will watch any program.* **2.** random or confused. —**in′dis·crim′i·nate·ly,** *adv.*

in·dis·pen·sa·ble (in′di spen′sə bəl) *adj.* that cannot be dispensed with; absolutely necessary or essential: *A balanced diet is indispensable for good health.* —**in′dis·pen′sa·bil′i·ty,** *n.* —**in′dis·pen′sa·bly,** *adv.* —For Synonyms, see **necessary.**

in·dis·pose (in′di spōz′) *v.t.,* **-posed, -pos·ing. 1.** to make unwilling or unreceptive. **2.** to make unfit or incapable. **3.** to make slightly ill.

in·dis·posed (in′di spōzd′) *adj.* **1.** slightly ill. **2.** not willing or receptive; disinclined: *to be indisposed to help someone.*

in·dis·po·si·tion (in dis′pə zish′ən, in′dis-) *n.* **1.** a slight illness. **2.** the condition of being unwilling; unwillingness.

in·dis·put·a·ble (in′di spū′tə bəl, in dis′pyə-) *adj.* not subject to dispute; unquestionable: *The facts are indisputable.* —**in′dis·put′a·bil′i·ty,** *n.* —**in′dis·put′a·bly,** *adv.*

in·dis·sol·u·ble (in′di sol′yə bəl) *adj.* that cannot be dissolved, destroyed, or abolished. —**in′dis·sol′u·bil′i·ty,** *n.* —**in′dis·sol′u·bly,** *adv.*

in·dis·tinct (in′di stingkt′) *adj.* not clear or distinct. [Latin *indistinctus.*] —**in′dis·tinct′ly,** *adv.* —**in′dis·tinct′ness,** *n.* —For Synonyms, see **faint.**

in·dis·tin·guish·a·ble (in′di sting′gwi shə bəl) *adj.* **1.** that cannot be told apart: *The two houses are so similar that they are indistinguishable from one another.* **2.** that cannot be seen or recognized: *an indistinguishable difference.*

in·dite (in dīt′) *v.t.,* **-dit·ed, -dit·ing.** to put into writing; compose. [Old French *enditer* to dictate, write down, going back to Latin *in* in + *dictāre* to dictate, write down.] —**in·dite′ment,** *n.* —**in·dit′er,** *n.*

in·di·um (in′dē əm) *n.* a soft, silvery, rare metallic element, used esp. in alloys for jewelry, bearings, and dentures, and to make semiconductors. Symbol: **In** For tables, see **element.** [Modern Latin *indium,* from Latin *indicum* blue pigment, indigo; the element was discovered by the two indigo lines in its spectrum.]

in·di·vid·u·al (in′də vij′ü əl) *adj.* **1.** being a solitary being or thing: *Each individual house has its own backyard.* **2.** for or by one only: *an individual portion, an individual effort.* **3.** relating to or characteristic of one only: *individual opinions.* —*n.* **1.** a person. **2.** a single person, being, or thing: *A herd of caribou may contain thousands of individuals.* [Middle English *individual,* from Medieval Latin *indīviduālis,* from Latin *indīviduus* indivisible, from *in-* not + *dīviduus* divided, from *dīvidere* to divide.] —**in′di·vid′u·al·ly,** *adv.*

in·di·vid·u·al·ism (in′də vij′ü ə liz′əm) *n.* **1.** the theory that individual interests are as important as the welfare of the community as a whole. **2.** any theory that emphasizes the worth, freedom, and well-being of the individual and one's right to think and live as one sees fit without the control or direction of others, esp. of a government. **3.** action or thought by each person for his or her own ends without regard for others. **4.** individuality.

in·di·vid·u·al·ist (in′də vij′ü ə list) *n.* **1.** a person who practices or advocates individualism. **2.** a person who has individuality. —*adj.* individualistic.

in·di·vid·u·al·is·tic (in′də vij′ü ə lis′tik) *adj.* of, relating to, or characteristic of individualism or individualists.

in·di·vid·u·al·i·ty (in′də vij′ü al′i tē) *n., pl.* **-ties. 1.** a quality that distinguishes one person or thing from others; individual character. **2.** the condition of being an individual.

in·di·vid·u·al·ize (in′də vij′ü ə līz′) *v.t.,* **-ized, -iz·ing. 1.** to make individual; give a distinct character to: *We individualized our house from the others in the development by painting our front door red.* **2.** to fit to a particular individual or to different individuals: *to individualize instruction.* **3.** to consider separately; particularize: *to individualize the features of a landscape.* —**in′di·vid′u·al·i·za′tion,** *n.*

in·di·vid·u·ate (in′də vij′ü āt′) *v.t.,* **-at·ed, -at·ing.** to make distinct from others; make individual.

in·di·vid·u·a·tion (in′də vij′ü ā′shən) *n.* the act or process of individuating or the state of being individuated.

in·di·vis·i·ble (in′də viz′ə bəl) *adj.* **1.** that cannot be divided. **2.** that cannot be divided without a remainder: *The number 5 is indivisible by 2.* —**in′di·vis′i·bil′i·ty,** *n.* —**in′di·vis′i·bly,** *adv.*

in·doc·tri·nate (in dok′trə nāt′) *v.t.,* **-nat·ed, -nat·ing.** to imbue (someone) with theories, beliefs, or principles, esp. of a particular sect or political group. [Latin *in* in + *doctrīna* learning, teaching + -ATE¹.] —**in·doc′tri·na′tion,** *n.*

In·do-Eu·ro·pe·an (in′dō yür′ə pē′ən) *n.* **1.** a family of languages that includes the majority of those spoken in Europe and the Americas and many of those spoken in Asia. English, Russian, Italian, Spanish, Persian, and Hindi are Indo-European languages. **2.** Proto-Indo-European. —*adj.* of or relating to this family of languages.

In·do-I·ra·ni·an (in′dō i rā′nē ən, -ī rā′-) *n.* a subfamily of the Indo-European family of languages, including Hindustani, Bengali, Persian, and other languages spoken predominantly in Afghanistan, India, Iran, and certain other Asian countries, as well as Sanskrit and other dead languages.

in·dole·a·ce·tic acid (in′dōl ə sē′tik, -ə set′ik) the chief auxin in most plants, which stimulates plant growth and development. Formula: $C_{10}H_9NO_2$

in·do·lence (in′də ləns) *n.* the state or quality of being indolent.

in·do·lent (in′də lənt) *adj.* having or showing a dislike or avoidance of work or exertion; lazy; idle. [Late Latin *indolēns* painless, from Latin *in-* not + *dolēns,* present participle of *dolēre* to feel pain.] —**in′do·lent·ly,** *adv.*

in·dom·i·ta·ble (in dom′i tə bəl) *adj.* that cannot be conquered or dominated: *an indomitable will.* [Late Latin *indomitābilis,* from Latin *in-* not + *domitāre* to tame.] —**in·dom′i·ta·bly,** *adv.*

In·do·ne·sian (in′də nē′zhən, -shən) *adj.* of, relating to, or characteristic of Indonesia or its people, language, or culture. —*n.* **1.** a native or citizen of Indonesia. **2.** a person of Indonesian ancestry. **3.** a form of Malay that is the official language of Indonesia.

in·door (in′dôr′) *adj.* **1.** used, done, or situated within a house or building: *an indoor swimming pool, an indoor sport.* **2.** meant to be used within a house or building: *indoor carpeting, indoor furniture.*

in·doors (in′dôrz′) *adv.* in or into a house or building: *We moved the party indoors when it began to rain.*

in·dorse (in dôrs′) *v.t.,* **-dorsed, -dors·ing.** endorse.

in·dor·see (in dôr sē′, in′dôr-) endorsee.

in·dorse·ment (in dôrs′mənt) endorsement.

In·dra (in′drə) *n.* one of the chief gods of the earliest Hindu religion, associated with rain and storms. In the present form of Hinduism, Indra is of minor rank.

in·du·bi·ta·ble (in dü′bi tə bəl, -dū′-) *adj.* not to be doubted; certain; unquestionable. —**in·du′bi·ta·bly,** *adv.*

in·duce (in düs′, -dūs′) *v.t.,* **-duced, -duc·ing. 1.** to lead by or as by persuasion or influence; motivate: *We tried to induce them to come with us.* **2.** to bring about; bring on; produce; cause: *The nurse gave me a drug to induce sleep.* **3.** to arrive at a general theory or conclusion through the observation and analysis of particular facts; reason by induction. **4.** to produce (electric current) by induction. [Latin *indūcere* to lead in, persuade.]

Synonyms **Induce** and **persuade** may both mean to move or coax someone to act in a particular way. **Induce** connotes offering something that overcomes hesitation or opposition: *I induced the children to go to bed by promising to tell them a story.* **Persuade** connotes moving someone by pleading or reasoning: *The salesperson's arguments persuaded me to buy the more expensive TV set.*

in·duce·ment (in düs′mənt, -dūs′-) *n.* **1.** something attractive that leads someone to do something: *The extra money was an inducement to work more hours.* **2.** the act of inducing or the state of being induced. —For Synonyms, see **incentive.**

in·duct (in dukt′) *v.t.* **1.** to take into military service: *to induct youths into the army.* **2.** to bring into a group formally; admit: *The club inducted four new members.* **3.** to install formally in an office: *to induct a new mayor.* [Latin *inductus,* past participle of *indūcere* to lead in.]

a	at	e	end	o	hot	u	up	hw	white	ə	about
ā	ape	ē	me	ō	old	ū	use	ng	song		taken
ä	far	i	it	ô	fork	ū	rule	th	thin		pencil
âr	care	ī	ice	oi	oil	ù	pull	th	this		lemon
				ir	pierce	ou	out	ûr	turn	zh	measure		circus

Synonyms **Induct, install,** and **initiate** mean to admit as a member or put in office through some formal procedure. **Induct** suggests a special ceremony that invests the person with the insignia of the office: *to induct a minister, to induct new members into an academy.* **Install** stresses the concept of seating someone in the official seat or office: *to install a bishop.* **Initiate** means to admit a new member into some group that has complex or arcane rules or rituals: *to initiate fraternity members.*

in·duc·tance (in duk′təns) *n.* the ability of an electric circuit to produce an electromotive force when the current in the circuit or in a neighboring circuit is changing.

in·duc·tee (in duk′tē, in′duk tē′) *n.* a person who is being inducted, esp. into military service.

in·duc·tion (in duk′shən) *n.* **1.a.** the process by which someone is made a member of the military service, including swearing in. **b.** the process or ceremony of being brought into a group or installed in an office formally. **2.** the act of inducing: *the induction of a hypnotized state.* **3.** *Electricity.* **a.** the act or process of giving an electric charge to an object by bringing it close to a charged object. **b.** the act or process of magnetizing an object by placing it in a magnetic field. **c.** the act or process of producing an electric current in a conductor by moving the conductor through a magnetic field, or by moving the field itself. **d.** any process by which a body having electric or magnetic properties produces electric or magnetic properties in another body. **4.** the method of supporting or of arriving at a general or universal statement by observing a limited number of particular cases. ➡ distinguished from **deduction**. **5.** *Mathematics.* a method of proving a law or theorem about numbers by showing that the law or theorem holds for the first number and then showing that if it holds for all the numbers preceding a given number, it also holds for the next following number.

induction coil, a transformer that converts low-voltage direct current into high-voltage pulses or into high-voltage alternating current. It is used to produce the spark in the spark plugs of an internal-combustion engine.

induction heating, the process of heating a material by causing an electric current to flow through it or its container by electromagnetic induction.

in·duc·tive (in duk′tiv) *adj.* **1.** of or relating to logical induction: *We attempted to reach a conclusion by the use of inductive reasoning.* **2.** of, relating to, producing, or produced by electrical or magnetic induction. —**in·duc′tive·ly,** *adv.*

in·duc·tor (in duk′tər) *n.* **1.** a person who inducts. **2.** an electrical device that possesses inductance, used to introduce inductance into a circuit.

in·due (in dü′, -dū′) *v.t.,* **-dued, -du·ing.** endue.

in·dulge (in dulj′) *v.,* **-dulged, -dulg·ing.** —*v.t.* **1.** to give way to; yield to: *I sometimes indulge my love for photography.* **2.** to yield to the whims or wishes of; give in to: *The grandparents indulge the child.* —*v.i.* to allow oneself to have, do, or enjoy something (with *in*): *to indulge in a special treat occasionally.* [Latin *indulgēre* to be kind to.] —For Synonyms, see **humor.**

in·dul·gence (in dul′jəns) *n.* **1.** the act of indulging. **2.** something that is indulged in. **3.** something granted by a person who is indulgent; favor. **4.** in the Roman Catholic Church, pardon from punishment that would otherwise remain due for a sin after the sin itself has been forgiven.

in·dul·gent (in dul′jənt) *adj.* characterized by or showing indulgence. —**in·dul′gent·ly,** *adv.*

in·du·rate (*v.,* in′də rāt′, -dyə-; *adj.,* in′dər it, -dyər-, in dur′-, -dyur′-) *v.t., v.i.,* **-rat·ed, -rat·ing.** **1.** to make or become unfeeling or callous. **2.** to make or become hard: *When mud or clay becomes indurated, it forms shale.* —*adj.* hard or unfeeling. [Latin *indūrātus,* past participle of *indūrāre* to harden.]

in·dus·tri·al (in dus′trē əl) *adj.* **1.** of, relating to, or produced by industry: *industrial wastes, industrial output.* **2.** relating to or engaged in industry: *industrial development, industrial workers.* **3.** having or characterized by highly developed industry: *an industrial society.* **4.** made for use in industry: *heavy machinery and other industrial products.* [Partly from French *industrial* relating to industry, from *industrie* work, manufacturing, from Latin *industria* diligence; partly from Latin *industria* + -AL¹.] —**in·dus′tri·al·ly,** *adv.*

industrial arts, skill or knowledge in the use of tools and machines, as in carpentry or metalworking, esp. as taught in schools. ➡ often used as singular.

in·dus·tri·al·ism (in dus′trē ə liz′əm) *n.* a social and economic system based chiefly on large-scale industries, mechanization, and production, rather than on agriculture or commerce.

in·dus·tri·al·ist (in dus′trē ə list) *n.* a person who conducts, owns, or engages in an industrial enterprise.

in·dus·tri·al·ize (in dus′trē ə līz′) *v.,* **-ized, -iz·ing.** —*v.t.*

1. to create a high proportion of mechanized industry in (a region or country). **2.** to organize as an industry. —*v.i.* to become industrial: *The country industrialized quickly.* —**in·dus′tri·al·i·za′tion,** *n.*

industrial park, a section of land with factories, warehouses, or other industrial buildings, usually located in a suburban or rural area.

Industrial Revolution, economic and social changes occurring first in England and later throughout Europe and the United States in the eighteenth and nineteenth centuries, resulting from innovations in technology and agriculture. The Industrial Revolution brought about a shift from an agrarian to an industrial society.

industrial union, a labor union to which all the workers in a given industry, regardless of particular occupation or skill, may belong. Also, **vertical union.**

in·dus·tri·ous (in dus′trē əs) *adj.* working hard and steadily; diligent. [Latin *industriōsus* diligent, from *industrius.*] —**in·dus′tri·ous·ly,** *adv.* —**in·dus′tri·ous·ness,** *n.*

in·dus·try (in′də strē) *n., pl.* **-tries. 1.** manufacturing plants and other businesses considered as a whole, esp. as constituting a highly mechanized system: *The future of the nation's industry is imperiled by the strike.* **2.** a particular branch of business, trade, or manufacture: *the tourist industry, the aircraft industry.* **3.** the owners or managers of manufacturing concerns: *Labor is for the new tax proposal, but industry is opposed.* **4.** hard work or steady effort; diligence: *to show much industry in performing a job.* [Latin *industria* diligence.]

in·dwell·ing (in′dwel′ing) *adj.* that dwells or is located within.

-ine¹ *suffix* (used to form adjectives from nouns) of, like, or relating to: *alpine, feline.* [Latin *-inus, -īnus,* from Greek *-inos,* sometimes through French *-in(e).*]

-ine² *suffix* used in chemistry to form nouns, esp. the names of basic substances or halogens: *purine, fluorine.* [Latin *-īna,* feminine of *-īnus,* sometimes through French *-ine.* See -INE¹.]

in·e·bri·ate (*v.,* i nē′brē āt′; *n.,* i nē′brē it, -āt′) *v.t.* **-at·ed, -at·ing.** to make inebriated. —*n.* a person who is drunk or habitually drunk. [Latin *inēbriātus,* past participle of *inēbriāre* to make drunk.] —**in·e′bri·a′tion,** *n.*

in·e·bri·at·ed (i nē′brē ā′tid) *adj.* **1.** intoxicated with liquor; drunk. **2.** excited or stupefied, as if with liquor: *inebriated with success.*

in·e·bri·e·ty (in′i brī′i tē) *n.* the condition of being inebriated or of being an inebriate.

in·ed·i·ble (in ed′ə bəl) *adj.* not fit as food; unsuitable for eating: *The burned meat was inedible.*

in·ef·fa·ble (in ef′ə bəl) *adj.* **1.** that cannot be fully described in words: *The view from here is one of ineffable beauty.* **2.** too sacred to be spoken aloud. [Latin *ineffābilis* unutterable, going back to *in-* not + *ex* out + *fārī* to speak.] —**in·ef′fa·bil′i·ty, in·ef′fa·ble·ness,** *n.* —**in·ef′fa·bly,** *adv.*

in·ef·face·a·ble (in′i fā′sə bəl) *adj.* that cannot be obliterated, erased, or rubbed out. —**in′ef·face′a·bly,** *adv.*

in·ef·fec·tive (in′i fek′tiv) *adj.* **1.** not able to bring about a desired effect; not effective. **2.** not able or competent: *an ineffective person.* —**in′ef·fec′tive·ly,** *adv.* —**in′ef·fec′tive·ness,** *n.*

in·ef·fec·tu·al (in′i fek′chü əl) *adj.* that cannot or does not produce a desired result or effect: *ineffectual action, ineffectual advice.* —**in′ef·fec′tu·al·ly,** *adv.*

in·ef·fi·ca·cious (in ef′i kā′shəs) *adj.* unable to produce an intended or desired effect; ineffective.

in·ef·fi·ca·cy (in ef′i kə sē) *n.* the inability to produce an intended or desired effect.

in·ef·fi·cien·cy (in′i fish′ən sē) *n.* the state, quality, or fact of being inefficient.

in·ef·fi·cient (in′i fish′ənt) *adj.* **1.** involving or resulting in too much effort or waste; not efficient: *The business failed because of inefficient management.* **2.** not working or accomplishing something efficiently: *an inefficient typist.* —**in′ef·fi′cient·ly,** *adv.*

in·e·las·tic (in′i las′tik) *adj.* not elastic. —**in′e·las·tic′i·ty,** *n.*

in·el·e·gance (in el′i gəns) *n.* **1.** the state or quality of being inelegant. **2.** something that is inelegant.

in·el·e·gan·cy (in el′i gən sē) *n., pl.* **-cies.** inelegance.

in·el·e·gant (in el′i gənt) *adj.* not elegant. —**in·el′e·gant·ly,** *adv.*

in·el·i·gi·ble (in el′i jə bəl) *adj.* not qualified or fit to be chosen: *I was ineligible for the team because of poor grades.* —*n.* a person who is ineligible. —**in·el′i·gi·bil′i·ty,** *n.* —**in·el′i·gi·bly,** *adv.*

in·e·luc·ta·ble (in′i luk′tə bəl) *adj.* that cannot be overcome or escaped from; inevitable: *an ineluctable force.* [Latin *inēluctābilis,* from *in-* not + *ēluctābilis* resistible by struggling, from *ēluctārī* to

resist by struggling.] —in′e·luc′ta·bil′i·ty, *n.* —in′e·luc′ta·bly, *adv.*

in·ept (i nept′) *adj.* **1.** lacking skill or ability; awkward or clumsy: *to be inept at changing a tire.* **2.** poorly done or chosen; not suitable; inappropriate: *an inept comparison.* **3.** lacking reason or logic; foolish; absurd: *an inept policy.* [Latin *ineptus* unsuitable, foolish.] —in·ept′ly, *adv.* —in·ept′ness, *n.*

in·ept·i·tude (i nep′ti tüd′, -tūd′) *n.* **1.** the quality of being inept. **2.** an inept act or remark.

in·e·qual·i·ty (in′i kwol′i tē) *n., pl.* **-ties. 1.** the fact or condition of not being equal; lack of equality: *There is great inequality between the rich and poor in that country.* **2.** a mathematical statement that a number or algebraic expression is greater or less than another.

in·eq·ui·ta·ble (in ek′wi tə bəl) *adj.* not fair and just; not equitable: *an inequitable settlement of a dispute.* —in·eq′ui·ta·bly, *adv.*

in·eq·ui·ty (in ek′wi tē) *n., pl.* **-ties. 1.** lack of justice; unfairness. **2.** something that is unfair and unjust.

in·e·rad·i·ca·ble (in′i rad′i kə bəl) *adj.* that cannot be eradicated. —in′e·rad′i·ca·bly, *adv.*

in·ert (i nûrt′) *adj.* **1.** without power to move or act; not moving: *a lifeless and inert body.* **2.** not reacting or combining readily with other substances; chemically inactive. **3.** slow to move or act; not active; sluggish: *an inert bureaucracy.* [Latin *iners* inactive.]

in·er·tia (i nûr′shə) *n.* **1.** the tendency not to move or change: *My inertia kept me from turning off the television.* **2.** *Physics.* resistance of a body to any change in its state of rest or motion. [Latin *inertia* inactivity.] —in·er′tial, *adj.*

inertial guidance system, a system of guidance for a space vehicle that uses gyroscopic devices to absorb and interpret information automatically, such as speed and position, and adjust the vehicle to a planned flight path.

in·es·cap·a·ble (in′e skā′pə bəl) *adj.* that cannot be escaped or avoided; certain: *an inescapable conclusion.* —in′es·cap′a·bly, *adv.*

in·es·sen·tial (in′i sen′shəl) *adj.* not essential.

in·es·ti·ma·ble (in es′tə mə bəl) *adj.* that cannot be completely assessed or estimated; very great: *Your friendship is of inestimable worth to me.* —in·es′ti·ma·bly, *adv.*

in·ev·i·ta·ble (in ev′i tə bəl) *adj.* that cannot be avoided; obvious or certain: *an inevitable result.* [Latin *inēvītābilis.*] —in·ev′i·ta·bil′i·ty, *n.* —in·ev′i·ta·bly, *adv.*

in·ex·act (in′eg zakt′) *adj.* not completely correct; not exact. —in′ex·act′ly, *adv.* —in′ex·act′ness, *n.*

in·ex·cus·a·ble (in′ek·skū′zə bəl) *adj.* that cannot or should not be excused or justified: *rude behavior that was inexcusable.* —in′ex·cus′a·bly, *adv.*

in·ex·haust·i·ble (in′eg zôs′tə bəl) *adj.* **1.** that cannot be depleted or used up easily: *The office seemed to have an inexhaustible supply of paper.* **2.** that does not become easily worn out or tired; tireless: *an inexhaustible swimmer.* —in′ex·haust′i·bil′i·ty, *n.* —in′ex·haust′i·bly, *adv.*

in·ex·o·ra·ble (in ek′sər ə bəl) *adj.* that does not change, stop, or yield, no matter what anyone does or says; unyielding: *inexorable fate.* [Latin *inexōrābilis,* going back to *in-* not + *exōrāre* to gain by entreaty + -ABLE.] —in·ex′o·ra·bil′i·ty, *n.* —in·ex′o·ra·bly, *adv.*

in·ex·pe·di·en·cy (in′ek spē′dē ən sē) *n.* the state or quality of being inexpedient. Also, **in′ex·pe′di·ence.**

in·ex·pe·di·ent (in′ek spē′dē ənt) *adj.* not promoting immediate results or advantage; not expedient.

in·ex·pen·sive (in′ek spen′siv) *adj.* involving little expense; not costly. —in′ex·pen′sive·ly, *adv.* —in′ex·pen′sive·ness, *n.*

in·ex·pe·ri·ence (in′ek spîr′ē əns) *n.* lack of experience or of the knowledge or skill that comes with experience.

in·ex·pe·ri·enced (in′ek spîr′ē ənst) *adj.* lacking experience, knowledge, or skill: *an inexperienced swimmer.*

in·ex·pert (in eks′pûrt, in′ek spûrt′) *adj.* lacking skill or ability; not expert.

in·ex·pi·a·ble (in eks′pē ə bəl) *adj.* that cannot be atoned for or made amends for: *an inexpiable offense.* [Latin *inexpiābilis.*]

in·ex·plic·a·ble (in′ek splik′ə bəl, in ek′spli kə-) *adj.* that cannot be explained: *The cat's odd behavior is inexplicable.* [Latin *inexplicābilis.*] —in′ex·plic′a·bil′i·ty, *n.* —in′ex·plic′a·bly, *adv.*

in·ex·plic·it (in′ek splis′it) *adj.* not clear or definite; not explicit.

in·ex·press·i·ble (in′ek spres′ə bəl) *adj.* that cannot be put into words, communicated, or shown outwardly: *inexpressible feelings.* —in′ex·press′i·bil′i·ty, in′ex·press′i·ble·ness, *n.* —in′ex·press′i·bly, *adv.*

in·ex·pres·sive (in′ek spres′iv) *adj.* conveying little feeling or meaning; not expressive.

in ex·ten·so (in′ek sten′sō) *Latin.* at full length; in full.

in·ex·tin·guish·a·ble (in′ek sting′gwi shə bəl) *adj.* that cannot be put out, destroyed, or obscured: *an inextinguishable flame, an inextinguishable memory.* —in′ex·tin′guish·a·bly, *adv.*

in ex·tre·mis (in′ek strē′mis) *Latin.* at the outermost limits, as of endurance, esp. at the point of death.

in·ex·tri·ca·ble (in ek′stri kə bəl, in′ek strik′ə bəl) *adj.* **1.** impossible to separate, disentangle, remove, or set free: *an inextricable tangle of threads.* **2.** impossible to solve, straighten out, or escape from: *an inextricable dilemma.* [Latin *inextricābilis* that cannot be disentangled.] —in′ex·tri′ca·bly, *adv.*

inf., infinitive.

in·fal·li·ble (in fal′ə bəl) *adj.* **1.** incapable of error: *No one is infallible.* **2.** that can be relied on; unfailing; sure: *an infallible solution.* [Medieval Latin *infallibilis* incapable of error, from Latin *in-* not + Late Latin *fallibilis.* See FALLIBLE.] —in·fal′li·bil′i·ty, *n.* —in·fal′li·bly, *adv.*

in·fa·mous (in′fə məs) *adj.* **1.** widely known and condemned for wrongdoing: *an infamous criminal.* **2.** having or deserving everyone's condemnation; extremely bad: *infamous crimes.* [Medieval Latin *infamosus* ill spoken of, from Latin *infāmis.*] —in′fa·mous·ly, *adv.*

in·fa·my (in′fə mē) *n., pl.* **-mies. 1.** the state or condition of being widely known and condemned for wrongdoing. **2.** the quality of being extremely bad: *the great infamy of these crimes.* **3.** an extremely bad act. [Latin *infāmia* bad reputation.]

in·fan·cy (in′fən sē) *n., pl.* **-cies. 1.** the state or period of being an infant. **2.** the earliest period of development of anything: *When computers were in their infancy, vacuum tubes were used to process data.* **3.** *Law.* the state of being under the age of legal responsibility, usually twenty-one, or the period before reaching this age. [Latin *infantia* early childhood; literally, inability to speak.]

in·fant (in′fənt) *n.* **1.** a child during the earliest period of his or her life; baby. **2.** *Law.* a person who has not reached the age of legal responsibility; minor. —*adj.* **1.** of, relating to, or for an infant: *infant care, infant toys.* **2.** in the earliest period of development: *an infant industry.* [Middle English *infaunt,* from Old French *enfant,* from Latin *infant-,* stem of *infans* mute, without speech, from *in-* not + *fans,* present participle of *fari* to speak.]

in·fan·ta (in fan′tə) *n.* a daughter of the monarch of Spain or Portugal. [Spanish and Portuguese *infanta,* feminine of *infante.* See INFANTE.]

in·fan·te (in fan′tā) *n.* a son of the monarch of Spain or Portugal other than the first son, who is not an heir to the throne. [Spanish and Portuguese *infante,* from Latin *infāns.* See INFANT.]

in·fan·ti·cide[1] (in fan′tə sīd′) *n.* the killing of an infant. [Late Latin *infanticīdium,* from Latin *infāns* baby + -cīdium. See -CIDE[1].]

in·fan·ti·cide[2] (in fan′tə sīd′) *n.* a person who kills an infant. [Late Latin *infanticīda,* from Latin *infāns* baby + -cīda. See -CIDE[2].]

in·fan·tile (in′fən tīl′, -təl) *adj.* **1.** too much like an infant or like that of an infant; childish: *Infantile behavior by an older person is very unattractive.* **2.** of, relating to, or belonging to infancy. [Late Latin *infāntilis* relating to an infant, from *infāns.* See INFANT.]

infantile paralysis, poliomyelitis.

in·fan·ti·lism (in′fən tī liz′əm, -tə-) *n.* a condition characterized by overly slow body development and persistence of childish physical, emotional, or intellectual traits in adult life.

in·fan·try (in′fən trē) *n., pl.* **-tries. 1.** soldiers trained and equipped to fight on foot. **2.** the branch of an army composed of such soldiers. [French *infanterie,* from Italian *infanteria,* from *infante* child, servant of a knight, foot soldier, from Latin *infāns* baby.]

in·fan·try·man (in′fən trē mən) *n., pl.* **-men** (-mən). a member of the infantry.

infant school *British.* a school for children who are under seven years of age.

in·farct (in färkt′) *n.* a circumscribed area of tissue that is dead or dying because the amount of blood supplying the area is no longer adequate. Also, **in·farc·tion** (in färk′shən). [Medieval Latin *infarctus,* from Latin *infartus,* past participle of *infarcire* to stuff in.]

in·fat·u·ate (in fach′ü āt′) *v.t.,* **-at·ed, -at·ing.** to cause to have a seemingly great passion or attraction that is actually childish or foolish and will pass quickly: *My friend was infatuated with*

a	at	e	end	o	hot	u	up	hw	white		about
ā	ape	ē	me	ō	old	ū	use	ng	song	ə	taken
ä	far	i	it	ô	fork	ü	rule	th	thin		pencil
âr	care	ī	ice	oi	oil	u̇	pull	th	this		lemon
		îr	pierce	ou	out	ûr	turn	zh	measure		circus

635

a rock singer. [Latin *īnfatuātus,* past participle of *īnfatuāre* to make a fool of, from *in* in + *fatuus* foolish.]

in·fat·u·at·ed (in fach′ü ā′tid) *adj.* affected with a passion or attraction that is childish or foolish and will pass quickly.

in·fat·u·a·tion (in fach′ü ā′shən) *n.* **1.** the act of infatuating or the state of being infatuated. **2.** a passion or attraction that passes quickly.

in·fect (in fekt′) *v.t.* **1.** to cause disease in by introducing certain microorganisms. **2.** to contaminate with microorganisms that cause disease: *The dirty bandage infected the wound.* **3.** to affect or influence, as with feelings or beliefs: *Your happiness infected all of us.* [Latin *īnfectus,* past participle of *īnficere* to put in, stain, taint.]

in·fec·tion (in fek′shən) *n.* **1.** the invasion of part of the body by certain microorganisms, such as bacteria, viruses, or fungi, whose growth cause disease. **2.** a disease or other harmful condition resulting from this. **3.** the fact or state of being infected. **4.** the communication of a feeling, belief, or state of mind.

in·fec·tious (in fek′shəs) *adj.* **1.** (of a disease) caused or transmitted by infection. **2.** capable of producing infection; containing disease-producing microorganisms. **3.** readily communicated to others; tending to spread: *infectious laughter.* —**in·fec′tious·ly,** *adv.* —**in·fec′tious·ness,** *n.*

infectious mononucleosis, a contagious, acute infectious disease caused by a herpeslike virus that most often affects young adults and adolescents, characterized by the presence of abnormal lymphocytes in the blood, fever, sore throat, and fatigue. Also, **glandular fever.**

in·fec·tive (in fek′tiv) *adj.* likely to produce infection; infectious.

in·fe·lic·i·tous (in′fə lis′i təs) *adj.* **1.** not suitable or appropriate; unfitting: *an infelicitous comment.* **2.** characterized by bad luck; unfortunate: *an infelicitous turn of events.*

in·fe·lic·i·ty (in′fə lis′i tē) *n., pl.* **-ties. 1.** the state or quality of being infelicitous. **2.** something that is inappropriate.

in·fer (in fûr′) *v.,* **-ferred, -fer·ring.** —*v.t.* to derive or conclude by reasoning from something known or assumed: *From your grades I inferred you were a good student.* —*v.i.* to draw inferences. [Latin *īnferre* to bring into, deduce.]

in·fer·ence (in′fər əns) *n.* **1.** something that is inferred; conclusion. **2.** the act or process of inferring: *to reason by inference.*

in·fer·en·tial (in′fə ren′shəl) *adj.* involving or depending on inference. —**in′fer·en′tial·ly,** *adv.*

in·fe·ri·or (in fîr′ē ər) *adj.* **1.** of poor quality; below average: *The food at that restaurant is inferior.* **2.** low or lower in quality, value, or importance: *to feel inferior to other people.* **3.** low or lower in place or rank; subordinate: *an inferior position.* **4.** *Anatomy.* (of an organ or part) lower in place or position or directed downward; below in relation to another structure: *inferior vena cava.* **5.** *Botany.* (of a plant part) growing below some other part: *inferior ovary.* **6.** between the earth and the sun: *Venus is an inferior planet.* —*n.* a person who is inferior to others, as in rank or achievement. [Latin *īnferior* lower, comparative of *īnferus* low.]

in·fe·ri·or·i·ty (in fîr′ē ôr′i tē, -or′-) *n.* the quality or condition of being inferior.

inferiority complex 1. *Psychology.* a general, intense feeling of personal unworthiness and inadequacy leading to shyness or aggressiveness. **2.** *Informal.* lack of self-confidence or esteem.

in·fer·nal (in fûr′nəl) *adj.* **1.** of, relating to, or characteristic of hell. **2.** like or appropriate to hell; hellish; diabolical: *infernal cruelty.* **3.** *Informal.* hateful; outrageous: *an infernal nuisance.* [Late Latin *īnfernālis* relating to the underworld, going back to Latin *īnfernus* low.] —**in·fer′nal·ly,** *adv.*

in·fer·no (in fûr′nō) *n., pl.* **-nos. 1.** hell. **2.** any place resembling hell, esp. one having intense heat: *The furnace room was an inferno.* [Italian *inferno,* from Latin *īnfernus* lying beneath.]

in·fer·tile (in fûr′təl) *adj.* not fertile; barren. —**in′fer·til′i·ty,** *n.* —For Synonyms, see **barren.**

in·fest (in fest′) *v.t.* to overrun or occur in large numbers so as to be harmful or troublesome: *Weeds infested the garden.* [Latin *īnfestāre* to attack, trouble.]

in·fes·ta·tion (in′fes tā′shən) *n.* the act of infesting or the state of being infested.

in·fi·del (in′fi dəl, -del′) *n.* **1.** a person who does not believe in any religion. **2.** among Muslims, a person who does not accept Islam. **3.** among Christians, a person who does not accept Christianity. —*adj.* **1.** having no religious beliefs. **2.** not accepting a particular faith, esp. Christianity or Islam. **3.** of or relating to unbelievers. [Latin *īnfidēlis* faithless, unbelieving.] —For Synonyms *(n.),* see **pagan.**

in·fi·del·i·ty (in′fi del′i tē) *n., pl.* **-ties. 1.** lack of faith; disloyalty. **2.** marital unfaithfulness; adultery. **3.** lack of belief in a particular religion, esp. Christianity or Islam. **4.** a disloyal or adulterous act.

infield

in·field (in′fēld′) *n. Baseball.* **1.** the area bounded by the paths connecting the bases. **2.** the first, second, and third basemen and shortstop, collectively.

in·field·er (in′fēl′dər) *n. Baseball.* a player who plays a position in the infield.

in·fight·ing (in′fī′ting) *n.* **1.** boxing or other fighting in which heavy blows are delivered at close range. **2.** *Informal.* conflict or dissension among members of a group or others who are closely associated, as in a business. —**in′fight′er,** *n.*

in·fil·trate (in fil′trāt, in′fil trāt′) *v.,* **-trat·ed, -trat·ing.** —*v.t.* **1.** to move members of a faction or group gradually and secretly into positions of power or responsibility within (an organization or government). **2.** (of troops) to move through (enemy lines) in order to attack the rear or engage in sabotage or espionage. **3.** to filter into or through; permeate. **4.** to cause (a liquid or gas) to pass through pores or openings. —*v.i.* to pass into or through a substance by filtering. —**in·fil·tra·tor** (in′fil trā′tər, in fil′trā-), *n.*

in·fil·tra·tion (in′fil trā′shən) *n.* **1.** the act of infiltrating or the state of being infiltrated. **2.** something that infiltrates.

infin., infinitive.

in·fi·nite (in′fə nit) *adj.* **1.** having no limits or end; boundless: *Space seems to be infinite.* **2.** immeasurably or extremely great; immense; vast: *We took infinite care in packing the china and crystal.* **3.** *Mathematics.* **a.** of or designating a quantity larger than any assigned number. **b.** of or relating to a set containing an unlimited number of elements. —*n.* **1.** something that is infinite. **2. the Infinite.** God. [Latin *īnfīnītus* unlimited.] —**in′fi·nite·ly,** *adv.* —**in′fi·nite·ness,** *n.*

in·fin·i·tes·i·mal (in′fi ni tes′ə məl) *adj.* **1.** so small as to be immeasurable or insignificant: *an infinitesimal speck of dust.* **2.** *Mathematics.* of, relating to, or designating a variable that becomes arbitrarily small, approaching zero as a limit. —*n. Mathematics.* an infinitesimal variable. [Modern Latin *infinitesimus* (from Latin *īnfīnītus* unlimited) + -AL[1].] —**in′fi·ni·tes′i·mal·ly,** *adv.*

in·fin·i·tive (in fin′i tiv) *n.* a form of a verb expressing existence or action, without indicating person or number. In English, it is often preceded by *to.* In the sentences *My dog likes to run* and *We must leave,* the verb forms *to run* and *leave* are infinitives. [Late Latin *īnfīnītīvus,* from Latin *īnfīnītus* unlimited (because it does not indicate definite persons or numbers).]

in·fin·i·tude (in fin′i tüd′, -tūd′) *n.* **1.** the quality of being infinite. **2.** an infinite quantity, number, or extent.

in·fin·i·ty (in fin′i tē) *n., pl.* **-ties. 1.** the state or quality of being infinite; boundlessness. **2.** something that is infinite, as space or time. **3.** an indefinitely or extremely great amount or number: *an infinity of details.* **4.** *Mathematics.* a quantity of unbounded magnitude, larger than any assigned number, represented by the symbol ∞. [Latin *īnfīnītās* boundlessness.]

in·firm (in fûrm′) *adj.* **1.** physically weak, esp. from old age. **2.** lacking firmness of will, purpose, or character; irresolute. [Latin *īnfirmus* feeble, sick.] —**in·firm′ly,** *adv.* —**in·firm′ness,** *n.*

in·fir·ma·ry (in fûr′mə rē) *n., pl.* **-ries**. a place, as in a school or factory, for the care or treatment of the sick or injured. [Medieval Latin *infirmaria* hospital, from Latin *infirmus* sick.]
in·fir·mi·ty (in fûr′mi tē) *n., pl.* **-ties**. **1.** the state or quality of being infirm; physical weakness; feebleness. **2.** a physical defect or ailment, esp. from old age. **3.** a moral weakness or failing.
in·flame (in flām′) *v.,* **-flamed, -flam·ing.** —*v.t.* **1.** to excite to great emotion; stir up: *The speaker inflamed the audience.* **2.** to make hot, red, swollen, or painful; cause inflammation in: *The infection inflamed my finger.* **3.** to set on fire; kindle. **4.** to increase or intensify, as anger or violence. —*v.i.* **1.** to become affected, as a part of the body, with inflammation. **2.** to become excited with great emotion. **3.** to catch on fire. [Old French *enflammer* to set on fire, excite, irritate, from Latin *inflammāre* to set on fire.]
in·flam·ma·ble (in flam′ə bəl) *adj.* **1.** capable of being set on fire easily; flammable. **2.** easily excited or aroused. —*n.* something that can be set on fire easily; combustible. —**in·flam′ma·bil′i·ty,** *n.* —**in·flam′ma·bly,** *adv.*

> **Usage** Because the prefix **in-** often means "not," **inflammable** is sometimes mistakenly thought to mean "not capable of being set on fire." In fact, the prefix **in** in **inflammable** is simply an intensifier that strengthens the meaning of the rest of the word, so that **inflammable** actually means "capable of being set on fire easily." In order to avoid any misunderstanding, **flammable**, which has the same meaning, is usually used instead in warnings and labels.

in·flam·ma·tion (in′flə mā′shən) *n.* **1.** a reaction of body tissue to injury, infection, or irritation, characterized by heat, redness, swelling, and pain. **2.** the act of inflaming or the state of being inflamed.
in·flam·ma·to·ry (in flam′ə tôr′ē) *adj.* **1.** tending to excite strong emotion or violent action: *an inflammatory statement.* **2.** of, relating to, or characterized by inflammation.
in·flat·a·ble (in flā′tə bəl) *adj.* that can be inflated: *an inflatable rubber raft.* —*n.* something, esp. a rubber or plastic boat, that can be inflated. —**in·fla′ta·bil′i·ty,** *n.*
in·flate (in flāt′) *v.,* **-flat·ed, -flat·ing.** —*v.t.* **1.** to cause to swell by filling with air or gas; distend: *to inflate the lungs.* **2.** to enhance or give a boost to: *Fame can inflate one's ego.* **3.** to increase beyond previous or usual levels, as prices or currency. —*v.i.* to become inflated. [Latin *inflātus,* past participle of *inflāre* to blow into.] —**in·flat′er;** *also,* **in·fla′tor,** *n.*
in·fla·tion (in flā′shən) *n.* **1.** the act of inflating or the state of being inflated. **2.** an economic condition characterized by a rise in the average price level, usually caused by an increase in money supply without a corresponding increase in the supply of goods and services.
in·fla·tion·ar·y (in flā′shə ner′ē) *adj.* of, relating to, or causing economic inflation.
in·fla·tion·ist (in flā′shə nist) *n.* a person who favors economic inflation.
in·flect (in flekt′) *v.t.* **1.** to change or vary the tone or pitch of (the voice); modulate. **2.** to vary the form of (a word) by inflection. **3.** to turn from a direct line or course; bend. [Latin *inflectere* to change, bend.]
in·flec·tion (in flek′shən) *also, British,* **inflexion**. *n.* **1.** a change or variation in the tone or pitch of the voice. **2.a.** a process by which the form of a word is changed to express grammatical or syntactical relationships. **b.** a word formed by this process. **3.** the act of inflecting or the state of being inflected. **4.** a bend or angle. **5.** *Mathematics.* (on a curve) a point at which the curvature changes from convex to concave or vice versa. Also *(def. 5),* **inflection point.**

> **Usage** In language, **inflection** is a change in the form of a word that indicates a change in its use or meaning. It is an economical process that allows the same word, with minor changes, to function in different ways. There are three types of **inflection** in English: declension, conjugation, and comparison. *Declension,* which applies to nouns and pronouns, gives information about number (singular or plural) and case (nominative, objective, possessive), as in *horse, horses, horse's, horses'* or *they, them, their, theirs. Conjugation,* which applies to verbs, gives information about time (present or past, for instance), person (first, second, third), and number (singular or plural), as in *dance, dances, danced, dancing* or *drink, drinks, drank, drunk, drinking. Comparison,* which applies to adjectives and adverbs, gives information on degree of intensity (positive, comparative, or superlative), as in *cold, colder, coldest* or *sad, sadder, saddest.* Whereas lower-level dictionaries show both regular and irregular inflected forms, high school and college dictionaries usually show only irregular inflections, such as *child, children* and *good, better, best.* For another Usage Note, see **comparison.**

in·flec·tion·al (in flek′shə nəl) *also, British,* **inflexional**. *adj.* of, relating to, or showing grammatical inflection.

in·flex·i·ble (in flek′sə bəl) *adj.* **1.** that cannot be bent; stiff; rigid. **2.** unyielding in mind or purpose; adamant: *An inflexible person never admits being wrong.* **3.** that cannot be changed or altered; immutable: *an inflexible rule.* [Latin *inflexibilis* that cannot be bent.] —**in·flex′i·bil′i·ty,** *n.* —**in·flex′i·bly,** *adv.* —For Synonyms, see **stiff.**
in·flex·ion (in flek′shən) *British.* inflection.
in·flex·ion·al (in flek′shə nəl) *British.* inflectional.
in·flict (in flikt′) *v.t.* **1.** to cause or administer by or as by striking: *to inflict pain, to inflict a wound, to inflict a blow.* **2.** to impose (something unwelcome) on someone: *to inflict punishment, to inflict a burden.* [Latin *inflictus,* past participle of *infligere* to dash against, impose upon.]
in·flic·tion (in flik′shən) *n.* **1.** the act of inflicting. **2.** something that is inflicted, such as pain, punishment, or suffering.
in-flight (in′flīt′) *adj.* happening, given, or shown during the flight of an aircraft: *in-flight meals, movies and other in-flight entertainment.*
in·flo·res·cence (in′flô res′əns) *n.* **1.a.** the mode of arrangement of a cluster of flowers in relation to the stem or stems in the cluster and in relation to each other. **b.** a flower cluster. **c.** flowers collectively. **d.** a solitary flower. **2.** the unfolding of blossoms; flowering. [Modern Latin *inflorescentia,* from Late Latin *inflōrēscere* to begin to blossom, going back to Latin *in* in + *flōs* flower.] —**in′flo·res′cent,** *adj.*

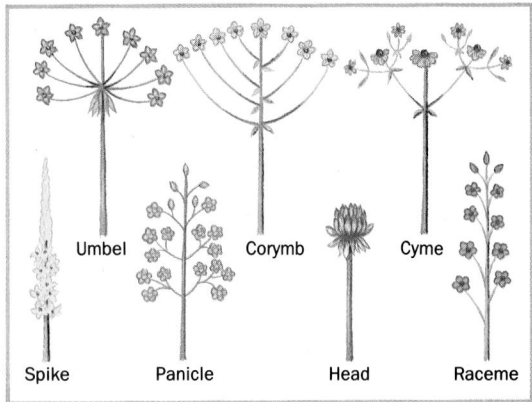

Umbel   Corymb   Cyme

Spike   Panicle   Head   Raceme

common types of **inflorescence**

in·flow (in′flō′) *n.* **1.** the act of flowing in. **2.** something that flows in.
in·flu·ence (in′flü əns) *n.* **1.a.** the power or capacity of persons or things to produce effects on others or to affect the outcome of events, esp. by indirect or invisible means: *The moon exerts an influence on the tides. Do you have any influence over your friend?* **b.** the power to produce effects by virtue of one's wealth, social position, or prestige: *He tried to use his political influence to get the contract for the municipal building.* **2.** an effect thus produced: *She had a great influence on my career.* **3.** a person or thing that possesses or exercises the power to affect others: *Those friends were a bad influence.* —*v.t.,* **-enced, -enc·ing. 1.** to change or affect the thought, nature, or behavior of; persuade; sway: *My friend influenced me to try out for the play.* **2.** to have or produce an effect on; modify: *Their opinions influenced my thinking.* [Old French *influence* power flowing from the stars, from Medieval Latin *influentia* literally, a flowing in, from Latin *influent-,* stem of *influens,* present participle of *influere* to flow in, from *in* in + *fluere* to flow; referring to the former belief that forces flowing in from stars and planets influenced human life.]
in·flu·en·tial (in′flü en′shəl) *adj.* having or exerting influence: *The banker is a very influential person in that community.*
in·flu·en·za (in′flü en′zə) *n.* a highly contagious viral infection characterized by fever, headache, coughing, exhaustion, and inflammation of the mucous membranes. Also, **flu**. [Italian *influenza* influence, influenza (because the disease was once believed to be caused by the *influence* of the stars), from Medieval Latin *influentia.* See INFLUENCE.]

a	at	e	end	o	hot	u	up	hw	white		about
ā	ape	ē	me	ō	old	ū	use	ng	song		taken
ä	far	i	it	ô	fork	ü	rule	th	thin	ə	pencil
âr	care	ī	ice	oi	oil	u̇	pull	t͟h	this		lemon
				ou	out	ûr	turn	zh	measure		circus
			î r	pierce							

I

in·flux (in′fluks′) *n.* **1.** a continual flow: *the influx of goods into a country.* **2.** the act of flowing in, as of a liquid or gas. **3.** the place at which a river flows into another body of water; mouth. [Late Latin *īnflūxus* a flowing in, from Latin *īnfluere* to flow in.]

in·fo (in′fō′) *n. Informal.* information. [Short for INFO(RMATION).]

in·fold (in fōld′) enfold.

in·form (in fôrm′) *v.t.* **1.** to give information to; make known to; tell: *The police informed the prisoners of their rights. Please inform me when the train arrives.* **2.** to inspire with a specific quality or character; animate. —*v.i.* to give or disclose incriminating information (with *on* or *against*): *The criminal informed on the other members of the gang.* [Old French *enformer* to give form to, tell, from Latin *informare,* from *in* + *forma* shape, pattern.]

in·for·mal (in fôr′məl) *adj.* **1.** not bound by or following fixed customs, rules, or ceremonies: *The meeting of the board of directors was informal.* **2.** characteristic of or suitable for everyday or ordinary use or occasions: *informal clothes, an informal speech.* **3.** lacking or not requiring ceremony or elaborate detail or dress: *an informal atmosphere, an informal wedding.* **4.** (of language) characteristic of or appropriate for everyday speech or writing. —**in·for′mal·ly,** *adv.*

Usage Informal language, as opposed to **formal** language, is our usual way of speaking and writing, the language we use in everyday conversations with family and friends, teachers and colleagues. Most of us use different words in different situations without being aware of it. We would most likely use the informal *Hi!* to greet a friend, but would be more apt to say *How do you do?* when introduced to the governor of our state. *Would you like to go to a movie with me?* is an example of an informal invitation, whereas *We request the pleasure of your company* is the more formal language we might find in a wedding invitation. If we were making a speech or writing a book report, it would be customary to use more formal language. The most formal language can be found in legal documents such as leases, in scholarly books and journals, or in formal, written invitations. Although there are no strict guidelines governing the use of informal or formal language, the distinction is not between spoken and written words. It is only a question of what kind of language is most appropriate for the situation.

in·for·mal·i·ty (in′fôr mal′i tē) *n., pl.* **-ties. 1.** the state or quality of being informal. **2.** an informal act.

in·form·ant (in fôr′mənt) *n.* a person who gives information.

in·for·ma·tion (in′fər mā′shən) *n.* **1.** facts given or learned about something: *I got my information on Aztec customs from the encyclopedia. We asked for information about the train schedule.* **2.** the act of informing or the state of being informed. **3.** a person or service that answers questions and provides facts for the public. **4.** a formal accusation filed by a prosecuting officer rather than by a grand jury. —**in′for·ma′tion·al,** *adj.*

information science, the study of the means by which information can be most efficiently collected, stored, processed, and distributed by computers.

information theory, the branch of mathematics concerned with analyzing factors, such as noise and distortion, that affect the transmission and reception of information, esp. in communications systems.

in·form·a·tive (in fôr′mə tiv) *adj.* giving information; instructive.

in·formed (in fôrmd′) *adj.* having or based on information or knowledge: *The reporter got the story from an informed source inside the mayor's office.*

informed consent, permission by a patient for a doctor to perform an operation or other medical procedure, given after the doctor has explained the dangers involved.

in·form·er (in fôr′mər) *n.* **1.** a person who informs on others, often for money: *an informer for the police.* **2.** informant.

infra- *prefix* below; beneath: *infrared.* [Latin *īnfrā.*]

in·frac·tion (in frak′shən) *n.* the act or an instance of breaking or violating something, such as a law or rule; infringement: *The driver was fined for a parking infraction.* [Latin *īnfrāctiō* a breaking.]

in·fra·hu·man (in′frə hū′mən, -ū′mən) *adj.* **1.** connoting a condition below the human level, usually said of primates at a lower stage of developmental evolution than hominids. **2.** subhuman. [INFRA- + HUMAN.]

in·fra·red (in′frə red′) *adj.* relating to, having, or using that portion of the spectrum of electromagnetic radiation whose wavelengths are longer than those of visible light but shorter than those of microwaves. When a body absorbs infrared radiation, its temperature rises. [INFRA- + RED.]

in·fra·son·ic (in′frə son′ik) *adj.* of or relating to a frequency of sound below the range heard by the human ear, or lower than 20 hertz. [INFRA- + SONIC.]

in·fra·struc·ture (in′frə struk′chər) *n.* a basic foundation or substructure on which the functioning of a system or organization depends, esp. the fundamental facilities and installations of a country, city, or state, such as transportation, schools, roads, communications, and public utilities. [INFRA- + STRUCTURE.]

in·fre·quen·cy (in frē′kwən sē) *n.* the state or quality of being infrequent. Also, **in·fre′quence.**

in·fre·quent (in frē′kwənt) *adj.* not happening or appearing often; not frequent; rare: *infrequent visits from a friend who lives far away.* [Latin *īnfrequēns.*] —**in·fre′quent·ly,** *adv.*

in·fringe (in frinj′) *v.,* **-fringed, -fring·ing.** —*v.i.* to trespass or intrude (with *on* or *upon*): *The proposed law would infringe on the rights of the people.* —*v.t.* to break or violate, as a law or agreement. [Latin *īnfringere* to break off, weaken.] —**in·fring′er,** *n.* —For Synonyms, see **intrude.**

in·fringe·ment (in frinj′mənt) *n.* the act or an instance of infringing.

in·fu·ri·ate (in fyūr′ē āt′) *v.t.,* **-at·ed, -at·ing.** to make furious; enrage. [Medieval Latin *infuriatus,* past participle of *infuriare,* from Latin *in* in + *furia* rage.] —**in·fu′ri·at′ing·ly,** *adv.* —**in·fu′ri·a′tion,** *n.*

in·fuse (in fūz′) *v.t.,* **-fused, -fus·ing. 1.** to instill, as principles or qualities: *The parents infused a sense of honor into their children.* **2.** to cause to have a specified thought or feeling; inspire; imbue: *The brave officer infused the troops with courage.* **3.** to steep or soak in a liquid: *to infuse tea leaves in boiling water.* [Latin *īnfūsus,* past participle of *īnfundere* to pour into, moisten.]

in·fu·si·ble (in fū′zə bəl) *adj.* incapable of being fused or melted.

in·fu·sion (in fū′zhən) *n.* **1.** the act or process of infusing. **2.** something that is infused in a liquid. **3.** a liquid extract obtained by steeping or soaking a substance in a liquid.

in·fu·so·ri·an (in′fū sôr′ē ən) *n.* ciliate. [Modern Latin *Infusoria* a class of protozoans, from Latin *īnfūsus,* past participle of *īnfundere* to pour into; referring to their presence in things soaked in a liquid.] —**in′fu·so′ri·al,** *adj.*

-ing¹ *suffix* **1.** (used to form nouns from verbs) **a.** the act, art, or process or instance of performing the action of the root verb: *her sewing, their meeting, our skating.* **b.** the product or result of such action: *to make a drawing, a reading of poems.* **c.** material used for a specific purpose as indicated by the root verb: *lining, roofing, scaffolding.* **d.** something that does the action of the root verb: *bedding, a covering for the head.* **2.** (used to form nouns from other nouns) of the nature of, belonging to, or involving the noun root: *bookkeeping, carpeting, ticking.* [Middle English *-ing, -yng,* from Old English *-ing, -ung,* suffix forming nouns of action from verbs.]

-ing² *suffix* **1.** used to form the present participle of verbs: *He is walking. We were talking.* **2.** used to form adjectives from the present participle of verbs: *a charming woman, a leading citizen.* **3.** used to form adjectives from words other than verbs: *swashbuckling.* [Middle English *-ing(e),* form of *-ind, -end,* from Old English *-ende,* suffix forming the present participle.]

in·gen·ious (in jēn′yəs) *adj.* **1.** conceived, made, or done with cleverness, originality, or imagination: *an ingenious plan, an ingenious contraption.* **2.** characterized by, showing, or having creative ability; imaginative; inventive: *an ingenious designer.* [Latin *ingeniōsus* clever, from *ingenium* natural ability, talent.] —**in·gen′ious·ly,** *adv.* —**in·gen′ious·ness,** *n.* —For Synonyms, see **clever.**

in·gé·nue (än′zhə nū′, -nū′, -jə-, an′-; *French* aN zhā NY′) *n., pl.* **-nues** (-nüz′, -nūz′; *French* -NY′). **1.** an innocent or unsophisticated girl or young woman. **2.a.** the role of such a person in a theatrical presentation. **b.** an actress who plays such a role. [French *ingénue,* feminine of *ingénu* artless, from Latin *ingenuus* freeborn, candid.]

in·ge·nu·i·ty (in′jə nū′i tē, -nū′-) *n., pl.* **-ties. 1.** cleverness, originality, or imagination shown in conceiving, making, or doing something. **2.** cleverness or originality of design or conception: *The ingenuity of the plan surprised us.* [Latin *ingenuitās* frankness; influenced in meaning by INGENIOUS.]

in·gen·u·ous (in jen′ū əs) *adj.* **1.** honest and frank; straightforward; candid: *an ingenuous reply.* **2.** innocent and simple; guileless; naive: *an ingenuous manner.* [Latin *ingenuus* freeborn, candid.] —**in·gen′u·ous·ly,** *adv.* —**in·gen′u·ous·ness,** *n.*

in·gest (in jest′) *v.t.* to put into the body, as food or liquid, for digestion. [Latin *ingestus,* past participle of *ingerere* to carry in.]

in·ges·tion (in jes′chən) *n.* the act or process of ingesting food or other substances. —**in·ges′tive,** *adj.*

in·gle·nook (ing′gəl nùk′) *n.* a corner beside a chimney or fireplace.

in·glo·ri·ous (in glôr′ē əs) *adj.* bringing no glory or honor; shameful; disgraceful: *an inglorious battle against a poorly armed enemy.* —**in·glo′ri·ous·ly,** *adv.* —**in·glo′ri·ous·ness,** *n.*

1,500 pounds (680 kilograms) of gold **ingots**

in·got (ing′gət) *n.* a mass of metal cast into a shape convenient for storage or further processing. [Old English *in* in + *goten* poured, past participle of *gēotan* to pour.]

in·graft (in graft′) engraft.

in·grain (*v.,* in grān′; *adj., n.,* in′grān′) *v.t.* to fix deeply or permanently: *to ingrain an idea in someone's mind.* —*adj.* **1.** (of yarn or fiber) dyed before weaving or knitting. **2.** made of yarn or fiber dyed before weaving or knitting. —*n.* yarn or fiber dyed before weaving or knitting. [IN-[2] + obsolete *grain* color, from Old French *graine* seed of plants, cochineal, going back to Latin *grānum* seed; with reference to the resemblance to seeds of the bodies of the insects from which cochineal is made.]

in·grained (in grānd′, in′grānd′) *adj.* **1.** deeply or permanently fixed; firmly established: *ingrained prejudice.* **2.** thorough or habitual: *an ingrained hypocrite.*

in·grate (in′grāt′) *n.* an ungrateful person. [Latin *ingrātus* ungrateful.]

in·gra·ti·ate (in grā′shē āt′) *v.t.,* -at·ed, -at·ing. to bring (oneself) deliberately into another's favor. [IN-[3] + Latin *grātia* favor + -ATE[1].] —**in·gra′ti·a′tion,** *n.* —**in·gra′ti·at′ing,** *adj.* —**in·gra′ti·at′ing·ly,** *adv.*

in·grat·i·tude (in grat′i tüd′, -tūd′) *n.* a lack of gratitude; ungratefulness.

in·gre·di·ent (in grē′dē ənt) *n.* **1.** any one of the component parts of a mixture: *Butter and eggs are two of the ingredients of this sauce.* **2.** a component part of anything. [Latin *ingrediēns,* present participle of *ingredī* to enter, begin.]

> **Synonyms** Ingredient, constituent, component, and element denote one of the parts or units of a composite or compound. **Ingredient** connotes any substance that is, or can be, but need not be, combined with others to form a mixture: *the ingredients of a cake, the ingredients of a successful campaign.* **Constituent** connotes an essential part, which helps to determine the nature of something: *One constituent of democracy is freedom of speech.* **Component** is generally used to describe a functional part of a compound that has a distinct identity: *the components of a radio.* **Element** broadly connotes what is thought of as basic or not further reducible: *to identify the elements in a mineral.*

in·gress (in′gres′) *n.* **1.** the act of going in; entrance. **2.** a place or means of entrance. **3.** the right to go in. [Latin *ingressus* an entrance.]

in·grow·ing (in′grō′ing) *adj.* growing inward or into something.

in·grown (in′grōn′) *adj.* **1.** grown into the flesh, as a hair or toenail. **2.** innate; inborn: *ingrown prejudice.*

in·gui·nal (ing′gwə nəl) *adj.* of, relating to, or located in or near the groin. [Latin *inguinālis,* from *inguen* groin.]

in·gulf (in gulf′) engulf.

in·hab·it (in hab′it) *v.t.* to live in or on: *Many birds inhabit the island.* —*v.i.* Archaic. to live; dwell. [Latin *inhabitāre* to dwell in.] —**in·hab′it·a·ble,** *adj.* —**in·hab′it·er,** *n.*

in·hab·it·ant (in hab′i tənt) *n.* a person or animal that lives in a specified place; resident. [Latin *inhabitāns,* present participle of *inhabitāre* to dwell in.]

in·hal·ant (in hā′lənt) *n.* a substance, esp. a medicine, to be or capable of being inhaled. —*adj.* used for inhaling.

in·ha·la·tion (in′hə lā′shən) *n.* the act of inhaling.

in·ha·la·tor (in′hə lā′tər) *n.* a device that mixes carbon dioxide and oxygen for breathing, used in artificial respiration.

in·hale (in hāl′) *v.,* -haled, -hal·ing. —*v.t.* to draw into the lungs. —*v.i.* to draw something, as air, into the lungs. [IN-[2] + (EX)HALE.]

in·hal·er (in hā′lər) *n.* **1.** a device used to promote the inhaling of a gas or spray, as an anesthetic or medicinal vapor. **2.** a device,

such as a face mask, used to filter air that is breathed in a particle-laden, noxious, or cold environment. **3.** a person who inhales something, esp. tobacco smoke.

in·har·mo·ni·ous (in′här mō′nē əs) *adj.* not in harmony or agreement: *inharmonious sounds.* Also, **in·har·mon·ic** (in′här-mon′ik). —**in′har·mo′ni·ous·ly,** *adv.* —**in′har·mo′ni·ous·ness,** *n.*

in·here (in hîr′) *v.i.,* -hered, -her·ing. to exist as or form a permanent or essential quality, element, or attribute; be inherent (with *in*): *Knowledge and perception inhere in mind alone* (Alexander Bain, 1855). [Latin *inhaerēre* to stick to.] —**in·her·ence** (in hîr′əns, -her′-), **in·her′en·cy,** *n.*

in·her·ent (in hîr′ənt, -her′-) *adj.* existing as or forming a permanent or essential quality, element, or attribute of a person or thing. [Latin *inhaerēns,* present participle of *inhaerēre* to stick to.] —**in·her′ent·ly,** *adv.*

> **Synonyms** Inherent, intrinsic, and innate refer to qualities or attributes thought of as part of the essential character of a person or thing. **Inherent** connotes the inseparability of the quality or attribute from the person or thing: *a person's inherent goodness, the inherent cold of the polar regions.* **Intrinsic** connotes the essential nature of a thing or attribute: *Whether or not you find it attractive, that antique clock has intrinsic value.* **Innate** is properly used only of living things, in referring to what is thought to have been bred in: *a horse's innate speed.*

in·her·it (in her′it) *v.t.* **1.** to receive, as property or a title, from a former owner at his or her death: *I inherited this jewelry from my aunt.* **2.** to receive (a characteristic) through genetic transmission from one's parent or parents. **3.** to receive or come into possession of in any way: *He inherited many of his predecessor's problems.* —*v.i.* to come into or take possession of an inheritance. [Old French *enheriter* to put in possession of an inheritance, from Late Latin *inhērēditāre* to appoint as heir, going back to Latin *in* in + *hērēs* heir.]

in·her·it·a·ble (in her′i tə bəl) *adj.* **1.** capable of being inherited: *an inheritable trait.* **2.** Archaic. capable of inheriting; qualified to inherit.

in·her·it·ance (in her′i təns) *n.* **1.** something that is or may be inherited; legacy: *to receive a large inheritance.* **2.** the act or fact of inheriting.

inheritance tax, a tax imposed on inherited property.

in·her·i·tor (in her′i tər) *n.* a person who inherits something; heir.

in·hib·it (in hib′it) *v.t.* to hold back, as from speaking or acting; check; restrain. [Latin *inhibitus,* past participle of *inhibēre.*] —**in·hib′i·tive, in·hib′i·to′ry,** *adj.*

in·hi·bi·tion (in′i bish′ən, in′hi-) *n.* **1.** a restraint or check on some activity or on one's natural impulses: *My inhibitions prevented me from speaking up.* **2.** the act of inhibiting or the state of being inhibited.

in·hib·i·tor (in hib′i tər) *n.* a substance that slows down or stops a chemical reaction.

in·hos·pi·ta·ble (in hos′pi tə bəl, in′ho spit′ə-) *adj.* **1.** not offering hospitality to guests or visitors; not hospitable; unfriendly. **2.** not providing food, shelter, or other necessities of life: *an inhospitable desert.* —**in·hos′pi·ta·bly,** *adv.*

in·hos·pi·tal·i·ty (in hos′pi tal′i tē, in′hos-) *n.* lack of hospitality.

in-house (*adj.,* in′hous′; *adv.,* in′hous′) *adj.* being, occurring, or done within a business firm or other organization: *an in-house job, a sensitive in-house report.* —*adv.* within or on the inside: *a report produced in-house.*

in·hu·man (in hū′mən, -ū′mən) *adj.* **1.** lacking the feelings or qualities that are considered natural to a human being; without kindness, pity, or compassion: *an inhuman tyrant.* **2.** causing extreme pain, grief, or suffering; savage; brutal: *an inhuman punishment.* **3.** not like or characteristic of a human being: *an inhuman ability, inhuman creatures from another galaxy.* [Latin *inhūmānus* savage, cruel.] —**in·hu′man·ly,** *adv.* —**in·hu′man·ness,** *n.*

in·hu·mane (in′hū mān′, -ū mān′) *adj.* not feeling or showing kindness, pity, or compassion for other human beings or animals; not humane. [Form of INHUMAN.] —**in′hu·mane′ly,** *adv.*

in·hu·man·i·ty (in′hū man′i tē, -ū man′-) *n., pl.* -ties. **1.** the quality or condition of being inhuman or inhumane; lack of kindness, pity, or compassion. **2.** an instance of this; inhuman act.

a	at	e	end	o	hot	u	up	hw	white		about
ā	ape	ē	me	ō	old	ū	use	ng	song	ə	taken
ä	far	i	it	ô	fork	ü	rule	th	thin		pencil
âr	care	ī	ice	oi	oil	u̇	pull	th	this		lemon
		îr	pierce	ou	out	ûr	turn	zh	measure		circus

I

639

in·im·i·cal (i nim′i kəl) *adj.* **1.** not friendly; antagonistic; hostile: *an inimical reaction to a suggestion.* **2.** causing harm; injurious: *Lack of sleep is inimical to good health.* [Late Latin *inimīcālis* hostile, from Latin *inimīcus* enemy.] —**in·im′i·cal·ly,** *adv.*

in·im·i·ta·ble (i nim′i tə bəl) *adj.* that cannot be imitated; matchless. —**in·im′i·ta·bil′i·ty,** *n.* —**in·im′i·ta·bly,** *adv.*

in·iq·ui·tous (i nik′wi təs) *adj.* characterized by iniquity; unjust or wicked: *an iniquitous law.* —**in·iq′ui·tous·ly,** *adv.* —**in·iq′ui·tous·ness,** *n.*

in·iq·ui·ty (i nik′wi tē) *n., pl.* **-ties. 1.** great injustice or wickedness: *the iniquity of slavery.* **2.** a wicked or unjust act. [Latin *inīquitās* injustice.]

i·ni·tial (i nish′əl) *adj.* of, relating to, or occurring at the beginning; first: *the initial letter of a word, the initial step in a process.* —*n.* **1.** the first letter of a person's name or of each part of a person's name: *Sara Ann Smith's initials are S.A.S.* **2.** the first letter of any name or word. —*v.t.,* **-tialed, -tial·ing;** *also, British,* **-tialled, -tial·ling.** to mark or sign with one's initial or initials: *The executive initialed the report after reading it.* [Latin *initiālis* incipient, from *initium* a beginning.]

i·ni·tial·ly (i nish′ə lē) *adv.* at the beginning.

i·ni·ti·ate (*v.,* i nish′ē āt′; *n., adj.,* i nish′ē it) *v.t.* **-at·ed, -at·ing. 1.** to bring into existence; introduce or begin: *to initiate changes in a law.* **2.** to admit (a person) into an organization or group, esp. with formal ceremonies or secret rites. **3.** to introduce to or instruct in some subject: *My father initiated me in the art of cooking.* —*n.* a person who has been initiated into an organization or group. —*adj.* initiated. [Latin *initiātus,* past participle of *initiāre* to begin.] —**i·ni′ti·a′tor,** *n.* —For Synonyms *(v.t.),* see **induct.**

i·ni·ti·a·tion (i nish′ē ā′shən) *n.* **1.** the act of initiating or the state of being initiated. **2.** ceremonies or special rites by which a person is admitted to an organization or group.

i·ni·tia·tive (i nish′ə tiv) *n.* **1.** the first step in doing or beginning something; active role; lead: *Take the initiative and introduce yourself to the new employee.* **2.** the power or ability to originate something or lead in an undertaking: *the initiative to start a business.* **3.a.** the power or right of the general public to introduce and enact a new law or constitutional amendment. **b.** the procedure by which the general public introduces and enacts legislation.

i·ni·ti·a·to·ry (i nish′ē ə tôr′ē, i nish′ə-) *adj.* **1.** introductory; initial. **2.** serving to initiate.

in·ject (in jekt′) *v.t.* **1.** to force (fluid), as with a syringe, through the skin into a muscle, vein, or the like: *to inject serum into the bloodstream.* **2.** to force or drive (fluid) into something: *to inject fuel into an engine.* **3.** to throw in; introduce: *to inject humor into a situation.* [Latin *injectus,* past participle of *injicere* to throw in.] —**in·jec′tor,** *n.*

in·jec·tion (in jek′shən) *n.* **1.** the act or process of injecting. **2.** fluid that is injected. **3.** the act or process of boosting a spacecraft into a desired trajectory or orbit.

in-joke (in′jōk′) *n.* a joke that can be appreciated only by those who have special knowledge through common association or interests.

in·ju·di·cious (in′jü dish′əs) *adj.* showing lack of judgment; not judicious. —**in′ju·di′cious·ly,** *adv.* —**in′ju·di′cious·ness,** *n.*

in·junc·tion (in jungk′shən) *n.* **1.** a court order requiring or forbidding some act. **2.** a command; order; directive: *The crowd ignored the repeated injunctions of the police to disperse.* **3.** the act of requiring or commanding, esp. officially or authoritatively. [Late Latin *injunctiō* command, from Latin *injungere* to join to, enjoin.]

in·jure (in′jər) *v.t.* **-jured, -jur·ing. 1.** to do or cause physical damage to; harm. **2.** to do injustice or wrong to: *The rumors injured the company's reputation.* **3.** to cause suffering to: *The unfair criticism injured my feelings.* [From INJURY.]

> **Synonyms** Injure, hurt, harm, and damage mean to cause someone or something to suffer pain or loss. **Injure** connotes causing temporary or permanent loss, as of function, and may suggest intent: *I injured my leg playing soccer. The neighbors' dog chased our cat and injured it.* **Hurt** may be used similarly, but may also describe pain without serious impairment: *I hurt my hand when I fell, but it wasn't serious.* **Harm,** however, connotes more serious distress or suffering and is often used in the abstract sense: *Thoughtless behavior can harm one's reputation.* **Damage** specifically connotes loss, even though no pain may be involved: *Listening to loud music can damage your hearing permanently.*

in·ju·ri·ous (in jûr′ē əs) *adj.* **1.** causing harm or damage. **2.** slanderous or abusive. [Latin *injūriōsus* harmful, from *injūria* harm.] —**in·ju′ri·ous·ly,** *adv.* —**in·ju′ri·ous·ness,** *n.*

in·ju·ry (in′jə rē) *n., pl.* **-ries. 1.** damage or harm inflicted on or suffered by a person or thing. **2.** injustice or wrong inflicted or suffered. [Latin *injūria.*]

in·jus·tice (in jus′tis) *n.* **1.** a lack of justice; unfairness. **2.** an unjust act.

ink (ingk) *n.* **1.** any of various colored fluids or pastes used esp. for writing, drawing, or printing. **2.** a dark pigment ejected by cuttlefish, squids, and other cephalopods when frightened in order to cloud the water and hide them from their enemies. —*v.t.* to mark, cover, or color with ink. [Old French *enque* liquid used for writing, from Late Latin *encaustum* purple ink, from Greek *enkauston,* from *enkaiein* to burn in; referring to the ancient Greek practice of burning in, or making colors of paintings fast, with heat.] —**ink′er,** *n.*

ink·ber·ry (ingk′ber′ē, -bə rē) *n., pl.* **-ries. 1.** an evergreen shrub, *Ilex glabra,* of the holly family, native to North America, bearing many branches and small, black fruit. **2.** the fruit itself. **3.** pokeweed.

ink·blot (ingk′blot′) *n. Psychology.* any of a group of irregular patterns made by blots of ink that are submitted for interpretation in a Rorschach test. [INK + BLOT.]

ink·horn (ingk′hôrn′) *n.* a small container made of horn or similar material, formerly used to hold ink.

ink-jet printer (ingk′jet′) a high-speed computer printer that forms characters by spraying ink under pressure onto paper through a very fine nozzle.

ink·ling (ing′kling) *n.* **1.** a vague idea or notion: *They had no inkling of what we were talking about.* **2.** a slight suggestion; hint: *They gave us no inkling as to their plans.* [Of uncertain origin.]

ink·stand (ingk′stand′) *n.* **1.** a stand or rack for holding containers of ink and pens. **2.** inkwell.

ink·well (ingk′wel′) *n.* a container for ink, esp. on a desk.

ink·y (ing′kē) *adj.* **ink·i·er, ink·i·est. 1.** dark or black in color: *the inky depths of the ocean.* **2.** marked, covered, or stained with ink. —**ink′i·ness,** *n.*

in·laid (*v.,* in lād′; *adj.,* in′lād′) *v.* the past tense and past participle of **inlay.** —*adj.* **1.** set flush into a surface as a decoration: *The box had inlaid ivory on the lid.* **2.** decorated with a material set flush in the surface: *The table has an inlaid border of thin squares of marble.*

in·land (*adj.,* in′lənd; *adv., n.,* in′land′, -lənd) *adj.* **1.** of, relating to, or located in the interior of a country or region; away from the coast or border: *an inland city.* **2.** carried on or operating within a country or region; domestic: *inland trade.* —*adv.* in or toward the interior of a country or region: *to drive inland from the coast.* —*n.* the interior part of a country or region.

in·land·er (in′lan′dər, -lən-) *n.* a person who lives inland.

in-law (in′lô′) *n. Informal.* a relative by marriage.

in·lay (*v.,* in lā′; *n.,* in′lā′) *v.t.* **-laid, -lay·ing. 1.** to set or embed a material, such as gold or ivory, into the surface of something so as to form a decorative design flush with that surface. **2.** to decorate with a material set flush in the surface: *to inlay a cabinet with ivory.* —*n.* **1.** an inlaid design or material. **2.** a filling of gold, porcelain, or the like cemented into a cavity in a tooth.

in·let (in′let′) *n.* **1.** a narrow channel of water between islands or leading inland from a larger body of water. **2.** an entrance or opening.

in lo·co pa·ren·tis (in lō′kō pə ren′tis) *Latin.* in place of a parent. ➡ used of a school or other organization responsible for a child's welfare away from home. [Latin *in loco parentis* in place of a parent.]

in·mate (in′māt′) *n.* a person confined in a prison, asylum, or similar institution. [IN-³ + MATE¹.]

inlay
detail of a Florentine
table inlaid with stone

in me·di·as res (in mā′dē äs räs′, in mē′dē əs rēz′) *Latin.* in the middle of an action or event, as in a narrative, rather than at the beginning. ➡ used esp. of a narrative that begins in the middle of the action rather than at the beginning. [Latin *in medias res* into the middle of things.]

in me·mo·ri·am (in′mə môr′ē əm) as a memorial (to); in memory (of). [Latin.]

in·most (in′mōst′) *adj.* **1.** farthest in: *the inmost regions of a country.* **2.** most intimate or private; innermost: *inmost feelings.*

[Old English *innemest,* superlative of *inne* in, within; influenced by MOST.]

inn (in) *n.* **1.** a small hotel, esp. in the country. **2.** a restaurant or tavern. [Old English *inn* dwelling.]

in·nards (in′ərdz) *pl. n.* **1.** the internal organs of the body, esp. those inside the chest and abdomen. **2.** the inner parts or workings of anything, such as a machine, building, or vehicle.

in·nate (i nāt′,in′āt) *adj.* **1.** possessed at birth; natural; inborn: *innate intelligence.* **2.** belonging to or forming the essential character of a person or thing. [Latin *innātus,* past participle of *innāscī* to be born in.] —**in·nate′ly,** *adv.* —**in·nate′ness,** *n.* —For Synonyms, see **inherent.**

in·ner (in′ər) *adj.* **1.** located farther in; interior: *an inner chamber.* **2.** of or relating to the mind or soul: *a rich and fulfilling inner life.* **3.** private or intimate; secret: *one's inner feelings.* **4.** not obvious; hidden: *inner meaning.* [Old English *innera,* comparative of *inne* in, within.]

inner city, an old, often central part of a city, characterized by overcrowding and poverty.

inner ear, the area behind the three bones of the middle ear, consisting, in humans, of the vestibule, the semicircular canals, and the cochlea, involved in hearing and maintaining balance. For illustration, see **ear**[1]. Also, **internal ear.**

in·ner·most (in′ər mōst′) *adj.* **1.** most private or intimate; deepest: *one's innermost feelings.* **2.** farthest from the outside; most inward: *the innermost part of a building.*

inner tube, an airtight rubber tube used within a pneumatic tire to maintain a specified air pressure.

in·ning (in′ing) *n.* **1.a.** a division of a baseball game in which both teams bat, the visiting team first, until three players on each team are put out. **b. innings.** a similar division of a cricket match. **2.** *usually,* **innings.** a chance for a person, group, or team to act: *After our opponents leave office, we'll get our innings.* ➡ **Innings** is used as singular or plural. [IN + -ING[1].]

inn·keep·er (in′kē′pər) *n.* a person who owns or manages an inn.

in·no·cence (in′ə səns) *n.* **1.** the state, quality, or fact of being innocent. **2.** *Botany.* bluets.

in·no·cent (in′ə sənt) *adj.* **1.a.** not guilty of a specific crime: *The defendant in the robbery trial was shown to be innocent.* **b.** free from guilt or wrongdoing: *Their seemingly suspicious behavior proved to be entirely innocent.* **2.** free from or unaware of moral wrong, sin, or evil. **3.** not arising from or involving any evil or malicious intent or motive; harmless: *an innocent prank, an innocent remark.* **4.** having or exhibiting the naiveté, ignorance, or unsuspecting nature of one who lacks experience or worldliness. —*n.* **1.** a person, esp. a child, who is free from or unaware of evil or sin. **2.** a simple, inexperienced, or unworldly person. [Latin *innocēns* harmless, blameless.] —**in′no·cent·ly,** *adv.*

in·noc·u·ous (i nok′ū əs) *adj.* harmless; innocent. [Latin *innocuus.*]

in·nom·i·nate bone (i nom′ə nit) hipbone. [Late Latin *innōmjnātus* having no specific name.]

in·no·vate (in′ə vāt′) *v.,* **-vat·ed, -vat·ing.** —*v.t.* to introduce (something new): *to innovate a technique.* —*v.i.* to introduce something new; make changes in something. [Latin *innovātus,* past participle of *innovāre* to renew, alter.] —**in′no·va′tor,** *n.*

in·no·va·tion (in′ə vā′shən) *n.* **1.** something newly introduced; change, as in practice or method: *Anesthesia was a great innovation in medicine.* **2.** the act of innovating.

in·no·va·tive (in′ə vā′tiv) *adj.* **1.** able or tending to innovate: *an innovative teacher.* **2.** characterized by innovation: *an innovative method of controlling pollution.* —**in′no·va′tive·ness,** *n.*

Inns of Court **1.** a group of four legal societies in Britain that have the exclusive right to train barristers and regulate their admission to the British bar. **2.** the buildings that house these societies.

in·nu·en·do (in′ū en′dō) *n., pl.* **-does.** a hint or suggestion, esp. one intended to harm or damage a person's reputation; insinuation. [Latin *innuendō* by nodding to, by intimating, ablative gerund of *innuere* to nod to, intimate; referring to the use of a nod to imply something.] —For Synonyms, see **insinuation.**

in·nu·mer·a·ble (i nü′mər ə bəl, i nū′-) *adj.* too numerous to be counted: *There are innumerable stars in the sky.* —**in·nu′mer·a·ble·ness,** *n.* —**in·nu′mer·a·bly,** *adv.*

in·oc·u·late (i nok′yə lāt′) *v.t.,* **-lat·ed, -lat·ing.** **1.** to inject (a person or animal) with a biological substance, such as a serum or vaccine, in order to produce immunity against a particular disease. **2.** to use (the organism that causes a disease) in the prevention or cure of a disease. [Middle English *enoculaten,* from Latin *inoculātus,* past participle of *inoculāre* to engraft, implant, from *in* in + *oculus* eye, bud; referring to the similarity between introducing a germ into the body to immunize and grafting a bud onto a plant.] —**in·oc′u·la′tive,** *adj.* —**in·oc′u·la′tor,** *n.*

in·oc·u·la·tion (i nok′yə lā′shən) *n.* **1.** the act of inoculating, esp. in order to produce immunity to a disease. **2.** an injection given in order to produce immunity to a disease.

in·of·fen·sive (in′ə fen′siv) *adj.* **1.** not causing resentment or anger; not giving offense: *an inoffensive person, an inoffensive act.* **2.** not injurious or damaging; harmless: *an inoffensive snake, inoffensive vapors.* **3.** not disagreeable to the senses: *an inoffensive smell.* —**in′of·fen′sive·ly,** *adv.* —**in′of·fen′sive·ness,** *n.*

in·op·er·a·ble (in op′ər ə bəl) *adj.* **1.** that cannot be cured or treated by surgery. **2.** not functioning; inoperative.

in·op·er·a·tive (in op′ər ə tiv, -op′ə rā′-) *adj.* not functioning or effective; not operative.

in·op·por·tune (in op′ər tün′, -tūn′) *adj.* coming or occurring at a bad time; untimely or inconvenient. —**in·op′por·tune′ly,** *adv.* —**in·op′por·tune′ness,** *n.*

in·or·di·nate (in ôr′də nit) *adj.* beyond what is necessary or proper; excessive; immoderate: *inordinate demands.* [Latin *inōrdinātus* not arranged, going back to *in-* not + *ōrdō* row, arrangement.] —**in·or′di·nate·ly,** *adv.* —For Synonyms, see **excessive.**

in·or·gan·ic (in′ôr gan′ik) *adj.* **1.** containing no carbon compounds of high molecular weight; not organic: *an inorganic compound.* **2.** not produced by animals or plants. **3.** not having the organized structure of animals and plants. —**in′or·gan′i·cal·ly,** *adv.*

inorganic chemistry, the branch of chemistry concerned with the study of inorganic compounds.

i·no·si·tol (i nō′si tôl′, -tōl′) *n.* a crystalline alcohol widely distributed in plants and animals, an isomer of which is one of the vitamins of the B complex. Formula: $C_6H_{12}O_6$.

in·pa·tient (in′pā′shənt) *n.* patient who remains in a hospital or similar institution while receiving care and treatment.

in·put (in′pùt′) *n.* **1.** anything put or taken in. **2.** the amount of power or energy that is put into something, such as a machine. **3.** information fed into a computer or any other information storage and retrieval system. **4.** information, such as electrical or sound signals, fed into a mechanical, electronic, or other device. —*v.t.* to enter (information) into a computer, as by a keyboard.

in·quest (in′kwest′) *n.* **1.a.** a judicial or official inquiry made by a jury or other body appointed by law. **b.** a jury or body appointed to make such an inquiry. **c.** the finding of such a jury or body. **2.** a coroner's inquest. [Old French *enqueste* official inquiry, going back to Latin *inquīrere* to search for.]

in·qui·e·tude (in kwī′i tüd′, -tūd′) *n.* restlessness or uneasiness.

in·quire (in kwīr′) *also,* **enquire.** *v.,* **-quired, -quir·ing.** —*v.i.* **1.** to seek knowledge or information by asking a question or questions: *The driver inquired about directions.* **2.** to make an investigation, search, or examination (with *into*): *The police inquired into the victim's background.* —*v.t.* to seek knowledge or information about: *to inquire the way.* [Latin *inquīrere* to search for.] —**in·quir′er,** *n.* —**in·quir′ing·ly,** *adv.*

·to inquire after. to ask about the health of.

·to inquire for. to ask to see or speak to: *Someone called inquiring for you.*

in·quir·y (in kwīr′ē, in′kwə rē) *also,* **enquiry.** *n., pl.* **-quir·ies.** **1.** the act of inquiring. **2.** an investigation, search, or examination. **3.** a question; query.

> **Synonyms** **Inquiry, investigation,** and **probe** may all denote an attempt to establish the truth about something. **Inquiry** suggests an orderly attempt to uncover facts: *a scientific inquiry, an inquiry into a job applicant's background.* **Investigation** connotes a systematic, careful search: *The government ordered a full investigation of the scandal.* **Probe** suggests a penetrating, critical investigation into a crime or a series of questionable actions: *a Congressional probe into price fixing.*

in·qui·si·tion (in′kwə zish′ən) *n.* **1.a.** a judicial or official inquiry; inquest. **b.** a document recording the finding of such an inquiry. **2.** any strict or thorough inquiry or questioning. **3. the Inquisition.** the Roman Catholic tribunal established in the thirteenth century for the discovery, examination, and trial of heretics. It was abolished in the early nineteenth century. [Latin *inquīsītiō* a searching for.]

in·quis·i·tive (in kwiz′i tiv) *adj.* **1.** eager for knowledge; curious. **2.** unduly curious; nosy; prying. —**in·quis′i·tive·ly,** *adv.* —**in·quis′i·tive·ness,** *n.*

in·quis·i·tor (in kwiz′i tər) *n.* **1.** a person who conducts an

a	at	e	end	o	hot	u	up	hw	white		about
ā	ape	ē	me	ō	old	ū	use	ng	song		taken
ä	far	i	it	ô	fork	ü	rule	th	thin	ə	pencil
âr	care	ī	ice	oi	oil	ù	pull	th	this		lemon
		îr	pierce	ou	out	ûr	turn	zh	measure		circus

inquisition or makes an inquiry. **2. Inquisitor.** an official of the Inquisition, esp. the head of the tribunal.

in·quis·i·to·ri·al (in kwiz′i tôr′ē əl) *adj.* **1.** of, relating to, or like an inquisitor or inquisition. **2.** unduly curious; inquisitive.

in re (in rē′, in rā′) *Latin.* in the matter of; concerning.

I.N.R.I., the first letters of the Latin words *Iesus Nazarenus, Rex Iudaeorum* (Jesus of Nazareth, King of the Jews) placed on the cross of Christ.

in·road (in′rōd′) *n.* **1.** a sudden, hostile attack or raid. **2.** *also,* **inroads.** an advance that causes loss or injury to a person or thing: *Paying our medical bills made inroads on our savings.*

in·rush (in′rush′) *n.* a sudden rushing or pouring in.

ins. 1. inches. **2.** insulated. **3.** insurance.

in·sane (in sān′) *adj.* **1.** mentally deranged; not sane. **2.** characteristic of or for insane people. **3.** extremely foolish; senseless. [Latin *īnsānus* not sane.] —**in·sane′ly,** *adv.*

in·san·i·tar·y (in san′i ter′ē) *adj.* injurious to health; not sanitary. —**in·san′i·ta′tion,** *n.*

in·san·i·ty (in san′i tē) *n., pl.* **-ties. 1.** the state of being insane; mental derangement. **2.** *Law.* weakness or unsoundness of mind sufficient to render a person incapable of distinguishing between right and wrong or of comprehending the nature and consequences of his or her acts. **3.** extreme folly or senselessness.

in·sa·tia·ble (in sā′shə bəl) *adj.* that cannot be satisfied: *an insatiable thirst.* Also, **in·sa·ti·ate** (in sā′shē it). —**in·sa′tia·bly,** *adv.*

in·scribe (in skrīb′) *v.t.* **-scribed, -scrib·ing. 1.** to write, carve, engrave, or mark (words or characters) on a surface: *The stonecutter inscribed the date on the tombstone.* **2.** to write, carve, engrave, or mark words or characters on (a surface): *The jeweler inscribed the locket with my initials.* **3.** to write a message or note on (something, such as a book) in presenting or giving it to someone. **4.** to draw (a geometric figure) within another figure so that the inner intersects the outer in as many points as possible: *to inscribe a circle within a square.* **5.** to enter (a name) on a list; enroll. [Latin *īnscrībere* to write in or on.] —**in·scrib′er,** *n.*

in·scrip·tion (in skrip′shən) *n.* **1.** something inscribed, esp. words or characters written, carved, engraved, or marked on a surface, as of metal or stone: *an inscription on a tombstone.* **2.** a message or note written on something, such as a book, in presenting or giving it to someone. **3.** the act of inscribing. [Latin *īnscrīptiō* a writing in or on.]

in·scru·ta·ble (in skrü′tə bəl) *adj.* that cannot be easily understood; mysterious; enigmatic: *an inscrutable person, an inscrutable look.* [Late Latin *īnscrūtābilis,* from Latin *in-* not + *scrūtārī* to examine.] —**in·scru′ta·bil′i·ty,** *n.* —**in·scru′ta·bly,** *adv.*

in·seam (in′sēm′) *n.* the seam sewn on the inner side of a trouser leg.

in·sect (in′sekt) *n.* **1.** any of a widely distributed group of arthropods, class Insecta, characterized by a body divided into three parts with three pairs of legs and, in the adult, usually two pairs of wings. Flies, ants, grasshoppers, and beetles are insects. **2.** any similar crawling animal, such as a spider or tick. [Latin *īnsectum* literally, (animal) cut into, from *īnsecāre* to cut into; referring to the segmented body of an insect.]

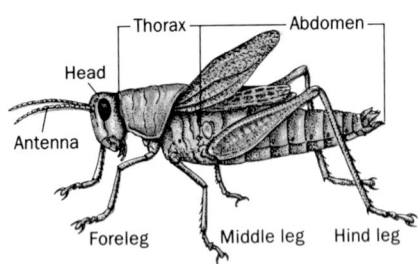

grasshopper, a representative **insect**

in·sec·ti·cide (in sek′tə sīd′) *n.* a chemical or other substance for killing insects and related pests. [Latin *īnsectum* insect + -CIDE².] —**in·sec′ti·cid′al,** *adj.*

in·sec·ti·vore (in sek′tə vôr′) *n.* **1.** any insect-eating animal or plant. **2.** any of certain insect-eating mammals, order Insectivora, such as hedgehogs, moles, and shrews. [French *insectivore,* from Modern Latin *insectivorus.* See INSECTIVOROUS.]

in·sec·tiv·o·rous (in′sek tiv′ər əs) *adj.* **1.** feeding chiefly on insects. **2.** of or relating to mammals belonging to the order Insectivora. [Modern Latin *insectivorus* literally, insect-eating (from Latin *īnsectum* insect + *vorāre* to devour) + -OUS.]

in·se·cure (in′si kyùr′) *adj.* **1.** liable to give way or fail; unstable or unsafe: *The knot was very insecure.* **2.** not assured; uncertain: *My position with the company was insecure.* **3.** lacking in self-confidence: *an insecure person.* —**in′se·cure′ly,** *adv.*

in·se·cu·ri·ty (in′si kyùr′i tē) *n., pl.* **-ties. 1.** the state or quality of being insecure. **2.** lack of self-confidence; self-doubt. **3.** something insecure.

in·sem·i·nate (in sem′ə nāt′) *v.t.* **-nat·ed, -nat·ing.** to introduce semen into the reproductive tract of (a female); impregnate.

in·sem·i·na·tion (in sem′ə nā′shən) *n.* the act of inseminating or the state of being inseminated.

in·sen·sate (sen′sāt, -sit) *adj.* **1.** without awareness or sensation; inanimate. **2.** having or showing a lack of feeling, sensitivity, or perception: *to be insensate to beautiful music.* **3.** lacking sense or reason; stupid; foolish. —**in·sen′sate·ly,** *adv.*

in·sen·si·bil·i·ty (in sen′sə bil′i tē) *n., pl.* **-ties.** the state or quality of being insensible.

in·sen·si·ble (in sen′sə bəl) *adj.* **1.** incapable of feeling, perceiving, or being affected by (with *to*): *insensible to pain, insensible to the suffering of others.* **2.** without knowledge; unaware: *We were insensible of the risks involved.* **3.** deprived of sensation; unconscious or numb: *The baseball player was insensible for several minutes after being struck on the head.* **4.** too slight, gradual, or subtle to be easily perceived; imperceptible: *insensible changes in temperature.* —**in·sen′si·bly,** *adv.*

in·sen·si·tive (in sen′si tiv) *adj.* **1.** incapable of feeling, perceiving, or being affected by (with *to*): *insensitive to beauty, insensitive to pain.* **2.** lacking feeling, sensitivity, or perception: *a cruel and insensitive person.* —**in·sen′si·tive·ly,** *adv.* —**in·sen′si·tive·ness, in·sen′si·tiv′i·ty,** *n.*

in·sen·ti·ent (in sen′shē ənt, -shənt) *adj.* without feeling, awareness, sensation, or consciousness; inanimate. —**in·sen′ti·ence,** *n.*

in·sep·a·ra·ble (in sep′ər ə bəl, -sep′rə-) *adj.* that cannot be separated: *inseparable friends.* —*n.* **inseparables.** inseparable persons or things. —**in·sep′a·ra·bil′i·ty,** *n.* —**in·sep′a·ra·bly,** *adv.*

in·sert (*v.,* in sûrt′; *n.,* in′sûrt) *v.t.* to put, set, or place in: *to insert a bookmark into a book.* —*n.* something inserted or to be inserted, such as an extra section or pamphlet inserted in a newspaper, magazine, or other printed matter. [Latin *insertus,* past participle of *īnserere* to put in.]

in·ser·tion (in sûr′shən) *n.* **1.** the act of inserting. **2.** something inserted. **3.** the point at which a muscle is attached to the bone that it moves. **4.** injection *(def. 3).* **5.** a band of lace or other material made so that it can be sewed at each edge between parts of other material.

in·ser·vice (in sûr′vis, in′sûr′-) *adj.* happening during the time a person is on a job: *in-service training.*

in·ses·so·ri·al (in′se sôr′ē əl) *adj.* **1.** adapted for perching: *insessorial claws.* **2.** habitually perching, as certain birds. [Modern Latin *Insessores* (plural) perching birds, from Latin *insessor* occupant; literally, one who sits in or on, from *insidere* to sit in or on.]

in·set (*v.,* in set′; *n.,* in′set′) *v.t.* **-set, -set·ting.** to set, put, or place in; insert. —*n.* **1.** something inset or to be inset; insertion. **2.** a small map, diagram, or other illustration inserted within the border of a larger one.

in·shore (in′shôr′) *adj.* **1.** near the shore. **2.** moving toward the shore. —*adv.* toward the shore.

in·side (in′sīd′, in sīd′, in′sīd′) *n.* **1.** an inner side, surface, or part; interior: *the inside of a car.* **2. insides.** *Informal.* **a.** the internal organs of the body. **b.** the internal parts of anything, such as a machine. —*adj.* **1.** situated on or in the inside. **2.** known to only a few; confidential: *The reporter got the inside story on the meeting.* **3.** working or done from within a place or organization: *The robbery was an inside job.* **4.** *Baseball.* (of a pitch) passing home plate between the batter and the plate. —*adv.* **1.** on, in, or toward the inside; within. **2.** indoors: *The children played inside all day.* —*prep.* in or into the inside of; within: *I looked inside the closet.*

• **inside of.** *Informal.* **a.** within; inside: *The dress is inside of the box.* **b.** within the space or limits of: *We'll finish this job inside of an hour.*

• **inside out. a.** so that the inside is facing out: *to turn a jacket inside out.* **b.** *Informal.* thoroughly; totally: *to know one's work inside out, to know a part of the country inside out.*

• **on the inside.** in a position of power or influence.

in·sid·er (in sī′dər) *n.* **1.** a person who is a member, as of a given group, society, or organization. **2.** a person who has or can obtain information that is not available to everyone.

insider trading, the illegal buying or selling of a company's stock based on secret or confidential information about the financial or business plans of the company.

in·sid·i·ous (in sid′ē əs) *adj.* **1.** slyly treacherous and deceitful: *an insidious manner.* **2.** working or proceeding in a hidden but harmful manner: *an insidious disease.* [Latin *īnsidiōsus* deceitful, from *īnsidiae* plot.] —**in·sid′i·ous·ly,** *adv.* —**in·sid′i·ous·ness,** *n.*

in·sight (in′sīt) *n.* **1.** the ability to see into and understand the inner character or hidden nature of things: *My friend had great insight into my problems.* **2.** an instance of such understanding.

in·sight·ful (in sīt′fəl) *adj.* having or showing insight; perceptive: *an insightful book reviewer, an insightful comment.*

in·sig·ni·a (in sig′nē ə) *also,* **in·sig·ne** (in sig′nē). *n., pl.* **-ni·a** or **-ni·as. 1.** an emblem, badge, medal, or other distinguishing mark, as of office, honor, or position. **2.** such marks collectively: *military insignia.* **3.** a distinguishing mark or sign of anything. [Latin *insignia,* plural of *insigne* mark, badge. Doublet of ENSIGN.]

in·sig·nif·i·cance (in′sig nif′i kəns) *n.* the state or quality of being insignificant.

in·sig·nif·i·can·cy (in′sig nif′i kən sē) *n., pl.* **-cies. 1.** insignificance. **2.** an insignificant person or thing.

in·sig·nif·i·cant (in′sig nif′i kənt) *adj.* **1.** being of or having little or no meaning or importance; not significant; trivial. **2.** small in size or amount; nominal: *an insignificant sum of money.* **3.** lacking distinction, power, or character: *an insignificant member of a committee.* —**in′sig·nif′i·cant·ly,** *adv.*

in·sin·cere (in′sin sîr′) *adj.* not sincere; hypocritical. —**in′sin·cere′ly,** *adv.*

in·sin·cer·i·ty (in′sin ser′i tē) *n., pl.* **-ties. 1.** the quality of being insincere. **2.** an instance of this.

in·sin·u·ate (in sin′ū āt′) *v.t.,* **-at·ed, -at·ing. 1.** to suggest indirectly; intimate: *The prosecutor insinuated that the witness was lying.* **2.** to get in or introduce by subtle or indirect means: *They insinuated themselves into families to betray them* (J. C. Sismonde de Sismondi, 1832). [Latin *īnsinuātus,* past participle of *īnsinuāre* to bring in by winding or turning, from *in* in + *sinus* curve, hollow.] —For Synonyms, see **hint.**

in·sin·u·a·tion (in sin′ū ā′shən) *n.* **1.** an indirect suggestion; sly hint. **2.** the act of insinuating.

> **Synonyms** **Insinuation** and **innuendo** denote the practice of hinting at or suggesting things one does not choose or dare to say directly. **Insinuation** connotes sly or artful comment, esp. of a derogatory nature: *The candidate used insinuation rather than direct attacks to question her opponent's integrity.* **Innuendo** has a more negative connotation, referring usually to deliberate but oblique and veiled disparagement conveyed through tone and gesture as much as through words: *He did not criticize me directly, but his expression let me know through innuendo how much he disapproved of my behavior.*

in·sip·id (in sip′id) *adj.* **1.** lacking qualities that arouse interest or excite; dull; colorless: *an insipid person.* **2.** without much taste or flavor; bland: *insipid food.* [Late Latin *īnsipidus* tasteless, from Latin *in-* not + *sapidus* savory[1].] —**in′si·pid′i·ty, in·sip′id·ness,** *n.* —**in·sip′id·ly,** *adv.*

in·sist (in sist′) *v.t.* **1.** to demand (something) firmly and strongly: *The doctor insisted that the patient get plenty of rest.* **2.** to maintain or assert persistently and positively: *to insist that one is right.* [Latin *īnsistere* to stand on, persist.]
 • **to insist on. a.** to demand firmly and strongly: *Our friend insists on our coming to the party.* **b.** to continue in a course of action: *If you insist on shouting, I shall leave.*

in·sis·tence (in sis′təns) *n.* **1.** an act or instance of insisting. **2.** the quality of being insistent. Also, **in·sis′ten·cy.**

in·sis·tent (in sis′tənt) *adj.* **1.** urgent or persistent, as in some demand. **2.** demanding attention or notice: *The insistent ringing of the doorbell woke us.* —**in·sis′tent·ly,** *adv.*

in si·tu (in sī′tü, -tū, sē′-) *Latin.* in its original place or position.

in·snare (in snâr′) *v.t.,* **-snared, -snar·ing.** ensnare.

in·so·bri·e·ty (in′sə brī′i tē) *n.* lack of sobriety.

in·so·far as (in′sō fär′) to such an extent as: *Insofar as we know, they are coming to the party.*

in·so·la·tion[1] (in′sə lā′shən) *n.* exposure to the light and heat of the sun. [Latin *insōlātiōn-,* stem of *insōlātiō* exposure to the sun, from *insōlātus,* past participle of *insōlāre* to expose to the sun, from *sōl* sun.]

in·so·la·tion[2] (in′sə lā′shən) *n.* the amount of solar radiation that a surface receives or the rate at which it is received per unit of surface area. [Short for *in(coming) sol(ar radi)ation.*]

in·sole (in′sōl′) *n.* **1.** the inner sole of a shoe or boot. **2.** a layer of material laid on the sole inside a shoe or boot for warmth, waterproofing, or a better fit.

in·so·lence (in′sə ləns) *n.* **1.** the quality of being insolent. **2.** insolent speech or behavior.

in·so·lent (in′sə lənt) *adj.* rude and without respect; arrogant. [Latin *insolēns,* from *in-* not + *solēre* to be accustomed.] —**in′so·lent·ly,** *adv.*

in·sol·u·ble (in sol′yə bəl) *adj.* **1.** that cannot be dissolved. **2.** that cannot be solved or explained: *an insoluble crime.* [Latin *insolūbilis* that cannot be loosed, going back to *in-* not + *solvere* to loose.] —**in·sol′u·bil′i·ty,** *n.* —**in·sol′u·bly,** *adv.*

in·solv·a·ble (in sol′və bəl) *adj.* incapable of being solved or explained.

in·sol·ven·cy (in sol′vən sē) *n., pl.* **-cies.** the state or condition of being unable to pay one's debts; bankruptcy.

in·sol·vent (in sol′vənt) *adj.* **1.** not able to pay one's debts. **2.** of or relating to insolvency or insolvent persons. —*n.* an insolvent person.

in·som·ni·a (in som′nē ə) *n.* restless sleep or an inability to fall asleep. [Latin *insomnia* sleeplessness.]

in·som·ni·ac (in som′nē ak) *n.* a person who suffers from insomnia.

in·so·much (in′sō much′) *adv.* to such an extent or degree.
 • **insomuch as.** inasmuch as; since.

in·sou·ci·ance (in sü′sē əns) *n.* the quality or condition of being insouciant.

in·sou·ci·ant (in sü′sē ənt) *adj.* free from care or worry; carefree; unconcerned. [French *insouciant,* going back to *in-* not (from Latin *in-*) + *soucier* to care (from Latin *sollicitāre* to move, excite).]

in·spect (in spekt′) *v.t.* **1.** to look at closely and critically, esp. for errors, faults, or flaws. **2.** to examine formally or officially: *to inspect troops.* [Latin *inspectus,* past participle of *inspicere* to look into.] —For Synonyms, see **examine.**

in·spec·tion (in spek′shən) *n.* **1.** the act of inspecting, esp. for errors, faults, or flaws. **2.** a formal or official examination.

in·spec·tor (in spek′tər) *n.* **1.** a person, esp. an appointed official, who inspects. **2.** a police officer ranking next below a superintendent. [Latin *inspector* examiner.]

in·spi·ra·tion (in′spə rā′shən) *n.* **1.** the stimulation of the mind, feelings, or imagination: *The beauty of nature gave inspiration to the painter.* **2.** a person or thing that inspires. **3.** something inspired, such as an idea or action. **4.** the state or quality of being inspired. **5.** *Theology.* a divine influence directly exerted upon the mind or soul. **6.** the act of breathing in; inhalation.

in·spi·ra·tion·al (in′spə rā′shə nəl) *adj.* **1.** giving inspiration; inspiring: *an inspirational sermon, an inspirational book.* **2.** resulting from inspiration; inspired: *an inspirational feeling.* **3.** of or relating to inspiration. —**in′spi·ra′tion·al·ly,** *adv.*

in·spire (in spīr′) *v.,* **-spired, -spir·ing.** —*v.t.* **1.** to have a rousing effect on; stimulate; stir: *The speaker's emotional words inspired the audience.* **2.** to be the force or influence that results in something: *The author's wife inspired his first novel.* **3.** to produce or arouse, as a thought or feeling: *Both my grandparents inspired love and respect.* **4.** to cause to have a specified thought or feeling: *Success inspired hope for the future.* **5.** to motivate, guide, or control by divine influence. **6.** to breathe in; inhale. —*v.i.* **1.** to inhale. **2.** to give inspiration. [Latin *inspīrāre* to breathe into.] —**in·spir′er,** *n.*

in·spir·it (in spir′it) *v.t.* to give life, courage, or spirit to.

in·spis·sate (in spis′āt) *v.t., v.i.,* **-sat·ed, -sat·ing.** *Medicine.* to thicken, as by evaporation or absorption of fluid; condense. [Latin *inspissātus,* past participle of *inspissāre* to thicken, from Latin *in* in + *spissus* thick.] —**in′spis·sa′tion,** *n.*

inst. 1. institute. **2.** institution.

in·sta·bil·i·ty (in′stə bil′i tē) *n.* lack of stability.

in·stal (in stôl′) *v.t.,* **-stalled, -stal·ling.** install.

in·stall (in stôl′) *also,* **in·stal.** *v.t.* **1.** to put in position for service or use: *to install an air conditioner.* **2.** to place (a person) in an office, rank, or position with ceremony: *We installed the new club president today.* **3.** to establish in a place or position; settle: *The office manager installed a receptionist at the front desk.* [Medieval Latin *installare* to introduce formally, from Latin *in* in + Late Latin *stallum* seat, stall[1]; of Germanic origin.] —**in·stall′er,** *n.* —For Synonyms, see **induct.**

in·stal·la·tion (in′stə lā′shən) *n.* **1.** the act of installing or the state of being installed. **2.** a mechanical system or apparatus placed in position for use. **3.** a military base, including its buildings and subsidiary facilities. **4.** military equipment, esp. equipment that is large and permanently placed: *antiaircraft installations.*

in·stall·ment[1] (in stôl′mənt) *also,* **in·stal·ment.** *n.* **1.** a portion of a sum of money owed, to be paid at regular intervals: *We paid for our car in ten installments.* **2.** any of several parts

a	at	e	end	o	hot	u	up	hw	white		about
ā	ape	ē	me	ō	old	ū	use	ng	song		taken
ä	far	i	it	ô	fork	ü	rule	th	thin	ə	pencil
âr	care	ī	ice	oi	oil	u̇	pull	th	this		lemon
		îr	pierce	ou	out	ûr	turn	zh	measure		circus

issued or presented at regular intervals: *The novel appeared in the magazine in installments.* [Modification (influenced by INSTALL) of obsolete *estallment* payment by installment, from *estall* to fix payments for, from Old French *estaler* to fix, set, from *estal* fixed place, stall, from Old High German *stal* stall.]

in·stall·ment² (in stôl′mənt) *also,* **in·stal·ment.** *n.* the act of installing or the state of being installed; installation. [INSTALL + -MENT.]

installment plan, a system of paying for goods or services at regular intervals.

in·stance (in′stəns) *n.* a specific occurrence; example or case: *This is one instance where you are wrong. We cannot be sure of the result in this instance.* [Medieval Latin *instantia,* from Latin *īnstantia* being present, urgency.]
 • **for instance.** by way of illustration; for example: *I enjoy team sports; for instance, I like baseball and basketball.*

in·stant (in′stənt) *n.* **1.** a very short period of time; moment: *I saw them for just an instant.* **2.** a particular moment or point in time: *If we don't leave this instant, we will be late.* —*adj.* **1.** without delay: *We received an instant reply.* **2.** of the greatest urgency; pressing; urgent: *an instant need.* **3.** (of food products) prepared beforehand and packaged, often in powdered form, and requiring only the addition of a liquid, such as water or milk, for quick, final preparation: *instant oatmeal, instant coffee.* **4.** *Archaic.* of or relating to the present month: *in my letter of the fifth instant.* [Latin *īnstāns,* present participle of *īnstāre* to be present, urge.]

in·stan·ta·ne·ous (in′stən tā′nē əs) *adj.* happening, done, or coming in an instant or without delay: *The reaction of the audience was instantaneous.* —**in′stan·ta·ne·ous·ly,** *adv.* —**in′stan·ta·ne·ous·ness,** *n.*

in·stant·ly (in′stənt lē) *adv.* without delay; at once.

instant re·play (rē′plā′) the immediate playback of part of a videotape to show a particular action, as in a televised sports event.

in·star (in′stär) *n.* any stage in the life of an insect or other arthropod between successive molts. [Modern Latin *instar,* from Latin *instar* shape, form, from *instare* to stand on or near.]

in·state (in stāt′) *v.t.,* **-stat·ed, -stat·ing.** to place in an office, rank, or position; install.

in·stead (in sted′) *adv.* in place of the person or thing mentioned; as a substitute or alternative: *The recipe called for butter, but we used margarine instead.* [Earlier *in stead* in place. See IN, STEAD.]
 • **instead of.** rather than; in place of: *We went for a walk instead of going straight home.*

in·step (in′step′) *n.* **1.** the arched upper surface of the human foot between the toes and the ankle. **2.** the part of a shoe, stocking, or other footwear that covers this part of the foot. **3.** the front part of the hind leg of a horse, from the hock to the pastern joint. [Probably IN + STEP.]

in·sti·gate (in′sti gāt′) *v.t.,* **-gat·ed, -gat·ing. 1.** to cause by arousing or stirring up; incite: *to instigate a riot.* **2.** to urge on to some action: *to instigate someone to commit a crime.* [Latin *īnstīgātus,* past participle of *īnstīgāre.*] —**in′sti·ga·tor,** *n.* —For Synonyms, see **incite.**

in·sti·ga·tion (in′sti gā′shən) *n.* the act of instigating.

in·still (in stil′) *also,* **in·stil.** *v.t.,* **-stilled, -stil·ling. 1.** to introduce gradually or by degrees: *The art teacher instilled a love of beauty into us.* **2.** to pour in by drops. [Latin *īnstīllāre* to pour in by drops, from *in* in + *stīlla* drop.] —**in′stil·la′tion,** *n.*

in·stinct¹ (in′stingkt′) *n.* **1.** an unlearned, inborn disposition, common to all members of a species, to behave in a fixed way in response to a particular set of stimuli. **2.** a natural aptitude or tendency; talent. [Latin *īnstinctus* impulse, from *īnstinctus,* past participle of *īnstinguere* to impel.] —**in·stinc·tu·al** (in stingk′chü əl), *adj.*

> **Synonyms** **Instinct¹** and **intuition** denote powers or faculties of the mind outside the level of conscious reasoning. **Instinct** refers to those impulses or predispositions a person or animal is born with: *the mating instinct, the instinct of self-preservation.* **Intuition,** on the other hand, connotes a human power to understand or respond to something in ways that cannot be rationally explained: *to know where a lost object is by intuition, to be guided by intuition in judging a person's character.*

in·stinct² (in stingkt′) *adj.* strongly charged or deeply imbued (with *with*): *to be instinct with a sense of justice.* [Latin *īnstinctus* impelled, past participle of *īnstinguere* to impel.]

in·stinc·tive (in stingk′tiv) *adj.* **1.** arising from or done by instinct. **2.** of, relating to, or of the nature of instinct. —**in·stinc′tive·ly,** *adv.*

in·sti·tute (in′sti tüt′, -tūt′) *v.t.,* **-tut·ed, -tut·ing. 1.** to set up or give form to; establish: *to institute an annual holiday, to institute a new set of rules.* **2.** to put into operation; initiate; start: *to*

institute an investigation. —*n.* **1.a.** an organization or society for the promotion of work in a particular field: *a music institute.* **b.** a building or buildings housing such an organization or society. **2.** an educational institution, often affiliated with a college or university, specializing in the research and teaching of a particular field or subject. **3.** something established, such as a principle or law. [Latin *īnstitūtus,* past participle of *īnstituere* to establish.]

in·sti·tu·tion (in′sti tü′shən, -tū′-) *n.* **1.a.** an organization, society, or similar establishment devoted to a particular purpose, esp. one of a social, educational, or religious nature. **b.** a building or buildings housing such an establishment. **2.** the act of instituting; establishment. **3.** an established practice, custom, law, or system: *Slavery was an institution in the South before the American Civil War.* **4.** a practice, custom, person, or thing that has become a traditional or established feature, as of a community: *The old doctor who still makes house calls is an institution in our town.*

in·sti·tu·tion·al (in′sti tü′shə nəl, -tū′-) *adj.* **1.** of, relating to, or having the nature of an institution. **2.** of or relating to an organization pursuing a particular purpose or the building or buildings in which it is housed. **3.** (of advertising) intended to promote a reputation and goodwill rather than increase immediate sales. —**in′sti·tu′tion·al·ly,** *adv.*

in·sti·tu·tion·al·ism (in′sti tü′shə nə liz′əm, -tū′-) *n.* **1.** a system of institutions or organized societies. **2.** a belief in established institutions, esp. of religion.

in·sti·tu·tion·al·ize (in′sti tü′shə nə līz′, -tū′-) *v.t.* **1.** to convert into or treat as an institution. **2.** to place in an institution, esp. one for the care and treatment of an illness. —**in′sti·tu′tion·al·i·za′tion,** *n.*

in·struct (in strukt′) *v.t.* **1.** to furnish with knowledge, information, or skill; teach. **2.** to give directions or orders to: *My employer instructed me to deliver the message.* [Latin *īnstructus,* past participle of *īnstruere* to build, provide, teach.] —For Synonyms, see **teach.**

in·struc·tion (in struk′shən) *n.* **1.** the act of teaching. **2. instructions.** explanations, directions, or orders. **3.** knowledge or skill that is taught. —**in·struc′tion·al,** *adj.*

in·struc·tive (in struk′tiv) *adj.* giving information; serving to instruct: *The lecture was instructive and interesting.* —**in·struc′tive·ly,** *adv.* —**in·struc′tive·ness,** *n.*

in·struc·tor (in struk′tər) *n.* **1.** a person who instructs; teacher. **2.** a teacher in a college or university who ranks next below an assistant professor. [Medieval Latin *īnstructor* teacher, from Latin *īnstructor* preparer.]

in·struc·tress (in struk′tris) *n.* a woman who instructs; teacher.

in·stru·ment (in′strə mənt) *n.* **1.** a device used to do something, esp. one designed or used for precise or exacting work: *surgical instruments.* **2.** a device for producing musical sounds: *a keyboard instrument, a wind instrument.* **3.** a device for measuring or monitoring the condition or progress of something: *navigational instruments.* **4.a.** a means by or through which something is done or brought about. **b.** a person used as such. **5.** a formal or legal document, such as a contract, deed, or will. [Latin *īnstrūmentum* tool, apparatus.]

in·stru·men·tal (in′strə men′təl) *adj.* **1.** serving as a means or agent; helpful: *The wealthy family was instrumental in getting a new hospital for our town.* **2.** of, relating to, composed for, or performed on musical instruments: *The musician composed both vocal and instrumental music.* **3.** of, relating to, or done with a tool. —*n.* a composition or part of a composition intended to be played by a musical instrument or instruments without voices. —**in′stru·men′tal·ly,** *adv.*

in·stru·men·tal·ist (in′strə men′tə list) *n.* a person who plays a musical instrument.

in·stru·men·tal·i·ty (in′strə men tal′i tē) *n., pl.* **-ties. 1.** the quality or condition of being instrumental. **2.** something that serves, or is used for, some purpose; means.

in·stru·men·ta·tion (in′strə men tā′shən) *n.* **1.** the arrangement or composition of music for instruments, esp. for an orchestra; orchestration. **2.** the use of scientific, surgical, or other instruments. **3.** instruments used for a particular purpose.

instrument flying, the navigation of an aircraft by instruments alone.

instrument landing, a landing in which the pilot relies solely on onboard instruments and radio signals from the ground.

instrument panel, a panel on or in which instruments are fixed for monitoring, as in an airplane. Also, **instrument board.**

in·sub·or·di·nate (in′sə bôr′də nit) *adj.* not submitting to authority; disobedient. —*n.* a person who is insubordinate. —**in′sub·or′di·nate·ly,** *adv.*

in·sub·or·di·na·tion (in′sə bôr′də nā′shən) *n.* the state, quality, or fact of being insubordinate; disobedience.

in·sub·stan·tial (in′səb stan′shəl) *adj.* **1.** not real; imaginary:

insubstantial hopes. **2.** not solid or firm; flimsy: *insubstantial evidence.*

in·suf·fer·a·ble (in suf′ər ə bəl) *adj.* not to be endured; not tolerable; unbearable: *insufferable pain, an insufferable bore.* —**in·suf′fer·a·ble·ness,** *n.* —**in·suf′fer·a·bly,** *adv.*

in·suf·fi·cien·cy (in′sə fish′ən sē) *n., pl.* **-cies.** a deficiency, as in amount or quality: *an insufficiency of supplies.*

in·suf·fi·cient (in′sə fish′ənt) *adj.* not sufficient; inadequate: *insufficient funds.* —**in′suf·fi′cient·ly,** *adv.*

in·su·lar (in′sə lər, ins′yə-) *adj.* **1.** of, relating to, or characteristic of an island or its people. **2.** inhabiting or situated on an island. **3.** composing or forming an island. **4.** standing alone; isolated. **5.** narrow-minded; provincial: *an insular way of thinking.* [Late Latin *īnsulāris* relating to an island, from Latin *īnsula* island.]

in·su·lar·i·ty (in′sə lar′i tē, ins′yə-) *n.* **1.** the state or condition of being an island. **2.** narrow-mindedness; provincialism. **3.** the condition of living on or as on an island.

in·su·late (in′sə lāt′, ins′yə-) *v.t.,* **-lat·ed, -lat·ing. 1.** to cover or surround with a nonconducting material, such as rubber: *to insulate an electric wire.* **2.** to install a layer of material, such as glass wool, within the walls of (a building, refrigerator, or other structure) to reduce the amount of heat or sound transferred. **3.** to protect or isolate: *Parents often try to insulate their children from the harshness of life.* [Late Latin *īnsulātus* made into an island, from Latin *īnsula* island.]

in·su·la·tion (in′sə lā′shən, ins′yə-) *n.* **1.** the material used in insulating. **2.** the act of insulating or the state of being insulated.

in·su·la·tor (in′sə lā′tər, ins′yə-) *n.* a material or device that prevents the conduction of electric current.

in·su·lin (in′sə lin, ins′yə-) *n.* **1.** a hormone, secreted by the islets of Langerhans in the pancreas, that regulates the body's use and storage of sugar and other carbohydrates. **2.** a preparation containing this hormone, used in treating diabetes. It is obtained from the pancreas of cattle, sheep, or pigs or is produced artificially. [Latin *īnsula* island + *in-*[1]; referring to its discovery in the *islets* of Langerhans.]

in·sult (*v.,* in sult′; *n.,* in′sult) *v.t.* to speak to or treat with scornful abuse, rudeness, or disrespect. —*n.* **1.** a rude, scornful, or disrespectful act or remark. **2.** an injury to the tissues or organs of the body, or something causing such an injury. [Latin *īnsultāre* to leap upon, scoff at.] —For Synonyms *(v.t.),* see **offend.**

in·su·per·a·ble (in sü′pər ə bəl) *adj.* that cannot be overcome or surmounted: *insuperable obstacles.* —**in·su′per·a·bil′i·ty,** *n.* —**in·su′per·a·bly,** *adv.*

in·sup·port·a·ble (in′sə pôr′tə bəl) *adj.* **1.** more than one can endure; unbearable; unendurable. **2.** not supportable by evidence: *insupportable charges of fraud.*

in·sur·a·ble (in shûr′ə bəl) *adj.* capable of being or fit to be insured.

in·sur·ance (in shûr′əns) *n.* **1.** protection against risk or loss by means of a contract between two parties, whereby the insurer guarantees to pay a sum of money to the insured in case of death, accident, fire, theft, or the like, in return for the prior regular payment of specified amounts by the insured. **2.** a contract guaranteeing such protection. **3.** the amount for which someone or something is insured. **4.** the amount paid for insurance; premium. **5.** the business of insuring persons or property. **6.** any protection against risk, harm, or loss.

in·sure (in shûr′) *v.,* **-sured, -sur·ing.** —*v.t.* **1.** to protect (someone or something) against risk or loss by means of insurance; cover with insurance. **2.** ensure. —*v.i.* to buy or sell insurance. [Form of ENSURE.]

in·sured (in shûrd′) *n.* a person who is covered by insurance.

in·sur·er (in shûr′ər) *n.* a person or company that insures.

in·sur·gence (in sûr′jəns) *n.* the act of rebelling against established authority; revolt.

in·sur·gen·cy (in sûr′jən sē) *n.* **1.** the state or quality of being insurgent. **2.** insurgence.

in·sur·gent (in sûr′jənt) *n.* **1.** a person who rebels against established authority. **2.** a member of a political party who rebels against the policies and decisions of the party. —*adj.* rising in revolt against authority; rebellious. [Latin *īnsurgēns,* present participle of *īnsurgere* to rise up.]

in·sur·mount·a·ble (in′sər moun′tə bəl) *adj.* that cannot be overcome: *insurmountable difficulties.* —**in′sur·mount′a·bly,** *adv.*

in·sur·rec·tion (in′sə rek′shən) *n.* an act or instance of rebelling against established authority, esp. of a government; revolt. [Late Latin *īnsurrēctiō,* from Latin *īnsurgere* to rise up.] —**in′sur·rec′tion·ar·y,** *adj., n.* —**in′sur·rec′tion·ist,** *n.* —For Synonyms, see **revolt.**

in·sus·cep·ti·ble (in′sə sep′tə bəl) *adj.* not easily affected or influenced by something; not susceptible (often with *to* or *of*): *insusceptible to criticism.* —**in′sus·cep′ti·bil′i·ty,** *n.*

int. 1. interest. **2.** interior. **3.** internal. **4.** international. **5.** intransitive.

in·tact (in takt′) *adj.* not missing anything or damaged in any way; untouched, whole, or unimpaired. [Latin *intāctus.*]

in·ta·glio (in tal′yō, -tăl′-) *n., pl.* **-glios. 1.** a design cut or carved deep into the surface of a hard material. **2.** the art or process of making such designs. **3.** something, esp. a gem, cut or ornamented with such a design. **4.** an incised design used as a mold for producing a design in relief. [Italian *intaglio* engraving, carving, from *intagliare* to cut into, engrave, going back to Latin *in* in + *tālea* stick, cutting.]

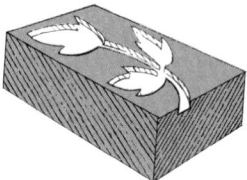

intaglio

in·take (in′tāk′) *n.* **1.** the act of taking in. **2.** an amount taken in: *The doctors restricted the patient's intake of liquids.* **3.** a place in a channel, pipe, or other narrow opening where air or fluids are taken in.

in·tan·gi·ble (in tan′jə bəl) *adj.* **1.** that cannot be easily defined or evaluated by the mind: *Morale is the intangible factor in warfare.* **2.** that cannot be perceived by the sense of touch: *The soul is intangible.* —*n.* something intangible. —**in·tan′gi·bil′i·ty,** *n.* —**in·tan′gi·bly,** *adv.*

in·te·ger (in′ti jər) *n.* **1.** any of the natural numbers, their additive inverses, or zero. For example, 16, −16, and 0 are integers. **2.** any whole or entire thing or entity. [Latin *integer* whole. Doublet of ENTIRE.]

in·te·gral (in′ti grəl) *adj.* **1.** necessary to the completeness of the whole; essential: *an integral part.* **2.** having no part or element missing; entire. **3.** relating to, produced by, or being an integer. —*n.* **1.** something entire; a whole. **2.** a mathematical quantity that is the limit of a sum. Symbol: ∫ [Late Latin *integrālis* whole, from Latin *integer* whole.]

integral calculus, see **calculus.**

in·te·grate (in′ti grāt′) *v.,* **-grat·ed, -grat·ing.** —*v.t.* **1.** to make accessible or available to all racial groups; desegregate. **2.** to bring (parts) together into a whole. **3.** to make whole by adding or bringing together all necessary parts. **4.** *Mathematics.* to find the integral of. —*v.i.* to become accessible or available to all racial groups. [Latin *integrātus,* past participle of *integrāre* to make whole.] —**in′te·gra′tor,** *n.*

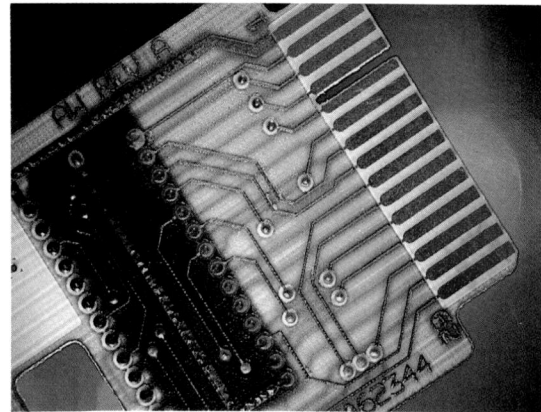

integrated circuit

integrated circuit, a microscopic electronic circuit formed on a minute slice of silicon called a chip, containing many thousands of transistors and other microelectronic devices. Integrated circuits are the basis of the microprocessors that are used in computers as well as in a wide and growing variety of machines and equipment.

a	at	e	end	o	hot	u	up	hw	white		about
ā	ape	ē	me	ō	old	ū	use	ng	song		taken
ä	far	i	it	ô	fork	ü	rule	th	thin	ə	pencil
âr	care	ī	ice	oi	oil	u̇	pull	th	this		lemon
		îr	pierce	ou	out	ûr	turn	zh	measure		circus

I

in·te·gra·tion (in'ti grā'shən) *n.* **1.** the elimination of racial segregation, as in schools or housing. **2.** the act of integrating parts into a whole. **3.** *Mathematics.* the process of integrating.

in·te·gra·tion·ist (in'ti grā'shə nist) *n.* a person who believes in or favors racial integration.

in·teg·ri·ty (in teg'ri tē) *n.* **1.** moral uprightness; honesty; sincerity. **2.** the state, quality, or condition of being complete; wholeness. [Latin *integritās.*] —For Synonyms, see **honesty.**

in·teg·u·ment (in teg'yə mənt) *n.* the natural covering of an animal or plant, such as a husk, skin, shell, or rind. Also, **tegument.** [Latin *integumentum* covering.] —**in·teg'u·men'tal, in·teg'u·men'ta·ry,** *adj.*

in·tel·lect (in'tə lekt') *n.* **1.** the power of the mind to know, understand, and reason. **2.** intelligence or mental ability, esp. when highly developed. **3.** a person of great intelligence. [Latin *intellēctus* understanding.]

in·tel·lec·tu·al (in'tə lek'chü əl) *adj.* **1.** of or relating to the intellect: *a person of great intellectual ability.* **2.** appealing to, involving, or using the intellect: *intellectual pursuits.* **3.** possessing or showing intellect. —*n.* an intellectual person. —**in'tel·lec'tu·al·ly,** *adv.*

in·tel·lec·tu·al·ism (in'tə lek'chü ə liz'əm) *n.* **1.** the exercise of the intellect. **2.** devotion to intellectual pursuits. **3.** the philosophical doctrine that knowledge is wholly or mainly derived from reason.

in·tel·lec·tu·al·i·ty (in'tə lek'chü al'i tē) *n., pl.* **-ties. 1.** the quality of being intellectual. **2.** intellectual power or force.

in·tel·lec·tu·al·ize (in'tə lek'chü ə līz') *v.,* **-ized, -iz·ing.** —*v.t.* to give an intellectual character to; make intellectual. —*v.i.* to think; reason.

in·tel·li·gence (in tel'i jəns) *n.* **1.** the ability to learn from experience, to solve problems rationally, and to modify behavior according to changes in environment; faculty of understanding and reasoning. **2.a.** secret information, esp. about an enemy: *Our intelligence shows that the enemy is advancing.* **b.** the agency or individuals of a military service engaged in the collection and evaluation of such information. **3.** *also,* **Intelligence.** an intelligent or rational being, esp. one that is incorporeal.

intelligence quotient, a number used to estimate a person's level of intelligence. It is obtained by dividing a person's mental age, as shown by tests, by his or her real age and multiplying by 100.

intelligence test, a test used to measure a person's mental development in relation to that of others. It may require answering questions or performing manual tasks.

in·tel·li·gent (in tel'i jənt) *adj.* **1.** having or showing a high degree of intelligence; bright: *an intelligent person, an intelligent question.* **2.** having or using the faculty of understanding and reasoning; having intelligence: *Humans are intelligent beings.* [Latin *intelligēns,* present participle of *intelligere* to understand, from *inter* between + *legere* to choose.] —**in·tel'li·gent·ly,** *adv.*

in·tel·li·gent·si·a (in tel'i jent'sē ə, -gent'-) *pl. n.* a well-educated group of persons having or regarded as having superior intelligence and noted for its influence and activity in cultural and intellectual affairs; intellectuals collectively. ➡ used as singular or plural. [Russian *intelligentsiya,* going back to Latin *intelligentia* understanding.]

in·tel·li·gi·bil·i·ty (in tel'i jə bil'i tē) *n.* the state or quality of being comprehensible.

in·tel·li·gi·ble (in tel'i jə bəl) *adj.* **1.** that can be understood; comprehensible. **2.** *Philosophy.* that can be known or understood by the intellect alone. [Latin *intelligibilis* comprehensible, from *intelligere* to understand.] —**in·tel'li·gi·bly,** *adv.*

in·tem·per·ance (in tem'pər əns) *n.* a lack of moderation or restraint, esp. in the use of alcoholic beverages.

in·tem·per·ate (in tem'pər it, -prit) *adj.* **1.** lacking temperance; excessive. **2.** not temperate: *a frigid, intemperate climate.* —**in·tem'per·ate·ly,** *adv.* —**in·tem'per·ate·ness,** *n.* —For Synonyms, see **excessive.**

in·tend (in tend') *v.t.* **1.** to have in mind as a purpose; plan: *I intend to call as soon as I arrive at the airport.* **2.** to make, design, or mean for a particular purpose, use, person, or group of persons: *The movie is intended for adults only. That remark was intended for you.* **3.** *Archaic.* to direct. —*v.i.* to have a purpose or plan in mind. [Latin *intendere* to stretch out, direct, apply oneself to.]

in·tend·an·cy (in ten'dən sē) *n., pl.* **-cies. 1.** the office, position, or function of an intendant. **2.** intendants collectively. **3.** formerly, a district under the control of an intendant.

in·tend·ant (in ten'dənt) *n.* **1.** formerly, a manager, director, or administrator under the French or Spanish monarchies. **2.** any

manager, director, or administrator, as of a public business. [French *intendant,* from Latin *intendēns,* present participle of *intendere.* See INTEND.]

in·tend·ed (in ten'did) *adj.* **1.** meant or planned; intentional. **2.** that is to be; prospective: *We met his intended wife.* —*n. Informal.* a prospective husband or wife.

in·tense (in tens') *adj.* **1.** of a very high degree; very strong: *an intense desire, intense heat.* **2.** having or showing strong emotion and earnest feeling: *an intense person, an intense look.* [Latin *intēnsus* stretched out, strained, past participle of *intendere.* See INTEND.] —**in·tense'ly,** *adv.* —**in·tense'ness,** *n.*

in·ten·si·fi·er (in ten'sə fī'ər) *n.* **1.** a person or thing that intensifies. **2.** *Grammar.* an intensive element, word, or phrase.

in·ten·si·fy (in ten'sə fī') *v.,* **-fied, -fy·ing.** —*v.t.* to make intense or more intense; increase greatly. —*v.i.* to become intense or more intense; grow in intensity. —**in·ten'si·fi·ca'tion,** *n.*

in·ten·si·ty (in ten'si tē) *n., pl.* **-ties. 1.** the state or quality of being intense. **2.** strength, amount, or degree, as of feeling or force: *The pain increased in intensity.* **3.** the strength of a form of energy, such as heat, light, or sound, per unit of area, volume, or mass.

in·ten·sive (in ten'siv) *adj.* **1.** thorough or concentrated: *intensive research, an intensive course in Russian religious art.* **2.** *Grammar.* giving or indicating force or emphasis. In the sentence *I myself did it, myself* is an intensive pronoun. —*n. Grammar.* an intensive element, word, or phrase. —**in·ten'sive·ly,** *adv.*

intensive care 1. the special services and equipment that a hospital offers critically ill patients, as continuous medical monitoring and the use of life-support systems for sustaining essential body functions. **2.** a facility in a hospital that treats patients requiring such services and equipment.

in·tent¹ (in tent') *n.* **1.** intention; aim. **2.** the act or fact of intending. [Old French *entent(e)* purpose, from Late Latin *intentus,* from Latin *intentus* an extending, from *intentus,* past participle of *intendere.* See INTEND.]

•**to (or for) all intents and purposes.** in almost every way; practically; virtually.

in·tent² (in tent') *adj.* **1.** having the mind firmly fixed on something: *He was intent on going. The student was intent on the book.* **2.** firmly directed or fixed: *an intent look.* [Latin *intentus,* past participle of *intendere.* See INTEND.] —**in·tent'ly,** *adv.*

in·ten·tion (in ten'shən) *n.* **1.** something that is intended; purpose; plan: *Her intention was to help you.* **2.** the act of intending. **3. intentions.** purposes with respect to marriage. —For Synonyms, see **purpose.**

in·ten·tion·al (in ten'shə nəl) *adj.* carefully thought out or planned; done on purpose. —**in·ten'tion·al·ly,** *adv.* —For Synonyms, see **deliberate.**

in·ter (in tûr') *v.t.,* **-terred, -ter·ring.** to put (a dead body) into a grave or tomb; bury. [Old French *enterrer,* going back to Latin *in in* + *terra* earth.]

inter- *prefix* **1.** one with the other; together: *interact.* **2.** between or among: *intercollegiate, interchange.* [Latin *inter* between, among, during.]

in·ter·act (in'tə rakt') *v.i.* to act on or influence each other. —**in'ter·ac'tive,** *adj.*

in·ter·ac·tion (in'tə rak'shən) *n.* reciprocal action or influence.

in·ter·ac·tive (in'tə rak'tiv) *adj.* of or relating to a computer or other system that prompts the user to enter data and responds by giving information or by prompting the user to enter other data.

in·ter a·li·a (in'tər ā'lē ə) *Latin.* among other things.

in·ter·a·tom·ic (in'tər ə tom'ik) *adj.* occurring, existing, or situated between atoms: *interatomic forces.*

in·ter·bor·ough (in'tər bûr'ō, -bur'ō) *adj.* between boroughs.

in·ter·breed (in'tər brēd') *v.t., v.i.,* **-bred, -breed·ing.** to crossbreed.

in·ter·ca·lar·y (in tûr'kə ler'ē) *adj.* **1.** (of a day or month) added to the calendar to make the calendar year correspond to the solar year. **2.** (of a year) having such a day or month added. **3.** interpolated; inserted. [Latin *intercalārius* relating to insertion, from *intercalāre* to insert.]

in·ter·ca·late (in tûr'kə lāt') *v.t.,* **-lat·ed -lat·ing. 1.** to add (a day or month) to the calendar. **2.** to interpolate; insert. [Latin *intercalātus,* past participle of *intercalāre* to insert.]

in·ter·ca·la·tion (in tûr'kə lā'shən) *n.* **1.** the act of intercalating. **2.** something that is intercalated.

in·ter·cede (in'tər sēd') *v.i.,* **-ced·ed, -ced·ing. 1.** to plead on behalf of another or others. **2.** to act as a mediator between opposing parties. [Latin *intercēdere* to go between.]

in·ter·cel·lu·lar (in'tər sel'yə lər) *adj. Biology.* situated among or occupying the area between cells.

in·ter·cept (*v.*, in'tər sept'; *n.*, in'tər sept') *v.t.* **1.** to seize, interrupt, or delay on the way. **2.** to stop the course or progress of; check: *to intercept a missile.* **3.** *Mathematics.* to meet at a point or points. —*n.* in a graph, the distance from the origin to a point at which a straight line or curve intersects a coordinate axis. [Latin *interceptus,* past participle of *intercipere* to interrupt; literally, to catch between.] —**in'ter·cep'tion,** *n.*

in·ter·cep·tor (in'tər sep'tər) *n.* **1.** a person or thing that intercepts. **2.** a fast-climbing airplane designed to intercept attacking enemy aircraft.

interceptor missile, a defensive missile designed to counter enemy forces in the air.

in·ter·ces·sion (in'tər sesh'ən) *n.* **1.** the act of interceding. **2.** a prayer or plea on behalf of another or others. [Latin *intercessiō* a going between.]

in·ter·ces·sor (in'tər ses'ər) *n.* a person who intercedes.

in·ter·ces·so·ry (in'tər ses'ə rē) *adj.* that intercedes on behalf of another or others.

in·ter·change (*v.*, in'tər chānj'; *n.*, in'tər chānj') *v.,* **-changed, -chang·ing.** —*v.t.* **1.** to put each of (two things) in the place or position of the other. **2.** to give and receive mutually. —*v.i.* to change places one with the other. —*n.* **1.** the act or an instance of changing places or positions, one with the other. **2.** the act or an instance of giving and receiving mutually: *an interchange of ideas.* **3.** an intersection, as a cloverleaf, where a vehicle may enter or leave a major highway without interfering with the flow of traffic on the highway. [Old French *entrechangier* to change, exchange, going back to Latin *inter* between + Late Latin *cambiāre.* See CHANGE.]

in·ter·change·a·ble (in'tər chān'jə bəl) *adj.* capable of being put or used in place of each other: *The machine parts are interchangeable.* —**in'ter·change'a·bil'i·ty,** *n.* —**in'ter·change'a·bly,** *adv.*

in·ter·col·le·giate (in'tər kə lē'jit, -jē it) *adj.* carried on or occurring between colleges or universities: *intercollegiate baseball.*

in·ter·com (in'tər kom') *n.* a radio or telephone system that affords internal communication, as between rooms or different areas, as of a building, ship, or aircraft. [Short for *intercommunication system.*]

in·ter·com·mu·ni·cate (in'tər kə mū'ni kāt') *v.i.* **-cat·ed, -cat·ing.** to communicate with each other or one another. —**in'ter·com·mu'ni·ca'tion,** *n.*

in·ter·con·nect (in'tər kə nekt') *v.t., v.i.* to connect or be connected one with the other. —**in'ter·con·nec'tion,** *n.*

in·ter·con·ti·nen·tal (in'tər kon'tə nen'təl) *adj.* **1.** traveling or capable of traveling from one continent to another: *an intercontinental missile.* **2.** of, relating to, or involving more than one continent: *intercontinental communications.*

in·ter·cos·tal (in'tər kos'təl) *adj.* between the ribs: *an intercostal artery.* —*n.* an intercostal organ or tissue, such as a blood vessel, muscle, or nerve. [Modern Latin *intercostalis,* from Latin *inter* between + *costa* rib.]

in·ter·course (in'tər kôrs') *n.* **1.** communication, relations, or dealings between individuals or groups; interchange, as of thoughts, ideas, or feelings: *social intercourse.* **2.** sexual intercourse. [Old French *entrecours* commerce, from Late Latin *intercursus,* from Latin *intercursus* a running between.]

in·ter·cross (*v.*, in'tər krôs'; *n.*, in'tər krôs') *v.t., v.i.,* **-crossed, -cross·ing.** hybridize. —*n.* hybrid *(def. 1).*

in·ter·de·nom·i·na·tion·al (in'tər di nom'ə nā'shə nəl) *adj.* between, among, or involving different religious denominations.

in·ter·de·part·men·tal (in'tər dē'pärt men'təl, -di pärt'-) *adj.* between or among departments.

in·ter·de·pen·dence (in'tər di pen'dəns) *n.* a dependence on each other or one another; mutual dependence.

in·ter·de·pen·dent (in'tər di pen'dənt) *adj.* dependent on each other or one another; mutually dependent. —**in'ter·de·pen'dent·ly,** *adv.*

in·ter·dict (*v.*, in'tər dikt'; *n.*, in'tər dikt') *v.t.* **1.** to prohibit, as by legal authority; forbid. **2.** to prevent or obstruct by heavy fire, as the advancement of enemy troops. **3.** in the Roman Catholic Church, to exclude from certain rites and sacraments. —*n.* **1.** an official or authoritative prohibition. **2.** in the Roman Catholic Church, a punishment in which a person, district, or country is excluded from certain rites and sacraments. [Latin *interdictum* prohibition.]

in·ter·dic·tion (in'tər dik'shən) *n.* **1.** the act of interdicting or the state of being interdicted. **2.** an interdict. —**in'ter·dic'to·ry,** *adj.*

in·ter·dig·i·tate (in'tər dij'i tāt') *v.i.* **-tat·ed, -tat·ing.** to interlock, like the fingers of hands that are clasped or folded together.

in·ter·dis·ci·pli·nar·y (in'tər dis'ə plə ner'ē) *adj.* involving different fields of knowledge or study: *Biochemistry is an interdisciplinary subject.*

in·ter·est (in'trist, -tər ist) *n.* **1.a.** a feeling of concern, involvement, or curiosity: *to have an interest in sports.* **b.** a cause or source of such feeling: *Her career is her primary interest at the moment. He was eager to know what my interests were.* **c.** the power to arouse such feeling: *Those books have little interest for me.* **2.** something that is advantageous, beneficial, or contributes to one's welfare. ➡ often used in the plural: *Some people care only about their own interests.* **3.** money paid for the use of borrowed money. **4.a.** a legal right, claim, or share: *to have a controlling interest in a business.* **b.** something in which a person has such a right, claim, or share. **5.** *usually,* **interests.** a group having a common concern, esp. in a business or industry: *mining interests.* **6.** anything given in excess of what is due: *to return someone's hospitality with interest.* —*v.t.* **1.** to stimulate or hold the curiosity or attention of: *The story interested me.* **2.** to cause (a person) to take an interest in something: *My friend tried to interest me in politics.* [Noun use of Latin *interest* it is of importance, it concerns.]
· **in the interest (or interests) of.** for the promotion, benefit, or advancement of; in behalf of.

in·ter·est·ed (in'trə stid, -tə res'tid) *adj.* **1.** having or showing interest: *an interested listener.* **2.** having a right, claim, or share: *Only interested parties can vote at the stockholders' meeting.* **3.** having a personal interest or prejudice: *an interested observer.* —**in'ter·est·ed·ly,** *adv.*

interest group, a group of people who share a common interest and organize to influence others in order to promote and protect that interest.

in·ter·est·ing (in'trə sting, -tə res'ting) *adj.* arousing curiosity or attention. —**in'ter·est·ing·ly,** *adv.*

Synonyms **Interesting, engrossing,** and **absorbing** mean engaging attention or arousing curiosity. **Interesting** is the general and least precise term: *an interesting book, an interesting idea, an interesting person.* **Engrossing** connotes controlling all one's attention: *The book was so engrossing that I didn't hear my friend come into the room.* **Absorbing** suggests a constant pull on one's attention: *The more I play chess, the more absorbing I find the game.*

interest rate **1.** the rate at which a borrower must pay interest on the amount of a loan remaining unpaid: *a car loan of $10,000 with an annual interest rate of 15% on the balance.* **2.** the rate at which an institution, such as a savings bank, pays interest on a deposit: *an interest rate of 5% on a savings account.*

in·ter·face (in'tər fās') *n.* **1.** the point at which different groups, systems, or devices, such as computers, interact, communicate, or exchange information. **2.** a means of allowing such interaction or exchange of information, such as a computer program. —*v.,* **-faced, -fac·ing.** —*v.i.* to act in coordination, communicate, or exchange information with another group, system, or device: *The company's domestic sales department interfaces with all international sales departments.* —*v.t.* to connect by an interface: *to interface computers.*

in·ter·faith (in'tər fāth') *adj.* of, for, or involving people of different religions: *an interfaith place of worship, an interfaith conference.*

in·ter·fere (in'tər fir') *v.i.,* **-fered, -fer·ing.** **1.** to concern oneself with or intrude in the affairs of others without having been asked; meddle (often with *in*): *to interfere in matters that don't concern one.* **2.** to interrupt, hinder, or disturb (with *with*): *Constant interruptions interfere with my work.* **3.** *Sports.* to obstruct the action of an opponent by illegal means. **4.** *Physics.* (of waves) to cause interference by acting upon one another. [Old French *(s')entreferir* to strike each other, going back to Latin *inter* between + *ferīre* to strike.]

Synonyms **Interfere** and **meddle** mean to involve oneself in or intrude in the affairs of others. **Interfere** is the more general term, and usually connotes hindering or frustrating: *By continually interfering, the parents created tension in the lives of the young couple.* **Meddle** is more negative than *interfere,* suggesting a completely unwanted involvement in someone else's personal concerns: *Because they tried to meddle in their neighbors' lives, everyone on the street learned to ignore them.*

a	at	e	end	o	hot	u	up	hw	white		about
ā	ape	ē	me	ō	old	ū	use	ng	song		taken
ä	far	i	it	ô	fork	ü	rule	th	thin	ə	pencil
âr	care	ī	ice	oi	oil	u̇	pull	th	this		lemon
				îr	pierce	ou	out	ûr	turn	zh	measure		circus

in·ter·fer·ence (in'tər fîr'əns) *n.* **1.** the act of interfering. **2.a.** disruption of a radio or television signal by other signals. **b.** radio or television signals that cause such disruption. **3.** *Football.* **a.** illegal hindering of the intended receiver of a pass. **b.** the blocking of opposing players in order to make way for the ball carrier. **c.** a player or players who provide such blocking. **4.** *Physics.* a phenomenon produced when two waves, as of light or sound, arrive at the same point. Where the waves are in phase, they reinforce one another; where they are out of phase, they weaken or neutralize one another, giving rise, in the case of light waves, to a pattern of alternating dark and light bands.

in·ter·fer·om·e·ter (in'tər fə rom'i tər) *n.* an instrument that uses interference patterns produced by light, sound, or radio waves to measure distances and wavelengths and to analyze spectra. [INTERFER(E) + -METER.] —**in'ter·fer·om'e·try,** *n.*

in·ter·fer·on (in'tər fîr'on) *n.* any of several proteins produced by the cells of humans and other mammals in response to infection by a virus. Interferon inhibits reproduction of the virus and helps protect the cells from further infection.

in·ter·fold (in'tər fōld') *v.t.* to fold together or one within another.

in·ter·fuse (in'tər fūz') *v.,* **-fused, -fus·ing.** —*v.t.* **1.** to mix together thoroughly; blend. **2.** to spread through; permeate. **3.** to cause to pass into or spread throughout. —*v.i.* to become blended. [Latin *interfūsus,* past participle of *interfundere* to pour between.] —**in'ter·fu'sion,** *n.*

in·ter·ga·lac·tic (in'tər gə lak'tik) *adj.* between or among galaxies: *intergalactic space.* [INTER- + GALACTIC.]

in·ter·gla·cial (in'tər glā'shəl) *adj. Geology.* of, relating to, or occurring during a warming interval between one period of glaciation and another. Some geologists regard the past 12,000 years as an interglacial episode and expect a resumption of ice age conditions a few thousand years from now. [INTER- + GLACIAL.]

in·ter·grade (*v.,* in'tər grād'; *n.,* in'tər grād') *v.i.* **-graded, -grading.** to change gradually into another form or kind through an unbroken series of intermediate stages, as one population of a subspecies into another. —*n.* an intermediate or transitional form, as between two distinct varieties of a plant or animal.

in·ter·im (in'tər im) *n.* the time intervening, as between events; meantime. —*adj.* for or occurring during an interim; temporary: *an interim settlement of a dispute.* [Latin *interim* in the meantime.]

in·te·ri·or (in tîr'ē ər) *n.* **1.** the inner side, surface, or part: *The interior of the cave was dark.* **2.** the part of a region or country that is away from the coast or border. **3.** a representation of the inside of a room or building, as in a painting. **4.** the internal or domestic affairs of a country: *a department of the interior.* —*adj.* **1.** of, relating to, or situated on the inside. **2.** away from the coast or border; inland. **3.** relating to the internal or domestic affairs of a country. [Latin *interior* inner.]

interior angle 1. any of the four angles formed inside two lines that are cut by a third line. For illustration, see **alternate angles.** **2.** an angle formed inside a polygon by two adjacent sides.

interior decoration, the art or business of planning, designing, and furnishing interiors, as of homes or offices, to provide beauty, comfort, and convenience. Also, **interior design.**

interior decorator, a person whose business is interior decoration.

interj., interjection.

in·ter·ject (in'tər jekt') *v.t.* to throw in between other things; insert abruptly: *to interject a comment.* [Latin *interjectus,* past participle of *interjicere* to throw between.]

in·ter·jec·tion (in'tər jek'shən) *n.* **1.** any of a class of words or phrases that express emotion or exclamation and are capable of standing alone. *Oh!* and *alas!* are interjections. **2.** the act of interjecting. **3.** something that is interjected, such as a remark or question. —**in'ter·jec'tion·al,** *adj.*

in·ter·lace (in'tər lās') *v.,* **-laced, -lac·ing.** —*v.t.* **1.** to unite by or as by weaving together; intertwine. **2.** to distribute at intervals; intersperse. —*v.i.* to intertwine.

in·ter·lard (in'tər lärd') *v.t.* to give variety to by mixing in or inserting something different: *to interlard a speech with quotations from Shakespeare.* [Middle French *entrelard,* going back to Old French *entre* (from Latin *inter* between, among) + *lard* bacon. See LARD.]

in·ter·leaf (in'tər lēf') *n., pl.* **-leaves** (-lēvz'). a sheet of paper, usually blank, placed between two regular printed leaves of a book, esp. to protect an engraving or color plate.

in·ter·leave (in'tər lēv') *v.t.,* **-leaved, -leav·ing.** to insert an interleaf or interleaves between the regular printed leaves of a book.

in·ter·leu·kin (in'tər lü'kin) *n.* any of a class of proteins, secreted by various lymphocytes, that help the cells of the immune

system to communicate with one another during regulation of the immune response. **Interleukin-2** stimulates the production and growth of T cells and is used in cancer therapy.

in·ter·line¹ (in'tər līn') *v.t.,* **-lined, -lin·ing.** to sew an interlining in (a garment). [INTER- + LINE².]

in·ter·line² (in'tər līn') *v.t.,* **-lined, -lin·ing.** **1.** to insert words between the written or printed lines of: *to interline a book.* **2.** to write or print between written or printed lines: *to interline a comment.* Also, **interlineate.** [Medieval Latin *interlineare* to write between lines, from Latin *inter* between + *līnea* line.]

in·ter·lin·e·ar (in'tər lin'ē ər) *adj.* **1.** inserted between written or printed lines. **2.** written or printed in different languages or versions in alternate lines.

in·ter·lin·e·ate (in'tər lin'ē āt') *v.t.,* **-at·ed, -at·ing.** interline².

in·ter·lin·e·a·tion (in'tər lin'ē ā'shən) *n.* **1.** the insertion of a word or words between printed or written lines. **2.** the word or words so inserted.

in·ter·lin·ing (in'tər lī'ning) *n.* an extra lining between the outer fabric and the ordinary lining of a garment.

in·ter·link (in'tər lingk') *v.t.* to link together.

in·ter·lock (in'tər lok') *v.t., v.i.* to lock or fit together closely. —*n.* the condition of being interlocked, or a mechanical device designed to create such a condition.

in·ter·loc·u·tor (in'tər lok'yə tər) *n.* **1.** a person who takes part in a conversation or dialogue. **2.** a performer in the middle of a line of performers in a minstrel show who exchanges jokes and puns with those on either end of the line. [Latin *interlocūtus,* past participle of *interloquī* to interrupt in speaking, converse + -OR.]

in·ter·loc·u·to·ry (in'tər lok'yə tôr'ē) *adj.* **1.** of, relating to, or occurring in conversation or dialogue. **2.** interjected into a narrative, conversation, or speech: *interlocutory observations.* **3.** coming between the beginning and end of a lawsuit or trial, as a temporary or provisional decree.

in·ter·lope (in'tər lōp') *v.i.,* **-loped, -lop·ing.** **1.** to interfere in the affairs of others; intrude. **2.** to encroach upon the rights or violate the domain of others, esp. in trade. [INTER- + LOPE.]

in·ter·lop·er (in'tər lō'pər) *n.* a person who interferes in the affairs of others; meddler; intruder.

in·ter·lude (in'tər lüd') *n.* **1.** an intervening time, space, or event: *a brief interlude of sleep.* **2.** a brief passage of music played between parts of a church service, acts of a play, or sections of a long musical composition. **3.** a short performance, such as a pantomime, between the acts of a play. [Medieval Latin *interludium* type of comic play given between the acts of a miracle or mystery play, from Latin *inter* between + *lūdus* a play.]

in·ter·lu·nar (in'tər lü'nər) *adj.* of or relating to the period between the old moon and the new moon, when the moon is invisible.

in·ter·mar·riage (in'tər mar'ij) *n.* marriage between persons of different religious faiths, races, or ethnic backgrounds.

in·ter·mar·ry (in'tər mar'ē) *v.i.,* **-ried, -ry·ing.** **1.** to marry outside one's religious, racial, or ethnic group. **2.** to become connected by marriage, as two families, tribes, or races. **3.** to marry within one's own family.

in·ter·me·di·ar·y (in'tər mē'dē er'ē) *n., pl.* **-ar·ies.** **1.** a person or group that comes between two or more opposing parties in order to bring about an agreement or compromise; mediator: *The state senator served as an intermediary in the negotiations.* **2.** the means by which something is brought about; instrument. **3.** an intermediate form or stage. —*adj.* **1.** acting as a mediator: *an intermediary agent.* **2.** located or occurring between; intermediate: *an intermediary step.* [Latin *intermedius* that which is between + -ARY¹.]

in·ter·me·di·ate¹ (in'tər mē'dē it) *adj.* located or occurring in the middle or between. —*n.* **1.** something intermediate. **2.** intermediary. **3.** *Chemistry.* a compound, such as one manufactured from raw materials, that is used as the basis for synthesizing a finished product. [Medieval Latin *intermediatus* lying between, from Latin *intermedius* that which is between.]

in·ter·me·di·ate² (in'tər mē'dē āt') *v.i.,* **-at·ed, -at·ing.** to act as an intermediary; mediate. [INTER- + MEDIATE.]

in·ter·ment (in tûr'mənt) *n.* the act or ceremony of interring; burial.

in·ter·me·tal·lic (in'tər mə tal'ik) *adj.* (of a chemical compound) consisting of two or more metallic elements, as certain alloys.

in·ter·mez·zo (in'tər met'sō, -med'zō) *n., pl.* **-mez·zos** or **-mez·zi** (-met'sē, -med'zē). **1.** a short musical or other entertainment performed between the acts of a play or opera. **2.** *Music.*

a. a short passage performed between longer movements of an extended composition. **b.** a short, independent instrumental composition. [Italian *intermezzo* interlude, interval, from Latin *intermedius* that which is between.]

in·ter·mi·na·ble (in tûr'mə nə bəl) *adj.* prolonged and seemingly endless; long and drawn out: *interminable controversy.* [Late Latin *interminābilis* endless, going back to Latin *in-* not + *terminus* end.] —**in·ter'mi·na·bly,** *adv.*

in·ter·min·gle (in'tər ming'gəl) *v.t., v.i.,* **-gled, -gling.** to mingle together.

in·ter·mis·sion (in'tər mish'ən) *n.* **1.** an interval between events or periods of activity: *There was a short intermission after the first act of the play.* **2.** the act or an instance of intermitting: *to work without intermission.* [Latin *intermissiō* interruption.]

in·ter·mit (in'tər mit') *v.t., v.i.,* **-mit·ted, -mit·ting.** to discontinue for a time; suspend; interrupt: *to intermit an action.* [Latin *intermittere* to leave off, pause.]

in·ter·mit·tent (in'tər mit'ənt) *adj.* alternately stopping and starting again; coming at intervals: *intermittent rain.* —**in'ter·mit'tence, in'ter·mit'ten·cy,** *n.* —**in'ter·mit·tent·ly,** *adv.* —For Synonyms, see **periodic.**

in·ter·mix (in'tər miks') *v.t., v.i.* to mix together; intermingle.

in·ter·mix·ture (in'tər miks'chər) *n.* **1.** the act of mixing together or the state of being mixed together. **2.** a mass of ingredients mixed together. **3.** something added: *intermixtures to the population.*

in·ter·mo·lec·u·lar (in'tər mə lek'yə lər) *adj.* existing, acting, or occurring between molecules: *Surface tension is caused by intermolecular forces.* —**in'ter·mo·lec'u·lar·ly,** *adv.*

in·tern[1] (in tûrn') *v.t.* to confine or restrict to a particular place, esp. during a war. [French *interner* to confine, from *interne* inward, from Latin *internus.*]

in·tern[2] (in'tûrn') *n.* also, **interne. 1.** an assistant resident doctor, esp. a recent graduate, serving in a hospital or clinic under the supervision of experienced doctors. **2.** a person who serves in an organization or profession, usually on a voluntary and temporary basis, to gain experience or training. —*v.i.* to be an intern. [French *interne* resident medical student in a hospital, from *interne* internal, from Latin *internus* inward.]

in·ter·nal (in tûr'nəl) *adj.* **1.** of, relating to, or existing on the inside; interior: *internal organs.* **2.** of or relating to the domestic matters or concerns of a country: *internal security, internal affairs.* **3.** to be taken internally: *internal medication.* **4.** of, relating to, or dependent upon the nature of a thing; intrinsic: *internal evidence.* **5.** of, relating to, or existing in the mind; subjective: *Sensations and ideas are both internal* (James Martineau, 1866). [Latin *internus* inward + -AL[1].] —**in·ter'nal·ly,** *adv.*

in·ter·nal-com·bus·tion engine (in tûr'nəl kəm bus'chən) **1.** a piston-driven engine of one or more cylinders, usually running on gasoline or diesel fuel. Unlike a steam engine, it produces power by burning fuel within the cylinder. **2.** any engine, including gas turbines and jet engines, in which fuel is burned within the engine itself.

in·ter·nal·ize (in tûr'nə līz') *v.t.,* **-ized, -iz·ing. 1.** to adopt or absorb (someone else's ideas, attributes, or standards) into one's personality or way of thinking: *to internalize an idea, to internalize a prevailing attitude.* **2.** to hold in; suppress: *to internalize one's angry feelings.* [INTERNAL + -IZE.] —**in·ter'nal·i·za'tion,** *n.*

internal medicine, the branch of medicine concerned with the diagnosis and nonsurgical treatment of diseases of the internal organs in adults.

internal respiration, the exchange of oxygen and carbon dioxide between blood or lymph and the various cells of the body. ➡ distinguished from **external respiration.**

internal revenue, governmental income that is derived from taxes other than customs duties.

Internal Revenue Service, an agency of the U.S. government in charge of collecting internal revenue, including personal income taxes.

internal rhyme, rhyme between words within a line or lines of poetry, rather than between words at the ends of lines.

in·ter·na·tion·al (in'tər nash'ə nəl) *adj.* **1.** of, relating to, or concerning two or more countries: *international cooperation.* **2.** of or relating to relations among countries. —*n.* **International.** any of several worldwide socialist or communist organizations. —**in'ter·na'tion·al·ly,** *adv.*

international candle, a unit of measure of light intensity, used internationally until 1948 and then superseded by the candela.

International Court of Justice, the judicial body of the United Nations, created in 1945. Also, **World Court.**

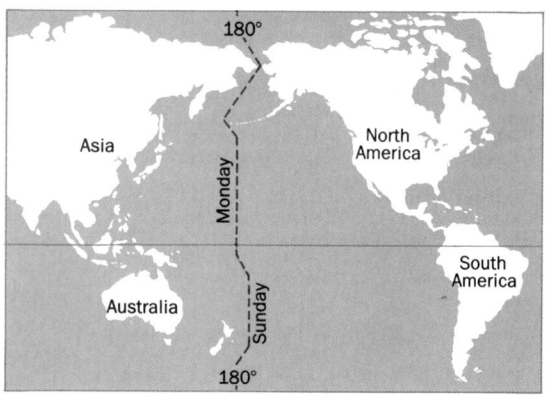

International Date Line

International Date Line also, **international date line.** an imaginary line running approximately along the 180th meridian, marking the time boundary between one day and the next. Also, **date line.**

In·ter·na·tio·nale (in'tər nash'ə nal', -näl') *n.* a revolutionary socialist anthem composed at the time of the Paris Commune of 1871.

in·ter·na·tion·al·ism (in'tər nash'ə nə liz'əm) *n.* **1.** the doctrine of mutual cooperation among countries and peoples for the benefit of all humanity. **2.** the state or quality of being international, as in character, interests, or outlook.

in·ter·na·tion·al·ist (in'tər nash'ə nə list) *n.* a person who supports internationalism.

in·ter·na·tion·al·ize (in'tər nash'ə nə līz') *v.t.,* **-ized, -iz·ing.** to bring under international control; make international.

international law, rules and conventions regulating the dealings of countries with one another.

International Phonetic Alphabet, an alphabet consisting of letters and symbols that are universally understood, developed to transcribe the sounds of any language.

International System of Units, a system of measurement, adopted worldwide, based on the meter as the unit of length, the kilogram as mass, the second as time, and using the ampere, kelvin, mole, and candela for measuring other fundamental quantities.

international unit, an amount of a vitamin, drug, or other substance needed to produce an effect in the body, accepted internationally as a standard measure.

in·terne (in'tûrn') *n.* intern[2].

in·ter·ne·cine (in'tər nes'ēn, -nē'sin, in tûr'nə sēn') *adj.* **1.** of or relating to conflict among groups or among people within a group: *Internecine squabbling between departments in the company made it difficult to do business.* **2.** mutually destructive: *an internecine struggle between two religious sects.* **3.** characterized by much bloodshed: *an internecine war.* [Latin *internecīnus* deadly.]

in·tern·ee (in'tûr nē') *n.* a person who is or has been interned.

in·ter·neu·ron (in'tər nûr'on, -nyûr'-) *n.* any nerve cell of the central nervous system that transmits impulses between sensory and motor neurons.

in·ter·nist (in'tûr nist) *n.* a doctor who specializes in the diagnosis and nonsurgical treatment of diseases of adults.

in·tern·ment (in tûrn'mənt) *n.* the act of interning or the state of being interned.

in·ter·node (in'tər nōd') *n.* the part of a plant stem between two successive nodes. [Latin *internodium.* See INTER-, NODE.] —**in'ter·nod'al,** *adj.*

in·tern·ship (in'tûrn ship') *n.* the period during which a person serves as an intern, as in a hospital or clinic.

in·ter·o·cep·tor (in'tər ō sep'tər) *n. Anatomy.* a sensory nerve receptor located in and transmitting impulses from the inner organs. —**in'ter·o·cep'tive,** *adj.*

in·ter·of·fice (in'tər ô'fis) *adj.* connecting or involving different offices or departments in a business or other organization: *interoffice telephones, an interoffice memo.*

a	at	e	end	o	hot	u	up	hw	white		about
ā	ape	ē	me	ō	old	ū	use	ng	song		taken
ä	far	i	it	ô	fork	ü	rule	th	thin	ə	pencil
âr	care	ī	ice	oi	oil	ù	pull	th	this		lemon
				îr	pierce	ou	out	ûr	turn	zh	measure	circus

I

in·ter·pel·late (in'tər pel'āt, in tûr'pə lāt') *v.t., v.i.,* -lat·ed, -lat·ing. to question formally or publicly an action or policy of the government. [Latin *interpellātus,* past participle of *interpellāre* to interrupt in speaking.] —**in·ter·pel·la·tion** (in'tər pə lā'shən, in tûr'-), *n.*

in·ter·pen·e·trate (in'tər pen'i trāt') *v.,* -trat·ed, -trat·ing. —*v.t.* to penetrate thoroughly; permeate; pervade. —*v.i.* to penetrate each other. —**in'ter·pen'e·tra'tion,** *n.* —**in'ter·pen'e·tra'tive,** *adj.*

in·ter·per·son·al (in'tər pûr'sə nəl) *adj.* **1.** between persons: *interpersonal relations.* **2.** wanting or needing contact with others: *Humans are interpersonal beings.* —**in'ter·per'son·al·ly,** *adv.*

in·ter·phase (in'tər fāz') *n.* the period in the life of a cell when it is not undergoing mitosis or meiosis.

in·ter·phone (in'tər fōn') *n.* an intercom system using telephones.

in·ter·plan·e·tar·y (in'tər plan'i ter'ē) *adj.* between the planets.

in·ter·play (in'tər plā') *n.* a reciprocal action or influence; interaction: *the interplay between two characters in a story.* —*v.i.* to act on each other; interact.

In·ter·pol (in'tər pōl') *n.* an international police agency that assists the police of member countries in their work. [Short for *inter(national) pol(ice).*]

in·ter·po·late (in tûr'pə lāt') *v.,* -lat·ed, -lat·ing. —*v.t.* **1.** to alter or falsify (a text) by inserting new material: *This ancient poem has been extensively interpolated by medieval scribes.* **2.** to insert (new or false material), as into a text: *The actors interpolated several lines of their own into the play.* **3.** *Mathematics.* to find the value of (a function, such as a logarithm) between two known values. —*v.i.* to make an insertion or insertions of new or false material. [Latin *interpolatus,* past participle of *interpolāre* to polish, give new form to, from *interpolis* refurbished, repaired, from *inter* between + *polire* to polish.]

in·ter·po·la·tion (in tûr'pə lā'shən) *n.* **1.** the act of interpolating or the state of being interpolated. **2.** something that is interpolated; insertion.

in·ter·pose (in'tər pōz') *v.,* -posed, -pos·ing. —*v.t.* **1.** to introduce into a conversation or speech: *to interpose an unnecessary remark.* **2.** to place between; insert: *to interpose an obstacle.* **3.** to assert in order to interfere or intervene: *to interpose authority.* —*v.i.* **1.** to interrupt. **2.** to come between; intervene. [French *interposer* to put between, a modification (influenced by French *poser* to place) of Latin *interpōnere.*] —**in'ter·pos'er,** *n.*

in·ter·po·si·tion (in'tər pə zish'ən) *n.* **1.** the act or an instance of interposing. **2.** something that is interposed.

in·ter·pret (in tûr'prit) *v.t.* **1.** to make clear or understandable; reveal the meaning of; elucidate. **2.** to translate orally: *The tourist guide interpreted the menu for us.* **3.** to understand or regard: *The police officer interpreted the suspect's offer as a bribe.* **4.** to render or perform so as to bring out the meaning of: *The pianist interpreted the sonata with great feeling.* —*v.i.* **1.** to act as an interpreter; translate: *During our trip abroad my friend offered to interpret for us.* **2.** to give an interpretation; explain. [Latin *interpretārī* to explain.]

Synonyms *v.t.* **Interpret, explain, expound,** and **elucidate** mean to make clear or understandable. **Interpret** connotes putting something unfamiliar into familiar terms, esp. through the use of special skill: *to interpret an abstract painting, to interpret a difficult piece of technical writing.* **Explain** is a more general term that may simply connote making something easier for someone to understand: *I had to explain the road signs to the children.* **Expound** connotes elaborating or expanding on something: *to expound a theory.* **Elucidate** suggests clearing up something confusing or obscure: *Would you care to elucidate your position on the new economic policy?*

in·ter·pre·ta·tion (in tûr'pri tā'shən) *n.* **1.** the act of interpreting. **2.** the sense that results from interpreting; meaning. **3.** a rendition or performance that brings out the meaning of something, as of a musical composition or dramatic role.

in·ter·pre·ta·tive (in tûr'pri tā'tiv) *adj.* interpretive.

in·ter·pret·er (in tûr'pri tər) *n.* **1.** a person who gives oral translations from one language to another. **2.** a person who renders or performs something, so as to bring out the meaning: *a leading interpreter of Bach's organ works.* **3.** *Computers.* a program that translates high-level language instructions into instructions that a computer can process directly.

in·ter·pre·tive (in tûr'pri tiv) *adj.* serving to interpret; explanatory. Also, **interpretative.**

in·ter·ra·cial (in'tər rā'shəl) *adj.* **1.** between or involving members of different races: *interracial marriage, interracial harmony.* **2.** of or for members of different races: *interracial community facilities.*

in·ter·reg·num (in'tər reg'nəm) *n., pl.* -nums or -na (-nə).

1. an interval between the end of a sovereign's reign and the accession of his or her successor. **2.** any period without the usual ruling power or authority. **3.** any break in continuity; pause. [Latin *interregnum* time between the end of a sovereign's reign and the accession of his successor, from *inter* between + *regnum* reign.]

in·ter·re·late (in'tər ri lāt') *v.t., v.i.,* -lat·ed, -lat·ing. to bring or come into mutual or close relation. —**in'ter·re·la'tion,** in'ter·re·la'tion·ship,** *n.*

in·ter·re·lat·ed (in'tər ri lā'tid) *adj.* closely or mutually related to each other: *interrelated laws.*

interrog. **1.** interrogation. **2.** interrogative.

in·ter·ro·gate (in ter'ə gāt') *v.,* -gat·ed, -gat·ing. —*v.t.* to examine by questioning formally and methodically: *The police interrogated the prisoner for hours.* —*v.i.* to ask questions: *They were granted permission to interrogate.* [Latin *interrogātus,* past participle of *interrogāre* to question.]

in·ter·ro·ga·tion (in ter'ə gā'shən) *n.* **1.** the act of interrogating or the state of being interrogated; questioning: *a defense attorney's lengthy interrogation of a witness.* **2.** a question.

interrogation point, question mark. Also, **interrogation mark.**

in·ter·rog·a·tive (in'tə rog'ə tiv) *adj.* **1.** of, relating to, or having the form of a question: *an interrogative sentence.* **2.** *Grammar.* expressing or introducing a question. *Who* is an interrogative pronoun in the sentence *Who is it?* —*n.* a word or construction used in asking a question. —**in'ter·rog'a·tive·ly,** *adv.*

in·ter·ro·ga·tor (in ter'ə gā'tər) *n.* a person who interrogates; questioner.

in·ter·rog·a·to·ry (in'tə rog'ə tôr'ē) *adj.* expressing or asking a question; questioning: *an interrogatory statement.* —*n., pl.* -ries. *Law.* a formal, written question sent by one side in a lawsuit to the other, to discover the other's factual and legal contentions: *to respond to interrogatories.*

in·ter·rupt (in'tər rupt') *v.t.* **1.** to break the continuity of; break off; cause to stop: *She interrupted her work to answer the phone.* **2.** to break in upon (someone) in the course of an action or speech: *Please do not interrupt me when I am talking.* **3.** to interfere with or make a break in: *The tall trees interrupted our view of the river.* —*v.i.* to break in upon an action or speech: *You always interrupt when someone is speaking.* [Latin *interruptus,* past participle of *interrumpere* to break up, break off.] —**in'ter·rup'tive,** *adj.*

in·ter·rupt·er (in'tə rup'tər) *n.* **1.** a person or thing that interrupts. **2.** a device for interrupting an electric circuit periodically and automatically.

in·ter·rup·tion (in'tə rup'shən) *n.* **1.** the act of interrupting or the state of being interrupted. **2.** something that interrupts. **3.** the period during which something is interrupted.

Synonyms **Interruption, interval,** and **hiatus** denote a break in continuity. **Interruption** is the most general term, which stresses the break itself: *an interruption from the audience, an interruption in service.* **Interval** refers to the distance in time or space between two things: *a ten-minute interval between the acts of a play, an interval of a foot or so between uprights of a fence.* **Hiatus** connotes an interval in which something is missing: *a hiatus in communications between the two cities.*

in·ter·scho·las·tic (in'tər skə las'tik) *adj.* between or among schools: *interscholastic rivalries.*

in·ter·sect (in'tər sekt') *v.t.* to divide by passing or lying across: *The river intersects the valley.* —*v.i.* to meet and lie across each other: *The two roads intersect at the bridge.* [Latin *intersectus,* past participle of *intersecāre* to cut apart.]

in·ter·sec·tion (in'tər sek'shən, in'tər sek'-) *n.* **1.** a place of intersecting, esp. where two or more roads or streets meet and cross. **2.** the act of intersecting or the state of being intersected. **3.** *Mathematics.* **a.** the points contained in common by two geometrical figures. **b.** the set of all the elements that are found in two or more given sets. —**in'ter·sec'tion·al,** *adj.*

in·ter·space (*n.,* in'tər spās'; *v.,* in'tər spās') *n.* the space between things; interval. —*v.t.,* -spaced, -spac·ing. **1.** to put a space between. **2.** to occupy or fill the space between.

in·ter·spe·ci·fic (in'tər spi sif'ik) *adj.* existing or arising between species. ➡ distinguished from **intraspecific.**

in·ter·sperse (in'tər spûrs') *v.t.,* -spersed, -spers·ing. **1.** to scatter at intervals among or between other things: *The author interspersed poems among the essays in the book.* **2.** to diversify by scattering at intervals among or between (with with): *to intersperse an article with literary quotations.* [Latin *interspersus* strewn, sprinkled upon.] —**in·ter·sper·sion** (in'tər spûr'shən, -zhən), *n.*

in·ter·state (in'tər stāt') *adj.* between or among two or more states, esp. in the United States: *interstate highways, interstate trade.* —*n.* an interstate highway that is part of the national highway system.

in·ter·stel·lar (in'tər stel'ər) *adj.* between or among the stars.

in·ter·stice (in tûr′stis) *n., pl.* **-sti·ces** (-stə siz, -sēz′). a narrow space or opening between things or parts; crevice; fissure. [Late Latin *interstitium,* from Latin *inter* between + *stāre* to stand.]

in·ter·sti·tial (in′tər stish′əl) *adj.* **1.** of, relating to, or forming an interstice or interstices: *interstitial spaces.* **2.** situated between the cellular elements of an organ or part: *interstitial tissue.* —**in′ter·sti′tial·ly,** *adv.*

in·ter·tid·al (in′tər tī′dəl) *adj.* inhabiting, occupying, or located within a zone extending from low to high tide; littoral. [INTER- + TIDAL.]

in·ter·trib·al (in′tər trī′bəl) *adj.* between tribes.

in·ter·twine (in′tər twīn′) *v.t., v.i.,* **-twined, -twin·ing.** to twine together.

in·ter·ur·ban (in′tər ûr′bən) *adj.* of or between different cities: *an interurban transit system, interurban commerce.*

in·ter·val (in′tər vəl) *n.* **1.** intervening time or space: *a year's interval between vacations, three-foot intervals between the fence posts.* **2.** a temporary stop or break in the course of something, as of an action or event: *After a brief interval we resumed our meeting.* **3.** a difference in pitch between any two notes. [Latin *intervallum* space between ramparts, space between, from *inter* between + *vallum* rampart.] —For Synonyms, see **interruption.**
·**at intervals. a.** with spaces between; here and there: *Signs were placed at intervals along the highway.* **b.** from time to time; now and then.

in·ter·vene (in′tər vēn′) *v.i.* **-vened, -ven·ing. 1.** to come between certain events or points in time: *Many years intervened before they met again.* **2.** to come in as a mediator; come between opposing parties; intercede: *to intervene to help end an argument.* **3.** to come in or between so as to affect, modify, or prevent: *We were ready to start the game when a storm intervened.* **4.** to interfere in the affairs of another, esp. of another country. [Latin *intervenīre* to come between.] —**in′ter·ven′er,** *n.*

in·ter·ven·tion (in′tər ven′shən) *n.* **1.** the act of intervening. **2.** interference in the affairs of another, esp. of another country.

in·ter·ven·tion·ist (in′tər ven′shə nist) *n.* **1.** a person who favors intervention, esp. in the affairs of another country. **2.** a person who advocates using medical techniques to affect the course of a disease. —*adj.* of, relating to, or favoring intervention: *an interventionist policy.*

in·ter·ver·te·bral (in′tər vûr′tə brəl) *adj.* located between the vertebrae: *an intervertebral disk.* —**in′ter·ver′te·bral·ly,** *adv.*

in·ter·view (in′tər vū′) *n.* **1.a.** a meeting between a writer or reporter and a person from whom information is sought. **b.** a broadcast or published report comprising or recording such a meeting. **2.** a meeting for a specific purpose, such as to discuss employment: *a job interview, an interview with a prospective client.* —*v.t.* to have an interview with or grant an interview to: *to interview applicants for a position, to interview a famous writer.* —*v.i.* **1.** to have or be granted an interview: *to interview with a company, to interview for a job.* **2.** to conduct an interview. [Old French *entrevue* meeting between people for discussion, from *entrevoir* to glimpse, going back to Latin *inter* between + *vidēre* to see.] —**in′ter·view′er,** *n.*

in·ter·weave (in′tər wēv′) *v.t., v.i.,* **-wove** (-wōv′) or **-weaved, -wo·ven** (-wō′vən) or **-wove** or **-weaved, -weav·ing.** to weave or blend together.

in·ter·wo·ven (in′tər wō′vən) *v.* a past participle of **interweave.** —*adj.* woven or mixed together; blended: *interwoven yarns in a quilt, the sun creating an interwoven pattern of light and shade through the trees.*

in·tes·tate (in tes′tāt, -tit) *adj.* without having made a will: *to die intestate.* —*n.* a person who dies without having made a will. [Latin *intestātus,* from *in-* not + *testārī* to make a will.] —**in·tes·ta·cy** (in tes′tə sē), *n.*

in·tes·ti·nal (in tes′tə nəl) *adj.* of, relating to, or affecting the intestines. —**in·tes′ti·nal·ly,** *adv.*

intestinal fortitude, courage and steadfastness. [A euphemism for the corresponding meaning of *guts.* See GUT.]

in·tes·tine (in tes′tin) *n. usually,* **intestines.** that part of the alimentary canal extending from the stomach to the anus. In mammals intestines are divided into the large intestine and the small intestine. —*adj.* of a domestic nature; internal: *intestine feuds and disorders.* [Latin *intestīnus* internal, and *intestīnum* gut, both from *intus* within.]

in·thrall (in thrôl′) *also,* **in·thral.** *v.t.,* **-thralled, -thrall·ing.** enthrall.

in·throne (in thrōn′) *v.t.* **-throned, -thron·ing.** enthrone.

in·ti (in′ti) *n.* the monetary unit of Peru.

in·ti·ma·cy (in′tə mə sē) *n., pl.* **-cies. 1.** the state of being intimate. **2.** an instance of this. **3.** *also,* **intimacies.** sexual liberties, esp. intercourse.

in·ti·mate [1] (in′tə mit) *adj.* **1.** closely or personally associated; well-acquainted: *intimate friends.* **2.a.** characterized by or result-

ing from a feeling of close personal association: *a long, intimate friendship.* **b.** of or resulting from great familiarity: *an intimate knowledge of a business.* **3.** personal or private: *A diary may contain a person's most intimate thoughts.* **4.** having or creating a feeling of privacy or romance: *an intimate little restaurant.* **5.** having sexual intercourse: *to be intimate with someone.* —*n.* a very close friend or associate. [Modification (influenced by IN-TIMATE [2]) of earlier *intime,* from French *intime* inward, close, from Latin *intimus* inmost, superlative of *in* in.] —**in′ti·mate·ly,** *adv.*

> **Synonyms** *adj.* **Intimate** [1], **familiar,** and **close,** used of relationships between persons, mean brought near to each other by regular association or by shared feelings or concerns. **Intimate** implies deep understanding or sympathy: *They were intimate friends with few secrets from each other.* **Familiar** suggests the easy give-and-take of family members: *We're so familiar by now that we know all each other's jokes.* **Close** suggests a relationship so near that others would find it hard to intrude upon: *They were so close in their thinking that neither would make a decision without consulting the other.*

in·ti·mate [2] (in′tə māt′) *v.t.,* **-mat·ed, -mat·ing. 1.** to make known indirectly; hint; imply. **2.** *Archaic.* to announce formally; declare. [Late Latin *intimātus,* past participle of *intimāre* to make known, bring into, from Latin *intimus* inmost. See INTIMATE [1].] —**in′ti·mat′er,** *n.* —**in′ti·ma′tion,** *n.* —For Synonyms, see **hint.**

in·tim·i·date (in tim′i dāt′) *v.t.,* **-dat·ed, -dat·ing. 1.** to make timid or fearful: *The fury of the storm intimidated the child.* **2.** to influence or deter by threats or violence. **3.** to fill with awe; disconcert: *The presence of the royal couple intimidated many of those in the audience.* [Medieval Latin *intimidatus,* past participle of *intimidare* to frighten, from Latin *in* in + *timidus* fearful.] —**in·tim′i·da′tion,** *n.* —**in·tim′i·da′tor,** *n.*

in·ti·tle (in tī′təl) *v.t.,* **-tled, -tling.** entitle.

in·to (in′tü, -tə) *prep.* **1.** to the inside of: *He bit into the apple. She came into the kitchen.* **2.** in the direction of; toward: *He rode off into the horizon. She looked into the sky.* **3.** against so as to meet head-on: *He bumped into the door. She drove into a pole.* **4.** to the state or form of: *The water turned into ice. The dish broke into many pieces.* **5.** to the midst of a period of time: *It rained into the night.* **6.** *Mathematics.* dividing: *8 into 16 is 2.* [Old English *intō* to the interior of, within the limits of, from *in* in + *tō* to.]

in·tol·er·a·ble (in tol′ər ə bəl) *adj.* not to be endured; not tolerable; insufferable; unbearable. [Latin *intolerābilis,* from *in-* not + *tolerābilis* bearable.] —**in·tol′er·a·bil′i·ty, in·tol′er·a·ble·ness,** *n.* —**in·tol′er·a·bly,** *adv.*

in·tol·er·ance (in tol′ər əns) *n.* **1.** an unwillingness to permit or endure differences of opinion or practice; lack of tolerance. **2.** the inability to resist or endure the effects of something; lack of resistance or abnormal sensitivity: *intolerance to penicillin.*

in·tol·er·ant (in tol′ər ənt) *adj.* **1.** unwilling to permit or endure differences of opinion or practice; not tolerant. **2.** unable to resist or endure the effects (usually with *of*): *My cat is intolerant of extreme heat.* —**in·tol′er·ant·ly,** *adv.*

in·tomb (in tüm′) entomb.

in·to·nate (in′tō nāt′, -tə-) *v.t.* **-nat·ed, -nat·ing. 1.** to utter or pronounce with a particular tone; modulate the voice. **2.** to intone.

in·to·na·tion (in′tō nā′shən, -tə-) *n.* **1.** the act of intonating. **2.** a manner of intonating; modulation of the voice in speaking; pitch. **3.** *Music.* the production of tones that are accurate in pitch.

in·tone (in tōn′) *v.t., v.i.,* **-toned, -ton·ing. 1.** to recite in a singing voice or monotone. **2.** to utter with a particular tone. [Medieval Latin *intonare* to utter in a musical tone, from Latin *in* in + *tonus* tone, sound. See TONE.] —**in·ton′er,** *n.*

in to·to (in tō′tō) *Latin.* as a whole; completely.

in·tox·i·cant (in tok′si kənt) *n.* any substance that intoxicates, esp. alcoholic liquor. —*adj.* intoxicating.

in·tox·i·cate (in tok′si kāt′) *v.t.* **-cat·ed, -cat·ing. 1.** to exhilarate, make unsteady, or put into a stupor by means of alcoholic liquor or a drug. **2.** to excite greatly or enrapture: *The sounds and smells of the city intoxicate me.* **3.** *Medicine.* to poison. [Medieval Latin *intoxicatus,* past participle of *intoxicare* to poison, from Latin *in* in + *toxicum* poison. See TOXIC.] —**in·tox′i·cat′ed·ly,** *adv.* —**in·tox′i·ca′tive,** *adj.* —**in·tox′i·ca′tor,** *n.*

in·tox·i·ca·tion (in tok′si kā′shən) *n.* **1.** the state of being drunk; drunkenness; inebriation. **2.** an act or instance of intoxicating or becoming intoxicated. **3.** mental excitement or emo-

a	at	e	end	o	hot	u	up	hw	white		about
ā	ape	ē	me	ō	old	ū	use	ng	song	ə	taken
ä	far	i	it	ô	fork	ů	rule	th	thin		pencil
âr	care	ī	ice	oi	oil	ŭ	pull	th	this		lemon
				ir	pierce	ou	out	ûr	turn	zh	measure		circus

I

651

tional frenzy. **4.** *Medicine.* poisoning, as by a drug, serum, alcohol, or any toxic substance.

intr., intransitive.

intra- *prefix* on the inside; within: *intravenous.* [Latin *intrā.*]

in·tra·cel·lu·lar (in′trə sel′yə lər) *adj. Biology.* located in or occurring within an individual cell or cells.

in·tra·coast·al (in′trə kōs′təl) *adj.* within a coastline or a coastal area: *an intracoastal waterway.* [INTRA- + COASTAL.]

in·trac·ta·ble (in trak′tə bəl) *adj.* **1.** not easily managed; not tractable; stubborn: *an intractable child.* **2.** not easily treated, handled, used, or worked: *an intractable problem, an intractable subject.* —**in·trac′ta·bil′i·ty, in·trac′ta·ble·ness,** *n.* —**in·trac′ta·bly,** *adv.*

in·tra·dos (in′trə dos′, -dōs′, in trā′dos) *n.* the interior curve or surface of an arch or vault. [French *intrados,* from Latin *intrā* within + French *dos* back (from Latin *dorsum*).]

in·tra·mo·lec·u·lar (in′trə mə lek′yə lər) *adj.* existing, acting, or occurring within a molecule or molecules: *Photochemical changes occur at the intramolecular level.* —**in′tra·mo·lec′u·lar·ly,** *adv.*

in·tra·mu·ral (in′trə myūr′əl) *adj.* consisting of or limited to participants from the same school or organization: *intramural basketball.* [INTRA- + Latin *mūrālis* relating to a wall, from *mūrus* wall.] —**in′tra·mur′al·ly,** *adv.*

in·tra·mus·cu·lar (in′trə mus′kyə lər) *adj.* located in or injected into muscle tissue. —**in′tra·mus′cu·lar·ly,** *adv.*

intrados

in·tran·si·gent (in tran′si jənt) *adj.* refusing to yield or compromise; uncompromising. —*n.* a person who is uncompromising. [French *intransigeant,* from Spanish *intransigente* (name given to a supporter of an extreme leftist party in Spain in 1873-74), going back to Latin *in-* not + *trānsigere* to come to an agreement.] —**in·tran′si·gence, in·tran′si·gen·cy,** *n.* —**in·tran′si·gent·ly,** *adv.*

in·tran·si·tive (in tran′si tiv) *adj. Grammar.* of or relating to an action that does not require a direct object. The verbs *exist* and *die* are intransitive. —**in·tran′si·tive·ly,** *adv.* —**in·tran′si·tive·ness,** *n.*

in·tra·spe·ci·fic (in′trə spi sif′ik) *adj.* existing within a species or involving members of one species. ➡ distinguished from **interspecific.**

in·tra·state (in′trə stāt′) *adj.* existing or occurring within a state, esp. of the United States.

in·tra·u·ter·ine (in′trə ū′tər in, -tə rīn′) *adj.* located within the uterus. [INTRA- + UTERINE.]

intrauterine device, any of various metal or plastic contraceptive devices placed and left in the uterus to prevent implantation of a fertilized ovum.

in·tra·ve·nous (in′trə vē′nəs) *adj.* **1.** existing or taking place within a vein. **2.** entering or introduced by way of a vein: *intravenous injection.* **3.** of, relating to, or used in administering an intravenous injection. [INTRA- + VENOUS.] —**in′tra·ve′nous·ly,** *adv.*

in·treat (in trēt′) entreat.

in·trench (in trench′) entrench.

in·trench·ment (in trench′mənt) entrenchment.

in·trep·id (in trep′id) *adj.* having or showing great bravery and valor; undaunted: *The intrepid explorers moved deeper into the jungle.* [Latin *intrepidus,* from *in-* not + *trepidus* alarmed.] —**in·tre·pid′i·ty** (in′trə pid′i tē), **in·trep′id·ness,** *n.* —**in·trep′id·ly,** *adv.*

in·tri·ca·cy (in′tri kə sē) *n., pl.* **-cies. 1.** the quality or state of being intricate. **2.** something intricate: *to understand the intricacies of a contract.*

in·tri·cate (in′tri kit) *adj.* **1.** perplexingly entangled or involved; very complicated: *an intricate pattern.* **2.** difficult to analyze or understand: *intricate reasoning.* [Latin *intrīcātus,* past participle of *intrīcāre* to entangle, perplex, from *in* in + *tricae* trifles, hindrances.] —**in′tri·cate·ly,** *adv.* —**in′tri·cate·ness,** *n.* —For Synonyms, see **complex.**

in·trigue (*n.,* in′trēg, in trēg′; *v.,* in trēg′) *n.* **1.** the use of underhanded and devious means to achieve a goal: *There was much plotting and intrigue before the outbreak of war.* **2.** an underhanded and devious scheme or plot: *a political intrigue.* **3.** a clandestine love affair. —*v.,* **-trigued, -trigu·ing.** —*v.i.* to carry on an underhanded and devious scheme or plot: *The military leaders intrigued against the government.* —*v.t.* to excite the

curiosity or interest of; fascinate: *The story of the sailor's adventures intrigued us.* [French *intrigue* plot, liaison, from Italian *intrigo* plot, from *intrigare* to plot, from Latin *intrīcāre.* See INTRICATE.] —**in·trigu′er,** *n.* —For Synonyms *(n.),* see **plot.**

in·trin·sic (in trin′zik, -sik) *adj.* belonging or basic to something by its very nature: *the intrinsic beauty of a sunset.* Also, **in·trin′si·cal.** [Old French *intrinseque* inner, from Late Latin *intrinsecus* inward, from Latin *intrinsecus* inwardly.] —**in·trin′si·cal·ly,** *adv.* —For Synonyms, see **inherent.**

in·tro (in′trō) *n., pl.* **-tros.** *Informal.* introduction. [Short for INTRO(DUCTION).]

intro- *prefix* into; inward; within: *introvert.* [Latin *intrō* to the inside, within.]

intro. 1. introduction. **2.** introductory.

in·tro·duce (in′trə düs′, -dūs′) *v.t.,* **-duced, -duc·ing. 1.** to bring into the formal acquaintance of a person or persons: *Our host introduced us to the other guests.* **2.** to bring into use, knowledge, or fashion; institute: *The inventor introduced a new procedure for manufacturing the product.* **3.** to bring into the acquaintance of something; give first knowledge or experience to: *My friend introduced me to the ballet.* **4.** to bring forward for consideration; propose: *The chair introduced a motion to adjourn.* **5.** to bring in and settle securely: *The botanist introduced a new species of plant to the region.* **6.** to add or put in as something new: *I introduced my observations into the discussion.* **7.** to place in or inside; insert. **8.** to get (something) going or in progress; start; open; begin: *to introduce a speech with a humorous anecdote.* [Latin *intrōdūcere* to bring in, originate.] —**in′tro·duc′er,** *n.*

in·tro·duc·tion (in′trə duk′shən) *n.* **1.** the act of introducing or the state of being introduced. **2.** something that serves to introduce, as a preface. **3.** something introduced: *The starling in North America was an introduction from England.* **4.** a beginning or elementary textbook or treatise. [Latin *intrōductiō* a leading in.]

> **Synonyms** Introduction, foreword, preface, and prologue are terms for something that serves as a preliminary to a book or artistic work. An **introduction** gives explanatory information about the subject: *The introduction includes a brief outline of the chapter content.* A **foreword** is a brief note, usually written by someone other than the author, which may be more personal than explanatory: *The foreword was written by a friend of the author.* A **preface,** which often serves as the introduction, is an opening discourse that stands apart from the work: *The preface describes the controversy that the book is designed to resolve.* A **prologue** usually appears before a dramatic work, esp. a play, and aims to set a mood or to introduce the audience to the conflict to come. *The play's prologue is suitably gloomy.*

in·tro·duc·to·ry (in′trə duk′tə rē) *adj.* serving to introduce; prefatory; preliminary. —**in′tro·duc′tor·i·ly,** *adv.*

in·tro·it (in′trō it, -troit, in trō′it) *n.* **1.** the opening portion of the Mass, usually consisting of an antiphon and Gloria Patri. **2.** a psalm or anthem sung at the beginning of the Communion service in the Anglican Church. **3.** any hymn, prayer, or response sung or played at the beginning of a religious service. [Latin *introitus* entrance.]

in·trorse (in trôrs′, in′trôrs) *adj. Botany.* facing or directed inward, as anthers that open toward the center of the flower. ➡ opposed to **extrorse.** [Latin *introrsus,* contraction of *introversus,* from *intro* inside + *vorsus* turned, variant of *versus,* past participle of *vertere* to turn.]

in·tro·spect (in′trə spekt′) *v.i.* to examine one's own thoughts or feelings; practice introspection.

in·tro·spec·tion (in′trə spek′shən) *n.* the examination of one's own thoughts or feelings. [Latin *intrōspectus,* past participle of *intrōspicere* to look into + -ION.]

in·tro·spec·tive (in′trə spek′tiv) *adj.* of, characterized by, or given to introspection. —**in′tro·spec′tive·ly,** *adv.* —**in′tro·spec′tive·ness,** *n.*

in·tro·ver·sion (in′trə vûr′zhən, -shən) *n.* a preoccupation with one's own inner experiences rather than with things outside oneself. ➡ opposed to **extroversion.** [INTRO- + Late Latin *versiō* a turning (from Latin *vertere* to turn).] —**in′tro·ver′sive,** *adj.*

in·tro·vert (*n.,* in′trə vûrt′; *v.,* in′trə vûrt′, in′trə vûrt′) *n.* **1.** a person whose attention is largely directed toward himself or herself. **2.** a shy, withdrawn person. ➡ opposed to **extrovert.** —*v.t.* to direct (one's attention) toward one's inner experiences. [INTRO- + Latin *vertere* to turn.]

in·tro·vert·ed (in′trə vûr′tid) *adj.* tending to be more concerned with one's own thoughts and feelings rather than with other people and what goes on around one.

in·trude (in trüd′) *v.,* **-trud·ed, -trud·ing.** —*v.i.* to come in as a disturbing or unwelcome addition; enter brusquely or obtrusively: *We were trying to study when a noisy crowd intruded.* —*v.t.*

1. to thrust or force in obtrusively. **2.** *Geology.* to penetrate into or between older rock. [Latin *intrūdere* to thrust in.] —**in·trud′·er,** *n.*

| **Synonyms** | **Intrude, trespass, encroach,** and **infringe** mean to violate the property or rights of another. |

Intrude generally connotes thrusting oneself in without right or welcome: *to intrude on a private conversation.* **Trespass** connotes an intrusion that violates property rights: *to trespass on someone's land.* **Encroach** suggests a gradual crossing over into another's rightful or private space: *to encroach on a neighbor's property.* **Infringe** suggests a more obvious interference and often applies to legal rights: *The proposed law would infringe on the rights of taxpayers.*

in·tru·sion (in trü′zhən) *n.* **1.** an act or instance of intruding or the state of being intruded upon. **2.** something that intrudes. **3.** the illegal entering into or seizing of another's property. **4.** *Geology.* **a.** the penetration of matter, as molten rock, into or between older rock. **b.** a body of rock thus formed. [Medieval Latin *intrūsiō* a thrusting in, from Latin *intrūsus,* past participle of *intrūdere* to thrust in.]

in·tru·sive (in trü′siv) *adj.* characterized by intrusion; tending to intrude: *intrusive questions.* —**in·tru′sive·ly,** *adv.* —**in·tru′sive·ness,** *n.*

in·trust (in trust′) entrust.

in·tu·i·tion (in′tü ish′ən, -tū-) *n.* **1.** a direct or immediate perception or understanding of truth without reasoning. **2.** the knowledge or insight resulting from such perception. **3.** the ability to conjecture correctly. [Late Latin *intuitiō* a looking into, from Latin *intuērī* to look upon, consider.] —**in′tu·i′tion·al,** *adj.* —**in′tu·i′tion·al·ly,** *adv.* —For Synonyms, see **instinct**[1].

in·tu·i·tive (in tü′i tiv, -tū′-) *adj.* **1.** of or relating to intuition: *intuitive ability.* **2.** derived from or characterized by intuition: *intuitive knowledge.* **3.** possessing intuition. —**in·tu′i·tive·ly,** *adv.* —**in·tu′i·tive·ness,** *n.*

in·tu·mes·cence (in′tü mes′əns) *n.* **1.** any swollen or enlarged organ or mass, as a tumor. **2.** the process of becoming swollen or enlarged, or the state of being swollen or enlarged. [French *intumescence,* from Latin *intumescere* to swell, swell up, from *in-* in + *tumescere* to begin to swell.] —**in·tu·mes′cent,** *adj.*

I·nu·it (in′ü it′, -ū it′) *n., pl.* **-it** or **-its.** **1.a.** a member of the Eskimo people living in North America. **b.** a member of the Eskimo people living in Greenland, Canada, and mainland Alaska, excluding the native people of the Aleutian Islands. **2.** the language spoken by these people. [Eskimo *inuit* people, plural of *inuk* person.] —For Usage Note, see **Eskimo.**

in·u·lin (in′yə lin) *n.* a white, starchy carbohydrate found in the roots and tubers of many plants, used in diagnostic tests of kidney function. Formula: $(C_6H_{10}O_5)_n$

in·un·date (in′ən dāt′, in un′dāt) *v.t.,* **-dat·ed, -dat·ing.** **1.** to cover with a flood: *The river overflowed its banks and inundated the valley.* **2.** to fill or overwhelm; swamp: *to inundate with requests.* [Latin *inundātus,* past participle of *inundāre,* from *in* upon + *unda* wave.] —**in′un·da′tion,** *n.* —**in′un·da′tor,** *n.*

in·ure (in yür′, i nür′) *v.t.,* **-ured, -ur·ing.** to make tough or hardy by experience; cause to withstand or endure (with *to*): *Living in an arctic climate will inure you to extreme cold.* [IN + obsolete *ure* use, work, from Old French *uevre* work, from Latin *opera.*] —**in·ure′ment,** *n.*

inv. **1.** invented. **2.** invention. **3.** inventor. **4.** invoice.

in va·cu·o (in vak′ū ō′) *Latin.* in a vacuum.

in·vade (in vād′) *v.,* **-vad·ed, -vad·ing.** —*v.t.* **1.** to enter and attack with an armed force, as for pillage or conquest: *Germany invaded France in 1940.* **2.** to enter and overrun as if to take possession: *Rabbits invaded the garden during the night.* **3.** to interfere with; infringe upon; violate: *to invade the privacy of others.* **4.** to penetrate and spread with harmful effects; infect: *Disease germs had invaded the patient's body.* —*v.i.* to make an invasion. [Latin *invādere* to go into, attack.] —**in·vad′er,** *n.*

in·vag·i·nate (in vaj′ə nāt′) *Biology.* *v.,* **-nat·ed, -nat·ing.** —*v.t.* to place or receive into a sheathlike covering, as within the body. —*v.i.* **1.** to become invaginated. **2.** to grow inward to form a hollow or pocket, as in formation of a gastrula. [Modern Latin *invaginatus,* past participle of *invaginare* to sheathe, from Latin *in-* in + *vāgina* sheath.] —**in·vag′i·na′tion,** *n.*

in·val·id[1] (in′və lid) *n.* a person who is disabled by disease or injury. —*adj.* **1.** disabled by disease or injury. **2.** of, relating to, or for invalids. —*v.t.* **1.** to make an invalid of; disable. **2.** *British.* to discharge or remove from active service because of disease or injury. [French *invalide* infirm, disabled, from Latin *invalidus* infirm, from *in-* not + *validus* strong, powerful.]

in·val·id[2] (in val′id) *adj.* without force, basis, or authority; not valid: *an invalid contract, invalid reasoning.* [Latin *invalidus* infirm, inadequate. See INVALID[1].] —**in·val′id·ly,** *adv.*

in·val·i·date (in val′i dāt′) *v.t.,* **-dat·ed, -dat·ing.** to make

invalid: *The contract invalidated a previous agreement.* —**in·val′i·da′tion,** *n.* —**in·val′i·da′tor,** *n.*

in·va·lid·ism (in′və li diz′əm) *n.* the condition of being disabled by disease or injury.

in·va·lid·i·ty (in′və lid′i tē) *n.* lack of validity.

in·val·u·a·ble (in val′ū ə bəl, -val′yə-) *adj.* of greater value or worth than can be measured; beyond valuation; incalculable; priceless: *invaluable information.* —**in·val′u·a·ble·ness,** *n.* —**in·val′u·a·bly,** *adv.*

in·var·i·a·ble (in vâr′ē ə bəl) *adj.* unchanging or unchangeable; not variable; uniform: *the invariable and oppressive heat of the tropics.* —*n.* something that is unchanging or unchangeable; constant: *the invariables in a mathematical function.* —**in·var′i·a·bil′i·ty, in·var′i·a·ble·ness,** *n.* —**in·var′i·a·bly,** *adv.*

in·var·i·ant (in vâr′ē ənt) *adj.* **1.** unchanging; constant. **2.** unaffected by a transformation or other mathematical operation. —*n.* an invariant quantity or expression. [IN-[1] + VARIANT.]

in·va·sion (in vā′zhən) *n.* **1.** the entrance of an armed force, as into a country, in order to pillage or conquer; military incursion. **2.** the act of invading or the state of being invaded. **3.** an intrusion or violation; infringement: *an invasion of one's rights.* [Late Latin *invāsiō* attack, from Latin *invādere.* See INVADE.]

| **Synonyms** | **Invasion, incursion,** and **raid** may all denote a military entrance onto territory owned or held by |

another country or group. An **invasion** is a large-scale armed attack aimed to conquer or occupy: *the Allied invasion of Normandy in June 1944.* An **incursion** is a brief or unexpected onslaught, which may be designed to harass or divert rather than to occupy or control: *The guerrillas made repeated incursions into enemy territory.* A **raid** is a swift, usually small-scale attack aimed at harassment: *A series of raids preceded the invasion.*

in·va·sive (in vā′siv) *adj.* **1.** tending to invade or spread: *An invasive disease may move from one organ to another.* **2.** *Medicine.* involving incision or insertion of an instrument, as a needle, into the body: *Surgery is an invasive form of treatment.* **3.** tending to intrude; intrusive: *Listening to private telephone conversations is invasive.*

in·vec·tive (in vek′tiv) *n.* a violent, railing accusation or verbal attack; vehement denunciation; vituperation: *The candidate for mayor directed an invective against the incumbent.* [Late Latin *invectīvus* abusive, from Latin *invehere.* See INVEIGH.]

in·veigh (in vā′) *v.i.* to utter or write a vehement denunciation; make a verbal attack (with *against*). [Latin *invehere* to carry in, attack.] —**in·veigh′er,** *n.*

in·vei·gle (in vā′gəl, -vē′-) *v.t.,* **-gled, -gling.** **1.** to lure or induce by deceit, blandishments, or cajolery: *The couple inveigled their friend into lending them a large sum of money.* **2.** to acquire by blandishments or cajolery: *The lawyer inveigled a response from the reluctant witness.* [Modification of French *aveugler* to blind, delude, going back to Latin *ab* without + *oculus* eye.] —**in·vei′gle·ment,** *n.* —**in·vei′gler,** *n.*

in·vent (in vent′) *v.t.* **1.** to conceive and produce by original thought and ingenuity; originate: *to invent a new part for a machine, to invent a new word.* **2.** to make up (something false or fictitious): *to invent rumors.* [Latin *inventus,* past participle of *invenīre* to come upon, find.] —For Synonyms, see **devise.**

in·ven·tion (in ven′shən) *n.* **1.** the act or process of inventing. **2.** something that is invented. **3.** a fictitious account; false statement. **4.** the ability to invent; inventiveness. **5.** *Music.* a short, contrapuntal composition written for a keyboard instrument.

in·ven·tive (in ven′tiv) *adj.* **1.** skillful and resourceful; able to invent: *an inventive person.* **2.** of, relating to, or characterized by invention: *inventive ability.* —**in·ven′tive·ly,** *adv.* —**in·ven′tive·ness,** *n.*

in·ven·tor (in ven′tər) *n.* a person who invents, esp. one who conceives and produces something new, as a process or device.

in·ven·to·ry (in′vən tôr′ē) *n., pl.* **-to·ries.** **1.** a descriptive list of articles in stock at a given time: *The inventory revealed that the store was overstocked.* **2.** any detailed list of articles: *an inventory of books in a library, an inventory of items in an estate.* **3.** the articles so listed. **4.** the act or process of compiling such a list: *The store was closed for inventory all week.* **5.** a list or account resulting from a survey or questionnaire: *a wildlife inventory, an inventory of personality traits.* —*v.t.,* **-to·ried, -to·ry·ing.** **1.** to make a detailed list of. **2.** to include in an inventory. [Medieval Latin *inventorium* list, modification of Late Latin *inventārium,*

a	at	e	end	o	hot	u	up	hw	white		about
ā	ape	ē	me	ō	old	ū	use	ng	song		taken
ä	far	i	it	ô	fork	ü	rule	th	thin	ə	pencil
âr	care	ī	ice	oi	oil	u̇	pull	th	this		lemon
		îr	pierce	ou	out	ûr	turn	zh	measure		circus

from Latin *inventus*, past participle of *invenīre* to find.] —in'ven·to'ri·al, *adj.* —in·ven·to'ri·al·ly, *adv.*

· to take inventory. a. to make an inventory of stock at a given time. b. to assess one's personal characteristics and skills.

in·verse (in vûrs', in'vûrs') *adj.* 1. reversed in sequence, position, or relation: *an inverse order.* 2. turned upside down; inverted. —*n.* 1. something that is the direct opposite; reverse. 2. *Mathematics.* an element in a set that when added to or multiplied by a given element yields the identity element for addition or multiplication respectively. The **additive inverse** of 3 is −3; the **multiplicative inverse** of 3 is ⅓. Also *(def. 2),* **inverse element.** [Latin *inversus,* past participle of *invertere* to turn about, reverse.] —in·verse'ly, *adv.*

in·ver·sion (in vûr'zhən, -shən) *n.* 1. the act of inverting or the state of being inverted. 2. something that is inverted. 3. (in the atmosphere) an increase of temperature with altitude, resulting from the entrapment of cool air by a blanket of warm air, a condition fostering the buildup of smog at lower altitudes. [Latin *inversiō* transposition, reverse order.]

in·vert (in vûrt') *v.t.* 1. to turn upside down: *The lens inverted the image.* 2. to reverse the sequence, position, or relation of. 3. to subject to or bring about inversion. [Latin *invertere* to turn about or upside down, reverse.] —in·vert'i·ble, *adj.*

in·ver·tase (in vûr'tās) *n.* an enzyme present in plants and animals that breaks down sucrose into glucose and fructose. Also, **sucrase.**

in·ver·te·brate (in vûr'tə brit, -brāt') *adj.* 1. having no backbone; not a vertebrate. 2. of or relating to an animal having no backbone. —*n.* an invertebrate animal.

in·vert·er (in vûr'tər) *n.* 1. a person or thing that inverts. 2. a device that converts direct current into alternating current.

invert sugar, a mixture of certain forms of glucose and fructose that is sweeter than sucrose, occurring naturally in fruit and honey and prepared commercially for use in foods and medicine by hydrolyzing sucrose.

in·vest (in vest') *v.t.* 1. to use (money) to acquire an interest in existing properties or to create new properties for the purpose of producing profit or income: *to invest one's savings in stocks.* 2. to expend or devote (something, as time, effort, or money), esp. for personal advantage or merit: *to invest time and effort in a project.* 3. to endow or furnish, as with power, authority, or privilege. 4. to formally install in an office, rank, or position. 5. to give a certain quality or attribute to: *The judge's manner of speaking invested every word with dignity.* 6. to cover; envelop: *Fog invested the harbor.* 7. to surround with armed forces in order to blockade or capture; lay siege to. —*v.i.* to make an investment: *to invest in a new business.* [Latin *investīre* to clothe, cover.] —in·ves'tor, *n.*

in·ves·ti·gate (in ves'ti gāt') *v.,* -gat·ed, -gat·ing. —*v.t.* to explore systematically in order to uncover facts or gain information; make a thorough examination of. —*v.i.* to make an investigation. [Latin *investīgātus,* past participle of *investīgāre* to trace out, search after, going back to *in* in + *vestīgium* track, footprint.]

in·ves·ti·ga·tion (in ves'ti gā'shən) *n.* the act or process of investigating; careful, thorough examination or search. —For Synonyms, see **inquiry.**

in·ves·ti·ga·tive (in ves'ti gā'tiv) *adj.* of, relating to, or engaged in investigating or an investigation: *an investigative reporter, investigative procedures.*

in·ves·ti·ga·tor (in ves'ti gā'tər) *n.* a person who investigates, as a detective.

in·ves·ti·ture (in ves'ti chər) *n.* 1. the act or ceremony of formally installing in an office, rank, or position. 2. anything that covers or envelops: *a bright investiture of light.*

in·vest·ment (in vest'mənt) *n.* 1. the act of investing, esp. the use of money to produce profit or income. 2. the amount of money that is invested. 3. something in which money is invested, as real estate, stocks, or bonds. 4. investiture *(def. 1).* 5. an outer covering.

in·vet·er·ate (in vet'ər it) *adj.* 1. confirmed in a habit or practice; habitual: *an inveterate complainer.* 2. firmly established by tradition or custom; deep-rooted: *inveterate prejudices.* [Latin *inveterātus,* past participle of *inveterāre* to make old, give duration to.] —in·vet'er·a·cy, in·vet'er·ate·ness, *n.* —in·vet'er·ate·ly, *adv.*

in·vid·i·ous (in vid'ē əs) *adj.* 1. arousing or liable to arouse ill will or hatred; odious: *an invidious task, an invidious remark.* 2. offensively or unfairly biased: *an invidious comparison.* [Latin *invidiōsus* envious, from *invidia* envy.] —in·vid'i·ous·ly, *adv.* —in·vid'i·ous·ness, *n.*

in·vig·or·ate (in vig'ə rāt') *v.t.,* -at·ed, -at·ing. to fill with strength and energy; give vigor to: *The mountain air invigorated and refreshed us.* [IN-² + VIGOR + -ATE¹.] —in·vig'or·at'-

ing·ly, *adv.* —in·vig'or·a'tion, *n.* —in·vig'or·a'tive, *adj.* —in·vig'o·ra'tor, *n.*

in·vin·ci·ble (in vin'sə bəl) *adj.* not capable of being vanquished or overcome; unconquerable: *an invincible army.* [Late Latin *invincibilis,* from Latin *in-* not + *vincere* to conquer.] —in·vin'ci·bly, *adv.* —in·vin'ci·bil'i·ty, in·vin'ci·ble·ness, *n.*

in·vi·o·la·ble (in vī'ə lə bəl) *adj.* 1. that must not be violated; sacrosanct: *an inviolable oath.* 2. not subject to harm or injury; indestructible or invulnerable: *an inviolable fortress.* —in·vi'o·la·bil'i·ty, *n.* —in·vi'o·la·bly, *adv.*

in·vi·o·late (in vī'ə lit, -lāt') *adj.* not broken or defiled; not violated: *Our friendship will remain strong and inviolate.* —in·vi'o·late·ly, *adv.* —in·vi'o·late·ness, *n.*

in·vis·i·ble (in viz'ə bəl) *adj.* 1. that cannot be seen; not visible: *invisible ink.* 2. hidden from view: *The house is invisible from the road.* 3. not evident to the mind: *invisible degrees of difference.* —*n.* an invisible being. —in·vis'i·bil'i·ty, in·vis'i·ble·ness, *n.* —in·vis'i·bly, *adv.*

in·vi·ta·tion (in'vi tā'shən) *n.* 1. the act of inviting. 2. the spoken or written form by which a person is invited.

in·vi·ta·tion·al (in'vi tā'shə nəl) *adj.* of or relating to an event in which participation is restricted to those who have been invited: *an invitational golf tournament.* —*n.* an invitational event.

in·vite (*v.,* in vīt'; *n.,* in'vīt') *v.t.,* -vit·ed, -vit·ing. 1. to make a courteous or formal request for the presence or participation of: *They invited us to their country house for the weekend.* 2. to ask for; solicit: *to invite confidences, to invite assistance.* 3. to tend to bring on; foster: *What you have done can only invite trouble.* 4. to attract or tempt: *The beauty of the place invited them to pause in their hike and rest awhile.* —*n. Informal.* invitation. [Latin *invītāre* to summon, entertain.] —in·vit'er, *n.*

in·vit·ing (in vī'ting) *adj.* tempting; attractive: *The cool, placid lake looked inviting.* —in·vit'ing·ly, *adv.* —in·vit'ing·ness, *n.*

in vi·tro (in vē'trō) (of a biological process) outside the living organism, as in a test tube: *The new drug shows good test results in vitro but has not yet been tried in animals or humans.* [Latin *in vitro* in glass.]

in vi·vo (in vē'vō) (of a biological process) inside a living organism: *After proving that the new drug killed bacteria in test tubes, the doctors tested it in vivo.* [Latin *in vivo* in something living.]

in·vo·ca·tion (in'vō kā'shən) *n.* 1. the act of invoking, esp. the calling upon in prayer for aid or protection; supplication. 2. a prayer used in invoking, esp. one spoken at the beginning of a public ceremony or formal religious service. 3. an incantation used to summon a devil or spirit. —in'vo·ca'tion·al, *adj.*

in·voice (in'vois') *n.* an itemized account of goods sent to a buyer, indicating the quantities shipped, prices, and other charges. —*v.t.,* -voiced, -voic·ing. to make an invoice of: *to invoice a shipment of goods.* [Earlier *invoyes,* plural of obsolete *invoy* something sent, from Old French *envoy* a sending, going back to Latin *in viam* on the way.]

in·voke (in vōk') *v.t.,* -voked, -vok·ing. 1. to call upon in prayer for aid or protection; make supplication to: *to invoke the Muses.* 2. to call or beg for earnestly; make supplication for: *to invoke a judge's mercy.* 3. to call forth by charms or incantation; conjure: *to invoke the spirits of the dead.* 4. to call upon as relevant or mandatory: *to invoke one's rights.* 5. to refer to as support, proof, or confirmation; cite: *to invoke a law.* [Latin *invocāre* to call on, implore.] —in·vok'er, *n.*

in·vo·lu·cre (in'vō lü'kər) *n.* a circle or circles of bracts surrounding a flower or flower cluster. [Latin *involūcrum* covering, case.] —in'vo·lu'cral, *adj.*

in·vol·un·tar·y (in vol'ən ter'ē) *adj.* 1. not done willingly or by choice; not voluntary: *an involuntary confession.* 2. occurring without control; unintentional or accidental: *I gave an involuntary shudder when I saw the snake.* 3. existing or acting without the control of the will: *Blinking is an involuntary action.* —in·vol'un·tar'i·ly, *adv.* —in·vol'un·tar'i·ness, *n.* —For Synonyms, see **automatic.**

involuntary muscle, a muscle not under direct voluntary control, generally consisting of smooth muscle tissue.

in·vo·lute (in'və lüt') *adj.* 1. involved or intricate: *an involute procedure.* 2. *Botany.* rolled inward toward the upper side from the edge or edges: *involute leaves.* 3. *Zoology.* rolled or curled inward around the axis: *an involute shell.* Also, **in'vo·lut'ed.** —*n. Geometry.* a spiral formed by the trace of the point at the end of a taut string as the string is unwound from a circular spool. [Latin *involūtus,* past participle of *involvere* to roll up, cover.]

in·vo·lu·tion (in'və lü'shən) *n.* 1. the act of involving or the state of being involved. 2. something involved or intricate. 3. *Biology.* a reduction in size, esp. as a result of the degenerative changes that occur with age. 4. *Mathematics.* the operation of raising a number to a given power, or of multiplying it by itself a

given number of times. ➡ opposed to **evolution** in def. 4. —**in′vo·lu′tion·al,** *adj.*

in·volve (in volv′) *v.t.,* **-volved, -volv·ing. 1.** to include as a necessary part, condition, or consequence: *Winning the game involves both skill and perseverance.* **2.** to have an effect on; affect: *The decision on tariffs involves more than just the economic well-being of the country.* **3.** to draw or bring, as into an unfortunate situation; cause to be associated or concerned: *Their heedless behavior involved them in a lawsuit. The youth was involved in the robbery.* **4.** to occupy completely; absorb: *I was involved in reading the book all evening.* **5.** to make intricate; complicate: *The lawyers involved their argument with numerous contradictions.* **6.** to surround; envelop: *Fog involved the quiet, ghostly city.* [Latin *involvere* to roll up, cover, envelop.] —**in·volve′ment,** *n.* —**in·volv′er,** *n.*

in·volved (in volvd′) *adj.* difficult to understand; complicated; complex: *an involved procedure.*

in·vul·ner·a·ble (in vul′nər ə bəl) *adj.* **1.** not subject to harm or injury; not vulnerable: *an invulnerable person.* **2.** not assailable; impregnable; unconquerable: *an invulnerable wall, an invulnerable argument.* —**in·vul′ner·a·bil′i·ty, in·vul′ner·a·ble·ness,** *n.* —**in·vul′ner·a·bly,** *adv.*

in·ward (in′wərd) *adv. also,* **inwards. 1.** toward the inside, interior, or center: *The door opened inward into the room.* **2.** into the mind; into one's own thoughts. —*adj.* **1.** directed toward the inside: *an inward motion.* **2.** situated within; inner; internal: *an inward vitality, an inward part.* **3.** of or relating to the mind or thought; mental: *inward vision, inward fears, an inward existence.* [Old English *inneweard* situated within.]

in·ward·ly (in′wərd lē) *adv.* **1.** in or on the inside; within: *Inwardly, I was seething with rage.* **2.** in the mind or thought; secretly; privately: *Although calm in appearance, the soldiers were inwardly terrified.* **3.** toward the inside.

in·ward·ness (in′wərd nis) *n.* **1.** the state of being inward. **2.** the inner nature, quality, or meaning. **3.** depth or intensity of feeling or thought. **4.** an inward preoccupation; spirituality.

in·wards (in′wərdz) *adv.* inward.

in·weave (in wēv′) *v.t.,* **-wove** or **-weaved, -wo·ven** or **-wove** or **-weaved, -weav·ing.** to weave in or weave together.

in·wrought (in rôt′) *adj.* **1.** having something worked in as a decoration: *a brocade inwrought with gold.* **2.** being worked into something: *a floral pattern inwrought on silk.*

I·o (ī′ō) *n.* in Greek mythology, a young maiden loved by Zeus, who changed her into a white heifer to protect her from Hera.

Io, the symbol for ionium.

i·o·dide (ī′ə dīd′) *n.* a binary compound of iodine with an element or radical, as potassium iodide.

i·o·dine (ī′ə dīn′, -din, -dēn′) *n.* **1.** a halogen element consisting of shiny, grayish crystals that vaporize in air, giving off a violet-colored vapor with a pungent, choking odor. Iodine is essential to the functioning of the thyroid gland and is used esp. in medicine, photography, and analytical chemistry. Symbol: I For tables, see **element. 2.** an antiseptic consisting of a dilute iodine solution. [French *iode* this element, from Greek *iōdēs* violet-colored, from *ion* violet + -INE².]

i·o·dize (ī′ə dīz′) *v.t.,* **-dized, -diz·ing.** to add or apply iodine or an iodide to (drinking water, table salt, photographic materials, or the like).

i·o·do·form (ī ō′də fôrm′, ī od′ə-) *n.* a yellow, crystalline iodine compound with a strong medicinal odor, formerly used as a local antiseptic. Formula: CHI₃ [IOD(INE) + (CHLOR)OFORM.]

i·o·dop·sin (ī′ə dop′sin) *n.* a violet, photosensitive pigment, similar to rhodopsin, that is present in the cones of the retina and plays an important part in daylight vision. [Modern Latin *iodum* iodine + Greek *opsis* eye + -IN¹.]

io moth *also,* **Io moth.** a large brownish yellow North American moth, *Automeris io,* marked with an eyelike spot on each hind wing. Length: 1 inch (3 centimeters). Wingspan: 3 inches (8 centimeters).

i·on (ī′ən, ī′on) *n.* an atom or group of atoms whose outer electron shell has gained or lost one or more electrons. **Positive ions** are formed by the loss of electrons. **Negative ions** are formed by the gain of electrons. [Greek *ion* going, neuter present participle of *ienai* to go.]

-ion *suffix* **1.** the act of: *notation, completion.* **2.** the state of being: *damnation, suspicion.* **3.** the result of: *pollution, solution.* [Latin *-iō* (stem *-iōn-*), suffix forming nouns, often through French *-ion.*]

I·o·ni·an (ī ō′nē ən) *adj.* of, relating to, or characteristic of Ionia or its people, language, or culture. —*n.* a member of one of the four major Greek tribes of antiquity. The Ionians settled in Attica, the Ionian Islands, and Ionia.

i·on·ic (ī on′ik) *adj.* of, relating to, or occurring in the form of ions.

I·on·ic (ī on′ik) *adj.* **1.** of or relating to one of the three orders of classical Greek architecture, characterized by columns having molded bases and capitals composed of spiral volutes or scrolls. **2.** of, relating to, or characteristic of Ionia or its people, language, or culture. —*n.* one of the three principal dialects of ancient Greece. [Latin *Iōnicus* relating to Ionia, from Greek *Iōnikos,* from *Iōn* legendary Greek hero after whom Ionia is named.]

ionic bond *Chemistry.* electrovalent bond.

i·o·ni·um (ī ō′nē əm) *n.* a radioactive isotope of thorium. Symbol: **Io** [From ION; with reference to its ionizing action.]

i·on·i·za·tion (ī′ə nə zā′shən) *n.* the process by which ions are formed, in which electrons are gained by or lost from the outer electron shells of atoms.

ionization chamber, a gas-filled vessel fitted with electrodes, used to detect and analyze ionizing radiation.

i·on·ize (ī′ə nīz′) *v.t., v.i.,* **-ized, -iz·ing.** to be converted into ions or to produce ions in. —**i′on·iz′er,** *n.*

ionizing radiation, electromagnetic radiation with enough energy to ionize the molecules of substances, esp. living tissue, through which it passes. X rays and gamma rays both have this potentially harmful or lethal capability.

i·on·o·sphere (ī on′ə sfir′) *n.* the highest region of ionized gases in the earth's atmosphere, beginning approximately 50 miles (80 kilometers) above the earth's surface and occupying the region above the stratosphere. The reflective properties of the ionosphere enable long-distance transmission of radio waves. [ION + SPHERE.] —**i·on·o·spher′ic,** *adj.*

i·o·ta (ī ō′tə) *n.* **1.** the ninth letter of the Greek alphabet (I, ι), corresponding to the English letter *I, i.* **2.** a very small quantity; bit: *They haven't an iota of proof.* [Greek *iōta* the Greek letter ι, the smallest letter of the Greek alphabet; of Semitic origin. Doublet of JOT.]

IOU (ī′ō′ū′) an informal written acknowledgment of a debt, usually containing only these letters, the amount owed, and the signature of the debtor. [Abbreviation of *I o(we) (yo)u.*]

IPA, International Phonetic Alphabet.

ip·e·cac (ip′i kak′) *n.* **1.** a drug obtained from the roots of a South American plant, *Cephaelis ipecacuanha,* used for medicinal purposes, esp. to induce vomiting in the treatment of poisoning. Also, **ip·e·cac·u·an·ha** (ip′i kak′ū an′ə). **2.** the plant itself. [Short for Portuguese *ipecacuanha,* from Tupi-Guarani *ipekaaguéne* literally, low leaves causing vomiting.]

Iph·i·ge·ni·a (if′i jə nī′ə) in Greek mythology, a daughter of Agamemnon offered as a sacrifice to the goddess Artemis in order to obtain favorable winds for sailing against Troy. She was saved by Artemis's intervention.

ip·se dix·it (ip′sē dik′sit) an assertion depending for its authority on the identity of the person making it; dogmatic assertion. [Latin *ipse dīxit* he himself said (it).]

ip·so fac·to (ip′sō fak′tō) *Latin.* by that very fact; by the fact itself.

IQ, intelligence quotient.

Ir, the symbol for iridium.

ir-¹, form of **in-¹** before *r,* as in *irregular.*

ir-², form of **in-²** before *r,* as in *irruption.*

IR, infrared.

IRA, a bank account, savings program, or other arrangement under which a person can set aside money that is not subject to taxes until after the person retires from work. ➡ distinguished from **Keogh plan.** [Abbreviation of *i(ndividual) r(etirement) a(ccount).*]

I·ra·ni·an (i rā′nē ən, i rä′-, ī rā′-) *adj.* of, relating to, or characteristic of Iran or its people, language, or culture. —*n.* **1.** a native or citizen of Iran. **2.** a person of Iranian ancestry. **3.** a subdivision of the Indo-Iranian branch of the Indo-European language family, which includes Persian, Kurdish, and other related languages.

i·ras·ci·ble (i ras′ə bəl) *adj.* **1.** easily irritated or provoked to anger; irritable: *an irascible person.* **2.** characterized by anger: *an irascible reply.* [Late Latin *īrāscibilis* irritable, from Latin *īrāscī* to become angry.] —**i·ras′ci·bil′i·ty, i·ras′ci·ble·ness,** *n.* —**i·ras′ci·bly,** *adv.*

i·rate (ī rāt′, ī′rāt) *adj.* very angry; incensed; enraged. [Latin *īrātus,* from *īra* anger.] —**i·rate′ly,** *adv.* —**i·rate′ness,** *n.*

IRBM, a ballistic missile with a range between 300 and 1,500 miles (483 and 2,414 kilometers). [Abbreviation of *i(ntermediate) r(ange) b(allistic) m(issile).*]

a	at	e	end	o	hot	u	up	hw	white		about
ā	ape	ē	me	ō	old	ū	use	ng	song		taken
ä	far	i	it	ô	fork	ü	rule	th	thin	ə	pencil
âr	care	ī	ice	oi	oil	u̇	pull	th	this		lemon
				îr	pierce	ou	out	ûr	turn	zh	measure		circus

ire (īr) *n.* anger; wrath. [Old French *ire,* from Latin *īra.*] —For Synonyms, see **anger.**

Ire., Ireland.

ire·ful (īr′fəl) *adj.* full of ire; angry; wrathful: *an ireful glance.* —**ire′ful·ly,** *adv.*

ir·i·des·cence (ir′i des′əns) *n.* a play of shimmering and changing colors; quality of being iridescent.

ir·i·des·cent (ir′i des′ənt) *adj.* displaying shimmering and changing colors, like those reflected by soap bubbles. [Latin *īrid-,* stem of *īris* rainbow + -ESCENT. See IRIS.] —**ir′i·des′cent·ly,** *adv.*

i·rid·i·um (i rid′ē əm) *n.* an extremely hard, brittle, silver-white metallic element of the platinum family, used esp. in alloys of platinum and for electrical contacts and chemical apparatus. Symbol: **Ir** For tables, see **element.** [Modern Latin *iridium,* from Latin *īris* rainbow; referring to the variety of its colors in solutions. See IRIS.]

i·ris (ī′ris) *n., pl.* **i·ris·es** or **ir·i·des** (ir′i dēz′, ī′ri-). **1.** the colored, contractile membrane between the cornea and the lens that controls the amount of light entering the eye. For illustration, see **eye**[1]. **2.** the showy flower of any of a large group of plants, genus *Iris,* usually growing directly from an underground bulb or rhizome and consisting of three erect petals and three drooping petals. **3.** the plant bearing this flower, cultivated as a house and garden plant, usually having long, sword-shaped leaves. **4. Iris.** the Greek goddess of the rainbow. **5.** rainbow. [Middle English *iris,* from Latin *īris* rainbow, from Greek *īris.*]

iris diaphragm *Optics.* an adjustable device consisting of a set of overlapping hinged blades, the movement of which enlarges or constricts a central opening, used to control the amount of light passing through a lens, as in a camera.

I·rish (ī′rish) *adj.* of, relating to, or characteristic of Ireland or its people, language, or culture. —*n.* **1. the Irish.** the people of Ireland or their close descendants. **2.** Irish Gaelic. **3.** Irish English. [Old English *Iras* inhabitants of Ireland.]

Irish English, the dialect of English spoken by the Irish.

Irish Gaelic, Gaelic as spoken in Ireland. Also, **Erse.** For table of words borrowed from Irish Gaelic, see **Gaelic.**

I·rish·man (ī′rish mən) *n., pl.* **-men** (-mən). **1.** a native of Ireland or a citizen of the Republic of Ireland or of Northern Ireland. **2.** a person of Irish ancestry.

Irish moss, a reddish or purple seaweed, *Chondrus crispus,* that is an edible variety of red algae found along the rocky Atlantic coasts of North America and northern Europe. Also, **carrageen.**

Irish potato, the common white potato.

Irish setter, a setter of a breed that originated in Ireland, having a coat of silky, reddish hair. Height: 27 inches (69 centimeters) at the shoulder.

Irish stew, a stew made of meat and various vegetables, as carrots, onions, and potatoes.

Irish terrier, a short-haired terrier having a reddish, wiry coat. Height: 18 inches (46 centimeters) at the shoulder.

Irish setter   Irish terrier

Irish wolfhound, a heavily built, tall hound having a rough, wiry, usually gray coat. Height: to 37 inches (94 centimeters) at the shoulder.

I·rish·wom·an (ī′rish wům′ən) *n., pl.* **-wom·en** (-wim′ən). **1.** a woman who is a native of Ireland or a citizen of the Republic of Ireland or of Northern Ireland. **2.** a woman of Irish ancestry.

irk (ûrk) *v.t.* to annoy; vex; bother. [Of uncertain origin.]

irk·some (ûrk′səm) *adj.* annoying; tiresome: *irksome tasks.* —**irk′some·ly,** *adv.* —**irk′some·ness,** *n.*

i·ron (ī′ərn) *n.* **1.** a lustrous, gray-white metallic element that is very ductile, highly magnetic, and a good conductor of heat and electricity. Iron and its alloys, esp. steel, are the most important and widely used of all metals, and it is an essential component of the hemoglobin of red blood cells. Symbol: **Fe** For tables, see **element.** **2.** anything that is hard, strong, resolute, or unyielding:

muscles of iron. **3.** something made from iron or an alloy of iron: *a branding iron, a curling iron.* **4.** an appliance having a flat surface that is heated and used to press or smooth fabrics, esp. clothing. **5.** a golf club with a metal head. Irons are numbered from one to ten according to their degree of loft. **6.** a dietary supplement or medication that contains iron. **7. irons.** fetters or shackles. —*adj.* **1.** of or relating to iron. **2.** resolute or unyielding: *an iron will.* **3.** cruel or harsh: *The conquered people had to submit to the iron rule of the tyrant.* **4.** hardy or robust: *an iron constitution.* —*v.t.* to smooth or press with a heated iron: *to iron a shirt.* —*v.i.* to iron fabric, esp. clothes. [Middle English *iren,* from Old English *īren, īse(r)n* the metal iron, tool made of iron.]

· **to have too many irons in the fire.** to be engaged in too many projects.

· **to iron out.** to settle, as differences.

· **to strike while the iron is hot.** to act at the most favorable moment.

Iron Age, the stage in the development of civilization following the Bronze Age, characterized by the widespread use of iron in tools and weapons and beginning around 1200 B.C.

i·ron·bound (ī′ərn bound′) *adj.* **1.** bound with iron. **2.** not easily changed; rigid; inflexible: *an ironbound society.* **3.** rocky; rugged: *an ironbound coast.*

i·ron·clad (ī′ərn klad′) *adj.* **1.** covered or protected with iron or steel plates. **2.** difficult to change or break: *an ironclad regulation, an ironclad alibi.* —*n.* a nineteenth-century warship covered wholly or partially with iron or steel plates for protection.

iron curtain *also,* **Iron Curtain.** a barrier of secrecy that separated the Soviet Union and allied communist countries of Eastern Europe from the noncommunist world following World War II, first described by Winston Churchill in a 1946 speech.

iron hand, very strict, harsh, or inflexible control: *The dictator ruled with an iron hand.* —**i′ron·hand′ed,** *adj.*

iron horse *Informal.* locomotive.

i·ron·ic (ī ron′ik) *adj.* **1.** of, relating to, or characterized by irony: *an ironic situation, an ironic remark.* **2.** given to the use of irony: *an ironic writer.* Also, **i·ron′i·cal.** [Late Latin *īrōnicus,* from Greek *eirōnikos* dissembling, from *eirōneiā* dissimulation.] —**i·ron′i·cal·ly,** *adv.* —**i·ron′i·cal·ness,** *n.*

i·ron·ing (ī′ər ning) *n.* **1.** the act or process of pressing or smoothing fabrics or clothing with a heated iron. **2.** something that has been or is to be ironed: *I have a lot of ironing to do.*

ironing board, a padded board, usually on a folding frame, on which fabrics or clothing may be ironed.

iron lung, an apparatus used to maintain breathing when normal respiration is impaired. An iron lung consists of a cylindrical tank that encloses the body, except the head, and air pumps that regulate the air pressure in the tank. It was formerly used to treat poliomyelitis.

i·ron·mon·ger (ī′ərn mung′gər, -mong′-) *n. British.* a dealer in ironware or hardware.

iron oxide, any of the various oxides of iron, esp. ferric oxide.

iron pyrites, pyrite.

I·ron·sides (ī′ərn sīdz′) *n.* **1.** the nickname of the English soldier Oliver Cromwell. **2.** the soldiers under Oliver Cromwell in the English Civil War. ➡ used as singular in def. 1, as plural in def. 2.

i·ron·stone (ī′ərn stōn′) *n.* **1.** a sedimentary rock containing large amounts of iron oxide minerals mixed with clay and other impurities. **2.** a type of hard, white stoneware.

i·ron·ware (ī′ərn wâr′) *n.* articles that are made of iron, as pots and kettles.

i·ron·weed (ī′ərn wēd′) *n.* any of a large group of plants, genus *Vernonia,* widely distributed in North America, having dark, very hard stems and clusters of usually purple flowers.

i·ron·wood (ī′ərn wůd′) *n.* **1.** any of a number of trees having hard, close-grained wood, esp. the hop hornbeam, *Ostrya virginiana.* **2.** the hard, durable wood of any of these trees, used esp. for making tool handles and similar equipment.

i·ron·work (ī′ərn wûrk′) *n.* an object or structure made of iron: *decorative ironwork.*

i·ron·work·er (ī′ərn wûr′kər) *n.* **1.** a person engaged in smelting iron or manufacturing iron objects. **2.** a person who constructs or repairs structures of metal.

i·ron·works (ī′ərn wûrks′) *pl. n.* an establishment where iron is smelted or where iron objects are manufactured. ➡ used as singular or plural.

i·ro·ny (ī′rə nē, ī′ər-) *n., pl.* **-nies. 1.a.** a form of expression in which the intended meaning is the opposite of that expressed in words. **b.** an instance of this: *to speak in subtle ironies.* **2.** an event or outcome of events opposite to what was, or might naturally have been, expected: *the irony of fate.* **3.** the incongruity

that results from such an outcome of events: *The firefighter whose home had burned down was unable to appreciate the irony of the situation.* **4.** feigned ignorance, esp. when used as part of an argument or a discussion. [Latin *īrōnīa* dissimulation, from Greek *eirōneiā.*]

Ir·o·quoi·an (ir′i kwoi′ən) *n.* **1.** a family of North American Indian languages, including Huron, Iroquois, Cherokee, and others. **2.** a member of a tribe speaking one of these languages. —*adj.* of or relating to this family of languages.

Ir·o·quois (ir′i kwoi′, -kwoiz′) *n., pl.* **-quois. 1.** a member of a confederation of North American Indian tribes speaking Iroquoian languages, formerly living in the state of New York. Originally called the Five Nations (the Seneca, Cayuga, Onondaga, Oneida, and Mohawk), the Iroquois became the Six Nations in 1722 when the Tuscarora joined the confederation. **2.** a member of a tribe belonging to this confederation. **3.** any of the Iroquoian languages spoken by these Indians. —*adj.* of or relating to the Iroquois, their tribes, or their languages. [French *Iroquois,* from Algonquian *Irinakhoiw* literally, real adders.]

ir·ra·di·ant (i rā′dē ənt) *adj.* emitting rays of light; shining brightly. —**ir·ra′di·ance, ir·ra′di·an·cy,** *n.*

ir·ra·di·ate (i rā′dē āt′) *v.,* **-at·ed, -at·ing.** —*v.t.* **1.** to shed light upon; brighten; illuminate: *Brilliant flashes of lightning irradiated the night sky.* **2.** to expose to or treat with radiation. **3.** to send out in or as in rays; radiate. —*v.i. Archaic.* to emit rays; shine. [Latin *irradiātus,* past participle of *irradiāre* to cast forth rays.] —**ir·ra′di·a′tion,** *n.* —**ir·ra′di·a′tor,** *n.*

ir·ra·tion·al (i rash′ə nəl) *adj.* **1.** deprived of or lacking reason; void of understanding; not rational: *to be in a confused and irrational state.* **2.** contrary to reason; illogical; absurd: *Their remarks were totally irrational.* **3.** *Mathematics.* not able to be expressed as a quotient of integers or as an integer. [Latin *irrationālis* without reason, going back to *in-* not + *ratiō* reason.] —**ir·ra′tion·al·ly,** *adv.*

ir·ra·tion·al·i·ty (i rash′ə nal′i tē) *n., pl.* **-ties. 1.** the condition or quality of being irrational. **2.** something that is irrational.

irrational number, a real number that cannot be expressed as a quotient of integers or as an integer. $\sqrt{2}$ and π are irrational numbers.

ir·re·claim·a·ble (ir′i klā′mə bəl) *adj.* that cannot be reclaimed: *irreclaimable land.* —**ir′re·claim′a·bil′i·ty,** *n.* —**ir′re·claim′a·bly,** *adv.*

ir·rec·on·cil·a·ble (i rek′ən sī′lə bəl, i rek′ən sī′-) *adj.* **1.** that cannot be restored to friendly relations; implacable or uncompromising; hostile: *irreconcilable enemies.* **2.** that cannot be brought into harmony or agreement; incompatible: *irreconcilable differences.* —*n.* a person who refuses to be reconciled. —**ir′rec′on·cil′a·bil′i·ty, ir′rec′on·cil′a·ble·ness,** *n.* —**ir′rec′on·cil′a·bly,** *adv.*

ir·re·cov·er·a·ble (ir′i kuv′ər ə bəl) *adj.* **1.** that cannot be recovered: *The money we lost is irrecoverable.* **2.** that cannot be remedied or restored; irreparable: *The flood caused irrecoverable damage.* —**ir′re·cov′er·a·ble·ness,** *n.* —**ir′re·cov′er·a·bly,** *adv.*

ir·re·deem·a·ble (ir′i dē′mə bəl) *adj.* **1.** that cannot be bought back or paid off: *an irredeemable mortgage.* **2.** that cannot be converted into coin, as certain kinds of paper money. **3.** beyond redemption or reform: *an irredeemable criminal.* **4.** that cannot be changed or remedied; hopeless: *an atmosphere of irredeemable gloom.* —**ir′re·deem′a·bly,** *adv.*

ir·re·den·tist (ir′i den′tist) *n.* **1.** *also,* **Irredentist.** a member of an Italian political party, formed in 1878, advocating the incorporation into Italy of neighboring territories with Italian populations. **2.** a person who advocates the incorporation into his or her country of a territory under foreign rule, claimed because of common linguistic, cultural, or racial characteristics. [Italian *irredentista* Irredentist, from *(Italia) irredenta* unredeemed (Italy), going back to Latin *in-* not + *redemptus,* past participle of *redimere* to buy back.] —**ir′re·den′tism,** *n.*

ir·re·duc·i·ble (ir′i dü′sə bəl, -dū′-) *adj.* that cannot be reduced or simplified; not reducible. —**ir′re·duc′i·bil′i·ty,** *n.* —**ir′re·duc′i·bly,** *adv.*

ir·ref·ra·ga·ble (i ref′rə gə bəl) *adj.* that cannot be contested or refuted; indisputable: *an irrefragable authority.* [Late Latin *irrefragābilis,* from Latin *in-* not + *refragārī* to oppose.] —**ir′ref′ra·ga·bil′i·ty,** *n.* —**ir′ref′ra·ga·bly,** *adv.*

ir·re·fran·gi·ble (ir′i fran′jə bəl) *adj.* that can or must not be violated or broken; inviolable: *an irrefrangible law.*

ir·ref·u·ta·ble (i ref′yə tə bəl, ir′i fū′-) *adj.* not able to be refuted; incontrovertible; indisputable: *irrefutable evidence.* —**ir·ref′u·ta·bly,** *adv.*

ir·re·gard·less (ir′i gärd′lis) *adj. Informal.* regardless.

Usage Irregardless uses two negative affixes meaning "without" (the prefix *ir-* and the suffix *-less*) to express a single negative meaning. The use of both affixes creates a redundancy. The word **irregardless** is generally considered nonstandard, although it is sometimes used for humorous effect. The preferred word is **regardless.**

ir·reg·u·lar (i reg′yə lər) *adj.* **1.** not conforming to convention or custom; deviating from the usual rule or practice; unusual: *These procedures are highly irregular.* **2.** not conforming to established law or morality; lawless: *an irregular and intemperate person.* **3.** not occurring at fixed or uniform intervals: *an irregular heartbeat.* **4.** not evenly or uniformly arranged or shaped; uneven: *an irregular surface.* **5.** (of goods) having slight imperfections; not perfect: *irregular towels.* **6.** not belonging to the regular army. **7.** *Grammar.* deviating from the usual or most common pattern of inflection. The verb *to be* is irregular. —*n.* a soldier not of the regular army. —**ir·reg′u·lar·ly,** *adv.*

ir·reg·u·lar·i·ty (i reg′yə lar′i tē) *n., pl.* **-ties. 1.** the quality or state of being irregular. **2.** something that is irregular. **3.** constipation.

ir·rel·e·vance (i rel′ə vəns) *n.* **1.** the quality or fact of being irrelevant. **2.** something that is irrelevant. Also, **ir·rel′e·van·cy.**

ir·rel·e·vant (i rel′ə vənt) *adj.* not bearing upon or connected with the matter at hand; not pertinent; inappropriate. —**ir·rel′e·vant·ly,** *adv.*

ir·re·li·gion (ir′i lij′ən) *n.* **1.** lack of religion. **2.** hostility to religion.

ir·re·li·gious (ir′i lij′əs) *adj.* **1.** indifferent to or lacking religion; not religious. **2.** showing disrespect or hostility to religious principles; profane. [Latin *irreligiōsus* impious.] —**ir′re·li′gious·ly,** *adv.*

ir·re·me·di·a·ble (ir′i mē′dē ə bəl) *adj.* not subject to remedy or cure; incurable. —**ir′re·me′di·a·ble·ness,** *n.* —**ir′re·me′di·a·bly,** *adv.*

ir·re·mis·si·ble (ir′ə mis′ə bəl) *adj.* that cannot be pardoned; not remissible; unpardonable: *an irremissible crime.* —**ir′re·mis′si·bil′i·ty,** *n.* —**ir′re·mis′si·bly,** *adv.*

ir·re·mov·a·ble (ir′i mü′və bəl) *adj.* that cannot be removed. —**ir′re·mov′a·bil′i·ty,** *n.* —**ir′re·mov′a·bly,** *adv.*

ir·rep·a·ra·ble (i rep′ər ə bəl) *adj.* that cannot be repaired, restored, or made good: *irreparable damage, irreparable loss.* —**ir′rep′a·ra·bil′i·ty, ir′rep′ar·a·ble·ness,** *n.* —**ir′rep′a·ra·bly,** *adv.*

ir·re·place·a·ble (ir′i plā′sə bəl) *adj.* that cannot be replaced: *irreplaceable works of art.*

ir·re·press·i·ble (ir′i pres′ə bəl) *adj.* that cannot be repressed or restrained: *irrepressible high spirits.* —**ir′re·press′i·bil′i·ty, ir′re·press′i·ble·ness,** *n.* —**ir′re·press′i·bly,** *adv.*

ir·re·proach·a·ble (ir′i prō′chə bəl) *adj.* free from blame or criticism; above reproach; faultless: *irreproachable conduct.* —**ir′re·proach′a·bly,** *adv.*

ir·re·sist·i·ble (ir′i zis′tə bəl) *adj.* **1.** that cannot be resisted or opposed: *an irresistible power, an irresistible temptation.* **2.** extremely charming or captivating: *an irresistible baby.* —**ir′re·sis′ti·bil′i·ty, ir′re·sist′i·ble·ness,** *n.* —**ir′re·sist′i·bly,** *adv.*

ir·res·o·lute (i rez′ə lüt′) *adj.* lacking steadfast determination; vacillating: *a spineless and irresolute character.* —**ir·res′o·lute′ly,** *adv.* —**ir·res′o·lute′ness, ir·res′o·lu′tion,** *n.*

ir·re·spec·tive (ir′i spek′tiv) *adv.* without regard to or consideration for; regardless of (with *of*): *We will proceed, irrespective of the consequences.* —**ir′re·spec′tive·ly,** *adv.*

ir·re·spon·si·ble (ir′i spon′sə bəl) *adj.* **1.** not trustworthy or dependable; unreliable: *a thoughtless and irresponsible person.* **2.** not carefully considered: *an irresponsible decision.* **3.** not answerable to a higher authority for conduct or action: *an irresponsible government.* **4.** not capable of managing one's affairs: *financially irresponsible.* —**ir′re·spon′si·bil′i·ty,** *n.* —**ir′re·spon′si·bly,** *adv.*

ir·re·triev·a·ble (ir′i trē′və bəl) *adj.* that cannot be retrieved. —**ir′re·triev′a·bil′i·ty, ir′re·triev′a·ble·ness,** *n.* —**ir′re·triev′a·bly,** *adv.*

ir·rev·er·ence (i rev′ər əns) *n.* **1.** the fact or quality of being irreverent; lack of reverence. **2.** an irreverent act or utterance.

ir·rev·er·ent (i rev′ər ənt) *adj.* not feeling or showing reverence; disrespectful: *an irreverent person, an irreverent attitude.* [Latin *irreverēns.*] —**ir·rev′er·ent·ly,** *adv.*

a	at	e	end	o	hot	u	up	hw	white		about
ā	ape	ē	me	ō	old	ū	use	ng	song		taken
ä	far	i	it	ô	fork	ū	rule	th	thin	ə	pencil
âr	care	ī	ice	oi	oil	ù	pull	th	this		lemon
		îr	pierce	ou	out	ûr	turn	zh	measure		circus

ir·re·vers·i·ble (ir′i vûr′sə bəl) *adj.* that cannot be reversed, repealed, or undone; irrevocable: *irreversible decisions.* —**ir′re·vers′i·bil′i·ty,** *n.* —**ir′re·vers′i·bly,** *adv.*

ir·rev·o·ca·ble (i rev′ə kə bəl) *adj.* that cannot be revoked or recalled; unalterable: *an irrevocable decision.* —**ir·rev′o·ca·bil′i·ty,** *n.* —**ir·rev′o·ca·bly,** *adv.*

ir·ri·ga·ble (ir′i gə bəl) *adj.* able to be irrigated.

ir·ri·gate (ir′i gāt′) *v.t.,* -**gat·ed, -gat·ing. 1.** to supply (land) with water by means of channels, streams, or pipes: *to irrigate a desert so that crops can be grown.* **2.** to cleanse (a wound or body cavity) with a constant flow of liquid. [Latin *irrigātus,* past participle of *irrigāre* to moisten.] —**ir′ri·ga′tion,** *n.* —**ir′ri·ga′tor,** *n.*

irrigate
irrigating crops

ir·ri·ta·bil·i·ty (ir′i tə bil′i tē) *n., pl.* -**ties. 1.** the quality or state of being irritable; petulance. **2.** (of a body organ or part) the condition of being excessively or morbidly sensitive, esp. to a slight stimulus. **3.** *Biology.* the ability to respond to a stimulus.

ir·ri·ta·ble (ir′i tə bəl) *adj.* **1.** easily excited to impatience or anger; petulant; irascible. **2.** excessively or morbidly sensitive. **3.** *Biology.* able to respond to a stimulus. [Latin *irrītābilis* easily excited or angered, from *irrītāre* to excite, provoke.] —**ir′ri·ta·ble·ness,** *n.* —**ir′ri·ta·bly,** *adv.*

ir·ri·tant (ir′i tənt) *n.* something that causes irritation. —*adj.* causing irritation; irritating. [Latin *irrītāns,* present participle of *irrītāre* to excite, provoke.]

ir·ri·tate (ir′i tāt′) *v.t.,* -**tat·ed, -tat·ing. 1.** to excite to impatience or anger; vex: *The couple's constant bickering irritated us.* **2.** to cause redness, pain, or swelling in; inflame: *The smoke irritates my eyes.* **3.** *Biology.* to stimulate (a body organ or part) to some characteristic action or function. [Latin *irrītātus,* past participle of *irrītāre* to excite, provoke.] —**ir′ri·tat′ing·ly,** *adv.* —**ir′ri·ta′tor,** *n.*

ir·ri·ta·tion (ir′i tā′shən) *n.* **1.** the act or process of irritating or the state of being irritated; vexation. **2.** a red, painful, or swollen condition.

ir·rupt (i rupt′) *v.i.* **1.** to burst or break in; enter forcibly or violently. **2.** *Zoology.* (of animals) to experience a sudden, unchecked increase in population. [Latin *irruptus,* past participle of *irrumpere* to break in.]

ir·rup·tion (i rup′shən) *n.* **1.** the act of bursting or breaking in; violent entry; invasion. **2.** *Zoology.* a sudden, unchecked increase in an animal population. [Latin *irruptiō* a bursting into.]

ir·rup·tive (i rup′tiv) *adj.* **1.** characterized by irruption. **2.** irrupting or tending to irrupt.

IRS, Internal Revenue Service.

is (iz) the third person singular present indicative of **be.** [Old English *is* is.]

is., island.

Is. 1. Isaiah. **2.** Island.

Isa., Isaiah.

I·sai·ah (ī zā′ə, ī zī′ə) *n.* a book of the Old Testament, attributed to the Hebrew prophet Isaiah. [Hebrew *Yeshaya* literally, salvation of Jehovah.]

is·che·mi·a (i skē′mē ə) *n.* a localized decrease in or lack of

blood supply due to a blocked artery or vasoconstriction. [Modern Latin *ischemia,* from Greek *ischaimos* stanching blood, from *ischein* to hold + *haima* blood.] —**is·che′mic,** *adj.*

is·chi·um (is′kē əm) *n., pl.* -**chi·a** (-kē ə). the lowest portion of the hipbone. For illustration, see **pelvis.** [Latin *ischium* hip joint, from Greek *ischion.*] —**is′chi·al,** *adj.*

-ise, form of **-ize.**

I·seult (i sült′) *n.* Isolde.

-ish *suffix* **1.** of, belonging to, or having to do with: *Irish, Polish.* **2.** of the nature or character of; like: *mannish, foolish.* **3.** tending or inclined to: *bookish.* **4.** somewhat: *bluish, youngish.* [Old English *-isc,* suffix forming adjectives.]

Ish·ma·el (ish′mē əl, -mā-) *n.* an outcast. [From *Ishmael,* in the Old Testament, the son of Abraham and Hagar, who was driven into the wilderness.]

Ish·ma·el·ite (ish′mē ə līt′, -mā-) *n.* **1.** a descendant of Ishmael. **2.** an outcast or wanderer.

Ish·tar (ish′tär) *n.* in Babylonian and Assyrian mythology, the goddess of fertility and love, identified with the Phoenician goddess Astarte.

i·sin·glass (ī′zən glas′, ī′zing-) *n.* **1.** a very pure form of gelatin obtained from the air bladders of fish, esp. sturgeon, used to make glue and clarify liquors. **2.** mica. [Modification (influenced by GLASS) of obsolete Dutch *huizenblas* sturgeon bladder.]

I·sis (ī′sis) *n.* in Egyptian mythology, the goddess of fertility, wife and sister of Osiris. [Latin *Isis,* from Greek *Isis;* of Egyptian origin.]

isl., island.

Is·lam (is′lam, iz′-, is läm′) *n.* **1.** a religion based on the teachings and writings of Muhammad, asserting that there is only one god, Allah, and that Muhammad is Allah's prophet. **2.** the whole of the Muslim world, including Muslim civilization and the countries under Muslim rule. [Arabic *islām* submission (to God).] —**Is·lam′ic,** *adj.*

Is·lam·ite (is′lə mīt′, iz′-) *n.* Muslim.

is·land (ī′lənd) *n.* **1.** a body of land entirely surrounded by water and smaller than a continent. **2.** anything resembling an island: *an island of floating ice.* —*v.t.* to make into or as into an island: *The mountains were islanded in the billowing mist.* [Old English *īgland* piece of land surrounded by water; Modern English spelling influenced by ISLE.]

is·land·er (ī′lən dər) *n.* a native or inhabitant of an island.

isle (īl) *n.* an island, esp. a small island. [Old French *isle,* from Latin *īnsula.*]

is·let (ī′lit) *n.* a very small island. [Middle French *islette,* diminutive of Old French *isle.* See ISLE.]

islet of Lang·er·hans (läng′ər häns′, -hänz′) any of several small masses of cells in the pancreas that function as endocrine glands by secreting insulin into the bloodstream. Also, **island of Langerhans.**

ism (iz′əm) *n.* a doctrine, theory, or system. [From words ending in -ISM.]

-ism *suffix* **1.** an action or practice: *criticism, nepotism.* **2.** a condition or state: *giantism, parallelism.* **3.** characteristic conduct or behavior: *patriotism, barbarism, heroism.* **4.** a distinguishing feature, aspect, or manner, as of style or language: *colloquialism, Hellenism, classicism.* **5.** a doctrine, system, or principle: *socialism, paganism, pragmatism.* [Greek *-ismos, -isma,* often through Latin *-ismus, -isma,* or French *-isme;* suffix used to form nouns.]

is·n't (iz′ənt) *contr.* is not.

iso- *combining form* **1.** equal: *isosceles, isogonic.* **2.** an isomer of: *isoleucine.* [Greek *isos* equal.]

i·so·bar (ī′sə bär′) *n.* **1.** a line on a weather map connecting points having the same barometric pressure. **2.** any of two or more atoms that have the same atomic weight but different atomic numbers. [Iso- + Greek *baros* weight.]

i·so·bar·ic (ī′sə bar′ik) *adj.* **1.** of, relating to, or containing isobars. **2.** having or indicating equal barometric pressure.

i·soch·ro·nal (ī sok′rə nəl) *adj.* **1.** equal in duration. **2.** characterized by, relating to, or occurring in equal intervals of time. Also, **i·soch′ro·nous.** [Greek *isochronos* equal in time + -AL[1].]

i·so·gam·ete (ī′sə gam′ēt, -gə mēt′) *n.* a mature reproductive cell that is similar in size, structure, and behavior to the one with which it unites during fertilization, as in some protists and fungi. ➡ opposed to **heterogamete.** [Iso- + GAMETE.] —**i·so·ga·met′ic,** *adj.*

i·sog·a·my (ī sog′ə mē) *n.* sexual reproduction by the fusion of isogametes. ➡ opposed to **heterogamy.** [Iso- + -GAMY.] —**i·sog′a·mous,** *adj.*

i·so·gon·ic (ī′sə gon′ik) *adj.* having equal angles. Also, **i·sog·o·nal** (ī sog′ə nəl). [Iso- + Greek *gōniā* angle, corner + -IC.]

isogonic line, a line connecting the points on a map where the earth's magnetic field has the same declination.

i·so·late (ī′sə lāt′, is′ə-) v.t., **-lat·ed, -lat·ing. 1.** to place or set apart; separate from others; detach: *The writer isolated himself in his study.* **2.** to separate (an infected person) from all contact with others; quarantine. **3.** to obtain (a chemical substance) in pure or uncombined form. [From *isolated,* from Italian *isolato* detached, from *isola* island, from Latin *īnsula.*]

Synonyms Isolate, segregate, and seclude mean to separate from others. **Isolate** implies a complete cutting off from the outside world: *The floodwaters isolated the town.* **Segregate** is applied to the separation of something or someone from the main group, as in the placing of people in unwilling confinement: *Refugees suspected of having radical political views were segregated in special camps.* **Seclude** implies a voluntary withdrawal from society or from outside influences: *Adherents of the religion were encouraged to seclude themselves for periods of meditation.*

i·so·la·tion (ī′sə lā′shən, is′ə-) n. **1.** the act of isolating. **2.** the state of being isolated; solitude: *The patient remained in isolation until she was no longer contagious.*

i·so·la·tion·ism (ī′sə lā′shə niz′əm, is′ə-) n. the policy of avoiding political, economic, or military involvements with foreign countries. —**i′so·la′tion·ist,** n.

I·sol·de (i zōl′də, i sōl′-) n. in medieval legend, an Irish princess loved by Tristan. Also, **I·seult, I·solt** (i sōlt′).

i·so·leu·cine (ī′sə lü′sēn, -sin) n. an essential amino acid similar to leucine that is present in fibrin, casein, and other proteins. Formula: $C_6H_{13}NO_2$ [Iso- + LEUCINE.]

i·so·mer (ī′sə mər) n. any of two or more chemical compounds that have the same molecular formula and thus the same composition but have different properties because their atoms are arranged differently. [Greek *isomerēs* equally divided, from *isos* equal + *meros* part.] —**i·so·mer·ic** (ī′sə mer′ik), adj.

i·som·er·ism (ī som′ə riz′əm) n. the relationship that characterizes isomers.

i·som·er·ous (ī som′ər əs) adj. having an equal number of markings, organs, or other parts.

i·so·met·ric (ī′sə met′rik) adj. **1.** of, relating to, or having all measurements equal to one another. **2.** relating to or denoting a system of crystalline forms characterized by three equal axes at right angles to one another. Also, **i′so·met′ri·cal. 3.** of or relating to the contraction of a muscle in which there is increased tension rather than change in length. —n. **isometrics.** isometric exercise. ➡ used as singular. [Greek *isometros* of equal measure, from *isos* equal + *metron* measure + -IC.] —**i′so·met′ri·cal·ly,** adv.

isometric exercise 1. a type of exercise accomplished by pitting any of the muscles or parts of the body against an immovable object, as a wall, or against an opposing set of muscles of either equal or greater strength. **2.** a specific exercise of this type.

i·so·morph (ī′sə môrf′) n. **1.** an organism that is similar in appearance or structure to another, but is of different ancestry. **2.** *Chemistry.* a substance isomorphous with another.

i·so·mor·phic (ī′sə môr′fik) adj. **1.** similar in appearance or structure, but of different ancestry; morphologically alike. **2.** isomorphous. [Iso- + Greek *morphē* form, shape + -IC.]

i·so·mor·phism (ī′sə môr′fiz əm) n. **1.** *Biology.* a similarity in structure or appearance between unrelated organisms, or between alternating generations in certain algae. **2.** *Chemistry.* the property of being isomorphous. [ISOMORPH(IC) + -ISM.]

i·so·mor·phous (ī′sə môr′fəs) adj. (of a substance) able to crystallize in the same or related form as another substance having a dissimilar chemical composition.

i·so·pod (ī′sə pod′) n. any of various insectlike crustaceans, order Isopoda, as the wood louse, having a flat, segmented body and seven pairs of legs. [Modern Latin *Isopoda* literally, equal-footed, from Greek *isos* equal + *pous* (stem *pod*-) foot.]

i·so·pro·pyl alcohol (ī′sə prō′pəl) a colorless, flammable, volatile liquid used as a solvent and in rubbing alcohol. Formula: C_3H_8O

i·sos·ce·les (ī sos′ə lēz′) adj. (of a plane figure, as a triangle or trapezoid) having two sides whose lengths are equal. [Late Latin *isoscelēs* having equal legs, from Greek *isoskelēs,* from *isos* equal + *skelos* leg.]

i·sos·ta·sy (ī sos′tə sē) n. **1.** *Geology.* a condition of equilibrium in the earth's crust maintained by the slow change in shape of deep rock to compensate for differences in density or changes in weight of the overlying load. Because of isostasy, the crust seems to float on the mantle, so that mountains, like icebergs, extend much deeper below the surface than they rise above it. **2.** a

state of equilibrium in which the pressure from all sides is equal. [Iso- + Greek *stasis* a standing still.] —**i·so·stat·ic** (ī′sə stat′ik), adj.

i·so·therm (ī′sə thûrm′) n. a line on a weather map connecting points having the same mean temperature. [Iso- + Greek *thermē* heat.]

i·so·ther·mal (ī′sə thûr′məl) adj. **1.** of, relating to, or indicating equal temperatures. **2.** of or relating to an isotherm.

i·so·ton·ic (ī′sə ton′ik) adj. **1.** (of solutions) having equal osmotic pressure on both sides of a membrane. **2.** denoting the contraction of a muscle encountering little resistance. [Greek *isotonos* of equal tension or tone (from *isos* equal + *tonos* stretching, tone) + -IC.] —**i′so·ton′i·cal·ly,** adv.

i·so·tope (ī′sə tōp′) n. any of two or more forms of the same chemical element having the same atomic number but differing mass number. [Iso- + Greek *topos* place.] —**i·so·top·ic** (ī′sə top′ik), adj. —**i′so·top′i·cal·ly,** adv.

i·so·trop·ic (ī′sə trop′ik, -trō′pik) adj. *Physics.* having the same physical properties in all directions. Also, **i·sot·ro·pous** (ī sot′rə pəs). [Iso- + Greek *tropos* turn, direction + -IC.] —**i·sot′ro·py,** n.

Is·ra·el (iz′rē əl, -rā-) n. the people descended from the biblical patriarch Jacob; the Hebrew people. [Latin *Isrāēl* another name of Jacob in the Old Testament, from Greek *Isrāēl,* from Hebrew *Yisrael* literally, he strives with God.]

Is·ra·el·ite (iz′rē ə līt′, -rā-) n. a descendant of the patriarch Jacob; Hebrew. —adj. of or relating to the Hebrews.

Is·sei (ēs′sā′) n., pl. **-sei.** a native of Japan who immigrated to the United States. [Japanese *issei* first generation.]

is·su·ance (ish′ü əns) n. the act of issuing.

is·sue (ish′ü) n. **1.a.** the act of sending or giving out: *an issue of licenses, an issue of supplies.* **b.** the act of going, passing, or flowing out: *the issue of blood from a wound.* **2.a.** something that is sent or given out, as a certain quantity of magazines, newspapers, stamps, or books, printed and distributed at one time: *the latest issue of the newspaper.* **b.** an individual copy of a magazine. **3.** a point in question or matter under consideration: *The raising of taxes was the issue under debate.* **4.** offspring. **5.** the outcome of an action or course of events; result; consequence. **6.** an opening or outlet. —v., **-sued, -su·ing.** —v.t. **1.a.** to send or give out: *to issue coins, to issue a statement.* **b.** to send forth; discharge; emit. **2.** to publish. —v.i. **1.** to go or come out; flow out; pour forth. **2.** to proceed as a result or outcome; be derived. [Old French *issue* way out, from *issir* to go out, from Latin *exīre.*] —**is′su·a·ble,** adj. —**is′su·er,** n.
• **at issue. a.** under discussion or consideration; in question. **b.** at variance; not in agreement.
• **to join issue.** to argue on a particular point; debate.
• **to take issue.** to disagree.

-ist suffix **1.** a person who does or makes: *tourist, novelist.* **2.** a person who practices or has as a profession: *bigamist, scientist, violinist.* **3.** a person who adheres to or advocates: *Buddhist, idealist, socialist.* [Greek *-istēs,* through Latin *-ista, -istēs* or French *-iste.*]

isth·mi·an (is′mē ən) adj. **1.** of or relating to an isthmus. **2. Isthmian.** of or relating to the isthmus of Corinth or of Panama.

isth·mus (is′məs) n., pl. **-mus·es.** a narrow strip of land bordered by water and connecting two larger bodies of land. [Latin *isthmus,* from Greek *isthmos* narrow passage.]

is·tle (ist′lē) n. a fiber obtained from certain tropical American plants, as the henequen, used in making bags, rope, and similar products. [Spanish *ixtle;* of Nahuatl origin.]

it (it) pron., sing. nominative, **it;** possessive, **its;** objective, **its;** pl. nominative, **they;** possessive, **their, theirs;** objective, **them. 1.** a thing or animal previously referred to: *Did you see that automobile? No, I didn't see it.* **2.** the subject of an impersonal verb: *It snowed last night.* **3.** the anticipatory subject of a verb introducing a phrase or dependent clause: *It is obvious that they like you.* **4.** an indefinite object without definite force: *Go to it! Flaunt it!* [Old English *hit,* neuter pronoun of the third person singular.]

It. 1. Italian. **2.** Italy.

ital., italic; italics.

Ital. 1. Italian. **2.** Italy.

I·tal·ian (i tal′yən) adj. of or relating to Italy or its people, language, or culture. —n. **1.** a native or citizen of Italy. **2.** a

a	at	e	end	o	hot	u	up	hw	white		about
ā	ape	ē	me	ō	old	ū	use	ng	song		taken
ä	far	i	it	ô	fork	ü	rule	th	thin	ə	pencil
âr	care	ī	ice	oi	oil	u̇	pull	th	this		lemon
		î	pierce	ou	out	ûr	turn	zh	measure		circus

I

Words from Italian

Italian, like all Romance languages, is descended from Latin and belongs to the Indo-European language family. A large number of Italian loanwords are in the areas of music, food, art, and politics. Below is a sampling of words that have entered English from or through Italian.

allegro	caricature	gondola	piano[2]
alto	carnival	graffiti	piccolo
andante	casino	grotto	pizza
aria	charlatan	inferno	portico
arpeggio	chiaroscuro	influenza	presto
arsenal	coda	intaglio	regatta
artichoke	coloratura	lagoon	relief[2]
ballerina	confetti	lasagne	ricotta
baluster	contralto	loggia	salami
bandit	contrapuntal	macaroni	spaghetti
basso	cupola	Madonna	squadron
belladonna	dilettante	maestro	staccato
bologna	ditto	malaria	stanza
broccoli	diva	minestrone	stiletto
cadenza	duet	motto	tempera
cameo	fantasia	oboe	tempo
cantata	fiasco	oratorio	vendetta
canto	fresco	pasta	viola
caprice	ghetto	patina	zany

person of Italian ancestry. **3.** the Romance language spoken predominantly in Italy and in parts of Switzerland.

I·tal·ian·ize (i tal′yə nīz′) *v.t., v.i.,* **-ized, -iz·ing.** to make or become Italian, esp. in style or character.

Italian sonnet, Petrarchan sonnet.

i·tal·ic (i tal′ik, ī tal′-) *adj.* **1.** relating to or designating a style of type whose letters slant to the right: *This sentence is printed in italic type.* **2. Italic.** of or relating to ancient Italy or its people, languages, or culture. —*n.* **1.** *also,* **italics.** italic type. **2. Italic.** a group of languages belonging to the Indo-European language family, including Umbrian, Latin, and the Romance languages. [Latin *Italicus* Italian, from Greek *Italikos,* from *Italia* Italy; so called because first used in an *Italian* edition (1501) of Vergil.]

i·tal·i·cize (i tal′ə sīz′, ī tal′-) *v.t.,* **-cized, -ciz·ing. 1.** to print in italics: *Foreign words are usually italicized.* **2.** to underscore with a single line to indicate italics.

itch (ich) *n.* **1.** a tickling or stinging sensation in the skin that is relieved by scratching or rubbing. **2.** a restless, uneasy desire for something: *The artist had an itch to travel to Europe.* **3. the itch.** scabies. —*v.i.* **1.** to have or cause a tickling or stinging sensation in the skin. **2.** to have a restless, uneasy desire: *to be itching for a fight.* [Old English *giccan* to feel irritation of the skin.]

itch·y (ich′ē) *adj.,* **itch·i·er, itch·i·est.** characterized by, having, or causing a tickling or stinging sensation in the skin: *itchy flannels, an itchy feeling.* —**itch′i·ness,** *n.*

-ite[1] *suffix* **1.** a native or resident of: *Muscovite, Israelite.* **2.** an advocate or adherent of: *pre-Raphaelite, Laborite.* **3.** a manufactured product: *dynamite.* **4.** a mineral compound of: *calcite.* **5.** a fossil: *trilobite.* [Greek *-itēs,* often through Latin *-īta, -ītēs* or French *-ite;* suffix forming adjectives and nouns.]

-ite[2] *suffix* salt of: *sulfite.* [French *-ite,* modification of *-ATE*[2].]

i·tem (ī′təm) *n.* **1.** a unit or article included in an assemblage, series, or list: *There are many valuable items in my stamp collection.* **2.** a bit of information, or a brief newspaper article or paragraph containing such information: *There was an item in Sunday's newspaper about the forthcoming convention.* —*adv.* also; likewise. ➡ formerly used before each listing except the first in an inventory. [Latin *item* likewise, also.]

i·tem·ize (ī′tə mīz′) *v.t.,* **-ized, -iz·ing.** to set down each item of; list by items: *The accountant itemized the tax deductions.* —**i′tem·i·za′tion,** *n.*

item veto, the power or right of a governor or other chief executive to veto specific parts of any legislation while approving and signing into law the other parts.

it·er·ate (it′ə rāt′) *v.t.,* **-at·ed, -at·ing.** to say or do again; repeat. [Latin *interātus,* past participle of *interāre.*] —**it′er·a′-tion,** *n.* —**it′er·a·tive,** *adj.*

i·tin·er·an·cy (ī tin′ər ən sē, i tin′-) *n.* **1.** the state or condition of traveling from place to place, esp. for business purposes or in the exercise of duty. **2.** the act of so traveling. Also, **i·tin·er·a·cy** (ī tin′ər ə sē, i tin′-).

i·tin·er·ant (ī tin′ər ənt, i tin′-) *adj.* traveling from place to place, esp. for business purposes or in the exercise of duty: *an*

itinerant judge, an itinerant preacher. —*n.* a person who travels from place to place, esp. for business or duty. [Late Latin *itiner-āns,* present participle of *itinerārī* to travel, from Latin *iter* journey.] —**i·tin′er·ant·ly,** *adv.*

i·tin·er·ar·y (ī tin′ə rer′ē, i tin′-) *n., pl.* **-ar·ies. 1.** a course or plan of travel, as for a journey: *Rome, Amsterdam, and New York were included in the itinerary.* **2.** an account or record of travel. **3.** a guidebook for travelers. —*adj.* of or relating to traveling or a route. [Late Latin *itinerārium* account of a journey, going back to Latin *iter* journey.]

i·tin·er·ate (ī tin′ə rāt′, i tin′-) *v.i.,* **-at·ed, -at·ing.** to travel from place to place. [Late Latin *itinerātus,* past participle of *itinerārī.* See ITINERANT.] —**i·tin′er·a′tion,** *n.*

-itis *suffix* inflammation of: *appendicitis.* [Modern Latin *-itis,* from Greek *-ītis,* feminine of *-ītēs* relating to.]

it'll (it′əl) *contr.* **1.** it will. **2.** it shall.

its (its) *adj.* (the possessive form of **it**) of, relating to, or belonging to it: *The cat licked its paw.* —*pron.* **1.** of, relating to, or belonging to it: *Each country claimed that the territory was its.* ➡ used with *of* after a noun or pronoun: *The library said the book was one of its.* **2.** the one or ones that relate or belong to it: *Other organizations have their problems just as ours has its.* ➡ **Its** is used as singular or plural, depending on the noun to which it refers.

it's (its) *contr.* **1.** it is. **2.** it has.

it·self (it self′) *pron.* **1.** the emphatic form of **it:** *The book itself is very poorly written.* **2.** the reflexive form of **it:** *The cat can wash itself.* **3.** its usual or normal state or condition: *The car is not itself this morning.*

-ity *suffix* the state, condition, or quality of being: *suavity, formality, animosity, inferiority.* [French *-ité,* from Latin *-itās.*]

IU, international unit; international units.

IUD, intrauterine device.

IV, intravenous.

I've (īv) *contr.* I have.

-ive *suffix* **1.** given or tending to: *active, demonstrative, inquisitive.* **2.** of or relating to: *infinitive, native.* [Latin *-īvus,* often through French *-if, -ive.*]

i·vied (ī′vēd) *adj.* covered or overgrown with ivy.

i·vo·ry (ī′və rē, īv′rē) *n., pl.* **-ries 1.** a smooth, hard, white substance composing the tusks of elephants, walruses, and certain other mammals. **2.** an object or objects made of this substance: *The museum has a fine collection of medieval ivories.* **3.** a creamy white color. **4. ivories.** *Slang.* **a.** piano keys. **b.** dice.

Nigerian **ivory** mask

—*adj.* **1.** of or resembling ivory. **2.** having the color ivory. [Anglo-Norman *ivorie* this substance, from Latin *eboreus* made of ivory, from *ebur* ivory; probably of Egyptian origin.]

ivory nut, the nutlike seed of a South American palm tree, *Phytelephas macrocarpa,* used to make imitation ivory buttons and other objects.

ivory tower, a situation, attitude, or condition of withdrawal from practical matters, as into a world of intellectual or artistic pursuits: *The writer lives in an ivory tower.*

i·vy (ī′vē) *n., pl.* **i·vies. 1.** any of several unrelated creeping vines widely cultivated as decorative coverings for walls and yards, as English ivy and Boston ivy. **2.** any of various climbing plants, as poison ivy. [Old English *īfig* climbing evergreen plant.]

Ivy League, an association of colleges and universities in the northeastern United States, having high scholastic standing and social prestige. —**Ivy Leaguer.**

i·wis (ē wis′, ī wis′) *adv. Archaic.* certainly; surely. [Old English *gewis* certain.]

Ix·i·on (ik sī′ən) *n.* in Greek mythology, the father of the centaurs. Zeus punished Ixion for making advances to Hera by having him bound to a perpetually revolving fiery wheel in Hades.

-ize *suffix* **1. a.** to act upon; make: *civilize, legalize, fertilize.* **b.** to treat like: *idolize.* **2.** to treat or affect with: *oxidize.* **3.** to form into; become: *crystallize.* **4.** to be concerned with or engaged in: *philosophize, characterize.* [Greek *-izein* to act in a certain way, often through Latin *-izāre* or French *-iser.*]

| | ancient Semitic | early Greek | later Greek | Etruscan | Latin |

J

J Because the letter J developed as a variation of the letter I, they share the same early history. The earliest ancestor of I and J was the ancient Semitic symbol called *yod*, meaning "hand." The Greeks simplified *yod*, called it *iota*, and used it to represent the sound of the short vowel *i*. By about the fifth century B.C., the Greeks were writing *iota* as a single vertical line. This form of *iota* was adopted by the Etruscans and the Romans. In the Latin alphabet, the letter I represented both the vowel sound *i* and the consonant sound *j*. In medieval manuscript writing, it became customary to lengthen the small letter *i* below the line when it was the initial letter of a word, resulting in two distinct forms of the letter. The new form was written much as the letter J is written today. Around the end of the sixteenth century, the letter I began to be used only for the vowel sound, and the letter J only for the consonant sound.

---

j, J (jā) *n., pl.* **j's, J's. 1.** the tenth letter of the English alphabet. **2.** the shape of this letter or something having this shape.

J *Physics.* joule.

J. 1. January. **2.** judge. **3.** July. **4.** June. **5.** justice.

Ja., January.

JA *also,* **J.A. 1.** joint account. **2.** judge advocate.

jab (jab) *v.t., v.i.,* **jabbed, jab·bing. 1.** to poke or thrust sharply, as with something pointed; stab. **2.** to punch or strike with short, quick blows. —*n.* a sharp, quick thrust or blow. [Form of archaic *job* to strike; possibly imitative.]

jab·ber (jab′ər) *v.i., v.t.* to talk rapidly, unintelligibly, or nonsensically; chatter. —*n.* rapid, unintelligible, or nonsensical talk; gibberish. [Imitative.] —**jab′ber·er,** *n.*

ja·bot (zha bō′, ja-) *n.* a ruffle or similar ornamentation of lace or other material, usually worn down the front of a dress or shirt. [French *jabot* originally, crop of a bird; of uncertain origin.]

jac·a·ran·da (jak′ə ran′də) *n.* any of a group of tropical American trees and shrubs bearing showy blue, violet, or white flowers.

ja·cinth (jā′sinth, jas′inth) *n.* hyacinth *(def. 3).* [Old French *jacinte,* from Latin *hyacinthus* larkspur, blue precious stone, from Greek *hyakinthos.* Doublet of HYACINTH.]

jack (jak) *n.* **1.** *also,* **Jack. a.** a man or boy; fellow. **b.** a worker who does manual labor or odd jobs; laborer. ➡ usually used in combination: *lumberjack, steeplejack, jack-of-all-trades.* **c.** a sailor; seaman. **2.** any of various mechanical or hydraulic devices, usually portable, used for lifting heavy objects a short distance. **3.** a playing card bearing the picture of a young man, in most games higher in value than a ten and lower than a queen. Also, **knave. 4.a. jacks.** a game played chiefly by children, the object of which is to pick up a number of small, six-pointed metal pieces or similar objects while bouncing and catching a small rubber ball with the same hand. Also, **jackstones.** ➡ used as singular. **b.** one of the playing pieces used in this game Also, **jackstone. 5.a.** a male donkey; jackass. **b.** jackrabbit. **6.** a small flag flown by a ship, usually to indicate nationality. **7.** an electrical socket into which a plug may be inserted to make a connection; receptacle: *a telephone jack.* **8.** *Slang.* money. —*v.t.* **1.** to lift or move with or as with a mechanical or hydraulic jack (often with *up*): *to jack up an automobile.* **2.** *Informal.* to increase, as prices (often with *up*): *stores that continually jack up prices.* [From the masculine proper name *Jack,* from *Jankin,* diminutive of JOHN; possibly influenced by French *Jacques* James.]

  •**every man jack.** everyone without exception.

jack·al (jak′əl, -ôl) *n.* **1.** any of various foxlike mammals, genus *Thos,* of Africa, Asia, and southeastern Europe, having a pointed face, bushy tail, and usually gray, buff, or reddish black fur. Jackals often feed on the remains of another animal's prey. Length: 32-38 inches (81-97 centimeters), including tail. **2.** a person who does menial or dishonest work for another. [Turkish *chakāl* the animal, from Persian *shaghāl.*]

jack·a·napes (jak′ə nāps′) *n., pl.* **-napes.** an impertinent, presumptuous, or conceited fellow; upstart. [From earlier *Jack Napes* ape, originally (about 1450) a nickname of the first Duke of Suffolk, whose badge was a ball and chain of the kind fastened on tame *apes.*]

jack·ass (jak′as′) *n.* **1.** a male donkey. **2.** a stupid or foolish person; blockhead.

jack·boot (jak′büt′) *also,* **jack boot.** *n.* a sturdy military boot reaching above the knee.

jackal

jack·daw (jak′dô′) *n.* a glossy black crow, *Corvus monedula,* of Europe, Asia, and northern Africa, having a gray band around the throat and a gray underside. Length: 13 inches (33 centimeters). Also, **daw.**

jack·et (jak′it) *n.* **1.a.** a short coat, usually not extending below the hips. **b.** a similar, usually lighter garment that is often part of a suit. **2.** an outer covering or casing, such as a removable paper or cardboard cover for a book or phonograph record, or the skin of a potato. —*v.t.* to cover with a jacket; put a jacket on. [Old French *jaquette,* diminutive of *jaque* sleeveless coatlike garment, possibly from *jacques* nickname given to French peasants of the fourteenth century who often wore the *jaque,* from *Jacques* James.]

Jack Frost, a figure thought of as representing frost or freezing cold weather.

jack·ham·mer (jak′ham′ər) *n.* a hand-held machine for drilling rock, pavement, or similar hard materials, powered by compressed air.

jack-in-the-box (jak′in thə boks′) *also,* **jack′-in-a-box′.** *n., pl.* **-box·es.** a toy consisting of a box containing a grotesque figure, often that of a clown, that springs up when the lid of the box is opened.

jack-in-the-pul·pit (jak′in thə púl′pit, -pul′pit) *n., pl.* **-pits.** a plant, *Arisaema triphyllum,* of eastern North America, bearing one or two long-stalked leaves that grow directly from an underground corm and tiny flowers that are enclosed within a green or white and purple striped spathe.

jack·knife (jak′nīf′) *n., pl.* **-knives** (-nīvz′). **1.** a large pocketknife. **2.** a dive in which the diver bends at the waist and, keeping the legs straight, touches the feet with the hands before straightening out and entering the water hands first. —*v.t., v.i.,* **-knifed, knif·ing.** to double up or bend like a jackknife. [Probably from *Jack,* nickname of King James I of England (because this knife was popular in England during his reign), + KNIFE.]

jack-of-all-trades (jak′əv ôl′trādz′) *n., pl.* **jacks-of-all-trades.** a person who can do many different kinds of work.

jack-o'-lan·tern (jak′ə lan′tərn) *n., pl.* **-terns. 1.** a pumpkin hollowed out and carved so as to resemble a human face, used as a decoration or lantern at Halloween. **2.** will-o'-the wisp *(def. 1).*

a	at	e	end	o	hot	u	up	hw	white		about
ā	ape	ē	me	ō	old	ū	use	ng	song		taken
ä	far	i	it	ô	fork	ü	rule	th	thin	ə	pencil
âr	care	ī	ice	oi	oil	ů	pull	th	this		lemon
		îr	pierce	ou	out	ûr	turn	zh	measure		circus

jack pine, a slender pine, *Pinus divaricata,* having stiff, paired needles, growing in Canada and the northeastern United States, used for wood pulp.

jack·pot (jak′pot′) *n.* the top prize or cumulative stakes in any of various games and contests: *a quiz show that offers a $100,000 jackpot.*

  ·to hit the jackpot. a. to win a jackpot. **b.** to have great success or unexpected good fortune.

jack·rab·bit (jak′rab′it) *n.* any of several North American hares, genus *Lepus,* having very long ears and long, powerful hind legs. Length: to 2 feet (0.6 meter).

jack·screw (jak′skrü′) *n.* a jack for lifting, operated by means of a screw.

Jack·so·ni·an (jak sō′nē ən) *adj.* of or relating to the U.S. president Andrew Jackson, his principles, or his policies. —*n.* a supporter of Andrew Jackson, his principles, or his policies.

jack·stone (jak′stōn′) *n.* **1. jackstones.** jack *(def. 4a).* ➡ used as singular. **2.** jack *(def. 4b).*

jack·straw (jak′strô′) *n.* **1. jackstraws.** a game in which a number of objects, usually thin sticks or light strips of wood or other material, are thrown into a pile and must be picked up one at a time without disturbing the rest of the pile. ➡ used as singular. **2.** one of the sticks or other objects used in this game.

jack-tar (jak′tär′) *also,* **Jack-tar, Jack Tar.** *n.* a sailor; seaman.

Jac·o·be·an (jak′ə bē′ən) *adj.* of, relating to, or characteristic of King James I of England or the period of his reign. —*n.* an English person who lived during the reign of King James I, esp. a statesman or writer. [Modern Latin *Jacobaeus,* from Latin *Jacobus* James, Jacob.]

Jac·o·bin (jak′ə bin) *n.* **1.** a member of a French revolutionary society organized in 1789 that dominated the government of France during the Reign of Terror, led by Robespierre. **2.** an extreme radical, esp. one who advocates violent upheavals to achieve political ends. **3.** a Dominican friar. [French *Jacobin,* from Medieval Latin *Jacobinus* relating to Jacob, from Latin *Jacobus.* The reference was to the meetings held by the revolutionary society in a building of the Dominican, or Jacobin, friars.] —**Jac′o·bin′ic;** *also,* **Jac′o·bin′i·cal,** *adj.*

Jac·o·bin·ism (jak′ə bə niz′əm) *n.* **1.** the political principles or practices of the society of Jacobins. **2.** extreme radicalism, esp. in politics.

Jac·o·bite (jak′ə bīt′) *n.* an English or Scottish supporter of James II after his expulsion in 1688, or of his descendants' claims to the throne. [From Latin *Jacobus* Jacob, James.]

Ja·cob's ladder (jā′kəbz) **1.** in the Old Testament, a ladder from earth to heaven that Jacob saw in a dream. **2.** a rope ladder used on ships, usually having wooden rungs. **3.** a sturdy, leafy member of the phlox family, *Polemonium caeruleum,* widely cultivated as a garden plant, having clusters of bell-shaped blue flowers and a ladderlike arrangement of leaves and leaflets.

Jac·que·rie (zhä′kə rē′, zhäk rē′) *n.* **1.** the revolt of the French peasants against the nobility in 1358. **2.** *also,* **jacquerie.** any peasants' revolt. [French *jacquerie,* from *jacques* scornful nickname given to French peasants by the nobility, from *Jacques* James.]

Ja·cuz·zi (jə kü′zē) *n. Trademark.* a bath incorporating a machine that circulates a current of water to provide massage.

jade¹ (jād) *n.* **1.** either of two very hard minerals, nephrite or jadeite, that are most commonly deep green to greenish white and are used for jewelry and carved ornaments. **2.** *also,* **jade green.** a deep green to greenish white color. —*adj.* having the color jade. [French *jade,* from Spanish *(piedra de la) ijada* (stone of the) loin, going back to Latin *īlia* abdomen, plural of *īleum* groin, flank. So called because it was once believed that jade could cure kidney stones.]

jade² (jād) *n.* **1.** an old, worn-out, worthless, or ill-tempered horse. **2.** a disreputable or worthless woman; hussy. —*v.t., v.i.,* **jad·ed, jad·ing.** to make or become tired or worn-out. [Middle English *jade,* probably from an unrecorded Anglo-Norman word, from Old Norse *jalda* mare, from Finnish *jalda.*]

jad·ed (jā′did) *adj.* **1.** worn-out; tired. **2.** dulled, as from overindulgence; satiated. —**jad′ed·ly,** *adv.* —**jad′ed·ness,** *n.*

jade·ite (jā′dīt) *n.* a mineral that is a variety of jade, usually green or greenish white, with a glassy or pearly luster. Formula: $NaAlSi_2O_6$

jae·ger (yā′gər, jā′-) *also,* **jäger.** *n.* any of several brown and white seabirds, genus *Stercorarius,* that resemble gulls. It pursues and harasses weaker birds, stealing their prey. Length: 18-22 inches (46-56 centimeters). [German *Jäger* hunter.]

jag¹ (jag) *n.* a sharp, projecting point. —*v.t.,* **jagged, jag·ging. 1.** to cut notches in. **2.** to make uneven or ragged by cutting or tearing. [Of uncertain origin.]

jag² (jag) *n. Informal.* an unrestrained outburst or period of overindulgence in some activity; spell; bout: *an eating jag.* [Of uncertain origin.]

Jag·an·nath (jug′ə nät′, -nôt′) *n.* Juggernaut.

jä·ger (yä′gər) jaeger.

jag·ged (jag′id) *adj.* having sharp, projecting points or uneven edges: *a jagged ridge of rocks.* —**jag′ged·ly,** *adv.* —**jag′ged·ness,** *n.*

jag·uar (jag′wär, -ü är′) *n.* a large mammal, *Felis onca,* of the cat family, native to Mexico and Central and South America, having a coat of short, tawny or golden fur with black spots. Length: to 9 feet (2.7 meters), including tail. [Tupi-Guarani *jaguara* carnivorous animal.]

jag·ua·run·di (jag′wə run′dē) *also,* **jag·ua·ron·di** (jag′wə ron′dē). *n.* a slender wildcat of Central and South America, *Herpailurus (Felis) yagouaroundi,* having black, brownish red, or gray fur. Length: 2 feet (0.6 meter), with a tail almost as long. [Spanish and Portuguese *jaguarundi,* from Tupi-Guarani *jaguarandi.*]

Jah·veh (yä′vā) *also,* **Jah·weh.** *n.* Yahweh.

jai a·lai (hī′lī′, -ə lī′) an extremely fast court game similar to handball, popular esp. in Spain and Latin America, in which the ball is hurled and caught with a long, curved basket strapped to the wrist. Also, **pelota.** [Spanish *jai alai,* from Basque *jai* festival + *alai* merry.]

jai alai

jail (jāl) *also, British,* **gaol.** *n.* **1.** a building for the confinement of persons accused or convicted of breaking the law. **2.** any place of confinement. —*v.t.* to put or keep in jail; imprison. [Old French *jaiole, gaole* prison, cage, from Medieval Latin *gabiola* cage, going back to Latin *cavea.*] —For Synonyms *(n.),* see **prison.**

jail·bird (jāl′bûrd′) *n. Informal.* a person who is or has been often confined in prison; prisoner or ex-convict.

jail·break (jāl′brāk′) *n.* an escape from a jail or prison.

jail·er (jā′lər) *also,* **jail·or;** *British,* **gaol·er.** *n.* the keeper of a jail.

Jain (jīn) *n.* a person who practices Jainism. —*adj.* of or relating to Jainism or the Jains. Also, **Jai·na** (jī′nə), **Jain′ist.** [Hindi *jaina* saint, going back to Sanskrit *jinas* literally, one who overcomes.]

Jain·ism (jī′niz əm) *n.* an ascetic Hindu religion founded in the sixth century B.C. that teaches immortality of the soul and respect for all living things.

jal·ap (jal′əp) *n.* **1.** a drug made from the dried roots of a plant, *Exogonium purga,* formerly used as a drastic cathartic. **2.** the plant yielding this drug, grown esp. in Mexico and India. [French *jalap,* from Spanish *jalapa* the plant, from *Jalapa,* Mexican town from which the plant was first obtained.]

ja·la·pe·ño (hä′lə pān′yō, -pēn′-) *n.* a cone-shaped, green or orange-red variety of hot pepper, commonly used in Mexican cooking. Also, **jalapeño pepper.** [Mexican Spanish *jalapeño* of or relating to *Jalapa,* city in eastern Mexico where the pepper originated.]

ja·lop·y (jə lop′ē) *n., pl.* **-lop·ies.** *Informal.* an old or broken-down automobile. [Of uncertain origin.]

jal·ou·sie (jal′ə sē′) *n.* **1.** a window made of a series of horizontal overlapping slats, often made of glass, that can be adjusted to regulate the passage of air and light. **2.** a blind or shade of similar design, made of wood, metal, or other material. [French *jalousie* literally, jealousy, from *jaloux* envious, from Old French *jalous;* because, supposedly, a jealous person can watch through it without being seen. See JEALOUS.]

jam¹ (jam) *v.,* **jammed, jam·ming.** —*v.t.* **1.** to squeeze, force, or press into or through a tight or close space: *We jammed all our clothes into one large suitcase.* **2.** to fill or crowd so as to make movement difficult or impossible: *Shoppers jammed the stores on the weekend.* **3.** to push, place, or thrust violently, esp. to apply (brakes) suddenly with maximum strength. **4.** to cause to become

stuck, wedged, or blocked up so as to be unworkable, as a machine or moving part: *Rust and dirt had jammed the gate's old latch.* **5.** to bruise or crush between two things: *She jammed her hand when she closed the drawer on it.* **6.** to interfere with a transmission, such as a broadcast or radar signal, often by sending out another signal at the same frequency. —*v.i.* **1.** to become stuck fast or wedged: *The key jammed in the lock.* **2.** to become unworkable through the sticking or wedging of some part: *The gears on his bicycle jammed.* **3.** to force one's way into a confined space: *Thousands of people jam into the subways during rush hour.* **4.** to take part in a jam session; improvise jazz. —*n.* **1.** a mass of people or things so tightly crowded together that movement is difficult or impossible. **2.** the act of jamming or the state of being jammed. **3.** *Informal.* a difficult or troublesome situation; fix. [Of uncertain origin.]

jam² (jam) *n.* a food made by boiling fruit with sugar to a thick consistency, used as a spread on bread and other foods. [Probably from JAM¹; referring to fruit pressed tightly together in making jam.]

Jam., Jamaica.

jamb (jam) *also,* **jambe.** *n.* a post or upright surface forming the side of a doorway, window, or other opening. [French *jambe* leg, side post of a door, from Late Latin *gamba* hoof, leg, going back to Greek *kampē* bend, joint.]

jam·ba·lay·a (jum'bə lī'ə, jam'-) *n.* **1.** a highly seasoned rice dish prepared with diced chicken, ham, shrimp, and other meat and seafood, mixed with onions, peppers, and tomatoes. **2.** *Informal.* any mixture or jumble of things. [Louisiana French *jambalaya,* from Portuguese *jambalaia.*]

jam·bo·ree (jam'bə rē') *n.* **1.** a noisy or festive gathering or celebration. **2.** a large national or international assembly of boy scouts or girl scouts. [Of uncertain origin.]

James (jāmz) *n.* an Epistle of the New Testament, often attributed to the Apostle James the Greater.

jam-pack (jam'pak') *v.t. Informal.* to fill or crowd to capacity: *We jam-packed the box with books and papers.* —**jam'-packed',** *adj.*

jam session, an informal gathering of jazz musicians, esp. to improvise on various themes.

Jan., January.

Jane Doe 1. an unknown or fictitious woman. ➡ used esp. in legal documents to designate a fictitious woman or a woman whose real name is not known. **2.** the average woman.

jan·gle (jang'gəl) *v.,* **-gled, -gling.** —*v.i.* **1.** to make a harsh or discordant sound. **2.** to quarrel peevishly; bicker. —*v.t.* **1.** to cause to make a harsh or discordant sound. **2.** to have an upsetting or irritating effect on: *The constant noise jangled my nerves.* —*n.* **1.** a harsh or discordant sound. **2.** a petty quarrel; bickering. [Old French *jangler* to chatter; of Germanic origin.] —**jan'gler,** *n.*

Jan·is·sar·y (jan'ə ser'ē) *also,* **jan·is·sar·y, Jan·i·zar·y, jan·i·zar·y.** *n., pl.* **-sar·ies. 1.** a soldier in an elite Turkish army corps, established about 1330 and abolished in 1826, that served as the sultan's guard and was also a powerful fighting force. **2.** any Turkish soldier. [French *janissaire,* from Italian *giannizzero,* from Turkish *yeñicheri* literally, new troop.]

jan·i·tor (jan'i tər) *n.* a worker employed to clean and service a building or establishment, as an apartment house, school, or office. [Latin *jānitor* doorkeeper, porter, from *jānua* door, from *Jānus* Roman god of gates and doors.] —**jan·i·to·ri·al** (jan'i tôr'ē əl), *adj.*

Jan·i·zar·y (jan'ə zer'ē) *also,* **jan·i·zar·y.** *n., pl.* **-zar·ies.** Janissary.

Jan·u·ar·y (jan'ū er'ē) *n., pl.* **-ar·ies.** the first month of the year, containing thirty-one days. [Middle English *Janyuere,* from Latin *Jānuārius (mēnsis)* (month) of the god Janus, from *Jānus;* because this month was dedicated to Janus.]

Ja·nus (jā'nəs) *n.* in Roman mythology, the god of gates and doors who presided over beginnings and endings, conventionally represented as having two faces looking in opposite directions. [Latin *Jānus.*]

Ja·nus-faced (jā'nəs fāst') *adj.* two-faced; hypocritical; deceitful.

Jap (jap) *n., adj. Slang.* Japanese. ➡ considered offensive.

Jap. 1. Japan. **2.** Japanese.

ja·pan (jə pan') *n.* **1.** any of various durable, glossy, black lacquers or varnishes, originally from Japan, used for coating objects. **2.** work varnished and decorated in this manner. —*adj.* relating to or varnished with japan. —*v.t.,* **-panned, -pan·ning.** to varnish or lacquer with or as with japan.

Jap·a·nese (jap'ə nēz', -nēs') *adj.* of, relating to, or characteristic of Japan or its people, language, or culture. —*n., pl.* **-nese. 1.** a native or citizen of Japan. **2.** a person of Japanese ancestry. **3.** the language of Japan.

Words from Japanese

Japanese, although it has adapted Chinese ideographic characters for its written form, is believed by many scholars to be unrelated linguistically to any other language. Many English words have been borrowed from Japanese, especially in such areas as politics, the martial arts, the fine arts, food, and religion. Below is a selection of loanwords that have come into English from or through Japanese.

banzai	hibachi	mikado	sukiyaki
bonsai	honcho	Nisei	sushi
bushido	Issei	origami	tempura
daimyo	jinricksha	sake²	teriyaki
futon	judo	samisen	tofu
geisha	jujitsu	samurai	torii
ginkgo	Kabuki	Sansei	tsunami
go²	kamikaze	sashimi	zaibatsu
haiku	karate	sayonara	Zen
hara-kiri	kimono	Shinto	zori

Japanese beetle, a small, destructive beetle, *Popillia japonica,* introduced into the United States from Japan, that has red wings and a greenish oval body and feeds on various plants.

Japanese lantern, Chinese lantern.

jape (jāp) *v.,* **japed, jap·ing.** —*v.i.* to joke; jest. —*v.t.* to make fun of; mock. —*n.* a joke; jest; gibe. [Probably blend of Old French *japer* to yelp (imitative) and Old French *gaber* to mock (from Old Norse *gabba*).] —**jap'er,** *n.*

jap·er·y (jā'pə rē) *n., pl.* **-er·ies.** a joke; jest.

ja·pon·i·ca (jə pon'i kə) *n.* **1.** a species of camellia, *Camellia japonica,* that blooms in a variety of colors. **2.** any of a number of flowering quinces, esp. *Camellia speciosa,* usually bearing scarlet, pink, or white flowers. Also, **Japanese quince.** [Modern Latin *japonica* literally, Japanese, from *Japonia* Japan.]

jar¹ (jär) *n.* **1.** a wide-mouthed, usually cylindrical container or vessel that is usually made of glass or earthenware. **2.** the amount contained in a jar; contents of a jar; jarful. [Middle English *jarre,* from French *jarre,* from Spanish *jarra* or Old Provençal *jarra,* from Arabic *jarra* large earthen vessel for storing water.]

jar² (jär) *v.,* **jarred, jar·ring.** —*v.t.* **1.** to cause to shake or vibrate; cause to move suddenly by impact or shock: *The explosion jarred the building.* **2.** to have a harsh, disturbing, or unpleasant effect on: *The sudden clatter jarred her nerves.* —*v.i.* **1.** to shake, vibrate, or move suddenly from impact or shock. **2.** to have an irritating or upsetting effect: *His snide remarks jar on my nerves.* **3.** to be in conflict; disagree; clash: *The evidence given by the two witnesses jars.* **4.** to make a harsh or discordant sound. —*n.* **1.** a shake or sudden movement; shock; jolt. **2.** a sudden disturbing effect on the mind or senses. **3.** a harsh or discordant sound or combination of sounds. [Probably imitative.]

jar³ (jär) *n.* **on the jar.** partially open; ajar. [Old English *c(i)err* turning.]

jar·di·niere (jär'də nîr', zhär'dən yâr') *n.* an ornamental pot or stand for flowers or plants. [French *jardinière,* feminine of *jardinier* of the garden, from *jardin* garden; of Germanic origin.]

jar·ful (jär'fŭl') *n., pl.* **-fuls.** the amount that a jar holds.

jar·gon (jär'gən, -gon) *n.* **1.** confused, unintelligible, or meaningless speech or writing; gibberish. **2.** the technical or specialized language or phraseology of a particular profession, sect, or other group: *legal jargon.* **3.** a mixture of two or more languages or dialects, esp. serving as a lingua franca. —*v.i.* to speak jargon. [Old French *jargon* chatter; probably of imitative origin.]

Usage **Jargon** is the specialized vocabulary used by a group of people who are in the same profession or share some special interest. Doctors, lawyers, musicians, government employees, and stamp collectors are examples of groups that have their own specialized language. Because **jargon** may be difficult for those outside the group to understand, the word is often used in a negative sense. **Jargon** is appropriate when it conveys infor-

a	at	e	end	o	hot	u	up	hw	white		about
ā	ape	ē	me	ō	old	ū	use	ng	song		taken
ä	far	i	it	ô	fork	ü	rule	th	thin	ə	pencil
âr	care	ī	ice	oi	oil	u̇	pull	th	this		lemon
		îr	pierce	ou	out	ûr	turn	zh	measure		circus

mation that simpler language could not. It would be natural for doctors to use medical **jargon** when discussing a disease, but inappropriate to use it when explaining the disease and its treatment to a patient unfamiliar with that terminology.

jarl (yärl) *n.* an ancient Scandinavian chieftain or nobleman. [Old Norse *jarl.*]

Jas., James.

jas·mine (jaz′min, jas′-) *n.* **1.** the usually fragrant bell-shaped flower of any of a large group of plants, genus *Jasminum,* of the olive family, growing in yellow, white, or pink clusters. **2.** the shrub bearing clusters of these flowers, widely cultivated throughout the world. **3.** any of several unrelated plants that bear sweet-scented flowers, as the **yellow jessamine,** *Gelsemium sempervirens,* or the **cape jasmine,** *Gardenia jasminoides.* Also, **jessamine.** [French *jasmin* the shrub, from Arabic *yāsamīn,* from Persian *yāsmīn.*]

Ja·son (jā′sən) *n.* in Greek legend, the hero who led the Argonauts in quest of the Golden Fleece.

jas·per (jas′pər) *n.* an opaque quartz, usually reddish, brown, or yellow. [Old French *jaspre,* from Latin *iaspis* a green precious stone prized by the ancients, from Greek *iaspis;* of Semitic origin.]

jaun·dice (jôn′dis, jän′-) *n.* **1.** a yellow discoloration of the skin, the whites of the eyes, and the mucous membranes, due to an excess of bile pigment in the blood. **2.** a state of mind or a negative feeling, as of envy or resentment, that colors the point of view or distorts the judgment. —*v.t.,* **-diced, -dic·ing.** to affect so as to color the point of view or distort the judgment; prejudice. [Old French *jaunice* yellowness, from *jaune* yellow, from Latin *galbinus* greenish yellow.]

jaun·diced (jôn′dist, jän′-) *adj.* **1.** affected with jaundice. **2.** affected or distorted by envy, jealousy, bitterness, or similar negative feeling; prejudiced.

jaunt (jônt, jänt) *n.* a short trip, esp. one taken for pleasure. —*v.i.* to take such a trip. [Of uncertain origin.]

jaun·ty (jôn′tē, jän′-) *adj.,* **-ti·er, -ti·est. 1.** lively, carefree, or self-confident in air or manner; sprightly. **2.** in style; fashionable; smart: *a jaunty cap and jacket.* [French *gentil* nice, pleasing, from Old French *gentil* nobly born, from Latin *gentīlis* of the same clan, from *gēns* race, clan. Doublet of GENTEEL, GENTILE, GENTLE.] —**jaun′ti·ly,** *adv.* —**jaun′ti·ness,** *n.*

Jav., Javanese.

Ja·va (jä′və, jav′ə) *n.* **1.** coffee grown on Java and other nearby islands. **2.** *also,* **java.** *Informal.* coffee.

Java man, an extinct primitive human being, able to walk erect, whose fossil remains, dating from the early Ice Age, were found in central Java. First classified as *Pithecanthropus erectus,* it is now generally classified as *Homo erectus,* together with Peking man and certain other human fossil remains. Also, **Pithecanthropus.**

Jav·a·nese (jav′ə nēz′, -nēs′) *adj.* of, relating to, or characteristic of Java or its people, language, or culture. —*n., pl.* **-nese. 1.** a native or citizen of Java. **2.** a person of Javanese ancestry. **3.** a language belonging to the Austronesian family of languages, spoken predominantly in Java.

jave·lin (jav′lin, jav′ə-) *n.* **1.** a light spear, used chiefly as a weapon. **2.a.** a lightweight, spearlike shaft, about 8 1/2 feet (2.6 meters) long and made of wood or metal, thrown for distance in athletic contests. **b.** the contest in which it is thrown. Also *(def. 2b),* **javelin throw.** [Middle French *javeline* long, thin dart; possibly of Celtic origin.]

Ja·velle water (zhə vel′) *also,* **Ja·vel water.** a solution of potassium or sodium hypochlorite in water, used as a bleach and disinfectant. [From French *(eau de) Javel* (water of) Javel, former French town, now part of Paris, where it was first produced.]

jaw (jô) *n.* **1.** either of the two bony structures forming the framework of the mouth and holding the teeth, esp. the lower of these structures. **2.** *also,* **jaws.** the part of the face covering these structures; the mouth and its related parts. **3.** either of a pair of parts, as of a tool, that can be closed to grasp or hold something: *the jaws of a vise.* **4. jaws.** any situation or position that suggests the closing or grasping action of a pair of jaws: *the jaws of danger, to snatch victory from the jaws of defeat.* **5.** one of the sides or walls of a pass, chasm, canyon, or similar opening. **6.** *Slang.* **a.** impudent or offensive talk. **b.** talk; chatter. —*v.i. Slang.* to talk; chatter. [Anglo-Norman *jowe,* from Old French *joe* cheek; of uncertain origin.] —**jaw′like′,** *adj.*

jaw·bone (jô′bōn′) *n.* one of the bones of the jaw, esp. the mandible. —*v.t., v.i.,* **-boned, -bon·ing.** *Informal.* to try to influence (a person or group), esp. in politics, by using strong persuasion: *The governor jawboned both sides in trying to end the strike.* —**jaw′bon′er,** *n.*

jaw·break·er (jô′brā′kər) *n.* **1.** a very hard, usually round piece of candy or chewing gum. **2.** *Informal.* a word that is difficult to pronounce.

jay (jā) *n.* **1.** any of various harsh-voiced birds, family Corvidae,

related to crows and magpies, often crested and having brightly colored plumage, as the blue jay or the **Canada jay,** *Perisoreus canadensis.* Length: 1 foot (0.3 meter). **2.** *Slang.* a silly, stupid, gullible, or inexperienced person. [Middle French *jay* the bird, from Late Latin *gaius;* probably imitative of the bird's sound.]

jay·walk (jā′wôk′) *v.i.* to cross a street without paying attention to traffic regulations or signals. [JAY in the sense of simpleton + WALK.] —**jay′walk′er,** *n.* —**jay′walk′ing,** *n.*

jazz (jaz) *n.* **1.** music originated by American blacks late in the nineteenth century, primarily in the southern United States, from blues, spirituals, and other sources. It has developed into a variety of styles, but is generally characterized by improvisation and strong, swinging rhythm. **2.** *Slang.* liveliness; animation: *to dance with a lot of jazz.* **3.** *Slang.* **a.** exaggerated, insincere, or idle talk: *The dealer gave us a lot of jazz about the car.* **b.** information or material of a related or miscellaneous nature: *a book on knights and castles and all that jazz.* —*v.t.* to play or arrange (music) as jazz. [Of uncertain origin.]

  · **to jazz up.** to make more lively or exciting: *to jazz up a lecture with some funny stories.*

jazz·y (jaz′ē) *adj.,* **jazz·i·er, jazz·i·est. 1.** resembling or characteristic of jazz music. **2.** *Slang.* lively; flashy. —**jazz′i·ly,** *adv.* —**jazz′i·ness,** *n.*

JCS, Joint Chiefs of Staff.

jct., junction.

JD, juvenile delinquent.

jeal·ous (jel′əs) *adj.* **1.** fearful or suspicious of losing to someone else what one wishes to gain or keep, esp. the love or affection of another. **2.** envious or resentful of a person or of that person's attainments or advantages: *to be jealous of a friend's success.* **3.** arising from feelings of apprehension, suspicion, envy, or resentment: *jealous anger.* **4.** watchful or careful in guarding or keeping something: *a people jealous of their liberties.* **5.** demanding exclusive worship and faithfulness: *a jealous god.* [Old French *jalous* fearful or suspicious of rivalry, from Late Latin *zēlōsus* full of fervor, from *zēlus* fervor, jealousy, from Greek *zēlos.*] —**jeal′ous·ly,** *adv.* —**jeal′ous·ness,** *n.* —For Synonyms, see **envious.**

jeal·ous·y (jel′ə sē) *n., pl.* **-ous·ies. 1.** the state or quality of being jealous. **2.** a jealous feeling or attitude: *Your petty jealousies are annoying.*

jean (jēn) *n.* **1.** a strong, twilled cotton fabric, used chiefly for sportswear and work clothes. **2. jeans.** trousers or overalls made of this fabric or of denim. [French *Gênes* Genoa, where this fabric was first produced.]

jeep (jēp) *n.* **1.** a rugged motor vehicle with four-wheel drive and usually a quarter-ton (227 kilograms) carrying capacity, used chiefly for transport, esp. by the armed forces. **2. Jeep.** *Trademark.* a similar vehicle for general use by civilians. [Supposedly from *G.P.,* abbreviation of general purpose, used by the U.S. Army to designate this vehicle.]

jeer (jir) *v.i.* to speak or shout in a derisive or mocking manner; scoff. —*v.t.* to treat or address with derision or mockery; taunt. —*n.* a derisive or mocking remark; taunt. [Of uncertain origin.] —**jeer′er,** *n.* —**jeer′ing·ly,** *adv.*

Synonyms *v.i.* Jeer, sneer, and scoff mean to show contempt for someone or something by word or gesture. Jeer means to mock or deride in a loud and coarse manner: *The fans jeered the opposing team.* Sneer connotes open or hinted contempt, and suggests a superior attitude: *They sneered at my ideas, calling them naive and simplistic.* Scoff generally connotes dismissing someone or something in an insulting manner: *Don't scoff at my plan until you've heard me out!*

Jef·fer·so·ni·an (jef′ər sō′nē ən) *adj.* of, relating to, or characteristic of the U.S. president and statesman Thomas Jefferson or his political principles. —*n.* a supporter of Thomas Jefferson or his political principles. —**Jef′fer·so′ni·an·ism,** *n.*

Je·ho·vah (ji hō′və) *n.* in the Old Testament, God. [Transliteration of Hebrew *JHVH* or *YHWH* (with the addition of vowels), used to refer to God.]

Jehovah's Witnesses, a proselytizing Christian sect, founded in the United States in the late nineteenth century, whose members are strongly opposed to war and to the authority of the government in matters of conscience.

je·june (ji jūn′) *adj.* **1.** lacking in nourishment; insubstantial; meager: *a jejune diet.* **2.** lacking interest, significance, or value; dull or empty: *a jejune speech.* **3.** not mature; childish; juvenile: *jejune behavior.* [Latin *jējūnus* fasting, barren, insignificant.] —**je·june′ly,** *adv.* —**je·june′ness, je·ju′ni·ty,** *n.*

je·ju·num (ji jū′nəm) *n., pl.* **-na** (-nə). the middle section of the small intestine, extending from the duodenum to the ileum. [Modern Latin *jejunum,* from Latin *jējūnus* fasting; referring to the belief of the ancient Greek physician Galen that it was empty after death.] —**je·ju′nal,** *adj.*

Jek·yll and Hyde (jek′əl, jē′kəl; hīd) **1.** two characters in a story by the American author Robert Louis Stevenson, the kindly Dr. Jekyll and the evil Mr. Hyde, who are actually opposing identities of the same person. **2.** *Informal.* a person who has or seems to have a personality distinctly split into a good side and an evil side. [From *The Strange Case of Dr. Jekyll and Mr. Hyde* (1886).] —**Jek·yll-and-Hyde,** *adj.*

jell (jel) *v.i.* **1.** to become the consistency of jelly. **2.** *Informal.* to assume definite form; become clear: *My career ambitions began to jell after I got my first job.* —*v.t.* **1.** to cause to become the consistency of jelly. **2.** *Informal.* to cause to assume definite form; make clear. —*n.* jelly. [From JELLY.]

jel·lied (jel′ēd) *adj.* **1.** having or brought to the consistency of jelly; congealed. **2.** spread or made with jelly or prepared in jelly.

Jel·lo (jel′ō) *n.* a gelatin dessert. *Trademark:* Jell-O.

jel·ly (jel′ē) *n., pl.* -**lies. 1.** any food preparation consisting mainly of gelatin or pectin and having a smooth, firm, somewhat elastic consistency and a semitransparent appearance, esp. such a preparation made of boiled fruit juice and sugar. **2.** anything having the consistency of or resembling jelly. —*v.,* -**lied, -ly·ing.** —*v.t.* **1.** to make into jelly. **2.** to spread or prepare with jelly. —*v.i.* to become the consistency of jelly. [Old French *gelee* frost, gelatin, going back to Latin *gelāta,* feminine past participle of *gelāre* to freeze, congeal.] —**jel′ly·like′,** *adj.*

jel·ly·bean (jel′ē bēn′) *also,* **jelly bean.** *n.* a small egg-shaped candy having a hard outer coating and a gelatinous center.

jel·ly·fish (jel′ē fish′) *n., pl.* -**fish** or -**fish·es. 1.** any of a group of free-swimming marine coelenterates, classes Hydrozoa and Scyphozoa, having a soft, gelatinous body with threadlike tentacles that are studded with stinging cells. **2.** *Informal.* a weak, fearful, or indecisive person.

jel·ly·roll (jel′ē rōl′) *n.* a thin piece of sponge cake covered with jelly and rolled into the shape of a log.

jen·net (jen′it) *n.* **1.** a small Spanish horse. **2.** a female donkey. [French *genet,* from Spanish *jinete* horseman, from Arabic *Zenāta* a Berber tribe noted for its horsemanship.]

jen·ny (jen′ē) *n., pl.* -**nies. 1.** spinning jenny. **2.** the female of certain animals, esp. a female wren or female donkey. [From *Jenny,* familiar form of the proper name *Jane.*]

jellyfish

jeop·ard·ize (jep′ər dīz′) *v.t.,* -**ized, -iz·ing.** to expose to loss or injury; endanger; imperil.

jeop·ard·y (jep′ər dē) *n.* **1.** danger of loss, injury, or death; peril: *The teenagers put their lives in jeopardy to save the child.* **2.** danger of conviction and punishment to which a defendant is exposed when put on trial for a crime. [Middle English *jeuparti,* from Old French *jeu parti* game in which the chances are even, even chance; literally, divided game, going back to Latin *jocus* jest, game + *partīre* to divide.]

Jer., Jeremiah.

jer·bo·a (jər bō′ə) *n.* any of various mouselike jumping rodents, family Dipodidae, of desert regions of Eurasia and Africa, having very long hind legs, a long tufted tail, and a silky buff-colored coat. Length: 6-18 inches (15-46 centimeters), including tail. [Modern Latin *jerboa,* from Arabic *yarbū̆* flesh of the loins; referring to the strong muscles in its hind legs.]

jer·e·mi·ad (jer′ə mī′ad) *n.* an anguished or doleful complaint or denunciation; lamentation; tale of woe. [French *jérémiade,* from *Jérémie* Jeremiah; referring to Lamentations, a book of the Old Testament attributed to the Hebrew prophet Jeremiah.]

Jer·e·mi·ah (jer′ə mī′ə) *also,* in the Douay Bible, **Jer·e·mi·as.** *n.* in the Old Testament, a book of prophecies attributed to the Hebrew prophet Jeremiah.

jerk¹ (jûrk) *n.* **1.** a sharp, abrupt pull, twist, push, or similar movement. **2.** a sudden, involuntary muscle contraction caused by reflex action. **3.** *Informal.* a stupid, dull, or unpleasant person. —*v.t.* **1.** to move or throw (something) with a sudden, sharp motion; give a sharp, abrupt pull, twist, or push to. **2.** to utter in an abrupt or sharply broken manner (with *out*). —*v.i.* **1.** to move with a sudden, sharp motion or series of such motions. **2.** to make spasmodic movements. [Probably a form of archaic *yerk* to pull tight; of uncertain origin.]

jerk² (jûrk) *v.t.* to cure (meat) by cutting it into strips and drying

it, usually in the sun. [Modification (influenced by JERK¹) of JERKY².]

jer·kin (jûr′kin) *n.* a short, close-fitting jacket or waistcoat, usually sleeveless and often made of leather, worn chiefly in the sixteenth and seventeenth centuries. [Of uncertain origin.]

jerk·wa·ter (jûrk′wô′tər, -wot′ər) *adj. Informal.* **1.** small and out-of-the-way: *a jerkwater town.* **2.** ridiculously or contemptibly insignificant: *some unknown jerkwater politician.* [Probably a form of archaic *yerk* to pull tight; of uncertain origin.]

jerk·y¹ (jûr′kē) *adj.,* **jerk·i·er, jerk·i·est. 1.** characterized by abrupt movements; moving with sudden starts and stops: *a jerky subway ride.* **2.** *Informal.* stupid; foolish: *a jerky idea.* [JERK¹ + -Y¹.] —**jerk′i·ly,** *adv.* —**jerk′i·ness,** *n.*

jerk·y² (jûr′kē) *n.* meat, esp. beef, that has been jerked. [Spanish *charqui,* from Quechua *charqui.*]

jer·o·bo·am (jer′ə bō′əm) *n.* a wine bottle having a capacity of about four fifths of a gallon (3 liters). [From *Jeroboam,* founder and first king of the northern kingdom of Israel in the tenth century B.C. So called because the large size of the bottle was likened to the many letters in his name.]

Jer·ry (jer′ē) *also,* **jer·ry.** *n., pl.* -**ries.** *Slang.* a German, esp. a German soldier. [Modification of GERMAN.]

jer·ry-built (jer′ē bilt′) *adj.* built or put together carelessly or hastily or with poor materials: *a jerry-built cottage.* [Possibly a blend of the proper name *Jerry* with JURY².]

jer·sey (jûr′zē) *n., pl.* -**seys. 1.** a machine-knitted fabric made of wool, cotton, silk, or synthetic fibers, used for clothing. **2.** a knitted sweater or shirt made of this or a similar fabric, usually a close-fitting pullover. **3. Jersey.** one of a breed of usually fawn-colored dairy cattle, the female of which produces milk with a very high butterfat content. Weight: to 1,500 pounds (680 kilograms) in bulls. [From *Jersey,* British island where the fabric and breed of cattle originated.]

Je·ru·sa·lem artichoke (jə rü′sə ləm, -zə-) **1.** a sunflower of the species *Helianthus tuberosus,* widely cultivated in North America and Europe, having large, rough leaves, yellow flower heads, and a potatolike tuber that is eaten as a vegetable. **2.** the tuber itself. [Modification of Italian *girasole* sunflower (going back to Latin *gȳrāre* to turn + *sōl* sun) + ARTICHOKE.]

Jerusalem cherry, a plant, *Solanum pseudocapsicum,* of the nightshade family, having white flowers and round, red or yellow poisonous fruit, widely grown as a houseplant.

jess (jes) *n.* in falconry, a strap that is fastened around a falcon's leg, to which a leash or bell may be attached. —*v.t.* to fasten a jess or jesses on. [Old French *ges* a throwing, going back to Latin *jactus.*]

jes·sa·mine (jes′ə min) *n.* jasmine.

jest (jest) *n.* **1.** something said or done to cause laughter; witticism or prank; joke. **2.** a frivolous or facetious mood or manner; playfulness; fun: *Many a true word is said in jest.* **3.** a mocking remark; jeer. **4.** an object of laughter or mockery; laughingstock. —*v.i.* **1.** to speak or act in a playful or facetious manner: *She was only jesting.* **2.** to utter gibes or taunts; scoff: *He jests at scars, that never felt a wound* (Shakespeare, *Romeo and Juliet*). [Old French *geste* exploit, tale, from Latin *gesta* (neuter plural) exploits.]

jest·er (jes′tər) *n.* a person who jests, esp. a clown formerly kept in royal and noble households to provide entertainment.

Jes·u·it (jezh′ü it, jez′-) *n.* a member of the Society of Jesus, a Roman Catholic religious order for men that was founded by Ignatius of Loyola in 1534. [Modern Latin *Jesuita,* from *Jesus.*]

jet¹ (jet) *n.* **1.** a stream of liquid, gas, or vapor, forcefully or suddenly emitted from a nozzle, spout, or narrow opening. **2.** something issued in or as in such a stream. **3.** a nozzle or spout for emitting such a stream: *the gas jets of a stove.* **4.a.** jet plane. **b.** jet engine. —*v.,* **jet·ted, jet·ting.** —*v.i.* **1.** to be shot forth in a stream. **2.** to travel by jet plane. —*v.t.* **1.** to shoot (something) forth in a stream. **2.** to transport by jet plane. [Medieval French *jeter* to throw, from Old French *jeter,* going back to Latin *jactāre,* form of *jacēre.*]

jet² (jet) *n.* **1.** a dense, deep black lignite coal capable of taking a high polish, used to make jewelry. **2.** a deep black color. —*adj.* **1.** made of or resembling jet. **2.** having the color jet; jet-black. [Middle English *get,* from Old French *jaiet* hard black mineral, from Latin *gagātēs,* from Greek *gagātēs* literally, stone of *Gagai,* an ancient town in Asia Minor where it was found.]

jet-black (jet′blak′) *adj.* black as jet; deep black.

a	at	e	end	o	hot	u	up	hw	white		about
ā	ape	ē	me	ō	old	ū	use	ng	song	ə	taken
ä	far	i	it	ô	fork	ū	rule	th	thin		pencil
âr	care	ī	ice	oi	oil	u̇	pull	th	this		lemon
				ou	out	ûr	turn	zh	measure		circus
		îr	pierce								

je·té (zhə tā′) *n.* in ballet, a leap in which the dancer pushes off the floor with one foot and lands on the other.

jet engine, a reaction engine that produces propulsive power by burning a mixture of fuel and air that is ejected to the rear as hot exhaust gases.

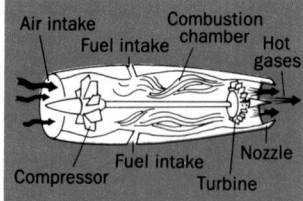

gas turbine **jet engine**

jet lag, the disruption of a person's sleeping and eating habits, often accompanied by fatigue, experienced after flying from one time zone to another.

jet·lin·er (jet′lī′nər) *n.* a large commercial jet plane designed to carry passengers.

jet plane, an airplane driven by jet propulsion.

jet-pro·pelled (jet′prə peld′) *adj.* driven by jet propulsion.

jet propulsion 1. propulsion by means of a jet of fluid, as hot gases, whose ejection in one direction generates a reactive motive force in the opposite direction. **2.** propulsion by means of one or more jet engines.

jet·sam (jet′səm) *n.* **1.** cargo or equipment cast overboard in order to lighten a ship in distress. **2.** such discarded cargo or equipment found washed ashore. ➡ distinguished from **flotsam. 3.** discarded, worthless, or miscellaneous things; odds and ends. [Modification of JETTISON.]

jet set, a social set composed of people who spend much of their time traveling, usually by jet, to various fashionable places around the world.

jet stream 1. a high-speed air current of the upper troposphere, usually 7 to 9 miles (11 to 14 kilometers) above the earth's surface, that moves generally west to east at speeds of from 100 to 300 miles (161 to 483 kilometers) per hour. **2.** a high-speed stream of gas or other fluid ejected from a jet engine.

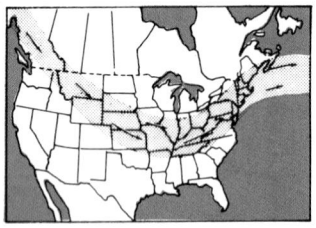

a **jet stream** across North America

jet·ti·son (jet′ə sən, -zən) *v.t.* **1.** to throw (cargo or equipment) overboard or off, esp. in order to lighten a ship or aircraft in distress. **2.** to cast off or discard (something unwanted, useless, or burdensome). —*n.* the act of jettisoning. [Old French *getaison* a throwing, from Latin *jactātiō.*]

jet·ty (jet′ē) *n., pl.* **-ties. 1.** a structure of timber, concrete, steel, or a combination of these materials, built out into a body of water in order to influence the current or protect a harbor or coast. **2.** a wharf; pier. [Old French *jetee* a throwing, structure "thrown out" to protect a harbor, from *jeter* to throw, going back to Latin *jactāre.*]

jeu d'es·prit (zhœ′ des prē′) *pl.* **jeux d'es·prit** (zhœ′ des prē′). *French.* a witty remark or piece of writing; witticism.

Jew (jü) *n.* **1.** a member of a people living in Israel and many other countries, descended from a group of Semitic tribes that lived in and around ancient Palestine and among whom the beliefs and laws of Judaism were developed and followed. **2.** a person whose religion is Judaism. [Old French *giu, juiu,* from Latin *Jūdaeus,* from Greek *Ioudaios,* going back to Hebrew *Yehuda* Judah (ancestor of the tribe of Judah in the Bible).]

jew·el (jü′əl) *n.* **1.** a precious stone; gem. **2.** an article of personal adornment, as a ring, bracelet, or brooch, usually made of cut and polished gems in a setting of precious metal. **3.** a person or thing of great value or rare excellence. **4.** a gem or substitute for a gem used as a bearing, as in a watch, because of its hardness. —*v.t.,* **-eled, -el·ing;** *also, British,* **-elled, -el·ling.** to set or adorn with or as with jewels. [Old French *jouel, joiel* gem, possibly from Late Latin *jocālia* gems, trinkets, from Latin *jocus* jest, game.]

jew·el·er (jü′ə lər) *also, British,* **jew·el·ler.** *n.* a person who makes, repairs, or deals in jewelry, watches, and the like.

jew·el·ry (jü′əl rē) *also, British,* **jew·el·ler·y.** *n.* precious stones or other articles, as of gold, silver, or glass, for personal ornamentation, collectively.

jew·el·weed (jü′əl wēd′) *n.* any of several species of impatiens, esp. *Impatiens capensis,* bearing orange-yellow flowers.

jew·fish (jü′fish′) *n., pl.* **-fish** or **-fish·es.** any of several dark green or black, rough-scaled sea bass, found in warm waters of the Atlantic and Pacific, valued as food fish.

Jew·ish (jü′ish) *adj.* of, relating to, or characteristic of Judaism, Jews, or their culture. —*n. Informal.* Yiddish.

Jewish calendar, Hebrew calendar.

Jew·ry (jü′rē) *n., pl.* **-ries. 1.** Jews collectively; the Jewish people. **2.** *Archaic.* ghetto. [Old French *juerie,* from *giu.* See JEW.]

Jew's harp, a small musical instrument, held between the teeth when played, that consists of a lyre-shaped metal frame and a flexible metal tongue and that produces a twanging tone when the free end of the metal tongue is plucked with the finger. [Modification of earlier *Jew's trump,* modification (influenced by JEW) of Dutch *jeugdtromp* literally, child's trumpet.]

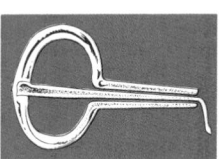

Jew's harp

Jez·e·bel (jez′ə bel′, -bəl) *n. also,* **jezebel.** a shameless or wicked woman. [From *Jezebel,* in the Old Testament, wife of Ahab, king of Israel.]

jib¹ (jib) *n.* any of various triangular sails set on a stay forward of the mast or foremast, usually smaller than the mainsail. For illustration, see **sloop.** [Of uncertain origin.]

• **the cut of one's jib.** *Informal.* one's appearance or manner.

jib² (jib) *v.,* **jibbed, jib·bing.** jibe¹. —*n.* jibe¹. [Possibly form of JIBE¹.]

jib³ (jib) *v.i.,* **jibbed, jib·bing.** to refuse to proceed or advance; balk. —*n.* a horse or other animal that jibs. Also, **jib′ber.** [Possibly from JIB².]

jib⁴ (jib) *n.* the boom of a crane or derrick. [Possibly short for GIBBET.]

jib boom, a spar that extends out from the bowsprit and to which a jib may be attached.

jibe¹ (jīb) *also,* **jib.** *v.,* **jibed, jib·ing.** —*v.i.* **1.** (of a fore-and-aft sail or its boom) to shift from one side of a boat or ship to the other when sailing before the wind. **2.** to change course so that the sail or boom shifts in this way: *The boat jibed back and forth several times.* —*v.t.* to cause to jibe: *to jibe the boom, to jibe a sailboat.* —*n.* the act of jibing. [Modification (influenced by *jib¹*) of obsolete Dutch *gijben,* form of Dutch *gijpen* to shift over (sails); literally, to gasp for air.]

jibe² (jīb) *n.* gibe. —*v.,* **jibed, jib·ing.** gibe. [Form of GIBE.] —**jib′er,** *n.*

jibe³ (jīb) *also,* **jive.** *v.i.,* **jibed, jib·ing.** *Informal.* to be in harmony or accord; agree. [Of uncertain origin.]

jif·fy (jif′ē) *n., pl.* **jif·fies.** *Informal.* a very short time; moment; instant. Also, **jiff.** [Of uncertain origin.]

jig (jig) *n.* **1.a.** a fast, lively dance, usually in triple time. **b.** the music for this dance. **2.** a device used for guiding a tool, as a drill, or for holding material to be worked on in place during the operation of such a tool. **3.** a fishhook, or set of fishhooks, attached to a colorful artificial lure and kept moving in the water to attract fish. —*v.,* **jigged, jig·ging.** —*v.i.* **1.** to dance or play a jig. **2.** to move with a rapid jerking or bobbing motion. **3.** to fish with a jig. **4.** to work with or operate a jig. —*v.t.* **1.** to dance (a jig or other lively dance). **2.** to move (something) with a rapid jerking or bobbing motion. **3.** to cut, form, or produce with the aid of a jig. [Possibly from Old French *giguer* to dance, frolic, from *gigue* fiddle; of Germanic origin.]

• **the jig is up.** *Informal.* all hope or chance of success is gone.

jig·ger¹ (jig′ər) *n.* **1.a.** a small glass or cup used to measure liquor, holding about an ounce and a half (44 milliliters). **b.** the amount contained in a jigger. **2.** jig (def. 3). **3.** any of various machines or mechanical devices that operate with a jerking motion. **4.a.** a light, general-purpose tackle used on a boat or ship. **b.** a small sail set in the stern of a yawl or similar boat. **c.** jiggermast. **5.** a person who jigs. **6.** *Informal.* any small device, article, or part that one is unable to name more precisely; thingamabob. [JIG + -ER¹.]

jig·ger² (jig′ər) *n.* chigger. [Form of CHIGGER.]

jig·ger·mast (jig′ər mast′) *n.* **1.** the aftermost mast of a ship having four or more masts. **2.** a mast in the stern of a yawl or similar boat.

jig·gle (jig′əl) *v.t., v.i.,* **-gled, -gling.** to move or shake up and down or to and fro with quick, slight jerking motions. —*n.* a jiggling movement. [JIG + -LE.]

jig·saw (jig′sô′) *n.* a saw with a narrow blade set in a frame, used to cut curved or irregular lines.

jigsaw puzzle, a puzzle consisting of a set of irregularly shaped cardboard or wooden pieces that can be fitted together to form a picture.

ji·had (ji häd′) *n.* **1.** a war waged by Muslims against those thought to be the enemies of Islam. **2.** an uncompromising strug-

gle or crusade for some belief or principle. [Arabic *jihād* struggle, holy war.]

jilt (jilt) *v.t.* to cast off or desert (a lover or sweetheart). —*n.* a person, esp. a woman, who jilts a lover or sweetheart. [Contraction of earlier *jillet* flirt, wench, diminutive of *Jill*, female proper name once used as a term for a girl or sweetheart.] —**jilt′er**, *n.*

Jim Crow (jim) *also*, **jim crow**. *Informal.* segregation or discrimination against blacks, esp. in the United States. Also, **Jim Crow′ism**. [From *Jim Crow*, the name of a nineteenth-century song sung in a minstrel show.]

jim·my (jim′ē) *n., pl.* **-mies.** a short crowbar, used esp. by burglars. —*v.t.,* **-mied, -my·ing.** to force or pry open with or as with a jimmy: *to jimmy a window.* [From *Jimmy*, familiar form of JAMES; example of the use of a nickname for a tool.]

jim·son·weed (jim′sən wēd′) *also*, **Jimson weed.** *n.* a poisonous, rank-smelling plant, *Datura stramonium*, of the nightshade family, found in the tropics and many parts of North America, having large oval leaves and white or purple trumpet-shaped flowers. Also, **stramonium.** [Modification of *Jamestown weed*, from *Jamestown*, Virginia.]

jin·gle (jing′gəl) *v.,* **-gled, -gling.** —*v.i.* **1.** to make a light, metallic tinkling or ringing sound: *The coins jingled in my pocket.* **2.** to be full of simple, catchy rhymes or repetitions. —*v.t.* to cause to make a tinkling or ringing sound: *to jingle keys.* —*n.* **1.** a light, metallic tinkling or ringing sound: *the jingle of spurs.* **2.** a catchy or repetitious succession of words or sounds, esp. a short, catchy song or piece of verse: *musical jingles used in advertising.* [Imitative.]

jin·gly (jing′glē) *adj.,* **-gli·er, -gli·est.** having, producing, or resembling a jingling sound.

jin·go (jing′gō) *n., pl.* **-goes.** a person whose behavior is characterized by jingoism. —*adj.* of, relating to, or characteristic of jingoes; characterized by jingoism. [From the phrase *by Jingo*, used in an English chauvinistic song of 1878 opposing Russian expansion; *Jingo* possibly a substitute for *Jesus* to avoid giving offense.]

jin·go·ism (jing′gō iz′əm) *n.* extreme, boastful patriotism or chauvinism, marked esp. by the advocacy of an aggressive, warlike foreign policy. —**jin′go·ist**, *n., adj.* —**jin′go·is′tic**, *adj.*

jin·ni (ji nē′, jin′ē) *n., pl.* **jinn** (jin). in Arab folklore and literature, a spirit having magic powers and capable of taking on the form of a human or animal. Also, **genie.**

jin·rick·sha (jin rik′shô) *also*, **jin·rik·i·sha.** *n.* ricksha. [Japanese *jinrikisha* literally, vehicle drawn by a man's strength, from *jin* man + *riki* strength + *sha* vehicle.]

jinx (jingks) *n.* **1.** a person or thing that is believed to bring bad luck. **2.** a spell of bad luck; hex: *to put a jinx on someone.* —*v.t.* to bring or try to bring bad luck to; hex. [Supposedly from Latin *iynx* wryneck (a bird used in witchcraft), from Greek *iynx*.]

jit·ney (jit′nē) *n., pl.* **-neys.** *Informal.* a car or bus that carries passengers for a small fare, usually over a short regular route. [Of uncertain origin.]

jit·ter (jit′ər) *Informal. v.i.* to be nervous or uneasy; fidget. —*n.* **the jitters.** a fit of nervousness; extreme anxiety. [Of uncertain origin.] —**jit′ter·y**, *adj.*

jit·ter·bug (jit′ər bug′) *Informal. n.* **1.** a lively dance, popular esp. during the 1930s and 1940s, consisting chiefly of improvised movements performed to swing music. **2.** a person who does this dance. —*v.i.,* **-bugged, -bug·ging.** to dance the jitterbug.

jiu·jit·su (jü jit′sü) *also*, **jiu·jut·su.** *n.* jujitsu.

jive¹ (jīv) *Slang. n.* **1.** jazz, esp. swing music of the late 1930s and 1940s. **2.** the jargon of jazz musicians and enthusiasts. **3.** deceptive, glib, or meaningless talk. —*v.t., v.i.,* **jived, jiv·ing.** to deceive by or as by glib talk. —*adj.* deceptive or insincere: *jive talk.* [Of uncertain origin.]

jive² (jīv) *v.i.,* **jived, jiv·ing.** *Informal.* jibe³. [Probably from JIBE³.]

jo (jō) *also*, **joe.** *n., pl.* **joes.** *Scottish.* sweetheart; dear. [Form of JOY.]

job (job) *n.* **1.** a position in which one is hired to work; employment: *a part-time job in a publishing company.* **2.** something that has to be done; task, duty, or responsibility: *It's your job to type the memo.* **3.** a specific piece of work, esp. when done for a set fee: *The repair job will cost $300.* **4.** a specific activity or function performed regularly, esp. a profession or occupation. **5.** the quality, product, or result of work: *You did a good job.* **6.** an object or material worked on. **7.** *Informal.* a criminal act, esp. a robbery. **8.** *Informal.* a difficult or exhausting task: *Waxing the car was quite a job.* **9.** a damaging or thoroughly destructive action or piece of work: *The storm did a job on our yard.* —*v.,* **jobbed, job·bing.** —*v.i.* **1.** to do odd or occasional pieces of work; work by the piece. **2.** to act as a middleman or jobber. —*v.t.* **1.** to buy

(goods) in large quantities and sell to dealers in smaller lots. **2.** to sublet (work) among different contractors or workers. —*adj.* of or for a particular task or piece of work; hired or done by the job. [Originally, a piece of work, possibly from obsolete *job* piece; of uncertain origin.]

• **on the job. a.** while working; at work: *to receive training on the job.* **b.** *Informal.* closely attentive to one's task, duty, or responsibility: *a dependable custodian who was always on the job.*

• **to lie down on the job.** *Informal.* to be lax about one's task, duty, or responsibility.

Synonyms *n.* **Job, task, duty,** and **chore** may all denote a piece of work that one does or is expected to do. **Job,** the most general term, often refers to work that is part of one's role or function: *Your job is to tidy up the house while I cook the food for the party. I have the job of opening the office every morning.* A **task** is a well-defined piece of work directed toward a goal, whether self-imposed or otherwise: *I set myself the task of getting all the phone numbers we needed.* **Duty** generally describes an obligatory labor done in the course of one's employment or occupation, or in order to meet some standard: *An officer's duty is to maintain order. Your duties include typing and filing.* **Chore** generally refers to a small job that keeps things going: *Can you help me with some garden chores?*

Job (jōb) *n.* a book of the Old Testament that tells the story of Job, a righteous man who patiently accepts the trials with which God tests his faith. [Late Latin *Iōb* the biblical character, from Greek *Iōb*, from Hebrew *Iyov* literally, persecuted.]

job action, a refusal to work by a group of employees in order to enforce a demand or to protest against some unsatisfactory working condition.

job·ber (job′ər) *n.* **1.** a merchant or business that buys goods, as from a manufacturer, and sells them to retailers; dealer in job lots. **2.** a person who does odd jobs.

job·hold·er (job′hōl′dər) *n.* a person who is regularly employed.

job·less (job′lis) *adj.* **1.** without a job; unemployed. **2.** of or relating to people who are unemployed: *an increase in the jobless rate.* —**job′less·ness**, *n.*

job lot 1. a miscellaneous collection of goods sold by a manufacturer or wholesaler, usually at reduced prices. **2.** any miscellaneous collection, esp. one composed of items of inferior quality.

Jo·cas·ta (jō kas′tə) *n.* in Greek legend, a queen of Thebes who unknowingly married her own son, Oedipus. When she later discovered his identity, she committed suicide.

jock (jok) *n. Slang.* an athlete, esp. an amateur male athlete. [From JOCKSTRAP.]

jock·ey (jok′ē) *n., pl.* **-eys.** a person who rides horses in races, esp. as a profession. —*v.,* **-eyed, -ey·ing.** —*v.i.* **1.** to maneuver, esp. to gain an advantage: *The sailboats in the race jockeyed for position.* **2.** to ride a horse in a race. —*v.t.* **1.** to maneuver or manipulate (a person or thing): *to jockey a car into a parking space.* **2.** to trick; cheat. **3.** to ride (a horse) in a race. [Diminutive of *Jock*, Scottish nickname for JOHN.]

jockey shorts, short, close-fitting underpants worn by boys and men; briefs. *Trademark:* **Jockey.**

jock·o (jok′ō) *n., pl.* **jock·os.** any ape or monkey.

jock·strap (jok′strap′) *also*, **jock strap.** *n.* an elastic support for the male genitals, worn esp. for athletics. Also, **athletic supporter.**

jo·cose (jō kōs′) *adj.* given to or characterized by joking and jesting; merry; playful. [Latin *jocōsus*, from *jocus* jest, game.] —**jo·cose′ly**, *adv.* —**jo·cose′ness**, *n.*

jo·cos·i·ty (jō kos′i tē) *n., pl.* **-ties. 1.** the state or quality of being jocose. **2.** a jocose act or remark; joke or jest.

joc·u·lar (jok′yə lər) *adj.* **1.** given to or characterized by joking and jesting; merry. **2.** of the nature of or intended as a joke; humorous: *a jocular remark.* [Latin *joculāris*, from *joculus* little jest, diminutive of *jocus* jest, game.] —**joc′u·lar·ly**, *adv.*

joc·u·lar·i·ty (jok′yə lar′i tē) *n., pl.* **-ties. 1.** the state or quality of being jocular; merriment. **2.** a jocular act or remark; joke or jest.

joc·und (jok′ənd, jō′kənd) *adj.* showing or feeling mirth and ease; cheerful; merry. [Old French *jocond* pleasant, going back to Latin *jūcundus*.] —**joc′und·ly**, *adv.*

jo·cun·di·ty (jō kun′di tē) *n., pl.* **-ties. 1.** the state or quality of being jocund; cheerfulness. **2.** a jocund act or remark; pleasantry.

a	at	e	end	o	hot	u	up	hw	white		about
ā	ape	ē	me	ō	old	ū	use	ng	song		taken
ä	far	i	it	ô	fork	ū̄	rule	th	thin	ə	pencil
âr	care	ī	ice	oi	oil	u̇	pull	th	this		lemon
		îr	pierce	ou	out	ûr	turn	zh	measure		circus

jodh·purs (jod′pərz) *pl. n.* breeches for horseback riding that are loose above the knee and close-fitting from knee to ankle. [From *Jodhpur,* India, where they were first widely used.]

joe (jō) jo.

Jo·el (jō′əl) *n.* a book of the Old Testament, attributed to the Hebrew prophet Joel.

jo·ey (jō′ē) *n., pl.* **-eys.** a young kangaroo. [From a native Australian name.]

jog¹ (jog) *v.,* **jogged, jog·ging.** —*v.i.* **1.** to run or move at a slow, steady, jolting pace or trot: *The runners jogged lazily around the track.* **2.** to proceed in a slow, steady, or monotonous manner (with *on* or *along*): *The last week of school just jogged along.* —*v.t.* **1.** to jolt or cause to move by shaking or jerking: *The rickety wagon jogged us up and down.* **2.** to give a slight shake or push to; nudge. **3.** to stir or stimulate, esp. the memory. —*n.* **1.** a shake, push, or nudge. **2.** a slow, steady, jolting pace or motion. [Possibly imitative.] —**jog′ger,** *n.*

jog² (jog) *n.* an irregularity in a line or surface; angle, projection, or recess. [Form of JAG¹.]

jodhpurs

jog·ging (jog′ing) *n.* a form of exercise in which a person runs at a slow, steady trot or pace for a distance.

jog·gle¹ (jog′əl) *v.t., v.i.,* **-gled, -gling.** to shake slightly. —*n.* an act or instance of joggling; shake or shaking. [JOG¹ + -LE.]

jog·gle² (jog′əl) *n.* **1.** a projection or a corresponding notch on either of two surfaces, fitted together in order to prevent slipping. **2.** a joint formed in this way. —*v.t.,* **-gled, -gling.** to join or fasten by means of a joggle or joggles. [Probably from JOG².]

jog trot **1.** a slow, regular trot; jog. **2.** a routine or humdrum habit or way of doing something.

john (jon) *n. Informal.* toilet; bathroom. [From JOHN, masculine proper name.]

John (jon) *n.* one of the four Gospels, the fourth book of the New Testament, attributed to the Apostle John. [Medieval Latin *Johannes,* masculine proper name, from Latin *Jōannēs,* from Greek *Iōannēs,* from Hebrew *Yochanan* literally, Jehovah is gracious.]

John Bar·ley·corn (bär′lē kôrn′) a personification of barley as used in malt liquor, of malt liquor itself, or of intoxicating liquors in general.

john·boat (jon′bōt′) *n.* a light, flat-bottomed, square-ended boat for use in shallow bays or rivers, propelled by poling or by rowing.

John Bull **1.** a personification of England or the English. **2.** the typical Englishman.

John Doe **1.** an unknown or fictitious person, esp. a man. ➡ used esp. in legal documents to designate a fictitious man or a man whose real name is not known. **2.** the average man.

John Do·ry (dôr′ē) *pl.* **John Do·rys.** any of several saltwater fish, family Zeidae, commonly found in coastal waters, having a large, pouting mouth and a thin, yellowish brown body marked on each side with a black spot ringed in yellow.

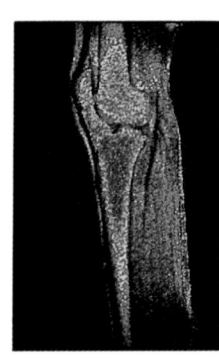

John Han·cock (han′kok) *Informal.* a person's signature or autograph. [From the large, prominent signature of *John Hancock,* 1737-93, American statesman who was the first signer of the Declaration of Independence.]

John Dory

John Hen·ry (hen′rē) in American legend, a black railroad worker of great strength who died proving that he could drive track spikes faster than a steam drill could.

john·ny·cake (jon′ē kāk′) *n.* a flat, crisp bread made of cornmeal, water or milk, flour, and, sometimes, eggs, often baked on a griddle.

John·ny-come-late·ly (jon′ē kum lāt′lē) *n., pl.* **John·ny-come-late·lies** or **John·nies-come-late·ly.** *Informal.* a person who has recently arrived on the scene, esp. someone who belatedly follows a trend.

John·ny-jump-up (jon′ē jump′up′) *n.* a wild pansy, *Viola tricolor,* of the violet family. [Referring to its rapid growth.]

John·ny-on-the-spot (jon′ē ôn thə spot′, -on-) *n. Informal.* a person who is on hand and ready to act whenever needed.

John·ny Reb (jon′ē reb′) *Informal.* a Confederate soldier.

joie de vi·vre (zhwä′ də vē′vRə) *French.* keen enjoyment of life.

join (join) *v.t.* **1.** to bring, put, or fasten together so as to become

one or as one: *a coupler that joins two boxcars, to join hands and form a circle.* **2.** to come into contact or union with: *This road joins the highway up ahead. This bone joins the other at the shoulder.* **3.** to become a member or part of: *to join a club.* **4.** to come or enter into the company of: *Join us at our table when you're done.* **5.** to participate with (someone) in some act or activity: *The rest of the family joins me in expressing our gratitude.* **6.** to unite, combine, or bring together in act, purpose, association, or relationship: *to join forces, to join a couple in marriage.* **7.** to take a place in, with, or among: *This recording now joins the year's top hits.* **8.** *Geometry.* to draw a straight or curved line segment between (points). **9.** *Informal.* adjoin. —*v.i.* **1.** to take part with others; participate (often with *in*): *to join in a conversation.* **2.** to combine or act together in close association; become united or associated (often with *with*): *All segments of the community joined to fight the epidemic.* **3.** to become a member of a group or organization; enlist, as in the armed forces (often with *up*): *They joined up in the last months of the war.* **4.** to come into or be in contact or union: *At what point do the rivers join?* **5.** to meet in battle or conflict: *Our troops joined with enemy forces just outside the city.* —*n.* a place or line of joining; seam; joint; junction. [Old French *joindre* to unite, connect, from Latin *jungere.*]

· **to join battle.** to enter into a battle or conflict: *The armies joined battle on the plain.*

join·er (joi′nər) *n.* **1.** *Informal.* a person who joins many clubs, committees, or other organized activities. **2.** a craftsperson or carpenter who makes woodwork and furniture, esp. one who constructs articles by joining pieces of wood. **3.** a person or thing that joins.

join·er·y (joi′nə rē) *n.* **1.** the skill or trade of a joiner. **2.** woodwork, furniture, or other articles made by a joiner.

joint (joint) *n.* **1.** a place or structure where two or more bones meet or join, usually freely movable. **2.** any place at which, or structure by which, two or more things or parts are joined or fitted together. **3.** a part or section between such places or structures. **4.** one of the portions into which a carcass is cut by a butcher, esp. one containing part of the bone. **5.** *Botany.* a point on a stem from which a leaf or branch grows; node. **6.** *Geology.* a fracture in a rock mass, usually transverse or vertical to the bedding, along which no movement has occurred. **7.** *Slang.* **a.** a cheap or disreputable gathering place: *a gambling joint.* **b.** any building, establishment, or place: *Let me out of this joint.* **8.** *Slang.* a marijuana cigarette. —*adj.* **1.** belonging to or used by two or more; held or shared together: *a joint interest in an enterprise.* **2.** performed or produced by two or more in conjunction: *joint efforts, a joint attack.* **3.** sharing or acting with another or others: *joint owners.* **4.** of or involving both houses or branches of a legislature: *a joint session of Congress.* —*v.t.* **1.** to connect by means of a joint or joints. **2.** to divide or cut at the joints, as meat. [Old French *joint* place where two things touch or join, yoke, from *joindre.* See JOIN.]

· **out of joint.** **a.** out of place at the joint, as a bone. **b.** in an unfavorable, disordered, or inharmonious state.

joint *(def. 1)*
MRI of a
human knee joint

joint account, a bank account in the name of two or more persons, each of whom may deposit or withdraw funds.

Joint Chiefs of Staff, the principal military advisory board to the president of the United States, consisting of a chairperson and the commanding officers of the Army, Air Force, Navy, and Marine Corps.

joint custody, custody of a child shared equally by parents after a divorce or during a separation. ➡ distinguished from **sole custody.**

joint·ed (join′tid) *adj.* having a joint or joints: *a jointed body.*

joint·ly (joint′lē) *adv.* in conjunction; unitedly; together: *The island is administered jointly by the two countries.*

joint resolution, a resolution passed by both houses of Congress and having the force of law if signed by the president.

joint-stock company, a business organization whose capital is held in transferable shares of stock by its joint owners, similar to a corporation, but differing in that the shareholders are personally liable for the debts of the business.

join·ture (join′chər) *n.* property settled on a married woman by her husband, to be given to her after his death. [Middle French

jointure a joining, yoking together, from Latin *jūnctūra* a joining. Doublet of JUNCTURE.]

joist (joist) *n.* one of a series of parallel beams to which the boards of a floor or the laths of a ceiling are fastened. [Old French *giste* such a beam, bed, going back to Latin *jacēre* to lie.]

jo·jo·ba (hō hō′bə) *n.* a shrub, *Simmondsia chinensis,* of the boxwood family, native to the southwestern United States, whose seed contains a cosmetic oil.

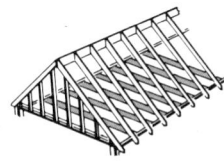

joists

joke (jōk) *n.* **1.** an anecdote or story, usually having a punch line or funny climax, intended to provoke laughter or amusement. **2.** anything said or done to provoke laughter or amusement, as a humorous remark or a prank: *She hid my keys as a joke.* **3.** a person or thing exciting amusement or ridicule; object of laughter or jesting; laughingstock: *The whole class thought the play was a joke.* **4.** something not to be taken seriously; matter of little or no importance; trifle: *He tried to treat his failure as a joke.* —*v.i.,* **joked, jok·ing. 1.** to tell or make jokes; speak or act in a playful, merry way (often with *around*): *Our predicament is nothing to joke about. You're always joking around when you should be working.* **2.** to say something in jest, rather than in earnest: *I'm not joking—I really do have measles.* [Latin *jocus* jest, game.] —**jok′ing·ly,** *adv.*

jok·er (jō′kər) *n.* **1.** a person who jokes or is given to joking. **2.** either of two extra playing cards provided with a standard deck, often bearing a picture of a jester and used in certain games as a wild card or as trump. **3.a.** a hidden, ambiguous, or seemingly unimportant clause, phrase, or wording in a document, as a piece of legislation, that partially or completely defeats its purpose or changes its original or intended meaning. **b.** any hidden or unexpected hindrance. **4.** *Informal.* **a.** a prankster, practical joker, or smart aleck: *Who's the joker who switched the name plates around?* **b.** a man or fellow, esp. one who seems unimpressive or worthy of contempt.

joke·ster (jōk′stər) *n.* a person who makes jokes or plays pranks.

jol·li·fi·ca·tion (jol′ə fi kā′shən) *n.* merrymaking; jollity.

jol·li·ty (jol′i tē) *n., pl.* **-ties. 1.** the state or quality of being jolly. **2.** *British.* a festive occasion or gathering.

jol·ly (jol′ē) *adj.,* **-li·er, -li·est. 1.** full of fun, good humor, and high spirits: *a jolly companion.* **2.** characterized by or causing mirth, gaiety, or good cheer: *a jolly song, jolly laughter.* **3.** *British. Informal.* **a.** pleasant; agreeable; delightful: *How jolly it will be to see them again!* **b.** great; large; remarkable: *You've gotten yourself into a jolly mess.* —*adv. British. Informal.* extremely; very; remarkably: *It was jolly good of you to help.* —*v.t.,* **-lied, -ly·ing.** *Informal.* to amuse, humor, or flatter so as to put or keep in a good mood (often with *up* or *along*): *We tried to jolly them up.* [Old French *joli(f)* gay, festive, pretty, from Old Norse *jōl* Yule, feast.] —**jol′li·ly,** *adv.* —**jol′li·ness,** *n.*

jolly boat, a small, general-purpose boat carried on a ship. [Possibly from Danish *jolle* yawl + BOAT.]

Jolly Rog·er (roj′ər) a flag with a skull and crossbones, usually white on a black field, esp. one flown by pirates.

jolt (jōlt) *v.t.* **1.** to cause to move with a rough, jerky motion; jar or shake up with or as with a sudden bump or blow: *The impact of the collision jolted us.* **2.** to shock or surprise: *The tragedy jolted us all.* **3.** to bring or put abruptly or roughly into a specified state or condition: *to jolt someone out of a daydream.* —*v.i.* to move with an abrupt jerk or in a succession of abrupt, bumpy jerks: *The train jolted forward. The carriage jolted along the dirt road.* —*n.* **1.** a rough, jerky motion: *The wagon stopped with a jolt.* **2.** an abrupt surprise or emotional shock: *The news gave me quite a jolt.* [Of uncertain origin.]

Jo·nah (jō′nə) *n.* **1.** a book of the Old Testament, containing the story and prophecies of Jonah. **2.** a person whose presence supposedly brings bad luck; jinx. [(*Def. 2*) From *Jonah,* an Old Testament figure who disobeyed God's command, causing a storm that endangered the ship he was on.]

Jon·a·than (jon′ə thən) *n.* an apple of a variety having a bright red color and ripening in the late autumn.

jon·gleur (jong′glər; *French* zhôn glœR′) *n.* in medieval France and England, a wandering minstrel, juggler, going back to Latin *joculātor* jester.]

jon·quil (jong′kwəl, jon′-) *n.* **1.** the fragrant yellow flower of a plant, *Narcissus jonquilla,* resembling the daffodil, having six petallike segments surrounding a shallow, cup-shaped structure. **2.** the slender plant bearing this flower, having shiny dark green leaves and grown from bulbs. [French *jonquille* this plant, from

Spanish *junquillo,* diminutive of *junco* reed, from Latin *juncus;* because of its reedlike leaves.]

Jor·dan almond (jôr′dən) **1.** a large almond of a variety from Spain, widely used in confectionery. **2.** an almond covered with a hard, colored sugar coating. [Modification of Middle English *jardyne almaunde* literally, garden almond, from Old French *jardin* garden + *almande* almond. See JARDINIERE, ALMOND.]

jo·rum (jôr′əm) *n.* **1.** a large drinking bowl. **2.** its contents: *a jorum of punch.* [From *Joram,* Old Testament character who brought metal vessels to David.]

jo·seph (jō′zəf, -səf) *n.* a long coat or cloak with a cape, worn chiefly by women in the eighteenth century for horseback riding. [From the many-colored coat of the Old Testament figure *Joseph.*]

josh (josh) *Informal. v.t.* to make good-natured fun of; tease playfully: *I'm only joshing you.* —*v.i.* to indulge in lighthearted, playful teasing. [Of uncertain origin.] —**josh′er,** *n.*

Josh., Joshua.

Josh·u·a (josh′ü ə) *n.* a book of the Old Testament, containing the history of the Israelites from the death of Moses to the settlement in Canaan. [Hebrew *Yehoshua* literally, Jehovah is salvation.]

Joshua tree, a tall, treelike plant, *Yucca brevifolia,* of arid or desert regions of the southwestern United States, having extended, forking branches and bearing clusters of white or greenish white flowers. [From the resemblance of its extended branches to the outstretched arms of *Joshua* as described in the Old Testament.]

Joshua tree

joss (jos) *n.* an image or idol of a Chinese god. [Pidgin English modification of Portuguese *deos* a god, from Latin *deus.*]

joss house, a Chinese temple or shrine containing idols.

joss stick, a slender stick of dried fragrant paste, burned as incense, as before a joss.

jos·tle (jos′əl) *also,* **justle.** *v.t., v.i.,* **-tled, -tling.** to bump, push, or shove roughly, as with the elbows in a crowd. —*n.* a bump, push, or shove; a jostling. [JOUST + -LE.] —**jos′tler,** *n.*

Jos·u·e (jos′ü ē′) *n.* in the Douay Bible, Joshua.

jot (jot) *n.* the least or smallest bit; iota; whit: *Their superior attitude didn't impress me a jot.* —*v.t.,* **jot·ted, jot·ting.** to make a brief and hasty note of (often with *down*): *Let me jot down your telephone number.* [Latin *iōta* iota, the Greek letter *ι,* from Greek *iōta* (the smallest letter of the Greek alphabet); of Semitic origin. Doublet of IOTA.] —**jot′ter,** *n.*

Jo·tun (yô′tün) *also,* **Jo·tunn, Jö·tunn.** *n.* in Norse mythology, one of a race of giants who were enemies of the gods. [Old Norse *jötunn* giant.]

Jo·tun·heim (yô′tün hām′) *also,* **Jo·tunn·heim, Jö·tunn·heim.** *n.* the home of the Jotuns.

joule (jül, joul) *n. Physics.* a unit of work or energy in the meter-kilogram-second system of units, equal to the work done by a force of 1 newton acting through a distance of 1 meter. The joule is equivalent to 10^7 ergs. [From James P. *Joule,* 1818-89, English physicist.]

a	at	e	end	o	hot	u	up	hw	white		about
ā	ape	ē	me	ō	old	ū	use	ng	song		taken
ä	far	i	it	ô	fork	ü	rule	th	thin	ə	pencil
âr	care	ī	ice	oi	oil	u̇	pull	th	this		lemon
		îr	pierce	ou	out	ûr	turn	zh	measure		circus

jounce (jouns) *v.t., v.i.,* **jounced, jounc·ing.** to move or shake up and down roughly; bounce; jolt. —*n.* a sudden, rough bump; bounce; jolt.

jour·nal (jûr′nəl) *n.* **1.** a record or account, esp. one kept daily, of occurrences, experiences, or observations. **2.** an official record, usually one kept daily, of proceedings or transactions, as the register of a legislative body. **3.** a magazine or periodical, esp. one dealing with matters of current interest in a particular area: *The study appeared in a leading medical journal.* **4.** a newspaper, esp. one published daily. **5.** the part of a shaft or axle turning within a bearing. **6.** daybook *(def. 1).* [French *journal* newspaper, diary, from Old French *jornal* daily, from Latin *diurnālis,* going back to *diēs* day. Doublet of DIURNAL.]

Synonyms **Journal** and **periodical** denote a publication that appears at stated intervals. **Journal** is generally used to describe publications that present the current news or views of a particular group or society: *a medical journal, the journal of a scientific society.* **Periodical** is used generally of publications that appear regularly but at intervals of more than a day: *Monthly magazines and weekly newsletters are two kinds of periodical.*

jour·nal·ese (jûr′nə lēz′, -lēs′) *n.* a slick, superficial style of writing that uses informal or colorful language, slang, fad expressions, and clichés, considered to be characteristic of newspapers and magazines.

jour·nal·ism (jûr′nə liz′əm) *n.* **1.** the collecting, interpreting, or presenting of facts and opinions about current events and topics of public interest, esp. in newspapers and magazines or over television and radio. **2.** the occupation or study of this.

jour·nal·ist (jûr′nə list) *n.* a person whose occupation is journalism.

jour·nal·is·tic (jûr′nə lis′tik) *adj.* of, relating to, or characteristic of journalism or journalists. —**jour′nal·is′ti·cal·ly,** *adv.*

jour·ney (jûr′nē) *n., pl.* **-neys. 1.** a trip, esp. one over a considerable distance or taking considerable time: *a journey across the United States.* **2.** a distance traveled, or that can be traveled, in a specified time: *The town is four days' journey from here.* —*v.,* **-neyed, -ney·ing.** —*v.i.* to make a trip; travel: *to journey through Europe.* —*v.t.* to travel over or through: *We journeyed Ireland last summer.* [Old French *journee* day, a day's travel, a day's work, going back to Latin *diurnus* daily, from *diēs* day.] —**jour′ney·er,** *n.*

Synonyms *n.* **Journey, voyage,** and **trip** denote travel from one place to another. **Journey** originally denoted one day's travel but now is used in a general sense: *a journey to the capital, a month-long journey.* **Voyage** implies length, and is used chiefly of travel by sea: *a voyage from Lisbon to Rio.* **Trip** is used chiefly of shorter travels, and implies a purpose: *a business trip, a trip to see the volcano.*

jour·ney·man (jûr′nē mən) *n., pl.* **-men** (-mən). **1.** a worker who has completed an apprenticeship in a trade, craft, or skill, but who is not yet eligible to become a master and works for another. **2.** an experienced, qualified, and competent worker. **3.** a worker who does competent but undistinguished work. [From obsolete *journey* a day's work (from Old French *journee*) + MAN. See JOURNEY.]

joust (joust) *also,* **just.** *n.* **1.** a formal combat, often part of a tournament, between two mounted knights or other individuals armed with lances and other weapons. **2. jousts.** a series of such confrontations; tournament. **3.** any combat, confrontation, or struggle resembling a joust. —*v.i.* to engage in a joust. [Old French *jouste,* from *jouster* to meet, joust, tourney, from Late Latin *iuxtāre* to approach, join, from Latin *iuxtā* near.] —**joust′er,** *n.*

Jove (jōv) *n.* **1.** Jupiter *(def. 1).* **2.** *Archaic.* the planet Jupiter. [Latin *Jov-,* stem of oblique cases of *Jupiter.*]

jo·vi·al (jō′vē əl) *adj.* characterized by hearty, good-natured humor and conviviality; merry; jolly. [Late Latin *Joviālis* relating to Jove or Jupiter, from Latin *Jov-.* See JOVE. From the belief that people born under the sign of the planet Jupiter were happy and jolly.] —**jo′vi·al·ly,** *adv.* —**jo′vi·al·ness,** *n.*

jo·vi·al·i·ty (jō′vē al′i te) *n.* the state or quality of being jovial; jollity; merriment.

Jo·vi·an (jō′vē ən) *adj.* of, relating to, or like Jove or the planet Jupiter.

jowl[1] (joul, jōl) *n.* **1.** flabby, sagging flesh hanging from or under the lower jaw. **2.** any fleshy part, as the dewlap of cattle or the wattle of fowl. [Old English *ceole* throat.]

jowl[2] (joul, jōl) *n.* **1.** the jawbone or jaw, esp. the lower jaw. **2.** cheek. [Old English *ceafl* jaw.]

joy (joi) *n.* **1.** a strong feeling of pleasure, happiness, or delight, as that arising from present or expected gratification or good. **2.** a person or thing that is the source or cause of such feeling. **3.** an expression or manifestation of happiness; outward rejoicing.

—*v.i.* to feel joy. [Old French *joie,* from Latin *gaudia,* plural of *gaudium.*]

joy·ance (joi′əns) *n. Archaic.* enjoyment; delight; gladness.

joy·ful (joi′fəl) *adj.* **1.** full of joy; feeling joy. **2.** showing joy: *a joyful look.* **3.** causing joy: *a joyful sight.* —**joy′ful·ly,** *adv.* —**joy′ful·ness,** *n.* —For Synonyms, see glad[1].

joy·less (joi′lis) *adj.* feeling, expressing, or causing no joy; completely lacking in joy: *a joyless smile, a joyless existence.* —**joy′less·ly,** *adv.* —**joy′less·ness,** *n.*

joy·ous (joi′əs) *adj.* feeling, showing, or causing joy; marked by rejoicing. —**joy′ous·ly,** *adv.* —**joy′ous·ness,** *n.*

joy·ride (joi′rīd′) *Informal. n.* **1.** a reckless automobile ride, esp. in a stolen vehicle, taken purely for fun or amusement. **2.** something, as a venture, resembling this, marked by recklessness, danger, or disregard for consequences. —*v.i.,* **-rode** (-rōd′), **-rid·den** (-rid′ən), **-rid·ing.** to take a joyride. —**joy′rid′er,** *n.*

joy·stick (joi′stik′) *n.* **1.** the flight control lever of an aircraft or other vehicle. **2.** a lever, usually connected to a computer or video game player, that can be moved in any direction to control the movement of a cursor in some programs or the movement of a character or playing piece in some games.

JP *also,* **J.P.** justice of the peace.

jr., junior.

ju·bi·lant (jü′bə lənt) *adj.* joyfully elated or triumphant; exultant: *After the contest, the victor was jubilant.* [Latin *jūbilāns,* present participle of *jūbilāre* to shout with joy.] —**ju′bi·lance, ju′bi·lan·cy,** *n.* —**ju′bi·lant·ly,** *adv.*

ju·bi·late (jü′bə lāt′) *v.i.,* **-lat·ed, -lat·ing.** to feel or express great joy; rejoice; exult. [Latin *jūbilātus,* past participle of *jūbilāre* to shout with joy.]

Ju·bi·la·te (ü′bi lä′tā; jü′-) *n.* **1.** in the Old Testament, the One-hundredth Psalm, or, in the Douay Bible, the Ninety-ninth Psalm. **2.** the third Sunday after Easter. [Latin *jūbilāte,* imperative of *jūbilāre* to shout with joy; the first word of the Latin version of the psalm.]

ju·bi·la·tion (jü′bə lā′shən) *n.* **1.** a feeling of elated or triumphant joy. **2.** the act of rejoicing; exultation.

ju·bi·lee (jü′bə lē′, jü′bə lē′) *n.* **1.a.** a special anniversary, esp. a twenty-fifth or fiftieth anniversary. **b.** the celebration of such an anniversary. **2.** a year, season, or occasion of joyful celebration and rejoicing. **3.** great joy; rejoicing. **4.** among the ancient Hebrews, a yearlong celebration held every fifty years, during which time slaves were freed, debts were forgiven, and fields were left uncultivated. **5.** in the Roman Catholic Church, a year in which punishment for sin is remitted after repentance and the fulfillment of certain conditions. It occurs every twenty-five years. [Old French *jubile,* from Late Latin *jūbilaeus* year of jubilee among the Hebrews, going back to Greek *iōbēlos,* from Hebrew *yovel,* originally, ram's horn; because such a horn was sounded to proclaim the year of jubilee on the Day of Atonement every fiftieth year.]

Judaeo-, form of **Judeo-.**

Ju·da·ic (jü dā′ik) *adj.* of or relating to Jews or Judaism. Also, **Ju·da′i·cal.**

Ju·da·ism (jü′dē iz′əm, -dā-) *n.* **1.** the monotheistic religion followed by the Jews, based chiefly on the Old Testament and the teachings of the Talmud and marked by the observance of the Mosaic law and adherence to certain principles of ethical conduct. Judaism has three branches: Orthodox, Conservative, and Reform. **2.** the observance of the practices and ceremonies of this religion. **3.** the cultural, social, and intellectual tradition and heritage associated with this religion. **4.** Jews collectively; Jewry.

Ju·da·ize (jü′dē īz′, -dā-) *v.,* **-ized, -iz·ing.** —*v.t.* to bring into conformity with Judaism. —*v.i.* to conform to Judaism.

Ju·das (jü′dəs) *also,* **ju·das.** *n.* a treacherous betrayer or traitor, esp. one who betrays under the guise of friendship. [From *Judas,* in the New Testament, the Apostle who betrayed Jesus.]

judas goat *also,* **Judas goat. 1.** a goat used to lead unsuspecting sheep or other animals to their slaughter. **2.** a person who betrays unsuspecting persons by leading them to their death or into a trap or ambush. [From *Judas,* in the New Testament, the Apostle who betrayed Jesus.]

Judas tree, redbud. [Because *Judas* Iscariot, according to legend, is said to have hanged himself from such a tree.]

Jude (jüd) *n.* a book of the New Testament, often attributed to the Apostle Jude.

Judeo- *also,* **Judaeo-.** *combining form* Jewish: *Judeo-Christian.* [Latin *Jūdaeus* Jewish, Jew. See JEW.]

Ju·de·o·Chris·tian (jü dā′ō kris′chən) *adj.* based on or relating to both Judaism and Christianity: *in the Judeo-Christian tradition.*

Judg., Judges.

judge (juj) *v.,* **judged, judg·ing.** —*v.t.* **1.** to hear and decide by official authority the merits or guilt of: *to judge a case impartially.* **2.** to settle or decide authoritatively, as a contest, competition, or

dispute: *Who's judging the first race?* **3.** to form an opinion, estimate, or evaluation of: *Judge them by their actions, not their appearance. I can't judge the distance in this light.* **4.** to criticize; condemn; censure. **5.** to think; suppose; consider: *I judge it to be midnight.* —*v.i.* **1.** to form an opinion, estimate, or critical evaluation: *Listen to both sides of the story and judge for yourself.* **2.** to act or decide as a judge: *You'll have to judge between four contestants.* —*n.* **1.** an appointed or elected official who has authority to hear and decide, or to preside over, cases in a court of law. **2.** a person appointed to decide in any contest, competition, or dispute; arbiter: *The judges awarded first prize to the mastiff.* **3.** anyone qualified to form and pronounce an opinion and make critical evaluations (about a particular subject): *I'm no judge when it comes to opera.* **4.** one of the rulers of Israel during the period between the death of Joshua and the reign of Saul. [Old French *juge* official who decides cases in a court of law, from Latin *jūdex* arbiter, juror, from *jūs* law + *dīcere* to say.] —**judg'er,** *n.*

judge advocate *pl.* **judge advocates.** a staff officer whose duty is to administer military law and advise the commanding officer on legal questions.

judge advocate general *pl.* **judge advocates general** or **judge advocate generals.** in the U.S. Army, Navy, and Air Force, the head of the legal department of each service.

Judg·es (juj'iz) *n.* a book of the Old Testament, containing the history of the Israelites from the death of Joshua to the birth of Samuel. ➡ used as singular.

judge·ship (juj'ship') *n.* the position, function, or term of office of a judge.

judg·ment (juj'mənt) *also,* **judge·ment.** *n.* **1.** the faculty of judging; ability to judge, discern, or make decisions wisely: *a person of judgment, to show good judgment.* **2.** the act of judging. **3.** the result of judging; opinion or conclusion reached through judging: *In my judgment, they've got nothing to worry about. Form your own judgment of what's going on.* **4.** *Law.* **a.** a decree, verdict, order, or sentence handed down by a court of law. **b.** an obligation arising from such a decree, verdict, or order, as a debt or the duty to fulfill a legal contract. **c.** a document embodying such a decree, verdict, or order. **5.** a misfortune considered to be sent by God as a punishment for sin. **6.** *also,* **Judgment.** Judgment Day. —For Synonyms, see **verdict.**

judg·men·tal (juj men'təl) *adj.* **1.** of, relating to, or using judgment. **2.** forming or tending to form subjective, moralistic judgments.

Judgment Day *also,* **judgment day.** in some religions, the day of God's final judgment of human beings, which is to occur on the day the world ends. Also, **Day of Judgment, Last Judgment, Doomsday.**

ju·di·ca·to·ry (jü'di kə tôr'ē) *adj.* of or relating to the administration of justice. —*n., pl.* **-ries. 1.** a body of persons having judicial authority; court of justice; tribunal. **2.** the system of administration of justice. [Late Latin *jūdicātōrius* relating to judging, from Latin *jūdicāre* to judge, decide.]

ju·di·ca·ture (jü'di kā'chər, -kə chûr') *n.* **1.** the administration of justice. **2.** the right, power, or authority to administer justice; extent of jurisdiction of a judge or court. **3.** a court of law. **4.** the system of courts of law; judges or courts of law collectively. [Medieval Latin *judicatura* office of a judge, from Latin *jūdicāre* to judge, decide.]

ju·di·cial (jü dish'əl) *adj.* **1.** of or relating to courts of law, to the administration of justice, or to the application and interpretation of the law: *judicial proceedings, the judicial branch of the government.* **2.** of, relating to, or appropriate to a judge, judges, or the office of a judge: *judicial robes, judicial authority.* **3.** decreed or enforced by a judge or a court: *a judicial decision.* **4.** inclined to make judgments; critical; discriminating; judicious. [Latin *jūdiciālis* relating to law courts, from *jūdicium* judgment, trial.] —**ju·di'cial·ly,** *adv.*

ju·di·ci·ar·y (jü dish'ē er'ē) *n., pl.* **-ar·ies. 1.** the branch of government that is invested with judicial power and that interprets and applies the law. **2.** the system of courts, as of a country. **3.** the judges of these courts collectively. —*adj.* of or relating to judges, courts of law, or to judgments made in courts of law.

ju·di·cious (jü dish'əs) *adj.* **1.** having or exercising good judgment; wise; sensible: *a judicious leader.* **2.** marked by or proceeding from good judgment: *a judicious plan of operations.* [French *judicieux,* going back to Latin *jūdicium* judgment, trial.] —**ju·di'cious·ly,** *adv.* —**ju·di'cious·ness,** *n.*

Ju·dith (jü'dith) *n.* a book of the Protestant Apocrypha and of the Douay Bible that relates the story of the Jewish heroine Judith.

ju·do (jü'dō) *n.* **1.** a method of unarmed combat and self-defense related to but less violent than jujitsu and karate. It developed from jujitsu. **2.** the sport of fighting by this method. [Japanese *jūdō,* from *jū* gentle + *dō* way.]

Ju·dy (jü'dē) *n.* the wife of the puppet Punch.

jug (jug) *n.* **1.** a rounded vessel of earthenware, glass, or other material, with a handle and a narrow neck that usually has a stopper or cap, used chiefly for holding liquids. **2.** a pitcher or similar vessel for liquids. **3.a.** a jug and its contents: *There are three jugs of cider on the shelf.* **b.** the contents of a jug: *We drank a jug of milk.* **4.** *Slang.* jail; prison. —*v.t.,* **jugged, jug·ging. 1.** to put or cook in a jug. **2.** *Slang.* to jail; imprison. [Possibly from *Jug,* an earlier nickname for the proper name *Joan* (used humorously to refer to such a vessel).]

jug band, a small band that uses simple or improvised instruments, such as jugs, washboards, and kazoos, esp. to play folk music or blues.

jug·ger·naut (jug'ər nôt') *n.* **1.** any overpowering force or object that advances relentlessly and destroys whatever is in its path. **2.** something, as a custom or belief, to which people blindly devote themselves or are ruthlessly sacrificed. [From JUGGERNAUT.]

Jug·ger·naut (jug'ər nôt') *n.* an idol of the Hindu god Krishna, annually drawn in procession on a huge car under whose wheels devotees of the god are said to have thrown themselves to be crushed to death. Also, **Jagannath.** [Hindi *Jagannāth* lord of the world, from Sanskrit *Jagannātha.*]

jug·gle (jug'əl) *v.,* **-gled, -gling.** —*v.t.* **1.** to keep (two or more balls or other objects) in continuous motion from the hands into the air by skillfully tossing and catching in rapid succession: *I can juggle four oranges at once.* **2.** to change or manipulate in order to deceive or defraud: *The embezzler juggled the firm's financial records.* **3.** to attempt to balance or handle; hold, balance, or handle precariously: *He juggled his books and the baseball bats as we walked down the block.* **4.** to deal with (two or more jobs, activities, or the like) at the same time: *This year she's juggling going to school, working part-time, and taking tennis lessons.* —*v.i.* **1.** to perform or entertain as a juggler. **2.** to practice artifice and trickery with the intent of deceiving or defrauding. —*n.* **1.** the act of juggling. **2.** a trick; deception; fraud. [Old French *jogler* to jest, from Latin *joculārī.*]

jug·gler (jug'lər) *n.* **1.** a person whose work or occupation is juggling or performing juggling feats: *a circus juggler.* **2.** a person who practices deception or fraud. [Old French *jougleor* jester, from Latin *joculātor.*]

jug·gler·y (jug'lə rē) *n., pl.* **-gler·ies. 1.** the skill or tricks of a juggler; sleight of hand. **2.** trickery; deception; fraud.

jug·u·lar (jug'yə lər) *adj.* **1.** of or relating to the neck or throat. **2.** of or relating to the jugular vein. —*n.* jugular vein. [Modern Latin *jugularis,* from Latin *jugulum* collarbone, diminutive of *jugum* yoke; because the jugular vein is near the *jugulum,* or collarbone, which *yokes* the shoulder and neck.]

jugular vein, either of the two large blood vessels on either side of the neck that return blood from the head and neck to the heart.

juice (jüs) *n.* **1.** fluid contained in a plant or in plant tissues, esp. that extracted from a fruit or vegetable for use as a drink. **2.** fluid contained in animal flesh or tissues: *Let the roast cook in its own juices.* **3.** fluid secreted in animal tissue: *gastric juices, intestinal juices.* **4.** *Slang.* electric current. **5.** *Slang.* vigor; vitality. **6.** *Slang.* gasoline, oil, or other liquid fuel. —*v.t.,* **juiced, juicing.** to extract the juice from. [Old French *jus* broth, sauce, from Latin *jūs.*]

• **to juice up.** to give life, spirit, or interest to: *to juice up a party with music.*

juic·er (jü'sər) *n.* an appliance for extracting juice from fruits and vegetables.

juic·y (jü'sē) *adj.,* **juic·i·er, juic·i·est. 1.** having much juice; succulent: *a juicy orange.* **2.** full of interest; colorful; lively: *juicy gossip.* —**juic'i·ly,** *adv.* —**juic'i·ness,** *n.*

ju·jit·su (jü jit'sü) *also,* **jiu·jit·su, jiu·jut·su.** *n.* a Japanese method of unarmed self-defense or combat, related to judo and karate, that employs skill and anatomical knowledge to turn the strength and weight of an opponent to one's own advantage. [Japanese *jūjutsu,* from *jū* gentle + *jutsu* art.]

ju·jube (jü'jüb') *n.* **1.** a fruit-flavored, gelatinous candy or lozenge. **2.** the edible plumlike fruit of a shrub or small tree, *Ziziphus jujuba* or *Z. mauritiana,* that is preserved in various ways and made into candy. **3.** the shrub or tree bearing this fruit, cultivated in warm regions throughout the world. [Old French *jujube* the plumlike fruit, going back to Latin *zizyphum,* from Greek *zizyphon.*]

juke·box (jük'boks') *n.* a phonograph, usually coin-operated

a	at	e	end	o	hot	u	up	hw	white		about
ā	ape	ē	me	ō	old	ū	use	ng	song	ə	taken
ä	far	i	it	ô	fork	ü	rule	th	thin		pencil
âr	care	ī	ice	oi	oil	u̇	pull	th	this		lemon
		îr	pierce	ou	out	ûr	turn	zh	measure		circus

and encased in a cabinet, that allows for a choice of records to be played, as by pushing one or more of a series of buttons. [From Gullah *juke* disorderly + BOX¹.]

Jul., July.

ju·lep (jŭ′ləp) *n.* **1.** mint julep. **2.** a sweet drink made of sugar or syrup, flavoring, and water, often taken with medicine. [French *julep,* through Spanish and Arabic, from Persian *gulāb* rose water.]

Jul·ian (jŭl′yən) *adj.* of, relating to, or named for the Roman statesman Julius Caesar.

Julian calendar, a calendar established by the Roman statesman Julius Caesar, providing for 365 days in a year with every fourth year having 366 days. The order of months in the year corresponded to the almost universally used present-day Gregorian calendar.

ju·li·enne (jŭ′lē en′) *adj.* cut into thin strips: *julienne carrots, julienne potatoes.* —*n.* a clear soup containing vegetables cut in such a manner. [French *julienne* the soup, possibly from a chef named *Julien.*]

Ju·liet (jŭl′yət, jŭ′lē ət, -et′) *n.* the heroine of Shakespeare's tragedy *Romeo and Juliet.*

Ju·ly (jŭ lī′) *n., pl.* **-lies.** the seventh month of the year, containing thirty-one days. [Middle English *Julie,* from Norman French *Julie,* from Latin *Jūlius,* from the Roman statesman *Julius* Caesar, who was born in this month.]

jum·ble (jŭm′bəl) *v.t.,* **-bled, -bling. 1.** to mix or throw in confusion and disorder: *All the toys were jumbled together in the box.* **2.** to confuse mentally; muddle. —*n.* **1.** a confused or disordered mixture, collection, or mass. **2.** a state of disorder or confusion. [Probably imitative.]

jum·bo (jŭm′bō) *Informal. adj.* extremely large: *a jumbo ice-cream cone.* —*n., pl.* **-bos.** a person, animal, or thing that is unusually large for its kind. [Probably from *Jumbo,* name of a huge circus elephant exhibited by the American showman P. T. Barnum, 1810-91.]

jump (jŭmp) *v.i.* **1.** to spring into the air, esp. to spring free from the ground or other surface by a sudden propelling effort, as of the feet and legs: *to jump to catch a ball.* **2.** to move or go suddenly or abruptly, as with a bounding movement: *They jumped under the table when they heard the shots.* **3.** to start involuntarily, as in surprise or fright: *She always jumps when the phone rings.* **4.** to move with a sudden, spasmodic jerk or twitch: *The needle jumped when we turned on the car's ignition.* **5.** to increase or rise suddenly: *His temperature jumped sharply.* **6.** to come or pass abruptly, as by omitting necessary intermediate points: *to jump to a hasty conclusion, to jump to the last page of a book.* **7.** to accept or grab hastily and eagerly (with *at*): *to jump at a chance, to jump at an offer.* **8.** to enter or join with eagerness or vigor (with *in* or *into*): *She jumped into the discussion as soon as the subject came up.* **9.** to attack with abuse; criticize or scold harshly (often with *at*): *He jumped at me for not agreeing to his proposal.* **10.** *Informal.* to respond, obey, or act without question or delay: *When the sergeant gives an order, we jump.* **11.** *Slang.* to be filled with or show signs of vigorous, pulsating activity; be lively or vibrant: *The club is jumping tonight.* **12.** in the game of checkers, to capture an opponent's piece by passing one's own directly over it to a vacant square. **13.** *Bridge.* to make a jump bid. —*v.t.* **1.** to spring over or across: *to jump a fence.* **2.** to cause to jump: *to jump a pony across a brook.* **3.** to pass over or by (something intermediate); skip; bypass: *The typewriter jumped three spaces.* **4.** to move or start before (the proper time or signal); anticipate: *The driver jumped the green light at the corner.* **5.** to leave or depart from (a usual course or track) abruptly: *The locomotive jumped the rails.* **6.** *Informal.* to attack by surprise; pounce upon: *The intruders jumped the victim at the door.* **7.** *Informal.* to board hastily or by jumping: *to jump a train.* **8.** in the game of checkers, to capture (an opponent's piece) by passing one's own piece directly over to a vacant square. **9.** *Bridge.* to make (a jump bid). **10.** jump-start. —*n.* **1.** an instance of jumping; spring; leap: *The dog cleared the stream with one jump.* **2.** a place or thing to be jumped over or across: *There were five jumps in the race. The second jump was a tall hedge.* **3.** the distance or space covered by a jump: *a jump of eight feet.* **4.** a sudden start or jerk, as in surprise or fright. **5.** a sudden increase or rise: *a jump in prices.* **6.** a sudden and abrupt transition, as with omission of something intermediate: *to make a jump from one subject to another.* **7.** any of a number of sports contests in jumping. **8.** a leap by parachute from an airplane. **9.** in the game of checkers, a move made by jumping. —*adj. Military.* of, relating to, or used by paratroops: *jump area, jump boots, jump school.* [Probably imitative.]

• **to get** (or **have**) **the jump on.** *Informal.* to get or have a head start or advantage over.

• **to jump a claim.** to take possession of something belonging to another, as a mining claim, by fraud or force.

• **to jump bail.** to forfeit one's bail by absconding when free on bail.

• **to jump on** (or **all over**). to berate or criticize, esp. hastily or without reflection.

• **to jump ship. a.** to desert from service in a ship's crew. **b.** to abandon or withdraw support from a particular group or cause; desert.

• **to jump the gun. a.** to start or act prematurely or too hastily. **b.** to leap to a premature conclusion.

Synonyms *v.i.* **Jump, leap, spring,** and **bound²** mean to move through space with a quick motion. **Jump,** the most common term, connotes propelling oneself upward, usually from one point to another: *to jump across a brook, to jump over a stool.* **Leap** suggests a greater or more strenuous jump: *The monkeys leaped from tree to tree.* **Spring** suggests grace and agility: *The tiger sprang on its unsuspecting prey.* **Bound** describes a series of leaps: *An enormous dog bounded into the room.*

jump ball, a basketball tossed up by the referee between two opposing players who jump up and try to tap it to a teammate to put it into play.

jump bid, a bid in bridge that is higher than necessary to reach the next level, usually made to show strength.

jump·er¹ (jŭm′pər) *n.* **1.** a person or thing that jumps. **2.a.** a cable, wire, or other conductor used, usually temporarily, to complete or bypass a circuit. **b.** jumper cable. [JUMP + -ER¹.]

jump·er² (jŭm′pər) *n.* **1.** a one-piece, sleeveless dress, usually worn over a blouse or sweater. **2.** a loose shirt, smock, or jacket worn over other clothes to protect them, as by sailors or workers. **3.** jumpers. rompers. [From dialectal *jump* kind of short coat, from French *jupe* petticoat, skirt, from Spanish *aljuba* kind of Moorish garment, from Arabic *al jubba* long outer garment.]

jumper cable, one of a pair of heavy, insulated wires used to start the engine of an automobile whose battery has lost its charge.

jumping bean, the beanlike seed of any of several plants native to Mexico, genera *Sebastiana* and *Sapium,* containing a small moth larva whose movements cause the seed to jump. Also, **Mexican jumping bean.**

jumping jack 1. a toy figure of a person or animal, usually of wood and having jointed limbs that can be made to move by pulling attached strings or a lever. **2.** an exercise that involves jumping from a standing position, spreading the legs and placing the hands together over the head, then jumping again and returning to the first position.

jump·ing-off place (jŭm′ping ôf′, -of′) **1.** the starting point for a trip or enterprise: *London will be the jumping-off place for our trip through England.* **2.** the utmost limit or extent, as of anything settled or civilized; remote or isolated place.

jump-off (jŭmp′ôf′, -of′) *n.* the start of an enterprise or activity, as of a planned military attack.

jump rope 1. a piece of rope, often with a handle at each end, used for skipping or jumping over as a game or exercise. **2.** a game or exercise using such a rope.

jump shot, a basketball shot in which a player jumps into the air and shoots the ball at the basket at the highest point of the jump.

jump-start (jŭmp′stärt′) *v.t.* to start (an automobile engine) by using jumper cables connected to the battery of another automobile. —*n.* an act or instance of jump-starting.

jump·suit (jŭmp′sūt′) *n.* **1.** a one-piece garment, combining shirt and trousers, designed to be worn as coveralls by paratroopers. **2.** any garment styled like this.

jump·y (jŭm′pē) *adj.,* **jump·i·er, jump·i·est. 1.** easily made to start, as in surprise or fright; nervous; jittery. **2.** moving by jumps or sudden variations. —**jump′i·ness,** *n.*

jun., junior.

Jun., June.

junc., junction.

jun·co (jŭng′kō) *n., pl.* **-cos.** any of various North American finches, genus *Junco,* usually having gray and white plumage. Length: 5-6½ inches (13-17 centimeters). [Modern Latin *Junco* literally, reed bird, from Spanish *junco* reed, from Latin *juncus.*]

junc·tion (jŭngk′shən) *n.* **1.** a place or station where railroad lines meet or cross. **2.** any place or point where two or more things join or meet. **3.** the act of joining or the state of being joined. [Latin *jūnctiō* a joining.]

junc·ture (jŭngk′chər) *n.* **1.** a point in time, esp. one made critical by a concurrence of circumstances or events: *At this juncture, the outbreak of war seems imminent.* **2.** a place at which, or a structure by which, two things are joined; joint. **3.** the act of joining or the state of being joined. [Latin *jūnctūra* a joining. Doublet of JOINTURE.]

June (jūn) *n.* the sixth month of the year, containing thirty days. [Old French *June,* from Latin *Jūnius,* shortening of *mensis Jūnius* Juno's month.]

June·ber·ry (jūn′ber′ē, -bə rē) *n., pl.* **-ries.** the shadbush or its fruit.

June bug 1. any of several stout, brown beetles, family Scarabaeidae, that emerge as adults in late spring or early summer and are destructive to shrubs and trees. Their larvae feed on the roots of many crops. Also, **June beetle. 2.** figeater.

Jung·i·an (yūng′ē ən) *adj.* of, relating to, or in accordance with the theories of the Swiss psychiatrist Carl Jung. —*n.* an adherent or advocate of the theories of Jung.

jun·gle (jung′gəl) *n.* **1.a.** a dense and tangled mass of tropical vegetation, usually consisting of vines, ferns, low bushes, and young trees. **b.** land overgrown with such a mass, usually inhabited by wild animals. **2.** any wild, confused, or tangled growth or mass: *a jungle of skyscrapers, a jungle of red tape.* **3.** a scene of ruthless competition or of a fierce struggle for survival: *the advertising jungle.* **4.** *Slang.* a place where hobos camp. [Hindi *jangal* forest, desert, Sanskrit *jāngala* desert.]

jungle fowl, any of various pheasants, genus *Gallus,* of southern Asia, the East Indies, and some Pacific islands, the male of which has a long, arched tail, two wattles, and a comb. Jungle fowl are considered to be the ancestors of the domestic chicken.

jungle gym, a structure of vertical and horizontal bars on which children can climb and play.

jungle rot, a skin condition or disease usually caused by a fungus and occurring in a tropical environment.

jun·ior (jūn′yər) *adj.* **1.** being the younger of two. ▶ distinguished from *senior*; often used after the name of a son whose father has the same name. **2.** of lower position or rank: *a junior member of a law firm.* **3.** (of a U.S. senator) of more recent appointment or election. **4.** relating to, enrolled in, or designating the third year of high school or college: *the junior class.* **5.** of or for younger people: *the junior department in a store.* **6.** smaller in size than others or than the usual. —*n.* **1.** a person who is younger than another: *She's his junior by three years.* **2.** a student in the third year of a four-year high school or college. **3.** a person who is of lower position, rank, or standing or of more recent appointment. [Latin *jūnior,* comparative of *juvenis* young.]

junior college, a school having a two-year course equivalent to the first two years of a four-year college, offering liberal arts courses and special or vocational training, and granting an associate's degree.

junior high school, a school usually including grades seven and eight, and sometimes six or nine; any school intermediate between elementary school and senior high school.

ju·ni·per (jū′nə pər) *n.* any of a group of evergreen shrubs or trees, genus *Juniperus,* of the cypress family, bearing berrylike cones, some of which yield an oil used as a flavoring agent in gin. [Latin *jūniperus.*]

junk¹ (jungk) *n.* **1.** old or discarded material, as metal, wood, or rags, that may be put to some use. **2.** *Informal.* anything regarded as worthless or useless; rubbish; trash. **3.** *Nautical.* **a.** old cable or rope used for making such items as mats, swabs, or gaskets. **b.** hard, salted meat used for food on shipboard. **4.** *Slang.* a narcotic drug, esp. heroin. —*v.t. Informal.* to throw away or discard as junk; scrap: *to junk an old car.* [Middle English *jonk* old, disused cable, possibly from *jonk* reed, from Old French *jonc,* from Latin *juncus* a rush.]

junk² (jungk) *n.* a large flat-bottomed sailing vessel developed in China, having a square prow and lugsails. [Portuguese *junco,* from Javanese *jong* large boat.]

junk bond, a high-yielding, high-risk security of low quality issued by a company to finance the takeover of another company.

Jun·ker (yùng′kər) *n.* formerly, a member of the German or Prussian landed aristocracy. [German *Junker,* going back to Old High German *junc* young + *hērro* lord.]

jun·ket (jung′kit) *n.* **1.** a trip or excursion, as one made by a government official or business executive, paid for by public or organizational funds and ostensibly for purposes of inspection or other

junk²

official business. **2.** a trip or tour, esp. one undertaken for pleasure. **3.** a custardlike food of flavored and sweetened milk curdled by rennet. **4.** a feast, banquet, or picnic. —*v.i.* **1.** to go on a junket, esp. at public expense. **2.** to feast, banquet, or picnic. [Probably from Italian *giuncata* originally, a cream cheese taken to market (or served) on reeds, going back to *giunco* reed, from Latin *juncus.*] —**jun′ket·er;** also, **jun·ket·eer** (jung′ki tîr′), *n.*

junk food, food that is low in nutritional value but high in calories.

junk·ie (jung′kē) *n., pl.* **-ies.** also, **junk·y. 1.** *Slang.* a narcotics addict, esp. one addicted to heroin. **2.** *Informal.* a person addicted to or excessively devoted to anything: *a television junkie.*

junk mail, unrequested mail, such as advertisements, circulars, and catalogs, sent to a large number of addresses.

junk·man (jungk′man′) *n., pl.* **-men** (-men′). a person who buys or sells scrap material, such as metal, glass, paper, and rags.

junk·yard (jungk′yärd′) *n.* a place where junk is collected, stored, or resold.

Ju·no (jū′nō) *n., pl.* **-nos** *(def. 2).* **1.** in Roman mythology, the goddess who was the wife and sister of Jupiter and queen of the gods, protector chiefly of women and marriage. Her Greek counterpart is Hera. **2.** a beautiful, stately woman. [Latin *Juno* this goddess.]

Ju·no·esque (jū′nō esk′) *adj.* having the regal bearing and stately beauty of the Roman goddess Juno.

jun·ta (hùn′tə, hūn′-, jun′-) *n.* **1.** a group, often consisting of military officers, that rules a country, without having been elected, after a coup d'état. **2.** a legislative or administrative council or committee, esp. in Latin America. [Spanish *junta* a council, assembly, from Latin *jūncta,* past participle of *jungere* to connect, unite.]

jun·to (jun′tō) *n., pl.* **-tos.** a small, usually secret group that gathers for some common purpose, esp. for purposes of political intrigue. [Spanish *junto,* modification of *junta.* See JUNTA.]

Jupiter (def. 2)

Ju·pi·ter (jū′pi tər) *n.* **1.** in Roman mythology, the god who was the ruler of gods and humans, associated esp. with rain and thunder. His Greek counterpart is Zeus. Also, **Jove. 2.** the largest planet of the solar system and fifth in order of distance from the sun. It has sixteen confirmed moons. [Latin *Jupiter* this god.]

ju·ral (jùr′əl) *adj.* **1.** of or relating to law; legal. **2.** of or relating to rights and obligations. [From Latin *jūr-,* stem of *jūs* right, law.] —**ju′ral·ly,** *adv.*

Ju·ras·sic (ju ras′ik) *n.* the middle geologic period of the Mesozoic era, during which time birds and flowering plants first appeared. For table, see **geologic time.** —*adj.* of, relating to, or characteristic of this period. [From the *Jura* Mountains, where fossils of the Jurassic period were found.]

ju·rid·i·cal (ju rid′i kəl) *adj.* of or relating to law and to the administration of justice. Also, **ju·rid′ic.** [Latin *jūridicus* (from *jūs* right, law + *dicere* to say) + -AL¹.] —**ju·rid′i·cal·ly,** *adv.*

ju·ris·dic·tion (jùr′is dik′shən) *n.* **1.** the limits within which judicial or other authority may be exercised; range or extent of

a	at	e	end	o	hot	u	up	hw	white		about
ā	ape	ē	me	ō	old	ū	use	ng	song		taken
ä	far	i	it	ô	fork	ü	rule	th	thin	ə	pencil
âr	care	ī	ice	oi	oil	ù	pull	th	this		lemon
		îr	pierce	ou	out	ûr	turn	zh	measure		circus

authority. **2.** the territory over which authority is exercised. **3.** the legal right to exercise authority, esp. the authority of a court to interpret or apply the law. **4.** the power of those in authority; authority; control. [Latin *jūrisdictiō* administration of justice, from *jūs* right, law + *dictiō* a saying.] —**ju′ris·dic′tion·al,** *adj.*

ju·ris·pru·dence (jŭr′is prū′dəns) *n.* **1.** the science or philosophy of law. **2.** a body or system of laws. **3.** a branch or department of law: *medical jurisprudence.* [Late Latin *jūrisprūdentia* the science of law, from Latin *jūs* right, law + *prūdentia* skill.]

ju·rist (jŭr′ist) *n.* a person who is versed or skilled in the law, such as a judge or a legal scholar. [Medieval Latin *jurista* lawyer, from Latin *jūs* right, law.]

ju·ris·tic (jŭ ris′tik) *adj.* of or relating to a jurist, to jurisprudence, or to the legal profession. Also, **ju·ris′ti·cal.** —**ju·ris′ti·cal·ly,** *adv.*

ju·ror (jŭr′ər) *n.* a member of a jury. [Anglo-Norman *jurour* a swearer, from Latin *jūrātor.*]

ju·ry[1] (jŭr′ē) *n., pl.* **ju·ries. 1.** a body of persons selected according to law to hear evidence on a matter submitted to them in a court of law and to render a decision or make a presentment according to the law and the evidence. **2.** a committee chosen to select the winners and award the prizes in a contest, exhibition, or other competition. [Old French *juree* oath, legal inquiry, from *jurer* to swear, from Latin *jūrāre.*]

ju·ry[2] (jŭr′ē) *adj. Nautical.* for temporary use, as in an emergency; makeshift: *a jury mast.* [Of uncertain origin.]

jury duty, service by a citizen as a juror in a court of law.

ju·ry-rig (jŭr′ē rig′) *v.t.,* **-rigged, -rig·ging.** to make or arrange for temporary use, as in an emergency. —**ju′ry-rigged′,** *adj.*

just[1] (just) *adj.* **1.** fair, upright, and reasonable in acting or judging; adhering to standards of honesty and morality: *a stern but just ruler, to be just in one's dealings.* **2.** consistent with standards of what is fair, upright, and moral: *a just cause, a legal system providing for just treatment of suspects.* **3.** rightly due or given; deserved; merited: *just punishment.* **4.** having sound, reasonable, or adequate grounds; well-founded: *just indignation.* **5.** legally valid; lawful; legitimate: *a just claim to a throne.* **6.** in accordance with truth or fact; accurate; correct: *The book presented a just picture of the incidents that led to the war.* **7.** conforming to standards or requirements; proper: *a just balance.* —*adv.* **1.** exactly; precisely: *That's just what we were looking for. It's just as I thought.* **2.** a very little while ago; very recently: *I just saw him. We just finished packing.* **3.** by very little; by a narrow margin: *They stopped just short of the edge of the cliff. She arrived just in the nick of time.* **4.** only; merely: *It's just a cold and nothing to worry about.* **5.** at a short distance; immediately: *It's just south of here.* **6.** *Informal.* simply; utterly; positively: *That movie was just awful.* [Middle English *just,* from Old French *just* fair, right, from Latin *jūstus* upright, righteous, true, from *jūs* right, law.] —**just′ly,** *adv.* —**just′ness,** *n.*

Synonyms *adj.* **Just**[1], **fair**[1], and **impartial** mean free from bias or influence in making a judgment. **Just** is the broadest of these terms, connoting adherence to larger standards of right and truth: *The judge's wisdom and reputation for honesty led us to expect a just ruling.* **Fair** is generally used of a decision that attempts to accommodate the reasonable demands of parties to a dispute: *The mediator was fair in deciding the case, taking account of everyone's needs.* **Impartial** means scrupulously objective and free from favoritism or prejudice: *In order to get an impartial judgment, the names of the contestants were concealed.*

just[2] (just) *n.* joust. —*v.i.* joust. [Form of JOUST.]

jus·tice (jus′tis) *n.* **1.** the maintenance of just treatment of or what is just; the administering of merited rewards and punishments or of what is due: *The proper function of government is justice.* **2.** something that is merited or due with regard to standards of what is fair, upright, or moral: *to right wrongs and secure social justice.* **3.** the quality of conforming to standards of what is fair, upright, and moral: *No one could deny the justice of their being punished.* **4.** the maintenance, administration, or procedure of law: *a court of justice.* **5.** conformity to reason, truth, or fact; correctness; rightfulness; validity: *There's much justice in your*

conclusion. **6.a.** a judge of the Supreme Court of the United States. **b.** in certain states, a judge of an appellate court. [Old French *justice* equity, righteousness, from Latin *jūstitia.*]

· **to bring to justice.** to cause to be tried or to be legally punished for wrongdoing.

· **to do justice (to). a.** to treat or deal (with something or someone) fittingly or in a manner showing due appreciation. **b.** to represent or show (something or someone) truly or well.

justice of the peace, a local public official empowered to try minor cases, hold inquests and hearings, perform civil marriages, and carry out other administrative and judicial duties.

jus·tice·ship (jus′tis ship′) *n.* the position, function, or term of office of a justice.

jus·ti·fi·a·ble (jus′tə fī′ə bəl) *adj.* capable of being justified; defensible: *justifiable homicide.* —**jus′ti·fi′a·bil′i·ty, jus′ti·fi′-a·ble·ness,** *n.* —**jus′ti·fi′a·bly,** *adv.*

jus·ti·fi·ca·tion (jus′tə fi kā′shən) *n.* **1.** the act of justifying or the state of being justified. **2.** a fact or circumstance that justifies: *Your rudeness was justification for their anger.*

jus·ti·fy (jus′tə fī′) *v.t.,* **-fied, -fy·ing. 1.** to show to be just, right, or reasonable; vindicate: *Her great success justified our faith in her.* **2.** to provide adequate grounds for; warrant: *Their dangerous negligence justified his firing them on the spot.* **3.** to declare or prove guiltless or blameless; absolve. **4.** *Law.* to show a sufficient reason for (an act or omission) in court. **5.** *Printing.* to adjust (lines of type) to the proper length by spacing. [Old French *justifier* to assert or prove the innocence of, going back to Latin *jūstus* upright, fair + *facere* to make.] —**jus′ti·fi′er,** *n.*

jus·tle (jus′əl) jostle.

jut (jut) *v.i.,* **jut·ted, jut·ting.** to stick out; project; protrude. —*n.* something that juts out; projection or protruding point. [Form of JET[1].]

jute (jūt) *n.* **1.** a strong flexible fiber obtained from either of two plants, genus *Corchorus,* chiefly used to make burlap and twine. **2.** either of the two plants yielding this fiber, grown chiefly in India and Pakistan. [Bengali *jhūto* from Sanskrit *jūta* braid of hair.]

Jute (jūt) *n.* a member of a Germanic tribe, some of whom, along with the Angles and Saxons, invaded and settled in Britain during the fifth century A.D. The Jutes founded the kingdom of Kent.

ju·ve·nes·cence (jū′və nes′əns) *n.* the state of growing young or youthful.

ju·ve·nes·cent (jū′və nes′ənt) *adj.* growing young or youthful. [Latin *juvenēscēns,* present participle of *juvenēscere* to grow young again, from *juvenis* young.]

ju·ve·nile (jū′və nəl, -nīl′) *adj.* **1.** designed or appropriate for children or young people: *a juvenile book, juvenile fashions.* **2.** characteristic of children or young people; childish; immature: *juvenile behavior.* **3.** young; youthful. —*n.* **1.** a young person; youth. **2.** an actor who plays youthful parts. **3.** a book for children. [Latin *juvenīlis* youthful, from *juvenis* young.] —**ju′ve-nile·ly,** *adv.* —**ju′ve·nile·ness,** *n.*

juvenile court, a court of law having special jurisdiction over persons under a specified age, usually eighteen, when they have been apprehended by the police or neglected by parents or legal guardians.

juvenile delinquency, antisocial or illegal behavior by a person or persons under a specified age, usually eighteen.

juvenile delinquent, a person of a specified age, usually under eighteen, who is guilty of antisocial or illegal behavior but is too young to be held criminally responsible.

ju·ve·nil·i·a (jū′və nil′ē ə, -nil′yə) *pl. n.* **1.** works, esp. writings, produced in childhood or youth. **2.** literary or artistic works designed or appropriate for children.

ju·ve·nil·i·ty (jū′və nil′i tē) *n., pl.* **-ties. 1.** the quality or state of being juvenile. **2.** an instance of being juvenile; juvenile act or idea.

jux·ta·pose (juk′stə pōz′) *v.t.,* **-posed, -pos·ing.** to place (two or more things) side by side or close together, esp. for contrast or comparison. [From JUXTAPOSITION.]

jux·ta·po·si·tion (juk′stə pə zish′ən) *n.* the act of juxtaposing or the state of being juxtaposed. [Latin *iuxtā* near + POSITION.]

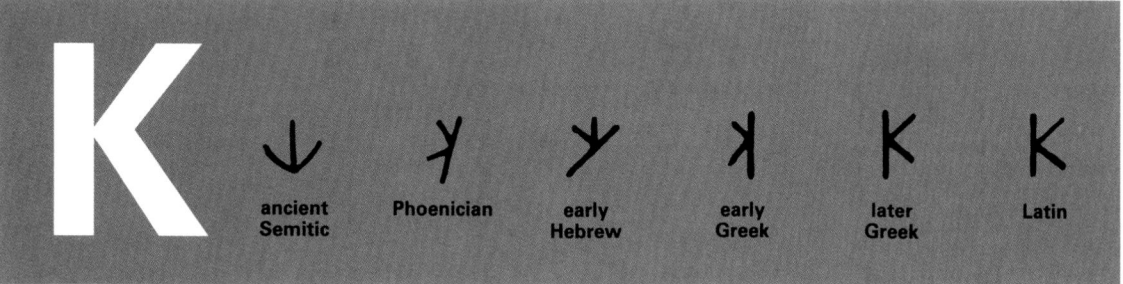

ancient Semitic	Phoenician	early Hebrew	early Greek	later Greek	Latin

K The history of the letter **K** goes back to the ancient Semitic alphabets, where an arrow pointing downward represented the *k* sound. This letter, called *kaph*, meant "hand" or "fist." When the Phoenicians and the early Hebrews borrowed *kaph*, they made some changes in its shape. In the ninth century B.C., the Greeks adopted *kaph* and called it *kappa*. The early Greeks wrote either from right to left or in alternating rows of right to left and left to right. Later, when their script became exclusively left to right, the shape of certain letters, including *kappa*, was reversed. The Romans borrowed this reversed form of *kappa* for the Latin alphabet but rarely used it, preferring the letter **C** as a symbol for the *k* sound. In modern English, we use both **C** and **K** to represent the *k* sound. The shape of the letter *k* has remained virtually unchanged for the last 2,400 years.

k, K (kā) *n., pl.* **k's, K's. 1.** the eleventh letter of the English alphabet. **2.** the shape of this letter or something having this shape.

K, the symbol for potassium.

k 1. karat. **2.** *also,* **k.** kilogram; kilograms. **3.** *also,* **k.** kilometer; kilometers.

k. 1. kopeck. **2.** krone.

K 1. Kelvin. **2.** kilobyte; kilobytes. **3.** *Chess.* king.

K. 1. king. **2.** knight.

Kaa·ba (kä′bə) *also,* **Caaba.** *n.* a sacred Islamic shrine at Mecca, toward which Muslims face when praying. It is a small cubical structure containing a black stone said to have been given to Abraham by the archangel Gabriel. [Arabic *ka'bah* square house, from *ka'b* cube.]

kab·a·la (kab′ə lə, kə bä′-) *also,* **kab·ba·la.** cabala.

ka·bob (kə bob′) *n.* kebab. [Arabic *kabāb*.]

Ka·bu·ki (kə bü′kē, kä′bü-) *n.* a form of Japanese drama, originating in the late sixteenth century, characterized by stylized acting, singing, and dancing, elaborate costuming, and the playing of both male and female roles by men. [Japanese *kabuki* literally, art of singing and dancing, from *kabu* singing and dancing + *ki* art.]

ka·chi·na (kə chē′nə) *n.* **1.** any of various supernatural

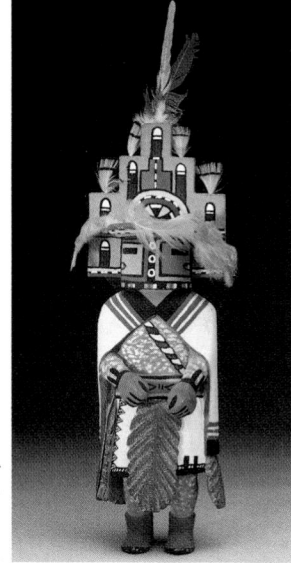

Hopi **kachina** doll

beings, esp. one associated with clouds and rain, worshiped by the Hopi, Zuñi, and other Pueblo Indian tribes. **2.** a masked and costumed male dancer who impersonates such a being. **3.** a doll that is carved and decorated to resemble such a dancer. Also *(def. 3),* **kachina doll.**

Kad·dish (kä′dish) *n. also,* **kad·dish.** a Jewish prayer in praise of God, recited by mourners or as part of a daily synagogue service. [Yiddish *kadesh,* from Hebrew-Aramaic *kadish,* from Aramaic *kadish* holy.]

Kaf·fir (kaf′ər) *also,* **Kaf·ir.** *n.* in South Africa, a black person. ➤ considered offensive. [Arabic *kāfir* infidel.]

kaf·ir (kaf′ər) *also,* **kaf·fir.** *n.* an edible sorghum, *Sorghum bicolor,* cultivated for its grain and as a source of forage. Also, **kafir corn.**

kaf·tan (kaf′tən, kaf tan′) caftan.

kai·ak (kī′ak) kayak.

Kai·ser (kī′zər) *n.* **1.a.** any of the emperors of Germany from 1871 to 1918. **b.** any of the emperors of Austria from 1804 to 1918. **c.** any of the emperors of the Holy Roman Empire from A.D. 962 to 1806. ➤ used as a title. **2. kaiser.** emperor. [Middle English *caiser* and German *Kaiser,* both going back to Gothic *kaisar,* from Latin *Caesar,* cognomen of the Roman dictator Gaius Julius *Caesar,* 100?-44 B.C., adopted as a title by certain Roman emperors.]

kal·an·cho·e (kal′ən kō′ē, -chō′ē, kə lan′chō) *n.* any of a number of tender, succulent plants, genus *Kalanchoe,* related to the stonecrops, grown as pot plants or in gardens for their ornamental flowers or foliage.

kale (kāl) *n.* **1.** the broad, curly, bluish green leaves of a plant, *Brassica oleracea acephala,* of the cabbage family, eaten cooked or raw as a vegetable. **2.** the plant itself, cultivated in many temperate regions of the world. [Form of COLE.]

ka·lei·do·scope (kə lī′də skōp′) *n.* **1.** a tube-shaped optical device containing loose bits of colored glass or other small objects which are reflected by a set of mirrors as a series of continually changing symmetrical patterns when the tube is rotated. **2.** anything exhibiting a succession of changing colors, patterns, or phases: *the perpetually shifting kaleidoscope of public opinion.* [Greek *kalos* beautiful + *eidos* form + -SCOPE.] —**ka·lei·do·scop·ic** (kə lī′də skop′ik), *adj.* —**ka·lei′do·scop′i·cal·ly,** *adv.*

kal·ends (kal′əndz) calends.

Ka·le·va·la (kä′lə vä′lä) *n.* the national epic poem of Finland, consisting of a compilation of traditional Finnish folktales.

kal·mi·a (kal′mē ə) *n.* any of a small group of broad-leafed, usually evergreen shrubs, genus *Kalmia,* of the heath family, native to North America and bearing clusters of cup-shaped flowers. The mountain laurel is a kalmia. [Modern Latin *Kalmia,* from Peter *Kalm,* 1715-79, Swedish botanist.]

Kal·muck (kal′muk) *also,* **Kal·muk, Kal·myk** (kal′mik). *n.* **1.** a member of a group of Mongol tribes, formerly nomadic herders, who settled in the region of the lower Volga River. **2.** their language, a member of the Ural-Altaic family of languages. [Turkish *Kalmuk* part of a Tatar tribe that was formerly nomadic.]

kal·so·mine (kal′sə mīn′, -min) calcimine.

kame (kām) *n.* a mound or hillock composed of beds of sand and gravel deposited by water from a melting glacier. [British dialectal form of COMBE.]

ka·mi·ka·ze (kä′mi kä′zē) *n.* **1.** one of a group of Japanese pilots in World War II whose mission was to dive their airplanes, which were carrying explosives, into a ship or other target in a suicidal attempt to destroy it. **2.** the airplane flown by such a pilot. **3.** a person or thing whose actions resemble those of a kamikaze. —*adj.* of, like, or behaving like a kamikaze: *a kamikaze driver.* [Japanese *kamikaze* literally, divine wind, from *kami* god + *kaze* wind, referring to the typhoon that destroyed a Mongol fleet in 1281 before it could invade Japan.]

a	at	e	end	o	hot	u	up	hw	white		about
ā	ape	ē	me	ō	old	ū	use	ng	song	ə	taken
ä	far	i	it	ô	fork	ü	rule	th	thin		pencil
âr	care	ī	ice	oi	oil	u̇	pull	th	this		lemon
		îr	pierce	ou	out	ûr	turn	zh	measure		circus

Kam·pu·che·an (kam′pù chē′ən) Cambodian.

Kan., Kansas.

Ka·nak·a (kə nak′ə, kan′ə kə) *n.* **1.** a Hawaiian. **2.** any South Sea islander. [Hawaiian *kanaka* man.]

kan·ga·roo (kang′gə rü′) *n., pl.* **-roos** or **-roo.** any of various marsupials, family Macropodidae, of Australia and neighboring islands, having small forelimbs, long hind feet, powerful hind legs adapted for leaping, and a long, muscular tail used for support and balancing and for giving greater force to the leap. For approximately six months after birth, the baby kangaroo is carried in the mother's abdominal pouch. Height: 1½-7 feet (0.5-2.1 meters). [Possibly of native Australian origin.]

kangaroo court, an unauthorized, irregular court in which trials are hastily arranged, verdicts often decided beforehand, and fair legal procedures ignored.

kangaroo rat, any of various burrowing rodents, genus *Dipodomys,* of the warm, sandy plains of western North America, having small, weak forelegs, strong hind legs which enable it to hop like a kangaroo, and a silky coat of tan or gray fur with white markings. Length: 9-14 inches (23-36 centimeters), including tail.

kangaroo

Kans., Kansas.

Kant·ian (kan′tē ən) *adj.* of or relating to the German philosopher Immanuel Kant or his philosophy. —*n.* a follower or adherent of Kant or his philosophy.

ka·o·lin (kā′ə lin) *also,* **ka·o·line.** *n.* a fine, white clay used chiefly to fill and coat paper and to make pottery and other ceramics. [French *Kaolin,* from Chinese *Kao-ling* name of a mountain (literally, high hill) in China where it was first obtained.]

ka·on (kā′on) *n. Physics.* a subatomic particle of the meson group. Also, **K-meson.** [*Ka* the letter *k* + (MES)ON.]

ka·pok (kā′pok) *n.* a light, fluffy fiber obtained from the pods of the silk-cotton tree, used as a stuffing for life preservers, pillows, and mattresses and as an insulating material. Also, **silk cotton.** [Malay *kāpoq* silk-cotton tree.]

Ka·po·si's sarcoma (kə pō′sēz) a malignant skin disease characterized by bluish red or brown nodules and plaques, a major AIDS-related disease that formerly appeared mostly in elderly men in a relatively benign form. [From Moritz K. *Kaposi,* 1837-1902, Hungarian dermatologist who described it.]

kap·pa (kap′ə) *n.* the tenth letter of the Greek alphabet (K, κ), corresponding to English *K, k* and sometimes *C, c.*

ka·put (kə püt′, kä-) *adj. Informal.* **1.** defeated, destroyed, or ruined: *Our hopes for an uneventful trip seemed kaput when our flight was canceled.* **2.** not capable of functioning or continuing: *The car has been kaput since the accident.* [German *Kaputt,* from French *capot* without tricks (in the game of piquet); literally, hoodwinked, from *capot* hooded cloak, going back to Late Latin *cappa.* See CAPE¹.]

kar·a·kul (kar′ə kəl) *n.* **1.** a sheep of a breed originally native to central Asia, having a narrow body and a broad tail. The young karakul has a coat of curled, gray or glossy black fur which becomes long, coarse, and gray or brown when the lamb matures. Height: to 3 feet (0.9 meter) at the shoulder. **2.** caracul. [From *Kara Kul,* lake in Turkestan, where it was first raised.]

kar·at (kar′ət) *also,* **carat.** *n.* a unit of measure used to express the degree of purity of gold, 24 karats equaling pure gold. Fourteen-karat gold is 14 parts gold and 10 parts alloy.

ka·ra·te (kə rä′tē) *n.* a Japanese system of unarmed self-defense in which the hands, elbows, knees, and feet are used to strike an opponent at various vulnerable points of the body. [Japanese *karate,* probably from *kara* empty + *te* hand; because no hand weapons are used.]

kar·ma (kär′mə) *n.* **1.** in Hinduism and Buddhism, the effect produced by a person's actions, supposed to determine the status of the person's reincarnation. **2.** fate; destiny. **3.** *Informal.* an atmosphere, feeling, or spirit, usually generated by a person or set of circumstances: *There's been bad karma at work since the company was sold.* [Sanskrit *karma* action, fate.]

kar·roo (kə rü′) *also,* **ka·roo.** *n., pl.* **-roos.** a dry tableland of southern Africa. [Afrikaans *karo,* probably from Khoikhoi *garo* desert.]

karst (kärst) *n.* a type of landscape that forms in areas underlain by limestone or dolomite, characterized by sinkholes, caverns, underground streams, and, in China, by spectacular pinnacles of

karst on the River Li, China

limestone. [German *karst,* from *Karst* (now *Kras,* region in Croatia), a limestone plateau characterized by this type of landscape.]

karyo- *combining form* the nucleus of a cell: *karyokinesis.* [Greek *karyon* kernel, nut.]

kar·yo·ki·ne·sis (kar′ē ō ki nē′sis, -kī-) *n.* mitosis. [KARYO- + Greek *kinēsis* movement, motion.] —**kar′y·o·ki·net′ic,** *adj.*

kar·y·o·type (kar′ē ə tīp′) *n.* the general appearance of the chromosome set of a cell or organism, including number, size, and shape. —*v.t.,* **-typed, -typ·ing.** to determine the karyotype of (a cell or organism). [KARYO- + TYPE.] —**kar·y·o·typ·ic** (kar′ē ə tip′ik); *also,* **kar′y·o·typ′i·cal,** *adj.*

Kash·mir goat (kash′mir, kazh′-) a goat native to India, Tibet, and other regions of Asia, raised esp. for its fine, soft undercoat, which is used to make cashmere wool. Also, **Cashmere goat.**

kat·a·bat·ic (kat′ə bat′ik) *adj. Meteorology.* moving downward, as an air current or wind. ➡ opposed to **anabatic.** [Greek *katabatikos,* from *katabasis* a stepping down, from *katabainein* to go down, from *kata-* down + *bainein* to go.]

ka·ty·did (kā′tē did′) *n.* any of a group of large, green grasshoppers, family Tettigoniidae, having long threadlike antennae. The male produces a shrill, rasping noise by rubbing its wings together. Length: 2 inches (5 centimeters). [Imitative of this sound.]

kau·ri (kour′ē) *n., pl.* **-ris.** *also,* **kaury.** **1.** any of several tall evergreen trees, genus *Agathis,* of the pine family, esp. *A. australis,* native to New Zealand. Also, **kauri pine. 2.** the fine, straight-grained wood of this tree, used in shipbuilding. **3.** a resin obtained from this tree, used esp. in making varnish and linoleum. [Of Maori origin.]

kau·ry (kour′ē) *n., pl.* **-ries.** kauri.

Kay, Sir (kā) in Arthurian legend, a rude and boastful knight of the Round Table who was the foster brother and steward of King Arthur.

kay·ak (kī′ak) *also,* **kaiak.** *n.* **1.** an Eskimo canoe made of animal skins stretched over a light framework of wood or whalebone, having a small opening in the center for a paddler. **2.** a light, highly maneuverable canoe resembling this, used esp. in sports and usually covered with canvas. —*v.i., v.t.* to travel in a kayak. [Of Eskimo origin.] —**kay′ak·er,** *n.*

kay·o (kā′ō′) *Slang. n., pl.* **kay·os.** KO. —*v.t.* KO.

ka·zoo (kə zü′) *n., pl.* **-zoos.** a toy musical instrument consisting of a tube containing a strip of catgut or a piece of paper that vibrates and produces a harsh buzzing sound when the player hums into the tube. [Probably imitative.]

kc *also,* **kc.** kilocycle; kilocycles.

K.C. *also,* **KC** Knights of Columbus.

kcal, kilocalorie; kilocalories.

ke·a (kē′ə) *n.* a New Zealand parrot, *Nestor notabilis,* having a sharp, hooked bill and predominantly olive-green plumage. [Of Maori origin.]

ke·bab (kə bob′) *also,* **ke·bob.** **1.** any of the small pieces of meat used in making shish kebab. **2. kebabs.** shish kebab.

kedge (kej) *v.,* **kedged, kedg·ing.** —*v.t.* to move (a boat or ship) by pulling on a rope attached to a small anchor that has been dropped at some distance. —*v.i.* (of a boat or ship) to move by kedging. —*n.* a small anchor used esp. in kedging. Also, **kedge anchor.** [Of uncertain origin.]

keel (kēl) *n.* **1.** the main beam extending lengthwise along the center of the bottom of a ship or boat and supporting the entire frame. **2.** a part in an aircraft, esp. an airship, corresponding to a ship's keel. **3.** any structure or part resembling a ship's keel. **4.** *Archaic.* a ship. —*v.i., v.t.* to capsize or nearly capsize; turn over: *The boat keeled when the wind came up.* [Old Norse *kjölr* lowest timber along the bottom of a ship.]

• **on an even keel.** steady, stable, or upright: *Your clearheadedness helped keep everyone on an even keel.*
• **to keel over. a.** to turn bottom up; capsize. **b.** to fall over suddenly; topple or collapse: *to keel over in a faint.*

keel·boat (kēl′bōt′) *n.* a flat-bottomed river boat having a keel but no sails, propelled by being rowed, towed, or poled, formerly used to carry freight in the western United States.

keel·haul (kēl′hôl′) *v.t.* **1.** to drag (a person) under the keel of a ship from one side or end to the other as a form of punishment. **2.** to rebuke or punish severely. [Dutch *kielhalen,* from *kiel* keel + *halen* to haul.]

keel·son (kel′sən, kēl′-) *also,* **kelson.** *n.* a long beam running parallel with and fastened to the main keel of a ship in order to strengthen it. [Of Germanic origin.]

keen[1] (kēn) *adj.* **1.** having a fine cutting edge or point; able to cut or pierce easily; sharp: *a keen sword.* **2.** having or showing great mental sharpness; clever; perceptive: *a keen mind, a keen understanding of a subject.* **3.** highly sensitive or developed, as a sense or sense organ: *keen eyes, a keen sense of smell.* **4.** vividly felt or experienced; intense; strong: *a keen sense of loss, a keen scent.* **5.** of a piercing, penetrating, or cutting nature: *A cold, keen wind blows in from the ocean.* **6.** enthusiastic; eager: *A tourist should be keen about traveling.* **7.** *Slang.* wonderful; excellent: *The children thought the movie was keen.* [Middle English *kene,* from Old English *cēne* wise, fierce, brave.] —**keen′ly,** *adv.* —**keen′ness,** *n.* —For Synonyms, see **eager.**

keen[2] (kēn) *Irish. n.* a wailing lament for the dead. —*v.i.* to wail loudly or lament for the dead. —*v.t.* to wail loudly or lament for (the dead). [Irish *caoine,* from *caoinim* I wail.] —**keen′er,** *n.*

keep (kēp) *v.,* **kept, keep·ing.** —*v.t.* **1.a.** to retain in one's possession, power, or control: *I told her she could borrow my sweater but not keep it.* **b.** to retain for one's use for a limited period of time: *Keep the book for a week.* **2.** to cause to continue in a certain place, condition, relation, or position: *to keep things in order, to keep the door open, to keep a child happy.* **3.** to put away in a usual or proper place; store: *Where do you keep your dictionary?* **4.** to have in stock or for sale: *That market keeps fine meats.* **5.** to have or maintain in one's service or for one's use or enjoyment: *to keep servants, to keep a boat at the lake.* **6.** to maintain by making regular entries in: *to keep account books, to keep a diary.* **7.** to set down so as to have a record: *to keep the score of a basketball game.* **8.** to cause to remain in a place or position; restrain from leaving; detain: *to keep a person in jail, to keep a sick child in bed.* **9.** to hold back; prevent; deter: *Cold weather may keep the plants from budding. He kept himself from laughing.* **10.** to withhold from present use; reserve; save: *to keep some for tomorrow.* **11.** to refrain from making known: *Can you keep a secret? The newspaper refused to keep the facts from the public.* **12.** to be faithful to; abide by; fulfill: *to keep one's word, to keep an appointment.* **13.** to observe or celebrate, as with certain rites or ceremonies: *to keep the Sabbath, to keep Christmas.* **14.** to look after the affairs of; manage: *to keep a shop.* **15.** to provide the necessities of life for; support: *to keep a large family.* **16.** to protect from harm; guard; defend: *The Lord bless thee, and keep thee* (Numbers 6:24). **17.** to take care of; watch over; tend: *to keep a flock of sheep.* **18.** to stay in, at, or on: *The spectators kept their seats.* —*v.i.* **1.** to stay in a specified place, condition, relation, or position: *to keep silent, to keep away.* **2.** to continue or persevere in some course or action (often with *on*): *to keep moving, to keep on driving despite the snow.* **3.** to restrain oneself; refrain (with *from*): *We couldn't keep from crying at the sad movie.* **4.** to remain in good condition; last without spoiling: *Will this meat keep until tomorrow?* **5.** to be able to last or endure until a later time: *The rest of my news will keep until I see you again.* —*n.* **1.** things needed to sustain a person or animal, as food and shelter; means of subsistence: *to earn one's keep.* **2.** the state of being watched over, supervised, and protected; care; custody: *The orphan is in our keep.* **3.** the strongest, usually innermost, part of a castle, serving as a last defense; donjon. [Old English *cēpan* to observe, seize.]

• **for keeps.** *Informal.* **a.** with the understanding that the winner will keep what he or she wins: *to play marbles for keeps.* **b.** with complete seriousness: *Tennis may be only a game, but I always play for keeps.* **c.** permanently: *You gave it to me for keeps and not as a loan.*
• **to keep at.** to continue with; persist in: *Keep at your studying and you'll be able to pass the test.*
• **to keep back. a.** to restrain, withhold, or conceal: *to keep back tears, to keep back important information.* **b.** to retard the growth or progress of: *A slow learner could keep back the whole class.* **c.** to withhold promotion to the next grade from: *The school will keep back all students who fail.*
• **to keep in with.** *Informal.* to remain in good favor with; continue a friendly relationship with.

• **to keep to. a.** to adhere to strictly; follow closely: *to keep to a diet.* **b.** to remain in or at: *to keep to one's bed.*
• **to keep to oneself. a.** to avoid the company of others; remain alone. **b.** to refrain from divulging (something); to keep (something) a secret: *Keep this bit of gossip to yourself.*
• **to keep up. a.** to maintain or continue: *Keep up the good work. The noise kept up all night.* **b.** to maintain the necessary pace or rate of progress: *Can you keep up, or should we walk more slowly?* **c.** to maintain in good order or condition: *The city keeps up the parks.* **d.** to cause to remain awake or out of bed: *The howling dog kept me up last night.*
• **to keep up on.** to continue to be informed about: *to keep up on the latest news.*
• **to keep up with. a.** to maintain the same rate of speed or rate of progress as: *to keep up with the fastest runner, to keep up with the rest of the French class.* **b.** to remain in contact with: *to keep up with old friends.* **c.** to continue to be informed about: *to keep up with the latest fashions, to keep up with local gossip.*

keep·er (kē′pər) *n.* **1.** a person who protects, tends, or is responsible for someone or something: *a keeper at a zoo, the keeper of an inn, a good keeper of secrets.* ➡ often used in combination: *a shopkeeper, a gamekeeper.* **2.** something that should or may be kept, such as fish that may legally be kept if landed. **3.** something that keeps or stores in a specified way: *This type of tomato is an excellent keeper.*

keep·ing (kē′ping) *n.* **1.** custody, or possession: *The jewels were placed in my keeping.* **2.** the celebration or observance: *the keeping of Thanksgiving.*

• **in keeping with.** in harmony with; consistent or appropriate: *Jokes are not in keeping with a solemn occasion.*

keep·sake (kēp′sāk′) *n.* something given or kept to remind one of the giver; memento.

Synonyms Keepsake, memento, souvenir, and remembrance refer to something that serves to remind. **Keepsake** denotes an article that reminds the keeper of the giver: *Please wear this ring as a keepsake while I am away.* A **memento** is usually something small that serves to renew or keep alive some memory: *I look at this memento of our trip whenever I'm feeling low.* **Souvenir** also suggests an article kept as a memento, but one that may have less evocative power: *I bought lots of souvenirs on my trip, but gave most of them away.* **Remembrance** is a rarer, general term: *I shall treasure this book as a remembrance of our friendship.*

keg (keg) *n.* **1.** a small barrel, usually holding 5 to 10 gallons (19-38 liters). **2.** a unit of weight for nails that is equal to 100 pounds (45 kilograms). [Old Norse *kaggi* cask.]

ke·loid (kē′loid) *n.* an elevated, irregular, fibrous overgrowth at the site of a scar. [French *kéloïde, chéloïde,* from Greek *chēlē* claw of a crab + *oeidēs* (see -OID).] —**ke·loi′dal,** *adj.*

kelp (kelp) *n.* **1.** any of a large group of brown seaweeds, order Laminariales, growing in great masses in cold coastal waters of the Atlantic and Pacific oceans. **2.** the ashes of such seaweed, formerly a major source of potassium and iodine, now used mainly as a fertilizer. [Of uncertain origin.]

kel·pie[1] (kel′pē) *n., pl.* **-pies.** *also,* **kel·py.** in Scottish folklore, a water spirit that usually appears as a horse, supposed to drown people or warn them of drowning.

kel·pie[2] (kel′pē) *n., pl.* **-pies.** *also,* **kel·py.** a breed of Australian sheep dog. [Supposedly from *Kelpie,* the name of a dog of this breed.]

kel·son (kel′sən) keelson.

Kelt (kelt) Celt.

Kelt·ic (kel′tik) Celtic.

kel·vin (kel′vin) *n.* the International System unit of temperature, equal to 1 degree on the Kelvin and Celsius scales.

Kel·vin (kel′vin) *adj.* of, according to, or designating the temperature scale on which a degree is equal in size to a Celsius degree and 0 degrees represents absolute zero (− 273.15 degrees Celsius). For illustration, see **Fahrenheit.** [From the English physicist William Thomson, Lord *Kelvin,* 1824-1907, who developed this scale.]

ken (ken) *n.* range of sight, knowledge, or understanding: *I'm afraid the subject under discussion is beyond my ken.* —*v.t., v.i.,* **kenned** or **kent, ken·ning.** *Scottish.* to know or understand. [Partly from Old English *cennan* to make known, declare; partly from Old Norse *kenna* to know.]

ke·naf (kə naf′) *n.* **1.** a tropical plant, *Hibiscus cannabinus,*

a	at	e	end	o	hot	u	up	hw	white		about
ā	ape	ē	me	ō	old	ū	use	ng	song		taken
ä	far	i	it	ô	fork	ü	rule	th	thin	ə	pencil
âr	care	ī	ice	oi	oil	u̇	pull	th	this		lemon
		îr	pierce	ou	out	ûr	turn	zh	measure		circus

related to the mallows, cultivated for its fiber and seeds that yield a flammable oil. **2.** the jutelike fiber obtained from this plant, used for rope and burlap. [Persian *kenaf* parallel to *kanab* hemp.]

ken·nel (ken'əl) *n.* **1.** a shelter for a dog or cat. **2.** *also,* **kennels.** an establishment where dogs or cats are bred, trained, or boarded. —*v.t.,* **-neled, -nel·ing;** *also, British,* **-nelled, -nel·ling.** to put or keep in a kennel. [Going back to Latin *canis* dog.]

Ken·nel·ly-Heav·i·side layer (ken'ə lē hev'ē sīd') Heaviside layer. [From Arthur Edwin *Kennelly,* 1861-1939, American electrical engineer, and Oliver *Heaviside,* 1850-1925, English physicist.]

ke·no (kē'nō) *n.* a gambling game derived from and resembling lotto. [Possibly from French *quine* five winning numbers in a lottery, from Latin *quīnī* five each; because the pieces used in the game are placed in rows of five.]

kent (kent) a past tense and past participle of **ken.**

Kent·ish (ken'tish) *adj.* of, relating to, or characteristic of Kent, its people, or the English dialects once spoken there. —*n.* the Old English or Middle English dialect spoken in the kingdom of Kent.

Ken·tuck·y Derby (kən tuk'ē) a race for three-year-old horses, established in 1875 and run annually at Churchill Downs in Louisville, Kentucky.

Ke·ogh plan (kē'ō) a retirement plan for self-employed individuals or unincorporated business owners and their employees. ➡ distinguished from **IRA.** [From Eugene J. *Keogh,* 1907-89, U.S. congressman.]

kep·i (kep'ē) *n.* a military cap having a flat, circular top inclined toward the front and a visor. [French *képi,* from Swiss German *Käppi,* diminutive of *Kappe* cap, from Late Latin *cappa* hood, cape. See CAP.]

kept (kept) the past tense and past participle of **keep.**

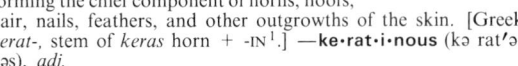

kepi

ker·a·tin (ker'ə tin) *n.* a tough, fibrous protein in the skin tissue of all vertebrates, forming the chief component of horns, hoofs, hair, nails, feathers, and other outgrowths of the skin. [Greek *kerat-,* stem of *keras* horn + -IN¹.] —**ke·rat·i·nous** (kə rat'ə-nəs), *adj.*

kerb (kûrb) *n. British.* curb *(def. 1).*

kerb·stone (kûrb'stōn') *British.* curbstone.

ker·chief (kûr'chif) *n.* **1.** a piece of cloth, usually square, worn over the head or around the neck; scarf. **2.** handkerchief *(def. 1).* [Old French *couvrechief* literally, to cover the head, from *couvrir* to cover + *chef* head (from Latin *caput*). See COVER.] —**ker'·chiefed,** *adj.*

kerf (kûrf) *n.* a cut or notch made by an ax, saw, or other tool. [Old English *cyrf* act of cutting.]

ker·mes (kûr'mēz) *n.* **1.** the dried bodies of females of certain scale insects of the genus *Kermes,* used for making a scarlet dye. **2.** this dye. **3.** a Mediterranean oak, *Quercus coccifera,* on which these insects are found. Also *(def. 3),* **kermes oak.** [French *kermès,* from Arabic *qirmiz* literally, crimson, from Sanskrit *krimija* insect-produced, from *krmi,* worm, insect.]

ker·mis (kûr'mis) *also,* **ker·mess, kir·mess.** *n.* **1.** an annual fair or festival held in the Low Countries. **2.** any similar fair or entertainment. [Dutch *kermis* church Mass; originally, a religious celebration including a fair, from *kerk* church (going back to Greek *kyriakon*) + *mis* Mass (going back to Late Latin *missa*). See CHURCH, MASS.]

kern¹ (kûrn) *also,* **kerne.** *n. Archaic.* a medieval Irish or Scottish foot soldier armed with light weapons. [Irish *ceatharn* troop, soldier.]

kern² (kûrn) *n. Printing.* the part of a typeface projecting beyond the body of the character, as at the bottom of an italic *j.* [French *carne* projecting angle, hinge, going back to Latin *cardinis,* genitive of *cardo* hinge.]

ker·nel (kûr'nəl) *n.* **1.** a grain or seed of various plants, as of wheat or corn. **2.** the softer, inner part of a seed or fruit. **3.** the central, most valuable, or most important part; core; nucleus. [Old English *cyrnel.*]

kern·ite (kûr'nīt) *n.* a white or clear, glassy mineral, the hydrous borate of sodium, found esp. in the Mojave Desert, where it is mined as an ore of boron and a source of borax. Formula: $Na_2 B_4 O_7 \cdot 4H_2 O$ [From *Kern* County, California, where it is mined + -ITE¹.]

ker·o·sene (ker'ə sēn', ker'ə sēn') *also,* **ker·o·sine.** *n.* a colorless, highly volatile liquid distilled from petroleum, widely used as a fuel and cleaning solvent. It consists of a mixture of hydrocarbons. Also, **coal oil.** [Greek *kēros* wax + -ENE; because paraffin is used in distilling it.]

Ker·ry (ker'ē) *n., pl.* **-ries.** one of a breed of small, black dairy cattle, often having white markings, originally developed in Ireland.

Kerry blue terrier, a terrier of a breed originally developed in Ireland, having a dark grayish blue coat of thick, wavy hair. Height: to 19 inches (48 centimeters) at the shoulder.

ker·sey (kûr'zē) *n., pl.* **-seys.** a coarse, ribbed, woolen fabric, woven with a cotton warp, used esp. for work clothes. [Probably from *Kersey,* village in Suffolk, England, once noted for its trade in woolens.]

kes·trel (kes'trəl) *n.* **1.** a small falcon, *Falco tinnunculus,* native to Europe and Asia, having predominantly brown plumage, noted for its ability to hover in the air against the wind. Length: about 13½ inches (34 centimeters). **2.** a small American falcon, *Falco sparvevius.* Length: 10 inches (25 centimeters). Also *(def. 2),* **sparrow hawk.** [Old French *cresserelle,* going back to Latin *crepitāculum* rattle; because its cry resembles the sound of a rattle.]

ketch (kech) *n.* a fore-and-aft-rigged sailing ship with two masts, similar to a yawl, but having the mizzenmast farther forward, ahead of the rudder post. [Possibly from CATCH.]

ketch·up (kech'əp) *also,* **catchup, catsup.** *n.* a thick, seasoned sauce that is usually made of tomatoes, vinegar, onions, salt, sugar, and spices and is used with many types of food. [Malay *kēchap* fish sauce, from dialectal Chinese *ke-tsiap* brine of fish.]

ke·tone (kē'tōn') *n.* any of a class of organic compounds in which a carbonyl group is attached to each of two carbon atoms that are contained in hydrocarbon radicals. [German *Keton,* short for *Aketon,* from French *acétone* acetone.] —**ke·ton·ic** (ki ton'-ik), *adj.*

ketone body, any of three ketone compounds, including acetone, that are produced by the liver during the breakdown of fatty acids and accumulate in the blood and urine as a result of extreme dieting, diabetes, pregnancy, or other conditions.

ket·tle (ket'əl) *n.* **1.** any metal container for boiling liquids or for cooking in liquid; pot. **2.** teakettle. **3.** a bowl-shaped depression formed in the surface of the land by the melting of a block of glacial ice. [Old Norse *ketill* caldron, from Latin *catillus* small bowl, diminutive of *catīnus* deep vessel for cooking food.]

· **kettle of fish.** a matter or situation for consideration, esp. a difficult, disagreeable, or awkward one: *The apparently simple job quickly became quite another kettle of fish.*

ket·tle·drum (ket'əl drum') *n.* a drum consisting of a hollow brass, copper, or fiberglass hemisphere with a parchment or plastic head that can be tuned to a definite pitch.

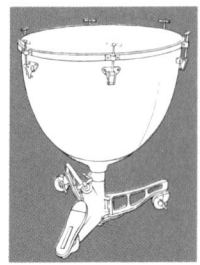

kettledrum

Kew·pie (kū'pē) *n. Trademark.* a small doll representing a plump cupid with a topknot of hair. Also, **kewpie doll.**

key¹ (kē) *n., pl.* **keys. 1.** an instrument that opens or closes a locking mechanism by moving a bolt or tumblers. **2.** anything like this instrument in use or shape: *a roller skate key, a key for a sardine can, a key for winding a clock.* **3.** something that serves to disclose, explain, or solve, as a clue in a mystery, a set of answers to problems in a textbook, or the legend of a map. **4.** something that leads to or is a means of attaining something: *The miser thought money was the key to happiness.* **5.** something, as a geographical location or position, which provides a means of control, esp. of entry or possession: *The Bosporus is the key to the Black Sea.* **6.** a person or thing that is considered the essential or controlling element or force of something: *The quarterback was the key to their team.* **7.** a finger-operated part that works by lever action or by making electrical contact, used in operating an instrument or machine: *a piano key, a telegraph key, a typewriter key.* **8.** a device, as a pin, bolt, or wedge, put in a hole or space to hold parts together; cotter. **9.** *Music.* a scale or system of notes in which all the notes bear a definite relationship to and are based on a given note, which is the keynote: *a symphony in the key of F sharp.* **10.** a tone or pitch of the voice: *to speak in a high key.* **11.** a characteristic or general tone or level of intensity, as of feeling, action, or expression: *The letter was written in an angry key. The actor's performance was in a subtle, low key.* **12.** samara. —*adj.* of great or chief importance; essential, major, or basic: *a key factor in one's success, a key battle in the war.* —*v.t.,* **keyed, key·ing. 1.** *Music.* to regulate the pitch or tone of: *to key an instrument to B flat.* **2.** to regulate or adjust (something) to suit a particular activity, occasion, or need: *to key a lecture to the interests of a youthful audience.* **3.** to lock or fasten with or as if with a key: *to key a door, to key parts together with a wedge.* **4.** to provide (something, as a machine or instrument) with a key or keys. **5.** to finish (an arch) by adding a keystone. **6.** to provide with an explanatory key, legend, table, or the like. [Old English *cæg* instrument that locks or unlocks something, explanation.]

•**to key up.** to make nervous, tense, or excited: *Just thinking about the exam keyed me up.*

key² (kē) *n., pl.* **keys.** a low, coastal island or reef, such as those along the southern tip of Florida; cay. [Spanish *cayo,* probably from Old French *cay* retaining wall; of Celtic origin.]

key·board (kē'bôrd') *n.* **1.** an arrangement or set of keys, as on a piano, harpsichord, typewriter, or computer terminal. **2.** a musical instrument played by means of a keyboard, esp. an electronic instrument. —*v.t.* to enter (data) into a computer by using a keyboard. —**key'board'er,** *n.*

key fruit, samara.

key·hole (kē'hōl') *n.* a hole through which a key is inserted into a lock.

keyhole saw, compass saw.

key·note (kē'nōt') *n.* **1.** *Music.* the note on which a scale or system of tones is based; tonic. **2.** the main or dominant idea, principle, theme, or mood: *Economic expansion was the keynote of the nation's foreign policy.* —*v.t.,* **-not·ed, -not·ing. 1.** to give or set the keynote of. **2.** to give the keynote speech at. —**key'not'er,** *n.*

keynote speech, a speech, as at the convention of a political party, in which important issues and the basic policy to be followed are presented. Also, **keynote address.**

key·pad (kē'pad') *n.* **1.** a small keyboard. **2.** a section of a computer keyboard with keys for numbers and mathematical symbols, usually arranged like the keys of a calculator. **3.** a small panel with keys or buttons marked by letters or numbers.

key·punch (kē'punch') *n.* a machine operated from a keyboard and used in data processing to record information by means of holes punched in cards. —**key'punch'er,** *n.*

key signature *Music.* the sharps or flats placed after the clef at the beginning of each staff, or at any point where there is a change of key, indicating the key of the music that follows.

key·stone (kē'stōn') *n.* **1.** the central, topmost stone of an arch, serving to lock the remaining stones of the arch together. It is usually the last stone to be set in place and is often distinguished from the other stones in some way. For illustration, see **arch¹. 2.** a fundamental element or part upon which associated parts depend: *Singapore was the keystone of British power in the Far East.*

key·stroke (kē'strōk') *n.* the striking of a key, as on the keyboard of a computer terminal or typewriter.

key·word (kē'wûrd') also, **key word.** *n.* a word or phrase that is used to index, catalog, or access book titles or other information.

kg *also,* **kg.** kilogram; kilograms.

khak·i (kak'ē, kä'kē) *n.* **1.** a dull, yellowish brown or tan color. **2.** a sturdy, twilled cotton fabric of this color. **3.** khakis. a garment made of this fabric, esp. a military uniform. —*adj.* **1.** having a dull, yellowish brown or tan color. **2.** made of khaki. [Hindi *khākī* dusty, from Persian *khāk* dust.]

khan¹ (kän, kan) *n.* **1.** a title formerly used by the rulers of Mongol, Tatar, and Turkish tribes and by the Mongol emperors of China. **2.** a title of respect in Iran, Afghanistan, and central Asia. [Turkish *khān* lord, prince.]

khan² (kän, kan) *n.* an inn or caravansary in Turkey and neighboring countries. [Arabic *khān,* from Persian *khān.*]

khe·dive (kə dēv') *n.* the title of the Turkish viceroys of Egypt from 1867 to 1914. [French *khédive,* going back to Persian *khedīv* prince, sovereign.]

Khmer (kə mer') *n.* **1.** a member of an ethnic group that makes up most of the population of Cambodia. Their civilization reached its greatest height in the twelfth century. **2.** the language of Cambodia. Also *(def. 2),* **Cambodian.**

Khoi·khoi (koi'koi') *n., pl.* **-khois** or **-khoi. 1.** a member of a southern African people, formerly nomadic raisers of sheep and cattle. **2.** the language of the Khoikhoi, belonging to the Khoisan language family. Also, **Hottentot.**

Khoi·san (koi'sän) *n.* a family of languages spoken in southwest Africa, including Khoikhoi and San.

kib·ble (kib'əl) *n.* dry animal feed, esp. for dogs and cats, pressed into bits from ground meal. —*v.t.,* **-bled, -bling.** to grind coarsely; crush or press into bits. [Of uncertain origin.]

kib·butz (ki büts', -büts') *n., pl.* **-but·zim** (-bùt sēm', -büt-). a collective farm or settlement in modern Israel. [Hebrew *kibuts* literally, a gathering, from *kibets* to gather, collect, from *kavats* to save up, lay by.]

kib·itz (kib'its) *v.i. Informal.* to act as a kibitzer. [Yiddish *kibetsn,* from German *kiebitzen* to look on (at cards); literally, to snoop, from *kiebitz* someone who looks on (at cards), nosy person; literally, lapwing; imitative.]

kib·itz·er (kib'it sər) *n. Informal.* **1.** a spectator at a card game who gives unwanted advice to the players. **2.** anyone who gives unwanted advice or meddles in the affairs of others. [Yiddish *kibitzer,* going back to German *kiebitzen* to look on.]

ki·bosh (kī'bosh, ki bosh') *n.* **put the kibosh on.** *Slang.* to put a stop to (an activity, project, undertaking, or the like): *to put the kibosh on roughhousing.* [Of uncertain origin.]

kick (kik) *v.t.* **1.** to strike with the foot or feet: *to kick the tires on a car.* **2.** to drive, impel, or move by striking with the foot or feet: *to kick a stone into the sewer.* **3.** *Sports.* to score (a goal or point) by kicking the ball over the goal posts or into the goal, as in football or soccer. **4.** (of firearms) to strike in recoiling: *The rifle kicked my shoulder.* —*v.i.* **1.** to strike out with the foot or feet: *The wild bronco kicked and bucked. The swimmer increased her speed by kicking faster.* **2.** *Sports.* to put the ball in play or attempt to score or gain ground by kicking the ball, as in football or soccer. **3.** (of firearms) to recoil when fired. **4.** *Informal.* to object strongly; complain; rebel: *He kicked at having so much work to do.* —*n.* **1.** the act or power of kicking the foot or feet: *I shut the door with a kick. The swimmer has a strong kick.* **2.** a sudden recoil, esp. of a gun when fired. **3.** *Sports.* **a.** the act or an instance of kicking a ball. **b.** a kicked ball: *to block a kick.* **c.** the distance a ball travels when kicked: *a 50-yard kick.* **4.** *Informal.* a complaint; objection: *What's your kick this time?* **5.** *Informal.* a pleasing or exciting feeling; thrill: *I get a kick out of riding my bicycle down a steep hill.* **6.** *Informal.* a stimulating or intoxicating power or effect, esp. of alcoholic drink. **7.** *Informal.* a temporary but intense period of interest or indulgence: *a knitting kick.* [Of uncertain origin.]

•**to kick around.** *Informal.* **a.** to treat roughly or inconsiderately. **b.** to wander from place to place: *The sailor had kicked around for years.* **c.** to give consideration or thought to: *to kick around a plan.*

•**to kick back. a.** (of firearms) to recoil in a sudden, unexpected way. **b.** *Slang.* to pay back (a portion of money received as a fee, commission, salary, or the like) as a secret or illegal payment.

•**to kick in.** *Slang.* to contribute as one's share: *Everyone was asked to kick in fifty cents.*

•**to kick off. a.** *Football.* to make a kickoff. **b.** to start; initiate: *to kick off a stage show with a rousing song.* **c.** *Slang.* to die.

•**to kick (someone) out.** *Informal.* to dismiss, expel, or eject (someone) forcefully or suddenly: *to kick a student out of school for cheating.*

•**to kick the bucket.** *Slang.* to die.

•**to kick the habit.** *Slang.* to free oneself of an addiction, esp. to narcotics or cigarettes.

•**to kick up.** *Informal.* **a.** to cause trouble, pain, or difficulty: *My arthritis kicks up in wet weather.* **b.** to cause or stir up (trouble, confusion, or the like): *The spoiled child kicked up a fuss.*

•**to kick (someone) upstairs.** *Informal.* to promote (someone) to a position that is higher but gives less responsibility or power.

Kick·a·poo (kik'ə pü') *n., pl.* **-poo** or **-poos.** a member of a North American Indian tribe formerly living in the southwestern Great Lakes area, now living in Kansas, Oklahoma, and Mexico.

kick·back (kik'bak') *n.* **1.** an illegal or secret payment made by a seller of goods or services to the person who referred a buyer or client. **2.** a portion of a worker's wages wrongfully and secretly returned to a supervisor or employer, as the condition under which the employee gets or keeps the job. **3.** a sudden or violent reaction, response, or movement: *Injury can result from a chain saw's kickback.*

kick·ball (kik'bôl') *n.* a game for children that is similar to baseball but is played with a large ball that is kicked and thrown.

kick·er (kik'ər) *n.* **1.** a person or thing that kicks. **2.** *Informal.* a surprising, controversial, or difficult part or point: *It's an easy job, but the kicker is the long hours.*

kick·off (kik'ôf', -of') *n.* **1.** a kick that puts the ball in play in football or soccer, as after points or a goal is scored. **2.** the beginning; commencement: *The dance marked the kickoff of the charity's fund drive.*

kick·shaw (kik'shô') *n.* **1.** a fancy or uncommon dish; delicacy. **2.** a trinket or trifle. [Modification of French *quelque chose* trifle, something, going back to Latin *quālis* of what kind + *qui* who + *causa* reason.]

kick·stand (kik'stand') *n.* a movable metal bar attached to the underside of a bicycle or motorcycle that can be lowered into position with the foot to prop the vehicle upright when not in use.

a	at	e	end	o	hot	u	up	hw	white		about
ā	ape	ē	me	ō	old	ū	use	ng	song		taken
ä	far	i	it	ô	fork	ü	rule	th	thin	ə	pencil
âr	care	ī	ice	oi	oil	ù	pull	th	this		lemon
		îr	pierce	ou	out	ûr	turn	zh	measure		circus

kid¹ (kid) *n.* **1.** a young goat. **2.** kidskin. **3.** *Informal.* a young person; child; youngster. **4.** *Informal.* a son or daughter; offspring. —*adj.* **1.** *Informal.* (of a brother or sister) younger: *a kid sister.* **2.** made of kidskin. [Old Norse *kith* young goat.]

kid² (kid) *v.,* **kid·ded, kid·ding.** —*v.t. Informal.* **1.** to make fun of; tease: *They kidded him about his freckles.* **2.** to deceive (someone) as a joke; fool: *Don't try to kid us into believing that story.* —*v.i.* to engage in good-humored fooling or teasing; joke. [Probably from *kid¹*, in the sense "make a kid of."] —**kid′der,** *n.*

Kid·dush (kid′əsh, ki düsh′) *n.* a Jewish prayer recited over wine on the eve of the Sabbath or a festival. [Yiddish *kidesh,* from Hebrew *kidush* literally, sanctification, from *kidesh* to sanctify.]

kid·dy (kid′ē) *also,* **kid·die.** *n., pl.* **-dies.** a young child. —*adj.* relating to or for young children: *a kiddy show on television.* [From KID¹.]

kid glove 1. a glove made of kidskin or similar leather. **2. kid gloves.** tactful, gentle, or cautious treatment: *The child is sensitive and unpredictable and must be handled with kid gloves.*

kid·nap (kid′nap′) *v.t.,* **-napped** or **-naped, -nap·ping** or **-nap·ing.** to seize or detain (a person) against his or her will, esp. for the purpose of receiving a ransom. [KID¹ child + *nap,* form of NAB.] —**kid′nap′per;** *also,* **kid′nap′er,** *n.*

> **Synonyms** Kidnap and abduct mean to carry off and hold someone illegally. **Kidnap** generally refers to seizing someone against his or her will, esp. for ransom: *to kidnap a child, to kidnap people to hold as hostages.* **Abduct** is narrower and is esp. used in its legal sense of carrying away a child or an underage woman: *to abduct a girl in order to marry her without her parents' consent.*

kid·ney (kid′nē) *n., pl.* **-neys. 1.** either of a pair of organs lying against the back of the abdominal cavity that filter urea, various salts, and other wastes out of the bloodstream, forming urine, which is collected in the bladder. For illustration, see **urinary system. 2.** the kidney of certain animals, used as food. **3.** nature; disposition; temperament. **4.** kind; sort; type. [Middle English *kidenei,* from *kiden-,* of uncertain meaning and origin + *ei* egg, from Old English *æg* egg.]

kidney bean 1. the kidney-shaped seed of any of various varieties of a plant, *Phaseolus vulgaris,* of the pea family, cooked and eaten as a vegetable. **2.** the plant itself, widely cultivated throughout the world.

kidney stone, a hard mineral deposit, or calculus, that sometimes forms in a kidney.

kid·skin (kid′skin′) *n.* a leather made from the skin of young goats, used for such items as gloves and shoes.

kiel·ba·sa (kil bä′sə, kēl-, kyel-) *n., pl.* **-sas** or **-sy** (-sē). a smoked sausage flavored with garlic and spices. Also, **Polish sausage.** [Polish *kielbasa* this sausage; of uncertain origin.]

Ki·ku·yu (ki kü′ū) *n., pl.* **-yu** or **-yus. 1.** a member of a Bantu tribe of northern Kenya. **2.** their language, a member of the Bantu family of languages.

kill¹ (kil) *v.t.* **1.** to cause the death of; deprive of life: *Car accidents kill thousands of Americans every year. The sergeant killed three enemy soldiers.* **2.** to put an end to; destroy; extinguish: *A drink of water killed the taste of the medicine.* **3.** to destroy or spoil the effect of: *The ugly fence kills the beauty of the house.* **4.** to destroy the active qualities of; neutralize: *Too many consecutive plantings killed the soil.* **5.** to cross out, cancel, or stop the publication of: *The editor killed the story in the late edition.* **6.** to defeat or veto: *to kill a proposed law.* **7.** (in tennis and some other sports) to hit (a ball) to an opponent with such force that it is impossible to return it. **8.** to pass (time) aimlessly or unproductively: *We killed an hour by wandering through the town.* **9.** *Informal.* to overcome completely, as with amusement or embarrassment: *The joke killed the audience. It kills you to admit you are wrong.* **10.** *Informal.* to affect with severe pain, discomfort, or fatigue: *My back is killing me.* **11.** *Informal.* to stop or turn off: *to kill a motor, to kill a light.* —*v.i.* **1.** to cause death; be fatal: *An overdose of this drug can kill.* **2.** to commit murder: *to kill without a motive.* —*n.* **1.** the act or an instance of killing, esp. in hunting: *The hunters moved in for the kill.* **2.** an animal or animals killed: *The tiger dragged its kill into the jungle.* **3.a.** the act of destroying an enemy aircraft or other target. **b.** the enemy aircraft or other target so destroyed. [Middle English *killen,* probably from an unrecorded Old English variant of *cuellan.*]

• **to kill off.** to cause the death of all or large numbers of: *What killed off the dinosaurs?*

> **Synonyms** *v.t.* **Kill¹, murder, slay,** and **assassinate** mean to deprive of life. **Kill** is the general term, meaning to cause the death of a person, animal, or plant: *to kill a plant by forgetting to water it, to kill a dog by running over it.* **Murder** refers to killing a person in a criminal manner and usually involves a motive and forethought: *The mobsters murdered the leader of a rival group.* **Slay** connotes killing someone violently. It now appears chiefly in literature and in tabloid headlines: *The knights slew six of the enemy.* ROBBERS SLAY WITNESS. **Assassinate** refers to killing a prominent person, esp. a political figure: *Religious zealots assassinated the prime minister.*

kill² (kil) *n.* a channel, creek, or stream. [Dutch *kil.*]

kill·deer (kil′dîr′) *n., pl.* **-deers** or **-deer.** a North American plover, *Charadrius vociferus,* having a brown back, a white throat, breast, and abdomen, and two black bands across the breast. Length: 9-11 inches (23-28 centimeters). [Imitative of its cry.]

kill·er (kil′ər) *n.* **1.** a person, animal, or thing that kills. **2.** killer whale.

killer bee, any of a variety of honeybee, *Apis mellifera,* noted for its especially aggressive behavior. Native to Africa, it was accidentally released in Brazil and has spread to North America.

killer whale, any of various black-and-white aquatic carnivores of the dolphin family, genus *Orcinus,* inhabiting all oceans of the world. The killer whale preys on fish, penguins, seals, sea lions, and other whales. Length: to 30 feet (9.1 meters). Also, **grampus.**

killer whale

kil·li·fish (kil′ē fish′) *n., pl.* **-fish** or **-fish·es.** any of a group of small, freshwater and brackish water fish, family Cyprinodontidae, usually barred or striped and often used as bait and in mosquito control. Also, **topminnow.** [Earlier *killie* (from KILL² + -IE) + FISH.]

kill·ing (kil′ing) *n.* **1.** the act of a person, animal, or thing that kills, esp. murder. **2.** *Informal.* a sudden great profit or success: *to make a killing in a real estate deal.* —*adj.* **1.** causing or likely to cause death or destruction; deadly; fatal: *a killing blow, a killing frost.* **2.** extremely tiring; exhausting: *a killing amount of work.*

kill·joy (kil′joi′) *n.* someone who spoils or lessens the enjoyment of others.

kiln (kil, kiln) *n.* a furnace or oven for burning, baking, or drying, as in making bricks, pottery, or charcoal. —*v.t.* to burn, bake, or dry in a kiln. [Old English *cylene* oven, from Latin *culīna* kitchen.]

ki·lo (kē′lō, kil′ō) *n., pl.* **-los.** kilogram.

kilo- *prefix* a thousand: *kilocycle, kiloliter.* [French *kilo-,* from Greek *chílioi.*]

kil·o·bar (kil′ə bär′) *n.* a unit of pressure equal to 1,000 bars.

kil·o·byte (kil′ə bīt′) *n. Computers.* 1,024 bytes.

kil·o·cal·o·rie (kil′ə kal′ə rē) *n.* a large calorie.

kil·o·cy·cle (kil′ə sī′kəl) *n.* **1.** a unit equal to 1,000 cycles. **2.** kilohertz.

kil·o·gram (kil′ə gram′) *also, British,* **kil·o·gramme.** *n.* a unit of mass and weight in the metric system, equal to 1,000 grams. [French *kilogramme,* going back to Greek *chílioi* thousand + *gramma* small weight.]

kil·o·gram-me·ter (kil′ə gram′mē′tər) *n.* the meter-kilogram-second unit of work or energy, equal to about 7.2 foot-pounds. A kilogram-meter is the amount of energy required to raise a mass of 1 kilogram to a height of 1 meter.

kil·o·hertz (kil′ə hûrts′) *n., pl.* **-hertz.** a unit equal to 1,000 hertz, used in measuring the frequency of electromagnetic waves. Also, **kilocycle.**

kil·o·li·ter (kil′ə lē′tər) *also, British,* **kil·o·li·tre.** *n.* a unit of capacity in the metric system equal to 1,000 liters. [French *kilolitre,* going back to Greek *chílioi* thousand + *litra* pound.]

ki·lom·e·ter (ki lom′i tər, kil′ə mē′-) *also, British,* **kil·o·me·tre** (kil′ə mē′tər). *n.* a unit of length in the metric system, equal to 1,000 meters. [French *kilomètre,* going back to Greek *chílioi* thousand + *metron* measure.] —**kil·o·met·ric** (kil′ə met′rik), *adj.*

kil·o·ton (kil′ə tun′) *n.* **1.** a unit of weight equal to 1,000 tons.

K

2. a unit of explosive force equivalent to that produced by the detonation of 1,000 tons of TNT.

kil·o·volt (kil′ə vōlt′) *n.* a unit of electromotive force equal to 1,000 volts.

kil·o·watt (kil′ə wot′) *n.* a unit of electrical power equal to 1,000 watts.

kil·o·watt-hour (kil′ə wot′our′) *n.* a unit of electrical energy equal to the energy consumed by a machine working at a steady rate of 1 kilowatt for 1 hour.

kilt (kilt) *n.* a pleated skirt usually made of tartan and reaching to the knees, esp. one worn by men in the Scottish Highlands. —*v.t.* *Scottish.* to tuck up or fasten (the skirts) around the body. [Of Scandinavian origin.]

kil·ter (kil′tər) *n.* *Informal.* good condition; order. ➡ now used chiefly in the phrase *out of kilter: That toaster is out of kilter.* [Of uncertain origin.]

ki·mo·no (ki mō′nə, -nō) *n., pl.* **-nos. 1.** a loose robe or gown tied with a sash, traditionally worn as an outer garment by the Japanese. **2.** a loose dressing gown similar to this. [Japanese *kimono* clothing.]

kin (kin) *n.* **1.** one's whole family; one's relatives; kindred; kinsfolk. **2.** a kinsman or kinswoman; relative: *She is no kin of mine.* —*adj.* **1.** related: *He is not kin to me.* **2.** closely similar; akin: *a parliament that is kin to Great Britain's.* [Old English *cynn* kind², family.]

• **next of kin.** the person or persons most closely related to one: *The police notified the victim's next of kin.*

• **of kin.** related: *We have the same surname, but we are not of kin.*

-kin *suffix* little; small: *lambkin.* [Middle Dutch *-kijn, -kin.*]

kind¹ (kīnd) *adj.* **1.** gentle, considerate, and friendly in nature or behavior; good-hearted: *a kind person, to be kind to animals.* **2.** proceeding from or characterized by good-heartedness: *kind words, a kind act.* [Middle English *kynde,* from Old English *gecynde* natural, inborn.]

Synonyms Kind¹ and benevolent mean disposed to do good or to be friendly and considerate. Kind is the common term, which connotes natural sympathy and goodness: *to be kind to everyone, to be kind to a stray dog.* Benevolent is less profound and less intrinsic to a person's character. It may suggest a position of superiority: *a benevolent ruler, benevolent people who give a lot to charity.*

kind² (kīnd) *n.* **1.** a group whose members are related or are the same or similar in some way; class: *This goose and others of its kind migrate every year.* **2.** a particular type or variety: *The whale is a kind of mammal.* **3.** an example of something that belongs to a group but that has a specified, individual character or characteristic: *a strange kind of hairdo, a rainy kind of day.* **4.** a questionable or imperfect example of a group or class: *The survivors built a kind of shelter from the wreckage of the boat.* **5.** fundamental character or nature: *The difference between ice and liquid water is one of degree and not of kind.* [Old English *cynd* nature.]

• **in kind. a.** in goods or services, rather than in money: *payment in kind.* **b.** with something comparable: *She insulted him, and he responded in kind.*

• **kind of.** *Informal.* somewhat; rather: *I'm getting kind of hungry. It's kind of late.*

• **of a kind. a.** of the same kind; alike: *A pair is the same as two of a kind.* **b.** of poor or imperfect quality; of sorts: *The poor nation began to enjoy prosperity of a kind.*

kin·der·gar·ten (kin′dər gär′tən, -dən) *n.* a class or division of school for children from four to six years old, preceding the first grade of elementary school. [German *kindergarten* literally, children's garden, from *kinder,* genitive plural of *kind* child + *garten* garden.]

kin·der·gart·ner (kin′dər gärt′nər, -gärd′-) *also,* **kin·der·gar·ten·er.** *n.* a child who attends kindergarten.

kind·heart·ed (kīnd′här′tid) *adj.* having or showing kindness or sympathy: *a kindhearted person, kindhearted actions.* —**kind′heart′ed·ly,** *adv.* —**kind′heart′ed·ness,** *n.*

kin·dle (kin′dəl) *v.,* **-dled, -dling.** —*v.t.* **1.a.** to set (something) on fire: *to kindle logs.* **b.** to start (a fire) burning: *to kindle a blaze in a fireplace.* **2.** to arouse, stir up, or excite: *to kindle a person's anger, to kindle a revolt.* **3.** to make bright or glowing; light up: *The setting sun kindled the evening sky.* —*v.i.* **1.** to catch fire; begin to burn: *A dry forest is likely to kindle with the smallest spark.* **2.** to become aroused or stirred up: *Her anger kindled when I told her of their lies.* **3.** to become bright or glowing: *His face kindled with excitement.* [Old Norse *kynda* to light a fire + -LE.] —**kin′dler,** *n.* —For Synonyms *(v.t.),* see **light¹.**

kin·dling (kind′ling) *n.* material for starting a fire, esp. small pieces of dry wood or twigs.

kind·ly (kīnd′lē) *adj.,* **-li·er, -li·est. 1.** having or showing kindness; kind; benevolent: *a kindly face, a kindly smile, kindly*

people. **2.** having a favorable effect; pleasant; agreeable: *a kindly breeze on a hot day.* —*adv.* **1.** in a kind or gentle manner: *to speak kindly to a child.* **2.** in a favorable or agreeable way: *Fate did not look kindly upon their venture.* **3.** as a favor; please: *Kindly remove your foot from the table.* **4.** with feeling or enthusiasm: *We thank you kindly.* [Old English *cyndelīc* natural.] —**kind′li·ness,** *n.*

• **to take kindly to.** to like or accept: *My boss does not take kindly to criticism.*

kind·ness (kīnd′nis) *n.* **1.** the quality or state of being kind; good will. **2.** a kind act; favor: *We thanked our hosts for their many kindnesses.*

kin·dred (kin′drid) *n.* one's whole family; one's relatives. —*adj.* **1.** having a similar character or qualities: *a kindred spirit, kindred pursuits.* **2.** related by birth, history, derivation, or evolution; having common ancestors: *kindred languages, kindred species.* [Old English *cynn* family, kind² + *rǣden* condition.]

kine (kīn) *pl. n. Archaic.* cows; cattle. [Old English *cȳna* of cows, genitive plural of *cū* cow¹.]

kin·e·mat·ics (kin′ə mat′iks) *n.* the branch of mechanics dealing with the motion of moving bodies, without reference to the mass or force involved in the motion. [Greek *kīnēma* motion + -ICS.] —**kin′e·mat′ic,** *adj.*

kin·e·scope (kin′ə skōp′) *n.* **1.** a motion-picture record of a television program. **2.** picture tube. —*v.t.,* **-scoped, -scop·ing.** to make a kinescope of. [Greek *kīnētos* moving + -SCOPE.]

ki·ne·sics (ki nē′siks, -ziks) *n.* the study of body language. ➡ used as singular. [Greek *kinēsis* motion (from *kīnein* to move) + -ICS.] —**ki·ne′sic,** *adj.*

ki·ne·si·ol·o·gy (ki nē′sē ol′ə jē, -zē-) *n.* the study of the principles of mechanics and anatomy in relation to human movement, esp. as applied to physical exercise. [Greek *kinēsis* motion (from *kīnein* to move) + -LOGY.]

kin·es·the·sia (kin′əs thē′zhə, -zē ə) *n.* the sensation of movement, weight, resistance, and position in the muscles and joints, perceived through the nerves. Also, **kin·es·the·sis** (kin′əs thē′sis). [Modern Latin *kinesthesia,* from Greek *kīnein* to move + *aisthēsis* perception.] —**kin·es·thet·ic** (kin′əs thet′ik), *adj.* —**kin′es·thet′i·cal·ly,** *adv.*

ki·net·ic (ki net′ik) *adj.* **1.** of or relating to motion. **2.** produced or caused by motion. **3.** full of energy; dynamic; lively: *The pianist gave a kinetic performance.* [Greek *kīnētikos* of putting in motion, going back to *kīnein* to move.] —**ki·net′i·cal·ly,** *adv.*

kinetic energy, energy possessed by a body because of its motion. ➡ distinguished from **potential energy.**

ki·net·ics (ki net′iks) *n. Physics.* the branch of mechanics that deals with the effects of forces in causing or changing the motion of bodies. ➡ used as singular.

kin·folk (kin′fōk′) *also,* **kin·folks, kinsfolk.** *pl. n.* a person's relatives collectively; family.

king (king) *n.* **1.** a male ruler who holds limited or absolute sovereignty over a nation or state for life, usually by hereditary rights. **2.** King. God or Jesus. **3.** a person or thing supreme or the best in a given sphere: *the king of the jungle, an oil king, the king of popular music.* **4.** a playing card bearing a picture of a king, in most games higher in value than a queen and lower than an ace. **5.** the principal piece in the game of chess, ordinarily capable of moving only one square in any direction. The object of the game is to checkmate the opponent's king. **6.** a piece in the game of checkers that has moved across the board to the opponent's side and been crowned, thus entitling it to move both forward and backward. [Old English *cyning* male ruler of a state.]

king
(def. 5)

king·bird (king′bûrd′) *n.* any of various flycatchers, genus *Tyrannus,* found throughout North and South America. Length: 8-9 inches (20-23 centimeters).

king·bolt (king′bōlt′) *n.* a vertical bolt connecting the body of a wagon or other vehicle with the front axle, or the body of a railroad car with a truck, and serving as a pivot in turning. Also, **kingpin.**

king cobra, a large cobra, *Ophiophagus hannah,* that feeds primarily on other snakes. It is the world's largest poisonous snake. Length: to 18 feet (5.5 meters).

king crab 1. the largest edible crab, *Paralithodes camtschatica,*

a	at	e	end	o	hot	u	up	hw	white		about
ā	ape	ē	me	ō	old	ū	use	ng	song		taken
ä	far	i	it	ô	fork	ü	rule	th	thin	ə	pencil
âr	care	ī	ice	oi	oil	u̇	pull	th	this		lemon
		îr	pierce	ou	out	ûr	turn	zh	measure		circus

having a small triangular body and very long legs. It is found in the northern Pacific Ocean and weighs 11 pounds (5 kilograms) or more. **2.** horseshoe crab.

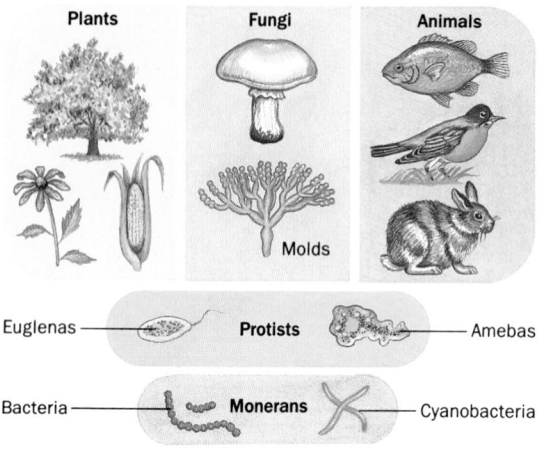

taxonomic **kingdoms**

king·dom (king′dəm) *n.* **1.** a nation or state ruled by a king or queen. **2.** a realm, region, or sphere in which some condition or quality is supreme or prevails: *a cattle kingdom, the kingdom of the intellect.* **3.** one of the three broad categories into which nature is traditionally divided: *the animal, vegetable, and mineral kingdoms.* **4.** in taxonomy, one of the primary categories into which all life is divided. Many biologists now use a system that assigns living things to the animal, plant, fungi, protist, and moneran kingdoms. **5.** *Religion.* the realm, in heaven and on earth, over which God has spiritual sovereignty. [Old English *cyningdōm* kingship.]

king·fish (king′fish′) *n., pl.* **-fish** or **-fish·es. 1.** any of several saltwater food and game fish of the drumfish family, esp. the northern kingfish, *Menticirrhus saxatilis,* found along the Atlantic coast of the United States, having a dark gray body, and weighing up to 3 pounds (1.4 kilograms). Length: to 18 inches (46 centimeters). **2.** *Informal.* a person, esp. a politician, who has undisputed power or supremacy in a group or area.

king·fish·er (king′fish′ər) *n.* any of various brightly colored birds, family Alcedinidae, found throughout temperate and tropical regions of the world, having a large, usually crested head and a long, pointed bill. It feeds on fish, insects, crayfish, and frogs. Length: to 18 inches (46 centimeters).

King James Version, an English translation of the Bible authorized by King James I and first published in 1611, widely used by Protestants. Also, **Authorized Version.**

king·let (king′lit) *n.* **1.** a weak or insignificant king. **2.** any of various greenish songbirds, genus *Regulus,* related to and resembling warblers, often having a somewhat concealed orange, yellow, or red crest. Length: 4 inches (10 centimeters).

king·ly (king′lē) *adj.,* **-li·er, -li·est. 1.** characteristic of, like, or suitable for a king; royal; regal: *a kingly bearing, kingly pride.* **2.** having the status of a king; of royal rank. —*adv.* in a kingly manner; regally; royally. —**king′li·ness,** *n.*

king·pin (king′pin′) *n.* **1.** the pin that is positioned in the center and in front of the other pins in bowling. **2.** kingbolt. **3.** *Informal.* the chief person in a group or sphere: *the kingpin of organized crime.*

king·post (king′pōst′) *n.* a vertical post connecting the apex of a triangular truss, as of a roof, with the tie beam. For illustration, see **tie beam.**

Kings (kingz) *n.* **1.** either of two books, I Kings and II Kings, of the Old Testament, containing the history of the Jewish monarchy from the reign of Solomon to the fall of Jerusalem in 586 B.C. **2.** in the Douay Bible, one of four books of the Old Testament, equivalent to I and II Samuel and I and II Kings of the Protestant Bible. ➡ used as singular in both defs.

king salmon, a large salmon, *Oncorhynchus tschawtscha,* found throughout the northern Pacific Ocean, commercially important as a food fish. Length: to 4 feet (1.2 meters). Also, **chinook.**

King's English, standard, correct, or accepted English usage or speech, esp. that of Great Britain. Also, **Queen's English.**

king·ship (king′ship′) *n.* **1.** the position, office, or dignity of a king. **2.** government by a king; monarchy.

king-size (king′sīz′) *also,* **king′-sized′.** *adj.* **1.** larger or longer

than is ordinary: *a king-size portion of meat.* **2.** of or relating to a bed measuring 76 inches (193 centimeters) wide by 80 inches (203 centimeters) long, a size larger than a queen-size bed: *a king-size blanket.*

king snake, any of a group of nonpoisonous constrictors, genus *Lampropeltis,* of varied marking and coloration, found from southern Canada to Ecuador. It feeds on other snakes and on rodents, lizards, frogs, and other small animals. Length: to 7 feet (2.1 meters).

ki·nin (kī′nin) *n.* **1.** any of a group of polypeptides that enable smooth muscles to contract, dilate blood vessels, and assist in a wide range of other biological functions. **2.** cytokinin. [KIN(ETIC) + -IN [1].]

kink (kingk) *n.* **1.** a tight curl or sharp twist, as in a hair, wire, or rope. **2.** a painful muscle spasm or cramp; crick: *I got a kink in my back from lifting the sofa.* **3.** an imperfection or flaw, as in the plan or operation of something: *The engineer got the kinks out of the design.* **4.** a mental quirk, eccentricity, or whim. —*v.i., v.t.* to form or cause to form a kink or kinks. [Dutch *kink* twist in a rope.]

kin·ka·jou (king′kə jü′) *n.* a small, slender, yellowish brown, arboreal mammal, *Potos flavus,* related to the raccoon, native to the tropical forests of Mexico and Central and South America, having a long prehensile tail and soft woolly fur. Length: 36 inches (91 centimeters), including tail. Also, **honey bear.** [French *kinkajou;* of Algonquian origin.]

kinkajou

kink·y (king′kē) *adj.,* **kink·i·er, kink·i·est. 1.** tightly curled or twisted; full of kinks: *kinky hair.* **2.** *Informal.* very strange or weird. —**kink′i·ness,** *n.*

kins·folk (kinz′fōk′) kinfolk.

kin·ship (kin′ship′) *n.* **1.** a family relationship. **2.** any relationship or close connection: *the kinship between botany and zoology.*

kins·man (kinz′mən) *n., pl.* **-men** (-mən). a male relative.

kins·wom·an (kinz′wŭm′ən) *n., pl.* **-wom·en** (-wim′ən). a female relative.

ki·osk (kē′osk, kē osk′) *n.* **1.** a small structure with one or more open sides, used esp. as a newsstand, bandstand, telephone booth, or subway entrance. **2.** a freestanding, cylindrical structure on which advertisements and notices are posted. **3.** a light, open pavilion or summerhouse, often having its roof supported by columns, common in Turkey and Iran. [French *kiosque,* from Turkish *kiūshk* pavilion, from Persian *kūshk* palace.]

Ki·o·wa (kī′ə wə) *n., pl.* **-wa** or **-was.** a member of a North American Indian tribe living on the southern Great Plains.

kip (kip) *n.* the untanned hide of a small or young animal. [Middle Dutch *kip* bundle of hides.]

kip·per (kip′ər) *v.t.* to cure (fish) by splitting, cleaning, and salting, and then drying, smoking, or preserving. —*n.* **1.** a fish, esp. herring, salmon, or sea trout, that has been kippered. **2.** a male salmon or sea trout during or shortly after the spawning season. [Old English *cypera* kind of salmon, possibly from *coper* copper (with reference to the coloring of the salmon). See COPPER.]

Kir·ghiz (kir gēz′) *n., pl.* **-ghiz** or **-ghiz·es. 1.** a member of a Turkic-speaking Mongolian people living mainly in west-central Asia. **2.** their language, a member of the Ural-Altaic family of languages.

kirk (kûrk) *n.* **1.** *Scottish.* a church. **2. the Kirk.** the established Presbyterian Church of Scotland, as distinguished from the Church of England or the Episcopal Church of Scotland. [Old Norse *kirkja* church, from Old English *cirice.* See CHURCH.]

kir·mess (kûr′mis) kermis.

kir·tle (kûr′təl) *n.* **1.** a woman's skirt, gown, or petticoat. **2.** a short coat or tunic formerly worn by men. [Old English *cyrtel,* going back to Latin *curtus* short.]

kis·met (kiz′met, -mət) *n.* fate; destiny. [Turkish *qismet,* from Arabic *qisma(t).*]

kiss (kis) *v.t., v.i.* **1.** to touch with the lips as a sign of greeting, affection, desire, or respect: *The mother kissed her son. They kissed and said good-bye.* **2.** to touch lightly or softly: *When the sweet wind did gently kiss the trees* (Shakespeare, *Merchant of Venice*). —*n.* **1.** a touching with the lips as a sign of greeting, affection, desire, or respect. **2.** a light or gentle touch. **3.** any of several small candies, esp. of chocolate, usually individually wrapped in foil or paper. [Old English *cyssan* to touch with the lips.] —**kiss′·a·ble,** *adj.*

kiss·er (kis′ər) *n.* **1.** a person who kisses. **2.** *Slang.* **a.** the face. **b.** the mouth.

Ki·swa·hi·li (kē'swä hē'lē) *also*, **ki-Swa·hi·li.** *n.* Swahili *(def. 2).*

kit¹ (kit) *n.* **1.** a set of tools, instruments, or equipment for a specific purpose: *a repair kit, a first-aid kit.* **2.** a collection of personal effects or articles, esp. for traveling. **3.** a bag, case, box, or other container for storing or carrying a kit. **4.** a set of parts or materials to be assembled: *I built a model of a rocket from a kit.* **5.** *Informal.* a collection of persons or things; lot. ➡ now used chiefly in the phrase *the whole kit and caboodle: We sold the whole kit and caboodle to a junk dealer.* [Middle Dutch *kitte* large wooden bowl, tankard.]

kit² (kit) *n.* **1.** kitten. **2.** a young or undersized animal of a species that bears fur, such as a fox or beaver.

kitch·en (kich'ən) *n.* **1.** a room or place specially equipped or set apart for the preparation and cooking of food. **2.** the facilities, equipment, or staff of a kitchen. **3.** cuisine: *This restaurant has an international kitchen that includes French and Italian dishes.* [Old English *cycene* place for cooking food, going back to Latin *coquīna,* from *coquere* to cook.]

kitch·en·ette (kich'ə net') *also,* **kitch·en·et.** *n.* a small, compactly arranged kitchen, frequently in an alcove off or a section of a larger room.

kitchen garden, a garden where vegetables and fruit are grown for home use.

kitchen midden, a mound of refuse consisting mainly of shells and bones, marking the prehistoric location of a human habitation. Also, **midden.** [Translation of Danish *kökkenmödding.*]

kitchen police *Military.* **1.** the duty of assisting the cook by performing kitchen chores. **2.** the enlisted persons assigned to such duty.

kitch·en·ware (kich'ən wâr') *n.* kitchen utensils, such as pots and pans.

kite (kīt) *n.* **1.** a lightweight frame, usually of wood covered with paper or cloth, flown in the air at the end of a long string for sport or recreation. **2.** any of various small hawks, family Accipitridae, having a forked tail, and long narrow wings, noted for graceful flight. **3.** any of several light, lofty sails spread only in a light wind. —*v.,* **kit·ed, kit·ing.** —*v.i. Informal.* to move or fly with or as with the swift, gliding motion of a kite. —*v.t.* to write (a check) against an account that does not have enough funds to cover all outstanding checks. [Old English *cȳta* a bird of prey.]

kith (kith) *n.* **kith and kin.** a person's friends, acquaintances, and relatives collectively. [Old English *cȳththu* relationship.]

kit·ten (kit'ən) *n.* a young cat. [Blend of dialectal *kitling* (of Scandinavian origin) and Old French *chaton,* diminutive of *chat* cat, from Late Latin *cattus.* See CAT.]

kit·ten·ish (kit'ə nish) *adj.* **1.** playful or cute, esp. in a coquettish manner. **2.** like or characteristic of a kitten. —**kit'ten·ish·ly,** *adv.* —**kit'ten·ish·ness,** *n.*

kit·ti·wake (kit'ē wāk') *n.* a sea gull, genus *Rissa,* native to Arctic regions, having white plumage with gray and black markings on the wings and a very short hind toe. Length: 16-18 inches (41-46 centimeters). [Imitative of its cry.]

kit·ty¹ (kit'ē) *n., pl.* **-ties.** a kitten or cat. [KIT² + -Y².]

kit·ty² (kit'ē) *n., pl.* **-ties. 1.a.** a pool in a card game into which each player contributes, used esp. to pay expenses or buy refreshments. **b.** the stakes in a card game, esp. poker; pot. **2.** money pooled by a group of people for some special purpose. [KIT¹ + -Y².]

kit·ty-cor·ner (kit'ē kôr'nər) *n.* cater-corner. Also, **kit'ty-cor'nered.**

Kitty Litter *Trademark.* an absorbent, granular material used for cats kept as household pets.

ki·va (kē'və) *n.* a round chamber in a Pueblo Indian dwelling, usually completely or partly underground, and entered by ladder from an opening in the roof, used esp. for religious ceremonies. [Of Hopi origin.]

Ki·wa·nis International (ki wä'nis) an international association of men's business and professional clubs, founded in Detroit in 1915, pledged to promote higher standards in business and professional life. —**Ki·wa·ni·an** (ki wä'nē ən), *n., adj.*

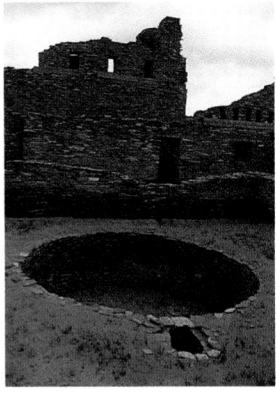

Pueblo Indian **kiva**

ki·wi (kē'wē) *n.* **1.** any of several flightless birds, genus *Apteryx,* native to the forests of New Zealand, having a rounded body, a very long, slender bill, and brownish gray, furlike feathers. Length: 19-33 inches (48-84 centimeters). Also, **apteryx. 2.** an oval, usually edible fruit having many seeds, green pulp, and usually a covering of reddish brown bristles when ripe. **3.** the climbing shrub, genus *Actinidia,* that bears this fruit. Also *(defs. 2, 3),* **Chinese gooseberry.** [Of Maori origin.]

KKK, Ku Klux Klan.

kl *also,* **kl.** kiloliter; kiloliters.

Klan (klan) *n.* Ku Klux Klan.

Kleen·ex (klē'nex) *n. Trademark.* a disposable paper tissue that serves as a handkerchief.

Klein bottle (klīn) *Geometry.* a one-sided edgeless surface formed by taking the neck of a bottle, passing it through the side of the bottle, and joining it to an opening at the bottom of the bottle.

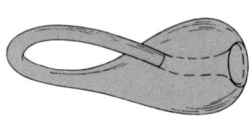

Klein bottle

klep·to·ma·ni·a (klep'tə mā'nē ə) *also,* **cleptomania.** *n.* an obsessive and uncontrollable impulse or tendency to steal, esp. items that one can afford to pay for or does not need. [Greek *kleptēs* thief + *maniā* madness.] —**klep'to·ma'ni·ac',** *n.*

klieg light (klēg) a bright arc lamp used esp. in filming motion pictures. [From the brothers John H. *Kliegl,* 1869-1959, and Anton T. *Kliegl,* 1872-1927, German-American developers of this light.]

klutz (kluts) *n. Slang.* an awkward or clumsy person. [Yiddish *klots* literally, (wooden) beam, from Middle High German *kloc* (wooden) beam.]

klys·tron (klis'tron, klīs'-) *n.* an electron tube in which the velocity of a beam of electrons is modulated to amplify or generate ultrahigh frequency radiation, such as an oscillator in radio and radar transmitters. *Trademark:* **Klystron.**

km *also,* **km.** kilometer; kilometers.

K-me·son (kā'mē'zon, -mez'on, -mē'son, -mes'on) *n.* kaon.

knack (nak) *n.* a special skill, ability, or method for doing something easily or proficiently: *a knack for writing, to have a knack for saying funny things.* [Possibly identical with obsolete *knack* sharp blow; imitative.]

knack·wurst (nok'wûrst') *also,* **knockwurst.** a short, thick, highly seasoned sausage.

knap·sack (nap'sak') *n.* a bag for carrying clothes, equipment, or other supplies, designed to be strapped over the shoulders and carried on the back. [Dutch *knapzak,* from *knappen* to eat + *zak* bag.]

knap·weed (nap'wēd') *n.* any of a number of plants, genus *Centaurea,* of the composite family, esp. black knapweed, *C. nigra,* widely distributed throughout North America and Europe, having a wiry stem and bearing oblong leaves and reddish purple flowers. [Archaic *knop* bud of a flower, knob (possibly from Old English *cnop* knob) + WEED¹.]

knave (nāv) *n.* **1.** an unprincipled, deceitful, or disloyal person; scoundrel. **2.** in card games, a jack. **3.** *Archaic.* **a.** a male servant. **b.** a man of humble birth. [Old English *cnafa* boy, servant.]

knav·er·y (nā'və rē) *n., pl.* **-er·ies.** an act or behavior characteristic of a knave; trickery; deceit.

knav·ish (nā'vish) *adj.* of, relating to, or characteristic of a knave; dishonest; deceitful. —**knav'ish·ly,** *adv.* —**knav'ish·ness,** *n.*

knead (nēd) *v.t.* **1.** to mix or work (a substance, as dough or clay) into a uniform mass, esp. by pressing and squeezing with the hands. **2.** to manipulate by pressing and squeezing with the hands; massage: *The team's trainer kneaded the pitcher's sore arm.* **3.** to make or shape by or as by kneading: *to knead a statue of clay, to knead a person's character.* [Old English *cnedan* to make into a dough.] —**knead'er,** *n.*

knee (nē) *n.* **1.a.** a joint of the human leg between the thigh and the lower leg. **b.** the region around this joint. **2.** any joint similar or corresponding to the human knee, as the carpal joint in the foreleg of hoofed mammals. **3.** the part of a garment, esp. trousers, covering the knee. **4.** anything resembling a bent knee. —*v.t.,* **kneed, knee·ing.** to strike or touch with the knee. [Old English *cnēo* joint between the thigh and lower leg.]

a	at	e	end	o	hot	u	up	hw	white	(	about
ā	ape	ē	me	ō	old	ū	use	ng	song		taken
ä	far	i	it	ô	fork	ü	rule	th	thin	ə	pencil
âr	care	ī	ice	oi	oil	ù	pull	th	this		lemon
		îr	pierce	ou	out	ûr	turn	zh	measure	(	circus

• **to bring to one's knees.** to force to submit or yield: *The siege brought the town to its knees.*

knee·cap (nē′kap′) *n.* a flat, triangular, movable bone at the front of the knee, protecting the joint from injury. Also, **patella.** For illustration, see **skeleton.**

knee-deep (nē′dēp′) *adj.* **1.** so deep as to reach the knees: *The river is only knee-deep at this point.* **2.** sunk to the knees: *knee-deep in mud.* **3.** deeply involved or concerned: *knee-deep in work.*

knee-high (nē′hī′) *adj.* so high or tall as to reach the knees: *The meadow was covered with knee-high grass.* —*n.* a stocking that covers the leg up to the knee.

knee jerk, a reflex of the leg produced by a sharp tap to the tendon below the kneecap.

kneel (nēl) *v.i.* **knelt** or **kneeled, kneel·ing.** to go down or rest on a bent knee or knees: *to kneel down to scrub the floor, to kneel before an altar.* [Old English *cnēowlian,* from *cnēo* knee.]

kneel·er (nē′lər) *n.* **1.** a person or thing that kneels. **2.** something on which one kneels, such as a cushion or padded part of a pew.

knee·pad (nē′pad′) *n.* a protective covering for the knee, worn esp. when engaging in certain sports, such as football or ice hockey.

knell (nel) *n.* **1.** the tolling of a bell, esp. the sound of a bell rung slowly and solemnly, as after a death or at a funeral. **2.** an omen of death, failure, or impending doom: *Not receiving the requested funds was the final knell for the project.* **3.** any mournful sound: *a knell of sobbing voices.* —*v.i.* **1.** (of a bell) to ring slowly and solemnly, as after a death or at a funeral; toll. **2.** to sound mournfully or ominously. —*v.t.* to summon or proclaim by or as by a knell. [Old English *cnyllan* to sound a bell.]

knelt (nelt) a past tense and past participle of **kneel.**

Knes·set (knes′et) *n.* the parliament of Israel. [Hebrew *kneset* literally, assembly, gathering, from *kanas* to gather, collect, assemble.]

knew (nū, nū) the past tense of **know.**

Knick·er·bock·er (nik′ər bok′ər) *n.* **1.** a descendant of the early Dutch settlers of New York. **2.** a native or resident of New York. [From Diedrich *Knickerbocker,* pseudonym used by the American author Washington Irving, 1783-1859, for his *History of New York.*]

knick·ers (nik′ərz) *pl. n.* loose-fitting trousers extending to and gathered just below the knee. Also, **knick·er·bock·ers** (nik′ər bok′ərz). [From KNICKERBOCKER; because of their resemblance to the breeches worn by the Dutch in the illustrations for Washington Irving's book.]

knick·knack (nik′nak′) *also,* **nicknack.** *n.* a small decorative object. [Repetition of obsolete *knack* toy (with vowel change); imitative.]

knife (nīf) *n., pl.* **knives. 1.** a cutting or stabbing instrument or weapon consisting of one or more usually sharp-edged blades attached to a handle. **2.** the cutting blade of a tool or machine. —*v.,* **knifed, knif·ing.** —*v.t.* **1.** to cut or stab with a knife. **2.** *Informal.* to slander, betray, or harm (someone), esp. in an underhanded way. —*v.i.* to move or cut a way through something with or as with a knife: *The boat knifed through the water.* [Old English *cnīf* a cutting tool with a blade and handle.]

knife-edge (nīf′ej′) *n.* **1.** the sharp, cutting part of the blade of a knife. **2.** anything very sharp or penetrating: *The knife-edge of analysis revealed the solution.* **3.** a wedge having a fine edge that is used as a fulcrum for a scale, beam, pendulum, or similar instrument.

knife pleat, one of a set of narrow pleats turned in the same direction.

knight (nīt) *n.* **1.a.** in the Middle Ages, a mounted soldier who gave military service to a king or lord in return for the right to hold land. **b.** such a soldier, usually of noble birth, who, after serving an apprenticeship as a page and squire, was raised to honorable military rank by a king or lord and was pledged to chivalrous behavior. **2.** a man upon whom an honorary, nonhereditary dignity has been conferred by a sovereign in recognition of personal merit or for services rendered to the crown or country. In Great Britain a knight ranks next below a baronet and is entitled to use *Sir* before his given name. **3.** a man devoted to the service or protection of another, esp. a lady; champion. **4.** a member of a society or brotherhood that refers to its members as knights. **5.** a piece in the game of chess that is shaped like a horse's head, which moves two squares forward or backward and then one square to either side or two squares to either side and then one square forward or backward. —*v.t.* to raise to the rank

knight
(def. 5)

of knight: *The queen knighted the soldier for his valor.* [Old English *cniht* boy, servant, vassal.]

knight-er·rant (nīt′er′ənt) *n., pl.* **knights-er·rant.** a medieval knight who traveled in search of adventure, esp. to display military skill, bravery, and chivalry.

knight-er·rant·ry (nīt′er′ən trē) *n., pl.* **knight-er·rant·ries. 1.** conduct, actions, or practices characteristic of a knight-errant. **2.** conduct inspired by noble but impractical ideals; quixotic behavior.

knight·hood (nīt′hůd) *n.* **1.** the rank, dignity, or vocation of a knight. **2.** the behavior or qualities befitting a knight; chivalry. **3.** knights collectively.

knight·ly (nīt′lē) *adj.* **1.** of, relating to, or characteristic of a knight: *knightly deeds, knightly valor.* **2.** composed of knights. —**knight′li·ness,** *n.*

Knights of Columbus, an international fraternal and service organization of Roman Catholic men founded in 1882.

Knight Templar *pl. (def. 1)* **Knights Templars** or *(def. 2)* **Knights Templar. 1.** Templar *(def. 1).* **2.** a member of an order of Freemasons.

knish (knish) *n., pl.* **knish·es.** a baked or fried dumpling containing mashed potato, cheese, meat, or other filling. [Yiddish *knish,* from Polish *knysz* and Ukrainian *knyš,* both probably from dialectal German *knitsch* something pressed together, from *knitschen* to press together.]

knit (nit) *v.,* **knit·ted** or **knit, knit·ting.** —*v.t.* **1.** to make (a fabric or garment) by interlocking loops of yarn or thread, either by hand, using knitting needles, or by machine. **2.** to join or fasten closely and securely: *Love knitted the family together.* **3.** to draw (the brows) together in wrinkles; furrow. —*v.i.* **1.a.** to make a fabric or garment by interlocking loops of yarn or thread. **b.** to make a basic stitch in knitting. **2.** to come together securely, as the parts of a broken bone. **3.** (of the brows) to come together in wrinkles. —*n.* a fabric or garment made by knitting. [Old English *cnyttan* to tie by knotting.] —**knit′ter,** *n.*

knit·ting (nit′ing) *n.* **1.** the action of a person or thing that knits. **2.** knitted work, such as a fabric or garment.

knitting needle, a long, slender rod, either straight or curved, having a blunt point at one or both ends, used in knitting.

knit·wear (nit′wâr′) *n.* clothing made of knitted fabric.

knives (nīvz) the plural of **knife.**

knob (nob) *n.* **1.** a rounded protuberance or lump. **2.** a rounded handle or dial, as for opening a door or drawer or for operating a radio or television. **3.** a rounded, usually isolated, hill or mountain. [Middle Low German *knobbe* knot, bud.] —**knobbed,** *adj.*

knob·by (nob′ē) *adj.,* **-bi·er, -bi·est. 1.** covered with knobs or lumps. **2.** shaped like a knob or knobs: *knobby knees.* —**knob′bi·ness,** *n.*

knock (nok) *v.t.* **1.** to strike with a sharp, hard blow; hit: *The falling branch knocked a passerby on the head.* **2.** to drive, push, or force by hitting: *The batter knocked the ball out of the park. The jostling crowd knocked the cup from my hand.* **3.** to drive or bring (something) violently against something else; cause to collide: *They accidentally knocked heads when they stood up. I knocked my knee against the leg of the table.* **4.** to hit or push so as to cause to fall: *to knock a glass over, to knock a book to the floor.* **5.** to make or cause by striking: *to knock a hole in the wall, to knock a person unconscious.* **6.** *Informal.* to find fault with; disparage: *The critics knocked the dramatist's latest play.* —*v.i.* **1.** to strike a resounding blow or series of blows, esp. with the fist; rap: *I knocked on the door but nobody answered.* **2.** to come into collision; bump: *Fear made their knees knock.* **3.** to make a pounding, clanking, or rattling sound, as an engine with faulty combustion. —*n.* **1.** the act or an instance of knocking; sharp, hard blow: *to get a knock on the head in a fight.* **2.** the sound produced by a blow or series of blows, as that produced by rapping on a door with the fist in order to gain admittance. **3.** a pounding, clanking, or rattling sound, esp. one caused by faulty combustion in an automobile engine. **4.** *Informal.* a misfortune or setback. **5.** *Informal.* harsh or hostile criticism; adverse remark: *The actor's performance received more knocks than praise.* [Old English *cnocian* to strike with a hard blow.]

• **to knock about** (or **around**). *Informal.* **a.** to treat roughly or inconsiderately. **b.** to wander from place to place.

• **to knock down. a.** to take apart, as for shipping or storage. **b.** to dispose of (an article) to a bidder at an auction by a knock with the auctioneer's gavel; sell to the highest bidder. **c.** *Informal.* to lower (a purchase price); reduce: *During the sale prices were knocked down twenty percent or more.* **d.** *Slang.* to receive as wages or salary; earn: *to knock down $150 a week.*

• **to knock it off.** *Slang.* to stop what one is doing.

• **to knock off. a.** *Informal.* to stop: *to knock off work for lunch.* **b.** *Informal.* to stop work: *to knock off every day at five o'clock.* **c.** *Informal.* to deduct (an amount or sum): *to knock off ten*

dollars from the retail price. **d.** *Informal.* to make or accomplish hastily, roughly, or easily: *The author knocked off the book in less than a month.* **e.** *Slang.* to kill. **f.** *Slang.* to rob or burglarize. **g.** *Slang.* to make a copy, esp. a cheap imitation, of (something), as of a designer garment.

•**to knock out. a.** to render unconscious: *A blow on the head knocked me out.* **b.** to defeat (an opposing boxer) by means of a blow that leaves the boxer down and unable to rise and stand before the referee counts to ten. **c.** *Informal.* to tire or exhaust completely: *The long drive really knocked me out.* **d.** *Informal.* to destroy the power, effectiveness, or functioning of: *The storm knocked out electricity in the town. Bombing raids knocked out the enemy's artillery.* **e.** *Informal.* to make or accomplish hastily, roughly, or easily: *The artist knocked out a sketch in fifteen minutes.*

•**to knock out of the box.** *Baseball.* to get so many hits against (an opposing pitcher) that the pitcher is removed from the game.

•**to knock over.** *Slang.* to rob or burglarize: *to knock over a bank.*

•**to knock together.** to make or put together hastily or roughly.

knock·a·bout (nok′ə bout′) *n.* **1.** a small, one-masted sailboat, rigged with a mainsail and a jib. **2.** something suitable or designed for rough use or wear, as an old car. —*adj.* **1.** suitable or designed for rough use or wear, as a garment. **2.** rough; noisy; boisterous: *knockabout comedy.*

knock·down (nok′doun′) *adj.* **1.** powerful enough to knock down or overwhelm: *a knockdown blow.* **2.** made so as to be easily taken apart or put together: *a knockdown bookcase.* —*n.* **1.** the act or an instance of knocking down, esp. in a boxing match. **2.** something, esp. a blow, powerful enough to knock down or overwhelm. **3.** something that is easily taken apart or put together, esp. a piece of furniture.

knock·er (nok′ər) *n.* **1.** someone or something that knocks. **2.** a hinged knob, ring, or other device, usually made of metal, fastened to a door for use in knocking.

knock-knee (nok′nē′) *n.* **1.** an abnormal condition of inward curvature of the leg or legs, causing the knees to knock or rub together in walking. **2. knock-knees.** the knees of a person whose legs are in this condition. —**knock′-kneed′,** *adj.*

knock·off (nok′ôf′, -of′) *n. Slang.* a copy, esp. a cheap imitation, as of a designer garment.

knock·out (nok′out′) *n.* **1.** the act of knocking out or the state of being knocked out. **2.** a victory in boxing by means of a blow that leaves the opponent down and unable to rise and stand before the referee counts to ten. **3.** a blow that causes unconsciousness. **4.** *Informal.* someone or something that is extremely attractive, striking, or impressive: *Your date at the party was a real knockout.* —*adj.* causing a knockout: *a knockout punch.*

knock·wurst (nok′wûrst′) knackwurst.

knoll (nōl) *n.* a small, rounded hill or mound; hummock; hillock. [Old English *cnoll.*]

knot[1] (not) *n.* **1.** a fastening formed by intertwining rope, string, or the like, esp. with one free end being passed through a loop and drawn tight. **2.** a lump, knob, or tangle formed by the intertwining of thread, cord, or the like: *to comb the knots out of a child's hair.* **3.** a piece of material, as ribbon or lace, folded or tied into a knot and worn as an ornament or accessory. **4.** a small group or cluster of persons or things: *A knot of people waited on the platform for the train.* **5.** something intricate, involved, or difficult to solve: *It is too hard a knot for me* (Shakespeare, *Twelfth Night*). **6.** something that forms or maintains a union; any tie or bond, esp. the bond of marriage. **7.a.** a hard, cross-grained lump of wood formed in a tree trunk at the point where a branch grows out from the tree. **b.** a cross section of such a lump, appearing as a roundish, cross-grained section in a piece of cut lumber. **8.** an enlargement or swelling, as in a muscle or gland; node; lump. **9.a.** a unit of speed of 1 nautical mile per hour, or 1.15 statute miles per hour. **b.** 1 nautical mile. —*v.,* **knot·ted, knot·ting.** —*v.t.* **1.** to tie in a knot; form a knot or knots in: *I knotted the string around the package.* **2.** to secure or fasten with or by a knot: *to knot one's hair with a ribbon.* **3.** to unite in a close or intertwined way. —*v.i.* to become tangled or snarled. [Old English *cnotta.*]

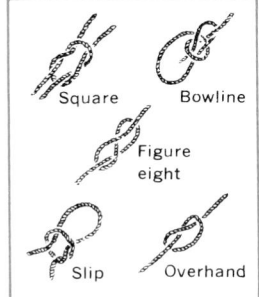

Square   Bowline

Figure eight

Slip   Overhand

knots

fastening formed by intertwining parts of rope, strings, or the like, something intricate.]

•**to tie the knot.** *Informal.* to get married.

knot[2] (not) *n.* any of several sandpipers, genus *Calidris,* that breed in Arctic regions, esp. *C. canutus,* having a reddish breast during the breeding season. [Of uncertain origin.]

knot·grass (not′gras′) *n.* a low-growing plant, *Polygonum aviculare,* of the buckwheat family, found as a weed throughout the world, having a wiry stem with a lump or swelling at each joint, and bearing small, bluish gray leaves and tiny, pink-edged flowers.

knot·hole (not′hōl′) *n.* a hole in a board or other piece of lumber where a knot has fallen out or been removed.

knot·ted (not′id) *adj.* **1.** having or covered with knots, knobs, or bumps. **2.** tied in or decorated with knots.

knot·ty (not′ē) *adj.,* **-ti·er, -ti·est. 1.** having, covered with, or full of knots or bumps, as wood: *knotty pine.* **2.** difficult to understand, solve, or explain; puzzling: *a knotty problem.* —**knot′ti·ness,** *n.*

knout (nout) *n.* a whip formerly used for flogging criminals, esp. in Russia. —*v.t.* to flog with a knout. [Russian *knut* (knotted) whip, from Old Norse *knūtr* knot.]

know (nō) *v.,* **knew, known, know·ing.** —*v.t.* **1.** to perceive or comprehend with certainty; understand clearly: *He refused to compromise because he knew that he was right.* **2.** to be conscious or aware of: *I knew what I was doing.* **3.** to have practical experience with or skill in, esp. through instruction, practice, or study: *She knows how to use a computer. I know how to speak French.* **4.** to have learned by committing to memory; be able to repeat: *The actors knew their lines.* **5.** to be acquainted or familiar with, as through experience: *Alas! poor Yorick. I knew him, Horatio* (Shakespeare, *Hamlet*). **6.** to be able to identify; recognize: *You won't know me with my beard.* **7.** to be able to distinguish: *to know good music from bad music.* **8.** to meet with; experience; undergo: *to know poverty and hunger.* —*v.i.* **1.** to have knowledge or clear understanding: *The goal of scientists is not to speculate but to know.* **2.** to have a clear idea; be conscious or aware (with *of*): *I know of the town but I've never been there.* [Old English *cnāwan* to recognize, be familiar with, understand.] —**know′a·ble,** *adj.* —**know′er,** *n.*

•**in the know.** *Informal.* having special or secret information.

Synonyms *v.t.* **Know, understand,** and **comprehend** may all mean to have a clear idea of something. **Know** is the general and common term. It stresses certainty: *I know what you mean. Do you know how to replace a gasket? Everyone in town knows what happened last night.* **Understand** adds to knowledge of the facts the suggestion of insight into their meaning or significance: *At last I understand what it means to be self-sufficient.* **Comprehend** stresses the process of grasping what is meant: *It took a while to comprehend the reasons for the prime minister's resignation.*

know·how (nō′hou′) *n. Informal.* knowledge of how to do something; practical skill.

know·ing (nō′ing) *adj.* **1.** suggesting secret or private knowledge about something: *a knowing smile.* **2.** showing discernment or cunning; clever; shrewd: *a knowing judge of human nature.* **3.** having knowledge; well-informed: *very knowing about horses.* **4.** deliberate; intentional: *a knowing mistake.* —**know′ing·ly,** *adv.*

know-it-all (nō′it ôl′) *n. Informal.* a person who claims to know a great deal about everything and who rejects the opinions and advice of others.

knowl·edge (nol′ij) *n.* **1.** familiarity, understanding, awareness, or information acquired through experience, study, or observation: *Her knowledge of zoology was limited.* **2.** the fact of knowing: *The knowledge that the car might skid made me drive more slowly.* **3.** something that is or can be perceived or learned; learning or information: *a scholar of great knowledge, to seek knowledge of someone's whereabouts.* **4.** the sum or range of that which is or can be perceived or learned. **5.** specific information or facts concerning a given matter: *Have you any knowledge of his whereabouts?* [Middle English *knowlche* fact of knowing, acquaintance, going back to Old English *cnāwan* to be familiar with, understand.]

•**to (the best of) one's knowledge.** so far as one is aware.

knowl·edge·a·ble (nol′i jə bəl) *adj.* having knowledge or

a	at	e	end	o	hot	u	up	hw	white	about
ā	ape	ē	me	ō	old	ū	use	ng	song	taken
ä	far	i	it	ô	fork	ü	rule	th	thin	ə pencil
âr	care	ī	ice	oi	oil	u̇	pull	th	this	lemon
		îr	pierce	ou	out	ûr	turn	zh	measure	circus

insight; well-informed or intelligent. —**knowl′edge·a·bil′i·ty, knowl′edge·a·ble·ness,** n. —**knowl′edge·a·bly,** adv.

known (nōn) the past participle of **know.**

know-noth·ing (nō′nuth′ing) n. **1.** an ignorant person. **2. Know-Nothing.** a member of a secretive American political party, prominent from 1853 to 1856, that was opposed to the political influence exercised by immigrants.

knuck·le (nuk′əl) n. **1.** a joint of a finger, esp. one connecting a finger to the rest of the hand. **2.** the rounded bump formed when such a joint is bent. **3.** a cut of meat, esp. of pork or veal, consisting of the knee or hock joint and the flesh immediately above and below it. **4. knuckles.** brass knuckles. —v., **-led, -ling.** —v.i. to put the knuckles on the ground when shooting a marble. —v.t. to press, rub, or hit with the knuckles. [Of Germanic origin.]
  ·**to knuckle down.** *Informal.* to apply oneself earnestly; work harder.
  ·**to knuckle under.** to give in; submit; yield.

knuck·le·bone (nuk′əl bōn′) n. **1.** either of the bones forming a knuckle in humans. **2.a.** in animals, a long limb bone having a knobbed end. **b.** the knob itself. [KNUCKLE + BONE.]

knurl (nûrl) n. **1.** a knot, knob, lump, or similar protuberance. **2.** one of a series of small ridges on the edge of a metal object, such as a coin or thumbscrew. —v.t. to make knurls on; mill. [Possibly diminutive of earlier *knur* gnarl (of uncertain origin).] —**knurled,** adj.

knurl·y (nûr′lē) adj., **knurl·i·er, knurl·i·est.** having knurls or knots; gnarled.

KO also, **kayo, K.O., k.o.** *Slang.* n., pl. **KO's** a knockout in boxing. —v.t., **KO'd, KO'ing.** to knock out in boxing.

ko·a·la (kō ä′lə) n. a tree-dwelling marsupial, *Phascolarctos cinereus,* native to Australia, having a chubby, tailless body covered with grayish blue fur, large, bushy ears, and a black nose. Length: to 2½ feet (0.8 meter). [Of native Australian origin.]

Ko·di·ak bear (kō′dē ak′) an especially large variety of brown bear found on Kodiak Island and adjacent areas in Alaska. Height: to 9 feet (2.7 meters) when standing erect.

K. of C., Knights of Columbus.

Koh·i·noor (kō′ə nûr′) also, **Koh·i·nor.** n. a very large diamond that was found in India, weighing 108.93 carats, now one of the British crown jewels. [Persian *kōh-i nūr* literally, mountain of light.]

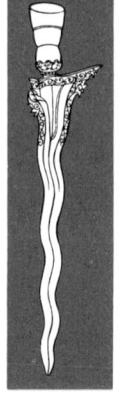
koala

kohl (kōl) n. a cosmetic preparation used by women in certain Middle Eastern and Asian countries to darken the skin around the eyes. [Arabic *kohl* powder of antimony.]

kohl·ra·bi (kōl rä′bē) n., pl. **-bies.** a cultivated plant, *Brassica oleracea gongylodes,* of the cabbage family, having a white or purple, thick, round stem that is eaten as a vegetable. [German *Kohlrabi,* through Italian, from Latin *caulis* cabbage + *rāpa* turnip.]

ko·la (kō′lə) also, **cola.** n. **1.** an evergreen tree, *Cola acuminata,* widely cultivated in tropical regions of the world, having leathery oval leaves, and bearing kola nuts and clusters of small bell-shaped yellow flowers. Also, **kola nut tree. 2.** kola nut. **3.** a dried extract of kola nuts, used chiefly to flavor soft drinks. [Of West African origin.]

kola nut also, **cola nut.** the bitter brown seed of the kola, borne in thick, fleshy pods.

ko·lin·sky (kə lin′skē) n., pl. **-skies. 1.** a yellow mink, *Mustela sibirica,* native to Asia and eastern Europe. Length: 18-21 inches (46-53 centimeters), including tail. **2.** the tawny fur of this animal, frequently dyed to resemble sable. [Russian *kolinski* relating to *Kola,* a region in the northwestern Soviet Union where the best grade of this fur is found.]

Kol Ni·dre (kōl nid′rə) a Jewish prayer of atonement recited in the service on the eve of Yom Kippur.

Ko·mo·do dragon (kə mō′dō) a monitor of Indonesia that is the largest lizard in the world. It grows to a length of 12 feet (3.7 meters) and can kill large animals. [From *Komodo,* island in Indonesia where it is found.]

koo·doo (kü′dü′) n., pl. **-doos.** kudu.

kook (kük) n. *Slang.* an odd, eccentric, or insane person: *People are staring at you because you're acting like a kook.*

kook·a·bur·ra (kük′ə bûr′ə, -bur′ə) n. an Australian kingfisher, *Dacelo novaeguineae,* having a large head, a stout, pointed bill, and a cry that sounds like loud, harsh laughter. Length: 17 inches (43 centimeters). [Of native Australian origin.]

kook·y (kü′kē) also, **kook·ie.** adj., **kook·i·er, kook·i·est.** *Slang.* of, relating to, or like a kook; odd, eccentric, or insane. —**kook′i·ness,** n.

ko·peck (kō′pek) also, **ko·pek, co·peck.** n. a monetary unit and coin equal to 1/100 of a ruble. [Russian *kopeika,* from *kop'e* spear; because the coin once depicted the czar holding a spear.]

Ko·ran (kô ran′, -rän′) n. the sacred book of the Muslims, containing the religious and moral code of Islam. [Arabic *Qur'ān* a reading, recitation.] —**Ko·ran′ic,** adj.

Ko·re·an (kə rē′ən, kô-) adj. of, relating to, or characteristic of Korea or its people, language, or culture. —n. **1.** a native or citizen of Korea. **2.** a person of Korean ancestry. **3.** the language of Korea, unrelated to any known language family.

Korean War, a war between North Korea, aided by the People's Republic of China, and South Korea, aided by the United States and other United Nations members, that lasted from June 1950 until July 1953.

ko·ru·na (kôr′ə nä′) n., pl. **ko·ru·nas** or **ko·ru·ny** (kôr′ə nē) or **ko·run** (kôr′ün). the monetary unit of Czechoslovakia. [Czech *koruna* literally, crown, from Latin *corōna.* See CROWN.]

ko·sher (kō′shər) adj. **1.** conforming to or in accordance with Jewish ceremonial law, esp. those laws affecting food and its preparation: *kosher meat.* **2.** selling, serving, or preparing food according to Jewish ceremonial law: *a kosher restaurant, a kosher butcher.* **3.** *Slang.* right; proper; legitimate: *Cheating is not kosher.* —v.t. to make kosher, esp. to prepare (food) in accordance with Jewish ceremonial law. —n. kosher food. [Yiddish *kosher,* from Hebrew *kasher* literally, fit, proper, from the root *ksr* to be fit, proper.]

ko·to (kō′tō) n., pl. **-tos.** a Japanese musical instrument consisting of a sounding board over which are stretched strings that are plucked with plectrums. [Japanese *koto.*]

kou·miss (kü′mis) also, **kou·mis.** n. kumiss.

kow·tow (kou′tou′, -tou′) v.i. **1.** to kneel and touch the forehead to the ground as an expression of deep respect, submission, or worship. **2.** to act in an obsequious manner; show servile deference: *The young worker refused to kowtow to the boss.* —n. the act of kowtowing. [Chinese (Mandarin) *kòutóu* to touch the forehead on the ground to show respect, from *kòu* to strike + *tóu* head.] —**kow′tow′er,** n.

KP, kitchen police.

Kr, the symbol for krypton.

kraal (kräl) n. **1.** a village of South African blacks, typically surrounded by a fence or stockade. **2.** a fenced enclosure in South Africa for livestock, as cattle or sheep. —v.t. to enclose (livestock) in a kraal. [Afrikaans *kraal* village, enclosure, pen, from Portuguese *curral* pen for cattle, from *correr* to run, from Latin *currere.*]

kraft (kraft) n. a strong brown paper or cardboard made from wood chips treated in an alkaline solution. Also, **kraft paper.** [Short for KRAFT PAPER, from Swedish *kraftpapper,* from *kraft* strength + *papper* paper.]

krait (krīt) n. any of several very poisonous snakes, genus *Bungarus,* related to the cobra and found in southeastern Asia and adjacent islands. [Hindi *karait.*]

K ration, a packaged emergency field ration used by U.S. military forces. [From Ancel *K(eys),* born 1904, U.S. physiologist.]

Krebs cycle (krebz) the cycle of enzymatic reactions that occur in plant and animal cells, by which carbohydrates, proteins, and fats are metabolized and carbon dioxide and ATP are produced. [From Hans Adolf *Krebs,* 1900-81, British biochemist.]

Krem·lin (krem′lin) n. **1.a.** the seat of government of the Soviet Union from 1922 to 1991. **b.** the seat of government of Russia. **2.** the citadel of Moscow, the former royal residence of the czars. **3. kremlin.** the citadel of any Russian city. [French *kremlin,* from Russian *kreml'* citadel; of Tatar origin.]

kreut·zer (kroit′sər) also, **kreu·zer.** n. a former coin of Germany or Austria. [German *Kreuzer,* from *Kreuz* cross, going back to Latin *crux;* because it originally bore the design of a cross.]

krill (kril) n., pl. **krill.** any of a group of small marine crustaceans that resemble shrimp. Krill are eaten by various fish, seals, whales, and other animals.

krim·mer (krim′ər) n. a loosely curled, usually gray fur resembling Persian lamb and astrakhan, made from the pelts of young lambs raised in the Crimean peninsula region. [German *Krimmer,* from Russian *Krim* Crimea; of Tatar origin.]

kris (krēs) also, **crease, creese.** n. a Malay dagger or short sword with a wavy, double-edged blade. [Malay *krīs.*]

kris

Krish·na (krish′nə) *n.* one of the most important Hindu gods, an incarnation, or avatar, of Vishnu. [Sanskrit *Krsnāh* literally, black, dark.]

Kriss Krin·gle (kris′ kring′gəl) Santa Claus. [German *Christkindl* little Christ child, from *Christ* Christ + *Kind* child. See CHRIST.]

kro·na (krō′nə) *n., pl.* **-nor** (-nôr). the monetary unit of Sweden. [Swedish *krona,* going back to Latin *corōna.* See CROWN.]

kró·na (krō′nə) *n., pl.* **-nur** (-nər). the monetary unit of Iceland. [Icelandic *kruna,* going back to Latin *corōna.* See CROWN.]

kro·ne[1] (krō′nə) *n., pl.* **-ner** (-nər). the monetary unit of Denmark and Norway. [Danish and Norwegian *krone,* going back to Latin *corōna.* See CROWN.]

kro·ne[2] (krō′nə) *n., pl.* **-nen** (-nən). **1.** a former gold coin of Germany. **2.** a former monetary unit and silver coin of Austria. [German *Krone,* going back to Latin *corōna.* See CROWN.]

Kro·nos (krō′nos) Cronus.

krul·ler (krul′ər) cruller.

kryp·ton (krip′ton) *n.* a colorless, inert, gaseous element used in some fluorescent light bulbs. Symbol: **Kr** For tables, see **element.** [Greek *krypton,* neuter of *kryptos* hidden; because it is colorless, tasteless, and odorless.]

KS, the postal abbreviation for Kansas.

Kt *Chess.* knight.

ku·dos (kü′dōs, -dos, kū′-) *n.* praise; renown. ➡ used as singular. [Greek *kydos.*]

ku·du (kü′dü) *also,* **koodoo.** *n.* an African antelope, genus *Tragelaphus,* the male of which has long, spirally twisted horns. There are two species: the **greater kudu,** *T. strepsiceros,* having a reddish or grayish body marked with vertical white stripes, and the **lesser kudu,** *T. imberbis,* having a dark gray, heavily striped body. Height: 4 feet (1.2 meters) at the shoulder. [Of Khoikhoi origin.]

kud·zu (kud′zü) *n.* a hairy, perennial vine, *Pueraria lobata,* of the pea family, native to China and Japan, and introduced into the United States. It is cultivated as fodder and for its edible roots, and is sometimes used for erosion control. [From *Kuzu,* the village in Japan where this vine was cultivated.]

greater **kudu**

Ku Klux Klan (kü′ kluks′ klan′, kū′) **1.** a secret society founded in the southern United States after the American Civil War that used acts of terrorism against blacks and their supporters in an effort to reestablish the political and social dominance that white Southerners lost under Reconstruction. **2.** a secret society founded in 1915 and modeled on the original Ku Klux Klan but national in membership and directed against Roman Catholics, Jews, and immigrants, as well as blacks. [Possibly a modification of Greek *kyklos* circle + CLAN.]

ku·lak (kü läk′, kü′läk) *n.* a wealthy or landed peasant in the Soviet Union who resisted the program of collectivization of agriculture of the Soviet government in the 1920s and 1930s. [Russian *kulak* rich peasant; literally, fist.]

ku·miss (kü′mis) *also,* **koumiss, koumis.** *n.* **1.** an alcoholic drink usually made from fermented mare's or camel's milk, drunk esp. by nomads in western and central Asia. **2.** a similar drink made from cow's milk. [Russian *kumys* fermented mare's milk; of Tatar origin.]

küm·mel (kim′əl, kūm′-) *n.* a colorless liqueur usually flavored with caraway seeds, cumin, or anise. [German *Kümmel* caraway seed, this liqueur, going back to Latin *cumīnum* cumin.]

kum·quat (kum′kwot) *also,* **cumquat.** *n.* **1.** a small, oval, orange or yellow fruit with a sweet rind and sour pulp, which grows on any of a group of evergreen shrubs or trees, genus *Fortunella.* **2.** the shrub or tree bearing this fruit, grown in many tropical and temperate regions of the world. [Chinese (Cantonese) *kam kwat* golden orange.]

kung fu (kung′fü′) a Chinese system of unarmed self-defense similar to karate. [Chinese *gōng fū* boxing principles; literally, skill.]

Kuo·min·tang (kwō′min′tang′, -täng′) *n.* a Chinese nationalist party organized in the early twentieth century by Sun Yat-sen and later led by Chiang Kai-shek. [Chinese (Mandarin) *kuo* nation + *min* people + *tang* party.]

kur·cha·to·vi·um (kûr′chə tō′vē əm) *n.* rutherfordium.

Kurd (kûrd, kürd) *n.* a member of a Muslim people, formerly nomadic, who live largely in southeastern Turkey, northern Iraq, and northwestern Iran.

Kurd·ish (kûr′dish, kür′-) *adj.* of, relating to, or characteristic of the Kurds or their language or culture. —*n.* the language of the Kurds, belonging to the Indo-Iranian branch of the Indo-European language family.

Kush·it·ic (kü shit′ik) Cushitic.

kV *also,* **kv** kilovolt.

kW *also,* **kw.** kilowatt; kilowatts.

Kwa·ki·u·tl (kwä′kē ü′təl) *n., pl.* **-tl** or **-tls.** a member of a North American Indian tribe living on the northern coast of Vancouver Island and on the coast of British Columbia.

Kwan·za (kwän′zə) *also,* **Kwan·zaa.** *n.* an annual festival, originally an African harvest festival, celebrated between December 26 and January 1 by some American blacks. [Swahili *kwanza* first fruits.]

kwash·i·or·kor (kwä′shē ôr′kər) *n.* a serious nutritional disease occurring in children, esp. in tropical areas of Africa, Latin America, and Asia, caused by a protein deficiency.

kWh *also,* **kwh, kwhr, kw.hr.** kilowatt-hour; kilowatt-hours.

Ky., Kentucky.

KY, the postal abbreviation for Kentucky.

ky·a·nite (kī′ə nīt′) *n.* a blue or green, glassy silicate mineral used in making refractory materials, esp. the porcelain insulation of spark plugs. Formula: Al_2SiO_5

kyat (chät) *n., pl.* **kyats.** the monetary unit of Burma.

ky·mo·graph (kī′mə graf′) *n.* an instrument used for measuring and recording variations in fluid pressure, as in blood pressure or the pulse. [Greek *kȳma* something swollen, wave + -GRAPH.]

Ky·ri·e e·le·i·son (kir′ē ā′e lā′ə son′) **1.** a liturgical prayer containing the words *Kyrie eleison* or *Lord, have mercy,* esp. part of the ordinary of the Mass, sung or said before the Gloria. **2.** a musical setting for this. Also, **Kyrie.** [Greek *Kyrie eleēson* Lord, have mercy.]

a	at	e	end	o	hot	u	up	hw	white	⎧	about
ā	ape	ē	me	ō	old	ū	use	ng	song	⎪	taken
ä	far	i	it	ô	fork	ü	rule	th	thin	ə ⎨	pencil
âr	care	ī	ice	oi	oil	ů	pull	th	this	⎪	lemon
		îr	pierce	ou	out	ûr	turn	zh	measure	⎩	circus

L The earliest form of **L** was the letter called *lamedh*, meaning "staff" or "rod," in the ancient Semitic alphabets. The early Greeks borrowed *lamedh* and, by reversing it and turning it upside down, formed a new letter that they called *lambda*. By about the fifth century B.C., *lambda* was being written as an inverted letter **V**. This shape was not adopted by the Etruscans, who wrote their letter **L** very much as *lamedh* had been written, although sometimes reversing it. The Romans, who adopted the Etruscan alphabet, also based their letter **L** on *lamedh* rather than *lambda*. Our modern English capital **L** is almost identical in shape to the Latin **L** as it was written around 400 B.C.

---

l, L (el) *n., pl.* **l's, L's. 1.** the twelfth letter of the English alphabet. **2.** the shape of this letter or something having this shape.

L (el) *also,* **l** *n., pl.* **L's.** the Roman numeral for 50.

l *also,* **L** liter; liters.

l. 1. lake. **2.** latitude. **3.** law. **4.** league. **5.** left. **6.** length. **7.** line. **8.** lira; lire.

L. 1. Lake. **2.** Latin. **3.** League.

la (lä) *n. Music.* the sixth of the series of syllables used to name the eight tones of the diatonic scale. For illustration, see **do²**.

La, the symbol for lanthanum.

La., Louisiana.

LA, the postal abbreviation for Louisiana.

L.A. *also,* **LA** Los Angeles.

lab (lab) *n. Informal.* laboratory.

Lab. 1. Labourite. **2.** Labrador.

la·bel (lā′bəl) *n.* **1.a.** any attachment, as a gummed piece of paper or a small square of cloth, affixed to an article to give information, as to its contents, owner, manufacturer, or destination. **b.** a statement on such an attachment. **2.** a brand identifying a product, as a phonograph record: *What label did that singer record on?* **3.** a short descriptive or characterizing phrase applied to a person, group, thing, or idea. —*v.t.,* **-beled, -bel·ing;** *also, British,* **-belled, -bel·ling. 1.** to put a label on. **2.** to describe or characterize by means of a label: *to label a product "flammable," to label a person "unteachable."* **3.** *Medicine.* to treat (a substance) with a radioisotope in order to trace its path through the body. [Old French *label* ribbon, strip²; of Germanic origin.] —**la′bel·er;** *also, British,* **la′bel·ler,** *n.*

la·bel·lum (lə bel′əm) *n., pl.* **-bel·la** (-bel′ə). *Botany.* the inner petal of an orchid, usually larger and different in shape and markings from the other two. [Latin *labellum* little lip, diminutive of *labrum* lip.]

la·bi·a (lā′bē ə) the plural of **labium.**

la·bi·al (lā′bē əl) *adj.* **1.** of, relating to, or characteristic of the lips. **2.** *Phonetics.* articulated primarily by the lips. **3.** of or relating to a labium or labia. —*n. Phonetics.* a vowel or consonant sound made by the lips. [Medieval Latin *labialis* relating to the lips, from *labium* lip.] —**la′bi·al·ly,** *adv.*

la·bi·ate (lā′bē āt′, -it) *adj.* having lips or parts resembling lips. —*n. Botany.* a plant in which the corolla or calyx is divided into labiate parts, as in members of the mint family. [Modern Latin *labiatus,* from Latin *labium* lip.]

la·bile (lā′bəl, -bīl) *adj.* **1.** likely or tending to change. **2.** (of a chemical compound) containing atoms or groups that are readily replaced, hence inherently unstable. [Late Middle English *labyl* changeable, unstable, from Late Latin *labilis,* from Latin *labi* to slip, fall.] —**la·bil·i·ty** (lə bil′i tē), *n.*

la·bi·o·den·tal (lā′bē ō den′təl) *Phonetics. adj.* articulated with the lower lip and upper front teeth, as in pronouncing *f* or *v.* —*n.* a sound made by the lower lip and upper front teeth. [Latin *labium* lip + DENTAL.]

la·bi·um (lā′bē əm) *n., pl.* **-bi·a. 1.** a lip or liplike part. **2.** *Anatomy.* any of the liplike folds of flesh that border the vulva. [Latin *labium* lip.]

la·bor (lā′bər) *also, British,* **labour.** *n.* **1.** physical or mental exertion; work; toil. **2.** a specific piece of work; task: *Hercules was given twelve labors to perform.* **3.** persons who perform manual work for wages, collectively. **4.** labor unions collectively. **5.** the exertion and contractions of childbirth. —*v.i.* **1.** to do work; perform labor: *Pickers labored in the field.* **2.** to move slowly and with difficulty: *The old truck labored up the steep hill.* **3.** to suffer from a disadvantage, burden, or trouble (with *under*): *to labor under extremely difficult circumstances.* **4.** to undergo the exertion and contractions of childbirth. —*v.t.* to spend too much time on or work out in too much detail; belabor: *The authors labored their argument against sales taxes.* [Old French *labour* toil, trouble, from Latin *labor* toil, pain.]

lab·o·ra·to·ry (lab′rə tôr′ē, lab′ər ə-) *n., pl.* **-ries. 1.** a room, building, or workshop designated and equipped for teaching science or for conducting scientific experiments or tests. **2.** a factory that develops and manufactures chemical or pharmaceutical products. **3.** an educational program involving practical experience, observation, or experimentation: *a writing laboratory.* [Medieval Latin *laboratorium* workshop, from Latin *laborāre* to work.]

Labor Day, a legal holiday in honor of workers, observed in the United States and Canada on the first Monday in September.

la·bored (lā′bərd) *adj.* done with effort; not easy; forced: *labored breathing, a labored style of writing.*

la·bor·er (lā′bər ər) *n.* a worker, esp. one who performs manual work for wages.

la·bor-in·ten·sive (lā′bər in ten′siv) *adj.* requiring a greater investment in labor than in machines, buildings, or materials: *The automobile industry is more labor-intensive than the computer industry.*

la·bo·ri·ous (lə bôr′ē əs) *adj.* **1.** requiring much work, esp. much tedious work: *Checking all the names was a slow, laborious job.* **2.** hard-working; industrious. [Latin *labōriōsus,* from *labor* toil.] —**la·bo′ri·ous·ly,** *adv.* —**la·bo′ri·ous·ness,** *n.* —For Synonyms, see **hard.**

la·bor·ite (lā′bə rīt′) *n.* a member or supporter of a labor party.

labor party, a political party that supports or represents the interests of labor.

la·bor-sav·ing (lā′bər sā′ving) *adj.* saving or designed to save work or effort, esp. manual work: *The dishwasher is a laborsaving appliance.*

labor union, an association of workers organized to advance their mutual interests, esp. in improving wages and working conditions.

la·bour (lā′bər) *British.* labor.

La·bour·ite (lā′bə rīt′) *n.* a member or supporter of the Labour Party.

Labour Party, a British political party that represents the laboring class and supports welfare legislation and the nationalizing of basic industry, formed by an alliance of trade union and intellectual socialist groups.

lab·ra·dor·ite (lab′rə dô-rīt′) *n.* an iridescent, blue feldspar mineral of the plagioclase group, quarried for use as an ornamental building stone. [From *Labrador,* region in Canada where it is found + *-ite¹*.]

Lab·ra·dor retriever (lab′rə dôr′) a sturdy breed of hunting dog commonly used to retrieve game birds and waterfowl, having a dense coat of short

Labrador retriever

688

black, brown, or yellowish hair and a thick tail. Height: 23 inches (58 centimeters) at the shoulder.

la·brum (lā′brəm) *n., pl.* -bra (-brə). *Zoology.* a lip or lip-shaped edge, esp. the frontmost mouthpart of insects and other arthropods. [Modern Latin *labrum,* from Latin lip.]

la·bur·num (lə bûr′nəm) *n.* any of a group of shrubs or small trees, genus *Laburnum,* of the pea family, bearing hanging clusters of yellow flowers and leaves divided into three leaflets. [Latin *laburnum.*]

lab·y·rinth (lab′ə rinth′) *n.* **1.** a set of winding, interconnected passages or pathways in which it is easy to get lost or lose one's way; maze. **2.** any intricate, complicated, and confusing arrangement, situation, or subject. **3.** Labyrinth. in Greek mythology, an underground maze in Crete designed by Daedalus to contain the Minotaur. **4.** *Anatomy.* inner ear. [Latin *labyrinthos* maze, from Greek *labyrinthos.*]

lab·y·rin·thine (lab′ə rin′thin, -thēn) *adj.* **1.** of or being a labyrinth. **2.** like a labyrinth; intricate; complicated. Also, **lab·y·rin·thi·an** (lab′ə rin′thē ən).

lac[1] (lak) *n.* a reddish brown, resinous substance deposited on trees, esp. in India and Burma, by the female lac insect, used to make shellac and varnish. [Hindi *lākh,* going back to Sanskrit *lākshā.*]

lac[2] (lak) *also,* **lakh.** *n.* **1.** in India, a sum or amount equal to 100,000, esp. 100,000 rupees. **2.** in India, any great number. [Hindi *lākh* 100,000, from Sanskrit *lākshā* originally, mark.]

lac·co·lith (lak′ə lith) *n.* a dome-shaped body of igneous rock intruded between layers of sedimentary rock, causing the sedimentary strata to bulge upward. For illustration, see **volcano.** [Greek *lakkos* cistern + -LITH.]

lace (lās) *n.* **1.** a long, thin piece of string, cord, or leather passed or threaded through holes or eyelets to pull or hold together the edges or parts of something. **2.** an ornamental, patterned, openwork fabric made by interweaving fine thread. **3.** an ornamental braid, usually of gold or silver, used for trimming such items as military uniforms and hats. —*v.,* **laced, lac·ing.** —*v.t.* **1.** to pull together or fasten with a lace or laces (often with *up*): *to lace up a corset, to lace one's shoes.* **2.** to ornament or trim with lace. **3.** to join by weaving together; interlace; intertwine: *to lace garlands of flowers together.* **4.** to add a dash of liquor to. **5.** to streak with or as if with lines of color: *brown fabric laced with white.* **6.** to beat; thrash. —*v.i.* to fasten by means of a lace or laces: *shoes that lace rather than button.* [Middle English *las,* from Old French *las* noose, snare, from Latin *laqueus.*] —**lac′er,** *n.*
· **to lace into.** to attack with or as if with blows.

lac·er·ate (las′ə rāt′) *v.t.,* -at·ed, -at·ing. **1.** to tear roughly or severely; mangle. **2.** to hurt or distress; wound: *to lacerate someone's feelings.* [Latin *lacerātus,* past participle of *lacerāre* to tear[1], rend.]

lac·er·a·tion (las′ə rā′shən) *n.* **1.** the act of lacerating. **2.** a jagged tear; wound.

lace·wing (lās′wing′) *n.* any of a group of brown or green insects, families Chrysopidae and Hemerobiidae, having four long, narrow, transparent wings veined in a lacelike pattern. Lacewing larvae feed on aphids and other insect pests.

lach·es (lach′iz) *n. Law.* delay in pursuing a legal claim that prejudices the rights of the other side to the degree that the law will no longer enforce the claim. [Old French *laschesse* neglect, from *lasche* loose, relaxed, going back to Latin *laxus* loose, open.]

Lach·e·sis (lak′ə sis) *n.* in Greek mythology, one of the three Fates. Lachesis determined the length of the thread of life. [Latin *Lachesis,* from Greek *Lachesis;* literally, disposer of lots, from *lanchanein* to obtain by lot.]

lach·ry·mal (lak′rə məl) *also,* **lacrimal.** *adj.* of or relating to tears. [Medieval Latin *lachrymalis* relating to tears, from Latin *lacrima* tear[2].]

lach·ry·ma·to·ry (lak′rə mə tôr′ē) *n., pl.* -ries. any of various small thin-necked vases found in ancient Roman tombs, formerly supposed to have been used to hold the tears of mourners. —*adj.* of, relating to, or producing tears.

lach·ry·mose (lak′rə mōs′) *adj.* shedding tears or causing the shedding of tears; tearful or sad. [Latin *lacrimōsus* tearful, weeping, from *lacrima* tear[2].] —**lach′ry·mose′ly,** *adv.*

lac·ing (lā′sing) *n.* **1.** lace. **2.** a beating; thrashing.

lac insect, a scale insect, *Laccifera lacca,* found esp. in India and Burma, the female of which deposits lac on trees.

lack (lak) *v.t.* **1.** to be without or have too little of; be deficient in; need: *a personality that lacks warmth.* **2.** to be missing, short of, or less than (a portion of a total): *My friend lacks an inch of being six feet tall.* —*v.i.* to be missing or needing (with *in*): *What the rookie lacks in experience is made up in hard work.* —*n.* **1.** the state of being without or having too little: *The poor harvest was caused by a lack of rain.* **2.** something that is needed. [Possibly from Middle Dutch *lac* fault.]

lack·a·dai·si·cal (lak′ə dā′zi kəl) *adj.* lifeless and uninterested; listless. [From earlier *lackadaisy,* lengthened form of LACKADAY.] —**lack′a·dai′si·cal·ly,** *adv.*

lack·a·day (lak′ə dā′) *interj. Archaic.* alas and alack. [Short for *alackaday.*]

lack·ey (lak′ē) *n., pl.* -eys. **1.** a servile subordinate or follower. **2.** a low-ranking male servant, esp. a footman. —*v.i., v.t.,* -eyed, -ey·ing. to serve as a lackey. [French *laquais* footman, flunky, possibly through Spanish, Italian, and Greek, going back to Turkish *ulak* courier.]

lack·ing (lak′ing) *prep.* not having; free from: *We went to the movies, lacking anything else to do.* —*adj.* not having enough; deficient: *to be found lacking in courage.*

lack·lus·ter (lak′lus′tər) *also, British,* **lack·lus·tre.** *adj.* lacking spirit, brilliance, or any other special qualities; dull: *a lackluster performance.*

la·con·ic (lə kon′ik) *adj.* characterized by the use of few words to express much; terse; concise. [Latin *Lacōnicus* relating to Laconia, a country of ancient Greece where the Spartans lived, from Greek *Lakōnikos,* from *Lakōn* a Spartan; referring to the supposedly concise speech of the Spartans.] —**la·con′i·cal·ly,** *adv.*

lac·o·nism (lak′ə niz′əm) *n.* **1.** a laconic style of expression. **2.** a laconic phrase or expression.

lac·quer (lak′ər) *n.* **1.** a fast-drying varnish usually consisting of a cellulose derivative in a mixture of solvents, plasticizers, and resins. **2.** a varnish obtained from the sap of an oriental sumac tree, *Rhus verniciflua,* formerly widely used on furniture. **3.** wooden articles or decorative work covered with such varnish. —*v.t.* to coat with or as with lacquer. [Obsolete French *lacre* sealing wax, from Portuguese *laca* lac[1], from Hindi *lākh.* See LAC[1].] —**lac′quer·er,** *n.*

lacquer
detail of a Chinese lacquered screen

lac·ri·mal (lak′rə məl) lachrymal.

lacrimal glands, a pair of small glands in the upper part of the eye socket that secrete tears.

lac·ri·ma·tion (lak′rə mā′shən) *n.* the secretion or shedding of tears, as in weeping. [Latin *lacrimationis,* genitive of *lacrimatio* a weeping, going back to *lacrima* tear[2].]

la·crosse (lə krôs′) *n.* a game for two teams of ten players each, played with lacrosse sticks whose netlike pockets are used for catching, carrying, or throwing the ball into the opponent's goal. [Canadian French *lacrosse,* from *la* the + *crosse* lacrosse stick; literally, hooked stick, from Old French *croce;* of Germanic origin.]

lacrosse stick, a stick used in playing lacrosse, consisting of a long handle that curves around a netlike pocket at one end.

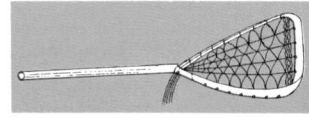

lacrosse stick

lact- *combining form* form of **lacto-** used before a vowel: *lactase, lactic.*

lac·tase (lak′tās) *n.* an enzyme present in yeast and the intestines of animals. It aids in digestion by hydrolyzing lactose into glucose and galactose. [LACTO- + -ASE.]

a	at	e	end	o	hot	u	up	hw	white		about
ā	ape	ē	me	ō	old	ū	use	ng	song		taken
ä	far	i	it	ô	fork	ü	rule	th	thin	ə	pencil
âr	care	ī	ice	oi	oil	u̇	pull	th	this		lemon
				îr	pierce	ou	out	ûr	turn	zh	measure		circus

lac·tate (lak′tāt) *n.* a salt or ester of lactic acid. —*v.i.,* **-tat·ed, -tat·ing.** to produce or secrete milk. [Latin *lactatus,* past participle of *lactare* to produce milk, from *lac* milk.]

lac·ta·tion (lak tā′shən) *n.* **1.** the formation and secretion of milk by the mammary glands. **2.** the act or period of giving an infant or young animal milk from the breast or udder. [Late Latin *lactation-,* stem of *lactatio* lactation, from Latin *lactatus.* See LAC-TATE.] —**lac·ta′tion·al,** *adj.*

lac·te·al (lak′tē əl) *n.* any of the lymphatic vessels of the small intestine that carry chyle to the blood. —*adj.* **1.** of or like milk; milky. **2.** of or relating to the lacteals. [Latin *lacteus* milky (from *lac* milk) + -AL[1].]

lac·tic (lak′tik) *adj.* of, relating to, or obtained from milk. [Latin *lact-,* stem of *lac* milk + -IC.]

lactic acid, a colorless, odorless syrupy compound formed in sour milk, in fermenting molasses, and in muscles, and also produced synthetically for use in food and medicine. Formula: $C_3H_6O_3$

lac·tif·er·ous (lak tif′ər əs) *adj.* **1.** conveying milk. **2.** yielding or secreting milk or a milky fluid. —**lac·tif′er·ous·ness,** *n.*

lacto- *combining form* **1.** of or relating to milk: *lactometer.* **2.** of or relating to lactic acid: *lactobacillus.* [Latin *lact-,* stem of *lac* milk.]

lac·to·ba·cil·lus (lak′tō bə sil′əs) *n., pl.* **-cil·li** (-sil′ī). any of a genus of bacteria, *Lactobacillus,* that ferment milk and various carbohydrates, producing lactic acid and carbon dioxide, found in the intestinal tract and vagina of humans and other mammals. [Modern Latin *lactobacillus,* from Latin *lact-,* stem of *lac* milk + *bacillus* bacillus.]

lac·to·fla·vin (lak′tō flā′vin, lak′tō flā′-) *n.* riboflavin.

lac·tose (lak′tōs) *n.* a white sugar present in milk. Formula: $C_{12}H_{22}O_{11}$ Also, **milk sugar.** [LACTO- + -OSE[2].]

la·cu·na (lə kū′nə) *n., pl.* **-nae** (-nē) or **-nas. 1.** a space in which something has been left out; gap. **2.** a small cavity in bone or tissue. [Latin *lacūna* hole, pond. Doublet of LAGOON.] —**la·cu′nal, la·cu′nar,** *adj.*

la·cus·trine (lə kus′trin) *adj.* **1.** of or relating to lakes. **2.** found or formed in or near lakes.

lac·y (lā′sē) *adj.,* **lac·i·er, lac·i·est.** of or resembling lace. —**lac′i·ness,** *n.*

lad (lad) *n.* **1.** a young fellow; boy. **2.** *Informal.* a fellow; man. [Of uncertain origin.]

lad·der (lad′ər) *n.* **1.** a device used for climbing, usually made of two parallel side pieces with a series of crosspieces, or rungs, connecting them. **2.** any means of rising from one step or stage to another: *The employee started in the business at the bottom of the ladder as a clerk but later became the manager.* **3.** an arrangement of ascending steps or levels: *a family prominent on the social ladder.* [Old English *hlǣder* frame with steps for ascending or descending.]

lad·die (lad′ē) *n. Scottish.* lad.

lade (lād) *v.,* **lad·ed, lad·ed** or **lad·en, lad·ing.** —*v.t.* **1.** to load, esp. cargo. **2.** ladle. —*v.i.* **1.** to take on a load, as of cargo. **2.** to ladle liquid. [Old English *hladan* to load, draw (water).]

lad·en (lā′dən) *v.* a past participle of **lade.** —*adj.* **1.** loaded: *a ship laden with riches.* **2.** weighed down; burdened: *laden with cares.*

lad·ing (lā′ding) *n.* **1.** the act of loading. **2.** something that is loaded; freight; cargo.

la·dle (lā′dəl) *n.* a long-handled spoon with a cup-shaped bowl for dipping liquids. —*v.t.,* **-dled, -dling.** to dip out with or carry in a ladle. [Old English *hlædel* large spoon, from *hladan* to draw (water).] —**la′dler,** *n.*

la·dy (lā′dē) *n., pl.* **-dies. 1.** a woman: *A lady answered the phone.* **2.** the mistress of a household. ➡ used esp. in the phrase *lady of the house.* **3.** a girl or woman with good manners or feminine qualities. **4.** Lady. in Great Britain, a marchioness, countess, viscountess, or baroness; a daughter of a duke, marquis, or earl; the wife of a baronet or knight; or the wife of a man holding the courtesy title of Lord. ➡ used as a title. **5.** formerly, a woman who exercised authority over a feudal manor. **6.** a woman who is the object of a man's love or devotion. **7.** wife. [Old English *hlǣfdige* mistress of a household; literally, loaf-kneader; with reference to the duties of the mistress of a house in early times.]

la·dy·bug (lā′dē bug′) *n.* any of a group of beetles, family Coccinellidae, that have a round, humped body, often bright red or orange with black spots, and feed chiefly on aphids and other insect pests. Also, **lady beetle, la·dy·bird** (lā′dē bûrd′), **lady-bird beetle.**

Lady Day, Annunciation.

la·dy·fin·ger (lā′dē fing′gər) *n.* a small sponge cake resembling a finger in size and shape.

la·dy-in-wait·ing (lā′dē in wā′ting) *n., pl.* **la·dies-in-wait-ing.** a woman who is an attendant of a queen or princess.

la·dy-kill·er (lā′dē kil′ər) *n. Informal.* a man who is very popular with women, esp. one who is insensitive to their feelings.

la·dy·like (lā′dē līk′) *adj.* like or suitable for a lady.

la·dy·love (lā′dē luv′) *n.* a woman who is the object of a man's love; sweetheart.

la·dy·ship (lā′dē ship′) *n.* **1.** the rank, status, or position of a lady. **2. Ladyship.** used as a form of address for a Lady, usually preceded by *Her* or *Your.*

la·dy's-slip·per (lā′dēz slip′ər) *also,* **la′dy-slip′per.** *n.* any of a group of hardy orchids, genus *Cypripedium,* that bear flowers having a lower petal or lip with a shoelike pouch, esp. *C. reginae,* whose flowers are white with a red lip.

la·dy's-thumb (lā′dēz thum′) *n.* a weedy plant, *Polygonum persicaria,* of the buckwheat family, found in damp regions in Europe and North America, having small pink flowers borne on spikes.

lady's-slipper

la·e·trile (lā′i tral) *n.* a drug derived from certain plant substances containing amygdalin, as apricot and almond seeds, and used as an unorthodox cancer treatment that is without proven effectiveness. [Short for *lae(vorotatory glycosidic ni)trile.*]

lag (lag) *v.i.,* **lagged, lag·ging. 1.** to fail to keep up or keep pace (often with *behind*): *The child lagged behind the rest of the family.* **2.** to drop or fall off; slump: *a business that lags in summer.* —*n.* an act, instance, or amount of lagging. [Probably of Scandinavian origin.]

la·ger (lä′gər) *n.* a light-bodied beer that is prepared by slow fermentation at low temperature and is aged for months before being used. [Short for German *Lagerbier* beer brewed for keeping, from *Lager* storehouse + *Bier* beer.]

lag·gard (lag′ərd) *n.* a person or thing that lags. —*adj.* that lags; slow; backward. —**lag′gard·ly,** *adv.* —**lag′gard·ness,** *n.*

la·gniappe (lan yap′, lan′yap) *also,* **la·gnappe.** *n.* **1.** a gift that comes with a purchase. **2.** anything given as an extra; bonus. [French *lagniappe* gift that comes with a purchase, from Spanish *la ñapa* the addition, going back to Latin *illa,* feminine of *ille* that + Quechua *yapa* addition.]

lag·o·morph (lag′ə môrf′) *n.* any of numerous mammals constituting the order Lagomorpha, having two pairs of upper incisors and comprising the hares, rabbits, and pikas. [Modern Latin *Lagomorpha,* from Greek *lagōs* hare + *morphē* form.] —**lag′o·mor′phic, lag′o·mor′phous,** *adj.*

la·goon (lə gün′) *n.* **1.** a shallow body of water partly or completely enclosed within an atoll. **2.** a shallow body of seawater partly cut off from the sea by a narrow strip of land. [Italian *laguna* pool, from Latin *lacūna* hole, pond. Doublet of LACUNA.]

la·ic (lā′ik) *adj.* of, relating to, or belonging to the laity. —*n.* a member of the laity. [Latin *lāicus* relating to the people. See LAY[3].] —**la′i·cal·ly,** *adv.*

laid (lād) the past tense and past participle of **lay[1].**

laid-back (lād′bak′) *adj. Slang.* casual; relaxed; easygoing. [From the phrase *lay back.*]

lain (lān) the past participle of **lie[2].**

lair (lâr) *n.* a home or resting place, esp. of a wild animal. [Old English *leger* bed.]

laird (lârd) *n. Scottish.* the owner of a large estate; lord. [Scottish form of LORD.]

lais·sez-faire (les′ā fâr′, lā′zā-) *adj.* **1.** of or based on laissez faire: *laissez-faire economics.* **2.** that does not interfere; hands-off: *a laissez-faire attitude.*

laissez faire, an economic theory developed in the eighteenth century that opposed mercantilism and supported the growth of free enterprise and capitalism. It claims that economic laws guarantee well-being as long as individuals are left alone to pursue their own interests with a minimum of interference or regulation by the government. [French *laissez faire* allow (people) to do (what they please), from *laissez,* imperative of *laisser* to allow (going back to Latin *laxāre* to loosen, relax) + *faire* to do (going back to Latin *facere.*)]

la·i·ty (lā′i tē) *n., pl.* **-ties. 1.** all persons who are members of a church but are not ordained for religious work. ➡ distinguished from **clergy. 2.** those who are not members of a certain profession or who are not trained in a certain specialty: *Lawyers use many terms not familiar to the laity.* [LAY³ + -ITY.]

La·ius (lā′əs) *n.* in Greek legend, the king of Thebes killed unknowingly by his son Oedipus.

lake¹ (lāk) *n.* **1.** an inland body of salt or fresh water. **2.** any large pool of liquid, as lava or tar. [Old French *lac* pond, from Latin *lacus* pond, large reservoir for water.]

lake² (lāk) *n.* **1.** any of various pigments and coloring compounds consisting of an organic dye, as cochineal, bonded to an inorganic base. **2.** a deep red or purplish red color. [Form of LAC¹.]

lake dweller, a member of a prehistoric people who lived in lake dwellings.

lake dwelling, a hut built on piles over water or marshland in prehistoric times.

lake herring, a North American fish, *Coregonus artedii*, of the trout family, found in the Great Lakes; cisco. Length: to 12 inches (30 centimeters).

lake trout, a large, fork-tailed trout, *Salvelinus namaycush*, grayish green in color with pale spots, found in lakes of North America. Weight: usually 9 pounds (4.1 kilograms) or less.

lakh (lak) lac².

lam (lam) *n. Slang.* **1. on the lam.** hiding or escaping, esp. from law enforcement officials. **2. to take it on the lam.** to escape or go into hiding, esp. from the law. [Of uncertain origin.]

Lam., Lamentations.

la·ma (lä′mə) *n.* a priest or monk of Lamaism. [Tibetan *blama* priest.]

La·ma·ism (lä′mə iz′əm) *n.* a religion centered in Tibet, Mongolia, and surrounding areas that is a mixture of Buddhism and the native religion, characterized by a strong organized hierarchy of monks. —**La′ma·ist,** *n.* —**La′ma·is′tic,** *adj.*

La·marck·i·an (lə mär′kē ən) *adj.* of or relating to the French naturalist Jean de Lamarck or his theory. —*n.* a supporter or follower of Lamarck or his theory.

La·marck·ism (lə mär′kiz əm) *n.* the biological theory of the French naturalist Jean de Lamarck, now widely believed to be false, that characteristics acquired or developed by individuals in response to the environment are passed on to their descendants.

la·ma·ser·y (lä′mə ser′ē) *n., pl.* **-ser·ies.** a monastery of lamas.

La·maze (lə mäz′) *n.* a training program for natural childbirth that emphasizes breathing and relaxation techniques to control pain and the encouraging assistance of the father or another person during labor. [From Fernand *Lamaze,* 1890-1927, French physician who developed it.]

lamb (lam) *n.* **1.** a young sheep. **2.** the meat from a lamb used as food. **3.** the skin of a lamb. **4. the Lamb.** Jesus. **5.** a person who is gentle, weak, or innocent. —*v.i.* to give birth to a lamb. [Old English *lamb* young of the sheep, innocent person.] —**lamb′like′,** *adj.*

lam·baste (lam bāst′, -bast′) *v.t.,* **-bast·ed, -bast·ing.** *Informal.* **1.** to beat or thrash. **2.** to abuse verbally. [Probably from earlier *lam* to thrash (of Scandinavian origin) + BASTE³.]

lamb·da (lam′də) *n.* **1.** the eleventh letter (Λ, λ) of the Greek alphabet, corresponding to the English letter *L, l.* **2.** *Physics.* a subatomic particle of the hyperon group.

lam·bent (lam′bənt) *adj.* **1.** shining with a soft, clear light; softly radiant: *lambent eyes, the lambent light of early morning.* **2.** (of a flame) flickering lightly over or on a surface. **3.** characterized by lightness and brilliance: *a lambent wit.* [Latin *lambēns,* present participle of *lambēre* to lick.] —**lam′ben·cy,** *n.* —**lam′-bent·ly,** *adv.*

lam·bert (lam′bərt) *n.* the centimeter-gram-second unit of brightness, equal to the brightness of a surface that emits or reflects 1 lumen per square centimeter.

lamb·kin (lam′kin) *n.* **1.** a little lamb. **2.** a person who is dearly loved, esp. a young child.

Lamb of God, Jesus.

lam·bre·quin (lam′bri kin, -bər-) *n.* drapery hanging from a shelf or covering the upper part of a window or door. [French *lambrequin* valance, going back to Middle Dutch *lamper* veil.]

lamb·skin (lam′skin′) *n.* **1.** the skin of a lamb, esp. when dressed with the wool left on it and used for clothing. **2.** leather made from the skin of a lamb. **3.** parchment made from this leather.

lamb's-quar·ters (lamz′kwôr′tərz) *n.* a weedy plant, *Chenopodium album,* related to the goosefoot, having small green flowers and edible leaves that are sometimes used as greens. ➡ used as singular or plural.

la·mé (la mā′, lä-) *n.* a fabric woven with metallic threads or with threads that appear metallic. [French *lamé* spangled with gold or silver, from *lame* metal leaf, gold or silver wire, from Latin *lāmina* thin plate or leaf of metal or wood.]

lame (lām) *adj.,* **lam·er, lam·est. 1.** unable to walk easily or properly; disabled in the leg or foot. **2.** stiff and painful: *a lame back.* **3.** ineffective; poor or weak: *The employee offered a lame excuse for being late.* —*v.t.,* **lamed, lam·ing.** to make lame. [Old English *lama* disabled, infirm.] —**lame′ly,** *adv.* —**lame′-ness,** *n.*

lame duck 1. a public official who has failed to win reelection but continues to hold office for a time after being defeated. **2.** a person who is weak or ineffectual.

la·mel·la (lə mel′ə) *n., pl.* **-mel·lae** (-mel′ē) or **-mel·las. 1.** a thin plate, scale, sheet, or layer of bone, tissue, or shell. **2.** *Botany.* **a.** any of various thin scales or scalelike parts of a plant. **b.** gill¹ *(def.* 2). [Latin *lāmella* small plate of metal, diminutive of *lāmina* thin plate or leaf of metal or wood.]

lam·el·late (lam′ə lāt′, -lit, lə mel′āt, -it) *adj.* like, having, composed of, or arranged in lamellas. Also, **la·mel·lar** (lə mel′ər, lam′ə lər). —**lam′el·la′tion,** *n.*

la·mel·li·branch (lə mel′i brangk′) *n.* pelecypod. [Modern Latin *Lamellibranchia,* from Latin *lāmella* (see LAMELLA) + Greek *branchia* gills.]

la·ment (lə ment′) *v.t.* **1.** to feel or express deep sorrow or grief for or about: *to lament the loss of a friend.* **2.** to feel or express deep regret over: *to lament a mistake.* —*v.i.* to feel or express deep sorrow or grief. —*n.* **1.** an expression of sorrow or grief. **2.** a literary form, as a song or poem, that expresses sorrow or grief. [Latin *lāmentārī* to wail, bewail.] —**la·ment′er,** *n.*

lam·en·ta·ble (lam′ən tə bəl, lə men′-) *adj.* **1.** causing or likely to cause sorrow or regret: *a lamentable tragedy, a lamentable oversight.* **2.** expressing sorrow; mournful. —**lam′en·ta·bly,** *adv.*

lam·en·ta·tion (lam′ən tā′shən) *n.* **1.** the act of lamenting. **2.** a mournful outcry of sorrow or grief. **3. Lamentations.** a book of the Old Testament, attributed by some to the Hebrew prophet Jeremiah. ➡ used as singular.

lam·i·na (lam′ə nə) *n., pl.* **-nae** (-nē′) or **-nas. 1.** a thin plate, scale, or layer. **2.** *Botany.* the flat or expanded part of a leaf or petal. [Latin *lāmina* thin plate or leaf of metal or wood.]

lam·i·nar (lam′ə nər) *adj.* **1.** like, having, composed of, or arranged in thin plates, scales, or layers; laminate. **2.** *Physics.* moving in a smooth, regular pattern, as air over or about an airfoil: *laminar flow.* ➡ opposed to **turbulent.**

lam·i·nate (*v.,* lam′ə nāt′; *n.,* lam′ə nit, -nāt′) *v.,* **-nat·ed, -nat·ing.** —*v.t.* **1.** to form by uniting or bonding different layers, as with glue or heat. **2.** to beat or roll (metal) into thin plates. **3.** to cover with thin sheets or layers. **4.** to split or separate (something) into thin layers. —*v.i.* to split or separate into thin layers. —*adj.* laminated or consisting of laminae; laminar: *Shale is a laminate rock.* —*n.* a product formed by laminating, as safety glass or plywood. —**lam′i·na′tor,** *n.*

lam·i·nat·ed (lam′ə nā′tid) *adj.* manufactured or formed by laminating.

lam·i·na·tion (lam′ə nā′shən) *n.* **1.** the process of laminating. **2.** the state of being laminated. **3.** a thin layer, esp. when bonded to something else: *A lamination of plastic makes the counter more durable.* **4.** a laminated structure; arrangement in thin layers.

Lam·mas (lam′əs) *n.* a harvest festival formerly celebrated in England and still observed in Scotland, during which newly baked loaves of bread are blessed at Mass. It is observed on August 1. Also, **Lam·mas·tide** (lam′əs tīd′).

lam·mer·gei·er (lam′ər gī′ər) *also,* **lam·mer·gey·er.** *n., pl.* **-geier.** a large, black Old World vulture, *Gypaetus barbatus,* of high mountain ranges. It has a tuft of bristles over the nostrils and under the bill. Length: 40-45 inches (102-114 centimeters). [German *lämmergeier,* from *lämmer,* plural of *lamm* lamb + *geier* vulture.]

lamp (lamp) *n.* **1.** a portable or freestanding device that produces light by the use of a light bulb or by burning a substance, as gas or oil. **2.** an electric bulb that gives off light or other radiation. **3.** a source of knowledge or spiritual guidance. [Old French *lampe* device for lighting, from Latin *lampas* torch, light, from Greek *lampas.*]

lamp·black (lamp′blak′) *n.* a black pigment, consisting of almost pure carbon soot, made by burning oil or gas in insufficient air.

lamp·light (lamp′līt′) *n.* the light from a lamp or lamps.

a	at	e	end	o	hot	u	up	hw	white		about
ā	ape	ē	me	ō	old	ū	use	ng	song	ə	taken
ä	far	i	it	ô	fork	u	rule	th	thin		pencil
âr	care	ī	ice	oi	oil	u	pull	th	this		lemon
		îr	pierce	ou	out	ûr	turn	zh	measure		circus

lamp·light·er (lamp′lī′tər) *n.* formerly, a person whose job was to light gas or oil street lights at night.

lam·poon (lam pün′) *n.* a piece of satirical writing, often scurrilous or malicious, directed against a person or an institution. —*v.t.* to satirize or attack in a lampoon. [French *lampon* usually satirical drinking song, probably from *lampons* let us drink (word often used in such songs), from *lamper* to drink; of imitative origin.] —**lam·poon′er, lam·poon′ist,** *n.* —**lam·poon′er·y,** *n.*

lamp·post (lamp′pōst′) *n.* a post supporting a lamp, esp. in a public place, as a street or a park.

lam·prey (lam′prē) *n., pl.* **-preys.** any of a group of primitive, brown or black eellike fish, family Petromyzontidae, found in salt and fresh water in temperate regions. The lamprey has a round mouth with a rasping tongue and sharp toothlike structures for attaching itself to fish and feeding parasitically on their blood. Length: 6-40 inches (15-102 centimeters). [Old French *lampreie,* from Medieval Latin *lampreda* lamprey, limpet; of uncertain origin.]

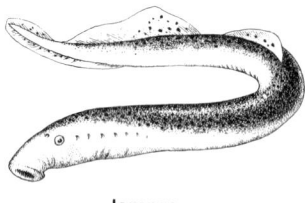

lamprey

lamp·shade (lamp′shād′) *n.* a covering for a lamp, used to reduce, diffuse, or direct the light.

lamp shell, brachiopod.

la·nai (lə nī′) *n.* a porch or veranda. [Hawaiian *lanai.*]

Lan·cas·ter (lang′kə stər) *n.* an English royal house in rivalry with York, descended from John of Gaunt, whose kings were Henry IV, Henry V, and Henry VI.

Lan·cas·tri·an (lang kas′trē ən) *adj.* of or relating to the English house of Lancaster. —*n.* a member or supporter of the house of Lancaster.

lance (lans) *n.* **1.** a long spear, usually consisting of a wooden shaft with a sharp metal head, carried by mounted soldiers or knights. **2.** any spearlike weapon or instrument. **3.** a soldier armed with a lance. **4.** lancet. —*v.t.,* **lanced, lanc·ing. 1.** to pierce with or as with a lance. **2.** to open with or as with a lancet: *The doctor lanced the abscess.* [Old French *lance* spear, from Latin *lancea* light spear; of Celtic origin.]

lance corporal 1. an enlisted man in the U.S. Marine Corps ranking above a private first class and below a corporal. **2.** *British.* a private acting as a corporal, without a pay increase.

lance·let (lans′lit) *n.* amphioxus.

Lan·ce·lot (lan′sə lot′) *n.* in Arthurian legend, an important knight of the Round Table and lover of Guinevere.

lan·ce·o·late (lan′sē ə lāt′, -lit) *adj. Botany.* narrow and tapering toward each end, like the head of a lance: *a lanceolate leaf.* [Latin *lanceolātus* shaped like a small spear, from *lanceola* small spear, diminutive of *lancea* light spear. See LANCE.]

lanc·er (lan′sər) *n.* a cavalry soldier armed with a lance, or one whose regiment was traditionally so armed.

lanc·ers (lan′sərz) *n.* **1.** a dance that is a form of quadrille. **2.** the music for such a dance ➡ used as singular in both defs.

lan·cet (lan′sit) *n.* a short surgical knife having two sharp edges. Also, **lance.** [Old French *lancette* surgeon's lancet, little spear, diminutive of *lance* spear. See LANCE.]

lance·wood (lans′wûd′) *n.* **1.** a tough, straight-grained, elastic wood, used mainly for fishing rods and billiard cues. **2.** any of various tropical trees yielding this wood, found esp. in South America.

land (land) *n.* **1.a.** the exposed, solid portion of the earth's surface, as distinguished from the submerged parts or the ocean: *to travel by land and by sea.* **b.** any similar surface on a planet or large natural satellite. **2.** ground or soil with reference to its qualities: *arable land, desert land.* **3.** rural or agricultural areas as distinguished from urban areas. **4.** a part of the earth's surface marked off by natural, political, or cultural boundaries; country; region: *China is a vast land.* **5.** the people of such a region; nation: *The whole land rejoiced when the war ended.* **6.** real estate; property: *to invest in land.* **7.** natural resources in their original, undeveloped state. **8.** territory or country; domain: *the land of the free.* —*v.i.* **1.a.** (of aircraft or spacecraft) to come down from the air or sky under control and alight on land, water, or another suitable surface, as an aircraft carrier deck. **b.** (of seagoing vessels) to come to land or shore. **2.** to come to rest, as after a fall or flight: *I dropped my glove, and it landed in a puddle.* **3.** to go or come ashore from a vessel; disembark. **4.** to arrive in a specific point, place, or situation, esp. one that is bad; end up: *The thief landed in jail. The letter landed in the wrong office.* —*v.t.* **1.** to

bring (an aircraft or spacecraft) down from the air or sky onto land, water, or another suitable surface, as the deck of a ship. **2.** to set ashore from a vessel; unload onto land: *to land a cargo, to land passengers.* **3.** to cause to end up: *Fishing without a license will land you in trouble.* **4.** to bring (a fish) to land or into a boat. **5.** *Informal.* to obtain possession of; win; get: *to land a good job.* **6.** *Informal.* to deliver (a blow). [Old English *land* solid part of the earth's surface, ground, nation.]

-land *combining form* place of; region of: *homeland, fairyland.*

lan·dau (lan′dou, -dô) *n.* **1.** a four-wheeled, two-seated carriage with a top that opens in the center and can be folded down in the back and front. **2.** a sedanlike automobile with a collapsible top over the rear seats. [From *Landau,* German town where this carriage was first made.]

lan·dau·let (lan′dô let′) *also,* **lan·dau·lette** *n.* **1.** a small landau, usually having only one seat. **2.** an automobile with an open driver's seat and a collapsible top over the back section.

land breeze, a breeze blowing toward the sea from the land.

land bridge, a low-lying neck or other strip of land connecting two landmasses, esp. one that enables plants and animals to migrate from one place to another.

land crab, any of various tropical crabs that live on beaches or mud flats.

land·ed (lan′did) *adj.* **1.** owning land: *landed gentry.* **2.** consisting of land: *landed property.*

land·er (lan′dər) *n.* a space probe or manned spacecraft designed to land on a planet or other solid celestial body. ➡ distinguished from **orbiter.**

land·fall (land′fôl′) *n.* **1.** an act or instance of reaching or sighting land, as after a long voyage. **2.** the land so reached or sighted.

land·fill (land′fil′) *n.* **1.** an area of land that has been filled in, usually by dumping refuse and mixing or covering it with soil: *These new houses were built on a landfill.* **2.** the refuse disposed of in this manner.

land·form (land′fôrm′) *n.* a feature on the earth's surface resulting from natural causes, as a valley or mountain range.

land grant, a gift of public land by the government for a public purpose, as establishing a college.

land·grave (land′grāv′) *n.* **1.** in medieval Germany, a count or prince, esp. one having authority over a large territory. **2.** the title of certain German princes. [German *Landgraf* count²; literally, land count, from *Land* land + *Graf* count².]

land·hold·er (land′hōl′dər) *n.* a person who owns land. —**land′hold′ing,** *adj., n.*

land·ing (lan′ding) *n.* **1.** the act or process of coming to the earth or land, or coming ashore. **2.** a space on a dock or pier for disembarking from or unloading a ship. **3.** a platform at the end of or between flights of stairs.

landing craft, any of various flat-bottomed naval vessels used for putting troops and equipment ashore, as during an attack launched from the sea.

landing field, an area of land designed or suited for the takeoff and landing of aircraft.

landing gear, the wheels, shock absorbers, and other structures on which an aircraft lands and on which it moves when not aloft.

landing net, a net to take a hooked fish from the water.

landing strip, airstrip.

land·la·dy (land′lā′dē) *n., pl.* **-dies. 1.** a woman who owns houses or apartments occupied by tenants. **2.** a woman who runs an inn, boarding house, or rooming house.

land·less (land′lis) *adj.* owning no land: *landless tenant farmers.*

land·locked (land′lokt′) *adj.* **1.** entirely or almost entirely surrounded by land, esp. having no harbor or seacoast: *a landlocked nation.* **2.** (of certain species of salmon) living out the entire life cycle in fresh water.

land·lord (land′lôrd′) *n.* **1.** a person, esp. a man, who owns houses or apartments occupied by tenants. **2.** a landowner or lord of a manor, who exacts rent or service for the use of his land. **3.** a person who runs an inn, boarding house, or rooming house.

land·lub·ber (land′lub′ər) *n.* a person who is awkward or inexperienced on ships. ➡ often used in mild scorn by experienced sailors.

land·mark (land′märk′) *n.* **1.** a prominent feature of a landscape, often used to determine direction or location. **2.** an historically important building or site: *The Civil War battlefield was declared a national landmark.* **3.** a prominent or historically important fact or event: *The court decision was a landmark in civil rights.* **4.** an object that marks a boundary line.

land·mass (land′mas′) *n.* a large area of land.

land mine, a device with an explosive charge, buried in the ground and set off when troops or vehicles pass over or near it.

land office, a government office that handles and records transfers and sales of public lands.

land·of·fice business (land′ô′fis, -of′is) a large amount or high rate of buying or selling: *The store did a land-office business during the sale.* [Referring to the many transactions made by land offices in the western United States during the nineteenth century.]

Land of Promise, in the Old Testament, Canaan, the land promised by God to Abraham and his descendants.

land·own·er (land′ō′nər) *n.* a person who owns land. —**land′own′ing,** *adj.*

land·poor (land′pur′) *adj.* owning much land, esp. nonproductive land, but not earning enough income from it to pay taxes or other expenses.

land reform, the redistribution of large holdings of agricultural land among small farmers, esp. as a government measure.

land·scape (land′skāp′) *n.* **1.** a stretch or expanse of scenery viewed from one place. **2.** a picture representing a view of natural scenery or land. **3.** a branch of painting, photography, or the like, dealing with natural scenery or land. —*v.,* **-scaped, -scap·ing.** —*v.t.* to beautify or improve (a piece of land), as by planting trees and shrubs. —*v.i.* to engage in landscape architecture or gardening. [Dutch *landschap* province, painting of a land scene, from *land* land + *-schap* -ship.] —**land′scap′er,** *n.*

Russian **landscape**
a painting by Boris Kustodiev

landscape architecture, the art or profession of arranging or changing the natural scenery of a place for aesthetic effect or some desired purpose. —**landscape architect.**

landscape gardening 1. the art or work of beautifying land, as the grounds around a house, by planting trees and other plants and designing gardens. **2.** the result or an example of this. —**landscape gardener.**

land·scap·ist (land′skā′pist) *n.* a painter of landscapes.

land·slide (land′slīd′) *n.* **1.** the sliding or falling of a mass of soil, rock, or debris down a slope. **2.** the mass that slides down. **3.** an overwhelming victory, esp. in an election.

land·slip (land′slip′) *n. British.* landslide *(defs. 1, 2).*

lands·man (landz′mən) *n., pl.* **-men** (-mən). a person who lives or works on land.

land·ward (land′wərd) *adj.* lying or going toward land. —*adv.* also, **land·wards.** toward land.

lane (lān) *n.* **1.** a narrow way or road, esp. in a rural area. **2.** any long, narrow way or passage between barriers. **3.** a course or route having definite boundaries: *a shipping lane, a traffic lane.* **4.** bowling alley *(def. 1).* [Old English *lane* narrow road.]

lang., language.

lan·gouste (lang güst′; län güst′) *n. French.* spiny lobster. [French *langouste,* from Provençal *langusta,* from Latin *locusta* kind of lobster.]

lan·guage (lang′gwij) *n.* **1.** an organized system of spoken sounds by which people communicate their thoughts and feelings to each other; human speech. **2.** written symbols representing these spoken sounds. **3.** all the spoken sounds, and the written symbols representing them, that make up a system by which the members of a nation, tribe, or other group communicate with each other. **4.** any means of communication, as through gestures,

signs, or symbols: *Algebra is a mathematical language.* **5.** the special vocabulary, uses, and forms characteristic of a particular group or profession: *military language, the language of medicine.* **6.** a style or kind of language; manner of expression: *earthy language, flowery language, Milton's majestic language.* **7.** a means of communication used by animals: *the language of dolphins.* **8.** *Law.* the exact wording of a document: *the language of a contract.* **9.** the study of language or languages; linguistics. **10.** computer language. [Old French *langage* speech of a country, expression of thought by words, from *langue* tongue, speech of a country, from Latin *lingua* tongue, speech.]

language arts, reading, spelling, grammar, composition, and literature taught in school to develop a student's skill in the use of language.

language laboratory, a room specially equipped with tape recordings or records to enable students to listen to and practice speaking a foreign language that they are studying.

langue d'oc (läNg dôk′) any of a group of dialects spoken in southern France in the Middle Ages, from which modern Provençal is descended. [Old French *langue d'oc* language of *oc.* The two principal dialects of Old French took their names from *oc* and *oïl,* their different words for "yes." See LANGUE D'OÏL, LANGUAGE.]

langue d'o·ïl (läNg dô ēl′, doil′) any of a group of dialects spoken in northern France in the Middle Ages, from which modern French is descended. [Old French *langue d'oïl* language of *oïl.* See LANGUE D'OC.]

lan·guid (lang′gwid) *adj.* **1.** lacking or showing a lack of energy or force; weak; sluggish. **2.** lacking interest or spirited concern; indifferent. [Latin *languidus* weak, sluggish.] —**lan′guid·ly,** *adv.* —**lan′guid·ness,** *n.*

lan·guish (lang′gwish) *v.i.* **1.** to grow weak or feeble; lose health or vitality: *The garden languished from lack of rain.* **2.** to live under conditions that lower the vitality or depress the spirits: *The people languished under dictatorial rule.* **3.** to be overlooked or neglected: *Our proposal languished on the president's desk.* **4.** to suffer with desire; pine (with *for*): *to languish for home.* **5.** to assume a languid look or expression, as an indication of sorrowful or tender emotion. [Old French *languiss-,* a stem of *languir* to be listless, pine, going back to Latin *languēre* to be weak.] —**lan′guish·er,** *n.* —**lan′guish·ment,** *n.*

lan·guish·ing (lang′gwi shing) *adj.* **1.** becoming weak or spiritless; pining away. **2.** indicating tender, sentimental emotion.

lan·guor (lang′gər) *n.* **1.** lack of vigor; weakness; fatigue. **2.** lack of activity; stagnation. **3.** tenderness or softness of mood or feeling. **4.** lack of spirit or interest; indifference. **5.** oppressive stillness. [Old French *languor* prolonged physical or emotional depression, from Latin *languor* faintness.]

lan·guor·ous (lang′gər əs) *adj.* **1.** languid. **2.** causing or tending to cause languor. —**lan′guor·ous·ly,** *adv.* —**lan′guor·ous·ness,** *n.*

lan·gur (lung gur′) *n.* any of various long-tailed monkeys, genus *Presbytis,* found in Asia, usually having a slender body and long limbs. [Hindi *langūr,* possibly from Sanskrit *lāngūlin* having a tail.]

lan·iard (lan′yərd) lanyard.

lank (langk) *adj.* **1.** long and lean; slender. **2.** (of hair) straight and flat. [Old English *hlanc* lean.] —**lank′ly,** *adv.* —**lank′ness,** *n.*

lank·y (lang′kē) *adj.,* **lank·i·er, lank·i·est.** ungracefully tall and thin: *a lanky youth.* —**lank′i·ly,** *adv.* —**lank′i·ness,** *n.*

lan·o·lin (lan′ə lin) *also,* **lan·o·line** (lan′ə lin, -lēn′). *n.* a fatty substance obtained from the wool of sheep, used in various ointments, cosmetics, and soaps. [Latin *lāna* wool + *oleum* oil + -IN[1].]

lan·ta·na (lan tan′ə) *n.* any of various mostly tropical shrubs and herbs, genus *Lantana,* related to the verbenas, bearing clusters of flowers of various colors.

lan·tern (lan′tərn) *n.* **1.** a light, as a kerosene light, with a protective, partly transparent casing, usually made to be carried in the hand. **2.** a casing or covering for a light, esp. a decorative paper covering. **3.** the chamber at the top of a lighthouse in which the light is placed. **4.** *Architecture.* a turret-shaped structure, esp. on the top of a roof, with windows or openings to admit light and air. [Old French *lanterne* box with transparent sides in which a

a	at	e	end	o	hot	u	up	hw	white		about
ā	ape	ē	me	ō	old	ū	use	ng	song		taken
ä	far	i	it	ô	fork	ü	rule	th	thin	ə	pencil
âr	care	ī	ice	oi	oil	ù	pull	th	this		lemon
		îr	pierce	ou	out	ûr	turn	zh	measure		circus

light is enclosed for protection, from Latin *lanterna* torch, lamp, from Greek *lamptēr*.]

lantern jaw, a long, thin projecting jaw.

lantern slide *Archaic.* photographic slide.

lan·tha·nide (lan′thə nīd′) *n.* any of a series of chemical elements that comprises the rare-earth elements, atomic numbers 57 through 71, beginning with lanthanum and ending with lutetium. [LANTHAN(UM) + -IDE.]

lan·tha·num (lan′thə nəm) *n.* a soft, white, metallic element belonging to the rare-earth group, used esp. in the manufacture of electronic devices. Symbol: La For tables, see **element.** [Modern Latin *lanthanum,* from Greek *lanthanein* to escape notice; because it was long undetected, having been mistaken for another element already discovered.]

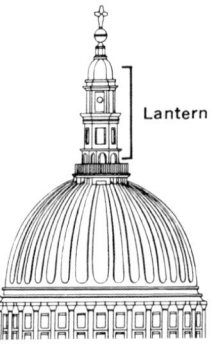

lantern (def. 4)

lan·yard (lan′yərd) *also,* **laniard.** *n.* **1.** a short rope or cord used on ships to fasten or tighten rigging. **2.** a cord worn around the neck, from which to hang something, as a whistle. **3.** a cord with a small hook at one end, used in firing certain types of cannon. [Earlier *lanyer,* from Old French *la(s)niere* thong, from *lasne* thong, noose, possibly from blend of *las* noose (see LACE) + *nasle* string (of Germanic origin).]

La·oc·o·ön (lā ok′ō on′) *n.* in Greek legend, a Trojan priest who was killed with his two sons by two sea serpents after he warned the Trojans against the Trojan horse.

La·o·tian (lā ō′shən) *adj.* of, relating to, or characteristic of Laos or its people, language, or culture. —*n.* **1.** a native or citizen of Laos. **2.** a person of Laotian ancestry. **3.** the language of the Laotians.

lap¹ (lap) *n.* **1.** the level area formed between the waist and the knees of a seated person. **2.** the clothing that covers this area. **3.** an area of responsibility or control: *Don't drop all your personal problems in my lap.* **4.** a place or condition in which a person is cared for: *to live in the lap of luxury.* [Old English *læppa* flap (of a garment).]

lap² (lap) *v.,* **lapped, lap·ping.** —*v.i.* **1.** to lie partly over or beside another; overlap. **2.** to extend beyond something in space or time (with *over*): *One meeting lapped over into the next.* **3.** to wind, wrap, or fold: *The long scarf lapped around my neck twice.* —*v.t.* **1.** to wind, wrap, or fold around something: *to lap a scarf around one's neck.* **2.** to wrap in something; swathe: *The nurse lapped the child in a blanket.* **3.** to lay (something) partly over or beside another: *to lap one shingle over another.* **4.** to get one or more lengths or circuits of something, as a racetrack, ahead of. **5.** to cut or polish (something, as glass or gems) with a revolving disk. —*n.* **1.** the act or fact of lapping over. **2.** a part that extends partly over another. **3.** the amount of overlapping. **4.** one length or circuit of something, as a swimming pool or racetrack. **5.** a revolving disk used to cut or polish something, as glass or gems. [Middle English *lapen,* from Old English *lapian* to lick, lap³.]

lap³ (lap) *v.,* **lapped, lap·ping.** —*v.t.* **1.** to drink (a liquid) by lifting it into the mouth with the tongue (often with *up*): *The cat lapped its milk.* **2.** to move or wash gently against with a splashing sound: *Waves lapped the dock.* —*v.i.* **1.** to drink a liquid by lifting it into the mouth with the tongue. **2.** to move or wash gently with a splashing sound. —*n.* **1.** the act of lapping. **2.** a gentle, splashing sound. [Old English *lapian* to take up liquid with the tongue.] —**lap′per,** *n.*

· **to lap up.** *Informal.* to accept eagerly or greedily: *to lap up compliments.*

lap·a·ro·scope (lap′ər ə skōp′) *n.* a long, slender optical instrument inserted through an incision in the abdominal wall to allow examination of internal organs or to conduct certain surgical procedures.

lap·board (lap′bôrd′) *n.* a board held on the lap and used as a table.

lap dog, a pet dog, small enough to be held easily on the lap.

la·pel (lə pel′) *n.* the part of the front of a coat or jacket folded back and forming a continuation of the collar. [From LAP¹.]

lap·ful (lap′fůl′) *n., pl.* **-fuls.** as much as the lap can hold.

lap·i·dar·y (lap′i der′ē) *n., pl.* **-dar·ies.** a person who engraves, cuts, or polishes precious stones. —*adj.* **1.** of or relating to the cutting or engraving of precious stones. **2.** engraved on stone, as an epitaph. [Latin *lapidārius* stonecutter, from *lapis* stone.]

lap·in (lap′in) *n.* **1.** a rabbit. **2.** rabbit fur, often dyed to resemble more valuable furs. [French *lapin* rabbit; possibly of Iberian origin.]

lap·is laz·u·li (lap′is laz′ə lē, lazh′-) **1.** a translucent semiprecious stone used for carvings or jewelry, usually azure blue or violet blue. For illustration, see **semiprecious. 2.** a deep, violet-blue color. [Medieval Latin *lapis lazuli* stone of azure, from Latin *lapis* stone + Medieval Latin *lazuli,* genitive of *lazulum* a blue semiprecious stone, azure (from Arabic *lāzward*). See AZURE.]

lap joint, a joint formed by overlapping one end or edge over another and fastening the two together.

Lapp (lap) *n.* **1.** a member of an ethnic group living in Lapland, formerly nomadic, now partly settled. **2.** the language of the Lapps, a member of the Ural-Altaic family of languages. [Possibly from Finnish *lapaan* nomad.]

lap·pet (lap′it) *n.* **1.** a loose flap on a garment or head covering. **2.** *Zoology.* any fleshy or membranous part hanging loosely, as the dewlap of a cow or the wattle of a turkey. [LAP¹ + -ET.]

lap robe, a fur robe or blanket used to protect the legs from the cold, as when riding in an open carriage or sleigh.

lapse (laps) *n.* **1.** a small error; mistake, esp. a trivial one: *a spelling lapse, a memory lapse.* **2.** a period or interval: *The wanderer returned after a lapse of ten years.* **3.** a slipping or falling away, as from a moral standard: *a lapse into former bad habits.* **4.** a gradual ending or falling into disuse: *a lapse in the use of a slang expression, a lapse of a holiday practice.* **5.** the termination of a right or privilege through failure to use or renew it or to meet stated obligations: *the lapse of an insurance policy.* —*v.i.,* **lapsed, laps·ing. 1.** to make an error or mistake, esp. by not doing what is moral or right. **2.** to slip or fall (with *into*): *to lapse into silence, to lapse into ruin.* **3.** (of time) to elapse. **4.** to stop, go out of effect, or fall into disuse: *My family's custom of spending Christmas together lapsed when the children grew older.* **5.** (of a right or privilege) to terminate or become void through failure to use or renew or to meet stated obligations: *The contract lapsed.* [Latin *lapsus* fall, slipping.]

lap·sus lin·guae (lap′səs ling′gwē) *Latin.* a slip of the tongue.

lap·top (lap′top′) *Informal.* a microcomputer as small, light, and compact as a portable typewriter.

lap·wing (lap′wing′) *n.* any of various crested plovers, family Charadriidae, noted for a slow, irregular wing beat in flight and a shrill, wailing cry. Length: 10-16 inches (25-41 centimeters). [Old English *hlēapewince,* from *hlēapan* to spring + *wincian* to blink; originally, to move from side to side; because it turns about when it flies.]

lapwing

lar·board (lär′bôrd′, -bərd) *n., adj. Nautical.* port². [Modification (influenced by STARBOARD) of earlier *ladeborde* literally, loading side, apparently from LADE + BOARD.]

lar·ce·ny (lär′sə nē) *n., pl.* **-nies.** the crime of unlawfully taking away another's property; theft. [Old French *larcin* theft, from Latin *latrōcinium* robbery.] —**lar′ce·nist,** *n.* —**lar′ce·nous,** *adj.* —For Synonyms, see **theft.**

larch (lärch) *n.* **1.** any of a group of tall, hardwood trees, genus *Larix,* of the pine family, found in the cold regions of the Northern Hemisphere, bearing needle-shaped leaves that are shed annually. **2.** the hard, strong, durable wood of this tree, used mainly in shipbuilding, for telephone poles, and for railroad ties. [German *Lärche* this tree, going back to Latin *larix.*]

lard (lärd) *n.* a soft, white, edible fat obtained by rendering fatty tissue from the body of a hog, used in cooking and as a base for certain ointments. —*v.t.* **1.** to add lard to or cover with lard. **2.** to stuff or cover (poultry or meat) with pieces of fat before cooking. **3.** to add extra material to (speech or writing): *to lard a passage with quotations.* [Old French *lard* bacon, from Latin *lār(i)dum.*] —**lard′like′,** *adj.* —**lard′y,** *adj.*

lar·der (lär′dər) *n.* **1.** a place where food is kept; pantry. **2.** a stock of provisions. [Anglo-Norman *larder* tub in which bacon is kept, from Old French *lard* bacon. See LARD.]

lar·es and penates (lâr′ēz) **1.** the household gods of the ancient Romans. **2.** the treasured possessions of a family or household. [Latin *lārēs et penātēs* household gods of the ancient Romans.]

large (lärj) *adj.,* **larg·er, larg·est. 1.** of considerable size or quantity; not small. **2.** exceeding the usual size or quantity: *a large ant.* **3.** wide in range or capacity: *The president's powers under the bill would be very large.* [Old French *large* broad, generous, from Latin *largus* abundant.] —**large′ness,** *n.* —For Synonyms, see **big.**

· **at large. a.** at liberty; free: *The suspect is still at large.* **b.** of,

by, or relating to an entire political unit, as a state: *Since the representatives were elected at large, they all had to campaign statewide.* **c.** as a whole; in general: *to talk about the world at large.* **d.** at length; in detail; fully: *to speak at large on a subject.*

large·heart·ed (lärj′här′tid) *adj.* generous; liberal; kindly. —**large′heart′ed·ness,** *n.*

large intestine, the lower part of the intestines, between the small intestine and the anus, consisting of the cecum, colon, and rectum. As digested food passes through the large intestine, water is absorbed from it and feces are formed.

large·ly (lärj′lē) *adv.* to a great extent; mostly; mainly: *The buildings in this area are largely two-bedroom homes.*

largemouth bass (lärj′mouth′) *also,* **large-mouth bass.** a blackish, North American game fish, *Micropterus salmoides,* having a mouth that extends back behind the eye; black bass. Weight: to 8 pounds (3.6 kilograms).

large-print (lärj′print′) *adj.* printed in large characters for easier readability by persons with poor eyesight: *the large-print edition of a newspaper.*

large-scale (lärj′skāl′) *adj.* **1.** of broad scope; extensive: *a large-scale strike.* **2.** drawn or made to a large scale: *a large-scale map, a large-scale graph.*

lar·gess (lär jes′, lär′jis) *also,* **lar·gesse.** *n.* **1.** generous giving. **2.** a gift or gifts so given. [Old French *largesse* bounty, going back to Latin *largus* abundant.]

lar·ghet·to (lär get′ō) *Music. adj., adv.* rather slow. —*n., pl.* **-tos.** a composition, movement, or part in such a tempo. [Italian *larghetto* somewhat slow, diminutive of *largo* slow, wide, from Latin *largus* abundant.]

larg·ish (lär′jish) *adj.* rather large.

lar·go (lär′gō) *Music. adj., adv.* very slow and dignified; stately. —*n., pl.* **-gos.** a largo composition, movement, or part. [Italian *largo* slow, wide, from Latin *largus* abundant.]

lar·i·at (lar′ē ət) *n.* **1.** a long rope with a loop secured in a running knot at one end, used esp. for roping livestock; lasso. **2.** tether. [Spanish *la reata* the rope, *reata* rope, from *reatar* to tie again, going back to Latin *re-* again + *aptāre* to adjust.]

lark[1] (lärk) *n.* **1.** any of various small songbirds, family Alaudidae, having a long, straight hind claw and predominantly gray-brown plumage, as the skylark, *Alauda arvensis,* found in Europe, and the **horned lark,** *Eremophila alpestris,* the only North American lark. Length: 5-9 inches (13-23 centimeters). **2.** any of various similar but unrelated birds, as the meadowlark. [Middle English *lark, laverke,* from Old English *laferce,* from earlier *læmerce* Old World lark.]

lark[2] (lärk) *n.* a playful, frivolous adventure or antic; something done just for fun: *We jumped in the fountain for a lark.* —*v.i.* to do things just for fun. [Possibly modification (influenced by LARK[1]) of dialectal English *lake* to play, from Old Norse *leika.*]

lark·spur (lärk′spûr′) *n.* delphinium. [LARK[1] + SPUR; because of its spur-shaped calyx.]

lar·rup (lar′əp) *v.t.,* **-ruped, -rup·ing.** *Informal.* to beat; flog; thrash. [Possibly from Dutch *larpen* to thrash.] —**lar′rup·er,** *n.*

lar·va (lär′və) *n., pl.* **-vae** (-vē). **1.** an insect in the early, worm-like stage of metamorphosis, after hatching from an egg and before becoming a pupa. Maggots and caterpillars are larvae. **2.** an early form of any animal that undergoes metamorphosis. The tadpole is the larva of a frog. [Latin *lārva* ghost, mask; because this stage was thought to mask the final form of the insect.] —**lar′val,** *adj.*

lar·vi·cide (lär′və sīd′) *n.* a substance used to kill harmful insect larvae, as some garden pests.

la·ryn·ge·al (lə rin′jē əl) *adj.* of, relating to, or located in or on the larynx: *laryngeal cartilage.* —**la·ryn′ge·al·ly,** *adv.*

lar·yn·gi·tis (lar′ən jī′tis) *n.* inflammation of the larynx, often characterized by hoarseness of the voice. [Modern Latin *laryngitis,* from Greek *larynx* throat + -ITIS.] —**lar′yn·git·ic** (lar′ən jit′ik), *adj.*

la·ryn·go·scope (lə ring′gə skōp′) *n.* a tubular telescopic and reflecting instrument for examining the larynx, as during surgery. —**la·ryn·go·scop·ic** (lə ring′gə skop′ik); *also,* **la·ryn·go·scop·i·cal,** *adj.* —**la·ryn·go·scop′i·cal·ly,** *adv.*

lar·ynx (lar′ingks) *n., pl.* **la·ryn·ges** (lə rin′jēz) or **lar·ynx·es.** **1.** a triangular, box-like chamber at the upper end of the human windpipe, containing the vocal cords and serving as the organ of speech. Also, **voice box. 2.** a similar organ in most other mammals and some other animals. [Modern Latin *larynx,* from Greek *larynx* throat.]

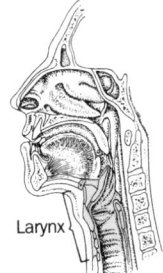

Larynx

la·sa·gne (lə zän′yə) *n.* **1.** a baked dish usually consisting of alternating layers of wide noodles, chopped meat, tomato sauce, cheese, and seasonings. **2.** a broad, flat noodle, sometimes having ruffled edges. [Italian *lasagne* (plural), going back to Latin *lasanum* cooking pot, from Greek *lasanon* chamber pot.]

las·car (las′kər) *n.* an East Indian sailor. [Hindi *lashkarī* sailor, soldier, going back to Persian *lashkar* army, from Arabic *al′askar* the army, possibly, through Greek, going back to Latin *exercitus* army.]

las·civ·i·ous (lə siv′ē əs) *adj.* **1.** feeling, showing, or characterized by lust. **2.** arousing lust. [Late Latin *lascīviōsus* lustful, from Latin *lascīvia* wantonness, playfulness.] —**las·civ′i·ous·ly,** *adv.* —**las·civ′i·ous·ness,** *n.*

lase (lāz) *v.i.,* **lased, las·ing.** to produce a laser beam; act as a laser. [From LASER.]

la·ser (lā′zər) *n. Physics.* a device that generates and amplifies visible radiation, producing an extremely powerful beam consisting of light waves that are of the same wavelength and are in phase. Lasers are used to cut steel, perform surgical procedures, and transmit communications signals. Also, **optical maser.** [Short for *l(ight) a(mplification by) s(timulated) e(mission of) r(adiation).*]

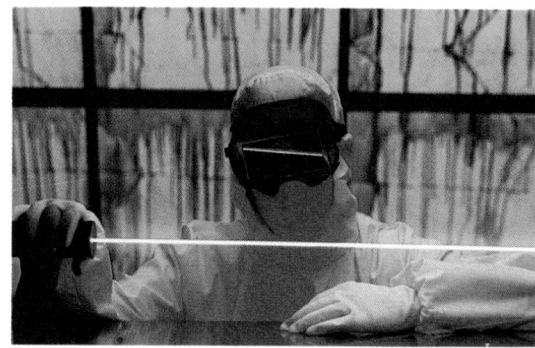

laser beam

laser disc *also,* **laser disk.** optical disc.

laser printer, a computer printer that uses a laser beam to form characters and graphics on paper.

lash[1] (lash) *n.* **1.** a stroke or blow with a whip, scourge, thong, or the like: *The slave was given ten lashes for insubordination.* **2.** the flexible, often braided, part of a whip. **3.** eyelash. **4.** a movement or impact like that of a whip: *the lash of an animal's tail.* **5.** anything that cuts or gives pain like a blow from a whip: *the lash of one's conscience.* —*v.t.* **1.** to beat or strike with a whip, scourge, or other flexible object. **2.** to beat or strike with violence; dash forcefully against: *The rain lashed the windows.* **3.** to wave or move to and fro like a whip; switch angrily: *The tiger lashed its tail.* **4.** to attack violently with words; assail: *The newspaper article lashed the politician.* **5.** to incite, as if by whipping: *The speaker lashed the crowd into violent action.* —*v.i.* **1.** to dash violently; rush: *The waves lashed against the rocks.* **2.** to beat or strike with or as with a whip or scourge (with *at*). [Middle English *laschen* to strike, beat.] —**lash′er,** *n.*

•**to lash out.** to make an attack with sudden violence or harsh, bitter words: *The writer lashed out against the critics.*

lash[2] (lash) *v.t.* to tie or fasten, as with a rope or cord: *The campers lashed logs together to make a raft.* [Middle English *lashen,* from Old French *lachier,* variant of *lacier* to lace, fasten, from Latin *laqueare* to ensnare, from *laquea* noose, snare[1].]

lash·ing[1] (lash′ing) *n.* **1.** an act or instance of whipping. **2.** a sharp rebuke or scolding. [LASH[1] + -ING[1].]

lash·ing[2] (lash′ing) *n.* something that fastens or ties, as a rope or cord. [LASH[2] + -ING[1].]

lass (las) *n.* **1.** a young woman; girl. **2.** sweetheart. [Of uncertain origin.]

las·sie (las′ē) *n.* a young girl; lass.

las·si·tude (las′i tüd′, -tūd′) *n.* a state or feeling of weariness or listlessness; languor; fatigue. [Latin *lassitūdō.*]

las·so (las′ō, la sü′) *n., pl.* **-sos** or **-soes.** a long rope with a running knot at one end, used esp. for roping livestock. —*v.t.,*

a	at	e	end	o	hot	u	up	hw	white		about
ā	ape	ē	me	ō	old	ū	use	ng	song	ə	taken
ä	far	i	it	ô	fork	ü	rule	th	thin		pencil
âr	care	ī	ice	oi	oil	u̇	pull	th	this		lemon
		îr	pierce	ou	out	ûr	turn	zh	measure		circus

las·soed, las·so·ing. to rope with a lasso. [Spanish *lazo* slip knot, snare, going back to Latin *laqueus* snare.]

last¹ (last) *adj.* **1.** following all others, as in order, time, or occurrence; furthest from the first; final: *the last one in line, the last day of the month.* **2.** being the only one remaining: *The vendor sold the last balloon.* **3.** next before the present; most recent; latest: *last night.* **4.** most unlikely; least probable: *She'd be the last person to go along with such a scheme.* **5.** least important; ranking lowest: *the last prize.* **6.** belonging to the end or final stages, esp. of life: *His last days were spent in bed.* **7.** of the greatest or highest; utmost: *to the last degree.* —*adv.* **1.** after all others in time or sequence; at the end: *Last came the clowns.* **2.** at a past time nearest to the present; most recently: *When did you last visit the dentist?* **3.** in conclusion; finally: *Last, I would like to summarize the points of my argument.* —*n.* **1.** a person or thing that is last: *I was the last in line. This is the last of the milk.* **2.** the end; conclusion: *They gave in at the last and told all they knew.* [Middle English *laste,* from Old English *latost, lætest,* superlative of *læt* late, slow, sluggish.]

· **at last.** finally: *At last, the dog stopped barking.*

· **to see** (or **hear**) **the last of.** to come in contact with for the last time; be rid of: *We'll never hear the last of it. You haven't seen the last of me.*

Synonyms *adj.* **Last¹, final,** and **ultimate** mean coming after all others in time or order. **Last** connotes occurring at the end of a series of similar or analogous things: *the last cracker in the box, the last train of the day.* **Final** connotes the termination or completion of a series or progression: *the final line of a poem, the final report of a commission.* **Ultimate** is similar to *final,* but may suggest a longer process: *the ultimate battle in a long-drawn-out war.*

last² (last) *v.i.* **1.** to go on; continue: *The play lasted three hours.* **2.** to stay in good condition: *These colors won't last if exposed to the sun.* **3.** to be enough not to give out or be depleted: *Our supplies should last until tomorrow.* [Middle English *lasten,* from Old English *læstan* to follow, continue.] —For Synonyms, see **continue.**

last³ (last) *n.* a wood or metal form, shaped like a human foot, on which footwear is made or repaired. —*v.t.* to form (footwear) on a last. [Old English *læste* this wooden form, from *læst* footprint.]

last-ditch (last'dich') *adj.* made or done as a final thing, esp. to prevent a crisis, failure, or disaster: *a last-ditch attempt to save an endangered species.*

Las·tex (las'teks) *n. Trademark.* an elastic yarn made with a core of rubber thread covered with any of various fibers, used for such items as bathing suits, girdles, and ski wear. [(E)LAST(IC) + TEX(TILE).]

last·ing (las'ting) *adj.* that lasts; permanent; enduring; durable. —**last'ing·ly,** *adv.* —**last'ing·ness,** *n.*

Last Judgment, Judgment Day.

last·ly (last'lē) *adv.* in the last place; in conclusion.

last-min·ute (last'min'it) *adj.* at the latest possible time; at the end; final: *last-minute arrangements for an extra guest.*

last quarter, the half moon that follows a full moon.

last rites, the sacraments administered by a Roman Catholic priest to someone in danger of death, consisting of confession, the viaticum, and anointing of the sick.

last straw, the added factor that finally makes something intolerable.

Last Supper, the final meal of Jesus and the Apostles on the night before the Crucifixion.

last word **1.** a final remark, as in an argument. **2.** ultimate authority: *Congress is supposed to have the last word in declaring war.* **3.** a final or definitive statement, treatment, or work: *This book is the last word on model airplanes.* **4.** *Informal.* the most recent style or development: *Those are the last word in ski boots.*

lat., latitude.

Lat., Latin.

latch (lach) *n.* any device for keeping a door, window, or gate closed, usually consisting of a bar that falls or slides into a notch, hole, or groove. —*v.t.* to secure the latch of (something): *to latch a gate.* —*v.i.* to be equipped with a latch; close with a latch: *Do the cabinet doors latch?* [Old English *læccan* to seize.]

· **to latch onto.** *Informal.* **a.** to attach oneself to; stick close to. **b.** to grasp or obtain.

latch·et (lach'it) *n. Archaic.* a thong used to fasten a shoe; shoelace. [Dialectal Old French *lachet* thong, lacing, diminutive of Old French *las* noose. See LACE.]

latch·key (lach'kē') *n.* a key for opening the latch of a door or gate.

latch·string (lach'string') *n.* a string passing through a door, used to open a latch.

late (lāt) *adj.,* **lat·er** or **lat·ter, lat·est** or **last.** **1.** coming after the proper, expected, or promised time: *I was late for our appointment.* **2.** coming or being after the usual or customary time: *a late lunch.* **3.a.** beginning or occurring at, or going on until, an advanced time, as of night: *to call at a late hour, a late movie.* **b.** of or relating to an advanced stage of history or development: *late Byzantine architecture.* **4.** most recent: *to fill someone in on the latest developments.* **5.** recently but no longer holding a position or office: *The late owners sold the store for several million dollars. The late governor returned to private life.* **6.** recently dead. —*adv.,* **lat·er, lat·est.** **1.** after the proper, expected, or usual time: *We arrived late at the party. The mail was delivered late today.* **2.** at or until an advanced time, as of night: *The children stayed up late.* **3.** at or to an advanced stage or period. **4.** not long since; recently. [Old English *læt* slow, tardy.] —**late'ness,** *n.*

· **of late.** lately; recently: *Our neighbor has been acting rather strangely of late.*

Synonyms *adj.* **Late** and **tardy** mean coming or happening after the expected or appointed time. **Late** is the general term for anything falling behind a schedule or a usual rate of progress: *The train was late. Our report to the board is late.* **Tardy** connotes a lack of punctuality and has a negative connotation: *Employees who are frequently tardy may be asked to make up for lost time.*

late bloomer, a person who is late in developing his or her talents or abilities.

late·com·er (lāt'kum'ər) *n.* **1.** a person who arrives late. **2.** a person or thing that has recently arrived; newcomer.

la·teen (la tēn', lə-) *adj.* of, relating to, or having a sailing rig characterized by a triangular sail that is suspended from a long slanting yard and extends both fore and aft of the mast. —*n.* a ship having such a rig, common esp. in the Mediterranean Sea. Also, **la·teen'er.** [French *(voile) latine* Latin (sail), feminine of *latin* Latin, from Latin *Latīnus* (see LATIN); because of its use in the Mediterranean Sea.]

Late Greek, a form of the Greek language used from about A.D. 300 to 600.

Late Latin, a form of the Latin language used from about A.D. 300 to 600.

late·ly (lāt'lē) *adv.* **1.** within a recent time; not long ago: *Have you seen them lately?* **2.** now and during a recent time; these days: *I haven't been feeling well lately.*

la·tent (lā'tənt) *adj.* present and actual, but not obvious, developed, or brought out; hidden: *the latent meaning of a ritual.* [Latin *latēns,* present participle of *latēre* to lie concealed.] —**la'ten·cy,** *n.* —**la'tent·ly,** *adv.*

latent heat, the amount of heat that must be absorbed or released by a substance undergoing a change of state, as from solid to liquid or from liquid to vapor, the temperature and pressure of the substance remaining constant.

latent image, image *(def. 8).*

lat·er (lā'tər) a comparative of **late.**

lat·er·al (lat'ər əl) *adj.* **1.** of or relating to the side; at, from, or toward the side. **2.** *Phonetics.* articulated with the breath passing over the sides of the tongue. **3.** descended from a brother or a sister of an ancestor: *a lateral relation.* —*n.* **1.** a lateral or side part, member, or object. **2.** *Football.* a pass thrown to the side or in a direction away from the opponent's goal, rather than forward. Also, **lateral pass.** **3.** *Phonetics.* a lateral consonant sound. In English, the only lateral is *l.* —*v.i. Football.* to throw a lateral. [Latin *laterālis* relating to the side, from *latus* side.] —**lat'er·al·ly,** *adv.*

lateral line, a long canal containing pressure-sensitive organs along each side of the body in fish and aquatic larval amphibians, serving for the detection of sound waves and currents. The two canals are generally connected across the head, where they may branch.

Lat·er·an (lat'ər ən) *n.* **1.** the church of St. John Lateran, the cathedral of the pope as bishop of Rome. **2.** the palace, formerly the official papal residence and now a museum, adjoining this church.

lat·er·ite (lat'ə rīt') *n.* a type of reddish soil, rich in iron or aluminum, formed by the intense weathering of igneous or metamorphic rocks, as in tropical rain forests. [Latin *later* brick, tile + -ITE¹; because its color is similar to that of red bricks.] —**lat·er·it·ic** (lat'ə rit'ik), *adj.*

la·tex (lā'teks) *n., pl.* **lat·i·ces** or **la·tex·es.** **1.** a milky liquid obtained from a rubber tree, esp. the tropical rubber tree, *Hevea brasiliensis,* that consists of small globules of pure rubber suspended in water. **2.** a similar milky liquid found in some other plants, as milkweeds and poppies. **3.** a liquid emulsion consisting of small globules of plastic or of synthetic rubber suspended in water, used esp. as a base for certain paints. [Latin *latex* liquid, probably from Greek *latax* wine lees.]

lath (lath) *n., pl.* **laths** (lathz, laths) or **lath.** **1.** any of the thin,

narrow strips of wood used esp. to make a lattice or as a base for a coat of plaster. **2.** a sheet or sheets of building material, esp. metal mesh, used for a similar purpose. Also, **lathing.** —*v.t.* to build or line with laths. [Old English *lætt* thin, narrow strip of wood used as a base for plaster of a building or for lattice work.]

lathe (lāth) *n.* a machine that holds a long piece of wood, metal, or other material at both ends and rotates it for shaping by a cutting tool. [Of Scandinavian origin.]

lath·er (lath′ər) *n.* **1.** foam, froth, or suds made esp. from soap moistened with water. **2.** foam caused by profuse sweating, esp. on a horse. **3.** *Informal.* a state of excitement or agitation. —*v.i.* **1.** to form a lather. **2.** to become covered with lather. —*v.t.* **1.** to cover with lather. **2.** *Informal.* to beat soundly; thrash. [Old English *lēathor* foam from soap and water.]

lath·ing (lath′ing) *n.* **1.** lath or laths. **2.** the act or process of putting laths in place for use.

lat·i·ces (lat′ə sēz′) a plural of **latex.**

Lat·in (lat′in) *n.* **1.** the language of the ancient Romans, a member of the Italic group of the Indo-European family of languages, the parent of the Romance languages. **2.** a member of any of the peoples, as Italians or Portuguese, whose languages are derived from Latin. **3.** a native or inhabitant of ancient Latium, which included Rome. **4.** a Roman Catholic of the Latin Rite. —*adj.* **1.** of, relating to, or composed in Latin. **2.** of or relating to the people or countries that use languages descended from Latin. **3.** of or relating to Latium or its people. **4.** of or relating to the Roman Catholic Church or its Latin Rite. **5.** of or relating to the alphabet used to write Latin and most European languages, including English. [Latin *Latīnus* Roman, from *Latium* the region in Italy in which ancient Rome was located.]

Words from Latin

Latin, the language from which French, Italian, Portuguese, Spanish, and other Romance languages are derived, is the largest contributor of root words to English. It is an extinct language that belongs to the Italic group of the Indo-European language family. Below are some of the loanwords that have entered English from or through Latin.

abdicate	corpuscle	herbivore	pessimism
abdomen	credo	hibernate	plebeian
act	deficit	human	pollen
aggression	dense	incur	population
agriculture	doctrine	insomnia	proletariat
album	education	intestine	prostrate
alias	equine	liberty	public
alumnus	fame	library	pulmonary
antenna	fanatic	ligament	reptile
aquarium	fatal	mammal	rupture
bonus	fauna	modest	suffocate
candidate	flora	municipal	terrarium
canine	fortune	nasal	tonsil
capsule	fume	nature	tribunal
collapse	fungus	objective	ulcer
communism	gestation	pagan	urbane
contagion	habitat	patrician	vaccine

Lat·in-A·mer·i·can (lat′in ə mer′i kən) *adj.* of, relating to, or characteristic of Latin America.

Latin American, a native or inhabitant of Latin America.

Lat·in·ate (lat′ə nāt′) *adj.* of, derived from, or resembling Latin.

Latin Church, the Roman Catholic Church.

Latin cross, a cross formed by one short horizontal bar that intersects a longer vertical bar near the top, used as a sacred symbol, esp. in certain Christian religions. For illustration, see **cross.**

Lat·in·ism (lat′ə niz′əm) *n.* a word, idiom, or expression borrowed from or modeled on Latin.

Lat·in·ist (lat′ə nist) *n.* a student of or expert in Latin.

La·tin·i·ty (lə tin′i tē) *n.* the use of Latin or its style or idioms.

Lat·in·ize (lat′ə nīz′) *v.t.*, **-ized, -iz·ing. 1.** to translate into Latin. **2.** to make (writings, customs, or rituals) conform to the Roman Catholic Church. **3.** to put into the Latin alphabet. —**Lat′in·i·za′tion,** *n.*

La·ti·no (la tē′nō) *n., pl.* **-nos.** a person living in the United States who is of Latin-American origin or descent. —*adj.* Latin-American: *Latino music.* [Short for Spanish *latinoamericano* Latin American.]

Latin Rite, the liturgy of the Roman Catholic Church, formerly in the Latin language.

lat·ish (lā′tish) *adj., adv.* somewhat late.

lat·i·tude (lat′i tūd′, -tūd′) *n.* **1.** the angular distance north or south of the equator, expressed as degrees measured from the earth's center. All points of a given latitude form a circle running east and west and parallel to the equator. **2.** a place or region marked by parallels of latitude: *temperate latitudes.* **3.** freedom from narrow restrictions: *The students were given great latitude in selecting topics for their essays.* **4.** *Astronomy.* celestial latitude. [Latin *lātitūdō* breadth.]

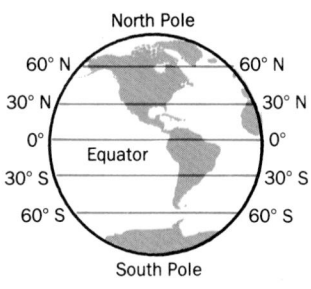

lines of **latitude**

lat·i·tu·di·nal (lat′i tü′də nəl, -tū′-) *adj.* of or relating to latitude. —**lat′i·tu′di·nal·ly,** *adv.*

lat·i·tu·di·nar·i·an (lat′ə tü′də när′ē ən, -tū′-) *adj.* demanding, promoting, or allowing others much freedom in beliefs and conduct, esp. in religious matters. —*n.* a person who is latitudinarian in thought and conduct. —**lat′i·tu′di·nar′i·an·ism,** *n.*

la·trine (lə trēn′) *n.* a toilet or privy, often temporary and without plumbing, as in an army camp. [French *latrines* (plural) privies, from Latin *lātrīna* privy, bath, going back to *lavāre* to wash.]

lat·ter (lat′ər) *adj.* **1.** the second of the two mentioned. **2.** nearer to the end or to the present time: *We spent the latter part of the evening at a party on the other side of town.* [Old English *lætra* slower, later, comparative of *læt* slow, tardy.]

> **Usage** **Latter** is used to refer to the second of two things mentioned, as in *I took Latin and French and found the latter more difficult.* The purpose of using **latter** is to avoid repetition. However, it is often preferable to repeat the name of the second reference, so that the reader does not have to look back to determine what **latter** means. The use of **latter** to refer to the last of three or more persons or things rather than the second of two, as in *I took Latin, French, and German and found the latter the most difficult,* is generally considered unacceptable. **Former,** which is often opposed to **latter,** is used to refer to the first of two things mentioned, as in *They looked up Alaska and Texas and found that the former was larger.* As with **latter,** it is often preferable to avoid **former** and instead repeat the name of the first reference. However, when used, **former** and **latter** are usually preceded by *the.*

lat·ter-day (lat′ər dā′) *adj.* of recent or present times; modern.

Latter-day Saint, a member of the Church of Jesus Christ of Latter-day Saints; Mormon.

lat·ter·ly (lat′ər lē) *adv.* at a late or recent time; lately.

lat·tice (lat′is) *n.* **1.** an openwork structure of crossed or interlaced strips, as of wood or metal, spaced to form a regular pattern of openings. **2.** something having a lattice, as a window. **3.** anything having an orderly arrangement like a lattice, as the ions or molecules in crystalline minerals. —*v.t.,* **-ticed, -tic·ing. 1.** to form into or arrange like a lattice. **2.** to furnish with a lattice. [Old French *lattis* lath work, from *latte* lath; of Germanic origin.] —**lat′tice·like′,** *adj.*

lat·tice·work (lat′is wûrk′) *n.* **1.** lattice. **2.** a structure made of lattices.

Lat·vi·an (lat′vē ən) *adj.* of, relating to, or characteristic of Latvia or its people, language, or culture. —*n.* **1.** a native or citizen of Latvia. **2.** a person of Latvian descent. **3.** the language of the Latvians; Lett.

lattice window

laud (lôd) *v.t.* to praise, extol. —*n.* **1.** a hymn or song of praise. **2. lauds.** one of the seven canonical hours, during which psalms and prayers of praise are recited, usually with matins. [Latin *laudāre* to praise, from *laus* praise.]

---

a	at	e	end	o	hot	u	up	hw	white		about
ā	ape	ē	me	ō	old	ū	use	ng	song	ə	taken
ä	far	i	it	ô	fork	ü	rule	th	thin		pencil
âr	care	ī	ice	oi	oil	u̇	pull	th	this		lemon
		îr	pierce	ou	out	ûr	turn	zh	measure		circus

laud·a·ble (lô′də bəl) *adj.* worthy of praise; commendable. —**laud′a·bil′i·ty, laud′a·ble·ness,** *n.* —**laud′a·bly,** *adv.*

lau·da·num (lô′də nəm) *n.* a medicinal solution of opium in alcohol.

lau·da·tion (lô dā′shən) *n.* the act of lauding; praise.

laud·a·to·ry (lô′də tôr′ē) *adj.* containing or expressing praise.

laugh (laf) *v.i.* **1.** to make the inarticulate sounds and the associated facial and body movements that show any of several emotions, such as amusement, joy, or scorn. **2.** to feel amusement or joy; be happy. —*v.t.* to produce a specified effect upon by laughing: *to laugh one's troubles away.* —*n.* **1.** the act, sound, or manner of laughing. **2.** something that provokes or tends to provoke laughter or amusement. **3. laughs.** *Informal.* amusement or fun: *to do something for laughs.* [Old English *hlæhhan, hliehhan* to indicate mirth by sound.] —**laugh′er,** *n.*
• **to have the last laugh.** to win or have one's way at the end of a dispute, esp. after apparently losing.
• **to laugh at.** to deride, ridicule, or fail to take seriously.
• **to laugh off.** to dismiss lightly; treat as not serious: *to laugh off an injury.*
• **to laugh up one's sleeve.** to laugh to oneself; be secretly amused.

laugh·a·ble (laf′ə bəl) *adj.* provoking or tending to provoke laughter, esp. laughter that is derisive. —**laugh′a·ble·ness,** *n.* —**laugh′a·bly,** *adv.*

laugh·ing (laf′ing) *adj.* **1.** that laughs or seems to laugh: *a laughing brook.* **2.** expressed with laughter: *a laughing comment.* —*n.* laughter. —**laugh′ing·ly,** *adv.*
• **no laughing matter.** a matter of serious concern.

laughing gas, nitrous oxide.

laugh·ing·stock (laf′ing stok′) *n.* an object of ridicule.

laugh·ter (laf′tər) *n.* the action or sound of laughing. [Old English *hleahtor* action of laughing.]

launch[1] (lônch) *v.t.* **1.** to put (a boat or ship) into the water. **2.** to push or propel forcibly into motion, esp. outward into the air: *to launch a spear, to launch a rocket.* **3.** to start (someone or something) on a course or career: *to launch a political career.* **4.** to put into operation; start: *The governor launched a new anti-poverty program.* —*v.i.* **1.** to throw oneself into or begin vigorously: *The journalist suddenly launched into intensive questioning.* **2.** to move outward into the water or air. —*n.* an act or instance of launching. [Middle English *launchen,* from Norman French *lancher,* from Old French *lanchier,* from Late Latin *lanceare* to throw a lance, from Latin *lancea* lance; of Celtic origin.] —**launch′er,** *n.*

launch[2] (lônch) *n.* **1.** an open or half-decked powerboat. **2.** formerly, the largest boat carried by a warship. [Spanish or Portuguese *lancha* pinnace, from Malay *lancharan* swift boat, from *lanchār* swift.]

launch pad, an area or structure from which a rocket or missile is launched. Also, **launching pad.**

laun·der (lôn′dər) *v.t.* **1.** to wash or wash and iron (clothes or linens). **2.** to make (money obtained illegally) appear to be lawfully gained by directing it through another person or organization. —*v.i.* **1.** to wash or wash and iron clothes or linens. **2.** to withstand washing or washing and ironing: *This material launders poorly.* [From Middle English *launder, lavender* one who washes (clothes), from Old French *lavandier,* going back to Latin *lavanda* things to be washed, from *lavāre* to wash.] —**laun′der·er,** *n.*

laun·dress (lôn′dris) *n.* a woman employed to do laundering.

Laun·dro·mat (lôn′drə mat′) *n. Trademark.* a self-service laundry that has coin-operated washing machines and dryers.

laun·dry (lôn′drē) *n., pl.* **-dries.** **1.** things that have been, are, or will be laundered. **2.** a place where laundering is done.

laun·dry·man (lôn′drē mən) *n., pl.* **-men** (-mən). **1.** a person who works in or runs a laundry. **2.** a person who collects and delivers laundry.

laun·dry·wom·an (lôn′drē wùm′ən) *n., pl.* **-wom·en** (-wim′ən). laundress.

lau·re·ate (lôr′ē it) *n.* **1.** a person singled out for special honor, esp. an honor relating to arts and sciences: *a Nobel laureate.* **2.** poet laureate. —*adj. Archaic.* crowned or decked with laurel as a mark of honor; greatly honored. [Middle English *laureate,* from Latin *laureātus* crowned with laurel, from *laurea (corona)* laurel (wreath); referring to the ancient Roman custom of honoring poets, athletes, and other heroes by crowning them with a laurel wreath.] —**lau′re·ate·ship,** *n.*

lau·rel (lôr′əl, lor′-) *n.* **1.** either of two medium-sized evergreen trees, genus *Laurus,* native to the Mediterranean area, bearing stiff lance-shaped leaves and clusters of tiny yellow flowers. **2.** any of various trees or shrubs of the same family, as the sassafras and avocado, or the mountain laurel of the heath family. **3.** the foliage of the laurel tree used as an emblem of victory or of distinction. **4. laurels.** an honor; distinction. —*v.t.,* **-reled, -rel·ing;** *also,*

British, **-relled, -rel·ling.** to honor by or as by crowning with laurel. [Old French *laurier* laurel tree, going back to Latin *laurus.*]
• **to look to one's laurels.** to be aware of having one's accomplishments excelled: *That country's antiquated steel industry had better look to its laurels.*
• **to rest on one's laurels.** to be satisfied with what one has already achieved or accomplished.

la·va (lä′və, lav′ə) *n.* **1.** molten material that flows from a volcano or a fissure in the earth's surface. **2.** volcanic rock of varied structure and texture formed by the cooling of such molten material. [Dialectal Italian *lava* torrent, avalanche, from Latin *lābēs* a fall.]

la·vage (lə väzh′, lav′ij) *n. Medicine.* the irrigation or washing out of an organ, as the stomach, intestines, bladder, or sinuses. [French *lavage,* from *laver* to wash (from Latin *lavāre*) + *-age* (see -AGE).]

lav·a·liere (lav′ə lîr′, lä′və-) *also,* **lav·a·lier.** *n.* an ornamental pendant on a small chain, worn around the neck. [French *lavallière* loose necktie, from the Duchess of *La Vallière,* a mistress of King Louis XIV of France.]

lav·a·to·ry (lav′ə tôr′ē) *n., pl.* **-ries.** **1.** a room with toilets and facilities for washing the hands and face. **2.** toilet. **3.** a bowl or basin for washing. [Late Latin *lavātōrium* place for washing, going back to Latin *lavāre* to wash. Doublet of LAVER.]

lava flow

lave (lāv) *v.,* **laved, lav·ing.** —*v.t.* **1.** to wash or bathe. **2.** to flow along or against: *The waves laved the shore.* —*v.i.* to wash or bathe. [Old English *lafian* to wash, going back to Latin *lavāre* to wash.]

lav·en·der (lav′ən dər) *n.* **1.** a pale reddish purple color. **2.** any of a group of plants and shrubs, genus *Lavandula,* of the mint family, cultivated throughout the world, esp. the common lavender, *L. augustifolia,* having narrow, grayish leaves and spikes of fragrant, pale purple flowers that yield an oil used in perfumes. For illustration, see **herb. 3.** the dried leaves and flowers of this plant, used mainly in sachets. —*adj.* **1.** having the color lavender. **2.** having the fragrance of lavender. [Anglo-Norman *lavendre* the plant, from Medieval Latin *lavendula,* possibly going back to Latin *lavāre* to wash; because of its use in perfuming laundered clothing and bath water.]

la·ver[1] (lā′vər) *n. Archaic.* a basin, bowl, or trough to wash in. [Old French *laveo(i)r* basin, from Late Latin *lavātōrium* place for washing, going back to Latin *lavāre* to wash. Doublet of LAVATORY.]

la·ver[2] (lā′vər) *n.* any of various edible seaweeds, esp. red algae of the genus *Porphyra.* [Modern Latin *laver,* from Latin *laver* water plant.]

lav·ish (lav′ish) *adj.* **1.** given or done extravagantly, out of or as if out of great wealth or abundance; expensive or ostentatious: *a lavish gift.* **2.** more than necessary; profuse; abundant: *lavish amounts of food.* —*v.t.* to give generously or profusely: *to lavish gifts on one's grandchildren.* [From obsolete *lavish* profusion, from Old French *lavasse* abundant rain, from *laver* to wash, from Latin *lavāre* to wash, shower.] —**lav′ish·ly,** *adv.* —**lav′ish·ness,** *n.*

law (lô) *n.* **1.** a rule that allows or prohibits certain conduct or activities, established by custom or by official adoption, as by a legislature, and applied to all members of a community: *to pass a new health-insurance law.* **2.** a particular set of such rules: *international law, tribal law.* **3.** the principle of regulating society by such rules: *respect for the law, the rule of law.* **4.** an agent or agency applying or enforcing such rules: *an officer of the law.* **5.** a legal action begun in a court of law to correct a grievance or settle a claim; lawsuit: *to resort to law.* **6.** the department of knowledge dealing with these rules: *a student of law.* **7.** the profession of being a lawyer: *to practice law.* **8.** the governing principle that regulates a certain area: *the laws of right conduct, the law of the jungle.* **9.** in science, a statement concerning the relation between two or more factors or variables that is universally accepted because it is observed to be true under all circumstances. **10.** a rule or principle that is applied throughout a body of mathematics or to all members of a set. **11.** something considered to be authoritative; something that must be obeyed: *Their word is law.* **12.** a

divine commandment or precept. **13. Law.** Law of Moses. [Old English *lagu* body of rules, a rule, custom; of Scandinavian origin.]
· **to lay down the law.** to command in an authoritative manner.
· **to read law.** to study to become a lawyer by serving as an apprentice in a law office rather than attending a law school.

> **Synonyms** **Law, regulation, statute,** and **ordinance** all denote an established rule governing conduct. **Law** is the general term for a rule established by authority, through legislation, or through court decision: *The judge interpreted the law for the jury. By exceeding the speed limit, you broke the law.* A **regulation** is a rule governing the operation of some system. It may be created within the system rather than by a legislative body: *school regulations, military regulations.* **Statute** connotes a legislative act: *The statute was passed and went into effect three years ago.* **Ordinance** is used of a law with local effect, esp. a law passed by a municipal government: *A town ordinance forbids driving on the beach.*

law·a·bid·ing (lô′ə bī′ding) *adj.* obedient to the law.

law·break·er (lô′brā′kər) *n.* a person who violates the law. —**law′break′ing,** *n., adj.*

law·ful (lô′fəl) *adj.* **1.** allowed by or not contrary to law: *a lawful act, exercising rights in a lawful manner.* **2.** according to or recognized by law: *a lawful marriage.* —**law′ful·ly,** *adv.* —**law′ful·ness,** *n.*

law·giv·er (lô′giv′ər) *n.* a person who establishes a law or code of laws for a country or people.

law·less (lô′lis) *adj.* **1.** not according to or obeying the law: *a lawless act, a lawless person.* **2.** not controlled by law; without laws: *a lawless society.* —**law′less·ly,** *adv.* —**law′less·ness,** *n.*

law·mak·er (lô′mā′kər) *n.* a person who makes laws; legislator.

law·mak·ing (lô′mā′king) *n.* the making of laws. —*adj.* responsible for making laws: *a lawmaking body.*

lawn[1] (lôn) *n.* a grassy area that is kept closely mowed, esp. around a house or building or in a park. [Middle English *launde,* from Old French *lande* grassy area, heath, from Breton *lann* heath, country.]

lawn[2] (lôn) *n.* a lightweight, sheer cotton fabric, used esp. for blouses and handkerchiefs. [From *Laon,* French town famous for the manufacture of linen.]

lawn bowling, bowls.

lawn mower, any of various machines with revolving blades used for cutting grass.

lawn tennis, tennis *(def. 1).*

Law of Moses, the first of the three divisions of the Jewish Scriptures, preceding the Prophets and the Hagiographa, comprising Genesis, Exodus, Leviticus, Numbers, and Deuteronomy. Also, **Pentateuch, Torah.**

law·ren·ci·um (lô ren′sē əm) *n.* a short-lived, radioactive element produced by bombarding a californium target with boron ions. Symbol: **Lr** For tables, see **element.** [From E. O. *Lawrence,* 1901-58, U.S. physicist who invented the cyclotron.]

law·suit (lô′süt′) *n.* an action instituted in a civil court or a court of equity.

law·yer (lô′yər) *n.* a person whose profession is representing clients in courts of law and advising them in other legal matters; attorney.

> **Synonyms** **Lawyer, counselor,** and **attorney** denote a person authorized to practice law. **Lawyer** is the general term: *a small-town lawyer, a property lawyer.* **Counselor** is used to refer to a lawyer representing clients in court: *the counselor for the defendant.* **Attorney** denotes a lawyer who serves as an agent in transacting business: *We spoke to the seller's attorney.*

lax (laks) *adj.* **1.** not careful or watchful enough; allowing too much latitude; negligent: *a lax inspection procedure.* **2.** not rigid, tense, or firm; slack. [Latin *laxus* loose.] —**lax′ly,** *adv.* —**lax′ness,** *n.*

lax·a·tive (lak′sə tiv) *n.* a drug that promotes the discharge of feces from the bowels. [Medieval Latin *laxativus* loosening, going back to Latin *laxus* loose.]

lax·i·ty (lak′si tē) *n.* the state or quality of being lax.

lay[1] (lā) *v.,* laid, lay·ing. —*v.t.* **1.** to put or place down on something; cause to lie: *to lay a plate on the table, to lay a baby in a crib.* **2.** to knock down; cause to fall: *The boxer laid his opponent low with a blow to the jaw.* **3.** to prepare for use; make ready; set: *to lay a trap, to lay plans, to lay a course for home.* **4.** to put down and fasten in place: *to lay a pipeline through a swamp, to lay a floor, to lay cinder blocks.* **5.** to produce and deposit (an egg or eggs): *The robin laid three eggs in the nest.* **6.** to assign or attribute (with *to*): *The food shortage was laid to a lack of rain.* **7.** to place or allocate (with *on*): *The detective lays great stress on details. She lays much emphasis on doing a job well.* **8.** to accuse or

impute; charge: *to lay the blame on someone.* **9.** to submit or present: *to lay a case before a judge.* **10.** to impose or establish: *The Congress shall have power to lay and collect taxes, duties, imposts, and excises* (U.S. Constitution, 1787). **11.** to place (a bet); bet. **12.** to place in the setting or location of: *The novel is laid in Chicago around the turn of the century.* **13.** to cause to settle, subside, or be still: *The rain laid the dust on the dirt road.* **14.** to apply (one's strength) energetically (with *to* or *into*): *The soldiers laid their backs to the truck and moved it out of the mud.* **15.** to arrange dishes, silverware, and other items upon (a table) in preparation for a meal. —*v.i.* to lay eggs. —*n.* the manner, direction, or position in which something lies or is arranged: *the lay of the land.* [Middle English *lai,* from Old English *lecgan* to put, place.]
· **to lay about one. a.** to strike out on all sides; deliver blows wildly. **b.** to begin energetically; act with vigor.
· **to lay aside. a.** to put down, esp. out of the way: *I laid my book aside last night, and now I can't find it.* **b.** to put away or save for future use; reserve: *to lay aside five dollars a week.* **c.** to do away with; abandon; discard: *The city council laid aside plans for the new building.*
· **to lay away.** to reserve for safekeeping, future delivery, or later use, esp. to hold (an item) until all payments on it have been made.
· **to lay bare.** to make known: *This special report lays bare all the facts in the case.*
· **to lay by.** to put away; reserve; save: *to lay by part of one's income.*
· **to lay down. a.** to assert or declare, esp. officially, dogmatically, or authoritatively: *The regime laid down a ban on travel abroad.* **b.** to give up; sacrifice; relinquish: *to lay down one's life to save another person's.* **c.** to bet; wager. **d.** to store away for future use: *to lay down wine in a cellar.*
· **to lay for.** to lie in wait to or as if to attack.
· **to lay in.** to get and store for the future: *to lay in provisions.*
· **to lay into.** to make a vigorous physical or verbal attack on.
· **to lay it on (thick).** *Slang.* to give excessive or overstated praise or criticism: *Your friend was really laying it on thick by calling that inexperienced actor the best in the play.*
· **to lay off. a.** to mark off; fix: *to lay off boundaries.* **b.** to dismiss from employment: *Workers were laid off in several plants.* **c.** *Slang.* to stop: *to lay off teasing someone.*
· **to lay out. a.** to spread out and arrange: *to lay out one's clothes for packing.* **b.** to arrange according to design; prepare: *to lay out a campaign strategy.* **c.** to prepare (a corpse) for burial. **d.** *Slang.* to spend: *We laid out twenty dollars for the gift.* **e.** *Slang.* to knock unconscious: *One punch laid the fighter out.*
· **to lay over.** to stop temporarily in the course of a trip.
· **to lay to. a.** to apply oneself with vigor. **b.** to bring a boat or ship into the wind and maintain it in a stationary or nearly stationary position.
· **to lay up. a.** to store or put aside for future use. **b.** to confine or incapacitate, as from illness or injury. **c.** to take (a boat or ship) out of service and put it in dock, as for repairs.

> **Usage** Forms of the verb **lay** *(lay, laid, laying)* are often used mistakenly for forms of the verb **lie**[2] *(lie, lay, lain, lying).* For example, some people say *Lay down until you feel better* instead of *Lie down until you feel better,* or *She laid on the couch and took a nap* instead of *She lay on the couch and took a nap,* or *They found him laying on the ground unconscious* instead of *They found him lying on the ground unconscious.* The use of the verb **lay** to mean *lie* is generally considered nonstandard.

lay[2] (lā) the past tense of **lie**[2].

lay[3] (lā) *adj.* **1.** of or relating to those who are not members of the clergy. **2.** of, relating to, or belonging to those not in a certain profession, such as medicine or law. [Old French *lai* secular, relating to the laity, from Latin *laïcus* relating to the people, from Greek *lāikos,* from *lāos* the people.]

lay[4] (lā) *n.* **1.** a short lyric or narrative poem originally intended to be sung. **2.** a melody; song. [Old French *lai* type of poem; of Breton origin.]

lay·a·way (lā′ə wā′) *n.* a system of buying goods in which an article is set aside for the purchaser until installment payments have been completed. —*adj.* of or designating such a system of purchase: *The store has a layaway plan.*

a	at	e	end	o	hot	u	up	hw	white		about
ā	ape	ē	me	ō	old	ū	use	ng	song	ə	taken
ä	far	i	it	ô	fork	ū	rule	th	thin		pencil
âr	care	ī	ice	oi	oil	u	pull	th	this		lemon
		îr	pierce	ou	out	ûr	turn	zh	measure		circus

699

lay·er (lā′ər) *n.* **1.** a single thickness laid on or over something or forming one level of a stack or series: *a layer of ice on the street, a wedding cake with four layers.* **2.** a person or thing that lays: *a cable layer.* **3.** a chicken that lays eggs. **4.** *Botany.* a shoot that is rooted without detaching it from its parent. —*v.t.* **1.** to make, arrange, or form in layers: *to layer a cake.* **2.** to propagate (a plant) by means of a layer. —**lay′er·ing,** *n.*

lay·er·ing (lā′ər ing) *n.* a method of propagating plants by placing part of a stem in soil or other rooting medium and allowing it to form roots while still attached to the parent plant.

lay·ette (lā et′) *n.* a complete outfit for a newborn baby, including clothes, toilet articles, and bedding. [French *layette* baby's garments, box, diminutive of Old French *laie* box, from Middle Dutch *laeye.*]

lay figure 1. a jointed model of a human body, usually of wood, used esp. by artists to show the arrangement of drapery. **2.** a person who lacks importance or individuality. [From obsolete *layman* jointed model of the body (from Dutch *leeman* jointed man, from Middle Dutch *led* joint + *man* man) + FIGURE.]

lay·man (lā′mən) *n., pl.* **-men** (-mən). **1.** a person who does not belong to a certain profession. **2.** a person who is not a member of the clergy. [LAY[3] + MAN.]

lay·off (lā′ôf′, -of′) *n.* **1.** the act of dismissing a relatively large number of employees. **2.** a period of enforced unemployment or inactivity.

lay·out (lā′out′) *n.* **1.** the act or process of laying out. **2.** the way in which the various parts of something are located or arranged; design: *the layout of a building.* **3.** a plan or design of material prepared for printing. **4.** an outfit or set, as of tools.

lay·o·ver (lā′ō′vər) *n.* a temporary stop in the course of a trip.

lay·peo·ple (lā′pē′pəl) *pl. n.* laypersons.

lay·per·son (lā′pûr′sən) *n.* **1.** a person who does not belong to a certain profession. **2.** a person who is not a member of the clergy.

lay·up (lā′up′) *n.* in basketball, a shot taken near the basket, often banking the ball off the backboard.

lay·wom·an (lā′wŭm′ən) *n., pl.* **-wom·en** (-wim′ən). **1.** a woman who does not belong to a certain profession. **2.** a woman who is not a member of the clergy.

laz·ar (laz′ər, lā′zər) *n. Archaic.* a poor person afflicted with a loathsome disease, esp. leprosy. [Medieval Latin *lazarus* leper, from *Lazarus,* name of the beggar in Luke 16:20.]

laze (lāz) *v.,* **lazed, laz·ing.** —*v.i.* to be lazy; loaf. —*v.t.* to pass (time) lazily. [From LAZY.]

la·zy (lā′zē) *adj.,* **-zi·er, -zi·est. 1.** unwilling to work or exert oneself. **2.** moving slowly; sluggish: *a lazy river.* **3.** causing laziness: *a lazy summer day.* [Of uncertain origin.] —**la′zi·ly,** *adv.* —**la′zi·ness,** *n.*

la·zy·bones (lā′zē bōnz′) *n. Informal.* a lazy person.

lazy su·san (sü′zən) a revolving tray for food or condiments placed in the center of a dining table.

lb *also,* **lb.** *pl.* **lbs** pound; pounds. [Abbreviation of Latin *libra* pound[1], scales.]

l.c., lower case.

l.c.d. *also,* **L.C.D.** least common denominator; lowest common denominator.

l.c.m. *also,* **L.C.M.** least common multiple; lowest common multiple.

Ld., Lord.

LDL a blood lipoprotein that transports cholesterol to cells that need it and deposits excess cholesterol in the cells lining the blood vessels, associated with a higher risk of atherosclerotic heart disease. [Abbreviation of *l(ow-)d(ensity) l(ipoprotein).*]

L-do·pa (el dō′pə) *n.* a drug, the levorotatory isomer of dopa, obtained esp. from broad beans or produced synthetically, used in the treatment of Parkinson's disease. [Short for *l(evorotatory)-dopa.*]

-le *suffix* (used to form verbs) repeatedly: *fizzle.* [Old English *-lian.*]

lea (lē) *n.* a meadow; pasture. [Old English *lēah* open ground.]

leach (lēch) *v.t.* **1.** to drain or wash by filtering with water or other liquid. **2.** to remove soluble or loose parts from (ashes, soils, ores, or other materials) by filtration with water or other liquid. —*v.i.* to lose soluble or other loose parts by the filtering through of water or other liquid. —*n.* **1.** a container used for leaching. **2.** an act, instance, or result of leaching. **3.** leachate. [Old English *leccan* to wet.]

leach·ate (lē′chāt) *n.* a soluble material that has been extracted from a substance by leaching, or a solution containing such materials. [LEACH + -ATE[3].]

lead[1] (lēd) *v.,* **led, lead·ing.** —*v.t.* **1.** to show the way to, esp. by going first: *Our guide led us through the ruins of the ancient city.* **2.** to conduct or guide by pulling or other contact: *The Seeing Eye dog led our blind neighbor across the street.* **3.** to be or show a

route or way for: *This road will lead you into town. The lights led us to the house.* **4.** to be ahead of or first in: *Which state leads the others in auto safety?* **5.** to be the head of; control or direct: *to lead a neighborhood cleanup committee, to lead an orchestra.* **6.** to cause to arrive at a particular opinion or to do a particular thing: *What led you to this conclusion? The doctor's advice led me to go on a diet.* **7.** to have or experience; live: *to lead a life of ease.* **8.** to aim or throw ahead of (a target) to allow for its motion: *A good quarterback leads receivers so they can catch passes on the run.* **9.** *Card Games.* to begin a round with (a card). —*v.i.* **1.** to go or be first, ahead of all others: *The burro leads, and the horses follow. Food leads on our list of necessities. Chile leads in copper production.* **2.** to be the head or director; exercise leadership or guidance. **3.** to be a route or way, as to a place or conclusion: *Poor sanitation leads to disease. This hall leads to the bedroom.* **4.** to submit to being led: *Some horses lead more easily than others.* **5.** to make the first play in a round, as in a card game. **6.** *Boxing.* to jab first at an opponent: *Lead with your left.* —*n.* **1.** the position or being ahead of all others. **2.** the measure or extent of being ahead: *a lead of several years in space technology.* **3.** an example or direction: *to follow someone's lead.* **4.** a clue or indication that may serve to locate someone or obtain something: *to follow a lead on a missing person.* **5.** a rope or leash, as for walking a dog. **6.** a conductor of electricity, as a wire, esp. one connecting a piece of apparatus to an antenna or other source of signals or to a power source. **7.** *Theater.* **a.** the principal part in a play, motion picture, or other theatrical presentation. **b.** a person who plays such a part. **8.** the introductory paragraph of a news story, usually giving a summary of the contents. **9.** *Baseball.* the position or distance of a base runner away from the base. **10.** *Card Games.* **a.** the right or duty of playing first in a round: *It is your lead.* **b.** the card so played. **11.** an open water channel through a field of ice. —*adj.* being or going first; leading: *The president rode in the lead car.* [Old English *lǣdan* to conduct, guide.]

• **to lead off. a.** to take the initiative; begin; open: *The speaker led off the talk with a joke.* **b.** *Baseball.* to be the first person to bat in an inning.

• **to lead on.** to draw or entice into foolish action or mistaken opinion: *to lead on an infatuated admirer.*

• **to lead up to.** to prepare the way for gradually: *The series of meetings and conferences led up to a trade agreement.*

lead[2] (led) *n.* **1.** a heavy, soft, poisonous, silver-gray metallic element that resists corrosion and conducts electricity poorly, used esp. in storage batteries and as a shield against radiation. Symbol: **Pb** For tables, see **element. 2.** a thin stick of graphite, as in a pencil. **3.** a weight attached to a line used to determine the depth of water. **4.** bullets or shot. **5.** *Printing.* a thin metal strip used to widen the space between lines of type. **6. leads. a.** *British.* sheets or strips of lead used to cover a roof. **b.** lead frames in which panes of glass are fixed. —*v.t.* **1.** *Printing.* to increase the space separating the lines of (print) by inserting leads. **2.** to cover, join, weight, or mix with lead. [Old English *lēad* the metallic element.]

lead acetate, a poisonous, white crystalline solid used as a mordant in dyeing textiles and as a desiccant in paints and varnishes. Formula: $Pb(C_2H_3O_2)_2 \cdot 3H_2O$

lead arsenate, a poisonous, crystalline compound, soluble in water, used as an insecticide. Formula: $Pb_3(AsO_4)_2$

lead·en (led′ən) *adj.* **1.** made of lead: *a leaden bucket.* **2.** dull gray like lead: *a leaden sky.* **3.** heavy like lead. **4.** dull; depressed; gloomy: *leaden spirits.*

lead·er (lē′dər) *n.* **1.** a person or thing that is ahead of others: *After the first lap, she was the leader. That corporation is a leader in preventing pollution.* **2.** a person who influences others, or shows or directs others: *a leader of the opposition, a leader of a marching band.* **3.** leading article: *The news about the assassination was the leader on the front page of the paper.* **4.** a short length of material, now usually nylon, connecting the lure or hook to a fish line. **5.** a horse or other draft animal at the front of a team. **6.** loss leader. **7. leaders.** a row or rows of dots or dashes used to guide the eye horizontally across a printed page. —**lead′er·less,** *adj.*

lead·er·ship (lē′dər ship′) *n.* **1.** the position or function of a leader: *to assume the leadership of a political party.* **2.** the ability to lead others. **3.** the act or fact of being a leader. **4.** leaders as a group: *the union leadership.*

lead glass (led) flint glass.

lead-in (lēd′in′) *n.* **1.** something that acts as an introduction or opening. **2.** a wire that conducts signals between an antenna and a radio or television receiver or transmitter.

lead·ing[1] (lē′ding) *adj.* **1.** chief; principal: *a leading cause of heart disease.* **2.** that is or goes first; forward; frontmost: *The leading marchers carried a banner.* **3.** that plays a lead: *the leading man in a theatrical production.* —*n.* the act of a person or thing that leads. [From LEAD[1].]

lead·ing² (led'ing) *n.* **1.** a frame or covering of lead. **2.** *Printing.* spacing created by using metal strips between lines of type. [From LEAD².]

lead·ing article (lē'ding) the article that begins in the upper right-hand column of the first page of a newspaper or is the first article in a magazine. Also, **leader.**

lead·ing edge (lē'ding) the forward edge of an airfoil or propeller blade.

lead·ing question (lē'ding) a question worded so as to suggest the desired answer.

lead·ing strings (lē'ding) **1.** strings or straps used to support a child learning to walk. **2.** excessive control or guidance.

lead line (led) *Nautical.* sounding line.

lead monoxide (led) litharge.

lead·off (lēd'ôf', -of') *n.* **1.** an opening action; beginning. **2.** *Baseball.* **a.** the first person on either team to come to bat in an inning. **b.** the player designated first in a team's batting order. —*adj.* beginning; starting: *a leadoff batter.*

lead pencil (led) an ordinary pencil, having a thin stick of graphite as its marking material.

lead poisoning (led) acute or chronic poisoning caused by the absorption of lead or substances containing lead, as certain paints, with symptoms that include colic, anemia, and brain and nerve damage.

lead time (lēd) the time that passes between a decision to do something and its execution: *Lead time from planning to production in the automobile industry is about five years.*

leaf (lēf) *n., pl.* **leaves. 1.** one of the flattened, usually green parts that grow as extensions of a plant's stem and serve as the plant's food manufacturing organs by means of photosynthesis. **2.** a sheet of paper, esp. in a book. **3.** a very thin sheet of metal, esp. gold, used for decoration. **4.** a layer of a leaf spring. **5.** an extra piece for extending a table, that drops out of place, slides in, or comes out when not in use. —*v.i.* **1.** to put forth leaves: *Many trees leaf in the spring.* **2.** to turn and glance at the pages of (with *through*): *to leaf through a book.* [Middle English *lefe,* from Old English *lēaf.*] —**leaf'like',** *adj.*

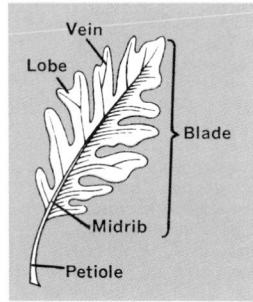

parts of a **leaf**

Labels: Vein, Lobe, Blade, Midrib, Petiole

• **to turn over a new leaf.** to act in a different and better way: *The student vowed to turn over a new leaf and study at least two hours every evening.*

leaf·age (lē'fij) *n.* leaves collectively; foliage.

leaf·hop·per (lēf'hop'ər) *n.* any of a group of tiny, jumping homopterous insects, family Cicadellidae, that suck the juices of grasses, flowers, shrubs, and trees. Many species are agricultural pests.

leaf insect, any of a group of Southeast Asian insects, family Phylliidae, related to stick insects, in which the flat-lying wings and extensions on the legs resemble leaves in color and form.

leaf·less (lēf'lis) *adj.* without leaves.

leaf·let (lēf'lit) *n.* **1.** a single sheet of printed matter, folded or unfolded, used in an information, advertising, or political campaign; handbill; flyer. **2.** a small, unbound book; booklet: *This leaflet contains operating instructions for the toaster.* **3.a.** a small or young leaf. **b.** one of the separate blades or divisions of a compound leaf.

leaf miner, any of various destructive insect larvae that burrow into the tissues of leaves, causing blisters, blotches, or the like.

leaf mold, humus or compost consisting mainly of decomposed leaves.

leaf spring, a spring made of layers of flexible metal strips.

leaf·stalk (lēf'stôk') *n.* petiole *(def. 1).*

leaf·y (lē'fē) *adj.,* **leaf·i·er, leaf·i·est.** covered with, consisting of, or resembling leaves. —**leaf'i·ness,** *n.*

league¹ (lēg) *n.* **1.** an association of individuals, groups, or countries formed to foster common interests. **2.** an association of athletic teams that compete regularly among themselves. —*v.t., v.i.* to form, join, or band together into a league. [Middle English *ligg,* from Old French *ligue,* from Italian *liga,* from *legare* to tie, bind, from Latin *legare.*] —For Synonyms *(n.),* see **alliance.**

• **in league with.** working together with; associated with: *Anybody on the road might be a robber or in league with robbers* (Charles Dickens, 1859).

league² (lēg) *n.* a measure of distance equal to about 3 miles (4.8 kilometers). [Middle English *lege,* from Old French *legue,* from Late Latin *leuga, leuca* Gallic mile; of Celtic origin.]

League of Nations, an association of nations established in 1920 and dissolved in 1946, designed to settle international disputes and promote world peace.

lea·guer¹ (lē'gər) *Archaic. v.t.* to besiege; beleaguer. —*n.* **1.** a siege. **2.** a camp, esp. of a besieging army. [Dutch *leger* lair, camp.]

lea·guer² (lē'gər) *n.* a member of a league. [LEAGUE¹ + -ER¹.]

leak (lēk) *n.* **1.** an accidental or unwanted passage, as of liquid or air, through a hole, fissure, or other small opening: *to stop a leak in a roof, a slow leak in a tire.* **2.** the hole or fissure itself: *We patched the leak in the rowboat.* **3.** a process or condition by which withheld information becomes known: *A security leak ended all hopes of secrecy.* —*v.i.* **1.** to have a leak: *The water pipes leak.* **2.** to pass through a small opening: *All the gasoline leaked out during the night.* **3.** to become known: *News leaked out of a plot to overthrow the government.* —*v.t.* **1.** to permit the accidental or unwanted passage of (something) through a small opening: *My fountain pen leaks ink.* **2.** to permit or cause to become known: *to leak a secret.* [Old Norse *leka* to drip.]

leak·age (lē'kij) *n.* **1.** the act or process or an instance of leaking. **2.** something that is leaking or has leaked. **3.** the amount that leaks. **4.** *Commerce.* an allowance for loss by leaking, as of liquids in shipment.

leak·y (lē'kē) *adj.,* **leak·i·er, leak·i·est.** having a leak or leaks. —**leak'i·ness,** *n.*

lean¹ (lēn) *v.,* **leaned** or **leant, lean·ing.** —*v.i.* **1.** to be at an angle from the upright: *The walls of the dilapidated shed lean outward.* **2.** (of a person) to bend or stretch the body: *The customer leaned over the counter. I leaned down to pet the dog.* **3.** to rest on or against something for support: *to lean against a fence.* **4.** to depend on or use, as for information or support; rely: *In evaluating applicants, some colleges lean heavily on interviews.* **5.** to tend, as in opinion, toward or against something; be inclined: *to lean toward socialism.* —*v.t.* **1.** to cause to bend or stretch: *to lean one's body over a railing.* **2.** to cause to be at an angle from the upright: *Lean the fishing rod against the tree.* —*n.* the act of leaning; inclination. [Old English *hleonian* to recline, incline, bend.]

lean² (lēn) *adj.* **1.** with little or no extra flesh or fat: *Our team's star center is tall and lean.* **2.** (of meat) containing little or no fat. **3.** lacking in substance, richness, or productiveness; poor; scanty: *a lean year for farmers, lean ore.* **4.** (of the fuel mixture of an engine) having a low fuel-to-air ratio. —*n.* a part of meat containing little or no fat. [Old English *hlǣne* thin.] —**lean'ness,** *n.*

Le·an·der (lē an'dər) *n.* see **Hero.**

lean·ing (lē'ning) *n.* a tendency to favor one thing over another; inclination.

Leaning Tower of Pisa, a bell tower at Pisa, Italy, that slants more than 17 feet (5.2 meters) from the perpendicular.

leant (lent) a past tense and past participle of **lean¹.**

lean-to (lēn'tū') *n., pl.* **-tos. 1.** a shed or building having a roof that slopes in one direction, supported by the wall of an adjoining structure. **2.** a crude, usually open shelter, consisting only of a sloping roof that extends to the ground.

leap (lēp) *v.,* **leaped** or **leapt, leap·ing.** —*v.i.* **1.** to make a big, impressive, or spectacular jump: *The dancers leaped into the air.* **2.** to move or act eagerly or quickly: *to leap into battle, to leap at an opportunity.* —*v.t.* **1.** to make a big or spectacular jump over: *The horse leaped the wall.* **2.** to cause to make a big jump: *The rider leaped the horse over the wall.* —*n.* **1.** a big, impressive, or spectacular jump. **2.** the distance covered in a leap. **3.** a sudden transition: *a leap from one topic to another.* **4.** a place for leaping. [Old English *hlēapan* to run, spring.] —**leap'er,** *n.* —For Synonyms *(v.i.),* see **jump.**

• **a leap of faith.** the act or fact of accepting something as true or real without proof.

• **by leaps and bounds.** with great speed; very fast; rapidly: *Our town is growing by leaps and bounds.*

leap·frog (lēp'frôg', -frog') *n.* a game in which players take turns jumping, with legs spread apart, over the backs of the other players. —*v.t.,* **-frogged, -frog·ging.** to leap over in or as in a game of leapfrog.

leap second, an extra second added each year to clock time in order to make navigational time signals coincide with the actual period of rotation of the earth.

leapt (lept, lēpt) a past tense and past participle of **leap.**

leap year, a calendar year containing an extra day, February 29,

a	at	e	end	o	hot	u	up	hw	white		about
ā	ape	ē	me	ō	old	ū	use	ng	song		taken
ä	far	i	it	ô	fork	ü	rule	th	thin	ə	pencil
âr	care	ī	ice	oi	oil	u̇	pull	th	this		lemon
		îr	pierce	ou	out	ûr	turn	zh	measure		circus

incorporated in the Gregorian calendar to compensate for the difference between the ordinary year of 365 days and the slightly longer solar year. Leap years occur in years divisible by 4, such as 1996, except for century years, which must be evenly divisible by 400, such as 1600 or 2000.

Lear (lîr) *n.* a legendary king of Britain, written of in early chronicles and histories and by Edmund Spenser in *The Faerie Queen* and by Shakespeare in the tragedy *King Lear.*

learn (lûrn) *v.,* **learned** or **learnt, learn·ing.** —*v.t.* **1.** to gain knowledge of or skill in (something) as a result of study or experience: *to learn algebra, to learn the history of the Cherokee, to learn how to ski.* **2.** to commit to memory; memorize: *to learn the lines in a play.* **3.** to become informed of; find out: *We tried to learn the truth of what really happened.* —*v.i.* **1.** to gain knowledge or skill: *Children learn at different rates.* **2.** to become informed: *to learn of a marriage.* [Old English *leornian* to acquire knowledge.] —**learn′er,** *n.*

learn·ed (lûr′nid) *adj.* **1.** having or displaying much knowledge: *a learned person.* **2.** produced by or for someone with much knowledge: *a learned study.*

learn·ing (lûr′ning) *n.* **1.** the act of acquiring knowledge or skill. **2.** knowledge, esp. when acquired by systematic study.

learning disability, a syndrome seen in persons of normal and above-normal intelligence, characterized by difficulty in understanding spoken or written language or learning basic academic skills.

learnt (lûrnt) a past tense and past participle of **learn.**

lear·y (lîr′ē) leery.

lease (lēs) *n.* **1.** a contract for the use of property for a specified period of time. **2.** the period of time specified in such a contract: *to have a two-year lease.* —*v.,* **leased, leas·ing.** —*v.t.* **1.** to take or hold a lease on: *They leased the property from the Smith family.* **2.** to grant possession or use of by a lease: *The Smith family leased the property to them.* —*v.i.* to be available for lease or require for lease: *The property leases for $5,000 a year.* [Anglo-Norman *les* a letting, leaving, from *lesser* to let[1], leave[1], from Latin *laxāre* to slacken.]

> **Synonyms** *v.t.* **Lease, rent, hire,** and **charter** may all mean to acquire temporary use and enjoyment of something by contract. **Lease** is used of contracting for possession and use of property, especially land or buildings: *to lease a garage, to lease a car for a year.* **Rent,** which is more often applied to arrangements for shorter periods, emphasizes regular payments: *to rent a furnished room by the week, to rent a car for the day.* **Hire** is used less formally of temporary arrangements for services or the use of goods: *to hire a cab, to hire a cleaning crew.* **Charter** is used especially of contracts to use ships or other conveyances: *to charter a plane for a tour group.*

lease·hold (lēs′hōld′) *n.* **1.** a tenure by lease. **2.** real estate held under a lease.

leash (lēsh) *n.* **1.** a strap, chain, or other line fastened to a dog or other animal to control it. **2.** *Hunting.* a group of three, as of hounds. —*v.t.* to control or hold with or as with a leash. [Old French *laisse* thong to hold an animal, from *laisser* to let[1], leave[1], loosen, from Latin *laxāre* to slacken, open.]

least (lēst) *adj.* (a superlative of **little**) smallest in size, degree, amount, or importance. —*n.* a person or thing that is least: *They are the least of my worries at this time. That is the least we can do.* —*adv.* (the superlative of **little**) in the smallest or lowest degree. [Old English *lǣst* smallest.]
  • **at least. a.** at the very minimum: *At least twenty people will come to the party.* **b.** at any rate; in any event: *They should at least let us know where they are.*
  • **not in the least.** not in the smallest degree; not at all: *I am not in the least interested.*

least common denominator, the smallest number that can be divided by each of the denominators of a given group of fractions without leaving a remainder. Also, **lowest common denominator.**

least common multiple, the smallest number that is an exact multiple of two or more given quantities. The least common multiple of 2, 3, and 4 is 12. Also, **lowest common multiple.**

least·wise (lēst′wīz′) *adv. Informal.* at least; at any rate. Also, **least′ways′.**

leath·er (leth′ər) *n.* a tough, flexible material made from animal skin or hide, usually with hair or fur removed, prepared for use by tanning or a similar process. —*adj.* of or made of leather. —*v.t.* **1.** to cover or furnish with leather. **2.** *Informal.* to beat with or as with a strap; thrash. [Old English *lether* hide[2], skin.]

leath·er·back (leth′ər bak′) *n.* a large, wide-ranging sea turtle, *Dermochelys coriacea,* having an upper shell composed of a mosaic of small bones embedded in a tough, leathery skin. It is the

leatherback

largest living turtle. Weight: 600-1,600 pounds (273-727 kilograms).

leath·er·ette (leth′ə ret′) *n.* any of various plastics or fabrics that resemble leather in appearance.

leath·ern (leth′ərn) *adj.* **1.** made of leather. **2.** resembling leather.

leath·er·neck (leth′ər nek′) *n. Slang.* a U.S. Marine. [From the stiff collars lined with *leather* on jackets worn by U.S. Marines in the mid-nineteenth century.]

leath·er·y (leth′ə rē) *adj.* resembling leather; tough like leather. —**leath′er·i·ness,** *n.*

leave[1] (lēv) *v.,* **left, leav·ing.** —*v.i.* **1.** to go to another place, after a stay in one place; go away: *I thought the guests would never leave.* **2.** to depart or set out: *Your plane leaves at ten o'clock. My cousin left for college last week.* —*v.t.* **1.** to go away from: *Alice left the table after dinner.* **2.** to separate, withdraw, or depart from; quit: *to leave one occupation for another.* **3.** to neglect to take along or remove; allow to stay: *Someone left the keys in the ignition.* **4.** to go away and allow to stay in a particular state or condition: *My roommate left the report unfinished and went bowling.* **5.** to place in the care of: *We left the dog with friends when we went on vacation.* **6.** to let remain; not use: *The food was left on the plate. I have $300 left.* **7.** to entrust, refer, or commit: *Leave them to their fate.* **8.** to have remaining at death: *The dead soldier leaves a wife and three children.* **9.** to transmit at death; give by will; bequeath: *How much property did the deceased leave the college?* **10.** to have remaining after subtraction: *Ten minus three leaves seven.* [Old English *lǣfan* to bequeath, to allow to remain.] —For Synonyms *(v.i.),* see **go**[1].
  • **to leave off.** to stop: *Where did we leave off in the discussion?*

leave[2] (lēv) *n.* **1.** permission to do something. **2.** permission to be absent, as from work or military duty. **3.** the period that such permission lasts. Also *(defs. 2, 3),* **leave of absence.** [Old English *lēaf* permission.]
  • **on leave.** absent from duty with permission.
  • **to take leave of.** to bid farewell to or leave behind.
  • **to take one's leave.** to go away.

leave[3] (lēv) *v.i.,* **leaved, leav·ing.** to put forth leaves; leaf. [Middle English *leven,* from *lef* leaf. See LEAF.]

leaved (lēvd) *adj.* having a specified kind or number of leaves.
  ➡ usually used in combination: *broad-leaved.*

leav·en (lev′ən) *n.* **1.** a substance, such as yeast or baking powder, that produces fermentation, esp. in dough or batter. **2.** a small portion of fermented dough reserved for this purpose. **3.** a pervasive and subtle influence that brings about significant change: *Without the leaven of wit, the speech would have been dull.* —*v.t.* **1.** to produce fermentation in (dough) by means of a leaven; raise and make light. **2.** to spread through and change subtly. [Old French *levain* fermented substance that causes dough to rise, going back to Latin *levāmen* alleviation; literally, a raising.]

leav·en·ing (lev′ə ning) *n.* something that leavens.

leave of absence, leave[2] *(defs. 2, 3).*

leaves (lēvz) the plural of **leaf.**

leave-tak·ing (lēv′tā′king) *n.* the act of taking leave; bidding farewell.

leav·ings (lē′vingz) *pl. n.* something that is left unused; remains; refuse: *The dogs ate the leavings from the table.*

Le·bens·raum (lā′bəns roum′) *n.* additional territory, esp. that claimed by Nazi Germany, desired by a nation in order to accom-

modate the growth of its economy and population. [German *Lebensraum* living space, from *Leben* life + *Raum* space.]

lech·er (lech′ər) *n.* a man given to or engaging in lechery. [Old French *lecheor* glutton, libertine; literally, one who licks, from *lechier* to lick; of Germanic origin.]

lech·er·ous (lech′ər əs) *adj.* given to, characterized by, or showing lechery. —**lech′er·ous·ly,** *adv.* —**lech′er·ous·ness,** *n.*

lech·er·y (lech′ə rē) *n.* excessive preoccupation with or indulgence of sexual desires.

lec·i·thin (les′ə thin) *n.* 1. any of a group of fatty compounds containing phosphorus, found in animal and plant tissues. 2. a form of this substance obtained usually from soybeans, egg yolks, or corn, used in making candy, ice cream, cosmetics, and other products.

lec·tern (lek′tərn) *n.* 1. a stand with an inclined shelf for holding the written speech or other papers of a speaker. 2. a reading desk in a church, esp. one from which scripture lessons are read during services. [Old French *letrun* reading desk, going back to Late Latin *lēctrum,* from Latin *legere* to read.]

lec·ture (lek′chər) *n.* 1. a prepared talk on a specific subject delivered before an audience for the purpose of instruction. 2. a lengthy reprimand or scolding. —*v.,* **-tured, -tur·ing.** —*v.i.* 1. to give a lecture or lectures: *to lecture on economics.* —*v.t.* 1. to give a lecture to; instruct by means of a lecture. 2. to reprimand or scold at length. [Late Latin *lēctūra* a reading, from Latin *legere* to read.]

lec·tur·er (lek′chər ər) *n.* 1. a person who lectures. 2. a person who holds a teaching position below that of assistant professor in a college or university.

led (led) the past tense and past participle of **lead**¹.

LED, a solid-state electronic device that emits light when a current is applied to its circuit, used to display numbers, letters, and symbols in watches, calculators, cameras, and other devices. [Short for *l(ight-)e(mitting) d(iode).*]

Le·da (lē′də) *n.* in Greek mythology, the mother of the Dioscuri, the mortal Castor and the immortal Pollux, and of Clytemnestra and Helen of Troy.

ledge (lej) *n.* 1. a narrow shelf or similar flat surface, projecting from a vertical plane. 2.a. a narrow rock shelf on the side of a mountain or the walls of a canyon. b. a submerged rock ridge or offshore reef. 3. a mineral-bearing vein or outcrop, usually of quartz. [Middle English *legge* bar, possibly going back to Old English *lecgan* to place.]

ledg·er (lej′ər) *n.* an account book in which all the financial transactions of a business are recorded. [Middle English *legger* record book, going back to Old English *lecgan* to place.]

ledger line, a short line added above or below a musical staff for the placement of notes too high or too low to be put on the staff.

lee (lē) *n.* 1. shelter or protection. 2. a side or part, esp. of a ship, sheltered or turned away from the wind. 3. the direction toward which the wind is blowing. —*adj.* of, relating to, located on, or moving toward the side or direction toward which the wind blows: *the lee side of an island.* [Old English *hlēo* protection, shelter.]

leech¹ (lēch) *n.* 1. any of a group of parasitic worms, class Hirudinea, found in salt water, fresh water, and damp soil, that suck the blood of animals, esp. the **medicinal leech,** *Hirudo medicinalis,* once used by physicians to bleed their patients. Length: 1-4 inches (2.5-10 centimeters). 2. a person who clings persistently to others for personal gain; parasite. —*v.t.* to bleed with leeches. [Old English *lǣce* bloodsucking worm, physician.]

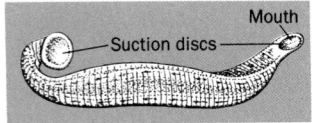

leech¹

leech² (lēch) *n.* 1. either of the vertical edges of a square sail. 2. the after edge of a fore-and-aft sail. [Probably from Middle Low German *līk* rope to which the sail is fastened.]

leek (lēk) *n.* 1. the narrow flat leaves, stalk, and bulb of a plant, *Allium ampeloprasum porrum,* of the lily family, eaten as a vegetable. 2. the plant itself, widely cultivated throughout the world, growing from a cylindrical bulb and bearing clusters of small pinkish flowers. [Old English *lēac* the plant.]

leer (lir) *n.* a sly look or sidelong glance expressing cunning, lust, or malice. —*v.i.* to look with a leer. [Old English *hlēor* cheek, face, look.] —**leer′ing·ly,** *adv.*

leer·y (lir′ē) *also,* **leary.** *adj. Informal.* feeling distrust; wary; suspicious.

lees (lēz) *pl. n.* sediment, esp. of wine; dregs. [Old French *lie;* of Celtic origin.]

lee shore, a shore lying off the leeward side of a vessel, toward which the vessel may be driven by the wind.

lee·ward (lē′wərd, lü′ərd) *adj.* located on or moving toward the side toward which the wind is blowing. —*n.* the side or direction toward which the wind is blowing; lee. —*adv.* toward the lee. ➡ opposed to **windward.**

lee·way (lē′wā′) *n.* 1. the sideways drift of a boat or ship to leeward, off its course. 2. time, space, or any other condition making freedom of action or movement possible: *My schedule isn't full; I have plenty of leeway to do what I want.*

left¹ (left) *adj.* 1. of, on, or toward the side of the body that is to the west when one is facing north: *the left side of a road.* 2. *also,* **Left.** relating to or applied to political views ranging from liberal to radical. —*n.* 1. the left side or direction: *They were seated on my left. The car skidded to the left.* 2. *also,* **Left.** a party or group characterized by political views ranging from liberal to radical. Also, **left wing.** 3. a blow delivered with the left hand, as in boxing. —*adv.* to or toward the left: *Walk three blocks and then turn left at the corner.* [Middle English *lift* left side, from Old English *lyft* weak.]

left² (left) the past tense and past participle of **leave**¹.

left field *Baseball.* 1. the left section of the outfield when viewed from home plate. 2. the position of the player stationed in this area. —**left fielder.**
 •**out in left field.** *Slang.* completely wrong.

left-hand (left′hand′) *adj.* 1. situated on or toward the left: *the top left-hand drawer of a desk.* 2. of, for, relating to, or with the left hand: *a left-hand glove.*

left-hand·ed (left′han′did) *adj.* 1. using the left hand more naturally and easily than the right. 2. done with the left hand. 3. made to be held in or used by the left hand. 4. turning or moving from right to left; counterclockwise. 5. doubtful, insincere, or ironic: *a left-handed compliment.* 6. lacking dexterity; clumsy; awkward. —*adv.* with the left hand: *to throw left-handed.*

left-hand·er (left′han′dər) *n.* a left-handed person, esp. an athlete who is left-handed.

left·ist (lef′tist) *n.* a person who has political views ranging from liberal to radical. —*adj.* of, relating to, or characterized by liberal to radical political views.

left·o·ver (left′ō′vər) *n. also,* **leftovers.** something that remains unused, esp. unconsumed food from a meal: *We ate leftovers for a week after Thanksgiving.* —*adj.* unused or uneaten; remaining.

left-wing (left′wing′) *adj.* of, relating to, or belonging to the left wing. —**left′-wing′er,** *n.*

left wing 1. left¹ *(n., def. 2).* 2. a portion of a political party or group characterized by a more liberal or radical outlook than the rest. [Because liberals and radicals in the French National Assembly of 1789 were seated to the left of the presiding officers. See RIGHT WING.]

left·y (lef′tē) *n., pl.* **left·ies.** *Informal.* 1. a left-handed person. 2. a person who has leftist political views.

leg (leg) *n.* 1. one of the paired limbs or appendages in vertebrates and various other animals, used chiefly for supporting the body and for locomotion. 2. that part of such a limb, esp. in human beings, between the knee and the ankle. 3. something resembling a leg in shape, position, or function: *the leg of a chair.* 4. the part of a garment, esp. of trousers, that covers a leg. 5. a distinct portion or stage of a journey or course: *The first leg of the voyage took them to Australia.* 6. the distance traveled by a sailing vessel on a single tack. 7. *Geometry.* either of the sides of a triangle other than the base or, in a right triangle, the hypotenuse. [Old Norse *leggr* this limb.]
 •**on one's last legs.** *Informal.* close to death, collapse, or failure.
 •**to give (someone) a leg up.** to assist or aid by boosting or providing support.
 •**to leg it.** *Informal.* to walk quickly or run: *We legged it home when the rain started.*
 •**to not have a leg to stand on.** to have no defense or justification.
 •**to pull someone's leg.** *Informal.* to trick or tease; make fun of.
 •**to shake a leg.** *Slang.* to make haste; hurry.
 •**to stretch one's legs.** to stand up or walk around, esp. after sitting for a long time.

a	at	e	end	o	hot	u	up	hw	white	(	about
ā	ape	ē	me	ō	old	ū	use	ng	song		taken
ä	far	i	it	ô	fork	ü	rule	th	thin	ə	pencil
âr	care	ī	ice	oi	oil	u̇	pull	th	this		lemon
		îr	pierce	ou	out	ûr	turn	zh	measure	(	circus

leg. 1. legal. **2.** legato. **3.** legislative. **4.** legislature.

leg·a·cy (leg′ə sē) *n., pl.* **-cies. 1.** money or property left in a will: *Her uncle left her a legacy of $5,000.* **2.** something handed down from previous generations or from the past; heritage: *Freedom of speech is part of the American legacy.* [Old French *legacie* office of a legate, going back to Latin *lēgāre* to appoint, bequeath.] —For Synonyms, see **tradition.**

le·gal (lē′gəl) *adj.* **1.** of, relating to, or concerned with law: *to be in need of legal advice, to raise a legal objection.* **2.** in conformity with or permitted by law; lawful: *the legal possession of firearms.* **3.** established or authorized by law: *to know one's legal rights, to be the legal owner of property.* **4.** recognized or enforced by or under the jurisdiction of courts of law, rather than courts of equity. **5.** of, relating to, or characteristic of lawyers or the practice of law: *legal ethics, a keen legal mind.* [Latin *lēgālis* relating to the law, from *lēx* law. Doublet of LOYAL.] —**le′gal·ly,** *adv.*

legal age, the age at which a citizen achieves full adult legal rights and responsibilities, such as the right to make contracts.

legal cap, thin, white writing paper, often ruled, usually measuring 8½ inches by 13 inches (22 centimeters by 33 centimeters) and having a fold at the top.

le·gal·ese (lē′gə lēz′ -lēs′) *n. Informal.* the specialized language used in legal documents, such as contracts.

legal holiday, a holiday established by law on which the usual work of government offices is suspended and schools, banks, and courts are closed.

le·gal·ism (lē′gə liz′əm) *n.* strict, literal adherence to law, esp. excessive conformity to the letter rather than the spirit of the law. —**le′gal·ist,** *n.* —**le′gal·is′tic,** *adj.*

le·gal·i·ty (li gal′i tē) *n., pl.* **-ties. 1.** the state or quality of being legal; lawfulness. **2.** *usually,* **legalities.** a procedure required by law: *the legalities of buying a house.*

le·gal·ize (lē′gə līz′) *v.t.,* **-ized, -iz·ing.** to make legal or lawful. —**le′gal·i·za′tion,** *n.*

legal pad, a pad of writing paper, usually lined, measuring 8½ inches by 14 inches (21.6 centimeters by 35.6 centimeters).

legal tender, coin or currency that, by law, must be accepted by a creditor when offered by the debtor in payment of a debt.

leg·ate (leg′it) *n.* **1.** a cardinal sent by the pope on a special diplomatic or ecclesiastical mission. **2.** an official envoy or representative. [Latin *lēgātus* envoy, ambassador, deputy.]

leg·a·tee (leg′ə tē′) *n.* a person to whom a legacy is left in a will.

le·ga·tion (li gā′shən) *n.* **1.** a diplomatic mission of a country, ranking below an embassy and consisting of a minister and his or her staff. **2.** the official residence and offices of such a mission in a foreign country where an embassy is not maintained. **3.** the office or rank of a legate. [Latin *lēgātio* embassy.]

le·ga·to (li gä′tō, le-) *Music. adj.* smooth and even, with no noticeable breaks between successive tones. —*adv.* in a legato manner. —*n., pl.* **-tos.** a legato style, performance, or passage. [Italian *legato* bound, past participle of *legare* to bind, from Latin *ligāre.*]

leg·end (lej′ənd) *n.* **1.** a story handed down by tradition and usually based on some facts, popularly regarded as true: *There are many legends about the exploits of Robin Hood.* **2.** such stories collectively, esp. of a nation or culture. **3.** a popular, often fictitious or romanticized concept of a well-known person: *the legends surrounding a movie star.* **4.** a person whose life or exploits have been the subject of many stories: *George Washington became a legend in his own time.* **5.** an inscription or motto, esp. on a coin, medal, or coat of arms. **6.** an explanatory description accompanying a chart, map, or other illustration. [Old French *legende* fable, myth, a writing, inscription on a coin, going back to Latin *legenda* things to be read, from *legere* to read.]

Synonyms	**Legend, myth,** and **fable** denote a story of unknown or obscure origin that is handed down from the past. **Legend** connotes a popularly accepted story that has grown around a real or supposed historical event: *the legend of Joan of Arc.* A **myth** is a story concerning a people's early religious or cultural development: *Myths explaining the origin of the earth are found everywhere in the world.* A **fable** involves supernatural or heroic beings that may be used to transmit traditional values: *Fables that endow animals with speech and wisdom are common to many cultures.*

leg·end·ar·y (lej′ən der′ē) *adj.* **1.** of, relating to, or characteristic of a legend or legends: *a legendary account of a battle.* **2.** celebrated or described in or as in a legend: *a legendary queen.*

leg·er·de·main (lej′ər də mān′) *n.* **1.** skill in using the hands in performing tricks; sleight of hand. **2.** artful trickery; deception. [Old French *legier de main* literally, light of hand, going back to Latin *levis* light + *dē* from + *manus* hand.]

le·ges (lē′jēz) the plural of **lex.**

leg·ged (leg′id) *adj.* having a certain kind or number of legs. ⇒ used in combination: *four-legged.*

leg·ging (leg′ing) *n.* **1.** a covering for the leg, esp. the lower part of the leg, often made of cloth or leather. **2. leggings.** close-fitting trousers, often heavily lined for cold weather, esp. for children.

leg·gy (leg′ē) *adj.,* **-gi·er, -gi·est. 1.** having very long, often awkward legs. **2.** having long, attractive legs: *a leggy model.* **3.** (of plants) having long, spindly stems with few leaves.

leg·horn (leg′hôrn′; *def. 1, also,* leg′ərn) *n.* **1.** *often,* **Leghorn.** any of a breed of small, hardy domestic fowl, raised primarily for their white-shelled eggs. **2.a.** a fine, braided wheat straw obtained principally from Italy and used in the manufacture of hats. **b.** a hat made of this straw.

leg·i·ble (lej′ə bəl) *adj.* capable of being read: *The address on the envelope was not legible.* [Late Latin *legibilis* readable, from Latin *legere* to read.] —**leg′i·bil′i·ty,** *n.* —**leg′i·bly,** *adv.*

le·gion (lē′jən) *n.* **1.** a military unit in the army of ancient Rome, varying from 3,000 to 6,000 infantrymen and from 300 to 700 cavalrymen. **2.** any large military unit; army. **3.** a vast number of persons or things; multitude: *a legion of stars in the night sky.* —*adj.* very great in number; innumerable. ⇒ used in the predicate: *The enemy's forces are legion.* [Old French *legion* a Roman legion, body of soldiers, from Latin *legiō,* from *legere* to gather, choose.] —For Synonyms, see **host**[2].

le·gion·ar·y (lē′jə ner′ē) *adj.* **1.** of or relating to a legion or army. **2.** constituting a legion or multitude; innumerable. —*n., pl.* **-ar·ies.** a soldier of a legion.

le·gion·naire (lē′jə nâr′) *n.* **1.** *also,* **Legionnaire.** a member of any of various military or honorary national organizations, as the American Legion or the Foreign Legion. **2.** legionary. [French *légionnaire* legionary, from Old French *legion.* See LEGION.]

Le·gion·naires′ disease (lē′jə nârz′) an acute respiratory infection usually characterized by pneumonia, with renal, intestinal, and neurological symptoms, caused by a small, gram-negative bacillus found in soil and water. [Because it was first described after an outbreak among *Legionnaires* at an American Legion convention in Philadelphia in July 1976.]

Legion of Honor 1. a French order of merit founded by Napoleon Bonaparte in 1802. **2.** the decoration awarded to members of this order.

leg·is·late (lej′is lāt′) *v.,* **-lat·ed, -lat·ing.** —*v.i.* to make or enact a law or laws: *Parliament legislates for the United Kingdom.* —*v.t.* to cause, regulate, or bring about by passing laws: *Congress legislated increased benefits for veterans.* [From LEGISLATOR.]

leg·is·la·tion (lej′is lā′shən) *n.* **1.** the making or enacting of laws. **2.** laws made or enacted. ⇒ used as singular. **3.** a proposed law or group of laws introduced in a legislative body for enactment.

leg·is·la·tive (lej′is lā′tiv) *adj.* **1.** of or relating to legislation: *legislative powers.* **2.** having the power to make or enact laws: *Congress is a legislative body.* **3.** of or relating to a legislature. —*n.* **the legislative.** the legislative branch of a government. —**leg′is·la′tive·ly,** *adv.*

leg·is·la·tor (leg′is lā′tər) *n.* a member of a legislative body, esp. a member of a state legislature or of Congress. [Latin *lēgis lātor* proposer of a law.]

leg·is·la·ture (lej′is lā′chər) *n.* a government body consisting of a group of persons invested with the power to make or pass laws for a country or state.

le·git (li jit′) *adj. Slang.* legitimate.

le·git·i·ma·cy (li jit′ə mə sē) *n.* the quality or state of being legitimate.

le·git·i·mate (*adj.,* li jit′ə mit; *v.,* li jit′ə māt′) *adj.* **1.** permitted by or according to law; lawful: *The judge ruled the claim was legitimate.* **2.** logically correct or valid: *a legitimate argument.* **3.** genuine or reasonable: *a legitimate excuse.* **4.** born or legally considered to have been born of parents who are legally married to each other. **5.** ruling by the principle of hereditary right: *a legitimate ruler.* **6.** of or relating to professionally produced stage plays, as distinguished from vaudeville, burlesque, motion pictures, or the like: *the legitimate theater.* —*v.t.,* **-mat·ed, -mat·ing. 1.** to make or show to be lawful: *to legitimate a claim.* **2.** to make (a child) legitimate. **3.** to show to be justified; serve as justification for. [Medieval Latin *legitimatus,* past participle of *legitimare* to make lawful, from Latin *lēgitimus* lawful.] —**le·git′i·mate·ly,** *adv.*

le·git·i·mist (li jit′ə mist) *n.* a supporter of legitimate authority, esp. of claims to rule based on the principle of hereditary right.

le·git·i·mize (li jit′ə mīz′) *v.t.,* **-mized, -miz·ing.** legitimate. —**le·git′i·mi·za′tion,** *n.*

leg·man (leg′man′) *n., pl.* **-men** (-men′). **1.** a newspaper reporter who is assigned to gather information. **2.** an assistant who gathers information and runs errands for an office.

leg-of-mut·ton (leg′əv mut′ən) *adj.* tapering sharply from a wide end to a narrow end or point, as a sleeve or sail.

leg·ume (leg′ūm, li gūm′) *n.* **1.** any of a large group of plants, family Leguminosae or Fabaceae, as peas, peanuts, and alfalfa. Legumes are cultivated as food crops, for fodder, and as natural fertilizers. **2.** a seed pod characteristic of such a plant, usually splitting along two sutures. [French *légume* vegetable, from Latin *legūmen* bean, pulse².]

le·gu·mi·nous (li gū′mə nəs) *adj.* **1.** of or relating to plants of the legume family: *leguminous crops.* **2.** of, relating to, or consisting of the seed pods of these plants: *leguminous vegetables.*

leg warmer, a covering for the leg, usually made of a bulky knitted fabric. Leg warmers are worn esp. for exercising or dance practice.

leg·work (leg′wûrk′) *n.* work that involves walking or traveling about, as in gathering information or running errands: *A newspaper reporter's job involves a lot of legwork.*

le·hu·a (lā hū′ä) *n.* **1.** the bright red flower of a tree or shrub, *Metrosideros collina,* of the myrtle family, native to Hawaii. **2.** the tree or shrub itself. [Hawaiian *lehua* the tree.]

lei (lā) *n., pl.* **leis.** a garland of flowers, leaves, or other material, often worn about the neck. [Hawaiian *lei.*]

lei·sure (lē′zhər, lezh′ər) *n.* **1.** time that one can spend as one pleases; free or unoccupied time: *After they retired, my grandparents had the leisure to travel.* **2.** freedom from the demands of work or duty: *a life of leisure.* —*adj.* **1.** free or unoccupied: *leisure hours.* **2.** not having to work for a living; having much leisure: *the leisure class.* [Old French *leisir* free time, from Latin *licēre* to be permitted.]
  • **at leisure. a.** having free time: *I am now at leisure to visit my friends.* **b.** without haste; slowly: *The new proposal should be considered at leisure.*
  • **at one's leisure.** when one has free time; at one's ease or convenience: *Visit us at your leisure.*

lei·sured (lē′zhərd, lezh′ərd) *adj.* characterized by or having leisure: *a leisured class of society.*

lei·sure·ly (lē′zhər lē, lezh′ər-) *adj.* characterized by leisure; unhurried; relaxed: *a leisurely drive in the country.* —*adv.* in a leisurely manner. —**lei′sure·li·ness,** *n.*

leit·mo·tif (līt′mō tēf′) *also,* **leit·mo·tiv.** *n.* **1.** a short theme recurring throughout a musical composition and associated with a certain person, situation, sentiment, or the like. **2.** any dominant, recurring theme, as in a literary work. [German *Leitmotiv* the musical passage or theme, from *leiten* to lead + *Motiv* theme (from French *motif*). See MOTIF.]

lek (lek) *n.* the monetary unit of Albania.

lem·an (lem′ən, lē′mən) *n. Archaic.* a sweetheart or lover. [Middle English *lemman,* from Old English *lēof* dear + *mann* human being.]

lem·ma (lem′ə) *n.* the lower of the two bracts beneath the floret or flower in a spikelet of grass. [Greek *lemma* husk, from *lepein* to peel.]

lem·ming (lem′ing) *n.* any of various arctic rodents, family Cricetidae, having a stout body and long, predominantly yellowish brown fur, esp. the **Norway lemming,** *Lemmus lemmus,* noted for recurrent mass migrations that sometimes result in drowning when they attempt to cross a large body of water. Length: 3-6 inches (8-15 centimeters). [Norwegian *lemming.*]

lem·on (lem′ən) *n.* **1.** the oval fruit of a citrus tree, *Citrus limon,* having a thick, yellow rind and a juicy, sour, edible pulp. **2.** the thorny evergreen tree bearing this fruit, cultivated in warm climates. **3.** a clear, bright yellow color characteristic of the lemon. **4.** *Slang.* a person or thing that is unsatisfactory, defective, or worthless: *My old car is a real lemon.* —*adj.* **1.** having the color lemon. **2.** made from or flavored with lemon: *lemon juice, a lemon cake.* [Old French *limon* a sour citrus fruit, going back to Persian *līmūn* fruit of the lemon tree.] —**lem′on·y,** *adj.*

lem·on·ade (lem′ə nād′) *n.* a drink made of lemon juice, water, and, usually, sugar.

lemon balm, a hardy, perennial herb, *Melissa officinalis,* of the mint family, cultivated for its lemon-flavored leaves that are used for seasoning, as in tea or liquors.

lem·pi·ra (lem pîr′ə) *n.* the monetary unit of Honduras. [From *Lempira,* Indian leader who opposed the Spaniards.]

le·mur (lē′mər) *n.* any of various monkeylike mammals, family Lemuridae, found chiefly in Madagascar,

lemur

usually having a foxlike face, soft, woolly fur, and a long tail. Length: to 3½ feet (1.1 meters), including tail. [From Latin (plural) *lemurēs* ghosts; with reference to the appearance and nocturnal habits of lemurs.]

lend (lend) *v.,* **lent, lend·ing.** —*v.t.* **1.** to grant the use of (something) with the understanding that it will be returned: *I'll lend you my cassettes for the party.* **2.** to give the temporary use of (money) on condition of repayment and at a specified rate of interest. **3.** to furnish or impart: *The rustic furnishings lent a certain charm to the cabin.* **4.** to make available for aid or support: *to lend assistance.* **5.** to adapt or suit (itself or oneself) to a specific use or purpose: *This novel lends itself to various interpretations.* —*v.i.* to make a loan or loans. [Old English *lænan* to give, grant temporarily.] —**lend′er,** *n.*

lending library 1. circulating library. **2.** a small library operated by a store, which lends books for a small daily fee.

lend-lease (lend′lēs′) *n.* during World War II, a system under which goods and services were provided to foreign countries whose defense was deemed vital to the security of the United States. —*v.t.,* **-leased, -leas·ing.** to supply with (goods and services) by lend-lease.

length (lengkth, length, lenth) *n.* **1.** the linear extent of anything as measured from end to end, esp. the greater or greatest dimension: *The length of the football field is 100 yards.* **2.** the extent from beginning to end: *the length of a vacation, the length of a book.* **3.** the state, quality, or fact of being long: *The length of the climb discouraged all but the professional mountaineers.* **4.** the measurement of anything considered as a unit: *We parked one car's length away from the hydrant.* **5.** in racing, the extent from front to back of a competing animal, vehicle, or the like, used to describe distance: *The horse won the race by 2½ lengths.* **6.** a piece or portion of anything, esp. of a certain or standard size: *a length of silk.* **7.** a long stretch or extent: *to drive down a length of highway.* [Old English *lengthu* linear extent.]
  • **at full length.** fully extended; completely stretched out: *to lie at full length.*
  • **at length. a.** in full; in detail: *We discussed the matter at length.* **b.** after a time; finally: *At length they reached their destination.*
  • **to go to any** (or **great**) **length** (or **lengths**). to do whatever is necessary: *The politician would go to any length to win the election. Our host went to great lengths to make sure we were comfortable.*
  • **to keep at arm's length.** to discourage from becoming too familiar.

length·en (lengk′thən, leng′-, len′-) *v.t., v.i.* to make or become longer. —**length′en·er,** *n.*

length·wise (lengkth′wīz′, length′-, lenth′-) *adj., adv.* in the direction of the length: *a lengthwise rip in a coat, to saw a board lengthwise.* Also, **length·ways** (lengkth′wāz′, length′-, lenth′-).

length·y (lengk′thē, leng′-, len′-) *adj.,* **length·i·er, length·i·est.** unusually or unduly long: *a lengthy trip, a lengthy speech.* —**length′i·ly,** *adv.* —**length′i·ness,** *n.*

len·i·en·cy (lē′nē ən sē, lēn′yən-) *n.* **1.** the quality or state of being lenient. **2.** a lenient action. Also, **len′i·ence.** —For Synonyms, see mercy.

len·i·ent (lē′nē ənt, lēn′yənt) *adj.* not severe or harsh; merciful; tolerant: *a lenient judge, lenient laws.* [Latin *lēniēns,* present participle of *lēnīre* to soften.] —**len′i·ent·ly,** *adv.*

Len·in·ism (len′ə niz′əm) *n.* the economic, political, and social theories and policies of Vladimir Ilyich Lenin, Russian revolutionary leader. —**Len′in·ist,** *n., adj.*

len·i·tive (len′i tiv) *adj.* capable of relieving pain or discomfort, as a medicine: *a lenitive ointment.* —*n.* something that is lenitive.

len·i·ty (len′i tē) *n.* leniency. [Latin *lēnitās* softness, mildness.]

lens (lenz) *n., pl.* **lens·es. 1.** a piece of glass or other transparent material, having two nonparallel surfaces, either both curved, or one plane and one curved, that cause the light rays passing through them to either diverge or converge. **2.** any combination of such lenses. **3.** a colorless, transparent body present in the eyes of vertebrates and cephalopods that focuses the image on the retina. For illustration, see **eye.** **4.** a device used to direct or

a	at	e	end	o	hot	u	up	hw	white		about
ā	ape	ē	me	ō	old	ū	use	ng	song		taken
ä	far	i	it	ô	fork	ū	rule	th	thin	ə	pencil
âr	care	ī	ice	oi	oil	u	pull	th	this		lemon
				ou	out	ûr	turn	zh	measure		circus
		îr	pierce								

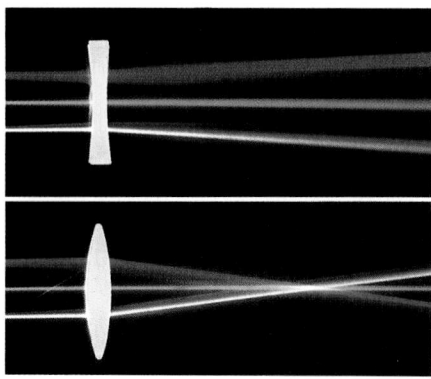

lens *(def. 1)*
biconcave lens (top), biconvex lens (bottom)

focus electromagnetic radiation, particle beams, or sound waves. [Latin *lēns* lentil; because the shape of a glass lens often resembles that of a lentil seed.]

lent (lent) the past tense and past participle of **lend.**

Lent (lent) *n.* the period of penitence and prayer observed in Christian churches beginning on Ash Wednesday and continuing for the forty weekdays before Easter. [Old English *lengten* spring, Lent, from *lang* long[1]; probably with reference to the lengthening of the days in spring.]

Lent·en (len'tən) *also,* **lent·en.** *adj.* **1.** of, relating to, or characteristic of Lent. **2.** suitable for Lent: *a Lenten diet.*

len·ti·cel (len'tə sel') *n.* a small elliptical pore in the corky layer of plant bark, analogous to stomata on the leaf of a plant, that permits the interchange of gases between the plant and the atmosphere. [Modern Latin *lenticella,* diminutive of Latin *lentis,* genitive of *lens* lentil.]

len·tic·u·lar (len tik'yə lər) *adj.* **1.** of or relating to a lens or lenses. **2.** resembling a lens, esp. a biconvex lens, in shape, as certain clouds; lens-shaped. [Latin *lenticularis,* from *lenticula,* diminutive of *lens* lentil.]

len·til (len'təl) *n.* **1.** the edible seed of a plant, *Lens culinaris,* of the pea family, cooked and eaten as a vegetable, esp. in soups and stews, ground into meal, or used as livestock feed. **2.** the plant itself, cultivated chiefly in Europe and Asia, bearing tiny white or pale blue flowers that ripen into broad pods containing one or two seeds. [Old French *lentille,* from Latin *lenticula* small lentil, diminutive of *lēns* the plant.]

len·to (len'tō) *Music. adj.* slow. —*adv.* slowly. [Italian *lento* slow, from Latin *lentus.*]

l'en·voy (len'voi, län'-) *also,* **l'en·voi.** *n.* envoy[2]. [Old French *l'envoy, l'envoi* the sending, the envoy. See ENVOY[2].]

Le·o (lē'ō) *n.* **1.** a constellation in the northern sky containing the bright star Regulus, conventionally depicted as a lion. **2.** the fifth sign of the zodiac. [Latin *leō.* See LION.]

le·one (lē ōn') *n.* the monetary unit of Sierra Leone.

Le·o·nid (lē'ə nid) *n.* one of the showers of meteors occurring on or about November 15 and appearing to come from the constellation Leo.

le·o·nine (lē'ə nīn') *adj.* relating to, characteristic of, or resembling a lion: *leonine courage.* [Latin *leōnīnus,* from *leō.* See LION.]

leop·ard (lep'ərd) *n.* **1.** a carnivorous mammal, *Panthera pardus,* of the cat family, found in Africa, India, and eastern Asia, having either a tawny coat marked with black spots or a solid black coat. Length: to 9 feet (2.7 meters), including tail. **2.** the fur of this mammal. **3.** any of various similar related felines, as the cheetah or jaguar. [Middle English *leoparde,* from Old French *leupart,* from Late Latin *leopardus,* from Late Greek *leopardos,* from *leōn* lion + *pardos* leopard, panther.]

leop·ard·ess (lep'ər dis) *n.* a female leopard.

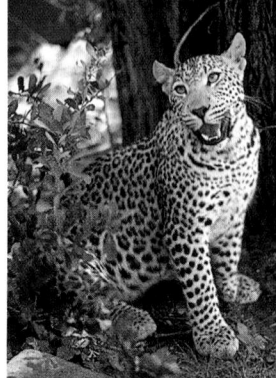

leopard

leopard frog, any of several species of North American frogs, genus *Rana,* having distinct, large, dark spots.

le·o·tard (lē'ə tärd') *also,* **le·o·tards.** *n.* a stretchable, close-fitting, one-piece garment extending from the neck or waist to the feet. [From Jules *Léotard,* 1830-70, French aerialist who made it popular.]

lep·er (lep'ər) *n.* **1.** a person who is afflicted with leprosy. **2.** a person who is rejected or shunned; pariah; outcast. [Old French *lepre* leprosy, from Latin *lepra,* from Greek *leprā,* from *lepros* scaly; because a leper's skin becomes scaly.]

lep·i·dop·ter·an (lep'i dop'tər ən) *n.* any member of the insect order Lepidoptera, consisting of butterflies and moths. These insects are characterized by two pairs of often brightly colored, scale-covered wings, and often have a maxilla that is adapted for siphoning nectar. They undergo complete metamorphosis, including a larval, or caterpillar, stage and a pupal, or chrysalis, stage. —*adj.* lepidopterous. [Modern Latin *Lepidoptera* (from Greek *lepid-,* stem of *lepis* scale + *pteron* wing) + -AN.]

lep·i·dop·ter·ist (lep'i dop'tə rist) *n.* a person specializing in the study of butterflies and moths.

lep·i·dop·ter·ous (lep'i dop'tər əs) *adj.* of, relating to, or belonging to the lepidopterans. [Modern Latin *Lepidoptera* (from Greek *lepid-,* stem of *lepis* scale + *pteron* wing) + -OUS.]

lep·re·chaun (lep'ri kon', -kôn') *n.* in Irish folklore, a mischievous fairy with the appearance of a little old man. [Irish *lupracān,* earlier *luchrupān* literally, very small body, from *lu* little + *corpān* small body (going back to Latin *corpus* body).]

lep·ro·sy (lep'rə sē) *n.* an infectious disease caused by a bacterium and affecting the body tissues, esp. the skin, nerves, and mucous membranes. Also, **Hansen's disease.** [LEPROUS + -Y[3].]

lep·rous (lep'rəs) *adj.* **1.** afflicted with leprosy. **2.** of, relating to, or characteristic of leprosy. [Late Latin *leprōsus* having leprosy, from Latin *lepra* leprosy. See LEPER.] —**lep'rous·ly,** *adv.*

lep·ton (lep'ton) *n.* any of a group of subatomic particles whose interaction is governed by the weak force, including the electron, the muon, the electron's neutrino, and the muon's neutrino. [Greek *leptos* thin, fine + -ON.]

les·bi·an (lez'bē ən) *n.* a woman who is a homosexual. —*adj.* of or relating to homosexuality between women. [From the supposed homosexuality of the ancient Greek poet Sappho, a native of Lesbos.] —**les'bi·an·ism,** *n.*

lese-maj·es·ty (lēz'maj'ə stē, lez'-) *also,* **lèse-ma·jes·té** (lez'-ma zhes tā'). *n.* **1.** *Law.* a crime or offense against the sovereign power of a state or against the dignity of a ruler; treason. **2.** lack of respect for or an affront to the dignity of an institution, person, custom, or the like that is widely held in esteem. [French *lèse-majesté* high treason, from Latin *laesa mājestās* literally, violated majesty.]

le·sion (lē'zhən) *n.* **1.** an injury; wound. **2.** a circumscribed abnormality resulting from disease or injury: *The X ray revealed a lesion on the left lung.* [Latin *laesiō.*]

les·pe·de·za (les'pi dē'zə) *n.* any of several herbs and low shrubs, genus *Lespedeza,* of the pea family, some of which are grown for hay, forage, or green manure, or as ornamentals. [Modern Latin *Lespedeza* from incorrect spelling of V. M. de *Zespedes,* an eighteenth-century Spanish governor of the eastern part of Florida.]

less (les) *adj.* a comparative of **little. 1.** not so much or as great in quantity, extent, or degree: *less trouble, less time, less money.* **2.** lower in rank, consequence, or importance: *No less a person than the boss made the request.* **3.** smaller in number: *less than a hundred people.* —*adv.* (the comparative of **little**) to a smaller extent or degree: *The movie was less funny than the book.* —*n.* a smaller amount or quantity: *I finished less of the work than I'd hoped.* —*prep.* with the subtraction of; minus: *Ten less seven is three.* [Old English *lǣsa* smaller, used as a comparative of *little.*]

> **Usage** In formal speech and writing, **fewer** is generally preferred to **less** when referring to things that can be counted as separate units: *fewer cars, fewer than twenty people.* However, **less** is usually used with plural nouns that are considered as a unit, such as those used to describe distance, time, or money: *less than two miles, less than thirty seconds, less than fifty dollars.*

-less *suffix* **1.** (used to form adjectives from nouns) having no; without: *hopeless.* **2.** (used to form adjectives from verbs) that does not: *tireless.* **3.** (used to form adjectives from verbs) that cannot be: *numberless.* [Old English *-lēas* without.]

les·see (le sē') *n.* a person to whom a lease is granted.

less·en (les'ən) *v.i.* to become less; decrease: *The value of money lessens during inflation.* —*v.t.* **1.** to make less; diminish. **2.** to degrade; belittle.

less·er (les'ər) *adj.* **1.** a comparative of **little. 2.** smaller or less, as in quantity, quality, extent, degree, or importance: *the lesser of two evils.*

lesser panda, panda *(def. 2).*

les·son (les′ən) *n.* **1.a.** a period or unit of instruction devoted to a particular subject or skill: *a French lesson, a riding lesson.* **b.** one of a series of such units, as in a textbook: *The French textbook has forty lessons.* **2.** a subject or skill learned or presented at one time: *Today's French lesson was not difficult.* **3.** an event or experience serving to guide or warn: *The accident has taught me a lesson I'll never forget.* **4.** a selection from the Scriptures or other sacred writings read during a church service. **5.** a rebuke; reprimand: *The judge gave the prisoner a stern lesson.* —*v.t.* **1.** to give a lesson to. **2.** to rebuke; reprimand. [Old French *leçon* a reading, lecture, part of a church service, from Latin *lēctiō* a reading.]

les·sor (les′ôr, le sôr′) *n.* a person who grants a lease.

lest (lest) *conj.* **1.** in order to prevent the possibility that; for fear that: *Let this be a reminder lest you forget.* **2.** that: *I feared lest the children would lose their way in the woods.* [Old English *thȳ lǣs the* literally, whereby less that.]

let¹ (let) *v.,* **let, let·ting.** —*v.t.* **1.** to give permission, leave, or opportunity to; not prevent; permit: *Father let me drive the car. A stroke of luck let us win the game.* **2.** to allow to pass, go, or come: *to let someone out of prison.* **3.** to cause; make: *I'll let you know my decision. Let me hear from you soon.* **4.** used as an auxiliary verb, usually in the imperative, to indicate: **a.** a suggestion, command, or warning: *Let's take a walk. Let's go! Just let her try to win!* **b.** a supposition or assumption: *Let x + y = a + b.* **5.** to rent or lease, as a house or room: *to let a cottage to vacationers.* **6.** to assign or give out, as a contract for work. **7.** to allow or cause to flow, as blood. —*v.i.* to be rented: *The apartment lets on a yearly basis.* [Old English *lǣtan* to allow, leave behind.]

• **to let alone** (or **be**). to leave undisturbed; not interfere with or bother: *Let the dog be.*
• **to let down. a.** to allow to fall or descend; lower: *to let down a hem.* **b.** to fail to fulfill the hopes of; disappoint: *When I needed help, you let me down.*
• **to let off. a.** to excuse from a duty or service: *The boss let us off an extra day at Christmas.* **b.** to give little or no punishment to; treat leniently: *The judge let the offender off with a warning.* **c.** to release, as from tension or pressure: *The volcano let off a cloud of gases.*
• **to let on.** *Informal.* **a.** to allow to become known; reveal: *Did you let on that you knew the answer, or did you feign ignorance?* **b.** to claim falsely; pretend: *The new neighbors let on that they were richer than they really were.*
• **to let out. a.** to give forth; release: *to let out a scream.* **b.** to enlarge or extend: *to let out a dress.* **c.** to dismiss or be excused: *School lets out at three o'clock.*
• **to let up.** to stop or lessen in intensity: *The storm let up about noon.*
• **to let up on.** *Informal.* to treat less severely; be gentler with.

Synonyms *v.t.* **Let¹, allow,** and **permit** mean not to prevent or forbid. **Let,** the most common of these terms, means to refrain from preventing either because of power or lack of inclination: *to let children be noisy, to let a faucet drip.* **Allow** suggests having the power to prevent but not doing so: *They allowed us to see the interior of their barn.* **Permit** implies formal or authoritative consent: *The town permits dumping here.*

let² (let) *n.* **1.** in tennis, volleyball, and similar games, a service or other stroke that must be repeated because of interference, esp. a service that touches the net. **2.** *Archaic.* a hindrance; obstacle; obstruction. —*v.t.,* **let·ted** or **let, let·ting.** *Archaic.* to prevent or hinder. [Old English *lettan* to hinder.]

-let *suffix* (used to form nouns) **1.** little: *booklet, kinglet.* **2.** an article worn on or around a (specified part of the body): *anklet, wristlet.* [Old French *-elet,* from *-el,* noun ending (sometimes from Latin *ellus,* diminutive suffix; sometimes from Latin *-āle,* neuter of *-ālis* -AL¹) + -ET.]

let·down (let′doun′) *n.* **1.** a disappointment or disillusionment: *It was a real letdown when our plan failed.* **2.** a lessening or slowing up; letup. **3.** the descent of an airplane from cruising altitude as it nears its destination.

le·thal (lē′thəl) *adj.* causing or capable of causing death; deadly: *a lethal wound, a lethal poison.* [Latin *lēt(h)ālis,* from *lētum* death.] —For Synonyms, see **deadly.**

lethal gene, a gene, usually recessive, that is capable of causing the premature death of an organism. Also, **lethal factor.**

le·thar·gic (li thär′jik) *adj.* **1.** feeling or showing lethargy; sluggish; apathetic. **2.** causing lethargy. Also, **le·thar′gi·cal.** —**le·thar′gi·cal·ly,** *adv.*

leth·ar·gy (leth′ər jē) *n., pl.* **-gies. 1.** the quality or state of being without strength, energy, or alertness; sluggish indifference or inactivity; apathy. **2.** an abnormal condition characterized by excessive drowsiness or by prolonged deep sleep. [Late Latin *lēthargia* drowsiness, from Greek *lēthargiā.*]

Le·the (lē′thē) *n.* **1.** in classical mythology, a river in Hades, where spirits about to be reborn drank to forget their former existence. **2.** forgetfulness; oblivion. —**Le·the·an** (li thē′ən), *adj.*

Le·to (lē′tō) *n.* in Greek mythology, the mother of Apollo and Artemis by Zeus.

let's (lets) *contr.* let us.

Lett (let) *n.* **1.** Latvian. **2.** the language of the Latvians, belonging to the Baltic group of the Indo-European family of languages. Also *(def. 2),* **Lettish.**

let·ted (let′id) a past tense and past participle of **let².**

let·ter (let′ər) *n.* **1.** a mark or character, usually printed or written, that represents one or more speech sounds; character of an alphabet. **2.** a written or printed message, usually of a personal or business nature, sent by one person or organization to another. **3.** an official or legal document granting a specific right, authority, or privilege to a person. ➡ usually used in the plural: *The explorer had letters from the crown granting a monopoly on trade.* **4.** the literal meaning or exact wording of something, esp. as distinguished from the general meaning or interpretation: *The judge's ruling was based on the letter of the law.* ➡ opposed to **spirit. 5. letters. a.** literary culture; literature: *a student of art and letters.* **b.** knowledge of or acquaintance with literature: *a person of letters.* **c.** the literary profession. **6.** the initial of a school or college given as an award, as for varsity participation in a particular sport. **7.** *Printing.* **a.** one piece of type producing a single character. **b.** a particular style of type: *The commercial artist printed the sign in block letters.* —*v.t.* **1.** to mark or inscribe with letters: *to letter a sign.* **2.** to inscribe (a word or words) in letters: *The word "exit" was lettered on the door.* —*v.i.* to form letters. [Old French *lettre* letter of the alphabet, written message, from Latin *littera* letter of the alphabet (in plural: written document, literature).] —**let′ter·er,** *n.*

• **to the letter.** exactly as written or spoken; precisely: *I followed your instructions to the letter.*

letter box, mailbox.

letter carrier, mail carrier.

let·tered (let′ərd) *adj.* **1.** able to read and write; literate. **2.** of, relating to, or characterized by learning or literary culture; learned. **3.** marked with or as with letters.

let·ter·head (let′ər hed′) *n.* **1.** information printed at the top of a sheet of paper, usually including the name and address of the sender. **2.** a sheet of paper with such a heading.

let·ter·ing (let′ər ing) *n.* **1.** the act or art of forming or inscribing letters, esp. by hand. **2.** the letters so formed or inscribed.

let·ter·man (let′ər man′) *n., pl.* **-men** (-men′). *Informal.* an athlete to whom a letter has been awarded for participation or achievement.

letter of credit, a letter issued by a bank, authorizing the person named to draw money or have credit established up to a specified amount at that bank, its branches, or a correspondent bank.

letter of marque *also,* **letters of marque.** formerly, documents issued by a government authorizing a private citizen to arm a ship for the purpose of capturing enemy ships and their cargo. Also, **letter of marque and reprisal.** [LETTER + OF + Old French *marque* arrest, seizure, from Old Provençal *marca* reprisal; of Germanic origin.]

let·ter·per·fect (let′ər pûr′fikt) *adj.* **1.** correct in every detail; completely accurate. **2.** knowing one's part or lesson perfectly, as an actor. —*adv.* perfectly.

let·ter·press (let′ər pres′) *n.* a printing produced from a plate on which the type or image to be reproduced is raised above the surface.

let·ter·qual·i·ty (let′ər kwol′i tē) *adj.* **1.** (of a computer printer) capable of producing printouts of a quality equal to that of copy typed on a typewriter. **2.** (of a printout) equal in quality to that of copy typed on a typewriter.

letters patent 1. formerly, in English law, a grant by a sovereign, conferring on a subject or subjects some right, property, franchise, or the like. **2.** *British.* patent *(def. 1).*

Let·tish (let′ish) *adj.* Latvian. —*n.* Lett *(def. 2).*

let·tuce (let′is) *n.* **1.** the large green or red leaves of a plant, *Lactuca sativa,* of the composite family, forming a round, oval, or long, loose head, eaten mainly as a raw vegetable in salads. **2.** the plant itself, widely cultivated in many parts of the world. [Old French *laitues,* plural of *laitue* this plant, from Latin *lactūca,* from *lac* milk; because of the plant's milky juice.]

a	at	e	end	o	hot	u	up	hw	white		about
ā	ape	ē	me	ō	old	ū	use	ng	song		taken
ä	far	i	it	ô	fork	ü	rule	th	thin	ə	pencil
âr	care	ī	ice	oi	oil	u̇	pull	th	this		lemon
		ir	pierce	ou	out	ûr	turn	zh	measure		circus

707

let·up (let′up′) *n. Informal.* a lessening or slackening, as of pace, force, or intensity; lull or cessation: *It snowed all day without letup.*

le·u (le′ù) *n., pl.* **lei** (lā). the monetary unit of Romania.

leu·cine (lü′sēn, -sin) *n.* an essential amino acid produced in the body as a result of the breakdown of dietary proteins by pancreatic enzymes. Formula: $C_6H_{13}NO_2$

leu·co·plast (lü′kə plast′) *n.* a colorless plastid found in the cells of roots and other underground plant parts, associated with the formation and storage of starch.

leuk- *also,* **leuc-.** form of **leuko-** before vowels, as in *leukemia.*

leu·ke·mia (lü kē′mē ə) *n.* a cancer of the bone marrow characterized by the development and proliferation of abnormal white blood cells and their spread to other organs, such as the lymph nodes, spleen, and liver. [Modern Latin *leukaemia,* from Greek *leukos* white + *haima* blood.] —**leu·ke′mic,** *adj.*

leuko- *also,* **leuco-.** *combining form* white or colorless: *leukocyte.* [Greek *leukos* white.]

leu·ko·cyte (lü′kə sīt′) *also,* **leu·co·cyte.** *n.* white blood cell. [Greek *leukos* white + *kytos* hollow container.]

lev (lev) *n., pl.* **le·va** (le′vä). the monetary unit of Bulgaria.

Lev., Leviticus.

Le·van·tine (lev′ən tīn′, -tēn′, lə van′tin) *adj.* of, relating to, or characteristic of the Levant. —*n.* a native or inhabitant of the Levant.

le·va·tor (li vā′tər) *n., pl.* **lev·a·to·res** (lev′ə tôr′ēz). any of various muscles that raise some part of the body. [Modern Latin *levator,* from Latin *levātus,* past participle of *levāre* to raise.]

lev·ee¹ (lev′ē) *n.* **1.** a wall of earth and other materials built along the bank of a river as protection from flooding. **2.** a landing place, esp. on a river; pier; quay. [French *levée* raising, embankment, from *lever* to raise, from Latin *levāre.*]

lev·ee² (lev′ē, le vē′) *n.* a reception held by a person of high rank, esp. a sovereign, upon rising in the morning. [French *levé* rising, from *(se) lever* to rise, from Latin *levāre* to raise.]

lev·el (lev′əl) *adj.* **1.** having no part higher than another; flat; even: *The steamroller made the road level.* **2.** parallel to the plane of the horizon; perpendicular to a plumb line; horizontal. **3.** being or situated at the same height or on the same plane as something else: *The two paintings were level with the window.* **4.** having the surface even with the rim or edge of a container: *a level teaspoon of flour.* **5.** equal to someone or something, as in degree, importance, rank, or stage of development: *Educationally the child is level with other children his age.* **6.** even or uniform, as in quality, tone, or style: *Even though she was getting angry, her voice remained level.* **7.** *Informal.* mentally well-balanced; sensible: *to keep a level head in a crisis.* —*n.* **1.** a relative position or degree in any scale or order: *a low level of economic development.* **2.** a horizontal surface, plane, or line, esp. as used to determine or measure the relative position of one or more points or surfaces: *The town is situated just ten feet above the level of the river.* **3.** height, depth, or altitude: *During the flood, the water in the basement rose to a level of three feet.* **4.** a relatively flat surface; horizontal area or expanse, as of land. **5.** an area lying in a horizontal plane and constituting a floor or story of a structure: *The car is parked on the lower level of the garage.* **6.** any of various devices, such as a carpenter's level or a surveyor's level, used to determine whether a surface is horizontal or to determine the degree of departure from the horizontal. —*v.,* **-eled, -el·ing;** *also, British,* **-elled, -el·ling.** —*v.t.* **1.a.** to make even, flat, or smooth: *The bulldozer leveled the mound of earth.* **b.** to make perpendicular to a plumb line; make horizontal: *to level a board before nailing it.* **2.** to bring to the level of the ground; destroy; raze: *The fire leveled the house.* **3.** *Informal.* to knock (someone) down with or as with a blow: *The punch leveled the boxer.* **4.** to reduce or bring to equality in degree, state, or condition; equalize: *to level the ranks of society.* **5.** to bring to and aim in a horizontal plane: *to level a gun on a target.* **6.** to direct (something, as words): *to level an accusation at someone.* **7.** in surveying, to measure or determine differences in elevation within (an area of land) with a surveyor's level. —*v.i.* **1.** to bring people and things to a common level. **2.** to level and aim a weapon: *The soldier*

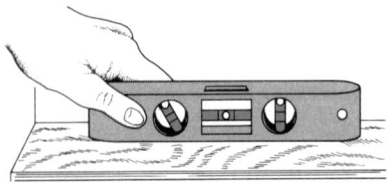

level *(n., def. 6)*

leveled and fired. **3.** *Slang.* to be candid and honest (often with *with*). [Old French *livel* carpenter's level, going back to Latin *lībella,* diminutive of *lībra* balance, scales.] —**lev′el·er;** *also, British,* **lev′el·ler,** *n.* —**lev′el·ly,** *adv.* —**lev′el·ness,** *n.*

• **one's level best.** one's very best: *The team did its level best to win the game.*

• **on the level.** *Informal.* upright, true, fair, and honest: *The teacher is on the level, and we can believe what he says.*

• **to find one's** (or **its**) **level.** to reach a natural or appropriate place or position: *The hard-working executive finally found her level as president of the corporation.*

• **to level off. a.** to continue on a horizontal course after gaining or losing altitude. **b.** to arrive at and maintain stability after a period of fluctuation: *Costs leveled off after a time of steep rises and declines.*

Synonyms *adj.* Level and flat¹, used of horizontal surfaces, mean having no part higher than any other. **Level** describes an absolutely even surface like the surface of still water: *To support the statue properly, the base must be absolutely level.* It is, however, often used loosely: *We stood on a broad, level plain.* **Flat** generally connotes a surface without easily observable irregularity: *If the lawn is flat we can play croquet on it.*

lev·el·head·ed (lev′əl hed′id) *adj.* having or showing common sense and sound judgment; sensible. —**lev′el·head′ed·ness,** *n.*

lev·er (lev′ər, lē′vər) *n.* **1.** a device, one of the simple machines, consisting of a rigid body, such as a rod or bar, that transmits force or motion from one point to another as it rotates about a fixed point, or fulcrum. There are three types of levers, defined by the relative positions of the applied and resisting forces and fulcrum. **2.** anything that operates in this way, as a crowbar or pry. **3.** a means of exerting effective power: *The friends of the senator tried to use their relationship as a lever for getting favors.* —*v.t.* to move or pry with or as with a lever. —*v.i.* to use a lever. [Old French *levier* crowbar, from *lever* to raise, from Latin *levāre.*]

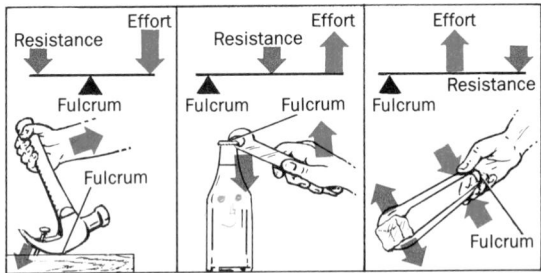

three types of **levers**

lev·er·age (lev′ər ij, lē′vər-) *n.* **1.** the action of a lever. **2.** the mechanical advantage or power gained by use of a lever. **3.** increased power to act or influence: *The governor's friendship gave the contractor political leverage when bidding on public works projects.* **4.** *Finance.* **a.** the effect on a corporation's common-stock earnings when a large part of the company's indebtedness is in the form of bonds with a fixed interest rate or when there are many preferred stocks outstanding with a fixed dividend rate. **b.** the purchase of an asset by borrowing part or most of the money needed for payment. —*v.t.,* **-aged, -ag·ing. 1.** to use increased power to act on or influence. **2.** to affect (a corporation's common-stock earnings) by the need to pay holders of bonds or preferred stock. **3.** to purchase (an asset, as common stock in a corporation) with part or most of the money borrowed from banks.

leveraged buyout, the acquiring of a public company by a group of investors, primarily through borrowed funds that are secured by the assets of the company being purchased.

lev·er·et (lev′ər it) *n.* a young hare, esp. one that is in its first year. [Anglo-Norman *leveret,* diminutive of *levre* hare, from Latin *lepus.*]

le·vi·a·than (li vī′ə thən) *n.* **1.** in the Old Testament, a huge sea monster. **2.** anything of huge size, such as a whale or large ship. **3.** a person or thing that has great power: *The Soviet leviathan controlled Eastern Europe for nearly forty-five years.* [Late Latin *leviathon* sea monster, from Hebrew *livyatan* dragon, sea monster, from *lava* to twist; because it twisted itself into coils.]

Le·vi's (lē′vīz) *pl. n. Trademark.* close-fitting trousers, esp. of blue denim.

lev·i·tate (lev′i tāt′) *v.,* **-tat·ed, -tat·ing.** —*v.i.* to rise or float in the air by or as by magnetic forces, buoyancy, or supernatural power. —*v.t.* to cause to rise or float in the air. [From LEVITY, on

the model of English GRAVITATE.] —lev′i·ta′tion, *n.* —lev′i-ta′tor, *n.*

Le·vite (lē′vīt) *n.* a member of the biblical tribe of Levi.

Le·vit·i·cal (lə vit′i kəl) *adj.* **1.** of or relating to the Levites. **2.** of or relating to the book of Leviticus or its laws.

Le·vit·i·cus (lə vit′i kəs) *n.* the third book of the Old Testament, containing the laws for the priests and Levites and the body of the Jewish ceremonial law.

lev·i·ty (lev′i tē) *n., pl.* -ties. **1.** an attitude or behavior lacking seriousness; lightness. **2.** a changeable and capricious nature; fickleness. [Latin *levitās* lightness.]

levo- *combining form* toward the left: *levorotatory.* [Latin *laevus,* left.]

le·vo·ro·ta·to·ry (lē′vō rō′tə tôr′ē) *adj.* **1.** turning toward the left or in a counterclockwise direction. **2.** *Physics, Chemistry.* turning the plane of polarization of light to the left, as a chemical solution, lens, or crystal. Also, **le·vo·ro·ta·ry** (lē′vō rō′tə rē). [LEVO- + ROTATORY.]

lev·u·lose (lev′yə lōs′) *n.* fructose. [From Latin *laevus* left; because the plane of polarization of polarized light passing through it is rotated to the left.]

lev·y (lev′ē) *v.,* **lev·ied, lev·y·ing.** —*v.t.* **1.** to impose or collect by force or authority: *Governments levy taxes.* **2.** to conscript (troops) for military service. **3.** to prepare for, commence, or wage (war). —*v.i. Law.* to seize and dispose of property in order to satisfy unpaid debts. —*n., pl.* **lev·ies.** **1.** anything collected by authority, such as troops or taxes. **2.** the act of levying. [French *levée* raising, embankment, raising of money or soldiers. See LE-VEE[1].]

lewd (lüd) *adj.* offending modesty or decency; obscene; bawdy; indecent. [Middle English *lewed* ignorant, uneducated, lay[3], secular, from Old English *lǣwede.*] —lewd′ly, *adv.* —lewd′ness, *n.*

lew·is·ite (lü′ə sīt′) a yellow, liquid arsenic compound used in vapor form during World War I as a blistering poison gas. Formula: $C_2H_2AsCl_3$. [From Winford Lee *Lewis,* 1878-1943, American chemist who developed it + -ITE[1].]

lex (leks) *n., pl.* **le·ges** (lē′jēz). law. [Latin *lēx.*]

lex·i·cal (lek′si kəl) *adj.* **1.** of or relating to the words of a language. **2.** of or relating to a lexicon.

lex·i·cog·ra·pher (lek′si kog′rə fər) *n.* a person whose profession is writing or compiling a dictionary. [Greek *lexikographos* (from *lexikon* dictionary + *graphein* to write) + -ER[1].]

lex·i·cog·ra·phy (lek′si kog′rə fē) *n.* the process or profession of writing or compiling a dictionary. —lex·i·co·graph·ic (lek′-si kə graf′ik); *also,* lex′i·co·graph′i·cal, *adj.*

lex·i·con (lek′si kən, -kon′) *n.* **1.** a dictionary, esp. of Greek, Hebrew, Latin, or another ancient language. **2.** the vocabulary of a specific field, profession, writer, speaker or group of speakers, or the like. [Greek *lexikon* dictionary, from *lexikos* relating to words, from *lexis* word, speech.]

Ley·den jar (lī′dən) a device for storing an electric charge, consisting of a glass jar that is coated almost to the top with metal foil inside and outside. The two coatings are equivalent to the two plates of a capacitor, and the glass wall of the jar serves as the dielectric. [From *Leiden,* city of the Netherlands where it was invented.]

LF, low frequency.

LG, Low German.

L.Gk., Late Greek.

Lha·sa ap·so (las′ə ap′sō) a small, shaggy breed of terrier having short legs, a thick coat of long, straight hair, and a tail curving over the back. Height: 10 inches (25 centimeters) at the shoulder. [From *Lhasa,* capital of Tibet + Tibetan *apso* sentinel.]

Li, the symbol for lithium.

L.I., Long Island.

li·a·bil·i·ty (lī′ə bil′i tē) *n., pl.* -ties. **1.** the state or condition of being liable. **2.** something for which a person is liable, esp. a financial obligation or debt. **3.** something that works to one's disadvantage; handicap: *Lack of education was a liability in getting a job.* **4. liabilities.** in account-

Lhasa apso

ing, the debts or financial commitments of a business, as entered on a balance sheet or stated in an annual report. ➡ opposed to **assets.**

li·a·ble (lī′ə bəl) *adj.* **1.** legally responsible; obligated by law: *The owner of the car is liable for damages to our fence.* **2.** naturally inclined; prone; subject (with *to*): *to be liable to migraines.* **3.** having or showing a possibility; apt; likely: *You are liable to fall on the*

icy *sidewalk if you are not careful.* [French *lier* to bind (from Latin *ligāre*) + -ABLE.]

li·ai·son (lē′ə zon′, lē ā′-) *n.* **1.** a line of communication between parts of an organization, such as military units, used to ensure coordination of actions. **2.** an agent or means of maintaining or improving communication between persons or groups. **3.** an illicit love affair. **4.** in certain languages, esp. French, the pronunciation of a silent final consonant of a word as the first letter of a following word that begins with a vowel or mute *h.* Example: The pronunciation in French of the *s* in *les* in *les amis* (lā zä mē′) or the *s* in *les* in *les hommes* (lā zôm′). [French *liaison,* from Late Latin *ligātiō* a binding, from Latin *ligāre* to bind.]

li·a·na (lē ä′nə, -an′ə) *also,* **li·ane** (lē än′) *n.* any of various climbing vines found esp. in tropical forests, having stems that wind around the trunks of trees. [French *liane,* probably from *lier* to bind. See LIABLE.]

li·ar (lī′ər) *n.* a person who tells lies.

lib. **1.** book. **2.** librarian. **3.** library. [Latin *liber.*]

li·ba·tion (lī bā′shən) *n.* **1.** the ritual of pouring out wine or other liquid as an offering to a deity. **2.** a liquid offered in this way. **3.** *Informal.* a drink, esp. an alcoholic beverage. [Latin *libātiō* liquid poured out as an offering to a deity.]

li·bel (lī′bəl) *n.* **1.** *Law.* the act or crime of damaging a person's reputation by printing, writing, or representing in a picture false and malicious information about that person. ➡ distinguished from **slander.** **2.** any false or malicious defamatory statement or picture. —*v.t.,* **-beled, -bel·ing;** *also, British,* **-belled, -bel·ling.** **1.** to write or publish a libel about. **2.** to defame or misrepresent, as by libel. [Latin *libellus* little book, pamphlet, lampoon, diminutive of *liber* book; because of the use of pamphlets or "little books" to damage reputations in ancient Rome.]

li·bel·er (lī′bə lər) *also, British,* **li·bel·ler.** *n.* a person who libels.

li·bel·ous (lī′bə ləs) *also, British,* **li·bel·lous.** *adj.* containing a libel: *a libelous accusation.* —li′bel·ous·ly; *also, British,* **li′bel-lous·ly,** *adv.*

lib·er·al (lib′ər əl, lib′rəl) *adj.* **1.** being open to change and disposed toward reform, as in politics, religion, or education. ➡ distinguished from **conservative.** **2.** free from prejudice; broad-minded; tolerant. **3.** characterized by generosity; bountiful: *to be liberal with one's money.* **4.** ample or plentiful; abundant: *a liberal supply of food, liberal spending.* **5.** not literal or strict: *a liberal interpretation of the law.* —*n.* **1.** a person who has liberal opinions. **2. Liberal.** a member of a Liberal Party, esp. in Great Britain, the United States, or Canada. [Latin *liberālis* befitting a free man, generous, from *liber* free.] —lib′er·al·ly, *adv.* —lib′er·al·ness, *n.*

liberal arts, the subjects stressed in an academic curriculum, including literature, languages, history, sciences, and philosophy.

lib·er·al·ism (lib′ər əl iz′əm, lib′rə-) *n.* **1.** liberal principles and ideals. **2.** *also,* **Liberalism.** principles and policies of a Liberal Party. —lib′er·al·ist, *adj., n.* —lib′er·al·is′tic, *adj.*

lib·er·al·i·ty (lib′ə ral′i tē) *n., pl.* -ties. **1.** willingness to give or share freely; generosity; magnanimity. **2.** a tolerant attitude; broad-mindedness. **3.** a generous gift.

lib·er·al·ize (lib′ər ə līz′, lib′rə-) *v.t., v.i.,* -ized, -iz·ing. to make or become liberal. —lib′er·al·i·za′tion, *n.* —lib′er·al-iz′er, *n.*

Liberal Party, a political party, as in Great Britain, the United States, or Canada, that favors change, with the hope that such change will result in progress and reform.

lib·er·ate (lib′ə rāt′) *v.t.,* -at·ed, -at·ing. **1.** to set free; release. **2.** *Chemistry.* to free (as a gas or liquid) from combination: *Heating mercuric oxide triggers an endothermic reaction that liberates oxygen.* [Latin *liberātus,* past participle of *liberāre* to set free.] —lib′er·a′tion, *n.* —lib′er·a′tor, *n.*

lib·er·tar·i·an (lib′ər târ′ē ən) *n.* **1.** a person who advocates liberty, esp. of thought or conduct. **2.** a person who believes in the doctrine of free will. —lib′er·tar′i·an·ism, *n.*

lib·er·tine (lib′ər tēn′, -tin) *n.* a person who is lacking in moral restraint; dissolute person. —*adj.* dissolute; immoral. [Latin *libertīnus* freed slave, going back to *liber* free; with reference to the loose morals associated with former slaves of ancient Rome.] —lib′er·tin·ism, *n.*

lib·er·ty (lib′ər tē) *n., pl.* -ties. **1.** freedom from tyranny or foreign domination; political independence. **2.** freedom from imprisonment, captivity, or other physical restraint: *The prisoners*

a	at	e	end	o	hot	u	up	hw	white		(	about
ā	ape	ē	me	ō	old	ū	use	ng	song		{	taken
ä	far	i	it	ô	fork	ü	rule	th	thin	ə		pencil
âr	care	ī	ice	oi	oil	u̇	pull	t͟h	this			lemon
		îr	pierce	ou	out	ûr	turn	zh	measure		(	circus

were finally given their liberty. **3.** the ability to act as one pleases; freedom of choice: *You have the liberty to say what you want.* **4.** freedom of thought and action possessed by the people of a state or nation, considered as a human right: *Freedom of speech is a precious liberty.* **5.** action, speech, or behavior that is too free or too familiar. **6.** permission to move freely (with *of*): *The dog had the liberty of the entire house.* **7.** in the navy, time off granted to a sailor to go ashore or to be off the post for a short period. [Old French *liberte* freedom, from Latin *lībertās.*] —For Synonyms, see **freedom.**

• **at liberty. a.** not restrained; free: *The former captives were finally at liberty.* **b.** having permission; permitted; allowed: *I am not at liberty to tell you.* **c.** not busy; without work: *The actor was at liberty and hoped to get a part in the new play.*

• **to take liberties (with). a.** to speak or act in a too familiar manner: *The stranger embarrassed us by taking liberties.* **b.** to misrepresent, as facts, data, or information: *The article took liberties with the facts of the case.*

Liberty Bell, a bell rung on July 8, 1776, in Philadelphia to proclaim the signing of the Declaration of Independence by the Continental Congress.

li·bid·i·nous (li bid′ə nəs) *adj.* characterized by or showing excessive sexual desires; lustful. [Latin *libīdinōsus,* from *libīdō* lust.] —**li·bid′i·nous·ly,** *adv.* —**li·bid′i·nous·ness,** *n.*

li·bi·do (li bē′dō) *n.* **1.** the sexual drive or instinct. **2.** in psychoanalysis, psychic energy that is derived from the instinctual drives of the id and is associated with sexual desire, creativity, and, sometimes, aggressiveness. [Latin *libīdō* lust, desire.] —**li·bid·i·nal** (li bid′ə nəl) *adj.* —**li·bid′i·nal·ly,** *adv.*

Li·bra (lē′brə, lī′-) *n.* **1.** a small, dim constellation in the southern sky just south of the celestial equator, conventionally depicted as a pair of scales. **2.** the seventh sign of the zodiac. [Latin *lībra* pound¹, balance, scales.]

li·brar·i·an (lī brer′ē ən, -brâr′-) *n.* **1.** a person who is in charge of a library. **2.** a person who is trained for work in a library. [LIBRARY + -AN.]

li·brar·y (lī′brer′ē, -brə rē) *n., pl.* **-brar·ies. 1.** a collection of books or other literary, artistic, or reference material. **2.** a room or building containing such a collection. **3.** a public or private institution that maintains and circulates such a collection. [Middle English *librarie* collection of books, from Old French *librairie,* going back to Latin *librārius* relating to books, from *liber* book.]

Library of Congress, the national library of the United States, in Washington, D.C.

li·bra·tion (lī brā′shən) *n. Astronomy.* a phenomenon arising from variations in the rate of rotation and orbital motion of the moon that makes it possible to see more of its surface than the half that would otherwise be visible from earth. [Latin *lībrātiō* oscillation, from *lībrātus,* past participle of *lībrāre* to weigh, from *lībra* balance.]

li·bret·tist (li bret′ist) *n.* a writer of a libretto.

li·bret·to (li bret′ō) *n., pl.* **-bret·tos** or **-bret·ti** (-bret′ē). **1.** the text of an opera or other long vocal composition. **2.** a book or pamphlet containing such a text. [Italian *libretto,* diminutive of *libro* book, from Latin *liber.*]

lice (līs) the plural of **louse.**

li·cense (lī′səns) *also,* **li·cence.** *n.* **1.** a document, plate, tag, or other object showing that the holder has official permission to do something, as drive a car, or to own something, as a dog. **2.** permission given by law or authority to do something: *a license to handle classified documents.* **3.** undisciplined and excessive freedom; abuse of liberty. **4.** the freedom to break or ignore certain rules to achieve an effect: *I took the license of changing historical facts in my short story.* —*v.t.,* **-censed, -cens·ing.** to grant a license to or for; permit or authorize. [Old French *licence* permission of action granted, unregulated freedom, from Latin *licentia.*] —**li·cens′a·ble,** *adj.* —**li·cens′er,** *n.*

licensed practical nurse, a nurse who has completed certain training and educational requirements and is licensed by a state to provide care as a practical nurse under the supervision of a doctor or a registered nurse.

li·cen·see (lī′sən sē′) *also,* **li·cen·cee.** *n.* a person to whom a license has been granted.

license plate, a plate bearing the number of a license granted to the owner of a registered motor vehicle, attached to the rear, and often the front, of the vehicle.

li·cen·ti·ate (lī sen′shē it, -āt′) *n.* **1.** a person who has a license, as from a board of examiners or a university, to practice a profession. **2.** in certain universities of Europe, a degree between bachelor and doctor, or the holder of such a degree.

li·cen·tious (lī sen′shəs) *adj.* **1.** lacking moral restraint; lewd. **2.** *Archaic.* disregarding commonly accepted rules. [Latin *licentiōsus* unrestrained, from *licentia* unrestrained liberty.] —**li·cen′tious·ly,** *adv.* —**li·cen′tious·ness,** *n.*

li·chee (lē′chē) litchi.

li·chen (lī′kən) *n.* any of numerous complex plantlike organisms, group Lichenes, found in all parts of the world, usually growing on tree trunks, rocks, or the ground. A lichen consists of a fungus that usually forms the outer layer and an inner supporting network, and an alga that contains chlorophyll and manufactures food. [Latin *līchēn,* from Greek *leichēn.*] —**li′chen·ous,** *adj.*

lich gate (lich) *also,* **lych gate.** a roofed gateway to a churchyard, sometimes used as a resting place for a bier. [Obsolete *lich* body (from Old English *līc*) + GATE.]

lic·it (lis′it) *adj.* lawful; permitted. [Latin *licitus,* past participle of *licēre* to be permitted.] —**lic′it·ly,** *adv.* —**lic′it·ness,** *n.*

lick (lik) *v.t.* **1.** to move the tongue over the surface of: *The kitten licked its paw. I licked the envelope and sealed it.* **2.** to taste, eat, or remove by moving the tongue over: *to lick an ice-cream cone.* **3.** to move over or touch lightly or quickly: *Flames from the campfire licked the coals.* **4.** *Informal.* to hit forcefully; thrash. **5.** *Informal.* to gain a victory over; defeat; overcome: *to lick a difficult problem, to lick an opponent.* —*n.* **1.** a stroke of the tongue while licking. **2.** a small quantity; bit: *They haven't done a lick of work all day.* **3.** salt lick. **4.** *Informal.* a sharp blow. **5.** *Slang.* a chance or turn: *to take a lick at fixing a leaky faucet.* **6.** *Informal.* speed; rate: *The horse galloped at a fast lick.* [Old English *liccian* to pass the tongue over, lap³.]

lich gate

• **a lick and a promise.** a hasty and superficial effort: *to give a task a lick and a promise.*

• **last licks.** *Informal.* the final chance or turn.

• **to lick (something) into shape.** *Informal.* to give an orderly or acceptable form to: *to lick a report into shape.*

• **to lick one's chops.** to show delighted anticipation.

• **to lick one's wounds.** to try to recover from sorrow or hurt after a defeat.

lick·er·ish (lik′ər ish) *adj. Archaic.* **1.** craving delicious food. **2.** lecherous. [Modification of obsolete *lickerous,* going back to Old French *lecherous* lecherous, from *lecheor.* See LECHER.]

lick·e·ty-split (lik′ə tē split′) *adv. Informal.* at great speed.

lick·ing (lik′ing) *n.* **1.** the act of a person or thing that licks. **2.** *Informal.* a thrashing; beating.

lick·spit·tle (lik′spit′əl) *n.* a servile flatterer or admirer; fawning person.

lic·o·rice (lik′ər is, -ish, lik′rish) *also,* **liquorice.** *n.* **1.** a candy or other confection flavored with the sweet juice or extract obtained from the root of a plant, *Glycyrrhiza glabra,* of the pea family. **2.** the plant yielding this juice or extract, widely cultivated in Europe and Asia, bearing spikes of pale blue flowers. **3.** the sweet juice or extract itself, used esp. as a flavoring agent in candy, liquor, and tobacco. [Old French *licorice* licorice plant or extract, from Late Latin *liquiritia,* going back to Greek *glykyrrhiza,* from *glykys* sweet + *rhiza* root.]

lic·tor (lik′tər) *n.* one of the officers or attendants who preceded the Roman magistrates and carried the fasces. [Latin *līctor.*]

lid (lid) *n.* **1.** a hinged or removable cover placed over the opening of a receptacle: *Put the lid on the garbage can.* **2.** eyelid. **3.** *Informal.* anything that restrains, restricts, or covers up: *The police put the lid on gambling in the town.* **4.** *Slang.* a hat; cap. [Old English *hlid* cover.]

lid·less (lid′lis) *adj.* **1.** having no lid. **2.** *Archaic.* watchful; vigilant: *a lidless watcher of the public weal* (Alfred, Lord Tennyson, 1847).

lie¹ (lī) *n.* **1.** a false statement made with the purpose of deceiving; falsehood. **2.** anything that gives a false impression: *Her smile was a lie that concealed her true feelings.* —*v.,* **lied, ly·ing.** —*v.i.* **1.** to make a false statement or statements with the purpose of deceiving: *He lied about his age.* **2.** to give a false impression: *Mirrors don't lie.* —*v.t.* to put or bring into a specified condition by lying. [Old English *lēogan* to make a false statement.]

• **to give the lie to. a.** to accuse of lying. **b.** to expose as false.

• **to lie in (or through) one's teeth.** to lie outrageously.

lie² (lī) *v.i.,* **lay, lain, ly·ing. 1.** to be or place oneself in a flat or reclining position: *to lie in bed.* **2.** to be placed upon or rest against a surface, esp. in a horizontal position: *The quilt is lying across the bed.* **3.** to remain in a particular state or condition: *The fields lay fallow throughout the winter.* **4.** to be located or placed: *Mexico lies to the south of Texas.* **5.** to extend or continue in a

specific direction: *The long road lay in front of us. A great future lies before you.* **6.** to be; exist: *The defendant's fate lies in the hands of the jury.* **7.** to be buried, as in a grave or tomb. **8.** *Archaic.* to reside temporarily; spend the night; lodge; sleep. —*n.* **1.** the manner, direction, or position in which something lies; lay: *the lie of the land.* **2.** *Golf.* the position in which a ball rests on the course. [Old English *licgan* to be in a prostrate position, to be placed in a horizontal position.]

• **to lie in.** to be confined for childbirth.

• **to lie in wait.** to wait for in concealment so as to attack by surprise.

• **to lie low.** *Slang.* **a.** to conceal oneself; hide: *The thief decided to lie low for a few days.* **b.** to refrain from action until the right moment.

• **to lie off.** (of a vessel) to keep near the shore or nearly alongside another vessel.

• **to lie over.** to be postponed: *Because of the weather, our outing will have to lie over until next weekend.*

• **to lie to.** to keep a vessel in a nearly stationary position by facing into the wind.

• **to lie with.** **a.** to be dependent upon; rest with: *The decision lies with the judge. The success of our plan lies with you.* **b.** *Archaic.* to have sexual intercourse with.

• **to take (something) lying down.** *Informal.* to accept without protest; submit to: *I won't take that kind of insult lying down!*

lie detector, an instrument that detects certain bodily changes considered to occur when a person lies; polygraph.

lief (lēf) *adv.* **as lief.** as willingly; as gladly: *I would as lief go there as stay here.* —*adj. Archaic.* **1.** beloved; dear. **2.** willing. [Old English *lēof* dear.]

liege (lēj) *n.* **1.** a feudal lord or sovereign entitled to the allegiance and service of his vassals or subjects. **2.** a vassal or subject bound to give allegiance and service to a feudal lord or sovereign. —*adj.* **1.** entitled to the allegiance and service of vassals or subjects. **2.** bound to give allegiance and service to a feudal lord or sovereign. **3.** of, relating to, or designating the relationship or bond between vassal and lord. **4.** loyal; faithful. [Old French *liege* relating to a vassal bound to a lord, from Late Latin *laeticus* relating to a serf, from *laetus* serf; probably of Germanic origin.]

liege·man (lēj′mən) *n., pl.* **-men** (-mən). **1.** a vassal. **2.** a faithful follower or subject: *foes of God and liegemen of the Devil* (Francis Parkman, 1865).

lien (lēn) *n.* a legal claim placed on the property of another for payment of a debt. [French *lien* bond, tie, from Latin *ligāmen.*]

lieu (lü) *n.* **1. in lieu of.** in place of; instead of: *The salesperson received commissions in lieu of salary.* **2.** *Archaic.* place; stead. [Old French *lieu* place, from Latin *locus.*]

Lieut., Lieutenant.

lieu·ten·an·cy (lü ten′ən sē) *n., pl.* **-cies.** the rank, status, or commission of a lieutenant.

lieu·ten·ant (lü ten′ənt; *British* lef ten′ənt) *n.* **1.a.** first lieutenant. **b.** second lieutenant. **2.** an officer in the U.S. Navy or Coast Guard ranking next below a lieutenant commander and above a lieutenant junior grade. **3.** a person who acts in the place of a superior; deputy. [Middle English *lutenand, luftenand,* from Middle French *lieutenant* officer who takes the place of his superior, from *lieu* place (from Latin *locus*) + *tenant,* present participle of *tenir* to hold (from Latin *tenēre*).]

lieutenant colonel, an officer in the U.S. Army, Air Force, and Marine Corps ranking next below a colonel and above a major.

lieutenant commander, an officer in the U.S. Navy or Coast Guard ranking next below a commander and above a lieutenant.

lieutenant general, an officer in the U.S. Army, Air Force, and Marine Corps ranking next below a general and above a major general.

lieutenant governor 1. the second-ranking executive officer in thirty-eight U.S. states who succeeds to the governorship when that office is declared vacant and in certain states presides over the state senate. **2.** the titular head of a district or province that is under the jurisdiction of a governor general.

lieutenant junior grade, an officer in the U.S. Navy or Coast Guard ranking next below a lieutenant and above an ensign.

life (līf) *n., pl.* **lives. 1.** the form or quality of existence that distinguishes organisms such as animals and plants from inorganic or inanimate things. The characteristics of life that are shared by all living organisms are growth, reproduction, metabolism, and the capacity to respond to stimuli. **2.** the state, condition, or fact of possessing this form or quality of existence: *to lose one's life.* **3.** spiritual existence regarded as transcending physical death. **4.** living organisms collectively: *No life has been found on the moon.* **5.** a living person: *The firefighters helped to save many lives.* **6.** the period from birth to death; duration of existence: *a long and happy life, to achieve success early in life.* **7.** a particular portion of this period: *adult life.* **8.** a particular aspect of exist-

ence: *one's private life.* **9.** the period during which something lasts or remains useful or effective: *Minor accidents can shorten the life of a car.* **10.** human activities, relationships, or pursuits collectively: *a common occurrence of everyday life.* **11.** a manner of existence, esp. characteristic activities of a group, location, time, or the like: *military life, city life.* **12.** a written account of the history of an individual; biography. **13.** something that supports, sustains, shapes, or is essential to the existence of someone or something: *Tourism is the life of the island.* **14.** a lively, fun-loving, vivacious manner: *jolly and full of life.* **15.** a source of liveliness or vitality; animating force: *to be the life of the party.* **16.** the living form or a model: *The portrait was painted from life.* [Old English *līf* quality of being alive, period from birth to death.]

• **a matter of life and (or or) death.** something extremely important, urgent, or critical.

• **as big (or large) as life.** in person: *I never expected to meet the great actor, but there he was as big as life.*

• **for dear life.** as or as if to save one's life; with great effort or urgency: *When the dog growled, we ran for dear life.*

• **for life.** for the remaining period of one's life: *The murderer was imprisoned for life.*

• **for the life of one.** *Informal.* under any circumstances; at all: *I can't for the life of me remember her name.*

• **not on your life.** *Informal.* under no circumstances; never: *Are you going? Not on your life.*

• **to bring to life. a.** to cause to regain consciousness; revive. **b.** to make lively. **c.** to cause to appear to be alive or real; make lifelike: *A great actor can bring a fictional character to life.*

• **to come to life. a.** to regain consciousness. **b.** to become lively: *The city comes to life at night.* **c.** to appear to be alive or real; become lifelike.

• **to take (someone's) life.** to kill (someone).

• **true to life.** corresponding to reality; faithfully representing real life: *a novel that is true to life.*

life-and-death (līf′ən deth′) *adj.* **1.** threatening to life: *a life-and-death crisis, a life-and-death struggle.* **2.** necessary for the maintenance of life: *a life-and-death operation.* **3.** of critical importance; crucial: *Success of the new product was a life-and-death matter for the failing company.* Also, **life-or-death** (līf′ər deth′).

life belt, a life preserver in the form of a belt.

life·blood (līf′blud′) *n.* **1.** blood necessary to life. **2.** something that supports, sustains, or is essential to the existence of a person or thing: *The participation of every citizen is the lifeblood of democracy.* Also *(def. 2),* **life's blood.**

life·boat (līf′bōt′) *n.* a strong, buoyant boat, usually carried on a larger ship, constructed and equipped for saving lives at sea in case of shipwreck or other emergency.

life buoy, a life preserver, often ring-shaped, used to keep afloat a person in danger of drowning.

life cycle *Biology.* the series of changes in form and function undergone by an organism from a particular stage in one generation to the development of the same stage in the next generation.

life expectancy, the predicted or average length of time that a person or animal will live or that an object will exist or function. A person's life expectancy is determined statistically and affected by such factors as age, sex, physical condition, and occupation.

life·guard (līf′gärd′) *n.* an expert swimmer employed at a beach or a swimming pool to protect and aid swimmers. Also, **life-saver.**

Life Guards, two regiments of British cavalry that, together with the Royal Horse Guards, form the Household Cavalry, the personal guard of the sovereign.

life history 1. the history of the developmental changes undergone by an organism from egg or spore to maturity and death. **2.** one series of these changes, constituting a life cycle. **3.** biography *(def. 1).*

life insurance 1. a contract between a person and an insurance company requiring the person to pay regular premiums over a specified period of time and providing for cash payment to a designated beneficiary upon the death of the insured or to the insured person upon reaching a certain age. **2.** the sum specified in such a contract. **3.** the premiums paid on such a contract.

life jacket, a life preserver in the form of a jacket or vest.

life·less (līf′lis) *adj.* **1.** not having life; inanimate: *lifeless statues.* **2.** no longer alive; dead. **3.** lacking animation or vigor;

a	at	e	end	o	hot	u	up	hw	white		about
ā	ape	ē	me	ō	old	ū	use	ng	song		taken
ä	far	i	it	ô	fork	th	thin	ə	pencil
âr	care	ī	ice	oi	oil	u̇	pull	th	this		lemon
		îr	pierce	ou	out	ûr	turn	zh	measure		circus

711

dull: *a lifeless speech.* **4.** devoid of living organisms: *a lifeless moon.* —**life′less·ly,** *adv.* —**life′less·ness,** *n.*

life·like (līf′līk′) *adj.* accurately resembling or imitating real life: *The doll was amazingly lifelike.* —**life′like′ness,** *n.*

life·line (līf′līn′) *n.* **1.** a rope used for rescue or security, esp. one attached to a life preserver and thrown to a person in the water. **2.** a line by which a diver is raised or lowered and used by the diver for signaling. **3.** a route that is the only one over which vital supplies are transported to a place.

life·long (līf′lông′) *adj.* lasting or continuing through a lifetime: *a lifelong struggle, a lifelong student of literature.*

life mask, a cast, usually of plaster, made of the face of a living person.

life net, a strong net or sheet of canvas, used to catch people falling or jumping from a great height, as from a burning building.

life preserver, a device, esp. in the form of a belt, jacket, or circular tube, inflated with air or filled with cork or other buoyant material, used by a person to keep afloat.

lif·er (lī′fər) *n. Slang.* a person sentenced to prison for life.

life raft, a floating structure, esp. an inflatable rubber raft or boat, used to rescue people, as from a sinking ship.

life·sav·er (līf′sā′vər) *n.* **1.** a person who saves another from death. **2.** lifeguard. **3.** *Informal.* a person or thing that provides help in a time of need or crisis. **4.** a life preserver in the form of a ring.

life·sav·ing (līf′sā′ving) *adj.* used in or designed for saving lives: *Ladders and nets are used by firefighters as lifesaving equipment.* —*n.* the skill and techniques used in saving a life or lives, esp. from drowning: *The lifeguard won awards for swimming and lifesaving.*

life's blood, lifeblood *(def. 2).*

life science, any of various sciences dealing with organisms and their life processes, as botany, zoology, or genetics. —**life scientist.**

life-size (līf′sīz′) *adj.* of the same size as the thing portrayed: *a life-size statue of a dancer.*

life span **1.** the period or length of time that a person or organism lives or that an object exists or functions. **2.** life expectancy.

life·style (līf′stīl′) *n.* a style or way of life that reflects the taste, attitudes, beliefs, and other values of a person or group.

life-sup·port system (līf′sə pôrt′) **1.** equipment, as a respirator, that artificially performs an essential body function, used to maintain the life of a patient who would be unable to survive without it. **2.** the equipment that provides oxygen, regulates air temperature and pressure, and performs other functions to maintain an environment that can sustain life, as in a spacecraft or submarine: *The astronauts double-checked each mechanism in the life-support system.*

life·time (līf′tīm′) *n.* the period of time that a person, animal, or plant lives or that a thing lasts or functions: *a lifetime devoted to learning, the lifetime of a television set.* —*adj.* lasting for such a period: *a lifetime guarantee.*

life·work (līf′wûrk′) *n.* the principal or entire work of a lifetime: *Betty chose medicine as her lifework.*

life zone, any of a series of zones into which a region is divided geographically according to the distribution of plant and animal life.

lift (lift) *v.t.* **1.** to bring up into the air from a surface; elevate: *to lift a box of books from the floor, to lift a heavy suitcase.* **2.** to direct upward: *The stranger lifted his eyebrows as we walked by. Several students lifted their hands in response to the teacher's question.* **3.** to raise in rank, condition, or estimation: *Good fortune lifted our spirits.* **4.** to protect, display, or support in the air; hold up: *The castle lifted turrets toward the sky.* **5.** to project in a clear, loud tone: *The choir members lifted their voices in song.* **6.** to revoke or remove; cancel: *The ban on parking was lifted temporarily.* **7.** to put an end to (something, as a siege or blockade), esp. by removing forces. **8.** to pay off (an obligation, as a debt or mortgage). **9.** *Golf.* to pick up (a ball) from an unplayable position and place it in a more favorable position. **10.** to remove or change (something, as wrinkles or the contours of a body part) by performing plastic surgery or a facelift. **11.** *Informal.* to steal: *The burglars lifted three radios.* **12.** *Informal.* to plagiarize: *The author lifted the paragraph from someone else's work.* —*v.i.* **1.** to rise or become raised; go up: *This box should lift easily.* **2.** to strain or exert effort in order to raise something. **3.** to rise or seem to rise and disperse; disappear: *The fog lifted.* **4.** to cease temporarily: *The storm lifted for a few hours.* **5.** to become raised or improved, as in condition: *His spirits lifted.* —*n.* **1.** the act or an instance of lifting or rising: *a lift of the eyebrow.* **2.** the distance, height, or extent to which a thing is lifted or raised: *The canal lock has a lift of ten feet.* **3.** a free ride: *to get a lift into town.* **4.** a good feeling resulting from having one's spirits lifted: *The compliment gave her a lift.* **5.** an elevated manner of carriage, as of the head

or neck: *a lift of the chin.* **6.** a mechanical device or apparatus that lifts, conveys, or hoists, as a ski lift. **7.** *British.* elevator. **8.** one of the layers of leather, rubber, or plastic at the bottom of the heel of a shoe. **9.** the component of aerodynamic force that opposes the force of gravity on an airfoil, such as a plane wing, and causes an aircraft to stay aloft. [Old Norse *lypta* to raise.] —**lift′er,** *n.* —For Synonyms *(v.t.),* see **raise.**

· **to not lift a finger.** to do nothing: *My relatives would not lift a finger to help me when I was broke.*

lift-off (lift′ôf′, -of′) *also,* **lift·off.** *n.* the action of a spacecraft or rocket as it rises from its launching pad.

lift pump, a pump that operates by lifting liquid on the top of a rising piston, rather than by forcing it up by downward movement of a piston.

lift pump

lig·a·ment (lig′ə mənt) *n.* **1.** a band of strong, fibrous tissue that connects two bones or cartilages or supports muscles. **2.** a connecting bond or tie. [Latin *ligāmentum* tie, bond.]

lig·and (lig′ənd, lī′gənd) *n.* an atom or molecule that, in donating a pair of electrons, has become bound to the central metal ion of a complex compound, as in a chelate. [Latin *ligandum,* gerundive of *ligāre* to bind.]

li·gate (lī′gāt) *v.t.* -gat·ed, -gat·ing. to bind up or tie off, as a blood vessel in surgery. [Latin *ligātus,* past participle of *ligāre* to bind, tie.] —**li·ga′tion,** *n.*

lig·a·ture (lig′ə chûr′, -chər) *n.* **1.** something that is used to bind, tie, or constrict, esp. thread, nylon filament, or wire used to tie off a blood vessel. **2.** the act of binding up or tying off; ligation. **3.** *Music.* a slur or a group of notes connected by a slur. **4.** *Printing.* two or more letters joined together to form one character. Æ is a ligature. Also *(def. 4),* diphthong. —*v.t.,* -tured, -tur·ing. to bind up or tie off with a ligature; ligate. [Late Latin *ligātūra* bond, tie, from Latin *ligāre* to bind, tie.]

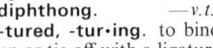

Si — lent — night

ligature *(def. 3)*

light¹ (līt) *n.* **1.a.** electromagnetic radiation that can be detected by the human eye and travels at a velocity of about 186,000 miles (300,000 kilometers) per second. **b.** invisible electromagnetic radiation, esp. ultraviolet or infrared radiation. **2.a.** the medium or condition that makes vision possible; illumination: *Is there enough light to read by?* **b.** a particular instance of such illumination: *a strong light, a bright light.* **3.** a sensation produced by stimulation of the organs of sight: *The light hurt my eyes when I came out of the darkroom.* **4.** a source of illumination or brightness, as a lamp or a traffic light: *Shut off the lights when you leave. Turn left at the light.* **5.** a portion or quantity of light: *The heavy curtains reduced the light in the room.* **6.** illumination that comes from the sun during the day; daylight: *Plants grow rapidly when exposed to light.* **7.** dawn; daybreak: *The farmer was up before light.* **8.** something, as a flame or spark, used to ignite a combustible substance: *I need a light for the candle.* **9.** something that admits light, as a window or a windowpane. **10.** mental or spiritual comprehension; enlightenment: *The investigation shed new light on the mystery.* **11.** public knowledge: *a political scandal that has recently come to light.* **12.** the manner in which something is seen or judged; aspect: *to see a person in a new light.* **13.** an outstanding or prominent person, esp. one serving as a model of excellence; luminary: *one of the leading lights in the field of medicine.* **14.** an animated facial expression, esp. in the eyes. **15.** *Art.* **a.** the representation of light, as in a painting. **b.** a bright portion, as in a painting or statue. —*adj.* **1.** having light; illuminated; not dark: *The room was lighter in the morning than in the afternoon.* **2.** pale or whitish: *a light pink, a light complexion.* —*v.,* **light·ed** or **lit, light·ing.** —*v.t.* **1.** to cause to catch fire; kindle; ignite: *to light a fire.* **2.** to cause to emit light or illumination: *He lighted the lamp every evening at six.* **3.** to give light to; illuminate: *One lamp lighted the room.* **4.** to make bright or animated: *a face lighted by happiness.* **5.** to show the way to by means of a light or lights; guide: *The beam lighted the ship into the harbor.* —*v.i.* **1.** to take fire; become ignited: *Wet wood doesn't light easily.* **2.** to become

radiant or bright: *Sue's face lighted up when she heard the good news.* [Old English *lēoht* illumination, source of illumination, daylight.]

· **in (the) light of.** because of: *In light of this new evidence, the defendant must be found not guilty.*

· **to see the light.** to come to understand something; comprehend.

· **to see the light of day. a.** to come into existence. **b.** to come to public notice; become widely known.

Synonyms *v.t.* **Light¹, kindle,** and **ignite** mean to set on fire. **Light** is the most general term, used of any action that causes something to catch fire: *to light a bonfire, to light a torch, to light a match.* **Kindle** suggests the process, sometimes gradual, of catching fire: *to kindle a fire with burning straw.* **Ignite** is often, but not always, used when the agent is a spark or an electric current, and suggests a sudden bursting into flame: *to ignite a rocket's engines.*

light² (līt) *adj.* **1.** having little weight; not heavy. **2.** possessing little weight in proportion to size or bulk; of low specific gravity: *Hydrogen is a light gas.* **3.** below the legal, standard, or usual weight: *a light coin.* **4.** having little pressure or force; gentle: *a light wind.* **5.** of low density, amount, or degree: *a light fog.* **6.** not hard to bear: *light punishment.* **7.** easy to do or perform; not difficult: *light housework.* **8.** moving easily; graceful; nimble; agile: *to be light on one's feet.* **9.** harmonious and delicate in form or appearance; airy: *The church had a small, light spire.* **10.** happy; cheerful: *light laughter, a light heart, light spirits.* **11.** intended chiefly to entertain; not serious: *light reading, light comedy.* **12.** characterized by levity; trivial: *to take seriously what was only a light remark.* **13.** few or slight, as in number, quantity, or consequence: *The army sustained light casualties.* **14.** containing a smaller percentage of alcohol than is normal, often with fewer calories than normal as well: *light beer.* **15.** easily eaten or digested; not rich or fatty: *a diet of light foods.* **16.** having an airy or spongy consistency: *The cake is moist and light.* **17.** having a loose consistency; porous; sandy: *light soil.* **18.** designed for swiftness and easy maneuverability: *a light ship.* **19.** designating troops or units with relatively little heavy equipment: *light cavalry.* **20.** designating any industry that produces relatively small products using relatively light equipment. **21.** unstressed or unaccented, as a syllable or vowel. —*adv.* lightly, esp. without unnecessary equipment: *to travel light.* [Middle English *light,* from Old English *lēoht* not heavy.]

· **light in the head. a.** giddy; dizzy. **b.** foolish.

· **to make light of.** to consider or treat as of little or no importance: *Don't make light of your friend's serious problem.*

light³ (līt) *v.i.,* **light·ed** or **lit, light·ing. 1.** to get down; alight: *to light from a carriage.* **2.** to settle or come to rest, esp. from flight: *The bee lighted on the flower.* **3.** to fall or strike suddenly, as a blow. [Old English *līhtan* to descend; literally, to make not heavy (with reference to removing the weight of a rider from a horse), from *līht* light².]

· **to light into.** *Informal.* **a.** to attack: *The collie lit into the coyote that was after the sheep.* **b.** to reprimand sharply; scold.

· **to light on.** to find by chance: *to light on a solution, to light on a scheme.*

· **to light out.** *Informal.* to leave suddenly and hastily.

light bulb, an incandescent or fluorescent lamp.

light-emit·ting diode (līt'ĭ mĭt'ĭng) see LED.

light·en¹ (līt'ən) *v.t.* **1.** to make lighter or brighter: *The painter lightened the color with white.* **2.** to make luminous; illuminate: *The distant glow from the city lightened the night sky.* —*v.i.* **1.** to grow or become light or bright: *When the storm ended, the sky lightened.* **2.** to brighten or gleam. **3.** to flash with lightning. [LIGHT¹ + -EN¹.]

light·en² (līt'ən) *v.t.* **1.** to reduce the weight or load of; make less heavy. **2.** to make less oppressive or burdensome: *Machines lighten our labor.* **3.** to make more cheerful; gladden: *The good news lightened our mood.* —*v.i.* **1.** to become less heavy, oppressive, or burdensome. **2.** to become more cheerful; gladden: *Their spirits lightened when they knew their friend was safe.* [Middle English *lighter,* from Middle Dutch *lichter,* from *lichten* to lighten, unload (from *licht* light².)]

light·er¹ (līt'ər) *n.* a person or thing that causes something to ignite, esp. a mechanical device used to light cigarettes, cigars, or the like. [LIGHT¹ + -ER¹.]

light·er² (līt'ər) *n.* a flat-bottomed barge usually used in a harbor for loading and unloading ships or for transporting goods for short distances. —*v.t., v.i.* to transport (goods) in a lighter. [Middle English *lighter,* from Middle Dutch *lichter,* from *lichten* to lighten, unload (from *licht* light².)]

light·er·age (līt'ər ĭj) *n.* **1.** the act of loading and unloading ships, or transporting goods, by means of a lighter. **2.** a charge made for this service.

light·er-than-air (līt'tər thən âr') *adj.* (of a gas) having specific gravity less than that of air.

lighter-than-air craft, an aircraft that maintains buoyancy by having compartments filled with a gas less dense than the air around it, as a blimp, balloon, or dirigible; airship.

light·face (līt'fās') *n.* a typeface whose characters have thin, light lines.

light-fin·gered (līt'fĭng'gərd) *adj.* skillful at stealing, esp. at picking pockets.

light-foot·ed (līt'fŏt'ĭd) *adj.* having a light and graceful step. Also, **light'-foot'.** —**light'-foot'ed·ly,** *adv.* —**light'-foot'ed·ness,** *n.*

light-head·ed (līt'hĕd'ĭd) *adj.* **1.** somewhat faint or delirious; dizzy. **2.** frivolous in attitude or behavior; flighty; giddy. —**light'head'ed·ly,** *adv.* —**light'head'ed·ness,** *n.*

light-heart·ed (līt'här'tĭd) *adj.* free from care or anxiety; cheerful; gay. —**light'heart'ed·ly,** *adv.* —**light'heart'ed·ness,** *n.*

light heavyweight, a boxer who competes in the weight class of up to 175 pounds (79 kilograms), or a competitor, as a wrestler, in a similar class.

light·house (līt'hous') *n., pl.* **-hous·es** (-hou'zĭz). a tower or similar structure equipped with a powerful light and other devices, erected to warn ships and guide them past hazards to navigation.

lighthouse in Nova Scotia

light·ing (līt'ĭng) *n.* **1.** the act of lighting or the state of being lighted; illumination. **2.** an arrangement or system of lights: *stage lighting.* **3.** a distribution of light and shadow, as in a painting.

light·ly (līt'lē) *adv.* **1.** with little weight or force; not heavily: *to pet a cat lightly.* **2.** in a small degree or amount: *to season food lightly.* **3.** with a light, buoyant, or graceful motion: *to step lightly.* **4.** in a carefree manner; cheerfully: *to accept defeat lightly.* **5.** with little concern; in a slighting manner; indifferently: *It is too serious a matter to be taken lightly.* **6.** with little or no consideration: *Their proposal is not to be turned down lightly.*

light meter *Photography.* a device used to measure the intensity of light in a certain place and thus determine the correct exposure. Also, **exposure meter.**

light-mind·ed (līt'mīn'dĭd) *adj.* characterized by a lack of seriousness; frivolous. —**light'-mind'ed·ly,** *adv.* —**light'-mind'ed·ness,** *n.*

light·ness¹ (līt'nĭs) *n.* **1.** the quality or state of being light; brightness. **2.** paleness of color. [Old English *līhtness* brightness, from *līht* bright + -*nes(s)* -ness.]

light·ness² (līt'nĭs) *n.* **1.** the quality or state of having relatively little weight, heaviness, force, or the like. **2.** the quality of being buoyant or graceful; agility. **3.** freedom from sorrow or care; gayness; blitheness. **4.** lack of seriousness; frivolity. [LIGHT² + -NESS.]

light·ning (līt'nĭng) *n.* a visible electrical discharge in the atmosphere, between two regions in the air or between the ground and a region in the air. —*adj.* having or moving with great speed or suddenness: *a lightning response to a crisis situation.* [LIGHTEN¹ + -ING¹.]

lightning arrester, a device for protecting radios, televisions, or the like from damage from lightning.

a	at	e	end	o	hot	u	up	hw	white		about
ā	ape	ē	me	ō	old	ū	use	ng	song	ə	taken
ä	far	i	it	ô	fork	ü	rule	th	thin		pencil
âr	care	ī	ice	oi	oil	ů	pull	th	this		lemon
		îr	pierce	ou	out	ûr	turn	zh	measure		circus

lightning bug, firefly.

lightning rod, a metal conductor used to protect a building from damage by lightning by conducting the electricity to the ground.

light pen, an input device resembling a pencil that is held in the hand and moved across a computer screen to enter commands or data.

light·plane (līt'plān') *n.* a small, lightweight passenger airplane, esp. one that is used for pleasure.

light·proof (līt'prūf') *adj.* not capable of being penetrated by light: *a lightproof container for undeveloped film.*

lights (līts) *pl. n.* the lungs of an animal, esp. a sheep or pig, used as food. [Because they weigh so little. See LIGHT².]

light·ship (līt'ship') *n.* a vessel equipped with lights and signals, moored at a place dangerous to navigation as a warning and guide to ships.

light·some (līt'səm) *adj.* **1.** having the quality of buoyancy or grace. **2.** lighthearted; gay; cheerful. **3.** flighty; frivolous. —**light'some·ly,** *adv.* —**light'some·ness,** *n.*

light·weight (līt'wāt') *n.* **1.** a person or thing of less than average weight. **2.** a boxer who competes in the weight class of up to 135 pounds (61 kilograms), or a competitor, as a wrestler, in a similar class. **3.** *Informal.* a person who has little intelligence, importance, or competence. —*adj.* **1.** light in weight. **2.** of or relating to a lightweight. **3.** lacking seriousness or importance: *a lightweight detective novel.*

light-year (līt'yîr') *n.* **1.** an astronomical unit of distance equal to the distance that light travels through space in one year; approximately 5.878 trillion miles (9.459 trillion kilometers). **2. light-years.** a great distance or extent, as in technological progress: *an innovative manufacturing process that is light-years ahead of present methods.*

lig·ne·ous (lig'nē əs) *adj.* of or resembling wood; woody. [Latin *ligneus,* from *lignum* wood.]

lig·ni·fy (lig'nə fī') *v.t., v.i.,* **-fied, -fy·ing.** to convert into or become wood or woody tissue. —**lig'ni·fi·ca'tion,** *n.*

lig·nin (lig'nin) *n.* a complex carbohydrate that strengthens the cell walls of woody plants and trees and, with cellulose, forms the greater part of woody tissue.

lig·nite (lig'nīt) *n.* a brownish black, low-quality coal, denser and with more carbon than peat, in which the texture of the original wood can be seen. Also, **brown coal.** [French *lignite,* from Latin *lignum* wood; because of its woody texture and color.]

lig·num vi·tae (lig'nəm vī'tē) **1.** any of a small group of evergreen trees and shrubs, genus *Guaiacum,* found in Central America, Mexico, and the West Indies, bearing leathery leaves and small pale purple flowers. **2.** the hard, heavy wood of this tree, having a dark brown color streaked with black and containing an oily resin. [Modern Latin *lignum vitae,* from Late Latin *lignum vītae* literally, wood of life; because it was once thought to have medicinal value.]

li·gro·in (lig'rō in) *n.* a volatile petroleum derivative used as a solvent.

lik·a·ble (lī'kə bəl) *also,* **likeable.** *adj.* of a nature to be liked; pleasing; genial: *a likable person.* —**lik'a·ble·ness,** *n.*

like¹ (līk) *prep.* **1.** having a close resemblance to; similar to: *My cousin looks like me. The house is exactly like the others on the street.* **2.** in the same manner as; with the characteristics of; similar to: *Don't act like a baby.* **3.** corresponding in character to; typical of: *It was like him to forget her birthday.* **4.** such as: *fruit like apples, oranges, and grapes.* **5.** mentally inclined to; desirous of: *I feel like taking a vacation.* **6.** giving promise of; indicative of: *It looks like a long, cold winter.* —*adj.* **1.** having identical or similar form, appearance, or characteristics. **2.** equal or equivalent: *Each child received a like amount.* **3.** bearing a faithful resemblance to the original: *a like portrait.* **4.** *Archaic.* alike: *They are like as twins.* **5.** *Archaic.* likely: *That horse is like to buck.* —*adv. Informal.* **1.** probably; likely: *Like enough she'll arrive today.* **2.** to some extent or degree; somewhat: *I'm tired like.* —*n.* **1.** a person or thing that is considered equal to another; match; counterpart: *We will never see the great actor's like again.* **2.** something of a similar nature (preceded by *the*): *We bought chairs, tables, and the like.* —*conj.* **1.** in a like way to how; as: *This doesn't taste like it should.* **2.** as if; as though: *It looks like I'll be late today.* ➡ The use of the conjunction is generally considered unacceptable in formal speech and writing. [Old English *(ge) līc* similar, alike, equal.]

adj. **Like¹, similar,** and **comparable** mean resembling or agreeing with each other when considered together. **Like** may connote anything from apparently exact correspondence to only slight resemblance: *like parts in a machine, two children of like disposition.* **Similar** means having prominent characteristics in common along with others that are different: *to have similar interests, to have similar tastes in music.*

Comparable connotes enough likeness to make a comparison appropriate: *two makes of car that are comparable in size and price.*

like² (līk) *v.,* **liked, lik·ing.** —*v.t.* **1.** to take pleasure in; enjoy: *to like school.* **2.** to feel affection, tenderness, or fondness for: *I like our new neighbors now that I know them better.* **3.** to wish or desire; prefer: *I'd like another glass of water.* —*v.i.* to have a desire or preference; choose; prefer: *Do what you like.* —*n.* inclination; preference: ➡ usually used in the plural: *to have strange likes and dislikes.* [Old English *līcian* to please.]

-like *suffix* (used to form adjectives from nouns) **1.** resembling or similar to; having the characteristics of: *childlike, squirrellike, shell-like.* **2.** appropriate or fit for; suited to: *ladylike.* [From LIKE¹.]

like·a·ble (lī'kə bəl) *adj.* likable. —**like'a·ble·ness,** *n.*

like·li·hood (līk'lē hŭd') *n.* the fact or condition of being likely to happen; probability: *In all likelihood, I will leave tomorrow.*

like·ly (līk'lē) *adj.,* **-li·er, -li·est. 1.** apparently true; credible; probable: *the most likely explanation.* **2.** having or showing a tendency or possibility: *likely to do something wrong.* **3.** suitable; appropriate: *a likely spot to build a house.* **4.** having a good chance for success; promising: *likely young horses.* —*adv.* probably: *Your friend is most likely very intelligent.* [Old Norse *līkligr* probable.]

like-mind·ed (līk'mīn'did) *adj.* having or sharing similar opinions, tastes, feelings, or ideas.

lik·en (lī'kən) *v.t.* to represent as like; compare.

like·ness (līk'nis) *n.* **1.** the state or quality of being alike; resemblance. **2.** a representation or facsimile, esp. a portrait: *A likeness of their daughter hung above the mantel.* **3.** a semblance or appearance; guise: *Zeus often took on the likeness of animals.*

like·wise (līk'wīz') *adv.* **1.** in a like manner; similarly: *You became angry, and I reacted likewise.* **2.** in addition; moreover.

lik·ing (lī'king) *n.* **1.** favorable regard; inclination; fondness: *a liking for hard-boiled eggs.* **2.** preference or taste: *Your humor is not much to my liking.* [Old English *līcung* pleasure.]

li·lac (lī'lək, -lăk, -lak) *n.* **1.** a purple, pink, or white flower cluster, composed of fragrant, tube-shaped flowers, borne by any of a group of plants, genus *Syringa,* of the olive family. **2.** the shrub or small tree bearing this flower, widely cultivated throughout the world, having oval, heart-shaped, or lance-shaped leaves. **3.** a pale, pinkish purple color characteristic of lilac blossoms. —*adj.* having the color lilac. [Middle French *lilac,* through Spanish and Arabic, from Persian *līlak* bluish, going back to Sanskrit *nīla* dark blue.]

Lil·li·pu·tian (lil'ə pū'shən) *adj.* **1.** of or relating to the island of Lilliput or its inhabitants. In Jonathan Swift's *Gulliver's Travels,* Lilliput is an island inhabited by tiny people, only 6 inches tall. **2. lilliputian.** of small size; tiny; dwarfed.

lilt (lilt) *v.t., v.i.* to sing or play (music) with a light, graceful rhythm. —*n.* **1.** a lively song or tune with a light, graceful rhythm. **2.** a lively, buoyant quality of voice or movement.

lilt·ing (lil'ting) *adj.* having a light, graceful quality: *a lilting tune, a lilting stride.*

lil·y (lil'ē) *n., pl.* **lil·ies. 1.** the showy, trumpet-shaped flower of any of a large group of plants, genus *Lilium,* growing singly or in clusters. Two of the best-known species are the Easter lily and the tiger lily. **2.** the hardy plant bearing this flower, found both wild and cultivated throughout the northern temperate regions of the world, growing directly from an underground bulb. **3.** any of various other plants, as the calla lily or the water lily. **4.** *Heraldry.* a fleur-de-lis, esp. as in the royal coat of arms of France. —*adj.* resembling a lily, as in whiteness, delicacy, or beauty. [Old English *lilie* flower or plant of the genus *Lilium,* from Latin *līlium.*]

lil·y-liv·ered (lil'ē liv'ərd) *adj.* not brave or courageous; cowardly.

lily of the valley *pl.* **lilies of the valley. 1.** a long cluster of small, fragrant, usually white, bell-shaped flowers that grow down one side of the stalk of either of two plants, genus *Convallaria,* of the lily family. **2.** the plant bearing this flower, found both wild and cultivated in many parts of the world, having long oval leaves that grow directly from a rootstock.

**lily of
the valley**

lily pad, a floating leaf of a water lily.

li·ma bean (lī'mə) **1.** the pale green, kidney-shaped seed of a plant, *Phaseolus limensis,* of the pea family, cooked and eaten as a vegetable. **2.** the dwarf bush or stout climbing plant itself,

widely cultivated in the tropics. [From *Lima,* Peru; because it originally came from tropical America.]

limb¹ (lim) *n.* **1.** a part of the body of an animal or human being distinct from the head and torso, used for support, locomotion, grasping, or the like, as an arm, leg, wing, or flipper. **2.** one of the large branches of a tree. **3.** an extension or projecting part or member. **4.** a person or thing that is regarded as a member, extension, or representative of a larger group: *Our group is a limb of the national organization.* **5.** *Informal.* a mischievous child; rascal; imp. [Old English *lim* the part of the body, branch of a tree.] —For Synonyms, see **branch.**
• **out on a limb.** *Informal.* in a difficult, vulnerable, or precarious position: *The newspaper went out on a limb by predicting the results of a close election.*

limb² (lim) *n.* **1.** the apparent edge of a heavenly body: *the southern limb of the sun.* **2.** the expanded upper part of the calyx or corolla of a flower. [Latin *limbus* border.]

lim·ber¹ (lim′bər) *adj.* **1.** bending or flexing easily; pliant: *Dancers keep their legs limber by exercising.* **2.** able to bend or move easily; lithe; nimble: *a limber acrobat.* —*v.t.* to make limber (usually with *up*): *The violinists limbered up their fingers.* —*v.i.* to become limber, esp. by exercising (with *up*): *The football player limbered up before the game.* [Of uncertain origin.] —**lim′ber·ness,** *n.*

lim·ber² (lim′bər) *n.* the detachable front part of a gun or caisson, formerly used to hold boxes of ammunition. [Possibly from French *limonière* wagon with shafts, from *limon* shaft; probably of Celtic origin.]

lim·bic system (lim′bik) a part of the vertebrate brain, believed to control emotion and motivation, located deep within the cerebrum in mammals. [From Latin *limbus* border, edge + -IC; because it is found around the hypothalamus.]

lim·bo (lim′bō) *n.* **1.** *also,* **Limbo.** in Roman Catholic theology, the abode of souls not entitled to enter heaven, but the punishment of hell, esp. those of infants who died before being baptized. **2.** a place or condition of oblivion or neglect to which unwanted, useless, or forgotten people or things are relegated: *The junkyard was a limbo of abandoned cars.* **3.** any place of confinement, esp. a prison. [Medieval Latin *(in) limbo* (on) the border of hell, going back to Latin *in* in + *limbus* border.]

Lim·burg·er (lim′bûr′gər) *n.* a semisoft white cheese having a strong odor and a mild flavor. Also, **Lim·burg cheese** (lim′-bûrg′). [From *Limburg,* Belgian province where it was first made.]

lime¹ (līm) *n.* a white, powdery compound consisting largely of calcium oxide, usually prepared by burning limestone, and used in making cement and as a fertilizer. Also, **quicklime.** —*v.t.,* **limed, lim·ing.** to treat with lime; apply lime to. [Middle English *lime,* from Old English *līm* cement, lime¹.]

lime² (līm) *n.* **1.** the small, oval or round fruit of a citrus tree, *Citrus aurantifolia,* having a thin rind and a juicy, tart pulp. **2.** the thorny evergreen tree bearing this fruit, cultivated in many tropical and subtropical areas of the world, esp. in the West Indies and southern Florida. [French *lime,* from Provençal *limo,* from Arabic *limah,* from citrus fruit.]

lime³ (līm) *n.* linden. [Earlier *line,* going back to Old English *lind* linden.]

lime·kiln (līm′kil′, -kiln′) *n.* a kiln or furnace in which lime is made by burning limestone, shells, or other materials.

lime·light (līm′līt′) *n.* **1.** a conspicuous position before the public; center of interest: *The election victory put the candidate's family in the limelight.* **2.** a strong light used in the theater to illuminate a performer, part of the stage, or the like, originally produced by heating lime to incandescence.

lim·er·ick (lim′ər ik) *n.* a humorous verse form of five anapestic lines of which the first, second, and fifth have three accents and the third and fourth have two accents. It has a rhyme scheme of *aabba.* Example: *There was a young lady of Niger/ Who smiled as she rode on a tiger;/ They returned from the ride/ With the lady inside,/ And the smile on the face of the tiger* (Anon.). [From *Limerick,* Ireland; possibly with reference to the practice at certain social gatherings of singing the refrain "Will you come up to Limerick?" after each guest extemporized nonsense verse.]

lime·stone (līm′stōn′) *n.* a sedimentary rock generally formed by deposition of the calcareous remains of shellfish, corals, and plankton and consisting chiefly of calcium carbonate, used for building stone, and yielding lime when burned.

lime·wa·ter (līm′wô′tər, -wot′ər) *n.* a water solution of calcium hydroxide, used medicinally as an antacid and in the laboratory to test for the presence of carbon dioxide.

lim·ey (lī′mē) *n., pl.* **-eys.** *Slang.* an Englishman, esp. an English sailor. [From the use of *lime* juice in the British navy to prevent scurvy.]

lim·it (lim′it) *n.* **1.** the furthest or utmost range, extent, or boundary; point at which something ends or must end: *to reach the limit of one's patience.* **2.** *also,* **limits.** the boundary of a specified area: *It is illegal to burn piles of leaves within the city limits.* **3.** an amount or quantity established as the maximum allowed: *a speed limit of 15 miles per hour in a school zone.* **4.** in certain gambling games, the maximum amount a player may bet at one time. **5.** *Mathematics.* a finite quantity that the terms of a converging series progressively approach but never reach. —*v.t.* to keep or set within a bound or bounds; restrict; confine: *to limit spending.* [Latin *limit-,* stem of *līmes* boundary.] —**lim′it·a·ble,** *adj.* —**lim′it·er,** *n.*
• **off limits.** prohibited or forbidden.
• **the limit.** *Informal.* a person or thing that approaches or exceeds certain limits, as of credibility or tolerance.

lim·i·ta·tion (lim′i tā′shən) *n.* **1.** something that limits, esp. a restrictive weakness or lack of capacity; limiting condition or circumstance: *to know one's limitations.* **2.** the act of limiting or the state of being limited. **3.** *Law.* a period of time, prescribed by statute, during which an action may be brought and after which no claim will be recognized.

lim·i·ta·tive (lim′i tā′tiv) *adj.* limiting; restrictive.

lim·it·ed (lim′i tid) *adj.* **1.** confined within or having a limit or limits; restricted: *The offer is good for a limited time only.* **2.** lacking imagination, independence, or originality; narrow: *a limited person with few interests.* **3.** having governing powers restricted, as by constitutional law: *a limited monarchy.* **4.** restricted in liability to the amount of capital invested by stockholders: *a limited company.* **5.** (of trains, buses, or other public conveyances) making a restricted number of stops instead of all those along a given route and usually carrying no more than a specified number of passengers. —*n.* a limited train, bus, or other public conveyance.

lim·it·less (lim′it lis) *adj.* having no limits; boundless.

limn (lim) *v.t.* **1.** to paint or draw: *to limn a portrait, to limn a subject in oils.* **2.** to portray in words. [Form of earlier *lumine* to light up, illuminate (manuscripts), modification of Middle French *enluminer,* going back to Latin *illūmināre* to light up, embellish.] —**lim·ner** (lim′nər), *n.*

lim·nol·o·gy (lim nol′ə jē) *n.* the branch of hydrology that deals with fresh waters, esp. lakes and ponds. [Greek *limnē* marsh + -LOGY.] —**lim·no·log·i·cal** (lim′nə loj′i kəl), *adj.* —**lim·nol′o·gist,** *n.*

lim·o (lim′ō) *n., pl.* **-os.** *Informal.* limousine.

Li·moges (li mōzh′) *n.* a variety of fine porcelain manufactured at Limoges, France.

li·mo·nite (lī′mə nīt′) *n.* a hydrous iron oxide mineral, amorphous and varying in color from brown to yellow, sometimes mined as a source of iron. [German *Limonit* literally, meadow ore, from Greek *leimōn* meadow.] —**li·mo·nit·ic** (lī′mə nit′ik), *adj.*

lim·ou·sine (lim′ə zēn′, lim′ə zēn′) *n.* **1.** a large sedan with a partition between the front and back seats, often driven by a chauffeur. **2.** formerly, a large automobile having a closed compartment for passengers, often with the roof extending out over an open driver's seat. **3.** a large automobile used as a commercial passenger vehicle to or from an airport, train station, or the like. [French *limousine* originally, a cloak worn by the people of *Limousin,* former province of central France.]

limp¹ (limp) *v.i.* **1.** to walk lamely, esp. by favoring one leg. **2.** to move or proceed slowly or with difficulty: *The old wagon limped along the dirt road.* —*n.* a lame movement or walk. [Middle English *lympen,* from Old English *limpan.*] —**limp′er,** *n.* —**limp′ing·ly,** *adv.*

limp² (limp) *adj.* **1.** lacking stiffness or firmness; wilted: *After three days, the flowers became limp.* **2.** without force or vigor; weak: *a limp argument.* [Of uncertain origin.] —**limp′ly,** *adv.* —**limp′ness,** *n.*

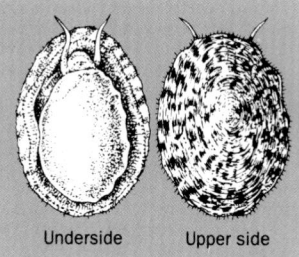

Underside   Upper side

limpet

lim·pet (lim′pit) *n.* any of a group of brownish green saltwater mollusks, order Prosobranchia, having a conical shell and a large muscular

foot that acts as a suction cup, enabling the limpet to cling firmly to rocks. [Old English *lempedu,* from Medieval Latin *lampreda* lamprey, limpet; of uncertain origin.]

lim·pid (lim′pid) *adj.* **1.** so clear as to be seen through; transparent: *a limpid pool of water.* **2.** characterized by clarity or lucidity, as of style: *limpid prose.* [Latin *limpidus* clear.] —**lim·pid′i·ty,** **lim′pid·ness,** *n.* —**lim′pid·ly,** *adv.*

limp·kin (limp′kin) *n.* a large, brown wading bird, *Aramus guarauna,* having a long neck and long bill, and found in Florida, Central America, and South America. Average length: 26 inches (66 centimeters). [LIMP[1] + -KIN; referring to its walk.]

lim·y (lī′mē) *adj.* **lim·i·er,** **lim·i·est.** consisting of, containing, or resembling lime or limestone.

lin·age (lī′nij) *n.* **1.** the number of lines in a piece of printed or written matter. **2.** payment for written work based on the number of such lines.

linch·pin (linch′pin′) *n.* **1.** a pin passed through the end of an axle to keep the wheel in place. **2.** anything that holds a group, argument, or structure together. [Old English *lynis* axle + *pinn* peg.]

Lin·coln's Birthday (ling′kənz) the anniversary of the birthday of Abraham Lincoln, observed as a legal holiday on February 12 or on the third Monday in February in some states of the United States.

lin·dane (lin′dān) a white, powdery, poisonous chemical used to kill weeds and insects. Formula: $C_6H_6Cl_6$ [From T. van der Linden, twentieth-century Dutch chemist + -ANE.]

lin·den (lin′dən) *n.* any of a large group of tall trees, genus *Tilia,* that grow throughout the northern temperate regions of the world, bearing broad, usually heart-shaped leaves and drooping clusters of small, fragrant, pale yellow or white flowers. Also, **lime.** [Probably from Middle English *linden* made of the wood of the linden, from Old English *linden,* from *lind* linden.]

line[1] (līn) *n.* **1.** a continuous mark or stroke, usually straight, having greater length than width: *White lines divided the lanes of the highway.* **2.** anything resembling such a mark, as a band of color, a furrow, or a wrinkle. **3.** the shape around the edge of something; outline, contour, or profile: *the line of someone's chin, the sleek lines of a sports car.* **4.** a limit or boundary, as between two areas; border: *The town is two miles from the state line.* **5.** the division or demarcation between contrasting ideas, qualities, conditions, or the like: *the line between illness and health.* **6.** a number of persons or things arranged in one continuous series; row: *a line outside a movie theater.* **7.** a continuous chronological succession of persons or things related by or as by direct descent: *Elizabeth I was the last ruler of the Tudor line.* **8.** a horizontal group of words or letters printed or written between the margins of a page or column: *Each page has fifty lines of type.* **9.** a short letter; note: *Drop me a line when you know your plans.* **10.** a series of words appearing together as a single unit in poetry: *There are six lines in each stanza of the poem.* **11.** a spoken or sung part of a theatrical presentation, esp. for a single performer: *I had the first line of the second act.* **12.** a course or direction of progress or movement: *a line of march, the line of fire.* **13.** a course of action, conduct, or thought; method: *I couldn't follow the author's line of reasoning.* **14.** *also,* **lines.** a general plan or concept, as of construction: *The house was designed along very simple lines.* **15.** a scope or field of interest, activity, ability, or the like: *Cooking just isn't my line.* **16.** a particular business or activity: *to be in the banking line.* **17.** the stock of merchandise of a particular or related type: *The department store is selling a new line of winter coats.* **18.a.** a wire or series of wires connecting points or stations in a telegraph or telephone system. **b.** a system of such connections. **c.** a connection or contact established between two points by such a system: *The lines between the two capitals were kept open during the crisis.* **19.a.** a system of transportation consisting of public conveyances traveling regularly over an established route: *a steamship line serving the Pacific.* **b.** one branch of such a system of transportation. **c.** a group or company that owns or manages such a system. **20.** the roadbed and track of a railroad: *to lay down a new line over the mountains.* **21.** a piece of rope, cord, or wire: *to hang wet clothes on the line.* **22.a.** *Nautical.* any rope, cable, hawser, or the like used for a specific purpose. **b.** a cord, wire, or tape used in surveying for taking measurements. **c.** a cord with one or more hooks, used for fishing. **23.** a channel, wire, pipe, or other conduit that carries a substance, as gas, water, or electricity, from one point to another: *The electric lines were knocked down in the thunderstorm.* **24.** *Mathematics.* a track thought of as having length but no thickness, as being generated by a moving point, and as consisting of a set of points. It may be straight or curved. **25.** *Music.* one of the five parallel, horizontal marks that form the staff. **26.** *Art.* **a.** the use of strokes and outlines as opposed to shading and color, as in a painting. **b.** the distinctive form or

contours of a work of art. **27.** *Football.* **a.** line of scrimmage. **b.** the row of players who are arranged along the line of scrimmage at the beginning of a play. **28.** *Sports.* the players arranged in parallel formation in any of various games, as hockey. **29.** **lines.** *Military.* the arrangement of fighting forces in closest contact with the opposing forces: *behind enemy lines.* **30.** *Military.* **a.** a formation in which the elements, as troops or ships, are arranged abreast. ➡ distinguished from **column. b.** an extended series of fortifications forming a front. **c.** formerly, military forces that do the actual fighting. **31.** *Informal.* glib, often insincere or untrue talk: *The con artist uses the same line on every potential victim. The thief gave the police a line about being out of town on the day of the burglary.* —*v.,* **lined, lin·ing.** —*v.t.* **1.** to cover with lines: *The student lined the paper.* **2.** to arrange or form a line along; border: *Trees lined the edge of the road.* **3.** *Baseball.* to hit (a ball) so that it travels through the air in an almost completely horizontal path. —*v.i. Baseball.* to hit a line drive: *The batter lined to right field.* [Middle English *line,* partly from Old English *līne* cord, rope, row[1] and partly from Old French *ligne* thread, cord, line of descent (both from Latin *līnea* string, linen thread, from *linum,* flax, linen.]

· **all along the line.** in every way or at every point; including everything: *Are these facts accurate all along the line?*

· **in line. a.** in agreement. **b.** under control: *to keep a large group of children in line.* **c.** among a number of persons arranged in a continuous series or row: *to wait in line for theater tickets.*

· **in line for.** in a deserving or promising position for: *to be in line for a raise.*

· **in line with.** in agreement or conformity with: *to act in line with regulations.*

· **into line.** into agreement or conformity: *to bring one's behavior into line with a policy, to bring a theory into line with the facts.*

· **on a line.** aligned evenly; level.

· **on line.** ready for use or in use: *The computer is now on line.*

· **on the line. a.** in a vulnerable or hazardous position: *The editors put their reputation on the line by defending an unpopular cause.* **b.** paid immediately: *cash on the line.*

· **out of line.** not in conformity with certain accepted standards: *You are out of line for criticizing them publicly.*

· **to draw a (or the) line.** to establish and not go beyond a certain limit.

· **to get (or have) a line on.** *Informal.* to acquire information about.

· **to hold the line.** to maintain a defense or opposition; remain firm or steadfast: *The government tried to hold the line against inflation.*

· **to lay (or put) it on the line.** to speak frankly.

· **to line out.** *Baseball.* to make an out by hitting a line drive that is caught by a fielder.

· **to line up. a.** to arrange in a line: *The teacher lined up the children according to height.* **b.** to form a line: *People lined up in front of the theater.* **c.** to get into a formation: *The football players lined up for the next play.* **d.** to gather or arrange for: *to line up support for a proposed law.* **e.** to get together, as in support of something: *to line up in support of a candidate.* **f.** to obtain the use or services of: *to line up a room for a meeting.*

· **to read between the lines.** to understand something that is implied but not actually stated.

· **to toe the line.** to conform to rules or policy.

line[2] (līn) *v.t.,* **lined, lin·ing. 1.** to cover the inner surface of: *The tailor lined the jacket with silk.* **2.** to supply or fill: *The shelves were lined with books.* **3.** to serve or be used as a lining for: *Family portraits lined the walls.* [Middle English *lynen* to cover the inner surface of, from *lin* flax, linen, from Old English *lin,* going back to Latin *linum* flax, linen; from the use of linen to line clothing.]

· **to line one's pockets.** to make money, esp. illegally.

lin·e·age (lin′ē ij) *n.* **1.** direct descent from an ancestor; pedigree. **2.** those persons descended from a common ancestor collectively; family. [Old French *lignage* all those descended from the same line, from *ligne* line of descent. See LINE[1].]

lin·e·al (lin′ē əl) *adj.* **1.** being in the direct line of descent: *a lineal heir to a throne.* **2.** of, relating to, or based upon direct descent; hereditary: *a lineal right to a title.* **3.** linear. [Late Latin *līneālis* relating to a line, from Latin *līnea* line[1], linen thread.] —**lin′e·al·ly,** *adv.*

lin·e·a·ment (lin′ē ə mənt) *n.* **1.** a feature, detail, or contour of the face or body. **2.** a distinctive feature or quality. [Latin *līneāmentum* feature, delineation, from *līneāre* to reduce to a straight line.]

lin·e·ar (lin′ē ər) *adj.* **1.** of or relating to a line or lines. **2.** consisting of or involving the use of lines. **3.** extended in a line or lines. **4.** extending in one dimension only; relating to length. **5.** resembling a line; long and narrow. **6.** *Mathematics.* **a.** (of the

relationship between two variables) directly proportional. **b.** having to do with linear equations. [Latin *lineāris* relating to a line, from *līnea* linen thread, line¹.] —**lin·e·ar·i·ty** (lĭn′ē ăr′ĭ tē), *n.* —**lin′e·ar·ly,** *adv.*

linear accelerator, a particle accelerator in which charged subatomic particles are propelled in a straight line by an electric field that accelerates the particles to increasingly higher energies.

linear equation *Mathematics.* an algebraic equation of the first degree, as $x + y + 5 = 0$ or $x + 6 = 0$. The graph of such an equation is a straight line.

linear function, a polynomial function in which the highest degree term in the variable or variables is of the first degree.

linear measure 1. measurement by length. **2.** a unit or system of units for measuring length. For Weights and Measures table, see **weight.**

linear programming, a method of solving operational problems by stating two or more variables simultaneously as linear functions and calculating the best solution subject to given limitations.

line·back·er (līn′băk′ər) *n. Football.* a defensive player whose position is directly behind the linemen. [LINE¹ + BACK¹ + -ER¹.]

line cut *Printing.* **1.** a printing plate made from a drawing consisting entirely of lines, done by photoengraving. **2.** an illustration printed from such a plate.

line drive *Baseball.* a strongly hit ball that travels through the air in an almost completely horizontal path. Also, **liner.**

line engraving 1. a style of engraving in which effects are produced by using lines of different widths and varying the closeness of their spacing. **2.** a metal plate engraved in this style. **3.** an illustration printed from such a plate.

line graph, a graph in which points representing specific values are plotted and then connected with a series of straight lines or a smooth curve. For illustration, see **graph.**

line·man (līn′mən) *n., pl.* **-men** (-mən). **1.** *also,* **linesman.** a worker who installs or repairs telegraph, telephone, or electric wires. **2.** a worker who inspects railroad tracks. **3.** *Football.* any of the players in the line. **4.** a worker who carries the line, tape, chain, or the like in surveying.

lin·en (lĭn′ən) *n.* **1.** a usually lustrous, durable fabric woven from flax fibers, used for such items as dresses, suits, and tablecloths. **2.** *also,* **linens.** garments or household articles, such as tablecloths, napkins, or sheets, made of linen or similar fabric. —*adj.* made of linen. [Old English *līnen* made of flax, from *līn* flax.]

  •**to wash dirty linen in public.** to make public information that is usually kept confidential because it is unflattering to a group or individual.

line of credit, the maximum amount of credit extended to a customer by a bank, store, or credit card institution.

line officer, an officer of the armed forces who is assigned to a combat unit. ➡ distinguished from **staff officer.**

line of force *Physics.* an imaginary line in a field of force, indicating the direction of force of the field.

line of scrimmage, an imaginary line running across a football field parallel to the goal lines, on which the ball is placed by the referee, a new line being established wherever the ball is ruled dead at the end of a play.

line of sight 1. an imaginary line from an observer's eye to a distant object. **2.** *Electronics.* a straight path, unobstructed by the horizon, between transmitting and receiving antennas.

line printer, a high-speed computer printer that produces an entire line of characters as a unit, rather than a character at a time.

lin·er¹ (lī′nər) *n.* **1.** a ship or airplane operated by a transportation line, esp. a transoceanic passenger ship. **2.** a person or thing that makes lines. **3.** *Baseball.* line drive. [LINE¹ + -ER¹.]

lin·er² (lī′nər) *n.* **1.** something serving as a lining: *a trash can liner.* **2.** a person who lines or fits a lining to something. [LINE² + -ER¹.]

line segment 1. the part of a line between two given points on the line. **2.** a line with a definite point at each end.

lines·man (līnz′mən) *n., pl.* **-men** (-mən). **1.** lineman *(def. 1).* **2.a.** an official in tennis who judges whether the ball falls inside or outside the lines marking the boundaries of the court. **b.** an official in football who measures and marks the yardage gained or lost on a play and keeps count of the downs. **c.** an official who assists the referee in certain other games, as hockey.

line·up (līn′ŭp′) *also,* **line-up.** *n.* **1.a.** an arrangement of persons or things in or as in a line or row. **b.** a number of suspects lined up by the police for the purpose of identification by a crime victim or witness. **2.a.** the players on a team actually participating

in play at any given time during a game. **b.** a list of the players on a team who will play at the start of a game. **c.** the arrangement of the players, as in football, when in position for play.

ling (lĭng) *n., pl.* **ling** or **lings. 1.** a saltwater fish, *Molva vulgaris,* found in the North Atlantic, the largest member of the cod family. Length: to 7 feet (2.1 meters). **2.** any of various related fish, esp. the burbot. [Possibly of Low German origin.]

-ling¹ *suffix* (used to form nouns) **1.** little or young: *duckling, princeling.* **2.** a person or thing that belongs to or is related to or concerned with: *earthling -ling.* [Old English *-ling.*]

-ling² *suffix* (used to form adverbs) in a specified direction, state, or condition: *sideling.* [Old English *-ling.*]

ling·cod (lĭng′kŏd′) *n.* a North Pacific game fish, *Ophiodon elongatus,* not a true cod, having greenish flesh and a long dorsal fin. Length: to 20 inches (51 centimeters). [LING + COD.]

lin·ger (lĭng′gər) *v.i.* **1.** to stay on as if reluctant to leave; delay leaving; tarry: *The fans lingered outside the theater after the concert.* **2.** to proceed at a slow pace; dawdle: *My parents told me not to linger on the way home.* **3.** to continue to exist; endure; persist: *The memory lingers.* **4.** to continue living although very close to death. **5.** to be tardy in action; hesitate; delay: *to linger in obeying an order.* [Middle English *lengeren* to tarry, from *lengen,* from Old English *lengan* to prolong) + -ER⁴.] —**lin′ger·er,** *n.* —**lin′ger·ing·ly,** *adv.*

lin·ge·rie (län′zhə rā′, -rē′, -jə-, lăn′-) *n.* women's underwear, nightgowns, robes, and similar garments. [French *lingerie* underclothing, linen garments, from Old French *linge* linen, from Latin *lineus* linen, from *linum* flax, linen.]

lin·go (lĭng′gō) *n., pl.* **-goes.** *Informal.* language or speech that is strange or difficult to understand by a person who is unfamiliar with it: *sports lingo, political lingo.* [Provençal *lingo, lengo* tongue, speech, from Latin *lingua.*]

ling·on·ber·ry (lĭng′ən bĕr′ē) *n., pl.* **-ries.** cowberry *(defs. 1, 2).* [Swedish *lingon* mountain cranberry (parallel to Old Norse *lyng* heather) + BERRY.]

lin·gua fran·ca (lĭng′gwə frăng′kə) *pl.* **lin·gua fran·cas** or **lin·guae fran·cae** (lĭng′gwē frăn′sē). **1.** a hybrid language, based on Italian, with elements of French, Spanish, Greek, Arabic, and Turkish, formerly used in Mediterranean ports. **2.** any hybrid language used by people who speak different languages, esp. for the purpose of transacting business. [Italian *lingua franca* literally, language of the Franks; *lingua* language, from Latin *lingua* speech, tongue. See FRANK.]

lin·gual (lĭng′gwəl) *adj.* **1.** of or relating to the tongue. **2.** *Phonetics.* articulated chiefly with the tongue. **3.** of language or languages. —*n. Phonetics.* a sound articulated chiefly with the tongue, as *l* or *t.* [Medieval Latin *lingualis* relating to the tongue, from Latin *lingua* speech, tongue.] —**lin′gual·ly,** *adv.*

lin·gui·ne (lĭng gwē′nē) *also,* **lin·gui·ni.** *n.* pasta shaped into long, thin, flat noodles. [Italian *linguine* literally, little tongues, from *lingua* tongue, from Latin *lingua* tongue.]

lin·guist (lĭng′gwĭst) *n.* **1.** a person who is fluent in several languages. **2.** an expert in linguistics. [Latin *lingua* tongue, speech + -IST.]

lin·guis·tic (lĭng gwĭs′tĭk) *adj.* of or relating to language or linguistics. —**lin·guis′ti·cal·ly,** *adv.*

linguistic form, any unit of speech that has meaning, as an affix, word, phrase, or sentence.

lin·guis·tics (lĭng gwĭs′tĭks) *n.* **1.** the comparative study of languages, including their origins, development, and interrelationships; science of language. **2.** the study of a given language, its structure and development, and its relationship to other languages. ➡ used as singular in both defs.

lin·i·ment (lĭn′ə mənt) *n.* a liquid rubbed on the skin to relieve pain or stiffness, as from a bruise or sprain. [Late Latin *linīmentum* ointment, from *linīre* to smear.]

lin·ing (lī′nĭng) *n.* **1.** a surface, layer, or coating covering the inside of something: *the silk lining of a jacket.* **2.** any material used or suitable for this purpose.

link¹ (lĭngk) *n.* **1.** one of the rings or loops of a chain. **2.** something resembling or joined like a link in a chain: *a link of sausage.* **3.** anything that serves to join or connect: *a link with the past.* **4.** a single segment of an interrelated series: *There is a weak link in your argument.* **5.a.** in surveying, a single division of a chain used

a	at	e	end	o	hot	u	up	hw	white		about
ā	ape	ē	me	ō	old	ū	use	ng	song		taken
ä	far	i	it	ô	fork	ü	rule	th	thin	ə	pencil
âr	care	ī	ice	oi	oil	u̇	pull	th	this		lemon
		îr	pierce	ou	out	ûr	turn	zh	measure		circus

as a measure of length, equal to 7.92 inches (20 centimeters). **b.** in engineering, a single division of a chain used as a measure of length, equal to 1 foot (30 centimeters). **6.** chemical bond. **7.** cuff link. —*v.t., v.i.* to join or be joined by or as by a link or links; unite; connect. [Of Scandinavian origin.]

link² (lingk) *n. Archaic.* torch. [Possibly from Medieval Latin *linchinus,* form of *lichinus* candle, wick, from Greek *lychnos* lamp.]

link·age (ling′kij) *n.* **1.** the act of linking or the state of being linked. **2.** a system of interconnected links or mechanical parts. **3.** *Biology.* **a.** sex linkage. **b.** an association of genes on the same chromosome that gives rise to closely related inherited characteristics.

linking verb, a verb that connects a subject with a predicate adjective or noun without expressing action; copula. *Appear, be,* and *seem* are linking verbs. Also, **copulative verb.**

links (lingks) *pl. n.* golf course. [Old English *hlinc* hill.]

link-up (lingk′up′) *n.* **1.** the act of connecting or state of being connected: *to complete the link-up of several TV stations, a link-up of two spacecraft.* **2.** anything that serves to connect or join; link.

Lin·ne·an (li nē′ən) *also,* **Lin·nae·an.** *adj.* of or relating to the Swedish botanist Carolus Linnaeus or to his system of binomial nomenclature.

lin·net (lin′it) *n.* a small finch, *Carduelis cannabina,* of Europe and Asia, having a reddish crown and breast. [Old French *linette,* from *lin* flax, from Latin *līnum* flax, linen; because it eats flaxseeds.]

lin·o·le·ic acid (lin′ə lē′ik) an unsaturated fatty acid, essential to human nutrition, obtained from linseed and peanut oil and other fats and oils and used commercially in paints, varnishes, and other industrial products. Formula: $C_{18}H_{32}O_2$ [Latin *linum* or Greek *linon* flax + OLEIC (ACID).]

lin·o·le·nic acid (lin′ə lē′nik) an unsaturated fatty acid, essential to human nutrition, often obtained in conjunction with linoleic acid and used commercially in paints, varnishes, and other industrial products. Formula: $C_{18}H_{30}O_2$ [LINOL(EIC ACID) + -EN(E) + -IC.]

lin·o·le·um (li nō′lē əm) *n.* **1.** a material used for covering floors, made into sheets or tiles from a mixture of linseed oil, finely ground cork or wood, resins, and pigments, that is applied to a fabric backing, as burlap, canvas, or felt. **2.** any floor covering resembling this material. [Latin *līnum* flax, linen + *oleum* oil.]

Li·no·type (lī′nə tīp′) *n. Trademark.* a typesetting machine, operated by a keyboard, that sets and casts entire lines of type in one piece. —**lin′o·typ′er, lin′o·typ′ist,** *n.*

lin·seed (lin′sēd′) *n.* flaxseed, the source of linseed oil. [Old English *līnsǣd,* from *līn* flax + *sǣd* seed.]

linseed oil, a yellow or brown oil obtained from the seed of certain flax plants, used in making such items as paints, varnish, printing ink, patent leather, and linoleum.

lin·sey-wool·sey (lin′zē wůl′zē) *n., pl.* **-wool·seys.** a strong, coarse, loosely woven fabric of linen and wool or of cotton and wool. [From *Lindsey,* English town where it was first produced + WOOL.]

lint (lint) *n.* **1.** tiny bits of thread or fluff. **2.** a soft, downy or fleecy material obtained by scraping linen fibers, formerly used as a dressing for wounds. [Latin *linteum* linen cloth, going back to *līnum* flax, linen.] —**lint′y,** *adj.*

lin·tel (lin′təl) *n.* a horizontal member spanning an opening, as of a door or window, and supporting the structure above it. [Old French *lintel,* going back to Latin *līmes* (stem *līmit-*) boundary.]

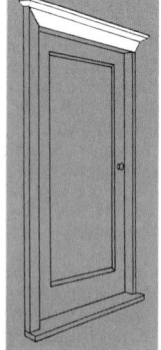

lintel

lint·er (lin′tər) *n.* **1.** a machine for removing the short cotton fibers remaining on cottonseeds after ginning. **2. linters.** the short fibers that adhere to cottonseeds after ginning.

li·on (lī′ən) *n.* **1.** a carnivorous mammal, *Panthera leo,* of the cat family, native to Africa and southern Asia, having a tawny coat of short, coarse hair and a tufted tail. The male has a shaggy mane encircling the neck, head, and shoulders. Length: to 10 feet (3 meters), including tail. **2.** any of various animals related or in some way similar to the lion, as the mountain lion and the sea lion. **3.** a man of great strength or courage. **4.** a famous person, esp. one much sought after socially; celebrity. [Old French *lion* the mammal *Panthera leo,* from Latin *leō* the mammal *Panthera leo,*

lions

courageous person, the constellation Leo, the sign of the zodiac Leo, from Greek *leōn.*]

• **to beard the lion in his den.** to defy or confront a person on his or her own territory.

li·on·ess (lī′ə nis) *n.* a female lion.

li·on·heart·ed (lī′ən här′ted) *adj.* brave; courageous.

li·on·ize (lī′ə nīz′) *v.t.,* **-ized, -iz·ing.** to treat (someone) as very important or as a hero. —**li′on·i·za′tion,** *n.*

lion's share, the largest or best portion.

lip (lip) *n.* **1.** either of the two fleshy folds forming the opening of the mouth. **2.** any projecting part resembling this: *the flared lip of a bell.* **3.** the edge or rim of any opening or cavity: *the lip of a crater, the lip of a glass.* **4.** the position and adjustment of the lips and tongue in playing a wind instrument; embouchure. **5.** *Botany.* a protruding part, occurring either singly or paired, in an unequally divided calyx or corolla, as in a snapdragon or orchid. **6.** *Slang.* insolent talk; impudence: *Don't give me any of your lip.* —*v.t.,* **lipped, lip·ping. 1.** to touch with the lips; apply the lips to: *to lip a glass.* **2.** to utter softly; murmur. **3.** to use the lips in playing (a wind instrument). **4.** *Golf.* to hit the ball so that it stops at the edge of (the hole). —*adj.* **1.** *Phonetics.* articulated primarily by the lips; labial: *a lip consonant.* **2.** of, relating to, or for the lips. **3.** spoken, but not felt or meant; insincere: *lip support.* [Old English *lippa* fleshy fold around the mouth.] —**lip′like′,** *adj.*

• **to button one's lips.** *Slang.* to stop talking.

• **to hang on the lips of.** to listen attentively to every word: *The audience hung on the lips of the speaker.*

• **to keep a stiff upper lip.** to face adversity with courage; show fortitude: *They kept a stiff upper lip during the crisis.*

• **to smack one's lips.** to show pleasure at the thought of something enjoyable.

lip-, form of **lipo-** before a vowel, as in *lipase.*

li·pase (lī′pās, lip′ās) *n.* an enzyme that aids in the breaking down of fats into glycerin and fatty acids. [LIP- + -ASE.]

lip·id (lip′id) *also,* **lip·ide** (lip′īd). *n.* any of a group of organic compounds that consist of the fats and other substances with similar properties and constitute, with proteins and carbohydrates, the principal structural components of living cells. Lipids are insoluble in water, soluble in fat solvents, and greasy to the touch. Also, **lipoid.** [LIP- + -ID².]

lipo- *combining form* of or relating to fat or fatty tissue: *lipoprotein.* [Greek *lipos* fat.]

li·poid (lī′poid, lip′oid) *adj.* of or resembling fat; fatty. Also, **li·poi·dal** (lī poi′dəl, li-). —*n.* lipid. [LIP(O)- + -OID.]

li·po·ma (lī pō′mə, li-) *n., pl.* **-mas** or **-ma·ta** (-mə tə). a benign tumor composed of mature fatty tissue cells. —**li·pom·a·tous** (lī pom′ə təs, -pō′mə-, li-), *adj.*

li·po·pro·tein (lī′pō prō′tēn, -tē in, lip′ō-) *n.* any of a group of compounds consisting of simple proteins joined to a lipid. Lipoproteins in the blood transport cholesterol and triglycerides throughout the body. [LIPO- + PROTEIN.]

lip-read (lip′rēd′) *v.i., v.t.,* **-read** (-red′), **-read·ing.** to interpret or understand (speech) by watching the movements of the speaker's lips.

lip reader, a person who lip-reads.

lip-read·ing (lip′rē′ding) *n.* the technique or practice of interpreting or understanding speech by watching the movements of the speaker's lips.

lip service, the insincere expression of devotion, respect, loyalty, or the like.

lip·stick (lip′stik′) *n.* a crayonlike cosmetic preparation used to color the lips, usually contained in a small cylinder.

lip-sync (lip′singk′) *also,* **lip-synch.** *v.t., v.i.,* **-synced, -sync·ing.** to move one's lips silently in synchronization with the words of (recorded speaking or singing) to give the impression of producing the sounds oneself. —*n.* the act or process of doing this.

liq. **1.** liquid. **2.** liquor.

liq·ue·fac·tion (lik′wə fak′shən) *n.* **1.** the act or process of liquefying or the state of being liquefied. **2.** a liquid state or condition.

liquefied petroleum gas, a mixture of propane, butane, and other volatile hydrocarbons compressed to form a liquid, used as a fuel.

liq·ue·fy (lik′wə fī′) *v.t., v.i.,* **-fied, -fy·ing.** to reduce to or become a liquid. [Middle French *liquefier* to make liquid, from Latin *liquefacere,* from *liquēre* to be fluid + *facere* to make.] —**liq′ue·fi′a·ble,** *adj.* —**liq′ue·fi′er,** *n.*

li·ques·cent (li kwes′ənt) *adj.* becoming or tending to become liquid; melting. [Latin *liquēscēns,* present participle of *liquēscere* to become liquid.] —**li·ques′cence, li·ques′cen·cy,** *n.*

li·queur (li kûr′, -kyūr′) *n.* a strong, sweet-flavored alcoholic beverage; cordial. [French *liqueur* liquid, liqueur, from Latin *liquor* fluid, liquid. Doublet of LIQUOR.]

liq·uid (lik′wid) *n.* **1.** a form of matter that is characterized by the ability of its atoms or molecules to move about freely within a restricted area, but not completely independently of the other atoms or molecules. A liquid can assume the shape of but not necessarily fill its container. ➡ distinguished from **gas** and **solid. 2.** *Phonetics.* the consonant sound of *l* or *r.* —*adj.* **1.** in the form of, or having the properties of, a liquid; capable of flowing or being poured; fluid: *The medicine comes either in a pill or liquid form.* **2.** clear or transparent; limpid. **3.** flowing musically and clearly: *a poet's liquid verses.* **4.** gracefully flowing and freely: *the liquid motion of a dancer's arms.* **5.** consisting of or readily convertible into cash: *liquid assets.* **6.** *Phonetics.* (of a consonant) frictionless and like a vowel. [Latin *liquidus* fluid, clear.] —**liq′uid·ly,** *adv.* —**liq′uid·ness,** *n.*

liquid air, a bluish, transparent or milky liquid mixture formed when air is subjected to great pressure and then cooled by its own expansion, used as a refrigerant.

liq·ui·date (lik′wi dāt′) *v.t.,* **-dat·ed, -dat·ing. 1.** to pay off or settle (a debt or obligation). **2.** to settle the accounts of (a business) by using the assets to pay off the liabilities, as in bankruptcy. **3.** to convert (assets) into cash. **4.** to do away with; dispose of: *Strong censorship helped liquidate opposition to the regime.* **5.** to murder: *The gangster was liquidated by a rival mob.* [Late Latin *liquidātus,* past participle of *liquidāre* to make clear or liquid, from Latin *liquidus* fluid, clear.] —**liq′ui·da′tion,** *n.*

liquid crystal, a substance that is fluid yet possesses some of the molecular order of a crystal. The molecular order and optical properties that depend on it are altered by applying an electrical field, allowing the substance to be used as the basis of display units in digital watches, pocket calculators, and miniature television sets.

li·quid·i·ty (li kwid′i tē) *n.* the state or quality of being liquid.

liquid measure, a system for measuring the volume of liquids. For Weights and Measures table, see **weight.**

liquid oxygen, a cold, highly compressed, liquid form of oxygen, used as an oxidizer for liquid rocket fuel.

liq·uor (lik′ər) *n.* **1.** any alcoholic beverage, esp. one produced by distillation rather than by fermentation. **2.** any liquid substance, as the natural liquid of certain shellfish or the broth or juice produced in cooking. —*v.t. Slang.* to cause to become intoxicated with alcohol (with *up*). [Old French *lic(o)ur* fluid, liquid, from Latin *liquor.* Doublet of LIQUEUR.]

liq·uo·rice (lik′ər is, -ish, lik′rish) licorice.

li·ra (lir′ə) *n., pl. (def. 1)* **li·re** (lir′ā), *(def. 2)* **li·ri** (lir′ē) or **li·ras. 1.** the monetary unit of Italy. **2.** the monetary unit of Malta. **3.** the monetary unit of Turkey. [Italian *lira* Italian monetary unit, from Latin *lībra* pound [1], scales.]

lisle (līl) *n.* **1.** a fine, strong thread, usually made of cotton fibers that have been tightly twisted and given a smooth finish, used principally for such knit items as socks, underwear, and gloves. **2.** a knit fabric made of this thread. —*adj.* made of lisle. [From *Lisle* (now Lille), French town where it was first produced.]

lisp (lisp) *n.* **1.** a speech defect or mannerism in which the sounds of *s* and *z* are mispronounced, as with the sounds of *th* in *think* and *them,* respectively. **2.** the act or habit of speaking with a lisp. **3.** a sound resembling lisping: *the lisp of leaves in the breeze.* —*v.t., v.i.* **1.** to speak or pronounce with a lisp. **2.** to speak or pronounce imperfectly, as a child does. [Middle English *lispen* to speak with a lisp, going back to Old English *wlisp* lisping.] —**lisp′er,** *n.* —**lisp′ing·ly,** *adv.*

lis·some (lis′əm) *also,* **lis·som.** *adj.* **1.** bending easily; limber;

supple. **2.** moving gracefully; nimble; agile. [Form of earlier *lithesome,* from LITHE + -SOME [1].] —**lis′some·ly,** *adv.* —**lis′some·ness,** *n.*

list[1] (list) *n.* an itemized series of names, numbers, words, or the like; catalog; roll: *a list of addresses.* —*v.t.* **1.** to make a list of; itemize: *List the items you want me to buy.* **2.** to enter or include in a list: *Are you listed in the telephone directory?* [French *liste* roll, catalog; of Germanic origin.]

list[2] (list) *n.* a border, edging, or selvage of cloth. —*v.t.* to edge with a list. [Old English *liste* border, strip [2].]

list[3] (list) *n.* an inclination or leaning to one side; tilt. —*v.t., v.i.* to tilt or cause to tilt to one side: *The ship listed 15 degrees in the storm.* [Of uncertain origin.]

list[4] (list) *Archaic. v.t.* to be pleasing to; please; gratify. —*v.i.* to be inclined; choose; wish. [Old English *lystan.*]

list[5] (list) *Archaic. v.i.* to listen. —*v.t.* to listen to; hear. [Old English *hlystan.*]

lis·ten (lis′ən) *v.i.* **1.** to give attention for the purpose of hearing; try to hear: *We listened for the sound of the bell.* **2.** to give heed; pay attention: *The child refused to listen to his mother and did as he pleased.* [Modification (influenced by LIST [5]) of Old English *hlysnan.*] —**lis′ten·er,** *n.*
  ·**to listen in. a.** to listen without participating, esp. to eavesdrop. **b.** to listen to a broadcast.

list·er (lis′tər) *n.* a plow equipped with a double moldboard that throws soil to both sides of the furrow. [From LIST [2].]

list·ing (lis′ting) *n.* **1.** the act of making or entering in a list. **2.** an entry in a list: *a new listing in the telephone directory.* **3.** a list: *They gave us a listing of supplies to buy.*

list·less (list′lis) *adj.* characterized by or exhibiting indifference or lack of energy; apathetic: *I remained weak and listless for weeks after my illness.* [Archaic *list* desire (from LIST [4]) + -LESS.] —**list′less·ly,** *adv.* —**list′less·ness,** *n.*

list price, the price of an item, as published in a catalog or price list, often subject to discounts.

lists (lists) *pl. n.* **1.** a field or area in which knights fought tournaments. **2.** the barriers enclosing such a field or area. **3.** any area or place of combat, controversy, or competition. [Plural of LIST [2]; influenced in meaning by Old French *lice* barrier (probably of Germanic origin).]
  ·**to enter the lists.** to enter a contest or controversy.

lit (lit) a past tense and past participle of light [1] and light [3].

lit. 1. liter. **2.** literal. **3.** literally. **4.** literary. **5.** literature.

lit·a·ny (lit′ə nē) *n., pl.* **-nies. 1.** a form of prayer consisting of a series of petitions spoken by the minister to which the choir or the congregation makes fixed responses. **2.** any long or repetitious series: *a litany of complaints.* [Old French *litanie,* from Late Latin *litanīa* form of prayer, from Greek *litaneiā* entreaty, prayer.]

li·tchi (lē′chē) *n., pl.* **-tchis.** *also,* **lichee. 1.** the small, round, edible fruit of a tree, *Litchi chinensis,* having a brittle, red outer shell and juicy, white flesh. Also, **litchi nut. 2.** the tree producing this fruit, widely cultivated in China. [Chinese (Mandarin) *li chih.*]

lite (līt) *adj.* **1.** having a lower than normal alcohol and, often, calorie content: *a lite wine.* **2.** having less than normal of any of various substances, including coloring or flavoring or substances considered harmful to good health, such as sugar, fat, or tobacco: *a lite cigarette, a lite soft drink.* ➡ considered unacceptable as a variant spelling of **light**[2] except in reference to food, beverages, or tobacco products or in extremely informal writing. [A form of LIGHT [2].]

-lite *combining form* rock or mineral: *rhyolite, cryolite.* [French *-lite,* form of *-lithe,* from Greek *lithos* stone.]

li·ter (lē′tər) *also, British,* **litre.** *n.* the basic unit of capacity in the metric system, equal to 1 cubic decimeter, 1.0567 U.S. liquid quarts, or 0.908 U.S. dry quart. [French *litre,* from obsolete *litron* measure of capacity, from Medieval Latin *litra,* from Greek *lītrī* pound [1].]

lit·er·a·cy (lit′ər ə sē) *n.* **1.** the ability to read and write: *Proof of literacy was a requirement for voting.* **2.** an understanding of a particular subject or field of knowledge: *computer literacy.*

lit·er·al (lit′ər əl) *adj.* **1.** following the exact words of the original; word for word: *The student prepared a literal translation of the German poem.* **2.** based on, following, or giving the exact meaning; not figurative or metaphorical: *the literal sense of a word.* **3.** having a tendency to regard what is said in an exact and unimaginative manner; using or having little imagination: *a literal*

a	at	e	end	o	hot	u	up	hw	white		about
ā	ape	ē	me	ō	old	ū	use	ng	song	ə	taken
ä	far	i	it	ô	oil	ü	rule	th	thin		pencil
âr	care	ī	ice	oi	oil	ū	pull	th	this		lemon
		îr	pierce	ou	out	ûr	turn	zh	measure		circus

person. **4.** restricted to or according to the facts; unexaggerated: *a literal description.* **5.** of, relating to, or expressed by letters. [Late Latin *litterālis* relating to a letter, from Latin *littera* letter of the alphabet.] —**lit′er·al·ness,** *n.*

lit·er·al·ism (lit′ər ə liz′əm) *n.* adherence to the exact meaning in a translation or interpretation. —**lit′er·al·ist,** *n.* —**lit′er·al·is′tic,** *adj.* —**lit′er·al·is′ti·cal·ly,** *adv.*

lit·er·al·ly (lit′ər ə lē) *adv.* **1.** in a literal manner or sense: *Don't take what they say about their fishing trip literally.* **2.** in actual fact; without exaggeration; actually; really: *The city was literally destroyed.* **3.** for all practical purposes; in effect; virtually. **4.** word for word: *to translate a story literally.*

> **Usage** Because **literally** is used to mean "in actual fact," some people consider it incorrect to use it for emphasis in statements such as *The spectators were literally glued to their seats.* In such statements, **literally** can usually be omitted without affecting the meaning or diluting the emphasis. The usage is best avoided except in informal speech and writing.

lit·er·ar·y (lit′ə rer′ē) *adj.* **1.** of or relating to literature: *literary history.* **2.** appropriate to or characteristic of literature: *literary effects.* **3.a.** well versed in or occupied with literature: *a literary family.* **b.** of or relating to literary people: *a literary society.* [Latin *litterārius* relating to reading and writing, from *littera* letter of the alphabet.]

lit·er·ate (lit′ər it) *adj.* **1.** able to read and write. **2.** familiar with literature; well-read; cultured. **3.** having an understanding of a particular subject or field of knowledge. —*n.* **1.** a person who can read and write. **2.** a person who is well-read. [Latin *litterātus* educated; literally, one who knows letters, from *littera* letter.] —**lit′er·ate·ly,** *adv.*

lit·e·ra·ti (lit′ə rä′tē, -rā′tē) *pl. n.* persons who have achieved distinction as scholars or writers.

lit·e·ra·tim (lit′ə rā′tim) *adv.* letter for letter; literally. [Medieval Latin *litteratim* letter by letter, from Latin *littera* letter.]

lit·er·a·ture (lit′ər ə chər, -chŭr′, lit′rə-) *n.* **1.** writings that have artistic merit rather than didactic or expository value; belles-lettres. **2.** a body of writings, as of a particular period, country, language, or style: *children's literature, classical literature, French literature.* **3.** writings dealing with a particular subject: *the literature of science.* **4.** the activity or profession of writing. **5.** printed matter of any kind: *The sales representative gave us some literature on the latest computers.* [Latin *litterātūra* learning, writing, grammar, going back to *littera* letter.]

-lith *combining form* stone; rock: *megalith, batholith.* [French *-lithe,* from Greek *lithos* stone.]

lith·arge (lith′ärj, li thärj′) *n.* a red or yellow oxide of lead, used in glass and pottery glazes. Formula: PbO Also, **lead monoxide.** [Old French *litarge,* from Latin *lithargyrus,* from Greek *lithargyros,* from *lithos* stone + *argyros* silver.]

lithe (līth) *adj.* easily bent; flexible; pliant. Also, **lithe′some.** [Old English *līthe* soft, mild.] —**lithe′ly,** *adv.* —**lithe′ness,** *n.*

lith·i·a (lith′ē ə) *n.* a white oxide of lithium. Formula: Li_2O [Modern Latin *lithia,* going back to Greek *lithos* stone.]

lith·ic (lith′ik) *adj.* **1.** of or relating to stone. **2.** of, relating to, or containing lithium. [Greek *lithikos* relating to stone, from *lithos* stone.]

lith·i·um (lith′ē əm) *n.* **1.** a soft, silvery, metallic element, lightest of the solid elements, used in a variety of metallurgical processes and, in the form of its salts, in medicine. Symbol: Li For tables, see **element.** **2.** a salt of lithium used to treat depression or manic-depressive psychosis, as lithium carbonate (Li_2CO_3). [Modern Latin *lithium,* going back to Greek *lithos* stone; because it was discovered in rock minerals.]

litho- *combining form* stone; rock: *lithograph, lithology.* [Greek *lithos* stone.]

lith·o·graph (lith′ə graf′) *n.* a print made by lithography. —*v.t.* to produce or reproduce by lithography. [From LITHOGRA-PHY.] —**lith′o·graph′ic;** *also,* **lith′o·graph′i·cal,** *adj.* —**lith′o·graph′i·cal·ly,** *adv.*

li·thog·ra·phy (li thog′rə fē) *n.* the art or process of printing from a flat surface, as a smooth stone, on which a design has been drawn with a special grease crayon and to which water and then ink are applied. The ink adheres to the crayon image and is repelled by the moist areas. [Greek *lithos* stone + -GRAPHY.] —**li·thog′ra·pher,** *n.*

li·thol·o·gy (li thol′ə jē) *n.* **1.** the branch of geology that deals with rocks. **2.** the composition or character of a rock. [LITHO- + -LOGY.] —**lith′o·log′ic** (lith′ə loj′ik); *also,* **lith′o·log′i·cal,** *adj.* —**lith′o·log′i·cal·ly,** *adv.*

lith·o·sphere (lith′ə sf ir′) *n.* the crust of the earth. For illustration, see **earth.** [Greek *lithos* stone + SPHERE.]

Lith·u·a·ni·an (lith′ü ā′nē ən) *adj.* of, relating to, or characteristic of Lithuania or its people, language, or culture. —*n.* **1.** a native or citizen of Lithuania. **2.** a person of Lithuanian ancestry. **3.** a language belonging to the Baltic branch of the Indo-European language family.

lit·i·ga·ble (lit′i gə bəl) *adj.* capable of being made the subject of a lawsuit.

lit·i·gant (lit′i gənt) *n.* a party to a lawsuit: *Neither litigant was pleased with the judge's ruling.* —*adj.* engaged in a lawsuit.

lit·i·gate (lit′i gāt′) *v.t.* to make the subject of a lawsuit: *The tenants litigated their complaints against the landlord.* —*v.i.* to engage in a lawsuit. [Latin *lītigātus,* past participle of *lītigāre* to dispute, from *līs* lawsuit, quarrel + *agere* to drive.] —**lit′i·ga′-tor,** *n.*

lit·i·ga·tion (lit′i gā′shən) *n.* **1.** the act or process of engaging in a lawsuit. **2.** a lawsuit.

li·ti·gious (li tij′əs) *adj.* **1.** of or relating to lawsuits. **2.** inclined to engage in lawsuits; fond of litigation. [Latin *lītigiōsus* contentious, from *lītigium* dispute.]

lit·mus (lit′məs) *n.* a dye obtained from any of various lichens that turns blue in alkaline solutions and red in acid solutions. [Old Norse *litmosi* herbs for dyeing, from *litr* color + *mosi* moss.]

litmus paper, paper impregnated with litmus, used as a chemical indicator.

li·to·tes (lī′tə tēz′, li tō′tēz) *n.* a figure of speech in which a positive statement about a person or thing is made by saying the opposite is not true; for example: *Winning the tennis championship was no small achievement.* [Greek *litotēs* literally, simplicity, plainness, from *litos* simple.]

li·tre (lē′tər) *British.* liter.

lit·ter (lit′ər) *n.* **1.** an accumulation of things scattered about carelessly; rubbish; mess. **2.** the young produced by an animal at one birth. **3.** loose straw, hay, or similar material used as bedding for animals. **4.** any absorbent, granular material used to soak up urine and moisture from feces, usually placed in a box or pan to be used by household pets, esp. cats, for urination and defecation. **5.** a vehicle consisting of a couch usually enclosed by curtains and carried by people on their shoulders or by animals. **6.** a stretcher for carrying a sick or injured person. —*v.t.* **1.** to make disordered or untidy by scattering things about carelessly: *to litter a park with trash.* **2.** to scatter carelessly. **3.** to give birth to (young). **4.** to provide (animals) with litter for bedding. —*v.i.* **1.** to scatter things about carelessly. **2.** to give birth to a litter: *The cat littered last night in the garage.* [Old French *litiere* bed, material for bedding, going back to Latin *lectus* bed.]

lit·te·ra·teur (lit′ər ə tûr′) *also,* **lit·té·ra·teur.** *n.* a literary person, such as a writer. [French *littérateur,* from Latin *litterātor* critic, grammarian.]

lit·ter·bug (lit′ər bug′) *n. Informal.* a person who litters public places.

lit·tle (lit′əl) *adj.,* **less** or **less·er** or **lit·tler, least** or **lit·tlest.** **1.** small in size: *A pebble is a little stone.* **2.** short in extent or duration; brief: *a little trip, a little while.* **3.** small in amount or degree; not much: *a little water.* **4.** not of great importance or interest; trivial: *Your problems seem very little.* **5.** lacking in force or intensity; weak: *The child had a plaintive little voice.* **6.** lacking in or having little power or influence: *the little people in society.* **7.** ignoble or petty in nature; mean; narrow: *bigots with pathetically little minds.* **8.** charming or endearing: *The child has the sweetest little smile!* —*adv.,* **less, least. 1.** to a small extent; not much; slightly: *I thought little about it.* **2.** not at all: *He little imagined the consequences.* ➡ used before a verb. —*n.* **1.** a small amount: *I'll have a little.* **2.** a short time or distance: *She walked a little down the road.* [Old English *lȳtel* small, few, trivial.] —**lit′tle·ness,** *n.*

·**in little.** on a small scale.

·**little by little.** by slow degrees; gradually.

·**not a little.** to a substantial degree; very much.

·**to make little of.** to treat as unimportant; disparage.

·**to think little of. a.** to regard as insignificant or worthless; have a low opinion of. **b.** to have no hesitation about: *They thought little of spending thousands of dollars for a vacation.*

Little Bear, Ursa Minor.

Little Dipper, a group of stars in the constellation Ursa Minor that forms the outline of a dipper.

little finger, the finger farthest from the thumb.

Little League, a baseball league for children under thirteen years of age. —**Little Leaguer.**

lit·tle·neck (lit′əl nek′) *n.* the young of the quahog clam, *Venus mercenaria,* usually served on the half shell and eaten raw.

little slam, the winning of twelve tricks in a round of bridge.

little theater, an amateur theater group established by a community or college for the production of live drama.

lit·to·ral (lit′ər əl) *adj.* of or relating to a shore. —*n.* a region lying along a shore, esp. the zone under water at high tide and exposed at low tide. [Latin *lītōrālis* relating to the seashore, from *lītus* seashore.]

li·tur·gi·cal (li tûr′ji kəl) *adj.* 1. of or relating to liturgies. 2. of, relating to, or used in the liturgy or communion service. Also, **li·tur′gic.** —**li·tur′gi·cal·ly,** *adv.*

lit·ur·gy (lit′ər jē) *n., pl.* -**gies.** 1. in various churches, the prescribed form of public worship, esp. the communion service. 2. *also,* **Liturgy.** the communion service. [Late Latin *lītūrgia* the service of the Mass, from Greek *leitourgiā* public service, public worship.]

liv·a·ble (liv′ə bəl) *also,* **liveable.** *adj.* 1. fit to live in; habitable: *The abandoned house is not livable.* 2. worth living; endurable.

live¹ (liv) *v.,* **lived, liv·ing.** —*v.i.* 1. to be alive; have life: *Beethoven lived two hundred years ago.* 2. to continue to exist; remain alive: *to live through a famine.* 3. to support oneself: *to live on one's income.* 4. to obtain needed food; subsist: *to live on fruit.* 5. to make one's home: *to live in a city.* 6. to pass or conduct one's life: *to live well.* 7. to get the fullest enjoyment from life: *After they retired, they really began to live.* 8. to persist in memory or remain in use: *These books will live throughout the ages.* —*v.t.* 1. to pass (one's life): *They lived a life of luxury.* 2. to practice or express in one's life: *to live one's philosophy.* [Old English *lifian, libban* to have life, pass life, maintain life.]

• **to live and let live.** to be tolerant, as of the behavior, customs, or beliefs of others.
• **to live down.** to live so as to atone for or remove the effects of (a careless or stupid remark or mistake).
• **to live in.** (of domestic help) to reside where one works.
• **to live it up.** *Informal.* to have a very good time.
• **to live out.** (of domestic help) to live away from where one works.
• **to live up to.** to abide by: *She tries to live up to her ideals. He will live up to his end of the bargain.*
• **to live with.** to bear with; endure: *You'll simply have to live with the results.*

live² (līv) *adj.* 1. possessing life; living: *The zoo exhibits live animals in their natural habitats.* 2.a. of or relating to the living state or a living being: *the live temperature of a body.* b. filled with life; energetic; lively: *a live party.* 3. of present interest or importance; timely: *a live topic.* 4. burning: *a live coal.* 5. containing an explosive charge: *live ammunition.* 6. carrying electric current. 7. seen or presented while actually occurring, as on the stage or on radio or television: *a live performance, a live broadcast.* 8. having or imparting movement: *a live pulley.* 9. in the natural state, without having been quarried or mined: *live rock.* 10. *Printing.* ready to be used, as type, plates, or copy. —*adv.* during, from, or at an actual performance: *The Olympics will be broadcast live from Europe.* [Short for ALIVE.]

live·a·ble (līv′ə bəl) livable.

live·bear·er (līv′bâr′ər) *n.* any of a group of small, tropical American, freshwater fish, family Poeciliidae, frequently kept as aquarium fish. Included are guppies, mollies, and platy. Also, **topminnow.** —*adj.* of or relating to this group of fish. [Because they bear live young rather than eggs.]

lived (līvd, livd) *adj.* having a certain kind of life or lives. ➡ used in combination, as in *long-lived.*

live·li·hood (līv′lē hůd′) *n.* that which serves to maintain or support life: *Fishing is their livelihood.* [Modification (influenced by LIVELY and -HOOD) of Middle English *livelode* course of life, maintenance, going back to Old English *līf* life + *lād* course.]

live·long (liv′lông′) *adj.* the whole period of; entire: *the livelong night.*

live·ly (līv′lē) *adj.,* -**li·er,** -**li·est.** 1. full of life, energy, or movement; vigorous; active: *a lively walk.* 2. suggesting cheerful energy; sprightly: *a lively tune.* 3. stimulating mental energy; exciting: *a lively debate.* 4. characterized by or indicative of mental keenness, brilliance, or creativity: *a lively imagination.* 5. intensely felt or perceived; vivid; striking: *a lively fear, lively colors.* 6. giving refreshment or vigor; invigorating: *a lively breeze.* 7. springing back quickly; resilient: *a lively tennis ball.* —*adv.* in a lively manner; energetically; vigorously: *to step lively.* [Old English *līflīc* living, vital.] —**live′li·ly,** *adv.* —**live′li·ness,** *n.*

liv·en (lī′vən) *v.t., v.i.* to make or become more cheerful, active, or exciting (usually with *up*).

live oak (līv) any of several evergreen oaks, esp. *Quercus virginiana,* native to the southeastern United States and Cuba.

liv·er¹ (liv′ər) *n.* 1. a large, reddish brown gland that secretes bile and performs metabolic functions. It is the largest gland in the human body. 2. the liver of certain other vertebrate animals, used as food. [Old English *lifer.*]

liv·er² (liv′ər) *n.* a person who lives in a certain manner: *a fast liver, an easy liver.* [LIVE¹ + -ER¹.]

liver fluke, any of various parasitic flatworms, esp. *Fasciola hepatica,* that invade the liver and bile ducts.

liv·er·ied (liv′ə rēd, liv′rēd) *adj.* dressed in livery: *liveried servants.*

liv·er·leaf (liv′ər lēf′) *n.* hepatica.

Diaphragm · Liver · Stomach · Small intestine

liver¹

liver spot, a flat, uniformly colored, brown, red, or black spot appearing on exposed skin areas starting in middle age. [Because it was erroneously believed to result from malfunctioning of the liver.]

liv·er·wort (liv′ər wûrt′) *n.* 1. any of various primitive, moss-like plants, class Hepaticae, mostly lacking stems and leaves, and found throughout the world, esp. in damp, shady areas. 2. hepatica.

liv·er·wurst (liv′ər wûrst′, -wûrst′) *n.* a sausage made of or consisting mostly of liver, esp. pork liver. [Partial translation of German *Leberwurst,* from *Leber* liver + *Wurst* sausage.]

liv·er·y (liv′ə rē, liv′rē) *n., pl.* -**er·ies.** 1. a uniform provided for servants. 2. any distinctive garb or uniform worn by members of a group or profession. 3. a characteristic dress or outward appearance. 4. the stabling and feeding of horses for pay. 5. livery stable. [Old French *livree* something delivered (as a servant's clothes), from *livrer* to deliver, from Late Latin *līberāre* to give freely, from Latin *līberāre* to set free.]

liv·er·y·man (liv′ə rē mən, liv′rē-) *n., pl.* -**men** (-mən). a person who owns or works in a livery stable.

livery stable, a stable where horses are cared for and let out for hire, with or without vehicles.

lives (līvz) the plural of **life.**

live·stock (līv′stok′) *n.* domestic animals raised or kept for use or profit, as cattle, sheep, or pigs. ➡ used as singular or plural.

live wire (līv) 1. a wire carrying electric current. 2. *Informal.* a vigorously energetic, forceful, or alert person.

liv·id (liv′id) *adj.* 1. having a pale coloration, as from strong emotion. 2. extremely angry; furious; enraged. 3. having a grayish blue coloration from a contusion; black-and-blue. [Latin *līvidus* bluish.] —**liv′id·ly,** *adv.* —**liv′id·ness,** *n.*

liv·ing (liv′ing) *adj.* 1. having life; being alive. 2. of or relating to life or suitable for life: *Living conditions in the city are sometimes unbearable.* 3. of or relating to persons now alive: *in living memory.* 4. still valid, active, or in use: *a living faith, a living language.* 5. very. ➡ used as an intensifier: *The noise scared the living daylights out of me.* 6. true to life; lifelike: *That statue is the living image of the mayor.* —*n.* 1. the fact or state of being alive. 2. that which serves to maintain or support life; livelihood: *to earn a living as a carpenter.* 3. a manner of life: *clean living, plain living.* 4. *British.* benefice. 5. **the living.** persons now alive.

living room, a room in a home for general family use or for receiving guests.

living wage, a wage sufficient to maintain one's existence and provide those things needed for the well-being of one's dependents.

living will, a document in which a person states whether he or she wishes to be kept alive by extraordinary medical treatment in case of incurable illness, permanent brain damage or unconsciousness, or the like. Some states recognize living wills as legal documents.

li·vre (lē′vər, -vrə) *n.* a former coin of France, replaced by the franc. [French *livre* pound¹, unit of money, from Latin *libra* pound¹, scales.]

liz·ard (liz′ərd) *n.* any of a group of scaly reptiles, suborder Sauria, typically having a long, narrow body, four legs, and a tapering tail, found in tropical and temperate regions. [Old French *lesard,* from Latin *lacertus.*]

-'ll *suffix* (used in contractions) 1. will: *I'll call you tonight.* 2. shall: *I'll be glad to help you.*

a	at	e	end	o	hot	u	up	hw	white	ə	about
ā	ape	ē	me	ō	old	ū	use	ng	song		taken
ä	far	i	it	ô	fork	ü	rule	th	thin		pencil
âr	care	ī	ice	oi	oil	u̇	pull	th	this		lemon
		îr	pierce	ou	out	ûr	turn	zh	measure		circus

ll., lines.

LL, Late Latin.

lla·ma (lä′mə) *n.* a cud-chewing, South American mammal, *Lama glama,* related to the camel, having a thick, woolly coat and used chiefly as a pack animal. Height: 4 feet (1.2 meters) at the shoulder. [Spanish *llama;* of Quechuan origin.]

lla·no (lä′nō) *n., pl.* **-nos.** a level grassland or plain, found esp. in South America. [Spanish *llano* level, level, from Latin *plānus* level.]

llama

LL.B., Bachelor of Laws.

LL.D., Doctor of Laws.

lo (lō) *interj.* look; see: *Lo and behold!* [Old English *lā.*]

loach (lōch) *n.* any of a group of freshwater fish, family Cobitidae, found in inland waters of Europe and Asia, used in aquariums. [Old French *loche;* of uncertain origin.]

load (lōd) *n.* **1.** something that is carried by a vehicle, as a truck, or borne by a person or animal. **2.** the amount or quantity that can be carried by any of these means, taken as a unit of measure. **3.** something wearisome, oppressive, or grievous: *a load of sorrow, a load of guilt.* **4.** the amount of work a person or machine is expected to do: *The secretary's typing load was twenty letters a day.* **5.** the weight or pressure supported by a structure or part. **6.** a charge for a firearm. **7.** the external resistance overcome by an engine or other power source. **8.** *usually,* **loads.** *Informal.* a great quantity or number: *My parents have loads of friends.* —*v.t.* **1.** to put a load on or in: *to load a shelf with books.* **2.** to place (something) on or in a conveyance: *to load cattle in a boxcar.* **3.** to weigh down; oppress: *The dictator loaded the people with taxes.* **4.** to supply abundantly or in excess: *Relatives loaded the graduate with gifts.* **5.** to alter or add weight to, esp. in order to deceive or commit fraud: *The manufacturer loaded the cereal with sugar and chemicals.* **6.** to slant so as to prejudice the response or outcome: *to load a question, to load evidence.* **7.a.** to place something, as film or a tape cartridge, into (an apparatus, as a camera or tape recorder). **b.** to place (something) into an apparatus: *to load film into a camera, to load a computer disk.* **c.** *Computers.* to transfer (a program or data) from storage into memory. **8.** to place a charge in (a firearm). —*v.i.* **1.** to put on or take on a load: *The ship has finished loading. This camera loads easily.* **2.** to place a charge in a firearm: *The gunners loaded and fired.* **3.** to enter, as in a mass: *We all loaded into the elevator.* —*adj.* of or relating to a sales commission paid on purchase of a mutual fund: *a low-fee load fund.* [Old English *lād* way, journey, carrying.] —**load′er,** *n.*

• **to get a load of.** *Slang.* to look at or listen to.

load·ed (lō′did) *adj.* **1.** carrying a load: *The cart was loaded with fruit.* **2.** holding something, as film or ammunition: *a loaded gun.* **3.** full of added accessories, features, ingredients, or the like: *an automobile loaded with optional equipment, a pizza loaded with onions, mushrooms, and sausage.* **4.** altered or weighted, as fraudulent dice. **5.** slanted so as to prejudice the response or outcome: *a loaded question.* **6.** *Slang.* intoxicated. **7.** *Slang.* extremely wealthy.

load·star (lōd′stär′) lodestar.

load·stone (lōd′stōn′) lodestone.

loaf[1] (lōf) *n., pl.* **loaves.** **1.** bread molded and baked as one mass. **2.** any molded portion of food: *a meat loaf.* [Middle English *lof,* from Old English *hlāf* bread, loaf of bread.]

loaf[2] (lōf) *v.i.* **1.** to spend time doing nothing; idle. **2.** to work lazily or inefficiently: *to loaf on the job.* —*v.t.* to spend (time) doing nothing (often with *away*): *The teenagers loafed the afternoon away.* [Possibly from LOAFER.]

loaf·er (lō′fər) *n.* **1.** a person who loafs; idler. **2.** a casual, moccasinlike shoe made to slip onto the foot easily. Trademark: **Loafer.** [Probably a contraction of *land-loafer,* from German *landläufer* vagabond, from *land* land + *läufer* runner.]

loam (lōm) *n.* **1.** a fertile soil that is a mixture of clay, sand, and silt, generally rich in humus and other forms of organic matter. **2.** a mixture of clay, sand, and straw used in making bricks and molds and in plastering walls. —*v.t.* to cover, fill, or coat with loam. [Old English *lām* clay, earth.] —**loam′i·ness,** *n.* —**loam′y,** *adj.*

loan (lōn) *n.* **1.** an act or instance of lending. **2.** something lent, esp. a sum of money lent at interest. —*v.t., v.i.* lend. [Old Norse *lān* a lending.]

• **on loan.** borrowed, as from a museum, for use or display at another location.

Usage Strictly speaking, **loan** is used only as a noun and **lend** as the verb: *We applied for a loan to buy a new car. The bank agreed to lend us the money.* Over time, however, **loan** has come to be used more frequently in the sense of "lend," as in *The bank has agreed to loan us the money to buy a new car,* and it is gradually becoming more acceptable.

loan shark *Informal.* a person who lends money at an excessive or illegal rate of interest.

loan·word (lōn′wûrd′) *also,* **loan-word, loan word.** *n.* a word taken into one language from another. *Pizza, mosquito, pecan,* and *shampoo* are loanwords from Italian, Spanish, Algonquian, and Hindi, respectively. [Translation of German *Lehnwort.*]

loath (lōth, lōth) *also,* **loth.** *adj.* reluctant; unwilling: *I'm loath to borrow money unless absolutely necessary.* [Old English *lāth* hateful, hostile.]

loathe (lōth) *v.t.,* **loathed, loath·ing.** to regard with disgust, hate, or strong dislike; feel repugnance toward; detest. [Old English *lāthian* to be hateful.] —For Synonyms, see **hate.**

loath·ing (lō′thing) *n.* a feeling of disgust, hatred, or strong dislike; repugnance; detestation. —**loath′ing·ly,** *adv.*

loath·ly[1] (lōth′lē, lōth′-) *adj.* loathsome. [Old English *lāthlīc.*]

loath·ly[2] (lōth′lē, lōth′-) *adv.* unwillingly. [Old English *lāthlīce* dreadfully, shockingly.]

loath·some (lōth′səm, lōth′-) *adj.* causing loathing; repulsive; offensive. —**loath′some·ly,** *adv.* —**loath′some·ness,** *n.*

loaves (lōvz) the plural of **loaf**[1].

lob (lob) *v.t.,* **lobbed, lob·bing.** **1.** in tennis, to hit (a ball) high and usually far to the back of the opponent's court. **2.** in some other games, to throw (a ball) slowly and sometimes in a high arc. —*n.* a ball hit or thrown in such a manner. [Possibly of Low German origin.]

lo·bar (lō′bər, -bär) *adj.* of or relating to a lobe, as of the lungs.

lo·bate (lō′bāt) *adj.* having or resembling a lobe.

lo·ba·tion (lō bā′shən) *n.* a lobe or lobate formation.

lob·by (lob′ē) *n., pl.* **lob·bies.** **1.** an entrance hall, as in an apartment house, hotel, or theater. **2.** a person or group of persons who seek to influence legislative and administrative decisions of government. —*v.,* **lob·bied, lob·by·ing.** —*v.i.* to try to influence legislators or government administrators to favor a particular group or interest. —*v.t.* **1.** to promote the passage of (legislation) or adoption of (a policy) by lobbying. **2.** to try to influence (legislators or government officials). [Medieval Latin *lobia* covered walk, portico; of Germanic origin.]

lob·by·ist (lob′ē ist) *n.* a person or organization that seeks to influence legislators or government officials to favor a particular group or interest. —**lob′by·ism,** *n.*

lobe (lōb) *n.* a rounded division or projection, as of a bodily organ, leaf, or external ear. [Late Latin *lobus* hull, pod, from Greek *lobos* lobe of the ear, liver[1], or lung.]

lobed (lōbd) *adj.* having a lobe or lobes.

lobe-fin (lōb′fin′) *n.* any of an ancient freshwater and marine group of fish, Crossopterygia, characterized by thick, fleshy paired fins, and extinct except for the coelacanth. The group is considered to include the freshwater ancestors of land vertebrates. Also, **lobe-finned fish.**

lo·bel·ia (lō bēl′yə) *n.* any of a large group of plants, genus *Lobelia,* found in many parts of the world, having oval or lance-shaped leaves and showy blue, red, white, violet, or yellow flowers. [Modern Latin *Lobelia,* from Matthias de *Lobel,* 1538-1616, Flemish botanist.]

lob·lol·ly pine (lob′lol′ē) **1.** an evergreen tree, *Pinus taeda,* of the pine family, growing in the southern United States. **2.** the wood of this tree.

lo·bot·o·my (lō bot′ə mē) *n., pl.* **-mies.** an operation that involves severing the nerve connections between one lobe of the brain and the lower brain center, performed to relieve certain mental disorders.

lob·ster (lob′stər) *n.* **1.** any of several edible saltwater crustaceans having five pairs of walking legs, including one pair of large pincer claws, and a hard, mottled, dark green body, esp. the American lobster, *Homarus americanus,* found in North Atlantic waters. **2.** spiny lobster. **3.** the flesh of a lobster, used as food. —*v.i.* to fish for lobsters. [Old English *loppestre* saltwater crustacean, from Latin *locusta* saltwater crustacean, locust.]

lobster pot, a slatted, usually wooden trap, used to catch lobsters.

lob·ule (lob′ūl) *n.* **1.** a small lobe. **2.** a subdivision of a lobe. —**lob·u·lar** (lob′yə lər), *adj.*

lo·cal (lō′kəl) *adj.* **1.** of, relating to, or involving a particular place: *a local newspaper, local politics.* **2.** limited or restricted in area; narrow: *The writer's fame is local rather than national.* **3.** (of

a means of public transportation) stopping at all stations: *a local train.* **4.** relating to or affecting a particular part or organ of the body: *a local inflammation, local anesthesia.* **5.** of or relating to position in space; spatial. —*n.* **1.** a train, bus, or other means of public transportation that stops at all the stations along its route. **2.** a branch or chapter of an organization, esp. a labor union. **3.** a person who lives in a particular area: *Ask one of the locals for directions.* [Late Latin *localis* relating to a place, from Latin *locus* place.] —**lo′cal·ly,** *adv.*

local color, the character or atmosphere of a particular place or period, as found in works of literature.

lo·cale (lō kal′) *n.* a particular place, esp. with reference to events or circumstances connected with it; setting. [French *local* place, relating to a place, from Late Latin *localis.* See LOCAL.]

local government **1.** the exercise of control or authority over the affairs of a county, town, or other small political unit by its own people. **2.** the elected officials of a county, town, or other small political unit.

lo·cal·ism (lō′kə liz′əm) *n.* **1.** a word, pronunciation, expression, or manner of speech peculiar to a particular place. **2.** a custom characteristic of a particular place. **3.** provincialism *(def. 1).*

lo·cal·i·ty (lō kal′i tē) *n., pl.* **-ties.** a place, region, or district and its surroundings.

lo·cal·ize (lō′kə līz′) *v.,* **-ized, -iz·ing.** —*v.t.* **1.** to restrict to a particular place: *to localize an infection.* **2.** to assign to a particular place; find the place of origin of: *to localize a folk song.* —*v.i.* to become localized: *Iodine localizes in the thyroid.* —**lo′cal·i·za′tion,** *n.*

local option, the right of a local government to allow or prohibit something, as the sale and distribution of liquor.

lo·cate (lō′kāt, lō kāt′) *v.,* **-cat·ed, -cat·ing.** —*v.t.* **1.** to discover the exact place of: *The police were able to locate the lost child.* **2.** to assign a particular place to; fix the position of: *The captain located the ship's position on the chart.* **3.** to establish in a particular place; settle: *The company located its branch office in the suburbs.* —*v.i.* to establish oneself in a particular place; settle: *to locate in California.* [Latin *locātus,* past participle of *locāre* to place, put.] —**lo·cat′a·ble,** *adj.* —**lo′cat·er,** *n.*

lo·ca·tion (lō kā′shən) *n.* **1.** the act of locating or the state of being located. **2.** an exact position; place: *The police discovered the location of the thief's hideout.* **3.** a place where something, as a store, factory, or home, might be established; site: *a perfect location for a drugstore.* **4.** a place away from a motion-picture studio, used in filming.

• **on location.** away from a motion-picture studio: *Two scenes were shot on location in Florida.*

loc·a·tive (lok′ə tiv) *n.* **1.** *Grammar.* the case in Latin and certain other Indo-European languages that indicates the place in which someone or something is located. **2.** a word or construction in this case. —*adj.* of, relating to, or designating this case. [From Latin *locus* place, on the model of VOCATIVE.]

loc. cit., in the place cited. ➡ used chiefly in footnotes. [Abbreviation of Latin *locō citātō.*]

loch (lok, loкн) *n. Scottish.* **1.** lake. **2.** a narrow arm of the sea, esp. one partially landlocked. [Gaelic *loch* lake.]

lo·ci (lō′sī) the plural of **locus.**

a **lock** in the Panama Canal

lock¹ (lok) *n.* **1.** a mechanical device used to fasten something, as a door. **2.** any device that fastens or secures something in place, as a brake to keep a wheel from turning. **3.** an enclosure in a canal

or other waterway with gates at each end, in which the water level can be changed to raise or lower vessels. **4.** gunlock. **5.** air lock. **6.** any of several holds in wrestling. —*v.t.* **1.** to fasten or secure with a lock or locks: *Don't forget to lock the door.* **2.** to shut up or confine securely (often with *up*): *I locked myself in my room to study. The guards locked the prisoners into their cells.* **3.** to join or link together firmly: *He locked his arm in hers.* **4.** to grip firmly, as in an embrace. —*v.i.* **1.** to become fastened or secured with a lock or locks: *This door locks automatically when closed.* **2.** to become joined or linked together firmly: *The bumpers of the two cars locked.* [Old English *loc* door fastener, bolt¹.]

• **lock, stock, and barrel.** *Informal.* entirely; completely.

• **to lock out.** **a.** to shut out by or as by locking. **b.** to keep (employees) from working by closing a plant or business.

• **under lock and key.** securely confined or put away.

lock² (lok) *n.* **1.** a tuft or strand of hair; tress. **2. locks.** the hair of the head. **3.** a tuft of wool, cotton, or flax. [Old English *locc* tress.]

lock·age (lok′ij) *n.* **1.** the operation of a lock or locks in a canal during the passage of a vessel. **2.** the toll for such passage.

locker (lok′ər) *n.* **1.** an enclosed compartment, cabinet, or chest, usually of metal, that can be locked. **2.** a refrigerated compartment used to store frozen foods. **3.** a person or thing that locks.

locker room, a room in a building, as in a gymnasium or clubhouse, equipped with lockers.

lock·et (lok′it) *n.* a small case holding a picture, a lock of hair, or other keepsake, usually worn on a chain. [Old French *loquet* door latch, diminutive of Old French *loc* latch; of Germanic origin.]

lock·jaw (lok′jô′) *n.* **1.** tetanus. **2.** spasms of the muscles of the jaw that make it difficult to open the mouth, an early symptom of tetanus.

lock·out (lok′out′) *n.* the closing of a plant or a business by an employer until certain conditions are met by employees.

lock·smith (lok′smith′) *n.* a person who makes, installs, and repairs locks.

lock·step (lok′step′) *n.* a marching step in which each person follows exactly the step of the person directly ahead.

lock stitch, a stitch made by a sewing machine in which two threads are interlocked at short intervals.

lock·up (lok′up′) *n.* **1.** jail. **2.** the act of locking up or the state of being locked up.

lo·co (lō′kō) *n., pl.* **-cos.** locoweed. —*adj. Informal.* crazy; insane. [Spanish *loco* insane; of uncertain origin.]

lo·co·mo·tion (lō′kə mō′shən) *n.* the act or capability of moving from place to place. [Latin *locō,* ablative of *locus* place + MOTION.]

lo·co·mo·tive (lō′kə mō′tiv) *n.* a self-propelled vehicle used to haul railroad cars. —*adj.* of, relating to, or capable of locomotion.

lo·co·mo·tor (lō′kə mō′tər) *adj.* **1.** locomotive. **2.** relating to or affecting the organs of the body involved in locomotion: *the locomotor system.*

locomotor ataxia, a disease of the spinal cord and other parts of the nervous system, usually caused by syphilis and characterized by loss of muscular control, atrophy of certain muscles and nerves, and sharp pains.

lo·co·weed (lō′kō wēd′) *n.* any of several plants of the pea family, genera *Astragalus* and *Oxytropis,* found in the Rocky Mountain and prairie regions of the western United States, containing a poison that is harmful to range animals. Also, **loco.** [Spanish *loco* insane (of uncertain origin) + WEED¹.]

loc·u·lus (lok′yə ləs) *n., pl.* **-li** (-lī′). any small cavity or compartment, esp. as in plant or animal tissue. Also, **loc·ule** (lok′ūl). [Modern Latin *loculus,* from Latin *loculus* small place, diminutive of *locus* place.]

lo·cum te·nens (lō′kəm tē′nənz) *pl.* **lo·cum te·nen·tes** (lō′kəm tə nen′tēz). *British.* a person who substitutes for another, esp. for a doctor or a member of the clergy. [Medieval Latin *locum tenens* deputy; literally, one holding the place (of another), going back to Latin *locus* place + *tenēre* to hold.]

lo·cus (lō′kəs) *n., pl.* **lo·ci.** **1.** place; locality. **2.** *Mathematics.* any set of points that satisfies one or more specified conditions. *The locus of all points in a plane that are equidistant from a given point is a circle.* [Latin *locus* place.]

lo·cust (lō′kəst) *n.* **1.** any of several short-horned grasshoppers,

a	at	e	end	o	hot	u	up	hw	white		about
ā	ape	ē	me	ō	old	ū	use	ng	song		taken
ä	far	i	it	ô	fork	ü	rule	th	thin	ə	pencil
âr	care	ī	ice	oi	oil	u̇	pull	th	this		lemon
				ou	out	ûr	turn	zh	measure		circus
			ir	pierce							

family Locustidae, often migrating in large swarms that destroy much of the vegetation in their path. **2.** any of certain cicadas, esp. the seventeen-year locust. **3.** any of a group of North American shrubs and trees, genus *Robinia,* of the pea family, having compound leaves and showy clusters of flowers. **4.** any of various related trees, as the honey locust. [Latin *locusta* grasshopper, lobster.]

lo·cu·tion (lō kū′shən) *n.* **1.** a form of verbal expression; phrase. **2.** a style or manner of verbal expression; phraseology. [Latin *locūtiō* way of speaking, speech.]

lode (lōd) *n.* a deposit containing valuable minerals, often found in a rock fissure. [Old English *lād* way, course.]

lode·star (lōd′stär′) *also,* **loadstar.** *n.* **1.** a star that serves as a guide to navigators, esp. the star Polaris. **2.** a focus of attention or hopes; guiding principle. [Middle English *lodesterre,* from *lode* way, course (from Old English *lād*) + *sterre* star. See STAR.]

lode·stone (lōd′stōn′) *also,* **loadstone.** *n.* a variety of magnetite possessing strong magnetic properties.

lodge (loj) *n.* **1.** a small house, cabin, or hut, often secluded and of rustic appearance, used esp. as a temporary abode during a vacation or hunting trip. **2.** a small house or cottage on the grounds of a park or estate: *a caretaker's lodge.* **3.a.** a branch of a fraternal or secret society. **b.** the meeting place for such a branch. **4.a.** a hut or dwelling of certain North American Indians. **b.** the inhabitants of a lodge. **5.** the den of certain wild animals, esp. beavers. —*v.,* **lodged, lodg·ing.** —*v.t.* **1.** to provide with a temporary place to stay, as for the night. **2.** to rent a room or rooms to: *to lodge students in one's home.* **3.** to bring formally to an authority: *to lodge a complaint in court.* **4.** to fix, settle, or embed: *to lodge an arrow in a tree.* **5.** to place for safekeeping: *to lodge money in a bank.* **6.** to confer (authority or power) on; vest (with *with* or *in*). —*v.i.* **1.** to have a temporary place to stay: *to lodge with friends for the night.* **2.** to occupy a rented room or rooms. **3.** to be deposited or embedded: *A pebble lodged in my shoe.* [Old French *loge* shed, small house; of Germanic origin.]

lodge·ment (loj′mənt) lodgment.

lodge·pole pine (loj′pōl′) any of several varieties of a tall, slender pine, *Pinus contorta,* of western North America, having stout, paired needles and short, egg-shaped cones.

lodg·er (loj′ər) *n.* a person who rents a room or rooms, as in a private home.

lodg·ing (loj′ing) *n.* **1.** a temporary place to stay, as for the night. **2. lodgings.** a rented room or rooms, as in a private home.

lodg·ment (loj′mənt) *also,* **lodgement.** *n.* **1.** the act of lodging or the state of being lodged. **2.** something deposited or embedded. **3.** *Military.* a position gained from the enemy.

loess (les, lō′əs, lus) *n.* a yellowish brown, fine-grained deposit of silt, commonly found in river valleys. [German *Löss,* from Swiss German *lösch* loose.] —**lo·ess·i·al** (lō es′ē əl), *adj.*

loft (lôft, loft) *n.* **1.** the upper story of a building, as a warehouse, often used as a storeroom or workroom. **2.** a room or space directly beneath a roof; attic. **3.** a gallery in a hall or church: *a choir loft.* **4.** hayloft. **5.a.** a large room or space, usually in a former commercial building, suitable for conversion into an apartment or artist's studio. **b.** a space so converted. **6.** *Golf.* **a.** the backward angle of a club's face that enables the golfer to hit the ball so that it rises in an arc. **b.** a stroke that accomplishes this. —*v.t.* **1.** to hit or throw (a ball or other object) so that it rises in an arc. **2.** to store in a loft. —*v.i.* to hit or throw a ball or other object in an arc. [Old Norse *lopt* sky, upper room.]

loft·y (lôf′tē, lof′-) *adj.,* **loft·i·er, loft·i·est. 1.** extending to a great height; towering: *We stood in awe of the lofty redwood trees.* **2.** exalted in dignity, rank, character, or quality: *lofty ideals.* **3.** having or showing excessive pride; haughty: *a lofty manner.* —**loft′i·ly,** *adv.* —**loft′i·ness,** *n.* —For Synonyms, see **high.**

log¹ (lôg, log) *n.* **1.** an unhewn portion of wood cut from a tree. **2.** an official daily record of the voyage of a ship. **3.** a record of the flight or flights of an aircraft. **4.** any record of progress, performance, or events: *the log of a scientific expedition.* **5.** a book in which such records are kept. Also, **logbook. 6.** a device for measuring the speed of a ship. —*v.,* **logged, log·ging.** —*v.t.* **1.** to cut down trees on (an area of land). **2.** to cut (trees) into logs. **3.** to record in a log. **4.** to cover (a certain distance), as in a ship or aircraft: *to log 150 air miles in three days.* —*v.i.* to chop down trees, cut them into logs, and transport the logs to a sawmill. —*adj.* made of logs: *a log cabin.* [Of uncertain origin.]

• **to log off.** to break off contact with a computer program or system, as by entering a command.

• **to log on.** to gain access to a computer program or system, as by entering a command.

log² (lôg, log) *n.* logarithm.

lo·gan·ber·ry (lō′gən ber′ē) *n., pl.* **-ries. 1.** the tart, reddish purple fruit of a variety of the shrub *Rubus loganbaccus,* widely

grown in the western United States. **2.** the thorny shrub bearing this fruit. [From James H. *Logan,* 1841-1928, American judge who first cultivated this shrub.]

log·a·rithm (lô′gə rith′əm, log′ə-) *n.* an exponent indicating the power to which a base must be raised in order to produce a given number. The logarithm of 9 to the base 3 is 2. Also, **log.** [Modern Latin *logarithmus,* from Greek *logos* word, reckoning, ratio + *arithmos* number.]

log·a·rith·mic (lô′gə rith′mik, log′ə-) *adj.* of or relating to a logarithm or logarithms: *logarithmic tables.* Also, **log′a·rith′-mi·cal.**

log·book (lôg′bŏŏk′, log′-) *n.* log¹ *(def. 5).*

loge (lōzh) *n.* **1.** a seating area in a theater, consisting of the first few rows of the lowest balcony. **2.** a box in a theater. [French *loge* small house, box at a theater; of Germanic origin.]

log·ger (lô′gər, log′ər) *n.* **1.** a person whose work is logging; lumberjack. **2.** a machine for handling logs.

log·ger·head (lô′gər hed′, log′ər-) *n.* **1.** a large-headed saltwater turtle, genus *Caretta,* whose flesh and eggs are valued as food. It may weigh as much as 850 pounds (386 kilograms) and have a flipper spread of 9 feet (2.7 meters). Also, **loggerhead turtle. 2.** a stupid person; blockhead. [Possibly from dialectal English *logger* block of wood used as a hobble for horses (from LOG¹) + HEAD.]

• **at loggerheads.** engaged in an apparently unresolvable dispute.

log·gia (loj′ə, lō′jē ə; *Italian,* lôd′jä) *n., pl.* **log·gias** or *Italian,* **log·gie** (lôd′je). an open gallery whose roof is supported by an arcade or colonnade. [Italian *loggia,* from French *loge* small house; of Germanic origin.]

log·ging (lô′ging, log′ing) *n.* the work or business of chopping down trees, cutting them into logs, and transporting the logs to a sawmill.

log·ic (loj′ik) *n.* **1.** the science of correct reasoning. **2.** a system or method of reasoning: *I can't follow your logic.* **3.** sound or correct thinking; reason: *There is much logic in your argument.* **4.** an agreement or connection between parts or elements found in something, as in a series of events or in a work of art. [Middle English *logike,* from Old French *logique,* from Latin *logica,* from Greek *logikē (technē)* (art of) logic, from *logikos* related to reasoning or speaking, from *logos* word, thought, reasoning, from *legein* to speak, read.]

log·i·cal (loj′i kəl) *adj.* **1.** of, relating to, or in accordance with logic: *logical thinking, a logical explanation.* **2.** following as a natural consequence; reasonably expected: *a logical result.* **3.** capable of reasoning correctly: *a logical mind.* —**log′i·cal·ly,** *adv.*

lo·gi·cian (lō jish′ən) *n.* a person, esp. a philosopher, who is skilled in logic.

lo·gis·tic (lō jis′tik) *adj.* of or relating to logistics. Also, **lo·gis′ti·cal.**

lo·gis·tics (lō jis′tiks) *n.* **1.** the branch of military science concerned with the movement, procurement, and maintenance of equipment, facilities, and personnel. ➤ used as singular. **2.** the organization and carrying out of the details of any undertaking. ➤ used as singular or plural. [French *logistique,* from *logis* lodging, from *loger* to lodge, from *loge* small house; with reference to finding quarters for soldiers. See LODGE.]

log·jam (lôg′jam′, log′-) *n.* **1.** an obstruction in a river caused by a mass of floating logs that have become pressed together. **2.** anything that obstructs; blockage: *The sale created a logjam of telephone orders.*

lo·go (lō′gō) *n., pl.* **-gos.** a distinctive name, symbol, or trademark used by a company to identify its products or services. [Short for LOGOTYPE.]

LOGO (lō′gō) *n.* a simple programming language that is especially suited for teaching children how to use computers.

log·o·type (lô′gə tīp′, log′ə-) *n.* a piece of type on which the letters of a word or syllable, as a trademark, are cast. [Greek *logos* word, speech + TYPE.]

log·roll (lôg′rōl′, log′-) *v.t.* to procure passage of (a bill) by logrolling. —*v.i.* to take part in logrolling. —**log′roll′er,** *n.*

log·roll·ing (lôg′rō′ling, log′-) *n.* **1.a.** political bargaining among legislators, whereby political aid is given in return for a similar favor. **b.** any exchange of praise, help, or favors. **2.** a sport in which two people stand on and rotate a floating log, each trying to get the other off balance and into the water. **3.** the act of rolling logs.

log·wood (lôg′wŏŏd′, log′-) *n.* **1.** a spiny, tropical tree, *Haematoxylon campechianum,* found esp. in Central America, having leaves composed of leaflets and bearing clusters of yellow flowers. **2.** the wood of this tree, which yields a purplish red dye.

lo·gy (lō′gē) *adj.,* **-gi·er, -gi·est.** acting or moving slowly;

heavy; sluggish. [Possibly from Dutch *log* heavy, cumbersome + -Y¹.] —**lo′gi·ly,** *adv.* —**lo′gi·ness,** *n.*

-logy *combining form* **1.** the study or science of: *astrology, theology, paleontology.* **2.** saying; speaking: *tautology.* [Greek *-logiā.*]

loin (loin) *n.* **1.** *usually,* **loins.** the part of the body of a person or a quadruped between the thorax and the pelvis. **2.** a cut of meat from this part of an animal with the flank removed. **3. loins.** the lower part of the abdomen and groin considered as the seat of physical strength or generative power. [Old French *loigne* the part of the body, going back to Latin *lumbus.*]

  •**to gird (up) one's loins.** to prepare for something difficult or strenuous.

loin·cloth (loin′klôth′) *n., pl.* **-cloths** (-klôthz′, -klôths′). a piece of cloth, skin, or other material worn around the hips and over the loins, as in very hot climates.

loi·ter (loi′tər) *v.i.* **1.** to linger idly or aimlessly about a place: *to loiter on a street corner.* **2.** to move sluggishly or with frequent pauses: *to loiter along a path.* —*v.t.* to waste (time); dawdle (with *away*): *The youths loitered away the hours.* [Possibly from Middle Dutch *loteren* to delay.] —**loi′ter·er,** *n.* —**loi′ter·ing·ly,** *adv.*

Lo·ki (lō′kē) *n.* in Norse mythology, the god of fire, strife, and evil, who provoked conflict among the gods.

loll (lol) *v.i.* **1.** to recline or lean in a careless, lazy, or relaxed manner: *The children lolled about on the park bench.* **2.** to hang down loosely; droop: *The weary animal's tongue lolled out.* —*v.t.* to allow to hang down; let droop. —*n. Archaic.* the act of lolling. [Possibly imitative.] —**loll′er,** *n.* —**loll′ing·ly,** *adv.*

lol·li·pop (lol′ē pop′) *also,* **lol·ly·pop.** *n.* a piece of hard candy placed on the end of a stick. [Possibly from dialectal English *lolly* tongue (of uncertain origin) + POP¹.]

Lom·bard (lom′bärd, -bərd, lum′-) *n.* **1.** a member of a Germanic tribe that invaded Italy in the sixth century A.D. and founded the kingdom of Lombardy. **2.** a native or inhabitant of Lombardy.

Lom·bard·y poplar (lom′bər dē, lum′-) a tall, slender, columnar or spire-shaped poplar, *Populus nigra,* variety *italica.*

lo·ment (lō′ment) *n.* a pod that has constrictions between the individual seeds, breaking apart into one-seeded units when ripe. [Late Middle English *lomente,* from Latin *lomentum* bean meal, face cream made of bean meal, from *lotus,* past participle of *lavāre* to wash.]

Lon·don broil (lun′dən) a boneless cut of beef, esp. from the round or flank, that is broiled and served thinly sliced.

lone (lōn) *adj.* **1.** without companions; alone; solitary: *a lone traveler.* **2.** standing apart from others; isolated: *a lone castle.* **3.** being the only one; single; sole: *the lone survivor of a shipwreck.* **4.** without a spouse; single or widowed. [Short for ALONE.] —For Synonyms, see **alone.**

lone·ly (lōn′lē) *adj.,* **-li·er, -li·est. 1.** without friendship or companionship; solitary; lone. **2.a.** depressed from lack of friendship or companionship; lonesome: *The young child felt very lonely in the new school.* **b.** causing or characterized by such depression: *a lonely room, a lonely evening.* **3.** lacking people; unfrequented; deserted: *a lonely road.* **4.** apart from others of its kind; lone; solitary: *a lonely hill.* —**lone′li·ness,** *n.*

lon·er (lō′nər) *n.* a person who prefers to do something alone or to be alone rather than with other people.

lone·some (lōn′səm) *adj.* **1.** depressed from lack of friendship or companionship. **2.** causing or characterized by such depression: *a lonesome journey.* **3.** unfrequented; deserted: *a lonesome road.* —**lone′some·ly,** *adv.* —**lone′some·ness,** *n.*

lone wolf *Informal.* a person who mixes little with others, preferring to live and work alone or independently.

long¹ (lông) *adj.,* **long·er** (lông′gər, -ər), **long·est** (lông′gist, -ist). **1.** having great extension in space: *long arms, a long road.* **2.** having great duration: *That was a long performance.* **3.** having a specified distance or duration: *The road is only two blocks long. The program was an hour long.* **4.** containing many items or entries: *a long list of rules.* **5.** exceeding the average or standard quantity or dimensions: *an extra rose in a long dozen.* **6.** seemingly prolonged; dull or tiring: *It's been a long day.* **7.** having an abundant supply of (with *on*): *The speaker was long on humorous anecdotes.* **8.** extending far into the past or future: *a long memory, to take the long view.* **9.** (of vowels) relatively prolonged in duration, as the *e* in *be.* **10.** *Finance.* holding large amounts of some commodity or stock in anticipation of a rise in prices: *The investor was long in grain.* —*adv.* **1.** for an extended period: *He did not stay long.* **2.** for or throughout the length of the specified period: *She works all day long.* **3.** far from the time indicated: *long after, long ago.* —*n.* **1.** a long time. **2.** a long vowel. [Old English *lang, long* extended, not short.]

  •**as (or so) long as.** since: *I'll go as long as you are going too.*

  •**before long.** soon.

  •**the long and the short of.** the main idea or point of: *The long and the short of it is that we finally found an inexpensive rug.*

long² (lông) *v.t., v.i.* to have a strong or persistent desire; wish earnestly; yearn: *to long for home.* [Old English *langian.*]

long., longitude.

long·boat (lông′bōt′) *n.* formerly, the largest boat carried by a sailing ship.

long·bow (lông′bō′) *n.* a large bow drawn by hand, used by the English during the Middle Ages as a primary military weapon.

long-dis·tance (lông′dis′təns) *adj.* **1.** covering or capable of covering a long distance: *a long-distance runner, a long-distance mover.* **2.** connecting distant locations: *a long-distance call.* —*adv.* by long-distance telephone: *to phone long-distance.*

long distance, an operator or exchange that handles long-distance telephone calls.

long division, mathematical division in which the divisor contains more than one digit or in which the process of division cannot be carried out mentally and must be written out.

long-drawn (lông′drôn′) *adj.* prolonged. Also, **long′-drawn′-out′.**

lon·gev·i·ty (lon jev′i tē, lôn-) *n.* **1.** long life. **2.** the length or duration of life: *Medical discoveries have increased average longevity.* **3.** length of service, as in an occupation. [Late Latin *longaevitās,* going back to Latin *longus* long + *aevum* age.]

long·hair (lông′hâr′) *Informal. adj.* **1.** of, relating to, or characteristic of intellectuals or their tastes. **2.** of or relating to classical music. Also, **long′-haired′.** —*n.* an intellectual.

long·hand (lông′hand′) *n.* writing by hand in which the words are written out in full. ➡ opposed to **shorthand.** —*adj.* **1.** using longhand: *longhand writing.* **2.** written in longhand: *a longhand account.*

long-head·ed (lông′hed′id) *adj.* discerning; shrewd; far-sighted.

long·horn (lông′hôrn′) *n.* one of a breed of cattle having very long horns, introduced by the Spanish to the southwestern United States and formerly common there.

long house, a communal dwelling of the Iroquois and certain other American Indian tribes.

long·ing (lông′ing) *n.* a strong or persistent desire; yearning. —*adj.* feeling or expressing such a desire. —**long′ing·ly,** *adv.*

long·ish (lông′ish) *adj.* somewhat long.

lon·gi·tude (lon′ji tüd′, -tūd′) *n.* **1.** the distance east and west of the prime meridian, measured in degrees and expressed by imaginary lines extending from the North Pole to the South Pole. **2.** *Astronomy.* celestial longitude. [Latin *longitūdō* length.]

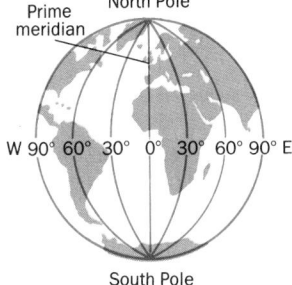

lines of **longitude**

lon·gi·tu·di·nal (lon′ji tü′də nəl, -tū′-) *adj.* **1.** of or relating to longitude. **2.** running lengthwise: *a longitudinal cross section.* —**lon′gi·tu′di·nal·ly,** *adv.*

long johns *Informal.* long underwear.

long jump 1. a field event in which the contestant jumps for distance from a running start or from a standing position. **2.** such a jump. Also, **broad jump.**

long·leaf pine (lông′lēf′) a pine, *Pinus palustris,* having long, densely crowded needles and long cones, native to the southern United States, used for lumber and wood pulp and an important source of turpentine. [LONG¹ + LEAF; referring to its long needles.]

long-lived (lông′līvd′, -livd′) *adj.* living or lasting a long time: *a long-lived illness.* —**long′-lived′ness,** *n.*

long-play·ing (lông′plā′ing) *adj.* of or relating to a phonograph record usually 12 inches (30 centimeters) in diameter and played at 33⅓ revolutions per minute.

long-range (lông′rānj′) *adj.* **1.** for or involving the future: *long-range plans.* **2.** capable of firing or traveling over long distances: *long-range guns, a long-range missile.*

a	at	e	end	o	hot	u	up	hw	white		about
ā	ape	ē	me	ō	old	ū	use	ng	song	ə	taken
ä	far	i	it	ô	fork	ü	rule	th	thin		pencil
âr	care	ī	ice	oi	oil	u̇	pull	th	this		lemon
		îr	pierce	ou	out	ûr	turn	zh	measure		circus

725

long·shore (lông′shôr′) *adj.* **1.** formed, existing, or taking place along a shore or shoreline, as a current or landform. Longshore currents move sand parallel to a coast, building up offshore bars and spits. **2.** working along the seacoast or on the waterfront. [Form of ALONGSHORE.]

long·shore·man (lông′shôr′mən) *n., pl.* **-men** (-mən). a person employed in loading or unloading ships. [Short for ALONGSHORE + MAN.]

long shot 1. an entry in a contest or race considered to have little chance of winning. **2.** a venture promising great rewards but having little chance of success. **3.** a television or motion-picture shot taken at some distance from the subject.

long·stand·ing (lông′stan′ding) *adj.* lasting a long time: *a longstanding friendship.*

long·suf·fer·ing (lông′suf′ər ing) *adj.* enduring wrongs, trouble, or pain patiently for a long time. —*n.* the long and patient endurance of wrongs, trouble, or pain.

long suit 1. in some card games, the suit in which a person holds the most cards. **2.** a valuable quality or ability; something in which a person excels.

long-term (lông′tûrm′) *adj.* **1.** planned for or involving a long period of time, as a project. **2.** requiring payment after a long period of time, as a loan.

long·time (lông′tīm′) *adj.* having lasted for a long time: *a longtime friend, a longtime interest.*

long ton, ton *(def. 1b).*

long·ways (lông′wāz′) *adv.* longwise.

long-wind·ed (lông′win′did) *adj.* **1.** speaking or writing at great length: *a long-winded speaker.* **2.** tediously long and wordy: *a long-winded speech.* **3.** capable of sustained effort or activity without loss of breath. —**long′-wind′ed·ly,** *adv.* —**long′-wind′ed·ness,** *n.*

long·wise (lông′wīz′) *adv.* lengthwise. Also, **longways.**

loo (lü) *n.* a card game in which each player who fails to win a trick must pay a specified number of chips into the next pool. [Short for earlier *lanterloo,* from French *lanturelu* originally, the refrain of a seventeenth-century French song.]

look (lŭk) *v.i.* **1.** to make use of the power of sight; use one's eyes; see. **2.** to direct one's eyes: *She looked toward the window.* **3.** to use one's eyes in making a search or examination: *We helped him look for his wallet.* **4.** to gaze or glance in a meaningful way: *I looked quizzically at him.* **5.** to give the impression of being; seem: *She looks tired.* **6.** to turn one's attention or regard; take notice: *We look at this situation in a different light now.* **7.** to face in a certain direction or have a certain view: *The windows looked north. The porch looks onto the neighbor's yard.* —*v.t.* **1.** to have an appearance befitting: *This building looks its age.* **2.** to direct one's eyes up or toward: *He looked me straight in the face.* **3.** to express or suggest with one's eyes: *Soft eyes looked love* (Lord Byron, 1811). —*n.* **1.** an act or instance of looking; glance: *Take a look at this car.* **2.** the impression a person or thing gives; air or appearance: *This room has a cheerful look.* **3.** **looks.** outward appearance: *She is endowed with good looks.* [Old English *lōcian* to see, direct one's eyes.]

· **to look after.** to take care of: *We looked after our neighbors' dog while they were away.*

· **to look back on.** to recall.

· **to look down on.** to consider beneath one; regard with contempt.

· **to look for.** to expect: *I'll look for you on Sunday.*

· **to look forward to.** to anticipate happily or eagerly.

· **to look in.** to make a brief visit.

· **to look into.** to make an examination of; investigate.

· **to look on. a.** to be a spectator. **b.** to think of; regard; consider: *I look on them as my best friends.*

· **to look oneself.** to seem to be one's normal self.

· **to look out.** to take care; watch out.

· **to look out for. a.** to protect. **b.** to be careful of; watch out for: *Look out for that loose board!*

· **to look over.** to examine, esp. hastily or superficially.

· **to look to. a.** to attend; take care of. **b.** to depend upon; rely on.

· **to look up. a.** to attempt to locate, as in a source: *I looked up the date in the encyclopedia.* **b.** to pay a visit to: *He looked her up when he got into town.* **c.** *Informal.* to improve: *Business is looking up.*

· **to look up to.** to respect or admire greatly.

look-a·like (lŭk′ə līk′) *also,* **look·a·like.** *n.* a person or thing that closely resembles another in appearance: *My cousin and I are look-alikes.* —*adj.* closely resembling each other: *look-alike hairdos.*

look·er (lŭk′ər) *n.* **1.** a person who looks. **2.** *Slang.* a person who is very attractive: *Your friend is a real looker!*

look·er-on (lŭk′ər ôn′, -on′) *n., pl.* **look·ers-on.** a person who looks on; spectator.

looking glass, mirror.

look·out (lŭk′out′) *n.* **1.a.** the act of looking out. **b.** an alert or careful watch for someone or something: *to maintain a lookout from a ship's crow's-nest.* **2.** a place where a watch is kept: *The tower was a lookout over the valley.* **3.** a person or group that keeps watch. **4.** *Informal.* a particular matter of interest or concern: *How you solve the problem is your lookout.*

loom¹ (lüm) *n.* a machine for weaving thread into cloth. [Middle English *lome* weaver's loom, tool, implement, from Old English *lōma* tool, implement, from *gelōma.*]

loom² (lüm) *v.i.* **1.** to appear indistinctly, esp. as a large, threatening shape: *A tall building loomed in the distance.* **2.** to appear to the mind as large or ominous; stand out prominently or threateningly: *Final exams loomed ahead.* [Earlier *lome, loam;* possibly of Scandinavian origin.]

loon¹ (lün) *n.* any of various web-footed diving birds, genus *Gavia,* of the Northern Hemisphere, having a slender pointed bill, small pointed wings, and short legs. the **common loon,** *G. immer,* noted for its laughlike call. Length: 26-37½ inches (66-95 centimeters). [Modification of earlier *loom,* from Old Norse *lōmr.*]

loon¹

loon² (lün) *n.* a crazy or foolish person. [Scottish English *lown, loun,* from Middle English *lowen,* possibly from Middle Dutch *loen* stupid person.]

loon·y (lü′nē) *Informal. adj.,* **loon·i·er, loon·i·est.** crazy or foolish. —*n., pl.* **loon·ies.** a crazy or foolish person. [Short for LUNATIC, -Y¹; influenced by LOON².]

loop (lüp) *n.* **1.** a portion of a string, wire, or other similar material that is doubled over itself, forming an elliptical or circular shape with an opening between the parts. **2.** anything resembling this: *the loop of the cursive letter "e."* **3.** a round or bent piece of material, as metal or cord, serving as a hook or ornament: *a belt loop.* **4.** a maneuver in which an airplane makes a complete turn in a vertical plane. **5.** a closed electric circuit. **6.** the repetition of a sequence of instructions in a computer program one or more times. —*v.t.* **1.** to form into a loop or loops: *Loop the rope around the tree.* **2.** to fasten with a loop or loops (often with *up*): *to loop a curtain up.* **3.** to encircle with a loop: *I looped my finger with a string.* **4.** to fly (an airplane) in a loop or loops. —*v.i.* **1.** to form a loop or loops. **2.** to move or fly in a loop or loops. [Of uncertain origin.]

· **to loop the loop.** to make loops in the air, as in an airplane.

loop·hole (lüp′hōl′) *n.* **1.** a means or method of escape or evasion, esp. one provided by an ambiguity or omission in a law or contract. **2.** a small opening in a wall, as the wall of a fortification, through which weapons may be fired or observations may be made. [Earlier *loop* opening (possibly from Middle Dutch *lupen* to watch) + HOLE.]

loose (lüs) *adj.,* **loos·er, loos·est. 1.a.** not attached or fastened: *There were several loose pages in the book.* **b.** not set tightly or firmly in position: *The diamond was loose in its setting.* **2.** free from physical restraint; not bound or confined; at liberty: *He got his arm loose from his assailant's grip.* **3.** not fitting tightly or snugly: *She wore loose garments in the summer.* **4.** not tight or firm; slack: *loose reins.* **5.** not tied or joined together: *loose keys.* **6.** not contained in something, as a package or receptacle: *loose candy.* **7.** spread out or apart in arrangement or structure; not compact: *loose gravel, a fabric of loose texture.* **8.** not careful, accurate, or precise: *loose reasoning, a loose translation.* **9.** not under control; unrestrained: *a loose tongue, a loose temper.* **10.** characterized by a lack of moral restraint; dissolute: *a loose person, loose behavior.* **11.** free from tension; relaxed: *The team was loose once the game started.* —*adv.* in a loose manner. —*v.t.,* **loosed, loos·ing. 1.** to set free from bonds or physical restraint; set at liberty: *to loose an animal from a cage.* **2.** to untie; unfasten: *to loose a knot.* **3.** to make less tight; loosen. **4.** to shoot or let fly: *to loose a dart.* [Old Norse *lauss* free, immoral.] —**loose′ly,** *adv.* —**loose′ness,** *n.*

· **on the loose.** *Informal.* **a.** free from captivity or restraint. **b.** behaving in an unrestrained manner.

· **to break loose.** to run away or get away: *to break loose from a corral.*

• **to cut loose. a.** to free or become free from control or domination. **b.** *Informal.* to celebrate or behave without restraint: *After the team's victory, the whole town cut loose.*
• **to let** (or **set** or **turn**) **loose.** to set free; release.

loose ends, matters, usually of a minor nature, yet to be taken care of.
• **at loose ends. a.** in an unorganized, undetermined, or confused state. **b.** without a job; unemployed: *to be at loose ends for the summer.*

loose-joint·ed (lüs′join′tid) *adj.* **1.** having joints that are loosely formed. **2.** having or capable of limber movement: *a loose-jointed dancer.* —**loose′-joint′ed·ly,** *adv.* —**loose′-joint′ed·ness,** *n.*

loose-leaf (lüs′lēf′) *adj.* **1.** containing or designed to contain specially perforated sheets that may be bound or removed easily. **2.** of or designed for use with a loose-leaf notebook, binder, or the like: *loose-leaf paper.*

loos·en (lü′sən) *v.t.* **1.** to make less tight: *to loosen a tie.* **2.** to detach or make detachable by unfastening or by rendering less fixed: *to loosen a stone in a wall.* **3.** to spread out or separate elements of (a substance); make less compact: *to loosen soil, to loosen the weave of a fabric.* **4.a.** to lessen or remove restraints upon: *The threat of jail loosened the suspect's tongue.* **b.** to relax the severity or strictness of: *to loosen discipline.* —*v.i.* to become loose or looser. —**loos′en·er,** *n.*
• **to loosen up.** *Informal.* to speak or act or cause to speak or act in a freer, more relaxed way.

loose·strife (lüs′strīf′) *n.* **1.** any of various plants, genus *Lysimachia,* having flowers that are usually yellow or white. **2.** any of various plants, genus *Lythrum,* having pink or purple flowers and growing in damp areas. [Translation of Latin *lysimachia,* going back to Greek *Lysimachos* name of its discoverer, from *lysis* loosing + *machē* strife.]

loot (lüt) *n.* **1.** valuables seized by thieves in a robbery. **2.** valuables taken from an enemy during a war; booty; plunder. **3.** *Slang.* money. —*v.t.* **1.** to rob by force, as during a war; plunder: *The soldiers looted the town. Thieves looted the building.* **2.** to steal or rob by fraud; expropriate; embezzle: *The treasurer looted most of the company's assets. Corrupt politicians looted the city treasury.* **3.** to carry off as loot: *Thieves broke into our neighbors' apartment and looted their belongings.* —*v.i.* to engage in plunder; take booty. [Hindi *lūt* plunder, from Sanskrit *lōtra* booty.] —**loot′er,** *n.*

lop[1] (lop) *v.t.,* **lopped, lop·ping. 1.** to cut off or remove as unnecessary (often with *off*): *to lop off dead branches from trees.* **2.** to cut off parts, as branches, from: *to lop trees.* [Middle English *loppen,* from Old English *loppian;* probably of Scandinavian origin.]

lop[2] (lop) *v.i., v.t.,* **lopped, lop·ping.** to hang or let hang loosely; droop. —*adj.* hanging loosely; drooping: *lop ears.* [Of uncertain origin.]

lope (lōp) *v.t., v.i.,* **loped, lop·ing.** to run or cause to run with a long, easy, often bounding stride: *The dog and its owner could be seen loping together in the park.* —*n.* a long, easy, often bounding stride. [Old Norse *hlaupa* to leap.] —**lop′er,** *n.*

lop-eared (lop′ird′) *adj.* having ears that hang down loosely.

lop·sid·ed (lop′sī′did) *adj.* **1.** larger or heavier on one side than the other; not symmetrical. **2.** leaning or slanting to one side. —**lop′sid′ed·ly,** *adv.* —**lop′sid′ed·ness,** *n.*

lo·qua·cious (lō kwā′shəs) *adj.* characterized by or disposed to excessive talking; talkative. [Latin *loquāc-,* stem of *loquāx* talkative + -ous.] —**lo·qua′cious·ly,** *adv.* —**lo·qua′cious·ness,** *n.* —For Synonyms, see **talkative.**

lo·quac·i·ty (lō kwas′i tē) *n.* an act or instance of talking excessively; talkativeness.

lo·quat (lō′kwot, -kwat) *n.* **1.** the yellow or orange, plumlike fruit of a tree, *Eriobotrya japonica,* of the rose family, having a slightly acid taste and used esp. in preserves. **2.** the tree itself, a small evergreen native to Japan and China. [Chinese (Cantonese) *lō kwat* literally, rush orange.]

lo·ran (lôr′an) *also,* **Loran.** *n.* a navigational system in which the geographical position of a ship or aircraft can be determined by using signals transmitted by two or more radio stations. [Short for *lo(ng) ra(nge) n(avigation).*]

lord (lôrd) *n.* **1.** a person who has power or authority over others, as a feudal superior. **2.** *British.* a titled nobleman or peer of the realm belonging to the House of Lords. **3. Lord.** *British.* **a.** a title or form of address for any of various noblemen or peers of the realm. The *Earl of Arran* would be referred to informally as *Lord Arran.* **b.** a title or form of address for certain high officials or members of the clergy: *Lord Mayor of London, Lord Archbishop of Canterbury.* **4. the Lord. a.** the Supreme Being; God. **b.** Jesus Christ. **5. Lords.** the House of Lords in the British Parliament. [Middle English *lord,* from Old English *hlāford* mas-

ter, ruler, husband, from earlier *hlāfweard,* from *hlāf* loaf + *weard* keeper; referring to the concept in earlier times of the master of a household as the keeper of the loaf of bread of his dependents. See LADY.]
• **to lord it over.** to behave in a grand, haughty, or domineering manner toward.

lord·ling (lôrd′ling) *n.* an insignificant lord, as a minor feudal noble.

lord·ly (lôrd′lē) *adj.,* **-li·er, -li·est. 1.** of, relating to, or suited for a lord: *a lordly estate.* **2.** haughty, imperious, or insolent: *a lordly manner.* —*adv.* in a lordly manner. —**lord′li·ness,** *n.*

lor·do·sis (lôr dō′sis) *n., pl.* **-ses** (-sēz) a forward curvature of the spine that produces a hollow in the back. [Modern Latin *lordosis,* from Greek *lordōsis,* from *lordos* bent backward.] —**lor·dot·ic** (lôr dot′ik), *adj.*

Lord's Day *also,* **Lord's day.** Sunday.

lord·ship (lôrd′ship′) *n.* **1.** *also,* **Lordship.** *British.* a title used in addressing or referring to a judge or nobleman other than a duke (preceded by *His* or *Your*). **2.** the rank, power, or authority of a lord. **3.** the territory over which a lord holds dominion.

Lord's Prayer, the prayer given by Jesus to his Apostles, which begins with the words "Our Father." Also, **Our Father, Paternoster.**

Lord's Supper 1. Last Supper. **2.** Holy Communion; Eucharist.

lore (lôr) *n.* **1.** a body of traditional or popular facts or beliefs on a particular subject: *nature lore.* **2.** learning or knowledge in general: *a writer of great lore.* [Old English *lār* teaching, doctrine.]

Lor·e·lei (lôr′ə lī′) *n.* in German legend, a siren of the Rhine who by her song lured sailors to their deaths by shipwreck.

lor·gnette (lôrn yet′) *n.* a pair of eyeglasses or opera glasses held by a short, usually ornate handle. [French *lorgnette* opera glasses, from *lorgner* to leer at, from *lorgne* squinting; of uncertain origin.]

lo·ris (lôr′is) *n., pl.* **-ris.** a small, tree-climbing, nocturnal prosimian, related to the lemur, having a small head, rounded ears, and large eyes. The **slender loris,** *Loris tardigradus,* is native to India, and the **slow,** or **gray, loris,** genus *Nycticebus,* inhabits Southeast Asia. Length: 5-18 inches (13-46 centimeters). [French *loris,* probably from obsolete Dutch *loeris* clown.]

lorn (lôrn) *adj. Archaic.* abandoned; lonely: *She might be despised by my lord's circle, and left lone and lorn* (Thomas Hardy, 1876). [Old English *loren,* past participle of -*lēosan* (used only in compounds) to lose.]

lor·ry (lôr′ē, lor′ē) *n., pl.* **-ries. 1.** a long, flat wagon without sides, drawn by a horse. **2.** *British.* truck[1] *(def. 1).* [Possibly from dialectal English *lurry* to pull; of uncertain origin.]

lo·ry (lôr′ē) *n., pl.* **-ries.** any of various brightly colored parrots of Australasia having a brushlike tip on the tongue, esp. **Swainson's lory,** *Trichoglossus haematodus.* [Malay *lūri.*]

lories

lose (lüz) *v.,* **lost, los·ing.** —*v.t.* **1.** to have no longer because of some act or accident: *My friend lost a book on the train. The investor lost a fortune on the stock market. We lost our belongings in the flood.* **2.** to put in a place afterward forgotten; misplace: *to lose one's car keys.* **3.** to be deprived of by death: *Mary lost her brother in the war.* **4.** to be defeated in; fail to win: *Our team lost the game.* **5.** to fail to preserve or maintain: *Don loses his temper*

a	at	e	end	o	hot	u	up	hw	white		about
ā	ape	ē	me	ō	old	ū	use	ng	song		taken
ä	far	i	it	ô	fork	ü	rule	th	thin	ə	pencil
âr	care	ī	ice	oi	oil	u̇	pull	th	this		lemon
		îr	pierce	ou	out	ûr	turn	zh	measure		circus

727

easily. **6.** to let pass unprofitably or wastefully; fail to take advantage of: *We lost valuable time waiting for our tardy friend.* **7.** to fail to keep up with, esp. in order to understand or see: *I lost the sense of what you were saying.* **8.** to wander from: *The explorers lost their way in the dark cavern.* **9.** to allow (oneself) to be engrossed (with *in*): *She lost herself in her reading.* **10.** to leave behind; outdistance: *The deer easily lost the hunters pursuing it.* **11.** to cause the loss of: *Arrogance lost the youth many friends.* **12.** to bring to destruction; kill, ruin, or destroy: ➡ used in the passive: *The ship was lost in the hurricane.* —*v.i.* **1.** to suffer loss: *The stockholders lost heavily when the company went bankrupt.* **2.** to be defeated: *I usually lose when I play chess.* [Old English *losian* to be lost, perish, escape.] —For Synonyms *(v.t.),* see **misplace.**

· **to lose out.** to fail to get or achieve something contended for: *to lose out in an election.*
· **to lose out on.** to fail to take advantage of: *We lost out on the special sale because we didn't see the advertisement announcing it.*

los·er (lü′zər) *n.* **1.** a person or thing that loses in a game or contest. **2.** *Informal.* **a.** a person or thing that seems destined to lose or fail: *The author's latest book is a loser.* **b.** a person or thing that always loses or fails, usually because of inability.

los·ing (lü′zing) *adj.* **1.** bringing about a loss: *a losing strategy.* **2.** that is defeated; failing to win: *the losing team.* —*n.* **losings.** losses, esp. gambling losses.

loss (lôs) *n.* **1.** the act or fact of losing or the state of being lost. **2.** something that is lost, as a person, thing, or amount: *The company's profits greatly outweighed its losses.* **3.** the damage or disadvantage that results from losing something. **4.** **losses.** soldiers lost in action; casualties. [Probably from *lost,* past participle of LOSE.]

· **at a loss. a.** puzzled; confused; perplexed: *The new rules left me completely at a loss.* **b.** in such a way as to cause a loss: *I sold my car at a loss.*
· **at a loss to.** not knowing how to: *to be at a loss to interpret a statement.*

loss leader, an item offered for sale by a retail store at a loss in order to attract customers.

lost (lôst) *v.* the past tense and past participle of **lose.** —*adj.* **1.** unable to be found; misplaced or missing: *a lost book, a lost dog.* **2.** no longer possessed or used: *a lost fortune, lost youth, lost skills.* **3.** resulting in defeat; not won: *a lost game.* **4.** not used to good purpose; wasted: *a lost opportunity, a lost weekend.* **5.** having gone astray: *We are lost in the woods.* **6.a.** harmed or damaged beyond help or repair; destroyed; ruined: *lost health, a lost reputation.* **b.** spiritually doomed or ruined: *a lost sinner.* **7.** resulting from being confused; bewildered: *a lost expression.* **8.** engrossed; absorbed (with *in*): *lost in meditation, lost in one's work.* **9.** unable to help oneself: *I'd be lost without my calculator.*

· **to be lost on** (or **upon**). to fail to have an effect on, as because not noticed or understood: *My ironic remarks were lost on them.*
· **to be lost to. a.** to be no longer possessed by. **b.** to be no longer possible: *Any bit of good fortune seemed lost to them.* **c.** insensible to: *lost to one's conscience.*

lot (lot) *n.* **1.** an object used to determine something by chance: *We drew lots to decide which team would bat first.* **2.** the casting or drawing of such an object or objects as a means of determining: *to choose by lot.* **3.** the choice resulting from this: *The lot fell on me to pay the bill.* **4.** something that one receives in this manner; portion or share. **5.** a portion of land, esp. one set aside for a particular purpose: *a building lot.* **6.** a motion-picture studio and its property. **7.** a portion or way of life believed to be determined by fate: *The lot of the poor is a hard one.* **8.** an item or items separated from others of the same kind for sale or auction: *The first three lots of furniture were sold this morning.* **9.** a number of persons or things considered as a unit or group: *They were a sorry lot of workers. Our entire lot of tomatoes spoiled.* **10.** *Informal.* (of a person) a specific type; sort: *That bully is a bad lot.* **11.** also, **lots.** *Informal.* a considerable number or amount; great deal: *We bought lots of clothes for school.* —*adv.* **a lot.** also, **lots.** considerably; very much: *You are a lot taller than I am.* —*v.,* **lot·ted, lot·ting.** —*v.t.* **1.** to portion out; allot: *His aunt's will lotted most of the estate to him.* **2.** to divide (something) into lots. —*v.i.* to cast or draw lots. [Old English *hlot* share, object used to determine something by chance.] —For Synonyms *(n.),* see **fate.**

· **to cast** (or **throw in**) **one's lot with.** to associate with and share the fortunes of.

loth (lōth, lō̟th) loath.

Lo·thar·i·o (lō thâr′ē ō′) *n., pl.* **-thar·i·os.** a man who seduces women; libertine; rake. [From *Lothario,* a libertine in *The Fair Penitent,* a play by Nicholas Rowe, 1674-1718, English writer.]

lo·tion (lō′shən) *n.* a liquid preparation containing medication or softening agents, used on the skin to heal, soothe, soften, or cleanse. [Latin *lōtiō* a washing.]

lo·tos (lō′təs) lotus.

lot·ter·y (lot′ə rē) *n., pl.* **-ter·ies.** a manner of raising money, distributing prizes, or selecting persons, as for military service, in which chances are sold or distributed and winners are decided or selected by a drawing. [Italian *lotteria,* from *lotto* lot, share. See LOTTO.]

lot·to (lot′ō) *n.* a game of chance in which a caller draws numbered disks or balls from a bag and the players cover squares on cards containing the corresponding numbers, the winner being the first player to cover a row of squares. [Italian *lotto* lot, share, from French *lot;* of Germanic origin.]

lo·tus (lō′təs) *also,* **lotos.** *n., pl.* **-tus·es. 1.** the large, showy flower of any of several plants of the water lily family, genus *Nymphaea* or *Nelumbo.* **2.** the plant bearing this flower. **3.** any of a small group of shrubby plants, genus *Lotus,* of the pea family. **4.** the fruit eaten by the lotus-eaters, thought to be the jujube. [Latin *lōtus* name of several plants, from Greek *lōtos;* of Semitic origin.]

lotus flowers

lo·tus-eat·er (lō′təs ē′tər) *n.* **1.** in Greek legend, one of a race of men who ate lotus fruit, which made them forget the past and live in indolence. **2.** one who leads a life of luxury and indolence.

loud (loud) *adj.* **1.** having great intensity of sound: *a loud cry, a loud noise.* **2.** producing great intensity of sound; resounding: *loud cymbals, a loud voice.* **3.** forceful and insistent; vehement: *loud denunciations, loud demands.* **4.** tastelessly bright; garish; flashy: *a loud red automobile.* **5.** obtrusive in appearance or manner: *a loud, vulgar person.* —*adv.* in a loud manner. [Old English *hlūd* sonorous, strongly audible.] —**loud′ly,** *adv.* —**loud′ness,** *n.*

loud·mouth (loud′mouth′) *n., pl.* **-mouths** (-mouthz′, -mouths′). a person who annoys other people by talking too loudly or too much. —**loud·mouthed** (loud′mouthd′, -moutht′), *adj.*

loud·speak·er (loud′spē′kər) *also,* **loud-speak·er.** *n.* a device that transforms a varying electrical signal into amplified sound.

lough (lok, loкн) *n. Irish.* **1.** lake. **2.** an arm of the sea.

lou·is d'or (lü′ē dôr′) formerly, a gold coin of France, used during the seventeenth and eighteenth centuries. Also, **lou′is.** [French *louis d'or* literally, louis of gold, from *Louis* XIII, 1601-43, in whose reign the coin was first issued.]

lounge (lounj) *v.,* **lounged, loung·ing.** —*v.i.* **1.** to lean, sit, or recline lazily; loll: *to lounge on a sofa.* **2.** to move lazily, listlessly, or unhurriedly: *The bored children lounged about the yard.* **3.** to spend time doing nothing; idle. —*v.t.* to pass (time) by lounging. —*n.* **1.** a public room where one may lounge, relax, or wait, as in a hotel, restaurant, or club. **2.** a sofa for reclining, provided with a headrest and sometimes having no back. [Of uncertain origin.] —**loung′er,** *n.*

lour (lour) lower².

louse (lous) *n., pl. (def. 1)* **lice** or *(def. 2)* **lous·es. 1.** any of a large number of tiny wingless insects that live as parasites on birds and mammals. They are divided into two groups, the **biting louse,** order Mallophaga, and the **sucking louse,** order Anoplura, which includes the human **body louse,** *Pediculus humanus.* **2.** *Slang.* a low, contemptible person. —*v.t.,* **loused, lous·ing.** to delouse. [Old English *lūs* the insect.]

· **to louse up.** *Slang.* to make a mess or muddle of; spoil.

lous·y (lou′zē) *adj.,* **lous·i·er, lous·i·est. 1.** infested with lice. **2.** *Slang.* **a.** disgusting or contemptible: *a lousy trick.* **b.** of wretched quality; terrible: *That was a lousy movie.* —**lous′i·ly,** *adv.* —**lous′i·ness,** *n.*

· **lousy with.** *Slang.* well provided with; loaded: *That family is lousy with money.*

lout (lout) *n.* an awkward, stupid person; oaf. [Possibly from Old Norse *lūtr* bent down.]

lout·ish (lou′tish) *adj.* resembling or characteristic of a lout; awkward; clumsy. —**lout′ish·ly,** *adv.* —**lout′ish·ness,** *n.*

lou·ver (lü′vər) *n.* **1.** a ventilator placed in a window, door, or other opening, consisting of a

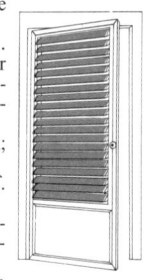

louver

series of horizontal slats fitted in a frame. **2.** in medieval architecture, a turret or turretlike structure, as on the roof of a church, that is provided with slanted slats for ventilation. **3.** any ventilating slit, as in the hood of an automobile. [Old French *lov(i)er* skylight; possibly of Germanic origin.] —**lou′vered,** *adj.*

Lou·vre (lü′vrə) *n.* an art museum in Paris.

lov·a·ble (luv′ə bəl) *also,* **loveable.** *adj.* worthy of being loved; endearing: *a lovable puppy.* —**lov′a·bil′i·ty, lov′a·ble·ness,** *n.* —**lov′a·bly,** *adv.*

lov·age (luv′ij) *n.* a perennial herb, *Levisticum officinale,* of the parsley family, cultivated for its aromatic seeds that are used as a flavoring, as in liqueurs, and for its leaves and stems that are eaten as a vegetable. [Middle English *loveache,* from Old French *levesche,* from Late Latin *levisticum,* equivalent to Latin *ligusticum* lovage, plant native to Liguria, from *Ligusticus* Ligurian, from *Liguria* Liguria, region of Italy.]

love (luv) *n.* **1.a.** a profound affection and deep devotion between persons: *love for one's children.* **b.** a passionate affection arising from sexual desire. **c.** compassion and concern for another or others: *love for one's neighbor.* **2.a.** a benevolence and concern of God for his creation. **b.** devotion to God. **3.** a beloved person; sweetheart. ➡ often used as a term of endearment. **4.** a strong liking for: *a love of music.* **5.** something loved or greatly liked: *Skiing is my great love.* **6.** sexual relations. **7. Love.** Eros; Cupid. **8.** in tennis, a score of zero. —*v.,* **loved, lov·ing.** —*v.t.* **1.** to have a profound affection for and deep devotion to; cherish. **2.** to have a passionate affection for; be in love with. **3.** to have a strong liking for; take great pleasure or interest in: *to love good books.* **4.** to show affection, as by embracing or caressing. **5.** to thrive upon or flourish in: *Plants love sunlight.* —*v.i.* to be in love. [Old English *lufu* profound affection, attachment.]

• **for love.** as a favor; for nothing.
• **for love or money.** under any circumstances: *I wouldn't go there for love or money.*
• **for the love of.** for the sake of; in consideration of: *For the love of mercy, please stop arguing.*
• **in love.** feeling love; enamored.
• **to fall in love.** to become enamored.
• **to make love. a.** to woo or embrace. **b.** to engage in sexual intercourse.

love·a·ble (luv′ə bəl) lovable.

love affair, a romantic or sexual relationship between two people.

love apple *Archaic.* tomato. [Probably a translation of French *pomme d'amour,* from Italian *pomo d'amore,* alteration of *pomo dei Mori* apple of the Moors; referring to the introduction of the tomato into Italy by the Moors.]

love·bird (luv′bûrd′) *n.* any of several small African parrots, genus *Agapornis,* having predominantly gray or green plumage. It is noted for its affectionate behavior with its mate.

love feast 1. among early Christians, a meal eaten together in token of brotherly love. **2.** a religious service in imitation of this, practiced today by some Christians. **3.** a banquet or other gathering held to honor someone or promote goodwill.

love-in-a-mist (luv′in ə mist′) *n.* an annual garden plant, *Nigella damascena,* of the buttercup family, bearing finely cut leaves, light blue or white flowers enveloped by threadlike bracts, and an inflated, globular fruit.

love knot, a knot tied as a token of love and loyalty.

love·less (luv′lis) *adj.* **1.** untouched by love; void of love: *a loveless marriage.* **2.** feeling or expressing no love; unloving: *a loveless person.* **3.** not loved.

love-lies-bleed·ing (luv′līz′blē′ding) *n.* a type of amaranth, *Amaranthus caudatus,* bearing spikes of showy, bright red flowers.

love·lock (luv′lok′) *n.* a lock of hair, usually tied separately from the rest of the hair, esp. a curl formerly worn by courtiers.

love·lorn (luv′lôrn′) *adj.* abandoned or rejected by one's lover; miserable because of love.

love·ly (luv′lē) *adj.,* -**li·er,** -**li·est. 1.** possessing beautiful qualities, such as an attractive appearance or a pleasing personality. **2.** *Informal.* very delightful; enjoyable; pleasing: *We had a lovely time!* —**love′li·ness,** *n.* —For Synonyms, see **beautiful.**

love·mak·ing (luv′mā′king) *n.* the act of making love.

lov·er (luv′ər) *n.* **1.** a person who loves another. **2. lovers.** two people involved in a love affair. **3.** a person who has a strong liking for or takes great pleasure or interest in: *a lover of art.* —**lov′er·ly,** *adj., adv.*

love seat, a small sofa seating two persons.

love·sick (luv′sik′) *adj.* **1.** pining or languishing because of love. **2.** expressing such feeling: *a lovesick ballad.*

lov·ing (luv′ing) *adj.* feeling or expressing love; affectionate; fond. —**lov′ing·ly,** *adv.*

loving cup 1. a large, often inscribed cup, usually with handles,

presented as a prize, trophy, or memento. **2.** formerly, a large wine cup passed from person to person.

lov·ing-kind·ness (luv′ing kīnd′nis) *n.* affectionate tenderness and consideration arising from or expressing love.

low[1] (lō) *adj.* **1.** rising only slightly above the surface; not high: *A low hedge surrounds the yard.* **2.** located close to the ground or to some other base: *a low leap, low branches of a tree.* **3.** lying below the average or natural level of the ground: *a low valley.* **4.** cut so as to expose the neck and shoulders: *a low neckline.* **5.** below the usual or desired level: *The river was low after the drought.* **6.** below the usual or desired amount: *The yield of corn was low that year.* **7.** below or inferior to others: *low intelligence.* **8.** having a place or position near the bottom, as of a scale or other means of measurement: *low wages, a low percentile, a low grade of meat.* **9.** full of or showing a mean or wicked nature; debased; corrupt: *low behavior, a low person.* **10.** lacking in dignity or refinement; vulgar: *low language.* **11.** not approving; critical; unfavorable: *to have a low opinion of something.* **12.** not having an adequate supply of (with *on* or *in*): *to be low on cash.* **13.** not loud; soft: *a low whisper.* **14.** (of musical sounds) produced or characterized by relatively slow vibrations: *a low note.* **15.** low in spirits; depressed: *Failing the test made them feel very low.* **16.** lacking in physical strength; feeble; weak: *The patient's condition is very low.* **17.** not highly advanced or organized. **18.** *Phonetics.* pronounced with the tongue lowered against the floor of the mouth. The *a* in *father* is a low vowel. —*adv.* **1.** near the ground or floor; not aloft: *The plane flew very low.* **2.** to, in, or at a low point, degree, or level: *Prices sank low.* **3.** in a quiet tone; gently; softly: *to speak low.* **4.** in or to a humble position: *to be born low.* **5.** at a cheap price; inexpensively. —*n.* **1.** a low level, place, or position. **2.** an arrangement of gears that produces the lowest speed and the greatest power. **3.** an area of low barometric pressure. [Old Norse *lāgr* not high, small, humble, base[2].] —**low′ness,** *n.*

low[2] (lō) *v.t., v.i.* to make the bellowing sound characteristic of cattle; moo. —*n.* such a sound. [Old English *hlōwan* to moo.]

low beam, the beam of a motor vehicle headlight aimed close to the ground to illuminate nearby objects.

low blood pressure, hypotension.

low-born (lō′bôrn′) *adj.* of humble birth.

low·boy (lō′boi′) *n.* a low chest of drawers on short legs.

low-bred (lō′bred′) *adj.* of poor breeding or inferior birth; vulgar.

low-brow (lō′brou′) *Informal. n.* a person who lacks cultivated tastes or who avoids intellectual pursuits. —*adj.* of, relating to, or suitable for a lowbrow.

Low Church, a group in the Anglican Church that minimizes the importance of church authority, liturgy, and sacraments.

low comedy, comedy relying on slapstick and broad humor rather than witty dialogue. ➡ opposed to **high comedy.**

low-den·si·ty lipoprotein (lō′den′si tē) see **LDL.**

low·down (*n.,* lō′doun′; *adj.,* lō′doun′) *n. Slang.* bare facts; truth. —*adj. also,* **low-down.** *Informal.* full of or showing meanness of spirit; base; contemptible: *a lowdown trick.*

low·er[1] (lō′ər) *adj.* **1.** the comparative of **low**[1]. **2.** less advanced in evolutionary development: *lower organisms.* **3.** *also,* **Lower.** designating an earlier part of a geological period or system: *lower Cretaceous.* —*v.t.* **1.** to take or bring down; let down: *to lower the flag, to lower a bucket into a well.* **2.** to reduce, as in height, amount, value, or degree: *to lower the water level, to lower prices.* **3.** to lessen the intensity of; diminish the volume of: *Lower your voice.* **4.** to bring down in value or estimation: *Don't lower yourself by cheating.* **5.** to lessen the force or effectiveness of; weaken: *A lack of sleep will lower your resistance to illness.* —*v.i.* to become lower. [**Low**[1] + -**ER**[1].]

low·er[2] (lou′ər) *v.i.* **1.** to frown; scowl. **2.** to appear dark, gloomy, or threatening. —*n.* **1.** a frown; scowl. **2.** a dark, gloomy, or threatening appearance, as in the sky. *Also,* **lour.** [Middle English *louren.*]

low·er·case (lō′ər kās′) *adj.* of or relating to or printed in small letters. ➡ distinguished from **upper-case.** —*v.t.,* -**cased,** -**cas·ing.** to set in or print with small letters.

lower case 1. small letters. **2.** a type case holding small letters.

low·er-class (lō′ər klas′) *adj.* of or relating to the lower class.

lower class, the portion of society, including the working class and the very poor, occupying a social and economic position below that of the middle class.

a	at	e	end	o	hot	u	up	hw	white	⟨ about
ā	ape	ē	me	ō	old	ū	use	ng	song	taken
ä	far	i	it	ô	fork	ü	rule	th	thin	ə⟨ pencil
âr	care	ī	ice	oi	oil	u̇	pull	th	this	lemon
		îr	pierce	ou	out	ûr	turn	zh	measure	⟨ circus

lower house *also,* **Lower House.** in a legislature having two branches, the larger and more representative branch, such as the House of Representatives in the U.S. Congress.

low·er·ing (lou′ər ing) *adj.* **1.** clouded over; dark; gloomy: *the steady rain falling from lowering sky* (Joseph Conrad, 1895). **2.** frowning or gloomy because of bad humor or anger; scowling. —**low′er·ing·ly,** *adv.*

low·er·most (lō′ər mōst′) *adj.* lowest.

lower world, the abode of the dead; Hades.

lowest common denominator, least common denominator.

lowest common multiple, least common multiple.

low frequency, any radio frequency between 30 and 300 kilohertz. —**low′-fre′quen·cy,** *adj.*

Low German 1. a form of the German language spoken predominantly in the lowlands of northern Germany. **2.** a group of Germanic languages, including Frisian, Dutch, and Flemish, spoken predominantly in the Low Countries. [Translation of German *Niederdeutsch;* because originally used mainly in the lowlands of northern Germany. Compare HIGH GERMAN.]

low-grade (lō′grād′) *adj.* **1.** of an inferior grade, worth, or quality: *low-grade ore.* **2.** at the end of a range that is lower or less: *a low-grade fever, a low-grade conflict.*

low-key (lō′kē′) *adj.* characterized by restraint or subtlety; quiet. Also, **low-keyed** (lō′kēd′).

low·land (lō′lənd) *n.* land that is on a lower level than its surroundings. —*adj.* **1.** of, relating to, or characteristic of such land. **2.** Lowland. of or relating to the Scottish Lowlands.

low·land·er (lō′lən dər) *n.* **1.** a native or inhabitant of a lowland. **2.** Lowlander. an inhabitant of the Scottish Lowlands.

low-lev·el language, (lō′lev′əl) a computer language made up entirely of patterns of zeros and ones.

low·ly (lō′lē) *adj.,* **-li·er, -li·est. 1.** humble in condition or quality; low in rank or importance: *a lowly cottage.* **2.** humble in manner or spirit; meek: *a lowly and unassuming person.* —*adv.* in a humble manner; humbly; meekly. —**low′li·ness,** *n.*

Low Mass, a simplified form of Mass that is said, not sung, by the celebrant, who is assisted by one or two servers. It is celebrated without the use of choir, music, or incense. ➡ distinguished from **High Mass.**

low-mind·ed (lō′mīn′did) *adj.* having a base or vulgar mind or nature.

low-necked (lō′nekt′) *adj.* (of a garment) cut so as to expose the neck and shoulders; décolleté.

low-pitched (lō′picht′) *adj.* **1.** having a low tone. **2.** (of a roof) having little slope.

low-pres·sure (lō′presh′ər) *adj.* **1.** having, using, or indicating a low degree of pressure: *low-pressure tires.* **2.** having a low barometric pressure. **3.** calm and unhurried; relaxed: *a low-pressure sales technique.*

low profile, a manner, attitude, or way of behaving that is deliberately restrained so as not to attract attention.

low relief, bas-relief.

low-spir·it·ed (lō′spir′i tid) *adj.* depressed; dispirited.

low tide 1. the tide at its lowest level. **2.** the time when this level is reached. **3.** the lowest point of anything.

low water 1. water that has reached its lowest level, as in a river or stream. **2.** low tide.

low-wa·ter mark (lō′wô′tər, -wot′ər) **1.** a mark indicating the lowest level reached by a body of water. **2.** the lowest point of anything.

lox[1] (loks) *n.* a kind of smoked, heavily cured salmon. [Yiddish *laks* salmon, from German *lachs,* from Middle High German *lahs.*]

lox[2] (loks) *n.* liquid oxygen. [Short for *l(iquid) ox(ygen).*]

loy·al (loi′əl) *adj.* **1.** steadfast in one's friendship, devotion, or regard; faithful to one's trust or duty: *a loyal friend.* **2.** constant in one's allegiance to one's monarch, government, or country. **3.** characterized by or expressing loyalty: *a loyal declaration.* [French *loyal* faithful, lawful, from Latin *lēgālis* relating to the law, from *lēx* law. Doublet of LEGAL.] —**loy′al·ly,** *adv.* —For Synonyms, see **faithful.**

loy·al·ist (loi′ə list) *n.* **1.** a person who supports the existing monarch, leader, or government, esp. during times of war or revolution. **2.** *also,* Loyalist. a colonist who remained loyal to the British government during the American Revolution. **3.** Loyalist. a person who supported the republic during the Spanish Civil War.

loy·al·ty (loi′əl tē) *n., pl.* **-ties. 1.** constant devotion or allegiance; faithful adherence: *loyalty to one's country.* **2.** an instance of being loyal: *to have loyalties to two schools.*

loz·enge (loz′inj) *n.* **1.** a small tablet of sugar and other flavoring, often containing medicine. **2.** a figure having two acute and two oblique angles and four equal sides; diamond. [Old French *losenge* figure or shape shaped like a diamond; probably of Celtic origin.]

LP *n., pl.* **LPs** or **LP's.** *Trademark.* a long-playing record.

LPG, liquefied petroleum gas.

LPN, licensed practical nurse.

Lr, the symbol for lawrencium.

LSAT, Law School Admission Test.

LSD, a psychedelic drug that produces hallucinations and temporary changes in personality. Continued use can produce depression, paranoia, or psychosis. [Abbreviation of *l(y)s(ergic acid) d(iethylamide).*]

l.t. 1. local time. **2.** long ton.

Lt., Lieutenant.

Ltd. *also,* **ltd.** *British.* limited.

Lu, the symbol for lutetium.

lu·au (lü′ou′) *n.* in Hawaii, a feast, often with entertainment. [Hawaiian *lu′au.*]

lub·ber (lub′ər) *n.* **1.** a heavy, clumsy, stupid person. **2.** an awkward or inexperienced sailor; landlubber. [Possibly of Scandinavian origin.] —**lub′ber·ly,** *adj., adv.*

lu·bri·cant (lü′bri kənt) *n.* any substance, as oil or grease, used to reduce friction, such as between moving parts of a machine. —*adj.* lubricating.

lu·bri·cate (lü′bri kāt′) *v.,* **-cat·ed, -cat·ing.** —*v.t.* **1.** to apply oil, grease, or other lubricant to (the moving parts of a machine) in order to reduce friction: *to lubricate a door hinge.* **2.** to make slippery or smooth: *to lubricate the skin with oil.* —*v.i.* to act as a lubricant. [Latin *lūbricātus,* past participle of *lūbricāre* to make slippery (from *lūbricus* slippery) + -ATE[1].] —**lu′bri·ca′tion,** *n.* —**lu′bri·ca′tor,** *n.*

lu·bric·i·ty (lü bris′i tē) *n., pl.* **-ties. 1.** the state or quality of being slippery; oiliness; smoothness. **2.** elusiveness or instability: *the lubricity of fame.* **3.** lewdness; lasciviousness. [Medieval Latin *lubricitas* lechery, from Late Latin *lūbricitās* slipperiness, from Latin *lūbricus* slippery.]

lu·bri·cous (lü′bri kəs) *adj.* **1.** smooth and slippery; oily: *a lubricous surface.* **2.** elusive or unstable: *a lubricous mobility, lubricous proof.* **3.** lewd; lascivious. Also, **lu·bri·cious** (lübrish′əs). [Latin *lūbricus* slippery.]

lu·cent (lü′sənt) *adj.* **1.** emitting light; shining; bright; luminous. **2.** clear or translucent. [Latin *lūcēns,* present participle of *lūcēre* to shine.] —**lu′cen·cy,** *n.* —**lu′cent·ly,** *adv.*

lu·cerne (lü sûrn′) *n. British.* alfalfa. [French *luzerne,* from Provençal *luzerno* glowworm, going back to Latin *lucerna* lamp; referring to its shiny seeds.]

lu·ces (lü′sēz) a plural of **lux.**

lu·cid (lü′sid) *adj.* **1.** easily understood; fully intelligible; clear: *a lucid explanation.* **2.** showing clear thinking or mental soundness; rational; sane: *a lucid person, lucid reasoning.* **3.** transparent: *the pure and lucid mountain air.* **4.** emitting light; shining; bright; luminous. [Latin *lūcidus* bright, shining.] —**lu·cid′i·ty, lu′cid·ness,** *n.* —**lu′cid·ly,** *adv.*

Lu·ci·fer (lü′sə fər) *n.* **1.** in Christianity, the rebellious archangel who was cast out of heaven with his followers; Satan. **2.** in poetry, the planet Venus when it appears as the morning star. [Latin *lūcifer* light-bringing, the planet Venus, from *lūx* light + *ferre* to bring.]

lu·cif·er·in (lü sif′ər in) *n.* a pigment present in bioluminescent organisms, as fireflies and glowworms, that produces an almost heatless light as it oxidizes. [Latin *lūcifer* morning star + -IN[1].]

Lu·cite (lü′sīt) *n. Trademark.* a transparent, acrylic resin available in solid or liquid form and having many uses, as in light fixtures. [Latin *lūc-,* stem of *lūx* + -ITE[1].]

luck (luk) *n.* **1.** an unpredictable factor influencing events or circumstances for good or ill: *Luck alone will not get you a job.* **2.** the events or circumstances so influenced: *a life filled with bad luck.* **3.** success or good fortune: *Did you have any luck in finding the glasses you had lost?* [Middle Dutch *luc* good fortune.]

· **to be down on one's luck.** to experience bad luck.

· **to be in luck.** to have good luck.

· **to be out of luck.** to have bad luck.

· **to luck out.** to be lucky.

· **to push (or crowd) one's luck.** to take additional risks when one already has had good fortune.

· **to try one's luck.** to see if one can do something; take a chance.

Synonyms *n.* **Luck, fortune,** and **chance** denote a factor often thought to be behind events that are not predictable and have no apparent cause. **Luck** is informal and suggests complete randomness: *By pure luck we left the building just before the fire broke out.* **Fortune** has its roots in Latin, where it was the name of a goddess of fate. It is more formal and suggests that there is a force controlling events: *It was my good fortune to meet you when I was most in need of a friend.* **Chance,**

somewhere between these extremes, suggests impersonality and the lack of any controlling force: *We'll be prepared and leave the rest to chance.*

luck·i·ly (luk′ə lē) *adv.* with or by a stroke of good luck; fortunately.

luck·less (luk′lis) *adj.* not having good luck; unlucky. —**luck′less·ly,** *adv.* —**luck′less·ness,** *n.*

luck·y (luk′ē) *adj.,* **luck·i·er, luck·i·est. 1.** having good luck; fortunate. **2.** occurring happily or fortunately: *a lucky meeting.* **3.** thought to bring good luck: *a lucky charm.* —**luck′i·ness,** *n.*

lu·cra·tive (lü′krə tiv) *adj.* bringing money or profit; profitable: *a lucrative business.* [Latin *lucrātivus,* going back to *lucrum* gain.] —**lu′cra·tive·ly,** *adv.* —**lu′cra·tive·ness,** *n.*

lu·cre (lü′kər) *n.* money or riches, esp. when thought of as evil: *filthy lucre.* [Latin *lucrum.*]

lu·cu·brate (lü′kyə brāt′) *v.i.,* **-brat·ed, -brat·ing. 1.** to write or study laboriously, esp. at night. **2.** to write in a learned or scholarly manner. [Latin *lūcubrātus,* past participle of *lūcubrāre* to work by lamplight at night.]

lu·cu·bra·tion (lü′kyə brā′shən) *n.* **1.** laborious writing or study, esp. done late at night. **2.** an elaborately written and scholarly literary work. [Latin *lūcubrātiō* a working at night.]

lu·di·crous (lü′di krəs) *adj.* laughably absurd; ridiculous: *to look ludicrous in a wig.* [Latin *lūdicrus* sportive, playful, from *lūdus* sport, play.] —**lu′di·crous·ly,** *adv.* —**lu′di·crous·ness,** *n.*

luff (luf) *n.* **1.** the sailing of a ship closer to the wind. **2.** the forward edge of a fore-and-aft sail. —*v.i.* to turn the bow of a ship nearer to the wind, so that the sails flap and do not fill with air. [Old French *lof* device to change the course of a ship; of Germanic origin.]

Luft·waf·fe (lüft′vä′fə) *n. German.* the German air force under the Nazis.

lug¹ (lug) *v.,* **lugged, lug·ging.** —*v.t.* to pull or carry with effort: *We lugged the heavy trunk down the stairs.* —*v.i.* to pull or tug. [Middle English *luggen;* probably of Scandinavian origin.]

lug² (lug) *n.* **1.** the projecting part by which something is gripped or held. **2.** a heavy nut fitting over a large bolt, used esp. to attach a wheel to an automobile axle. Also, **lug nut. 3.** *Slang.* a clumsy, doltish person. [Middle English *lugge;* of uncertain origin.]

lug³ (lug) *n.* lugsail.

luge (lüzh) *n.* a type of sled on which one or two persons lie face up, used esp. in racing. —*v.i.,* **luged, lug·ing.** to race or ride on such a sled.

lug·gage (lug′ij) *n.* bags, boxes, trunks, or suitcases used by a traveler for transporting belongings. [LUG¹ + -AGE.]

lug·ger (lug′ər) *n.* a small boat having two or three masts and rigged with lugsails.

lug nut, lug² *(def. 2).*

lug·sail (lug′sāl′, -səl) *n.* a four-sided sail without a boom, held by a yard that hangs obliquely to the mast. Also, **lug.** [Dialectal English *lug* pole (of uncertain origin) + SAIL.]

lu·gu·bri·ous (lù gü′brē əs, -gü′-) *adj.* excessively mournful or sorrowful: *The disappointed child had a lugubrious look.* [Latin *lūgubris* mournful + -OUS.] —**lu·gu′bri·ous·ly,** *adv.* —**lu·gu′bri·ous·ness,** *n.*

lug·worm (lug′wûrm′) *n.* a marine worm, genus *Arenicola,* having tufted gills in two rows on its back, that burrows in the sand along the seashore. [Of uncertain origin.]

Luke (lük) *n.* the third book and Gospel of the New Testament, attributed to the Evangelist Luke.

luke·warm (lük′wôrm′) *adj.* **1.** moderately warm; tepid: *lukewarm bath water.* **2.** having or expressing little warmth or enthusiasm; lacking zeal; indifferent: *a lukewarm welcome.* [Dialectal English *luke* (of uncertain origin) + WARM.] —**luke′warm′ly,** *adv.* —**luke′warm′ness,** *n.*

lull (lul) *v.t.* **1.** to calm with soothing sounds or caresses: *The sound of the rain lulled me to sleep.* **2.** to calm by deception: *to be lulled into a false sense of security.* —*v.i.* to become calm; diminish in force gradually: *The storm lulled.* —*n.* **1.** a brief calm or period of quiet. **2.** a brief lessening or cessation of activity: *There was a lull in business.* [Imitative.]

lul·la·by (lul′ə bī′) *n., pl.* **-bies.** a song sung to lull a child to sleep.

lum·ba·go (lum bā′gō) *n.* a pain in the region of the back between the chest cavity and the pelvis. [Late Latin *lumbāgō,* from Latin *lumbus* loin.]

lum·bar (lum′bər, -bär) *adj.* of, relating to, or near the loins. —*n.* a lumbar vertebra, artery, nerve, or the like. [Modern Latin *lumbaris,* from Latin *lumbus* loin.]

lum·ber¹ (lum′bər) *n.* **1.** timber cut as planks and boards. **2.** useless articles, as old furniture or worn-out household items, taking up space. —*v.i.* to cut timber into lumber and prepare it for market. —*v.t.* **1.** to cut down the trees in: *to lumber a forest.*

2. to cut down (trees) for lumber. **3.** to take up space or encumber (something, as a room) with useless articles. [Of uncertain origin.]

lum·ber² (lum′bər) *v.i.* to move in a clumsy or noisy manner: *The old wagon lumbered down the dirt road.* [Middle English *lomeren;* probably of Scandinavian origin.]

lum·ber·ing¹ (lum′bər ing) *n.* the business or work of cutting and preparing timber for market. [LUMBER¹ + -ING¹.]

lum·ber·ing² (lum′bər ing) *adj.* moving in a clumsy or noisy manner: *a lumbering gait.* [LUMBER² + -ING².]

lum·ber·jack (lum′bər jak′) *n.* a person who cuts down trees and prepares logs for transportation to a sawmill.

lum·ber·man (lum′bər mən) *n., pl.* **-men** (-mən). **1.** lumberjack. **2.** a person who works in or manages a lumberyard.

lum·ber·yard (lum′bər yärd′) *n.* a business concern that stores and sells lumber.

lu·men (lü′mən) *n.* a unit of luminous flux equal to the amount of light falling on 1 square unit of surface area, of which each point is at a distance of 1 unit from a light source with an intensity of 1 candela. [Latin *lūmen* light.]

lu·mi·nance (lü′mə nəns) *n.* **1.** the quality or condition of being luminous. **2.** the brightness or intensity of light reflected or emitted by a surface of a given area, esp. as measured in candelas per square meter. [Latin *lūminis,* genitive of *lūmen* light + -ANCE.]

lu·mi·nar·y (lü′mə ner′ē) *n., pl.* **-nar·ies. 1.** a person who is recognized or noted for high achievement: *A group of luminaries discussed the future of space travel.* **2.** a light-giving body, esp. the sun or the moon. [Medieval Latin *luminarium* light, lamp, going back to Latin *lūmen* light.]

lu·mi·nesce (lü′mə nes′) *v.i.,* **-nesced, -nesc·ing.** to display the property of luminescence; emit light without heat, as a phosphorescent or fluorescent substance.

lu·mi·nes·cence (lü′mə nes′əns) *n.* **1.** the emission of visible light without heat, as by means of some chemical reaction or some electrical action within or upon the emitting body. Phosphorescence and fluorescence are two forms of luminescence. **2.** the light thus emitted. [Latin *lūmen* light + -ESCENCE.] —**lu′mi·nes′cent,** *adj.*

lu·mi·nif·er·ous (lü′mə nif′ər əs) *adj.* producing or transmitting light. [Latin *lūmen* light + -FEROUS.]

lu·mi·nos·i·ty (lü′mə nos′i tē) *n., pl.* **-ties. 1.** the quality or condition of being luminous. **2.** something luminous.

lu·mi·nous (lü′mə nəs) *adj.* **1.** emitting light; shining: *luminous flames.* **2.** full of light; bright; resplendent. **3.** clear to the mind; easily understood: *luminous prose.* [Latin *lūminōsus* full of light, from *lūmen* light.] —**lu′mi·nous·ly,** *adv.* —**lu′mi·nous·ness,** *n.* —For Synonyms, see **bright.**

luminous flux, the rate of transmission of light energy.

lum·mox (lum′əks) *n.* a clumsy, foolish person.

lump¹ (lump) *n.* **1.** a solid, usually shapeless piece or mass: *a lump of iron ore, a lump of clay.* **2.** a small cube: *a lump of sugar.* **3.** a swelling; protuberance: *to have a lump on the head.* **4.** a heavy, often dull person. **5. lumps.** *Informal.* a deserved rebuke or punishment: *to take one's lumps.* —*adj.* **1.** formed in a lump or lumps: *lump sugar.* **2.** not divided into parts; whole or total: *We paid for the used car in a lump sum.* —*v.t.* **1.** to put or bring together, as in one pile or collection. **2.** to consider or deal with as a whole. —*v.i.* to form into a lump or lumps; become lumpy: *The oatmeal lumped when it cooled.* [Of uncertain origin.]

•**a lump in one's throat.** a feeling of tightness in the throat, esp. from emotion.

lump² (lump) *v.t. Informal.* to endure despite one's displeasure: *If you don't like it, lump it.* [Of uncertain origin.]

lum·pen (lum′pən) *adj.* of, relating to, or belonging to a group of people who are generally considered the lowest segment of their class in society as a result of being uprooted or dispossessed: *street people, the homeless, and other members of the lumpen proletariat.* [Short for German *Lumpenproletariat* the dregs of the proletariat, from *Lumpen* rags + *Proletariat* proletariat.]

lump·ish (lum′pish) *adj.* **1.** like a lump. **2.** heavy and awkward. **3.** stupid; dull.

lump·y (lum′pē) *adj.,* **lump·i·er, lump·i·est. 1.** covered or filled with lumps: *lumpy oatmeal.* **2.** heavy and awkward; lumpish. —**lump′i·ly,** *adv.* —**lump′i·ness,** *n.*

Lu·na (lü′nə) *n.* in Roman mythology, the goddess of the moon. Her Greek counterpart is Selene. [Latin *lūna* moon.]

lu·na·cy (lü′nə sē) *n., pl.* **-cies. 1.a.** mental illness; madness; insanity. **b.** formerly, periodic insanity thought to be caused by

a	at	e	end	o	hot	u	up	hw	white	⟨	about
ā	ape	ē	me	ō	old	ū	use	ng	song		taken
ä	far	i	it	ô	fork	ü	rule	th	thin	ə	pencil
âr	care	ī	ice	oi	oil	u̇	pull	th	this		lemon
		îr	pierce	ou	out	ûr	turn	zh	measure		circus

changes of the moon. **2.** senseless or reckless conduct; utter folly. [LUNA(TIC) + -CY.]

lu·na moth (lü′nə) *also,* **Luna moth.** a large green moth, *Actias luna,* having wings with transparent spots and, on the hind wings, graceful taillike extensions.

lu·nar (lü′nər) *adj.* **1.** of or relating to the moon: *the lunar orbit.* **2.** measured by the revolutions of the moon. [Latin *lūnāris* relating to the moon, from *lūna* moon.]

luna moth

lunar eclipse, see **eclipse** *(def. 1).*

lunar module, a self-contained section of the manned spacecraft that flew to the moon, designed to separate from the spacecraft as it orbited the moon and to carry two astronauts to and from the moon's surface.

lunar month, see **month** *(def. 4).*

lunar year, year *(def. 3).*

lu·nate (lü′nāt) *adj. Anatomy.* crescent-shaped: *lunate bone.* —*n.* a bone of the wrist. [Latin *lūnātus,* from *lūna* moon.]

lu·na·tic (lü′nə tik) *n.* **1.** an insane person. **2.** a senseless or reckless person. —*adj.* **1.** not mentally sound; insane. **2.** of or for insane people: *a lunatic asylum.* **3.** extremely senseless or reckless. [Middle English *lunatik,* from Old French *lunatique,* from Late Latin *lūnāticus* insane, moonstruck, from *lūna* moon, from Latin *lūna;* referring to the earlier belief that a form of insanity was related to or caused by the phases of the moon.]

lunatic fringe, the members of a movement or society who express extremist views.

lunch (lunch) *n.* **1.** a light meal between breakfast and supper, usually eaten around noon. **2.** the food prepared for such a meal. —*v.i.* to eat lunch. [Short for LUNCHEON.] —**lunch′er,** *n.*

lunch·box (lunch′boks′) *n.* a small metal or plastic box with a handle used to carry one's lunch to work or school.

lunch counter, an area where light meals are served, consisting of a counter and a row of stools, as found in a store or restaurant.

lunch·eon (lun′chən) *n.* lunch, esp. a formal one. [Possibly a modification of dialectal English *nuncheon* light noon snack, going back to Old English *nōn* (see NOON) + *scenc* a drink.]

lunch·eon·ette (lun′chə net′) *n.* a small restaurant or lunch counter where light meals, esp. breakfast and lunch, are served.

lunch·room (lunch′rüm′, -ru̇m′) *n.* a place where light meals are served, esp. a cafeteria in a school or factory, or where one may eat one's lunch.

lune (lün) *n.* a crescent-shaped plane figure or figure on the surface of a sphere bounded by two arcs of circles. [Latin *lūna* moon.]

lu·nette (lü net′) *n.* **1.** a curved or crescent-shaped window or other opening in a vaulted ceiling or dome. **2.** a wall area bounded by the curve of a rounded or pointed arch, often decorated with paintings or sculpture. [French *lunette,* diminutive of *lune* moon, from Latin *lūna.*]

lung (lung) *n.* **1.** in air-breathing vertebrates, one of a pair of spongy, cone-shaped organs of respiration that supply the blood with oxygen and rid it of carbon dioxide. For illustration, see **respiratory system. 2.** a similar organ in certain invertebrates, as the freshwater snail or the land snail. [Old English *lungen* the organ of respiration in vertebrates.]

lunge (lunj) *n.* **1.** any sudden forward movement: *The catcher made a lunge for the ball.* **2.** a sudden forward thrust, as with a sword. —*v.i.,* **lunged, lung·ing.** to make a sudden forward movement: *I lunged for the falling platter.* —*v.t.* to thrust or cause to thrust. [Short for obsolete *allonge,* from French *allonger* to lengthen, going back to Latin *ad* to + *longus* extended; referring to the extension of the body when lunging.] —**lung′er,** *n.*

lung·fish (lung′fish′) *n., pl.* **-fish** or **-fish·es.** any of several fish, order Dipnoi, that inhabit freshwater swamps and marshes in Africa, South America, and Australia, having a brown or tan body with two pairs of ribbonlike fins. Lungfish have lunglike air bladders and, in hatchlings, gills that enable the young to breathe under water. Length: 2-4 feet (0.6-1.2 meters).

lung·wort (lung′wûrt′) *n.* any of a small group of plants, genus *Pulmonaria,* found in Europe and Asia, bearing clusters of large blue or purple, funnel-shaped flowers, esp. the **blue lungwort,** *P. officinalis,* grown as a garden plant.

Lu·per·ca·li·a (lü′pər kā′lē ə) *n.* an ancient Roman fertility festival, celebrated on February 15.

lu·pine¹ (lü′pīn) *n.* any of a group of plants, genus *Lupinus,* of the pea family, bearing spikes of white, yellow, blue, or purple flowers. [Latin *lupīnum,* from *lupus* wolf; referring to the belief that the plant exhausts the soil.]

lu·pine² (lü′pīn) *adj.* **1.** related to the wolf. **2.** of or resembling a wolf; fierce; ravenous. [Latin *lupīnus,* from *lupus* wolf.]

lu·pus (lü′pəs) *n.* any of several chronic, autoimmune, tubercular diseases of the skin, often affecting other parts and systems of the body. [Latin *lupus* wolf; referring to the resemblance of its sores to wolf bites.]

lurch¹ (lûrch) *n.* a sudden rolling or swaying to one side or from side to side: *The ship gave a lurch in the choppy water.* —*v.i.* **1.** to move jerkily and unsteadily; stagger: *to lurch to one's feet after suddenly awakening.* **2.** to roll or sway suddenly to one side or from side to side. [Of uncertain origin.]

lurch² (lûrch) *n.* the situation of the loser at the end of various games when he or she fails to score or is far behind an opponent. [French *lourche* name of a game resembling backgammon; probably of Germanic origin.]

·**to leave in the lurch.** to leave (someone) in a difficult or embarrassing situation.

lurch·er (lûr′chər) *n. Archaic.* a petty thief; poacher.

lure (lu̇r) *n.* **1.** a powerful or irresistible attraction: *the lure of the unknown.* **2.** something that attracts. **3.** bait, as an artificial fly used in fishing. —*v.t.,* **lured, lur·ing.** to attract powerfully; tempt: *I was lured into not going to class by the nice weather.* [Old French *loirre* bait; of Germanic origin.]

lu·rid (lu̇r′id) *adj.* **1.** shockingly terrible or repellent; sensational: *a lurid crime.* **2.** shining with a reddish glow or fiery glare: *a lurid fire.* **3.** extremely pale; wan. [Latin *lūridus* pale yellow, wan.] —**lu′rid·ly,** *adv.* —**lu·rid·ness,** *n.*

lurk (lûrk) *v.i.* **1.** to lie hidden: *A lion lurked in the underbrush.* **2.** to move about in a furtive manner; sneak. [Middle English *lurken,* from *luren* to frown; of uncertain origin.]

lus·cious (lush′əs) *adj.* **1.** sweet and pleasing to the taste or smell; delicious: *ripe, luscious pears.* **2.** pleasing to the other senses or to the mind: *luscious music.* [Possibly a shortening and modification of DELICIOUS.] —**lus′cious·ly,** *adv.* —**lus′cious·ness,** *n.*

lush¹ (lush) *adj.* **1.** rich and abundant; luxuriant: *a lush growth of ferns.* **2.** characterized by or covered with luxuriant growth: *lush forests.* **3.** juicy and tender: *lush oranges.* **4.** extremely comfortable and pleasant; luxurious; sumptuous; rich: *a lush carpet.* [Possibly a form of obsolete *lash* soft, watery, from Old French *lasche* slack, loose, from Latin *laxus* loose.] —**lush′ly,** *adv.* —**lush′ness,** *n.*

lush² (lush) *n. Slang.* a person who drinks alcoholic beverages often and to excess. [Of uncertain origin.]

lust (lust) *n.* **1.** intense sexual appetite or desire. **2.** any strong or excessive desire: *The miser had a lust for money.* —*v.i.* to have a strong or excessive desire, as a sexual desire (often with *for* or *after*): *to lust after power.* [Old English *lust* pleasure, desire.]

lus·ter (lus′tər) *also, British,* **lustre.** *n.* **1.** the quality of shining by reflected light; luminous glow; sheen: *The wax gave the floor a bright luster.* **2.** a radiant or glowing brightness: *tired eyes that have lost their luster.* **3.** exalted honor or glory; splendor; renown: *Brave deeds add luster to one's reputation.* **4.** the reflective quality of the surface of a mineral. **5.** a shiny, often iridescent, metallic glazed surface, as on pottery. **6.** any of several substances, as a polish, used to give a glossy finish or appearance. **7.** a fabric that has a glossy appearance. [French *lustre* brightness, from Italian *lustro,* from *lustrare* to illuminate, from Latin *lūstrāre.*]

> **Synonyms** **Luster, sheen,** and **gloss¹** denote a shiny, usually smooth quality observable when light falls on a surface. **Luster** connotes brilliance: *to burnish brass to a high luster.* **Sheen** suggests a softer, more subdued luster: *the sheen on someone's freshly washed hair, the sheen on the surface of water in the moonlight.* **Gloss** is a more superficial sheen, which may be obtained through a process: *the gloss on a newly waxed floor, a cheap fabric with high gloss.*

lus·ter·ware (lus′tər wâr′) *n.* pottery having a shiny, often iridescent, glazed surface.

lust·ful (lust′fəl) *adj.* full of or characterized by lust. —**lust′ful·ly,** *adv.* —**lust′ful·ness,** *n.*

lus·tral (lus′trəl) *adj.* **1.** of, relating to, or used in rites of purification. **2.** occurring every five years. [Latin *lustrālis,* from *lustrum* rites of purification performed in ancient Rome once every five years.]

lus·trate (lus′trāt) *v.t.,* **-trat·ed, -trat·ing.** to purify by a rite or ceremony. [Latin *lūstrātus,* past participle of *lūstrāre* to illuminate, purify.] —**lus·tra′tion,** *n.*

lus·tre (lus′tər) *British.* luster.

lus·trous (lus′trəs) *adj.* having a glossy surface; shining: *lustrous hair, lustrous fabric.* —**lus′trous·ly,** *adv.*

lus·trum (lus′trəm) *n., pl.* **-trums** or **-tra** (-trə). **1.** a purification ceremony performed by the censors for the people of ancient Rome every five years. **2.** a period of five years. [Latin *lūstrum.*]

lust·y (lus'tē) *adj.*, **lust·i·er, lust·i·est. 1.** full of strength and vigor; healthy: *a lusty cry from a newborn baby.* **2.** strong or abundant: *a lusty wine.* —**lust'i·ly,** *adv.* —**lust'i·ness,** *n.*

lu·ta·nist (lü'tə nist) *also,* **lu·te·nist.** *n.* a person who plays the lute. Also, **lutist.** [Medieval Latin *lutanista* lutanist, from *lutana* lute, probably from Old French *lëut.* See LUTE.]

lute (lüt) *n.* a stringed musical instrument having a pear-shaped body and a long fretted neck, played with the fingers or a plectrum. The lute's number and arrangement of strings vary. [Old French *lëut,* going back to Arabic *al-'ūd* the wood, the lute.]

lute
a painting of Elizabeth I playing a lute

lu·te·al (lü'tē əl) *adj.* of or relating to the corpus luteum or to the hormone it secretes, progesterone.

lu·te·in·ize (lü'tē ə nīz') *v.,* **-ized, -iz·ing.** —*v.t.* to stimulate development of corpora lutea. —*v.i.* to become transformed into or a part of a corpus luteum. —**lu'te·in·i·za'tion,** *n.*

luteinizing hormone (lü'tē ə nī'zing) a hormone secreted by the pituitary gland that is essential to the production of progesterone in females and testosterone in males.

lu·te·ti·um (lü tē'shē əm) *n.* a heavy, silvery white metallic element, one of the rare-earth elements. Symbol **Lu** For tables, see **element.** [Modern Latin *lutetium,* from Latin *Lūtētia* ancient name for Paris, the birthplace of Georges Urbain, 1872-1938, French chemist who discovered the element.]

Lu·ther·an (lü'thər ən) *adj.* of or relating to the German theologian Martin Luther, his doctrines, or the Protestant denomination named after him. —*n.* a member of the Lutheran denomination.

Lu·ther·an·ism (lü'thər ə niz'əm) *n.* the doctrines, beliefs, and practices of the Lutherans.

lut·ist (lü'tist) *n.* **1.** lutanist. **2.** a person who makes lutes.

lux (luks) *n., pl.* **lux** or **lux·es** or **lu·ces** (lü'sēz). the International System unit of illumination, equal to the illumination produced by 1 lumen distributed over an area of 1 square meter. [Latin *lux* light.]

lux·u·ri·ance (lug zhùr'ē əns, luk shùr'-) *n.* the state or quality of being luxuriant. Also, **lux·u'ri·an·cy.**

lux·u·ri·ant (lug zhùr'ē ənt, luk shùr'-) *adj.* **1.** thick or abundant: *a luxuriant growth of rosebushes.* **2.** rich in detail or ornament: *a luxuriant imagination, luxuriant decoration.* **3.** producing in great abundance: *luxuriant soil.* [Latin *luxuriāns,* present participle of *luxuriāre* to abound.] —**lux·u'ri·ant·ly,** *adv.*

lux·u·ri·ate (lug zhùr'ē āt', luk shùr'-) *v.i.,* **-at·ed, -at·ing. 1.** to indulge oneself in pleasure or luxury; live luxuriously. **2.** to take great delight (with *in* or *on*): *The dictator luxuriated in power.* **3.** to grow in great abundance: *The plants luxuriated in the warm, moist climate.* [Latin *luxuriātus,* past participle of *luxuriāre* to abound.] —**lux·u'ri·a'tion,** *n.*

lux·u·ri·ous (lug zhùr'ē əs, luk shùr'-) *adj.* **1.** given to or liking pleasure or luxury: *to have luxurious tastes.* **2.** characterized by luxury: *a luxurious mansion.* —**lux·u'ri·ous·ly,** *adv.* —**lux·u'ri·ous·ness,** *n.*

lux·u·ry (luk'shə rē, lug'zhə-) *n., pl.* **-ries. 1.** something that is conducive to a person's comfort or pleasure but not regarded as a necessity. **2.** a way of life that gives great comfort or pleasure.

—*adj.* providing luxury: *a luxury hotel.* [Latin *luxuria* excess, abundance, extravagance.]

-ly[1] *suffix* (used to form adverbs) **1.** in a particular manner or to a particular extent: *gladly, greatly.* **2.** in a particular position or at a particular time: *secondly, hourly, annually.* [Old English *-līce.*]

-ly[2] *suffix* (used to form adjectives) **1.** like, of the nature of, or suited to: *brotherly, sisterly.* **2.** happening at specified periods of time: *weekly.* [Old English *-līc.*]

ly·can·thrope (lī'kən thrōp', lī kan'thrōp) *n.* werewolf. [Greek *lykanthrōpos,* from *lykos* wolf + *anthrōpos* man.]

ly·cée (lē sā') *n., pl.* **-cées** (-sāz'; *French* -sā'). a preparatory school in France supported by the government. [French *lycée,* from Latin *Lycēum* gymnasium near Athens, where Aristotle taught, from Greek *Lykeion.* Doublet of LYCEUM.]

ly·ce·um (lī sē'əm, lī'sē-) *n.* **1.** a public hall in which educational programs, such as concerts or lectures, are presented. **2.** an organization devoted to such educational programs. [Latin *Lycēum* gymnasium near Athens, where Aristotle taught, from Greek *Lykeion;* so called from the nearby temple of *(Apollōn) lykeios* (Apollo the) Wolfslayer, from Greek *lykos* wolf. Doublet of LYCÉE.]

lych gate (lich) lich gate.

ly·co·pod (lī'kə pod') *n.* any of various small, green, creeping or erect, mosslike plants of the genus *Lycopoda,* as the club moss.

ly·co·po·di·um (lī'kə pō'dē əm) *n.* **1.** lycopod. **2.** a yellow powder made from the spores of certain lycopods and used in pyrotechnics and pharmacology. [Modern Latin *Lycopodium,* from Greek *lykos* wolf + *pous* foot; referring to its claw-shaped root.]

lydd·ite (lid'īt) *n.* an explosive whose chief ingredient is picric acid.

Lyd·i·an (lid'ē ən) *n.* **1.** a native, inhabitant, or citizen of Lydia. **2.** the language spoken in Lydia. —*adj.* of, relating to, or characteristic of Lydia or its people, language, or culture.

lye (lī) *n.* **1.** commercial sodium hydroxide, used to make soap and detergents. **2.** a solution obtained from leaching wood ashes, consisting mostly of potassium carbonate, used in making soap and glass. [Old English *lēag* strong alkaline solution.]

ly·ing[1] (lī'ing) *v.* the present participle of **lie**[1]. —*n.* the act of telling lies. —*adj.* untruthful or deceitful.

ly·ing[2] (lī'ing) the present participle of **lie**[2].

ly·ing-in (lī'ing in') *n., pl.* **ly·ings-in** or **ly·ing-ins.** the condition of a woman during and immediately following childbirth. —*adj.* of or relating to childbirth: *a lying-in hospital.*

Lyme disease (līm) a disease characterized by tiredness, chills, fever, headache, and a stiff neck, sometimes followed weeks or months later by heart and nerve abnormalities and arthritis. It is caused by a bacterium that is transmitted by the bite of a tick. [From *Lyme,* the town in Connecticut where it was first described.]

lymph (limf) *n.* a clear, colorless fluid, similar to blood in composition, that bathes the body cells, bringing nutrients and oxygen to the cells and carrying away wastes. [Latin *lympha* water.]

lym·phat·ic (lim fat'ik) *adj.* **1.** of, relating to, or containing lymph. **2.** lacking energy; dull; sluggish. —*n.* a lymphatic vessel.

lymphatic system, the system in the body that forms white blood cells and carries lymph from the tissues to the bloodstream. The lymphatic system includes the lymphatic vessels and the lymph nodes.

lymph node, any of the small nodes or bodies in the lymphatic vessels that filter out harmful substances and produce lymphocytes. Also, **lymph gland.**

lym·pho·cyte (lim'fə sīt') *n.* either of the two kinds of white blood cells, T cells and B cells, formed in the lymph nodes, that play an essential role in the body's immune reaction to infection. [Latin *lympha* water + Greek *kytos* hollow vessel.] —**lym·pho·cyt·ic** (lim'fə sit'ik), *adj.*

lym·phoid (lim'foid) *adj.* of, relating to, or resembling lymph or the tissue of the lymph nodes.

lym·pho·ma (lim fō'mə) *n., pl.* **-mas** or **-ma·ta** (-mə tə). any progressive enlargement of lymphatic tissue, usually due to malignant cell growth.

lynch (linch) *v.t.* to seize by mob action and put to death, usually by hanging, without due process of law. [From LYNCH LAW.] —**lynch'er,** *n.*

a	at	e	end	o	hot	u	up	hw	white	⌠	about
ā	ape	ē	me	ō	old	ū	use	ng	song		taken
ä	far	i	it	ô	fork	ü	rule	th	thin	ə ⟨	pencil
âr	care	ī	ice	oi	oil	ù	pull	th	this		lemon
		îr	pierce	ou	out	ûr	turn	zh	measure	⌡	circus

lynch law, the administration of punishment, usually death by hanging, without due process of law. [Earlier *Lynch's law,* possibly from Charles *Lynch,* 1736-86, a Virginia planter who organized bands of patriots to punish British sympathizers during the American Revolution.]

lynx (lingks) *n., pl.* **lynx** or **lynx·es.** any of various wildcats, genus *Lynx,* characterized by long legs, a short tail, and usually tufted ears. [Latin *lynx,* from Greek *lynx.*]

lynx-eyed (lingks′īd′) *adj.* having sharp vision.

ly·on·naise (lī′ə nāz′) *adj.* cooked with finely chopped onions: *lyonnaise potatoes.* [Probably short for French *à la lyonnaise* in the manner of *Lyon,* French city.]

Ly·ra (lī′rə) *n.* a constellation in the northern sky containing the bright star Vega. [Latin *lyra.* See LYRE.]

ly·rate (lī′rāt) *adj.* resembling a lyre in shape. Also, **ly′rat·ed.**

lyre (līr) *n.* a stringed musical instrument, used by the ancient Greeks to accompany singing and recitation. [Old French *lyre,* from Latin *lyra,* from Greek *lyrā.*]

lyre·bird (līr′bûrd′) *n.* an Australian bird, genus *Menura,* having predominantly brown plumage and known for its ability to mimic the calls of other birds. The male has a long tail that is lyre-shaped when spread. There are two species: *M. superba* and *M. alberti.* Length: to 38 inches (97 centimeters).

lyr·ic (lir′ik) *adj.* **1.** of or relating to a type of poetry that expresses strong personal emotion. **2.** like a lyric poem: *a lyric quality, lyric prose.* **3.** intended to be sung. **4.** of, relating to, or adapted to the lyre. **5.** having a light, flexible singing voice: *a lyric soprano.* Also, **lyr′i·cal.** —*n.* **1.** a lyric poem or lyric poetry.

lyrebird

2. lyrics. words written for a song. [Latin *lyricus* relating to the lyre, from Greek *lyrikos,* from *lyrā* lyre; originally referring to songs or poems accompanied by the lyre.] —**lyr′i·cal·ly,** *adv.*

lyr·i·cism (lir′ə siz′əm) *n.* **1.** the qualities or characteristics of lyric poetry. **2.** an outpouring of personal feeling; lyric expression.

lyr·i·cist (lir′ə sist) *n.* a person who writes lyrics, esp. for popular songs.

ly·sin (lī′sin) *n.* an antibody capable of bringing about the destruction of tissues, bacteria, or cells, esp. red blood cells. [Greek *lysis* a releasing, dissolution + -IN[1].]

ly·sine (lī′sēn, -sin) *n.* an essential amino acid produced by the hydrolysis of certain proteins, important for human and animal growth. Formula: $C_6H_{14}N_2O_2$ [Greek *lysis* a releasing, dissolution + -INE[2].]

ly·sis (lī′sis) *n., pl.* **-ses** (-sēz). the disintegration of a living cell, esp. through the action of specific antibodies. [Modern Latin *lysis,* from Greek *lysis* a loosening, separation into parts.]

Ly·sol (lī′sôl) *n. Trademark.* an oily liquid containing soap and cresols, used as an antiseptic and disinfectant. [Greek *lysis* a releasing + Latin *oleum* oil.]

ly·so·some (lī′sə sōm′) *n.* a membrane-bound cellular organelle, formed from the Golgi apparatus, that contains hydrolytic enzymes which break down proteins, polysaccharides, and lipids into their component parts. [Greek *lysis* a releasing, dissolution + -SOME[3].] —**ly′so·so′mal,** *adj.*

ly·so·zyme (lī′sə zīm′) *n.* an enzyme present in tears, saliva, mucus, and other body fluids that destroys a wide variety of bacteria.

lyt·ic (lit′ik) *adj.* **1.** of, relating to, or causing lysis. **2.** of or relating to a lysin. [Greek *lytikos* able to loosen, from *lysis.* See LYSIS.]

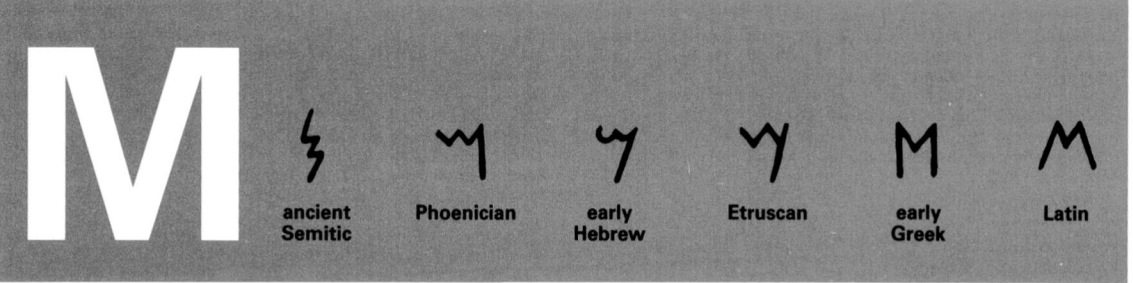

| ancient Semitic | Phoenician | early Hebrew | Etruscan | early Greek | Latin |

M The earliest form of the letter **M** was the ancient Semitic letter *mem*, meaning "water." The early Phoenician and early Hebrew alphabets altered the shape of *mem* by turning it on its side and making the last stroke longer. This was the form of **M** that the Etruscans borrowed about 2,800 years ago. The early Greeks also adopted the letter *mem*, and called it *mu*. But in writing *mu*, the Greeks made the first and last strokes of the letter nearly vertical. This shape was only slightly changed in the following centuries when the Romans borrowed *mu*. Our modern capital letter **M** closely resembles both the Latin and Greek forms of the letter.

m, M (em) *n., pl.* **m's, M's. 1.** the thirteenth letter of the English alphabet. **2.** the shape of this letter or something having this shape.

M (em) *also,* **m** *n., pl.* **M's.** the Roman numeral for 1,000.

M'- *prefix* Mac-; Mc.

m *also,* **m. 1.** *Physics.* mass. **2.** meter; meters. **3.** mile; miles. **4.** mill; mills. **5.** minute; minutes.

m. 1. male. **2.** married. **3.** masculine. **4.** meridian. **5.** month. **6.** morning.

M. 1. March. **2.** Master. **3.** May. **4.** Monday. **5.** Monsieur.

ma (mä) *n. Informal.* mother. [Short for MAMA.]

MA, the postal abbreviation for Massachusetts.

M.A., Master of Arts. Also, **A.M.**

ma'am (mam; *unstressed* məm) *n. Informal.* madam *(def. 1).*

Mab, Queen (mab) in English and Celtic folklore, the queen of the fairies.

Mac- *also,* **Mc-, M'-.** *prefix* son of. ➡ used in certain Scottish and Irish family names. [Irish and Gaelic *mac* son.]

ma·ca·bre (mə kä′brə, -bər, -käb′) *adj.* suggesting or dealing with death in a ghastly or ghoulish way; gruesome: *a macabre tale of a haunted cemetery.* [French *macabre* gruesome, ghastly (from the phrase *danse macabre* dance of death), possibly modification of Old French *Macabe* Maccabaeus; referring to the martyrdom of the Maccabees.]

mac·ad·am (mə kad′əm) *n.* **1.** a pavement or road surface consisting largely or entirely of layers of crushed stone. **2.** the crushed stone used in such pavements or roads. [From John L. *McAdam,* 1756-1836, Scottish engineer who introduced such roads.]

mac·a·da·mi·a (mak′ə dā′mē ə) *n.* **1.** any of a small genus, *Macadamia,* of trees and shrubs having hard fruit, esp. *M. integrifolia,* an Australian tree widely cultivated in Hawaii for its edible seeds. **2.** the round, sweet seed of this tree. Also *(def. 2),* **macadamia nut.** [From John *Macadam,* 1827-65, a Scottish chemist living in Australia.]

mac·ad·am·ize (mə kad′ə mīz′) *v.t.,* **-ized, -iz·ing.** to construct or pave (a road) with macadam. **—mac·ad′am·i·za′tion,** *n.*

ma·caque (mə kak′, -käk′) *n.* any of various short-tailed Old World monkeys, as the rhesus, genus *Macaca,* having cheek pouches in which food is stored. Length: 15-30 inches (38-76 centimeters) without the tail. [French *macaque,* from Portuguese *macaco* monkey, macaque; of Bantu origin.]

mac·a·ro·ni (mak′ə rō′nē) *n., pl.* **-nis** or **-nies. 1.** food made from a wheat-flour paste or dough, usually in the shape of short, hollow tubes, prepared for eating by boiling. **2.** an affected fop or dandy of eighteenth-century England. [Dialectal Italian *maccaroni,* plural of *maccarone* dumpling, small cake, paste with cheese; of uncertain origin.]

mac·a·roon (mak′ə rün′) *n.* a small cake or cookie made chiefly of ground almonds or coconut, egg whites, and sugar. [French *macaron,* from dialectal Italian *maccarone.* See MACARONI.]

ma·caw (mə kô′) *n.* any of several long-tailed parrots, family Psittacidae, found in Central and South America, esp. genus *Ara,* which is brilliantly colored. Length: to 3 feet (0.9 meter). [Portuguese *macau,* probably from *macaúba* a kind of palm tree, from Tupi-Guarani *macauba;* supposedly because it eats the fruit of this tree.]

Mac·beth (mək beth′) *n.* the main character in Shakespeare's play *Macbeth.*

Mac·ca·be·an (mak′ə bē′ən) *adj.* of, relating to, or characteristic of Judas Maccabeus or the Maccabees. [From the Jewish patriot Judas *Maccabeus,* died 160 B.C.]

macaw

Mac·ca·bees (mak′ə bēz′) *pl. n.* **1.** members of the family of Judas Maccabeus, who led a revolt in Judea against the Syrian ruler Antiochus IV, 215?-164 B.C., and themselves ruled Judea until 37 B.C. **2.** the last two books in the Old Testament of the Douay Bible, which recount the history of the Maccabean revolt.

mace[1] (mās) *n.* **1.** a heavy war club, usually having a spiked metal head, used esp. in the Middle Ages for crushing armor. **2.** an ornamental scepter or staff resembling such a club in shape, used as a ceremonial symbol of office or authority. [Middle English *mace,* from Old French *mace* large mallet, going back to Latin *matteola* mallet.]

mace[2] (mās) *n.* a delicately flavored, aromatic spice made by grinding the dried outer covering of the seed of the nutmeg. [Middle English *mace,* from Old French *macis,* from Medieval Latin *macis,* probably a scribe's error for Latin *macir* red spicy bark from India, from Greek *makir* a spice from India.]

Mace (mās) *n. Trademark.* a chemical mixture containing tear gas, used chiefly in riot control. **—v.t., Maced, Mac·ing.** to subject to Mace; use Mace against. [From MACE[1].]

mac·é·doine (mas′ā dwän′) *n.* **1.** a mixture of raw or cooked vegetables or fruits, sometimes jellied. **2.** any mixture or medley; hodgepodge. [French *macédoine* medley, hodgepodge, from Latin *Macedonia* Macedonia; referring to the mixture and variety of peoples living in Macedonia.]

mac·er·ate (mas′ə rāt′) *v.,* **-at·ed, -at·ing. —v.t. 1.** to soften or separate into constituent parts by or as by soaking in liquid. **2.** to cause (the body) to waste away or grow thin. **3.** to soak (food) in a liquid, such as wine: *to macerate currants.* **—v.i.** to become macerated. [Latin *mācerātus,* past participle of *mācerāre* to soften.] **—mac′er·a′tion,** *n.*

Mach (mäk, mak) *also,* **mach.** *n.* Mach number.

mach. 1. machine. **2.** machinery. **3.** machinist.

ma·chet·e (mə shet′ē, -chet′ē) *n.* a broad heavy knife used as a tool and weapon. [Spanish *machete,* from *macho* hammer, from Latin *marculus* small hammer.]

Mach·i·a·vel·li·an (mak′ē ə vel′ē ən) *adj.* **1.** characterized by subtle or sinister cunning, unscrupulous deception, and a tendency

a	at	e	end	o	hot	u	up	hw	white		about
ā	ape	ē	me	ō	old	ū	use	ng	song		taken
ä	far	i	it	ô	fork	ü	rule	th	thin	ə	pencil
âr	care	ī	ice	oi	oil	u̇	pull	th	this		lemon
		îr	pierce	ou	out	ûr	turn	zh	measure		circus

to do what is expedient rather than what is moral. **2.** acting in accordance with or characterized by the principles of government set forth by the Florentine statesman Niccolò Machiavelli in his book *The Prince,* whereby expediency is placed above morality and the use of unscrupulous means of acquiring and maintaining power is justified. **3.** of, relating to, or resembling Machiavelli or his political theories. —*n.* a follower of the political methods and theories advocated by Machiavelli. —**Mach′i·a·vel′li·an·ism, Mach′i·a·vel′lism,** *n.*

ma·chic·o·la·tion (mə chik′ə lā′shən) *n.* **1.** an opening, as in the base of a parapet or in the roof of a portal or entrance of a castle, through which missiles or molten lead could be dropped on attackers. **2.** a projecting gallery or parapet supported on corbels, with or without such openings.

mach·i·nate (mak′ə nāt′) *v.t., v.i.,* **-nat·ed, -nat·ing.** to scheme or contrive, esp. slyly or with evil purpose: *The rebels machinated to overthrow the government.* [Latin *māchinātus,* past participle of *māchinārī* to contrive.] —**mach′i·na′tor,** *n.*

mach·i·na·tion (mak′ə nā′shən) *n.* an artful, secret, or elaborate plot or scheme, often for some evil purpose.

machicolation

ma·chine (mə shēn′) *n.* **1.** an apparatus consisting of a number of integrated, usually moving, parts having specific functions, used in the performance of work, esp. a mechanical apparatus used to perform mechanical work. **2.** a device, such as a lever, pulley, or screw, that is used to perform work by directing, transmitting, or modifying force or motion. Also, **simple machine. 3.** a complex system or organization coordinated to function efficiently and smoothly: *The nation built up a powerful war machine.* **4.** a political organization, usually headed by a boss or clique, that controls a political party in an area: *the Democratic machine.* **5.** a person who behaves in a rigid or mechanical manner without emotion, thought, or will. **6.** a person who performs a particular activity or functions within a particular area with great efficiency and precision: *That boxer is the local fighting machine.* —*v.t.,* **-chined, -chin·ing.** to make, shape, or finish with a machine. [French *machine* engine, contrivance, from Latin *māchina,* going back to Greek *mēchanē.*]

ma·chine-gun (mə shēn′gun′) *v.t.,* **-gunned, -gun·ning.** to fire at or shoot with a machine gun.

machine gun, an automatic weapon that uses small-arms ammunition and fires continuously while pressure on the trigger is maintained.

machine language, the lowest-level computer programming language, written with only the binary digits 0 and 1, used directly by a computer without translation.

ma·chine-read·a·ble (mə shēn′rē′də bəl) *adj.* in a form that can be processed directly by a computer.

ma·chin·er·y (mə shē′nə rē) *n., pl.* **-er·ies. 1.** machines or machine parts, collectively: *a factory equipped with the latest machinery.* **2.** the working parts of a particular machine, collectively: *the machinery of an elevator.* **3.** the means or working parts by which something is kept in motion or a desired result is obtained: *the machinery of government.*

machine shop, a workshop where metal or other material is cut, shaped, and finished with machine tools.

machine tool, a power-driven, automatic or semiautomatic metalworking machine, as a lathe or drill press, designed to cut, shape, and perform similar operations.

ma·chin·ist (mə shē′nist) *n.* **1.** a person whose job is to operate machine tools. **2.** a person who designs, assembles, installs, or repairs machinery.

ma·chis·mo (mä chēz′mō) *n.* an exaggerated concept of masculinity, characterized by excessive pride, aggressiveness, and a sense of male superiority. Also, **macho.** [Spanish *machismo* virility, manhood, from *macho.* See MACHO.]

Mach·me·ter (mäk′mē′tər, mak′-) *also,* **mach·me·ter.** *n.* a device that indicates the speed of an aircraft in Mach numbers.

Mach number *also,* **mach number.** a number expressing the ratio of the speed of a body in a given atmosphere to the speed of sound in the same atmosphere. An aircraft traveling at Mach 3 is moving three times faster than sound; at Mach 1, its speed equals that of sound. Also, **Mach.** [From Ernst *Mach,* 1838-1916, Austrian physicist.]

ma·cho (mä′chō) *n., pl.* **-chos. 1.** machismo. **2.** in Spanish cultures, a strong, brave, and virile man. —*adj.* having or showing machismo; strongly masculine. [Spanish *macho* male, going back to Latin *masculus.* See MASCULINE.]

mac·in·tosh (mak′in tosh′) mackintosh.

mack·er·el (mak′ər əl, mak′rəl) *n., pl.* **-els** or **-el.** any of a group of commercially important food and game fish, family Scombridae, related to the tuna, having a silvery body that is marked in metallic blue on its upper surface. [Old French *makerel, maquerel;* of uncertain origin.]

mackerel sky, a sky covered with rows of small, white, fleecy clouds resembling the patterns on the back of a mackerel.

mack·i·naw (mak′ə nô′) *n.* **1.** a short coat made of a heavy woolen fabric that is usually napped on both sides and woven in a plaid. Also, **Mackinaw coat. 2.** a thick blanket made of a heavy woolen fabric, often woven in wide bands of different colors. Also, **Mackinaw blanket.** [From *Mackinac* Island, Michigan, where these items were traded in the nineteenth century.]

mack·in·tosh (mak′in tosh′) *also,* **macintosh.** *n.* **1.** a raincoat, esp. one made of a waterproof, rubberized fabric. **2.** the waterproof fabric itself. [From Charles *Macintosh,* 1766-1843, Scottish chemist who invented the fabric.]

mac·ra·mé (mak′rə mā′, mak′rə mā′) *n.* coarse lace made by knotting thread or cord, often in geometric patterns. [French *macramé,* from Italian *macrame,* from Turkish *makrama* towel, napkin, from Arabic *miqrama* embroidered cloth, from *rqm* to embroider.]

macro- *combining form* large; long; great: *macrocosm, macroeconomics.* [Greek *makros.*]

mac·ro·bi·ot·ic (mak′rō bī ot′ik) *adj.* of or relating to a diet, consisting primarily of whole grains, vegetables, and beans, that is intended to promote long life, good health, and harmony with nature. —*n.* **macrobiotics.** a method of promoting longevity by means of such a diet. ➡ used as singular. [Greek *makrobiotos* long-lived (from *makros* long + *bios* life) + -IC.]

mac·ro·ceph·a·ly (mak′rō sef′ə lē) *n.* a condition characterized by an abnormally large head or cerebrum. ➡ distinguished from **microcephaly.** —**mac·ro·ce·phal·ic** (mak′rō sə fal′ik), **mac′ro·ceph′a·lous,** *adj.*

mac·ro·cosm (mak′rə koz′əm) *n.* **1.** the whole world or universe, esp. in contrast to the human race. **2.** a great complex regarded as representing on a large scale the nature or structure of one of its constituents. ➡ opposed to **microcosm** in both defs. [French *macrocosme* universe, through Medieval Latin, from Greek *makros* large, long, great + *kosmos* world.] —**mac′ro·cos′mic,** *adj.*

mac·ro·ec·o·nom·ics (mak′rō ek′ə nom′iks, -ē′kə-) *n.* the branch of economics concerned with the broad and general aspects of an economy, as the national income, and the relationship between various sectors of an economy. ➡ used as singular.

mac·ro·ev·o·lu·tion (mak′rō ev′ə lü′shən) *n.* the evolutionary process responsible for the appearance of new major groups among existing organisms, as new species or genera.

mac·ro·mol·e·cule (mak′rō mol′ə kūl′) *n.* a very large molecule, containing thousands of atoms, as a molecule of a protein or rubber. —**mac′ro·mo·lec′u·lar,** *adj.*

ma·cron (mā′kron, mak′ron) *n.* a short horizontal line (‾) placed over a vowel to show that it has a long sound. [Greek *makron,* neuter of *makros* large, long, great.]

mac·ro·nu·cle·us (mak′rō nü′klē əs, -nū′-) *n.* the larger of two types of nuclei in the cells of ciliate protozoans, believed to control metabolism and protein synthesis.

mac·ro·nu·tri·ent (mak′rō nü′trē ənt, -nū′-) *n.* **1.** a chemical element, as carbon or calcium, that plants require substantial amounts of for growth. **2.** a nutrient that the body requires relatively large amounts of, as fat, protein, or carbohydrate. [MACRO- + NUTRIENT.]

mac·ro·phage (mak′rō fāj′) *n.* any of various large phagocytes found in the tissues of vertebrates, esp. connective, bone marrow, and lymphatic tissues. [MACRO- + -PHAGE.] —**mac·ro·phag·ic** (mak′rō faj′ik), *adj.*

mac·ro·scop·ic (mak′rə skop′ik) *adj.* large enough to be visible to the naked eye. Also, **mac′ro·scop′i·cal.**

mac·u·la (mak′yə lə) *n., pl.* **-lae** (-lē′) or **-las. 1.** any of various anatomical structures having the form of a spot distinguishable from surrounding tissue, as the yellowish, cone-filled spot on the retina of the eye. **2.** macule. [Latin *macula* spot, stain.] —**mac′u·lar,** *adj.*

mac·u·la·tion (mak′yə lā′shən) *n.* the pattern of spots or other markings characteristic of an animal or plant. [Middle English *maculation,* from Latin *maculātiōn-,* stem of *maculātiō* a staining, from *macula* spot, stain.]

mac·ule (mak′ūl) *n.* a small, flat, circumscribed spot on the skin, such as a freckle, a flat mole, or a rash in certain diseases, such as rubella. Also, **macula.** [Middle English *macule* spot, blemish, from Latin *macula.* See MACULA.]

mad (mad) *adj.,* **mad·der, mad·dest. 1.** feeling or exhibiting

anger, resentment, or irritation. **2.** suffering from or exhibiting mental disorder; insane. **3.** totally lacking in reason, prudence, or judgment; wildly foolish or rash: *You'd be mad to turn down that good an offer.* **4.** marked by confusion, agitation, or frantic activity: *Because all tickets were for general admission, there was a mad scramble for seats when the doors opened.* **5.** going beyond bounds or limits: *to have a mad passion for chocolate ice cream.* **6.** violently affected or moved; frantic: *mad with jealousy.* **7.** *Informal.* feeling or exhibiting intense eagerness, liking, and desire; wildly enthusiastic or fond (with *about, for,* or *over*): *to be mad about football.* **8.** (of dogs and other animals) having rabies; rabid. **9.** (of animals) enraged to the point of being murderous; dangerously violent: *a mad bull.* [Old English *(ge)mǣded* maddened.]
· **like mad.** *Informal.* with great speed, vigor, or energy; furiously: *The audience cheered like mad when the Senator finished speaking.*
· **to have a mad on.** *Informal.* to be angry or ill-tempered: *He's had a mad on all day.*

mad·am (mad′əm) *n., pl. (def. 1)* **mes·dames** or *(def. 2)* **mad·ams. 1.** lady; mistress. ➡ used as a form of respectful or polite address to a woman: *Madam Gandhi, Madam Chairman. Madam, may I help you?* **2.** a woman who runs a brothel. [Old French *ma dame* my lady, going back to Latin *mea,* feminine of *meus* my + *domina* mistress, lady.]

mad·ame (mə dam′, ma-, mad′əm) *n., pl.* **mes·dames.** Mrs. ➡ French form of address for a married woman; also used as a title of distinction.

mad·cap (mad′kap′) *adj.* wildly impulsive, reckless, or eccentric: *a madcap idea.* —*n.* a person who is madcap. [MAD + CAP.]

mad·den (mad′ən) *v.t.* **1.** to drive to frenzy or violent, uncontrollable rage. **2.** to cause to feel anger, resentment, or irritation. —*v.i.* to become maddened.

mad·den·ing (mad′ə ning) *adj.* **1.** tending to provoke anger, resentment, or irritation: *a maddening traffic jam, a maddening habit.* **2.** tending to drive to frenzy, hysteria, or madness: *a maddening desire for revenge.* —**mad′den·ing·ly,** *adv.*

mad·der[1] (mad′ər) *n.* **1.** a climbing plant, *Rubia tinctorum,* found in Asia and southern Europe, having long, fleshy red roots. **2.** a red dye made from the roots of this plant. **3.** a brilliant red color. [Middle English *mad(d)er,* from Old English *mæd(e)re;* of Germanic origin.]

mad·der[2] (mad′ər) the comparative of **mad.**

mad·ding (mad′ing) *adj. Archaic.* acting as if mad; frenzied: *far from the madding crowd's ignoble strife* (Thomas Gray, 1749).

made (mād) *v.* the past tense and past participle of **make.** —*adj.* produced, constructed, or shaped. ➡ often used in combination: *a well-made chair, a handmade sweater.*
· **to have it made.** *Informal.* to be assured of success.

Ma·dei·ra (mə dîr′ə, -dâr′ə) *also,* **ma·dei·ra.** *n.* any of a group of white wines, esp. a sweet, amber-colored wine originally made on the island of Madeira.

mad·e·moi·selle (mad′ə mə zel′, mad′mwə-) *n., pl.* **mad·e·moi·selles** or **mes·de·moi·selles.** miss. ➡ French form of address for an unmarried girl or woman. [French *mademoiselle* literally, my young lady, going back to Latin *mea,* feminine of *meus* my + *domina* mistress, lady.]

made-to-order (mād′tü ôr′dər, -tə-) *adj.* **1.** made in accordance with specified instructions, measurements, or requirements; custom-made: *a made-to-order suit.* **2.** perfectly suited to tastes, abilities, desires, or requirements: *a made-to-order vacation.*

made-up (mād′up′) *adj.* **1.** not real or true; fictitious: *a made-up name.* **2.** having cosmetics or makeup applied: *a heavily made-up face.* **3.** put together; finished: *a made-up bed.*

mad·house (mad′hous′) *n., pl.* **-hous·es** (-hou′ziz). **1.** formerly, a hospital or asylum for the mentally ill. **2.** a place or scene of wild uproar or confusion: *After our team won, the locker room was a madhouse.*

Mad·i·son Avenue (mad′ə sən) the U.S. advertising industry or its practices, methods, and attitudes. [From *Madison Avenue* in New York City, where the offices of many advertising firms are located.]

mad·ly (mad′lē) *adv.* **1.** in an insane or hysterical manner. **2.** with great speed, vigor, or energy; furiously: *The men worked madly to reinforce the dam in time.* **3.** to an excessive degree: *to be madly in love.* **4.** in a foolish or rash manner.

mad·man (mad′man′, -mən) *n., pl.* **-men** (-men′, -mən). a person who is, acts, or seems to be insane.

mad·ness (mad′nis) *n.* **1.** mental illness; insanity. **2.** extreme imprudence, foolishness, or rashness; utter folly. **3.** a violent, frenzied, or uncontrollable rage. **4.** wild excitement or enthusiasm.

Ma·don·na (mə don′ə) *n.* **1.** Mary, the mother of Jesus. **2.** a representation of the mother of Jesus, as in painting or sculpture.

[Italian *Madonna,* going back to Latin *mea,* feminine of *meus* my + *domina* mistress, lady.]

Madonna lily, a lily, *Lilium candidum,* cultivated for its white flowers.

mad·ras (mad′rəs, mə dras′) *n.* a cotton fabric usually having a plaid, checked, or striped pattern. [From *Madras,* India, where it was first produced.]

mad·re·pore (mad′rə pôr′) *n.* any of various solitary and reef-building polyps, order Scleractinia, having cup-shaped, stony, external skeletons divided by radial partitions. [French *madrépore,* from Italian *madrepora* literally, mother-stone, from *madre* mother (from Latin *mater*) + *poro* pore[1] (from Latin *porus*).] —**mad′re·po′ri·an,** *adj.*

mad·re·por·ite (mad′rə pôr′īt) *n.* a porous, calcareous plate through which water enters the circulatory system of starfish and other echinoderms. [MADREPORE + -ITE[1].]

mad·ri·gal (mad′ri gəl) *n.* **1.** a short, lyric medieval poem suitable for setting to music. **2.** an unaccompanied song with parts for several voices, usually with elaborate counterpoint and secular lyrics. **3.** any song, esp. a song with parts for several voices. [Italian *madrigale* the short lyric poem, from Medieval Latin *matricalis* simple, from Late Latin *mātricālis* relating to the womb, from Latin *mātrix* womb, source.]

mad·ri·lène (mad′rə lān′, -len′) *also,* **mad·ri·lene.** *n.* a tomato-flavored consommé served hot or cold. [Short for French *consommé madrilène* literally, consommé of Madrid, from Spanish *madrileño* relating to Madrid, from *Madrid.*]

ma·dro·ña (mə drōn′yə) *also,* **ma·dro·ne** (mə drō′nə), **ma·dro·ño** (mə drōn′yō). *n.* an evergreen tree, *Arbutus menziesii,* having leathery leaves, edible orange-red berries, and red bark, growing on the Pacific coast of North America.

mad·wom·an (mad′wùm′ən) *n., pl.* **-wom·en** (-wim′ən). a woman who is, acts, or seems to be insane.

Mae·ce·nas (mi sē′nəs, mī-) *n.* a generous patron, esp. of literature or art. [From Gaius Cilnius *Maecenas,* 70?-8 B.C., Roman statesman and literary patron.]

mael·strom (māl′strəm) *n.* **1.** a violent or turbulent whirlpool. **2.** something resembling such a whirlpool in intensity, violence, or destructive force: *the maelstrom of war.* [Obsolete Dutch *maelstrom* literally, grinding stream, from *malen* to grind + *strom* stream.]

mae·nad (mē′nad) *also,* **menad.** *n.* **1.** a priestess or female worshiper of Dionysus, esp. one taking part in the frenzied, orgiastic rites that characterized his worship; bacchante. **2.** a woman who is in a frenzy. [Latin *maenas,* from Greek *mainas.*]

mae·sto·so (mī stō′sō) *Music. adj.* with majesty or stateliness. —*adv.* in a majestic, stately manner. [Italian *maestoso* majestic, stately, from *maesta* majesty, from Latin *mājestās* dignity, authority.]

maes·tro (mīs′trō) *n., pl.* **-tros** or **-tri** (-trē). **1.** an eminent conductor, composer, or teacher of music. **2.** an eminent master of any art. [Italian *maestro* master, teacher, from Latin *magister.*]

Mae West (mā′west′) an inflatable vestlike life jacket, used esp. by aviators. [From *Mae West,* 1892-1980, buxom U.S. actress.]

Ma·fi·a (mä′fē ə, -fē ä′) *also,* **Maf·i·a.** *n.* **1.** a secret criminal society in Sicily operating in opposition to legal and governmental authority. **2.** a criminal organization or syndicate believed to be related to this society and active in the United States and other countries. [Italian *mafia,* from dialectal Italian *maffia* boldness, possibly from Arabic *mahyah* boasting.]

Ma·fi·o·so (mä′fē ō′sō, -zō) *n., pl.* **-si** (-sē, -zē) or **-sos.** a member of the Mafia. [Italian *mafioso,* from *mafia.* See MAFIA.]

mag. 1. magazine. **2.** magnetism. **3.** magnitude.

mag·a·zine (mag′ə zēn′, mag′ə zēn′) *n.* **1.** a periodical publication, often issued weekly or monthly, usually bound in a paper cover, containing articles, stories, pictures, and other features. **2.** a building or place for storing ammunition and explosives, such as a storeroom in a ship or fort. **3.** a building or place for storing military supplies, such as arms or provisions. **4.** a metal container for holding bullets or cartridges so that they can be fed into the chamber of a gun for firing. **5.** a supply chamber, such as the receptacle for film in a camera. [French *magasin* storehouse, store, from Italian *magazzino* storehouse, from Arabic *makhzan.*]

mag·da·lene (mag′də lēn′) *also,* **mag·da·len** (mag′də lən). *n.* a reformed and repentant prostitute. [From Mary *Magdalene,* in the New Testament, a repentant sinner.]

a	at	e	end	o	hot	u	up	hw	white	⎧	about
ā	ape	ē	me	ō	old	ū	use	ng	song		taken
ä	far	i	it	ô	fork	ü	rule	th	thin	ə	pencil
âr	care	ī	ice	oi	oil	ù	pull	<u>th</u>	this		lemon
		îr	pierce	ou	out	ûr	turn	zh	measure	⎩	circus

mage (māj) *n. Archaic.* magician. [Latin *magus.* See MAGI.]

Ma·gel·lan·ic Clouds (maj′ə lan′ik) two galaxies that are visible as faintly glowing areas in the heavens south of the equator and are the galaxies closest to ours. [From Ferdinand *Magellan,* 1480?-1521, Portuguese explorer.]

Ma·gen Da·vid (mô′gən dô′vid, dā′-, mä′-) *also,* **Mogen David.** Star of David. [Hebrew *magen-david* literally, shield of David, biblical king of Israel.]

ma·gen·ta (mə jen′tə) *n.* **1.** a purplish red color. **2.** fuchsin. —*adj.* having the color magenta. [From the Battle of *Magenta,* 1859; because the dye fuchsin was discovered at about that time.]

mag·got (mag′ət) *n.* **1.** the wormlike larva of a fly, usually legless and having a thick body. **2.** an odd or fantastic notion; whim. [Middle English *magot, magat, magotte,* probably a variant of *mathek* a kind of worm, from Old English *matha* worm, maggot, from Old Norse *mathkr.*]

mag·got·y (mag′ə tē) *adj.* infested with maggots; rotten.

Ma·gi (mā′jī, maj′ī) *pl. n., sing.* **Ma·gus. 1.** in the New Testament, the three wise men from the East who brought gifts to the infant Jesus. **2.** priests of ancient Persia. [Latin *magī,* plural of *magus* magician, from Greek *magos* priest of ancient Persia, magician, from Old Persian *magush* magician, seer.]

mag·ic (maj′ik) *n.* **1.** the art or practice that claims to produce marvelous physical phenomena and influence or control the course of events by invoking or directing supernatural forces. **2.** the art or skill of performing tricks or producing baffling effects or illusions, esp. for entertainment. **3.** an overpowering or mysteriously enchanting influence: *the magic of the first snowfall of winter.* —*adj.* **1.** relating to, produced by, possessing, or used in magic: *a magic trick, a magic wand.* **2.** producing extraordinary or startling effects, as if by supernatural power: *a magic touch.* **3.** mysteriously impressive or enchanting: *a magic moment.* [Latin *magicē* sorcery, from Greek *magikē (technē)* magic (art), going back to *magos.* See MAGI.]

Synonyms *n.* **Magic, sorcery, witchcraft,** and **wizardry** denote an art or practice purported to produce phenomena or to influence events by means of supernatural powers. **Magic** is the most general term, and is usually applied to the invoking of supernatural power to perform miraculous acts: *to move large objects through the air by magic, to employ magic to see the future.* **Sorcery** is more specific, connoting the use of incantations or spells, esp. to harm or enthrall: *The evil fairy used sorcery to transform the prince into a frog.* **Witchcraft** refers to the art of someone possessed by evil spirits or possessing occult powers: *Puritans in New England used to burn those accused of witchcraft.* **Wizardry** is like *witchcraft,* but is used generally of a power exercised by males, and suggests mastery: *the dazzling wizardry of a pagan priest.* In a more colloquial sense, it is used to describe a seemingly magical skill or power or a dazzling effect: *the wizardry of satellite technology.*

mag·i·cal (maj′i kəl) *adj.* of, relating to, or produced by or as if by magic. —**mag′i·cal·ly,** *adv.*

ma·gi·cian (mə jish′ən) *n.* **1.** an entertainer who performs tricks of illusion or sleight of hand. **2.** a person who is skilled in the use of magic; sorcerer; wizard. **3.** a person whose ability or skill is seemingly magical: *to be a magician on the basketball court.* [Old French *magicien* one skilled in magic, from *magique* sorcery, from Latin *magicē.* See MAGIC.]

magic lantern, an early kind of projector for showing slides.

Ma·gi·not Line (mazh′ə nō′) a system of French fortifications built along the eastern border of France in the 1930s as a defense against a future German invasion, outflanked by the Germans in May 1940. [From André *Maginot,* 1877-1932, French minister of war when its construction began.]

mag·is·te·ri·al (maj′ə stîr′ē əl) *adj.* **1.** relating to or befitting a person in a position of authority; commanding: *a magisterial manner.* **2.** like a dictator; imperious; domineering. **3.** of or relating to a magistrate or the office or duties of a magistrate. [Medieval Latin *magisterialis* relating to authority, going back to Latin *magister* master.] —**mag′is·te′ri·al·ly,** *adv.*

mag·is·tra·cy (maj′ə strə sē) *n., pl.* **-cies. 1.** the office, duties, or term of a magistrate. **2.** magistrates collectively. **3.** a district under the jurisdiction of a magistrate.

mag·is·trate (maj′ə strāt′, -strit) *n.* **1.** a government officer empowered to administer and enforce the law. **2.** a judge having limited jurisdiction, empowered to try minor civil and criminal cases and issue marriage licenses and traffic summonses, as a justice of the peace. [Latin *magistrātus* civil office, public official, from *magister* master.]

mag·lev (mag′lev′) *adj.* of or relating to an electrically powered railroad or train in which the cars are suspended above the tracks by powerful magnetic forces that allow them to move at speeds of several hundred miles per hour. [Short for MAG(NETIC) + LEV(ITATION).]

mag·ma (mag′mə) *n., pl.* **-mas** or **-ma·ta.** molten rock that exists beneath the surface of the earth and from which lava and igneous rocks are formed. For illustration, see **volcano.** [Latin *magma* the dregs of an unguent, from Greek *magma* thick unguent.] —**mag·mat·ic** (mag·mat′ik) *adj.*

Mag·na Car·ta (mag′nə kär′tə) *also,* **Mag·na Char·ta. 1.** the charter that King John of England was compelled to grant to his barons at Runnymede on June 15, 1215. The Magna Carta guaranteed certain civil rights and liberties to the barons, merchants, and clergy of England by limiting the power of the king. **2.** any document guaranteeing or securing liberties and rights. [Medieval Latin *magna c(h)arta* literally, great charter, going back to Latin *magnus* great, large + *charta* paper. See CHART.]

mag·na cum lau·de (mag′nə kům lou′də, kum lô′dē) with high honors or praise. ▸ used to signify graduation with high honors from a university or college. [Modern Latin *magna cum laude.*]

mag·na·nim·i·ty (mag′nə nim′i tē) *n., pl.* **-ties. 1.** the quality of being magnanimous. **2.** a magnanimous act.

mag·nan·i·mous (mag nan′ə məs) *adj.* **1.** generous and noble of mind and heart, esp. in forgiving insults or injuries; free from pettiness: *a magnanimous ruler.* **2.** characterized by or arising from magnanimity: *a magnanimous gesture of clemency.* [Latin *magnanimus* great-souled, high-minded, from *magnus* great, large + *animus* soul, mind.] —**mag·nan′i·mous·ly,** *adv.* —**mag·nan′i·mous·ness,** *n.*

mag·nate (mag′nāt, -nit) *n.* a person of great power, importance, or wealth in a field of activity, esp. in business or industry: *a railroad magnate, a shipping magnate.* [Late Latin *magnās* (stem *magnāt-*) great man, from Latin *magnus* great, large.]

mag·ne·sia (mag nē′shə, -zhə) *n.* magnesium oxide. [Modern Latin *magnesia (alba)* (white) magnesia, going back to Greek *(hē) Magnēsiā (lithos)* (the stone from) Magnesia, a region in Thessaly noted for metals.] —**mag·ne′sian,** *adj.*

mag·ne·site (mag′nə sīt′) *n.* a glassy, white carbonate mineral from which magnesia is made and magnesium was formerly obtained. Formula: $MgCO_3$ [MAGNES(IUM) + -ITE[1].]

mag·ne·si·um (mag nē′zē əm, -zhəm) *n.* a tough, very light, silver-white metallic element that burns with a brilliant light, used esp. in the production of lightweight alloys. The magnesium in chlorophyll plays a role similar to that of iron in hemoglobin. Symbol: **Mg** For tables, see **element.** [Modern Latin *magnesium,* from MAGNESIA.]

magnesium carbonate, a white, powdery compound, insoluble in water, that occurs naturally as the mineral magnesite, used in toothpaste and in medicine. Formula: $MgCO_3$

magnesium chloride, a colorless salt found in seawater, from which it is extracted, used as a source of magnesium or as a laxative. Formula: $MgCl_2$

magnesium hydroxide, a white, crystalline compound used in refining sugar and as an antacid and laxative. Formula: $Mg(OH)_2$

magnesium oxide, a white, powdery compound used in firebricks and pharmaceuticals; magnesia. Formula: MgO

magnesium sulfate, a white, bitter, crystalline salt used in leather tanning, as a mordant in dyeing textiles, and medicinally, in the hydrated form, as Epsom salts. Formula: $MgSO_4$

mag·net (mag′nit) *n.* **1.a.** a body, as a piece of lodestone, that attracts iron by means of the permanent magnetic field that it generates outside itself. The field also enables such bodies to attract and repel other magnetic bodies. **b.** electromagnet. **2.** a person or thing that attracts: *That monument is a magnet for tourists.* [Latin *magnet-,* stem of *magnēs* lodestone, from Greek *Magnētis lithos* stone from Magnesia (a region in Thessaly where it was first found by the ancient Greeks), lodestone.]

mag·net·ic (mag net′ik) *adj.* **1.** having the properties of a magnet; able to exert magnetism. **2.** of, relating to, producing, or caused by magnetism. **3.** capable of being magnetized or of being attracted or repelled by a magnet. **4.** of or relating to the magnetism of the earth. **5.** possessing power to attract, influence, or charm: *a magnetic speaker.* Also, **mag·net′i·cal.** —**mag·net′i·cal·ly,** *adv.*

magnetic disk, disk *(def. 4).*

magnetic equator, an imaginary line around the earth, encircling it nearly halfway between the magnetic poles, along which a magnetic needle is in horizontal balance. Also, **aclinic line.**

magnetic field, the region around a magnet or magnetic object, or around an electric current, in which a magnetic force can be detected. For illustration, see **magnetosphere.**

magnetic flux, the total number of lines of force in a magnetic field. Also, **flux.**

magnetic induction 1. induction *(def. 3b).* **2.** the amount of magnetic flux within a given area, a measure of the strength and direction of a magnetic field. Also *(def. 2),* **magnetic flux density.**

magnetic levitation, the suspension of an object above or below another object by means of magnetic repulsion or attraction, as in a maglev train.

magnetic mine, an underwater mine that is detonated by an electric current induced by the magnetic field of a passing ship.

magnetic needle, a bar magnet shaped like a needle. In a compass, it indicates the approximate direction of the earth's north and south magnetic poles.

magnetic north, the direction toward which the north-seeking end of a compass needle points, usually differing from true north.

magnetic pole 1. either of the two poles of a magnet, from which or toward which the lines of force of the magnet diverge or converge. **2.** either of two points on the earth's surface that are the poles of the earth's magnetic field and toward which a compass needle points. The north magnetic pole is at approximately 75 degrees north latitude and 101 degrees west longitude. The south magnetic pole is at approximately 69 degrees south latitude and 14 degrees east longitude.

magnetic recording, the process or result of recording sound, images, or other data on magnetic media, esp. tape or disks.

magnetic storm, a sudden and intense disturbance of the earth's magnetic field, caused by sunspots and other solar disturbances.

magnetic tape, a thin tape coated with magnetically sensitive material, used to record sound, images, and data.

mag·net·ism (mag'nə tiz'əm) *n.* **1.** the property of certain materials and of all electric currents enabling them to produce a magnetic field external to themselves, attract iron, steel, and certain other materials, and both to attract and repel materials like themselves. **2.** the branch of physics dealing with magnets, their fields of force, and their magnetic properties. Also, **mag·net′ics. 3.** an extraordinary power to attract, influence, or charm.

mag·net·ite (mag'ni tīt') *n.* a black magnetic iron mineral, mined as an ore, common in some igneous and metamorphic rocks. Formula: Fe_3O_4

mag·net·ize (mag'ni tīz') *v.t.,* **-ized, -iz·ing. 1.** to give magnetic properties to; make into a magnet. **2.** to attract as if by a magnet; charm. —**mag′net·i·za′tion,** *n.* —**mag′net·iz′er,** *n.*

mag·ne·to (mag nē'tō) *n., pl.* **-tos.** a small generator of alternating current, using permanent magnets rather than electromagnets. [Short for *magneto(electric machine).*]

magneto- *combining form* of or relating to magnetism, magnetic force, or magnets: *magnetometer, magnetosphere.*

mag·ne·to·e·lec·tric (mag nē'tō i lek'trik) *adj.* of or relating to electricity produced by magnets.

mag·ne·tom·e·ter (mag'ni tom'i tər) *n.* an instrument for measuring the intensity of magnetic forces, esp. the regular and irregular variations of the earth's magnetic field.

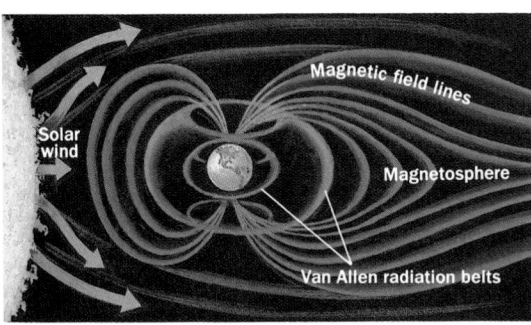

magnetosphere

mag·ne·to·sphere (mag nē'tə sfîr') *n.* the region of space around the earth in which the earth's magnetic field affects the movement of charged particles from the solar wind. It contains the Van Allen radiation belts.

magnet school, a public school with particularly good, often specialized programs and instruction designed to attract students from all groups within a district, esp. in order to bring about desegregation.

magni- *combining form* great; large: *magnify.* [Latin *magnus.*]

mag·nif·ic (mag nif'ik) *adj. Archaic.* **1.** magnificent. **2.** pompous. Also, **mag·nif′i·cal.** [Latin *magnificus* splendid, noble, from *magnus* great + *facere* to make, do.]

Mag·nif·i·cat (mag nif'i kat', män yif'i kät') *n.* **1.** a hymn honoring Mary, the mother of Jesus, consisting of her words at the Visitation, beginning "My soul doth magnify the Lord." **2.** the musical setting for this hymn. **3. magnificat.** any song or hymn of praise. [Latin *magnificat* it magnifies; the first word of the Latin form of the hymn of the Virgin Mary.]

mag·ni·fi·ca·tion (mag'nə fi kā'shən) *n.* **1.** the act, process, or degree of magnifying. **2.** the state of being magnified. **3.** something that has been magnified; enlarged copy or representation.

mag·nif·i·cence (mag nif'ə səns) *n.* the state or quality of being magnificent. [Latin *magnificentia* splendor, nobleness.]

mag·nif·i·cent (mag nif'ə sənt) *adj.* **1.** presenting a breathtaking or imposing appearance; surpassingly beautiful or splendid: *a magnificent view, magnificent tapestries.* **2.** having a nobility or grandeur of character; inspiring: *a magnificent victory over a seemingly invincible enemy.* **3.** extraordinarily good; exceptional; outstanding: *a magnificent opportunity.* [Old French *magnificent* splendid, grand, from Latin *magnificentior,* comparative of *magnificus* splendid, noble. See KAGNIFIC.] —**mag·nif′i·cent·ly,** *adv.*

Synonyms Magnificent and splendid mean greatly impressive because of size, beauty, or excellence. Magnificent usually implies dignity as well as a grandeur that overwhelms the senses: *a magnificent palace, a magnificent range of mountains.* Splendid, on the other hand, usually stresses glorious or shining properties: *a monarch's splendid robes, a splendid display of horsemanship.*

mag·nif·i·co (mag nif'i kō') *n., pl.* **-coes. 1.** formerly, a Venetian nobleman. **2.** a person of high rank, great importance, or distinguished appearance. [Italian *magnifico* splendid, from Latin *magnificus* splendid, noble. See KAGNIFIC.]

mag·ni·fy (mag'nə fī') *v.,* **-fied, -fy·ing.** —*v.t.* **1.** to increase the apparent size of, as by means of a lens: *This microscope can magnify things up to 1,000 times.* **2.** to cause to seem greater or more important than is really so; exaggerate: *Many people magnify the dangers of plane travel.* **3.** to increase the size or extent of; add to; enlarge: *The brisk wind magnified the cold.* **4.** *Archaic.* to praise; glorify. —*v.i.* to increase or have the power to increase the apparent size of an object. [Latin *magnificāre* to make large, praise highly, going back to *magnus* great, large + *facere* to make, do.] —**mag′ni·fi′er,** *n.*

magnifying glass, a lens or combination of lenses that increases the apparent size of an object seen through it.

mag·nil·o·quent (mag nil'ə kwənt) *adj.* lofty, pompous, or high-flown in speech or style of expression. [Latin *magniloquus* pompous, lofty + -ENT.] —**mag·nil′o·quence,** *n.* —**mag·nil′o·quent·ly,** *adv.*

mag·ni·tude (mag'ni tūd', -tūd') *n.* **1.** size or extent, esp. greatness of size or extent: *to determine the magnitude of an angle, a conflict of great magnitude.* **2.** greatness of importance: *The splitting of the atom was an achievement of great magnitude.* **3.** *Astronomy.* the relative brightness of a star or other celestial body, as expressed on a numerical scale. **Apparent magnitude** refers to the relative brightness of a celestial body as observed from the earth. **Absolute magnitude** refers to the relative brightness of a body as it would appear at a distance of 10 parsecs from the observer. **4.** *Mathematics.* a number assigned to a quantity to enable comparison with other quantities of the same set or class. [Latin *magnitūdō* greatness.]

mag·no·lia (mag nōl'yə, -nō'lē ə) *n.* **1.** any of a group of ornamental trees and tall shrubs, genus *Magnolia,* often cultivated for their large, showy, fragrant flowers. **2.** the flower itself, growing in white, rose, purple, or yellow. [Modern Latin *Magnolia,* from Pierre Magnol, 1638-1715, French botanist.]

magnolia

mag·num (mag'nəm) *n.* **1.** a bottle for various wines, often holding two quarts or two fifths of a gallon. **2.** the amount that such a bottle holds. [Latin *magnum,* neuter of *magnus* great, large.]

mag·num o·pus (mag'nəm ō'pəs) a great work, esp. the greatest single work or achievement of a writer, artist, or composer; masterpiece. [Latin *magnum opus* great work.]

Ma·gog (mā'gog) see **Gog and Magog.**

a	at	e	end	o	hot	u	up	hw	white		about
ā	ape	ē	me	ō	old	ū	use	ng	song		taken
ä	far	i	it	ô	fork	ü	rule	th	thin	ə	pencil
âr	care	ī	ice	oi	oil	u̇	pull	th	this		lemon
		îr	pierce	ou	out	ûr	turn	zh	measure		circus

739

mag·pie (mag′pī′) *n.* **1.** any of various noisy, long-tailed birds, family Corvidae, esp. genus *Pica,* having black-and-white feathers. The **black-billed magpie,** *P. pica,* has iridescent patches of blue and green on its wings and tail. **2.** a person who chatters incessantly. [*Mag,* familiar form of *Margaret* female proper name + PIE².]

mag·uey (mag′wā) *n.* **1.** any of several Mexican agave plants, esp. *Agave americana,* some of which yield long, tough fibers used for making cord and rope and sap used in medicine and in alcoholic beverages. **2.** the fiber obtained from such a plant. [Spanish *maguey* the plant; of Taino origin.]

Ma·gus (mā′gəs, mag′əs) *n., pl.* **Ma·gi. 1.** *also,* **magus.** a person who practices magic or is knowledgeable about the stars or the occult; sorcerer; wizard. **2.** one of the Magi. [Latin *magus* magician. See MAGI.]

Mag·yar (mag′yär, mäg′-) *n.* **1.** a member of a tribe speaking a Ural-Altaic language that settled in Hungary in the ninth century. **2.** Hungarian *(def. 2).* —*adj.* of, relating to, or characteristic of the Magyars or their language or culture. [Magyar *Magyar* a Magyar, of Magyars.]

Ma·ha·bha·ra·ta (mə hä′bär′ə tə) *n.* one of the two great Sanskrit epic poems of ancient India. It includes the Bhagavad-Gita.

ma·ha·ra·jah (mä′hə rä′jə) *also,* **ma·ha·ra·ja.** *n.* formerly, a ruling prince of an Indian state. [Sanskrit *mahārājā* great king, from *mahā* great + *rājā* king.]

ma·ha·ra·ni (mä′hə rä′nē) *also,* **ma·ha·ra·nee.** *n.* **1.** the wife of a maharajah. **2.** formerly, a ruling princess of an Indian state. [Hindi *mahārānī* great queen, from *mahā* great + *rānī* queen.]

ma·ha·ri·shi (mä′hə rē′shē) *n.* **1.** Maharishi. the title of a Hindu guru. **2.** any person who is a respected leader or teacher. [Sanskrit *mahārisi,* from *mahā* great + *rsi* sage, holy man.]

ma·hat·ma (mə hät′mə, -hat′-) *n.* a venerated wise and holy person. ➡ often used as a Hindu title of respect: *Mahatma Gandhi.* [Sanskrit *mahātman* great-souled, wise, from *mahā* great + *ātman* soul.]

Mah·di (mä′dē) *n., pl.* **-dis. 1.** in Islam, a messianic spiritual and temporal leader expected to lead the Muslims to salvation, convert all people to Islam, and establish a reign of righteousness. **2.** any of several persons who have claimed to be this leader. [Arabic *mahdīy* one who is guided aright.]

Ma·hi·can (mə hē′kən) *n., pl.* **-can** or **-cans.** a member of a tribe of North American Indians of the Algonquian language family, formerly living in the area of the upper Hudson River. Also, **Mohican.**

ma·hi·ma·hi (mä′hē mä′hē) *also,* **mahi-mahi.** *n., pl.* **-hi.** a dolphin, *Coryphaena hippuris,* of warm Atlantic and Hawaiian coastal waters, valued as a food fish. [Hawaiian *mahimahi.*]

mah jongg (mä′ jong′, zhong′) *also,* **mah-jongg, mah-jong. 1.** a game of Chinese origin for two to four players, played with 152 decorated tiles, the object being to obtain any of various winning combinations of tiles. **2.** a winning hand or combination in this game. [Chinese (Mandarin) *ma chiang* this game; literally, sparrow; referring to the bird depicted on some of the tiles used in the game.]

ma·hog·a·ny (mə hog′ə nē) *n., pl.* **-nies. 1.a.** the strong, hard, reddish brown or yellowish wood of any of several tropical evergreen trees, genus *Swietenia,* widely used for making such items as furniture, cabinets, and musical instruments. **b.** the tree yielding this wood. **2.** any of several similar trees of other genera, as **African mahogany,** *Khaya ivorensis,* or their wood. **3.** any of various reddish brown colors, esp. a rich reddish brown. —*adj.* having the color mahogany. [From earlier *mohogeney,* from earlier Spanish *mahogani;* of uncertain origin.]

Ma·hom·et·an (mə hom′ə tən) *adj., n.* Muslim.

ma·hout (mə hout′) *n.* in India or the East Indies, an elephant driver or trainer. [Hindi *mahāwat,* from Sanskrit *mahāmātra* high official; literally, great in measure.]

maid (mād) *n.* **1.** a female servant. **2.** a girl or young unmarried woman. [Short for KAIDEN.]

maid·en (mā′dən) *n.* **1.** a girl or young unmarried woman. **2.** a virgin. —*adj.* **1.** of, relating to, or befitting a maiden. **2.** unmarried: *a maiden aunt.* **3.** first or earliest: *a ship's maiden voyage.* **4.** untried or unused; fresh. [Old English *mægden* young unmarried woman, virgin.]

maid·en·hair (mā′dən hâr′) *n.* any of a large group of delicate ferns, genus *Adiantum,* having slender stems and feathery fronds. Also, **maidenhair fern.**

maid·en·head (mā′dən hed′) *n.* hymen.

maid·en·hood (mā′dən hůd′) *n.* the state or time of being a maiden.

maid·en·ly (mā′dən lē) *adj.* of or befitting a maiden. —**maid′·en·li·ness,** *n.*

maiden name, a woman's surname before she is married.

maid-in-wait·ing (mād′in wā′ting) *also,* **maid in waiting.** *n., pl.* **maids-in-wait·ing.** an unmarried woman, esp. a noblewoman, who attends a queen or princess.

maid of honor *pl.* **maids of honor. 1.** the chief unmarried female attendant of the bride at a wedding. **2.** maid-in-waiting.

maid·serv·ant (mād′sûr′vənt) *n.* a female servant.

mail¹ (māl) *n.* **1.a.** letters, other written or printed matter, and packages, collectively, that are sent, distributed, or received by post. **b.** similar material sent, distributed, or received in a similar way: *interoffice mail.* **2.** such material as sent or delivered at a specific time: *The check should arrive in today's mail.* **3.** *also,* **mails.** a system, usually operated by the national government, by which mail is collected, transported, and delivered; postal system. —*v.t.* to send by mail; deposit in a mailbox or at a post office. [Middle English *male* bag, pouch (referring to the bag in which letters were carried), from Old French *male,* from Middle High German *malhe* traveling bag, from Old High German *malaha* wallet.]

mail² (māl) *n.* **1.** flexible armor made of interlinked rings of metal, usually iron or steel. **2.** any protective or defensive covering, as the shell of a turtle. —*v.t.* to cover or protect with or as with mail. [Middle English *maile,* from Old French *maille* metal link, mesh, from Latin *macula* mesh; literally, spot.]

mail·bag (māl′bag′) *n.* **1.** a canvas or leather bag or pouch to be worn suspended from the shoulder, used by mail carriers for carrying mail. **2.** a large canvas bag or sack in which mail is transported.

mail·box (māl′boks′) *n.* **1.** a box into which mail is deposited by the public for collection by the post office. **2.** a box into which mail is delivered.

mail carrier, a person who carries and delivers mail.

mailed fist, the use or threat of aggressive force, esp. between nations.

mail·er (mā′lər) *n.* **1.** a person who mails or prepares a package or letter for mailing. **2.** a machine that automatically addresses mail. **3.** a container, such as a cardboard tube or padded envelope, used to protect something being sent by mail.

Mail·gram (māl′gram′) *n. Trademark.* a letter sent by telegraph to a local post office from which it is delivered with regular mail.

mailing list, a list of people, businesses, or organizations to whom a business or organization mails advertisements and other literature.

mail·man (māl′man′) *n., pl.* **-men** (-men′). a person who carries and delivers mail. Also, **mail carrier, postman.**

mail order, an order for merchandise that is received and filled by mail. —**mail′-or′der,** *adj.*

mail-order house, a business that sells its merchandise primarily through the mail by filling mail orders received.

maim (mām) *v.t.* **1.** to seriously injure or disfigure, esp. to deprive of a limb. **2.** to render defective or less powerful; impair. [Old French *mahaignier* to wound; possibly of Germanic origin.]

main (mān) *adj.* **1.** greatest or foremost in some capacity, as size, extent, or importance; principal; chief: *the main branch of a library.* **2.** fully exerted; sheer: *by main force.* **3.** *Nautical.* of, near, or connected with the mainmast or mainsail. —*n.* **1.** a principal pipe, duct, conduit, or cable for the passage of water, gas, sewage, or electricity. **2.** a principal or chief part or point: *The main of life is composed of small incidents* (Samuel Johnson, 1750). **3.** the open sea: *over the bounding main.* **4.** physical strength or effort; force; power. ➡ used chiefly in the phrase *with might and main.* **5.** *Archaic.* mainland. [Partly from Old English *mægen* strength; partly from Old Norse *megn* strong.]

·**in the main.** for the most part; on the whole; chiefly: *We enjoyed the show in the main.*

Synonyms *adj.* **Main, chief,** and **principal** mean something preeminent or leading. **Main,** in this sense, implies having the greatest importance because of size or capacity: *Our main contributor donates 75% of the funds we receive.* **Chief** connotes leadership in or predominance over a group because of rank or power: *the chief engineer, the chief designer for a clothing company.* **Principal** generally describes something or someone who is directing or controlling: *the company's principal office, the principal violinist of an orchestra.* In general usage, however, these three terms are widely interchanged.

main clause, independent clause.

main·frame (mān′frām′) *n.* a large, powerful computer that can quickly perform numerous complicated calculations as well as support more than one user.

main·land (mān′land′, -lənd) *n.* a body of land forming the principal or largest landmass of a region, country, or continent, as distinguished from an island or peninsula: *the mainland of Greece.*

main·line (mān′līn′) *v.t., v.i.,* **-lined, -lin·ing.** *Slang.* to inject (a narcotic or other illegal drug) into a vein. —**main′lin′er,** *n.*

main·ly (mān′lē) *adv.* for the most part; chiefly: *The coin collector was interested mainly in old dimes.*

main·mast (mān′mast′, -məst) *n.* **1.** the principal mast of a vessel, usually the second mast from the bow, as in a schooner or a brig. **2.** a mast nearer the bow, as in a ketch or a yawl.

main·sail (mān′sāl′, -səl) *n.* **1.** in a fore-and-aft-rigged vessel, the principal sail set on the mainmast. For illustration, see **sloop**. **2.** in a square-rigged vessel, the sail bent to the main yard.

main·sheet (mān′shēt′) *n.* a sheet or rope by which the mainsail is trimmed and secured. For illustration, see **sloop**.

main·spring (mān′spring′) *n.* **1.** the principal spring in a mechanism, esp. in a watch or clock. **2.** the chief motivating force: *The mainspring of their lives was a desire for wealth and comfort.*

main·stay (mān′stā′) *n.* **1.** a rope extending forward from the head of the mainmast, used to support and steady the mast. **2.** a person or thing that is the chief support or part of something: *Fishing is the mainstay of their economy.*

main·stream (mān′strēm′) *n.* **1.** the principal or prevailing direction or trend of development: *The senator's political beliefs are in the mainstream of American politics.* **2.** an area or part regarded as having the most activity, vitality, or importance: *to be in the mainstream of a profession.* —*v.t.* to place (a disabled person) in a regular school, class, job, or the like. —*adj.* conforming to or influenced by the principal or prevailing attitudes or trends of a particular group.

main·stream·ing (mān′strē′ming) *n.* the act of placing disabled people in regular schools, classes, jobs, or the like.

Main Street **1.** a principal street, esp. the main business street of a small American town. **2.** American middle-class attitudes, esp. those regarded as complacent, provincial, or conservative.

main·tain (mān tān′) *v.t.* **1.** to keep in existence or continuance; carry on, go on with, or persevere in: *Maintain this speed on the highway, but slow up when you approach the exit.* **2.** to keep or hold on to; retain; preserve: *It was hard for me to maintain my balance on the icy path.* **3.** to keep in force, operation, or proper condition; keep from declining: *The city maintains public roads.* **4.** to keep, sustain, or hold on to against, or as if against, attack or opposition: *The senators maintained their position on tax increase.* **5.** to state positively or firmly; claim; declare: *No matter what you think, I still maintain that they are wrong.* **6.** to insist on the truth of; uphold or assert against dispute: *to maintain one's innocence.* **7.** to provide for the support or upkeep of; bear the expenses of: *They maintain a house in the country as well as an apartment in the city.* [Middle English *mainteinen,* from Old French *maintenir,* from Medieval Latin *manūtenēre,* from Latin *manū tenēre* to hold in one's hand, from *manus* hand + *tenēre* to hold.]

main·te·nance (mān′tə nəns) *n.* **1.** the act of maintaining or the state of being maintained. **2.** the work of keeping something in desirable or proper condition. **3.** a means of support or subsistence; livelihood.

main·top (mān′top′) *n.* a platform at the head of the lower section of a mainmast.

main·top·gal·lant (mān′top′gal′ənt, -tə gal′-) *n.* a mast, sail, or yard above the maintopmast.

main·top·mast (mān′top′mast′, -məst) *n.* the section of the mast next above the lower section of the mainmast.

main·top·sail (mān′top′sāl′, -səl) *n.* a sail above the mainsail, set on the maintopmast.

main yard, the lower yard on the mainmast.

maî·tre d' (mā′tər dē′, mā′trə) *pl.* **maî·tre d's.** *Informal.* maître d'hôtel.

maî·tre d'hô·tel (mā′tər dō tel′, mā′trə; *French* me′tRə dō tel′) *pl.* **maî·tres d'hô·tel** (mā′tərz dō tel′, mā′trə; *French* me′tRə dō-tel′). **1.** a headwaiter. **2.** the manager of a hotel. **3.** a majordomo. [French *maître d'hôtel* headwaiter, butler; literally, master of the house, going back to Latin *magister* master + *dē* from + Medieval Latin *hospitale,* place to receive guests. See HOTEL.]

maize (māz) *n.* **1.** corn¹ *(defs. 1, 2).* **2.** the color of ripe corn; deep yellow. —*adj.* having the color maize. [Spanish *maíz* Indian corn, from Taino *mahiz.*]

maj., major.

ma·jes·tic (mə jes′tik) *adj.* having or exhibiting majesty: *a majestic mountain.* Also, **ma·jes′ti·cal.** —**ma·jes′ti·cal·ly,** *adv.* —For Synonyms, see **grand**.

maj·es·ty (maj′ə stē) *n., pl.* **-ties.** **1.** impressive or awesome dignity or splendor; stateliness; grandeur: *The king and queen were seated on their thrones in all their majesty.* **2.** sovereign power or authority: *the majesty of the law.* **3. Majesty.** used as a form of address for a sovereign and preceded by *His, Her,* or *Your.* [Old French *majeste,* from Latin *mājestās* dignity, authority.]

ma·jol·i·ca (mə jol′i kə, mə yol′-) *n.* **1.** glazed earthenware that is richly colored and decorated over a surface of opaque, white

enamel, such as that made in Renaissance Italy. **2.** pottery made in imitation of this. [Italian *maiolica,* from *Majolica,* earlier name of Majorca, where such pottery was first made.]

ma·jor (mā′jər) *adj.* **1.** great or greater in extent, size, amount, or degree: *He spent the major part of a year abroad. The Rockies are a major mountain system in North America.* **2.** of great or comparatively great importance, value, or rank: *a major French novelist.* **3.** designating or relating to the subject or field of study specialized in by a student in a college or university: *Her major field is economics.* **4.** of or relating to a majority. **5.** *Music.* **a.** of or relating to an interval equivalent to the distance between the tonic and the second or third or sixth or seventh degrees of a major scale. **b.** based on a major scale: *a major chord.* **c.** of or relating to a

majolica pitcher

triad in which the third tone above the fundamental is a whole step above the second tone. **6.** *Law.* having reached majority. —*n.* **1.** in the U.S. Army, Air Force, and Marine Corps, an officer ranking below a lieutenant colonel and above a captain. **2.a.** the subject or field of study in which a student in a college or university specializes: *My major is physics.* **b.** a student specializing in a specified subject or field of study: *a history major.* **3.** *Music.* a major scale, key, mode, or interval. **4. the majors.** *Sports.* the major leagues collectively. **5.** *Law.* a person who has reached legal age, or majority. —*v.i.* (of a college or university student) to have a major subject or field of study; specialize (with *in*): *to major in English.* [Latin *mājor* greater, comparative of *magnus* great. Doublet of KAYOR.]

ma·jor-do·mo (mā′jər dō′mō) *n., pl.* **-mos.** **1.** the chief steward in a royal, noble, or great household. **2.** a butler; steward. [Spanish *mayordomo,* from Medieval Latin *major domus* chief of the house, going back to Latin *mājor* greater + *domus* house.]

ma·jor·ette (mā′jə ret′) *n.* drum majorette.

major general, in the U.S. Army, Air Force, and Marine Corps, an officer ranking below a lieutenant general and above a brigadier general.

ma·jor·i·ty (mə jôr′i tē, -jor′-) *n., pl.* **-ties.** **1.** the larger number or part of a whole; portion constituting more than half of a total: *The majority of the students voted to have a dance.* **2.** the number of votes or of persons casting votes that are in agreement and compose more than half of a total number or group: *This referendum received a majority.* **3.** the amount by which a larger number exceeds a smaller number; margin. **4.** a party, group, or faction with the largest number of votes or greatest representation, as in a legislature. **5.** *Law.* the age at which a person is legally entitled to manage his or her own affairs and has full legal rights and responsibilities, usually twenty-one. **6.** the military rank of a major. [French *majorité,* going back to Latin *mājor* greater. See KAJOR.]

majority leader, the member of the party that holds a majority of seats in a legislative body, who organizes the members of the party regarding party tactics and measures to be voted on.

major league **1.** either of the two main groups of professional baseball teams in the United States. **2.** any league of principal importance in certain other professional sports, as ice hockey. —**ma′jor-league′,** *adj.* —**ma′jor-lea′guer,** *n.*

major premise, the premise in a syllogism that contains the major term. See **syllogism**.

major scale, a diatonic musical scale having half steps between the third and fourth and the seventh and eighth tones.

major term, the term in a syllogism that forms the predicate of the conclusion. In the syllogism *All men are mortal; Socrates is a man; therefore Socrates is mortal,* the word *mortal* is the major term.

M

a	at	e	end	o	hot	u	up	hw	white		about
ā	ape	ē	me	ō	old	ū	use	ng	song	ə	taken
ä	far	i	it	ô	fork	ü	rule	th	thin		pencil
âr	care	ī	ice	oi	oil	ú	pull	th	this		lemon
		îr	pierce	ou	out	ûr	turn	zh	measure		circus

ma·jus·cule (mə jus′kūl, maj′ə skūl′) *n.* a large letter of the alphabet, such as is found in medieval manuscripts. —*adj.* (of a letter of the alphabet) of a large size. [French *majuscule*, from Latin *majusculus* somewhat larger, diminutive of *major* greater.]

make (māk) *v.*, **made, mak·ing.** —*v.t.* **1.** to form or bring into being by shaping, altering, or combining material; construct; fashion: *The birds made a nest in the tree.* **2.** to cause to exist or occur; be the cause or occasion of; bring about: *to make a change in plans.* **3.** to produce, achieve, or accomplish, as through exertion or activity: *The two countries made peace.* **4.** to cause to appear; give shape or form to; form: *You don't make your capital letters large enough.* **5.** to bring to a specified state or condition; cause to be or become: *The smell of food made us hungry.* **6.** to cause to act or behave in a specified manner: *Peeling the onions made my eyes water.* **7.** to cause to seem or appear in a specified way: *Those jeans make you look thin.* **8.** to induce or compel: *The police could not make the prisoner confess.* **9.** to deliver in words; utter; express: *to make an announcement.* **10.** to frame, hold, or arrive at in one's mind; entertain or formulate mentally: *to make plans, to make a decision.* **11.** to perform (an action); execute: *to make a phone call, to make a curtsy.* **12.** to carry out; engage in: *to make war.* **13.** to earn or gain: *to make ten dollars an hour.* **14.** to win, acquire, or obtain, as through one's behavior or actions: *I made many friends this year.* **15.** to prepare or put together, such as a meal: *to make breakfast.* **16.** to arrange or put into proper condition for use (often with *up*): *to make a bed.* **17.** to draw or set up; frame; enact; establish: *to make a will, to make rules.* **18.** to cause to be available; provide: *We'll make room for you in the back of the car.* **19.** to put forward or present: *to make demands.* **20.** to put into a specified rank, position, or office; appoint, designate, or elect: *They made me head of the committee.* **21.** to regard as or conclude as to the meaning or nature (with *of*): *What do you make of this letter?* **22.** to fit or intend, as if by destiny or deliberate creation: *You were made to be a writer.* **23.** to amount to; add up to; form as a total: *Five and five make ten.* **24.** to constitute or be equivalent to in effect or significance: *This paragraph doesn't make sense.* **25.** to bring the total to; count as: *That makes the fourth time I've seen that movie.* **26.** to be sufficient to constitute; be the essential criterion, element, or determinant of: *Do clothes make the man?* **27.** to serve as; act as: *Nervous people make poor subjects in this type of experiment.* **28.** to have or turn out to have the necessary or essential qualities of: *You'll make a good doctor.* **29.** to afford what is necessary for: *Fresh vegetables make a good soup.* **30.** to cause or assure the success of: *Your singing makes the show.* **31.** to appear in or on or succeed in getting recognition in or on: *Their breakthrough made the headlines.* **32.a.** *Informal.* to succeed in winning a place or position in or on; succeed in becoming a member of: *She made the basketball team.* **b.** to achieve the rank or status of: *He made lieutenant.* **33.** to cause to be complete or totally satisfactory: *The two days in Paris really made the trip.* **34.** to judge or calculate to be; estimate: *I make the wall's height to be 9 feet.* **35.** to arrive in time for or in time for the departure of: *They barely made the train.* **36.** to arrive at; reach: *We made the city in four hours.* **37.** to travel at the rate of: *That racing car can easily make 200 miles an hour.* **38.** to cover by traveling; traverse: *We can make 300 miles before dark.* **39.** to close or complete (an electric circuit). **40.** to shuffle (a deck of cards). —*v.i.* **1.** to move or set out; proceed; head: *The ship made for shore.* **2.** to cause oneself to be in a specified state or condition: *to make ready for battle, to make sure of something.* **3.** to act or behave in a certain manner: *to make bold.* —*n.* **1.a.** a class or kind of manufactured article with reference to the maker; brand: *I wouldn't buy any other make.* **b.** such a class or kind with reference to the time or place of manufacture: *a camera of Japanese make.* **2.** the manner in which a thing is made: *I like the make of that dress.* **3.** physical, mental, or moral constitution; nature; character. [Old English *macian* to fashion, frame, produce, cause.] —**mak′a·ble,** *adj.*

• **on the make. a.** *Informal.* aggressively eager to obtain social, professional, or financial success or advancement. **b.** *Slang.* in search of sexual relations.

• **to make after.** to chase; pursue.

• **to make as if** (or **as though**). to begin or pretend to begin; act as if: *The forward made as if to pass, then took a jump shot instead.*

• **to make away with. a.** to steal. **b.** to kill. **c.** to get rid of or consume.

• **to make do.** to manage, function, or get along (with what is available, however unsatisfactory or inadequate): *I'll have to make do with my old coat this winter.*

• **to make for. a.** to be conducive or favorable to; help promote or maintain; further: *Thoughtfulness makes for closer relation-*

ships. **b.** to afford, provide, or constitute: *This book makes for very enjoyable reading.* **c.** to go in the direction of: *The ship made for port.* **d.** to charge or lunge at; attack.

• **to make it.** *Informal.* to succeed in doing, achieving, or attaining something: *They'll never make it across the desert.*

• **to make off.** to depart suddenly; run away.

• **to make off with.** to carry off; steal.

• **to make out. a.** to create or complete by writing: *to make out a shopping list, to make out a check.* **b.** to see or read clearly; distinguish; discern: *I can't make out this handwriting.* **c.** to grasp the meaning, nature, or drift of (something); understand; comprehend. **d.** to get along; manage; succeed: *How did you make out at the interview?* **e.** to attempt to prove or show; represent or portray: *The newspaper made me out to be a hero.* **f.** *Informal.* to make love by kissing and caressing.

• **to make over. a.** to change or redo; renovate. **b.** to transfer title or ownership of: *to make over an account to someone.*

• **to make up. a.** to be the parts or components of; constitute: *Nine players make up a baseball team.* **b.** to put together or prepare from parts or ingredients; compose; assemble: *to make up a prescription.* **c.** to be reconciled, as after a dispute; resolve differences and become friendly or loving again. **d.** to settle (a dispute); reconcile. **e.** to create in the mind; concoct fictionally or falsely: *to make up an excuse.* **f.** to make suitable or equal return, payment, or amends; compensate: *to make up for one's rudeness by apologizing.* **g.** to supply an equivalent to or for (a loss or deficiency); make good. **h.** to supply what is lacking in; complete: *We need one more to make up the dozen.* **i.** to apply cosmetics to (the face). **j.** to put on a costume, cosmetics, and the like for a dramatic performance. **k.** to take (an examination one has missed) at a later time. **l.** to take (a course or examination one has failed) again. **m.** *Printing.* to arrange or decide the arrangement of type, illustrations, or other material for (something to be printed, as a book or page).

• **to make up to.** to try to win favor with by flattery or a show of affection, admiration, or friendliness.

> **Synonyms** *v.t.* **Make, build,** and **construct** may all mean to bring into being by starting with some existing material and ending with something new. **Make** is the common term. It connotes imposing some shape or fashion onto something: *to make a bowl out of clay.* **Build** implies putting together parts into a whole: *to build a shed out of timber and shingles.* **Construct** implies more distinctly than *build* the existence of a pattern or plan in the bringing together of materials: *to construct a chair out of wood, canvas, and metal, to construct a new conference center.*

make-be·lieve (māk′bi lēv′) *n.* a playful or fanciful pretense; imaginative belief or invention; fantasy: *The story about ghosts in the house is only make-believe.* —*adj.* resembling, involving, or produced by make-believe; imaginary: *The cardboard box became a make-believe rocket ship.*

mak·er (mā′kər) *n.* **1.** a person or thing that makes something. ➡ often used in combination, as in *noisemaker, shoemaker, troublemaker.* **2. Maker.** God.

• **to meet one's Maker.** to die.

make·shift (māk′shift′) *n.* a temporary or expedient substitute for the proper or desired thing: *We used a carton as a makeshift for a table.* —*adj.* of the nature of or used as a makeshift: *The sofa was a makeshift bed.*

make·up (māk′up′) *n.* **1.** cosmetics collectively, esp. those applied to the face: *You're wearing too much eye makeup.* **2.** the cosmetics, wigs, or other articles used by a performer for the portrayal of a role. **3.** the way in which something is put together or organized; composition: *The firm's makeup is complex and involves an elaborate hierarchy of management.* **4.** physical, mental, or moral constitution; nature: *It isn't in my makeup to be rude to people.* **5.** *Informal.* an examination to be taken by a student in substitution for a previous examination he or she has missed or failed. **6.** *Printing.* the arrangement of type, illustrations, or other material into columns or pages.

make-work (māk′wûrk′) *n.* work designed to keep a person or a group busy or regularly employed. —*adj.* designed to keep people busy or regularly employed: *a government make-work program.*

mak·ing (mā′king) *n.* **1.** the act of a person or thing that makes or the process of being made: *a dilemma of one's own making, to witness news in the making.* **2.** a means or cause of improvement, advancement, or success: *Winning the case will be the making of your career as a lawyer.* **3.** *usually,* **makings.** materials or qualities from which something can be made; components: *to have the makings of a great athlete.* **4.** a quantity made at one time.

mal- *prefix.* **1.** bad or badly; wrong or wrongly: *malpractice.*

2. defective or defectively; inadequate or inadequately: *malnutrition*. **3.** not: *malcontent*. [French *mal-* badly, bad, from Latin *male* badly, ill and *malus* bad, evil.]

Ma·lac·ca (mə lak′ə) *n.* the stem of a rattan palm, used for making such items as canes and walking sticks. [From *Malacca,* a city and political subdivision in Malaysia.]

Mal·a·chi (mal′ə kī′) *n.* the last book of the Protestant Old Testament, attributed to the Hebrew prophet Malachi. Also, in the Douay Bible, **Mal·a·chi·as** (mal′ə kī′əs).

mal·a·chite (mal′ə kīt′) *n.* a bright green translucent copper mineral, used for making ornaments and jewelry and mined as an ore of copper. Formula: $Cu_2Co_3(OH)_2$ [Greek *malachē* mallow + -ITE[1]; because its color is similar to that of the mallow's leaves.]

mal·a·col·o·gy (mal′ə kol′ə jē) *n.* the zoological science that deals with the study of mollusks. [French *malacologie,* from Greek *malakos* soft + -LOGY.] —**mal′a·col′o·gist,** *n.*

mal·ad·just·ed (mal′ə jus′tid) *adj.* poorly adjusted, esp. in relationship to the conditions or requirements of one's environment or the circumstances of one's life.

mal·ad·just·ment (mal′ə just′mənt) *n.* poor or faulty adjustment, esp. to one's surroundings or circumstances.

mal·ad·min·is·ter (mal′ad min′ə stər) *v.t.* to administer or manage inefficiently or improperly. —**mal′ad·min′is·tra′tion,** *n.*

mal·a·droit (mal′ə droit′) *adj.* lacking in skill or dexterity; awkward; clumsy: *a maladroit dancer.* [French *maladroit,* from *mal-* (see KAL-) + *adroit* skillful. See ADROIT.] —**mal′a·droit′ly,** *adv.* —**mal′a·droit′ness,** *n.*

mal·a·dy (mal′ə dē) *n., pl.* -dies. **1.** a sickness; illness. **2.** any disturbed or unwholesome condition. [Old French *maladie* sickness, from *malade* sick, from Latin *male habitus* literally, badly kept.]

Mál·a·ga (mal′ə gə) *n.* **1.** a rich, sweet, white wine, originally made in Málaga, Spain. **2.** muscat.

Mal·a·gas·y (mal′ə gas′ē) *n., pl.* -gas·y or -gas·ies. **1.** a native or inhabitant of Madagascar. **2.** the language belonging to the Austronesian family of languages, spoken predominantly on Madagascar.

ma·laise (mə lāz′) *n.* **1.** an indefinite feeling of ennui or dissatisfaction. **2.** a vague feeling of physical discomfort, as at the onset of an illness. [French *malaise,* from *mal-* (see KAL-) + *aise* comfort. See EASE.]

ma·la·mute (mal′ə mūt′) *also,* **malemute.** *n.* Alaskan malamute. [From *Malemute,* the Eskimo tribe that developed this dog.]

mal·a·pert (mal′ə pûrt′) *Archaic. adj.* impudent; forward; bold. —*n.* an impudent, bold person. [Old French *mal apert* insolent, from *mal-* (see KAL-) + *apert,* form of *espert* clever, from Latin *expertus* tested.]

mal·a·prop (mal′ə prop′) *n.* a malapropism *(def. 2).* —*adj.* using or characterized by malapropisms.

mal·a·prop·ism (mal′ə prop iz′əm) *n.* **1.** a humorously ridiculous misuse of words, esp. the use of one word for another having a similar sound but a different meaning. **2.** an instance of this, for example: *What are you incinerating (insinuating) by that last remark?* [From Mrs. *Malaprop,* character who misused words in the play *The Rivals* by the Irish dramatist Richard Brinsley Sheridan, 1751-1816; from KALAPROPOS.]

mal·ap·ro·pos (mal′ap rə pō′) *adj.* out of place; inappropriate. —*adv.* inappropriately. [French *mal à propos* inappropriately, improperly, from *mal-* (see KAL-) + *à propos* to the purpose. See APROPOS.]

ma·lar (mā′lər) *adj.* of or relating to the region of the cheek. —*n.* cheekbone; zygomatic bone. [Modern Latin *malaris* of the cheek, from Latin *mala* cheek, cheekbone, jawbone.]

ma·lar·i·a (mə lâr′ē ə) *n.* any of a group of diseases characterized by recurring attacks of chills, high fever, and sweating, caused by microscopic parasites introduced into the bloodstream by the bite of female anopheles mosquitoes. [Italian *mal'aria,* contraction of *mala aria* bad air (because it was once believed that the foul air of swamps caused or spread this disease), going back to Latin *malus* bad + *āēr* atmosphere.]

ma·lar·i·al (mə lâr′ē əl) *adj.* **1.** relating to or caused by malaria. **2.** having malaria. Also, **ma·lar′i·an, ma·lar′i·ous.**

ma·lar·key (mə lär′kē) *also,* **ma·lar·ky.** *n. Informal.* insincere talk; nonsense. [Of uncertain origin.]

mal·a·thi·on (mal′ə thī′on, -ən) *n.* a phosphate compound of moderate toxicity, used as an insecticide in applications where the risk to people, pets, or livestock must be minimized. Formula: $C_{10}H_{19}O_6PS_2$

Ma·lay (mā′lā, mə lā′) *n.* **1.** a member of a people of Southeast Asia speaking an Austronesian language, living in the Malay Peninsula, eastern Sumatra, parts of Borneo, Singapore, and some adjacent islands. **2.** a language belonging to the Austronesian

Words from Malay			

Malay belongs to the Austronesian family of languages, along with such languages as Indonesian, Malagasy, and Tagalog. Below are words that have come into English from or through Malay.

amok	dugong	ketchup	pangolin
bamboo	gecko	kris	rattan
caddy[1]	gingham	launch[2]	sago
cassowary	gong	lory	sarong
cockatoo	gutta-percha	orangutan	
compound[2]	kapok	paddy	

family of languages, spoken predominantly in the Malay Peninsula and the East Indies. —*adj.* of, relating to, or characteristic of the Malays or their language or culture.

Mal·a·ya·lam (mal′ə yä′ləm) *n.* a language belonging to the Dravidian family of languages, spoken predominantly in southwestern India.

Ma·lay·an (mə lā′ən) *adj.* Malay. —*n.* Malay *(def. 1).*

Ma·lay·o-Pol·y·ne·sian (mə lā′ō pol′ə nē′zhən) *n., adj.* Austronesian.

mal·con·tent (mal′kən tent′) *adj.* discontented or dissatisfied, esp. with a government or established or existing conditions. —*n.* a person who is malcontent.

male (māl) *adj.* **1.** of or relating to the sex that fathers young or produces sperm. **2.** masculine *(def. 1).* **3.** consisting of men or boys: *a male chorus.* **4.** of or relating to a plant that bears staminate flowers. **5.** (of an object or device) having a part designed to be inserted into a corresponding hollow part: *a male electric plug.* —*n.* a male person, animal, or plant. [Old French *ma(s)le* masculine, manly, from Latin *masculus,* diminutive of *mās* male creature.] —**male′ness,** *n.*

mal·e·dic·tion (mal′ə dik′shən) *n.* **1.** a curse or the utterance of a curse against someone. **2.** malicious talk; slander. [Latin *maledictiō* abuse, curse, going back to *male* badly + *dīcere* to speak. Doublet of KALISON.]

mal·e·dic·to·ry (mal′ə dik′tə rē) *adj.* containing, expressing, or of the nature of a malediction.

mal·e·fac·tion (mal′ə fak′shən) *n.* an evil deed; wrongdoing.

mal·e·fac·tor (mal′ə fak′tər) *n.* **1.** a person who commits a crime; criminal. **2.** evildoer. [Latin *malefactor* evildoer, going back to *male* badly + *facere* to do.]

ma·lef·ic (mə lef′ik) *adj.* producing or causing evil. [Latin *maleficus* evildoing, wicked, going back to *male* badly + *facere* to do.]

ma·lef·i·cence (mə lef′ə səns) *n.* **1.** the doing of evil, mischief, or harm. **2.** the state or quality of being maleficent. [Latin *maleficentia* evildoing, harm, going back to *male* badly + *facere* to do.]

ma·lef·i·cent (mə lef′ə sənt) *adj.* causing or doing evil, mischief, or harm. [From KALEFICENCE.]

ma·le·mute (mal′ə mūt′) *n.* Alaskan malamute.

ma·lev·o·lence (mə lev′ə ləns) *n.* a disposition to do or wish evil or harm to others.

ma·lev·o·lent (mə lev′ə lənt) *adj.* **1.** doing or desiring to do evil or harm to others. **2.** tending to exert an evil or harmful influence. [Latin *malevolēns* ill-disposed, envious, going back to *male* badly + *velle* to wish.] —**ma·lev′o·lent·ly,** *adv.*

mal·fea·sance (mal fē′zəns) *n. Law.* the performance of a wrongful act, esp. by a public official; official misconduct: *Police officers are guilty of malfeasance if they accept bribes.* ➡ distinguished from **misfeasance** and **nonfeasance.** [MAL- + Anglo-Norman *fesance* a doing, from Old French *faire* to do, from Latin *facere.*] —**mal·fea′sant,** *adj., n.*

mal·for·ma·tion (mal′fôr mā′shən) *n.* an irregular, defective, or abnormal formation or structure, esp. in an organism.

mal·formed (mal fôrmd′) *adj.* irregularly, defectively, or abnormally formed; misshapen.

mal·func·tion (mal fungk′shən) *n.* a failure to function or work properly: *A malfunction in the carburetor caused the car to stall repeatedly.* —*v.i.* to fail to function or work properly.

mal·ic acid (mal′ik, mā′lik) an organic acid found in apples and many other fruits. Formula: $C_4H_6O_5$ [French *(acide) malique* malic (acid), from Latin *mālum* apple, from dialectal Greek *mālon.*]

M

a	at	e	end	o	hot	u	up	hw	white		about
ā	ape	ē	me	ō	old	ū	use	ng	song	ə	taken
ä	far	i	it	ô	fork	ü	rule	th	thin		pencil
âr	care	ī	ice	oi	oil	u̇	pull	th	this		lemon
		îr	pierce	ou	out	ûr	turn	zh	measure		circus

mal·ice (mal′is) *n.* **1.** a desire to cause injury or pain to another; desire to take pleasure in the misfortune of another: *With malice toward none; with charity for all* (Abraham Lincoln, 1865). **2.** *Law.* the willful, deliberate committing of an unlawful act, with the intent to inflict injury or under conditions that imply an evil intent. [Old French *malice* wickedness, from Latin *malitia.*]

ma·li·cious (mə lish′əs) *adj.* **1.** characterized by, showing, or resulting from malice: *a malicious person, malicious gossip.* **2.** *Law.* involving or caused by malice. —**ma·li′cious·ly,** *adv.* —**ma·li′cious·ness,** *n.*

ma·lign (mə līn′) *v.t.* to tell damaging lies about; slander: *to malign someone's character.* —*adj.* **1.** having or showing an evil disposition toward others; malevolent: *malign thoughts.* **2.** evil or harmful in nature or effect; injurious: *a malign influence.* [Late Latin *malignāre* to act maliciously, from Latin *malignus* malicious, wicked.]

ma·lig·nan·cy (mə lig′nən sē) *n., pl.* **-cies. 1.** the state or quality of being malignant. Also, **ma·lig′nance. 2.** any malignant disease, process, or condition, esp. a cancerous tumor.

ma·lig·nant (mə lig′nənt) *adj.* **1.** *Medicine.* **a.** (of a growth or tumor) tending to grow and spread uncontrollably or to recur after removal. **b.** (of a disease) tending to become progressively worse or to result in death unless halted by treatment. **2.** viciously evil or harmful in nature, influence, or effect: *a malignant being.* **3.** feeling or showing a desire to do harm or evil to another or others. [Late Latin *malignāns,* present participle of *malignāre.* See KALIGN.] —**ma·lig′nant·ly,** *adv.*

ma·lig·ni·ty (mə lig′ni tē) *n., pl.* **-ties. 1.** the state or quality of being malign. **2.** something evil or harmful.

ma·lines (mə lēn′) *also,* **ma·line.** *n.* **1.** Mechlin. **2.** a very fine, stiff net, similar to tulle, used chiefly in millinery trimming. [French *malines* Mechlin, from *Malines,* the French name for Mechlin, the Belgian town where this lace was originally made.]

ma·lin·ger (mə ling′gər) *v.i.* to attempt to avoid or shirk work or duty, esp. by pretending to be sick or injured. [From French *malingre* sickly, possibly from *mal-* (see KAL-) + Old French *haingre* thin (probably of Germanic origin).] —**ma·lin′ger·er,** *n.*

mal·i·son (mal′ə sən, -zən) *n.* *Archaic.* malediction; curse. [Old French *maleison,* from Latin *maledictiō* abuse, curse, going back to *male* badly + *dīcere* to speak. Doublet of KALEDICTION.]

mall (môl, mal) *n.* **1.** a walk or promenade, usually public and lined with trees. **2.** a street or number of streets closed off to vehicles and consisting of retail stores and shops, restaurants, and other facilities. **3.** a completely enclosed complex of buildings that house various retail stores and shops, restaurants, and other facilities. Also *(def. 3),* **shopping mall.** [Old French *mail* hammer, from Latin *malleus;* development of meaning from the hammer or mallet used to play the game pall-mall, to the alley in which the game was played, to an alley or lane.]

mal·lard (mal′ərd) *n., pl.* **-lards** or **-lard.** a wild duck, *Anas platyrhynchos,* of freshwater ponds and marshes throughout temperate northern regions. The male has a green head, a white band around the neck, a reddish brown breast, and a grayish back. Length: 28 inches (71 centimeters). [Middle English *mallard,* from Middle French *mallard,* from Old French *malart* wild drake, going back to Latin *masculus* male.]

mallard

mal·le·a·ble (mal′ē ə bəl) *adj.* **1.** capable of being hammered, pressed, or beaten into various shapes without breaking. **2.** capable of being molded, changed, or influenced; flexible: *a malleable personality.* [Old French *malleable* capable of being hammered, going back to Latin *malleus* hammer.] —**mal′le·a·bil′i·ty, mal′le·a·ble·ness,** *n.* —**mal′le·a·bly,** *adv.* —For Synonyms, see **pliable.**

mal·let (mal′it) *n.* **1.** a short-handled hammer with a heavy, cylindrical, usually wooden, head. **2.** a long-handled wooden hammer used to strike the ball in certain games, as croquet or polo. [Old French *maillet* hammer, diminutive of *mail,* from Latin *malleus.*]

mal·le·us (mal′ē əs) *n., pl.* **mal·le·i** (mal′ē ī′). *Anatomy.* the largest and outermost of the three small bones in the middle ear, shaped like a hammer. For illustration, see **ear**[1]. Also, **hammer.** [Latin *malleus* hammer.]

mal·low (mal′ō) *n.* **1.** any of a group of plants, genus *Malva,* having small pink, purple, or white flowers and lobed or cut leaves. **2.** any plant of the family that this group belongs to, Malvaceae, usually having large, showy flowers, as the hollyhock or okra.

[Old English *mealewe* plant of the genus *Malva,* from Latin *malva.* Doublet of KAUVE.]

malm·sey (mäm′zē) *n.* an aromatic, sweet white wine. [Medieval Latin *Malmasia* Monemvasia, Greek town near which this wine was first made, from Greek *Monembasiā.*]

mal·nour·ished (mal nûr′isht, -nur′-) *adj.* suffering from malnutrition; poorly fed; undernourished.

mal·nu·tri·tion (mal′nü trish′ən, -nū-) *n.* a condition caused by a lack of nutrients in the body tissues, as from insufficient food or improper diet.

mal·oc·clu·sion (mal′ə klü′zhən) *n.* a condition in which the teeth of the upper and lower jaws do not meet properly.

mal·o·dor·ous (mal ō′dər əs) *adj.* having a disagreeable odor. —**mal·o′dor·ous·ly,** *adv.* —**mal·o′dor·ous·ness,** *n.*

Mal·pigh·i·an body (mal pig′ē ən) the part of a nephron in the kidney consisting of a glomerulus together with its surrounding Bowman's capsule. Also, **Malpighian corpuscle.** [From Marcello *Malpighi,* 1628-94, Italian physiologist.]

Malpighian tubule, any of a group of slender tubes that open into the hind end of the alimentary canal of many insects and some other arthropods, and function to excrete waste. Also, **Malpighian vessel.** [From Marcello *Malpighi,* 1628-94, Italian physiologist.]

mal·prac·tice (mal prak′tis) *n.* **1.** injurious, improper, or culpably negligent treatment of a patient by a doctor. **2.** improper or unethical conduct in any professional or official position.

malt (môlt) *n.* **1.** a cereal grain, esp. barley, steeped in warm water until it germinates and then kiln-dried, used chiefly in brewing and distilling. **2.** an alcoholic beverage or liquor brewed from malt, as beer or ale. **3.** *Informal.* malted milk. —*v.t.* **1.** to cause (grain) to become malt. **2.** to treat or mix with malt. —*v.i.* to become malt. [Old English *mealt* barley or other grain specially prepared for brewing or distilling.]

malt·ase (môl′tās) *n.* an enzyme present in saliva and pancreatic juice that breaks down maltose into glucose. [MALT + -ASE.]

malt·ed milk (môl′tid) **1.** a powdered preparation consisting chiefly of dried milk and malted cereals. **2.** a drink made by mixing this preparation with milk and sometimes ice cream. Also *(def. 2),* **malt′ed.**

Mal·tese (môl tēz′, -tēs′) *adj.* of, relating to, or characteristic of Malta or its people, language, or culture. —*n., pl.* **-tese. 1.** a native or citizen of Malta. **2.** a person of Maltese ancestry. **3.** the language of Malta, an Arabic dialect containing Italian elements.

Maltese cat, a short-haired, bluish gray domestic cat.

Maltese cross, an eight-pointed cross resembling four arrowheads pointed inward and meeting at a central point. For illustration, see **cross.**

malt extract, a thick, sugary substance obtained by soaking malt in water.

Mal·thu·si·an (mal thü′zē ən, -zhən) *adj.* of or relating to the English economist Thomas R. Malthus or his theory that population tends to increase at a faster rate than its means of subsistence unless it is checked by some natural disaster or a voluntary limitation of the birthrate. —*n.* a believer in the theories of Malthus.

malt liquor, an alcoholic liquor made by fermenting malt.

malt·ose (môl′tōs) *n.* a colorless crystalline compound similar to sucrose, produced by the enzymatic action of diastase on starch, used esp. as a foodstuff and as a sweetening agent. Formula: $C_{12}H_{22}O_{11} \cdot H_2O$ Also, **malt sugar.**

mal·treat (mal trēt′) *v.t.* to treat badly or cruelly; abuse. —**mal·treat′ment,** *n.*

ma·ma (mä′mə, mə mä′) *also,* **mam·ma.** *n.* *Informal.* mother. [Repetition of *ma,* a sound commonly uttered by infants.]

mam·ba (mäm′bə) *n.* any of a group of aggressive and extremely poisonous arboreal African snakes, genus *Dendroaspis,* related to cobras, but not hooded. [Zulu *imamba.*]

mam·bo (mäm′bō) *n., pl.* **-bos. 1.** a social dance of Latin-American origin resembling the rumba. **2.** the music for this dance. —*v.i.* to dance the mambo. [Cuban Spanish *mambo* this dance, possibly from Haitian *mambo* voodoo priestess.]

Mam·e·luke (mam′ə lük′) *n.* a member of a military class that ruled Egypt from about 1250 to 1517 and remained powerful until 1811. [French *mameluk,* from Arabic *mamlūk* slave, from *malaka* to own.]

mam·ma (mam′ə) *n., pl.* **mam·mae** (mam′ē). a mammary gland. [Latin *mamma* breast.]

mam·mal (mam′əl) *n.* any animal of a class, Mammalia, of warm-blooded vertebrates, including humans, dogs, elephants, porcupines, and whales, the females of which have mammary glands and, with the exception of the monotremes, give birth to live young. Mammals are the only animals that have hair. [Modern Latin *Mammalia,* neuter plural of Latin *mammālis* relating to

the breast, from Latin *mamma* breast; because this class of vertebrates feeds its young on milk produced by the mammary glands.] —**mam·ma·li·an** (mə mā′lē ən, -māl′yən), *adj., n.*

mam·mal·o·gy (mə mal′ə je) *n.* the branch of zoology dealing with mammals. —**mam·mal′o·gist,** *n.*

mam·ma·ry (mam′ə rē) *adj.* of, relating to, or of the nature of a mammary gland.

mammary gland, a gland that produces milk, with which female mammals nourish their young.

mam·mil·la (ma mil′ə) *n., pl.* **-mil·lae** (-mil′ē). **1.** a nipple or teat. **2.** any nipple-shaped structure or protuberance. [Latin *mamilla* nipple, teat, diminutive of *mamma* breast.]

mam·mil·lar·y (mam′ə ler′ē) *adj.* of or relating to a mammilla or nipple.

mam·mo·gram (mam′ə gram′) *n.* an X ray of the breast.

mam·mog·ra·phy (ma mog′rə fē) *n.* an X-ray technique for examining the breast for tumors.

Mam·mon (mam′ən) *n.* **1.** *also,* **mammon.** the personification of riches and worldly gain. **2.** *usually,* **mammon.** riches regarded as an evil influence or as an object of worship and greedy pursuit. [Latin *mammōna* riches, from Greek *mamōnás,* from Aramaic *māmōnā.*]

mam·moth (mam′əth) *n.* any of various extinct, prehistoric elephants, genus *Mammuthus,* that had long, upward-curving tusks and shaggy, blackish hair. Height: to 14 feet (4.3 meters) at the shoulder. —*adj.* of immense size; huge; gigantic. [Russian *mamont,* possibly going back to Yakut *mamma* earth; because mammoths were thought to burrow in the earth.]

mammoth

mam·my (mam′ē) *also,* **mam·mie.** *n., pl.* **-mies. 1.** *Informal.* mother. **2.** formerly, esp. in the southern United States, a black woman serving as a nurse to white children. ➡ now usually considered offensive. [Dialectal form of KAKA.]

man (man) *n., pl.* **men. 1.** an adult male human being. **2.** a member of the human race; human being; person: *All men are created equal.* **3.** human beings collectively; the human race: *the study of man through the ages.* **4.** any of various extinct, prehistoric hominids that were the evolutionary ancestors of modern human beings, as Java man and Neanderthal man. **5.** a male human being distinguished by qualities commonly considered manly, such as strength and courage. **6.a.** a male human being considered to be in some way under the control, supervision, or leadership of another: *Our platoon lost two officers and twenty men.* **b.** a male employee; worker; hand: *The boss assigned four men to do the job.* **c.** a male servant, esp. a valet. **d.** one of the members of a team; player: *The coach had to send a new man in after the first quarter.* **7.** one of the pieces used to play certain games, as chess and checkers. **8.** a husband, lover, or sweetheart. ➡ now chiefly used informally, except in the phrase *man and wife.* **9.** *Slang.* fellow. ➡ used as a term of address: *Hey, man, how've you been?* —*interj. Slang.* used to express surprise or excitement or to emphasize what is said: *Man, it's freezing out there!* —*v.t.,* **manned, man·ning. 1.** to supply with people, as for work or defense: *to man a work station.* **2.** to take one's place or station at: *Man the torpedoes.* **3.** to summon up strength or fortitude: *to man oneself for an ordeal.* [Old English *mann* human being, adult male.]

• **as one man.** in unison; unanimously: *They answered the question as one man.*

• **to a man.** without exception: *We all feel the same way on this issue to a man.*

• **to be one's own man.** to be one's own master; be independent.

Man., Manitoba.

man about town, a sophisticated man who frequents fashionable places.

man·a·cle (man′ə kəl) *n.* **1.** a handcuff. **2.** anything that restrains or binds. —*v.t.,* **-cled, -cling. 1.** to put manacles on: *Guards manacled the prisoners.* **2.** to restrain; hamper. [Old French *manicle* handcuff, from Latin *manicula* little hand, handle, diminutive of *manus* hand.]

man·age (man′ij) *v.,* **-aged, -ag·ing.** —*v.t.* **1.** to direct, guide, or control the affairs or operation of: *to manage a department store, to manage a political campaign.* **2.** to succeed in doing or accomplishing; be able: *I'll manage to see you before I leave.* **3.** to exert control or influence over, so as or as if to make submissive or docile: *The politician knows how to manage people.* **4.** to control the use, movement, or behavior of; handle: *The rider managed the horse well. Can you manage all those heavy bundles?* —*v.i.* **1.** to be able to succeed or get along: *I don't know how the team will manage without you.* **2.** to direct, guide, or control affairs; carry on business; act as a manager. [Italian *maneggiare* to control (a horse), handle, from *mano* hand, from Latin *manus.*]

Synonyms *v.t.* **Manage, direct,** and **administer** mean to exercise authority over an organization or a project. **Manage** connotes the closest kind of involvement or supervision: *to manage a hotel, to manage a political campaign.* **Direct** suggests overall but less immediate control: *The board directs the company, but does not get involved in day-to-day operations.* **Administer** connotes performing executive duties directed toward achieving the objectives of an organization: *The chancellor administers the university.*

man·age·a·ble (man′i jə bəl) *adj.* capable of being managed; controllable. —**man′age·a·bil′i·ty, man′age·a·ble·ness,** *n.* —**man′age·a·bly,** *adv.*

man·age·ment (man′ij mənt) *n.* **1.** the act, art, or practice of managing. **2.a.** a person or persons who manage a business, institution, or other enterprise: *I'm going to complain to the management about the poor service in this hotel.* **b.** such persons collectively, esp. in relation to workers or unions: *A strike was called because labor and management could not agree upon a settlement.*

man·ag·er (man′i jər) *n.* **1.** a person who manages a business, institution, organization, or other enterprise. **2.** a person who takes care of or who is in charge of the business or professional affairs of an entertainer, athlete, or similar client. **3.** a person who is skilled in managing, as business, monetary, or household affairs. —**man′ag·er·ship′,** *n.*

man·a·ge·ri·al (man′i jir′ē əl) *adj.* of or relating to a manager or management: *managerial duties.* —**man′a·ge′ri·al·ly,** *adv.*

ma·ña·na (mən yä′nə, mä nyä′nä) *Spanish. adv.* **1.** tomorrow. **2.** at some future time: *We'll do all that work mañana.* —*n.* some future time. [Spanish *mañana* morning, tomorrow, going back to Latin *māne* in the morning.]

Ma·nas·seh (mə nas′ə) *n.* one of the twelve tribes of Israel, descended from Manasseh, the elder son of Joseph.

man-at-arms (man′ət ärmz′) *n., pl.* **men-at-arms. 1.** a soldier. **2.** in the Middle Ages, a heavily armed soldier, usually mounted.

man·a·tee (man′ə tē′) *n.* any of various aquatic, plant-eating mammals, genus *Trichechus,* having two broad front flippers and a flat, paddlelike tail, found in the warm coastal waters of the Atlantic Ocean. Length: 7 feet (2.1 meters). [Spanish *manatí;* of Carib origin.]

Man·chu (man chü′) *n., pl.* **-chu** or **-chus. 1.** a member of a Mongolian people speaking a Tungus language, living in Manchuria, who completed a conquest of China in 1644 and established a dynasty that ruled until 1912. **2.** a language belonging to the Ural-Altaic family of languages, spoken predominantly in Manchuria. —*adj.* **1.** of, relating to, or characteristic of the Manchus or their dynasty, language, or culture. **2.** of, relating to, or characteristic of Manchuria or its people, language, or culture.

man·ci·ple (man′sə pəl) *n.* an officer or steward, as of a college or monastery, authorized to purchase provisions. [Old

manatee

M

French *mancip(l)e* slave, from Latin *mancipium* legal purchase (as of a slave), slave, going back to *manus* hand + *capere* to take.]

man·da·mus (man dā′məs) *n.* a written order from a higher court to a lower court, or from a court to an official or organization, commanding that an act be performed. [Latin *mandāmus* we command, from *mandāre* to command.]

Man·dan (man′dan) *n., pl.* **-dan** or **-dans.** a member of a North American Indian tribe, formerly living in the northern Great Plains and speaking a Siouan language.

man·da·rin (man′dər in) *n.* **1.** in imperial China, a member of any of the nine ranks of high public officials. **2. Mandarin.** the principal dialect of Chinese that is the official national language of the People's Republic of China. **3.** a member of any elite or influential group, esp. one who is elderly or conservative or whose power seems unduly unrestricted. **4.** mandarin orange. —*adj.* of, relating to, or characteristic of a mandarin. [Portuguese *mandarim* high-ranking Chinese official, modification (influenced by Portuguese *mandar* to order) of Malay *mantrī* counselor, going back to Sanskrit *mantrin.*]

mandarin orange, a small, sweet orange, *Citrus reticulata,* having a thin rind that is easy to peel. [Probably because its color is reminiscent of that of a mandarin's robe.]

man·da·tar·y (man′də ter′ē) *also,* **mandatory.** *n., pl.* **-tar·ies.** a person or nation holding or receiving a mandate.

man·date (man′dāt) *n.* **1.** instruction, authorization, or support given by an electorate to its representative in government, as regarding a program or policy, expressed or implied by the results of an election or vote. **2.** an authoritative or official command, order, or charge. **3.a.** a commission from the League of Nations to a member nation for the administration of a former German colony or other conquered territory until the territory was ready for self-government. **b.** a territory so administered. **4.** *Law.* an order from a higher court or judicial officer directing that action be taken by a lower court or judicial officer. —*v.t.,* **-dat·ed, -dat·ing. 1.** to administer or assign (a territory) under a mandate. **2.** to make mandatory; order or require: *The new state law mandates the use of seat belts in cars.* [Latin *mandātum* order, commission.]

man·da·tor (man dā′tər, man′dā-) *n.* a person who gives a mandate.

man·da·to·ry (man′də tôr′ē) *adj.* **1.** required by or as if by a mandate; compulsory; obligatory: *Fastening your seat belt when the plane takes off is mandatory.* **2.** of, relating to, or conveying a mandate. **3.** holding a mandate over some territory. —*n.* mandatary.

man·di·ble (man′də bəl) *n.* **1.** the bone of the lower jaw. **2.** either the upper or lower part of a bird's beak. **3.** one of a pair of jawlike parts used for seizing and biting, located on either side of the mouth opening in insects and other arthropods. [Latin *mandibula* jaw, from *mandere* to chew.] —**man·dib·u·lar** (man-dib′yə lər), *adj.*

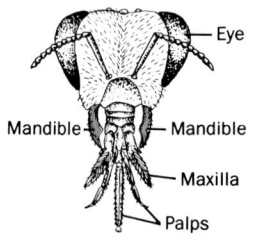

mandible *(def. 3)*

Labels: Eye, Mandible, Mandible, Maxilla, Palps

Man·din·go (man ding′gō) *n., pl.* **-go** or **-gos** or **-goes. 1.** a member of an African people of Negroid stock, living primarily in western Africa in the region of the Niger River. **2.** any of a group of languages spoken predominantly in western Africa, esp. in Liberia and Sierra Leone.

man·do·lin (man′də lin′, man′də lin′) *n.* a musical instrument having a pear-shaped body, a fretted neck, and metal strings, usually played by plucking with a plectrum. [French *mandoline,* from Italian *mandolino,* diminutive of *mandola* lute, from Late Latin *pandura* kind of lute, from Greek *pandoura* three-stringed musical instrument.]

man·drake (man′drāk′) *n.* **1.** a low-growing plant, *Mandragora officinarum,* of the nightshade family, having thick fleshy roots, wavy-edged oval leaves, and cup-shaped flowers. Also, **man·drag·o·ra** (man drag′ər ə). **2.** the root of this plant, formerly believed to have magical powers. **3.** May apple. [Modification (probably influenced by obsolete *drake* dragon) of Old English *madragora* this plant, from Latin *mandragoras,* from Greek *mandragoras.*]

man·drel (man′drəl) *also,* **man·dril.** *n.* **1.** a shaft, spindle, or similar piece for holding material to be shaped or worked, as on a lathe. **2.** a metal rod or core around which material may be shaped, cast, or bent. [Earlier *manderil,* probably from French *mandrin,* from Provençal *mandre* spindle, from Latin *mamphur* kind of drill.]

man·drill (man′dril) *n.* a large ground-dwelling baboon, *Mandrillus sphinx,* of tropical western Africa, having a long, ridged nose. The male has a pale blue nose with a red streak in the center, a black mask around the eyes, a scarlet rump shading into blue or black, and an olive-brown and gray body. Length: 3 feet (0.9 meter). [MAN + DRILL[4]; because of its resemblance to *man.*]

mandrill

mane (mān) *n.* **1.** the long, heavy hair along the back of and around the neck of certain animals, as the horse and lion. **2.** a long or abundant growth of hair on a person's head. [Middle English *mane,* from Old English *manu* mane of an animal.]

man·eat·ing (man′ē′ting) *adj.* likely to attack and eat human beings; that eats, or is said to eat, human flesh: *a man-eating tiger, man-eating sharks.* —**man′eat′-er,** *n.*

ma·nège (ma nezh′, -nāzh′, mə-) *also,* **ma·nege.** *n.* **1.** the art or practice of training, managing, or riding horses; horsemanship. **2.** the movements or paces of a trained horse. **3.** a school for training horses and teaching horsemanship. [French *manège,* from Italian *maneggio,* from *maneggiare* to control (a horse), handle. See KANAGE.]

ma·nes (mā′nēz) *also,* **Ma·nes.** *pl. n.* **1.** among the ancient Romans, the good spirits of the dead, esp. of dead ancestors, regarded as gods. **2.** a spirit or shade of a particular dead person. ➡ used as plural in def. 1, as singular in def. 2. [Middle English *manes,* from Latin *mānēs* the gods of the lower world, the deified souls of the dead.]

ma·neu·ver (mə nü′vər) *also, British,* **manoeuvre.** *n.* **1.** *Military.* **a.** a planned tactical or strategic movement, as of ships, troops, or firepower. **b.** *usually,* **maneuvers.** a large-scale tactical exercise simulating combat. **2.** any skillful move, procedure, or stratagem, as one executed to gain a desired goal: *political maneuvers.* **3.** physical movement showing or marked by agility or skill. —*v.t.* **1.** to cause (troops or ships) to perform a maneuver or maneuvers. **2.** to move or manage skillfully, as into a desired position or toward a desired goal: *I maneuvered my way through the crowded entrance.* —*v.i.* **1.** to perform a maneuver or maneuvers. **2.** to use skillful movements, procedures, or stratagems; craftily shift position, ground, or tactics: *to maneuver for a position of power.* [From earlier *manoeuvre,* from French *manoeuvre* originally, manual labor, from Middle French *manuevre,* from Vulgar Latin *manuopera,* from Latin *manū operāre* to work by hand, from *manus* hand + *operāre* to work.] —**ma·neu′ver·er,** *n.*

ma·neu·ver·a·ble (mə nü′vər ə bəl) *adj.* capable of being maneuvered, esp. easily: *That small airplane is more maneuverable than a big airliner.* —**ma·neu′ver·a·bil′i·ty,** *n.*

man Friday 1. a dependable, faithful servant, aide, or follower. **2.** a male employee, esp. in an office, with a wide variety of duties. [From *Friday,* the faithful servant and companion in the novel *Robinson Crusoe* by the English author Daniel Defoe, 1660?-1731.]

man·ful (man′fəl) *adj.* having or showing manly spirit; brave; resolute. —**man′ful·ly,** *adv.* —**man′ful·ness,** *n.*

man·ga·nese (mang′gə nēz′, -nēs′) *n.* a brittle, silver-gray metallic element that is readily oxidized, like iron, but not magnetic, used esp. in the production of steel. Symbol: Mn For tables, see element. [French *manganèse,* from Italian *manganese,* from Medieval Latin *magnesia,* going back to Greek *magnēsiā* any of various ores from Magnesia, a region in Thessaly noted for metals.]

manganese dioxide, a black, powdery compound extracted from manganese ores, used in dry-cell batteries and in making glass. Formula: MnO_2

man·gan·ic (mang gan′ik) *adj.* of, relating to, or containing manganese, esp. in the trivalent state.

mange (mānj) *n.* a contagious skin disease of cattle, horses, dogs, and other domestic animals, caused by certain mites and marked by scaly pimples and often by a loss of hair. [Old French *manjue* itching, from *mangier* to eat, from Latin *mandūcāre.*]

man·gel-wur·zel (mang′gəl wûr′zəl) *n.* a large, sweet beet cultivated in Europe and western North America for its sweet, fleshy roots, used as food for livestock. [German *Mangoldwurzel* beet root, from *Mangold* beet + *Wurzel* root.]

man·ger (mān′jər) *n.* a box or trough designed to hold feed, as

for horses or cows. [Middle English *manger*, from Old French *mangeure*, from *mangier* to eat, from Latin *mandūcāre*.]

man·gle¹ (mang′gəl) *v.t.*, **-gled, -gling. 1.** to disfigure or mutilate, as by tearing or crushing. **2.** to render imperfect or mar in the making or performing; botch: *The inexperienced translator mangled the author's novel.* [Middle English *manglen*, from Norman French *mangler* to maim; of uncertain origin.] **—man′gler,** *n.*

man·gle² (mang′gəl) *n.* a machine for pressing and smoothing cloth by passing it between rollers. **—***v.t.*, **-gled, -gling.** to press or smooth with a mangle. [Dutch *mangel*, from German *mangel*, from Middle High German *mangel*, diminutive of *mange*, from Latin *manganum*, from Greek *manganon*, axis of a pulley, war engine.]

man·go (mang′gō) *n.*, *pl.* **-goes** or **-gos. 1.** the yellowish red, oval, edible fruit of any of a group of trees, genus *Mangifera* and esp. *M. indica*, of the cashew family, having a sweet, spicy taste. **2.** the tropical evergreen tree bearing this fruit. [Portuguese *manga* this fruit, from Malay *mangā*, from Tamil *mānkāy*.]

man·go·nel (mang′gə nel′) *n.* formerly, a machine used in war to hurl large stones and other missiles at the enemy. [Old French *mangonel*, from Late Latin *mangonellus*, diminutive of *manganum*, from Greek *manganon* axis of a pulley, war engine.]

man·go·steen (mang′gə stēn′) *n.* **1.** the reddish purple edible fruit of a small tree, *Garcinia mangostana*, having a juicy white pulp. **2.** the tree bearing this fruit, cultivated in tropical regions. [Malay *mangustan* this fruit.]

man·grove (mang′grōv′) *n.* **1.** any of several trees, genus *Rhizophora*, found in tropical marshy and coastal regions. **2.** any of various other trees, as the **black mangrove,** *Avicennia marina.* [Modification (influenced by GROVE) of *man-growe*, from Portuguese *mangue*, from Spanish *mangle* mangrove tree; of Taino origin.]

mangrove

man·gy (mān′jē) *adj.*, **-gi·er, -gi·est. 1.** affected with, resembling, or caused by mange: *a mangy cat.* **2.** worn, dirty, and squalid in appearance; shabby; seedy: *a mangy old coat.* **—man′gi·ly,** *adv.* **—man′gi·ness,** *n.*

man·han·dle (man′han′dəl) *v.t.*, **-dled, -dling. 1.** to use the hands on with gruff force; handle roughly: *The prisoners charged that the guards had manhandled them.* **2.** to accomplish by human strength alone, without mechanical aids.

man·hat·tan (man hat′ən, mən-) *also,* **Man·hat·tan.** *n.* a cocktail consisting of whiskey, vermouth, and, sometimes, bitters.

Manhattan Project, an atomic research project established in the United States in August 1942 that developed the first atomic bomb.

man·hole (man′hōl′) *n.* an opening, usually with a removable cover, through which a sewer, steam boiler, or other structure may be entered, esp. for purposes of inspection or repair.

man·hood (man′hửd′) *n.* **1.** the state or time of being an adult male human being. **2.** character or qualities, such as strength and courage, considered to be manly. **3.** men collectively.

man·hour (man′our′, -ou′ər) *n.* the amount of work that can be done by one person in one hour, used as a unit or standard of measurement in industry.

man·hunt (man′hunt′) *n.* an organized, large-scale, and intensive search for a person, usually a fugitive criminal.

ma·ni·a (mā′nē ə, mān′yə) *n.* **1.** enthusiasm or desire so excessive as to resemble madness: *The miser had a mania for gold coins.* **2.** a form of mental illness characterized by great excitability, elation, and agitation. [Latin *mania* madness, from Greek *maniā.*]

-mania *combining form* **1.** madness; insanity: *kleptomania, megalomania.* **2.** abnormally excessive or intense interest, desire, or liking: *Anglomania.* [Greek *maniā* madness.]

ma·ni·ac (mā′nē ak′) *n.* **1.** a person who is or acts as if wildly or violently insane; lunatic. **2.** a person who has excessive enthusiasm or desire for something: *a sports maniac.* **—***adj.* wildly or violently insane.

-maniac *combining form* a person affected by a specified mania: *pyromaniac.* [Greek *maniakos* like a madman, from *maniā* madness.]

ma·ni·a·cal (mə nī′ə kəl) *adj.* **1.** of, relating to, or characteristic of mania or a maniac: *maniacal laughter.* **2.** wildly or violently insane: *a maniacal dictator.* **—ma·ni′a·cal·ly,** *adv.*

ma·nic (man′ik) *adj.* relating to, resembling, or affected by mania: *a manic personality, a manic mood.*

man·ic-de·pres·sive (man′ik di pres′iv) *adj.* designating a mental disorder in which periods of extreme excitement alternate with periods of extreme depression and, often, periods of normal, even mood. **—***n.* a person who suffers from this disorder.

Man·i·chae·an (man′i kē′ən) *also,* **Man·i·che·an.** *n.* a follower of or believer in Manichaeism. Also, **Man′i·chee.** **—***adj.* of or relating to Manichaeism.

Man·i·chae·ism (man′i kē′iz′əm) *also,* **Man·i·che·ism.** *n.* an Oriental religious system originating in Persia in the third century A.D., whose basic doctrine was belief in a dualistic universe where spiritual forces of light and goodness were in conflict with material forces of darkness and evil. Also, **Man′i·chae′an·ism.**

man·i·cot·ti (man′i kot′ē) *n.* **1.** hollow round pieces of pasta. **2.** a dish consisting of this pasta stuffed with cheese and baked in a tomato sauce. ➡ usually used as singular. [Italian *manicotti,* plural of *manicotto* literally, muff, going back to Latin *manica* sleeve, from *manus* hand.]

man·i·cure (man′i kyửr′) *n.* a treatment for the hands chiefly consisting of cleaning, shaping, and polishing the nails. **—***v.t.,* **-cured, -cur·ing. 1.** to clean, shape, and polish (the fingernails); give a manicure to. **2.** to trim evenly, closely, or elaborately: *The gardener manicured the lawns of the estate.* [French *manicure* treatment for the care of the hands, from Latin *manus* hand + *cūra* care.]

man·i·cur·ist (man′i kyửr′ist) *n.* a person who gives manicures.

man·i·fest (man′ə fest′) *v.t.* **1.** to make obvious or clear; show plainly. **2.** to be evidence of; prove: *The firefighter's daring rescue of the child manifested great courage.* **—***adj.* plainly apparent; evident; obvious. **—***n.* a list of cargo or passengers for a ship or plane. [Latin *manifēstus* evident.] **—man′i·fest′ly,** *adv.*

man·i·fes·ta·tion (man′ə fes tā′shən) *n.* **1.** the act of manifesting or the state of being manifested. **2.** something that manifests; indication; sign. **3.** a public demonstration or display, as for political effect.

manifest destiny *also,* **Manifest Destiny.** a nineteenth-century doctrine that the United States was inevitably destined to expand territorially from the Atlantic to the Pacific.

man·i·fes·to (man′ə fes′tō) *n.*, *pl.* **-tos** or **-toes.** a public declaration of principles or objectives, as that issued by a political party. [Italian *manifesto,* going back to Latin *manifēstus* evident.]

man·i·fold (man′ə fōld′) *adj.* **1.** of many kinds or varieties; multiple; diverse: *This job has manifold duties.* **2.** having many parts or features: *The novel is a manifold portrait of society.* **3.** consisting of or operating several things of one kind at once. **—***n.* **1.** a pipe fitting having several openings for connecting one pipe with others, as in the exhaust system of an automobile. **2.** something that is manifold. **—***v.t.* **1.** to make more than one copy of, as with carbon paper. **2.** to make manifold; multiply. [Old English *manigfeald* various, varied, numerous.]

man·i·kin (man′i kin) *also,* **mannikin.** *n.* **1.** a little man; dwarf. **2.** an anatomical model of the human body, such as one used for teaching anatomy. **3.** mannequin. [Middle Dutch *manneken* little man, diminutive of *man* man.]

ma·nil·a (mə nil′ə) *also,* **Ma·nil·a, ma·nil·la.** *n.* **1.** Manila hemp. **2.** Manila paper. **3.** a cheroot made in Manila. **—***adj.* made of Manila paper: *a manila envelope.*

Manila hemp, a fiber obtained from the leaves of the abaca, widely used in the manufacture of rope, cord, and paper. Also, **abaca.**

Manila paper, a strong, brown or yellow paper originally made from Manila hemp, used esp. for bags and file folders.

man in the street, the ordinary person; ordinary citizen.

man·i·oc (man′ē ok′) *n.* cassava.

man·i·ple (man′ə pəl) *n.* **1.** in ancient Rome, a subdivision of a legion, consisting of 60 or 120 men. **2.** a silk band worn on the left arm as a Eucharistic vestment. [Old French *maniple* handful, handkerchief, from Latin *manipulus* handful, bundle of hay serving as a standard, company of soldiers.]

ma·nip·u·late (mə nip′yə lāt′) *v.t.,* **-lat·ed, -lat·ing. 1.** to try to influence, adapt, or manage to one's own advantage: *to manipulate public opinion.* **2.** to manage or work with or as with the hands, esp. with dexterity or skill: *By manipulating a few wires, I repaired the telephone.* **3.** to change, falsify, or tamper with for

a	at	e	end	o	hot	u	up	hw	white		about
ā	ape	ē	me	ō	old	ū	use	ng	song		taken
ä	far	i	it	ô	fork	ü	rule	th	thin	ə	pencil
âr	care	ī	ice	oi	oil	ủ	pull	th	this		lemon
		îr	pierce	ou	out	ûr	turn	zh	measure		circus

747

one's own purpose or profit: *The cashier manipulated bank funds so that the theft would not be discovered.* [From MANIPULATION.] —**ma·nip′u·la·tive, ma·nip·u·la·to·ry** (mə nip′yə lə tôr′ē), *adj.* —**ma·nip′u·la′tor,** *n.* —For Synonyms, see **handle.**

ma·nip·u·la·tion (mə nip′yə lā′shən) *n.* the act of manipulating or the state of being manipulated. [French *manipulation* handling, clever trick, from Latin *manipulus* handful.]

man·i·tou (man′i tü′) *also,* **man·i·to, man·i·tu.** *n.* among the Algonquian Indians, a spirit worshiped as a governing force of life and nature. [Algonquian *manito* spirit.]

man·kind (*def. 1* man′kīnd′; *def. 2* man′kīnd′) *n.* **1.** human beings collectively; the human race. **2.** men collectively.

man·like (man′līk′) *adj.* **1.** befitting a man; manly. **2.** resembling a man. **3.** resembling a human being: *manlike apes.*

man·ly (man′lē) *adj., -li·er, -li·est.* **1.** having the qualities generally attributed to or characteristic of men. **2.** relating to or appropriate for a man. —**man′li·ness,** *n.*

man-made (man′mād′) *adj.* made by human beings, rather than by natural processes; synthetic; artificial: *man-made snow.*

man·na (man′ə) *n.* **1.** in the Old Testament, the food miraculously supplied to the Israelites during their flight from Egypt. **2.** anything that is badly needed and is unexpectedly or miraculously supplied: *The praise from classmates was manna for the shy student.* [Late Latin *manna* the food miraculously supplied to the Israelites, from Greek *manna,* from Aramaic *mannā,* from Hebrew *mān.*]

manned (mand) *adj.* carrying or controlled by human beings: *a manned spacecraft.*

man·ne·quin (man′i kin) *also,* **manikin.** *n.* **1.** a full-sized, usually jointed model of a human figure, used esp. for displaying clothes. **2.** a person who models clothing; model. **3.** a person who seems devoid of animation, warmth, or spontaneity. [French *mannequin,* from Middle Dutch *manneken* little man. See MANIKIN.]

man·ner (man′ər) *n.* **1.** the way in which something happens or is done; mode; fashion: *Please put a heading on your paper in the usual manner.* **2.** a way of acting or behaving, esp. one that is customary or characteristic: *His gruff manner frightens some people.* **3.** a typical or characteristic way of doing things; customary mode: *the manner of life in the eighteenth century.* **4. manners. a.** ways of behaving in society, esp. with reference to standards of politeness: *Her reply showed a lack of manners.* **b.** forms of polite or socially correct behavior in society; etiquette: *to have good table manners.* **c.** prevailing social conditions, customs, or rules of behavior: *a novel of manners.* **5.** a distinctive artistic style or method. **6.** kind or sort: *What manner of dog is that?* [Anglo-Norman *manere* way of behaving, going back to Latin *manuārius* handy, relating to the hand, from *manus* hand.]

· **in a manner of speaking.** in a way or to a certain extent.

man·nered (man′ərd) *adj.* **1.** having (a specified kind of) manner or manners. ➡ used in combination: *mild-mannered.* **2.** having or marked by mannerisms, as in writing or speech; stilted: *The actor gave a mannered performance.*

man·ner·ism (man′ə riz′əm) *n.* **1.** a characteristic manner of speaking or behaving; trait peculiar to a person. **2.** exaggerated or affected use of a particular manner or style, esp. in literature or art: *The author's novel was full of mannerisms.* **3.** *usually,* **Mannerism.** a style of sixteenth-century European art that stressed emotional expression and boldly dramatic effects. —**man′ner·is′tic,** *adj.*

man·ner·ly (man′ər lē) *adj.* having or showing good manners; polite. —*adv.* with good manners; politely. —**man′ner·li·ness,** *n.*

man·ni·kin (man′i kin) manikin.

man·nish (man′ish) *adj.* **1.** thought to be suited to a man or men: *mannish furniture.* **2.** in a manner thought to resemble a man or men: *to speak in a mannish voice.* —**man′nish·ly,** *adv.* —**man′nish·ness,** *n.*

man·ni·tol (man′i tôl′) *n.* a slightly sweet, crystalline alcohol present in many plants, used nutritionally as a sugar substitute and medicinally as a diuretic. Formula: $C_6H_{14}O_6$

ma·noeu·vre (mə nü′vər) *British. n.* maneuver. —*v.t., v.i., -vred, -vring.* maneuver.

man of God 1. a clergyman. **2.** a holy man, as a saint or prophet.

man of letters 1. a writer; author. **2.** a scholar, esp. one with a wide knowledge of literature.

man of the world, a worldly, sophisticated, cosmopolitan man.

man-of-war (man′əv wôr′) *n., pl.* **men-of-war.** an armed naval ship, usually rigged with sails.

ma·nom·e·ter (mə nom′i tər) *n.* an instrument used to measure the pressure exerted by a gas. [French *manomètre,* from Greek *mānos* thin + *metron* measure.]

man·or (man′ər) *n.* **1.** under the feudal system, a self-sufficient estate under the authority of a lord, in which part of the land was

divided among serfs who were bound to the estate. **2.** manor house. **3.** a land unit or landed estate, as one largely farmed by tenants who pay rent to the owner. **4.** a mansion, esp. the main house on an estate. [Old French *manoir* mansion, dwelling, from *manoir* to dwell, from Latin *manēre* to remain.]

manor house, the residence of the lord of a manor.

ma·no·ri·al (mə nôr′ē əl) *adj.* of or like a manor.

man-o′-war bird (man′ə wôr′) frigate bird.

man·power (man′pou′ər) *n.* **1.** the total number of persons available to work, as in industry or the armed forces: *the manpower of the automobile industry.* **2.** *also,* **man power.** power or force supplied by the physical exertion of people.

man·qué (mäN kā′) *adj. French.* aspiring but unsuccessful. ➡ placed after the noun it modifies: *an author manqué.*

man·sard (man′särd) *n.* **1.** a roof having two slopes on all sides, with the lower slope almost vertical and the upper slope almost horizontal. Also, **mansard roof. 2.** a room or story under such a roof. [French *mansarde* garret, and *toit en mansarde* mansard roof, from François *Mansart* (or *Mansard*), 1598-1666, French architect.]

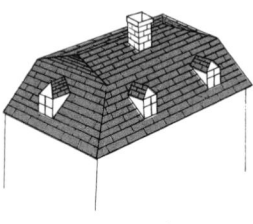

mansard

manse (mans) *n.* the residence of a minister, esp. of a Presbyterian minister; parsonage. [Medieval Latin *mansus* farm, dwelling, from Latin *manēre* to remain.]

man·serv·ant (man′sûr′vənt) *n., pl.* **men·serv·ants.** a male servant.

man·sion (man′shən) *n.* a very large, stately, or imposing house. [Old French *mansion* dwelling, from Latin *mānsiō.*]

man-sized (man′sīzd′) *adj. Informal.* **1.** suited to or large enough for a man. **2.** requiring the capabilities of an adult: *a man-sized problem.* Also, **man′-size′.**

man·slaugh·ter (man′slô′tər) *n.* **1.** *Law.* the unlawful killing of a human being, without cold-blooded intent. **2.** the slaying of a human being by another.

man·ta (man′tə) *n.* **1.** any of a group of rays, family Mobulidae, having a flat, diamond-shaped body and pectoral fins resembling wings. The largest of all rays, it may weigh more than 3,000 pounds (1,361 kilograms). Also, **manta ray, devilfish. 2.a.** a coarse cotton cloth, used esp. in Latin America for cloaks and blankets. **b.** something made of this, as a cloak. [Spanish *manta* cape, blanket, going back to Late Latin *mantum* cloak, from Latin *mantellum;* referring to the blanket-shaped trap with which a manta ray is caught.]

man·teau (man′tō, man tō′) *n., pl.* **-teaus** or **-teaux** (-tōz, -tōz′). a loose cloak, usually without sleeves, worn as an outer garment. [French *manteau,* from Old French *mantel* cloak. See MANTLE.]

man·tel (man′təl) *also,* **mantle.** *n.* **1.** a structure of stone, brick, or other material, surrounding the opening of a fireplace. **2.** the upper, horizontal portion of this, usually in the form of a projecting shelf. Also *(def. 2),* **man′tel·piece′.**

man·tel·et (man′tə let′, mant′lit) *n.* **1.** a short cloak or mantle. **2.** a movable shelter, screen, or shield, formerly used esp. to protect soldiers when besieging an enemy. Also *(def. 2),* **mantlet.**

man·til·la (man til′ə, -tē′ə) *n.* a scarflike covering for the head, usually made of black or white lace, worn by women, esp. in Spain and Latin America. [Spanish *mantilla,* going back to Latin *mantellum* cloak.]

man·tis (man′tis) *n., pl.* **-tis·es** or **-tes** (-tēz). praying mantis. [Modern Latin *mantis,* from Greek *mantis* prophet; because it often holds its forelegs in a position suggesting hands folded in prayer.]

man·tis·sa (man tis′ə) *n. Mathematics.* the decimal part of a logarithm.

man·tle (man′təl) *n.* **1.** a loose, usually sleeveless cloak. **2.** something that covers or envelops: *under the mantle of night.* **3.** mantel. **4.** the layer of the earth's interior between the crust and the core. For illustration, see **earth. 5.** in mollusks, a fleshy fold of tissue that encloses the internal organs and secretes the shell. **6.** the plumage of the back and folded wings of a bird, esp. when differently colored from the rest of the body. **7.** gas mantle. —*v.,* **-tled, -tling.** —*v.t.* **1.** to cover with or as with a mantle; conceal; envelop: *The snow mantled the countryside in white.* —*v.i.* **1.** to cover or spread over the surface of something. **2.** to be or become covered with a coating or scum. **3.** to blush. [Partly from Old French *mantel* cloak; partly from Old English *mentel* cloak; both from Latin *mantellum* cloak, napkin.]

man·tle·rock (man′təl rok′) *n.* regolith.

mant·let (mant′lit) *n.* mantelet *(def. 2).*

man·tra (man′trə) *n.* in Hinduism and Buddhism, a prayer or incantation, often thought to possess magical power.

man·tu·a (man′chü ə) *n.* a loose gown worn by women in the seventeenth and eighteenth centuries. [Modification of French *manteau* cloak, from Latin *mantellum.*]

man·u·al (man′ū əl) *adj.* **1.** relating to, done by, or involving the use of the hand or hands: *manual crafts.* **2.** operated by hand: *a manual control.* **3.** involving or requiring physical exertion or work with the hands: *manual labor.* —*n.* **1.** a concise book of instructions or other information on a particular subject. **2.** a prescribed drill in the handling of a weapon. Also, **manual of arms. 3.** an organ keyboard played with the hands, as distinguished from one that is played with the feet. [Respelling (influenced by Latin *manuālis*) of Middle English *manuel,* from Old French *manuel,* from Latin *manuālis,* from Latin *manus* hand.] —**man′u·al·ly,** *adv.*

manual alphabet, an alphabet used to communicate with the deaf, consisting of a series of signs made with the fingers, each sign representing a letter of the written alphabet.

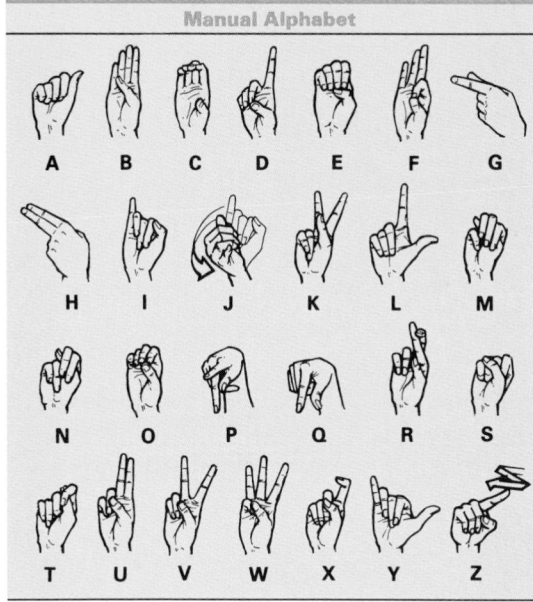

Manual Alphabet

manual training, practical training in various manual crafts, as woodworking or machine and tool operation, esp. as given in schools.

ma·nu·bri·um (mə nü′brē əm) *n., pl.* **-bri·a** (-brē ə) or **-bri·ums.** any handlike process or anatomical part, esp. the uppermost of the three bony segments forming the breastbone in mammals. [Latin *manubrium* handle, from *manus* hand.]

man·u·fac·to·ry (man′yə fak′tə rē) *n., pl.* **-ries.** *Archaic.* a factory.

man·u·fac·ture (man′yə fak′chər) *v.,* **-tured, -tur·ing.** —*v.t.* **1.** to make or produce (a product), esp. on a large scale by means of machinery and a division of labor. **2.** to make or process (a raw material) into a form or product suitable for use: *to manufacture wool into cloth.* **3.** to make up or concoct; invent; fabricate: *to manufacture excuses.* **4.** to produce or turn out, as a literary work, in a mechanical way, without evidence of originality or individuality. —*v.i.* to make, produce, or process something. —*n.* **1.** the act or process of manufacturing. **2.** something manufactured; product. [French *manufacture* a making, workmanship, from Medieval Latin *manufactura* handiwork, going back to Latin *manū factūra* a making by hand, from *manus* hand + *facere* to make.]

man·u·fac·tur·er (man′yə fak′chər ər) *n.* a person or company whose business is manufacturing; owner of a factory.

man·u·mis·sion (man′yə mish′ən) *n.* liberation from slavery or bondage; emancipation. [Latin *manūmissiō* the freeing of a slave.]

man·u·mit (man′yə mit′) *v.t.,* **-mit·ted, -mit·ting.** to release from slavery or bondage; emancipate; liberate. [Latin *manūmittere,* from *manū* from the hand + *mittere* to send.]

ma·nure (mə nůr′, -nyůr′) *n.* any natural organic material, esp.

the waste matter from domestic animals, used as fertilizer. —*v.t.,* **-nured, -nur·ing.** to put manure in or on. [Middle English *mainouren* to till, from Norman French *meinoverer* to manage; literally, to work with one's hands, going back to Latin *manū operāre* to work by hand, from *manus* hand + *operāre* to work.]

man·u·script (man′yə skript′) *n.* **1.** a version of a book, article, or other work written by hand or on a typewriter or computer and prepared for a publisher or printer. **2.** a book or document written by hand, esp. one written before the invention of printing. —*adj.* written by hand or on a typewriter or computer; not printed. [Medieval Latin *manuscriptum* something written by hand, going back to Latin *manū scriptus* written by hand.]

Manx (mangks) *n.* **1. the Manx.** the people of the Isle of Man. **2.** a language belonging to the Celtic branch of the Indo-European family of languages, spoken on the Isle of Man, now nearly extinct. —*adj.* of, relating to, or characteristic of the Isle of Man or its people, language, or culture.

Manx cat, a short-haired breed of domestic cat having long hind legs, a high, rounded rump, and, usually, no tail.

Manx·man (mangks′mən) *n., pl.* **-men** (-mən). a native or inhabitant of the Isle of Man.

man·y (men′ē) *adj.,* **more, most.** consisting of or amounting to a large number; numerous: *The library has many books on history.* —*n.* **1.** a large number (of persons or things): *Many of the delegates vetoed the plan.* **2. the many.** the majority of people. —*pron.* a large number of persons or things: *Many were late for the party because of the storm.* [Old English *manig* a great number, numerous.]

man·y·plies (men′ē plīz′) *n.* omasum. [MANY + *plies,* plural of PLY².]

man·y·sid·ed (men′ē sī′did, -sī′-) *adj.* **1.** having many sides. **2.** having many aspects or possibilities: *a many-sided problem.* **3.** having many interests or capabilities: *a many-sided athlete.*

man·za·ni·ta (man′zə nē′tə) *n.* any of several evergreen shrubs or small trees, genus *Arctostaphylos,* of the heath family, native mostly to western North America, bearing thick leaves and white or pink urn-shaped flowers. [Spanish *manzanita* little apple, diminutive of *manzana* apple, from Latin *Matiāna (māla)* (apples) of Matius; possibly from Caius *Matius* Calvena, a Roman who wrote a cookbook in the first century A.D.]

Mao·ism (mou′iz əm) *n.* the political theories, principles, and practices of the Chinese communist leader Mao Zedong.

Mao·ist (mou′ist) *n.* a person who believes in or supports Maoism. —*adj.* of or relating to Mao Zedong or Maoism.

Ma·o·ri (mä′ôr ē, mour′ē) *n., pl.* **-ris. 1.** a member of a Polynesian people living in New Zealand. **2.** their language, a member of the Austronesian family of languages. —*adj.* of, relating to, or characteristic of the Maoris or their language or culture.

map (map) *n.* **1.** a drawing or other representation of an area, as of the earth's surface, typically showing the relative position and size of the features represented. **2.** a drawing or representation of the sky, usually showing the stars and planets. Also, **star chart.** —*v.t.,* **mapped, map·ping. 1.** to make a map of; represent on a map. **2.** to plan in detail (often with *out*): *to map out a political campaign.* **3.** *Mathematics.* to assign (an element of one set) to an element of the same or another set. [Medieval Latin *mappa (mundi)* map (of the world), from Latin *mappa* napkin, (painted) cloth; possibly of Punic origin.] —**map′per,** *n.*

•**off the map.** out of existence; into oblivion: *The enemy threatened to wipe the region off the map.*

•**to put on the map.** *Informal.* to make well-known: *The discovery of oil in the area will put this town on the map.*

Synonyms *n.* Map, chart, and diagram denote a graphic representation of information. A **map** depicts the relative position and size of features, as well as other characteristics: *a map of the moon's surface, a map of the city.* A **chart** generally presents variations in data by means of tables, symbols, or graphs: *a chart of temperature changes, a chart of bus service.* A **diagram** is similar to a *map,* but is used for graphic representations of how things are organized or work: *a diagram of a car's engine, a diagram of a group of muscles in the arm.*

ma·ple (mā′pəl) *n.* **1.** any of a large group of trees and some shrubs, genus *Acer,* growing throughout the Northern Hemisphere, usually having lobed leaves and winged fruits. **2.** the

a	at	e	end	o	hot	u	up	hw	white	⎧	about
ā	ape	ē	me	ō	old	ū	use	ng	song		taken
ä	far	i	it	ô	fork	ü	rule	th	thin	ə	pencil
âr	care	ī	ice	oi	oil	ů	pull	th	this		lemon
		îr	pierce	ou	out	ûr	turn	zh	measure	⎩	circus

wood of this tree, used in the manufacture of furniture. **3.** the flavor of maple syrup or of maple sugar. [Middle English *mapel,* short for Old English *mapultrēow, mapulder* maple tree.]

maple sugar, a sugar made by boiling down maple syrup.

maple syrup, a syrup obtained by boiling and concentrating the sap of the sugar maple or of any of several other maple trees.

map·ping (map′ing) *n.* **1.** the process or activity of making maps; cartography. **2.** *Mathematics.* function *(def. 4b).*

mar (mär) *v.t.,* **marred, mar·ring. 1.** to spoil the appearance of; deface; disfigure: *to mar a table top.* **2.** to damage the quality or character of; impair: *Their rude behavior marred an otherwise enjoyable evening.* —*n.* something that mars. [Old English *merran.*] —For Synonyms, see **deface.**

Mar., March.

mar·a·bou (mar′ə bü′) *n.* **1.** any of several storks, genus *Leptoptilus,* of Africa, India, and Southeast Asia, having white, black, and gray plumage. Height: to 6 feet (1.8 meters). Also, **adjutant stork. 2.** the soft, downy feathers from this bird, often used in trimming hats. **3.** the trimming or material made from such feathers. **4.** a lightweight fabric, woven with a white silk thread. [French *marabout,* through Portuguese, from Arabic *murābit* hermit; because the bird tends to be solitary.]

ma·ra·ca (mə rä′kə) *n.* an instrument made of a dried gourd or gourd-shaped rattle that contains seeds or pebbles, often played in pairs. [Portuguese *maracá* this instrument; probably from Tupi-Guarani.]

marabou

mar·a·schi·no (mar′ə skē′nō, -shē′nō) *n.* a sweet cordial or liqueur made from the fermented juice of certain cherries. [Italian *maraschino,* from *(a)maracsa* a sour cherry, going back to Latin *amārus* sour.]

maraschino cherry, a cherry preserved in real or imitation maraschino.

ma·ras·mus (mə raz′məs) *n.* a chronic wasting of body tissue, esp. in infants and children, usually the result of severe malnutrition. [Modern Latin *marasmus,* from Greek *marasmos* a weakening, wasting away, from *marainein* to make weak, cause to waste away.] —**ma·ras′mic,** *adj.*

Ma·ra·thi (mə rä′tē, -rat′ē) *n.* an Indo-Iranian language spoken chiefly in central and western India.

mar·a·thon (mar′ə thon′) *n.* **1.** a foot race of 26 miles, 385 yards (42.2 kilometers), run over an open course. **2.** any long-distance race or other competition or activity testing the stamina of the participants; endurance contest: *a dance marathon.* [From a Greek soldier's legendary run from *Marathon* to Athens, about 25 miles (40 kilometers), to announce his country's defeat of Persia at Marathon.] —**mar′a·thon′er,** *n.*

ma·raud (mə rôd′) *v.i.* to rove in search of plunder; make raids for booty. —*v.t.* to plunder; raid. [French *marauder* to pilfer, from *maraud* rascal, vagabond; of uncertain origin.]

ma·raud·er (mə rô′dər) *n.* a person who roams in search of booty or plunder, esp. one who is part of a wandering band of plunderers.

mar·ble (mär′bəl) *n.* **1.** a metamorphosed limestone, usually mottled or streaked with variously colored swirls, widely used in architecture and sculpture. **2.** a piece, block, or slab of marble. **3.** a piece of sculpture in marble. **4.** something resembling marble, as in hardness or smoothness. **5.** a small hard ball of glass or other material, used in children's games. **6. marbles.** any of various games played with a number of these balls. ➡ used as singular. **7. marbles.** *Slang.* common sense; wits. —*adj.* made of or resembling marble. —*v.t.,* **-bled, -bling.** marbleize. [Old French *marbre* the limestone, from Latin *marmor,* from Greek *marmaros.*] —**mar′ble·like′,** *adj.*

marble cake, a cake made of dark and light batter mixed so as to give a streaked or marblelike appearance.

mar·ble·ize (mär′bə līz′) *v.t.,* **-ized, -iz·ing.** to color, mottle, or streak in imitation of marble; give the appearance of marble to.

mar·ca·site (mär′kə sīt′) *n.* **1.** an opaque yellow or white iron sulfide mineral with a metallic luster. Formula: FeS_2 **2.** this mineral cut and polished for ornamental use, esp. in jewelry: *a marcasite ring.* [French *marcassite,* through Spanish and Arabic; of Persian origin.]

mar·cel (mär sel′) *n.* a series of deep, even waves put in the hair with a curling iron. —*v.t.,* **-celled, -cel·ling.** to put a series of deep, even waves in (the hair) with a curling iron. [From *Marcel Grateau,* died 1936, French hairdresser.]

march[1] (märch) *v.i.* **1.** to walk or move in time with regular, measured steps, esp. in a group or formation: *The soldiers marched by the reviewing stands.* **2.** to walk or move in a steady, deliberate, or solemn manner: *The children marched off to bed soon after supper.* **3.** to go or advance steadily; proceed with regularity: *Time marches on.* —*v.t.* to cause (someone) to march: *to march troops up and down.* —*n.* **1.** the act of marching. **2.** the distance covered by a march: *a 20-mile march.* **3.** a steady forward movement: *the march of time.* **4.** a regular measured step, esp. of a body of soldiers. **5.** a musical composition, usually in duple time and with a strong rhythmical accent, suitable for marching. [Middle English *marchen,* from Middle French *march-(i)er,* from Old French *marchier* to trample; of Germanic origin.] —**march′er,** *n.*

• **on the march.** moving or advancing at a steady pace.

• **to steal a march on.** to gain an advantage over in a quiet but clever way: *The new advertising agency stole a march on its larger competitors by getting the big account.*

march[2] (märch) *n. usually,* **marches.** a region along the border of a country; frontier. [Old French *marche* frontier, boundary; of Germanic origin.]

March (märch) *n.* the third month of the year, containing thirty-one days. [Middle English *March(e),* from dialectal Old French *Marche,* from Latin *Martius (mēnsis)* (month) of *Mars;* referring to the ancient Roman practice of waging war during the month of March.]

mar·chion·ess (mär′shə nis) *n. British.* marquise *(defs. 1, 2).* [Medieval Latin *marchionissa,* feminine of *marchio* marquis; literally, ruler of a march, from *marca* march[2]; of Germanic origin.]

march·pane (märch′pān′) *n.* marzipan.

Mar·di Gras (mär′dē grä′) **1.** the last day before Lent. Also, **Shrove Tuesday. 2.** a celebration held in honor of this day, marked by parades and festivities. [French *mardi gras* Shrove Tuesday; literally, fat Tuesday, going back to Latin *Martis diēs* Tuesday (literally, day of Mars) + *crassus* fat, thick; supposedly referring to its being the last day of feasting before Lent.]

Mar·duk (mär′dùk′) *n.* in Babylonian mythology, the chief god.

mare[1] (mâr) *n.* a mature female of various equine animals, such as the horse, donkey, or zebra. [Old English *mere,* feminine of *mearh* horse.]

ma·re[2] (mär′ā, mâr′ē) *n., pl.* **maria.** any of various dark smooth plains on the moon or on Mars. [Latin *mare* sea; because the Italian astronomer Galileo, 1564-1642, thought they resembled seas.]

mare's-nest (mârz′nest′) *n.* **1.** a discovery that seems to be great or important but turns out to be a hoax or mistake. **2.** a confusing and disorderly situation.

mare's-tail (mârz′tāl′) *n.* **1.** a long, feathery cirrus cloud, resembling a horse's tail. **2.** a water plant, *Hippuris vulgaris,* having whorls of narrow tapered leaves and tiny, pale green flowers.

mar·ga·rine (mär′jər in, -jə rēn′) *also,* **mar·ga·rin** (mär′jər in). *n.* a food product usually made from vegetable oil with milk or water and salt, used as a substitute for butter. Also, **oleomargarine.** [French *margarine,* from Greek *margaron* pearl; referring to the pearllike sheen of an acid found in some fats.]

mar·gay (mär′gā) *n.* a small, spotted wildcat, *Felis wiedii,* resembling a small ocelot and ranging from southernmost Texas to Brazil. Length: 22 inches (56 centimeters), excluding tail. [French *margay,* from Portuguese *maracajá,* from Tupi *maracaja.*]

marge (märj) *n. Archaic.* a border; margin. [French *marge,* from Latin *margō.*]

mar·gin (mär′jin) *n.* **1.** a blank space around the body of written or printed matter on a page. **2.** an amount allowed or available in addition to what is necessary or needed: *a margin for error.* **3.** an amount or degree of difference: *We won the game by a narrow margin.* **4.** an edge or border: *the margin of a river.* **5.** the difference between the cost and selling price of merchandise. **6.** the minimum return necessary for an enterprise to continue to be profitable. **7.** the percentage of the total purchase price of a security that is lent by a broker to a client. The broker holds the security purchased as collateral against the loan. —*v.t.* **1.** to provide with a margin; border. **2.** to enter in the margin of a page, as notes. **3.** to buy (securities) on margin. [Latin *margin-,* stem of *margō* edge, border.]

mare's-tail

•**on margin.** with only a percentage of the total purchase price: *to buy stocks on margin, to trade on margin.*

mar·gin·al (mär′jə nəl) *adj.* **1.** written or printed in the margin of a page: *marginal notes.* **2.** of, relating to, constituting, or situated near a margin: *the marginal territories of an empire.* **3.** barely adequate, acceptable, or desirable; minimal: *marginal ability.* **4.** close to the point below which an investment is considered unprofitable; making very little profit. —**mar′gin·al′i·ty,** *n.* —**mar′gin·al·ly,** *adv.*

mar·gi·na·li·a (mär′jə nā′lē ə, -nāl′yə) *pl. n.* notes written or printed in the margin; marginal notes.

mar·grave (mär′grāv′) *n.* **1.** formerly, a prince of any of certain states of the Holy Roman Empire and Germany. **2.** formerly, a military governor of a German border province. [Middle Dutch *markgrave* count of a march², from *mark* march². + *grave* count².]

mar·gra·vine (mär′grə vēn′) *n.* the wife or widow of a margrave.

mar·gue·rite (mär′gə rēt′) *n.* **1.** the common daisy, *Chrysanthemum leucanthemum* or *C. frutescens,* bearing white or yellow ray flowers and yellow disk flowers. **2.** any of several other plants bearing daisylike flower heads. [French *marguerite* pearl, daisy, going back to Latin *margarīta* pearl, from Greek *margarítēs.*]

ma·ri·a (mär′ē ə, mâr′-) the plural of **mare².**

mar·i·gold (mar′i gōld′) *n.* **1.** the fragrant yellow, orange, or red flower head of any of a group of plants, genus *Tagetes,* of the composite family, such as the **African marigold,** *T. erecta.* **2.** the plant bearing this flower head. **3.** any of various other plants, such as the pot marigold and the marsh marigold. [*Mary* + GOLD; named after the Virgin Mary and referring to the gold-colored or yellow flowers of the plant.]

mar·i·jua·na (mar′ə wä′nə) *also,* **mar·i·hua·na.** *n.* **1.** the dried flowering tops and leaves of the hemp plant, *Cannabis sativa,* used as a drug, usually smoked in the form of cigarettes. **2.** hemp (*def. 2*). [Spanish *marihuana* kind of hemp with narcotic properties; of uncertain origin.]

ma·rim·ba (mə rim′bə) *n.* a musical percussion instrument resembling a large xylophone, consisting of a series of wooden bars, usually mounted over resonators, played by striking the bars with hand-held hammers. [Of Bantu origin.]

ma·ri·na (mə rē′nə) *n.* a dock or basin where slips, moorings, and, often, supplies, repairs, and other services are available for small boats. [Italian or

marimba

Spanish *marina* seashore, going back to Latin *marīnus* relating to the sea, from *mare* sea.]

mar·i·nade (*n.,* mar′ə nād′, mar′ə nād′, -näd′; *v.,* mar′ə nād′) *n.* a mixture, usually containing vinegar or wine and various spices, in which food is soaked before cooking. —*v.t.,* **-nad·ed, -nad·ing.** to soak (food) in this mixture; marinate. [French *marinade* liquid used for marinating, something marinated in this liquid, from *mariner* to marinate, from *marin* relating to the sea, from Latin *marīnus.* See MARINE.]

mar·i·nate (mar′ə nāt′) *v.t.,* **-nat·ed, -nat·ing.** to soak (food) in a marinade. [French *mariner* to marinate + -ATE¹. See MARINADE.] —**mar′i·na′tion,** *n.*

ma·rine (mə rēn′) *adj.* **1.** of or relating to the sea: *marine geology.* **2.** existing in or formed by the sea: *marine life, marine shells.* **3.** of, relating to, or used in sea navigation; nautical: *a marine barometer.* **4.** of or relating to commerce or shipping on the sea; maritime. **5.** of or relating to the navy or naval affairs. —*n.* **1. Marine.** a member of the U.S. Marine Corps. **2.** a soldier serving on a ship. **3.** a picture representing a sea scene; seascape. [Middle English *maryne,* from Old French *marin* relating to the sea, from Latin *marīnus,* from *mare* sea.]

Synonyms *adj.* **Marine, maritime,** and **nautical** mean of or relating to the sea or to navigation. **Marine** is the most general term: *marine engineering, marine biology.* **Maritime** is used mainly in reference to commerce on the seas: *maritime trade, maritime laws.* **Nautical** refers to the art or practice of navigation: *nautical skills, a nautical handbook.* Any of these terms may appear in loose usage in reference to large bodies of water other than seas: *a maritime history of the Great Lakes.*

marine biologist, a person who is a student of or an expert in marine biology.

marine biology, the scientific study of plants and animals living in the sea.

Marine Corps, a branch of the armed forces of the United States, under the Department of the Navy, that provides amphibious forces for overseas campaigns and detachments for other naval duties.

mar·i·ner (mar′ə nər) *n.* a person who navigates or assists in navigating a ship; sailor. [Anglo-Norman *mariner,* from Medieval Latin *marinarius,* from Latin *marīnus* relating to the sea, from *mare* sea.]

mar·i·o·nette (mar′ē ə net′) *n.* a small jointed figure, often of wood, moved by strings, wires, or rods held from above. [French *marionette,* diminutive of *Marion* Marian, from *Marie* Mary.]

Mar·i·po·sa lily (mar′ə pō′sə, -zə) **1.** a showy tulip-shaped flower of any of a group of plants, genus *Calochortus,* of the lily family, with flowers ranging from white to yellow and brown to purple. **2.** the plant bearing this flower, found in western North America. [Spanish *mariposa* butterfly (of uncertain origin) + LILY; referring to the resemblance of its multicolored flowers to butterflies.]

mar·ish (mar′ish) *Archaic. n.* a marsh. —*adj.* marshy.

mar·i·tal (mar′i təl) *adj.* of or relating to marriage. [Latin *marītālis,* from *marītus* husband.] —**mar′i·tal·ly,** *adv.*

mar·i·time (mar′i tīm′) *adj.* **1.** bordering on, close to, or living near the sea: *a maritime town, a maritime people.* **2.** of or relating to the sea or its navigation, commerce, or shipping: *maritime law.* [Latin *maritimus* relating to the sea, from *mare* sea.] —For Synonyms, see **marine.**

mar·jo·ram (mär′jər əm) *n.* **1.** the dried leaves of an aromatic plant, *Origanum majorana,* of the mint family, used as a spice. **2.** the plant itself, cultivated as a garden herb, bearing small, fuzzy, round leaves and clusters of tiny pink, white, or lilac flowers. Also, **sweet marjoram.** [Old French *majorane* the plant, from Medieval Latin *maiorana,* possibly through Latin, from Greek *amārakos.*]

mark¹ (märk) *n.* **1.** any visible trace left by a material object when it comes into contact with the surface of another. **2.** any sign or symbol used in writing or printing. **3.** a cross or other sign made in place of a signature by a person who cannot write. **4.** a number or letter used to show the level or quality of a person's work. **5.** a visible indication of some quality, feature, or characteristic: *a mark of intelligence.* **6.** a permanent or distinct impression: *a writer who left a mark on literature.* **7.** something, such as a seal, label, or inscription, placed on or attached to an object, esp. to indicate ownership, origin, quality, or authenticity. **8.** something, such as a line or object, used as a guide, indicator, or point of reference; bench mark: *a high-water mark.* **9.** a target or other object aimed at. **10.** something that a person desires or strives for; goal. **11.** an accepted standard or criterion, as of quality, performance, or propriety. **12.** distinction; note; importance: *a fellow of no mark, nor likelihood* (Shakespeare, *Henry IV, Part I*). **13.** in medieval Germany, a tract of land held in common by a village community. **14.** *Archaic.* boundary; frontier. **15.** *Informal.* a person who is easily fooled or victimized: *an easy mark for swindlers.* **16.** the starting line of a race. —*v.t.* **1.** to make or put a mark or marks on (a surface): *The children marked the sidewalk with chalk.* **2.** to trace, form, or indicate the limits or boundaries of (often with *out* or *off*): *to mark off an area on a map.* **3.** to indicate or represent, as by a sign or symbol: *The editor marked corrections in green.* **4.** to distinguish; characterize: *Solemnity marked the occasion.* **5.** to give or assign a mark to: *The teacher marked the papers.* **6.** to pay attention to; heed: *Mark my words.* **7.** to write (often with *down*): *I marked down the date of the party on my calendar.* **8.** to single out, designate, or select as if by marking; destine: *to be marked for death.* **9.** to provide with a mark, such as a label or tag, to indicate something, such as price, content, or quality: *They marked all the merchandise before displaying it.* **10.** in various games, to keep (the score): *to mark the score on a card.* **11.** to make obvious or clear; manifest: *A smile marked her happiness.* [Old English *mearc* boundary, trace, sign.]

•**beside** (or **wide of**) **the mark. a.** missing what is aimed at. **b.** not to the point; not relevant: *Too many comments and suggestions at the meeting were wide of the mark.*

•**to hit the mark. a.** to be accurate; be right. **b.** to attain one's goal; be successful.

a	at	e	end	o	hot	u	up	hw	white		about
ā	ape	ē	me	ō	old	ū	use	ng	song		taken
ä	far	i	it	ô	fork	ü	rule	th	thin	ə	pencil
âr	care	ī	ice	oi	oil	u̇	pull	th	this		lemon
				îr	pierce	ou	out	ûr	turn	zh	measure		circus

· **to make one's mark.** to become famous or successful.

· **to mark down. a.** to write down: *to mark down a phone number on a pad.* **b.** to reduce the price of.

· **to mark time. a.** to move the feet as in marching, but without going forward. **b.** to perform the actions of something without really accomplishing anything: *I felt I was simply marking time at that job and started looking for another with more challenge.*

· **to mark up. a.** to write or draw all over something: *The editor marked up the manuscript.* **b.** to increase the price of.

· **to miss the mark. a.** to be inaccurate; be wrong. **b.** to fail to attain one's goal; be unsuccessful.

mark² (märk) *n.* **1.** deutsche mark. **2.** ostmark. **3.** reichsmark. [German *Mark;* of Old Norse origin.]

Mark (märk) *n.* one of the four Gospels, the second book of the New Testament, attributed to the Evangelist Mark.

mark·down (märk′doun′) *n.* **1.** a reduction in the selling price of an item. **2.** the amount of reduction in price.

marked (märkt) *adj.* **1.** easily seen or noticed; obvious: *a marked similarity between two dresses.* **2.** singled out and watched as an object of suspicion, vengeance, punishment, or death: *a marked person.* **3.** having a mark or marks. —**mark′ed·ness,** *n.*

mark·ed·ly (mär′kid lē) *adv.* in a marked manner; clearly; obviously.

mark·er (mär′kər) *n.* **1.** a person who marks, esp. one who keeps score in a game or grades test papers. **2.** something that marks, esp. a writing implement, bookmark, milestone, or gravestone. **3.** a person who removes a target, marks the hits, and puts up a new target for the next round.

mar·ket (mär′kit) *n.* **1.** an open space or building where food products or goods are bought and sold; marketplace: *The farmer took vegetables to the market every week.* **2.** a shop or store, esp. one where food products are sold: *a fish market.* **3.** a region or country where commodities can be bought and sold; area of demand for commodities: *the foreign market.* **4.** trade and commerce, esp. in a specified service or commodity: *the grain market.* **5.** demand (for a commodity): *There is very little market for buggy whips today.* **6.** the rate or value (of a stock or commodity): *What is the current market for utilities?* **7.** the state of trading: *an active market, a bull market.* **8.** the available supply of a particular service or commodity: *a large labor market.* **9.** stock market. —*v.i.* **1.** to buy food products and other household items in a market. **2.** to deal in a market; buy and sell. —*v.t.* to sell or offer for sale: *The farmer markets vegetables in town.* [Anglo-Norman *market* trade, bargain, place for commercial transactions, from Latin *mercātus* trade, marketplace, going back to *merx* merchandise.] —**mar′ket·er,** *n.*

· **on the market.** available for purchase: *That company makes the best television sets on the market.*

· **to be in the market for.** to be interested in buying: *I'm in the market for a good used car.*

· **to play the market.** to speculate on the stock market.

· **to pull** (or **take**) **off the market.** to make unavailable for purchase.

mar·ket·a·ble (mär′ki tə bəl) *adj.* fit to be or capable of being sold; salable. —**mar′ket·a·bil′i·ty,** *n.*

mar·ket·place (mär′kit plās′) *also,* **market place.** *n.* **1.** a place where food products or other consumer goods are bought and sold. **2.** the world of business, commerce, and economics.

market price, the current or prevailing price of goods, services, or securities on the open market.

market research, a study of the buying habits and attitudes of consumers toward a particular product or line of products.

market value, the current value of goods, services, or securities as established by sales on the open market. ➡ distinguished from **book value.**

mark·ing (mär′king) *n.* **1.** a mark or marks. **2.** *also,* **markings.** the arrangement of marks and colors on a plant or animal: *a bird with red markings.* **3.** the act of making a mark or marks on something.

mark·ka (mär′kä) *n.* the monetary unit of Finland. [Finnish *markka,* from German *Mark.*]

marks·man (märks′mən) *n., pl.* **-men** (-mən). **1.** a person skilled in shooting a gun or other weapon. **2.a.** in the U.S. Armed Forces, the lowest category of qualification in target shooting. **b.** a person who has qualified in this category.

marks·man·ship (märks′mən ship′) *n.* skill in shooting a gun or other weapon.

mark·up (märk′up′) *n.* **1.** an amount added to the cost of an item in determining the selling price, usually taking into account overhead and profit. **2.** an increase in price. **3.** the amount of increase in price.

marl (märl) *n.* a clay containing calcium carbonate and, often, fragments of seashells, used in making portland cement and as a

fertilizer. —*v.t.* to fertilize or otherwise prepare (land) for cultivation by applying marl. [Old French *marle* this clay, from Medieval Latin *margila,* diminutive of Latin *marga;* possibly of Celtic origin.] —**marl′y,** *adj.*

mar·lin (mär′lin) *n., pl.* **-lin** or **-lins.** any of a group of saltwater game fish, genus *Makaira,* related to the sailfish and having a long, spearlike bill. Length: to 14 feet (4.3 meters). [Short for MARLINESPIKE; referring to its spearlike upper jaw.]

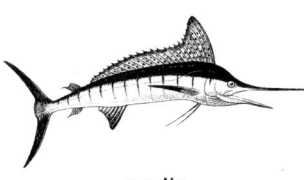

marlin

mar·line (mär′lin) *n.* a small cord of two strands loosely twisted together, used, as on ships, for winding around the ends of ropes or cables to prevent fraying. [Dutch *marlijn,* from *marren* to tie + *lijn* line (from French *ligne* cord). See LINE¹.]

mar·line·spike (mär′lin spīk′) *also,* **mar·lin·spike, mar·lingspike** (mär′ling spīk′). *n.* a pointed iron pin used to separate strands of rope, as in splicing.

mar·ma·lade (mär′mə lād′) *n.* a jam made by boiling the peel and flesh of fruit, usually citrus fruit, with sugar. [French *marmelade* from Portuguese *marmelada* quince jelly, marmalade, from *marmelo* quince, through Latin, from Greek *melimēlon* apple grafted on a quince, from *meli* honey + *mēlon* apple; because this jam was originally made of quinces.]

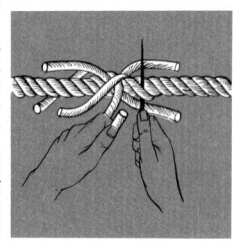

marlinespike

mar·mo·re·al (mär môr′ē əl) *adj.* made of, relating to, or like marble: *the cold, marmoreal beauty of a Greek statue.* Also, **mar·mo′re·an.** [Latin *marmoreus* (from *marmor* marble) + -AL¹. See MARBLE.]

mar·mo·set (mär′mə zet′) *n.* any of various tree-dwelling monkeys, family Callithricidae, of Central and South America, having shaggy or soft and fine fur, long, curved claws except on the big toe, and a long tail. Length: to 14 inches (36 centimeters), including tail. [Old French *marmoset* grotesque image; of uncertain origin.]

mar·mot (mär′mət) *n.* any of various plump, short-legged rodents, genus *Marmota,* having a gray or brown, thick, coarse coat and a short, bushy tail. Marmots, which hibernate during the cold months, are found in North America, Europe, and Asia. Length: to 30 inches (76 centimeters). [French *marmotte,* possibly going back to Latin *mūs* (stem *mūr-*) mouse + *montānus* of the mountains.]

ma·roon¹ (mə rün′) *n.* a dark brownish red color. —*adj.* having the color maroon. [French *marron* chestnut, from Italian *marrone;* of uncertain origin.]

ma·roon² (mə rün′) *v.t.* **1.** to put ashore and leave on a desolate island or coast. **2.** to leave helpless and alone; abandon. —*n.* a fugitive slave or his or her descendant living in the West Indies and Dutch Guiana in the seventeenth and eighteenth centuries. [French *marron* wild, runaway (slave), from Spanish *cimarrón* wild, from Old Spanish *cimarra* thicket.]

marque (märk) *n. Archaic.* letter of marque.

mar·quee (mär kē′) *n.* **1.** a canopy or other rooflike shelter, as of metal or canvas, over an entrance, esp. to a theater. **2.** a large tent, esp. one put up for an outdoor party or reception. [French *marquise* (mistaken for plural) awning, large tent, probably from *marquise,* feminine of *marquis* (see MARQUIS); possibly referring to the use of a tent or awning to protect a lady of rank from bad weather.]

mar·quess (mär′kwis) *British.* marquis.

mar·que·try (mär′ki trē) *n., pl.* **-tries.** inlaid work consisting of pieces of wood, often with the addition of other materials, such as ivory or metal. [French *marqueterie,* from *marqueter* to inlay, from *marque* sign, mark¹; of Germanic origin.]

mar·quis (mär′kwis, mär kē′) *also, British,* **marquess.** *n., pl.* **-quis·es** or **-quis** (-kēz′). a nobleman ranking next below a duke and above an earl or count. [Old French *marquis, marchis* originally, governor of a frontier, from *marche* frontier; of Germanic origin.]

mar·quis·ate (mär′kwi zit) *n.* the status or rank of a marquis.

mar·quise (mär kēz′) *n.* **1.** the wife or widow of a marquis. **2.** a woman holding in her own right the rank equal to that of a marquis. Also *(defs. 1, 2), British,* **marchioness. 3.** a gem, esp. a diamond, cut in an oval, pointed shape. **4.** a ring set with such

a gem or a cluster of such gems. [French *marquise,* feminine of *marquis.* See MARQUIS.]

mar·qui·sette (mär′kə zet′, -kwə-) *n.* a sheer, lightweight, mesh fabric made of various fibers, used esp. for curtains. [French *marquisette,* diminutive of *marquise* awning, large tent. See MARQUEE.]

mar·riage (mar′ij) *n.* **1.a.** the state of being married; wedlock. **b.** the legal union of a man and woman. **2.a.** the act of marrying. **b.** the ceremony or procedure accompanying this; wedding. **3.** any close relationship or union: *an interesting marriage of comedy and drama in a play.* **4.** in pinochle, a meld of the king and queen of the same suit. [Old French *mariage* the legal union of a man and woman, from *marier* to wed. See MARRY¹.]

mar·riage·a·ble (mar′i jə bəl) *adj.* fit or suitable for marriage. —**mar′riage·a·bil′i·ty,** *n.*

mar·ried (mar′ēd) *adj.* **1.** joined in marriage. **2.** having a husband or wife. **3.** of or relating to marriage or married persons: *married life.* **4.** closely united. —*n.* a married person. ➡ used chiefly in the phrase *young marrieds.*

mar·row (mar′ō) *n.* **1.** the soft tissue that fills the cavities and spongy parts of bones and produces most blood cells. For illustration, see **bone. 2.** the inmost, best, or vital part. [Old English *mearh, mærg* the tissue in the cavities of bones.] —**mar′row·y,** *adj.*

marrow bean, a thick, white variety of kidney bean.

mar·row·bone (mar′ō bōn′) *n.* **1.** a bone containing edible marrow, used for making soups and stews. **2. marrowbones. a.** *Informal.* knees. **b.** crossbones.

mar·row·fat (mar′ō fat′) *n.* a kind of pea with a large, rich seed.

mar·ry¹ (mar′ē) *v.,* -ried, -ry·ing. —*v.t.* **1.** to take as a husband or wife; wed. **2.** to join as husband and wife; unite in wedlock: *A judge will marry the couple.* **3.** to give in marriage (often with *off*): *The parents married off their last child.* **4.** to obtain or establish oneself with by marriage: *My friend married money.* **5.** to unite closely: *The sauce marries the flavors of many herbs.* —*v.i.* **1.** to take a husband or wife: *to marry young.* **2.** to enter into a close union. [Middle English *marien,* from Old French *marier,* from Latin *maritāre* to marry, from *maritus* husband.]

mar·ry² (mar′ē) *interj. Archaic.* an exclamation, as of anger, surprise, or indignation. [Euphemism for the Virgin *Mary* (used as an exclamation).]

Mars (märz) *n.* **1.** in Roman mythology, the god of war. His Greek counterpart is Ares. **2.** the seventh largest planet of the solar system and fourth in order of distance from the sun, having two moons and a tenuous atmosphere.

image of the surface of **Mars** taken by *Viking I* lander

mar·seilles (mär sālz′) *also,* **mar·seille.** *n.* a thick cotton cloth woven with raised figures or stripes, used esp. for bedspreads and quilts. [From *Marseilles,* France, where it was first made.]

marsh (märsh) *n.* a tract of low, wet land covered with grasses and grasslike plants, such as reeds. [Old English *mersc.*]

mar·shal (mär′shəl) *n.* **1.** an officer of a federal court who is appointed to a judicial district to carry out orders and perform other duties similar to those of a sheriff. **2.** in some states, a law officer of a city or borough having powers similar to those of a

sheriff. **3.** the head of a city police or fire department. **4.** field marshal. **5.** a person in charge of arranging and regulating processions and ceremonies. **6.** a high official of a royal household or court, esp. one in charge of protocol and official ceremonies. —*v.t.,* -shaled, -shal·ing; *also, British,* -shalled, -shal·ling. **1.** to arrange in methodical order: *to marshal one's arguments for a debate.* **2.** to organize or place (soldiers) in proper order, as for battle. **3.** to usher or lead ceremoniously. [Old French *mareschal* high official; originally, groom, farrier, going back to Old High German *marah* horse + *scalc* servant. The medieval marshal's prestige grew with the rise in importance of the cavalry.]

Marshall Plan, a U.S. plan for economic aid to western Europe after World War II. Also, **European Recovery Program.** [From George C. *Marshall,* 1880-1959, U.S. general and statesman who initiated the plan.]

marsh gas, methane.

marsh hawk, a slender North American bird of prey, *Circus cyaneus,* gray above in the male and brown in the female. Length: 17-23 inches (43-58 centimeters). Also, **northern harrier.**

marsh·land (märsh′land′) *n.* an area characterized by marshes or swamps.

marsh·mal·low (märsh′mel′ō, -mal′ō) *n.* a soft, usually white, spongy confection made from starch, sugar, gelatin, and corn syrup and covered with powdered sugar. [Because this confection was once made from the root of the marsh mallow.]

marsh mallow, a tall, leafy plant, *Althaea officinalis,* found growing wild in eastern Europe and the eastern United States, bearing downy, oval or heart-shaped leaves and bluish to pink flowers. [Old English *merscmealwe.* See MARSH, MALLOW.]

marsh marigold, any of several fleshy plants, genus *Caltha,* that grow in damp areas and bear heart- or kidney-shaped leaves and yellow, pink, or white flowers resembling buttercups. Also, **cowslip.**

marsh·y (mär′shē) *adj.,* marsh·i·er, marsh·i·est. **1.** like a marsh; swampy. **2.** of, relating to, or containing a marsh or marshes. **3.** growing or occurring in a marsh. —**marsh′i·ness,** *n.*

mar·su·pi·al (mär sü′pē əl) *n.* any of various mammals, order Marsupialia, such as kangaroos, wombats, and opossums, the female of which has an abdominal pouch in which the young continue to develop after birth. —*adj.* **1.** of, relating to, or designating a marsupial. **2.** of, like, or relating to a marsupium.

mar·su·pi·um (mär sü′pē əm) *n., pl.* -pi·a (-pē ə). **1.** a pouch on the abdomen of a female marsupial, used for carrying the newborn offspring. **2.** a similar pouch on certain fish and crustaceans, used for carrying eggs or young. [Latin *marsūpium* pouch, from Greek *marsypion,* diminutive of *marsypos* pouch, purse.]

mart (märt) *n.* a trading center; market: *a food mart.* [Obsolete Dutch *mart,* form of *markt* market.]

mar·ten (mär′tən) *n., pl.* -tens or -ten. **1.** any of various weasellike mammals, genus *Martes,* having thick, soft fur ranging in color from golden brown to blackish brown. Length: to 30 inches (76 centimeters), including tail. **2.** its fur, made into coats, stoles, and trimmings; sable. [Old French *martrine* the fur of the marten, from *martre* marten (animal); of Germanic origin.]

marten

mar·tial (mär′shəl) *adj.* **1.** of, relating to, or suitable for war or military life: *martial music.* **2.** of or characteristic of a warrior; warlike. [Middle English *martialle,* from Latin *mārtiālis* relating to Mars, from *Mārs* the Roman god of war.] —**mar′tial·ly,** *adv.*

martial art, any of the Oriental methods of unarmed combat or self-defense, such as karate or jujitsu.

martial law, military rule or authority imposed on a civilian population, as when the civil authorities cannot maintain law and order, in a time of war, or during an emergency.

Mar·tian (mär′shən) *adj.* of or relating to the planet Mars. —*n.*

a	at	e	end	o	hot	u	up	hw	white		about
ā	ape	ē	me	ō	old	ū	use	ng	song	ə	taken
ä	far	i	it	ô	fork	ü	rule	th	thin		pencil
âr	care	ī	ice	oi	oil	u̇	pull	th	this		lemon
		îr	pierce	ou	out	ûr	turn	zh	measure		circus

753

a supposed inhabitant of the planet Mars. [Latin *mārtius* relating to Mars (from *Mārs* Mars) + -AN.]

mar·tin (mär′tən) *n.* any of various dark-colored swallows widely distributed throughout the world, such as the **sand martin,** *Riparia riparia.* [From *Saint Martin;* supposedly referring to its migration around Saint Martin's Day on November 11.]

mar·ti·net (mär′tə net′) *n.* a strict disciplinarian, esp. a military one. [From Jean *Martinet,* died 1672, French general under Louis XIV, who originated a system of military drill.]

mar·tin·gale (mär′tən gāl′, -ting-) *n.* **1.** a strap of a horse's harness attached under the belly at one end to the girth, passing between the forelegs, and secured to the noseband. It prevents the horse from rearing or throwing back its head. **2.** *Nautical.* **a.** a lower stay that supports the jib boom or flying jib boom. **b.** a small spar projecting down from the end of the bowsprit, designed to spread such stays. [French *martingale,* supposedly going back to *Martigue,* a town in Provence; with reference to its inhabitants' practice of fastening trousers in the back.]

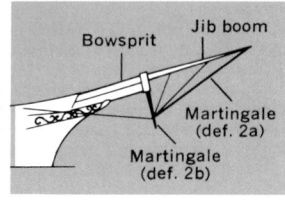

martingales

mar·ti·ni (mär tē′nē) *n., pl.* **-nis.** a cocktail made of gin or vodka and dry vermouth. [Possibly from *Martini* Italian proper name.]

Martin Luther King Day, the third Monday in January or January 15, observed as a legal holiday in almost all states of the United States in honor of Martin Luther King, Jr., U.S. civil rights leader.

Mar·tin·mas (mär′tən məs) *n.* a Christian festival held in honor of Saint Martin, observed on November 11.

mar·tyr (mär′tər) *n.* **1.** a person who suffers death rather than deny a religious faith. **2.** a person who dies, suffers greatly, or sacrifices all for a belief, principle, or cause. **3.** a person who suffers greatly or sacrifices much, often for attention or to arouse sympathy. —*v.t.* **1.** to make a martyr of, esp. by killing. **2.** to cause to suffer greatly; torture or persecute. [Old English *martyr* one who dies or suffers for the Christian faith, from Late Latin *martyr* one who, in dying for that faith, bears witness to its truth, witness, from Greek *martys.*]

mar·tyr·dom (mär′tər dəm) *n.* **1.** the state or condition of being a martyr. **2.** the death or suffering of a martyr. **3.** extreme pain or suffering; torture; torment.

mar·vel (mär′vəl) *n.* a wonderful or astonishing thing: *the marvels of modern medicine.* —*v.i.,* -**veled, -vel·ing;** *also, British,* -**velled, -vel·ling.** to be or become filled with wonder or astonishment: *We marveled at the acrobat's skill and grace.* [Old French *merveille* wonder, going back to Latin *mīrābilia* (plural) wonderful things.]

mar·vel·ous (mär′və ləs) *also, British,* **mar·vel·lous.** *adj.* **1.** causing wonder or astonishment: *marvelous and daring feats, a marvelous invention.* **2.** very good; splendid: *We had a marvelous vacation.* **3.** extremely improbable; incredible: *the marvelous adventures of a legendary hero.* —**mar′vel·ous·ly,** *adv.* —**mar′vel·ous·ness,** *n.*

Marx·ism (märk′siz əm) *n.* the economic theories of the German socialists Karl Marx and Friedrich Engels.

Marx·ist (märk′sist) *n.* a person who believes in or supports Marxism. —*adj.* of or relating to Marxism. Also, **Marx·i·an** (märk′sē ən). [From Karl *Marx,* 1818-83, German economist and philosopher.]

mar·zi·pan (mär′zə pan′) *n.* a confection made of ground almonds, sugar, and egg whites, often molded into various forms. Also, **marchpane.** [German *Marzipan,* from Italian *marzapane* marzipan, container for sweets, from Arabic *martabān* container.]

masc., masculine.

mas·ca·ra (mas kar′ə) *n.* a cosmetic preparation used to color the eyelashes and make them appear longer. [Spanish *máscara* mask, possibly from Arabic *maskharah* buffoon, person in masquerade.]

mas·con (mas′kon′) *n.* an area of unusually dense material under the surface of the mare areas of the moon, believed to be responsible for the uneven gravitational pull on spacecraft orbiting the moon. [Short for *mas(s) con(centration).*]

mas·cot (mas′kot) *n.* an animal, person, or thing supposed to bring good luck, esp. a pet animal kept by a sports team: *The school mascot was a bulldog.* [French *mascotte,* from Provençal *mascoto* sorcery, from *masco* witch; of uncertain origin.]

mas·cu·line (mas′kyə lin) *adj.* **1.** of, relating to, or thought to be characteristic of a man. **2.** having characteristics regarded as manly. **3.** (of a woman) having a mannish appearance or nature. **4.** *Grammar.* of the gender that includes words applying to things regarded as male. —*n. Grammar.* **1.** the masculine gender. **2.** a word or other element belonging to the masculine gender. [Latin *masculīnus* male, manly, from *masculus.* See MALE.]

masculine rhyme, a rhyme consisting of a single stressed syllable, as *sakes* and *lakes* or *maroon* and *baboon.*

mas·cu·lin·i·ty (mas′kyə lin′i tē) *n.* the quality or state of being masculine.

ma·ser (mā′zər) *n.* any of several devices that produce or amplify coherent microwave radiation using the excess energy from an excited atomic or molecular system and operating on the same principle as the laser. Masers are used in atomic clocks and in radio astronomy. [Short for *m(icrowave) a(mplification by) s(timulated) e(mission of) r(adiation).*]

mash (mash) *n.* **1.** a feed that consists of a mixture of ground grains and is fed either wet or dry to livestock or poultry. **2.** ground or crushed malt or meal combined with water, used to make beer. **3.** any soft, pulpy mass or mixture. —*v.t.* **1.** to make into a soft, pulpy mass or mixture: *to mash potatoes.* **2.** to mix thoroughly (ground barley malt) with hot water to produce wort. **3.** to damage or hurt by crushing or squeezing: *I mashed my finger in the door.* [Old English *māsc-* malt mixed with hot water for brewing.] —**mash′er,** *n.*

mash·ie (mash′ē) *also,* **mash·y.** *n., pl.* **mash·ies.** a golf club with a metal head having a short sloping face and giving a moderate amount of loft; number five iron.

wooden masks
Inuit mask (left); Papuan mask (right)

mask (mask) *n.* **1.** a covering worn over all or part of the face, used to conceal or disguise one's identity. **2.** a covering, as of metal, plastic, wire, or gauze, worn over all or part of the face for protection, as in certain sports or occupations: *a catcher's mask, a surgical mask.* **3.** a covering worn over the face of an actor, as in ancient Greek and Roman drama. **4.** a molded or sculptured likeness of a face, often made of plaster, clay, or papier-mâché. **5.** anything that hides or disguises something from view. **6.** a distinctive marking on the face of certain animals, esp. dogs. **7.** gas mask. —*v.t.* **1.** to cover with a mask. **2.** to conceal or disguise, as from view or notice: *A high stone wall masked the house from the road. A smile masked my disappointment.* [French *masque* visor, disguise for the face, masked person, from Italian *maschera,* possibly from Arabic *maskharah* buffoon, person in masquerade.]

> **Synonyms** *v.t.* **Mask, cloak,** and **disguise** mean to conceal by covering over in some way. **Mask** connotes simply hiding something from view: *to mask one's emotions with a poker face.* **Cloak** suggests a covering up intended to hide one's real intent: *to cloak one's curiosity in apparent indifference.* **Disguise** more clearly connotes change than covering up: *to adopt a brash manner in order to disguise one's insecurity.*

masked ball, a ball at which masks, and often costumes, are worn by the guests.

masking tape, an adhesive tape that can be removed easily, used esp. to cover and protect surfaces, as during painting.

mas·o·chism (mas′ə kiz′əm) *n.* **1.** an abnormal tendency to derive sexual pleasure from inflicting pain or punishment on oneself or from having it inflicted on oneself by others. **2.** gratification of any sort derived from physical or emotional pain, either

self-inflicted or inflicted by others. —**mas'o·chist,** *n.* —**mas'o·chis'tic,** *adj.* [From Leopold von Sacher-*Masoch*, 1836-95, Austrian novelist who described it.]

ma·son (mā′sən) *n.* **1.** a person whose occupation is building with stone, brick, or concrete. **2. Mason.** Freemason. [Old French *masson* worker in stone; of Germanic origin.]

Ma·son-Dix·on line (mā′sən dik′sən) part of the boundary line between Maryland and Pennsylvania, regarded as the dividing line between free and slave states before the American Civil War. It is now a symbolic boundary between the North and the South.

Ma·son·ic (mə son′ik) *adj.* of, relating to, or characteristic of Freemasons or Freemasonry.

Ma·son·ite (mā′sə nīt′) *n. Trademark.* any of several fiberboards, used esp. for paneling or insulation.

Mason jar, a glass jar used for home canning and preserving. It has a wide mouth and a metal top consisting of a lid with a rubber rim that makes an airtight seal when a separate fastener is screwed on. [From John L. *Mason*, nineteenth-century American inventor who patented it.]

ma·son·ry (mā′sən rē) *n., pl.* **-ries. 1.** something built by a mason, esp. in stone. **2.** the art, skill, or occupation of a mason. **3. Masonry.** Freemasonry.

masque (mask) *n.* **1.** a form of dramatic entertainment popular in the sixteenth and seventeenth centuries, often using masks and based on allegory. **2.** a literary work written for such a performance. **3.** masquerade *(def. 1).* [French *masque* visor, disguise for the face, masked person. See MASK.] —**mas′quer,** *n.*

mas·quer·ade (mas′kə rād′) *n.* **1.** a social gathering at which masks and fancy costumes are worn. **2.** a false outward show; pretense: *Their concern was just a masquerade.* —*v.i.* **-ad·ed, -ad·ing. 1.** to take part in a masquerade. **2.** to assume a false appearance or identity; disguise oneself; pose: *The jewelry thief masqueraded as an aristocrat.* [French *mascarade* band of masked persons, false pretense, from Italian *mascherata* band of masked persons, from *maschera* disguise for the face, masked person. See MASK.] —**mas′quer·ad′er,** *n.*

mass (mas) *n.* **1.** a body of matter holding or sticking together without a particular shape: *a mass of snow, a mass of clay.* **2.** a large quantity, amount, or number: *a mass of people.* **3.** a collection of individual parts or elements that together compose a single body: *a mass of rocks.* **4.** great size or extent; bulk: *the mass of an adult hippopotamus.* **5.** the main or greater part; majority: *the great mass of humanity.* **6.** *Physics.* a fundamental property of matter, measurable in terms of the inertia of a body, and used as a measure of the quantity of matter a body contains. **7. the masses.** the common people; populace. —*v.t., v.i.* to form or gather into a mass; assemble: *The herders massed the sheep behind the fence. Fans massed in front of the theater to see the rock star.* —*adj.* **1.** of, relating to, or for the masses. **2.** consisting of or involving a large number of people: *a mass walkout.* **3.** done on a large scale or in large quantities: *mass packaging.* [Latin *massa* lump, from Greek *māza* lump, barley cake.]
  • **in the mass.** as a whole or group; collectively.

Mass (mas) *also,* **mass.** *n.* **1.** the main ceremony of worship in the Roman Catholic and parts of the Anglican churches. **2.** a musical setting for certain parts of this service. [Old English *mæsse* celebration of the Eucharist, from Late Latin *missa*, from Latin *mittere* to send (away); supposedly from *Ite, missa est* Go, it is the dismissal (spoken at the end of the Mass).]

Mass., Massachusetts.

Mas·sa·chu·set (mas′ə chü′sit) *also,* **Mas·sa·chu·sett.** *n., pl.* **-set** or **-sets.** a member of a North American Indian tribe formerly living in what is now Massachusetts and speaking an Algonquian language.

mas·sa·cre (mas′ə kər) *n.* **1.** a brutal, indiscriminate slaughter, esp. of people. **2.** *Informal.* an overwhelming defeat, as in sports. —*v.t.,* **-cred, -cring. 1.** to kill brutally and in large numbers. **2.** *Informal.* to defeat overwhelmingly, as in sports. [French *massacre* slaughter; of uncertain origin.] —**mas·sa·crer** (mas′ə krər), *n.*

mas·sage (mə säzh′) *n.* the rubbing or kneading of parts of the body, esp. to increase circulation or relax muscles. —*v.t.,* **-saged, -sag·ing.** to give a massage to. [French *massage* manipulation of parts of the body, from *masser* to give a massage to, from Arabic *mass* to touch.]

mass-en·er·gy equation (mas′en′ər jē) an equation, $E = mc^2$, expressing the relation of mass and energy. In the equation E = energy, m = mass, and c = the velocity of light. Also, **Einstein's equation.**

mas·se·ter (ma sē′tər) *n.* either of a pair of large muscles that raise the lower jaw, as in talking or chewing. They arise from the cheek region and insert in the angle of the jawbone. [Modern Latin *masseter*, from Greek *masētēr* chewer, from *masathai* to chew.] —**mas·se·ter·ic** (mas′i ter′ik), *adj.*

mas·seur (mə sûr′, ma-) *n.* a man whose occupation is giving massages and other body-conditioning treatments. [French *masseur*, from *masser* to give a massage to. See MASSAGE.]

mas·seuse (mə süs′, -süz′) *n.* a woman whose occupation is giving massages and other body-conditioning treatments. [French *masseuse*, feminine of *masseur.* See MASSEUR.]

mas·sif (ma sēf′, mas′if) *n.* a group of connected peaks forming the main mass or backbone of a mountain range. [French *massif.* See MASSIVE.]

mas·sive (mas′iv) *adj.* **1.** consisting of or forming a large mass; having great size and weight: *The vault had massive steel doors.* **2.** imposing or exceedingly large, as in scope, scale, degree, or intensity: *a massive bombing raid.* [French *massif* bulky, heavy, going back to Latin *massa* lump. See MASS.] —**mas′sive·ly,** *adv.* —**mas′sive·ness,** *n.*

mass media *pl., sing.* **mass medium.** the various forms of public communication, such as television, newspapers, and magazines, that reach large audiences.

mass meeting, a large public gathering of people to discuss, listen to discussion of, or act on some matter of common interest.

mass noun, a noun that names a general thing or idea that cannot be counted and is not used with the indefinite articles *a* and *an*. *Mud* and *snow* are mass nouns; *hat, car,* and *dog* are not.

mass number, the total number of protons and neutrons in the nucleus of an atom; atomic weight rounded off to the nearest whole number.

mass-pro·duce (mas′prə düs′, -dūs′) *v.t.,* **-duced, -duc·ing. 1.** to manufacture or produce (goods) in large quantities, esp. by the use of machinery and assembly lines. **2.** to produce or turn out anything in large quantities.

mass production, the act or process of mass-producing.

mass spectrograph, an instrument that identifies ionized particles by their atomic mass. A beam of ions is passed through a magnetic field, which separates them according to mass into a spectrum that is photographically recorded.

mass spectrometer, an electronic instrument that uses the principle of the mass spectrograph but produces a digital record.

mass transit, public transportation in a large city or urban area, usually consisting of some combination of buses, subways, and trains.

mass·y (mas′ē) *adj.,* **mass·i·er, mass·i·est.** *Archaic.* massive.

mast[1] (mast) *n.* **1.** a vertical pole set upright in a sailing boat or ship to support the yards, sails, and rigging. **2.** any upright pole, as of a crane. —*v.t.* to supply with a mast or masts. [Old English *mæst* the vertical pole of a ship.]
  • **before the mast.** as a common sailor: *to sail before the mast.*

mast[2] (mast) *n.* the fruit of certain trees, such as the chestnut, esp. when used as food for animals. [Old English *mæst.*]

mas·tec·to·my (mas tek′tə mē) *n., pl.* **-mies.** the surgical removal of a breast, sometimes involving removal of muscles and other tissues surrounding the breast. [Greek *mastos* breast + *ektomē* a cutting out.]

mas·ter (mas′tər) *n.* **1.** a person who has power, control, or authority over someone or something: *a dog's master, to be the master of one's emotions.* **2.** a person who has great skill, ability, or knowledge in something; expert: *That author is a master of the short story.* **3.** a skilled craftsman or worker qualified to practice a craft or trade independently and to train apprentices. **4.** a teacher or leader, as in religion or philosophy. **5.** *also,* **Master.** a person who has received a master's degree. **6. Master.** a title of address appearing before the name of a boy not considered old enough to be addressed as *Mister.* **7.** a person who overcomes or defeats another, esp. a winner of chess or bridge tournaments: *a chess master.* **8.** a person who is appointed as a representative of the court to assist the judge by hearing evidence in a dispute, as between labor and management. **9.** something, such as a phonograph recording, from which duplicates can be made. —*adj.* **1.** being a master in one's craft or trade: *a master plumber.* **2.** main; principal: *a master bedroom.* **3.** of, relating to, or characteristic of a master; skilled. **4.** designating a device or mechanism that controls, operates, or fits any of various similar devices or mechanisms: *a master switch.* —*v.t.* **1.** to gain control over; overcome; defeat: *to master one's fears.* **2.** to acquire complete knowledge or understanding of; become expert in: *to master French, to master a trade.* [Middle English *maistre, maister,* from Old English *magister* chief, teacher, from Latin *magister* superior, chief, teacher.] —**mas′ter·less,** *adj.*

a	at	e	end	o	hot	u	up	hw	white	⟨	about
ā	ape	ē	me	ō	old	ū	use	ng	song		taken
ä	far	i	it	ô	fork	u̇	rule	th	thin	ə	pencil
âr	care	ī	ice	oi	oil	u̇	pull	th	this		lemon
		îr	pierce	ou	out	ûr	turn	zh	measure	⟨	circus

755

mas·ter-at-arms (mas'tər ət ärmz') *n., pl.* **mas·ters-at-arms.** a member of a ship's crew who is responsible for maintaining order and discipline.

mas·ter·ful (mas'tər fəl) *adj.* **1.** forceful or authoritative; domineering. **2.** having or exhibiting mastery; expert; skillful: *The violinist gave a masterful performance.* —**mas'ter·ful·ly,** *adv.*

master key, a key designed to open all the locks of a certain type or in a given location. Also, **passkey.**

mas·ter·ly (mas'tər lē) *adj.* characteristic of a master; expert. —*adv.* in a masterly manner. —**mas'ter·li·ness,** *n.*

mas·ter·mind (mas'tər mīnd') *n.* a person who has or displays great intelligence and ingenuity, esp. in devising or directing a course of action. —*v.t.* to devise or direct a course of action for (something): *to mastermind the election of a governor, to mastermind an insurrection.*

Master of Arts 1. a master's degree granted by a college or university to a person who has completed an advanced course of study in the arts or social sciences. **2.** a person who has received this degree.

master of ceremonies, a person who is in charge of a formal gathering or entertainment and usually introduces the speakers or performers.

Master of Science 1. a master's degree granted by a college or university to a person who has completed an advanced course of study in science or mathematics. **2.** a person who has received this degree.

mas·ter·piece (mas'tər pēs') *n.* **1.** something, such as a work of art, done with supreme skill or artistry. **2.** something regarded as a person's greatest achievement.

master's degree, a graduate degree that usually represents one year of study beyond the bachelor's degree. The most commonly awarded forms of this degree are Master of Arts and Master of Science.

master sergeant, a noncommissioned officer of the second highest rank in the U.S. Army and Marine Corps, and of the third highest rank in the U.S. Air Force.

mas·ter·ship (mas'tər ship') *n.* **1.** the office, status, or function of a master. **2.** the state or condition of being a master; rule; control. **3.** the skill, knowledge, or ability of a master.

mas·ter·stroke (mas'tər strōk') *n.* a masterly or ingenious act or achievement.

mas·ter·work (mas'tər wûrk') *n.* masterpiece.

mas·ter·y (mas'tə rē) *n., pl.* **-ter·ies. 1.** the state of being master; rule; control. **2.** expert skill or knowledge. **3.** superiority or victory in competition; the upper hand. **4.** the act of mastering something, such as a craft or subject.

mast·head (mast'hed') *n.* **1.** the head or top of a ship's mast. **2.** a notice printed in a newspaper or magazine giving the title, publisher's name, subscription rates, and other information.

mas·tic (mas'tik) *n.* **1.** a thick yellowish resin obtained from an evergreen tree, *Pistacia lentiscus,* used to make dental cement, incense, and varnish. **2.** the tree yielding this resin. **3.** any of various coal tar or asphalt mixtures used for setting windows, repairing roofs, or paving. [Old French *mastic* the resin, through Latin, from Greek *mastichē.*]

mas·ti·cate (mas'ti kāt') *v.t.,* **-cat·ed, -cat·ing. 1.** to chew. **2.** to grind, crush, or knead to a pulp, as rubber. [Late Latin *masticātus,* past participle of *masticāre* to chew, from Greek *masti-chān* to grind the teeth.] —**mas'ti·ca'tion,** *n.* —**mas'ti·ca'tor,** *n.*

mas·ti·ca·to·ry (mas'ti kə tôr'ē) *adj.* **1.** of, relating to, or used in chewing. **2.** adapted for chewing. —*n., pl.* **-ries.** a substance chewed to increase salivation.

mas·tiff (mas'tif) *n.* a large, powerful breed of dog having a heavy head, a predominantly light brown, short-haired coat, dark ears and muzzle, and a long, tapering tail. Height: 32 inches (81 centimeters) at the shoulder. [Modification (influenced in spelling by Old French *mestif* mongrel) of Old French *mastin,* going back to Latin *mānsuētus* tame.]

mas·ti·tis (mas tī'təs) *n.* an inflammation of the mammary glands, as of the breast or udder. [Greek *mastos* breast + -ITIS.]

mas·to·don (mas'tə don') *n.* any of various extinct, elephantlike mammals, genus *Mammut,* that originated in Africa and inhabited the Northern Hemisphere and South America during the Ice Age. [Modern Latin *mastodon,* from Greek *mastos* breast + *odōn* tooth; referring to the nipple-shaped projections on its molars.]

mas·toid (mas'toid) *n.* the lower, projecting part of the tempo-

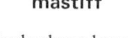
mastiff

ral bone behind and below each ear. Also, **mastoid bone.** —*adj.* **1.** of, relating to, designating, or near the mastoid. **2.** breast-shaped. [Greek *mastoeidēs* like a breast, from *mastos* breast + *eidos* form.]

mas·toid·i·tis (mas'toi dī'tis) *n.* an inflammation of the mastoid.

mas·tur·bate (mas'tər bāt') *v.i.,* **-bat·ed, -bat·ing.** to engage in masturbation.

mas·tur·ba·tion (mas'tər bā'shən) *n.* stimulation of the genital organs, usually by self-manipulation, for sexual pleasure.

mat¹ (mat) *n.* **1.** a small, flat piece of material, such as rubber or woven straw, usually used as a floor covering or placed in front of a door. **2.** a small, flat piece of material placed on a table under a vase or other object for protection or decoration. **3.** a large, thick pad or covering placed on the floor to protect wrestlers, boxers, or gymnasts. **4.** any thick, tangled mass: *a mat of hair.* —*v.,* **mat·ted, mat·ting.** —*v.t.* **1.** to cover with or as with a mat or mats. **2.** to entangle or entwine into a thick mass. —*v.i.* to become entangled into a thick mass. [Middle English *matte,* from Old English *matte,* from Late Latin *matta;* probably of Phoenician origin.]

mat² (mat) *n.* a piece of cardboard or other material serving as a mount or frame for a picture, or as a border between a picture and its frame. Also, **matting.** —*v.t.,* **mat·ted, mat·ting.** to provide (a picture) with a mat. [French *mat* dull color, from *mat* dull, faded. See MAT³.]

mat³ (mat) *adj.* matte. —*n.* matte. —*v.t.,* **mat·ted, mat·ting.** matte. [French *mat* dull, faded, from Old French *mat* conquered, from Late Latin *mattus* stupid, drunk.]

mat·a·dor (mat'ə dôr') *n.* the person who kills the bull in a bullfight. [Spanish *matador* killer, bullfighter who kills the bull, from Latin *mactātor* killer.]

match¹ (mach) *n.* **1.** a short piece of wood, cardboard, or other material coated on one end with a substance, such as a compound of sulfur and phosphorus, that is easily ignited by friction. **2.** a wick prepared to burn at a uniform rate, formerly used to fire guns and cannon. [Middle English *macche* wick, from Middle French *meiche,* from Old French *mesche,* going back to Latin *myxa,* from Greek *myxā* wick; literally, mucus.]

match² (mach) *n.* **1.a.** a person or thing that corresponds exactly to another; facsimile: *These fingerprints are a perfect match.* **b.** either of two things that correspond to each other; one of a pair: *I lost the match to this glove.* **2.** a person or thing that can compete with or oppose another as an equal: *The champion has yet to meet her match.* **3.** a person or thing that is similar to another in some respect; counterpart. **4.** two persons or things that are suitable for each other: *The blue coat and the gray suit are a good match.* **5.** a game or contest between two or more persons, animals, or teams: *a wrestling match.* **6.** a matrimonial agreement or union; marriage: *She made a bad match when she married him.* —*v.t.* **1.** to be like, suitable for, or a counterpart of: *The pattern on this material matches that of the sofa.* **2.a.** to find, select, or produce (things) that are equal to or suitable for one another: *to match socks.* **b.** to find, select, or produce something that is a counterpart of or is suitable for (another): *I'm trying to match this fabric.* **3.** to compete with or oppose as an equal; be a match for: *No one can match the mayor in oratory.* **4.** to place in competition or opposition, esp. in order to determine superiority (often with *against*): *to match wits.* **5.** to cause to correspond: *I will match my donation to yours.* **6.a.** to flip (a coin or coins) and bet on or compare the faces that are revealed. **b.** to flip coins in this way with (another person). **7.** to join in marriage; marry. —*v.i.* to be equal or correspond. [Middle English *macche,* from Old English *(ge)mæcca* mate¹, companion, spouse, from *macian* to make.]

match·book (mach'buk') *n.* a small cardboard folder containing two or more rows of safety matches and a surface for striking them.

match·box (mach'boks') *n.* a small box for holding safety matches, usually with a surface for striking them.

match·less (mach'lis) *adj.* having no equal; peerless; unrivaled. —**match'less·ly,** *adv.* —**match'less·ness,** *n.*

match·lock (mach'lok') *n.* formerly, a type of gun fired by igniting the powder with a slow-burning wick.

match·mak·er (mach'mā'kər) *n.* **1.** a person who arranges or tries to arrange marriages for others. **2.** a person who arranges sports contests, such as boxing matches. [MATCH² + MAKER.] —**match'mak'ing,** *adj., n.*

match play, a method of scoring in golf in which the total number of holes won determines the winner. ➡ distinguished from **medal play.**

match point, in certain games, the final point that is needed to win a match.

match·wood (mach'wud') *n.* **1.** wood used or suitable for making matches. **2.** splinters.

mate¹ (māt) *n.* **1.** one of a pair: *the mate to a sock.* **2.** a husband or wife. **3.** the male or female of a pair of animals that have paired or been paired for propagation. **4.** an officer on a merchant ship, ranking next below the captain. **5.** an assistant to a warrant officer in the U.S. Navy. **6.** a close associate; companion. —*v.*, **mat·ed, mat·ing.** —*v.t.* **1.** to join together or match. **2.** to cause (animals) to produce offspring; pair. **3.** to join in marriage. —*v.i.* **1.** (of animals) to pair for propagation: *Birds mate in the spring.* **2.** to become joined in marriage. [Middle Low German *mate* companion.]

mate² (māt) *Chess. v.t.*, **mat·ed, mat·ing.** checkmate. —*n.* checkmate. [From Old French chess term *eschec et mat* literally, check and conquered. See CHECKMATE.]

ma·té (mä′tā, mat′ā) *n.* **1.** a greenish tealike beverage made from the dried leaves of an evergreen shrub, *Ilex paraguariensis,* of the holly family, containing caffeine and having a slightly bitter taste. **2.** the leaves and shoots used to make this beverage. **3.** the shrub itself, found in South America. [Argentine Spanish *mate* this tealike beverage, vessel in which maté is made, from Quechua *mati* calabash vessel.]

ma·ter (mā′tər) *n.* mother. ➡ often used as an affectation or in humorous contexts. [Latin *māter.*]

ma·te·ri·al (mə tîr′ē əl) *n.* **1.** a substance or substances of which something is or may be made or composed. **2.** fabric. **3.** something that may be used, developed, or elaborated on, esp. in making something: *The author is gathering material for a new novel.* **4.** a person or thing that is especially suited for, or has great potential for succeeding in, a particular field or endeavor: *excellent executive material.* **5. materials.** things, such as tools or implements, needed to make or do something: *writing materials.* —*adj.* **1.** of, relating to, or consisting of matter; physical: *a material object.* **2.** of or relating to the body or physical well-being: *material needs.* **3.** concerned with or caring primarily for the physical rather than the intellectual or spiritual things of life; materialistic. **4.** essential; important. **5.** *Law.* likely to influence the outcome of a case or the character of a document: *a material witness.* **6.** relevant; pertinent (with *to*): *material to the present discussion.* **7.** *Philosophy.* of or relating to matter or substance, as opposed to form. [Late Latin *māteriālis* relating to matter, from Latin *māteria* wood, matter, topic.]

Synonyms *n.* **Material** and **substance** mean the matter of which something is made. **Material** is used more of matter that goes into a thing: *The material covering this sofa combines synthetic and natural fabrics.* **Substance** connotes something more basic, the specific matter that gives something its character: *an object made of some hard, dense substance.*

ma·te·ri·al·ism (mə tîr′ē ə liz′əm) *n.* **1.** the philosophical doctrine that everything that exists is either composed of matter or depends on matter for its existence. **2.** the tendency to be unduly concerned with material rather than intellectual or spiritual things.

ma·te·ri·al·ist (mə tîr′ē ə list) *n.* **1.** a believer in philosophical materialism. **2.** a person who is unduly or solely concerned with the material rather than the intellectual or spiritual things of life.

ma·te·ri·al·is·tic (mə tîr′ē ə lis′tik) *adj.* relating to or characteristic of materialism or materialists. —**ma·te′ri·al·is′ti·cal·ly,** *adv.*

ma·te·ri·al·ize (mə tîr′ē ə līz′) *v.*, **-ized, -iz·ing.** —*v.i.* **1.** to come into being; become actual fact; be realized: *dreams of success that failed to materialize.* **2.** to assume or appear in bodily or visible form: *During the séance, spirits seemed to materialize.* —*v.t.* to give material form or character to. —**ma·te′ri·al·i·za′tion,** *n.*

ma·te·ri·al·ly (mə tîr′ē ə lē) *adv.* **1.** with regard to material or physical things: *to be well-off materially.* **2.** to a great degree; considerably; substantially. **3.** *Philosophy.* in matter, content, or substance, not only in form.

ma·te·ri·a med·i·ca (mə tîr′ē ə med′i kə) **1.** drugs and similar substances used in the treatment of disease. **2.** the branch of medicine that deals with the origin, preparation, and administration of drugs and similar substances. [Modern Latin *materia medica* healing matter.]

ma·té·ri·el (mə tîr′ē el′) *also,* **ma·te·ri·el.** *n.* **1.** the equipment, apparatus, and supplies used by a military force. **2.** the equipment, apparatus, and supplies of any organized body. [French *matériel* equipment, from Late Latin *māteriālis* relating to matter. See MATERIAL.]

ma·ter·nal (mə tûr′nəl) *adj.* **1.** of, relating to, or like a mother; motherly: *maternal instincts.* **2.** inherited or derived from one's mother. **3.** related through one's mother: *a maternal aunt.* [Latin *māternus* relating to a mother (from *māter* mother) + -AL¹.] —**ma·ter′nal·ly,** *adv.*

ma·ter·ni·ty (mə tûr′ni tē) *adj.* **1.** for pregnant women: *a maternity dress.* **2.** designed for the care of newborn babies and women during and after childbirth: *a maternity ward.* —*n.* **1.** the

state of being a mother; motherhood. **2.** the qualities or characteristics of a mother; motherliness.

math (math) *n.* mathematics.

math·e·mat·i·cal (math′ə mat′i kəl) *adj.* **1.** of, relating to, like, or concerned with mathematics. **2.** rigorously exact; precise: *mathematical certainty.* Also, **math′e·mat′ic.** —**math·e·mat′i·cal·ly,** *adv.*

mathematical induction, induction *(def. 5).*

math·e·ma·ti·cian (math′ə mə tish′ən) *n.* a person who is an expert in or student of mathematics.

math·e·mat·ics (math′ə mat′iks) *n.* **1.** the science dealing with numbers, quantities, shapes, sets, and operations, and with their properties and relationships. Mathematics includes arithmetic, algebra, geometry, trigonometry, and calculus. ➡ used as singular. **2.** mathematical operations, procedures, or properties: *There is an error in your mathematics.* ➡ used as singular or plural. [Latin *mathēmatica,* from Greek *mathēmatikē (technē)* mathematical (art), from *mathēma* something learned, science.]

mat·i·nee (mat′ə nā′) *also,* **mat·i·née.** *n.* a theatrical presentation performed in the afternoon. [French *matinée,* from *matin* morning; in medieval France, morning was considered to be from sunrise until three o'clock.]

ma·tins (mat′inz) *pl. n.* **1.** the first of the canonical hours in the breviary, usually recited with Lauds. **2.** in the Church of England, the morning service prescribed by the Book of Common Prayer. **3.** *also,* **matin.** *Archaic.* any morning song. [French *matins* morning prayer, from *matin* morning, from Latin *mātūtīnum,* going back to *Mātūta* ancient Roman goddess of dawn.]

ma·tri·arch (mā′trē ärk′) *n.* **1.** a woman who is the head of a family or tribe. **2.** a woman who dominates or has great authority in any group. [Latin *mātr-,* stem of *māter* mother; on the model of PATRIARCH.]

ma·tri·ar·chal (mā′trē är′kəl) *adj.* **1.** relating to, like, or based on a matriarchy: *a matriarchal society.* **2.** of or relating to a matriarch.

ma·tri·ar·chy (mā′trē är′kē) *n., pl.* **-chies.** a form of society in which the woman is the head of a family or tribe and descent is traced through the maternal line.

ma·tri·ces (mā′trə sēz′, mat′rə-) a plural of **matrix.**

mat·ri·cid·al (mat′rə sī′dəl, mā′trə-) *adj.* of or relating to matricide or to a person who commits matricide.

mat·ri·cide¹ (mat′rə sīd′, mā′trə-) *n.* the act of killing one's mother. [Latin *mātricīdium,* from *māter* mother + -cīdium. See -CIDE¹.]

mat·ri·cide² (mat′rə sīd′, mā′trə-) *n.* a person who kills his or her mother. [Latin *mātricīda,* from *māter* mother + -cīda. See -CIDE².]

ma·tric·u·lant (mə trik′yə lənt) *n.* a person who has matriculated or is a candidate for matriculation.

ma·tric·u·late (mə trik′yə lāt′) *v.t., v.i.,* **-lat·ed, -lat·ing.** to admit or enroll in a college or university as a candidate for a degree. [Late Latin *mātriculātus* past participle of *mātriculāre* to register, enroll, going back to Latin *mātrix* womb, list, register.] —**ma·tric′u·la′tion,** *n.*

mat·ri·lin·e·al (mat′rə lin′ē əl, mā′trə-) *adj.* of, relating to, or tracing descent through the maternal line.

mat·ri·mo·ni·al (mat′rə mō′nē əl) *adj.* of or relating to marriage. —**mat′ri·mo′ni·al·ly,** *adv.*

mat·ri·mo·ny (mat′rə mō′nē) *n., pl.* **-nies.** **1.** the state or condition of being married. **2.** the rite or ceremony of marriage. [Latin *mātrimōnium* marriage, from *māter* mother.]

ma·trix (mā′triks, mat′riks) *n., pl.* **ma·tri·ces** or **ma·trix·es.** **1.** the place or thing in which something originates, develops, or is contained. A mold for casting metal is a matrix. **2.a.** the grains of smaller size in a rock in which some grains are much larger than others. **b.** the natural material in which something, such as a fossil, pebble, crystal, or mineral, is embedded. **3.a.** the intercellular substance of living tissue. **b.** the formative cells from which a structure, such as a tooth or nail, grows. **4.** formerly, the womb. **5.** *Printing.* a shallow mold, usually of paper, lead, or brass, in which typefaces are cast. **6.** *Mathematics.* a rectangular array of elements enclosed in parentheses or brackets and multiplied or added according to certain rules. [Latin *mātrix* womb, source, from *māter* mother.]

ma·tron (mā′trən) *n.* **1.** a married woman, esp. one who has children or is mature in age and manner. **2.** a woman who supervises or guards the inmates of an institution, such as a hospital or

a	at	e	end	o	hot	u	up	hw	white		about
ā	ape	ē	me	ō	old	ū	use	ng	song		taken
ä	far	i	it	ô	fork	ü	rule	th	thin	ə	pencil
âr	care	ī	ice	oi	oil	u̇	pull	th	this		lemon
		îr	pierce	ou	out	ûr	turn	zh	measure		circus

jail. **3.** a female rest room attendant, as in a restaurant. [Old French *matrone* married woman, from Latin *mātrōna*, from *māter* mother.]

ma·tron·ly (mā′trən lē) *adj.* characteristic of, suitable for, or like a matron. —**ma′tron·li·ness,** *n.*

matron of honor, a married woman who is the chief attendant of the bride at a wedding.

Matt., Matthew.

matte (mat) *also,* **mat, matt.** *adj.* having a dull, lusterless finish or surface. —*n.* a dull, lusterless finish or surface, as on glass or paper. —*v.t.,* **mat·ted, mat·ting.** to produce a dull, lusterless finish or surface on. [Form of MAT[3].]

mat·ted (mat′id) *adj.* **1.** entangled or entwined in a thick mass: *matted hair.* **2.** covered with a dense growth. **3.** covered with or made of matting. [MAT[1] + -ED[2].] —**mat′ted·ly,** *adv.* —**mat′-ted·ness,** *n.*

mat·ter (mat′ər) *n.* **1.** anything that occupies space and has weight. The three common states or phases of matter are solid, liquid, and gaseous. **2.** a particular kind or form of substance: *inorganic matter.* **3.** something that is the subject of discussion, concern, feeling, or action: *a legal matter.* **4.** a difficult, unpleasant, or unsatisfactory condition; trouble; problem: *What is the matter with my report?* **5.** importance; significance: *It's of no matter to me what you do.* **6.** a specific example or instance; case (with *of*): *a matter of opinion, a matter of preference.* **7.** written or printed material: *reading matter.* **8.** the content of something written or spoken: *The matter of the politician's speech was lost in the emotional oratory.* **9.** an indefinite amount, quantity, or extent (with *of*): *The police arrived in a matter of minutes.* **10.** anything sent by mail: *third-class matter.* **11.** a substance excreted by the body, such as feces, or discharged from a wound or abscess, such as pus. **12.** *Printing.* type or plates set up or to be set up. —*v.i.* to be of importance: *It matters to me what they say.* [Old English *mat(i)ere* substance, subject, pus, from Latin *māteria* wood, substance, subject.]

•**as a matter of course.** as something to be expected.

•**no matter.** regardless of; despite: *No matter what you say, I still disagree with you.*

mat·ter-of-course (mat′ər əv kôrs′) *n.* something to be expected as a natural or logical result.

mat·ter-of-fact (mat′ər əv fakt′) *adj.* **1.** dealing with facts; unimaginative; practical: *a matter-of-fact narrative.* **2.** having or exhibiting no emotion or feeling; disinterested. —**mat′-ter-of-fact′ly,** *adv.* —**mat′ter-of-fact′ness,** *n.*

Mat·thew (math′ū) *n.* one of the four Gospels, the first book of the New Testament, attributed to the Evangelist Matthew.

mat·ting[1] (mat′ing) *n.* **1.** a coarse, woven fabric of grass, straw, hemp, or other fiber, used esp. for making mats and as a packing material. **2.** mats collectively. [MAT[1] + -ING[1].]

mat·ting[2] (mat′ing) *n.* mat[2].

mat·ting[3] (mat′ing) *n.* **1.** matte. **2.** the act or process of producing a matte finish or surface on something. [MAT[3] + -ING[1].]

mat·tock (mat′ək) *n.* a tool consisting of a handle and a two-bladed head, used for loosening soil and cutting roots. [Middle English *mattok,* from Old English *mattuc,* going back to Latin *mateola.*]

mat·tress (mat′ris) *n.* a pad covered with strong cloth or other material and often stuffed with hair, cotton, batting, or rubber, designed to fit on the frame of a bed, esp. on top of a box spring. [Old French *materas* quilt to lie on, through Italian, from Arabic *matrah* place where something is thrown, cushion.]

mat·u·rate (mach′ə rāt′) *v.i.,* **-rat·ed, -rat·ing.** to ripen; mature. —**mat′u·ra′tion,** *n.*

ma·ture (mə chùr′, -tùr′, -tyùr′) *adj.* **1.** having reached full growth or development: *mature fruit, a physically mature person.* **2.** having the qualities or characteristics of a person who has reached full physical and mental development: *mature behavior, a mature attitude.* **3.** fully or thoroughly developed or thought out: *a mature scheme.* **4.** due for payment, as a loan or bond. **5.** having reached maximum development and form as produced by erosion: *a mature river.* —*v.,* **-tured, -tur·ing.** —*v.i.* **1.** to become fully grown or developed; reach maturity. —*v.t.* **1.** to bring to full growth or development. **2.** to develop or think out fully; complete. [Latin *mātūrus* ripe.] —**ma·ture′ly,** *adv.* —**ma·ture′ness,** *n.*

ma·tu·ri·ty (mə chùr′i tē, -tùr′-, -tyùr′-) *n., pl.* **-ties. 1.** the state or quality of being mature: *Accepting responsibility is a sign*

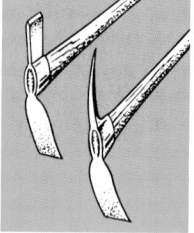

mattocks

of maturity. **2.a.** the time at which something, such as a bond, is due for payment. **b.** the state of being due for payment.

ma·tu·ti·nal (mə tü′tə nəl, -tū′-) *adj.* of, relating to, or occurring in the morning; early in the day. [Late Latin *mātūtinālis,* from Latin *mātūtīnus,* from *Mātūta.* See MATINS.]

mat·zoh (mät′sə) *also,* **mat·zo.** *n.* a thin, flat piece of unleavened bread, traditionally eaten at Passover. [Yiddish *matse,* from Hebrew *matsa.*]

maud·lin (môd′lin) *adj.* excessively and foolishly sentimental. [From *Maudlin,* an early Modern English name, from Middle English *Maudelen,* from Late Latin *Magdalēnē,* from Greek *Magdalēnē* Mary Magdalene, a New Testament figure who is often depicted as weeping over her sins.]

maul (môl) *n.* a heavy mallet or hammer used for driving wedges, stakes, or piles. —*v.t.* **1.** to injure, as by beating, knocking about, biting, or tearing. **2.** to handle roughly or clumsily; abuse: *The small child mauled the book.* [Old French *mail* hammer, from Latin *malleus.*] —**maul′er,** *n.*

maun·der (môn′dər) *v.i.* **1.** to talk in a rambling, confused manner. **2.** to move or act in an aimless, dreamy, or puzzled manner. [Of uncertain origin.] —**maund′er·er,** *n.*

Maun·dy Thursday (môn′dē) Thursday of Holy Week, commemorating the Last Supper. Also, **Holy Thursday.** [Old French *mande* command (from Latin *mandātum*) + THURSDAY; referring to the first word, *mandātum,* of a Latin anthem sung on the Thursday before Good Friday.]

mau·so·le·um (mô′sə lē′əm, -zə-) *n., pl.* **-le·ums** or **-le·a** (-lē′ə). a stately building housing a tomb or tombs. [Latin *mausōlēum* magnificent tomb, from Greek *Mausōleion* the splendid tomb of *Mausolus,* king in ancient Asia Minor.]

mauve (mōv) *n.* any of various pale, purplish blue or rose colors. —*adj.* having the color mauve. [French *mauve* mallow, the color of the flower of the mallow, from Latin *malva* mallow. Doublet of MALLOW.]

ma·ven (mā′vən) *also,* **ma·vin.** *n.* a person with special knowledge of and enthusiasm for something; connoisseur: *a baseball maven, a modern dance maven.* [Yiddish *maven,* from Hebrew *mēvin.*]

mav·er·ick (mav′ər ik) *n.* **1.** an unbranded animal, esp. a calf, traditionally belonging to the first person to find and brand it. **2.** *Informal.* a person who takes an unorthodox or unpopular stand, esp. in politics. [From Samuel A. *Maverick,* 1803-70, Texan who decided not to brand his calves because his ranch was on an island.]

ma·vis (mā′vis) *n.* song thrush. [Old French *mauvis;* of uncertain origin.]

ma·vour·neen (mə vùr′nēn) *also,* **ma·vour·nin.** *n.* my darling. [Irish *mo* my + *muirnín* darling.]

maw (mô) *n.* **1.** the jaws, mouth, throat, gullet, or stomach of an animal, esp. one that is voracious. **2.** a gaping opening that is seemingly voracious. [Old English *maga* stomach.]

mawk·ish (mô′kish) *adj.* **1.** excessively and foolishly sentimental. **2.** having a sickly, insipid flavor; nauseating. [Obsolete *mawk* maggot (from Old Norse *mathkr*) + -ISH.] —**mawk′ish·ly,** *adv.* —**mawk′ish·ness,** *n.*

max (maks) *Slang. n.* the highest degree or number; greatest amount; maximum: *Prices have reached the max.*

•**to max out.** to reach the greatest or highest degree or amount: *Before retirement, my salary maxed out at $40,000 a year.*

max., maximum.

max·i (mak′sē) *n., pl.* **max·is.** a long skirt, dress, or coat that usually reaches to the ankles.

max·il·la (mak sil′ə) *n., pl.* **max·il·lae** (mak sil′ē). **1.** the bone of the upper jaw. **2.** in arthropods, either of a pair of appendages, just behind the mandibles, often modified to perform other functions, but usually acting as accessory jaws. [Latin *maxilla* jawbone, jaw.]

max·il·lar·y (mak′sə ler′ē) *adj.* of, relating to, or situated near the bone of the upper jaw: *maxillary artery.* —*n., pl.* **-lar·ies.** maxilla *(def. 1).*

max·im (mak′sim) *n.* a concise statement expressing a general truth or doctrine; precept. *Haste makes waste* is a maxim. [French *maxime,* from Late Latin *maxima (prōpositiō)* greatest (proposition), axiom, feminine of Latin *maximus* greatest. See MAXIMUM.] —For Synonyms, see proverb.

max·i·mal (mak′sə məl) *adj.* of or being a maximum; greatest or highest possible. —**max′i·mal·ly,** *adv.*

max·i·mize (mak′sə mīz′) *v.t.,* **-mized, -miz·ing.** to make as great as possible; raise or increase to the maximum.

max·i·mum (mak′sə məm) *n., pl.* **-mums** or **-ma** (-mə). **1.** the greatest possible amount, degree, or quantity: *The trip will take a maximum of three hours.* **2.** the highest point, degree, or number reached or recorded: *The temperature reached a maximum of 90 degrees today.* —*adj.* greatest possible; highest: *The maximum*

speed on this road is 60 miles per hour. [Latin *maximum,* neuter of *maximus* greatest, superlative of *magnus* great.]

max·well (maks′wel′) *n.* the centimeter-gram-second unit of magnetic flux, equal to the flux through 1 square centimeter perpendicular to a magnetic field of 1 gauss. [From James Clerk *Maxwell,* 1831-79, Scottish physicist.]

may (mā) *auxiliary verb* (followed by an infinitive without *to* or elliptically with the infinitive understood) Present: **may** or *(archaic second person sing.)* **mayest** or **mayst.** Past: **might.** **1.** used to ask for or express permission: *You may leave the table.* **2.** used to express possibility or likelihood: *It may snow.* **3.** used to express desire, hope, or wish: *May you have many happy years together.* **4.** used to express contingency, esp. in clauses expressing condition, concession, purpose, or result: *If you really want to go to the party, I may change my mind and go with you.* **5.** used to express opportunity or chance: *I will pay the expenses so that you may go on the trip.* [Old English *mæg* I can or may.]

May (mā) *n.* the fifth month of the year, containing thirty-one days. [Old French *Mai,* from Latin *Māius (mēnsis)* (month) of Maia, Roman earth goddess.]

Ma·ya (mä′yə) *n., pl.* **Ma·ya** or **Ma·yas.** **1.** a member of an Indian people of southern Mexico and parts of Central America who had a highly developed civilization for hundreds of years before they were conquered by the Spanish in the sixteenth century. **2.** their language, a branch of the Mayan family of languages. —*adj.* of or relating to the Maya or their language, culture, or civilization: *a calendar inscribed on a Maya stele.*

Maya pottery (c.600-900 A.D.)

Ma·yan (mä′yən) *adj.* Maya. —*n.* **1.** Maya. **2.** a family of Central American Indian languages, including that of the Maya.

May·ap·ple 1. a small North American plant, *Podophyllum peltatum,* having a white cup-shaped flower that grows in the center of a forked stem. Also, **mandrake. 2.** the yellowish, egg-shaped fruit of this plant, used mainly to make preserves.

may·be (mā′bē) *adv.* possibly; perhaps.

May·day (mā′dā′) *n.* an international signal used by ships or aircraft as a call for help. [French *m'aidez* help me, going back to Latin *mē* me + *adjūtāre* to help.]

May Day, a holiday traditionally celebrated as a spring festival. Some countries commemorate the growth of the international labor movement on this day with parades and other demonstrations. It is observed on May 1.

may·est (mā′ist) *Archaic.* a second person singular present tense of **may.** ➡ used with *thou.*

may·flow·er (mā′flou′ər) *n.* **1.** any of various plants whose flowers blossom in May, such as the trailing arbutus. **2. Mayflower.** the ship on which the Pilgrims came to America in 1620.

may·fly (mā′flī′) *n., pl.* **-flies.** any of a group of short-lived insects, order Ephemeroptera, having two pairs of finely veined wings and taillike filaments attached to the end of the body. Length: to 1 inch (3 centimeters).

may·hap (mā′hap′, mā′hap′) *adv. Archaic.* perhaps. [Shortened from the phrase *it may hap.*]

may·hem (mā′hem, mā′əm) *n.* **1.a.** the crime of intentionally and violently inflicting a serious, permanent wound. **b.** the commission of such a crime. **2.** a state of confusion and disorder, often noisy and sometimes accompanied by violence and the destruction of property: *There was utter mayhem in the theater when the fire alarm sounded.* [Anglo-Norman *mahaym* injury, from Old French *mahaignier* to injure. See MAIM.]

may·n't (mā′ənt, mānt) *contr.* may not.

may·o (mā′ō) *n. Informal.* mayonnaise.

may·on·naise (mā′ə nāz′, mā′ə nāz′) *n.* a thick, creamy sauce

made of egg yolks, olive oil, vinegar or lemon juice, and seasoning. [French *mayonnaise,* from *Mahón* chief town of Minorca; possibly in honor of the capture of *Mahón* by the French in 1756.]

may·or (mā′ər, mâr) *n.* the official head of a municipal government. [Old French *maire,* from Latin *mājor* greater, comparative of *magnus* great. Doublet of MAJOR.] —**may′or·al,** *adj.*

may·or·al·ty (mā′ər əl tē, mâr′-) *n., pl.* **-ties.** the office or term of office of a mayor.

May·pole (mā′pōl′) *also,* **may·pole.** *n.* a pole decorated with flowers and ribbons, around which people dance on May Day.

mayst (māst) *Archaic.* a second person singular present tense of **may.** ➡ used with *thou.*

May·time (mā′tīm′) *n.* the month of May. Also, **May′tide′.**

Maz·da·ism (maz′də iz′əm) *also,* **Maz·de·ism.** *n.* Zoroastrianism.

maze (māz) *n.* **1.** a confusing network of paths or passageways, usually bordered by high walls or shrubs, through which it is difficult to find one's way. **2.** a bewildering network of pathways used in psychological experiments, as with rats, to study learning. **3.** any confusing network or situation. **4.** a state of bewilderment, indecision, or confusion. [From archaic *maze* to daze, confuse, form of AMAZE.]

ma·zur·ka (mə zûr′kə, -zùr′-) *also,* **ma·zour·ka.** *n.* **1.** a lively Polish dance resembling the polka. **2.** the music for such a dance. [Polish *mazurka* a Polish dance; literally, woman of *Mazovia,* a Polish province.]

maz·y (mā′zē) *adj.,* **maz·i·er, maz·i·est.** like a maze.

MB, the postal abbreviation for Manitoba.

M.B.A., Master of Business Administration.

Mc- *prefix* son of. ➡ used in certain Irish and Scottish family names.

Mc, megacycle; megacycles.

M.C. 1. Master of Ceremonies. **2.** Member of Congress.

Mc·Car·thy·ism (mə kär′thē iz′əm) *n.* the practice of making reckless, indiscriminate public accusations, as of disloyalty or subversion, against persons so as to suppress political opposition and nonconformity. [From U.S. Senator Joseph R. *McCarthy,* 1909-57, who used these tactics.]

Mc·Coy (mə koi′) *n.* **the real McCoy.** the genuine person or thing: *My diamond is glass, but that one is the real McCoy.* [Possibly the expression originated to distinguish the famous U.S. boxer Kid *McCoy,* 1873-1940, from a minor fighter having the same last name.]

Mc·In·tosh (mak′in tosh′) *n.* a juicy red apple with white flesh. [From the Canadian John *McIntosh,* 1771-1845, who first cultivated it.]

Md, the symbol for mendelevium.

Md., Maryland.

MD, the postal abbreviation for Maryland.

M.D., Doctor of Medicine.

mdse., merchandise.

me (mē) *pron.* the objective case of **I.**

> **Usage** According to the rules of traditional grammar, **I,** rather than **me,** should be used after the verb *to be,* as in *It is I.* However, **me** is commonly used and generally considered acceptable in speech or informal writing: *Who's there? It's only me.* Similarly, in such informal constructions, **him** is considered acceptable in place of **he; her** in place of **she; us** in place of **we;** and **them** in place of **they.**

Me., Maine.

ME 1. the postal abbreviation for Maine. **2.** Middle English.

M.E. 1. Master of Education. **2.** Master of Engineering. **3.** Mechanical Engineer. **4.** Methodist Episcopal. **5.** Mining Engineer.

mead¹ (mēd) *n.* an alcoholic drink made from fermented honey and water and flavored with herbs. [Middle English *mede,* from Old English *me(o)du;* of Germanic origin.]

mead² (mēd) *n. Archaic.* meadow. [Middle English *medu,* from Old English *mǣd.*]

mead·ow (med′ō) *n.* **1.** a piece of grassy land, used as a pasture or for growing hay. **2.** a tract of low, well-watered grassland, usually near a river or stream. [Old English *mǣdwe,* oblique case of *mǣd* grassy land used for growing hay.] —**mead′ow·y,** *adj.*

mead·ow·lark (med′ō lärk′) *n.* a North American songbird, genus *Sturnella,* having a pointed, cone-shaped bill, predominantly mottled brown plumage, and a yellow breast with a black crescent across it. There are two species: the **eastern meadow-**

M

a	at	e	end	o	hot	u	up	hw	white		about
ā	ape	ē	me	ō	old	ū	use	ng	song	ə	taken
ä	far	i	it	ô	fork	ü	rule	th	thin		pencil
âr	care	ī	ice	oi	oil	ù	pull	th	this		lemon
				ir	pierce	ou	out	ûr	turn	zh	measure		circus

lark, *S. magna*, and the **western meadowlark**, *S. neglecta.* Length: 8½-11 inches (22-28 centimeters).

mead·ow·sweet (mĕd′ō swĕt′) *n.* **1.** either of two North American shrubs, *Spiraea alba* and *Spiraea latifolia*, of the rose family, grown for their dense clusters of small, fragrant pink or white flowers. **2.** any of a related group of tall, hardy plants, genus *Filipendula*, found in north temperate regions, grown for their showy clusters of small white, pink, or purple flowers.

mea·ger (mē′gər) *also*, **mea·gre** *adj.* **1.** scarcely adequate in amount or quantity; insufficient: *a meager meal of toast and broth.* **2.** thin; lean: *a meager figure.* [Old French *maigre* thin, from Latin *mācer.*] —**mea′ger·ly**, *adv.* —**mea′ger·ness**, *n.*

Synonyms **Meager, scanty**, and **skimpy** mean not sufficient in some respect. **Meager** suggests a conspicuous deficiency in something that affords fullness, richness, or completeness: *a meager diet, a meager salary, a meager supply of textbooks.* **Scanty** implies being barely adequate in quantity or extent: *a scanty supply of emergency medicine.* **Skimpy** connotes insufficiency resulting from penury or exaggerated thrift: *That restaurant serves very skimpy portions. My clothes allowance was skimpy, but it was all my parents could afford.*

meal[1] (mēl) *n.* **1.** food or drink served or eaten at one time. **2.** any of the times during which such food or drink is regularly served or eaten. [Middle English *meel* appointed time, mealtime, feast, from Old English *mæl* appointed time, measure; of Germanic origin.]

meal[2] (mēl) *n.* **1.** the edible part of any grain, coarsely ground and unsifted. **2.** any similar ground substance. [Middle English *mele*, from Old English *melu*; of Germanic origin.]

meal ticket **1.** a ticket or card entitling the owner to meals at a specified restaurant or cafeteria, esp. at reduced prices. **2.** *Slang.* a person or thing depended on as a source of livelihood or support.

meal·time (mēl′tīm′) *n.* the customary time for a meal.

meal·worm (mēl′wûrm′) *n.* the wormlike larva of any of a group of beetles, genus *Tenebrio*, that feeds on grain and flour.

meal·y (mē′lē) *adj.*, **meal·i·er**, **meal·i·est**. **1.** resembling meal; dry and powdery. **2.** of or containing meal. **3.** sprinkled or covered with or as with meal. **4.** pale: *a mealy complexion.* **5.** mealy-mouthed. —**meal′i·ness**, *n.*

meal·y·bug (mē′lē bug′) *n.* any of a group of destructive, plant-sucking homopterous insects, family Pseudococcidae, having a soft, oval body covered by a powdery or mealy white wax.

meal·y-mouthed (mē′lē mouthd′, -moutht′) *also*, **meal·y-mouthed.** *adj.* not speaking in a direct, straightforward, honest, and open way; unwilling to say plainly what is meant. —**meal·y-mouth·ed·ly** (mē′lē mou″thid lē, -thid-), *adv.*

mean[1] (mēn) *v.*, **meant**, **mean·ing**. —*v.t.* **1.** to have in mind as a purpose or intention: *I did not mean to hurt you.* **2.** to intend to express or indicate: *I do not know what you mean by that remark.* **3.** to have as a particular sense; be defined as: *These words mean exactly the same thing.* **4.** to intend or design for a particular person, purpose, use, or end: *Fate meant us for each other.* **5.** to represent or serve as an indication or sign of: *Smoke usually means fire.* **6.** to bring about or have as a consequence: *Your promotion means a raise in salary.* —*v.i.* **1.** to be of or have a specified importance or value: *Your friendship means a lot to me.* **2.** to have intentions of a particular kind; be disposed: *to mean well.* [Middle English *menen*, from Old English *mǣnan* to intend; of Germanic origin.]

mean[2] (mēn) *adj.* **1.** lacking in kindness, compassion, or understanding: *My friend apologized for having been so mean to me.* **2.** full of or showing spite; malicious: *a mean look.* **3.** dangerous or vicious: *a mean dog.* **4.** miserly; stingy: *a mean person who spends little money.* **5.** of low social origin or position: *of mean birth.* **6.** of little importance or worth: *no mean achievement.* **7.** inferior in quality or grade; poor. **8.** *Informal.* hard to cope with; difficult: *a mean curve in the road.* **9.** *Slang.* expert; excellent: *to play a mean game of tennis.* [Middle English *mene* common, from Old English *mǣne*; of Germanic origin.] —**mean′ly**, *adv.*

mean[3] (mēn) *n.* **1.** something that is midway between two extremes. **2. means.** **a.** the method, agency, or way by which something is or may be accomplished: *by devious means.* **b.** money, property, or other resources; wealth: *a person of means.* **3.** *Mathematics.* **a.** a number or algebraic expression having a value intermediate between the values of a set of other numbers or algebraic expressions; arithmetic mean; average. **b.** either the second or third term of a mathematical proportion of four terms. In $a/b = c/d$, *b* and *c* are the means. ➡ distinguished from **extreme.** —*adj.* **1.** intermediate, as in size, quality, or degree. **2.** midway between two extremes: *The mean temperature this month was 60 degrees.* [Middle English *mene*, from Middle French *me(i)en*, from Latin *mediānus*, from *medius* middle.]

•**by all means.** without fail or hesitation: *Go, by all means.*

•**by means of.** with the help or use of: *We crossed the river by means of the bridge.*

•**by no means. a.** in no way; not at all. **b.** on no account: *By no means should the baby be left in the house alone.*

•**not by any means.** not at all.

me·an·der (mē an′dər) *v.i.* **1.** to follow a winding course: *The river meanders across a broad floodplain.* **2.** to wander aimlessly or idly: *I meandered slowly through the gardens.* —*n.* **1.** *also*, **meanders.** a winding, indirect journey or movement. **2. meanders.** windings or turnings, as of a stream or river. **3.** an ornamental geometric pattern of interlocking or crisscrossing lines. [Latin *maeander* a winding, winding pattern, from Greek *maiandros*, from *Maiandros* a river in Asia Minor proverbial for its unusually winding course.]

mean·ing (mē′ning) *n.* **1.** something that is meant as a goal or purpose; intention: *What is the meaning of this disgraceful behavior?* **2.** that which is intended to be expressed or understood, as by language: *What is the meaning of this poem? We looked up the word in the dictionary to find its meaning.* **3.** something that is intended to be or actually is conveyed or indicated; significance: *the meaning of a dream.* —*adj.* having meaning; expressive; significant: *a meaning smile.* —**mean′ing·ly**, *adv.*

Usage Words have no absolute or fixed **meanings**. Each word in our language originally had only one **meaning**, but as the need arose to define new concepts, objects, and actions, new words were coined or borrowed from other languages, or new **meanings** were created for existing words. A new **meaning** is easier to grasp than a coinage or borrowing, because the existing word is familiar and its original **meaning** provides a clue to the new one. The word *arm*, for example, originally meant "the upper limb of the human body." Other senses, such as "the arm of a chair" and "an arm of government," developed later. Similarly, the word *mouse* recently acquired the new **meaning** of "a device used to move the cursor on a computer screen." Some words gradually broaden in **meaning**, as in the case of *barn*, which originally meant "a storehouse for barley" and now means "a storehouse for any kind of grain or a place for livestock." Other words become more restrictive, as with *starve*, which once meant "to die" and now means "to die of hunger," or become more specialized, as with *base*, which generally refers to "the part on which something stands or rests," but to a soldier may mean "military headquarters or camp," to a chemist "a type of chemical compound," and to an athlete "a corner of a baseball diamond." For another Usage Note, see **neologism.**

mean·ing·ful (mē′ning fəl) *adj.* full of meaning; significant. —**mean′ing·ful·ly**, *adv.*

mean·ing·less (mē′ning lis) *adj.* without meaning or significance; senseless. —**mean′ing·less·ly**, *adv.* —**mean′ing·less·ness**, *n.*

mean·ness (mēn′nis) *n.* **1.** the state or quality of being mean. **2.** a mean or spiteful act.

meant (ment) past tense and past participle of **mean**[1].

mean·time (mēn′tīm′) *n.* the time between. —*adv.* **1.** in or during the time between. **2.** at the same time: *You were watching TV; meantime, the roast overcooked.*

mean·while (mēn′hwīl′, -wīl′) *adv.* **1.** in or during the time between: *The train doesn't leave for an hour; meanwhile, I'm going to get something to eat.* **2.** at the same time: *My cousin went shopping; meanwhile, I cleaned the house.* —*n.* the time between.

meas., measure.

mea·sles (mē′zəlz) *n.* **1.** a highly infectious virus disease characterized by cold symptoms, fever, and a rash. Also, **rubeola.** **2.** rubella. ➡ used as singular in both defs. [Probably from Middle Dutch *māsel* spot on the skin associated with measles; influenced by Middle English *mesel* leper, from Old French *mesel*, going back to Latin *miser* wretched.]

mea·sly (mēz′lē) *adj.*, **-sli·er**, **-sli·est**. **1.** of, like, or having measles; spotted. **2.** *Slang.* contemptibly scanty; worthless: *That store pays a measly $3.50 an hour for full-time work.*

meas·ur·a·ble (mezh′ər ə bəl) *adj.* that can be measured: *a measurable distance.* —**meas′ur·a·bil′i·ty**, **meas′ur·a·ble·ness**, *n.* —**meas′ur·a·bly**, *adv.*

meas·ure (mezh′ər) *v.*, **-ured**, **-ur·ing**. —*v.t.* **1.** to ascertain the dimensions, weight, extent, duration, quantity, or capacity of, esp. by comparison with a fixed standard: *to measure a person's height, to measure the speed of sound, to measure someone for a dress.* **2.** to mark off, set apart, or allot by or as by measuring: *to measure out two cups of flour, to measure off 6 feet of fabric for curtains.* **3.** to bring into opposition, comparison, or competition (with *with* or *against*): *to measure one's strength against another's.* **4.** to serve as a standard or unit of measurement for: *Degrees measure temperature.* **5.** to estimate by comparison; judge; appraise: *to measure the difficulty of a task.* **6.** to think over care-

fully and choose: *to measure one's words.* **7.** *Archaic.* to travel over or through; traverse. —*v.i.* **1.** to take measurements: *A carpenter must measure accurately.* **2.** to have a specific measurement: *The room measures 10 feet by 12 feet.* **3.** to be measurable, as to a particular degree: *Fabric measures best if you use a tape measure.* —*n.* **1.** the dimensions, weight, extent, duration, quantity, or capacity of anything as determined by measuring. **2.** the act or process of measuring; measurement. **3.** a unit or standard of measurement, such as an inch, quart, or minute. **4.** any standard or basis of comparison, estimation, or judgment: *the measure of one's strength.* **5.** a system of measuring, such as linear measure or square measure. For Weights and Measures table, see **weight.** **6.** an instrument, container, or other device used for measuring: *a gallon measure.* **7.** an amount or degree that should not or cannot be exceeded; limit: *Your generosity knows no measure.* **8.** a definite amount or degree: *The children were given a great measure of independence.* **9.** a quantity, degree, or proportion: *to take a measure of pride in one's work.* **10.** *also,* **measures.** a course of action used as a means to an end: *to take drastic measures.* **11.** a legislative proposal or enactment. **12.** *Poetry.* **a.** rhythm; meter. **b.** metrical unit; foot. **13.** the music contained between two bar lines; bar. **14.** **measures.** *Geology.* a series of strata that share some common characteristic; facies: *coal measures.* **15.** a dance or dance movement, esp. one that is slow and stately. [Old French *mesure* dimensions, moderation, degree, from Latin *mēnsūra* quantity, degree, proportion, extent.] —**meas′ur·er,** *n.*

　• **for good measure.** in addition to what is needed or called for.
　• **to measure up.** to have the needed qualifications: *Do you measure up for the job?*
　• **to measure up to.** to fulfill or meet: *The movie didn't measure up to what we expected.*

meas·ured (mezh′ərd) *adj.* **1.** characterized by uniformity of rhythm: *measured lines of verse.* **2.** in a slow, restrained, and dignified manner: *The graduates walked down the aisle with measured steps.* **3.** carefully weighed and chosen: *measured remarks.* **4.** regulated or determined by some standard.

meas·ure·less (mezh′ər lis) *adj.* that cannot be measured; immeasurable.

meas·ure·ment (mezh′ər mənt) *n.* **1.** the act or process of measuring. **2.** something that is found or determined by measuring, such as dimensions or quantity. **3.** measure *(def. 5).*

measuring worm, inchworm.

meat (mēt) *n.* **1.** parts of an animal used as food. **2.** the edible part of anything: *the meat of a coconut.* **3.** the main idea or most important part; substance: *the meat of a story.* **4.** anything eaten for nourishment: *meat and drink.* [Old English *mete* food.]

meat·ball (mēt′bôl′) *n.* ground meat, usually beef, mixed with bread crumbs and seasoning and rolled into a small ball for cooking.

meat packing 1. the business of slaughtering animals for food. **2.** the processing, packing, and distributing of meat and meat by-products.

me·a·tus (mē ā′təs) *n., pl.* **-tus·es** or **-tus.** a passage or opening in the body, as in the nose or ear. [Latin *meātus* path.]

meat·y (mē′tē) *adj.,* **meat·i·er, meat·i·est. 1.** of, relating to, or like meat. **2.** full of meat; fleshy; plump. **3.** full of substance or significance: *a meaty dialogue on a controversial topic.*

Mec·ca (mek′ə) *also,* **mecca.** *n.* **1.** any place that is visited by many people or has a special attraction. **2.** a goal of one's hopes. [From *Mecca,* Saudi Arabian city to which Muslims try to make a pilgrimage at least once in their life.]

me·chan·ic (mə kan′ik) *n.* **1.** a person skilled in designing, repairing, or operating machinery: *an auto mechanic.* **2.** formerly, any person skilled in working with tools. [Latin *mēchanicus* inventive, relating to machines, from Greek *mēchanikos,* from *mēchanē* device, contrivance.]

me·chan·i·cal (mə kan′i kəl) *adj.* **1.** of, relating to, or involving machinery or tools. **2.** produced or operated by a machine. **3.** like or suitable for a machine; lacking spontaneity or originality; automatic: *The actor's movements were very mechanical.* **4.** of, relating to, or in accordance with the science of mechanics. —*n.* a layout from which plates for printing are prepared, showing text and art copy as it will appear when printed. —**me·chan′i·cal·ly,** *adv.*

mechanical advantage, the ratio of the force produced by a machine to the force applied in using the machine; number of times that a machine multiplies effort: *a lever positioned so as to provide a mechanical advantage of 10.*

mechanical drawing 1. a drawing, usually of machinery or mechanical parts, done with the aid of rulers, scales, compasses, and similar instruments. **2.** the art or process of making such a drawing.

me·chan·ics (mə kan′iks) *n.* **1.** the branch of physics that deals with the conditions under which bodies and fluids move or remain

at rest. **2.** the body of knowledge dealing with the design, construction, operation, and care of machinery. **3.** the mechanical or technical aspects of anything: *the mechanics of painting.* ➡ used as singular in defs. 1 and 2, as plural in def. 3.

mech·a·nism (mek′ə niz′əm) *n.* **1.** the working parts, or arrangement of parts, of a machine: *The jeweler fixed the broken mechanism of my watch.* **2.** a system of parts resembling those of a machine in structure or function: *the mechanism of government, the mechanism of the nervous system.* **3.** the agency, means, or process by which an effect is produced or a purpose accomplished. **4.** *Philosophy.* the theory that the universe is like a great machine and that everything in it moves and changes in accordance with natural laws.

mech·a·nist (mek′ə nist) *n.* a person who believes in philosophical mechanism.

mech·a·nis·tic (mek′ə nis′tik) *adj.* **1.** of or relating to mechanics. **2.** of or relating to philosophical mechanism. —**mech′a·nis′ti·cal·ly,** *adv.*

mech·a·nize (mek′ə nīz′) *v.t.,* **-nized, -niz·ing. 1.** to equip with or convert to machinery as a means of production: *Much industry has been mechanized.* **2.** to equip (a military unit or army) with tanks, armored personnel carriers, and other vehicles. **3.** to give a mechanical character to; make automatic. —**mech′a·ni·za′tion,** *n.* —**mech′a·niz′er,** *n.*

mech·a·no·re·cep·tor (mek′ə nō ri sep′tər) *n.* any sensory nerve ending or specialized sensory structure that responds to mechanical stimuli, as those sensitive to touch, sound, or pressure.

Mech·lin (mek′lin) *n.* lace with the pattern, often a floral design, clearly outlined by a fine, but distinct, thread, used for such items as scarfs and veilings. Also, **malines.** [From *Mechlin* Mechelen, Belgium.]

med. **1.** medical. **2.** medicine. **3.** medieval. **4.** medium.

med·al (med′əl) *n.* a flat piece of metal bearing a design or inscription, often given as an award in recognition of merit,

Mechlin

achievement, or distinguished service. [French *médaille,* from Italian *medaglia,* going back to Latin *metallum* metal. See METAL.]

med·al·ist (med′ə list) *also, British,* **med·al·list.** *n.* **1.** a person who engraves, designs, or makes medals. **2.** a person who has been awarded a medal.

me·dal·lion (mə dal′yən) *n.* **1.** a large medal. **2.** anything resembling a medallion or medal, such as an ornamental object or design. [French *médaillon* large medal, locket, from Italian *medaglione,* from *medaglia* medal. See MEDAL.]

Medal of Honor, the highest U.S. military decoration, awarded by the president in the name of Congress to military personnel cited for conspicuous gallantry above and beyond the call of duty. Also, **Congressional Medal of Honor.**

medal play, a method of scoring in golf in which the lowest total number of strokes determines the winner. ➡ distinguished from **match play.**

med·dle (med′əl) *v.i.,* **-dled, -dling. 1.** to concern oneself with or intrude in the affairs of others without having been asked. **2.** to handle something without permission; tamper: *Someone has meddled with the lock on this door.* [Old French *medler, mesler* to mix, interfere with, going back to Latin *miscēre* to mix.] —**med′dler,** *n.* —For Synonyms, see **interfere.**

med·dle·some (med′əl səm) *adj.* tending to meddle. —**med′dle·some·ness,** *n.*

Mede (mēd) *n.* a member of the people who inhabited ancient Media.

Me·de·a (mi dē′ə) *n.* in Greek legend, an enchantress who helped Jason get the Golden Fleece in return for marrying her.

Med·fly (med′flī′) *n., pl.* **-flies.** Mediterranean fruit fly. [Short for *Med(iterranean fruit) fly.*]

me·di·a (mē′dē ə) a plural of **medium.**

me·di·ae·val (mē′dē ē′vəl, mid′ē-, med′ē-, mid ē′vəl) medieval.

me·di·al (mē′dē əl) *adj.* **1.** of, relating to, or located in the middle. **2.** of, relating to, or being a mathematical mean; average. [Late Latin *mediālis* middle, from Latin *medius.*] —**me′di·al·ly,** *adv.*

a	at	e	end	o	hot	u	up	hw	white		about
ā	ape	ē	me	ō	old	ū	use	ng	song	ə	taken
ä	far	i	it	ô	fork	ü	rule	th	thin		pencil
âr	care	ī	ice	oi	oil	u̇	pull	th	this		lemon
		îr	pierce	ou	out	ûr	turn	zh	measure		circus

me·di·an (mē′dē ən) *n.* **1.** the middle number in a set of numbers or, where there is no middle number, the average of the two middle numbers. In the set *11, 25, 41, 65*, the median is *33*. **2.a.** a line segment from a vertex of a triangle to the midpoint of the opposite side. **b.** a line segment joining the midpoints of the nonparallel sides of a trapezoid. —*adj.* of, relating to, or located in the middle; medial. [Latin *mediānus* middle, from *medius*.]

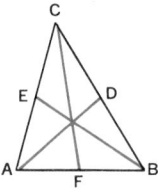

Median (mē′dē ən) *adj.* of or relating to ancient Media, the Medes, or their language or culture. —*n.* **1.** a native, inhabitant, or citizen of ancient Media. **2.** the Iranian language of ancient Media.

median strip, a raised strip, usually landscaped or paved, that separates opposing lanes of traffic on some roads or highways.

medians
AD, BE, CF, and *GH* are medians

me·di·ate (*v.,* mē′dē āt′; *adj.,* mē′dē it) *v.,* **-at·ed, -at·ing.** —*v.t.* **1.** to bring about by coming between disputing or opposing parties: *The government official mediated a settlement between the union and the owners of the factory.* **2.** to settle (differences or disputes) by coming between and working with disputing or opposing parties. **3.** to serve as the medium for bringing about (a result) or for conveying (an object or information). —*v.i.* **1.** to act as a mediator in order to bring about an agreement or settlement. **2.** to occupy an intermediate place or position. —*adj.* acting through or involving another person or agency; indirect. [Latin *mediātus,* past participle of *mediāre* to halve, be in the middle, from *medius* middle.] —**me′di·a′tive,** *adj.*

me·di·a·tion (mē′dē ā′shən) *n.* the act of mediating; intervention.

me·di·a·tor (mē′dē ā′tər) *n.* a person or group that comes between disputing or opposing parties in order to bring about a settlement.

me·di·a·to·ry (mē′dē ə tôr′ē) *adj.* **1.** of, relating to, or of the nature of mediation. **2.** serving to mediate. Also, **me′di·a·to′ri·al.**

med·ic¹ (med′ik) *n. Informal.* **1.** in the armed services, an enlisted person trained to give medical assistance; corpsman. **2.** a physician. **3.** a medical student or intern. [Latin *medicus* physician.]

med·ic² (med′ik) *also,* **medick.** *n.* any of a group of plants, genus *Medicago,* of the pea family, most of which bear purple or yellow cloverlike flower heads and are grown for fodder, such as alfalfa. [Latin *Mēdica* kind of clover, lucerne, from Greek *Mēdikē (poā)* Median (grass), lucerne.]

med·i·ca·ble (med′i kə bəl) *adj.* tending to respond to medical treatment, esp. with drugs; curable; treatable. [Latin *medicabilis.*]

Med·i·caid (med′i kād′) *n.* a U.S. government program of health insurance for persons of all ages within certain income limits, financed by local, state, and federal funds. [MEDIC(AL) + AID.]

med·i·cal (med′i kəl) *adj.* of or relating to doctors, medicine, or the study or practice of medicine. [Late Latin *medicālis* relating to a physician, from Latin *medicus* physician.] —**med′i·cal·ly,** *adv.*

me·dic·a·ment (mə dik′ə mənt, med′i kə-) *n.* a healing application, as used in therapy; medicine. [Latin *medicāmentum.*]

Med·i·care (med′i kâr′) *n.* a U.S. federal program of health insurance for persons aged sixty-five and over and certain disabled people under sixty-five. [MEDI(CAL) + CARE.]

med·i·cate (med′i kāt′) *v.t.,* **-cat·ed, -cat·ing.** **1.** to treat with medicine. **2.** to fill with medicine; put medicine on or in: *to medicate an ointment.* [Latin *medicātus,* past participle of *medicārī* to heal.]

med·i·ca·tion (med′i kā′shən) *n.* **1.** a substance used to treat disease or relieve pain; medicine. **2.** the act or process of medicating or the state of being medicated.

me·dic·i·nal (mə dis′ə nəl) *adj.* **1.** having the properties of medicine; able to heal, cure, or relieve: *medicinal baths.* **2.** characteristic of or resembling medicine: *The hospital room had a medicinal smell.* —**me·dic′i·nal·ly,** *adv.*

med·i·cine (med′ə sin) *n.* **1.** a drug or other substance used to treat disease or relieve pain. **2.** the science that deals with the cause, prevention, and treatment of disease and the preservation of health. **3.** the medical profession. **4.** among North American Indians, any object or ceremony thought to have magical or curative powers. [Latin *medicīna* healing art, remedy.]

 • **to take one's medicine.** to accept or endure punishment for something one has done.

medicine ball, a large, heavy stuffed ball thrown from one person to another for exercise.

medicine man, among North American Indians, a person believed to possess magical powers through communication with supernatural beings; shaman.

med·ick (med′ik) medic².

med·i·co (med′i kō′) *n., pl.* **-cos.** *Informal.* a medical doctor or medical student. [Spanish *médico* and Italian *medico* physician, both from Latin *medicus.*]

me·di·e·val (mē′dē ē′vəl, mid′ē-, med′ē-, mid ē′vəl) *also,* **mediaeval.** *adj.* of, relating to, belonging to, or characteristic of the Middle Ages: *medieval literature.* [Latin *medius* middle + *aevum* age + -AL¹; referring to its occurrence in the middle of, or between, early and recent times.] —**me′di·e′val·ly,** *adv.*

medieval illustration

me·di·e·val·ism (mē′dē ē′və liz′əm, mid′ē-, med′ē-, mid ē′və-) *n.* **1.** the spirit, beliefs, customs, and practices of the Middle Ages. **2.** devotion to or adoption of the beliefs, customs, and practices of the Middle Ages. **3.** anything, such as a belief or custom, surviving from the Middle Ages.

me·di·e·val·ist (mē′dē ē′və list, mid′ē-, med′ē-, mid ē′və-) *n.* **1.** a scholar of or specialist in medieval history, literature, or art. **2.** a person devoted to the spirit, beliefs, and customs of the Middle Ages.

Medieval Latin, Latin, esp. as a literary language, from the eighth to the fifteenth centuries A.D. Also, **Middle Latin.**

me·di·o·cre (mē′dē ō′kər) *adj.* not exceptional; ordinary; commonplace. [French *médiocre* middling, from Latin *mediocris* literally, halfway up a mountain, from *medius* middle + *ocris* rugged mountain.]

me·di·oc·ri·ty (mē′dē ok′ri tē) *n., pl.* **-ties.** **1.** the state or quality of being mediocre. **2.** mediocre ability, accomplishment, or performance. **3.** a person of mediocre talents or ability.

med·i·tate (med′i tāt′) *v.,* **-tat·ed, -tat·ing.** —*v.i.* **1.** to think seriously and carefully; reflect: *to meditate on a problem.* **2.** to reflect deeply on matters of spiritual importance, often as a religious practice. —*v.t.* to have in the mind; consider or intend: *to meditate one's next move.* [Latin *meditātus,* past participle of *meditārī* to consider, reflect.] —**med′i·ta′tor,** *n.*

Synonyms *v.i.* Meditate, ponder, muse, and reflect may all mean to consider something deliberately. **Meditate** connotes concentrating on something so as to comprehend it in all its aspects: *I meditated on my plan, trying to anticipate all possible consequences.* **Ponder** suggests deep, sober thought: *I pondered for days before deciding to take the job.* **Muse** connotes less intense or less directed thought: *On graduation day, I mused about what the future would bring me.* **Reflect** may connote serious thought, but suggests a limited focus: *to reflect on a friend's remark.*

med·i·ta·tion (med′i tā′shən) *n.* **1.** serious and careful thought. **2.** deep reflection on matters of spiritual importance, often as a religious practice. **3.** a discourse based on spiritual meditation.

med·i·ta·tive (med′i tā′tiv) *adj.* given to, expressing, or characterized by meditation: *a meditative mood.* —**med′i·ta′tive·ly,** *adv.* —**med′i·ta′tive·ness,** *n.*

Med·i·ter·ra·ne·an (med′i tə rā′nē ən) *adj.* of, relating to, or characteristic of the Mediterranean Sea or the nearby countries

and their people. [Latin *mediterrāneus,* from *medius* middle + *terra* land.]

Mediterranean fruit fly, a small fruit fly, *Ceratitis capitata,* the larvae of which infest and destroy citrus fruits, peaches, plums, and the like. It was introduced into the United States from the Mediterranean region.

me·di·um (mē′dē əm) *n., pl.* **-di·a** (-dē ə) (except def. 5) or **-di·ums.** **1.** something that is midway between two extremes; mean. **2.** an enveloping substance in which something exists or functions; environment: *Most bacteria grow best in a slightly acid medium.* **3.** a means or form of communication or expression: *Television is a medium that reaches a large audience.* **4.** a substance, means, or agency through, in, or by which something may act, be carried, or accomplished: *The atmosphere is a medium for sound waves.* **5.** a person through whom the spirits of the dead allegedly communicate with the world of the living. ➡ For def. 5, only the plural form **mediums** is used. **6.** a material or technique used as a means of artistic expression: *The artist's medium is watercolor.* **7.** in painting, a liquid with which pigments are mixed and made sufficiently fluid for application. Also, **vehicle.** —*adj.* intermediate, as in quantity, amount, or degree: *a girl of medium height.* [Latin *medium* the midst, the middle.]

medium frequency, a radio frequency between 300 and 3,000 kilohertz.

med·lar (med′lər) *n.* **1.** a thorny tree, *Mespilus germanica,* of the rose family, growing in Europe and Asia. **2.** the apple-shaped fruit of the medlar, having an acid taste and used to make preserves or eaten raw after it is somewhat decayed. [Old French *medler, meslier,* from *mesle* the fruit of the medlar, through Latin, from Greek *mespilon.*]

med·ley (med′lē) *n., pl.* **-leys.** **1.** a confused and disordered mass of things; jumble; hodgepodge. **2.** a musical composition made up of various tunes or parts from other compositions. —*adj. Archaic.* made up of varied parts. [Old French *medlee, meslee* a mixing, mixture, fight, from *medler, mesler* to mix, going back to Latin *miscēre.*]

me·dul·la (mə dul′ə) *n., pl.* **-dul·lae** (-dul′ē). **1.** medulla oblongata. **2.** *Anatomy, Botany.* the inner substance of an organ or part. [Latin *medulla* marrow, pith.] —**med·ul·lar·y** (med′ə ler′ē, mej′-), *adj.*

medulla ob·lon·ga·ta (ob′lông gä′tə) the lowest and hindmost part of the brain, connected with the top of the spinal cord. It controls breathing and other involuntary functions. [Modern Latin *medulla oblongata* literally, oblong marrow.]

med·ul·lar·y ray (med′ə ler′ē, mej′ə-, mə dul′ə rē) a vertical band of woody tissue extending radially from the pith to the cortex between the vascular bundles in the stems of plants.

me·du·sa (mə dü′sə, -zə, -dū′-) *n., pl.* **-sas** or **-sae** (-sē, -zē). jellyfish. [From *Medusa;* referring to the resemblance between some types of jellyfish and a head with snakelike hair.] —**me·du′san,** *adj., n.*

Me·du·sa (mə dü′sə, -zə, -dū′-) *n.* in Greek mythology, one of the three Gorgons, slain by Perseus.

meed (mēd) *n. Archaic.* well-deserved recompense. [Old English *mēd.*]

meek (mēk) *adj.* **1.** patient and mild in manner or disposition; gentle. **2.** unduly submissive or lacking in spirit: *The clerk was too meek to insist on an overdue raise in salary.* [Middle English *meke,* from *meoc,* from Old Norse *mjūkr* soft, mild, meek.] —**meek′ly,** *adv.* —**meek′ness,** *n.*

meer·schaum (mîr′shəm, -shôm′) *n.* **1.** a soft, porous, light, white clay mineral that is heat-resistant, used to make tobacco pipes. **2.** a tobacco pipe that has a bowl made of meerschaum. [German *Meerschaum* this mineral; originally, a variety of coral; literally, sea foam; supposedly because this coral was once believed to be sea foam hardened into stone.]

meet[1] (mēt) *v.,* **met, meet·ing.** —*v.t.* **1.** to come face to face with; come upon or across: *I met them just as I was leaving.* **2.** to make the acquaintance of; be introduced to: *Haven't I met you before?* **3.** to keep an appointment with: *I'll meet you by the information booth.* **4.** to go to or be present at the arrival of: *Will you be able to meet my plane on Monday?* **5.** to satisfy, fulfill, or comply with: *to meet the qualifications for a job.* **6.** to come into contact or conjunction with: *The Hudson River meets the Atlantic Ocean at New York City.* **7.** to come into the presence or company of, as for a meeting: *The judge met the lawyers in her chambers.* **8.** to come into the perception, observation, or notice of: *There is more to this job than meets the eye.* **9.** to pay: *I couldn't meet my bills this month.* **10.** to oppose or fight with, as in battle: *to meet an adversary.* **11.** to deal or cope with effectively; confront: *We met their criticism with indifference.* **12.** to experience: *to meet a cold reception.* —*v.i.* **1.** to come face to face: *We met in the elevator.* **2.** to be introduced; become acquainted: *We met him at a party.* **3.** to come into contact, conjunction, or union; join: *Oh,*

East is East, and West is West, and never the twain shall meet (Rudyard Kipling, 1889). **4.** to assemble, as for business or worship: *The committee met for two hours.* **5.** to be opposed, as in battle: *to meet on the battlefield.* —*n.* an assembly or gathering, esp. for an athletic contest: *a swimming meet.* [Old English *mētan* to find.]

•**to meet with. a.** to receive: *My suggestion met with opposition.* **b.** to experience; undergo: *to meet with adversity.*

meet[2] (mēt) *adj. Archaic.* suitable; proper. [Middle English *mete,* from Old English *(ge)mǣte* fitting, proper; of Germanic origin.] —**meet′ly,** *adv.*

meet·ing (mē′ting) *n.* **1.a.** a gathering or assembly of people: *The chairperson of the committee adjourned the meeting for the day.* **b.** the persons so gathered: *The committee meeting set the date for the party.* **2.** the act of coming together: *a meeting of minds.* **3.** a place or point where things come together; junction: *the meeting of two rivers.* **4.** an assembly of people, esp. Quakers, for worship.

Synonyms Meeting, assembly, and gathering denote a group of people coming together for some purpose. **Meeting** is used of a company of persons who come together for either a social or business purpose: *a club meeting, a meeting of sales representatives.* **Assembly** is more formal, and suggests an important procedure: *the annual assembly of a political organization.* **Gathering** suggests the arrival of participants from many directions, and may be used generally: *a family gathering, a gathering of townspeople to erect a barn.*

meet·ing·house (mē′ting hous′) *also,* **meeting house.** *n., pl.* **-hous·es** (-hou′ziz). a building or house used for worship, esp. by Quakers.

mega- *combining form* **1.** large; great: *megalith.* **2.** multiplied by a million; a million of: *megacycle.* [Greek *megas* great, large.]

meg·a·buck (meg′ə buk′) *n. Slang.* **1.** a million dollars. **2.** megabucks. very large amounts of money.

meg·a·byte (meg′ə bīt′) *n.* 1,024 kilobytes, or 1,048,576 bytes.

meg·a·cy·cle (meg′ə sī′kəl) *n.* **1.** 1 million cycles. **2.** megahertz. [MEGA- + CYCLE.]

meg·a·hertz (meg′ə hûrts′) *n., pl.* **-hertz.** a unit equal to 1 million hertz, used in measuring the frequency of electromagnetic waves. Also, **megacycle.**

meg·a·lith (meg′ə lith′) *n.* a huge stone, esp. one that is used in prehistoric monuments or other ancient constructions. [MEGA- + Greek *lithos* stone.] —**meg′a·lith′ic,** *adj.*

megaliths on Easter Island

megalo- *combining form* large, abnormally large, excessive, or exaggerated: *megalopolis, megalomania.* [Greek *megal-,* stem of *megas* great, large.]

meg·a·lo·ma·ni·a (meg′ə lō mā′nē ə) *n.* **1.** a mental disorder characterized by delusions of greatness, power, or wealth. **2.** the tendency to exaggerate. [MEGALO- + MANIA.]

meg·a·lo·ma·ni·ac (meg′ə lō mā′nē ak′) *n.* a person suffering

a	at	e	end	o	hot	u	up	hw	white		about
ā	ape	ē	me	ō	old	ū	use	ng	song	ə	taken
ä	far	i	it	ô	fork	ü	rule	th	thin		pencil
âr	care	ī	ice	oi	oil	u̇	pull	th	this		lemon
				îr	pierce	ou	out	ûr	turn	zh	measure		circus

M

from megalomania. —**meg·a·lo·ma·ni·a·cal** (meg′ə lō mə nī′ə-kəl), *adj.*

meg·a·lop·o·lis (meg′ə lop′ə lis) *n.* a densely populated urban complex made up of a number of adjoining metropolitan areas. [MEGALO- + Greek *polis* city.]

meg·a·phone (meg′ə fōn′) *n.* a funnel-shaped device used to amplify or direct the sound of the voice. [MEGA- + Greek *phōnē* sound, voice.]

meg·a·spore (meg′ə spôr′) *n.* the larger of the two types of plant spores that develop into a female gametophyte. ➡ distinguished from **microspore**. [MEGA- + SPORE.]

meg·a·ton (meg′ə tun′) *n.* a unit used to measure the explosive force of nuclear bombs, equivalent to the force produced by the detonation of 1 million tons (907,000 metric tons) of TNT. [MEGA- + TON.] —**meg′a·ton′nage,** *n.*

meg·a·watt (meg′ə wot′) *n.* a unit of electrical or mechanical power equal to 1 million watts (1,341 horsepower).

me·gil·lah (mə gil′ə) *n. Slang.* a long and involved story or explanation. [Yiddish *megile* literally, scroll, roll, from Hebrew *megila* scroll, roll, from *galal* to roll, roll up, from *gal* wave.]

me·grim (mē′grim) *n.* **1.** migraine. **2.** megrims. low spirits. **3.** whim; fancy. [Middle English *migreime,* from Old French *migraine.* See MIGRAINE.]

mei·o·sis (mī ō′sis) *n.* in organisms that reproduce sexually, the process of cell division, occurring only during the formation of sex cells, by which the number of chromosomes is halved. ➡ distinguished from **mitosis**. [Modern Latin *meiosis,* from Greek *meiō-sis* diminution, lessening, from *meioun* to make smaller, from *meiōn* less.] —**mei·ot′ic,** *adj.*

Meis·ter·sing·er (mīs′tər sing′ər, -zing′-) *n., pl.* **-sing·er.** a member of one of the German guilds of the fifteenth and sixteenth centuries that specialized in the composition of poems and songs. [German *Meistersinger* literally, master singer.]

mel·a·mine (mel′ə mēn′) *n.* any of several amino resins used to make strong, chemical-resistant, thermosetting plastics for tableware and plywood adhesives.

mel·an·cho·li·a (mel′ən kō′lē ə) *n.* a mental disorder characterized by severe depression and self-criticism. [Late Latin *melancholia* the humor thought to cause gloominess, a kind of madness, going back to Greek *melās* black + *cholē* bile. See HUMOR.]

mel·an·chol·ic (mel′ən kol′ik) *adj.* **1.** low in spirits; melancholy; sad; dejected. **2.** of, relating to, or suffering from melancholia.

mel·an·chol·y (mel′ən kol′ē) *adj.* **1.** low in spirits; sad; depressed. **2.** suggestive of or causing sadness; depressing; dismal: *melancholy music.* **3.** soberly thoughtful; meditative; pensive. —*n., pl.* **-chol·ies. 1.** a gloomy or depressed state of mind; sadness. **2.** sober thoughtfulness; pensiveness. [Old French *melancolie* gloominess, humor thought to cause gloominess, from Late Latin *melancholia.* See MELANCHOLIA.]

Mel·a·ne·sian (mel′ə nē′zhən, -shən) *n.* **1.** a member of a Negroid people living in Melanesia. **2.** a subfamily of the Austronesian family of languages, consisting of a number of languages that are spoken predominantly in Melanesia. —*adj.* of, relating to, or characteristic of Melanesia or its peoples, languages, or cultures.

mé·lange (mā länzh′) *n.* a mixture; medley: *a mélange of antique and modern furniture.* [French *mélange,* from *mêler* to mix, from Old French *mesler.* See MEDLEY.]

mel·a·nin (mel′ə nin) *n.* a dark brown pigment present in skin, hair, and other animal tissues, which helps to determine the color of the skin, hair, and eyes. [Greek *melan-,* stem of *melās* black + -IN¹.]

mel·a·nism (mel′ə niz′əm) *n.* excessive or abnormal pigmentation of the skin, hair, or other animal tissues. Also, **mel·a·no·sis** (mel′ə nō′sis). [Greek *melan-,* stem of *melās* black + -ISM.] —**mel′a·nis′tic,** *adj.*

mel·a·no·ma (mel′ə nō′mə) *n.* a malignant tumor of the melanin-producing cells of the skin. [Modern Latin *melanoma,* from Greek *melan-,* stem of *melās* black + -ōma, mass, lump.]

Mel·ba toast (mel′bə) very thin, dry slices of toast. [From Nellie *Melba,* 1861-1931, Australian operatic soprano.]

meld¹ (meld) *v.t., v.i.* in card games, to place (one or more cards) on the table in a set or on another set. —*n.* **1.** the act of melding. **2.** the cards melded. [German *melden* tell, inform.]

meld² (meld) *v.t., v.i.* to merge or cause to be merged; blend.

me·lee (mā′lā′, mā lā′) *also,* **mê·lée.** *n.* a confused fight involving a number of people. [French *mélée,* from *mêler* to mix, from Old French *mesler,* going back to Latin *miscēre.*]

mel·io·rate (mēl′yə rāt′, mē′lē ə-) *v.t., v.i.,* **-rat·ed, -rat·ing.** to make or become better; ameliorate. [Late Latin *meliorātus,* past participle of *meliōrāre* to improve, from Latin *melior* better.] —**mel′io·ra′tive,** *adj.* —**mel′io·ra′tor,** *n.*

mel·lif·lu·ent (me lif′lü ənt) *adj.* mellifluous. —**mel·lif′lu·ence,** *n.* —**mel·lif′lu·ent·ly,** *adv.*

mel·lif·lu·ous (me lif′lü əs) *adj.* sweetly or smoothly flowing: *a mellifluous voice.* [Late Latin *mellifluus* flowing with honey, from Latin *mel* honey + *fluere* to flow.] —**mel·lif′lu·ous·ly,** *adv.*

mel·low (mel′ō) *adj.* **1.** (of fruit) soft, sweet, and juicy from ripeness. **2.** (of cheese and wine) rich, delicate, and fully aged: *a mellow cheese.* **3.** softened and made wise, gentle, and understanding by age and experience. **4.** full, rich, and soft: *a mellow color, a mellow tone.* **5.** (of soil) rich and loamy. —*v.t., v.i.* to make or become mellow. [Probably from Old English *melu* flour, meal².] —**mel′low·ly,** *adv.* —**mel′low·ness,** *n.*

me·lo·de·on (mə lō′dē ən) *n.* a small reed organ. [From MELODY.]

me·lod·ic (mə lod′ik) *adj.* **1.** of, relating to, or containing melody. **2.** melodious. —**me·lod′i·cal·ly,** *adv.*

me·lo·di·ous (mə lō′dē əs) *adj.* **1.** pleasant to hear; musical: *a melodious voice.* **2.** of, relating to, containing, or producing melody. —**me·lo′di·ous·ly,** *adv.* —**me·lo′di·ous·ness,** *n.*

mel·o·dra·ma (mel′ə drä′mə -dram′ə) *n.* **1.a.** a dramatic performance or play characterized by exaggerated appeal to the emotions, sensational or overly sentimental incidents, and usually having a happy ending. **b.** such plays collectively. **2.** sensational or overly emotional writing, speech, or behavior. [French *mélodrame* such a play, from Greek *melos* song + *drāma* play; referring to the inclusion of songs and music in the original melodramas.] —**mel·o·dram·a·tist** (mel′ə dram′ə tist, -drä′mə-), *n.*

mel·o·dra·mat·ic (mel′ə drə mat′ik) *adj.* **1.** of, relating to, or characteristic of melodrama: *melodramatic acting.* **2.** sensational or overly emotional: *a melodramatic plea.* —**mel′o·dra·mat′i·cal·ly,** *adv.*

mel·o·dra·mat·ics (mel′ə drə mat′iks) *pl. n.* melodramatic behavior.

mel·o·dy (mel′ə dē) *n., pl.* **-dies. 1.** a pleasing arrangement or succession of sounds. **2.** *Music.* **a.** a succession of single tones constituting a complete phrase or idea; tune. **b.** the principal part in a harmonized composition. [Late Latin *melōdia* pleasant song, from Greek *melōidiā* a singing, going back to *melos* song + *ōidē* song.]

mel·on (mel′ən) *n.* a large, edible fruit of any of several leafy vines, having a sweet, soft, juicy pulp, as the watermelon, cantaloupe, or casaba. [Old French *melon,* through Latin, from Greek *mēlopepōn.*]

Mel·pom·e·ne (mel pom′ə nē) *n.* in Greek mythology, the Muse of tragedy.

melt (melt) *v.,* **melt·ed, melt·ed** or *(archaic)* **mol·ten, melt·ing.** —*v.i.* **1.** to be changed from a solid to a liquid state, esp. by heating. **2.** to dissolve, as in water. **3.** to disappear gradually; disperse (often with *away*): *The crowd melted away once the excitement was over.* **4.** to pass or change by gradual and imperceptible degrees; blend (with *into*): *The blue of the sky melted into the green landscape.* **5.** to become gentle, tender, or more understanding: *My heart melted when the child began to cry.* —*v.t.* **1.** to change (something) from a solid to a liquid state, esp. by heating. **2.** to dissolve (something), as in water. **3.** to make gentle, tender, or more understanding. **4.** to cause (something) to disappear gradually. **5.** to cause (something) to pass or change by gradual and imperceptible degrees. —*n.* **1.** something melted, as a metal. **2.** a quantity melted at one time. **3.** a sandwich or other dish covered with a layer of melted cheese: *a tuna melt.* [Old English *meltan* to liquefy or become liquefied by heat, dissolve, be overwhelmed.] —**melt′a·ble,** *adj.* —**melt′er,** *n.*

melt·down (melt′doun′) *n.* an accident in a nuclear reactor, as one in which the cooling system fails, causing a portion of the fuel or core to melt and radiation to escape. [MELT + DOWN¹.]

melting point, the temperature at which a given solid changes into a liquid. It is identical to its freezing point. The melting point of ice is 32 degrees Fahrenheit (0 degrees Celsius), which is also the freezing point of water.

melting pot, a country, city, or region in which people of various races and nationalities become part of an existing culture.

mel·ton (mel′tən) *n.* a heavyweight woolen fabric having a close weave and napped on both sides, used esp. for overcoats and pea jackets. [From *Melton* Mowbray, English town famous for hunting; referring to Melton hunting jackets and their woolen cloth.]

melt·wa·ter (melt′wô′tər, -wot′ər) *n.* water coming from melting snow or from glacial ice. [MELT + WATER.]

mem·ber (mem′bər) *n.* **1.** a person, animal, or thing belonging to a group or organization: *The club has 200 members. The wolf is a member of the dog family.* **2.** *also,* **Member.** a person who is part of a legislative body: *a member of Congress.* **3.** *Mathematics.* **a.** either of the sides of an algebraic equation. **b.** one of the collection of objects comprising a set; element. **4.** a part of a human or animal body, esp. a limb. **5.** a constituent part of a

whole: *a steel structural member of a bridge.* [Old French *membre* limb, from Latin *membrum* limb, part.]

mem·ber·ship (mem′bər ship′) *n.* **1.** the state of being a member of a group or organization. **2.** the members of a group or organization collectively: *The union membership voted to strike.* **3.** the number of members in a group or organization: *The club's membership increased this year.*

mem·brane (mem′brān) *n.* **1.** a thin layer of tissue that lines a cavity or passage in the body or covers a body surface. **2.** a thin structure that covers a cell or part of a cell. [Latin *membrāna.*]

mem·bra·nous (mem′brə nəs) *adj.* **1.** of, relating to, or resembling a membrane. **2.** characterized by the formation of a membrane.

me·men·to (mə men′tō) *n., pl.* **-tos** or **-toes. 1.** anything serving as a reminder of someone or something; keepsake; souvenir: *The pennant is a memento of my high school days.* **2.** anything serving as a reminder or warning. [Latin *mementō* remember, imperative of *meminisse* to remember.] —For Synonyms, see **keepsake.**

memento mo·ri (môr′ī) anything serving as a reminder of death, such as a skull. [Latin *mementō mori* remember that you must die.]

Mem·non (mem′non) *n.* **1.** in Greek legend, an Ethiopian king killed by Achilles in the Trojan War. **2.** a colossal statue at Thebes, Egypt, said to give forth a musical sound when touched by the rays of the sun at dawn.

mem·o (mem′ō) *n., pl.* **mem·os.** memorandum.

mem·oir (mem′wär, -wôr) *n.* **1.** *usually,* **memoirs. a.** a record of facts and events concerning a particular subject or period, usually written from the writer's personal knowledge, experiences, and observations: *a Confederate general's memoirs of the American Civil War.* **b.** a written account of the incidents and experiences of one's life; autobiography. **2.** a written account of a person's life; biography. **3. memoirs.** a report of the proceedings of a learned society. **4.** a report or dissertation on a scientific or scholarly subject; monograph. [French *mémoire* remembrance, record, from Latin *memoria* remembrance, historical account. Doublet of MEMORY.]

mem·o·ra·bil·i·a (mem′ər ə bil′ē ə, -bil′yə) *pl. n.* things worthy of remembrance or record. [Latin *memorābilia,* neuter plural of *memorābilis* worthy of remembrance. See MEMORABLE.]

mem·o·ra·ble (mem′ər ə bəl) *adj.* not to be forgotten; worthy of remembrance; notable: *a memorable event in history.* [Latin *memorābilis,* going back to *memor* mindful.] —**mem′o·ra·bly,** *adv.*

mem·o·ran·dum (mem′ə ran′dəm) *n., pl.* **-dums** or **-da** (-də). **1.** a brief note written as a reminder. **2.** an informal letter, record, or communication, such as that sent between departments in a business office. **3.** *Law.* a short document stating the terms of a contract or transaction. **4.** in business, a statement of goods sent to the buyer by the seller. **5.** in diplomacy, a brief statement, summary, or outline, usually of a subject under discussion between governments. [Latin *memorandum* something to be remembered, neuter of *memorandus* to be remembered, gerundive of *memorāre* to remember.]

me·mo·ri·al (mə môr′ē əl) *n.* **1.** something serving as a remembrance of some person or event, such as a monument, plaque, or holiday: *The town built a memorial to honor the famous general.* **2.** a written request or statement of facts sent to a government, legislative body, or other group in authority. —*adj.* serving as a memorial; commemorative: *a memorial plaque.* [Latin *memoriālis* relating to memory, from *memoria* ability to remember, remembrance, historical account.]

Memorial Day, a legal holiday in memory of members of the military killed in all American wars. It was originally observed on May 30, and is now usually observed on the last Monday in May. Some southern states observe it on April 26, May 10, or June 3. Also, **Decoration Day.**

me·mo·ri·al·ize (mə môr′ē ə līz′) *v.t.,* **-ized, -iz·ing. 1.** to preserve or honor the memory of. **2.** to submit a memorial to; petition.

mem·o·rize (mem′ə rīz′) *v.t.,* **-rized, -riz·ing.** to commit to memory; learn by heart. [MEMORY + -IZE.] —**mem′o·ri·za′·tion,** *n.* —**mem′o·riz′er,** *n.*

mem·o·ry (mem′ə rē) *n., pl.* **-ries. 1.** the mental power or capacity to recall or reconstruct past experiences. **2.** all that one can or does recall: *to recite a poem from memory.* **3.** a person or thing remembered: *The accident is an unpleasant memory.* **4.** something that is remembered of a person or thing: *to honor the memory of those who died in war.* **5.** a period of time during or within which a person or thing can be or is remembered: *an ancient time beyond the memory of the living.* **6.** the act of remembering or the state of being remembered. **7.a.** the capacity of a computer to store information for later recall. **b.** the components

of a computer in which this information is stored. **8.** a remembrance or commemoration: *a prayer in memory of a grandparent.* [Latin *memoria* ability to remember, remembrance, time of remembrance, historical account. Doublet of MEMOIR.]

> **Synonyms** **Memory, recollection,** and **remembrance** denote the power or faculty of bringing things past to mind. **Memory** is the general term: *to have a good memory, to have memory play tricks on one.* **Recollection** often implies a deliberate calling up of events from the past: *Many years later the two friends compared recollections of their school days.* **Remembrance,** though similar to *recollection,* is less common in this use: *I have only a faint remembrance of my early childhood.*

mem·sa·hib (mem′sä′ib, -ēb, mem sä′-) *n.* in colonial India, a European woman. ➡ formerly used as a term of address. [Hindi *memsāhib,* from *mem* lady (from English MA'AM) + *sāhib* master (from Arabic *sahib* master, friend).]

men (men) the plural of **man.**

men·ace (men′is) *n.* **1.** a person or thing that is a threat; danger: *The underwater reefs are a menace to ships entering the harbor.* **2.** a very annoying or troublesome person. —*v.,* **-aced, -ac·ing.** —*v.t.* to threaten; endanger: *The storm menaced the small ship.* —*v.i.* to be or pose a threat. [Old French *menace* threat, from Latin *minācia.*] —**men′ac·ing·ly,** *adv.*

me·nad (mē′nad) maenad.

mé·nage (mā näzh′) *also,* **me·nage.** *n.* **1.** a domestic establishment; household. **2.** the management of a household; housekeeping. [French *ménage,* going back to Latin *mānsiō* a staying, dwelling.]

me·nag·er·ie (mə naj′ə rē, -nazh′-) *n.* **1.** a collection of wild or unusual animals kept in cages or other enclosures, usually for exhibition. **2.** the enclosure where such animals are kept. [French *ménagerie* originally, place for keeping animals of a household, from *ménage* household, housekeeping. See MÉNAGE.]

men·ar·che (mə när′kē) *n.* the beginning of menstruation; first menstrual period. [Modern Latin *menarche,* from Greek *mēn* month + *archē* beginning. See MENSES.]

mend (mend) *v.t.* **1.** to restore to a sound condition or working order: *to mend a broken vase, to mend a torn curtain.* **2.** to reform, correct, or improve (something): *We were warned to mend our mischievous ways.* —*v.i.* **1.** to knit, as a broken bone; heal. **2.** to regain one's health; recover. **3.** to improve: *Things will mend in time.* —*n.* a mended place: *a mend in the sole of a shoe.* [Short for AMEND.]

·**on the mend.** getting better, esp. in health; improving.

> **Synonyms** *v.t.* **Mend, repair**[1], and **fix** mean to restore to whole or unbroken condition. **Mend** suggests removing defects and restoring to usefulness without the replacement of materials: *to mend a torn shirt.* **Repair** may suggest the replacement or rehabilitation of parts and possibly the use of greater skill: *to repair a broken vase, to repair the workings of a clock.* **Fix** is informal and general, and may also suggest complexity: *to fix a car's transmission, to fix the air conditioning.*

men·da·cious (men dā′shəs) *adj.* **1.** given to lying; untruthful: *a mendacious person.* **2.** false; untrue: *mendacious reports.* [Latin *mendāc-,* stem of *mendāx* lying + -OUS.] —**men·da′cious·ly,** *adv.* —**men·da′cious·ness,** *n.*

men·dac·i·ty (men das′i tē) *n., pl.* **-ties. 1.** the quality of being mendacious; untruthfulness. **2.** a falsehood; lie.

men·de·le·vi·um (men′də lē′vē əm) *n.* a radioactive metallic element that does not occur in nature, produced by bombarding an isotope of einsteinium with helium ions. Symbol: **Md** For tables, see **element.** [From D. I. *Mendeleev,* 1834-1907, Russian chemist.]

Men·de·li·an (men dē′lē ən) *adj.* **1.** of or relating to the Austrian botanist Gregor Mendel. **2.** of, relating to, or in accordance with Mendel's laws.

Men·del·ism (men′də liz′əm) *n.* the theory of heredity according to Gregor Mendel's genetic principles, as established in Mendel's laws.

Men·del's laws (men′dəlz) the principles that govern the transmission of characteristics from parents to offspring, forming the basis for modern genetic theory, discovered and formulated by the Austrian botanist Gregor Mendel.

men·di·cant (men′di kənt) *adj.* **1.** given to or characterized by begging; living on alms. **2.** of, relating to, or characteristic of a religious order, as the Franciscans, that formerly lived on alms. —*n.* **1.** a person who lives on alms; beggar. **2.** a mendicant friar.

M

a	at	e	end	o	hot	u	up	hw	white		about
ā	ape	ē	me	ō	old	ū	use	ng	song		taken
ä	far	i	it	ô	fork	u̇	rule	th	thin	ə	pencil
âr	care	ī	ice	oi	oil	u̇	pull	th	this		lemon
				îr	pierce	ou	out	ûr	turn	zh	measure		circus

[Latin *mendīcāns,* present participle of *mendīcāre* to beg.] —**men′di·can·cy, men·dic·i·ty** (men dis′i tē), *n.*

Men·e·la·us (men′ə lā′əs) *n.* in Greek legend, the king of Sparta whose wife, Helen, was carried off to Troy by Paris.

men·folk (men′fōk′) *also,* **men·folks.** *pl. n. Informal.* males collectively, esp. the male members of a group.

men·ha·den (men hā′dən) *n., pl.* **-den.** a saltwater fish, *Brevoortia tyrannus,* of the herring family, found in the western Atlantic from Nova Scotia to Brazil, used as a source of animal feed, fertilizer, and oil. [Modification of Narragansett *munnawhatteaũg,* from *munnawhat* fertilizer; referring to its use as a fertilizer by the Indians.]

men·hir (men′hir) *n.* a prehistoric monument consisting of a single, tall, rough-hewn stone standing upright, either alone or in a group. [French *menhir,* going back to Breton *men* stone + *hir* long.]

me·ni·al (mē′nē əl, mēn′yəl) *adj.* **1.** degrading; servile: *menial tasks.* **2.** of, relating to, or suitable for a servant. —*n.* a servant who performs very lowly or humble tasks. [Middle English *meineal* of a servant, from *meine(e)* household, from Old French *mesnie, meinie,* going back to Latin *mānsiō* dwelling.] —**me′ni·al·ly,** *adv.*

me·nin·ges (mi nin′jēz) *pl. n., sing.* **meninx.** the three membranes that enclose and protect the brain and spinal cord. [Modern Latin *meninges,* plural of *meninx,* from Greek *mēninx* membrane.] —**me·nin′ge·al,** *adj.*

men·in·gi·tis (men′in jī′tis) *n.* a serious illness characterized by inflammation of the meninges, esp. as a result of bacterial or viral infection. [Modern Latin *meningitis,* from Greek *mēninx* membrane + -ITIS.] —**men·in·git·ic** (men′in jit′ik), *adj.*

me·ninx (mē′ningks) the singular of **meninges.**

me·nis·cus (mi nis′kəs) *n., pl.* **-nis·cus·es** or **-nis·ci** (-nis′ī). **1.** a crescent or crescent-shaped body. **2.** *Physics.* the curved upper surface of a liquid in a container. Certain liquids, as water, have a concave meniscus; others, as mercury, have a convex meniscus. **3.** a lens that is convex on one side and concave on the other. [Modern Latin *meniscus,* from Greek *mēniskos* crescent, diminutive of *mēnē* moon.]

Men·non·ite (men′ə nīt′) *n.* a member of a Protestant sect founded in Holland in the sixteenth century, that rejects infant baptism, the taking of oaths, the holding of public office, and military service. [German *Mennonit,* from *Menno* Simons, 1496?-1559, religious reformer from Friesland who founded this sect.]

men-of-war (men′əv wôr′) the plural of **man-of-war.**

Me·nom·i·nee (mə nom′ə nē′) *n., pl.* **-nee** or **-nees.** a member of a North American Indian tribe living in Wisconsin and speaking an Algonquian language.

men·o·pause (men′ə pôz′) *n.* the final cessation of menstruation; change of life. [Greek *mēn* month + *pausis* a stopping. See MENSES.] —**men′o·pau′sal,** *adj.*

me·no·rah (mə nôr′ə) *n.* **1.** a candelabrum, traditionally with seven branches, used in Jewish religious services. **2.** a candelabrum with nine branches, used in the celebration of Hanukkah. [Hebrew *menōrāh* candlestick.]

mensch (mensh, mench) *n., pl.* **mensch·en** (men′shən, -chən). *Slang.* a respected or honorable person. [Yiddish *mensch,* from German *Mensch* man, human being.]

men·ser·vants (men′sûr′vənts) the plural of **manservant.**

men·ses (men′sēz) *n.* menstruation. ➡ used as singular or plural. [Latin *mēnsēs,* plural of *mēnsis* month; because it follows a monthly cycle.]

Men·she·vik (men′shə vik′) *n., pl.* **-viks** or **-vi·ki** (-vē′kē). a member of the more moderate wing of the Russian Social Democratic Party that was opposed to the Bolsheviks. [Russian *menshevik* minority, from *menshe* less; because this wing was originally in the minority.]

men·stru·al (men′strü əl) *adj.* **1.** of or relating to menstruation. **2.** *Archaic.* monthly.

menstrual cycle, in humans and certain other primates, the approximately monthly cycle of hormone-regulated changes in the female reproductive system, extending from the beginning of one menstrual period to the next.

men·stru·ate (men′strü āt′) *v.i.,* **-at·ed, -at·ing.** to undergo menstruation. [Late Latin *mēnstruātus,* past participle of *mēnstruāre* to menstruate, from Latin *mēnstruus* monthly, from *mēnsis* month. See MENSES.]

men·stru·a·tion (men′strü ā′shən) *n.* **1.** the periodic discharge of blood and bloody fluid from the uterus through the genital tract, usually occurring every twenty-eight days in a woman between puberty and menopause. **2.** an instance of this. Also, **menses.**

men·stru·um (men′strü əm) *n., pl.* **-stru·ums** or **-stru·a** (-strü ə). solvent *(def. 1).*

men·su·ra·bil·i·ty (men′shər ə bil′i tē) *n.* the state or quality of being mensurable.

men·su·ra·ble (men′shər ə bəl, -sər ə-) *adj.* that can be measured; measurable.

men·su·ra·tion (men′shə rā′shən, -sə-) *n.* **1.** the act, art, or process of measuring. **2.** the branch of mathematics dealing with the determination of lengths, areas, and volumes. [Late Latin *mēnsūrātio* act of measuring, going back to Latin *mēnsūra.* See MEASURE.] —**men·su·ra·tive** (men′shə rā′tiv, -sə-, -shər ə-, sər ə-), *adj.*

-ment *suffix* (used to form nouns) **1.** the act or process of: *accomplishment, abridgment.* **2.** the state or condition of being: *involvement, amazement.* **3.** the product or result of: *pavement, improvement.* **4.** a means or instrument of: *inducement.* [Old French *-ment,* from Latin *-mentum.*]

men·tal (men′təl) *adj.* **1.** of or relating to the mind: *one's mental state, mental awareness.* **2.** carried on in or performed by the mind: *mental arithmetic.* **3.** mentally ill: *a mental patient.* **4.** for the care of the mentally ill: *a mental hospital.* [Late Latin *mentālis* relating to the mind, from Latin *mēns* mind.]

mental age, the level of mental development as measured by performance on an intelligence test. A child who does as well on an intelligence test as an average ten-year-old child is said to have a mental age of ten.

mental deficiency, mental retardation.

men·tal·i·ty (men tal′i tē) *n., pl.* **-ties. 1.** mental capacity or power. **2.** a manner or way of thinking; outlook: *a snobbish mentality.*

men·tal·ly (men′tə lē) *adv.* **1.** with regard to the mind: *mentally ill.* **2.** in or with the mind: *to add a column of figures mentally without pencil and paper.*

mental retardation, a condition arising from faulty development of intelligence, characterized by difficulty in learning and in adapting to the demands of society.

men·thol (men′thôl) *n.* a white, crystalline, organic alcohol derived from peppermint oil by freezing. Formula: $C_{10}H_{20}O$ [Latin *ment(h)a* mint [1] + -OL. See MINT [1].]

men·tho·lat·ed (men′thə lā′tid) *adj.* containing or treated with menthol.

men·tion (men′shən) *v.t.* to speak about or refer to incidentally or briefly: *I mentioned them in my last letter.* —*n.* an incidental or brief remark or reference: *There was no mention of the robbery in today's paper.* [Latin *mentiō* a calling to mind.]

 •**not to mention.** without needing to mention or consider: *That student is good-looking and smart, not to mention popular in school.*

Men·tor (men′tər) *n.* **1.** in Greek mythology, a loyal friend of Odysseus, left in charge of Odysseus' household and son. **2. mentor.** any wise and trusted counselor. —*v.t., v.i.* to act as a mentor (to); counsel. —**men′tor·ship′,** *n.*

men·u (men′ū, mā′nū) *n.* **1.** a list of the food served or available, as in a restaurant. **2.** the food served or available. **3.** a list of options, such as commands or functions, that a program offers to a computer user. [French *menu* minute detail, bill of fare, small, from Latin *minūtus* small.]

me·ow (mē ou′) *also,* **mi·aow, mi·aou.** *n.* the cry of a cat. —*v.i.* to make such a sound. [Imitative.]

me·per·i·dine (mə per′i dēn′, -din) *n.* a bitter-tasting, crystalline, synthetic narcotic, used as a sedative and painkiller. Formula: $C_{15}H_{21}NO_2$

Meph·is·to·phe·le·an (mef′ə stə fē′lē ən) *also,* **Meph·is·to·phe·li·an.** *adj.* of, relating to, or like Mephistopheles; fiendish and crafty.

Meph·i·stoph·e·les (mef′ə stof′ə lēz′) *n.* **1.** in German legend, the devil to whom Faust sold his soul. **2.** any crafty, evil person.

me·phit·ic (mə fit′ik) *adj.* having an offensive odor. [Late Latin *mephīticus* pestilential, from Latin *mephītis* stench.]

me·pro·ba·mate (mə prō′bə māt′) *n.* a tranquilizer having muscle relaxant and sedative properties. Formula: $C_9H_{18}N_2O_4$

mer·can·tile (mûr′kən tēl′, -til′) *adj.* **1.** of, relating to, or characteristic of merchants or commerce; commercial. **2.** of or relating to mercantilism. [French *mercantile* commercial, from Italian *mercantile,* going back to Latin *mercārī* to trade.]

mer·can·til·ism (mûr′kən tē liz′əm, -tī-) *n.* **1.** an economic system developed in France and England in the sixteenth and seventeenth centuries that stressed strict government regulation of the national economy and believed that an excess of exports over imports was favorable because it brought in gold and silver from abroad. Also, **mercantile system. 2.** the spirit or practice of a mercantile life; devotion to trade; commercialism. —**mer′can·til·ist,** *n., adj.*

Mer·ca·tor projection (mər kā′tər) a conformal map projection in which the distances between parallels of latitude gradually

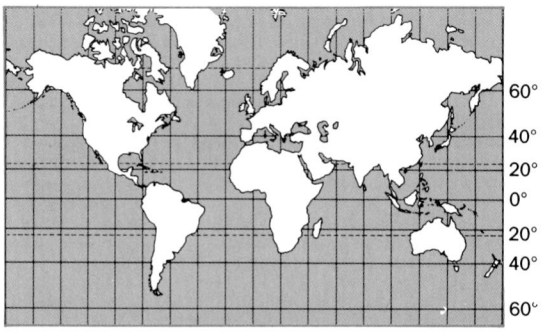

Mercator projection

increase north and south of the equator. Though distorting relative sizes of areas in the higher latitudes, it shows compass directions as straight lines, which makes it useful for navigation and for plotting the path of satellites in oblique earth orbit. [From Gerhardus *Mercator,* 1512-94, Flemish geographer, map maker, and mathematician.]

mer·ce·nary (mûr′sə ner′ē) *adj.* **1.** working or acting for money or material gain only. **2.** (of a soldier) serving in a foreign army for pay. —*n., pl.* **-nar·ies.** a mercenary soldier. [Latin *mercēnārius* hired for pay, from *mercēs* wages, reward.]

mer·cer (mûr′sər) *n. British.* a dealer in textiles. [Old French *mercier* trader, going back to Latin *merx* merchandise.]

mer·cer·ize (mûr′sə rīz′) *v.t.,* -ized, -iz·ing. to treat (cotton thread or fabric) by immersing in a caustic soda solution so as to increase the luster, strength, and absorbency of the fibers and make them more receptive to dyes. [From John *Mercer,* 1791-1866, English calico printer who developed the process + -IZE.]

mer·chan·dise (*n.,* mûr′chən dīz′, -dīs′; *v.,* mûr′chən dīz′) *also,* **merchandize.** *n.* articles bought and sold; commodities; wares. —*v.,* -dised, -dis·ing. —*v.t.* **1.** to buy and sell; trade. **2.** to promote the sale of, as through advertising. —*v.i.* to carry on commerce; trade. [Old French *marcheandise* goods, trading, from *marcheant* trader, going back to Latin *mercārī* to trade.] —**mer′·chan·dis′er,** *n.*

mer·chan·dize (mûr′chən dīz′) *v.t., v.i.,* -dized, -diz·ing. merchandise.

mer·chant (mûr′chənt) *n.* **1.** a person whose business is buying and selling merchandise for profit. **2.** a person who owns or runs a retail store; storekeeper. —*adj.* **1.** of or relating to merchants or commerce. **2.** of or relating to the merchant marine. [Old French *marcheant* trader, shopkeeper, going back to Latin *mercārī* to trade.]

mer·chant·a·ble (mûr′chən tə bəl) *adj.* marketable; salable.

mer·chant·man (mûr′chənt mən) *n., pl.* -men (-mən). a ship used in commerce.

merchant marine 1. all the commercial or trading ships of a nation collectively. **2.** the officers and crew of such ships.

Mer·ci·an (mûr′shē ən, -shən) *n.* **1.** a member of the people who inhabited Mercia. **2.** the Old English dialect spoken in Mercia. —*adj.* of, relating to, or characteristic of Mercia or its people, dialect, or culture.

mer·ci·ful (mûr′si fəl) *adj.* feeling, exhibiting, or characterized by mercy; compassionate. —**mer′ci·ful·ly,** *adv.* —**mer′ci·ful·ness,** *n.*

mer·ci·less (mûr′si lis) *adj.* without mercy; pitiless; unrelenting. —**mer′ci·less·ly,** *adv.* —**mer′ci·less·ness,** *n.*

mer·cu·ri·al (mər kyûr′ē əl) *adj.* **1.** likely or tending to change; erratic; changeable: *a mercurial personality.* **2.** of, relating to, containing, or caused by the action of mercury: *mercurial compounds, mercurial poisoning.* **3.** lively or quick. —*n.* a medicinal preparation containing mercury. —**mer·cu′ri·al·ly,** *adv.*

mer·cu·ric (mər kyûr′ik) *adj.* (of compounds) containing mercury, esp. bivalent mercury.

mercuric chloride, a white, poisonous, water-soluble compound used as a mordant, antiseptic, and preservative. Formula: $HgCl_2$

Mer·cu·ro·chrome (mər kyûr′ə krōm′) *n. Trademark.* a red antiseptic liquid solution containing mercury.

mer·cu·rous (mər kyûr′əs, mûr′kyər-) *adj.* (of compounds) containing mercury, esp. monovalent mercury.

mercurous chloride, calomel.

mer·cu·ry (mûr′kyə rē) *n., pl.* -ries. **1.** a heavy, lustrous, silvery, poisonous metallic element, the only metal that is liquid at room temperature. It is used in electrical switches, thermometers, and barometers. Symbol: **Hg** Also, **quicksilver.** For tables, see **element. 2.** the column of mercury in a thermometer or barometer, used as an indication of temperature or pressure: *The mercury rose today.* [Middle English *mercurie,* from Medieval Latin *mercurius,* from Latin *Mercurius* the god Mercury; so called because of its fluidity. See MERCURY.]

Mer·cu·ry (mûr′kyə rē) *n.* **1.** in Roman mythology, the messenger of the gods and patron of commerce. His Greek counterpart is Hermes. **2.** the second smallest planet of the solar system (after Pluto), the closest to the sun, and the fastest moving, orbiting the sun in just eighty-eight days. [Middle English *Mercurie,* from Latin *Mercurius;* of Etruscan origin.]

mer·cy (mûr′sē) *n., pl.* -cies. **1.** kindness, forbearance, or compassion toward another or others where severity is expected or merited; leniency: *The criminal begged the judge for mercy.* **2.** the disposition or power to be kind, forbearing, or forgiving: *The convicted thieves threw themselves on the mercy of the court.* **3.** something to be thankful for; blessing: *Your help was a real mercy.* [Old French *merci* thanks, pity, from Latin *mercēs* wages, reward.]

• **at the mercy of.** wholly in the power of: *We were at the mercy of the enemy.*

> **Synonyms** **Mercy, clemency,** and **leniency** denote the quality of being kind and compassionate toward others, esp. those over whom one has power, as to punish. **Mercy** is the most general term, implying compassion that tempers the exercise of justice: *to have mercy toward defeated enemies, to treat all with equal mercy.* **Clemency** suggests refusing to punish, or being slow to punish: *The judge was known for her clemency toward first offenders.* **Leniency** suggests mildness in punishing: *He was indulgent toward the children, treating their antics with leniency.*

mercy killing, euthanasia.

mercy seat 1. in the Old Testament, the solid gold covering on the Ark of the Covenant, regarded by the Hebrews as the resting place of God. **2.** the throne of God.

mere[1] (mîr) *adj., superlative* **mer·est.** being nothing more or other than what is specified; only: *a mere trifle, a mere child.* [Latin *merus* pure, not mixed.]

mere[2] (mîr) *n. Archaic.* lake; pond. [Old English *mere* sea, lake.]

-mere *combining form* a part or segment: *blastomere.* [Greek *meros* part.]

mere·ly (mîr′lē) *adv.* and nothing more; only: *Your explanations are merely poor excuses.*

mer·e·tri·cious (mer′i trish′əs) *adj.* attractive or plausible in a vulgar or deceitful way. [Latin *meretrīcius* relating to a harlot, from *meretrīx* harlot.] —**mer′e·tri′cious·ly,** *adv.* —**mer′e·tri′cious·ness,** *n.*

mer·gan·ser (mər gan′sər) *n.* any of several fish-eating diving ducks, native to the colder regions of the Northern Hemisphere, having a long, slender bill with saw-toothed edges and usually a crested head. [Modern Latin *merganser,* from Latin *mergus* diving bird + *anser* goose.]

merganser

merge (mûrj) *v.,* merged, merg·ing. —*v.i.* **1.** to be united so as to become one: *The two lanes merge going into the tunnel.* **2.** (of corporations) to be joined in a merger. —*v.t.* to unite so as to become one and lose individual identity: *The library merged the two rare book collections.* [Latin *mergere* to dip, plunge.]

a	at	e	end	o	hot	u	up	hw	white		about
ā	ape	ē	me	ō	old	ū	use	ng	song		taken
ä	far	i	it	ô	fork	ü	rule	th	thin	ə	pencil
âr	care	ī	ice	oi	oil	u̇	pull	th	this		lemon
		îr	pierce	ou	out	ûr	turn	zh	measure		circus

merg·er (mûr′jər) *n.* **1.** a union of two or more corporations in which one corporation continues to retain its identity while absorbing all the rights, privileges, franchises, and properties of the other corporation or corporations. **2.** the act of merging.

me·rid·i·an (mə rid′ē ən) *n.* **1.a.** an imaginary great circle on the earth's surface passing through the North and South poles. **b.** half of such a circle extending from pole to pole; line or parallel of longitude. **2.** celestial meridian. **3.** the highest or culminating point; zenith: *the meridian of a person's career.* —*adj.* of or relating to a meridian. [Latin *merīdiānus* relating to midday, relating to the south, from *merīdiēs* midday, south.]

me·rid·i·o·nal (mə rid′ē ə nəl) *adj.* **1.** of, relating to, or resembling a meridian. **2.** of, relating to, or characteristic of the south or the people inhabiting the south, esp. the south of France. **3.** situated in the south; southerly. —*n.* an inhabitant of the south, esp. the south of France. [Late Latin *merīdiōnālis* relating to midday, southern, from Latin *merīdiēs* midday, south.] —**me·rid′i·o·nal·ly,** *adv.*

me·ringue (mə rang′) *n.* **1.** a mixture of stiffly beaten egg whites and sugar, usually baked and used as a topping, as on cakes or pies. **2.** a small cake or pastry shell made of this mixture. [French *meringue;* of uncertain origin.]

me·ri·no (mə rē′nō) *n., pl.* **-nos. 1.** a sheep of a breed originally developed in Spain, having a light colored fleece and a white face, raised for its wool. **2.** the wool of this sheep. **3.** a fine, soft yarn or fabric made from this wool, used for such items as suits or dresses. **4.** a knitted fabric woven from a blend of cotton and wool fibers, used for such items as hosiery and underwear. [Spanish *merino;* probably from Berber *(Benī) Merīn* the Berber tribe that developed this sheep.]

merino

mer·i·stem (mer′ə stem′) *n.* unspecialized plant tissue containing cells capable of division and differentiation into specialized tissues or organs.

mer·it (mer′it) *n.* **1.** quality, worth, or excellence: *The author's latest book has great merit.* **2.** *also,* **merits.** something deserving praise or reward; commendable quality: *You may not like the plan, but it has its merits.* **3. merits.** the actual facts of a matter under consideration, whether good or bad or right or wrong: *The judge will decide the case on its merits.* —*v.t.* to be deserving of. [Latin *meritum* value, worth, desert[3], from *merēre* to earn, deserve.] —**mer′it·less,** *adj.*

Synonyms *(v.t.)* **Merit, earn,** and **deserve** mean to be worthy of or qualified for. **Merit** may connote being entitled to a reward or liable for censure or punishment, often because of intrinsic qualities: *a positive attitude that merits praise, an unkind remark that merits criticism.* **Earn** stresses the specific effort which entitles one to get something in return: *service that earned our gratitude, a story that earned the writer a reputation.* **Deserve,** like *merit,* suggests that something is owed, although it may or may not be received: *You have worked so hard that you deserve to succeed. I didn't deserve to be treated so badly.*

mer·i·to·ri·ous (mer′i tôr′ē əs) *adj.* worthy of reward or praise; having merit: *The soldier was given a medal for meritorious service.* —**mer′i·to′ri·ous·ly,** *adv.* —**mer′i·to′ri·ous·ness,** *n.*

merit system, a system in which people are hired or promoted on the basis of competence or performance, rather than strictly on the basis of seniority.

merle (mûrl) *also,* **merl.** *n.* blackbird *(def. 2).* [Old French *merle* blackbird, from Latin *merula.*]

mer·lin (mûr′lin) *n.* pigeon hawk. [Anglo-Norman *merilun,* from Old French *esmerillon;* of Germanic origin.]

Mer·lin (mûr′lin) *n.* in Arthurian legend, the wise magician who protected and counseled King Arthur.

mer·lon (mûr′lən) *n.* the solid part of a battlement between any two embrasures. For illustration, see **battlement.** [French *merlon,* from Italian *merlone,* from *merlo* battlement; of uncertain origin.]

mer·maid (mûr′mād′) *n.* in folklore, a sea creature having the head and body of a woman and the tail of a fish instead of legs. [MERE[2] + MAID.]

mer·man (mûr′man′) *n., pl.* **-men** (-mən′). in folklore, a sea creature having the head and body of a man and the tail of a fish instead of legs. [MERE[2] + MAN.]

Mer·o·vin·gi·an (mer′ə vin′jē ən) *adj.* of, relating to, or desig-

nating the first Frankish dynasty, reigning from A.D. 500? to 751? —*n.* one of the Merovingian kings.

Mer·ri·mac (mer′ə mak′) *also,* **Mer·ri·mack.** *n.* a U.S. steam-driven wooden frigate salvaged and converted to an ironclad by the Confederates during the American Civil War, and renamed the *Virginia.* It engaged in a historic battle with the *Monitor* at Hampton Roads, Virginia, on March 9, 1862.

mer·ri·ment (mer′i mənt) *n.* playfulness and gaiety; fun.

mer·ry (mer′ē) *adj.,* **-ri·er, -ri·est. 1.** festive and cheerful; full of merriment: *a merry group of people.* **2.** characterized by festivity and rejoicing; joyous: *a merry song.* **3.** *Archaic.* pleasant; delightful. [Old English *myrge* pleasant.] —**mer′ri·ly,** *adv.*
·**to make merry.** to be festive and jovial; engage in or have fun.

mer·ry-an·drew (mer′ē an′drü) *n.* a clown or buffoon.

mer·ry-go-round (mer′ē gō round′) *n.* **1.** a revolving circular platform equipped with wooden animals, esp. horses, and often having benchlike seats, ridden for amusement. Also, **carousel. 2.** a circular platform that revolves when pushed, found in playgrounds. **3.** a rapid round; whirl: *a merry-go-round of parties during the holidays.*

mer·ry·mak·ing (mer′ē mā′king) *n.* **1.** the act of engaging in or having fun; making merry. **2.** boisterous or gay festivity: *The merrymaking after the wedding went on until late at night.* —*adj.* full of joy and fun; gay and festive. —**mer′ry·mak′er,** *n.*

Mer·thi·o·late (mər thī′ə lāt′) *n. Trademark.* a bactericidal compound used in solution as an antiseptic for surface wounds and as a preservative in pharmaceutical products. Formula: $C_9H_9HgNaO_2S$ [Short for *(sodium ethyl-)mer(curi-)thio (salicy)late.*]

me·sa (mā′sə) *n.* a flat-topped hill or mountain with steep sides descending to the plain below; high plateau. [Spanish *mesa* literally, table, from Latin *mēnsa* table.]

mé·sal·li·ance (mā zal′ē əns, mā′zə lī′əns; *French,* mā zål yäns′) *n., pl.* **mé·sal·li·anc·es** (mā zal′ē ən siz, mā′zə lī′ən siz; *French,* mā zål yäns′). a marriage with a person of inferior social position. [French *mésalliance,* from *més-* + *alliance.* See MIS-, ALLIANCE.]

mes·cal (mes kal′) *n.* **1.** a colorless alcoholic beverage distilled from the fermented juice of certain agave plants. **2.** peyote. [Spanish *mescal* the alcoholic beverage, from Nahuatl *mexcalli,* from *metl* maguey + *ixcalli* stew.]

mes·ca·line (mes′kə lēn′, -lin) *n.* a crystalline drug that produces hallucinations, derived from the dried, button-shaped tops of the peyote cactus. Formula: $C_{11}H_{17}NO_3$ [MESCAL + -INE[2].]

mes·dames (mā däm′) **1.** a plural of **madam. 2.** the plural of **madame.**

mes·de·moi·selles (mād mwä zel′) the plural of **mademoiselle.**

mes·en·ceph·a·lon (mes′en sef′ə lon′, mez′-) *n., pl.* **-la** (-lə). midbrain. [Modern Latin *mesencephalon,* from Greek *mesos* middle + ENCEPHALON.] —**mes·en·ce·phal·ic** (mes′en sə fal′ik, mez′-), *adj.*

mes·en·chyme (mes′eng kīm′, mez′-) *n.* the part of the mesoderm in vertebrate embryos that gives rise to connective tissue, bone, and cartilage, and all the parts of the circulatory system. [Greek *mesos* middle + Modern Latin *-enchyma* type of cell tissue (from Greek *enchyma* infusion).] —**mes·en·chy·mal** (mes eng′kə məl, mez′-), *adj.*

mes·en·ter·y (mes′ən ter′ē, mez′-) *n., pl.* **-ter·ies.** a fold of the peritoneum that attaches the small intestine and most of the large intestine to the abdominal wall. [Modern Latin *mesenterium,* from Greek *mesenterion* membrane connecting all the intestines, from *mesos* middle + *enteron* intestine.] —**mes·en·ter′ic,** *adj.*

mesh (mesh) *n.* **1.** one of the open spaces between the cords, threads, or wires of a net or netting. **2. meshes.** the cords, threads, or wires bounding such a space or spaces. **3.** an open network consisting of interlaced cords, threads, or wires; netting. **4.** any of various fabrics consisting of an open network of interlaced threads. **5.** *also,* **meshes.** anything that entangles or ensnares. **6.** the interlocking or engagement of the teeth of a gear. —*v.t., v.i.* **1.** to catch or be caught in or as in a net; enmesh or become enmeshed. **2.** to engage or become engaged, as the teeth of a gear; interlock. [Middle Dutch *maesche* net, opening of a net.]
·**in mesh.** fitted together; in gear; interlocked.

mes·mer·ism (mez′mə riz′əm, mes′-) *n.* hypnotism. [From F. A. *Mesmer,* 1734-1815, Austrian physician associated with hypnotism + -ISM.] —**mes·mer·ic** (mez mer′ik, mes-), *adj.* —**mes′mer·ist,** *n.*

mes·mer·ize (mez′mə rīz′, mes′-) *v.t.,* **-ized, -iz·ing. 1.** hypnotize. **2.** to put as if into a trance; fascinate: *We were mesmerized by the performance.* —**mes′mer·i·za′tion,** *n.* —**mes′mer·iz′er,** *n.*

mes·o·blast (mez′ə blast′, mes′ə-) *n.* the portion of the blastula that gives rise to mesoderm. [Greek *mesos* middle + *blastos* germ, embryo.] —**mes′o·blas′tic,** *adj.*

mes·o·carp (mez′ə kärp′, mes′-) *n.* the middle layer of the pericarp, as the fleshy part of certain fruits. [Greek *mesos* middle + *karpos* fruit.] —**mes′o·car′pic**, *adj.*

mes·o·derm (mez′ə dûrm′, mes′-) *n.* the middle of the three primary germ layers of an animal embryo, from which the skeletal, muscular, connective, and reproductive tissues develop. [Greek *mesos* middle + *derma* skin.] —**mes′o·der′mal**, *adj.*

mes·o·gle·a (mez′ə glē′ə, mes′ə-) *also,* **mes·o·gloe·a**. *n.* a noncellular jellylike layer located between the ectoderm and endoderm of coelenterates, as in jellyfish and sea anemones. [Modern Latin *mesoglea* from Greek *mesos* middle + Late Greek *gloia* glue.] —**mes′o·gle′al** or **mes′o·gloe′al**, *adj.*

Mes·o·lith·ic (mez′ə lith′ik, mes′ə-) *adj.* of, relating to, or designating the middle part of the Stone Age, a long period of transition that marked the interval between the Paleolithic and Neolithic periods.

mes·o·morph (mez′ə môrf′, mes′-) *n.* a person having a muscular body. ➡ distinguished from **ectomorph** and **endomorph**. [Greek *mesos* middle + *morphē* form, shape.] —**mes′o·mor′phic**, *adj.*

me·son (mē′zon, mez′on, mē′son, mes′on) *n.* any of a group of subatomic particles whose mass is intermediate between that of a muon and a proton and is subject to the strong force, one of the four basic types of physical interaction. [Greek *mesos* middle + (ELECTR)ON.]

mes·o·pause (mez′ə pôz′, mes′ə-) *n.* the uppermost limit of the mesosphere, where the ionosphere begins, at an altitude of about 50 miles (80 kilometers) above the earth's surface.

mes·o·phyll (mez′ə fil, mes′-) *n.* the inner tissue of a leaf, lying between the upper and lower layers of the epidermis and consisting of cells that generally contain chloroplasts.

mes·o·phyte (mez′ə fīt′, mes′-) *n.* a plant requiring a moderate supply of water from the soil and atmosphere and thus generally not tolerant of environmental extremes. —**mes·o·phyt·ic** (mez′ə fit′ik, mes′-), *adj.*

mes·o·sphere (mez′ə sfîr′, mes′-) *n.* the layer of the atmosphere above the stratosphere, from about 30 to 50 miles (48 to 80 kilometers) above the earth's surface. For illustration, see **atmosphere**. [Greek *mesos* middle + SPHERE.] —**mes′o·spher′ic**, *adj.*

mes·o·the·li·um (mez′ə thē′lē əm, mes′ə-) *n., pl.* **-li·a** (-lē ə). any layer of epithelium derived from mesoderm, esp. the layer lining the various body cavities of vertebrates. [Modern Latin *mesothelium,* from Greek *mesos* middle + (EPI)THELIUM.]

mes·o·tho·rax (mez′ə thôr′aks, mes′ə-) *n., pl.* **-tho·rax·es** or **-tho·ra·ces** (-thôr′ə sēz′). the middle of the three segments constituting an insect's thorax. —**mes′o·tho·rac′ic** (mez′ə thô ras′-ik, mes′ə-), *adj.*

Mes·o·zo·ic (mez′ə zō′ik, mes′-) *n.* one of the major geologic eras, comprising the Cretaceous, Jurassic, and Triassic periods; age of reptiles. For table, see **geologic time**. —*adj.* of, relating to, or characteristic of this era. [Greek *mesos* middle + *zōē* life + -IC.]

mes·quite (mes kēt′, mes′kēt) *also,* **mes·quit.** *n.* **1.** any of several small thorny trees or shrubs, genus *Prosopis,* of the pea family, that grows in desert regions from the southwestern United States to Chile, bearing pinnate leaves, small flowers, and slender seed pods containing beans used for forage. **2.** the wood of this tree, used as fuel in grilling food. [Spanish *mezquite,* from Nahuatl *mizquitl.*]

mess (mes) *n.* **1.a.** an untidy, disorderly, or dirty state or condition: *The closet is in a mess.* **b.** a person or thing that is in such a state or condition: *The room was a mess after the party.* **2.** an unpleasant, difficult, embarrassing, or confusing situation or state of affairs; muddle: *to make a mess of one's life.* **3.** an untidy or confused mass or collection; jumble: *a mess of newspapers on the floor.* **4.** an indefinite amount: *to catch a mess of fish.* **5.a.** a group of people who take meals together regularly, esp. in the army or navy. **b.** the meal eaten by such a group. **c.** the place where such a meal is eaten; mess hall. **6.** an unappetizing or disagreeable concoction: *I can't eat this mess.* **7.** a portion of soft, partly liquid food. —*v.t.* **1.** to make dirty or untidy (often with *up*): *to mess up a room.* **2.** to make a mess of; confuse or spoil (often with *up*): *Your late arrival messed up our plans.* **3.** to treat or handle roughly (often with *up*): *The thieves messed up their victim pretty badly.* **4.** *Military.* to provide with a meal or meals. —*v.i.* **1.** to interfere or tamper (often with *around*): *Don't mess with the radio.* **2.** to take one's meals in a military mess. [Old French *mes* course of food, from Late Latin *missus,* from *mittere* to place, from Latin *mittere* to send.]

· **to mess around** (or **about**). to waste time or busy oneself by puttering: *We messed around the house all day.*

mes·sage (mes′ij) *n.* **1.** a communication sent from one person or group to another. **2.** a formal or official communication: *The president's message to Congress was televised.* **3.** a point of view or idea meant to be communicated: *The movie's message was that crime doesn't pay.* [Old French *message* information transmitted orally or in writing, going back to Latin *missus,* past participle of *mittere* to send.]

mes·sa·line (mes′ə lēn′) *n.* a soft, lightweight fabric woven of rayon or silk and having a satinlike finish. [French *messaline,* possibly from *Messalina,* a wife of the Roman emperor Claudius.]

Mes·sei·gneurs (me se nyœR′) the plural of **Monseigneur.**

mes·sen·ger (mes′ən jər) *n.* **1.** a person who picks up and delivers messages or runs errands. **2.** a person employed to deliver telegrams, letters, or parcels. **3.** a person whose work is carrying official dispatches. **4.** *Archaic.* a person or thing that tells of something to come; harbinger; forerunner. [Old French *messag-(i)er* bearer of a message, from *message.* See MESSAGE.]

messenger RNA, see RNA.

mess hall, a place where a group of people take meals together regularly, esp. in the army or navy.

Mes·si·ah (mə sī′ə) *n.* **1.** in Judaism, the expected deliverer of the Jews promised by God. **2.** in Christianity, Jesus, regarded as the savior of humankind. **3.** *also,* **messiah.** any savior or deliverer. [Hebrew *mashiach* anointed, from *mashach* to anoint; literally, to oil.]

Mes·si·an·ic (mes′ē an′ik) *adj.* **1.** of or relating to the Messiah. **2.** *also,* **messianic.** characteristic of a messiah.

mes·sieurs (mes′ərz; *French* me syœ′) the plural of **monsieur.**

mess kit, a compactly arranged kit consisting of eating utensils and a metal container that opens to make two separate compartments, used by a soldier or camper.

mess·mate (mes′māt′) *n.* a regular companion at meals, esp. in a ship's mess.

Messrs. (mes′ərz) **1.** Messieurs. **2.** the plural of **Mr.:** *Messrs. Holmes and Watson.*

mess·y (mes′ē) *adj.,* **mess·i·er, mess·i·est.** being in, characterized by, or causing a mess: *a messy room, a messy job.* —**mess′i·ly,** *adv.* —**mess′i·ness,** *n.*

mes·ti·za (me stē′zə) *n.* a woman of mixed racial ancestry, esp. one of Spanish and American Indian descent.

mes·ti·zo (me stē′zō) *n., pl.* **-zos** or **-zoes.** a person of mixed racial ancestry, esp. one of Spanish and American Indian descent. [Spanish *mestizo* mongrel, from Late Latin *mixtīcius* of mixed race, from Latin *mixtus* mixed, past participle of *miscēre* to mix.]

met (met) the past tense and past participle of **meet**[1].

met·a·bol·ic (met′ə bol′ik) *adj.* of, relating to, involving, or characterized by metabolism. —**met′a·bol′i·cal·ly,** *adv.*

me·tab·o·lism (mə tab′ə liz′əm) *n.* the total of all the biochemical processes that occur in a living organism. It is the means by which food is converted into protoplasm and by which the organism is provided with the energy necessary to carry on all basic life processes, such as respiration, digestion, and cell division. [Greek *metabolē* change + -ISM.]

me·tab·o·lite (mə tab′ə līt′) *n.* any chemical substance that participates in or is produced during a metabolic process.

me·tab·o·lize (mə tab′ə līz′) *v.,* **-lized, -liz·ing.** —*v.t.* to subject (food or nutrients) to metabolism. —*v.i.* to undergo or perform metabolism, as a cell or organism. —**me·tab′o·liz′a·ble,** *adj.*

met·a·car·pal (met′ə kär′pəl) *adj.* of or relating to the metacarpus. —*n.* one of the bones of the metacarpus. For illustration, see **hand.**

met·a·car·pus (met′ə kär′pəs) *n., pl.* **-pi** (-pī). **1.** the part of the hand between the wrist and the fingers, having five bones. **2.** a corresponding part of the forelimb of an animal. [Modern Latin *metacarpus,* going back to Greek *meta* between, after + *karpos* wrist.]

met·al (met′əl) *n.* **1.** any of a class of chemical elements, as iron, silver, copper, or lead, that exhibit certain typical properties, as luster, ductility, malleability, and conductivity of heat and electricity. **2.** a mixture of such elements, as brass or bronze; alloy. **3.** road metal. **4.** molten glass, esp. as used in making glass. **5.** an intrinsic quality or substance; mettle. [Latin *metallum* mine[2], substance such as gold or copper, from Greek *metallon.*]

me·tal·lic (mə tal′ik) *adj.* **1.** of, relating to, or having the

a	at	e	end	o	hot	u	up	hw	white		about
ā	ape	ē	me	ō	old	ū	use	ng	song		taken
ä	far	i	it	ô	fork	ü	rule	th	thin	ə	pencil
âr	care	ī	ice	oi	oil	u̇	pull	th	this		lemon
		îr	pierce	ou	out	ûr	turn	zh	measure		circus

properties of metal. **2.** containing or yielding metal. **3.** resembling, characteristic of, or suggestive of metal: *a metallic sound.* —**me·tal′li·cal·ly,** *adv.*

met·al·lif·er·ous (met′ə lif′ər əs) *adj.* containing or yielding metal: *metalliferous deposits.* [Latin *metallifer* (from *metallum* metal + *ferre* to bear) + -OUS. See METAL.]

met·al·log·ra·phy (met′ə log′rə fē) *n.* the study of the structure of metals, esp. with the aid of a microscope. [French *métallographie.* See METAL, -GRAPHY.]

met·al·loid (met′ə loid′) *n.* any of a class of chemical elements, such as boron and arsenic, that exhibit both metallic and nonmetallic properties. Metalloids, such as silicon and germanium, are important semiconductors. Also, **semimetal.** —*adj.* **1.** of, relating to, or having the properties of a metalloid. **2.** resembling a metal. Also, **met′al·loi′dal.**

met·al·lur·gist (met′ə lûr′jist) *n.* a student of or an expert in metallurgy.

met·al·lur·gy (met′ə lûr′jē) *n.* the science and technology of separating metals from ores and preparing them for use, as by refining or fabricating. [Modern Latin *metallurgia,* from Greek *metallourgos* working in metals, from *metallon* metal + *ergon* work.] —**met′al·lur′gic;** *also,* **met′al·lur′gi·cal,** *adj.*

metal oxide semiconductor 1. a transistor in which an oxide of a semiconductor, acting as an insulator, is sandwiched between a metal and the semiconductor itself. **2.** an integrated circuit composed of such transistors, used extensively in computers.

met·al·work (met′əl wûrk′) *n.* **1.** objects or structures made of metal. **2.** metalworking.

met·al·work·ing (met′əl wûr′king) *n.* the act, process, or business of making metal objects or structures. —**met′al·work′er,** *n.*

met·a·mere (met′ə mîr′) *n.* any one of the similar segments that repeat along the length of the bodies of annelid worms, larval arthropods, and, to some degree, embryonic vertebrates.

met·a·mor·phic (met′ə môr′fik) *adj.* **1.** of, relating to, or characterized by change in form or biological metamorphosis. **2.** *Geology.* of, relating to, exhibiting, or produced by metamorphism of rocks or minerals.

met·a·mor·phism (met′ə môr′fiz əm) *n.* **1.** a change in the texture, structure, and mineral composition of rock caused by processes operating deep within the earth. **2.** metamorphosis.

met·a·mor·phose (met′ə môr′fōz, -fōs) *v.t., v.i.,* **-phosed, -phos·ing.** to undergo or cause to undergo metamorphosis or metamorphism.

met·a·mor·pho·sis (met′ə môr′fə sis) *n., pl.* **-ses** (-sēz′). **1.** the process by which certain animals undergo changes in form, structure, or function as they develop from an immature form at birth or hatching to an adult, as the change from a tadpole to a frog or a caterpillar to a moth. **2.a.** any change in form, shape, or structure; transformation, as by sorcery. **b.** a person or thing that results from such a change. **3.** a complete or marked change, as of appearance, character, or condition. [Latin *metamorphosis* transformation, from Greek *metamorphōsis.*]

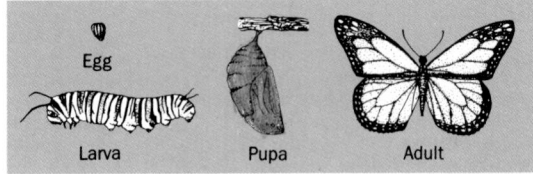

metamorphosis of a butterfly

Egg — Larva — Pupa — Adult

met·a·phase (met′ə fāz′) *n.* in cell division, the stage during which the chromosomes are arranged along the equatorial plate of the spindle. For illustration, see **mitosis.**

met·a·phor (met′ə fôr′, -fər) *n.* **1.** a figure of speech in which one object or idea is implicitly compared or identified with another in order to suggest a similarity between the two; for example: *to be a pillar of strength.* **2.** mixed metaphor. [Latin *metaphora* this figure of speech, from Greek *metaphorā* transference.]

met·a·phor·i·cal (met′ə fôr′i kəl) *adj.* relating to or containing metaphors. Also, **met′a·phor′ic.** —**met′a·phor′i·cal·ly,** *adv.*

met·a·phys·i·cal (met′ə fiz′i kəl) *adj.* **1.** of, relating to, treated by, or characteristic of metaphysics. **2.** difficult to understand; highly abstract; abstruse. —**met′a·phys′i·cal·ly,** *adv.*

met·a·phy·si·cian (met′ə fə zish′ən) *n.* a person who is skilled or expert in metaphysics.

met·a·phys·ics (met′ə fiz′iks) *n.* **1.** a branch of philosophy that deals with the nature and meaning of existence and investigates such aspects of reality as the fundamental unity underlying all particular things, their nature and form, and their relationships. **2.** a theoretical or speculative philosophy, esp. the principles underlying a branch of knowledge. **3.** any obscure or intricate speculation or discussion. ➡ used as singular in all defs. [Medieval Latin *metaphysica,* from Greek *ta meta ta physika* the (works) after the physics; because in one particular arrangement of the works of Aristotle, his works on abstract philosophy followed his works on physics. See PHYSICS.]

met·a·se·quoi·a (met′ə si kwoi′ə) *n.* dawn redwood.

met·a·sta·ble (met′ə stā′bəl) *adj.* having or characterized by a precarious stability, as a chemical that readily becomes either stable or unstable or a physical system that requires only a small input of energy to disrupt it.

me·tas·ta·sis (mə tas′tə sis) *n., pl.* **-ses** (-sēz′). the spread of a disease, disease-producing organism, or cancerous cells from one part of the body to another. [Greek *metastasis* change, removal, transference.] —**met·a·stat·ic** (met′ə stat′ik), *adj.* —**met′a·stat′i·cal·ly,** *adv.*

me·tas·ta·size (mə tas′tə sīz′) *v.i.,* **-sized, -siz·ing.** to spread from one part of the body to another, as certain types of cancer.

met·a·tar·sal (met′ə tär′səl) *adj.* of or relating to the metatarsus. —*n.* one of the bones of the metatarsus.

met·a·tar·sus (met′ə tär′səs) *n., pl.* **-si** (-sī). **1.** the part of the foot between the ankle and the toes, consisting of five bones. **2.a.** the corresponding part of the hind foot of a quadruped. **b.** the corresponding part of the foot of a bird. [Modern Latin *metatarsus,* from Greek *meta* between, after + *tarsos* flat of the foot, ankle.]

me·tath·e·sis (mə tath′ə sis) *n., pl.* **-ses** (-sēz′). **1.** the transposition of sounds or letters within a word. The Old English word *bridd* became *bird* in English through metathesis. **2.** any change or reversal. [Late Latin *metathesis* transposition of the letters of a word, from Greek *metathesis* change of position.]

met·a·zo·an (met′ə zō′ən) *n.* any animal, division Metazoa, whose body is composed of specialized cells grouped to form tissues and organs. All animals are metazoans except the sponges. —*adj.* of, relating to, or characteristic of the metazoans. Also, **met′a·zo′ic.** [Modern Latin *Metazoa* (from Greek *meta* after + *zōia,* plural of *zōion* animal) + -AN.]

mete¹ (mēt) *v.t.,* **met·ed, met·ing. 1.** to distribute by or as by measuring; apportion; allot (often with *out*): *to mete out punishment.* **2.** *Archaic.* to measure. [Old English *metan* to measure.]

mete² (mēt) *n.* a boundary or limit: *to know the metes and bounds of one's abilities.* [Old French *mete,* from Latin *mēta* goal, boundary.]

me·tem·psy·cho·sis (mə tem′sə kō′sis, -temp′-, met′əm sī-) *n., pl.* **-ses** (-sēz). the passage of the soul at death into a new body, either human or animal. [Greek *metempsȳchosis* transmigration of souls.]

me·te·or (mē′tē ər) *n.* a body from space that enters the earth's atmosphere, where it is heated by friction and burns with a bright light as it falls to earth. Also, **falling star, shooting star.** [Modern Latin *meteorum,* from Greek *meteōron* thing in the air, from *meteōros* high in the air.]

me·te·or·ic (mē′tē ôr′ik) *adj.* **1.** of, relating to, or containing meteors. **2.** resembling a meteor; brilliant and swift: *a meteoric rise in politics.* **3.** of, relating to, or occurring in the earth's atmosphere: *meteoric phenomena.* —**me′te·or′i·cal·ly,** *adv.*

me·te·or·ite (mē′tē ə rīt′) *n.* a meteor that has fallen to earth. —**me·te·or·it·ic** (mē′tē ə rit′ik), *adj.*

me·te·or·oid (mē′tē ə roid′) *n.* a meteor that is still in space, before entering earth's atmosphere.

me·te·or·o·log·i·cal (mē′tē ər ə loj′i kəl) *adj.* of or relating to meteorology. Also, **me′te·or·o·log′ic.** —**me′te·or·o·log′i·cal·ly,** *adv.*

me·te·or·ol·o·gist (mē′tē ə rol′ə gist) *n.* a student of or an expert in meteorology.

me·te·or·ol·o·gy (mē′tē ə rol′ə jē) *n.* the science dealing with the study of the atmosphere and the changes that take place within it. An important branch of meteorology is the study of weather. [Greek *meteōrologiā,* from *meteōron* thing in the air + *-logiā* -logy. See METEOR, -LOGY.]

meteor shower, a swarm of meteors that appear together, as at certain times of the year when the earth's orbit passes within range of debris from a comet.

me·ter¹ (mē′tər) *also, British,* **metre.** *n.* the fundamental unit of length in the metric system, equivalent to 3.28 feet. [French *mètre,* from Greek *metron* measure, rule.]

me·ter² (mē′tər) *also, British,* **metre.** *n.* **1.** the rhythmic

arrangement of accented and unaccented or short and long syllables in a line of verse. **2.** the basic rhythmic pattern of accented notes or beats in a musical composition: *duple meter, triple meter.* [Middle English *metre,* from Old English *mētre,* from Latin *metrum* literally, measure, from Greek *métron* measure, rule.]

Meter in English Poetry

In English poetry, meter, or poetic rhythm, is measured in feet and lines. Within a foot, a stressed, or accented, syllable is indicated by the symbol ´, while an unstressed, or unaccented, syllable is represented by the symbol ˘. The names of the feet in poetry and patterns of accented and unaccented syllables are shown below:

POETIC FOOT	PATTERN OF STRESS	
iambic	˘ ´	as in *delay*
trochaic	´ ˘	as in *river*
anapestic	˘ ˘ ´	as in *intersperse*
dactylic	´ ˘ ˘	as in *happiness*

A line is classified according to the number of feet it contains. Below are the types of lines and the number of feet in each type:

METRICAL LINE—FEET

monometer— one foot	pentameter — five feet
dimeter— two feet	hexameter — six feet
trimeter— three feet	heptameter — seven feet
tetrameter— four feet	octameter — eight feet

EXAMPLES OF POETIC METER

IAMBIC TETRAMETER:

˘ ´ ˘ ´ ˘ ´ ˘ ´
My life / closed twice / before / its close
— *Emily Dickinson*

TROCHAIC DIMETER:

´ ˘ ´ ˘
Wave of / sorrow — *Langston Hughes*

ANAPESTIC TRIMETER:

˘ ˘ ´ ˘ ˘ ´ ˘ ˘ ´
Were it ev/er so air/y a tread
— *Alfred Lord Tennyson*

DACTYLIC DIMETER:

´ ˘ ˘ ´ ˘ ˘
What is our / innocence — *Marianne Moore*

me·ter^3 (mē′tər) *n.* **1.** an instrument or device for measuring and recording the amount of something used or rate of flow: *a gas meter, an electric meter.* **2.** any of various similar instruments or devices for measuring and recording time, speed, distance, or degree of intensity: *a light meter.* **3.** parking meter. **4.** postage meter. —*v.t.* to measure or record by means of a meter. [From -METER.]

-meter *combining form* **1.** a device for measuring: *speedometer.* **2.** having a specified amount of meters: *kilometer.* **3.** having a specified number of poetic feet: *tetrameter.* [Latin *metrum* measure, from Greek *metron.*]

me·ter-kil·o·gram-sec·ond (mē′tər kil′ə gram′sek′ənd) *adj.* of, relating to, or being a system of measurement in which the meter is the unit of length, the kilogram is the unit of mass, and the second is the unit of time.

Meth., Methodist.

meth·ac·ryl·ate resin (meth ak′rə lāt′) a thermoplastic resin used as a substitute for glass because it is tough, hard, and highly transparent.

meth·a·done (meth′ə dōn′) *n.* a synthetic narcotic used as a painkiller and as a substitute for heroin in treating heroin addiction.

meth·ane (meth′ān) *n.* a colorless, odorless, highly flammable gas of the alkane, or paraffin, series. The simplest of the hydrocarbons, methane is the main constituent of natural gas and is present in small but increasing amounts in the atmosphere. Formula: CH_4 Also, **marsh gas.** [METHYL + -ANE.]

meth·a·nol (meth′ə nôl′) *n.* a clear, volatile, poisonous, liquid alcohol compound, used in antifreeze, shellac, and rocket fuel. Formula: CH_3OH Also, **methyl alcohol, wood alcohol.** [METHANE + -OL.]

meth·aq·ua·lone (meth ak′wə lōn′) *n.* a sedative and sleep-inducing drug that is not a barbiturate but can be habit-forming. Formula: $C_{16}H_{14}N_2O$

me·theg·lin (mə theg′lin) *n.* an alcoholic beverage made from fermented honey and water. [Welsh *meddyglyn,* from *meddyg* medicinal (from Latin *medicus* curative) + *llyn* liquor.]

me·thinks (mi thingks′) *v. impersonal, past tense* **me·thought.** *Archaic.* it seems to me. [Old English *mē thynceth* to me it seems, from *mē,* dative of *ic* I + *thynceth,* third person singular present of *thyncan* to seem.]

me·thi·o·nine (me thī′ə nēn′, -nin) *n.* an essential amino acid that provides the sulfur needed for metabolism, used medicinally in the prevention and treatment of certain liver disorders. Formula: $C_5H_{11}NO_2S$

meth·od (meth′əd) *n.* **1.** a way, means, or manner of doing something, esp. so as to be systematic or orderly. **2.** orderliness and regularity in thought, action, or activity: *Your plan lacks method.* **3.** a systematic and orderly arrangement, as of thoughts or topics. **4.** principles and techniques applied in or characteristic of a particular field. **5. the Method.** an introspective approach to acting in which an actor may draw on his or her own experiences in order to give a more truthful interpretation of a part. [Latin *methodus* way of proceeding, from Greek *methodos* pursuit, investigation, system.] —For Synonyms, see **process.**

me·thod·i·cal (mə thod′i kəl) *adj.* **1.** performed, arranged, or carried on in a systematic or orderly manner: *The police made a methodical search of the house.* **2.** characterized by systematic or orderly habits or behavior: *a very methodical housekeeper.* Also, **me·thod′ic.** —**me·thod′i·cal·ly,** *adv.* —**me·thod′i·cal·ness,** *n.* —For Synonyms, see **orderly.**

Meth·od·ism (meth′ə diz′əm) *n.* the faith, doctrines, and practices of the Methodists.

Meth·od·ist (meth′ə dist) *n.* a member of any of several branches of a Protestant denomination that had its origin in the teachings and work of the English religious reformer John Wesley. —*adj.* of, relating to, or characteristic of the Methodists or Methodism.

meth·od·ize (meth′ə dīz′) *v.t.,* **-ized, -iz·ing.** to reduce to or arrange according to a method; systematize.

meth·od·ol·o·gy (meth′ə dol′ə jē) *n., pl.* **-gies. 1.** an orderly system of principles or methods of inquiry applied to a particular body of knowledge. **2.** a branch of logic dealing with the examination and analysis of the principles or methods of inquiry as applied to a particular branch of knowledge. [Greek *methodos* pursuit, investigation, system + -LOGY.] —**meth′od·o·log′i·cal,** *adj.* —**meth′od·o·log′i·cal·ly,** *adv.* —**meth′od·ol′o·gist,** *n.*

M

me·thought (mi thôt′) the past tense of **methinks.**

Me·thu·se·lah (mə thü′zə lə) *n.* any very old man. [From *Methuselah,* biblical character who, according to Genesis, lived 969 years.]

meth·yl (meth′əl) *n.* an organic group or radical formed from methane. Formula: CH_3 [French *méthyle,* going back to Greek *methy* wine + *hȳlē* wood, matter; supposedly because methyl alcohol is obtained by treating wood.]

methyl alcohol, methanol.

meth·yl·ene blue (meth′ə lēn′) an organic dye used as a stain to test for bacteria, as in milk, and as an antidote for cyanide poisoning. Formula: $C_{16}H_{18}ClN_3S$

me·tic·u·lous (mə tik′yə ləs) *adj.* characterized by or exhibiting extreme or excessive concern about details; exacting: *a meticulous dresser.* [Latin *metīculōsus* full of fear, from *metus* fear.] —**me·tic′u·lous·ly,** *adv.* —**me·tic′u·lous·ness,** *n.* —For Synonyms, see **careful.**

mé·tier (mā tyā′) *n.* **1.** a trade, occupation, or profession. **2.** work or activity for which one is particularly suited. [French *métier* business, profession, going back to Latin *ministerium* service, occupation.]

met·o·nym (met′ə nim′) *n.* a word used in metonymy.

met·o·nym·i·cal (met′ə nim′i kəl) *adj.* **1.** relating to or of the nature of metonymy. **2.** used in metonymy. Also, **met′o·nym′ic.** —**met′o·nym′i·cal·ly,** *adv.*

me·ton·y·my (mə ton′ə mē) *n.* the use of the name of one thing for that of another associated with or related to it; for example: *crown* is a metonym for *monarch.* [Late Latin *metōnymia,* from Greek *metōnymiā* literally, change of names.]

met·o·pe (met′ə pē, met′ōp) *n.* one of the square spaces, either sculptured or

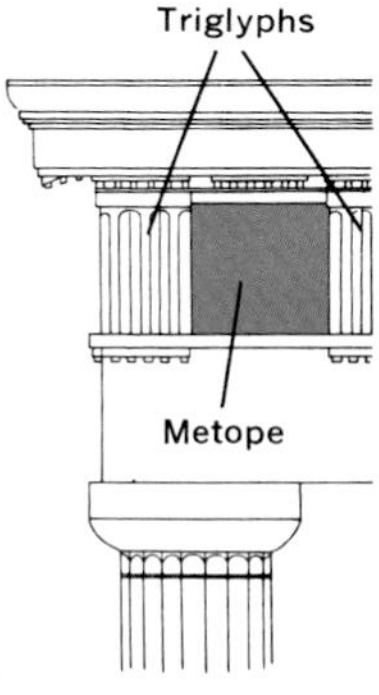

metope

a	at	**e**	end	**o**	hot	**u**	up	**hw**	white	ə	about, taken, pencil, lemon, circus
ā	ape	**ē**	me	**ō**	old	**ū**	use	**ng**	song		
ä	far	**i**	it	**ô**	fork	**ü**	rule	**th**	thin		
âr	care	**ī**	ice	**oi**	oil	**u̇**	pull	**th̲**	this		
		îr	pierce	**ou**	out	**ûr**	turn	**zh**	measure		

plain, between the triglyphs in a Doric frieze. [Greek *metopē*, from *meta* between + *opē* hole.]

me·tre¹ (mē′tər) *British.* meter¹.

me·tre² (mē′tər) *British.* meter².

met·ric¹ (met′rik) *adj.* of, relating to, or designating the metric system: *metric measurement.* [French *métrique*, from *mètre*. See METER¹.]

met·ric² (met′rik) *adj.* metrical. [Latin *metricus* metrical, from Greek *metrikos* of measure, from *métron* measure, rule.]

met·ri·cal (met′ri kəl) *adj.* **1.** of, relating to, or composed in poetic meter. **2.** of, relating to, or used in measurement. [Latin *metricus* (from Greek *metrikos*, from *metron* measure, rule, poetic meter) + -AL¹.] —**met′ri·cal·ly,** *adv.*

met·ri·cate (met′ri kāt′) *v.t.* **-cat·ed, -cat·ing.** to change to the metric system. —**met′ri·ca′tion,** *n.*

metric system, a decimal system of measurement in which the meter is the fundamental unit of length and the kilogram is the fundamental unit of mass, with the liter as the unit of volume. For Weights and Measures table, see **weight**.

metric ton, a measure of weight equal to 1,000 kilograms or 2,204.62 pounds avoirdupois. Also, **tonne.**

met·ro (met′rō) *also,* **Met·ro.** *n., pl.* **-ros.** a subway system in any of several cities, as in Washington, D.C., or Paris, France. [French *métro,* short for *(chemin de fer) métro(politain)* metropolitan railway.]

me·trol·o·gy (mi trol′ə jē) *n., pl.* **-gies. 1.** the science of weights and measures. **2.** a system of weights and measures. [Greek *metron* measure + -LOGY.]

met·ro·nome (met′rə nōm′) *n.* a mechanical device used for indicating the exact tempo to be maintained in music. [Greek *metron* measure + *nomos* law, rule.] —**met′ro·nom′ic,** *adj.*

me·trop·o·lis (mə trop′ə lis) *n., pl.* **-lis·es. 1.** a large city, esp. one that is an important center of commerce, culture, or other activity. **2.** the principal city of a particular country, state, or region, esp. one that is the capital or the largest. **3.** a city that is the seat of a metropolitan archbishop. [Late Latin *mētropolis* mother city (that established colonies), from Greek *mētropolis,* from *mētēr* mother + *polis* city.]

metronome

met·ro·pol·i·tan (met′rə pol′i tən) *adj.* **1.** relating to, characteristic of, or belonging to a metropolis: *a metropolitan police force.* **2.** consisting of or constituting a metropolis and its surrounding regions: *the New York metropolitan area.* **3.** in the Roman Catholic Church and certain Anglican and Orthodox churches, of or relating to an archbishop who is the head of a church province. —*n.* a metropolitan archbishop.

-metry *combining form* the art, science, or process of measuring: *geometry, optometry.* [Greek *-metriā* measurement, from *metron* measure.]

met·tle (met′əl) *n.* **1.** spirit and courage. **2.** an intrinsic quality or substance, as of a person's character. [Form of METAL; difference in spelling developed to distinguish literal from figurative meaning.]

•**on one's mettle.** ready or eager to do one's best.

met·tle·some (met′əl səm) *adj.* full of mettle; spirited or courageous.

Mev (mev) *n.* 1 million electron volts.

mew¹ (mū) *n.* the cry of a cat; meow. —*v.i.* to make such a sound. [Imitative.]

mew² (mū) *n.* a gull, esp. the common gull, *Larus canus,* of Europe. Also, **sea mew.** [Middle English *mewe,* from Old English *mǣw;* of Germanic origin.]

mew³ (mū) *n.* a cage for hawks, esp. when they are molting. —*v.t. Archaic.* to shut up in or as in a cage (often with *up*). [Old French *mue* cage for hawks, a molting, a change, from *muer* to molt, change, from Latin *mūtāre* to change.]

mewl (mūl) *v.i.* to cry feebly like a baby; whimper. [Imitative.]

mews (mūz) *n.* **1.** stables built around a court or alley. **2.** a narrow street or alley, usually having houses that have been converted from stables. ➡ used as singular or plural in both defs. [Plural of MEW³; because the royal stables in London were originally built on the site where the mews of the royal falcons were kept.]

Mex. 1. Mexican. **2.** Mexico.

Mex·i·can (mek′si kən) *adj.* of, relating to, or characteristic of Mexico or its people or culture. —*n.* **1.** a native or citizen of Mexico. **2.** a person of Mexican ancestry.

Mexican jumping bean, jumping bean.

Mexican Spanish, the variety of the Spanish language that is used in Mexico.

Mexican War, the war fought between the United States and Mexico from 1846 to 1848.

me·zu·zah (mə zúz′ə) *also,* **me·zu·za.** *n.* in Judaism, a small tubelike container containing parchment inscribed with biblical passages, usually affixed to a doorpost or worn as an amulet. [Hebrew *mezūzāh* literally, doorpost; because affixed to doorposts.]

mez·za·nine (mez′ə nēn′) *n.* **1.** an intermediate story between two main floors of a building, usually just above the ground floor. **2.** the lowest balcony in a theater or the first few rows of the balcony. [French *mezzanine* intermediate story, from Italian *mezzanino,* diminutive of *mezzano* middle, from Latin *mediānus.*]

mez·zo (met′sō, med′zō, mez′ō) *Music. adj.* half; medium; moderate. —*adv.* moderately. [Italian *mezzo* middle, from Latin *medius.*]

mez·zo-so·pran·o (met′sō sə pran′ō, -prä′nō, med′zō-, mez′ō-) *n., pl.* **-pran·os. 1.** a female voice intermediate between soprano and contralto. **2.** a singer having such a voice. **3.** a part composed for a mezzo-soprano. —*adj.* of or relating to a mezzo-soprano.

mez·zo·tint (met′sō tint′, med′zō-, mez′ō-) *n.* **1.** a method of engraving in which the entire surface of a copper or steel plate is uniformly roughened and then partially scraped or burnished to produce effects of light and shade. **2.** a print made from such a plate. —*v.t.* to engrave in mezzotint. [Italian *mezzotinto* half-tone, going back to Latin *medius* middle + *tinctus,* past participle of *tingere* to wet, dye.]

mf. *Music.* moderately loud. [Abbreviation of Italian *mezzo forte,* from Latin *medius* middle + *fortis* strong.]

MF, medium frequency.

mfg., manufacturing.

mfr., manufacture; manufacturer.

Mg, the symbol for magnesium.

mg *also,* **mg.** milligram; milligrams.

Mgr. 1. Manager. **2.** Monseigneur. **3.** Monsignor.

MHG, *also,* **M.H.G.** Middle High German.

mho (mō) *n., pl.* **mhos.** the meter-kilogram-second unit of electrical conductance, equal to the reciprocal of the ohm. [OHM spelled backward.]

MHz, megahertz.

mi (mē) *n. Music.* the third of the series of syllables used to name the eight tones of the diatonic scale. For illustration, see **do².** [See GAMUT.]

mi *also,* **mi.** mile; miles.

MI, the postal abbreviation for Michigan.

MIA (em′ī′ā′) a member of the armed forces who cannot be found after a battle or war, either alive or dead. [Abbreviation of *m(issing) i(n) a(ction).*]

mi·aow (mē ou′) *also,* **mi·aou.** *n., v.* meow.

mi·as·ma (mī az′mə, mē-) *n., pl.* **-mas** or **-ma·ta** (-mə tə). **1.** noxious or poisonous emanations formerly believed to rise from the earth and decaying matter and pollute the air. **2.** any noxious or harmful influence, effect, or atmosphere. [Modern Latin *miasma,* from Greek *miasma* pollution, from *miainein* to pollute.] —**mi·as′mal, mi·as′mic,** *adj.*

mi·ca (mī′kə) *n.* any of a group of silicate minerals, as muscovite or biotite, that can be separated into thin sheets, often used as insulators in electric devices. Also, **isinglass.** [Latin *mīca* crumb; influenced by Latin *micāre* to shine.] —**mi·ca·ceous** (mī kā′shəs), *adj.*

Mi·cah (mī′kə) *n.* a book of the Old Testament, attributed to the Hebrew prophet Micah.

mice (mīs) the plural of **mouse.**

mi·celle (mī sel′, mi-) *n.* an electrically charged clump of colloidal molecules, formed when soap or other detergents dissolve in water. [Modern Latin *micella,* diminutive of Latin *mica* grain, crumb.] —**mi·cel′lar,** *adj.*

Mich., Michigan.

Mi·chael (mī′kəl) *n.* in the Bible, an archangel. In Christian tradition, Michael cast Satan out of heaven.

Mich·ael·mas (mik′əl məs) *n.* the Christian feast in honor of the archangel Michael, observed on September 29.

Mi·che·as (mī kē′əs) *n.* in the Douay Bible, Micah.

mick·le (mik′əl) *Archaic.* much. [Middle English *mikel,* from Old English *micel.*]

Mic·mac (mik′mak′) *n., pl.* **-mac** or **-macs. 1.** a member of a tribe of North American Indians of the Algonquian language family, living in Newfoundland, Nova Scotia, and New Brunswick. **2.** the Algonquian language of this tribe. [Micmac *Migmac* literally, allies.]

mi·cra (mī′krə) a plural of **micron.**

micro- *combining form* **1.** very small; minute: *microorganism.* **2.** enlarging, magnifying, or amplifying: *microscope, microphone.* **3.** (of a science) relying on or using a microscope: *microbiology.*

4. in systems of measurement, one millionth of a: *microfarad.* [Greek *mīkros* small.]

mi·cro·bar (mī′krə bär′) *n.* a unit of pressure equal to 1 millionth of a bar. [MICRO- + BAR².]

mi·crobe (mī′krōb) *n.* a microscopic living thing; microorganism, esp. one that causes disease. [MICRO- + *bios* life.] —**mi·cro·bi·al** (mī krō′bē əl), *adj.*

mi·cro·bi·ol·o·gy (mī′krō bī ol′ə jē) *n.* the branch of biology that studies microorganisms. [MICRO- + BIOLOGY.] —**mi′cro·bi′o·log′i·cal,** *adj.* —**mi′cro·bi·ol′o·gist,** *n.*

mi·cro·cap·sule (mī′krō kap′səl) *n.* a tiny capsule containing a substance, as a medicine or glue, that is released when the capsule disintegrates or is broken. [MICRO- + CAPSULE.]

mi·cro·ceph·a·ly (mī′krō sef′ə lē) *n.* a condition characterized by an abnormally small head or cerebrum. ➡ distinguished from macrocephaly. —**mi·cro·ce·phal·ic** (mī′krō sə fal′ik), **mi′·cro·ceph′a·lous,** *adj.*

mi·cro·chip (mī′krə chip′) *n.* chip *(def. 7).*

mi·cro·cir·cuit (mī′krō sûr′kit) *n.* integrated circuit. [MICRO- + CIRCUIT.] —**mi′cro·cir′cuit·ry,** *n.*

mi·cro·cli·mate (mī′krō klī′mit) *n.* the climate characteristic of a particular place, a specific habitat, or a small area, esp. as distinguished from that of the surrounding region: *the microclimate of an urban park.* [MICRO- + CLIMATE.]

mi·cro·cline (mī′krō klīn′) *n.* a glassy, white feldspar mineral, dimorphous with orthoclase, that is a common constituent of granite and pegmatite. Formula: $KAlSi_3O_8$ [German *mikroklin,* from Greek *mikros* small + *klinein* to incline; because the angles formed by its cleavage planes diverge slightly from 90 degrees.]

mi·cro·coc·cus (mī′krō kok′əs) *n., pl.* **-coc·ci** (-kok′sī). any of several varieties of bacteria that are spherical or egg-shaped. [Modern Latin *micrococcus,* from MICRO- + COCCUS.] —**mi′cro·coc′cal,** *adj.*

mi·cro·com·put·er (mī′krō kəm pū′tər) *n.* a desktop computer having less memory and capability than a minicomputer, used in homes, schools, businesses, and institutions to perform routine operations, such as word processing, work with graphics, and computerized mailings. Also, **personal computer.**

mi·cro·cop·y (mī′krə kop′ē) *n., pl.* **-cop·ies.** a greatly reduced photographic copy of printed or graphic matter, as on or reproduced from microfilm.

mi·cro·cosm (mī′krə koz′əm) *n.* **1.** a little world; universe in miniature. **2.** anything thought of as being a miniature representation of a large whole: *The small town was a microcosm of all of the nation.* ➡ opposed to **macrocosm** in both defs. [French *microcosme,* through Late Latin, going back to Greek *mīkros* small + *kosmos* world.] —**mi′cro·cos′mic,** *adj.* —**mi′cro·cos′mi·cal·ly,** *adv.*

mi·cro·ec·o·nom·ics (mī′krō ek′ə nom′iks, -ē′kə-) *n.* the branch of economics concerned with specific aspects of an economy, such as the relative prices of a particular commodity. ➡ used as singular. [MICRO- + ECONOMICS.]

mi·cro·e·lec·trode (mī′krō i lek′trōd) *n.* a minute electrode, esp. one implanted in biological research to stimulate specific areas of the brain.

mi·cro·e·lec·tron·ics (mī′krō i lek tron′iks) *n.* the branch of electronics that deals with extremely small circuits and devices. ➡ used as singular. [MICRO- + ELECTRONICS.] —**mi′cro·e·lec·tron′ic,** *adj.*

mi·cro·en·cap·su·la·tion (mī′krō en kap′sə lā′shən) *n.* a process in which tiny amounts of a substance are enclosed in separate microcapsules for controlled release, as to prolong the action of a drug.

mi·cro·far·ad (mī′krə far′əd, -ad) *n. Electricity.* a unit of capacitance equal to $1/1,000,000$ of a farad. [MICRO- + FARAD.]

mi·cro·fiche (mī′krə fēsh′) *n.* a sheet of microfilm containing an array of pages of microcopy. Also, **fiche.**

mi·cro·film (mī′krə film′) *n.* **1.** a photographic film, usually 35 or 16 millimeters wide, on which a newspaper or other printed matter is reproduced in miniature. **2.** a reproduction made on such film. —*v.t.* to make a microfilm of.

mi·cro·gram (mī′krə gram′) *n.* one millionth of a gram. [MICRO- + GRAM.]

mi·cro·graph (mī′krə graf′) *n.* photomicrograph.

mi·cro·groove (mī′krə grüv′, -krō-) *n.* the very fine, narrow groove cut or pressed into the playing surface of a long-playing phonograph record.

mi·cro·me·te·o·rite (mī′krō mē′tē ə rīt′) *n.* a tiny meteorite that, because of its size, encounters no air resistance in falling to earth.

mi·crom·e·ter¹ (mī krom′i tər) *n.* **1.** any of a group of instruments that use a finely threaded screw, the head of which is divided

into equal parts forming a scale, to measure very small dimensions, distances, or angles to a high degree of precision, as on microscopes or telescopes. **2.** micrometer caliper. [MICRO- + -METER.]

mi·cro·me·ter² (mī′krō mē′tər) *n.* micron. [MICRO- + METER¹.]

micrometer caliper, a precision instrument with two jaws, one fixed and the other moved by a finely threaded screw, used by machinists for measuring thickness or diameter. Also, **micrometer.**

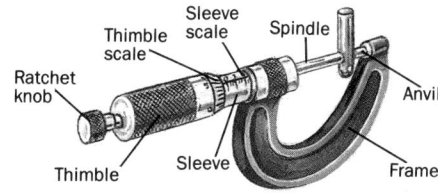

micrometer caliper

mi·cro·min·i·a·ture (mī′krō min′ē ə chər, -min′ə-) *adj.* smaller in size than miniature; extremely small: *microminiature electronic equipment.* [MICRO- + MINIATURE.]

mi·cro·min·i·a·tur·ize (mī′krō min′ē ə chə rīz′, -min′ə-) *v.t.,* **-ized, -iz·ing.** to make smaller than miniature in size: *to microminiaturize electronic equipment.*

mi·cron (mī′kron) *n., pl.* **mi·crons** or **mi·cra** (mī′krə). a unit of length equal to $1/1,000,000$ of a meter. Symbol: μ Also, **micrometer.** [Greek *mīkron,* neuter of *mīkros* small.]

Mi·cro·ne·sian (mī′krə nē′zhən, -shən) *n.* **1.** a native or inhabitant of Micronesia. **2.** a subfamily of the Austronesian family of languages, consisting of a number of languages, spoken predominantly in Micronesia. —*adj.* of, relating to, or characteristic of Micronesia or its peoples, languages, or cultures.

mi·cro·nu·cle·us (mī′krō nü′klē əs, -nū′-) *n., pl.* **-cle·i** (-klē ī′) or **-cle·us·es.** the smaller of the two types of nuclei present in various ciliate protozoans, believed to control the process of reproduction.

mi·cro·nu·tri·ent (mī′krō nü′trē ənt, -nū′-) *n.* any essential nutrient, as a trace element or vitamin, that is required in minute quantities for the growth, repair, and maintenance of a living organism. [MICRO- + NUTRIENT.]

mi·cro·or·gan·ism (mī′krō ôr′gə niz′əm) *n.* an organism, such as a bacterium, that is too small to be seen with the naked eye.

mi·cro·phone (mī′krə fōn′) *n.* a device that converts sound waves to an electrical signal, used to record, transmit, or amplify sound. [MICRO- + Greek *phōnē* sound.]

mi·cro·pho·to·graph (mī′krō fō′tə graf′) *n.* **1.** a photograph that requires magnification for viewing, as an image on microfilm. **2.** photomicrograph. [MICRO- + PHOTOGRAPH.]

mi·cro·print (mī′krō print′) *n.* a microphotograph of newspapers, records, or other printed matter reproduced in print for reading with a magnifying device. [MICRO- + PRINT.]

mi·cro·proc·es·sor (mī′krō-pros′es ər, -ə sər, -prō′ses ər, -sə-sər) *n. Computers.* a central processing unit contained on a single microchip. [MICRO- + PROCESSOR.]

mi·cro·pyle (mī′krə pīl′) *n.* the tiny pore at the apex of the ovule of seed plants through which a male reproductive cell must pass for fertilization to occur. [French *micropyle,* from Greek *mīkros* small + *pylē* gate.]

mi·cro·scope (mī′krə skōp′) *n.* **1.** an optical instrument with a lens or combination of lenses providing a clear magnified image of a small object viewed through it. **2.** an instrument, such as an electron microscope,

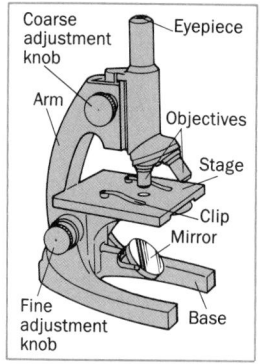

microscope

a	at	e	end	o	hot	u	up	hw	white		about
ā	ape	ē	me	ō	old	ū	use	ng	song		taken
ä	far	i	it	ô	fork	ü	rule	th	thin	ə	pencil
âr	care	ī	ice	oi	oil	u̇	pull	th	this		lemon
		ir	pierce	ou	out	ûr	turn	zh	measure		circus

that uses something other than light to achieve magnification. [Modern Latin *microscopium*, from MICRO- + -SCOPE.]

mi·cro·scop·ic (mī′krə skop′ik) *adj.* **1.** so small as not to be seen without using a microscope; too small to be visible to the naked eye. **2.** extremely small; minute. **3.** of, relating to, or performed with a microscope: *a microscopic lens, a microscopic observation of cells.* **4.** resembling, suggestive of, or functioning like a microscope; very detailed: *The jury made a microscopic examination of the evidence.* Also, **mi′cro·scop′i·cal.** —**mi′cro·scop′i·cal·ly,** *adv.*

mi·cros·co·py (mī kros′kə pē, mī′krə skō′pē) *n.* **1.** the process or technique of using a microscope. **2.** an investigation with a microscope. —**mi·cros′co·pist,** *n.*

mi·cro·sec·ond (mī′krō sek′ənd) *n.* $^1/_{1,000,000}$ of a second.

mi·cro·some (mī′krə sōm′) *n.* any of various minute granular structures, consisting of fragmented organelles, obtained from cellular material that has been separated in an ultracentrifuge. [MICRO- + -SOME[3].] —**mi′cro·so′mal,** *adj.*

mi·cro·spore (mī′krə spôr′) *n.* a small spore that develops into a male gametophyte, the pollen grain of seed plants. ➡ distinguished from **megaspore.**

mi·cro·sur·ger·y (mī′krō sûr′jə rē) *n.* delicate surgery on tiny structures of the body, such as nerves and blood vessels, performed under a microscope with the use of miniaturized instruments and laser beams.

mi·cro·tome (mī′krə tōm′) *n.* a precision instrument for cutting thin sections, esp. of organic tissue, for examination under a microscope. [MICRO- + Greek *tomon* instrument for cutting, from *tomos* section, piece cut off, from *temnein* to cut.]

mi·cro·vil·lus (mī′krō vil′əs) *n., pl.* **-vil·li** (-vil′ī). any of various microscopic fingerlike projections of a tissue, cell surface, or cell organelle. They are abundant on intestinal tissue, where they help to increase the absorptive area. —**mi′cro·vil′lar,** *adj.*

mi·cro·wave (mī′krə wāv′) *n.* a high-frequency electromagnetic wave having a wavelength ranging from about 1 millimeter to 30 centimeters. It is used in radar and telecommunications. —*v.t.* **-waved, -wav·ing.** to cook or heat in a microwave oven.

microwave oven, an electronic oven in which food is quickly cooked with the heat produced by the action of microwaves entering the food.

mic·tu·rate (mik′chə rāt′) *v.i.* **-rat·ed, -rat·ing.** urinate. [Latin *micturitus*, past participle of *micturīre* to want to urinate, going back to *meiere* to urinate.]

mid[1] (mid) *adj.* being at or near the middle: *the mid part of a year.* [Old English *midd* middle.]

mid[2] (mid) *also,* ′**mid.** *prep. Archaic.* amid. [Short for AMID.]

mid- *combining form* **1.** middle part of: *mid-January, midbrain.* **2.** being in the middle or center: *midpoint.* [From MID[1].]

mid·air (mid′âr′) *n.* a point or region high above the ground: *The acrobat did a spectacular flip in midair.*

Mi·das (mī′dəs) *n.* in Greek legend, a king of Phrygia to whom Dionysus gave the power of turning to gold all that he touched.

mid-At·lan·tic (mid′at lan′tik) *adj.* designating or characterized by a fusion of British and American speech habits, customs, and tastes.

mid·brain (mid′brān′) *n.* the middle part of the embryonic brain, or the parts of the adult brain that develop from it. For illustration, see **brain.** Also, **mesencephalon.**

mid·day (*n.,* mid′dā′; *adj.,* mid′dā′) *n.* the middle part of the day; noon. —*adj.* of, relating to, or occurring during the middle part of the day: *midday heat, a midday meal.* [Old English *middæg* noon.]

mid·den (mid′ən) *n.* **1.** kitchen midden. **2.** a dunghill or refuse heap.

mid·dle (mid′əl) *adj.* **1.** equally distant from the sides, extremities, or exterior points: *We sat in the middle row.* **2.** being or occurring halfway between two things, as in time, position, or amount: *a middle child, middle income.* **3.** average or medium: *A person of middle height.* **4. Middle.** of, relating to, or designating an intermediate stage or division, as of a language or geologic period. —*n.* **1.** a point, part, or area equally distant from the sides, extremities, or exterior points of anything: *the middle of a street.* **2.** a part or portion approximately halfway between the beginning and the end: *We left in the middle of the movie.* **3.** the middle part of the body; waist. [Old English *middel* midst, central part.]

middle age, the time of life between youth and old age, usually thought of as being between forty and sixty-five years of age.

mid·dle-aged (mid′əl ājd′) *adj.* **1.** in or of middle age. **2.** of, relating to, or characteristic of middle-aged persons.

Middle Ages, the period of European history between the fall of the Western Roman Empire and the beginning of the Renaissance, from about the fifth century to the middle of the fifteenth century.

Middle America 1. the American middle class considered as

being politically conservative and conventional. **2.a.** the inhabitants of the Midwest. **b.** the Midwest. **3.** the lands south of the United States and north of South America, usually taken to include the countries of the Caribbean.

mid·dle·brow (mid′əl brou′) *Informal. adj.* characteristic of or suitable for a person with a mild interest in culture and some concern for education; not highbrow or lowbrow. —*n.* a person of middlebrow interests and concerns.

middle C *Music.* **1.** the note written on the first ledger line below the treble staff and the first ledger line above the bass staff. **2.** the corresponding tone or key.

mid·dle-class (mid′əl klas′) *adj.* of, relating to, or characteristic of the middle class.

middle class, the part of society occupying an intermediate social and economic position.

middle distance, the area, as in a painting or photograph, between the foreground and the background. Also, **middle ground.**

Middle Dutch, the Dutch language from the twelfth to the sixteenth centuries.

middle ear, the cavity between the eardrum and the inner ear, containing, in humans, the incus, malleus, and stapes. For illustration, see **ear**[1]. Also, **tympanum.**

Middle English, the English language from the twelfth to the fifteenth centuries.

Middle French, the French language from the fourteenth to the sixteenth centuries.

Middle Greek, the Greek language from the seventh to the fifteenth centuries.

middle ground 1. middle distance. **2.** a position of compromise, or between two extremes: *to take the middle ground in a dispute.*

Middle High German, High German from the twelfth to the sixteenth centuries.

Middle Latin, Medieval Latin.

Middle Low German, Low German from the twelfth to the sixteenth centuries.

mid·dle·man (mid′əl man′) *n., pl.* **-men** (-men′). **1.** a person who buys goods directly from the producer and sells them to the retailer or consumer. **2.** any intermediary; go-between.

mid·dle·most (mid′əl mōst′) *adj.* being exactly in or nearest the middle.

mid·dle-of-the-road (mid′əl əv the rōd′) *adj.* not taking or advocating any extreme position or side; neither liberal nor conservative; moderate: *a middle-of-the-road politician.* —**mid′dle-of-the-road′er,** *n.*

middle school, a school with classes for grades between elementary school and high school, usually from grade five or six through grade eight or nine.

middle term, a term that appears in the major and minor premises of a syllogism but not in the conclusion. In the syllogism *All men are mortal; Socrates is a man; therefore Socrates is mortal,* the words *men* and *man* are the middle terms.

mid·dle·weight (mid′əl wāt′) *n.* **1.** a boxer competing in the weight class of up to 160 pounds (73 kilograms), or another competitor, as a wrestler, in a similar class. **2.** a person or animal of average weight.

mid·dling (mid′ling) *adj.* **1.** medium or average as in size or amount: *a person of middling height.* **2.** mediocre or second-rate: *a play with only middling performances by the actors.* —*adv. Informal.* moderately; fairly. —*n., pl.* **middlings. 1.** products that are regarded as being average, as in size, quality, grade, or price. **2.** a mixture of bran and coarsely ground particles of wheat, used esp. as a feed for poultry, hogs, and other livestock. [MID[1] + -LING[2].]

 ·**fair to middling.** moderately good; moderately well: *to feel fair to middling.*

mid·dy (mid′ē) *n., pl.* **-dies. 1.** *Informal.* midshipman. **2.** middy blouse.

middy blouse, a loosely fitting blouse designed to resemble a sailor's blouse.

Mid·gard (mid′gärd) *n.* in Norse mythology, the home of human beings; earth.

midge (mij) *n.* **1.** any of various tiny North American flies that often gather in large swarms in cool, damp areas. Some midges can inflict a painful bite. **2.** a very small person. [Old English *mycg(e)* gnatlike insect.]

midg·et (mij′it) *n.* **1.** a very small but normally proportioned person. **2.** anything that is very small for its kind. —*adj.* very small; diminutive. [MIDGE + -ET.]

mid·gut (mid′gut′) *n.* **1.** the middle portion of the embryonic digestive tract in vertebrates, usually considered as the anterior portion of the hindgut, which develops into the small intestine. **2.** the intermediate portion of an arthropod's digestive system, as in insects and crustaceans.

Mid·i·an·ite (mid′ē ə nīt′) *n.* in the Old Testament, one of a wandering tribe of Arabs that warred with the Israelites.

mid·land (mid′lənd) *n.* the central or interior part of a region or country. —*adj.* of, relating to, or situated in the midland: *a midland village.*

mid·life crisis (mid′līf′) a time of anxiety in middle age when a person is confused about goals and actual achievements in life and about relationships with friends and family.

mid·line (mid′līn′) *n.* a median line: *the midline of a trapezoid.*

mid·most (mid′mōst′) *adj.* being exactly in or nearest the middle; middlemost. —*adv.* in the middle or midst.

mid·night (mid′nīt′) *n.* twelve o'clock at night; the middle of the night. —*adj.* 1. of, relating to, or occurring at midnight: *a midnight train.* 2. resembling midnight; very dark: *The dress was midnight blue.*

midnight sun, the sun seen at midnight during summer in the arctic and antarctic regions.

mid·point (mid′point′) *n.* a point that is exactly in the middle of something, as a line.

mid·rib (mid′rib′) *n. Botany.* the central vein of a leaf. For illustration, see **leaf.**

mid·riff (mid′rif) *n.* 1. that part of the body below the breast and above the waist. 2. that part of a woman's garment that covers this part of the body. 3. a woman's blouse or blouselike garment that exposes this part of the body. 4. diaphragm *(def. 1).* [Old English *midhrif* diaphragm, from *midd* middle + *hrif* belly.]

mid·sec·tion (mid′sek′shən) *n.* 1. the middle part or section of anything: *the midsection of a country, the midsection of the human body.* 2. midriff *(def. 1).*

mid·ship (mid′ship′) *adj.* of, relating to, or situated in or near the middle of a ship.

mid·ship·man (mid′ship′mən) *n., pl.* -men (-mən). 1. in the U.S. Navy, a student in training at the U.S. Naval Academy for commission as an officer. 2. *British.* a second-year student in training on board ship for commission as an officer. [MIDSHIP + MAN; with reference to the earlier stationing of cadets in the British navy *amidships* when on duty.]

mid·ships (mid′ships′) *adv.* amidships.

mid·size (mid′sīz′) *also,* **mid-size.** *adj.* being a size between large and small; intermediate: *a midsize car that is larger than a compact car.* Also, **mid′sized′, mid′-sized′.**

midst¹ (midst) *n.* 1. the condition or position of being surrounded by, involved in, or beset by. ➡ used chiefly in the phrase *in the midst of: We were in the midst of dinner when you called.* 2. a gathering or association of people; company: *There is a traitor in our midst.* 3. a central or interior part: *Someone shouted in the midst of the speech.* [Partly from MID¹ + -EST¹; partly from Middle English *middes* middle, from the phrase *in middes* in the midst, from Old English *(on) middan* (in) the middle.]

midst² (midst) *also,* ′**midst.** *prep.* amid; amidst. [Form of AMIDST.]

mid·stream (mid′strēm′) *n.* 1. the middle of a stream: *to keep a boat in midstream.* 2. the middle part of a course of action: *The debate was confusing because several of the participants changed their opinions in midstream.* [MID¹ + STREAM.]

mid·sum·mer (mid′sum′ər) *n.* 1. the middle of summer. 2. the summer solstice, occurring about June 21. —*adj.* of, relating to, or occurring in the middle of summer.

mid·term (mid′tûrm′) *n.* 1. the middle of a school term or semester. 2. an examination taken during the middle of a school term or semester. —*adj.* taking place during the middle of a school term or semester: *a midterm vacation.*

mid·town (mid′toun′) *n.* the central part of a city or town. —*adj.* relating to or located in midtown.

mid-Vic·to·ri·an (mid′vik tôr′ē ən) *adj.* 1. of or relating to the middle period of Queen Victoria's reign in Great Britain, from about 1850 to 1880. 2. relating to, resembling, or characteristic of the culture, fashions, ideas, and rigid moral and social standards of this period. —*n.* 1. a person who is prudish or old-fashioned, as in thinking or matters of morality. 2. a person who lived during the mid-Victorian period.

mid·way (*adj., adv.,* mid′wā′; *n.,* mid′wā′) *adj., adv.* in or to the middle of the way or distance; halfway: *the midway point of a journey, to live midway between two places.* —*n.* a place where side shows and other amusements are located, as at a carnival, circus, or fair.

mid·week (*n.,* mid′wēk′; *adj.,* mid′wēk′) *n.* 1. the middle of the week. 2. Midweek. among the Quakers, Wednesday. —*adj.* in the middle of the week. —**mid′week′ly,** *adj., adv.*

mid·wife (mid′wīf′) *n., pl.* -wives (-wīvz′). a woman who is trained to assist women in childbirth. [Middle English *midwif,* from Old English *mid* with + *wīf* woman.]

mid·wife·ry (mid wif′ə rē, -wif′rē, mid′wī′fə rē, -wīf′rē) *n.* the work of a midwife.

mid·win·ter (mid′win′tər) *n.* 1. the middle of winter. 2. the winter solstice, occurring around December 22. —*adj.* of, relating to, or occurring in the middle of winter.

mid·year (*n., def. 1,* mid′yîr′; *n., def. 2, adj.,* mid′yîr′) *n.* 1. the middle of the year. 2. an examination taken during the middle of a school year. —*adj.* taking place during the middle of a school or calendar year.

mien (mēn) *n.* a person's manner or appearance, esp. as expressive of character or mood; bearing: *a person of gentle mien.* [Modification (influenced by French *mine* appearance, look) of obsolete *demean* behavior, from DEMEAN².]

miff (mif) *v.t. Informal.* to cause to be offended or annoyed. [Of uncertain origin.]

MIG (mig) *also,* **MiG, Mig.** *n.* any of various jet fighter planes designed and built by the former Soviet Union. [From Artem *Mi(koyan)* and Mikhail *G(urevich),* Soviet airplane designers.]

might¹ (mīt) *auxiliary verb* 1. the past tense of may. 2. used to express possibility: *What you say might be true, but I'm not sure.* 3. used to ask permission: *Might I use your dictionary for a day or two?* 4. used to offer a suggestion: *You might try starting over and doing it a different way.*

might² (mīt) *n.* 1. great power, force, or influence: *the might of a nation.* 2. physical power or strength: *to slam a door with all one's might, the might of a storm.* 3. the power or ability to do or accomplish something: *I tried with all my might not to laugh at the dumb joke.* [Middle English *myghte,* from Old English *miht, meaht;* of Germanic origin.]

might·i·ly (mī′tə lē) *adv.* 1. with great force, power, or strength. 2. to a great degree; very much; greatly.

might·y (mī′tē) *adj.,* **might·i·er, might·i·est.** 1. having or showing great power, strength, or ability: *a mighty foe.* 2. very great in amount, degree, intensity, or extent: *a mighty task.* —*adv. Informal.* very; greatly: *It was mighty nice of them to call.* —**might′i·ness,** *n.*

mi·gnon (min yon′, min′yon) *adj.* delicately small and pretty. [French *mignon;* of uncertain origin.]

mi·gnon·ette (min′yə net′) *n.* any of various erect or trailing plants, genus *Reseda,* found mostly in the Mediterranean region, bearing narrow spoon-shaped leaves and tiny yellowish white or greenish yellow often fragrant flowers in long spikes or clusters. [French *mignonette* type of flower, diminutive of *mignon* delicate, pretty. See MIGNON.]

mi·graine (mī′grān) *n.* a severe headache, usually affecting only one side of the head and tending to recur periodically. [Old French *migraine,* from Late Latin *hēmicrānia* pain on one side of the head, from Greek *hēmikrāniā,* from *hēmi* half + *kranion* skull.]

mi·grant (mī′grənt) *n.* 1. a person or thing that migrates. 2. a farm laborer who moves from one region to another in search of work. Also, **migrant worker.** —*adj.* characterized by or involving migration; migratory.

mi·grate (mī′grāt) *v.i.,* -grat·ed, -grat·ing. 1. to move from one country or region to another in order to settle there. 2. to move seasonally or periodically from one region or climate to another, as certain birds, mammals, and fish. [Latin *migrātus,* past participle of *migrāre* to move from one place to another.]

mi·gra·tion (mī grā′shən) *n.* 1. an act or instance of migrating. 2. a group, as of people, animals, or fish, that migrate together. 3. *Physics.* diffusion *(def. 3).*

mi·gra·to·ry (mī′grə tôr′ē) *adj.* 1. characterized by or given to migration; migrating: *migratory birds.* 2. of or relating to migration. 3. tending to wander; nomadic; roving.

mi·ka·do (mi kä′dō) *also,* **Mi·ka·do.** *n., pl.* -dos. an emperor of Japan. [Japanese *mikado* literally, exalted gate, from *mi* exalted + *kado* gate.]

mike (mīk) *n. Informal.* microphone. —*v.t.,* miked, mik·ing. to provide with a microphone: *There was no need to mike the singer, whose strong voice could be heard throughout the theater.*

mil (mil) *n.* a unit of length equal to $1/1,000$ of an inch (0.25 millimeter), used in measuring the diameter of wires. [Short for Latin *millēsimus* thousandth, from *mille* thousand.]

mil. 1. mileage. 2. military. 3. militia.

mi·la·dy (mi lā′dē) *also,* **mi·la·di.** *n., pl.* -dies. 1. my lady. ➡ a title of respect used in speaking or referring to an English gentlewoman or noblewoman. 2. a fashionable, well-dressed woman: *styles designed especially for milady.*

M

a	at	e	end	o	hot	u	up	hw	white		about
ā	ape	ē	me	ō	old	ū	use	ng	song		taken
ä	far	i	it	ô	fork	ü	rule	th	thin	ə	pencil
âr	care	ī	ice	oi	oil	u̇	pull	th	this		lemon
		îr	pierce	ou	out	ûr	turn	zh	measure		circus

mil·age (mī′lij) mileage.

milch (milch) *adj.* (of a cow) giving milk. [Old English *-milce*; used in *thrimilce* month of May; literally, (month of) milking three times (a day).]

mild (mīld) *adj.* **1.** not extreme, harsh, or severe, as in intensity, degree, or effect; moderate: *a mild winter, a mild headache.* **2.** not sharp, strong, or bitter in taste or odor: *a mild cheese.* **3.** gentle or kind in disposition, manners, or behavior. [Old English *milde* kind, gentle.] —**mild′ly,** *adv.* —**mild′ness,** *n.*

mil·dew (mil′dū′, -dū′) *n.* **1.** any of various parasitic fungi that attack plants, appearing as a usually white, fine powder or fuzzy down and causing dwarfing, deformation, and loss of the affected parts of the plant. **2.** any of various fungi that appear as discolored areas on leather or other materials. —*v.t., v.i.* to affect or be affected with mildew. [Old English *meledēaw* honeydew; probably referring to the resemblance of certain blights to sticky honey.] —**mil′dew′y,** *adj.*

mile (mīl) *n.* a unit of linear measure equal to 5,280 feet or 1,760 yards (1.609 kilometers). Also, **statute mile.** [Old English *mīl,* from Latin *mīlia (passuum),* plural of *mīlle (passuum)* Roman unit of measure; literally, one thousand (paces).]

mile·age (mī′lij) *also,* **milage.** *n.* **1.** the total number of miles covered or traveled in a specified period of time: *We put a lot of mileage on the car during our vacation.* **2.** the number of miles traveled, as by an automobile, on a certain amount of fuel: *Thirty miles per gallon is good mileage.* **3.** the total length, extent, or distance, given or measured in miles. **4.** the amount of use, service, or wear yielded by something: *The comedian got plenty of mileage from those old jokes.* **5.** an allowance for traveling expenses, estimated at a certain rate per mile. **6.** a rate charged per mile, as for the use of a rented car.

mile·post (mīl′pōst′) *n.* a post set up, as on a highway, to mark the distance in miles to or from a specified place.

mil·er (mī′lər) *n.* a person or animal specially conditioned to run a race of one mile.

mile·stone (mīl′stōn′) *n.* **1.** a stone set up, as on a highway, to mark the distance in miles to or from a certain place. **2.** an important or significant event or development: *The invention of the telephone was a milestone in the history of communications.*

mil·foil (mil′foil′) *n.* yarrow. [Old French *milfoil,* from Latin *mīllefolium,* from *mīlle* thousand + *folium* leaf; referring to the many sections of its leaf.]

mi·lieu (mil yū′, mil ū′, mēl-; *French,* mē lyœ′) *n., pl.* **mi·lieus** (mil yūz′, -ūz′, mēl-) *or French,* **mi·lieux** (mē lyœ′). surroundings or environment. [French *milieu* midst, environment; literally, middle place, going back to Latin *medius* middle + *locus* place.]

mil·i·tant (mil′i tənt) *adj.* **1.** active or aggressive in support of a cause: *The militant protesters occupied the building.* **2.** engaged in war or fighting: *militant nations.* —*n.* a militant person. [Latin *mīlitāns,* present participle of *mīlitāre* to serve as a soldier, from *mīles* soldier.] —**mil′i·tan·cy,** *n.* —**mil′i·tant·ly,** *adv.*

mil·i·ta·rism (mil′i tə riz′əm) *n.* **1.** the glorification of war and the military class and its ideals and policies. **2.** a national policy that emphasizes the power, influence, and predominance of the military.

mil·i·ta·rist (mil′i tər ist) *n.* a person who supports or upholds militarism. —**mil′i·ta·ris′tic,** *adj.*

mil·i·ta·rize (mil′i tə rīz′) *v.t.,* **-rized, -riz·ing. 1.** to change to a military system or adapt for military use. **2.** to train and equip for war. **3.** to imbue with militarism. —**mil′i·ta·ri·za′tion,** *n.*

mil·i·tar·y (mil′i ter′ē) *adj.* **1.** of, relating to, or involving armed forces, soldiers, or war: *a military career.* **2.** composed of or for members of the armed forces: *a military uniform, a military unit.* —*n., pl.* **-tar·ies. 1.** all the military forces of a country, taken as a whole. **2.** the members of the military collectively, esp. officers. [Latin *mīlitāris* relating to a soldier or to war, from *mīles* soldier.] —**mil′i·tar′i·ly,** *adv.*

military academy, an educational institution equivalent to a college, in which men and women are prepared for careers as officers in the armed forces.

military police, members of the army assigned to police duties.

military school, a school in which students follow some of the routines and disciplines typical of military life.

mil·i·tate (mil′i tāt′) *v.i.,* **-tat·ed, -tat·ing.** to act, operate, or have influence (often with *against*): *This testimony will militate against an acquittal.* [Latin *mīlitātus,* past participle of *mīlitāre* to serve as a soldier, from *mīles* soldier.]

mi·li·tia (mi lish′ə) *n.* a nonprofessional military force, such as the National Guard, called for service in time of emergency. [Latin *mīlitia* troops, warfare, from *mīles* soldier.]

mi·li·tia·man (mi lish′ə mən) *n., pl.* **-men** (-mən). a member of a militia.

milk (milk) *n.* **1.a.** a white liquid secreted by the mammary glands of female mammals for the nourishment of their young.

b. this liquid, esp. as secreted by cows, used as food by human beings. **2.** any liquid resembling this: *coconut milk.* —*v.t.* **1.** to draw milk from (a cow, goat, or other female mammal). **2.** to extract juice, poison, or other liquid from, by, or as by milking: *to milk a snake.* **3.** to extract or take (something), as by milking: *to milk information from someone.* **4.** to take advantage of for one's own benefit; exploit: *The blackmailer milked the couple of their savings.* —*v.i.* **1.** to draw milk from a cow, goat, or other female mammal. **2.** to give or yield milk. [Middle English *milk,* from Old English *meolc* white liquid secreted by female mammals; of Germanic origin.]

milk·er (mil′kər) *n.* **1.** a person who milks. **2.** a machine that milks cows. **3.** a cow or other animal that gives milk.

milk·ing (mil′king) *n.* **1.** the act of a person who draws milk from an animal, esp. a cow. **2.** the amount of milk obtained at one time.

milk·maid (milk′mād′) *n.* a woman or girl who milks cows or works in a dairy.

milk·man (milk′man′) *n., pl.* **-men** (-men′). a person who sells or delivers milk.

milk of magnesia, a milky white mixture of magnesium hydroxide in water, used as an antacid and laxative.

milk run *Slang.* a routine flight or mission of an aircraft, usually of short duration and relative safety.

milk shake, a frothy, cold drink made of milk, flavoring, and sometimes ice cream, shaken or whipped together.

milk snake, any of several yellowish brown or pale gray king snakes marked with red or reddish brown blotches. It is harmless to people and feeds chiefly on rodents and other snakes. [Early American; because it was believed they sucked milk from cows.]

milk·sop (milk′sop′) *n.* an unmanly or cowardly man or boy; sissy.

milk sugar, lactose.

milk tooth, in humans and other mammals, one of the temporary teeth that fall out and are replaced by permanent teeth.

milk·weed (milk′wēd′) *n.* any of a large group of plants, genus *Asclepias,* often containing a milky juice and bearing white, red, yellow, or purple flowers and seed pods with a tuft of hairs.

milk·white (milk′hwīt′, -wīt′) *adj.* having the white or bluish white color of milk.

milk·y (mil′kē) *adj.,* **milk·i·er, milk·i·est. 1.** resembling milk, esp. in color. **2.** containing or yielding milk or a milklike substance. **3.** insipid or timid. —**milk′i·ness,** *n.*

Milky Way, a galaxy made up of more than 100 billion stars, of which our sun and solar system are a part, appearing as a bright white path across the heavens. Also, **Galaxy.**

milkweed

mill¹ (mil) *n.* **1.a.** a building or establishment containing machinery for grinding or crushing grain: *flour mill, corn mill.* **b.** a machine or apparatus that grinds or crushes grain. **2.** any of various machines or devices for grinding or crushing substances: *a pepper mill, a coffee mill.* **3.** a building or group of buildings containing machinery for manufacturing or processing materials: *a paper mill.* **4.** milling machine. **5.** an establishment or process that operates in a routine or mechanical manner: *This school is a diploma mill.* —*v.t.* **1.** to subject to the mechanical operations performed by a mill, such as grinding, stamping, pressing, or polishing. **2.a.** to stamp or cut a series of notches or ridges around the edge of (a coin or other piece of metal). **b.** to make a raised edge around (a coin or other piece of metal). —*v.i.* to move in an aimless or confused manner: *The crowd milled around outside the stadium after the game was over.* [Middle English *melle,* from Old English *mylen,* going back to Late Latin *molīnae,* plural of *molīna* mill, from Latin *mola* millstone.] **·through the mill.** through a difficult and trying experience or period.

mill² (mil) *n.* a unit of monetary value used in calculating tax rates in certain U.S. states, equal to ¹⁄₁₀ of a cent. [Short for Latin *mīllesīmus* thousandth, from *mīlle* thousand.]

mill·dam (mil′dam′) *n.* **1.** a dam built across a stream to raise the water level sufficiently to supply water power for a mill. **2.** millpond.

mil·len·ni·al (mi len′ē əl) *adj.* **1.** of or relating to a thousand years. **2.** of, relating to, or suggestive of the millennium.

mil·len·ni·um (mi len′ē əm) *n., pl.* **-len·ni·a** (-len′ē ə) *or* **-len·ni·ums. 1.** a period of a thousand years. **2.** according to the New Testament, the period of a thousand years during which Jesus will

reign on earth. **3.** a period of happiness, peace, and prosperity. [Modern Latin *millennium* period of a thousand years, from Latin *mīlle* thousand + *annus* year.]

mil·le·pede (mil′ə pēd′) millipede.

mil·le·pore (mil′ə pôr′) *n.* any of a group of pink or yellow branching corals, genus *Millipora,* found in tropical reefs. [Modern Latin *Millepora,* from Latin *mīlle* thousand + *porus* pore[1]; with reference to its many pores. See PORE[1].]

mill·er (mil′ər) *n.* **1.** a person who owns or operates a mill, esp. one for grinding grain. **2.** any white or grayish moth whose wings look as if they were powdered with flour.

mill·er's-thumb (mil′ərz thum′) *n.* sculpin.

mil·les·i·mal (mi les′ə məl) *adj.* **1.** thousandth. **2.** of, relating to, or consisting of a thousandth. —*n.* a thousandth. [Latin *millēsimus* thousandth (from *mīlle* thousand) + -AL[1].] —**mil·les′i·mal·ly,** *adv.*

mil·let (mil′it) *n.* **1.** any of several wheatlike grasses widely cultivated for their small, edible grains or as a forage crop, such as **bread millet,** *Panicum miliaceum,* and **foxtail millet,** *Setaria italica.* **2.** the small grain of any of these grasses. [Old French *millet,* diminutive of *mil,* from Latin *milium.*]

milli- *combining form* a thousandth part of: *milligram.* [Latin *mīlle* thousand.]

mil·li·am·pere (mil′ē am′pîr) *n.* $\frac{1}{1,000}$ of an ampere.

mil·liard (mil′yərd, -yärd′) *n. British.* a thousand millions; billion. [French *milliard,* from MILLION.]

mil·li·bar (mil′ə bär′) *n.* a centimeter-gram-second unit for measuring atmospheric pressure, equal to $\frac{1}{1,000}$ of a bar or 1,000 dynes per square centimeter.

mil·li·gram (mil′i gram′) *also, British,* **mil·li·gramme.** *n.* a metric unit of weight equal to $\frac{1}{1,000}$ of a gram.

mil·li·li·ter (mil′ə lē′tər) *also, British,* **mil·li·li·tre.** *n.* a metric measure of capacity equal to $\frac{1}{1,000}$ of a liter.

mil·li·me·ter (mil′ə mē′tər) *also, British,* **mil·li·me·tre.** *n.* a metric measure of length equal to $\frac{1}{1,000}$ of a meter.

mil·li·mi·cron (mil′ə mī′kron) *n.* a metric unit of length equal to $\frac{1}{1,000}$ of a micrometer.

mil·li·ner (mil′ə nər) *n.* a person who designs, makes, trims, or sells women's hats. [Earlier *milaner* dealer in fancy wares, from *Milan,* Italian city famous for its fabrics, hats, gloves, and similar articles.]

mil·li·ner·y (mil′ə ner′ē, -nə rē) *n.* **1.** the articles, esp. hats, sold by a milliner. **2.** the business of a milliner.

mill·ing (mil′ing) *n.* **1.** the act or process of subjecting to the mechanical operations performed by a mill. **2.a.** the process of stamping or cutting notches or ridges around the edge of a piece of metal, as a coin. **b.** the notches or ridges so produced.

milling machine, a machine tool used to cut plane surfaces on metal by means of a rotating cutter.

mil·lion (mil′yən) *n.* **1.** the cardinal number that is one thousand times one thousand. **2.** a symbol representing this number, such as 1,000,000. **3.** a million monetary units, as dollars. **4.** an indefinitely large number: *That store stocks millions of hats.* —*adj.* numbering one million: *a million dollars.* [Old French *million* one thousand times one thousand, through Italian, from Latin *mīlle* thousand.]

mil·lion·aire (mil′yə nâr′) *n.* a person who has a million or more units of a particular currency, as of dollars. [French *millionnaire* one who has more than a million francs, from *million.* See MILLION.]

mil·lion·air·ess (mil′yə nâr′is) *n.* a woman who has a million or more units of a particular currency, as of dollars.

mil·lionth (mil′yənth) *adj.* **1.** (the ordinal of million) being last in a series of one million. **2.** being one of a million equal parts. —*n.* **1.** something that is last in a series of one million. **2.** one of a million equal parts.

mil·li·pede (mil′ə pēd′) *also,* **millepede.** *n.* any of a group of wormlike arthropods, class Diplopoda, having a body of twenty to over sixty segments, each with two legs, and feeding chiefly on decaying plant matter. [Latin *millepeda* wood louse; literally, thousand feet, from *mīlle* thousand + *ped-,* stem of *pēs* foot.]

mil·li·sec·ond (mil′ə sek′ənd) *n.* $\frac{1}{1,000}$ of a second.

mill·pond (mil′pond′) *n.* a pond, usually formed by a dam, for supplying water power to a mill. Also, **milldam.**

mill·race (mil′rās′) *n.* **1.** a current of water leading into and driving a mill wheel. **2.** the channel through which such a current runs.

mill·stone (mil′stōn′) *n.* **1.** either of a pair of circular stones between which grain or similar substances are placed for grinding. **2.** a heavy burden: *a millstone of debt.*

mill·stream (mil′strēm′) *n.* **1.** a stream whose water is used to run a mill. **2.** the water in a millrace.

mill wheel, a large wheel, usually turned by the force of falling

water, that supplies mechanical power to run the machinery of a mill.

mill·work (mil′wûrk′) *n.* **1.** ready-made products, esp. woodwork, finished or processed in a mill. **2.** the work done in a mill. —**mill′work′er,** *n.*

mill·wright (mil′rīt′) *n.* a person who designs or builds mills or installs and repairs machinery for mills.

mi·lo (mī′lō) *n., pl.* **-los.** a variety of grain sorghum bearing compact clusters of soft, white or yellow seeds, used as animal feed. [Bantu *maili.*]

mi·lord (mi lôrd′) *n.* my lord. ➡ a title of respect used in speaking or referring to an English gentleman or nobleman.

milque·toast (milk′tōst′) *n.* a weak, timid, apologetic person. [From Caspar *Milquetoast,* U.S. comic-strip character.]

milt (milt) *n.* in male fish, the sperm cells and the milky fluid containing them. [Probably from Middle Dutch *milte* milt of fish, spleen.]

Mil·ton·ic (mil ton′ik) *adj.* **1.** of or relating to the English poet John Milton or his works. **2.** characteristic of Milton's literary style; lofty and majestic. Also, **Mil·to·ni·an** (mil tō′nē ən).

mime (mīm) *n.* **1.** a performer who portrays characters or conveys an idea or story by body movements, facial expressions, and gestures rather than by the use of speech. **2.** the art of pantomime. **3.a.** a farcical drama popular among the ancient Greeks and Romans, in which actual persons and events were mimicked or ludicrously portrayed. **b.** an actor in such a drama. —*v.,* **mimed, mim·ing.** —*v.t.* to act out in mime; portray by pantomime. —*v.i.* to act or perform as a mime. [Latin *mīmus* actor, farce, from Greek *mīmos* imitator, actor, farce.] —**mim′er,** *n.*

mim·e·o·graph (mim′ē ə graf′) *n.* **1.** a machine for printing copies of material written, typed, or drawn on a stencil. **2.** a copy made by such a machine. —*v.t.* to reproduce on a mimeograph: *to mimeograph a financial report.* [From *Mimeograph,* the trademark for this machine.]

mi·met·ic (mi met′ik, mī-) *adj.* **1.** relating to, characterized by, or exhibiting mimicry: *a mimetic portrayal, the mimetic coloration of certain insects.* **2.** make-believe; mimic. [Greek *mīmētikos* imitative, from *mīmeisthai* to imitate.] —**mi·met′i·cal·ly,** *adv.*

mim·ic (mim′ik) *v.t.,* **-icked, -ick·ing. 1.** to imitate the speech, manners, or gestures of, esp. so as to ridicule. **2.** to copy closely or reproduce: *to mimic a painter's style.* **3.** to resemble closely, as in form or color; simulate: *The insect mimicked a dead twig.* —*n.* **1.** a person who mimics, esp. a performer skilled in mime. **2.** something that is a copy; imitation. —*adj.* **1.** of the nature of or characterized by mimicry; imitative. **2.** make-believe; pretended; mock: *mimic rivalry.* [Latin *mīmicus* farcical, from Greek *mīmikos* imitative, relating to farce, from *mīmos* actor, imitator, farce.] —**mim′ick·er,** *n.* —For Synonyms *(v.t.),* see **imitate.**

mim·ic·ry (mim′i krē) *n., pl.* **-ries. 1.** the act, practice, or art of mimicking. **2.** *Biology.* close external resemblance of one kind of organism to another or to an object in its natural environment, esp. as evolved for concealment or protection, as among certain plants and insects.

mi·mo·sa (mi mō′sə, -zə) *n.* **1.** any of a large group of plants, genus *Mimosa,* of the pea family, found esp. in tropical America, bearing fernlike leaves and dense heads or spikes of small white, pink, or purple flowers. **2.** a cocktail consisting of orange juice and champagne. [Modern Latin *Mimosa,* going back to Greek *mīmos* imitator, actor, farce; because in folding its leaves when touched, the mimosa mimics the reactions of animals.]

min *also,* **min.** minute; minutes.

min. 1. mineralogical. **2.** mineralogy. **3.** minimum. **4.** mining.

mi·na[1] (mī′nə) *n., pl.* **-nas** or **-nae** (-nē). an ancient unit of weight and money of varying amount and value. [Latin *mina* Greek unit of weight or money, from Greek *mnā;* of Semitic origin.]

mi·na[2] (mī′nə) *n.* myna.

mi·nae (mī′nē) a plural of **mina**[1].

min·a·ret (min′ə ret′) *n.* a tall, slender tower attached to a mosque and having one or more projecting balconies. [Spanish *minarete,* from Arabic *manārat.*]

min·a·to·ry (min′ə tôr′ē) *adj.* expressing or uttering a threat; menacing. Also, **min′a·to′ri·al.** [Late Latin *minātōrius,* from Latin *minārī* to threaten.]

mince (mins) *v.,* **minced, minc·ing.** —*v.t.* **1.** to cut or chop into very small, fine pieces: *to mince an onion.* **2.** to weaken or

a	at	e	end	o	hot	u	up	hw	white		about
ā	ape	ē	me	ō	old	ū	use	ng	song		taken
ä	far	i	it	ô	fork	ü	rule	th	thin	ə	pencil
âr	care	ī	ice	oi	oil	u̇	pull	th	this		lemon
		îr	pierce	ou	out	ûr	turn	zh	measure		circus

restrain the force or effect of (words) for the sake of politeness or decorum: *I don't mince words when I am angry.* **3.** to utter, express, or do with affected elegance, politeness, or refinement. —*v.i.* **1.** to walk in an affectedly dainty way with very short steps. **2.** to act or speak with affected elegance, politeness, or refinement. —*n.* mincemeat. [Old French *mincier* to cut into small pieces, going back to Latin *minūtia* smallness.] —**minc′er,** *n.*

mince·meat (mins′mēt′) *n.* a mixture of finely chopped apples, suet, raisins, currants, sugar, spices, and sometimes meat, used for pies.
· **to make mincemeat out of.** to destroy completely.

mince pie, a pie made with mincemeat.

minc·ing (min′sing) *adj.* affectedly dainty, refined, or polite, as in speech or manner. —**minc′ing·ly,** *adv.*

mind (mīnd) *n.* **1.** the totality of functions, associated with or involving the brain and related nerve cells, that deal with the conscious and unconscious processes of thought, perception, memory, imagination, will, and reason. **2.** the mind regarded as the source or repository of cognition and the intellectual aspects of consciousness. ➡ opposed to **heart** *(def. 5).* **3.** intellectual powers or mental ability; intelligence: *the mind of a five-year-old child.* **4.** a sound or healthy mental state or condition; sanity: *to lose one's mind.* **5.** imagination: *It's all in your mind.* **6.** a way of thinking or feeling; disposition: *to have an open mind.* **7.** what one thinks or feels; opinion or attitude: *I always try to speak my mind.* **8.** the fixing of one's thoughts on something; attention: *I can't keep my mind on what I'm doing.* **9.** a person regarded as having a highly developed intellect: *one of the great minds of the century.* —*v.t.* **1.** to pay careful attention to; concern or occupy oneself with: *Mind what the doctor says. Mind your own affairs. Tell the children to mind their manners.* **2.** to take care of; look after: *The baby-sitter will mind the children while I go shopping.* **3.** to obey: *The children always mind the teacher.* **4.** to object to: *I don't mind eating alone. I hope you won't mind mailing some letters for me.* **5.** to look or watch out for: *Mind the broken chair.* —*v.i.* **1.** to object or care: *Do you mind if I call you later?* **2.** to pay careful attention: *Mind now, this is the important part of the story.* **3.** to be obedient: *The puppy must learn to mind.* **4.** to be careful or wary: *If you don't mind, you'll fall.* [Old English *gemynd* memory, thought.] —**mind′er,** *n.*
· **a piece of one's mind. a.** a severe rebuke or scolding. **b.** one's harsh opinion.
· **never mind.** disregard or forget it; it doesn't matter.
· **on one's mind.** occupying one's thoughts.
· **to bear** (or **keep**) **in mind.** to remember.
· **to be of one mind.** to be in agreement.
· **to be of two minds.** to be undecided or uncertain.
· **to blow one's mind.** *Slang.* to astound or overwhelm, as with intense pleasure, amazement, excitement, or confusion.
· **to call to mind.** to serve as a reminder of.
· **to have a** (**good**) **mind.** to feel strongly inclined (to do something): *I have a good mind to go see them right now.*
· **to have in mind. a.** to be thinking of or about. **b.** to intend or plan: *What do you have in mind for us to do?*
· **to make up one's mind.** to come to a judgment or conclusion.
· **to slip one's mind.** to be forgotten.

mind-al·ter·ing (mīnd′ôl′tər ing) *adj.* having an effect on the mind or normal state of consciousness: *a mind-altering drug.*

mind-blow·ing (mīnd′blō′ing) *Slang. adj.* causing intense pleasure, amazement, excitement, or the like; astounding or overwhelming: *The roller-coaster ride was a mind-blowing experience.* [From *to blow (one's) mind* to amaze.] —**mind′-blow′er,** *n.*

mind-bog·gling (mīnd′bog′ling) *adj.* causing confusion or lack of comprehension, often because of great size, extent, or complexity: *a mind-boggling math problem.*

mind·ed (mīn′did) *adj.* **1.** favorably disposed; inclined: *Make those revisions if you are so minded.* **2.** having or marked by a (specified kind of) mind. ➡ used in combination in def. 2, as in *open-minded, narrow-minded.*

mind·ful (mīnd′fəl) *adj.* conscious, aware, or careful (with *of*): *Are you mindful of the risks involved?* —**mind′ful·ly,** *adv.* —**mind′ful·ness,** *n.*

mind·less (mīnd′lis) *adj.* **1.** lacking intelligence; stupid or foolish: *a mindless person.* **2.** without thought; heedless (with *of*): *to appear mindless of courtesy.* —**mind′less·ly,** *adv.* —**mind′less·ness,** *n.*

mind reader, a person who professes to have or is thought to have the ability to know or perceive the thoughts of others without normal or apparent communication. —**mind reading.**

mind·set (mīnd′set′) *n.* a state of mind that is rigidly fixed; point of view firmly held.

mind's eye, imagination or recollection: *I can see our old house in my mind's eye.*

mine¹ (mīn) *pron.* **1.** of, relating to, or belonging to me: *That*

coat is mine. ➡ used with *of* after a noun or pronoun: *a friend of mine.* **2.** the one or ones that relate or belong to me: *Your cat is three years old and mine is four.* ➡ **Mine** is the absolute form of the possessive adjective *my,* used when no noun follows. It is used as singular or plural depending on the noun to which it refers. —*adj. Archaic.* my. ➡ used before a word beginning with a vowel or *h,* or after a noun: *mine eyes, mine heart, mother mine.* [Old English *mīn* my, of me.]

mine² (mīn) *n.* **1.a.** an excavation from which coal, mineral ores, or other materials are extracted. **b.** the site of such an excavation, including shafts, buildings, and mining equipment. **2.** a deposit of coal, mineral ore, or other material that may be extracted from the earth. **3.** any abundant source or supply: *a mine of information.* **4.** an encased explosive charge placed underground or in water and designed to be detonated, used to destroy enemy personnel or equipment. **5.** formerly, a tunnel beneath the walls of an enemy fortification, as for the placement of explosives. —*v.,* **mined, min·ing.** —*v.t.* **1.** to extract from the earth: *to mine coal.* **2.** to excavate (the earth), as for coal or mineral ores. **3.** to make by digging, as a tunnel. **4.** to place explosive mines in or under: *The enemy mined the harbor.* **5.** to dig a tunnel beneath the surface of, as for the placement of explosives. **6.** to attack, weaken, or destroy by gradual or secret means; undermine. **7.** to make use of in order to obtain something: *to mine a book for information.* —*v.i.* **1.** to excavate the earth, as for coal or precious stones; dig a mine: *to mine for coal.* **2.** to work in a mine. **3.** to dig a tunnel or tunnels, as for the placement of explosives: *The enemy mined under the wall.* **4.** to place explosive mines underground or in water. [Old French *miner* to dig under, excavate, undermine, from Medieval French *mine* mine²; of Celtic origin.]

mine detector, an electromagnetic device used for locating the position of explosive mines.

mine·field (mīn′fēld′) *n.* an area of land or water in which explosive mines have been laid.

mine·lay·er (mīn′lā′ər) *n.* a ship equipped to place explosive mines in the water.

min·er (mī′nər) *n.* **1.** a person who mines, esp. one whose occupation is excavating the earth for coal or other materials. Also, **mineworker. 2.** a machine used in automated mining.

min·er·al (min′ər əl) *n.* **1.** any of various inorganic substances that occur in nature, having a characteristic composition that can be expressed by a chemical formula, as well as an orderly atomic structure that gives rise to a characteristic crystal form. **2.** a substance obtained by excavating or drilling into the earth, such as iron ore or petroleum. **3.** any inorganic substance, such as iron or calcium, ingestion of which is required for the proper functioning of an organism. —*adj.* **1.** of, relating to, consisting of, or of the nature of a mineral or minerals: *mineral ores.* **2.** impregnated with minerals. **3.** not vegetable or animal; nonliving or inorganic: *Is it animal, vegetable, or mineral?* [Old French *mineral* substance that contains a metal, from *miniere* mine of metals, from *miner.* See MINE².]

min·er·al·ize (min′ər ə līz′) *v.t.,* **-ized, -iz·ing. 1.** to convert or transform (a metal or other substance) into a mineral. **2.** to impregnate or supply with minerals. —**min′er·al·i·za′tion,** *n.*

min·er·al·o·gist (min′ə rol′ə jist, -ral′-) *n.* a person who is a specialist or expert in mineralogy.

min·er·al·o·gy (min′ə rol′ə jē, -ral′-) *n.* the science or study of minerals, esp. with regard to their origin, structure, characteristics, and classification. —**min·er·al·og·i·cal** (min′ər ə loj′i kəl), *adj.* —**min′er·al·og′i·cal·ly,** *adv.*

mineral oil, any of a group of colorless, nearly odorless, and tasteless oils obtained as a by-product of petroleum refining, often used as a laxative.

mineral spring, a spring that contains natural mineral water.

mineral water, water containing dissolved mineral salts and gases, used as a beverage and for medicinal purposes, esp. bathing.

mineral wool, a fibrous material resembling wool, made by forcing air or steam through molten rock or slag, used like glass wool for thermal insulation and soundproofing in building construction. Also, **rock wool.**

Mi·ner·va (mi nur′və) *n.* in Roman mythology, the goddess of wisdom, arts, crafts, and warfare. Her Greek counterpart is Athena.

min·e·stro·ne (min′ə strō′nē) *n.* a thick soup containing vegetables, beans, pasta, barley, and seasonings in a chicken or meat broth. [Italian *minestrone,* from *minestra* soup; literally, something served, going back to Latin *ministrāre* to serve.]

mine·sweep·er (mīn′swē′pər) *n.* a ship or device used to detect, remove, or destroy marine mines.

mine·work·er (mīn′wûr′kər) *n.* miner *(def. 1).*

Ming (ming) *n.* a Chinese dynasty that ruled from 1368 to 1644, a period noted for artistic achievement. —*adj.* of or relating to this dynasty or the art of this period: *a Ming porcelain.*

min·gle (ming′gəl) *v.,* -gled, -gling. —*v.i.* **1.** to be or become mixed or joined together. **2.** to associate, join in, or come into contact (often with *with*): *to mingle with the other guests at a party.* —*v.t.* to mix or join (something) together: *to mingle joy with sadness.* [Middle English *menglen* to join together, going back to Old English *mengan* to mix.] —**min′gler,** *n.*

Ming vase

min·i (min′ē) *n., pl.* -is. something that is smaller or shorter than usual, such as a minicomputer or miniskirt. —*adj.* smaller or shorter than usual: *a mini refrigerator, a mini umbrella.* [From MINI-.]

mini- *combining form* smaller or shorter than usual: *miniskirt.* [Probably short for MINIATURE or MINIMUM.]

min·i·a·ture (min′ē ə chər, min′ə-) *adj.* existing or represented on a small or greatly reduced scale; diminutive: *a miniature poodle.* —*n.* **1.** a copy or representation on a small or greatly reduced scale: *a miniature of the Statue of Liberty.* **2.a.** a painting, usually a portrait, done on a very small scale and in minute detail, as on ivory. **b.** the art or technique of doing such paintings. **3.** a small, highly detailed drawing or painting in an illuminated manuscript. [Italian *miniatura* small picture, illumination of manuscripts, going back to Latin *miniāre* to paint with red lead, from *minium* red lead; referring to the decorating of medieval manuscripts with *minium* and to the small size of the illustrations so done. See MINIUM.]

·in miniature, on a small scale.

min·i·a·tur·ize (min′ē ə chə rīz′, min′ə-) *v.t.,* -ized, -iz·ing. to make or design on a very small scale. —**min′i·a·tur·i·za′tion,** *n.*

min·i·bike (min′ē bīk′) *n.* a small, light motorcycle.

min·i·bus (min′ē bus′) *n.* a small bus, usually used for transporting a small number of people short distances.

min·i·cam (min′ē kam′) *n.* a lightweight, portable television camera. [MINI- + CAM(ERA).]

min·i·com·put·er (min′ē kəm pū′tər) *n.* a computer larger than a microcomputer but smaller than a mainframe, used in business, manufacturing, and scientific research.

min·im (min′im) *n.* **1.** an apothecaries' measure for very small amounts of liquid, equal to ¹⁄₆₀ of a fluid dram, or approximately one drop. **2.** a very small or insignificant portion or thing. **3.** *Music.* half note. [Latin *minimus* smallest, least.]

min·i·ma (min′ə mə) a plural of **minimum.**

min·i·mal (min′ə məl) *adj.* of a minimum amount or degree; least possible or smallest; very small. —**min′i·mal·ly,** *adv.*

min·i·mize (min′ə mīz′) *v.t.,* -mized, -miz·ing. **1.** to reduce to the smallest or least possible amount or degree; make as small as possible: *Hostility on both sides minimized the chance of reaching an agreement.* **2.** to represent or treat as being of small importance, value, amount, or degree: *Don't minimize your contribution to the success of the project.* —**min′i·mi·za′tion,** *n.* —**min′i·miz′er,** *n.*

min·i·mum (min′ə məm) *n., pl.* -mums or -ma (-mə). **1.** the least possible or smallest amount or degree: *We will need a minimum of one week to drive there.* **2.** the lowest point, degree, or number reached or recorded: *The temperature was at its minimum for the day at six o'clock this morning.* —*adj.* least, lowest, smallest, or fewest possible, allowable, or reached: *to meet the minimum qualifications for a loan.* [Latin *minimum,* neuter of *minimus* smallest, least.]

minimum wage, the lowest hourly wage, fixed by law, that an employer may pay an employee of a specified category.

min·ing (mī′ning) *n.* **1.** the act, process, or business of excavating and working mines for coal, ores, gems, or other materials. **2.** the act or process of laying explosive mines.

min·ion (min′yən) *n.* **1.** a favorite, follower, or dependent, esp. one who acts servile. ➡ often used contemptuously. **2.** a subordinate or minor official: *minions of the government.* [French *mignon* delicate, pretty; of uncertain origin.]

min·i·se·ries (min′ē sîr′ēz) *n.* a television drama broadcast in several episodes: *a six-part miniseries about the American Civil War.*

min·i·skirt (min′ē skûrt′) *n.* a short skirt, usually ending several inches above the knee. [MINI- + SKIRT.]

min·is·ter (min′ə stər) *n.* **1.** a person who is authorized to perform religious functions in a church, esp. in a Protestant church. **2.** a person who heads an executive governmental department: *a minister of finance.* **3.** a diplomatic agent ranking below an ambassador and acting as a government's chief representative in a foreign country to which an ambassador is not sent. **4.** a person or thing that acts as the agent or instrument of another person or thing. —*v.i.* to give aid, care, or attention (often with *to*): *to minister to someone's needs.* —*v.t.* **1.** to administer, apply, or dispose: *to minister a sacrament.* **2.** *Archaic.* to provide; furnish. [Old French *ministre* servant, minister, from Latin *minister* servant, helper, priest's assistant, going back to Latin *minor* minor.]

min·is·te·ri·al (min′ə stîr′ē əl) *adj.* **1.** of, relating to, or characteristic of religion or the ministry. **2.** of, relating to, or characteristic of a minister of state or executive functions of government. **3.** *Law.* of or relating to actions of a public official in carrying out orders, rather than in making policy, or discretionary, decisions. **4.** acting as an agent. —**min′is·te′ri·al·ly,** *adv.*

minister plenipotentiary *pl.* **ministers plenipotentiary.** plenipotentiary.

min·is·trant (min′ə strənt) *adj.* serving as a minister. —*n.* a person who ministers. [Latin *ministrāns,* present participle of *ministrāre* to serve.]

min·is·tra·tion (min′ə strā′shən) *n.* **1.** the act or process or an instance of giving aid. **2.** the act of serving as a minister of religion.

min·is·try (min′ə strē) *n., pl.* -tries. **1.** the profession, duties, functions, or time of service of a minister of religion. **2.** ministers of religion collectively; the clergy. **3.a.** a governmental department headed by a minister. **b.** the offices or building of such a department. **c.** governmental ministers collectively. **d.** the duties, functions, or term of office of a governmental minister. **4.** the act of ministering; ministration. [Latin *ministerium* service, office.]

min·i·um (min′ē əm) *n.* red lead. [Latin *minium;* probably of Iberian origin.]

min·i·van (min′ē van′) *n.* a small van designed primarily for passengers, usually taller than a station wagon, with several rows of seats and side and rear windows. [MINI- + VAN¹.]

min·i·ver (min′ə vər) *n.* fur, usually white or white mixed with gray or black, formerly used for trimming and lining garments. [Old French *menu vair* literally, small vair, going back to Latin *minūtus* small + *varius* of various colors. See VAIR.]

mink (mingk) *n., pl.* **mink** or **minks.** **1.** a weasellike, semiaquatic mammal, genus *Mustela,* native to northern woodlands, having soft, lustrous brown fur. There are two species: the **American mink,** *M. vison,* and the **European mink,** *M. lutreola.* Length: 2½ feet (0.8 meter), including tail. **2.** the valuable fur of this animal. [Middle English *minke;* of Scandinavian origin.]

mink

min·ke whale (ming′kē) *also,* **Min·ke whale.** a small, widely distributed finback whale, *Balaenoptera acutorostrata.* Length: to 30 feet (9.1 meters). [Possibly from *Meincke,* the name of a crew member on a 19th-century Norwegian whaling ship, who thought these whales were blue whales.]

Minn., Minnesota.

min·ne·sing·er (min′ə sing′ər) *n.* one of a group of poet-musicians of twelfth- to fourteenth-century Germany. [German *Minnesinger,* from *Minne* love + *Singer* singer; because love was the main theme of the poems and songs they composed.]

min·now (min′ō) *n.* **1.** any of a large number of small freshwater fish of the carp family, Cyprinidae, such as the dace and shiner, found in temperate and tropical regions and widely used as bait. **2.** any very small fish. [Middle English *menow,* from Old English *myne* any of various small fish.]

Mi·no·an (mi nō′ən) *adj.* of or relating to the civilization of Crete from about 2500 B.C. to about 1100 B.C. —*n.* a native or inhabitant of ancient Crete. [MINOS + -AN.]

a	at	e	end	o	hot	u	up	hw	white		about
ā	ape	ē	me	ō	old	ū	use	ng	song		taken
ä	far	i	it	ô	fork	ü	rule	th	thin	ə	pencil
âr	care	ī	ice	oi	oil	ů	pull	th	this		lemon
		îr	pierce	ou	out	ûr	turn	zh	measure		circus

mi·nor (mī′nər) *adj.* **1.** of small or comparatively small importance or rank: *minor details, one of Shakespeare's minor plays.* **2.** lesser in seriousness, risk, or danger: *minor injuries.* **3.** lesser or limited in extent, size, amount, or degree: *The invention was ingenious but of only minor usefulness.* **4.** under legal age. **5.** *Music.* **a.** of or relating to an interval less by a half step than the corresponding major interval. **b.** based on a minor scale. **c.** of or relating to a triad in which the third tone above the fundamental is less by half a step than the corresponding major tone. —*n.* **1.** a person who is under legal age. ➡ opposed to **adult** *(def. 3).* **2.a.** a subject or field of study in which a college or university student takes a large number of courses or credits, but not enough to qualify that subject as a major. **b.** a student studying a minor: *to be a philosophy minor.* **3.** *Music.* a minor scale, key, mode, or interval. **4.** *Sports.* **a.** minor league. **b. minors.** minor leagues collectively. —*v.i.* to take courses in a specified academic minor (with *in*): *to minor in English literature.* [Latin *minor* less, smaller.]

Mi·nor·ca (mi nôr′kə) *n.* one of a breed of black or white domestic fowl. [From *Minorca*, one of the Balearic Islands.]

mi·nor·i·ty (mə nôr′i tē, -nor′-, mī-) *n., pl.* **-ties. 1.** a number or group smaller than another number or group with which it makes up a whole; portion constituting less than half of a total: *Only a minority of students attended the dance.* **2.** a racial, religious, political, or other group differing in some way from the larger group of which it is a part. **3.** the state or period of being under legal age. **4.** a group or political party having fewer than half the votes or members, as in a legislature: *the Republican minority in Congress.* [Medieval Latin *minoritas* a being less, from Latin *minor* smaller, less.]

minority leader, a member of the political party that holds a minority of seats in a legislative body who organizes the members of the party regarding party tactics and measures to be voted on.

minor league, any league of professional sports clubs, esp. baseball, other than the major leagues. —**mi′nor-league′,** *adj.*

minor premise, the premise in a syllogism that contains the minor term. See **syllogism.**

minor scale, a diatonic scale consisting of eight tones. There are three forms of the minor scale: the **natural minor scale,** having half steps between the second and third and the fifth and sixth tones ascending and between the sixth and fifth and the third and second descending; the **melodic minor scale,** having half steps between the second and third and the seventh and eighth ascending and between the sixth and fifth and the third and second descending; the **harmonic minor scale,** having half steps between the second and third, the fifth and sixth, and the seventh and eighth ascending and between the eighth and seventh, the sixth and fifth, and the third and second descending.

minor term, the term of a syllogism that forms the subject of the conclusion. In the syllogism *All men are mortal; Socrates is a man; therefore, Socrates is mortal,* the name *Socrates* is the minor term.

Mi·nos (mī′nəs, -nos) *n. Greek Legend.* **1.** a king of Crete who became a judge of the dead in Hades. **2.** a grandson of Minos and husband of Pasiphaë who kept the Minotaur in a labyrinth.

Min·o·taur (min′ə tôr′) *n.* in Greek legend, a monster, half bull and half man, the offspring of Pasiphaë and a bull. It was confined by Minos in a labyrinth until killed by Theseus. [Latin *Mīnōtaurus,* from Greek *Mīnōtauros,* from *Mīnōs* (see MINOS) + *tauros* bull.]

min·ox·i·dil (mi nok′si dil) *n.* a vasodilator used to treat hypertension and certain kinds of baldness. Formula: $C_9H_{15}N_5O$

min·ster (min′stər) *n.* **1.** a church attached to a monastery. **2.** a cathedral or other large or important church. [Old English *mynster,* going back to Church Latin *monastērium* monastery, from Late Greek *monastērion,* from *monazein* to live alone. Doublet of MONASTERY.]

min·strel (min′strəl) *n.* **1.** in the Middle Ages, a traveling musician who sang or recited poems, usually to the accompaniment of a harp, lute, or similar instrument. **2.** any musician, singer, or lyric poet. **3.** a performer in a minstrel show. [Old French *menestrel* entertainer, servant, from Late Latin *ministeriālis* official, servant, from Latin *ministerium* service.]

minstrel show, a variety show popular in the United States during the nineteenth and early twentieth centuries, in which performers in blackface presented songs, dances, comic dialogues, and sketches.

min·strel·sy (min′strəl sē) *n., pl.* **-sies. 1.** the art or occupation of a minstrel. **2.** a collection of songs, lyrics, and ballads, such as those sung by minstrels. **3.** a company or group of minstrels.

mint[1] (mint) *n.* **1.** any of a large number of plants of the mint family, esp. those of the genus *Mentha,* such as the peppermint or spearmint, used as a flavoring or scent. For illustration, see **herb. 2.** a piece of candy flavored with mint. —*adj.* designating a family, Labiatae, also known as Lamiaceae, of widely distributed herbs and shrubs, many of which are cultivated for their flavor or odor, such as thyme and lavender. [Middle English *mynte,* from Old English *minte* the plant, going back to Latin *menta;* possibly of Greek origin.] —**mint′y,** *adj.*

mint[2] (mint) *n.* **1.** a place where money is coined by authority of the government. **2.** a very large amount, esp. of money: *We spent a mint getting our car repaired.* **3.** a place where something is made or created. —*adj.* unused or seeming as if unused: *in mint condition, a mint stamp.* —*v.t.* **1.** to coin (money). **2.** to create or invent, esp. a phrase or word. [Middle English *mynt,* from Old English *mynet* coin, money, going back to Latin *monēta* mint, coin, from *Monēta,* epithet of Juno, in whose temple money was coined in ancient Rome.] —**mint′er,** *n.*

mint·age (min′tij) *n.* **1.** the act or process of coining money. **2.** the money manufactured by a mint. **3.** the cost of, or charge for, minting or coining. **4.** an impression stamped on a coin.

mint julep, an alcoholic beverage usually made with bourbon, sugar, and ice, flavored with mint leaves. Also, **julep.**

min·u·end (min′ū end′) *n.* a number from which another is to be subtracted. In the equation $31 - 7 = 24$, 31 is the minuend. ➡ distinguished from **subtrahend.** [Latin *minuendus* to be made smaller, gerundive of *minuere* to make smaller.]

min·u·et (min′ū et′) *n.* **1.** a slow, stately dance for couples, introduced in seventeenth-century France. **2.** music for, or in the rhythm of, this dance. [French *menuet,* diminutive of *menu* small, from Latin *minūtus;* referring to the short steps characteristic of this dance.]

mi·nus (mī′nəs) *prep.* **1.** decreased by; less: *Ten minus seven is three.* **2.** without; lacking. —*adj.* **1.** negative. **2.** somewhat lower than; less than: *a grade of A minus.* —*n.* **1.** minus sign. **2.** a negative quantity. **3.** a deficiency or loss. [Latin *minus,* neuter of *minor* smaller, less.]

min·us·cule (min′ə skūl′, mi nus′kūl) *adj.* very small; tiny.

minus sign, a symbol ($-$) used to indicate subtraction or a negative quantity. Also, **minus.**

min·ute[1] (min′it) *n.* **1.** a unit of time equal to 1/60 of an hour; sixty seconds. **2.** a short period of time; moment: *This phone call will just take a minute.* **3.** a specific point in time: *I recognized you the minute you entered the room.* **4.** a measure of distance in terms of the time needed to cover it: *The park is only a few minutes from my house.* **5. minutes.** an official record of proceedings at a meeting or conference. **6.** a unit of angular measurement equal to 1/60 of a degree. [Old French *minute* 1/60 of an hour, short time, from Medieval Latin *minuta* 1/60 of an hour, 1/60 of a degree, going back to Latin *minūtus* small. See MINUTE[2].]

• **up to the minute.** conforming to or reflecting the very latest, as in style or thought.

mi·nute[2] (mī nūt′, -nūt′, mi-) *adj.* **1.** very small; tiny: *minute grains of salt.* **2.** of small importance; trifling: *minute details.* **3.** characterized by close attention to details: *a minute examination.* [Middle English *minute,* from Latin *minūtus* small, past participle of *minuere* to lessen, make fewer, from *minor* less, smaller.] —**mi·nute′ness,** *n.*

minute hand (min′it) the hand, usually longer than the hour hand, that indicates minutes on a clock or watch.

min·ute·ly[1] (min′it lē) *adv.* every minute. [MINUTE[1] + -LY[1].]

mi·nute·ly[2] (mī nūt′lē, -nūt′-, mi-) *adv.* in a minute manner or degree; in minute detail. [MINUTE[2] + -LY[2].]

min·ute·man (min′it man′) *also,* **Min·ute·man.** *n., pl.* **-men** (-men′). a volunteer militiaman during the American Revolution, ready to fight at a minute's notice.

minute steak, a boneless, thin piece of beef that can be quickly cooked.

mi·nu·ti·ae (mi nü′shē ē′, -nū′-) *pl. n., sing.* **-ti·a** (-shē ə). small or unimportant details. [Late Latin *minūtiae,* plural of Latin *minūtia* smallness.]

minx (mingks) *n.* a pert or flirtatious girl. [Possibly from Low German *minsk* female servant.]

Mi·o·cene (mī′ə sēn′) *n.* **1.** the fourth geologic epoch of the Tertiary period of the Cenozoic era, during which ruminants and other grazing animals, such as the horse, giraffe, and elephant, evolved and multiplied rapidly. For table, see **geologic time. 2.** the strata formed during this epoch. —*adj.* of or relating to this epoch: *Miocene fish fossils.* [Greek *meiōn* less + *kainos* new, recent.]

mir·a·cle (mir′ə kəl) *n.* **1.** an event that cannot be explained scientifically and is therefore often attributed to a divine or supernatural power. **2.** an amazing or marvelous occurrence or thing: *the miracle of spring.* **3.** an outstanding or remarkable example: *a miracle of wisdom.* **4.** miracle play. [Old French *miracle* act of divine power contrary to the laws of nature, from Latin *mīrāculum* wonderful thing, marvel, going back to *mīrus* wonderful.]

miracle play, a religious drama popular in the Middle Ages, based on legends and stories about the saints.

mi·rac·u·lous (mi rak′yə ləs) *adj.* **1.** brought about by a divine or supernatural power; of the nature of a miracle. **2.** amazing; extraordinary; incredible: *a miraculous escape.* **3.** working or having the power to work wonders: *a miraculous medicine.* —**mi·rac′u·lous·ly,** *adv.* —**mi·rac′u·lous·ness,** *n.*

mi·rage (mi räzh′) *n.* **1.** an optical illusion, such as the appearance of a sheet of water on a highway, caused by differences in the way that layers of air having different densities and temperatures refract light. **2.** something that seems real but is only illusory. [French *mirage,* from *mirer* to look at, from Late Latin *mīrāre* to behold, from Latin *mīrārī* to wonder at.]

Mi·ran·da warning (mə ran′də) a warning that officers of the law must give to anyone arrested or taken into custody. It must include mention of the right to remain silent, the right to consult an attorney, and the fact that anything said may be used in court against the person in custody. [From Ernesto A. *Miranda,* the defendant in the case of *Miranda* v. *Arizona,* that resulted in a ruling by the U.S. Supreme Court in 1966.]

mire (mīr) *n.* **1.** an area of wet, soft ground; bog. **2.** deep, soft mud; muck. —*v.,* **mired, mir·ing.** —*v.t.* **1.** to cause to sink or get stuck in mire. **2.** to soil with mud or muck. **3.** to entangle or involve, as in difficulties. —*v.i.* to sink or get stuck in mire. [Old Norse *mȳrr* bog, swamp.]

mirk (mûrk) murk.

mirk·y (mûr′kē) murky.

mir·ror (mir′ər) *n.* **1.** a smooth surface that forms images by reflecting light, esp. such a surface made of glass coated on the back with a highly reflective material. **2.** something that gives a true representation, expression, or description: *Literature is a mirror of its time.* **3.** a model to be imitated; pattern. —*v.t.* to reflect in, or as if in, a mirror: *The poet's moods are mirrored in the lyric poems.* [Old French *mireor* implement made of metal or glass and designed to reflect images, going back to Late Latin *mīrare* to behold, from Latin *mīrārī* to wonder at.]

mirror image, an image or representation of something as it would appear when reflected in a mirror, with right and left sides reversed.

mirth (mûrth) *n.* merriment or gaiety. [Old English *myrgth.*]

mirth·ful (mûrth′fəl) *adj.* full of, expressing, or characterized by mirth; merry. —**mirth′ful·ly,** *adv.* —**mirth′ful·ness,** *n.*

mirth·less (mûrth′lis) *adj.* without mirth; joyless. —**mirth′less·ly,** *adv.* —**mirth′less·ness,** *n.*

MIRV (mûrv) *n.* a long-range missile having several warheads that can be guided from beyond the atmosphere toward different enemy targets. [Short for *m(ultiple) i(ndependently) targeted) r(eentry) v(ehicle).*]

mir·y (mīr′ē) *adj.,* **mir·i·er, mir·i·est. 1.** like a mire; swampy or boggy. **2.** covered with mire; muddy. —**mir′i·ness,** *n.*

mis- *prefix* **1.** bad or wrong: *misconduct, misconception.* **2.** badly or wrongly: *mismanage, misquote.* **3.** lack of: *mistrust.* [Partly from Old English *mis-* bad, badly, wrong, wrongly; partly from Old French *mes-,* prefix with a disparaging or negative sense; of Germanic origin.]

mis·ad·ven·ture (mis′əd ven′chər) *n.* an unfortunate accident; mishap; misfortune.

mis·ad·vise (mis′əd vīz′) *v.t.,* **-vised, -vis·ing.** to give bad or wrong advice to; advise wrongly.

mis·al·li·ance (mis′ə lī′əns) *n.* an improper or unsuitable alliance or association, esp. in marriage.

mis·an·thrope (mis′ən thrōp′, miz′-) *n.* a person who hates or bitterly distrusts the human race. Also, **mis·an·thro·pist** (mis-an′thrə pist, miz-). [Greek *mīsanthrōpos* hating mankind, from *mīsein* to hate + *anthrōpos* man.] —**mis·an·throp·ic** (mis′ən-throp′ik, miz′-); *also,* **mis′an·throp′i·cal,** *adj.* —**mis′an-throp′i·cal·ly,** *adv.*

mis·an·thro·py (mis an′thrə pē, miz-) *n.* hatred or bitter distrust of the human race.

mis·ap·ply (mis′ə plī′) *v.t.,* **-plied, -ply·ing. 1.** to apply or use incorrectly or badly: *to misapply a mathematical principle.* **2.** to apply or use illegally or dishonestly: *to misapply public money.* —**mis′ap·pli·ca′tion,** *n.*

mis·ap·pre·hend (mis′ap ri hend′) *v.t.* to fail to understand; misunderstand.

mis·ap·pre·hen·sion (mis′ap ri hen′shən) *n.* a failure to understand; misunderstanding.

mis·ap·pro·pri·ate (mis′ə prō′prē āt′) *v.t.,* **-at·ed, -at·ing.** to take or use wrongly or dishonestly, esp. money with which one is entrusted. —**mis′ap·pro′pri·a′tion,** *n.*

mis·be·come (mis′bi kum′) *v.t.,* **-came (-kām′), -come, -com·ing.** to be inappropriate to; be unfit for.

mis·be·got·ten (mis′bi got′ən) *adj.* **1.** unlawfully or irregularly begotten, esp. illegitimate. **2.** poorly conceived, made, or done: *The misbegotten attempt to free the hostages failed.* Also, **mis′be·got′.**

mis·be·have (mis′bi hāv′) *v.,* **-haved, -hav·ing.** —*v.i.* to behave badly or improperly. —*v.t.* to conduct (oneself) badly or improperly.

mis·be·hav·ior (mis′bi hāv′yər) *also, British,* **mis·be·hav·iour.** *n.* bad or improper behavior.

mis·be·lief (mis′bi lēf′) *n.* a false, erroneous, or unorthodox belief.

mis·be·liev·er (mis′bi lē′vər) *n.* a person who holds or is regarded as holding a false, erroneous, or unorthodox belief, esp. in religion.

misc. 1. miscellaneous. **2.** miscellany.

mis·cal·cu·late (mis kal′kyə lāt′) *v.t., v.i.,* **-lat·ed, -lat·ing.** to calculate or estimate wrongly; misjudge. —**mis′cal·cu·la′-tion,** *n.*

mis·call (mis kôl′) *v.t.* to call by a wrong name; misname.

mis·car·riage (mis kar′ij) *n.* **1.** a failure to reach a proper, just, or desired end, often because of mismanagement. **2.** the expulsion of a nonviable fetus; spontaneous abortion.

mis·car·ry (mis kar′ē) *v.i.,* **-ried, -ry·ing. 1.** to fail to reach a proper, just, or desired end. **2.** to bring forth a fetus before it is viable; suffer a miscarriage; abort. **3.** to fail to reach an intended destination; go astray or be lost in transit, as a letter or package.

mis·cast (mis kast′) *v.t.,* **-cast, -cast·ing. 1.** to cast (an actor) in an unsuitable role. **2.** to select an unsuitable actor or actors for (a role or a dramatic or theatrical production): *to miscast a play.*

mis·ce·ge·na·tion (mis′ə jə nā′shən) *n.* interbreeding, marriage, or cohabitation between members of different races. [From Latin *miscēre* to mix + *genus* race, kind.]

mis·cel·la·ne·ous (mis′ə lā′nē əs) *adj.* **1.** of different kinds; having various characteristics or aspects: *miscellaneous items scattered all over the floor, miscellaneous arguments against a proposal.* **2.** composed of various things, elements, or members: *a miscellaneous collection.* **3.** dealing with or interested in a variety of subjects: *a miscellaneous author.* [Latin *miscellāneus* mixed, from *miscellus.*] —**mis′cel·la′ne·ous·ly,** *adv.* —**mis′cel·la′ne·ous·ness,** *n.*

a	at	e	end	o	hot	u	up	hw	white		about
ā	ape	ē	me	ō	old	ū	use	ng	song	ə	taken
ä	far	i	it	ô	fork	ū	rule	th	thin		pencil
âr	care	ī	ice	oi	oil	u̇	pull	th	this		lemon
		îr	pierce	ou	out	ûr	turn	zh	measure		circus

M

The following list contains a selection of compounds that can be formed with the prefix **mis-**. The meaning of a word on the list can be understood by combining the appropriate sense of the prefix with the root word.

misadapt	misarrangement	misclassify	misdescribe	misindex	misreckon
misadaptation	misassemble	miscommunicate	misdiagnose	misinstruct	misregister
misaddress	misassign	miscommunication	misdiagnosis	miskick	misregistration
misadjust	misassignment	miscomputation	misdial	mislabel	misreport
misadminister	misattribute	miscompute	misestimate	mislearn	misroute
misalign	misattribution	misconnect	misestimation	mismeasure	misserve
misalignment	misbutton	misconnection	misevaluate	misnumber	missort
misallocate	miscaption	miscopy	misevaluation	misorganize	misthrow
misallocation	miscatalog	miscorrelate	misfocus	mispair	mistitle
misallotment	miscategorize	miscorrelation	misfunction	misperceive	mistune
misalphabetize	mischannel	misdate	misgauge	misperception	misutilization
misapplication	mischaracterization	misdefine	misgrade	misplan	misutilize
misappoint	mischaracterize	misdeliver	misidentify	misplot	miswire
misarrange	misclassification	misdelivery	misimpression	misprescribe	miswrite

Miscellaneous and **assorted** mean made up of dissimilar or unrelated things. **Miscellaneous** implies a mixture that defies classification: *The basement was filled with miscellaneous objects that had accumulated over the years.* **Assorted** suggests a group of different elements that nonetheless fall within the same category: *assorted chocolates, assorted pieces of furniture.*

mis·cel·la·ny (mis′ə lā′nē) *n., pl.* **-nies. 1.** a mixture of various things. **2.** *also,* **miscellanies.** a collection of various literary works brought together to form a book. [Latin *miscellānea* hodgepodge, various things, from *miscellāneus* mixed. See MISCELLANEOUS.]

mis·chance (mis chans′) *n.* bad luck or an instance of bad luck.

mis·chief (mis′chif) *n.* **1.** an act or conduct that is often playful but causes harm or annoyance: *The child was always involved in some mischief.* **2.** a disposition to annoy, tease, or play pranks: *The student was full of mischief.* **3.** harm, evil, or damage. **4.** a cause or source of harm, annoyance, or trouble. [Old French *meschief* misfortune, damage, from *meschever* to be unfortunate, going back to *mes-* (see MIS-) + Latin *caput* head.]

mis·chie·vous (mis′chə vəs) *adj.* **1.** disposed to or characterized by conduct that is often playful but causes harm or annoyance. **2.** characteristic of or suggesting a disposition to such conduct; playful: *a mischievous smile.* **3.** causing harm; damaging: *mischievous rumors.* —**mis′chie·vous·ly,** *adv.* —**mis′chie·vous·ness,** *n.*

mis·ci·ble (mis′ə bəl) *adj.* capable of being mixed: *Oil and water are not miscible.* [Latin *miscēre* to mix + -IBLE.] —**mis′ci·bil′i·ty,** *n.*

mis·con·ceive (mis′kən sēv′) *v.t.* **-ceived, -ceiv·ing.** to have a wrong conception of; misunderstand.

mis·con·cep·tion (mis′kən sep′shən) *n.* a false or mistaken idea.

mis·con·duct (*n.,* mis kon′dukt; *v.,* mis′kən dukt′) *n.* **1.** improper behavior. **2.** unlawful conduct, esp. by a public official. **3.** failure to handle properly or honestly; mismanagement: *misconduct of financial affairs.* —*v.t.* **1.** to behave (oneself) improperly. **2.** to manage badly, improperly, or dishonestly; mismanage.

mis·con·struc·tion (mis′kən struk′shən) *n.* a false or incorrect interpretation; misunderstanding.

mis·con·strue (mis′kən strü′) *v.t.* **-strued, -stru·ing.** to mistake the meaning or intention of; misinterpret.

mis·count (*v.,* mis kount′; *n.,* mis′kount′) *v.t., v.i.* to count incorrectly; miscalculate. —*n.* an incorrect count.

mis·cre·ant (mis′krē ənt) *n.* **1.** a wicked person; villain. **2.** *Archaic.* infidel; heretic. —*adj.* **1.** villainous; vile. **2.** *Archaic.* infidel; heretical. [Old French *mescreant* disbelieving, infidel, present participle of *mescroire* to disbelieve, going back to *mes-* (see MIS-) + Latin *crēdere* to believe.]

mis·cue (mis kū′) *n.* **1.** a stroke in pool or billiards in which the cue slips and glances off or misses the ball. **2.** a mistake; error; slip. —*v.i.* **-cued, -cu·ing.** to make a miscue.

mis·deal (*v.,* mis dēl′; *n.,* mis′dēl′) *v.t., v.i.* **-dealt** (-delt′), **-deal·ing.** *Card Games.* to deal (cards) incorrectly or improperly. —*n.* an incorrect or improper deal.

mis·deed (mis dēd′) *n.* a wicked, immoral, or criminal act.

mis·de·mean·or (mis′di mē′nər) *also, British,* **mis·de·mean·our.** *n.* **1.** an illegal act less serious than a felony, usually punishable by a fine or a short term of imprisonment. **2.** misbehavior or an instance of it.

mis·di·rect (mis′di rekt′, -dī-) *v.t.* to direct wrongly or badly: *to misdirect a traveler.* —**mis′di·rec′tion,** *n.*

mis·do (mis dü′) *v.t.,* **-did** (-did′), **-done** (-dun′), **do·ing.** to do (something) wrongly or improperly. [Old English *misdōn* to act wrongly.] —**mis·do′er,** *n.*

mis·doubt (mis dout′) *v.t.* **1.** to doubt; distrust. **2.** to fear; suspect. —*n.* doubt; suspicion.

mise en scène (mēz äɴ sen′) *French.* **1.a.** the scenery, properties, and other physical equipment used in staging a theatrical or dramatic production. **b.** the arrangement of the actors, scenery, and properties. **2.** physical surroundings; environment.

mis·em·ploy (mis′em ploi′) *v.t.* to use wrongly or ineffectively; put to poor or improper use. —**mis′em·ploy′ment,** *n.*

mi·ser (mī′zər) *n.* a person who greedily saves or hoards money. [Latin *miser* wretched.]

mis·er·a·ble (miz′ər ə bəl, miz′rə-) *adj.* **1.** very unhappy; wretched: *I felt so miserable I wanted to cry.* **2.** causing or marked by great discomfort or unhappiness: *a miserable toothache, miserable weather.* **3.** pitifully or pathetically poor, inadequate, or unfortunate; deserving pity: *the miserable starving children of a war-ravaged country.* **4.** of little or no value; of very poor quality: *The actor gave a miserable performance.* **5.** deserving contempt; deplorable; shameful. [Latin *miserābilis* pitiable, going back to

miser wretched.] —**mis′er·a·ble·ness,** *n.* —**mis′er·a·bly,** *adv.*

Mis·e·re·re (miz′ə rär′ē, -rîr′ē) *n.* **1.** the Fifty-first Psalm in the Old Testament (the Fiftieth in the Douay Bible). **2.** a musical setting for this psalm. [Latin *miserēre* have mercy (first word of this psalm in the Vulgate), imperative of *miserērī* to have mercy.]

mi·ser·ly (mī′zər lē) *adj.* of, like, or characteristic of a miser; stingy. —**mi′ser·li·ness,** *n.*

mis·er·y (miz′ə rē) *n., pl.* **-er·ies. 1.** the state or condition of physical or mental suffering caused esp. by pain, privation, or extreme unhappiness; prolonged or intense distress: *the silent, hidden misery of childhood* (D. H. Lawrence, 1915). **2.** a cause or source of such suffering. [Latin *miseria* wretchedness.]

mis·fea·sance (mis fē′zəns) *n. Law.* the improper performance of a lawful act, as the wrongful exercise of lawful authority. ➡ distinguished from **malfeasance** and **nonfeasance.** [Old French *mesfaisance* offense, misdemeanor, from *mesfaire* to do wrong, going back to *mes-* (see MIS-) + Latin *facere* to do.]

mis·file (mis fīl′) *v.t.* **-filed, -fil·ing.** to file (papers, documents, or the like) incorrectly.

mis·fire (mis fīr′) *v.i.* **-fired, -fir·ing. 1.** to fail to fire, ignite, or explode at the proper time, as an internal-combustion engine. **2.** to fail to have the intended effect or result: *The plan misfired.* —*n.* a failure to fire, ignite, or explode at the proper time.

mis·fit (*n., defs. 1, 3* mis′fit, mis fit′; *n., def. 2* mis′fit′; *v.,* mis fit′) *n.* **1.** something that does not fit properly, as a garment of the wrong size. **2.** a person who does not fit in with other people or is poorly adjusted to his or her environment. **3.** the act or condition of fitting improperly. —*v.t., v.i.* **-fit·ted, -fit·ting.** to fit badly.

mis·for·tune (mis fôr′chən) *n.* **1.** bad luck; ill fortune. **2.** an instance of this; unlucky accident; mishap.

mis·give (mis giv′) *v.,* **-gave** (-gāv′), **-giv·en** (-giv′ən), **-giv·ing.** —*v.t.* to make doubtful, suspicious, or apprehensive. —*v.i.* to be doubtful, suspicious, or apprehensive.

mis·giv·ing (mis giv′ing) *n.* a feeling of doubt, distrust, or apprehension.

mis·gov·ern (mis guv′ərn) *v.t.* to govern or manage badly. —**mis·gov′ern·ment,** *n.*

mis·guide (mis gīd′) *v.t.,* **-guid·ed, -guid·ing.** to guide or direct wrongly; lead astray in action or thought. —**mis·guid′ance,** *n.*

mis·guid·ed (mis gī′did) *adj.* directed or influenced by or resulting from mistaken ideas or bad guidance: *to give well-intentioned but misguided advice.* —**mis·guid′ed·ly,** *adv.*

mis·han·dle (mis han′dəl) *v.t.,* **-dled, -dling.** to handle, treat, or manage badly.

mis·hap (mis′hap′, mis hap′) *n.* an unfortunate accident.

mis·hear (mis hîr′) *v.t.* **-heard** (-hûrd′), **-hear·ing.** to hear incorrectly or poorly.

mish·mash (mish′mash′, -mosh′) *n.* a confused mixture; jumble. [Repetition of MASH with vowel change in the first syllable.]

Mish·nah (mish′nə) *also,* **Mish·na.** *n., pl.* **Mish·na·yoth** (mish′nä yôt′). **1.** the first part of the Talmud, consisting of a collection of Jewish oral law and legal interpretations. **2.** a paragraph or section of this collection. [Hebrew *mishnāh* repetition, (oral) instruction.]

mis·in·form (mis′in fôrm′) *v.t.* to give false, inaccurate, or misleading information to. —**mis′in·for·ma′tion,** *n.*

mis·in·ter·pret (mis′in tûr′prit) *v.t.* to interpret wrongly; explain or understand incorrectly: *Our guest misinterpreted my compliment and felt insulted.* —**mis′in·ter′pre·ta′tion,** *n.*

mis·judge (mis juj′) *v.t., v.i.* **-judged, -judg·ing.** to judge incorrectly or unfairly: *to misjudge someone's character.* —**mis·judg′ment;** *also,* **mis·judge′ment,** *n.*

mis·la·bel (mis lā′bəl) *v.t.,* **-beled, -bel·ing;** *also, British,* **-belled, -bel·ling.** to label incorrectly or deceptively.

mis·lay (mis lā′) *v.t.,* **-laid** (-lād′), **-lay·ing. 1.** to put in a place that is later forgotten; lose temporarily. **2.** to lay or put down incorrectly, as a carpet. —For Synonyms, see **misplace.**

mis·lead (mis lēd′) *v.t.,* **-led** (-led′), **-lead·ing. 1.** to lead or guide in the wrong direction. **2.** to lead into error of thought, judgment, or action.

mis·lead·ing (mis lē′ding) *adj.* causing or tending to cause error of thought, judgment, or action: *a misleading speech, misleading instructions.* —**mis·lead′ing·ly,** *adv.*

Misleading and **deceptive** mean tending to give one the wrong idea or impression. **Misleading** is more general, applying to something that leads one astray, intentionally or otherwise: *The sales pitch was misleading. Because the weather report was misleading, I left my umbrella at home.* **Deceptive** is more properly used where there is intent to confuse or

lead astray: *deceptive advertising.* But it is loosely used as well when an unintentional or a nonhuman agency is involved: *Appearances are deceptive. A deceptive calm preceded the storm.*

mis·like (mis līk′) *Archaic. v.t.,* -liked, -lik·ing. 1. dislike. 2. displease. —*n.* disapproval; dislike.

mis·man·age (mis man′ij) *v.t.,* -aged, -ag·ing. to manage or handle badly, improperly, or dishonestly. —**mis·man′age·ment,** *n.*

mis·match (mis mach′) *v.t.* to match or join together unwisely or unsuitably: *The two boxers were mismatched in ability. These socks are mismatched.* —*n.* a bad or unsuitable match.

mis·mate (mis māt′) *v.t.,* -mat·ed, -mat·ing. to mate unsuitably.

mis·name (mis nām′) *v.t.,* -named, -nam·ing. to call by a wrong or inappropriate name.

mis·no·mer (mis nō′mər) *n.* 1. a name or designation incorrectly or unsuitably applied: *"Yacht" was a misnomer for the small boat.* 2. an error in naming a person or thing. [From Old French *mesnommer* to misname, going back to *mes-* (see MIS-) + Latin *nōmināre* to name.]

mi·sog·a·my (mi sog′ə mē) *n.* hatred of marriage. [Greek *mīsos* hatred + *gamos* marriage.] —**mi·sog′a·mist,** *n.*

mi·sog·y·ny (mi soj′ə nē) *n.* hatred of women. [Greek *mīsogyniā,* going back to *mīsos* hatred + *gynē* woman.] —**mi·sog′y·nist,** *n.* —**mi·sog′y·nous,** *adj.*

mis·place (mis plās′) *v.t.,* -placed, -plac·ing. 1. to put in a place that is later forgotten; mislay. 2. to put or locate in a wrong place: *to misplace an apostrophe.* 3. to give to an unsuitable person or thing; place unwisely: *to misplace one's trust.* —**mis·place′ment,** *n.*

Synonyms Misplace, mislay, and lose mean to be unable to find something. **Misplace** may be used when one has put something in a wrong or unaccustomed place: *I misplaced the file and couldn't find it for three days.* **Mislay** suggests putting something in a forgotten or unaccustomed place so that one is less likely to find it: *I mislaid that book years ago, but maybe it will show up some day.* **Lose** connotes no hope of recovery: *I lost my keys and had to get a new set made.*

mis·play (*v.,* mis plā′; *n.,* mis plā′, mis′plā′) *v.t.* to play (something) badly or incorrectly, as in a game or sport: *to misplay a poker hand.* —*n.* a bad or incorrect play in a game or sport.

mis·print (*n.,* mis′print, mis print′; *v.,* mis print′) *n.* an error in printing. —*v.t.* to print incorrectly.

mis·pri·sion (mis prizh′ən) *n. Law.* wrongful action or conduct, esp. maladministration by a public official or failure of a citizen to report or try to prevent a crime. [Old French *mesprision* error, wrongdoing, from *mesprendre* to do wrong, going back to *mes-* (see MIS-) + Latin *prehendere* to seize, grasp.]

mis·prize (mis prīz′) *v.t.,* -prized, -priz·ing. to undervalue; despise; scorn. [Old French *mesprisier,* from *mes-* (see MIS-) + *prisier* to value (going back to Latin *pretium* value).]

mis·pro·nounce (mis′prə nouns′) *v.t., v.i.,* -nounced, -nounc·ing. to pronounce (words or sounds) incorrectly. —**mis′pro·nun′ci·a′tion,** *n.*

mis·quote (mis kwōt′) *v.t.,* -quot·ed, -quot·ing. to quote incorrectly or inaccurately. —*n.* an incorrect or inaccurate quotation. —**mis′quo·ta′tion,** *n.*

mis·read (mis rēd′) *v.t.,* -read (-red′), -read·ing. to read, understand, or interpret incorrectly: *to misread a sign.*

mis·re·mem·ber (mis′ri mem′bər) *v.t., v.i.* to remember incorrectly.

mis·rep·re·sent (mis′rep ri zent′) *v.t.* 1. to represent, describe, or portray falsely or inaccurately: *The company misrepresented its product in the advertisement.* 2. to serve inadequately or improperly as the official delegate or agent of. —**mis′rep·re·sen·ta′tion,** *n.* —**mis′rep·re·sen′ta·tive,** *adj.*

mis·rule (mis rül′) *n.* 1. bad, unjust, or unwise rule or government. 2. disorder; tumult. —*v.t.,* -ruled, -rul·ing. to rule or govern badly, unjustly, or unwisely.

miss[1] (mis) *v.t.* 1. to fail to hit, reach, or land on: *The batter missed the ball. The falling limb just missed the roof of our house.* 2. to fail to catch, meet, or get: *to miss a bus.* 3. to fail to notice or find: *to miss a turnoff on a highway.* 4. to fail to accomplish, attain, achieve, or obtain: *The golfer missed sinking the short putt.* 5. to fail to attend, perform, keep, or be present for: *to miss an appointment.* 6. to fail to understand, perceive, or grasp: *You've missed the author's point.* 7. to feel or regret the absence or loss of: *I miss my friend who is away at college.* 8. to discover or realize the absence or loss of: *It was a long time before I missed my ring.* 9. to fail to take advantage of; let slip by: *to miss an opportunity.* 10. to leave out; omit; skip: *to miss a name in calling attendance.* 11. to escape or avoid: *to miss being struck by debris falling from a building.* 12. to be without; lack: *This coat is missing a button.* 13. to do or answer incorrectly; get wrong: *to miss a question.*

—*v.i.* 1. to fail to hit something: *Several arrows were shot, but they all missed.* 2. to be unsuccessful; fail: *Your ingenious plan can't miss.* 3. to misfire. —*n.* a failure to hit or reach. [Old English *missan* to fail to hit.]

·**to miss out on. a.** to fail to take advantage of: *to miss out on a free trip to Hawaii.* **b.** to fail to get, have, or attain: *I missed out on a raise. You missed out on getting that job because you didn't finish school.*

miss[2] (mis) *n., pl.* **miss·es.** 1. **Miss.** a form of address used before the name of a girl or unmarried woman: *Miss Beck.* 2. *also,* **Miss.** a form of address used in place of the name of a girl or unmarried woman: *May I help you, miss?* 3. a girl or young unmarried woman. [Short for MISTRESS.]

Miss., Mississippi.

mis·sal (mis′əl) *n.* a book containing the prescribed prayers and liturgical form for celebrating Mass throughout the year. [Medieval Latin *missale,* from Late Latin *missa.* See MASS.]

mis·shape (mis shāp′) *v.t.,* -shaped, -shaped or -shap·en, -shap·ing. to shape badly; deform.

mis·shap·en (mis shā′pən) *v.* a past participle of **misshape.** —*adj.* badly shaped or having an ugly or distorted shape; deformed.

mis·sile (mis′əl) *n.* 1. an object, esp. a weapon, designed to be thrown, shot, or otherwise projected or propelled, such as a bullet, arrow, or stone; projectile. 2. guided missile. 3. ballistic missile. [Latin *missile* weapon that can be thrown, going back to *missus,* past participle of *mittere* to send, throw.]

mis·sile·ry (mis′əl rē) *also,* **mis·sil·ry.** *n.* the technology of building and operating guided and ballistic missiles.

miss·ing (mis′ing) *adj.* 1. not to be found; lost: *to report a missing person to the police.* 2. absent or lacking: *a missing button.*

missing link 1. a hypothetical primate thought to have been a transitional form between the anthropoid apes and human beings in the evolutionary process. 2. something needed for the completion of a series.

mis·sion (mish′ən) *n.* 1. a group of persons sent or officially assigned to perform a task or service: *a rescue mission, a special diplomatic mission.* 2. the task or service that a person or group of persons is sent or officially assigned to perform: *The spy was sent on a dangerous mission.* 3. a diplomatic office in a foreign country; embassy; legation. 4. a military operation, task, or duty assigned to an individual or unit, esp. a combat flight by one or more aircraft: *a reconnaissance mission.* 5. a spaceflight designed to carry out specified tasks. 6. a group of missionaries sent to do religious, humanitarian, or educational work, esp. in a foreign country. 7. a church, headquarters, or other place used by missionaries in the performance of their work. 8. **missions.** organized missionary work or activities. 9. an establishment or institution set up to perform social services for the needy, as in a poor area of a large city. 10. a church or church district without its own priest or minister and served by a neighboring member of the clergy. 11. a special series of religious services for gaining converts or increasing the piety of believers. 12. the duty or task in life that a person feels destined to perform. —*adj.* 1. of or resembling the style of the churches and buildings of early Spanish missions in the southwestern United States. 2. of, relating to, or characteristic of a style of heavy, plain wood furniture originating in the late nineteenth century in the United States. [Latin *missiō* a sending.]

mis·sion·ar·y (mish′ə ner′ē) *n., pl.* -ar·ies. 1. a person who is sent by a church to spread its religion, esp. in a foreign country: *a Protestant missionary in India.* 2. a person who chooses or is sent to do humanitarian or educational work, esp. in a foreign country: *The doctor served as a medical missionary in Africa.* 3. a person who advocates and works to gain support for some idea or cause. —*adj.* of, relating to, or characteristic of missionaries or religious missions: *missionary zeal.*

mis·sis (mis′iz) *also,* **missus.** *n. Informal.* 1. wife. 2. the mistress of a household. [Modification of MISTRESS.]

Mis·sis·sip·pi·an (mis′ə sip′ē ən) *n.* 1. a native or inhabitant of Mississippi. 2. the earlier of the two geologic subdivisions of the Carboniferous period, during which tropical forests appeared and extensive limestone deposits formed. For table, see **geologic time.** —*adj.* 1. of or relating to Mississippi or the Mississippi River. 2. of or relating to the earlier of the two subdivisions of the Carboniferous period.

M

a	at	e	end	o	hot	u	up	hw	white		about
ā	ape	ē	me	ō	old	ū	use	ng	song		taken
ä	far	i	it	ô	fork	ü	rule	th	thin	ə	pencil
âr	care	ī	ice	oi	oil	ú	pull	th	this		lemon
				îr	pierce	ou	out	ûr	turn	zh	measure		circus

mis·sive (mis′iv) *n.* a written message; letter. [Middle French *missive,* short for *lettre missive* a letter sent, going back to Latin *missus,* past participle of *mittere* to send.]

mis·speak (mis spēk′) *v.t., v.i.,* **-spoke** (-spōk′), **-spo·ken** (-spō′kən), **-speak·ing. 1.** to say or pronounce wrongly or incorrectly: *The child misspoke the hard word.* **2.** to speak in error or in haste: *I misspoke, for I don't really know the correct answer.*

mis·spell (mis spel′) *v.t., v.i.,* **-spelled** or **-spelt, -spell·ing.** to spell (a word) incorrectly.

mis·spell·ing (mis spel′ing) *n.* an incorrect spelling.

Misspelling

The following are among the most frequently misspelled words in English:

accessory	fascinate	prevalent
accommodation	fulfill	privilege
acquire	grammar	procedure
adolescence	height	proceed
aggravate	heroes	prominent
apparent	indict	receive
beneficial	irrelevant	recommend
boundary	irresistible	reminisce
calendar	leisure	repetition
category	medicine	roommate
comparative	morale	seize
compatible	necessary	shepherd
conscientious	occasion	similar
conscious	occurred	succeed
curriculum	paid	supersede
definitely	parallel	surprise
devastate	personal	undoubtedly
embarrass	personnel	unnecessary
environment	playwright	vengeance
exaggerate	precede	weird
existence	prejudice	write

mis·spend (mis spend′) *v.t.,* **-spent, -spend·ing.** to spend or use wrongly or wastefully; squander.

mis·state (mis stāt′) *v.t.,* **-stat·ed, -stat·ing.** to state incorrectly or falsely: *to misstate one's intentions.* —**mis·state′ment,** *n.*

mis·step (mis step′) *n.* **1.** a wrong or careless step. **2.** a mistake in conduct; improper act.

mis·sus (mis′əz, -əs) *n. Informal.* missis.

miss·y (mis′ē) *n., pl.* **miss·ies.** *Informal.* miss².

mist (mist) *n.* **1.** a suspension of water in the air, at or near the earth's surface, consisting of tiny droplets that are finer than those in fog and therefore permit greater visibility. **2.** water vapor condensed on and clouding a surface: *All the windows in the steamy room were covered with a thin mist.* **3.** something resembling mist, such as a thin cloud of smoke or a fine spray from a pressurized can. **4.** a thin film or haze before the eyes that blurs the vision: *a mist of tears.* **5.** something that dims, clouds, or obscures: *The ancient ruler's true deeds were lost in the mist of legend.* —*v.i.* **1.** to be or become covered with or clouded by mist: *The child's eyes misted with tears.* **2.** to rain in very fine drops; drizzle. —*v.t.* **1.** to cover or cloud with mist. **2.** to spray with fine drops of water: *to mist clothes before ironing them.* [Old English *mist* darkness.]

mis·tak·a·ble (mis tā′kə bəl) *adj.* capable of being mistaken or misunderstood. —**mis·tak′a·bly,** *adv.*

mis·take (mis tāk′) *n.* something incorrectly done, believed, or stated. —*v.t.,* **-took** (-tůk′), **-tak·en** (-tā′kən), **-tak·ing. 1.** to regard, identify, or recognize (a person or thing) incorrectly; take (someone or something) to be another (often with *for*): *I mistook you for your twin sister. Tyrants often mistake fear for respect.* **2.** to make an error in understanding or interpreting: *He must have mistaken my intentions.* —*v.i.* to make a mistake; err. [Old Norse *mistaka* to take in error.]

Synonyms *n.* **Mistake, error,** and **blunder** denote a thought or act that is wrong, inaccurate, or not according to custom. **Mistake** suggests a lack of knowledge or judgment, to which no blame may be attached: *to make a mistake about a train schedule, to make a mistake in speaking Spanish.* **Error** more often suggests blameworthiness, as for negligence or insufficient effort: *You are making too many errors in your calculations.* **Blunder** implies stupidity or clumsiness: *Arriving at the party so early was a social blunder. Revealing our game plan in advance was a blunder that helped our opponents.*

mis·tak·en (mis tā′kən) *v.* the past participle of **mistake.** —*adj.* **1.** based on error or misjudgment; wrong: *a mistaken belief, a mistaken conclusion.* **2.** (of a person) wrong in action, thought, judgment, or perception: *You are mistaken if you think that no one will find out you lied.* —**mis·tak′en·ly,** *adv.*

mis·teach (mis tēch′) *v.t.,* **-taught** (-tôt′), **-teach·ing.** to teach (a subject) poorly or incorrectly.

mis·ter (mis′tər) *n.* **1.** Mister. a form of address used before a man's name, usually written *Mr.: Mr. Smith, Mr. Chairman.* **2.** *also,* **Mister.** a form of address used in place of a man's name: *Want a paper, mister?* [Form of MASTER.]

mis·time (mis tīm′) *v.t.,* **-timed, -tim·ing. 1.** to say or do at an inappropriate or wrong time. **2.** to misjudge the time of.

mis·tle·toe (mis′əl tō′) *n.* **1.** any of a large group of parasitic plants that live on the branches of various trees and have yellowish green leaves and white, poisonous berries, such as *Phoradendron flavescens,* the best-known U.S. species. **2.** a sprig of such a plant, often used for Christmas decoration. [Old English *misteltān* the plant.]

mis·took (mis tůk′) the past tense of **mistake.**

mis·tral (mis′trəl, mis träl′) *n.* a cold, dry wind, often of great intensity, that blows from the north or northwest toward the Mediterranean coast of France. [French *mistral,* from Provençal *mistral* literally, masterly wind, from Latin *magistrālis* relating to a master, from *magister* master.]

mis·trans·late (mis′trans lāt′, -tranz-, mis trans′lāt, -tranz′-) *v.t.,* **-lat·ed, -lat·ing.** to translate incorrectly. —**mis′trans·la′tion,** *n.*

mis·treat (mis trēt′) *v.t.* to treat badly or abusively. —**mis·treat′ment,** *n.*

mis·tress (mis′tris) *n.* **1.** a woman in a position of authority or control, such as the head of a household or estate. **2.a.** a woman who owns an animal. **b.** formerly, the female owner of a slave. **3.** a woman having complete control over something: *Her beauty made her mistress of men's hearts.* **4.** *also,* **Mistress.** something that is thought of as female and as having authority or control over something else: *England's mighty navy made her mistress of the high seas.* **5.** a woman who has a continued sexual relationship with and is often supported by a man to whom she is not married. **6.** a woman who has mastered an art or skill. **7.** Mistress. *Archaic.* a form of address used before the name of a woman. **8.** *Archaic.* sweetheart. **9.** *British.* a female schoolteacher. [Middle English *maistresse,* from Old French *maistresse,* feminine of *maistre* one in charge, chief. See MASTER.]

mis·tri·al (mis trī′əl, mis′trī′-) *n. Law.* **1.** a trial that is invalid because of some error in the proceedings. **2.** an inconclusive trial in which the jury fails to agree on a verdict.

mis·trust (mis trust′) *n.* a lack of trust or confidence. —*v.t.* to regard with suspicion or doubt. —*v.i.* to be suspicious or wary. —**mis·trust′ful,** *adj.*

mist·y (mis′tē) *adj.,* **mist·i·er, mist·i·est. 1.** of, resembling, or characterized by mist: *a misty spring morning.* **2.** clouded or obscured by or as by mist: *misty mountains in the distance.* **3.** blurred or clouded with a mist of tears; tearful. **4.** lacking clarity; vague; indistinct: *a misty recollection.* —**mist′i·ly,** *adv.* —**mist′i·ness,** *n.*

mis·un·der·stand (mis′un dər stand′) *v.t., v.i.,* **-stood, -stand·ing.** to understand incorrectly or fail to understand; misinterpret.

mis·un·der·stand·ing (mis′un dər stan′ding) *n.* **1.** a failure to understand correctly; error in interpretation. **2.** a disagreement or quarrel.

mis·un·der·stood (mis′un dər stůd′) *v.* the past tense and past participle of **misunderstand.** —*adj.* **1.** incorrectly understood. **2.** not properly appreciated.

mis·us·age (mis ū′sij, -zij) *n.* **1.** a wrong or improper use or application, as of words. **2.** bad treatment or ill use; abuse.

mis·use (*n.,* mis ūs′; *v.,* mis ūz′) *n.* a wrong or improper use; misapplication: *the misuse of a word, misuse of funds.* —*v.t.,* **-used, -us·ing. 1.** to use wrongly or improperly; misapply. **2.** to treat badly or abusively.

mis·word (mis wûrd′) *v.t.* to word incorrectly or poorly.

mite¹ (mīt) *n.* any of a group of tiny arachnids, order Acarina, having piercing, sucking mouthparts. Mites often damage stored foods or infest plants or animals. [Middle English *mite, myte,* from Old English *mīte* any tiny insect; of Germanic origin.]

mite² (mīt) *n.* **1.** a very small amount, object, or creature. **2.** a very small sum of money or contribution. **3.** a coin of very small value. [Middle Dutch *mīte* coin of small value.]

mi·ter¹ (mī′tər) *also,* **mitre.** *n.* **1.** a liturgical headdress worn by bishops and other prelates, consisting of a tall, peaked cap that

can be folded flat, with two fringed strips of material hanging from the back. **2.** the official headdress of the ancient Jewish high priest, wrapped in folds around the head. —*v.t.* to bestow a miter upon. [Latin *mītra* cap, from Greek *mitra* headband.]

mi·ter² (mī′tər) *n.* **1.** miter joint. **2.** the beveled edge on either of the pieces used to form a miter joint. —*v.t.* **1.** to join with a miter joint. **2.** to cut or shape for forming a miter joint; cut to a miter. [Probably from MITER¹.]

miter¹

miter box, a device used to guide a saw when making miter joints, esp. an open-ended, trough-shaped box with slotted sides.

miter joint, a joint formed by two pieces of wood or other material, whose joined edges have been beveled to form angles.

miter square, a tool having a blade set at a 45-degree angle or an adjustable blade, used to mark the angles of miter joints.

Mith·ra·ism (mith′rə iz′əm) *n.* an ancient Persian religion based on the worship of Mithras. —**Mith·ra·ic** (mith rā′ik), **Mith′ra·is′tic,** *adj.* —**Mith′ra·ist,** *n., adj.*

Mith·ras (mith′ras) *also,* **Mith·ra** (mith′rə). *n.* the Persian god of light and truth, associated with the sun.

mit·i·gate (mit′i gāt′) *v.t.,* -**gat·ed,** -**gat·ing.** to make milder or less severe, intense, or painful: *to mitigate anger, to mitigate suffering.* [Latin *mītigātus,* past participle of *mītigāre* to make soft, calm.] —**mit·i·ga·ble** (mit′i gə bəl), *adj.* —**mit′i·ga′tion,** *n.* —**mit′i·ga′tor,** *n.*

mit·i·ga·tive (mit′i gā′tiv) *adj.* tending to mitigate. Also, **mit·i·ga·to·ry** (mit′i gə tôr′ē).

mi·to·chon·dri·a (mī′tə kon′drē ə, mit′ə-) *pl. n., sing.* -**dri·on** (-drē ən). *Biology.* the assemblage of microscopic rods, filaments, or granules found in the cytoplasm of nearly all cells and serving as centers of cellular respiration and the sites of energy production. For illustration, see **cell.** [From Greek *mitos* thread + *chondrion* small grain.] —**mi′to·chon′dri·al,** *adj.*

mi·to·sis (mī tō′sis) *n.* a four-stage process of cell division utilized by most plant and animal cells, in which the nucleus of the cell divides into two identical nuclei and the cytoplasm divides equally, forming two identical daughter cells, each with the same number of chromosomes as the parent cell. ➡ distinguished from **meiosis.** [Modern Latin *mitosis,* from Greek *mitos* thread.] —**mi·tot·ic** (mī tot′ik), *adj.* —**mi·tot′i·cal·ly,** *adv.*

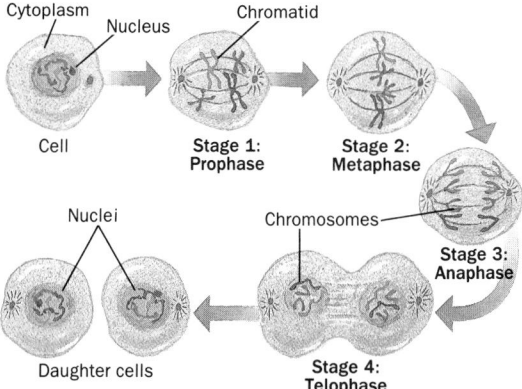

Cytoplasm
Nucleus
Chromatid

Cell

Stage 1: Prophase

Stage 2: Metaphase

Nuclei

Chromosomes

Stage 3: Anaphase

Daughter cells

Stage 4: Telophase

mitosis

mi·tral (mī′trəl) *adj.* **1.** of, relating to, or resembling a miter. **2.** of or relating to the mitral valve.

mitral valve, the heart valve located between the left atrium and left ventricle, consisting of two flaps.

mi·tre (mī′tər) *n.* miter¹. —*v.t.,* **mi·tred, mi·tring.** miter¹.

mits·vah (mits′və) *n., pl.* **mits·voth** (mits vôt′) or **mits·vahs.** mitzvah.

mitt (mit) *n.* **1.** a baseball glove, esp. that worn by the catcher or the person playing first base. **2.** mitten *(def. 1).* **3.** a woman's glove, often of lace, that may cover the forearm, wrist, and part of the hand, but does not extend over the fingers. **4.** *Slang.* hand. [Short for MITTEN.]

mit·ten (mit′ən) *n.* **1.** a covering for the hand enclosing the four fingers together and the thumb separately. **2.** mitt *(def. 3).* [Old French *mitaine,* from *mite;* of uncertain origin.]

mitz·vah (mitz′və) *also,* **mitsvah.** *n., pl.* **mitz·voth** (mits vôt′) or **mitz·vahs. 1.** a commandment or precept in Judaism. **2.** a good or praiseworthy deed; act of kindness. [Hebrew *mitzwāh* commandment.]

mix (miks) *v.,* **mixed** or **mixt, mix·ing.** —*v.t.* **1.** to put together into one mass or compound: *to mix lemon juice, sugar, and water to make lemonade.* **2.** to make or prepare by combining different ingredients (often with *up*): *to mix cement, to mix up a batch of pancakes.* **3.** to put or add, as an ingredient: *to mix herbs into a soup.* **4.** to stir or shake. **5.** to join or bring together: *to mix red and yellow roses in a bouquet.* **6.** to change the order or arrangement of at random (often with *up*): *For our history test, the teacher mixed up ten important events and then asked us to list them in order.* **7.** to crossbreed. **8.** to produce (an audio recording) by electronically combining sounds from various sources. —*v.i.* **1.** to become mixed or be capable of being mixed: *Oil and water will not mix.* **2.** to go or belong together. **3.** to associate, join in, or get along: *to mix with people from all walks of life.* **4.** to get involved; take part: *to mix in another person's affairs.* **5.** to be crossbred. —*n.* **1.** the product, result, or act of mixing; mixture. **2.** a mixture or combination of ingredients that is prepared and sold commercially: *a cake mix.* **3.** mixer *(def. 4).* [From obsolete *mixt* mixed, from Latin *mixtus,* past participle of *miscēre* to mingle.] —**mix′a·ble;** *also,* **mix′i·ble,** *adj.*

•**to mix it up.** *Slang.* to fight.

•**to mix up. a.** to confuse or disorder: *The files are all mixed up.* **b.** to involve: *Government officials may have been mixed up in the crime.*

Synonyms *v.t.* **Mix, blend,** and **stir¹** mean to combine or merge different elements. **Mix,** the most general term, suggests the combining of diverse elements into a cohesive mass or compound: *The workers mixed cement, gravel, sand, and water to make concrete.* **Blend** means to mix so thoroughly that the ingredients become indistinguishable: *The food processor blended the vegetables into a smooth paste.* **Stir** describes a continuous, circular movement: *to stir a sauce, to stir a can of paint.*

mixed (mikst) *adj.* **1.** put together or formed by mixing; blended together into one mass or compound: *a mixed salad dressing, mixed ingredients.* **2.** of or composed of different or incongruous elements or qualities: *to have mixed feelings about something.* **3.** made up of or involving persons of both sexes: *a mixed cooking class.* **4.** made up of or involving persons of different races, religions, national origins, or social classes: *a mixed marriage, a mixed neighborhood.*

mixed bag *Informal.* a group of persons or things with few characteristics in common; odd mixture or assortment: *This week has been a mixed bag, with some great days and a few not so good.*

mixed media 1. the use of a combination of media to produce some type of effect, such as the display of flashing lights and pictures projected on a screen to accompany musicians performing on a stage. **2.** a combination of different media, such as watercolors and ink, in one piece of art.

mixed metaphor, an expression in which two or more metaphors are combined in an illogical and contradictory manner; for example: *to take arms against a sea of troubles* (Shakespeare, *Hamlet*).

mixed number, a number consisting of an integer and a proper fraction. The numbers $4\frac{7}{8}$ and $-7\frac{2}{3}$ are mixed numbers.

mixed-up (mikst′up′) *adj.* confused or disordered.

mix·er (mik′sər) *n.* **1.** a person or thing that mixes, esp. a machine or device for mixing. **2.** a person with regard to his or her ability to associate or get along with others: *You are a good mixer at parties.* **3.** a dance, party, or other social gathering for the purpose of getting people acquainted. **4.** a beverage, such as soda or ginger ale, that is added to an alcoholic drink.

mixt (mikst) a past tense and past participle of **mix.**

mix·ture (miks′chər) *n.* **1.** a product or result of mixing; combination; blend: *This batter is a mixture of milk, eggs, and flour. My first reaction was a strange mixture of joy and anger.* **2.** a combination of two or more substances in which each retains its individual properties and does not join in forming a chemical compound. **3.** the act or process of mixing or the state of being mixed. [Latin *mixtūra* a mixing.]

M

a	at	e	end	o	hot	u	up	hw	white		about
ā	ape	ē	me	ō	old	ū	use	ng	song		taken
ä	far	i	it	ô	fork	ü	rule	th	thin	ə	pencil
âr	care	ī	ice	oi	oil	u̇	pull	th	this		lemon
		îr	pierce	ou	out	ûr	turn	zh	measure		circus

mix-up (miks'up') *n.* a state or instance of confusion.

miz·zen (miz'ən) *also,* **miz·en.** *n.* **1.** a fore-and-aft sail set on the mizzenmast. **2.** mizzenmast. —*adj.* of or relating to the mizzenmast. [Middle French *misaine* foresail, going back to Arabic *mazzān* mast.]

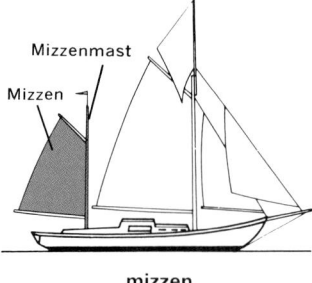

Mizzenmast

Mizzen

mizzen

miz·zen·mast (miz'ən-mast', -məst) *also,* **miz·en·mast.** *n.* **1.** the mast nearest the stern in a ship having two or three masts. **2.** the third mast from the bow of a ship having more than three masts.

mks *also,* **MKS** meter-kilogram-second.

mkt., market.

ml *also,* **ml.** milliliter; milliliters.

Mlle., Mademoiselle.

Mlles., Mesdemoiselles.

mm *also,* **mm.** millimeter; millimeters.

MM., Messieurs.

Mme., Madame.

Mmes., Mesdames.

Mn, the symbol for manganese.

MN, the postal abbreviation for Minnesota.

mne·mon·ic (ni mon'ik) *adj.* **1.** aiding or intended to aid the memory. **2.** of or relating to memory. —*n.* a device, such as a formula or phrase, that aids one in remembering. [Greek *mnēmonikos* relating to memory, going back to *mnēmē* memory.] —**mne·mon'i·cal·ly,** *adv.*

mne·mon·ics (ni mon'iks) *n.* a technique or system for improving or developing the memory. ➡ used as singular.

Mne·mos·y·ne (ni mos'ə nē) *n.* in Greek mythology, the goddess of memory.

Mo, the symbol for molybdenum.

mo., month.

Mo., Missouri.

MO, the postal abbreviation for Missouri.

M.O. 1. medical officer. **2.** modus operandi. **3.** *also,* **m.o.** money order.

mo·a (mō'ə) *n.* any of several extinct flightless birds, resembling the ostrich, family Dinornithidae, once numerous in New Zealand. Height: 10 feet (3 meters). [Of Maori origin.]

Mo·ab·ite (mō'ə bīt') *adj.* of, relating to, or characteristic of Moab or its people, language , or culture. —*n.* **1.** a native or inhabitant of the ancient kingdom of Moab. **2.** the language spoken by the people of Moab, belonging to the Semitic group of the Semito-Hamitic family of languages and closely related to ancient Hebrew.

moan (mōn) *n.* **1.** a low, prolonged, mournful sound, usually expressive of grief or pain. **2.** any sound resembling this: *the wind's eerie moan in the silent night.* **3.** *Archaic.* a lamentation; complaint. —*v.i.* **1.** to utter or produce a moan or moans. **2.** to complain, lament, or grieve: *The students moaned about having too much homework.* —*v.t.*

moa

1. to utter or express with a moan or moans: *The wounded soldiers moaned their distress.* **2.** to complain about; bemoan. [Probably from an unrecorded Old English word.]

moat (mōt) *n.* a deep, wide ditch, usually filled with water, surrounding a castle, fortress, or town as a protection against assault. —*v.t.* to surround with or as with a moat. [Old French *mote* dike, mound; possibly of Celtic origin.]

mob (mob) *n.* **1.** a disorderly, often menacing, crowd or throng. **2.** any crowd. **3. the mob.** common people collectively; the masses. **4.** *Informal.* an organized group of gangsters. —*v.t.,* **mobbed, mob·bing. 1.** to crowd around and jostle or annoy, as in curiosity: *Fans mobbed the actors wherever they went.* **2.** to crowd to capacity: *Shoppers mobbed the store during the big sale.* **3.** to attack in or as in a mob. [Short for Latin *mōbile vulgus* fickle crowd.]

mob·cap (mob'kap') *n.* a large, loose, ruffled cap covering the hair and ears, formerly worn indoors by women. [Probably from Middle Dutch *mop* woman's cap + CAP.]

mo·bile (*adj.,* mō'bəl, -bēl; *n.,* mō'bēl) *adj.* **1.** capable of moving or being moved, esp. easily or readily movable: *a mobile cannon.* **2.** able or tending to change, respond, or adapt easily or quickly, as in response to different moods or feelings: *a clown's mobile facial features.* **3.** flowing freely: *a mobile liquid.* **4.a.** capable of or permitting movement from one social class or group to a higher one: *a mobile society.* **b.** characterized by the mixing of social groups. —*n.* a construction or sculpture, as of metal, plastic, or cardboard, consisting of movable parts that are usually suspended from thin wires and can be set in motion, as by air currents. [Latin *mōbilis* movable, fickle, from *movēre* to move.] —**mo·bil'i·ty** (mō bil'ə tē), *n.*

-mobile *combining form* a vehicle for a specialized purpose: *bookmobile.*

mobile home, a large trailer designed and fully equipped for use as a permanent home.

mo·bi·lize (mō'bə līz') *v.,* **-lized, -liz·ing.** —*v.t.* **1.** to summon, assemble, or prepare (armed forces) for active military service, or put into such service: *to mobilize reserves in time of national emergency.* **2.** to prepare, organize, or adapt for use or action, or put into operation or active service, as for an emergency: *to mobilize backing for a political candidate.* —*v.i.* to become organized or prepared, as for war or an emergency. [French *mobiliser* to prepare the military, economic, and governmental resources of a country for war, going back to Latin *mōbilis* movable. See MOBILE.] —**mo'bi·li·za'tion,** *n.*

Mö·bi·us strip (mœ'bē-əs, mō'-, mā'-) a continuous surface having only one side and one edge, formed by turning one end of a rectangular strip 180 degrees and then attaching it to the other end.

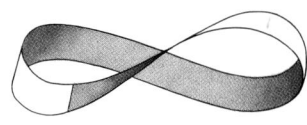

Möbius strip

[From A. F. *Möbius,* 1790-1868, German mathematician who invented it.]

mob·ster (mob'stər) *n. Slang.* a member of a criminal gang; gangster.

moc·ca·sin (mok'ə sin, -zən) *n.* **1.** a shoe having a soft sole and no heel, generally constructed from one piece of leather, originally worn by American Indians. **2.** any shoe or slipper resembling an Indian moccasin. **3.** water moccasin. [Of Algonquian origin.]

moccasin flower, a North American orchid, *Cypripedium acaule,* bearing a solitary moccasin-shaped flower with a pink lip.

mo·cha (mō'kə) *n.* **1.** a choice coffee originally grown in Arabia. **2.** a flavoring made from an infusion of coffee or a mixture of coffee and chocolate. **3.** a soft leather made from sheepskin and processed to have a suede finish on both sides, used chiefly for gloves. **4.** a chocolate-brown color. —*adj.* **1.** flavored with coffee or with a mixture of coffee and.chocolate. **2.** having the color mocha. [From *Mocha,* a port in Yemen, from which this coffee was first obtained.]

mo·chi·la (mō chē'lə) *n.* a saddle covering made of hide or leather. Mochilas equipped with pockets at each corner were used by pony express riders. [Spanish *mochila* cover for a horse, knapsack, from *mochil* errand boy, from Basque *motxil* servant, youth, from Latin *mutilus* maimed, shortened (from the custom of cutting the hair of children).]

mock (mok) *v.t.* **1.** to speak to or treat with ridicule or contempt; deride: *The newspaper article mocked the government's policies.* **2.** to imitate or mimic, as in sport or derision: *to mock the way someone speaks.* **3.** to scoff at or defy: *The criminal mocked the law.* **4.** to disappoint or deceive. —*v.i.* to express ridicule or contempt; scoff. —*adj.* not real; pretended; sham: *a mock battle, mock humility.* —*n.* **1.** an act of mocking or ridicule or an expression of mockery. **2.** a person or thing that is or deserves to be mocked or ridiculed. **3.** something that is an imitation or counterfeit. [Old French *mocquier* to deride, scoff; possibly imitative.] —**mock'er,** *n.* —**mock'ing·ly,** *adv.*

Synonyms *v.t.* **Mock, ridicule,** and **deride** mean to make someone or something appear foolish. **Mock** implies an attitude of contempt or scorn, often expressed through imitation: *The students mocked their classmate's accent.* **Ridicule** denotes an attempt to make someone or something the object of contemptuous laughter: *That comedian often ridicules members of his audience.* **Deride** emphasizes malice or bitterness: *After her team lost the game, the captain derided their performance on the field.*

mock·er·y (mok′ə rē) *n., pl.* **-er·ies. 1.** the act of mocking; ridicule; contempt; derision. **2.** a mocking or derisive speech or action. **3.** a person or thing that is or deserves to be an object of ridicule or contempt. **4.** a false, ridiculous, or offensive imitation: *The trial was a mockery of justice.* **5.** something that is absurdly or offensively futile or unsuitable.

mock-he·ro·ic (mok′hi rō′ik) *adj.* satirizing or burlesquing heroic style, action, or character: *a mock-heroic poem, mock-heroic courage.* —*n.* a satirical or burlesque imitation of something heroic, esp. a mock-heroic literary work. —**mock′-he·ro′i·cal·ly,** *adv.*

mock·ing·bird (mok′ing bûrd′) *n.* any of several North and South American birds, family Mimidae, usually having gray plumage, that can imitate the calls of various other birds. Length: 9-11 inches (23-28 centimeters).

mockingbird

mock orange, any of a group of ornamental shrubs, genus *Philadelphus,* found throughout Europe, Asia, and North America, bearing showy, creamy white flowers. Also, **syringa.**

mock turtle soup, a soup made from calf's head or other meat and flavored to taste like green turtle soup.

mock-up (mok′up′) *also,* **mock·up.** *n.* a model, as of an airplane or machine, usually full-scale, used for study, testing, or display.

mod (mod) *also,* **Mod.** *adj.* **1.** of or relating to anything that is stylish and up-to-date, esp. in an unconventional way. **2.** of or relating to a stylish, youth-oriented mode of dress first worn and popularized in England in the 1960s. [From MODERN.]

mod. 1. moderate. **2.** moderato. **3.** modern.

mod·a·cryl·ic (mod′ə kril′ik) *adj.* of, relating to, or designating a type of flame-resistant fiber composed of a polymer derived from acrylonitrile and used to make carpets and a variety of textiles. [Short for *mod(ified) acrylic.*]

mo·dal (mō′dəl) *adj.* **1.** of or relating to a mode. **2.** in grammar, of or relating to mood. [Medieval Latin *modalis,* from Latin *modus* measure, manner.] —**mo′dal·ly,** *adv.*

modal auxiliary, an auxiliary verb used to indicate the mood of the verb with which it is used. *May, must,* and *would* are modal auxiliaries.

mo·dal·i·ty (mō dal′i tē) *n., pl.* **-ties.** the fact, quality, or state of being modal.

mode¹ (mōd) *n.* **1.a.** a manner, way, or method of doing something or of acting: *to adopt a new mode of procedure.* **b.** a particular form or variety: *Automobiles are a popular mode of transportation.* **2.** *Grammar.* mood². **3.** *Music.* **a.** any of various arrangements of the diatonic tones of an octave, derived by beginning on any one of the various tones of a given scale and proceeding through an octave. **b.** any of the eight, later twelve, scales thus derived, used in ancient and medieval music. **c.** either of the two forms, major and minor, of the modern diatonic scale. **4.** *Statistics.* the value, number, or item occurring most often in a given series. [Latin *modus* measure, manner, melody.]

mode² (mōd) *n.* a current or prevailing style or fashion, as of dress. [French *mode,* from Latin *modus* measure, manner.]

mod·el (mod′əl) *n.* **1.** a reproduction or representation of something, usually constructed to scale or in miniature: *to build airplane models from kits, a working model of a new kind of engine.* **2.** an image or figure in clay, wax, or plaster of something to be reproduced in a more durable material, such as marble. **3.** a person or thing that serves as an example or standard for imitation or comparison: *a model of rectitude.* **4.** a person or thing that serves as the subject for an artist, photographer, or writer: *The famous senator was the model for a character in the novel. The artist hired a model to pose for a series of figure drawings.* **5.** a person who is employed to display merchandise, esp. a person employed to display or advertise clothing by wearing it. **6.** a style, design or type: *The car was a very old model.* **7.** a simplified representation of something actually or theoretically existing in nature: *a model of the DNA molecule.* **8.** a mathematical representation of a system or theory for study or analysis: *an economic model, a model describing stress on a steel framework.* —*v.,* **-eled, -el·ing;** *also, British,* **-elled, -el·ling.** —*v.t.* **1.** to fashion or plan according to or in imitation of a particular model, example, or pattern: *to model a statue after an ancient Greek one.* **2.** to make a model or representation of: *to model a nude figure in wax.* **3.** to form or shape; make: *to model clay into a figure of a horse.* **4.** to display

(clothing or other merchandise) by wearing: *to model dresses.* **5.** to simulate or represent (something, such as the operation of a process or system), esp. using a computer: *to model atmospheric circulation as an aid in weather forecasting.* **6.** to give a three-dimensional appearance to (a figure or object in painting or drawing), as by use of light and shadow. —*v.i.* **1.** to make a model or models: *to model in plastic.* **2.** to serve, be employed, or pose as a model: *to model at a fashion show.* —*adj.* **1.** designed or made as a model of something: *to build a model airplane.* **2.** designed as a display of things for sale or study: *The store has a model kitchen.* **3.** worthy of serving as a model: *a model teacher.* [Middle French *modelle* pattern, mold¹, from Italian *modello,* going back to Latin *modulus* small measure, diminutive of *modus* measure, manner.] —**mod′el·er;** *also, British,* **mod′el·ler,** *n.*

mod·el·ing (mod′ə ling) *also,* **mod·el·ling.** *n.* **1.** the act or art of making or constructing a model or models. **2.** the act or occupation of serving or posing as a model. **3.** the rendering of three-dimensional form in painting or drawing, as by use of light and shadow. **4.** the simulation or representation of something, such as the operation of a process or a system, esp. on a computer. **5.** a form or shape made by sculpture.

Model T, a Ford automobile in production from 1908 to 1927.

mo·dem (mō′dəm) *n.* an electronic device that enables computers to communicate over telephone lines by converting binary digital data into audio tone signals for transmission and back into digital data for reception. [Short for *mo(dulator-)dem(odulator).*]

mod·er·ate (*adj., n.,* mod′ər it; *v.,* mod′ə rāt′) *adj.* **1.** keeping or kept within reasonable or proper limits; not excessive or extreme: *moderate prices.* **2.** of medium or average amount, degree, or quality: *moderate traffic on a highway, to have moderate success as an actor.* **3.** not violent or intense; mild; calm: *moderate weather.* **4.** having or characterized by a viewpoint that is not radical or extreme, esp. in politics: *Most of the moderate senators voted against the bill.* —*n.* a person who holds moderate views, esp. in politics. —*v.,* **-at·ed, -at·ing.** —*v.t.* **1.** to make less excessive, extreme, violent, or intense: *The protesters were urged to moderate their demands.* **2.** to preside over: *to moderate a discussion.* —*v.i.* **1.** to become less excessive, extreme, violent, or intense. **2.** to act as a moderator; preside. [Latin *moderātus,* past participle of *moderārī* to regulate, control, from *modus* measure, limit.] —**mod′er·ate·ly,** *adv.* —**mod′er·ate·ness,** *n.*

mod·er·a·tion (mod′ə rā′shən) *n.* **1.** the state or quality of being moderate; avoidance of excess or extremes. **2.** the act of moderating.

·in moderation. within reasonable limits; without excess: *The doctor advised me to exercise, but in moderation.*

mod·e·ra·to (mod′ə rä′tō) *Music. adj.* in moderate tempo. —*adv.* at a moderate tempo. —*n.* a moderato passage or movement. [Italian *moderato* restrained, from Latin *moderātus* controlled. See MODERATE.]

mod·e·ra·tor (mod′ə rā′tər) *n.* **1.** a person or thing that moderates, esp. one who presides, as over a meeting or discussion. **2.** *Physics.* graphite, heavy water, or another substance used in a nuclear reactor to slow down neutrons without absorbing them, thereby increasing the efficiency of the reaction.

mod·ern (mod′ərn) *adj.* **1.a.** of, relating to, or characteristic of the present or recent time: *modern habits, modern attitudes toward the past.* **b.** of, relating to, or characteristic of certain contemporary trends in art, music, literature, and the like, esp. those that break with the past and explore new forms of expression: *modern jazz.* **2.** of or relating to the period of history following the Middle Ages, since about 1450: *modern history.* **3.** up-to-date; not old-fashioned: *The kitchen had modern appliances.* —*n.* **1.** a person who lives in modern times. **2.** a person who has modern views or standards. [Late Latin *modernus* of the present, from Latin *modō* just now.] —**mod′ern·ly,** *adv.* —**mod′ern·ness,** *n.*

Synonyms *adj.* **Modern, contemporary,** and **current** mean of recent origin. **Modern** is often used to emphasize the present in contrast to the past: *Some people prefer eighteenth-century music to modern music.* **Contemporary** stresses up-to-dateness, esp. of design or fashion: *The room was furnished in a contemporary style.* **Current** is applied to something that is the most recent of a series: *The current car models are a great improvement over last year's.*

a	at	e	end	o	hot	u	up	hw	white		about
ā	ape	ē	me	ō	old	ū	use	ng	song		taken
ä	far	i	it	ô	fork	ü	rule	th	thin	ə	pencil
âr	care	ī	ice	oi	oil	u̇	pull	th	this		lemon
		îr	pierce	ou	out	ûr	turn	zh	measure		circus

modern dance, a form of dance originating in the United States in the early twentieth century, characterized by less formal steps and movements than those of classical ballet.

modern dance

Modern English, the English language as it has been written and spoken since about 1500.

mod·ern·ism (mod′ər niz′əm) *n.* **1.** modern character, thought, attitudes, or practices. **2.** something characteristic of modern times, such as a newly introduced word or practice. **3.** also, **Modernism.** a late nineteenth- and early twentieth-century movement in Christianity and Judaism to interpret religious doctrine in accordance with current ideas in philosophy and science, denounced as heretical by the Roman Catholic Church. **4.** a movement in late nineteenth- and twentieth-century artistic, architectural, and literary styles characterized by a break with the past and the exploration of new forms of expression. —**mod′-ern·ist,** *n., adj.* —**mod′ern·is′tic,** *adj.*

mo·der·ni·ty (mo dûr′ni tē, mō-) *n., pl.* **-ties.** the quality or state of being modern.

mod·ern·ize (mod′ər nīz′) *v.,* **-ized, -iz·ing.** —*v.t.* to make modern, as in appearance, style, or character; change to suit present needs or tastes: *to modernize a hospital by installing the latest equipment.* —*v.i.* to become modern; adopt modern ways. —**mod′ern·i·za′tion,** *n.* —**mod′ern·iz′er,** *n.*

Modern Latin, a form of the Latin language used after 1500, esp. in scientific terminology.

modern pentathlon, an athletic contest in which all contestants must compete in each of five events: swimming, cross-country running, horseback riding, fencing, and pistol shooting.

mod·est (mod′ist) *adj.* **1.** tending to avoid praise or credit; humble; unassuming: *A modest person does not brag about accomplishments.* **2.** bashful and retiring; reserved: *a quiet, modest person.* **3.** having or showing a regard for propriety, esp. in behavior or dress: *a modest swimsuit, to be modest in one's dress.* **4.** not grand or showy; unpretentious; simple: *modest furnishings, a modest house.* **5.** not excessive or extreme; moderate: *a modest sum of money.* [Latin *modestus* unassuming, moderate, keeping within bounds, from *modus* measure.] —**mod′est·ly,** *adv.* —For Synonyms, see **humble.**

mod·es·ty (mod′ə stē) *n.* the quality or state of being modest.

mod·i·cum (mod′i kəm) *n.* a small or moderate amount or portion. [Latin *modicum,* neuter of *modicus* moderate, from *modus* measure.]

mod·i·fi·ca·tion (mod′ə fi kā′shən) *n.* **1.** the act of modifying or the state of being modified. **2.** a small or partial change, alteration, or adjustment: *The plan requires a few slight modifications.* **3.** the result of modifying; modified form: *The law passed by Congress was a modification of the original bill.*

mod·i·fi·er (mod′ə fī′ər) *n.* **1.** *Grammar.* a word, phrase, or clause that limits or qualifies the meaning of another word or group of words. Adjectives and adverbs are modifiers. **2.** a person or thing that modifies.

mod·i·fy (mod′ə fī′) *v.,* **-fied, -fy·ing.** —*v.t.* **1.** to change or alter, as in form, usually to a small extent: *The inventor modified the original design to increase the machine's efficiency.* **2.** to make less severe or extreme; moderate: *The mediator attempted to get both sides to modify their positions.* **3.** *Grammar.* to limit or qualify the meaning of. In the phrase *a quiet evening,* the adjective *quiet* modifies the noun *evening.* —*v.i.* to be or become modified. [Old French *modifier* to change, moderate, from Latin *modificāre* to limit, control, from *modus* measure, limit + *facere* to make.] —**mod′i·fi′a·ble,** *adj.* —For Synonyms, see **change.**

mod·ish (mō′dish) *adj.* following a current style or fashion; fashionable. —**mod′ish·ly,** *adv.* —**mod′ish·ness,** *n.*

mo·diste (mō dēst′) *n.* a person who makes or deals in women's fashions. [French *modiste* milliner, from *mode.* See MODE².]

Mo·dred (mō′drid) *also,* **Mordred.** *n.* in Arthurian legend, King Arthur's treacherous nephew.

mod·u·lar (moj′ə lər) *adj.* **1.** of or relating to a module or modulus. **2.** composed or constructed of modules.

mod·u·late (moj′ə lāt′) *v.,* **-lat·ed, -lat·ing.** —*v.t.* **1.** to change or vary the tone, volume, or pitch of (the voice). **2.** to adjust, adapt, or regulate to a certain degree or proportion. **3.** to vary the amplitude, frequency, or phase of (a carrier wave) for the transmission of a signal. —*v.i. Music.* to pass from one key to another. [Latin *modulātus,* past participle of *modulārī* to measure off properly, to measure rhythmically, going back to *modus* measure.] —**mod·u·la·to·ry** (moj′ə lə tôr′ē), *adj.*

mod·u·la·tion (moj′ə lā′shən) *n.* **1.** the act of modulating or the state of being modulated. **2.** *Music.* a passing from one key to another. **3.** *Electronics.* the process or result of modulating a carrier wave.

mod·u·la·tor (moj′ə lā′tər) *n.* **1.** a device or circuit for modulating carrier waves. **2.** a person or thing that modulates.

mod·ule (moj′ül, mod′ūl) *n.* **1.** any component or unit that may be combined with others in various arrangements, as in some sofas. **2.** a self-contained unit of a spacecraft, having a specific function, such as the lunar module of the Apollo spacecraft. **3.** a compact functional assembly used as a component part or unit, as in a computer. **4.** an instructional unit on a single topic or part of a broad topic. **5.** a standard or unit of measurement. **6.** *Architecture.* the size of some part, as of a building, taken as a unit of measurement, used to regulate the proportion among the other parts. [Latin *modulus* small measure, diminutive of *modus* measure. Doublet of MOLD¹.]

mod·u·lus (moj′ə ləs) *n., pl.* **-li** (-lī′). **1.** *Physics.* a quantity or number that is the measure of some function, property, force, or effect. **2.** *Mathematics.* an integer that leaves the same remainder when divided into different numbers. [Modern Latin *modulus,* from Latin *modulus.* See MODULE.]

mo·dus op·e·ran·di (mō′dəs op′ə ran′dē, -ran′dī) *pl.* **mo·di op·e·ran·di** (mō′dē op′ə ran′dē, mō′dī op′ə ran′dī). *Latin.* a manner of working or accomplishing something; method of operation: *The firm implemented a more efficient modus operandi.*

mo·dus vi·ven·di (mō′dəs vi ven′dē, -ven′dī) *pl.* **mo·di vi·ven·di** (mō′dē vi ven′dē, mō′dī vi ven′dī). *Latin.* **1.** a manner of living. **2.** a temporary agreement between contending parties pending a final settlement of matters in debate.

Mo·gen Da·vid (mô′gən dô′vid, mō′gən dā′-) Magen David.

mo·gul (mō′gəl) *n.* a bump or mound on a ski slope. [Possibly of Scandinavian origin.]

Mo·gul (mō′gul, -gəl) *n.* **1.** *also,* **Mughul.** a member or descendant of the Mongol conquerors of India who founded a Muslim empire that existed from 1526 to 1857. **2.** a Mongol or Mongolian. **3. mogul.** a powerful or important person: *The president of the studio was a mogul of the movie industry.*

mogul skiing, a type of downhill skiing done on a slope with moguls.

mo·hair (mō′hâr′) *n.* **1.** the long, silky hair of the Angora goat. **2.** a woven fabric or yarn made from this hair, sometimes mixed with cotton. [Modification (influenced by English *hair*) of earlier *mocayare,* from Italian *moccaiaro* cloth of goat's hair, from Arabic *mukhayyar* literally, choice, select.]

Mo·ham·me·dan (mō ham′i dən) *adj., n.* Muslim.

Mo·ham·med·an·ism (mō ham′i də niz′əm) *n.* Islam *(def. 1).*

Mo·ha·ve (mō hä′vē) *also,* **Mojave.** *n., pl.* **-ve** or **-ves.** a member of a tribe of North American Indians formerly living chiefly along the Colorado River. —*adj.* of or relating to the Mohave or their language or culture.

Mo·hawk (mō′hôk) *n., pl.* **-hawk** or **-hawks.** a member of a tribe of Iroquois Indians formerly living along the Mohawk River. —*adj.* of or relating to the Mohawk or their culture.

Mo·he·gan (mō hē′gən) *n., pl.* **-gan** or **-gans.** a member of a tribe of North American Indians of the Algonquian language family, originally a branch of the Mahicans, formerly living in Connecticut. —*adj.* of or relating to the Mohegan or their language or culture.

Mo·hi·can (mō hē′kən) *n., pl.* **-can** or **-cans.** **1.** Mahican. **2.** Mohegan.

Mo·ho·ro·vi·čić discontinuity (mō′hə rō′vi chich′) the boundary between the earth's crust and mantle, at a depth of 20-25 miles (32-40 kilometers) beneath the continents and 3-8 miles (5-13 kilometers) beneath the ocean floor. Also, **Mo·ho** (mō′hō). [From Andrija *Mohorovičić,* 1857-1936, Croatian geophysicist who discovered it.]

Mohs scale (mōz) a scale for judging the hardness of substances, esp. minerals, by comparing them with ten standard minerals arranged in order of increasing hardness from talc, with a

value of 1, to diamond, with a value of 10. [From Friedrich *Mohs,* 1773-1839, German mineralogist who devised it.]

moi·dore (moi'dôr) *n.* a former gold coin of Portugal or Brazil. [Portuguese *moeda d'ouro* literally, money of gold, going back to Latin *monēta* mint[2], coin + *dē* from, of + *aurum* gold.]

moi·e·ty (moi'i tē) *n., pl.* **-ties. 1.** a half. **2.** a portion; part; share. [Old French *moitie* half, from Latin *medietās* half.]

moil (moil) *v.i.* to work hard; toil. —*n.* **1.** hard work; toil; drudgery. **2.** confusion; turmoil. [Middle English *moillen* to moisten, make dirty (with mud), from Old French *moillier* to moisten, going back to Latin *mollis* soft.] **—moil'er,** *n.*

moi·ré (mwä rā', mô-) *n.* **1.** a fabric having a wavy or rippling pattern. **2.** such a pattern, pressed into fabric with engraved rollers. —*adj.* having a wavy or rippling appearance. [French *moiré,* past participle of *moirer* to water, from *moire* watered silk.]

moist (moist) *adj.* **1.** slightly or moderately wet; damp: *a moist cloth.* **2.** characterized by or containing moisture: *moist air.* **3.** (of eyes) tearful. [Old French *moiste* wet, going back to a blend of Latin *mūcidus* moldy, musty, and *musteus* fresh, new.] **—moist'ly,** *adv.* **—moist'ness,** *n.*

mois·ten (moi'sən) *v.t.* to make moist; wet slightly: *to moisten the lips.* —*v.i.* to become moist. **—mois'ten·er,** *n.*

mois·ture (mois'chər) *n.* **1.** water or other liquid diffused in the air or condensed on a surface. **2.** slight wetness; dampness.

mois·tur·ize (mois'chə rīz') *v.t.,* **-ized, -iz·ing.** to add or restore moisture to: *This cream moisturizes dry skin.* **—mois'-tur·iz'er,** *n.*

Mo·ja·ve (mō hä'vē) Mohave.

mol (mōl) mole[4].

mo·lal (mō'ləl) *adj.* (of a solution) containing 1 mole of solute per 1,000 grams of solvent. ➡ distinguished from **molar**[2] *(def. 1).* [MOLE[4] + -AL[1].]

mo·lal·i·ty (mō lal'i tē) *n.* the number of moles of solute dissolved in 1,000 grams of solvent, a measure of molal concentration. [MOLAL + -ITY.]

mo·lar[1] (mō'lər) *n.* in human beings and most mammals, any of the largest teeth in the mouth, having a broad, irregular surface for grinding food. Humans have twelve molars. —*adj.* **1.** used or adapted for grinding. **2.** of or relating to the molars. [Latin *molā-ris* molar tooth, from *mola* millstone; referring to the similarity between the grinding action of molars and that of millstones.]

mo·lar[2] (mō'lər) *adj. Chemistry.* **1.** (of a solution) containing 1 mole of solute per liter of solution. ➡ distinguished from **molal. 2.** relating to a mole or expressed in moles. [MOLE[4] + -AR[1].]

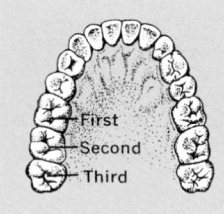

molars[1]

mo·lar·i·ty (mō lar'i tē) *n.* the number of moles of solute dissolved in 1 liter of solution, a measure of molar concentration. [MOLAR[2] + -ITY.]

mo·las·ses (mə las'iz) *n.* a sweet, thick, brownish syrup obtained from sugarcane as a by-product of the refining process. [Portuguese *melaço,* from Late Latin *mellāceum* must[2], from Latin *mel* honey.]

mold[1] (mōld) *also, British,* **mould.** *n.* **1.** a hollow form or matrix for giving a particular shape to something in a fluid or plastic state. **2.** a frame on or about which something is formed or made. **3.** something that is formed or made in or on a mold: *We served a gelatin mold for dessert.* **4.** the shape given by a mold. **5.** the general form; shape: *the mold of a baby's face.* **6.** a distinctive nature, character, or type: *brave people of rugged mold.* —*v.t.* **1.** to work into a particular shape; form: *to mold clay with the hands.* **2.** to form or make with or as with the use of a mold. **3.** to determine the form or nature of; influence or direct: *My parents helped mold my personality.* [Middle English *molde,* from Old French *modle* hollow form for giving a particular shape to something, from Latin *modulus* small measure, diminutive of *modus* measure. Doublet of MODULE.] **—mold'a·ble,** *adj.* **—mold'er,** *n.*

mold[2] (mōld) *also, British,* **mould.** *n.* **1.** any of various woolly or furry growths that form on food and other organic matter. **2.** any of a number of fungi that cause such a growth. —*v.i.* to become covered with mold; grow moldy. [Middle English *mold, moul, mowlde* mold, mildew; of Germanic origin.]

mold[3] (mōld) *also, British,* **mould.** *n.* a loose, crumbly soil that is rich in humus and suitable for plant growth. [Middle English *mold,* from Old English *molde* dust, earth; of Germanic origin.]

mold·board (mōld'bôrd') *also, British,* **mouldboard.** *n.* the curved metal plate or board on a plow that turns over the soil as it is plowed.

mold·er (mōl'dər) *also, British,* **moulder.** *v.i.* to turn to dust by natural decay; waste away; crumble. —*v.t.* to cause to crumble or decay. [MOLD[2] + -ER[4].]

mold·ing (mōl'ding) *also, British,* **moulding.** *n.* **1.** the act or process of forming or making something. **2.** something that is formed or made by molding; molded object. **3.** a shaped strip of wood, plaster, or other material that serves as a decorative edge, as along the upper part of a wall or other surface. **4.** a decoratively molded surface, contour, or projection.

mold·y (mōl'dē) *also, British,* **mouldy.** *adj.,* **mold·i·er, mold·i·est. 1.** covered with or containing fungus mold: *old, moldy biscuits.* **2.** stale, as from age or decay; musty: *the moldy odor in an old house.* **—mold'i·ness,** *n.*

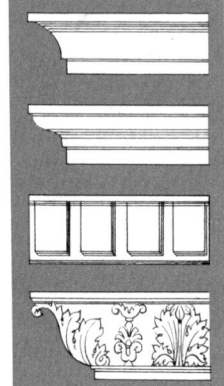

moldings

mole[1] (mōl) *n.* a congenital brownish spot on the skin. [Middle English *mole,* from Old English *māl* spot, stain; of Germanic origin.]

mole[2] (mōl) *n.* **1.** any of various mammals, family Talpidae, of temperate regions of the Northern Hemisphere, that live in underground burrows. They have long claws used for digging, very small eyes, a pointed snout, and velvety fur. Length: 6-7 inches (15-18 centimeters), including tail. **2.** a spy who has established over time an identity as a trustworthy person and usually occupies a position vital to an enemy nation's security, as in an intelligence agency. [Middle English *molle;* of Germanic origin.]

mole[3] (mōl) *n.* **1.** a massive structure, esp. of stone, that serves as a breakwater or pier. **2.** an anchorage or harbor formed by such a structure. [French *môle,* from Latin *mōlēs* mass, load, pier.]

mole[4] (mōl) *also,* **mol.** *n. Chemistry.* the quantity of an element or compound having a weight in grams numerically equal to the molecular weight. Also, **gram molecule, gram-molecular weight.** [German *Mol,* short for *Molekulargewicht* molecular weight.]

Mo·lech (mō'lek) Moloch.

mo·lec·u·lar (mə lek'yə lər) *adj.* relating to, caused by, or consisting of molecules.

molecular biology, a branch of biology that deals with the molecular structure of living organisms and with the chemical processes that operate within living cells. **—molecular biologist.**

molecular formula, the simplest type of chemical formula, showing the exact number and kinds of atoms in a molecule without regard to how the atoms are arranged.

molecular weight, the sum of the atomic weights of the atoms in a molecule.

mol·e·cule (mol'ə kūl') *n.* **1.a.** the smallest particle of an element that retains all the chemical properties of the element, consisting of either one atom, as in the monatomic gases, or of two or more identical atoms. **b.** the smallest particle of a compound that retains all of the compound's properties, consisting of atoms of two or more different elements joined by a covalent bond. **2.** any very small particle or bit. [Modern Latin *molecula,* diminutive of Latin *mōlēs* mass.]

mole·hill (mōl'hil') *n.* a small mound or ridge of earth formed by a mole burrowing under the ground.

 •**to make a mountain out of a molehill.** to give too much importance or emphasis to something relatively insignificant.

mole·skin (mōl'skin') *n.* **1.** the soft, dark gray pelt of a mole, used as fur. **2.** a strong, heavy cotton fabric with a short nap on one side, used chiefly for work and sports clothes.

mo·lest (mə lest') *v.t.* **1.** to annoy or disturb; bother. **2.** to make improper sexual advances to or abuse sexually. [Latin *molestāre* to annoy, trouble.] **—mo·les·ta·tion** (mō'les tā'shən), *n.* **—mo·lest'er,** *n.*

moll (mol) *n. Slang.* a female companion or accomplice of a gangster. [From *Moll,* familiar form of *Mary.*]

a	at	e	end	o	hot	u	up	hw	white		about
ā	ape	ē	me	ō	old	ū	use	ng	song	ə	taken
ä	far	i	it	ô	fork	ü	rule	th	thin		pencil
âr	care	ī	ice	oi	oil	u̇	pull	th	this		lemon
		îr	pierce	ou	out	ûr	turn	zh	measure		circus

mol·lie (mol′ē) *n., pl.* -lies. molly.

mol·li·fy (mol′ə fī′) *v.t.,* -fied, -fy·ing. 1. to reduce the anger or strong feelings of; pacify: *to mollify an enraged person.* 2. to reduce the intensity, severity, or harshness of: *to mollify someone's fury, to mollify his demands.* [Latin *mollificāre* to soften, from *mollis* soft + *facere* to make.] —**mol′li·fi·ca′tion,** *n.* —**mol′li·fi′er,** *n.*

mol·lus·can (mə lus′kən) *also,* **mol·lus·kan.** *adj.* of or relating to mollusks. —*n.* mollusk.

mol·lusk (mol′əsk) *also,* **mol·lusc.** *n.* any of a large group of invertebrates, phylum Mollusca, found chiefly in salt water, including clams, oysters, and snails. In most mollusks the soft, unsegmented body is protected by a hard, limy outer shell; the squid and octopus, however, lack such a shell. [Modern Latin *Mollusca,* neuter plural of Latin *molluscus* soft.]

mol·ly (mol′ē) *also,* **mollie.** *n., pl.* -lies. any of a group of tropical fish, genus *Mollienisia,* that bear their young alive. [From Modern Latin *Mollienisia,* from François N. *Mollien,* 1758-1850, French statesman.]

mol·ly·cod·dle (mol′ē kod′əl) *n.* a man or boy of an unmanly or meek nature, who needs to be or has always been pampered. —*v.t.,* -dled, -dling. to pamper; overprotect. [Obsolete *molly* milksop (from *Molly,* familiar form of *Mary*) + CODDLE.] —**mol′ly·cod′dler,** *n.*

Mo·loch (mō′lok, mol′ək) *also,* **Molech.** *n.* 1. in the Old Testament, the chief god of the Ammonites, to whom parents sacrificed their children by fire. 2. anything regarded as requiring frightful sacrifice. [Late Latin *Moloch,* from Greek *Moloch,* from Hebrew *molech, moloch,* probably the name of the sacrificial ceremony (mistaken by the translators of the Septuagint to be the name of a god), from Phoenician *moloch,* from *mulch* a sacrifice.]

Mo·lo·tov cocktail (mol′ə tôf′, mō′lə-) a makeshift bomb consisting of a bottle filled with gasoline or other flammable liquid and a wick made of cloth or other material. [Translation of Finnish *molotovin cocktaili;* referring to Vyacheslav M. Molotov, 1890-1986, Russian minister for foreign affairs during the war between Finland and the USSR (1939-40).]

molt (mōlt) *also, British,* **moult.** *v.i.* to shed the hair, feathers, skin, or shell and replace with a new growth. —*v.t.* to shed (an outer covering). —*n.* 1. the act or process of molting. 2. something that is shed by molting. [Middle English *mouten* to shed feathers, through Old English, from Latin *mūtāre* to change.] —**molt′er,** *n.*

mol·ten (mōl′tən) *v. Archaic.* a past participle of **melt.** —*adj.* 1. melted or liquefied by heat: *Lava is molten rock.* 2. made by melting and casting.

mol·to (mōl′tō) *adv. Music.* much; very. [Italian *molto,* from Latin *multum.*]

mo·ly (mō′lē) *n., pl.* -lies. a legendary herb with magical powers, having milk-white flowers and a black root, given to Odysseus by Hermes to counteract the spells of Circe. [Latin *mōly,* from Greek *mōly.*]

mo·lyb·de·nite (mə lib′də nīt′) *n.* a soft, graphitelike molybdenum sulfide mineral, the principle ore of molybdenum. Formula: MoS_2

mo·lyb·de·num (mə lib′də nəm) *n.* a heavy, very hard, silver-white metallic element, used esp. to make high-strength alloys. Symbol: **Mo** For tables, see **element.** [Modern Latin *molybdenum,* from *molybdaena* molybdenite (so called because it is similar to lead ore), from Latin *molybdaena* lead, galena, from Greek *molýbdaina* chunk of lead, from *mólybdos* lead.]

mom (mom) *n. Informal.* mother.

mom-and-pop (mom′ən pop′) *adj.* being or relating to a small retail business managed by the couple or family that owns it: *a mom-and-pop delicatessen.*

mo·ment (mō′mənt) *n.* 1. a short, indefinite period of time: *I'll be back in a moment.* 2. a particular point in time, esp. the present time: *They're not here at the moment. The moment you spoke I recognized your voice.* 3. a particular period or stage, as in a course of events: *a critical moment in a country's political development.* 4. a period or time distinguished by some quality, such as excellence or enjoyment: *It was a pretty dull party, but it did have its moments.* 5. importance; consequence: *This is a question of great moment.* 6. *Physics.* the turning effect of a force about a pivot point, measured as the product of the force and the distance between the point where the force is applied and the pivot point; torque. [Latin *mōmentum* movement, motion, short period of time, importance.]

mo·men·tar·i·ly (mō′mən ter′ə lē) *adv.* 1. for a moment: *Our train was momentarily delayed.* 2. at any moment; very soon: *An announcement is expected momentarily.* 3. from moment to moment; at every moment: *The swelling on my leg increased momentarily.*

mo·men·tar·y (mō′mən ter′ē) *adj.* 1. lasting only a very short time: *a momentary lull in a storm.* 2. occurring at every moment. 3. occurring at any moment. —**mo′men·tar′i·ness,** *n.*

Momentary, ephemeral, and evanescent mean lasting only a very short time. **Momentary** is the most general of these terms: *a momentary pause in one's work, a momentary break in the clouds.* **Ephemeral** is applied to something short-lived or fleeting or, more specifically, to existence that lasts only a day: *an ephemeral insect, the ephemeral quality of an improvised melody.* **Evanescent** suggests something unsubstantial and seeming almost unreal: *the evanescent beauty of a rainbow.*

mo·ment·ly (mō′mənt lē) *adv.* 1. from moment to moment; every moment. 2. for a moment. 3. at any moment.

mo·men·tous (mō men′təs) *adj.* of great importance or consequence: *a momentous event.* —**mo·men′tous·ly,** *adv.* —**mo·men′tous·ness,** *n.*

mo·men·tum (mō men′təm) *n., pl.* -ta (-tə) or -tums. 1. *Physics.* a measure of the motion of a moving body, equal to the product of its mass and its velocity. 2. the force or speed resulting from motion; impetus. [Latin *mōmentum* movement, motion.]

mom·ma (mom′ə) *n. Informal.* mama.

mom·my (mom′ē) *n., pl.* -mies. *Informal.* mother.

mon-, form of **mono-** before vowels, as in *monandrous.*

Mon., Monday.

mon·ad (mon′ad, mō′nad) *n.* 1. the ultimate indivisible unit of existence; simplest living entity. According to the German philosopher Gottfried Wilhelm von Leibniz, reality consists of an infinite number of these units. 2. *Biology.* any single-celled organism. 3. *Chemistry.* an atom or element with a valence of one. [Late Latin *monad-,* stem of *monas* unit, from Greek *monas,* from *monos* alone.] —**mo·nad′ic** (mə nad′ik), *adj.*

mo·nad·nock (mə nad′nok) *n.* an isolated hill or mountain standing conspicuously above the surrounding country, left over by the process of erosion. [From Mt. *Monadnock,* in New Hampshire.]

mo·nan·drous (mə nan′drəs) *adj.* of, relating to, or characterized by monandry. [Greek *monandros* having only one husband, from *monos* alone + *anēr* (stem *andr*-) man.]

mo·nan·dry (mə nan′drē) *n.* the practice, custom, or condition of having only one husband at a time.

mon·arch (mon′ərk) *n.* 1. a hereditary, usually constitutional ruler, such as a king or queen, having more or less limited powers. 2. the sole and absolute ruler of a state. 3. a person or thing suggesting, resembling, or of the nature of a monarch: *Mt. Everest is the monarch of mountains.* 4. a large orange and black butterfly, *Danaus plexippus,* that breeds in North America and is known for making southward migrations of several thousand miles in the fall. [Late Latin *monarcha* absolute ruler, from Greek *monarchēs* sole ruler, from *monos* alone + *archein* to rule.] —**mo·nar·chal** (mə när′kəl), **mo·nar′chi·al,** *adj.*

monarch butterflies

mo·nar·chi·cal (mə när′ki kəl) *adj.* 1. of, relating to, or characteristic of a monarch or monarchy. 2. ruled by or favoring a monarch or monarchy: *a monarchical society, a monarchical movement.* Also, **mo·nar′chic.** —**mo·nar′chi·cal·ly,** *adv.*

mon·ar·chism (mon′ər kiz′əm) *n.* 1. the principles of monarchy. 2. advocacy of or belief in monarchy as a form of government. —**mon′arch·ist,** *n., adj.* —**mon′ar·chis′tic,** *adj.*

mon·ar·chy (mon′ər kē) *n., pl.* -chies. 1. government by a monarch: *to favor monarchy over democracy.* 2. a nation, state, or

M

system of government ruled or headed by a monarch. [Late Latin *monarchia* absolute rule, from Greek *monarchia* government by one ruler, going back to *monos* alone + *archein* to rule.]

mon·as·te·ri·al (mon'ə stîr'ē əl) *adj.* of, relating to, or of the nature of a monastery or monastic life.

mon·as·ter·y (mon'ə ster'ē) *n., pl.* **-ter·ies. 1.** a house or other place of residence occupied by a community of persons, esp. monks, living under religious vows and according to fixed rules. **2.** the community of persons living in such a place. [Church Latin *monastērium,* from Late Greek *monastērion,* from *monazein* to live alone, from *monos* alone. Doublet of MINSTER.]

mo·nas·tic (mə nas'tik) *adj.* of, relating to, characteristic of, or of the nature of a monastery, its inhabitants, or their way of life: *monastic seclusion, monastic vows.* Also, **mo·nas'ti·cal.** —*n.* a monk or other member of a religious order. [Late Latin *monasticus* solitary, from Late Greek *monastikos* living alone, going back to *monos* alone.]

mo·nas·ti·cism (mə nas'tə siz'əm) *n.* a monastic system or way of life.

mon·a·tom·ic (mon'ə tom'ik) *adj.* (of a chemical element) occurring as a single atom rather than combined in a molecule.

mon·au·ral (mon ôr'əl) *adj.* of or relating to a system of sound reproduction in which the sound is heard from a single source. Also, **mono, monophonic.** ➡ distinguished from **stereophonic.**

mon·a·zite (mon'ə zīt') *n.* a brown or yellow phosphate mineral mined as an ore of thorium and a source of rare-earth elements. [German *monazit,* from Greek *monazein* to be alone, from *monos* alone; because its crystals occur in isolation.]

Mon·day (mun'dē, -dā) *n.* the second day of the week. [Middle English *Monday,* from Old English *mōnandæg* literally, moon's day; translation of Latin *lūnae diēs.*]

mo·ne·cious (mə nē'shəs) monoecious.

Mo·nel metal (mō nel') *Trademark.* a silvery alloy consisting principally of nickel, copper, and iron. It is highly resistant to corrosion and is used to make equipment for the chemical industry, for kitchens, and for boats.

mo·ne·ran (mə nîr'ən) *n.* any of a kingdom (Monera) of one-celled organisms, the prokaryotes, that lack a nucleus enclosed by a membrane, such as bacteria and cyanobacteria. For illustration, see **kingdom.**

mon·e·ta·rism (mon'i tə riz'əm, mun'-) *n.* an economic theory stating that the stable growth of a nation's economy is determined by controlling and maintaining the steady growth of its money supply. [MONETARY + -ISM.] —**mon'e·tar·ist,** *n., adj.*

mon·e·tar·y (mon'i ter'ē, mun'-) *adj.* **1.** of or relating to the currency or coinage of a country. **2.** of or relating to money: *monetary matters, a monetary gift.* [Late Latin *monētārius* relating to a mint², from Latin *monēta* mint², money. See MONEY.] —**mon'e·tar'i·ly,** *adv.*

monetary unit, the standard unit of value of a currency: *The peseta is the monetary unit of Spain.*

mon·e·tize (mon'i tīz', mun'-) *v.t.,* **-tized, -tiz·ing.** to establish as legal tender; legalize as money: *to monetize copper.* —**mon'e·ti·za'tion,** *n.*

mon·ey (mun'ē) *n., pl.* **mon·eys** or *(def. 7)* **mon·ies. 1.** coins and paper currency issued by government authority to serve as a medium of exchange and a standard of value, generally used as payment for goods and services; legal tender. **2.** any article or substance used or serving as money, such as checks. **3.** payment, gain, profit, or loss in terms of money: *The company made money on that deal.* **4.** wealth measured in terms of money, property, or possessions: *They tried to give the impression that their family had money.* **5.** a sum of money, esp. a definite amount of money needed for something: *to need money for college.* **6.** a form or denomination of money. **7. moneys** or **monies.** funds collected or stored, as by a government. [Old French *moneie* coin, from Latin *monēta* place for coining money, coin, from *Monēta,* epithet of Juno, in whose temple money was coined in ancient Rome. Doublet of MINT².]
 • **in the money.** *Slang.* **a.** having a lot of money; wealthy. **b.** in a winning position in a race, esp. a horse or dog race: *to finish in the money.*
 • **to put** (or **place**) **money on.** to place a bet on: *to put money on the outcome of a race.*

mon·ey·bag (mun'ē bag') *n.* **1.** a bag for holding money. **2. moneybags.** *Informal.* a wealthy, often miserly person. ➡ used as singular.

mon·ey·chang·er (mun'ē chān'jər) *n.* **1.** a person whose business is exchanging money, usually that of one country for that of another. **2.** a device that holds and dispenses coins.

mon·eyed (mun'ēd) *also,* **monied.** *adj.* **1.** having much money; wealthy. **2.** representing or derived from money or wealth: *moneyed influence.*

mon·ey·lend·er (mun'ē len'dər) *n.* a person whose business is lending money at interest.

mon·ey·mak·ing (mun'ē mā'king) *adj.* **1.** designed or likely to earn money, or successful in earning money: *a moneymaking scheme.* **2.** engaged in or intent on acquiring money or wealth: *a moneymaking spirit.* —*n.* the acquisition of money or wealth. —**mon'ey·mak'er,** *n.*

money market, a system for the investing of funds, esp. by governments, corporations, and banks, on a short-term basis.

money of account, a monetary denomination used in keeping accounts, esp. one not issued as a coin, as the U.S. mill.

money order, an order for the payment of a specified sum of money, esp. one issued by one bank or post office and payable at another.

mon·ger (mung'gər, mong'-) *n.* **1.** a person who engages in or promotes something contemptible, discreditable, or harmful. ➡ usually used in combination, as in *scandalmonger, warmonger.* **2.** a dealer in some commodity. ➡ usually used in combination, as in *fishmonger.* [Old English *mangere* dealer, going back to Latin *mangō.*]

Mon·gol (mong'gəl, -gōl) *n.* **1.** a member of one of the Mongolian-speaking nomadic tribes now living in Mongolia and nearby parts of China and southern Siberia. **2.** Mongolian *(defs. 1-3).* —*adj.* Mongolian.

Mon·go·li·an (mong gō'lē ən) *adj.* of, relating to, or characteristic of Mongolia or its people, language, or culture. —*n.* **1.** a native or citizen of Mongolia. **2.** a person of Mongolian ancestry. **3.** a member of the Mongoloid division of the human race. **4.** a subfamily of the Ural-Altaic family of languages, spoken predominantly in Mongolia and central Asia.

mon·gol·ism (mong'gə liz'əm) *also,* **Mon·gol·ism.** *n.* a word formerly used for **Down syndrome.**

Mon·gol·oid (mong'gə loid') *adj.* **1.** of or relating to one of the major divisions traditionally used to classify the human race, usually characterized by yellowish skin, brown, slanted eyes, and straight, dark hair. The Mongoloid division includes most of the peoples of eastern Asia and Japan, the Eskimo, and the North American Indians. **2.** of, resembling, or characteristic of Mongols or Mongolians. **3.** of, relating to, or characteristic of mongolism. —*n.* **1.** a member of the Mongoloid division of the human race. **2.** a person with mongolism.

mon·goose (mong'gūs') *n., pl.* **-goos·es.** a slender, carnivorous mammal, family Viverridae, native to Africa, southern Asia, and parts of southern Europe, having a pointed face, a long tail, and rough, shaggy fur. It is noted for its ability to kill certain poisonous snakes, esp. cobras. Length: 1½-3½ feet (0.5-1.1 meters), including tail. [Marathi *maṅgūs.*]

mon·grel (mung'grəl, mong'-) *n.* **1.** an animal of mixed breed, esp. a dog. **2.** a person or thing that is a mixture of different or incongruous elements. —*adj.* of mixed breed, origin, or nature. [From obsolete *mong* mixture, from Old English *gemang* a mingling.]

mon·ied (mun'ēd) moneyed.

mon·ies (mun'ēz) a plural of **money.**

mon·i·ker (mon'i kər) *also,* **mon·ick·er.** *n. Slang.* a name or nickname. [Of uncertain origin.]

mon·ism (mon'iz əm, mō'niz-) *n.* the philosophical theory that everything consists of or is reducible to one substance. ➡ distinguished from **dualism** and **pluralism.** [Modern Latin *monismus,* from Greek *monos* single, alone.] —**mon'ist,** *n.*

mo·nis·tic (mə nis'tik, mō-) *adj.* of or relating to monism. Also, **mo·nis'ti·cal.**

mo·ni·tion (mə nish'ən) *n.* **1.** a warning, admonition, or admonitory counsel. **2.** an official, legal, or formal notice. [Latin *monitiō* a reminding, warning.]

mon·i·tor (mon'i tər) *n.* **1.** a student in school given a special duty or responsibility, such as distributing materials or taking attendance. **2.** a receiver used for checking, watching, or listening to transmissions, such as those of television or radio. **3. Monitor.** a Union ironclad warship with a low, flat deck and a revolving turret with two guns. It fought the Confederate ironclad *Virginia* (the rebuilt *Merrimac*) at Hampton Roads, Virginia, in a historic battle of the American Civil War on March 9, 1862. **4.** any of a group of large, tropical Old World lizards, genus *Varanus,* such as the Komodo dragon, having a heavy, scaly, brown or black body, believed to give warnings of crocodiles. **5.** a person or thing that warns, advises, or reminds. **6.** the part of a computer terminal

a	at	e	end	o	hot	u	up	hw	white		about
ā	ape	ē	me	ō	old	ū	use	ng	song		taken
ä	far	i	it	ô	fork	ü	rule	th	thin	ə	pencil
âr	care	ī	ice	oi	oil	u̇	pull	th	this		lemon
		îr	pierce	ou	out	ûr	turn	zh	measure		circus

that contains the screen on which data are displayed. —*v.t.* **1.** to check, watch, or listen to (transmissions) with a receiver. **2.** to keep track of with or as with an electronic device. **3.** to watch over or supervise; oversee. —*v.i.* to serve as a monitor, receiver, or supervisor. [Latin *monitor* admonisher, adviser, overseer, from *monēre* to warn.]

mon·i·to·ri·al (mon'i tôr'ē əl) *adj.* **1.** of, relating to, or performed by a monitor or monitors. **2.** monitory.

mon·i·to·ry (mon'i tôr'ē) *adj.* serving to warn or admonish: *a monitory look.* —*n., pl.* **-ries.** a letter of admonition, as from a religious superior.

monk (mungk) *n.* a man who has entered a religious order devoted to prayer and contemplation and is bound by religious vows. [Old English *munuc,* going back to Late Latin *monachus,* from Late Greek *monachos,* from Greek *monos* alone.]

mon·key (mung'kē) *n.* **1.** any mammal of the order Primates, except humans, anthropoid apes, tarsiers, and lemurs, of Asia, Africa, and North and South America, having long limbs and hands and feet adapted for grasping and climbing, such as capuchins, marmosets, baboons, and rhesus monkeys. **2.** a person who resembles a monkey in behavior or appearance, esp. a mischievous, playful, or imitative child. **3.** *Informal.* a person who is made to appear foolish or ridiculous: *They really made a monkey out of me.* —*v.i.,* **-keyed, -key·ing.** *Informal.* to play, fool, or meddle (often with *around* or with): *Don't monkey with the machinery.* [Possibly from Middle Low German *Moneke,* name of an ape in medieval tales about Reynard the Fox.]

monkey bread 1. the gourdlike fruit of the baobab tree. **2.** the tree itself.

monkey business *Informal.* playful, foolish, mischievous, or deceitful activity or behavior.

mon·key·shines (mung'kē shīnz') *pl. n. Informal.* mischievous or playful acts; antics; pranks.

monkey suit *Slang.* a man's formal dress suit. [Variant of *monkey jacket* jacket worn by an organ grinder's monkey.]

monkey wrench 1. a wrench with an adjustable jaw and a fixed jaw, used on nuts and bolts of different sizes. **2.** something that disrupts or hinders: *This unexpected development throws a monkey wrench into our plans.*

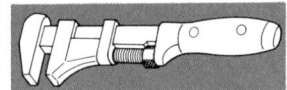

monkey wrench

monk·ish (mung'kish) *adj.* of, relating to, characteristic of, or like a monk or monks.

monks·hood (mungks'hдd') *n.* aconite *(def. 1).*

mon·o[1] (mon'ō) *n. Informal.* infectious mononucleosis.

mon·o[2] (mon'ō) *adj.* monaural.

mono- *combining form* one; single; alone: *monogamy, monotheism.* [Greek *monos.*]

mon·o·ba·sic (mon'ə bā'sik) *adj.* (of an acid) yielding only one hydrogen ion.

mon·o·chord (mon'ə kôrd') *n.* an acoustical instrument for measuring and determining musical intervals, consisting of a sounding board over which is stretched a single string that can be divided at any point by a movable bridge. [Old French *monocorde,* through Medieval Latin, going back to Greek *monos* single + *chordē* string.]

mon·o·chro·mat·ic (mon'ə krō mat'ik, mon'ō krə-) *adj.* **1.** of or having only one color. **2.** consisting of or producing light of one wavelength. —**mon'o·chro·mat'i·cal·ly,** *adv.*

mon·o·chrome (mon'ə krōm') *n.* **1.** a painting, drawing, or other representation in a single color or in various shades of a single color. **2.** the art or technique of producing such pictures. —*adj.* **1.** in one color or in shades of a single color. **2.** lacking variety; monotonous. [Greek *monochrōmos* of one color, from *monos* single + *chrōma* color.] —**mon'o·chrom'ic,** *adj.*

mon·o·cle (mon'ə kəl) *n.* an eyeglass for one eye. [French *monocle,* from Late Latin *monoculus* one-eyed, from Greek *monos* single + Latin *oculus* eye.]

mon·o·cled (mon'ə kəld) *adj.* wearing a monocle.

mon·o·cline (mon'ə klīn') *n.* a geologic structure consisting of sedimentary strata that all dip in the same direction. [MONO- + *-cline,* as in ANTICLINE.] —**mon'o·cli'nal,** *adj.*

mon·o·clin·ic (mon'ə klin'ik) *adj. Mineralogy.* of, relating to, or designating a system of crystalline forms characterized by three unequal axes, two of which intersect obliquely.

mon·o·cli·nous (mon'ə klī'nəs) *adj. Botany.* having both stamens and pistils in the same flower. [Modern Latin *monoclinus,* from Greek *monos* single + *klinē* bed.]

mon·o·clo·nal antibody (mon'ə klō'nəl) a laboratory-grown antibody for a specific antigen, produced in large quantities by a hybridoma and used in biologic research and in the manufacture of vaccines.

mon·o·cot·y·le·don (mon'ə kot'ə lē'd'n) *n.* any plant belonging to the class Monocotyledones, one of the two main groups of flowering plants, characterized by having only one cotyledon in the embryo. ➡ distinguished from **dicotyledon.** Also, **mon·o·cot** (mon'ə kot'). —**mon'o·cot'y·le'don·ous,** *adj.*

mo·noc·u·lar (mə nok'yə lər) *adj.* **1.** having only one eye. **2.** of, relating to, using, or intended for use by one eye: *a monocular microscope.* —*n.* any device intended for use with one eye. [Late Latin *monoculus* one-eyed + -AR[1]. See MONOCLE.]

mon·o·cul·ture (mon'ō kul'chər) *n.* the use of land to cultivate a single crop or plant, to the exclusion of others.

mon·o·cy·cle (mon'ə sī'kəl) *n.* unicycle.

mon·o·cyte (mon'ə sīt') *n.* a large, nongranular white blood cell that has a kidney-shaped nucleus and actively absorbs and destroys bacteria and other foreign material. —**mon'o·cyt'ic,** *adj.*

mon·o·dy (mon'ə dē) *n., pl.* **-dies. 1.** in ancient Greek literature, an ode sung by a single voice, as in a tragedy, esp. a lament or dirge. **2.** a poem in which the poet laments someone's death. **3.** *Music.* **a.** a homophonic style of composition. **b.** a composition in this style. [Greek *monōdidiā* solo, lament, going back to *monos* alone + *õidē* song.] —**mo·nod'ik** (mə nod'ik), *adj.*

mo·noe·cious (mə nē'shəs) *also,* **monecious.** *adj. Botany.* having male and female reproductive organs (in flowering plants, the stamen and pistil) in separate structures on the same plant. [MONO- + Greek *oikos* house + -OUS.] —**mo·noe·cism** (mə nē'siz əm), *n.*

mon·o·fil·a·ment (mon'ə fil'ə mənt) *n.* a single strand of synthetic fiber, as of nylon.

mo·nog·a·mist (mə nog'ə mist) *n.* a person who practices or believes in monogamy.

mo·nog·a·mous (mə nog'ə məs) *adj.* of, relating to, or practicing monogamy. Also, **mon·o·gam·ic** (mon'ə gam'ik). —**mo·nog'a·mous·ly,** *adv.*

mo·nog·a·my (mə nog'ə mē) *n.* **1.** the condition or practice of being married to only one person at a time. **2.** *Zoology.* the habit of having only one mate. **3.** the practice of marrying only once during life. [Late Latin *monogamia* the marrying of only one wife, going back to Greek *monos* single, alone + *gamos* marriage.]

mon·o·gram (mon'ə gram') *n.* a character consisting of two or more letters, esp. the initials of a person's name, combined or interlaced into one design, used on clothing, stationery, and other items. —*v.t.,* **-grammed** or **-gramed,** **-gram·ming** or **-graming.** to mark with a monogram. [Late Latin *monogramma* character consisting of several letters, from Greek *monos* single, alone + *gramma* letter.] —**mon·o·gram·mat·ic** (mon'ə grə mat'ik), *adj.*

mon·o·graph (mon'ə graf') *n.* a book, treatise, or article, usually of a scholarly nature, written on a single subject or on a particular aspect of a subject. —**mon'o·graph'ic,** *adj.*

mon·o·hy·brid (mon'ō hī'brid) *n.* an individual or variety that is the offspring of a cross between parents that are heterozygous in respect to one specific factor or gene. —*adj.* of or relating to a monohybrid.

mon·o·lay·er (mon'ə lā'ər) *n.* **1.** a monomolecular layer or film. **2.** a single layer, esp. a tissue culture consisting of a single layer of cells.

mon·o·lin·gual (mon'ə ling'gwəl) *adj.* **1.** capable of speaking only one's native language. **2.** expressed or written in only one language: *This is a monolingual dictionary.*

mon·o·lith (mon'ə lith') *n.* **1.** a single, usually very large block of stone, used in architecture and sculpture. **2.** a monument or other structure formed of such a block of stone, such as an obelisk. **3.** something that is like such a stone or monument, as in being massive and unmovable. [Latin *monolithus* made of one stone, from Greek *monolithos,* from *monos* single, alone + *lithos* stone.]

mon·o·lith·ic (mon'ə lith'ik) *adj.* **1.** formed of, relating to, or resembling a monolith. **2.** of the nature of a monolith; massive or uniform. **3.** *Electronics.* of or relating to an integrated circuit fabricated on a single silicon chip.

mo·nol·o·gist (mə nol'ə jist) *n.* a person, esp. an entertainer, who gives a monologue or monologues.

mon·o·logue (mon'ə lôg', -log') *also,* **mon·o·log.** *n.* **1.** a long speech made by one person, often monopolizing conversation. **2.** soliloquy. **3.** a dramatic or literary composition involving or performed by only one speaker. **4.** an entertainment consisting of a series of jokes, anecdotes, or humorous stories presented by a single speaker. [French *monologue* soliloquy, from Late Greek *monologos* speaking alone, from Greek *monos* alone + *logos* word, discourse.] —**mon·o·log·ic** (mon'ə loj'ik); *also,* **mon'o·log'i·cal,** *adj.*

mon·o·ma·ni·a (mon'ə mā'nē ə) *n.* **1.** a mental disorder in which a person has an obsession with one idea but otherwise appears sane. **2.** an excessive preoccupation with or enthusiasm

for one idea or subject. —**mon′o·ma′ni·ac′**, *n.* —**mon·o·ma·ni·a·cal** (mon′ə mə nī′ə kəl), *adj.*

mon·o·mer (mon′ə mər) *n.* one of the small simple molecules making up a polymer. —**mon·o·mer·ic** (mon′ə mer′ik), *adj.*

mon·o·met·al·lism (mon′ə met′ə liz′əm) *n.* the theory or system of using only one metal, usually gold, as the standard of currency. —**mon·o·me·tal·lic** (mon′ə mi tal′ik), *adj.* —**mon′o·met′al·list**, *n.*

mo·no·mi·al (mə nō′mē əl, mō-) *n.* **1.** an algebraic expression consisting of a single term. **2.** in taxonomy, a one-word plant or animal name. —*adj.* consisting of a single term or word. [MONO- + (BIN)OMIAL.]

mon·o·mo·lec·u·lar (mon′ō mə lek′yə lər) *adj.* having a thickness of only one molecule: *a monomolecular film.*

mon·o·nu·cle·ar (mon′ō nü′klē ər, -nū′-) *adj.* *Biology.* (of a cell) having only one nucleus.

mon·o·nu·cle·o·sis (mon′ə nü′klē ō′sis, -nū′-) *n.* infectious mononucleosis.

mon·o·phon·ic (mon′ə fon′ik) *adj.* **1.** *Music.* having a single melodic line with no accompaniment. **2.** monaural.

Mo·noph·y·sit·ism (mə nof′ə sī tiz′əm) *n.* the doctrine that the nature of Christ was divine only, not both human and divine. This doctrine is held by certain Eastern Christian churches, esp. the Coptic Church. [Greek *monos* single + *physis* nature.] —**Mo·noph·y·site** (mə nof′ə sīt′), *n.* —**Mo·noph·y·sit·ic** (mə nof′ə sit′ik), *adj.*

mon·o·plane (mon′ə plān′) *n.* an airplane with only one main supporting surface or only one pair of wings.

mon·o·ploid (mon′ə ploid′) *adj.* haploid. [MONO- + -*ploid,* on the model of DIPLOID, HAPLOID.]

mo·nop·o·list (mə nop′ə list) *n.* **1.** a holder of a monopoly. **2.** a person who favors monopoly. —**mo·nop′o·lis′tic**, *adj.*

mo·nop·o·lize (mə nop′ə līz′) *v.t.,* -**lized,** -**liz·ing.** **1.** to obtain or exercise a monopoly of: *an attempt to monopolize the automobile industry.* **2.** to take or acquire exclusive control or possession of: *to monopolize a conversation, to monopolize someone's attention.* —**mo·nop′o·li·za′tion**, *n.* —**mo·nop′o·liz′er**, *n.*

mo·nop·o·ly (mə nop′ə lē) *n., pl.* -**lies. 1.** exclusive control of a commodity or service in a particular market, or sufficient control to fix prices and eliminate competition. **2.** the right or privilege of such control conferred by a government. A patent gives an inventor a monopoly over the invention for a limited number of years. **3.** a commodity or service that is controlled by a monopoly. **4.** a company or group that has a monopoly. **5.** exclusive control or possession of something. [Latin *monopōlium* privilege of exclusive dealing or sale, from Greek *monopōlion,* going back to *monos* single, alone + *pōlein* to sell.]

mon·o·rail (mon′ə rāl′) *n.* **1.** a railway system in which the cars travel along a single rail, usually elevated above ground traffic. Cars may either ride upon the rail or be suspended beneath it. **2.** the single rail for such a system.

mon·o·sac·cha·ride (mon′ō sak′ə rīd′) *n.* any of a group of sugars, as glucose or fructose, that cannot be broken down by hydrolysis. Formula: $C_6H_{12}O_6$ Also, **simple sugar.**

mon·o·so·di·um glu·ta·mate (mon′ə sō′dē əm glü′tə māt′) a white powder added to many prepared foods to improve their flavor. Formula: $C_5H_8O_4NaN$ Also, **MSG.**

mon·o·some (mon′ə sōm′) *n.* an unpaired chromosome in an otherwise diploid cell, esp. a single X chromosome. [MONO- + -SOME³.] —**mon′o·so′mic**, *adj.*

mon·o·syl·lab·ic (mon′ə si lab′ik) *adj.* **1.** having only one syllable: *a monosyllabic suffix.* **2.** consisting of or using monosyllables: *a curt, monosyllabic reply.* —**mon′o·syl·lab′i·cal·ly**, *adv.*

mon·o·syl·la·ble (mon′ə sil′ə bəl) *n.* a word of one syllable.

mon·o·the·ism (mon′ə thē iz′əm) *n.* the doctrine or belief that there is only one God. [MONO- + Greek *theos* god + -ISM.] —**mon′o·the′ist**, *n.* —**mon′o·the·is′tic**, *adj.*

mon·o·tone (mon′ə tōn′) *n.* **1.** the utterance of a succession of words or sounds with no variation in pitch or key; single, unvaried tone in speaking, singing, or sound: *The lecturer spoke in a dull monotone.* **2.** sameness of style, manner, or color. **3.** *Music.* **a.** a single tone that does not change pitch. **b.** a musical passage sung in such a tone. **c.** a singer who sings in such a tone. —*adj.* **1.** monotonous. **2.** of, relating to, or characterized by a sameness or lack of variation, as in color or sound.

mo·not·o·nous (mə not′ə nəs) *adj.* **1.** unvaried in tone, sound, or cadence: *a monotonous voice, a monotonous rhythm.* **2.** tiresome or uninteresting due to a lack of change or variety: *I quickly became bored with the monotonous job.* —**mo·not′o·nous·ly**, *adv.* —**mo·not′o·nous·ness**, *n.*

mo·not·o·ny (mə not′ə nē) *n.* **1.** tiresome sameness; lack of variety: *the monotony of prison life.* **2.** a lack of variation in tone,

sound, or cadence. [Greek *monotoniā* sameness of tone, going back to *monos* single, alone + *tonos* sound.]

mon·o·treme (mon′ə trēm′) *n.* a member of the most primitive order of mammals, Monotremata, consisting of only the platypus and echidna and found chiefly in Australia and New Guinea. Monotremes lay eggs but nurse their young. [Modern Latin *Monotremata,* from MONO- + Greek *trēma* hole; referring to the single opening it has for its digestive, excretory, and reproductive organs.]

mon·o·type (mon′ə tīp′) *n.* **1.** a machine consisting of a keyboard unit and a typecasting unit, that casts and sets individual types for each character and assembles them into lines of proper length. Trademark: **Monotype. 2.** the type produced by such a machine: *The book was set in monotype.* **3.** *Biology.* the sole representative of its group, such as a single species that constitutes a genus.

mon·o·typ·ic (mon′ə tip′ik) *adj. Biology.* having only one member or subgroup, as a genus consisting of a single species, or a family of only one genus.

mon·o·va·lent (mon′ə vā′lənt) *adj. Chemistry.* univalent. —**mon′o·va′lence, mon′o·va′len·cy**, *n.*

mon·ox·ide (mon ok′sīd, mə nok′-) *n.* an oxide containing only one atom of oxygen in each molecule.

mon·o·zy·got·ic (mon′ō zī got′ik) *adj.* having developed from a single fertilized egg, as identical twins. Also, **mon·o·zy·gous** (mon′ə zī′gəs).

Mon·roe Doctrine (mən rō′) a declaration of U.S. foreign policy made by President James Monroe in 1823 that opposed further European colonization or interference with independent states in the Western Hemisphere.

Mon·sei·gneur (môn se nyœR′) *n., pl.* **Mes·sei·gneurs. 1.** a French title of honor given to men of eminence, such as members of the higher nobility, bishops, and cardinals. **2.** *also,* **monseigneur.** a man who bears this title. [French *monseigneur* my lord, from *mon* my (from Latin *meus*) + *seigneur* lord (from Latin *senior* older).]

mon·sieur (mə syœ′) *n., pl.* **mes·sieurs.** mister; sir. ➡ the French form of respectful or polite address for a man. [French *monsieur,* from *mon* my (from Latin *meus*) + *sieur* lord (from Latin *senior* older).]

Mon·si·gnor (mon sēn′yər; *Italian* môn′sē nyôR′) *n., pl.* **Mon·si·gnors** or *Italian* **Mon·si·gno·ri** (môn′sē nyô′Rē). **1.** a title given to certain Roman Catholic dignitaries, esp. those of the papal court and household. **2.** *also,* **monsignor.** a man who bears this title. [Italian *monsignore,* from French *monseigneur.* See MONSEIGNEUR.]

mon·soon (mon sün′) *n.* **1.** a seasonal wind of the Indian Ocean and southern Asia, which blows from the southwest toward the land in summer and from the northeast toward the ocean in winter. **2.** the season of the summer monsoon, characterized by heavy rains. **3.** any wind system that seasonally reverses its direction. [Middle Dutch *monssoen* periodic wind, from Portuguese *monção,* from Arabic *mausim* season.] —**mon·soon′al**, *adj.*

mon·ster (mon′stər) *n.* **1.** an animal or plant that is abnormal in structure or appearance. **2.** an imaginary creature that combines various animal and human features, such as a centaur or griffin. **3.** anything that is abnormal or grotesque in shape or character. **4.** a person or thing that is unusually large. **5.** a person whose behavior is inhumanly wicked, cruel, or immoral. —*adj.* enormous; gigantic. [Old French *monstre* something abnormal in nature, from Latin *mōnstrum* portent, monstrosity, from *monēre* to warn.]

mon·strance (mon′strəns) *n.* in Roman Catholicism, a vessel in which the consecrated host is exposed for adoration, consisting of a glass receptacle surrounded by a frame of gold or silver rays. [Medieval Latin *monstrantia,* from Latin *mōnstrāre* to show.]

mon·stros·i·ty (mon stros′i tē) *n., pl.* -**ties. 1.** a monstrous person or thing. **2.** the quality or condition of being monstrous.

mon·strous (mon′strəs) *adj.* **1.** abnormal or grotesque in appearance or character. **2.** unusually large; enormous: *an error of monstrous proportions.* **3.** hideously evil; horrible; shocking: *monstrous lies.* **4.** horribly wrong: *a monstrous error in planning.* —*adv. Archaic.* extremely. —**mon′strous·ly**, *adv.* —**mon′strous·ness**, *n.*

Mont., Montana.

mon·tage (mon täzh′) *n.* **1.** a composite picture made by superimposing or combining several different pictorial elements.

M

a	at	e	end	o	hot	u	up	hw	white		about
ā	ape	ē	me	ō	old	ū	use	ng	song		taken
ä	far	i	it	ô	fork	ü	rule	th	thin	ə	pencil
âr	care	ī	ice	oi	oil	u̇	pull	th	this		lemon
		îr	pierce	ou	out	ûr	turn	zh	measure		circus

793

2. the art or process of making such pictures. **3.** *Motion Pictures.* **a.** a rapid succession of scenes or images, used esp. to create atmosphere or to illustrate a group of associated ideas. **b.** the revolving or flashing of images into focus or around a focused area. **4.** a similar composite technique in radio, literature, music, and other arts. [French *montage* a putting together, from *monter* to put together, climb. See MOUNT[1].]

mon·tane (mon′tān) *adj.* of, relating to, or found in an ecologic zone characterized by cool, moist, upland slopes below the timberline, usually forested with large evergreen trees: *a montane plant community.* [Latin *montānus* relating to mountains. See MOUNTAIN.]

mon·te (mon′tē) *n.* a card game of Spanish origin played with a special pack of forty cards, in which players bet against the dealer. Also, **monte bank.** [Spanish *monte* the game, pile of cards left after dealing, mountain, from Latin *mōns* heap, mountain.]

Mon·tes·so·ri method (mon′tə sôr′ē) a method of preschool and primary education developed by the Italian educator Maria Montessori, emphasizing sensory and motor training, individual expression, and the development of self-discipline and independence.

month (munth) *n.* **1.** one of the twelve parts into which the calendar year is divided. Also, **calendar month. 2.** the time from any day of one calendar month to the corresponding day of the next month. **3.** a period of about four weeks or thirty days. **4.** the period of a complete revolution of the moon around the earth, esp. the period from one new moon to the next, a **lunar month,** about 29½ days, or the period from one conjunction with a star to the next, a **sidereal month,** about 27⅓ days. **5.** one twelfth of the solar year. Also *(def. 5),* **solar month.** [Old English *mōnath.*]

month·ly (munth′lē) *adj.* **1.** done, happening, or appearing once a month. **2.** of or relating to a month. **3.** continuing or lasting a month. —*adv.* once a month; every month. —*n., pl.* **-lies. 1.** a periodical published once a month. **2. monthlies.** *Informal.* menstruation.

mon·u·ment (mon′yə mənt) *n.* **1.** a building, statue, arch, or other structure erected to commemorate a person or event. **2.** a memorial stone or marker placed at a grave; tombstone. **3.** anything that serves as a memorial of a person, period, or event: *The Colosseum remains as a monument to ancient Rome's greatness.* **4.** a work or achievement of enduring significance: *The discovery of penicillin was a monument in medical research.* **5.** an area or site of special significance set aside and preserved by a government. **6.** a marker or other object, either occurring naturally or placed intentionally, that indicates a surveyed boundary. [Latin *monumentum* memorial, tomb.]

mon·u·men·tal (mon′yə men′təl) *adj.* **1.** of enduring significance; notable: *a monumental decision of the Supreme Court.* **2.** of great size or scope; huge; colossal: *a monumental traffic jam.* **3.** like a monument; imposing: *a monumental structure.* **4.** of, for, or serving as a monument. —**mon′u·men′tal·ly,** *adv.*

moo (mü) *n.* the sound made by a cow. —*v.i.,* **mooed, mooing.** to make such a sound; low. [Imitative.]

mooch (müch) *Slang. v.t.* **1.** to get without paying; beg: *to mooch a meal.* **2.** to steal; pilfer. —*v.i.* **1.** to get things without paying. **2.** to move stealthily; sneak; skulk: *to mooch around looking for trouble.* [Possibly from Old French *muchier* to hide, skulk; possibly of Celtic origin.] —**mooch′er,** *n.*

mood[1] (müd) *n.* **1.** a person's state or frame of mind or feeling at a particular time: *I was in a happy mood.* **2.** a state of mind disposing a person to action: *Some artists work only when they are in the mood.* **3. moods.** fits of bad temper, sudden anger, or depression. [Old English *mōd* mind, spirit, feeling.]

mood[2] (müd) *n. Grammar.* the form of a verb that shows whether the speaker thinks of the statement as fact, command, wish, or possibility. There are three moods in English: indicative, imperative, and subjunctive. Also, **mode.** [Modification (influenced by *mood*[1]) of MODE[1].]

mood·y (mü′dē) *adj.,* **mood·i·er, mood·i·est. 1.** given to or governed by changing moods, esp. gloomy or sullen moods. **2.** characterized by or expressing a gloomy mood: *a moody face, a moody film.* —**mood′i·ly,** *adv.* —**mood′i·ness,** *n.*

Synonyms **Moody** and **temperamental** mean having a changeable disposition. **Moody** suggests sudden and sharp changes of states of mind, which often lead to feelings of gloom and depression: *She is so moody that you never know what to expect from her.* **Temperamental** denotes erratic, unpredictable behavior arising from a high-strung, excitable nature: *He is a wonderful actor, but is known to be temperamental and difficult to work with.*

Moog (mōg, müg) *n. Trademark.* a type of synthesizer used to produce a wide range of musical sounds. Also, **Moog synthesizer.** [From R. A. *Moog,* born 1934, American engineer who invented it.]

moon (mün) *n.* **1.** the earth's natural satellite, visible by the sun's reflected light, orbiting the earth from west to east once in about 29½ days with reference to the sun and in about 27⅓ days with reference to the stars at a mean distance of about 238,857 miles (384,321 kilometers). The moon has a mean diameter of 2,160 miles (3,475 kilometers) or about ¼ that of the earth. Its mass is about ⅟81 and its volume about ⅟49 that of the earth. **2.** any one of the phases of the moon. **3.** anything resembling the moon in any of its phases, such as a crescent. **4.** a satellite of any other planet: *Mars has two small moons.* **5.** a month, esp. a lunar month. **6.** moonlight: *White in the moon the long road lies* (A. E. Housman, 1896). —*v.i.* to move or look about dreamily or aimlessly. —*v.t.* to spend (time) dreamily or aimlessly: *to moon an evening away.* [Middle English *mone,* from Old English *mōna.*]

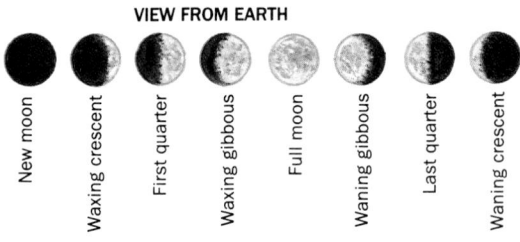

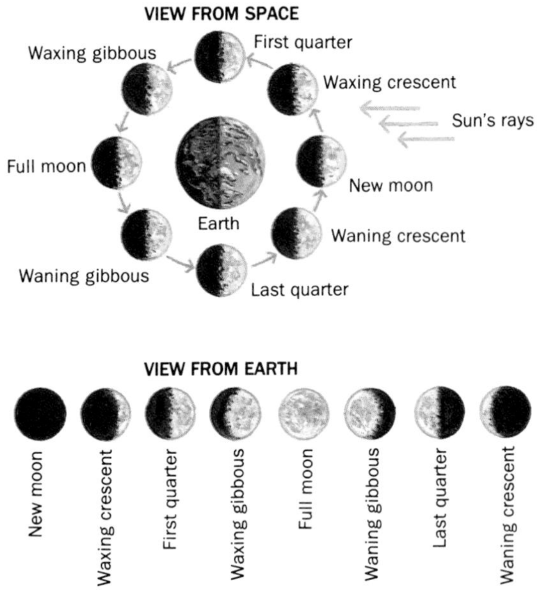

VIEW FROM SPACE

Waxing gibbous — First quarter — Waxing crescent — Sun's rays — New moon — Waning crescent — Last quarter — Waning gibbous — Full moon — Earth

VIEW FROM EARTH

New moon — Waxing crescent — First quarter — Waxing gibbous — Full moon — Waning gibbous — Last quarter — Waning crescent

phases of the **moon**

moon·beam (mün′bēm′) *n.* a ray of light from the moon.

moon·calf (mün′kaf′) *n., pl.* **-calves** (-kavz′). **1.** a person who is born deformed. **2.** an idiot. [From a belief that the influence of the moon can have a harmful effect.]

moon·fish (mün′fish′) *n., pl.* **-fish** or **-fish·es. 1.** any of a group of deep-bodied, flattened, Atlantic fish, genus *Selene,* with deeply forked tails, found off North and South America. **2.** a large, shiny, brightly colored, elliptical fish, *Lampris guttatus,* found in all oceans.

moon·flow·er (mün′flou′ər) *n.* a tropical American climbing morning glory, *Ipomoea alba,* grown for its large, fragrant flowers that bloom at night.

moon·let (mün′lit) *n.* a small artificial or natural satellite; small moon: *the moonlets embedded in Saturn's rings.* [MOON + -LET.]

moon·light (mün′līt′) *n.* the light shining from the moon. —*adj.* **1.** illuminated by the moon; moonlit. **2.** occurring or performed by the light of the moon: *a moonlight raid.* —*v.i.* to work at a second job, esp. at night, in addition to one's regular job. —**moon′light′er,** *n.* —**moon′light′ing,** *n.*

moon·lit (mün′lit′) *adj.* lighted by the moon.

moon·rock (mün′rok′) *n.* a loose piece of the moon's crust, esp. as sampled and returned to earth by an astronaut.

moon·scape (mün′skāp′) *n.* a picture or view of the moon's surface with the horizon in the background, or the surface depicted.

moon·shine (mün′shīn′) *n.* **1.** moonlight. **2.** empty talk or ideas; nonsense. **3.** liquor distilled secretly and illegally. —*v.t., v.i.,* **-shined, -shin·ing.** to distill (liquor) illegally. —**moon′shin′er,** *n.*

moon·stone (mün′stōn′) *n.* a pearly, opalescent gemstone, an ornamental variety of feldspar.

moon·struck (mün′struk′) *adj.* romantically dazed or slightly crazy, supposedly because of the influence of the moon.

moon·walk (mün′wôk′) *n.* an excursion on the moon's surface by an astronaut on foot.

moon·y (mü′nē) *adj.*, **moon·i·er, moon·i·est. 1.** affected by or expressing a dreamy mood; moonstruck. **2.** of, relating to, or like the moon. —**moon′i·ly,** *adv.* —**moon′i·ness,** *n.*

moor[1] (mûr) *v.t.* to secure (a ship or other craft) in place, as at a dock or berth. —*v.i.* **1.** to secure or anchor a ship or other craft. **2.** to be secured, as by ropes and anchors. [Middle English *moren;* of Germanic origin.]

moor[2] (mûr) *n.* a tract of open, rolling, wild land, often covered with heath, and having bogs and marshes. [Middle English *more,* from Old English *mōr;* of Germanic origin.]

Moor (mûr) *n.* **1.** a member of a people of mixed Arab and Berber descent living in northern Africa. **2.** a member of one group of this people that invaded and conquered Spain in the eighth century A.D. [Old French *More,* from Latin *Maurus* inhabitant of Mauretania, from Greek *Mauros.*]

moor·age (mûr′ij) *n.* **1.** a place for mooring. **2.** the act of mooring or the state of being moored. **3.** a charge for the use of a mooring.

moor cock, the male of the moorfowl.

moor·fowl (mûr′foul′) *n.* red grouse.

moor·hen (mûr′hen′) *n.* **1.** the female of the moorfowl. **2.** the common gallinule.

moor·ing (mûr′ing) *n.* **1.** the act of a person or thing that moors. **2.** a device, such as a cable line or anchor, by which a ship is moored. **3.** a place where a boat or ship can be moored. **4. moorings.** the elements of one's life, such as beliefs and habits, that make one feel stable and secure: *For a short while I lost my moorings.*

Moor·ish (mûr′ish) *adj.* **1.** of or relating to the Moors. **2.** characteristic of the artistic style of the Moors. Also, **Moresque.**

moor·land (mûr′land′, -lənd) *n. British.* a tract of land consisting of moors.

moose (müs) *n., pl.* **moose. 1.** a large, heavily built mammal, *Alces alces,* the largest member of the deer family, native to the northern forests of North America, having a massive head, a short neck, humped shoulders, and a blackish brown coat with gray markings. The male has enormous antlers that may measure more than 6½ feet (1.9 meters) across. Height: to 6 feet (1.8 meters) at the shoulder. **2.** the European elk. [Of Algonquian origin.]

moose

moot (müt) *adj.* **1.** subject to dispute or discussion; debatable: *a moot observation.* **2.** without practical significance or value; purely academic. —*v.t.* **1.** to bring up for discussion or debate. **2.** to make purely academic or unimportant. —*n.* in Anglo-Saxon England, an assembly of freemen to administer justice and discuss local problems. [Old English *mōt* assembly, discussion.]

moot court, a teaching court in which law students plead imaginary cases and instructors evaluate their legal knowledge and abilities.

mop (mop) *n.* **1.** a cleaning device consisting of a bundle of coarse yarn, cloth, sponge, or other absorbent material, fastened at the end of a handle. **2.** any thick, tangled mass resembling this, such as a head of hair. —*v.t., v.i.,* **mopped, mop·ping.** to clean with or as with a mop. [Possibly from Old French *mappe* napkin, from Latin *mappa.*]

• **to mop up. a.** to finish a project. **b.** *Military.* to clear out remaining enemy troops from (a captured area).

mope (mōp) *v.i.,* **moped, mop·ing.** to be gloomy, apathetic, and sad. —*n.* a person who mopes or is inclined to mope. [Of uncertain origin.] —**mop′er,** *n.* —**mop′ing·ly,** *adv.*

mo·ped (mō′ped) *n.* a lightweight motorbike that can be driven at low speeds or pedaled. [Short for *mo(tor)* and *ped(al).*]

mop·pet (mop′it) *n.* a little child. [Obsolete English *mop* fool, child (of uncertain origin) + -ET.]

mop-up (mop′up′) *n.* the act or an instance of mopping up.

mo·quette (mō ket′) *n.* a fabric having a thick velvety pile, used for upholstery or carpeting. [French *moquette* Wilton carpet,

modification of earlier *moucade* imitation velvet; of uncertain origin.]

mo·raine (mə rān′) *n.* a raised landform consisting of accumulated rock debris carried and deposited by a glacier. [French *moraine,* from dialectal French *morêna;* of uncertain origin.] —**mo·rain′al, mo·rain′ic,** *adj.*

mor·al (môr′əl, mor′-) *adj.* **1.** good according to a standard of right and wrong: *a moral person, the moral thing to do.* **2.** of, relating to, or concerned with a standard of right conduct: *the moral climate of a society.* **3.** promoting, aiding, or on the side of right conduct: *moral teachings.* **4.** acting on or relating to feelings or character: *moral support.* **5.** probable although not proven by evidence: *a moral certainty.* **6.** capable of conforming to a standard of right conduct: *Animals are not moral beings.* —*n.* **1.** a lesson or inner meaning taught by a fable, a story, or an event. **2. morals.** principles, standards, or behavior in regard to right or wrong conduct, esp. sexual conduct. [Latin *mōrālis* relating to manners, from *mōs* custom, manner.] —**mor′al·ly,** *adv.*

> **Synonyms** *adj.* **Moral** and **ethical** mean conforming to a system of right behavior. **Moral,** the more general term, emphasizes the distinction between right and wrong as dictated by one's own conscience: *Their moral beliefs would not allow them to cheat on the test.* **Ethical** implies adherence to objectively defined principles, esp. as embodied in a professional code laying down standards of honesty and integrity: *Refusing to betray a client's confidence is part of the ethical code of the legal profession.*

mo·rale (mə ral′) *n.* the attitude or condition of an individual or group, as when faced with a challenge, with respect to such qualities as courage, confidence, and discipline: *Scoring first boosted the team's morale.* [Modification of French *moral* spirit (as of troops), going back to Latin *mōrālis* relating to manners. See MORAL.]

mor·al·ism (môr′ə liz′əm, mor′-) *n.* **1.** adherence to or advocacy of strict or rigid moral standards. **2.** a moral saying or maxim.

mor·al·ist (môr′ə list, mor′-) *n.* **1.** a person who teaches or writes on morality. **2.** a person whose behavior or talk is characterized by moralism.

mor·al·is·tic (môr′ə lis′tik, mor′-) *adj.* characterized by moralism, esp. tending to preach or urge morality. —**mor′al·is′ti·cal·ly,** *adv.*

mo·ral·i·ty (mə ral′i tē) *n., pl.* **-ties. 1.** the state or quality of being moral. **2.** moral conduct. **3.** a system of conduct embodying principles of right and wrong; ethics: *Victorian morality.* **4.** a discourse or instruction intended to teach a lesson in right conduct or ethics. **5.** morality play.

morality play, any of a group of moralistic dramatic works popular during the fifteenth and sixteenth centuries, in which the characters represent abstract qualities, such as envy or fortitude.

mor·al·ize (môr′ə līz′, mor′-) *v.,* **-ized, -iz·ing.** —*v.i.* to make judgments on matters of right and wrong, esp. to tell people what to do in a moralistic fashion. —*v.t.* **1.** to explain or interpret the lesson or moral of. **2.** to view in moral terms; regard as a question of right and wrong. **3.** to improve the morals of. —**mor′al·iz′er,** *n.*

moral philosophy, ethics.

moral victory, a defeat that is felt to be a victory, esp. because of hopeful circumstances accompanying it.

mo·rass (mə ras′) *n.* **1.** a piece of low, soft, wet ground; marsh; swamp. **2.** any state or situation that is entangling, perplexing, or hindering: *a political morass.* [Dutch *moeras* marsh, from Old French *mareis;* of Germanic origin.]

mor·a·to·ri·um (môr′ə tôr′ē əm, mor′-) *n., pl.* **-to·ri·ums** or **-to·ri·a** (-tôr′ē ə). **1.** a suspension for a specified period of time of the obligations of a debtor or debtors. **2.** the period of such a suspension. **3.** any authorized temporary suspension or cessation of some activity. [Modern Latin *moratorium,* going back to Latin *morārī* to delay.]

Mo·ra·vi·an (mô rā′vē ən) *adj.* **1.** of, relating to, or characteristic of Moravia or its people, language, or culture. **2.** of or relating to the Moravian Church. —*n.* **1.** a native or inhabitant of Moravia. **2.** a member of the Moravian Church. **3.** a dialect of Czech spoken in Moravia.

a	at	e	end	o	hot	u	up	hw	white		about
ā	ape	ē	me	ō	old	ū	use	ng	song	ə	taken
ä	far	i	it	ô	fork	ü	rule	th	thin		pencil
âr	care	ī	ice	oi	oil	u̇	pull	th	this		lemon
				îr	pierce	ou	out	ûr	turn	zh	measure		circus

Moravian Church, a Protestant denomination that originated in Germany in the eighteenth century among followers of the Bohemian religious reformer John Huss.

mo·ray (môr′ā, mô rā′) *n.* any of various, often brilliantly colored saltwater eels, family Muraenidae, found in warm waters and having strong jaws and sharp teeth. Also, **moray eel.** [Portuguese *moreia* eel, from Latin *mūrena,* from Greek *myraina.*]

moray

mor·bid (môr′bid) *adj.* **1.** overly sensitive to or dwelling upon death, disease, decay, and the like; not cheerful or wholesome. **2.** of or relating to death, disease, decay, and the like; gruesome; grisly: *a morbid graveyard scene.* **3.** relating to, caused by, or characteristic of disease: *a morbid condition of the liver.* [Latin *morbidus* sickly, from *morbus* disease.] —**mor′bid·ly,** *adv.* —**mor′bid·ness,** *n.*

mor·bid·i·ty (môr bid′i tē) *n.* **1.** the quality or state of being morbid. **2.** the rate of disease or proportion of diseased persons, as in a particular population or area.

mor·da·cious (môr dā′shəs) *adj.* **1.** given to biting; biting. **2.** sarcastic; caustic. [Latin *mordāc-,* stem of *mordāx* biting + -OUS.] —**mor·da′cious·ly,** *adv.* —**mor·dac·i·ty** (môr das′i tē), *n.*

mor·dan·cy (môr′dən sē) *n.* the quality of being sarcastic or biting.

mor·dant (môr′dənt) *adj.* **1.** caustic, cutting, or sarcastic. **2.** acting or capable of acting as a color fixative in dyeing. —*n.* **1.** any substance, such as tannin, that when combined with a dye serves to fix the color in the cloth. **2.** an acid or other corrosive used in etching to eat into metal. [Old French *mordant* biting, present participle of *mordre* to bite, going back to Latin *mordēre.*] —**mor′dant·ly,** *adv.*

mor·dent (môr′dənt) *n. Music.* the quick alternation of a principal tone with a half or whole tone below it, used as an ornament; downward trill. [Italian *mordente* literally, a bite, from *mordere* to bite, from Latin *mordēre;* with reference to the sharp manner of its playing.]

Mor·dred (môr′drid) Modred.

more (môr) *adj.* the comparative of **much** or **many.** **1.** greater in number, quantity, intensity, or degree: *more cars, more flour.* **2.** being an additional amount; further: *Try it one more time. I'll need a minute more.* —*adv.* the comparative of **much.** **1.** in or to a greater extent or degree: *Be more careful. He exercises more regularly than I do.* **2.** in addition; further; again: *Spell it once more.* —*n.* **1.** a greater number, quantity, amount, or degree: *The more I work, the more I accomplish.* **2.** an additional amount: *Say no more.* [Old English *māra* greater, larger.]

· **more or less. a.** in or to a greater or lesser degree or extent: *The patient's condition has more or less improved.* **b.** just about; approximately: *She paid me more or less on time.*

mo·reen (mə rēn′) *n.* a medium to heavy wool or cotton fabric, woven with a lengthwise rib and given a moiré finish, used esp. for upholstery and men's suits.

mo·rel (mə rel′) *n.* any of a group of edible mushrooms, genus *Morchella,* having a brittle hollow stalk and a spongelike cap, esp. *M. esculenta.* [French *morille;* of Germanic origin.]

more·o·ver (môr ō′vər, môr′ō′-) *adv.* in addition to what has been said; also: *The day was dark and cold, and moreover it was raining.*

mo·res (môr′āz, -ēz) *pl. n.* customs that are considered essential for the preservation of a social system or community, such as particular standards of moral behavior. [Latin *mōrēs,* plural of *mōs* custom, manner.]

Mo·resque (mə resk′) *adj.* Moorish.

Mor·gan (môr′gən) *n.* a light horse of a breed originally developed in New England, having short legs and powerful shoulders, and noted for its stamina and gentle disposition. [From Justin *Morgan,* 1747-98, U.S. owner of the horse that was the sire of the breed.]

mor·ga·nat·ic (môr′gə nat′ik) *adj.* of or designating a form of marriage between a person of royal or noble rank and a commoner in which the person of lower rank and any children of the marriage do not share in the titles and estates of the person of higher rank. [Modern Latin *morgenatica* morning gift (from Medieval Latin *matrimonium ad morganaticam* marriage with morning gift), going back to Old High German *morgan* morning; referring to the traditional gift given by a husband to a wife of lower rank on the morning after their wedding with the understanding that this gift was to be her sole share in her husband's estate.]

Mor·gan le Fay (môr′gən lə fā′) in Arthurian legend, a fairy, the evil half sister of King Arthur.

morgue (môrg) *n.* **1.** a place, such as one run by the police or a municipality, in which the bodies of persons who were the victims of accidents or violence or who were found dead are kept for identification or examination. **2.a.** a reference library, as in a newspaper office, in which old clippings and other sources of information are stored. **b.** a file of such information. [French *morgue* place where unknown dead persons are kept for identification; of uncertain origin.]

mor·i·bund (môr′ə bund′, mor′-) *adj.* in a dying state; nearly lifeless or outmoded: *a moribund empire.* [Latin *moribundus* dying, from *morī* to die.] —**mor′i·bun′di·ty,** *n.* —**mor′i·bund′ly,** *adv.*

mo·ri·on (môr′ē on′) *n.* a metal helmet with a brim that comes to a peak in the front and back and has no visor or other part to protect the face, worn esp. by European soldiers of the sixteenth and seventeenth centuries. [French *morion,* from Spanish *morrión,* from *morra* crown of the head; of uncertain origin.]

Mor·mon (môr′mən) *n.* a member of the Church of Jesus Christ of Latter-day Saints, a Christian denomination founded in 1830 in New York by Joseph Smith. The Mormons' religious beliefs are based on revelations from God, some of which are contained in their holy book, the *Book of Mormon.* —*adj.* of or relating to the Mormons, their beliefs, or their church.

Mor·mon·ism (môr′mə niz′əm) *n.* the religious beliefs and practices of the Mormons.

morn (môrn) *n.* morning. [Old English *morgen.*]

morn·ing (môr′ning) *n.* **1.** the first part of the day, beginning at midnight or daybreak and ending at noon. **2.** daybreak; dawn: *Morning began to streak the sky.* **3.** the first part of anything; beginning: *the morning of life.* —*adj.* of, relating to, or occurring in the morning: *a morning chill, morning coffee.* [Middle English *morwening* beginning of morn, from *morwen* morning, from Old English *morgen.*]

morning glory 1. the trumpet-shaped flower of any of a large group of vines, shrubs, or trees, genus *Ipomoea* or *Convolvulus,* growing mainly in purple, blue, pink, yellow, or white. **2.** the plant, esp. a twining vine, bearing this flower, widely cultivated in gardens and having oval or heart-shaped leaves.

morning sickness, the nausea and vomiting that affect some women during the first months of pregnancy, usually in the morning.

morning star, a planet, esp. Venus, visible in the eastern sky before sunrise.

Mo·ro (môr′ō) *n., pl.* **Mo·ros. 1.** a member of any of the various Muslim Malay tribes living in the southern Philippine Islands. **2.** the language of these people, belonging to the Austronesian language family. —*adj.* of, relating to, or characteristic of the Moros or their language or culture. [Spanish *moro* Moor, Muslim, from Latin *Maurus.* See MOOR.]

mo·roc·co (mə rok′ō) *n., pl.* **-cos. 1.** a kind of leather that originally came from Morocco, made from goatskin tanned with sumac. It is often used for the bindings of fine books. **2.** any leather finished in imitation of this. [From *Morocco.*]

mo·ron (môr′on) *n.* **1.** a very foolish or stupid person. **2.** a person who is mentally retarded, having a mental age of up to twelve years. ➡ now considered obsolete in def. 2. [Greek *mōron,* neuter of *mōros* dull, stupid.]

mo·rose (mə rōs′) *adj.* bad-tempered, gloomy, and withdrawn. [Latin *mōrōsus* peevish, particular, from *mōs* manner, custom.] —**mo·rose′ly,** *adv.* —**mo·rose′ness,** *n.*

mor·pheme (môr′fēm) *n.* the smallest meaningful unit of language. A morpheme can be a word, a word element, or an affix. *Tri-, angle-,* and *-s* are the three morphemes in the word *triangles.* [French *morphème,* from Greek *morphē* shape, form.] —**mor·phem′ic,** *adj.*

Mor·phe·us (môr′fē əs, -fūs) *n.* in classical mythology, the god of dreams, son of Hypnos.

mor·phine (môr′fēn) *n.* a powerful narcotic derived from opium, valuable as a painkiller. Formula: $C_{17}H_{19}NO_3H_2O$ Also, **mor·phi·a** (môr′fē ə). [German *Morphin,* from *Morpheus* god of dreams; because it causes sleep.]

mor·phin·ism (môr′fē niz′əm) *n.* a pathological condition caused by addiction to morphine.

mor·pho·gen·e·sis (môr′fə jen′ə sis) *n. Biology.* the embryological development of form and structure in an organism. [Greek *morphē* shape, form + GENESIS.] —**mor·pho·ge·net·ic** (môr′fō-jə net′ik), **mor′pho·gen′ic,** *adj.*

mor·pho·log·i·cal (môr′fə loj′i kəl) *adj.* of, relating to, or part of morphology. Also, **mor′pho·log′ic.** —**mor′pho·log′i·cal·ly,** *adv.*

mor·phol·o·gy (môr fol′ə jē) *n.* **1.** the branch of biology devoted to the study of the structure and form of animals and plants. **2.** the structure of an organism considered as a whole. **3.** the branch of linguistics that studies how groups of sounds are joined together to make words. [Greek *morphē* shape, form + -LOGY.] —**mor·phol′o·gist,** *n.*

mor·ris (môr′is, mor′-) *n.* a vigorous English dance performed in fancy costumes, often representing Robin Hood and his men. Also, **morris dance.** [Form of MOORISH.]

Mor·ris chair (môr′is, mor′-) an easy chair with removable cushions and an adjustable back. [From William *Morris,* 1834-96, English furniture maker who designed it.]

mor·row (mor′ō, môr′ō) *n.* **1.** tomorrow: *I shall say good night till it be morrow* (Shakespeare, *Romeo and Juliet*). **2.** *Archaic.* morning. [Middle English *morwe,* form of *morwen* morning. See MORNING.]

Morse code (môrs) a code used chiefly in radiotelegraphy and signaling in which combinations of dots and dashes are used to represent the letters of the alphabet, numerals, and punctuation marks. [From Samuel F. B. *Morse,* 1791-1872, U.S. inventor who invented it.]

mor·sel (môr′səl) *n.* **1.** a small bite or portion, as of food. **2.** a small quantity or piece; fragment. [Old French *morsel* a small bite, diminutive of *mors* a bite, from Latin *morsus,* from *mordēre* to bite.]

mor·tal (môr′təl) *adj.* **1.** subject to death; destined to die: *All things that live are mortal.* **2.** causing or capable of causing death; fatal: *a mortal blow, a mortal disease.* **3.** that precedes, accompanies, or brings death. **4.** fought, pursued, or existing to the death; relentless; implacable: *mortal combat, mortal enemies.* **5.** very great or intense: *to live in mortal fear of snakes.* **6.** limited and human; earthly. **7.** possible; conceivable: *What mortal reason can you have for saying that?* **8.** *Informal.* excessive or extremely great in some respect: *We worked on that car for three mortal hours.* —*n.* a human being; person. [Latin *mortālis* subject to death, human, from *mors* death.] —**mor′tal·ly,** *adv.* —For Synonyms *(adj.),* see **deadly.**

mor·tal·i·ty (môr tal′i tē) *n.* **1.** the state or condition of being subject to death. **2.** the number or rate of deaths in a given time in a given place, sometimes from a given cause; death rate: *In the case of tuberculosis, a decrease in mortality has been accompanied by an increase in morbidity.* **3.** large-scale death or destruction, as from war. **4.** humanity; mankind.

mortal sin, in Roman Catholic theology, a sin so serious as to separate the sinner from the favor and love of God and to result in damnation to hell unless forgiven. ➡ distinguished from **venial sin.**

mor·tar[1] (môr′tər) *n.* a mixture of sand and water with lime or cement that hardens as it dries, used esp. for binding bricks or stones together, as in a wall. [Old French *mortier* cement, from Latin *mortārium* vessel in which substances are pounded, pounded material.]

mor·tar[2] (môr′tər) *n.* **1.** a thick bowl, as of marble, in which substances are crushed to a powder by means of a pestle. **2.** a muzzle-loading, smooth-bored, short-barreled cannon for firing shells in a high trajectory. [French *mortier* mortar[1], vessel in which substances are pounded, type of cannon resembling this vessel, from Latin *mortārium.* See MORTAR[1].]

mor·tar·board (môr′tər bôrd′) *n.* **1.** a square, flat plate of wood or metal with a centered handle, used by masons to hold mortar. **2.** a skullcap attached to a square, cloth-covered piece of wood or cardboard, worn at graduations and other academic exercises by teachers and students.

mort·gage (môr′gij) *n.* **1.** a right to claim real property, given as security for the payment of a debt or for the performance of some obligation. **2.** a document proving that such security has been given. —*v.t.,* **-gaged, -gag·ing. 1.** to pledge (real property) as security for the payment of a debt or for the performance of some obligation. **2.** to put under obligation or pledge in advance: *to mortgage one's future for the sake of present enjoyment.* [Old French *mortgage* literally, dead pledge (because the pledge is lost or "dead" to the mortgager if he or she fails to meet the conditions of the contract), from *mort* dead (from Latin *mortuus*) + *gage* pledge (of Germanic origin).]

mort·ga·gee (môr′gə jē′) *n.* a person or organization to whom property is mortgaged: *The bank is our mortgagee.*

mort·ga·gor (môr′gə jər) *also,* **mort·gag·er.** *n.* a person or organization that mortgages property.

mor·tice (môr′tis) *n.* mortise. —*v.t.,* **-ticed, -tic·ing.** mortise.

mor·ti·cian (môr tish′ən) *n.* undertaker *(def. 1).* [From Latin *mors* (stem *mort-*) death, on the model of English *physician.*]

mor·ti·fi·ca·tion (môr′tə fi kā′shən) *n.* **1.** a feeling of shame, humiliation, or embarrassment. **2.** anything causing such feelings. **3.** *Religion.* the practice of suppressing desires and passions, as by austere living or by inflicting pain on oneself. **4.** the death and decay of one part of a living animal organism; gangrene; necrosis.

mor·ti·fy (môr′tə fī′) *v.,* **-fied, -fy·ing.** —*v.t.* **1.** to subject to shame, humiliation, or embarrassment. **2.** *Religion.* to subject to mortification: *to mortify the desires of the flesh.* —*v.i.* to become gangrenous; decay. [Old French *mortifier* to torment the body by austerities, put to death, from Late Latin *mortificāre* to kill, from Latin *mors* death + *facere* to make.] —**mor′ti·fi′er,** *n.*

mor·tise (môr′tis) *also,* **mortice.** *n.* a shaped hole, as in a piece of wood, to receive a tenon or projecting part of a second piece so as to form a strong joint. —*v.t.,* **-tised, -tis·ing. 1.** to join or fasten securely, esp. by a mortise and tenon: *to mortise a rung to a chair.* **2.** to cut or make a mortise in. [Middle French *mortaise* hole in a piece of timber to receive the tenon, going back to Arabic *murtazz* fixed in.]

mort·main (môrt′mān′) *n.* the transfer of real property to any corporate body, such as a religious order, in perpetuity. [Old French *mortemain* the state of being inalienable; literally, dead hand, from Medieval Latin *mortua manus* dead hand; probably because the property could not be disposed of.]

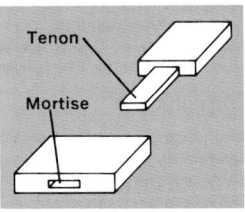

mortise

mor·tu·ar·y (môr′chü er′ē) *n., pl.* **-ar·ies.** a place where corpses are prepared, as by embalming, and kept until burial or cremation. —*adj.* of or relating to death or burial. [Late Latin *mortuārius* relating to the dead, from Latin *mortuus* dead.]

mor·u·la (môr′yə lə, mor′ə-) *n., pl.* **-lae** (-lē′). a globular, solid mass of cells formed by early divisions of the fertilized egg in the embryonic development of many kinds of animals, usually developing into a blastula by the formation of an internal cavity. [Modern Latin *morula,* diminutive of Latin *mōrum* mulberry fruit.] —**mor′u·lar,** *adj.* —**mor′u·la′tion,** *n.*

mos., months.

MOS *Electronics.* metal oxide semiconductor, a type of integrated circuit.

mo·sa·ic (mō zā′ik) *n.* **1.** an inlaid surface decoration composed of variously colored bits of stone, glass, or other hard material forming a picture or design. **2.** the technique or process of making such designs. **3.** anything that is similar to a mosaic: *The seaport was a mosaic of cultures.* [French *mosaïque* the inlaid surface decoration, through Italian and Medieval Latin, from Late Latin *mūsīvum,* from Latin *Mūsa.* See MUSE.]

Mo·sa·ic (mō zā′ik) *adj.* of or relating to Moses or the writings or laws ascribed to him.

Mosaic law 1. the ancient civil and ceremonial law of the Hebrews, ascribed to Moses. **2.** the first five books of the Old Testament, containing this law; the Pentateuch.

Mo·selle (mō zel′) *n.* a light, dry white wine produced in the valley along the Moselle River in Germany.

mo·sey (mō′zē) *v.i.,* **-seyed, -sey·ing.** *Informal.* to shuffle along or move in a leisurely way. [Probably from VAMOOSE.]

Mos·lem (moz′ləm, mos′-) Muslim.

mosque (mosk) *n.* a Muslim temple or place of worship. [French *mosquée,* through Italian and Spanish, from Arabic *masjid*

a	at	e	end	o	hot	u	up	hw	white		about
ā	ape	ē	me	ō	old	ū	use	ng	song		taken
ä	far	i	it	ô	fork	ü	rule	th	thin	ə	pencil
âr	care	ī	ice	oi	oil	u̇	pull	th	this		lemon
		îr	pierce	ou	out	ûr	turn	zh	measure		circus

mosque
Dome of the Rock mosque in Jerusalem

temple, place of worship, from *sajada* to worship; literally, to bow down.]

mos·qui·to (mə skē'tō) *n., pl.* **-toes** or **-tos.** any of a group of two-winged insects related to the gnat and fruitfly, family Culicidae, having a long proboscis that the female uses to pierce the skin of humans and animals and suck their blood. The resulting bite causes itching and can transmit such diseases as malaria and yellow fever. [Spanish *mosquito,* diminutive of *mosca* fly, from Latin *musca.*]

mosquito net, a screen or covering of gauzelike material that keeps out mosquitoes.

moss (môs) *n.* **1.** any of a large group of primitive, nonflowering plants, division Bryophyta, that grow in colonies and often form soft, dense mats. Mosses are found throughout the world, growing mostly in damp, shady places, as on rocks, next to streams, on tree trunks, and on the ground. **2.** any of various other plants that resemble moss in appearance or in the way they grow, such as club moss, Spanish moss, or Iceland moss. [Middle English *mos, mosse,* from Old English *mos* bog, marsh; of Germanic origin.]

moss agate, a variety of translucent chalcedony in which dark mineral inclusions form dendritic, or treelike, patterns, used for jewelry.

moss·back (môs'bak') *n. Informal.* a person who is extremely old-fashioned or conservative.

moss pink, a low, mat-forming perennial phlox, *Phlox subulata,* grown for its abundant pink, white, or purple flowers.

moss rose 1. a variety of rose, *Rosa centifolia muscosa,* having mosslike hair on the stem and buds. **2.** any of a number of garden plants, genus *Portulaca,* with mostly red, yellow, or white flowers.

moss·y (mô'sē) *adj.,* **moss·i·er, moss·i·est. 1.** covered with or having much moss. **2.** resembling moss. **3.** covered with something like moss. —**moss'i·ness,** *n.*

most (mōst) *adj.* the superlative of **much** and **many. 1.** greatest in number, quantity, or degree: *Who picked the most apples?* **2.** the greatest part or number of; majority of: *Most children like weekends.* —*n.* **1.** the greatest number, quantity, or degree: *That is the most I can do.* **2.** the greatest part or number of persons: *You did more to help than most would.* —*adv.* the superlative of **much. 1.** very: *to be a most gracious person.* **2.** in or to the greatest extent or degree. **3.** *Informal.* almost; nearly: *I'm most all tuckered out. Most everyone who was invited came to the party.* [Old English *mǣst* greatest.]
   ·**at (the) most.** at or to the greatest extent or degree; not more than: *At most, I'll be away two days.*
   ·**for the most part.** in general; mainly: *Things have been quiet here, for the most part.*
   ·**to make the most of.** to employ to the best advantage: *Make the most of each opportunity.*

-most *suffix* (used to form adjectives in the superlative degree) most or closest to: *uppermost, topmost.* [Old English *-mest.*]

most·ly (mōst'lē) *adv.* for the greatest part of the time, place, or the like being considered; mainly; chiefly: *Our weather has been mostly warm.*

mot (mō) *n.* a brief, witty saying or remark. [French *mot* word, going back to Latin *muttum* grunt, mutter.]

mote (mōt) *n.* a particle or speck, as of dust. [Old English *mot.*]

mo·tel (mō tel') *n.* a hotel for motorists, usually situated near a main road or highway, with parking space convenient to the guest rooms. [Blend of MOTOR and HOTEL.]

mo·tet (mō tet') *n. Music.* a solo or choral vocal composition, often with no instrumental accompaniment, usually meant to be sung in church. [Old French *motet,* diminutive of *mot* word. See MOT.]

moth (môth) *n., pl.* **moths** (môthz, môths). **1.** any of a group of broad-winged insects, order Lepidoptera, found throughout the world. Moths are distinguished from butterflies by flying mostly at night, by being less brightly colored, by having stouter bodies, and, in the male, by having comblike antennae. **2.** clothes moth. [Old English *moththe* clothes moth.]

moth·ball (môth'bôl') *n.* a small ball of naphthalene or camphor, used to repel clothes moths from fabrics and furs. —*v.t.* to put into storage.
   ·**in mothballs.** in storage, because no longer being used or because outdated: *a ship in mothballs.*

moth·eat·en (môth'ē'tən) *adj.* **1.** eaten away or damaged by clothes moths. **2.** worn-out. **3.** old-fashioned.

moth·er[1] (muth'ər) *n.* **1.** a female that has given birth to an offspring. **2.a.** a female that principally cares for a child or offspring. **b.** an adoptive mother or stepmother. **c.** a mother-in-law. **3.** something that has given birth to or nurtures another thing; origin; source. **4.** a woman who has a role like that of a mother. **5.** the qualities characteristic of a mother, such as affection, concern, or protectiveness: *The helpless kitten brought out the mother in me.* **6.** mother superior. —*adj.* **1.** that is a mother: *a mother hen.* **2.** relating to or characteristic of a mother: *mother love.* **3.** native: *mother wit.* **4.** bearing a relationship like that of a mother: *the mother church of a sect.* —*v.t.* **1.** to be the mother of. **2.** to treat in a motherly way, esp. by being too protective toward. [Old English *mōdor*] —**moth'er·less,** *adj.*

moth·er[2] (muth'ər) *n.* a scum that forms on the surface of wine or cider that is turning to vinegar, used as a starter in making vinegar. Also, **mother of vinegar.** [Modification (influenced by MOTHER[1]) of Middle Dutch *moeder* dregs.]

Mother Car·ey's chicken (kâr'ēz) storm petrel.

mother country 1. one's native country. **2.** a colonizing country in relation to its colonies: *The American colonies rose against their mother country.*

Mother Goose, the imaginary author of various fairy tales and nursery rhymes.

moth·er·hood (muth'ər hud') *n.* **1.** the state or role of being a mother. **2.** mothers collectively.

Mother Hub·bard (hub'ərd) **1.** the main character in an old nursery rhyme. **2.** *also,* **mother hubbard.** a full, loose gown worn by women.

mother-in-law (muth'ər in lô') *n., pl.* **moth·ers-in-law.** the mother of one's husband or wife.

moth·er·land (muth'ər land') *n.* **1.** one's native land. **2.** the country of one's ancestors.

mother lode, the principal, broad vein of ore that runs through a district or particular section of country.

moth·er·ly (muth'ər lē) *adj.* characteristic of or befitting a mother: *motherly concern.* —*adv.* in the manner of a mother. —**moth'er·li·ness,** *n.*

Mother Nature, nature in a pure or unspoiled condition, including the earth, seas, atmosphere, and organic life, esp. when thought of as a source of generation.

moth·er-of-pearl (muth'ər əv pûrl') *n.* a hard, rainbow-colored layer lining the shells of pearl oysters, abalone, and certain other mollusks, used for making buttons and ornaments. Also, **nacre.**

mother of vinegar, mother[2].

Mother's Day, a day set aside in honor of mothers, observed annually on the second Sunday of May.

mother ship, a vessel or craft providing services, as fuel or provisions, to a fleet of smaller craft operating far from a home port.

mother superior, a nun who is head of a female religious community.

mother tongue 1. one's native language. **2.** a language from which other languages are derived: *Latin is the mother tongue of the Romance languages.*

moth·proof (môth'prüf') *v.t.* to make resistant to or free from clothes moths, as by treatment with insecticide: *The storage closet has been mothproofed.* —*adj.* resistant to or free of clothes moths: *a mothproof sweater.*

moth·y (mô'thē) *adj.,* **moth·i·er, moth·i·est.** containing or damaged by moths.

mo·tif (mō tēf') *n.* **1.** an idea, situation, incident, problem, or the like that serves as a major, and usually repeated, theme or subject in a work of art, literature, or drama. **2.** a distinctive, usually repeated figure, design, or color, as in a decoration or printed pattern: *The wallpaper had a floral motif.* **3.** *Music.* a short and easily recognizable fragment of music that may be associated with a particular character or idea. Also, **motive.** [French

motif theme, cause, from Medieval Latin *motivum* that which causes an action. See MOTIVE.]

mo·tile (mō′təl) *adj. Biology.* having the power to move itself: *a motile flagellum.* [Latin *mōtus,* past participle of *movēre* to set in motion + -ILE.] —**mo·til·i·ty** (mō til′i tē), *n.*

mo·tion (mō′shən) *n.* **1.** the fact or process of changing position or place or of not staying still: *the continual motion of the sea, the forward motion of a car.* **2.** the act or an instance of moving the body or one of its parts, esp. in a meaningful manner: *The police officer signaled with a motion of his hand.* **3.** a formal proposal or suggestion made in a law court or other meeting or assembly: *She made a motion to take a vote.* —*v.i.* to make a significant or meaningful movement of a part of the body: *The guide motioned to me silently.* —*v.t.* to direct with a movement or gesture: *The usher motioned me to a seat.* [Latin *mōtiō* movement, moving.]

mo·tion·less (mō′shən lis) *adj.* **1.** not moving. **2.** not capable of moving or being moved.

motion picture **1.** a presentation or show created by projecting a sequence of still photographs onto a white screen or the like at high speed, thus producing the illusion of movement or reproducing the movement originally photographed. Also, **moving picture.** **2.** a specific story or other subject matter photographed as a motion picture. —**mo′tion-pic′ture,** *adj.*

motion sickness, a disorder that results from being subjected to continuous motion, as in a car, ship, or aircraft, characterized by nausea, vomiting, and dizziness.

mo·ti·vate (mō′tə vāt′) *v.t.,* -**vat·ed, -vat·ing.** to provide with a motive; move to effort or action.

mo·ti·va·tion (mō′tə vā′shən) *n.* **1.** the act or process of motivating or the state of being motivated. **2.** anything that motivates.

mo·tive (mō′tiv) *n.* **1.** a mental state, internal need, or outward goal that causes one to act; motivation: *The motive for the attack was a fear of being attacked first.* **2.** motif. —*adj.* of, relating to, or producing motion: *Wind is the motive power of sailboats.* [Medieval Latin *motivum* that which causes an action, from *motivus* moving, from Latin *movēre* to set in motion.] —For Synonyms, see **reason.**

mot juste (mō zhyst′) *pl.* **mots justes** (mō zhyst′). *French.* a word or phrase that is exactly appropriate to the situation.

mot·ley (mot′lē) *adj.* **1.** made up of diverse or varied elements; heterogeneous: *a motley blend of images, a motley group of people on a train.* **2.** of different colors; mottled: *the motley hues of autumn leaves.* —*n.* **1.** a suit or costume of many different colors, esp. one worn by a clown or court jester. **2.** a mixture of incongruous or varied elements. [Of uncertain origin.]

mo·to·neu·ron (mō′tə nûr′on, -nyûr′-) *n.* motor neuron.

mo·tor (mō′tər) *n.* **1.** a machine that converts electrical energy to mechanical energy: *the motor of a fan.* Also, **electric motor.** **2.** a small engine, esp. an internal-combustion engine. **3.** *British.* automobile. **4.** something that causes or imparts motion. —*adj.* **1.** producing or imparting motion: *motor power.* **2.** equipped with or driven by a motor. **3.** of, relating to, used, or designed for motor vehicles: *motor oil.* **4.** *Physiology.* **a.** of or relating to that part of the nervous system that sends out impulses to control the functioning, coordination, and behavior of glands and muscles. **b.** of or relating to muscular movement: *motor reflex.* —*v.i.* to ride in or travel by motor vehicle, esp. by automobile. [Latin *mōtor* mover.]

mo·tor·bike (mō′tər bīk′) *n.* **1.** a bicycle powered by a small motor. **2.** motorcycle.

mo·tor·boat (mō′tər bōt′) *n.* a boat powered by a motor, esp. a small, open boat.

mo·tor·bus (mō′tər bus′) *n.* bus.

mo·tor·cade (mō′tər kād′) *n.* a procession of automobiles. [MOTOR + (CAVAL)CADE.]

mo·tor·car (mō′tər kär′) *n.* automobile.

motor court, motel.

mo·tor·cy·cle (mō′tər sī′kəl) *n.* a two-wheeled, motorized vehicle, built like a bicycle though larger and heavier, and propelled by an internal-combustion engine. —*v.i.,* -**cled, -cling.** to ride or travel by motorcycle. —**mo′tor·cy′clist,** *n.*

mo·tor·ist (mō′tər ist) *n.* a person who drives a car.

mo·tor·ize (mō′tə rīz′) *v.t.,* -**ized, -iz·ing. 1.** to equip or furnish with a motor: *to motorize a wheelchair.* **2.** to supply with motor-driven vehicles in place of horses and horse-drawn vehicles: *to motorize a farm.* —**mo′tor·i·za′tion,** *n.*

mo·tor·man (mō′tər mən) *n., pl.* -**men** (-mən). a person who drives or operates a subway train, streetcar, or similar vehicle.

motor neuron, a kind of nerve cell that conducts impulses that trigger movement or activity, as muscular contraction or glandular secretion. Also, **motoneuron.**

motor scooter, a two-wheeled vehicle similar to a child's scooter but with a motor and a seat for the driver.

mo·tor·ship (mō′tər ship′) *also,* **motor ship.** *n.* a ship propelled by an internal-combustion engine. ➡ distinguished from **steamship.**

motor vehicle, any wheeled conveyance, such as a truck, bus, automobile, or motorcycle, powered by a motor for use on roads and highways.

mot·tle (mot′əl) *v.t.,* -**tled, -tling.** to mark or cover with irregular spots or streaks of different colors. —*n.* **1.** a mottled coloring or pattern. **2.** a spot or streak, as in such a pattern. [Probably from MOTLEY.]

mot·to (mot′ō) *n., pl.* -**toes** or -**tos. 1.** a maxim or proverb that expresses a principle: *My motto is "Nothing ventured, nothing gained."* **2.** a short, appropriate statement added to something to express or symbolize its content or nature. [Italian *motto* word, saying, going back to Latin *muttum* grunt, mutter.]

moue (mü) *n.* a pouting grimace. [French *moue;* of Germanic origin.]

mouf·lon (müf′lon) *also,* **mouf·flon.** *n.* a wild sheep, *Ovis musimon,* native to Corsica and Sardinia, having a dark reddish brown coat, and large curving horns in the male. Height: 27 inches (69 centimeters) at the shoulder. [French *mouflon,* from Italian *mufflone,* going back to Late Latin *mufrō* wild sheep; of uncertain origin.]

mould (mōld) *British.* mold.

mould·board (mōld′bôrd′) *British.* moldboard.

mould·er (mōl′dər) *British.* molder.

mould·ing (mōl′ding) *British.* molding.

mould·y (mōl′dē) *adj.,* **mould·i·er, mould·i·est.** *British.* moldy. —**mould′i·ness,** *n.*

moult (mōlt) *British.* molt.

mound (mound) *n.* **1.** an artificial elevation or bank of earth or stones: *a fortress surrounded by mounds and trenches.* **2.** any heap or pile: *a mound of leaves, a mound of garbage.* **3.** a small, natural elevation; hillock. **4.** *Baseball.* the slightly raised area in the center of the diamond from which the pitcher pitches. —*v.t.* **1.** to heap up in a mound. **2.** to fortify or enclose with a mound. [Possibly from Middle Dutch *mond* protection.]

Mound Builders, various early Indian peoples of southeastern North America who built burial mounds and fortifications.

mount[1] (mount) *v.t.* **1.** to go up; climb: *to mount a small hill.* **2.** to get up on top of: *to mount a horse.* **3.** to place on or attach to a support or stand: *to mount a camera on a tripod.* **4.** to set in place, as for display or examination: *to mount stamps in an album, to mount a specimen on a microscope slide.* **5.** to prepare and begin to carry out: *The candidate mounted an attack on the incumbent's voting record.* **6.** to provide (a theatrical presentation) with the accessories or equipment of production, such as scenery, costumes, and lighting. **7.** to furnish with a horse or other animal for riding. **8.** *Military.* **a.** to have or carry (armaments): *a ship that mounts two machine guns.* **b.** to post (someone) as a guard. —*v.i.* **1.** to increase or accumulate (often with *up*): *Tension mounts up.* **2.** to get up on something, such as the back of a horse: *The outlaws mounted and rode off.* **3.** to rise; ascend. —*n.* **1.** a horse or other animal for riding. **2.** that in which or on which anything is mounted; mounting. [Old French *monter* to go up, climb, going back to Latin *mōns* mountain, heap.] —**mount′a·ble,** *adj.* —**mount′er,** *n.* —For Synonyms *(v.t.),* see **climb.**

mount[2] (mount) *n.* mountain. ➡ archaic except before a proper name: *Mount Rushmore.* [Old English *munt* mountain, hill, from Latin *mōns* mountain, heap; influenced by Old French *mont* mountain, hill.]

moun·tain (moun′tən) *n.* **1.** a mass of land rising considerably above the surrounding country, usually to a peak, and produced by movements of the earth's crust, volcanic action, erosion of surrounding land areas, or a combination of these processes. **2.** a huge heap or pile; towering mass: *a mountain of ice.* **3.** a great quantity or amount: *a mountain of trouble.* [Old French *montaigne* high hill, going back to Latin *montānus* relating to mountains, from *mōns* high hill, heap.]

mountain ash, any of a group of trees or tall shrubs, genus *Sorbus,* of the rose family, bearing foul-smelling white flowers and red or orange berrylike fruits, such as the rowan.

mountain chain, mountain range.

moun·tain·eer (moun′tə nîr′) *n.* **1.** a person who lives in or is part of the culture of a mountainous region. **2.** a person who is skilled at mountain climbing. —*v.i.* to climb mountains.

mountain goat, Rocky Mountain goat.

a	at	e	end	o	hot	u	up	hw	white		about
ā	ape	ē	me	ō	old	ū	use	ng	song		taken
ä	far	i	it	ô	fork	ü	rule	th	thin	ə	pencil
âr	care	ī	ice	oi	oil	u̇	pull	th	this		lemon
						îr	pierce	ou	out	ûr	turn	zh	measure		circus

M

mountain laurel, an ornamental North American evergreen shrub, *Kalmia latifolia,* of the heath family, having glossy oblong leaves and large clusters of flowers in white or shades of rose.

mountain lion, cougar.

moun·tain·ous (moun′tə nəs) *adj.* **1.** having many mountains: *a mountainous country.* **2.** like a mountain in size or shape; huge; enormous: *a mountainous pile of old cars.* —**moun′tain·ous·ly,** *adv.* —**moun′tain·ous·ness,** *n.*

mountain range, a chain of connected mountains, usually alike in origin, geologic age, and form. Also, **mountain chain, range.**

mountain laurel

mountain sheep, any of various wild sheep found in mountainous regions, such as the bighorn.

moun·tain·side (moun′tən sīd′) *n.* the side or slope of a mountain.

Mountain Standard Time, the local civil time of the 105th meridian west of Greenwich, England, used in the west-central United States and Canada. It is 7 hours earlier than Greenwich Time.

moun·tain·top (moun′tən top′) *n.* the top of a mountain.

moun·te·bank (moun′tə bank′) *n.* **1.** a person who is deceitful or unscrupulous; trickster; charlatan. **2.** formerly, an impostor who sold quack medicines, jumping on a bench to attract a crowd. [Italian *montambanco* quack[2], short for *monta in banco* literally, climb on a bench (in order to address an audience), from *montare* to climb (going back to Latin *mōns* mountain) + *in* in + *banco.* See BANK[2].]

mount·ed (moun′tid) *adj.* **1.** seated or riding on a mount or mounts: *We saw five mounted hunters.* **2.** serving on mounts, esp. horses: *mounted police.* **3.** in or on a stable support or a stand: *Use that mounted saw to cut a perfectly straight line.* **4.** set in place, as for display: *a ring with mounted rubies, an album of mounted stamps.*

Moun·tie (moun′tē) *n. Informal.* a member of the Royal Canadian Mounted Police.

mount·ing (moun′ting) *n.* **1.** anything that serves as a support or setting: *The trophy is in its mounting on the wall.* **2.** the act or process of a person or thing that mounts.

mourn (môrn) *v.i.* **1.** to feel sorrow or grief: *We mourn for the trees we lost in the storm.* **2.** to lament the death of someone, esp. by exhibiting conventional signs of grief. —*v.t.* **1.** to feel or express sorrow or grief over (someone who has died): *We all mourn our friend.* **2.** to feel or express grief or sadness at; complain about or bemoan: *They mourned their great misfortunes.* [Old English *murnan* to feel sorrow, lament.]

mourn·er (môr′nər) *n.* a person who mourns, esp. one attending a funeral: *The mourners walked slowly from the grave.*

mourners' bench, the front row of seats at a revival meeting, reserved for those who are repenting their sins.

mourn·ful (môrn′fəl) *adj.* **1.** feeling grief or sorrow: *the mournful family of someone who has died.* **2.** expressing or filled with sadness or sorrow: *a mournful song, a mournful face.* —**mourn′ful·ly,** *adv.* —**mourn′ful·ness,** *n.*

mourn·ing (môr′ning) *n.* **1.** the acts or feelings of anyone who mourns. **2.** a conventional display of sorrow over a person's death, esp. the wearing of black. **3.** the customary clothes, draperies, and other furnishings worn or used to express such sorrow: *dressed in mourning.* **4.** the period during which such garments or furnishings are worn or displayed: *The family is still in mourning.*

mourning cloak, a common butterfly, *Nymphalis antiopa,* with purple-brown, yellow-bordered wings, found throughout the Northern Hemisphere.

mourning dove, a wild North American pigeon, *Zenaidura macroura,* having a mournful-sounding, cooing call. Length: 12 inches (30 centimeters).

mouse (*n.,* mous; *v.,* mouz, mous) *n., pl.* **mice. 1.** any of numerous small rodents, families Muridae and Cricetidae, usually having pointed snouts, relatively small ears, and thin tails with little or no hair. **2.** a person who is quiet or timid. **3.** *Computers.* a hand-held device used to move the cursor on a computer screen. **4.** *Slang.* a bruise under the eye, usually from a punch; black eye. —*v.i.* **1.** **moused** (mouzd, moust), **mous·ing** (mou′zing, -sing) to hunt for or catch mice. [Old English *mūs* the small rodent.]

mous·er (mou′zər, -sər) *n.* an animal, esp. a cat, that is good at catching mice.

mouse·trap (mous′trap′) *n.* a trap for catching mice.

mous·sa·ka (mü sä′kə, mü′sä kä′) *n.* a Greek dish made with layers of ground beef or lamb and sliced eggplant or zucchini covered with a white custard sauce and baked with a topping of cheese. [Modern Greek *mousakâs,* from Turkish *musakka* this dish.]

mousse (müs) *n.* **1.** a dessert consisting of whipped cream or beaten egg whites combined with a flavoring and chilled. **2.** a dish made of finely chopped or puréed meat, poultry, or fish and stock and chilled in a mold until jelled. **3.** a foamy substance used to style the hair. [French *mousse* froth, foam; probably of Germanic origin.]

mousse·line (müs lēn′) *n. French.* a fine, lightweight muslin.

mous·tache (mus′tash, mə stash′) mustache.

mous·y (mou′sē) *adj.,* **mous·i·er, mous·i·est. 1.** of, resembling, or suggesting a mouse, esp. in color; drab or dirty: *mousy brown hair.* **2.** timid and quiet as a mouse. **3.** infested with mice. —**mous′i·ness,** *n.*

mouth (*n.,* mouth; *v.,* mou<u>th</u>) *n., pl.* **mouths** (mou<u>th</u>z). **1.a.** the opening through which an animal takes in food. **b.** the cavity bounded in front by the lips and teeth and in the back by the pharynx, which in higher vertebrates encloses the teeth, gums, and tongue and through which sounds are uttered. **2.** the parts of this that are outwardly visible on the face, esp. the lips. **3.** an opening resembling a mouth: *the mouth of a jar, the mouth of a volcano.* **4.** a living thing considered as needing food: *many mouths to feed.* **5.** the power, quality, or manner of speech. **6.** the part of a river where it empties into another body of water. **7.** *Archaic.* a disapproving or derisive expression; grimace. —*v.t.* **1.** to pronounce or speak without believing or understanding; say or repeat automatically: *to mouth popular opinions.* **2.** to appear to sing or speak (something) by silently moving the lips: *Some choir members never sang but only mouthed their parts.* **3.** to speak or say (something) in a pompous, affected manner: *to mouth one's lines instead of acting convincingly.* **4.** to mumble or garble (one's speech). **5.** to take, grasp, or touch with the mouth. [Old English *mūth* body opening for the functions of eating and speaking.]

·**down in** (or **at**) **the mouth.** *Informal.* dejected; depressed: *down in the mouth because of defeat.*

·**to mouth off.** *Slang.* to talk too much: *Stop mouthing off and let us hear this song.*

mouth·breed·er (mouth′brē′dər) *n.* any of various fish that carry their eggs or young in their mouths, as certain cichlids and catfish.

mouth·ful (mouth′fül′) *n., pl.* **-fuls. 1.** the amount, as of food, that is or can be held in the mouth at one time. **2.** a word or phrase that is difficult to pronounce: *That name is quite a mouthful.*

·**to say a mouthful.** to say something important, perceptive, or revealing.

mouth organ 1. harmonica. **2.** panpipe.

mouth·part (mouth′pärt′) *n.* any of the structures and appendages surrounding the mouth of insects and other arthropods, variously adapted for biting, sucking, piercing, and chewing.

mouth·piece (mouth′pēs′) *n.* **1.** a piece or part, as of a musical instrument or telephone, that is placed between or next to the lips. **2.** a person who speaks on behalf of an individual or group. **3.** *Slang.* a criminal defense lawyer.

mouth-to-mouth (mouth′tə mouth′) *adj.* of, relating to, or designating a first-aid method of artificial respiration in which a person exhales from his or her mouth directly into the mouth of the person being resuscitated to force air into that person's lungs.

mouth·wash (mouth′wôsh′, -wosh′) *n.* a liquid preparation used to clean the mouth or to sweeten the breath.

mouth·y (mou′<u>th</u>ē, -thē) *adj.,* **mouth·i·er, mouth·i·est.** ranting or railing; bombastic: *a mouthy bore.*

mov·a·ble (mü′və bəl) *also,* **moveable.** *adj.* **1.** able to be moved. **2.** changing from one date to another in different years: *Thanksgiving is a movable holiday.* **3.** able to be broken down and reused: *movable type.* —*n.* **1.** any furnishing or piece of furniture that can be moved. **2. movables.** personal property. —**mov′a·bil′i·ty, mov′a·ble·ness,** *n.* —**mov′a·bly,** *adv.*

move (müv) *v.,* **moved, mov·ing.** —*v.i.* **1.** to change posture, position, or direction: *Don't move from your seat. If you move, you will frighten the bird.* **2.a.** to change the location of a residence or business: *Our office moved downtown.* **b.** to establish residence (with *in*): *to move in next door.* **3.** to go forward; advance; progress: *The book moves slowly. Time moves quickly.* **4.** to live or circulate; have associations: *The crime reporter moved in a world of courts and police stations.* **5.** to undertake action: *to move on an issue.* **6.** (of merchandise) to be sold. **7.** to make a formal motion, as in a court or legislative assembly: *to move for adjournment.* **8.** to be alive with activity: *The club is really moving tonight.* **9.** (of the bowels) to discharge feces. **10.** *Games.* to change the position of a playing piece: *Each player must move within two minutes.* —*v.t.* **1.** to change the location, position, or direction of: *Move*

the light away from your eyes. **2.** to put or keep in motion: *Water moves the waterwheel.* **3.** to cause or urge: *I was moved by curiosity to open the box.* **4.** to affect with emotion; stir the feelings of: *The speech moved us deeply.* **5.** to put forward (a motion). **6.** to cause (the bowels) to evacuate. **7.** to sell (merchandise). —*n.* **1.** an action calculated to secure a result; piece of strategy: *A wise move was to remain silent.* **2.** *Games.* **a.** the act of moving a playing piece: *The wrong move of a pawn cost the challenger the game.* **b.** a turn to move a playing piece. **3.** the act of changing one's posture or position, esp. in an accomplished or controlled way: *All the moves of the dancer were graceful.* **4.** a change of location of a business or residence. [Anglo-Norman *mover* to set in motion, change the place of, cause, excite, propose, from Latin *movēre* to set in motion, cause.]

· **on the move.** **a.** not staying in any one place very long; moving about. **b.** progressing; advancing: *Science is always on the move.*

· **to get a move on.** to hurry up; get started.

· **to move in on.** *Informal.* **a.** to advance toward (someone or something) with the intention of capturing or controlling. **b.** to attempt to usurp (something) from someone: *The company's new ad campaign is designed to move in on their competitor's customers.*

move·a·ble (mü′və bəl) *adj.* movable. —**move′a·bil′i·ty, move′a·ble·ness,** *n.* —**move′a·bly,** *adv.*

move·ment (müv′mənt) *n.* **1.** the act or process or an instance of moving. **2.** a mechanism consisting of many closely associated moving parts, as in a watch. **3.** *Music.* one of the principal divisions or sections of a sonata, symphony, or other extended musical composition. **4.** a group of people working together to achieve some specific end, or all their endeavors and actions together: *the civil rights movement.* **5.** a course or tendency in a particular field; trend: *a movement toward greater liberalism in education.* **6.** the act of elimination through the bowels, or the matter so eliminated. **7.** *Music.* **a.** tempo. **b.** rhythm. **8.** a condition or action of moving about; activity: *There was too much movement in the room for me to concentrate.*

mov·er (mü′vər) *n.* **1.** a person or thing that moves. **2.** a person or business that moves furniture and belongings from one place to another, as from a former residence or office to a new one.

mov·ie (mü′vē) *n. Informal.* **1.** motion picture. **2.** *usually,* **movies.** a motion-picture theater: *We went to the movies up the street.* **3.** **movies.** the motion-picture industry: *to work in the movies.* [Short for MOVING PICTURE.]

mov·ing (mü′ving) *adj.* **1.** that moves: *a moving target.* **2.** causing or producing action or motion: *the moving force behind a revolution.* **3.** stirring or affecting the emotions, esp. evoking tender feelings; touching: *a moving story, a moving experience.* **4.** used or hired to move a residence or business: *a moving van, a moving company.* —**mov′ing·ly,** *adv.* —For Synonyms, see **touching.**

moving picture, motion picture *(def. 1).*

mow[1] (mō) *v.,* **mowed, mowed** or **mown, mow·ing.** —*v.t.* **1.** to cut (grass, hay, grain, or the like) with a scythe or machine. **2.** to cut grass, grain, or hay from: *The gardener mowed the lawn.* **3.** to kill or destroy with or as with a single sweeping stroke; cut down (with *down*): *The machine gun mowed down a line of soldiers.* —*v.i.* to cut grass, grain, hay, or the like. [Old English *māwan* to cut down crops with a scythe.] —**mow′er,** *n.*

mow[2] (mou) *n.* **1.** the part of a barn where hay and grain are stored. **2.** a pile or stack of hay or grain. [Old English *mūga* heap, stack.]

mow[3] (mō, mou) *Archaic. n.* a grimace. —*v.i.* to grimace. [Old French *moe* mouth, grimace; of Germanic origin.]

mox·ie (mok′sē) *n. Slang.* **1.** a combination of energy and initiative; drive; pep. **2.** a combination of courage and audacity; nerve. [From *Moxie,* trademark for a U.S. soft drink.]

moz·za·rel·la (mot′sə rel′ə, mōt′-) *n.* a soft, white cheese having a mild flavor. [Italian *mozzarella,* diminutive of *mozza* a kind of cheese; literally, a cut, from *mozzare* to cut off, from *mozzo* not sharp.]

mp *also,* **m.p.** melting point.

MP **1.** the postal abbreviation for the Northern Mariana Islands. **2.** Member of Parliament. **3.** military police. **4.** mounted police.

mpg, miles per gallon.

mph, miles per hour.

Mr. (mis′tər) *pl.* **Messrs.** Mister. ➡ a form of address used before a man's name, as in *Mr. Simpson,* or in polite address, as in *Mr. Chairman.*

MRI, a medical technique that produces detailed pictures of organs and tissues in the body by recording the nuclear magnetic resonance of hydrogen atoms in the molecules of living cells. It is

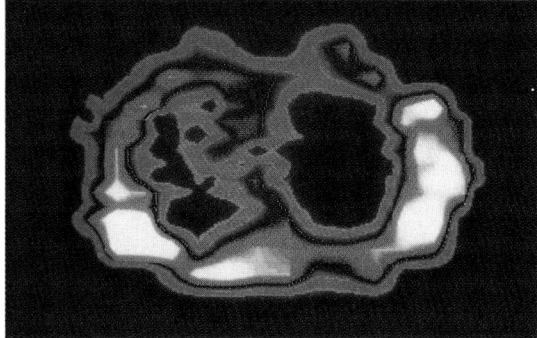

MRI of diseased lung (left) and healthy lung (right)

used to study and diagnose diseases. [Abbreviation of *m(agnetic) r(esonance) i(maging).*]

Mrs. (mis′iz, miz′-) *pl.* **Mmes.** a form of address used before a married woman's name: *Mrs. Simpson.*

Ms. (miz) *pl.* **Mses** (miz′iz). a form of address used before a woman's name: *Ms. Simpson.*

MS **1.** *pl.,* **MSS.** manuscript. **2.** the postal abbreviation for Mississippi. **3.** multiple sclerosis.

M.S. **1.** *also,* **M.Sc.** Master of Science. Also, **S.M. 2.** Master of Surgery.

MSG, monosodium glutamate.

Msgr., Monsignor.

MST, Mountain Standard Time.

Mt. **1.** Mount. **2.** *also,* **Mtn.** mountain.

MT, the postal abbreviation for Montana.

mu (mū, mü) *n.* the twelfth letter of the Greek alphabet (M, μ), corresponding to the English letter *M, m.*

much (much) *adj.,* **more, most.** great in quantity, amount, or degree: *much trouble, not much power.* —*adv.,* **more, most. 1.** to a great extent or degree: *much the worse for wear.* **2.** just about; nearly; largely: *to leave something much as you found it.* —*n.* **1.** a great deal: *Much has been said.* **2.** a good, noteworthy, or impressive example: *not much of a speech.* **3.** *Informal.* a person or thing that is impressive or important: *I visited the place last year, and it's not much.* [Middle English *muche(l)* great, great quantity of, from Old English *micel.*]

· **much as.** **a.** in the same or nearly the same way as: *Much as spiders scare you, snakes frighten me.* **b.** even though; although: *Much as I would like to go, I have work to do.*

· **not much for.** *Informal.* not inclined to; not likely to want to: *I'm not much for walking in the rain.*

· **not much of a.** not a very good example of a: *That's not much of a tree house.*

· **to make much of.** to treat as of great importance: *to make much of trivial details.*

mu·ci·lage (mū′sə lij) *n.* **1.** a clear, brownish glue used esp. on paper and cardboard and usually sold in a bottle topped with a rubber applicator. **2.** any of several sticky adhesive substances produced by certain plants, such as the seaweed Irish moss. [Late Latin *mūcilāgō* musty juice, from Latin *mūcus* mucus.]

mu·ci·lag·i·nous (mū′sə laj′ə nəs) *adj.* **1.** of or like mucilage; slimy and sticky. **2.** producing or containing mucilage.

mu·cin (mū′sin) *n.* any of various viscous protein compounds present in mucus, saliva, and other secretions that protect and lubricate body tissues. [French *mucine* (from Latin *mūcus* mucus) + French *-ine* -ine[2].] —**mu′cin·ous,** *adj.*

muck (muk) *n.* **1.** any dirty, moist, sticky or slimy substance, such as mud or manure. **2.** *Informal.* anything messy or disgusting. **3.** *Informal.* an unclean or untidy condition; mess. **4.** a black humus consisting chiefly of highly decomposed plant matter. —*v.t.* **1.** to soil, make dirty, or cover with or as with muck (often with *up*). **2.** *Informal.* to make a mess of; ruin or spoil (with *up*): *The director mucked the film up by changing the ending.* [Of Scandinavian origin.]

· **to muck about** (or **around**). *Slang.* to waste time.

muck·rake (muk′rāk′) *v.i.,* **-raked, -rak·ing.** to search for and expose, as in the newspapers, real or alleged corruption in govern-

a	at	e	end	o	hot	u	up	hw	white		about
ā	ape	ē	me	ō	old	ū	use	ng	song		taken
ä	far	i	it	ô	fork	ü	rule	th	thin	ə	pencil
âr	care	ī	ice	oi	oil	u̇	pull	<u>th</u>	this		lemon
		îr	pierce	ou	out	ûr	turn	zh	measure		circus

ment or society. [From U.S. President Theodore Roosevelt's reference to the man with the *muck rake* in the allegory *Pilgrim's Progress* by the English writer John Bunyan, 1628-86.] —**muck′·rak′er,** *n.*

muck·y (muk′ē) *adj.*, **muck·i·er, muck·i·est.** of, containing, or like muck: *a mucky river bottom.*

mu·co·sa (mū kō′sə, -zə) *n., pl.* **-sae** (-sē, -zē) or **-sas.** mucous membrane. [Modern Latin *mucosa,* going back to Latin *mūcōsus* slimy, from *mūcus* mucus.]

mu·cous (mū′kəs) *adj.* **1.** containing or secreting mucus. **2.** of or like mucus. [Latin *mūcōsus* slimy, from *mūcus* mucus of the nose.]

mucous membrane, a membrane that secretes mucus and lines body passages and cavities open to the outside, esp. the respiratory and digestive tracts.

mu·cus (mū′kəs) *n.* a viscous fluid secreted by the mucous membranes, which serves as a lubricant and protective coating for the inner surfaces of the mouth and throat and other body passages and cavities. [Latin *mūcus* mucus of the nose.]

mud (mud) *n.* **1.** soft, wet, sticky clay or dirt. **2.** this mixture after it has dried and hardened: *a house of mud and straw.* **3.a.** scandalous, often libelous charges: *to throw mud in a magazine article.* **b.** disgrace caused by such charges: *to drag someone's name through the mud.* [Probably of Low German origin.]

mud dauber, any of various wasps, family Sphecidae, that build nests of many cells of hardened mud, usually stocked with paralyzed spiders for their larvae to eat.

mud·dle (mud′əl) *n.* a cause or condition of bewilderment or confusion. —*v.,* **-dled, -dling.** —*v.t.* **1.** to bring into a state of confusion; mix up; bungle. **2.** to make bewildered or confused, as with liquor; befuddle. **3.** to mix; stir. —*v.i.* to act or think in a confused or aimless way: *to muddle around without a plan.* [MUD + -LE.] —**mud′dler,** *n.*

·**to muddle through.** to achieve an objective despite bungling or incompetence.

mud·dle·head·ed (mud′əl hed′did) *adj.* bungling or confused.

mud·dy (mud′ē) *adj.*, **-di·er, -di·est. 1.** covered or spattered with mud; full of mud: *a muddy raincoat, a muddy road.* **2.** of or resembling mud: *a muddy consistency.* **3.** clouded or dull with or as if with mud; not clear or pure: *a muddy pond.* **4.** vague or unclear; muddled: *a muddy prose style.* —*v.,* **-died, -dy·ing.** —*v.t.* **1.** to cover or spatter with mud; get mud on: *Don't muddy your new shoes.* **2.** to make confusing or bewildering: *to muddy an issue.* **3.** to make cloudy or dull: *to muddy the waters of a stream.* —*v.i.* to become muddy. —**mud′died,** *adj.* —**mud′di·ly,** *adv.* —**mud′di·ness,** *n.*

mud flat, a low, muddy coastal area that is submerged at high tide and exposed at low tide.

mud·guard (mud′gärd′) *n.* **1.** splash guard. **2.** fender *(def. 1).*

mud hen, any of various marsh-dwelling water birds, such as the coot or gallinule.

mud puppy *also,* **mud·pup·py** (mud′pup′ē). a large salamander, *Necturus maculosus,* found in fresh waters of North America, having three pairs of red, external gills. Length: to 17 inches (43 centimeters).

mud·sill (mud′sil′) *n.* the lowest sill, block, or timber of a structure, usually placed even with the ground.

mud·sling·ing (mud′sling′ing) *n.* the practice of making malicious charges against an opponent, esp. against a political rival. —**mud′sling′er,** *n.*

mud·stone (mud′stōn′) *n.* an unlayered shale formed of hardened silty mud, consisting of roughly equal proportions of silt and clay. [MUD + STONE.]

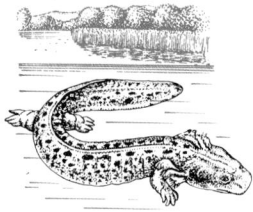

mud puppy

mud turtle, any of a group of small freshwater turtles, family Kinosternidae, found on the bottoms of ponds, rivers, and streams throughout North and South America.

Muen·ster (mun′stər, mun′-) *n.* a mild, semisoft cheese having a creamy yellow color and smooth texture. [From *Munster,* French city where it was first made.]

mu·ez·zin (mū ez′in, mü-) *n.* in Muslim communities, the public crier who announces the hours of prayer from the minaret of a mosque. [Arabic *mu'adhdhin.*]

muff (muf) *n.* **1.** a fluffy cylinder of fur or other material, designed so that one hand can be slipped in at each end for warmth. **2.** a mistake or missed opportunity. —*v.t.* to fail at or miss: *You had your chance, and you muffed it.* —*v.i.* to make a mistake or miss an opportunity. [Dutch *mof* covering for the

hands, from Middle Dutch *moffel* mitten, thick glove, from Medieval Latin *muffula* fur-lined glove; of uncertain origin.]

muf·fin (muf′in) *n.* **1.** a light bread made of batter containing eggs, baked in individual portions and often served hot. **2.** English muffin. [Of uncertain origin.]

muf·fle (muf′əl) *v.t.,* **-fled, -fling. 1.** to deaden or soften (a sound): *to muffle a cry.* **2.** to deaden or soften the sound of (something) by or as if by wrapping it in thick, heavy material: *The enemy muffled the oars with wool in order to slip by the sentry.* **3.** to deaden, repress, or cut off; muzzle: *to muffle criticism.* **4.** to wrap up or cover for protection or warmth; bundle (with *up*): *a child all muffled up in a sweater, scarf, and heavy blankets.* —*n.* a cover or wrap used to deaden sound or for protection or warmth. [Possibly short for Old French *enmoufler* to wrap up, from *moufle* thick glove, from Medieval Latin *muffula* fur-lined glove. See MUFF.]

muf·fler (muf′lər) *n.* **1.** a scarf, as of wool, worn around the neck for warmth. **2.** a device that reduces the noise from an engine exhaust, as in an automobile, by reducing the pressure of the escaping gases.

muf·ti¹ (muf′tē) *n. Islam.* an interpreter of religious law. [Arabic *muftī,* from *āftā* to judge.]

muf·ti² (muf′tē) *n.* street dress or plain clothes, esp. when worn by a person who usually wears a uniform: *The undercover police officer was in mufti.* [Of unknown origin.]

mug (mug) *n.* **1.** a large, heavy drinking cup. **2.** the contents of a mug; as much as a mug holds: *a mug of cocoa.* **3.** *Slang.* face. **4.** *Slang.* a person, esp. a hoodlum. —*v.,* **mugged, mug·ging.** —*v.t.* **1.** to assault (a person) with intent to rob. **2.** to photograph the face of (a suspect or criminal) for police files. —*v.i.* to make faces or exaggerated expressions; grimace: *to mug for the camera.* [Probably of Scandinavian origin.]

mug·ger (mug′ər) *n.* **1.** a person who assaults someone with intent to rob. **2.** a person who makes faces or exaggerated expressions.

mug·ging (mug′ing) *n.* a crime in which someone is assaulted and robbed.

mug·gy (mug′ē) *adj.*, **-gi·er, -gi·est.** warm, humid, and stifling: *a hot, muggy day with no breeze.* [Dialectal English *mug* drizzle (of Scandinavian origin) + -Y¹.] —**mug′gi·ly,** *adv.* —**mug′gi·ness,** *n.*

Mu·ghul (mü′gəl) *n.* Mogul *(def. 1).*

mug shot *Slang.* a police photograph of the face of a suspect or criminal.

mug·wump (mug′wump′) *n.* **1.** in U.S. politics, a person who leaves one party in order to support an opposition candidate. **2.** any of the Republicans who refused to support the party ticket in 1884. [Algonquian *mugkuomp* great chief.]

Mu·ham·ma·dan·ism (mu ham′ə də niz′əm) *n.* Islam *(def. 1).*

mu·jik (mü zhēk′, mü′zhik) muzhik.

muk·luk (muk′luk) *n.* **1.** a winter boot worn by Eskimos, made of caribou or sealskin with waterproof seams and sole. **2.** any similar soft boot or slipper. [Eskimo *muklok* large seal¹.]

mu·lat·to (mə lat′ō, -lä′tō, mū-) *n., pl.* **-toes. 1.** a person who is of mixed white and black ancestry. **2.** a person who has one white and one black parent. [Spanish *mulato* one of mixed race, from *mulo* mule (because it is a hybrid animal), from Latin *mūlus.*]

mul·ber·ry (mul′ber′ē, -bə rē) *n., pl.* **-ries. 1.** any of various trees of the genus *Morus,* such as the **white mulberry,** *M. alba,* having thin, oval leaves used as food for silkworms, and the **black mulberry,** *M. nigra,* bearing black fruits used to make preserves and wines. **2.** the sweet, edible fruit of the black mulberry, similar to a blackberry. **3.** a dark reddish purple color. —*adj.* having the color mulberry. [Old English *mōrberie* the fruit, from Latin *mōrum* + Old English *berie* berry.]

mulch (mulch) *n.* any of various materials, such as straw, shredded bark, stones, or sheets of black plastic, spread around plants to protect them against loss of moisture or sharp changes in temperature, to help prevent soil erosion, and to slow the growth of weeds. —*v.t., v.i.* **1.** to cover (the ground) with mulch. **2.** to cover the ground around (plants) with mulch. [From obsolete *mulch* soft, from Old English *myl(i)sc* mellow.]

mulct (mulkt) *v.t.* **1.** to punish by a fine or penalty. **2.** to swindle (someone) out of something. —*n.* a fine or penalty. [Latin *mulc(t)a* penalty, fine².]

mule¹ (mūl) *n.* **1.** a large-eared domestic animal produced by crossbreeding a female horse with a male donkey. Mules are frequently used as pack animals and for farm work and are usually barren. Height: to 6 feet (1.8 meters) at the shoulder. **2.** *Informal.* a person who is very stubborn. **3.** a machine that spins fiber into yarn or thread and winds it on spindles. **4.** a small tractor or engine. [Old English *mūl* and Old French *mule* this animal, both from Latin *mūlus.*]

mule² (mūl) *n.* a slipper that leaves the back of the heel uncovered. [French *mule* slipper, from Latin *mulleus* red shoe worn by high magistrates.]

mule deer, a deer, *Odocoileus hemionus,* native to western North America, having a tawny gray coat and large ears. Height: 42 inches (107 centimeters) at the shoulder.

mule skinner *Informal.* a person who drives mules; muleteer.

mu·le·teer (mū′li tîr′) *n.* a person who is in charge of mules. [French *muletier,* from *mulet* mule¹, diminutive of Old French *mul.* See MULE¹.]

mul·ish (mū′lish) *adj.* stubborn; obstinate. —**mul′ish·ly,** *adv.* —**mul′ish·ness,** *n.*

mull¹ (mul) *v.t.* to think about or reflect on; ponder (often with *over*): *The witness mulled the question over carefully.* [Possibly form of MUDDLE.]

mull² (mul) *v.t.* to sweeten, heat, and add spices to (a beverage, such as wine or cider). [Of uncertain origin.]

mull³ (mul) *n.* a soft, sheer fabric woven of silk, cotton, and other fibers, used esp. for dresses and millinery. [Short for earlier *mulmul* muslin, from Hindi *malmal.*]

mul·lah (mul′ə, mŭl′ə) *n.* a Muslim religious leader, esp. one versed in religious law. [Turkish, Persian, and Urdu *mullā,* from Arabic *maulā* judge, master.]

mul·lein (mul′ən) *also,* **mul·len.** *n.* any of several tall plants with velvety, gray-green, coarsely toothed leaves that are oblong or oval, such as the **common mullein,** *Verbascum thapsus,* a widespread weed that bears yellow flowers. [Anglo-Norman *moleine,* probably from Old French *mol* soft, from Latin *mollis;* because of the soft down on its leaves.]

mul·let (mul′it) *n., pl.* -lets or -let. any of a group of saltwater and freshwater food fish, family Mugilidae, found throughout tropical and temperate regions, having a gray, red, or striped torpedo-shaped body with a spiny dorsal fin. [Old French *mulet,* from Latin *mullus.*]

mul·li·gan stew (mul′i gən) a stew of fish, poultry, or meat and vegetables, often put together from leftovers. Also, **mul′li·gan.** [Possibly from the proper name *Mulligan.*]

mul·li·ga·taw·ny (mul′i gə tô′nē) *n.* a soup, originally of India, usually made with chicken stock and highly seasoned with curry. [Tamil *miakutannil* a spicy soup, from *milaku* pepper + *tanni* water.]

mul·lion (mul′yən) *n.* a vertical bar dividing panels, as of windows, doors, or screens. —*v.t.* to divide with mullions. [Modification of obsolete *monial,* from Old French *moinel* middle, from *moien, meien.* See MEAN³.]

multi- *prefix* **1.** more than one or two; many: *a multicolored cloak.* **2.** many times over: *a multimillionaire.* [Latin *multus* much, many.]

mul·ti·cel·lu·lar (mul′ti sel′yə lər) *adj.* composed of more than one cell; many-celled.

mul·ti·col·ored (mul′ti kul′ərd) *adj.* of many or various colors. Also, **mul′ti·col′or.**

mullions

mul·ti·di·men·sion·al (mul′ti di men′shə nəl) *adj.* of, relating to, or having several dimensions.

mul·ti·far·i·ous (mul′tə fâr′ē əs) *adj.* having many aspects or forms; varied; diversified. [Latin *multifārius* manifold, various.] —**mul′ti·far′i·ous·ly,** *adv.* —**mul′ti·far′i·ous·ness,** *n.*

mul·ti·form (mul′tə fôrm′) *adj.* having many different forms or appearances. —**mul′ti·form′i·ty,** *n.*

Mul·ti·graph (mul′ti graf′) *n. Trademark.* a machine with a rotary drum that reproduces typewritten material by means of metal type.

mul·ti·lat·er·al (mul′ti lat′ər əl) *adj.* **1.** involving or participated in by three or more nations or governments: *a multilateral treaty.* **2.** many-sided. —**mul′ti·lat′er·al·ly,** *adv.*

Mul·ti·lith (mul′ti lith′) *n. Trademark.* a small offset printing press.

mul·ti·me·di·a (mul′ti mē′dē ə) *adj.* of, relating to, or using several media of communication, art, or entertainment at the same time, such as television and newspapers for advertising or photographs and watercolors for a collage. —*n.* the employment of or a combination of several media of communication, art, or entertainment at the same time.

mul·ti·mil·lion·aire (mul′ti mil′yə nâr′) *n.* a person who has holdings worth several millions of some unit of currency, esp. dollars.

mul·ti·na·tion·al (mul′ti nash′ə nəl) *adj.* **1.** of or relating to more than two nations or nationalities: *a multinational project.* **2.** having business divisions or operations in more than two countries: *a multinational corporation.* —*n.* a business enterprise that has divisions in more than two countries.

mul·ti·nu·cle·ate (mul′ti nū′klē it, -āt′, -nū′-) *adj.* having more than two nuclei, as the cells of striated muscle tissue. Also, **mul′ti·nu′cle·ar, mul′ti·nu′cle·at′ed.**

mul·tip·a·rous (mul tip′ər əs) *adj.* producing or capable of producing more than one offspring at one time. [Modern Latin *multiparus,* from Latin *multus* much, many + *parere* to bring forth.]

mul·ti·phase (mul′ti fāz′) *adj.* polyphase. Also, **mul′ti·pha′sic.**

mul·ti·ple (mul′tə pəl) *adj.* consisting of or characterized by many or by more than one part or individual: *multiple fractures, a multiple birth.* —*n.* a number or algebraic expression that is a product of a given number or algebraic expression. The number 16 is a multiple of 8; $4x^2y$ is a multiple of xy. [French *multiple,* from Late Latin *multiplus* manifold, from Latin *multus* much, many.]

mul·ti·ple-choice (mul′tə pəl chois′) *adj.* offering a variety of answers from which the correct one or ones are to be chosen: *a multiple-choice exam, a multiple-choice question.*

multiple fruit, a fruit formed from the matured ovaries of separate flowers in a cluster, as the pineapple or mulberry.

multiple personality, a rare mental disorder in which parts of a personality become so severely dissociated that two or more entirely separate personalities develop in the same person.

multiple sclerosis, a disease of the nervous system characterized by patchy destruction of the sheath of myelin that covers the nerves of the brain and spinal cord, leading to spasms, speech disorders, and paralysis.

mul·ti·plex (mul′tə pleks′) *adj.* **1.a.** manifold; multiple. **b.** having many parts: *a multiplex theater.* **2.** of or relating to a telecommunications line and equipment that can transmit several messages at once. [Latin *multiplex* manifold.]

mul·ti·pli·cand (mul′tə pli kand′) *n.* a number or algebraic expression that is to be multiplied by another, the multiplier. [Latin *multiplicandus* to be increased, gerundive of *multiplicāre* to increase, multiply (in arithmetic).]

M

a	at	e	end	o	hot	u	up	hw	white		about
ā	ape	ē	me	ō	old	ū	use	ng	song	ə	taken
ä	far	i	it	ô	fork	ǔ	rule	th	thin		pencil
âr	care	ī	ice	oi	oil	u̇	pull	th	this		lemon
		îr	pierce	ou	out	ûr	turn	zh	measure		circus

The following list contains a selection of compounds that can be formed with the prefix **multi-**. The meaning of a word on the list can be understood by combining the sense of the prefix and the root word.

multiagency	multicultural	multifamily	multilevel	multipolar	multistep
multiarmed	multidenominational	multifilament	multilobed	multipower	multistory
multibarreled	multidirectional	multifocal	multimegaton	multiproblem	multisyllabic
multibladed	multidisciplinary	multifunctional	multimember	multipronged	multitalented
multibranched	multidivisional	multigenerational	multimetallic	multipurpose	multitiered
multicausal	multidwelling	multigrade	multimillennial	multiroomed	multitone
multichambered	multielement	multiheaded	multimillion	multiseasonal	multitowered
multichannel	multiengined	multihued	multimodal	multiservice	multitrack
multicharacter	multienvironmental	multiindustrial	multimolecular	multisided	multiunit
multichord	multiethnic	multiinstitutional	multiparameter	multisized	multiuse
multicomponent	multifaceted	multilane	multipart	multiskilled	multiwarhead
multicrested	multifactional	multilayered	multiparty	multispeed	multiyear

mul·ti·pli·ca·tion (mul′tə pli kā′shən) *n.* **1.** the process of adding a number to itself a certain number of times. **2.** the act or process of multiplying or increasing. —**mul′ti·pli·ca′tive,** *adj.*

multiplicative inverse, see **inverse** *(def. 2).*

mul·ti·plic·i·ty (mul′tə plis′i tē) *n., pl.* **-ties.** a great number or variety. [Late Latin *multiplicitās,* from Latin *multiplex* manifold.]

mul·ti·pli·er (mul′tə plī′ər) *n.* **1.** a number or algebraic expression by which another, the multiplicand, is to be multiplied. **2.** a person or thing that multiplies or causes an increase.

mul·ti·ply (mul′tə plī′) *v.,* **-plied, -ply·ing.** —*v.i.* **1.** to perform multiplication. **2.** to reproduce: *Rabbits multiply rapidly.* **3.** to grow in number, quantity, or extent; increase: *In a few months the guerrilla army had multiplied tenfold.* —*v.t.* **1.** to perform multiplication with (numbers or algebraic expressions): *to multiply the height by the width to determine the area.* **2.** to cause to increase in number, quantity, or extent: *The war greatly multiplied the possibility of dying violently.* [Old French *multiplier,* from Latin *multiplicāre.*]

mul·ti·ra·cial (mul′ti rā′shəl) *adj.* of, relating to, or composed of several races, peoples, or ethnic groups: *Hawaii has a multiracial society.*

mul·ti·stage (mul′ti stāj′) *adj.* (of a rocket or guided missile) having more than one section that is self-propelling and can separate from the rest of the rocket or missile.

mul·ti·tude (mul′ti tūd′, -tūd′) *n.* **1.** a great number, as of people or things, esp. when collected together in one place or regarded collectively: *a multitude listening to a speech, a multitude of problems.* **2.** **the multitude.** the masses; populace. [Latin *multitūdō* a great number.] —For Synonyms, see **host**[2].

mul·ti·tu·di·nous (mul′ti tū′də nəs, -tū′-) *adj.* of, like, or being a multitude: *a multitudinous herd of wild horses.* —**mul′ti·tu′di·nous·ly,** *adv.* —**mul′ti·tu′di·nous·ness,** *n.*

mul·ti·va·lent (mul′ti vā′lənt, mul tiv′ə-) *adj. Chemistry.* having a valence of three or more, or more than one valence. Also, **polyvalent.** —**mul′ti·va′lence,** *n.*

mul·ti·vi·ta·min (mul′ti vī′tə min, mul′tē vī′-) *adj.* containing or employing several vitamins: *a multivitamin tablet.*

mum[1] (mum) *adj.* silent; quiet: *to keep mum.* [Probably imitative.]
• **mum's the word.** keep silent. ➡ usually used in the imperative.

mum[2] (mum) *n. Informal.* chrysanthemum.

mum·ble (mum′bəl) *v.t., v.i.,* **-bled, -bling. 1.** to speak (words) softly and indistinctly with or as if with the mouth closed: *The shy child mumbled the words.* **2.** *Archaic.* to chew or bite (something, such as food) with or as if with toothless gums. —*n.* a soft, indistinct sound, esp. of speech. [Middle English *momelen* to speak indistinctly, from *mom* inarticulate sound; of imitative origin.] —**mum′bler,** *n.* —**mum′bling,** *n.*

mum·ble·ty-peg (mum′bəl tē peg′) *also,* **mum·ble·dy-peg** (mum′bəl dē peg′). *n.* a game played by one or more persons, consisting of throwing or dropping a knife from various positions in such a way that it sticks in the ground. Also, **mum′bly-peg′.** [Because the loser formerly had to MUMBLE *the peg,* which had been driven into the ground, removing it from the ground with his teeth.]

mum·bo jum·bo (mum′bō jum′bō) **1.** meaningless, ritualistic words or actions; gibberish: *the secretive mumbo jumbo of an initiation ceremony.* **2.** *also,* **Mumbo Jumbo.** an idol or image superstitiously worshiped or feared. [Modification of Mandingo *Mama Dyumbo* a tribal deity.]

mu meson, muon.

mum·mer (mum′ər) *n.* **1.** a person who wears a mask or costume, as for a parade or celebration. **2.** *Archaic.* actor. [Old French *momeur* masker, mountebank, from *momer* to go in a mask; of uncertain origin.]

mum·mer·y (mum′ə rē) *n., pl.* **-mer·ies. 1.** any ridiculous or hypocritical ritual or ceremony. **2.** a performance or the actions of a mummer. [Old French *mommerie* masquerade, from Old French *momeur* mummer. See MUMMER.]

mum·mi·fy (mum′ə fī′) *v.,* **-fied, -fy·ing.** —*v.t.* **1.** to make into a mummy by embalming. **2.** to preserve in a rigid, dead, or lifeless state. —*v.i.* to dry, shrivel up, or become lifeless like a mummy. —**mum′mi·fi·ca′tion,** *n.*

mum·my (mum′ē) *n., pl.* **-mies. 1.** a dead body embalmed and dried for preservation, esp. in the manner of the ancient Egyptians. **2.** a dead body similarly preserved by nature. [Old French *momie,* going back to Arabic *mūmiyā,* from Persian *mūm* wax (used for embalming).]

mumps (mumps) *n.* a contagious disease caused by a virus, characterized by painful swelling of the salivary glands at the side

of the face. ➡ used as singular or plural. [Plural of obsolete *mump* grimace; of imitative origin.]

munch (munch) *v.t., v.i.* to chew or eat, esp. noisily: *to munch on a sandwich, to munch a carrot.* [Imitative.]

mun·dane (mun dān′, mun′dān) *adj.* **1.** of or relating to what is common, ordinary, or usual; prosaic: *We were bored by the mundane week we were having.* **2.** of this world; earthly. [Late Latin *mundānus* relating to the world, from Latin *mundus* world.] —**mun·dane′ly,** *adv.* —**mun·dane′ness,** *n.*

mung bean (mung) **1.** the edible green or yellow seed of a legume, *Vigna radiata,* grown esp. as the chief source of bean sprouts. **2.** the plant bearing this seed.

Mu·nich Pact (mū′ nik) an agreement signed at Munich in September 1938, in which France and Great Britain sought to appease Adolf Hitler by allowing Germany to annex the Sudetenland region of Czechoslovakia.

mu·nic·i·pal (mū nis′ə pəl) *adj.* **1.** of or relating to the local government or affairs of a city, town, or other community: *a municipal transportation commission.* **2.** having local self-government. [Latin *mūnicipālis* relating to a township, going back to *mūnia* official duties + *capere* to take.] —**mu·nic′i·pal·ly,** *adv.*

mu·nic·i·pal·i·ty (mū nis′ə pal′i tē) *n., pl.* **-ties.** an incorporated city, town, or other community.

mu·nic·i·pal·ize (mū nis′ə pə līz′) *v.t.,* **-ized, -iz·ing. 1.** to bring under municipal ownership or control: *to municipalize bus service.* **2.** to give (a city or town) municipal institutions; make a municipality of. —**mu·nic′i·pal·i·za′tion,** *n.*

mu·nif·i·cent (mū nif′ə sənt) *adj.* **1.** very lavish and generous in giving: *a munificent benefactor.* **2.** showing or indicating lavish generosity: *a munificent gesture.* [Latin *mūnificēns,* going back to *mūnus* duty, gift + *facere* to make.] —**mu·nif′i·cence,** *n.* —**mu·nif′i·cent·ly,** *adv.*

mu·ni·tion (mū nish′ən) *n. usually,* **munitions.** military supplies, such as guns, ammunition, or bombs. —*v.t.* to provide with munitions. [French *munition* provision, military supply, from Latin *mūnītiō* fortification, defense.]

mu·on (mū′on) *n. Physics.* a subatomic particle whose mass is greater than that of an electron but less than that of a meson. Also, **mu meson.** [MU + (MES)ON.]

mu·ral (myur′əl) *n.* a picture, photograph, or the like applied directly to or painted directly on a wall or ceiling. —*adj.* **1.** placed, fixed, or executed on or in a wall. **2.** of, relating to, or resembling a wall. [French *mural* relating to a wall, from Latin *mūrālis,* from *mūrus* wall.]

mu·ral·ist (myur′ə list) *n.* an artist who executes murals.

mur·der (mur′dər) *n.* **1.** the unlawful and intentional killing of a human being, usually premeditated but sometimes without specific intent but in the course of committing another felony. **2.** *Informal.* a person or thing that is very difficult, trying, or dangerous: *It was murder to travel on the overcrowded trains. My piano teacher can be murder about the need to practice.* —*v.t.* **1.** to kill (a human being) unlawfully and intentionally, with premeditation or in the course of committing another felony. **2.** to kill or slaughter, esp. in a brutal manner. **3.** to abuse, mangle, or mar: *to murder the English language.* **4.** *Informal.* to defeat decisively; trounce: *We murdered the other team, 65-0.* **5.** *Informal.* to impress (someone, esp. an audience) greatly. —*v.i.* to commit murder. [Old English *morthor* willful homicide.] —**mur′der·er,** *n.* —For Synonyms *(v.t.),* see **kill**[1].
• **to get away with murder.** to be allowed to do something wrong without being punished.

mur·der·ous (mur′dər əs) *adj.* **1.** of, relating to, or characterized by murder: *a murderous plot.* **2.** capable of, given to, or threatening murder: *a murderous attack, a murderous gleam in an attacker's eyes, a murderous tyrant.* **3.** *Informal.* very difficult, trying, or dangerous: *a murderous mountain road.* —**mur′der·ous·ly,** *adv.* —**mur′der·ous·ness,** *n.*

mu·rex (myur′iks) *n.* a marine gastropod, genus *Murex,* found in tropical seas, having a spiny shell and yielding a purple dye. [Modern Latin *Murex,* from Latin *mūrex* a shellfish yielding a purple dye.]

mu·ri·at·ic acid (myur′ē at′ik) a commercial term for hydrochloric acid. [Latin *muriāticus* pickled in brine, from *muria* brine.]

mu·rine (myur′īn, -in) *adj.* of or relating to the Muridae, the family of rodents that includes the Old World rats and mice commonly associated with human habitation. [Latin *murinus,* from *mus* mouse.]

murk (murk) *also,* **mirk.** *n.* darkness or gloom, as caused by fog or smoke. —*adj. Archaic.* murky. [Probably from Old Norse *myrkr.*]

murk·y (mur′kē) *adj.,* **murk·i·er, murk·i·est. 1.** dark, ob-

scured, or gloomy: *the murky waters of a muddy river.* **2.** dark and obscure to the mind; hard to understand. —**murk′i·ly,** *adv.* —**murk′i·ness,** *n.*

mur·mur (mûr′mər) *n.* **1.** a low, continuous, rising and falling sound: *the murmur of the wind in the trees.* **2.** a soft, low, nearly indistinct voice or speech: *The listener gave a murmur of approval. The child spoke in a murmur.* **3.** an abnormal rumbling or blowing sound in the heart, lungs, or arteries that indicates some malfunction. **4.** an expression of discontent; complaint; protest: *to accept a rebuke without a murmur.* —*v.i.* **1.** to make a murmur. **2.** to complain or protest. —*v.t.* to say in a soft, low, nearly indistinct voice. [Latin *murmur* a humming, rumbling, crashing.] —**mur′mur·er,** *n.*

mur·rain (mûr′in) *n.* **1.** any of several infectious, usually fatal diseases of cattle and other animals. **2.** *Archaic.* a pestilence or plague. [Old French *morine,* from *morir* to die, going back to Latin *morī.*]

murre (mûr) *n., pl.* **murres** or **murre.** any of a group of black and white, diving and swimming shorebirds, genus *Uria,* related to auks and puffins. The **common murre,** *U. aalge,* of the Northern Hemisphere, about 12 inches (30 centimeters) long, nests in dense colonies on rocky cliffs.

mus. 1. museum. **2.** music. **3.** musician.

mus·ca·dine (mus′kə din, -dīn′) *n.* a grape, *Vitis rotundifolia,* native to the southeastern United States and Mexico.

mus·cat (mus′kat, -kət) *n.* a large, pale green grape having seeds, used esp. to make raisins and muscatel. [French *muscat* this grape, wine from this grape, going back to Old Provençal *muscat* musky, going back to Late Latin *muscus* musk. See MUSK.]

mus·ca·tel (mus′kə tel′) *n.* a rich, sweet wine made from the muscat grape.

mus·cle (mus′əl) *n.* **1.** a body tissue composed of bundles of elongated cells, capable of contracting upon stimulation to produce motion. **2.** one of the or-

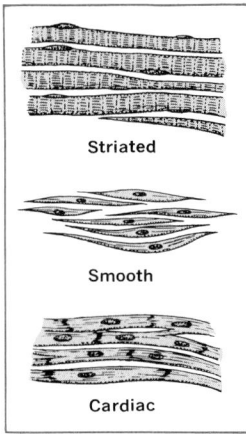

Striated

Smooth

Cardiac

types of **muscle**

gans of the body composed of this tissue, esp. one that is attached by tendons to bones and that functions to move part of the body. **3.** strength or force, esp. bodily strength. —*v.,* **-cled, -cling.** *Informal.* —*v.i.* to force one's way into an activity or organization against resistance, by or as by sheer physical strength or power (with *in* or *into*): *Racketeers muscled in on the business.* —*v.t.* to force in some direction: *to muscle people out of one's way, to muscle a piano into position on a stage.* [Latin *mūsculus* little mouse, the organ of the body, diminutive of *mūs* mouse; because certain muscles supposedly resemble a mouse in form and action.]

mus·cle-bound (mus′əl bound′) *adj.* having overdeveloped or tight muscles, as from too much exercise.

mus·cle·man (mus′əl man′) *n., pl.* **-men** (-men′). **1.** *Informal.* a musclebound man. **2.** *Slang.* a man hired to threaten or beat up others: *a muscleman for the mob.*

mus·co·vite (mus′kə vīt′) *n.* a light yellow, brown, green, red, or colorless mineral that is the most common form of mica.

Mus·co·vite (mus′kə vīt′) *n.* a native or resident of Moscow or, formerly, of Russia: *The nineteenth-century poet and dramatist Pushkin was a famous Muscovite.*

Mus·co·vy duck (mus′kə vē) a duck, *Cairina moschata,* usually having black-and-white plumage, native to Mexico and Central and South America, now widely raised for its meat. Length: 28-30 inches (71-76 centimeters).

mus·cu·lar (mus′kyə lər) *adj.* **1.** of, relating to, or involving muscles: *muscular coordination.* **2.** having well-developed muscles; strong: *a muscular athlete.* **3.** composed or consisting of muscle. —**mus′cu·lar·ly,** *adv.*

muscular dys·tro·phy (dis′trə fē) a genetically inherited disease of unknown origin characterized by progressive weakening and wasting of the skeletal muscles. It usually begins in early childhood.

mus·cu·lar·i·ty (mus′kyə lar′i tē) *n.* the strength, development, or condition of the muscles.

muscular system, the system of muscles that move the parts of the body of an animal. Some parts of the muscular system, such

as the smooth muscles of the heart and arteries, work automatically. Others, such as the skeletal or striated muscles, are under voluntary control.

mus·cu·la·ture (mus′kyə lə chər) *n.* the arrangement of the muscles in the body or in a particular part of the body. [French *musculature,* from Latin *mūsculus* muscle of the body. See MUSCLE.]

muse (mūz) *v.,* **mused, mus·ing.** —*v.i.* to think, reflect, or meditate, esp. in an idle or detached manner: *to muse on the events of the day.* —*v.t.* to say or think in a reflective or detached manner. [Old French *muser* to ponder, linger, from *muse* snout of an animal (suggesting a dog's sniffing about); of uncertain origin.] —**mus′er,** *n.* —For Synonyms *(v.i.),* see **meditate.**

Muse (mūz) *n.* **1.** in Greek mythology, one of the nine goddesses who presided over the arts and sciences and were daughters of Zeus and Mnemosyne: Calliope, Clio, Erato, Euterpe, Melpomene, Polyhymnia, Terpsichore, Thalia, or Urania. **2.** *muse.* a spirit or other source of genius or artistic inspiration. [Latin *Mūsa* one of these nine goddesses, from Greek *Mousa.*]

mu·sette bag (mū zet′) a small bag carried over the shoulder by hikers, and formerly by soldiers, for small personal items. [Middle French *musette* a kind of bagpipe; from its shape.]

mu·se·um (mū zē′əm) *n.* a building, place, or institution where a collection of objects of value or interest, as in the fields of art, science, history, or natural history, is preserved and displayed. [Latin *mūsēum* library, study, museum, from Greek *mouseion* shrine of the Muses, philosophical school and library, from *Mousa* any of the nine ancient Greek Muses.]

mush¹ (mush) *n.* **1.** a thick porridge made by boiling cornmeal. **2.** any soft, thick, or pulpy mass. **3.** *Informal.* anything overly sentimental or romantic. [Form of MASH.]

mush² (mush) *interj.* go or go faster. ➡ used as a command to a team of dogs pulling a sled. —*v.i.* to travel on foot with a dogsled over snow. —*n.* a journey made with a dogsled. [Probably from *mush on,* from French *marchons,* first person plural imperative of *marcher* to go.] —**mush′er,** *n.*

mush·room (mush′rüm′, -rüm′) *n.* **1.** any of various fungi shaped like an umbrella, a sponge, or a ball, some of which are edible and others poisonous. **2.** anything resembling a mushroom, esp. in shape or rapid growth. —*adj.* **1.** made of or with mushrooms: *a mushroom omelet.* **2.** like or suggestive of a mushroom or mushrooms: *a mushroom pattern.* —*v.i.* **1.** to spring up or grow suddenly and rapidly: *Buildings mushroomed all over the area.* **2.** to spread out or flatten at one end into the shape of a mushroom: *The cloud of smoke mushroomed in the sky.* [Middle French *muscheron* from Old French *moisseron,* from Late Latin *mussirion-,* stem of *mussirio;* of uncertain origin.]

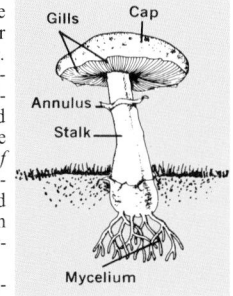

Gills   Cap
Annulus
Stalk
Mycelium

mushroom

mushroom cloud, a mushroom-shaped cloud resulting from an explosion, esp. of a nuclear weapon, either on the ground or at a low altitude.

mush·y (mush′ē) *adj.,* **mush·i·er, mush·i·est. 1.** having a soft and pulpy consistency like mush. **2.** *Informal.* overly sentimental or romantic. —**mush′i·ly,** *adv.* —**mush′i·ness,** *n.*

mu·sic (mū′zik) *n.* **1.** a pleasing or harmonious succession or combination of sounds. **2.** the art of producing and arranging aesthetically pleasing and emotionally expressive combinations of sounds, usually according to principles of rhythm, melody, harmony, tonality, and dynamics. **3.** a musical composition as represented by graphic symbols, or the written or printed score of a musical composition: *Can you read music?* **4.** any pleasant sound or series of sounds: *Her words of welcome were music to his ear.* **5.** the business or occupation of composing or performing music: *to study for a career in music.* [Latin *mūsica* art of music, from Greek *mousikē* any art over which the Muses presided, esp. music, from *Mousa.* See MUSE.]

a	at	e	end	o	hot	u	up	hw	white		about
ā	ape	ē	me	ō	old	ū	use	ng	song		taken
ä	far	i	it	ô	fork	ü	rule	th	thin	ə	pencil
âr	care	ī	ice	oi	oil	u̇	pull	th	this		lemon
				ir	pierce	ou	out	ûr	turn	zh	measure		circus

• **to face the music.** *Informal.* to face consequences bravely, no matter what they are.

• **to set to music.** to provide (a poem or other text) with a written musical accompaniment.

mu·si·cal (mū′zi kəl) *adj.* **1.** of, relating to, or producing music. **2.** set to or accompanied by music: *a musical show.* **3.** similar to music in beauty or expression: *the musical sounds of laughter.* **4.** fond of or gifted in music: *a very musical family.* —*n.* a musical comedy or other musical play or film. —**mu·si·cal·i·ty** (mū′zi kal′i tē), **mu′si·cal·ness,** *n.* —**mu′si·cal·ly,** *adv.*

musical chairs, a children's game in which the players march to music around a row of chairs having one fewer than the number of players. When the music suddenly stops, the players rush to sit down, and the one left standing is eliminated. The game continues until only one player is left.

musical comedy, a light theatrical work or motion picture combining songs, dances, and spoken dialogue.

mu·si·cale (mū′zi kal′) *n.* a party or other social gathering featuring musical entertainment. [French *(soirée) musicale* musical (evening), from *musique* art of music, from Latin *mūsica.* See MUSIC.]

music box, a box or case containing a device that produces a tune mechanically.

music hall 1. an auditorium or hall for musical performances. **2.** *British.* vaudeville theater.

mu·si·cian (mū zish′ən) *n.* a person skilled in or professionally engaged in the performance or composition of music. —**mu·si′·cian·ship′,** *n.*

mu·si·col·o·gy (mū′zi kol′ə jē) *n.* the study of the history, theory, and forms of music. —**mu·si·co·log·i·cal** (mū′zi kə loj′i kəl), *adj.* —**mu′si·col′o·gist,** *n.*

music video, a dramatized or stylized performance of a popular song recorded on videotape.

mu·sing (mū′zing) *n.* the act of thinking or reflecting in a detached manner; meditation. —*adj.* engaged in musing; meditative. —**mu′sing·ly,** *adv.*

musk (musk) *n.* **1.** an oily, strong-smelling substance secreted by an abdominal gland in the male musk deer, used in making perfumes, medicine, and soaps. **2.** any similar substance made synthetically or processed from secretions of muskrat, musk ox, or civet. **3.** the odor of musk. [Late Latin *muscus* the substance obtained from the musk deer, through Persian, from Sanskrit *muskah* testicle similar in shape to the bag of the musk deer containing musk.]

musk deer, a small, hornless deer, *Moschus moschiferus,* of central and eastern Asia, the male of which has a gland that secretes musk. Height: 2 feet (0.6 meter) at the shoulder.

mus·keg (mus′keg) *n.* a kind of bog found in the taiga of subarctic North America, underlain by thick layers of decaying sphagnum moss, with a layer of living moss on top. [Cree *maskeek* swamp.]

mus·kel·lunge (mus′kə lunj′) *n., pl.* **-lunge.** a large, greenish brown, freshwater game fish, *Esox masquinongy,* of the pike family, found esp. in the Great Lakes. Length: to 5 feet (1.5 meters). Weight: to 70 pounds (31.7 kilograms). Also, **muskie.** [Algonquian *maskinonge* large pike.]

mus·ket (mus′kit) *n.* any of several types of guns fired from the shoulder, esp. one having a smooth bore, used before the general adoption of rifles. [Middle French *mousquet,* from Italian *moschetto* musket; earlier, arrow for a crossbow, from *mosca* fly, from Latin *musca.*]

mus·ket·eer (mus′ki tîr′) *n.* **1.** a soldier armed with a musket, or one whose regiment was traditionally so armed. **2.** a member of the king's guard in seventeenth-century France.

mus·ket·ry (mus′ki trē) *n.* **1.** the art or science of firing muskets. **2.** muskets collectively. **3.** musketeers collectively: *to call out the musketry.* **4.** the firing of muskets: *They could hear the musketry over the hill.*

mus·kie (mus′kē) *n.* muskellunge.

musk·mel·on (musk′mel′ən) *n.* **1.** any of several large, edible fruits having a netted rind, sweet juicy flesh, and small flat seeds in the center. **2.** any of several trailing or climbing vines, *Cucumis melo reticulatus,* of the gourd family, native to Central and North America and Europe and bearing these fruits.

Mus·ko·ge·an (mus kō′gē ən, -jē-) *n.* a family of American Indian languages, including Chickasaw, Choctaw, and Seminole, spoken predominantly in the southern United States. —*adj.* belonging to this language family.

musk ox, a buffalolike mammal, *Ovibos moschatus,* native to the tundra of northern Canada and Greenland, having a shaggy, dark brown or black coat. It gives off a musky odor during the mating season. Height: 4-6 feet (1.2-1.8 meters) at the shoulder.

musk ox

musk·rat (musk′rat′) *n., pl.* **-rat** or **-rats. 1.** any of various North American aquatic rodents, genus *Ondatra,* having webbed hind feet, a flat tail, a musky odor, and a thick, soft coat of glossy, dark brown fur. Length: to 26 inches (66 centimeters), including tail. **2.** its fur.

musk·y (mus′kē) *adj.,* **musk·i·er, musk·i·est.** of, relating to, resembling, or smelling like musk. —**musk′i·ness,** *n.*

Mus·lim (muz′lim, mu̇z′-, mus′-) *also,* **Mus·lem, Mos·lem.** *adj.* of, relating to, or characteristic of Islam or its culture. —*n.* a follower of Islam. Also, **Islamite, Mohammedan, Mahometan, Mussulman.** [Arabic *muslim* follower of Islam, one who has submitted (to God).]

mus·lin (muz′lin) *n.* any of a large group of cotton fabrics, varying from lightweight, sheer materials used for such items as blouses to heavyweight materials used for sheets and pillowcases. —*adj.* made of muslin. [French *mousseline* thin fine cotton cloth, from Italian *mussolino,* from *Mosul,* city in Iraq where it was first produced.]

muss (mus) *Informal. v.t.* to make disordered or untidy; rumple (often with *up*): *The wind mussed up my hair.* —*n.* a state of disorder; mess. [Probably modification of MESS.]

mus·sel (mus′əl) *n.* **1.** any saltwater bivalve mollusk of the family Mytilidae, having a soft body encased in a bluish black shell, esp. the common edible mussel, *Mytilus edulis,* found primarily along the coasts of Europe and North America. Length: to 14 inches (36 centimeters). **2.** any of the related freshwater mollusks of the family Unionidae, found in lakes and streams of the central United States. [Middle English *mussel,* from Old English *muscle* a saltwater mollusk, going back to Latin *mūsculus* a saltwater mollusk, muscle of the body. See MUSCLE.]

Mus·sul·man (mus′əl mən) *n., pl.* **-mans.** *Archaic.* Muslim. [Persian *musulmān,* from Arabic *muslim.* See MUSLIM.]

muss·y (mus′ē) *adj.,* **muss·i·er, muss·i·est.** *Informal.* disordered; untidy; rumpled. —**muss′i·ly,** *adv.* —**muss′i·ness,** *n.*

must[1] (must) *auxiliary verb* (followed by an infinitive without *to*) **1.** to be obliged or bound: *I must return their call today.* **2.** to be forced or required by necessity, compulsion, or command: *Many wild animals must fight to survive.* **3.** to be reasonably or certainly expected: *The sun must set soon. My request must seem strange to you.* —*n. Informal.* anything vital, necessary, or essential: *Insect repellent is a must in the swamp.* —*adj. Informal.* vital, essential, or necessary: *a must movie for fans of 1950s comedies.* [Old English *mōste,* past tense of *mōtan* to have to, be permitted to, be able to.]

Synonyms	**Must**[1], **ought**[1], and **should** mean to be obliged to. **Must** emphasizes necessity or determination: *They must finish the assignment this week.* **Ought** implies being bound by a promise or duty: *I ought to return the book to the library.* **Should** also stresses duty or obligation and is often used interchangeably with *ought.* But it can also express propriety or expediency: *You should be more polite to your grandparents. You should brush your teeth regularly.*

must[2] (must) *n.* the unfermented or not completely fermented juice of fruit, esp. grapes, before it becomes wine. [Old English *must,* from Latin *mustum,* from *mustus* fresh, new.]

must[3] (must) *n.* a moldy condition; mustiness. [From MUSTY.]

mus·tache (mus′tash, mə stash′) *also,* **moustache.** *n.* **1.** *also,* **mustaches.** a growth of hair on the upper lip. **2.** a growth of hairs or bristles around the mouth in certain animals. [French *moustache,* from Italian *mostaccio* ugly face, snout (in plural, hair on upper lip), going back to Greek *mystax* upper lip, hair on upper lip.]

mus·ta·chio (mə stash′ō, -stash′e ō′) *n., pl.* **-chios.** mustache. —**mus·ta′chioed,** *adj.*

mus·tang (mus′tang) *n.* a wild horse of the American plains, believed to be descended from stock brought by the Spanish. [Spanish *mestengo* stray, from *mesta* company of owners of cattle who disposed of strays, from Medieval Latin *mixta (animalia)* mixed (animals), including both stray and herd animals, from Latin *miscēre* to mix.]

mus·tard (mus′tərd) *n.* **1.** a pungent, yellowish paste or powder made from the seeds of any of various plants, genus *Brassica*, used as a spice or medicinally as a stimulant and emetic. **2.** the plant itself, esp. **black mustard**, *B. nigra* and **white mustard**, *B. hirta*. **3.** the color of mustard paste or powder; dark or brownish yellow. —*adj.* **1.** designating a family, Cruciferae or Brassicaceae, of plants growing in temperate parts of the world, including mustard, many common vegetables, such as broccoli, cabbage, radish, and turnip, and plants with ornamental flowers, such as the candytuft and wallflower. **2.** having the color mustard. [Old French *mostarde* the plant of the genus *Brassica*, going back to Latin *mustum* must²; because must was once an ingredient of mustard paste.]
  • **to cut the mustard.** to perform up to expectations; meet a standard, as in doing a job.
mustard gas, a deadly poison gas that burns and blisters the skin and eyes and damages the bronchial tubes and lungs, made from ethylene or from hydrogen chloride and produced for chemical warfare. Formula: $C_4H_8Cl_2S$
mustard plaster, a poultice made of a cloth covered with a mixture of mustard, flour, and water, used as a counterirritant.
mus·ter (mus′tər) *v.t.* **1.** to find and gather together; collect or summon: *to muster strength, to muster arguments in defense of a theory.* **2.** to gather or call (troops) together. **3.** to dismiss or discharge (someone), esp. from military service (with *out*): *They mustered me out last winter, and I still haven't found a job.* —*v.i.* to gather together in a group; assemble: *The platoon mustered for roll call.* —*n.* **1.** the act or an instance of assembling troops or others for military inspection or service. **2.** the list or number of those so assembled. Also, **muster roll. 3.** any assembly or collection. [Old French *monstrer* to show, from Latin *mōnstrāre.*]
  • **to pass muster.** to meet a standard; live up to expectations.
must·n't (mus′ənt) *contr.* must not.
mus·ty (mus′tē) *adj.,* **-ti·er, -ti·est. 1.** having a stale or moldy odor or taste: *a damp cellar with boxes of musty books.* **2.** old-fashioned; antiquated: *musty conventions that do not fit modern times.* [Possibly from obsolete *moisty* wet, damp, from MOIST.] —**mus′ti·ly,** *adv.* —**mus′ti·ness,** *n.*
mu·ta·ble (mū′tə bəl) *adj.* **1.** liable or subject to change or alteration; variable; changeable. **2.** liable to change one's mind; fickle. [Latin *mūtābilis,* from *mūtāre* to change.] —**mu′ta·bil′i·ty, mu′ta·ble·ness,** *n.* —**mu′ta·bly,** *adv.*
mut·a·gen (mū′tə jən) *n.* any agent or substance, as X rays or certain chemicals, producing increases in the rate of mutation. [MUTA(TION) + -GEN.] —**mu′ta·gen·ic** (mū′tə jen′ik), *adj.*
mu·tant (mū′tənt) *n.* mutation *(def. 2).*
mu·tate (mū′tāt) *v.,* **-tat·ed, -tat·ing.** —*v.i.* to undergo change, esp. by mutation. —*v.t.* **1.** to cause to undergo change, esp. by mutation. **2.** *Linguistics.* to change (a vowel) by use of an umlaut.
mu·ta·tion (mū tā′shən) *n.* **1.** a sudden change in a gene or chromosome that affects the form or qualities of offspring and is inheritable. **2.** an individual or species resulting from such a change. **3.** any act or process of changing in form or qualities; change. **4.** umlaut. [Latin *mūtātiō* change.]
mu·ta·tis mu·tan·dis (mū tā′tis mū tan′dis) *Latin.* with the necessary changes.
mute (mūt) *adj.* **1.a.** not able to speak or make vocal sounds as a result of an inborn defect or an injury. **b.** making no vocal sounds by nature: *a mute species.* **2.** refusing to speak; not speaking: *The prisoner stood mute.* **3.** that gives out or is accompanied by no sound or direct statement; silent: *The rows of graves were a mute reminder of the effects of war.* **4.** *Linguistics.* not pronounced; silent. The *b* in *lamb* is mute. —*n.* **1.** a person who is unable to speak, as because of an inborn defect or an injury. **2.** a device inserted in or put on a musical instrument, esp. a brass instrument, to muffle or soften the tone. **3.** a silent letter, such as the *e* in *mate.* —*v.t.,* **mut·ed, mut·ing. 1.** to muffle or soften the sound of (a musical instrument). **2.** to make less brilliant, strident, or strong; restrain; soften: *to mute criticism, to mute the colors of a painting.* [Latin *mūtus* dumb.] —**mute′ly,** *adv.* —**mute′ness,** *n.*
mu·ti·late (mū′tə lāt′) *v.t.,* **-lat·ed, -lat·ing. 1.** to deform or injure seriously, as by the loss of a limb or member; maim. **2.** to damage or disfigure; mar: *The desk was mutilated by deep scratches.* **3.** to make incomplete, imperfect, or less effective by removing an important part or parts: *to mutilate a play by cutting out scenes.* [Latin *mutilātus,* past participle of *mutilāre* to maim.] —**mu′ti·la′tion,** *n.* —**mu′ti·la′tor,** *n.*
mu·ti·neer (mū′tə nîr′) *n.* a person who is guilty of mutiny. [Middle French *mutinier,* from *mutin* rebellious, unruly. See MU-TINY.]

mu·ti·nous (mū′tə nəs) *adj.* **1.** engaged in or disposed to engage in mutiny: *The mutinous sailors seized the ship.* **2.** of, relating to, or characterized by something like mutiny; rebellious: *a mutinous spirit among the students.* —**mu′ti·nous·ly,** *adv.* —**mu′ti·nous·ness,** *n.*
mu·ti·ny (mū′tə nē) *n., pl.* **-nies.** the act or an instance of open rebellion against authority, esp. by sailors or soldiers against their commanding officers. —*v.i.,* **-nied, -ny·ing.** to engage in mutiny; revolt against authority. [From obsolete *mutine* rebellion, from French *mutin* rebellious, from Old French *muete* revolt, going back to Latin *movēre* to move.]
mutt (mut) *n. Informal.* a dog, esp. a mongrel.
mut·ter (mut′ər) *v.i.* **1.** to speak in low, indistinct tones with the mouth nearly closed: *If you mutter, I can't understand you.* **2.** to complain without confronting the source of one's discontent; grumble: *The soldiers muttered angrily when they heard that all leaves had been canceled.* **3.** to make a low, indistinct sound: *The storm muttered in the distance.* —*v.t.* to utter (words) in low, indistinct tones. —*n.* a low, indistinct utterance or sound. [Middle English *moteren* to speak low and indistinctly; probably imitative.] —**mut′ter·er,** *n.*
mut·ton (mut′ən) *n.* flesh from a sheep, esp. a sheep between one and two years of age, used as food. [Old French *moton* ram; of Celtic origin.] —**mut′ton·y,** *adj.*
mutton chop, a piece of mutton from the rib or loin, usually for broiling.
mut·ton·chops (mut′ən chops′) *pl. n.* side whiskers that are narrow at the temples and broad and rounded at the bottom, often worn with a mustache but not with a beard.
mu·tu·al (mū′chü əl) *adj.* **1.** done, felt, or expressed by each of two toward the other; reciprocal: *She disliked him immediately, and the feeling was mutual.* **2.** affecting or involving both or all parties: *mutual defense, mutual benefits.* **3.** possessed by both or all; shared; common: *They met each other through a mutual friend.* **4.** of or relating to a kind of insurance in which the policyholders form the membership of the insurance company and indemnify one another against loss. [Old French *mutuel* reciprocal, from Latin *mūtuus.*] —**mu′tu·al′i·ty,** *n.* —**mu′tu·al·ly,** *adv.*

> **Synonyms** **Mutual** and **reciprocal** mean done or experienced in common. **Mutual** suggests that two persons or things share something in equal measure: *The two friends have a mutual interest in jazz.* **Reciprocal** indicates the equal or comparable return of what has been offered or given: *Under a reciprocal arrangement, if you join one of these clubs you automatically become a member of the other.*

mutual fund, an investment company that sells an unlimited number of shares to the public and invests the proceeds in a variety of securities. ➡ distinguished from **closed-end investment company.**
mu·tu·al·ism (mū′chü ə liz′əm) *n. Biology.* a relationship in which two different kinds of organisms live together in a condition of symbiosis that benefits both of them, as between a fungus and alga in a lichen.
Mu·zak (mū′zak) *n.* **1.** *Trademark.* a system of recorded background music transmitted by telephone lines or radio to offices, restaurants, and other subscribers. **2.** the music transmitted by this system. **3. muzak.** any bland and undistinguished music regarded as similar to this.
mu·zhik (mü zhik′, mü′zhik) *also,* **mujik.** *n.* a peasant in Russia under the czars. [Russian *muzhik,* diminutive of *muzh* man.]
muz·zle (muz′əl) *n.* **1.** the projecting part of the head of an animal, including the nose, mouth, and jaws; snout. **2.** a device, usually made of straps or wires, that is put over an animal's mouth to keep it from biting or eating. **3.** the opening at the front end of a gun, out of which the bullet or other projectile leaves the weapon. **4.** anything that discourages or restrains comments or spoken opinions, esp. of subordinates: *to put a muzzle on criticism.* —*v.t.,* **-zled, -zling. 1.** to put a muzzle on. **2.** to restrain or discourage (someone) from speaking; silence. [Old French *musel* snout, nose of an animal, from *muse* snout; of uncertain origin.] —**muz′zler,** *n.*
muz·zle·load·er (muz′əl lō′dər) *n.* a gun loaded through the muzzle. —**muz′zle·load′ing,** *adj.*

a	at	e	end	o	hot	u	up	hw	white		about
ā	ape	ē	me	ō	old	ū	use	ng	song		taken
ä	far	i	it	ô	fork	ü	rule	th	thin	ə	pencil
âr	care	ī	ice	oi	oil	u̇	pull	th	this		lemon
		îr	pierce	ou	out	ûr	turn	zh	measure		circus

muzzle velocity, the speed at which a projectile, such as a bullet, leaves the muzzle of a gun.

MVP, in sports, most valuable player.

MW, megawatt.

my (mī) *adj.* (the possessive form of **I**) of, relating to, or belonging to me: *my best friend, my good fortune, my raincoat.* —*interj.* used to express surprise, awe, disapproval, or other emotion: *My! Look at that outfit!* [Old English *mīn.*]

my·as·the·ni·a (mī′əs thē′nē ə) *n.* a weakness of the muscles. [Modern Latin *myasthenia,* from Greek *myos,* genitive of *mys* muscle + *astheneia* weakness (from *a-* without + *sthenos* strength).] —**my′as·then′ic,** *adj.*

myasthenia gra·vis (grav′is, grä′vis, grā′-) a fluctuating, chronic disease of neurological origin, characterized by weakness and quick fatigue of certain voluntary muscles, esp. those of the face and neck. [Modern Latin *myasthenia gravis,* from MYASTHE-NIA + *gravis* painful, severe.]

my·ce·li·um (mī sē′lē əm) *n., pl.* **-li·a** (-lē ə) the part of a mushroom or other fungus that consists of a tangle of tiny fibers, called hyphae, usually embedded in whatever material, such as wood, earth, or the like, that the mushroom is growing on. For illustration, see **mushroom.** [Modern Latin *mycelium,* from Greek *mykēs* fungus + *hēlos* nail, wart.] —**my·ce′li·al,** *adj.*

My·ce·nae·an (mī′sə nē′ən) *adj.* of or relating to the ancient civilization located at Mycenae.

my·co·bac·te·ri·um (mī′kō bak tîr′ē əm) *n., pl.* **-te·ri·a** (-tîr′ē ə). any of a genus, *Mycobacterium,* of rod-shaped, gram-positive bacteria, including those producing tuberculosis and leprosy. [Modern Latin *mycobacterium,* from Greek *mykēs* fungus + Latin *bacterium* bacterium. See BACTERIA.]

my·col·o·gy (mī kol′ə jē) *n.* the branch of science that studies fungi. [Greek *mykēs* fungus + -LOGY.] —**my·co·log·i·cal** (mī-kə loj′i kəl), *adj.* —**my·col′o·gist,** *n.*

my·co·plas·ma (mī′kō plaz′mə) *n.* any of a genus, *Mycoplasma,* of minute, gram-negative bacteria that lack cell walls. The smallest of free-living cells, some cause diseases of the lungs and joints in humans and domestic animals, and some infect plants. [Modern Latin *mycoplasma,* from Greek *mykēs* fungus + Late Latin and Greek *plasma* mold [1], image. See PLASMA.]

my·cor·rhi·za (mī′kə rī′zə) *n.* a symbiotic association between a fungus and the roots of a plant. —**my′cor·rhi′zal,** *adj.*

my·co·sis (mī kō′sis) *n., pl.* **-ses.** any infection or disease caused by a fungus. —**my·cot·ic** (mī kot′ik), *adj.*

my·e·lin (mī′ə lin) *n.* a white, fatty substance forming a sheath around certain nerve fibers. For illustration, see **neuron.** [Greek *myelos* marrow + -IN [1].] —**my′e·lin′ic,** *adj.*

my·e·li·tis (mī′ə lī′tis) *n.* inflammation of the spinal cord or of the bone marrow.

My·lar (mī′lär) *n.* Trademark. a thin, strong film of polyester resin, used for magnetic tape and photographic materials.

my·na (mī′nə) *also,* **my·nah, mi·na.** *n.* any of several black or brown starlings, family Sturnidae, native to Asia, esp. the **hill myna,** *Gracula religiosa,* of India and Sri Lanka, a skillful mimic of the human voice. [Hindi *mainā.*]

Myn·heer (mīn hâr′, -hîr′) *n.* Mister; Sir. ➡ Dutch form of address for a man. [Dutch *mijnheer,* from *mijn* my + *heer* lord.]

my·o·car·di·um (mī′ō kär′dē əm) *n., pl.* **-di·a** (-dē ə). the muscular tissue of the heart. [Modern Latin *myocardium,* from Greek *myos,* genitive of *mys* muscle + *kardion,* diminutive of *kardía* heart.] —**my·o·car′di·al,** *adj.*

my·o·fi·bril (mī′ō fī′brəl, -fib′rəl) *n.* any of the alternating thick and thin contractile filaments of a skeletal muscle cell or fiber that slide into one another, and give the muscle its striated appearance. [Modern Latin *myo-* muscle + FIBRIL.] —**my·o·fi·bril·lar** (mī′ō fī′brə lər, -fib′rə-), *adj.*

my·o·glo·bin (mī′ə glō′bin, mī′ō glō′-) *n.* a form of hemoglobin present in muscle fibers that transports oxygen from red blood cells to muscle cells.

my·o·pi·a (mī ō′pē ə) *n.* **1.** an inability to see things that are far away; nearsightedness. ➡ opposed to **hyperopia. 2.** an inability or unwillingness to see beyond narrow attitudes. [Modern Latin *myopia,* from Greek *myōpiā,* going back to *myein* to shut + *ops* eye.] —**my·op·ic** (mī op′ik), *adj.* —**my·op′i·cal·ly,** *adv.*

my·o·sin (mī′ə sin) *n.* a muscle protein that in conjunction with actin produces muscular contraction. [Greek *my-,* stem of *mys* muscle + -OSE [2] + -IN [1].]

myr·i·ad (mir′ē əd) *n.* a great or countless number: *Myriads of tiny fish swarmed in the pond.* —*adj.* of indefinitely large number; countless; innumerable: *myriad possibilities.* [Greek *mȳriad-,* stem of *mȳrias* ten thousand, from *mȳrios* countless.] —For Synonyms, see **host** [2].

myr·i·a·pod (mir′ē ə pod′) *n.* any of a group of arthropods of the group Myriapoda, formerly regarded as a class comprising the centipedes and millipedes, having a wormlike, segmented body and many legs. [Modern Latin *Myriapoda,* from Greek *mȳrias* ten thousand + *pod-,* stem of *pous* foot.]

Myr·mi·don (mûr′mi don′) *n.* **1.** in Greek legend, one of a group of warriors from ancient Thessaly who formed the army of Achilles in the Trojan War. **2. myrmidon.** any blindly faithful follower.

myrrh (mûr) *n.* a fragrant, yellowish brown resin obtained from any of several tropical trees, esp. *Commiphora myrrha,* having a bitter taste and used esp. in the manufacture of dentifrices and perfumes. [Middle English *mirre,* from Old English *myrre,* from Latin *myrrha,* from Greek *myrrā,* going back to Akkadian *murru.*]

myr·tle (mûr′təl) *n.* **1.** any of a group of fragrant evergreen shrubs and trees, genus *Myrtus,* widely grown for ornament, bearing shiny oval or lance-shaped leaves and white or pink flowers. **2.** common periwinkle. —*adj.* designating a family, Myrtaceae, of semitropical trees and shrubs having aromatic leaves, such as clove, myrtle, and eucalyptus. [Old French *myrtille* myrtle berry, going back to Latin *myrtus* myrtle tree, from Greek *myrtos;* of Semitic origin.]

my·self (mī self′) *pron., pl.* **our·selves. 1.** the emphatic form of **me** and **I:** *I will do this myself.* **2.** the reflexive form of **me** and **I:** *I don't pamper myself.* **3.** my usual, normal, or true self: *I haven't been myself since the accident.*

> **Usage** **Myself** is sometimes used in constructions where **I** or **me** would be grammatically correct, as in *Harry and myself were the leaders of the group* or *They were very kind to my parents and myself.* Similarly, **yourself** and **yourselves** are sometimes used instead of **you,** as in *I would prefer that either Carol or yourself do the job.* Although these constructions may be considered acceptable in informal speech, they should be avoided in writing.

mys·te·ri·ous (mi stîr′ē əs) *adj.* **1.** full of, shrouded in, or suggesting mystery; impossible or difficult to explain or understand; puzzling; obscure: *a mysterious incident.* **2.** suggesting these qualities: *a mysterious smile.* —**mys·te′ri·ous·ly,** *adv.* —**mys·te′ri·ous·ness,** *n.*

mys·ter·y (mis′tə rē) *n., pl.* **-ter·ies. 1.** something that is not or cannot be known, explained, or understood: *The identity of the thief is still a mystery.* **2.** a thing or event that arouses curiosity or suspense because it is not fully explained or revealed: *It is a mystery to me how you knew I was here.* **3.** a book, play, motion picture, or the like involving a mysterious crime, esp. a narrative that gradually leads to the discovery of the criminal. **4.** a mysterious, obscure, or secret character or quality: *An air of mystery surrounded the events leading up to the accident.* **5.** a religious doctrine or truth that cannot be understood by reason and can be known only through divine revelation. **6.** *usually,* **mysteries. a.** any of various ancient religious cults practicing secret rites to which uninitiated persons were not admitted. **b.** a secret rite practiced by such a group. **7.a.** a sacrament of the Christian religion, esp. the Eucharist. **b.** any of fifteen events connected with the lives of Jesus and the Virgin Mary that serves as a subject for meditation during recitation of the rosary. **8.** mystery play. [Latin *mystērium* secret worship, from Greek *mystērion* secret rite, going back to *myein* to close (lips and eyes).]

> **Synonyms** **Mystery, enigma,** and **riddle** [1] mean something puzzling that invites attempts at explanation. **Mystery** can be applied generally to inexplicable phenomena: *Why the dinosaurs disappeared from the earth remains a mystery.* **Enigma** designates something cryptic and obscure: *The significance of these ancient artifacts is one of history's enigmas.* **Riddle** is a puzzling problem to be solved or a question to be answered: *The characters in fairy tales are often required to answer riddles.*

mystery play, a medieval religious drama based on events in the Bible, esp. in the life of Jesus, often performed by trade guilds.

mys·tic (mis′tik) *adj.* **1.** of or relating to beliefs or practices that have hidden or secret meanings, such as the ancient religious mysteries: *mystic rites.* **2.** having hidden or secret meaning or character; mysterious; enigmatic: *the mystic prophecies of an oracle.* **3.** of or relating to mystics or mysticism. **4.** mystical *(def. 1).* —*n.* a person who seeks to achieve an intimate knowledge of God or absolute truth through personal spiritual experience. [Latin *mysticus* relating to secret rites, from Greek *mystikos,* from *mystēs* person who is initiated.]

mys·ti·cal (mis′ti kəl) *adj.* **1.** having a spiritual meaning that is beyond human knowledge or understanding. **2.** of or relating to a direct knowledge of God or absolute truth achieved through personal spiritual experience: *a mystical philosophy.* **3.** mystic *(defs. 1, 2).* —**mys′ti·cal·ly,** *adv.*

mys·ti·cism (mis′tə siz′əm) *n.* **1.** the doctrines, beliefs, or ideas of mystics. **2.** the doctrine that knowledge of God or absolute truth may be achieved through personal spiritual experience, esp. by contemplation. **3.** vague, confused, or illogical thinking.

mys·ti·fi·ca·tion (mis′tə fi kā′shən) *n.* **1.** the act of mystifying or the state of being mystified. **2.** something that mystifies.

mys·ti·fy (mis′tə fī′) *v.t.,* **-fied, -fy·ing. 1.** to bewilder or confuse, esp. intentionally: *The banker mystified the police by disappearing suddenly.* **2.** to make obscure or difficult to understand; involve in mystery. [French *mystifier* to hoax, going back to Latin *mysticus* relating to secret rites + *facere* to make. See MYSTIC.] —**mys′ti·fy′ing·ly,** *adv.*

mys·tique (mi stēk′) *n.* **1.** an air or feeling of mystery or suspense about a person or thing: *the mystique of a guru.* **2.** a spiritually symbolic way of explaining life and the world by the teachings of some doctrine or cult: *the mystique of Buddhism.* [French *mystique* this attitude, from *mystique* mystic, from Latin *mysticus* relating to secret rites.]

myth (mith) *n.* **1.** a traditional story of unknown authorship that expresses a belief of a particular people, usually involving gods and heroes. A myth is an attempt to explain a phenomenon of nature, an event in history, or the origin of a particular custom, practice, or religious belief. **2.** such accounts or stories collectively; mythology. **3.** any imaginary or fictitious person, story, or thing: *That story about my vacation was pure myth.* **4.** an opinion, belief, or ideal that has no basis in truth or fact, esp. one held uncritically by the members of a group. [Late Latin *mȳthos* fable, from Greek *mȳthos* word, fable, story.] —For Synonyms, see **legend.**

myth·i·cal (mith′i kəl) *adj.* **1.** of, resembling, based on, or existing only in myths: *a mythical underworld.* **2.** having no basis in fact or reality; imaginary; fictitious: *a purely mythical account of one's early life.* Also, **myth′ic.** —**myth′i·cal·ly,** *adv.*

myth·o·log·i·cal (mith′ə loj′i kəl) *adj.* of, relating to, or found in mythology: *a mythological being.* —**myth′o·log′i·cal·ly,** *adv.*

my·thol·o·gist (mi thol′ə jist) *n.* **1.** a person who collects or records myths. **2.** a person who studies or is an expert in mythology.

my·thol·o·gy (mi thol′ə jē) *n., pl.* **-gies. 1.** myths and legends collectively, esp. a body of myths belonging to a specific ancient religion or culture or relating to a particular hero or event: *Egyptian mythology.* **2.** the study and interpretation of myths and legends. [Late Latin *mȳthologia,* from Greek *mȳthologiā* legend, storytelling, from *mȳthos* word, fable, story + *logos* word, discourse.]

myx·e·de·ma (mik′si dē′mə) *n.* a condition resulting from decreased activity of the thyroid gland, characterized by swelling, esp. of the hands and face, dryness of hair and skin, and sluggishness.

myx·o·my·cete (mik′sō mī′sēt, -mī sēt′) *n.* any of a group of protists, class Myxomycetes, comprising the slime molds.

a	at	e	end	o	hot	u	up	hw	white		about
ā	ape	ē	me	ō	old	ū	use	ng	song		taken
ä	far	i	it	ô	fork	ü	rule	th	thin	ə	pencil
âr	care	ī	ice	oi	oil	u̇	pull	th	this		lemon
				îr	pierce	ou	out	ûr	turn	zh	measure	circus

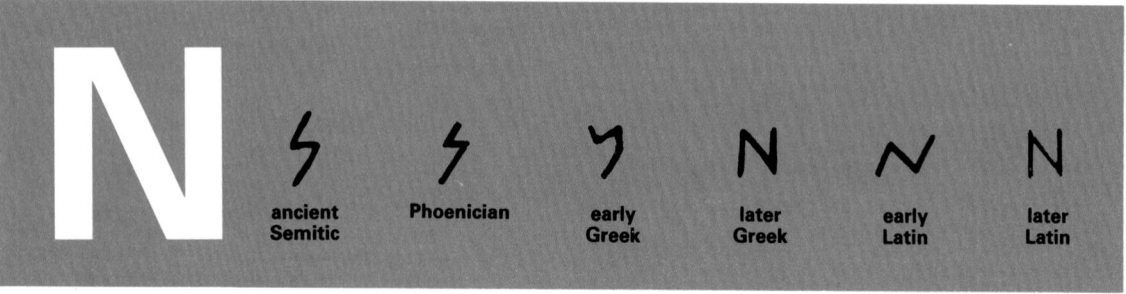

ancient Semitic | Phoenician | early Greek | later Greek | early Latin | later Latin

N The earliest form of **N** was used in the ancient Semitic alphabets as the letter *nun*, meaning "fish." The early Greeks borrowed *nun* around the ninth century B.C. and called it *nu. Nu* was close in shape to some of the earlier forms of the letter, such as Phoenician, but differed from them in that the crossbar connecting the bottom of the first vertical stroke with the top of the second was drawn on a slant. By about the fifth century B.C., the direction of the slant of *nu* had been reversed. This altered form of *nu* was adopted by the Romans and it came down almost unchanged into the English alphabet.

---

n, N (en) *n., pl.* **n's, N's. 1.** the fourteenth letter of the English alphabet. **2.** the shape of this letter or something having this shape.

n (en) *n.* any indefinite number.

n. 1. born. **2.** name. **3.** neuter. **4.** new. **5.** nominative. **6.** noon. **7.** north. **8.** northern. **9.** noun. **10.** number.

N, the symbol for nitrogen.

N 1. *Chess.* knight. **2.** *also,* **N.** North. **3.** *also,* **N.** Northern.

N. 1. Nationalist. **2.** Navy. **3.** New. **4.** Noon. **5.** Norse. **6.** November.

Na, the symbol for sodium.

N.A., North America.

NAACP, National Association for the Advancement of Colored People.

nab (nab) *v.t.,* **nabbed, nab·bing.** *Informal.* **1.** to capture or arrest: *The police nabbed the thieves before they could escape.* **2.** to snatch or steal: *The thief nabbed my camera.* [Probably of Scandinavian origin.]

na·bob (nā′bob) *n.* **1.** a rich and important person. **2.** a native ruler in India under the Mogul empire. [Hindi *nawwâb* governor of a province, from Arabic *nuwwâb,* plural of *nâ′ib* governor.]

na·celle (nə sel′) *n.* a separate, enclosed part of an aircraft that carries the engines and sometimes the crew. [French *nacelle* nacelle, little boat, from Late Latin *navicella* little boat, diminutive of Latin *nāvis* ship.]

na·cho (nä′chō) *n., pl.* **-chos.** a tortilla chip topped with cheese, chilies, or other toppings and broiled, eaten as a snack or appetizer. [Mexican Spanish *nacho.*]

na·cre (nā′kər) *n.* mother-of-pearl. [French *nacre,* going back to Arabic *naqrah* cavity (as of a shell).] —**na·cre·ous** (nā′krē əs), *adj.*

na·dir (nā′dər, -dîr) *n.* **1.** the point on the celestial sphere directly below the position of the observer. ➡ opposed to **zenith. 2.** the lowest point: *The loss of the election marked the nadir of the politician's career.* [Middle French *nadir,* from Medieval Latin *nadir,* from Arabic *nazīr (as-samt)* literally, opposite (to the zenith).]

nae (nā) *adj., adv. Scottish.* no.

nae·vus (nē′vəs) *n.* nevus. —**nae′void,** *adj.*

nag[1] (nag) *v.,* **nagged, nag·ging.** —*v.t.* **1.** to annoy (someone) with repeated urging or complaining; badger: *My parents never have to nag me about my homework.* **2.** to cause continual discomfort or worry to; trouble: *His conscience nagged him for lying.* —*v.i.* **1.** to annoy with continual urging or complaining. **2.** to be a persistent source

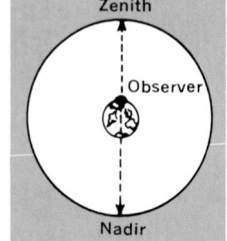

nadir

of discomfort or worry (often with *at*): *The pain nagged at her.* —*n.* a person who nags. [Of Scandinavian origin.] —**nag′ger,** *n.* —**nag′ging·ly,** *adv.*

nag[2] (nag) *n.* **1.** an old, broken-down horse. **2.** *Informal.* any horse. [Middle English *nagge* horse, pony.]

Na·hua·tl (nä′wä·təl) *n.* a language belonging to the Uto-Aztecan language family, spoken predominantly in central Mexico and parts of Central America by various Indian tribes. Also, **Aztec.**

Na·hum (nā′əm, -həm) *n.* a book of the Old Testament, containing the prophecies of the Hebrew prophet Nahum.

nai·ad (nā′ad, nī′-) *n., pl.* **-ads** or **-a·des** (-ə dēz′). in Greek and Roman mythology, a water nymph living in a fountain, spring, or brook.

nail (nāl) *n.* **1.** a slender piece of metal, usually pointed at one end and enlarged at the other, used chiefly to penetrate wood and other materials so as to hang things on a vertical surface or to hold or fasten parts together. **2.a.** a hard, horny structure, consisting chiefly of keratin, that grows on the upper side at the end of a finger or toe in humans and other primates. **b.** a similar or corresponding structure in other animals, such as a claw or talon. —*v.t.* **1.** to fasten, attach, or close with a nail or nails. **2.** to hold fast or keep fixed as if with a nail: *Fear nailed him to the spot.*

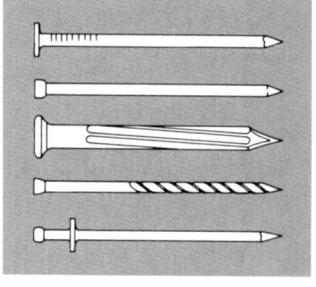

nails

3. *Informal.* **a.** to catch or capture: *The police nailed the car thief.* **b.** to intercept and delay: *Reporters nailed the mayor on her way in.* [Old English *naegel* metal spike, horny structure growing at the end of a finger or toe.]

·**hard as nails. a.** showing little or no emotion; unfeeling; cold. **b.** in good physical condition; rugged; tough.

·**to hit the nail on the head.** to say or do something exactly right.

·**to nail down.** to make certain of; secure: *to nail down a job.*

nail·set (nāl′set′) *also,* **nail set.** *n.* a tool in the shape of a short rod, used for driving nails flush with or below a surface.

nain·sook (nān′sùk′, nan′-) *n.* a soft, lightweight cotton fabric, used for such items as infants' wear, blouses, and lingerie. [Hindustani *nainsukh* literally, pleasure to the eye, from *nain* eye + *sukh* pleasure.]

na·ive (nä ēv′) *also,* **na·ïve.** *adj.* having or showing a lack of knowledge of the ways of the world; unsophisticated; innocent: *a naive youth, a naive faith in human goodness.* [French *naïve,* feminine of *naïf* natural, from Latin *nātīvus* innate, natural. Doublet of NATIVE.] —**na·ive′ly;** *also,* **na·ïve′ly,** *adv.* —**na·ive′ness;** *also,* **na·ïve′ness,** *n.*

na·ive·té (nä′ēv tā′, nä ēv′ə-) *also,* **na·ïve·té.** *n.* **1.** the quality or condition of being naive. **2.** a naive remark or action. [French *naïveté* artlessness, from *naïf* natural. See NAIVE.]

na·ive·ty (nä ēv′tē, -ē′və-) *n., pl.* **-ties.** *also,* **na·ïve·ty.** naiveté.

na·ked (nā′kid) *adj.* **1.** without clothing or similar covering; nude. **2.** stripped, as of vegetation, furnishings, or decoration; bare: *a naked room, a naked branch.* **3.** without a cover or case; exposed: *a naked light bulb, a naked wire, a naked sword.* **4.** without addition or concealment; plain: *the naked truth, naked jealousy.* **5.** without protection; vulnerable: *With its walls destroyed,*

the city lay naked to attack. [Old English *nacod* bare, unclothed.] —**na′ked·ly,** *adv.* —**na′ked·ness,** *n.*

Synonyms *adj.* **Naked** and **nude,** used of persons, mean without clothing or covering. **Naked,** used of part of the body or the entire body, suggests physical exposure and in some cases a natural state of being: *The members of the tribe went naked even in cold weather.* **Nude,** used almost always of the entire body, is most often employed in artistic contexts: *a painter of nude figures.*

naked eye, the human eye unaided by a magnifying glass, telescope, or microscope: *The ameba was not visible to the naked eye.*

nam·a·ble (nā′mə bəl) nameable.

nam·by-pam·by (nam′bē pam′bē) *adj.* **1.** foolishly sentimental; insipid. **2.** weak and indecisive; wishy-washy. —*n., pl.* **-bies. 1.** a namby-pamby person. **2.** namby-pamby speech or writing. [Modification of *Ambrose* Philips, 1674-1749, English poet, whose sentimental poems and style were mocked by Alexander Pope and others.]

name (nām) *n.* **1.** a word or group of words by which a person, animal, place, thing, or class of things is known or referred to: *My brother's name is Michael.* **2.** a word or phrase, usually derogatory, used to describe or characterize a person or thing: *to call someone names.* **3.a.** public estimation; reputation; character: *Her actions had given her a bad name.* **b.** distinguished reputation; fame; eminence: *He had earned a name for himself as a blues singer.* **4.** official designation or outward appearance, as opposed to fact or reality: *The country was a democracy in name only.* **5.** a person or thing that is famous or outstanding in some way: *She is one of the big names in American theater.* **6.** a person or group of persons with the same name; family; clan: *all the clans hostile to the name of Campbell* (Thomas B. Macaulay, 1849). —*v.t.,* **named, nam·ing. 1.** to give a name or names to; designate by a particular name: *They named their son Anthony.* **2.** to mention or refer to by name: *The newspaper article named the people who won scholarships.* **3.** to identify correctly; call by the right name or names: *Can you name all the presidents of the United States?* **4.** to speak of; mention: *Name something you'd like for your birthday.* **5.** to make definite or specific; specify; fix: *Name the time and I'll meet you.* **6.** to nominate, appoint, or assign: *The president named her to head the commission.* —*adj.* **1.** having a well-known name: *a name brand, a name actor.* **2.** containing a name: *to put name tags on luggage.* [Old English *nama* specific designation.] —**nam′er,** *n.*

· **in the name of. a.** with appeal or reference to: *What in the name of heaven are you doing here?* **b.** on behalf of; for the sake of: *The ambassadors met in the name of peace.* **c.** by the authority or as the representative of: *The prime minister spoke in the name of the sovereign.*

· **to name names.** to mention specific names, esp. in accusation or criticism.

· **to one's name.** in one's possession; belonging to one: *I don't have a cent to my name.*

name·a·ble (nā′mə bəl) *also,* **namable.** *adj.* **1.** capable of being named. **2.** worthy of being mentioned; memorable.

name-brand (nām′brand′) *adj.* bearing a trade name: *name-brand running shoes.*

name-drop·ping (nām′drop′ing) *n. Informal.* the act or practice of attempting to impress others by referring to famous or important people in a casual and familiar manner. —**name′-drop′per,** *n.*

name·less (nām′lis) *adj.* **1.** not identified by a name; without a name: *a nameless tomb.* **2.** not known or mentioned by name; anonymous: *The donation was from a nameless benefactor. The culprit shall remain nameless.* **3.** not known to fame; obscure: *a nameless inventor.* **4.** incapable of being identified or described; inexpressible: *nameless fears.* **5.** too horrible to be mentioned or described: *nameless atrocities.* —**name′less·ly,** *adv.*

name·ly (nām′lē) *adv.* that is to say; specifically: *We visited two southern states, namely, Florida and Georgia.*

name·plate (nām′plāt′) *n.* a strip of metal, plastic, or wood on which a name is printed and displayed.

name·sake (nām′sāk′) *n.* a person or thing named after or having the same name as another.

nan·keen (nan kēn′) *also,* **nan·kin.** *n.* **1.** a durable brownish yellow or buff cotton fabric, formerly used for trousers and other articles of clothing. **2.** nankeens. trousers made of this fabric. [Modification of *Nanking,* China, where the cloth was originally produced.]

nan·ny (nan′ē) *n., pl.* **-nies.** nursemaid. [Baby talk for *Anna,* a woman's name.]

nanny goat *Informal.* female goat.

nano- *combining form* one billionth (10^{-9}) part of. [Greek *nanos* a dwarf.]

nan·o·sec·ond (nan′ə sek′ənd) *n.* one billionth of a second. [NANO- + SECOND.]

Nantes, Edict of (nants; *French* näNt) a proclamation granting a substantial amount of religious freedom and political equality to French Protestants, issued in 1598 by Henry IV and revoked in 1685 by Louis XIV.

nap[1] (nap) *n.* a short sleep. —*v.i.,* **napped, nap·ping. 1.** to sleep for a short time. **2.** to be off guard or unprepared: *The question caught me napping.* [Old English *hnappian* to sleep for a short time.] —**nap′per,** *n.*

nap[2] (nap) *n.* a downy or fuzzy finish on fabric, formed by short fibers that are raised on the surface. —*v.t.,* **napped, nap·ping.** to raise a nap on (fabric). [Middle Dutch *noppe* the downy finish on fabric.]

na·palm (nā′päm) *n.* **1.** an aluminum soap compound used to thicken and jell gasoline. **2.** gasoline that has been thickened and jelled with napalm, used in incendiary bombs that break on impact and spread the flaming contents in all directions. —*v.t.* to attack with napalm.

nape (nāp, nap) *n.* the back of the neck. [Of uncertain origin.]

na·per·y (nā′pə rē) *n.* household linens, esp. tablecloths, napkins, and other table linens. [Old French *naperie* table linen, from *nappe* linen, going back to Latin *mappa* cloth, napkin; of Semitic origin.]

naph·tha (naf′thə, nap′-) *n.* any of several liquids made from petroleum or coal tar, whose boiling points are higher than gasoline but lower than kerosene. Naphtha is used in cleaning fluid, fuel mixtures, and solvents, and in the manufacture of rubber, paints, and varnishes. [Latin *naphtha,* from Greek *naphtha;* of Persian origin.]

naph·tha·lene (naf′thə lēn′, nap′-) *also,* **naph·tha·line.** *n.* a white, crystalline compound with a strong coal-tar odor, used in making mothballs. Formula: $C_{10}H_8$ [NAPHTHA + -ENE.]

naph·thol (naf′thôl, nap′-) *n.* either of two crystalline substances obtained from naphthalene and caustic soda, used esp. in making dyes. Formula: $C_{10}H_7OH$ [NAPHTH(ALENE) + -OL.]

nap·kin (nap′kin) *n.* **1.** a piece of cloth or paper, usually square, used at meals for protecting clothing or for wiping the lips, hands, or fingers. **2.** a small cloth or towel. [Diminutive of Old French *nappe* linen. See NAPERY.]

na·po·le·on (nə pō′lē ən, -pōl′yən) *n.* **1.** a former French gold coin equivalent to twenty francs. **2.** a rich pastry, usually rectangular, having cream or custard between layers of pastry dough, and frequently icing. [From the French emperor *Napoleon* I, 1769-1821.]

Na·po·le·on·ic (nə pō′lē on′ik) *adj.* of, relating to, or characteristic of the French emperor Napoleon I or his reign.

nappe (nap) *n.* **1.** *Geometry.* one of the two parts of a conical surface extending in opposite directions from the vertex, as in a hyperbolic conic section. **2.** *Geology.* a large sheet of rock that has been thrust or has slid a considerable distance from its original position. [French *nappe* literally, linen. See NAPERY.]

nar·cis·sism (när′sə siz′əm) *n.* **1.** excessive admiration for or fascination with oneself; self-love. **2.** *Psychoanalysis.* the arresting of development at, or regression to, the infantile stage of development in which one's own body is the object of one's erotic interest. [From *Narcissus.*] —**nar′cis·sist,** *n.* —**nar′cis·sis′tic,** *adj.*

nar·cis·sus (när sis′əs) *n., pl.* **-cis·sus** or **-cis·sus·es** or **-cis·si** (-sis′ī). **1.** a showy yellow or white flower of any of several plants, genus *Narcissus,* consisting of a star of petals around a central tube. **2.** the plant bearing this flower, having long, slender leaves that grow directly from an underground bulb. **3. Narcissus.** in Greek mythology, a handsome youth who was made to fall in love with his own reflection in a pool and stayed gazing at it until he pined away and was transformed into the narcissus flower. [Latin *narcissus,* from Greek

narcissus

a	at	e	end	o	hot	u	up	hw	white		about
ā	ape	ē	me	ō	old	ū	use	ng	song		taken
ä	far	i	it	ô	fork	ü	rule	th	thin	ə	pencil
âr	care	ī	ice	oi	oil	ù	pull	th	this		lemon
		îr	pierce	ou	out	ûr	turn	zh	measure		circus

narkissos, allegedly from *narkē* numbness; because of its supposed narcotic effect.]

nar·co·lep·sy (när′kə lep′sē) *n.* a condition marked by attacks of uncontrollable drowsiness or sleep in the daytime, sometimes accompanied by sudden loss of muscular power. [Latin *narcosis* (see NARCOSIS) + (EPI)LEPSY.]

nar·co·lep·tic (när′kə lep′tik) *adj.* of, relating to, or having narcolepsy.

nar·co·sis (när kō′sis) *n.* a deep stupor produced by a drug. [Modern Latin *narcosis,* from Greek *narkōsis* a benumbing, going back to *narkē* numbness.]

nar·cot·ic (när kot′ik) *n.* **1.** a drug, such as opium or morphine, that dulls the senses, produces sleep or unconsciousness, relieves pain, and, with prolonged use, usually becomes addictive. **2.** anything that has a calming or dulling effect. —*adj.* **1.** of, relating to, or caused by a narcotic or narcotics: *narcotic addiction, a narcotic stupor.* **2.** relating to, of the nature of, or inducing narcosis. **3.** having the properties of a narcotic. [Old French *narcotique* benumbing, from Greek *narkōtikos,* going back to *narkē* numbness.] —**nar·cot′i·cal·ly,** *adv.*

nar·co·tize (när′kə tīz′) *v.t.,* **-tized, -tiz·ing. 1.** to put under the influence of, or make unconscious with, a narcotic. **2.** to dull the senses of or deaden the awareness of. [NARCOT(IC) + -IZE.] —**nar′co·ti·za′tion,** *n.*

nard (närd) *n.* spikenard *(def. 2).* [Latin *nardus,* from Greek *nardos;* of Semitic origin.]

nares (når′ēz) *pl. n., sing.* **nar·is** (når′is). the nostrils or nasal passages. [Latin *nārēs,* plural of *nāris* nostril.]

nar·ghi·le (när′gə lē, -lā′) *also,* **nar·gi·le.** *n.* an Oriental pipe with a long flexible tube through which smoke passes and is cooled by water contained in a bowl or similar receptacle. [From Persian *nārgīl* coconut (from which the bowls of these pipes were once made).]

Nar·ra·gan·sett (nar′ə gan′sit) *n.* **1.** a member of a North American Indian tribe formerly living in the western woodlands of Rhode Island. **2.** the Algonquian language of this tribe.

nar·rate (når′āt, na rāt′) *v.t., v.i.,* **-rat·ed, -rat·ing. 1.** to give a detailed account of (something, such as a story, sequence of events, or experience); tell. **2.** to speak in accompaniment to (a motion picture or the like). [Latin *narrātus,* past participle of *narrāre* to tell, relate.] —**nar′ra·tor;** *also,* **nar′rat·er,** *n.*

nar·ra·tion (na rā′shən) *n.* **1.** the act of narrating. **2.** something that is narrated; narrative. **3.** a literary form, such as fiction or history, relating a story or sequence of events.

nar·ra·tive (når′ə tiv) *n.* **1.** an account, as of an experience or sequence of events. **2.** the act, art, or process of narrating: *This novelist is better at description than at narrative.* —*adj.* of, relating to, or containing narration: *narrative skill, a narrative poem.*

nar·row (når′ō) *adj.* **1.** having little width; not broad: *a narrow aisle, a narrow stream.* **2.** limited in extent; restricted: *She has a narrow range of interests.* **3.** lacking tolerance, imagination, or breadth of view; narrow-minded: *He is a poorly educated man with a narrow outlook on life.* **4.** barely successful or adequate; with little margin: *a narrow escape, a narrow victory.* **5.** with careful attention to detail; thorough; close: *a narrow search.* **6.** limited in income or other resources; straitened: *narrow circumstances.* **7.** *Phonetics.* articulated with muscular tension of the vocal organs. —*v.t., v.i.* to make or become smaller in width or extent: *We've narrowed the choices down to three. The river narrows at the bridge.* —*n. also,* **narrows.** a narrow part, as of a body of water or a mountain pass: *A bridge was built across the narrows.* ➡ **Narrows** is used as singular or plural. [Old English *nearu* having little width, small.] —**nar′row·ly,** *adv.* —**nar′row·ness,** *n.*

nar·row-gauge (når′ō gāj′) *also,* **nar·row·gauge.** *adj.* **1.** (of railroad track) having a width less than the standard gauge of 56½ inches (144 centimeters) between rails. **2.** designed for use on a narrow-gauge railroad track.

narrow gauge, a narrow-gauge railroad, locomotive, or car.

nar·row-mind·ed (når′ō mīn′did) *adj.* having or showing rigid and prejudiced attitudes; illiberal. —**nar′row-mind′ed·ly,** *adv.* —**nar′row-mind′ed·ness,** *n.*

nar·thex (när′theks) *n.* **1.** in early Christian and Byzantine churches, a vestibule or portico extending across the ends of the nave and side aisles, forming an entrance. **2.** any vestibule leading to the nave of a church. [Late Greek *narthēx* portico, from Greek *narthēx* fennel; supposedly because the porch resembled the hollow stem of fennel.]

nar·whal (när′wəl) *n.* a toothed whale, *Monodon monoceros,* native to the Arctic and North Atlantic oceans, having shiny, black skin with pale yellow spots, the male of which has a twisted tusk that may be as long as 9 feet (2.7 meters). It is widely hunted by Eskimo for food and oil. Length: 12-15 feet (3.7-4.6 meters).

[Probably from Danish *narhval,* going back to Old Norse *nār* corpse + *hvalr* whale; because of its coloration.]

nar·y (når′ē) *adj. Informal.* not one (often with *a*): *There's nary a hope that we'll win.* [Modification of earlier *ne'er a* never a.]

NASA (nas′ə) National Aeronautics and Space Administration.

na·sal (nā′zəl) *adj.* **1.** of, from, or relating to the nose: *the nasal passages.* **2.** *Phonetics.* pronounced with the sound passing through the nose, as in the sounds of *m, n,* and *ng.* **3.** characterized by or resembling such a sound: *the nasal drone of a bagpipe.* —*n.* a nasal sound or letter. [French *nasal* relating to the nose, from Latin *nāsus* nose.] —**na·sal·i·ty** (nā zal′i tē), *n.* —**na′sal·ly,** *adv.*

na·sal·ize (nā′zə līz′) *v.t., v.i.,* **-ized, -iz·ing.** to pronounce or speak with a nasal tone or quality. —**na′sal·i·za′tion,** *n.*

nas·cent (nas′ənt, nā′sənt) *adj.* in the process of coming into being; beginning to exist or develop. [Latin *nāscēns,* present participle of *nāscī* to be born.] —**nas′cence, nas′cen·cy,** *n.*

na·so·phar·ynx (nā′zō far′ingks) *n., pl.* **-pha·ryn·ges** (-fə rin′-jēz) or **-phar·ynx·es.** the upper part of the pharynx, located directly behind the nasal passages. [Latin *nāsus* nose + PHARYNX.] —**na·so·pha·ryn·ge·al** (nā′zō fə rin′jē əl), *adj.*

nas·tic (nas′tik) *adj.* of, relating to, or characterized by movement in plants in response to, but not directed by, an external stimulus, as the opening and closing of many flowers in response to changes in light or temperature. [Greek *nastos* pressed close, from *nassein* to press.]

na·stur·tium (nə stûr′shəm) *n.* **1.** a showy funnel-shaped flower of any of a small group of plants, genus *Tropaeolum,* growing in a variety of colors and often spotted or striped. It has sharp-tasting buds and seeds that are sometimes used in pickling. **2.** the climbing plant bearing this flower, having rounded or lobed leaves with heavy veins branching out from the center. [Latin *nasturtium* a kind of cress, from *nāsus* nose + *torquēre* to twist; because its strong odor irritates the nose.]

nas·ty (nas′tē) *adj.,* **-ti·er, -ti·est. 1.** characterized by or resulting from hostility or cruelty; malicious; spiteful: *a nasty personality, a nasty rumor.* **2.** disagreeable or annoying; unpleasant: *nasty weather.* **3.** seriously harmful; severe: *a nasty fall.* **4.** morally offensive; obscene; indecent: *nasty language.* **5.** repulsive to taste or smell; nauseating: *a nasty odor, a nasty medicine.* **6.** physically dirty; filthy. [Of uncertain origin.] —**nas′ti·ly,** *adv.* —**nas′ti·ness,** *n.*

nat. 1. national. **2.** native. **3.** natural. **4.** naturalist.

na·tal (nā′təl) *adj.* **1.** of, relating to, or dating from one's birth. **2.** *Archaic.* (of places) native. [Latin *nātālis* relating to one's birth, from *nātus,* past participle of *nāscī* to be born.]

na·tal·i·ty (nā tal′i tē) *n., pl.* **-ties.** birthrate.

na·tant (nā′tənt) *adj.* swimming or floating. [Latin *natāns,* present participle of *natāre* to swim, float.]

na·ta·tion (nā tā′shən) *n.* the act or art of swimming.

na·ta·to·ri·al (nā′tə tôr′ē əl) *adj.* of, relating to, characterized by, or adapted for swimming. Also, **na′ta·to′ry.** [Late Latin *natātōrius* relating to swimming (from Latin *natāre* to swim) + -AL¹.]

na·ta·to·ri·um (nā′tə tôr′ē əm) *n., pl.* **-to·ri·ums** or **-to·ri·a** (-tôr′ē ə). swimming pool. [Late Latin *natātōrium,* from Latin *natāre* to swim.]

Natch·ez (nach′iz) *n.* a member of a tribe of North American Indians, formerly living in southwestern Mississippi, speaking a Muskogean language.

na·tes (nā′tēz) *pl. n.* the buttocks. [Latin *natēs,* plural of *natis* rump.]

nathe·less (nāth′lis, nath′-) *also,* **nath·less.** *Archaic. adv.* nevertheless. —*prep.* notwithstanding. [Old English *nā thē lǣs* never the less.]

na·tion (nā′shən) *n.* **1.a.** a large group of people living in a particular land under one government and usually forming an independent political entity: *The nation mourned the death of its leader.* **b.** the land occupied by a nation: *The candidate campaigned throughout the nation.* **c.** the political entity formed by a nation; country: *The ship flew the flag of the nation of Venezuela.* **2.** a group of people having a common origin, language, and history; nationality: *a member of the Irish nation.* **3.** a tribe or federation of tribes, esp. of North American Indians. [Latin *nātiō* race, people.] —For Synonyms, see **state.**

na·tion·al (nash′ə nəl) *adj.* **1.** of, belonging to, involving, or affecting a nation as a whole: *the national employment rate, a national treasure.* **2.** characteristic of or peculiar to a particular nation: *a national language, a national costume.* **3.** established or maintained by the government of a nation: *a national wildlife preserve.* —*n.* a person under the protection of a particular nation; citizen or subject: *The government ordered all foreign nationals to leave the country.* —**na′tion·al·ly,** *adv.* —For Synonyms *(n.),* see **citizen.**

U.S. National Parks

NATIONAL PARK (location)	AREA		FEATURES
	acres	hectares	
Acadia (Maine)	41,888	16,965	Rugged maritime coastline; islands
Arches (Utah)	73,379	29,719	Natural stone arches; Colorado River gorge
Badlands (South Dakota)	242,756	98,316	Eroded ravines; fossils; wildlife
Big Bend (Texas)	801,163	324,471	Rio Grande canyons; desert
Biscayne (Florida)	173,467	70,254	Coral reefs; marine life
Bryce Canyon (Utah)	35,835	14,513	Multicolored rock formations
Canyonlands (Utah)	337,570	136,716	Canyons; mesas; Anasazi rock art
Capitol Reef (Utah)	241,904	97,971	Dome-shaped rock; canyons
Carlsbad Caverns (New Mexico)	46,775	18,944	Stalactites; stalagmites
Channel Islands (California)	249,354	100,988	Marine wildlife
Crater Lake (Oregon)	183,224	74,206	Lake in extinct volcano crater
Denali (Alaska)	4,716,726	1,910,274	Mt. McKinley
Everglades (Florida)	1,506,499	610,132	Wetlands; subtropical plants and animals
Gates of the Arctic (Alaska)	7,523,888	3,047,175	Tundra wilderness
Glacier (Montana)	1,013,572	410,497	Glaciers; alpine lakes; wildlife
Glacier Bay (Alaska)	3,225,284	1,306,240	Glaciers; mountains; forests
Grand Canyon (Arizona)	1,218,375	493,442	Vast mile-deep canyon; trails
Grand Teton (Wyoming)	309,994	125,548	Mountains towering above valley floor
Great Basin (Nevada)	77,100	31,226	Caves; forests; mountains
Great Smoky Mountains (North Carolina, Tennessee)	520,269	210,709	Ancient mountains, among Earth's oldest; lush forests
Guadalupe Mountains (Texas)	86,416	34,998	Fossil reef; evergreen forests
Haleakala (Hawaii)	28,655	11,605	Haleakala volcano (dormant)
Hawaii Volcanoes (Hawaii)	229,177	92,817	Active volcanoes
Hot Springs (Arkansas)	5,839	2,365	Hot mineral springs
Isle Royale (Michigan)	571,790	231,575	Island wilderness; wolves and moose herds
Katmai (Alaska)	3,716,000	1,504,980	Wilderness area on volcanic eruption site
Kenai Fjords (Alaska)	669,541	271,164	Major U.S. icecap; whale watching
Kings Canyon (California)	461,901	187,070	Giant sequoias; canyons
Kobuk Valley (Alaska)	1,750,421	708,921	Arctic wildlife; sand dunes
Lake Clark (Alaska)	2,636,839	1,067,920	Glaciers and active volcanoes; wildlife
Lassen Volcanic (California)	106,372	43,081	Active volcano; hot springs
Mammoth Cave (Kentucky)	52,419	21,230	Limestone caverns; underground river
Mesa Verde (Colorado)	52,122	21,109	Prehistoric cliff dwellings
Mount Rainier (Washington)	235,612	95,423	Glacier system; forests
North Cascades (Washington)	504,781	204,436	Mountain wilderness; alpine scenery
Olympic (Washington)	922,654	373,675	Mt. Olympus; rain forest
Petrified Forest (Arizona)	93,533	37,881	Petrified wood; Painted Desert
Redwood (California)	110,132	44,603	Redwood forest; tallest known tree
Rocky Mountain (Colorado)	265,190	107,405	High mountain peaks
Sequoia (California)	402,482	163,005	Sequoias; Mt. Whitney
Shenandoah (Virginia)	196,039	79,396	Blue Ridge Mountains
Theodore Roosevelt (North Dakota)	70,447	28,531	Badlands; Theodore Roosevelt's ranch
Virgin Islands (Virgin Islands)	14,689	5,949	Reefs; beaches; marine life
Voyageurs (Minnesota)	218,035	88,304	Lakes; forests; glacial features
Wind Cave (South Dakota)	28,295	11,459	Limestone formations carved by winds
Wrangell-St. Elias (Alaska)	8,331,604	3,374,300	High mountain peaks; glaciers
Yellowstone (Idaho, Montana, Wyoming)	2,219,791	899,015	Geysers; hot springs; waterfalls; oldest national park
Yosemite (California)	761,170	308,274	Mountain gorges; high waterfalls
Zion (Utah)	146,598	59,372	Colorful rock formations; mesas

N

national bank **1.** in the United States, a commercial bank chartered by the federal government. **2.** a bank associated with the finances of a nation, such as the Federal Reserve Bank.

national debt, the total amount owed by a national government. The U.S. Department of the Treasury finances the national debt by selling securities backed by the credit of the government.

National Guard, a reserve military force supported by each state of the United States. It is under the control of the governor of the state but may be put under federal control by the president in time of war or national emergency.

national income, the total income earned in a nation during a specified period, including rent from property, wages and salaries, interest from loans, and business profits.

na·tion·al·ism (nash′ə nə liz′əm) *n.* **1.a.** devotion to one's nation and its interests. **b.** excessive patriotism; chauvinism. **2.** beliefs and policies stressing the different interests of different nations and opposed to international cooperation. **3.** a desire or movement for national independence.

na·tion·al·ist (nash′ə nə list) *adj.* favoring or supporting nationalism. Also, **na′tion·al·is′tic.** —*n.* a person who favors or supports nationalism. —**na′tion·al·is′ti·cal·ly,** *adv.*

na·tion·al·i·ty (nash′ə nal′i tē) *n., pl.* **-ties. 1.** the fact or state of belonging to a particular nation: *to be proud of one's national-*

ity. **2.** a group of people sharing a common origin, language, and history: *Various nationalities were represented at the conference.* **3.** the condition of being a politically independent nation: *Many former colonies have achieved nationality.*

na·tion·al·ize (nash′ə nə līz′) *v.t.,* **-ized, -iz·ing. 1.** to place (something, such as an industry) under the control or ownership of a national government: *The new socialist government nationalized many industries.* **2.** to extend throughout a nation; make nationwide: *to nationalize a television network.* —**na′tion·al·i·za′tion,** *n.*

national monument, a natural formation, place of historic interest, or notable structure maintained by the U.S. government for public use.

national park, an area of land, usually with great natural beauty or historical importance, maintained by a national government for public use.

a	at	e	end	o	hot	u	up	hw	white		about
ā	ape	ē	me	ō	old	ū	use	ng	song		taken
ä	far	i	it	ô	fork	ü	rule	th	thin	ə	pencil
âr	care	ī	ice	oi	oil	u̇	pull	th	this		lemon
		îr	pierce	ou	out	ûr	turn	zh	measure		circus

National Security Council, a group of high officials of the executive branch of the U.S. government who advise the president on integrating domestic, foreign, and military policies for more effective national security.

National Socialism, Naziism.

National Weather Service, an agency of the U.S. Department of Commerce that observes and forecasts the weather.

na·tion·wide (nā′shən wīd′) also, **na·tion-wide.** adj. extending throughout a nation. —adv. throughout a nation.

na·tive (nā′tiv) n. **1.** a person who was born in a particular place or country: a native of France, a native of Cleveland. **2.** an original inhabitant of a region or country, as distinguished from a foreigner, settler, or the like. **3.** an animal or plant that lives or grows naturally in a particular place: That bird is a native of South Carolina. **4.** a permanent or lifelong resident of a place, country, or region. —adj. **1.** born in a particular place or country: a native New Yorker. **2.** connected with or belonging to one by birth or birthplace: French is not my native tongue. **3.** possessed from birth; inherent; innate; natural: native intelligence. **4.** living or growing naturally in a particular place; indigenous: Cacti are native to the Americas. **5.** of, relating to, or characteristic of the original inhabitants of a country or region or their descendants: native Zulu customs. **6.** of, relating to, or characteristic of a region or its inhabitants: native cuisine. **7.** free from artificiality; natural; simple; unaffected: native sweetness. **8.** occurring in nature in an uncombined or pure state: Native silver has been found in volcanic rocks. **9.** found in a natural state; not produced artificially: native sulfur. [Latin nātīvus born, innate, natural. Doublet of NAIVE.] —na′tive·ly, adv. —na′tive·ness, n.

·**to go native.** to adopt the manner and style of living of a particular place, esp. to become more relaxed in dress and behavior: We went native on our vacation in the Caribbean.

Synonyms adj. **Native** and **indigenous** mean belonging to a particular place by birth or origin. **Native** is the more general term, indicating that a person or thing originates in a given locality: Jane and Tim are native Michiganders. The statue is carved from native stone. **Indigenous** is usually applied to a species or race that occurs naturally in a large region: The gorilla is indigenous to equatorial Africa.

Native American 1. a member of any of the tribes of people inhabiting North and South America when the Europeans arrived. **2.** of, relating to, or characteristic of Native Americans, their languages, or their cultures: Native American customs. Also, **American Indian, Amerind, Amerindian, Indian.** For table of words borrowed from languages spoken by Native Americans, see **American Indian.**

na·tive-born (nā′tiv bôrn′) adj. born in the place or country specified or understood: a native-born Austrian.

na·tiv·i·ty (nə tiv′ə tē, nā-) n., pl. **-ties. 1. Nativity. a.** the birth of Jesus. **b.** a representation of the birth of Jesus, as in painting. **c.** Christmas; December 25. **2.** birth. **3.** the position of the stars at the date of one's birth; horoscope. [Old French nativite, from Latin nātīvitās.]

natl., national.

NATO (nā′tō) North Atlantic Treaty Organization, established in 1949, a military alliance of Western nations.

nat·ter (nat′ər) v.i. **1.** to find fault; complain or scold. **2.** British. to chatter, esp. at length. —n. idle chatter. [Of uncertain origin.]

nat·ty (nat′ē) adj., **-ti·er, -ti·est.** neat, trim, and stylish: a natty new suit. [Possibly form of NEAT[1] + -Y[1].] —nat′ti·ly, adv.

nat·u·ral (nach′ər əl, nach′rəl) adj. **1.** produced or existing in nature; not artificial: a natural rock formation. **2.** based on or derived from nature: a natural growth process, the natural beauty of the Rocky Mountains. **3.** of, relating to, or dealing with nature or its study: a natural scientist. **4.** belonging to or existing in a person from birth; innate: a woman with natural beauty. **5.** having innate talents or abilities; born: She is a natural athlete. **6.** happening in the normal course of things: to die from natural causes. **7.** to be expected; reasonable or logical: Anger was a natural reaction to the insult. **8.** closely imitating or resembling nature; realistic; lifelike: The portrait is very natural. **9.** free from artificiality or constraint; not forced or contrived: to speak in a natural voice. **10.** based on an innate feeling of morality; instinctively felt to be right and fair: natural justice, natural rights. **11.** based on what is observable in nature or has physical existence, rather than on faith or revelation: natural religion. **12.** illegitimate: The king's natural child could not succeed to the throne. **13.** related by birth rather than by adoption: The adopted child never knew his natural parents. **14.** having had little or no processing and containing no artificial substances or chemical additives: natural foods. **15.** Music. **a.** having neither sharps nor flats; without accidentals: the natural scale of C major. **b.** neither sharp nor flat: She played F sharp instead of F natural. **c.** having the pitch

changed by the sign ♮. —n. **1.** something that is natural or occurs in the normal course of things: the natural and the supernatural. **2.** Music. **a.** a sign (♮) used to cancel the effect of a preceding sharp or flat. **b.** a tone or note changed by this sign. **c.** in keyboard instruments, a white key. **3.** Informal. **a.** a person who is endowed with a specific talent: Some people have to study acting, but he's a natural. **b.** a person who seems exceptionally qualified or well-suited: a natural for the job. **c.** a person or thing that seems highly likely to succeed. [Latin nātūrālis by birth, in accordance with nature, from nātūra character, disposition, course of things, the world.] —nat′u·ral·ness, n.

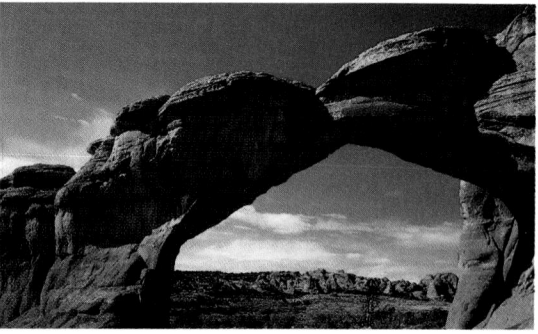

natural bridge

natural bridge, a geologic formation that resembles a bridge.

natural childbirth, the manner of giving birth to a baby using a minimum of drugs and anesthetics, in which the mother remains conscious and assists throughout labor and delivery of the baby. Exercises and training prepare expectant mothers for natural childbirth.

natural food, food that contains no additives, such as preservatives or artificial coloring.

natural gas, a highly flammable mixture of the gaseous hydrocarbons (mainly methane, and lesser amounts of ethane, propane, and butane) with other gases, found in underground deposits that are commercially exploited as a source of fuel.

natural history, the observation and study of natural organisms, objects, and processes.

nat·u·ral·ism (nach′ər ə liz′əm, nach′rə-) n. **1.** in art and literature, faithful representation of or close adherence to nature or reality. **2.** a style and set of principles of fiction writing developed in the mid-nineteenth century, in which environment, which is considered the strongest force in shaping a character's existence, is depicted realistically and in great detail. **3.** an action or moral system based on or arising from natural instincts. **4.** the philosophical view that the real world is that of nature as studied by science, and is governed by natural mechanical laws and forces rather than by supernatural ones. **5.** the belief that all religious truth can be derived from the study of nature without the aid of divine revelation.

nat·u·ral·ist (nach′ər ə list, nach′rə-) n. **1.** a person who studies natural science, esp. a botanist or zoologist. **2.** an adherent of or believer in naturalism, esp. in art or literature.

nat·u·ral·is·tic (nach′ər ə lis′tik, nach′rə-) adj. **1.** of, relating to, or characteristic of naturalism, esp. in art or literature. **2.** imitating or resembling nature: The lighting on the stage set produced a naturalistic effect. —nat′u·ral·is′ti·cal·ly, adv.

nat·u·ral·ize (nach′ər ə līz′, nach′rə-) v., **-ized, -iz·ing.** —v.t. **1.** to make a citizen of (an alien); grant citizenship to. **2.** to adopt (a foreign word or custom) into common use: The German word "kindergarten" has been naturalized in English. **3.** to adapt (an animal or plant) to another environment; acclimate. **4.** to make lifelike; free from artificiality: The photographer asked her to naturalize her pose. —v.i. to adapt oneself to a place; become like a native: The immigrant tried to naturalize in his new country. —nat′u·ral·i·za′tion, n.

natural logarithm, a logarithm that has e (2.7182818 . . .) as its base.

nat·u·ral·ly (nach′ər ə lē, nach′rə-) adv. **1.** as would be expected; of course: Naturally I'll help you. **2.** by nature; inherently: to be naturally shy. **3.** in a natural manner; without artificiality: to act naturally. **4.** by natural processes: Coconuts grow naturally on the island. He didn't die naturally—he was murdered.

natural number, the number one or any number produced by repeatedly adding one to it. The numbers 1, 4, 37, and 592 are natural numbers.

natural philosophy *Archaic.* physical sciences collectively, esp. physics.

natural resource, a material or growth found in nature that is useful to humans or necessary for their survival, such as water, wood, or any of various minerals.

natural science, any or all of the sciences concerned with the physical universe, including biology, chemistry, physics, and geology.

natural selection, the evolutionary process by which those animals and plants having characteristics best adapted to their environment tend to survive to reproduce and thereby pass those characteristics on to their progeny.

na·ture (nā′chər) *n.* **1.** the essential quality of a thing; inherent character: *What is the nature of your request? It is the nature of fire to burn.* **2.** *also,* **Nature.** the forces that create and control all things in the universe: *the laws of nature.* **3.** the entire physical universe. **4.** a fundamental disposition; temperament: *He has a gentle nature.* **5.** *also,* **Nature.** an inherent power or impulse that directs or controls the behavior of a person or animal; instinct. **6.** sort; kind; variety: *A rumor of this nature should not be published.* **7.** a primitive or simple way of life or system of social organization: *to live in a state of nature, to go back to nature.* **8.** natural scenery or plant and animal life: *a walk through the woods to observe nature.* **9.** *Theology.* the state of the human soul without divine grace. [Latin *nātūra* character, disposition, course of things, the world.] —For Synonyms, see **disposition.**

• **by nature.** as a result of the essential character of a person or thing; innately: *She is by nature a happy person.*

• **of** (or **in**) **the nature of.** having the nature, character, or qualities of; being; like: *The invitation was of the nature of a command.*

nature study, the elementary study of plant and animal life, esp. through field trips.

nature trail, a path maintained in a park or other area, along which trees, plants, rocks, and other natural features are often marked for study.

na·tur·op·a·thy (nā′chə rop′ə thē, nach′ə-) *n.* a method of medical treatment that avoids using drugs or surgery and depends only on natural healing agents, such as herbs, massage, sunshine, and water. —**na·tur·o·path** (nā′chər ə path′), *n.* —**na′tur·o·path′ic,** *adj.*

naught (nôt) *also,* **nought.** *n.* **1.** nothing: *All our plans came to naught.* **2.** zero: *Five plus naught equals five.* [Old English *nāwiht* mischief, nothing, from *nā* no + *wiht* thing.]

naugh·ty (nô′tē) *adj.,* **-ti·er, -ti·est. 1.** characterized by misbehavior; mischievous; disobedient: *a naughty child.* **2.** in bad taste; improper: *a naughty word.* [NAUGHT + -Y¹.] —**naugh′ti·ly,** *adv.* —**naugh′ti·ness,** *n.*

nau·pli·us (nô′plē əs) *n., pl.* **-pli·i** (-plē ī′). the first, tiny, unsegmented larval stage of many crustaceans, having a single median eye and three pairs of appendages on the head. [Latin *nauplius* kind of shellfish, from Greek *nauplios,* from *naus* ship + *plerein* to sail; because it was thought to sail in its shell.]

nau·se·a (nô′zē ə, -shə, -zhə) *n.* **1.** a sick feeling in the stomach; the feeling that one is going to vomit. **2.** extreme disgust; revulsion. [Latin *nausea* seasickness, nausea, from Greek *nausiē* seasickness, from *naus* ship.]

nau·se·ate (nô′zē āt′, -shē-, -zhē-) *v.,* **-at·ed, -at·ing.** —*v.t.* to produce nausea in: *The rolling of the ship nauseated the passengers.* —*v.i.* to become affected with nausea (often with *at*). [Latin *nauseātus,* past participle of *nauseāre* to be seasick, vomit, from *nausea* seasickness. See NAUSEA.] —**nau′se·at′ing·ly,** *adv.* —**nau′se·a′tion,** *n.*

nau·seous (nô′shəs, -zē əs) *adj.* **1.** causing nausea; repulsive to the taste or smell; nauseating: *a nauseous odor.* **2.** affected by nausea; sickened; nauseated: *to feel nauseous during an automobile ride.* [Latin *nauseōsus* that produces nausea, from *nausea* seasickness. See NAUSEA.] —**nau′seous·ly,** *adv.* —**nau′seous·ness,** *n.*

| Usage | **Nauseous** is often used instead of **nauseated** to mean "affected by nausea." Since the original meaning was "causing nausea" or "repulsive," a statement such as *I was nauseous after lunch* may be unintentionally humorous. Although this usage is becoming widespread, it is best avoided except in informal speech and writing. |

Nau·sic·a·ä (nô sik′ā ə, -ē ə) *n.* in Greek legend, a maiden who helped the shipwrecked Ulysses by taking him to her father's palace.

naut., nautical.

nautch (nôch) *n.* in India, an exhibition of dancing performed by professional dancing girls. [Hindi *nāch* a dance, from Prakrit *nachcha* dancing, from Sanskrit *nritja.*]

nau·ti·cal (nô′ti kəl) *adj.* of or relating to ships, sailors, or

navigation. [Latin *nauticus* (from Greek *nautikos,* going back to *naus* ship) + -AL¹.] —**nau′ti·cal·ly,** *adv.* —For Synonyms, see **marine.**

nautical mile, a unit of distance used in navigation, now based on the length of 1 minute of arc of a great circle on the earth's surface, or about 6,076 feet (1,852 meters). Also, **sea mile.**

nau·ti·lus (nô′tə ləs) *n., pl.* **-ti·lus·es** or **-ti·li** (-tə lī′). **1.** any of several species of saltwater cephalopods, genus *Nautilus,* found in tropical waters, having a flattened spiral shell divided into chambers. The nautilus lives in the outermost chamber of its shell. Diameter: to 8 inches (20 centimeters). Also, **chambered nautilus, pearly nautilus. 2.** paper nautilus. [Latin *nautilus,* from Greek *nautilos* nautilus, sailor, going back to *naus* ship; because it was once thought to use its shell as a sail.]

nav. 1. naval. **2.** navigation.

Nav·a·ho (nav′ə hō′) *n., pl.* **-ho** or **-hos** or **-hoes. 1.** a member of the largest tribe of North American Indians, living in New Mexico, Arizona, and Utah. **2.** the Athapascan language of this tribe. **3. the Navaho.** the members of this tribe collectively.

Navaho rug

Nav·a·jo (nav′ə hō′) *n., pl.* **-jo** or **-jos** or **-joes.** Navaho.

na·val (nā′vəl) *adj.* **1.** of or relating to warships: *naval maneuvers.* **2.** of or relating to a navy: *naval supplies, naval discipline.* **3.** of or relating to ships: *naval engineering.* **4.** possessing or based on the possession of a navy: *naval strength, a great naval power.* [Latin *nāvālis* relating to ships, from *nāvis* ship.] —**na′val·ly,** *adv.*

nave¹ (nāv) *n.* the main part of a church interior. In a church built in a cruciform plan, it is located between the side aisles and extends from the main entrance to the chancel or transept. [Medieval Latin *navis,* from Latin *nāvis* ship; referring to the old comparison of the Christian church to a storm-tossed ship.]

nave² (nāv) *n.* the hub of a wheel. [Old English *nafu.*]

na·vel (nā′vəl) *n.* a rounded depression or scar in the middle of the surface of the abdomen that remains after the umbilical cord is cut. Also, **umbilicus.** [Old English *nafela.*]

navel orange, the large, usually seedless, sweet fruit of an evergreen tree, *Citrus sinensis,* having a navellike formation at one end that contains a small, undeveloped secondary fruit.

nav·i·ga·ble (nav′i gə bəl) *adj.* **1.** able to be traveled on or through by ships or other water vessels: *a navigable waterway.* **2.** capable of being steered. —**nav′i·ga·bil′i·ty,** *n.*

nav·i·gate (nav′i gāt′) *v.,* **-gat·ed, -gat·ing.** —*v.t.* **1.** to direct the course of or operate (a water vessel or aircraft); pilot. **2.** to plan or direct the course of (a voyage, flight, or the like). **3.** to sail on or across (a body of water). **4.** to move through, on, or over: *It was impossible to navigate the snow-covered highway until a snowplow cleared a path.* —*v.i.* **1.** to direct the course of or operate a water vessel or aircraft. **2.** to plan or direct the course of a voyage, flight, or the like. **3.** to travel on water; sail. **4.** to walk or find one's way: *to navigate through a crowd.* [Latin *nāvigātus,* past participle of *nāvigāre* to sail, from *nāvis* ship + *agere* to drive.]

a	at	e	end	o	hot	u	up	hw	white		about
ā	ape	ē	me	ō	old	ū	use	ng	song		taken
ä	far	i	it	ô	fork	ü	rule	th	thin	ə	pencil
âr	care	ī	ice	oi	oil	ù	pull	th	this		lemon
		îr	pierce	ou	out	ûr	turn	zh	measure		circus

815

nav·i·ga·tion (nav′i gā′shən) *n.* **1.** the act or practice of navigating a ship or aircraft. **2.** the art or science of determining the position and directing the course of ships and aircraft. **3.** commerce by ship; shipping. —**nav′i·ga′tion·al,** *adj.*

navigation satellite, an earth satellite intended to provide navigational data for ships or aircraft.

nav·i·ga·tor (nav′i gā′tər) *n.* **1.** a person who navigates. **2.** a person who has skill in or practices navigation, esp. of a ship or aircraft. **3.** formerly, an explorer of the seas. [Latin *nāvigātor* sailor, from *nāvigāre* to sail. See NAVIGATE.]

nav·vy (nav′ē) *n., pl.* **-vies.** *British.* an unskilled laborer, esp. one who works on railways, roads, or the like. [Short for NAVIGA-TOR; referring to a laborer who worked on (dialectal English) *navigations* or canals.]

na·vy (nā′vē) *n., pl.* **-vies. 1.** all the warships of a country, collectively. **2.a.** *also,* **Navy.** the entire military sea force of a country, including ships, land bases, equipment, and personnel. **b.** the department of government in charge of this. **3.** navy blue. **4.** *Archaic.* any large group of ships. [Old French *navie* ships, fleet, going back to Latin *nāvis* ship.]

navy bean, a small, dried white bean related to the kidney bean.

navy blue, a very dark blue color.

navy yard, a land base with docking facilities and dry docks where naval vessels are built, fitted out, and repaired.

nay (nā) *adv.* **1.** no. **2.** not only that, but even: *They were disappointed, nay, heartbroken by the news.* —*n.* **1.** a negative vote or voter. **2.** a refusal, denial, or prohibition. [Old Norse *nei* no, from *ne* not + *ei* ever.]

nay·say (nā′sā′) *v.t.,* **-said** (-sed′) or **-sayed, -say·ing.** to say no to, often repeatedly; refuse; oppose. [From *to say nay*.] —**nay′say′er,** *n.*

Naz·a·rene (naz′ə rēn′, naz′ə rēn′) *n.* **1.** a native or inhabitant of Nazareth. **2.** a member of a sect of early Christians who observed the Mosaic law. **3. the Nazarene.** Jesus.

Naz·a·rite (naz′ə rīt′) *also,* **Nazirite.** *n.* in the Old Testament, one of a group of Israelites who took certain strict vows as a symbol of service to God.

Na·zi (nät′sē, nat′-) *n., pl.* **Na·zis. 1.** a member or follower of the fascist political party that controlled Germany under the leadership of Adolf Hitler from 1933 to 1945. **2.** a person holding views similar to those of the Nazis. —*adj.* of, relating to, or characteristic of Nazis.

Na·zi·ism (nät′sē iz′əm, nat′-) *also,* **Na·zism** (nät′siz əm, nat′-). *n.* the theories and beliefs of the Nazis, including racism, militarism, totalitarianism, and extreme nationalism. Also, **National Socialism.**

Naz·i·rite (naz′ə rīt′) Nazarite.

Nb, the symbol for niobium.

NB, the postal abbreviation for New Brunswick.

N.B. 1. note well. [Latin *notā bene*.] **2.** New Brunswick.

NC, the postal abbreviation for North Carolina.

N.C., North Carolina.

NCAA, National Collegiate Athletic Association.

NCO *also,* **N.C.O.** noncommissioned officer.

Nd, the symbol for neodymium.

ND, the postal abbreviation for North Dakota.

N.D. 1. no date. **2.** North Dakota.

N. Dak., North Dakota.

Ne, the symbol for neon.

NE 1. the postal abbreviation for Nebraska. **2.** northeast. **3.** northeastern.

N.E., New England.

NEA 1. National Education Association. **2.** National Endowment for the Arts.

Ne·an·der·thal (nē an′dər thôl′, -täl′) *adj.* of, relating to, or characteristic of Neanderthal man. —*n.* **1.** Neanderthal man. **2.** *Informal.* an extremely conservative or old-fashioned person.

Neanderthal man, any of an extinct species of prehistoric human being, *Homo neanderthalensis,* that lived during the early Stone Age. [From *Neanderthal,* the valley of the Neander River in Germany, where bones of this human being were found.]

Ne·a·pol·i·tan (nē′ə pol′i tən) *adj.* **1.** of, relating to, or characteristic of Naples. **2.** (of ice cream) having layers of different colors and flavors. —*n.* a native or inhabitant of Naples.

neap tide (nēp) the tide occurring at the first and third quarters of the moon, when there is the least difference between the levels of high and low tide. [Old English *nēp,* possibly meaning "lacking" + TIDE.]

near (nîr) *adv.* **1.** to, within, or at a short distance; not far in time, place, or degree: *Night is drawing near.* **2.** very close to being; almost; nearly: *We were near frantic with worry.* **3.** in a close relationship; closely. —*adj.* **1.** not distant in time, place, or degree: *Will we see you in the near future?* **2.** achieved or avoided by only a slight margin: *a near disaster, a near miss.* **3.** closely

related or associated: *They are near relatives of ours.* **4.** closely resembling or approximating an original: *a near copy.* **5.** short and direct: *the near route into the city.* **6.** less distant; closer: *the near side of the house.* **7.** left: *the near horse of a pair.* ➡ opposed to **off.** —*prep.* close to or by: *a house near the beach.* —*v.t.* to come or draw near to; approach. —*v.i.* to come or draw near or nearer. [Old English *nēar* closer, nearer, comparative of *nēah* nigh.] —**near′ness,** *n.*

Synonyms *adj.* **Near** and **close** mean not far away or apart. **Near** suggests being separated by a short interval of space, time, or relationship: *The school was conveniently near, only a few blocks from their house.* **Close** suggests an extreme nearness, to the point of being almost or actually in contact: *The shrubs were so close together that they had little room in which to grow.*

near·by (nîr′bī′) *adj., adv.* a short distance away; not far off: *They moved to a nearby town. We'll stop nearby for lunch.*

near·ly (nîr′lē) *adv.* **1.** almost, but not quite; practically. **2.** closely: *We are nearly associated in business.* —For Synonyms, see **almost.**

near·sight·ed (nîr′sī′tid) *adj.* unable to see distant objects clearly; myopic. ➡ opposed to **farsighted.** —**near′sight′ed·ly,** *adv.* —**near′sight′ed·ness,** *n.*

neat¹ (nēt) *adj.* **1.** clean and orderly; tidy: *to keep a room neat.* **2.** inclined to keep oneself or one's things clean and orderly: *a neat person.* **3.** done in a clever or skillful way: *a neat trick.* **4.** well-shaped or well-proportioned: *a neat profile.* **5.** without anything mixed in it, as an alcoholic beverage. **6.** (of money) remaining after deductions; net: *a neat profit.* **7.** *Informal.* wonderful; fine; swell: *We had a neat time at the party.* [Old French *net* clean, pure, from Latin *nitidus* shining, clear, elegant.] —**neat′ly,** *adv.* —**neat′ness,** *n.*

neat² (nēt) *n., pl.* **neat.** *Archaic.* cattle. [Old English *nēat.*]

neat·en (nē′tən) *v.t.* *Informal.* to make neat; tidy (usually with *up*): *Neaten up the room before you leave.*

neath (nēth, nēth) *prep.* *Archaic.* beneath.

neat·herd (nēt′hûrd′) *n.* *Archaic.* cowherd.

neat's-foot oil (nēts′fût′) a yellow oil obtained by boiling the feet and shinbones of cattle, used chiefly to soften leather.

neb (neb) *n.* *Scottish.* **1.** a bill or beak, as of a bird. **2.** the snout of an animal. **3.** the nose or mouth of a person. **4.** the tip or point of anything, esp. of a pen. [Old English *nebb* beak, nose.]

Neb., Nebraska.

neb·bish (neb′ish) *n.* *Slang.* a pitiful, unfortunate, timid person. [Yiddish *nebach* poor thing; from Slavic.]

Nebr., Nebraska.

neb·u·la (neb′yə lə) *n., pl.* **-lae** (-lē′) or **-las. 1.** a bright, cloudlike mass visible in the night sky, composed of dust and gases. **2.** galaxy *(def. 1).* [Latin *nebula* mist, cloud.] —**neb′u·lar,** *adj.*

nebular hypothesis, any of various theories of the origin of the solar system according to which the sun and planets condensed from a rotating nebula.

neb·u·lize (neb′yə līz′) *v.t.,* **-lized, -liz·ing.** to reduce (a liquid) to a misty spray; atomize. —**neb′u·li·za′tion,** *n.* —**neb′u·liz′er,** *n.*

neb·u·los·i·ty (neb′yə los′i tē) *n., pl.* **-ties. 1.** the state or quality of being nebulous. **2.** nebula.

neb·u·lous (neb′yə ləs) *adj.* **1.** vague or confused; indistinct; unclear: *nebulous ideas.* **2.** like a cloud or clouds; cloudy. **3.** resembling or characterized by the presence of a nebula or nebulae. [Latin *nebulōsus* misty, cloudy, from *nebula* mist, cloud.] —**neb′u·lous·ly,** *adv.* —**neb′u·lous·ness,** *n.*

nec·es·sar·i·ly (nes′ə ser′ə lē) *adv.* **1.** as an inevitable consequence: *Tall, strong persons are not necessarily good athletes.* **2.** because of an obligation or necessity: *You don't necessarily have to leave now.*

nec·es·sar·y (nes′ə ser′ē) *adj.* **1.** that cannot be omitted or done without; needed; required: *Proper food and rest are necessary for good health.* **2.** that cannot be avoided; certain; inevitable: *Failure was a necessary result of their lack of preparation.* —*n., pl.* **-sar·ies.** something that cannot be done without; necessity; essential. [Latin *necessārius* unavoidable, needful, from *necesse* unavoidable.]

Synonyms *adj.* **Necessary, indispensable,** and **essential** mean strongly required. **Necessary** often implies a need that, although important, is not an absolute requirement: *To get a good job, it is necessary to have a high school diploma.* **Indispensable** indicates something that cannot be done without: *A visa is an indispensable document for travel in many countries.* **Essential** suggests a requirement that is not only absolute but inherent in the nature of what requires it: *Oxygen is essential to life.*

ne·ces·si·tar·i·an·ism (nə ses′i târ′ē ə niz′əm) *n.* the philosophical belief that all events are determined beforehand by a fixed sequence of causes. —**ne·ces·si·tar·i·an**, *adj., n.*

ne·ces·si·tate (nə ses′i tāt′) *v.t.,* **-tat·ed, -tat·ing. 1.** to cause (something) to be needed or unavailable; make necessary: *The crime necessitated punishment. Your reasoning necessitates certain conclusions.* **2.** to force or compel (someone) to do something. —**ne·ces·si·ta′tion,** *n.*

ne·ces·si·tous (nə ses′i təs) *adj.* **1.** lacking basic requirements for living; destitute; needy. **2.** urgent; demanding; compelling. —**ne·ces′si·tous·ly,** *adv.* —**ne·ces′si·tous·ness,** *n.*

ne·ces·si·ty (nə ses′i tē) *n., pl.* **-ties. 1.** something that cannot be done without; requirement: *Sturdy shoes are a necessity for hiking. The poor family could afford only the basic necessities, such as food and shelter.* **2.** the fact or condition of being necessary: *I realize the necessity of finishing school.* **3.** the fact or a state of extreme or urgent need; exigency: *Necessity is the mother of invention.* **4.** circumstances making a certain course of action compulsory: *I went only out of necessity.* **5.** something unavoidable, as because of natural or logical conditions. **6.** a condition of poverty; neediness. [Latin *necessitās* inevitability, destiny.]
· **of necessity.** necessarily.

neck (nek) *n.* **1.** the part of the body of a human being or animal connecting the head and the trunk. **2.** the part of a garment that fits around the neck. **3.** a narrow portion of certain organs or parts of the body: *the neck of the bladder.* **4.** a narrow upper part of a bottle, vase, or other container. **5.** a narrow strip of land, such as an isthmus or peninsula. **6.** a narrow body of water, such as a channel or inlet. **7.** the part of a stringed musical instrument, such as a violin or guitar, extending from the main body and carrying the fingerboard, strings, and tuning pegs. **8.** the upper part of the shaft of a column, just below the capital. **9.** the part of a tooth between the crown and the root. —*v.i. Informal.* to make love by kissing and caressing. [Old English *hnecca* part of the body connecting the head and the trunk.]
· **neck and neck.** at an equal pace; even or very close: *A poll showed the two candidates running neck and neck.*
· **neck of the woods.** *Informal.* area; neighborhood: *Come to see me if you're in my neck of the woods.*
· **to break one's neck.** *Informal.* to try very hard: *I broke my neck to get to the meeting on time.*
· **to risk one's neck.** *Informal.* to take a chance on losing one's career, reputation, or other thing of great value.
· **to stick one's neck out.** *Informal.* to risk one's well-being and interests, esp. by making a commitment; take a chance.
· **up to one's neck.** having an abundance or excess: *By August we were up to our necks in tomatoes from the garden.*

neck·band (nek′band′) *n.* **1.** a band of material around the neck of a shirt or other garment, to which a collar may be attached. **2.** a band worn around the neck.

neck·cloth (nek′klôth′) *n., pl.* **-cloths** (-klôthz′, -klôths′) a piece of cloth worn around the neck, esp. a cravat.

necked (nekt) *adj.* having the kind of neck specified. ➡ usually used in combination: *a narrow-necked bottle.*

neck·er·chief (nek′ər chif) *n.* a scarf or kerchief worn around the neck.

neck·lace (nek′lis) *n.* an ornament worn around the neck, such as a string or chain of beads or gems.

neck·line (nek′līn′) *n.* the line or contour formed by the upper edge of a garment at or near the neck: *This dress has a scalloped neckline.*

neck·tie (nek′tī′) *n.* a strip of fabric designed to be worn around the neck, usually under the collar, and knotted in front. Also, **tie.**

neck·wear (nek′wâr′) *n.* any of various articles of clothing that are worn around the neck, such as scarves and neckties.

ne·crol·o·gy (ne krol′ə jē) *n., pl.* **-gies. 1.** a list of persons who have died, as at a given time or place. **2.** a notice of a person's death; obituary. [Greek *nekros* corpse + -LOGY.]

nec·ro·man·cy (nek′rə man′sē) *n.* **1.** the act or practice of predicting the future by supposedly communicating with the dead. **2.** black magic; sorcery. [Late Latin *necromantīa* prophecy by invoking the dead, from Greek *nekromanteiā,* from *nekros* corpse + *manteiā* prophecy.] —**nec′ro·man·cer,** *n.*

ne·crop·o·lis (ne krop′ə lis) *n., pl.* **-lis·es.** cemetery. [Greek *nekropolis* literally, city of the dead, from *nekros* corpse + *polis* city.]

ne·cro·sis (ne krō′sis) *n., pl.* **-ses** (-sēz). the death or decay of plant or animal cells or tissue. [Greek *nekrōsis* state of death, going back to *nekros* corpse.] —**ne·crot·ic** (ni krot′ik, ne-), *adj.*

nec·tar (nek′tər) *n.* **1.** in Greek mythology, the drink of the gods that made anyone who drank it immortal. **2.** the thick, undiluted juice from any of various fruits, such as peaches, pears, or apricots. **3.** a sweet liquid secreted by the nectaries and glands of plants, used by bees in making honey. **4.** any sweet and delicious drink. [Latin *nectar* the drink of the gods, from Greek *nektar.*] —**nec′tar·ous,** *adj.*

nec·tar·ine (nek′tə rēn′) *n.* **1.** a variety of peach having a smooth, downless skin and firm pulp. **2.** the tree, *Prunus persica nucipersica,* that bears this fruit. [NECTAR + -INE¹.]

nec·ta·ry (nek′tə rē) *n., pl.* **-ries.** a nectar-secreting part or organ of a plant.

née (nā) *also,* **nee.** *adj. French.* born. ➡ used chiefly in designating the maiden name of a married woman: *Susan Brown, née Smith.*

need (nēd) *n.* **1.** a lack or absence of something necessary, useful, or desired: *The team's defeat showed their need of practice.* **2.** a necessity or obligation: *There is no need to stay any longer.* **3.** an intense desire or urgent requirement: *a need for recognition.* **4.** something necessary, useful, or desired: *Food is a basic human need.* **5.** a condition of poverty or hardship: *His need led him to crime.* **6.** a time or condition in which something is missing: *We are in need of help on the project.* **7.** a time or condition of difficulty or trouble: *a friend in need.* —*v.t.* **1.** to have need of; lack; require: *to need new shoes, to need a room for the night.* **2.** to be obliged; must: *I need to study harder.* —*v.i.* to be in want: *Those who need are often reluctant to speak.* —*auxiliary verb* to be obliged to. ➡ used in questions and with the negative, always in the form *need* rather than *needs: Need I wait for you? She need not wait. Nothing need be done.* [Old English *nēd* necessity, distress.]

need·ful (nēd′fəl) *adj.* needed; required; necessary. —**need′ful·ly,** *adv.* —**need′ful·ness,** *n.*

nee·dle (nē′del) *n.* **1.** a thin, pointed instrument, usually of steel, with a hole at one end through which thread is passed, used in sewing. **2.** a slender pointer, as on a compass or dial. **3.** a sharp, hollow tube attached to a hypodermic syringe to puncture the skin. **4.a.** a slender rod tapered at one or both ends, used in knitting. **b.** a slender rod with a hook at one end, used in crocheting. **5.** a small, slender instrument of steel, diamond, sapphire, or other material, mounted in a phonograph cartridge, that rides the grooves in a record and transmits sound vibrations. Also, **stylus. 6.** a fine-pointed instrument used in etching, esp. dry point. **7.** a slender rod used to control the opening of a valve. **8.** something resembling a needle in shape, such as an obelisk or pinnacle. **9.** *Botany.* the needle-shaped leaf of a fir, pine, or other conifer. —*v.t.,* **-dled, -dling.** *Informal.* to annoy, as by teasing repeatedly. [Old English *nǣdl* pointed instrument used in sewing.] —**nee′dle·like′,** *adj.*
· **needle in a haystack.** something impossible or almost impossible to find.

nee·dle·point (nē′dəl point′) *n.* **1.** embroidery done on canvas, often used as upholstery fabric. **2.** lace made entirely with a sewing needle and worked with a buttonhole stitch over a paper pattern. Also *(def. 2),* **point lace, point.**

need·less (nēd′lis) *adj.* not needed; unnecessary. —**need′less·ly,** *adv.* —**need′less·ness,** *n.*

needle valve, a valve with a narrow opening controlled by a needle-shaped plug, used esp. to control the flow of a gas.

nee·dle·wom·an (nē′dəl wǔm′ən) *n., pl.* **-wom·en** (-wim′ən). seamstress.

nee·dle·work (nē′dəl wûrk′) *n.* **1.** something made by using a needle, such as embroidery. **2.** the occupation or process of sewing, embroidering, or the like: *to be skilled at needlework.*

need·n't (nēd′dənt) need not.

needs (nēdz) *adv. Archaic.* of necessity; necessarily (with *must*): *We must needs be leaving now.* [Old English *nēdes,* genitive of *nēd* necessity.]

need·y (nē′dē) *adj.,* **need·i·er, need·i·est.** experiencing or being in need, want, or poverty: *The agency gives clothes to needy families.* —**need′i·ness,** *n.*

ne'er (nâr) *adv. Archaic.* **1.** never: *For ne'er was flattery lost on poet's ear* (Sir Walter Scott, 1805). **2.** not; nary (with *a*): *ne'er a one.*

ne'er-do-well (nâr′dü wel′) *n.* a worthless person; good-for-nothing. —*adj.* worthless; good-for-nothing.

ne·far·i·ous (ni fâr′ē əs) *adj.* causing or inclined to cause harm; wicked; evil; villainous: *nefarious deeds, a nefarious scoundrel.* [Latin *nefārius,* going back to *ne-* not + *fās* divine law.] —**ne·far′i·ous·ly,** *adv.* —**ne·far′i·ous·ness,** *n.*

neg., negative.

ne·gate (ni gāt′) *v.t.,* **-gat·ed, -gat·ing. 1.** to make ineffective;

a	at	e	end	o	hot	u	up	hw	white		about
ā	ape	ē	me	ō	old	ū	use	ng	song		taken
ä	far	i	it	ô	fork	ů	rule	th	thin	ə	pencil
âr	care	ī	ice	oi	oil	ů	pull	th	this		lemon
		îr	pierce	ou	out	ûr	turn	zh	measure		circus

N

817

nullify: *That one mistake negated all our efforts.* **2.** to deny the validity of: *The new evidence negated the prisoner's alibi.* [Latin *negātus,* past participle of *negāre* to deny, refuse.]

ne·ga·tion (ni gā'shən) *n.* **1.** the act of negating. **2.** something that negates; denial. **3.** the absence or opposite of something positive: *A lie is the negation of truth.* [Latin *negātiō* denial.]

neg·a·tive (neg'ə tiv) *adj.* **1.** expressing, containing, or implying denial or refusal: *a negative reply.* **2.** lacking positive qualities, such as helpfulness, hope, or confidence; destructive or pessimistic: *negative criticism, a negative attitude.* **3.** less than zero: *a negative number.* **4.** *Electricity.* of a lower electric potential than others in the same system: *a negative electrode.* **5.** *Physics.* (of ions) having more electrons than protons. **6.** *Photography.* having the areas that were light in the original subject dark, and those that were dark, light. **7.** not indicating the presence of a given condition, disease, or the like: *The tests for tuberculosis were negative.* —*n.* **1.** a negative image on a photographic plate or film from which prints can be made. **2.** a word or phrase that expresses denial or refusal: *"No" and "not" are negatives.* **3.** the side that argues against the proposition in a debate. **4.** a negative number or algebraic expression. **5.** *Electricity.* the plate or element in an electric cell having the lower electric potential. **6.** *Archaic.* the right to veto. [Late Latin *negātīvus* that denies, from Latin *negāre* to deny.] —**neg'a·tive·ly,** *adv.* —**neg'a·tive·ness, neg'a·tiv'i·ty,** *n.*

· **in the negative.** in a way that expresses refusal or denial: *to answer in the negative.*

neg·a·tiv·ism (neg'ə tə viz'əm) *n.* **1.** a tendency to deny, contradict, or oppose anything that others want, say, or suggest. **2.** an inclination to doubt or deny traditional beliefs; skepticism. —**neg'a·tiv·ist,** *adj., n.* —**neg'a·tiv·is'tic,** *adj.*

neg·lect (ni glekt') *v.t.* **1.** to fail to give proper attention or care to: *She neglected her friends because she was busy. The children neglected their pets.* **2.** to fail to do, esp. through carelessness; leave undone: *You've neglected your chores in the kitchen.* —*n.* **1.** an act or instance of neglecting; negligence: *His neglect of the business caused it to go bankrupt.* **2.** the condition of being neglected: *The old house fell into neglect.* [Latin *neglectus,* past participle of *negligere* to disregard.] —**neg·lect'er,** *n.* —For Synonyms *(v.t.),* see **ignore.**

neg·lect·ful (ni glekt'fəl) *adj.* characterized by or showing neglect: *We were neglectful of the time and arrived late.* —**neg·lect'ful·ly,** *adv.* —**neg·lect'ful·ness,** *n.*

neg·li·gee (neg'li zhā') *n.* **1.** a woman's loose, flowing dressing gown. **2.** any informal, incomplete, or careless attire. [French *négligée,* feminine past participle of *négliger* to be careless of, disregard, from Latin *negligere* to disregard.]

neg·li·gence (neg'li jəns) *n.* **1.** the state or quality of being negligent. **2.** the act or an instance of being negligent. **3.** *Law.* failure to give proper attention or care when such failure results in injury or damage to a person or persons. [Latin *negligentia* carelessness, neglect.]

neg·li·gent (neg'li jənt) *adj.* **1.** habitually neglecting to do what ought to be done; neglectful: *a negligent parent.* **2.** showing carelessness or casual indifference: *a negligent reply.* **3.** *Law.* failing to exercise the degree of care the law says a reasonable person would exercise in a given situation. [Latin *negligēns,* present participle of *negligere* to disregard.] —**neg'li·gent·ly,** *adv.*

neg·li·gi·ble (neg'li jə bəl) *adj.* so small or limited that it can be disregarded; not worth considering: *Their impact on the project is negligible.* —**neg'li·gi·bil'i·ty,** *n.* —**neg'li·gi·bly,** *adv.*

ne·go·tia·ble (ni gō'shə bəl, -shē ə bəl) *adj.* **1.** able to be sold or transferred, as a bond. **2.** open to discussion: *a negotiable demand.* **3.** able to be traveled on or over: *The mountain roads are not negotiable in winter.* —**ne·go'tia·bil'i·ty,** *n.*

ne·go·ti·ate (ni gō'shē āt') *v.,* **-at·ed, -at·ing.** —*v.t.* **1.** to bring about or arrange the terms of: *to negotiate a settlement of a strike, to negotiate a loan.* **2.** to sell or transfer: *to negotiate securities.* **3.** to succeed in traveling over or on: *The car could not negotiate the icy road.* **4.** to bring about or deal with successfully. —*v.i.* to confer in order to bring about an agreement: *The two warring nations refused to negotiate.* [Latin *negōtiātus,* past participle of *negōtiārī* to carry on business, from *negōtium* business.] —**ne·go'ti·a'tor,** *n.* —**ne·go·ti·a·to·ry** (ni gō'shē ə tôr'ē), *adj.*

ne·go·ti·a·tion (ni gō'shē ā'shən) *n.* **1.** the act of negotiating. **2.** a discussion for the purpose of bringing about an agreement or transaction.

Ne·gri·to (ni grē'tō) *n., pl.* **-tos** or **-toes.** a member of one of the Pygmy peoples of Southeast Asia, esp. those of the Philippine and Andaman islands and the Malay Peninsula. [Spanish *negrito* young or small black person, diminutive of *negro* black. See NEGRO.]

Ne·gro (nē'grō) *n., pl.* **-groes.** a member of the Negroid divi-

sion of the human race, which includes many of the native peoples of Africa. —*adj.* of or relating to a Negro or Negroes. [Spanish or Portuguese *negro* black man, black, from Latin *niger* black.]

Ne·groid (nē'groid) *adj.* of or relating to one of the major divisions traditionally used to classify the human race, whose members often are characterized by dark skin, tightly curled hair, and broad features. —*n.* a member of the Negroid race.

ne·gus (nē'gəs) *n.* a drink made of wine, hot water, sugar, lemon juice, and spices. [From Colonel Francis *Negus,* died 1732, who originated it.]

Neh., Nehemiah.

Ne·he·mi·ah (nē'ə mī'ə) *n.* a book of the Old Testament, containing the story of the Hebrew leader Nehemiah.

Ne·he·mi·as (nē'ə mī'əs) *n.* in the Douay Bible, Nehemiah.

neigh (nā) *n.* the characteristic cry of a horse; whinny. —*v.i.* to utter a neigh; whinny. [Old English *hnǣgan* to utter a neigh.]

neigh·bor (nā'bər) *also, British,* **neighbour.** *n.* **1.** a person who lives near another, esp. one who lives in a house next to one's own. **2.** a person, place, or thing located next to another: *Mexico is a neighbor of the United States.* **3.** a fellow human being: *Thou shalt love thy neighbor as thyself* (Mark 12:31). —*adj.* living or situated nearby: *neighbor countries.* [Old English *nēahgebūr* one who lives near another.]

neigh·bor·hood (nā'bər hŏŏd') *n.* **1.** a small residential area or district: *a tough neighborhood.* **2.** people living in the same district: *The whole neighborhood is talking about the fire.*

· **in the neighborhood of.** somewhere near; close to; approximately: *Lunch cost in the neighborhood of ten dollars.*

neigh·bor·ing (nā'bər ing) *adj.* located or living nearby; adjacent: *My friend comes from a neighboring town.*

neigh·bor·ly (nā'bər lē) *adj.* having or showing the characteristics of a good neighbor; friendly; sociable. —**neigh'bor·li·ness,** *n.*

neigh·bour (nā'bər) *British.* neighbor.

nei·ther (nē'thər, nī'-) *conj.* **1.** not either. ➧ used with **nor** to introduce two or more negative alternatives: *When I was sick, I could neither eat nor drink.* **2.** nor: *They don't want to go; neither do I.* —*adj.* not the one (person or thing) nor the other; not either: *Neither team played well.* —*pron.* not either one: *I tried on two hats, but neither fit me.* [Middle English *neither* not either, from *ne* not (from Old English *ne*) + EITHER.]

> **Usage** Although the conjunction **neither** is sometimes used with *or* rather than **nor,** many people consider *or* unacceptable in formal speech and writing. When **neither** and **nor** (or *or*) are used to join two or more subjects, the verb agrees in number with the subject closest to it: *Neither the students nor the teacher was able to attend.* However, sometimes a singular verb form sounds awkward, and it may be preferable to place the plural subject closer to the verb: *Neither the teacher nor the students were able to attend.* For another Usage Note, see **anybody.**

nek·ton (nek'ton) *n.* all animals that swim freely in the ocean, including fish, octopuses, squid, and whales. ➧ distinguished from **plankton.** —**nek·ton'ic,** *adj.*

nel·son (nel'sən) *n.* any of several wrestling holds, such as the half nelson. [Of uncertain origin.]

nem·a·to·cyst (nem'ə tə sist') *n.* a stinging cell, as on the tentacles of a jellyfish or other coelenterate, that ejects a poisonous thread when triggered, used to immobilize prey or fend off an attack. [Greek *nēmat-,* stem of *nēma* thread + CYST.] —**nem'a·to·cys'tic,** *adj.*

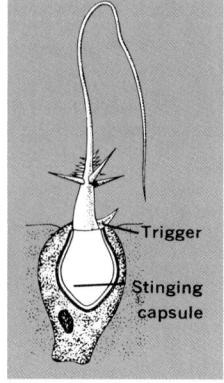

nem·a·tode (nem'ə tōd') *adj.* of or relating to a large group of worms, phylum Nematoda, having an unsegmented, cylindrical body tapering to a point at each end, including many crop pests and parasites, such as the hookworm; roundworm. —*n.* a nematode worm. [Modern Latin *Nematoda,* from *nēmat-,* stem of Greek *nēma* thread + *-ōdēs* like.]

Nem·bu·tal (nem'byə tôl') *n. Trademark.* a barbiturate drug, a pentobarbital salt, used as a hypnotic and a sedative, esp. prior to anesthesia.

nematocyst

Ne·me·an games (ni mē'ən, nē'mē-) one of the main festivals of the ancient Greeks, held every two years and including athletic and musical competitions.

Nemean lion, a lion strangled by Hercules as the first of his twelve labors.

Nem·e·sis (nem'ə sis) *n., pl.* (*defs. 2, 3*) **-ses** (-sēz'). **1.** in Greek

mythology, the goddess of vengeance. **2. nemesis. a.** a person or thing that punishes wrongdoing. **b.** just punishment for wrongdoing. **3. nemesis.** a person or thing that causes one's defeat or failure: *Spelling has always been my nemesis.* [Greek *nemesis* retribution.]

ne·o- *combining form* new, recent: *neoplasm, neoclassicism.* [Greek *neos.*]

ne·o·clas·si·cal (nē′ō klas′i kəl) *also,* **Ne·o·clas·si·cal.** *adj.* of or relating to neoclassicism. Also, **ne′o·clas′sic, Ne′o·clas′-sic.**

ne·o·clas·si·cism (nē′ō klas′ə siz′əm) *also,* **Ne·o·clas·si·cism.** *n.* a revival of classical style in art, music, literature, or architecture, esp. that in Europe in the late seventeenth and eighteenth centuries. [NEO- + CLASSICISM.]

ne·o·dym·i·um (nē′ō dim′ē əm) *n.* a yellowish metallic element of the rare-earth group, used esp. to make lavender-colored glass for a type of laser. Symbol: **Nd** For tables, see **element.** [Modern Latin *neodymium,* from NEO- + (DI)DYMIUM.]

Ne·o·lith·ic (nē′ə lith′ik) *adj.* of, relating to, or characteristic of the last period of the Stone Age, at the end of the Ice Age, when human beings began to develop agriculture, domesticate animals, and use tools and weapons made from shaped and polished stone. [NEO- + Greek *lithos* stone + -IC.]

ne·ol·o·gism (nē ol′ə jiz′əm) *n.* **1.** a new word or new meaning for an existing word. **2.** the use of such words or meanings. Also, **ne·ol·o·gy** (nē ol′ə jē). [French *néologisme* new word, going back to Greek *neos* new + *logos* word.] —**ne·ol′o·gist,** *n.*

> **Usage** Neologisms, or new words, are being added to our language all the time. Only a short time ago many people had never heard of AIDS or Lyme disease, compact disks or colorization, networking or disinformation. As new concepts are introduced or objects or processes invented, new words are developed to describe them. Neologisms develop in many different ways, among them, combining existing words (*computer virus, spacewalk, voiceprint*); blending words (*brunch,* from breakfast + lunch; *camcorder,* from camera + recorder; *smog,* from smoke + fog); and borrowing words from foreign languages (*karate* and *tofu* from Japanese; *macho* and *taco* from Spanish; *croissant* and *quiche* from French; *dungaree* and *yoga* from Hindi). Neologisms are also derived from proper names (*cardigan,* from the Earl of Cardigan, *saxophone* from Antoine Joseph Sax) and from the development of acronyms (*AIDS, laser, yuppie*). Other common sources are slang, jargon, and advertising. Although many **neologisms** become part of our permanent vocabulary, others quickly become dated or fall out of use.

ne·o·my·cin (nē′ō mī′sin) *n.* an antibiotic drug used esp. as an antiseptic in surgery and to treat skin and eye infections. [NEO- + Greek *mykēs* fungus + -IN[1].]

ne·on (nē′on) *n.* **1.** a colorless, odorless, inert, gaseous element that makes up a very small percentage of the air, best known for its use in neon lamps. Symbol: **Ne** For tables, see **element.** **2.** neon lamp. —*adj.* made of or using neon or neon lamps. [Modern Latin *neon* literally, the new (element), from Greek *neon,* neuter of *neos* new.]

neon sign

ne·o·nate (nē′ə nāt′) *adj.* a newborn infant. [Modern Latin *neonatus,* from Latin *neo-* neo- + *natus* born.] —**ne′o·na′tal** *adj.*

ne·o-Na·zi·ism (nē′ō nät′sē iz′əm, -nat′-) *also,* **ne·o-Na·zism** (nē′ō nät′siz əm, -nat′-). *n.* a present-day movement promoting the theories and beliefs of National Socialism.

neon lamp 1. a neon-filled discharge tube in which the gas glows red when ionized by an electric current. Color variations are achieved by altering the tubes or gas pressure or by adding other gases. **2.** a sign made up of such tubes, used esp. in advertising displays.

ne·o·phyte (nē′ə fīt′) *n.* **1.** a person recently admitted to a religion or denomination; new convert. **2.** a beginner in any area; novice. [Church Latin *neophytus* new convert, newly planted, from Greek *neophytos,* from *neos* new + *phyton* plant.]

ne·o·plasm (nē′ə plaz′əm) *n.* any new growth of abnormal tissue in the body, such as a tumor. [NEO- + -PLASM.] —**ne′o·plas′tic,** *adj.*

Ne·o·pla·to·nism (nē′ō plā′tə niz′əm) *n.* a mystical philosophy of the third century A.D., which combined Platonic ideas with Oriental mysticism and greatly influenced early Christian theology. —**Ne·o·pla·ton·ic** (nē′ō plə ton′ik), *adj.* —**Ne′o·pla′to·nist,** *n.*

ne·o·prene (nē′ə prēn′) *n.* a polymer compound made by polymerizing the monomer chloroprene, used as a substitute for rubber where resistance to oil, chemicals, sunlight, or oxidation is needed.

Ne·o-Scho·las·ti·cism (nē′ō skə las′tə siz′əm) *n.* a revival of Scholasticism begun in the late nineteenth century under Pope Leo XIII, emphasizing Thomism and the application of Scholastic thought to contemporary problems. —**Ne′o-Scho·las′tic,** *adj., n.*

Ne·pa·li (nə pô′lē, -pä′-) *n.* a language belonging to the Indo-Iranian branch of the Indo-European language family, spoken predominantly in Nepal.

ne·pen·the (ni pen′thē) *n.* **1.** in Greek mythology, a drug that brought forgetfulness of pain or sorrow. **2.** anything bringing forgetfulness of pain or sorrow. [Greek *nēpenthes,* neuter of *nē-penthēs* free from sorrow.] —**ne·pen′the·an,** *adj.*

neph·ew (nef′ū, nev′ū) *n.* **1.** the son of one's brother or sister. **2.** the son of one's brother-in-law or sister-in-law. [Old French *neveu,* from Latin *nepōs* nephew, grandson.]

ne·phrid·i·um (ni frid′ē əm) *n., pl.* **-phrid·i·a** (-frid′ē ə). a tubular excretory organ in mollusks, crustaceans, flatworms, and various other invertebrates.

neph·rite (nef′rīt) *n.* a type of jade that is a mineral of the amphibole group, ranging in color from green to white and having a glassy luster. [German *Nephrit,* going back to Greek *nephros* kidney; because formerly believed to be a remedy for kidney diseases.]

ne·phrit·ic (ni frit′ik) *adj.* **1.** of, relating to, or suffering from nephritis. **2.** of or relating to the kidney or kidneys.

ne·phri·tis (ni frī′tis) *n.* inflammation of the kidneys. [Late Latin *nephrītis,* from Greek *nephrītis,* from *nephros* kidney.]

neph·ron (nef′ron) *n.* any of a large number of tiny structures in the kidney that filter water, wastes, and other substances from the blood and send them to the bladder to be excreted as urine.

ne plus ultra (nē′plus′ul′trə, nā′) *Latin.* the extreme or utmost point attainable; height of excellence: *an evening gown that was the ne plus ultra of fashion.*

nep·o·tism (nep′ə tiz′əm) *n.* the giving of jobs or special privileges to relatives by a person in a high or official position. [French *népotisme,* from Italian *nepotismo,* from *nepote* nephew, grandson, from Latin *nepōs.* Nepotism originally referred to the practice of certain popes who advanced their "nephews" (often actually their sons) to high positions.] —**ne·pot·ic** (nə pot′ik), *adj.* —**nep′o·tist,** *n.*

Nep·tune (nep′tün, -tūn) *n.* **1.** in Roman mythology, the god of the sea and brother of Jupiter. His Greek counterpart is Poseidon. **2.** the fourth largest planet of the solar system and eighth in order of distance from the sun, having eight confirmed satellites and a system of rings. It is invisible to the naked eye, but appears green when viewed through a telescope. [Latin *Neptūnus* the Roman god.] —**Nep·tu′ni·an,** *adj.*

nep·tu·ni·um (nep tü′nē əm, -tū′-) *n.* a silvery, radioactive metallic element chemically similar to uranium, produced by bombarding uranium with neutrons. Symbol: **Np** For tables, see **element.** [Modern Latin *neptunium,* from the planet *Neptune;* because it follows uranium in the periodic table and the planet Neptune comes after Uranus, after which uranium was named, in the solar system.]

nerd (nûrd) *n. Slang.* a clumsy, silly, or ineffectual person; jerk. [Of uncertain origin.]

Ne·re·id (nîr′ē id) *n.* in Greek mythology, a water nymph living in the sea.

Ne·re·us (nîr′ē əs, nîr′ūs) *n.* in Greek mythology, a sea god, father of the Nereids.

ne·rit·ic (ni rit′ik) *adj.* of, relating to, or inhabiting the shallow

N

a	at	e	end	o	hot	u	up	hw	white		about
ā	ape	ē	me	ō	old	ū	use	ng	song		taken
ä	far	i	it	ô	fork	ü	rule	th	thin	ə	pencil
âr	care	ī	ice	oi	oil	u̇	pull	th	this		lemon
		îr	pierce	ou	out	ûr	turn	zh	measure		circus

waters of a shoreline. [Greek *nērítēs* a sea snail (from *Nēreus* Nereus) + -IC.]

ner·o·li (ner′ə lē, nîr′-) *n.* an oil distilled from orange blossoms, used esp. in making perfume. Also, **neroli oil.** [French *néroli,* from Italian *neroli, nerolo,* after the Princess of *Nerola,* who is said to have discovered it around 1670.]

ner·va·tion (nûr vā′shən) *n. Botany, Zoology.* venation.

nerve (nûrv) *n.* **1.** a bundle of fibers carrying impulses between the brain and spinal cord and other parts of the body. **2.** courage; bravery: *I didn't have the nerve to jump off the high diving board.* **3. nerves.** the nervous system considered as the source of a person's state of mind: *Her nerves were unsteady after the accident.* **4.** the part of a tooth sensitive to pain; pulp. **5.** *Informal.* rude boldness; presumption; audacity: *You've got a lot of nerve to ask such a personal question!* **6.** *Informal.* a source of sensitivity, such as a painful subject: *The speaker's attack on social security hit a nerve in the elderly audience.* **7. nerves.** emotional or physical tension; nervousness: *I always have a bad case of nerves before an exam.* —*v.t.,* **nerved, nerv·ing.** to give courage or strength to: *The boxer nerved himself for the fight.* [Latin *nervus* sinew, bowstring, strength.]

· **to get on (someone's) nerves.** to make (someone) annoyed or irritated.

· **to strain every nerve.** to make the greatest possible physical effort.

nerve cell, neuron.

nerve center 1. a group of neurons closely connected with one another and acting together in the performance of some specific function, such as hearing or breathing. **2.** a center of operations; headquarters.

nerve cord 1. the spinal cord of vertebrates. **2.** a pair of closely united strands of nerve tissue running the length of the body below the intestine in many invertebrates.

nerve fiber, any of the threadlike fibers that constitute neurons; axon or dendrite.

nerve gas, in chemical warfare, any of several poisonous, gaseous compounds that attack the involuntary nervous system, often causing convulsions and death.

nerve impulse, an electrochemical change in a nerve fiber by means of which messages are transmitted from sense organs to the central nervous system and from the central system to muscles and glands.

nerve·less (nûrv′lis) *adj.* **1.** lacking courage or determination; spineless. **2.** lacking energy or strength; feeble; weak. **3.** controlled and calm; not easily unnerved; poised. **4.** *Anatomy.* having no nerves. —**nerve′less·ly,** *adv.* —**nerve′less·ness,** *n.*

nerve-rack·ing (nûrv′rak′-ing) *also,* **nerve-wrack·ing.** *adj.* extremely irritating, upsetting, or frustrating: *The accident was a nerve-racking experience.*

nerv·ous (nûr′vəs) *adj.* **1.** having or showing mental or emotional restlessness or strain; tense; jumpy. **2.** having or showing apprehension or fear: *She's very nervous about that exam. He gave a nervous glance over his shoulder.* **3.** of, affecting, or originating in the nerves or nervous system: *a nervous disorder.* **4.** *Archaic.* vigorous; muscular; powerful. [Latin *nervōsus* sinewy, vigorous, from *nervus* sinew, strength.] —**nerv′ous·ly,** *adv.* —**nerv′ous·ness,** *n.*

nervous breakdown, any mental or emotional disturbance so severe as to be disabling, often requiring hospitalization. ➡ not used as a medical term.

nervous system, the system of nerve tissue and nerve cells which, in vertebrates, includes the brain, spinal cord,

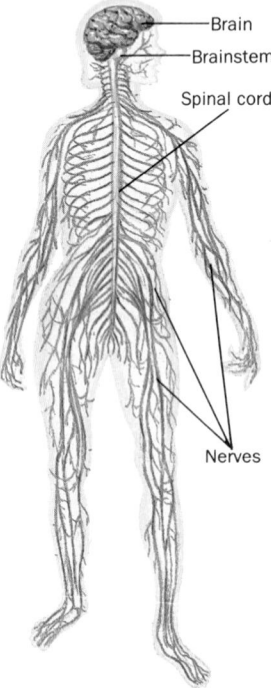

Brain
Brainstem
Spinal cord

Nerves

human **nervous system**

ganglia, nerves, and nerve centers. The nervous system controls and coordinates all the activities of the body.

ner·vure (nûr′vyûr) *n.* vein *(defs. 2, 3).* [French *nervure,* from Latin *nervus* sinew, bowstring, strength.]

nerv·y (nûr′vē) *adj.,* **nerv·i·er, nerv·i·est. 1.** characterized by or showing rude boldness; presumptuous; impudent: *a nervy person, a nervy remark.* **2.** without fear; courageous; brave. **3.** *Archaic.* vigorous and powerful; strong; sinewy. **4.** *British. Informal.* nervous. —**nerv′i·ly,** *adv.* —**nerv′i·ness,** *n.*

nes·cience (nesh′əns, -ē əns, nes′ē-) *n.* **1.** a lack of knowledge; ignorance. **2.** agnosticism. [Late Latin *nescientia* ignorance, from Latin *nescīre* to be ignorant, from *ne-* not + *scīre* to know.] —**nes′cient,** *adj.*

-ness *suffix* **1.** the quality, state, or condition of being: *wilderness, lightness.* **2.** an act or instance of being: *kindness.* [Old English *-nes(s).*]

nes·sel·rode (nes′əl rōd′) *n.* a mixture of cream or custard, preserved fruits, and nuts, eaten as a pudding or used as a pie filling. [From Count Karl *Nesselrode,* 1780-1862, Russian statesman, whose chef supposedly invented it.]

nest (nest) *n.* **1.** a structure or place in which birds lay their eggs and raise their young. **2.** a place or structure used by insects, fish, turtles, mice, or other animals for depositing eggs or raising young: *a hornet's nest.* **3.** a group of birds, animals, insects, or the like living in a nest. **4.** a cozy place or shelter. **5.a.** a place where something dangerous, bad, or illegal goes on: *a smugglers' nest.* **b.** the occupants of such a place. **6.** a set of similar objects designed so that they can be stacked together, esp. so that each fits into the next largest one: *a nest of tables.* —*v.i.* **1.** to build or occupy a nest: *The birds nested in the oak tree.* —*v.t.* **1.** to settle or house in or as in a nest. **2.** to arrange (objects) in a stack, esp. with each fitting into the next largest one. [Old English *nest* bird's nest.]

nest egg 1. a reserve of money saved up, as for an emergency or retirement. **2.** a natural or artificial egg left in a nest to induce a hen to continue laying eggs there.

nes·tle (nes′əl) *v.,* **-tled, -tling.** —*v.i.* **1.** to press or lie close; cuddle: *The foal nestled up to its mother.* **2.** to settle oneself snugly and cozily: *We nestled by the fire.* **3.** to be located in a snug and sheltered spot: *The cabin nestled among the hills.* —*v.t.* **1.** to hold or press closely; snuggle: *I nestled the kitten in my arms. She nestled her face against his collar.* **2.** to give protection to; shelter: *The thick forest nestled the family of deer.* [Old English *nestlian* to make a nest.] —**nes′tler,** *n.*

nest·ling (nest′ling, nes′-) *n.* a bird too young to leave the nest.

Nes·tor (nes′tər) *n.* in Greek legend, the oldest and wisest of the Greek chieftains in the Trojan War.

net¹ (net) *n.* **1.** any of various fabrics made of threads, cords, or ropes that are knotted, twisted, or woven into an open, crisscross pattern. **2.** something made of such fabric, used for various purposes, as to catch, hold, protect, or divide: *a butterfly net, a hair net, a mosquito net, a badminton net.* **3.** something that captures or entangles like a net: *caught in a net of lies.* **4.** a fine, openwork fabric, such as that used for veils. **5.** anything forming an open, crisscross pattern; network: *a net of veins.* **6.** net ball. —*v.t.,* **net·ted, net·ting. 1.** to catch with or as with a net: *to net a fish, to net a criminal.* **2.** to make into net: *to net string.* **3.** to protect or hold with a net: *to net one's hair.* **4.** to hit (a ball) into the net. [Old English *net(t)* openwork fabric, snare.]

net² (net) *adj.* **1.** remaining after all deductions or allowances have been made: *net profit, net weight.* **2.** after everything is considered; final: *The net result of the meeting was a decision to go ahead with the project.* —*v.t.,* **net·ted, net·ting.** to produce or earn as a final yield or profit: *After taxes I netted only $10,000.* —*n.* what remains after all deductions or allowances have been made: *The business produced a yearly net of $50,000.* [Middle English *net* literally, pure, fine, from French *net* pure, clean, from Latin *nitidus* bright, neat, trim, from *nitēre* to shine, be bright. See NEAT¹.]

net ball, in racket games, a ball hit into the net.

Neth., Netherlands.

neth·er (neth′ər) *adj.* lower: *Hell is sometimes called the nether world.* [Old English *neothera,* from *nither* downward.]

neth·er·most (neth′ər mōst′) *adj.* lowest.

net·ting (net′ing) *n.* netted material, such as fabric or wire mesh.

net·tle (net′əl) *n.* any of a group of weedy plants, genus *Urtica,* whose leaves are covered with tiny hairs which, when touched, secrete a substance that irritates the skin. —*v.t.,* **-tled, -tling.** to cause annoyance to; irritate; rile. [Old English *netele* the plant.]

net·tle·some (net′əl səm) *adj.* **1.** causing annoyance; irritating: *a nettlesome complainer, a nettlesome problem.* **2.** easily provoked or annoyed; irritable. [NETTLE + -SOME¹.]

net·work (net'wûrk') *n.* **1.** a system of lines or structures that cross or interlace: *a network of wires, a network of tunnels.* **2.** an interconnected organization, group, or system: *a network of spies.* **3.** openwork material; net; netting. **4.a.** a group of radio or television stations connected so that they may all broadcast the same program. **b.** a company that broadcasts programs for such a group, usually during certain specified hours. **5.** a system of computers linked by telephone lines. **6.** any interconnected system of electrical elements.

net·work·ing (net'wûr'king) *n.* **1.** the sharing of information or services among individuals, groups, or organizations having a common purpose or interest. **2.** the making of personal contacts by individuals seeking to further their own careers or other interests. **3.** the state of being connected or linked to a system of computers and data banks.

Neuf·châ·tel (nü'shə tel', nū-) *n.* a soft, white, uncured cheese similar to cream cheese, made from skim or whole milk, to which cream is added. [From *Neufchâtel,* French town where it is made.]

neur-, form of **neuro-** before vowels, as in *neurasthenia.*

neu·ral (nûr'əl, nyûr'-) *adj.* of or relating to a nerve, neuron, or nervous system. [Greek *neuron* nerve + -AL[1].]

neu·ral·gia (nù ral'jə, nyû'-) *n.* a recurrent sharp pain along the path of a nerve. [NEURO- + Greek *algos* pain.] —**neu·ral'gic,** *adj.*

neu·ras·the·ni·a (nûr'əs thē'nē ə, nyûr'-) *n.* a condition characterized by excessive tiredness, depression, weakness, and inability to concentrate and remember, with no discernible physical cause. ➡ not used as a medical term. [NEURO- + Greek *astheneia* weakness.] —**neu·ras·then·ic** (nûr'əs then'ik, nyûr'-), *adj., n.*

neu·ri·lem·ma (nûr'ə lem'ə, nyûr'-) *n.* the thin protective layer covering the myelin sheath of certain nerve fibers. [Modern Latin *neurilemma,* modification (influenced by Greek *lemma* husk, peel) of *neurilema,* from Greek *neuron* nerve + *eilēma* covering, veil.]

neu·ri·tis (nù rī'tis, nyû-) *n.* inflammation of a nerve or nerves. [NEURO- + -ITIS.]

neuro- *combining form* nerve: *neurology, neurosis.* [Greek *neuron* sinew, nerve.]

neu·ro·gen·ic (nûr'ə jen'ik, nyûr'-) *adj.* originating in the nerves or controlled by the nervous system. [NEURO- + -GEN + -IC.] —**neu·ro·gen'i·cal·ly,** *adv.*

neu·rog·li·a (nù rog'lē ə, nyû-) *n.* the connective tissue that supports the essential elements of nervous tissue in the central nervous system. —**neu·rog'li·al,** *adj.*

neur·o·hor·mone (nûr'ō hôr'mōn, nyûr'ō-) *n.* any hormone produced by nerve cells and secreted into the bloodstream, as noradrenaline. [NEURO- + HORMONE.] —**neur·o·hor·mo·nal** (nûr'ō hôr mō'nəl, nyûr'ō-), *adj.*

neur·o·lep·tic (nûr'ə lep'tik, nyûr'-) *adj.* having a tranquilizing effect, esp. on someone with a mental or nervous disorder. —*n.* a tranquilizing drug, esp. one used to treat psychoses. [French *neuroleptique,* from Greek *neuron* nerve + *lēptos* a seizing (from *lambanein* to seize).]

neu·ro·log·i·cal (nûr'ə loj'i kəl, nyûr'-) *adj.* of, relating to, or affecting the nervous system. Also, **neu'ro·log'ic.**

neu·rol·o·gy (nù rol'ə jē, nyû-) *n.* the branch of medicine concerned with the nervous system and its disorders. [NEURO- + -LOGY.] —**neu·rol'o·gist,** *n.*

neu·ro·ma (nù rō'mə, nyû-) *n., pl.* **-ma·ta** (-mə tə) a tumor formed from nerve tissue.

neu·ro·mus·cu·lar (nûr'ō mus'kyə lər, nyûr'-) *adj.* of or involving both nerves and muscles: *neuromuscular disease.* [NEURO- + MUSCULAR.]

neu·ron (nûr'on, nyûr'-) *also,* **neu·rone** (nûr'ōn, nyûr'-). *n.* the basic structural unit of the nervous system, consisting of a cell body and its fibers, that receives nerve impulses and conveys them to other cells. Also, **nerve cell.** [Greek *neuron* sinew, nerve.] —**neu·ron·al** (nûr'ə nəl, nyûr'-), *adj.*

neu·rop·ter·an (nù rop'tər ən, nyû-) *n.* any of a group of carnivorous insects, order Neuroptera, having four elongate, deli-

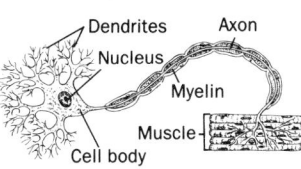

Dendrites
Axon
Nucleus
Myelin
Muscle
Cell body

neuron

cately veined, membranous wings. Included are lacewings and ant lions. —*adj.* of or relating to this insect order. Also *(adj.),* **neu·rop·ter·ous** (nù rop'tər əs, nyû-). [Modern Latin *Neuroptera,* from Greek *neuron* nerve + *pteron* wing; because of its membranous wings.]

neu·ro·sis (nù rō'sis, nyû-) *n., pl.* **-ses** (-sēz) an emotional disorder in which a person deals with the normal anxieties, con-

flicts, and concerns of life in inappropriate ways. [NEURO- + -OSIS.]

neu·ro·sur·geon (nûr'ō sûr'jən, nyûr'-) *n.* a physician who specializes in neurosurgery. [NEURO- + SURGEON.]

neu·ro·sur·ger·y (nûr'ō sûr'jə rē, nyûr'-) *n.* **1.** surgery of the brain and nervous system. **2.** the branch of medicine concerned with this type of surgery. [NEURO- + SURGERY.] —**neu'ro·sur'gi·cal,** *adj.*

neu·rot·ic (nú rot'ik, nyù-) *adj.* characteristic of or suffering from neurosis: *neurotic symptoms, a neurotic person.* —*n.* a person who is neurotic.

neu·ro·tox·in (nûr'ō tok'sin, nyûr'-) *n.* any toxin, as rattlesnake venom, damaging to nerves or nervous tissue. [NEURO- + TOXIN.] —**neu'ro·tox'ic,** *adj.*

neu·ro·trans·mit·ter (nûr'ō trans mit'ər, -tranz-, nyûr'-) *n.* any of several chemical substances that transmit impulses from one nerve cell to another.

neut., neuter.

neu·ter (nü'tər, nū-) *adj.* **1.** *Grammar.* of or relating to the gender that is neither masculine nor feminine. **2.** having no sex organs or having sex organs that are undeveloped or nonfunctioning, as certain insects or castrated animals. **3.** *Archaic.* taking no side; neutral. —*n.* **1.** a neuter animal or plant. **2.** the neuter gender. **3.** a word belonging to the neuter gender. —*v.t.* to castrate or spay (an animal). [Latin *neuter* neither, from *ne-* not + *uter* either.]

neu·tral (nü'trəl, nū-) *adj.* **1.** taking neither side in a conflict: *Switzerland was neutral in World War II.* **2.** belonging to neither side in a conflict: *a neutral zone.* **3.** having no particular shade or tint: *Gray is a neutral color.* **4.** falling into no particular category; having no marked characteristics. **5.** *Chemistry.* neither acid nor base. **6.** *Electricity.* neither positive nor negative. —*n.* **1.** a person or thing that is neutral. **2.** the position of gears when they are not engaged and do not transmit motion from the engine to working parts, such as the wheels of a car. [Latin *neutrālis* neuter, from *neuter* neither. See NEUTER.] —**neu'tral·ly,** *adv.*

Synonyms *adj.* **Neutral** and **nonaligned,** in reference to nations, mean not participating or taking a side in actual or potential hostilities. **Neutral** is the broader term, implying a general policy of removal from conflict: *Switzerland has remained neutral throughout the twentieth century.* **Nonaligned** suggests a refusal to line up with either side in a particular set of circumstances: *Finland remained nonaligned in the cold war.*

neu·tral·ism (nü'trə liz'əm, nū-) *n.* a policy or advocacy of remaining neutral, esp. in foreign affairs. —**neu'tral·ist,** *adj., n.*

neu·tral·i·ty (nü tral'i tē, nū-) *n.* the state or quality of being neutral.

neu·tral·ize (nü'trə līz', nū-) *v.t.,* **-ized, -iz·ing. 1.** to destroy by counteracting the force or effect of; make ineffective: *to neutralize an enemy's strength, to neutralize an opponent's argument.* **2.** to exclude (a nation, territory, or the like) from a conflict; declare neutral. **3.** *Chemistry.* to make neutral. An acid and a base neutralize each other and form a salt and water. **4.** *Electricity.* to make neutral by balancing the positive and negative charges. —**neu'tral·i·za'tion,** *n.* —**neu'tral·iz'er,** *n.*

neutral spirits, ethyl alcohol of at least 190 proof, frequently used in alcoholic beverage blends.

neutral vowel, schwa.

neu·tri·no (nü trē'nō, nū-) *n., pl.* **-nos.** either of two stable subatomic particles in the lepton group, having no detectable mass or electric charge.

neu·tron (nü'tron, nū'-) *n.* a subatomic nuclear particle having no electric charge and slightly more mass than a proton. Neutrons occur in every atomic nucleus except that of hydrogen. For illustration, see atom. [NEUTR(AL) + -*on,* as in ELECTRON, ION.]

neutron activation analysis, activation analysis.

neutron bomb, a hydrogen bomb designed to produce an intense burst of neutrons, but little blast or fire damage and only slight fallout.

neutron star, a small, dense stellar body formed by gravitational collapse of a large star, believed to consist mostly of tightly packed neutrons. Pulsars may be neutron stars that are rotating at an extremely rapid rate.

neu·tro·phil (nü'trə fil, nū'-) *also,* **neu·tro·phile** (nü'trə fīl', nū'-). *n.* a type of phagocytic white blood cell that can be stained with neutral dyes for microscopic observation.

Nev., Nevada.

N

a	at	e	end	o	hot	u	up	hw	white		about
ā	ape	ē	me	ō	old	ū	use	ng	song		taken
ä	far	i	it	ô	fork	ü	rule	th	thin	ə	pencil
âr	care		ice	oi	oil	ů	pull	th	this		lemon
		îr	pierce	ou	out	ûr	turn	zh	measure		circus

né·vé (nā vā′) *n.* a mass of accumulated snow partly converted to ice, forming the upper part of a glacier. [French *névé,* going back to Latin *nix* (stem *niv-*) snow.]

nev·er (nev′ər) *adv.* **1.** at no time; not ever: *I have never been to Europe.* **2.** in no way or degree; not at all: *This kind of behavior will never do.* [Old English *nǣfre* at no time, from *ne* not + *ǣfre* always.]

nev·er·more (nev′ər môr′) *adv.* never again.

nev·er-nev·er land (nev′ər nev′ər) an imaginary or unrealistic condition or place; world of illusion and fantasy.

nev·er·the·less (nev′ər thə les′) *adv.* in spite of all; however; yet: *They thought it might rain; nevertheless, they went to the beach.*

ne·vus (nē′vəs) *also,* **naevus.** *n., pl.* **-vi** (-vī). birthmark or mole. [Latin *naevus* mole[1], wart.] **—ne′void,** *adj.*

new (nü, nū) *adj.* **1.** having existed only a short time; recently grown or made: *The tree has new buds. Have you been to the new mall?* **2.** made or brought into existence for the first time; not existing before; original: *The scientist developed a new synthetic fiber.* **3.** previously existing, but recognized, observed, discovered, or experienced for the first time: *I found a new way to get to your house.* **4.** *also,* **New.** the more or most recent form, period, or development of something, such as a language. **5.** not seen or known before; unfamiliar, strange: *There were many new faces at the party.* **6.** not yet accustomed or experienced: *new to a job.* **7.** having recently come into a certain state, position, relationship, or the like: *The new recruits were assigned to their barracks.* **8.** replacing another of its kind: *I'll need a new pair of shoes when these wear out.* **9.** not yet used or worn out: *The store sells both new and used furniture.* **10.** further; additional: *The police found new evidence of her guilt.* **11.** physically or mentally changed, esp. for the better: *After his vacation he felt like a new man.* **12.** coming or beginning again: *a new dawn.* —*adv.* newly; recently; freshly. ➡ usually used in compounds: *new-fallen snow, a new-found friend.* —*n.* something that is new: *The design of the house combines the old and the new.* [Old English *nīwe* not existing before, starting afresh, of recent origin.] **—new′ness,** *n.*

Synonyms **New, novel[2],** and **original** mean unlike what previously existed. **New** stresses recentness of origin rather than distinctiveness: *They trade their car in for a new model each year.* **Novel** adds to **new** the idea of being strikingly different from what was known before: *The young director's novel stage techniques astonished critics and audiences.* **Original** indicates that something is so unusual as to be without precedent: *The composer wrote several imitative works before developing an original style.*

New Age *also,* **new age.** **1.** of or relating to a cultural trend of the 1980s characterized by a rejection of such elements of the American mainstream as traditional medicine and established religion, and embracing such spiritual concerns as the interpretation of past lives or of cosmic omens. **2.** of or relating to arts or practices associated with this trend: *New Age music.*

new blood, people who have not previously belonged to a group or organization, considered as a possible source of new ideas, renewed interest or vitality, and the like.

new·born (nü′bôrn′, nū′-) *adj.* **1.** born very recently: *The parents took their newborn baby home from the hospital.* **2.** born again; revived or regenerated: *newborn confidence.* —*n.* a newborn baby.

new·com·er (nü′kum′ər, nū′-) *n.* a person who has recently arrived: *a newcomer in our town, a newcomer to national politics.*

New Deal, the domestic program of President Franklin D. Roosevelt during the 1930s, which emphasized social and economic reforms.

New Economic Policy, a policy adopted by the Soviet government under V. I. Lenin from 1921 to 1928 that permitted limited capitalistic practices.

new·el (nü′əl, nū′-) *n.* **1.** a post at the head or foot of a flight of stairs, supporting the handrail. Also, **newel post. 2.** the central, upright pillar of a spiral staircase. [Old French *nouel* stone of a fruit, newel (because it is the center of a spiral staircase as a fruit stone is of its fruit), from Late Latin *nucālis* like a nut, from Latin *nux* nut.]

newels

new·fan·gled (nü′fang′gəld, nū′-) *adj.* recently come into fashion; modern: *a newfangled invention.* ➡ often derogatory. [From Middle English *newefangel* fond of novelty, going back to Old English *nīwe* new + *fangen,* past participle of *fōn* to take.]

new-fash·ioned (nü′fash′ənd, nū′-) *adj.* of or in a new fashion; recently come into style.

New·found·land (nü′fənd lənd, nū′-, nü found′-, nū-) *n.* a large, heavily built dog of a breed developed in Newfoundland for pulling sleds and carrying packs, having a massive head and a dense, usually black coat. Height: 28 inches (71 centimeters) at the shoulder.

New·gate (nü′gāt′, nū′-) *n.* a prison in London, torn down in 1902.

New Jerusalem, in the New Testament, heaven.

New Latin, Modern Latin.

New Left, a political movement in the United States and other Western countries that began in the 1960s, made up chiefly of college students and other young adults who advocated an end to the war in Vietnam and radical changes in existing political, economic, and social systems.

new·ly (nü′lē, nū′-) *adv.* **1.** lately; recently: *a newly elected senator.* **2.** in a new or different way; anew: *an old idea newly applied.* **3.** once more; again: *The house was newly painted after the fire.*

new·ly·wed (nü′lē wed′, nū′-) *n.* a person who has recently married.

new math, a modern method of teaching mathematics that uses set theory and stresses understanding of basic mathematical concepts. Also, **new mathematics.**

new moon, 1. the moon when it is not visible or when, after a day or two, it appears as a thin crescent with the hollow side on the left. **2.** the period during which the new moon appears. For illustration, see **moon.**

news (nüz, nūz) *n.* **1.a.** a report of or information about a recent event or development, esp. when important or unusual: *We read the news of the signing of the treaty in the newspaper. Have you had any news from home lately?* **b.** a person or thing important enough to be included in such a report. **2.** information recently discovered or disclosed: *Their marriage was news to me!* **3.** a recent event or events: *a report of the news.* **4.** newscast: *We watch the news on television every night.* ➡ used as singular. [Plural of NEW.]

news agency, an organization that gathers and supplies news to subscribing newspapers, television stations, or the like. Also, **news service.**

news·boy (nüz′boi′, nūz′-) *n.* a boy who sells or delivers newspapers.

news·cast (nüz′kast′, nūz′-) *n.* a radio or television program on which news items are broadcast. **—news′cast′er,** *n.*

news conference, a meeting of reporters with a public official, celebrity, or spokesperson at which news or information is released, usually in the form of answers to reporters' questions.

New Scotland Yard, see **Scotland Yard.**

news·deal·er (nüz′dē′lər, nūz′-) *n.* a person who sells newspapers and magazines.

news·girl (nüz′gûrl′, nūz′-) *n.* a girl who sells or delivers newspapers.

news·let·ter (nüz′let′ər, nūz′-) *n.* a printed report of news, usually published periodically and relating to a particular field of interest: *The university sent out a monthly newsletter to all alumni.*

news·mak·er (nüz′mā′kər, nūz′-) *n.* a person or event considered newsworthy.

news·man (nüz′man′, nūz′-) *n., pl.* **-men** (-men′). a person, esp. a man, who reports news, as for a newspaper or radio or television station.

news·mon·ger (nüz′mung′gər, -mong′-, nūz′-) *n.* a gossip.

news·pa·per (nüz′pā′pər, nūz′-, nüs′-, nūs′-) *n.* a publication printed on sheets of paper that are folded but not bound, containing news, editorials, feature articles, advertising, and other information of interest, issued regularly, esp. every day or every week.

news·pa·per·man (nüz′pā′pər man′, nūz′-, nüs′-, nūs′-) *n., pl.* **-men** (-men′). a man who owns a newspaper or works for one, esp. as a reporter or editor.

news·pa·per·wom·an (nüz′pā′pər wùm′ən, nūz′-, nüs′-, nūs′-) *n., pl.* **-wom·en** (-wim′ən). a woman who owns a newspaper or works for one, esp. as a reporter or editor.

news·print (nüz′print′, nūz′-) *n.* thin paper made chiefly from wood pulp, on which newspapers are usually printed.

news·reel (nüz′rēl′, nūz′-) *n.* a short motion picture dealing with recent events, formerly shown in a motion-picture theater.

news service, news agency.

news·stand (nüz′stand′, nūz′-) *n.* a stand where newspapers and, often, magazines and books are sold.

New Style, the method of calculating the months and days of the year according to the Gregorian calendar.

news·wom·an (nüz′wùm′ən, nūz′-) *n., pl.* **-wom·en** (-wim′ən). a woman who reports news, as for a newspaper or radio or television station.

news·wor·thy (nūz′wûr′thē, nūz′-) *adj.* significant or interesting enough to be reported in a newscast or newspaper.

news·y (nū′zē, nū′-) *adj.*, **news·i·er**, **news·i·est.** *Informal.* chatty and full of news; gossipy: *to receive a newsy letter from home.*

newt (nūt, nūt) *n.* any of various small, brightly colored salamanders, family Salamandridae, found living in or around water in North America, Europe, and Asia. Length: to 6 inches (15 centimeters), including tail. [From the incorrect division of Middle English *an ewt(e)* (from Old English *efeta*) into *a newt(e)*.]

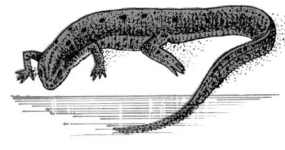

newt

New Testament, the second part of the Christian Bible, containing the life and teachings of Jesus and his disciples.

new·ton (nū′tən, nū′-) *n.* the basic unit of force in the meter-kilogram-second system. It is equal to the amount of force that must be applied to a mass of 1 kilogram to produce an acceleration of 1 meter per second per second. [From Isaac *Newton*, 1642-1727, English physicist.]

New·to·ni·an (nū tō′nē ən, nū-) *adj.* of, relating to, or in accordance with Isaac Newton or his theories or discoveries. —*n.* a follower of Isaac Newton or his theories or discoveries.

new wave, a movement or trend, as in the arts or politics, to create or achieve something different: *Abstract painting was once the new wave in art.* ➡ often **New Wave** when referring to a specific movement.

New World, the Western Hemisphere, esp. North and South America and their surrounding islands.

New Year's Day, the first day of the calendar year, Jan 1, usually observed as a legal holiday. Also, **New Year, New Year's.**

New Year's Eve 1. the night beginning on December 31, just before New Year's Day. **2.** December 31.

next (nekst) *adj.* immediately following or nearest in time, space, or order: *next week, in the next room, the next name on the list.* —*adv.* **1.** immediately afterward: *The children's choir sang next.* **2.** on the first subsequent occasion: *when we next meet.* —*prep.* closest to or beside. [Old English *nēhst* nearest in time, place, or order, superlative of *nēah* nigh.]
·**next door. a.** adjacent: *She lives in the house next door.* **b.** in, at, or to the building, house, apartment, or the like that is nearest: *Let's go next door. He lives next door to me.*
·**next to. a.** almost; nearly: *Fixing the toaster was next to impossible.* **b.** beside: *He stood next to his wife.*

next-door (nekst′dôr′) *adj.* in or at the nearest building, house, apartment, or the like: *Our next-door neighbors share a driveway with us.*

next of kin 1. a person's nearest relative or relatives. **2.** *Law.* the nearest relative or relatives of a person who died without having made a will, who are entitled to share in his or her estate.

nex·us (nek′səs) *n.*, *pl.* **-us·es** or **-us. 1.** the factor or point connecting members of a group or series; bond; link: *The nexus of the diverse factions was opposition to higher taxes.* **2.** a connected group or series. [Latin *nexus* a binding together.]

Nez Percé (nez′ pûrs′; *French* nā peʀ sā′) *pl.* **Nez Percé** or **Nez Per·cés** (nez′ pûr′siz; *French* nā peʀ sā′). a member of a North American Indian tribe formerly living in what is now the northwestern United States and southwestern Canada. [French *nez percé* pierced nose, going back to Latin *nāsus* nose + *pertundere* to make a hole in; supposedly because of their custom of piercing noses.]

NF 1. the postal abbreviation for Newfoundland. **2.** Norman French.

Nfld., Newfoundland.

N.G. 1. National Guard. **2.** New Guinea. **3.** no good.

NH, the postal abbreviation for New Hampshire.

N.H., New Hampshire.

Ni, the symbol for nickel.

N.I., Northern Ireland.

ni·a·cin (nī′ə sin) *n.* a vitamin of the vitamin B complex occurring esp. in liver, yeast, beans, and grains, that helps to prevent and cure pellagra. Formula: $C_6H_5NO_2$ Also, **nicotinic acid.** [NI(COTINIC) AC(ID) + -IN[1].]

nib (nib) *n.* **1.** the tip or point of a pen, esp. a fountain pen. **2.** the projecting point of anything. **3.** a bird's bill or beak. [Form of NEB.]

nib·ble (nib′əl) *v.*, **-bled, -bling.** —*v.t.* **1.** to eat by taking small, quick bites: *The mouse nibbled the cheese.* **2.** to take small,

gentle bites on; bite softly: *A fish nibbled our bait.* —*v.i.* **1.** to take small, gentle bites: *to nibble on the end of a pencil.* **2.** to eat something with small, quick bites: *to nibble on an apple.* —*n.* **1.** a small, quick bite, such as that taken by a fish at bait. **2.** a small piece; morsel: *There's not even a nibble of the cake left.* [Of uncertain origin.] —**nib′bler,** *n.*

Ni·be·lung (nē′bə lung′) *n. Teutonic Mythology.* **1.** one of a family of evil dwarfs who possessed a treasure and a magic ring that were stolen from them by the hero Siegfried. **2.** any of the followers of Siegfried. **3.** any of the Burgundian kings in the *Nibelungenlied.*

Ni·be·lung·en·lied (nē′bə lung′ən lēt′) *n.* a medieval German epic poem by an unknown author, probably written in the early thirteenth century, telling stories of Siegfried, Kriemhild, and the Burgundian kings.

nib·lick (nib′lik) *n.* a golf club having a metal head with a short sloping face and giving much loft; number nine iron. [Of uncertain origin.]

nibs (nibz) *n.* an excessively demanding or dictatorial person. ➡ used as singular with the possessive pronouns *his, her,* or *your,* frequently expressing mock admiration: *His nibs would like this done in* exactly *the right way.* [Of uncertain origin.]

nice (nīs) *adj.*, **nic·er, nic·est. 1.** giving pleasure or satisfaction; agreeable; pleasant: *The weather was nice yesterday.* **2.** kind; considerate: *It was nice of you to invite us.* **3.** highly satisfactory; good: *a nice turnout at a meeting, to do a nice job.* **4.** showing or requiring accuracy, skill, or delicacy: *Archaeologists examining objects recovered from the earth must make nice distinctions.* **5.** respectable or well-bred: *Her fiancé is from one of the nicest families in town.* **6.** *Archaic.* virtuous; pure. **7.** *Archaic.* particular; fastidious; fussy. [Middle English *nice* odd, lazy, stupid, from Old French *nice, nisce,* stupid, foolish, from Latin *nescius* ignorant, from *nescire* not to know, from *ne-* not + *scīre* to know.] —**nice′ly,** *adv.* —**nice′ness,** *n.*
·**nice and.** very: *The test was nice and easy.*

Ni·cene Council (nī sēn′, nī′sēn) either of two general church councils held at Nicaea, in Asia Minor, in A.D. 325 and 787, esp. the first, which condemned the Arian heresy.

Nicene Creed, a formal statement of the chief doctrines of Christian belief, expanded from the one adopted by the first Nicene Council and generally accepted in varying forms throughout Christendom.

ni·ce·ty (nī′si tē) *n.*, *pl.* **-ties. 1.** an elegant or refined feature. ➡ usually used in the plural: *Having a chauffeur is one of the niceties of life.* **2.** a small or subtle detail; fine point. ➡ usually used in the plural: *the niceties of etiquette.* **3.** the quality of requiring delicacy, subtlety, or accuracy: *The nicety of the problem was a challenge.* **4.** the quality of being exact; accuracy; precision. **5.** the quality of being particular; fastidiousness. [Old French *nicete* simplicity, foolishness, from *nice* foolish, simple. See NICE.]
·**to a nicety.** exactly; perfectly.

niche (nich) *n.* **1.** a decorative recess in a wall, often used as a setting for statues or other ornaments, such as vases or glassware. **2.** a place, position, or situation for which a person is especially suited: *to find one's niche in a new school.* **3.** *Biology.* in ecology, the place and function of an organism in an ecosystem. —*v.t.*, **niched, nich·ing.** to place in a niche. [French *niche* recess, corner, going back to Latin *nīdus* nest.]

nick (nik) *n.* a cut or chip in a surface or edge: *The table top was full of nicks.* —*v.t.* to make a nick or nicks in or on: *The razor nicked my skin.* [Of uncertain origin.]
·**in the nick of time.** at the last critical moment; just in time.

nick·el (nik′əl) *n.* **1.** a hard, silvery metallic element, used esp. as a constituent of alloys because of its resistance to corrosion. Symbol: Ni For tables, see **element. 2.** a coin of the United States equal to five cents, or one twentieth of a dollar. [Swedish *nickel* the metallic element, going back to German *kupfernickel* false copper; literally, copper devil (because the ore yielding nickel is copper-colored but contains no copper), from *kupfer* copper + *nickel* devil, goblin.]

nick·el-and-dime (nik′əl ən dīm′) *Informal. adj.* **1.** amounting to or involving only small sums of money: *a nickel-and-dime business, nickel-and-dime debts.* **2.** of little or no significance; trivial. —*v.,* **-el-and-dimed** or **-eled-and-dimed, -el-and-dim·ing** or **-el·ing-and-dim·ing.** —*v.i.* to be careful about money; be frugal or stingy. —*v.t.* **1.** to be stingy to; treat cheaply: *a company that nickel-and-dimes its employees.* **2.** to

a	at	e	end	o	hot	u	up	hw	white		about
ā	ape	ē	me	ō	old	ū	use	ng	song		taken
ä	far	i	it	ô	rule	th	thin	ə	pencil
âr	care	ī	ice	oi	oil	u	pull	th	this		lemon
		ir	pierce	ou	out	ûr	turn	zh	measure		circus

N

823

weaken, damage, or destroy gradually, as by persistent small expenses or harassments: *A series of fines by the health department nickel-and-dimed the restaurant out of business.*

nick·el·o·de·on (nik′ə lō′dē ən) *n.* **1.** a motion-picture theater charging an admission price of five cents. **2.** a player piano or jukebox. [NICKEL + (MEL)ODEON.]

nick·el-plate (nik′əl plāt′) *v.t.*, -plat·ed, -plat·ing. to coat with nickel by electroplating.

nickel plate, a thin coating of nickel deposited on a metal surface by electroplating, used esp. to prevent corrosion or improve appearance.

nickel silver, any of a group of silver-colored alloys of copper, nickel, and zinc that have low electrical conductivity and good resistance to corrosion. Also, **German silver.**

nick·er (nik′ər) *n.* neigh. —*v.i.* neigh. [Probably imitative.]

nick·nack (nik′nak′) knickknack.

nick·name (nik′nām′) *n.* **1.** a descriptive word or phrase used in addition to or instead of a name: *Chicago's nickname is the "Windy City."* **2.** a familiar, usually shortened form of a name: *Kathy is a nickname for Katherine.* —*v.t.*, -named, -nam·ing. to give a nickname to: *They nicknamed him Rusty because he had red hair.* [From the incorrect division into *a nekename* of Middle English *an ekename* literally, an additional name (going back to Old English *ēaca* addition + *nama* name).]

ni·co·ti·a·na (ni kō′shē an′ə) *n.* any of several flowering tobaccos of the nightshade family, genus *Nicotiana,* grown for their fragrant flowers. [Modern Latin *nicotiana (herba),* Nicot's (plant); from Jean *Nicot,* 1530-1600, French ambassador to Portugal who first introduced tobacco into France.]

nic·o·tin·a·mide (nik′ə tin′ə mīd′) *n.* a member of the vitamin B complex that occurs in coenzymes and is similar to, and found in virtually the same foods as, niacin, but lacks niacin's vasodilation properties. Formula: $C_6H_6N_2O$

nic·o·tine (nik′ə tēn′) *n.* a poisonous, addictive, oily alkaloid found in the leaves, roots, and seeds of the tobacco plant. Formula: $C_{10}H_{14}N_2$ [From Jean *Nicot,* 1530-1600, French ambassador to Portugal, who introduced tobacco into France.]

nic·o·tin·ic (nik′ə tin′ik) *adj.* of or relating to niacin or nicotine. [NICOTIN(E) + -IC.]

nicotinic acid, niacin. [NICOTINE + -IC; because obtained by the oxidation of nicotine.]

nic·ti·tate (nik′ti tāt′) *v.i.,* -tat·ed, -tat·ing. to blink rapidly, as with a nictitating membrane. Also, **nic·tate** (nik′tāt). [Medieval Latin *nictitatus,* past participle of *nictitare.*] —**nic′ti·ta′tion,** *n.*

nictitating membrane, a transparent, movable fold of skin lying below the outer eyelids and attached at the inner corner of the eye. It occurs in amphibians, reptiles, birds, and some mammals, and functions to wipe the eye clean.

niece (nēs) *n.* **1.** the daughter of one's brother or sister. **2.** the daughter of one's brother-in-law or sister-in-law. [Old French *n(i)ece,* going back to Latin *neptis* niece, granddaughter.]

niels·bohr·i·um (nēlz bôr′ē əm) *n.* hahnium.

nif·ty (nif′tē) *adj.,* -ti·er, -ti·est. *Informal.* fine, dandy, or stylish: *a nifty idea, a nifty party.* [Possibly from MAGNIFICENT.]

nig·gard (nig′ərd) *n.* a stingy person; skinflint; miser. —*adj.* niggardly. [Of Scandinavian origin.]

nig·gard·ly (nig′ərd lē) *adj.* **1.** tight-fisted; miserly; penurious. **2.** small or scanty; paltry; meager: *a niggardly amount.* —*adv.* in a niggardly manner; stingily. —**nig′gard·li·ness,** *n.*

nig·gling (nig′ling) *adj.* **1.** having or showing too much concern with details or trivial matters: *the niggling manner of bureaucrats.* **2.** demanding close attention to details: *niggling work.* —*n.* too much concern with details or trivial matters. [From *niggle* to trifle, carp[1] + -ING[2].]

nigh (nī) *Archaic. adv.* **1.** near; close: *The carriage drew nigh.* **2.** practically; almost: *It's nigh onto midnight.* —*adj.,* **nigh·er, nigh·est** or **next.** near; close: *the hour is nigh.* —*prep.* near; close to. [Old English *nēah* near.]

night (nīt) *n.* **1.** the period of darkness between the setting and the rising of the sun; time from sunset to sunrise. **2.** the beginning of night; nightfall. **3.** the darkness of night; the dark; darkness. **4.** a state or time of mental or spiritual darkness: *In the real dark night of the soul it is always three o'clock in the morning* (F. Scott Fitzgerald, 1936). [Old English *niht* period of darkness between evening and morning.]

night blindness, an inability to see normally in dim light, often caused by a deficiency of vitamin A. —**night-blind** (nīt′blīnd′), *adj.*

night-bloom·ing cereus (nīt′blü′ming) any of several American cactuses of the genera *Hylocereus, Nyctocereus,* or *Selenicereus,* bearing large, fragrant, usually white flowers that open at night.

night·cap (nīt′kap′) *n.* **1.** a soft cloth cap worn esp. in bed.

2. *Informal.* an alcoholic drink taken just before going to bed. **3.** *Informal.* the last event in a sports program, esp. the second game in a baseball double-header.

night·clothes (nīt′klōz′, -klōthz) *also,* **night clothes.** *pl. n.* garments worn in bed, such as pajamas.

night·club (nīt′klub′) *also,* **night club.** *n.* a place of entertainment open until late at night, usually serving food and drink and offering a show.

night crawler, any large earthworm, esp. one that appears at night.

night·dress (nīt′dres′) *n.* **1.** nightgown. **2.** nightclothes.

night·fall (nīt′fôl′) *n.* the end of the day; beginning of night.

night·gown (nīt′goun′) *n.* **1.** a loose gown worn in bed by women or children. **2.** nightshirt.

night·hawk (nīt′hôk′) *n.* **1.** any of various American nightjars, genus *Chordeiles,* related to and resembling the whippoorwill, and having mottled, predominantly gray plumage. Length: 10 inches (25 centimeters). **2.** night owl.

night·in·gale (nī′tən gāl′, nī′ting-) *n.* a small, migratory European thrush, *Luscinia megarhyncha,* having predominantly reddish brown plumage and a whitish breast, noted for the rich, melodious song of the male.

nighthawk

Length: 6½ inches (17 centimeters). [Old English *nihtegale,* from *niht* night + *galan* to sing.]

night·jar (nīt′jär′) *n.* any of various mostly nocturnal, insect-eating birds, family Caprimulgidae, related to the whippoorwill and found in temperate and tropical regions throughout the world, having plumage that is a mixture of buff, gray, black, and white. Length: 7½-11½ inches (19-29 centimeters). Also, **goatsucker.** [NIGHT + JAR[2]; because the male makes a jarring noise.]

night latch, a door latch opened from the inside by a knob and from the outside only by a key.

night letter, a telegram sent at night at a reduced rate and delivered the following morning.

night-light (nīt′līt′) *n.* a small light kept burning all night, as in a bedroom, hall, or bathroom.

night·long (*adj.,* nīt′lông′; *adv.,* nīt′lông′) *adj.* lasting through the whole night: *a nightlong vigil.* —*adv.* through the whole night.

night·ly (nīt′lē) *adj.* done, occurring, or appearing at night or every night. —*adj.* at night or every night.

night·mare (nīt′mâr′) *n.* **1.** a dream producing feelings of great anxiety or intense fear. **2.** any experience or condition resembling a nightmare; something horrible or frightening. **3.** an evil spirit formerly thought to oppress people during sleep. [NIGHT + obsolete *mare* horrible dream, from Old English *mare.*] —**night′mar·ish,** *n.*

night owl *Informal.* a person who often stays up late at night.

night-rid·er (nīt′rī′dər) *n.* a member of any of various vigilante groups that perform acts of violence at night for the purpose of intimidation, terrorizing, or revenge, esp. a member of such a group in the southern United States after the American Civil War.

night school, a school held in the evening, esp. for those unable to attend during the day.

night·shade (nīt′shād′) *n.* **1.** any of various plants, genus *Solanum,* of the family Solanaceae, having lobed leaves and small five-petaled flowers of various colors, esp. the bittersweet and black nightshade. **2.** any of various related plants, such as belladonna. —*adj.* designating a large family, Solanaceae, of herbs, trees, and shrubs of warm regions, including the potato, tomato, eggplant, petunia, morning glory, tobacco, and belladonna. [Old English *nihtscada* literally, shade of night; probably because it was used to induce sleep.]

night·shirt (nīt′shûrt′) *n.* a long shirt worn in bed, esp. by a man or boy.

night soil, human excrement gathered for use as fertilizer. [Because it was originally collected at night.]

night·stick (nīt′stik′) *n.* a long, slender club carried by a police officer. Also, **billy, billy club.**

night·time (nīt′tīm′) *n.* the period of time between dusk and dawn.

night·walk·er (nīt′wô′kər) *n.* a person who roves about during the night, esp. for criminal purposes.

night watch 1. a watch or guard kept during the night. **2.** a person who keeps such a watch. **3.** a period of watch at night.

ni·hil·ism (nī′ə liz′əm) *n.* **1.** the total rejection of all existing political and social institutions and traditional religious and moral values. **2.** *also,* **Nihilism.** a revolutionary movement in Russia in the late nineteenth century that opposed existing social and

political institutions and advocated the use of assassination and terrorism. **3.** any violent revolutionary movement advocating terrorism or anarchy. **4.** *Philosophy.* **a.** the doctrine that nothing exists. **b.** the doctrine that there is no basis for knowledge or truth. [Latin *nihil* nothing + -ISM.] —**ni′hil·ist,** *n.* —**ni′hil·is′·tic,** *adj.*

-nik *suffix* (used to form nouns) a person who is, has to do with, or advocates: *beatnik, peacenik.* [Yiddish *-nik* and Russian *-nik.*]

Ni·ke (nī′kē) *n.* in Greek mythology, the goddess of victory, usually represented as a winged figure.

nil (nil) *n.* nothing; zero. —*adj.* nonexistent: *My knowledge of the subject is nil.* [Latin *nil,* contraction of *nihil* nothing.]

nil·gai (nil′gī) *n., pl.* -**gais** or -**gai.** a large, Indian antelope, *Boselaphus tragocamelus,* mostly gray, the male having a throat tuft and short horns. Height: 6 1/2 feet (1.9 meters) at the shoulder. Also, **nil·gau** (nil′gô). [Persian *nilgāw* literally, blue cow, from *nil* blue + *gāw* cow.]

nim·ble (nim′bəl) *adj.,* -**bler,** -**blest. 1.** light and quick in movement: *a nimble dancer.* **2.** quick to perceive, understand, or respond: *a nimble mind.* [Middle English *nymel* quick, agile, going back to Old English *niman* to take.] —**nim′ble·ness,** *n.* —**nim′bly,** *adv.*

nim·bo·stra·tus (nim′bō strā′təs, -strat′əs) *n., pl.* -**tus.** a low, dark gray, shapeless cloud layer, usually bringing rain or snow. For illustration, see **cloud.**

nim·bus (nim′bəs) *n., pl.* -**bi** (-bī) or -**bus·es. 1.** a disk or ring of light surrounding the head of a deity, saint, or other sacred person in a painting. **2.** a bright cloud thought to surround a deity when on earth. **3.** an aura of splendor or glory surrounding a person or thing. **4.** a gray rain cloud that covers the sky; nimbostratus. [Latin *nimbus* cloud.]

nim·rod (nim′rod) *also,* **Nim·rod.** *n.* a great hunter. [From *Nimrod,* in the Old Testament, a mighty hunter.]

Ni·ña (nēn′yə) *n.* one of the three ships of the Italian explorer Christopher Columbus on his first voyage to the New World, in 1492.

nin·com·poop (nin′kəm püp′, ning′-) *n. Informal.* a silly or stupid person; fool; blockhead. —**nin′com·poop′er·y,** *n.*

nine (nīn) *n.* **1.** the cardinal number that is one more than eight. **2.** a symbol representing this number, such as 9 or IX. **3.** something having this many units or members, such as a playing card or a baseball team. —*adj.* numbering one more than eight. [Old English *nigon.*]

nine days′ wonder, something that creates great excitement or interest for a short time.

nine·fold (nīn′fōld′) *adj.* **1.** nine times as great or numerous. **2.** having or consisting of nine parts. —*adv.* so as to be nine times greater or more numerous.

nine·pin (nīn′pin′) *n.* **1.** ninepins. a bowling game using nine bottle-shaped wooden pins and a large ball. ➡ used as singular. **2.** a pin used in this game.

nine·teen (nīn′tēn′) *n.* **1.** the cardinal number that is nine more than ten. **2.** a symbol representing this number, such as 19 or XIX. **3.** something having this many units or members. —*adj.* numbering nine more than ten. [Old English *nigontȳne.*]

nine·teenth (nīn′tēnth′) *adj.* **1.** (the ordinal of nineteen) next after the eighteenth. **2.** being one of nineteen equal parts. —*n.* **1.** something that is next after the eighteenth. **2.** one of nineteen equal parts; 1/19. —*adv.* in the nineteenth place.

nine·ti·eth (nīn′tē ith) *adj.* **1.** (the ordinal of ninety) next after the eighty-ninth. **2.** being one of ninety equal parts. —*n.* **1.** something that is next after the eighty-ninth. **2.** one of ninety equal parts; 1/90. —*adv.* in the ninetieth place.

nine·ty (nīn′tē) *n.* **1.** the cardinal number that is nine times ten. **2.** a symbol representing this number, such as 90 or XC. **3. the nineties.** the number series from ninety through ninety-nine. ➡ used esp. in reference to the tenth decade of a century or of a person's life. —*adj.* numbering nine times ten. [Old English *nigontig.*]

nin·ja (nin′jə) *n., pl.* -**jas** or -**ja.** a member of a Japanese society in feudal times that practiced martial arts and engaged in secret activities including assassination. [From Japanese *ninja;* of Chinese origin.]

nin·ny (nin′ē) *n., pl.* -**nies.** a fool; simpleton.

ninth (nīnth) *adj.* **1.** (the ordinal of nine) next after the eighth. **2.** being one of nine equal parts. —*n.* **1.** something that is next after the eighth. **2.** one of nine equal parts; 1/9. —*adv.* in the ninth place.

Ni·o·be (nī′ō bē′) *n.* in Greek legend, a queen of Thebes who angered the gods by boasting of the number and beauty of her children. Apollo and Artemis killed her children, causing her to weep unceasingly. She was then turned into a stone from which tears continued to flow.

ni·o·bi·um (nī ō′bē əm) *n.* a steel-gray or silvery white metallic

element that is used in alloys and superconductors. Symbol: **Nb** For tables, see **element.** [Modern Latin *niobium,* from *Niobe,* who was the daughter of Tantalus; referring to the element's similarity to tantalum.]

nip[1] (nip) *v.,* **nipped, nip·ping.** —*v.t.* **1.** to seize, as between two surfaces, and pinch or bite: *The parrot nipped its owner's finger.* **2.** to sever by pinching, cutting, or biting (usually with *off* or *out*): *The gardener nipped the dead leaves off the bush.* **3.** to cause (something) to smart or sting: *The cold night air nipped my fingers.* **4.** to check or destroy the development or growth of: *The late frost nipped the fruit trees. We nipped the rumor before it spread.* —*v.i. Informal.* to move or go quickly: *I'll nip around the corner to the store for some milk.* —*n.* **1.** the act or an instance of nipping. **2.** a small portion or quantity; little bit. **3.** sharp, biting cold; chill: *There is a nip in the air today.* **4.** a sharp or pungent flavor; tang: *The chili sauce has quite a nip.* [Middle English *nippen, nyppe* to pinch, from Middle Low German *nippen* or Old Norse *hnippa.*]

·**nip and tuck.** *Informal.* so close or even as to leave the outcome in doubt: *The game was nip and tuck until the last inning.*

nip[2] (nip) *n.* a little drink of liquor: *a nip of brandy.* —*v.t., v.i.,* **nipped, nip·ping.** to drink (liquor) in nips. [Short for obsolete *nipperkin* small vessel for measuring liquors, from Dutch *nippertje* small measure for liquids, from *nippen* to sip.]

ni·pa (nē′pə) *n.* a palm, *Nipa fruticans,* native from East India to Australia, having leaves that are used for thatching, basketry, and cigarette wrappers and an inflorescence that is tapped for sugar. [Modern Latin *nipa,* from Spanish *nipa,* from Malay *nīpah.*]

nip·per (nip′ər) *n.* **1.** a person or thing that nips. **2. nippers.** any of various tools that seize and hold or cut, such as pincers or pliers. **3.** one of the large claws of a crustacean. **4.** *Informal.* a small boy.

nip·ple (nip′əl) *n.* **1.** a small conical projection at the center of the breast or udder that, in the female, contains the opening of the milk ducts. **2.** the rubber mouthpiece of a baby's bottle. **3.** anything resembling a nipple in shape or function, such as a short piece of pipe threaded at each end for use as a coupling. [Possibly diminutive of NIB, NEB.]

Nip·pon·ese (nip′ə nēz′, -nēs′) *n., pl.* -**ese.** Japanese. —*adj.* Japanese.

nip·py (nip′ē) *adj.,* -**pi·er,** -**pi·est. 1.** cold or chilling in a sharp, biting way: *The air is a bit nippy tonight.* **2.** tending or likely to nip: *a nippy dog.*

nir·va·na (nir vä′nə, -van′ə) *also,* **Nir·va·na.** *n.* **1.** in Buddhism, the highest attainable state of bliss, in which all desire and suffering are extinguished and the soul becomes a part of the supreme universal soul. **2.** any place or condition free from care or pain. [Sanskrit *nirvāna* extinction.]

Ni·sei (nē′sā′) *n., pl.* -**sei.** a person born and educated in the United States or Canada, whose parents were immigrants from Japan. [Japanese *nisei* literally, second generation, from *ni* second + *sei* generation.]

nit (nit) *n.* the egg or young of a parasitic insect, such as a louse. [Old English *hnitu.*]

ni·ter (nī′tər) *also,* **nitre.** *n.* **1.** potassium nitrate. **2.** sodium nitrate. [French *nitre,* from Latin *nitrum,* from Greek *nitron,* possibly from Hebrew *netr* or Egyptian *ntr.*]

nit·pick (nit′pik′) *v.i.* to be overly concerned with minor faults or unimportant details. —**nit′pick′er,** *n.* —**nit′pick′ing,** *n.*

ni·trate (nī′trāt) *n.* **1.** a salt or ester of nitric acid. **2.** sodium nitrate or potassium nitrate used as a fertilizer. **3.** sodium nitrate used as a preservative in processed meats. —*v.t.,* -**trat·ed,** -**trat·ing.** to treat or combine with nitric acid or a nitrate. —**ni·tra′·tion,** *n.*

ni·tre (nī′tər) niter.

ni·tric (nī′trik) *adj.* of or containing nitrogen, esp. of a higher valence. [French *nitrique,* from *nitre* saltpeter. See NITER.]

nitric acid, a colorless, highly corrosive liquid compound that is one of the strongest known oxidizing agents, used in the manufacture of explosives, nitrate fertilizers, and dyes. Formula: HNO_3

nitric oxide, a colorless gas that is liberated when nitric acid reacts with copper. Formula: NO

ni·tride (nī′trīd, -trid) *n.* a compound of nitrogen with another element that is more electropositive, such as calcium, boron, or lithium.

ni·tri·fi·ca·tion (nī′trə fi kā′shən) *n.* the oxidation of ammonia into nitrites or nitrates, esp. by the action of bacteria in the soil.

a	at	e	end	o	hot	u	up	hw	white		about
ā	ape	ē	me	ō	old	ū	use	ng	song		taken
ä	far	i	it	ô	fork	ü	rule	th	thin	ə	pencil
âr	care	ī	ice	oi	oil	u̇	pull	th	this		lemon
		îr	pierce	ou	out	ûr	turn	zh	measure		circus

825

ni·tri·fy (nī′trə fī′) *v.t.*, **-fied, -fy·ing. 1.** to oxidize into nitrites or nitrates, esp. by the action of bacteria in the soil. **2.** to cause to be permeated with nitrates. —**ni′tri·fi′er,** *n.*

ni·trite (nī′trīt) *n.* **1.** a salt or ester of nitrous acid. **2.** sodium nitrite used as a preservative in processed meats.

ni·tro (nī′trō) *n. Informal.* nitroglycerin. —*adj.* (of a chemical compound) containing the group —NO_2.

ni·tro·bac·te·ri·a (nī′trō bak tîr′ē ə) *n.* any of various soil bacteria that are involved in nitrification.

ni·tro·ben·zene (nī′trō ben′zēn, -ben zēn′) *n.* a poisonous, yellow liquid compound, used esp. to make aniline. Formula: $C_6H_5NO_2$.

ni·tro·cel·lu·lose (nī′trə sel′yə lōs′) *n.* any of a number of flammable organic compounds produced by adding a mixture of concentrated sulfuric and nitric acids to cellulose, used in the manufacture of plastics, lacquers, and explosives. Also, **cellulose nitrate.**

ni·tro·gen (nī′trə jən) *n.* a colorless, odorless, tasteless, gaseous element that makes up about 78% of the volume of the air at sea level. Nitrogen is essential to all forms of life and is used in making ammonia, nitric acid, and fertilizers. Symbol: **N** For tables, see **element.** [French *nitrogène,* from Greek *nitron* (see NITER) + *-genēs* (see -GEN).] —**ni·trog·e·nous** (nī troj′ə nəs), *adj.*

nitrogen balance, the global circulation and reutilization of nitrogen, largely by metabolic processes. Atmospheric nitrogen, converted by bacteria into compounds used by plants and animals to form proteins, is returned to the atmosphere through the bacterial decomposition of decaying organic matter.

nitrogen cycle, a continuous series of chemical changes by which nitrogen circulates between air, soil, and living organisms. Free nitrogen in the atmosphere passes into the soil, where it is converted by nitrogen-fixing bacteria into soluble compounds for use by plants and animals. When the plant and animal matter decays or burns, nitrogen is released to the atmosphere, completing the cycle.

nitrogen dioxide, a poisonous, brown gas that dissolves in water to form nitric acid and is an atmospheric pollutant produced by automobile engines. Formula: NO_2

nitrogen fixation 1. the conversion of free nitrogen in the atmosphere into nitrogenous compounds that can be utilized by plants, through the action of certain bacteria living in soil or on the roots of such plants as peas or beans. **2.** the conversion of free nitrogen to useful nitrogen compounds by any of various other processes, esp. by chemical means in the production of industrial products.

ni·tro·gen-fix·ing (nī′trə jən fik′sing) *adj.* assisting or involved in the process of nitrogen fixation: *nitrogen-fixing bacteria.*

ni·trog·en·ize (nī troj′ə nīz′) *v.t.*, **-ized, -iz·ing.** to combine with nitrogen or with a nitrogen compound. [NITROGEN + -IZE.] —**ni·trog′en·i·za′tion,** *n.*

nitrogen mustard, any of a class of toxic compounds similar to mustard gas but containing nitrogen instead of sulfur, used to treat certain kinds of cancer.

ni·tro·glyc·er·in (nī′trə glis′ər in) *also,* **ni·tro·glyc·er·ine.** *n.* a colorless, oily, liquid organic compound that is poisonous and very explosive. Weak alcohol solutions of nitroglycerin are used to treat heart disease. Formula: $C_3H_5N_3O_9$

ni·tros·a·mine (nī tros′ə mēn′, nī′trəs am′in) *n.* any of a group of organic compounds that contain a nitrate linked to an amine. Certain nitrosamines produced by the metabolism of nitrite preservatives, as used in bacon and other processed meats, are carcinogenic.

ni·trous (nī′trəs) *adj.* **1.** of or containing nitrogen, esp. of a lower valence. **2.** of or containing niter. [Latin *nitrōsus* full of natron, from *nitrum* natron. See NITER.]

nitrous acid, an unstable compound of nitrogen occurring only in solution or in the form of its salts. Formula: HNO_2

nitrous oxide, a gas with a sweetish odor and taste that produces an exhilarating effect when breathed in small amounts. It is used as an anesthetic. Formula: N_2O Also, **laughing gas.**

nit·ty-grit·ty (nit′ē grit′ē) *n.* the basic part or parts; practical essentials; fundamental details: *Let's concentrate on the nitty-gritty of this plan and ignore the unimportant factors.* [A rhyming formation from GRITTY.]

nit·wit (nit′wit′) *n.* a stupid or foolish person. [Dialectal German *nit,* form of *nicht* not + WIT¹.]

nix¹ (niks) *Slang. n.* nothing. —*adv.* no. —*interj.* watch out! stop! —*v.t.* to reject or put a stop to: *The boss nixed our proposals.* [German *nix,* informal form of *nichts* nothing.]

nix² (niks) *n., pl.* **nix·es.** in German mythology, a water sprite who can change shape at will, appearing at times as part fish and part human. [German *Nix.*]

NJ, the postal abbreviation for New Jersey.

N.J., New Jersey.

NLRB, National Labor Relations Board.

NM, the postal abbreviation for New Mexico.

N. Mex. *also,* **N.M.** New Mexico.

NMR, nuclear magnetic resonance.

NNE, north-northeast.

NNW, north-northwest.

no¹ (nō) *adv.* **1.** certainly not; not so. ➡ used to express denial, disagreement, dissent, or refusal: *No, I don't want to do it. No, that's not right.* ➡ opposed to **yes. 2.** not at all. **3.** used with a comparative: *That one is no worse than the others.* **3.** not: *whether or no.* —*interj.* used to express amazement, bewilderment, or skepticism. —*n., pl.* **noes. 1.** the saying of the word "no"; negative response; refusal; denial. ➡ opposed to **yes. 2.** a negative vote or voter: *The noes have it.* [Old English *nā* never, from *ne* not + *ā* ever.]

no² (nō) *adj.* **1.** not any: *There were no mistakes in my addition. They've had no food all day.* **2.** not a: *The candidate is no financial expert.* [Form of NONE.]

No, the symbol for nobelium.

No. 1. north. **2.** northern. **3.** *also,* **no.** number.

no-ac·count (nō′ə kount′) *Informal. adj.* worth no respect or consideration; good-for-nothing: *a no-account loafer.* —*n.* a person who deserves no respect or consideration because he or she is idle or shiftless.

no·be·li·um (nō bē′lē əm) *n.* an artificial radioactive metallic element produced by bombarding curium. Symbol: **No** For tables, see **element.** [Modern Latin *nobelium,* from Alfred B. Nobel, 1833-96, Swedish chemist and industrialist.]

No·bel prize (nō bel′) any of various international prizes originally established by the will of the Swedish industrialist Alfred Nobel, awarded annually for accomplishments in the fields of physics, chemistry, physiology or medicine, economics, and literature, and for the promotion of peace.

no·bil·i·ty (nō bil′i tē) *n., pl.* **-ties. 1.** a class of people in a society having hereditary title, rank, and privileges: *A duke and duchess are members of the nobility.* **2.** the state or quality of being distinguished by superior birth or rank. **3.** the state or quality of having or showing greatness of character or superior merit. [Latin *nōbilitās.*]

no·ble (nō′bəl) *adj.,* **-bler, -blest. 1.** distinguished by superior birth, rank, or title; aristocratic. **2.** having or showing greatness of character: *a noble mind.* **3.** having superior merit; worthy: *noble sentiments, a noble cause, noble conduct.* **4.** impressive in appearance; splendid; magnificent: *a noble oak tree.* **5.** chemically inert or inactive. —*n.* **1.** a person who is distinguished by superior birth, rank, or title; nobleman or noblewoman. **2.** a former English gold coin. [Old French *noble* relating to the upper classes, superior in dignity and merit, from Latin *nōbilis* famous, of noble birth.] —**no′ble·ness,** *n.* —**no′bly,** *adv.*

noble gas, any of a group of six chemically nonreactive gaseous elements that, in order of increasing atomic weight, consists of helium, neon, argon, krypton, xenon, and radon. Also, **rare gas.**

no·ble·man (nō′bəl mən) *n., pl.* **-men** (-mən). a man of noble birth, rank, or title.

no·blesse o·blige (nō bles′ ō blēzh′) the obligation of those of noble birth or rank to behave nobly toward others. [French *noblesse oblige* literally, rank is under an obligation, going back to Latin *nōbilis* (see NOBLE) + *obligāre* (see OBLIGATE).]

no·ble·wom·an (nō′bəl wŭm′ən) *n., pl.* **-wom·en** (-wim′ən). a woman of noble birth, rank, or title.

no·bod·y (nō′bod′ē, -bə dē) *pron.* no person; no one. —*n., pl.* **-bod·ies.** a person of no importance, authority, or social position. —For Usage Note, see **anybody.**

nock (nok) *n.* **1.** a notch at either end of a bow that holds the bowstring. **2.** a notch at the end of an arrow for receiving the bowstring. —*v.t.* **1.** to put a notch in (an arrow or bow). **2.** to fit (an arrow) to the bowstring ready for shooting. [Middle Dutch *nocke* notch.]

noc·tur·nal (nok tûr′nəl) *adj.* **1.** of or occurring at night: *nocturnal sounds, a nocturnal walk.* **2.** active at night: *The raccoon is a nocturnal animal.* **3.** (of a flower) opening at night and closing during the day. ➡ opposed to **diurnal** in defs. 2 and 3. [Late Latin *nocturnālis* for night use, from Latin *nocturnus* relating to night, from *nox* night.] —**noc·tur′nal·ly,** *adv.*

noc·turne (nok′tûrn′) *n.* **1.** a musical composition of a dreamy or romantic character appropriate to the evening. **2.** a painting of a night scene. [French *nocturne,* from Latin *nocturnus* relating to night.]

nod (nod) *v.,* **nod·ded, nod·ding.** —*v.i.* **1.** to lower briefly and then raise the head, as in greeting or agreement. **2.** to let the head fall forward with a quick, involuntary motion, as when sleepy: *The student sat nodding over the dull book.* **3.** to bend forward with a swaying motion: *The grasses nodded as the breeze swept over the field.* —*v.t.* **1.** to lower briefly and then raise (the head), as in

greeting or agreement. **2.** to show or express by nodding: *to nod approval.* **3.** to summon, invite, or send away by nodding. —*n.* a lowering and raising of the head, as in greeting or agreement. [Of uncertain origin.] —**nod′der,** *n.*

•**to nod off.** to fall asleep, esp. while in a sitting position.

nod·dy (nod′ē) *n., pl.* **-dies. 1.** a fool; simpleton. **2.** any of several tropical terns, genus *Anous,* having dark brown plumage and a short tail. [Of uncertain origin.]

node (nōd) *n.* **1.** a knot, knob, or swelling. **2.** a mass of tissue that resembles a knot, such as a lymph node. **3.** a point on a stem from which a leaf or branch grows; joint. For illustration, see **wheat. 4.** *Physics.* a point, line, or plane in a vibrating body where there is no motion. **5.** *Astronomy.* either of two points at which the orbit of a celestial body intersects the ecliptic. [Latin *nōdus* knot.] —**nod′al,** *adj.*

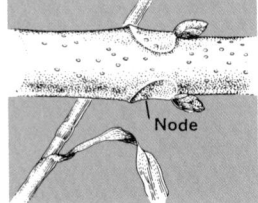

Node

nod·ule (noj′ūl) *n.* **1.** a small knot, swelling, or growth, as on plant or animal tissue. **2.** a small, rounded mass or lump, as of some mineral substance. [Latin *nōdulus* little knot, diminutive of *nōdus* knot.] —**nod·u·lar** (noj′ə lər), *adj.*

no·ël (nō el′) *n.* **1.** a Christmas carol. **2. Noël.** Christmas. [French *noël,* going back to Latin *nātālis* relating to one's birth (with reference to the birthday of Christ), from *nāsci* to be born.]

no-fault (nō′fôlt′) *adj.* **1.** of or relating to a form of automobile insurance under which compensation for injury or damage suffered in an accident is provided by an insurance company regardless of whether the holder of the insurance was responsible for the accident. **2.** of or relating to a form of divorce that requires only that the husband and wife desire to end the marriage, with no finding of blame.

no-frills (nō′frilz′) *adj.* basic and unadorned; without extras or embellishments: *a no-frills airline flight without refreshments.*

nog·gin (nog′in) *n.* **1.** a small mug or cup. **2.** a small quantity of drink, esp. liquor, equal to about one fourth of a pint. **3.** *Informal.* a person's head. [Of uncertain origin.]

no-good (*adj.* nō′gŭd′, -gŭd′; *n.* nō′gŭd′) *adj.* useless or worthless. —*n.* a person who is idle, useless, or worthless.

no-hit·ter (nō′hit′ər) *n.* a baseball game in which a pitcher does not allow the opposing team to make any base hits.

no·how (nō′hou′) *adv. Slang.* in no way; not at all.

noise (noiz) *n.* **1.** a sound that is loud, harsh, or unpleasant: *The noise of the traffic made it difficult to sleep.* **2.** any sound: *I heard a noise outside the window.* **3.** a loud outcry or shouting, as of many voices; uproar; disturbance. **4.** unwanted electrical interference, as in a radio signal. —*v.t.,* **noised, nois·ing.** to spread by rumor or report (usually with *abroad* or *about*): *It was noised about that you were leaving the company.* [Old French *noise* uproar, noise, from Latin *nausea.* See NAUSEA.]

noise·less (noiz′lis) *adj.* making no noise; silent; quiet: *noiseless movements, a noiseless fan.* —**noise′less·ly,** *adv.* —**noise′less·ness,** *n.*

noise·mak·er (noiz′mā′kər) *n.* something that makes noise, esp. a horn, rattle, or other device used to make noise at a celebration.

noise pollution, environmental noise, such as that made by jet airplanes, traffic, or machinery, that is harmful or annoying.

noi·some (noi′səm) *adj.* **1.** offensive to the sense of smell: *a noisome odor.* **2.** harmful to health; injurious: *noisome fumes.*

[Obsolete *noy* to vex (short for ANNOY) + -SOME[1].] —**noi′some·ly,** *adv.* —**noi′some·ness,** *n.*

nois·y (noi′zē) *adj.,* **nois·i·er, nois·i·est. 1.** making noise: *noisy children.* **2.** full of or characterized by noise: *a noisy argument.* —**nois′i·ly,** *adv.* —**nois′i·ness,** *n.*

no-load (nō′lōd′) *adj.* sold without charging a sales commission: *a no-load mutual fund.*

no·mad (nō′mad) *n.* **1.** a member of a group or tribe that has no permanent home and moves from place to place in search of food. **2.** any person who wanders from place to place. —*adj.* nomadic. [Latin *nomad-,* stem of *nomas* wanderer, from Greek *nomas* wandering, as in search of pasture, from *nomos* pasture.] —**no′mad·ism,** *n.*

no·mad·ic (nō mad′ik) *adj.* of, relating to, or resembling nomads; wandering: *nomadic tribes.* —**no·mad′i·cal·ly,** *adv.*

no-man's-land (nō′manz′land′) *n.* **1.** a tract of unowned or barren land. **2.** the land between two opposing armies, not controlled by either one. **3.** an area of thought or activity that is indefinite or uncertain: *the no-man's-land between fact and fiction.*

nom de guerre (nom′də gâr′; *French* nôɴ də geʀ′) *pl.* **noms de guerre** (nomz′də gâr′; *French* nôɴ də geʀ′). pseudonym.

nom de plume (nom′ də plüm′; *French* nôɴ də plʏm′) *pl.* **noms de plume** (nomz′də plüm′; *French* nôɴ də plʏm′). pen name. [Translation into French of English *pen name.*]

no·men·cla·ture (nō′mən klā′chər, nō men′klə-) *n.* a system of names or special terms, esp. in an art or science: *the nomenclature of biology.* [Latin *nōmenclātūra* calling by name, going back to *nōmen* name + *calāre* to call.]

nom·i·nal (nom′ə nəl) *adj.* **1.** being so in name but not in fact; not real or actual: *a nominal peace, a nominal ruler.* **2.** small compared with the actual value: *a nominal cost.* **3.** of, relating to, or containing a name or names: *a nominal list, a nominal account.* **4.** *Grammar.* of, relating to, or used as a noun: *a nominal adjective.* [Latin *nōminālis* relating to a name, from *nōmen* name.] —**nom′i·nal·ly,** *adv.*

nom·i·nate (nom′ə nāt′) *v.t.,* **-nat·ed, -nat·ing. 1.** to propose as a candidate for an office or honor. **2.** to appoint to an office or duty: *The mayor nominated the captain as police chief.* [Latin *nōminātus,* past participle of *nōmināre* to name, from *nōmen* name.] —**nom′i·na′tor,** *n.*

nom·i·na·tion (nom′ə nā′shun) *n.* **1.** the act or an instance of nominating. **2.** the state of being nominated: *to place a name in nomination.*

nom·i·na·tive (nom′ə nə tiv) *Grammar. adj.* of, relating to, or designating the case of the subject of a verb or of words agreeing with the subject. —*n.* **1.** the nominative case. **2.** a word in the nominative case. *I, they,* and *who* are nominatives. [Latin *nōminātīvus (cāsus)* nominative (case), from *nōmināre* to name.]

nom·i·nee (nom′ə nē′) *n.* a person who is nominated, esp. as a candidate for office.

non- *prefix* opposite or lack of; not. [Latin *nōn* not.]

non·age (non′ij, nō′nij) *n.* **1.** the period of being legally underage. **2.** any period of immaturity. [Old French *nonage* state of being under age, going back to Latin *nōn* not + *aetās* age.]

non·a·ge·nar·i·an (non′ə jə nâr′ē ən, nō′nə-) *n.* a person who is ninety or between ninety and one hundred years old. —*adj.*

N

a	at	e	end	o	hot	u	up	hw	white		about
ā	ape	ē	me	ō	old	ū	use	ng	song		taken
ä	far	i	it	ô	fork	ū	rule	th	thin	ə	pencil
âr	care	ī	ice	oi	oil	ů	pull	th	this		lemon
		îr	pierce	ou	out	ûr	turn	zh	measure		circus

The following list contains a selection of compounds that can be formed with the prefix **non-**. The meaning of a word on the list can be understood by combining the sense of the prefix and the root word.

nonabrasive	nonaffluent	nonauthoritative	noncellular	noncombustible	nonconflicting
nonabsorbent	nonaggression	nonautomatic	nonchallenging	noncommercial	nonconforming
nonacademic	nonaggressive	nonbacterial	nonchauvinist	noncommunicable	noncongenital
nonacceptance	nonagreement	nonbearing	non-Christian	noncommunicative	nonconsecutive
nonactive	nonagricultural	nonbeliever	nonchurchgoer	noncommunist	nonconservative
nonadaptive	nonallergenic	nonbelieving	noncitizen	non-Communist	nonconstructive
nonaddicting	nonallergic	nonbelligerent	nonclassical	noncompetitive	nonconsumption
nonaddictive	nonanalytic	nonbinding	nonclassified	noncomplaisant	noncontagious
nonadherence	nonaquatic	nonbiodegradable	nonclerical	nonconciliatory	noncontemporary
nonadhesive	nonaromatic	nonbreakable	nonclinical	nonconcurrence	noncontiguous
nonadjacent	nonaspirated	noncaking	noncohesive	nonconcurrent	noncontinuous
nonadjustable	nonassertive	noncaloric	noncollapsible	noncondensing	noncontributory
nonadministrative	nonassessable	noncancerous	noncollectible	nonconducting	noncontributory
nonadult	nonathletic	noncarbonated	noncollegiate	nonconductive	noncontrolling
nonaffiliated	nonattendance	noncarnivorous	noncombat	nonconfidential	noncontroversial

being ninety or between ninety and one hundred years old. [Latin *nōnāgēnārius* containing ninety (going back to *nōnāginta* ninety) + -AN.]

non·a·gon (non′ə gon′) *n.* a polygon with nine sides and nine angles. [Latin *nōnus* ninth + Greek *gōniā* angle.]

non·al·co·hol·ic (non′al kə hô′lik, -hol′ik) *adj.* containing no alcohol: *a nonalcoholic beverage.*

non·a·ligned (non′ə līnd′) *adj.* not allied with or following any major power in foreign affairs; committed to neutrality as a foreign policy. —**non′a·lign′ment,** *n.* —For Synonyms, see **neutral.**

non·ap·pear·ance (non′ə pîr′əns) *n.* a failure to appear, esp. in court as a witness or party to a suit.

nonce (nons) *n.* the present time, purpose, or occasion. ➡ used chiefly in the phrase *for the nonce.* [From the incorrect division of Middle English *(for then) ones* literally, (for the) once, into *(for the) nones.* See ONCE.]

nonce word, a word coined and used for a particular purpose or occasion.

non·cha·lance (non′shə läns′, -chə-) *n.* the state of being nonchalant.

non·cha·lant (non′shə länt′, -chə-) *adj.* characterized by or showing a lack of interest, concern, or enthusiasm; casually indifferent: *a nonchalant response.* [French *nonchalant* careless, going back to Latin *nōn* not + *calēre* to be warm.] —**non′cha·lant′ly,** *adv.*

non·com (non′kom′) *n. Informal.* a noncommissioned officer.

non·com·bat·ant (non′kəm bat′ənt, non kom′bə tənt) *n.* **1.** a member of the armed forces whose normal duties do not include fighting, such as a doctor, nurse, or chaplain. **2.** a civilian in wartime. —*adj.* not involving or engaged in combat.

non·com·mis·sioned officer (non′kə mish′ənd) an enlisted person in the armed forces promoted to a rank above other enlisted people, but who has not received a commission from the president. A sergeant and a corporal are noncommissioned officers.

non·com·mit·tal (non′kə mit′əl) *adj.* not involving or showing commitment to a particular opinion, view, or course of action: *The politician made a noncommittal statement on the issue.* —**non′com·mit′tal·ly,** *adv.*

non·com·pli·ance (non′kəm plī′əns) *n.* failure or refusal to comply: *Noncompliance with the terms of the agreement will result in court action.* —**non′com·pli′ant,** *adj., n.*

non com·pos men·tis (non′ kom′pəs men′tis) not mentally able to manage one's affairs; of unsound mind. [Latin *nōn compos mentis* literally, not having control of the mind.]

non·con·duc·tor (non′kən duk′tər) *n.* a substance that does not readily conduct some form of energy, such as heat or electricity. —**non′con·duct′ing,** *adj.*

non·con·form·ist (non′kən fôr′mist) *n.* **1.** a person who does not conform to the thoughts, actions, or beliefs held or approved by most people; unconventional person. **2.** *also,* **Nonconformist.** *British.* any Protestant who is not a member of the Church of England.

non·con·form·i·ty (non′kən fôr′mi tē) *n.* **1.** refusal to conform to conventional thought, action, or belief. **2.** a lack of conformity or agreement. **3.** *also,* **Nonconformity.** *British.* refusal to conform to the principles and requirements of the Church of England.

non·co·op·er·a·tion (non′kō op′ə rā′shən) *also,* **non·co·op·er·a·tion.** *n.* **1.** failure or refusal to cooperate with a person, group, or organization. **2.** resistance to government through civil disobedience, such as a refusal to pay taxes or perform other civic duties. —**non′co·op′er·a′tion·ist, non′co·op′er·a′tor,** *n.* —**non·co·op·er·a·tive** (non′kō op′ər ə tiv, -ə rā′tiv), *adj.*

non·dair·y (non dâr′ē) *adj.* containing no milk or milk products: *a nondairy whipped topping for desserts.*

non·de·nom·i·na·tion·al (non′di nom′ə nā′shə nəl) *adj.* not restricted to a particular religious denomination: *a nondenominational wedding ceremony.*

non·de·script (non′di skript′) *adj.* without interesting or striking characteristics or features; not distinctive; colorless: *a nondescript dress, a nondescript personality, a nondescript performance.* —*n.* a nondescript person or thing. [NON- + Latin *dēscrīptus,* past participle of *dēscrībere* to write down, represent.]

non·dis·junc·tion (non′dis jungk′shən) *n. Biology.* the failure of chromatids to separate during cell division, resulting in extra chromosomes in some sex cells and correspondingly fewer in others, sometimes resulting in certain genetic conditions, as Down syndrome.

none (nun) *pron.* **1.** no one; not one: *Several senators criticized the bill, but none voted against it.* **2.** not any: *None of the stolen money was ever recovered.* **3.** no part; nothing: *He has none of his brother's bad habits.* —*adv.* by no means; not at all; to no extent: *Help came none too soon.* [Old English *nān* no one, not any, from *ne* not + *ān* one.]

> **Usage** Traditionally, **none** has been followed by a singular verb when used to mean "not one": *None of the books was in its proper place.* Now, however, it is acceptable to use **none** with a plural verb in such constructions: *None of the passengers were aware of their narrow escape.*

non·e·lec·tro·lyte (non′i lek′trə līt′) *n.* a substance that does not ionize when dissolved in water and thus will not conduct an electric current. [NON- + ELECTROLYTE.] —**non·e·lec·tro·lyt·ic** (non′i lek′trə lit′ik), *adj.*

non·en·ti·ty (non en′ti tē) *n., pl.* -ties. **1.** a person or thing of little or no importance. **2.** something that does not exist or exists only as a figment of the imagination, such as a mermaid or unicorn.

nones¹ (nōnz) *n.* in the ancient Roman calendar, the seventh day of March, May, July, or October, and the fifth day of the other months. ➡ used as singular. [Latin *nōnae,* originally feminine plural of *nōnus* ninth, from *novem* nine; because it was the ninth day before the ides.]

nones² (nōnz) *also,* **Nones.** *pl. n.* the fifth of the seven canonical hours, or the service for it. [From Latin *nōna hōra* ninth hour (after sunrise).]

non·es·sen·tial (non′i sen′shəl) *adj.* not necessary; not essential. —*n.* a nonessential person or thing.

none·such (nun′such′) *also,* **nonsuch.** *n.* a person or thing that has no equal or is beyond comparison; paragon.

none·the·less (nun′thə les′) *adv.* nevertheless; however.

non-Eu·clid·e·an (non′ū klid′ē ən) *also,* **non-Eu·clid·i·an.** *adj.* of, relating to, or designating any geometry that is not based on the postulates of Euclid's geometry.

non·ex·ist·ent (non′eg zis′tənt, -ig-) *adj.* not existing in reality; unreal: *a nonexistent problem, a nonexistent place.* —**non′ex·ist′ence,** *n.*

non·fat (non′fat′) *adj.* (of food) having fat or fat solids removed; containing no fats: *nonfat dry milk.*

non·fat·ten·ing (non′fat′ə ning) *adj.* (of food) relatively low in carbohydrates or fats.

non·fea·sance (non fē′zəns) *n. Law.* the failure, esp. by a public official, to perform some act required by law or official duty. ➡ distinguished from **malfeasance** and **misfeasance.**

nonconvertible	nondestructive	nonecclesiastical	nonexclusive	nonfulfillment	nonimmune
noncorporate	nondetachable	nonedible	nonexempt	nonfunctional	noninclusive
noncorrectable	nondiabetic	noneducational	nonexpendable	nonfusible	nonindependent
noncorrosive	nondictatorial	noneffervescent	nonexperimental	nongaseous	nonindictable
noncriminal	nondifferentiation	nonelected	nonexplosive	nongovernmental	nonindustrial
noncritical	nondigestible	nonelection	nonfactual	nongranular	noninfectious
noncrystalline	nondiplomatic	nonelective	nonfading	nonhabitual	noninflammable
noncumulative	nondirectional	nonelectric	nonfatal	nonhazardous	noninflationary
noncyclic	nondirective	nonelectrical	nonfederal	nonhereditary	noninjurious
noncyclical	nondisclosure	noneligible	nonfederated	nonhistoric	noninstantaneous
nondeciduous	nondiscriminatory	nonemergency	nonfilterable	nonhistorical	noninstinctual
nondeductible	nondistinctive	nonemotional	nonfinite	nonhomogeneous	noninstitutional
nondeferrable	nondoctrinal	nonempirical	nonfiscal	nonhostile	nonintellectual
nondefining	nondogmatic	nonenforceable	nonfissionable	nonhuman	noninterchangeable
nondegradable	nondramatic	nonenforcement	nonflexible	nonidentical	noninterference
nondelivery	nondrinker	nonentanglement	nonflowering	nonideological	nonintersecting
nondemocratic	nondrying	nonethical	nonfluid	nonidiomatic	nonintoxicant
nondepartmental	nondurable	nonexchangeable	nonfreezing	nonimmigrant	nonintoxicating

non·fer·rous (non fer′əs) *adj.* **1.** (of a metal) containing little or no iron. **2.** relating to or designating metals other than iron or steel, such as copper or tin.

non·fic·tion (non fik′shən) *n.* prose literature other than fiction, such as essays or biographies, dealing with real or historical characters, circumstances, or events. —**non·fic′tion·al,** *adj.*

non·flam·ma·ble (non flam′ə bəl) *adj.* not likely to catch fire easily; not flammable.

no·nil·lion (nō nil′yən) *n.* **1.** in the United States, the cardinal number that is represented by 1 followed by thirty zeros. **2.** in Great Britain, the cardinal number that is represented by 1 followed by fifty-four zeros. —*adj.* numbering one nonillion. [French *nonillion* one followed by thirty zeros (from Latin *nōnus* ninth), on the model of *million.* See MILLION.] —**no·nil′lionth,** *adj., n.*

non·in·ter·ven·tion (non′in tər ven′shən) *n.* a failure or refusal to intervene, esp. the systematic practice of noninterference by a nation in the affairs of other nations. —**non′in·ter·ven′-tion·ist,** *adj., n.*

non·judg·men·tal (non′juj men′təl) *adj.* avoiding judgment based on one's personal principles or opinions; objective: *a nonjudgmental decision.*

non·ju·ror (non jūr′ər) *n.* **1.** a person who refuses to take an oath, as of allegiance. **2.** *usually,* **Nonjuror.** one of the clergymen of the Church of England who refused to swear allegiance to William III and Mary II after their accession in 1688.

non·met·al (non met′əl) *n.* a chemical element not having the character of a metal, esp. an element that tends to gain electrons and form negatively charged ions.

non·me·tal·lic (non′mə tal′ik) *adj.* **1.** not of or like metal. **2.** *Chemistry.* of, relating to, or having the characteristics of a nonmetal: *a nonmetallic element.*

non·mor·al (non môr′əl, -mor′-) *adj.* not relating to or involving morality or moral judgments; neither moral nor immoral; amoral.

non·neg·a·tive (non neg′ə tiv) *adj.* of, relating to, or designating a real number either greater than or equal to zero.

non·nu·cle·ar (non nü′klē ər, -nū′-) *adj.* **1.** not utilizing or operated by nuclear energy or power: *a nonnuclear power station, nonnuclear weapons.* **2.** not having nuclear weapons: *a nonnuclear country.*

no-no (nō′nō′) *n., pl.* **no-nos** or **no-no′s.** *Informal.* something unacceptable or improper: *Talking out loud in the library is a no-no.* [Baby-talk for NO.]

non·ob·jec·tive (non′əb jek′tiv) *adj.* characteristic of or designating a style of art in which objects are not shown as they appear in nature; abstract; nonrepresentational.

no-non·sense (nō′non′sens, -səns) *adj.* not involving or tolerating anything frivolous or impractical; practical, serious, or businesslike: *a no-nonsense approach to investment, a no-nonsense person.*

non·pa·reil (non′pə rel′) *adj.* having no equal; incomparable; matchless. —*n.* **1.** a person or thing that has no equal; paragon. **2.** a small disk of chocolate candy covered with white pellets of sugar. **3.** a 6-point blank space between lines of print. [French *nonpareil* matchless, from *non* not (from Latin *nōn*) + *pareil* equal (going back to Latin *pār*).]

non·par·ti·san (non par′tə zən) *also,* **non·par·ti·zan.** *adj.* **1.** not supporting, belonging to, or influenced by any single political party or its interests: *a nonpartisan political ticket.* **2.** not partisan; objective; disinterested: *a nonpartisan view of current issues.* —**non′par′ti·san·ship′;** *also,* **non′par′ti·zan·ship′,** *n.*

non·plus (non plus′) *v.t.,* **-plused, -plus·ing;** *also, British,* **-plussed, -plus·sing.** to put at a loss for what to say, think, or do; bewilder; perplex: *to be nonplused by an outburst of anger.* —*n.* a state of bewilderment or perplexity. [Latin *nōn plūs* no more, no further.]

non·pos·i·tive (non poz′i tiv) *adj.* of, relating to, or designating a real number either less than or equal to zero.

non·pro·duc·tive (non′prə duk′tiv) *adj.* **1.** not involved directly in the production of goods, such as managerial or sales personnel. **2.** producing or yielding little or nothing: *nonproductive soil.* —**non′pro·duc′tive·ly,** *adv.* —**non′pro·duc′tive·ness,** *n.*

non·prof·it (non prof′it) *adj.* not operated for profit: *a nonprofit organization.*

non·re·new·a·ble (non′ri nü′ə bəl, -nū′-) *adj.* not readily replaced or capable of renewal after being used up or exhausted: *Fossil fuels are nonrenewable natural resources.*

non·re·peat·ing decimal (non′ri pē′ting) an irrational number in decimal form, characterized by an infinite number of digits that do not form a sequence that repeats infinitely.

non·rep·re·sen·ta·tion·al (non′rep ri zen tā′shə nəl, -zən-) *adj.* nonobjective.

non·res·i·dent (non rez′i dənt) *adj.* not residing in a particular place, esp. not residing permanently where one works, attends school, or owns property, as for tax or voting purposes. —*n.* a person who is nonresident. —**non·res′i·dence, non·res′i·den·cy,** *n.*

non·re·sist·ance (non′ri zis′təns) *n.* **1.** the policy or practice of refusing to use force or violence to resist authority, however unjust or arbitrary. **2.** the policy or practice of refusing to use force or violence even in self-defense. —**non′re·sist′ant,** *adj., n.*

non·re·stric·tive (non′ri strik′tiv) *adj.* *Grammar.* designating a word, clause, or phrase that describes a modified element without limiting or changing the essential meaning of the sentence. In the sentence *Mr. Bridges, who is a captain in the army, has been sent to Japan,* the clause *who is a captain in the army* is nonrestrictive. ➡ opposed to **restrictive.**

non·rig·id (non rij′id) *adj.* **1.** not rigid. **2.** of, relating to, or being a type of airship whose shape is maintained by the pressure of the gas within it, rather than by the support of a framework.

non·sec·tar·i·an (non′sek târ′ē ən) *adj.* not restricted to or affiliated with any specific religious denomination or sect: *a nonsectarian service, a nonsectarian college.*

non·sense (non′sens, -səns) *n.* **1.** something that makes or has no sense, esp. language or behavior that is meaningless; absurdity: *Since we didn't know the code, the message was mere nonsense to us.* **2.** language or conduct that is annoying or lacking in good sense; foolishness: *I won't put up with any more of your nonsense.* **3.** things of no importance or value; trifles: *Don't waste your money on that nonsense.* [NON- + SENSE.]

non·sen·si·cal (non sen′si kəl) *adj.* having or making no sense; foolish; absurd: *a nonsensical statement.* —**non·sen′si·cal·ly,** *adv.*

non seq., non sequitur.

non se·qui·tur (non sek′wi tər) a statement or conclusion that does not follow logically from the statements already made or the facts given. [Latin *nōn sequitur* it does not follow, from *non* not + *sequor* to follow.]

N

a	at	e	end	o	hot	u	up	hw	white		about
ā	ape	ē	me	ō	old	ū	use	ng	song		taken
ä	far	i	it	ô	fork	ü	rule	th	thin	ə	pencil
âr	care	ī	ice	oi	oil	u̇	pull	th	this		lemon
		îr	pierce	ou	out	ûr	turn	zh	measure		circus

noninvolvement	nonmarine	nonmunicipal	nonparochial	nonpossession	nonrealistic
nonirritant	nonmarital	nonmythical	nonparticipant	nonprescriptive	nonreality
nonkosher	nonmarketable	nonnavigable	nonparticipating	nonproducer	nonreciprocal
nonlaminated	nonmaterialistic	nonnegotiable	nonparticipation	nonprofessional	nonrecognition
nonlethal	nonmathematical	nonnutritious	nonpaying	nonprogressive	nonrecoverable
nonlinear	nonmechanistic	nonnutritive	nonpayment	nonproportional	nonrecurrent
nonliquid	nonmedical	nonoccurrence	nonperformance	nonproprietary	nonrecurring
nonliterary	nonmedicinal	nonodorous	nonperishable	nonpunitive	nonredeemable
nonliturgical	nonmelodious	nonofficial	nonperishables	nonrabbinic	nonreducible
nonliving	nonmember	nonoily	nonpermanent	nonrabbinical	nonreducing
nonluminous	nonmembership	nonoperable	nonpermissive	nonracial	nonrefillable
nonmagnetic	nonmetrical	nonoperative	nonphonetic	nonradical	nonreflective
nonmalicious	nonmigratory	nonorganic	nonphysical	nonradioactive	nonregistered
nonmalignant	nonmilitant	nonorthodox	nonphysiological	nonrandom	nonregulation
nonmalleable	nonmilitary	nonowner	nonpoisonous	nonrated	nonreligious
nonmammalian	nonministerial	nonparallel	nonpolitical	nonrational	nonremovable
nonmanagerial	nonmolecular	nonparasitic	nonpolluting	nonreactive	nonremunerative
nonmanufacturing	nonmotile	nonparliamentary	nonporous	nonreader	nonrepresentative

non·skid (non′skid′) *adj.* made or designed to prevent skidding: *nonskid tires, a nonskid floor wax.*

non·stan·dard (non stan′dərd) *adj.* **1.** of or relating to usage or language that is not considered acceptable by educated users of the language. **2.** varying from the standard; not standard.

non·stick (non′stik′) *adj.* having a special coating to which food does not readily stick during cooking and that easily washes clean: *a nonstick frying pan.*

non·stop (non′stop′) *adj.* not making stops en route: *a nonstop flight.* —*adv.* without stops en route: *We flew nonstop to Rome.*

non·stri·a·ted muscle (non strī′ā tid) smooth muscle.

non·such (nun′such′) nonesuch.

non·suit (non′sūt′) *n. Law.* a judgment given against a plaintiff who fails to prosecute or provide sufficient evidence for a case. —*v.t.* to subject to a nonsuit.

non·sup·port (non′sə pôrt′) *n. Law.* failure to provide financial support for a legal dependent.

non trop·po (non trop′ō, -trō′pō, nōn-) *Music.* not too much; moderately. ➡ used to modify a direction: *allegro non troppo.* [Italian *non troppo,* from *non* not (from Latin *nōn*) + *troppo* too much (of Germanic origin).]

non·un·ion (non ūn′yən) *adj.* **1.** not employing union members; not recognizing any trade or labor unions: *a nonunion shop.* **2.** not belonging to a trade or labor union: *nonunion electricians, a nonunion profession.* **3.** not made by union labor or according to union regulations.

non·vi·a·ble (non vī′ə bəl) *adj.* **1.** not able to live or survive: *a nonviable fetus.* **2.** not practicable or workable: *a nonviable solution to a problem.*

non·vi·o·lence (non vī′ə ləns) *n.* the philosophy or practice of opposing the use of all physical force or violence. —**non·vi·o·lent,** *adj.* —**non·vi·o·lent·ly,** *adv.*

non·white (non hwīt′, -wīt′) *n.* a person who is not a light-skinned member of the Caucasoid division of the human race. —*adj.* of or relating to a nonwhite or nonwhites.

non·ze·ro (non zîr′ō) *adj.* not equal to zero.

noo·dle[1] (nü′dəl) *n.* a narrow, flat, or cylindrical strip of dried dough made from a mixture of flour, water, and eggs. [German *Nudel.*]

noo·dle[2] (nü′dəl) *n.* **1.** a silly or stupid person; fool. **2.** *Slang.* the head. [Of uncertain origin.]

nook (nůk) *n.* **1.** any small recess or corner: *a breakfast nook.* **2.** a secluded or sheltered place: *a shady nook in the woods.* [Middle English *nok,* of Scandinavian origin.]

noon (nün) *n.* **1.** twelve o'clock in the daytime; the middle of the day. **2.** the highest point: *in the bright wisdom of youth's breathless noon* (Percy Bysshe Shelley, 1817). [Old English *nōn* ninth hour after sunrise, from Latin *nōna (hōra)* ninth (hour), feminine of *nōnus* ninth, from *novem* nine. When the time of the nones was changed from three P.M. to midday, the word *noon* also came to mean midday.]

noon·day (nün′dā′) *n.* noon. —*adj.* of or occurring at noon.

no one, nobody. —For Usage Note, see **anybody.**

noon·time (nün′tīm′) *n.* noon. Also, **noon′tide′.**

noose (nüs) *n.* **1.** a loop of rope with a slipknot that allows the loop to tighten when the end of the rope is pulled. **2.** a trap or snare. —*v.t.,* **noosed, noos·ing. 1.** to capture with a noose; entrap. **2.** to tie a noose with or in. [Provençal *nous* knot, from Latin *nōdus.*]

nope (nōp) *adv. Informal.* no. [A form of NO.]

nor (nôr; *unstressed* nər) *conj.* **1.** used with a preceding *neither* or other negative to introduce another element in a series: *Neither she nor I have seen it.* **2.** used in place of *and . . . not* to continue the force of a negative: *He was not at work today, nor will he be*

there tomorrow. [Contraction of obsolete *nother,* form of NEITHER; influenced in spelling by OR.]

> **Usage** Or is generally used instead of **nor** to introduce a second negative idea in a series, if it is clear that the idea is negative: *The employee would not go on a vacation or even take a day off.*

Nor. 1. Norman. **2.** North. **3.** Norway. **4.** Norwegian.

nor·ad·ren·a·line (nôr′ə dren′ə lin) *also,* **nor·ad·ren·a·lin.** *n.* a hormone, closely related to adrenaline, that is secreted by the medulla of the adrenal glands and from nerve endings in the central and peripheral nervous systems. It constricts blood vessels and acts as a neurotransmitter. Formula: $C_8H_{11}NO_3$ Also, **norepinephrine.**

Nor·dic (nôr′dik) *adj.* **1.** of or relating to one of the divisions of the Caucasoid people, characterized by tall stature, long heads, fair skin, and blond hair, and living mainly in northern Europe, esp. Scandinavia. **2.** of or relating to skiing activities involving ski jumping or cross-country skiing. —*n.* a member of the Nordic people. [French *nordique* relating to the north, from *nord* north, going back to Old English *north.*]

nor′east·er (nôr′ēs′tər) northeaster.

nor·ep·i·neph·rine (nôr′ep ə nef′rin, -rēn) *also,* **nor·ep·i·neph·rin** (nôr′ep ə nef′rin). *n.* noradrenaline.

Nor·folk jacket (nôr′fək) a single-breasted, belted jacket having box pleats in the front and back and extending to the hips.

norm (nôrm) *n.* **1.** a rule, standard, or pattern, as of behavior: *cultural norms.* **2.** an average derived from the organization and analysis of data: *statistical norms.* [Latin *nōrma* carpenter's square, rule, pattern.]

nor·mal (nôr′məl) *adj.* **1.** conforming to an accepted standard, model, or pattern; usual; standard; typical: *Heavy traffic is normal during rush hour.* **2.** having or showing average intellectual or emotional development, as at a particular age: *According to various tests, the student's performance is normal for his age.* **3.** free from mental or emotional disturbance. **4.** *Mathematics.* perpendicular. **5.** *Chemistry.* (of a solution) containing 1 gram equivalent weight of solute per liter. —*n.* **1.** anything that is normal. **2.** a usual or standard condition or level: *Her temperature is 2 degrees above normal.* **3.** *Mathematics.* a line or plane that is perpendicular to another. [Late Latin *nōrmālis* in conformity with rule, going back to Latin *nōrma* carpenter's square, rule, pattern.]

nor·mal·cy (nôr′məl sē) *n.* normality.

normal distribution *Statistics.* a hypothetical frequency distribution represented graphically by a symmetrical, bell-shaped curve.

nor·mal·i·ty (nôr mal′i tē) *n.* the state, quality, or condition of being normal.

nor·mal·ize (nôr′mə līz′) *v.,* **-ized, -iz·ing.** —*v.t.* to cause to conform to the usual or standard condition; make normal. —*v.i.* to become normal. —**nor′mal·i·za′tion,** *n.* —**nor′mal·iz′er,** *n.*

nor·mal·ly (nôr′mə lē) *adv.* **1.** under normal circumstances; ordinarily; usually: *Normally the train takes twenty minutes to reach the next town.* **2.** in a normal manner; to behave normally.

normal school, a school that trains high school graduates to be teachers. [Partial translation of French *école normale* training school, going back to Late Latin *normālis* (see NORMAL) + Latin *schola* (see SCHOOL).]

Nor·man (nôr′mən) *n.* **1.** a member of the Scandinavian people who invaded and conquered Normandy in the tenth century A.D. **2.** one of the descendants of these people and the French who conquered England in 1066. **3.** a native or inhabitant of Normandy. **4.** Norman French. —*adj.* **1.** of or relating to Normandy or the Normans. **2.** relating to or designating a style of architecture that developed in Normandy and England in the

nonresidential	nonsegregated	nonspecific	nonsymbiotic	nontransferable	nonvibratory
nonrespondent	nonselective	nonspeculative	nonsymbolic	nontransparent	nonvintage
nonrestricted	non-self-governing	nonspiritual	nonsymmetrical	nontropical	nonviolation
nonretroactive	nonsensual	nonstaining	nonsympathizer	nontypical	nonviral
nonreturnable	nonsensuous	nonstandardized	nonsynchronous	nontyrannical	nonviscous
nonreusable	nonsexual	nonstarter	nonsystematic	nonulcerous	nonvisual
nonreversible	nonshrinkable	nonstatistical	nontarnishable	nonuniform	nonvocal
nonrural	nonsignificant	nonstrategic	nontaxable	nonurban	nonvocational
nonrusting	nonskilled	nonstriker	nontechnical	nonuser	nonvolatile
nonsalable	nonsmoker	nonstructural	nontemporal	nonutilitarian	nonvolcanic
nonsalaried	nonsmoking	nonsubscriber	nonterritorial	nonvariable	nonvoluntary
nonscheduled	nonsocial	nonsupporter	nontheatrical	nonvascular	nonvoter
nonscholastic	nonsoluble	nonsupporting	nonthreatening	nonvenomous	nonvoting
nonscientific	nonspeaking	nonsurgical	nontitular	nonverbal	nonworker
nonseasonal	nonspecialist	nonsusceptible	nontoxic	nonverifiable	nonworking

eleventh and twelfth centuries, characterized by massive construction with short, heavy columns supported by semicircular arches.

Norman Conquest, the conquest of England by the Normans under William the Conqueror in 1066.

Norman French, a dialect of French spoken by the people of Normandy in the Middle Ages. **—Nor′man-French′,** *adj.*

nor·ma·tive (nôr′mə tiv) *adj.* **1.** establishing or attempting to establish a standard or pattern: *normative rules of language usage.* **2.** derived from or based on a standard or pattern: *a normative principle.* **—nor′ma·tive·ly,** *adv.* **—nor′ma·tive·ness, nor′-ma·tiv′i·ty,** *n.*

Norse (nôrs) *adj.* **1.** of or relating to ancient Scandinavia or its people, language, or culture. **2.** Norwegian. **—n. 1. the Norse. a.** people of ancient Scandinavia. **b.** Norwegians. **2.** Old Norse. **3.** the language of Norway; Norwegian. [Dutch *Noorsch* Scandinavian, from *noord* north.]

Norse·man (nôrs′mən) *n., pl.* **-men** (-mən). a member of the people of ancient Scandinavia. Also, **Northman.**

north (nôrth) *n.* **1.** the direction to one's right as one faces the sunset. **2.** one of the four cardinal points of the compass, directly opposite south, and at zero degrees. **3.** *also,* **North.** any region situated toward this direction in relation to a specified point of reference. **—adj. 1.** toward or in the north. **2.** coming from the north: *the north wind.* **—adv.** toward the north: *to walk north.* [Old English *north* toward the region farthest from sun at noon.]

north·bound (north′bound′) *adj.* going northward: *northbound traffic.*

north·east (nôrth′ēst′; *Nautical* nôr′ēst′) *n.* **1.** the direction halfway between north and east. **2.** the point of the compass indicating this direction. **3.** *also,* **Northeast.** any region situated toward this direction in relation to a specified point of reference. **—adj. 1.** toward or in the northeast; northeastern. **2.** coming from the northeast: *a northeast wind.* **—adv.** toward the northeast.

north·east·er (nôrth′ēs′tər; *Nautical* nôr′ēs′tər) *n. also,* **nor′-east·er.** a strong wind or storm from the northeast.

north·east·er·ly (nôrth′ēs′tər lē; *Nautical* nôr′ēs′tər lē) *adj., adv.* **1.** toward the northeast. **2.** from the northeast: *northeasterly winds.*

north·east·ern (nôrth′ēs′tərn; *Nautical* nôr′ēs′tərn) *adj.* **1.** to, toward, or in the northeast. **2.** *also,* **Northeastern.** of, relating to, or characteristic of the northeast or Northeast. **3.** coming from the northeast. **—North′east′ern·er,** *n.*

north·east·ward (nôrth′ēst′wərd; *Nautical* nôr′ēst′wərd) *adv.* also, **north·east·wards.** toward the northeast. **—adj.** toward or in the northeast. **—n.** the northeastward direction, point, or part.

north·east·ward·ly (nôrth′ēst′wərd lē; *Nautical* nôr′ēst′wərd-lē) *adj., adv.* **1.** toward the northeast. **2.** from the northeast.

north·er (nôr′thər) *n.* a strong wind or storm from the north.

north·er·ly (nôr′thər lē) *adj., adv.* **1.** toward the north. **2.** from the north. **—n., pl.** **-lies.** a wind blowing from the north.

north·ern (nôr′thərn) *adj.* **1.** to, toward, or in the north. **2.** *also,* **Northern.** of, relating to, or characteristic of the north or North. **3.** coming from the north.

Northern Cross *Astronomy.* a group of five major stars and one minor star that form a cross in the constellation Cygnus.

north·ern·er (nôr′thər nər) *n.* **1.** a person who was born or lives in the north. **2.** *usually,* **Northerner.** a person who was born or lives in the northern part of the United States.

northern harrier, marsh hawk.

Northern Hemisphere, the half of the earth north of the equator.

northern lights, aurora borealis.

north·ern·most (nôr′thərn mōst′) *adj.* farthest north.

north·land (nôrth′lənd) *n.* **1.** any land in the north, such as the northern region of a country. **2. Northland.** Scandinavia. **—north′land·er,** *n.*

North·man (nôrth′mən) *n., pl.* **-men** (-mən). Norseman.

north-north·east (nôrth′nôrth′ēst′; *Nautical* nôr′nôr′ēst′) *n.* a point on the compass halfway between north and northeast. **—adj., adv.** toward the north-northeast.

north-north·west (nôrth′nôrth′west′; *Nautical* nôr′nôr′west′) *n.* a point on the compass halfway between north and northwest. **—adj., adv.** toward the north-northwest.

North Pole 1. the northernmost point on earth; the northern end of the earth's axis. **2. north pole.** the pole of a magnet that points to the north when the magnet swings freely.

North Star, Polaris.

North·um·bri·an (nôr thum′brē ən) *adj.* of or relating to Northumbria, its people, or their dialect. **—n. 1.** a member of the people inhabiting ancient Northumbria. **2.** the Old English dialect spoken in Northumbria.

north·ward (nôrth′wərd; *Nautical* nôr′thərd) *adv.* also, **north-**

wards. toward the north. **—adj.** toward or in the north. **—n.** a northward direction, point, or part.

north·ward·ly (nôrth′wərd lē; *Nautical* nôr′thərd lē) *adj., adv.* **1.** toward the north. **2.** from the north.

north·west (nôrth′west′; *Nautical* nôr′west′) *n.* **1.** the direction halfway between north and west. **2.** the point of the compass indicating this direction. **3.** *also,* **Northwest.** any region situated toward this direction in relation to a specified point of reference. **—adj. 1.** toward or in the northwest; northwestern. **2.** coming from the northwest: *a northwest wind.* **—adv.** toward the northwest.

north·west·er (nôrth′wes′tər; *Nautical* nôr′wes′tər) *n.* a strong wind or storm from the northwest.

north·west·er·ly (nôrth′wes′tər lē; *Nautical* nôr′wes′tər lē) *adj., adv.* **1.** toward the northwest. **2.** from the northwest.

north·west·ern (nôrth′wes′tərn; *Nautical* nôr′wes′tərn) *adj.* **1.** to, toward, or in the northwest. **2.** *also,* **Northwestern.** of, relating to, or characteristic of the northwest or Northwest. **3.** coming from the northwest. **—North′west′ern·er,** *n.*

north·west·ward (nôrth′west′wərd; *Nautical* nôr′west′wərd) *adv.* also, **north·west·wards.** toward the northwest. **—adj.** toward or in the northwest. **—n.** a northwestward direction, point, or part.

north·west·ward·ly (nôrth′west′wərd lē; *Nautical* nôr′west′-wərd lē) *adj., adv.* **1.** toward the northwest. **2.** from the northwest.

Nor·way maple (nôr′wā) a maple, *Acer platanoides,* native to Europe and the Caucasus, widely planted in the United States for shade and ornament.

Nor·we·gian (nôr wē′jən) *adj.* of, relating to, or characteristic of Norway or its people, language, or culture. **—n. 1.** a native or citizen of Norway. **2.** a person of Norwegian descent. **3.** the language of Norway, belonging to the northern group of the Germanic branch of the Indo-European language family.

nose (nōz) *n.* **1.** the part of the human face that contains the organ of smell and the breathing passages. **2.** the corresponding part of the head in other animals. **3.** the sense of smell. **4.** a prominent or projecting part of something, such as the bow of a ship or the front end of an airplane. **5.** the ability to perceive or detect: *a reporter with a nose for news.* **6.** *Informal.* the nose considered as a means of interfering or meddling: *Keep your nose out of this.* **—v., nosed, nos·ing. —v.t. 1.** to touch or rub with the nose; nuzzle. **2.** to push slowly or gently with or as with the nose: *Tugboats nosed the ship into the harbor.* **—v.i. 1.** to sniff: *The puppy nosed at my arm.* **2.** to move forward, esp. with caution: *The ship slowly nosed through the narrow channel.* **3.** to pry or meddle: *They tend to nose about in matters that don't concern them.* **4.** to look for: *Reporters nosed around for a good story.* [Old English *nosu* this part of the face.]

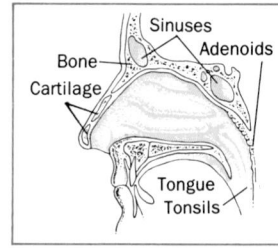

nose

- **by a nose.** by a small margin: *to win by a nose.*
- **on the nose.** *Informal.* exactly or precisely: *The play starts at eight o'clock on the nose.*
- **to count noses.** to determine the number of people present.
- **to follow one's nose. a.** to go straight ahead. **b.** to be guided by instinct.
- **to lead by the nose.** to be completely dominant over; control absolutely.
- **to look down one's nose at.** *Informal.* to hold a superior attitude toward; disdain.
- **to nose out. a.** to defeat by a small margin. **b.** to discover: *The reporter nosed out the details of the scandal.*
- **to pay through the nose.** to pay too much.
- **to put (someone's) nose out of joint.** to displease (someone).
- **to turn up one's nose at.** to express scorn or contempt for; show disdain toward.
- **under one's nose.** within one's immediate view; plainly or easily visible.

a	at	e	end	o	hot	u	up	hw	white		about
ā	ape	ē	me	ō	old	ū	use	ng	song		taken
ä	far	i	it	ô	fork	ü	rule	th	thin	ə	pencil
âr	care	ī	ice	oi	oil	u̇	pull	th	this		lemon
		îr	pierce	ou	out	ûr	turn	zh	measure		circus

nose·band (nōz′band′) *n.* the strap on a bridle or halter that passes over the animal's nose.

nose·bleed (nōz′blēd′) *n.* a bleeding from the nose.

nose cone, the conical front section of a rocket that carries the payload and is often equipped with a heat shield.

nose·dive (nōz′dīv′) *v.i.,* -dived or -dove, -diving. to take a rapid or abrupt plunge downward. —*n.* **1.** a rapid plunge downward by an aircraft, with the nose pointing toward the earth. **2.** any rapid or abrupt plunge downward, as in prices or profits.

nose·gay (nōz′gā′) *n.* a small bunch of flowers; bouquet. [NOSE + obsolete *gay* ornament (from GAY).]

nose·piece (nōz′pēs′) *n.* **1.** the part of a helmet that protects the nose. **2.** the part of a microscope, often rotatable, on which the objective lens or lenses are mounted. **3.** noseband.

nos·ey (nō′zē) *adj.,* nos·i·er, nos·i·est. nosy.

nosh (nosh) *Slang. n., pl.* nosh·es. a light meal; snack: *to have a nosh with some friends.* —*v.i.,* noshed, nosh·ing. to eat a snack. [Yiddish *nashm* a light meal, from Middle High German *naschen* to eat secretly.]

no-show (nō′shō′) *n.* **1.** a person who does not show up to take a reserved seat or use a passenger reservation, meet an appointment, or fulfill some other obligation: *The plane had empty seats because there were several no-shows.* **2.** an act or instance of failing to show up at some scheduled time.

nos·tal·gia (nos tal′jə, nas-) *n.* **1.** sentimental longing for what is past or far away: *The faded mementos of my youth filled me with nostalgia.* **2.** homesickness. [Modern Latin *nostalgia,* from Greek *nostos* return home + *algos* pain.] —nos·tal′gic, *adj.* —nos·tal′gi·cal·ly, *adv.*

nos·tril (nos′trəl) *n.* either of the two outer openings of the nose. [Middle English *nosethirl,* from Old English *nosthyrl,* from *nosu* nose + *thyrel* hole.]

nos·trum (nos′trəm) *n.* **1.** a patent medicine, esp. one that is a quack remedy. **2.** a pet scheme or favorite remedy, as for curing social ills. [Latin *nostrum,* neuter of *noster* our, ours; referring to the former use of the label *nostrum* (suggesting medicines of "our own preparation") for quack medicines.]

nos·y (nō′zē) *also,* nosey. *adj.,* nos·i·er, nos·i·est. *Informal.* unduly curious about other people's business; prying. —nos′i·ly, *adv.* —nos′i·ness, *n.*

not (not) *adv.* at no time; in no way. ➡ used to express negation, denial, refusal, or prohibition: *They are not home. You may not go.* [Contraction of NAUGHT, NOUGHT.]

no·ta be·ne (nō′tä be′ne; nō′tə bā′nē, ben′ē) *Latin.* note well; take notice.

no·ta·bil·i·ty (nō′tə bil′i tē) *n., pl.* -ties. the state or quality of being notable.

no·ta·ble (nō′tə bəl) *adj.* worthy of notice; noteworthy; remarkable: *The novelist's first book was a notable achievement.* —*n.* a person who is worthy of notice; person of eminence or distinction. [Latin *notābilis* remarkable, from *notāre* to mark.] —no′ta·ble·ness, *n.* —no′ta·bly, *adv.*

no·tar·i·al (nō târ′ē əl) *adj.* of, relating to, or carried out by a notary public.

no·ta·rize (nō′tə rīz′) *v.t.,* -rized, -riz·ing. to certify (a document) as authentic; attest to as a notary public: *to notarize a will.* —no′ta·ri·za′tion, *n.*

no·ta·ry (nō′tə rē) *n., pl.* -ries. notary public. [Latin *notārius* stenographer, clerk, from *nota* mark.]

notary public, *pl.* notaries public or notary publics. a public officer authorized to administer oaths, certify documents as authentic, and take affidavits.

no·ta·tion (nō tā′shən) *n.* **1.** a system of signs or symbols used to represent values, quantities, or other facts or information: *musical notations, chemical notations.* **2.** the act or process of using such signs or symbols. **3.** a brief note, as in the margin of a book. **4.** the act of making notes in writing. [Latin *notātiō* designation, shorthand, from *notāre* to mark.] —no·ta′tion·al, *adj.*

notch (noch) *n.* **1.** a wedge-shaped nick or other indentation cut into the surface or along the edge of something. **2.** a narrow pass between mountains. **3.** *Informal.* a step or degree: *That politician has come down several notches in my estimation.* —*v.t.* **1.** to cut a notch or notches in. **2.** to keep count of by or as if by cutting notches. [Probably from the incorrect division into *a notch* of *an otch,* from Old French *osche* a nick, cut, from Old French *oschier* to nick, cut; of uncertain origin.]

note (nōt) *n.* **1.** *usually,* notes. a brief record, as of a lecture, written down to assist the memory: *The student took notes in class. The professor spoke without notes.* **2.** an explanatory or critical comment added to a text, as at the bottom of a page. **3.** a brief message or letter: *The teacher sent a note to the boy's mother.* **4.** a formal, written diplomatic communication. **5.** careful notice; regard: *Your opinions are worthy of note.* **6.** distinction, importance, or significance: *The judge is a person of note.* **7.** indication or suggestion, as of an emotion: *a note of bitterness.* **8.** promissory note. **9.** a piece of paper currency or a certificate of payment issued by a government or bank, serving as legal tender: *a one-pound note.* **10.** *Music.* **a.** a tone of definite pitch. **b.** the sign representing such a tone and indicating its pitch and duration. **c.** a key of a piano or other similar instrument. **11.** *Archaic.* melody; tune; song. —*v.t.,* not·ed, not·ing. **1.** to set down in writing; make a note of: *to note someone's phone number on a slip of paper.* **2.** to take careful notice of; regard: *Please note the enclosed instructions.* **3.** to mention specially; remark about: *The critic noted several of the young artist's paintings in the review.* [Latin *nota* mark, sign, musical note.] —not′er, *n.*

· **to compare notes.** to exchange points of view or ideas.

· **to hit (or strike) a sour note.** to do or say what is inappropriate: *The speaker hit a sour note when she criticized social security at the banquet for retired workers.*

· **to strike the right note.** to do or say what is appropriate: *My friend struck just the right note when he praised the host's taste in art.*

musical **notes**	
Whole note	𝅝
Half note	𝅗𝅥
Quarter note	𝅘𝅥
Eighth note	𝅘𝅥𝅮
Sixteenth note	𝅘𝅥𝅯

note·book (nōt′bûk′) *n.* a book containing blank or lined pages for notes.

not·ed (nō′tid) *adj.* well-known; famous; celebrated; distinguished: *Several noted authors attended the reception.*

Synonyms Noted, distinguished, and eminent mean widely known for a particular ability or achievement. **Noted** is usually applied to broad accomplishments, as within a profession: *a noted surgeon.* **Distinguished** implies significant individual achievements: *The distinguished author had written novels, short stories, and essays.* **Eminent** gives even more emphasis to individual achievement, esp. in relation to one's peers: *Only one composer in the country's history is considered truly eminent.* For other Synonyms, see **famous**.

note·pa·per (nōt′pā′pər) *n.* paper used for writing notes.

note·wor·thy (nōt′wûr′thē) *adj.* worthy of notice or special attention. —note′wor′thi·ly, *adv.* —note′wor′thi·ness, *n.*

not-for-prof·it (not′fər prof′it) *adj.* not operated or organized to make a profit; nonprofit: *a not-for-profit organization.*

noth·ing (nuth′ing) *n.* **1.** no thing; not anything: *We bought nothing at the store.* **2.** no part or share: *to be left nothing in a will.* **3.** an obscure or unimportant state or condition: *to rise from nothing to a position of power.* **4.** a person or thing that is of no value or significance. **5.** the absence of matter or existence; nothingness. **6.** zero. —*adv.* in no way; not at all: *He looks nothing like his sister.* [NO + THING.]

· **for nothing. a.** without cost; free. **b.** for no benefit or gain: *We went to all that trouble for nothing.*

· **nothing doing.** *Informal.* absolutely not.

noth·ing·ness (nuth′ing nis) *n.* **1.a.** the absence of matter; empty space; emptiness. **b.** the absence of existence; nonexistence. **c.** the absence of consciousness; unconsciousness or death. **2.** insignificance or worthlessness. **3.** a thing of no value or significance.

no·tice (nō′tis) *n.* **1.** the act of observing or the state of being observed: *to escape notice, to bring something to notice.* **2.** an announcement or warning: *to attack without notice.* **3.** a printed announcement: *There were notices posted all over town about the sale.* **4.** a formal announcement, as of the end of an agreement: *I gave my employer two weeks' notice that I was leaving to take another job.* **5.** a critical review: *The play received very poor notices.* —*v.t.,* -ticed, -tic·ing. **1.** to become aware of visually; observe: *I noticed Fred's car parked outside. She noticed the changes in her friend's personality.* [Middle French *notice* acquaintance, from Latin *nōtitia* knowledge, acquaintance, information.]

· **to serve notice.** to give warning or information; announce.

· **to take notice of.** to become aware of; pay attention to: *Take notice of the new parking restrictions.*

no·tice·a·ble (nō′ti sə bəl) *adj.* easily seen or noticed: *There is a noticeable difference in your appearance today.* —no′tice·a·bly, *adv.*

no·ti·fi·ca·tion (nō′tə fi kā′shən) *n.* **1.** the act of notifying or the state of being notified. **2.** a written or printed notice.

no·ti·fy (nō′tə fī′) *v.t.,* -fied, -fy·ing. to give notice to; inform: *to notify the police of an accident, to notify customers of a sale.* [Old French *notifier* to make known, from Latin *nōtificāre,* from *nōtus* known + *facere* to make.] —no′ti·fi′er, *n.*

no·tion (nō′shən) *n.* **1.** a mental image; conception; idea: *I*

haven't the faintest notion of what you meant by that remark. **2.** a theory, belief, or opinion: *the superstitious notion that breaking a mirror causes seven years' bad luck.* **3.** an intention or whim; desire: *I had a sudden notion to leave.* **4. notions.** small useful items, such as ribbons, pins, needles, and thread. [Latin *nōtiō* becoming acquainted, idea.] —**no′tion·al,** *adj.* —For Synonyms, see **idea.**

no·to·chord (nō′tə kôrd′) *n.* a stiff, supportive, rodlike structure that extends lengthwise below the spinal cord in primitive chordates and is present during the early embryonic stages in the development of higher vertebrates. [Greek *nōtos* back + CHORD².]

no·to·ri·e·ty (nō′tə rī′i tē) *n., pl.* **-ties.** the state or quality of being notorious.

no·to·ri·ous (nō tôr′ē əs) *adj.* well-known for something bad; widely and unfavorably known: *a notorious criminal, a notorious affair.* [Medieval Latin *notorious* well-known, from Latin *nōtus* known.] —**no·to′ri·ous·ly,** *adv.* —**no·to′ri·ous·ness,** *n.*

no-trump (nō′trump′) *n.* **1.** a bid in bridge in which no suit is named as trump. **2.** a hand played without a trump suit. —*adj.* of or designating such a bid or hand.

not·with·stand·ing (not′with stan′ding, -with-) *prep.* in spite of: *The tennis match was completed notwithstanding the bad weather.* —*adv.* all the same; nevertheless. —*conj.* in spite of the fact that; although.

nou·gat (nü′gət) *n.* a confection made mainly of sugar or honey and nuts. [French *nougat,* through Provençal, going back to Latin *nux* nut.]

nought (nôt) naught.

noun (noun) *n.* any of a class of words that name or denote something, such as a person, animal, place, thing, action, or quality, and function as the subject or object of a verb or the object of a preposition. Most English nouns have a plural formed by adding *-s* or *-es,* and many have a possessive formed by adding *-'s.* [Anglo-Norman *noun* name, noun, going back to Latin *nōmen.*]

nour·ish (nûr′ish, nur′-) *v.t.* **1.** to furnish with food and other substances necessary to life and growth. **2.** to promote the development of; foster: *to nourish a deep affection for someone.* [Old French *noris-,* a stem of *norir* to bring up, nurture, from Latin *nūtrīre* to bring up, feed.]

nour·ish·ing (nûr′ə shing, nur′-) *adj.* promoting health and growth; providing nourishment; nutritious: *Milk, cereals, and fresh fruit and vegetables are nourishing foods.*

nour·ish·ment (nûr′ish mənt, nur′-) *n.* **1.** that which nourishes; sustenance. **2.** the act of nourishing or the state of being nourished.

nou·veau (nü vō′, nü′vō) *adj.* newly arrived, developed, or formed: *the nouveau millionaires in their expensive foreign cars.* [French *nouveau,* from Old French *novel* new, from Latin *novellus* new, young. See NOVEL².]

nou·veau riche (nü′vō rēsh′) *pl.* **nou·veaux riches** (nü′vō-rēsh′). a person who has recently become rich, esp. one who flaunts or displays this wealth in a showy or vulgar way. [French *nouveau riche* literally, new rich, from *nouveau* new (going back to Latin *novus*) + *riche* rich (of Germanic origin).]

nou·velle cuisine (nü vel′) a style of French cooking that uses the finest and freshest ingredients and little fat or starch, emphasizing light sauces and artful presentation of food. [French *nouvelle cuisine* literally, new cooking, going back to Latin *novus* new + *coquere* to cook.]

Nov., November.

no·va (nō′və) *n., pl.* **-vas** or **-vae** (-vē). a star that rapidly increases in brightness and then gradually fades to its original magnitude. [Modern Latin *nova (stella)* new (star), from Latin *novus* new.]

nov·el¹ (nov′əl) *n.* **1.** a fictional prose narrative, usually of considerable length and containing detailed treatment of character and plot. **2.** the literary form represented by this type of fiction: *to study the novel.* [Short for Italian *novella (storia)* new kind of (story).]

nov·el² (nov′əl) *adj.* new and unusual: *a novel idea, a novel technique.* [Old French *novel,* from Latin *novellus* new, young, diminutive of *novus* new.] —For Synonyms, see **new.**

nov·el·ette (nov′ə let′) *n.* a short novel. [NOVEL¹ + -ETTE.]

nov·el·ist (nov′ə list) *n.* a person who writes novels.

nov·el·is·tic (nov′ə lis′tik) *adj.* of, relating to, or characteristic of novels. —**nov′el·is′ti·cal·ly,** *adv.*

nov·el·ize (nov′ə līz′) *v.t.,* **-ized, -iz·ing.** to make into or redo as a novel. —**nov′el·i·za′tion,** *n.* —**nov′el·iz′er,** *n.*

no·vel·la (nō vel′ə) *n., pl.* **-vel·las** or **-vel·le** (-vel′ā). **1.** a short prose narrative of the type developed by the Italian humanist Giovanni Boccaccio in the *Decameron,* usually containing a moral or satire. **2.** a short novel; novelette. [Italian *novella* short story, news. See NOVEL¹.]

nov·el·ty (nov′əl tē) *n., pl.* **-ties. 1.** the quality of being new; newness. **2.** something that is new or unusual, such as a thing or event. **3. novelties.** small, inexpensive, manufactured articles, such as small ornaments or toys. [Old French *novelete* something new, innovation, change, from Late Latin *novellitās* newness, from Latin *novellus* new. See NOVEL².]

No·vem·ber (nō vem′bər) *n.* the eleventh month of the year, containing thirty days. [Latin *November* ninth month in the early Roman calendar (in which March was the first month), from *novem* nine.]

no·ve·na (nō vē′nə) *n., pl.* **-nas** or **-nae** (-nē). a Roman Catholic devotion consisting of prayers said for nine consecutive days. [Medieval Latin *novena,* going back to Latin *novem* nine.]

nov·ice (nov′is) *n.* **1.** a person who is new to an occupation, activity, or the like; beginner. **2.** a person who is admitted into a religious order for a probationary period before taking vows. [Old French *novice,* going back to Latin *novīcius* new, from *novus.*]

no·vi·ti·ate (nō vish′ē it, -āt′) *also,* **no·vi·ci·ate.** *n.* **1.** the state or period of being a novice. **2.** a novice; beginner. **3.** quarters housing novices in a religious order. [Medieval Latin *novitiatus* the state of being a novice, going back to Latin *novus* new.]

No·vo·cain (nō′və kān′) *n. Trademark.* procaine. [Latin *novus* new + (CO)CAINE.]

now (nou) *adv.* **1.** at the present time: *She is now living in London.* **2.** without delay; at once; immediately: *We must leave now if we hope to catch our train.* **3.** a very short while ago: *He arrived just now, while you were out.* **4.** in a moment; shortly: *The teacher is going to read now.* **5.** under the present circumstances: *Since I lost my keys, I must now wait until my parents come home.* **6.** at the point of time referred to; then: *The war was now over.* —*conj.* since (usually with *that*): *Now that we are alone, we can speak freely.* —*n.* the present time; present: *The time to act is now.* —*interj.* used to express warning, sympathy, or reproach: *Now, be careful! Now, don't worry.* [Old English *nū* at the present time, immediately.]

• **now and again** (or **then**). from time to time; occasionally.

NOW, National Organization for Women.

now·a·days (nou′ə dāz′) *adv.* at the present time; during these days.

no·way (nō′wā′) *also,* **no·ways.** *adv.* in no way; not at all.

no·where (nō′hwâr′, -wâr′) *adv.* to, in, or at no place; not anywhere. —*n.* **1.** a place that is remote, nonexistent, or unknown: *We moved to a little town in the middle of nowhere. The tourists stopped for the night at a motel miles from nowhere.* **2.** a place or state of obscurity: *The young writer appeared out of nowhere and had a bestseller.* [Old English *nāhwǣr* in no place.]

• **nowhere near.** *Informal.* not nearly; not at all: *We have nowhere near enough money to cover our expenses.*

• **to get nowhere.** to make absolutely no progress: *I got nowhere with my research project for the first two weeks.*

no-win (nō′win′) *adj.* **1.** not likely to be successful or won; not able to overcome or achieve a victory: *a no-win policy of retaliation.* **2.** affording no chance for victory or success: *a no-win situation.*

no·wise (nō′wīz′) *adv.* in no way; noway.

nox·ious (nok′shəs) *adj.* **1.** very harmful to the health; injurious: *noxious gases.* **2.** morally harmful. [Latin *noxius* injurious, from *noxa* harm, hurt.] —**nox′ious·ly,** *adv.* —**nox′ious·ness,** *n.*

noz·zle (noz′əl) *n.* a projecting, often adjustable, spout at the end of a hose, pipe, or the like that serves as an outlet for a liquid or gas. [Diminutive of NOSE.]

Np, the symbol for neptunium.

N.P., Notary Public.

NS, the postal abbreviation for Nova Scotia.

N.S. 1. New Style. **2.** Nova Scotia.

N.S.P.C.A., National Society for the Prevention of Cruelty to Animals.

-n't *suffix* (used to form contractions) not: *haven't.*

NT, the postal abbreviation for the Northwest Territories.

N.T., New Testament.

nth (enth) *adj.* relating to or denoting an indefinitely large or small number or value.

N

a	at	e	end	o	hot	u	up	hw	white		about
ā	ape	ē	me	ō	old	ū	use	ng	song		taken
ä	far	i	it	ô	fork	ü	rule	th	thin	ə	pencil
âr	care	ī	ice	oi	oil	u̇	pull	-th	this		lemon
		îr	pierce	ou	out	ûr	turn	zh	measure		circus

•**to the nth degree** (or **power**). **a.** to any degree or power, usually a high one. **b.** to the greatest extreme; to the utmost.

nt. wt., net weight.

nu (nü, nū) *n.* the thirteenth letter of the Greek alphabet (N, ν), corresponding to the English letter N, n.

nu·ance (nü′äns, nū′-, nü äns′, nū-) *n.* a gradual, subtle, or slight change or difference, as of tone, expression, or meaning. [French *nuance,* from *nuer* to shade, cloud, from *nue* cloud, going back to Latin *nūbēs.*]

nub (nub) *n.* **1.** a knob or protuberance. **2.** a small piece or lump: *a nub of a pencil, a nub of coal.* **3.** *Informal.* the main point or part, as of a story; gist. [Form of dialectal English *knub* small lump, swelling, from Middle Low German *knubbe* knot of a tree, knob.]

nub·bin (nub′in) *n.* **1.** a small or imperfect ear of corn. **2.** any small or imperfect fruit. **3.** a small, usually projecting piece. [Diminutive of NUB.]

nub·by (nub′ē) *adj.,* **-bi·er, -bi·est.** having a rough, lumpy texture: *a nubby fabric, a nubby sweater.* [NUB + -Y¹.]

Nu·bi·an (nü′bē an, nū′-) *n.* **1.** a member of the people of Nubia. **2.** the language spoken in Nubia. —*adj.* of or relating to Nubia, its people, or their language or culture.

nu·bile (nü′bəl, -bīl, nū′-) *adj.* of an age suitable for marriage; marriageable. [Latin *nūbilis,* from *nūbere* to marry.] —**nu·bil′i·ty,** *n.*

nu·cel·lus (nü sel′əs, nū-) *n., pl.* **-cel·li** (-sel′ī). the tissue composing the chief part of the young ovule of flowering plants, in which the embryo sac develops. [Modern Latin *nucellus,* modification of Latin *nucella* small nut, diminutive of *nux* nut.] —**nu·cel′lar,** *adj.*

nu·cle·ar (nü′klē ər, nū′-) *adj.* **1.** of, relating to, or forming a nucleus. **2.** of, relating to, or involving the use of atomic nuclei or energy derived from them: *nuclear arms, nuclear fuel.* **3.** relating to, involving, or having nuclear weapons: *nuclear warfare, a nuclear power.*

nuclear energy, energy obtained from controlled nuclear fission or fusion. Also, **atomic energy.**

nuclear family, a social unit consisting of a mother and father and their child or children, as opposed to an extended family.

nuclear fission, fission *(def. 2).*

nuclear fusion, fusion *(def. 6).*

nuclear magnetic resonance, a phenomenon characterized by the absorption or emission of a quantum of radiation by an atomic nucleus when an external magnetic field is applied, used in spectroscopy to determine the structure of complex molecules and in medicine to produce three-dimensional images of internal body tissues.

nuclear medicine, the branch of medicine concerned with the use of radioisotopes in diagnosis and therapy.

nuclear membrane, the double-layered membrane surrounding the nucleus of a eukaryotic cell.

nuclear physics, a branch of physics that deals with the structure and properties of atomic nuclei. ➡ used as singular. —**nuclear physicist.**

nuclear power, power produced by a nuclear reactor; heat, electricity, or other forms of power obtained from nuclear energy. Also, **atomic power.**

nuclear reactor, a device in which a nuclear chain reaction can be initiated, sustained, and controlled, used for generating heat or producing useful radiation. Also, **atomic pile, atomic reactor.**

nuclear winter, a period of worldwide cold, darkness, and destruction of life that some scientists believe would follow large-scale nuclear warfare as a result of the formation of vast clouds of dust and smoke blocking the sun's heat and light.

nu·cle·ase (nü′klē ās′, nū′-) *n.* any of a group of enzymes that break down nucleic acids by hydrolysis, forming nucleotides or nucleosides.

nu·cle·ate (*v.,* nü′klē āt′, nū′-; *adj.,* nü′klē it, -āt′, nū′-) *v.,* **-at·ed, -at·ing.** —*v.t.* to form into a nucleus. —*v.i.* to form a nucleus. —*adj.* having a nucleus. [Late Latin *nucleātus,* past participle of *nucleāre* to become like a kernel, from Latin *nucleus* kernel, nut, diminutive of *nux* nut.] —**nu′cle·a′tion,** *n.* —**nu′cle·a′tor,** *n.*

nu·cle·i (nü′klē ī′, nū′-) a plural of **nucleus.**

nu·cle·ic acid (nü klē′ik, nū-) any of a group of long, complex organic macromolecules, consisting of linked nucleotides and found in all living cells, that carry genetic information and control the functions of the cell. The two main types of nucleic acid are DNA and RNA.

nu·cle·o·lus (nü klē′ə ləs, nū-) *n., pl.* **-li** (-lī′). a small round body in the nucleus of a cell that contains genetic material and is involved in reproduction. For illustration, see **cell.** [Latin *nucleolus* little nut, diminutive of *nucleus* nut, kernel, diminutive of *nux* nut.]

nu·cle·on (nü′klē on′, nū′-) *n.* a proton or neutron, esp. one constituting a part of an atomic nucleus.

nu·cle·on·ics (nü′klē on′iks, nū′-) *n.* the branch of science that deals with atomic nuclei, esp. with the production and application of nuclear energy. ➡ used as singular.

nu·cle·o·plasm (nü′klē ə plaz′əm, nū′-) *n.* the protoplasm of which a cell nucleus is composed. [NUCLE(US) + -PLASM.]

nu·cle·o·pro·tein (nü′klē ō prō′tēn, -tē in, nū′-) *n.* any of a group of compounds consisting of a protein joined to a nucleic acid, forming the principal component in chromosomes and viruses.

nu·cle·o·side (nü′klē ə sīd′, nū′-) *n.* any of various organic compounds, as adenosine, consisting of a sugar combined with a purine or pyrimidine base, chemically similar to nucleotides but lacking phosphoric acid.

nu·cle·o·tide (nü′klē ə tīd′, nū′-) *n.* any of various organic compounds, such as ADP, AMP, or ATP, consisting of phosphoric acid, a sugar, and a purine or pyrimidine base. Nucleotides are the fundamental building blocks of the nucleic acids.

nu·cle·us (nü′klē əs, nū′-) *n., pl.* **-cle·i** (-klē ī′) or **-cle·us·es.** **1.** the central or essential part around which other parts are grouped or collected; core: *The nucleus of the building is a large open court. There is a nucleus of truth in the story.* **2.** a basis for further growth and development: *These volumes form the nucleus of a fine library.* **3.** a small, dense, usually round or oval body located near the center of a plant or animal cell, surrounded by a delicate membrane and containing most of the cell's hereditary material. The nucleus is essential to growth, reproduction, metabolism, and other vital activities. For illustration, see **cell. 4.** the positively charged central portion of an atom, containing most of the atom's mass and consisting of protons and neutrons, except in the case of hydrogen, whose nucleus consists of one proton only. For illustration, see **atom. 5.** the dense, central portion of the head of a comet. [Latin *nucleus* kernel, nut, diminutive of *nux* nut.]

nu·clide (nü′klīd, nū′-) *n.* an atomic nucleus or a type of atom, characterized by both the atomic number and number of neutrons or mass number. [NUCL(EUS) + -ide from Greek *eidos* form.]

nude (nüd, nūd) *adj.* without clothing or other covering; unclothed; bare. —*n.* **1.** the unclothed human figure, esp. one represented in a painting or other work of art. **2.** the state of being unclothed: *in the nude.* [Latin *nūdus* naked.] —**nude′ly,** *adv.* —**nude′ness,** *n.* —For Synonyms, see **naked.**

nudge (nuj) *v.t.,* **nudged, nudg·ing.** to push gently or touch, esp. to attract attention: *He nudged her with his elbow.* —*n.* a gentle push or touch. [Form of dialectal *nidge, knidge,* of Germanic origin.] —**nudg′er,** *n.*

nu·di·branch (nü′di brangk′, nū′-) *n.* any of a group of marine mollusks, order Nudibranchia, related to snails but without a shell and bearing branching, often brightly colored, external gills. [Modern Latin *Nudibranchia,* from Latin *nūdus* naked + *branchia* gill, from Greek *branchion;* referring to their extended gills.]

nud·ism (nü′diz əm, nū′-) *n.* a belief in or the practice of living in the nude.

nud·ist (nü′dist, nū′-) *n.* a person who believes in or practices nudism. —*adj.* of or relating to nudism or nudists.

nu·di·ty (nü′di tē, nū′-) *n., pl.* **-ties. 1.** the state of being nude; nakedness. **2.** something nude.

nu·ga·to·ry (nü′gə tôr′ē, nū′-) *adj.* **1.** of little importance; insignificant; trifling: *Don't waste time making nugatory comments.* **2.** without force or authority; ineffective; invalid. [Latin *nūgātōrius* trifling, going back to *nūgae* trifles.]

nug·get (nug′it) *n.* **1.** a lump, esp. a lump of native gold. **2.** something small but useful or valuable: *nuggets of information.* **3.** a small piece of cooked chicken, fish, or the like, esp. one that has been batter-coated and fried. [Possibly from dialectal English *nug* lump; of uncertain origin.]

nui·sance (nü′səns, nū′-) *n.* **1.** a person or thing that annoys or offends. **2.** *Law.* something that annoys or offends another or others, as by obstructing the use of property or by creating a dangerous or disturbing condition. [Old French *nuisance* offense, hurt, from *nuire* to harm, from Latin *nocēre.*]

nuisance tax, a tax collected in small amounts from the consumer.

nuke (nük, nūk) *Slang. n.* **1.** a nuclear weapon. **2.** a nuclear power plant or nuclear reactor. **3.** a nuclear-powered vessel or vehicle. —*v.t.,* **nuked, nuk·ing.** to attack or destroy with nuclear weapons. [From NUCLEAR.]

null (nul) *adj.* **1.** having no or very little value, effect, or importance; insignificant; ineffective: *an argument based on evidence now considered null.* **2.** amounting to nothing; nonexistent; nil: *Positive and negative forces, if equal, make each other null when brought together.* **3.** *Mathematics.* of, relating to, or designating a set that contains no elements or members. [Latin *nūllus* not any, from *ne* not + *ūllus* any.]
　·**null and void.** without legal force or authority; not binding; invalid: *The judge ruled that the property agreement, never put in writing, was null and void.*
nul·li·fi·ca·tion (nul′ə fi kā′shən) *n.* **1.** the act of nullifying or the state of being nullified. **2.** the refusal of a state to recognize or enforce a federal law within its borders.
nul·li·fy (nul′ə fī′) *v.t.,* **-fied, -fy·ing. 1.** to make void; declare invalid; annul: *to nullify a law.* **2.** to make useless or worthless; destroy: *Their mistake was so serious that it nullified all the good work they had done.* [Late Latin *nūllificāre* to despise, from Latin *nūllus* not any + *facere* to make.] —**nul′li·fi′er,** *n.*
nul·li·ty (nul′i tē) *n., pl.* **-ties. 1.** the quality or state of being null; nothingness. **2.** something that is null, esp. an act that has no legal force or authority. [Medieval Latin *nullitas* nothingness, invalidity, from Latin *nūllus* not any.]
Num., Numbers.
numb (num) *adj.* not having or deprived of sensation or movement: *numb with cold, numb with fear.* —*v.t.* to make numb. [Middle English *nomen,* past participle of *nimen* to take, seize, from Old English *niman.*] —**numb′ly,** *adv.* —**numb′ness,** *n.*
num·ber (num′bər) *n.* **1.a.** a mathematical concept that indicates how many units or objects are contained in a certain group; something that tells how many members there are in a set. **b.** a word or symbol, or group of words or symbols, representing such a concept; numeral. **2.** a specified amount, as of persons or things; total; sum: *We decided to increase the number of invited guests to thirty.* **3.** an unspecified amount, as of persons or things; quantity: *A number of people gathered in front of the display. I have read a number of books on the subject.* **4.** a numeral given to or identifying a person or thing: *What is the number of your room?* **5.** one of a series that has been given numbers: *The football team was rated number one in all the polls.* **6.** one of the songs or other musical compositions on a program. **7.** a single issue of a newspaper or periodical. **8.** *Informal.* a person or thing that arouses interest. **9.** *Grammar.* the form or property of a word that indicates whether the word is singular or plural. **10. numbers. a.** numerical superiority: *The army overpowered the invaders by force of numbers.* **b.** arithmetic. **c.** metrical lines; poetry. **d.** numbers racket. —*v.t.* **1.** to ascertain the number of; count. **2.** to give a number or numbers to. **3.** to amount to or include: *The freshman class numbers over a thousand students.* **4.** to limit the number of: *The days are numbered before summer vacation ends.* —*v.i.* **1.** to amount to a group or total: *The contest winners numbered in the hundreds.* **2.** to list or recite numbers: *Number from one to ten on your papers.* [Old French *nombre* unit (in counting), indefinite quantity, from Latin *numerus.*] —**num′ber·er,** *n.*
　·**beyond** (or **without**) **number.** too many to be counted.
　·**to get** (or **have**) **someone's number.** *Informal.* to discover or know someone's true motives or character.
num·ber·less (num′bər lis) *adj.* **1.** too numerous to be counted; innumerable. **2.** without a number.
number line, a line on which points are identified with real numbers.
number one *Informal.* oneself: *to look after number one and no one else.*
Num·bers (num′bərz) *n.* the fourth book of the Old Testament, containing the census of the Israelites after their escape from Egyptian bondage. ➡ used as singular.
numbers racket, an illegal lottery in which bets are made that a particular number will appear in an unpredictable statistical total, such as the amount of money wagered at a racetrack in a single day. Also, **numbers, numbers game, policy.**
number theory, a branch of mathematics dealing with the properties and relations of integers.
numb·ing (num′ing) *adj.* inducing the loss of the power of sensation or movement: *a numbing blow.* —**numb′ing·ly,** *adv.*
numb·skull (num′skul′) numskull.
nu·mer·a·ble (nü′mər ə bəl, nū′-) *adj.* capable of being counted.
nu·mer·al (nü′mər əl, nū′-) *n.* **1.** a symbol or a group of symbols representing a number, such as 7 or VII. **2.** a word standing for such a symbol, such as *seven.* **3. numerals.** cloth numbers, usually the last two numbers of a student's year of graduation, awarded by a school for excellence in some sport.

Numerals

The following table shows several of the many systems of numeration that have been developed throughout history. The modern numerals, now used almost universally, were developed in Europe and are based primarily on Hindu and Arabic sources.

MODERN	EGYPTIAN	BABYLONIAN	GREEK	ROMAN	MAYAN	HINDU	EARLY ARABIC
1	I	ᛉ	I	I	•	I	I
2	II	ᛉᛉ	II	II	••	२	૨
3	III	ᛉᛉᛉ	III	III	•••	३	३
4	IIII	ᛉᛉᛉᛉ	IIII	IIII	••••	୪	૪
5	IIII I	ᛉᛉᛉᛉᛉ	Γ	V	—	५	৬
6	III III	ᛉᛉᛉ	Γι	VI	⊥	६	५
7	IIII III	ᛉᛉᛉᛉ	Γιι	VII	••	৩	৺
8	IIII IIII	ᛉᛉᛉᛉ	Γιιι	VIII	•••	८	∧
9	IIIII IIIII	ᛉᛉᛉᛉᛉ	Γιιιι	IX	••••	९	९
10	∩	⟨	Δ	X	═	۱0	۱0
20	∩∩	⟨⟨	ΔΔ	XX	⊛	२0	२0
50	∩∩∩∩∩	⟨⟨⟨	Ͷ	L	≣	५0	৬0
60	∩∩∩ ∩∩∩	⟨	Ͷ Δ	LX	⊛⊛	ৎ0	५0
70	∩∩∩∩ ∩∩∩	⟨⟨	Ͷ ΔΔ	LXX	⊛≡	⟩0	৺0
100	⌐	⟨⟨⟨⟨	Η	C	⊛	۱00	۱00
300	⌐⌐⌐	⟨⟨⟨	ΗΗΗ	CCC	≣≣	३00	३00
500	⌐⌐⌐⌐⌐	⟨⟨⟨⟨⟨	⊢Η	D	⊛••	५00	৬00

—*adj.* of, relating to, or representing a number or numbers. [Late Latin *numerālis* relating to number, from Latin *numerus* unit (in counting), quantity.]
nu·mer·ate (nü′mə rāt′, nū′-) *v.i.,* **-at·ed, -at·ing.** to number; count. [Latin *numerātus,* past participle of *numerāre* to count, *numerus* unit (in counting), quantity.]
nu·mer·a·tion (nü′mə rā′shən, nū′-) *n.* **1.** the act or process of numbering: *a numeration of a town's inhabitants.* **2.** a system of representing numbers by symbols.
nu·mer·a·tor (nü′mə rā′tər, nū′-) *n.* **1.** the number above or to the left of the line in a fraction, indicating the number of equal parts that are being considered; dividend. In the fraction ½, 1 is the numerator. ➡ distinguished from **denominator. 2.** a person or thing that numbers. [Late Latin *numerātor* one who numbers, from *numerāre* to count, number.]
nu·mer·i·cal (nü mer′i kəl, nü-) *adj.* of, relating to, or represented by numbers. Also, **nu·mer′ic.** —**nu·mer′i·cal·ly,** *adv.* —**nu·mer′i·cal·ness,** *n.*
nu·mer·ol·o·gy (nü′mə rol′ə jē, nū′-) *n.* the study of numbers as a means of analyzing character, telling fortunes, and foretelling future events. —**nu·mer·o·log·i·cal** (nü′mər ə loj′i kəl, nū′-), *adj.* —**nu·mer·ol′o·gist,** *n.*

a	at	e	end	o	hot	u	up	hw	white		about
ā	ape	ē	me	ō	old	ū	use	ng	song		taken
ä	far	i	it	ô	fork	ü	rule	th	thin	ə	pencil
âr	care	ī	ice	oi	oil	ú	pull	th	this		lemon
		îr	pierce	ou	out	ûr	turn	zh	measure		circus

nu·mer·ous (nü′mər əs, nū′-) *adj.* **1.** forming a large number; many: *We visited them on numerous occasions.* **2.** containing a large number; abundant: *a numerous collection of antiques.* [Latin *numerōsus* plentiful, from *numerus* unit (in counting), quantity.] —**nu′mer·ous·ly,** *adv.* —**nu′mer·ous·ness,** *n.*

nu·mis·mat·ics (nü′miz mat′iks, -mis-, nū′-) *n.* the collection or study of coins, paper money, or medals. ➡ used as singular. [French *numismatique* numismatics, from Latin *numisma* coin, from Greek *nomisma* custom, coin.] —**nu′mis·mat′ic,** *adj.* —**nu·mis·ma·tist** (nü miz′mə tist, -mis′-, nü-), *n.*

num·skull (num′skul) *also,* **numbskull.** *n.* a stupid person; blockhead. [NUMB + SKULL.]

nun (nun) *n.* a member of a religious order for women, living under vows in a convent and leading a life of prayer and good works. [Old English *nunne,* from Late Latin *nonna,* feminine of *nonnus* monk.]

nun·ci·o (nun′shē ō′) *n., pl.* **-ci·os.** an ambassador representing the pope in a foreign country. [Obsolete Italian *nuncio* ambassador, from Latin *nūntius* messenger.]

nun·ner·y (nun′ə rē) *n., pl.* **-ner·ies.** the residence of a society of nuns.

nup·tial (nup′shəl) *adj.* of or relating to marriage or the marriage ceremony: *nuptial bliss, the nuptial feast.* —*n. usually,* **nuptials.** a marriage ceremony; wedding. [Latin *nuptiālis* relating to a wedding, from *nuptiae* wedding.]

nurse (nûrs) *n.* **1.** a person who is trained to attend the sick or injured, usually under the direction of a physician. **2.** a woman employed to attend children; nursemaid. **3.** a woman employed to feed babies by suckling; wet nurse. —*v.,* **nursed, nurs·ing.** —*v.t.* **1.** to attend (the sick or injured); act as a nurse for. **2.** to feed (a baby) from the breast; suckle. **3.** to try to cure or heal (an illness or injury): *to nurse a sore throat with aspirin and plenty of rest.* **4.** to handle or use with care: *I nursed my weak knee by limping slightly.* **5.** to promote the growth or development of; foster: *to nurse a small tree, to nurse a talent.* **6.** to keep in the mind; harbor: *to nurse an idea, to nurse a grudge.* **7.** to consume slowly: *to nurse a drink, to nurse a small amount of pocket money.* —*v.i.* **1.** to be employed or work as a nurse. **2.** to suckle a baby. **3.** to be fed from the breast. [Old French *nurrice* one who nurses an infant or takes care of a child, from Late Latin *nūtrīcia* governess, wet nurse, going back to Latin *nūtrīx* wet nurse, nourisher.]

nurse·maid (nûrs′mād′) *n.* a woman employed to attend children.

nurs·er·y (nûr′sə rē) *n., pl.* **-ries. 1.** a room set apart for small children, esp. a baby's bedroom. **2.** a place where plants, esp. trees and shrubs, are raised for sale.

nurs·er·y·man (nûr′sə rē mən) *n., pl.* **-men** (-mən). a person who owns or works in a nursery that raises and sells plants.

nursery rhyme, a short, rhymed verse for young children.

nursery school, preschool.

nursing home, an institution for the long-term housing and care of people who cannot care for themselves, such as those who are chronically ill.

nurs·ling (nûrs′ling) *n.* **1.** a person who is nursed, such as a baby. **2.** a person or thing that receives careful and loving attention.

nur·ture (nûr′chər) *v.t.,* **-tured, -tur·ing. 1.** to take care of; nourish; feed. **2.** to develop, educate, or foster: *to nurture a talent.* —*n.* **1.** something that nourishes; food. **2.** an act or instance of developing, educating, or fostering. [Anglo-Norman *nurture* nourishment, from Late Latin *nūtrītūra* a nursing, suckling, from Latin *nūtrīre* to feed, bring up.] —**nur′tur·er,** *n.*

nut (nut) *n.* **1.** a dry, usually one-seeded fruit of a plant, having a hard, woody shell. **2.** the kernel of such a fruit. **3.** a block of metal or wood with a screw thread around a central opening into which the threaded end of a bolt fits. **4.** *Slang.* an eccentric or crazy person. **5.** *Slang.* a person who follows or engages in something with much enthusiasm; enthusiast; devotee; buff. —*v.i.* **nut·ted, nut·ting.** to hunt for or gather nuts. [Middle English *note* this fruit, from Old English *hnutu.*] —**nut′like′,** *adj.*

· **a hard** (or **tough**) **nut to crack.** *Informal.* a person or thing that is difficult to understand or deal with.

nut·crack·er (nut′krak′ər) *n.* **1.** a utensil for cracking nuts. **2.** any of various birds, genus *Nucifraga,* of the crow family, found in northern evergreen forests, having a long, pointed bill, and feeding on pine seeds and nuts.

nut·gall (nut′gôl′) *n.* a nutlike gall, esp. on oaks. Also, **gallnut.**

nut·hatch (nut′hach′) *n.* any of various small, lively birds related to the titmouse and creeper, esp. the **common nuthatch,** family Sittidae, found chiefly in the Northern Hemisphere, having a straight, pointed bill and a short tail, and feeding on insects,

nuts, and seeds. Length: 3¾-7½ inches (10-19 centimeters). [Middle English *notehach,* from *note* (see NUT) + *hache* ax (from Old French *hache* battle-ax; of Germanic origin); referring to the way it hacks nuts open for food.]

nut·meat (nut′mēt′) *n.* the edible kernel of a nut.

nut·meg (nut′meg′) *n.* **1.** the hard, aromatic seed of an ever-

nuthatch

green tree, *Myristica fragrans,* dried and ground or grated and used as a spice. **2.** the tree that yields this seed, bearing light green or yellowish green leaves and yellow flowers. [Partial translation and modification of Old French *nois muguete* nutmeg seed; literally, nut with the smell of musk, going back to Latin *nux* nut + *muscus* (see MUSK).]

nu·tri·a (nü′trē ə, nū′-) *n.* **1.** a large South American rodent, *Myocastor coypus,* that lives near water and closely resembles the muskrat, valued for its thick, light brown to black fur. Length: 3 feet (0.9 meter), including tail. Also, **coypu. 2.** the soft, thick, velvety fur of this animal, often dyed to resemble beaver. [Spanish *nutria* otter, from Latin *lutra.*]

nu·tri·ent (nü′trē ənt, nū′-) *adj.* providing nourishment; nutritious. —*n.* a nutritious substance that is essential for body functioning. Proteins, fats, carbohydrates, minerals, and vitamins are all nutrients. [Latin *nūtriēns,* present participle of *nūtrīre* to feed, bring up.]

nu·tri·ment (nü′trə mənt, nū′-) *n.* anything that nourishes; food. [Latin *nūtrīmentum,* from *nūtrīre* to feed, bring up.]

nu·tri·tion (nü trish′ən, nū-) *n.* **1.** the process by which essential nutrients are taken in and absorbed into body tissues. **2.** the study of human nutrition. **3.** nourishment: *A balanced diet should provide proper nutrition.* [Late Latin *nūtrītiō* nourishment, from Latin *nūtrīre* to feed.] —**nu·tri′tion·al,** *adj.* —**nu·tri′tion·al·ly,** *adv.*

nu·tri·tion·ist (nü trish′ə nist, nū-) *n.* a person who specializes or is trained in the study of nutrition.

nu·tri·tious (nü trish′əs, nū-) *adj.* containing or giving nourishment; nourishing. [Latin *nūtrītius,* going back to *nūtrīre* to feed, bring up.] —**nu·tri′tious·ly,** *adv.* —**nu·tri′tious·ness,** *n.*

nu·tri·tive (nü′tri tiv, nū′-) *adj.* **1.** giving nourishment; nutritious: *a nutritive diet.* **2.** of or relating to nutrition: *the nutritive functions.* —**nu′tri·tive·ly,** *adv.*

nuts (nuts) *adj. Slang.* **1.** eccentric or crazy. **2.** in love with or very enthusiastic about.

nuts and bolts, the basic facts and details; practicalities: *to learn the nuts and bolts of a business.* —**nuts′-and-bolts′,** *adj.*

nut·shell (nut′shel′) the hard shell of a nut.

· **in a nutshell.** in a few words: *That's what happened, in a nutshell.*

nut·ty (nut′ē) *adj.,* **-ti·er, -ti·est. 1.** filled with or producing nuts. **2.** having the flavor of nuts. **3.** *Slang.* eccentric or crazy; nuts. —**nut′ti·ly,** *adv.* —**nut′ti·ness,** *n.*

nux vom·i·ca (nuks vom′i kə) **1.** a drug obtained from the seed of an East Indian tree, *Strychnos nux-vomica,* containing strychnine and other alkaloids, used in medicine. **2.** the tree itself. [Modern Latin *nux vomica* literally, vomiting nut, going back to Latin *nux* nut + *vomere* to vomit.]

nuz·zle (nuz′əl) *v.t., v.i.,* **-zled, -zling. 1.** to touch or rub with the nose: *The dog nuzzled its master.* **2.** to press or lie close; nestle; cuddle: *The child nuzzled against my shoulder.* [NOSE + -LE.]

NV, the postal abbreviation for Nevada.

NW, northwest; northwestern.

N.W.T., Northwest Territories.

NY, the postal abbreviation for New York.

N.Y., New York.

N.Y.C., New York City.

ny·lon (nī′lon) *n.* **1.** any of a group of thermoplastic resins used in making strong, durable, synthetic fiber and a variety of plastic articles. **2.** fabric woven with threads made from this substance. **3. nylons.** stockings made of nylon.

nymph (nimf) *n.* **1.** in classical mythology, any of various female deities represented esp. in forests, hills, or rivers, and usually represented as beautiful maidens. **2.** a beautiful young woman; damsel. **3.** an insect in the larval stage in incomplete metamorphosis, resembling the adult but lacking wings. [Latin *nympha,* from Greek *nymphē.*]

nym·pho·ma·ni·a (nim′fə mā′nē ə) *n.* excessive and uncontrollable sexual desire on the part of a woman. [Modern Latin *nymphomania,* from Greek *nymphē* bride + *-mania* madness.]

N.Z., New Zealand.

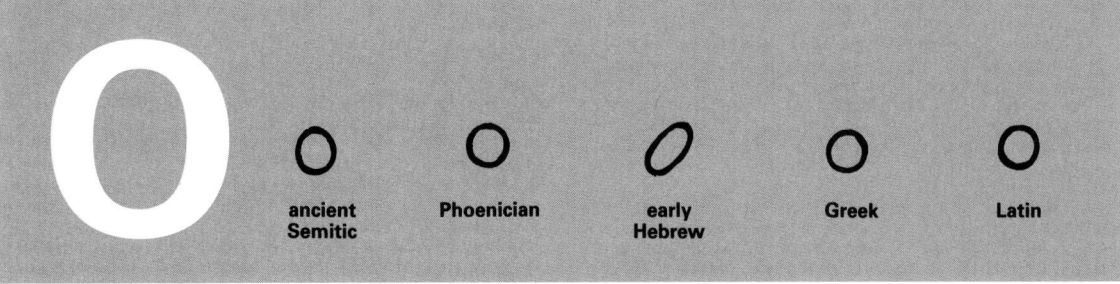

ancient
Semitic

Phoenician

early
Hebrew

Greek

Latin

O is one of the few letters whose written form has remained almost unchanged throughout the centuries. The earliest form of **O** was the ancient Semitic letter *ayin*, meaning "eye," which stood for a breathing sound. A similar letter appeared in the Phoenician and early Hebrew alphabets, both of which made the **O** smaller than the other letters. When the Greeks adopted *ayin* for their alphabet, they used it to represent the short *o* sound and called it *omicron*, meaning "small *o*." This was to distinguish it from the Greek letter for the long *o* sound, called *omega* and meaning "great *o*." The Romans borrowed *omicron* from the Greeks and used it for both the short and long *o* sounds. Our capital letter **O** is almost identical in shape to the Latin **O** of the fourth century B.C.

o, O (ō) *n., pl.* **o's, O's. 1.** the fifteenth letter of the English alphabet. **2.** the shape of this letter or something having this shape.

o' (ə, ō) *prep.* **1.** of: *man-o'-war.* **2.** *Archaic.* on.

O (ō) *interj.* **1.** used in direct address, esp. to express earnestness or solemnity: *O heart, how fares it with thee now?* (Alfred, Lord Tennyson, 1850). **2.** oh.

O (ō) *n., pl.* **O's. 1.** one of the four principal blood groups. For table, see **blood group. 2.** zero.

O, the symbol for oxygen.

o-, form of **ob** before *m*, as in *omit.*

O. 1. ocean. **2.** October.

oaf (ōf) *n., pl.* **oafs.** a stupid, clumsy person. [Old Norse *ālfr* elf.] **—oaf′ish,** *adj.*

oak (ōk) *n.* **1.** any of a large group of trees or shrubs, genus *Quercus,* of the beech family, bearing acorns and found esp. in northern temperate regions. **2.** the hard, sturdy wood of this tree, among the most important of all timber woods. [Old English *āc* the tree.]

oak apple, a boillike swelling that occurs on the leaves and stems of oak trees, caused by insects. Also, **oak gall.**

oak·en (ō′kən) *adj.* made of oak.

oa·kum (ō′kəm) *n.* a loose fiber obtained by untwisting and picking apart old ropes, often used for filling up seams and cracks in a boat or ship. [Old English *ācumba* tow²; literally, off combing; referring to *combing* the tow out of the flax before spinning.]

oar (ôr) *n.* **1.** a long, usually wooden, pole with a flat or curved blade at one end, used to propel or steer a boat. **2.** a person who rows a boat; rower. *—v.t.* to propel with or as with oars; row. *—v.i.* to advance by or as by rowing. [Old English *ār* implement for propelling a boat.]

oar·lock (ôr′lok′) *n.* a device, often U-shaped, for holding an oar in place while rowing. Also, *British,* **rowlock.** [Old English *ārloc.*]

oars·man (ôrz′mən) *n., pl.* **-men** (-mən). a person who rows a boat.

OAS, Organization of American States.

o·a·sis (ō ā′sis) *n., pl.* **-ses** (-sēz). **1.** a place in the desert made fertile by a permanent or nearly permanent supply of water. **2.** something that offers relief or a welcome change from that which is dull, annoying, or otherwise unpleasant: *The library was an oasis of quiet in the bustling city.* [Late Latin *oasis* name of fertile spots in the Libyan desert, from Greek *oasis;* of Egyptian origin.]

oat (ōt) *n.* **1.** *also,* **oats.** a cereal grain of the plant *Avena sativa,* of the grass family, enclosed in a thick hull, cultivated mainly for animal feed. **2.** *also,* **oats.** the plant itself, having flat grasslike leaves of bluish green. **3.** any of various related grasses, such as the wild oat. [Old English *āte* grain of a cereal plant.]

• **to feel one's oats.** *Informal.* **a.** to be lively, high-spirited, or frisky. **b.** to feel self-assured or important and act accordingly.

oat·cake (ōt′kāk′) *n.* a thin, hard oatmeal cake.

oat·en (ō′tən) *adj.* relating to, containing, or made of oats, oatmeal, or oat straw.

oath (ōth) *n., pl.* **oaths** (ōthz, ōths). **1.** a formal declaration bound by an appeal to God or a person or thing considered sacred to witness the truth of a statement or the binding character of a promise: *The president takes an oath to uphold the Constitution.* **2.** a careless or irreverent use of the name of God or a person or thing considered sacred to add emphasis or express anger. **3.** a profane expression or utterance; swearword. [Old English *āth* formal statement bound by an appeal to God or something held sacred.]

oat

oat·meal (ōt′mēl′) *n.* **1.** a meal made from oats; ground or rolled oats. **2.** a porridge prepared from this.

ob- *prefix* **1.** in opposition to; against: *obstruct.* **2.** over; upon: *obscure.* **3.** toward; to: *obtrude.* **4.** completely: *obsolete.* **5.** contrary to the usual position; inversely: *oblate.* [Latin *ob* toward, against.]

ob., obiit.

O·ba·di·ah (ō′bə dī′ə) *n.* a book of the Old Testament, containing prophecies attributed to the Hebrew prophet Obadiah. Also, in the Douay Bible, **Abdias.**

ob·bli·ga·to (ob′li gä′tō) *also,* **obligato.** *Music. adj.* (of an accompaniment or part) essential to the performance of a composition. *—n., pl.* **-tos.** an accompaniment or part of independent importance, esp. an instrumental solo accompanying a vocal piece. [Italian *obbligato* obligatory, past participle of *obbligare* to compel, bind, from Latin *obligāre* to bind; referring to music essential to a performance, such as an accompaniment.]

ob·du·ra·cy (ob′dər ə sē, ob′dyər-) *n.* the state or quality of being obdurate.

ob·du·rate (ob′dər it, ob′dyər-) *adj.* **1.** not yielding; stubborn; obstinate. **2.** unmoved by feelings of pity or regret; hardhearted: *an obdurate criminal.* [Latin *obdūrātus,* past participle of *obdūrāre* to harden.] **—ob′du·rate·ly,** *adv.* **—ob′du·rate·ness,** *n.*

o·be·di·ence (ō bē′dē əns) *n.* the act of obeying or the state of being obedient.

o·be·di·ent (ō bē′dē ənt) *adj.* tending or willing to obey or comply with something, as a rule, order, or law; submissive to authority. [Old French *obedient,* from Latin *obēdiēns,* present participle of *obēdīre* to hearken, serve.] **—o·be′di·ent·ly,** *adv.*

Synonyms **Obedient, compliant,** and **submissive** mean inclined to yield to the will of others. **Obedient** indicates a willingness to follow the orders of persons or institutions in authority: *The student was obedient to the wishes of the teacher.* **Compliant** implies an inclination to give in meekly to the demands of other persons: *The bully would take advantage of*

O

a	at	e	end	o	hot	u	up	hw	white		about
ā	ape	ē	me	ō	old	ū	use	ng	song		taken
ä	far	i	it	ô	fork	ü	rule	th	thin	ə	pencil
âr	care	ī	ice	oi	oil	u̇	pull	th	this		lemon
			ir	pierce	ou	out	ûr	turn	zh	measure		circus

anyone with a compliant personality. **Submissive** goes further than *compliant,* suggesting an inability to assert one's own will: *The submissive employee never dreamed of asking for a raise.*

o·bei·sance (ō bā′səns, ō bē′-) *n.* **1.** a bodily movement or gesture, such as a bow or curtsy, indicating or expressing obedience or respect. **2.** deference, respect, or reverent regard given or shown; homage: *to pay obeisance to one's elders.* [Old French *obeissance* obedience, from *obeir* to obey, from Latin *obēdīre* to hearken, yield, serve.] —**o·bei′sant,** *adj.* —**o·bei′sant·ly,** *adv.*

ob·e·lisk (ob′ə lisk′) *n.* a four-sided, usually monolithic, stone pillar that tapers as it rises and terminates in a pyramid, often used as a monument in ancient Egypt. [Latin *obeliscus* small spit², obelisk, from Greek *obeliskos,* diminutive of *obelos* a spit², obelisk.]

O·ber·on (ō′bə ron′) *n.* in medieval legend and literature, the king of the fairies and husband of Titania.

o·bese (ō bēs′) *adj.* extremely fat or fleshy. [Latin *obēsus* fat; literally, that has eaten himself fat, past participle of *obedere* to eat, eat away.] —**o·bese′ness,** *n.*

o·bes·i·ty (ō bē′si tē) *n.* the condition of being obese.

o·bey (ō bā′) *v.t.* **1.** to comply with or carry out the orders, commands, requests, or instructions of: *The child obeyed the baby-sitter.* **2.** to comply with or carry out: *to obey the law, to obey orders.* **3.** to be guided, controlled, or motivated by: *to obey one's conscience.* —*v.i.* to be obedient. [Old French *obeir,* from Latin *obēdīre* to hearken, yield, serve.] —**o·bey′er,** *n.*

ob·fus·cate (ob′fə skāt′, ob fus′kāt) *v.t.,* -**cat·ed,** -**cat·ing.** **1.** to make unclear; confuse; muddle. **2.** to make obscure or indistinct; darken or cloud over. [Late Latin *obfuscātus,* past participle of *obfuscāre* to darken, going back to Latin *ob-* (see OB-) + *fuscus* dark.] —**ob′fus·ca′tion,** *n.* —**ob·fus′ca·to′ry,** *adj.*

o·bi (ō′bē) *n.* a broad sash worn with a Japanese kimono.

Japanese kimonos with **obis**

o·bi·it (ō′bē it, ob′ē-) *Latin.* he (or she) died.

o·bit (ō′bit, ob′it) *n. Informal.* obituary.

ob·i·ter dic·tum (ob′i tər dik′təm) *pl.* **ob·i·ter dic·ta** (ob′i tər dik′tə). **1.** an opinion expressed by a judge, not directly related to the case in question and therefore not binding. **2.** any incidental statement or remark. [Latin *obiter dictum* something said in passing.]

o·bit·u·ar·y (ō bich′ü er′ē) *n., pl.* -**ar·ies.** a notice of a death, esp. in a newspaper, often including a short biography of the deceased. —*adj.* relating to or recording a death. [Medieval Latin *obituarius* record of a death, relating to death, from Latin *obitus* death.]

obj. **1.** object. **2.** objection. **3.** objective.

ob·ject (*n.,* ob′jikt, -jekt; *v.,* əb jekt′) *n.* **1.** anything that can be seen or touched and differentiated from things around it; material thing. **2.** a person or thing that is the focus of feeling, thought, or action: *The proposal was the object of much criticism.* **3.** a thing aimed at; goal: *The object of their visit was not clear.* **4.** *Grammar.* **a.** a word or group of words that receive or are affected by the action of the verb. **b.** a word or group of words expressing a relationship to a preposition. **5.** *Philosophy.* anything that is conceived of or apprehended by the mind. —*v.i.* **1.** to offer a reason or argument against; have or raise an objection (with *to*): *The defense lawyer objected to the prosecutor's badgering of the witness.* **2.** to express or feel disapproval: *We objected to their*

rudeness. —*v.t.* to bring forward or offer in opposition or criticism; state as an objection. [Latin *objectus* a casting before, something presented to the sight, from *obicere* to cast before or in the way of, oppose.] —**ob·jec′tor,** *n.* —For Synonyms *(n.),* see **subject.**

ob·jec·ti·fy (əb jek′tə fī′) *v.t.,* -**fied,** -**fy·ing.** to express in concrete form; make objective; externalize. —**ob·jec′ti·fi·ca′tion,** *n.*

ob·jec·tion (əb jek′shən) *n.* **1.** a cause or reason for opposing, disliking, or disapproving of something: *The committee listed its objections to the budget cuts.* **2.** a statement or feeling of opposition, dislike, or disapproval: *They showed their objection to the speech by walking out of the auditorium.* **3.** the act of objecting.

ob·jec·tion·a·ble (əb jek′shə nə bəl) *adj.* deserving of or arousing dislike or disapproval; offensive: *a highly objectionable decision.* —**ob·jec′tion·a·bly,** *adv.*

ob·jec·tive (əb jek′tiv) *adj.* **1.** unaffected by personal feelings or prejudices; without emotional or intellectual bias; detached: *The reporter tried to be as objective as possible in the article on the trial.* **2.** concerned with or emphasizing external or observable phenomena rather than personal thoughts or feelings. **3.** having actual existence independent of the mind; real: *the objective universe.* **4.** *Grammar.* designating the case of the object of a transitive verb or preposition. **5.** being the object toward which effort is directed: *The walled city was the army's objective point.* —*n.* **1.** something toward which effort is directed; aim. **2.** *Grammar.* **a.** the objective case. **b.** a word in this case; object. **3.** the lens or lenses that are the first to receive light from the object being viewed through an optical instrument, such as a telescope, microscope, or camera. [Medieval Latin *objectivus* relating to an object, from Latin *objectus* object. See OBJECT.] —**ob·jec′tive·ly,** *adv.* —**ob·jec′tive·ness,** *n.*

n. **Objective, goal,** and **end** mean what one intends to accomplish by some effort. **Objective** designates a clearly defined, attainable purpose: *The team's objective was to have a winning season.* **Goal** suggests an aim that may not be easily attainable: *The organization's goal is to eliminate air pollution.* **End** suggests a remote outcome, distinguished from the process of attaining it: *The candidate argued that means were as important as ends in foreign policy.*

objective complement, a word or phrase that modifies the object of a transitive verb, such as *guilty* in *The jury found the defendant guilty.*

ob·jec·tiv·i·ty (ob′jek tiv′i tē) *n.* **1.** the state or quality of being objective. **2.** external or material reality.

object lesson, a practical illustration of some principle or truth.

ob·jet d'art (ôb zhā där′) *pl.* **ob·jets d'art** (ôb zhā däʀ′). *French.* an object that has artistic value.

ob·jur·gate (ob′jər gāt′, əb jûr′gāt) *v.t.,* -**gat·ed,** -**gat·ing.** to rebuke severely; scold harshly. [Latin *objurgātus,* past participle of *objurgāre* to scold.] —**ob′jur·ga′tion,** *n.*

ob·jur·ga·to·ry (əb jûr′gə tôr′ē) *adj.* conveying or containing a sharp rebuke.

ob·late (ob′lāt, ob lāt′) *adj.* (of a spheroid) flattened at the poles. ➡ opposed to **prolate.** [Modern Latin *oblatus* stretched, from Latin *ob* (see OB-) + *lātus* carried, past participle of *ferre* to bring, carry.]

ob·la·tion (ob lā′shən) *n.* **1.** the act of offering a gift, sacrifice, or worship to God or another sacred being, esp. the offering of bread and wine in the Holy Communion service. **2.** anything offered as a gift or sacrifice, esp. the bread and wine of Holy Communion. [Late Latin *oblātiō* offering, from Latin *oblātus,* past participle of *offerre* to present, bring before, from *ob* toward + *ferre* to bring, carry.]

ob·li·gate (ob′li gāt′) *v.t.,* -**gat·ed,** -**gat·ing.** to bind morally or legally, as by a contract, promise, or sense of duty. [Latin *obligātus,* past participle of *obligāre* to bind.]

ob·li·ga·tion (ob′li gā′shən) *n.* **1.** a binding or constraining power, as of a law, promise, or sense of duty: *We are under no obligation to them.* **2.** something that a person is morally or legally bound to do: *It is the obligation of all citizens to vote.* **3.** the fact, state, or condition of being grateful or indebted to another for a favor or service: *We feel a sense of obligation to them for their help.* **4.** something by which one is bound, such as a promise or sense of duty or responsibility: *to fulfill an obligation.* **5.** something owed in payment or return for a favor or service received: *to repay a financial obligation.* **6.** *Law.* **a.** a binding agreement acknowledging indebtedness or promising to perform some act. **b.** a document containing the terms of such an agreement. —For Synonyms, see **duty.**

ob·li·ga·to (ob′li gä′tō) obbligato.

ob·lig·a·to·ry (ə blig′ə tôr′ē, ob′li gə-) *adj.* of the nature of or constituting an obligation; mandatory; compulsory.

o·blige (ə blīj′) *v.t.*, **o·bliged, o·blig·ing. 1.** to bind, compel, or constrain, as by moral or legal force. **2.** to place under an obligation, as for a favor or service; make indebted or grateful (with *to*): *I'm obliged to you for all you've done.* **3.** to do a favor or service for: *Please oblige me by returning this book to the library.* [Old French *obliger* to bind, tie, from Latin *obligāre* to bind, make liable, pledge.] —**o·blig′er,** *n.* —For Synonyms, see **force.**

ob·li·gee (ob′li jē′) *n.* **1.** *Law.* a person to whom one is obligated by contract or bond. **2.** a person who is under obligation to another.

o·blig·ing (ə blī′jing) *adj.* willing to do favors or to be of service; helpful. —**o·blig′ing·ly,** *adv.* —**o·blig′ing·ness,** *n.*

o·blique (ə blēk′, ō blēk′) *adj.* **1.** having a slanting or sloping direction, position, or course; inclined. **2.** not straightforward or direct: *to give an oblique answer to a question.* **3.** neither perpendicular nor parallel. —*n.* something that is oblique, such as a line. [Latin *oblīquus* slanting, indirect.] —**o·blique′ly,** *adv.* —**o·blique′ness,** *n.*

oblique angle, an angle that is not a right angle; acute or obtuse angle.

oblique case, any case of a declension other than the nominative and vocative.

o·bliq·ui·ty (ə blik′wi tē) *n., pl.* **-ties. 1.** the state, quality, or condition of being oblique. **2.a.** an inclination from a vertical or horizontal line, plane, or position. **b.** the amount of such inclination. **3.** a turning away from accepted standards of morality or sound thinking.

ob·lit·er·ate (ə blit′ə rāt′) *v.t.*, **-at·ed, -at·ing. 1.** to destroy completely; remove all traces of. **2.** to blot or rub out, such as writing; erase. [Latin *oblīterātus,* past participle of *oblīterāre* to strike out, erase, from *ob* over + *littera* letter.] —**ob·lit′er·a′tion,** *n.* —**ob·lit′er·a′tive,** *adj.* —**ob·lit′er·a′tor,** *n.*

ob·liv·i·on (ə bliv′ē ən) *n.* **1.** the state or condition of being entirely forgotten: *That author's works have passed into oblivion.* **2.** the state or condition of forgetting completely; forgetfulness. [Old French *oblivion* forgetfulness, from Latin *oblīviō.*]

ob·liv·i·ous (ə bliv′ē əs) *adj.* **1.** not aware or conscious; unmindful (with *of* or *to*): *The child ran into the street, oblivious of the dangers involved.* **2.** lacking memory; forgetful (with *of*). [Latin *oblīviōsus* forgetful, from *oblīviō* forgetfulness.] —**ob·liv′i·ous·ly,** *adv.* —**ob·liv′i·ous·ness,** *n.*

ob·long (ob′lông′) *adj.* having greater length than width, as an ellipse and certain rectangles. —*n.* an oblong figure. [Latin *oblongus* rather long.]

ob·lo·quy (ob′lə kwē) *n., pl.* **-quies. 1.** abusive, slanderous language addressed to or aimed at another, esp. by a large number of people. **2.** the disgrace or shame resulting from such abuse. [Late Latin *obloquium* contradiction, from Latin *obloquī* to speak against.]

ob·nox·ious (ob nok′shəs) *adj.* **1.** extremely annoying and offensive: *an obnoxious person.* **2.** extremely disagreeable; odious; repugnant: *an obnoxious smell.* [Latin *obnoxius* liable to injury, from *ob-* (see OB-) + *noxa* injury.] —**ob·nox′ious·ly,** *adv.* —**ob·nox′ious·ness,** *n.* —For Synonyms, see **offensive.**

o·boe (ō′bō) *n.* a double-reed woodwind instrument having a high, penetrating tone and a range of three octaves. [Italian *oboè,* from French *hautbois.* See HAUTBOY.] —**o·bo·ist** (ō′bō ist), *n.*

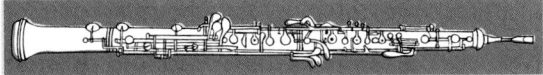

oboe

ob·o·lus (ob′ə ləs) *n., pl.* **-li** (-lī′). a silver coin of ancient Greece. Also, **ob·ol** (ob′əl). [Latin *obolus,* from Greek *obolos.*]

obs. 1. observatory. **2.** obsolete.

ob·scene (əb sēn′) *adj.* **1.** offensive to accepted standards of modesty or decency; indecent. **2.** causing disgust; repulsive. [Latin *obscēnus* of bad omen, repulsive.] —**ob·scene′ly,** *adv.*

ob·scen·i·ty (əb sen′i tē, -sē′ni-) *n., pl.* **-ties. 1.** the state or quality of being obscene; indecency. **2.** something obscene, as an act, expression, or word.

ob·scur·ant (əb skyūr′ənt) *n.* a person who opposes and tries to prevent inquiry, enlightenment, reform, and the advancement of knowledge. —*adj.* of, relating to, or characteristic of an obscurant. [Latin *obscūrāns,* present participle of *obscūrāre* to darken.]

ob·scur·ant·ism (əb skyūr′ən tiz′əm) *n.* opposition to inquiry, enlightenment, reform, and the advancement of knowledge; principles or practices of obscurants. —**ob·scur′ant·ist,** *n.*

ob·scu·ra·tion (ob′skyə rā′shən) *n.* the act of obscuring or the state of being obscured.

ob·scure (əb skyūr′) *adj.*, **-scur·er, -scur·est. 1.** not clearly expressed; difficult to understand: *an obscure explanation.* **2.** not clear or distinct; barely perceived by the senses: *an obscure figure in a photograph.* **3.** not well known; undistinguished: *an obscure writer.* **4.** not easily seen or discovered; remote; hidden: *an obscure mountain village.* **5.** having little or no light; dark; dim: *an obscure corner of an attic.* —*v.t.* **-scured, -scur·ing. 1.** to hide from view; darken or conceal: *Fog obscured the stars.* **2.** to lessen the glory of; overshadow. **3.** to make unintelligible or difficult to understand. [Old French *o(b)scur* dark, sinister, from Latin *obscūrus* dark, indistinct, from *ob-* over + *-scūrus* covered.] —**ob·scure′ly,** *adv.* —**ob·scure′ness,** *n.* —For Synonyms *(adj.),* see **vague.**

ob·scu·ri·ty (əb skyūr′i tē) *n., pl.* **-ties. 1.** the state or quality of being obscure. **2.** a person or thing that is obscure.

ob·se·quies (ob′si kwēz) *pl. n., sing.* **-quy** (-kwē). funeral rites or ceremonies. [Anglo-Norman *obsequie(s),* from Late Latin *obsequiae* (plural), modification (influenced by Latin *obsequium* service) of Latin *exsequiae.*]

ob·se·qui·ous (əb sē′kwē əs) *adj.* too ready or eager to serve, please, or obey; fawning. [Latin *obsequiōsus* full of compliance, from *obsequium* compliance, service.] —**ob·se′qui·ous·ly,** *adv.* —**ob·se′qui·ous·ness,** *n.*

ob·serv·a·ble (əb zûr′və bəl) *adj.* **1.** capable of being observed; perceptible: *an observable difference in attitude.* **2.** that may, should, or must be observed, celebrated, followed, or kept: *Certain formalities are observable in a court of law.* —**ob·serv′a·bly,** *adv.*

ob·serv·ance (əb zûr′vəns) *n.* **1.** the act or practice of following, adhering to, or complying with something, such as a rule or law. **2.** the act or practice of keeping or celebrating a customary rite, ceremony, or holiday: *the observance of Easter.* **3.** a customary rite, ceremony, or celebration: *Birthdays are annual observances.* **4.** the act of noticing or perceiving; observation.

ob·serv·ant (əb zûr′vənt) *adj.* **1.** quick to notice or perceive; alert. **2.** carefully attentive in observing anything required or prescribed, such as a rule, law, or custom (often with *of*): *observant of the laws.* [Latin *observāns,* present participle of *observāre* to watch, note, guard.] —**ob·serv′ant·ly,** *adv.*

ob·ser·va·tion (ob′zər vā′shən) *n.* **1.a.** the act, practice, or faculty of noticing or perceiving. **b.** the fact of being observed; notice: *The thief escaped observation.* **2.a.** the act of examining, noting, and recording facts or phenomena, esp. for scientific study. **b.** the record or data resulting from this. **3.** a remark or comment in reference to something that has been observed: *observations about a basketball game.*

ob·ser·va·tion·al (ob′zər vā′shə nəl) *adj.* of, relating to, resulting from, or based on observation. —**ob′ser·va′tion·al·ly,** *adv.*

ob·serv·a·to·ry (əb zûr′və tôr′ē) *n., pl.* **-ries. 1.a.** a place or building furnished with instruments and facilities for observing, studying, and collecting information on astronomical phenomena. **b.** a similarly equipped place for making meteorological or geophysical observations. **2.** an institution in which such work is carried on. **3.** any place or structure affording an extensive view.

ob·serve (əb zûrv′) *v.*, **-served, -serv·ing.** —*v.t.* **1.** to become aware of; notice or perceive. **2.** to watch carefully; regard with attention: *Observe how I make the sauce.* **3.** to make a careful observation of, esp. for a scientific purpose: *The scientist observed the behavior of the mice after they were given the drug.* **4.** to follow or comply with, as a rule or law: *to observe the speed limit.* **5.** to keep or celebrate according to custom, such as a holiday. **6.** to comment; remark: *"That concert was quite good," my friend observed.* —*v.i.* **1.** to attend or watch without taking an active role, as at a meeting; act as an observer. **2.** to take notice. **3.** to make a comment (often with *on* or *upon*). [Old French *observer* examine, keep, from Latin *observāre* to watch, note, guard.]

ob·serv·er (əb zûr′vər) *n.* **1.** a person who observes. **2.** a person who attends a meeting, assembly, or convention to observe and report on the proceedings, rather than to participate as an official delegate. **3.** a member of an airplane crew who maintains observation during flight. —For Synonyms, see **spectator.**

ob·sess (əb ses′) *v.t.* to occupy or trouble the mind of excessively, esp. as a fixed idea: *A fear of failure obsessed the student.* [Latin *obsessus,* past participle of *obsidēre* to sit at, besiege.]

a	at	e	end	o	hot	u	up	hw	white		about
ā	ape	ē	me	ō	old	ū	use	ng	song	ə	taken
ä	far	i	it	ô	fork	ü	rule	th	thin		pencil
âr	care	ī	ice	oi	oil	u̇	pull	t͡h	this		lemon
				ou	out	ûr	turn	zh	measure		circus
		î	pierce								

839

ob·ses·sion (əb sesh′ən) *n.* **1.** something that obsesses, such as a fixed idea or desire: *Making a great deal of money was an obsession of the executive.* **2.** the act of obsessing or the state of being obsessed.

ob·ses·sive (əb ses′iv) *adj.* of, relating to, causing, or caused by an obsession: *an obsessive interest in clothes.* —*n.* a person who has obsessive thoughts or behavior. —**ob·ses′sive·ly,** *adv.* —**ob·ses′sive·ness,** *n.*

ob·sid·i·an (əb sid′ē ən, ob-) *n.* a hard, glassy igneous rock, usually black, formed when molten lava cools so rapidly that there is not enough time for crystallization to occur. [Latin *obsidiānus (lapis)* manuscript error for *obsiānus (lapis)* (stone) of Obsius, a Roman traveler who, according to Pliny the Elder, A.D. 23?-79, found a similar stone in Ethiopia.]

ob·so·les·cent (ob′sə les′ənt) *adj.* going out of use or date; becoming obsolete. [Latin *obsolēscēns,* present participle of *obsolēscere* to grow old, fall into disuse.] —**ob′so·les′cence,** *n.* —**ob′so·les′cent·ly,** *adv.*

ob·so·lete (ob′sə lēt′, ob′sə lēt′) *adj.* **1.** no longer in use or practice: *Stagecoaches are obsolete.* **2.** out-of-date; outmoded; old-fashioned. [Latin *obsolētus,* past participle of *obsolēscere* to grow old, fall into disuse, from *ob* (see OB-) + *solēre* to be accustomed.] —**ob′so·lete′ly,** *adv.* —**ob′so·lete′ness,** *n.*

> **Usage** **Obsolete** and **archaic** words are words that are no longer part of everyday vocabulary. When a concept or object becomes **obsolete,** the word or words that refer to it also gradually disappear from current use. For example, many words that referred to medieval knighthood have become **obsolete.** **Archaic** words are words that were in current use for a long time but are no longer part of the spoken vocabulary. These words, such as *thou, thee, shalt, doth, quoth,* and *spake,* have become old-fashioned or are now used in a different form. **Obsolete** words, however, are not necessarily old. Slang terms, for example, often become **obsolete** within a short time, and technical words generally fall out of use when the technology itself becomes outdated. Because readers come across **archaic** and **obsolete** words in great works from the past, such as the Bible or the writings of Shakespeare, many of these words continue to be listed in contemporary dictionaries.

ob·sta·cle (ob′stə kəl) *n.* a person or thing that opposes, stands in the way of, or blocks progress. [Old French *o(b)stacle,* from Latin *obstāculum,* from *obstāre* to stand in the way.]

> **Synonyms** **Obstacle, obstruction,** and **impediment** mean something that prevents or hinders progress. **Obstacle** suggests an object or condition that must be removed or gotten around before progress can resume: *Their parents' opposition was a serious obstacle to the marriage.* **Obstruction** is stronger and implies making a way impassable: *The landslides created many obstructions on the mountain roads.* **Impediment** is used of something that interferes with or delays a process or normal functioning: *The engineer's injury was an impediment to construction of the bridge.*

ob·stet·ric (ob stet′rik) *adj.* of or relating to obstetrics and childbirth. Also, **ob·stet′ri·cal.**

ob·ste·tri·cian (ob′sti trish′ən) *n.* a physician specializing in obstetrics.

ob·stet·rics (ob stet′riks) *n.* the branch of medicine that deals with the care of women from the first sign of pregnancy until a few weeks after delivery. ➡ used as singular. [Plural of *obstetric,* from Modern Latin *obstetricus* relating to a midwife, from Latin *obstētrīx* midwife; literally, she who stands by.]

ob·sti·na·cy (ob′stə nə sē) *n., pl.* -cies. **1.** the state or quality of being obstinate. **2.** an act or instance of this.

ob·sti·nate (ob′stə nit) *adj.* **1.** not yielding to argument, persuasion, or reason; stubborn; inflexible. **2.** difficult to overcome, control, or cure: *an obstinate cough.* [Latin *obstinātus* stubborn, past participle of *obstināre* to persist.] —**ob′sti·nate·ly,** *adv.* —**ob′sti·nate·ness,** *n.*

ob·strep·er·ous (əb strep′ər əs) *adj.* noisy, boisterous, or unruly, esp. in resisting control. [Latin *obstreperus* clamorous.] —**ob·strep′er·ous·ly,** *adv.* —**ob·strep′er·ous·ness,** *n.*

ob·struct (əb strukt′) *v.t.* **1.** to block or fill with obstacles or impediments that prevent passage: *Large boulders obstructed the entrance to the cave.* **2.** to be or come in the way of: *The column obstructed my view of the stage.* **3.** to interrupt, interfere with, or retard the action, passage, course, or progress of: *to obstruct justice.* [Latin *obstructus,* past participle of *obstruere* to block up, hinder, from *ob* against + *struere* to pile up.] —**ob·struct′er;** *also,* **ob·struc′tor,** *n.* —**ob·struc′tive,** *adj.* —For Synonyms, see **hinder**[1].

ob·struc·tion (əb struk′shən) *n.* **1.** something that obstructs. **2.** the act of obstructing or the state of being obstructed. —For Synonyms, see **obstacle.**

ob·struc·tion·ist (əb struk′shə nist) *n.* a person who systematically obstructs or impedes work or progress, esp. in a legislative body. —**ob·struc′tion·ism,** *n.*

ob·tain (əb tān′) *v.t.* to gain possession of, esp. as a result of effort; acquire: *to obtain permission to do something.* —*v.i.* to be widespread, established, or customary: *The custom still obtains in many parts of the country.* [Old French *obtenir* to acquire, succeed in getting, going back to Latin *obtinēre* to take hold of.] —**ob·tain′a·ble,** *adj.* —**ob·tain′ment,** *n.* —For Synonyms *(v.t.),* see **gain.**

ob·trude (əb trūd′) *v.,* -**trud·ed,** -**trud·ing.** —*v.t.* **1.** to force or thrust, as an opinion or oneself, upon another or others in a rude or bold manner. **2.** to push out; thrust forward. —*v.i.* to force oneself upon another or others. [Latin *obtrūdere* to thrust against, from *ob* against + *trūdere* to thrust.] —**ob·trud′er,** *n.*

ob·tru·sion (əb trū′zhən) *n.* **1.** the act of obtruding. **2.** something obtruded.

ob·tru·sive (əb trū′siv) *adj.* **1.** tending to obtrude; overly assertive; forward: *obtrusive behavior.* **2.** protruding; projecting. **3.** unpleasantly noticeable. —**ob·tru′sive·ly,** *adv.* —**ob·tru′sive·ness,** *n.*

ob·tuse (əb tūs′, -tūs′) *adj.* **1.** slow in understanding or perceiving: *an obtuse person.* **2.** not sharp or pointed; blunt: *an obtuse leaf.* **3.** (of a triangle) having an obtuse angle. [Latin *obtūsus* blunted, past participle of *obtundere* to beat against, blunt.] —**ob·tuse′ly,** *adv.* —**ob·tuse′ness,** *n.*

obtuse angle, an angle that is greater than 90 degrees but less than 180 degrees. For illustration, see **angle**[1].

ob·verse (*n.,* ob′vûrs; *adj.,* ob vûrs′, ob′vûrs) *n.* **1.** the side of a coin or medal that bears the principal design. ➡ opposed to **reverse. 2.** the front or principal surface of anything. **3.** counterpart. **4.** *Logic.* a proposition that is logically equivalent to another proposition from which it is formed by changing a positive predicate to a negative and vice versa, for example: *No one is immortal* is the obverse of *Everyone is mortal.* —*adj.* **1.** turned toward or facing the observer. **2.** narrower at the base than at the top: *an obverse leaf.* **3.** serving as or being a counterpart. [Latin *obversus,* past participle of *obvertere* to turn toward or against.] —**ob·verse′ly,** *adv.*

ob·ver·sion (ob vûr′zhən, -shən) *n.* **1.** the act of obverting or the state of being obverted. **2.** something that results from obverting.

ob·vert (ob vûrt′) *v.t.* **1.** *Logic.* to derive or state the obverse of (a proposition). **2.** to turn (something) so as to show another surface. [Latin *obvertere* to turn toward or against.]

ob·vi·ate (ob′vē āt′) *v.t.,* -at·ed, -at·ing. to prevent or remove by anticipatory measures; anticipate and dispose of: *to obviate the risks involved in shipping explosives.* [Late Latin *obviātus,* past participle of *obviāre* to meet, prevent, going back to Latin *ob* (see OB-) + *via* way.] —**ob′vi·a′tion,** *n.*

ob·vi·ous (ob′vē əs) *adj.* **1.** easily seen or understood; clearly evident: *It was obvious that they didn't want to go.* **2.** not trying to hide one's feelings; without pretense: *to be obvious about one's dislikes.* [Latin *obvius* in the way, at hand, from *ob* (see OB-) + *via* way.] —**ob′vi·ous·ly,** *adv.* —**ob′vi·ous·ness,** *n.*

oc-, form of **ob-** before *c,* as in *occasion.*

oc·a·ri·na (ok′ə rē′nə) *n.* a musical wind instrument having ten finger holes and producing a whistlelike tone when air is blown through the mouthpiece. [Italian *ocarina,* diminutive of *oca* goose (because of its shape), going back to Latin *avis* bird.]

oc·ca·sion (ə kā′zhən) *n.* **1.** a particular time at which something occurs: *I can't recall the occasion, but I've met you before.* **2.** an event or occurrence: *We congratulated them on the occasion of their marriage.*

ocarina

3. an event or function regarded as being special or significant: *My parents' fiftieth wedding anniversary was a very happy occasion.* **4.** a favorable or suitable time; opportunity: *I don't have many occasions to be alone.* **5.** an immediate cause or reason: *Our teacher's departure was the occasion of much sadness.* **6.** need or requirement: *I never had occasion to reprimand them.* —*v.t.* to be the cause of; bring about. [Latin *occāsiō* opportunity, going back to Latin *oc-* for *ob* (see OB-) + *cadere* to fall.] —For Synonyms, see **opportunity.**

•**on occasion.** now and then; as opportunity or need arises.

oc·ca·sion·al (ə kā′zhə nəl) *adj.* **1.** happening or appearing at varying intervals of time; infrequent: *an occasional visitor, an occasional smile.* **2.** produced, intended, or used for some special occasion or event: *occasional verse.* **3.** (of furniture) not part of a set: *an occasional chair.*

oc·ca·sion·al·ly (ə kā′zhə nə lē) *adv.* at varying intervals of time; once in a while.

Oc·ci·dent (ok′si dənt) *n.* the countries of Europe and the Western Hemisphere. ➡ distinguished from **Orient.** [Latin *occidēns* quarter of the setting sun, west.]

Oc·ci·den·tal (ok′si den′təl) *also,* **oc·ci·den·tal.** *adj.* of, relating to, or characteristic of the Occident. ➡ distinguished from **Oriental.** —*n.* a member or close descendant of a people native to the Occident.

oc·cip·i·tal (ok sip′i təl) *adj.* of, relating to, or near the occiput or occipital bone. —*n.* occipital bone.

occipital bone, a bone forming the back of the skull and part of its base. For illustration, see **parietal.**

oc·ci·put (ok′si pət) *n., pl.* **oc·cip·i·ta** (ok sip′i tə). the back part of the head. [Latin *occiput,* from *ob* (see OB-) + *caput* head.]

oc·clude (ə klüd′) *v.,* **-clud·ed, -clud·ing.** —*v.t.* **1.** to stop up, close, or block, such as a passage or pore. **2.** to shut in, out, or off. **3.** (of a solid chemical compound, as some metals) to absorb and retain (a gas, liquid, or other solid). **4.** (of a mass of cold air) to force (warm air) upward from the surface of the earth. —*v.i.* (of the teeth in the upper and lower jaws) to meet closely. [Latin *occlūdere* to shut up.]

occluded front, an air mass formed when a cold air mass occludes a warm air mass.

oc·clu·sion (ə klü′zhən) *n.* **1.** the act or process of occluding or the state of being occluded. **2.** occluded front. **3.** blockage of a blood vessel.

oc·cult (ə kult′, ok′ult) *adj.* **1.** of, relating to, or concerned with certain mystical arts or practices, such as astrology or alchemy. **2.** beyond the realm of human understanding; mysterious. **3.** communicated only to the initiated; secret. —*n.* occult arts or practices. ➡ usually preceded by *the: a follower of the occult.* —*v.t.* **1.** to conceal from view; hide. **2.** *Astronomy.* to conceal by occultation. —*v.i.* to become concealed from view. [Latin *occultus* hidden, past participle of *occulere* to cover up, hide.] —**oc·cult′ly,** *adv.* —**oc·cult′ness,** *n.*

oc·cul·ta·tion (ok′ul tā′shən) *n.* **1.** an eclipse of one celestial body by the passing of another between it and the observer. **2.** a disappearance from view or notice.

oc·cult·ism (ə kul′tiz əm, ok′ul tiz′-) *n.* **1.** a belief in the existence of mysterious or hidden spiritual powers. **2.** the study or practice of occult arts. —**oc·cult′ist,** *n.*

oc·cu·pan·cy (ok′yə pən sē) *n., pl.* **-cies. 1.** the act of occupying or the state of being occupied. **2.** a period of time during which something is occupied. **3.** the condition of being an occupant or tenant. **4.** *Law.* the act of taking possession of ownerless property with the intention of acquiring right of ownership to it.

oc·cu·pant (ok′yə pənt) *n.* **1.** a person who occupies a place or position. **2.** a person, group, or organization having legal control or possession of a property; tenant or owner. [Latin *occupāns,* present participle of *occupāre* to seize.]

oc·cu·pa·tion (ok′yə pā′shən) *n.* **1.** work or activity pursued as the source of one's livelihood. **2.** the act of occupying or the state of being occupied. **3.** the act or process of seizing and maintaining control of enemy territory by a military force. [Latin *occupātiō* a seizing, employment.]

oc·cu·pa·tion·al (ok′yə pā′shə nəl) *adj.* of, relating to, or resulting from one's occupation: *Miners are at risk of getting an occupational disease of the lungs.* —**oc′cu·pa′tion·al·ly,** *adv.*

occupational therapy, a type of therapy that promotes the recovery or rehabilitation of patients by teaching them a skill or providing them with creative activity, such as arts and crafts.

oc·cu·py (ok′yə pī′) *v.t.,* **-pied, -py·ing. 1.** to take up (time or space): *Meetings occupied most of the morning.* **2.** to seize and maintain control of by military force. **3.** to live in; inhabit. **4.** to be the main consideration or interest of: *Vacation plans occupied my thoughts all morning.* **5.** to have and retain possession; hold: *to occupy a high position in a company.* [Old French *occuper* to keep busy, take possession of, from Latin *occupāre* to seize.] —**oc′cu·pi′er,** *n.*

oc·cur (ə kûr′) *v.i.,* **-curred, -cur·ring. 1.** to take place; come to pass: *The accident occurred yesterday.* **2.** to appear or be found: *The same theme occurs in much of the author's work.* **3.** to come to mind; suggest itself: *It did not occur to me to take an umbrella today.* [Latin *occurrere* to run to meet, present itself.] —For Synonyms, see **happen.**

oc·cur·rence (ə kûr′əns) *n.* **1.** the act or fact of occurring. **2.** something that occurs; incident: *an everyday occurrence.* —For Synonyms, see **event.**

o·cean (ō′shən) *n.* **1.** the whole body of salt water that covers nearly three fourths of the earth's surface. **2.** any of the major subdivisions of this body of water, such as the Atlantic, Pacific,

Indian, or Arctic Ocean. **3.** a vast expanse or quantity: *an ocean of light.* [Latin *ōceanus* the great sea around the earth, from Greek *ōkeanos.*]

ocean current, a large-scale movement of ocean water flowing continuously in approximately the same path, such as the Gulf Stream.

o·cean·go·ing (ō′shən gō′ing) *adj.* of, relating to, or designed for operation on the open sea.

o·ce·an·ic (ō′shē an′ik) *adj.* **1.** of, relating to, or inhabiting the ocean. **2.** resembling the ocean; vast.

O·ce·a·nid (ō sē′ə nid) *n.* in Greek mythology, any one of the ocean nymphs who were the daughters of Oceanus.

o·cean·og·ra·phy (ō′shə nog′rə fē) *n.* the science of the oceans, dealing with the structure of the ocean basins, composition and movement of the waters, and oceanic life. —**o′cean·og′ra·pher,** *n.* —**o·cean·o·graph·ic** (ō′shə nə graf′ik); *also,* **o′cean·o·graph′i·cal,** *adj.*

ocean sunfish, a large fish, *Mola mola,* found in temperate and tropical seas, having a flattened, oval body and weighing up to 2,000 pounds (907 kilograms). Length: to 11 feet (3.4 meters).

O·ce·a·nus (ō sē′ə nəs) *n.* in Greek mythology, a Titan who was the father of the Oceanids and the ruler of the great river that the ancient Greeks believed surrounded the earth.

o·cel·lus (ō sel′əs) *n., pl.* **o·cel·li** (ō sel′ī). **1.** in insects and certain other invertebrates, a simple eye consisting of sensory cells, pigment-containing cells, and sometimes a lens that can concentrate light rays. **2.** an eyelike spot, as on a peacock feather. [Latin *ocellus* little eye, diminutive of *oculus* eye.]

o·ce·lot (os′ə lot′, ō′sə-) *n.* a wildcat, *Felis pardalis,* native to Texas and Central and South America, having a yellowish coat marked with black spots, rings, and stripes. Height: 16 inches (41 centimeters) at the shoulder. [French *ocelot,* from Nahuatl *ocelotl* tiger, jaguar.]

o·cher (ō′kər) *also,* **o·chre.** *n.* **1.** any of several mixtures of clay and iron oxides used as pigments. Yellow or brown ochers consist of limonite; red ochers consist of hematite. **2.** a reddish yellow or brownish yellow color. —*adj.* having the color ocher. [Old French *ocre* friable clay (yellow or red) used as a pigment, from Latin *ōchra* yellow ocher, from Greek *ōchrā,* from *ōchros* pale yellow.] —**o′cher·ous,** *adj.*

o'clock (ə klok′) *adv.* **1.** of or according to the clock: *two o'clock.* **2.** according to the direction indicated by a num-

ocelot

ber on an imaginary clock with the observer at the center of the clock, facing or heading toward twelve o'clock horizontally or directly beneath twelve o'clock vertically. To such an observer something directly behind would be at six o'clock. [Contraction of *of the clock.*]

o·co·til·lo (ō′kə tē′yō) *n., pl.* **-los.** a spiny shrub, *Fouquieria splendens,* found in arid parts of southwestern North America, bearing red, tubular flowers. [Mexican Spanish *ocotillo,* diminutive of *ocote* Mexican pine, from Nahuatl *okotl* pine.]

oct-, form of **octa-** or **octo-** before vowels.

Oct., October.

octa- *combining form* eight: *octahedron.* [Greek *oktō.*]

oc·ta·gon (ok′tə gon′, -gən) *n.* a polygon having eight sides and eight angles. [Latin *octagōnum,* from Greek *oktagonon,* going back to *oktō* eight + *gōniā* angle, corner.]

oc·tag·o·nal (ok tag′ə nəl) *adj.* having the geometric properties of an octagon. —**oc·tag′o·nal·ly,** *adv.*

oc·ta·he·dral (ok′tə hē′drəl) *adj.* having the geometric properties of an octahedron.

oc·ta·he·dron (ok′tə hē′drən) *n., pl.* **-drons** or **-dra** (-drə). a

a	at	e	end	o	hot	u	up	hw	white		about
ā	ape	ē	me	ō	old	ū	use	ng	song	ə	taken
ä	far	i	it	ô	fork	ü	rule	th	thin		pencil
âr	care	ī	ice	oi	oil	u̇	pull	th	this		lemon
		îr	pierce	ou	out	ûr	turn	zh	measure		circus

841

polyhedron having eight faces. [Greek *oktaedron,* from *oktō* eight + *hedra* seat, base[1].]

oc·tal (ok′tәl) *adj.* **1.** relating to or based on the number 8. **2.** of or relating to a system of computation having the number 8 as its base.

oc·tane (ok′tān) *n.* **1.** a colorless, liquid hydrocarbon of the alkane, or paraffin, series. Formula: C_8H_{18} **2.** octane number. [Greek *oktō* eight + -ANE.]

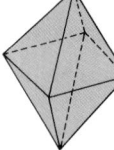

octahedron

octane number, a number that indicates the antiknock quality of a fuel. Also, **octane rating.**

oc·tant (ok′tәnt) *n.* **1.** an aircraft navigation instrument used to measure the angle of elevation of heavenly bodies up to 80 degrees above the horizon. **2.** any of the eight parts into which space is divided by three mutually perpendicular planes having a common point of intersection. **3.** an eighth of a circle or its circumference. [Late Latin *octāns* eighth part of a circle, from Latin *octō* eight.]

oc·tave (ok′tiv, -tāv) *n.* **1.** *Music.* **a.** the interval between a given tone or note and another that is eight diatonic degrees above or below it. **b.** a tone or note at this interval having twice or half as many vibrations per second as the one below or above it. **c.** a harmonic combination of two tones or notes at this interval sounded together. **d.** a series of tones or notes or of keys of an instrument contained within this interval: *The singer's vocal range is two octaves.* **e.** an organ stop giving tones an octave above those corresponding to the keys used. **2.a.** a group or stanza of eight lines of verse, esp. the ottava rima. **b.** the first Petrarchan eight lines of a sonnet. Also, **octet.** ➡ distinguished from **sestet. 3.a.** a major religious feast and the week after it, totaling eight days. **b.** the last of the eight days of such a period. **4.** any group of eight. [Latin *octāva,* feminine of *octāvus* eighth, from *octō* eight.]

oc·ta·vo (ok tā′vō, -tä′-) *n., pl.* **-vos. 1.** a page or paper size, as of a book, usually measuring from 5 by 8 inches (13 by 20 centimeters) to 6 by 9½ inches (15 by 24 centimeters), formerly ⅛ of a whole printer's sheet. **2.** a book having pages this size. [Latin *octāvō,* ablative of *octāvus* eighth. See OCTAVE.]

oc·tet (ok tet′) *also,* **oc·tette.** *n.* **1.a.** a musical composition for eight voices or instruments. **b.** a musical ensemble of eight performers. **2.** any group or set of eight persons or things. **3.** octave *(def. 2).* [Latin *octō* eight, on the model of DUET.]

oc·til·lion (ok til′yәn) *n.* **1.** in the United States, the cardinal number that is represented by 1 followed by twenty-seven zeros. **2.** in Great Britain, the cardinal number that is represented by 1 followed by forty-eight zeros. —*adj.* numbering one octillion. [French *octillion* unit followed by twenty-seven zeros, from Latin *octō* eight, on the model of *million.* See MILLION.] —**oc·til′lionth,** *adj., n.*

octo- *combining form* eight: *octopus.* [Greek *oktō* or Latin *octō.*]

Oc·to·ber (ok tō′bәr) *n.* the tenth month of the year, containing thirty-one days. [Middle English *October,* from Old French *Octobre,* from Latin *October* eighth month in the early Roman calendar, in which March was the first month, from *octō* eight.]

oc·to·ge·nar·i·an (ok′tә jә när′ē әn) *n.* a person who is eighty or between eighty and ninety years old. —*adj.* being eighty or between eighty and ninety years old. [Latin *octōgēnārius* containing eighty (going back to *octōgintā* eighty) + -AN.]

oc·to·pus (ok′tә pәs) *n., pl.* **-pus·es** or **-pi** (-pī′). **1.** any of a widespread group of saltwater cephalopods, family Octopodidae, having a soft, rounded body and eight tentacles that bear suckers and are used to move along the ocean bottom and to capture prey. **2.** a corporation or other organization having much power and far-reaching influence. [Modern Latin *octopus,* from Greek *oktōpous* eight-footed, from *oktō* eight + *pous* foot.]

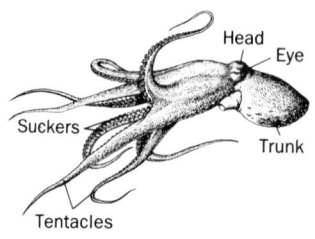

Head

Eye

Suckers

Trunk

Tentacles

octopus

oc·to·roon (ok′tә rün′) *n.* a person who is one-eighth black. ➡ often considered offensive. [OCTO- + (QUAD)ROON.]

oc·u·lar (ok′yә lәr) *adj.* **1.** of, relating to, or like the eye or eyesight. **2.** seen by the eye; visual. —*n.* the eyepiece of a telescope, microscope, or other optical instrument. [Late Latin *oculāris* relating to the eye, from Latin *oculus* eye.]

oc·u·list (ok′yә list) *n.* **1.** ophthalmologist. **2.** optometrist. [French *oculiste,* from Latin *oculus* eye.]

OD (ō′dē′) *n., pl.* **OD's.** *Slang.* an overdose of a drug, esp. a narcotic. —*v.i.,* **OD'ed, OD'ing.** to take or receive an overdose of a drug.

O.D. 1. officer of the day. **2.** olive drab. **3.** overdraft. **4.** overdrawn.

o·da·lisque (ō′dә lisk′) *also,* **o·da·lisk.** *n.* a female slave or concubine in a harem. [French *odalisque,* from Turkish *ōdalīq* chambermaid, from *ōdah* chamber in a harem.]

odd (od) *adj.* **1.** differing from the usual or ordinary, as in appearance or behavior; strange; peculiar. **2.** not belonging or relating to any particular total, set, or group; mixed; miscellaneous: *odd bits of information.* **3.** being one of a pair or set of which the rest is missing: *an odd shoe, an odd glove.* **4.** differing from or in addition to the routine, habitual, or planned; irregular; occasional: *I often think of them at odd moments.* **5.** (of a number) having a remainder of one when divided by two, as 5, 7, and 187. ➡ opposed to **even**[1]. **6.** with an indefinite amount in addition to a specified round number; plus a few more. ➡ often connected to a numerical adjective by a hyphen: *I have 500-odd dollars in the bank. The company was founded some forty-odd years ago.* **7.** left over; extra: *The odd guest at the dinner party made thirteen at the table.* [Old Norse *oddi* triangle, third or odd number.] —**odd′ly,** *adv.* —**odd′ness,** *n.* —For Synonyms, see **strange.**

odd·ball (od′bôl′) *Informal. n.* a person whose behavior or way of thinking is odd; eccentric. —*adj.* eccentric or outlandish: *an oddball idea.*

odd·i·ty (od′i tē) *n., pl.* **-ties. 1.** a person or thing that is odd or peculiar. **2.** an odd characteristic or trait; peculiarity. **3.** the state or quality of being odd; strangeness.

odd·ment (od′mәnt) *n. usually,* **oddments.** something that remains; leftover; remnant: *some oddments that didn't fit in the trunk.*

odds (odz) *pl. n.* **1.** the probability in favor of or against something being true or happening, often stated in the form of a ratio: *The odds are ten to one against your winning.* **2.** an allowance or advantage given to the weaker opponent in a contest in order to equalize the competitors. **3.** a difference that favors one side and is against another; advantage: *The odds are with the stronger team.* **4.** *Archaic.* unequal matters or conditions; inequalities. [From ODD.]

·**at odds.** in disagreement; quarreling.

odds and ends, miscellaneous or leftover articles, items, or matters: *I bought a few odds and ends at the hardware store.*

odds-on (odz′ôn′, -on′) *adj.* having a good chance to win or succeed: *the odds-on candidate in an election.*

ode (ōd) *n.* **1.** a lyric poem, usually rhymed, often in the form of an address, and usually dignified or lofty in subject, feeling, and style. **2.** formerly, a lyric poem intended or adapted to be sung. [French *ode,* from Late Latin *ōdē* song, from Greek *ōidē.*]

-ode *combining form* way; path: *cathode.* [Greek *-odos,* from *hodos.*]

O·din (ō′din) *n.* in Norse mythology, the king of the gods and god of wisdom and war. His Teutonic counterpart is Woden.

o·di·ous (ō′dē әs) *adj.* causing hate, disgust, or repugnance; detestable: *an odious crime.* [Latin *odiōsus,* from *odium* hatred.] —**o′di·ous·ly,** *adv.* —**o′di·ous·ness,** *n.* —For Synonyms, see **offensive.**

o·di·um (ō′dē әm) *n.* **1.** extreme hatred, disgust, or repugnance; detestation: *We view cruelty to animals with odium.* **2.** reproach, shame, or stigma attached to something hateful: *the odium of being a traitor.* **3.** the state or quality of being odious. [Latin *odium* hatred.]

o·dom·e·ter (ō dom′i tәr) *n.* a device for measuring the distance traveled by a vehicle. [French *odomètre* pedometer, going back to Greek *hodos* way, path + *metron* measure.]

o·don·tol·o·gy (ō′don tol′ә jē) *n.* a branch of anatomy dealing with the structure, growth, and diseases of the teeth. [Greek *odont-,* stem of *odōn* tooth + -LOGY.] —**o′don·tol′o·gist,** *n.*

o·dor (ō′dәr) *also, British,* **odour.** *n.* **1.** the property of a thing or substance that makes it perceptible to the sense of smell; scent. **2.** a general estimation or reputation: *The outgoing mayor was in bad odor with the voters.* [Old French *odeur* smell, from Latin *odor.*] —For Synonyms, see **smell.**

o·dor·if·er·ous (ō′dә rif′әr әs) *adj.* having or giving forth an odor. [Latin *odōrifer* fragrant, bringing odors (from *odor* smell + *ferre* to bear) + -OUS.] —**o′dor·if′er·ous·ly,** *adv.* —**o′dor·if′er·ous·ness,** *n.*

o·dor·ous (ō′dәr әs) *adj.* having or giving forth an odor. [Latin *odōrus* fragrant, from *odor* smell.] —**o′dor·ous·ly,** *adv.* —**o′dor·ous·ness,** *n.*

o·dour (ō′dәr) *British.* odor.

O·dys·se·us (ō dis′ē әs, ō dis′ūs) *n.* in Greek legend, a king of Ithaca and a Greek leader in the Trojan War. He was forced to wander for ten years after the fall of Troy until the gods finally

permitted him to return home. He was called Ulysses by the Romans.

Od·ys·sey (od′ə sē) *n., pl.* **-seys. 1.** an ancient Greek epic poem describing the adventures of Odysseus after the Trojan War. **2.** **odyssey.** a long, adventurous journey.

OE, Old English.

oec·u·men·i·cal (ek′yə men′i kəl) *British.* ecumenical. Also, **oec·u·men′ic.**

Oed·i·pus (ed′ə pəs, ē′də-) *n.* in Greek legend, a king who fulfilled a prophecy by unknowingly killing his father and marrying his mother.

Oedipus complex *Psychology.* a strong, unconscious sexual attraction of a son toward his mother, characterized by feelings of jealousy and hostility toward his father.

Oe·no·ne (ē nō′nē) *n.* in Greek mythology, a nymph who was the wife of Paris and was later deserted by him for Helen of Troy.

o′er (ôr) *prep., adv. Archaic.* over.

oer·sted (ûr′sted) *n.* the centimeter-gram-second unit used to measure the strength of a magnetic field equal to a force of 1 dyne acting in a vacuum on a magnetic pole, one of a pair, separated from the other by a space of 1 centimeter. [From Hans Christian *Oersted,* 1777-1851, Danish physicist.]

oe·soph·a·gus (i sof′ə gəs, e sof′-) *n., pl.* **-gi** (-jī′). esophagus.

of (uv, ov; *unstressed* əv) *prep.* **1.** belonging to or possessed by: *the cover of a book, the leg of a chair.* **2.** descended or coming from: *people of noble lineage, a citizen of France.* **3.** away or at a distance from: *within a yard of the finish line.* **4.** that is or is called; specified as: *the city of New York.* **5.** having as a quality or attribute; characterized by: *news of importance.* **6.** in or with regard to; concerning: *to be in fear of one's life, to be innocent of a crime.* **7.** as a result of; caused by: *to die of suffocation.* **8.** having; possessing: *a family of wealth.* **9.** filled with or containing: *a book of poetry, a pitcher of milk.* **10.** from the whole number, amount, or group comprising: *Three members of the class were absent. They always gave freely of their time.* **11.** associated with as a member or adherent: *They are of our faith.* **12.** made, created, or produced by; emanating from: *the sweet fragrance of the flowers.* **13.** made from or with: *a ring of diamonds and emeralds.* **14.** so as to be without or separated from: *to be cured of a cold, to be robbed of one's money.* **15.** situated at or in: *the deserts of Arabia.* **16.** focused upon or directed toward; for: *a love of life.* **17.** set aside for; devoted to: *an evening of music, a day of meditation.* **18.** on the part of: *It was kind of you to help my child.* **19.** before. ➡ used in telling time: *We are meeting at five minutes of twelve.* **20.** *Archaic.* by: *beloved of the Lord.* **21.** distinguished or characterized by: *a dancer of extraordinary talent.* [Old English of belonging to, made from, by, about, out of.]

of-, form of **ob-** before *f,* as in *offer.*

OF, Old French.

off (ôf, of) *prep.* **1.** so as to be no longer on, in contact with, or connected with: *to take a book off a shelf, to jump off a horse, to keep off the grass.* **2.** not engaged in or occupied with; free from: *to be off duty.* **3.** deviating from or less than the usual or normal: *to be off one's game, to be off balance.* **4.a.** by eating or consuming: *The prisoners lived off bread and water for many days.* **b.** on or with that which is provided by: *to live off the land.* **5.** branching or leading out or away from: *The house is on a road a couple of miles off the main highway.* **6.** abstaining from: *to be off liquor.* **7.** *Informal.* from the hands, charge, or possession of; from: *She bought the book off me.* **8.** seaward of: *The submarine was a mile off the coast.* —*adv.* **1.** so as to be separated, removed, or detached: *to break off a piece of bread, to take off one's coat.* **2.** so as to be no longer operating, continuing, or functioning: *to break off negotiations, to turn the motor off.* **3.** at or to a distance; away: *The dog scared off the intruder.* **4.** to or at a (specified) distance in time or space: *The party was put off for a week. The house is 3 miles off in the opposite direction.* **5.** so as to be smaller, fewer, or diminished in amount or degree: *Business dropped off during the winter.* **6.** so as to exhaust, eliminate, or finish: *The dictator killed off all those who opposed him.* **7.** so as to be away from work or duty: *to take the day off.* **8.** so as to divide, set apart, or delineate: *to mark off an area on a map.* **9.** so as not to hesitate or falter: *to rattle off a list of dates.* **10.** on the way: *to start off on a trip.* —*adj.* **1.** no longer in operation, existence, or effect: *Their engagement is off. The motor is off.* **2.** not occupied with work or duty: *The students were off for the holidays.* **3.** in a specified state or condition: *to be badly off financially.* **4.** inaccurate or incorrect: *My calculation was off by three decimal places.* **5.** on the way; going: *The children are off to bed.* **6.** not up to the usual or normal level or standard; below average: *an off year for grapes.* **7.** unlikely; slight; remote: *an off chance.* **8.** right: *to mount a horse on the off side.* ➡ opposed to **near. 9.** farther from the shore; seaward: *the off side of the ship.* [Old English *of* away, away from, from.]

•off and on. now and then; at times.

•off of. off: *Get that wet towel off of the bed!*

•off with. remove: *Off with their heads!* ➡ used as an imperative.

off. 1. office. **2.** officer. **3.** official.

of·fal (ô′fəl, of′əl) *n.* **1.** the waste parts of a butchered animal. **2.** garbage; refuse. [OFF + FALL; originally referring to the fact that a butcher, when cutting up an animal, would cut off and throw away the refuse parts.]

off·beat (*adj.,* ôf′bēt′, of′-; *n.,* ôf′bēt′, of′-) *adj. Informal.* not conforming to the usual or ordinary; strange; unconventional: *an offbeat movie, an offbeat sense of humor.* —*n. Music.* any weak or unaccented beat in a measure.

off-Broad·way (ôf′brôd′wā′, of′-) *adj.* **1.** located outside of the Broadway theater district: *an off-Broadway theater.* **2.** of, relating to, or designating theatrical productions, often experimental or low-budget, produced in theaters outside of the Broadway theater district.

off Broadway, theatrical productions produced in off-Broadway theaters or as off-Broadway presentations.

off-cen·ter (ôf′sen′tər, of′-) *adj.* **1.** not in the center or centered. **2.** not conventional; eccentric: *off-center sense of humor.*

off-color (ôf′kul′ər, of′-) *adj.* **1.** slightly improper; risqué: *an off-color joke.* **2.** without the usual or desired color.

of·fence (ə fens′) *British.* offense.

of·fend (ə fend′) *v.t.* **1.** to cause or arouse resentment, anger, or hostility in; insult or hurt the feelings of: *They were offended at not being invited to the party.* **2.** to be displeasing, disagreeable, or repugnant to: *The crude remark offended my sense of modesty.* —*v.i.* **1.** to cause resentment, anger, or displeasure. **2.** to commit an offense; do wrong. [Old French, *offendre* to hurt, from Latin *offendere* to strike against, hurt, commit a fault.] —**of·fend′er,** *n.*

Synonyms *v.t.* **Offend, affront,** and **insult** may all mean to cause resentment in or damage the self-respect of someone. **Offend** indicates the violation of a sense of pride or honor, either intentionally or not: *Sarah was offended when she was not appointed to the committee.* **Affront** is a more formal word that implies open and deliberate disrespect: *The dictator's disregard of the principle of diplomatic immunity affronted other countries.* **Insult** suggests an intention to anger and humiliate: *One of the candidates insulted the other by calling him a coward.*

of·fense (*defs. 1-5,* ə fens′; *def. 6,* ô′fens, of′ens) *also, British,* **offence.** *n.* **1.** the act of breaking or violating a moral or social code of conduct. **2.a.** the act of breaking the law. **b.** a criminal act; crime. **3.** the act of causing or arousing resentment, anger, or displeasure. **4.** something that offends. **5.** the act of attacking or assaulting. **6.** *Sports.* the side, team, or players in possession of the ball or puck, as in basketball or hockey. [Old French *offense* injury by word or deed, from Latin *offēnsa* a striking against, wrong, displeasure.]

•to give offense. to cause anger, resentment, or displeasure.

•to take offense. to feel anger, resentment, or displeasure.

of·fense·less (ə fens′lis) *adj.* **1.** harmless. **2.** incapable of offense or attack.

of·fen·sive (ə fen′siv) *adj.* **1.** causing resentment, anger, or displeasure; giving offense: *offensive behavior.* **2.** unpleasant to the senses; repugnant; disagreeable: *an offensive smell.* **3.** relating to, characterized by, or used for attack: *an offensive team, offensive tactics.* —*n.* a position, attitude, or course of attack: *The enemy took the offensive and attacked the town.* —**of·fen′sive·ly,** *adv.* —**of·fen′sive·ness,** *n.*

Synonyms *adj.* **Offensive, obnoxious, hateful,** and **odious** mean arousing great dislike or distaste. **Offensive** is the broadest of these terms: *an offensive remark, an offensive speaker.* **Obnoxious** suggests being so offensive as to cause discomfort: *Everyone was relieved when the obnoxious guests left.* **Hateful** implies arousing actual hostility: *Their hateful behavior made them outcasts in the community.* **Odious** stresses the unpleasant or disgusting quality of what is disliked: *The accusation was too odious to repeat.*

of·fer (ô′fər, of′ər) *v.t.* **1.** to present for acceptance or rejection: *to offer an apology.* **2.** to express one's willingness or readiness (to do or give something); volunteer: *We offered our help.* **3.** to put forth or propose for consideration: *to offer an opinion.* **4.** to attempt or make a show of: *to offer resistance.* **5.** to suggest or

O

a	at	e	end	o	hot	u	up	hw	white		about
ā	ape	ē	me	ō	old	ū	use	ng	song		taken
ä	far	i	it	ô	fork	ü	rule	th	thin	ə	pencil
âr	care	ī	ice	oi	oil	u̇	pull	th	this		lemon
				îr	pierce	ou	out	ûr	turn	zh	measure		circus

propose as payment: *We offered ten dollars for the book.* **6.** to present for sale: *He offered the car for a good price.* **7.** to present as an act of religious worship or devotion: *to offer prayers in thanksgiving.* —*v.i.* **1.** to present itself; occur: *She travels whenever the opportunity offers.* **2.** to make an offering in religious worship or devotion. —*n.* **1.** the act of offering. **2.** something offered, such as a suggestion, bid, or opinion. [Old English *offrian* to present a sacrifice or offering, from Latin *offerre* to bring before, present, from *of-* for *ob* (see OB-) + *ferre* to bring.]

of·fer·ing (ô′fər ing, of ′ər-) *n.* **1.** a contribution or gift, as at a religious service. **2.** something offered or presented, esp. in religious worship or devotion. **3.** the act of making an offer.

of·fer·to·ry (ô′fər tôr′ē, of ′ər-) *n., pl.* **-ries. 1.** the part of the Mass or Communion service at which the unconsecrated bread and wine are offered to God. **2.** the collection of the congregation's offerings at a religious service. **3.** the verses said by the celebrant or sung by the choir during the offerings at Mass or other religious services. [Church Latin *offertōrium* place to which offerings were brought, going back to Latin *offerre* to bring before, present.]

off·hand (ôf′hand′, of ′-) *adv.* without previous thought or preparation: *I cannot say offhand when I will arrive.* —*adj.* **1.** done, made, or said offhand: *offhand comments.* **2.** casual; informal: *an offhand manner.*

off·hand·ed (ôf′han′did, of ′-) *adj.* offhand. —**off′hand′ed·ly,** *adv.* —**off′hand′ed·ness,** *n.*

of·fice (ô′fis, of ′is) *n.* **1.a.** a place in which business, professional services, or clerical duties are carried on. **b.** all the people who work in such a place: *The office is having a New Year's party.* **2.** a position or post of authority, trust, or responsibility, esp. in a government or corporation: *the office of vice president.* **3.** a duty, service, or charge undertaken by or assigned to someone: *to exercise the offices of teacher and counselor.* **4.** *also,* **Office.** an administrative unit or branch of a government. **5.** *also,* **offices.** something done for another; kindness, service, or favor: *We got the information we needed through the good offices of a friend.* **6.** *also,* **Office.** a prescribed religious ceremony or service for a particular occasion or purpose, esp. the canonical hours. **7. offices.** *British.* the rooms or buildings of a house or estate devoted to household or farm duties. [Old French *office* duty, position, religious service, from Latin *officium* duty, service, ceremony, kindness, from *opificium* doing work, from *opifex* worker, from *opus* work + *facere* to make.]

office boy, a man or boy hired to run errands and do odd jobs in a business office.

of·fice·hold·er (ô′fis hōl′dər, of ′is-) *n.* a person who holds a public office.

office hours 1. the hours during which an office is normally open for business. **2.** the number of hours spent at work in an office.

of·fi·cer (ô′fə sər, of ′ə-) *n.* **1.** a person appointed to a particular rank and position of authority in a military service, esp. one holding a commission. **2.** a person appointed or elected to a position or post of authority, trust, or responsibility, as in a club or business. **3.** the captain or any of the captain's chief assistants on a boat or ship. **4.** a police officer or constable. **5.** a member above the lowest rank in some honorary societies. —*v.t.* **1.** to provide with officers. **2.** to command as officer; direct. [Old French *officier* one who has an office or employment, from Medieval Latin *officiarius* one who performs an office, from Latin *officium* service, duty.]

officer of the day, a military officer who is in charge, for a specified period of time, of the buildings, equipment, and personnel, esp. the guards, of a unit.

of·fi·cial (ə fish′əl) *n.* **1.** a person who holds an office or position. **2.** a person who referees or umpires a sport or game. —*adj.* **1.** of or relating to an office or position of authority: *official duties.* **2.** coming from or authorized by a proper authority: *an official statement.* **3.** holding an office or authorized to carry out some specific function: *an official representative, an official scorekeeper.* **4.** characteristic of or suitable for a person of authority; formal: *an official reception for a governor.* [Late Latin *officiālis* relating to duty or service, public servant, from Latin *officium* duty, service.] —**of·fi′cial·ly,** *adv.*

of·fi·cial·dom (ə fish′əl dəm) *n.* **1.** officials collectively. **2.** officialism.

of·fi·cial·ism (ə fish′ə liz′əm) *n.* the attitudes and practices characteristic of officials, esp. excessive adherence to regulations and routine.

of·fi·ci·ate (ə fish′ē āt′) *v.i.,* **-at·ed, -at·ing. 1.** to perform the duties and functions of an office or position: *The mayor officiated at the last town meeting.* **2.** to perform the duties of a member of the clergy, esp. at a religious service. **3.** to act as umpire or referee in any of various sports. [Medieval Latin *officiatus,* past participle

of *officiare* to perform a religious service, from Latin *officium* service.]

of·fic·i·nal (ə fis′ə nəl) *adj.* (of drugs) available or sold without prescription. —*n.* an officinal drug. [Medieval Latin *officinalis* relating to a workshop (as of an apothecary), from Latin *officīna* workshop, laboratory.]

of·fi·cious (ə fish′əs) *adj.* too forward in offering services or advice to others; meddlesome. [Latin *officiōsus* dutiful, obliging, from *officium* service, duty.] —**of·fi′cious·ly,** *adv.* —**of·fi′cious·ness,** *n.*

off·ing (ô′fing, of ′ing) *n.* that part of the visible sea lying between the shore and the horizon.
  · **in the offing. a.** in the near future. **b.** at a distance but within sight.

off·ish (ô′fish, of ′ish) *adj. Informal.* inclined to keep aloof; distant or cool in manner; reserved. —**off′ish·ness,** *n.*

off-key (ôf′kē′, of ′-) *adj.* **1.** higher or lower in pitch than the correct tone; out of tune: *Several people in the chorus were off-key.* **2.** not conforming to what is expected, usual, or customary; somewhat unusual: *an off-key remark.* [OFF + KEY[1].]

off-lim·its (ôf′lim′its, of ′-) *adj.* prohibited as a place to be entered or patronized, esp. by a particular group; out of bounds: *The school's boiler room is off-limits to students.*

off-put·ting (ôf′pŭt′ing, of ′-) *adj.* offensive, disagreeable, or annoying: *an off-putting remark, an off-putting manner.* [From *to put off* to offend.] —**off′put′ting·ly,** *adv.*

off-sea·son (ôf′sē′zən, of ′-) *n.* a time of the year that is not a busy season for a particular activity or business: *Summer is the off-season for the ski resort.*

off·set (*v.,* ôf′set′, of ′-; *n.,* ôf′set′, of ′-) *v.,* **-set, -set·ting.** —*v.t.* **1.** to balance or make up for: *The product's virtues offset its faults.* **2.** to reproduce (something) by offset printing. —*v.i.* to develop or project as a branch or shoot. —*n.* **1.** something that balances or makes up for something else; compensation. **2.** a small plant or bulb growing from the base or shoot of a plant or larger bulb. **3.** offshoot *(def. 2).* **4.a.** offset printing. **b.** an image or impression made by offset printing. **c.** an accidental smudge produced on a clean sheet of paper that is in contact with a freshly inked or printed page. **5.** a ledge formed on a wall by narrowing the thickness above. **6.** a bend or angle made in a pipe or bar to enable it to bypass an obstacle.

offset printing, a printing process in which an inked impression is transferred from a metal or paper plate to a cylinder covered with rubber, which in turn transfers it onto paper.

off·shoot (ôf′shūt′, of ′-) *n.* **1.** a shoot that grows from the main stem of a plant. **2.** anything that develops, derives, or branches off from something else.

off·shore (ôf′shôr′, of ′-) *adj.* **1.** moving or directed away from the shore: *an offshore breeze.* **2.** situated, existing, or operating at a distance from the shore: *offshore fishing.* —*adv.* **1.** in a direction away from the shore: *The wind was blowing offshore.* **2.** at a distance from the shore: *to anchor a ship offshore.*

off·side (ôf′sīd′, of ′-) *also,* **off side.** *adj.* **1.** in football, illegally ahead of the ball before a play begins. **2.** in certain games, esp. hockey or soccer, illegally ahead of the puck or ball in an attacking zone or area. —*adv.* in or to a position that is offside. —*n.* an act or instance of being offside.

off·spring (ôf′spring′, of ′-) *n., pl.* **-spring. 1.** a living organism born or produced as a result of the reproductive process. **2.** any result or product. [Old English *ofspring* progeny.]

off·stage (ôf′stāj′, of ′-) *adj.* located in or coming from that part of the stage that is not visible to the audience: *an offstage voice.* —*adv.* away from that part of the stage that is visible to the audience: *to go offstage.*

off-the-cuff (ôf′thə kuf′, of ′-) *adj. Informal.* not planned in advance; spontaneous.

off-the-record (ôf′thə rek′ərd, of ′-) *adj., adv.* not for publication or quotation: *a politician's off-the-record remarks, to speak off-the-record.*

off-the-wall (ôf′thə wôl′, of ′-) *adj. Informal.* strange, unusual, or unconventional: *off-the-wall behavior, an off-the-wall idea.*

off-track (ôf′trak′, of ′-) *adj.* (of legalized betting) carried on away from a racetrack: *off-track betting.*

off-white (ôf′hwīt′, -wīt′, of ′-) *n.* a grayish or yellowish white color. —*adj.* having the color off-white: *an off-white dress.*

off-year (ôf′yîr′, of ′-) *n.* **1.** a year in which conditions, production, yield, or activity is below average: *an off-year for car sales.* **2.** a year in which elections are not held for major executive offices, such as governor or president. —*adj.* of or happening in an off-year: *an off-year election campaign for Congress.*

oft (ôft, oft) *adv. Archaic.* often. ➡ sometimes used in combination, as in *oft-repeated.* [Old English *oft.*]

of·ten (ô′fən, of ′ən) *adv.* many times; repeatedly; frequently. [Middle English *often,* from *oft.* See OFT.]

of·ten·times (ô′fən tīmz′, of′ən-) *adv.* often. Also, **oft·times** (ôft′tīmz′, oft′-).

o·gee (ō′jē) *n.* **1.** an S-shaped curve or line. **2.** a molding having an S-shaped curve in profile. **3.** ogee arch. [French *ogive* pointed arch; of uncertain origin.]

ogee arch, a pointed arch each side of which is formed by a convex curve on the bottom and a concave curve on the top.

o·gle (ō′gəl) *v.,* **o·gled, o·gling.** —*v.t.* to look or stare at in a leering manner or with desire. —*v.i.* to look or stare in a leering or amorous manner. —*n.* a leering or amorous look. [Probably from Low German *oegeln,* from *oegen* to look at, from *oog* eye.] —**o′gler,** *n.*

o·gre (ō′gər) *n.* **1.** in fairy tales and legends, a fearsome giant or monster. **2.** any person or thing that is cruel, brutal, or dreaded: *The dictator soon acquired a reputation as an ogre.* [French *ogre* the giant, possibly going back to Latin *Orcus* Roman god of the lower world, Pluto.] —**o′gre·ish, o′grish,** *adj.*

o·gress (ō′gris) *n.* a female ogre.

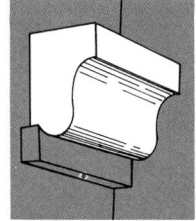

ogee

oh (ō) *also,* **O.** *interj.* **1.** used to express an emotion or feeling, as of surprise, joy, grief, or pain. **2.** used to address a person directly: *Oh, waiter! Please bring us the check.* —*n., pl.* **oh's** or **ohs.** the exclamation "oh" or an instance of it.

OH, the postal abbreviation for Ohio.

OHG, Old High German.

ohm (ōm) *n.* a unit of electrical resistance equal to the resistance of a conductor in which a potential difference of 1 volt produces a current of 1 ampere. [From Georg S. *Ohm,* 1787-1854, German physicist.] —**ohm′ic,** *adj.*

ohm·me·ter (ōm′mē′tər) *n.* a device that indicates the electrical resistance in a circuit, as measured in ohms.

Ohm's law (ōmz) the law stating that in electric circuits the current, measured in amperes, is directly proportional to the voltage and inversely proportional to the resistance, measured in ohms. [From the German physicist Georg S. *Ohm,* 1787-1854, who formulated this law.]

o·ho (ō hō′) *interj.* used to express surprise, astonishment, or exultation.

-oid *suffix* (used to form adjectives from nouns) having the form, nature, or appearance of; like or resembling: *spheroid, planetoid.* [Greek *-oeidēs,* from *eidos* form, shape, sometimes through French *-oïde* and Latin *-oīdēs.*]

oil (oil) *n.* **1.** any of a large group of greasy substances that are insoluble in water but soluble in ether and that are liquid at normal temperatures or liquefy readily when warmed. **2.** petroleum. **3.** oil paint. **4.** an oil painting. **5.** any of various substances having an oily consistency. —*v.t.* **1.** to cover, smear, lubricate, supply, or polish with oil: *to oil a hinge, to oil furniture.* **2.** to bribe or flatter. [Old French *huile* the greasy substance, from Latin *oleum* olive oil, oily substance, from Greek *elaion.*]

· **to burn the midnight oil.** to work or study until very late at night.

· **to pour oil on troubled waters.** to settle differences or a dispute, or calm a disturbance; pacify.

· **to strike oil.** to come upon a source of wealth suddenly or unexpectedly.

oil burner, a furnace or heating unit that burns fuel oil.

oil cake, livestock feed consisting of a mass of seeds, such as linseed, from which most of the oil has been pressed out.

oil·can (oil′kan′) *n.* a can with a long spout, used for applying lubricating oil, as to machinery.

oil·cloth (oil′klôth′) *n.* a waterproof fabric made by coating cloth with oil or a similar substance, used for such items as tablecloths, shelf lining, and cushion covers.

oil color, oil paint.

oil·er (oi′lər) *n.* **1.** a person or thing that oils, esp. a person who oils machinery and engines. **2.** oilcan.

oil field, an area where subterranean deposits of petroleum of economic value have been found.

oil of turpentine, turpentine *(def. 2).*

oil of vitriol, sulfuric acid.

oil paint, paint that is made of pigment ground in linseed or other oil.

oil painting 1. a painting done in oil paints. **2.** the art of painting in oil paints.

oil shale, shale that will yield liquid or gaseous hydrocarbons, as by distillation.

oil·skin (oil′skin′) *n.* **1.** a fabric that has been treated with oil or a similar substance to make it waterproof, used esp. for rainwear. **2.** a garment made of this fabric.

oil slick, a film of oil floating on the surface of water.

oil·stone (oil′stōn′) *n.* a smooth, fine-grained stone treated with oil, used for sharpening blades.

oil well, a well that is dug or drilled in the earth to extract petroleum.

oil·y (oi′lē) *adj.,* **oil·i·er, oil·i·est. 1.** of, relating to, or containing oil. **2.** covered, smeared, or soaked with oil; greasy. **3.** too smooth or suave in speech or manner; disagreeably unctuous. —**oil′i·ness,** *n.*

oink (oingk) *n.* the sound made by a pig. —*v.i.* to make such a sound.

oint·ment (oint′mənt) *n.* a soft, semifluid or jellylike substance, often medicated, applied to the skin to soothe, protect, or heal it; salve. [Old French *oignement,* going back to Latin *unguentum.*]

O·jib·wa (ō jib′wä′) *also,* **O·jib·way.** *n., pl.* **-wa** or **-was. 1.** a member of a large tribe of North American Indians formerly living in the Great Lakes region, now living primarily in Minnesota, Wisconsin, and North Dakota. **2.** the language of this tribe, belonging to the Algonquian language family. Also, **Chippewa.**

OK[1] (ō′kā′) *also,* **okay.** *Informal. adj., adv., interj.* all right. ➡ used to express endorsement, approval, or agreement. —*n., pl.* **OK's.** endorsement, agreement, or approval. —*v.t.,* **OK'd, OK'ing.** to endorse, approve, or agree to, esp. by signing with an OK. [Abbreviation of *oll korrect,* supposed folk spelling of *all correct.* The abbreviation was first used no later than March 23, 1839, and was popularized during the 1840 U.S. presidential campaign.]

OK[2], the postal abbreviation for Oklahoma.

o·ka·pi (ō kä′pē) *n., pl.* **-pis** or **-pi.** a rare African mammal, *Okapia johnstoni,* related to the giraffe and native to tropical forests of western equatorial Africa, with buff markings on the face and zebralike black and white stripes on the upper legs and hindquarters. Height: to 6 feet (1.8 meters) at the shoulder. [From a Central African language.]

okapi

o·kay (ō′kā′) *Informal. adj., adv., interj.* OK[1]. —*n., pl.* **o·kays.** OK[1]. —*v.t.,* **o·kayed, o·kaying.** OK[1]. [Form of OK[1].]

O·kie (ō′kē) *n. Informal.* a migrant farm worker. [Referring originally to farmers from *Oklahoma* who had to leave their farms because of the depression of the 1930s.]

Okla., Oklahoma.

o·kra (ō′krə) *n.* **1.** the soft, green pods of a plant, *Abelmoschus esculentus,* having a waxy texture, eaten as a vegetable either cooked or pickled. **2.** the plant itself, cultivated in warm regions of the world, having broad oval leaves with coarsely toothed edges and bearing bell-shaped flowers. Also, **gumbo.** [From a West African language.]

-ol *suffix* (used in chemistry to form nouns) alcohol: *glycerol.* [From (ALCOH)OL.]

OL, Old Latin.

old (ōld) *adj.,* **old·er** or **eld·er, old·est** or **eld·est. 1.** having lived or existed for a long time: *an old couple.* **2.** of a specified age or length of existence: *Our car is three years old.* **3.** not new, recent, or current; made, produced, or created in the past: *an old song, an old joke.* **4.** familiar through having been acquainted with, known, or used in the past or for a long time: *It's the same old story. We're old friends.* **5.** of or belonging to antiquity or the remote past; ancient: *an old classmate.* **6.** worn with age or use; worn-out: *We gave our old clothes to charity.* **7.** possessing or exhibiting the characteristics of age or aged persons: *old beyond one's years.* **8.** of, relating to, or belonging to the latter part of life: *to live to a ripe old age.* **9.** experienced, skilled, or practiced: *an old hand at sailing.* **10.** *Informal.* cherished; dear: *It's a grand old flag.* ➡ used as a term of affection or endearment. **11.** *Informal.* excellent; fine: *We had a high old time at the party.* ➡ used as an intensive. —*n.* former times: *the knights of old.* [Old English *ald, eald* having existed long, of a specified age, of the past, earlier.] —**old′ness,** *n.*

a	at	e	end	o	hot	u	up	hw	white	⎧	about
ā	ape	ē	me	ō	old	ū	use	ng	song	⎪	taken
ä	far	i	it	ô	fork	ü	rule	th	thin	ə ⎨	pencil
âr	care	ī	ice	oi	oil	ù	pull	th	this	⎪	lemon
				îr	pierce	ou	out	ûr	turn	zh	measure	⎩	circus

O

Old, aged, and **elderly,** used of a person, mean at a late stage in life. **Old** is a general term. Its implication depends on how it is used, and it does not necessarily imply a decline in physical or mental powers: *Several of the old people told stories of their youth.* **Aged** suggests extreme old age with signs of decline: *I helped the aged couple put their groceries in their car.* **Elderly** suggests the period past middle age, and may imply accompanying dignity or physical decline: *The gathering listened respectfully to several elderly speakers.*

Old Church Slavonic, a Slavic language used in translations of the Bible as early as the ninth century A.D., and still used in some Orthodox liturgies. Also, **Old Slavonic.**

old country, a country, esp. one in Europe, from which a person has emigrated.

old·en (ōl′dən) *adj. Archaic.* old; ancient.

Old English 1. a West Germanic language of the Indo-European language family, spoken by the Anglo-Saxon people until about the twelfth century. Also, **Anglo-Saxon. 2.** an elaborate, angular typeface, used esp. in printing formal documents or invitations.

Old English

English is derived from the languages spoken by Germanic tribes who settled in Britain during the fifth century. Although there have been many influences on English since then, much of the basic vocabulary of the language is derived from Old English. Below are some modern English terms and their Old English equivalents.

MODERN — OLD ENGLISH	MODERN — OLD ENGLISH
bird — bridd	father — fæder
boat — bāt	fish — fisc
book — bōc	food — fōda
bread — brēad	friend — frēond
church — cirice	horse — hors
crop — cropp	house — hūs
devil — dēofol	mother — mōdor
dog — docga	sun — sunne
drink — drincan	tree — trēo(w)
earth — eorthe	water — wæter

Old English sheepdog, a breed of dog developed in England for herding sheep and cattle, having a long, shaggy, gray or bluish gray coat with white markings. Height: 2 feet (0.6 meter) at the shoulder.

Old Faithful, a famous geyser in Yellowstone National Park that erupts approximately every 65 minutes.

old-fash·ioned (ōld′fash′ənd) *adj.* **1.** keeping to or favoring old ways, ideas, or customs. **2.** of, relating to, or characteristic of former times; out-of-date.

old fo·gy (fō′gē) *also,* **old fo·gey.** a person who is old-fashioned and very conservative.

old-fo·gy·ish (ōld′fō′gē ish) *also,* **old-fo·gey·ish.** *adj.* of, like, or characteristic of an old fogy; behind the times.

Old French, the French language from the ninth to the thirteenth centuries A.D.

Old Glory, the flag of the United States.

Old Guard 1. a select group of soldiers serving the French emperor Napoleon I. **2. old guard.** the most conservative element, as of a political party, country, or community.

old hand, a person with a great deal of experience or skill in something: *The mayor is an old hand at campaigning.*

old hat *Informal.* out-of-date; old-fashioned.

Old High German, the German language of southern Germany from the eighth through the eleventh centuries A.D. Modern standard German is descended from Old High German.

Old Icelandic, the Icelandic language from the mid-twelfth century through the fourteenth century A.D.

old·ie (ōl′dē) *n. Informal.* a song, movie, joke, or the like from the past, esp. one that was well known or popular.

Old Irish, the Irish language from the seventh to the thirteenth centuries A.D.

old·ish (ōl′dish) *adj.* somewhat old.

Old Latin, the Latin language before the second century B.C.

old-line (ōld′līn′) *adj.* **1.** conservative or traditional in one's actions or way of thinking. **2.** firmly established; traditional.

old maid 1. a woman who has never married. ➡ now usually considered offensive. **2.** *Informal.* a person who is prim, fussy, and prudish. **3.** a card game in which two or more players discard matched pairs of cards and the one holding the odd queen at the end is the loser. **—old′-maid′ish,** *adj.*

old master 1. any of the great European painters, esp. of Italy and the Low Countries, who lived between the thirteenth and seventeenth centuries. **2.** a painting by such a painter.

old moon, the moon when seen as a thin crescent before the appearance of the new moon.

Old Nick, the devil; Satan.

Old Norse, the North Germanic language of Scandinavia from the eighth to the fourteenth centuries A.D., esp. in its Norwegian and Icelandic forms.

Old North French, any of several dialects of Old French that were spoken in the northern provinces of France, esp. Normandy and Picardy.

Old Persian, the earliest form of the Persian language, found in inscriptions dating from the sixth century B.C.

Old Provençal, the Provençal language from the tenth to the thirteenth centuries A.D.

Old Saxon, a dialect of Low German written and spoken by the Saxons in northwestern Germany from the ninth to the twelfth centuries A.D.

old school, any group of people regarded as having or clinging to conservative or traditional ideas, methods, or points of view.

Old Slavonic, Old Church Slavonic.

old·ster (ōld′stər) *n. Informal.* an old or elderly person.

Old Style 1. a method of reckoning time according to the Julian calendar. **2. old style.** a style of printing type characterized by slanting, rounded serifs and uniformly thick strokes.

Old Testament, the collection of writings that makes up the first part of the Christian Bible and is the Jewish Bible. It contains an account of the Creation and early human history, the sacred agreements between God and the Hebrews, and the laws, prophecies, and religious literature of the Hebrew nation up to the second century B.C.

old-time (ōld′tīm′) *adj.* of, belonging to, or characteristic of former times.

old-tim·er (ōld′tī′mər) *n. Informal.* **1.** a person who has been a member of a group or organization for a long time. **2.** a person who is old or elderly.

old wives' tale, a belief not founded on fact, esp. a superstition.

old-world (ōld′wûrld′) *adj.* belonging to or characteristic of former times: *The inn had an old-world charm.*

Old World, the Eastern Hemisphere, esp. Europe, Asia, and Africa.

o·lé (ō lā′) *interj.* well done; bravo. **—n.** a shout of "olé." [Spanish *olé;* probably imitative.]

o·le·ag·i·nous (ō′lē aj′ə nəs) *adj.* **1.** of, relating to, or containing oil: *oleaginous juices.* **2.** too smooth in speech or manner; oily; unctuous. [Latin *oleāginus* relating to the olive or olive tree, from *olea* olive, olive tree, from Greek *elaiā.*]

o·le·an·der (ō′lē an′dər) *n.* an extremely poisonous evergreen shrub, *Nerium oleander,* cultivated throughout the world, bearing narrow, lance-shaped leaves and clusters of fragrant, funnel-shaped red, purple, or white flowers. [Medieval Latin *oleander,* possibly modification (influenced by Latin *olea* olive tree) of Late Latin *lōrandrum,* possibly modification of Latin *rhododendron* oleander. See RHODODENDRON.]

o·le·ate (ō′lē āt′) *n.* a salt or ester of oleic acid.

o·le·fin (ō′lə fin) *also,* **o·le·fine** (ō′lə fin, -fēn′). *n.* alkene. **—o′le·fin′ic,** *adj.*

o·le·ic (ō lē′ik, ō′lē-) *adj.* **1.** of, derived from, or contained in oil. **2.** of or relating to oleic acid. [Latin *oleum* oil + -IC.]

oleic acid, an unsaturated fatty acid derived from animal fat and vegetable oil by hydrolysis, used as a basis for soaps and ointments. Formula: $C_{18}H_{34}O_2$

o·le·in (ō′lē in) *also,* **o·le·ine** (ō′lē in, -ēn′). *n.* an oily, yellow liquid compound found in most oils and fats; glycerin ester of oleic acid. Formula: $C_{57}H_{104}O_6$ [French *oléine,* from Latin *oleum* (see OIL).]

o·le·o·mar·ga·rine (ō′lē ō mär′jər in, -jə rēn′) *also,* **o·le·o·mar·ga·rin** (ō′lē ō mär′jər in). *n.* margarine. Also, **o′le·o′.** [Latin *oleum* (see OIL) + MARGARINE.]

o·le·o·res·in (ō′lē ō rez′in) *n.* a naturally occurring mixture of a resin and an oil, such as turpentine. [Latin *oleum* (see OIL) + RESIN.]

ol·fac·tion (ol fak′shən, ōl-) *n.* **1.** the act or process of smelling. **2.** the sense of smell. [Latin *olfactus,* past participle of *olfacere* to smell + -ION.]

ol·fac·to·ry (ol fak′tə rē, ōl-) *adj.* of or relating to the sense of smell. **—n., pl. -ries.** an olfactory organ. ➡ usually used in the plural.

olfactory lobe, the portion of the frontal lobe of the vertebrate brain in which olfactory sensations are received.

olfactory nerve, either of the first pair of cranial nerves in vertebrates, consisting of nerve fibers that extend from sensory cells in the lining of the nose to the olfactory centers of the brain.

ol·i·garch (ol′i gärk′) *n.* any of the rulers in an oligarchy.

ol·i·gar·chic (ol′i gär′kik) *adj.* of, relating to, or governed by an oligarchy. Also, **ol′i·gar′chi·cal.**

ol·i·gar·chy (ol′i gär′kē) *n., pl.* **-chies.** **1.** a form of government in which power is held by only a few people. **2.** a state having such a government. **3.** the body of persons composing such a government. [Greek *oligarchiā* government by a few, going back to *oligos* few + *archein* to rule.]

Ol·i·go·cene (ol′i gō sēn′) *n.* the third geologic epoch of the Tertiary period, during which primates first appeared. For table, see **geologic time.** —*adj.* of, relating to, or characteristic of this epoch. [Greek *oligos* few, little + *kainos* new.]

ol·i·gop·o·ly (ol′i gop′ə lē) *n., pl.* **-lies.** a state of limited competition in which a market is shared by so few producers that they can affect the prices and other conditions of the marketplace for their product or products without having a marketing agreement among themselves. [Greek *oligos* few + (MON)OPOLY.]

ol·ive (ol′iv) *n.* **1.** the small, oily, edible fruit of any of a group of evergreen shrubs and trees, genus *Olea,* usually having a single hard seed and firm flesh, esp. the fruit of the common olive, *O. europaea,* often eaten pickled and widely used as a source of edible oil. **2.** the shrub or tree bearing this fruit, esp. the common olive, cultivated in warm regions, having gray-green leaves and clusters of fragrant white flowers. **3.** a dull yellowish green color. Also (*def. 3*), **olive green.** —*adj.* having the color olive. [Old French *olive* the tree, the fruit, from Latin *olīva,* from Greek *elaiā.*]

olive branch **1.** a branch of the olive tree, regarded as a symbol of peace. **2.** anything offered as a token of peace or goodwill.

olive drab **1.** a dull greenish brown color. **2.** a woolen fabric of this color. **3.** *also,* **olive drabs.** a military uniform made of this fabric.

olive green, olive (*def. 3*). —**ol′ive-green′,** *adj.*

olive oil, a clear yellow or greenish yellow oil obtained by pressing olives, widely used as a salad and cooking oil.

ol·i·vine (ol′ə vēn′, ol′ə vēn′) *n.* a transparent to translucent, rock-forming silicate mineral ranging from olive to brown in color, transparent green varieties of which, such as chrysolite and peridot, are used as gems. It is found in dark igneous rocks, such as basalt. Formula: $(Mg, Fe)_2SiO_4$ [German *Olivin,* from Latin *olīva* (see OLIVE); referring to its color.]

ol·la (ol′ə) *n.* a wide-mouthed earthenware jar or pot, used esp. for holding water or for cooking. [Spanish *olla,* from Latin *ōlla.*]

Ol·mec (ol′mek, ōl′-) *n., pl.* **-mec** or **-mecs.** a member of a pre-Columbian North American Indian tribe that lived in what is now southern Mexico and built large ceremonial centers.

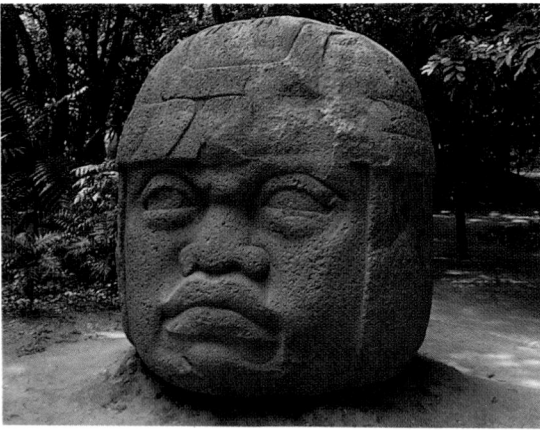

Olmec sculpture

ol·o·gy (ol′ə jē) *n., pl.* **-gies.** *Informal.* any science or branch of knowledge. [From *-ology,* as in BIOLOGY, SOCIOLOGY. See -LOGY.]

O·lym·pi·ad (ō lim′pē ad′) *n.* **1.** the period of four years from one celebration of the Olympic games to another, by which the ancient Greeks computed time. **2.** the celebration of the modern Olympic games.

O·lym·pi·an (ō lim′pē ən) *adj.* **1.** of or relating to Mount Olympus or the gods who, in Greek mythology, lived there. **2.** of or relating to Olympia. **3.** of or relating to the Olympic games. **4.** like a god; majestic; exalted. —*n.* **1.** one of the twelve major Greek gods who lived on Mount Olympus. **2.** a person who competes in the Olympic games.

O·lym·pic (ō lim′pik) *adj.* **1.** of or relating to Mount Olympus or the plain of Olympia. **2.** of or relating to the Olympic games: *an Olympic event.* —*n.* **Olympics.** Olympic games.

O·lym·pic games **1.** in ancient Greece, a Panhellenic festival consisting of a series of competitions in athletics, poetry, music, and oratory, held every four years at Olympia in honor of Zeus. Also, **Olympian games.** **2.** the modern international athletic contests modeled on the ancient athletic games, held winter and summer every four years in a different country.

O·ma·ha (ō′mə hô′, -hä′) *n.* a member of a tribe of North American Indians speaking a Siouan language, formerly living in Nebraska and Iowa, now living in Nebraska.

o·ma·sum (ō mā′səm) *n., pl.* **-sa** (-sə). the third stomach of a cud-chewing animal. Also, **manyplies.** For illustration, see **ruminant.** [Latin *omāsum* tripe of a bullock; probably of Celtic origin.]

om·buds·man (om′bədz mən, om bŭdz′-) *n., pl.* **-men** (-mən). an official employed by a government or institution to investigate and resolve complaints. [Swedish *ombudsman* commissioner, attorney.]

o·me·ga (ō meg′ə, ō mē′gə, ō mā′-) *n.* **1.** the twenty-fourth and last letter of the Greek alphabet (Ω, ω), corresponding to the English long *o.* **2.** the last in a group or series; end. **3.** a subatomic particle of the baryon group. [Greek *ō mega* literally, great *o.*]

om·e·let (om′lit, om′ə-) *also,* **om·e·lette.** *n.* a dish consisting of beaten eggs cooked in a pan and folded over, often having a filling, as of cheese, vegetables, or meat. [French *omelette,* going back to Latin *lāmella* thin metal plate; supposedly referring to its resemblance to a thin flat plate.]

o·men (ō′mən) *n.* a sign or occurrence supposed to foretell good or bad luck. —*v.t.* to be an omen of; foretell; portend. [Latin *ōmen* sign of a future happening.]

o·men·tum (ō men′təm) *n., pl.* **-ta** (-tə) or **-tums.** a fold of the peritoneum that suspends and interconnects the stomach and associated visceral organs within the body cavity of vertebrates. [Latin *omentum.*] —**o·men′tal,** *adj.*

om·i·cron (om′i kron′, ō′mi-) *n.* the fifteenth letter of the Greek alphabet (O, o), corresponding to the English short *o.* [Greek *o micron* literally, small *o.*]

om·i·nous (om′ə nəs) *adj.* foreboding trouble or misfortune; threatening: *Ominous black clouds came in from the sea.* [Latin *ōminōsus,* from *ōmen* omen.] —**om′i·nous·ly,** *adv.* —**om′i·nous·ness,** *n.*

o·mis·si·ble (ō mis′ə bəl) *adj.* capable of being omitted.

o·mis·sion (ō mish′ən) *n.* **1.** the act of omitting or the state of being omitted. **2.** something that is omitted.

o·mit (ō mit′) *v.t.,* **o·mit·ted, o·mit·ting.** **1.** to leave out; fail to include: *to omit an item on a shopping list.* **2.** to fail to do or perform; neglect: *to omit mailing a letter.* [Latin *ōmittere* to let go, neglect.]

omni- *combining form* all; everywhere; universally: *omnifarious.* [Latin *omnis* all, every.]

om·ni·bus (om′nə bus′) *n.* **1.** a public motor vehicle having rows of seats to accommodate passengers and sometimes having two decks, used esp. along a fixed, regular route; bus. **2.** a collection of works written by the same author or of writings relating to the same subject. —*adj.* including or covering a number of different items, cases, or instances: *an omnibus bill in a legislature.* [French *omnibus* public vehicle, from Latin *omnibus* for all, dative plural of *omnis* all; because the vehicle was intended for all classes of society.]

om·ni·di·rec·tion·al (om′nē di rek′shə nəl, -dī-) *adj.* sending or receiving signals or sound in every direction: *an omnidirectional radio antenna.* [OMNI- + DIRECTIONAL.]

om·ni·far·i·ous (om′nə fâr′ē əs) *adj.* of all forms, varieties, or kinds. [Late Latin *omnifārius,* from Latin *omnis* all + *-fārius* -fold.]

om·nip·o·tence (om nip′ə təns) *n.* **1.** infinite or unlimited power or authority. **2.** Omnipotence. God.

om·nip·o·tent (om nip′ə tənt) *adj.* having infinite or unlimited power or authority; all-powerful. —*n.* the Omnipotent. God. [Latin *omnipotēns* almighty, from *omnis* all + *potēns* powerful.] —**om·nip′o·tent·ly,** *adv.*

om·ni·pres·ent (om′nə prez′ənt) *adj.* present in all places at the same time. [Medieval Latin *omnipraesens,* from Latin *omnis* all, every + *praesēns* that is before one.] —**om′ni·pres′ence,** *n.*

om·ni·range (om′ni rānj′) *n.* a radio navigational system in which airplane pilots determine their position by reference to omnidirectional radio signals from a ground station. [Short for *omni(directional radio) range.*]

a	at	e	end	o	hot	u	up	hw	white		about
ā	ape	ē	me	ō	old	ū	use	ng	song		taken
ä	far	i	it	ô	fork	ū	rule	th	thin	ə	pencil
âr	care	ī	ice	oi	oil	ů	pull	th	this		lemon
		îr	pierce	ou	out	ûr	turn	zh	measure		circus

om·nis·cience (om nish′əns) *n.* **1.** infinite or unlimited knowledge. **2. Omniscience.** God. [Medieval Latin *omniscientia* infinite knowledge, from Latin *omnis* all, every + *scientia* knowledge.]

om·nis·cient (om nish′ənt) *adj.* having infinite or unlimited knowledge; knowing everything. —*n.* **the Omniscient.** God. —**om·nis′cient·ly,** *adv.*

om·ni·um-gath·er·um (om′nē əm gath′ər əm) *n.* a miscellaneous collection; confused mixture. [Latin *omnium* of all (genitive of *omnis* all) + *gatherum,* Latinized form based on English *gather.*]

om·ni·vore (om′nə vôr′) *n.* an organism that eats both animal and vegetable food. [French *omnivore,* from Latin *omnivorous.* See OMNIVOROUS.]

om·niv·o·rous (om niv′ər əs) *adj.* **1.** eating both animal and vegetable food. **2.** taking in everything: *an omnivorous reader.* **3.** eating all kinds of food indiscriminately. [Latin *omnivorus* all-devouring, from *omnis + vorāre* to devour.] —**om·niv′o·rous·ly,** *adv.* —**om·niv′o·rous·ness,** *n.*

Om·pha·le (om′fə lē) *n.* in Greek legend, a queen of Lydia whom Hercules voluntarily served as a slave to atone for having murdered a friend.

on (ôn, on) *prep.* **1.** in a position above and supported by; above and in contact with: *The coats are on the bed.* **2.** so as to be in contact with any surface: *Please put butter on both sides of the bread.* **3.** fastened to or suspended from: *a watch on a chain, a chandelier on the ceiling.* **4.** in a position at, near, or adjacent to: *Their cabin is on the lake.* **5.** in the direction of; toward; to: *Our house is on the left.* **6.** directed toward, esp. in the way of attack; against: *to make war on one's enemies.* **7.** in the state, condition, or process of: *I bought the dress on sale.* **8.** in regard to; about; concerning: *The lecture was on the fall of the Roman Empire.* **9.** during the time, course, or occasion of: *We left on Thursday.* **10.** at the precise point or moment of: *The chimes ring every hour on the hour.* **11.** connected or associated with as a member: *to be on a board of trustees.* **12.** by means or use of: *to leave on the last train.* **13.** so as to use as a source or means of support or sustenance: *You can never depend on that person to keep a secret.* **14.** bound by: *on one's honor.* **15.** in such a position as to be supported or borne by: *to stand on one's toes.* **16.** for the purpose of: *to go away on business.* **17.** engaged in; occupied with: *to be on duty all day.* **18.** as a result or consequence of: *We made money on the deal.* **19.** available by means of: *The doctor is on call twenty-four hours a day.* **20.** coming after; following. **21.** in addition to. **22.** *Informal.* in the possession of; with: *Do you have a match on you?* **23.** *Informal.* at the expense of: *The joke's on me.* —*adv.* **1.** in or into a position in contact with, attached to, supported by, or covering something: *to put one's shoes on.* **2.** in the direction of; toward. **3.** forward, in space or time; onward: *to move on.* **4.** in a continuous course; without stop: *The party went on until midnight.* **5.** in or into action, operation, or movement: *to turn the water on.* **6.** in or at the present place or position: *If you don't hang on, you'll fall.* **7.** in or into place or position for use or action: *The star of the show was ill, so the understudy went on. Bring on the food.* **8.** *Baseball.* on base. —*adj.* **1.** taking place; happening: *The war is still on.* **2.** operating: *The radio is on.* **3.** *Informal.* planned; scheduled: *What's on for tonight?* **4.** performing at an optimum level of competence: *The singer was really on last night.* [Old English *on, an* above, upon, touching, near, toward.]
- **and so on.** and more of the same; and so forth.
- **on and off.** from time to time; occasionally.
- **on and on.** without stopping; continuously.
- **to be on to.** *Informal.* to have uncovered knowledge, usually of an unflattering or unfavorable kind, about someone or something: *to be on to a person's unethical behavior, to be on to a fraud.*
- **to have something on (someone).** *Informal.* to have damaging or unfavorable information about someone: *The crooked businessman's assistant had something on her boss and attempted to blackmail him.*

-on *suffix* **1.** a subatomic particle: *proton, neutron.* **2.** an inert gas: *neon, krypton.* **3.** a genetic unit: *operon, codon.*

ON 1. the postal abbreviation for Ontario. **2.** Old Norse.

on·a·ger (on′ə jər) *n.* a wild ass, *Equus hemionus onager,* native to central Asia, uniformly gray in color with a short blackish mane. Height: 4½ feet (1.4 meters) at the shoulder. [Middle English *onager,* from Latin *onager,* from Greek *onagros,* from *onos* ass + *agrios* wild.]

on-air (ôn′âr′, on′-) *adj.* broadcast or broadcasting over the airwaves: *an on-air political debate.*

on·board (ôn′bôrd′, on′-) *also,* **on-board.** *adj.* on or in a vehicle or aircraft, or in a spacecraft: *an onboard computer.*

once (wuns) *adv.* **1.** one time: *I have a piano lesson once every*

two weeks. **2.** in time past; previously: *She was once a beautiful woman.* **3.** at any time; ever: *Once I pay the loan, I will never borrow money again.* —*n.* one single time: *Once should be enough.* —*adj.* former. —*conj.* as soon as; when; whenever: *It's easy, once you learn the basic rules.* [Middle English *ōnes, ānes,* one time only, ever, formerly, genitive of *ōn, ān* one, from Old English *ān.* See ONE.]
- **all at once. a.** suddenly: *All at once, I remembered where I had left my keys.* **b.** all at the same time: *Don't try to do everything all at once.*
- **at once. a.** without delay; immediately: *Come here at once.* **b.** at the same time: *Everything happened at once.*
- **once and for all.** finally or for the last time.
- **once in a while.** occasionally.
- **once upon a time.** at some time in the past; long ago.

once-o·ver (wuns′ō′vər) *n. Informal.* **1.** a quick look or examination. **2.** a quick, superficial cleaning or putting in order: *He gave the room a once-over.*

on·col·o·gy (on kol′ə jē, ong-) *n.* the study and medical treatment of neoplasms, esp. malignant tumors. [Greek *onkos* mass + -LOGY.] —**on·co·log·ic** (on′kə loj′ik, ong′-), *adj.* —**on·col′o·gist,** *n.*

on·com·ing (ôn′kum′ing, on′-) *adj.* approaching: *an oncoming train.* —*n.* approach: *the oncoming of summer.*

one (wun) *n.* **1.** the first and lowest cardinal number. **2.** a symbol representing this number, such as 1 or I. **3.** a single person or thing. —*adj.* **1.** being a single object, unit, or individual: *one loaf of bread, one important point.* **2.** being a specific person, thing, or group, as contrasted with another or others: *The child ran from one side of the room to the other.* **3.** some: *They will probably marry one day.* **4.** single in kind; the same: *all the children of one family.* **5.** characterized by harmony, unity, or agreement: *They were of one mind.* **6.** a certain: *The visitor was one Chris Jones.* —*pron.* **1.** a specific person or thing: *I'll take that one.* **2.** any person or thing: *One could see that you were very upset.* **3.** the same person or thing: *The student didn't know that water and H$_2$O are one.* [Old English *ān* the lowest cardinal number, a single.] —For Usage Note, see **each.**
- **all one.** the same, as in thought or opinion; united: *Then we are all one on the matter.*
- **at one.** in harmony or agreement.
- **one and all.** everyone.
- **one another.** each other: *They loved one another.*
- **one by one.** one at a time in succession.

-one *suffix* designating a ketone or related compound: *acetone.*

one-horse (wun′hôrs′) *adj.* **1.** drawn by or made for one horse: *a one-horse sleigh.* **2.** *Informal.* of little significance, importance, or interest: *a one-horse town.*

O·nei·da (ō nī′də) *n., pl.* **-da** or **-das. 1.** a member of a tribe of Iroquois Indians formerly living in central New York, now living primarily in Wisconsin and New York. **2.** the language of this tribe.

one-lin·er (wun′lī′nər) *n.* a very brief joke or witty remark.

one·ness (wun′nis) *n.* **1.** the state or quality of being one; singleness or sameness. **2.** agreement, as of thought or purpose; harmony.

one-night stand (wun′nīt′) **1.** a performance given in a specific place on one night only. **2.** a place in which such a performance is given.

one-on-one (wun′ôn wun′, -on-) *adj., adv.* **1.** in sports, competing as an individual against a single opposing player. **2.** involving direct communication between one person and another: *to have a one-on-one discussion, to debate one-on-one.*

on·er·ous (on′ər əs, ō′nər-) *adj.* difficult to bear; burdensome; oppressive. [Latin *onerōsus,* from *onus* burden.] —**on′er·ous·ly,** *adv.* —**on′er·ous·ness,** *n.*

one·self (wun self′) *also,* **one's self.** *pron.* the reflexive form of **one:** *Seeing oneself on television is exciting.*
- **to be oneself. a.** to feel mentally or physically the way one usually does. **b.** to behave in a natural or sincere manner: *to relax and be oneself.*

one-sid·ed (wun′sī′did) *adj.* **1.** favoring, dealing with, or presenting only one side; biased; partial: *a one-sided account of an incident.* **2.** unequal or uneven: *a one-sided game.* **3.** having or on one side only.

one-step (wun′step′) *n.* **1.** a ballroom dance consisting of a series of rapid walking steps. **2.** the music for such a dance. —*v.i.,* **-stepped, -step·ping.** to dance the one-step.

one-time (wun′tīm′) *adj.* former: *our one-time associate.*

one-to-one (wun′tə wun′) *adj.* **1.** proportionately equal on both sides: *a one-to-one correspondence.* **2.** *Mathematics.* relating to the pairing of each element of one set with one and only one element from another set.

one-track (wǔn'trǎk') *adj.* **1.** obsessed with or limited to one idea or purpose; narrow: *a one-track mind.* **2.** having one track.

one-up·man·ship (wǔn'ǔp'mən ship') *also,* **one-ups·man·ship** *n. Informal.* the art or practice of taking advantage of an opportunity to gain superiority over another or others.

one-way (wǔn'wā') *adj.* **1.** moving or allowing movement in one direction only: *one-way traffic, a one-way street.* **2.** allowing travel in one direction only: *a one-way ticket.* **3.** without mutual or reciprocal involvement: *a one-way conversation.*

on·go·ing (ôn'gō'ing, on'-) *adj.* in progress or continuing.

on·ion (ǔn'yən) *n.* **1.** the bulb of a plant, *Allium cepa,* having a pungent taste and smell, eaten as a vegetable either raw or cooked. For illustration, see **bulb. 2.** the plant itself, widely cultivated, having clusters of pink or white, bell-shaped flowers. [Old French *oignon* the plant, from Latin *ūniō* oneness, type of onion plant; because it forms a united whole despite its many layers.]

onions

on·ion·skin (ǔn'yən skin') *n.* a thin, strong, translucent paper.

on-line (ôn'līn', on'-) *adj.* (of a work station, terminal, or the like) operating under the direct control of or directly connected to a central computer: *an on-line airline reservations system.*

on·look·er (ôn'lǔk'ər, on'-) *n.* a person who looks on; spectator. —For Synonyms, see **spectator.**

on·look·ing (ôn'lǔk'ing, on'-) *adj.* looking on; watching; observing.

on·ly (ōn'lē) *adj.* **1.** alone of its kind or class; without others; solitary: *an only child.* **2.** being the most suitable or excellent of all; best: *the only person for a job.* —*adv.* **1.** no more than; nothing but: *I have only two dollars. It's only a minor error.* **2.** no one or nothing other than: *Only you remembered that it was my birthday.* **3.** exclusively; solely: *This bus runs only on weekends.* **4.** as recently in the past as: *I saw them only last week.* —*conj.* except that; but: *I would have come, only it was raining.* [Old English *ānlīc* unique, solitary, from *ān* one + *-līc* (see -LY²).] —For Synonyms *(adj.),* see **sole².**

•**only too.** very; exceedingly: *I am only too happy to help.*

Usage To avoid ambiguity, **only** is generally placed just before the word or words to which it refers. For example, the sentence *Many people watch sports only on television* implies that they never attend sporting events in person. *Many people watch only sports on television* implies that they do not watch any programs other than sports. And *Many people only watch sports on television* implies either that they do little else other than watch sports on television, or that they do not participate in sports themselves, but are just spectators.

on·o·mat·o·poe·ia (on'ə mat'ə pē'ə, -mä'tə-) *n.* **1.** the formation of a name or word by imitating the natural sound associated with the thing designated. *Crackle, roar,* and *sizzle* are examples of onomatopoeia. **2.** a word formed in this way. **3.** the use of such words, as in poetry or rhetoric. [Greek *onomatopoiiā* formation of a word in imitation of a sound, from *onoma* name + *poiein* to make.]

on·o·mat·o·po·et·ic (on'ə mat'ə pō et'ik, -mä'tə-) *adj.* of, relating to, or of the nature of, or characterized by onomatopoeia. Also, **on·o·mat·o·poe·ic** (on'ə mat'ə pē'ik, -mä'tə-). —**on'o·mat'o·po·et'i·cal·ly,** *adv.*

On·on·da·ga (on'ən dô'gə, -dä'gə) *n., pl.* **-ga** or **-gas. 1.** a member of a tribe of Iroquois Indians formerly living in central New York, now living primarily in Canada. **2.** the language of this tribe.

on·rush (ôn'rush', on'-) *n.* a rapid or violent forward flow or rush.

on·set (ôn'set', on'-) *n.* **1.** beginning; start: *the onset of winter.* **2.** attack; assault.

on·shore (ôn'shôr', on'-) *adv., adj.* on or toward the shore.

on·side (ôn'sīd', on'-) *adj., adv.* in various sports, not offside.

on-site (ôn'sīt', on'-) *adj.* carried out or located at the site where a particular activity or event takes place: *an on-site inspection, on-site training of hospital workers.*

on·slaught (ôn'slôt', on'-) *n.* a vigorous or destructive attack.

Ont. Ontario.

on-the-job (ôn'thə job', on'-) *adj.* done or received while working at a job: *on-the-job training.*

on·to (ôn'tü, on'-, on'-) *prep.* **1.** to a position on: *The door opens onto the street.* **2.** aware of: *I'm onto your tricks.*

on·tog·e·ny (on toj'ə nē) *n., pl.* **-nies.** the history of the development of an individual organism from fertilization to hatch-ing or birth. [Greek *ont-,* stem of *ōn* being + *-geneia* birth.] —**on·to·ge·net·ic** (on'tə jə net'ik), *adj.*

on·tol·o·gy (on tol'ə jē) *n.* the branch of philosophy that deals with the nature of being. [Modern Latin *ontologia,* from Greek *ont-,* stem of *ōn* being + -LOGY.]

o·nus (ō'nəs) *n.* burden; responsibility. [Latin *onus.*]

on·ward (ôn'wərd, on'-) *adv. also,* **on·wards.** toward a position that is ahead or in front. —*adj.* moving or directed toward a point in front; forward: *an onward course.* —For Synonyms *(adv.),* see **forward.**

on·yx (on'iks) *n.* a variety of quartz consisting of different colored layers, esp. white, yellow, black, or red. [Latin *onyx,* from Greek *onyx.*]

o·o·cyte (ō'ə sīt') *n.* a cell that gives rise to a mature egg, or ovum, by meiosis. [Greek *ōion* egg¹ + *kytos* hollow vessel.]

oo·dles (ü'dəlz) *pl. n. Informal.* a large number; a lot. [Of uncertain origin.]

o·og·a·mous (ō og'ə məs) *adj.* reproducing by the fusion of a large, nonmotile sex cell, the egg or ovum, and a small, active sex cell, the sperm; heterogamous. [Greek *ōion* egg¹ + -GAMOUS.] —**o·og'a·my,** *n.*

o·o·gen·e·sis (ō'ə jen'ə sis) *n.* the process of the origin and growth of the ovum or ova. [Greek *ōion* egg¹ + GENESIS.] —**o·o·ge·net·ic** (ō'ə jə net'ik), *adj.*

o·o·go·ni·um (ō'ə gō'nē əm) *n.* **1.** a female reproductive structure of certain algae and fungi, consisting of a single large cell in which one or more eggs are developed. **2.** any of the descendants of a primordial germ cell that give rise to oocytes. [Greek *ōion* egg¹ + Modern Latin *gonium* cell, seed (from Greek *gonos* seed, procreation).]

o·o·lite (ō'ə līt') *n.* **1.** a pinhead-sized sphere consisting of concentric layers of calcium carbonate, silica, or iron, often surrounding a particle of sand or some other substance. **2.** a rock composed of such spheres. [Modern Latin *oölites,* from Greek *ōion* egg + *lithos* stone.]

oo·long (ü'lông') *n.* a variety of tea prepared from leaves that were partially fermented before being dried. [Chinese (Mandarin) *wu lung* literally, black dragon.]

oomph (ùmf) *n. Slang.* vitality or energy. [Imitative.]

ooze¹ (üz) *v.,* **oozed, ooz·ing.** —*v.i.* **1.** to pass out slowly through or as through small openings; seep. **2.** to disappear slowly or imperceptibly: *My enthusiasm oozed away.* **3.** to exude moisture or a liquid. —*v.t.* to emit or give off slowly or gradually. —*n.* **1.** a slow, gradual leak or flow. **2.** something that oozes. [Old English *wōs* juice, sap¹; of Germanic origin.]

ooze² (üz) *n.* a soft, wet mud or slime, esp. at the bottom of a body of water, such as a sea or lake. [Old English *wāse.*]

oo·zy¹ (ü'zē) *adj.,* **-zi·er, -zi·est.** slowly leaking; dripping. [OOZE¹ + -Y¹.]

oo·zy² (ü'zē) *adj.,* **-zi·er, -zi·est.** composed of or resembling ooze; slimy. [Middle English *wosie,* from *wose* mud, from Old English *wāse.*] —**oo'zi·ness,** *n.*

op-, form of **ob-** before *p,* as in *oppose.*

op. 1. opera. **2.** operation. **3.** opposite. **4.** opus.

o·pac·i·ty (ō pas'i tē) *n., pl.* **-ties. 1.** the state or quality of being opaque. **2.** something that is opaque. [Latin *opācitās* shadiness.]

o·pal (ō'pəl) *n.* a transparent to translucent mineral, an amorphous, hydrated form of silica, found in igneous and sedimentary rocks and in deposits from hot springs. Iridescent white, milky blue, yellow, or black varieties are used as gems. [Latin *opalus,* through Greek, from Sanskrit *upala* precious stone.]

opal

o·pal·esce (ō'pə les') *v.i.,* **-esced, -esc·ing.** to exhibit an iridescent play of colors like that of opal: *The pearl necklace opalesced in the sunlight.* [From OPALESCENT.]

o·pal·es·cence (ō'pə les'əns) *n.* an iridescent play of colors like that of opal.

o·pal·es·cent (ō'pə les'ənt) *adj.* having a milky iridescence; exhibiting opalescence. [OPAL + -ESCENT.]

a	at	e	end	o	hot	u	up	hw	white		about
ā	ape	ē	me	ō	old	ū	use	ng	song		taken
ä	far	i	it	ô	fork	ü	rule	th	thin	ə	pencil
âr	care	ī	ice	oi	oil	ù	pull	th	this		lemon
		îr	pierce	ou	out	ûr	turn	zh	measure		circus

o·pal·ine (ō′pə lin, -līn′) *adj.* of or resembling opal.

o·paque (ō pāk′) *adj.* **1.** not letting light through; not transparent or translucent. **2.** not shining or lustrous; dull: *a table with an opaque finish.* **3.** difficult to understand; obscure: *an opaque essay.* **4.** lacking intelligence or understanding; obtuse: *an opaque student.* —*n.* something that is opaque. [Latin *opācus* shady, dark.] —**o·paque′ly,** *adv.* —**o·paque′ness,** *n.*

op art (op) *also,* **Op Art.** a style of abstract art in which geometrical patterns and other devices are used to create various optical effects, esp. illusions. [From OPTICAL.]

op. cit., in the work cited. [Latin *opere citātō.*]

ope (ōp) *v.t., v.i.,* **oped, op·ing.** *Archaic.* open.

OPEC (ō′pek) Organization of Petroleum Exporting Countries.

op-ed (op′ed′) *also,* **Op-ed.** *n.* a newspaper page, usually appearing opposite the editorial page, that carries articles by columnists and other writers. Also, **op-ed page.** [Short for *op(posite) ed(itorial page).*]

o·pen (ō′pən) *adj.* **1.** allowing free passage through; not shut: *an open door.* **2.** not sealed, wrapped, or otherwise done up: *an open package.* **3.** having no surrounding barriers or obstructions; unenclosed: *an open meadow.* **4.** having no lid or other covering: *an open manhole.* **5.** free from obstructions or hindrances: *Only one highway lane is open because of the accident.* **6.** having spaces, holes, or gaps between the component parts or elements: *an open weave, an open formation of troops.* **7.** not drawn, folded, or rolled together; spread out; expanded: *an open hand, an open flower.* **8.** liable or subject to something; exposed (with *to*): *open to attack.* **9.** that can be used; available (often with *to*): *There are two courses open to us.* **10.** not yet taken; unfilled: *The doctor has two appointments open.* **11.a.** receptive, as to new ideas, facts, or views; agreeable (often with *to*): *open to suggestions.* **b.** having no prejudices or biases; unprejudiced: *an open mind.* **12.** unreserved in expressing one's thoughts or feelings; outspoken; candid: *She was very open with him.* **13.** exposed to general view or knowledge; not secret or hidden: *open defiance.* **14.** ready or prepared to do business: *The store is not open after lunch.* **15.** accessible to the general public: *an open meeting.* **16.** not settled or decided; undetermined: *an open question.* **17.** having no prohibition or restriction: *open season on ducks.* **18.** generous; liberal: *to give with an open hand.* **19.a.** (of a vowel) articulated with the tongue held relatively low in the mouth. The *a* in *calm* is an open vowel. **b.** (of a syllable) ending in a vowel or diphthong. **20.** not guarded by an opposing player: *The quarterback threw to the open receiver.* **21.** free from ice or other navigational hazards, as a body of water or a harbor. **22.** (of an electrical circuit) incomplete; broken. **23.** *Informal.* characterized by ineffective or unenforced legal restrictions, as on gambling or drinking: *an open town.* —*v.t.* **1.** to cause to be open; move from a closed position: *to open a door, to open a drawer, to open one's mouth.* **2.a.** to remove a lid or other covering from: *to open a jar.* **b.** to unwrap, unseal, or otherwise undo: *to open the mail.* **3.** to disclose the secrets of; lay bare: *to open one's heart.* **4.** to make more receptive, as to new ideas: *to open one's mind.* **5.** to unfold or unroll so as to expose that which is contained within: *to open a map.* **6.** to clear of obstructions or hindrances; make passable: *After the landslide, the road was not opened for three days.* **7.** to make or render accessible or available to the general public, as for use or settlement: *The city parks department opened the pool today.* **8.** to establish or set into operation: *to open a new office, to open an account.* **9.** to begin (something); start: *to open negotiations, to open a meeting with a roll call.* **10.** to expand or spread out the component parts or elements of, so as to leave spaces, holes, or gaps: *to open the ranks.* **11.** to cause to separate, burst open, or otherwise come apart: *to open a wound.* **12.** to make or form (a passage, hole, or other opening). —*v.i.* **1.** to become open: *The door opened.* **2.** to afford access or view; have an opening or passage: *The rooms open onto the pool.* **3.** to become ready to do business; begin operations: *The new store opens next week.* **4.** to become accessible or available to the general public, as for use. **5.** to begin; commence: *The exhibition opens tomorrow.* **6.** to spread apart; expand: *Most flowers open in the spring.* **7.** to separate or burst open: *The wound opened when I fell.* **8.** to begin to appear; become disclosed or revealed. —*n.* **1.** an athletic contest, such as a golf tournament, in which both amateurs and professionals may participate. **2. the open. a.** any clear or unenclosed space or area. **b.** public or general knowledge: *Their secret is now in the open.* [Old English *open* not shut, not secret, exposed.] —**o′pen·ly,** *adv.* —**o′pen·ness,** *n.*

• **to open up. a.** to make or become open. **b.** to start firing: *The guerrillas opened up on the troops.* **c.** *Informal.* to disclose one's innermost thoughts or feelings: *The psychiatrist got the patient to open up.* **d.** to cut open or an opening in: *The surgeon opened up the patient's heart.*

open admission, the admission to a college or university of any high school graduate, without regard for the level of his or her academic grades.

o·pen-air (ō′pən âr′) *adj.* located outdoors: *an open-air theater.*

open air, the outdoors.

o·pen-and-shut (ō′pən ən shut′) *adj.* easily settled or decided; obvious: *The lawsuit was an open-and-shut case.*

open dating, the practice of stamping on packaged food the date after which it should not be sold or consumed.

open door 1. free admission or easy access: *Vocational training may or may not provide an open door to employment.* **2.** a policy of admission to a country of all people on equal terms, as for immigration. **3.** a policy whereby a country allows all other countries an equal opportunity to trade with it. Also *(defs. 2, 3),* **open-door policy** (ō′pən dôr′).

o·pen-end·ed (ō′pən en′did) *adj.* **1.** having no fixed limit or restrictions: *open-ended negotiations.* **2.** open to future change or revision: *an open-ended trade agreement.* **3.** having no predetermined answer: *an open-ended question.* —**o′pen-end′ed·ness,** *n.*

o·pen-end investment company (ō′pən end′) mutual fund.

o·pen·er (ō′pə nər) *n.* **1.** any of various instruments or devices for opening tightly closed or sealed containers, such as cans or bottles. **2.** the first item or introductory part in any series: *Our team won the opener in the play-offs.* **3.** a person or thing that opens.

o·pen-eyed (ō′pən īd′) *adj.* **1.** having eyes wide open, as in amazement or surprise. **2.** very watchful; alert or observant.

o·pen-faced (ō′pən fāst′) *adj.* **1.** having a face or expression that shows frankness and honesty. **2.** without an upper slice of bread: *an open-faced sandwich.*

o·pen·hand·ed (ō′pən han′did) *adj.* liberal in giving; generous. —**o′pen·hand′ed·ly,** *adv.* —**o′pen·hand′ed·ness,** *n.*

o·pen·heart·ed (ō′pən här′tid) *adj.* **1.** candid; frank. **2.** generous. —**o′pen·heart′ed·ly,** *adv.* —**o′pen·heart′ed·ness,** *n.*

o·pen-hearth (ō′pən härth′) *adj.* **1.** relating to, designating, or used in a process for making steel, in which a furnace reflects heat from a low roof onto the raw material and in which brickwork on either side of the furnace retains heat that is then reutilized. **2.** of or relating to steel made by this process.

o·pen-heart surgery (ō′pən härt′) surgery performed on the heart, which has been opened for that purpose, the blood being circulated by mechanical means.

open house 1. a party that is open to all who wish to come. **2.** an occasion when an institution, school, or the like is open to visitors.

o·pen·ing (ō′pə ning) *n.* **1.** a vacant or empty space: *an opening in a fence.* **2.** the initial steps or stage; first part: *the opening of a long campaign.* **3.** an unfilled position; job vacancy. **4.** the first performance or occasion, as of a play. **5.** the act of becoming open or of causing to open. **6.** an open space in a forest; clearing. **7.** a favorable opportunity or chance.

open letter, a statement of protest, appeal, or belief written in the form of a personal letter but intended to be published, as in a newspaper or magazine.

open market, a market that is open or accessible to all buyers and sellers.

o·pen-mind·ed (ō′pən mīn′did) *adj.* having or showing a willingness to consider new facts, ideas, views, or beliefs; impartial; unprejudiced: *an open-minded approach.* —**o′pen-mind′ed·ly,** *adv.* —**o′pen-mind′ed·ness,** *n.*

o·pen-mouthed (ō′pən mouthd′, -moutht′) *adj.* **1.** having the mouth open. **2.** gaping, as in wonder, amazement, or surprise. **3.** greedy; ravenous. **4.** speaking freely and loudly; vociferous; clamorous.

open primary, a direct primary election in which any registered voter may vote for a candidate of any political party.

open season 1. the period, prescribed by state or local law, when a particular animal may be hunted, trapped, or fished: *The open season for salmon begins tomorrow.* **2.** a period during which someone or something may be, or is being, criticized, attacked, or ridiculed: *Journalists seem to have declared open season on the mayoral candidates.*

open sesame, any miraculous, swift, or unfailing means of attaining a desired result or goal: *They believed that money was the open sesame to happiness.* [From *open sesame,* the magic words used by Ali Baba to open the door of a robbers' cave in a story of the *Arabian Nights.*]

open shop 1. a factory or other establishment in which belonging to or becoming a member of a union is not a requirement for employment. **2.** an establishment that employs only nonunion labor. ▶ distinguished from **closed shop** and **union shop** in both definitions.

o·pen·work (ō′pən wûrk′) *n.* any ornamental work, as of metal, wood, or cloth, containing numerous small openings.

op·e·ra¹ (op′ər ə, op′rə) *n.* **1.** a play having all or most of its text sung, usually performed by solo voices, chorus, and orchestra, and presented with costumes, scenery, acting, and, sometimes, dancing. **2.** the branch of musical and dramatic art represented by such plays: *to prefer opera to symphonic music.* **3.** the score or libretto of an opera. **4.** a performance of an opera. **5.** opera house. [Italian *opera* work, musical drama, short for *opera in musica* work set to music, from Latin *opera* work, labor.]

op·e·ra² (ō′pər ə, op′ər ə) a plural of **opus.**

op·er·a·ble (op′ər ə bəl) *adj.* **1.** capable of being done, carried out, or used. **2.** capable of being treated by a surgical procedure.

o·pé·ra bouffe (op′ər ə büf′, op′rə; *French* ô pā ʀä büf′) *French.* comic opera, usually dealing with average human beings in farcical situations.

o·pé·ra co·mique (op′ər ə kо̄ mēk′, kō mēk′, op′rə; *French* ô pā ʀä kô mēk′) *French.* opera having spoken dialogue.

opera glasses, small, low-power binoculars for use at theatrical entertainments, such as operas, plays, or concerts.

opera hat, a silk top hat with a collapsible crown, worn by a man in formal dress.

opera house, a theater specially designed for the performance of operas. Also, **opera.**

op·er·ate (op′ə rāt′) *v.*, **-at·ed, -at·ing. —v.i. 1.** to perform or be at work: *The staff operates well as a unit.* **2.** to produce an effect, esp. the intended or proper one: *The antibiotic operated at once.* **3.** to perform a surgical procedure: *The surgeon operated on me to remove my appendix.* **4.** to carry on military operations: *The commandos operated behind enemy lines.* **—v.t. 1.** to cause to perform or work: *to operate a machine.* **2.** to manage or direct the affairs of: *to operate a business.* **3.** to bring about; accomplish. [Latin *operātus*, past participle of *operārī* to work.]

op·er·at·ic (op′ə rat′ik) *adj.* of, relating to, like, or suitable for the opera.

operating system, a group of programs that control the basic functioning of a computer, including the operation of other programs.

op·er·a·tion (op′ə rā′shən) *n.* **1.** the act or process of performing or being at work. **2.** the way in which something operates. **3.** the state or condition of performing or being at work: *The machine is in operation.* **4.** a surgical procedure performed on the body for the purpose of relieving, removing, or repairing some diseased or malfunctioning part. **5.** any specific act or process, esp. one that is part of a series. **6.** a military movement, attack, or campaign. **7.** *Mathematics.* something done to one or more numbers or algebraic expressions to produce a single number or algebraic expression. Addition, subtraction, multiplication, and division are binary operations. [Latin *operātiō* a working.]

op·er·a·tion·al (op′ə rā′shə nəl) *adj.* **1.** of or relating to working, performing, or directing: *a company's operational headquarters, a machine's operational efficiency.* **2.** capable of operating or being used; ready to perform some intended function: *Our new computer has been installed and is now operational.* **—op′er·a′tion·al·ly,** *adv.*

op·er·a·tive (op′ər ə tiv, op′rə-, op′ə rā′-) *adj.* **1.a.** in operation; in force: *a law that is no longer operative.* **b.** functioning effectively or producing effects: *an operative dose of medicine.* **2.** concerned with, engaged in, or relating to practical or physical work or operations: *operative expenses.* **3.** of, resulting from, or relating to a surgical operation. **—n. 1.** a skilled worker: *a political operative.* **2.** a private or secret agent or investigator. **—op′er·a·tive·ly,** *adv.* **—op′er·a·tive·ness,** *n.*

op·er·a·tor (op′ə rā′tər) *n.* **1.** a person who operates a machine or other mechanical device. **2.** a person or company that owns or runs a business or other enterprise. **3.** *Informal.* a person who is shrewd, crafty, and often unscrupulous in obtaining what he or she wants.

operator gene, that part of an operon that determines whether its associated genes will function and form messenger RNA.

o·per·cu·lar (ō pûr′kyə lər) *adj.* of, relating to, or of the nature of an operculum.

o·per·cu·late (ō pûr′kyə lit) *adj.* having an operculum. Also, **o·per·cu·lat·ed** (ō pûr′kyə lā′tid).

o·per·cu·lum (ō pûr′kyə ləm) *n., pl.* **-la** (-lə) or **-lums.** any flaplike part or organ over an opening, esp. a bony protective covering over the gills of bony fish. [Latin *operculum* cover, lid, from *operīre* to cover + *-culum* -cle.]

op·er·et·ta (op′ə ret′ə) *n., pl.* **-tas.** a form of opera, usually of a light and amusing character, in which music and song are combined with spoken dialogue and dancing. [Italian *operetta,* diminutive of *opera.* See OPERA.]

op·er·on (op′ə ron′) *n.* a region on a chromosome, consisting of an operator gene and the genes that it regulates in order to form messenger RNA. [French *opéron,* from *opérer* to work.]

o·phid·i·an (ō fid′ē ən) *adj.* of, relating to, or belonging to either of two reptilian suborders, Ophidia and Serpentes, that include all snakes. **—n.** a member of either of these suborders; snake. [Modern Latin *Ophidia* (from Greek *ophis* snake) + -AN.]

oph·thal·mi·a (of thal′mē ə, op-) *n.* a severe inflammation of the eye or the membrane that surrounds the eye and lines the eyelids. [Late Latin *ophthalmia,* from Greek *ophthalmiā,* from *ophthalmos* eye.]

oph·thal·mic (of thal′mik, op-) *adj.* **1.** of or relating to the eye or eyes. **2.** relating to or affected with ophthalmia.

oph·thal·mol·o·gist (of′thal mol′ə jist, -thə-, op′-) *n.* a doctor who specializes in ophthalmology. Also, **oculist.**

oph·thal·mol·o·gy (of′thal mol′ə jē, -thə-, op′-) *n.* the branch of medicine that deals with the treatment of diseases and disorders of the eye and includes eye surgery. [Greek *ophthalmos* eye + -LOGY.] **—oph·thal·mo·log·i·cal** (of thal′mə loj′i kəl, op-), *adj.*

oph·thal·mo·scope (of thal′mə skōp′, op-) *n.* an instrument for examining the interior of the eye, esp. the retina. [Greek *ophthalmos* eye + -SCOPE.]

o·pi·ate (ō′pē it, -āt′) *n.* **1.** a drug that contains or is prepared from opium. **2.** anything that soothes, quiets, pacifies, or induces sleep. **—adj. 1.** made with or containing opium. **2.** inducing sleep or relaxation. [Medieval Latin *opiātus* bringing sleep, from Latin *opium.* See OPIUM.]

o·pine (ō pīn′) *v.t., v.i.,* **o·pined, o·pin·ing.** to hold or express (an opinion); think. [French *opiner,* from Latin *opīnārī.*]

o·pin·ion (ə pin′yən) *n.* **1.** a belief or conclusion based on what a person thinks rather than on what is proven or known to be true: *Everyone has an opinion on the mayor's chances for reelection.* **2.** an impression, evaluation, or estimation formed of a person or thing with reference to worth, excellence, or quality: *What is your opinion of the book?* **3.** a formal conclusion or judgment given by an expert or professional: *I got an opinion on the need for treatment from another doctor.* **4.** *Law.* the formal statement of a judge or court giving the legal reasons and principles used in reaching a conclusion in a case. [Old French *opinion* belief, from Latin *opīniō.*]

Synonyms	Opinion, view, and belief mean a personal judgment. Opinion describes a subjective conclusion

that is open to debate: *The speaker expressed the opinion that the sales tax should be reduced.* **View** is usually applied to a broad opinion colored by a personal bias: *The losing candidate took a gloomy view of the party's future.* **Belief** emphasizes the personal acceptance of a position or doctrine: *At the time Columbus sailed, most people shared the belief that the earth was flat.*

o·pin·ion·at·ed (ə pin′yə nā′tid) *adj.* stubbornly and unreasonably holding to one's opinions; dogmatic. **—o·pin′ion·at′ed·ly,** *adv.* **—o·pin′ion·at′ed·ness,** *n.*

o·pin·ion·a·tive (ə pin′yə nā′tiv) *adj.* **1.** opinionated. **2.** relating to or of the nature of opinion. **—o·pin′ion·a′tive·ly,** *adv.* **—o·pin′ion·a′tive·ness,** *n.*

o·pi·um (ō′pē əm) *n.* a powerful drug obtained from the white fluid contained in the unripe seed capsules of the opium poppy. Opium and its derivatives, including morphine and codeine, are valuable for relieving pain and inducing sleep, but they are addictive. [Latin *opium,* from Greek *opion,* diminutive of *opos* juice.]

opium poppy, an annual Eurasian poppy, *Papaver somniferum,* having grayish green leaves and white or purple flowers, grown esp. as the source of opium.

o·pos·sum (ə pos′əm) *n., pl.* **-sums** or **-sum.** any of various marsupials, family Didelphidae, native to North, Central, and South America, having a white, pointed snout, a hairless prehensile tail, and long, coarse, usually gray-and-white fur. When it is frightened, the opossum suffers temporary paralysis and lies motionless, as if it were dead. Length: 3-15 inches (8-38 centimeters). [Algonquian *âpäsûm* literally, white animal.]

opossum

op·po·nent (ə pō′nənt) *n.* a person or thing that opposes, fights, or competes with another, as in a game or discussion. **—adj.** acting or behaving in opposition; opposing or antagonistic: *opponent teams, opponent principles.* [Latin *oppōnēns,* present participle of *oppōnere* to set or place against.]

a	at	e	end	o	hot	u	up	hw	white		about
ā	ape	ē	me	ō	old	ū	use	ng	song		taken
ä	far	i	it	ô	fork	ü	rule	th	thin	ə	pencil
âr	care	ī	ice	oi	oil	u̇	pull	<u>th</u>	this		lemon
		îr	pierce	ou	out	ûr	turn	zh	measure		circus

Synonyms *n.* **Opponent, antagonist,** and **adversary** mean someone who contends with or opposes another. **Opponent** describes someone who is on the opposing side of a contest or controversy: *The champion was defeated by an inexperienced opponent.* **Antagonist** implies a sharper opposition and a desire for supremacy: *For the defense attorney, the acquittal represented a satisfying victory over a prosecutor who was her longtime antagonist.* **Adversary** suggests a determined and implacable opposition manifested in hostility and animosity: *Every speech the candidate tried to deliver was drowned out by shouts of abuse from his adversaries.*

op·por·tune (op′ər tün′, -tün′) *adj.* **1.** suitable or appropriate for a particular purpose: *Wait for an opportune time to discuss it.* **2.** well-timed; timely: *an opportune offer of help.* [Latin *opportūnus* convenient; literally, toward the harbor (referring to favorable winds) from *ob* (see OB-) + *portus* harbor.] —**op′por·tune′-ly,** *adv.* —**op′por·tune′ness,** *n.*

op·por·tun·ist (op′ər tü′nist, -tū′-) *n.* a person who takes advantage of every opportunity in furthering his or her own interests or achieving some end, regardless of the consequences or of moral principles. —**op′por·tun′ism,** *n.*

op·por·tun·is·tic (op′ər tü nis′tik, -tū-) *adj.* **1.** using or characterized by the use of every opportunity to further one's interests or achieve some end, regardless of the consequences or of moral principles. **2.** *Medicine.* of or relating to illness caused by organisms that are usually harmless but are disease-producing when the body's immune system is impaired: *an opportunistic infection.* —**op′por·tun·is′ti·cal·ly,** *adv.*

op·por·tu·ni·ty (op′ər tü′ni tē, -tū′-) *n., pl.* **-ties. 1.** a time or circumstance that is favorable or suitable for the achievement of some purpose. **2.** a good chance, as to advance oneself: *a job with many opportunities.*

Synonyms **Opportunity, occasion, chance,** and **break** mean favorable conditions. **Opportunity** is applied generally to a situation that is in accord with a person's purposes or desires: *The prisoner had an opportunity to escape.* **Occasion** suggests a situation that is a convenient time or excuse for a specific action: *A business trip gave the executive the occasion to see Japan.* **Chance** implies luck or accident: *The unexpected spring snow gave me a chance to use my new skis.* **Break** is a less formal term indicating a stroke of luck: *The stretch of good weather was the break the farmer had been hoping for.*

op·pos·a·ble (ə pō′zə bəl) *adj.* **1.** capable of being resisted or opposed. **2.** capable of being placed opposite or in opposition to something else, as the human thumb. —**op·pos′a·bil′i·ty,** *n.*

op·pose (ə pōz′) *v.,* **-posed, -pos·ing.** —*v.t.* **1.** to be or struggle against; offer resistance to: *to oppose change.* **2.** to place in opposition; contrast: *If we oppose these two slides, the differences leap out at us.* —*v.i.* to act or be in opposition to something. [Old French *opposer* to cause to face, put in the way of; modification (influenced by French *poser* to put, place) of Latin *oppōnere* to set or place against.] —**op·pos′er,** *n.*

op·po·site (op′ə zit, -sit) *adj.* **1.** situated face to face with, against, or on the other side of an intervening space or thing: *opposite sides of a street.* **2.** turned or moving the other way: *to travel in opposite directions.* **3.** of a totally or radically different nature, character, or tendency: *Hot is opposite to cold.* **4.** growing in opposite directions from one node, as leaves. ➡ distinguished from **alternate.** —*n.* **1.** a person or thing that is opposite or contrary to another. **2.** a word that has a meaning opposite from that of another word; antonym. —*prep.* across from or facing: *Sit opposite your friend.* —*adv.* **1.** to or on the opposite side. **2.** in an opposite direction. [Old French *opposite* placed facing, contrary, from Latin *oppositus,* past participle of *oppōnere* to set or place against.] —**op′po·site·ly,** *adv.* —**op′po·site·ness,** *n.*

op·po·si·tion (op′ə zish′ən) *n.* **1.** the act of being or struggling against. **2.** the state of being opposed or opposite. **3.** contrary or hostile action or feeling: *Our plan met with fierce opposition.* **4.** a position that is opposite to another. **5.** *also,* **Opposition.** a political party opposed to the party in power. **6.** a group of people, such as a team, that opposes someone or something: *Our basketball team beat the opposition.* **7.** *Astronomy.* the situation of a planet when its celestial longitude differs by 180 degrees from that of the sun. [Latin *oppositiō* an opposing.] —**op′po·si′tion·al,** *adj.*

op·press (ə pres′) *v.t.* **1.** to control or govern by the cruel and unjust use of force or authority; tyrannize: *The army oppressed the people.* **2.** to affect with a feeling of pressure, constraint, or distress; weigh heavily on: *Our failure oppressed us.* [Old French *oppresser* to torment, harass, from Medieval Latin *oppressāre* to bear down on, suppress, from *oppriməre* to press against, suppress.] —**op·pres′sor,** *n.*

Synonyms **Oppress, suppress,** and **repress** mean to control someone or something by the use or threat of force. **Oppress** implies the imposing of cruel or tyrannical burdens: *The occupying army oppressed the population with requisitions of food and fuel.* **Suppress** suggests a complete blocking or overcoming of something that seeks expression or an outlet: *The police used tear gas and mass arrests to suppress the demonstration.* **Repress,** a more moderate term, indicates simple restraint: *The arrival of the security guards repressed the crowd's exuberance.*

op·pres·sion (ə presh′ən) *n.* **1.** the act of oppressing or the state of being oppressed. **2.** cruel and unjust use of power or authority, as by a military government: *to fight against oppression.* **3.** a feeling of being mentally or physically weighed down.

op·pres·sive (ə pres′iv) *adj.* **1.** cruel and unjust; tyrannical: *an oppressive law.* **2.** producing a state or feeling of oppression: *The hot, muggy day was oppressive.* —**op·pres′sive·ly,** *adv.* —**op·pres′sive·ness,** *n.*

op·pro·bri·ous (ə prō′brē əs) *adj.* **1.** expressing or conveying reproach, disapproval, or disgrace; abusive: *an opprobrious epithet.* **2.** deserving reproach or disapproval; disgraceful: *opprobrious conduct.* [Late Latin *opprobriōsus* full of reproach, from Latin *opprobrium* reproach, disgrace.] —**op·pro′bri·ous·ly,** *adv.* —**op·pro′bri·ous·ness,** *n.*

op·pro·bri·um (ə prō′brē əm) *n.* **1.** disgrace or reproach arising from conduct considered shameful. **2.** a cause, object, or occasion of disgrace or reproach. **3.** reproach or contempt. [Latin *opprobrium* reproach, disgrace.]

op·so·nin (op′sə nin) *n.* any of various antibodies in the blood serum that cause bacteria to be less resistant to the action of white blood cells. [Latin *opsōnium* victuals (from Greek *opsōnion* prepared food) + -IN[1].]

opt (opt) *v.i.* to make a choice; choose: *I opt to have the picnic at the seashore instead of at the lake.* [French *opter* to choose, from Latin *optāre.*]

•**to opt out.** to choose not to join in something (often with *of*): *We decided to opt out of the trip.*

op·ta·tive (op′tə tiv) *adj.* of, relating to, or designating the verbal mood in certain languages, such as Greek, that expresses a wish. —*n.* **1.** the optative mood. **2.** a verb or construction in this mood. [Late Latin *optātīvus* expressing a wish, from Latin *optāre* to wish.]

op·tic (op′tik) *adj.* of or relating to vision or the eye. [Old French *optique* relating to vision, from Greek *optikos.*]

op·ti·cal (op′ti kəl) *adj.* **1.** of or relating to vision. **2.** designed to aid vision. **3.** of or relating to the science of optics. —**op′ti·cal·ly,** *adv.*

optical disc *also,* **optical disk.** a disk on which sounds, images, or computer data are stored in microscopic pits. The information can be read by a laser beam and played back through a speaker, television receiver, or computer. Also, **laser disc, laser disk.**

optical fiber, transparent glass or plastic fiber, surrounded by a less refractive material, that conducts light by repeatedly reflecting light waves along its inner surface, used to transmit images and for long-distance transmission of telephone messages and computer data. For illustration, see **fiber optics.**

optical illusion 1. a false impression of the appearance of something, caused by a misinterpretation of what is seen. **2.** a design, pattern, or the like that gives such a false impression.

optical illusion
(the three players are the same height)

optical maser, laser.

optic axis, a line passing through the center of a lens or spherical mirror.

op·ti·cian (op tish′ən) *n.* a person who fills prescriptions written by an ophthalmologist or optometrist for eyeglasses and contact lenses and specializes in fitting and adjusting the glasses or lenses. An optician may also make or sell binoculars, magnifying glasses, and other optical instruments. [French *opticien,* from Medieval Latin *optica* optics, from Greek *ta optika.*]

optic nerve, the nerve that carries impulses from the retina of the eye to the brain. For illustration, see **eye.**

op·tics (op′tiks) *n.* the branch of physics dealing with the nature and behavior of light. ➡ used as singular.

op·ti·mal (op′tə məl) *adj.* best or most favorable: *The weather conditions today are optimal for sailing.* —**op′ti·mal·ly,** *adv.*

op·ti·mism (op′tə miz′əm) *n.* **1.** the belief that things will turn out for the best and are not hopeless: *Before the meeting, both parties expressed optimism about an eventual solution.* **2.** a tendency or disposition to hope for or expect the best or to look on the bright side of things: *Your optimism has blinded you to many problems.* **3.** the philosophical view, as stated by the German philosopher Gottfried Wilhelm von Leibniz, that the existing world is the best of all possible worlds. [French *optimisme,* from Latin *optimum* the best.] —**op′ti·mist,** *n.* —**op′ti·mis′tic, op′ti·mis′ti·cal,** *adj.* —**op′ti·mis′ti·cal·ly,** *adv.*

op·ti·mize (op′tə mīz′) *v.t.,* **-mized, -miz·ing.** to make as good or as favorable as possible; make the best or the most of: *to optimize a poor situation.* —**op′ti·mi·za′tion,** *n.* —**op′ti·miz′er,** *n.*

op·ti·mum (op′tə məm) *n., pl.* **-ma** (-mə) or **-mums.** the best, highest possible, or most favorable point or level: *During the boom, business profits were at an optimum.* —*adj.* the best, highest possible, or most favorable: *In wartime, many industries work at optimum efficiency.* [Latin *optimum* the best.]

op·tion (op′shən) *n.* **1.** the right, ability, or opportunity to choose: *You have the option of leaving or staying.* **2.** the act of choosing or course of action chosen: *My option is to stay.* **3.** something chosen or available for choosing, such as an extra feature on an automobile that is added at the buyer's request. **4.** a negotiable right to buy, sell, rent, or use something for a specified price within a stated period of time: *The new owner obtained an option to sell back the business if it didn't make money.* [Latin *optiō* choice.] —For Synonyms, see **choice.**

op·tion·al (op′shə nəl) *adj.* left to one's choice; not required or automatic: *Attendance at the meeting is optional.* —**op′tion·al·ly,** *adv.*

op·tom·e·trist (op tom′i trist′) *n.* a person licensed to practice optometry.

op·tom·e·try (op tom′i trē) *n.* the practice or profession of testing the eyes for defects of vision and prescribing corrective lenses. [Greek *optos* seen, visible + -METRY.] —**op·to·met·ric** (op′tə met′rik), *adj.*

op·u·lent (op′yə lənt) *adj.* **1.** having much wealth; wealthy; affluent. **2.** indicating or showing wealth or affluence: *an opulent gift, an opulent apartment.* **3.** existing in abundance; plentiful; abundant: *the opulent vegetation of the jungle.* [Latin *opulentus* rich, from *ops* might, riches, aid.] —**op′u·lence,** *n.* —**op′u·lent·ly,** *adv.*

o·pun·ti·a (ō pun′shē ə) *n.* any of various cacti, genus *Opuntia,* including the chollas and prickly pears, divided into groups according to growth habit. [Modern Latin *opuntia,* from Latin *(herba) Opuntia* (plant of) Opus, an ancient Greek city.]

o·pus (ō′pəs) *n., pl.* **op·er·a** or **o·pus·es.** a musical or literary work or composition. ➡ often abbreviated **op.** and used with numbers to identify a composer's musical works according to the order in which they were composed or published: *Beethoven's Symphony No. 9, op. 125.* [Latin *opus* work, labor.]

or[1] (ôr; *unstressed* ər) *conj.* **1.** used to indicate an alternative of two or more: *hot or cold; red, blue, or green ink.* **2.** used to introduce the second of two alternatives when the first is introduced by *either* or *whether: Either write or phone me. We didn't know whether to stay or leave.* **3.** used to introduce a word meaning the same thing: *aeronautics, or the science of flight.* **4.** otherwise: *You had better eat lunch, or you will be hungry.* [Shortened from Middle English *other,* modification of Old English *oththe.*]

or[2] (ôr) *n. Heraldry.* gold or yellow, represented in engraving by small dots powdered over a plain field. [Old French *or* gold, from Latin *aurum.*]

-or *suffix* **1.** (used to form nouns from verbs) a person or thing that performs the action of: *inventor, governor, elevator.* **2.** (used to form nouns) a state, condition, or quality: *stupor, color, tremor.* [Latin *-or.*]

OR, the postal abbreviation for Oregon.

or·a·cle (ôr′ə kəl, or′-) *n.* **1.** a priest, priestess, or other medium through whom certain ancient gods, such as Apollo, were believed to answer the questions of their worshipers. **2.** a shrine or temple of a god, such as that at Delphi, where answers were given. **3.** an answer given by a medium at such a shrine, often having a vague or hidden meaning. **4.** a person or thing that has, pretends to have, or is believed to have great knowledge, wisdom, or authority: *That newspaper is their oracle.* **5.** any wise or authoritative statement. [Old French *oracle* divine announcement, place where a divine announcement is given, from Latin *ōrāculum,* from *ōrāre* to speak, pray.]

o·rac·u·lar (ô rak′yə lər) *adj.* **1.** of, relating to, or like an oracle. **2.** with vague or hidden meaning: *an author whose writings are mysterious and oracular.* —**o·rac′u·lar·ly,** *adv.*

o·ral (ôr′əl) *adj.* **1.** uttered or communicated in words; spoken: *to give an oral report.* **2.** of or relating to the mouth: *oral surgery.* **3.** taken into the body through the mouth: *an oral vaccine.* **4.** *Phonetics.* produced by the mouth without the nasal passage. —*n. also,* **orals.** an examination, as given by a college, with spoken questions and answers. [Latin *ōr-,* stem of *ōs* mouth + -AL[1].] —**o′ral·ly,** *adv.*

Synonyms Oral and verbal mean related to communication through the use of words. **Oral** refers to spoken rather than written communication: *Although the tribe lacked a system of writing, it had an extensive oral literature.* **Verbal** applies to the use of words in either speech or writing: *Traffic signs direct motorists through a combination of pictorial and verbal symbols.*

oral history 1. a historical account obtained by recording interviews with people who can give firsthand descriptions of past events: *an oral history of the civil rights movement.* **2.** the study or collection of oral histories. —**oral historian.**

or·ange (ôr′inj, or′-) *n.* **1.** a round, edible citrus fruit having a thick orange or yellow rind and a juicy, sweetish or acid pulp. **2.** the tropical evergreen tree, genus *Citrus,* bearing this fruit, having waxy white flowers. **3.** a reddish yellow color. —*adj.* **1.** having the color orange. **2.** made from or flavored with oranges: *orange juice, orange icing.* **3.** of, relating to, or containing oranges: *an orange grove.* [Old French *orenge* the citrus fruit, through Arabic, from Persian *nārang,* from Sanskrit *nāranga* the tree of the genus *Citrus.*]

or·ange·ade (ôr′in jād′, or′-) *n.* a drink made of orange juice and water and sweetened with sugar.

O·range·man (ôr′inj mən, or′-) *n., pl.* **-men** (-mən). **1.** a member of a secret political and religious society formed in the north of Ireland in 1795 to oppose Roman Catholicism and support Protestant control of Ireland. **2.** any Protestant native or inhabitant of Northern Ireland.

orange pekoe, a fine quality black tea processed from small leaves.

or·ange·wood (ôr′inj wŭd′, or′-) *n.* the wood of the orange tree, used esp. in carving.

o·rang·u·tan (ə rang′ŭ tan′, ô rang′-) *also,* **o·rang·ou·tang** (ə rang′ŭ tang′, ô rang′-). *n.* a tree-dwelling anthropoid ape, *Pongo pygmaeus,* native to the forests of Borneo and Sumatra, having very long powerful arms, short legs, and a shaggy coat of reddish brown hair. Height: 4½ feet (1.4 meters). [Dutch *orang outang,* going back to Malay *oran utan* wild man, from *oran* man + *utan* forest.]

orangutan

o·rate (ô rāt′, ôr′āt) *v.i.,* **o·rat·ed, o·rat·ing.** to speak in a grandiose, pompous, or formal manner: *a boring meeting characterized by tiresome orating.* [From ORATION.]

o·ra·tion (ô rā′shən) *n.* a long, elaborate formal speech, usually prepared for delivery before a large audience. [Latin *ōrātiō* speech, prayer. Doublet of ORISON.]

or·a·tor (ôr′ə tər, or′-) *n.* **1.** a person who delivers orations or an oration. **2.** any skilled public speaker. [Latin *ōrātor.*]

or·a·tor·i·cal (ôr′ə tôr′i kəl, or′ə tor′-) *adj.* **1.** overly pompous,

O

a	at	e	end	o	hot	u	up	hw	white		about
ā	ape	ē	me	ō	old	ū	use	ng	song	ə	taken
ä	far	i	it	ô	fork	ü	rule	th	thin		pencil
âr	care	ī	ice	oi	oil	u̇	pull	th	this		lemon
		ir	pierce	ou	out	ûr	turn	zh	measure		circus

grandiose, or formal like oratory. **2.** of or relating to orators or oratory. —**or′a·tor′i·cal·ly,** *adv.*

or·a·to·ri·o (ôr′ə tôr′ē ō′, or′-) *n., pl.* **-ri·os.** a long, dramatic musical composition, usually set to a religious text and performed by solo voices, chorus, and orchestra, without action, costumes, or scenery. [Italian *oratorio* oratorio, oratory², from Church Latin *ōrātōrium* place of prayer.]

or·a·to·ry¹ (ôr′ə tôr′ē, or′-) *n.* **1.** eloquent or grandiose public speaking, often in an artificial style, designed to persuade or edify an audience: *campaign oratory.* **2.** the art of public speaking. [Latin *(ars) ōrātōria* (art) of public speaking, from *ōrātor* speaker.]

or·a·to·ry² (ôr′ə tôr′ē, or′-) *n., pl.* **-ries.** a place set aside for prayer, as a room in a convent. [Church Latin *ōrātōrium* place of prayer, from Latin *ōrātor* orator, from *ōrāre* to plead, argue.]

orb (ôrb) *n.* **1.** something round, such as a sphere or globe. **2.** the sun, moon, or any other heavenly body. **3.** the eye or eyeball. ➡ used in literature. **4.** a small globe having a cross on top, used as a symbol of royal power. —*v.t.* **1.** to form (something) into a circle or sphere. **2.** *Archaic.* to encircle or surround (something). [Latin *orbis* circle, disk.]

or·bic·u·lar (ôr bik′yə lər) *adj.* round or rounded. Also, **or·bic·u·late** (ôr bik′yə lit, -lāt′). [Late Latin *orbiculāris* circular, from Latin *orbiculus* small disk, diminutive of *orbis* circle, disk.] —**or·bic′u·lar′i·ty,** *n.* —**or·bic′u·lar·ly,** *adv.*

or·bit (ôr′bit) *n.* **1.** the path in space of one body revolving around another: *the earth's orbit around the sun.* **2.** one complete trip of a spacecraft or artificial satellite along such a path. **3.** orbital. **4.** the range of one's life, activities, or knowledge: *one's intellectual orbit.* **5.** either of the bony hollows or cavities in the skull in which the eyeballs are located; eye socket. —*v.t.* **1.** to move in an orbit around: *Mercury orbits the sun.* **2.** to put (a spacecraft or satellite) into an orbit. —*v.i.* to move in an orbit. [Latin *orbita* path, track made by a wheel, from *orbis* circle, disk.]

or·bit·al (ôr′bi təl) *adj.* **1.** of, relating to, in, or required for an orbit: *orbital docking, orbital velocity.* **2.** of or relating to an ocular orbit: *orbital cavity.* —*n.* the area of space or fixed path through which an electron moves about the nucleus of an atom.

or·bit·er (ôr′bi tər) *n.* a device that orbits in space, as a spacecraft or satellite. ➡ distinguished from **lander.**

or·ca (ôr′kə) *n.* killer whale. [Latin *orca* kind of whale, modification (influenced by *orca* large tub) of Greek *oryga,* accusative of *oryx* large fish.]

or·chard (ôr′chərd) *n.* **1.** an area where fruit or nut trees are grown. **2.** the trees themselves. [Old English *ortgeard* garden, from Latin *hortus* garden + Old English *geard* yard¹.]

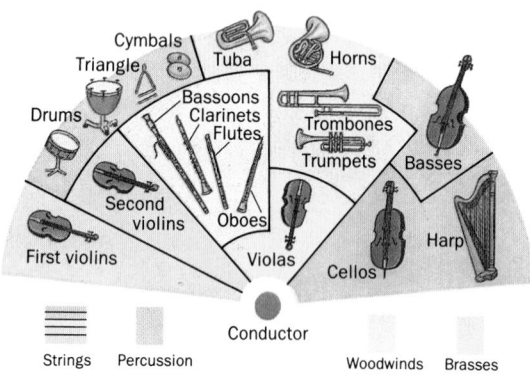

typical arrangement of an **orchestra**

or·ches·tra (ôr′kə strə) *n.* **1.** a comparatively large group of instrumentalists performing as an organized unit, usually under the direction of a conductor. **2.** the instruments played by such a group, usually including strings, woodwinds, brasses, and percussion instruments. **3.** the main floor of a theater. **4.** the usually lowered or sunken area just in front of a stage, in which the orchestra plays at the performance of an opera, ballet, or other musical show. Also *(def. 4),* **orchestra pit.** [Latin *orchēstra* place where the Senate sat in the theater, from Greek *orchēstra* space in the Greek theater where the chorus danced; literally, dancing place, from *orcheisthai* to dance.]

or·ches·tral (ôr kes′trəl) *adj.* **1.** of, relating to, or like an orchestra. **2.** composed for or performed by an orchestra. —**or·ches′tral·ly,** *adv.*

orchestra pit, orchestra *(def. 4).*

or·ches·trate (ôr′kə strāt′) *v.t.,* **-trat·ed, -trat·ing. 1.** to compose or arrange (music) for an orchestra, esp. to decide which instruments are to play each part. **2.** to arrange or organize in order to achieve the best or desired result: *to orchestrate the colors in a painting, to orchestrate a campaign rally.* —**or′ches·tra′tion,** *n.* —**or′ches·tra′tor** *also,* **or′ches·trat′er,** *n.*

or·chid (ôr′kid) *n.* **1.** any of various flowers, often pale purple or white, having three petallike sepals, two similar outer petals, and an inner petal or lip. **2.** any of various plants, family Orchidaceae, bearing this flower. **3.** a bluish or rosy purple color. —*adj.* having the color orchid. [From Modern Latin *Orchideae,* from Latin *orchis* the plant, from Greek *orchis* the plant, testicle; because of the shape of the root.]

orchids

or·chis (ôr′kis) *n.* an orchid, esp. any of a number of terrestrial forms, genus *Orchis,* having tuberous roots and small, showy flowers. [Modern Latin *Orchis,* from Latin *orchis.* See ORCHID.]

or·dain (ôr dān′) *v.t.* **1.** to fix, decide, or command by or as by decree or authority: *Fate ordained that they would meet again.* **2.** to appoint formally to the ministry or another religious office. [Anglo-Norman *ordeiner,* from Latin *ordināre* to set in order.] —**or·dain′er,** *n.* —**or·dain′ment,** *n.*

or·deal (ôr dēl′, ôr′dēl) *n.* **1.** a circumstance or experience that is painful or difficult to endure. **2.** formerly, the subjection of an accused person to some danger, such as poison or fire. If the person was unharmed, it was believed to be proof of innocence. [Old English *ordāl* form of trial in which the accused is forced to take a test of a dangerous nature.]

or·der (ôr′dər) *n.* **1.** *also,* **orders.** a statement that tells someone what to do, esp. one backed by force or authority; command or direction: *orders from headquarters.* **2.** a command or direction of a court or judge entered or made in writing, but not included in a judgment: *to obtain a court order releasing a prisoner from jail.* **3.** an arrangement of things; position in a series: *You will pass a school, a church, and a bus station, in that order.* **4.** any fixed, lawful, or logical system, scheme, or condition: *the order of the universe.* **5.** a set of established, usual, or normal practices, institutions, activities, or rules: *to destroy the old order of society.* **6.** a condition in which laws and rules are obeyed: *to restore order after a riot.* **7.** a clean, neat, proper, or manageable condition: *to put a room in order, to put one's life in order.* **8.** a certain condition or state: *working order, in good order.* **9.** a request for something, such as food: *Has the waitress taken your order?* **10.** something requested or supplied in response to a request: *The company shipped my order last week.* **11.** a single portion or serving of food: *two orders of French fried potatoes.* **12.** kind; type; sort: *Find an old bed sheet or something of that order to use as a tourniquet.* **13.** a rank or level: *work of the highest order of excellence, people of all orders of society.* **14.** *Biology.* a category in the classification of living things that ranks higher than a family but lower than a class; for example, the order Carnivora includes the cat, dog, bear, and other families, and is included in the class of mammals. **15.** any of the grades or ranks of the Christian clergy: *He was a member of the order of deacons.* **16.** a body of persons living under the same regulations, esp. a religious group. **17.** a society or institution into which a person is admitted as an honor. **18.** a body of persons united by some special interest or purpose; fraternal organization. **19.** a decoration, such as a medal or badge, awarded to persons admitted into an order. **20.** *Architecture.* **a.** any one of several major styles of classical architecture, esp. Doric, Ionic, or Corinthian styles of classical Greek architecture, usually distinguished from each other by the general character of the columns, including proportion and capital types. **b.** a column with its entablature, forming the basic unit of such a style. **21.** *Algebra.* degree. **22.** *also,* **orders.** the rite of ordination. **23.** a prescribed form for the performance of a religious service: *the order for the consecration of a bishop.* —*v.t.* **1.** to command or direct (someone) to do something, esp. with force or authority: *to order soldiers to retreat.* **2.** to command or direct (someone) to come or go to or from a specified place: *She ordered him out of the house.* **3.** to give an order that (something) be done: *to order that a flag be flown at half-mast.* **4.** to place an order for; request: *to order wine with dinner.* **5.** to put into a fixed, logical, or proper order;

give order to: *Here all things in their place remain, as all were ordered, ages since* (Tennyson, 1842). —*v.i.* to place or give an order or orders. [Old French *ordre* regular disposition of things, grade in the hierarchy of the church, each of a group making up a classification, from Latin *ordō* row[1], methodical arrangement, rank[1].] —**or′der·er,** *n.* —For Synonyms *(v.t.),* see **command.**

• **a tall order.** *Informal.* a very difficult or demanding task or requirement.

• **by order (of).** according to an order (given by a person with the proper authority): *by order of the president.*

• **in order. a.** in the right or proper position or condition: *The books were in order on the shelf.* **b.** in working condition. **c.** permitted by or in accordance with the rules: *Nominations for class president are now in order.* **d.** called for; appropriate; suitable: *An apology for your behavior is in order.*

• **in order that.** for the purpose that; so that.

• **in order to.** so as to: *to climb a tree in order to see over a wall.*

• **in short order.** without delay; quickly.

• **made to order. a.** made according to the purchaser's wishes or requirements: *a suit made to order.* **b.** ideally suited; just right: *a sunny day made to order for a picnic.*

• **on order.** having been requested but not yet delivered: *The new recording is on order.*

• **on the order of. a.** similar to; like: *Can you design a kitchen on the order of the one pictured here?* **b.** approximately; about: *It takes on the order of forty minutes to drive to town.*

• **out of order. a.** not in the right or proper position or condition: *The encyclopedias are out of order.* **b.** not in working condition: *the telephone is out of order.* **c.** not permitted by or in accordance with the rules: *The council president ruled that the motion was out of order.* **d.** not suitable; inappropriate: *Their sad faces seemed out of order at the party.*

• **to be in orders.** to be a member of the ordained clergy.

• **to call to order.** to ask for quiet and begin the business of (a meeting or the like).

• **to order (someone) about** (or **around**). to treat (someone) as a subordinate: *The bully is always ordering others about.*

• **to take orders. a.** to do what is ordered; obey. **b.** to become a member of the ordained clergy.

ordered pair *Mathematics.* a pair of numbers or elements in which one of the pair is considered the first and the other the second. The ordered pair one, two is written as (1, 2). Also, **ordered couple.**

or·der·ly (ôr′dər lē) *adj.* **1.** in a certain order or having order: *to march in an orderly line, an orderly room.* **2.** free from disturbances, trouble, or violence: *an orderly demonstration.* —*n., pl.* **-lies. 1.** a soldier assigned to an officer or officers for the purpose of carrying messages and performing various other tasks. **2.** a hospital worker who assists doctors and nurses. **3.** a hospital attendant. —*adv.* in a regular or systematic manner. —**or′der·li·ness,** *n.*

Synonyms *adj.* **Orderly, methodical,** and **systematic** mean arranged or carried out according to a particular system. **Orderly** suggests neatness and lack of confusion: *The office manager maintained an orderly filing system.* **Methodical** emphasizes the following of a logical, definite plan: *The detective's methodical search for clues began at the front door and continued from room to room.* **Systematic** is close to *methodical* in meaning but puts a greater stress on thoroughness and complexity: *A systematic study of the state's prisons produced detailed recommendations for reforms in sentencing and parole policies.*

order of magnitude, the number of times that 10 is multiplied by itself in expressing a particular value. 10^4 is 2 orders of magnitude less than 10^6.

Order of the Garter, the oldest and most important order of knighthood in England, founded about 1350.

or·di·nal (ôr′də nəl) *adj.* **1.** of, relating to, or indicating order or position in a series. **2.** of or relating to an order of animals or plants. —*n.* **1.** ordinal number. **2.** *also,* **Ordinal.** a book containing the directions for the performance of various ceremonies, esp. ordinations. [Late Latin *ordinālis* denoting an order of succession, from Latin *ordō* row[1], methodical arrangement, rank[1].]

ordinal number, a number that shows sequence or position in a set or collection, as first, second, third, and so forth. Ordinal numbers break down a set or collection one by one rather than dealing with its members all at once: *The first kitten is black, the second buff, the third gray.* ➡ distinguished from **cardinal number.**

or·di·nance (ôr′də nəns) *n.* **1.** a regulation or law, esp. one made by a municipal government. **2.** a prescribed religious cere-

mony. [Old French *ordenance* rule, government, going back to Latin *ōrdināre* to set in order.] —For Synonyms, see **law.**

or·di·nar·i·ly (ôr′də ner′ə lē) *adv.* **1.** in most cases; usually; commonly: *Ordinarily, the museum is open on Sundays.* **2.** in a normal or commonplace way: *a simple couple who were rather ordinarily dressed.*

or·di·nar·y (ôr′də ner′ē) *adj.* **1.** commonly used; habitual or regular; usual: *a person's ordinary tone of voice.* **2.** not distinguished in any way from others; not outstanding or exceptional: *an ordinary, unexceptional performance.* **3.** below average, as in quality or ability; inferior. —*n., pl.* **-nar·ies. 1.** a person who has power and jurisdiction attached directly to his or her position, esp. a bishop or a judge. **2.** *also,* **Ordinary.** the prescribed form for saying Mass, esp. the prayers that do not change from day to day. [Latin *ōrdinārius* usual, regular, from *ōrdō* row[1], rank[1], methodical arrangement.] —**or′di·nar′i·ness,** *n.* —For Synonyms, see **common.**

• **in ordinary.** in regular, steady service: *a physician in ordinary to the royal family.*

• **out of the ordinary.** unusual; exceptional.

ordinary seaman, a seaman who is not skilled enough to be considered an able-bodied seaman.

or·di·nate (ôr′də nit, -nāt′) *n.* **1.** on a line graph, the distance of a point from the horizontal axis measured parallel to the vertical axis, used to define the point in the system of Cartesian coordinates and commonly referred to as the *y* coordinate. ➡ distinguished from **abscissa. 2.** a line, number, or algebraic expression representing this distance. [Latin *ōrdinātus,* past participle of *ōrdināre* to set in order.]

ordinate

or·di·na·tion (ôr′də nā′shən) *n.* **1.** the act or ceremony of ordaining or being ordained: *A bishop officiated at the priest's ordination.* **2.** the state of being ordained. [Latin *ōrdinātiō* a setting in order, appointing to office.]

ord·nance (ôrd′nəns) *n.* **1.** military weapons and equipment. **2.** artillery. **3.** the branch of a military service that procures, stores, and issues weapons and equipment. [Form of ORDINANCE.]

Or·do·vi·cian (ôr′də vish′ən) *n.* the second geologic period of the Paleozoic era, when the first vertebrates, the fish, appeared. For table, see **geologic time.** —*adj.* of, relating to, or characteristic of this period. [Latin *Ordovicēs* an ancient Celtic tribe of Wales + -IAN; because this period was studied intensively in Wales.]

or·dure (ôr′jər, -dyər) *n.* **1.** filth; dung; excrement. **2.** something morally degrading or offensive. [Old French *ordure* filth, from *ord* filthy, from Latin *horridus* rough, frightful.]

ore (ôr) *n.* a substance in the earth's crust that can be profitably mined for its content of metals or useful minerals. [Old English *ōra* crude metal.]

ö·re (œ′Rə) *n., pl.* **ö·re.** a unit of currency in Scandinavia, equal to $1/100$ of a krona or a krone. [Danish and Norwegian *Øre* and Swedish *öre,* all going back to Latin *aureus* gold coin.]

Ore. *also,* **Oreg.** Oregon.

o·re·ad (ôr′ē ad′) *n.* in Greek mythology, a nymph who lived in a mountain or grotto. [Latin *Orēas,* from Greek *Oreias,* from *oros* mountain.]

o·reg·a·no (ə reg′ə nō′, ô reg′-) *n.* any of various plants, genus *Origanum,* of the mint family, whose fragrant leaves are used for seasoning.

Or·e·gon Trail (ôr′i gən, -gon′, or′-) an overland route between the Missouri River near Independence, Missouri, and the Columbia River in northwestern Oregon, widely used esp. from about 1840 to 1849.

O·res·tes (ô res′tēz) *n.* in Greek legend, the brother of Electra, who killed his mother Clytemnestra and her lover because they had murdered his father Agamemnon.

or·gan (ôr′gən) *n.* **1.** a musical instrument consisting of ranks of pipes of different lengths that are sounded by air blown from a bellows, played by means of one or more keyboards. Also, **pipe organ. 2.** a similar instrument whose tones are produced and amplified electrically. **3.** reed organ. **4.** hand organ. **5.** mouth

a	at	e	end	o	hot	u	up	hw	white		about
ā	ape	ē	me	ō	old	ū	use	ng	song		taken
ä	far	i	it	ô	fork	ü	rule	th	thin	ə	pencil
âr	care	ī	ice	oi	oil	u̇	pull	t͟h	this		lemon
		îr	pierce	ou	out	ûr	turn	zh	measure		circus

organ; harmonica. **6.** *Biology.* any specialized structure, such as a kidney, that is composed of several kinds of tissue and performs a specific function or functions. Organs are present in all higher plants and animals. **7.** a newspaper, newsletter, or magazine published by a political party, business, or some other group or organization. **8.** a means or instrument by which something is performed or accomplished, esp. a government institution: *A city council is an organ of municipal government.* [Latin *organum* implement, musical instrument, from Greek *organon.*]

or·gan·dy (ôr′gən dē) *also,* **or·gan·die.** *n., pl.* **-dies.** a sheer, lightweight fabric, usually made of cotton and given a crisp finish, used esp. for dresses and curtains. [French *organdi;* of uncertain origin.]

or·gan·elle (ôr′gə nel′) *n. Biology.* a structure inside a cell that has a specialized function. Mitochondria, vacuoles, and ribosomes are typical organelles in animal cells; chloroplasts are organelles in plant cells.

organ grinder, a street musician who plays a hand organ.

or·gan·ic (ôr gan′ik) *adj.* **1.** of, relating to, including, or derived from living things: *to use decayed leaves as an organic fertilizer.* **2.a.** of or relating to a body organ. **b.** adversely affecting the structure of an organ or part: *an organic disorder.* ➡ distinguished from **functional. 3.** of, using, raised, or grown by methods that avoid the use of chemical fertilizers or insecticides or other artificial substances: *organic farming, organic foods.* **4.** of, relating to, or part of the fundamental makeup of a person or thing; not accidental or superficial; inherent; basic: *art that has an organic connection with religious faith.* **5.** made up of interconnected and related parts: *The life of the pond formed an organic whole because each living thing performed a function that supported others.* **6.** of, relating to, or belonging to a class of chemical compounds including most of the compounds of carbon. [Latin *organicus* relating to implements, going back to Greek *organon* implement.] —**or·gan′i·cal·ly,** *adv.*

organic chemistry, the branch of chemistry that deals with organic compounds.

or·gan·ism (ôr′gə niz′əm) *n.* **1.** a living animal or plant having organs that function together to maintain vital activities. **2.** something comparable to a living thing in having parts that function together to form a whole: *the economic organism.*

or·gan·ist (ôr′gə nist) *n.* a person who plays the organ.

or·gan·i·za·tion (ôr′gə nə zā′shən) *n.* **1.** the act or process of organizing: *Who's responsible for the organization of the dance?* **2.** the state or manner of being organized: *the organization of books by subject matter or by author.* **3.** a group composed of individuals united or organized for a particular purpose: *a labor organization.* **4.** the administrative personnel or executive branch of a company, political party, or the like, as distinguished from the rest of the employees or membership. —**or′gan·i·za′tion·al,** *adj.* —**or′gan·i·za′tion·al·ly,** *adv.*

Organization of American States, a regional organization composed of thirty-one Latin American and Caribbean countries and the United States, established in 1948 to provide collective security, economic cooperation, and peaceful settlement of disputes.

or·gan·ize (ôr′gə nīz′) *v.,* **-ized, -iz·ing.** —*v.t.* **1.a.** to arrange in an orderly, systematic fashion: *to organize files.* **b.** to plan and arrange for: *to organize a trip.* **2.** to put or bring together; bring into being; create: *to organize an amateur theater group.* **3.** to cause (employees) to form or join a labor union: *to organize steelworkers.* **4.** to cause employees of (a business or an industry) to form or join a labor union: *to organize a factory.* —*v.i.* to form or join a labor union or other organization. [Medieval Latin *organizare* to arrange, form, from Latin *organum* implement. See ORGAN.] —**or′gan·iz′a·ble,** *adj.* —**or′gan·iz′er,** *n.*

organized labor, all the members of labor unions, considered collectively.

or·gan·za (ôr gan′zə) *n.* a transparent, lightweight fabric that resembles organdy, usually made of rayon, nylon, or silk and given a stiff finish.

or·gasm (ôr′gaz əm) *n.* the point of highest sexual excitement; climax. [French *orgasme,* from Greek *orgasmos,* from *organ* to swell (with lust).] —**or·gas·mic** (ôr gaz′mik), *adj.*

or·gi·as·tic (ôr′jē as′tik) *adj.* of, relating to, or resembling an orgy: *orgiastic abandon, orgiastic rites.* —**or′gi·as′ti·cal·ly,** *adv.*

or·gy (ôr′jē) *n., pl.* **-gies. 1.** a wild, drunken, unrestrained revelry or party. **2.** an instance or activity marked by excessive or unbridled indulgence: *an orgy of sentiment.* **3. orgies.** in ancient Greece and Rome, secret rites or ceremonies dedicated to certain gods, such as Bacchus or Ceres, and accompanied by drunkenness, dancing, and singing. [Latin *orgia* wild rites connected esp. with the worship of Bacchus, secret, frantic revels, from Greek *orgia* secret rites.]

o·ri·el (ôr′ē əl) *n.* a bay window built outward from a wall, resting on corbels or brackets. [Old French *oriol* porch, corridor; of uncertain origin.]

o·ri·ent (*n., adj.,* ôr′ē ənt, -ent′; *v.,* ôr′ē ent′) *n.* **the Orient.** the countries of Asia, esp. the Far East. ➡ distinguished from **Occident.** —*v.t.* **1.** to make familiar with new surroundings or a situation: *It took a while for the new students to orient themselves.* **2.** to get or fix the location or bearings of: *The sailors oriented themselves by the North Star.* **3.** to fix so as to be pointed or directed: *to orient a tennis court north and south, to orient fashions toward youthful buyers.* **4.** to place so as to face the east, esp. to build (a church) with the main altar at the eastern end. —*adj.* **1.** *Archaic.* Oriental; Eastern. **2.** glowing; radiant; shining. **3.** *Archaic.* rising; ascending: *the orient moon.* [Old French *orient* east, countries of Asia, from Latin *oriēns* rising sun, east, from *orīrī* to rise.]

oriel

O·ri·en·tal (ôr′ē en′təl) *also,* **o·ri·en·tal.** *adj.* of, relating to, or characteristic of the Orient or its peoples or cultures. ➡ distinguished from **Occidental.** —*n.* **1.** a native or inhabitant of the Orient. **2.** a person of Oriental ancestry. ➡ often considered offensive in def. 2.

oriental carpet, oriental rug.

O·ri·en·tal·ism (ôr′ē en′tə liz′əm) *also,* **o·ri·en·tal·ism.** *n.* **1.** any quality, characteristic, custom, or the like associated with the peoples of the Orient. **2.** the study of Oriental languages, literature, history, and culture. —**O′ri·en·tal·ist;** *also,* **o′ri·en′tal·ist,** *n.*

oriental rug, a handwoven rug or carpet having a geometric or floral design, made in the Orient. Also, **oriental carpet.**

o·ri·en·tate (ôr′ē ən tāt′) *v.t., v.i.,* **-tat·ed, -tat·ing.** to orient or become oriented.

o·ri·en·ta·tion (ôr′ē ən tā′shən) *n.* **1.** the act or process of orienting. **2.** the state or manner of being oriented, esp. with relation to points of the compass: *The building has an east-west orientation.* **3.** an introduction to or familiarization with new surroundings or circumstances, or the period of time of this: *The college sponsored a weekend orientation for all new students.* **4.** *Psychology.* awareness of one's surroundings or environment with reference to time, place, and people.

or·i·fice (ôr′ə fis, or′-) *n.* a passage or opening, esp. in the body; aperture: *The ears, nose, and mouth are orifices.* [Old French *orifice,* from Late Latin *ōrificium* opening, from Latin *ōr-,* stem of *ōs* mouth + *facere* to make.]

or·i·flamme (ôr′ə flam′, or′-) *n.* **1.** a banner of red silk used in battle by the early kings of France. **2.** a banner or symbol for any struggle or enterprise. [Old French *oriflambe* old banner of France, going back to Latin *aurum* gold + *flamma* blaze; because it was originally a red banner attached to a gilded pole.]

o·ri·ga·mi (ôr′i gä′mē) *n.* **1.** the traditional Japanese art of folding paper into the form of an animal, flower, or other object. **2.** something made in this way. [Japanese *origami,* going back to *ori* a folding + *kami* paper.]

or·i·gin (ôr′i jin, or′-) *n.* **1.** the source from which something begins or derives; root or cause: *The basement was the place of origin of the fire. What is the origin of the rumor?* **2.** the act or process of beginning or coming into existence: *The earth was here long before the origin of the human species.* **3.** parentage or ancestry; extraction: *an American of Korean origin.* **4.** *Mathematics.* the point of intersection of the x-axis and the y-axis of a Cartesian coordinate system, with coordinates (0,0). **5.** *Anatomy.* the point of attachment of a muscle to a bone, which serves as a relatively fixed basis of movement. [Latin *orīgō* beginning, source.]

Synonyms **Origin** and **source** mean the point at which something begins its existence. **Origin** designates the beginning of a specific thing or concept: *The origin of the rumor was an overheard remark.* **Source** is often applied to primary, ultimate beginnings: *The sun is the source of all energy on earth.*

o·rig·i·nal (ə rij′ə nəl) *adj.* **1.** not made, done, thought of, or used before; new or unusual: *an original suggestion, original research.* **2.** capable of producing, doing, or thinking of something new or unusual; inventive; creative: *an original thinker.* **3.** of, relating to, or belonging to the origin or beginning of something; first; starting: *The original owner still lives in the house.* **4.** being that from which copies are made: *an original birth certificate.* **5.** conceived and made by the creator; not copied, imitated, or translated: *an original painting by Van Gogh.* —*n.* **1.** something that is original and not a print, copy, imitation, or translation:

The original hangs in a New York museum. **2.** the first form or type from which variations develop or derive: *The eohippus is the original of the horse.* **3.** a person who is unusual or eccentric. **4.** a person who is creative or inventive. —For Synonyms, see **new.**

o·rig·i·nal·i·ty (ə rij′ə nal′i tē) *n.* **1.** the quality of being original. **2.** the ability to be inventive or creative.

o·rig·i·nal·ly (ə rij′ə nə lē) *adv.* **1.** at or from the start; at first; initially: *Originally, we were going to meet at noon.* **2.** in a new, fresh, or unusual manner; with originality: *an experimental poet who writes most originally.* **3.** with reference to origin or source: *Many houseplants were originally tropical plants.*

original sin, in Christian theology, an innate tendency in humanity toward evil, inherited from Adam as a result of his sin. Some Christians, esp. Roman Catholics, believe that original sin deprives a person of divine grace, unless removed by baptism or other means.

o·rig·i·nate (ə rij′ə nāt′) *v.,* **-nat·ed, -nat·ing.** —*v.t.* to start or bring into existence. —*v.i.* to come into existence; begin: *That airplane flight originates in San Francisco.* —**o·rig′i·na′tion,** *n.* —**o·rig′i·na′tive,** *adj.* —**o·rig′i·na′tor,** *n.*

o·ri·ole (ôr′ē ōl′) *n.* **1.** any of various songbirds, family Oriolidae, related to crows, of Eurasia, Africa, the East Indies, and Australia. The male is usually bright orange or yellow and has black markings on the head, wings, and tail, while the female is dull greenish yellow. Length: 6-12 inches (15-30 centimeters). **2.** any of various similar songbirds, family Icteridae, of North, Central, and South America, such as the Baltimore oriole. [Old French *oriol* European bird with golden feathers, from Latin *aureolus* golden, going back to *aurum* gold; referring to the color of its plumage.]

O·ri·on (ō rī′ən) *n.* a constellation on the celestial equator containing the bright star Betelgeuse, conventionally depicted as a hunter wearing a belt with a sword at his side.

or·i·son (ôr′i zən, or′-) *n.* a prayer. [Old French *orison,* from Latin *ōrātiō* speech, prayer. Doublet of ORATION.]

Or·lan·do (ôr lan′dō) *n.* in Italian literature, Roland.

Or·lon (ôr′lon) *n. Trademark.* an acrylic fiber that resists stretching, mildew, acids, and moths, does not absorb water, and is not discolored by sunlight, widely used in the manufacture of clothing, bedding, and other textile products.

Or·mazd (ôr′mazd) *n.* Ahura Mazda.

or·mo·lu (ôr′mə lü′) *n.* an alloy of copper, zinc, and tin that looks like gold, used for gilding articles and making inexpensive jewelry. [French *or moulu* literally, ground gold, going back to Latin *aurum* gold + *molere* to grind.]

or·na·ment (*n.,* ôr′nə mənt; *v.,* ôr′nə ment′) *n.* **1.** a small, often brightly colored or shiny decorative object, such as a colored ball for decorating a Christmas tree. **2.** a person who adds grace, dignity, or luster to his or her time, sphere, or group. **3.** ornamentation. **4.** *Music.* extra notes, such as a trill, added to the notes of a simple melody for interest or expressiveness. **5.** any accessory used in church services, such as the organ, vestments, or the like. —*v.t.* **1.** to add an ornament or ornaments to: *to ornament a dress with silver buttons.* **2.** to be an ornament to: *A clock ornamented the mantelpiece.* [Old French *ornement* adornment, from Latin *ōrnāmentum* decoration, trinket.]

or·na·men·tal (ôr′nə men′tal) *adj.* of, relating to, or used as an ornament: *an ornamental design on a blouse.* —*n.* an ornamental object, such as a tree or shrub cultivated and used for decoration. —**or′na·men′tal·ly,** *adv.*

or·na·men·ta·tion (ôr′nə men tā′shən) *n.* **1.** the act of ornamenting or the state of being ornamented. **2.** something, such as a decorative design, that ornaments another thing. **3.** ornaments collectively. Also, **ornament.**

or·nate (ôr nāt′) *adj.* **1.** having much ornamentation: *an ornate room.* **2.** characterized by showy or flowery language: *an ornate way of speaking.* [Latin *ōrnātus,* past participle of *ōrnāre* to adorn.] —**or·nate′ly,** *adv.* —**or·nate′ness,** *n.*

> **Synonyms** **Ornate, florid,** and **flamboyant** mean extravagantly decorated or designed. **Ornate** can be applied to anything heavily adorned or embellished: *an ornate table, an ornate prose style.* **Florid** implies ostentatious or pretentious richness of detail: *The florid carving of the frame detracted from the painting's simple beauty.* **Flamboyant** suggests a bold, vigorous, daring effect intended to draw attention: *The dancers' flamboyant costumes dazzled the audience.*

or·ner·y (ôr′nə rē) *adj.,* **-ner·i·er, -ner·i·est. 1.** stubborn and difficult to control; unruly: *an ornery mule.* **2.** having or showing a mean or ugly disposition: *an ornery person, an ornery mood.* **3.** inferior. [Modification of ORDINARY.] —**or′ner·i·ness,** *n.*

or·ni·thine (ôr′nə thēn′) *n.* a nonessential amino acid, found in the urine of some birds. In mammals, it serves as an intermediate in the formation of urea from ammonia and carbon dioxide. Formula: $C_5H_{12}N_2O_2$

or·ni·thol·o·gist (ôr′nə thol′ə jist) *n.* a person who is a student of or expert in ornithology.

or·ni·thol·o·gy (ôr′nə thol′ə jē) *n.* the branch of zoology that deals with birds. [Modern Latin *ornithologia,* from Greek *ornith-,* stem of *ornis* bird + -LOGY.] —**or·ni·tho·log·i·cal** (ôr′nə thə loj′i kəl), *adj.*

o·rog·e·ny (ô roj′ə nē) *n., pl.* **-nies.** *Geology.* the process of mountain building, as by folding, faulting, and other diastrophic crustal movements. Also, **or·o·gen·e·sis** (ôr′ə jen′ə sis). [Greek *oros* mountain + -*geneia* birth, origin.] —**or·o·gen·ic** (ôr′ə jen′-ik), *adj.*

o·ro·tund (ôr′ə tund′) *adj.* **1.** (of the voice) strong, full, resonant, and mellow. **2.** pompous; bombastic: *an orotund speech.* [Modification of Latin phrase *ōre rotundō* with polished speech; literally, with round mouth.]

or·phan (ôr′fən) *n.* **1.a.** a child whose natural parents are absent or dead and who must be brought up in an orphanage or by foster parents. **b.** a child who has lost one parent. **2.** a young animal that has lost its mother or its parents. —*adj.* **1.** being an orphan: *orphan children.* **2.** of or for orphans: *an orphan home.* —*v.t.* to make an orphan of: *The war orphaned thousands of children.* [Late Latin *orphanus* child without parents, from Greek *orphanos* without parents, fatherless.]

or·phan·age (ôr′fə nij) *n.* **1.** an institution that takes in and cares for orphans. **2.** the state of being an orphan. [ORPHAN + -AGE.]

Or·phe·us (ôr′fē əs, ôr′fūs) *n.* in Greek mythology, a musician renowned for his beautiful lyre playing, which enchanted trees and stones and tamed wild beasts.

Or·phic (ôr′fik) *adj.* **1.** of, relating to, attributed to, or like Orpheus or his music. **2.** of or relating to mystical religious cults, esp. in ancient Greece and Rome, based on poems supposedly written by Orpheus. **3.** *also,* **orphic.** mystical or oracular.

or·pi·ment (ôr′pə mənt) *n.* a yellow or orange mineral that is a sulfide of arsenic, used as a pigment. Formula: As_2S_3 [Old French *orpiment,* from Latin *auripigmentum,* from *aurum* gold + *pigmentum* pigment.]

or·rer·y (ôr′ə rē) *n., pl.* **-rer·ies.** a mechanical apparatus designed to represent the motion of the planets and moons of the solar system. [From Charles Boyle, Earl of *Orrery,* 1676-1731, patron of the inventor.]

or·ris (ôr′is, or′-) *n., pl.* **or·ris·es.** any of several varieties of iris having a fragrant root. [Form of IRIS.]

or·ris·root (ôr′is rüt′, -rút′, or′-) *n.* the violet-scented root of the orris, dried and powdered for use in perfume, sachets, and tooth powder.

ortho- *combining form* straight, upright, right, or correct: *orthodox.* [Greek *orthos.*]

or·tho·cen·ter (ôr′thə sen′tər) *n.* the point at which the three altitudes of a triangle all intersect. [ORTHO- + CENTER.]

or·tho·clase (ôr′thə klās′, -klāz′) *n.* a variety of the mineral feldspar, a silicate of potassium and aluminum, characterized by a tendency to split along right-angled planes, used chiefly in the manufacture of porcelain and glass. [German *Orthoklas,* from Greek *orthos* (see ORTHO-) + *klasis* a breaking.]

or·tho·don·tics (ôr′thə don′tiks) *n.* the branch of dentistry that deals with the correction and prevention of abnormalities in the growth or position of the teeth and jaws, as by means of braces. ➡ used as singular. Also, **or·tho·don·tia** (ôr′thə don′-shə). [Modern Latin *orthodontia* (from ORTHO- + Greek *odont-,* stem of *odōn* tooth) + -ICS.]

or·tho·don·tist (ôr′thə don′tist) *n.* a dentist who specializes in orthodontics.

or·tho·dox (ôr′thə doks′) *adj.* **1.a.** established or accepted as correct: *orthodox doctrine, an orthodox economic theory.* **b.** adhering to that which is so established or accepted: *an orthodox Marxist.* **2.** marked by or limited to widely used or already proven methods or practices: *an orthodox approach to education.* **3. Orthodox. a.** of, relating to, or characteristic of the Orthodox Church. **b.** of, relating to, or designating Orthodox Judaism. [Late Latin *orthodoxus* having the right faith, from Greek *orthodoxos* having the right opinion, from *orthos* straight, right + *doxa* opinion.]

Orthodox Church, a group of Christian churches that developed from the church of the Byzantine Empire. The Orthodox Church does not recognize the supremacy of the pope and accords special honor to the patriarch of Constantinople. Also, **Eastern**

a	at	e	end	o	hot	u	up	hw	white		about
ā	ape	ē	me	ō	old	ū	use	ng	song		taken
ä	far	i	it	ô	fork	ü	rule	th	thin	ə	pencil
âr	care	ī	ice	oi	oil	ú	pull	th	this		lemon
		îr	pierce	ou	out	ûr	turn	zh	measure		circus

Church, Eastern Orthodox Church, Greek Orthodox Church.

Orthodox Judaism, the branch of Judaism that adheres to a strict interpretation and observance of the Torah.

or·tho·dox·y (ôr′thə dok′sē) *n., pl.* **-dox·ies. 1.** the quality or character of being orthodox: *the orthodoxy of a belief.* **2.** something that is orthodox, such as a religious belief or practice.

or·tho·e·py (ôr thō′ə pē) *n.* **1.** the branch of grammar dealing with pronunciation of words. **2.** the standard or customary pronunciation of a word. [Greek *orthoepeia* correctness of diction, from *orthos* straight, right + *epos* word.] —**or·tho′e·pist,** *n.*

or·tho·gen·e·sis (ôr′thə jen′ə sis) *n.* a theory in biology that species evolve along single straight lines that are predetermined, without disruption or alteration by random mutations or by any independent outside forces or conditions. [ORTHO- + GENESIS.]

or·thog·o·nal (ôr thog′ə nəl) *adj.* of, relating to, composed of, or employing right angles or perpendicular lines. [Latin *orthogōnius* rectangular (from Greek *orthogōnios,* from *orthos* right + *gōniā* angle) + -AL¹.] —**or·thog′o·nal·ly,** *adv.*

orthogonal projection, orthographic projection.

or·thog·ra·pher (ôr thog′rə fər) *n.* a student of or expert in orthography.

or·tho·graph·ic (ôr′thə graf′ik) *adj.* **1.** of or relating to orthography. **2.** correct in spelling. Also, **or′tho·graph′i·cal.** —**or′tho·graph′i·cal·ly,** *adv.*

orthographic projection 1. a technique of mechanical drawing in which each principal face of an object is isolated and drawn separately, showing the exact outlines but no depth, as though each face were projected onto a transparent surface. **2.** any drawing produced in this way. Also, **orthogonal projection.**

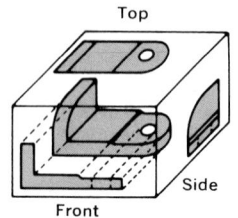
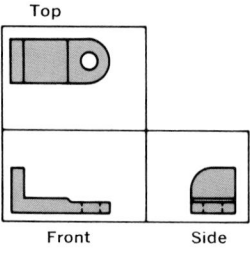

orthographic projections

or·thog·ra·phy (ôr thog′rə fē) *n., pl.* **-phies. 1.** a manner of representing the sounds of a language by written or printed symbols; system of spelling: *Japanese orthography.* **2.** the spelling of words according to an accepted standard of correctness. **3.** the study of letters and spelling. [Latin *orthographia* writing correctly, from Greek *orthographia,* going back to *orthos* right + *graphein* to write.]

or·tho·pe·dic (ôr′thə pē′dik) *adj.* of, relating to, or used in orthopedics.

or·tho·pe·dics (ôr′thə pē′diks) *n.* the branch of medicine that deals with injuries, disorders, and diseases of bones, tendons, ligaments, muscles, and joints. ➡ used as singular. [ORTHO- + Greek *paid-,* stem of *pais* child + -ICS.]

or·tho·pe·dist (ôr′thə pē′dist) *n.* a physician who specializes in orthopedics.

or·thop·ter·an (ôr thop′tər ən) *n.* any of a group of insects, order Orthoptera, including the grasshopper, roach, and praying mantis, characterized by incomplete metamorphosis, biting mouth parts, and two pairs of wings, the thicker, narrower forewings held folded over the hind wings when at rest. [Modern Latin *Orthoptera* literally, straight wings (from ORTHO- + Greek *pteron* wing).]

or·thop·ter·ous (ôr thop′tər əs) *adj.* of, relating to, or belonging to the orthopterans.

or·tho·rhom·bic (ôr′thə rom′bik) *adj.* (of crystals) having three unequal axes at right angles to one another.

or·to·lan (ôr′tə lən) *n.* **1.** a European bunting, *Emberiza hortulana,* having predominantly blue-gray and brown plumage, valued for its meat, which is considered a delicacy. **2.** any of various small New World birds, such as the bobolink. [French *ortolan* the bunting, from Provençal *ortolan* gardener, going back to Latin *hortus* garden; because it is found in gardens.]

Or·well·i·an (ôr wel′ē ən) *adj.* **1.** of, relating to, or characteristic of the English writer George Orwell or his writings. **2.** characteristic of or resembling the totalitarian society depicted in Orwell's novel *1984.*

-ory *suffix* **1.** (used to form adjectives from verbs or from nouns that end in *-ion*). **a.** of, relating to, or doing: *contradictory.* **b.** serving to or characterized by: *illusory, compulsory, contributory.* **2.** (used to form nouns from verbs or from other nouns) a

place or instrument for: *observatory, purgatory.* [Latin *-ōrius, -oria, -orium.*]

o·ryx (ôr′iks) *n., pl.* **o·ryx** or **o·ryx·es.** any of several straight-horned antelopes, genera *Oryx* and *Aegoryx,* of desert regions of Africa and Arabia, having a gray or brown coat with striking black or brown markings. Height: to 7 feet (2.1 meters) at the shoulder. [Latin *oryx* gazelle, from Greek *oryx* pickax, antelope; because of its pointed horns.]

os (os) *n., pl.* **os·sa** (os′ə). a bone. [Latin *os.*]

Os, the symbol for osmium.

O.S., Old Style.

O·sage (ō′sāj, ō sāj′) *n., pl.* **O·sage** or **O·sag·es. 1.** a member of a tribe of North American Indians, originally inhabiting parts of Kansas, Missouri, and Illinois, now living in Oklahoma. **2.** the language of this tribe, a member of the Siouan language family. —*adj.* of, relating to, or characteristic of these people or their language.

Osage orange 1. a thorny American shrub or tree, *Maclura pomifera,* of the mulberry family, widely cultivated as a hedge and for its strong wood that yields a yellowish orange dye. **2.** the yellow, inedible fruit of this shrub or tree, having a green, pebbly outer covering.

Os·car (os′kər) *n. Trademark.* **1.** a gold statuette given to the winner of an Academy Award. **2.** *Informal.* Academy Award. [Supposedly from the comment, "It looks just like my Uncle Oscar," made by a member of the awarding society when shown one of the statuettes.]

os·cil·late (os′ə lāt′) *v.,* **-lat·ed, -lat·ing.** —*v.i.* **1.** to vibrate, fluctuate, or move back and forth between two points: *The compass needle oscillates between north and east.* **2.** to waver between contrary feelings, thoughts, or courses of action: *to oscillate between conservatism and liberalism.* **3.** *Physics.* to produce oscillation. —*v.t.* to cause to move or vibrate back and forth. [Latin *ōscillātus,* past participle of *ōscillāre* to swing, from *ōscillum* swing.]

os·cil·la·tion (os′ə lā′shən) *n.* **1.** the act, condition, or process of oscillating. **2.** a single movement from one point, limit, or extreme to another. **3.** *Physics.* **a.** a periodic fluctuation between two extremes of a quantity, such as voltage, or two extreme positions, as in a vibrating tuning fork. **b.** one complete cycle in which a vibrating object or particle starts at any given point, passes through maximum and minimum positions, and returns to the starting point.

os·cil·la·tor (os′ə lā′tər) *n.* **1.** a person or thing that oscillates. **2.** a device that produces electrical oscillations, or alternating current, used in radio and television transmitters and receivers. —**os·cil·la·to·ry** (os′ə lə tôr′ē), *adj.*

os·cil·lo·scope (ə sil′ə skōp′) *n.* an electronic instrument that produces, on the fluorescent screen of a cathode-ray tube, a luminous visible wave pattern corresponding to the electric signals fed into it. [Latin *ōscillāre* to swing + -SCOPE.]

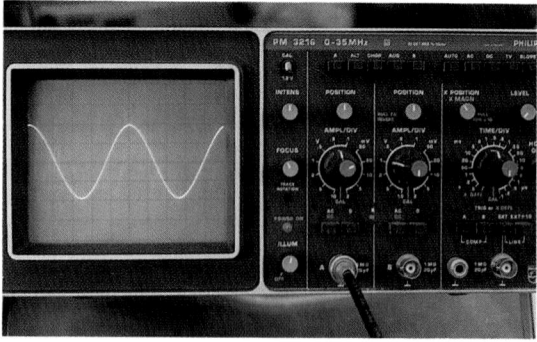

oscilloscope

os·cine (os′in, -īn) *adj.* of or relating to a large suborder of birds, Oscines, including those having the most highly developed vocal organs, such as finches, thrushes, sparrows, and larks. —*n.* an oscine bird. [From Modern Latin *Oscines,* from Latin *oscinēs,* plural of *oscen* a singing bird.]

os·cu·late (os′kyə lāt′) *v.i., v.t.,* **-lat·ed, -lat·ing.** to kiss. [Latin *osculātus,* past participle of *osculārī* to kiss, going back to *ōs* mouth.] —**os′cu·la′tion,** *n.*

-ose¹ *suffix* (used to form adjectives) full of, given to, or like: *grandiose, bellicose.* [Latin *-ōsus* full of.]

-ose² *suffix* used in chemistry to indicate a carbohydrate: *dextrose, sucrose.* [From *-ose,* last syllable of GLUCOSE.]

o·sier (ō′zhər) *n.* **1.** any of various species of willow, having pliable twigs and branches that are used in making baskets and wicker furniture. **2.** a twig of such a willow. **3.** any of several varieties of dogwood. [Old French *osier* willow, from Medieval Latin *auseria* bed of willows; of uncertain origin.]

O·si·ris (ō sī′ris) *n.* in Egyptian mythology, the god of the lower world and judge of the dead, husband and brother of Isis.

-osis *suffix* (used to form nouns) the process or pathological condition of: *metamorphosis, tuberculosis.* [Greek *-ōsis.*]

Os·man·li (oz man′lē, os-) *n., pl.* **-lis. 1.** Ottoman *(def. 1).* **2.** the Turkish language, esp. when written in Arabic script. —*adj.* Ottoman *(def. 2).*

os·mi·um (oz′mē əm) *n.* a very hard, heavy, bluish white metallic element, used to make alloys for pen points and electrical contacts. Symbol: **Os** For tables, see **element.** [Modern Latin *osmium,* from Greek *osmē* odor; because one of its oxides has a strong smell.]

os·mose (oz mōs′, os-) *v.,* **-mosed, -mos·ing.** —*v.i.* **1.** to spread by osmosis. **2.** to undergo osmosis. —*v.t.* to subject to osmosis. [From OSMOSIS.]

os·mo·sis (oz mō′sis, os-) *n.* **1.** the movement of a fluid through a semipermeable membrane, such as the wall of a plant or animal cell, into a solution that contains the same fluid; movement of a more concentrated solution toward a less concentrated one, thereby equalizing the pressure on both sides of a membrane. **2.** any gradual process of assimilation that seems to occur without conscious effort: *Young children learn their native language by osmosis.* [Modern Latin *osmosis,* from Greek *ōsmos* thrust + -OSIS.] —**os·mot·ic** (oz mot′ik, os-), *adj.* —**os·mot′i·cal·ly,** *adv.*

os·prey (os′prē) *n., pl.* **-preys** or **-prey.** a fish-eating hawk, *Pandion haliaetus,* having brownish black plumage with a white head and undersides. Wingspan: 5½ feet (1.7 meters). Also, **fish hawk.** [From an unrecorded Old French form, from Latin *ossifraga* osprey; literally, bone-breaking, from *os* bone + *frangere* to break; referring to the bird's great strength.]

os·se·ous (os′ē əs) *adj.* made of, containing, or resembling bone; bony. [Latin *osseus,* from *os* bone.]

os·si·cle (os′i kəl) *n.* a small bone or bonelike structure, esp. any of the three small bones of the middle ear. [Latin *ossiculum,* diminutive of *os* bone.] —**os·sic·u·lar** (o sik′yə lər), *adj.*

os·si·fi·ca·tion (os′ə fi kā′shən) *n.* **1.** an abnormal hardening, as of muscle or other soft tissue, into bonelike tissue. **2.** the normal process of bone formation. **3.** the fact or process of becoming overly rigid, conservative, or conventional, as in an attitude or custom.

os·si·fy (os′ə fī′) *v.,* **-fied, -fy·ing.** —*v.t.* **1.** to cause to change into bone. **2.** to cause to become very rigid, conservative, or conventional: *An old quarrel had ossified the cousins' dislike for each other.* —*v.i.* **1.** to change into bone. **2.** to become very rigid, conservative, or conventional: *Some of my opinions have ossified over the years.* [Latin *os* bone + -FY.]

os·ten·si·ble (os ten′sə bəl) *adj.* put forth as being or seeming to be actual; declared or apparent: *an ostensible victory that was in fact a defeat.* [French *ostensible,* going back to Latin *ostendere* to show.] —**os·ten′si·bly,** *adv.*

os·ten·sive (os ten′siv) *adj.* **1.** directly pointing out; clearly demonstrative. **2.** ostensible. —**os·ten′sive·ly,** *adv.*

os·ten·ta·tion (os′tən tā′shən) *n.* a showy, excessive, or overly ceremonial display meant to impress others or attract attention: *the ostentation of a victorious army's entry into a conquered city.* [Middle French *ostentation* display, from Latin *ostentātio.*]

os·ten·ta·tious (os′tən tā′shəs) *adj.* **1.** done with the intent of impressing others or attracting attention: *an ostentatious contempt of the law.* **2.** characterized or marked by ostentation: *an ostentatious mansion.* —**os·ten·ta′tious·ly,** *adv.* —**os′ten·ta′tious·ness,** *n.*

osteo- *combining form* of or relating to bone: *osteopathy.* [Greek *osteon* bone.]

os·te·o·ar·thri·tis (os′tē ō är thrī′tis) *n.* a progressive degenerative disease of the joints, esp. of the legs and fingers, occurring mainly in the elderly and characterized by painful swelling and stiffness. [OSTEO- + ARTHRITIS.]

os·te·ol·o·gy (os′tē ol′ə jē) *n.* the branch of anatomy dealing with bones and bone structure. [OSTEO- + -LOGY.]

os·te·o·my·e·li·tis (os′tē ō mī′ə lī′tis) *n.* an infection of the bone, esp. the marrow, usually caused by a bacterium.

os·te·o·path (os′tē ə path′) *n.* a doctor who is trained to practice osteopathy. Also, **os·te·op·a·thist** (os′tē op′ə thist).

os·te·op·a·thy (os′tē op′ə thē) *n.* a system of treating patients by manipulating the bones and muscles. Osteopathy also includes other methods of medical treatment, such as the use of drugs and surgery. [OSTEO- + -PATHY.] —**os·te·o·path·ic** (os′tē ə path′ik), *adj.*

os·te·o·po·ro·sis (os′tē ō pə rō′sis) *n.* a disorder in which the bones gradually become porous and brittle because of a loss of calcium and other minerals. It occurs esp. among women who have experienced menopause. [OSTEO- + Latin *porus* pore[1] + -OSIS. See PORE[1].]

os·tler (os′lər) *n.* hostler.

ost·mark (ôst′märk′, ost′-) *n.* the former monetary unit of East Germany. [German *Ostmark,* from *Ost* east + *Mark* mark[2].]

os·tra·cism (os′trə siz′əm) *n.* **1.** the act of ostracizing or the state of being ostracized. **2.** in ancient Greece, temporary banishment by vote of the people.

os·tra·cize (os′trə sīz′) *v.t.,* **-cized, -ciz·ing. 1.** to cut off or exclude from a group or from society: *to ostracize a classmate for cheating.* **2.** in ancient Greece, to banish temporarily by vote of the people. [Greek *ostrakízein* to banish through a vote recorded on potsherds, from *óstrakon* tile, potsherd.]

os·tra·cod (os′trə kod′) *n.* any of a group of tiny freshwater or marine crustaceans, subclass Ostracoda, having the body enclosed in a clamlike shell. [Modern Latin *ostracoda,* from Greek *ostrakon* shell, potsherd.]

os·trich (ôs′trich, os′-) *n.* **1.** a two-toed, flightless bird, *Struthio camelus,* of central Africa, the largest of all living birds. It has a long neck, long, powerful legs, a small, flat head, and, in the male, large, white plumes on the wings and tail that are used to trim hats and other apparel. Height: 8 feet (2.4 meters). **2.** a person who tries to avoid danger or a disagreeable situation by refusing to acknowledge it. [Old French *ostruce,* going back to Latin *avis* bird + Greek *strouthiōn* ostrich.]

ostrich

Os·tro·goth (os′trə goth′) *n.* a member of the eastern branch of the Goths, who controlled Italy A.D. 493 to 554. [Late Latin *Ostrogothus;* of Germanic origin.] —**Os′tro·goth′ic,** *adj.*

O.T., Old Testament.

O·thel·lo (ə thel′ō) *n.* the principal character of Shakespeare's tragedy *Othello,* who, driven to suspicion and jealousy by Iago's insinuations and lies, murders his faithful wife, Desdemona.

oth·er (uth′ər) *adj.* **1.** different from the one or ones already mentioned or implied; not the same: *If you won't do it, some other friend will.* **2.a.** indicating the remaining one of two or more: *Now I'll look in the other ear.* **b.** indicating the remaining ones of several: *The other guests have not arrived yet.* **3.** additional; further: *We have no other choice.* **4.** different in kind or quality: *I cannot be other than I am.* **5.** recently past (with *the*): *the other morning, the other night.* —*n.* **1.** a different or additional person or thing: *No other has a key to the vault. Did many others travel with you?* **2.** the remaining one of two or more: *If the first store is closed, the other will be open. The others will join us later.* —*pron.* **1.** a different or additional person or thing: *The business failed for some reason or other.* **2. others.** additional or different people or things: *Some children laughed, but others didn't.* —*adv.* otherwise (with *than*): *I could not feel other than surprised.* [Old English *ōther* remaining, additional, different.]

• **every other.** every second or alternate: *The team practices every other day.*

oth·er·wise (uth′ər wīz′) *adv.* **1.** apart from that; in other respects: *The food ran out early, but otherwise the party was a success.* **2.** under any different circumstances; if not for that: *The sailors would have otherwise fallen into the sea.* **3.** in a different way or in any other way: *I cannot believe otherwise but that we shall succeed.* —*adj.* otherwise; other: *The facts are otherwise.* —*conj.* because if not; or else: *The shingles must be fixed, otherwise the roof will leak.* [Old English *(on) ōthre wīsan* (in) other manner. See OTHER, WISE[2].]

other world, a world or existence beyond death or beyond earthly reality.

oth·er·world·ly (uth′ər wûrld′lē) *adj.* **1.** of, belonging to, or preoccupied with a future life, heaven, an ideal world, or the like: *an otherworldly religion.* **2.** not seeming to be of this world or of

a	at	e	end	o	hot	u	up	hw	white		about
ā	ape	ē	me	ō	old	ū	use	ng	song		taken
ä	far	i	it	ô	fork	ü	rule	th	thin	ə	pencil
âr	care	ī	ice	oi	oil	u̇	pull	th	this		lemon
		îr	pierce	ou	out	ûr	turn	zh	measure		circus

life in this world; unearthly; strange: *music that is eerie and other-worldly.* —**oth′er·world′li·ness,** *n.*

o·tic (ō′tik) *adj.* of, related to, or located in or around the ear. [Greek *ōtikos,* from *ous* ear[1].]

o·ti·ose (ō′shē ōs′, ō′tē-) *adj.* **1.** performing no work; lazy or idle. **2.** producing no useful effect or result; futile. **3.** serving no useful purpose; superfluous or useless. [Latin *ōtiōsus* at leisure, idle, from *ōtium* leisure.]

o·ti·tis (ō tī′tis) *n., pl.* **o·tit·i·des** (ō tit′i dēz′). inflammation of the ear. [Modern Latin *otitis,* from Greek *ōtos,* genitive of *ous* ear[1] + *-itis* (see -ITIS).]

o·to·lar·yn·gol·o·gy (ō′tō lar′ing gol′ə jē) *n.* the branch of medicine that deals with diseases of the ear, nose, and throat.

o·tol·o·gy (ō tol′ə jē) *n.* the branch of medicine that deals with diseases of the ear. —**o·to·log·i·cal** (ō′tə loj′i kəl), *adj.* —**o·tol′o·gist,** *n.*

ot·ta·va ri·ma (ō tä′və rē′mə) a stanza form of Italian origin, consisting of eight lines of ten or eleven syllables each, having the rhyme scheme *ababbcc.* [Italian *ottava rima* the stanza; literally, eighth rhyme, going back to Latin *octāvus* eighth + Old High German *rīm* series, row, number.]

Ot·ta·wa (ot′ə wə) *n., pl.* **-wa** or **-was.** a member of a tribe of Algonquian Indians who lived near the Great Lakes in what is now southern Ontario.

ot·ter (ot′ər) *n., pl.* **-ters** or **-ter. 1.** any of various web-footed aquatic mammals, family Mustelidae, esp. genus *Lutra,* related to and resembling the weasel and mink, and having a long, slightly flattened tail. Length: 32-64 inches (81-163 centimeters), including tail. **2.** its brown, glossy fur, used in making coats and trimmings. [Old English *otor* the animal.]

otter

Ot·to·man (ot′ə mən) *n., pl.* **-mans. 1.** a Turk of the Ottoman Empire, esp. a member of the tribe whose ruling family founded and ruled the empire. Also, **Osmanli. 2. ottoman. a.** a low, boxlike, upholstered seat or footstool resembling a hassock. **b.** a couch or sofa, esp. one without back or arms. **3. ottoman.** a medium-weight to heavyweight fabric woven with a broad, flat, rib effect, used for such items as coats and upholstery. —*adj.* **1.** Turkish. **2.** of or relating to the Ottoman Empire or the family that ruled it. Also *(def. 2),* **Osmanli.**

ouch (ouch) *interj.* used to express pain or sympathy for being hurt.

ought[1] (ôt) *auxiliary verb* (followed by an infinitive) **1.** to be bound by a promise or duty or by values of right and wrong: *You ought to obey the rules.* **2.** to be expected or likely: *I put in new batteries, so the radio ought to work.* **3.** to be compelled by what is sensible or wise: *You ought to take care of your cold.* **4.** to be bound by desirability: *You ought to read this book; it is very good.* [Old English *ahte,* past tense of *āgan* to own, owe.] —For Synonyms, see **must**[1].

ought[2] (ôt) **aught**[1].

ought[3] (ôt) **aught**[2].

oui·ja board (wē′jə, -jē) a board used in spiritualism, printed with letters, numbers, and other signs that are used to form messages as indicated by a special pointing device, or planchette. Trademark: **Ouija.** [French *oui* yes + German *ja* yes.]

ounce[1] (ouns) *n.* **1.** a unit of weight equal to $\frac{1}{16}$ pound avoirdupois (28.35 grams), or $\frac{1}{12}$ pound troy, or 8 drams apothecaries′. **2.** in liquid measure, fluid ounce. **3.** a small quantity: *The dancers didn't have an ounce of energy left.* [Old French *once, unce* unit of weight, from Latin *uncia* a twelfth part. Doublet of INCH.]

ounce[2] (ouns) *n.* snow leopard. [Middle English *once* lynx, from Old French *once,* from a mistaken interpretation of *lonce* lynx (as if it were *l'once* the lynx), from Latin *lynx,* from Greek *lynx.*]

our (our, är) *adj.* (the possessive form of **we**) of, relating to, or belonging to us: *our house.* [Old English *ūre* of us (genitive plural of first personal pronoun), belonging to us.]

Our Father, Lord′s Prayer.

Our Lady, Mary, the mother of Jesus.

ours (ourz, ärz) *pron.* the one or ones belonging to us: *Their dog is larger than ours. Ours is a miniature poodle.* ➡ used as singular or plural.

our·self (our′self′, är-) *pron.* myself. ➡ used with we when *we* is singular: *"We declare ourself opposed,"* the senator announced.

our·selves (our′selvz′, är-) *pl. pron.* **1.** the emphatic form of **we** or **us:** *We ourselves decided to go.* **2.** the reflexive form of **us:**

We took it upon ourselves to tell you. **3.** our normal, average, or true selves: *We haven't been ourselves since the accident.* —For Usage note, see **myself.**

-ous *suffix* **1.** (used to form adjectives from nouns) of, full of, characterized by, like, or having: *religious, dangerous, bulbous, famous.* **2.** used in chemistry to indicate a lower valence than that indicated by *-ic: cuprous.* [Latin *-ōsus* full of (often through Old French *-ous, -eus*); also representing adjectival endings *-us* in Latin and *-os* in Greek.]

ou·sel (ü′zəl) ouzel.

oust (oust) *v.t.* to force or drive out from a place or position: *The people rebelled and ousted the dictator.* [Anglo-Norman *ouster* to remove, take away, going back to Latin *obstāre* to oppose, hinder.]

oust·er (ous′tər) *n.* **1.** the act or an instance of ousting. **2.** the state of being ousted.

out (out) *adv.* **1.** from within or the inside; away from the center: *Roads radiated out from the plaza. The water rushed out.* **2.** away from a place, esp. one's home or business: *The doctor went out on a call.* **3.** into the open air; outdoors: *The children went out to play.* **4.** from a source or container: *to draw out a sword, to pour out orange juice.* **5.** so as to project or extend: *I stretched out my hand. The rocks jutted out into the sea.* **6.** to an end or conclusion: *Hear me out.* **7.** into or in a condition of inactivity or extinction: *The firefighters put out the flames. The injured player is out for three weeks.* **8.** so as to be exhausted or consumed: *The flow of water petered out.* **9.** completely or thoroughly: *Dry out your clothes. Write your full name out.* **10.** into existence or a state of activity: *Riots broke out. An epidemic of flu broke out.* **11.** into or within view, public notice, or circulation: *The sun came out. The secret was out.* **12.** from or not at a proper, necessary, or usual place or position: *He put his shoulder out at football practice. You left a word out in this sentence.* **13.** aloud, esp. with power or force: *The sergeant called out the names of the soldiers. The bells rang out.* **14.** to others: *to deal out cards, to rent out rooms.* **15.** from among others: *We picked out a new car.* **16.** into or in a state of annoyance or dispute: *She felt put out because the train was so late. The two friends fell out.* **17.** on strike: *The factory workers went out for higher wages.* **18.** Baseball. in such a way as to cause a batter or base runner to be unsuccessful in reaching a base: *The batter grounded out.* **19.** Informal. into or in a condition of being unfashionable or unpopular: *That style went out two years ago.* —*adj.* **1.** not in control, power, or office: *The losers in the election will be out in January.* **2.** without any: *Last week we had bananas, but now we're out.* **3.** at a financial loss: *I am out five dollars.* **4.** bared or threadbare: *This sweater is out at the elbow.* **5.** no longer skillful because of lack of practice: *My backhand is out.* **6.** in error; wrong: *You were out in your estimate.* **7.** not in working order or condition: *That road is out because of the flood.* **8.** considered unacceptable or impossible: *That plan is definitely out.* **9.** going outward or used for things going outward: *an out train, an out basket for mail.* **10.** external; exterior; outer: *the out edge.* **11.** outlying: *out islands.* **12.** (in sports) outside the prescribed playing area: *The ball is out when it crosses the white line.* **13.** Baseball. (of a batter or base runner) unsuccessful in reaching a base. —*prep.* **1.** from within; out from: *I looked out the window.* **2.** outward on; out along: *Drive out the dirt road until you come to the highway.* —*n.* **1.** a person or thing that is out. **2.** a way or means of escaping or avoiding: *I didn't want to go, but I couldn't think of an out.* **3.** Baseball. **a.** the act or an instance of putting out a batter or base runner. **b.** a batter or base runner who is to be put out: *Their catcher is an easy out.* **4.** a serve or return that falls outside the proper part of the court, as in tennis or squash. **5.** a person out of office or out of power. ➡ opposed to **in;** usually used in the plural. **6.** Printing. **a.** the omission of a word or words. **b.** the word or words omitted. —*v.i.* to be disclosed or revealed; come out: *The truth will out.* —*interj.* away; begone. [Old English *ūt, ūte* forth, away, into the open air, from the usual place or condition, into activity.]

• **on the** (or **at) outs.** in disagreement; not friendly: *They have been on the outs since their quarrel.*

• **out and away.** to a great degree; by far: *This car is out and away the best on the market.*

• **out for.** trying hard to get or do: *an ambitious worker out for a promotion.*

• **out from under.** free or away from (a difficult situation): *I was eager to start anew and get out from under my debts.*

• **out of. a.** from within: *She went out of the room.* **b.** at the outside from or through: *He looked out of the window.* **c.** beyond the limits, scope, reach, range, or influence of: *The jet flew out of sight. My friend was out of hearing.* **d.** without: *We're out of butter, so please buy some.* **e.** so as to deprive or be deprived of: *to be swindled out of $500.* **f.** from, as material: *a house built out of stone.* **g.** from among: *to choose one out of*

three. **h.** as a result of; because of: *to do something out of kindness.* **i.** (of horses) born of: *a foal out of a good mare.*
• **out to.** trying hard to please: *tourists out to see all the sights.*

out- *prefix* **1.** external, outside, or outward: *outline, outcry.* **2.** more than or better than: *outgrow, outshine, outshoot.* **3.** beyond the usual or normal: *outsize.* [From OUT.]

out·age (ou′tij) *n.* an interruption in some service or operation, as of electric power.

out-and-out (out′ən out′) *adj.* **1.** thorough; complete: *an out-and-out liar.* **2.** easily seen; obvious; unconcealed: *an out-and-out fake.*

out·back (out′bak′) *n.* **1.** *also,* **Out·back.** the wild or largely undeveloped rural part of Australia. **2.** any similar area.

out·bid (out′bid′) *v.t.* **-bid, -bid** or **-bid·den, -bid·ding.** to offer a higher price than (someone else), as at an auction.

out·board (out′bôrd′) *adj.* outside the hull or farther away from the center of a ship, boat, or aircraft. —*n.* **1.** outboard motor. **2.** a boat equipped with an outboard motor.

outboard motor, an engine and propeller externally mounted on the stern of a small boat. Also, **outboard.**

out·bound (out′bound′) *adj.* outward bound: *trains outbound from Detroit.*

out·break (out′brāk′) *n.* **1.** a sudden occurrence or eruption: *the outbreak of World War II.* **2.** a sudden increase in the occurrence of something: *There was an outbreak of flu among the students.*

out·build·ing (out′bil′ding) *n.* a separate building, such as a woodshed, barn, or garage, associated with a main building.

out·burst (out′bûrst′) *n.* a sudden, noisy, or violent outpouring: *a person given to sudden outbursts of anger, an outburst of flames.*

out·cast (out′kast′) *n.* a person who is rejected or forced out of a group. —*adj.* rejected or forced out of a group.

out·class (out′klas′) *v.t.* to surpass in rank or skill.

out·come (out′kum′) *n.* a result or consequence: *the outcome of an election.*

> **Synonyms** Outcome, effect, result, and consequence mean something that can be traced to a cause. **Outcome** suggests a final and overall state but does not imply a necessary connection with a cause as strongly as the other terms do: *The outcome of the meeting was more confusion.* **Effect** stresses a connection: *One effect of applying electrical current is movement of the muscles.* **Result** more strongly suggests finality: *As a result of our complaint, the store changed its policy.* **Consequence** refers to anything that follows a cause, whether immediately or at some length: *One consequence of the flood was a poor crop the next year.*

out·crop (*n.,* out′krop′; *v.,* out′krop′) *n.* *Geology.* **1.** the part of a rock layer that comes up or out to the surface of the ground so as to be visible or easily mined. **2.** the process or fact of so coming out. —*v.i.* to form an outcrop.

out·cry (out′krī′) *n., pl.* **-cries. 1.** a strong objection or complaint, esp. of many people: *The proposed tax caused an outcry.* **2.** a shout or crying out.

out·dat·ed (out′dā′tid) *adj.* obsolete; out-of-date.

out·dis·tance (out′dis′təns) *v.t.,* **-tanced, -tanc·ing.** to leave behind in or as in a race: *The fast horse easily outdistanced the others.*

out·do (out′dü′) *v.t.,* **-did** (-did′), **-done** (-dun′), **-do·ing.** to do better than; surpass; exceed. —For Synonyms, see **excel.**
• **to outdo oneself.** to do better than one usually does: *Our hosts outdid themselves in planning this party.*

out·door (out′dôr′) *adj.* **1.** performed, located, or intended for use out in the open rather than inside a building: *outdoor furniture.* **2.** liking or preferring life outdoors: *an outdoor person.*

out·doors (out′dôrz′) *adv.* outside a house or other building; out under the sky: *to take a walk outdoors.* —*n.* the world that is outside or distant from houses or other buildings. ➡ used as singular. Also, **out-of-doors.**

out·er (ou′tər) *adj.* **1.** far or farther away from the center: *the outer reaches of the universe.* **2.** located on or more toward the outside; external: *outer garments.* —For Synonyms, see **exterior.**

outer ear, external ear.

out·er·most (ou′tər mōst′) *adj.* most distant or external or farthest out: *the outermost layer of an onion, the outermost island.*

outer space, space beyond the outermost layer of the earth's atmosphere; interplanetary and interstellar space.

out·er·wear (ou′tər wâr′) *n.* clothing worn over other clothes, esp. sweaters, coats, and hats worn outdoors for warmth or protection against the weather.

out·face (out′fās′) *v.t.,* **-faced, -fac·ing. 1.** to stare down or overcome. **2.** to confront boldly; defy.

out·field (out′fēld′) *n.* *Baseball.* **1.** the part of the field beyond the infield and between the foul lines. For illustration, see **infield. 2.** the players who play in this area.

out·field·er (out′fēl′dər) *n.* *Baseball.* a player who plays a position in the outfield.

out·fit (out′fit′) *n.* **1.** a set of articles or equipment needed for doing something: *a camping outfit.* **2.** a set of clothes worn together; ensemble: *dressed in a red outfit.* **3.** *Informal.* a group or team that works together, such as a business office or military unit. —*v.t.,* **-fit·ted, -fit·ting.** to provide with articles or equipment: *to outfit an expedition to the North Pole.* —**out′fit′ter,** *n.*

out·flank (out′flangk′) *v.t.* **1.** to outmaneuver (an opposing army) by getting around its side. **2.** to get the better of (an opponent), esp. by outmaneuvering and avoiding a direct assault.

out·flow (out′flō′) *n.* **1.** the act or process of flowing out. **2.** something that flows out: *an outflow of lava from a volcano.* **3.** the amount that flows out.

out·fox (out′foks′) *v.t.* to trick or outsmart (someone).

out·gen·er·al (out′jen′ər əl) *v.t.,* **-aled, -al·ing;** *also, British,* **-alled, -al·ling.** to outmaneuver, esp. by superior military skill.

out·go (out′gō′) *n., pl.* **-goes.** something that goes or is paid out, esp. money spent.

out·go·ing (out′gō′ing) *adj.* **1.** sociable, open, and talkative; not withdrawn or private: *an outgoing person who makes friends quickly.* **2.** going out or departing: *an outgoing flight.* **3.** leaving a position, as by retiring: *an outgoing president.*

out·grow (out′grō′) *v.t.,* **-grew** (-grü′), **-grown** (-grōn′), **-grow·ing. 1.** to grow too large for: *to outgrow one's clothing.* **2.** to leave behind or lose in the process of developing or maturing: *to outgrow a fear of the dark.* **3.** to surpass in growth; grow taller or faster than: *She outgrew her older brother by 4 inches.*

out·growth (out′grōth′) *n.* **1.** a product, result, or development: *The author's pacifism is a natural outgrowth of seeing war's effects.* **2.** something that grows out; growth. **3.** the act or process of growing out or forth.

out·guess (out′ges′) *v.t.* to guess correctly the plans of; outwit.

out·house (out′hous′) *n., pl.* **-hous·es** (-hou′ziz). **1.** a small shed or stall outdoors that is used as a toilet. **2.** an outbuilding.

out·ing (ou′ting) *n.* a short pleasure trip; excursion.

out·laid (out′lād′) the past tense and past participle of **outlay.**

out·land·er (out′lan′dər) *n.* a stranger or foreigner.

out·land·ish (out′lan′dish) *adj.* strange, unfamiliar, or bizarre. —**out′land′ish·ly,** *adv.* —**out′land′ish·ness,** *n.*

out·last (out′last′) *v.t.* to last longer than.

out·law (out′lô′) *n.* **1.** a person who habitually breaks or defies the law; criminal. **2.** formerly, a person who has been deprived of the benefits and protection of the law; fugitive or exile. —*v.t.* **1.** to make illegal; prohibit: *to outlaw the sale of certain drugs.* **2.** to declare (someone) an outlaw. **3.** to deprive (a debt or contract) of legal force, as because of the statute of limitations. [Old English *ūtlaga* one put outside of the law, going back to Old Norse *ūtlagr* banished.]

out·law·ry (out′lô′rē) *n., pl.* **-ries. 1.** constant defiance or disregard of the law. **2.** the act of outlawing or the state of being outlawed. **3.** formerly, the practice of putting a person beyond the protection of the law, esp. as a punishment.

out·lay (*n.,* out′lā′; *v.,* out′lā′) *n.* **1.** an investment or expenditure of money: *They started their business with only a small initial outlay.* **2.** any expenditure, as of time or effort. —*v.t.,* **-laid, -lay·ing.** to spend (money); expend.

out·let (out′let′, -lit) *n.* **1.** a place at which something escapes or comes out: *the outlet of a swimming pool.* **2.** a means of expression or gratification: *Sports are a good outlet for a young person's energy.* **3.** a place in an electrical wiring system having a female fitting, where appliances can be plugged in and the current tapped. **4.** a place where products are sold, esp. a store that sells the goods of a single manufacturer at a discount. Also, **factory outlet. 5.** a stream, river, or other channel through which the water of an enclosed body flows out. **6.** an end of a street or other passage that opens onto another.

out·line (out′līn′) *n.* **1.** *also,* **outlines. a.** a line that traces the outer edges of an object. **b.** the shape of an object formed by its outer edges: *Through the fog they saw the barely visible outline of a passing ship.* **2.** *also,* **outlines.** a description without precise details; general idea: *to give a rough outline of expenses for next year.* **3.** a summary, often with separate parts marked off with Roman numerals and alphabet letters, that organizes the contents

a	at	e	end	o	hot	u	up	hw	white		about
ā	ape	ē	me	ō	old	ū	use	ng	song		taken
ä	far	i	it	ô	fork	ū	rule	th	thin	ə	pencil
âr	care	ī	ice	oi	oil	u̇	pull	th	this		lemon
		îr	pierce	ou	out	ûr	turn	zh	measure		circus

of a story, composition, or speech. **4.a.** a style of drawing in which an object or scene is represented merely by lines of contour without shading: *to show a bridge in outline.* **b.** a drawing made in this way. —*v.t.,* **-lined, -lin·ing. 1.** to set off, make visible, or mark the outlines of: *Dawn outlined the skyscrapers against the sky.* **2.** to summarize or give a general description of: *to outline travel plans.* **3.** to draw the outline of.

Synonyms *n.* **Outline, profile, silhouette,** and **contour** mean the outer edge of a figure or mass. **Outline,** the most general of these terms, may refer to any object or mass: *The outline of an ameba changes constantly.* **Profile** emphasizes the contrast of an outline with its background and is used esp. of the side view of a head: *The monarch's profile appears on the nation's coins.* **Silhouette** indicates the edge of a dark shape clearly delineated against a light background, esp. a likeness of a head or body: *Its distinctive silhouette made the plane easy to identify.* **Contour** refers either to the shape of a landmass or to any graceful, curving outline: *the contours of a plowed field, the pleasing contour of the dancer's extended arm.*

out·live (out′liv′) *v.t.,* **-lived, -liv·ing. 1.** to live or last longer than. **2.** to live through; survive; endure: *to outlive a serious automobile accident.*

out·look (out′lŏŏk′) *n.* **1.** a view into the future; expectation or prospect: *The outlook for a good corn crop is favorable.* **2.** a point of view or set of opinions or beliefs: *persons of different religious outlooks.* **3.a.** a place from which a view is obtained; lookout. **b.** the view from such a place: *the dreary outlook of chimney tops and smoke* (Charles Kingsley, 1850).

out·ly·ing (out′lī′ing) *adj.* located far from the center, as of a city: *a large park in an outlying suburb.*

out·ma·neu·ver (out′mə nü′vər) *v.t.,* **-vered, -ver·ing.** to maneuver better than or defeat by maneuvering.

out·mod·ed (out′mō′did) *adj.* no longer in style or no longer suitable or useful: *an outmoded computer.*

out·most (out′mōst′) *adj.* farthest out; outermost.

out·num·ber (out′num′bər) *v.t.* to be greater in number than; exceed in number.

out-of-bounds (out′əv boundz′) *adv., adj. Sports.* outside the legal area of play: *to hit a ball out-of-bounds, an out-of-bounds part of a soccer field.*

out-of-date (out′əv dāt′) *adj.* no longer fashionable or being used; belonging to a former time. —**out′-of-date′ness,** *n.*

out-of-doors (out′əv dôrz′) *adj.* Also, **out-of-door. out-door.** ⇒ used as singular. —*adv.* outdoors.

out-of-pock·et (out′əv pok′it) *adj.* paid directly in cash: *out-of-pocket expenses incurred while traveling.*

out-of-the-way (out′əv thə wā′) *adj.* **1.** not easily accessible; off the beaten track: *an out-of-the-way spot that is ideal for fishing.* **2.** not usually met with; little known or unusual: *a few out-of-the-way facts of history.*

out·pace (out′pās′) *v.t.,* **-paced, -pac·ing. 1.** to go faster than: *to outpace other runners.* **2.** to go beyond; surpass; exceed: *Their spending outpaced their income.*

out·pa·tient (out′pā′shənt) *n.* a patient who receives care or treatment from a hospital, clinic, or similar institution without being confined or kept in a bed there.

out·place·ment (out′plās′mənt) *n.* **1.** the act or process of finding or helping to find a job in another company for an employee who has been or soon will be discharged. **2.** services and other assistance, such as counseling, provided in outplacement.

out·play (out′plā′) *v.t.* to play better than.

out·point (out′point′) *v.t.* to score more points than.

out·post (out′pōst′) *n.* **1.** a small military installation, usually at some distance from the main force, established to maintain control over the area and to guard against attack. **2.** the military personnel assigned to such an installation. **3.** any settlement lying outside a border or boundary or on a frontier. **4.** anything beyond a border, far off, or in advance.

out·pour·ing (out′pôr′ing) *n.* **1.** the act of pouring out something, esp. thoughts or feelings: *A great outpouring of emotion accompanied the end of the war.* **2.** something that is poured or pours out: *The outpouring of mail overwhelmed the small post office.*

out·put (out′pŏŏt′) *n.* **1.** anything put or taken out: *Much of the output of a fire is in the form of light and heat.* **2.** the amount produced, as of work, energy, or goods: *a large output.* **3.** the information made available by a computer or any other storage and retrieval system.

out·rage (out′rāj′) *n.* **1.** an act of such violence, viciousness, or excessive cruelty that it arouses, or should arouse, general rage or anger. **2.** great anger or rage: *The peasants felt outrage at the attacks on their villages.* **3.** a deeply felt insult, indignity, or offense: *Such behavior is an outrage.* —*v.t.,* **-raged, -rag·ing. 1.** to cause great anger in: *The editorial outraged the senator.* **2.** to

subject to an outrage; abuse or injure greatly. **3.** to rape. [Old French *outrage* excess, presumption, going back to Latin *ultrā* beyond.]

out·ra·geous (out rā′jəs) *adj.* **1.** exceeding proper limits; unconventional or immoderate: *an outrageous request, outrageous behavior.* **2.** of the nature of or resembling an outrage: *an outrageous murder.* —**out·ra′geous·ly,** *adv.* —**out·ra′geous·ness,** *n.*

out·ran (out′ran′) the past tense of **outrun.**

out·rank (out′rangk′) *v.t.* to be of a higher rank than: *A major outranks a captain.*

ou·tré (ü trā′) *adj. French.* beyond the bounds of what is usual or considered proper; eccentric; bizarre.

out·reach (*v.,* out′rēch′; *n., adj.,* out′rēch′) *v.t.* to reach further than; exceed. —*v.i.* to reach out. —*n.* **1.** the act of reaching out. **2.** the act of offering or providing services, benefits, or the like to people who do not usually or readily have access to them. —*adj.* engaged in, consisting of, or provided through outreach: *an outreach office, outreach work, outreach services.*

out·rid·er (out′rī′dər) *n.* **1.** a person who rides out or forth, esp. a guide or escort. **2.** a cowboy who rides on the edge of a moving herd of cattle. **3.** a mounted servant or attendant who goes in advance of or beside a vehicle, such as a carriage.

out·rig·ger (out′rig′ər) *n.* **1.a.** an extra float and its supporting frame that can be fixed to the side of a canoe or boat to extend out into the water and prevent capsizing. **b.** a canoe or boat having an outrigger. **2.** any projecting support. **3.** a bracket projecting outward from either side of a rowboat or racing shell to support an oarlock.

Spar
Float
outrigger

out·right (out′rīt′) *adj.* **1.** not qualified or changed by the addition or lack of anything; complete; thorough: *outright viciousness, an outright lie.* **2.** having no conditions or restrictions: *an outright grant for scientific research.* —*adv.* **1.** in a direct or straightforward way; openly: *to say outright what you mean.* **2.** completely and all at once: *Rather than lease the farm, the couple sold it outright for a large amount of cash.* **3.** at once; immediately: *to be fired outright for stealing.*

out·run (out′run′) *v.t.,* **-ran, -run, -run·ning. 1.** to run farther or faster than. **2.** to escape the pursuit of by or as by running: *The fugitive outran the police for more than a year.* **3.** to go beyond the limits of; exceed: *to allow zeal to outrun discretion.*

out·sell (out′sel′) *v.t.,* **-sold** (-sōld′), **-sel·ling. 1.** to sell more merchandise than: *to outsell the other salespeople.* **2.** to be sold in greater quantities than: *The red shoes outsell the others.*

out·set (out′set′) *n.* the beginning; start: *at the outset of a journey.*

out·shine (out′shīn′) *v.t.,* **-shone** (-shōn′), **-shin·ing. 1.** to shine more brightly than. **2.** to be or do better than; surpass: *to outshine other students in math.*

out·shoot (*v.,* out′shüt′; *n.,* out′shüt′) *v.t.,* **-shot** (-shot′), **-shoot·ing. 1.** to shoot beyond. **2.** to surpass in shooting. —*n.* something that shoots out; projection or protrusion: *an outshoot of rock.*

out·side (out′sīd′, out′sīd′, out′sīd′) *n.* **1.** the outer side, surface, or part; exterior: *The outside of the house was painted white.* **2.** the aspect, part, or side that is external, superficial, or able to be seen easily: *Although I was angry inside, I didn't show it on the outside.* **3.** the area or world beyond the walls or boundaries of an enclosed place, such as a prison. —*adj.* **1.** situated on the outside; outer: *The outside layer of paint was peeling.* **2.** coming from or acting from without; not originating or situated within: *outside influences, an outside observer.* **3.** directed or going outward: *an outside call, an outside line.* **4.** extremely slight; remote: *an outside chance.* **5.** reaching the utmost limit possible: *It is an outside estimate of expenses, and the actual amount will probably be much less.* **6.** *Baseball.* (of a pitch) passing home plate on the side away from the batter, but not over the plate. —*adv.* **1.** on, to, or toward the outside. **2.** outdoors: *The children played outside all day.* —*prep.* **1.** beyond the walls, surfaces, or boundaries of: *They live just outside Philadelphia.* **2.** beyond the range or limits of: *The matter falls outside the jurisdiction of this court.* **3.** *Informal.* with the exception of; besides. —For Synonyms *(adj.),* see **exterior.**

·at the outside. at the maximum; at most: *The mechanic said the job would take an hour at the outside.*

·outside of. a. outside the walls, surfaces, or boundaries of; outside: *outside of Chicago.* **b.** beyond the range or limits of; outside. **c.** with the exception of.

out·sid·er (out′sī′dər) *n.* **1.** a person who is not a member, as of a certain group, society, or organization. **2.** a person who has no special interest in or who is not acquainted with a particular matter: *We had to call in an outsider to settle the dispute.*

out·size (out′sīz′) *adj.* also, **out·sized.** irregularly or unusually large: *an outsize head, outsize shoes.* —*n.* **1.** an irregular size, esp. an unusually large size. **2.** a garment or other item of such a size.

out·skirts (out′skûrts′) *pl. n.* regions or sections surrounding or at the edge of a specified area, such as a city.

out·smart (out′smärt′) *v.t.* to get the better of (someone) by cunning or cleverness.
　•**to outsmart (oneself).** to cause (oneself) to fail by being too cunning or clever.

out·sold (out′sōld′) the past tense and past participle of **outsell.**

out·spo·ken (out′spō′kən, out′spō′-) *adj.* **1.** open or unreserved in speech: *The young senator was very outspoken on the issues.* **2.** expressed without reserve or evasion: *outspoken disapproval.* —**out′spo′ken·ly,** *adv.* —**out′spo′ken·ness,** *n.* —For Synonyms, see **frank**[1].

out·spread (*adj.,* out′spred′; *v.,* out′spred′) *adj.* spread out; extended: *outspread arms.* —*v.t., v.i.,* **-spread, -spread·ing.** to spread out; extend.

out·stand·ing (out′stan′ding) *adj.* **1.** so excellent as to stand out from others of its kind: *an outstanding surgeon, an outstanding example.* **2.** remaining to be done, settled, or paid: *an outstanding obligation, an outstanding check.* **3.** (of stocks and bonds) issued, sold, and still in circulation. —**out′stand′ing·ly,** *adv.* —**out′stand′ing·ness,** *n.*

out·stay (out′stā′) *v.t.* to remain longer than or beyond the time or duration of: *to outstay one's welcome.*

out·stretch (out′strech′) *v.t.* **1.** to stretch out; extend. **2.** to stretch beyond. —**out′stretched′,** *adj.*

out·strip (out′strip′) *v.t.,* **-stripped, -strip·ping. 1.** to do or be better than; surpass; excel: *to outstrip other nations in coal production.* **2.** to run farther or faster than, as in a race. **3.** to be greater than; exceed: *The island's population outstripped its food supply.*

out·talk (out′tôk′) *v.t.* to talk louder or with more skill than.

out·vote (out′vōt′) *v.t.,* **-vot·ed, -vot·ing.** to overcome or defeat in voting: *The governor's proposal was outvoted in the legislature.*

out·ward (out′wərd) *adv.* also, **outwards.** from the inside to or toward the outside; away; out: *The door opens outward.* —*adj.* **1.** of or relating to the outside, the visible, the apparent, or the external: *There were outward changes, but the city remained essentially the same.* **2.** directed, turned, or proceeding toward the outside: *an outward flow of goods.* [Old English *ūteweard* outer, on the outside.] —**out′ward·ness,** *n.*

out·ward·ly (out′wərd lē) *adv.* **1.** on or toward the outside or outer surface: *The secret door was not outwardly visible.* **2.** in appearance or outward manifestation; seemingly: *outwardly happy.*

out·wards (out′wərdz) *adv.* outward.

out·wear (out′wâr′) *v.t.,* **-wore, -worn, -wear·ing. 1.** to last longer or wear better than: *This fabric outwears most other materials.* **2.** to wear out or exhaust.

out·weigh (out′wā′) *v.t.* **1.** to be greater in weight than. **2.** to mean more than; be more important than; exceed in value or significance: *The advantages of the new system outweigh its disadvantages.*

out·wit (out′wit′) *v.t.,* **-wit·ted, -wit·ting.** to get the better of by being smarter, more ingenious, or more clever: *The fox outwitted the pursuing hounds and escaped safely.*

out·wore (out′wôr′) the past tense of **outwear.**

out·work (*v.,* out′wûrk′; *n.,* out′wûrk′) *v.t.,* **-worked** or **-wrought** (-rôt′), **-work·ing.** to work better or faster than; outdo in working. —*n.* a part of a castle, fortress, or stockade that is beyond the walls or parapet.

out·worn (*v.,* out′wôrn′; *adj.,* out′wôrn′) *v.* the past participle of **outwear.** —*adj.* **1.** worn out: *an outworn coat.* **2.** no longer in use; out-of-date: *an outworn political slogan.*

ou·zel (ū′zəl) also, **ousel.** *n.* **1.** any of various European thrushes, such as the blackbird or the **ring ouzel,** *Turdus torquatus,* which is black with a white band on the neck and breast. **2.** water ouzel. [Old English *ōsle* blackbird.]

o·va (ō′və) the plural of **ovum.**

o·val (ō′vəl) *adj.* **1.** shaped like an egg. **2.** shaped like an ellipse. —*n.* something having an oval shape. [Modern Latin *ovalis,* from Latin *ōvum* egg.] —**o′val·ly,** *adv.* —**o·val·i·ty** (ō val′i tē), **o′val·ness,** *n.*

Oval Office, the office of the president of the United States, located in the White House. [From its oval shape.]

o·var·i·an (ō vâr′ē ən) *adj.* of, relating to, or affecting an ovary.

o·va·ry (ō′və rē) *n., pl.* **-ries. 1.** the female reproductive organ

that produces eggs and, in mammals, certain hormones. **2.** *Botany.* the enlarged, saclike part of a pistil that encloses the ovules or young seeds and later develops into the fruit. For illustration, see **flower.** [Modern Latin *ovarium,* from Latin *ōvum* egg.]

o·vate (ō′vāt) *adj.* having an oval shape: *an ovate leaf.* [Latin *ōvātus* egg-shaped, from *ōvum* egg.]

o·va·tion (ō vā′shən) *n.* an enthusiastic burst of applause or other demonstration of public acclaim: *The pianist received a standing ovation from the audience.* [Latin *ōvātiō* celebration honoring a victorious general; literally, rejoicing.]

ov·en (uv′ən) *n.* an enclosed chamber, as in a stove, that is used to heat, bake, roast, or dry objects placed within. [Old English *ofen,* of Germanic origin.]

ovate leaf

ov·en·bird (uv′ən bûrd′) *n.* **1.** a brownish warbler, *Seiurus aurocapillus,* of North America, that builds an ovenlike, domed nest on the ground. **2.** any of numerous Central and South American birds, family Furnariidae, esp. genus *Furnarius,* generally having brownish plumage, that build a thick-walled, often dome-shaped, nest.

ov·en·ware (uv′ən wâr′) *n.* heat-resistant containers of glass, ceramic, or metal, suitable for use in a hot oven.

o·ver (ō′vər) *prep.* **1.** in or to a place or position higher than; above: *Clouds moved over the lake. The roof jutted over the street.* **2.** upon so as to cover or close: *to put a blanket over a sleeping child, to put a lid over a jar.* **3.** on or across the surface of: *to spread butter over bread.* **4.** above or on top and to the other side of; across: *The horse jumped over the fence. They walked over the bridge.* **5.** forward and down from: *to fall over a precipice, to trip over a log.* **6.** from one end of to the other; along: *We drove over the whole road looking for the place we remembered.* **7.** on the other side of (some boundary); beyond: *That city is over the border.* **8.** on or in all or most parts of; everywhere on: *Corn is raised over the Midwest.* **9.** from place to place on or in; to and fro upon: *to travel over the countryside.* **10.** through all parts of; all through: *I pored over my notes.* **11.** until the end of: *School is closed over the holidays.* **12.** all through; during: *I recorded the rainfall over a number of months.* **13.** at or up to a higher level than: *The water came over the tops of our boots.* **14.** above in authority, power, or rank: *to take a position over a working group.* **15.** above or beyond in degree, amount, quality, or extent; more than: *I spent over twenty dollars on groceries.* **16.** in preference to: *The two winners were chosen over all other candidates.* **17.** upon, as an effect or influence: *A sudden change came over the audience when the winner was announced.* **18.** while engaged in or occupied with: *They discussed the plan over dinner.* **19.** with reference to; concerning; about: *to worry over details.* **20.** through the medium of; by means of: *The news came over the radio.* —*adv.* **1.** above: *a ledge that projects over.* **2.** down or forward and down: *The ball rolled over the edge of the terrace and fell over.* **3.** above and beyond the top, brim, or edge: *The water boiled over.* **4.** from an erect or upright position: *The cat knocked the vase over.* **5.** so as to cover or be covered: *The lake froze over.* **6.** from one side to the other; across any intervening space: *Come over for a cup of coffee.* **7.** on or at the other side of some intervening space; at some distance: *I was over in Spain for three months.* **8.** from one opinion, attitude, or side to another: *to be won over by someone's arguments.* **9.** from one person to another: *to will property over to one's children.* **10.** so as to show the other or a different side: *Turn the book over to the back cover.* **11.** once more; again: *You'll have to do the job over.* **12.** in repetition or succession: *three times over.* **13.** in all parts or directions; throughout: *to travel the whole world over.* **14.** from beginning to end; through: *I read the document over.* **15.** through or beyond a period of time: *Stay over through the weekend. I worked two hours over on Friday.* **16.** in excess; in addition; remaining: *Four goes into ten twice with two left over.* —*adj.* **1.** ended: *The game is over.* **2.** upper or higher: *an over layer of insulation.* **3.** in excess; extra: *We earned thirty-five dollars to cover expenses, and there is ten dollars over.* —*interj.* in radio communication, used to indicate that the sender has stopped transmitting and is leaving the channel open for a reply. [Old English *ofer* above, to or on the other side, exceeding in quantity.]
　•**over again.** once more: *I will sing the song over again.*

a	at	e	end	o	hot	u	up	hw	white		about
ā	ape	ē	me	ō	old	ū	use	ng	song		taken
ä	far	i	it	ô	fork	ü	rule	th	thin	ə	pencil
âr	care	ī	ice	oi	oil	u̇	pull	th	this		lemon
		îr	pierce	ou	out	ûr	turn	zh	measure		circus

•**over and above.** besides; in addition to: *There are reasons over and above the ones I have given you.*

•**over and over.** repeatedly.

over- *prefix* **1.** too much or too highly; excessively: *overload, overrate, overdeveloped.* **2.** above; higher: *overhead.* **3.** around, covering, or on top: *overgrowth, overcoat, overshoe.* **4.** from above to below; down: *overthrow, overturn.* [Old English *ofer-*.]

o·ver·a·bun·dance (ō′ver ə bun′dəns) *n.* too great an amount; excess. —**o′ver·a·bun′dant,** *adj.* —**o′ver·a·bun′dant·ly,** *adv.*

o·ver·a·chieve (ō′ver ə chēv′) *v.i.* **-chieved, -chiev·ing.** to do more or better than one is thought capable of. —**o′ver·a·chiev′er,** *n.*

o·ver·act (ō′ver akt′) *v.i., v.t.* to act (a role or part) too emotionally or unrealistically; exaggerate in acting.

o·ver·ac·tive (ō′ver ak′tiv) *adj.* excessively or abnormally active: *a dreamer with an overactive imagination.* —**o′ver·ac′tive·ly,** *adv.* —**o′ver·ac′tive·ness, o′ver·ac·tiv′i·ty,** *n.*

o·ver·age¹ (ō′ver āj′) *adj.* **1.** too old: *overage fruit.* **2.** beyond the usual or normal age: *to be overage for a youth group.*

o·ver·age² (ō′ver ij) *n.* the portion that is over the requested amount, as in weighing; surplus.

o·ver·all (*adj.,* ō′ver ôl′; *adv.,* ō′ver ôl′) *adj.* **1.** taking everything into account; general or total: *My overall impression of them was favorable.* **2.** from one end to the other: *the overall length of a car.* —*adv.* as a whole; generally.

o·ver·alls (ō′ver ôlz′) *pl. n.* loose-fitting trousers, often with a chest piece and suspenders attached, worn esp. by farmers and laborers.

o·ver·anx·ious (ō′ver angk′shəs, ō′ver-) *adj.* excessively anxious.

o·ver·arch (ō′ver ärch′) *v.t., v.i.* to form an arch over (something).

o·ver·arm (ō′ver ärm′) *adj., adv.* performed with the arm raised above the shoulder: *an overarm throw, to throw overarm.*

o·ver·ate (ō′ver āt′) the past tense of **overeat.**

o·ver·awe (ō′ver ô′) *v.t.,* **-awed, -aw·ing.** to overcome, subdue, or restrain by inspiring awe.

o·ver·bal·ance (ō′ver bal′əns) *v.t.,* **-anced, -anc·ing. 1.** to cause to lose balance. **2.** to be greater than in weight or importance.

o·ver·bear (ō′ver bâr′) *v.t.,* **-bore, -borne, -bear·ing.** to oppress or drive down, as by weight, power, or force.

o·ver·bear·ing (ō′ver bâr′ing) *adj.* **1.** that oppresses, drives down, or overrules others; arrogantly superior. **2.** of greatest importance; overriding: *an overbearing issue.* —**o′ver·bear′ing·ly,** *adv.*

o·ver·bid (*v.,* ō′ver bid′; *n.,* ō′ver bid′) *v.,* **-bid, -bid** or **-bidden** (-bid′ən), **-bid·ding.** —*v.t.* **1.** to bid higher than (a person); outbid. **2.** to bid higher than the value of (a thing). —*v.i.* to bid too high. —*n.* a higher or excessive bid.

o·ver·bite (ō′ver bīt′) *n.* a condition in which the upper front teeth project out abnormally over the lower when the jaws are closed.

o·ver·blown¹ (ō′ver blōn′) *adj.* blown up or inflated, as with vanity or conceit; overdone and bombastic: *overblown rhetoric.* [OVER + BLOWN¹.]

o·ver·blown² (ō′ver blōn′) *adj.* **1.** excessively large in size; obese. **2.** (of flowers or blossoms) past the stage of full bloom; withered. [OVER + BLOWN².]

o·ver·board (ō′ver bôrd′) *adv.* over the side of a ship into the water: *to fall overboard, to throw a net overboard.*

•**to go overboard.** *Informal.* to go to extremes, esp. because of enthusiasm or affection: *The critic went overboard in praising the new play.*

o·ver·book (ō′ver bůk′) *v.t., v.i.,* **-booked, -book·ing.** to make reservations (for more than can be accommodated by the space available): *The airline overbooked our flight. Ten passengers were overbooked.*

o·ver·bore (ō′ver bôr′) the past tense of **overbear.**

o·ver·borne (ō′ver bôrn′) the past participle of **overbear.**

o·ver·build (ō′ver bild′, ō′ver-) *v.t., v.i.,* **-built** (-bilt′), **-build·ing. 1.** to build too many houses or buildings in (an area). **2.** to build (something) too elaborately or too large. **3.** to build over or on top of (something).

o·ver·bur·den (*v.,* ō′ver bûr′dən; *n.,* ō′ver bûr′dən) *v.t.* to put too great a weight or burden on; overload. —*n.* **1.** too great a burden. **2.** a layer of rock, earth, or other material under which an ore deposit is buried.

o·ver·came (ō′ver kām′) the past tense of **overcome.**

o·ver·cap·i·tal·ize (ō′ver kap′i tə līz′) *v.t.,* **-ized, -iz·ing. 1.** to invest more capital in (a company) than is warranted by actual prospects. **2.** to fix the nominal value of the capital of (a corporation) higher than is justified by legal limits or by actual market value. **3.** to overestimate the capital value of (a property or company). —**o′ver·cap′i·tal·i·za′tion,** *n.*

o·ver·cast (*adj.,* ō′ver kast′, ō′ver kast′; *v.,* ō′ver kast′, ō′ver-kast′; *n.,* ō′ver kast′) *adj.* **1.** clouded over; cloudy; dark; gloomy: *an overcast sky.* **2.** sewn over and over with long stitches to prevent unraveling. —*v.t., v.i.,* **-cast, -cast·ing. 1.** to make or become clouded over. **2.** to sew (fabric, esp. raw edges of fabric) over and over with long stitches to prevent unraveling. —*n.* **1.** a covering of clouds. **2.** an overcast stitch.

o·ver·cau·tious (ō′ver kô′shəs) *adj.* too cautious.

o·ver·charge (*v.,* ō′ver chärj′; *n.,* ō′ver chärj′) *v.,* **-charged, -charg·ing.** —*v.t.* **1.** to charge (someone) more than the established, usual, or proper price. **2.** to load, supply, or fill to excess: *to overcharge an electric battery.* —*v.i.* to charge more than the established, usual, or proper price. —*n.* an act, instance, or amount of overcharging.

o·ver·cloud (ō′ver kloud′) *v.t., v.i.* to cover or be covered with or as with clouds.

o·ver·coat (ō′ver kōt′) *n.* a heavy outer coat worn over a suit or other clothing for added warmth.

o·ver·come (ō′ver kum′) *v.,* **-came, -come, -com·ing.** —*v.t.* **1.** to get the better of, as in a contest or conflict; conquer: *The enemy army overcame all opposition.* **2.** to rise above or get over: *I finally overcame my fear of heights.* **3.** to exhaust or make helpless: *Many in the crowd were overcome by the heat.* —*v.i.* to be victorious; conquer. [Old English *ofercuman.*] —For Synonyms, see **defeat.**

o·ver·com·pen·sate (ō′ver kom′pən sāt′) *v.,* **-sat·ed, -sat·ing.** —*v.i.* to engage in psychological overcompensation. —*v.t.* to give excessive compensation to; overpay.

o·ver·com·pen·sa·tion (ō′ver kom′pən sā′shən) *n.* **1.** *Psychology.* the process of reacting to a feeling of real or imagined deficiency, as inferiority or guilt, by an exaggerated or excessive drive to compensate for it, as when a short person who is self-conscious about height engages in bragging and aggressive and arrogant behavior. **2.** any process of excessive compensation.

o·ver·con·fi·dent (ō′ver kon′fi dənt) *adj.* too confident. —**o′ver·con′fi·dence,** *n.*

o·ver·cook (ō′ver kůk′) *v.t.* to cook (something) too much or too long.

o·ver·crowd (ō′ver kroud′) *v.t.* to cause to have too many people or things: *They overcrowded the small apartment with furniture.*

o·ver·de·vel·op (ō′ver di vel′əp) *v.t.* **1.** to develop too much. **2.** to submerge (a photographic film or plate) in developing solution too long, so that it becomes too dark. —**o′ver·de·vel′op·ment,** *n.*

The following list contains a selection of compounds that can be formed with the prefix over-. The meaning of a word on the list can be understood by combining the appropriate sense of the prefix with the root word.

overaccumulation	overappreciative	overbreed	overcivil	overconciliatory	overdecorate
overadorned	overapprehensive	overbright	overcivilized	overconscientious	overdefensive
overadventurous	overassertive	overbulky	overclean	overconservative	overdeferential
overaffect	overassessment	overbusy	overcolor	overconsiderate	overdelicate
overaggressive	overassured	overcareful	overcompetitive	overconsumption	overdemand
overambitious	overattached	overcareless	overcomplacent	overcool	overdemanding
overamplify	overattentive	overcasual	overcomplex	overcount	overdependent
overanalytical	overattentiveness	overcaustic	overcompliant	overcourteous	overdesirous
overanalyze	overbill	overcentralization	overconcentrate	overcritical	overdestructive
overanimated	overbold	overcharitable	overconcentration	overcultivate	overdestructiveness
overappraise	overbounteous	overchill	overconcern	overcurious	overdetailed

o·ver·do (ō'vər dü') v., **-did** (-did'), **-done** (-dun'), **-do·ing.** —v.t. **1.** to do or use too much or carry too far: *They overdid the joke and it stopped being funny.* **2.** to cook (food) too much. —v.i. to do too much or go too far.

o·ver·dose (n., ō'vər dōs'; v., ō'vər dōs') n. too large a dose, as of a drug, esp. with fatal consequences. —v., **-dosed, -dos·ing.** —v.t. to give too large a dose to. —v.i. to take or die from too large a dose, esp. of a narcotic: *to overdose on heroin.*

o·ver·draft (ō'vər draft') n. **1.** an act or instance of overdrawing a bank account. **2.** the amount of the shortage in an overdrawn account.

o·ver·draw (ō'vər drô') v.t., **-drew** (-drü'), **-drawn** (-drôn'), **-draw·ing. 1.** to write a check against (a bank account) that is larger than the account's balance or credit. **2.** to exaggerate, as in drawing or describing: *Their description of the danger they were in was overdrawn.*

o·ver·dress (ō'vər dres') v.i., v.t. to dress in clothes that are too formal, fancy, or warm for the occasion.

o·ver·drive (ō'vər drīv') n. an additional set of gears in some motor vehicles that enables the drive shaft to turn faster than the engine or crankshaft, for use at high cruising speeds.

o·ver·due (ō'vər dü', -dū') adj. **1.** remaining unpaid past the assigned date of payment: *an overdue bill.* **2.** that has not yet happened or arrived, though the expected or scheduled time is past: *The train is overdue.* **3.** that should have happened sooner: *An apology from you is long overdue.*

o·ver·eat (ō'vər ēt') v.i., **-ate** (-āt'), **-eat·en** (-ē'tən), **-eat·ing.** to eat too much.

o·ver·em·pha·size (ō'vər em'fə sīz') v.t., **-sized, -siz·ing.** to place too much emphasis on; stress too much. —o'ver·em'pha·sis, n.

o·ver·es·ti·mate (v., ō'vər es'tə māt'; n., ō'vər es'tə mit) v.t., v.i., **-mat·ed, -mat·ing.** to make too high an estimate of (something): *to overestimate a person's ability, to always overestimate when predicting costs.* —n. an estimate that is too high. —o'ver·es'ti·ma'tion, n.

o·ver·ex·cite (ō'vər ek sīt') v.t., **-cit·ed, -cit·ing.** to excite excessively. —o'ver·ex·cit'a·ble, adj. —o'ver·ex·cite'ment, n.

o·ver·ex·pose (ō'vər ek spōz') v.t., **-posed, -pos·ing. 1.** to display or expose (someone or something) too much. **2.** to expose (a photographic film or plate) for too long a time. —o'ver·ex·po'sure, n.

o·ver·ex·tend (ō'vər ek stend') v.t. **1.** to extend (something) beyond what is safe, reasonable, or prudent. **2.** to extend (oneself) beyond one's ability to fulfill obligations or commitments, esp. in financial matters. —o'ver·ex·ten'sion, n.

o·ver·feed (ō'vər fēd') v.t., v.i., **-fed** (-fed'), **-feed·ing.** to feed or eat to excess.

o·ver·fish (ō'vər fish') v.t., **-fished, -fish·ing.** to fish to excess in (a body of water), so that fish in general, or a certain kind of fish, are depleted.

o·ver·flight (ō'vər flīt') n. a passage of an aircraft over an area without landing, as for spying.

o·ver·flow (v., ō'vər flō'; n., ō'vər flō') v., **-flowed, -flowed** or **-flown** (-flōn'), **-flow·ing.** —v.i. **1.** to flow beyond the usual limits: *Water from the kitchen sink overflowed onto the floor.* **2.** to be so full that the contents flow over: *The bathtub overflowed.* **3.** to be so full as to seem to flow over: *Their hearts overflowed with love.* —v.t. **1.** to flow over the top edge or rim of: *The rainwater overflowed the barrel.* **2.** to flow or spread over; flood. **3.** to cause to overflow; fill too full: *Don't overflow the bathtub.* **4.** to be larger than (something) can hold; fill to overflowing: *The large crowd overflowed the small auditorium.* —n. **1.** the act or process of overflowing. **2.** something that overflows. **3.** an outlet for excess liquid, as in a sink.

o·ver·graze (ō'vər grāz') v.t., **-grazed, -graz·ing.** to allow livestock to graze in (a field or pasture) so excessively that the grass cover is damaged or destroyed.

o·ver·grow (ō'vər grō') v., **-grew** (-grü'), **-grown, -grow-**ing. —v.t. **1.** to cover with growth; grow over: *Weeds overgrew the yard.* **2.** to grow too large for; outgrow. —v.i. to grow too much or too fast.

o·ver·grown (ō'vər grōn', ō'vər grōn') v. the past participle of **overgrow.** —adj. **1.** grown too large or beyond normal size. **2.** covered with foliage, such as weeds or vines: *The vacant lot is overgrown.*

o·ver·growth (ō'vər grōth') n. **1.** excessive growth. **2.** a growth spreading over or covering something: *an overgrowth of vines.*

o·ver·hand (ō'vər hand') adj. **1.** performed with the hand raised above the elbow or the arm raised above the shoulder: *an overhand pitch.* Also, **o'ver·hand'ed. 2.** sewn with closely spaced stitches that pass over and over, as in joining finished edges: *an overhand seam.* —adv. in an overhand style or manner: *to throw overhand.* Also, **o'ver·hand'ed.** —v.t. to sew with overhand stitches. —n. an overhand stroke or delivery, as in tennis.

overhand knot, a knot made by forming a loop and passing the end of the rope or other material through it.

o·ver·hang (v., ō'vər hang'; n., ō'vər hang') v., **-hung** (-hung'), **-hang·ing.** —v.t. **1.** to hang out over (something): *Tall bushes overhung the walk.* **2.** to loom over threateningly; menace. —v.i. to hang or project over something. —n. **1.** a part or section that overhangs; projection. **2.** the extent or amount of projection of something.

o·ver·haul (ō'vər hôl') v.t. **1.** to examine thoroughly and make needed repairs or adjustments in: *to overhaul an engine.* **2.** to investigate thoroughly and make far-reaching changes in: *The new governor introduced legislation to overhaul the prison system.* **3.** to catch up with; overtake: *The coast guard cutter quickly overhauled the fishing boat.* —n. the act or process of overhauling.

o·ver·head (adv., ō'vər hed'; n., adj., ō'vər hed') adv. above the level of the head: *a light burning overhead, birds flying overhead.* —n. **1.** the general operating expenses of a business, as rent, taxes, heating, lighting, and repair, as opposed to costs of materials and labor. **2.** a stroke made above the level of the head in tennis and other racket games. —adj. **1.** situated, operating, or moving overhead: *overhead lights.* **2.** of or relating to overhead in business: *overhead expenses.*

o·ver·hear (ō'vər hîr') v.t., **-heard** (-hûrd'), **-hear·ing.** to hear without the speaker's intention or knowledge.

o·ver·heat (ō'vər hēt') v.t., v.i. **1.** to make or become too hot: *The engine overheats in low gear.* **2.** to make or become too excited or angry.

o·ver·in·dulge (ō'vər in dulj') v.t., v.i., **-dulged, -dulg·ing.** to indulge too much. —o'ver·in·dul'gence, n. —o'ver·in·dul'gent, adj.

o·ver·joy (ō'vər joi') v.t. to make very joyful.

o·ver·joyed (ō'vər joid', ō'vər-) adj. very happy or joyful.

o·ver·kill (ō'vər kil') n. **1.** the capacity to kill more of an enemy or inflict greater damage than is necessary for victory, esp. by using nuclear weapons. **2.** more of something than is suitable or required, as force, zeal, or publicity; excess: *The ad agency engaged in promotional overkill.*

o·ver·land (ō'vər land', -lənd) adv., adj. by, on, or across land: *to travel overland, an overland mail route.*

o·ver·lap (v., ō'vər lap'; n., ō'vər lap') v., **-lapped, -lap·ping.** —v.t. **1.** to rest on top of (something) and partially cover it up; lap over: *One feather overlaps another on a bird's wing.* **2.** to coincide partly with or extend over part of: *The Renaissance overlapped the later Middle Ages.* —v.i. **1.** to rest on top of something, partially covering it. **2.** to coincide partly: *Our ski*

a	at	e	end	o	hot	u	up	hw	white		about
ā	ape	ē	me	ō	old	ū	use	ng	song	ə	taken
ä	far	i	it	ô	fork	ü	rule	th	thin		pencil
âr	care	ī	ice	oi	oil	u̇	pull	th	this		lemon
				îr	pierce	ou	out	ûr	turn	zh	measure		circus

overdiligent	overeffusive	overexert	overfatigued	overharvest	overinfluential
overdilute	overelaborate	overexertion	overfearful	overhasty	overinsistent
overdistant	overembellish	overexpand	overfill	overhunt	overinsure
overdiversification	overembroider	overexpansion	overfond	overidealistic	overintense
overdiversify	overemotional	overexplain	overformal	overidealize	overinvest
overdramatic	overemphatic	overexplicit	overfrequent	overimaginative	overinvolve
overdrink	overenergetic	overexpressive	overgeneralization	overimpressionable	overjealous
overeager	overenthusiastic	overexuberant	overgeneralize	overindustrialize	overkeen
overedit	overexacting	overfamiliar	overgenerous	overinflate	overkind
overeducate	overexercise	overfastidious	overharsh	overinfluence	overladen

trips overlapped by a day. —*n.* **1.** an instance of overlapping. **2.** a part that overlaps. **3.** the extent or amount of overlapping.

o·ver·lay (*v.,* ō′vər lā′; *n.,* ō′vər lā′) *v.t.,* **-laid** (-lād′), **-lay·ing.** **1.** to place (something) over or on another thing: *to overlay shingles on a roof.* **2.** to cover or spread with something, as a layer of protective or decorative material: *to overlay painted wood with shellac.* —*n.* **1.** a decorative or protective layer: *an overlay of gold.* **2.** any added, superficial front or veneer: *a violent society with an overlay of civility.* **3.** *Printing.* a transparent sheet placed over art work in order to add letters, lines, or other elements or to modify color or shading.

o·ver·leap (ō′vər lēp′) *v.t.,* **-leaped** or **-leapt, -leap·ing. 1.** to leap over or across. **2.** to fail because of leaping too far. **3.** to pass over; ignore.

o·ver·lie (ō′vər lī′) *v.t.,* **-lay** (-lā′), **-lain** (-lān′), **-ly·ing. 1.** to lie over or upon: *The layer of Cenozoic rocks overlies Paleozoic strata.* **2.** to cause the death of, as an infant, by lying upon and smothering.

o·ver·load (*v.,* ō′vər lōd′; *n.,* ō′vər lōd′) *v.t.* to put an excessive load or burden in or on: *to overload a car, to overload an electrical circuit.* —*n.* an excessive load or burden.

o·ver·long (ō′vər long′) *adj., adv.* too long.

o·ver·look (ō′vər lŭk′) *v.t.* **1.** to fail to see, observe, or think of: *The burglars overlooked the possibility of the alarm going off.* **2.** to regard (something) as never having happened; ignore: *to overlook an insult.* **3.** to allow or treat indulgently; excuse: *to overlook a person's faults.* **4.a.** to look over or down upon from a higher place or position: *We overlooked the ocean from the tower.* **b.** to offer a view of: *The house on the hill overlooks the valley.* —*n.* a high place that provides a view of the landscape below.

o·ver·lord (ō′vər lôrd′) *n.* a person who is the lord of other lords or rulers.

o·ver·ly (ō′vər lē) *adv.* excessively; too: *overly generous.*

o·ver·mas·ter (ō′vər mas′tər) *v.t.* to gain mastery or control over; overcome; overpower; subdue.

o·ver·match (ō′vər mach′) *v.t.* **1.** to be more than a match for; surpass or defeat. **2.** to match (someone) against a superior opponent.

o·ver·much (ō′vər much′) *adj., adv.* too much. —*n.* too great an amount; excess.

o·ver·night (*adv.,* ō′vər nīt′, ō′vər-; *adj.,* ō′vər nīt′) *adv.* **1.** during or through the night: *to keep watch overnight.* **2.** very quickly; suddenly: *The new buildings sprang up overnight.* **3.** in the space of one night: *to move a camp overnight.* —*adj.* **1.** for one night: *an overnight guest.* **2.** of, lasting through, or occurring during the night: *an overnight storm, an overnight flight to Japan.* **3.** suitable, used, or made for short trips: *an overnight bag.* **4.** occurring suddenly: *There was an overnight change in public opinion.*

o·ver·pass (*n.,* ō′vər pas′; *v.,* ō′vər pas′) *n.* a bridge, road, or other passage that crosses above a railroad or another roadway or passage. —*v.t.* **1.** to pass over, across, or through. **2.** to not pay attention to; disregard; ignore. **3.** to go beyond; exceed; surpass.

o·ver·pay (ō′vər pā′) *v.t., v.i.,* **-paid** (-pād′), **-pay·ing. 1.** to pay (someone) too much. **2.** to pay more than (the amount required or due). —**o′ver·pay′ment,** *n.*

o·ver·play (ō′vər plā′) *v.t.* **1.** to overestimate the value, importance, or strength of; emphasize or use too much: *The tennis player overplayed her backhand.* **2.** to play (a part or role) in an exaggerated manner; overact.

o·ver·plus (ō′vər plus′) *n.* more of something than required; excess; surplus.

o·ver·pop·u·late (ō′vər pop′yə lāt′) *v.t.,* **-lat·ed, -lat·ing.** to fill (an area) with more people or things than can be supported: *The state is overpopulated with deer.* —**o′ver·pop′u·la′tion,** *n.*

o·ver·pow·er (ō′vər pou′ər) *v.t.* **1.** to overcome by greater strength or power; overwhelm. **2.** to make helpless or ineffective; overcome. **3.** to supply with too much power. —**o′ver·pow′er·ing,** *adj.* —**o′ver·pow′er·ing·ly,** *adv.*

o·ver·praise (ō′vər prāz′) *v.t.,* **-praised, -prais·ing.** to praise too highly.

o·ver·price (ō′vər prīs′) *v.t.,* **-priced, -pric·ing.** to set too high a price or value upon.

o·ver·pro·duce (ō′vər prə düs′, -dūs′) *v.t., v.i.,* **-duced, -duc·ing.** to produce (goods) in excess of demand. —**o′ver·pro·duc′tion,** *n.*

o·ver·pro·tect (ō′vər prə tekt′) *v.t.* to protect or shelter to too great a degree: *The parents overprotected their child.* —**o′ver·pro·tec′tive,** *adj.*

o·ver·ran (ō′vər ran′) the past tense of **overrun.**

o·ver·rate (ō′vər rāt′) *v.t.,* **-rat·ed, -rat·ing.** to rate, value, or estimate at too high a level: *The general overrated the army's ability to achieve a quick victory. That movie is overrated.*

o·ver·reach (ō′vər rēch′) *v.t.* **1.** to reach or extend over or beyond. **2.** to get the better of by cunning. **3.** to reach past and miss. —*v.i.* to reach too far. —**o′ver·reach′er,** *n.* •**to overreach oneself.** to fail because of trying to do something beyond one's ability.

o·ver·re·act (ō′vər rē akt′) *v.i.* to react to something too strongly or emotionally: *It would be overreacting to give up baseball just because you weren't chosen for the school team.* —**o′ver·re·ac′tion,** *n.*

o·ver·ride (*v.,* ō′vər rīd′; *n.,* ō′vər rīd′) *v.t.,* **-rode** (-rōd′), **-rid·den** (-rid′ən), **-rid·ing. 1.** to set aside (something), as by superior authority; cancel (an action or decision): *The legislature overrode the governor's veto and the bill became law.* **2.** to be more important than, so as to exclude; prevail over; supersede: *This problem overrides all other matters.* **3.** to ride (a horse or other animal) until it becomes exhausted. **4.** to ride over or across. **5.** to trample down. **6.** to extend or pass over: *The floodwaters overrode the valley.* —*n.* a mechanism or design feature that allows for manual control of an otherwise automatic system or device.

o·ver·ripe (ō′vər rīp′) *adj.* past the peak of ripeness; becoming rotten.

o·ver·rule (ō′vər rül′) *v.t.,* **-ruled, -rul·ing. 1.** to invalidate or supersede (a prior judicial decision): *The Supreme Court overruled the decision of the lower court.* **2.** to reject (an objection to evidence offered at a trial). **3.** to decide against or prevail over: *I thought we should stay, but I was overruled by the rest of the group.*

o·ver·run (*v.,* ō′vər run′; *n.,* ō′vər run′) *v.,* **-ran, -run, -run·ning.** —*v.t.* **1.** to swarm or spread over or throughout, esp. with harmful intent or effects: *Invaders overran the countryside. Poison ivy overran the park grounds.* **2.** to flow over: *The river overran its banks.* **3.** to run or go beyond: *The batter overran second base.* **4.** to go beyond or exceed (a limit): *The actual costs overran the budget by a large amount.* —*v.i.* **1.** to exceed a limit. **2.** to overflow; run over. —*n.* **1.** an act or instance of overrunning. **2.** the amount by which something overruns.

o·ver·seas (ō′vər sēz′) *also,* **o·ver·sea.** *adv.* over, across, or beyond the sea; abroad: *to travel overseas.* —*adj.* **1.** employed, situated, or serving overseas: *a company's overseas representative.* **2.** of or relating to countries across the sea; foreign: *overseas trade.*

o·ver·see (ō′vər sē′) *v.t.,* **-saw** (-sô′), **-seen** (-sēn′), **-see·ing. 1.** to watch over and manage; have charge of; direct: *to oversee the building of a canal.* **2.** to see or notice in secret or by accident: *The burglars were overseen leaving the building.*

o·ver·se·er (ō′vər sē′ər) *n.* a person who oversees, esp. one who supervises the work of laborers.

o·ver·sell (ō′vər sel′) *v.t.,* **-sold** (-sōld′), **-sel·ling. 1.** to take orders for or sell more of than is available. **2.** to try to sell (something) too aggressively. **3.** to praise or promote (something or someone) so highly as to have the opposite effect: *The critics so oversold the movie that I was disappointed by it.*

o·ver·set (*v.,* ō′vər set′; *n.,* ō′vər set′) *v.t.,* **-set, -set·ting. 1.** to turn or knock over; overthrow: *to overset a lamp.* **2.** to cause to lose composure or balance; upset: *They were overset by the unpleasant incident.* **3.** *Printing.* to set too much type or copy for (a given space). —*n.* the act or fact of oversetting.

o·ver·sexed (ō′vər sekst′) *adj.* characterized by an unusually strong sexual drive or by excessive interest in sex.

o·ver·shad·ow (ō′vər shad′ō) *v.t.* **1.** to be more important or significant than: *The continuing war overshadowed all the country's other problems.* **2.** to cast a pall or shadow over: *Dark clouds overshadowed the sun. The bad news overshadowed our weekend.*

o·ver·shoe (ō′vər shü′) *n.* a protective shoe or boot, often made of rubber, worn over an ordinary shoe to protect against cold, snow, water, or mud.

o·ver·shoot (ō′vər shüt′) *v.,* **-shot** (-shot′), **-shoot·ing.** —*v.t.* **1.** to go or pass over, above, or beyond (a target, mark, or goal):

overlaudatory	overluxurious	overnice	overpatriotic	overprivileged	overrigorous
overlavish	overmagnification	overnourish	overpermissive	overprominent	overromanticize
overliberal	overmagnify	overoptimistic	overpessimistic	overpromote	oversalt
overlively	overmedicate	overornamented	overpolite	overpublicize	overscrupulous
overloud	overmodest	overparticular	overpossessive	overqualified	oversensitive
overluxuriant	overmoist	overpassionate	overprecise	overrationalize	oversensual

The aircraft overshot the landing field. **2.** to shoot or project (something) over or beyond a target or goal. —*v.i.* to shoot or go too far.

o·ver·shot (ō′vər shot′) *v.* the past tense and past participle of **overshoot.** —*adj.* **1.** having the upper jaw projecting beyond the lower. **2.** (of a waterwheel) driven by water falling down from above, rather than by water flowing past.

o·ver·sight (ō′vər sīt′) *n.* **1.** a careless, unintentional mistake: *The omission of your name from the guest list was an oversight.* **2.** watchful care or management; supervision.

o·ver·sim·pli·fy (ō′vər sim′plə fī′) *v.t., v.i.,* **-fied, -fy·ing.** to make (something) appear to be much simpler than it really is. —**o′ver·sim′pli·fi·ca′tion,** *n.*

o·ver·size (ō′vər sīz′) *adj.* also, **o·ver·sized.** larger than the normal or usual size. —*n.* **1.** a size larger than the normal or usual size. **2.** something that is oversize.

o·ver·skirt (ō′vər skûrt′) *n.* a skirt worn over another skirt.

o·ver·sleep (ō′vər slēp′) *v.,* **-slept** (-slept′), **-sleep·ing.** —*v.i.* to sleep beyond one's intended or usual time for waking up. —*v.t.* to sleep beyond (a particular time or event): *I overslept my morning class.*

o·ver·spread (ō′vər spred′) *v.t.,* **-spread, -spread·ing.** to spread or extend over: *Trees overspread the tiny cabin.*

o·ver·state (ō′vər stāt′) *v.t.,* **-stat·ed, -stat·ing.** to state or stress too strongly; exaggerate. —**o′ver·state′ment,** *n.*

o·ver·stay (ō′vər stā′) *v.t.* to stay beyond the time or limit of: *to overstay a visa.*

o·ver·step (ō′vər step′) *v.t.,* **-stepped, -step·ping.** to go over or beyond the limits of; exceed: *to overstep one's authority.*

o·ver·stock (ō′vər stok′) *v.t.* **1.** to supply with more than is needed: *to overstock a store with a particular product.* **2.** to stock (a commodity) to excess. —*n.* too large a stock or supply.

o·ver·strung (ō′vər strung′) *adj.* too highly strung; too tense.

o·ver·stuff (ō′vər stuf′) *v.t.* to stuff to excess.

o·ver·stuffed (ō′vər stuft′) *adj.* **1.** stuffed to excess. **2.** (of furniture) having the frame covered over with a thick padding or large amount of stuffing.

o·ver·sub·scribe (ō′vər səb skrīb′) *v.t.,* **-scribed, -scrib·ing.** to subscribe for more of (something) than is available or necessary: *The theater series was oversubscribed.* —**o′ver·sub·scrip′tion,** *n.*

o·ver·sup·ply (*v.,* ō′vər sə plī′; *n.,* ō′vər sə plī′) *v.t.,* **-plied, -ply·ing.** to supply in excess. —*n., pl.* **-plies.** an excessive supply.

o·vert (ō vûrt′, ō′vûrt) *adj.* open and unconcealed; easily observed; not secret: *overt hostility.* [Old French *overt,* past participle of *ovrir* to open, going back to Latin *aperīre.*] —**o·vert′ly,** *adv.* —**o·vert′ness,** *n.*

o·ver·take (ō′vər tāk′) *v.t.,* **-took** (-tůk′), **-tak·en** (-tā′kən), **-tak·ing.** **1.a.** to catch up with: *The cheetah overtook the fleeing antelope.* **b.** to catch up with and then pass: *The company has overtaken its chief competitor in sales.* **2.** to come upon unexpectedly or suddenly.

o·ver·tax (ō′vər taks′) *v.t.* **1.** to place too heavy a burden on or draw too much from: *The country's resources were overtaxed by years of war.* **2.** to charge too great a tax on. —**o′ver·tax·a′tion,** *n.*

o·ver-the-coun·ter (ō′vər thə koun′tər) *adj.* **1.** of or relating to the buying and selling of securities that are not listed on an organized stock exchange and are not sold on the floor of an exchange. **2.** (of a drug) able to be sold legally without a doctor's prescription: *Aspirin is an over-the-counter painkiller.* ➡ distinguished from **prescription.**

o·ver·throw (*v.,* ō′vər thrō′; *n.,* ō′vər thrō′) *v.t.,* **-threw** (-thrū′), **-thrown** (-thrōn′), **-throw·ing.** **1.** to remove from power or dominance, esp. by force or struggle: *to overthrow a government.* **2.** to throw or knock down; overturn; upset: *to overthrow a table in rage.* **3.** to throw something, as a baseball, beyond (the intended place). —*n.* **1.** the act of overthrowing or the fact of being overthrown. **2.** a throw that goes beyond the intended place.

o·ver·time (*n., adv., adj.,* ō′vər tīm′; *v.,* ō′vər tīm′) *n.* **1.** time worked beyond the regular working hours. **2.** the pay for such extra time. **3.** *Sports.* an extra period of play, after regulation time has expired, to decide the winner of a contest that has ended in a

tie. —*adv., adj.* of, for, or during overtime: *to work overtime, overtime pay.* —*v.t.* **-timed, -tim·ing.** to allow too much time for: *to overtime a photographic exposure.*

o·ver·tone (ō′vər tōn′) *n.* **1.** a fainter and higher tone heard along with the fundamental tone produced by a musical instrument; harmonic. **2.** a secondary or implicit meaning or quality; suggestion; hint: *My friend's congratulatory remarks carried an overtone of envy.*

o·ver·top (ō′vər top′) *v.t.,* **-topped, -top·ping.** **1.** to rise over or above the top of; be higher than: *The new building overtops the highest of the existing structures.* **2.** to exceed in some quality; surpass; excel.

o·ver·train (ō′vər trān′) *v.t., v.i.* to train beyond the point of best condition or readiness.

o·ver·trick (ō′vər trik′) *n.* a card trick taken in excess of the number bid.

o·ver·trump (ō′vər trump′) *v.t., v.i.* in card games, to play a trump higher than one previously played.

o·ver·ture (ō′vər chůr′, -chər) *n.* **1.** an orchestral musical composition serving as a prelude, preview, or introduction to a larger, usually dramatic, musical work, as an opera. **2.** a suggestion or proposal meant to lead to some new action; offer intended to begin something: *The negotiators made overtures toward settling the strike.* [Old French *overture* opening, beginning, going back to Latin *apertūra* opening. Doublet of APERTURE.]

o·ver·turn (ō′vər tûrn′) *v.t.* **1.** to turn or throw over or upside down; upset: *Heavy winds overturned the sailboat.* **2.** to force from a position of power; overthrow. —*v.i.* to be or become turned over: *The car overturned on the wet highway.*

o·ver·use (*v.,* ō′vər ūz′; *n.,* ō′vər ūs′) *v.t.,* **-used, -us·ing.** to use too much or too often. —*n.* too heavy or too frequent use: *The composer's overuse of the same theme is tiresome.*

o·ver·val·ue (ō′vər val′ū) *v.t.,* **-val·ued, -val·u·ing.** to place too high a value on.

o·ver·view (ō′vər vū′) *n.* a broad, general view or survey.

o·ver·ween·ing (ō′vər wē′ning) *adj.* having or showing exaggerated arrogance, conceit, or self-importance. [Present participle of *overween* to be conceited, from Old English *oferwenian* to become insolent.]

o·ver·weigh (ō′vər wā′) *v.t.* **1.** to be greater in weight than; outweigh. **2.** to weigh down; burden; oppress.

o·ver·weight (*adj.,* ō′vər wāt′, -wāt′; *n.,* ō′vər wāt′; *v.,* ō′vər·wāt′) *adj.* above the normal, desirable, or allowed weight. —*n.* more weight than is normal, desirable, or allowed. —*v.t.* **1.** to give too much emphasis or importance to. **2.** to weigh down; burden.

o·ver·whelm (ō′vər hwelm′, -welm′) *v.t.* **1.** to overcome completely in mind or spirit; make helpless: *to be overwhelmed by the death of a parent.* **2.** to completely overcome physically; overpower; crush: *The enemy forces overwhelmed the camp.* **3.** to cover or bury completely: *The big wave overwhelmed the swimmers.* [OVER- + WHELM.]

o·ver·whelm·ing (ō′vər hwel′ming, -wel′-) *adj.* that overcomes by great power or intensity; irresistible; overpowering: *The force of the tornado was overwhelming. The candidate was elected by an overwhelming majority.* —**o′ver·whelm′ing·ly,** *adv.*

o·ver·win·ter (ō′vər win′tər) *v.i.,* **-tered, -ter·ing.** to pass or last through the winter: *Some animals overwinter in hibernation.* [Translation of German *überwintern.*]

o·ver·work (*v.,* ō′vər wûrk′; *n.,* ō′vər wûrk′) *v.t.* **1.** to cause to work too hard; weary or exhaust with too much work. **2.** to use too often; make excessive use of: *to overwork a literary theme.* **3.** to work too hard or too long on: *to overwork a speech.* —*n.* more work than one should do or can be expected to do.

o·ver·write (ō′vər rīt′) *v.,* **-wrote** (-rōt′), **-writ·ten** (-rit′ən), **-writ·ing.** —*v.t.* **1.** to write too much or in too elaborate or

a	at	e	end	o	hot	u	up	hw	white		about
ā	ape	ē	me	ō	old	ū	use	ng	song		taken
ä	far	i	it	ô	fork	ü	rule	th	thin	ə	pencil
âr	care	ī	ice	oi	oil	ů	pull	th	this		lemon
		îr	pierce	ou	out	ûr	turn	zh	measure		circus

pretentious a style about (a subject). **2.** to write over or on top of (other writing). —*v.i.* to write too much or in too elaborate or pretentious a style.

o·ver·wrought (ō′vər rôt′) *adj.* **1.** worked up to an unhealthy degree of excitement or nervousness: *a child overwrought with anticipation before a holiday.* **2.** decorated or worked all over: *a dress overwrought with embroidered flowers.* **3.** too elaborate or fancy; overdone.

ovi- also, **ovo-**. *combining form* egg or ovum: *oviduct.* [Latin *ovum* egg[1].]

o·vi·duct (ō′vi dukt′) *n.* a tube through which an egg cell passes from the ovary. The female of higher mammals has a pair of oviducts called fallopian tubes. [Modern Latin *oviductus,* from Latin *ōvum* egg + *ductus* a leading.]

o·vi·form (ō′və fôrm′) *adj.* egg-shaped; ovoid. [Latin *ōvum* egg + -FORM.]

o·vip·a·rous (ō vip′ər əs) *adj.* producing eggs that hatch after leaving the body of the female. All birds, most fish and reptiles, and certain primitive mammals, as the platypus, are oviparous. ➡ distinguished from **ovoviviparous** and **viviparous**. [Latin *ōviparus,* from *ōvum* egg + *parere* to bring forth.]

o·vi·pos·i·tor (ō′və poz′i tər) *n.* **1.** an organ at the end of the abdomen of the female of certain insects, by which eggs are deposited. **2.** a similar organ in certain fish and other animals. [Latin *ōvum* egg + *positor* placer.]

ovo-, ovi-.

o·void (ō′void) *adj.* egg-shaped. Also, **o·void·al** (ō voi′dəl). —*n.* something shaped like an egg. [Modern Latin *ovoides,* from Latin *ōvum* egg.]

o·vo·vi·vip·a·rous (ō′vō-vī vip′ər əs) *adj.* producing eggs that develop inside the body of the female and hatch either inside the mother or soon after they are laid. Certain reptiles and fish and many insects are ovoviviparous. ➡ distinguished from **oviparous** and **viviparous**. [Latin *ōvum* egg + VIVIPA-ROUS.]

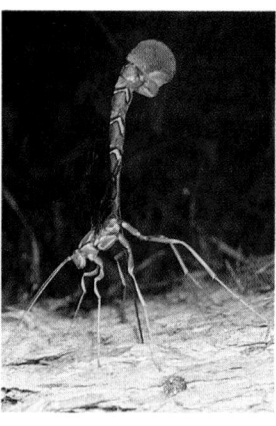

ovipositor of a female wasp

ov·u·late (ov′yə lāt′, ō′vyə-) *v.i.,* -lat·ed, -lat·ing. to produce egg cells or discharge them from the ovary. —**ov′u·la′tion,** *n.*

ov·ule (ov′ūl, ō′vūl) *n.* **1.** a small egg, esp. one in an early stage of growth. **2.** the part of the ovary of a plant that develops into a seed after fertilization. For illustration, see **flower.** [Modern Latin *ovulum,* diminutive of Latin *ōvum* egg.] —**ov·u·lar** (ov′yə-lər, ō′vyə-), *adj.*

o·vum (ō′vəm) *n., pl.* **o·va.** egg[1] *(def. 3).*

owe (ō) *v.,* **owed, ow·ing.** —*v.t.* **1.** to be under obligation to pay or repay: *to owe a friend ten dollars, to owe two months' rent.* **2.** to be under social or moral obligation to offer or give: *to owe someone an apology.* **3.** to attribute (something) to as the cause or source: *To what do I owe the honor of your visit? We owe the general theory of relativity to Einstein.* —*v.i.* to be in debt. [Old English *āgan* to have to pay, possess, own.]

ow·ing (ō′ing) *adj.* due to be paid; unpaid; owed.
• **owing to.** because of: *Owing to bad weather, today's game was postponed.*

owl (oul) *n.* any of numerous birds of prey, order Strigiformes, having a rounded head with large, staring eyes and a hooked bill, a short, square tail, rounded wings, and soft, downy plumage. Owls usually hunt at night and feed chiefly on rodents and other small mammals. Height: 5½-27 inches (14-69 centimeters). [Old English *ūle;* of Germanic origin.]

owl·et (ou′lit) *n.* **1.** a young owl. **2.** a member of any species of small owl.

owl·ish (ou′lish) *adj.* like or resembling an owl in features or characteristics. —**owl′ish·ly,** *adv.* —**owl′ish·ness,** *n.*

own (ōn) *adj.* of, relating to, or belonging to oneself or itself: *It was my own fault. Her own brother testified against her.* ➡ used to intensify a possessive pronoun. —*n.* something

owl

that belongs exclusively to oneself or itself: *My time isn't my own.* —*v.t.* **1.** to have as one's property; have ownership of: *We own all the land between here and the river.* **2.** to acknowledge or admit: *I own that the mistake was my fault.* —*v.i.* to confess; admit (with to): *He owned to having played the prank.* [Old English *āgen* possessed, originally past participle of *āgan* to possess, have, owe.]
• **of one's own.** belonging exclusively to oneself.
• **on one's own. a.** relying only on oneself for support or success. **b.** through one's personal efforts or initiative: *She got the job on her own.*
• **to come into one's own.** to receive that which rightfully belongs to one, esp. success or recognition.
• **to hold one's own.** to maintain one's standing, as against opposition or competition.
• **to own up.** to confess frankly and fully: *They owned up to their part in the crime.*

Synonyms *v.t.* **Own** and **possess** may mean to have something as one's property. **Own** stresses the right to use or dispose of something as one wishes: *The teacher owns a portfolio of securities.* **Possess** stresses the sense of control or exclusiveness: *The collector's greatest wish was to possess a painting by Picasso.*

own·er (ō′nər) *n.* a person or organization that owns something.

own·er·ship (ō′nər ship′) *n.* **1.** the state of being an owner. **2.** the legal title or right to something, esp. property.

ox (oks) *n., pl.* **ox·en. 1.** a domesticated cow or bull, esp. a castrated adult male used as a draft animal or for beef. **2.** any member of a family of large mammals that have hollow horns and chew their cuds, including buffaloes, bison, cattle, and yaks. [Old English *oxa;* of Germanic origin.]

ox·a·late (ok′sə lāt′) *n.* a salt or ester of oxalic acid.

ox·al·ic acid (ok sal′ik) a poisonous organic acid that occurs as oxalates in plants such as the wood sorrel but is usually prepared synthetically, used to remove stains, ink, and rust and as a bleaching agent. Formula: $C_2H_2O_4$ [French *oxalique* extracted from sorrel[1] (from Latin *oxālis* sorrel[1]) + ACID; because it is found in the sorrel plant. See OXALIS.]

ox·al·is (ok sal′is, ok′sə lis) *n.* any of a large group of plants, genus *Oxalis,* having an acid juice and bearing small, round, pink, red, white, or yellow flowers and cloverlike leaves that fold up at night. [Latin *oxālis* sorrel[1], from Greek *oxalis,* from *oxys* sharp, acid, sour.]

ox·blood (oks′blud′) *n.* a deep red color. —*adj.* having the color oxblood.

ox·bow (oks′bō′) *n.* **1.** the wooden, U-shaped part of a yoke, placed as a collar under and around the neck of an ox. **2.** a U-shaped meander in a river. **3.** a lake formed when such a meander is cut off from the river. Also *(def. 3),* **oxbow lake.**

ox·cart (oks′kärt′) *n.* a cart pulled by an ox or oxen.

ox·en (ok′sən) the plural of **ox.**

ox·eye (oks′ī′) *n.* **1.** any of several plants of the composite family, esp. those of the genera *Buphthalmum* and *Heliopsis.* **2.** oxeye daisy.

oxeye daisy, see **daisy.**

ox·ford (oks′fərd) *n.* **1.** a shoe that comes up to just below the ankle and laces across the instep. Also, **oxford shoe. 2.** a soft, medium-weight cotton fabric, used chiefly for shirts and blouses. Also, **oxford cloth.** [From *Oxford,* England.]

Oxford gray, a very dark gray color.

Oxford University, a university located in Oxford, England, established in the twelfth century.

ox·i·dant (ok′si dənt) *n.* oxidizer *(def. 2).* [French *oxidant* (now *oxydant*), from the present participle of *oxider* to oxidize, from *oxide* OXIDE.]

ox·i·dase (ok′si dās′) *n.* any of a number of plant and animal enzymes that promote oxidation. [OXID(IZE) + -ASE.]

ox·i·da·tion (ok′si dā′shən) *n.* the act of oxidizing or the state of being oxidized.

oxidation number, the number of electrons lost, gained, or shared by an atom in forming a chemical bond, expressed as a positive or negative number equal to the charge of its ion; valence. Oxidation causes an increase in oxidation number, and reduction causes a decrease. Also, **oxidation state.**

ox·i·da·tion-re·duc·tion (ok′si dā′shən ri duk′shən) *n.* a chemical reaction in which electrons are transferred from one atom or molecule to another or in which the oxidation numbers of the reactants change. Also, **redox.**

ox·ide (ok′sīd) *n.* a compound of oxygen with some other element or with a radical. [French *oxide* (now *oxyde*), from *ox(ygène)* (see OXYGEN) + *(ac)ide* acid (from Latin *acidus* sour).]

ox·i·dize (ok'si dīz') *v.,* **-dized, -diz·ing.** —*v.t.* **1.** to cause the atoms of (a chemical substance) to lose electrons, increasing the oxidation number. **2.** to combine (a chemical substance) with oxygen; cause to form an oxide. —*v.i.* to become oxidized. [OXIDE + -IZE.]

ox·i·diz·er (ok'si dī'zər) *n.* **1.** a substance that yields oxygen for the burning of rocket fuel or a propellant, as nitric acid or liquid oxygen. **2.** any substance that causes oxidation. Also *(def. 2),* **oxidant.**

ox·lip (oks'lip') *n.* any of a species of primrose, *Primula elatior,* bearing clusters of yellow flowers and resembling the cowslip. [Old English *oxanslyppe,* from *oxan* ox's + *slyppe* slime.]

Ox·o·ni·an (ok sō'nē ən) *adj.* of or relating to Oxford University or Oxford, England. —*n.* **1.** a member or graduate of Oxford University. **2.** a native or inhabitant of Oxford, England. [Medieval Latin *Oxonia* Oxford (from Old English *Oxenaford* literally, ford of oxen) + -AN.]

ox·tail (oks'tāl') *n.* the skinned tail of an ox or steer, used in cooking.

ox·y·a·cet·y·lene (ok'sē ə set'ə lēn') *n.* a mixture of oxygen and acetylene that burns with a very hot flame, used in cutting or welding steel.

ox·y·gen (ok'sə jən) *n.* a colorless, odorless, gaseous element that makes up about one fifth of the air and, in compounds, about one half the weight of the earth's crust. Oxygen is essential to life and combustion. Symbol: **O** For tables, see **element.** [French *oxygène* oxygen; literally, producing acids, from Greek *oxys* sharp, acid + *-genēs* (see -GEN).] —**ox·y·gen·ic** (ok'sə jen'ik), *adj.*

ox·y·gen·ate (ok'sə jə nāt') *v.t.,* **-at·ed, -at·ing.** to treat, supply with, or mix with oxygen. —**ox'y·gen·a'tion,** *n.* —**ox'·y·gen·a'tor,** *n.*

oxygen debt, a deficiency of oxygen resulting from intensive muscular exertion which must be restored during recovery in order to oxidize metabolic wastes and to replenish depleted stores of energy.

oxygen mask, a device worn over the nose and mouth, through which oxygen is supplied from a storage container.

oxygen tent, a tentlike structure, usually of a clear plastic material, placed over a patient's head and supplied with a flow of oxygen to assist breathing.

ox·y·he·mo·glo·bin (ok'sē hē'mə glō'bin) *n.* a bright red substance found in red blood cells, consisting of hemoglobin combined with oxygen and carried to tissues by the arteries.

ox·y·mo·ron (ok'si môr'on) *n., pl.* **-mo·ra** (-môr'ə). a figure of speech in which contradictory or incongruous terms are combined, usually for emphasis, as in *bitterly happy* and *idiotic wisdom.* [Greek *oxymōron* witty paradoxical saying, from *oxys* sharp + *mōros* foolish.] —**ox'y·mo·ron'ic,** *adj.*

ox·y·to·cin (ok'si tō'sin) *n.* a hormone secreted by the pituitary gland that induces contractions of the uterus during childbirth and stimulates the secretion of milk by the mammary glands. Formula: $C_{43}H_{66}N_{12}O_{12}S_2$

o·yez (ō'yes, ō'yez, ō'yā) *interj.* hear ye! ➡ used to announce that court is in session and to demand silence. [Anglo-Norman *oyez,* imperative plural of *oyer* to hear, from Latin *audīre.*]

oys·ter (ois'tər) *n.* any of a group of commercially important mollusks, family Ostreidae, widely found in shallow coastal waters, having a soft body enclosed in two irregular, ear-shaped shells hinged at the narrow end. Oysters of the genus *Ostrea* are highly valued as food, while those of the genus *Pinctada* are raised for the fine pearls they produce. [Old French *oistre,* from Latin *ostrea,* from Greek *ostreon.*]

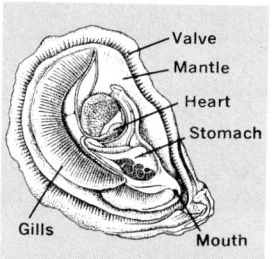

oyster

oyster bed, an area on the bottom of shallow coastal waters where oysters breed or are cultivated.

oys·ter·catch·er (ois'tər-kach'ər) *also,* **oyster catcher.** *n.* any of a group of chunky shorebirds, family Haematopodidae, with side-to-side, flattened, heavy, orange-red bills used to pry open mollusk shells. The **American oystercatcher,** *Haematopus palliatus,* about 19 inches (48 centimeters) long, is black and white above and white below.

oyster crab, any of a group of small crabs, family Pinnotheridae, the female of which lives inside an oyster's shell in a commensal relationship with the live oyster.

oyster cracker, a small, salted cracker usually served with shellfish dishes, such as oysters, or with soup.

oyster drill, drill[1] *(def. 5).*

oyster farm, a place where oyster beds are seeded and maintained for commercial purposes.

oys·ter·man (ois'tər mən) *n., pl.* **-men** (-mən). a person who gathers, raises, or sells oysters.

oyster plant, salsify.

oz *also,* **oz.** *pl.* **ozs** ounce.

o·zone (ō'zōn) *n.* **1.** a pale blue gas with a distinctive odor, formed when an electric discharge passes through the air. Ozone is an allotropic form of oxygen in which three atoms, rather than two, combine to form the molecule. It is used esp. as a bleach, disinfectant, and deodorant. Formula: O_3. **2.** *Informal.* pure, refreshing air. [German *Ozon* the gas, from Greek *ozōn* smelling, present participle of *ozein* to smell.] —**o·zon·ic** (ō zon'ik, ō zō'nik), *adj.*

ozone layer, a layer of ozone concentrated in the stratosphere, 10-30 miles (16-48 kilometers) above the earth. The ozone layer absorbs harmful ultraviolet rays, preventing them from reaching the earth's surface. Also, **ozonosphere.** For illustration, see **atmosphere.**

o·zo·nif·er·ous (ō'zə nif'ər əs) *adj.* containing ozone.

o·zo·no·sphere (ō zō'nə sf îr') *n.* ozone layer.

a	at	e	end	o	hot	u	up	hw	white		about
ā	ape	ē	me	ō	old	ū	use	ng	song		taken
ä	far	i	it	ô	fork	ü	rule	th	thin	ə	pencil
âr	care	ī	ice	oi	oil	u̇	pull	th	this		lemon
		îr	pierce	ou	out	ûr	turn	zh	measure		circus

O

| ancient Semitic | Phoenician | early Hebrew | Greek | early Latin | later Latin |

P The earliest ancestor of our modern letter **P** was an ancient Semitic letter that looked like a hook. This hook-shaped letter, which was called *pe*, meaning "mouth," was changed only slightly in the Phoenician and early Hebrew alphabets. The ancient Greeks borrowed *pe* and called it *pi*, writing it much as it had been written in the preceding alphabets, but in two different directions. The Romans originally adopted one of the Greek forms of *pi* and later changed its shape by closing the hook at the top of the letter to form a loop. This later Latin version, which came into use about 2,400 years ago, is the form of the letter **P** we use today.

---

p, P (pē) *n., pl.* **p's, P's. 1.** the sixteenth letter of the English alphabet. **2.** the shape of this letter or something having this shape.
• **to mind one's P's and Q's.** to be careful, esp. of one's behavior.
P, the symbol for phosphorus.
p 1. *Music.* piano. **2.** *also,* **p.** pint.
p. 1. page. **2.** part. **3.** participle. **4.** past. **5.** penny. **6.** per. **7.** *Baseball.* pitcher. **8.** population. **9.** post.
P 1. *Chess.* pawn. **2.** *Physics.* pressure.
P. 1. pastor. **2.** president. **3.** priest. **4.** prince.
pa (pä) *n. Informal.* father. [Short for PAPA.]
Pa, the symbol for protactinium.
p.a. 1. participial adjective. **2.** per annum.
Pa., Pennsylvania
PA 1. the postal abbreviation for Pennsylvania. **2.** press agent. **3.** public-address (system).
P.A., public administration.
PABA (pä′bə, pab′ə) para-aminobenzoic acid.
Pab·lum (pab′ləm) *n.* **1.** *Trademark.* a soft, bland cereal used as food for infants. **2. pablum.** speaking or writing that is oversimplified; bland, dull language or ideas: *The politician's speech was nothing but pablum.* [Contraction of PABULUM.]
pab·u·lum (pab′yə ləm) *n.* any substance that gives nourishment; food. [Latin *pābulum*.]
Pac., Pacific.
pa·ca (pä′kə, pak′ə) *n.* any of a genus, *Agouti* or *Cuniculus,* of stubby-tailed, burrowing, Central and South American rodents related to agoutis and having spotted, brownish-black coats. Length: 24-32 inches (61-81 centimeters). [Portuguese and Spanish *paca,* from Tupi *páca.*]
pace (pās) *n.* **1.** a single step. **2.** the distance covered in a step, often used as a variable measure of length averaging from 2½ to 3½ feet (0.8 to 1.1 meters). **3.a.** a rate of speed in walking or running: *to quicken one's pace.* **b.** a rate of speed in any movement, activity, or progression: *They worked at a hectic pace to meet the deadline.* **4.** a particular manner of stepping, as in walking or running; gait; walk. **5.** a gait of a horse, in which both feet on the same side are lifted and put down together. —*v.,* **paced, pac·ing.** —*v.t.* **1.** to walk back and forth across, esp. with a slow, steady gait: *He paced the room while he waited.* **2.** to measure by paces (often with *off*): *She paced off 20 feet from the wall.* **3.** to set or regulate the rate of speed for: *The coach paced the runner.* **4.** to train (a horse) to move at a certain gait, esp. the pace. —*v.i.* **1.** to walk with slow, steady steps. **2.** (of a horse) to move with the gait of the pace. [Old French *pas* step, rate, from Latin *passus* step.]
• **to keep pace with. a.** to maintain the same speed of movement as: *The child ran along, trying to keep pace with the adults.* **b.** to maintain the same rate of progress or development as.
• **to put (someone) through his (or her) paces.** to test or

exhibit the talents or abilities of: *The animals were put through their paces for the judges.*
• **to set the pace. a.** to set the speed for others to maintain or go beyond. **b.** to be an example for others to follow: *Our store set the pace in book sales.*
pace·mak·er (pās′mā′kər) *n.* **1.** a person who sets the pace in a race. **2.** a person who leads a trend or sets an example for others. **3.** any of several small electronic devices implanted under the skin that control the rhythm of the heart, used in the treatment of heart disorders.
pac·er (pā′sər) *n.* **1.** a person who paces or measures by paces. **2.** a horse that paces, esp. one whose natural gait is a pace. **3.** pacemaker *(def. 1).*
pace·set·ter (pās′set′ər) *n.* pacemaker *(defs. 1, 2).*
pa·cha (pə shä′, pash′ə, pä′shə) pasha.
pach·y·derm (pak′ə dûrm′) *n.* **1.** any of several large, thick-skinned, hoofed mammals, such as the elephant or rhinoceros. **2.** a stolid, thick-skinned, insensitive person. [French *pachyderme* the animal, from Greek *pachydermos* thick-skinned.] —**pach′y·der′mal, pach·y·der·ma·tous** (pak′ə dûr′mə təs), *adj.*
pach·y·san·dra (pak′ə san′drə) *n.* any of various plants, genus *Pachysandra,* of the boxwood family, esp. *P. terminalis,* cultivated as a ground cover. [Modern Latin *Pachysandra* literally, having thick stamens, going back to Greek *pachys* thick + *andr-,* stem of *anēr* man.]
pa·cif·ic (pə sif′ik) *adj.* **1.** making or tending to make peace; conciliatory: *pacific gestures.* **2.** of a peaceful nature; calm; tranquil: *pacific waters.* [Latin *pācificus* peacemaking.] —**pa·cif′i·cal·ly,** *adv.*
Pa·cif·ic (pə sif′ik) *adj.* **1.** of, relating to, or designating the Pacific Ocean. **2.** on, along, or near the coast of the Pacific Ocean.
pac·i·fi·ca·tion (pas′ə fi kā′shən) *n.* the act of pacifying or the state of being pacified.
pa·cif·i·ca·to·ry (pə sif′i kə tôr′ē) *adj.* tending to make peace; conciliatory. —**pa·cif′i·ca·tor** (pə sif′i kā′tər), *n.*
Pacific Standard Time, the local civil time of the 120th meridian west of Greenwich, England, used in the western coastal region of the United States and Canada. It is 8 hours earlier than Greenwich Time.
pac·i·fi·er (pas′ə fī′ər) *n.* **1.** a person or thing that pacifies. **2.** a rubber nipple or similar object for babies to suck on.
pac·i·fism (pas′ə fiz′əm) *n.* the principle of opposition to war or other violence; belief that peaceful methods should be used to settle differences among nations.
pac·i·fist (pas′ə fist) *n.* a person who opposes war or other violence; advocate of pacifism. —**pac′i·fis′tic,** *adj.*
pac·i·fy (pas′ə fī′) *v.t.,* **-fied, -fy·ing. 1.** to allay the anger, excitement, or agitation of; calm; quiet: *The mayor tried to pacify the angry crowd.* **2.** to bring peace to; end the fighting in. **3.** to make submissive, esp. by military force; subdue. [Latin *pācificāre* to make peace.] —For Synonyms, see **appease.**
pack¹ (pak) *n.* **1.** a collection of things enclosed in wrapping or tied together, esp. for carrying on the back by a person or animal. **2.** a package containing a standard number of similar things: *a pack of matches, a pack of gum.* **3.** a set or group of similar persons or things: *a pack of cards, a pack of tourists.* **4.** a large quantity or amount: *a pack of lies.* **5.** a group of animals living or hunting together: *a pack of wolves.* **6.** the total amount of something, as fruits or vegetables, processed at one time, esp. in one season. **7.** an absorbent material, as a cloth or sheet, soaked in water or medicinal liquid and applied to the body or a part of the body as a treatment. **8.** a thick preparation applied in a layer to the skin, esp. the face, for cosmetic purposes. —*v.t.* **1.** to place in a receptacle for storing or carrying: *We packed the books in boxes.* **2.** to fill (something) with objects: *to pack a suitcase.* **3.** to make into a compact bundle or pack. **4.** to compress tightly; press closely together: *The child packed the sand down with the shovel.*

5. to fill by crowding or pressing together: *Capacity crowds packed the hall.* **6.** to crowd closely together: *We packed everyone in the car and went to the beach.* **7.** to prepare and put into a suitable container to be marketed or stored: *to pack beans for consumer use.* **8.** to fill or surround tightly with something in order to make airtight, leakproof, or impervious to damage: *to pack a pipe joint with lead.* **9.** to load (an animal) with a pack. **10.** to treat with a pack: *to pack a wound.* **11.** *Informal.* to carry or wear on one's person regularly: *to pack a gun.* **12.** *Informal.* to deliver or be able to deliver: *to pack a wallop.* **13.** to send away (with *off*): *We packed the children off to camp.* —*v.i.* **1.** to place articles in a receptacle, as a suitcase or box, for carrying or storing. **2.** to admit of being placed into a receptacle; be stored: *This dress packs easily.* **3.** to compress into a compact mass. **4.** to press together tightly; crowd together: *People packed into the subway car.* **5.** to go away quickly; depart hastily (with *off*). [Middle Dutch and Middle Low German *pak* bundle.]

· **to pack it in.** give up one's efforts: *I worked late into the night before I finally packed it in and went home.*
· **to send (someone) packing.** to send (someone) away summarily.

pack² (pak) *v.t.* to select, arrange, or manipulate fraudulently or to one's own advantage: *to pack a jury.* [Possibly from PACT.]

pack·age (pak′ij) *n.* **1.** a thing or group of things packed, wrapped up, or bound together; parcel. **2.** a box, case, or other receptacle in which things are packed. **3.** the act or process of packing. **4.** a group of items considered as a unit: *The travel package included several tours.* —*v.t.,* -**aged,** -**ag·ing.** to make or put into a package, as for storage, transportation, or marketing. —**pack′ag·er,** *n.*

Synonyms

n. **Package** and **parcel** mean something wrapped or packed for convenience in carrying, storing, or shipping. **Package** is used of something packed, especially to sell or transport: *packages of food on a store's shelves, packages shipped overseas.* **Parcel** suggests the way something is packed, wrapped, tied, or otherwise put together: *The clerk put all my purchases in one parcel. What a neat parcel you made of these things!*

---

package deal 1. an arrangement under which a group of items or services is offered or sold only as a unit: *a package deal for a trip to Canada, with transportation and meals included.* **2.** the items or services offered or sold in this way.

package store, a store that sells bottled or canned alcoholic beverages for consumption off the premises; liquor store.

pack animal, an animal, as a horse or mule, used for carrying loads.

pack·er (pak′ər) *n.* a person or thing that packs, esp. someone who owns or is employed in a business where produce or products are processed and packaged for sale: *a meat packer.*

pack·et (pak′it) *n.* **1.** a small package or parcel: *a packet of letters.* **2.** packet boat. [PACK¹ + -ET.]

packet boat, a boat that conveys mail, passengers, and freight at fixed times over a regular route, esp. along a coast or river.

pack ice, a large, uneven layer of floating ice formed by pieces of ice that are pressed together and frozen into a single mass. Also, **ice pack.**

pack·ing (pak′ing) *n.* **1.** the act or work of a person or thing that packs. **2.** the processing and packaging of meat, vegetables, fruit, or other produce and products. **3.** material used to make something airtight, watertight, or otherwise secure: *We carefully removed the packing from the box of glassware.*

packing house, an establishment where produce or products are processed and packaged for sale. Also, **packing plant.**

pack rat 1. a small, squirrellike North American rodent, genus *Neotoma,* noted for its habit of collecting small shiny objects and leaving other objects, such as nuts or pine cones, in exchange. **2.** *Informal.* a person who saves miscellaneous, often unneeded items.

pack·sad·dle (pak′sad′əl) *n.* a saddle designed to carry the load transported by a pack animal.

pack·thread (pak′thred′) *n.* a strong thread or twine used for tying up packages.

pact (pakt) *n.* an agreement between persons or countries, such as a treaty: *The two warring nations signed a peace pact.* [Latin *pactum.*]

pad¹ (pad) *n.* **1.** a soft piece of dense or stuffed material, used as a filling or covering for the purpose of protection or comfort: *a gauze pad, a back pad.* **2.** a number of sheets of paper fastened together along one edge; tablet: *a sketch pad.* **3.** one of the cushionlike parts on the underside of the toes of dogs, foxes, and certain other animals. **4.** the foot of a dog, fox, or certain other animals. **5.** a small ink-soaked block of cloth or other material, used to ink a rubber stamp. **6.** a large floating leaf of a water plant, such as a water lily. **7.** launch pad. **8.** a soft, cushionlike

saddle. **9.** *Slang.* the place where a person lives, such as a room or apartment. —*v.t.,* **pad·ded, pad·ding. 1.** to cover, fill, or line with a pad or padding. **2.** to lengthen (a speech or piece of writing) by adding unnecessary material (often with *out*): *to pad out an essay with quotations.* **3.** to add to dishonestly: *to pad an expense account with false expenditures.* [Possibly of Low German origin.]

pad² (pad) *v.i.,* **pad·ded, pad·ding. 1.** to move with dull, muffled, barely audible steps: *We took our shoes off and padded across the room.* **2.** to travel on foot; walk. —*n.* **1.** a dull, muffled sound, as of a footstep. **2.** a slow-paced horse used for riding on roads. [Possibly imitative.]

pad·ding (pad′ing) *n.* **1.** any soft material, as cotton or foam rubber, used to make a pad. **2.** extraneous matter used to expand a speech or written material. **3.** the act of a person or thing that pads.

pad·dle¹ (pad′əl) *n.* **1.** a short oar with a blade at one or both ends, used to propel a canoe or other small boat. **2.** a round or rectangular board with a handle, used to strike the ball in table tennis and similar games. **3.** a flat, wooden board used for inflicting punishment by spanking. **4.** any of various devices used for beating, stirring, or mixing. **5.** any of various paddle-shaped instruments used for stirring or mixing in industrial processes, as glassmaking or metalworking. **6.** one of the broad boards set on the circumference of a paddle wheel or waterwheel. **7.** the act of paddling. —*v.,* -**dled,** -**dling.** —*v.t.* **1.** to propel (a canoe or other small boat) by means of a paddle or paddles. **2.** to convey by paddling: *The campers paddled supplies to their camp further up the river.* **3.** to punish by striking with or as with a paddle; spank. **4.** to beat, stir, or mix with a paddle. —*v.i.* **1.** to propel a canoe or other small boat by means of a paddle. **2.** to row lightly or gently. [Of uncertain origin.] —**pad′dler,** *n.*

pad·dle² (pad′əl) *v.i.,* -**dled,** -**dling. 1.** to move about or splash in shallow water; wade. **2.** to toddle. [Possibly PAD² + -LE.] —**pad′dler,** *n.*

pad·dle·boat (pad′əl bōt′) *n.* a boat propelled by a paddle wheel or paddle wheels.

pad·dle·fish (pad′əl fish′) *n., pl.* -**fish** or -**fish·es.** any of several gray large-mouthed fish, family Polyodontidae, having a long, paddlelike snout, that are native to the Mississippi and yield roe used for caviar. Length: to 12 feet (3.7 meters), including the snout.

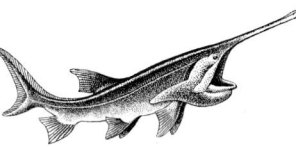

paddlefish

paddle tennis, a game of tennis played with wooden paddles and a smooth rubber ball on an enclosed court about half the size of a standard tennis court and with a lower net.

paddle wheel, a wheel having projecting floats or paddles around its circumference, used to propel a steamboat.

pad·dock (pad′ək) *n.* **1.** a small field or enclosure in which an animal can graze and exercise. **2.** an area at a race track in which the horses are saddled and mounted. [Modification of dialectal English *parrock,* from Old English *pearroc* enclosure.]

pad·dy (pad′ē) *n., pl.* -**dies. 1.** a field where rice is grown. **2.** rice, esp. when not yet milled. [Malay *pādī* rice in the husk.]

Pad·dy (pad′ē) *n., pl.* -**dies.** Irishman. ➡ considered offensive. [Familiar form of *Patrick,* masculine proper name.]

paddy wagon *Slang.* patrol wagon. [Probably from PADDY.]

pad·lock (pad′lok′) *n.* a detachable lock with a curved bar that is made to be passed through an opening. —*v.t.* to fasten with or as with a padlock.

pa·dre (pä′drā) *n.* **1.** father. ➡ used in addressing or referring to a priest, esp. in Italy, Spain, Portugal, or Latin America. **2.** *Informal.* a military chaplain. [Italian, Spanish, or Portuguese *padre* father, from Latin *pater.*]

pae·an (pē′ən) *also,* **pean.** *n.* a song of praise, joy, thanksgiving, or triumph. [Latin *paeān,* from Greek *paiān* hymn to Apollo (one of whose names was *Paiān*).]

pa·el·la (pä yel′ə, -äl′yə) *n.* a dish consisting of rice with chicken, seafood, meat, and vegetables flavored with saffron. [Spanish *paella,* from Catalan *paella* frying pan, the name of this food, going back to Latin *patella* a small pan or dish.]

pa·gan (pā′gən) *n.* **1.** a person who is not a Christian, Jew, or

---

a	at	e	end	o	hot	u	up	hw	white		about
ā	ape	ē	me	ō	old	ū	use	ng	song		taken
ä	far	i	it	ô	fork	ü	rule	th	thin	ə {	pencil
âr	care	ī	ice	oi	oil	u̇	pull	th	this		lemon
				îr	pierce	ou	out	ûr	turn	zh	measure		circus

P

Muslim. **2.** formerly, a person who was not a Christian and worshiped many gods. The ancient Greeks and Romans were pagans. **3.** a person who has no religion. —*adj.* **1.** of or relating to pagans or paganism. **2.** not religious; idolatrous. [Latin *pāgānus* villager, civilian (from the early Christian concept of heathens as civilians and members of the faith as soldiers of Christ), from *pāgus* village.] —**pa′gan·dom,** *n.*

Synonyms **Pagan, heathen,** and **infidel** mean a person who does not accept a certain faith, esp. Christianity, Judaism, or Islam. **Pagan** is most often used of ancient peoples who worshiped many gods: *Early converts to Christianity included both Jews and pagans.* **Heathen,** a more derogatory term, is applied esp. to a person who worships idols and is regarded as primitive or uncivilized: *The missionary appealed for funds to help educate and convert heathens.* **Infidel** is used derogatorily of a person who does not share one's own religious beliefs: *The two neighbors, one Muslim and the other Christian, regarded each other as infidels.*

pa·gan·ism (pā′gə niz′əm) *n.* **1.** the beliefs, practices, and customs of pagans. **2.** the state of being a pagan. —**pa′gan·is′tic,** *adj.*

page[1] (pāj) *n.* **1.a.** one side of a leaf of a book, letter, or similar article. **b.** an entire leaf. **2.** the print, writing, or type used on one side of a leaf: *to read six pages of a book.* **3.** *also,* **pages.** a written record: *in the pages of medical science.* **4.** an event, series of events, or period of time worthy of recording: *The Civil War was a tragic page in American history.* —*v.,* **paged, pag·ing.** —*v.t.* to number the pages of; paginate. —*v.i.* to turn the pages steadily: *to page through a catalog to find an item.* [Old French *page* side of a leaf (of a book), from Latin *pāgina* leaf for writing.]

page[2] (pāj) *n.* **1.** a servant or attendant, esp. a boy who attends a person of rank, as in a royal household. **2.** a young person employed to serve as an attendant to members of Congress or other legislatures while in session. **3.** a person employed to run errands or carry messages, as in a hotel. **4.** formerly, a boy in training for knighthood. —*v.t.,* **paged, pag·ing.** to seek or summon (someone) by calling out the person's name or sending signals to a beeper. [Old French *page* young boy, valet, going back to Greek *paidíon* young boy, diminutive of *pais* child.]

pag·eant (paj′ənt) *n.* **1.** a theatrical presentation that dramatizes or is based on historical or legendary events. **2.** an elaborate spectacle, procession, or parade. [Medieval Latin *pagina* scene of a play, stage, from Latin *pāgina* leaf for writing.]

pag·eant·ry (paj′ən trē) *n., pl.* **-ries. 1.** pageants collectively. **2.** ceremonial splendor or spectacular display: *We enjoyed the pageantry of the parade.*

page·boy (pāj′boi′) *n.* a hair style in which the hair is worn long and straight with the ends curled inward into a roll.

pag·er (pā′jər) *n.* beeper.

pag·i·nal (paj′ə nəl) *adj.* **1.** of, relating to, or consisting of pages. **2.** page for page: *a paginal reprint.*

pag·i·nate (paj′ə nāt′) *v.t.,* **-nat·ed, -nat·ing.** to number the pages of (a book or other writing).

pag·i·na·tion (paj′ə nā′shən) *n.* **1.** the numbers or figures with which pages are marked. **2.** the arrangement or sequence of such figures or marks. **3.** the act of paginating or the state of being paginated.

pa·go·da (pə gō′də) *n.* **1.** in the Far East, a temple or memorial tower, usually pyramidal in form, often with a series of boldly projecting roofs. **2.** any building resembling this, as an ornamental structure in a formal garden. [Portuguese *pagode* temple, probably going back to Persian *butkada* temple of idols.]

paid (pād) *v.* the past tense and past participle of **pay**[1]. —*adj.* **1.** receiving pay: *a paid adviser.* **2.** having been paid for: *a paid political advertisement.*

pail (pāl) *n.* **1.** an open cylindrical container, usually with a handle, used for carrying liquid, sand, or other materials. **2.** the amount that a pail holds; pailful. [Partly from Old English *pægel* gill[2], wine measure; partly from Old French *paelle* pan, liquid measure, from Latin *patella* small pan[1]. See PATELLA.]

pail·ful (pāl′fŭl′) *n., pl.* **-fuls.** the capacity of a pail.

pain (pān) *n.* **1.** an unpleasant physical sensation resulting from or accompanying an injury, illness, or other physical disorder. **2.** emotional distress or suffering; anxiety; grief: *the pain of loneliness.* **3. pains.** care or trouble: *The caterers took great pains with*

pagoda

the table arrangements. **4. pains.** the pangs or labor of childbirth. **5.** *Informal.* a person or thing that is a nuisance; annoyance. —*v.t.* to cause pain to; make suffer: *My knee pains me on damp days.* —*v.i.* to have or cause pain. [Old French *peine* punishment, suffering, from Latin *poena,* from Greek *poinē* punishment.] •**on** (or **upon** or **under**) **pain of.** at the risk of or subject to (a specified punishment).

Synonyms *n.* **Pain** and **ache** mean a sensation of bodily discomfort or suffering. **Pain** is the general term: *The fracture caused the player intense pain.* **Ache** refers to a dull, steady pain: *The ache in my bruised shoulder lasted for two days.*

pained (pānd) *adj.* **1.** affected with pain; hurt or distressed. **2.** showing pain: *a pained expression on one's face.*

pain·ful (pān′fəl) *adj.* **1.** causing or affected with pain; hurting: *a painful wound, a painful knee.* **2.** causing mental pain; distressing: *painful memories.* **3.** requiring effort or care; laborious; irksome: *a painful decision.* —**pain′ful·ly,** *adv.* —**pain′fulness,** *n.*

pain·kill·er (pān′kil′ər) *n.* a substance, such as a drug, that relieves pain.

pain·less (pān′lis) *adj.* free from or not causing pain: *a painless operation.* —**pain′less·ly,** *adv.* —**pain′less·ness,** *n.*

pains·tak·ing (pānz′tā′king) *adj.* characterized by or requiring close, careful labor or attention: *painstaking work.* —*n.* the act of taking pains; careful effort; diligence. —**pains′tak′ing·ly,** *adv.*

paint (pānt) *n.* **1.a.** a liquid coloring material consisting of one or more solid pigments mixed with a liquid, such as oil or water, that dries to form a hard layer or film when applied to surfaces, and is used as a protective or decorative coating. **b.** a layer or coating of such material. **c.** the solid pigment alone. **2.** a cosmetic, such as rouge or lipstick, used to add color. —*v.t.* **1.** to represent on a surface with paints: *to paint a landscape on canvas.* **2.** to make (something), such as a picture, by applying paints: *The artist painted two large canvases in four days.* **3.** to cover the surface of or decorate with paint: *to paint a house.* **4.** to depict or describe vividly in words. **5.** to color with cosmetics; apply cosmetics to: *to paint one's face with rouge.* **6.a.** to apply (medicine) with a brush or swab. **b.** to treat (a wound) in such a way. —*v.i.* **1.** to practice the art of painting; make pictures: *I learned to paint in art class.* **2.** to use cosmetics. [Old French *peint,* past participle of *peindre* to color, represent pictorially, from Latin *pingere.*]

paint·brush (pānt′brush′) *n.* **1.** a brush for applying paint. **2.** Indian paintbrush.

paint·ed (pān′tid) *adj.* **1.** covered or adorned with or as with paint. **2.** represented in paint. **3.** wearing too much or highly colored makeup. **4.** having no reality; artificial; sham: *their painted expressions.*

painted bunting, a brightly colored songbird, *Passerina ciris,* breeding in the southern United States. The male is red-breasted with a green back and purple head. Length: 5½ inches (14 centimeters).

paint·er[1] (pān′tər) *n.* **1.** an artist who paints pictures. **2.** a person who paints surfaces, esp. a person whose work is painting the interiors or exteriors of houses. [Old French *peintour,* going back to Latin *pictor.*]

paint·er[2] (pān′tər) *n.* a rope attached to the bow of a boat for securing it to something. [Possibly from Old French *pentoir* rope for hanging things, from *pendre* to hang, from Latin *pendēre.*]

paint·er[3] (pān′tər) *n.* cougar. [Form of PANTHER.]

paint·ing (pān′ting) *n.* **1.** the act of covering with paint. **2.** the art of applying paints to a surface in order to create an image or effect. **3.** a picture or image produced in paint.

pair (pâr) *n., pl.* **pairs** or **pair. 1.** a set of two identical, similar, or corresponding things intended for use together or associated in some way: *a pair of slippers, a pair of oars.* **2.** a single thing consisting of two identical or similar connected parts: *a pair of pliers, a pair of pants.* **3.** two persons who have something in common or are associated together: *a pair of police officers.* **4.** a married or engaged couple. **5.a.** two animals mated together: *a pair of doves.* **b.** two animals working together. **6.a.** two members of a legislative body who, because they would vote differently and offset each other, arrange not to vote on a certain issue or issues. **b.** the arrangement thus made. **7.** in some card games, esp. poker, two cards of the same denomination: *a pair of aces.* —*v.t.* **1.** to join or match (two persons or things) in a pair (often with *off*): *They paired John and Marsha for the dance.* **2.** to arrange in pairs. **3.** to arrange a partner for (with *with*): *The teacher paired Marsha with John.* —*v.i.* **1.** to form a pair or pairs. **2.** to separate into pairs (usually with *off*): *The students paired off for dancing.* **3.** to join in marriage. **4.** to join to produce offspring; mate. [Old French *paire* a set of two, from Latin *paria,* neuter plural of *pār* like[1], equal.]

pais·ley (pāz′lē) *n., pl.* **-leys**. **1.** a distinctive, usually colorful design that incorporates curved forms on a patterned background. **2.** a fabric having such a design. —*adj.* **1.** made of or resembling such fabric: *a paisley shirt.* **2.** designating or having the characteristic design of paisley. [From *Paisley,* city in Scotland once famous for woolen shawls in this pattern.]

Pai·ute (pī ūt′, pī′ūt) *n., pl.* **-ute** or **-utes**. **1.** a member of any of a group of North American Indian tribes formerly living in Arizona, California, Nevada, and Utah. **2.** their language, belonging to the Shoshonean language family.

paisley design

pa·ja·mas (pə jä′məz, -jam′əz) *also, British,* **pyjamas**. *pl. n.* **1.** a loose-fitting two-piece garment for sleeping or informal wear, consisting of a jacketlike top and trousers. **2.** loose trousers worn by men and women in Oriental countries. [Urdu *pāē jāmah* trousers; literally, leg garment, from Persian *pāē* leg + *jāmah* garment.]

pal (pal) *Informal. n.* a close friend. —*v.i.,* **palled, pal·ling**. to associate as pals. [Gypsy *pal* brother, going back to Sanskrit *bhrātar.*]

pal·ace (pal′is) *n.* **1.** the official residence of a sovereign, member of royalty, or high dignitary, such as a bishop. **2.** any large, grand residence or building. **3.** a large, often ornate, public building, esp. one used for exhibitions or entertainment: *a movie palace.* [Old French *palais* royal residence, from Latin *palātium,* from *Palātium* Palatine Hill in Rome, site of the first imperial palace of Rome, which was built by the emperor Augustus.]

pal·a·din (pal′ə din) *n.* **1.** in medieval legend, one of the twelve peers or famous warriors who accompanied Charlemagne. **2.** any heroic champion. [French *paladin,* from Italian *paladino,* from Latin *palātīnus* officer of the palace. See PALATINE.]

pa·laes·tra (pə les′trə) palestra.

pal·an·quin (pal′ən kēn′) *also,* **pal·an·keen**. *n.* a covered litter, usually for one person, carried on the shoulders of two or more people by means of poles, used esp. in Eastern countries. [Portuguese *palanquim,* going back to Sanskrit *palyanka* couch.]

pal·at·a·ble (pal′ə tə bəl) *adj.* **1.** agreeable to the taste or palate; savory. **2.** agreeable to the mind or feelings; acceptable: *a palatable solution to a problem.* —**pal′at·a·bil′i·ty,** *n.* —**pal′at·a·bly,** *adv.*

pal·a·tal (pal′ə təl) *adj.* **1.** of or relating to the palate. **2.** (of a speech sound) articulated with the tongue close to or touching the hard palate, as the *y* in *young.* —*n.* a palatal sound.

pal·a·tal·ize (pal′ə tə līz′) *v.t.,* **-ized, -iz·ing**. to pronounce as a palatal sound. —**pal′a·tal·i·za′tion,** *n.*

pal·ate (pal′it) *n.* **1.** the roof of the mouth, consisting of the bony hard palate in the front of the mouth and the fleshy soft palate in the back of the mouth. **2.** the sense of taste: *food that is pleasing to the palate.* **3.** intellectual taste; liking. [Latin *palātum* roof of the mouth.]

pa·la·tial (pə lā′shəl) *adj.* of, resembling, or befitting a palace: *a palatial home.* [Latin *palātium* palace + -AL¹. See PALACE.] —**pa·la′tial·ly,** *adv.*

pa·lat·i·nate (pə lat′ə nāt′, -nit) *n.* a territory under the jurisdiction of a palatine.

pal·a·tine (pal′ə tīn′, -tin) *adj.* **1.** having royal privileges and prerogatives on one's own territory: *a count palatine.* **2.** of or relating to a lord having royal privileges and prerogatives on his own territory. **3.** of or relating to a palace; palatial. **4. Palatine.** of or relating to the Palatinate in Germany. —*n.* **1.** a palatine lord. **2. Palatine.** a native or inhabitant of the Palatinate in Germany. [Latin *palātīnus* officer of the palace, relating to the imperial palace, from *palātium* palace. See PALACE.]

pa·lav·er (pə lav′ər, -lä′vər) *n.* **1.** idle talk; chatter. **2.** a parley or conference, esp. one between explorers or traders and native inhabitants. —*v.i.* to talk idly and profusely. [Portuguese *palavra* word, talk, from Latin *parabola* comparison, parable, from Greek *parabolē.* Doublet of PARABLE, PAROLE.]

pa·laz·zo (pə lät′sō) *n., pl.* **-laz·zos** or **-laz·zi** (-lät′sē). a palace or other large and stately building, esp. in a city in Italy. [Italian *palazzo,* from Latin *palatium* royal residence. See PALACE.]

pale¹ (pāl) *adj.,* **pal·er, pal·est**. **1.** whitish or lacking natural or healthy color; pallid: *a pale complexion.* **2.** lacking intensity or depth of color: *pale green.* **3.** lacking in brightness or brilliance of light; dim: *pale moonlight.* **4.** lacking strength or intensity; feeble; weak: *a pale imitation.* —*v.,* **paled, pal·ing**. —*v.i.* **1.** to turn pale: *They paled when they heard the scream.* **2.** to become or appear to be of less importance: *My problems pale when I think of*

yours. —*v.t.* to make pale. [Old French *pale* lacking color, from Latin *pallidus.* Doublet of PALLID.] —**pale′ly,** *adv.* —**pale′ness,** *n.*

adj. **Pale¹, pallid,** and **wan¹** mean having a complexion with little or deficient color. **Pale** suggests whiteness or lack of bright colors, often under normal circumstances: *People with pale skin usually sunburn easily.* **Pallid** suggests a lack of color resulting from an abnormal condition: *The child was pallid from lack of sleep.* **Wan** implies a paleness caused by ill health: *The patient looked wan after the operation.*

pale² (pāl) *n.* **1.** a pointed, narrow piece of wood used in fences; stake; picket. **2.** a place, district, or territory enclosed within bounds. **3.** any boundary, barrier, or limit: *behavior that is beyond the pale of recognized propriety.* **4.** a broad, vertical stripe through the middle of the shield on a coat of arms. —*v.t.,* **paled, pal·ing**. to enclose with pales; fence in. [Old French *pal* stake, from Latin *pālus.*]

pa·le·a (pā′lē ə) *n., pl.* **-le·ae** (-lē ē′). the upper of the two bracts beneath a flower in the spikelet of a grass. [Modern Latin *palea,* from Latin *palea* chaff.]

pale·face (pāl′fās′) *n.* a white person as opposed to a North American Indian.

paleo- *combining form* ancient; old: *paleography.* [Greek *palaios.*]

pa·le·o·bot·a·ny (pā′lē ō bot′ə nē) *n.* the branch of paleontology that deals with the study of fossil plants. [PALEO- + BOTANY.] —**pa·le·o·bo·tan·i·cal** (pā′lē ō bə tan′i kəl), *adj.* —**pa′le·o·bot′a·nist,** *n.*

Pa·le·o·cene (pā′lē ə sēn′) *n.* the earliest geologic epoch of the Tertiary period of the Cenozoic era, when mammalian life began to proliferate. For table, see **geologic time.** —*adj.* of or relating to this epoch. [PALEO- + Greek *kainos* new.]

pa·le·og·ra·pher (pā′lē og′rə fər) *n.* a person who studies or is an expert in paleography.

pa·le·og·ra·phy (pā′lē og′rə fē) *n.* **1.** ancient forms of writing or ancient writings collectively. **2.** the study of ancient writings and inscriptions. [PALEO- + -GRAPHY.] —**pa·le·o·graph·ic** (pā′lē ə graf′ik), *adj.*

Pa·le·o·lith·ic (pā′lē ə lith′ik) *adj.* of, relating to, or designating the earliest part of the Stone Age, which began with the Pleistocene epoch, characterized by tools made of crudely chipped stone and by cave art. [PALEO- + Greek *lithos* stone + -IC.]

Paleolithic cave art, Lascaux, France

pa·le·o·mag·net·ism (pā′lē ō mag′ni tiz′əm) *n. Geology.* **1.** the natural remanence of magnetic mineral grains in rock, aligned with the earth's magnetic poles as they existed when the rock formed. **2.** the study of such remanence as a way of charting the movements of the magnetic poles throughout the course of geologic time. [PALEO- + MAGNETISM.] —**pa′le·o·mag·net′ic,** *adj.*

pa·le·on·tol·o·gy (pā′lē on tol′ə jē) *n.* the science that deals with fossils and extinct forms of life. [PALEO- + Greek *ont-,* stem of *ōn* being + -LOGY.] —**pa·le·on·to·log·ic** (pā′lē on′tə loj′ik), *adj.* —**pa′le·on·tol′o·gist,** *n.*

Pa·le·o·zo·ic (pā′lē ə zō′ik) *n.* the geologic era comprising all the periods from the Cambrian through the Permian, characterized by the advent of land plants, fish, amphibians, and reptiles. For table, see **geologic time.** —*adj.* of, relating to, or characteristic of this era. [PALEO- + Greek *zōē* life + -IC.]

Pal·es·tine Liberation Organization (pal′ə stīn′) a coalition

a	at	e	end	o	hot	u	up	hw	white		about
ā	ape	ē	me	ō	old	ū	use	ng	song	ə	taken
ä	far	i	it	ô	fork	u̇	rule	th	thin		pencil
âr	care	ī	ice	oi	oil	u̇	pull	th	this		lemon
		îr	pierce	ou	out	ûr	turn	zh	measure		circus

P

of Arab political and military groups formed with the purpose of establishing a Palestinian state.

pa·les·tra (pə les'trə) *also,* **palaestra.** *n.* a school in ancient Greece for exercise and physical training, esp. in wrestling. [Latin *palaestra,* from Greek *palaistrā*.]

pal·ette (pal'it) *n.* **1.** a thin board or tablet, usually having a hole for the thumb, on which artists place and mix their paints. **2.** the range or system of colors characteristic of a particular artist, painting, or school of painting. [French *palette,* going back to Latin *pāla* spade[1].]

palette knife, an implement with a thin, flexible blunt blade set in a handle, used by artists to mix and apply colors and to clean the palette.

pal·frey (pôl'frē) *n., pl.* **-freys.** *Archaic.* a saddle horse, esp. one for a woman. [Old French *palefrei,* going back to Late Latin *paraverēdus* post horse, from Greek *para* beside + Late Latin *verēdus* post horse (of Celtic origin).]

pal·i·mo·ny (pal'ə mō'nē) *Informal. n.* an amount of money or property given as a settlement to one member of an unmarried couple by the other after they have separated.

pal·imp·sest (pal'imp sest') *n.* parchment or other writing material written upon two or more times, the earlier writing having been erased partially or completely to make room for the next. [Latin *palimpsēstus,* from Greek *palimpsēstos* scraped again.]

pal·in·drome (pal'in drōm') *n.* a word, verse, phrase, sentence, or number that reads the same forward and backward. The word *madam,* the sentence *Was it a cat I saw?* and *2992* are palindromes. [Greek *palindromos* running back again.]

pal·ing (pā'ling) *n.* **1.** a fence made of pales. **2.** pales collectively. **3.** one of the pales forming a fence.

pal·i·sade (pal'ə sād') *n.* **1.** a fence of strong, pointed stakes placed closely together and set firmly in the ground, used for defense or protection. **2.** one of the long, pointed stakes used in such a fence. **3.** **palisades.** a line of steep, columnar cliffs, usually rising along the edge of a body of water. **4.** palisade parenchyma. —*v.t.,* **-sad·ed, -sad·ing.** to enclose or fortify with a palisade. [French *palissade* fence of stakes, going back to Latin *pālus*.]

palisade parenchyma, the usually upper layer in the mesophyll of certain leaves, composed of elongated chloroplast-bearing cells, in which most of the photosynthesis occurs. Also, **palisade layer, palisade mesophyll.**

pall[1] (pôl) *n.* **1.** a heavy covering of soft black or purple cloth, laid over a bier, coffin, hearse, or tomb. **2.** something that covers or conceals with an atmosphere of darkness and gloom: *a thick pall of black smoke.* **3.** a piece of linen, or a square piece of cardboard covered with linen, used to cover a chalice in the Mass. —*v.t.* to cover with or as with a pall. [Old English *pæll* robe, cloak, purple cloth, from Latin *pallium* cloak, covering.]

pall[2] (pôl) *v.i.* **1.** to become insipid or boring: *After ten minutes the television show began to pall.* **2.** to have a dulling or displeasing effect (with *on*). —*v.t.* to cause to become tired or bored; satiate; cloy: *to pall the senses.* [Short for APPALL.]

pal·la·di·um (pə lā'dē əm) *n.* a soft, heavy, silver-white metallic element of the platinum family, used esp. as a catalyst in hydrogenation processes. Symbol: **Pd** For tables, see **element.** [Modern Latin *palladium,* from the asteroid *Pallas*.]

Pal·la·di·um (pə lā'dē əm) *n., pl.* **-di·a** (-dē ə). **1.** in ancient Greece and Rome, a statue of Pallas Athena, esp. one in Troy on which the preservation of the city was supposed to depend. **2. palladium.** anything regarded as essential to the safety or preservation of a community or institution. [Latin *Palladium* statue of Pallas in Troy, from Greek *Palladion,* from *Pallas* Pallas.]

Pal·las (pal'əs) *n.* **1.** in Greek mythology, Athena. Also, **Pallas Athena. 2.** one of the asteroids.

pall·bear·er (pôl'bâr'ər) *n.* a person who carries or escorts the coffin at a funeral.

pal·let[1] (pal'it) *n.* **1.** a straw bed or mattress. **2.** any small, hard, or temporary bed, often on the floor. [Anglo-Norman *paillete* straw, diminutive of *paille,* from Latin *palea.*]

pal·let[2] (pal'it) *n.* **1.** a wooden tool with a flat blade and a handle, esp. one used by potters for mixing and shaping clay. **2.** palette (*def. 1*). **3.** a movable platform for storing and transporting goods, as in a warehouse. **4.** a projection on a pawl that engages the teeth of a ratchet wheel. For illustration, see **ratchet.** [Old French *palette* small shovel, diminutive of *pale* shovel, spade[1], from Latin *pāla* spade[1].]

pal·li·ate (pal'ē āt') *v.t.,* **-at·ed, -at·ing. 1.** to make (an offense or fault) appear less serious; extenuate. **2.** to alleviate the symptoms or pain of (a disease) without effecting a cure. [Latin *palliātus* covered with a cloak, from *pallium* cloak.] —**pal'li·a'tion,** *n.*

pal·li·a·tive (pal'ē ā'tiv, -ə tiv) *adj.* serving or tending to

palliate: *palliative drugs, a palliative influence.* —*n.* something that palliates.

pal·lid (pal'id) *adj.* lacking natural or healthy color; pale. [Latin *pallidus.* Doublet of PALE[1].] —For Synonyms, see **pale**[1].

pall-mall (pel'mel') *n.* **1.** a game formerly played in England, in which a ball was struck by a mallet and hit through a ring hung at the end of an alley. **2.** the alley in which this game was played. [Middle French *pallemaille* the game, from Italian *pallamaglio,* from *palla* ball (of Germanic origin) + *maglio* mallet (from Latin *malleus* hammer).]

pal·lor (pal'ər) *n.* lack of natural or healthy color; paleness. [Latin *pallor.*]

palm[1] (päm) *n.* **1.** the flexible inner surface of the hand, extending from the wrist to the base of the fingers. **2.** a measure of length equivalent either to the width of a hand (3-4 inches; 8-10 centimeters) or the length of a hand (about 8½ inches; 22 centimeters). **3.** the part of a glove or mitten covering the palm. **4.** anything resembling or corresponding to the palm, as the blade of a paddle. —*v.t.* **1.** to conceal in the palm or hand: *to palm cards.* **2.** to hold or handle with the palm of the hand. [Old French *paume* the inner surface of the hand, from Latin *palma.* See PALM[2].]

·**to grease (someone's) palm.** to bribe.
·**to palm off.** to pass off or dispose of by deceit or fraud.

palm[2] (päm) *n.* **1.** any of a group of tropical and subtropical trees, shrubs, or vines, family Palmae or Arecaceae, usually having large, featherlike or fan-shaped leaves growing in a cluster at the top of a tall, branchless trunk. **2.** a leaf or branch of such a tree, esp. when considered or used as a symbol of victory or success. **3.** a representation of such a leaf or branch given to indicate the second award for the same military decoration of honor. **4.** victory or success; triumph. [Old English *palm* the tree, from Latin *palma* palm tree and leaf, palm of the hand (from the resemblance of the palm leaf to the outspread palm of the hand).]

·**to bear (or carry) off the palm.** to be the winner.

pal·mar (pal'mər, päl'mər) *adj.* of, relating to, or located in the palm of the hand. [Latin *palmaris.*]

pal·mate (pal'māt, päl'-) *adj.* **1.** resembling a hand with the fingers spread or extended: *the palmate antlers of the reindeer.* **2.** (of a compound leaf) composed of leaflets that originate from a common point. **3.** webbed, as the toes of a bird. [Latin *palmātus* shaped like the palm of the hand, from *palma* palm of the hand. See PALM[1].] —**pal'mate·ly,** *adv.*

palm·er (pä'mər, päl'-) *n.* **1.** in the Middle Ages, a pilgrim who went to the Holy Land and brought back a palm branch as a token. **2.** any pilgrim. [Anglo-Norman *palmer* pilgrim returning from the Holy Land, going back to Latin *palma* palm tree, palm leaf.]

palmate
compound leaf

pal·met·to (pal met'ō, päl'-) *n., pl.* **-tos** or **-toes.** any of a group of hardy palms, genus *Sabal,* widely cultivated as ornamentals and as a source of leaves for thatching, grown in the southern United States and other warm areas. [Spanish *palmito,* diminutive of *palma* palm tree, from Latin *palma.*]

palm·ist (pä'mist) *n.* a person who practices palmistry.

palm·is·try (pä'mə strē) *n.* the art or practice of telling fortunes and describing personal character by examining the lines and configurations in the palm of the hand. [Middle English *pawmestry,* possibly from *palme* palm of the hand (see PALM[1]) + *mestry* mastery (from Old French *maistrie,* from *maistre* one in charge). See MASTER.]

pal·mit·ic acid (pal mit'ik, päl'-) a saturated fatty acid, glycerides of which are contained in palm oil and many animal fats. [French *palmitique* referring to palm oil, from *palme* palm[2] + *-ite* -ite[1] + *-ique* -ic.]

palm oil, a yellowish butterlike edible oil obtained from the fruit of several species of palm, used in the manufacture of many products, such as soap, candles, and cosmetics.

Palm Sunday, the Sunday before Easter Sunday, commemorating Jesus' entry into Jerusalem, when people spread palm branches before him.

palm·y (pä'mē) *adj.,* **palm·i·er, palm·i·est. 1.** full of or shaded by palm trees: *palmy beaches.* **2.** characterized by prosperity; flourishing: *the palmy days of one's career.* **3.** of or like a palm.

pal·my·ra (pal mī'rə) *n.* a tropical Asian palm, *Borassus flabellifer,* having large, fanlike fronds. Its wood is used for rafters, its leaves for thatch, baskets, brushes, and paper, its sap for sugar, and its fruit for food. [Portuguese *palmeira,* from *palma,* from Latin *palma.* See PALM.]

pal·o·mi·no (pal'ə mē'nō) *n., pl.* **-nos.** a light tan or golden

horse having a cream-colored or white mane and tail. [Spanish *palomino* dove-colored, going back to Latin *palumbes* dove.]

palp (palp) *n.* a jointed sensory organ attached to the mouth of insects and other arthropods. Also, **palpus.** For illustration, see **mandible.**

pal·pa·ble (pal'pə bəl) *adj.* **1.** capable of being touched or felt; tangible. **2.** easily perceived by the senses or mind; obvious; noticeable: *a palpable difference, a palpable error.* [Late Latin *palpābilis* capable of being touched, from Latin *palpāre* to touch.] —**pal'pa·bil'i·ty,** *n.* —**pal'pa·bly,** *adv.*

pal·pate (pal'pāt) *v.t.,* **-pat·ed, -pat·ing.** to examine by touching, esp. for medical diagnosis. [Latin *palpātus,* past participle of *palpāre* to touch.] —**pal·pa'tion,** *n.*

pal·pi·tate (pal'pi tāt') *v.i.,* **-tat·ed, -tat·ing. 1.** to beat irregularly or at an abnormally rapid rate: *My heart palpitated from overexertion.* **2.** to quiver, tremble, or vibrate. [Latin *palpitātus,* past participle of *palpitāre* to throb.] —**pal·pi·tant** (pal'pi tənt), *adj.*

pal·pi·ta·tion (pal'pi tā'shən) *n.* **1.** an abnormally rapid and often irregular beating of the heart. **2.** a quivering, trembling, or vibrating motion.

pal·pus (pal'pəs) *n., pl.* **-pi** (-pī). palp. [Modern Latin *palpus,* from Latin *palpāre* to touch.]

pal·sied (pôl'zēd) *adj.* **1.** paralyzed. **2.** trembling; shaking.

pal·sy (pôl'zē) *n., pl.* **-sies. 1.** weakness or paralysis of a muscle, usually characterized by trembling. **2.** any impairment of the power to feel or to control movement of any part of the body. —*v.t.,* **-sied, -sy·ing. 1.** to paralyze. **2.** to make helpless or cause to tremble, as from fear. [Old French *paralysie* paralysis, from Latin *paralysis,* from Greek *paralysis* paralysis, disabling of the nerves. Doublet of PARALYSIS.]

pal·ter (pôl'tər) *v.i.* **1.** to talk or act insincerely; equivocate; lie. **2.** to deal carelessly or capriciously; trifle. **3.** to haggle, as in bargaining. [Of uncertain origin.]

pal·try (pôl'trē) *adj.,* **-tri·er, -tri·est. 1.** having little or no value; insignificant: *a paltry sum of money.* **2.** low-minded or contemptible; mean; petty: *a paltry, hypocritical person.* [Possibly from dialectal English *palt* trash; possibly of Low German origin.] —**pal'tri·ness,** *n.* —For Synonyms, see **petty.**

pal·y·nol·o·gy (pal'ə nol'ə jē) *n.* the study of living and fossil pollen grains and spores. [Greek *palynein* to strew, sprinkle, from *palē* fine meal, dust + -LOGY.] —**pal'y·no·log'i·cal** (pal'ə nə-loj'i kəl), *adj.* —**pal'y·nol'o·gist,** *n.*

pam·pas (pam'pəz) *also,* **pam·pa.** *pl. n.* vast, treeless plains extending from the Atlantic Ocean to the Andes Mountains in Argentina and in certain other areas of South America. [Spanish *pampas,* plural of *pampa* plain, from Quechua *pampa.*]

pam·per (pam'pər) *v.t.* to treat with extreme indulgence or care; cater to the needs or desires of; coddle: *to pamper one's children.* [Probably of Flemish origin.] —**pam'per·er,** *n.* —For Synonyms, see **humor.**

pam·phlet (pam'flit) *n.* **1.** a printed publication stitched or fastened together but not bound, usually enclosed in a paper cover. **2.** a short essay or treatise, usually on a current or controversial issue, published in this form. [Medieval Latin (in England) *panfletus* a little book, from Old French *Pamphilet,* popular name of *Pamphilus seu de Amore* Pamphilus or About Love, a medieval Latin poem that was first published as a small booklet containing a few pages.]

pam·phlet·eer (pam'fli tîr') *n.* a person who writes or publishes pamphlets. —*v.i.* to write or issue pamphlets.

pan[1] (pan) *n.* **1.** a broad, shallow container, usually made of metal and without a cover, used for cooking, holding liquids, and other household purposes. **2.** any similar vessel or receptacle, as the container used to separate precious minerals from gravel by washing with water, or either of the two dishes for holding objects on a pair of scales. **3.** the amount a pan will hold. **4.** a layer of hard subsoil; hardpan. **5.** a hollow depression in the ground. —*v.,* **panned, pan·ning.** —*v.t.* **1.** to cook in a pan. **2.** *Informal.* to give an unfavorable review to; criticize harshly: *The critics panned the new musical comedy.* **3.a.** to separate (gold or other precious minerals) from gravel by washing in a pan. **b.** to wash (earth, gravel, or other material) in a pan to separate the gold or other precious minerals. —*v.i.* **1.** to wash earth or gravel in a pan in search for gold or other precious minerals: *The prospector panned for gold.* **2.** (of gravel) to yield gold or other precious minerals when washed in a pan. [Old English *panne* the container, possibly going back to Latin *patina* broad, shallow dish, from Greek *patanē* flat dish.]

· **to pan out.** *Informal.* to turn out well; succeed.

pan[2] (pan) *v.i., v.t.,* **panned, pan·ning.** (of a motion picture or television camera) to move or be moved so as to take in a wide area or follow a moving object. —*n.* the act of panning. [From PANORAMA.]

Pan (pan) *n.* in Greek mythology, the god of forests, fields, flocks, and shepherds, characteristically depicted as a man with the horns, ears, legs, and tail of a goat.

pan- *combining form* **1.** all; every: *panchromatic.* **2.a.** *usually,* **Pan-.** of, including, or applying to all (members of a specified group or area): *Pan-American, Panhellenic.* **b.** advocating or designating the cooperation or union of all (members of a specified group or area): *Pan-Americanism.* [Greek *pān,* neuter of *pās* all, every.]

pan·a·ce·a (pan'ə sē'ə) *n.* a remedy for all diseases or evils; cure-all. [Latin *panacēa,* from Greek *panakeia.*]

pa·nache (pə nash', -näsh') *n.* **1.** a dashing or flamboyant manner; elegance or flair. **2.** an ornamental plume, usually worn on a helmet or cap. [French *panache* plume, swagger, going back to Latin *penna* wing, feather.]

pan·a·ma (pan'ə mä') *also,* **Pan·a·ma.** *n.* a hat made from the young leaves of a palmlike tropical American plant.

Pan-A·mer·i·can (pan'ə mer'i kən) *adj.* including or relating to all the countries or people of North, Central, and South America.

Pan-A·mer·i·can·ism (pan'ə mer'i kə niz'əm) *n.* a policy promoting cooperation in social, cultural, economic, and peacekeeping activities among nations of the Western Hemisphere.

pan-broil (pan'broil') *v.t.,* **-broiled, -broil·ing.** to cook in a skillet over direct heat, using little or no fat.

pan·cake (pan'kāk') *n.* **1.** a thin, flat cake of batter, cooked in a pan or on a griddle; griddlecake; flapjack. **2.** a landing in which an airplane levels off in the air and drops flat onto the landing surface. Also, **pancake landing.** —*v.,* **-caked, -cak·ing.** —*v.i.* (of an airplane) to make a pancake landing. —*v.t.* to cause (an airplane) to make a pancake landing.

pan·chro·mat·ic (pan'krō mat'ik) *adj.* sensitive to light of all colors, as a photographic film. —**pan·chro·ma·tism** (pan krō'mə tiz'əm), *n.*

pan·cre·as (pan'krē əs) *n.* a long, narrow gland below the stomach that secretes enzymes into the small intestine and the hormone insulin into the bloodstream. [Modern Latin *pancreas,* from Greek *pankreas,* from *pān-* (see PAN-) + *kreas* flesh; because it is all meat without any bone.] —**pan'cre·at'ic,** *adj.*

pan·cre·at·ic juice (pan'krē at'ik) a clear, watery fluid containing the digestive enzymes secreted by the pancreas.

pan·da (pan'də) *n.* **1.** a bearlike mammal, *Ailuropoda melanoleuca,* native to the bamboo forests of the mountains of southwestern China, having a shaggy white coat with black markings. Length: 5 feet (1.5 meters). Also, **giant panda.** **2.** a reddish brown, raccoon-like mammal, *Ailurus fulgens,* native to the Himalayas, having short legs, a long, bushy, ringed tail, and a white face. Length: 3 feet (0.9 meter), including tail. Also, **lesser panda, red panda.** [From a Nepali word for the animal.]

panda

pan·dect (pan'dekt) *n.* **1.** *usually,* **pandects.** a complete body of laws. **2.** any comprehensive digest. **3. Pandects.** a digest of Roman civil law made by order of the Emperor Justinian in the sixth century A.D., consisting of fifty books. [Late Latin *pandectēs* Pandects, going back to Greek *pandektēs* comprehensive.]

pan·dem·ic (pan dem'ik) *adj.* (of a disease) epidemic over a large area and affecting all or a majority of a population. —*n.* a widespread epidemic that afflicts most of the population in the affected area. [Greek *pandēmos* relating to all the people + -IC.]

pan·de·mo·ni·um (pan'də mō'nē əm) *n.* **1.** wild disorder or uproar: *There was pandemonium in the arena when our team won.* **2.** a place or gathering of wild disorder or uproar. **3.** *also,* **Pandemonium. a.** the abode of all the demons. **b.** hell. [Modern Latin *Pandemonium,* from Greek *pan-* (see PAN-) + *daimōn* demon; coined by the English poet John Milton, 1608-74, as the name for the capital of hell.]

pan·der (pan'dər) *n.* **1.** a go-between in sexual intrigues; procurer; pimp. **2.** a person who indulges or exploits the weaknesses, vices, or prejudices of others. Also, **pan'der·er.** —*v.i.* to act as

a	at	e	end	o	hot	u	up	hw	white		(about
ā	ape	ē	me	ō	old	ū	use	ng	song		taken
ä	far	i	it	ô	fork	ü	rule	th	thin	ə	pencil
âr	care	ī	ice	oi	oil	u̇	pull	th	this		lemon
		îr	pierce	ou	out	ûr	turn	zh	measure		circus

a pander: *That writer panders to the public taste for violence in this novel.* [From *Pandarus,* a character in medieval legend who procured Cressida for Troilus.]

pan·dit (pun′dit) *n.* **1.** a Hindu scholar or learned man, knowledgeable in philosophy and Sanskrit. **2. Pandit.** a title of respect in India for such a person. [Hindi *pansit,* from Sanskrit *pansita.*]

Pan·do·ra (pan dôr′ə) *n.* in Greek mythology, the first mortal woman, whose curiosity led her to open a box into which Zeus had put all human evils and miseries, thus allowing them to escape into the world.

Pandora's box, a source of many unforeseen troubles.

pan·dow·dy (pan dou′dē) *n., pl.* **-dies.** a deep pie or pudding having only a top crust: *apple pandowdy.* [Of uncertain origin.]

pane (pān) *n.* **1.** one of the divisions of a window or door, filled with a sheet of glass or similar material. **2.** a sheet of glass or similar material for such a division. **3.** a panel, as in a door or ceiling. [Old French *pan* piece, part, from Latin *pannus* piece of cloth, rag.]

pan·e·gyr·ic (pan′ə jir′ik, -jī′rik) *n.* **1.** a formal speech or writing praising a person or thing; eulogy. **2.** elaborate praise; laudation. [Latin *panēgyricus* public eulogy, from Greek *panēgyrikos* relating to public assembly, praising, going back to *pān-* (see PAN-) + *agyris* assembly.] —**pan′e·gyr′i·cal,** *adj.* —**pan′e·gyr′i·cal·ly,** *adv.* —For Synonyms, see **eulogy.**

pan·e·gyr·ist (pan′ə jir′ist, -jī′rist) *n.* a person who speaks or writes panegyrics.

pan·e·gy·rize (pan′i jə rīz′) *v.,* **-rized, -riz·ing.** —*v.t.* to deliver or write a panegyric about; eulogize. —*v.i.* to write or deliver panegyrics.

pan·el (pan′əl) *n.* **1.** a section of a door, cabinet, or other surface, distinguished from the surrounding surface by being raised, recessed, or bordered. **2.** a flat piece of material, as of wood or plastic, made to be joined with others. **3.** a lengthwise section of fabric in a garment, as a skirt. **4.a.** a thin wooden board used as the surface for an oil painting. **b.** a painting on such a board. **c.** any picture or photograph much longer than it is wide. **5.** a board or other surface on which controls, instruments, or dials are mounted, as in an automobile or airplane. **6.** a group of persons selected for some purpose, such as to hold a discussion, judge a contest, or participate in something as a team: *a panel of experts.* **7.a.** a list of persons summoned for jury duty on a single case. **b.** the members of a jury. —*v.t.* to furnish or decorate with panels: *We paneled the living room with dark mahogany.* [Old French *panel* piece, piece of cloth, going back to Latin *pannus* piece of cloth, rag.]

panel discussion, a discussion of a specific topic by a selected group of speakers, usually before an audience.

pan·el·ing (pan′ə ling) *n.* **1.** wood or other material used to make panels. **2.** panels collectively.

pan·el·ist (pan′ə list) *n.* a person who serves on a panel or participates in a panel discussion.

panel truck, a small truck, pickup, or van with a fully enclosed cargo section, used esp. to make deliveries and to carry small loads.

pan·fish (pan′fish′) *n., pl.* **-fish.** any edible fish that can be fried whole in a pan.

pan·fry (pan′frī′, -frī′) *v.t.,* **-fried, -fry·ing.** to fry in a skillet over direct heat.

pang (pang) *n.* **1.** a sudden, sharp feeling of discomfort or pain: *pangs of hunger.* **2.** a sharp feeling of mental distress: *I felt pangs of guilt after lying to my friend.* [Of uncertain origin.]

pan·go·lin (pang gō′lin) *n.* any of several scale-covered, toothless mammals, order Pholidota, native to Asia, Africa, and certain Pacific islands, having sharp claws, a long extensile tongue, and usually a long tail. Length: 3-6 feet (0.9-1.8 meters), including tail. Also, **scaly anteater.** [Malay *peng-gōling* roller; referring to its habit of rolling itself into a ball.]

pan·han·dle[1] (pan′han′dəl) *n.* **1.** the handle of a pan. **2.** *also,* **Panhandle.** a narrow strip of projecting land that is attached to a larger landmass: *the Oklahoma panhandle.*

pan·han·dle[2] (pan′han′dəl) *v.,* **-dled, -dling.** —*v.i. Informal.* to beg, esp. in the streets. —*v.t.* to get by panhandling. [Of uncertain origin.] —**pan′han′dler,** *n.*

Pan·hel·len·ic (pan′hə len′ik) *also,* **pan·hel·len·ic.** *adj.* **1.** of or relating to all Greek people. **2.** of or relating to all Greek-letter fraternities and sororities.

pan·ic (pan′ik) *n.* **1.** a sudden, overpowering fear, esp. when affecting a number of persons at once. **2.** an instance of such fear: *There was a panic when the fire broke out.* **3.** a sudden and widespread financial crisis caused by a collapse of public confidence in banks, the stock market, foreign currencies, or other investments. **4.** *Slang.* a person or thing considered to be very amusing. —*v.,* **-icked, -ick·ing.** —*v.i.* to become affected with panic: *The children panicked when they realized they were lost.*

—*v.t.* **1.** to affect with panic. *The thunder and lightning panicked the horses.* **2.** *Slang.* to amuse greatly. —*adj.* of the nature of or resulting from panic; showing panic. [French *panique* sudden fear, from Greek *Pānikos* relating to Pan, who was said to inspire unreasoning fear by unexpected appearances.] —**pan′ick·y,** *adj.* —For Synonyms *(n.),* see **terror.**

panic button *Slang.* **to push** (or **hit** or **press**) **the panic button.** to react excitedly or in an irrational way to a situation.

pan·i·cle (pan′i kəl) *n.* a bushy flower cluster consisting of tiny stalked flowers that grow from secondary stems off the main stem. For illustration, see **inflorescence.** [Latin *pānicula,* diminutive of *pānus* thread wound round a bobbin.]

pan·ic-strick·en (pan′ik strik′ən) *adj.* overcome by panic.

pa·nic·u·late (pə nik′yə lāt′, -lit) *adj.* (of flowers) growing in a panicle.

pan·ni·er (pan′ē ər) *also,* **pan·ier.** *n.* **1.** a large basket for carrying goods, esp. one of a connected pair designed to be slung across the back of a pack animal or hung over the wheel of a bicycle. **2.** a framework of hoops formerly used to give fullness to the sides of a woman's skirt. **3.** a gathering of material at the sides of a skirt, used to give the effect of a pannier. [Old French *panier* basket, from Latin *pānārium* breadbasket, from *pānis* bread.]

pa·no·cha (pə nō′chə) *n.* **1.** a coarse Mexican sugar. **2.** penuche. [Spanish *panocha,* diminutive of *pan* bread, from Latin *pānis;* because they come in chunks that resemble small loaves of bread.]

pan·o·ply (pan′ə plē) *n., pl.* **-plies. 1.** any magnificent array or covering: *The lakes were surrounded by a panoply of mountains.* **2.** a complete suit of armor. [Greek *panopliā* complete suit of armor, from *pān-* (see PAN-) + *hopla* arms.] —**pan′o·plied,** *adj.*

pan·o·ram·a (pan′ə ram′ə, -rä′mə) *n.* **1.** a complete or unbroken view of an area in every direction: *From the mountaintop we could see the vast panorama of the valley below us.* **2.** a complete and comprehensive survey or presentation of a subject: *a panorama of the current political scene.* **3.** a picture or series of pictures representing a continuous scene, unrolled and passed continuously before the spectators. **4.** a continuously passing or changing scene. [PAN- + Greek *horāma* view.]

pan·o·ram·ic (pan′ə ram′ik, -rä′mik) *adj.* of or like a panorama. —**pan′o·ram′i·cal·ly,** *adv.*

pan·pipe (pan′pīp′) *also,* **Pan·pipe.** *n.* a primitive wind instrument consisting of a graduated series of reeds or tubes bound together, played by blowing across the top.

pan·sy (pan′zē) *n., pl.* **-sies. 1.** a velvety flower of a common garden plant, *Viola tricolor,* of the violet family, having five flat, overlapping petals and growing in a variety of colors. **2.** the plant bearing this flower, having many branching stems. [Old French *pensee* the flower, thought, from *penser* to think, from Latin *pēnsāre* to consider.]

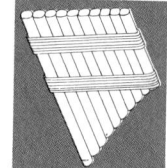

panpipe

pant[1] (pant) *v.i.* **1.** to breathe quickly, spasmodically, or heavily; gasp for breath: *I panted after running up the stairs.* **2.** to emit steam, smoke, or the like in loud puffs, as from an engine. **3.** to desire breathlessly; long eagerly; yearn (with *for* or *after*): *to pant for success.* **4.** to throb or pulsate rapidly, as the heart. —*v.t.* to utter breathlessly: *The drowning swimmer panted, "Help me!"* —*n.* **1.** a short or labored breath; gasp. **2.** a puff, as from an engine. **3.** a throb or pulsation, as of the heart. [Probably from Old French *pantaisier* to gasp, through an unrecorded Vulgar Latin word meaning "to gasp from a nightmare," going back to Greek *phantasiā* imagination, appearance.]

pant[2] (pant) *adj.* of, relating to, or including pants: *pant legs.* —*n.* pants.

pan·ta·lets (pan′tə lets′) *also,* **pan·ta·lettes.** *pl. n.* long ruffled drawers formerly worn by women and girls. [Diminutive of PANTALOON.]

pan·ta·loon (pan′tə lün′) *n.* **1. pantaloons.** tight-fitting trousers formerly worn by men. **2. Pantaloon.** a stock character in sixteenth-century Italian commedia dell'arte, usually a foolish old man wearing pantaloons and slippers. **3.** any similar stock character in modern pantomime, usually the object of the clown's jokes. [French *pantalon* the trousers, from Italian *Pantalone* Pantaloon, who represented Venetians, from *Pantaleone* Venetian saint and nickname given to Venetians.]

pan·the·ism (pan′thē iz′əm) *n.* **1.** the religious and philosophical theory that God and the universe are identical. **2.** a belief in and worship of all gods. —**pan′the·ist,** *n.* —**pan′the·is′tic;** *also,* **pan′the·is′ti·cal,** *adj.* —**pan′the·is′ti·cal·ly,** *adv.*

pan·the·on (pan′thē on′, -ən) *n.* **1. Pantheon.** a temple built at Rome by Agrippa in 27 B.C., rebuilt by Hadrian in A.D. 120-124 and, since A.D. 609, used as a Christian church. **2.** any temple dedicated to all the gods. **3.** all the gods of a people collectively.

4. a public building serving as a memorial or mausoleum for the famous people of a nation. [Latin *Panthēon* the Roman temple, going back to Greek *pantheios* common to all the gods, from *pān-* (see PAN-) + *theos* a god.]

pan·ther (pan′thər) *n., pl.* **-thers** or **-ther. 1.** a leopard, esp. one having a black coat. **2.** cougar. **3.** jaguar. [Old French *panthere* large wild animal of the cat family with spotted skin, from Latin *panthēra,* from Greek *panthēr.*]

pant·ies (pan′tēz) *also,* **pantie, panty.** *pl. n.* short underpants worn by girls and women. [From PANTS.]

pan·to·graph (pan′tə graf′) *n.* an instrument used for copying plane figures on any scale desired. It has a framework of four rods jointed in parallelogram form. [Greek *pant-,* stem of *pās* all + -GRAPH.]

pan·to·mime (pan′tə mīm′) *n.* **1.** a technique of conveying meaning or a story without speech, through the use of gestures, body movements, and facial expressions. **2.** a dramatic performance using this technique. **3.** a traditional English Christmas entertainment using stock characters, originally without speech, but later expanded to include dialogue. —*v.t., v.i.,* **-mimed, -mim·ing.** to act or express in pantomime. [Latin *pantomīmus* pantomimic actor, from Greek *pantomīmos,* from *pant-,* stem of *pās* all + *mīmos* imitator.] —**pan·to·mim·ic** (pan′tə mim′ik), *adj.* —**pan·to·mim·ist** (pan′tə mī′mist), *n.*

pan·to·then·ic acid (pan′tə then′ik) a yellow oily compound of the vitamin B complex required for obtaining energy from carbohydrates in the body, found esp. in eggs and liver. Formula: $C_9H_{17}O_5N$ [Greek *pantothen* on every side (from *pant-,* stem of *pās* all) + -IC + ACID.]

pan·try (pan′trē) *n., pl.* **-tries.** a room or closet in which food and articles connected with the preparation and serving of food are kept. [Old French *paneterie* place where bread is kept, from Medieval Latin *panetaria* place where bread is made, going back to Latin *pānis* bread.]

pants (pants) *pl. n.* **1.** trousers. **2.** underpants. [Short for *pantaloons,* plural of PANTALOON.]

pant·suit (pant′süt′) *also,* **pants suit.** *n.* a woman's outfit consisting of matching jacket and slacks.

pant·y (pan′tē) panties.

pan·ty·hose (pan′tē hōz′) *n.* a one-piece undergarment for women, combining panties and stockings.

pan·ty·waist (pan′tē wāst′) *n.* **1.** a child's two-piece undergarment buttoning at the waist. **2.** *Informal.* a weak or effeminate man or boy.

pan·zer (pan′zər) *adj.* of, relating to, or designating an armored military unit: *a panzer division.* [German *Panzer* armor, from Old French *panciere* coat of mail; literally, piece for the belly, from Latin *pantex* belly.]

pap (pap) *n.* **1.** soft or semiliquid food for infants or invalids. **2.** ideas, speech, or writing without real substance or value: *That magazine contains nothing but worthless pap.* **3.** money or favors given as political patronage. [Probably imitative of baby talk.]

pa·pa (pä′pə, pə pä′) *n.* father. [French *papa,* from Latin *pāpa.*]

pa·pa·cy (pā′pə sē) *n., pl.* **-cies. 1.** the office or authority of the pope. **2.** the tenure of a pope's reign. **3.** the line of the popes; popes collectively. **4.** the government of the Roman Catholic Church in which the Pope is supreme ruler. [Medieval Latin *papatia* dignity or authority of the pope, from Late Latin *pāpa.* See POPE.]

pa·pa·in (pə pā′in, -pī′-) *n.* an enzyme derived from unripe papaya that hydrolyzes protein, used primarily as a digestive aid and as a meat tenderizer. [PAPA(YA) + -IN¹.]

pa·pal (pā′pəl) *adj.* **1.** of or relating to the pope or the papacy: *papal influence, papal reforms.* **2.** of or relating to the Roman Catholic Church. [Medieval Latin *papalis* relating to the pope, from Late Latin *pāpa.* See POPE.]

pa·pa·raz·zi (pä′pə rät′sē) *pl. n., sing.* **-zo** (-rät′sō). newspaper or free-lance photographers who aggressively follow celebrities to obtain sensational pictures of their activities. [Italian *paparazzi,* plural of *paparazzo* this photographer, from the family name of such a photographer in *La Dolce Vita,* a 1959 film by the Italian film director Federico Fellini, born 1920, who had found the name in the Italian translation of *By the Ionian Sea,* by George Gissing, 1857-1903, English novelist.]

pa·paw (pə pô′, pô′pô′) *n.* **1.** pawpaw. **2.** papaya.

pa·pa·ya (pə pä′yə) *n.* **1.** the edible green to yellowish orange fruit of an evergreen tree, *Carica papaya,* having a thick rind, many small black seeds, and a fleshy pulp with a sweet musky flavor. **2.** the tree bearing this fruit, raised in warm regions, having a trunk crowned by a cluster of seven-lobed leaves. [Spanish *papaya* the fruit; of Carib origin.]

pa·per (pā′pər) *n.* **1.** a material made from matted fibers, such as those obtained from wood pulp, rags, and certain grasses, usually formed in thin flexible sheets, used for writing, printing, wrapping,

and many other purposes. **2.** a piece or sheet of this material: *I wrote my name at the top of the paper.* **3.** a sheet or sheets of this material bearing writing or printing; document: *We signed the adoption papers at the lawyer's office.* **4.** a written discourse, report, or essay: *to present a paper at a medical conference.* **5.** a written piece of schoolwork, such as an essay or examination: *a paper on the Spanish Civil War.* **6.** newspaper. **7. papers.** a collection of letters, journals, and other writings, esp. of one person: *the Churchill papers.* **8. papers.** a collection of documents that identify a person; credentials. **9.** a negotiable written or printed note, such as a check or promissory note. **10.** paper money. **11.** a card or sheet of paper holding something: *a paper of pins.* **12.** wallpaper. —*v.t.* to cover or decorate with paper, esp. wallpaper: *to paper a room.* —*v.i.* to hang wallpaper. —*adj.* **1.** made of or consisting of paper: *paper flowers.* **2.** like paper in thinness; flimsy: *These apartments have paper walls.* **3.** existing only in writing; never realized in actuality: *paper promises.* **4.** used to make paper: *paper pulp.* [Old French *papier* the material made from matted fibers, sheet for writing, from Latin *papȳrus* paper made of papyrus, papyrus plant, from Greek *papȳros* papyrus plant. Doublet of PAPYRUS.] —**pa′per·er,** *n.* —**pa′per·y,** *adj.*

• **on paper. a.** in written or printed form. **b.** in theory: *The idea looked good on paper, but it never worked out.*

pa·per·back (pā′pər bak′) *n.* a book bound in paper. —*adj.* paperbound.

pa·per·board (pā′pər bôrd′) *n.* a stiff material made of sheets of heavy paper pasted together or of paper pulp pressed together. —*adj.* made of paperboard: *a paperboard book cover.*

pa·per·bound (pā′pər bound′) *adj.* (of a book) bound in paper.

pa·per·boy (pā′pər boi′) *n.* a boy who sells or delivers newspapers, esp. to the home.

paper clip, a device made of bent wire or molded plastic, used to hold sheets of paper together.

pap·er·girl (pā′pər gûrl′) *n.* a girl who sells or delivers newspapers, esp. to the home.

pa·per·hang·er (pā′pər hang′ər) *n.* a person whose work is hanging wallpaper.

paper knife, a thin, dull knife used for cutting open sealed envelopes or the uncut pages of books.

paper money, currency printed on paper, issued by a government or authorized banks.

paper nautilus, a type of saltwater cephalopod, genus *Argonauta,* related to the octopus, the female of which secretes a delicate shell-like cradle in which her eggs are hatched.

paper profit, profit that can be realized only by the sale of something, as a stock, that has appreciated in value.

paper tiger, a person, organization, or country that gives the appearance of being strong and threatening but is actually weak or unable to act.

pa·per·weight (pā′pər wāt′) *n.* a small, heavy object, often ornamental, placed on top of papers to hold them down.

pa·per·work (pā′pər wûrk′) *n.* **1.** routine clerical work, esp. the keeping of administrative records: *The job involves a lot of paperwork.* **2.** work done on paper, esp. written forms or records: *We made sure that all the paperwork for the sale of the house was in order.*

pa·pier-mâ·ché (pā′pər mə shā′) *n.* a substance made of paper mixed with glue and other materials, which can be molded when moist and which hardens when dry. [French *papier-mâché* literally, chewed paper, going back to Latin *papȳrus* (see PAPYRUS) + Late Latin *masticātus,* past participle of *masticāre.* See MASTICATE.]

pa·pil·la (pə pil′ə) *n., pl.* **-pil·lae** (-pil′ē). **1.** a small knoblike projection of a hair follicle, containing tiny blood vessels that nourish the root of the hair. For illustration, see **hair. 2.** any of certain small protuberances located in or on the surface of various parts of the body, as on the tongue. Many are connected with the senses of touch, taste, or smell. **3.** any small, nipplelike projection. [Latin *papilla* nipple.] —**pap·il·lar·y** (pap′ə ler′ē), *adj.*

pap·il·lo·ma (pap′ə lō′mə) *n., pl.* **-ma·ta** (-mə tə) or **-mas.** a benign tumor, such as a wart, of the skin or adjoining mucous membrane, consisting of an overgrowth of epithelial tissue on papillae. —**pap′il·lo′ma·tous,** *adj.*

pa·pist (pā′pist) *n.* Roman Catholic. —*adj.* of, relating to, or like the Roman Catholic Church. ➡ used disparagingly. [Modern Latin *papista,* from Late Latin *pāpa.* See POPE.]

a	at	e	end	o	hot	u	up	hw	white		about
ā	ape	ē	me	ō	old	ū	use	ng	song	ə	taken
ä	far	i	it	ô	fork	ü	rule	th	thin		pencil
âr	care	ī	ice	oi	oil	u̇	pull	th	this		lemon
		îr	pierce	ou	out	ûr	turn	zh	measure		circus

P

pa·poose (pa püs′) *also,* **pap·poose.** *n.* a North American Indian baby or small child. [Algonquian *papoos* child.]

pap·pus (pap′əs) *n., pl.* **pap·pi** (pap′ī). an appendage on the seeds of certain plants, as the dandelion, consisting of scales, bristles, hairs, or similar structures that help keep the seed aloft as it is carried by the wind. [Modern Latin *pappus,* from Latin *pappus,* from Greek *pappos* old man, grandfather; referring to its resemblance to gray hairs.]

pap·py (pap′ē) *n., pl.* **-pies.** *Informal.* father. [Diminutive of PAPA.]

pap·ri·ka (pa prē′kə, pə-, pap′ri-) *n.* a reddish orange spice made from the powdered fruits of the sweet red pepper. [German *Paprika* red pepper, through Magyar and Serbo-Croatian, from Greek *peperi* pepper. See PEPPER.]

Pap smear (pap) a medical test in which a small sample of cells is wiped from the cervix or vagina and studied under a microscope for abnormalities. Also, **Pap test.** [From the Greek-American physician George Nicolas *Papanicolaou,* 1883-1962, who developed the test.]

Pap·u·an (pap′ū ən) *adj.* of, relating to, or characteristic of Papua New Guinea or its people, languages, or cultures. —*n.* **1.** a member of any of the indigenous peoples inhabiting Papua New Guinea and adjacent islands. **2.** any of a number of languages spoken predominantly in the southwest Pacific islands, constituting a separate language family.

pa·py·rus (pə pī′rəs) *n., pl.* **-ri** (-rī). **1.** a stiff grasslike plant, *Cyperus papyrus,* found growing in swamps and along rivers in northern Africa and southern Europe, having dark green hollow stalks. **2.** a writing material made from the stems of this plant by the ancient Egyptians. **3.** an ancient manuscript or document written on this material. [Latin *papyrus* the plant and the paper, from Greek *papyros* the plant. Doublet of PAPER.]

par (pär) *n.* **1.** an average or normal amount, degree, quality, or condition: *Your performance is above par.* **2.** an equal or common level: *Her work is on a par with his.* **3.** a state of equality between the face value and the market value of bonds, shares of stock, and other financial instruments. If a stock is selling at par, it is selling at the value actually printed on the stock certificate. **4.** a ratio of the monetary unit of one country to the monetary unit of another country, based on the same standard of value. **5.** *Golf.* the number of strokes set as a standard minimum of skillful play for a hole or course. —*adj.* **1.** average or normal. **2.** in commerce, of or at par: *the par value of a bond.* [Latin *pār* equal.]

par-, form of **para-**[1] before vowels and *h,* as in *parody, parhelion.*

par. **1.** paragraph. **2.** parallel. **3.** parenthesis. **4.** parish.

para-[1] *prefix* **1.** beside; near; along with: *parallel, paraphrase, parasympathetic.* **2.** beyond; aside from: *paradox.* **3.** disordered; abnormal; malfunctioning: *paranoia, paraplegia.* **4.** similar to; resembling: *paratyphoid.* **5.** subordinate to: *paraprofessional.* [Greek *para* beside, beyond.]

para-[2] *combining form* **1.** protection against: *parachute, parasol.* **2.** using a parachute: *paratroops.* [French *para-* guarding against, from Italian *para* ward off, imperative of *parare* to ward off, from Latin *parāre* to make ready.]

par·a·a·mi·no·ben·zo·ic acid (par′ə ə mē′nō ben zō′ik, -am′ə-nō-) a member of the vitamin B complex that is essential for growth, used in suntan lotion to absorb ultraviolet rays and in the manufacture of dyes and pharmaceuticals. Formula: $C_7H_7NO_2$ Also, **PABA.**

par·a·ble (par′ə bəl) *n.* a short allegorical story illustrating some truth or moral lesson. [Latin *parabola* allegory, comparison, proverb, from Greek *parabolē* comparison, proverb; literally, a throwing beside, from *para* beside + *ballein* to throw. Doublet of PALAVER, PAROLE.]

pa·rab·o·la (pə rab′ə lə) *n., pl.* **-las.** an open curve consisting of

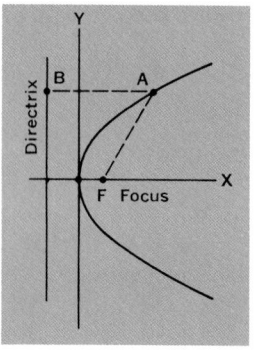

parabola

a set of points in a plane that lie at equal distances from a fixed point, or focus, and a fixed line, or directrix; conic section formed by the intersection of a cone and a plane parallel to a side of the cone. [Modern Latin *parabola,* from Greek *parabolē* juxtaposition, comparison. See PARABLE.]

par·a·bol·ic[1] (par′ə bol′ik) *adj.* of, resembling, or expressed in a parable. Also, **par′a·bol′i·cal.** [Late Latin *parabolicus,* from Late Greek *parabolikos* figurative, from *parabolē.* See PARABLE.] —**par′a·bol′i·cal·ly,** *adv.*

par·a·bol·ic[2] (par′ə bol′ik) *adj.* of, relating to, or having the form of a parabola. [PARABOLA + -IC.]

par·a·chute (par′ə shüt′) *n.* **1.** an umbrellalike device for retarding the speed of a body falling through air from a great height, usually used to drop a person or object safely to the ground from an aircraft and sometimes used for recreation. **2.** any similar device for retarding speed, as of an aircraft in landing. —*v.,* **-chut·ed, -chut·ing.** —*v.i.* to descend by parachute: *The soldiers parachuted into the war zone.* —*v.t.* to drop, as troops or supplies, by parachute. [French *parachute* the device, from *para-* guarding against (see PARA-[2]) + *chute* fall. See CHUTE.]

parachute

par·a·chut·ist (par′ə shü′tist) *n.* a person who uses a parachute or is skilled in parachuting.

pa·rade (pə rād′) *n.* **1.** an organized, often ceremonial march or procession in honor of a person or special occasion: *a circus parade, a Memorial Day parade.* **2.** a long line or succession, as of people; array. **3.** a pretentious display; exhibition: *to make a parade of one's wealth.* **4.** a public place where people promenade. **5.** the people who promenade. **6.** a procession or assembly of troops for inspection, display, or review. —*v.,* **-rad·ed, -rad·ing.** —*v.i.* **1.** to march publicly in an organized procession: *The band paraded through town.* **2.** to walk about to show oneself off. **3.** to march or assemble for military review or inspection. —*v.t.* **1.** to walk through or down, as in an organized procession. **2.** to display ostentatiously; make a show of: *to parade one's knowledge before everyone.* **3.** to cause (troops) to march in review or assemble for inspection: *The company commander paraded the troops before the visiting dignitaries.* [French *parade* military review, display, through Spanish, going back to Latin *parāre* to make ready.] —**pa·rad′er,** *n.*

·on parade. on display; in review.

parade rest, in military drill, a formal position of rest in which the feet are placed 12 inches (30 centimeters) apart, the hands are clasped behind the back, and the head faces forward and is held motionless.

par·a·digm (par′ə dīm′, -dim) *n.* **1.** a pattern or example. **2.** *Grammar.* a list of all the inflectional forms of a word, used as a pattern for other words of the same class. [Late Latin *paradīgma* example, from Greek *paradeigma* example, model.] —**par·a·dig·mat·ic** (par′ə dig mat′ik), *adj.*

par·a·dise (par′ə dīs′, -dīz′) *n.* **1.** the abode of God, the angels, and those who are saved; heaven. **2.** any place of extreme beauty or delight. **3.** a state of supreme happiness or bliss. **4. Paradise.** Garden of Eden. [Late Latin *paradīsus* heaven, Garden of Eden, park, from Greek *paradeisos;* of Persian origin.] —**par·a·dis·i·ac** (par′ə dis′ē ak′, -diz′-); *also,* **par·a·di·si·a·cal** (par′ə di sī′ə kəl, -zī′-), *adj.* —**par·a·di·si·a·cal·ly,** *adv.*

par·a·dox (par′ə doks′) *n.* **1.** a statement that seems to be contradictory or absurd, but in fact may be true. The statement *Liberty is the only thing you cannot have unless you are willing to give it to others* is a paradox. **2.** a statement that is in fact self-contradictory and therefore untrue: *I puzzled my friends with this paradox: "All that I say is false, including this statement."* **3.** any seemingly contradictory person or thing. [Latin *paradoxum* something unexpected, from Greek *paradoxos* contrary to or beyond expectation, incredible.] —**par′a·dox′i·cal,** *adj.* —**par′a·dox′i·cal·ly,** *adv.*

par·af·fin (par′ə fin) *n.* **1.** a solid, waxy, white substance obtained from petroleum and used esp. in the making of candles, waxed paper, and cosmetics. **2.** alkane. —*v.t.* to treat or saturate with paraffin. [German *Paraffin* the waxy substance, from Latin *parum* too little + *affinis* related; because it has little affinity for other materials.] —**par·af·fin·ic** (par′ə fin′ik), *adj.*

par·a·gon (par′ə gon′) *n.* a model or pattern of excellence or perfection: *You are a paragon of virtue.* [Obsolete French *paragon,* from Italian *paragone* touchstone, going back to Greek *para* beside + *akonē* whetstone.]

par·a·graph (par′ə graf′) *n.* **1.** a distinct unified section of a chapter, article, or other written matter, usually consisting of a number of sentences on one particular point or idea, and begun on a new, usually indented, line. **2.** a brief article or item, as in a

newspaper. **3.** a mark (¶) used in printing and writing to indicate the beginning of a paragraph or to refer to other material, such as a footnote or appendix. —*v.t.* **1.** to arrange in or divide into paragraphs: *The editor paragraphed the story.* **2.** to write about or express in a paragraph. [Medieval Latin *paragraphus* mark indicating a section of writing, from Greek *paragraphos* line in the margin (indicating a break in sense), from *para* beside + *graphein* to write.] —**par′a·graph′er,** *n.*

par·a·keet (par′ə kēt′) *also,* **paraquet, parrakeet.** *n.* any of various small parrots, usually having brightly colored plumage, able to imitate speech, and often kept as cage birds. Length: 7-12 inches (18-30 centimeters). [Old French *paroquet* parrot, possibly modification of *Perrot,* diminutive of *Pierre* Peter. See PARROT.]

par·a·le·gal (par′ə lē′gəl) *n.* a person who is trained to assist lawyers and to perform certain legal tasks but who does not have a license to practice law. —*adj.* of or relating to a paralegal or paralegals.

Par·a·li·pom·e·non (par′ə li pom′ə non′) *n.* in the Douay Bible, either of two books of the Old Testament corresponding to I and II Chronicles.

par·al·lac·tic (par′ə lak′tik) *adj.* of or relating to a parallax: *parallactic shift.*

par·al·lax (par′ə laks′) *n.* the apparent shift in the position of an object, relative to its background, that occurs when an observer changes position. In astronomy, parallax is used to determine the distances of nearby stars. [Greek *parallaxis* alternation, change.]

par·al·lel (par′ə lel′, -ləl) *adj.* **1.** extending in the same direction and always the same distance apart at every point, so as never to meet, such as lines or planes: *The rails of a railroad track are parallel.* **2.** closely similar or corresponding, as in direction, meaning, or development: *parallel opinions, parallel careers.* **3.** having statements expressed in the same grammatical form: *parallel wording.* —*n.* **1.** a parallel line, plane, or surface. **2.** close similarity or correspondence: *We can find many parallels in the customs of those two tribes.* **3.** a person or thing that closely resembles or corresponds to another; counterpart. **4.** a comparison to show similarity or correspondence: *The teacher drew a parallel between the two wars.* **5.a.** any of the imaginary lines that circle the earth parallel to the equator, designating degrees of latitude. **b.** a marking on a map, globe, or chart representing such a line. —*v.t.,* **-leled, -lel·ing;** *also, British,* **-lelled, -lel·ling. 1.** to be or lie in a direction parallel to: *The railroad tracks paralleled the highway.* **2.** to cause to be or lie in a parallel direction; make parallel. **3.** to be similar or equal to; correspond to: *The growth of the town paralleled that of the country.* **4.** to show, find, or furnish a parallel or equal for. **5.** to compare in order to show similarity of; liken. —*adv.* in a parallel manner or direction (often with *to* or *with*): *The highway runs parallel with the river.* [Latin *parallēlus* extending in the same direction and equidistant, from Greek *parallēlos* side by side.]

• **in parallel.** (of electric circuits) connected so as to form separate paths between the positive and negative terminals of the current source for each object, as each light, in the circuit. ➡ opposed to **in series.**

parallel bars, two poles set parallel to each other and supported by adjustable uprights, used in gymnastics.

par·al·lel·e·pi·ped (par′ə lel′ə pī′ped) *n.* a polyhedron with six faces that are all parallelograms. Also, **par·al·lel·e·pip·e·don** (par′ə lel′ə pip′i don′). [Greek *parallēlepipedon* body with parallel surfaces, from *parallēlos* side by side + *epipedon* plane surface.]

par·al·lel·ism (par′ə le liz′əm) *n.* **1.** the state or condition of being parallel. **2.** a close similarity or resemblance; correspondence. **3.** a similarity in grammatical form of the elements of a phrase or sentence.

par·al·lel·o·gram (par′ə lel′ə gram′) *n.* a polygon with four sides whose opposite sides are parallel and equal in length. Squares, rectangles, and rhombuses are parallelograms. [Greek *parallēlogrammon,* from *parallēlos* side by side + *grammē* line[1].]

pa·ral·y·sis (pə ral′ə sis) *n., pl.* **-ses** (-sēz′). **1.** a loss of the power of motion or sensation in a part of the body due to disease of, or an injury to, the nervous system. **2.** a state of inactivity or inability to act: *The war caused a paralysis of normal trade.* [Latin *paralysis* the medical condition, from Greek *paralysis* disabling of the nerves. Doublet of PALSY.]

par·a·lyt·ic (par′ə lit′ik) *adj.* **1.** of, relating to, or characteristic of paralysis. **2.** having paralysis. —*n.* a person who has paralysis.

par·a·lyze (par′ə līz′) *v.t.,* **-lyzed, -lyz·ing. 1.** to affect with paralysis; make paralytic. **2.** to make helpless, powerless, or ineffective: *The bus strike paralyzed the city.*

par·a·me·ci·um (par′ə mē′shē əm, -sē əm) *n., pl.* **-ci·a** (-shē ə, -sē ə). a microscopic, slipper-shaped freshwater protozoan, genus *Paramecium,* having cilia that provide locomotion and help to sweep food into its oral groove. [Modern Latin *paramecium,* from Greek *paramēkēs* oblong.]

Contractile vacuole · Macronucleus · Cilia · Micronucleus · Cytoplasm · Food vacuole

paramecium

par·a·med·ic (par′ə med′ik) *n.* a person who is specially trained to help a doctor and to administer first aid at the site of an emergency.

par·a·med·i·cal (par′ə med′i kəl) *adj.* of, relating to, or designating personnel whose work is auxiliary to that of medical professionals, as paramedics or laboratory technicians. [PARA-[1] + MEDICAL.]

pa·ram·e·ter (pə ram′i tər) *n.* **1.** a quantity in a mathematical expression that is constant in a particular case under consideration but varies in different cases. In the equation for a circle, $x^2 + y^2 = a^2$, the quantity a^2 is a parameter determining the radius and varies with the size of the circle. **2.** any constant in a given situation that determines or limits other conditions of that situation. **3.** *usually,* **parameters.** a limit or boundary. **4.** a characteristic or element; factor. [PARA-[1] + Greek *metron* measure.] —**par·a·met·ric** (par′ə met′rik), *adj.*

par·a·mil·i·tar·y (par′ə mil′i ter′ē) *adj.* **1.** organized on a military basis but not officially part of a country's military forces: *paramilitary guerrilla fighters.* **2.** of, relating to, or composed of a paramilitary force: *a paramilitary expedition.*

par·a·mount (par′ə mount′) *adj.* above all others, as in influence or importance; preeminent; supreme: *The children's welfare was my paramount consideration.* [Anglo-Norman *par amont* at the top, above, going back to Latin *per* through, beyond + *ad montem* to a mountain, upward.]

par·a·mour (par′ə mùr′) *n.* a lover, esp. of a person who is married to someone else. [Old French *par amour* by love, from Latin *per* by + *amor* love.]

par·a·noi·a (par′ə noi′ə) *n.* **1.** a psychotic condition marked by feelings of grandeur or persecution. **2.** a tendency to distrust others and to regard everyone as an enemy. [Modern Latin *paranoia,* from Greek *paranoia* derangement, going back to *para* beyond + *nous* mind.]

par·a·noid (par′ə noid′) *adj.* relating to, characteristic of, or affected with paranoia. —*n.* a person who is affected with paranoia. Also, **par·a·noi·ac** (par′ə noi′ak).

par·a·nor·mal (par′ə nôr′məl) *adj.* outside the range of human knowledge or comprehension; beyond normal perception: *paranormal powers of communication.*

par·a·pet (par′ə pit, -pet′) *n.* **1.** a low wall of earth or stone, esp. on a rampart, to protect troops from observation or fire. **2.** a low wall or railing around the edge of a balcony, roof, or other structure. [Italian *parapetto* breast-high wall, from *para* (see PARA-[2]) + *petto* breast (from Latin *pectus*).] —**par′a·pet·ed,** *adj.*

par·a·pher·nal·ia (par′ə fər nāl′yə) *n.* **1.** personal belongings. **2.** equipment used for a particular purpose or activity; gear. ➡ used as singular or plural. [Medieval Latin *paraphernalia* (goods) of a bride in addition to her dowry, through Latin, from Greek *parapherna,* from *para* beyond, beside + *phernē* dowry.]

parapet

par·a·phrase (par′ə frāz′) *n.* a restatement of the meaning of a phrase or passage. —*v.t., v.i.,* **-phrased, -phras·ing.** to express in or make a paraphrase. [Latin *paraphrasis* restatement of the meaning of a passage, from Greek *paraphrasis.*]

par·a·ple·gi·a (par′ə plē′jē ə, -plē′jə) *n.* paralysis of both legs and the lower part of the trunk. [Modern Latin *paraplegia,* from Greek *paraplēgiā* paralysis of one side (of the body).]

a	at	e	end	o	hot	u	up	hw	white		about
ā	ape	ē	me	ō	old	ū	use	ng	song	ə	taken
ä	far	i	it	ô	fork	ü	rule	th	thin		pencil
âr	care	ī	ice	oi	oil	ů	pull	th	this		lemon
		îr	pierce	ou	out	ûr	turn	zh	measure		circus

par·a·ple·gic (par′ə plē′jik) *adj.* paralyzed in both legs and the lower part of the trunk. —*n.* a person who is paraplegic.

par·a·pro·fes·sion·al (par′ə prə fesh′ə nəl) *n.* a person who works with and assists a lawyer, teacher, or other professional, but is not licensed to practice alone.

par·a·psy·chol·o·gy (par′ə sī kol′ə jē) *n.* the study of extrasensory perception and other psychic phenomena. —**par′a·psy·cho·log·i·cal** (par′ə sī′kə loj′i kəl), *adj.* —**par′a·psy·chol′o·gist,** *n.*

par·a·quat (par′ə kwot′) *n.* a highly toxic, volatile herbicide, used esp. as a weed killer.

par·a·quet (par′ə ket′) parakeet.

par·a·sang (par′ə sang′) *n.* an ancient Persian measure of length, varying from 2 to 4 miles (3.2 to 6.4 kilometers). [Latin *parasanga,* from Greek *parasangēs;* of Persian origin.]

par·a·site (par′ə sīt′) *n.* **1.** an animal or plant that lives on or in another organism of a different species and obtains all or part of its food from that organism while contributing nothing to its survival. Fleas, tapeworms, and mistletoe are parasites. **2.** a person who lives off another or who associates with another for personal gain while providing nothing in return. [Latin *parasītus* one who lives off another, from Greek *parasītos* one who eats at the table of another, from *para* beside + *sītos* food; with reference to the men in ancient Greece and Rome who offered flattery in return for food or support.]

par·a·sit·ic (par′ə sit′ik) *adj.* **1.** of or relating to a parasite. **2.** caused by a parasite: *a parasitic disease.* Also, **par′a·sit′i·cal.** —**par′a·sit′i·cal·ly,** *adv.*

par·a·sit·i·cide (par′ə sit′ə sīd′) *n.* any substance or agent capable of destroying parasites, esp. those living on or in the skin. [PARASIT(E) + -CIDE².] —**par′a·sit′i·cid′al,** *adj.*

par·a·sit·ism (par′ə sī tiz′əm) *n.* **1.** *Biology.* a close and intimate association between two organisms of different species in which one benefits and the other is often harmed; relationship between a parasite and its host. **2.** *Medicine.* the condition of being infected with parasites.

par·a·si·tize (par′ə si tīz′, -sī-) *v.t.,* **-tized, -tiz·ing.** to infest or live on or with as a parasite. —**par′a·sit′i·za′tion,** *n.*

par·a·si·tol·o·gy (par′ə sī tol′ə jē, -si-) *n.* the branch of biology dealing with parasites and parasitism. —**par′a·si·to·log′i·cal,** *adj.* —**par′a·si·tol′o·gist,** *n.*

par·a·sol (par′ə sôl′, -sol′) *n.* a small, light, decorative umbrella, used esp. by women for protection from the sun. [French *parasol,* from Italian *parasole,* from *para* (see PARA-²) + *sole* sun (from Latin *sōl*).]

par·a·sym·pa·thet·ic nervous system (par′ə sim′pə thet′-ik) the part of the autonomic nervous system that opposes the actions of the sympathetic nervous system. Its functions include slowing the heart rate, dilating blood vessels, contracting the pupils, and inducing secretion in the digestive glands. ➡ distinguished from **sympathetic nervous system.**

par·a·thi·on (par′ə thī′on) *n.* a colorless or brown toxic liquid used in agriculture as an insecticide. Formula: $C_{10}H_{14}NO_5PS$

par·a·thy·roid gland (par′ə thī′roid) any of several small endocrine glands behind the thyroid gland, producing a hormone that regulates the body's use of calcium and phosphorus.

par·a·troop (par′ə trüp′) *adj.* of or relating to paratroops.

par·a·troop·er (par′ə trü′pər) *n.* a member of the paratroops. [PARA(CHUTE) + TROOPER.]

par·a·troops (par′ə trüps′) *pl. n.* a group of soldiers trained to parachute from airplanes into the area of their objective.

par·a·ty·phoid fever (par′ə tī′foid) a disease resembling typhoid fever but usually milder, caused by a different species of salmonella than the one that causes typhoid. [PARA-¹ + TYPHOID.]

par a·vion (pär ä vyôN′) *French.* by air mail.

par·boil (pär′boil′) *v.t.* to cook partially by boiling, usually for a short time. [Old French *parbouillir* to cook thoroughly, from Late Latin *perbullīre,* from Latin *per* through + *bullīre* to boil; meaning influenced by association with PART.]

Par·cae (pär′sē) *pl. n.* in Roman mythology, the three Fates.

par·cel (pär′səl) *n.* **1.** a thing or group of things packed together; package; bundle: *A parcel of books arrived in the mail.* **2.** a distinct portion of land. **3.** a group of similar persons or things; pack; bunch: *a parcel of fools.* **4.** a quantity of merchandise put up for sale. —*v.t.,* **-celed** or **-celled, -cel·ing** or **-cel·ling.** to divide into sections or distribute in portions: *to parcel up land.* [Old French *parcelle* small part, going back to Latin *particula,* diminutive of *pars* portion.] —For Synonyms, see **package.**

parcel post 1. a classification of mail, used esp. for packages weighing 16 ounces (0.5 kilogram) or more. **2.** the branch of the postal service handling such mail. **3.** mail handled by this service.

parch (pärch) *v.t.* **1.** to make very dry or shriveled, as by exposure to heat: *The summer sun parched the lawn.* **2.** to make very thirsty. **3.** to dry by roasting slightly: *to parch peanuts.* —*v.i.* **1.** to become very dry or hot, as by exposure to heat. **2.** to become very thirsty. [Of uncertain origin.]

Par·chee·si (pär chē′zē) *n. Trademark.* a board game in which each player tries to be the first to move his or her tokens into a home square, with the moves governed by throws of the dice.

parch·ment (pärch′mənt) *n.* **1.** the skin of sheep, goats, or other animals, prepared for writing or painting upon. **2.** a manuscript or document written on this material. **3.** any of several types of paper made to resemble this material. [Old French *parchemin* such skin, modification (influenced by Latin *Parthica pellis* Parthian leather) of Latin *pergamīna,* from Greek *pergamēnē,* from *Pergamon,* city in Asia Minor where it was first produced.]

pard¹ (pärd) *n. Archaic.* leopard; panther. [Latin *pardus* male panther, from Greek *pardos.*]

pard² (pärd) *n. Slang.* a close friend; partner. [Short for PARD-NER.]

pard·ner (pärd′nər) *n. Slang.* a close friend; chum. [Modification of PARTNER.]

par·don (pär′dən) *v.t.* **1.** to release (a person) from punishment for an offense: *The governor pardoned the condemned prisoner.* **2.** to pass over (an offense) without exacting penalty or placing blame; forgive. **3.a.** to overlook as a courtesy: *Please pardon my interruption.* **b.** to grant courteous tolerance to: *Pardon me if I appeared rude.* —*n.* **1.** a release from punishment for an offense. **2.** a document or official warrant granting such a release. **3.** polite forbearance, as for a discourtesy. **4.** the act of passing over without exacting penalty or placing blame: *You have my pardon for your recent actions.* **5.** in the Roman Catholic Church, a release from temporal punishment due to sin; indulgence. [Old French *pardonner* to forgive, bestow, from Late Latin *perdōnāre* to remit, give wholeheartedly, from Latin *per* through + *dōnāre* to give.] —**par′don·a·ble,** *adj.* —**par′don·a·bly,** *adv.* —For Synonyms *(v.t.),* see **excuse.**

par·don·er (pär′də nər, pärd′nər) *n.* **1.** in the Middle Ages, a person who was authorized to grant ecclesiastical indulgences. **2.** a person who pardons.

pare (pâr) *v.t.,* **pared, par·ing. 1.** to cut or peel off the outer layer or skin of: *to pare an apple.* **2.** to cut, trim, or shave off (an outer layer or part): *to pare the bark from a twig.* **3.** to reduce or lessen (often with *down*): *to pare down an essay, to pare expenses.* [Old French *parer* to trim, from Latin *parāre* to make ready.]

par·e·gor·ic (par′ə gôr′ik) *n.* a medicine containing opium and camphor, used primarily to treat diarrhea. [Late Latin *parēgoricus* assuaging, from Greek *parēgorikos* soothing, going back to *para* beside + *agorā* public assembly.]

paren., parenthesis.

pa·ren·chy·ma (pə reng′kə mə) *n.* **1.** the basic tissue in plants, consisting of unspecialized thin-walled cells that are able to differentiate into other specialized types of cells. **2.** the basic tissue of an animal organ, contained in and supported by connective tissue. [Modern Latin *parenchyma,* from Greek *parenchyma* tissue of internal organs, from *parenchein* to pour in beside; referring to the belief that the tissues of these organs were poured in by their blood vessels.] —**pa·ren′chy·mal, par·en·chym·a·tous** (par′əng-kim′ə təs), *adj.*

par·ent (pâr′ənt) *n.* **1.** a person who produces offspring; father or mother. **2.** a person who performs the functions of a father or mother. **3.** any organism that produces offspring. **4.** anything regarded as a cause; origin or source: *Virtue is the parent of good deeds.* —*adj.* **1.** of or designating a predecessor or original: *a parent group.* **2.** of or designating a corporation in relation to a subsidiary: *a parent company.* —*v.i., v.t.* to raise (a child or children). [Latin *parēns* father or mother.]

par·ent·age (pâr′ən tij) *n.* **1.** descent from parents; origin. **2.** the state of being a parent; parenthood.

pa·ren·tal (pə ren′təl) *adj.* **1.** of, relating to, or characteristic of a parent or parents: *parental duties.* **2.** *Genetics.* relating to or designating the generation that precedes the filial one. —**pa·ren′tal·ly,** *adv.*

par·en·ter·al (pa ren′tər əl) *adj.* **1.** situated or occurring outside the intestine, but within the body. **2.** introduced by any way other than through the digestive system, as intramuscularly or intravenously. —*n.* a drug or solution intended for parenteral use. [PAR- + ENTERO- + -AL¹.] —**par·en′ter·al·ly,** *adv.*

pa·ren·the·sis (pə ren′thə sis) *n., pl.* **-ses** (-sēz′). **1.** a word, phrase, or clause inserted as an explanation or qualification in a sentence that would be grammatically complete without it, usually set off by curved marks. **2.** either of the curved marks ( ) used to set off such material, or to enclose symbols or numbers to be considered as a single entity. **3.** a remark or comment that digresses from a main theme. **4.** an episode that is a break in continuity. [Medieval Latin *parenthesis* insertion, from Greek *parenthesis.*]

pa·ren·the·size (pə ren′thə sīz′) *v.t.*, **-sized, -siz·ing. 1.** to enclose within marks of parentheses. **2.** to insert or express as a parenthesis. **3.** to insert parentheses in, as a speech.

par·en·thet·i·cal (par′ən thet′i kəl) *adj.* **1.** inserted as qualifying or explanatory material: *a parenthetical remark.* **2.** using or containing parentheses: *a parenthetical style.* **3.** placed within parentheses: *Each foreign word was followed by a parenthetical translation.* Also, **par′en·thet′ic.** —**par′en·thet′i·cal·ly,** *adv.*

par·ent·hood (pâr′ənt hud′) *n.* the state of being a parent.

par·ent·ing (pâr′ən ting) *n.* **1.** the raising of a child or children. **2.** the methods used in raising children: *a course in parenting.*

pa·re·sis (pə rē′sis, par′ə-) *n.* **1.** a partial paralysis in which movement, but not sensation, is impaired. **2.** general paresis. [Modern Latin *paresis,* from Greek *paresis* a letting go.]

pa·ret·ic (pə ret′ik) *adj.* relating to, affected with, or caused by a paresis. —*n.* a person who is affected with a paresis.

par ex·cel·lence (pär ek′sə läns′) in the highest degree; beyond comparison: *a musician par excellence.* [French *par excellence* literally, by way of excellence, going back to Latin *per* through + *excellentia* excellence.]

par ex·em·ple (pär eg zän′plə) *French.* for example.

par·fait (pär fā′) *n.* **1.** a dessert made of layers of ice cream, syrup, and sometimes fruit, usually served in a tall slender glass. **2.** a dessert made of custard or whipped cream and syrup frozen together. [French *parfait* perfect, going back to Latin *perficere* to finish.]

par·he·lion (pär hēl′yən) *n., pl.* **-he·lia** (-hēl′yə). a bright spot resembling the sun, seen on a solar halo. [Latin *parēlion,* from Greek *parēlion,* from *para* beside + *hēlios* sun.] —**par·he·lic** (pär hē′lik), *adj.*

pa·ri·ah (pə rī′ə) *n.* **1.** a person who is shunned or despised by others; outcast. **2.** *also,* **Pariah.** a member of a low caste in India and Burma, traditionally considered untouchable by some Hindus. [Tamil *paraiyan* member of a low caste, from *parai* drum; with reference to the traditional task of drum beating performed by this caste.]

Par·i·an (pâr′ē ən) *adj.* **1.** of, relating to, or characteristic of Paros or the white marble found there. **2.** relating to or designating a coarse, unglazed porcelain resembling the marble of Paros. —*n.* **1.** a native or inhabitant of Paros. **2.** a coarse, unglazed, ivory-colored porcelain resembling the marble of Paros, used esp. for making statuettes.

pa·ri·e·tal (pə rī′i təl) *adj.* of or relating to the wall of any body cavity. —*n.* either of a pair of bones that form part of the sides and top of the skull, lying between the frontal and the occipital bones. [Late Latin *parietālis* relating to a wall, from Latin *paries* wall.]

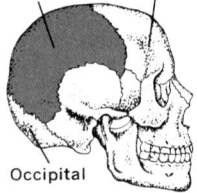

Parietal / Frontal / Occipital

parietal

par·i·mu·tu·el (par′i mū′chü əl) *n.* **1.** a system of betting in which the odds are automatically adjusted according to the betting and in which the winners share the total amount wagered minus a percentage for the operators of the contests and for the state. **2.** a computer for recording and showing the odds of such bets. Also *(def. 2),* **totalizator.** [French *pari mutuel* literally, mutual bet, going back to Latin *pār* equal + *mūtuus* reciprocal.]

par·ing (pâr′ing) *n.* **1.** something that has been pared off: *vegetable parings.* **2.** the act of a person who pares.

pa·ri pas·su (par′ē pas′ü) *Latin.* at the same rate; equally.

Par·is (par′is) *n.* in Greek legend, the son of Priam, whose abduction of Helen brought on the Trojan War, in which he himself was killed.

Paris green, an extremely poisonous, emerald-green copper compound containing arsenic, used as a pigment and in insecticides.

par·ish (par′ish) *n.* **1.** in the Anglican, Roman Catholic, and certain other churches, an administrative district having its own church and one or more resident members of the clergy. **2.** in Louisiana, a civil district corresponding to a county. **3.** in Great Britain, a civil district that is a subdivision of a county. **4.** the people of a parish. [Old French *paroisse* ecclesiastical district, from Late Latin *parochia,* from Greek *paroikiā,* going back to *para* beside + *oikos* house.]

pa·rish·ion·er (pə rish′ə nər) *n.* a member of a parish.

par·i·ty (par′i tē) *n.* **1.** the state or quality of being equal or equivalent, as in power, position, value, or degree: *The two countries reached parity in military strength.* **2.** an equivalence in value between farmers' present purchasing power and their purchasing power at a given base period, maintained by government price supports. **3.** an equivalence in value of one kind of currency or

security with respect to another currency or security. [Latin *paritās* equality.]

park (pärk) *n.* **1.** an area of land set apart for the pleasure and use of the public, such as a small area in a city with paths, benches, and playgrounds or a large expanse of scenic land preserved in its natural state. **2.** the spacious grounds of a country estate, often having woods, lakes, and fields. **3.** a stadium and surrounding facilities, used esp. for athletic contests. —*v.t.* **1.** to leave or situate (a vehicle) in a certain place where it may remain temporarily. **2.** *Informal.* to place, leave, or situate: *The guards parked themselves at the entrance to the hall.* —*v.i.* to leave or situate a vehicle temporarily: *You parked too close to the fire hydrant.* [Old French *parc* enclosure, from Medieval Latin *parricus;* of uncertain origin.]

par·ka (pär′kə) *n.* **1.** a hooded fur outer garment worn by the Eskimo. **2.** any similar hooded garment for outdoor wear.

parking lot, an area set aside for cars to be parked.

parking meter, a timer mounted on a pole, into which coins are inserted to pay for the use of a parking space by a motor vehicle for a limited period of time.

Par·kin·son's disease (pär′kin sənz) a disease of the central nervous system, characterized by rhythmic tremor, stiffness of the muscles, and slowing of movement, thought to be caused by the gradual loss of brain cells that produce the neurotransmitter dopamine. Also, **par′kin·son·ism.** [From James *Parkinson,* 1755-1824, English physician who first described it.]

park ranger, an officer who patrols and supervises the use of a public park, esp. a national or state park. Also, **ranger.**

park·way (pärk′wā′) *n.* a highway or wide thoroughfare divided by or bordered with landscaped trees, bushes, or grass.

par·lance (pär′ləns) *n.* a style or manner of speech; language: *medical parlance.* [Old French *parlance,* from *parler* to speak. See PARLEY.]

par·lay (pär′lā, -lē) *v.t.* **1.** to bet (the money from a first bet plus the winnings) on one or more successive races or contests. **2.** to exploit, utilize, or increase (an asset or talent) successfully: *to parlay a small inheritance into a fortune.* —*n.* a bet made by parlaying. [French *paroli* double stake, from dialectal Italian *paroli,* from *paro* equal, pair, from Latin *pār* equal.]

par·ley (pär′lē) *n., pl.* **-leys.** a conference, esp. one between enemies to determine the terms of a truce or agreement. —*v.i.* **-leyed, -ley·ing.** to hold a parley. [Old French *parlee* conversation, from *parler* to speak, from Late Latin *parabolāre,* from Latin *parabola* comparison, allegory. See PARABLE.]

par·lia·ment (pär′lə mənt) *n.* **1. Parliament. a.** the legislature of Great Britain, made up of the House of Commons and the House of Lords. **b.** the legislature of Canada, made up of the House of Commons and the Senate. **2.** any of various legislatures in other countries, based on the British system. **3.** any formal assembly or conference dealing with governmental affairs. [Old French *parlement* a speaking, conference, from *parler* to speak. See PARLEY.]

par·lia·men·tar·i·an (pär′lə men târ′ē ən) *n.* **1.** a person who is an expert in parliamentary procedure or debate. **2. Parliamentarian.** a person who supported the Long Parliament during the reign of Charles I in England.

par·lia·men·ta·ry (pär′lə men′tə rē, -men′trē) *adj.* **1.** of, relating to, or characteristic of a parliament. **2.** based on or according to the rules of a parliament or other deliberative body: *parliamentary procedure.* **3.** enacted or issued by a parliament: *a parliamentary act.* **4.** having or governed by a parliament: *a parliamentary democracy.*

par·lor (pär′lər) *also, British,* **par·lour.** *n.* **1.** a room in a home in which visitors are received and entertained. **2.** a small, semiprivate sitting room for relaxation or conversation in a hotel, club, or other public facility. **3.** a room, group of rooms, or a building used as a business establishment, often having special equipment or decor: *a dog-grooming parlor, an ice-cream parlor.* [Old French *parleor* reception room; literally, place for conversation, from *parler* to speak. See PARLEY.]

parlor car, a railroad passenger car equipped with individual chairs and other equipment, affording more comfort than ordinary passenger cars.

par·lous (pär′ləs) *Archaic. adj.* **1.** full of danger; perilous. **2.** clever or shrewd. —*adv.* exceedingly; extremely. [Form of PERILOUS.] —**par′lous·ly,** *adv.*

Par·me·san (pär′mə zän′, -zan′, -zən) *n.* a pale yellow, hard,

a	at	e	end	o	hot	u	up	hw	white		about
ā	ape	ē	me	ō	old	ū	use	ng	song		taken
ä	far	i	it	ô	fork	ü	rule	th	thin	ə	pencil
âr	care	ī	ice	oi	oil	u̇	pull	th	this		lemon
		îr	pierce	ou	out	ûr	turn	zh	measure		circus

dry Italian cheese made from skim milk, usually grated and used in soups, sauces, and other dishes. [French *parmesan,* from Italian *parmegiano* relating to Parma, from *Parma,* Italy, where it is made.]

par·mi·gia·na (pär′mi zhä′nə, -jä′-) *adj.* made or covered with Parmesan cheese: *veal parmigiana, eggplant parmigiana.* [Italian *Parmigiana,* feminine of *Parmigiano* relating to Parma, from *Parma* city in northern Italy.]

Par·nas·sus (pär nas′əs) *n.* **1.** poetry or poets collectively. **2.** any center of poetic or literary activity. —**Par·nas′si·an,** *adj.* [From *Mount Parnassus,* in Greek mythology, a mountain sacred to Apollo and the Muses.]

pa·ro·chi·al (pə rō′kē əl) *adj.* **1.** of, relating to, or supported by a parish. **2.** limited in point of view; narrow; provincial: *parochial ideas.* [Late Latin *parochiālis* relating to a parish, from *parochia* parish. See PARISH.] —**pa·ro′chi·al·ly,** *adv.*

pa·ro·chi·al·ism (pə rō′kē ə liz′əm) *n.* the quality of being parochial in thinking; narrowness of viewpoint; provincialism.

parochial school, a school maintained and controlled by a church or other religious organization.

par·o·dy (par′ə dē) *n., pl.* **-dies. 1.** an imitation of something serious, such as a literary or artistic work, a style of composition, or a way of life, presented for comic effect or ridicule. **2.** a poor or weak imitation: *The dress was a parody of the latest fashions.* —*v.t.,* **-died, -dy·ing.** to make a parody of: *The film parodied old silent movies.* [Greek *parōidiā* burlesque poem.] —**pa·rod·ic** (pə rod′ik); *also,* **pa·rod′i·cal,** *adj.* —**par′o·dist,** *n.*

pa·role (pə rōl′) *n.* **1.** *Law.* **a.** the conditional release of a prisoner before the expiration of the full sentence. **b.** the period of such conditional release. **2.** conditional freedom granted instead of imprisonment. **3.** a promise, esp. the pledge of a prisoner of war to his or her captors to not take part in any further fighting. —*v.t.,* **-roled, -rol·ing.** to release (a prisoner) on the conditions of parole. [Old French *parole* word, promise, going back to Latin *parabola* comparison, allegory, proverb, from Greek *parabolē* comparison, proverb. Doublet of PALAVER, PARABLE.]
 •**on parole.** out of prison on the conditions of parole.

pa·ro·lee (pə rō lē′, -rō′lē) *n.* a person who is released from prison on parole.

pa·rot·id (pə rot′id) *adj.* of or designating one of the paired salivary glands situated below and in front of each ear. —*n.* a parotid gland. [Modern Latin *parotis,* from Latin *parōtis,* tumor near the ear, from Greek *parōtis.*]

par·ox·ysm (par′ək siz′əm) *n.* **1.** a sudden outburst or fit, as of laughter or rage. **2.** a sudden attack or intensification of a disease or a symptom, usually of a recurring nature: *to suffer paroxysms of malaria every few years.* [Medieval Latin *paroxysmus* irritation, from Greek *paroxysmos* irritation, fit (of a disease).] —**par′ox·ys′mal,** *adj.*

par·quet (pär kā′, -ket′) *n.* **1.** flooring made of parquetry. **2.** the main floor of a theater, esp. the section from the orchestra pit to the parquet circle; orchestra. —*adj.* made of parquetry: *parquet floors.* —*v.t.,* **-queted, -quet·ing.** to make or furnish with parquetry. [French *parquet* wooden floor; earlier, small enclosure, from Old French *parc* enclosure. See PARK.]

parquet circle, the part of the main floor of a theater at the rear of the parquet and under the balcony.

par·quet·ry (pär′ki trē) *n., pl.* **-ries.** an inlaid mosaic of wood, usually in geometric patterns, used esp. for floors. [French *parqueterie* inlaid floor, from *parquet* wooden floor. See PARQUET.]

parr (pär) *n., pl.* **parr** or **parrs.** a young salmon before it is mature enough to begin its migration downstream to the sea. [Of uncertain origin.]

parquetry

par·ra·keet (par′ə kēt′) parakeet.

par·ri·cide[1] (par′ə sīd′) *n.* the murder of a parent or other close relative. [Latin *pārricīdium.* See -CIDE[1].] —**par′ri·cid′al,** *adj.*

par·ri·cide[2] (par′ə sīd′) *n.* a person who murders a parent or other close relative. [Latin *parricīda.* See -CIDE[2].]

par·rot (par′ət) *n.* **1.** any of numerous hook-billed birds, family Psittacidae, found throughout the Southern Hemisphere and in warmer parts of the Northern Hemisphere, having a large head and glossy, usually brightly colored plumage, capable of imitating speech and other sounds, and popular as a pet. Length: 3½-39 inches (9-99 centimeters). **2.** a person who repeats or imitates the words or actions of others without thinking. —*v.t.* to repeat or imitate without thinking. [Obsolete French *Perrot* man's proper name, diminutive of *Pierre* Peter, from Latin *Petrus,* from Greek *Petros.*] —**par′rot·like′,** *adj.*

parrot fever, psittacosis.

par·rot·fish (par′ət fish′) *n., pl.* **-fish** or **-fish·es.** any of a group of tropical, reef-dwelling fish, family Scaridae, having parrotlike jaws lined with rows of fused teeth adapted for scraping algae and breaking off pieces of coral.

par·ry (par′ē) *v.t., v.i.,* **-ried, -ry·ing. 1.** to stop or deflect an opponent's attack, as in fencing. **2.** to ward off or divert (any attack or threatened danger); evade: *The speaker deftly parried the questions from the audience.* —*n., pl.* **-ries.** an act or instance of parrying. [French *parez,* imperative of *parer* to defend, from Latin *parāre* to make ready.]

parse (pärs) *v.t.* **parsed, pars·ing. 1.** to analyze (a sentence) grammatically, describing the parts of speech, their functions, and their relation to each other. **2.** to analyze (a word in a sentence) by stating its part of speech, its function, and its relation to the other words in the sentence. [Latin *pars (orātiōnis)* part (of speech).]

par·sec (pär′sek′) *n.* a unit of measure used in astronomy to express the distance between stars, equal to 19.2 trillion miles (31 trillion kilometers), or 3.26 light-years. [PAR(ALLAX) + SEC(OND).]

Par·see (pär′sē) *also,* **Par·si.** *n.* a member of a Zoroastrian sect located chiefly in India, descended from Persians who fled from Muslim persecution in the eighth century A.D. [Persian *Pārsī* Persian, from *Pārs* Persia.]

par·si·mo·ni·ous (pär′sə mō′nē əs) *adj.* extremely cautious in spending money; stingy. —**par′si·mo′ni·ous·ly,** *adv.* —**par′si·mo′ni·ous·ness,** *n.*

par·si·mo·ny (pär′sə mō′nē) *n.* extreme cautiousness in spending money; excessive frugality; stinginess. [Latin *parsimōnia.*]

pars·ley (pär′slē) *n., pl.* **-leys.** a low-branching plant, *Petroselinum crispum,* having finely divided, fragrant leaves used to flavor and garnish food. —*adj.* designating a large family of plants, Umbelliferae or Apiaceae, grown throughout most parts of the world, bearing tiny flowers in round, mostly flat-topped clusters, and including vegetables, as celery, carrots, and parsnips, and many herbs, as caraway, dill, and parsley. [Old French *peresil* the plant parsley, going back to Latin *petroselīnum,* from Greek *petroselīnon.*]

pars·nip (pär′snip) *n.* **1.** the thick, white, edible root of a plant, *Pastinaca sativa,* of the parsley family, having a sweet flavor, cooked and eaten as a vegetable. **2.** the plant itself, having a hollow grooved stem and clusters of greenish yellow flowers. [Modification (influenced by Middle English *nepe* turnip) of Old French *pasnaie* the plant parsnip, from Latin *pastināca.*]

par·son (pär′sən) *n.* **1.** a member of the clergy in charge of a parish; pastor; rector. **2.** any member of the clergy, esp. a Protestant minister. [Medieval Latin *persona* parish priest, from Latin *persōna* mask, character, personage, probably from Etruscan *phersu* mask. Doublet of PERSON.]

par·son·age (pär′sə nij) *n.* the residence of a parson, usually provided by the church.

part (pärt) *n.* **1.** a portion constituting a whole or into which a whole can be divided; something less than the whole: *The cat finished only part of the milk. The last part of the movie is very exciting.* **2.** *Mathematics.* one of several equal portions or quantities into which a whole may be divided; an aliquot part: *An inch is a twelfth part of a foot.* **3.** a component of a machine or other system, esp. one that can be separated or replaced: *automobile parts.* **4.** a portion of assigned or assumed responsibility; share: *I'll do my part to make the plan work.* **5.** participation; interest; concern: *I had no part in the dispute.* **6.** one of the sides in a contest, dispute, or question. **7.** a member or organ of a plant or animal body. **8.** a line made by separating one's hair: *I always wear a center part.* **9.** *usually,* **parts.** a region, area, or place: *to travel to foreign parts.* **10.** *usually,* **parts.** ability or attribute; accomplishment; talent: *a person of many parts.* **11.a.** a role in a film, play, opera, or other dramatic presentation. **b.** the lines or actions assigned to a character in a dramatic presentation. **12.** *Music.* **a.** one of the voices or instruments in concerted music. **b.** a melody or melodic line for such a voice or instrument. **c.** the written or printed musical score for such a voice or instrument. —*v.t.* **1.** to separate by coming between; draw or hold apart: *The referee parted the fighters.* **2.** to comb (the hair) so as to make a part. **3.** to divide into two or more portions or sections. —*v.i.* **1.** to become separated or divided into two or more pieces: *The shirt parted at the seams.* **2.** to go in different directions; go apart from one another: *The friends parted at the corner. The paths parted at the river.* **3.** to separate or leave; depart (with *from*): *I parted from the company last May. The boat parted from the dock.* —*adv.* in part; partly. —*adj.* not full or complete; partial: *part owner of a store.* [Latin *part-,* stem of *pars* portion, share.]
 •**for one's part.** as far as one is concerned.
 •**for the most part.** to the greatest extent; generally.
 •**in good part.** in a friendly or good-natured way.

• **in part.** to some extent; partly.
• **part and parcel.** an essential part: *Travel is part and parcel of the job.*
• **to part company.** to dissolve or end a relationship.
• **to part with.** to give up; surrender: *to part with one's money.*
• **to take part.** to have a share; join (usually with *in*): *They refused to take part in the game.*
• **to take someone's part.** to support someone in an argument or dispute.

Synonyms **Part, portion,** and **piece** mean something that together with other things makes up a whole. **Part,** the most general of these terms, designates anything that is or can be thought of as separate from a whole: *I liked the first part of the movie.* **Portion** usually implies a well-defined share: *A large portion of the millionaire's estate was left to charitable institutions.* **Piece** refers to a distinct, detached part of a whole or group: *a piece of cake, a piece of a puzzle, a piece of silverware.*

part. 1. participle. 2. particular.

par·take (pär tāk´) *v.i.,* **-took, -tak·en, -tak·ing. 1.** to take part; participate (with *in*): *She partook in the festivities.* **2.** to take or have a portion: *The meal was ready, but they refused to partake.* —**par·tak´er,** *n.*
• **to partake of. a.** to take or have a portion of: *to partake of dinner.* **b.** to have the character of; resemble: *His wild acts partake of madness.*

par·terre (pär târ´) *n.* **1.** the section of a theater under the balcony and behind the parquet; parquet circle. **2.** a flower garden having the beds separated by paths and arranged in patterns. [French *parterre,* from *par terre* along the ground, going back to Latin *per* through + *terra* earth.]

par·the·no·gen·e·sis (pär´thə nō jen´ə sis) *n.* reproduction in which a new organism develops from an egg cell without fertilization. [Greek *parthenos* virgin + GENESIS.] —**par·the·no·ge·net·ic** (pär´thə nō jə net´ik), *adj.* —**par·the·no·ge·net´i·cal·ly,** *adv.*

Par·the·non (pär´thə non´) *n.* the temple of Athena on the Acropolis in Athens, built in the fifth century B.C. It is considered the finest existing example of Greek Doric architecture. [Latin *Parthenon,* from Greek *Parthenōn,* from *parthenos* virgin (because Athena was a virgin).]

the **Parthenon** in Athens, Greece

Par·thi·an shot (pär´thē ən) a remark or attack made in parting or fleeing. [From the custom of the Parthian cavalry of shooting arrows as it was fleeing.]

par·tial (pär´shəl) *adj.* **1.** not complete or total; of or involving a part only: *a partial payment.* **2.** favoring one side, person, or group more than another; prejudiced; biased. [Middle French *partial* biased, incomplete, from Late Latin *partiālis* relating to a part, incomplete, from Latin *pars* share, portion.] —**par´tial·ly,** *adv.*
• **partial to.** having a strong liking for; fond of: *Our whole family is partial to traveling.*

par·ti·al·i·ty (pär´shē al´i tē, pär shal´-) *n., pl.* **-ties. 1.** the quality or state of favoring one side, person, or group more than another; bias; prejudice: *The jury considered the case without partiality.* **2.** a strong liking or fondness: *a partiality for water sports.*

par·tic·i·pant (pär tis´ə pənt) *n.* a person who participates. —*adj.* taking part; participating.

par·tic·i·pate (pär tis´ə pāt´) *v.i.,* **-pat·ed, -pat·ing.** to take part or have a share with others: *to participate in sports.* [Latin

participātus, past participle of *participāre* to share in, going back to *pars* share + *capere* to take.] —**par·tic´i·pa´tor,** *n.*

par·tic·i·pa·tion (pär tis´ə pā´shən) *n.* the act or condition of taking part or sharing.

par·tic·i·pa·to·ry (pär tis´ə pə tôr´ē) *adj.* characterized by or involving active participation, esp. on an individual basis: *a participatory democracy.*

par·ti·cip·i·al (pär´tə sip´ē əl) *adj.* of, based on, or used as a participle: *a participial phrase.*

par·ti·ci·ple (pär´tə sip´əl) *n.* a verb form used as an adjective and possessing certain qualities of both verbs and adjectives. Participles are like verbs in that they may take an object (*leaving his books behind him*), they may be modified by adverbs (*having quickly used up her supplies*), and that they are formed in tenses. The present participle ends in *-ing* (*speaking*), the past participle ends in *-ed, -en,* or other forms (*spoken*), and the perfect participle is formed by adding *having* before the past participle (*having spoken*). Participles may also function as pure adjectives (*a broken dish*). [Old French *participle,* form of *participe,* from Latin *participium* a sharing, participle (from its sharing of the uses of a noun).]

par·ti·cle (pär´ti kəl) *n.* **1.** a very small bit or minute amount; trace; speck: *a particle of soot, a particle of truth.* **2.** subatomic particle. **3.a.** a short, indeclinable part of speech, such as a preposition, conjunction, or article. **b.** a prefix or suffix. [Latin *particula* small part, diminutive of *pars* share, portion.] —For Synonyms, see bit[2].

particle accelerator, accelerator *(def. 2).*

particle beam *Nuclear Physics.* a stream of subatomic particles generated for use in studying nuclear structure and the interactions between particles.

particle board, a building material made from small bits of wood bonded together with glue or resin, used for wall panels, partitions, furniture, and other items usually constructed from wood.

particle physics, a branch of physics that deals with the properties and structure of subatomic particles, as neutrons, protons, and electrons, esp. as shown in experiments with accelerators.

par·ti·col·ored (pär´ti kul´ərd) *also,* **party-colored.** *adj.* **1.** having different colors in different parts: *a parti-colored flower.* **2.** characterized by variation or diversity. [Old French *parti* divided, past participle of *partir* to divide (from Latin *partīre*) + COLORED. See COLOR.]

par·tic·u·lar (pər tik´yə lər) *adj.* **1.** distinct or separate from others; specific; individual: *This particular suitcase is too small for a long trip.* **2.** belonging to or characteristic of a single specified person or thing: *My particular strength is in science.* **3.** special in some way; exceptional; noteworthy: *That news item is of particular interest to me.* **4.** attentive to details; careful or exacting; fastidious: *to be particular about one's clothes.* **5.** precise or detailed, as a description. **6.** *Logic.* of or relating to a proposition that includes or treats its predicate in part or with qualification. *Some horses are ponies* is a particular proposition. ➡ opposed to **universal.** —*n.* **1.** a single and distinct instance, fact, or item: *The story is correct in every particular.* **2. particulars.** specific items of information; details: *The article included all the particulars of the murder trial.* [Old French *particuler* characteristic, special, from Late Latin *particulāris* relating to a small part, partial, from Latin *particula* small part. See PARTICLE.]
• **in particular.** specifically; especially: *I like all kinds of fruit, but I like peaches in particular.*

par·tic·u·lar·i·ty (pər tik´yə lar´i tē) *n., pl.* **-ties. 1.** the quality or condition of being distinct from others; individuality. **2.** attentiveness to details; carefulness; fastidiousness. **3.** precision or exactitude of detail, as in a description. **4.** a distinctive, individual quality or trait. **5.** an individual instance or item; particular.

par·tic·u·lar·ize (pər tik´yə lə rīz´) *v.,* **-ized, -iz·ing.** —*v.t.* to state in detail; treat individually; specify. —*v.i.* to give particulars; go into detail. —**par·tic´u·lar·i·za´tion,** *n.*

par·tic·u·lar·ly (pər tik´yə lər lē) *adv.* **1.** to an unusual degree; especially: *a particularly hot day.* **2.** in a precise manner; item by item; in detail: *to discuss a problem particularly.* —For Synonyms, see **especially.**

par·tic·u·late (pär tik´yə lit, -lāt´, pər-) *n.* a small, distinct particle: *smog created by particulates in the atmosphere.* —*adj.* of, relating to, or consisting of small, distinct particles: *particulate*

---

a	at	e	end	o	hot	u	up	hw	white	⎧	about
ā	ape	ē	me	ō	old	ū	use	ng	song	⎪	taken
ä	far	i	it	ô	fork	th	rule	th	this	⎬	pencil
âr	care	ī	ice	oi	oil	u̇	pull	th	this	⎪	lemon
		îr	pierce	ou	out	ûr	turn	zh	measure	⎩	circus

P

fallout from soot and ash. [Latin *particula* small part + -ATE[3]. See PARTICLE.]

part·ing (pär′ting) *n.* **1.** a departure or leave-taking: *The children cried at their parents' parting.* **2.** the act of separating or the state of being separated. **3.** a line, point, or place of division or separation. **4.** death. —*adj.* **1.** given, spoken, or performed at parting: *a parting request.* **2.** leaving; departing: *The parting train disappeared down the track.* **3.** serving to separate or divide: *a parting layer of rock.*

par·ti·san (pär′tə zən) *also,* **partizan.** *n.* **1.** a person who strongly supports a person, idea, cause, or side, esp. someone who is an overly zealous adherent. **2.** a member of a body of soldiers usually engaged in resistance work within enemy lines; guerrilla. —*adj.* **1.** of, relating to, or characteristic of a partisan or partisans: *to take a partisan stand on an issue, an attack of partisan troops.* **2.** composed of, proposed by, or controlled by one party, faction, or group: *partisan politics.* [Middle French *partisan* supporter of a side, from Italian *partigiano* protector, partner, from *parte* part, faction, from Latin *pars* portion.] —**par′ti·san·ship′**, *n.*

par·ti·tion (pär tish′ən) *n.* **1.** a dividing or being divided into shares or distinct parts; division and distribution of portions: *the partition of territory between rival nations.* **2.** a section or part into which a thing is divided. **3.** something that divides, such as an interior wall separating parts of a room. —*v.t.* **1.** to divide into shares or distinct parts: *to partition land for sale, to partition office space into small cubicles.* **2.** to separate by a partition (with *off*): *to partition off a space for storage.* [Latin *partitio* division.]

par·ti·tive (pär′ti tiv) *Grammar.* *n.* a word that expresses part of a collective whole. —*adj.* denoting or used as part of a whole. —**par′ti·tive·ly**, *adv.*

par·ti·zan (pär′tə zən) partisan.

part·ly (pärt′lē) *adv.* in some degree; not wholly or completely: *I am only partly responsible for the damage.*

part·ner (pärt′nər) *n.* **1.** a person who joins or associates with another or others in some action or enterprise; sharer: *partners in crime.* **2.** a member of a business partnership: *partners in a law firm.* **3.** a player on the same side in a game, usually when there are only two players on a side, as in bridge or tennis. **4.** either of two persons dancing together. **5.** a wife or husband. —*v.t.* **1.** to join or associate as partners: *The coach partnered them for the game.* **2.** to be or act as the partner of: *I'll partner you in the tennis match.* [Modification (influenced by *part*) of earlier *parcener,* from Old French *parçoner* one who shares, from Medieval Latin *partionarius* one who has a share, going back to Latin *partitio* sharing, division.]

part·ner·ship (pärt′nər ship′) *n.* **1.** the state of being a partner; association. **2.a.** a form of business organization in which two or more persons are associated in carrying on commercial or professional activities, usually sharing the profits and losses in specified proportions. **b.** a contract creating such an association. **c.** the persons so associated.

part of speech, any of the major classes into which words of a language can be divided. The traditional parts of speech for English are noun, pronoun, adjective, verb, adverb, preposition, conjunction, and interjection.

par·took (pär tŏok′) the past tense of **partake.**

par·tridge (pär′trij) *n., pl.* -tridge or -tridg·es. **1.** any of several plump-bodied game birds,

partridge

family Phasianidae, native to temperate regions of Europe, Asia, and Africa, having plumage patterned with gray, brown, and white markings. Length: 12-14 inches (30-36 centimeters). **2.** any of various similar or related birds of the United States, esp. the ruffed grouse and the bobwhite. [Old French *perdris* the game bird, going back to Latin *perdīx,* from Greek *perdīx.*]

par·tridge·ber·ry (pär′trij ber′ē) *n., pl.* -ries. **1.** a trailing evergreen plant, *Mitchella repens,* found in North America, having round, dark green leaves, white flowers, and bright red berries. **2.** the edible berry itself.

part song, a song having two or more voice parts, esp. one without an accompaniment.

part-time (pärt′tīm′) *adj.* for or during part of the normal time: *a part-time job.* —*adv.* on a part-time basis: *to work part-time.*

par·tu·ri·ent (pär tŏor′ē ənt, -tyŏor′-) *adj.* **1.** giving birth or about to give birth to young. **2.** of or relating to parturition.

par·tu·ri·tion (pär′tŏo rish′ən, pär′chŏo-) *n.* the act of giving

birth; childbirth. [Late Latin *parturitiō,* from Latin *parturīre* to be in labor.]

part·way (pärt′wā′, -wā′) *adv.* to some extent; part of the way; not completely: *Rewind the tape partway. The sun is partway out.*

par·ty (pär′tē) *n., pl.* -ties. **1.** a social gathering or entertainment: *a birthday party.* **2.** a group of people gathered together for a specific purpose or engaged in a common activity: *a search party.* **3.** a group of people organized to gain control of or influence the government, esp. through the election of its candidates: *a political party.* **4.** a person who takes part in or is involved with an action or plan: *I refused to be a party to such underhanded schemes.* **5.** a person or organization directly participating in a lawsuit, contract dispute, or other legal matter. **6.** person: *Certain unnamed parties have informed us of your plan.* —*adj.* **1.** of, for, or relating to a social party: *party hats.* **2.** of, relating to, or characteristic of a political party: *party politics.* —*v.i.*, -tied, -ty·ing. **1.** to attend or give social parties. **2.** to participate in social activities without restraint. [Old French *partie* side, contract, share, from *partir* to divide, from Latin *partīre.*] —For Synonyms *(n.),* see **company.**

par·ty-col·ored (pär′tē kul′ərd) parti-colored.

party line 1. a single telephone circuit with two or more subscribers on it, arranged so that only one call at a time can be made or received. **2.** the official views and policies of a political party, esp. the Communist Party. —**par′ty lin′er.**

party politics, political actions and views strictly supporting the policies and interests of one political party without regard for public interests.

party wall, a common wall between adjoining properties or structures, in which each owner has a partial right of use.

par value, the value printed on the face of a stock, bond, or other financial instrument; nominal or face value.

par·ve·nu (pär′və nü′, -nū′) *n.* a person who has recently or suddenly attained wealth or importance and is not yet fit for his or her new position; upstart. [French *parvenu,* from *parvenir* to arrive, from Latin *pervenīre.*]

par·vo·vi·rus (pär′vō vī′rəs) *n.* **1.** any of a group of small, DNA-containing viruses, sometimes associated with adenoviruses and thought to cause infectious hepatitis in humans. **2.** a highly contagious disease of dogs, caused by a parvovirus and marked by bloody diarrhea, vomiting, and sometimes death. [Latin *parvus* small + VIRUS.]

pas (pä) *n., pl.* **pas.** **1.** a dance step or series of dance steps. **2.** the right of precedence. [French *pas,* from Latin *passus* step.]

pas·cal (pas kal′) *n.* the International System unit of pressure, equal to 1 newton per square meter. [From Blaise *Pascal,* 1623-62, French physicist, philosopher, and mathematician.]

PASCAL (pas kal′) *also,* **Pascal.** *n.* a powerful, high-level computer language with a modular structure suitable for business applications and general use. [Probably from Blaise *Pascal,* 1623-62, French physicist, philosopher, and mathematician.]

Pasch (pask) *n.* **1.** Passover. **2.** Easter. [Old French *pasche* Passover, Easter, from Late Latin *pascha.* See PASCHAL.]

pas·chal (pas′kəl) *adj.* **1.** of or relating to Passover. **2.** of or relating to Easter. [Old French *pascal,* from Late Latin *paschālis,* from Latin *pascha* Passover, Easter, from Greek *paschā* Passover, going back to Hebrew *pesakh.*]

paschal lamb 1. in ancient times, the lamb eaten at Passover. **2.** Paschal Lamb. **a.** Jesus. **b.** Agnus Dei *(def. 3).*

pas de deux (*French* pä də dœ′) *pl.* **pas de deux.** in ballet, a dance for two performers. [French *pas de deux* step for two.]

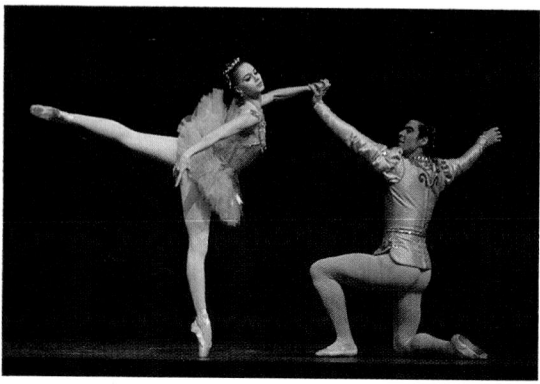

pas de deux

pa·sha (pə shä′, pash′ə, pä′shə) *also,* **pacha.** *n.* the title formerly placed after the name of high-ranking Turkish civil or military officials. Also, **bashaw.** [Turkish *pasa.*]

Pash·to (push′tō) *also,* **Pushtu.** *n.* an Indo-Iranian language that is the official language of Afghanistan, also spoken in parts of Pakistan. Also, **Afghan.**

Pa·siph·a·ë (pə sif′ə ē′) *n.* in Greek mythology, the wife of Minos and mother of the Minotaur.

pasque·flow·er (pask′flou′ər) *n.* any of several early-blooming plants of the genus *Anemone,* esp. *A. patens* and *A. pulsatilla,* that bear purple, reddish, or white bell-shaped flowers and narrowly divided, fan-shaped leaves. [Modification (influenced by Middle French *Pasque* Easter, from Latin *pascha* Easter, Passover) of French *passe-fleur* an anemone, from *passer* to move on, surpass + *fleur* flower (from Old French *flo(u)r*); referring to its blooming around Easter. See PASS, FLOWER, PASCHAL.]

pas·quin·ade (pas′kwə nād′) *n.* a satire or lampoon posted in a public place. —*v.t.,* **-ad·ed, -ad·ing.** to attack or satirize in a pasquinade; lampoon. [French *pasquinade* a lampoon, from Italian *pasquinata,* from *Pasquino* a statue in Rome to which lampoons were once attached.]

pass (pas) *v.i.* **1.** to go or move; proceed: *The hosts passed from table to table. Several thoughts passed through my mind.* **2.** to go or move by: *A flock of birds passed overhead.* **3.** to make one's way: *The politician passed through the throng of reporters.* **4.** to extend, run, or lead: *The new subway passes under the park.* **5.** (of time) to go by; elapse: *The hours passed slowly.* **6.** to get away or by without notice or action; slip by: *You let a good opportunity pass.* **7.** to come to an end; cease: *The illness quickly passed.* **8.** to die (often with *on* or *away*). **9.** to undergo transition, as from one state or form to another: *The ice passed into water and steam.* **10.** to get through or complete an examination, trial, or course of study successfully or satisfactorily: *to pass by five points.* **11.** to be accepted or taken (with *for* or *as*): *The counterfeit painting could not pass for the original.* **12.** to be approved or ratified: *The bill passed easily in the Senate.* **13.** to go without censure, challenge, or notice: *It was a thoughtless remark, but we let it pass.* **14.** to be exchanged or transacted, as between two persons: *Angry words passed between them.* **15.** to take place; happen; occur: *We had no idea of what had passed at the meeting.* **16.** to go or be handed about; circulate: *The story passed from person to person.* **17.** to be transferred to another, as by a will: *The couple's property passed to their children.* **18.a.** to pronounce or express a judgment, opinion, or sentence (with *on* or *upon*): *The judge could not pass on the matter without more facts.* **b.** to sit in inquest or judgment (with *on* or *upon*): *A jury will be selected to pass upon this question.* **19.** to be discharged from the body, as waste or a kidney stone. **20.** *Sports.* to transfer the ball or puck to a teammate. **21.** *Card Games.* to decline to bid. —*v.t.* **1.** to go or move by (something): *I pass the park on my way to school.* **2.a.** to get through or complete (an examination, trial, or course of study) successfully or satisfactorily: *to pass a physical, to pass a spelling test.* **b.** to cause or allow to get through or complete an examination, trial, or course of action successfully or satisfactorily: *The teacher passed all the students in the class.* **3.** to transfer, hand over, or spread (something) from one person or place to another: *Please pass the salt. Did you pass the word?* **4.** to give out, issue, or distribute (often with *out* or *around*): *to pass bad checks, to pass out leaflets.* **5.** to cause or allow (something) to move or go in a specified way: *to pass thread through the eye of a needle.* **6.** to cause to go or march by: *to pass soldiers in review.* **7.** to go beyond; exceed; surpass: *This year's attendance may pass that of last year.* **8.** to go through, across, or over. **9.** to cause or allow to elapse; spend (often with *away*): *to pass the summer traveling, to pass away the hours sitting in the sun.* **10.** to undergo, experience, or endure: *They passed a sleepless night in the old house.* **11.a.** to approve or ratify: *Congress passed the resolution.* **b.** to be approved or ratified by: *The bill passed the Senate by three votes.* **12.** to pronounce or express: *The judge passed sentence.* **13.** to discharge (something, as waste or a kidney stone) from the body. **14.** to omit payment of (a dividend). **15.** *Sports.* to throw (the ball) or propel (the puck) to a teammate. **16.** *Baseball.* to walk (a batter) intentionally. —*n.* **1.a.** a permit or written authorization to come, go, or move about freely: *to enter the building after showing a pass.* **b.** a ticket entitling the holder to admission or transportation: *two free passes to a baseball game, to buy a bus pass.* **c.** written authorization to be absent from military duty, esp. for a specified period of time. **2.** a natural passage, esp. a narrow gap in a mountain range or ridge. **3.** a condition or situation; state of affairs: *Events were at a critical pass.* **4.** a sweep or dive made by an aircraft at a particular target. **5.** a thrusting or lunging movement, as in fencing. **6.** a movement of the hand or hands over or along anything, esp. such a motion as used in magic or hypnotism. **7.** the act of passing; passage. **8.** *Sports.* a

successful or unsuccessful attempt to throw the ball or propel the puck to a teammate. **9.** *Baseball.* a walk, esp. an intentional walk. **10.** *Card Games.* the act of declining to bid. **11.** *Informal.* a flirtatious or sexually inviting action or proposal. [Old French *passer* to go across, go beyond, spend (time), ratify, going back to Latin *passus* step.]

•**to bring to pass.** to cause to happen; bring about.
•**to come to pass.** to happen; come about.
•**to pass off.** to cause to be accepted, regarded, or received, esp. by deception: *to pass off the fur as mink.*
•**to pass out.** to lose consciousness; faint.
•**to pass over.** to overlook or ignore.
•**to pass up. a.** to reject or allow to get away: *to pass up a chance to be famous.* **b.** to overlook or ignore.

pass. **1.** passage. **2.** passenger. **3.** passive.

pass·a·ble (pas′ə bəl) *adj.* **1.** fairly good; adequate; acceptable: *to speak passable French.* **2.** capable of being traveled through, across, or over: *The dense jungle was barely passable.* **3.** acceptable as currency. [Old French *passable* capable of being traversed, from *passer* to move on, walk, cross. See PASS.]

pass·a·bly (pas′ə blē) *adv.* fairly well; adequately: *to play the piano passably.*

pas·sa·ca·glia (pä′sə käl′yə) *n.* a musical composition having one theme, usually in the bass, that is repeated over and over. [Italian *passacaglia,* through Spanish, going back to Latin *passus* step + *callis* street; because frequently played in the street.]

pas·sage (pas′ij) *n.* **1.a.** a portion, usually short, of a written work or speech: *The author read a passage from a new story to the class.* **b.** *Music.* a phrase or other short section of a composition. **2.** a route, path, or other way through or by which someone or something may pass, go, or move: *air passages in a mine, a mountain passage.* **3.** a passageway in a building; corridor. **4.** the right, permission, or freedom to pass, go, or travel: *The government granted them passage through the country.* **5.** a journey, esp. by sea or air: *Our passage across the Pacific was uneventful.* **6.** passenger accommodations: *to book passage on an ocean liner.* **7.** course, progress, or advance: *the passage of time.* **8.** the act or process of passing, moving, or changing, as from one place or state to another. **9.** approval or enactment by a legislative body: *Congressional passage of such a resolution seemed unlikely.* **10.** an exchange between persons, as of blows or words. [Old French *passage* a going across, portion of a speech or book, from *passer* to move on, walk, cross. See PASS.]

pas·sage·way (pas′ij wā′) *n.* a way through or by which someone or something can pass, go, or move, as a corridor or alley.

pas·sant (pas′ənt) *adj. Heraldry.* (of a beast) walking and looking to the right side with the right forepaw raised. [Old French *passant,* present participle of *passer* to move on, walk. See PASS.]

pass·book (pas′bŭk′) *n.* bankbook.

pas·sé (pa sā′) *adj.* no longer in style; out-of-date. [French *passé,* past participle of *passer* to go, fade, expire. See PASS.]

passed ball *Baseball.* a pitch that gets away from the catcher even though it was within reach, allowing one or more base runners to advance.

pas·sel (pas′əl) *n. Informal.* a large number; group: *a passel of troubles.* [Modification of PARCEL.]

passe·men·terie (pas men′trē) *n.* a heavy ornamental trimming made of beads, braid, or cord.

pas·sen·ger (pas′ən jər) *n.* a person who travels in an automobile, train, airplane, or other conveyance. [Old French *passager* passenger on a ship, passing, from *passage* a going across. See PASSAGE.]

passenger pigeon, an extinct wild pigeon, *Ectopistes migratorius,* of North America, having chiefly blue-gray plumage and a wine-colored breast.

passe-par·tout (pas′pär tü′) *n.* **1.** a picture frame usually consisting of a pasteboard back and a piece of glass, often with a plain or ornamented mat, held together by strips of gummed paper attached to the backing. **2.** the gummed paper used for this purpose. **3.** a mat used for mounting a picture. **4.** something that enables one to pass, enter, or go everywhere, esp. a master key. [French *passe-partout* a frame; literally, pass everywhere, from *passer* to go, move on + *partout* everywhere (going back to Latin *per* through + *tōtus* all). See PASS.]

P

a	at	e	end	o	hot	u	up	hw	white		about
ā	ape	ē	me	ō	old	ū	use	ng	song		taken
ä	far	i	it	ô	fork	ü	rule	th	thin	ə	pencil
âr	care	ī	ice	oi	oil	ú	pull	th	this		lemon
		îr	pierce	ou	out	ûr	turn	zh	measure		circus

pass·er·by (pas′ər bī′) *also*, **pass·er-by.** *n., pl.* **pass·ers·by.** a person who passes or goes by.

pas·ser·ine (pas′ər in, -ə rīn′) *adj.* of, belonging to, or relating to an order of perching birds, Passeriformes, including all songbirds and more than half of all living birds. —*n.* a passerine bird. [Latin *passerīnus* relating to the sparrow, from *passer* sparrow.]

pass-fail (pas′fāl′) *adj.* of or relating to a method of grading schoolwork in which a student either passes or fails without being given a specific letter or number grade.

pas·sim (pas′im) *adv. Latin.* here and there; in different places. ➡ used as a reference note to indicate the occurrence of something, as a phrase, in various places throughout a book.

pass·ing (pas′ing) *adj.* **1.** going or moving by: *to grow wiser with the passing years.* **2.** of brief duration; not lasting; transitory: *a passing fancy.* **3.** given or done casually; cursory: *a passing glance.* **4.** allowing one to pass an examination, trial, or course of study; satisfactory: *a passing grade.* —*n.* **1.** the act of a person or thing that passes. **2.** death; dying. **3.** a means or place of passing or crossing; way through, across, or over: *The speaker remarked in passing that our town had many lovely parks.* —*adv. Archaic.* exceedingly; very: *strange, passing strange indeed* (Benjamin Disraeli, 1837).
· **in passing.** in the course of proceeding; incidentally.

pas·sion (pash′ən) *n.* **1.** a strong or intense feeling, as love, hate, joy, or anger, esp. when overwhelming or violent. **2.** a strong or ardent liking, desire, or enthusiasm: *a passion for baseball.* **3.** an object of strong feeling, liking, desire, or enthusiasm: *Painting was the artist's only passion.* **4.** an amorous feeling; love. **5.** sexual desire. **6.** an outburst or fit of strong or violent feeling, esp. of rage: *to fly into a passion.* **7.** *also*, **Passion. a.** the sufferings of Jesus following the Last Supper and ending with the Crucifixion. **b.** the chapters in the Gospels that relate these sufferings. [Old French *passion* suffering, from Late Latin *passiō* suffering, affection, from Latin *patī* to suffer.]

pas·sion·ate (pash′ə nit) *adj.* **1.** characterized by or tending to display strong or intense feeling; ardent: *The senator is a passionate defender of freedom of speech.* **2.** expressing, revealing, or arising from such feeling: *a passionate plea for forgiveness.* **3.** (of an emotion) overwhelming or vehement: *a passionate fury.* **4.** easily angered; hot-tempered. [Medieval Latin *passionatus* enraged, having strong feelings, from Late Latin *passiō* suffering, affection. See PASSION.] —**pas′sion·ate·ly,** *adv.*

> **Synonyms** **Passionate, ardent,** and **fervent** mean experiencing or showing intense feeling. **Passionate** connotes emotion that strains against, and may overcome, reason: *His passionate desire for adventure blinded him to danger.* **Ardent** suggests continued intensity and commitment and is used esp. where feeling is displayed in action: *Her ardent love of nature led her to become an environmental activist.* **Fervent,** on the other hand, may be used of similar emotions held in or not displayed: *The tourists kept their fervent patriotism to themselves in conversations with the natives.*

pas·sion·flow·er (pash′ən flou′ər) *n.* **1.** the large, showy flower of any of a group of climbing vines, genus *Passiflora,* esp. the **wild passionflower,** *P. incarnata,* having white petals and a pinkish crown. **2.** the vine that bears this flower. [Because parts of the flower supposedly resemble the instruments of the crucifixion of Christ.]

passion fruit *also,* **pas·sion·fruit** (pash′ən früt′). *n.* the edible fruit of the passionflower.

pas·sion·less (pash′ən lis) *adj.* without feeling; unemotional.

Passion play *also,* **passion play.** a dramatic representation of the Passion, death, and Resurrection of Jesus.

Passion Sunday, the second Sunday before Easter and fifth Sunday in Lent.

Passion Week, the fifth week in Lent, beginning with Passion Sunday.

pas·sive (pas′iv) *adj.* **1.** acted upon or tending to be acted upon without responding or reacting. **2.** submitting without opposition or resistance; submissive: *The prisoner was passive as the judge pronounced the sentence.* **3.** not taking part, acting, or oper-

passionflower

ating: *a passive observer.* **4.** *Grammar.* relating to or designating the voice of a verb whose subject is represented as receiving the action expressed by the verb. In the sentence *The child was bitten by a dog, was bitten* is in the passive voice. ➡ opposed to **active.** —*n.* **1.** the passive voice. **2.** a verb form or construction in this voice. [Latin *passīvus* capable of suffering.] —**pas′sive·ly,** *adv.* —**pas′sive·ness,** *n.*

passive immunity, the immunity to disease possessed by an individual by virtue of having received antibodies, as by injection or from one's mother while in the uterus. ➡ distinguished from **active immunity.**

passive resistance, a method of resisting authority or protesting against some law or act by nonviolent means, as by refusing to comply or by staging a sit-in.

passive smoking, the unavoidable inhalation of smoke in the air from another person's cigarette, cigar, or pipe, esp. by a nonsmoker.

pas·siv·i·ty (pa siv′i tē) *n.* the state or condition of being passive.

pass·key (pas′kē′) *n.* **1.** master key. **2.** any of various other keys, as a skeleton key or latchkey.

Pass·o·ver (pas′ō′vər) *n.* the annual Jewish feast commemorating the Exodus of the Jews from Egypt. Also, **Pesach.** [PASS + OVER; referring to the episode in the Bible in which God *passed over* the houses of the Jews in Egypt when he killed the first-born children of the Egyptians.]

pass·port (pas′pôrt′) *n.* **1.** a document issued by the government of a citizen's own country, certifying citizenship and identity and granting permission to travel abroad. **2.** something that enables a person to gain acceptance or admission or achieve an end: *A clever mind can be a passport to success.* [French *passeport* the document, from *passer* to move on, go + *port* harbor. See PASS, PORT[1].]

pass·word (pas′wûrd′) *n.* **1.** a secret word or phrase that identifies the speaker as someone to be allowed to pass. **2.** a secret code used to gain access to a computer system, program, or file.

past (past) *adj.* **1.** gone by; ended; over: *The days of our childhood are past.* **2.** having occurred or existed in or belonging to time gone by: *to learn from past mistakes.* **3.** gone by immediately before the present time: *We have been on the phone for the past hour.* **4.** having served formerly: *a past mayor.* **5.** *Grammar.* indicating a state or action in time gone by. —*n.* **1.** a time that has gone by: *Dinosaurs lived in the remote past.* **2.** something that was done or has happened in the past. **3.a.** a past life, career, history, or reputation: *to investigate someone's past.* **b.** a concealed, questionable, or disreputable former period of a person's life: *to live down one's past.* **4.** *Grammar.* the past tense or a verb in the past tense. —*prep.* **1.** beyond in place; farther than: *The pitcher threw the ball past the catcher.* **2.** beyond in time; after: *It's past your bedtime.* **3.** beyond the power, scope, limits, or reach of: *This poetry is past comprehension.* **4.** beyond in amount, number, or degree: *My grandparents are both past ninety.* —*adv.* so as to pass or go by: *We watched the train rumble past.* [Middle English *past,* past participle of *passen* to pass. See PASS.]

pas·ta (pä′stə) *n.* **1.** a paste or dough made with semolina and flour, used to make macaroni, ravioli, and similar food products. **2.** a dish or food product consisting of cooked pasta. [Italian *pasta,* from Late Latin *pasta* dough. See PASTE.]

paste (pāst) *n.* **1.** a mixture, as of flour and water, used as an adhesive. **2.** any similar soft, smooth, often moist substance. **3.** a soft, creamy food preparation: *tomato paste.* **4.** a dough, esp. one made with butter or lard and used for pastry. **5.a.** a hard, glass-like material used to make artificial or imitation gems. **b.** a gem made of this material. **6.** a moistened clay mixture used in making pottery and porcelain. —*v.t.,* **past·ed, past·ing. 1.** to fasten with or as with paste: *She pasted the photographs in her album.* **2.** to cover or fill with something that is pasted on: *He pasted the walls of his room with posters.* **3.** *Slang.* to strike with a hard blow; punch. [Old French *paste* dough, from Late Latin *pasta,* from Greek *pasta* barley porridge.] —**past′er,** *n.*

paste·board (pāst′bôrd′) *n.* **1.** a stiff material made of sheets of paper pasted together or of paper pulp pressed together. **2.** *Informal.* any of various cards made of such material, as a playing card, calling card, or ticket. —*adj.* **1.** made of pasteboard: *a pasteboard box.* **2.** having little or no substance or credibility; flimsy; sham.

pas·tel (pa stel′, pas′tel) *n.* **1.** a crayon consisting of dried paste made by mixing ground pigment with resin, gum, or a similar binding material. **2.** a picture drawn with such crayons. **3.** the art or process of drawing with such crayons. **4.** any pale, soft shade of color. —*adj.* **1.** of, relating to, or drawn with pastels. **2.** (of a color) having a pale, soft shade: *a dress of pastel blue.* [French *pastel* crayon, from Italian *pastello,* from Late Latin *pastellus*

woad, diminutive of *pasta* dough; referring to the paste for pigment made from woad. See PASTE.]

pas·tern (pas′tərn) *n.* **1.** the part of a horse's foot between the fetlock and the hoof. **2.** a similar part on the foot of another animal, such as a cow or dog. [Old French *pasturon,* from *pasture* tether (tied around the *pastern* of a horse at pasture), pasture, food, from Late Latin *pāstūra* feeding. See PASTURE.]

pas·teur·ize (pas′chə rīz′, pas′tə-) *v.t.,* **-ized, -iz·ing.** to subject (milk or other food) to a temperature high enough to destroy microorganisms that cause disease or food spoilage. [From Louis *Pasteur,* 1822-95, French chemist and bacteriologist who discovered this process + -IZE.] —**pas′teur·i·za′tion,** *n.* —**pas′teur·iz′er,** *n.*

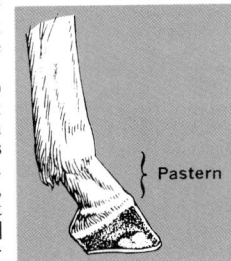

Pastern

pas·tiche (pa stēsh′) *n.* **1.** an artistic, literary, or musical work composed of excerpts from various sources, often intended to satirize other artists. **2.** any incongruous or varied combination; hodgepodge. [French *pastiche,* from Italian *pasticcio* hodgepodge, pasty², going back to Late Latin *pasta.* See PASTE.]

pas·tille (pa stēl′) *also,* **pas·til** (pas′təl). *n.* **1.** a flavored lozenge, often containing medicine; troche. **2.** a small roll or cone of benzoin or other aromatic paste, burned as a disinfectant or deodorizer. [French *pastille* lozenge, from Latin *pastillus* little roll or loaf, lozenge, diminutive of *pānis* bread.]

pas·time (pas′tīm′) *n.* something that serves to make time pass pleasantly, as a hobby; diversion. [PAS(S) + TIME.] —For Synonyms, see *amusement.*

past master 1. a person who is highly skilled or thoroughly experienced in something, as an art or profession; expert. **2.** a person who was formerly a master in a guild, lodge, or similar organization.

pas·tor (pas′tər) *n.* a member of the clergy in charge of a parish or congregation. [Latin *pāstor* shepherd; literally, feeder, from *pāscere* to feed.]

pas·tor·al (pas′tər əl) *adj.* **1.** of, relating to, or portraying rural life, esp. idealized rural life: *pastoral poetry.* **2.** of or relating to shepherds or their way of life: *a pastoral tribe.* **3.** having the simplicity, peacefulness, charm, and other qualities usually associated with idealized rural life or the country: *pastoral scenery.* **4.** of or relating to a pastor or his or her duties. —*n.* **1.** a literary work, esp. a poem or play, that deals with rural life, usually in an idealized or artificial manner. **2.** a picture or scene depicting rural life. **3.** a letter from a bishop or pastor to those under his or her spiritual care. **4.** pastorale. [Latin *pāstōrālis* relating to shepherds, from *pāstor* shepherd. See PASTOR.] —**pas′tor·al·ly,** *adv.*

pas·to·rale (pas′tə ral′, -räl′) *n., pl.* **-rales** or **-ra·li** (-rä′lē). a musical composition, such as an opera, based on or suggestive of a pastoral theme or subject. [Italian *pastorale* pastoral, from Latin *pāstōrālis.* See PASTORAL.]

pas·tor·ate (pas′tər it) *n.* **1.** the office, position, or jurisdiction of a pastor. **2.** the tenure of service of a pastor with one parish or congregation. **3.** pastors collectively.

past participle, a participle expressing a past action or state, used esp. in English with auxiliary verbs to form perfect tenses of the active voice and all tenses of the passive voice. In the sentence *The decision was made in haste,* the word *made* is a past participle.

past perfect 1. a verb tense expressing past action completed before another past action or before a specified past time. In the sentence *Steve had returned by the time Frieda arrived,* the phrase *had returned* is in the past perfect. **2.** a verb in this tense. Also, **pluperfect.**

pas·tra·mi (pə strä′mē) *n.* a variety of highly seasoned smoked beef, usually from a shoulder cut.

pas·try (pās′trē) *n., pl.* **-tries. 1.** any of several flour doughs used in making pie crusts, tarts, and other items. **2.** baked foods made with such a dough, collectively. **3.** any sweet, baked food. [PASTE + -RY.]

past tense 1. a verb tense expressing an action or state that occurred or existed in the past. In the sentence *The bird flew away,* the word *flew* is in the past tense. **2.** a verb in this tense.

pas·tur·age (pas′chər ij) *n.* **1.** grass and other growing herbage that animals feed on. **2.** land used or suitable for grazing livestock. **3.** the action or business of grazing livestock. [Old French *pasturage* food, from *pasture.* See PASTURE.]

pas·ture (pas′chər) *n.* **1.** a field or other tract of land suitable for the grazing of cattle, sheep, or other animals. **2.** grass and other herbage that animals feed on. —*v.,* **-tured, -tur·ing.**

—*v.t.* to put (animals) in a pasture to graze. —*v.i.* to graze: *The farmer put the sheep out to pasture.* [Old French *pasture* food, grass, from Late Latin *pāstūra* feeding, from Latin *pāscere* to feed.]

past·y¹ (pās′tē) *adj.,* **past·i·er, past·i·est. 1.** resembling paste, as in consistency: *a pasty mixture.* **2.** pale and sickly: *a pasty complexion.* [PASTE + -Y¹.] —**past′i·ness,** *n.*

pas·ty² (pas′tē) *n., pl.* **-ties.** a small pie with a filling, usually of meat. [Old French *pastee,* from *paste* dough. See PASTE.]

PA system, public-address system.

pat¹ (pat) *v.t.,* **pat·ted, pat·ting. 1.** to stroke or tap gently, usually with the hand, esp. in affection or approval: *I patted the dog.* **2.** to shape or smooth by striking gently with a flat surface. —*n.* **1.** a gentle tap or stroke. **2.** the sound made by such a tap or stroke. **3.** a small slice or molded mass of butter. [Imitative.] •**pat on the back.** *Informal.* praise or approval.

pat² (pat) *adj.* **1.** exactly suitable for the purpose or occasion; fitting. **2.** contrived or superficial; glib; insincere: *You had a pat answer to every question.* **3.** needing no change: *a pat hand in poker.* —*adv.* in an appropriate or suitable way; aptly; suitably. [From PAT¹.]
•**to have down pat.** to know perfectly or thoroughly: *I have all the answers down pat.*
•**to know pat.** to know perfectly or thoroughly.
•**to stand pat.** to stay firm without changing.

pat., patent; patented.

pa·ta·gi·um (pə tā′jē əm) *n.* a web of skin between the body and wing of a bird or a fold of skin between the forelimb and hind limb of certain arboreal animals, such as the flying squirrel. [Modern Latin *patagium,* from Latin *patagium* gold border on a tunic, from Greek *patageion.*]

patch (pach) *n.* **1.** a piece of material used to mend or cover a hole, strengthen a worn spot, or ornament a garment. **2.** a pad, piece of material, or other covering worn or put over a wound or injured part, usually for protection: *an eye patch.* **3.** any of the pieces of material used in making patchwork. **4.** a small piece of black silk or court plaster formerly worn on the face or neck to enhance beauty or cover a blemish. **5.** a small area, as of a surface, that differs or stands out from the whole: *Only a tiny patch of blue was visible in the cloudy sky.* **6.** a small piece or section of ground, esp. one in which a specific kind of plant is grown: *a lettuce patch.* **7.** a small scrap, piece, or area of anything. —*v.t.* **1.** to put a patch or patches of material on, esp. to mend, cover, strengthen, or ornament: *to patch a hole in the elbow of a jacket.* **2.** to make by joining pieces together: *to patch a quilt.* [Possibly from Old French *pieche,* form of *piece* part of a whole, period of time. See PIECE.]
•**to patch up. a.** to repair or put back together, esp. in a hasty or makeshift way: *to patch up a roof after a bad storm.* **b.** to smooth over; settle: *to patch up a quarrel.*

patch·ou·li (pach′ů lē, pə chü′lē) *also,* **patch·ou·ly.** *n.* **1.** either of two East Indian plants, *Pogostemon heyneanus* and *P. cablin,* of the mint family. **2.** a strong perfume derived from the dried leaves of either of these plants. [Tamil *pacculi* the plant, from *paccu* green + *ilai* leaf.]

patch test, any of several skin tests used chiefly for determining the presence of an allergy.

patch·work (pach′wûrk′) *n.* **1.** needlework consisting of pieces of material, usually of varying colors or shapes, that are sewed together. **2.** any surface divided into sections of varying colors or shapes. **3.** something composed of miscellaneous or incongruous parts; jumble: *The report was a patchwork of many unrelated facts.* —*adj.* made of or covered with patchwork: *a patchwork quilt.*

patch·y (pach′ē) *adj.,* **patch·i·er, patch·i·est. 1.** made up of, marked by, or occurring in patches: *patchy fog.* **2.** lacking uniformity, consistency, or completeness: *Only patchy reports were received from the battlefront.* —**patch′i·ly,** *adv.* —**patch′i·ness,** *n.*

patd., patented.

pate (pāt) *n.* the head, esp. the crown of the head.

pâ·té (pä tā′) *n. French.* **1.** a small pie or pastry shell with a filling usually of meat or fish paste. **2.** a paste, usually of finely ground and highly seasoned meat, used as a filling or spread.

pâté de foie gras (də fwä grä′) *French.* a paste made from livers of specially fattened geese, often with truffles added.

pa·tel·la (pə tel′ə) *n., pl.* **-tel·las** or **-tel·lae** (-tel′ē). **1.** kneecap. **2.** in ancient Rome, a small pan or dish. [Latin

a	at	e	end	o	hot	u	up	hw	white		about
ā	ape	ē	me	ō	old	ū	use	ng	song		taken
ä	far	i	it	ô	fork	ü	rule	th	thin	ə	pencil
âr	care	ī	ice	oi	oil	ů	pull	th	this		lemon
		îr	pierce	ou	out	ûr	turn	zh	measure		circus

P

patella small pan[1] or dish, diminutive of *patina* pan[1], dish. See PATEN.] —**pa·tel′lar,** *adj.*

pa·tel·li·form (pə tel′ə fôrm′) *adj. Biology.* having the shape of a pan or saucer, as the shell of a limpet. [PATELLA + -FORM.]

pat·en (pat′ən) *n.* **1.** a plate, esp. the small circular plate, usually of gold or silver, on which the bread is placed during the celebration of the Eucharist. **2.** a metal disk. [Latin *patina, patena* dish, pan[1], from Greek *patanē* flat dish.]

pa·ten·cy (pā′tən sē) *n.* the state or quality of being obvious or evident.

pat·ent (pat′ənt, pā′tənt) *n.* **1.** a government grant to an individual or organization conferring, for a certain period of time, the exclusive right of making, using, or selling a new invention. **2.** an invention that is protected by such a grant. **3.** an official document granting a right or privilege: *a patent of nobility.* **4.a.** a grant of public land by a government to an individual. **b.** the land so granted. **5.** any exclusive right or privilege. —*adj.* **1.** conferred or protected by a patent. **2.** of, relating to, or dealing with patents: *a patent attorney.* **3.** easily seen or understood; clearly evident; obvious: *patent arrogance, a patent lie.* —*v.t.* **1.** to obtain a patent for (an invention); protect with a patent. **2.** to grant a patent to. [Latin *patēns* open, present participle of *patēre* to lie open; because the official document granting a patent is *open* to public inspection.] —**pat′ent·a·ble,** *adj.*

pat·ent·ee (pat′ən tē′) *n.* a person to whom a patent is granted.

pat·ent leather (pat′ənt) a smooth, soft leather that is finished to a very high gloss.

pa·tent·ly (pā′tənt lē, pat′ənt-) *adv.* in an obvious or clear way: *behavior that patently offends everyone.*

patent medicine, any medicine that is patented and can be purchased without a prescription.

Patent Office, a U.S. government office that issues patents and administers federal patent and trademark laws.

pat·en·tor (pat′ən tər) *n.* a person who grants a patent.

pa·ter (pā′tər) *n.* father. ➡ often used as an affectation or for humorous effect. [Latin *pater.*]

pa·ter·fa·mil·i·as (pā′tər fə mil′ē əs) *n.* the father or head of a family or household. [Latin *paterfamiliās,* from *pater* father + *familiās,* archaic genitive of *familia* household.]

pa·ter·nal (pə tûr′nəl) *adj.* **1.** of, relating to, or like a father; fatherly: *paternal affection.* **2.** related through one's father: *a paternal grandparent.* **3.** inherited or derived from one's father. [Late Latin *paternālis* relating to a father, going back to Latin *pater* father.] —**pa·ter′nal·ly,** *adv.*

pa·ter·nal·ism (pə tûr′nə liz′əm) *n.* the principle or practice of regulating the life and supplying the needs of a country or group of people in a way suggestive of a father handling his children. —**pa·ter′nal·is′tic,** *adj.*

pa·ter·ni·ty (pə tûr′ni tē) *n.* **1.** the state of being a father. **2.** paternal origin. [Late Latin *paternitās,* going back to Latin *pater* father.]

pat·er·nos·ter (pā′tər nos′tər, pat′ər-) *n.* **1.** *also,* **Paternoster, Pater Noster.** the Lord's Prayer, esp. the Latin version. **2.** one of several beads of a rosary, often distinct in size, shape, or spacing from the other beads, on which the Lord's Prayer is said. **3.** any formulaic recitation used as a prayer or incantation. [Latin *pater noster* our father (the first two words of the Latin version of the Lord's Prayer).]

path (path) *n., pl.* **paths** (pathz, paths). **1.** a trail or way that has been trodden or worn, as through a forest. **2.** a way or road constructed for a specific purpose: *to shovel a path through the snow.* **3.** a route along which a person or thing travels: *the path of a projectile.* **4.** a way or line of action, behavior, or procedure: *a path to fame.* [Old English *paeth.*]

path. **1.** pathological. **2.** pathology.

Pa·than (pə tän′, pət hän′) *n.* **1.** a member of any of various Muslim peoples living in Afghanistan and West Pakistan. **2.** Afghan.

pa·thet·ic (pə thet′ik) *adj.* **1.** arousing or expressing pity, sadness, or compassion: *a pathetic tale of misery and woe.* **2.** extremely or pitifully inadequate or ineffective: *a pathetic attempt at acting.* Also, **pa·thet′i·cal.** [Late Latin *pathēticus* full of pathos, from Greek *pathētikos* capable of emotion, going back to *pathein* to suffer.] —**pa·thet′i·cal·ly,** *adv.*

pathetic fallacy, an attribution of human feelings or characteristics to nature or inanimate objects, for example: *an angry sea.*

path·find·er (path′fīn′dər) *n.* a person who discovers or leads the way: *a pathfinder in space exploration.*

path·o·gen (path′ə jən) *also,* **path·o·gene** (path′ə jēn′). *n.* any disease-causing microorganism or the toxic secretion of such a microorganism. [Greek *pathos* suffering + -GEN.]

path·o·gen·e·sis (path′ə jen′ə sis) *n.* the origin and development of a disease. Also, **pa·thog·e·ny** (pə thoj′ə nē). [Modern Latin *pathogenesis,* from Greek *pathos* suffering + GENESIS.]

path·o·gen·ic (path′ə jen′ik) *adj.* producing disease or relating to the production of disease. Also, **path·o·ge·net·ic** (path′ə jə net′ik).

pathol. **1.** pathological. **2.** pathology.

path·o·log·i·cal (path′ə loj′i kəl) *adj.* **1.** of, relating to, or concerned with pathology. **2.** characteristic of, caused by, or accompanying disease. Also, **path′o·log′ic.** —**path′o·log′i·cal·ly,** *adv.*

pa·thol·o·gist (pə thol′ə jist) *n.* a doctor who specializes in pathology.

pa·thol·o·gy (pə thol′ə jē) *n., pl.* **-gies. 1.** the science that deals with the nature, cause, and development of disease. **2.** the abnormal condition and bodily change resulting from a disease. [Modern Latin *pathologia,* from Greek *pathos* suffering, emotion + -LOGY.]

pa·thos (pā′thos, -thōs) *n.* **1.** a quality in an event or work of art or literature that arouses a feeling of pity, sadness, or compassion. **2.** pity, sadness, or compassion. [Greek *pathos* suffering, emotion.]

path·way (path′wā′) *n.* path.

-pathy *combining form* **1.** feeling: *sympathy, empathy.* **2.** disease: *psychopathy.* **3.** treatment of disease: *osteopathy.* [Greek -*patheia* suffering, feeling.]

pa·tience (pā′shəns) *n.* **1.** the quality, state, or fact of being patient or the ability to be patient. **2.** solitaire *(def. 1).*

pa·tient (pā′shənt) *adj.* **1.** capable of waiting calmly or without complaint: *We must be patient until our turn comes.* **2.** able to endure annoyance, hardship, or difficulty without complaining or losing one's composure: *The baby-sitter needed to be patient with the unruly child.* **3.** exhibiting or characterized by such an ability to wait or endure: *a patient smile.* **4.** calm and sympathetic; understanding: *It was a difficult lesson, but the professor was very patient with the class.* **5.** quietly careful and diligent: *a patient worker.* —*n.* a person who is undergoing medical care or treatment. [Old French *patient* waiting, enduring troubles, one who is undergoing medical treatment, from Latin *patiēns* suffering, present participle of *patī* to suffer.] —**pa′tient·ly,** *adv.*

pat·i·na (pat′ə nə) *n.* **1.** a green film or encrustation produced by oxidation on the surface of bronze. **2.** surface appearance, such as a change in color or finish, usually produced gradually by age and use, as on wood or silver. [Italian *patina* incrustation, coating, from Latin *patina* dish, pan[1]. See PATEN.]

pat·i·o (pat′ē ō′) *n., pl.* **-i·os. 1.** a paved, outdoor area next to a house or other building, used for cooking, eating, or lounging; terrace. **2.** an inner court open to the sky, as in a Spanish or Spanish-American house. [Spanish *patio* courtyard, possibly going back to Latin *patēre* to lie open.]

pa·tis·se·rie (pə tis′ə rē) *n.* a store that sells, and usually makes, baked goods, esp. pastries. [French *pâtisserie,* from Middle French *pastiserie,* going back to Late Latin *pasta* dough.]

pat·ois (pat′wä) *n., pl.* **pat·ois** (pat′wäz). a dialect, esp. a substandard form of a language, spoken in a particular region. [French *patois* rustic speech, from *patte* paw (of uncertain origin); referring to the clumsy style of the speakers.]

pat. pend., patent pending.

pa·tri·arch (pā′trē ärk′) *n.* **1.** the paternal head of a family or tribe. **2.** a person who is regarded as the founder or father of something, as a philosophy, religion, or order. **3.** an

patio *(def. 2)*

old man who is venerated by a group and whose opinions have great influence or authority. **4.** in the Roman Catholic, Orthodox, and various other Christian churches in the Middle East, a prelate who exercises the highest authority over all archbishops, bishops, clergy, and laity of his territory. **5.** in the early Christian church, a bishop of one of the five major sees of Christendom. **6.** in the Mormon Church, a member of the higher priesthood who administers church affairs. [Late Latin *patriarcha* father of a tribe, bishop of high rank, from Greek *patriarchēs,* from *patria* lineage, family + *-archēs* ruler.]

pa·tri·ar·chal (pā′trē är′kəl) *adj.* **1.** of, relating to, or characteristic of a patriarch: *patriarchal authority.* **2.** of, relating to, or of the nature of a patriarchy: *a patriarchal form of government.* **3.** ruled by a patriarch: *a patriarchal tribe.*

pa·tri·ar·chate (pā′trē är′kit, -kāt) *n.* **1.** the office, jurisdiction, or territory of an ecclesiastical patriarch. **2.** patriarchy.

pa·tri·ar·chy (pā′trē är′kē) *n., pl.* **-chies. 1.** a system of social organization in which the father or eldest male is head of the family or tribe and descent is traced through the paternal line. **2.** rule or government of a family, tribe, or the like by men.

pa·tri·cian (pə trish′ən) *n.* **1.** a member of one of the aristocratic families in ancient Rome who were descended from the original settlers of the city. **2.** a person who is of high birth or social status; aristocrat. —*adj.* **1.** of or relating to the aristocracy, *esp.* that of ancient Rome. **2.** of, relating to, characteristic of, or befitting a patrician; aristocratic; noble. [Latin *patricius* noble, of senatorial rank (from *patrēs* senators, fathers, plural of *pater* father) + -AN.]

pat·ri·cid·al (pat′rə sī′dəl) *adj.* of or relating to patricide or a person who commits patricide.

pat·ri·cide[1] (pat′rə sīd′) *n.* the act of killing one's father. [Latin *pater* father + *-cīdium* (see -CIDE[1]).]

pat·ri·cide[2] (pat′rə sīd′) *n.* a person who kills his or her father. [Latin *pater* father + *-cīda* (see -CIDE[2]).]

pat·ri·lin·e·al (pat′rə lin′ē əl, pā′trə-) *adj.* of, relating to, or tracing descent through the paternal line. —**pat′ri·lin′e·al·ly,** *adv.*

pat·ri·mo·ny (pat′rə mō′nē) *n., pl.* **-nies. 1.** an inheritance from one's father or ancestors. **2.** anything inherited; heritage: *Americans enjoy a patrimony of freedom of speech.* **3.** the property or endowment of a church or other religious institution. [Old French *patrimoine* inheritance, from Latin *patrimōnium,* from *pater* father.] —**pat′ri·mo′ni·al,** *adj.*

pa·tri·ot (pā′trē ət) *n.* a person who loves and enthusiastically and loyally supports his or her country. [Middle French *patriote,* from Late Latin *patriōta* fellow countryman, from Greek *patriōtēs.*]

pa·tri·ot·ic (pā′trē ot′ik) *adj.* characterized by, displaying, or inspired by patriotism. —**pa′tri·ot′i·cal·ly,** *adv.*

pa·tri·ot·ism (pā′trē ə tiz′əm) *n.* a love for and enthusiastic support of one's country.

pa·tris·tic (pə tris′tik) *adj.* of or relating to the fathers of the early Christian church or to their doctrines or writings. Also, **pa·tris′ti·cal.**

Pa·tro·clus (pə trō′kləs) *n.* in Greek legend, a friend of Achilles. When Patroclus took Achilles' place in battle, he was killed by Hector.

pa·trol (pə trōl′) *v.t., v.i.,* **-trolled, -trol·ling.** to go through or around (an area or place) for the purpose of guarding or inspecting: *Several police cars patrolled the neighborhood.* —*n.* **1.** one or more persons who patrol or are assigned to patrol. **2.** a detachment of ground, sea, or air forces sent out for reconnaissance, combat, or some other purpose: *All the soldiers in the patrol returned safely.* **3.** the act of patrolling: *Sentries maintained an all-night patrol.* **4.** a unit of a Boy or Girl Scout troop usually consisting of eight scouts. [French *patrouiller* to paddle in mud (because sentries often had to walk back and forth in mud), from *patte* paw; of uncertain origin.] —**pa·trol′ler,** *n.*

patrol car, a police car assigned to patrol a particular area. Also, **squad car.**

pa·trol·man (pə trōl′mən) *n., pl.* **-men** (-mən). a police officer assigned to patrol a certain area.

patrol wagon, a specially equipped truck used by the police for conveying prisoners.

pa·trol·wom·an (pə trōl′wùm′ən) *n., pl.* **-wom·en** (-wim′ən). a female police officer assigned to patrol a certain area.

pa·tron (pā′trən) *n.* **1.** a person who supports, promotes, or protects a person, cause, organization, or undertaking by the use of money or influence: *a patron of the arts.* **2.** a regular customer: *a patron of a restaurant.* **3.** patron saint. [Old French *patron* protector, from Latin *patrōnus,* from *pater* father.] —**pa′tron·al,** *adj.*

> **Synonyms** **Patron** and **sponsor** mean a person or organization that promotes the cause of or contributes financial support to someone or something. **Patron** designates a wealthy and influential supporter, *esp.* a benefactor of the arts: *The prodigy's musical training was paid for by a patron.* **Sponsor** is applied to a person or organization that supports another through promotion, endorsement, or financial backing: *The foundation acted as sponsor of the research study.*

pa·tron·age (pā′trə nij, pat′rə-) *n.* **1.** the support or assistance provided by a patron. **2.** the financial support given to a commercial establishment by customers. **3.** a condescending manner or treatment. **4.a.** the power, right, or system of distributing jobs, government contracts, or other political favors: *the patronage of a senator.* **b.** the jobs or favors so distributed.

pa·tron·ess (pā′trə nəs) *n.* a woman who is a patron.

pa·tron·ize (pā′trə nīz′, pat′rə-) *v.t.,* **-ized, -iz·ing. 1.** to be a customer of (a commercial establishment), *esp.* on a regular basis. **2.** to treat as inferior or in a condescending manner: *Don't patron-*

ize the younger children. **3.** to give support or assistance to; act as a patron toward. —**pa′tron·iz′er,** *n.* —**pa′tron·iz′ing·ly,** *adv.*

patron saint, a saint chosen as the special guardian or protector of a person, place, or group.

pat·ro·nym·ic (pat′rə nim′ik) *n.* **1.** a name derived from the name of a person's father or other male ancestor, *esp.* by the addition of a prefix or suffix, as *Ericson,* son of Eric. **2.** a family name; surname. —*adj.* **1.** relating to or derived from the name of a person's father or other male ancestor: *a patronymic surname.* **2.** indicating such descent: *a patronymic suffix.* [Late Latin *patrōnymicus* derived from the name of a father, from Greek *patrōnymicos,* from *patēr* father + (dialectal) *onyma* name, word.]

pa·troon (pə trün′) *n.* a proprietor of a feudal estate in the former Dutch colony of New Netherland. [Dutch *patroon* employer, master, from Latin *patrōnus* protector.]

pat·sy (pat′sē) *n., pl.* **-sies.** *Slang.* a person who is easily tricked, taken advantage of, or made a fool of; dupe. [Of uncertain origin.]

pat·ten (pat′ən) *n.* any of various types of footwear, including shoes, overshoes, and sandals, having thick, often wooden soles and formerly worn to protect the feet from dampness. [Old French *patin* a clog, wooden shoe, from *patte* paw, foot; of uncertain origin.]

pat·ter[1] (pat′ər) *v.i.* **1.** to make a rapid succession of soft taps: *I like the sound of raindrops as they patter on the roof.* **2.** to move with soft, rapid steps: *We heard the children pattering down the stairs.* —*n.* a rapid succession of soft taps. [PAT[1] + -ER[4].]

pat·ter[2] (pat′ər) *n.* **1.** any rapid, glib speech, *esp.* the fast, fluent talk of a salesperson, barker, or the like. **2.** the jargon of a particular class or group; cant. —*v.t., v.i.* to speak rapidly, glibly, or mechanically. [Short for PATERNOSTER; referring to the effect of the rapid repetition of the *paternoster* by priests in earlier times.]

pat·tern (pat′ərn) *n.* **1.** a decorative or artistic design: *The wallpaper was printed with a pretty flower pattern.* **2.** any natural or accidental arrangement or design of colors, shapes, or lines: *The trees cast an intricate pattern of shadows on the ground.* **3.** something designed or used as a guide, *esp.* in the making of some article: *I cut the cloth according to a pattern.* **4.** an example worthy of or proposed for imitation; model: *You were the pattern of politeness.* **5.** a set of habitual or representative actions or characteristics: *The scientist studied the pattern of the monkey's behavior.* **6.** a set path or route, as for an airplane about to land: *a flight pattern.* **7.** a style or form, as of a literary or musical work. **8.** a representative sample, specimen, or instance. —*v.t.* **1.** to make or fashion according to or in imitation of a particular pattern, guide, or example: *The author patterned the novel after a famous legend.* **2.** to mark or decorate with a pattern or design. [Old French *patron* protector, model, from Latin *patrōnus* protector.]

pat·ty (pat′ē) *also,* **pat·tie.** *n., pl.* **-ties. 1.** a small, round, flattened cake of ground or chopped food: *a hamburger patty.* **2.** a small pie. **3.** a small, flat piece, *esp.* of candy: *a mint patty.* [French *pâté* pie, pastry, from Old French *pastee* pie, from *paste* dough. See PASTE.]

pat·ty·cake (pat′ē kāk′) *n.* a game for very young children, played by patting the hands together, *esp.* while singing a nursery rhyme. —*v.i.,* **-caked, -cak·ing.** to play pattycake. [From *pat a cake,* the opening lines of a children's rhyme.]

patty shell, a small shell of puff paste, used to serve creamed meat, fish, vegetables, or fruit.

pau·ci·ty (pô′si tē) *n.* **1.** a small number; fewness: *this theory's paucity of supporters.* **2.** a scarcity or insufficiency: *a paucity of evidence.* [Latin *paucitās.*]

Paul Bun·yan (pôl′ bun′yən) in American folklore, a giant lumberjack who performed superhuman feats.

Paul·ine (pô′līn) *adj.* of or relating to Saint Paul or to his doctrines or writings.

paunch (pônch, pänch) *n.* **1.** the belly or stomach, *esp.* when large and protruding; potbelly. **2.** the first stomach of a cud-chewing animal; rumen. [Dialectal Old French *panche* belly, from Latin *pantex.*]

paunch·y (pôn′chē, pän′-) *adj.,* **-chi·er, -chi·est.** having a large, protruding belly. —**paunch′i·ness,** *n.*

pau·per (pô′pər) *n.* a very poor person, *esp.* one supported by charity. [Latin *pauper.* Doublet of POOR.]

pau·per·ism (pô′pə riz′əm) *n.* the state of being very poor; poverty.

a	at	e	end	o	hot	u	up	hw	white		about
ā	ape	ē	me	ō	old	ū	use	ng	song	ə	taken
ä	far	i	it	ô	fork	ü	rule	th	thin		pencil
âr	care	ī	ice	oi	oil	ù	pull	th	this		lemon
		îr	pierce	ou	out	ûr	turn	zh	measure		circus

P

pau·per·ize (pô′pə rīz′) *v.t.,* **-ized, -iz·ing.** to make a pauper of. —**pau′per·i·za′tion,** *n.*

pause (pôz) *v.i.,* **paused, paus·ing.** to stop for a short time. —*n.* **1.** a brief or temporary stop, hesitation, or delay: *After a pause because of rain, the game continued.* **2.** a brief stop or break in speaking, reading, or writing, esp. to clarify meaning or add expression: *The speaker continued after a pause for applause.* **3.** *Music.* a sign (⌒ or ⌣) placed above or below a note or rest to indicate that it is to be prolonged. [Latin *pausa* a stop, ceasing, from Greek *pausis.*]
 •**to give someone pause.** to cause someone to hesitate or be uncertain.

pa·vane (pə vän′, -van′) *also,* **pav·an** (pav′ən). *n.* **1.** a slow, stately dance of the sixteenth century. **2.** the music for this dance.

pave (pāv) *v.t.,* **paved, pav·ing. 1.** to cover (a road or other surface) with pavement: *to pave a driveway with concrete.* **2.** to cover as if with pavement. [Old French *paver* to cover ground with paving stones, going back to Latin *pavīre* to strike, tread down.]
 •**to pave the way.** to prepare or lead the way; make progress easier: *This research will pave the way for future discoveries.*

pave·ment (pāv′mənt) *n.* **1.** a covering or surface of concrete, asphalt, brick, or similar material, as for a road or sidewalk. **2.** the material used to make such a covering or surface. **3.** sidewalk. [Old French *pavement* floor, going back to Latin *pavīmentum* hard floor.]

pa·vil·ion (pə vil′yən) *n.* **1.** an open, often ornamental building, as in a park or public garden, used for exhibition, entertainment, recreation, or shelter. **2.** a large tent, often with a pointed top. **3.** one of a group of related buildings or an extension of a main building, as of a hospital. **4.** a projecting part of a building, often elaborately decorated. —*v.t.* to shelter or enclose in or as if in a pavilion. [Old French *pavillon* tent, canopy, from Latin *pāpiliō* butterfly, tent; because it resembles a butterfly with outspread wings.]

pav·ing (pā′ving) *n.* **1.** the act of laying a pavement. **2.** a paved surface; pavement. **3.** the material used for pavement.

paw (pô) *n.* **1.** the foot of an animal having nails or claws. **2.** *Informal.* a human hand, esp. when used in a rough or clumsy way. —*v.t.* **1.** to strike or scrape (something) with the paws or hooves: *The angry bull pawed the ground.* **2.** to touch or handle roughly, clumsily, or in too familiar a manner. —*v.i.* **1.** to strike or scrape something with the paws or hooves: *The dog pawed at the spot where the bone had been buried.* **2.** to make rough or clumsy movements with the hands. [Old French *powe* foot of an animal or bird, claw; possibly of Germanic origin.]

pawl (pôl) *n.* a catch or bar on a pivot that engages the teeth of a ratchet wheel, permitting the wheel to revolve in only one direction. For illustration, see **ratchet.** [Possibly modification of Dutch *pal.*]

pawn¹ (pôn) *v.t.* **1.** to deposit (something valuable) as security for a loan, esp. with a pawnbroker. **2.** to risk or wager; pledge: *to pawn one's life.* —*n.* **1.** the condition of being held as security, as for a loan. **2.** something that is given or held as security, as for a loan. **3.** a person being held as security; hostage. [Old French *pan* pledge, security; of Germanic origin.] —**pawn′er;** *also,* **paw·nor** (pô′nər, -nôr), *n.*

pawn² (pôn) *n.* **1.** *Chess.* any of the sixteen chess pieces of lowest value, eight to each player, that is usually able to move only one square forward at a time and captures by moving one square diagonally. **2.** a person or thing that is manipulated by another, esp. a person who is exploited or used for another's purposes or personal gain. [Old French *paon, peon* the chess piece, from Medieval Latin *pedo* foot soldier, from Latin *pēs* foot. Doublet of PEON.]

pawn²

pawn·bro·ker (pôn′brō′kər) *n.* a person licensed to lend money at interest on articles of personal property left as security.

Paw·nee (pô nē′) *n., pl.* **-nee** or **-nees. 1.** a member of any of a group of North American Indian tribes formerly living in the valley of the Platte River in Nebraska, now living in Oklahoma. **2.** the language of the Pawnee.

pawn·shop (pôn′shop′) *n.* a pawnbroker's shop.

paw·paw (pə pô′, pô′pô′) *also,* **pa·paw.** *n.* **1.** the strong-smelling, edible oblong fruit of a tree, *Asimina triloba,* having yellow flesh and a bananalike taste. **2.** the tree bearing this fruit, growing mainly in the central United States. [Spanish *papaya* fruit; of Carib origin.]

Pax (paks) *n.* in Roman mythology, the goddess of peace. [Latin *pāx* peace.]

pax vo·bis·cum (vō bis′kəm) *Latin.* peace be with you.

pay¹ (pā) *v.,* **paid, pay·ing.** —*v.t.* **1.** to give (money) in return for goods or services or to settle a debt: *We paid fifty dollars to have the stereo fixed.* **2.** to give (a person, company, or organization) what is due for services rendered or goods received: *I paid the salesclerk for the coat.* **3.** to give, provide, or hand over the amount or cost of: *to pay a bill.* **4.** to yield as return or compensation: *This job pays $200 a week.* **5.** to be profitable or worthwhile for: *It will pay you to plan now for the future.* **6.** to give, render, or bestow: *to pay a compliment.* **7.** to make (a visit or call). **8.** to undergo, suffer, or bear: *to pay the consequences of one's actions.* —*v.i.* **1.** to give something, esp. money, in buying something or settling a debt or obligation; make payment: *Can I pay by check?* **2.** to be profitable or worthwhile: *It pays to eat a balanced diet.* **3.** to undergo suffering; be punished: *to pay for one's crimes.* —*n.* **1.** something given in return or compensation, esp. money given for work done: *The workers demanded higher pay.* **2.** paid employment: *in the pay of the government.* —*adj.* **1.** (of earth) yielding valuable minerals in mining: *a pay lode.* **2.** operated by or made available for use by the deposit of a coin or coins: *a pay toilet, a pay telephone.* **3.** requiring regular payments for use or service. [Old French *paier* to appease, satisfy (as with money), discharge a debt, from Latin *pācāre* to appease, pacify.]
 •**to pay back. a.** to repay: *Please pay back the money I lent you.* **b.** to return: *to pay back a favor.*
 •**to pay off. a.** to pay all that is owed on or to; pay in full: *to pay off a debt, to pay off a creditor.* **b.** to yield favorable or desired results; be profitable: *My hard work paid off when I got the promotion.* **c.** to get even with or for: *to pay off an enemy, to pay off an old grudge.* **d.** to bribe.
 •**to pay one's dues.** to earn a right or position through experience, hard work, or suffering: *to pay one's dues in regional theater before getting a role on Broadway.*
 •**to pay one's way.** to pay one's own share of expenses.
 •**to pay out. a.** to expend; disburse. **b.** to slacken or let out (a rope or line): *The sailor payed out the rope.* ➡ For def. b, past tense and past participle: **payed out.**
 •**to pay up.** to pay all that is owed.

Synonyms *n.* **Pay, wage,** and **salary** mean the money a person is given in return for labor or services. **Pay** is the general term for money paid to an employee: *The company did not withhold taxes from its employees' pay.* **Wage** usually refers to money paid at a weekly, daily, or hourly rate, often for manual or mechanical labor: *The waiters and waitresses were paid the minimum wage.* **Salary** indicates a specific sum, often annual, paid in installments for professional or managerial services: *The marketing director received an increase in salary.*

pay² (pā) *v.t.,* **payed** or **paid, pay·ing.** to cover with tar, pitch, or other waterproof material, as the seams of a boat or ship. [Old French *peier* to cover with pitch, from Latin *picāre.*]

pay·a·ble (pā′ə bəl) *adj.* **1.** to be paid; due: *The bill is payable within ninety days.* **2.** capable of being paid; that can be paid: *I made the check payable to the manager.* **3.** profitable, as a mine.

pay·check (pā′chek′) *n.* a check given to an employee for work done.

pay·day (pā′dā′) *n.* the day on which wages are paid.

pay dirt 1. earth, ore, or similar material containing enough valuable metal to make mining profitable. **2.** any source of profit or success: *The toy company really hit pay dirt with its new talking dolls.*

pay·ee (pā ē′) *n.* a person to whom money has been or is to be paid.

pay·er (pā′ər) *n.* a person who pays or is responsible for paying something, such as a bill.

pay·load (pā′lōd′) *n.* **1.** a cargo or part of a cargo, as on a ship or truck, that produces revenue. **2.** in a rocket, aircraft, or spacecraft, anything carried in addition to what is essential to the operation of the craft: *The rocket carried a payload of scientific instruments for collecting data.* **3.** the warhead of a guided or ballistic missile.

pay·mas·ter (pā′mas′tər) *n.* a person in charge of paying wages.

pay·ment (pā′mənt) *n.* **1.** the act of paying: *The company required that payment be made on time.* **2.** something that is paid: *to receive weekly payment for one's work.* **3.** reward or punishment; requital: *The long jail sentence was just payment for that crime.*

pay·nim (pā′nim) *n. Archaic.* **1.** heathen. **2.** a non-Christian, esp. a Muslim. [Old French *paienisme* heathendom, from Late Latin *pāgānismus,* from Latin *pāgānus* heathen, villager, civilian. See PAGAN.]

pay·off (pā′ôf′, -of′) *n.* **1.** payment, as of wages. **2.** a reward or punishment. **3.** *Informal.* a climax or outcome, as of a narrative or series of events. **4.** *Informal.* a bribe.

pay·o·la (pā ō′lə) *n. Informal.* a payment made as a bribe, esp. for illegal favors. [From PAY¹.]

pay·roll (pā′rōl′) *also,* **pay roll.** *n.* **1.** a list of employees to be paid, with the amounts to which each is entitled. **2.** the total amount of money to be paid to employees.

payt., payment.

pay TV, a service that provides subscribers with certain television programs for a monthly payment. Cable TV is a form of pay TV. Also, **pay television.**

Pb, the symbol for lead. [Latin *plumbum.*]

PBB, any one of a group of chemicals related to the polychlorinated biphenyls, used in industry and regarded as poisonous environmental pollutants.

PBS, Public Broadcasting Service.

pc., piece.

p.c. 1. percent. **2.** petty cash. **3.** postcard.

PC, personal computer.

P.C., Privy Council.

PCB, any of a family of highly toxic, carcinogenic chlorinated hydrocarbons that are used in paints, inks, and plastics and as heat exchangers in electrical transformers, regarded as being among the most dangerous of environmental pollutants. [Abbreviation of *p(oly)c(hlorinated) b(iphenyl).*]

pct., percent.

Pd, the symbol for palladium.

pd., paid.

p.d., per diem.

P.D., Police Department.

PE, the postal abbreviation for Prince Edward Island.

P.E., Protestant Episcopal.

pea (pē) *n.* **1.** the round, usually green seed of a pod-bearing plant, *Pisum sativum,* eaten as a vegetable, either raw or cooked. **2.** the plant itself, having oval or oblong leaflets and white flowers with winglike petals. **3.** any of various pod-bearing plants of the same family as the pea, such as the cowpea, or their seeds. [Taken as singular of earlier *pease* pea, mistakenly thought to be plural. See PEASE.]

peace (pēs) *n.* **1.** freedom from or cessation of war or hostilities: *years of peace between world wars.* **2.** an agreement, treaty, or settlement to end a war or hostilities. **3.** freedom from lawlessness or other strife; public order and security: *Law officers were assigned to keep the peace.* **4.** an absence of or freedom from disturbance or agitation; calmness: *the peace and quiet of the country.* **5.** mental, emotional, or spiritual tranquility or contentment: *to find inner peace through meditation.* —*interj.* **1.** be quiet; keep silent. **2.** peace be with you. [Old French *pais* untroubled state, absence of war, agreement to end war, from Latin *pāx.*]

•**at peace.** free from war or other strife.

•**to hold** (or **keep**) **one's peace.** to be or remain silent.

•**to make one's peace with.** to have a reconciliation with.

peace·a·ble (pē′sə bəl) *adj.* **1.** inclined to avoid strife and disturbance; disposed to peace. **2.** characterized by peace; peaceful: *The ruler had a long and peaceable reign.* —**peace′a·ble·ness,** *n.* —**peace′a·bly,** *adv.*

Peace Corps, a U.S. government agency that trains and sends volunteer workers to aid developing countries.

peace·ful (pēs′fəl) *adj.* **1.** free from war, strife, or other disturbance. **2.** not violent, warlike, or quarrelsome: *to decide a dispute by peaceful means.* **3.** free from worry or agitation; tranquil; serene; calm: *a peaceful atmosphere.* —**peace′ful·ly,** *adv.* —**peace′ful·ness,** *n.*

peace·keep·ing (pēs′kē′ping) *n.* the maintenance of peace and order between hostile countries or groups within a country by an outside military force: *to use UN troops for peacekeeping.* —*adj.* relating to or charged with peacekeeping: *a peacekeeping force.*

peace·mak·er (pēs′mā′kər) *n.* a person who brings about or tries to bring about a reconciliation between warring or disputing parties. —**peace′mak′ing,** *n., adj.*

peace offering 1. an offering, such as a gift, made to appease anger or bring about reconciliation or peace. **2.** in the Old Testament, an offering of thanksgiving to God, prescribed by Levitical law.

peace officer, a civil officer, such as a sheriff or police officer, whose duty is the preservation of public order and security.

peace pipe, a tobacco pipe with a long ornamented stem, used by North American Indians on ceremonial occasions as a symbol of peace. Also, **calumet.** For illustration, see **calumet.**

peace·time (pēs′tīm′) *n.* a period when a nation is not involved in war. —*adj.* of, for, or characteristic of such a period: *a peacetime army.*

peach¹ (pēch) *n.* **1.** the sweet, juicy fruit of a tree, *Prunus persica,* of the rose family, having a large rough stone or pit, thick fleshy pulp, and a velvety yellow or yellow-red skin. **2.** the tree bearing this fruit, having pink flowers, widely cultivated in temper-

ate climates. **3.** a yellowish pink color. **4.** *Slang.* an exceptionally beautiful, pleasing, or excellent person or thing. —*adj.* **1.** made with peaches. **2.** having the color peach. [Old French *pesche* the fruit, from Latin *Persicum* literally, Persian; referring to the Romans' importing of peaches from Persia.]

peach² (pēch) *v.i. Slang.* to inform on an accomplice; turn informer. [Short for obsolete *appeach* to accuse, from Anglo-Norman *apecher,* form of Old French *empecher* to hinder. See IMPEACH.] —**peach′like′,** *adj.*

peach·blow (pēch′blō′) *n.* a pale pinkish purple glaze used on some Chinese porcelain.

peach·y (pē′chē) *adj.,* **peach·i·er, peach·i·est. 1.** resembling a peach, esp. in color or texture. **2.** *Slang.* fine; wonderful: *a peachy idea.* —**peach′i·ness,** *n.*

pea·coat (pē′kōt′) *also,* **pea coat.** *n.* pea jacket.

pea·cock (pē′kok′) *n.* **1.** the male of the peafowl, having a fan-shaped crest, shiny blue plumage on the head, neck, and body, and a train of bright, metallic green feathers covered with large eyelike spots. When the train is raised and spread, it is fan-shaped. Length: to 92 inches (234 centimeters), including train. **2.** any peafowl. **3.** a vain and ostentatious person. [Old English *pēa, pāwa* peafowl (from Latin *pāvō*) + *cocc* (see COCK¹).]

peacock

peacock blue, a bright greenish blue color.

pea·fowl (pē′foul′) *n., pl.* **-fowl** or **-fowls.** any of several pheasants, family Phasianidae, esp. genus *Pavo,* native to India and Southeast Asia, noted for the brilliant ornamental feathers of the male. [PEA(COCK) + FOWL.]

pea green, a medium yellowish green color.

pea·hen (pē′hen′) *n.* the female peafowl.

pea jacket, a short, double-breasted coat of thick woolen cloth, such as that originally worn by sailors. Also, **peacoat.** [Modification of Dutch *pijjekker,* from *pij* thick cloth + *jekker* jacket (going back to Old French *jaque*). See JACKET.]

peak (pēk) *n.* **1.** the pointed top of a mountain. **2.** a mountain having a pointed summit. **3.** a sharp, tapering, or projecting point or end: *the peak of a skyscraper.* **4.** the maximum point or greatest level, as of development or intensity: *Traffic reaches its peak during rush hour.* **5.** the projecting brim of a cap. **6.a.** the narrow part of a ship's hull at the bow or stern. **b.** the upper after corner of a fore-and-aft sail that is attached to a gaff. —*adj.* of, relating to, or constituting the maximum: *the peak hours of production.* —*v.i.* to reach the maximum point or greatest level: *Sales peak during this time of year.* [Form of PIKE².]

Synonyms *n.* **Peak, summit,** and **pinnacle** mean the highest point or level. **Peak** designates the maximum point of development: *Sales hit their peak in the week before Christmas.* **Summit** implies the highest level of accomplishment that can be reached: *Appointment to the corporation's presidency was the summit of her career.* **Pinnacle** suggests a dizzying and often precarious height: *The twenty-five games he won in his first major-league season were a pinnacle the pitcher never equaled.*

a	at	e	end	o	hot	u	up	hw	white		about
ā	ape	ē	me	ō	old	ū	use	ng	song		taken
ä	far	i	it	ô	fork	ü	rule	th	thin	ə	pencil
âr	care	ī	ice	oi	oil	u̇	pull	th	this		lemon
		îr	pierce	ou	out	ûr	turn	zh	measure		circus

P

891

peaked¹ (pēkt, pē′kid) *adj.* having or ending in a peak; pointed: *a peaked roof.* [PEAK + -ED².]

peak·ed² (pē′kid) *adj.* pale and emaciated; sickly: *You looked rather peaked after your illness.* [From earlier *peak* to look wan, fade (of uncertain origin) + -ED².] —**peak′ed·ness,** *n.*

peal (pēl) *n.* **1.** a loud, sonorous, often prolonged sound or succession of sounds, as of a bell or laughter. **2.** a set of bells tuned to one another. —*v.t., v.i.* to sound or give forth in a peal or peals. [Short for APPEAL.]

pe·an (pē′ən) paean.

pea·nut (pē′nut′) *n.* **1.** the edible, nutlike seed of a plant, *Arachis hypogaea,* of the pea family, developing in an underground pod and having a thin brownish skin. **2.** such a pod, usually containing two of these seeds. **3.** the bush or runner-type plant bearing these pods, widely cultivated in warm climates, having short-lived, yellow flowers. **4.** peanuts. *Slang.* a small or insignificant sum of money. [PEA + NUT.]

peanut brittle, a hard candy containing peanuts.

peanut butter, a soft, creamy food made by grinding blanched, roasted peanuts, usually used as a spread.

peanut oil, an oil extracted from peanuts by pressing or by means of solvents, used in cooking and in the manufacture of margarine.

peanut plant

pear (pâr) *n.* **1.** the sweet, usually bell-shaped, edible fruit of any of a group of trees, genus *Pyrus,* of the rose family, having a firm, juicy, sandy-textured flesh and a smooth yellow, brown, or reddish skin. **2.** the tree bearing this fruit. [Old English *pere* the fruit, going back to Latin *pirum.*]

pearl (pûrl) *n.* **1.** a lustrous, rounded, usually white or cream-colored gem, the only precious stone of organic origin, formed from a secretion around a foreign substance inside the shell of a mollusk, esp. an oyster of the genus *Pinctada.* **a cultured pearl** is one that forms when the foreign body is introduced by hand rather than entering naturally. **2.** something resembling a pearl in appearance, as a drop of water. **3.** a person or thing that is choice, precious, or the finest example of something: *pearls of wisdom.* **4.** mother-of-pearl. **5.** pearl gray. —*adj.* **1.** relating to, consisting of, or adorned or set with a pearl or pearls. **2.** made of or inlaid with mother-of-pearl: *pearl buttons.* **3.** having the color or shape of a pearl. —*v.i.* **1.** to form drops or beads resembling pearls. **2.** to dive or fish for pearls. [Old French *perle* the gem, a very fine example, going back to Latin *perna* ham, a sea mussel (in which pearls were sometimes found).] —**pearl′er,** *n.*

· **to cast pearls before swine.** to offer or give something of great value to someone who cannot appreciate it and may defile or abuse it.

pearl gray, a clear, pale, bluish gray color.

pearl·y (pûr′lē) *adj.,* **pearl·i·er, pearl·i·est. 1.** resembling a pearl or pearls: *pearly teeth.* **2.** adorned with pearls or mother-of-pearl. —**pearl′i·ness,** *n.*

pearly nautilus, nautilus *(def. 1).*

pear-shaped (pâr′shāpt′) *adj.* **1.** having the shape of a pear. **2.** (of a vocal tone) clear, mellow, and full of resonance.

peas·ant (pez′ənt) *n.* **1.** a member of a class of persons, as in Europe or Asia, who work as small-scale farmers or as farm laborers. **2.** an unsophisticated or boorish person. [Old French *païsant* native, dweller in rural areas, from *païs* country, district, going back to Latin *pāgus* village, district.]

peas·ant·ry (pez′ən trē) *n.* **1.** peasants considered collectively or as a social class. **2.** the rank, condition, or behavior of a peasant.

pease (pēz) *n., pl.* **peas·es, peas·en** (pē′zən). *Archaic.* pea. [Old English *pise* pea plant or its seed, from Latin *pīsum,* from Greek *pison.*]

pease·cod (pēz′kod′) *also,* **peas·cod.** *n. Archaic.* the pod of the pea plant.

pea·shoot·er (pē′shü′tər) *n.* a toy consisting of a tube through which small pellets may be blown.

peat (pēt) *n.* a deposit of decomposed plant matter that accumulates in bogs and similar poorly drained areas, used to improve soil or as a mulch. [Medieval Latin (in England) *peta;* possibly of Celtic origin.]

peat moss 1. any of a group of pale green mosses, genus *Sphagnum,* that grow in swamps and bogs and are the major source of peat. **2.** the residue of such mosses and other plants, used to improve garden soil and as a mulch.

pea·vey (pē′vē) *n., pl.* **-veys.** a heavy pole having a strong metal spike at the tip and a hinged hook near the end, used by lumberjacks to handle logs. [From Joseph *Peavey,* nineteenth-century American blacksmith, who supposedly invented it.]

pea·vy (pē′vē) *n., pl.* **-vies.** peavey.

peb·ble (peb′əl) *n.* **1.** a small, usually round, stone that is worn or eroded by the action of water or sand. **2.** a rough, irregular surface, as on leather or paper. —*v.t.,* **-bled, -bling.** to give a rough, irregular surface to (leather or paper). [Old English *papol(stān)* small stone.] —**peb′bly,** *adj.*

pe·can (pi kän′, -kan′) *n.* **1.** the sweet, edible nut of a large North American tree, *Carya illinoensis,* of the walnut family, having a thin, brittle shell and an outer husk. **2.** the tree producing this nut, having a deeply ridged, gray or brown bark, hard, strong wood, and leaves composed of many leaflets. [Algonquian *pakan* hard-shelled nut.]

pec·ca·dil·lo (pek′ə dil′ō) *n., pl.* **-loes** or **-los.** a slight fault or sin. [Spanish *pecadillo,* diminutive of *pecado* sin, from Latin *peccātum.*]

pec·cant (pek′ənt) *adj.* **1.** guilty of a moral offense; sinning. **2.** violating a rule or principle; faulty. [Latin *peccāns,* present participle of *peccāre* to sin.] —**pec′can·cy,** *n.* —**pec′cant·ly,** *adv.*

pec·ca·ry (pek′ə rē) *n., pl.* **-ries.** a wild, piglike mammal, genus *Tayassu,* native to brush and forest country from the southern United States to Argentina, having coarse, bristly hair and straight tusks that point downward. Length: 3 feet (0.9 meter). [Carib *pakira.*]

peck¹ (pek) *n.* **1.** a unit of dry measure, equal to 8 quarts or ¼ of a bushel (8.8 liters). **2.** a vessel for measuring or holding a peck. **3.** *Informal.* a great deal; considerable amount: *I got myself into a peck of trouble when I broke the window.* [Old French *pek* unit of measure for oats; of uncertain origin.]

peccary

peck² (pek) *v.t.* **1.** to strike (something) with the beak in a short, rapid movement: *The parakeet pecked the bars of its cage.* **2.** to make by striking with the beak: *to peck a hole.* **3.** to strike at and pick up with the beak: *to peck grains of corn.* —*v.i.* **1.** to strike or try to strike with the beak in a short, rapid movement (often with *at*): *The chick pecked at my finger.* **2.** to eat in small amounts, esp. without appetite or interest (with *at*): *to peck at one's food.* —*n.* **1.** a short, rapid stroke made with the beak. **2.** a hole or mark made by such a stroke. **3.** *Informal.* a quick, light kiss: *a peck on the cheek.* [Possibly form of PICK¹.] —**peck′er,** *n.*

pecking order 1. a social hierarchy within a flock of birds composed of a single species, esp. of poultry, in which each member is able to peck at and dominate weaker members and is in turn pecked and dominated by those stronger than it is. **2.** any similar social hierarchy having definite levels of rank, esp. one in which rank is determined by aggressive behavior. Also, **peck order.**

Pe·cos Bill (pā′kəs, -kōs) in American folklore, a cowboy hero known for his superhuman exploits.

pec·ten (pek′tən) *n., pl.* **pec·ti·nes** (-tə nēz′). *Zoology.* **1.** a comblike part, esp. a fan-shaped membrane in the eyes of birds and reptiles, that has folds resembling the teeth of a comb. **2.** a scallop, esp. one of the genus *Pecten.* [Latin *pecten* comb.]

pec·tin (pek′tin) *n.* any of several gelatinous substances found esp. in certain ripe fruits and used to gel jams and jellies. [Greek *pēktos* congealed, curdled + -IN¹.]

pec·to·ral (pek′tər əl) *adj.* **1.** of, relating to, or situated in or on the chest. **2.** worn on the chest or breast: *a pectoral cross.* —*n.* **1.** pectoral fin. **2.** a medicine, as an expectorant, used to treat a disorder of the respiratory tract. **3.** a pectoral organ, as a muscle. **4.** something worn on the breast. [Latin *pectorālis* relating to the breast, from *pectus* breast.]

pectoral fin, in fish, one of a pair of fins behind the head, corresponding to the forelimbs of higher vertebrates.

pectoral girdle 1. in vertebrates, the ring of bones to which the forelimbs or arms are attached. **2.** in humans, the bony structure to which the arms are attached, consisting of the shoulder blades and collarbones. Also, **pectoral arch.**

pec·u·late (pek′yə lāt′) *v.t., v.i.,* **-lat·ed, -lat·ing.** to steal (money or property entrusted to one, esp. public funds); embezzle. [Latin *pecūlātus,* past participle of *pecūlārī* to embezzle public money, going back to *pecu* money, cattle (because wealth in ancient times was often thought of in terms of cattle).] —**pec′u·la′tion,** *n.* —**pec′u·la′tor,** *n.*

pe·cul·iar (pi kūl′yər) *adj.* **1.** strange or unusual; odd: *a peculiar habit.* **2.** belonging exclusively to a certain person, group, place, or thing: *The koala bear is peculiar to Australia.* **3.** distinct

from others; special; particular: *This discovery is of peculiar interest to students of Greek history.* [Latin *peculiaris* one's own, from *peculium* property (in cattle), private property, from *pecu*. See PECULATE.] —**pe·cul′iar·ly,** *adv.* —For Synonyms, see **strange.**

pe·cu·li·ar·i·ty (pi kū′lē ar′i tē) *n., pl.* **-ties. 1.** a strange or unusual feature or characteristic. **2.** a special or particular characteristic: *A long tail is a peculiarity of that breed of dog.* **3.** the quality or state of being peculiar: *The peculiarity of your answer puzzled them.*

pe·cu·ni·ar·y (pi kū′nē er′ē) *adj.* **1.** of, relating to, or consisting of money: *a pecuniary reward.* **2.** (of a legal offense) involving a fine. [Latin *pecūniārius* relating to money, from *pecūnia* money, from *pecu* money, cattle. See PECULATE.]

-ped, form of **-pede,** as in *biped.*

ped·a·gog·ic (ped′ə goj′ik, -gō′jik) *adj.* of, relating to, or characteristic of a pedagogue or pedagogy. Also, **ped′a·gog′i·cal.** —**ped′a·gog′i·cal·ly,** *adv.*

ped·a·gog·ics (ped′ə goj′iks, -gō′jiks) *n.* pedagogy. ➡ used as singular.

ped·a·gogue (ped′ə gog′, -gôg′) also, **ped·a·gog.** *n.* **1.** any teacher. **2.** a teacher who is pedantic and narrow-minded. [Latin *paedagōgus* slave who led a boy to school, teacher, from Greek *paidagōgos,* from *pais* boy + *agōgos* leader.]

ped·a·go·gy (ped′ə goj′ē, -gō′jē) *n.* the art, science, or profession of teaching.

ped·al (ped′əl) *n.* **1.** a foot-operated part or lever that activates or controls a machine or part of a machine, as on a bicycle or automobile. **2.** a similar part or lever worked by the foot that modifies the sound of a musical instrument, as a piano. —*v.,* -aled, -al·ing; *also, British,* -alled, -al·ling. —*v.t.* to work the pedals of; operate by working pedals: *to pedal a bicycle.* —*v.i.* to work or use a pedal or pedals: *to peddle slowly.* —*adj.* **1.** of or relating to a foot or the feet. **2.** of, relating to, or operated by a pedal or pedals. [Latin *pedālis* relating to the foot, from *pēs* foot.]

ped·al·board (ped′əl bôrd′) *n.* an organ keyboard played with the feet.

pedal point *Music.* a note or tone sustained, usually in the bass, while the other parts progress harmonically and melodically.

pedal pushers, women's slacks that extend to, or just below, the knee.

ped·ant (ped′ənt) *n.* a person who presents his or her knowledge in an ostentatious, dogmatic, or dull manner, often placing excessive emphasis on trivial details and formal rules. [Italian *pedante* schoolmaster, teacher; of uncertain origin.]

pe·dan·tic (pi dan′tik) *adj.* of, like, characteristic of, or of the nature of a pedant or pedantry: *a pedantic lecturer.* —**pe·dan′ti·cal·ly,** *adv.*

ped·ant·ry (ped′ən trē) *n., pl.* **-ries. 1.** the qualities, characteristics, manner, or practices of a pedant. **2.** an instance of being pedantic.

ped·ate (ped′āt) *adj.* **1.** having feet: *pedate animals.* **2.** resembling or serving as a foot or feet; footlike. **3.** *Botany.* (of a leaf) having the two lateral lobes divided into smaller segments. [Latin *pedātus,* past participle of *pedāre* to furnish with feet, from *pēs* foot.]

ped·dle (ped′əl) *v.,* -dled, -dling. —*v.t.* **1.** to sell (merchandise), usually in small quantities, esp. by traveling from place to place: *to peddle vegetables from door to door.* **2.** to dispense, deal out, or distribute: *to peddle rumors.* —*v.i.* to travel from place to place offering merchandise for sale. [From PEDDLER.]

ped·dler (ped′lər) *also,* **pedlar.** *n.* a person who peddles. [Modification of obsolete *pedder,* from (dialectal) *ped* basket; of uncertain origin.]

-pede *combining form* foot; feet: *centipede.* [Latin *ped-,* stem of *pēs* foot.]

ped·er·ast (ped′ə rast′) *n.* a man who engages in pederasty.

ped·er·as·ty (ped′ə ras′tē) *n.* sexual relations between males, esp. between a man and a boy. [Greek *paiderastiā* love of boys, going back to *pais* boy + *erān* to love.]

ped·es·tal (ped′ə stəl) *n.* **1.** an architectural support for a column, statue, or similar upright structure. **2.** any base or supporting structure, as for a bust, sculpture, or urn. —*v.t.,* -taled, -tal·ing; *also, British,* -talled, -tal·ling. to place on or support with a pedestal. [French *piédestal* support, from Italian *piedistallo* base¹, support, from *pie* foot (from Latin *pēs*) + *di* of (from Latin *dē* from) + *stallo* stall (of Germanic origin).]

   • **on a pedestal.** in a position or state of high, often excessive or exaggerated regard or estimation: *The children put the movie star on a pedestal.*

pe·des·tri·an (pə des′trē ən) *n.* a person who travels on foot, esp. as opposed to a motorist; walker. —*adj.* **1.** of or for people traveling on foot: *a pedestrian path.* **2.** lacking originality, imagination, or excitement; commonplace or dull: *a pedestrian style of*

writing. [Latin *pedester* (from *pēs* foot) + -IAN.] —**pe·des′tri·an·ism,** *n.*

pedi- *combining form* foot; feet: *pedicure.* [Latin *ped-,* stem of *pēs* foot.]

pe·di·at·ric (pē′dē at′rik) *adj.* of or relating to pediatrics.

pe·di·a·tri·cian (pē′dē ə trish′ən) *n.* a doctor specializing in pediatrics. Also, **pe·di·at·rist** (pē′dē ə trist′).

pe·di·at·rics (pē′dē at′riks) *n.* the branch of medical science that deals with the care of babies and children and the treatment of their diseases. ➡ used as singular. [Greek *paid-,* stem of *pais* child + *iātreiā* medical treatment + -ICS.]

ped·i·cel (ped′ə səl) *also,* **ped·i·cle** (ped′i kəl). *n.* **1.** *Botany.* a small stem, esp. one supporting a single flower in a flower cluster. **2.** *Zoology.* peduncle. [Modern Latin *pedicellus,* from Latin *pedīculus,* diminutive of *pēs* foot.]

pe·dic·u·lo·sis (pi dik′yə lō′sis) *n.* the state or condition of being infested with lice; lousiness. [Modern Latin *pediculosis,* from Latin *pedīculus* louse, diminutive of *pedis.*]

ped·i·cure (ped′i kyūr′) *n.* a cosmetic treatment of the feet, esp. trimming and polishing of the toenails. [French *pédicure,* from Latin *pēs* foot + *cūra* care.] —**ped′i·cur′ist,** *n.*

ped·i·gree (ped′i grē′) *n.* **1.** a line of ancestors; descent; lineage. **2.** a detailed record or list of ancestry or descent, esp. of an animal: *the pedigree of a champion dog.* **3.** a distinguished or pure ancestry. [Probably from Middle French *pie de grue* foot of a crane (from Latin *pēs* foot + *dē* from + *grūs* crane); referring to the resemblance to a crane's foot of a mark used to indicate descent in genealogies.]

ped·i·greed (ped′i grēd′) *adj.* having a recorded or known pedigree, esp. one that is distinguished: *a pedigreed cat.*

ped·i·ment (ped′ə mənt) *n.* **1.** a low-pitched, triangular, gable-like part on the front of a building, as over a portico. **2.** a similar decorative part, not necessarily triangular in shape, as over a door, screen, or window. [Earlier *periment,* probably a modification of PYRAMID.] —**ped′i·men′tal,** *adj.*

ped·i·palp (ped′ə palp′) *n.* one of the second pair of appendages in spiders and other arachnids, located on either side of the mouth, and adapted in different groups for grasping prey, chewing, feeling, or fertilizing. [Modern Latin *pedipalpus,* from Latin *pedi-* PEDI- + *palpus* soft palm of the hand.]

ped·lar (ped′lər) peddler.

pe·dol·o·gy (pi dol′ə jē) *n.* the science that deals with the origin, nature, and classification of soils. [Greek *pedon* soil¹ + -LOGY.] —**pe·do·log·i·cal** (pē′də loj′i kəl), *adj.* —**pe·dol′o·gist,** *n.*

pe·dom·e·ter (pi dom′i tər) *n.* an instrument that measures the distance covered in walking by counting the number of steps taken and multiplying by the length of a single step. [French *pédomètre,* from Latin *pēs* foot + Greek *metron* measure.]

pe·dun·cle (pi dung′kəl) *n.* **1.** *Botany.* the main stem supporting a flower cluster or an individual flower. **2.** *Zoology.* a stemlike part or structure. In brachiopods, the peduncle is used for attachment to rocks or other solid surfaces. Also, **pedicel. 3.** *Anatomy.* one of several bundles of nerve fibers connecting parts of the central nervous system. [Modern Latin *pedunculus,* diminutive of Latin *pēs* foot.] —**pe·dun·cu·lar** (pi dung′kyə lər), **pe·dun′cled,** *adj.*

pe·dun·cu·late (pi dung′kyə lit) *adj.* growing on or having a peduncle. Also, **pe·dun·cu·lat·ed** (pi dung′kyə lā′tid).

peek (pēk) *v.i.* to look quickly, furtively, or cautiously. —*n.* a quick, furtive, or cautious look. [Of uncertain origin.]

peek·a·boo (pēk′ə bü′) *n.* a game played with a young child in which one person hides his or her face, then suddenly uncovers it and says "peekaboo." —*adj.* made of openwork or a nearly transparent material; partially revealing: *a peekaboo blouse.* [PEEK + BOO.]

peel¹ (pēl) *n.* the skin or outer covering that has been or can be removed from certain fruits and vegetables: *a banana peel.* —*v.t.* **1.** to remove the skin or outer covering from: *to peel a potato.* **2.** to remove or strip off: *to peel a stamp off an envelope, to peel wallpaper from a wall.* —*v.i.* **1.** to come off, as in pieces or strips:

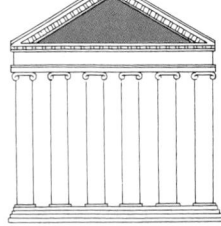

pediment

P

a	at	e	end	o	hot	u	up	hw	white		about
ā	ape	ē	me	ō	old	ū	use	ng	song		taken
ä	far	i	it	ô	fork	ū	rule	th	thin	ə	pencil
âr	care	ī	ice	oi	oil	u̇	pull	th	this		lemon
		îr	pierce	ou	out	ûr	turn	zh	measure		circus

The paint is peeling off the walls. **2.** to lose or shed an outer covering or layer, as of skin: *Your sunburned back is peeling.* **3.** *Slang.* to undress. [Old French *peler* to strip off, as skin, from Latin *pilāre* to deprive of hair, from *pilus* hair.]

· **to keep one's eye(s) peeled.** *Informal.* to be watchful; keep alert: *Keep your eyes peeled for any sign of trouble.*

· **to peel off.** (of aircraft) to veer off from a flight formation, esp. in order to make a dive.

peel² (pēl) *n.* a long-handled, shovellike implement used by bakers to put bread or other items into an oven or remove them. [Old French *pele* shovel, from Latin *pāla* shovel, spade¹.]

peel·er (pē′lər) *n.* **1.** a person or thing that peels. **2.** a device for peeling the skin or outer covering from certain fruits and vegetables: *a potato peeler.*

peel·ing (pē′ling) *n.* something that has or has been peeled off: *paint peelings, apple peelings.*

peen (pēn) *n.* the cone-shaped, hemispherical, or ball-shaped end of the head of a hammer opposite the face. [Probably of Scandinavian origin.]

peep¹ (pēp) *v.i.* **1.** to look furtively or cautiously, as through a narrow opening or from a concealed place; peek: *to peep through a crack in a wall.* **2.** to come gradually or partially into view: *The moon peeped through the clouds.* —*v.t.* to cause to become visible; put forth: *to peep one's head out a door.* —*n.* **1.** a furtive, cautious, or quick look. **2.** a first appearance: *the peep of dawn.* [Possibly from of PEEK.]

peep² (pēp) *n.* **1.** a short, sharp sound, as that made by a young bird; cheep. **2.** a slight sound; utterance; sound: *Not another peep out of you!* —*v.i.* to utter a peep. [Imitative.]

peep·er¹ (pē′pər) *n.* **1.** a person who peeps or spies. **2.** *Informal.* eye. [PEEP¹ + -ER¹.]

peep·er² (pē′pər) *n.* any of several tree frogs, family Hylidae, that make a shrill, peeping noise, esp. the **spring peeper,** *Hyla crucifer,* found in the United States and Canada. [PEEP² + -ER¹.]

peep·hole (pēp′hōl′) *n.* a small hole or opening through which one may look, esp. in a door.

peep·ing Tom (pē′ping) *also,* **Peep·ing Tom.** a person who spies on others, esp. in order to derive sexual pleasure. [From *Peeping Tom,* in English legend, a tailor who attempted to look at the naked Lady Godiva during her ride through Coventry and was instantly struck blind.]

peep show, an exhibition of pictures or objects viewed through a small opening that is usually fitted with a magnifying glass.

peer¹ (pîr) *n.* **1.** a person who is equal to another, as in status, social class, or ability; equal: *to be tried by a jury of one's peers.* **2.** in Great Britain, a member of one of the five degrees of nobility: duke, marquis, earl, viscount, or baron. **3.** any titled member of the nobility. [Old French *per* one of equal rank, from Latin *pār* equal.]

peer² (pîr) *v.i.* **1.** to look closely or searchingly, as in an effort to see clearly: *to peer through the darkness, to peer at the small print in a newspaper.* **2.** to come into view; be partially visible: *The sun peered over the mountain.* [Possibly short for APPEAR.]

peer·age (pîr′ij) *n.* **1.** the rank or dignity of a peer or other member of the nobility. **2.** the peers or other members of the nobility of a country collectively: *The peerage controlled the wealth of the country.* **3.** a book containing a list of the peers of a country and their genealogies.

peer·ess (pîr′is) *n.* **1.** the wife or widow of a peer or nobleman. **2.** a woman who holds the rank of a peer in her own right.

peer group, a group of people sharing approximately the same age, social status, education, value system, or other characteristic.

peer·less (pîr′lis) *adj.* without equal; matchless: *a peerless performance.* —**peer′less·ly,** *adv.* —**peer′less·ness,** *n.*

peeve (pēv) *v.t.,* **peeved, peev·ing.** to annoy; irritate; vex. —*n.* a cause of annoyance; grievance: *Rude people are one of my biggest peeves.* [From PEEVISH.]

pee·vish (pē′vish) *adj.* **1.** hard to please; irritable and ill-tempered; cranky. **2.** displaying or marked by annoyance or irritation: *a peevish expression, a peevish mood.* [Of uncertain origin.] —**pee′vish·ly,** *adv.* —**pee′vish·ness,** *n.*

pee·wee (pē′wē′) *n. Informal.* **1.** an unusually small person or thing. **2.** pewee.

peg (peg) *n.* **1.** a piece of wood, metal, or other hard substance, usually cylindrical and tapered, that can be fitted or driven into a surface, as to fasten parts together, hang something on, or serve as a marker. **2.** a wooden, plastic, or metal pin in a stringed instrument that secures and regulates the tension of a string. **3.** a step or degree: *Ever since he lied to me he's come down a peg in my estimation.* **4.** an alcoholic drink, esp. brandy and soda or whiskey and soda. **5.** *Informal.* a throw, esp. a fast and accurate throw in baseball. —*v.,* **pegged, peg·ging.** —*v.t.* **1.** to fasten or mark with a peg or pegs. **2.** to fix the price of, as a stock, by keeping it at or close to a certain figure. **3.** *Informal.* to throw: *to peg a ball.*

4. *Informal.* to recognize or classify; identify: *I had her pegged as a cheat from the very beginning.* —*v.i.* *Informal.* to work hard and persistently (often with *away*). [Possibly from Middle Dutch *pegge* little wooden pin for fastening.]

· **to take down a peg.** to lower the self-opinion of; humble.

Peg·a·sus (peg′ə səs) *n.* **1.** in Greek mythology, a winged horse that sprang from the blood of Medusa when she was killed by Perseus. **2.** a constellation in the northern sky, usually depicted as a winged horse.

Peg-Board (peg′bôrd′) *n.* **1.** *Trademark.* a boardlike material having rows of holes into which pegs or hooks can be inserted for holding or displaying items, such as tools. **2. pegboard.** a board having rows of holes into which pegs can be inserted, as for playing games or keeping score.

peg leg *Informal.* **1.** an artificial leg, esp. one made of wood. **2.** a person having such a leg.

peg·ma·tite (peg′mə tīt′) *n.* a coarse-grained granitic rock often found in dikes, the source of rare elements such as beryllium and lithium. [Greek *pēgmat-,* stem of *pēgma* framework + -ITE¹.] —**peg·ma·tit·ic** (peg′mə tit′ik), *adj.*

peg-top (peg′top′) *adj.* wide or full at the top and tapering toward the bottom: *peg-top trousers.*

P.E.I., Prince Edward Island.

peign·oir (pān wär′, pen-, pān′wär, pen′-) *n.* a woman's dressing gown or negligee. [French *peignoir,* from *peigner* to comb the hair, from Latin *pectināre* to comb.]

pej·o·ra·tion (pej′ə rā′shən, pē′jə-) *n.* a deterioration, as in quality or worth.

pe·jo·ra·tive (pi jôr′ə tiv, -jor′-, pej′ə rā′tiv) *adj.* having a derogatory or unfavorable meaning or effect; disparaging: *to use a word in its pejorative sense.* —*n.* a pejorative word or form. [Latin *pejōrātus,* past participle of *pejōrāre* to make worse + -IVE.] —**pe·jo′ra·tive·ly,** *adv.*

Pe·kin (pē′kin) *n.* any of a breed of large, white ducks, originally domesticated in China. Also, **Pek·ing** (pe′king′). [From *Peking* (now Beijing), China.]

Pe·king·ese (pē′kə nēz′, -nēs′, pē′king ēz′, -ēs′) *also,* **Pe·kin·ese** (pē′kə nēz′, -nēs′). *n., pl.* **-ese. 1.** a small dog of a breed originally developed in China, having a wrinkled, flat face, bulging eyes, and a long, silky coat. Height: 6 inches (15 centimeters) at the shoulder. **2.** a native or inhabitant of Peking. **3.** the Chinese dialect spoken in Peking. —*adj.* of, relating to, or characteristic of Peking or its people.

Pe·king man (pē′king′) an extinct primitive human being whose fossil remains were found near Peking (Beijing), China. First classified as *Sinanthropus pekinensis,* it is now generally classified with Java man as *Homo erectus.*

pe·koe (pē′kō) *n.* a superior grade of black tea from India, Sri Lanka, and Java, made from the smallest tea leaves. [Chinese *pek-ho* white down²; because only the young tea leaves that still have down are picked.]

pel·age (pel′ij) *n.* the hair, fur, wool, or other soft covering of a mammal. [French *pelage* coat of an animal, from Old French *pel* hair, from Latin *pilus.*]

pe·lag·ic (pə laj′ik) *adj.* of, relating to, or inhabiting the open sea, usually near the surface of the water. [Latin *pelagicus* relating to the sea, from Greek *pelagikos,* from *pelagos* sea.]

pel·ar·go·ni·um (pel′är gō′nē əm) *n.* geranium *(def. 1).* [Modern Latin *Pelargonium,* from Greek *pelargos* stork; because its carpels resemble a stork's bill.]

pe·lec·y·pod (pə les′ə pod′) *n.* any of a large group of mollusks, class Pelecypoda, having two hinged shells and usually a hatchetlike, digging extension on the bottom side of the body; bivalve. Also, **lamellibranch.** [Greek *pelekys* ax, hatchet + *pous* (stem *pod-*) foot.]

pel·er·ine (pel′ə rēn′) *n.* a waist-length cape, usually having long ends hanging down in front, worn by women during the seventeenth and eighteenth centuries. [French *pèlerine,* from *pèlerin* pilgrim. See PILGRIM.]

pelf (pelf) *n.* money or wealth. ➡ usually used disparagingly. [Old French *pelfre* booty; of uncertain origin.]

pel·i·can (pel′i kən) *n.* any of various web-footed water birds, genus *Pelecanus,* having predominantly white plumage and a large, distensible pouch beneath the bill that is used for storing fish. Length: 4-6 feet (1.2-1.8 meters). [Late Latin *pelicānus,* from Greek *pelekan,* from *pelekys* ax; referring to the appearance of its bill.]

pelican

pe·lisse (pə lēs′) *n.* a woman's coat or cloak, usually lined or trimmed with fur, worn in the eighteenth and nineteenth centuries. [Old French *pelisse* fur, fur coat, going back to Late Latin *pelliceus* made of skins, from Latin *pellis* skin, pelt [2].]

pel·la·gra (pə lag′rə, -lā′grə) *n.* a disease usually caused by a deficiency of niacin in the diet, characterized by skin eruptions, diarrhea, and mental disorders, including depression and hallucinations. [Italian *pellagra,* from *pelle* skin, from Latin *pellis.*] —**pel·la′grous,** *adj.*

pel·let (pel′it) *n.* **1.** a small ball, as of food, medicine, or paper. **2.** a bullet or piece of shot. **3.** a ball, usually of stone, formerly used as a missile, as in a cannon. [Old French *pelote* small ball, going back to Latin *pila* ball.]

pel·let·ize (pel′i tīz′) *v.t.,* **-ized, -iz·ing.** to make or form into pellets: *to pelletize ore.* [PELLET + -IZE.] —**pel′let·i·za′tion,** *n.*

pel·li·cle (pel′i kəl) *n.* a thin skin or film, as on the surface of a liquid. [Latin *pellicula* small skin, diminutive of *pellis* skin.] —**pel·lic·u·lar** (pe lik′yə lər), *adj.*

pell-mell (pel′mel′) *also,* **pell·mell.** *adv.* **1.** in great, often disorderly haste; headlong: *The people ran pell-mell from the burning building.* **2.** in a jumbled or confused manner; without order: *Papers were scattered pell-mell about the room.* —*adj.* disorderly or hasty; headlong; tumultuous. —*n.* a confused mixture; jumble; disorder. [French *pêle-mêle* disorder, confusedly, earlier *pesle-mesle* (rhyming repetition with change of consonant of *mesle,* imperative of *mesler* to mix, going back to Latin *miscēre).*]

pel·lu·cid (pə lü′sid) *adj.* **1.** transparent or translucent, as glass: *a pellucid stream.* **2.** easy to understand; lucid: *a pellucid writing style.* [Latin *pellūcidus* transparent, going back to *per* through + *lūcēre* to shine.] —**pel·lu·cid·i·ty** (pel′ü sid′i tē), **pel·lu′cid·ness,** *n.* —**pel·lu′cid·ly,** *adv.*

Pel·o·pon·ne·sian War (pel′ə pə nē′zhən, -shən) a war fought between Athens and Sparta from 431 to 404 B.C., ending in a victory for Sparta.

Pe·lops (pē′lops) *n.* in Greek mythology, the son of Tantalus, served to the gods as food by his father but later restored to life by them.

pe·lo·ta (pe lō′tə) *n.* **1.** jai alai. **2.** the ball used in jai alai. [Spanish *pelota* ball, going back to Latin *pila* ball.]

pelt[1] (pelt) *v.t.* **1.** to attack or strike repeatedly with or as if with something thrown: *The children pelted each other with snowballs.* **2.** to beat against continuously or repeatedly: *Hail pelted the roof.* **3.** to throw or hurl (missiles) repeatedly: *We pelted stones against the wall.* —*v.i.* to beat or strike heavily or continuously: *The rain pelted against the windows.* —*n.* a hard blow, as from something thrown. [Of uncertain origin.]
• **full pelt.** maximum speed: *The car was moving at full pelt.*

pelt[2] (pelt) *n.* the skin of an animal with its fur or hair, esp. when removed to be used for making garments or other items. [Possibly from PELTRY.]

pel·try (pel′trē) *n.* pelts collectively. [Anglo-Norman *pelterie,* going back to Old French *pel* skin, from Latin *pellis* skin.]

pel·vic (pel′vik) *adj.* of or relating to the pelvis.

pelvic fin, in fish, one of a pair of hind fins on the lower body, corresponding to the hind limbs of higher vertebrates.

pelvic girdle 1. in quadrupeds, the bony arch to which the hind limbs are attached. **2.** in human beings, the arch to which the lower limbs are attached. Also, **pelvic arch.**

pel·vis (pel′vis) *n., pl.* **-vis·es** or **-ves** (-vēz). **1.** a large, basin-shaped ring of bone that protects and supports the organs in the lower abdomen, consisting in humans of the sacrum and coccyx and the ilium, ischium, and pubis of both hipbones. **2.** a similar structure in many vertebrates. [Latin *pēlvis* basin; referring to its resemblance to a basin.]

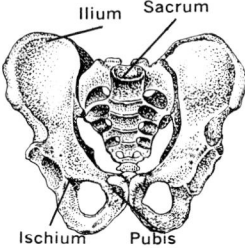

Ilium | Sacrum | Ischium | Pubis

pelvis

pem·mi·can (pem′i kən) *also,* **pem·i·can.** *n.* **1.** a food preparation consisting of lean meat that is dried, pounded, mixed with melted fat to form a paste, and pressed into cakes. **2.** a similar concentrated food preparation made of dried meat, dried fruit, flour, and sugar, used as emergency rations. [Cree *pimecan* the food preparation of lean meat, from *pime* fat.]

pen[1] (pen) *n.* **1.** any of various instruments for writing or drawing with ink. **2.** a detachable metal point of certain pens.

3. fountain pen. **4.** ballpoint pen. **5.** the pen regarded as a means of expression or instrument of authorship: *The pen is mightier than the sword* (Edward George Bulwer-Lytton, 1839). **6.** writing style or ability: *an author's scathing pen.* **7.** the profession of writing. **8.** writer; author. **9.** the internal shell of a squid and certain other cephalopods; cuttlebone. —*v.t.,* **penned, pen·ning.** to write with or as with a pen: *to pen a letter.* [Old French *penne* quill, feather pen for writing, from Latin *penna* feather; because the earliest pens were made from feathers.]

pen[2] (pen) *n.* **1.** a small enclosure used to confine animals. **2.** the animals confined in such an enclosure. **3.** any of various small or relatively small enclosures, as a playpen or a bullpen. —*v.t.,* **penned** or **pent, pen·ning.** to confine in or as in a pen. [Old English *penn* fold [2].]

pen[3] (pen) *n. Slang.* penitentiary.

pen[4] (pen) *n.* female swan. [Of uncertain origin.]

pe·nal (pē′nəl) *adj.* **1.** of, relating to, or prescribing punishment, esp. legal punishment: *penal laws.* **2.** for or serving as punishment: *penal servitude.* **3.** liable to punishment; punishable: *a penal offense.* [Latin *poenālis* relating to punishment, from *poena* punishment, from Greek *poinē* penalty.]

pe·nal·ize (pē′nə līz′) *v.t.,* **-ized, -iz·ing. 1.** to subject to a penalty or punishment: *The coach penalized two team members for being late.* **2.** to declare (an action) liable to penalty or punishment: *That type of violation is penalized in all sports.* **3.** to put at a disadvantage: *My lack of education penalized me in the business world.* —**pe′nal·i·za′tion,** *n.*

pen·al·ty (pen′əl tē) *n., pl.* **-ties. 1.** a punishment established or imposed for violating a law or regulation. **2.** a sum of money required to be paid as punishment for a violation or offense committed; fine: *There is a penalty of fifty dollars for missing a monthly payment on the loan.* **3.** an unpleasant or painful consequence of an action or condition: *to pay the penalty for one's foolishness.* **4.** *Sports.* a disadvantage or punishment imposed on a player or side for an infraction of the rules. [Medieval Latin *poenalitas* punishment, from Latin *poenālis* relating to punishment. See PENAL.]

penalty box, an area alongside an ice-hockey rink where a player must sit for a certain amount of time as a penalty for breaking a rule.

pen·ance (pen′əns) *n.* **1.** punishment, usually self-inflicted, undergone to express or demonstrate repentance for a sin or offense. **2.** in some Christian churches, a sacrament administered by a priest that includes sorrow for and confession of sin, acceptance of prescribed penalties, and absolution. [Old French *peneance,* from Latin *paenitentia* repentance. Doublet of PENITENCE.]
• **to do penance.** to express or demonstrate repentance by undergoing punishment.

pe·na·tes (pə nā′tēz) *pl. n.* the household gods of the ancient Romans. [Latin *Penātēs.*]

pence (pens) *British.* the plural of **penny** (def. 2).

pen·chant (pen′chənt) *n.* a strong liking or inclination: *a penchant for gardening.* [French *penchant* inclination, from *pencher* to lean, incline, going back to Latin *pendēre* to hang.]

pen·cil (pen′səl) *n.* **1.** a marking, drawing, or writing implement usually consisting of a stick of graphite, chalk, or similar substance enclosed in a case of wood, metal, or plastic. **2.** something like a pencil in shape or use, esp. an implement or stick having a cosmetic or medicinal use, as a styptic pencil. **3.** a style, ability, or technique in drawing or writing. —*v.t.,* **-ciled, -cil·ing;** *also, British,* **-cilled, -cil·ling.** to write, draw, mark, or color with or as if with a pencil. [Old French *pincel* painter's brush, going back to Latin *penicillus* little tail, painter's brush (which resembled a little tail), diminutive of *pēnis* tail.]
• **to pencil in.** to schedule, list, or include on a tentative basis: *Let's pencil in a date for the meeting and finalize it later.*

pend·ant (pen′dənt) *n.* **1.** a piece of jewelry or other ornamental object that is suspended, as from a necklace or bracelet. **2.** an ornament or fixture, often elaborately decorated, hanging down, as from a roof or ceiling. **3.** something that is a match, parallel, companion, or addition to something else: *The narrative of the historian forms a fitting pendant to that of the satirist* (Charles Merivale, 1862). —*adj.* pendent. [Old French *pendant,* present participle of *pendre* to hang, going back to Latin *pendēre* to hang.]

a	at	e	end	o	hot	u	up	hw	white	⟨	about
ā	ape	ē	me	ō	old	ū	use	ng	song		taken
ä	far	i	it	ô	fork	u̇	rule	th	thin	ə	pencil
âr	care	ī	ice	oi	oil	u̇	pull	th	this		lemon
		îr	pierce	ou	out	ûr	turn	zh	measure	⟨	circus

P

895

pend·ent (pen′dənt) *adj.* **1.** hanging or held from above; suspended: *pendent glass beads.* **2.** jutting out; overhanging. **3.** not yet decided or settled; pending. —*n.* pendant. [Latin *pendēns,* present participle of *pendēre* to hang.] —**pen′dent·ly,** *adv.*

pen·den·tive (pen den′tiv) *n.* a spherical triangular member between each pair of arches supporting a dome. [French *pendentif,* from Latin *pendēns.* See PENDENT.]

pend·ing (pen′ding) *adj.* **1.** awaiting decision or settlement; remaining undecided: *The decision on that question is still pending.* **2.** about to happen; impending; imminent: *a pending disaster.* —*prep.* **1.** while awaiting; until: *We postponed our picnic pending a change in the weather.* **2.** during the course of. [Obsolete *pend* to hang (going back to Latin *pendēre*) + -ING².]

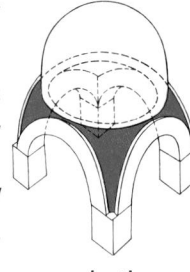

pendentives

pen·drag·on (pen drag′ən) *n.* in ancient Britain, a supreme leader or chief. [Welsh *pendragon* supreme leader in war, from *pen* chief + *dragon* dragon, leader in war (from Latin *dracō* dragon); referring to the dragon on the leader's banner. See DRAGON.]

pen·du·lous (pen′jə ləs, -dyə ləs, -də ləs) *adj.* **1.** hanging in a loose or drooping manner: *a pendulous branch of a tree.* **2.** swinging freely: *a pendulous motion.* **3.** characterized by doubt or uncertainty; wavering; vacillating. [Latin *pendulus* hanging, from *pendēre* to hang.] —**pen′du·lous·ly,** *adv.* —**pen′du·lous·ness,** *n.*

pen·du·lum (pen′jə ləm, -dyə ləm, -də ləm) *n.* **1.** a suspended body that can be set in motion to swing back and forth or oscillate about a fixed point. **2.** such a device used to regulate the movement of a clock. [Modern Latin *pendulum,* from Latin *pendulus* hanging. See PENDULOUS.]

Pe·nel·o·pe (pə nel′ə pē) *n.* in Greek and Roman legend, the wife of Ulysses, noted for her faithfulness during her husband's long absence.

pe·ne·plain (pē′nə plān′) *also,* **pe·ne·plane.** *n. Geology.* a land surface reduced by erosion to an almost flat plain. [Latin *paene* almost + PLAIN¹.]

pe·nes (pē′nēz) a plural of **penis.**

pen·e·tra·ble (pen′i trə bəl) *adj.* capable of being penetrated. [Latin *penetrābilis,* from *penetrāre* to enter, pierce.] —**pen′e·tra·bil′i·ty,** *n.*

pen·e·trate (pen′i trāt′) *v.,* **-trat·ed, -trat·ing.** —*v.t.* **1.** to pass into or through, esp. by force or with difficulty: *The bullet penetrated the steel plate.* **2.** to seep or spread through; permeate: *The rain penetrated my sleeping bag.* **3.** to discover the meaning of; understand: *Science endeavors to penetrate the mysteries of nature.* **4.** to have a strong effect on; affect deeply. —*v.i.* **1.** to pass or force a way into or through something. **2.** to have a strong effect on someone. [Latin *penetrātus,* past participle of *penetrāre* to enter, pierce.] —For Synonyms, see **permeate.**

pen·e·trat·ing (pen′i trā′ting) *adj.* **1.** having a strong effect, as on the senses or emotions; piercing: *a penetrating wind, a penetrating stare.* **2.** mentally keen and discerning; acute: *a penetrating analysis.* —**pen′e·trat′ing·ly,** *adv.*

pen·e·tra·tion (pen′i trā′shən) *n.* **1.** the act or power of penetrating or making a way into or through something. **2.** the degree or extent to which something penetrates. **3.** mental acuteness; insight; discernment.

pen·e·tra·tive (pen′i trā′tiv) *adj.* tending or able to penetrate. —**pen′e·tra′tive·ly,** *adv.* —**pen′e·tra′tive·ness,** *n.*

pen·guin (pen′gwin, peng′-) *n.* any of various flightless seabirds, family Spheniscidae, native to Antarctica and to the shores of other regions of the Southern Hemisphere, having webbed feet, flipperlike wings used for swimming, and dense plumage that is typically black or gray on the back and white on the chest, stomach, and legs. Height: to 4 feet (1.2 meters). [Possibly from Welsh *pen* head + *gwyn* white; name originally applied by sailors to the great auk, now extinct, a flightless bird with a white patch

penguin

on its face, and later applied to the penguin, also flightless, but usually having a black head.]

pen·i·cil·lin (pen′ə sil′in) *n.* a powerful antibiotic made from certain penicillium molds, used in the treatment of a wide variety of bacterial infections. [From PENICILLIUM.]

pen·i·cil·li·um (pen′ə sil′ē əm) *n., pl.* **-cil·li·a** (-sil′ē ə) or **-cil·li·ums.** any of a group of fungi, class Ascomycetes, commonly found as a blue-green mold on bread, cheese, and other foods. Certain penicillium molds are a source of the drug penicillin. [Modern Latin *penicillium,* from Latin *pēnicillus* painter's brush; referring to its brushlike spore case. See PENCIL.]

pen·in·su·la (pə nin′sə lə, -syə-) *n.* a body of land almost entirely surrounded by water, usually connected with the mainland by an isthmus. [Latin *paeninsula,* from *paene* almost + *īnsula* island.]

pen·in·su·lar (pə nin′sə lər, -syə-) *adj.* of, relating to, or like a peninsula.

pe·nis (pē′nis) *n., pl.* **-nis·es** or **-nes** (-nēz). the male organ of urination and copulation. [Latin *pēnis* penis, tail.] —**pe·ni·al** (pē′nē əl), **pe·nile** (pē′nīl), *adj.*

pen·i·tence (pen′i təns) *n.* the state of being penitent; repentance; contrition. [Old French *penitence,* from Latin *paenitentia.* Doublet of PENANCE.]

pen·i·tent (pen′i tənt) *adj.* feeling or expressing sorrow or regret for sin or wrongdoing and resolved on atonement; repentant: *I wrote a penitent letter apologizing for my rudeness.* —*n.* **1.** a person who is penitent. **2.** a person who confesses to a sin and receives the sacrament of penance. [Latin *paenitēns,* present participle of *paenitēre* to repent.] —**pen′i·tent·ly,** *adv.*

pen·i·ten·tial (pen′i ten′shəl) *adj.* **1.** of, relating to, or expressing penitence or repentance. **2.** of or relating to penance. —**pen′i·ten′tial·ly,** *adv.*

pen·i·ten·tia·ry (pen′i ten′shə rē) *n., pl.* **-ries. 1.** an institution, esp. a state or federal institution, for the confinement of persons convicted of major crimes. **2.** in the Roman Catholic Church, a tribunal of the Holy See, headed by a cardinal, that is concerned with special dispensations, problems of conscience, and certain other matters. —*adj.* **1.** (of an offense) punishable by imprisonment in a penitentiary. **2.** relating to or used for imprisonment, punishment, discipline, or reformation. **3.** of or relating to penance. —For Synonyms, see **prison.**

pen·knife (pen′nīf′) *n., pl.* **-knives** (-nīvz′). a small pocketknife, originally used for making or sharpening quill pens.

pen·man (pen′mən) *n., pl.* **-men. 1.** a writer; author. **2.** a person skilled in penmanship.

pen·man·ship (pen′mən ship′) *n.* **1.** the style or quality of handwriting. **2.** the art or skill of handwriting.

Penn. *also,* **Penna.** Pennsylvania. Also, **Pa.**

pen name, an assumed name under which an author writes; pseudonym; nom de plume. —For Synonyms, see **pseudonym.**

pen·nant (pen′ənt) *n.* **1.** a long flag, usually triangular, used esp. as a school or team emblem or, on a ship, for signaling or identification. **2.** such a flag symbolizing a victory or championship, esp. in professional baseball. [Blend of PENNON and PENDANT.]

pen·nate (pen′āt) *adj.* having wings or feathers. Also, **pen′nat·ed.** [Latin *pennātus* winged, from *penna* feather, wing.]

pen·ni·less (pen′ē lis) *adj.* having no money; extremely poor. —**pen′ni·less·ness,** *n.*

pen·non (pen′ən) *n.* **1.** a long, triangular or swallow-tailed flag or streamer borne on the head of a knight's lance in the Middle Ages. **2.** any flag or banner. **3.** a wing or pinion. [Middle French *penon* flag, streamer, from *pene* feather, wing, from Latin *penna.*]

Penn·syl·va·nia Dutch (pen′səl vān′yə, -vā′nē ə) **1.** the descendants of German immigrants who settled in southeastern Pennsylvania in the seventeenth and eighteenth centuries. **2.** a High German dialect heavily mixed with English, spoken by these people.

Penn·syl·va·nian (pen′səl vān′yən, -vā′nē ən) *n.* **1.** a native or

inhabitant of Pennsylvania. **2.** the later of the two geologic subdivisions of the Carboniferous period, a time of widespread coal-forming, swampy forests when the earliest form of conifers and reptiles appeared. For table, see **geologic time.** —*adj.* **1.** of or relating to Pennsylvania. **2.** of or relating to the later of the two geologic subdivisions of the Carboniferous period.

pen·ny (pen′ē) *n., pl.* **pen·nies** or *(def. 2)* **pence. 1.** a coin of the United States and Canada, equal to one cent or ¹/₁₀₀ of a dollar. **2.** a coin of the United Kingdom equal to ¹/₁₀₀ of a pound, formerly equal to ¹/₁₂ of a shilling. **3.** a sum of money: *to earn a penny.* [Old English *pening* British coin equal to ¹/₁₂ of a shilling.]
•**a pretty penny.** *Informal.* a large sum of money.

penny ante 1. a poker game having very low stakes. **2.** *Informal.* any transaction of little significance. —**pen′ny-an′te,** *adj.*

penny arcade, a place or area, as in an amusement park, made up principally of coin-operated games and entertainment devices.

penny pincher, a stingy or miserly person. —**pen′ny-pinch′-ing,** *adj., n.*

pen·ny·roy·al (pen′ē roi′əl) *n.* any of several fragrant plants of the mint family, esp. the **Eurasian pennyroyal,** *Mentha pulegium,* which yields an aromatic oil used chiefly in making soaps, and the **American pennyroyal,** *Hedeoma pulegioides,* a common weed bearing aromatic leaves used in home remedies. [Modification of earlier *puliol real* from Old French *puliol* pennyroyal (going back to Latin *pūlēium*) + *real* kingly (going back to Latin *rēgālis* relating to a king). See ROYAL.]

pen·ny·weight (pen′ē wāt′) *n.* a measure of weight equal to 24 grains or ¹/₂₀ of a troy ounce.

pen·ny-wise (pen′ē wīz′) *adj.* prudent or thrifty in small matters.
•**to be penny-wise and pound-foolish.** to be cautious or thrifty in small matters but wasteful in large ones.

pen·ny·worth (pen′ē wûrth′) *n.* **1.** as much as can be bought for a penny. **2.** a small amount of anything.

Pe·nob·scot (pə nob′skot) *n., pl.* **-scot** or **-scots.** a member of an American Indian tribe of the Algonquian language family, living in central Maine.

pe·nol·o·gy (pē nol′ə jē) *n.* the study of the punishment and rehabilitation of criminals and the management of prisons. [Greek *poinē* punishment + -LOGY.] —**pe·no·log·i·cal** (pē′nə loj′i kəl), *adj.* —**pe·nol′o·gist,** *n.*

pen pal, a person with whom one exchanges letters, esp. without ever having met or when living so far apart that a personal meeting is not possible.

pen·sile (pen′səl, -sīl) *adj.* **1.** suspended from above; hanging. **2.** (of birds) having a hanging nest. [Latin *pēnsilis* hanging down, from *pendēre* to hang.]

pen·sion¹ (pen′shən) *n.* a periodic payment, other than wages, made by a former employer to a retired or disabled person who has fulfilled certain requirements or conditions. —*v.t.* to give a pension to. [Old French *pension* payment, from Latin *pēnsiō.*] —**pen′sion·a·ble,** *adj.*
•**to pension off.** to retire or dismiss with a pension: *The company pensioned off its veteran employees.*

pen·sion² (päN syôN′) *n.* in France and other European countries, a boarding house or boarding school. [French *pension,* from Latin *pēnsiō* payment.]

pen·sion·er (pen′shə nər) *n.* **1.** a person who receives a pension. **2.** hireling.

pen·sive (pen′siv) *adj.* **1.** engaged in deep and serious thought, often concerning matters of a sad nature. **2.** characterized by or showing deep, often sad thoughtfulness: *a pensive look, a pensive mood.* [Old French *pensif* preoccupied by thought, from *penser* to think, from Latin *pēnsāre* to weigh, ponder.] —**pen′sive·ly,** *adv.* —**pen′sive·ness,** *n.*

pen·stock (pen′stok′) *n.* **1.** a gate or sluice for regulating the flow of water. **2.** a pipe or conduit for carrying water. [PEN² + STOCK.]

pent (pent) *v.* a past tense and past participle of **pen².** —*adj.* closely confined; shut up.

penta- *combining form* five: *pentagon, pentameter.* [Greek *pente* five.]

pen·ta·cle (pen′tə kəl) *n.* a star with five points, used as a symbolic figure in magic. Also, **pentagram.** [Medieval Latin *pentaculum,* from Greek *pente* five.]

pen·ta·gon (pen′tə gon′) *n.* **1.** a polygon with five sides and five angles. **2. the Pentagon. a.** a five-sided building in Arlington, Virginia, that is the headquarters of the U.S. Department of Defense. **b.** the power and influence of the military as represented by this building; the U.S. military establishment. [Late Latin *pen-*

the Pentagon

tagōnum the polygon, from Greek *pentagōnon,* from *pente* five + *gōniā* angle.]

pen·tag·o·nal (pen tag′ə nəl) *adj.* having the geometric properties of a pentagon. —**pen·tag′o·nal·ly,** *adv.*

pen·ta·gram (pen′tə gram′) *n.* pentacle.

pen·ta·he·dron (pen′tə hē′drən) *n., pl.* **-drons** or **-dra** (-drə). a polyhedron with five faces. [Modern Latin *pentahedron,* Greek *pente* five + *hedrā* base¹, seat.] —**pen′ta·he′dral,** *adj.*

pen·tam·er·ous (pen tam′ər əs) *adj. Biology.* divided into or composed of five parts. [PENTA- + Greek *meros* part.]

pen·tam·e·ter (pen tam′i tər) *n.* **1.** a line of verse consisting of five metrical feet. **2.** a verse composed of such lines. —*adj.* consisting of five metrical feet. [Latin *pentameter,* from Greek *pentametros,* from *pente* five + *metron* measure.]

pen·tane (pen′tān) *n.* a colorless, volatile hydrocarbon of the alkane series, used as an anesthetic and a solvent. Formula: C_5H_{12} [Greek *pente* five + -ANE; referring to the *five* carbon atoms in its molecule.]

Pen·ta·teuch (pen′tə tük′, -tūk′) *n.* the first five books of the Old Testament collectively, ascribed to Moses, and consisting of Genesis, Exodus, Leviticus, Numbers, and Deuteronomy. In Judaism this group is called the Torah.

pen·tath·lon (pen tath′lən, -lon) *n.* **1.** a track and field contest in which each contestant participates in five different events. **2.** modern pentathlon. [Greek *pentathlon,* from *pente* five + *āthlon* contest.]

pen·ta·ton·ic (pen′tə ton′ik) *adj.* of, designating, or relating to a musical scale consisting of only five tones.

pen·ta·va·lent (pen′tə vā′lənt) *adj.* having a valence of five.

Pen·te·cost (pen′tə kôst′, -kost′) *n.* **1.** a Christian feast observed on the seventh Sunday after Easter, commemorating the possession of the Apostles by the Holy Ghost, considered by many the beginning of the Christian religion. Also, **Whitsunday. 2.** Shavuoth. [Latin *pentēcostē,* from Greek *pentēkostē (hēmera)* fiftieth (day).] —**pen′te·cos′tal,** *adj.*

pent·house (pent′hous′) *n., pl.* **-hous·es** (-hou′ziz). **1.** an apartment or other dwelling on the roof of a building. **2.** a shed, sloping roof, or similar structure attached to a wall or building. [Modification (influenced by English *house*) of earlier *pentice,* from Old French *apentis* shed with sloping roof forming part of a building, from Late Latin *appendicium* appendage, from Latin *appendēre* to hang on something.]

pent·land·ite (pent′lən dīt′) *n.* a bronze-colored sulfide mineral mined as an ore of nickel. Formula: $(Fe, Ni)_9S_8$ [French *pentlandite,* from Joseph B. *Pentland,* 1797-1873, Irish mineralogist.]

pen·to·bar·bi·tal (pen′tə bär′bi tôl′) *n.* a bitter barbiturate compound used as a sedative and a hypnotic. Formula: $C_{11}H_{17}N_2O_3$

pen·tode (pen′tōd) *n.* an electron tube with five electrodes. [PENTA- + -ODE.]

pen·tose (pen′tōs) *n.* any monosaccharide, as ribose, that contains five carbon atoms in each molecule. Formula: $C_5H_{10}O_5$ [PENTA- + -OSE².]

Pen·to·thal (pen′tə thôl′) *n. Trademark.* a short-acting barbiturate used as an anesthetic and, in psychiatry, to facilitate the recall of forgotten or repressed events and emotions. Formula: $C_{11}H_{17}N_2NaO_2S$

a	at	e	end	o	hot	u	up	hw	white		about
ā	ape	ē	me	ō	old	ū	use	ng	song	ə	taken
ä	far	i	it	ô	fork	ü	rule	th	thin		pencil
âr	care	ī	ice	oi	oil	u̇	pull	th	this		lemon
		îr	pierce	ou	out	ûr	turn	zh	measure		circus

pent-up (pent′up′) *adj.* not expressed or released; restrained; held in: *pent-up feelings, pent-up hostility.*

pe·nu·che (pi nü′chē) *n.* a candy, resembling fudge, usually made of brown sugar, milk or cream, butter, and nuts. Also, **panocha.** [Form of PANOCHA.]

pe·nult (pē′nult, pi nult′) *n.* the second to last syllable in a word. Also, **pe·nul·ti·ma** (pi nul′tə mə). [Latin *paenultima (syllaba)* last (syllable) but one, from *paene* almost + *ultimus* last.]

pe·nul·ti·mate (pi nul′tə mit) *adj.* **1.** next to the last. **2.** of, relating to, or occurring on the penult of a word: *penultimate stress.* —*n.* the second to last.

pe·num·bra (pi num′brə) *n., pl.* **-bras** or **-brae** (-brē) **1.** *Astronomy.* **a.** in an eclipse, the partial shadow between the region of total eclipse and the region of complete illumination. For illustration, see **eclipse. b.** a grayish fringe around the dark central portion of a sunspot. **2.** the partially darkened region surrounding the completely dark central region of a shadow. ➡ distinguished from **umbra** in all defs. [Modern Latin *penumbra,* from Latin *paene* almost + *umbra* shadow.] —**pe·num′bral,** *adj.*

pe·nu·ri·ous (pi nùr′ē əs, -nyùr′-) *adj.* **1.** greatly reluctant to spend or part with money; miserly. **2.** extremely poor; poverty-stricken: *a penurious existence.* —**pe·nu′ri·ous·ly,** *adv.* —**pe·nu′ri·ous·ness,** *n.*

pen·u·ry (pen′yə rē) *n.* extreme poverty. [Latin *pēnūria* want.]

pe·on (pē′on, -ən) *n.* **1.** in Spanish America, an unskilled worker or farm laborer. **2.** formerly, a person forced to work to pay off a debt. **3.** an unskilled worker of low status. [Spanish *peón* foot soldier, day laborer, from Medieval Latin *pedō* foot soldier, going back to Latin *pēs* foot. Doublet of PAWN².]

pe·on·age (pē′ə nij) *n.* **1.** the condition of being a peon. **2.** the practice of forcing people to work in exchange for the payment of debts.

pe·o·ny (pē′ə nē) *n., pl.* **-nies. 1.** the large, showy flower of any of a group of hardy plants, genus *Paeonia.* **2.** the plant bearing this flower, widely cultivated in gardens. [Old English *peonie,* from Latin *paeōnia,* from Greek *paiōnia,* from *Paiōn* physician of the Greek gods who supposedly discovered the plant.]

peo·ple (pē′pəl) *n., pl.* **-ple** or *(def. 2)* **-ples. 1.** persons, esp. when considered indefinitely or collectively; men, women, and children: *People think of some of the strangest inventions. This theater can seat 500 people.* **2.** the body of persons comprising a nation, race, tribe, or community: *the Israeli people, primitive peoples, the peoples of Asia.* **3.** a body of persons considered as or comprising a distinct group: *rich people, thin people, people of New England.* **4.** the body of citizens of a state or other political unit: *Members of Congress are elected by the people.* **5.** the body or mass of common persons as distinguished from persons of some special group or class. **6.** persons in relation to a superior, as the subjects of a ruler: *The king and queen loved their people.* **7.** human beings as distinguished from animals: *Distemper is not a disease affecting people.* **8.** *Informal.* one's family; relatives. —*v.t.,* **-pled, -pling.** to fill with inhabitants; populate: *the myriad of human beings who people the earth.* [Old French *pueple* body of persons, nation, the public, from Latin *populus.*]

  • **the little** (or **good) people.** leprechauns; fairies.

People's Party, Populist Party.

pep (pep) *n.* liveliness and high spirits; energy: *She's always full of pep in the morning.* —*v.t.,* **pepped, pep·ping.** to make lively or cheerful; fill with energy (with *up*): *The good news pepped him up.* [Short for PEPPER.]

pep·er·o·ni (pep′ə rō′nē) *n., pl.* **-nis** or **-ni.** pepperoni.

pep·los (pep′ləs) *also,* **pep·lus.** *n.* a garment resembling a shawl, draped over the upper part of the body by women of ancient Greece. [Greek *peplos.*]

pep·lum (pep′ləm) *n.* **1.** a short overskirt or ruffle attached at the waistline and extending over the hips. **2.** peplos. [Latin *peplum* upper garment, from Greek *peplos* upper garment, mantle.]

pe·po (pē′pō) *n., pl.* **-pos.** a many-seeded fruit with fleshy pulp and a hard rind, as the watermelon, gourd, or squash. [Latin *pepō* melon, from Greek *pepōn.*]

pep·per (pep′ər) *n.* **1.a.** a hot, pungent spice consisting of the berries, either whole or ground, of a tropical Asian plant, *Piper nigrum.* **Black pepper** consists of entire dried berries, and **white pepper** the dried seeds of the berries with the outer coat and pulp removed. **b.** any plant of the genus *Piper,* family Piperaceae. **2.a.** the usually red, green, or yellow, sweet or hot, edible fruit of a tropical American plant, *Capsicum annuum.* **b.** the plant bearing this fruit. **c.** any plant of the genus *Capsicum.* **d.** cayenne or any other spice or sauce prepared from a plant of the genus *Capsicum.* —*v.t.* **1.** to sprinkle or season with pepper. **2.** to cover or sprinkle as if with pepper: *The tweed was peppered with flecks of red and blue.* **3.** to shower or pelt with bullets or other small missiles.

4. to add spice or variety to: *to pepper a speech with humorous expressions.* [Old English *pipor* the spice, from Latin *piper* the plant, from Greek *peperi,* from Sanskrit *pippalī* berry, peppercorn.]

pep·per-and-salt (pep′ər ən sôlt′) *adj.* composed of a fine mixture of black and white: *a pepper-and-salt tweed.* Also, **salt-and-pepper.**

pep·per·corn (pep′ər kôrn′) *n.* the dried berry or seed of the pepper plant, *Piper nigrum,* used as a spice, either whole or ground.

pep·per·grass (pep′ər gras′) *n.* any of a large group of plants, genus *Lepidium,* of the mustard family, whose leaves have a pungent flavor.

pepper mill, a utensil used to grind peppercorns.

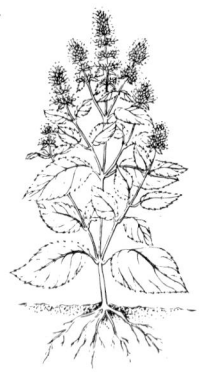

peppermint plant

pep·per·mint (pep′ər mint′) *n.* **1.** a fragrant plant, *Mentha piperita,* of the mint family, having small purple or white flowers and tooth-edged leaves. **2.** the pungent oil obtained from this plant, having a minty aroma and taste and used in medicine and as a flavoring, esp. in candy, chewing gum, and toothpaste. **3.** a candy or lozenge flavored with peppermint oil.

pep·per·o·ni (pep′ə rō′nē) *also,* **pep·eroni.** *n., pl.* **-nis** or **ni.** a highly seasoned, hard sausage. [Italian *peperoni* literally, chilies, augmentative form of *pepe* pepper, from Latin *piper.* See PEPPER.]

pepper tree, either of two evergreen trees of tropical America, the **California pepper tree,** *Schinus molle,* and the **Brazilian pepper tree,** *S. terebinthifolius,* bearing clusters of small white or yellowish flowers and red or rose-colored berries.

pep·per·y (pep′ə rē) *adj.* **1.** of, like, or relating to pepper; pungent: *a peppery taste.* **2.** sharp or fiery; stinging: *a peppery speech, peppery writing.* **3.** easily angered; hot-tempered; testy. —**pep′per·i·ness,** *n.*

pep pill *Informal.* a tablet or capsule containing a stimulant, esp. amphetamine.

pep·py (pep′ē) *adj.,* **-pi·er, -pi·est.** *Informal.* full of pep or energy; lively. —**pep′pi·ness,** *n.*

pep·sin (pep′sin) *n.* **1.** an enzyme produced in the stomach that aids in the digestion of proteins. **2.** a medicine used to relieve indigestion, containing pepsin taken from the stomach of certain animals. [German *Pepsin,* from Greek *pepsin* digestion.]

pep·sin·o·gen (pep sin′ə jən) *n.* an inactive precursor of pepsin that is produced in the stomach and is converted to the enzyme by hydrochloric acid. [PEPSIN + -GEN.]

pep talk, a speech given to an individual or group for the purpose of increasing enthusiasm or confidence or bolstering morale.

pep·tic (pep′tik) *adj.* **1.** of, relating to, or promoting digestion; digestive. **2.** of or relating to pepsin or other digestive secretions or resulting from their action: *a peptic ulcer.* —*n.* a substance that promotes digestion. [Greek *peptikos* able to digest, from *peptein* to digest, cook.]

pep·tide (pep′tīd) *n.* any of a group of amide compounds formed by the linking together of amino acids into a long chain. [PEPT(ONE) + -IDE.]

peptide bond, the chemical bond that links the amino acids in proteins, joining the carboxyl group of one amino acid to the amino group of another.

pep·tone (pep′tōn) *n.* any of a class of soluble substances derived from proteins during the process of digestion. [German *Pepton,* going back to Greek *peptein* to cook, digest.]

Pe·quot (pē′kwot) *n., pl.* **-quots** or **-quot.** a member of a tribe of Algonquian Indians living in Connecticut.

per (pûr; *unstressed* pər) *prep.* **1.** for each: *The speed limit is forty miles per hour.* **2.** by means of; by; through: *a message sent per a representative.* **3.** according to: *as per instructions.* [Latin *per* through, by.]

per- *prefix* **1.** through; throughout: *perforate, perfume.* **2.** thoroughly; completely: *perfect, perceive.* **3.** *Chemistry.* containing a relatively large or the largest possible proportion of a specified element: *hydrogen peroxide.* [Latin *per* through, by.]

per·ad·ven·ture (pûr′əd ven′chər) *Archaic. adv.* perhaps; maybe; perchance. —*n.* chance or uncertainty; doubt; question. [Old French *par aventure* perchance, perhaps, from *par* by (from Latin *per* through, by) + *aventure* chance. See ADVENTURE.]

per·am·bu·late (pər am′byə lāt′) *v.,* **-lat·ed, -lat·ing.** —*v.t.* to walk through, around, or about, esp. so as to survey, inspect, or examine: *The tourists perambulated the castle grounds.* —*v.i.* to walk about; stroll: *The two friends perambulated aimlessly*

about the park. [Latin *perambulātus,* past participle of *perambulāre* to ramble through.] —**per·am·bu·la′tion,** *n.*

per·am·bu·la·tor (pər am′byə lā′tər) *n.* **1.** baby carriage. **2.** a person who perambulates.

per an·num (pər an′əm) for each year; per year; annually: *an income that exceeds $30,000 per annum.* [Latin *per annum.*]

per·cale (pər kāl′) *n.* a closely woven, lightweight cotton fabric with a smooth, dull finish, used esp. for sheets, pajamas, and shirts. [French *percale,* going back to Persian *pargālah* shred, scrap.]

per cap·i·ta (pər kap′i tə) for, from, or by each person: *Per capita income in the city has risen this year by approximately $300.* [Latin *per capita* literally, by heads.]

per·ceive (pər sēv′) *v.t.,* -ceived, -ceiv·ing. **1.** to be or become aware of through the senses; see, hear, taste, smell, or feel: *to perceive a change in the temperature.* **2.** to take in or grasp mentally; comprehend: *I perceived that it would be a long wait.* [Old French *percevoir,* from Latin *percipere* to take possession of, observe.] —For Synonyms, see **discern.**

per·cent (pər sent′) *also,* **per cent.** *n.* **1.** the number of parts in or to every hundred. Two percent of 50 is ²/₁₀₀ × 50, or 1. ⇒ The symbol for percent (%) is often used with figures, as in *6% interest.* **2.** percentage. —*adj.* paying a specified percentage in interest, as of a loan. [Latin *per centum* by the hundred.]

per·cent·age (pər sen′tij) *n.* **1.** the rate or proportion of to every hundred: *What percentage of registered voters actually voted?* **2.** a part or proportion in regard to the whole: *A great percentage of our pilots retire early.* **3.** an amount calculated by percent, such as an allowance, commission, or rate of interest. **4.** *Informal.* advantage; profit: *There's no percentage in getting upset.*

per·cen·tile (pər sen′tīl, -təl) *n.* any value in a series of values on a scale found by dividing a group into a hundred equal parts. A person scoring in the eightieth percentile on a test has done as well as or better than eighty percent of the people taking the test.

per centum, percent.

per·cept (pûr′sept) *n.* **1.** something that is perceived. **2.** knowledge or understanding that results from perceiving. [From PER-CEPTION.]

per·cep·ti·ble (pər sep′tə bəl) *adj.* capable of being perceived; noticeable: *There has been a perceptible change in the child's behavior lately.* —**per·cep′ti·bil′i·ty,** *n.* —**per·cep′ti·bly,** *adv.*

per·cep·tion (pər sep′shən) *n.* **1.** the act or process of perceiving. **2.** the result or product of perceiving; percept. **3.** awareness, insight, or information gained by perceiving. **4.** the power or faculty of perceiving: *Since I am color-blind, my perception of certain patterns in fabric is poor.* [Latin *perceptiō* collecting, comprehending.]

per·cep·tive (pər sep′tiv) *adj.* **1.** capable of or characterized by keen perception: *a perceptive judge of human nature, perceptive and intelligent advice.* **2.** having the power or faculty of perceiving. **3.** of or relating to perception. —**per·cep′tive·ly,** *adv.* —**per·cep′tive·ness, per′cep·tiv′i·ty,** *n.*

per·cep·tu·al (pər sep′chü əl) *adj.* of or relating to the power or faculty of perceiving. —**per·cep′tu·al·ly,** *adv.*

Per·ce·val (pûr′sə vəl) *also,* Percival, Percivale. *n.* in Arthurian legend, the knight of the Round Table who, along with Galahad, sought the Holy Grail.

perch[1] (pûrch) *n.* **1.** anything on which a bird can alight or come to rest, esp. a horizontal bar or branch. **2.** any elevated place or position, esp. for sitting or standing: *The lifeguard watched the swimmers from a perch above the pool.* **3.a.** a measure of length equal to 1 rod; 5½ yards (5 meters). **b.** a measure of area equal to 1 square rod; 30¼ square yards (25 square meters). —*v.i.* to alight or rest on something; sit on or as on a perch; settle: *Spectators perched on the fence.* —*v.t.* to set or place on or as on a perch: *to perch a glass on a mantelpiece.* [Old French *perche* place where a bird alights, long piece of wood, from Latin *pertica* pole[1], bar.]

perch[2] (pûrch) *n., pl.* perch or perch·es. any of a large group of North American or European freshwater food fish, family Percidae, such as the **yellow perch,** *Perca flavescens,* found in shallow lakes and slow-moving streams of the United States and Canada and having a yellow body marked with blackish bands. Length: 4-15 inches (10-38 centimeters). [Old French *perche* a small freshwater fish, from Latin *perca,* from Greek *perkē.*]

per·chance (pər chans′) *adv.* by chance; possibly; perhaps: *To sleep; perchance to dream* (Shakespeare, *Hamlet*). [Old French *par* by (from Latin *per* through, by) + *ch(e)ance* a falling. See CHANCE.]

perch·er (pûr′chər) *n.* **1.** a person or thing that perches. **2.** a bird whose feet are adapted for perching.

Per·che·ron (pûr′chə ron′, -shə-) *n.* one of a breed of strong, very heavy draft horses, usually having a gray or black coat.

[French *Percheron* horse or mare, from *Le Perche,* region in France noted for its horses.]

per·chlo·rate (pər klôr′āt) *n.* a salt or ester of perchloric acid. [PER- + CHLORATE.]

per·chlo·ric acid (pər klôr′ik) an unstable liquid acid, highly oxidizing, used in the laboratory to decompose organic matter before subjecting it to chemical analysis. Formula: $HClO_4$

per·cip·i·ent (pər sip′ē ənt) *adj.* capable of perceiving; discerning: *the percipient mind of a philosopher.* —*n.* a person who perceives. [Latin *percipiēns,* present participle of *percipere* to take possession of, observe.]

Per·ci·val (pûr′sə vəl) *also,* Per·ci·vale. *n.* Perceval.

per·co·late (pûr′kə lāt′) *v.,* -lat·ed, -lat·ing. —*v.t.* **1.** to prepare (coffee) in a percolator. **2.** to cause (a liquid) to filter through small spaces or holes. —*v.i.* **1.** to drip or filter through small spaces or holes: *The water purifies as it percolates through the tiny pebbles of the streambed.* **2.** to become percolated: *The coffee is percolating.* [Latin *percōlātus,* past participle of *percōlāre* to strain through.] —**per′co·la′tion,** *n.* —**per′co·la′tive,** *adj.*

per·co·la·tor (pûr′kə lā′tər) *n.* **1.** a kind of coffeepot in which boiling water rises through a tube to a perforated basket containing ground coffee, and then filters back down to the bottom. **2.** something that percolates.

per·cuss (pər kus′) *v.t. Medicine.* to tap (a part of the body) with the finger or an instrument for diagnostic purposes.

per·cus·sion (pər kush′ən) *n.* **1.** the striking of one body with or against another with great force; collision. **2.** the shock or impact resulting from a collision. **3.** the striking of sound waves upon the ear. **4.** the act of striking the percussion cap of a firearm. **5.** *Medicine.* the tapping of a part of the body with the finger or an instrument for diagnostic purposes. **6.** percussion instruments collectively. [Latin *percussiō* a striking.]

percussion cap, a small cap containing powder in a cavity at the bottom. It explodes to set off a larger charge when it is struck by a sharp blow, as from the hammer of a gun.

percussion instrument, any of various musical instruments in which tones are produced by striking or shaking, such as the drum, cymbal, xylophone, triangle, castanets, gong, and piano.

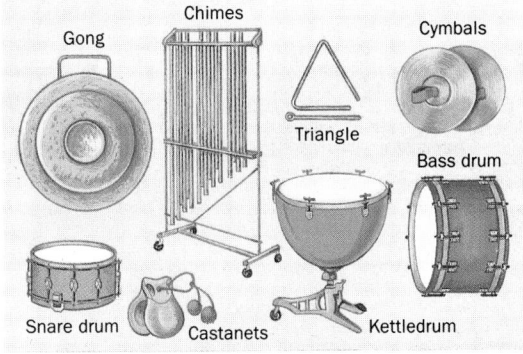

percussion instruments

per·cus·sion·ist (pər kush′ə nist) *n.* a musician who plays a percussion instrument.

per·cus·sive (pər kus′iv) *adj.* of, relating to, or characterized by percussion. —**per·cus′sive·ly,** *adv.* —**per·cus′sive·ness,** *n.*

per di·em (pər dē′əm, dī′əm) **1.** for each day; per day; daily. **2.** a daily allowance for expenses. [Latin *per diem* daily.]

per·di·tion (pər dish′ən) *n.* **1.** the loss of one's soul and of heavenly salvation; eternal damnation. **2.** hell. **3.** utter ruin; complete destruction. [Late Latin *perditiō* destruction, ruin, from Latin *perdere* to destroy.]

per·e·gri·nate (per′i grə nāt′) *v.,* -nat·ed, -nat·ing. —*v.i.* to travel, esp. by walking. —*v.t.* to travel through or over, esp. by walking. [Latin *peregrīnātus,* past participle of *peregrīnārī* to travel abroad.] —**per′e·gri·na′tion,** *n.* —**per′e·gri·na′tor,** *n.*

a	at	e	end	o	hot	u	up	hw	white		about
ā	ape	ē	me	ō	old	ū	use	ng	song		taken
ä	far	i	it	ô	fork	ü	rule	th	thin	ə	pencil
âr	care	ī	ice	oi	oil	u̇	pull	th	this		lemon
		îr	pierce	ou	out	ûr	turn	zh	measure		circus

per·e·grine (per′i grin, -grēn′, -grīn′) *also,* **per·e·grin** (per′i-grin). *n.* a falcon, *Falco peregrinus,* having predominantly bluish gray plumage and formerly much used in falconry. Length: to 19 inches (48 centimeters). Also, **peregrine falcon, peregrin falcon.** *—adj.* wandering or migratory: *peregrine faunas.* [Latin *peregrīnus* foreign, going back to *per* through, beyond + *ager* *(Rōmānus)* (Roman) territory.]

per·emp·to·ry (pə remp′tə rē) *adj.* **1.** absolutely settled or determined; unconditional; final: *a peremptory court action.* **2.** not to be disobeyed, refused, or questioned; imperative: *The orders of the president were peremptory.* **3.** authoritative or arrogant; dictatorial; dogmatic: *a peremptory expert on everything, a peremptory manner.* [Latin *peremptōrius* destructive, decisive.] **—per·emp′to·ri·ly,** *adv.* **—per·emp′to·ri·ness,** *n.*

per·en·ni·al (pə ren′ē əl) *adj.* **1.** lasting or continuing through the year or many years: *a perennial stream that doesn't dry up in summer.* **2.** lasting for a long time; enduring: *the perennial optimism of youth.* **3.** *Botany.* living more than two years. *—n.* a perennial plant. [Latin *perennis* lasting through the year (from *per* through + *annus* year) + -AL¹.] **—per·en′ni·al·ly,** *adv.*

pe·re·stroi·ka (per′ə stroi′kə) *n.* *Russian.* a basic reorganization of the economy and society of the Soviet Union, associated with the policies of Mikhail Gorbachev from 1986 to 1991. [Russian *perestroika* reconstruction, restructuring.]

perf. **1.** perfect. **2.** perforated.

per·fect *(adj., n.,* pûr′fikt; *v.,* pər fekt′) *adj.* **1.** free from any defect or flaw; faultless: *perfect weather for a picnic, a perfect diamond.* **2.** having all the proper or essential qualities or characteristics; fully developed, formed, or done; complete: *perfect happiness, a perfect house for a big family.* **3.** corresponding exactly to the original; accurate; correct: *That photo is a perfect likeness of you.* **4.** highly trained or skilled; accomplished: *a perfect goldsmith.* **5.** very great; absolute; utter: *a perfect fool.* **6.** *Grammar.* of, relating to, or designating the verb tenses that express action completed in the past or at the time of speaking. There are three perfect tenses in English: present perfect, past perfect (or pluperfect), and future perfect. *—n.* *Grammar.* **1.** a perfect tense. **2.** a verb form in such a tense. *—v.t.* **1.** to make faultless or complete: *to perfect a new surgical technique.* **2.** to bring to a high level of achievement; make fully expert: *to perfect oneself as a computer programmer.* [Latin *perfectus* completed, excellent, past participle of *perficere* to complete, do thoroughly.]

Synonyms *adj.* **Perfect, ideal,** and **flawless** mean without defect. **Perfect** suggests not only the absence of flaws but also the presence of all required characteristics: *The car was perfect for driving on unpaved roads.* **Ideal** implies a standard of perfection beyond what normally exists: *The party's ideal candidate would be equally acceptable to all of its factions.* **Flawless** describes something that is perfect within its limits: *Although not the best all-around musician, the singer had a flawless delivery.*

per·fect·i·ble (pər fek′tə bəl) *adj.* capable of becoming or being made perfect: *The technique involved in shaping this utensil is perfectible with practice.* **—per·fect′i·bil′i·ty,** *n.*

per·fec·tion (pər fek′shən) *n.* **1.** the quality or state of being perfect or faultless; excellence: *I always strive for perfection in my work. The food was cooked to perfection.* **2.** a person or thing that is the embodiment of excellence: *The chocolate mousse is sheer perfection.* **3.** the act or process of perfecting: *The perfection of the gymnast's technique took years of practice.*

per·fec·tion·ism (pər fek′shə niz′əm) *n.* **1.** the belief that moral perfection is possible and that human beings should strive for it. **2.** the practice of setting extremely high standards for oneself and others.

per·fec·tion·ist (pər fek′shə nist) *n.* **1.** a person who sets extremely high standards and goals for himself or herself and others; person who demands perfection. **2.** a person who believes in perfectionism. *—adj.* relating to or characteristic of a perfectionist or perfectionism. Also *(adj.),* **per·fec′tion·is′tic.**

per·fect·ly (pûr′fikt lē) *adv.* **1.** in a perfect manner; faultlessly: *This dress fits perfectly.* **2.** completely; entirely: *Today was a perfectly awful day. You are perfectly correct.*

perfect number, a number that is equal to the sum of its divisors, not including the number itself. 28, which can be divided by 1, 2, 4, 7, and 14, is a perfect number.

per·fec·to (pər fek′tō) *n., pl.* **-tos.** a thick, medium-length cigar tapering almost to a point at both ends. [Spanish *perfecto* complete, faultless, from Latin *perfectus* completed. See PERFECT.]

perfect participle, a participle that denotes action completed prior to the time of the main verb. In the sentence *Having finished my work, I left, having finished* is a perfect participle.

perfect pitch, absolute pitch.

per·fer·vid (pər fûr′vid) *adj.* very fervid; ardent: *a perfervid reformer.*

per·fid·i·ous (pər fid′ē əs) *adj.* given to or characterized by perfidy; faithless; treacherous. **—per·fid′i·ous·ly,** *adv.* **—per·fid′i·ous·ness,** *n.*

per·fi·dy (pûr′fi dē) *n., pl.* **-dies.** a deliberate betrayal of trust; base treachery; faithlessness. [Latin *perfidia* treachery.]

per·fo·li·ate (pər fō′lē it, -āt′) *adj.* (of a leaf) growing around the stem so that the stem appears to pass through it. [Modern Latin *perfoliatus,* from Latin *per* through + *folium* leaf.]

per·fo·rate *(v.,* pûr′fə rāt′; *adj.,* pûr′fər-it, -fə rāt′) *v.t.* **-rat·ed, -rat·ing.** **1.** to make a hole or holes through, as by cutting or punching: *We perforated the cardboard box so the kittens could breathe.* **2.** to make a row or series of small holes through (something): *The edge of the order blank in the catalog was perforated so that it could be torn out easily.* *—adj.* pierced with a hole or holes. [Latin *perforātus,* past participle of *perforāre* to pierce through.] **—per′fo·ra′tor,** *n.* —For Synonyms *(v.t.),* see **pierce.**

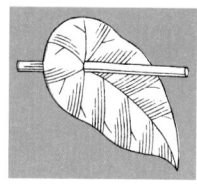

perfoliate leaf

per·fo·ra·tion (pûr′fə rā′shən) *n.* **1.** the act or process of perforating or the state of being perforated. **2.** a hole made by boring or piercing through something: *perforations in a sheet of postage stamps.*

per·force (pər fôrs′) *adv.* *Archaic.* of or by necessity; necessarily: *The reader must perforce . . . make his own inferences* (Edward Edwards, 1868). [Old French *par force* by force, from *par* by (from Latin *per*) + *force.* See FORCE.]

per·form (pər fôrm′) *v.t.* **1.** to begin and carry out to completion; execute; do: *A noted surgeon performed the operation.* **2.** to meet or satisfy the requirements of; fulfill; discharge: *to perform one's duty.* **3.** to give a performance of: *to perform a play by Shakespeare.* *—v.i.* **1.** to carry out a task, duty, job, or the like; function: *She performs well under pressure.* **2.** to give a performance: *The singer has never performed in New York before.* [Anglo-Norman *parformer* to accomplish, form of Old French *parfournir,* from *par* thoroughly (from Latin *per* through) + *fournir* to provide (of Germanic origin).]

Synonyms *v.t.* **Perform** and **execute** mean to carry out a task. **Perform** is used in reference to the actions involved, usually formal, lengthy, or complicated ones: *Computers can quickly perform calculations that would take a person hours or days.* **Execute** emphasizes an often complex plan of action: *The troops executed the rescue mission efficiently.*

per·for·mance (pər fôr′məns) *n.* **1.** a public presentation, as of a play, musical program, or other entertainment: *The show closed after ten performances.* **2.** the act of performing or the state of being performed. **3.** the way in which someone or something performs; manner of performing: *to test a car's performance in icy conditions.* **4.** something performed; action; deed.

per·form·er (pər fôr′mər) *n.* a person who performs, esp. a person who gives or takes part in public entertainment.

performing arts, the art forms, such as drama or dance, that require public performance.

per·fume *(n.,* pûr′fūm, pər fūm′; *v.,* pər fūm′) *n.* **1.** a liquid with a pleasing fragrance, worn on the body or added as a scent to various products. **2.** a sweet or pleasant odor; fragrance: *the perfume of a flower garden.* *—v.t.,* **-fumed, -fum·ing.** to make fragrant: *The roses perfumed the room. I perfume my hair with a scented spray.* [French *parfumer* to fill with a pleasant odor, fumigate, through Italian, going back to Latin *per* through + *fūmāre* to smoke.]

per·fum·er (pər fū′mər) *n.* a person who makes or sells perfumes.

per·fum·er·y (pər fū′mə rē) *n., pl.* **-er·ies.** **1.** the art of making perfumes or the business of selling them. **2.** a place where perfumes are made or sold. **3.** perfume or perfumes collectively.

per·func·to·ry (pər fungk′tə rē) *adj.* **1.** done hurriedly or as a matter of routine; mechanical; superficial: *to be too busy to give a newspaper more than a perfunctory glance.* **2.** acting in such a manner; halfhearted; indifferent: *a perfunctory salesperson.* [Late Latin *perfunctōrius* careless, done superficially, from Latin *perfungī* to perform.] **—per·func′to·ri·ly,** *adv.* **—per·func′to·ri·ness,** *n.*

per·fuse (pər fūz′) *v.t.,* **-fused, -fus·ing.** **1.** to permeate, suffuse, or sprinkle with (something, such as a liquid, color, or light). **2.** to spread or pour (a liquid) over or through something. [Latin *perfūsus,* past participle of *perfundere* to pour over.] **—per·fu′sion,** *n.* **—per·fu′sive** (pər fū′siv), *adj.*

per·go·la (pûr′gə lə) *n.* a structure resting on columns or other supports and having an open roof, used esp. as a trellis for vines. [Italian *pergola,* from Latin *pergula* vine arbor, shed.]

per·haps (pər haps′) *adv.* possibly but not certainly; maybe:

Perhaps your friend would like to join us. [Per- + *haps,* plural of HAP.]

pe·ri (pîr′ē) *n.* in Persian mythology, a beautiful fairylike being composed of fire, descended from fallen angels and excluded from paradise until penance has been done. [Persian *parī* fairy.]

per·i·anth (per′ē anth′) *n.* the external part or envelope of a flower, including the calyx and the corolla. [Modern Latin *perianthium,* from Greek *peri* around + *anthos* flower.]

per·i·car·di·al (per′i kär′dē əl) *adj.* of, relating to, or affecting the pericardium. Also, **per′i·car′di·ac.**

per·i·car·di·tis (per′i kär dī′tis) *n.* inflammation of the pericardium.

per·i·car·di·um (per′i kär′dē əm) *n., pl.* **-di·a** (-dē ə). the thin membranous sac that surrounds and protects the heart. [Modern Latin *pericardium,* from Greek *perikardion,* neuter of *perikardios* around the heart, from *peri* around + *kardiā* heart.]

per·i·carp (per′i karp′) *n.* the wall of a ripened ovary, sometimes consisting of three layers, the exocarp, mesocarp, and endocarp; seedcase. [Greek *perikarpion* shell, husk, from *peri* around + *karpos* fruit.]

per·i·cra·ni·um (per′i krā′nē əm) *n., pl.* **-ni·a** (-nē ə). a membrane covering the external surface of the skull. [Modern Latin *pericranium,* from Greek *perikrānion,* neuter of *perikrānios* around the skull, from *peri* around + *krānion* skull.] —**per′i·cra′ni·al,** *adj.*

per·i·cy·cle (per′ə sī′kəl) *n.* the outermost layer of the stele in the stems and roots of most plants, composed mostly of parenchyma. [French *péricycle,* from Greek *perikyklos* spherical, from *peri-* around + *kyklos* circle, wheel.]

per·i·dot (per′i dot′) *n.* a yellowish green, transparent variety of olivine used as a gem. [French *péridot,* from Middle French *péritot;* of uncertain origin.]

per·i·gee (per′i jē) *n.* the point in the orbit of the moon, an artificial satellite, or a spacecraft at which it is closest to the earth. ➡ opposed to **apogee.** For illustration, see **apogee.** [French *périgée,* from Modern Latin *perigēum,* from Late Greek *perigeion,* going back to Greek *peri* around, near + *gē* earth.] —**per′i·ge′al, per′i·ge′an,** *adj.*

pe·rig·y·nous (pə rij′ə nəs) *adj. Botany.* having sepals, petals, and stamens attached to the margin of a cuplike receptacle surrounding but not attached to the ovary, as in a rose.

per·i·he·li·on (per′ə hē′lē ən, -hēl′yən) *n., pl.* **-he·li·a** (-hēl′ē ə, -hēl′yə). the point in the orbit of a planet or other heavenly body at which it is closest to the sun. ➡ opposed to **aphelion.** [Greek *peri* around + *hēlios* sun.] —**per′i·he′li·al, per′i·he′li·an,** *adj.*

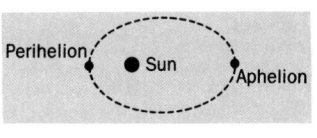

perihelion

per·il (per′əl) *n.* **1.** the chance or risk of injury, loss, or destruction; danger: *a time of peril.* **2.** something that may cause injury or damage: *Icy roads are a peril to motorists.* —*v.t.,* **-iled, -il·ing;** *also, British,* **-illed, -il·ling.** to expose to danger; imperil. [Old French *peril* danger, from Latin *perīculum.*] —For Synonyms, see **danger.**

per·il·ous (per′ə ləs) *adj.* full of or involving peril; hazardous; dangerous: *a perilous journey.* [Old French *perillous,* from Latin *perīculōsus,* from *perīculum* danger.] —**per′il·ous·ly,** *adv.* —**per′il·ous·ness,** *n.*

pe·rim·e·ter (pə rim′i tər) *n.* **1.** the boundary of an area or a closed plane figure: *the perimeter of a backyard, the perimeter of a square.* **2.** the measure or length of such a boundary. **3.** a boundary area where military defenses are set up. [Latin *perimetros,* from Greek *perimetros,* from *peri* around + *metron* measure.]

per·i·na·tal (per′ə nā′təl) *adj.* of, relating to, or occurring during the period shortly before and after the time of birth, commonly regarded as beginning when the fetus attains a weight of about 14 ounces (500 grams) and ending 28 days after birth.

per·i·ne·um (per′ə nē′əm) *n., pl.* **-ne·a** (-nē′ə). the region of the body between the thighs, extending from the anus to the genitals. [Modern Latin *perineum,* going back to Greek *perīneos.*] —**per′i·ne′al,** *adj.*

pe·ri·od (pîr′ē əd) *n.* **1.** a portion of time of a given length or marked by certain conditions or events: *a period of mild weather, a period of three months.* **2.a.** a portion of time regarded as a phase of development; stage: *This painting is from the artist's last period.* **b.** a span of historical time; era: *the colonial period, the Victorian period.* **3.** a portion of time marked off by some recurring action or event; cycle: *The tides of the ocean . . . flow in periods* (James McCosh, 1850). **4.** *Physics.* the time of one complete cycle of an oscillation or other recurring motion or phenomenon. **5.** the time that it takes a planet or satellite to make one complete revolu-

tion. **6.** a timed portion of certain games and sports: *Our team scored in the second period.* **7.** one of the divisions of time in a school day. **8.** a fundamental unit of the standard geologic time scale, a primary subdivision of an era, characterized by certain kinds of rock formations and usually named for the place where such formations were discovered or are particularly prominent. **9.** menstruation *(def. 2).* **10.** the duration or a stage in the duration of a disease. **11.** a mark of punctuation (.) indicating the end of a declarative sentence or an abbreviation. **12.** a pause at the end of a sentence. **13.** a complete sentence, esp. one consisting of several clauses. **14.** the end, completion, or conclusion. **15.** a series of chemical elements, arranged in order of increasing atomic number, forming one of the seven horizontal rows of the periodic table. ➡ distinguished from **group** *(def. 4a).* —*adj.* of, relating to, or characteristic of a certain era or time: *The actors were dressed in period costumes. This chair is a period piece and quite valuable.* —*interj.* ➡ used to emphasize the finality or absoluteness of a statement: *They have no money, period.* [Latin *periodus* sentence, cycle, from Greek *periodos.*]

Synonyms **Period, era, epoch,** and **age** all mean a division of time. **Period** refers to any time regarded separately, whether by one person or generally: *that period of my life, the colonial period of American history.* **Era** indicates a period of historical change: *the era of the Renaissance.* **Epoch** is used of an era that begins with some momentous change: *The French revolutionary epoch lasted a quarter century after the events of 1789.* **Age** is a general term for an extended period, esp. one marked by great developments or associated with a great figure or figures: *the age of electricity, the age of Alexander the Great.*

pe·ri·od·ic (pîr′ē od′ik) *adj.* **1.** happening on occasion; intermittent: *periodic shifts in public opinion.* **2.** happening or appearing at regular intervals; recurrent: *periodic audits of a bank's records.* **3.** of, relating to, or characterized by periods or cycles; cyclical: *the periodic rise and fall of the tide.* —**pe′ri·od′i·cal·ly,** *adv.*

Synonyms **Periodic, sporadic,** and **intermittent** mean happening in an interrupted sequence. **Periodic** is usually used of something that happens at more or less regular and predictable intervals: *The geyser Old Faithful is named for its periodic eruptions.* **Sporadic** describes events that are widely scattered and unpredictable: *We had generally good weather, with only sporadic thunderstorms.* **Intermittent** stresses the lack of continuity in an irregular succession of happenings: *The intermittent nature of their income made it hard for the family to follow a budget.*

pe·ri·od·i·cal (pîr′ē od′i kəl) *n.* a publication issued at regular intervals, such as every two weeks or every month. —*adj.* **1.** of or relating to periodicals. **2.** published at regular intervals, such as every two weeks or every month. **3.** periodic. —For Synonyms *(n.),* see **journal.**

periodic decimal, repeating decimal.

pe·ri·o·dic·i·ty (pîr′ē ə dis′i tē) *n., pl.* **-ties. 1.** the tendency to appear or occur at regular intervals. **2.** the tendency of the chemical elements to exhibit the same or similar properties at regular intervals when arranged in order of increasing atomic numbers.

periodic law, the scientific principle that the properties of the chemical elements vary at regular intervals with their atomic numbers.

periodic sentence, a sentence so constructed that its meaning and grammatical structure are not complete until the very end, for example: *The jury, after much deliberation, found the defendant in the case to be not guilty.*

periodic table, a table in which the chemical elements are arranged in order of increasing atomic numbers, with elements having similar properties arranged in vertical columns called groups. For tables, see **element.**

per·i·o·don·tal (per′ē ə don′təl) *adj.* **1.** surrounding a tooth. **2.** of or affecting the tissues surrounding the teeth, as the gums: *periodontal infection.*

per·i·os·te·um (per′ē os′tē əm) *n., pl.* **-te·a** (-tē ə). a dense, fibrous membrane consisting of two layers, that covers the surface of bones except at the joints and supplies the bones with blood vessels and nerves. For illustration, see **bone.** [Modern Latin *periosteum,* going back to Greek *periosteon,* neuter of *periosteos* around the bones.] —**per′i·os′te·al,** *adj.*

per·i·pa·tet·ic (per′ə pə tet′ik) *adj.* **1.** walking or traveling from place to place; rambling; itinerant: *a peripatetic peddler.*

a	at	e	end	o	hot	u	up	hw	white		about
ā	ape	ē	me	ō	old	ū	use	ng	song		taken
ä	far	i	it	ô	fork	ü	rule	th	thin	ə	pencil
âr	care	ī	ice	oi	oil	u̇	pull	th	this		lemon
		îr	pierce	ou	out	ûr	turn	zh	measure		circus

P

2. Peripatetic. of, relating to, or adhering to the philosophy of the Greek philosopher Aristotle, who taught while walking in the Lyceum of ancient Athens. —*n.* **1.** a person who walks or travels from place to place; itinerant. **2. Peripatetic.** one of Aristotle's followers. [Latin *peripatēticus* relating to the philosophy of the Greek philosopher Aristotle, 384-322 B.C., from Greek *peripatētikos* given to walking about.] —**per′i·pa·tet′i·cal·ly,** *adv.*

pe·riph·er·al (pə rif′ər əl) *adj.* **1.** relating to, situated at, or forming a periphery: *peripheral vision, a peripheral area, peripheral expansion.* **2.** of or relating to the peripheral nervous system. —*n. Computers.* any input or output device, such as a printer or keyboard. Peripherals are controlled by the central processing unit, to which they are linked by cables. —**pe·riph′er·al·ly,** *adv.*

peripheral nervous system, the part of the nervous system that connects the central nervous system (the brain and spinal cord) to the rest of the body, consisting of the nerves that connect the brain with the voluntary muscles, sense organs, and skin, and the autonomic nerves, which regulate the internal organs.

peripheral vision, vision of objects outside the area that the eye is directly focusing on, in which the image is formed outside the central area of the retina.

pe·riph·er·y (pə rif′ə rē) *n., pl.* **-er·ies. 1.** the external boundary or surface of an area or object. **2.** a surrounding area or region; environs. [Late Latin *peripheria,* from Greek *periphereia* circumference of a circle.]

pe·riph·ra·sis (pə rif′rə sis) *n., pl.* **-ses** (-sēz′) **1.** a roundabout or needlessly wordy way of saying something; circumlocution. **2.** an instance of this. Also, **per·i·phrase** (per′ə frāz′). [Latin *periphrasis,* from Greek *periphrasis.*]

per·i·phras·tic (per′ə fras′tik) *adj.* **1.** of, characterized by, or expressed by periphrasis. **2.** *Grammar.* denoting a construction using an auxiliary word rather than an inflectional form, as *more rich* rather than *richer* or *of Jan* rather than *Jan's.* —**per′i·phras′ti·cal·ly,** *adv.*

per·i·scope (per′ə skōp′) *n.* an optical instrument, as in a submarine or tank, for viewing objects not directly in the observer's line of sight, consisting of a tube with an arrangement of prisms or mirrors that reflect the images through the tube to the eye of the observer. [Greek *peri* around + -SCOPE.] —**per·i·scop·ic** (per′ə skop′ik), *adj.*

per·ish (per′ish) *v.i.* **1.** to die, esp. in a violent or untimely way: *Many people perished when the ship sank.* **2.** to pass from existence; disappear: *Government of the people, by the people, and for the people, shall not perish from the earth* (Abraham Lincoln, 1863). [Old French *periss-,* a stem of *perir* to die, from Latin *perīre.*]

per·ish·a·ble (per′i shə bəl) *adj.* likely to spoil or decay: *Perishable foods should be refrigerated.* —*n.* something, esp. an item of food, that is likely to spoil or decay. —**per′ish·a·bil′i·ty, per′ish·a·ble·ness,** *n.*

pe·ris·so·dac·tyl (pə ris′ə dak′təl) *n.* any of a group of hoofed mammals, order Perissodactyla, having an odd number of toes, with the weight-bearing axis of the foot centered on the middle toe. Included are tapirs, rhinoceroses, and horses. [Modern Latin *perissodactyus,* from Greek *perissos* uneven, from *peri* over + *daktylos* finger.] —**pe·ris′so·dac′tyl·ous,** *adj.*

per·i·stal·sis (per′ə stôl′sis, -stal′-) *n., pl.* **-ses** (-sēz) the successive waves of contractions in the walls of the intestine or another tubular organ, which propel the contents of the organ onward. [Modern Latin *peristalsis,* from Greek *peri* around + *stalsis* checking.] —**per′i·stal′tic,** *adj.*

per·i·style (per′ə stīl′) *n.* **1.** a row of columns surrounding a building or open space. **2.** a building or area so enclosed. [French *péristyle,* from Latin *peristylum,* from Greek *peristylon,* from *peri* around + *stȳlos* pillar.] —**per′i·sty′lar,** *adj.*

peristyle of the Jefferson Memorial, Washington, D.C.

per·i·to·ne·um (per′i tə nē′əm) *n., pl.* **-ne·ums** or **-ne·a** (-nē′ə). a transparent serous membrane that lines the walls of the abdominal cavity and covers the organs in it. [Late Latin *peritonaeum,* from Greek *peritonaion,* going back to *peri* around + *teinein* to stretch.] —**per′i·to·ne′al,** *adj.*

per·i·to·ni·tis (per′i tə nī′tis) *n.* inflammation of the peritoneum. [Modern Latin *peritonitis,* from Greek *peritonaion* peritoneum + *-itis* -ITIS.]

per·i·wig (per′i wig′) *n.* a wig or peruke. [Modification of PERUKE.]

per·i·win·kle¹ (per′i wing′kəl) *n.* any of a group of erect or trailing plants, genus *Vinca,* esp. the **common periwinkle,** *V. minor,* commonly having lilac-blue, trumpet-shaped flowers and oval leaves. [Latin *pervinca.*]

per·i·win·kle² (per′i wing′kəl) *n.* any of a group of small sea snails, genus *Littorina,* found in shallow waters along the coasts of Europe and northeastern North America, esp. the **common periwinkle,** *L. littorea,* having a cone-shaped spiral shell that is usually olive-green, sometimes banded with red or brown. Length: ³/₄ inch (2 centimeters). Also, **winkle.** [Of uncertain origin.]

per·jure (pûr′jər) *v.t.,* **-jured, -jur·ing.** to make (oneself) guilty of perjury: *The district attorney proved that the witness had perjured herself.* [Old French *parjurer,* from Latin *perjūrāre.*] —**per′jur·er,** *n.*

per·ju·ry (pûr′jə rē) *n., pl.* **-ries.** the act or an instance of lying in court or in any situation in which one is under oath. [Anglo-Norman *perjurie,* from Latin *perjūrium.*] —**per·ju′ri·ous,** *adv.*

perk¹ (pûrk) *v.i.* **1.** to become lively, vigorous, or cheerful (with *up*): *The patient perked up when the doctor said he could go home.* **2.** to move or lift one's head and carry oneself in a jaunty manner. **3.** to rise smartly or briskly: *The dog's ears perked when it saw me.* —*v.t.* **1.** to raise smartly or briskly: *The fox perked its ears.* **2.** to make lively, vigorous, or cheerful: *I felt depressed, but my friend's letter perked me up.* **3.** to make spruce, bright, or smart: *A yellow tie perked up her drab suit. The children were perked out in their best clothes.* [Dialectal Old French *perquer* to perch, from *perque* perch, from Latin *pertica* pole, bar.]

perk² (pûrk) *n. Informal.* perquisite. [From PERQUISITE.]

perk·y (pûr′kē) *adj.,* **perk·i·er, perk·i·est.** lively and vigorous; jaunty; pert. —**perk′i·ly,** *adv.* —**perk′i·ness,** *n.*

perm (pûrm) *n. Informal.* permanent wave.

perm·a·frost (pûr′mə frôst′) *n.* a layer of permanently frozen earth found in arctic and antarctic regions.

per·ma·nence (pûr′mə nəns) *n.* the state or quality of being permanent; durability; endurance.

per·ma·nen·cy (pûr′mə nən sē) *n., pl.* **-cies. 1.** permanence. **2.** something permanent.

per·ma·nent (pûr′mə nənt) *adj.* lasting or intended to last indefinitely without change; durable; enduring: *a permanent dye, permanent employment.* —*n.* permanent wave. [Latin *permanēns,* present participle of *permanēre* to endure, continue.] —**per′ma·nent·ly,** *adv.*

permanent magnet, a magnet that retains its magnetism after the magnetizing force has been removed.

permanent press, (of a fabric or garment) finished in such a manner that little or no ironing is required after washing.

permanent tooth, any of the set of teeth that replace the milk teeth in mammals, numbering thirty-two in humans, including eight incisors, four canines, eight premolars, and twelve molars.

permanent wave, a curl lasting several months, set in the hair with a chemical solution or with heat.

per·man·ga·nate (pər mang′ə nāt′) *n.* a salt of permanganic acid, as potassium permanganate.

per·man·gan·ic acid (pûr′man gan′ik) an unstable liquid acid, used in aqueous solution as an oxidizing agent. Formula: $HMnO_4$ [PER- + MANGANIC.]

per·me·a·bil·i·ty (pûr′mē ə bil′i tē) *n.* **1.** the quality or state of being permeable. **2.** *Physics.* a measure of the ability of a substance to conduct magnetic lines of force. **3.** the rate at which a fluid will diffuse through a porous body.

per·me·a·ble (pûr′mē ə bəl) *adj.* capable of being permeated: *a permeable membrane, permeable defenses.* [Late Latin *permeābilis,* from Latin *permeāre* to pass through.]

per·me·ate (pûr′mē āt′) *v.,* **-at·ed, -at·ing.** —*v.t.* **1.** to pass through the pores or openings of: *Water can permeate sand.* **2.** to spread throughout; pervade: *The fragrance of the lilacs permeated the room.* —*v.i.* to spread or diffuse itself: *Fear permeated throughout the entire community.* [Latin *permeātus,* past participle of *permeāre* to pass through.] —**per′me·a′tion,** *n.* —**per′me·a′tive,** *adj.*

Synonyms *v.t.* **Permeate, pervade,** and **penetrate** mean to pass into and spread through something in either a physical or an abstract sense. **Permeate** emphasizes spreading throughout all parts, often through holes or openings: *Water permeated the sponge.* **Pervade** also stresses spreading widely and is often used in a nonphysical sense: *A feeling of optimism pervaded the conference.* **Penetrate** emphasizes the entry of something that goes deep and spreads extensively: *The termites penetrated the house's foundation.*

Per·mi·an (pûr′mē ən) *n.* the seventh and last geologic period of the Paleozoic era, when mammallike reptiles appeared and many species of plants and animals became extinct. For table, see **geologic time.** —*adj.* of, relating to, or characteristic of the Permian. [From *Perm,* area in the Ural Mountains.]

per·mis·si·ble (pər mis′ə bəl) *adj.* that may be permitted; allowable. —**per·mis′si·bly,** *adv.*

per·mis·sion (pər mish′ən) *n.* **1.** the act of permitting. **2.** formal consent; authorization; leave: *Do I have your permission to go?* [Latin *permissiō* a giving up, leave.]

per·mis·sive (pər mis′iv) *adj.* **1.** allowing much freedom; not strict; lenient or tolerant: *a permissive parent.* **2.** granting permission: *a permissive proclamation.* **3.** permitted; optional: *permissive legislative powers.* —**per·mis′sive·ly,** *adv.* —**per·mis′sive·ness,** *n.*

per·mit (*v.,* pər mit′; *n.,* pûr′mit, pər mit′) *v.,* **-mit·ted, -mit·ting.** —*v.t.* **1.** to allow (a person) to do something; give leave to: *Permit me to be of assistance to you.* **2.** to allow (something) to be done; give consent or authorization to: *This county permits the sale of alcoholic beverages in restaurants.* **3.** to give an opportunity for: *The large window permitted a panoramic view of the land.* —*v.i.* to give an opportunity; allow: *I'll call you today if time permits.* —*n.* **1.** *Law.* a written order or license issued by a competent authority, granting permission to a party to perform some action not otherwise allowed. **2.** permission, esp. in written form. [Latin *permittere* to allow.] —For Synonyms *(v.t.),* see **let**[1].

per·mu·tate (pûr′myů tāt′) *v.t.,* **-tat·ed, -tat·ing. 1.** to cause to change; alter. **2.** to rearrange the sequence of. [Latin *permutatus,* past participle of *permutare* to change radically.]

per·mu·ta·tion (pûr′myů tā′shən) *n.* **1.** a complete change or alteration: *permutations in American life as a result of shifts in population.* **2.** *Mathematics.* **a.** a change in the order or sequence of the elements of a set. **b.** any ordered arrangement of the elements of a set. The sequences *abc, acb, bac,* and *cab* are permutations of *a, b,* and *c.* [Latin *permūtātiō* a changing.] —**per′mu·ta′tion·al,** *adj.*

per·mute (pər mūt′) *v.t.,* **-muted, -mut·ing. 1.** to bring about a change in; alter. **2.** *Mathematics.* to subject to permutation. —**per·mut′a·ble,** *adj.* —**per·mut′a·bil′i·ty,** *n.*

per·ni·cious (pər nish′əs) *adj.* **1.** causing or likely to cause harm, injury, or destruction; malicious: *Pernicious gossip can ruin a reputation.* **2.** causing injury or death; severe or fatal: *a pernicious disease.* [Latin *perniciosus* destructive, from *perniciēs* destruction.] —**per·ni′cious·ly,** *adv.* —**per·ni′cious·ness,** *n.*

pernicious anemia, severe anemia caused by an inability of the digestive system to absorb vitamin B_{12}, characterized by weakness, shortness of breath, and a greatly decreased number of red blood cells.

per·nick·e·ty (pər nik′i tē) *adj.* persnickety.

per·o·rate (per′ə rāt′) *v.i.,* **-rat·ed, -rat·ing. 1.** to speak at length; make a speech. **2.** to deliver a peroration. [Latin *perōrātus,* past participle of *perōrāre* to speak from beginning to end.]

per·o·ra·tion (per′ə rā′shən) *n.* **1.** the concluding part of a speech, repeating key points and summing up what has been said. **2.** a high-sounding, pompous speech. [Latin *perōrātiō.*]

per·ox·ide (pə rok′sīd) *n.* **1.** an oxide whose molecules contain more than the usual number of oxygen atoms. In peroxides, the oxygen atoms form a weak bond with each other. **2.** an oxide containing the highest possible proportion of oxygen. **3.** hydrogen peroxide. —*v.t.,* **-id·ed, -id·ing.** to bleach (hair) using hydrogen peroxide. [PER- + OXIDE.]

per·pen·dic·u·lar (pûr′pən dik′yə lər) *adj.* **1.** at right angles to the plane of the horizon; upright; vertical. **2.** *Mathematics.* at right angles to a given line, plane, or surface. The sides of a square are perpendicular to the base. —*n.* **1.** a perpendicular line or plane. **2.** a perpendicular position. [Latin *perpendiculāris* vertical, from *perpendiculum* plumb line.]

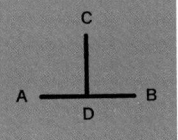

perpendicular lines

per·pen·dic·u·lar·i·ty (pûr′pən dik′yə lar′i tē) *n.* the state or quality of being perpendicular.

per·pe·trate (pûr′pi trāt′) *v.t.,* **-trat·ed, -trat·ing.** to do, perform, or commit (a crime, misdeed, or the like): *The two students perpetrated a hoax that fooled even the newspaper reporters.* [Latin *perpetrātus,* past participle of *perpetrāre* to perform, accomplish.] —**per′pe·tra′tion,** *n.*

per·pe·tra·tor (pûr′pi trā′tər) *n.* a person who commits a crime, misdeed, or the like, esp. a person sought or arrested for a crime.

per·pet·u·al (pər pech′ü əl) *adj.* **1.** lasting or enduring forever; eternal: *a mountaintop enveloped in perpetual snow.* **2.** continuing throughout one's lifetime; permanent: *perpetual vows, perpetual ownership.* **3.** continuing without interruption; unceasing: *the perpetual ebb and flow of the tide.* **4.** *Botany.* blooming continuously throughout the growing season or year. [Latin *perpetuālis* permanent, from *perpetuus* continuous.] —**per·pet′u·al·ly,** *adv.*

perpetual motion, constant motion, esp. that of a hypothetical machine that, once set in motion, would continue moving indefinitely without any additional energy being supplied to it.

per·pet·u·ate (pər pech′ü āt′) *v.t.,* **-at·ed, -at·ing.** to cause to last or endure; keep in memory or existence: *History perpetuates the deeds of our ancestors.* [Latin *perpetuātus,* past participle of *perpetuāre* to make perpetual.] —**per·pet′u·a′tion,** *n.* —**per·pet′u·a′tor,** *n.*

per·pe·tu·i·ty (pûr′pi tü′i tē, -tū′-) *n., pl.* **-ties. 1.** the quality or state of being perpetual; endless existence or duration. **2.** something perpetual. **3.** *Law.* **a.** a condition or limitation under which land or property cannot be transferred during the life of a certain living person or for twenty-one years thereafter. **b.** property so limited. [Latin *perpetuitās* continuity.]

•**in perpetuity.** forever: *The deed grants full ownership of the property in perpetuity.*

per·plex (pər pleks′) *v.t.* **1.** to trouble or fill with doubt or uncertainty; bewilder: *Contradictory news reports perplexed the public.* **2.** to make (something) intricate, complex, or difficult to understand; complicate; muddle. [Latin *perplexus* involved, confused, entangled.] —**per·plex′ing,** *adj.* —**per·plex′ing·ly,** *adv.* —For Synonyms, see **puzzle.**

per·plex·i·ty (pər plek′si tē) *n., pl.* **-ties. 1.** the state or condition of being perplexed; bewilderment; confusion. **2.** a perplexing situation or circumstance.

per·qui·site (pûr′kwə zit) *n.* **1.** any additional profit or benefit received for work besides regular salary: *Free room and board was a perquisite of the job.* **2.** a particular right or privilege to which a person, group, or organization is entitled; prerogative: *Members of Congress may send mail without paying postage as one of the perquisites of office.* [Medieval Latin *perquisitum* acquisition, from Latin *perquīrere* to search diligently.]

per se (pər sā′, sē′) *Latin.* by or in itself; intrinsically.

per·se·cute (pûr′si kūt′) *v.t.,* **-cut·ed, -cut·ing. 1.** to subject to cruel, harmful, or oppressive treatment: *a minority group that was persecuted for centuries.* **2.** to harass, vex, or annoy constantly: *Some unknown person persecuted me with telephone calls.* [Old French *persecuter,* going back to Latin *persequī* to follow after, prosecute.] —**per′se·cu′tor,** *n.*

per·se·cu·tion (pûr′si kū′shən) *n.* the act of persecuting or the state of being persecuted. [Latin *persecūtiō* pursuit, prosecution.]

Per·seph·o·ne (pər sef′ə nē) *n.* in Greek mythology, the goddess of vegetation and of death. She was the daughter of Zeus and Demeter and wife of Hades, the god of the underworld. Her Roman counterpart is Proserpina.

Per·se·us (pûr′sē əs, pûr′sūs) *n.* **1.** in Greek mythology, the hero who killed Medusa and rescued Andromeda from a sea monster. **2.** a constellation in the northern celestial hemisphere, between Taurus and Cassiopeia.

per·se·ver·ance (pûr′sə vîr′əns) *n.* the act or quality of persevering; persistence. —For Synonyms, see **persistence.**

per·se·vere (pûr′sə vîr′) *v.i.,* **-vered, -ver·ing.** to continue steadfastly in a course of action or pursuit in spite of difficulties or obstacles; persist: *Despite the failure of some early experiments, the scientists persevered with their research project.* [Old French *perseverer,* from Latin *perseverāre.*] —**per′se·ver′ing·ly,** *adv.*

a	at	e	end	o	hot	u	up	hw	white		about
ā	ape	ē	me	ō	old	ū	use	ng	song		taken
ä	far	i	it	ô	fork	ü	rule	th	thin	ə	pencil
âr	care	ī	ice	oi	oil	ů	pull	th	this		lemon
		îr	pierce	ou	out	ûr	turn	zh	measure		circus

P

903

Per·sian (pûr′zhən) *adj.* of, relating to, or characteristic of Persia or its people, language, or culture. —*n.* **1.** a native, inhabitant, or citizen of Persia. **2.** the language of Persia, belonging to the Indo-Iranian branch of the Indo-European language family.

Words from Persian			

Persian, which is now often known as Farsi, is the language of Iran and West Afghanistan. Many Persian words originally came from Sanskrit and passed through Arabic before entering English. Below is a selection of loanwords that have come into English from or through Persian.

arsenic	cheese[2]	Magi	rice
attar	dervish	magic	rook[2]
ayatollah	divan	marcasite	satrap
azure	gherkin	mullah	scimitar
bazaar	Hindi	mummy	seersucker
bulgur	Hindustani	orange	shah
calabash	jackal	pajamas	shawl
caravan	jasmine	paradise	sherbet
caravansary	julep	percale	spinach
carboy	khaki	peri	tabor
cassock	khan[2]	pilaf	taffeta
check	khedive	pistachio	turban
checkmate	lemon	purdah	zircon

Persian cat, a cat of a breed originally raised in Persia and Afghanistan, having a round head and long, silky fur.

Persian lamb, the tightly curled fur from newborn karakul lambs.

per·si·flage (pûr′sə fläzh′) *n.* light, flippant speech or writing; banter. [French *persiflage,* from *persifler* to jeer, going back to Latin *per* through + *sībilāre* to hiss.]

per·sim·mon (pər sim′ən) *n.* **1.** the fleshy, edible berry of any of a group of trees and shrubs, genus *Diospyros,* having thin, orange or yellow skin and containing from one to ten flat seeds. **2.** the tree or shrub bearing this berry. [Algonquian *pasimenan* dried fruit.]

per·sist (pər sist′, -zist′) *v.i.* **1.** to continue firmly and steadily in spite of opposition or difficulty; persevere: *If you persist in misbehaving, you will be punished.* **2.** to insist, as by repeating a statement: *"But I'm innocent," the prisoner persisted.* **3.** to continue to exist; endure: *The rain persisted all week.* [Latin *persistere* to continue steadfastly.]

per·sist·ence (pər sis′təns, -zis′-) *n.* **1.** the act of persisting: *My persistence finally brought them around to my point of view.* **2.** the quality or state of being persistent; tenacity. **3.** the power or condition of lasting, as of an effect after its cause is removed: *the persistence of a sensory impression.* Also, **per·sist′en·cy.**

Synonyms Persistence and perseverance mean continuing to do something in spite of obstacles or difficulties. **Persistence** often has a negative connotation, implying stubbornness or the continuation of something undesirable: *The parents were disturbed by the child's persistence in lying even after punishment.* **Perseverance** stresses patience and courage in pursuit of a goal: *After years of delay due to financial hardship, the student's perseverance was rewarded with a diploma.*

per·sist·ent (pər sis′tənt, -zis′-) *adj.* **1.** persisting in the face of difficulty or opposition: *a persistent campaigner for reform.* **2.** enduring; continual: *persistent interruptions, a persistent cough.* **3.** (of plant or animal structures) not shed or modified in maturation; retained permanently. —**per·sist′ent·ly,** *adv.*

per·snick·e·ty (pər snik′i tē) *adj. Informal.* **1.** very fussy about trivial matters; hard to please. **2.** requiring strict attention to detail. Also, **pernickety.**

per·son (pûr′sən) *n.* **1.** a man, woman, or child; human being; individual. **2.a.** the living body of a human being: *to have something on one's person.* **b.** bodily appearance: *to be careless and sloppy about one's person.* **3.** *Grammar.* **a.** any of three categories of personal pronouns or verb inflections indicating the person speaking (first person), the person spoken to (second person), or the person or thing spoken of (third person). **b.** any of the pronoun forms or verb inflections giving such an indication. **4.** *Law.* any individual or corporation having certain legal rights and duties. **5.** *also,* **Person.** one of the three modes of being in the Trinity. The Father is the First Person, the Son is the Second Person, and the Holy Spirit is the Third Person. [Old French *persone* human being, creature, from Latin *persōna* mask used by an actor, character, personage, probably from Etruscan *phersu* mask. Doublet of PARSON.]

•**in person.** in the flesh; physically present: *The actor looked older in person.*

per·so·na (pər sō′nə) *n., pl.* **-nae** (-nē) **-nas.** a character in a drama, novel, or the like. [Latin *persōna* mask used by an actor, character.]

per·son·a·ble (pûr′sə nə bəl) *adj.* having a pleasing or attractive appearance and manner: *a personable youngster.* —**per′son·a·ble·ness,** *n.* —**per′son·a·bly,** *adv.*

per·son·age (pûr′sə nij) *n.* **1.** a person of distinction or importance. **2.** any person; individual. **3.** persona. [Old French *personage* person, from *persone.* See PERSON.]

per·so·na gra·ta (pər sō′nə grä′tə, grat′ə) a person who is acceptable or welcome. [Latin *persōna grāta.*]

per·son·al (pûr′sə nəl) *adj.* **1.** of or relating to a particular person; individual; private: *a personal matter that shouldn't be discussed in public.* **2.** done, made, or performed in person: *The mayor made a personal appearance at the fair.* **3.** involving or carried on directly between persons: *a personal interview.* **4.** of or relating to the body or physical appearance: *personal hygiene, personal adornments.* **5.** making or inclined to make remarks about or inquiries into private matters: *The reporters became very personal in their questions.* **6.** relating or directed to a particular person or persons, esp. in a disparaging or offensive sense or manner: *a personal insult, a personal attack.* **7.** of, relating to, or having the characteristics of a person considered as a self-conscious, rational being, as opposed to a thing or abstraction: *a personal god.* **8.** *Law.* relating to or designating temporary or movable things: *personal property.* ➡ distinguished from **real.** **9.** *Grammar.* indicating person. —*n.* a short paragraph or item in a newspaper relating to a particular person or persons, or to private matters. [Late Latin *persōnālis* relating to a person, from Latin *persōna* mask, character, personage.]

personal computer, microcomputer.

personal equation, an individual tendency for error in seeing or judging someone or something, for which allowance must be made.

personal foul, any of various infractions of the rules in certain team sports, such as basketball, usually involving body contact.

per·son·al·i·ty (pûr′sə nal′i tē) *n., pl.* **-ties. 1.** the sum of the traits, habits, attitudes, and behavior of a person that makes him or her different from all others. **2.** distinctive personal characteristics or attributes, esp. those that are pleasing socially: *Her personality rather than her appearance made her popular.* **3.** a well-known or distinguished person; celebrity: *He is a famous stage and screen personality.* **4.** the quality, fact, or condition of being a person, not a thing; personal existence; identity. **5.** a remark or reference, often disparaging, made about or to some person: *a gossip who frequently indulged in personalities.*

per·son·al·ize (pûr′sə nə līz′) *v.t.* **-ized, -iz·ing. 1.** to make personal: *I personalized each invitation by adding a short note.* **2.** personify. **3.** to mark (property or possessions) with the name or initials of a person: *The stationery was personalized with my monogram.* —**per′son·al·i·za′tion,** *n.*

per·son·al·ly (pûr′sə nə lē) *adv.* **1.** not by the aid of or through others; in person: *The senator visited the war zone personally.* **2.** as far as oneself is concerned; for oneself: *Personally, I am in favor of the new policy.* **3.** as an individual: *They are friends of my parents, but I don't know them personally.* **4.** as though directed toward or intended for one as a person: *to take a remark personally.*

personal name, a name given to a person or by which a person is known.

personal pronoun, one of a group of pronouns indicating the speaker, the person or persons addressed, or any other persons, places, or things spoken about. *I, you, he, she, it, we,* and *they* are personal pronouns.

per·son·al·ty (pûr′sə nəl tē) *n., pl.* **-ties.** personal, movable property.

per·so·na non gra·ta (pər sō′nə non grä′tə, grat′ə) a person who is not acceptable or welcome. [Latin *persōna nōn grāta.*]

per·son·ate (pûr′sə nāt′) *v.t.,* **-at·ed, -at·ing. 1.** to act the part of (a character in a play or the like). **2.** *Law.* to impersonate or assume the identity of (someone) with intent to deceive. [Latin *persōnātus* masked, pretended, from *persōna* mask, character.] —**per′son·a′tion,** *n.* —**per′son·a′tor,** *n.*

per·son·i·fi·ca·tion (pər son′ə fi kā′shən) *n.* **1.** a figure of speech in which human characteristics are attributed to an animal, inanimate object, or quality, for example: *The sun smiled down on the green meadows.* **2.** a person or thing that typifies a particular quality or idea; embodiment: *a hero who is the personification of bravery.* **3.** an imaginary or ideal person or creature conceived as representing a thing or abstraction: *In Greek mythology, Neptune was the personification of the sea.* —**per·son′i·fi·ca′tor,** *n.*

per·son·i·fy (pər son′ə fī′) *v.t.,* **-fied, -fy·ing. 1.** to regard or

represent as having human characteristics. **2.** to be an embodiment of; typify in one's own person: *The dictator personified evil.* **3.** to represent or conceive as representing (an abstract quality or idea) by a human figure: *The figures in the painting personify the forces of good and evil.*

per·son·nel (pûr′sə nel′) *n.* **1.** the persons employed in a business or other place of employment: *doctors, nurses, and all the other personnel of a hospital.* **2.** the department in a business or other organization that hires the employees, maintains their records, and handles most aspects of employee relations. ➡ used as singular or plural in def. 1, as singular in def. 2. [French *personnel* persons employed in an organization, going back to Late Latin *personālis* relating to a person. See PERSONAL.]

per·spec·tive (pər spek′tiv) *n.* **1.a.** the art or theory of representing objects on a flat surface in such a way as to give the appearance of having three dimensions, depth, and distance. **b.** a picture that represents objects in this way. **2.** the effect of distance on the appearance of objects: *Perspective creates the illusion that parallel railroad tracks meet on the horizon.* **3.** a point of view: *Let's try to think about the problem from a different perspective.* **4.** the relation of events, ideas, facts, or the like to one another: *If you keep things in their proper perspective, you will quickly see what is important.* **5.** a scene or view from a distance; vista. —*adj.* of, relating to, seen, or represented according to the art or theory of perspective: *a perspective drawing.* [Medieval Latin *perspectiva (ars)* optical (science), from Late Latin *perspectīvus* optical, from Latin *perspicere* to see through, look at closely.] —**per·spec′tiv·al,** *adj.*

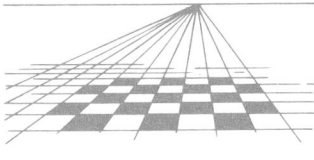
perspective *(def. 1)*

per·spi·ca·cious (pûr′spi kā′shəs) *adj.* having keen powers of observation and judgment; discerning. [Latin *perspicāc-,* stem of *perspicāx* sharp-sighted, acute + -OUS.] —**per′spi·ca′cious·ly,** *adv.* —**per′spi·ca′cious·ness,** *n.*

per·spi·cac·i·ty (pûr′spi kas′i tē) *n.* keenness in observation and judgment; discernment.

per·spi·cu·i·ty (pûr′spi kū′i tē) *n.* the quality of being perspicuous; lucidity.

per·spic·u·ous (pər spik′ū əs) *adj.* clearly expressed; easily understood; lucid: *a long but perspicuous speech.* [Latin *perspicuus* transparent, clear.] —**per·spic′u·ous·ly,** *adv.* —**per·spic′u·ous·ness,** *n.*

per·spi·ra·tion (pûr′spə rā′shən) *n.* **1.** the moisture given off through the pores of the skin by the sweat glands; sweat. **2.** the act or process of giving off this moisture.

per·spire (pər spīr′) *v.,* -spired, -spir·ing. —*v.i.* to give off perspiration; sweat. —*v.t.* to give off or expel through the pores; exude. [Latin *perspīrāre* literally, to breathe through.]

per·suade (pər swād′) *v.t.,* -suad·ed, -suad·ing. **1.** to induce (someone) to do something, as by argument, entreaty, or reasoning: *The salesperson persuaded us to buy the new product.* **2.** to lead (someone) to believe something; convince: *I am thoroughly persuaded of your loyalty.* [Latin *persuādēre.*] —**per·suad′er,** *n.*

| **Synonyms** | **Persuade** and **convince** mean to cause someone to believe something. **Persuade** suggests an approach that appeals as much to the emotions as to the intellect: *The public relations firm used slogans and statistics to persuade voters that the referendum proposal would result in a tax increase.* **Convince** implies influence by means of logical argument: *The publication of the study convinced the scientific community that the theory was valid.* For other Synonyms, see **induce.** |

per·sua·si·ble (pər swā′sə bəl) *adj.* capable of being persuaded; open to persuasion. Also, **per·suad·a·ble** (pər swā′də bəl).

per·sua·sion (pər swā′zhən) *n.* **1.** the act of persuading: *He won her support by persuasion, not force.* **2.** the power or ability to persuade; persuasiveness. **3.** a firm belief; conviction: *We are of different political persuasions.* **4.** religious belief; creed. **5.** a religious sect or denomination: *a minister of the Methodist persuasion.* [Latin *persuāsiō* act of persuading, belief.]

per·sua·sive (pər swā′siv, -ziv) *adj.* able or tending to persuade: *The lawyer presented a persuasive argument for the acquittal of the defendant.* —**per·sua′sive·ly,** *adv.* —**per·sua′sive·ness,** *n.*

pert (pûrt) *adj.* **1.** showing disrespect in speech or behavior; saucy; impudent: *The fresh student made a pert reply to the*

teacher's question. **2.** trim, stylish, and smart: *a pert outfit.* **3.** in good health or spirits; lively; vivacious. [Short for Old French *apert* open, from Latin *apertus;* partly also from Old French *aspert* able, from Latin *expertus* experienced.] —**pert′ly,** *adv.* —**pert′ness,** *n.*

per·tain (pər tān′) *v.i.* **1.** to have reference; refer; relate: *The president's advisers discussed matters that pertained to the war.* **2.** to belong or be connected as an adjunct, accessory, or the like: *The children inherit the business and all that pertains to it.* **3.** to be fitting or appropriate: *all the goodwill pertaining to the Christmas season.* [Old French *partenir* to belong, from Latin *pertinēre* to belong, concern.]

per·ti·na·cious (pûr′tə nā′shəs) *adj.* resolute in holding to a purpose, action, or opinion; stubbornly persistent. [Latin *pertināc-,* stem of *pertinā-* tenacious, steadfast + -OUS.] —**per′ti·na′cious·ly,** *adv.* —**per′ti·na′cious·ness,** *n.*

per·ti·nac·i·ty (pûr′tə nas′i tē) *n.* the quality or state of being pertinacious.

per·ti·nence (pûr′tə nəns) *n.* the quality or state of being pertinent. Also, **per′ti·nen·cy.**

per·ti·nent (pûr′tə nənt) *adj.* belonging or appropriate to the matter at hand; relevant: *Reporters were only permitted to ask questions that were pertinent to the president's speech.* [Latin *pertinēns,* present participle of *pertinēre* to belong, concern.] —**per′ti·nent·ly,** *adv.*

| **Synonyms** | **Pertinent, relevant,** and **germane** mean related to the matter being considered. **Pertinent** implies a strong logical relationship that contributes to an immediate understanding of the subject: *The fingerprint was the clue most pertinent to the thief's identity.* **Relevant** indicates a general logical connection: *The professor argued that ancient philosophy is still relevant to modern life.* **Germane** suggests a natural and obvious appropriateness: *The opinions of teachers are highly germane to the planning of the school curriculum.* |

per·turb (pər tûrb′) *v.t.* to disturb or disquiet greatly; make uneasy or anxious; trouble: *The monarch was perturbed by reports of unrest among the people.* [Latin *perturbāre.*] —**per·turb′a·ble,** *adj.* —For Synonyms, see **disturb.**

per·tur·ba·tion (pûr′tər bā′shən) *n.* **1.** the act of perturbing or the state of being perturbed. **2.** something that causes disquiet or anxiety. **3.** the deviation of a celestial body from a regular orbit, caused by the gravitational attraction of other celestial bodies.

per·tus·sis (pər tus′is) *n.* whooping cough. [Modern Latin *pertussis,* from Latin *per-* denoting intensification + *tussis* cough.] —**per·tus′sal, per·tus′soid,** *adj.*

pe·ruke (pə rük′) *n.* a wig, esp. of the type worn by men in the seventeenth and eighteenth centuries. [French *perruque,* from Italian *parrucca;* of uncertain origin.]

pe·rus·al (pə rü′zəl) *n.* the act or process of perusing, esp. with great care: *A careful perusal of the documents revealed inconsistencies.*

pe·ruse (pə rüz′) *v.t.,* -rused, -rus·ing. **1.** to read through or examine carefully; scrutinize thoroughly: *to peruse an old manuscript.* **2.** to read: *to peruse the newspaper before dinner.* [Middle English *perusen* to use up, from PER- + *usen* to use. See USE.]

Pe·ru·vi·an bark (pə rü′vē ən) cinchona *(def. 2).*

per·vade (pər vād′) *v.t.,* -vad·ed, -vad·ing. to spread or diffuse through every part of: *The odor of jasmine pervaded the room. A strong sense of patriotism pervades that novelist's writings.* [Latin *pervādere* to go through.] —**per·va′sion,** *n.* —For Synonyms, see **permeate.**

per·va·sive (pər vā′siv) *adj.* having the power of or tending to pervade; thoroughly penetrative. —**per·va′sive·ly,** *adv.* —**per·va′sive·ness,** *n.*

per·verse (pər vûrs′) *adj.* **1.** willfully going against what is right or moral; corrupt; perverted. **2.** stubbornly determined to continue doing what is harmful or wrong: *a perverse child who refused to obey anyone.* **3.** characterized by or arising from such a determination or disposition: *perverse behavior, a perverse opinion.* **4.** morally wrong or erring; wicked; corrupt: *O faithless and perverse generation* (Matthew 17:17). [Latin *perversus,* past participle of *pervertere* to turn around, corrupt.] —**per·verse′ly,** *adv.* —**per·verse′ness,** *n.*

a	at	e	end	o	hot	u	up	hw	white		about
ā	ape	ē	me	ō	old	ū	use	ng	song		taken
ä	far	i	it	ô	fork	ü	rule	th	thin	ə	pencil
âr	care	ī	ice	oi	oil	u̇	pull	th	this		lemon
		îr	pierce	ou	out	ûr	turn	zh	measure		circus

P

per·ver·sion (pər vûr′zhən, -shən) *n.* **1.** the act of perverting or the state of being perverted. **2.** any abnormal form, act, or practice, esp. a sexual deviation.

per·ver·si·ty (pər vûr′si tē) *n., pl.* **-ties. 1.** the quality or state of being perverse. **2.** an instance of this; wrong or abnormal act, habit, or thing.

per·vert (*v.,* pər vûrt′; *n.,* pûr′vûrt) *v.t.* **1.** to lead or turn from what is considered right or moral; lead astray; corrupt. **2.** to distort the meaning of; misconstrue: *to pervert the truth.* **3.** to divert from proper purposes; misuse: *to pervert one's talents.* **4.** to bring into a worse or inferior condition; debase. — *n.* a person who is perverted or given to perversion, esp. sexual perversion. [Latin *pervertere* to turn around, corrupt.] —**per·vert′er,** *n.*

per·vi·ous (pûr′vē əs) *adj.* **1.** allowing passage or entrance; permeable: *a fiber pervious to heat.* **2.** open to influence, reasoning, or argument: *stubbornly old-fashioned and not pervious to suggestions for improvement.* [Latin *pervius* passable.]

Pe·sach (pä′säk; *Hebrew* pe′säкн) *n.* Passover.

pe·se·ta (pə sā′tə) *n.* the monetary unit of Spain. [Spanish *peseta,* diminutive of *pesa* weight, from Latin *pēnsa,* plural of *pēnsum* weight.]

pes·ky (pes′kē) *adj.,* **-ki·er, -ki·est.** *Informal.* troublesome; annoying. [Modification of PEST + -Y¹.] —**pesk′i·ly,** *adv.* —**pesk′i·ness,** *n.*

pe·so (pā′sō) *n., pl.* **-sos.** the monetary unit of Mexico, several South and Central American countries, Cuba, the Dominican Republic, and the Philippines. [Spanish *peso* weight, Latin-American monetary unit, from Latin *pēnsum* weight.]

pes·si·mism (pes′ə miz′əm) *n.* **1.** the tendency to take a gloomy or cynical view of life or to see only the bad side of things. **2.** the doctrine or belief that everything naturally tends to evil and that this is the worst possible world. [Latin *pessimus* worst + -ISM.] —**pes′si·mist,** *n.* —**pes′si·mis′tic,** *adj.* —**pes′si·mis′ti·cal·ly,** *adv.*

pest (pest) *n.* **1.** a person or thing that is troublesome, annoying, or destructive; nuisance: *Locusts, gnats, and mosquitoes are insect pests. The reporter made a pest of himself by repeatedly asking personal questions.* **2.** an epidemic disease; pestilence. [Latin *pestis* plague.]

pes·ter (pes′tər) *v.t.* to give trouble to in a persistent manner; bother repeatedly: *The children were always pestering their parents with demands.* [Short for Middle French *empestrer* to hobble, entangle, tether a horse at pasture, going back to Latin *in* in + Medieval Latin *pastōrium* clog (for a horse at pasture), from Latin *pastus* pasture, food.] —**pes′ter·er,** *n.*

pest·house (pest′hous′) *n., pl.* **-hous·es** (-hou′ziz). *Archaic.* a hospital for those suffering from an epidemic disease.

pes·ti·cide (pes′tə sīd′) *n.* a chemical or other substance used to destroy harmful plants or animals. —**pes′ti·cid′al,** *adj.*

pes·tif·er·ous (pes tif′ər əs) *adj.* **1.** producing or carrying disease or plague: *a pestiferous swamp.* **2.** morally corrupt or corrupting; evil. **3.** *Informal.* mischievous; troublesome; annoying: *a pestiferous young prankster.* [Latin *pestiferus* bringing pestilence, destructive, from *pestis* plague + *ferre* to bring.]

pes·ti·lence (pes′tə ləns) *n.* any highly infectious, epidemic disease, esp. bubonic plague.

pes·ti·lent (pes′tə lənt) *adj.* **1.** producing or tending to produce infectious disease. **2.** harmful or destructive to peace, morals, or society. **3.** troublesome; annoying. [Latin *pestilēns* unhealthy.] —**pes′ti·lent·ly,** *adv.*

pes·ti·len·tial (pes′tə len′shəl) *adj.* **1.** of, relating to, causing, or resembling a pestilence. **2.** harmful; pernicious. **3.** troublesome; annoying. —**pes′ti·len′tial·ly,** *adv.*

pes·tle (pes′əl, -təl) *n.* a blunt tool for pounding, grinding, or mixing substances in a mortar. — *v.t., v.i.,* **-tled, -tling.** to pound, grind, or mix with or as if with a pestle. [Old French *pestel* the tool, from Latin *pistillum,* going back to *pinsere* to pound.]

pes·to (pes′tō) *n.* a sauce usually made with basil, garlic, pine nuts, grated cheese, and olive oil, often served with pasta.

pet¹ (pet) *n.* **1.** a tame animal that is kept chiefly for amusement and companionship, such as a dog or cat. **2.** any person who is indulged or treated with special favor or kindness; favorite: *That student is the teacher's pet.* —*adj.* **1.** kept or treated as a pet: *a pet frog.* **2.** expressing fondness or familiarity; affectionate: *a pet name.* **3.** best liked; favorite; cherished: *a pet charity.* **4.** most important; greatest: *a pet peeve.* —*v.,* **pet·ted, pet·ting.** —*v.t.* to stroke, pat, or caress: *I petted the cat, and it purred.* —*v.i. Informal.* to make love by kissing and caressing. [Of uncertain origin.]

pet² (pet) *n.* a fit of peevishness or ill humor; discontent. [Of uncertain origin.]

pet·al (pet′əl) *n.* one of the usually colored divisions or leaflike parts of the corolla of a flower. For illustration, see **flower.** [Modern Latin *petalum,* from Greek *petalon* leaf, from *petalos* spread out.] —**pet′aled;** *also,* **pet′alled,** *adj.*

pe·tard (pi tärd′) *n.* formerly, an explosive device used to blow in a door or gate or to make a breach in a wall, consisting of a bell-shaped or boxlike structure fastened against the surface of the obstacle and ignited by a fuse. [French *pétard,* from *péter* to break wind, from *pet* a breaking wind, from Latin *pēditum.*]
  · **to be hoist with** (or **by**) **one's own petard.** to be caught or victimized by one's own actions.

pet·cock (pet′kok′) *n.* a small valve or faucet.

pe·ter (pē′tər) *v.i.* **to peter out.** *Informal.* **a.** to diminish gradually and disappear: *The tennis player's strength petered out toward the end of the game.* **b.** to become exhausted: *I petered out on the last mile of the hike.* [Of uncertain origin.]

Pe·ter (pē′tər) *n.* either of two books, I Peter and II Peter, of the New Testament, attributed to the Apostle Peter.

pet·i·o·late (pet′ē ə lāt′) *adj.* having a petiole. Also, **pet′i·o·lat′ed.**

pet·i·ole (pet′ē ōl′) *n.* **1.** a stalk that attaches a leaf to a stem. Also, **leafstalk. 2.** a slender, stalklike structure, such as the waist of an ant or wasp connecting the thorax and abdomen. [Late Latin *petiolus* stalk of fruits, diminutive of Latin *pēs* foot.]

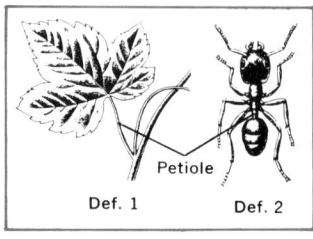

Def. 1   Def. 2

petioles

pet·it (pet′ē) *also,* **petty.** *adj. Law.* small; lesser; minor. [Old French *petit;* of uncertain origin.]

pe·tite (pə tēt′) *adj.* (usually of a woman or girl) of small size; little; tiny. [French *petite,* feminine of *petit;* of uncertain origin.] —**pe·tite′ness,** *n.*

pet·it four (pet′ē fôr′) *pl.* **pet·its fours** (pet′ē fôrz′). a small cake covered with decorative icing. [French *petit four* literally, small oven, from *petit* small (of uncertain origin) + *four* oven (from Latin *furnus*).]

pe·ti·tion (pə tish′ən) *n.* **1.** a formal request made to a person in a position of authority: *We signed a petition asking our senator to support the proposed legislation.* **2.** a prayer or entreaty; supplication. **3.** something that is formally requested or entreated: *to accede to a petition.* **4.** *Law.* a written application made to a court requesting the court to take some action. —*v.t.* **1.** to make a petition to. **2.** to pray or ask for; request. —*v.i.* to make a petition: *The defendant's lawyer petitioned for a new trial.* [Latin *petītiō* request, solicitation.] —**pe·ti′tion·ar′y,** *adj.* —**pe·ti′tion·er,** *n.*

pet·it jury (pet′ē) *also,* **petty jury.** a jury, usually composed of twelve persons, selected to hear a civil or criminal case in a court of law. ➡ distinguished from **grand jury.**

pet·it larceny (pet′ē) petty larceny.

pe·tit mal (pet′ē mäl′, mal′, pə tē′) a mild form of epilepsy, most common in children and adolescents, characterized by numerous brief attacks of unconsciousness and often by slight twitching. [French *petit mal* literally, small sickness, from *petit* small (of uncertain origin) + *mal* sickness (going back to Latin *malus* bad).]

pet·it point (pet′ē) **1.** a small stitch used in needlepoint. **2.** work done with this stitch.

Pe·trar·chan sonnet (pi trär′kən) a sonnet form developed by the Italian poet Petrarch, consisting of an eight-line stanza rhyming *abbaabba* and a six-line stanza often rhyming *cdecde.* Also, **Italian sonnet.**

pet·rel (pet′rəl) *n.* any of various hook-billed seabirds, order Procellariiformes, usually having blackish or brownish plumage with white markings. There are three families of petrels, the best known being the storm petrels. [Possibly diminutive of Saint *Peter;* because it seems to walk on water like Saint Peter.]

pe·tri dish (pē′trē) a round, shallow dish of plastic or glass with a slightly larger cover, used in the laboratory for growing bacteria and other microorganisms. [From the German bacteriologist Julius *Petri,* 1852-1921, who suggested using this type of dish.]

pet·ri·fac·tion (pet′rə fak′shən) *n.* **1.** the act or process of petrifying or the state of being petrified. **2.** something that is petrified. Also, **pet·ri·fi·ca·tion** (pet′rə fi kā′shən).

petrified wood, a hard, stony material formed when silica replaces the cellulose in wood, preserving the plant's structure.

petrified wood

pet·ri·fy (pet′rə fī′) v., -fied, -fy·ing. —v.t. **1.** to convert (organic material) into stone or a stony substance. **2.** to paralyze with fear, astonishment, or horror: *The growling dog petrified the child.* **3.** to harden or stiffen; deaden. —v.i. to become stone or like stone. [French *pétrifier* to turn into stone, amaze, from Latin *petra* rock (from Greek *petrā*) + *facere* to make.]

pet·ro·chem·i·cal (pet′rō kem′i kəl) n. a chemical substance obtained from petroleum or natural gas, such as gasoline or kerosene. —adj. of or relating to such substances or the industry producing them.

pet·ro·dol·lars (pet′rō dol′ərz) pl. n. money, expressed in dollars, earned by oil-producing countries in the Middle East from the export of petroleum. [PETRO(LEUM) + DOLLAR.]

pe·trog·ra·phy (pi trog′rə fē) n. the branch of geology that deals with the systematic classification and description of rocks. [Greek *petrā* rock + -GRAPHY.] —**pe·trog′ra·pher,** n. —**pet·ro·graph·ic** (pet′rə graf′ik); also, **pet′ro·graph′i·cal,** adj.

pet·rol (pet′rəl) n. British. gasoline. [French *pétrole* petroleum, oil, from Medieval Latin *petroleum.* See PETROLEUM.]

pet·ro·la·tum (pet′rə lā′təm) n. a jellylike substance obtained from petroleum, used as a lubricant, rust preventive, and base for ointments and dressings. Also, **petroleum jelly.** [Modern Latin *petrolatum,* from English PETROLEUM.]

pe·tro·le·um (pi trō′lē əm) n. a viscous, flammable liquid, occurring naturally in the sedimentary materials of the earth's crust, consisting of a mixture of hydrocarbons, with traces of organic sulfur, nitrogen, and oxygen compounds. Petroleum yields various products, such as gasoline, diesel fuel, and lubricants, and many derivatives used in the manufacture of various products. [Medieval Latin *petroleum* literally, rock oil, from Latin *petra* rock (from Greek *petrā*) + *oleum* oil (from Greek *elaion*).]

petroleum jelly, petrolatum.

pe·trol·o·gy (pi trol′ə jē) n. the branch of geology that deals with the study of the origin, structure, and characteristics of rocks. [Greek *petrā* rock + -LOGY.] —**pet·ro·log·ic** (pet′rə loj′ik); also, **pet′ro·log′i·cal,** adj. —**pe·trol′o·gist,** n.

pet·rous (pet′rəs, pē′trəs) adj. **1.** of or like rock; stony; rocky. **2.** Anatomy. of or relating to the part of the temporal bone that contains the inner ear.

PET scan (pet) an image produced by a medical diagnostic technique that pinpoints areas of unusual metabolic activity in the brain or other parts of the body by recording bursts of energy given off by the body as it absorbs an injected radioactive substance. [Short for *p(ositron) e(mission) t(omography)* + SCAN.]

pet·ti·coat (pet′ē kōt′) n. **1.** a skirtlike undergarment, esp. one designed to be worn under and add fullness to a skirt. **2.** formerly, a skirt. **3.** Informal. a woman; girl. —adj. of, relating to, or influenced by women: *to be engaged in petticoat politics.* [Earlier PETTY COAT literally, little coat; because it originally was a short coat for men worn under armor or a doublet.]

pet·ti·fog (pet′ē fôg′, -fog′) v.i., -fogged, -fog·ging. to act like a pettifogger.

pet·ti·fog·ger (pet′ē fô′gər, -fog′ər) n. **1.** a lawyer who deals with small, unimportant matters and who uses underhanded or dishonest methods. **2.** a person who fusses over trivial things. [PETTY + obsolete *fogger* pettifogger; of uncertain origin.] —**pet′ti·fog′ger·y,** n.

pet·tish (pet′ish) adj. ill-tempered; cross; peevish. [PET² + -ISH.] —**pet′tish·ly,** adv.

pet·ty (pet′ē) adj., -ti·er, -ti·est. **1.** of little value or importance; insignificant: *a petty complaint.* **2.** mean, spiteful, or ungenerous: *Only a very petty person could get angry over so small a mistake.* **3.** having little importance or authority; minor; subordinate: *a petty government official.* **4.** having or marked by a small range of interests or sympathies; narrow-minded. **5.** Law. petit.

[Old French *petit* small, little; of uncertain origin.] —**pet′ti·ly,** adv. —**pet′ti·ness,** n.

Synonyms Petty, trivial, paltry, and trifling mean small in size or significance. **Petty** is often used in comparing something with others of its kind: *Most of the patients' complaints were petty, but a few were more serious.* **Trivial** suggests something commonplace and ordinary: *The conversation was mostly about the weather and other trivial topics.* **Paltry** implies that a thing is ridiculously or offensively small or insufficient: *The employer offered a paltry salary for the demanding job.* **Trifling** suggests that something is so unimportant or small that it is unworthy of attention: *The teacher marked the paper as "excellent" despite a few trifling errors.*

petty cash, a small cash fund kept on hand to pay minor or incidental expenses, as in a business office: *The secretary took money for postage stamps and envelopes out of petty cash.*

petty jury, petit jury.

petty larceny also, **petit larceny.** larceny in which the goods stolen do not exceed an amount set by law. ➡ distinguished from **grand larceny.**

petty officer, any enlisted person in the U.S. Navy or Coast Guard of a rank corresponding to any of the noncommissioned ranks in the U.S. Army.

pet·u·lance (pech′ə ləns) n. the quality or state of being petulant; peevishness. Also, **pet′u·lan·cy.**

pet·u·lant (pech′ə lənt) adj. having or showing a tendency to be easily irritated or angered. [Latin *petulāns* pert, saucy.] —**pet′u·lant·ly,** adv.

pe·tu·nia (pi tün′yə, -tūn′-) n. **1.** the funnel-shaped flower of any of a group of plants, genus *Petunia,* of the nightshade family, sometimes having fringed or ruffled petals. **2.** the plant bearing this flower, widely cultivated in the United States, having hairy branches and smooth, soft leaves. [Modern Latin *Petunia,* from French *petun* tobacco plant, through Portuguese, from Tupi-Guarani *petyn* tobacco.]

pew (pū) n. a long, immovable bench with a back, used to seat worshipers in a church. [Old French *puie* elevated place, from Latin *podia,* plural of *podium* elevated place. See PODIUM.]

pe·wee (pē′wē′) also, **pee·wee.** n. any of various small flycatchers, family Tyrannidae, that are native to the temperate and tropical regions of the Western Hemisphere, having dull olivebrown or gray plumage. [Imitative.]

pe·wit (pē′wit′, pū′it) n. any of several birds with a shrill cry, esp. the lapwing. [Imitative.]

pew·ter (pū′tər) n. **1.** an alloy, formerly made of tin, lead, and copper, now 90% to 95% tin, copper, and antimony, used to make tableware, utensils, and ornamental objects. **2.** articles made of this alloy. —adj. made of pewter. [Old French *peautre* tin; of uncertain origin.]

pey·o·te (pā ō′tē) n. **1.** a small cactus, *Lophophora williamsii,* found in dry regions from Texas to Central America. Also, **mes·cal.** **2.** mescaline. [Spanish *peyote* the cactus, from Nahuatl *peyotl* caterpillar; referring to the plant's hairy center.]

pf. 1. pfennig. **2.** preferred.

pfc also, **Pfc, Pfc.** private first class.

pfen·nig (pfen′ig) n. a unit of currency of Germany, equal to ¹/₁₀₀ of a deutsche mark. [German *Pfennig.*]

pfg., pfennig.

pg., page.

Pg. 1. Portugal. **2.** Portuguese.

pH, the chemical symbol for the unit that measures the acidity or alkalinity of a solution in terms of its hydrogen ion concentration. On a scale of 0 to 14, a pH of 7 is neutral, a pH of less than 7 is acid, and a pH of more than 7 is alkaline. [Abbreviation of *p(otential of) h(ydrogen).*]

P.H., public health.

Phae·dra (fē′drə, fā′-) n. in Greek mythology, the daughter of Minos and wife of Theseus, king of Athens. She fell in love with her stepson Hippolytus, but he resisted her advances. She falsely accused him of seducing her and hanged herself.

Pha·ë·thon (fā′ə thon′, -thən) n. in Greek mythology, the mortal son of Helios, god of the sun. He tried to drive the chariot of the sun across the sky, but couldn't control it and scorched the earth before Zeus could stop him with a deadly thunderbolt.

pha·e·ton (fā′ə tən) n. **1.** a light, low, open, four-wheeled carriage. **2.** an open automobile whose body resembles that of the

a	at	e	end	o	hot	u	up	hw	white		about
ā	ape	ē	me	ō	old	ū	use	ng	song		taken
ä	far	i	it	ô	fork	ü	rule	th	thin	ə	pencil
âr	care	ī	ice	oi	oil	u̇	pull	th	this		lemon
			ir	pierce	ou	out	ûr	turn	zh	measure	circus

phaeton carriage. [French *phaéton* light, open carriage, from PHA-ĒTHON.]

phage (fāj) *n.* bacteriophage.

-phage *combining form* a person or thing that eats, devours, or consumes: *bacteriophage.* [Greek *phagein* to eat.]

phag·o·cyte (fag'ə sīt') *n.* any cell, esp. a white blood cell, or leucocyte, that can absorb and destroy bacteria and other harmful material in the body. [Greek *phagos* eating + *kytos* hollow vessel.] —**phag·o·cyt·ic** (fag'ə sit'ik), *adj.*

phag·o·cy·to·sis (fag'ō sī tō'sis) *n., pl.* -**ses.** the engulfment and destruction by phagocytes of foreign cells or other foreign substances in the blood and tissues. —**phag·o·cy·tot·ic** (fag'ō-sī tot'ik), *adj.*

pha·lan·ger (fə lan'jər) *n.* any of various small, arboreal, nocturnal marsupials, family Phalangeridae, native to Australia, having small, round ears and a long, bushy tail. [Modern Latin *phalanger*, from Greek *phalanx* bone between two joints of the fingers or toes; with reference to the formation of its toes.]

pha·lanx (fā'langks, fal'angks) *n., pl.* **pha·lanx·es** or **pha·lan·ges** (fə lan'jēz). **1.** in ancient Greek and Macedonian armies, a battle formation of infantry standing in close ranks with their shields and long spears overlapping each other. **2.** a compact body of persons, animals, or things massed together, as for attack or for defense: *A phalanx of police held back the crowd.* **3.** a number of persons united for a common purpose, esp. in support of some cause. **4.** *Anatomy.* any of the bones in the fingers or toes. For illustration, see **hand.** [Latin *phalanx* multitude, battalion, battle array, from Greek *phalanx* line of battle, battle array, bone between two joints of the fingers or toes.]

phal·a·rope (fal'ə rōp') *n.* any of a family of small, aquatic shorebirds, genus *Phalaropus,* having partially lobed feet. The female, larger and more brightly colored than the male, initiates the courting. [French *phalarope,* from Modern Latin *phalaropus* the genus name, from Greek *phalaris* coot + *pous* foot.]

phal·lus (fal'əs) *n., pl.* **phal·li** (fal'ī) or **phal·lus·es.** **1.** a representation of the male sexual organs, symbolizing in certain religions the generative power in nature. **2.** penis. [Late Latin *phallus,* from Greek *phallos.*] —**phal'lic,** *adj.*

Phan·er·o·zo·ic (fan'ər ə zō'ik) *n.* the eon of geologic time during which rocks containing abundant fossils were deposited, comprising the Paleozoic, Mesozoic, and Cenozoic eras. —*adj.* of, relating to, or characteristic of the Phanerozoic. [Greek *phaneros* visible (from *phainein* to appear) + *zōē* life + -IC.]

phan·tasm (fan'taz əm) *n.* **1.** something seen in the imagination; unreal or fantastic idea or fancy: *the bizarre phantasms of a nightmare.* **2.** ghost; phantom; apparition. [Latin *phantasma* apparition, from Greek *phantasma.* Doublet of PHANTOM.]

phan·tas·ma·go·ri·a (fan taz'mə gôr'ē ə) *n.* **1.** a shifting series of imaginary figures, such as those seen in a dream: *Milton's genius has filled the atmosphere with a brilliant phantasmagoria of contending angels* (E. G. White, 1875). **2.** formerly, a magic lantern show. [French *fantasmagorie,* from Greek *phantasma* apparition + *agora* assembly.] —**phan·tas·ma·gor·ic** (fan taz'mə gôr'ik, -gor'-); *also,* **phan·tas'ma·gor'i·cal,** *adj.*

phan·tas·mal (fan taz'məl) *adj.* of or like a phantasm; unreal; imaginary.

phan·ta·sy (fan'tə sē, -zē) *n., pl.* -**sies.** fantasy.

phan·tom (fan'təm) *n.* **1.** something that appears to be real but is not; ghost; apparition. **2.** something that exists only as an image in the mind; illusion. **3.** mere show or appearance lacking force or substance: *The president had only the phantom of authority.* —*adj.* resembling a phantom; unreal; illusive: *a tale of a phantom ship.* [Old French *fanto(s)me* ghost, from Latin *phantasma* apparition, from Greek *phantasma.* Doublet of PHANTASM.]

Phar·aoh (fâr'ō) *n.* the title of the kings of ancient Egypt. [Late Latin *Pharaō,* through Greek and Hebrew, from Egyptian *per-o* literally, great house.]

Phar·i·sa·ic (far'ə sā'ik) *adj.* **1.** of or relating to the Pharisees. **2. pharisaic. a.** stressing a strict

gilded wooden statue of a **Pharaoh**

public observance of religious or moral laws or principles without regard for their real or spiritual meaning. **b.** assuming a moral superiority; self-righteous; hypocritical. —**Phar'i·sa'i·cal·ly;** *also,* **phar'i·sa'i·cal·ly,** *adv.*

Phar·i·sa·ism (far'ə sā iz'əm) *n.* **1.** the doctrines and practices of the Pharisees. **2. pharisaism.** the character, principles, or behavior of a pharisee.

Phar·i·see (far'ə sē') *n.* **1.** a member of an ancient Jewish sect that was very strict in observing both the written law and the oral tradition of Judaism. **2. pharisee.** a pharisaic person. [Middle English *pharise,* from Old English *fariseus,* from Late Latin *pharisaeus,* from Greek *pharisaios,* from Aramaic *perīshayyā* (plural) literally, separated.]

phar·ma·ceu·ti·cal (fär'mə sü'ti kəl) *adj.* of or relating to pharmacy or drugs. Also, **phar'ma·ceu'tic.** —*n.* a medicinal product; drug. [Late Latin *pharmaceuticus* (from Greek *pharmakeutikos,* going back to *pharmakon* drug) + -AL[1].]

phar·ma·ceu·tics (fär'mə sü'tiks) *n.* pharmacy (def. 2). ⇒ used as singular.

phar·ma·cist (fär'mə sist) *n.* a person who is licensed to prepare drugs and fill prescriptions.

phar·ma·col·o·gist (fär'mə kol'ə jist) *n.* a person who is skilled or an expert in pharmacology.

phar·ma·col·o·gy (fär'mə kol'ə jē) *n.* the branch of science that deals with the sources, qualities, preparation, uses, and esp. the effects of drugs. [Greek *pharmakon* drug + -LOGY.] —**phar·ma·co·log·i·cal** (fär'mə kə loj'i kəl), *adj.*

phar·ma·co·poe·ia (fär'mə kə pē'ə) *n.* **1.** a book that lists and describes drugs, their sources, qualities, and uses, esp. one published by a government agency. **2.** a stock of drugs. [Modern Latin *pharmacopoeia,* from Greek *pharmakopoiiā* preparation of drugs, from *pharmakon* drug + *poiein* to make.]

phar·ma·cy (fär'mə sē) *n., pl.* -**cies. 1.** drugstore. **2.** the science, practice, or profession of preparing and dispensing drugs. Also *(def. 2),* **pharmaceutics.** [Old French *pharmacie* treatment with drugs or medicines, through Late Latin, from Greek *pharmakeiā* use of drugs, from *pharmakon* drug.]

Phar·os (fâr'os) *n.* a huge lighthouse constructed on an island in the harbor of Alexandria, Egypt, in the third century B.C.

pha·ryn·ge·al (fə rin'jē əl, -jəl, far'in jē'əl) *adj.* of, relating to, near, or affecting the pharynx.

phar·yn·gi·tis (far'in jī'tis) *n.* inflammation of the mucous membrane of the pharynx. [Modern Latin *pharyngitis,* from Greek *pharynx* throat + -ITIS.]

phar·ynx (far'ingks) *n., pl.* **pha·ryn·ges** (fə rin'jēz) or **phar·ynx·es.** a short, muscular tube that connects the mouth and nasal cavity with the esophagus and windpipe. [Modern Latin *pharynx,* from Greek *pharynx* throat.]

phase (fāz) *n.* **1.** a stage of development of a person or thing: *Digging the foundation is the first phase of our building project. The child went through a rebellious phase.* **2.** one side, view, or aspect of a subject or phenomenon: *The president received a report covering all phases of the proposed poverty program.* **3.** *Astronomy.* one of the recurring variations in the appearance of the illuminated visible portion of the moon or of a planet. **4.** *Chemistry.* a distinct homogeneous part of a heterogeneous system that is mechanically separable from the other parts: *the solid, liquid, and gaseous phases of water.* **5.** *Physics.* any stage or point in a periodic motion, as a sound wave, usually reckoned with reference to an arbitrarily fixed starting point or moment of starting. [Modern Latin *phasis,* from Greek *phasis* appearance, phase of the moon.] —**pha'sic,** *adj.*

· **in phase.** *Physics.* being at the same point or stage in a cycle, thereby reinforcing one another, as two or more sound waves.

· **out of phase.** *Physics.* being at different points or stages in a cycle, thereby weakening or neutralizing one another, as two or more sound waves.

· **to phase in.** to introduce in stages: *The company is phasing in new production methods.*

· **to phase out.** to eliminate in stages: *The army plans to phase out that weapon.*

phase-con·trast microscope (fāz'kon'trast) a compound microscope that provides an image with enhanced contrast, produced by interference between light waves passing through different parts of a transparent specimen, used esp. in examining biological materials. Also, **phase microscope.**

Ph.B., Bachelor of Philosophy.

Ph.C., pharmaceutical chemist.

Ph.D., Doctor of Philosophy.

pheas·ant (fez'ənt) *n., pl.* -**ants** or -**ant. 1.** any of various long-tailed birds, family Phasianidae, originally native to Asia and

now found in most parts of the world, the male of which often has brilliantly colored and patterned plumage, while the female is generally brownish. Length: 1½-8 feet (0.5-2.4 meters), including tail. **2.** any of various similar birds, esp. the ruffed grouse. [Anglo-Norman *fesaunt,* from Latin *phasiāna,* from Greek *phasianos* literally, of *Phasis,* a river in Colchis associated with the Asian bird.]

golden **pheasant**
of eastern Asia

phe·nix (fē′niks) phoenix.

phe·no·bar·bi·tal (fē′nō-bär′bi tôl′) *n.* a long-acting barbiturate, used as a sedative and hypnotic. Formula: $C_{12}H_{12}N_2O_3$

phe·nol (fē′nôl) *n.* **1.** a poisonous, crystalline organic compound used in plastics, explosives, weed killers, and pharmaceuticals. It was formerly used as an antiseptic and disinfectant. Formula: C_6H_5OH Also, **carbolic acid. 2.** any compound that contains one or more hydroxyl groups attached to a benzene ring. [Greek *phainein* to show, shine + -OL.]

phe·no·lic (fi nō′lik) *adj.* of, containing, or obtained from phenol. —*n.* any of a large group of plastics or resins made from a phenol and an aldehyde. [PHENOL + -IC.]

phe·nol·phthal·e·in (fē′nôl thal′ē in, -thal′ēn) *n.* a crystalline, powdery organic compound, used esp. in alcohol solution as an indicator to test whether a substance is an acid or base. Formula: $C_{20}H_{14}O_4$

phe·nom·e·nal (fə nom′ə nəl) *adj.* **1.** of or relating to a phenomenon or phenomena. **2.** remarkable or extraordinary; prodigious: *phenomenal strength.* **3.** *Philosophy.* capable of being perceived by the senses. —**phe·nom′e·nal·ly,** *adv.*

phe·nom·e·non (fə nom′ə non′, -nən) *n., pl.* **-na** (-nə) or **-nons. 1.** a fact, event, or condition that can be perceived by the senses: *Rain and snow are phenomena of the weather.* **2.** a person or thing that is remarkable or extraordinary: *a phenomenon in the business world.* **3.** *Philosophy.* something that is perceived by the senses. [Late Latin *phaenomenon* appearance, from Greek *phainomenon,* neuter present participle of *phainesthai* to appear.]

phe·no·type (fē′nə tīp′) *n.* the physical characteristics of an individual organism, determined through interaction of the genotype with environmental factors, such as nutrition or health care. ➡ opposed to **genotype.** [PHENO(MENON) + TYPE.] —**phe·no·typ·ic** (fē′nə tip′ik), *adj.*

phen·yl (fen′əl, fē′nəl) *n.* a radical or group left when one atom of hydrogen is taken away from benzene. Formula: C_6H_5 [Greek *phainein* to show, shine + -YL.]

phen·yl·al·a·nine (fen′əl al′ə nēn′, -nin, fē′nəl-) *n.* an essential amino acid obtained from eggs, milk, and other foods, converted in the body into tyrosine. Formula: $C_9H_{11}NO_2$

phen·yl·ke·to·nu·ri·a (fen′əl kē′tə nùr′ē ə, -nyùr′ē ə) *n.* a genetic disorder of protein metabolism, leading to excess phenylalinine in the blood, and causing nerve damage and severe mental retardation if not treated in infancy. —**phen′yl·ke′to·nu′ric,** *adj.*

pher·o·mone (fer′ə mōn′) *n.* any chemical substance excreted by certain animals, esp. insects, that serves as a signal or stimulus to other members of the same species. [Greek *pherein* to bear + (HOR)MONE.] —**pher′o·mo′nal,** *adj.*

phew (fū, hwū) *interj.* used to express disgust, weariness, or surprise.

phi (fī, fē) *n.* the twenty-first letter of the Greek alphabet (Φ, φ), corresponding to English *Ph, ph* and *F, f.*

phi·al (fī′əl) vial.

Phi Beta Kappa 1. an American honor society founded in 1776 for college and university students of high academic achievement. **2.** a member of this society. [From the initial letters of the society's Greek motto *philosophia biou kubernētēs* philosophy the guide of life.]

Phid·i·an (fid′ē ən) *adj.* of, relating to, or following the style of the Greek sculptor Phidias.

Phil. 1. Philippians. **2.** Philippine.

Phila., Philadelphia.

phi·lan·der (fi lan′dər) *v.i.* (of a man) to make love without serious intentions. [From the use of *Philander* as the name of a

lover in plays and romances, from Greek *philandros* loving men, from *philos* loving + *anēr* man.] —**phi·lan′der·er,** *n.*

phi·lan·thro·py (fi lan′thrə pē) *n., pl.* **-pies. 1.** a love of or a desire to help humanity expressed by the giving of time or money to charities and other good causes. **2.** a charitable action, service, or agency. [Late Latin *philanthrōpia* benevolence, from Greek *philanthrōpia,* going back to *philos* loving + *anthrōpos* man.] —**phil·an·throp·ic** (fil′ən throp′ik); *also,* **phil′an·throp′i·cal,** *adj.* —**phil′an·throp′i·cal·ly,** *adv.* —**phi·lan′thro·pist,** *n.* —For Synonyms, see **charity.**

phi·lat·e·ly (fə lat′ə lē) *n.* the collecting, arranging, and studying of postage stamps and related items, such as stamped envelopes, postcards, or revenue stamps, as a hobby. [French *philatélie,* from Greek *philos* loving + *ateleiā* tax exemption; because postage stamps allow people to receive mail free of charge, it having been the custom before the introduction of postage stamps that recipients of mail paid for its delivery.] —**phil·a·tel·ic** (fil′ə-tel′ik); *also,* **phil′a·tel′i·cal,** *adj.* —**phi·lat′e·list,** *n.*

-phile *combining form* a person who has a strong liking or love for: *Anglophile.* [Greek *philos* friend, loving, dear.]

Phi·le·mon (fi lē′mən) *n.* **1.** a book of the New Testament, consisting of an Epistle written by the Apostle Paul. **2.** in classical mythology, the husband of Baucis.

phil·har·mon·ic (fil′här mon′ik, fil′ər-) *adj.* **1.** fond of or devoted to music. **2.** of, relating to, or presented by a musical society or an orchestra, esp. a symphony orchestra: *a philharmonic concert.* —*n.* a philharmonic orchestra, concert, or society. [French *philharmonique* loving music, through Italian, from Greek *philos* loving + *harmonia* music.]

Phi·lip·pi·ans (fi lip′ē ənz) *n.* a book of the New Testament, consisting of an Epistle written by the Apostle Paul to the Christians of Philippi. ➡ used as singular.

Phi·lip·pic (fi lip′ik) *n.* **1.** any of a series of orations by the Greek orator Demosthenes against Philip of Macedon warning the Athenians of Philip's growing power and of his threat to Athenian political freedom. **2.** **philippic.** a bitter verbal denunciation or attack.

Phil·ip·pine (fil′ə pēn′) *adj.* of, relating to, or characteristic of the Philippines or their inhabitants. Also, **Filipino.**

Phil·is·tine (fil′ə stēn′, -stīn′, fə lis′tin) *n.* **1.** in the Bible, a member of an ancient people of Philistia, often mentioned in the Old Testament as enemies of the Israelites. **2.** *also,* **philistine.** a person who is ignorant, uncultured, or smugly conventional in ideas and tastes. —*adj.* **1.** of or relating to the Philistines. **2.** *also,* **philistine.** uncultured, unrefined, or narrow-minded in ideas or tastes. —**Phil′is·tin′ism,** *n.*

phil·o·den·dron (fil′ə den′drən) *n.* any of various tropical American plants, family Araceae, often with heart-shaped, glossy leaves, commonly grown as houseplants.

phi·lol·o·gist (fə lol′ə jist) *n.* a student of or an expert in philology.

phi·lol·o·gy (fə lol′ə jē) *n.* **1.** the study, criticism, and interpretation of literature and other written records. **2.** linguistics. [Latin *philologia* love of learning, love of letters, from Greek *philologiā,* going back to *philos* loving + *logos* word.] —**phil·o·log·i·cal** (fil′ə loj′i kəl), *adj.*

phil·o·mel (fil′ə mel′) *also,* **Phil·o·mel.** *n. Archaic.* nightingale. [Latin *philomēla,* from PHILOMELA.]

Phil·o·me·la (fil′ə mē′lə) *n.* **1.** in classical mythology, a princess of Athens who was raped by her sister Procne's husband, the king of Thrace, who then tore out her tongue. In revenge the two sisters murdered his son, and when the enraged king threatened to kill them, they were changed by the gods into birds, Philomela into a nightingale and Procne into a sparrow. **2.** **philomela.** philomel.

phi·los·o·pher (fi los′ə fər) *n.* **1.** a person who studies or is an expert in philosophy. **2.** a person who develops or lives by a particular system of philosophy. **3.** a person who accepts life and its difficulties with serenity and composure. [Anglo-Norman *philosofre* one who studies philosophy, from Latin *philosophus,* from Greek *philosophos* lover of wisdom, one who speculates on philosophical subjects, from *philos* loving + *sophos* wise.]

philosophers' stone, an imaginary substance believed by alchemists to have the power to transmute elements, esp. to change base metals into gold or silver.

phil·o·soph·i·cal (fil′ə sof′i kəl) *adj.* **1.** of or relating to philosophy: *a philosophical treatise.* **2.** of, relating to, or characteristic of a philosopher: *a philosophical mind.* **3.** accepting life

a	at	e	end	o	hot	u	up	hw	white		about
ā	ape	ē	me	ō	old	ū	use	ng	song		taken
ä	far	i	it	ô	fork	ü	rule	th	thin	ə	pencil
âr	care	ī	ice	oi	oil	ù	pull	th	this		lemon
		îr	pierce	ou	out	ûr	turn	zh	measure		circus

P

and its difficulties with serenity and composure. Also, **phil′o·soph′ic**. —**phil′o·soph′i·cal·ly**, *adv.*

phi·los·o·phize (fə los′ə fīz′) *v.i.*, **-phized**, **-phiz·ing**. to think or reason as a philosopher does, esp. to speculate about fundamental concepts. —**phi·los′o·phiz′er**, *n.*

phi·los·o·phy (fə los′ə fē) *n., pl.* **-phies**. **1**. the study of or search for the fundamental nature, function, and purpose of human beings, the universe, and life itself, as well as most general causes and principles of the universe. **2**. a system of thought of a particular school or philosopher: *the philosophy of Plato.* **3**. the study of the fundamental principles of a particular branch of knowledge, an activity, or a field of experience: *the philosophy of history.* **4**. a system for guiding life or conduct, esp. personal principles and beliefs: *My philosophy is "live and let live."* **5**. a calm, philosophical attitude. [Latin *philosophia* study of wisdom, from Greek *philosophiā* love of wisdom, study of wisdom.]

phil·ter (fil′tər) *also,* **phil·tre**. *n.* **1**. a magic drug or potion supposed to arouse sexual passion. **2**. any magic drug or potion. [French *philtre* love potion, from Latin *philtrum*, from Greek *philtron.*]

phle·bi·tis (flə bī′tis) *n.* inflammation of a vein, frequently accompanied by the formation of a blood clot. [Modern Latin *phlebitis*, from Greek *phleps* vein + -ITIS.]

phle·bot·o·my (flə bot′ə mē) *n.* the practice of opening a vein in order to draw blood, used as a therapeutic measure. Also, **venesection**. [Late Latin *phlebotomia*, from Greek *phlebotomiā*, from *phleps* vein + *tomos* a cutting.] —**phle·bot′o·mist**, *n.*

phlegm (flem) *n.* **1**. mucus, esp. in the nose or throat during a respiratory infection. **2**. a sluggish, unexcitable disposition; indifference; apathy. **3**. calmness; equanimity. [Old French *fleume,* from Late Latin *phlegma* clammy humor of the body, from Greek *phlegma* the humor thought to cause sluggishness. See HUMOR.]

phleg·mat·ic (fleg mat′ik) *adj.* **1**. sluggish in disposition; indifferent; apathetic. **2**. calm; self-possessed. Also, **phleg·mat′i·cal**. [Late Latin *phlegmaticus* full of phlegm, from Greek *phlegmatikos,* from *phlegma* the humor thought to cause sluggishness. See HUMOR.] —**phleg·mat′i·cal·ly**, *adv.*

phlo·em (flō′em) *n.* the layer of vascular plant tissue that conducts food made in the leaves down to the other parts of the plant. In woody plants, it lies just under the hard, outer bark. Also, **bast.** [German *Phloem,* from Greek *phloos* bark.]

phlo·gis·ton (flō jis′tən) *n.* the basic substance that, according to a theory of combustion held in the seventeenth and eighteenth centuries, was present in all combustible materials and given off by them when they burned. [Modern Latin *phlogiston,* from Greek *phlogiston,* neuter of *phlogistos* inflammable, going back to *phlox* flame.]

phlox (floks) *n.* any of a group of erect or trailing plants, genus *Phlox,* bearing showy clusters of small tubular flowers. [Latin *phlox,* from Greek *phlox.*]

-phobe *suffix* (used to form nouns) a person who fears or dreads: *Anglophobe.* [Greek *-phobos* fearing, from *phobos* panic, fear.]

pho·bi·a (fō′bē ə) *n.* an excessive, irrational dread or fear, esp. of a specific object, situation, phenomenon, or the like. [Greek *-phobiā* (from *phobos* panic, fear), often through Latin *-phobia.*] —**pho′bic**, *adj.*

phoe·be (fē′bē) *n.* any of several small flycatchers, family Tyrannidae, native to tropical and temperate regions of the Western Hemisphere, such as the **eastern phoebe**, *Sayornis phoebe,* having

phlox

gray-brown plumage with white underparts and named for the sound of its two-note song. Length: 7 inches (18 centimeters). [Imitative, but influenced by the proper name *Phoebe.*]

Phoe·be (fē′bē) *n.* in Greek mythology, Artemis, esp. as goddess of the moon.

Phoe·bus (fē′bəs) *n.* in Greek mythology, Apollo, esp. as god of the sun. Also, **Phoebus Apollo.**

Phoe·ni·cian (fə nish′ən, -nē′shən) *adj.* of, relating to, or characteristic of Phoenicia or its people, language, or culture. —*n.* **1**. a native, inhabitant, or citizen of Phoenicia. **2**. the extinct language of Phoenicia, belonging to the Semito-Hamitic language family.

phoe·nix (fē′niks) *also,* **phenix**. *n.* in Egyptian and Greek mythology, a beautiful and miraculous bird believed to live for 500 years, to die in the flames of a funeral pyre, and then to rise again from its own ashes. [Latin *phoenix,* from Greek *phoinix.*]

phone[1] (fōn) *n. Informal.* telephone. [Short for TELEPHONE.]

phone[2] (fōn) *n. Phonetics.* a single speech sound. [Greek *phōnē* sound.]

pho·neme (fō′nēm) *n. Phonetics.* the smallest unit of speech sound that can distinguish one word from another. The words *hat* and *rat* are distinguished by the different phonemes *h* and *r.* The *t* of *tip* and the *t* of *stop* are different allophones because of the influence of the adjacent sounds, but belong to the same phoneme *t.* [Greek *phōnēma* sound.]

pho·nem·ic (fə nē′mik) *adj.* of or relating to a phoneme or phonemes.

pho·net·ic (fə net′ik) *adj.* **1**. of or relating to speech sounds or phonetics. **2**. representing speech sounds with a set of symbols, each of which stands for a single speech sound: *a phonetic alphabet, phonetic spelling.* Also, **pho·net′i·cal**. [Modern Latin *phoneticus,* from Greek *phōnētikos* relating to speaking, going back to *phōnē* sound.] —**pho·net′i·cal·ly**, *adv.*

pho·ne·ti·cian (fō′ni tish′ən) *n.* a person who studies or is an expert in phonetics. Also, **pho·net·i·cist** (fə net′ə sist).

pho·net·ics (fə net′iks) *pl. n.* **1**. the branch of linguistics that deals with speech sounds and their use, and their representation by symbols. **2**. the system of speech sounds of a particular language. ➧ used as singular in both defs.

phon·ic (fon′ik, fō′nik) *adj.* of, relating to, or of the nature of sound, esp. speech sound. [Greek *phōnē* sound + -IC.]

phon·ics (fon′iks, fō′niks) *n.* **1**. any of various methods employing phonetics in the teaching of reading. **2**. acoustics *(def. 2).* ➧ used as singular in both defs. [Greek *phōnē* sound + -ICS.]

phono- *also,* **phon-**. *combining form* sound; voice; speech: *phonograph.*

pho·no·gram (fō′nə gram′) *n.* a symbol that represents a single speech sound, syllable, or word, esp. one used in shorthand. [Greek *phōnē* sound + -GRAM[1].]

pho·no·graph (fō′nə graf′) *n.* a device that reproduces sounds recorded on a disc of plastic or other material. Also, **record player**. [Greek *phōnē* sound + -GRAPH.]

pho·no·graph·ic (fō′nə graf′ik) *adj.* **1**. of, relating to, or produced by a phonograph. **2**. of, relating to, or written in phonography. —**pho′no·graph′i·cal·ly**, *adv.*

pho·nog·ra·phy (fō nog′rə fē) *n.* **1**. spelling based on sound or pronunciation; phonetic spelling or transcription. **2**. any system of shorthand that uses symbols to represent letters, syllables, and words. —**pho·nog′ra·pher, pho·nog′ra·phist**, *n.*

pho·nol·o·gist (fō nol′ə jist) *n.* a person who studies or is an expert in phonology.

pho·nol·o·gy (fō nol′ə jē) *n.* **1**. the system of speech sounds of a language. **2**. the science that studies the special sounds of a language. [Greek *phōnē* sound + -LOGY.] —**pho′no·log′ic**; *also,* **pho·no·log·i·cal** (fō′nə loj′i kəl), *adj.* —**pho′no·log′i·cal·ly**, *adv.*

pho·non (fō′non) *n. Physics.* a quantum of sound wave energy, which, like its analog the photon, can be considered a discrete particle. [PHONO- + -ON.]

pho·ny (fō′nē) *Informal. adj.,* **-ni·er**, **-ni·est**. not genuine; spurious; counterfeit; fake: *a phony diamond.* —*n., pl.* **-nies**. **1**. something that is not genuine; fake. **2**. a person who pretends or tries to be what he or she is not. [Of uncertain origin.] —**pho′ni·ness**, *n.*

phos·gene (fos′jēn) *n.* a colorless, lethal poison gas that acts on the respiratory system, used in chemical warfare. Formula: $COCl_2$ [Greek *phōs* light + *-genēs* born, produced.]

phos·pha·tase (fos′fə tās′) *n.* any of a large number of enzymes in body tissues and fluids that break down esters of phosphoric acid, liberating phosphate ions. Phosphatases are important in the metabolism of carbohydrates and nucleotides and in the calcification of young bones. [PHOSPHAT(E) + -ASE.]

phos·phate (fos′fāt) *n.* **1**. any salt of phosphoric acid. **2**. a fertilizer having a high phosphorus content. **3**. a beverage made with carbonated water and fruit syrup. [PHOSPH(ORUS) + -ATE[2].] —**phos·phat·ic** (fos fat′ik), *adj.*

phosphate rock, phosphorite.

phos·phide (fos′fīd) *n.* a compound of phosphorus and a single metallic element.

phos·phite (fos′fīt) *n.* a salt of phosphorous acid.

phos·pho·lip·id (fos′fō lip′id) *n.* any of a group of fatty compounds, or lipids, as lecithin, that are esters of phosphoric acid and are present in all living cells.

phos·phor (fos′fər) *n.* a substance that emits light when stimulated by a form of radiant energy, such as ultraviolet light; phosphorescent substance. [French *phosphore,* from Modern Latin *phosphorus.* See PHOSPHORUS.]

Phos·phor (fos′fər) *n. Archaic.* the morning star, esp. Venus.

phosphor bronze, a hard, corrosion-resistant bronze that has been deoxidized by the addition of phosphorus to the molten metal, used esp. for fittings on boats and ships.

phos·pho·resce (fos′fə res′) v.i., **-resced, -resc·ing.** to give off faint light without noticeable heat, as phosphorus does; exhibit phosphorescence.

phos·pho·res·cence (fos′fə res′əns) n. **1.** the emission of light by an organism or organic compound as a result of slow, cool oxidation, as in fireflies. **2.** Physics. the luminescence exhibited by a substance that is absorbing radiant energy and, after a time delay, emitting it as visible light. Phosphorescence continues after the source of energy is removed. ➡ distinguished from **fluorescence. 3.** a light so produced.

phos·pho·res·cent (fos′fə res′ənt) adj. exhibiting phosphorescence.

phos·phor·et·ed (fos′fə ret′id) also, **phos·phor·et·ted.** adj. combined with phosphorus.

phos·phor·ic (fos fôr′ik, -for′-) adj. of, relating to, or containing phosphorus, esp. in a higher oxidation state than in phosphorous compounds.

phosphoric acid, any of three acids containing phosphorus. Formulas: HPO_3; H_3PO_4; $H_4P_2O_7$

phos·pho·rite (fos′fə rīt′) n. a sedimentary rock rich enough in phosphate minerals to be worth mining, esp. for use as a chemical fertilizer in agriculture. Also, **phosphate rock.** [PHOSPHORUS + -ITE[1].] **—phos·pho·rit·ic** (fos′fə rit′ik), adj.

phos·pho·rous (fos′fər əs, fos fôr′-) adj. of, relating to, or containing phosphorus, esp. in a lower oxidation state than in phosphoric compounds.

phosphorous acid, a crystalline acid, used as a reducing agent and to make phosphites. Formula: H_3PO_3

phos·pho·rus (fos′fər əs) n. a solid, nonmetallic element existing in three allotropic forms. **Yellow phosphorus** is a poisonous, waxy solid that glows faintly in the dark. **Red phosphorus** is a less reactive, reddish brown, crystalline powder. **Black phosphorus** is prepared by heating yellow phosphorus under very high pressure. Phosphorus is one of the elements essential to life. Symbol: P For tables, see **element.** [Modern Latin phosphorus, from Greek phōsphoros bringing light; because it glows in the dark.]

pho·tic (fō′tik) adj. **1.** of or relating to light. **2.** (of the waters of a lake or the sea) receiving enough light for photosynthesis; penetrated by light: marine organisms of the photic zone. [Greek phōtos, genitive of phōs light + -IC.]

pho·to (fō′tō) n., pl. **-tos.** Informal. photograph.

photo- combining form **1.** of, relating to, or produced by light: photosynthesis, photometry. **2.** of, relating to, or produced by photography; photographic: photogravure, photomechanical. [Greek phōt-, stem of phōs light.]

pho·to·cell (fō′tō sel′) n. photoelectric cell.

pho·to·chem·is·try (fō′tō kem′ə strē) n. the branch of science that deals with the chemical changes brought about by the action of electromagnetic radiation, esp. visible light and ultraviolet radiation, on matter. **—pho′to·chem′i·cal,** adj. **—pho′to·chem′i·cal·ly,** adv. **—pho′to·chem′ist,** n.

pho·to·co·ag·u·la·tion (fō′tō kō ag′yə lā′shən) n. the production of scar tissue by a controlled and intense beam of light, as a laser, used in treating certain eye disorders.

pho·to·com·po·si·tion (fō′tō kom′pə zish′ən) n. Printing. a typesetting method in which images of type or graphics are photographed, producing negatives that are used to make printing plates.

pho·to·cop·i·er (fō′tə kop′ē ər) n. a device that makes photocopies.

pho·to·cop·y (fō′tə cop′ē) v.t., v.i., **-cop·ied, -cop·y·ing.** to make copies of (printed matter or the like) by a photographic process. —n., pl. **-cop·ies.** a copy produced by such a process.

pho·to·e·lec·tric (fō′tō i lek′trik) adj. of or relating to the emission of electrons from a surface due to the action of light. **—pho′to·e·lec′tri·cal·ly,** adv.

photoelectric cell, an electronic device that produces or regulates a flow of current photoelectrically, used esp. in electric eyes, television cameras, and light meters. Also, **photocell.**

pho·to·e·mis·sive (fō′tō i mis′iv) adj. Physics. (of a metal) emitting electrons in response to irradiation; exhibiting a photoelectric effect.

pho·to·en·grav·ing (fō′tō en grā′ving) n. **1.** the process by which engraved plates for relief printing are produced from photographs of illustrations. **2.** the plate or print so produced. **3.** a print or engraving made from this.

photo finish 1. in horse racing, a finish so close that a photograph of the horses as they cross the finish line is needed to decide on the winner. **2.** the finish of any contest that is extremely close or not decided until the last minute.

pho·to·flash (fō′tə flash′) n. flashbulb.

pho·to·flood lamp (fō′tə flud′) a floodlight used for taking pictures.

pho·to·gen·ic (fō′tə jen′ik) adj. **1.** suitable for or being a good

subject for photographing; that photographs well: a photogenic person. **2.** Biology. emitting light; luminescent; phosphorescent. [PHOTO- + -GEN + -IC.] **—pho′to·gen′i·cal·ly,** adv.

pho·to·gram·me·try (fō′tə gram′i trē) n. the art or process of using data from photographs for making maps or for architectural and engineering construction work. **—pho·to·gram·met·ric** (fō′tō grə met′rik), adj. **—pho·to·gram·met′ri·cal·ly,** adv.

pho·to·graph (fō′tə graf′) n. a picture or reproduction made by photography. —v.t. to take a photograph of. —v.i. **1.** to take photographs. **2.** to appear or look in a photograph: That model always photographs well.

pho·tog·ra·pher (fə tog′rə fər) n. a person who takes photographs, esp. as a profession.

pho·to·graph·ic (fō′tə graf′ik) adj. **1.** used in or produced by photography: photographic equipment. **2.** relating to or resembling photography: a photographic style of painting. **3.** capable of remembering or reproducing as precisely as a photograph, esp. with respect to minor details: a photographic memory. Also, **pho′to·graph′i·cal. —pho′to·graph′i·cal·ly,** adv.

pho·tog·ra·phy (fə tog′rə fē) n. **1.** the technique of recording the image of someone or something by the photochemical action of light on a light-sensitive surface. **2.** the art or practice of taking photographs.

pho·to·gra·vure (fō′tə grə vyür′, -grāv′yər) n. **1.** a photoengraving process in which a printing plate is made by reproducing a photographic negative of the image to be printed in an acid-resistant coating on a metal plate and then etching the image into the plate using an acid bath. **2.** a plate or picture produced by this method. Also, **gravure.**

pho·to·jour·nal·ism (fō′tō jûr′nə liz′əm) n. journalism in which the basic presentation of the news is through photography rather than through the accompanying written account. **—pho′to·jour′nal·ist,** n.

pho·to·li·thog·ra·phy (fō′tō li thog′rə fē) n. a lithographic printing method in which the printing plates are prepared using photographic images. **—pho·to·lith·o·graph·ic** (fō′tō lith′ə graf′ik), adj.

pho·tol·y·sis (fō tol′ə sis) n. chemical decomposition triggered by the exposure of a substance to light. **—pho·to·lyt·ic** (fō′tə lit′ik), adj.

pho·to·me·chan·i·cal (fō′tō mi kan′i kəl) adj. of or relating to any process by which printed material is produced from a photograph.

pho·tom·e·ter (fō tom′i tər) n. any device for determining the intensity of a light source by comparing it to a source of known intensity. A light meter is a photometer designed to be used in or with a camera.

pho·to·met·ric (fō′tə met′rik) adj. of or relating to photometry or a photometer. **—pho′to·met′ri·cal·ly,** adv.

pho·tom·e·try (fō tom′i trē) n. the branch of physics that deals with the measurement of the intensity of light.

pho·to·mi·cro·graph (fō′tə mī′krə graf′) n. a photograph taken through a microscope. Also, **micrograph, microphotograph. —pho·to·mi·crog·ra·phy** (fō′tə mī krog′rə fē), n.

pho·to·mul·ti·pli·er (fō′tō mul′tə plī′ər) n. an electron tube with a series of supplementary electrodes between the cathode and the anode that uses the multiplication of electrons by secondary emission to detect and measure small amounts of light and other radiation.

photomicrograph of Velcro

pho·ton (fō′ton) n. a basic quantum, or unit, of light or other electromagnetic radiant energy, considered a discrete particle. [PHOTO- + -ON.]

pho·to·off·set (fō′tō ôf′set′, -of′-) n. offset printing in which plates prepared by photolithography are used.

pho·to·pe·ri·od (fō′tō pir′ē əd) n. **1.** the length of the period

P

a	at	e	end	o	hot	u	up	hw	white		about
ā	ape	ē	me	ō	old	ū	use	ng	song		taken
ä	far	i	it	ô	fork	ü	rule	th	thin	ə	pencil
âr	care	ī	ice	oi	oil	u̇	pull	th	this		lemon
		îr	pierce	ou	out	ûr	turn	zh	measure		circus

of daylight to which an organism adjusts its annual cycle of growth and activity. **2.** the number of daylight hours best suited to the growth and maturation of an organism, esp. flowering in plants. —**pho·to·pe·ri·od·ic** (fō′tō pir′ē od′ik), *adj.* —**pho′·to·pe′ri·od′i·cal·ly,** *adv.*

pho·to·play (fō′tə plā′) *n.* a script for a motion picture; screenplay.

pho·to·re·cep·tor (fō′tō ri sep′tər) *n.* a cell or sense organ specialized for the detection of light, as the cells of the retina, or the eye itself.

pho·to·sen·si·tive (fō′tō sen′si tiv) *adj.* **1.** *Physics.* liable to undergo chemical change or to exhibit a photoelectric effect when exposed to light. **2.** *Biology.* **a.** capable of reacting to or being stimulated by radiant energy, esp. light. **b.** abnormally sensitive to ultraviolet radiation. —**pho′to·sen′si·tiv′i·ty,** *n.*

pho·to·sphere (fō′tə sfir′) *n.* **1.** the visible surface of the sun, consisting of a layer of hot gases about 250 miles (402 kilometers) thick. For illustration, see **sun. 2.** a similar surface on any star.

Pho·to·stat (fō′tə stat′) *n.* **1.** *Trademark.* a device for making photographic copies of graphic matter directly on specially prepared paper. **2.** *also,* **photostat.** a copy made by Photostat. —*v.t. also,* **photostat.** to make a photostat of. [PHOTO- + Greek *-statēs* that causes to stand, that stands.]

pho·to·stat·ic (fō′tə stat′ik) *adj.* of or relating to a Photostat, the process by which it operates, or copies made by this process: *a photostatic print.*

pho·to·syn·the·sis (fō′tə sin′thə sis) *n.* the manufacture of organic compounds, such as sugar and starch, from inorganic substances, including water and carbon dioxide, by the living cells of green plants, using the energy of light absorbed by the plant pigment chlorophyll. —**pho·to·syn·thet·ic** (fō′tə sin thet′ik), *adj.* —**pho′to·syn′thet′i·cal·ly,** *adv.*

pho·to·tax·is (fō′tō tak′sis) *n.* the movement of a cell or of a freely moving organism in response to light, either toward or away from it, as in certain protozoans. —**pho·to·tac·tic** (fō′tō tak′tik), *adj.*

pho·to·te·leg·ra·phy (fō′tō tə leg′rə fē) *n.* facsimile *(def. 2).*

pho·tot·ro·pism (fō tot′rə piz′əm, fō′tō trō′piz-) *n.* the tendency of a plant or other organism to turn toward or away from light. [PHOTO- + TROPISM.] —**pho·to·trop·ic** (fō′tə trop′ik, -trō′pik), *adj.*

pho·to·type (fō′tə tīp′) *n. Printing.* **1.** a plate with a relief surface for printing produced by photography. **2.** the process for making such a plate. **3.** a picture printed from such a plate.

pho·to·vol·ta·ic (fō′tō vol tā′ik) *adj.* capable of generating an electric current when exposed to light or other radiation. [PHOTO- + VOLTAIC.]

pho·to·vol·ta·ics (fō′tō vol tā′iks) *n.* the technology of converting sunlight into electricity using devices, such as the solar cell, that depend on a photovoltaic effect. ➡ used as singular.

phras·al (frā′zəl) *adj.* of, like, or consisting of a phrase or phrases.

phrase (frāz) *n.* **1.** a group of words taken as a grammatical unit or expressing a single thought, but not containing a subject and predicate. In the sentence *To achieve success is our goal, To achieve success* is a phrase. **2.** a particular or characteristic expression; slogan. **3.** a short, distinct division of a musical composition, forming an independent unit of melody. **4.** a series of movements regarded as a complete unit in a dance pattern. —*v.t.,* **phrased, phras·ing. 1.** to express in a particular or distinctive way: *The defense attorney phrased the question very carefully.* **2.** to divide or mark off (a melody, musical composition, or the like) into phrases. [Latin *phrasis* diction, from Greek *phrasis* speech, expression.]

phra·se·ol·o·gy (frā′zē ol′ə jē) *n., pl.* **-gies.** a particular style or manner of expression; choice and arrangement of words: *a document written in complex legal phraseology.*

phras·ing (frā′zing) *n.* **1.** phraseology. **2.** a way of marking off musical phrases.

phra·try (frā′trē) *n., pl.* **-tries. 1.** a subdivision of an ancient Greek phyle. **2.** any similar tribal subdivision, such as a clan, among primitive peoples. [Greek *phrātriā* tribe, clan.]

phre·net·ic (fri net′ik) *adj.* frenetic. [Latin *phrenēticus* mad, from Greek *phrenētikos,* from *phrēnītis* delirium.]

phren·ic (fren′ik) *adj.* of or relating to the diaphragm: *a phrenic nerve or artery.* [Greek *phrēn* midriff, diaphragm, mind + -IC.]

phre·nol·o·gy (fri nol′ə jē) *n.* the study of the bumps and depressions on a person's skull, based on the belief that they are indicative of character and intelligence. [Greek *phrēn* mind + -LOGY.] —**phren·o·log·i·cal** (fren′ə loj′i kəl), *adj.* —**phre·nol′o·gist,** *n.*

phthis·ic (tiz′ik) *n.* phthisis. —*adj.* phthisical.

phthis·i·cal (tiz′i kəl) *adj.* of, relating to, or suffering from phthisis.

phthi·sis (thī′sis) *n.* the atrophy of any part of the body, esp.

tuberculosis of the lungs. [Latin *phthisis* consumption, from Greek *phthisis* consumption, a wasting away.]

phy·co·my·cete (fī′kō mī′sēt, -mī sēt′) *n.* in older classifications, any of a class of primitive fungi, Phycomycetes, some of which resemble algae, such as the molds that grow on bread and fruit. —**phy′co·my·ce′tous,** *adj.*

phy·lac·ter·y (fi lak′tə rē) *n., pl.* **-ter·ies. 1.** a small leather case with straps attached, containing texts from the Old Testament. Orthodox Jews fasten one around the forehead and one around the left arm during prayer as a reminder to them to keep the Mosaic law. **2.** a charm worn as a protection or safeguard; amulet. [Late Latin *phylactērium* amulet, from Greek *phylaktērion* amulet, safeguard.]

phyle (fīl) *n.* the largest political subdivision in ancient Athens. [Greek *phȳlē* tribe.]

phy·let·ic (fī let′ik) *adj.* of or relating to the evolutionary line of descent of a species or other group. [Modern Latin *phyleticus,* from Greek *phȳletikós* relating to a tribesman, from *phȳlétēs* tribesman, from *phȳlē* tribe.]

phyl·lo·tax·is (fil′ə tak′sis) *n., pl.* **-tax·es** (tak′sēz). phyllotaxy.

phyl·lo·tax·y (fil′ə tak′sē) *n., pl.* **-tax·ies.** *also,* **phyllotaxis.** the arrangement of leaves on a stem.

phyl·lox·e·ra (fil′ək sîr′ə, fi lok′sər ə) *n.* any of a group of destructive plant lice, genus *Phylloxera,* esp. *P. vitifoliae,* which attacks the roots and leaves of European grapevines. [Modern Latin *phylloxera,* from Greek *phyllon* leaf + *xēros* dry.]

phy·log·e·ny (fī loj′ə nē) *n., pl.* **-nies.** the history of the evolution of a species or group. Also, **phy·lo·gen·e·sis** (fī′lə jen′ə sis). [Greek *phȳlon* tribe, race + *-geneia* birth, origin.] —**phy·lo·ge·net·ic** (fī′lō jə net′ik); *also,* **phy′lo·gen′ic,** *adj.*

phy·lum (fī′ləm) *n., pl.* **-la** (-lə). a primary subdivision in the classification of the animal kingdom. In botany, phylum is sometimes used to denote a division, a similar classification in the plant kingdom. [Modern Latin *phylum,* from Greek *phȳlon* class, tribe, race.]

phys·ic (fiz′ik) *n.* **1.** any medicine, esp. one that purges. **2.** *Archaic.* the science, practice, or profession of medicine. —*v.t.,* **-icked, -ick·ing.** *Archaic.* to treat with or as with a physic; relieve; cure. [Medieval Latin *physica* medical science, from Latin *physica* natural science, from Greek *physikē,* going back to *physis* nature.]

phys·i·cal (fiz′i kəl) *adj.* **1.** of or relating to the body: *physical strength.* **2.** of, relating to, or containing matter. **3.** of or relating to matter and energy or the relationship between them. **4.** of or relating to physics. —*n.* physical examination. —**phys′i·cal·ly,** *adv.*

physical anthropology, the branch of anthropology that studies the physical evolution, variation, and classification of human beings. ➡ distinguished from **cultural anthropology.**

physical chemistry, the branch of chemistry that is concerned with how the properties of a substance are related to its chemical composition and that studies chemical reactions in terms of the changes they produce in physical properties.

physical education, instruction in physical activities and the care of the body.

physical examination, a medical examination to determine a person's general state of health or fitness for certain activities. Also, **physical.**

physical geography, the study of the physical features of the earth, such as land formation, climate, and vegetation. Also, **physiography.**

physical science, any natural science concerned with inanimate matter, such as physics, chemistry, or astronomy.

physical therapy, the treatment of disease or injury by physical methods, such as heat, massage, or exercise. Also, **physiotherapy.**

phy·si·cian (fə zish′ən) *n.* a person who is licensed to practice medicine, such as a general practitioner; medical doctor. [Old French *fisicien,* from *fisique* medicine, from Latin *physica* natural science. See PHYSIC.]

phys·i·cist (fiz′ə sist) *n.* a person who is a student of or expert in physics.

phys·ics (fiz′iks) *pl. n.* **1.** the science concerned with matter and energy and the relationships between them, encompassing the fields of mechanics, light, heat, sound, optics, electricity and magnetism, and nuclear physics. ➡ used as singular. **2.** physical properties or processes: *the physics of space flight.* ➡ used as singular or plural. [Plural of PHYSIC (to represent neuter plural of Latin *physica,* from Greek *ta physika,* title given to the works on physics by the Greek philosopher Aristotle, 384-322 B.C.).]

phys·i·og·no·my (fiz′ē og′nə mē, -on′ə mē) *n., pl.* **-mies. 1.** the features or appearance of the face, esp. when considered as an indication of character. **2.** the art of judging character from the

features or appearance of the face. **3.** the general appearance of something: *the physiognomy of a landmass.* [Old French *phisonomie* art of judging character by the features, through Medieval Latin, going back to Greek *physiognōmoniā*, going back to *physis* nature + *gnōmōn* interpreter.] —**phys·i·og·nom·ic** (fiz′ē og·nom′ik, fiz′ē ə-); also, **phys′i·og·nom′i·cal,** *adj.* —**phys′i·og′no·mist,** *n.*

phys·i·og·ra·phy (fiz′ē og′rə fē) *n.* physical geography. [Greek *physis* nature + -GRAPHY.] —**phys′i·og′ra·pher,** *n.* —**phys·i·o·graph·ic** (fiz′ē ə graf′ik); also, **phys′i·o·graph′i·cal,** *adj.*

phys·i·o·log·i·cal (fiz′ē ə loj′i kəl) *adj.* **1.** of or relating to physiology. **2.** characteristic of or promoting the normal functioning of an organism. Also, **phys′i·o·log′ic.** —**phys′i·o·log′i·cal·ly,** *adv.*

phys·i·ol·o·gy (fiz′ē ol′ə jē) *n.* **1.** the science concerned with the functions and processes of living organisms. **2.** the functions or processes of an organism or of any of its aspects or parts: *the physiology of the frog, the physiology of respiration.* [Latin *physiologia* study of nature, from Greek *physiologiā.*] —**phys′i·ol′o·gist,** *n.*

phys·i·o·ther·a·py (fiz′ē ō ther′ə pē) *n.* physical therapy. [Greek *physis* nature + THERAPY.]

phy·sique (fi zēk′) *n.* the structure, development, or appearance of the body: *a muscular physique.* [French *physique* physical, from Latin *physicus* natural, from Greek *physikos,* from *physis* nature.]

-phyte *combining form* a plant, esp. one having a specified environment or nature: *saprophyte, zoophyte.* [Greek *phyton* plant.]

phy·to·plank·ton (fī′tō plangk′tən) *n.* the plant or plantlike portion of plankton that undergoes photosynthesis, esp. microscopic forms of algae, as diatoms. [Greek *phyton* plant + PLANKTON.] —**phy′to·plank·ton′ic,** *adj.*

pi¹ (pī) *n., pl.* **pis. 1.** the sixteenth letter of the Greek alphabet (Π, π), corresponding to the English letter *P, p.* **2.** the ratio of the circumference of a circle to its diameter, denoted by the Greek letter π. Pi is approximately 3.1415926. [Middle Greek *pī* sixteenth letter of the Greek alphabet, from Greek *peī;* of Semitic origin.]

pi² (pī) *also,* **pie.** *n. Printing.* type that has been mixed together. —*v.t.,* **pied, pi·ing.** to mix or jumble up (type). [Of uncertain origin.]

P.I., Philippine Islands.

pi·a ma·ter (pī′ə mā′tər, pē′ə) a thin, delicate membrane, the innermost of the three coverings of the brain and spinal cord. [Medieval Latin *pia mater (cerebrī)* literally, pious mother (of the brain).]

pi·a·nis·si·mo (pē′ə nis′ə mō′, pyä-) *Music. adj.* very soft. —*adv.* very softly. —*n., pl.* **-mos.** a very soft passage of music. [Italian *pianissimo* very softly, superlative of *piano* softly. See PIANO².]

pi·an·ist (pē an′ist, pyan′-, pē′ə nist) *n.* a person who plays the piano, especially one who is a skilled performer.

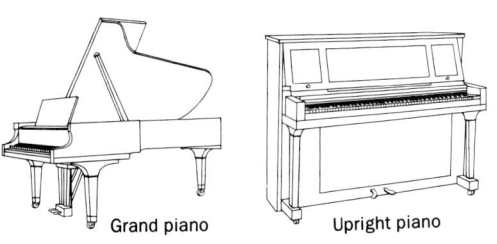

Grand piano   Upright piano

pi·an·o¹ (pē an′ō, pyan′ō) *n., pl.* **-an·os.** a stringed musical instrument that produces tones when felt-covered hammers, operated by a keyboard, strike the strings. Also, **pianoforte.** [Short for PIANOFORTE.]

pi·a·no² (pē ä′nō, pyä′-) *Music. adj.* soft. —*adv.* softly. —*n., pl.* **-nos.** a soft passage of music. [Italian *piano* softly, from Late Latin *plānus* smooth, from Latin *plānus* flat, level.]

pi·an·o·for·te (pē an′ə fôr′tē, -tā, -fôrt′, pyan′-) *n.* piano¹. [Italian *pianoforte,* from *piano* (see PIANO²) + *forte* loud (from Latin *fortis* strong); referring to the ability of the instrument to produce both soft and loud sounds.]

pi·as·ter (pē as′tər) *also,* **pi·as·tre.** *n.* **1.** a unit of currency of Egypt, Lebanon, Sudan, and Syria, equal to ¹⁄₁₀₀ of a pound. **2.** the former monetary unit of South Vietnam. [French *piastre,* from Italian *piastra* metal plate, coin, going back to Latin *emplastrum* medical plaster. See PLASTER.]

pi·az·za (pē az′ə, -ä′zə, -ät′sə) *n.* **1.** a public square in a town, esp. in Italy. **2.** a covered porch or veranda. [Italian *piazza* marketplace, square, from Latin *platēa* broad way, from Greek *plateia (hodos)* broad (way). Doublet of PLACE, PLAZA.]

pi·broch (pē′brok) *n.* a musical composition originating in the Scottish Highlands, performed on the bagpipe and consisting of variations on a basic, usually martial or dirgelike theme. [Scottish Gaelic *piobaireachd,* going back to *piob* pipe, bagpipe.]

pi·ca¹ (pī′kə) *n.* **1.** a unit of measure used in printing, equal to twelve points, or about ¹⁄₆ inch (0.42 centimeter). **2.** a size of type for typewriters, providing ten characters to the linear inch. [Medieval Latin *pica* book of rules regarding religious services (said to have been written in *pica* lettering), from Latin *pīca* magpie; because the black lettering on white paper recalled the colors of the magpie.]

pi·ca² (pī′kə) *n.* a craving for or compulsive eating of nonfood substances, such as clay, paint, or starch. [Modern Latin *pica,* from Latin *pīca* magpie; because of its omnivorous eating habits.]

pic·a·dor (pik′ə dôr′) *n.* any of the participants mounted on horseback who pricks the neck of the bull with a lance in a bullfight in order to weaken the bull's neck muscles so that the bull will keep its head lower during the rest of the fight. [Spanish *picador* literally, pricker, from *picar* to prick, probably going back to Latin *pīcus* woodpecker.]

pic·a·resque (pik′ə resk′) *adj.* of or relating to rogues and their adventures, esp. as described in fiction. [Spanish *picaresco* roguish, from *pícaro* rogue, from *picar* to prick. See PICADOR.]

pic·a·roon (pik′ə rūn′) *n.* **1.** rogue; scoundrel; adventurer. **2.** pirate. [Spanish *picarón* great rogue, villain, from *pícaro* rogue. See PICARESQUE.]

pic·a·yune (pik′ə ūn′) *adj.* **1.** of little value or significance; paltry: *a picayune sum.* **2.** narrow-minded; mean; petty: *That was a picayune thing to do.* —*n.* a person or thing that is of little importance. [French *picaillon* copper coin of small value, from Provençal *picaioun;* of uncertain origin.]

pic·ca·lil·li (pik′ə lil′ē) *n., pl.* **-lis.** a relish made of chopped vegetables, sugar, hot spices, and vinegar. [Modification (possibly influenced by CHILI) of PICKLE.]

pic·co·lo (pik′ə lō′) *n., pl.* **-los.** a small flute pitched one octave higher than the ordinary flute. [Italian *piccolo* small, small flute; of uncertain origin.]

pick¹ (pik) *v.t.* **1.** to select from a number; choose: *The city picked the site for the new museum.* **2.** to gather with the fingers; pluck: *to pick flowers.* **3.a.** to use the fingers or something pointed to remove matter from: *to pick one's teeth.* **b.** to remove bit by bit with the fingers or something pointed: *to pick the meat from a bone.* **4.** to prepare by removing feathers, hulls, leaves, or other parts: *to pick a chicken.* **5.** to pierce, dig into, or break up (the surface of anything) with something pointed: *to pick frozen ground.* **6.** to make or form (a hole) with something pointed. **7.** to pull apart or to pieces, as rags or fibers. **8.** (of birds) to take up (food) with the beak or bill. **9.a.** to pluck with the fingers or a plectrum, as the strings of a guitar. **b.** to play (a stringed instrument) by plucking the strings with the fingers or a plectrum. **10.** to provoke deliberately: *He picked a fight with his brother.* **11.** to look for critically and point out: *She picked many flaws in the plan.* **12.** to steal the contents of: *The thief picked the tourist's pocket.* **13.** to open (a lock) with a pointed instrument or wire instead of a key. —*v.i.* **1.** to use or work with something pointed. **2.** to eat sparingly or without appetite: *Why don't you eat a full meal rather than pick?* **3.** to select, esp. very fastidiously and carefully: *to pick and choose.* **4.** (of birds) to take up food with the beak or bill. —*n.* **1.** the act or right of selecting; choice: *Take your pick of these books.* **2.** a person or thing that is selected: *That student is my pick for class treasurer.* **3.** the best or choicest part or example: *That puppy is the pick of the litter.* **4.** the quantity of a crop gathered by hand at one time: *a large pick of corn.* **5.** a stroke with something pointed. **6.** plectrum. [Possibly from Middle French *piquer* to prick, strike. See PIKE¹.] —For Synonyms (*v.t.*), see **choose.**

  • **to pick apart. a.** to pull, break, or tear into small pieces. **b.** to point out faults or flaws in, esp. in detail: *to pick apart a proposal.*

  • **to pick at. a.** to pull on; toy with; handle: *She picked at her necklace nervously.* **b.** *Informal.* to find fault with constantly; nag. **c.** to eat sparingly or without appetite: *He picked at his dinner.*

a	at	e	end	o	hot	u	up	hw	white		about
ā	ape	ē	me	ō	old	ū	use	ng	song		taken
ä	far	i	it	ô	fork	u̇	rule	th	thin		pencil
âr	care	ī	ice	oi	oil	u̇	pull	th	this		lemon
		îr	pierce	ou	out	ûr	turn	zh	measure		circus

P

• **to pick off. a.** to shoot after taking careful aim: *The hunters picked off the ducks as they flew over the pond.* **b.** *Baseball.* to tag (a base runner) out after he or she has taken a lead off a base.

• **to pick on. a.** *Informal.* to find fault with; criticize: *The mayor picked on the plan from every angle.* **b.** to bully or annoy; harass: *The older children picked on the younger ones.*

• **to pick one's way.** to walk carefully so as to avoid obstacles or dangers: *to pick one's way along an icy sidewalk.*

• **to pick out. a.** to select from all that are available; choose: *Have you picked out the movie you want to see?* **b.** to distinguish from a group or mass: *to pick out a friend's face in a crowd.* **c.** to make out or gather (the sense or meaning); discern. **d.** to play (a tune) by ear or note by note.

• **to pick over.** to examine (a group of things) in order to make a selection: *to pick over some pears to find the ripest ones.*

• **to pick someone's brain.** to get (someone's) advice, suggestions, or opinions.

• **to pick up. a.** to take up; lift: *The campers picked up sticks and small branches for firewood.* **b.** to take (someone or something) into a vehicle or ship: *The driver picked up a hitchhiker. A passing liner picked up the shipwrecked sailors. The freighter picked up its cargo from the loading dock.* **c.** to acquire casually or by chance: *He picked up a few dollars by doing odd jobs. She picks up languages easily.* **d.** to bring into range of sight or hearing: *I can pick up London on my shortwave radio.* **e.** to stop to buy or claim: *to pick up some toothpaste at the drugstore, to pick up a suit from the dry cleaner.* **f.** to make neat; tidy: *to pick up a room before guests arrive.* **g.** *Slang.* to take into custody: *The police picked up the suspected thief for questioning.* **h.** to gain speed. **i.** *Informal.* to change for the better; improve; recover: *Business picked up after the brief recession. My spirits picked up after they told me the good news.* **j.** to go faster; accelerate: *The tempo of the music picks up after the slow passage.* **k.** *Informal.* to make a casual acquaintance with (a stranger), esp. for sexual purposes. **l.** to sense and follow: *to pick up the scent of a fox.* **m.** to begin traveling on (a route): *We picked up the trail a few miles downstream.* **n.** to resume after an interruption or pause: *to pick up the main subject after a brief digression.* **o.** to become ill with; catch: *to pick up a virus while on vacation.* **p.** to take responsibility for paying: *The company picked up the bill for employees' health insurance.*

• **to pick up on. a.** to become aware of; perceive: *to pick up on someone's insecurities.* **b.** to begin to use or do; adopt: *to pick up on the latest fads.*

pick² (pik) *n.* **1.** a chipping or breaking tool that has a metal head, usually with one or two tips sharpened to a point, attached to a wooden handle. Also, **pickax.** **2.** any of various sharp-pointed tools without a head, as an ice pick. [Form of PIKE².]

pick·a·back (pik′ə bak′) *adv., adj.* piggyback.

pick·ax (pik′aks′) *also,* **pick·axe.** *n.* pick² *(def. 1).* [Modification (influenced by AX) of Middle English *pikois,* from Old French *picois,* from *pic,* probably going back to Latin *pīcus* woodpecker.]

pick² *(def. 1)*

picked (pikt) *adj.* **1.** specially selected: *picked troops.* **2.** cleaned or cleared: *a picked chicken.*

pick·er (pik′ər) *n.* **1.** a person who picks: *migrants who work as apple pickers.* **2.** a machine that picks.

pick·er·el (pik′ər əl, pik′rəl) *n., pl.* **-el** or **-els.** any of several freshwater game and food fish related to the pike, genus *Esox,* found in North America, having a slender body and long snout. Length: to 2 feet (0.6 meter). [Diminutive of PIKE³.]

pick·er·el·weed (pik′ər əl wēd′, pik′rəl-) *n.* a North American water plant, *Pontederia cordata,* found in the shallow waters of ponds or streams, having a heart-shaped leaf and dense spikes of funnel-shaped, violet-blue flowers with two yellow or white spots.

pick·et (pik′it) *n.* **1.** a pointed stake or slat usually driven into the ground to secure or build something, as a fence or stockade. **2.** a person who walks or stands outside a place of business, school or university building, or government office to draw attention to a grievance or discourage workers or customers from entering, as in a labor dispute or protest. **3.** a guard or body of troops stationed ahead of an army or outside a camp to watch for and give warning of the enemy's approach. —*v.t.* **1.** to act as or station a picket or pickets outside: *to picket a store, to picket an embassy.* **2.** to guard with a picket or pickets. **3.** to post (troops) as a picket. **4.** to fasten to a picket, as a horse. **5.** to enclose or fortify with pickets. —*v.i.* to act as a picket. [Partly from French

piquet pointed stake, diminutive of *pic* pick, going back to Latin *pīcus* woodpecker; partly from French *piquer* to prick. See PIKE¹.] —**pick′et·er,** *n.*

picket fence, a fence made of upright pickets attached to horizontal rails.

picket line, a line of people picketing an establishment.

pick·ing (pik′ing) *n.* **1.** the act of a person who picks. **2. pickings. a.** something that is or can be picked or picked up: *We carried home our pickings from the sale.* **b.** the amount or quality of something that is or can be picked or picked up: *slim pickings, good pickings.* **c.** something that is left over to be picked; scraps: *the pickings of a turkey.* **d.** something acquired by effort, esp. dishonestly; spoils.

pick·le (pik′əl) *n.* **1.** any food, esp. a cucumber, that has been preserved in a solution of salt water or vinegar. **2.** a solution of salt water or vinegar used to preserve or flavor food. **3.** an acid solution for removing oxides from metal surfaces. **4.** *Informal.* a difficult or disagreeable situation. —*v.t.,* **-led, -ling. 1.** to preserve or flavor in a solution of salt water or vinegar. **2.** to remove oxides from (metal) by means of an acid solution. [Middle Dutch *pekel* solution for preserving food, food preserved in such a solution.]

pick·pock·et (pik′pok′it) *n.* a thief who steals from pockets or purses.

pick·up (pik′up′) *n.* **1.** an act or instance of picking up: *a pickup of mail.* **2.** the capacity for quick acceleration: *The old car doesn't have much pickup.* **3.** cartridge *(def. 3).* **4.** in radio and television, the reception of sound or light waves by the transmitter for conversion into electric waves. **5.** a small truck with an open body. Also, **pickup truck. 6.** *Baseball.* an act or instance of fielding a ball that has just bounced. **7.** *Informal.* **a.** a casual acquaintance with a stranger, esp. for sexual purposes. **b.** a person with whom such an acquaintance is made. **8.** *Informal.* an increase or improvement, as in activity or business. —*adj.* organized using whoever or whatever is at hand: *a pickup basketball game.*

pick·y (pik′ē) *adj.,* **pick·i·er, pick·i·est.** hard to please; finicky; fussy.

pic·nic (pik′nik) *n.* **1.** an outing that includes a meal eaten out-of-doors. **2.** *Slang.* a pleasant experience or easy job. —*v.i.,* **-nicked, -nick·ing.** to go on or have a picnic: *We picnicked in the park.* [French *piquenique* meal taken on the grass out-of-doors, from *piquer* to forage, prick (see PIKE¹) + Old French *nique* thing without value (of uncertain origin).] —**pic′nick·er,** *n.*

pico- *combining form* one trillionth (10^{-12}) part of. [Possibly from Italian *piccolo* small.]

pi·co·sec·ond (pē′kə sek′ənd) *n.* one trillionth of a second. [PICO- + SECOND².]

pi·cot (pē′kō) *n.* one of a series of small loops forming part of an ornamental edging on a piece of material, such as ribbon or lace. —*v.t.,* **-coted** (-kōd), **-cot·ing** (-kō ing). to finish or ornament with such loops. [French *picot* literally, small point, diminutive of *pic* point, pickax. See PICKAX.]

pic·ric acid (pik′rik) a poisonous, very bitter, organic acid, used esp. in explosives. Formula: $C_6H_3N_3O_7$ [Greek *pikros* bitter + -IC + ACID.]

Pict (pikt) *n.* a member of an ancient people formerly living in northern and central Scotland. [Middle English *Pictes* (plural), from Old English *Peohtas, Pihtas,* from Late Latin *Picti.*]

Pict·ish (pik′tish) *n.* the language spoken by the Picts. —*adj.* of or relating to the Picts or their language or culture.

pic·to·graph (pik′tə graf′) *n.* **1.** a picture that stands for a word or idea in a system of picture writing. **2.** a diagram, graph, or chart using pictures to represent data. [Latin *pictus,* past participle of *pingere* to paint + -GRAPH.] —**pic′to·graph′ic,** *adj.* —**pic′to·graph′i·cal·ly,** *adv.*

pictographs, ancient (left) and modern (right)

pic·tog·ra·phy (pik tog′rə fē) *n.* the use of pictographs; picture writing.

pic·to·ri·al (pik tôr′ē əl) *adj.* **1.** of, relating to, or of the nature of pictures: *pictorial art, pictorial writing.* **2.** illustrated by or containing pictures: *The school library subscribes to several pictorial publications.* **3.** vividly descriptive; graphic: *a pictorial account of an adventure.* —*n.* a periodical containing many illustrations. [Late Latin *pictōrius* relating to painters (from Latin *pictor* painter) + -AL¹.] —**pic·to·ri·al·ly,** *adv.*

pic·ture (pik′chər) *n.* **1.** a visual representation of something on a flat surface, as a drawing, painting, or photograph. **2.** something presented to the eye, as an image on a motion-picture or television screen. **3.a.** a description in words: *The lecturer gave an excellent picture of living conditions in China.* **b.** an impression or idea: *He already had a mental picture of how she looked.* **4.** a typical example; embodiment: *She looks the picture of health.* **5.** a close likeness; exact image: *John is the picture of his grandfather.* **6.** motion picture. **7.** everything about a particular subject or event; situation: *Here's the economic picture as I see it.* —*v.t.,* -tured, -tur·ing. **1.** to represent visually, as in a drawing or painting; depict: *The artist pictured her sitting in a chair.* **2.** to give a description of; describe. **3.** to form an impression or idea of: *Can you picture them playing football?* [Latin *pictūra* art of painting, a painting.]

pic·tur·esque (pik′chə resk′) *adj.* **1.** having pleasing visual qualities suitable for a picture: *a picturesque cottage.* **2.** graphic or vivid: *picturesque language.* [French *pittoresque,* from Italian *pittoresco* in the style of a painter, from *pittore* painter, from Latin *pictor;* influenced by PICTURE.] —**pic′tur·esque′ly,** *adv.* —**pic′tur·esque′ness,** *n.*

picture tube, a cathode-ray tube with a phosphor coating at one end, which serves as the screen of a television receiver. Also, **kinescope.**

picture window, a large window, usually with a single pane of glass, that is intended to allow a wide view of the outdoors.

picture writing 1. the use of pictures or pictorial symbols to represent a word or idea in writing. **2.** the pictures or symbols so used.

pid·dle (pid′əl) *v.,* -dled, -dling. —*v.i.* to waste time; dawdle; trifle. —*v.t.* to waste (usually with *away*): *to piddle away time.* [Of uncertain origin.]

pid·dling (pid′ling) *adj.* of little importance; trivial; insignificant. Also, **pid′dly.**

pidg·in (pij′ən) *n.* a mixture of two or more languages, having a simplified grammar and vocabulary and used for communication between people who speak different languages. [Chinese modification of BUSINESS.]

pidgin English, a pidgin based on English, esp. a mixture of English with Chinese or Melanesian languages.

pie¹ (pī) *n.* a baked dish made of pastry with a filling of fruit, meat, fish, or other food. [Possibly from PIE²; referring to the magpie's habit of collecting odds and ends (which the contents of a pie resemble) in its nest.]

• **as easy as pie.** very easy.

pie² (pī) *n.* magpie. [Old French *pie,* from Latin *pīca.*]

pie³ (pī) *n.* [Of uncertain origin.]

pie·bald (pī′bôld′) *adj.* having spots or patches, esp. of black and white. —*n.* a piebald animal, esp. a horse. [PIE² + BALD; referring to the variegated coloring of the magpie.]

piece (pēs) *n.* **1.** a separated part; fragment: *a piece of broken glass.* **2.** a part of something forming a single unit or whole: *a piece of land, a piece of cake.* **3.** a single object belonging to a category or group: *a piece of luggage, a piece of china.* **4.** an artistic composition or production: *a piece of music, a literary piece.* **5.** a standard or fixed quantity or amount, as of fabric sold or work done: *to be paid by the piece.* **6.** instance; example; specimen: *That car is a piece of junk.* **7.** a coin: *a ten-cent piece.* **8.** any of the small objects, as disks or figures, used in playing checkers, chess, or other board games. **9.** a gun or cannon. —*v.t.,* pieced, piec·ing. **1.** to construct or make complete by joining the pieces of; assemble (usually with *together*): *to piece together a quilt, to piece a story together from scattered information.* **2.** to join (parts or pieces) into a whole (usually with *together*): *The archaeologist attempted to piece together the fragments of the jaw bone.* **3.** to complete or mend by adding a piece or pieces; patch: *to piece a dress.* [Old French *piece* part of a whole; of Celtic origin.] —For Synonyms (*n.*), see **part.**

• **a piece of the action.** *Informal.* a share of an activity or profits: *If you're thinking of starting a business, I'd like a piece of the action.*

• **of a piece.** of the same sort; alike.

• **to go to pieces. a.** to break or fall apart. **b.** to break down mentally or emotionally: *They went all to pieces when they heard the tragic news.*

• **to speak one's piece.** to express one's views.

pièce de ré·sis·tance (pyes′də RÄ zēs täns′) *French.* **1.** the main dish of a meal. **2.** the main or most important event, incident, item, or accomplishment, as in a series.

piece·meal (pēs′mēl′) *adv.* **1.** piece by piece; not all at one time: *The book was written piecemeal over several years.* **2.** into pieces or fragments: *to be torn piecemeal.* —*adj.* made or done piece by piece: *piecemeal changes in a law.* [Middle English *pecemele* by piece, from *pece* piece + Old English *mǣlum,* dative plural of *mǣl* measure. See PIECE.]

piece of cake *Informal.* something very easy; cinch: *The test was a piece of cake for those who had studied.*

piece of eight, an obsolete Spanish silver coin equal to eight reals.

piece·work (pēs′wûrk′) *n.* work done and paid for by pieces completed rather than by the hour or the day. —**piece′work·er,** *n.*

pie chart, pie graph.

pie·crust (pī′krust′) *n.* pastry for the bottom or top of a pie.

pied (pīd) *adj.* having large spots of different colors; mottled. [PIE² + -ED²; originally referring to the variegated coloring of the magpie.]

pied-à-terre (pyä′də târ′, pye′dä-) *n., pl.* **pieds-à-terre** (pyä′də târ′, pye′dä-). a place to live, often a small apartment, that is used only temporarily or part-time. [French *pied-à-terre* literally, foot to the ground.]

pie graph, a graph in which a circle is divided into wedge-shaped sections of various sizes, resembling pieces of a pie, each piece representing a percentage of the whole. For illustration, see **graph.**

pie·plant (pī′plant′) *n.* rhubarb *(def. 1).*

pier (pîr) *n.* **1.** a structure secured by piles over the water, used esp. as a landing place for boats or ships. **2.** a solid support on which an arch rests, as in a bridge. For illustration, see **arch¹. 3.** the solid part of a wall between openings, as windows. [Medieval Latin (in England) *pera* pier (of a bridge); of uncertain origin.]

pierce (pîrs) *v.,* pierced, pierc·ing. —*v.t.* **1.** to penetrate or pass into or through, as with a sharp-pointed instrument: *The splinter pierced my finger.* **2.** to make a hole or opening into or through; perforate: *The pick pierced the ice.* **3.** to make (a hole or opening) as by perforating: *to pierce a hole in ice.* **4.** to force or break a way into or through: *The enemy's offensive pierced our line of defense.* **5.** to perceive with the mind or senses; see into or through; discern: *to pierce a mystery.* **6.** to affect (the emotions) keenly; touch or move deeply: *The sad tale pierced our hearts.* **7.** to penetrate with a sharp sound: *A scream pierced the stillness of the night.* —*v.i.* to pass into or through something; penetrate: *The splinter did not pierce very deeply into the skin.* [Old French *perc(i)er* to make a hole in, going back to Latin *pertūsus,* past participle of *pertundere* to bore through.] —**pierc′er,** *n.* —**pierc′ing·ly,** *adv.*

Synonyms *v.t.* **Pierce, perforate,** and **puncture** mean to make a hole in or through something. **Pierce** describes the passing of a pointed instrument deeply into a thing or through its entire thickness: *The bullet pierced the door and hit the opposite wall.* **Perforate** is often used to describe the making of small holes mechanically: *The device perforates the checks to indicate cancellation.* **Puncture** suggests penetration by a sharp, pointed instrument, usually causing the penetrated object to deflate or collapse: *The tire went flat when the nail punctured it.*

pierc·ing (pîr′sing) *adj.* penetratingly sharp: *a piercing scream.*

Pi·e·ri·an spring (pī ir′ē ən) in Greek mythology, a fountain sacred to the Muses, considered a source of poetic inspiration.

Pi·er·rot (pē′ə rō′) *n.* a comic character in French pantomime, usually having a whitened face and costumed in loose white pantaloons and jacket. [French *Pierrot,* diminutive of *Pierre* Peter.]

Pie·tà (pē′ä tä′, pyä tä′) *also,* **pie·tà.** *n.* a representation in a work of art, as a painting or sculpture, of the Virgin Mary holding the dead body of Jesus. [Italian *pietà* compassion, piety, from Latin *pietās.* See PIETY.]

pi·e·tism (pī′i tiz′əm) *n.* **1.** religious devotion or godliness; piety. **2.** exaggerated or pretended piety. **3. Pietism.** a reform movement within the Lutheran Church in Germany, begun in the late seventeenth century, which emphasized personal piety rather than formal doctrine and ritual. [German *Pietismus* form of evangelical devotional piety, from Latin *pietās* dutiful conduct, devo-

a	at	e	end	o	hot	u	up	hw	white		about
ā	ape	ē	me	ō	old	ū	use	ng	song	ə	taken
ä	far	i	it	ô	fork	ū	rule	th	thin		pencil
âr	care	ī	ice	oi	oil	ů	pull	th	this		lemon
		îr	pierce	ou	out	ûr	turn	zh	measure		circus

tion.] —**pi′e·tist,** *n.* —**pi′e·tis′tic;** *also,* **pi·e·tis′ti·cal,** *adj.* —**pi·e·tis′ti·cal·ly,** *adv.*

pi·e·ty (pī′i tē) *n., pl.* **-ties. 1.** reverence for God; religious devoutness; godliness. **2.** loyalty and obedience, as to one's parents. **3.** a pious act or belief. [Old French *piete* dutiful conduct, compassion, from Latin *pietās* dutiful conduct, devotion, kindness. Doublet of PITY.]

pi·e·zo·e·lec·tric·i·ty (pī ē′zō i lek tris′i tē) *n.* electricity produced on the opposite faces of certain crystals, as quartz or tourmaline, when they are subjected to stress. A variety of devices have been designed to operate on the principle of this phenomenon, as timepieces, microphones, oscillators, and phonograph cartridges. [Greek *piezein* to squeeze, press¹ + ELECTRICITY.] —**pi·e′zo·e·lec′tric,** *or,* **pi·e′zo·e·lec′tri·cal·ly,** *adv.*

pif·fle (pif′əl) *n. Informal.* foolish talk; nonsense. —*v.i.,* **-fled, -fling.** to talk or act in a foolish way. [Of uncertain origin.]

pig (pig) *n.* **1.** a hoofed mammal, genus *Sus,* esp. one of various breeds widely raised for food, typically having a stout, roundish body, short legs, and a blunt snout. Length: to 4 feet (1.2 meters). **2.** a young swine, esp. one weighing less than 120 pounds (54 kilograms). **3.** the flesh of a pig used as food; pork. **4.a.** an oblong mass of metal, esp. iron from a blast furnace, that has been cast in a mold. **b.** any mold used for casting such metal. **c.** pig iron. **5.** guinea pig. **6.** *Informal.* a person who is dirty, greedy, or very fat. [Probably from an unrecorded Old English word.]
  · **pig in a poke.** something that is offered for sale or bought without the buyer seeing it or knowing its real value.
  · **to pig out.** *Slang.* to eat too much or in large amounts; gorge.

pi·geon (pij′ən) *n.* **1.a.** any of numerous wild or domesticated birds, family Columbidae, native to temperate or tropical regions throughout the world, having a stout body, a small head, and thick, soft plumage. Certain smaller or medium-sized birds of this family are called doves. **b.** a blue and gray domesticated bird of this family, a variety of *Columba livia,* found commonly in cities and sometimes raised for food. **2.** *Slang.* a person who is easily cheated or fooled; dupe. [Old French *pijon* young bird, from Late Latin *pīpiō* squab, young chirping bird, from Latin *pīpīre* to chirp.]

pigeon breast, a chest with a projecting sternum, like that of a bird, often a result of rickets. —**pi′geon-breast′ed,** *adj.*

pigeon hawk, a falcon, *Falco columbarius,* that feeds on small birds. Also, **merlin.**

pi·geon·heart·ed (pij′ən här′tid) *adj.* easily frightened; timid.

pi·geon·hole (pij′ən hōl′) *n.* **1.** a small compartment, as in a cabinet or desk, for holding papers or other articles. **2.** a small hole or place for pigeons to nest in. —*v.t.,* **-holed, -hol·ing. 1.** to put into a small compartment or compartments; file: *to pigeonhole mail.* **2.** to lay aside or put away as if to forget or ignore until some future time; shelve: *The committee pigeonholed the project.* **3.** to put into a category; classify: *We pigeonholed them as troublemakers.*

pi·geon-toed (pij′ən tōd′) *adj.* having the toes or feet turned inward.

pig·ger·y (pig′ə rē) *n., pl.* **-ger·ies.** *British.* pigpen.

pig·gish (pig′ish) *adj.* like a pig in habits or manners, esp. in being greedy or dirty. —**pig′gish·ly,** *adv.* —**pig′gish·ness,** *n.*

pig·gy (pig′ē) *n., pl.* **-gies.** a little pig; piglet. —*adj.,* **-gi·er, -gi·est.** like a pig, esp. in habits or manners; piggish.

pig·gy·back (pig′ē bak′) *adv.* **1.** on the back or shoulders: *The father carried his daughter piggyback.* **2.** by or in truck trailers that are carried on railroad flatcars: *to transport goods piggyback.* —*adj.* **1.** on the back or shoulders: *a piggyback ride.* Also, **pickaback. 2.** of or relating to the carrying of one vehicle by another, as truck trailers by railroad flatcars or cars by specially designed trucks. **3.** attached to or carried by something larger or more important: *a piggyback provision in a law, piggyback cargo on a spacecraft.* —*v.t.* **1.** to carry on the back or shoulders. **2.** to transport piggyback. **3.** to attach to something larger or more important: *to piggyback an increase in the minimum wage on a tax bill.* —*v.i.* **1.** to transport truck trailers on railroad flatcars. **2.** to be attached to or carried by something larger or more important.

piggy bank, a small bank, often in the shape of a pig, used esp. by children for saving coins.

pig·head·ed (pig′hed′id) *adj.* unreasonably obstinate; stubborn: *a pigheaded person, a pigheaded refusal.* —**pig′head′ed·ly,** *adv.* —**pig′head′ed·ness,** *n.*

pig iron, iron from which the impurities have been removed in a blast furnace, used to make commercial iron or steel.

pig Latin, a code language used esp. by children, in which the first consonant or group of consonants in each word is placed at the end of the word and followed by -ay, as *irlgay* for *girl.*

pig·let (pig′lit) *n.* a little pig, esp. a baby pig.

pig·ment (pig′mənt) *n.* **1.** a substance used for coloring, esp. a powdered substance that is mixed with a liquid to produce a paint

or dye. **2.** any substance, as melanin or chlorophyll, that is the coloring matter of animal or plant tissues. —*v.t.* to color by adding pigment to. [Latin *pigmentum* substance used for coloring, paint. Doublet of PIMENTO.] —**pig′men·tar′y,** *adj.*

pig·men·ta·tion (pig′mən tā′shən) *n.* **1.** the coloration in plant or animal tissues caused by pigment. **2.** the deposition of pigment in plant or animal tissues.

Pig·my (pig′mē) *n., pl.* **-mies.** Pygmy.

pig·nut (pig′nut′) *n.* **1.** the small brown nut of either of two North American hickory trees of the genus *Carya.* **2.** the trees that produce this nut, having a strong, tough wood, used in making tool handles, as a fuel, and for smoking meats. **3.** the edible tuberous root of an herb, *Conopodium majus,* of the parsley family.

pig·pen (pig′pen′) *n.* **1.** a pen for pigs. **2.** a dirty or messy place. Also, **pigsty.**

pig·skin (pig′skin′) *n.* **1.** the skin of a pig. **2.** leather made of this. **3.** *Informal.* football *(def. 1b).*

pig·sty (pig′stī′) *n., pl.* **-sties.** pigpen.

pig·tail (pig′tāl′) *n.* **1.** hair that has been pulled and fastened or braided so as to hang down the back or from either side of the head. **2.** tobacco twisted into a thin rope.

pig·weed (pig′wēd′) *n.* **1.** goosefoot. **2.** any of several weedy plants, genus *Amaranthus,* sometimes used as salad greens.

pi·ka (pī′kə) *n.* any of various rabbitlike mammals, genus *Ochotona,* native to mountain ranges of western North America and Eurasia, having a gray or buff-colored coat. Length: 6 inches (15 centimeters). Also, **cony.**

pike¹ (pīk) *n.* a weapon consisting of a long wooden shaft with a pointed tip of iron or steel, formerly used by foot soldiers. [Old French *pique,* from *piquer* to prick, pierce, probably going back to Latin *picus* woodpecker.]

pike² (pīk) *n.* a sharp point, as the tip of a spear. [Old English *pīc;* possibly of Celtic origin.]

pike³ (pīk) *n.* **1.** a large, carnivorous, freshwater game and food fish, *Esox lucius,* found in Europe, Asia, and northern North America, having a slim, tapering, olive-green body, with a duck-billed snout and many sharp teeth. Length: to over 4 feet (1.2 meters). **2.** any of several related fish, as the pickerel, or similar fish of the perch group, as the walleye. [Possibly from PIKE²; referring to the pointed shape of the head.]

pike⁴ (pīk) *n.* turnpike.

pike·man (pīk′mən) *n., pl.* **-men** (-mən). a soldier armed with a pike.

pike perch, any of several perches superficially resembling pikes, as the sauger and walleye.

pik·er (pī′kər) *n. Slang.* a person who is miserly, overly cautious, or petty, esp. in dealings with others. [Of uncertain origin.]

pike·staff (pīk′staf′) *n., pl.* **-staves** (-stāvz′). **1.** the shaft of a pike. **2.** a walking stick with a metal tip at the lower end, used by walkers.

pi·laf (pi läf′, pē′läf) *also,* **pi·laff.** *n.* a dish of Middle Eastern origin that consists mainly of rice boiled with meat or fish and seasoned with spices. Also, **pi·lau, pi·law** (pi läf′, pē′läf, pi lô′, pē′lô). [Persian *pilāw.*]

pi·las·ter (pi las′tər) *n.* a rectangular column projecting slightly from a wall. [French *pilastre,* from Italian *pilastro,* going back to Latin *pīla* pillar.]

pil·chard (pil′chərd) *n.* any of several small, herringlike fish of the family Clupeidae, found in ocean waters in the temperate zones, as the **Pacific pilchard,** *Sardinops caerulea.* [Of uncertain origin.]

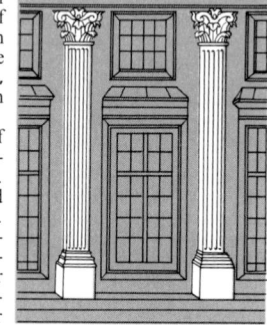

pilasters

pile¹ (pīl) *n.* **1.a.** a number of things laid or lying one upon another; heap: *a pile of newspapers.* **b.** a quantity of material heaped together; mound: *a pile of dirt.* **2.** a heap of wood or other material on which a dead body or sacrifice is burned; pyre. **3.** a high or large building or group of buildings. **4.** *Informal.* a large mass or quantity: *a pile of troubles, a pile of work.* **5.** *Informal.* a large amount of money; fortune: *He made his pile in the stock market.* **6.** nuclear reactor. **7.** voltaic pile. —*v.,* **piled, pil·ing.** —*v.t.* **1.** to form into a heap or mass (often with *up*): *She piled the fallen leaves in a corner of the yard.* **2.** to amass; accumulate (often with *up*): *to pile up debts.* **3.** to cover or load with a pile: *to pile a wagon with hay.* **4.** to heap a large quantity of: *to pile books on a desk.* —*v.i.* **1.** to form or rise in a heap or mass: *The snow piled in drifts.* **2.** to accumulate

(often with *up*): *The evidence piled up against them.* **3.** *Informal.* to move in a confused or disorderly mass; crowd: *to pile into a car, to pile out of an elevator.* **4.** to move violently; crash (with *into*): *The truck skidded and piled into the car ahead of it.* [Old French *pile* heap, from Latin *pīla* pillar.]

pile² (pīl) *n.* a strong, slender beam of wood, steel, or concrete, driven vertically into the ground to support a structure, as a bridge or wharf. —*v.t.*, **piled, pil·ing. 1.** to furnish or support with piles. **2.** to drive piles into. [Old English *pīl* pointed stick, from Latin *pīlum* javelin.]

pile³ (pīl) *n.* **1.** the raised cut or uncut loops of yarn that form the surface of a fabric, as velvet, or of a carpet. **2.** fine, soft hair or fiber. [Latin *pilus* hair.]

pi·le·ate (pī′lē it) *also,* **pi·le·a·ted** (pī′lē ā′tid). *adj.* **1.** *Botany.* having a pileus. **2.** *Zoology.* having a crest covering the top of the head from the bill to the nape, as certain woodpeckers. [Latin *pileatus* wearing a felt cap, from *pileus* felt cap.]

pi·le·at·ed woodpecker (pī′lē ā′tid, pil′ē-) a large black-and-white North American woodpecker, *Dryocopus pileatus*, with a marked red crest, which does not extend all the way to the bill in the female. Length: 16 inches (41 centimeters).

pile driver, a machine for driving piles into the ground, usually consisting of a frame in which a heavy weight is lifted and then dropped on the pile or in which a steam- or air-driven hammer pounds the pile.

piles (pīlz) *pl. n.* hemorrhoids. [Latin *pila* ball; referring to the shape.]

pile·up (pīl′up′) *n.* **1.** an accumulation: *There was quite a pileup of work during my illness.* **2.** a traffic accident involving several vehicles.

pi·le·us (pī′lē əs) *n.* the umbrella-shaped cap or fruiting structure of certain fungi, as the mushroom. [Latin *pileus* felt cap, from Greek *pilos*.]

pil·fer (pil′fər) *v.t., v.i.* to steal in small quantities. [Old French *pelfrer*, from *pelfre* booty. See PELF.] —**pil′fer·age,** *n.* —**pil′fer·er,** *n.* —For Synonyms, see **steal.**

pil·grim (pil′grəm) *n.* **1.** a person who travels to a sacred place for a religious purpose, as for penance or devotion. **2.** any traveler. **3. Pilgrim.** one of the group of English Puritans that founded Plymouth Colony in 1620. [Old French *peligrin, pelerin* one who travels to a sacred place for penance or religious devotion, going back to Latin *peregrīnus* foreigner, foreign; with reference to a pilgrim's wandering away from home.]

pil·grim·age (pil′grə mij) *n.* **1.** a journey to a sacred place for a religious purpose, as for penance or devotion. **2.** a long journey, esp. to a place regarded as having spiritual or cultural significance: *a pilgrimage to the museums of Europe.*

pil·ing (pī′ling) *n.* piles collectively or a structure composed of piles.

pill (pil) *n.* **1.** a pellet of medicine that is swallowed whole or chewed; tablet, capsule, or the like. **2.** something that is disagreeable but must be endured: *The loss of the election was a bitter pill for the party.* **3.** *Slang.* a disagreeable, difficult, or boring person. **4. the pill.** an oral contraceptive. —*v.i.* to form into balls, as fuzz on a sweater; ball. [Latin *pilula* small ball, pellet of medicine, diminutive of *pila* ball.]

pil·lage (pil′ij) *v.*, **-laged, -lag·ing.** —*v.t.* **1.** to rob by force, as during a war; plunder: *to pillage a town.* **2.** to carry off as booty: *to pillage valuables.* —*v.i.* to take booty. —*n.* **1.** the act of plundering. **2.** something carried off as booty; plunder. [Old French *pillage* plunder, from *piller* to plunder, going back to Late Latin *pilleus* rag, from Latin *pilleus* cap of felt.] —**pil′lag·er,** *n.*

pil·lar (pil′ər) *n.* **1.** a detached, upright structure that supports a building or stands alone as a monument. **2.** something resembling a pillar in shape or function. **3.** a person who is a chief supporter or important member of something, as an institution: *a pillar of society.* [Old French *pil(i)er* column, vertical support for a building, going back to Latin *pīla* column.]

· **from pillar to post. a.** aimlessly from one place or situation to another. **b.** from one predicament or misfortune to another.

pill·box (pil′boks′) *n.* **1.** a small box for pills. **2.** a small, low, concrete gun emplacement. **3.** a small cylindrical woman's hat without a brim and with a flat top.

pill bug, any of a group of small, land-dwelling crustaceans, family Armadillidae, related to wood lice, that roll up in a ball when disturbed. [Because they look like small pills when rolled up.]

pil·lion (pil′yən) *n.* a pad or cushion attached behind the saddle of a horse or the seat of a motorcycle for another rider. [Scottish Gaelic *pillean* cushion, diminutive of *peall* skin, from Latin *pellis.*]

pil·lo·ry (pil′ə rē) *n., pl.* **-ries.** a wooden frame fitted with openings to hold the head and hands, formerly used to expose a person to public ridicule as punishment for an offense. —*v.t.*, **-ried, -ry·ing. 1.** to put in a pillory. **2.** to expose to public

ridicule or abuse: *The newspapers pilloried the corrupt politician.* [Old French *pilori* the wooden frame; of uncertain origin.]

pil·low (pil′ō) *n.* **1.** a bag or casing filled with soft or flexible material, as feathers, down, or foam rubber, used to support a part of the body, esp. the head of a reclining person. **2.** something resembling a pillow in shape or function, as a pad on which bobbin lace is made. —*v.t.* **1.** to rest (something) on or as on a pillow: *He pillowed his head on his hand.* **2.** to serve as a pillow for: *Her arm pillowed the baby's head.* [Old English *pyle, pylu* cushion for the head, going back to Latin *pulvīnus.*] —**pil′low·y,** *adj.*

pil·low·case (pil′ō kās′) *n.* a removable cover, usually of cloth, for a pillow. Also, **pil·low·slip** (pil′ō slip′).

pillow lace, bobbin lace.

pi·lose (pī′lōs) *adj.* covered with fine or soft hair. [Latin *pilōsus* hairy, from *pilus* hair.] —**pi·los·i·ty** (pī los′i tē), *n.*

pi·lot (pī′lət) *n.* **1.** a person who operates the flight controls of an aircraft or spacecraft. **2.** a person who steers a ship, esp. in coastal waters or into or out of a harbor. **3.** any person who guides or leads. **4.** pilot light. **5.** a television program made as a test for a proposed series of programs. **6.** cowcatcher. —*v.t.* **1.** to act as the pilot of; steer. **2.** guide. —*adj.* preliminary, trial, or sample: *a pilot study.* [French *pilote* steersman, from Italian *pilota,* form of obsolete Italian *pedota,* going back to Greek *pēdon* rudder.]

PILOT (pī′lət) *n.* a computer language designed for beginners, esp. for use in the classroom.

pi·lot·age (pī′lə tij) *n.* **1.** the act of piloting. **2.** a fee paid to a pilot. **3.** navigation of a ship or aircraft by observation of landmarks.

pilot biscuit, hardtack. Also, **pilot bread.**

pilot fish, *also,* **pi·lot·fish** (pī′lət fish′). a small fish, *Naucrates ductor,* found in temperate seas, that usually swims alongside sharks or other large fish to feed on leftover scraps of their food.

pi·lot·house (pī′lət hous′) *n., pl.* **-hous·es** (-hou′ziz). an enclosed structure on the deck of a ship that shelters the steering equipment and the pilot. Also, **wheelhouse.**

pilot lamp, a small lamp that indicates that a circuit or motor is in operation.

pilot light 1. a small flame kept burning so as to light a gas burner when it is turned on, as in a gas stove. **2.** pilot lamp.

Pilt·down man (pilt′doun′) a hypothetical primitive human species whose existence was presumed from remains that were discovered in Piltdown, England, around 1911, but in 1953 were shown to be a hoax.

Pi·ma (pē′mə) *n., pl.* **-ma** or **-mas. 1.** a member of a tribe of American Indians living in southern Arizona. **2.** the language spoken by the Pima, belonging to the Uto-Aztecan language family. —**Pi′man,** *adj.*

Pima cotton, a variety of strong, fine cotton developed from Egyptian cotton, grown in the southwestern United States.

pi·men·to (pi men′tō) *n., pl.* **-tos. 1.** an evergreen tree, *Pimenta dioica,* of the myrtle family, from which allspice is derived. **2.** pimiento. [Spanish *pimiento* capsicum, from Medieval Latin *pigmentum* spice, from Late Latin *pigmentum* juice of plants, from Latin *pigmentum* substance used for coloring. Doublet of PIGMENT.]

pi meson, pion.

pi·mien·to (pi myen′tō, -men′tō) *also,* **pimento.** *n., pl.* **-tos.** a mild, sweet red pepper used as a garnish or as a stuffing for olives. [Spanish *pimiento* capsicum. See PIMENTO.]

pimp (pimp) *n.* a person, esp. a man, who solicits customers for a prostitute or prostitutes and often receives a share of their payments in return; procurer. —*v.i.* to act as a pimp. [Of uncertain origin.]

pim·per·nel (pim′pər nel′, -pər nəl) *n.* **1.** the small, bell-shaped, scarlet, purple, or white flower of any of a group of plants, genus *Anagallis,* of the primrose family, esp. the **scarlet pimpernel,** *A. arvensis.* **2.** the plant bearing this flower. [Old French *pimpernelle* the plant, going back to Latin *piper* pepper plant; referring to the resemblance of its fruit to that of the pepper plant. See PEPPER.]

pim·ple (pim′pəl) *n.* a small, inflamed swelling of the skin, often containing pus. [Of uncertain origin.] —**pim′pled, pim′ply,** *adj.*

pin (pin) *n.* **1.** a short, straight, stiff piece of wire with a point at one end and a head at the other, used to fasten or attach things. **2.** an ornament or emblem that has a pin or clasp for attaching it to clothing: *a fraternity pin.* **3.** a peg of wood, plastic, or metal

a	at	e	end	o	hot	u	up	hw	white	(	about
ā	ape	ē	me	ō	old	ū	use	ng	song		taken
ä	far	i	it	ô	fork	ü	rule	th	thin	ə	pencil
âr	care	ī	ice	oi	oil	u̇	pull	th	this		lemon
		îr	pierce	ou	out	ûr	turn	zh	measure	(	circus

P

used for various purposes, as to fasten things together, hold something in place, or hang something on. **4.** anything like a pin in form or use, as a safety pin, a clothespin, a hairpin, a bobby pin, or a cotter pin. **5.** a long, thin piece of metal used to join the ends of a broken bone. **6.** *Bowling.* any of the usually bottle-shaped pieces set up as a target to be knocked down by the ball. **7.** *Wrestling.* the act of forcing an opponent's shoulder to the mat for a specified length of time; fall. **8.** *Nautical.* **a.** thole. **b.** belaying pin. **9.** *Music.* peg *(def. 2).* **10.** *Golf.* the staff of the pennant that marks the hole on a green. **11.** something very small or of little value or significance; trifle: *not worth a pin.* **12. pins.** *Informal.* legs. —*v.t.,* **pinned, pin·ning. 1.** to fasten or attach with or as with a pin or pins: *She pinned her hopes on going to medical school.* **2.** to hold fast in one spot or position: *The fighter pinned his opponent against the ropes.* **3.** *Wrestling.* to force the shoulders of (an opponent) to touch the mat for a specified length of time. [Old English *pinn* peg.]
　•**to pin down. a.** to get or force (someone) to make a decision or commitment. **b.** to fix or establish clearly: *to pin down the source of a quotation.*
　•**to pin (something) on (someone).** *Slang.* to place the blame for (something) on (someone): *The police tried to pin the burglary on a former servant.*
pin·a·fore (pin′ə fôr′) *n.* a garment resembling an apron, covering most of a dress, worn esp. by young girls. [PIN + AFORE; referring to the fact that it was formerly pinned on the front of a dress.]
pi·ña·ta (pēn yä′tə) *also,* **pi·na·ta.** *n.* a colorfully decorated container, originally used in Latin-American Christmas and birthday celebrations, that is filled with fruit, candy, and gifts and hung from the ceiling to be broken with a stick by a child who is blindfolded. [Spanish *piñata* literally, pot, jug.]
pin·ball (pin′bôl′) *n.* a game played on a machine in which the player uses a spring to drive a steel ball onto a slanted board, where it scores points by hitting pins or other targets that record the score electronically.
pinball machine, a machine for playing pinball, often used for gambling.
pince-nez (pans′nā′, pins′-) *n., pl.* **pince·nez.** eyeglasses held on the nose by a spring. [French *pince-nez,* from *pincer* to nip (of uncertain origin) + *nez* nose (from Latin *nāsus).*]
pin·cers (pin′sərz, -chərz) *also,* **pinchers.** *pl. n.* **1.** a gripping implement having a pair of jaws and handles that are fastened on a pivot. **2.** a grasping claw, as of a crab or lobster, resembling this. [From an unrecorded Old French word, from Old French *pincier* to nip. See PINCH.]
pinch (pinch) *v.t.* **1.** to squeeze between two surfaces or edges, as between the forefinger and thumb. **2.** to press or squeeze painfully: *His new shoes pinched his toes.* **3.** to afflict with physical or mental hardship: *to be pinched by poverty.* **4.** to make haggard or wrinkled: *Her face was pinched with grief.* **5.** to subject to severe restrictions; limit greatly: *Paying all our debts pinched us for a while.* **6.** *Slang.* to steal. **7.** *Slang.* to arrest. **8.** to remove the buds from (a plant or shoot), esp. to increase branching or bud development (usually with *off* or *back*): *to pinch back chrysanthemums.* —*v.i.* **1.** to press or squeeze painfully; hurt. **2.** to be frugal or miserly: *The young couple pinched and saved in order to buy a house.* —*n.* **1.** the act of pinching. **2.** the quantity that can be taken up between the forefinger and thumb; very small amount: *Add a pinch of salt.* **3.** a physical or mental hardship: *Everyone felt the pinch of the new taxes.* **4.** a time of stress or need; emergency: *I can loan you money in a pinch.* **5.** *Slang.* theft. **6.** *Slang.* arrest. [Old French *pincier* to nip; of uncertain origin.]
　•**to pinch pennies.** to be frugal; manage economically.
pinch bar, a crowbar with a pointed end, used as a lever, esp. to move heavy objects.
pinch·beck (pinch′bek′) *n.* **1.** an alloy of zinc and copper, used in cheap imitation gold. **2.** something counterfeit or imitative. —*adj.* **1.** made of pinchbeck. **2.** not genuine; counterfeit; imitative. [From Christopher *Pinchbeck,* died 1732, English watchmaker who invented the alloy.]
pinch·cock (pinch′kok′) *n.* a clamp attached to a flexible tube to regulate the flow of fluid through the tube. [PINCH + COCK¹.]
pinch·er (pin′chər) *n.* **1.** a person or thing that pinches. **2. pinchers.** pincers.
pinch·hit (pinch′hit′) *v.i.,* **-hit, -hit·ting. 1.** *Baseball.* to bat in place of another player. **2.** to take someone's place; be a substitute. —**pinch hitter.**
pin·cush·ion (pin′kŭsh′ən) *n.* a small cushion into which pins and needles are stuck until needed.
Pin·dar·ic (pin dar′ik) *adj.* of, relating to, or characteristic of the style of the Greek lyric poet Pindar.
Pindaric ode, an ode composed in a series of triads, each triad consisting of three stanzas: the strophe, antistrophe, and epode.

pine¹ (pīn) *n.* **1.** any of a large group of evergreen trees, genus *Pinus,* found in all temperate regions of the world, bearing cones and needlelike leaves. **2.** the wood of this tree, widely used in building and as a source of turpentine. —*adj.* designating a widely distributed family of trees and shrubs often bearing needle-like leaves and male and female cones and including larches, hemlocks, pines, and spruces. [Old English *pīn* the tree, from Latin *pīnus.*]
pine² (pīn) *v.i.,* **pined, pin·ing. 1.** to long intensely; yearn: *The exiles pined for their homeland.* **2.** to become unhealthy, as from grief or longing (usually with *away*): *After its owner's death, the old dog pined away.* [Old English *pīnian* to torment, going back to Latin *poena* penalty, from Greek *poinē.*]
pin·e·al (pin′ē əl) *adj.* **1.** shaped like a pine cone. **2.** of or relating to the pineal body.
pineal body, a small organ in the brain of vertebrates. Its function in humans is not fully determined, but in lower mammals it serves as an endocrine gland, secreting hormones that influence reproduction. Also, **epiphysis, pineal gland.**
pine·ap·ple (pīn′ap′əl) *n.* **1.** the large, oval, edible fruit of a tropical American plant, *Ananas comosus,* having firm, juicy, yellow flesh and a hard, scaly, reddish outer covering with a crown of stiff, narrow leaves. **2.** the plant bearing this fruit, having jagged-edged leaves and clusters of reddish or violet flowers. [PINE¹ + APPLE.]
pine cone, the fruit of the pine tree, covered with hard, overlapping scales.
pine needle, the slender, usually very small, needlelike leaf of a pine tree.
pine nut, the edible seed found in the cone of any of several pine trees, as the piñon.
pine tar, a substance prepared by the destructive distillation of pine wood, used in paints and varnishes and in medicines for treating skin diseases.
pine·y (pī′nē) *adj.,* **pin·i·er, pin·i·est.** piny.
pin·feath·er (pin′feth′ər) *n.* an undeveloped feather, esp. one that is just beginning to break through the skin.
pin·fold (pin′fōld′) *n.* a place in which stray animals are penned. [Old English *pundfald* pound³.]
ping (ping) *n.* a sudden, high-pitched sound, as of a bullet striking a metal surface. —*v.i.* to produce a ping. [Imitative.]
Ping-Pong (ping′pong′, -pông′) *n. Trademark.* table tennis. [Imitative.]
pin·head (pin′hed′) *n.* **1.** the head of a pin. **2.** something of very small size or value. **3.** *Informal.* a stupid person.
pin·hole (pin′hōl′) *n.* a tiny hole made by or as by a pin.
pin·ion¹ (pin′yən) *n.* **1.** the last segment of a bird's wing, including the carpus, metacarpus, and phalanges. **2.** the wing of a bird. **3.** a feather; quill. —*v.t.* **1.** to prevent (a bird) from flying by cutting off the pinions or binding the wings. **2.** to cut off the pinions of or bind (the wings). **3.** to bind or hold firmly: *to pinion someone's arms.* **4.** to restrain or confine by binding the arms of: *The police pinioned the suspect with handcuffs.* [Old French *pignon* feather, wing, going back to Latin *pinna.*]
pin·ion² (pin′yən) *n.* a small cogwheel that engages a larger cogwheel or rack and transmits motion to it. [French *pignon* cogwheel; earlier, battlement, going back to Latin *pinna* wing, pinnacle.]
pink¹ (pingk) *n.* **1.** a light red color. **2.** the most perfect condition or highest degree: *in the pink of health.* **3.a.** the showy, fragrant flower of any of a group of plants, genus *Dianthus,* having five or more petals that are often fringed, as the carnation. **b.** the plant bearing this flower, having grayish green leaves. **4.** *Informal.* a person who holds moderately leftist political or economic views. ➡ used disparagingly. —*adj.* **1.** having the color pink. **2.** *Informal.* holding moderately leftist political or economic views. ➡ used disparagingly. **3.** designating a family, Caryophyllaceae, of widely distributed plants, many of which are cultivated for their flowers, as the carnation, sweet william, and baby's breath. [Of uncertain origin.]

Pinion

pinion²

pink² (pingk) *v.t.* **1.** to pierce slightly or stab with a sharp, pointed weapon, as a sword. **2.** to cut and finish the edge of (fabric) with a series of small notches, esp. with pinking shears. **3.** to ornament (cloth, paper, or the like) with a pattern of small holes. [Possibly of Low German origin.]
pink·eye (pingk′ī′) *n. Medicine.* an acute form of conjunctivitis that is highly contagious.
pink·ie (ping′kē) *also,* **pinky.** *n., pl.* **pink·ies.** *Informal.* the smallest finger on each hand.
pinking shears, scissors having notched blades, used to pink fabric.

pink·ish (ping′kish) *adj.* somewhat pink: *The sky took on a pinkish hue at sunset.*

pink·o (ping′kō) *n., pl.* **-os** or **-oes**. *Slang.* pink¹ (*def.* 4).

pink slip *Informal.* a notice of dismissal given to an employee.

pink·y (ping′kē) *n., pl.* **pink·ies**. pinkie.

pin money, a small sum of money for minor expenses or purchases, originally an allowance given by a man to his wife for her personal expenses.

pin·na (pin′ə) *n., pl.* **pin·nae** (pin′ē) or **pin·nas**. **1.** a feather, wing, fin, or winglike part. **2.** the cartilaginous part of the external ear that protrudes from the skull. **3.** one of the primary divisions of a pinnate leaf; leaflet. [Latin *pinna* feather, wing, fin.]

pin·nace (pin′is) *n.* **1.** a small boat, usually schooner-rigged with two masts, formerly attending a larger vessel. **2.** any of various ships' boats. [French *pinasse* small boat, from Italian *pinaccia,* going back to Latin *pīnus* pine¹; because it was originally made of pine wood.]

pin·na·cle (pin′ə kəl) *n.* **1.** a high, pointed formation, as a mountain peak. **2.** the highest point; peak: *the pinnacle of success.* **3.** *Architecture.* a small, vertical structure, usually set above a buttress or parapet. —*v.t.* **-cled, -cling**. **1.** to put on or as on a pinnacle. **2.** to furnish with a pinnacle or pinnacles. [Late Latin *pinnāculum* peak of a building, diminutive of *pinna* peak, from Latin *pinna* feather, wing.] —For Synonyms, see **peak**.

pin·nate (pin′āt) *adj.* **1.** resembling a feather in shape or structure. **2.** of a compound leaf, having leaflets on both sides of a stalk. [Latin *pinnātus* feathered, winged, from *pinna* feather, wing.] —**pin′nate·ly**, *adv.*

pin·ni·ped (pin′ə ped′) *adj.* belonging to the Pinnipedia, an order of carnivorous mammals having limbs shaped like fins or flippers, comprising seals, sea lions, and walruses. —*n.* a pinniped mammal. [Modern Latin *pinnipedia,* from Latin *pinnapes, pinnipes* having winged feet, from *pinna* feather, wing + *pēs* foot.]

pinnacle
(def. 3)

pin·nule (pin′ūl) *n.* **1.** *Botany.* any of the smallest divisions of a doubly compound leaf, esp. in fern fronds. **2.** *Zoology.* any of the slender, side extensions branching from the upward-reaching rays of crinoids. [Modern Latin *pinnula,* from Latin *pinnula,* diminutive of *pinna* feather, wing.]

pi·noch·le (pē′nuk′əl, -nok′-) *also,* **pi·noc·le**. *n.* **1.** a game played with a special deck of forty-eight cards consisting of two of the ace, king, queen, jack, ten, and nine in each suit. Players score points by taking tricks and putting together particular combinations of cards. **2.** the combination of the jack of diamonds and the queen of spades in this game. [Of uncertain origin.]

pin·o·cy·to·sis (pin′ə sī tō′sis) *n., pl.* **-ses** (-sēz). the process by which a living cell engulfs a drop of liquid and then ingests it. —**pin·o·cyt·ic** (pin′ə sit′ik), **pin·o·cy·tot·ic** (pin′ə sī tot′ik), *adj.*

pi·ñon (pin′yon, pēn yōn′) *also,* **pinyon**. *n.* **1.** any of several small, evergreen pine trees, genus *Pinus,* found in the southwestern United States. **2.** the edible nut of this tree; pine nut. [Spanish *piñon* pine nut, from *piña* pine nut, pine cone, from Latin *pīnea.*]

pin·point (pin′point′) *v.t.* **1.** to locate or identify precisely: *to pinpoint a source of trouble.* **2.** to aim at with great accuracy: *to pinpoint a target.* —*adj.* strict; exact: *pinpoint accuracy.* —*n.* **1.** the point of a pin. **2.** something very small or insignificant: *a pinpoint of light.*

pin·prick (pin′prik′) *n.* **1.** a small puncture made by a pin. **2.** a small irritation or annoyance.

pins and needles, a tingling, prickling sensation in a part of the body recovering from numbness.

 • **on pins and needles.** in a state of nervous or anxious anticipation.

pin·stripe (pin′strīp′) *n.* **1.** a very narrow stripe on a fabric. **2.** fabric or an article of clothing having such stripes.

pint (pīnt) *n.* **1.** a unit of liquid measure equal to ½ of a quart or ⅛ of a gallon (473 milliliters). **2.** a unit of dry measure equal to ½ of a quart or 1/16 of a peck (551 milliliters). **3.** an apothecaries' measure of fluid equal to 16 fluid ounces of ½ of a quart. **4.** a container that holds a pint. [Old French *pinte* old measure of capacity; of uncertain origin.]

pin·ta (pin′tə) *n.* an infectious disease found predominantly in Latin America, characterized by sores and patches of discoloration on the skin. [Spanish *pinta* spot, mark, going back to Latin *picta,* feminine of *pictus.* See PINTO.]

Pin·ta (pin′tə) one of the three ships of the Italian explorer Christopher Columbus on his first voyage to the New World, in 1492.

pin·tail (pin′tāl′) *n., pl.* **-tail** or **-tails**. **1.** a long-necked duck,

Anas acuta, having long, pointed central tail feathers. Length: 25-30 inches (64-76 centimeters), including tail. **2.** a North American grouse, *Pedioecetes phasianellus,* having a long, pointed tail.

pin·to (pin′tō) *adj.* having spots or patches, esp. of two colors; mottled; piebald. —*n., pl.* **-tos**. **1.** a pinto horse or pony. **2.** pinto bean. [Obsolete Spanish *pinto* spotted, going back to Latin *pictus,* past participle of *pingere* to paint.]

pinto bean, a variety of kidney bean noted for its mottled seeds, grown in the western United States.

pin·up (pin′up′) *n.* **1.** a large photograph that can be fastened to a wall, esp. one of a very attractive person. **2.** a person pictured in a pinup. —*adj.* **1.** of, relating to, or pictured in a pinup: *a pinup model.* **2.** designed to be fastened to a wall: *a pinup lamp.*

pin·wheel (pin′hwēl′, -wēl′) *n.* **1.** a toy made of curved strips of paper or plastic pinned to a stick so as to revolve when spun by hand or blown upon. **2.** a firework supported by a pin upon which it revolves when lighted.

pin·worm (pin′wûrm′) *n.* a small, white, threadlike roundworm, *Enterobius vermicularis,* infesting the lower intestinal tract, esp. of children.

pin·y (pī′nē) *also,* **piney**. *adj.,* **pin·i·er, pin·i·est**. **1.** of, relating to, or suggestive of pine trees. **2.** covered with or abounding in pine trees.

Pin·yin (pin′yin′) *n.* a system for transliterating Chinese words into the Latin alphabet. [Chinese *pinyin* transliteration.]

pin·yon (pin′yən, pēn yōn′) *n.* piñon. [Anglicized respelling of PIÑON.]

pi·on (pī′on) *n.* a subatomic particle of the meson group. Also, **pi meson**. [Contraction of PI MESON.]

pi·o·neer (pī′ə nîr′) *n.* **1.** a person who is first or among the first to explore or settle a region. **2.** a person who is first or among the first to open up or develop an area of thought, research, or activity: *a pioneer in psychiatry.* —*v.t.* **1.** to explore or settle: *Settlers from the East pioneered the Northwest Territory.* **2.** to open up or develop. —*v.i.* to be a pioneer: *American industry pioneered in the development of mass production.* [French *pionnier* settler of previously unsettled land, soldier who goes ahead to clear the way for an army, from Old French *peon* foot soldier, from Medieval Latin *pedo,* from Latin *pēs* foot.]

pi·ous (pī′əs) *adj.* **1.** having reverence for God; devoutly religious: *a pious family.* **2.** of, relating to, or resulting from religious devotion: *pious writings.* **3.** characterized by a false or hypocritical religious devoutness. **4.** showing loyalty to or reverence for one's parents, friends, or the like. [Latin *pius* devout, dutiful.] —**pi′ous·ly**, *adv.* —**pi′ous·ness**, *n.*

Synonyms **Pious, devout,** and **religious** mean having a sincere dedication to religion. **Pious** emphasizes the faithful performance of religious obligations, esp. the outward acts of worship: *The more pious members of the congregation attend services every day.* **Devout** stresses inward devotion to one's God and the tenets of one's religion: *to lead a quietly devout life.* **Religious,** a more general term, implies belief in a religion or adherence to the way of life sanctioned by a religion: *The religious couple brought up their children in the faith.*

pip¹ (pip) *n.* **1.** the seed of a fruit, as an apple or orange. **2.** *Slang.* a person or thing that is excellent: *You sure are a pip!* [Short for PIPPIN.]

pip² (pip) *n.* a contagious disease of poultry and other birds, characterized by the secretion of thick mucus in the mouth and throat or the formation of a scale on the tongue. [Middle Dutch *pippe* the disease of birds, slime, going back to Latin *pītuīta* phlegm.]

pip³ (pip) *n.* **1.** any of the spots or marks on dominoes, dice, or playing cards. **2.** a rhizome of various flowering plants, esp. the lily of the valley. **3.** one of the small, diamond-shaped segments on the surface of a pineapple. [Of uncertain origin.]

pip⁴ (pip) *v.,* **pipped, pip·ping**. —*v.i.* to peep. —*v.t.* to break through (an eggshell), as a chick when hatching. [Form of PEEP².]

pip⁵ (pip) *n.* blip. [Imitative.]

pipe (pīp) *n.* **1.** a hollow cylinder for carrying a gas or liquid; tube. **2.a.** a tube with a bowl made of briar, clay, or other material at one end, used for smoking. **b.** the amount of tobacco that fills the bowl of a pipe. **3.** a wind instrument, as a flute. **4.** one of the tubes in an organ in which tones are produced. **5. pipes. a.** an instrument consisting of a series of tubes bound together; panpipe. **b.** bagpipe. **6.a. pipes.** the vocal cords or voice, esp. when used in singing. **b.** the song or note of a bird.

a	at	e	end	o	hot	u	up	hw	white		about
ā	ape	ē	me	ō	old	ū	use	ng	song	ə	taken
ä	far	i	it	ô	fork	ü	rule	th	thin		pencil
âr	care	ī	ice	oi	oil	u̇	pull	th	this		lemon
		îr	pierce	ou	out	ûr	turn	zh	measure		circus

P

7. any natural formation resembling a tube, as a cylindrical passage opening into the crater of a volcano. **8.** a boatswain's whistle. **9.a.** a cask for wine holding 126 gallons (477 liters). **b.** a unit of measure equivalent to this. —*v.t.* **1.** to convey by means of a pipe or pipes: *to pipe water.* **2.** to supply with pipes: *to pipe a new house for gas.* **3.** to play (music) on a pipe. **4.** to say or sing in a loud, shrill voice. **5.** to summon by sounding a boatswain's whistle: *The boatswain piped all hands on deck.* **6.** to finish or trim (fabric) with piping. **7.** to transmit by electric wire or cable. —*v.i.* **1.** to make a loud, shrill sound. **2.** to play on a pipe. **3.** to summon the crew or give orders by sounding a boatswain's whistle. [Old English *pīpe* tube, musical wind instrument, going back to Latin *pīpāre* to chirp.]

· **to pipe down.** *Slang.* to be quiet.

· **to pipe up. a.** to begin to play, sing, or speak, esp. in a loud, shrill voice. **b.** to speak out in an assertive way.

pipe cleaner, a tufted wire used esp. to clean the stem of a tobacco pipe.

pipe dream, a vain or fanciful notion or wish.

pipe·fish (pīp′fish′) *n., pl.* **-fish** or **-fishes.** any of various small to medium-size, slender, elongate marine fish, family Syngnathidae, related to sea horses and with a similar tubelike snout.

pipe fitter, a person who installs and repairs pipe systems.

pipe fitting 1. a piece, as a coupling or elbow, used to connect pipes in a pipe system. **2.** the work done by a pipe fitter.

pipe·ful (pīp′fůl′) *n., pl.* **-fuls.** the amount of tobacco sufficient to fill the bowl of a pipe.

pipe·line (pīp′līn′) *n.* **1.** a line of pipes for carrying a gas or liquid. **2.** a route by which information or supplies are carried, often secretly: *Party leaders have a direct pipeline to the governor's office. The stolen goods were smuggled out of the country through an elaborate pipeline.*

pipe organ, organ *(def. 1).*

pip·er (pī′pər) *n.* a person who plays on a pipe, esp. a bagpipe.

· **to pay the piper.** to endure the consequences of one's actions.

pipe·stem (pīp′stem′) *n.* the stem of a tobacco pipe.

pi·pette (pī pet′) *also,* **pi·pet.** *n.* a slender glass tube, usually marked with units of measure, for transferring or measuring liquids. [French *pipette,* diminutive of *pipe* pipe, going back to Latin *pīpāre* to chirp.]

pip·ing (pī′ping) *n.* **1.** a system or array of pipes. **2.** the music of a pipe or pipes: *the piping of a flute.* **3.** a loud, shrill sound: *the piping of a bird.* **4.** a tubular strip of material used for trimming items made of fabric, as garments or cushions, along the seams or edges. —*adj.* shrill: *a piping voice.*

· **piping hot.** very hot.

pip·it (pip′it) *n.* any of various small, sparrowlike birds, genus *Anthus,* having a thin bill and predominantly brown plumage. Also, **titlark.** [Imitative.]

pip·kin (pip′kin) *n.* a small earthenware pot. [Probably PIPE (cask) + -KIN.]

pip·pin (pip′in) *n.* any of various kinds of yellowish green apple. [Old French *pepin* seed of a fruit; of uncertain origin.]

pip·sis·se·wa (pip sis′ə wə) *n.* a woody, evergreen herb, *Chimaphila umbellata,* found in Europe, Asia, and North America, bearing white or pinkish flowers, used in medicine as a diuretic or tonic. [Cree *pipisisikweu* literally, it separates (a bladder stone) into small particles; referring to its use by American Indians as a medicine to treat gallstones.]

pip·squeak (pip′skwēk′) *n. Informal.* a small or unimportant person or thing: *Compared with that tugboat, our little rowboat is just a pipsqueak.*

pi·quant (pē′kənt) *adj.* **1.** agreeably sharp to the taste; pungent; tart: *a piquant sauce.* **2.** stimulating, provocative, or charming: *piquant comments, a piquant face.* [French *piquant,* present participle of *piquer* to prick, pierce, sting. See PIKE¹.] —**pi′quan·cy, pi′quant·ness,** *n.* —**pi′quant·ly,** *adv.*

pique (pēk) *n.* resentment resulting from hurt feelings or wounded pride: *I returned the gift in a fit of pique.* —*v.t.,* **piqued, pi·quing. 1.** to arouse resentment in; wound the vanity of; offend: *She was piqued by his thoughtless remark.* **2.** to stimulate; arouse; excite: *The locked closet piqued my curiosity.* **3.** *Archaic.* to pride (oneself) (with *on* or *upon*). [French *piquer* to prick, pierce, sting. See PIKE¹.]

pi·qué (pi kā′, pē-) *n.* a fabric usually made of cotton, woven with narrow, lengthwise ribs. [French *piqué* quilting, from *piquer* to prick, quilt, stitch. See PIKE¹.]

pi·quet (pi kā′, -ket′) *n.* a card game played by two people, requiring a deck of thirty-two cards, with no cards below the seven. [French *piquet* the card game, peg, diminutive of *pic* pickax, probably going back to Latin *pīcus* woodpecker.]

pi·ra·cy (pī′rə sē) *n., pl.* **-cies. 1.** robbery of ships at sea. **2.** unauthorized publication, reproduction, or use of another's work, invention, or ideas, esp. in violation of a copyright. [Medie-

val Latin *piratia* robbery on the high seas, from Late Greek *peirāteiā,* from Greek *peirātēs* pirate.]

pi·ra·nha (pi ran′yə, -rän′-) *n.* any of several voracious fish, genus *Serrasalmus,* found in the rivers and streams of tropical South America, that travel in schools and feed on other fish. Piranhas will also attack large animals, including humans. Average length: less than 1 foot (0.3 meter). [Portuguese *piranha,* from Tupi-Guarani *piranha* literally, toothed fish, from *pirá* fish + *sainha* tooth.]

piranha

pi·rate (pī′rit) *n.* **1.** a person who robs ships at sea or plunders in coastal regions. **2.** a ship used by pirates. **3.** a person who appropriates the work, invention, or ideas of another without permission or authorization. —*v.,* **-rat·ed, -rat·ing.** —*v.t.* **1.** to rob (ships) at sea. **2.** to publish, reproduce, or use (another's work, invention, or ideas) without permission or authorization. —*v.i.* to practice piracy. [Latin *pīrāta* robber on the high seas, from Greek *peirātēs* one who attacks, adventurer, robber on the high seas.] —**pi·rat·ic** (pī rat′-ik); *also,* **pi·rat′i·cal,** *adj.* —**pi·rat′i·cal·ly,** *adv.*

pi·rogue (pi rōg′) *n.* **1.** a canoe or boat made by hollowing out a large log. **2.** any small boat or canoe that resembles this. [French *pirogue,* from Spanish *piragua;* of Carib or Arawak origin.]

pir·ou·ette (pir′ü et′) *n.* a rapid turning about on the toes, esp. in dancing. —*v.i.,* **-et·ted, -et·ting.** to perform a pirouette. [French *pirouette* spinning top, a whirling about; of uncertain origin.]

pis·ca·to·ry (pis′kə tôr′ē) *adj.* **1.** of or relating to fish or fishing. **2.** employed in or devoted to fishing: *piscatory tribes.* Also, **pis′ca·to′ri·al.** [Latin *piscātōrius* relating to fishermen or fishing, going back to *piscis* fish.]

Pis·ces (pī′sēz, pis′ēz) *n.* **1.** a constellation in the northern sky, conventionally depicted as two fish. **2.** the twelfth sign of the zodiac. [Latin *Piscēs* literally, the Fish, plural of *piscis* fish.]

pis·cine (pī′sēn, pis′īn) *adj.* of, relating to, or resembling fish. [Modern Latin *piscinus,* from Latin *piscis* fish.]

pis·mire (pis′mīr, piz′-) *n.* ant. [Middle English *pissemire,* from *pisse* urine + *mire* ant; referring to the odor of formic acid, which is secreted by ants.]

pis·ta·chi·o (pi stash′ē ō′, -stä′shē ō′) *n., pl.* **-chi·os. 1.** the small, edible, greenish seed of a tree, *Pistacia vera,* of the cashew family, having a thin purple skin and covered by a hard gray shell. **2.** the small tree bearing this seed, native to the Mediterranean region and the Middle East. **3.** the flavor of the seed. **4.** a light yellowish green color. —*adj.* having the color or flavor of pistachio. [Italian *pistacchio* the nut, the tree, from Latin *pistācium* the nut, from Greek *pistakion,* from Persian *pistah.*]

pis·til (pis′təl) *n.* the part of a flower where seeds are produced, consisting of the ovary, style, and stigma; carpel. [Latin *pistillum* pestle; referring to its shape.]

pis·til·late (pis′tə lāt′) *adj.* (of a flower) having a pistil or pistils, esp. having pistils but no stamens.

pis·tol (pis′təl) *n.* a small firearm designed to be held and fired with one hand. [French *pistole,* from German *Pistole,* from Czech *pišt'al* tube, firearm.]

pis·tole (pi stōl′) *n.* any of various old European gold coins, esp. one of Spain. [French *pistole* coin, pistol. See PISTOL.]

pis·ton (pis′tən) *n.* **1.** a disk or cylinder that fits closely inside a sleeve or hollow cylinder, where it moves back and forth. **2.** *Music.* in a brass instrument, a sliding valve used to change the pitch of tones. [French *piston,* from Italian *pistone,* from *pistare* to pound²; going back to Latin *pistus,* past participle of *pīnsere.*]

piston ring, an expandable metal ring that fits into a groove near the top of a piston, sealing the gap between the piston and the surrounding cylinder.

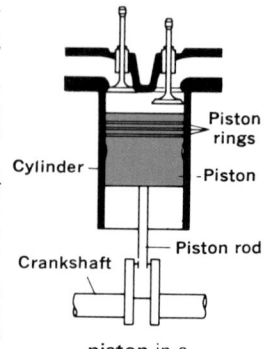

piston in a gasoline engine

piston rod, a rod connected to the underside of a piston that transfers the reciprocal motion of the piston to a rotating shaft.

pit¹ (pit) *n.* **1.** a hole in the ground, either natural or dug. **2.a.** a

very small indentation or scar on a surface, as a pockmark on the skin. **b.** a natural hollow or depression in the body: *the pit of the stomach.* **3.** a sunken or enclosed area for staging fights between animals. **4.** a sunken area in front of the stage of a theater, used for the orchestra. **5.a.** the lowest or deepest part or point; abyss; depth: *the pit of despair.* **b.** hell. **6.** the area of an exchange where a particular commodity is traded: *the wheat pit.* **7.** an area beside a racetrack for servicing cars in a race. **8. the pits.** *Slang.* an unpleasant situation, place, or thing: *Cold, rainy weather is the pits.* —*v.t.,* **pit·ted, pit·ting. 1.** to make small holes or indentations in; mark with pits: *a windshield pitted by gravel.* **2.** to place in opposition or rivalry; match: *to pit a challenger against the champion.* [Old English *pyt(t)* hole in the ground, well, from Latin *puteus* well, shaft.]

pit² (pit) *n.* the hard stone of a fruit, as of a peach or cherry. —*v.t.,* **pit·ted, pit·ting.** to remove stones from (fruit). [Dutch *pit* kernel.]

pi·ta (pē′tə) *n.* a round, flat bread with a hollow center, often sliced in half to form a pocket that can be stuffed with meat, vegetables, and other fillings. Also, **pita bread.** [Modern Greek *pita* this bread.]

pit·a·pat (pit′ə pat′) *adv.* with a quick succession of beats or taps: *My heart went pitapat.* —*n.* a quick beating or tapping, or the sound made by this. —*v.i.,* **-pat·ted, -pat·ting.** to go pitapat. [Imitative.]

pit bull, American Staffordshire terrier.

pitch¹ (pich) *v.t.* **1.** to throw, hurl, or toss: *to pitch horseshoes, to pitch pennies.* **2.** *Baseball.* **a.** to throw (the ball) to the batter. **b.** to be the pitcher in (a game or part of one). **3.** to fix or set firmly in the ground, as a peg or stake. **4.** to set up; erect: *to pitch a camp, to pitch a tent.* **5.a.** to set at a particular point or angle: *The carpenters pitched the roof steeply.* **b.** to set at a degree or level, as a goal or hope: *Don't pitch your hopes too high, or you may be disappointed.* **6.** *Music.* to set the key of, as a tune, the voice, or an instrument. **7.** *Informal.* to try to sell or gain approval for: *The company pitched its new products in radio commercials.* —*v.i.* **1.** to fall or plunge forward or headlong: *to lose balance and pitch off a ladder.* **2.** to settle temporarily; encamp. **3.** to stagger around; lurch. **4.** to throw or toss something. **5.** *Baseball.* **a.** to throw the ball to the batter. **b.** to play the position of pitcher. **6.a.** (of a boat or ship) to plunge so that the bow and stern alternately rise and fall. **b.** (of an aircraft or spacecraft) to turn about a lateral axis so that the nose rises and falls. **7.** to incline or slope downward; dip: *The vein of ore pitched at a 45-degree angle.* —*n.* **1.a.** the act or way of throwing. **b.** a throw; hurl; toss. **2.** *Baseball.* **a.** the act or way of throwing the ball to the batter. **b.** the ball so thrown. **3.** a degree or level: *a high pitch of excitement.* **4.** the highest point or degree: *the pitch of happiness.* **5.** height: *the pitch of an arch.* **6.** a downward slope or inclination: *The road takes a pitch around the bend.* **7.** the amount of slope or inclination: *the 30-degree pitch of a roof.* **8.** something that is pitched: *a pitch of hay.* **9.** the highness or lowness of a sound or musical tone, depending on the relative rapidity of the vibrations by which it is produced. A high pitch results from rapid vibrations and a low pitch from slow vibrations. **10.** the alternate rise and fall of the bow and stern of a ship in a rough sea. **11.** the movement of the lateral axis of an aircraft or spacecraft up or down from the horizontal plane. **12.** the distance that an aircraft propeller moves forward in one revolution. **13.a.** the distance between corresponding points of two adjacent gear teeth. **b.** the distance between any two adjacent things in a machine, as the threads of a screw. **14.** *Informal.* an attempt to sell something or persuade someone: *a sales pitch.* [Possibly from an unrecorded Old English word.] —For Synonyms *(v.t.),* see **throw.**

· **to pitch in.** *Informal.* **a.** to begin to work with promptness and energy: *Pitch in so we can get the job done quickly.* **b.** to contribute money toward a common purpose: *We all pitched in to rent a boat.*

· **to pitch into.** *Informal.* **a.** to attack with words or physical force: *My boss pitched into me for being late.* **b.** to begin to work on with promptness and energy: *to pitch into an assignment.*

pitch² (pich) *n.* **1.** a dark, thick, sticky substance obtained by the distillation of such substances as petroleum, coal tar, or wood tar, used for waterproofing, insulating, or paving. **2.** a resin produced by pine trees. —*v.t.* to cover or smear with or as with pitch. [Old English *pic* dark resinous substance, from Latin *pix.*]

pitch-black (pich′blak′) *adj.* extremely black.

pitch·blende (pich′blend′) *n.* a massive, black, lumpy variety of uraninite. [German *Pechblende,* from *Pech* pitch² (from Latin *pix*) + *Blende.* See BLENDE.]

pitch-dark (pich′därk′) *adj.* extremely dark.

pitched battle 1. a battle in which the troops have been specially positioned in advance. **2.** any heatedly fought battle.

pitch·er¹ (pich′ər) *n.* **1.** a vessel with a handle and a lip or spout, used chiefly for holding and pouring liquids. **2.** the amount contained by a pitcher. **3.** the leaf of a pitcher plant; ascidium. [Old French *pichier* container for liquids, going back to Late Latin *bīcārium* goblet, possibly from Greek *bīkos* jar.]

pitcher² (pich′ər) *n.* **1.** a person who pitches, esp. the player on a baseball team who throws the ball to the batter. [PITCH¹ + -ER¹.]

pitcher plant, any of several plants having pitcher-shaped leaves that capture and digest insects, esp. *Sarracenia purpura,* found in North America, bearing long, drooping yellow or purple flowers.

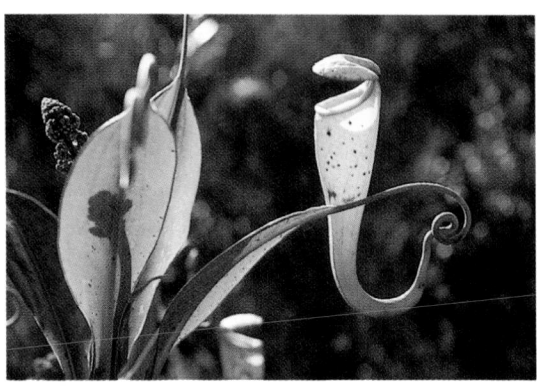

pitcher plant

pitch·fork (pich′fôrk′) *n.* a long-handled tool with projecting prongs, used esp. to lift and pitch hay. —*v.t.* to lift and pitch with or as with a pitchfork.

pitch·man (pich′mən) *n., pl.* **-men** (-mən). *Informal.* **1.** a person who tries to sell or gain approval for a product, service, or cause, as on television or radio. **2.** a person who tries to sell merchandise to passersby, as at a carnival or on a city street.

pitch·out (pich′out′) *n.* **1.** *Baseball.* a pitch intentionally thrown too wide of home plate for the batter to hit, in order to make it easier for the catcher to throw out a base runner attempting to steal. **2.** *Football.* a lateral pass behind the line of scrimmage, usually from the quarterback to another back.

pitch pine, any of several pines that yield pitch, esp. *Pinus rigida,* native to eastern North America, now valued esp. for their wood.

pitch pipe, a small pipe that produces a fixed note when it is blown into, used to give the pitch for a singer or instrumentalist.

pitch·y (pich′ē) *adj.,* **pitch·i·er, pitch·i·est. 1.** full of or covered with pitch: *a pitchy roadbed.* **2.** resembling pitch, as in color or consistency.

pit·e·ous (pit′ē əs) *adj.* deserving or arousing pity; pitiable; pathetic. [Old French *pitos, piteus,* going back to Latin *pietās* dutiful conduct, kindness.] —**pit′e·ous·ly,** *adv.* —**pit′e·ous·ness,** *n.*

pit·fall (pit′fôl′) *n.* **1.** a trap dug into the ground and hidden, used to catch animals. **2.** any hidden danger or unforeseen difficulty.

pith (pith) *n.* **1.** the soft, spongy tissue in the center of the stems of certain plants. **2.** a soft plant tissue resembling this. **3.** the important or essential part; essence; substance: *the pith of an essay.* [Old English *pitha* medulla of plants, essential part.]

Pith·e·can·thro·pus (pith′ə kan′thrə pəs, -kan thrō′pəs) *n., pl.* **-pi** (-pī′, -pī). Java man. [Modern Latin *pithecanthropus,* from Greek *pithēkos* ape + *anthrōpos* man.]

pith·y (pith′ē) *adj.,* **pith·i·er, pith·i·est. 1.** of, like, or full of pith. **2.** short and full of meaning: *a pithy remark.* —**pith′i·ly,** *adv.* —**pith′i·ness,** *n.*

pit·i·a·ble (pit′ē ə bəl) *adj.* **1.** deserving or arousing pity; lamentable. **2.** deserving or arousing contempt; mean. —**pit′i·a·ble·ness,** *n.* —**pit′i·a·bly,** *adv.*

pit·i·ful (pit′i fəl) *adj.* **1.** arousing pity: *a pitiful look.* **2.** arousing contempt; paltry: *a pitiful excuse.* **3.** *Archaic.* full of pity; compassionate. —**pit′i·ful·ly,** *adv.* —**pit′i·ful·ness,** *n.*

pit·i·less (pit′i lis) *adj.* without pity; showing no mercy: *a*

a	at	e	end	o	hot	u	up	hw	white		about
ā	ape	ē	me	ō	old	ū	use	ng	song		taken
ä	far	i	it	ô	fork	ü	rule	th	thin	ə	pencil
âr	care	ī	ice	oi	oil	u̇	pull	th	this		lemon
		îr	pierce	ou	out	ûr	turn	zh	measure		circus

pitiless villain, a pitiless attack. —**pit′i·less·ly,** *adv.* —**pit′i-less·ness,** *n.*

Pi·tot tube (pē′tō, pē tō′) the L-shaped, tubular component of a device, incorporating a manometer, that measures fluid velocity in order to provide an indication of the air speed of an aircraft. [From Henri *Pitot,* 1695-1771, French physicist who invented it.]

pit stop 1. a stop made by a racing car for servicing during a race. **2.** *Informal.* **a.** a stop to eat, rest, get fuel, or the like during a trip, esp. by automobile. **b.** the place where such a stop is made.

pit·tance (pit′ əns) *n.* a small or meager amount or allowance, as of money: *I was paid only a pittance for mowing the lawn.* [Old French *pi(e)tance* allowance of food, pity, going back to Latin *pietās* dutiful conduct, kindness.]

pit·ter-pat·ter (pit′ər pat′ər) *n.* a quick succession of light taps or beats: *the pitter-patter of footsteps.* —*adv.* with a quick succession of light taps or beats. [Imitative.]

pi·tu·i·tar·y (pi tü′i ter′ē, -tü′-) *n.* **1.** pituitary gland. **2.** *Medicine.* an extract from the pituitary glands of cattle, used in treating a variety of disorders. —*adj.* of or relating to the pituitary gland. [Latin *pītuītārius* relating to or secreting phlegm, from *pītuīta* phlegm, slime.]

pituitary gland, a small, oval endocrine gland, located beneath the brain, that secretes hormones that regulate growth and the functions of many parts of the body. Also, **pituitary body.** For illustration, see **brain.**

pit viper, any of several poisonous snakes, family Crotalidae, of the New World and Asia, including the bushmaster, rattlesnake, copperhead, and water moccasin, having a deep, heat-sensitive pit on each side of the head.

pit·y (pit′ē) *n., pl.* **pit·ies. 1.** a feeling of sorrow and sympathy aroused by the unhappiness or suffering of another; commiseration. **2.** a cause for sympathy or regret: *What a pity you can't go.* —*v.t.,* **pit·ied, pit·y·ing.** to feel pity for. [Old French *pite* dutifulness, compassion, from Latin *pietās* dutiful conduct, devotion, kindness. Doublet of PIETY.] —**pit′y·ing·ly,** *adv.* —For Synonyms, see **sympathy.**

· **to have** (or **take**) **pity on.** to be merciful to.

piv·ot (piv′ət) *n.* **1.** a point, shaft, or pin about which something turns. **2.** a person or thing of importance on which something depends. **3.** the act of turning on or as on a pivot. —*v.t.* to place on or furnish with a pivot. —*v.i.* to turn on or as on a pivot: *I pivoted around when I heard my name.* [French *pivot* hinge, pin; of uncertain origin.]

piv·ot·al (piv′ə təl) *adj.* **1.** of, relating to, or serving as a pivot. **2.** of central or vital importance; crucial: *a pivotal matter.* —**piv′ot·al·ly,** *adv.*

pix (piks) *pl. n. Slang.* **1.** motion pictures. **2.** photographs. [Shortened form of PICT(URE)S.]

pix·el (pik′səl) *n.* one of the small, luminous dots on a television or computer screen that are arranged in groups to form pictures, characters, and symbols. [From *pix* (shortened form of *picture*) + *el*(ement).]

pix·ie (pik′sē) *also,* **pix·y.** *n., pl.* **pix·ies. 1.** an imaginary small or mischievous being; fairy; elf. **2.** a mischievous child. [Of uncertain origin.]

pi·zazz (pə zaz′) *also,* **piz·zazz.** *n. Slang.* **1.** an exciting or lively quality; vigor; spirit: *a band that plays with lots of pizazz.* **2.** a flamboyant or flashy quality; dash: *a sports car full of pizazz.* [Of uncertain origin.]

piz·za (pēt′sə) *n.* a baked dish of Italian origin made of a thin layer of dough topped with tomatoes, cheese, and sometimes other ingredients, as sausages or mushrooms. [Italian *pizza,* possibly from *pizza* edge, point; of uncertain origin.]

piz·ze·ri·a (pēt′sə rē′ə) *n.* a place where pizzas are prepared and sold.

piz·zi·ca·to (pit′si kä′tō) *Music. adj.* (of a stringed instrument, as a violin) played by plucking the strings with a finger. —*n., pl.* **-ca·ti** (-kä′tē). a note or passage played in this way. [Italian *pizzicato* plucked, past participle of *pizzicare* to pluck, pinch, from *pizzare* to prick, sting, from *pizza* edge, point; of uncertain origin.]

pk *also,* **pk.** *pl.* **pks** peck.

pk. *pl.* **pks. 1.** pack. **2.** park. **3.** peak.

pkg. *pl.* **pkgs.** package.

pl. 1. place. **2.** plate. **3.** plural.

PL/1, a computer programming language oriented toward solving both scientific and business problems. [Short for *p(rogramming) l(anguage)/one.*]

plac·a·ble (plak′ə bəl, plā′kə-) *adj.* easily placated; forgiving. [Latin *plācābilis,* from *plācāre* to appease.] —**plac′a·bil′i·ty, plac′a·ble·ness,** *n.* —**plac′a·bly,** *adv.*

plac·ard (plak′ärd, -ərd) *n.* a large sign or notice made of paper or cardboard for displaying in a public place. —*v.t.* **1.** to display placards on or in: *to placard the wall of a building.* **2.** to make known by means of placards. **3.** to display as a placard. [French

placard poster, from *plaquer* to stick on, plaster, from Middle Dutch *placken* to patch, plaster.]

pla·cate (plā′kāt, plak′āt) *v.t.,* **-cat·ed, -cat·ing.** to calm the hostility or anger of; pacify: *The salesclerk tried to placate the unhappy customer.* [Latin *plācātus,* past participle of *plācāre* to appease.] —**pla′cat·er,** *n.* —**pla·ca′tion,** *n.* —**pla·ca·tive** (plā′kā tiv, plak′ā-), **plac·a·tor·y** (plak′ə tôr′ē), *adj.*

place (plās) *n.* **1.** a portion of space; location: *a place to hang one's coat.* **2.** the particular part of space normally occupied by something or someone: *to put everything in its place.* **3.** space in general: *time and place.* **4.** an area or locality, as a city or town: *I don't know the name of this place.* **5.** a building, part of a building, or location set apart for any purpose: *a place of worship, a place of amusement.* **6.** a house or other residence: *We have a place in the country.* **7.** a particular part or spot: *a sore place, a wet place on the floor.* **8.** the point reached by a reader in a book or other writing: *He looked up from his book and lost his place.* **9.** a space or seat for one person, as in a train or theater, or at a table: *Save a place for me at the movies.* **10.** the right or appropriate position, time, or location: *A crowded bus is not the place for a private conversation.* **11.** the present condition or state of affairs; situation or circumstances: *If I were in your place, I wouldn't go.* **12.** a position or standing in a social scale, hierarchy of power, or other order of rank: *to have friends in high places, an author with a secure place in the history of English literature.* **13.** a position of work; job: *She found a place as a sales manager.* **14.** duty or business: *It is not your place to criticize.* **15.** a position in a line, list, or the like: *in first place.* **16.a.** a position among the first three or top three contestants at the finish of a race or competition. **b.** the position of the horse that finishes second in a race. **17.** *Mathematics.* the relative position of a figure in a series, as in decimal notation. In .347, 4 is in the second decimal place. **18.** a short street, open space, or public square, as in an urban area. **19.** the position customarily or otherwise occupied by another; stead: *Will you go in my place?* —*v.,* **placed, plac·ing.** —*v.t.* **1.** to put or set in a particular place or position: *to place the fork to the left of the plate.* **2.** to put in the proper relation, position, or order; arrange: *Place the books in alphabetical order.* **3.** to arrange or make provision for: *to place an order, to place a bet.* **4.** to identify by connecting with the proper location, circumstances, or time: *I finally placed you as someone from my old neighborhood.* **5.** to assign to a position, rank, or category. **6.** to find employment or a home for: *The school claimed to place all its graduates in high-paying jobs. The agency placed the orphans with good families.* —*v.i.* **1.** to finish among the first three contestants or in a specified position in a race or competition. **2.** to finish second in a horse race. ➡ distinguished from **show** and **win.** [Old French *place* space occupied by a person or thing, spot, room, court, rank, going back to Latin *platēa* broad way, from Greek *plateia (hodos)* broad (way). Doublet of PIAZZA, PLAZA.] —For Synonyms *(v.t.),* see **put.**

· **in place.** in the original, proper, or natural location or position: *The books were in place on the shelves.*

· **in place of.** instead of: *Use cream in place of milk in the recipe.*

· **out of place. a.** not in the original, proper, or natural place or position. **b.** not proper; unsuitable.

· **to go places.** *Slang.* to become increasingly successful.

· **to know one's place.** to behave in a way considered appropriate for one's inferior position.

· **to put (someone) in (his or her) place.** to humble (someone), esp. an arrogant person.

· **to take place.** happen; occur: *The opening of the play will take place tomorrow night.*

pla·ce·bo (plə sē′bō) *n., pl.* **-bos** or **-boes.** a preparation having no medicinal value, given to soothe or humor a patient or used as a control in an experiment. [Latin *placēbō* I shall please.]

place-kick (plās′kik′) *also,* **place·kick.** *v.t., v.i.* to give a place kick (to). —**place′-kick′er;** *also,* **place′kick′er,** *n.*

place kick *Football.* a kick in which the ball is placed or held nearly upright on the ground, as in kicking off or attempting a field goal.

place mat, a mat laid on a table under each place setting for protection or decoration.

place·ment (plās′mənt) *n.* **1.** an act or instance of putting or setting in a particular place: *The placement of our furniture in the new house took all day.* **2.** the way in which something is placed; positioning or arrangement: *The placement of the windows made the room dark.* **3.** the finding or assigning of suitable employment, education, or housing for people: *The company hired an agency to help in the placement of the laid-off workers.* **4.** *Football.* **a.** the placing of the ball for a place kick. **b.** the position of a ball so placed. **c.** place kick.

pla·cen·ta (plə sen′tə) *n., pl.* **-tas** or **-tae** (-tē). **1.** an organ attached to the wall of the uterus and to the umbilical cord

through which the embryo receives food and oxygen and gives off waste. **2.** *Botany.* the place in the ovary of a flowering plant where ovules are borne. [Latin *placenta* cake, from Greek *plakoenta*, accusative of *plakoeis* flat cake; referring to the shape.] —**pla-cen′tal,** *adj.*

plac·er (plas′ər) *n.* an alluvial deposit, as of gravel or sand, that contains particles of gold or other valuable heavy minerals. [Spanish *placer* mass or ridge of sand, from *plaza* square, market, from Latin *plātea* broad way. See PLACE.]

plac·er mining (plas′ər) mining in which gravel or sand is washed to sort out gold or other valuable heavy minerals.

place setting, the dishes, silverware, and other items needed to set a place for one person at a table.

place value, the value given to a digit, based on the place it occupies in a number. In the number 368, 3 is in the hundreds place and has a place value of 300; 6 is in the tens place and has a place value of 60; and 8 is in the ones place and has a place value of 8.

plac·id (plas′id) *adj.* having or showing no excitement or disturbance; calm or peaceful: *a placid cow, a placid temperament.* [Latin *placidus* gentle, pleasing.] —**pla·cid′i·ty, plac′id·ness,** *n.* —**plac′id·ly,** *adv.* —For Synonyms, see **calm.**

plack·et (plak′it) *n.* **1.** a usually concealed opening or slit in a garment, as at the neckline or wrists, that makes it easy to put the garment on or take it off. **2.** *Archaic.* a pocket in a woman's skirt. [Possibly a form of PLACARD.]

plac·o·derm (plak′ə dûrm′) *n.* any of an extinct class, Placodermi, of primitive jawed fishes, usually heavily armored, living in Devonian geologic time. [Modern Latin *Placodermi* taxonomic class of these fishes, from Greek *plakos,* genitive of *plax* flat plate (referring to the fishes' armorlike plating) + *derma* skin.]

plac·oid (plak′oid) *adj.* of or having toothlike, enamel-covered scales that are periodically shed and replaced, as in sharks and rays. [Greek *plax* flat plate, tablet + -OID; because the scales look like flat plates.]

pla·gia·rism (plā′jə riz′əm) *n.* **1.** an act or instance of passing off someone else's work or ideas as one's own. **2.** the work or ideas of another passed off as one's own. [Earlier *plagiary* plagiarist, plagiarism (from Latin *plagiārius* kidnapper, literary thief) + -ISM.] —**pla′gia·rist,** *n.* —**pla′gia·ris′tic,** *adj.*

pla·gia·rize (plā′jə rīz′) *v.,* **-rized, -riz·ing.** —*v.t.* **1.** to pass off (someone else's work or ideas) as one's own: *to plagiarize a passage from an essay.* **2.** to pass off the work or ideas of (someone else) as one's own: *to plagiarize an author.* —*v.i.* to commit plagiarism. —**pla′gia·riz′er,** *n.*

pla·gio·clase (plā′jē ə klās′) *n.* any of a group of plentiful feldspar minerals, silicates of sodium, calcium, and aluminum, characterized by a tendency to split along smooth planes that are oblique to each other. Albite and labradorite are common varieties. [German *plagioklas,* from Greek *plagios* oblique, slanting (from *plagos* side) + *klasis* a breaking, fracture (from *klaein* to break).]

plague (plāg) *n.* **1.** a highly infectious, often fatal disease that occurs in several forms and is characterized by high fever and the swelling of the lymph glands, esp. bubonic plague. **2.** a great misfortune, disaster, or evil: *The land was ravaged by a plague of locusts.* **3.** a source of trouble or annoyance: *Having to clean my room is the plague of my existence.* —*v.t.,* **plagued, plagu·ing. 1.** to afflict with or as with a plague: *Smallpox once plagued much of the world. After the riots, looting plagued the city.* **2.** to trouble or annoy: *Injuries plagued the team.* [Latin *plāga* blow¹, pestilence.]

pla·guy (plā′gē) *also,* **pla·guey.** *adj. Informal.* troubling or annoying.

plaice (plās) *n., pl.* **plaice** or **plaic·es. 1.** a European flatfish, *Pleuronectes platessa,* found in the North Atlantic and valued as a food fish. **2.** any of various American flatfish. [Old French *plaïs* the European flatfish, going back to Late Latin *platessa,* possibly from Greek *platys* flat.]

plaid (plad) *n.* **1.** a pattern consisting of alternating narrow and wide stripes of varying colors that cross one another at right angles. **2.** a shawl having such a pattern. It is part of the traditional Scottish Highland dress. **3.** a fabric made with such a pattern. —*adj.* having such a pattern. [Scottish Gaelic *plaide* blanket.] —**plaid′ed,** *adj.*

plain¹ (plān) *adj.* **1.** clearly seen or heard; distinct: *She was in plain sight.* **2.** clearly understood; evident; obvious: *He made it plain that he would not change his mind.* **3.** complete or downright; sheer; utter: *That's just plain nonsense!* **4.** straightforward or direct; outspoken; frank: *I will be plain with you and tell you the truth.* **5.** without ornament or embellishment; unadorned: *plain*

clothes, a dress with a plain neckline. **6.** without pattern or figure: *fabric with a plain weave, plain dishes.* **7.** not rich or highly seasoned: *plain cooking.* **8.** without position or pretensions; unsophisticated or ordinary: *plain people.* **9.** not beautiful or striking in appearance; homely: *a plain face.* —*n. also,* **plains.** an expanse of level or nearly level land. —*adv.* in a plain manner; clearly; simply: *I fell asleep because I was just plain exhausted.* [Old French *plain* flat, level, from Latin *plānus.*] —**plain′ly,** *adv.* —**plain′ness,** *n.*

plain² (plān) *v.i. Archaic.* to complain. [Old French *plaindre* to mourn, from Latin *plangere* to lament aloud, beat (the breast).]

plain·chant (plān′chant′) *n.* plainsong.

plain·clothes·man (plān′klōz′mən, -klōthz′-) *n., pl.* -men (-mən). a police officer who wears civilian clothes while on duty.

plain sailing, easy progress, as in an endeavor.

Plains Indian, a member of any of various American Indian tribes who formerly inhabited the Great Plains.

plains·man (plānz′mən) *n., pl.* -men (-mən). an inhabitant of the plains, esp. the Great Plains.

plain·song (plān′sông′) *n.* vocal music in a style that originated in the medieval Roman Catholic Church, having a simple melody and an irregular rhythm and sung in unison without accompaniment. Also, **Gregorian chant, plainchant.**

plain-spo·ken (plān′spō′kən) *adj.* open or unreserved in speech; outspoken; frank: *a plain-spoken adviser, plain-spoken advice.*

plains·wom·an (plānz′wŭm′ən) *n., pl.* -wom·en (-wim′ən). a woman who lives on the plains, esp. the Great Plains.

plaint (plānt) *n.* **1.** complaint. **2.** *Archaic.* lament. [Old French *plaint,* from Latin *planctus* lamentation.]

plain·tiff (plān′tif) *n.* the person that brings a suit in a court of law. [Old French *plaintif,* from *plaintif* complaining, lamenting. See PLAINTIVE.]

plain·tive (plān′tiv) *adj.* expressing sorrow; mournful; sad: *a plaintive face, a plaintive song.* [Old French *plaintif* lamenting, complaining, going back to Latin *planctus* lamentation.] —**plain′tive·ly,** *adv.* —**plain′tive·ness,** *n.*

plait (plāt, plat) *n.* **1.** a braid, as of hair. Also, **plat². 2.** pleat. —*v.t.* **1.** to braid. **2.** to make by braiding: *to plait a rug.* Also (*defs. 1, 2*), **plat². 3.** pleat. [Old French *pleit* fold¹, going back to Latin *plicitus,* past participle of *plicāre* to fold¹.] —**plait′er,** *n.*

plan (plan) *n.* **1.** a method or way that has been thought out beforehand, as for doing or making something: *The general's plan of attack was brilliant.* **2.** something that a person intends to do: *My plans for the weekend are still tentative.* **3.** a drawing or diagram, often made to scale, that shows the relative position of parts, as of a building or a section of land. —*v.,* **planned, plan·ning.** —*v.t.* **1.** to prepare a method, program, or outline for. **2.** to have in mind; intend: *We plan to go shopping tomorrow.* **3.** to make a drawing or diagram of; design: *The architect planned a house for us.* —*v.i.* to make a plan or plans: *to plan for a celebration.* [French *plan* ground plan (drawn on a flat surface), design, scheme, going back to Latin *plānus* flat, level.] —**plan′ner,** *n.*

pla·nar (plā′nər, -när) *adj.* **1.** of or relating to a plane. **2.** flat. [Late Latin *plānāris* flat, from *plānum.* See PLANE¹.]

pla·nar·i·an (plə nâr′ē ən) *n.* any of various small, free-swimming flatworms of the class Turbellaria that inhabit freshwater lakes, streams, or ponds. It has the power of regenerating injured body parts. Length: to 4 inches (10 centimeters). [Modern Latin *Planaria,* going back to Latin *plānus* flat.]

pla·na·tion (plā nā′shən) *n.* the reduction of a land surface to a nearly flat plain, or peneplain, through the combined effects of erosion and deposition by rivers and streams. Also, **gradation.** [PLAN(E)¹ + -ATION.]

plan·chette (plan shet′) *n.* a small three-cornered or heart-shaped wooden board supported by a pencil and two short legs resting on casters, used in divination. A modified planchette is used as the pointing device on a ouija board. [French *planchette* planchette, small board, diminutive of *planche* board, from Latin *planca.*]

plane¹ (plān) *n.* **1.** a flat or level surface. **2.** a level or degree, as of development, character, or existence: *to reach a high plane of*

a	at	e	end	o	hot	u	up	hw	white		about
ā	ape	ē	me	ō	old	ū	use	ng	song		taken
ä	far	i	it	ô	fork	ü	rule	th	thin	ə	pencil
âr	care	ī	ice	oi	oil	u̇	pull	th	this		lemon
		îr	pierce	ou	out	ûr	turn	zh	measure		circus

achievement. **3.** airplane or hydroplane. **4.** (on an airplane) the flat or curved supporting surface of a wing or other airfoil. **5.** *Geometry.* a flat surface that wholly contains every line connecting any two points on it. —*adj.* **1.** level; flat. **2.** of, relating to, or designating a plane or planes or a figure contained in a plane: *a plane curve.* —*v.i.,* **planed, plan·ing. 1.** to glide or soar. **2.** to ride in an airplane. **3.** to rise partly out of the water when moving at a high speed, as a motor boat. [Latin *plānum* level surface.]

plane² (plān) *n.* a hand tool with an adjustable, inclined blade that projects from the bottom, used for leveling or smoothing wood. —*v.,* **planed, plan·ing.** —*v.t.* **1.** to level or smooth with or as with a plane. **2.** to remove with or as with a plane: *to plane the rough edges of a plank.* —*v.i.* **1.** to work with a plane. **2.** to do the work of a plane: *A knife will not plane adequately.* [Old French *plane* the tool, going back to Late Latin *plāna,* from Latin *plānāre* to level.]

plane³ (plān) *n.* plane tree. [Old French *plane,* from Latin *platanus,* from Greek *platanos,* from *platys* broad; referring to its broad leaves.]

plane angle, an angle formed by two intersecting straight lines in the same plane.

plane geometry, the branch of geometry that deals with plane figures.

plan·er (plā′nər) *n.* a person or machine tool that planes.

plan·et (plan′it) *n.* **1.a.** any one of the nine large spherical bodies that revolve around the sun and shine by reflected light. The planets in order of their distance from the sun are Mercury, Venus, Earth, Mars, Jupiter, Saturn, Uranus, Neptune, and Pluto. **b.** a similar body revolving around another star. **2.** *Astrology.* a heavenly body supposed to influence people and events. [Late Latin *planēta* wandering star (as it appeared to the ancient astronomers), from Greek *planētēs* wanderer, wandering star.]

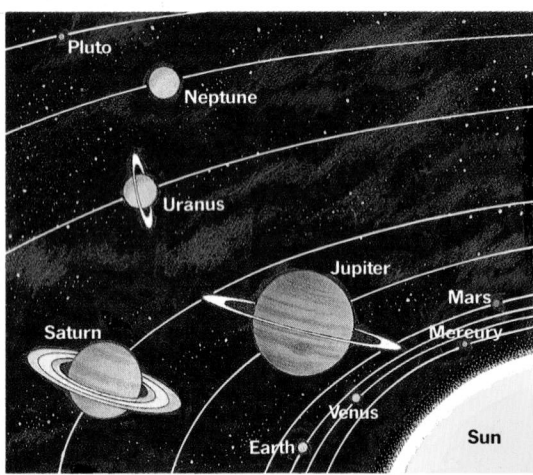

planets of the solar system

plan·e·tar·i·um (plan′i târ′ē əm) *n., pl.* **-i·ums** or **-i·a** (-ē ə). **1.** an apparatus designed to display the positions and motions of celestial bodies by projecting their images on the inside of a hemispherical dome. **2.** a room or building housing such an apparatus. **3.** orrery. [Modern Latin *planetarium,* going back to Latin *planēta* wandering star. See PLANET.]

plan·e·tar·y (plan′i ter′ē) *adj.* **1.** of, relating to, or resembling a planet. **2.** wandering; erratic: *to lead a planetary life.* **3.a.** of or relating to the earth; terrestrial. **b.** extending throughout the earth; worldwide; global: *Pollution is an issue of planetary importance.* **4.** of, relating to, or designating a gear train consisting of several gears placed around and meshed with a central gear, as in the automatic transmission or differential of an automobile.

plan·e·tes·i·mal (plan′i tes′ə məl) *adj.* of or relating to a class of small, cold, solid bodies that are thought to have existed in the early solar system. —*n.* one of these bodies. [PLANET + (IN-FINIT)ESIMAL.]

planetesimal hypothesis, the hypothesis that planetesimals gradually coalesced to form the planets and the satellites of the solar system.

plan·et·oid (plan′i toid′) *n.* asteroid. [PLANET + -OID.]

plane tree, any of a group of trees, genus *Platanus,* esp. *P. orientalis,* found in parts of Europe and Asia, and *P. occidentalis,* found in North America, having smooth, brown bark that flakes off in thin layers and bearing dense, round clusters of tiny flowers at the ends of the branches. The plane tree of North America is also called the sycamore. Also, **plane.**

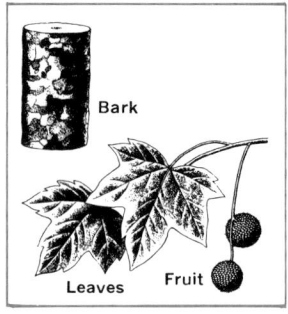

Bark
Leaves   Fruit

plane tree

plank (plangk) *n.* **1.** a long, flat piece of sawed wood thicker than a board. **2.** a statement of a goal or principle forming part of the platform of a political party. —*v.t.* **1.** to cover or lay with planks: *to plank a floor.* **2.** to cook and serve (steak or fish) on a board. **3.** *Informal.* to put or set down quickly or forcefully: *I planked down the money for my share of the bill.* [Dialectal Old French *planke* board, from Latin *planca.*]

•**to walk the plank.** to walk blindfolded off a plank extending over the water from the side of a ship, as prisoners of pirates were sometimes forced to do.

plank·ing (plang′king) *n.* **1.** planks collectively: *the planking on a floor.* **2.** the act of covering or laying with planks.

plank·ton (plangk′tən) *n.* the group of minute plants and animals that drift or float in the sea or in bodies of fresh water, made up mostly of microscopic algae and protozoans. Plankton, an important link in the marine food chain, is the principal food source of many fish and crustaceans. ➡ distinguished from **nekton.** [German *Plankton,* from Greek *plankton,* neuter of *planktos* wandering; referring to their wandering or drifting habits.] —**plank·ton·ic** (plangk ton′ik), *adj.*

pla·no·con·cave (plā′nō kon′kāv) *adj.* flat on one side and concave on the other, as a lens. [Latin *plānus* flat, level + CONCAVE.]

pla·no·con·vex (plā′nō kon′veks) *adj.* flat on one side and convex on the other, as a lens. [Latin *plānus* flat, level + CONVEX.]

pla·nog·ra·phy (plā nog′rə fē, plə-) *n.* any process for printing from a flat or smooth surface, as lithography or offset printing. [Latin *plānus* flat, level + -GRAPHY.] —**pla·no·graph·ic** (plā′nə graf′ik), *adj.*

plant (plant) *n.* **1.** any of a large kingdom of living organisms, Plantae, that characteristically lack locomotive power and sensory organs and have cellulose cell walls. Green plants, in addition, have chlorophyll, which enables them to produce their own food by photosynthesis. **2.** a small plant having a soft stem, as distinguished from a tree or shrub. **3.** a young tree, vine, shrub, or herb recently planted or ready for planting. **4.** the buildings, machinery, tools, and the like used in an industrial or manufacturing process: *an automobile plant.* **5.** the apparatus or equipment for a specific mechanical operation or process: *a heating plant for an office building.* **6.** the buildings, equipment, and grounds of an institution, as a college or hospital. **7.** a person placed in an audience and rehearsed to react in a seemingly spontaneous way to the speaker or performance. **8.** *Informal.* a person placed in a group or organization as a spy or source of disruption. **9.** *Informal.* any person, thing, or scheme intended to deceive or trap. —*v.t.* **1.** to set or place in the ground to take root and grow. **2.a.** to furnish or stock (land) with growing plants. **b.** to introduce (a breed of animals) into a country. **c.** to stock (a body of water) with fish or spawn. **3.** to introduce or instill (principles or ideas): *to plant ideas in people's minds.* **4.** to place or set firmly in position: *to plant a signpost in the ground, to plant one's feet and refuse to budge.* **5.** *Informal.* to deliver with force, as a blow or kiss. **6.** to establish or found, as a colony, city, or church. **7.** *Informal.* to hide or conceal, as something stolen. **8.** *Informal.* to place (someone or something) as a trick or trap or with a concealed purpose: *to plant fake evidence at the scene of a crime, to plant an informer in a revolutionary group, to plant favorable stories about a candidate in the news media.* [Old English *plante* young tree or shrub ready for planting or recently planted, from Latin *planta* sprout, shoot (for planting).]

plan·tain¹ (plan′tən) *n.* **1.** the large, greenish yellow fruit of a tropical plant, *Musa paradisiaca,* resembling a banana. **2.** the plant bearing this fruit. [Spanish *plantano* the plant, going back to Latin *platanus* plane tree. See PLANE³.]

plan·tain² (plan′tən) *n.* any of a group of plants, genus *Plantago,* found as a common weed in Europe, Asia, and North America, bearing clusters of tiny flowers on slender spikes and large,

heavily ribbed leaves. [Old French *plantain,* from Latin *plantāgō,* from *planta* sole of the foot; referring to the appearance of its leaves, which are broad and flat.]

plantain lily, any of a number of hardy, perennial plants, genus *Hosta,* of the lily family, bearing white, blue, or purple flowers, grown for their ornamental foliage. Also, **hosta.**

plan·tar (plan′tər) *adj.* of, relating to, or located on the sole of the foot: *a plantar wart.* [Latin *plantaris,* from *planta* sole of the foot.]

plan·ta·tion (plan tā′shən) *n.* **1.** a large estate or farm that is usually devoted to a single crop and cultivated by workers who live on it. **2.** a group of plants, as rubber trees, that has been planted. **3.** formerly, a newly established colony or settlement. [Latin *plantātiō* planting.]

plant·er (plan′tər) *n.* **1.a.** a person who plants. **b.** any of various mechanical devices used for planting. **2.** a person who owns or manages a plantation. **3.** a decorative container for growing plants. **4.** formerly, a colonist.

plan·ti·grade (plan′ti grād′) *adj.* walking on the entire sole of the foot, as a human being or a bear. ➡ distinguished from **digitigrade.** [French *plantigrade,* from Latin *planta* sole of the foot + *gradī* to walk.]

plant louse, aphid.

plaque (plak) *n.* **1.** a flat plate or slab of hard material, as wood or metal, that is ornamented or inscribed for mounting on a wall or other surface, as for identification or commemoration. **2.** a platelike ornament worn as a badge. **3.** a thick, white film that forms on teeth as a result of bacterial growth. **4.** a fatty deposit on an arterial wall. [French *plaque,* from Dutch *plak* tablet.]

plash (plash) *n.* splash. —*v.t., v.i.* splash. [Old English *plæsc* puddle, pool.]

-plasm *combining form* molded or formed cellular material: *cytoplasm.* [Greek *plasma* something molded or formed.]

plas·ma (plaz′mə) *n.* **1.** blood plasma. **2.** the thin liquid that forms the fluid portion of milk; whey. **3.** cytoplasm or protoplasm. **4.** a hot, highly ionized gas that is electrically neutral, found on the sun and in interstellar space or formed by lightning bolts. Plasma is sometimes considered to be a fourth state of matter. [Late Latin *plasma* mold[1], image, from Greek *plasma* something molded or formed.]

plasma cell, any of the antibody-producing lymphocytes into which a B cell differentiates when bound to an antigen and sensitized by a T cell.

plasma membrane, cell membrane.

plasma physics, a branch of physics that deals with ionized gas, or plasma.

plas·mid (plaz′mid) *n.* a small, circular piece of DNA that exists and replicates independently of the chromosomes in a cell. Bacterial plasmids are used in genetic engineering to produce recombinant DNA. For illustration, see **gene-splicing.** [PLASMA + -ID[2].]

plas·mo·di·um (plaz mō′dē əm) *n., pl.* **-di·a** (-dē ə). **1.** any of several parasitic protozoans, esp. one that causes malaria in humans. **2.** the mobile, amoebalike mass of protoplasm characteristic of some stages of various organisms, as the slime molds.

plas·mol·y·sis (plaz mol′ə sis) *n. Biology.* the separation of protoplasm from a cell wall because of the loss of water by osmosis, causing the cell to shrink and die.

plas·ter (plas′tər) *n.* **1.** a mixture of lime, sand, and water that becomes a hard, smooth material when dry, used for coating walls, ceilings, or partitions. **2.** plaster of Paris. **3.** a medical preparation that is spread on cloth and then applied to the body for healing purposes, as a mustard plaster. —*v.t.* **1.** to cover or coat with plaster. **2.** to cover thoroughly or thickly, as if with plaster: *The workers plastered the fence with posters.* **3.** to spread thickly or abundantly: *to plaster butter on a piece of bread.* **4.** to cause to adhere or lie flat: *The rain has plastered your hair to your head.* [Old English *plaster* medical plaster, going back to Latin *emplastrum,* from Greek *emplastron,* from *emplassein* to daub on.] —**plas′ter·er,** *n.*

plas·ter·board (plas′tər bôrd′) *n.* a thin, firm board composed of layers of paper and plaster, used for walls or partitions; drywall.

plaster cast **1.** a cast or copy, as of a work of art, made with plaster of Paris. **2.** a rigid form made of plaster of Paris and gauze, used to immobilize a broken bone or badly sprained muscle.

plaster of Paris, powdered gypsum that is mixed with water to form a paste, which dries rapidly into a hard, solid mass. It is used for making molds, casts, or reproductions of works of art. Also, **plaster.** [Middle English *plaster of parys;* referring to the fact that in the Middle Ages the highest grade of gypsum for making plaster came from *Paris.*]

plas·tic (plas′tik) *n.* **1.** any of a group of synthetic materials, made from organic compounds by polymerization, that can be molded or shaped when softened. Most plastics are poor conductors of electricity and heat, resist chemical attack, and are waterproof. **2.** *Informal.* a credit card or credit cards or the use of credit: *to live on plastic.* —*adj.* **1.** capable of being molded or shaped: *a plastic material.* **2.** of or relating to molding or shaping: *Ceramics is a plastic art.* **3.** made of plastic. **4.** capable of molding or shaping material; creative: *a plastic artist.* **5.** easily changed, modified, or influenced; impressionable; adaptable. **6.** superficial or artificial; lacking originality or sincerity: *Their world is very plastic. The salesclerk had a plastic smile.* [Latin *plasticus* relating to molding or forming, from Greek *plastikos,* going back to *plassein* to mold[1], form.] —**plas′ti·cal·ly,** *adv.* —**plas·tic·i·ty** (plas tis′i tē), *n.*

plas·ti·cize (plas′tə sīz′) *v.t.,* -**cized, -ciz·ing. 1.** to make soft or pliable. **2.** to treat or impregnate with plastic, as a porous or fibrous material. [PLASTIC + -IZE.]

plas·ti·ciz·er (plas′tə sī′zər) *n.* any of a group of substances that is added to a plastic to make it softer or more flexible.

plastic surgery, surgery for the purpose of repairing or restoring injured or malformed parts of the body. —**plastic surgeon.**

plas·tid (plas′tid) *n.* any of various organelles in the cytoplasm of most plant cells, as leukoplasts and chromoplasts, that either store food or manufacture it. [German *plastide,* from Greek *plastis,* feminine of *plastēs* modeler, creator, from *plassein* to mold[1], form.]

plas·tron (plas′trən) *n.* **1.** a protective pad worn over the chest in fencing. **2.** a metal breastplate worn under a coat of mail. **3.** the part of a turtle's or tortoise's shell that covers the belly. [French *plastron* breastplate, fencer's chest pad, from Italian *piastrone,* from *piastra* breastplate, metal plate, from Latin *emplastrum* medical plaster. See PLASTER.]

plat[1] (plat) *n.* **1.** a small piece of ground; plot. **2.** a map, chart, or plan. —*v.t.,* **plat·ted, plat·ting.** to make a plat of. [Partly a form of PLOT; partly from Old French *plat* flat, going back to Greek *platys* flat, broad.]

plat[2] (plat) *n.* plait *(def. 1).* —*v.t.* **plat·ted, plat·ting.** plait *(defs. 1, 2).* [Form of PLAIT.]

plate (plāt) *n.* **1.** a shallow dish from which food is served or eaten.

plastron *(def. 3)*

2. the contents of such a dish: *to eat a plate of spaghetti.* **3.a.** food and service for one person at a meal: *The banquet cost twenty dollars a plate.* **b.** an entire course served on one plate: *to order the luncheon plate.* **4.** a dish passed to take collections, as in a church. **5.a.** dishes and table utensils coated with a thin layer of silver or gold. **b.** dishes and table utensils made of silver or gold. **6.a.** a flat, comparatively thin piece of metal of uniform thickness and even surface: *a plate of steel.* **b.** armor made of such pieces of metal. **7.** a piece of metal, usually thin and flat, on which something is or can be engraved. **8.** a print made from an engraved piece of metal, as an illustration in a book. **9.** *Printing.* a cast of a page of type to be printed from, as an electrotype or a stereotype. **10.** *Photography.* a thin sheet of glass, metal, or other material coated with a photosensitive substance, used to take photographs. **11. the plate.** home plate. **12.** *Biology.* a thin, flat part, organ, or structure, as the bony structures protecting the armadillo. **13.** a piece of metal, plastic, or similar material implanted with a set of artificial teeth, fitted to the gums to replace missing natural teeth; denture. **14.** a thin cut of beef from the lower end of the breast or brisket. **15.** the anode in a vacuum tube, toward which electrons flow because of its positive charge. **16.** a horizontal timber supporting the ends of other timbers, as one of the wall supports for a girder or roof. **17.** *Geology.* one of the huge sections, according to the theory of plate tectonics, that make up the landmasses of the earth and the floors of the oceans. Movement of the plates gives rise to continental drift. —*v.t.,* **plated, plat·ing. 1.** to coat with a thin layer of metal, as silver, gold, or chromium. **2.** to cover with metal plates for protection. **3.** *Printing.* to make an electrotype or stereotype from (type). [Old French *plate* sheet of metal, from *plat* flat, going back to Greek *platys* flat, broad.]

a	at	e	end	o	hot	u	up	hw	white		about
ā	ape	ē	me	ō	old	ū	use	ng	song		taken
ä	far	i	it	ô	fork	u̇	rule	th	thin	ə {	pencil
âr	care	ī	ice	oi	oil	u̇	pull	th	this		lemon
		îr	pierce	ou	out	ûr	turn	zh	measure		circus

pla·teau (pla tō′) *n., pl.* **-teaus** or **-teaux** (-tōz′). **1.** an area of relatively flat land elevated above the surrounding land. **2.** a relatively stable or inactive period or stage, as in development: *to reach a plateau in one's career.* [French *plateau* tableland, from Old French *plat* flat. See PLATE.]

plate·ful (plāt′fùl′) *n., pl.* **-fuls.** as much as a plate will hold.

plate glass, a strong glass made in clear, flat sheets, used for windowpanes or mirrors.

plate·let (plāt′lit) *n.* blood platelet.

plat·en (plat′ən) *n.* **1.** the flat metal plate in a printing press that presses the paper against the inked type. **2.** the roller in a typewriter or computer printer around which paper is fed and that holds the paper in place during typing or printing. [Old French *platine* flat plate, from *plat* flat. See PLATE.]

plate tectonics **1.** the theory that the earth's crust is made of separate rigid plates that are in slow, constant motion, giving rise to continental drift, volcanic activity, and earthquakes. **2.** the branch of geology that deals with continental drift, volcanic and seismic activity, and other geologic processes in light of this theory. ➡ used as singular in both defs. —**plate′·tec·ton′ic,** *adj.*

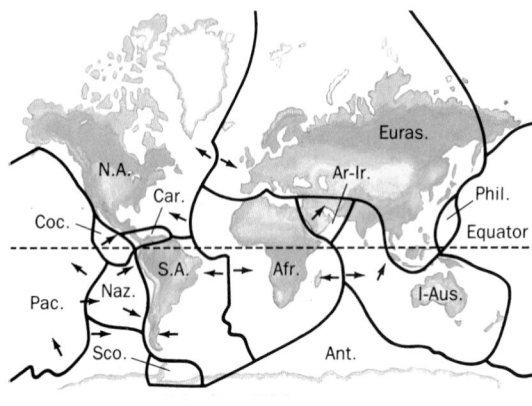

N.A. = North American plate	Ar-Ir. = Arabian-Iranian plate
Coc. = Cocos plate	Euras. = Eurasian plate
Car. = Caribbean plate	Phil. = Philippine plate
Pac. = Pacific plate	I-Aus. = Indo-Australian plate
Naz. = Nazca plate	Ant. = Antarctic plate
Sco. = Scotia plate	S.A. = South American plate
Afr. = African plate	

plate tectonics
map of the earth's plates

plat·form (plat′fôrm′) *n.* **1.** a raised, flat structure or flooring, as for a speaker in an auditorium. **2.** a raised area alongside the tracks at a railroad or subway station. **3.** a declaration of principles, esp. a public statement of the principles and policies of a political party. [French *plateforme*, from *plat* flat + *forme* form, shape. See PLATE, FORM.]

platform car, flatcar.

platform tennis, a form of tennis played with wooden paddles and a rubber ball on a wooden platform surrounded by a high wire fence.

plat·ing (plā′ting) *n.* **1.** a thin coating or layer of metal, esp. of gold or silver. **2.** an external layer or covering of metal plates. **3.** the act of a person or thing that plates: *the plating of steel with chromium.*

pla·tin·ic (pla tin′ik) *adj.* of, relating to, or containing platinum, esp. in its higher oxidation state of +4.

plat·i·nize (plat′ə nīz′) *v.t.*, **-nized, -niz·ing.** to plate (a metal) with platinum or apply a coat of platinum to (a surface or object).

plat·i·nous (plat′ə nəs) *adj.* of, relating to, or containing platinum, esp. in its lower oxidation state of +2.

plat·i·num (plat′ə nəm) *n.* a heavy, soft, silver-white metallic element that is ductile, malleable, and resistant to corrosion. It is used in jewelry and catalytic converters. Symbol: **Pt** For tables, see **element.** [Modern Latin *platinum* (referring to its silvery color), going back to Spanish *plata* silver, from Old French *plate* sheet of metal. See PLATE.]

plat·i·tude (plat′i tüd′, -tūd′) *n.* **1.** a dull, trite, or commonplace remark, esp. one meant to sound original or important. **2.** the state or quality of being dull, trite, or commonplace.

[French *platitude*, from *plat* flat. See PLATE.] —For Synonyms, see **truism.**

plat·i·tu·di·nous (plat′i tü′də nəs, -tū′-) *adj.* **1.** of, relating to, or having the nature of a platitude; trite: *a platitudinous comment.* **2.** given to or full of platitudes: *a platitudinous speaker, a platitudinous book.* —**plat′i·tu′di·nous·ly,** *adv.*

Pla·ton·ic (plə ton′ik) *adj.* **1.** of or relating to the Greek philosopher Plato or his philosophy. **2.** *also,* **platonic.** of or designating a relationship between two people that is spiritual or intellectual rather than sexual. —**Pla·ton′i·cal·ly,** *adv.*

Pla·to·nism (plā′tə niz′əm) *n.* **1.** the philosophy of Plato or his followers. **2.** a Platonic doctrine or saying. **3.** *also,* **platonism.** the theory or practice of Platonic love.

Pla·to·nist (plā′tə nist) *n.* **1.** a follower of Plato or of his philosophy. **2.** a person who tends to think and act on the basis of intuition and ideals rather than of conclusions drawn from experience.

pla·toon (plə tün′) *n.* **1.** a military unit forming part of a company, usually commanded by a lieutenant. **2.** any similar group or unit: *a platoon of volunteers.* **3.** a group of football players who specialize in either offensive or defensive play and enter or leave the game as a unit. —*v.t.* **1.** *Sports.* to use (a player or players) in alternation with another player or players at the same position: *to platoon Smith with Rodriguez at third base.* **2.** *Sports.* to use (two different groups of players) in alternation for offense and defense. **3.** to divide into platoons. —*v.i. Sports.* **1.** to alternate players or be alternated with another player at a position. **2.** to use different groups of players for offense and defense. [French *peloton* group, little ball, from *pelote* ball. See PELLET.]

plat·ter (plat′ər) *n.* **1.** a large, usually oval dish for holding or serving food. **2.** food served on a platter: *a platter of roast beef.* [Anglo-Norman *plater* dish, from Old French *plat*, from *plat* flat. See PLATE.]

plat·y¹ (plā′tē) *adj.*, **plat·i·er, plat·i·est.** *Geology.* consisting of or separating into thin, platelike layers, as mica or shale. [PLATE + -Y¹.]

plat·y² (plat′ē) *n., pl.* **plat·y, plat·ys,** or **plat·ies.** any of a group of colorful, livebearer aquarium fish, genus *Xiphophorus*, of tropical America, having a swordlike lower tail fin. Also, **swordtail.** [Contraction of Modern Latin *Platypoecilus* genus name of fish, from Greek *platys* broad, flat + *poikilos* many-colored.]

plat·y·hel·minth (plat′ē hel′minth) *n.* flatworm. [Greek *platys* broad, flat + *helminth-*, stem of *helmins* worm.]

plat·y·pus (plat′ə pəs) *n.* a primitive, aquatic egg-laying mammal, or monotreme, *Ornithorhynchus anatinus*, native to Australia and Tasmania, having a flat, wide bill, webbed feet, a tail like a beaver's, and soft, brown fur. Length: to 2 feet (0.6 meter), including tail. Also, **duckbill, duck-billed platypus.** [Greek *platypous* flat-footed.]

platypus

plau·dit (plô′dit) *usually,* **plau·dits.** *n.* an expression of praise or approval, as enthusiastic applause. [Latin *plaudite* applaud, plural imperative of *plaudere* to applaud (request for applause made by ancient Roman actors at the end of a performance).]

plau·si·ble (plô′zə bəl) *adj.* **1.** apparently true or acceptable; likely: *a plausible excuse.* **2.** seemingly honest or worthy of confidence, but often deceptively so. [Latin *plausibilis* praiseworthy, from *plausus*, past participle of *plaudere* to applaud.] —**plau′si·bil′i·ty, plau′si·ble·ness,** *n.* —**plau′si·bly,** *adv.*

play (plā) *n.* **1.** something done for recreation, pleasure, or amusement: *children at play.* **2.a.** the act of carrying on a game: *Play resumed after the time-out.* **b.** a manner or style of carrying on a game: *There was some rough play in that hockey game.* **3.** a move or turn to move in a game: *It's your play.* **4.a.** a literary work written to be performed on a stage; drama. **b.** the performance of such a work. **5.** behavior of a specified kind: *fair play.* **6.** action or operation; working: *The engine was in full play.* **7.** light, rapid, or fluttering movement or change, esp. of light or color: *the play of shadows on a wall.* **8.** free or unimpeded motion or action: *the play of a wheel, too much play in a door handle.* **9.** movement, or space or room for it, as of a part of a mechanism. **10.** gambling. —*v.i.* **1.** to do something for recreation, pleasure, or amusement: *The children played in the backyard.* **2.** to act or deal carelessly (usually with *with*): *Don't play with a loaded gun.* **3.** to do something that is not to be taken seriously: *I was only*

playing when I acted angry. **4.** to perform in a play, movie, or television program. **5.** to act or behave (in a specified way): *That politician plays rough.* **6.** to perform on a musical instrument: *to play in an orchestra.* **7.** to give out sound, esp. musical sound: *The band is playing. Is the stereo playing?* **8.** to move in a light, rapid, or fluttering way: *A smile played on her lips. The wind played among the leaves.* **9.** to operate with continuous or repeated action: *The hose played on the fire.* **10.** to engage in a game: *They played for three innings.* **11.** to gamble; bet: *to play at the races.* **12.** to lend itself to performance: *The third act plays well.* **13.** to be performed or exhibited: *The movie was playing at the local theater.* —*v.t.* **1.** to act the part of in a dramatic performance: *The young actor played an old person.* **2.** to behave like; act as: *to play the fool, to play the hostess.* **3.** to give a performance of: *The theater is playing a very good film. The orchestra will play a Brahms symphony this evening.* **4.** to give performances in: *The troupe will play New York next week.* **5.** to imitate or pretend to be, as for amusement: *The children were playing pirates.* **6.** to do; perform, esp. in fun or to deceive: *to play a trick on someone.* **7.** to direct continuously or repeatedly: *to play a hose on a burning building.* **8.** to cause to move lightly or rapidly: *to play lights on a fountain.* **9.** to bet or speculate on: *to play the horses, to play the stock market.* **10.** to engage in (a game or other activity): *to play a round of golf, to play baseball.* **11.** to contend against in a game: *New York played Chicago for the championship.* **12.** to occupy or perform in (a specified position) in a game: *Smith will play first base.* **13.** to use in a game or sport: *The coach played him at center. Play your jack of clubs.* **14.** to perform or produce (music) on an instrument: *to play a Beethoven sonata.* **15.** to perform on (a musical instrument): *to play the piano.* **16.** to cause to give out sound, esp. of music: *to play a phonograph.* **17.** to let (a hooked fish) tire itself by pulling on the line. [Old English *pleg(i)an* to sport, play (a game), amuse oneself.] —**play'a·ble,** *adj.*
 •**in play.** *Sports.* (of a ball or the like) in a condition or position for play to continue without interruption.
 •**out of play.** *Sports.* (of a ball or the like) in a condition or position that interrupts play, as outside the playing field.
 •**played out. a.** exhausted; tired. **b.** too worn or used to be useful; worn out: *a new stereo to replace one that was played out.* **c.** used up: *The mine closed after the vein of ore was played out.*
 •**to play along. a.** to agree or cooperate, esp. without enthusiasm or sincerity: *I knew their plan was unrealistic, but I played along with it.* **b.** to take part; participate: *I played along with the joke.*
 •**to play at. a.** to take part in; participate in: *to play at cards.* **b.** to do halfheartedly or insincerely: *to play at being a writer.*
 •**to play back.** to play (a recording, esp. one that has just been made).
 •**to play both ends against the middle.** to manipulate opposing interests to benefit oneself.
 •**to play down.** to treat as of little or no importance; understate the importance of: *You always play down your accomplishments.*
 •**to play for time.** to prolong or delay something deliberately; stall.
 •**to play into the hands of.** to act in a way that unintentionally benefits (someone, esp. an opponent).
 •**to play it by ear.** to act or do something without prior preparation; improvise.
 •**to play it cool.** *Slang.* to keep one's composure; be calm.
 •**to play off. a.** to break (a tie) by playing an extra game, round, or the like. **b.** to set into conflict for one's own advantage: *a country that maintained its independence by playing off one powerful neighbor against another.*
 •**to play on** (or **upon**). to take advantage of, esp. unfairly or selfishly: *to play on someone's sympathies.*
 •**to play one's cards right** (or **well**). to act in a careful and effective way.
 •**to play out. a.** to perform to the end: *to play out a drama.* **b.** to release (a rope, fishing line, or the like) gradually. **c.** to become used up or exhausted.
 •**to play up.** to treat as important; emphasize or highlight: *to play up one's experience on a résumé.*
 •**to play up to.** to try to gain the favor of, as by flattery.
pla·ya (plī′ə) *n.* a flat-floored desert basin, esp. in the southwestern United States, occupied by a shallow, temporary lake after heavy rains. [Spanish *playa* literally, beach, from Provençal *playa,* from Vulgar Latin *plagia* coast, side, from or akin to Greek *plagia* sides, from *plagos* side.]
play·act (plā′akt′) *v.i.* **1.** to perform in a theatrical production. **2.** to make believe; pretend. **3.** to behave in an affected or exaggerated manner. —*v.t.* to act out; dramatize; portray. —**play'·ac′tor,** *n.*
play·back (plā′bak′) *n.* the act or process of playing a recording

again, esp. an audio or video recording that has just been made on tape.
play·bill (plā′bil′) *n.* an announcement or program of a play.
play·boy (plā′boi′) *n.* a man, esp. a wealthy man, who spends much of his time seeking pleasure.
play-by-play (plā′bī plā′) *adj.* of, relating to, or giving a description of a sports or news event as it takes place.
play·er (plā′ər) *n.* **1.** a person who participates in a sport or game: *a baseball player, a chess player.* **2.** a person who performs in a theater; actor. **3.** a person who performs on a musical instrument; musician: *a piano player.* **4.** a mechanical device that operates a player piano. **5.a.** a record player. **b.** any machine that reproduces images or sound, as a tape player.
player piano, a piano played by a mechanical device.
play·fel·low (plā′fel′ō) *n.* playmate.
play·ful (plā′fəl) *adj.* **1.** spirited and full of fun; lively; frolicsome: *a playful puppy.* **2.** characterized or motivated by humor; humorous; joking: *a playful remark.* —**play'ful·ly,** *adv.* —**play'ful·ness,** *n.*
play·go·er (plā′gō′ər) *n.* a person who attends the theater often.
play·ground (plā′ground′) *n.* an area used for outdoor recreation, esp. by children.
play·house (plā′hous′) *n., pl.* -**hous·es** (-hou′ziz). **1.** theater. **2.** a small house for children to play in. [Old English *pleghūs* theater.]
playing card, a card used in playing games, esp. one of a deck of fifty-two cards divided into four suits (clubs, diamonds, hearts, and spades) and thirteen ranks (jacks, queens, kings, aces, and the numbers from two to ten).
play·let (plā′lit) *n.* a short dramatic work.
play·mate (plā′māt′) *n.* a companion in recreation or amusement. Also, **playfellow.**
play-off (plā′ôf′, -of′) *n.* **1.** a game played to break a tie. **2.** one or more games played to decide a championship or who will play for a championship.
play·pen (plā′pen′) *n.* a small, usually portable enclosure for a baby or small child to play in.
play·room (plā′rüm′, -rum′) *n.* a room, esp. in a home, used for recreation.
play·thing (plā′thing′) *n.* a thing to play with; toy.
play·time (plā′tīm′) *n.* time for recreation or amusement.
play·wright (plā′rīt′) *n.* a person who writes plays.
pla·za (plä′zə, plaz′ə) *n.* **1.** a public square or open space in a city or town. **2.** a shopping area or shopping center. **3.** a service area along a superhighway, usually having a restaurant and gas station. [Spanish *plaza,* going back to Latin *platēa* broad way, from Greek *plateia* (*hodos*) broad (way). Doublet of PLACE, PIAZZA.]
plea (plē) *n.* **1.** an earnest request or appeal: *a plea for help.* **2.** a reason given as an explanation; excuse: *a plea of ignorance.* **3.** *Law.* the answer given by the defendant in a criminal trial to the formal charge against him or her: *a plea of not guilty.* **4.** *Law.* the allegation made by a plaintiff or the answer given by a defendant in a civil suit. [Old French *plaid* lawsuit, discussion, from Medieval Latin *placitum* lawsuit, from Latin *placitum* opinion, from *placēre* to be pleasing.]
plea-bar·gain (plē′bär′gin) *n.* an agreement reached through plea bargaining. —*v.i.* to engage in plea bargaining.
plea bargaining, the practice of allowing the defendant in a criminal case to plead guilty to a less serious charge in order to avoid a long, costly, or difficult trial on the original charge or to obtain the defendant's testimony in prosecuting other persons accused of crimes.
pleach (plēch) *v.t.* to interlace, as growing vines; interweave. [Old French *plessier,* going back to Latin *plectere* to weave, plait.]
plead (plēd) *v.,* **plead·ed** or **pled, plead·ing.** —*v.i.* **1.** to make an earnest request or appeal; beg: *to plead for mercy.* **2.** to act as an appeal or argument: *Their youth and inexperience plead for them.* **3.** to conduct or argue a case in a court of law: *to plead before a jury.* —*v.t.* **1.** to give as an excuse or justification: *to plead illness to get out of an engagement.* **2.** to argue or present (a case or cause) in or as in a court of law. **3.** to give as answer to a charge or allegation in a court of law: *to plead guilty.* [Old French *plaidier* to argue a case in court, from *plaid* lawsuit, discussion. See PLEA.]
plead·ing (plē′ding) *n.* **1.** the act of a person who pleads. **2.** *Law.* **a.** the system of filing formal, written statements of the position of each side in a lawsuit. **b.** a written statement by a party

a	at	e	end	o	hot	u	up	hw	white		about
ā	ape	ē	me	ō	old	ū	use	ng	song		taken
ä	far	i	it	ô	fork	ü	rule	th	thin	ə	pencil
âr	care	ī	ice	oi	oil	u̇	pull	th	this		lemon
				îr	pierce	ou	out	ûr	turn	zh	measure		circus

to a lawsuit stating a claim or defense. ➡ often used in the plural: *There was nothing about negligence in the pleadings.*

pleas·ant (plez′ənt) *adj.* **1.** giving pleasure or satisfaction; pleasing; agreeable: *pleasant surroundings.* **2.** having or showing pleasing manners or behavior: *a pleasant personality.* [Old French *plaisant* pleasing, present participle of *plaisir* to be agreeable to, delight. See PLEASE.] —**pleas′ant·ly**, *adv.* —**pleas′ant·ness**, *n.*

pleas·ant·ry (plez′ən trē) *n., pl.* **-ries. 1.** a pleasant, courteous remark. **2.** a good-naturedly playful remark or action.

please (plēz) *v.*, **pleased, pleas·ing.** —*v.t.* **1.** to give pleasure or satisfaction to; be agreeable to. **2.** to be so kind or obliging as to. ➡ used in the imperative to indicate a request or politely expressed command: *Please close the door.* **3.** to be the will or pleasure of: *May it please Your Honor to hear this testimony.* —*v.i.* **1.** to give pleasure or satisfaction; be agreeable: *to try hard to please.* **2.** to have the will or desire; choose: *You may leave whenever you please.* [Old French *plaisir* to be agreeable to, delight, from Latin *placēre* to be pleasing.]

Synonyms *v.t.* **Please, gratify,** and **delight** mean to make someone happy. **Please** suggests a conscious attempt to give pleasure or satisfaction: *The hosts went to great lengths to please their guests.* **Gratify** implies the production of a deep and intense satisfaction through fulfillment of a need, expectation, or desire: *The actors were gratified by the standing ovation.* **Delight** suggests the production of intense but perhaps short-lived joy: *The postponement of the exam delighted the students.*

pleas·ing (plē′zing) *adj.* giving pleasure or satisfaction; agreeable. —**pleas′ing·ly**, *adv.* —**pleas′ing·ness**, *n.*

pleas·ur·a·ble (plezh′ər ə bəl) *adj.* giving pleasure or enjoyment: *a pleasurable experience, a pleasurable sensation.* —**pleas′ur·a·ble·ness**, *n.* —**pleas′ur·a·bly**, *adv.*

pleas·ure (plezh′ər) *n.* **1.** an enjoyable sensation or emotion. **2.** a source or cause of such a sensation or emotion: *It was a pleasure to see her again.* **3.** worldly or sensual amusement or gratification: *a life devoted to pleasure.* **4.** something that one wishes or chooses; desire or will: *It is His Majesty's pleasure that you join him.* —*v.i.* to feel pleasure; delight: *We pleasured in their visit.* [Old French *plaisir,* noun use of *plaisir* to be agreeable to, delight. See PLEASE.]

pleat (plēt) *n.* a lengthwise fold in cloth or other material, made by doubling the material upon itself and then pressing, stitching, or otherwise fastening it into place. —*v.t.* to make a pleat or pleats in; arrange in pleats. Also, **plait.** [Form of PLAIT.]

plebe (plēb) *n.* a member of the freshman class at the U.S. Military Academy or Naval Academy. [Short for PLEBEIAN.]

ple·be·ian (pli bē′ən) *n.* **1.** a member of the common people in ancient Rome. **2.** one of the common people in any society. **3.** a person who is coarse or vulgar. —*adj.* **1.** of or relating to the common people of ancient Rome. **2.** relating to, belonging to, or characteristic of the common people; ordinary. **3.** coarse; vulgar. [Latin *plēbēius* relating to the common people (from *plēbs* the common people) + -AN.]

pleb·i·scite (pleb′ə sīt′, -sit) *n.* a direct vote by the people of a country or territory on a specific political question or issue submitted to them, such as one concerning national self-determination or a choice of government or ruler. [Latin *plēbiscītum* decree of the people, from *plēbs* the common people + *scītum* decree.]

plebs (plebz) *n., pl.* **ple·bes** (plē′bēz). **1.** the common people of ancient Rome. **2.** the common people in any society; the masses. [Latin *plēbs* the common people.]

plec·trum (plek′trəm) *also,* **plec·tron** (plek′trən). *n., pl.* **-trums** or **-tra** (-trə). a small, thin implement of horn, plastic, or other material, used for plucking the strings of a guitar or similar instrument. Also, **pick.** [Latin *plectrum,* from Greek *plēktron.*]

pled (pled) a past tense and past participle of **plead.**

pledge (plej) *n.* **1.** a formal, binding guarantee that something will be done; promise: *a pledge of secrecy, a pledge to contribute to a charity.* **2.** something given or held as security: *He left his watch as a pledge that he would pay the debt.* **3.** the state of being given or held as security: *She left her necklace in pledge for the loan.* **4.** something given as a sign of affection or favor; token: *a ring given as a pledge of love.* **5.** a person who is undergoing a trial period before attaining full membership in a fraternity or similar organization. **6.** an expression of goodwill made by drinking to a person's health; toast. —*v.t.*, **pledged, pledg·ing. 1.** to offer or guarantee with a pledge: *We pledged our help.* **2.** to bind or commit by or as if by a pledge: *We were all pledged to secrecy.* **3.** to give (something) as security. **4.** to drink a toast to. **5.** to undergo a trial period before attaining full membership in (a fraternity or similar organization). [Old French *plege* surety, security, from Late Latin *plebium* security; of Germanic origin.] —**pledg′er,** *n.* —For Synonyms *(v.t.),* see **promise.**

•**to take the pledge.** to promise not to drink alcoholic beverages.

Ple·ia·des (plē′ə dēz′) *pl. n., sing.* **Ple·iad** (plē′əd). **1.** in Greek mythology, the seven daughters of Atlas, who were placed in the sky as stars by Zeus. **2.** a group of approximately 200 stars in the constellation Taurus that, to the naked eye, appears to number six or seven stars.

Plei·o·cene (plī′ə sēn′) Pliocene.

Pleis·to·cene (plīs′tə sēn′) *n.* the first of the two geologic epochs of the Quaternary period of the Cenozoic era, during which ice sheets advanced and receded over large areas of North and South America, Europe, and Asia, and human beings appeared. Also, **Ice Age.** For table, see **geologic time.** —*adj.* of, relating to, or belonging to this epoch. [Greek *pleistos* most + *kainos* recent, new.]

ple·na·ry (plē′nə rē, plen′ə-) *adj.* **1.** attended by all qualified members: *a plenary session of a legislative assembly.* **2.** complete; absolute; full: *The revolutionary committee assumed plenary powers.* [Late Latin *plēnārius* entire, full, from Latin *plēnus* full.]

plen·i·po·ten·ti·a·ry (plen′i pə ten′chə rē, -chē er′ē) *n., pl.* **-ar·ies.** an ambassador or other diplomatic agent having full power in representing a government and negotiating with other countries. —*adj.* having or bestowing full power. [Medieval Latin *plenipotentiarius,* from Latin *plēnus* full + *potentia* power.]

plen·i·tude (plen′i tūd′, -tüd′) *n.* **1.** a plentiful amount; abundance. **2.** the quality or state of being full. [Latin *plēnitūdō.*] —**plen′i·tu′di·nous,** *adj.*

plen·te·ous (plen′tē əs) *adj.* plentiful. —**plen′te·ous·ly,** *adv.* —**plen′te·ous·ness,** *n.*

plen·ti·ful (plen′ti fəl) *adj.* **1.** existing in great or sufficient quantity; abundant; ample. **2.** providing or yielding an abundance: *a plentiful harvest.* —**plen′ti·ful·ly,** *adv.* —**plen′ti·ful·ness,** *n.*

Synonyms **Plentiful, abundant,** and **copious** mean more than sufficient. **Plentiful** is the most general of these terms: *plentiful rainfall, plentiful stones to build with.* **Abundant** suggests a supply so great as to be close to the point of overflowing: *The rivers were abundant with fish.* **Copious** stresses the amount of the supply more than its relation to a need: *The diary provides copious information about life at the court.*

plen·ty (plen′tē) *n., pl.* **-ties. 1.** a full or totally sufficient supply or amount; more than enough: *There's plenty of food for everybody.* **2.** the quality or state of being plentiful; abundance: *Resources in plenty can be found in this territory.* **3.** an abundance of the necessities and comforts of life; general prosperity: *an era of peace and plenty.* —*adj.* enough or more than enough; ample: *Half a watermelon is plenty for me.* —*adv. Informal.* as much as or more than needed; quite; very: *You'd be plenty quick if you were being chased by a swarm of bees.* [Old French *plente* abundance, from Latin *plēnitās* fullness.]

ple·o·nasm (plē′ə naz′əm) *n.* **1.** the use of more words than are necessary to express an idea; redundancy. **2.** an instance of this, for example: *overly excessive.* [Late Latin *pleonasmus* excess, surplus, from Greek *pleonasmos* excess, surplus.] —**ple·o·nas·tic** (plē′ə nas′tik), *adj.* —**ple′o·nas′ti·cal·ly,** *adv.*

ple·si·o·saur (plē′sē ə sôr′) *n.* any of a group of extinct aquatic reptiles, suborder Plesiosauria, of the Mesozoic era, having a small head, long neck, and four paddlelike limbs. Also, **plesiosaurus.** [Greek *plēsios* near + *sauros* lizard.]

ple·si·o·sau·rus (plē′sē ə sôr′əs) *n., pl.* **-sau·ri** (-sôr′ī) or **-sau·rus·es.** plesiosaur.

pleth·o·ra (pleth′ər ə) *n.* **1.** more than is needed; too much; excess; superabundance. **2.** *Medicine.* an excess of a body fluid, esp. blood. [Modern Latin *plēthōra,* from Greek *plēthōrē.*]

ple·thor·ic (ple thôr′ik, -thor′-, pleth′ər ik) *adj.* **1.** excessively full; inflated; turgid. **2.** *Medicine.* relating to, characteristic of, or affected by plethora.

pleu·ra (plūr′ə) *n., pl.* **pleu·rae** (plūr′ē). the thin, serous membrane enclosing the lungs and lining the inner walls of the chest cavity. [Modern Latin *pleura,* from Greek *pleurā* side, rib.] —**pleu′ral,** *adj.*

pleu·ri·sy (plūr′ə sē) *n.* inflammation of the pleura, often accompanied by fever, difficulty in breathing, and a painful cough. Also, **pleu·ri·tis** (plù rī′tis). [Old French *pleurisie,* from Late Latin *pleurisis,* going back to Greek *pleurītis,* from *pleurā* side, rib.] —**pleu·rit·ic** (plù rit′ik), *adj.*

pleu·ro·pneu·mo·nia (plūr′ō nü mōn′yə, -nü-) *n.* a disease characterized by inflammation of both the lungs and the pleura; combined pneumonia and pleurisy.

Plex·i·glas (plek′si glas′) *n. Trademark.* a transparent acrylic resin used for such items as aircraft canopies and windows.

plex·us (plek′səs) *n., pl.* **-us·es** or **-us.** a network or interlacing, as of nerves or blood vessels. [Latin *plexus* a twining.]

pli·a·ble (plī′ə bəl) *adj.* **1.** readily yielding to force or pressure

without breaking; flexible: *pliable twigs.* **2.** easily influenced or persuaded; yielding: *a pliable personality.* **3.** readily adjusting to change; adaptable. [French *pliable* flexible, from *plier* to bend, fold [1], from Latin *plicāre* to fold [1].] —**pli·a·bil·i·ty, pli·a·ble·ness,** *n.* —**pli·a·bly,** *adv.*

Synonyms Pliable, pliant, ductile, and malleable mean capable of being literally or figuratively modified in form. **Pliable** suggests enough flexibility to be easily bent or twisted: *The pliable branches were woven into baskets.* **Pliant** also indicates flexibility and is often used figuratively: *The child has a pliant personality.* **Ductile** implies being pliable enough to be easily processed into various shapes, especially drawn out into wire: *Copper is a ductile metal.* **Malleable** refers to the capacity for being shaped by beating or pressing: *The sculptor formed the malleable clay into a human figure.*

pli·an·cy (plī′ən sē) *n.* the quality or state of being pliant.

pli·ant (plī′ənt) *adj.* **1.** bending or capable of being bent with ease; supple. **2.** easily influenced or controlled; yielding; docile. [Old French *pliant,* present participle of *plier* to bend, fold [1]. See PLIABLE.] —**pli′ant·ly,** *adv.* —For Synonyms, see **pliable.**

pli·cate (plī′kāt) *adj.* **1.** arranged in folds, as the cell walls of certain plants. **2.** folded like a fan, as the leaves of the birch. [Latin *plicātus,* past participle of *plicāre* to fold [1].] —**pli′cate·ly,** *adv.*

pli·ers (plī′ərz) *pl. n.* small pincers with parallel, often toothed jaws, used chiefly for gripping or bending objects. [From PLY [1].]

plight [1] (plīt) *n.* an unfortunate, distressing, or dangerous situation or condition: *the plight of the homeless.* [Anglo-Norman *plit* a fold, going back to Latin *plicitus,* past participle of *plicāre* to fold [1].]

plight [2] (plīt) *v.t.* to bind by a pledge; pledge; promise. [Old English *plihtan* to endanger, from *pliht* danger.]

• **to plight one's troth.** to promise oneself in marriage.

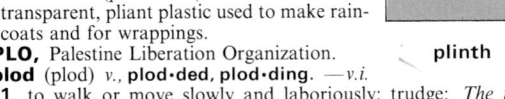

pliers

plink (plingk) *n.* a light, sharp, high sound, such as one made on a piano. —*v.i.* **1.** to make such a sound. **2.** to throw or shoot at a target that produces such a sound when hit: *to plink at tin cans.* —*v.t.* **1.** to cause to make such a sound: *to plink a banjo.* **2.** to hit (a target) so as to make such a sound: *to plink cans with a slingshot.* [Imitative.]

plinth (plinth) *n.* **1.** a slab, block, stone, or other projecting member, usually square, forming the lowest part of a base upon which a column, pedestal, or the like rests. **2.** a horizontal projecting course of masonry at the base of a wall or building. [Latin *plinthus* base of a column, from Greek *plinthos* brick.]

Pli·o·cene (plī′ə sēn′) *also,* **Pleiocene.** *n.* the fifth and last geologic epoch of the Tertiary period of the Cenozoic era, during which the Himalayas and Alps were uplifted and herbaceous plants appeared. For table, see **geologic time.** —*adj.* of, relating to, or belonging to this epoch. [Greek *pleiōn* more + *kainos* new, recent.]

Pli·o·film (plī′ə film′) *n. Trademark.* a transparent, pliant plastic used to make raincoats and for wrappings.

PLO, Palestine Liberation Organization.

plod (plod) *v.,* **plod·ded, plod·ding.** —*v.i.* **1.** to walk or move slowly and laboriously; trudge: *The tired children plodded through the snowdrifts.* **2.** to work or proceed slowly but steadily: *to plod through a difficult book.* —*v.t.* to trudge slowly and heavily along, over, or through. —*n.* the act of walking or moving slowly and laboriously. **2.** the sound made by a plodding step or steps. [Imitative.] —**plod′der,** *n.* —**plod′ding·ly,** *adv.*

plop (plop) *v.,* **plopped, plop·ping.** —*v.i.* to drop or fall heavily with or as with a sound like that of an object dropping into water: *She plopped on the bed and kicked off her shoes.* —*v.t.* to drop or let fall so as to make such a sound. —*n.* the act or sound of plopping. —*adv.* with a plop: *He fell plop into the puddle.* [Imitative.]

plinth

plo·sive (plō′siv, -ziv) *Phonetics. adj.* pronounced with a sudden letting go of breath, as the consonants *p, b, d,* and *k.* —*n.* a plosive speech sound. Also, **explosive.**

plot (plot) *n.* **1.** a secret plan, esp. to accomplish some evil or illegal purpose: *a plot to take over the government.* **2.** the main

story in a play, novel, or other literary work. **3.** a small piece of ground, usually used for a specific purpose: *a cemetery plot.* **4.** a chart, diagram, or map, as of a building or estate. —*v.,* **plot·ted, plot·ting.** —*v.t.* **1.** to devise a plot for: *to plot the downfall of a regime.* **2.** to make a diagram or map of; chart: *to plot a ship's course.* **3.** to mark the position of or show on a diagram or map: *All the fireboxes are plotted on this map of the city.* **4.** *Mathematics.* **a.** to locate and mark (a point or set of points) in a plane or in space by means of coordinates. **b.** to draw (a curve) by joining points so marked. **c.** to represent (an equation) by drawing such a curve. —*v.i.* to form a plot; scheme. [Partly from Old English *plot* piece of ground; partly short for earlier *complot* secret plan (from Old French *complot;* of uncertain origin); partly modification of PLAT [1].] —**plot′ter,** *n.*

Synonyms *n.* Plot, intrigue, conspiracy, and scheme mean a secret plan devised to achieve an evil, treacherous, or destructive end. **Plot** suggests a treacherous, carefully constructed plan: *The documents detailed a plot to discredit the governor.* **Intrigue** implies a more complex plan that may be far-reaching and involve many people: *The clerk was involved in many international intrigues during the war.* **Conspiracy,** a more sinister term, refers to a plot by two or more people to commit treason or a major crime: *The drug ring's leader was involved in a conspiracy to assassinate the president.* **Scheme** emphasizes the elaborateness or ingenuity of the plan and the craftiness of the planner: *The scheme involved the use of sophisticated computer technology to defraud the bank.*

plough (plou) plow.

plough·boy (plou′boi′) plowboy.

plough·man (plou′mən) *n., pl.* **-men** (-mən). plowman.

plough·share (plou′shâr′) plowshare.

plo·ver (pluv′ər, plō′vər) *n.* any of various shorebirds, family Charadriidae, having a straight, pointed bill. Length: 6-16 inches (15-41 centimeters). [Anglo-Norman *plover,* going back to Latin *pluvia* rain; because it was thought to be seen most often during a rainy season.]

plow (plou) *also,* **plough.** *n.* **1.** a farm implement for turning over or breaking up the soil in preparation for sowing or planting, usually drawn by animals or a tractor. **2.** any of various devices resembling a plow in shape or function, such as a snowplow. —*v.t.* **1.** to break and turn up the surface of with a plow: *to plow a field.* **2.** to form or make with or as if with a plow: *We plowed our way through the crowd.* **3.** to furrow, tear, or gash with or as if with a plow (often with *up*): *The plane plowed up the field during its forced landing.* **4.** to dig out, remove, or expose with or as if with a plow (often with *up*): *Farmers occasionally plow up old Indian relics.* **5.** to cleave the surface of or move through (water) like a plow: *The liner plowed the surface of the ocean.* **6.** to clear with a snowplow or similar device: *to plow a driveway.* —*v.i.* **1.** to break and turn up soil with a plow: *The farmer spent the morning plowing.* **2.** to be capable of being plowed: *Hard earth doesn't plow well.* **3.** to move forward steadily, forcefully, or with difficulty: *to plow through an assigned book.* [Old English *plōg* area of land that can be tilled by eight oxen in a year, from Old Norse *plōgr* the farm implement.]

plover

• **to plow back.** to put back into the same business or enterprise: *to plow profits back into a firm.*

• **to plow into. a.** *Informal.* to crash into: *The bus plowed into a truck.* **b.** to use money as capital to start or expand a business or enterprise: *The investors plowed millions of dollars into the development of a microchip.*

• **to plow under. a.** to cover or bury by plowing. **b.** *Informal.* to overwhelm: *to be plowed under with work.*

plow·boy (plou′boi′) *also,* **ploughboy.** *n.* **1.** a boy who leads or guides the animal or animals drawing a plow. **2.** a country boy.

plow·man (plou′mən) *also,* **ploughman.** *n., pl.* **-men** (-mən). **1.** a man who guides or operates a plow. **2.** a farmer or farm worker; rustic.

a	at	e	end	o	hot	u	up	hw	white		about
ā	ape	ē	me	ō	old	ū	use	ng	song		taken
ä	far	i	it	ô	fork	ü	rule	th	thin	ə	pencil
âr	care	ī	ice	oi	oil	u̇	pull	th	this		lemon
		îr	pierce	ou	out	ûr	turn	zh	measure		circus

P

plow·share (plou′shâr′) *also*, **ploughshare**. *n.* the edge or blade of a plow, which cuts the soil. Also, **share**.

ploy (ploi) *n.* a tricky maneuver or piece of strategy: *Those tears are only a ploy to gain attention.* [Scottish *ploy* enterprise, trick, possibly short for EMPLOY.]

pluck (pluk) *v.t.* **1.** to pull out or off; pick: *to pluck the feathers from a chicken.* **2.** to pull feathers or hair from (something): *to pluck one's eyebrows.* **3.a.** to pull quickly or with force; snatch: *He plucked the letter from her hands.* **b.** to pull, grasp, or tug at: *to pluck someone's sleeve.* **4.** to pull on and quickly release (the strings of a musical instrument), causing them to sound. **5.** *Slang.* to rob; swindle; cheat. —*v.i.* to give a pull; grasp; tug (with *at*): *The child plucked at my coat sleeve.* —*n.* **1.** courage, spirit, and determination, esp. as shown in the face of danger or difficulty. **2.** the act of pulling; tug; jerk. [Old English *pluccian* to pull off, pick[1].] —**pluck′er,** *n.*

• **to pluck up.** to summon or gather up; rouse: *to pluck up one's courage.*

pluck·y (pluk′ē) *adj.*, **pluck·i·er, pluck·i·est.** having or showing courage, spirit, and determination, esp. in the face of danger or difficulty. —**pluck′i·ly,** *adv.* —**pluck′i·ness,** *n.*

plug (plug) *n.* **1.** a piece of wood, rubber, or other material used to stop up a hole or fill a gap. **2.** *Electricity.* a male fitting, usually having prongs, attached to the end of a wire or cable and inserted into a female outlet or receptacle to make a connection. **3.** a cake of pressed or twisted tobacco, or a piece of it cut off for chewing. **4.** spark plug *(def. 1).* **5.** fireplug. **6.** *Informal.* a favorable mention of or piece of publicity about someone or something, esp. one that is unrelated to the subject under discussion: *The actor sneaked in a plug for the new movie during the interview.* **7.** a fishing lure with hooks attached, used in casting. **8.** *Slang.* an old, worn-out, or inferior horse. —*v.*, **plugged, plug·ging.** —*v.t.* **1.** to stop or fill with or as if with a plug (often with *up*): *The coffee grains plugged up the kitchen drain.* **2.** *Informal.* **a.** to make favorable public mention of. **b.** to publicize frequently or insistently, as by repeated performances or advertisements: *The disc jockey keeps plugging that record.* **3.** *Slang.* to hit with a bullet; shoot. —*v.i.* **1.** *Informal.* to work doggedly or persistently: *Keep on plugging for that raise.* [Middle Dutch *plugge* wooden peg.] —**plug′ger,** *n.*

• **to plug in. a.** to insert the plug of (an electrical device) into an outlet: *to plug in a toaster.* **b.** *Informal.* to insert or incorporate; put in: *to plug in new statistics in a report.*

• **to plug into.** to connect or become connected to by or as by a plug: *an appliance that plugs into a standard electrical outlet, an office that is plugged into a national computer network.*

• **to pull the plug.** *Informal.* to disconnect electrical medical equipment that is keeping a seriously ill person alive.

• **to pull the plug on.** *Informal.* to put an end to; end: *My parents pulled the plug on my party plans.*

plug-ug·ly (plug′ug′lē) *n., pl.* **-lies.** *Slang.* a hoodlum; thug.

plum (plum) *n.* **1.** the edible, round or oval fruit of a tree, genus *Prunus,* of the rose family, having a flattened pit, soft, juicy flesh, and smooth skin that may be purple, red, yellow, or green. **2.** the tree bearing this fruit, having oval leaves and small white or pink flowers. **3.** something choice or desirable, such as a fine job or position. **4.** a dark, reddish purple or bluish red color. **5.** a raisin, when added to a pudding or other dish. **6.** sugarplum. —*adj.* having the color plum. [Old English *plūme* the fruit, going back to Latin *prūnum,* from Greek *proumnon.* Doublet of PRUNE.]

plum·age (plü′mij) *n.* the feathers of a bird, collectively. [Old French *plumage,* from *plume* feather. See PLUME.]

plumb (plum) *v.t.* **1.** to test or adjust by a plumb line. **2.** to measure the depth of (a body of water) with or as with a plumb line; sound: *They plumbed the river to find a channel for ships.* **3.** to discover or examine closely the dimensions, nature, or contents of; get to the bottom of: *to plumb a mystery.* **4.** to make vertical; straighten (often with *up*). **5.** to install plumbing in (a house or other building). **6.** to seal with lead. —*adj.* **1.** vertical. **2.** *Informal.* complete; absolute: *He's a plumb fool. That's plumb nonsense.* —*adv.* **1.** in a vertical direction or line; vertically: *The wall must run plumb.* **2.** *Informal.* completely; absolutely: *She's plumb crazy.* —*n.* plumb bob. [Old French *plomb* lead, plumb bob, from Latin *plumbum* lead.]

• **out of** (or **off) plumb.** not vertical.

plum·ba·go (plum bā′gō) *n.* graphite. [Latin *plumbāgō* lead ore, from *plumbum* lead.]

plumb·er (plum′ər) *n.* a person who installs and repairs plumbing. [Old French *plommier,* from Latin *plumbārius,* from *plumbum* lead; because plumbers originally worked with lead.]

plumb·ing (plum′ing) *n.* **1.** the pipes, fixtures, and other apparatus involved in the use of water and the disposal of sewage in a building or other structure. **2.** the work or trade of a plumber.

plumb line, a line from which a weight is suspended, used to measure depths, as of excavations or bodies of water, or to determine whether something is vertical. Also, **plummet.**

plumb bob, a weight, often pointed, at the end of a plumb line. Also, **plumb, plummet.**

plume (plüm) *n.* **1.** a large, fluffy, showy feather. **2.** an ornament consisting of a plume or cluster of plumes, or of a feathery tuft of fluffy material, often worn as a token of honor or distinction, as on a hat. **3.** any token of honor or distinction. **4.** something resembling a plume: *a plume of smoke.* —*v.t.,* **plumed, plum·ing. 1.** to adorn or furnish with or as with a plume or plumes. **2.** (of a bird) to smooth or dress (itself) with the beak; preen. **3.** to feel pride in (oneself), as for an achievement. [Old French *plume* feather, from Latin *plūma.*]

plumb line

plum·met (plum′it) *v.i.* to fall or drop straight downward; plunge. —*n.* **1.** plumb bob. **2.** plumb line. [Old French *plommet* plumb bob, diminutive of *plomb* lead. See PLUMB.]

plu·mose (plü′mōs) *adj.* **1.** having feathers or plumes. **2.** like a plume or feather; feathery. [Latin *plūmōsus* full of feathers, from *plūma* feather.] —**plu′mose·ly,** *adv.* —**plu·mos·i·ty** (plü mos′i tē), *n.*

plump¹ (plump) *adj.* having a full or rounded form; somewhat fat or well filled out: *a plump child, a plump cushion.* —*v.t.* to make plump (often with *up* or *out*): *to plump up pillows.* —*v.i.* to become plump (with *up* or *out*). [Possibly from Middle Dutch *plomp* blunt, stupid.] —**plump′ly,** *adv.* —**plump′ness,** *n.*

plump² (plump) *v.i.* **1.** to fall or drop heavily, suddenly, or with abrupt impact: *She plumped down onto the sofa.* **2.** to support someone or something completely and enthusiastically (with *for*): *to plump for the election of a candidate.* —*v.t.* to throw, put, or let fall heavily or abruptly. —*adv.* **1.** directly; exactly; straight: *The shed was built plump in the middle of the oil field.* **2.** with an abrupt impact; heavily; suddenly: *He fell plump on the bed.* **3.** with no qualifications; bluntly. —*adj.* downright; blunt: *a plump denial.* —*n.* **1.** a heavy or abrupt fall. **2.** the sound made by such a fall. [Imitative.]

plum pudding, a boiled or steamed pudding containing flour, suet, eggs, raisins, currants, and spices.

plu·mule (plü′mūl) *n.* **1.** a small, downy feather. **2.** a bud that is part of the embryo in a seed or the part of a young shoot that is above the cotyledons. [Latin *plūmula* little feather, diminutive of *plūma* feather.]

plum·y (plü′mē) *adj.* **1.** covered or adorned with feathers or plumes. **2.** like a plume; feathery.

plun·der (plun′dər) *v.t.* **1.** to ravage or rob by open force, as during a war: *to plunder a town.* **2.** to take wrongfully or by force; steal or rob: *to plunder goods.* —*v.i.* to engage in plundering. —*n.* **1.** something that is taken by plundering; booty; loot. **2.** the act of plundering. [German *plündern* to pillage, from Middle High German *plunder* household effects.] —**plun′der·er,** *n.*

plunge (plunj) *v.,* **plunged, plung·ing.** —*v.t.* **1.** to put forcefully or suddenly; thrust: *to plunge one's hand into water.* **2.** to force or place suddenly into some condition or course of action: *A power failure plunged the room into darkness.* —*v.i.* **1.** to dive, fall or move suddenly or sharply in a downward direction: *The elevator plunged three stories when the cable snapped.* **2.** to move quickly or suddenly; lunge: *The thief plunged into the crowd and disappeared from sight.* **3.** to enter or fall headlong into some condition or course of action: *to plunge into war.* **4.** to dip suddenly: *The road plunges toward the beach.* —*n.* **1.** the act or motion of plunging. **2.** an instance of plunging; dive. [Old French *plongier* to dive, sink, going back to Latin *plumbum* lead.] —For Synonyms *(v.t.),* see dip.

• **to take a** (or **the) plunge. a.** to do or begin to do something difficult or unfamiliar, esp. after hesitating. **b.** *Slang.* to get married.

plung·er (plun′jər) *n.* **1.** a device consisting of a rubber suction cup attached to the end of a long handle, used to unclog toilets and drains. **2.** any device or machine that works with a plunging or thrusting motion, esp. a piston when it is part of a pump. **3.** a person or thing that plunges.

plunk (plungk) *Informal. v.t.* **1.** to pluck or strum the strings of (a musical instrument). **2.** to throw or put heavily or abruptly (often with *down*): *I plunked down all my change on the counter.* —*v.i.* **1.** to drop or fall heavily or abruptly. **2.** to give out a twanging sound, as a banjo. —*n.* **1.** the act or sound of plunking. **2.** a heavy, direct blow. —*adv.* **1.** directly; exactly: *The arrow hit plunk in the center of the target.* **2.** with a plop or a twanging or thudding sound. [Imitative.] —**plunk′er,** *n.*
•**to plunk down.** *Informal.* to pay: *We plunked down fifty dollars for repairing the radio.*

plu·per·fect (plü pûr′fikt) *Grammar. n.* the past perfect. —*adj.* of, relating to, or designating the past perfect. [Short for Latin *(tempus) plūs quām perfectum* more than perfect (tense).]

plupf., pluperfect.

plur., plural.

plu·ral (plŏŏr′əl) *adj.* **1.** containing, consisting of, or relating to more than one. **2.** of or relating to a grammatical form that denotes more than one. *Doors* and *women* are plural nouns. —*n.* **1.** a form of a word denoting more than one. **2.** a word in the plural form. [Latin *plūrālis* relating to more than one, from *plūs* more.] —**plu′ral·ly,** *adv.*

plu·ral·ism (plŏŏr′ə liz′əm) *n.* **1.a.** the existence within a nation or society of a number of different ethnic, religious, racial, or social groups, who have individual interests and who often form diverse institutions and organizations representing these respective interests. **b.** a policy fostering the existence of such groups. **2.** the quality or state of being plural. **3.** *Philosophy.* the theory that reality or the universe has many basic elements or aspects. ➡ distinguished from **dualism** and **monism.** —**plu′ral·ist,** *n., adj.* —**plu′ral·is′tic,** *adj.*

plu·ral·i·ty (plŏŏ ral′i tē) *n., pl.* **-ties. 1.a.** the number of votes that a winning candidate receives over and above the number cast for the nearest opponent. **b.** a number of votes cast for any one candidate in a contest of more than two candidates, that is greater than the number cast for anyone else, but not greater than one half of the total votes cast. **2.** the state or fact of being plural. **3.** more than half of a total; greater number; majority: *A plurality of citizens want better schools.*

plus (plus) *prep.* **1.** increased by; added to: *Two plus two is four.* **2.** with the addition of; together with: *The set consists of a table plus chairs.* —*adj.* **1.** somewhat higher than: *a grade of C plus.* **2.** involving or characterized by advantage or desirability: *The low price of the used car is a plus factor.* **3.** *Mathematics.* of, relating to, or being a quantity that is greater than zero; positive. **4.** *Electricity.* positive. **5.** *Informal.* and more: *a kid with personality plus.* —*n., pl.* **plus·es. 1.** plus sign. **2.** an added, favorable, or advantageous factor or quality: *Your good record is a plus in getting the job.* **3.** a positive quantity. —*conj. Informal.* in addition; and: *The car is in good condition, plus it's cheap.* [Latin *plūs* more.]

plus fours, loose knickers that extend below the knee, formerly worn for sports activities, such as golf.

plush (plush) *adj.* exhibiting or characteristic of an abundance of wealth; luxurious: *a plush hotel.* —*n.* a fabric similar to but having a deeper pile than velvet, used esp. for upholstery. [French *peluche* the fabric, going back to Latin *pilus* hair.] —**plush′ness,** *n.* —**plush′y,** *adj.*

plus sign, the symbol (+), used to indicate addition or a positive quantity.

Plu·to (plü′tō) *n.* **1.** in Greek mythology, the god of the dead and ruler of the underworld. His Roman counterpart is Dis. Also, **Hades. 2.** the smallest and most remote planet in the solar system, ninth in order of distance from the sun and the slowest moving, taking 248.53 years to orbit the sun.

plu·toc·ra·cy (plü tok′rə sē) *n., pl.* **-cies. 1.** government by the wealthy. **2.** a government or state in which the wealthy rule. **3.** a controlling or influential class of wealthy persons, esp. a wealthy class that rules such a government or state. [Greek *ploutokratiā* government by the wealthy, from *ploutos* wealth + *-kratiā* power, rule.]

plu·to·crat (plü′tə krat′) *n.* **1.** a person who has power or influence because of wealth. **2.** a wealthy person.

plu·to·crat·ic (plü′tə krat′ik) *adj.* of, relating to, or resembling plutocrats or plutocracy. Also, **plu′to·crat′i·cal.** —**plu′to·crat′i·cal·ly,** *adv.*

Plu·to·ni·an (plü tō′nē ən) *adj.* of, relating to, or suggesting Pluto or the underworld.

plu·ton·ic (plü ton′ik) *adj.* **1.** (of igneous rocks) formed and crystallized far beneath the earth's crust. **2. Plutonic.** Plutonian. [From *Pluto* Greek god of the underworld.]

plu·to·ni·um (plü tō′nē əm) *n.* a silvery, poisonous, radioactive metallic element produced from uranium in breeder reactors and used as the fission material in atomic bombs. Symbol: **Pu** For

tables, see **element.** [Modern Latin *plutonium,* from *Pluto* the planet.]

Plu·tus (plü′təs) *n.* in classical mythology, the god of wealth, blinded by Zeus so he would distribute riches without regard to merit.

plu·vi·al (plü′vē əl) *adj.* **1.a.** of or relating to rain. **b.** characterized by much rain; rainy. **2.** caused by the action of rain. [Latin *pluviālis* rainy, from *pluvia* rain.]

plu·vi·om·e·ter (plü′vē om′i tər) *n.* rain gauge. [Latin *pluvia* rain + -METER.]

plu·vi·ous (plü′vē əs) *adj.* of or characterized by much rain; rainy.

ply¹ (plī) *v.,* **plied, ply·ing.** —*v.t.* **1.** to use, wield, or apply diligently or vigorously: *The crew plied their oars.* **2.** to work at or pursue busily or steadily; practice: *to ply one's trade.* **3.** to act upon; work on: *to ply clay with a potter's tools.* **4.** to provide frequently or persistently with something: *Our hosts plied us with good food and drink.* **5.** to address or harass repeatedly or in a pressing way: *The lawyer plied the witness with questions.* **6.** to travel or traverse regularly: *The boat plies the route from the island to the mainland.* —*v.i.* **1.** to travel or traverse the same course regularly. **2.** to work busily or steadily. [Short for APPLY.]

ply² (plī) *n., pl.* **plies. 1.** a fold or layer, as of cloth or wood. **2.** one of the strands twisted together to make yarn, rope, or similar material. ➡ Both defs. are used in combination to indicate a specified number of layers or strands: *two-ply tissues, three-ply yarn.* [Old French *pli* a fold¹, bend, from *plier* to fold¹, bend, from Latin *plicāre* to fold¹.]

Plym·outh Rock (plim′əth) **1.** a rock at Plymouth, Massachusetts, on which the Pilgrims, according to tradition, landed in 1620. **2.** one of an American breed of domestic chickens, having white, buff, or blue plumage sometimes barred with gray.

ply·wood (plī′wŏŏd′) *n.* a construction material consisting of a number of thin layers of wood glued together, with the grain of one layer at right angles to the grain of the next. [PLY² + WOOD.]

Pm, the symbol for promethium.

p.m. 1. post meridiem. **2.** postmortem.

P.M. also, **PM 1.** Postmaster. **2.** post meridiem. **3.** Prime Minister.

PMS, premenstrual syndrome.

plywood

pneu·mat·ic (nŏŏ mat′ik, nū-) *adj.* **1.** operated by or using the force of compressed air: *a pneumatic drill.* **2.** containing or filled with air, esp. compressed air: *a pneumatic tire.* **3.** of or relating to air or other gases or to pneumatics. [Latin *pneumaticus* relating to air or wind, from Greek *pneumatikos,* from *pneuma* air, wind.] —**pneu·mat′i·cal·ly,** *adv.*

pneumatic caisson, a large boxlike or cylindrical structure for laying underwater foundations, having an airtight work chamber at the bottom that is entered through an air lock. Compressed air is pumped into this chamber to force out the water.

pneu·mat·ics (nŏŏ mat′iks, nū-) *n.* the branch of physics that deals with the physical properties of air and other gases and with their action on stationary objects. ➡ used as singular.

pneu·mo·coc·cus (nŏŏ′mō kok′əs, nū′-) *n., pl.* **-coc·ci** (-kok′sī). a gram-positive bacterium, genus *Streptococcus,* found normally in the upper respiratory tract of humans and other mammals. Various strains are known to cause pneumonia, meningitis, and middle ear infections. [Modern Latin *pneumococcus,* from *pneumo-* lung (going back to Greek *pneumōn* lung) + *coccus* (see COCCUS).] —**pneu·mo·coc·cal** (nŏŏ′mə kok′əl, nū′-), **pneu·mo·coc·cic** (nŏŏ′mə kok′sik, nū′-), *adj.*

pneu·mo·nia (nŏŏ mōn′yə, nū-) *n.* any of several diseases characterized by inflammation of the lungs, resulting esp. from a bacterial or viral infection. [Modern Latin *pneumonia,* from Greek *pneumoniā,* from *pneumōn* lung.]

pneu·mon·ic (nŏŏ mon′ik, nū-) *adj.* **1.** of or relating to pneumonia. **2.** pulmonary *(def. 1).* [Modern Latin *pneumonicus,* from Greek *pneumonikos* relating to the lungs, from *pneumōn* lung.]

Po, the symbol for polonium.

P.O., post office.

poach¹ (pōch) *v.t.* **1.** to cook (an egg) without the shell in

a	at	e	end	o	hot	u	up	hw	white		about
ā	ape	ē	me	ō	old	ū	use	ng	song		taken
ä	far	i	it	ô	fork	ŭ	rule	th	thin	ə	pencil
âr	care	ī	ice	oi	oil	ù	pull	th	this		lemon
				ir	pierce	ou	out	ûr	turn	zh	measure		circus

P

simmering water or in a receptacle placed above simmering water. **2.** to cook in simmering liquid: *to poach fish.* [Old French *pochier* originally, to put in a bag, from *poche* pocket, bag; of Germanic origin; because the white of the egg forms a pouchlike bag around the yolk.]

poach² (pōch) *v.i.* **1.** to hunt or fish illegally, as on another's property. **2.** to trespass for the purpose of taking game or fish. —*v.t.* **1.** to take (game or fish) illegally. **2.** to trespass on (property) for hunting or fishing. [Middle French *pocher* to encroach on, gouge; of Germanic origin.]

pock (pok) *n.* **1.** a pustule on the skin, caused by such diseases as smallpox and acne. **2.** a scar or pit left by such a pustule. —*v.t.* to mark with or as if with pocks. [Old English *pocc* pustule.]

pock·et (pok′it) *n.* **1.** a pouch sewn into or on a garment, used esp. to hold small objects. **2.** something resembling a pocket in shape or function: *There are pockets inside the briefcase for loose notes.* **3.** an isolated, usually small area or group that is different in some manner from a surrounding area or group: *a poverty pocket.* **4.** financial means or resources: *Inflation becomes a drain on everyone's pocket.* **5.** any of the pouches at the corners and sides of a pool or billiard table, into which the balls are driven. **6.** air pocket. **7.a.** a cavity in the earth containing ore. **b.** a small body or deposit of ore. —*adj.* **1.** adapted or intended to be carried in a pocket: *a pocket radio.* **2.** small for its class or kind: *a pocket battleship.* —*v.t.* **1.** to put in or as if in a pocket: *I pocketed my change and left.* **2.** to take for one's own, esp. dishonestly: *The salesclerk pocketed the day's receipts.* **3.** to give no indication of; suppress: *They pocketed their pride and asked for help.* **4.** to accept meekly or without protest, as an insult. **5.** to hit (a ball) into a pocket, as in pool. [Anglo-Norman *pokete* little bag, diminutive of *poke* bag, sack; of Germanic origin.]

· **in one's pocket.** under one's control: *I have the other members of the committee in my pocket.*

· **out of pocket. a.** paid directly, rather than charged to an account: *My expenses out of pocket were later reimbursed.* **b.** having lost money: *Investors were out of pocket millions of dollars when the business folded.*

· **to line one's pocket.** to enrich oneself while supposedly serving the public or another employer: *Crooked contractors lined their pockets at the city's expense.*

pocket billiards, pool² *(def. 1).*

pock·et·book (pok′it bùk′) *n.* **1.** a bag or case, often of leather, used for carrying a wallet, credit cards, and other small articles. **2.** financial means, resources, or interests: *The company's failure will affect every stockholder's pocketbook.* **3.** *also,* **pocket book.** a book, usually paperbound, small enough to be carried in a pocket.

pock·et·ful (pok′it fûl′) *n., pl.* **-fuls.** the amount that a pocket holds.

pocket gopher, gopher *(def. 1).*

pock·et·knife (pok′it nīf′) *n., pl.* **-knives** (-nīvz′). a small knife with one or more blades that fold into the handle.

pocket money, money carried for small personal expenses.

pock·et·size (pok′it sīz′) *adj.* **1.** small enough to fit in a pocket: *a pocket-size calculator.* **2.** small: *a pocket-size park.* Also, **pock′et-sized′.**

pocket veto 1. the power of the president of the United States to veto a bill passed by Congress during the last ten days of a session by simply retaining the bill unsigned until Congress adjourns. **2.** a similar power exercised by a chief executive, such as a state governor.

pock·mark (pok′märk′) *n.* a pit or scar left on the skin, as by smallpox or acne. —*v.t.* to mark with or as with pockmarks. —**pock′marked′,** *adj.*

pod (pod) *n.* **1.** a seed vessel, esp. of a leguminous plant, such as a pea, that usually splits along two seams when it is ripe. **2.** any container or covering resembling this, such as a cocoon. **3.** a separate enclosure on an aircraft, usually located beneath a wing, for housing fuel, an engine, cargo, or weapons. —*v.i.,* **pod·ded, pod·ding. 1.** to produce pods. **2.** to swell out into or as if into a pod. [Of uncertain origin.]

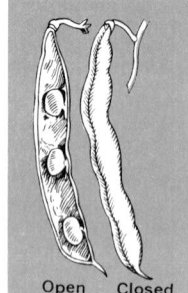

Open   Closed

pods

pod- *combining form* foot: *podiatry.* [Greek *pod-,* stem of *pous* foot.]

-pod *combining form* having a specified number or kind of feet: *pseudopod.* [Modern Latin *-pod,* from Greek *pod-,* stem of *pous* foot.]

po·di·a·trist (pə dī′ə trist) *n.* a doctor who is trained in and licensed to practice podiatry. Also, **chiropodist.**

po·di·a·try (pə dī′ə trē) *n.* a medical specialty that includes the diagnosis and treatment of diseases and injuries of the foot. Also, **chiropody.** [Greek *pod-,* stem of *pous* foot + *iātreiā* art of healing.] —**po·di·at·ric** (pō′dē at′rik), *adj.*

po·di·um (pō′dē əm) *n., pl.* **-di·ums** or **-di·a** (-dē ə). **1.** the raised platform from which a conductor leads an orchestra. **2.** a place or structure from which to address a group; lectern; rostrum. **3.** *Biology.* a foot or any structure serving as or resembling a foot. [Latin *podium* elevated place, from Greek *podion,* diminutive of *pous* foot.]

Po·dunk (pō′dungk′) *n. Informal.* any small, backward, or insignificant town. [From *Podunk,* name of places in Massachusetts and Connecticut.]

po·em (pō′əm) *n.* **1.** a composition usually designed to convey a complex, emotive, and intense sense of experience, written in some rhythmic scheme, and characterized by language regarded as more condensed and vivid than that of prose, often employing such devices as rhyme, meter, and metaphor. **2.a.** any literary composition written with an intensity or lyricism of language thought to be more characteristic of poetry than of prose. **b.** a musical work or other composition having an intensity of feeling or expression like that of a poem: *an orchestral poem.* **3.** something having qualities or effects similar or likened to those of poetry. [Latin *poēma* composition in verse, from Greek *poiēma* a work, composition in verse.]

po·e·sy (pō′ə sē, -zē) *n. Archaic.* **1.** poems collectively; poetry. **2.** the art of writing poetry. [Old French *poēsie* poetry, going back to Latin *poēsis,* from Greek *poiēsis* a making, poetry.]

po·et (pō′it) *n.* **1.** a person who writes poetry. **2.** a person who is greatly sensitive to beauty and who expresses thoughts, impressions, and ideas with imagination and lyricism. [Latin *poēta* maker, composer of verse, from Greek *poiētēs.*]

po·et·as·ter (pō′it as′tər) *n.* a person who writes poor poetry; inferior or would-be poet. [Modern Latin *poetaster,* from Latin *poēta* poet + *-aster* (suffix indicating inferiority).]

po·et·ess (pō′i tis) *n.* a woman who writes poetry. ➡ **Poet,** rather than **poetess,** is now generally used for a woman who writes poetry.

po·et·ic (pō et′ik) *adj.* **1.** of or relating to poetry: *poetic genius, poetic works.* **2.** having a quality or style characteristic of poetry: *poetic diction, a poetic description.* **3.** characteristic of or showing the qualities of a poet. Also, **po·et′i·cal.** —**po·et′i·cal·ly,** *adv.*

poetic justice, an ideal or appropriate distribution of reward for good and punishment for evil, as often represented in literature.

poetic license, a deviation from a rule, standard, or fact for the sake of effect, as in works of literature.

po·et·ics (pō et′iks) *n.* the branch of literary criticism that deals with the theory, nature, and forms of poetry. ➡ used as singular.

poet laureate *pl.* **poets laureate** or **poet laureates. 1.** in Great Britain, a poet appointed for life by the sovereign as official poet of the royal household, and whose duties formerly included writing verses to commemorate state occasions. **2.** the poet acclaimed as the most eminent of a locality or group. In the United States, the poet laureate is appointed for one year by the head of the Library of Congress and may be reappointed. Many states also have poets laureate.

po·et·ry (pō′i trē) *n.* **1.** poems collectively: *a volume of poetry.* **2.** writing or language characteristic of poems. **3.** the art of writing poems. **4.** a quality or effect considered characteristic of poetry: *the poetry of the dancer's movements.* **5.** something having such quality or effect. [Medieval Latin *poetria* poetic art, from Latin *poēta.* See POET.]

po·go stick (pō′gō) a stiltlike device consisting of a stick with footrests and a spring at its base, on which one may move along by propelling oneself in a series of bounds.

po·grom (pō grom′, pō′grəm) *n.* an organized, often officially initiated persecution and massacre of a minority group, esp. of Jews. [Russian *pogrom* devastation.]

poi (poi) *n.* a food of Hawaiian origin, made from taro root that is cooked, pounded into a paste, and fermented. [Hawaiian *poi.*]

poign·ant (poin′yənt) *adj.* **1.a.** evoking emotions, esp. sadness or melancholy; touching: *a poignant story of people separated by war.* **b.** evoking strong interest: *a matter of poignant concern.* **2.** deeply or painfully felt; severe: *a poignant sense of loss.* **3.** to the point; relevant: *poignant comments.* **4.** sharp; penetrating: *a poignant critique.* **5.** sharp or biting to the taste or smell; pungent. [Old French *poignant,* present participle of *poindre* to prick, from Latin *pungere.*] —**poign′ance, poign′an·cy,** *n.* —**poign′ant·ly,** *adv.* —For Synonyms, see **touching.**

poi·ki·lo·ther·mic (poi′kə lō thûr′mik) *adj.* cold-blooded *(def. 1).* Also, **poi′ki·lo·ther′mal.**

poin·ci·a·na (poin′sē an′ə) *n.* any of several tropical trees, genus *Delonix,* that bear clusters of large red, yellow, or orange flowers. [Modern Latin *Poinciana,* from M. de *Poinci,* a seventeenth-century governor of the French West Indies.]

poinciana

poin·set·ti·a (poin set′ē ə, -set′ə) *n.* a tropical American shrub, *Euphorbia pulcherrima,* bearing oval-shaped leaves and small flowers surrounded by showy red, pink, or white leaflike parts that resemble flower petals. It is widely used as a Christmas decoration. [Modern Latin *poinsettia,* from Joel Roberts *Poinsett,* 1779?-1851, U.S. diplomat who discovered it in Mexico.]

point (point) *n.* **1.** a tapering, often sharp, end: *the point of a pencil, the point of a knife.* **2.** something that has a tapering or sharp end, such as a sword. **3.** a tapering projection of land; cape. **4.** a dot or other small mark used in writing or printing as a diacritical mark or punctuation mark, esp. a period. **5.** decimal point. **6.** *Geometry.* something having position, but no length, width, or height: *to draw a line between two points.* **7.** a definite position; place; spot: *We stopped at all the points of interest.* **8.** a definite position in or as in a scale: *the point at which a metal melts, to work to the point of exhaustion.* **9.** a particular moment or time, as when something happens or is about to happen: *At that point, I got up and left the room.* **10.** the central topic under consideration: *to keep to the point in a discussion.* **11.** the main or most important idea: *the point of a story.* **12.** an impressive or effective fact, idea, or argument: *You've got a point there.* **13.** the reason for doing something; object; purpose: *What's the point in arguing with someone whose mind is made up?* **14.** an individual part or step; item; detail: *to explain a plan point by point.* **15.a.** a distinguishing mark or quality; trait; characteristic: *Being on time is not my strong point.* **b.** a physical characteristic of an animal, esp. one by which the excellence or purity of the breed is judged. **16.** a unit of scoring in a game: *Our team won by ten points.* **17.** *Finance.* **a.** a unit equal to one dollar, used to quote current prices of stocks and commodities. **b.** a unit or amount equal to one percent, used esp. to quote the fee paid in advance on a mortgage by the mortgagor. **18.** a unit of academic credit, equal to a certain number of hours of class work. **19.** *Printing.* a unit for measuring type, approximately ¹/₇₂ inch (0.4 millimeter). **20.a.** one of the thirty-two marks showing direction on a compass card. **b.** the interval between any two such marks, equal to 11 degrees 15 minutes. **21.** needlepoint *(def. 2).* **22.** *British.* a railroad switch. **23.** either of two electrical contacts that make or break the flow of current in a distributor, as in an automobile engine. **24.** a branch of a deer's antler. **25.** a small group that goes ahead of an advance unit in a military maneuver. **26.** a helpful suggestion; pointer. **27.a.** any of various positions in certain sports. **b.** a player occupying such a position. **28.** pointe. —*v.t.* **1.** to direct or aim, as a finger or weapon: *to point a flashlight into a cellar.* **2.** to indicate with or as with the finger; direct attention to (usually with *out*): *to point out someone's mistakes, to point the way.* **3.** to give a point to; sharpen, as a pencil. **4.** to mark or separate with points or dots; punctuate: *to point a sentence.* **5.** to separate (figures) with points or dots (with *off*): *to point off two decimal places.* **6.** to give force or emphasis to (often with *up*): *to point one's remarks, to point up a moral.* **7.** (of a hunting dog) to indicate the presence and position of (game) by freezing in a rigid stance with the nose and body facing the quarry. **8.** to fill the joints of (brickwork) with mortar. —*v.i.* **1.** to direct attention or indicate position or direction with or as with the finger: *to point at something unusual.* **2.** to direct the mind or thought in a specified direction: *All the evidence points to arson.* **3.** to face, aim, or be extended in a specified direction: *The house points toward the bay.* **4.** (of a

hunting dog) to point game. **5.** (of a ship) to sail close to the wind. [Old French *point* mark, a pricking, and *pointe* something pointed, both going back to Latin *pungere* to prick.]

· **beside the point.** not related to the subject under discussion; irrelevant: *What you say is probably true, but it is entirely beside the point.*

· **in point.** related to the subject; relevant; apt: *a case in point.*

· **in point of.** as regards; with respect to: *in point of fact.*

· **to make a point of.** to be determined to; insist upon: *I make a point of being always on time.*

· **to stretch a point.** to free from narrow restrictions; make an exception: *I'll stretch a point in your case and give you extra time to finish the project.*

· **to the point.** related to the subject; relevant; apt: *Your arguments were short and to the point.*

point-blank (point′blangk′) *adv.* **1.** from so close a range that missing a target is unlikely or impossible: *to fire point-blank at a target.* **2.** without hesitation or qualification; plainly and bluntly; flatly: *They asked me point-blank if I was responsible for the error.* —*adj.* **1.** pointed or aimed directly or straight at the mark, esp. from close range: *to be exposed to point-blank fire.* **2.** so close that missing a target is unlikely or impossible: *to shoot from point-blank range.* **3.** plain and blunt: *a point-blank denial.*

pointe (point; *French* pwaⁿt) *also,* **point** (point). *n.* in ballet, a position on the tip of the toe. [French *pointe* point. See POINT.]

point·ed (poin′tid) *adj.* **1.** having or coming to a point or points: *a pointed stick.* **2.** pertinent and incisive; to the point: *The reporter's pointed questions got to the heart of the story.* **3.** clearly or particularly aimed at or referring to a person, group, or thing: *a pointed comment.* **4.** clearly evident; conspicuous; marked: *a pointed display of anger.* —**point′ed·ly,** *adv.* —**point′ed·ness,** *n.*

point·er (poin′tər) *n.* **1.** a long, tapered stick used to point out things, as on a blackboard, chart,

pointer *(def. 2)*

or map. **2.** a short-haired breed of dog having long ears, a long, tapering tail, and a smooth, solid-color or spotted coat. It hunts game birds by scent and points to their location. Height: 25 inches (64 centimeters) at the shoulder. **3.** a needle, hand, or similar device, as on a scale or meter, indicating a recording or measurement; indicator. **4.** *Informal.* a useful or instructive piece of information or advice; hint; suggestion. **5.** a person or thing that points.

poin·til·lism (pwan′tə liz′əm, -tē iz′-, poin′tə liz′-) *n.* a technique in painting originating in France during the 1880s and 1890s, consisting of applying to canvas or a similar surface small dots or dashes of pure, unmixed colors, the dots blending into recognizable forms and patterns through the optical process of the spectator. [French *pointillisme,* from *pointiller* to dot, from *point* a dot, a mark. See POINT.]

point lace, needlepoint *(def. 2).*

point·less (point′lis) *adj.* **1.** without force, purpose, or concrete result; useless; ineffective: *a pointless attempt.* **2.** without meaning or relevance; inane: *a pointless remark.* **3.** without a point or sharp or tapering end. —**point′less·ly,** *adv.* —**point′less·ness,** *n.*

point of honor, a matter regarded as vitally affecting or relating to one's honor, reputation, or principles.

point of order, a question raised as to whether the correct or appropriate parliamentary procedure is being observed, as in legislative debate.

point of view **1.** a manner of thinking, feeling, or acting; attitude. **2.** a position from which something is considered or evaluated.

point·y (poin′tē) *adj.,* **point·i·er, point·i·est.** coming to a point; pointed: *a pointy nose.*

poise[1] (poiz) *n.* **1.** relaxed and self-possessed composure, assurance, and dignity, esp. as expressed in one's manner or bearing. **2.** a state or condition of balance; equilibrium. —*v.,* **poised,**

a	at	e	end	o	hot	u	up	hw	white		about
ā	ape	ē	me	ō	old	ū	use	ng	song		taken
ä	far	i	it	ô	fork	ü	rule	th	thin	ə	pencil
âr	care	ī	ice	oi	oil	u̇	pull	th	this		lemon
		îr	pierce	ou	out	ûr	turn	zh	measure		circus

P

933

pois·ing. —*v.t.* to place, carry, or hold in equilibrium: *The juggler poised a plate on the end of the stick.* —*v.i.* to be balanced, suspended, or held in equilibrium: *The diver poised on the edge of the board.* [Old French *poiser, peser* to weigh, going back to Latin *pēnsāre* to weigh out.]

poise² *n.* the centimeter-gram-second unit used to measure viscosity, equal to a stress of 1 dyne per second per square centimeter. [French *poise,* from J.L.M. *Poiseuille,* 1799-1869, French anatomist.]

poised (poizd) *adj.* **1.** having a relaxed assurance and dignity of manner or bearing; composed; self-possessed. **2.** suspended, balanced, or hovering in or as in midair: *an eagle poised in flight.* **3.** being in a state of balance or equilibrium: *a diver poised on the edge of the pool.*

poi·son (poi'zən) *n.* **1.** any substance dangerous to life and health and causing serious injury, illness, or death by its chemical action on an organism. **2.** something to be detested or shunned as harmful, corrupting, or destructive. —*v.t.* **1.** to administer poison to; injure or kill with poison. **2.** to put poison in, on, or into; cause to become harmful or deadly: *These chemicals have poisoned the water.* **3.** to have a harmful, corrupting, or destructive effect on: *to poison someone's mind with ideas of hate and revenge.* —*adj.* poisonous. [Old French *poison* magic potion, poisonous drink, drink, from Latin *pōtiō.* Doublet of POTION.] —**poi'son·er,** *n.*

poison gas, any of various toxic gases, as phosgene or mustard gas, esp. one used as a weapon in chemical warfare.

poison ivy 1. a woody vine, *Toxicodendron radicans,* of North America, having shiny leaves composed of three jagged oval leaflets and containing an oil in the stems, leaves, and roots that causes a rash when it comes in contact with the skin. **2.** the rash caused by contact with any of these plants.

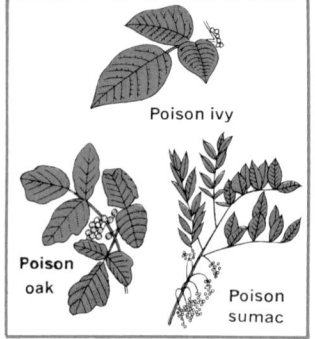

Poison ivy

Poison oak

Poison sumac

poison oak 1. a slender woody plant, *Toxicodendron toxicarium,* growing in dry barrens and sandy regions of North America, related to poison ivy and causing a similar rash, and having leaves composed of three usually oval, often lobed leaflets. **2.** the rash caused by contact with this plant.

poi·son·ous (poi'zə nəs) *adj.* **1.a.** full of, containing, or constituting a poison: *a poisonous concoction.* **b.** causing or capable of causing serious injury, illness, or death by poison; venomous: *a poisonous snake.* **2.** having a harmful, corrupting, or destructive effect: *a poisonous influence.* **3.** full of malice, spite, or ill will; malevolent: *a poisonous look.* —**poi'son·ous·ly,** *adv.* —**poi'son·ous·ness,** *n.*

poison sumac 1. a shrub or small tree, *Toxicodendron vernix,* growing in swamps of eastern North America, related to poison ivy and causing a similar rash, and having leaves that consist of from seven to thirteen oblong or oval leaflets. **2.** the rash caused by contact with this plant.

poke¹ (pōk) *v.,* poked, pok·ing. —*v.t.* **1.** to push into or against, as with something pointed; prod: *He poked the frog with a stick to make it jump.* **2.** to push or thrust through or out of: *She poked her head out of the window.* **3.** to make by or as if by pushing or thrusting: *The stick poked a hole in the drum.* **4.** *Informal.* to hit with the fist; strike; punch. —*v.i.* **1.** to make a pushing, thrusting, or prodding movement. **2.** to thrust forward or stick out; protrude; appear: *A tall tree trunk poked up out of the water.* **3.** to look, search, or investigate: *The police poked around looking for clues.* **4.** to intrude or meddle; pry: *to poke into someone else's business.* **5.** to move or proceed slowly or lazily; dawdle: *We'll be late if you don't stop poking along.* —*n.* **1.** a pushing, thrusting, or prodding movement. **2.** *Informal.* a blow with the fist; punch. **3.** slowpoke. [Possibly from Middle Dutch *poken* to thrust, prick².]

poke² (pōk) *n.* a small bag; sack. [Dialectal Old French *poque;* of Germanic origin.]

poke·ber·ry (pōk'ber'ē, -bə rē) *n., pl.* -ries. **1.** the berry of the pokeweed. **2.** the pokeweed itself.

poke bonnet, a bonnet having a large, deep, projecting brim in front.

pok·er¹ (pō'kər) *n.* **1.** a metal rod for stirring a fire. **2.** a person or thing that pokes. [POKE¹ + -ER¹.]

pok·er² (pō'kər) *n.* any of several card games in which the players bet on the value of their hands, the winner being the player having the hand of highest value of those who have stayed in the game. [Possibly from German *Pochspiel* a card game similar to poker, from *pochen* to brag.]

poker face *Informal.* a face held expressionless, such as that of an expert poker player who does not want to reveal the nature of his or her hand. —**pok'er-faced',** *adj.*

poke·weed (pōk'wēd') *n.* any of several coarse plants, genus *Phytolacca,* esp. *P. americana,* which is poisonous except for the edible young shoots, having fleshy roots and bearing pale green flowers that ripen into juicy, deep purple berries. Also, **poke-berry, inkberry.**

pok·ey (pō'kē) *n., pl.* -eys. *Slang.* a jail. [Modification (possibly under the influence of POKY) of earlier *pogey, pogie, pogy;* of unknown origin.]

pok·y (pō'kē) *also,* **pok·ey.** *adj.,* pok·i·er, pok·i·est. extremely slow; dawdling. [POKE¹ + -Y¹.]

pol (pol) *n. Informal.* a politician. [Short for POL(ITICIAN).]

Pol. 1. Poland. **2.** Polish.

Po·land China (pō'lənd) one of an American breed of black hogs having white markings on the feet, face, and tail.

po·lar (pō'lər) *adj.* **1.** of or relating to a pole or poles, as of a magnet, battery, or sphere. **2.** relating to, near, coming from, or going to the North or South Pole: *the polar icecap, a polar expedition.* **3.** directly opposite in character, action, or tendency: *the debaters' polar arguments.* **4.** resembling a pole around which all other things revolve; central; pivotal: *a polar principle.* **5.** *Chemistry.* **a.** (of a compound) ionizing when dissolved, as sodium chloride. **b.** (of a molecule) dipolar. **6.** serving to guide or direct, as a polestar. [Modern Latin *polaris,* from Latin *polus* end of an axis. See POLE².]

polar bear, a large, white bear, *Ursus maritimus,* native to arctic regions. Length: to 9 feet (2.7 meters).

polar body, one of three small, immature cells produced and discarded during the meiosis of egg cells, containing a nucleus and very little cytoplasm.

polar bear

polar circle, either of two parallels of latitude each at a distance of about 23 degrees 27 minutes from a pole of the earth; Arctic Circle or Antarctic Circle.

polar coordinate *Mathematics.* in analytic geometry, either of two coordinates locating a point in a plane, one being the distance of the point from a fixed point on a fixed line and the other being the angle made by this fixed line with the line connecting the two points.

Po·lar·is (pə lar'is) *n.* a star of the second magnitude, located very near the north celestial pole. It is the outermost star in the handle of the Little Dipper. Also, **North Star, polestar.**

po·lar·i·scope (pō lar'ə skōp') *n.* an instrument for measuring or exhibiting the polarization of light, or for studying substances in polarized light.

po·lar·i·ty (pō lar'i tē) *n.* **1.** the possession by a body of two poles at opposite extremities, the properties of one pole being an opposite or contrasting nature to the other, as in a magnet. **2.** the condition of being either positive or negative with respect to electric or magnetic poles. **3.** the condition of having or showing two opposite tendencies, tendencies, or qualities: *political polarity.*

po·lar·i·za·tion (pō'lər ə zā'shən) *n.* **1.** *Optics.* the condition, or the production of a condition, in which the transverse vibrations of light waves are confined to a single plane or direction. **2.** an increase in the internal resistance of a voltaic cell, resulting in a drop in voltage, usually caused by the production of gases around the electrodes of the cell during electrolysis. **3.** the state of having polarity or the act of producing polarity, such as the concentration of groups or forces about two opposing positions.

po·lar·ize (pō'lə rīz') *v.,* -ized, -iz·ing. —*v.t.* **1.** to cause polarization in; give polarity to: *to polarize light.* **2.** to cause to separate into opposing groups: *Disagreement over the government's policies threatened to polarize the country.* —*v.i.* to become polarized. [French *polariser* to cause polarization, from Modern Latin *polaris.* See POLAR.]

Po·lar·oid (pō′lə roid′) *n. Trademark.* **1.** a transparent plastic material capable of polarizing light, used esp. in lamps and eyeglasses to reduce glare. **2.a.** a portable camera that produces a finished print within seconds after exposure. Also, **Polaroid Land Camera. b.** a photograph produced by such a camera.

pol·der (pōl′dər) *n.* an area of low land reclaimed from the sea or another body of water and protected by dikes, esp. in the Netherlands. [Dutch *polder.*]

pole[1] (pōl) *n.* **1.** a long, slender, usually cylindrical piece of wood, metal, or other material: *a fishing pole.* **2.a.** a unit of length equal to 5½ yards (5 meters); rod. **b.** a unit of area equal to 30¼ square yards (25 square meters); square rod. **3.** the starting lane or position on the inside front of a racetrack, as in an automobile race: *The favorite has the pole.* —*v.t.,* **poled, pol·ing.** to propel, push, or strike with a pole: *to pole a boat down a river.* [Old English *pāl* stake, from Latin *pālus.*]

pole[2] (pōl) *n.* **1.a.** either end of the earth's axis; North Pole or South Pole. **b.** one of the two points where the axis of any rotating sphere intersects the surface of the sphere. **c.** celestial pole. **2.** either of two regions or parts at which opposite forces are concentrated or appear to originate, such as the ends of a magnet or the terminals of an electric battery. **3.** *Biology.* **a.** either end of the main axis of a nucleus, cell, or ovum, at or near which certain parts are symmetrically arranged. **b.** (in a cell) either end of the spindle-shaped structure that forms during cell division. **4.** *Mathematics.* the point of origin, or fixed point, in a system of polar coordinates. **5.** any fixed point of reference or guidance. **6.** either of two directly opposed opinions, principles, or ideas: *Their political beliefs are at opposite poles.* [Latin *polus* end of an axis, from Greek *polos* pivot, axis.]
  • **poles apart.** differing widely or completely opposite in nature, opinions, beliefs, or values: *The two candidates are poles apart on many of the issues.*

Pole (pōl) *n.* **1.** a native or citizen of Poland. **2.** a person of Polish ancestry.

pole·ax (pōl′aks′) *also,* **pole·axe.** *n.* a battle-ax having a long handle, esp. one with a hook, spike, or hammer opposite the blade. —*v.t.,* **-axed, -ax·ing.** to knock down or kill with or as if with a poleax. [Middle English *pollax* literally, head ax, from *pol* head (see POLL) + *ax.* See AX.]

pole bean, any of various cultivated climbing beans having long vinelike stems that twine around poles or other supports.

pole·cat (pōl′kat′) *n.* **1.** a small, carnivorous European mammal, *Mustela putorius,* closely related to the weasel and ferret and having long, soft, buff-gray fur. It sprays a foul-smelling liquid when attacked or frightened. Length: to 30 inches (76 centimeters), including tail. **2.** skunk. [Middle English *polcat,* possibly from Old French *po(u)le* hen (going back to Latin *pullus* young fowl) + CAT; possibly because it steals chickens.]

po·lem·ic (pə lem′ik) *n.* **1.** an argument or controversial discussion, esp. a refutation of or attack on a particular opinion, doctrine, or theory. **2. polemics.** the art or practice of disputation or controversy. ➡ used as singular. **3.** a person, such as a writer, who engages in controversy or argument. —*adj.* of, relating to, or involving controversy or dispute. Also *(adj.),* **po·lem′i·cal.** [Greek *polemikos* warlike, from *polemos* war.] —**po·lem′i·cal·ly,** *adv.*

po·lem·i·cist (pə lem′ə sist) *n.* a person who is skilled in, inclined toward, or engaged in polemics.

pole·star (pōl′stär′) *n.* **1.** Polaris. **2.** something that guides or directs; guiding principle. **3.** something that is a center of attention.

pole-vault (pōl′vôlt′) *v.i.* to make a pole vault. —**pole′-vault′er,** *n.*

pole vault 1. an athletic field event in which the contestant jumps for height from a running start, vaulting over a horizontal bar with the aid of a long pole. **2.** such a vault.

po·lice (pə lēs′) *n.* **1.** an official force or department established and empowered, usually by a local government, to prevent and detect crime, enforce the law, and maintain public order, peace, and safety. **2.** the members of such a force collectively. ➡ used as plural. **3.** any group officially employed to enforce regulations or maintain order and safety: *campus police.* —*v.t.,* **-liced, -lic·ing. 1.** to patrol, regulate, or keep orderly by or as by means of police: *to police a city, to police a demonstration.* **2.** to make (an area, such as a military or other campsite) clean and tidy. [Middle French *police* civil administration, from Late Latin *polītīa* government, from Latin *polītīa* the state, from Greek *polīteiā* citizenship, government.]

police dog 1. German shepherd. **2.** any dog used in policing.

po·lice·man (pə lēs′mən) *n., pl.* **-men** (-mən). a member of the police.

police officer, a member of the police.

police state, a country or other political unit in which the government exercises repressive, often arbitrary, control over political, social, and economic activity, esp. by means of a secret police force.

police station, the headquarters of a local or district police force. Also, **station house.**

po·lice·wom·an (pə lēs′wŭm′ən) *n., pl.* **-wom·en** (-wim′ən). a female member of the police.

pol·i·cy[1] (pol′ə sē) *n., pl.* **-cies. 1.** a guiding principle, course, or method of action followed or adhered to habitually or consistently: *a nation's foreign policy, a college's policy on admissions.* **2.** prudence, sagacity, or shrewdness in the management of affairs. [Old French *policie* government, administration, from Late Latin *polītīa.* See POLICE.]

pol·i·cy[2] (pol′ə sē) *n., pl.* **-cies. 1.** a written contract of insurance between an insurance company and the party or parties insured. **2.** numbers racket. Also *(def. 2),* **policy racket.** [French *police* the contract, through Italian and Latin, from Greek *apodeixis* proof.]

pol·i·cy·hold·er (pol′ə sē hōl′dər) *n.* a person who holds a policy of insurance; person insured.

po·li·o (pō′lē ō′) *n.* poliomyelitis.

po·li·o·my·e·li·tis (pō′lē ō mī′ə lī′tis) *n.* a highly contagious disease caused by a virus and occurring mainly in children, that, in its mild forms, is characterized by headache, sore throat, and fever, and, in its severe forms, attacks the central nervous system and is characterized by the destruction of nervous tissue, muscular weakness, and paralysis. Also, **infantile paralysis.** [Modern Latin *poliomyelitis,* from Greek *polios* gray + *myelos* marrow + -ITIS.]

po·li·o·vi·rus (pō′lē ō vī′rəs, pō′lē ō vī′-) *n.* any of various forms of an RNA-bearing virus that cause poliomyelitis. [POLIO + VIRUS.]

po·lis (pō′lis) *n., pl.* **-leis** (-līs). a city-state of ancient Greece. [Greek *polis* city, state.]

pol·ish (pol′ish) *v.t.* **1.** to shine, clean, or smooth, as by rubbing or by applying a special preparation: *to polish silverware.* **2.** to make more finished or complete; free from imperfections; improve (often with *up*): *to polish up a speech.* **3.** to make more elegant; refine: *to polish one's manners.* —*v.i.* **1.** to become smooth or glossy. —*n.* **1.** smoothness or glossiness of surface or finish, such as that produced by rubbing or by the application of a special preparation; bright, shiny appearance; luster: *The floor was buffed to a high polish.* **2.** a preparation or substance used to shine, clean, or smooth a surface: *shoe polish.* **3.** smooth elegance of manner or style; refinement: *a performer with polish and poise.* **4.** the act or an instance of polishing or the state of being polished. [Old French *poliss-,* a stem of *polir* to make smooth, make elegant, from Latin *polīre* to make smooth.] —**pol′ish·er,** *n.*
  • **to polish off.** *Informal.* **a.** to finish completely and quickly: *to polish off a meal, to polish off an assignment.* **b.** to subdue, overcome, or eliminate quickly: *to polish off an opponent.*

Pol·ish (pō′lish) *adj.* of, relating to, or characteristic of Poland or its people, language, or culture. —*n.* a language belonging to the western division of the Slavic branch of the Indo-European language family, spoken predominantly in Poland.

pol·ished (pol′isht) *adj.* **1.** having or showing social refinement or good taste; elegant; cultured: *polished manners, a polished host.* **2.** free from flaws or imperfections: *a polished performance.* **3.** having a smooth, glossy, shiny surface.

Polish sausage, kielbasa.

Po·lit·bu·ro (pol′it byůr′ō, pə lit′-) *n.* the highest policy-making and executive committee of a Communist Party, esp. in the Soviet Union.

po·lite (pə līt′) *adj.* **1.** having or exhibiting good manners, a tactful consideration for others, and a regard for correct social behavior; courteous. **2.** characterized by correct social behavior; refined: *polite society.* **3.** showing or characterized by cultivation or refined taste: *polite letters.* [Latin *polītus,* past participle of *polīre* to make smooth.] —**po·lite′ly,** *adv.* —**po·lite′ness,** *n.*

pol·i·tic (pol′i tik) *adj.* **1.** characterized by prudence or shrewd good judgment; skillfully or judiciously contrived: *politic advice.* **2.** having or using a shrewd awareness of what is expedient or

a	at	e	end	o	hot	u	up	hw	white		about
ā	ape	ē	me	ō	old	ū	use	ng	song		taken
ä	far	i	it	ô	fork	ü	rule	th	thin	ə	pencil
âr	care	ī	ice	oi	oil	ů	pull	th	this		lemon
		îr	pierce	ou	out	ûr	turn	zh	measure		circus

P

advantageous; artful: *a politic negotiator.* **3.** using shrewdness to clever or questionable ends; scheming; crafty; cunning. [Middle French *politique* political, from Latin *politicus* relating to the state, from Greek *politikos* civic, civil, going back to *polis* city, state.]

po·lit·i·cal (pə lit′i kəl) *adj.* **1.** of, relating to, or concerned with the science or activities of government or the administering of governmental affairs. **2.** of, relating to, or involved in politics: *a political campaign, a political party.* **3.** of, relating to, or characteristic of politicians. **4.** having a definite, organized system of government. —**po·lit′i·cal·ly,** *adv.*

political science, the study of the origin, organization, principles, and manner of operation of government. —**political scientist.**

pol·i·ti·cian (pol′i tish′ən) *n.* **1.** a person who is active in politics, esp. one holding public office. **2.** a person who is skilled in political maneuvering.

pol·i·tick (pol′i tik) *v.i. Informal.* to engage in campaigning or other political activity.

po·lit·i·co (pə lit′i kō′) *n., pl.* **-cos.** a person active in or shrewdly knowledgeable about politics; politician.

pol·i·tics (pol′i tiks) *pl. n.* **1.** the activities or affairs involved in the administering of a government or relating to governmental or state matters. **2.** the dealings, methods, or maneuvers involved in controlling, administering, or seeking to control a government. **3.** the science, art, or occupation of government or of the management of state or public affairs. **4.** political opinions, convictions, or affiliations: *What are your politics?* **5.** factional scheming, intrigues, or competition for positions of power within a group: *office politics.* ➡ usually used as singular or plural in defs. 1, 2, 3, 5, as plural in def. 4.

pol·i·ty (pol′i tē) *n., pl.* **-ties. 1.** a form, system, or method of government. **2.** any community living under some form or system of government. [Late Latin *politīa* government. See POLICE.]

pol·ka (pōl′kə, pō′kə) *n.* **1.** a lively dance of Bohemian origin that is danced in couples and whose basic movement consists of three steps and a hop in duple time. **2.** the music for this dance. —*v.i.,* **-kaed, -ka·ing.** to dance the polka. [French *polka* the dance, the music, from Czech *pùlka* half step, from *pul* half.]

pol·ka dot (pō′kə) **1.** one of a series of round dots spaced to form a pattern on fabric or other materials. **2.** a pattern or material with such dots. —**pol′ka-dot′, pol′ka-dot′ted,** *adj.*

poll (pōl) *n.* **1.** a survey of public opinion on a given subject, usually obtained by questioning a sample group of people. **2.** the casting and recording of votes in an election. **3.** the total number of votes cast or recorded. **4. polls,** a place where votes are cast and recorded. Also, **polling place. 5.** a list of persons, esp. of eligible voters. **6.** the head, esp. that part of it on which the hair grows. **7.** the blunt or flat end of certain tools, such as a hammer or ax. —*v.t.* **1.** to receive (a given number of votes) in an election: *The winner polled twice as many votes as all other candidates combined.* **2.** to question (a sample group of people) to obtain a survey of public opinion. **3.** to record or register the votes of: *to poll a district.* **4.** to cut off, trim, or crop: *to poll the horns of a cow.* **5.** to cut off, trim, or crop the hair, horns, branches, or other growth of: *to poll the sheep at shearing time.* —*v.i.* to cast one's vote in an election. [Middle English *pol(le)* head, possibly from Middle Dutch *pol(le);* referring to the counting of heads.] —**poll′er,** *n.*

pol·lack (pol′ək) *also,* **pollock.** *n.* either of two species of food fish, *Pollachius virens* or *P. pollachius,* related to the cod, found in coastal waters of the North Atlantic. Length: to over 40 inches (102 centimeters). [Of uncertain origin.]

pol·len (pol′ən) *n.* a fine, usually powdery material produced in the anthers of flowering plants that acts as a fertilizing element in plant reproduction. For illustration, see **flower.** [Latin *pollen* fine flour.]

pollen count, a measurement of the number of grains of pollen, esp. ragweed pollen, present in a given volume of air at a specified time and place.

pol·li·nate (pol′ə nāt′) *v.t.,* **-nat·ed, -nat·ing.** to carry or transfer pollen from an anther to a stigma of (a flower or plant).

pol·li·na·tion (pol′ə nā′shən) *n.* the transfer of pollen from the anther of a flower to the stigma of the same or another flower, which is usually followed by fertilization.

pol·li·na·tor (pol′ə nā′tər) *n.* an insect, bird, or other agent, as wind or water, that pollinates plants.

polling place, poll *(def. 4).*

pol·li·wog (pol′ē wog′) *also,* **pollywog.** *n.* tadpole. [Middle English *polywygle,* from *pol* head (see POLL) + *wigelen* to move to and fro. See WIGGLE.]

pol·lock (pol′ək) pollack.

poll·ster (pōl′stər) *n.* a person whose work is conducting public opinion polls.

poll tax, a tax levied on persons, rather than on property, income, or transactions, esp. one payable as a prerequisite to voting, now unconstitutional as a prerequisite to voting in U.S. elections.

pol·lut·ant (pə lü′tənt) *n.* something that pollutes, esp. industrial waste or other material that contaminates air, water, or soil.

pol·lute (pə lüt′) *v.t.,* **-lut·ed, -lut·ing. 1.** to contaminate or make impure or foul, as with industrial waste, esp. to a degree disturbing or harmful to plant or animal life. **2.** to destroy the purity of; sully; corrupt. [Latin *pollūtus,* past participle of *polluere* to defile.] —**pol·lut′er,** *n.*

> **Synonyms** **Pollute, contaminate,** and **defile**[1] mean to make something dirty or impure. **Pollute** suggests that something clean and pure has been made completely filthy or debased: *The air was so polluted that it was hard to breathe.* **Contaminate** stresses the agent that causes the foulness or impurity: *The fruit was contaminated by pesticides.* **Defile,** unlike the other two terms, is used more often in a spiritual or moral than in a physical sense and implies the violation or corruption of something regarded as a symbol of purity: *The invading army defiled the church by turning it into a barracks.*

pol·lu·tion (pə lü′shən) *n.* **1.** the act or process of polluting or the state of being polluted. **2.** something that pollutes, esp. something that contaminates air, water, or soil.

Pol·lux (pol′əks) *n.* see **Castor and Pollux.**

Pol·ly·an·na (pol′ē an′ə) *n.* an excessively or blindly optimistic person who tends to find good in everything. [From *Pollyanna,* the young heroine of *Pollyanna,* a novel by Eleanor H. Porter, 1868-1920, U.S. writer.]

pol·ly·wog (pol′ē wog′) *n.* tadpole.

po·lo (pō′lō) *n.* **1.** a game played on horseback by two teams of four riders each, using long-handled mallets, with which they attempt to hit a wooden ball through the opponent's goal posts. **2.** water polo. [Probably from dialectal Tibetan *polo* ball.] —**po′lo·ist,** *n.*

pol·o·naise (pol′ə nāz′, pō′lə-) *n.* **1.** a stately, majestic dance of Polish origin, in three-quarter time, characterized by slow, gliding steps. **2.** the music for this dance. **3.** a woman's dress popular in the eighteenth century, having a fitted bodice and a full skirt, worn over a separate skirt and open in the front so that the sides could be looped up to form three panels. [French *polonaise,* feminine of *polonais* Polish, from *Pologne* Poland, from Medieval Latin *Polonia* Poland, from Polish *Polanie.*]

po·lo·ni·um (pə lō′nē əm) *n.* a heavy, poisonous, radioactive metallic element, the first radioactive element to be discovered. It occurs naturally as a decay product of pitchblende. Symbol: Po For tables, see **element.** [Modern Latin *polonium,* from Medieval Latin *Polonia* Poland; because one of its discoverers, Marie Curie, 1867-1934, was born in Poland. See POLONAISE.]

polo shirt, a pullover sport shirt of knitted cotton, usually close-fitting and having short sleeves.

pol·ter·geist (pōl′tər gīst′) *n.* a ghost or supernatural presence, traditionally regarded as mischievous, that supposedly makes its presence known through unexplained sounds and the moving of inanimate objects. [German *Poltergeist,* from *poltern* to make a noise + *Geist* ghost.]

polonaise
(def. 3)

pol·troon (pol trün′) *n.* a contemptible, spiritless coward. [French *poltron,* from Italian *poltrone,* from *poltro* colt, going back to Latin *pullus* young animal.]

poly- *combining form* more than one; many; much: *polychrome, polygon.* [Greek *polys* much, many.]

pol·y·an·drous (pol′ē an′drəs) *adj.* **1.** of, relating to, or characterized by the practice, custom, or condition of having more than one husband at a time. **2.** *Botany.* marked by or having many stamens.

pol·y·an·dry (pol′ē an′drē) *n.* **1.** the practice, custom, or condition of having more than one husband at a time. **2.** *Botany.* the condition of being polyandrous. [Greek *polyandriā* condition of having many men, going back to *polys* much, many + *anēr* (stem *andr-*) man, husband.] —**pol′y·an′dric,** *adj.* —**pol′y·an′drist,** *n.*

pol·y·an·thus (pol′ē an′thəs) *n., pl.* **-thus·es. 1.** a hardy

primrose, *Primula polyantha,* that bears flowers of many colors. **2.** a widely cultivated narcissus, *Narcissus tazetta,* that bears small clusters of fragrant white flowers. [Modern Latin *polyanthus,* from Greek *polyanthos* having many flowers, from *polys* much, many + *anthos* flower.]

pol·y·car·pous (pol′ē kär′pəs) *adj.* having two or more carpels.

pol·y·chaete (pol′i kēt′) *n.* any of a class, Polychaeta, of aquatic annelid worms, such as the lugworm, that have bristly appendages used for locomotion.

pol·y·chlo·ri·nat·ed bi·phen·yl (pol′ē klôr′ə nā′tid bī fen′əl) see PCB.

pol·y·chro·mat·ic (pol′ē krō mat′ik) *adj.* having or showing several colors or changes of color. Also, **pol·y·chro·mic** (pol′ē-krō′mik).

pol·y·chrome (pol′ē krōm′) *adj.* having several colors. —*n.* a work of art executed or decorated in several colors. [French *polychrome* of many colors, from Greek *polys* much, many + *chrōma* color.]

pol·y·clin·ic (pol′ē klin′ik) *n.* a clinic or hospital for the study and treatment of a wide variety of diseases.

pol·y·es·ter (pol′ē es′tər) *n.* any of several thermosetting polymeric resins, used esp. in making textile fibers. [POLY(MER) + ESTER.]

pol·y·eth·yl·ene (pol′ē eth′ə lēn′) *n.* any of several thermoplastic resins produced by the polymerization of ethylene, used esp. in making bags, containers, and insulation. [POLY(MER) + ETHYLENE.]

po·lyg·a·mous (pə lig′ə məs) *adj.* **1.** of, relating to, or practicing polygamy. **2.** *Botany.* bearing unisexual and bisexual flowers on the same plant or on separate plants of the same kind. —**po·lyg′a·mous·ly,** *adv.*

po·lyg·a·my (pə lig′ə mē) *n.* the practice, custom, or condition of having more than one spouse or mate at a time. [Greek *polygamiā,* from *polys* much, many + *gamos* marriage.] —**po·lyg′a·mist,** *n.*

pol·y·gene (pol′ē jēn′) *n.* any of a group of genes that together control the expression of a certain complex inheritable character, as size or color. [POLY- + GENE.] —**pol·y·gen·ic** (pol′ē jen′ik), *adj.*

pol·y·glot (pol′ē glot′) *n.* **1.** a person who speaks, understands, or writes several languages. **2.** a book containing versions of the same text in several different languages. **3.** a mixture of several languages. —*adj.* **1.** speaking, understanding, or writing several languages. **2.** of, composed of, or expressed in several languages. [Greek *polyglōttos* speaking many languages, from *polys* much, many + *glōtta* tongue, language.]

pol·y·gon (pol′ē gon′) *n.* a closed plane figure having three or more straight sides. [Late Latin *polygōnum,* from Greek *polygō-non,* from *polys* much, many + *gōniā* angle.] —**po·lyg·o·nal** (pə lig′ə nəl), *adj.*

pol·y·graph (pol′ē graf′) *n.* an instrument that simultaneously measures and records changes in heartbeat, blood pressure, respiration, and other physiological processes, used esp. as a lie detector. [Greek *polygraphos* writing much.]

po·lyg·y·ny (pə lij′ə nē) *n.* the practice, custom, or condition of having more than one wife at a time. [POLY- + Greek *gynē* woman.] —**po·lyg′y·nous,** *adj.*

pol·y·he·dron (pol′ē hē′drən) *n., pl.* **-drons** or **-dra** (-drə) a closed solid figure that is the union of plane polygons, each two adjoining polygons having a common edge. [Greek *polyedron,* neuter of *polyedros* having many bases or sides, from *polys* much, many + *hedrā* base[1], side.] —**pol′y·he′dral,** *adj.*

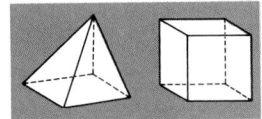

polyhedrons

Pol·y·hym·ni·a (pol′ē him′nē ə) *n.* in Greek mythology, the Muse of sacred poetry. [Latin *Polyhymnia,* from Greek *Polymnia,* going back to *polys* much, many + *hymnos* hymn.]

pol·y·mer (pol′ə mər) *n.* **1.** any large molecule formed of smaller simple molecules linked together in long chains of repeating units. The number of molecules that unite to form a polymer may vary from a few to thousands. **2.** a substance made of polymers. [Greek *polymerēs* having many parts, from *polys* much, many + *meros* part.]

pol·y·mer·ic (pol′ə mer′ik) *adj.* of, relating to, or consisting of a polymer.

po·lym·er·i·za·tion (pə lim′ər ə zā′shən, pol′ə mər ə-) *n.* the uniting of two or more monomers to form a polymer.

po·lym·er·ize (pə lim′ə rīz′, pol′ə mə-) *v.t., v.i.,* **-ized, -iz·ing.** to subject to or undergo polymerization.

polymorphism
two forms of carbon: graphite (left) and diamond (right)

pol·y·mor·phism (pol′ē môr′fiz əm) *n.* the state or quality of being polymorphous.

pol·y·mor·phous (pol′ē môr′fəs) *adj.* having, assuming, or occurring in many or various forms, stages, or characters. Also, **pol·y·mor′phic.** [Greek *polymorphos* multiform, from *polys* much, many + *morphē* form, shape.] —**pol′y·mor′phous·ly,** *adv.*

Pol·y·ne·sian (pol′ə nē′zhən, -shən) *n.* **1.** a member or close descendant of the people inhabiting Polynesia. **2.** a subfamily of the Austronesian family of languages, spoken predominantly in Polynesia and including Hawaiian, Maori, and Tahitian. —*adj.* of, relating to, or characteristic of Polynesia or its people, languages, or culture.

pol·y·no·mi·al (pol′ē nō′mē əl) *n. Mathematics.* an expression consisting of two or more terms. —*adj.* consisting of or characterized by two or more names or terms. [POLY- + (BI)NOMIAL.]

pol·yp (pol′ip) *n.* **1.** any small, sedentary coelenterate with a cup-shaped or saclike body, having a mouth opening at one end of the body surrounded by stinging tentacles. Some polyps, such as hydras, are solitary; others, such as coral, grow in colonies. **2.** *Medicine.* any mass of projecting tissue, esp. a growth on a mucous or serous surface. [French *polype,* from Latin *polypus* octopus, from Greek *polypous* literally, many-footed, from *polys* much, many + *pous* foot.] —**pol·yp·oid** (pol′ə poid′), *adj.*

pol·y·pep·tide (pol′ē pep′tīd) *n.* a peptide containing ten or more amino acids, having a characteristically high molecular weight. [POLY- + PEPTIDE.]

pol·y·phase (pol′ē fāz′) *adj.* having, producing, or using more than one phase, as a set of alternating currents. Also, **multi-phase.**

Pol·y·phe·mus (pol′ə fē′məs) *n.* in Greek mythology, a Cyclops who imprisoned Ulysses and his men in a cave until Ulysses blinded him and they were able to escape.

pol·y·phon·ic (pol′ē fon′ik) *adj.* **1.** consisting of or producing many sounds or voices. **2.** *Music.* of, relating to, or composed of the simultaneous combination of two or more independent melodic voices or parts, with harmonious effect; contrapuntal. ➡ opposed to homophonic. —**pol′y·phon′i·cal·ly,** *adv.*

po·lyph·o·ny (pə lif′ə nē) *n., pl.* **-nies. 1.** a multiplicity of sounds or voices, as in an echo. **2.** *Music.* a polyphonic composition or music; counterpoint. [Greek *polyphōniā* variety of tones, from *polys* much, many + *phōnē* sound, voice.]

pol·y·ploi·dy (pol′ē ploi′dē) *n. Genetics.* a condition, far more common in plants than in animals, in which an organism has one or more extra sets of chromosomes. Polyploidy is often purposely bred into plants, such as wheat, to make them larger or hardier. —**pol′y·ploid′,** *adj.*

pol·y·pro·pyl·ene (pol′ē prō′pə lēn′) *n.* any of several thermoplastic resins produced by the polymerization of propylene, used in packaging materials and carpet backing. [POLY(MER) + PROPYLENE.]

pol·y·sac·cha·ride (pol′ē sak′ə rīd′) *n.* any of a group of carbohydrates made up of long chains of monosaccharide molecules, as starch, glycogen, and cellulose. [POLY- + SACCHARIDE.]

pol·y·sty·rene (pol′ē stī′rēn) *n.* a clear plastic often used in packaging and insulation, as in refrigerators.

pol·y·syl·lab·ic (pol′ē si lab′ik) *adj.* **1.** consisting of three or

P

a	at	e	end	o	hot	u	up	hw	white		about
ā	ape	ē	me	ō	old	ū	use	ng	song		taken
ä	far	i	it	ô	fork	ü	rule	th	thin	ə	pencil
âr	care	ī	ice	oi	oil	u̇	pull	th	this		lemon
		îr	pierce	ou	out	ûr	turn	zh	measure		circus

more syllables. **2.** characterized by words of three or more syllables.

pol·y·syl·la·ble (pol′ē sil′ə bəl) *n.* a word of three or more syllables.

pol·y·tech·nic (pol′ē tek′nik) *adj.* of, relating to, or devoted to many arts or sciences and their practical application. Also, **pol′y·tech′ni·cal.** —*n.* a school offering instruction and training in applied science and technology. [French *polytechnique,* going back to Greek *polys* many, much + *technē* art.]

pol·y·the·ism (pol′ē thē iz′əm) *n.* belief in or worship of more than one god. [French *polythéisme,* going back to Greek *polys* many, much + *theos* god.] —**pol′y·the′ist,** *n.* —**pol′y·the·is′tic,** *adj.*

pol·y·un·sat·u·rate (pol′ē un sach′ər it, -ə rāt′) *n.* a polyunsaturated fat or oil.

pol·y·un·sat·u·rat·ed (pol′ē un sach′ə rā′tid) *adj.* (of a fat or oil molecule) containing many double or triple bonds, as certain vegetable and animal fats and oils. Diets high in polyunsaturated fats have been associated with low levels of cholesterol in the blood.

pol·y·u·re·thane (pol′ē yùr′ə thān′) *n.* any of several synthetic polymers, esp. a foam variety used as an insulating material and an elastic variety used in textiles that stretch.

pol·y·va·lent (pol′ē vā′lənt) *adj.* multivalent. —**pol′y·va′lence,** *n.*

pol·y·vi·nyl (pol′ē vī′nəl) *adj.* of, relating to, or derived from one of the odorless, tasteless, thermoplastic polymers of vinyl or vinyl compounds.

polyvinyl chloride, a tough, white plastic resistant to weather, chemicals, and fire, used as a substitute for iron and copper in indoor and outdoor pipe.

pom·ace (pum′is) *n.* **1.** the residue of fruit and plant parts after the juice or oil has been extracted, esp. the crushed pulp of apples, used for making cider. **2.** any similar pulpy material. [Medieval Latin *pomacium* cider, from Latin *pōmum* apple, fruit.]

po·ma·ceous (po mā′shəs) *adj.* **1.** of or relating to a pome or a plant bearing a pome, such as the apple. **2.** of, relating to, or consisting of apples. [Modern Latin *pomaceus,* from Latin *pōmum* apple, fruit.]

po·made (po mād′, -mäd′, pə-) *n.* a perfumed ointment, esp. one for dressing the hair. —*v.t.,* **-mad·ed, -mad·ing.** to anoint or dress with pomade. [French *pommade* ointment, from Italian *pomata,* from *pomo* apple, from Latin *pōmum* apple, fruit; because formerly made with the pulp of apples.]

po·man·der (pə man′dər, pō′man′-) *n.* a mixture of aromatic substances, often shaped into a ball, that gives off a pleasing scent, formerly worn esp. as a guard against infection but now placed in closets and dresser drawers. [Middle French *pome d'ambre* apple or ball of amber. See POME, AMBER.]

pome (pōm) *n.* a fleshy, firm fruit having several seeds rather than a stone, such as the apple or pear. [Old French *pome* apple, going back to Latin *pōmum* apple, fruit.]

pome·gran·ate (pom′gran′it, pom′ə-, pum′-) *n.* **1.** the round, edible fruit of a shrub or small tree, *Punica granatum,* having a golden red, leathery rind and containing many small seeds, each of which is enclosed by a juicy, reddish pulp. **2.** the shrub or tree bearing this fruit, having red or orange, trumpet-shaped flowers. [Old French *pome grenate* the fruit, going back to Latin *pōmum* apple, fruit + *grānātum,* neuter of *grānātus* having many grains.]

pom·e·lo (pom′ə lō′) *n., pl.* **-los.** shaddock.

Pom·er·a·ni·an (pom′ə rā′nē ən) *n.* **1.** a native or inhabitant of Pomerania. **2.** a small, long-haired breed of dog having a foxlike head and a bushy tail that lies flat on the back. Height: 7 inches (18 centimeters) at the shoulder. —*adj.* of, relating to, or characteristic of Pomerania or its people or culture.

pom·mel (pum′əl, pom′-) *n.* **1.** the upward-projecting front part of a saddle, consisting of a knob that is used chiefly as a grip. For illustration, see **saddle. 2.** the rounded knob on the hilt of some swords, daggers, or similar weapons. —*v.t.* pummel. [Old French *pomel* knob on the hilt of a sword; literally, small apple, going back to Latin *pōmum* apple, fruit.]

po·mol·o·gy (pō mol′ə jē) *n.* the branch of botany that deals with fruits and their cultivation. [Modern Latin *pomologia,* from Latin *pōmum* apple, fruit + -LOGY.] —**po·mo·log·i·cal** (pō′mə loj′i kəl), *adj.* —**po·mol′o·gist,** *n.*

Po·mo·na (pə mō′nə) *n.* in Roman mythology, the goddess of fruit trees.

pomp (pomp) *n.* **1.** stately and splendid ceremony or display; splendor; pageantry: *the pomp and ritual of a coronation.* **2.** any vain, ostentatious show or display. [Latin *pompa* procession, display, from Greek *pompē*.]

pom·pa·dour (pom′pə dôr′, -dùr′) *n.* **1.** a man's hair style in which the hair is combed up high from the forehead. **2.** a woman's hair style in which the hair is combed back from the forehead and puffed high in front, often over a pad. [From the Marquise de *Pompadour,* 1721-64, the mistress of Louis XV of France.]

pom·pa·no (pom′pə nō′) *n., pl.* **-nos.** any of several food and game fish, family Carangidae, found in temperate and tropical waters of the Americas, having a flattened, roundish or oval body that is usually silver in color. Length: to 18 inches (46 centimeters). [Spanish *pampano* a kind of fish, tendril of a vine, from Latin *pampinus* tendril of a vine.]

pom·pom (pom′pom′) *also,* **pom-pom.** *n.* **1.** an ornamental ball or tuft of wool or other material, used esp. as a decoration on hats and other clothing. **2.** pompon *(def. 1).* [French *pompon* ornamental tuft; of uncertain origin.]

pom·pon (pom′pon′) *n.* **1.** a small, round, globe-shaped flower, such as a chrysanthemum. **2.** pompom *(def. 1).*

pom·pos·i·ty (pom pos′i tē) *n., pl.* **-ties. 1.** the state or quality of being pompous. **2.** an instance of being pompous; pompous action, remark, or display.

pom·pous (pom′pəs) *adj.* **1.** exhibiting or characterized by an exaggerated or complacent sense of dignity or self-importance. **2.** excessively lofty or ornate, as language. **3.** characterized by or full of pomp or stately ceremony. [Late Latin *pompōsus* stately, from Latin *pompa* procession, display. See POMP.] —**pom′pous·ly,** *adv.* —**pom′pous·ness,** *n.*

pon·cho (pon′chō) *n., pl.* **-chos. 1.** a cloaklike garment consisting of a piece of cloth with a slit or hole in the middle so that it can be slipped over the head. **2.** a waterproof garment resembling this, worn chiefly as a raincoat. [Spanish *poncho,* from Araucanian *pontho* woolen cloth.]

pond (pond) *n.* a body of still or standing water, sometimes artificial and usually smaller than a lake. [Form of POUND³.]

pon·der (pon′dər) *v.t.* to weigh in the mind; consider or think over carefully: *The prisoners pondered the fate awaiting them.* —*v.i.* to think or deliberate; muse; reflect: *to ponder over a problem.* [Latin *ponderāre.*] —**pon′der·er,** *n.* —For Synonyms *(v.i.),* see **meditate.**

pon·der·a·ble (pon′dər ə bəl) *adj.* capable of being weighed or evaluated; appreciable.

pon·der·o·sa pine (pon′də rō′sə) a tall pine, *Pinus ponderosa,* of western North America, valued for its timber. [Modern Latin *Pinus ponderosa* literally, heavy pine; possibly referring to its strong wood.]

pon·der·ous (pon′dər əs) *adj.* **1.** having great weight or bulk; heavy; unwieldy: *The statue is too ponderous to be moved easily.* **2.** clumsy, slow, or labored, as if because of weight: *ponderous movements.* **3.** lacking grace or interest; tedious and labored: *a ponderous style of writing.* [Latin *ponderōsus* heavy, weighty, from *pondus* weight.] —**pon′der·os′i·ty** (pon′də ros′i tē), **pon′der·ous·ness,** *n.* —**pon′der·ous·ly,** *adv.* —For Synonyms, see **heavy.**

pond lily, any of a group of water plants, genus *Nuphar* or *Nymphaea,* including the spatterdock and common water lily.

pond scum, any freshwater algae that form a slimy or frothy floating mass on the surface of still or stagnant water, esp. any green algae of the genus *Spirogyra.*

pond·weed (pond′wēd′) *n.* any of a large group of water plants, genus *Potamogeton,* found growing in large numbers in ponds and streams, bearing dense spikes of tiny flowers just above the water's surface.

pone (pōn) *n.* corn pone. [Of Algonquian origin.]

pon·gee (pon jē′) *n.* a brownish yellow, lightweight fabric having an uneven surface, originally woven by hand in China from silk. [Dialectal Chinese *pun-chī* own loom.]

pon·gid (pon′jid) *n.* ape *(def. 1).* —*adj.* of or relating to the apes. [Modern Latin *Pongidae,* from Kongo (an African language) *mpongi* + Modern Latin *-idae* (see -ID²).]

pon·iard (pon′yərd) *n.* dagger. —*v.t.* to stab with a poniard. [French *poignard* dagger, from *poing* fist, from Latin *pugnus.*]

pons (ponz) *n., pl.* **pon·tes** (pon′tēz). a band of nerve fibers in the brain connecting the cerebellum, cerebrum, and medulla oblongata. For illustration, see **brain.** [Latin *pōns* bridge.]

pon·ti·fex (pon′tə feks′) *n., pl.* **pon·tif·i·ces** (pon tif′i sēz′). in ancient Rome, a member of the principal college of priests in charge of the state religion. [Latin *pontifex.*]

pon·tiff (pon′tif) *n.* **1.** pope. **2.** any high priest. **3.** *Archaic.* any bishop. [French *pontif* high priest of ancient Rome, ecclesiastical dignitary, from Latin *pontifex* high priest of ancient Rome.]

pon·tif·i·cal (pon tif′i kəl) *adj.* **1.** of, relating to, or suitable for a pope; papal. **2.** of or relating to a bishop. **3.** characterized by a haughty and pompous sense of self-importance or authority. —*n.* **pontificals. 1.** the vestments and insignia of office worn by bishops, cardinals, and the pope at certain ecclesiastical ceremonies. **2.** a book containing forms for the rites performed by bishops. —**pon·tif′i·cal·ly,** *adv.*

pon·tif·i·cate (*v.*, pon tif′i kāt′; *n.*, pon tif′i kit, -kāt′) *v.i.*, -cat·ed, -cat·ing. **1.** to speak or act with haughty, pompous self-importance or authority. **2.** to discharge the duties or officiate in the capacity of a pontiff, esp. of a pope. —*n.* the office or term of office of a pontiff, esp. of a pope.

pon·toon (pon tün′) *n.* **1.** a flat-bottomed boat or similar floating structure used as a support, as in the construction of floating bridges over water or in the raising of submerged vessels. **2.** the float of a seaplane. [French *ponton* bridge of boats, low flat boat, from Latin *pontō*, from *pōns* bridge.]

pontoon bridge, a bridge, often temporary, that is supported in the water by pontoons.

pontoon bridge

po·ny (pō′nē) *n.*, *pl.* -nies. **1.** a horse of any of various small breeds, such as the Shetland pony, less than 5 feet high (1.5 meters) at the shoulder. **2.** any horse, esp. one small in size. **3.** *Informal.* a synopsis of a literary work, or any other prepared text or aid, esp. a literal translation of a work in a foreign language, used by students, usually illicitly, in doing schoolwork or in preparing for an exam. Also, **trot. 4.** *Informal.* **a.** a small glass for liquor. **b.** the amount such a glass will hold. [Old French *poulenet* little colt, diminutive of *poulain* colt, going back to Latin *pullus* young animal.]
· **to pony up.** *Slang.* to pay, as in settling an account: *I ponied up ten dollars as my share of the bill.*

pony express, a rapid postal service in which mail was carried in relays by riders mounted on fast horses, in operation between Missouri and California from 1860 to 1861.

po·ny·tail (pō′nē tāl′) *also,* **pony tail.** *n.* a hair style in which the hair is drawn tightly back from the face and fastened at the back of the head, so as to hang down like a pony's tail.

pooch (püch) *n. Slang.* a dog. [Of uncertain origin.]

pood (püd) *n.* a unit of weight used in Russia, equal to approximately 36 pounds (16 kilograms). [Russian *pood,* going back to Latin *pondō* by weight.]

poo·dle (pü′dəl) *n.* a curly-haired breed of dog having a dense, usually solid-colored coat that is often clipped in elaborate styles. There are three varieties, which differ only in size: the **toy poodle,** to 10 inches (25 centimeters) at the shoulder; the **miniature poodle,** 10-15 inches (25-38 centimeters) at the shoulder; and the **standard poodle,** over 15 inches (38 centimeters). [German *Pudel,* from *pudeln* to splash in water; because the poodle was originally used in hunting to retrieve waterfowl.]

pooh (pü) *interj.* used to express disbelief, disdain, or impatience. [Imitative.]

pooh-pooh (pü′pü′) *v.t.* to express contempt or disdain for, or disbelief in: *to pooh-pooh an idea, to pooh-pooh a story.* [Repetition of POOH.]

pool¹ (pül) *n.* **1.** a small body of still or standing water, usually fresh. **2.** an indoor or outdoor tank designed for swimming, often rectangular in shape and usually built of concrete and furnished with water-filtering equipment. Also, **swimming pool. 3.** a small, shallow body or accumulation of liquid on a surface: *a pool of blood, a pool of spilt milk.* **4.** a still, deep place in a stream or river. [Old English *pōl* small body of water.]

pool² (pül) *n.* **1.** any of various games played on a pool table, with the object being to drive balls numbered from one to fifteen into the table's pockets by using the cue to hit the cue ball in such a way that it will strike the other balls. Also, **pocket billiards. 2.** any collective fund or endeavor or combining of resources or effort for the common benefit of the participants: *a day-care pool.* **3.** a group of workers whose labor or skills are shared by a group: *an office typing pool.* **4.** the persons or parties contributing to or participating in a pool. **5.** the accumulation, as of antes and bets, that the winner gets in certain gambling games; pot. **6.** a group of business firms or competitors that cooperate with each other to eliminate competition by fixing prices and establishing controls over the production and market of a commodity. **7.** a temporary association of persons or organizations working together to manipulate or speculate in the prices of securities. —*v.t.* to combine or put together and share in common for common benefit: *They pooled their money to get some new equipment.* [French *poule* stake in a game; literally, hen, going back to Latin *pullus* young fowl.]

pool·room (pül′rüm′, -rüm′) *n.* a room or place of business equipped for the playing of pool or billiards. Also, **pool hall.**

pool table, a rectangular table used in playing pool, having a felt-covered surface and six pockets, one in each of the four corners and one in the center of each of the longer sides.

poop¹ (püp) *n.* poop deck. —*v.t.* **1.** (of a wave) to break over the stern of (a boat or ship). **2.** (of a boat or ship) to receive (a wave) over the stern. [French *poupe* stern of a ship, going back to Latin *puppis.*]

poop² (püp) *v.t. Slang.* to cause to become exhausted or thoroughly fatigued: *Playing tennis in such heat pooped us all.* [Of uncertain origin.]
· **to poop out.** *Slang.* **a.** to make or become exhausted or nonfunctioning: *That last game of volleyball pooped me out. Our old refrigerator finally pooped out.* **b.** to back out of a commitment, esp. at the last minute: *One of our volunteers pooped out.*

poop deck, a short deck above the main deck at the stern of a boat or ship, often forming the roof of a cabin.

poor (pur) *adj.* **1.** lacking wealth, material possessions, or means of subsistence; having little or no money; needy: *a poor family struggling to make ends meet.* **2.** characterized by or indicating such a lack: *a poor neighborhood.* **3.** lacking or deficient in proper, necessary, or desirable qualities; inferior in quality or value: *poor health, poor housing, a poor candidate for a job.* **4.** being less than is wanted, needed, or expected; scanty; insufficient: *a poor wheat crop.* **5.** lacking skill, ability, application, or proficiency; not capable, persistent, or talented: *a poor writer, a poor student.* **6.** arousing or deserving pity or compassion; unhappy: *The poor dog hasn't eaten all day.* **7.** not favorable or positive: *to have a poor opinion of someone, to have a poor chance of recovery.* —*n.* **the poor.** poor or needy persons collectively. [Old French *povre* needy man, needy, from Latin *pauper.* Doublet of PAUPER.] —**poor′ness,** *n.*

poor·house (pur′hous′) *n.*, *pl.* -hous·es (-hou′ziz). formerly, an establishment or institution maintained at public expense to shelter and aid poor people.

poor law, a law providing for public relief or support of the poor.

poor·ly (pur′lē) *adv.* in a poor manner; badly: *You have performed rather poorly this term.* —*adj. Informal.* somewhat ill; ailing; indisposed: *I've been poorly lately.*

poor-spir·it·ed (pur′spir′i tid) *adj.* lacking spirit or courage; cowardly.

poor white, a white person, esp. in the southern United States, of very low social and economic status and having little educational or cultural background. ➡ usually considered offensive.

pop¹ (pop) *v.*, popped, pop·ping. —*v.i.* **1.** to make a short, sharp, explosive sound: *The cork popped when the bottle was opened.* **2.** to burst open or explode with such a sound: *The corn popped quickly.* **3.** to move, go, appear, or come quickly or suddenly: *to pop out of bed, to pop in to see someone.* **4.** (of the eyes) to open wide suddenly: *Their eyes popped when they heard the news.* **5.** *Baseball.* to hit the ball into the air into or near the infield (often with *up*). —*v.t.* **1.a.** to cause to burst open with a short, sharp, explosive sound: *The child popped the balloon with a pin.* **b.** to pull so as to release with such a sound: *to pop the tab from a can of soda.* **2.** to put or thrust quickly or suddenly: *He popped the bread into the oven. She popped her head out the window.* **3.** *Baseball.* to hit (the ball) high into the air into or near the infield, esp. so that an opposing player has a chance to catch it before it touches the ground. —*n.* **1.** a short, sharp, explosive sound. **2.** pop fly. —*adv.* **1.** with a pop. **2.** suddenly or unexpectedly. [Imitative.]
· **to pop off.** *Informal.* **a.** to die. **b.** to express oneself angrily or emotionally: *to pop off about someone's behavior.*
· **to pop the question.** *Informal.* to propose marriage.

pop² (pop) *adj. Informal.* **1.** of, relating to, or designating popular music: *a pop singer, a pop concert.* **2.** of, relating to, or designating anything for the popular taste: *a pop novel.* [Short for POPULAR.]

pop³ (pop) *n. Informal.* father. [A form of *papa.*]

pop⁴ (pop) *n. Informal.* soda *(def. 2b).* [From *pop¹.*]

pop. 1. popular. **2.** popularly. **3.** population.

pop art 1. an art movement or style of art in which subjects, image, themes, and techniques are taken from advertising, comic strips, motion pictures, and other forms of popular culture. **2.** art

a	at	e	end	o	hot	u	up	hw	white	⎧	about
ā	ape	ē	me	ō	old	ū	use	ng	song		taken
ä	far	i	it	ô	fork	u̇	rule	th	thin	ə	pencil
âr	care	ī	ice	oi	oil	u̇	pull	th	this		lemon
		îr	pierce	ou	out	ûr	turn	zh	measure	⎩	circus

P

of this movement: *a gallery full of pop art.* [Short for *popular art;* because it deals with subjects taken from popular culture.]

pop·corn (pop′kôrn′) *n.* **1.** a variety of corn, *Zea mays everta,* having small, hard kernels that, when heated, burst open and puff out to form white, fluffy masses. **2.** the white, fluffy masses so formed, eaten as a snack.

pope (pōp) *also,* **Pope.** *n.* the bishop of Rome and supreme head of the Roman Catholic Church, who, according to Catholic doctrine, derives his authority from, and acts as vicar of, Christ. [Old English *pāpa,* from Church Latin *pāpa* pope, bishop, from Latin *pāpa* father, from Greek *papās* bishop, father.]

pop·er·y (pō′pə rē) *n.* the doctrines and practices of the Roman Catholic Church. ➤ usually considered offensive.

pop·eyed (pop′īd′) *adj.* having large, protruding eyes.

pop fly *Baseball.* a high fly ball hit into or near the infield so that an opposing player has a chance to catch it before it touches the ground. Also, **pop-up, pop.**

pop·gun (pop′gun′) *n.* any toy gun that produces a loud pop when fired, esp. one that fires pellets or corks by means of air compressed in the barrel.

pop·in·jay (pop′in jā′) *n.* a vain, foppish person given to unthinking chatter. [Old French *popingay, papegai* parrot, from Arabic *babaghā;* influenced by JAY.]

pop·ish (pō′pish) *adj.* of or relating to popes or the Roman Catholic Church. ➤ usually considered offensive. —**pop′ish·ly,** *adv.* —**pop′ish·ness,** *n.*

pop·lar (pop′lər) *n.* **1.** any of a small group of fast-growing trees, genus *Populus,* of the willow family, found throughout the Northern Hemisphere, having pale, ridged bark and broad leaves and widely cultivated as ornamentals and in windbreaks. **2.** the soft white wood of this tree, often used to make shipping boxes and pulp. [Old French *poplier* the tree, going back to Latin *pōpulus.*]

pop·lin (pop′lin) *n.* a durable fabric woven with a pronounced crosswise rib, often made of cotton, and used for such items as shirts, dresses, curtains, and pajamas. [Obsolete French *papeline,* possibly from *Poperinge,* a Flemish city famous for its fabrics in the Middle Ages.]

pop·o·ver (pop′ō′vər) *n.* a very light muffin, made of flour, eggs, milk, and shortening, that puffs up and becomes hollow when baked. [POP¹ + OVER; because it *pops* up *over* the edge of the pan while baking.]

pop·per (pop′ər) *n.* **1.** a device used for popping popcorn, usually a covered wire basket or metal pan. **2.** a person or thing that pops.

pop·pet (pop′it) *n.* an intake or exhaust valve that works by being lifted up and down, rather than by turning or pivoting. Also, **poppet valve.** [Form of PUPPET.]

pop·py (pop′ē) *n., pl.* **-pies. 1.** the round, showy flower of any of a small group of plants, genus *Papaver,* often cultivated as a garden flower. **2.** any of the annual or perennial plants bearing this flower, containing a milky juice. One species, *P. somniferum,* is the source of the drug opium. **3.** any of various other plants related to the poppy, such as the **California poppy,** *Eschscholzia californica.* **4.** a bright orange-red color. —*adj.* having a bright orange-red color. [Old English *popæg* the plant and flower of the genus *Papaver,* going back to Latin *papāver.*]

poppies

pop·py·cock (pop′ē kok′) *n.* utterly foolish or empty talk; nonsense. [Dialectal Dutch *pappekak* literally, soft dung.]

Pop·si·cle (pop′si kəl) *n. Trademark.* a frozen confection consisting of a bar of flavored ice or ice cream on a stick.

pop-top (pop′top′) *adj.* (of a can or other container) having a tab on a ring that is pulled to open the top. —*n.* **1.** a can or container that opens by pulling such a tab. **2.** the tab itself.

pop·u·lace (pop′yə lis) *n.* **1.** the common people, as distinguished from the higher classes; the masses. **2.** all the inhabitants of a place; population. [French *populace* the common people, from Italian *popolaccio,* going back to Latin *populus* the people.]

pop·u·lar (pop′yə lər) *adj.* **1.** pleasing to or favored by very many or most people: *a popular actor.* **2.** having many friends and acquaintances; generally liked, admired, or beloved by others: *the most popular student in the class.* **3.** of, relating to, or representing the general public: *a popular election, popular government.* **4.** accepted or widespread among the general public; common; prevalent: *a popular misconception.* **5.** suited to or intended for the taste and intelligence of the average person or the general public: *popular music.* **6.** suited to or within the means of ordinary people; moderate: *This model is now available at popular prices.* **7.** arising from or originating among the common people: *an old legend of popular origin.* [Latin *populāris* relating to the people, from *populus* the people.] —**pop′u·lar·ly,** *adv.*

popular front, a coalition, as in the 1930s, of communist, socialist, and moderate political groups behind a common platform opposed to fascism.

pop·u·lar·i·ty (pop′yə lar′i tē) *n.* the quality or state of being widely liked, admired, or favored.

pop·u·lar·ize (pop′yə lə rīz′) *v.t.,* **-ized, -iz·ing.** to make popular, esp. to cause to become intelligible to the general public or widely known or accepted: *a writer who popularized the history of science.* —**pop′u·lar·i·za′tion,** *n.* —**pop′u·lar·iz′er,** *n.*

popular vote 1. the total vote of those citizens eligible to participate in an election, esp. of the ones who actually do vote. **2.** this vote as opposed to the vote of the electoral college: *to win the popular vote but lose the election.*

pop·u·late (pop′yə lāt′) *v.t.,* **-lat·ed, -lat·ing. 1.** to live in; inhabit. **2.** to furnish with inhabitants, as by colonization; people. [Medieval Latin *populatus,* past participle of *populare* to people, going back to Latin *populus* the people.]

pop·u·la·tion (pop′yə lā′shən) *n.* **1.** the total number of people living in a particular area or place: *The population of that state has doubled in the past decade.* **2.** the people themselves: *The entire population was opposed to the tax increase.* **3.** a segment of such people considered as a distinct group or distinguished in some way from the rest: *the English-speaking population of Montreal.* **4.** all the organisms living in a given area. **5.** the act or process of populating; furnishing with inhabitants. **6.** *Statistics.* a group of individuals or items to be studied. [Late Latin *populātiō* the people, from Latin *populus.*]

Pop·u·list (pop′yə list) *adj.* **1.** of, relating to, or characteristic of the Populist Party. **2. populist.** resembling the politics of the Populist Party or in similar ways appealing to the common people: *populist rhetoric.* —*n.* **1.** a member or supporter of the Populist Party. **2. populist.** a person, such as a politician, who appeals to the interests of the common people. —**Pop′u·lism;** *also,* **pop′u·lism,** *n.* —**Pop′u·lis′tic;** *also,* **pop′u·lis′tic,** *adj.*

Populist Party, a profarmer and prolabor political party active in the United States in the 1890s, chiefly advocating a graduated income tax, public ownership of railroads, direct election of senators, and free coinage of silver to increase the amount of currency in circulation. Also, **People's Party.**

pop·u·lous (pop′yə ləs) *adj.* having many inhabitants; heavily populated. [Latin *populōsus* full of people, from *populus* the people.] —**pop′u·lous·ly,** *adv.* —**pop′u·lous·ness,** *n.*

pop-up (pop′up′) *n.* pop fly. —*adj.* having or being something that pops up: *a pop-up toaster, a pop-up toy.*

por·ce·lain (pôr′sə lin, pôrs′lin) *n.* **1.** a fine ceramic ware that is hard, white, translucent, and nonporous. **2.** objects made of this, collectively. [French *porcelaine* china, a kind of shell whose polished surface resembled that of china, from Italian *porcellana,* going back to Latin *porcus* pig; because the shell supposedly resembled a pig's back.]

porch (pôrch) *n.* **1.** a roofed, sometimes partly or totally enclosed area attached to and extending along and outward from the outside of a house. **2.** a structure forming an entrance to a building, often covered. [Old French *porche,* from Latin *porticus* arcade, colonnade. Doublet of PORTICO.]

por·cine (pôr′sīn) *adj.* **1.** of or relating to pigs. **2.** resembling a pig or pigs. [Latin *porcīnus* relating to a pig, from *porcus* pig.]

por·cu·pine (pôr′kyə pīn′) *n.* any of various large rodents, families Erethizontidae and Hystricidae, whose body and tail are covered with spines or quills that serve as protection. Length: to 3 feet (0.9 meter). [Old French *porc espin* literally, thorny pig, going back to Latin *porcus* pig + *spīna* thorn.]

pore[1] (pôr) *n.* **1.** a very small opening, as in the skin of an animal, serving as an outlet for perspiration, or as in the surface of a leaf, serving as a means of absorption. **2.** a similar opening, as in the surface of rocks or soil. [Old French *pore,* from Latin *porus,* from Greek *poros.*]

porcupine

pore[2] (pôr) *v.i.,* **pored, por·ing. 1.** to read or study with great attention, application, care, or absorption (with *over*): *I pored over my notes while awaiting my turn to speak.* **2.** to consider carefully; ponder (with *over*): *to pore over a problem.* **3.** to gaze earnestly or steadily. [Of uncertain origin.]

por·gy (pôr′gē) *n., pl.* **-gies. 1.** any of a group of commercially important food and game fish, family Sparidae, found chiefly in coastal waters of the Atlantic Ocean, having a flattened, oval, usually silvery gray body with a stiff, spined dorsal fin. Length: 1-2½ feet (0.3-0.8 meter). **2.** any of various other fish, such as the menhaden. [Modification of earlier *pargo,* from Spanish *pargo,* from Latin *pagarus* sea bream, from Greek *phagros.*]

po·rif·er·an (pô rif′ər ən) *n.* sponge *(def. 1).* —*adj.* of or relating to sponges. [Latin *porus* PORE[1] + *ferre* to bear.]

pork (pôrk) *n.* **1.** the meat of a pig or hog used as food. **2.** *Informal.* government funds, jobs, or favors that benefit or enrich only one local district, given to gain political advantage for the representative of the district. [Old French *porc* pig, meat of a pig, from Latin *porcus* pig.]

pork-bar·rel (pôrk′bar′əl) *adj. Informal.* designating a government project or appropriation favoring one locality, meant to ingratiate the representative of that area with local voters.

pork barrel *Informal.* a pork-barrel project or appropriation or any appropriation of public money for local projects that may be considered unnecessary or extravagant.

pork·er (pôr′kər) *n.* a pig or hog, esp. one fattened for slaughter.

pork·pie (pôrk′pī′) *n.* a hat having a low, flat crown. Also, **porkpie hat.**

por·no (pôr′nō) *Slang. n.* pornography. —*adj.* pornographic: *porno books.* Also, **porn.** [Short for PORN(OGRAPHY).]

por·nog·ra·phy (pôr nog′rə fē) *n.* **1.** material, such as pictures or writings, intended to arouse sexual desires or excitement. **2.** the making of such material. [Greek *pornographos* writing about harlots (from *pornē* harlot + *-graphos* writing) + -Y[3].] —**por·nog′ra·pher,** *n.* —**por·no·graph·ic** (pôr′nə graf′ik), *adj.* —**por′no·graph′i·cal·ly,** *adv.*

po·ros·i·ty (pô ros′i tē) *n., pl.* **-ties. 1.** the quality or condition of being porous. **2.** a pore or similar opening.

po·rous (pôr′əs) *adj.* **1.** having or full of pores. **2.** permeable by liquids, air, or light. —**po′rous·ly,** *adv.* —**po′rous·ness,** *n.*

por·phy·ry (pôr′fə rē) *n., pl.* **-ries.** an igneous rock composed of two or more minerals, one of which, usually a feldspar, occurs in much larger crystals than the groundmass in which it is embedded. [Old French *porfire* a purple stone, through Latin, going back to Greek *porphyrītēs,* from *porphyra* a shellfish from which a purple dye was obtained.] —**por·phy·rit·ic** (pôr′fə rit′ik), *adj.*

por·poise (pôr′pəs) *n., pl.* **-pois·es** or **-poise. 1.** any of various fishlike mammals, family Phocaenidae, closely related to and resembling the dolphin, inhabiting all oceans except those in polar regions, having a torpedo-shaped body that is usually black with white undersides or with a large white patch on the side. Unlike most dolphins, most porpoises have a rounded head without a beak. Length: 4-6 feet (1.2-1.8 meters). [Old French *porpeis, porpois,* going back to Latin *porcus* pig + *piscis* fish.]

por·ridge (pôr′ij, por′-) *n.* a soft food made by boiling oatmeal or other meal in water or milk until thickened, usually served as a breakfast dish. [Form of POTTAGE.]

por·rin·ger (pôr′in jər, por′-) *n.* a small, shallow bowl, usually with a short handle, for holding porridge, soup, or other food, esp. such a bowl of silver or other material used by children. [Modification of earlier *pottinger,* going back to Old French *potager* relating to pottage, from *potage.* See POTTAGE.]

port[1] (pôrt) *n.* **1.** a place where boats or ships can anchor and be protected from storms; harbor. **2.** a city or town with a harbor having facilities for loading and unloading boats or ships. **3.** port of entry. [Old English *port,* from Latin *portus* harbor.] —For Synonyms, see **harbor.**

port[2] (pôrt) *n.* the left side of a boat or ship as one faces forward. ➡ opposed to **starboard.** —*adj.* of, relating to, or located on the left side of a boat or ship. Also, **larboard** (*n., adj.*). —*v.t., v.i.* to turn or shift to the port side. [Possibly once referring to the side of the ship facing the harbor or *port.*]

port[3] (pôrt) *n.* a strong, sweet wine, usually dark red in color. [From *Oporto,* Portuguese city from which this wine was shipped.]

port[4] (pôrt) *n.* **1.** porthole. **2.** a covering for a porthole. **3.** an opening in a piece of machinery for the passage of fluids, often controlled by a valve. **4.** a fixture on a computer for plugging in cables that connect to peripheral devices. [Old French *porte* gate, from Latin *porta.*]

port[5] (pôrt) *v.t. Military.* to bring (a rifle, sword, or other weapon) to a diagonal position in front of the chest and close to the body, with the muzzle or blade near the left shoulder. —*n.* **1.** *Military.* the position of a rifle or other weapon when ported. **2.** the manner in which one carries oneself; bearing. [Old French *port* carriage, demeanor, from *porter* to carry, from Latin *portāre.*]

Port. 1. Portugal. **2.** Portuguese.

port·a·ble (pôr′tə bəl) *adj.* capable of being carried, esp. easily carried, as in or with the hand: *a portable radio, a portable phonograph.* —*n.* something that is portable, such as a lightweight typewriter. [Late Latin *portābilis* capable of being carried, from Latin *portāre* to carry.]

por·tage (pôr′tij) *n.* **1.** the act of transporting boats or goods overland between navigable waters. **2.** a route or place over which this is done. **3.** the act or work of carrying or transporting. **4.** a cost or charge for this. —*v.t., v.i.,* **-taged, -tag·ing.** to carry (boats or goods) over a portage. [French *portage* act of carrying, going back to Latin *portāre* to carry.]

por·tal (pôr′təl) *n.* a door, gate, or entrance, esp. a large and imposing one. [Medieval Latin *portale,* from *portalis* relating to a gate, from Latin *porta* gate.]

por·tal-to-por·tal pay (pôr′təl tə pôr′təl) wages computed from the time an employee enters the door of an employer's place of business to begin work until the employee passes through the door after work.

portal vein, a large vein that carries blood from the veins of the pancreas, spleen, stomach, and intestines to the liver.

port authority, a commission charged with regulating and administering the transportation facilities and the water, rail, and other traffic of a port.

port·cul·lis (pôrt kul′is) *n.* a heavy grating constructed so as to slide up and down in grooves cut in the sides of the gateway of a castle or fortress, capable of being lowered quickly as a defense against assault. [Anglo-Norman *porte colice* literally, sliding gate, going back to Latin *porta* gate + *colāre* to strain, filter.]

Porte (pôrt) *n.* the government of the Ottoman Empire.

porte-co·chere (pôrt′kō shâr′) *also,* **porte-co·chère.** *n.* **1.** a covered passage or entrance for carriages or other vehicles, leading into a courtyard. **2.** a large porch at the entrance of a building, extending over the driveway, for sheltering persons entering or leaving vehicles. [French *porte-cochère* carriage entrance, from *porte* gate + *cochère* for carriages (from *coche* carriage). See PORT[4], COACH.]

portcullis

por·tend (pôr tend′) *v.t.* to be a warning, sign, or indication of, esp. beforehand; forebode. [Latin *portendere* to predict.]

por·tent (pôr′tent) *n.* **1.** a warning or indication of what is to come, esp. of something momentous or calamitous; omen. **2.** ominous or prophetic significance: *a development with portent.* [Latin *portentum* sign, omen.]

por·ten·tous (pôr ten′təs) *adj.* **1.** of the nature of or constituting a portent; ominous; threatening. **2.** exciting or causing wonder or awe; very remarkable or important: *a portentous achievement.* **3.** pretentious or pompous: *a portentous statement.* —**por·ten′tous·ly,** *adv.* —**por·ten′tous·ness,** *n.*

por·ter[1] (pôr′tər) *n.* **1.** a person employed to carry baggage at a transportation terminal, such as a railroad station, or in a hotel.

a	at	e	end	o	hot	u	up	hw	white		about
ā	ape	ē	me	ō	old	ū	use	ng	song		taken
ä	far	i	it	ô	fork	ü	rule	th	thin	ə	pencil
âr	care	ī	ice	oi	oil	u̇	pull	th	this		lemon
		îr	pierce	ou	out	ûr	turn	zh	measure		circus

2. an attendant on a train, esp. in a sleeping or parlor car. [Old French *porteur* bearer, from Late Latin *portātor,* from Latin *portāre* to carry.]

por·ter² (pôr′tər) *n.* **1.** a person employed to do cleaning and maintenance work in a building or establishment, as in an apartment house; janitor. **2.** a doorkeeper or gatekeeper. [Old French *portier* gatekeeper, from Late Latin *portārius* doorkeeper, from Latin *porta* gate, door.]

por·ter³ (pôr′tər) *n.* a dark brown, heavy, bitter beer brewed from partly charred malt. [Short for *porter's ale;* supposedly because this beer was popular among porters.]

por·ter·house (pôr′tər hous′) *n., pl.* **-hous·es** (-hou′ziz). a choice cut of beef taken from the loin, including a large part of the tenderloin. Also, **porterhouse steak**. [Supposedly from earlier *porterhouse* a place where porter and other malt beverages were sold and where steaks were also served.]

port·fo·li·o (pôrt fō′lē ō′) *n., pl.* **-li·os**. **1.** a portable case for holding or carrying loose papers, drawings, documents, and similar materials. **2.** the office, position, and duties of a cabinet member or a minister of state in charge of a department. **3.** a list or group of stocks, bonds, and the like of a bank, investment company, or private investor. **4.** a representative collection of an artist's or writer's works. [Italian *portafoglio* wallet, office of a cabinet minister, going back to Latin *portāre* to carry + *folium* leaf, leaf of paper.]

port·hole (pôrt′hōl′) *n.* **1.** a small opening in the side of a boat or ship, usually circular and fitted with a hinged glass cover, chiefly for admitting air and light. **2.** an opening in a wall, as of a fort, through which to shoot; embrasure. Also, **port**.

portico

por·ti·co (pôr′ti kō′) *n., pl.* **-coes** or **-cos**. a roofed structure forming a covered walk, usually attached to a building, supported by columns or piers, and open on at least one side. [Italian *portico,* from Latin *porticus* arcade, colonnade. Doublet of PORCH.]

por·tiere (pôr tyâr′) *also,* **por·tière**. *n.* a curtain, usually of a heavy material, hung at a doorway, used either instead of a door or as a decoration. [French *portière,* from *porte* door, gate, from Latin *porta*.]

por·tion (pôr′shən) *n.* **1.** a limited amount, piece, or segment of something. **2.** a segment of a whole that is allotted or belongs to one person or group; share. **3.** a quantity of food served to or for one person. **4.** a share of an estate received through inheritance or by gift. **5.** dowry *(def. 1)*. **6.** that which is allotted to a person or group by providence; lot; fate; destiny. —*v.t.* **1.** to divide into portions or shares; distribute; parcel (often with *out*). **2.** to furnish with a share, inheritance, or dowry. [Old French *portion* share, from Latin *portiō*.] —For Synonyms *(n.),* see **part**.

port·land cement (pôrt′lənd) *also,* **Portland cement**. a bluish gray construction cement composed chiefly of a mixture of calcined clay and limestone, that, when mixed with water, sand, and gravel, forms concrete that will harden under water as well as in the air. [From its resemblance to *Portland* stone, a limestone quarried on the Isle of *Portland,* a peninsula of southern England.]

port·ly (pôrt′lē) *adj.* **-li·er, -li·est**. **1.** having a heavy or stout but usually dignified appearance. **2.** *Archaic.* stately or imposing, esp. in bearing. [PORT⁵ + -LY².] —**port′li·ness,** *n.*

port·man·teau (pôrt man′tō) *n., pl.* **-teaus** or **-teaux** (-tōz). a suitcase or traveling bag, esp. a stiff leather one hinged at the back so as to open like a book into two compartments. [French *portemanteau* suitcase; literally, cloak bearer (originally, the official who carried the king's cloak or mantle in a case), from *porter* to

carry + *manteau* cloak (from Latin *mantellum* cloak). See PORT⁵, MANTLE.]

port of call *pl.* **ports of call**. a port where vessels stop, esp. regularly, in the course of voyages to obtain supplies, undergo repairs, or take on or discharge cargo or passengers.

port of entry *pl.* **ports of entry**. a place, designated by law, at which persons or goods may enter or leave a country under official supervision of customs.

por·trait (pôr′trit, -trāt) *n.* **1.** a painting, photograph, or other visual representation of a person or group of persons, usually drawn or otherwise produced from life, often showing the face and upper body only. **2.** a verbal picture or description, esp. of a person. [French *portrait,* from Old French *portraire* to draw, depict. See PORTRAY.]

por·trait·ist (pôr′tri tist, -trā-) *n.* a person who makes portraits, esp. a portrait painter or photographer.

por·trai·ture (pôr′tri chŭr′, -chər) *n.* **1.** the art or practice of making portraits. **2.** portrait. **3.** portraits collectively. [Old French *portraiture* likeness, representation, from *portrait,* from *portraire*. See PORTRAY.]

por·tray (pôr trā′) *v.t.* **1.** to set forth a picture of in words; describe. **2.** to make a visual likeness or representation of. **3.** to play the part of, as on the stage. [Old French *portraire,* from Late Latin *prōtrahere* to depict, from Latin *prōtrahere* to draw forth.] —**por·tray′er,** *n.*

Synonyms **Portray, delineate,** and **depict** mean to create a visual representation of a person or thing. **Portray** often suggests the revealing of an individual's characteristics: *The photograph portrays the subject's forceful, optimistic personality.* **Delineate** emphasizes accuracy and attention to detail: *The engravings delineate the differences between the two related species.* **Depict** usually refers to a broader subject than do the other two terms: *The movie depicts life in rural America.*

por·tray·al (pôr trā′əl) *n.* **1.** the act or process of portraying. **2.** a product of portraying; representation.

Por·tu·guese (pôr′chə gēz′, -gēs′) *adj.* of, relating to, or characteristic of Portugal or its people, language, or culture. —*n., pl.* **-guese**. **1.** a native or citizen of Portugal. **2.** a person of Portuguese ancestry. **3.** a Romance language of the Indo-European language family, spoken predominantly in Portugal and Brazil.

Words from Portuguese

Portuguese, a Romance language related to Spanish, is in the Italic group of the Indo-European language family. Below are words that have come into English from or through Portuguese.

auto-da-fé	cobra	macaque	piranha
banian	Creole	macaw	port³
betel	dodo	mango	samba
bossa nova	emu	marmalade	sargasso
carbonado	flamingo	molasses	teak
cashew	grouper	pagoda	yam
caste	junk²	palaver	zebra

Portuguese man-of-war, a floating colony of marine hydrozoans, *Physalia pelagica,* found in tropical and subtropical waters, in which one individual much larger than the others forms a gas-filled, floating sac and other individuals form long tentacles bearing stinging cells for stunning and holding its prey. Its stings are dangerous, sometimes even fatal, to human beings.

por·tu·lac·a (pôr′chə lak′ə) *n.* any of a group of plants, genus *Portulaca,* bearing clusters of showy flowers that have notched petals and that open only in full sunlight. [Modern Latin *Portulaca,* from Latin *portūlāca* purslane, going back to *porta* gate; because the covering on its capsule opens like a gate.]

pose¹ (pōz) *n.* **1.** an arrangement or position of the body or of part of the body, esp. as held for or depicted by an artist or photographer. **2.** an attitude or behavior assumed for effect; pretense: *a pose of sophistication.* —*v.,* **posed, pos·ing**. —*v.i.* **1.** to assume or hold a particular position or attitude, as for a photograph. **2.** to assume a false appearance or identity: *The thieves posed as guards to enter the museum.* —*v.t.* **1.** to place in a particular position. **2.** to cause or put forward: *to pose a question, a situation that poses a problem.* [Old French *poser* to place, put, halt, from Late Latin *pausāre* to cease, cause to rest, from Latin *pausa* cessation; influenced in meaning by Latin *pōnere* (past participle *positus*) to place. See PAUSE.]

pose² (pōz) *v.t.,* **posed, pos·ing**. to puzzle or confuse, as with

a difficult question; perplex. [Short for obsolete *appose,* form of OPPOSE; meaning influenced by Latin *appōnere* to put to.]

Po·sei·don (pə sī′dən) *n.* in Greek mythology, the god of the sea and the brother of Zeus and Pluto. His Roman counterpart is Neptune.

pos·er¹ (pō′zər) *n.* a person who poses. [POSE¹ + -ER¹.]

pos·er² (pō′zər) *n.* a puzzling question or problem. [POSE² + -ER¹.]

po·seur (pō zœr′) *n.* a person who assumes a particular attitude, manner, or role in order to impress or deceive others. [French *poseur,* from *poser* to place, pose. See POSE¹.]

posh (posh) *adj. Informal.* extremely fashionable, luxurious, or elegant. [Possibly from obsolete *posh* a dandy; of uncertain origin.] —**posh′ly,** *adv.* —**posh′ness,** *n.*

pos·it (poz′it) *v.t.* **1.** to propose or assume as a fact or basis of argument. **2.** to place in position. [Latin *positus,* past participle of *pōnere* to place.]

po·si·tion (pə zish′ən) *n.* **1.** the place occupied by a person or thing: *I can't see the door from my position.* **2.a.** the manner in which something is placed or arranged: *If you change the position of the chairs around the table, there will be more room.* **b.** an arrangement of the body or of its parts: *an uncomfortable position, to lie in a horizontal position.* **3.** the proper or appropriate place: *The members of the band were in position.* **4.** the way in which one looks upon or views a particular issue or subject; point of view: *Before the debate, both sides made their positions clear.* **5.** social standing or rank: *a high position in society.* **6.** the place and level of work in which one engages or is employed; post of employment: *to hold the same position with a company for ten years.* **7.** a state or situation in relation to circumstances: *Your request for a loan puts me in an awkward position. I'm not in a position to pass judgment.* —*v.t.* to put in a particular location or arrangement: *to position oneself in front of the television set.* [Latin *positiō* a placing, situation.] —**po·si′tion·er,** *n.* —For Synonyms *(n.),* see **rank.**

pos·i·tive (poz′i tiv) *adj.* **1.a.** leaving no room for question or doubt; undeniable: *positive proof.* **b.** clearly expressed or stated; definite; emphatic: *a positive refusal.* **2.a.** confident in opinion or assertion; fully assured; convinced: *Are you positive that this is the right address?* **b.** too sure of oneself; overconfident; opinionated. **3.** expressing, containing, or implying affirmation or acceptance; of an affirmative nature: *a positive reply to a request.* **4.** doing or able to do some good or adding something; constructive or practical: *a positive contribution to a discussion.* **5.** tending or moving in a direction considered to be one of increase, improvement, progress, or forward motion: *a positive change in someone's behavior.* **6.** possessing or characterized by the presence of real or particular qualities: *Sound is positive, silence negative.* **7.** having actual existence or effect: *The disease is a positive threat to children.* **8.** *Mathematics.* of or relating to a quantity that is greater than zero. **9.** indicating the presence of a particular disease, condition, or the like. **10.** *Physics.* (of ions) having more protons than electrons. **11.** *Electricity.* **a.** of or having the kind of electricity exhibited by a glass rod when rubbed with silk; having a deficiency of electrons. **b.** of or relating to the part of a circuit or device toward which current flows: *a positive electrode.* **12.** *Photography.* showing light and shade as they appear in the original. **13.** *Grammar.* designating the simple form or degree of an adjective or adverb. *Fast* is the positive degree of the adjective *fast.* ➡ distinguished from **comparative** and **superlative.** **14.** *Informal.* without qualification; out-and-out: *You are a positive idiot to go out in this weather without a coat.* —*n.* **1.** a positive photographic print or transparency. **2.** the positive form or degree of an adjective or adverb. **3.** something positive: *A sense of humor is a positive for a teacher.* [Latin *positīvus* settled by agreement, from *positus,* past participle of *pōnere* to place.] —**pos′i·tive·ly,** *adv.* —**pos′i·tive·ness,** *n.* —For Synonyms *(adj.),* see **sure.**

pos·i·tiv·ism (poz′i tə viz′əm) *n.* **1.** a philosophical view formulated in the 1800s, holding that all valid knowledge is limited to that obtained from observation of phenomena, and rejecting metaphysical speculations for which no definite proof can be obtained. **2.** great or too great certainty; dogmatism. —**pos′i·tiv·ist,** *n.* —**pos′i·tiv·is′tic,** *adj.*

pos·i·tron (poz′i tron′) *n.* the antiparticle of the electron. [POSI(TIVE) + (ELEC)TRON.]

poss. 1. possession. **2.** possessive.

pos·se (pos′ē) *n.* **1.** a group of persons summoned by a sheriff to assist in an action, such as the capture of a criminal. **2.** a group of persons temporarily organized to make a search. [Medieval Latin *posse* power, from Latin *posse* to be able.]

pos·sess (pə zes′) *v.t.* **1.** to hold as property; own: *to possess much land and money.* **2.** to have as a quality, characteristic, or attribute: *to possess talent.* **3.** to exert an overwhelming power or influence over: *What possessed you to buy that hat? A desire to find the truth possessed the reporter.* **4.** to put in possession; make master or owner (with *of*): *They possessed themselves of the gold.* **5.** *Law.* to take physical possession of; occupy: *We possessed the apartment on November 20th.* [Latin *possessus,* past participle of *possidēre* to own.] —**pos·ses′sor,** *n.* —For Synonyms, see **own.**

pos·sessed (pə zest′) *adj.* **1.** in possession of; having (with *of*): *possessed of a quick temper.* **2.** controlled by or as by an evil spirit or demon. **3.** self-possessed.

pos·ses·sion (pə zesh′ən) *n.* **1.** the act or fact of holding or owning. **2.** the state of being possessed. **3.** something that is held or owned. **4. possessions.** wealth or property. **5.** a territory under the rule of a foreign country but not participating in its government. **6.** domination by or as by an evil spirit or demon. **7.** the ability to control one's emotions; self-control; composure. **8.** *Law.* the fact of physically holding or occupying something: *Possession of property does not prove ownership.*

pos·ses·sive (pə zes′iv) *adj.* **1.** characterized by or displaying a strong desire to own, keep, or dominate: *I'm very possessive about my books.* **2.** denoting, or in a grammatical case that expresses, possession. —*n.* **1.** the possessive case. **2.** a possessive form or construction. In the sentence *I met Karen's brother, Karen's* is a possessive. —**pos·ses′sive·ly,** *adv.* —**pos·ses′sive·ness,** *n.*

possessive adjective, an adjective that shows possession. In the sentence *This is your book, your* is a possessive adjective.

possessive pronoun, a pronoun that shows possession. In the sentence *This book is mine, mine* is a possessive pronoun.

pos·set (pos′it) *n.* a hot drink made of milk curdled with ale or wine and usually spiced. [Of uncertain origin.]

pos·si·bil·i·ty (pos′ə bil′i tē) *n., pl.* -ties. **1.** the state or condition of being possible; likelihood. **2.** something possible.

pos·si·ble (pos′ə bəl) *adj.* **1.** capable of existing, happening, being done, or being proven true: *It's possible that it will rain. It is possible that we can find an answer to your problem.* **2.** that can be used, chosen, or considered; potential: *The senator is a possible candidate for the presidency.* [Latin *possibilis* that may be done, from *posse* to be able.]

pos·si·bly (pos′ə blē) *adv.* **1.** by any chance; in any way: *Our plan can't possibly succeed.* **2.** with some probability; perhaps: *I'll see you today, or possibly tomorrow.*

pos·sum (pos′əm) *n. Informal.* opossum. [Form of OPOSSUM.] **·to play possum,** to pretend to be dead or asleep.

post¹ (pōst) *n.* **1.** an upright piece of wood, stone, or other solid material, used esp. as a support or marker. **2.** the point at which a horse race begins. —*v.t.* **1.** to put up (an announcement or notice), esp. in a public place. **2.** to announce by or as by putting up a notice: *to post a reward for finding a lost kitten, to post grades.* **3.** to put up signs or notices warning against trespassing on (property). **4.** to enter the name of one on a list. [Old English *post* piece of timber used as a support, from Latin *postis* doorpost.]

post² (pōst) *n.* **1.** a place where someone, such as a soldier or police officer, is stationed for duty: *The guards were ordered not to leave their posts except in an emergency.* **2.a.** a place where one or more military units are stationed; military base. **b.** the buildings and grounds of such a place. **3.** a position of employment, esp. a public office to which one is appointed: *The ambassador has been assigned a new post.* **4.** trading post. **5.** a local unit or chapter of a veterans' organization. —*v.t.* **1.** to station at or assign to a post. **2.** to provide or put up (bail). [French *poste* station, from Italian *posto,* going back to Latin *positum,* neuter participle of *pōnere* to place.]

post³ (pōst) *n.* **1.** a system by which mail is collected, transported, and delivered, usually operated by a national government. **2.** *British.* **a.** a single delivery of mail. **b.** the mail delivered. **c.** a mailbox. **d.** a post office. **3.a.** formerly, one of a series of stations furnishing relays of people and horses for the carrying and delivery of mail. **b.** a rider who carried and delivered mail on such a route; postrider. —*v.t.* **1.** to deposit in a mailbox or at a post office: *to post a letter.* **2.** *Informal.* to supply with information or the latest news; inform: *Keep me posted on what happens while I'm*

a	at	e	end	o	hot	u	up	hw	white		about
ā	ape	ē	me	ō	old	ū	use	ng	song		taken
ä	far	i	it	ô	fork	ū	rule	th	thin	ə	pencil
âr	care	ī	ice	oi	oil	u̇	pull	th	this		lemon
		îr	pierce	ou	out	ûr	turn	zh	measure		circus

away. **3.** *Bookkeeping.* **a.** to transfer (accounts or items) from a journal to a ledger. **b.** to make the proper or necessary entries in (a ledger). —*v.i.* **1.** to travel with speed or haste; hurry. **2.** to travel with post horses. **3.** to rise and fall in the saddle in rhythm with the horse's gait when trotting. —*adv. Archaic.* posthaste. [Middle French *poste* relay station, courier, from Italian *posta,* going back to Latin *posita,* feminine past participle of *pōnere* to place; referring to the early transporting of mail by *posts,* or relay stations with couriers.]

post- *prefix* coming after in time or order; later: *postlude.* [Latin *post* behind, after.]

post·age (pōs′tij) *n.* the amount charged for sending something by mail.

postage meter, a machine that prints labels indicating the amount of postage paid on each piece of mail.

postage stamp, a small adhesive piece of paper with an imprint showing denomination, officially issued and sold by a national government to be placed on mail to show payment of postage.

post·al (pōs′təl) *adj.* of, relating to, or involving mail or the way in which it is collected, transported, and delivered. —*n.* postal card *(def. 1).*

postal card **1.** a card issued and sold by a government and bearing an official, imprinted postage stamp. It can be sent through the mail without an envelope. **2.** postcard *(def. 1).*

postal service, an agency or department of a national government in charge of handling and delivering mail. Also, **post office.**

post·bel·lum (pōst bel′əm) *adj.* occurring after a war, esp. the American Civil War. [Latin *post* after + *bellum* war.]

post·card (pōst′kärd′) *n.* **1.** a card, usually with a picture on one side, that can be sent through the mail without an envelope. **2.** postal card *(def. 1).*

post chaise, a four-wheeled carriage drawn by post horses, used to carry mail and passengers from station to station.

post·date (pōst dāt′) *v.t.,* **-dat·ed, -dat·ing. 1.** to date (a check, letter, or the like) with a date that is later then the actual one. **2.** to occur later than; follow in time.

post·er (pōs′tər) *n.* **1.** a large sign that carries a public notice or advertisement, often with a colorful illustration. **2.** a person who posts bills, advertisements, or notices.

pos·te·ri·or (pos tîr′ē ər, pōs-) *adj.* **1.** located at or toward the back; rear. ▶ opposed to **anterior. 2.** later in time; subsequent. **3.** coming after in a series. —*n.* the rear; buttocks. [Latin *posterior,* comparative of *posterus* coming after.]

pos·ter·i·ty (pos ter′i tē) *n.* **1.** generations of the future collectively. **2.** all of one's descendants collectively. [Latin *posteritās.*]

pos·tern (pōs′tərn, pos′-) *n.* a back door or gate, esp. in a castle or fortification. —*adj.* located at the back or side: *a postern door.* [Old French *posterne* back door to a fort, going back to Latin *posterus* coming after.]

post exchange, a nonprofit government store at a military installation that sells tax-free goods to military personnel, their families, and civilian employees.

post·gla·cial (pōst glā′shəl) *adj.* occurring after or following an ice age or other period of glaciation.

post·grad·u·ate (pōst graj′ū it) *adj.* of, relating to, or taking a course of study after graduation from a college or university, esp. after receiving a bachelor's degree. —*n.* a postgraduate student.

post·haste (pōst′hāst′) *adv.* as quickly as possible; with utmost haste. [POST³ + HASTE.]

post horse, a horse kept for use by postriders or for hire to travelers.

post·hu·mous (pos′chə məs) *adj.* **1.** published after the death of the author. **2.** coming or happening after one's death: *a posthumous award, posthumous fame.* **3.** (of a child) born after the death of the father. [Latin *posthumus,* modification of *postumus* last, superlative of *post* after; *h* of *posthumus* due to incorrect association with *humus* ground (as if *post humum* after (burial) in the ground).] —**post′hu·mous·ly,** *adv.*

post·hyp·not·ic (pōst′hip not′ik) *adj.* of or relating to the time following a hypnotic trance: *posthypnotic suggestion.*

pos·til·ion (pōs til′yən, pos-) *also,* **pos·til·lion.** *n.* a person who guides the team of a horse-drawn carriage by riding the left lead horse. [French *postillon,* from Italian *postiglione,* from *posta* messenger, relay station. See POST³.]

post·im·pres·sion·ism (pōst′im presh′ə niz′əm) *also,* **Post′-im·pres′sion·ism.** *n.* a style in French painting, beginning in the late nineteenth century and lasting until the early twentieth century, characterized by the work of such painters as Vincent van Gogh and Paul Cézanne and by an emphasis on the emotional content of subject matter, the expression of intensely personal

postimpressionism
a painting by Paul Gauguin

views, and the free use of color. —**post′im·pres′sion·ist;** *also,* **Post′im·pres′sion·ist,** *n., adj.* —**post′im·pres′sion·is′tic;** *also,* **Post′im·pres′sion·is′tic,** *adj.*

post·lude (pōst′lüd′) *n.* a concluding musical piece or movement, such as that played at the end of a religious service. [POST- + (PRE)LUDE.]

post·man (pōst′mən) *n., pl.* **-men** (-mən). mail carrier.

post·mark (pōst′märk′) *n.* an official mark stamped on mail to cancel the postage stamp and usually to show the place and date of mailing. —*v.t.* to stamp with a postmark.

post·mas·ter (pōst′mas′tər) *n.* a government official in charge of a post office.

postmaster general *pl.* **postmasters general. 1.** the head of the postal service of a country. **2. Postmaster General.** the head of the postal service of the United States, appointed by the president with the approval of the Senate.

post·me·rid·i·an (pōst′mə rid′ē ən) *adj.* of, relating to, or occurring during the afternoon.

post me·rid·i·em (pōst′mə rid′ē əm) between noon and midnight. [Latin *post merīdiem* after midday.]

post·mis·tress (pōst′mis′tris) *n., pl.* **-tress·es.** a female government official in charge of a post office.

post·mod·ern (pōst mod′ərn) *adj.* of or relating to late twentieth-century painting, sculpture, architecture, literature, dance, and various other art forms that reject or depart from strict modernism, and incorporate elements of various classical and historical styles.

post·mod·ern·ism (pōst mod′ər niz′əm) *n.* a movement in various art forms, such as painting, dance, and literature, that uses or incorporates postmodern styles and techniques. —**post·mod′ern·ist,** *n., adj.*

post·mor·tem (pōst môr′təm) *adj.* **1.** taking place or done after a person's death. **2.** of or relating to an autopsy. —*n.* **1.** a postmortem examination; autopsy. **2.** *Informal.* a discussion reviewing an event that has recently taken place: *The party leaders held a postmortem after their defeat in the primary.* [Latin *post mortem* after death.]

post·na·sal (pōst nā′zəl) *adj.* situated or occurring behind the nose.

post·na·tal (pōst nā′təl) *adj.* occurring after birth; subsequent to birth: *postnatal care.*

post·o·bit (pōst ō′bit) *n.* a written agreement by which a borrower promises to repay a debt upon the death of a specified person from whom he or she expects to inherit. Also, **post-obit bond.** —*adj.* made or taking effect after a person's death. [Latin *post obitum* after death.]

post office **1.** postal service. **2.** a local branch of the postal service.

post·op·er·a·tive (pōst op′ər ə tiv) *adj.* **1.** occurring or intended for use after a surgical operation: *postoperative care, a postoperative recovery room.* **2.** having had an operation: *a postoperative patient.*

post·paid (pōst′pād′) *adj.* having the postage prepaid.

post·par·tum (pōst pär′təm) *adj.* following childbirth: *postpartum care.* [Latin *postpartum,* from *post-* after + *partum,* accusative of *partus* a bringing forth, from *parere* to bear.]

post·pone (pōst pōn′) *v.t.,* **-poned, -pon·ing.** to put off to a later time: *The game was postponed until next week because of*

rain. [Latin *postpōnere* to put after.] —**post·pone′ment,** *n.*
—For Synonyms, see **defer**[1].

post·pran·di·al (pōst pran′dē əl) *adj.* after a meal, esp. after dinner. [Post- + PRANDIAL.]

post·rid·er (pōst′rī′dər) *n.* formerly, a person who carried and delivered mail on horseback on a fixed route.

post road, formerly, a road over which mail was carried by riders, with stations along the way that provided fresh horses.

post·script (pōst′skript′) *n.* **1.** a message or note added to a letter after the closing signature. **2.** a supplement or appendix of any composition or literary work. [Latin *postscrīptum,* neuter past participle of *postscrībere* to write after.]

pos·tu·lant (pos′chə lənt) *n.* a person who is a candidate, esp. for admission to a religious order. [Latin *postulāns,* present participle of *postulāre* to demand, request.]

pos·tu·late (*n.,* pos′chə lit; *v.,* pos′chə lāt′) *n.* **1.** a statement or principle accepted as true without proof: *A postulate of monotheistic religions is that there is only one God.* **2.** in logic or geometry, an established rule or principle or a truth held to be self-evident. —*v.t.,* **-lat·ed, -lat·ing. 1.** to accept (something) as true without proof. **2.** to require, demand, or claim. **3.** to claim the truth or existence of. [Latin *postulātus,* past participle of *postulāre* to demand, request.] —**pos′tu·la′tion,** *n.*

pos·ture (pos′chər) *n.* **1.** the way of carrying or holding the head and body; carriage. **2.a.** a position of the body or of parts of the body. **b.** such a position taken, as in posing for an artist. **3.** an attitude, condition, or situation: *The soldiers took a defensive posture.* —*v.,* **-tured, -tur·ing.** —*v.i.* to take or assume a certain bodily position, esp. for effect. —*v.t.* to put in a certain position; pose. [French *posture* attitude, situation, from Italian *postura* attitude, position, from Latin *positūra* position.] —**pos′tur·al,** *adj.* —**pos′tur·er,** *n.*

post·vo·cal·ic (pōst′vō kal′ik) *adj.* following immediately after a vowel.

post·war (pōst′wôr′) *adj.* after a war.

po·sy (pō′zē) *n., pl.* **-sies. 1.** a single flower. **2.** a bouquet of flowers; nosegay. **3.** *Archaic.* a motto or inscription engraved on a ring, knife, or the like. [Form of POESY.]

pot[1] (pot) *n.* **1.** a container of metal, earthenware, or other material, usually round and having one or two handles, used in cooking, for holding growing plants, and for many other purposes. **2.a.** a pot and its contents: *a pot of fresh coffee.* **b.** the amount contained in a pot; potful. **3.** the stakes in a card game, esp. poker. **4.** lobster pot. **5.** *Informal.* a large sum of money. —*v.t.,* **pot·ted, pot·ting. 1.** to put into a flowerpot: *to pot a plant.* **2.** to preserve (food) in a pot or jar. **3.** to cook in a pot; stew: *to pot beef.* **4.** to shoot (game) for food rather than for sport. **5.** *Informal.* to win, seize, or capture; bag. [Old English *pott* round, deep container.]

• **to go to pot.** to become run-down or ruined: *The beautiful old house went to pot after the owners died.*

pot[2] (pot) *n. Slang.* marijuana. [Short for Mexican Spanish *potiguaya* marijuana leaves, supposedly from *potación de guaya* brandy or wine in which marijuana buds are steeped; literally, drink of woe.]

po·ta·ble (pō′tə bəl) *adj.* fit or suitable for drinking. —*n.* something drinkable; drink. [Late Latin *pōtābilis* drinkable, from Latin *pōtāre* to drink.]

po·tage (pō täzh′) *n. French.* soup. [Old French *potage,* from *pot* pot; of Germanic origin.]

pot·ash (pot′ash′) *n.* **1.** potassium carbonate. **2.** any of various other potassium compounds, used esp. in fertilizers and soaps, and in making glass. [Earlier *pot ashes,* translation of obsolete Dutch *potasschen* literally, pot ashes; because it was formerly obtained from the ashes of vegetable substances burned in iron pots.]

potash alum, alum *(def. 2).*

po·tas·si·um (pə tas′ē əm) *n.* a very soft, light, silver-white metallic element that is highly reactive and an essential element for plant and animal life. Potassium compounds include some of the most important fertilizers and industrial chemicals. Symbol: **K** For tables, see **element.** [Modern Latin *potassium,* from *potassa,* from POTASH.] —**po·tas′sic** (pə tas′ik), *adj.*

po·tas·si·um-ar·gon dating (pə tas′ē əm är′gon) a method used in geochronology to determine the age of a mineral, fossil, or rock by measuring the amount of argon it contains in proportion to the potassium isotope from which the argon formed by radioactive decay.

potassium bi·tar·trate (bī tär′trāt) cream of tartar.

potassium bromide, a white, crystalline compound widely used in photographic developers, formerly used as a sedative. Formula: KBr

potassium carbonate, a white, powdery compound obtained from potassium chloride, used esp. as a fertilizer and in the manu-

facture of explosives, chemicals, glass, soap, textiles, and ceramics. Formula: K_2CO_3 Also, **potash.**

potassium chlorate, a poisonous crystalline substance obtained from potassium carbonate, used in the manufacture of explosives, fireworks, and matches. Formula: $KClO_3$

potassium chloride, a white crystalline compound that is the principal source of potassium for other applications and is used esp. as a fertilizer. Formula: KCl

potassium cyanide, an extremely poisonous solid compound that smells like bitter almonds, used in extracting gold and silver from ore and in electroplating. Formula: KCN

potassium dichromate, a red, toxic, crystalline compound used as an oxidizing agent and in a variety of industrial processes. Formula: $K_2Cr_2O_7$

potassium hydroxide, a white, caustic compound, used esp. in the manufacture of soap. Formula: KOH Also, **caustic potash.**

potassium iodide, a white, crystalline compound with a bitter taste, used as a reagent in chemical analysis, in photography, and as an additive in table salt to prevent goiter. Formula: KI

potassium nitrate, a colorless crystalline compound, used in gunpowder and explosives and as an oxidizing agent in solid rocket fuels. Formula: KNO_3 Also, **niter, saltpeter.**

potassium permanganate, a dark purple crystalline compound, used as a disinfectant, an oxidizing agent to purify water and air, and a bleaching agent. Formula: $KMnO_4$

po·ta·tion (pō tā′shən) *n.* **1.** the act of drinking. **2.** a drink, esp. of liquor. [Latin *pōtātiō* a drinking.]

po·ta·to (pə tā′tō) *n., pl.* **-toes. 1.** the edible tuber of a leafy, low-growing plant, *Solanum tuberosum,* first grown in South America. It is a basic food in Europe, the Americas, and other parts of the world, and is used to make a wide variety of products, such as starch, flour, and vodka. Also *(def. 1),* **white potato. 2.** the plant itself, having dull green leaves and white, blue, or purple flowers. **3.** sweet potato. [Spanish *patata,* from Taino *batata* sweet potato.]

potato beetle, Colorado potato beetle. Also, **potato bug.**

potato chip, a very thin slice of potato, fried crisp and usually salted.

pot·bel·ly (pot′bel′ē) *n., pl.* **-lies. 1.** a large, bulging belly. **2.** a person who has such a belly. —**pot′bel′lied,** *adj.*

potbelly stove, a stove having bulging, rounded sides, that burns coal or wood. Also, **potbellied stove.**

pot·boil·er (pot′boi′lər) *n. Informal.* a work of literature or art, usually inferior, produced merely to earn money.

pot cheese, cottage cheese, esp. a form having large curds and a dry consistency.

po·ten·cy (pō′tən sē) *n., pl.* **-cies. 1.** the state or quality of being potent. **2.** the degree of this. **3.** a capacity for development; potentiality. [Latin *potentia* power.]

potbelly
stove

po·tent (pō′tənt) *adj.* **1.** having force, effectiveness, strength, or power: *a potent medicine, a potent argument.* **2.** (of males) capable of engaging in sexual intercourse. [Latin *potēns* powerful, present participle of *posse* to be able.] —**po′tent·ly,** *adv.*

po·ten·tate (pō′tən tāt′) *n.* a person who has great power or authority, esp. a monarch or ruler. [Late Latin *potentātus,* from Latin *potentātus* power, rule.]

po·ten·tial (pə ten′shəl) *adj.* **1.** capable of being or becoming; possible but not actual: *a potential leader, a potential source of trouble.* **2.** denoting that aspect of the subjunctive mood that expresses possibility by the use of such auxiliary verbs as *may, might,* and *can.* —*n.* **1.** a quality or ability capable of being developed or advanced: *a novelist with great potential.* **2.** that aspect of the subjunctive mood that expresses possibility. **3.** the amount of electrification of a point in a circuit or field in relation to some standard reference point in that circuit or field. [Late Latin *potentiālis* possessing power, from Latin *potentia* power.] —**po·ten′tial·ly,** *adv.*

potential difference, the amount of work, measured in volts, required to move a unit charge of electricity between two points.

potential energy, the energy a body or system possesses because of its position or form. ➡ distinguished from **kinetic energy.**

a	at	e	end	o	hot	u	up	hw	white		about
ā	ape	ē	me	ō	old	ū	use	ng	song	ə	taken
ä	far	i	it	ô	fork	ü	rule	th	thin		pencil
âr	care	ī	ice	oi	oil	u̇	pull	th	this		lemon
		îr	pierce	ou	out	ûr	turn	zh	measure		circus

po·ten·ti·al·i·ty (pə ten′shē al′i tē) *n., pl.* **-ties. 1.** a quality or ability capable of being developed or advanced; potential. **2.** something potential; possibility.

po·ten·ti·ate (pə ten′shē āt′) *v.t.,* **-at·ed, -at·ing.** to increase the effect or activity of (a substance, as a drug or toxin) by the addition of another substance. [Latin *potentia* power + -ATE¹.] —**po·ten′ti·a′tion,** *n.*

po·ten·ti·om·e·ter (pə ten′shē om′i tər) *n.* a device for measuring electromotive force or potential difference. [POTENTI(AL) + -METER.]

pot·ful (pot′fŏŏl′) *n., pl.* **-fuls.** the amount that a pot can hold.

poth·er (poth′ər) *n.* **1.** a confused or excited state; commotion; uproar. **2.** a choking cloud of dust or smoke. —*v.t., v.i.* to worry or bother. [Of uncertain origin.]

pot·herb (pot′ûrb′, -hûrb′) *n.* any plant whose leaves, stems, or flowers are cooked and eaten as a vegetable, such as spinach, or used as a seasoning, such as sage or thyme.

pot·hold·er (pot′hōl′dər) *n.* a thick cloth pad used to handle hot cooking utensils safely.

pot·hole (pot′hōl′) *n.* **1.** a deep hole worn in the rock bed of a river or stream by stones and gravel whirled around by the force of the current. **2.** any deep hole, esp. in the surface of a road.

pot·hook (pot′hŏŏk′) *n.* **1.** a hook used to hang a pot over an open fire. **2.** an iron rod with a hook at the end, used to lift hot pots, irons, or stove lids. **3.** an S-shaped stroke in writing.

pot·hunt·er (pot′hun′tər) *n.* **1.** a person who hunts for food or money rather than for sport and shows little or no regard for the rules of hunting. **2.** a person who takes part in a contest merely for the sake of winning a prize. **3.** *Informal.* an amateur archaeologist, esp. one who unearths and removes artifacts illegally.

po·tion (pō′shən) *n.* a drink, esp. one supposedly having magical properties. [Latin *pōtiō.* Doublet of POISON.]

pot·latch (pot′lach′) *n.* a feast held by certain American Indian tribes of the Pacific Northwest at which the host gives away and sometimes destroys valuable objects as a show of wealth. [Chinook jargon *potlach* literally, giving.]

pot liquor, liquid left in a pot after meat and vegetables have been cooked in it.

pot·luck (pot′luk′) *n.* **1.** whatever food may be available for a meal for which no special preparation was made: *If you come for dinner tonight, you'll have to take potluck.* **2.** a meal to which all guests bring a dish to be shared by all. Also *(def. 2),* **potluck dinner, potluck supper.**

pot marigold 1. the showy yellow or orange flower head of a plant, *Calendula officinalis,* of the composite family, formerly used for seasoning. **2.** the plant bearing this flower head, having thick oblong leaves.

pot·pie (pot′pī′) *n.* **1.** a pie filled with meat or poultry and usually vegetables, encased in a pastry dough and baked in a deep dish. **2.** a meat stew with dumplings.

pot·pour·ri (pō′pŏŏ rē′, pot pŏŏr′ē) *n.* **1.** a mixture of dried flower petals and spices, and often other dried plant parts, kept in a jar and used for fragrance. **2.** a medley or anthology: *a musical potpourri.* **3.** any mixture or collection of miscellaneous things. [French *potpourri* hodgepodge, medley; literally, rotten pot, translation of Spanish *olla podrida* dish of meat and vegetables; literally, rotten pot (because cooked till "rotten"), going back to Latin *ōlla* pot + *pūtridus* rotten.]

pot roast, meat, usually beef, browned in a pot, covered, and cooked slowly in a small amount of water, often with vegetables.

pot·sherd (pot′shûrd′) *also,* **pot·shard** (pot′shärd′). *n.* a fragment of pottery, esp. one found at the site of an archaeological expedition. [POT + *sherd,* form of SHARD.]

pot·shot (pot′shot′) *n.* **1.** a shot fired at random or without careful aim from close range. **2.** a shot fired to kill game for food or money, with little or no regard for the rules of hunting. **3.** an apparently careless or thoughtless criticism: *The reviewer took several unnecessary potshots at the town the movie was filmed in.*

pot·tage (pot′ij) *n.* a thick soup or broth with vegetables and sometimes meat. [Old French *potage,* from *pot* pot; of Germanic origin.]

pot·ted (pot′id) *adj.* **1.** put or kept in a pot: *a potted plant.* **2.** cooked or preserved in a pot or can: *potted meat.* **3.** *Slang.* intoxicated; drunk.

pot·ter¹ (pot′ər) *n.* a person who makes pottery. [Old English *pottere,* from *pott* pot.]

pot·ter² (pot′ər) *v.i., v.t.* putter. [Dialectal English *pote* to poke (from Old English *potian* to push) + -ER⁴.] —**pot′ter·er,** *n.*

potter's field, a piece of ground used as a burial place for the poor and the unknown.

potter's wheel, a rotating level disk that is turned by a motor or by pumping with the foot, used by a potter to make objects from soft clay.

pot·ter·y (pot′ə rē) *n., pl.* **-ter·ies. 1.** pots, vases, and other objects made from soft clay and hardened by heat. **2.** the art or technique of making pottery. **3.** a place where pottery is made. [Old French *poterie,* from *potier* potter¹, from *pot* pot; of Germanic origin.]

forming **pottery** on a potter's wheel

pot·to (pot′ō) *n., pl.* **-tos.** either of two small, slow-moving prosimians of tropical Africa, related to lemurs, lorises, and galagos: *Perodictis potto,* about 14 inches (36 centimeters) long excluding the short tail, or the **golden potto,** *Arctocebus calabriensis,* somewhat smaller and tailless. [Of African origin.]

pouch (pouch) *n.* **1.** a bag, sack, or other container, usually made of a soft, flexible material, such as leather or canvas. **2.** anything resembling this. **3.** mailbag. **4.** a baglike structure on the abdomen of female marsupials, such as kangaroos and opossums, in which the young are carried after birth. **5.** any baglike cavity or part, as under the bill of a pelican. [Old French *po(u)che* bag, pocket; of Germanic origin.]

poul·ter·er (pōl′tər ər) *n.* a person who deals in poultry. [Obsolete *poulter* (from Old French *pouletier,* from *poulet* young chicken) + -ER¹. See POULTRY.]

poul·tice (pōl′tis) *n.* a soft, moist mass of an absorbent substance, such as a mustard plaster, heated and applied to a part of the body as a medicine for soreness or inflammation. —*v.t.,* **-ticed, -tic·ing.** to apply a poultice to. [Earlier *pultes,* from Latin *pultes,* plural of *puls* thick pap, pottage.]

poul·try (pōl′trē) *n.* any domestic fowl, such as chickens, turkeys, geese, and ducks, usually raised for their meat or eggs. [Old French *pouleterie,* from *poulet* young chicken, diminutive of *poule* hen, going back to Latin *pullus* young fowl, young animal.]

pounce¹ (pouns) *v.i.,* **pounced, pounc·ing. 1.** to swoop down, spring, or leap suddenly in or as in attack. **2.** to seize and put to advantage: *The student pounced on the chance to study abroad.* —*n.* **1.** the act of pouncing. **2.** the claw or talon of a bird of prey. [Probably from Middle English *ponson* sharp tool, from Old French *poinçon, poinchon.* See PUNCHEON².]

pounce² (pouns) *n.* **1.** a fine powder, as of cuttlebone, formerly used to soak up excess ink in writing or to prepare a smooth surface, as of parchment, for writing. **2.** a fine powder, as of charcoal, dusted over a stencil to transfer the design to the surface beneath. —*v.t.,* **pounced, pounc·ing. 1.** to trace or transfer (a design) with pounce. **2.** to sprinkle, smooth, or rub with pounce. [French *ponce* pumice stone, going back to Latin *pūmex.*]

pound¹ (pound) *n., pl.* **pounds** or **pound. 1.a.** a unit of weight equal to 16 ounces avoirdupois (0.4536 kilogram). **b.** a unit of weight equal to 12 ounces troy, or 5,760 grains apothecaries' weight (0.3732 kilogram). **2.** the monetary unit of the United Kingdom, equal to 100 pence, formerly equal to 20 shillings. Also, **pound sterling. 3.** the monetary unit of various other countries, including Egypt, Ireland, Lebanon, Sudan, and Syria. [Old English *pund* a measure of weight, an English monetary unit, from Latin *pondō* by weight.]

pound² (pound) *v.t.* **1.** to strike or hit with heavy, repeated blows: *to pound a nail into a wall.* **2.** to reduce to a powder or pulp by pounding; pulverize: *to pound garlic into paste with a pestle, to pound grain into meal.* **3.** to force or cause to give way by beating or hitting (often with *down*): *The angry mob pounded down the door.* **4.** to force or instill, as by repetition or drill. **5.** to produce by or as by hitting (often with *out*): *to pound out a letter on a typewriter.* —*v.i.* **1.** to strike heavy, repeated blows: *to pound on a door.* **2.** to beat heavily: *The runner's heart was pounding.* **3.** to walk or move with heavy steps; plod: *The children pounded into the house.* —*n.* **1.a.** a heavy blow. **b.** the sound of this; thump; thud. **2.** the act of pounding. [Old English *pūnian* to bruise, pulverize.] —For Synonyms *(v.t.),* see **beat.**

pound³ (pound) *n.* **1.** an enclosure for confining animals, esp. stray dogs, often maintained by a city or town. **2.** a place of confinement, as for prisoners. **3.** a compartment or net for catching or confining fish. [Old English *pund* enclosure.]

pound·age (poun′dij) *n.* a tax, commission, rate, or the like calculated per pound sterling or per pound weight.

pound·al (poun′dəl) *n.* the foot-pound-second unit of force, equal to the amount of force that gives an acceleration of 1 foot per second per second to a mass of 1 pound.

pound cake, a rich cake made with whole eggs and originally containing 1 pound each of butter, sugar, and flour.

pound·er[1] (poun′dər) *n.* a person or thing that pounds. [POUND[2] + -ER[1].]

pound·er[2] (poun′dər) *n.* a person or thing that weighs or is worth a certain number of pounds. ➡ used in combination: *This fish is a three-pounder.* [POUND[2] + -ER[1].]

pound-fool·ish (pound′fü′lish) *adj.* unwise or careless about spending large sums of money.

pound sterling, pound[1] *(def. 2).*

pour (pôr) *v.t.* **1.** to cause to flow, as from a container, in a continuous stream: *to pour water from a bucket.* **2.** to speak of or reveal freely and openly: *to pour out one's fury.* —*v.i.* **1.** to flow in a continuous stream: *The stream pours into the river.* **2.** to rain hard: *It poured all day.* **3.** to move or come forth in great numbers; swarm: *The people poured out of the train.* **4.** to act as host or hostess by pouring beverages for guests. —*n.* a heavy rainfall; downpour. [Of uncertain origin.] —**pour′a·ble,** *adj.* —**pour′er,** *n.*

pour·boire (pür bwär′) *n. French.* tip; gratuity.

pout[1] (pout) *v.i.* **1.** to thrust out the lips, as in displeasure or sullenness. **2.** to be sullen; sulk: *The spoiled child pouted when she was scolded.* **3.** to swell out; protrude. —*v.t.* to thrust out or protrude. —*n.* **1.** a protrusion of the lips, as when displeased. **2.** a fit of sullenness: *to be in a pout.* [Of uncertain origin.] —**pout′y,** *adj.*

pout[2] (pout) *n.* **1.** any of various catfish, such as the bullhead. **2.** an eelpout. [Old English *-pūte,* ǣlepūte eelpout.]

pout·er (pou′tər) *n.* **1.** a person who pouts. **2.** any of a breed of domestic pigeons having an enlarged esophagus and crop that can be inflated with air and puffed out.

pov·er·ty (pov′ər tē) *n.* **1.** the state or condition of being poor: *to live in poverty.* **2.** a deficiency or lack of what is needed or desired: *the poverty of the soil in a desert area.* **3.** a smallness of amount; scarcity; dearth: *The poem shows a poverty of imagination.* [Old French *poverte* state of being poor, need, from Latin *paupertās.*]

poverty level, a level of income below which a person or family is classified as living in poverty.

pov·er·ty-strick·en (pov′ər tē strik′ən) *adj.* very poor; destitute.

POW (pē′ō dub′əl ū′) a person who is taken and held as a prisoner of war, esp. one who is a member of the armed forces. [Abbreviation of *p(risoner) o(f) w(ar).*]

pow·der (pou′dər) *n.* **1.** fine particles produced by grinding, crushing, pounding, or crumbling a dry substance. **2.** any of various preparations or substances in such a form: *soap powder.* **3.** gunpowder. —*v.t.* **1.** to reduce to powder; pulverize. **2.** to sprinkle or cover with or as with powder: *He powdered the rolling pin with flour. Snow powdered the steps.* **3.** to use or apply powder as a cosmetic on (the face or body). —*v.i.* **1.** to be reduced to powder. **2.** to apply cosmetic powder to the face or body. [Old French *poudre,* earlier *pol(d)re* dust, solid substance reduced to fine particles, explosive, from Latin *pulvis* dust.]

·**to take a powder.** *Slang.* to run away; leave quickly.

powder blue, a pale blue color.

powder burn, a superficial burn suffered by skin exposed to the explosion of gunpowder at close range.

powder flask, a flask, usually of leather or metal, used for carrying gunpowder.

powder horn, the horn of a cow or other animal, used for carrying gunpowder.

powder keg 1. a small barrel containing explosives, such as gunpowder or blasting powder. **2.** a situation or condition that is likely to produce anger, a quarrel, or violence.

powder magazine, a room or compartment where gunpowder and other explosives are stored.

powder puff, a soft pad for applying powder to the skin.

powder room 1. a lavatory for women in a restaurant or public building. **2.** a lavatory for guests, located in the main part of a house.

pow·der·y (pou′də rē) *adj.* **1.** consisting of or resembling powder. **2.** sprinkled or covered with or as with powder. **3.** capable of being easily reduced to powder; friable.

powdery mildew 1. any of a number of parasitic fungi that produce a powdery mass of mycelia on the leaves and stems of host plants. **2.** a plant disease caused by such a fungus.

pow·er (pou′ər) *n.* **1.** the ability to do or effect something: *It is not in my power to help you.* **2.** the ability or right to command, control, or make decisions; authority: *A struggle for power took place within the company.* **3.** *also,* **powers.** a particular mental or physical ability or faculty: *the power of speech.* **4.** a person or thing that possesses or exercises influence, control, or authority over others: *The United States is a major world power.* **5.** the political or military strength of a nation. **6.** the legal ability or authority to do or act: *The president has the power to veto bills.* **7.** physical strength; force: *There was no power behind the tired boxer's punch.* **8.** *Mathematics.* **a.** the number of times, indicated by an exponent, that a given number or algebraic expression is multiplied by itself. The power of 4^3 is 3. **b.** the product found by multiplying a number or algebraic expression by itself a given number of times as indicated by an exponent. The second power of 5 is 25 since $5^2 = 5 \times 5 = 25$. **9.** energy or force that can do work, esp. electrical energy. **10.** the rate at which work is done or energy is used, measured in units such as the watt or horsepower. The power of a source is equal to the force exerted, multiplied by the distance through which it acts, divided by the time during which it acts. **11.** the capacity of a lens or lens system to magnify the apparent size of an object. **12.** *Informal.* a large number or quantity. —*v.t.* to provide with power, esp. mechanical power. —*adj.* **1.** operated or driven by a motor or by the energy produced by electricity, air, water, or steam: *a power saw, a power loom, a power lawn mower.* **2.** operating with the assistance of an auxiliary engine-driven system so as to require less effort: *power steering, power brakes.* [Anglo-Norman *poër* ability to act, authority, going back to Latin *potis* able.]

pow·er·boat (pou′ər bōt′) *n.* motorboat.

power brake, a brake in a motor vehicle that uses engine power to augment pressure exerted on the brake pedal in order to slow or stop the vehicle.

pow·er·bro·ker (pou′ər brō′kər) *also,* **power broker.** *n.* a person who has influence with or power over certain important people, and who makes use of this to get things done.

power dive, a dive made by an airplane under full or nearly full power.

pow·er·ful (pou′ər fəl) *adj.* **1.** having great strength or force: *a powerful machine, a powerful athlete.* **2.** having great influence or effect: *a powerful argument.* **3.** having or showing great power, authority, or control over others: *a powerful nation.* —*adv. Informal.* to a great degree; very: *We're powerful hungry.* —**pow′er·ful·ly,** *adv.* —**pow′er·ful·ness,** *n.*

pow·er·house (pou′ər hous′) *n., pl.* **-hous·es** (-hou′ziz). **1.** power plant *(def. 1).* **2.** *Informal.* someone or something possessing a great deal of strength, energy, or power.

pow·er·less (pou′ər lis) *adj.* **1.** lacking the ability or authority to do or bring about something. **2.** lacking power or strength; weak. —**pow′er·less·ly,** *adv.* —**pow′er·less·ness,** *n.*

power of attorney 1. a written document authorizing one person to act as the attorney or legal agent for another. **2.** the legal authority granted by such a document.

power pack, an electrical unit used to convert the voltage of a power supply to a voltage suitable for an electric or electronic device.

power plant 1. a generating station for electrical power. Also, **power station. 2.** any system that produces mechanical or electrical energy in useful form from fuels or other sources, as the internal-combustion engine of an automobile.

power play, a play in hockey in which a team having more players on the ice than the opposition concentrates its players in the offensive zone in an attempt to score a goal.

power politics, the use or threatened use of force by countries in order to strengthen their positions and increase their power.

power saw, a saw with a cutting blade driven by a motor. Circular saws and band saws are common kinds of power saw.

power shovel, a power-driven excavator with a bucket or scoop at the end of a long beam.

power station, power plant *(def. 1).*

power steering, a steering mechanism in a motor vehicle that uses engine power to reduce the effort required to steer the vehicle.

pow·wow (pou′wou′) *n.* **1.** a conference of or with North American Indians. **2.** a North American Indian ceremony characterized by feasting, dancing, and rites performed by a medicine man, esp. for the cure of disease or success in war or hunting. **3.** a North American Indian medicine man or priest. **4.** *Informal.* any conference or meeting. —*v.i.* to hold a powwow. [Algonquian *powwaw* magician; literally, he dreams.]

pox (poks) *n.* **1.** any of several diseases characterized by skin eruptions, such as chickenpox or smallpox. **2.** syphilis. [Form of earlier *pocks,* plural of POCK.]

pp, pianissimo.

pp. 1. pages. **2.** past participle.

a	at	e	end	o	hot	u	up	hw	white		about
ā	ape	ē	me	ō	old	ū	use	ng	song		taken
ä	far	i	it	ô	fork	ü	rule	th	thin	ə	pencil
âr	care	ī	ice	oi	oil	ù	pull	th	this		lemon
		îr	pierce	ou	out	ûr	turn	zh	measure		circus

p.p. 1. *also,* **P.P.** parcel post. **2.** past participle. **3.** postpaid.

ppd. 1. postpaid. **2.** prepaid.

ppr. *also,* **p.pr.** present participle.

PQ, the postal abbreviation for the Province of Quebec.

P.Q., Province of Quebec.

Pr, the symbol for praseodymium.

pr. 1. pair; pairs. **2.** power. **3.** present. **4.** price. **5.** pronoun.

PR 1. Public Relations. **2.** the postal abbreviation for Puerto Rico.

P.R., Puerto Rico.

prac·ti·ca·ble (prak′ti kə bəl) *adj.* **1.** capable of being put into practice; feasible: *a practicable plan.* **2.** able to be used: *a practicable road.* [Modification (influenced by earlier *practic* practice) of French *praticable,* going back to Middle French *pratique* practice, through Latin, from Greek *praktikē* practical (as opposed to theoretical) science.] —**prac′ti·ca·bil′i·ty, prac′ti·ca·ble·ness,** *n.* —**prac′ti·ca·bly,** *adv.*

prac·ti·cal (prak′ti kəl) *adj.* **1.** of, relating to, derived from, or concerned with experience, action, or use rather than theory or speculation: *practical knowledge.* **2.** capable of being done, used, or carried out: *a practical method of solving a problem.* **3.** having or showing good judgment or good sense; sensible: *Let's be practical and save our money.* **4.** tending or preferring to act rather than to theorize or speculate. **5.** to all intents and purposes; virtual: *a practical necessity.* **6.** actively engaged in the practice of a profession or occupation: *a practical psychologist.* [Late Latin *practicus* relating to action (from Greek *prāktikos,* from *prāssein* to do, accomplish) + -AL¹.] —**prac′ti·cal·ness,** *n.*

prac·ti·cal·i·ty (prak′ti kal′i tē) *n., pl.* -ties. **1.** the state or quality of being practical. **2.** something practical.

practical joke, a prank, trick, or other joke played on someone, esp. in order to cause embarrassment.

prac·ti·cal·ly (prak′ti klē) *adv.* **1.** to all intents or purposes; virtually. **2.** nearly; almost: *The work is practically finished.* **3.** in a practical manner; through actual experience or use. —For Synonyms, see **almost.**

practical nurse, a person with training and experience in performing certain nursing duties, but lacking the training and education of a registered nurse.

prac·tice (prak′tis) *also, British,* **practise.** *n.* **1.a.** repeated or continuous performance or exercise of an action in order to attain knowledge, skill, or proficiency: *Practice makes perfect.* **b.** a session during which such an action is performed: *If we don't hurry, we'll be late for football practice.* **c.** the condition of being skilled or proficient through repeated or continuous performance or exercise of an action: *to be out of practice.* **2.** the act or process of doing, using, or carrying out something; execution: *The idea is not good in practice.* **3.** the usual way of doing something; habit: *I make a practice of calling whenever I'm going to be late.* **4.** the established way of doing something; tradition: *It is the army's practice to play taps every night.* **5.** the active working at or pursuit of a profession or occupation: *the practice of medicine.* **6.** a professional business, esp. of a doctor or lawyer: *The doctor has a lucrative practice.* **7.** an established method of conducting legal proceedings. **8. practices.** schemes or plots. —*v.,* **-ticed, -tic·ing.** —*v.t.* **1.** to perform (something) repeatedly or continuously in order to attain knowledge or skill: *to practice playing the violin.* **2.** to carry out in action; put into practice: *Practice what you preach.* **3.** to make a habit or custom of: *to practice caution.* **4.** to work at or pursue: *to practice law.* **5.** to train or instruct by practice. —*v.i.* **1.** to perform something repeatedly or continuously in order to gain knowledge or skill. **2.** to work at or pursue a profession or occupation: *The doctor practiced in New York City.* [Old French *practiser* to do often, exercise, going back to Late Latin *prācticus* relating to action. See PRACTICAL.] —**prac′tic·er,** *n.*

n. **Practice, exercise,** and **drill¹** mean activities carried out repeatedly to improve or maintain one's proficiency or condition. **Practice** usually suggests an activity repeated to perfect a skill: *The gymnast attends practice six days a week.* **Exercise** is most often applied to activities intended to improve or maintain a person's physical condition: *Exercise hastened the patient's recovery.* However, it is also used of activities with other purposes: *vocal exercise, exercises to train one's memory, algebra exercises.* **Drill** designates a type of training often carried out by a group and fostering discipline or reinforcing a habit: *Lifeguards have intensive drills in rescue procedures.* For other Synonyms (*n.*), see **habit.**

prac·ticed (prak′tist) *also, British,* **prac·tised.** *adj.* **1.** skilled through practice; experienced: *a practiced carpenter.* **2.** learned or perfected through practice: *a practiced art.*

practice teacher, student teacher. —**practice teaching.**

prac·tise (prak′tis) *British. n.* practice. —*v.t., v.i.,* **-tised, -tis·ing.** practice.

prac·ti·tion·er (prak tish′ə nər) *n.* **1.** a person who practices a profession. **2.** in Christian Science, a person who is authorized to heal.

prae·fect (prē′fekt) prefect.

prae·no·men (prē nō′mən) *n., pl.* -nom·i·na (-nom′i nə). the first name of an ancient Roman citizen. [Latin *praenōmen.*]

prae·tor (prē′tər) *also,* **pretor.** *n.* in ancient Rome, an elected magistrate or judge ranking next below a consul. [Latin *praetor.*]

prae·to·ri·an (prē tôr′ē ən) *also,* **pretorian.** *adj.* **1.** of or relating to a praetor. **2. Praetorian.** of or relating to the Praetorian Guard. —*n.* **1.** praetor or ex-praetor. **2. Praetorian.** a member of the Praetorian Guard.

Praetorian Guard 1. the bodyguard of the ancient Roman emperors or military commanders. **2.** a member of this bodyguard.

prag·mat·ic (prag mat′ik) *adj.* **1.** concerned with practical results or values rather than theory or speculation. **2.** of or relating to philosophical pragmatism. Also, **prag·mat′i·cal.** [Latin *prāgmaticus* skilled in business, from Greek *prāgmatikos* businesslike, statesmanlike, from *prāgma* deed, affair.] —**prag·mat′i·cal·ly,** *adv.*

pragmatic sanction, an edict or decree issued by a sovereign and having the force of law.

prag·ma·tism (prag′mə tiz′əm) *n.* **1.** the philosophical theory set forth in the late nineteenth century by the American philosophers William James and Charles S. Peirce and further developed by John Dewey, American educator, holding that the validity of an idea should be determined by its practical consequences. **2.** a pragmatic quality or character. —**prag′ma·tist,** *n.*

prai·rie (prâr′ē) *n.* a vast, treeless, level or gently rolling grassland. [French *prairie* meadow, going back to Latin *prātum.*]

prairie chicken, a henlike grouse, genus *Tympanuchus,* of the prairies of North America, having brownish plumage heavily barred with black, and, in the male, inflatable air sacs on each side of the neck. The **greater prairie chicken,** *T. cupido,* has orange air sacs, and the **lesser prairie chicken,** *T. pallidicinctus,* has red air sacs. Also, **prairie hen.**

prairie dog, any of various burrowing rodents, genus *Cynomys,* that live in large colonies on the Great Plains and have a short tail, a coarse, buff-colored coat, and a cry like a dog's bark. Length: to 15 inches (38 centimeters), including tail.

prairie schooner, a covered wagon, smaller and more compact than the Conestoga wagon, used by pioneers in crossing the prairies westward to the Pacific coast.

prairie wolf, coyote.

praise (prāz) *n.* **1.** the expression of admiration, commendation, or approval. **2.** the glorification of a god, ruler, or hero, esp.

prairie dog

worship of God when expressed in words or song. —*v.t.,* **praised, prais·ing. 1.** to express admiration or approval of; commend: *The critics praised the author's latest novel.* **2.** to worship or glorify in words or song: *to praise God.* [Old French *preisier* to price, value, going back to Latin *pretium* price.] —**prais′er,** *n.*

•**to sing someone's praises.** to praise highly or with enthusiasm; extol.

v.t. **Praise, commend,** and **extol** mean to express admiration or approval of someone or something. **Praise,** the broadest of these terms, is often applied to the admiration expressed by a superior: *The supervisor praised the employee's work.* **Commend** frequently indicates official or public praise: *The government commended the conservationist's efforts.* **Extol** implies praise that glorifies and exalts: *The speaker extolled the president as a visionary leader.*

praise·wor·thy (prāz′wûr′t͟hē) *adj.* worthy of praise; commendable. —**praise′wor′thi·ly,** *adv.* —**praise′wor′thi·ness,** *n.*

Pra·krit (prä′krit) *n.* any of the various ancient or medieval Indic dialects spoken predominantly in northern and central India. Many languages and dialects spoken in modern India developed from them. [Sanskrit *prākrta* natural, vulgar.]

pra·line (prä′lēn, prā′-) *n.* a crisp candy made of brown sugar and nut meats, usually pecans or almonds, boiled together and formed into patties. [French *praline,* from Marshal Duplessis-*Praslin,* 1598-1675, French nobleman whose cook supposedly invented it.]

pram (pram) *n. Informal.* a baby carriage; perambulator.

prance (prans) *v.i.,* **pranced, pranc·ing. 1.** to move in a proud,

lively, or arrogant manner; strut; swagger: *The drum major pranced across the football field.* **2.** (of a horse) **a.** to spring forward from the hind legs. **b.** to move by a succession of such springs. **3.** to ride on a horse that is prancing. **4.** to run, leap, or skip about in play; gambol. —*n.* **1.** the act or an instance of prancing. **2.** a prancing movement. [Of uncertain origin.]

pran·di·al (prăn′dē əl) *adj.* of or relating to a meal, esp. dinner. [Latin *prandium* lunch, meal¹ + -AL¹.]

prank¹ (prăngk) *n.* something done to provoke laughter or amusement; mischievous or playful act. [Of uncertain origin.] —**prank′ish,** *adj.* —**prank′ish·ly,** *adv.* —**prank′ish·ness,** *n.*

prank² (prăngk) *v.t.* to dress or adorn in a showy way; decorate. —*v.i.* to make a show or display. [Possibly from Dutch *pronken* to show off.]

prank·ster (prăngk′stər) *n.* a person who plays tricks or practical jokes; mischievous person.

pra·se·o·dym·i·um (prā′zē ō dĭm′ē əm) *n.* a soft, slightly yellowish metallic element of the rare-earth group, used in small amounts to color glass, enamel, and synthetic emeralds. Symbol: **Pr** For tables, see **element.** [Modern Latin *praseodymium,* from Greek *prasios* leek + Modern Latin *didymium* didymium. So called because its salts are usually green.]

prate (prāt) *v.,* **prat·ed, prat·ing.** —*v.i.* to talk at length and to little purpose; chatter; babble. —*v.t.* to utter in an idle or foolish manner. —*n.* idle or foolish talk; prattle. [Middle Dutch *praten* to chatter; probably of imitative origin.] —**prat′er,** *n.* —**prat′ing·ly,** *adv.*

prat·fall (prăt′fôl′) *n.* a fall on the buttocks: *The clown took a pratfall.*

prat·tle (prăt′əl) *v.,* **-tled, -tling.** —*v.i.* to talk childishly or foolishly; babble. —*v.t.* to utter or tell in a childish or foolish manner. —*n.* **1.** idle or simple talk. **2.** a sound that is similar to baby talk. [Middle Low German *pratelen* to chatter, from *praten.*] —**prat′tler,** *n.*

prau (prou) proa.

prawn (prôn) *n.* any of various edible, shrimplike crustaceans found in salt and fresh waters throughout warm and temperate regions of the world. Length: 3-4 inches (8-10 centimeters). [Of uncertain origin.]

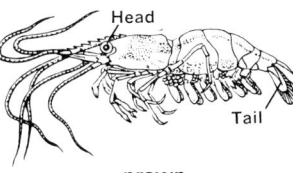

Head

Tail

prawn

pray (prā) *v.i.* **1.** to speak to God with adoration, thanksgiving, or appeal. **2.** to ask something from God or a god: *to pray for divine guidance.* —*v.t.* **1.** to ask of earnestly; beg; entreat: *I pray you to stay.* **2.** to ask for by entreaty; implore: *I know not how to pray your patience* (Shakespeare, *Much Ado About Nothing*). **3.** to say (a prayer): *to pray the Lord's Prayer.* **4.** to be so kind or obliging as to; please. ➡ used in the imperative to indicate a request or politely expressed command: *Pray don't do that.* [Old

French *prier* to worship God, ask earnestly (for), from Latin *precārī* to entreat, call upon.]

pray·er¹ (prā′ər) *n.* a person who prays. [PRAY + -ER¹.]

prayer² (prâr) *n.* **1.** the act of praying, esp. to God. **2.** something prayed for: *Their prayers were granted.* **3.** a set form of words used in praying: *a book of prayers.* **4.** *also,* **prayers.** a form of worship consisting entirely or mainly of prayers: *morning prayers.* **5.** an earnest request; supplication; entreaty. **6.** *Informal.* a possible chance or hope: *I don't have a prayer of getting that scholarship.* [Old French *priere* act of worshiping God, earnest request, going back to Latin *precārius* obtained by entreaty. See PRECARIOUS.]

prayer book (prâr) **1.** a book of formal prayers and other forms of religious devotion. **2.** *also,* **Prayer Book.** Book of Common Prayer.

prayer·ful (prâr′fəl) *adj.* characterized by, given to, or used in prayer; devout. —**prayer′ful·ly,** *adv.* —**prayer′ful·ness,** *n.*

prayer meeting (prâr) a Protestant service of prayer and worship, often held on a weekday night.

prayer plant (prâr) a Brazilian plant, *Maranta leuconeura,* having variegated leaves, often purple or red on the underside, commonly grown as a houseplant. [Because its leaves turn upward, suggesting hands in prayer, at night.]

praying mantis, any of a group of brown or green insects, family Mantidae, related to the grasshopper, most numerous in the tropics, having stout, spiny forelegs for grasping its prey. Length: 1-5 inches (3-13 centimeters). Also, **mantis.** [See MANTIS.]

pre- *prefix* **1.** before in place, time, order, position, or rank: *prewar, pretest, prehistoric.* **2.** in preparation for; preliminary to: *preschool.* [Latin *prae* before, often through French *pré-.*]

preach (prēch) *v.i.* **1.** to speak publicly on a religious subject, such as a Scriptural text; deliver a sermon. **2.** to give advice, esp. in a bossy, boring, or interfering way: *My cousin is always preaching to me about saving money.* —*v.t.* **1.** to set forth or proclaim by preaching: *to preach the word of God.* **2.** to deliver (a sermon or other religious discourse). **3.** to recommend strongly: *to preach legislative reform.* [Old French *prechier* to make known or teach the word of God, exhort, from Latin *praedicāre* to declare publicly, proclaim.]

preach·er (prē′chər) *n.* a person who preaches, esp. a member of the Protestant clergy.

preach·i·fy (prē′chə fī′) *v.i.,* **-fied, -fy·ing.** *Informal.* to preach or moralize in a bossy, boring, or interfering way.

preach·ment (prēch′mənt) *n.* **1.** the act of preaching. **2.** a sermon or speech, esp. a boring one.

preach·y (prē′chē) *adj.,* **preach·i·er, preach·i·est.** *Informal.* given to or suggestive of preaching. —**preach′i·ness,** *n.*

a	at	e	end	o	hot	u	up	hw	white		about
ā	ape	ē	me	ō	old	ū	use	ng	song	ə	taken
ä	far	i	it	ô	fork	ü	rule	th	thin		pencil
âr	care	ī	ice	oi	oil	u̇	pull	th	this		lemon
		îr	pierce	ou	out	ûr	turn	zh	measure		circus

The following list contains a selection of compounds that can be formed with the prefix **pre-**. The meaning of a word on the list can be understood by combining the appropriate sense of the prefix with the root word.

preaddiction	prebreakfast	predefine	prefeudal	premodern	presale
preaddress	prebuilt	predelinquent	prefight	premodify	preselect
preadmission	precalculate	predelivery	profile	premoisten	preselection
preadult	precampaign	predeparture	prefilter	premold	presoak
preagricultural	precertification	predesignate	pregame	prenotification	presort
prealign	precertify	predesignation	prehiring	prenotify	prestamp
preallocate	precheck	prediagnosis	prehung	preoperational	presterilize
preanesthetic	pre-Christian	predischarge	preimmunization	prepack	prestrike
prearraignment	precivilization	prediscovery	preimmunize	preplace	presuggest
prearrange	precode	prediscussion	preinaugural	preplan	presuggestion
prearrangement	precollege	predrill	preincorporate	preproduction	presurgical
preascertain	precollegiate	predug	preincorporation	preprogram	presweeten
preassign	precolonial	predusk	preindustrial	prepublication	presymptomatic
preattack	precombat	preedit	preinoculate	prepunch	pretape
preaudit	precombustion	preeducation	preinoculation	prepurchase	pretournament
preauthorization	precommitment	preelection	preinterview	prequalification	pretreat
preauthorize	precompute	preelementary	preinvasion	prequalify	pretreatment
preautomation	preconfinement	preemployment	preinvestigation	prerace	preuniversity
prebattle	preconvention	preendorse	prelaunch	preregister	prevacation
prebiblical	precool	preendorsement	prelaunder	preregistration	prewar
prebirth	precoordinate	preestablish	prelife	prerehearsal	prewash
prebleach	precoordination	preexamination	preload	prerelease	preweigh
preblend	precrash	preexperiment	premigratory	preretirement	prewrap
preboarding	predawn	preexperimental	premix	prerevolutionary	prewriting

pre·ad·o·les·cence (prē'ad ə les'əns) *n.* the period of human development immediately before adolescence, esp. the time of life between the ages of nine and twelve. —**pre'ad·o·les'cent,** *adj., n.*

pre·am·ble (prē'am'bəl) *n.* **1.** a preliminary statement or introduction, esp. one giving reasons or purposes, as in a statute. **2.** an introductory fact or circumstance. [Old French *preambule* preface, going back to Late Latin *praeambulus* walking in front, from Latin *prae* before + *ambulāre* to walk.]

We the People *of the United States,*

in Order to form a more perfect Union, establish Justice, insure domestic Tranquility, provide for the common defence, promote the general Welfare, and secure the Blessings of Liberty to ourselves and our Posterity, do ordain and establish this Constitution for the United States of America.

preamble to the Constitution of the United States (original spelling and capitalization)

pre·am·pli·fi·er (prē am'plə fī'ər) *n.* an electronic device in a sound reproduction system that contains the volume, tone, and other controls, and amplifies and directs signals to the main amplifier.

pre·ar·range (prē'ə rānj') *v.t.,* **-ranged, -rang·ing.** to arrange beforehand. —**pre'ar·range'ment,** *n.*

pre·a·tom·ic (prē'ə tom'ik) *adj.* of or relating to the time before the first use of atomic energy.

preb·end (preb'ənd) *n.* **1.** a part of the income of a cathedral church given as a stipend to a member of the clergy serving that church. **2.** church property or a tax that supplies money for this stipend. **3.** prebendary. [Medieval Latin *praebenda* church living, from Late Latin *praebenda* pension, allowance, going back to Latin *praebēre* to furnish.]

preb·en·dar·y (preb'ən der'ē) *n., pl.* **-dar·ies.** a member of the clergy who receives a prebend.

Pre·cam·bri·an (prē kam'brē ən) *n.* the first geologic era, comprising four fifths of the history of the earth, during which the earliest forms of life—bacteria and algae—appeared and the earth's atmosphere evolved. For table, see **geologic time.** —*adj.* of, relating to, or characteristic of the Precambrian.

pre·can·cer·ous (prē kan'sər əs) *adj.* of or relating to any pathological tissue condition that may develop into cancer: *a precancerous wart.*

pre·car·i·ous (pri kâr'ē əs) *adj.* **1.** involving great risk or uncertainty; risky; insecure: *a precarious investment.* **2.** exposed to danger; hazardous; perilous: *a precarious position on a cliff.* **3.** based on insufficient or doubtful evidence; unfounded: *a precarious theory.* [Latin *precārius* obtained by entreaty, doubtful, going back to *prex* prayer, entreaty.] —**pre·car'i·ous·ly,** *adv.* —**pre·car'i·ous·ness,** *n.*

pre·cau·tion (pri kô'shən) *n.* **1.** a measure taken beforehand to avoid danger, failure, loss, or harm: *to take precautions against burglary.* **2.** caution or care taken beforehand; wise foresight. [Late Latin *praecautiō,* from Latin *praecavēre* to guard against beforehand.]

pre·cau·tion·ar·y (pri kô'shə ner'ē) *adj.* relating to, advising, or using precaution.

pre·cede (pri sēd') *v.,* **-ced·ed, -ced·ing.** —*v.t.* **1.** to go or come before or ahead of, as in time, order, or importance. **2.** to introduce, as with a preface. —*v.i.* to go or come before. [Latin *praecēdere* to go before.]

prec·e·dence (pres'i dəns, pri sē'-) *n.* **1.** the act, right, or fact of preceding, as in time, rank, or order. **2.** the right to precede others because of superiority of rank or position, esp. at ceremonial or formal occasions: *the precedence of a senator over a representative.* —For Synonyms, see **priority.**

prec·e·dent (*n.,* pres'i dənt; *adj.,* pri sē'dent, pres'i-) *n.* **1.** an act or instance that may serve as an example, pattern, or rule for similar future actions. **2.** a decision or ruling of a court of law that serves as an example for deciding future similar cases. —*adj.* preceding. [Latin *praecēdēns,* present participle of *praecēdere* to go before.]

pre·ced·ing (pri sē'ding) *adj.* going or coming before; that precedes; previous.

pre·cen·tor (pri sen'tər) *n.* a person who directs the singing of a church choir or congregation, esp. a member of the clergy in charge of a cathedral choir. [Late Latin *praecentor,* going back to Latin *prae* before + *canere* to sing.]

pre·cept (prē'sept) *n.* **1.** a rule intended as a guide for conduct or action. **2.** a short statement expressing a general truth or doctrine; maxim. [Latin *praeceptum* rule, maxim, direction.]

pre·cep·tor (pri sep'tər, prē'sep-) *n.* a teacher; instructor. [Latin *praeceptor.*] —**pre·cep·to·ri·al** (prē'sep tôr'ē əl), *adj.*

pre·ces·sion (prē sesh'ən) *n.* **1.** the act or fact of preceding; precedence. **2.** the wobbling motion of a spinning body, such as a top, whose axis of rotation has been shifted by an external force. **3.** precession of the equinoxes. [Late Latin *praecessiō* a going before, from Latin *praecēdere* to go before.]

pre·ces·sion·al (prē sesh'ə nəl) *adj.* of, relating to, or resulting from the precession of the equinoxes.

precession of the equinoxes, the earlier occurrence of the equinoxes in each successive sidereal year, caused by the gradual westward movement of the equinoxes as a result of the slight wobbling of the earth as it rotates on its axis. It takes about 26,000 years for the equinoxes to move westward through 360 degrees and return to their starting points.

pre·cinct (prē'singkt') *n.* **1.** a subdivision or district of a city or town: *a police precinct, an election precinct.* **2.** a police station in such a district. Also, **precinct house. 3.** *also,* **precincts.** an enclosed or bounded space. **4. precincts.** neighborhood; environs. [Medieval Latin *praecinctum* boundary, originally neuter past participle of Latin *praecingere* to enclose.]

pre·ci·os·i·ty (presh'ē os'i tē) *n., pl.* **-ties.** an artificial manner of acting or speaking; affected refinement. [French *préciosité* affectation, from Latin *pretiōsitās* preciousness.]

pre·cious (presh'əs) *adj.* **1.** having great cost or value; costly: *precious heirlooms.* **2.** held in high esteem; cherished: *precious beliefs.* **3.** beloved; dear. **4.** affecting or showing too much delicacy or refinement: *precious manners.* **5.** *Informal.* very great. —*adv.* extremely; very: *The campers had precious little food remaining.* —*n.* loved one; dear; darling. [Old French *precios* expensive, from Latin *pretiōsus* valuable, from *pretium* price, value.] —**pre'cious·ly,** *adv.* —**pre'cious·ness,** *n.*

precious stone, a rare, valuable gem, such as a diamond or emerald.

prec·i·pice (pres'ə pis) *n.* **1.** a high, steep, often vertical or overhanging face of rock. **2.** the brink of a hazardous or perilous situation. [Latin *praecipitium* a steep place.]

pre·cip·i·tance (pri sip'i təns) *n.* the quality of being precipitant. Also, **pre·cip'i·tan·cy.**

pre·cip·i·tant (pri sip'i tənt) *adj.* **1.** falling or rushing rapidly or headlong. **2.** acting without thought or caution; rash; impetuous. **3.** very sudden or unexpected; abrupt. —*n.* a chemical substance that reacts with ions in a solution to form a solid, insoluble compound. [Latin *praecipitāns,* present participle of *praecipitāre* to throw down headlong.] —**pre·cip'i·tant·ly,** *adv.*

pre·cip·i·tate (*v.,* pri sip'i tāt'; *n., adj.,* pri sip'i tit, -tāt') *v.,* **-tat·ed, -tat·ing.** —*v.t.* **1.** to cause to happen before expected, needed, or desired: *to precipitate the failure of a business by poor bookkeeping.* **2.** to throw down violently from or as from a height; hurl downward. **3.** *Chemistry.* to cause (a substance in a solution) to combine to form a solid, insoluble substance. **4.** to cause (atmospheric water vapor) to condense and fall as rain, snow, or dew. —*v.i.* **1.** (of vapor) to be condensed and fall, as in the form of rain, snow, or dew. **2.** *Chemistry.* to be precipitated. **3.** to fall headlong. —*n.* a solid, insoluble chemical compound formed in a solution by the reaction of ions of a dissolved compound or element with ions of a compound or element added to the solution. —*adj.* **1.** falling or rushing rapidly or headlong. **2.** acting or done in a hasty or rash manner; impetuous: *a precipitate decision later regretted.* **3.** coming on suddenly or unexpectedly; abrupt: *a precipitate change in the weather.* [Latin *praecipitātus,* past participle of *praecipitāre* to throw down headlong.] —**pre·cip'i·tate·ly,** *adv.* —**pre·cip'i·tate·ness,** *n.* —**pre·cip'i·ta'tor,** *n.*

pre·cip·i·ta·tion (pri sip'i tā'shən) *n.* **1.a.** any form of water, such as rain, hail, or snow, that falls to earth. **b.** the depositing of such moisture on the earth. **c.** the amount deposited. **2.** the chemical process of forming solid substances in a solution. **3.** the act of precipitating or the state of being precipitated. **4.** rash or sudden haste.

pre·cip·i·tin (pri sip'i tin) *n.* an antibody that forms an insoluble precipitate when combined with its soluble antigen, thereby removing the antigen from the blood. [PRECIPITATE + -IN[1].]

pre·cip·i·tous (pri sip'i təs) *adj.* **1.** of the nature of or having a precipice or precipices; very steep: *precipitous cliffs.* **2.** hasty or rash; precipitate. —**pre·cip'i·tous·ly,** *adv.* —**pre·cip'i·tous·ness,** *n.*

pré·cis (prā'sē, prā sē') *n., pl.* **-cis.** a concise summary, as of a book or article; abstract. —*v.t.* to make a précis of. [French *précis,* from Latin *praecīsus* cut off, brief, past participle of *praecīdere* to cut off in front.] —For Synonyms *(n.),* see **summary.**

pre·cise (pri sīs′) *adj.* **1.** strictly accurate or clearly defined; exact; definite: *Those instructions were not very precise.* **2.** being exactly what is called for or needed; neither more nor less: *the precise amount.* **3.** distinguished from others; particular; very: *At that precise moment the teacher entered the room.* **4.** very strict or careful, as in following rules or standards: *a precise taskmaster.* [Latin *praecīsus* cut off, brief, past participle of *praecīdere* to cut off in front.] —**pre·cise′ly**, *adv.* —**pre·cise′ness**, *n.*

Synonyms Precise, definite, and explicit mean unmistakably clear. **Precise** stresses detailed accuracy: *The precise directions included a map.* **Definite** emphasizes certainty and the absence of ambiguous elements: *Their reply to the invitation was a definite refusal.* **Explicit** indicates that something is directly expressed rather than implied: *The package carried an explicit warning against taking the medicine during pregnancy.*

pre·ci·sion (pri sizh′ən) *n.* the state or quality of being precise; accuracy; exactness. —*adj.* marked by or designed for a high degree of fineness or accuracy: *a precision tool.*

pre·clude (pri klüd′) *v.t.*, -**clud·ed**, -**clud·ing.** to make impossible by previous action; prevent. [Latin *praeclūdere* to close, shut off, hinder from access.] —**pre·clud′a·ble**, *adj.* —**pre·clu·sion** (pri klü′zhən), *n.* —**pre·clu·sive** (pri klü′siv), *adj.* —**pre·clu′sive·ly**, *adv.*

pre·co·cial (pri kō′shəl) *adj.* of or relating to animals that mature quickly and can begin caring for themselves shortly after birth, esp. birds that are born feathered and sighted. [PRECO-CI(OUS) + -AL¹.]

pre·co·cious (pri kō′shəs) *adj.* **1.** developed or matured earlier than usual; displaying maturity at an unusually early age: *a precocious child.* **2.** characterized by or displaying premature development. [Latin *praecoc-*, stem of *praecox* ripe before its time + -OUS.] —**pre·co′cious·ly**, *adv.* —**pre·co′cious·ness**, *n.*

pre·coc·i·ty (pri kos′i tē) *n.* the state or quality of being precocious; early development or maturity.

pre·cog·ni·tion (prē′kog nish′ən) *n.* prior knowledge of specific future events. —**pre·cog·ni·tive** (prē kog′ni tiv), *adj.*

pre-Co·lum·bi·an (prē′kə lum′bē ən) *adj.* of, relating to, or belonging to the time before the Italian explorer Christopher Columbus arrived in the Western Hemisphere: *The museum has a collection of pre-Columbian art from Central America.*

pre-Columbian
gold mask from Peru

pre·con·ceive (prē′kən sēv′) *v.t.*, -**ceived**, -**ceiv·ing.** to form an idea or opinion of beforehand.

pre·con·cep·tion (prē′kən sep′shən) *n.* **1.** an idea or opinion formed beforehand. **2.** the act of preconceiving.

pre·con·cert (prē′kən sûrt′) *v.t.* to arrange by previous agreement.

pre·con·di·tion (prē′kən dish′ən) *v.t.* to put in proper condition or order beforehand. —*n.* something required or necessary beforehand; prerequisite.

pre·con·scious (prē kon′shəs) *adj.* of or relating to that portion of one's mental experiences outside the realm of consciousness but easily recalled: *a preconscious memory.* —*n.* the preconscious part of one's mental experiences.

pre·cook (prē kük′) *v.t.* **1.** to cook beforehand for later reheating. **2.** to cook partially before the final cooking.

pre·cur·sor (pri kûr′sər, prē′kûr′-) *n.* **1.** a person or thing that precedes and announces or indicates the approach of another; forerunner. **2.** a chemical compound or biological substance that gives rise to another compound or substance in a series of reactions or a biochemical process. [Latin *praecursor.*]

pre·cur·so·ry (pri kûr′sə rē) *adj.* **1.** announcing or indicating something to follow. **2.** preliminary or introductory. Also, **pre·cur′sive.**

pred., predicate.

pre·da·cious (pri dā′shəs) *also,* **pre·da·ceous.** *adj.* predatory. [From Latin *praedārī* to plunder.] —**pre·da′cious·ness, pre·dac·i·ty** (pri das′i tē), *n.*

pre·date (prē dāt′) *v.t.*, -**dat·ed**, -**dat·ing.** **1.** to give a date earlier than the correct one: *to predate a check.* **2.** to be or occur earlier than; precede in time.

pre·da·tion (pri dā′shən) *n.* **1.** the act of preying on others. **2.** the means by which predatory animals acquire food. [Latin *praedatio*, from *praedatus*, past participle of *praedārī* to plunder, from *praeda* prey.]

pred·a·tor (pred′ə tər) *n.* **1.** an animal that lives by preying on other animals, such as a wolf, lion, or hawk. **2.** a predatory person.

pred·a·to·ry (pred′ə tôr′ē) *adj.* **1.** living by preying on other animals. **2.** addicted to or living by plundering, robbing, or exploiting others: *a predatory outlaw.* **3.** of, relating to, or characterized by plundering or pillage: *predatory instincts.* [Latin *praedātōrius* plundering, going back to *praedārī* to plunder.]

pre·de·cease (prē′di sēs′) *v.t.*, -**ceased**, -**ceas·ing.** to die before (another person): *She predeceased her husband by only a few years.*

pred·e·ces·sor (pred′ə ses′ər) *n.* **1.** a person who precedes or has preceded another person in time, esp. in an office or position. **2.** something that precedes another thing. **3.** ancestor. [Late Latin *praedēcessor* forerunner in office, from Latin *prae* before + *dēcessor* retiring official.]

pre·des·ti·nate (*v.*, prē des′tə nāt′; *adj.*, prē des′tə nit, -nāt′) *v.t.*, -**nat·ed**, -**nat·ing.** **1.** to foreordain by divine decree or purpose. **2.** predestine. —*adj.* predestined. [Latin *praedestinātus*, past participle of *praedestināre* to determine beforehand.]

pre·des·ti·na·tion (prē des′tə nā′shən) *n.* **1.** the act of predestining or the state of being predestined. **2.a.** a doctrine held by certain Christian churches that God has ordained from all eternity the salvation or damnation of each soul. **b.** a divine decree wherein God has ordained for all eternity whatever is to happen.

pre·des·tine (prē des′tin) *v.t.*, -**tined**, -**tin·ing.** to determine, decree, or decide beforehand.

pre·de·ter·mine (prē′di tûr′min) *v.t.*, -**mined**, -**min·ing.** **1.** to determine, decree, or decide beforehand; predestine. **2.** to give direction to or influence beforehand; prejudice. —**pre′de·ter′mi·na′tion**, *n.*

pred·i·ca·ble (pred′i kə bəl) *adj.* capable of being predicated or affirmed. —*n.* something that is predicable. —**pred′i·ca·bil′i·ty, pred′i·ca·ble·ness**, *n.* —**pred′i·ca·bly**, *adv.*

pre·dic·a·ment (pri dik′ə mənt) *n.* an unpleasant, trying, or difficult situation. [Late Latin *praedicāmentum* category, quality, from Latin *praedicāre* to proclaim.]

pred·i·cate (*n., adj.*, pred′i kit; *v.*, pred′i kāt′) *n.* **1.** that part of a sentence or clause, consisting of the verb with its objects and modifiers, that expresses what is said about the subject, such as *laughed* in *She laughed*, *ran home* in *The dog ran home*, or *is of the essence* in *Time is of the essence.* **2.** *Logic.* that which is stated about the subject in a proposition. *Mortal* is the predicate in the proposition *Socrates is mortal.* —*v.t.*, -**cat·ed**, -**cat·ing.** **1.** to found or base (something, such as an action or statement): *to predicate a belief on one's experiences.* **2.** to affirm or assert as an attribute, quality, or property of something. **3.** to involve in direct association; connote; imply. **4.** to assert or affirm. —*adj. Grammar.* of or belonging to the predicate. [Latin *praedicātus*, past participle of *praedicāre* to declare publicly, proclaim.] —**pred′i·ca′tive**, *adj.* —**pred′i·ca′tive·ly**, *adv.*

predicate adjective, an adjective that follows a linking verb and refers to the subject of the verb. In the sentence *The woods are lovely, lovely* is a predicate adjective.

predicate nominative, a noun or pronoun that follows a linking verb and refers to the subject of the verb. In the sentence *You are a student, student* is a predicate nominative.

predicate noun, a noun that is a predicate nominative.

pred·i·ca·tion (pred′i kā′shən) *n.* **1.** the act of predicating. **2.** *Logic.* predicate.

pre·dict (pri dikt′) *v.t.* to announce beforehand; prophesy. —*v.i.* to make a prediction. [Latin *praedictus*, past participle of *praedīcere* to foretell.] —**pre·dict′a·bil′i·ty**, *n.* —**pre·dict′a·ble**, *adj.* —**pre·dict′a·bly**, *adv.*

a	at	e	end	o	hot	u	up	hw	white		about
ā	ape	ē	me	ō	old	u̇	use	ng	song		taken
ä	far	i	it	ô	fork	ü	rule	th	thin	ə	pencil
âr	care	ī	ice	oi	oil	u̇	pull	th	this		lemon
		îr	pierce	ou	out	ûr	turn	zh	measure		circus

P

Synonyms *v.t.* **Predict, forecast,** and **prognosticate** mean to state beforehand what is going to happen. **Predict** implies reasoning from known facts: *On the basis of historical patterns, the economist predicted a recession this year.* **Forecast** often adds to *predict* an emphasis on precise estimating of future events: *The weather service forecasts three days of rain for next week.* **Prognosticate** implies the use of symptoms or specific indications as the basis for prediction: *After getting the results of the tests, the doctor prognosticated that the patient would recover.* For other Synonyms *(v.t.),* see **foretell.**

pre·dic·tion (pri dik′shən) *n.* **1.** the act of predicting. **2.** something predicted; prophecy.

pre·dic·tive (pri dik′tiv) *adj.* **1.** of or relating to prediction: *The fortuneteller claimed to have predictive ability.* **2.** serving as a sign of future conditions or events; prophetic: *The appearance of crocus buds was predictive of spring.* —**pre·dic′tive·ly,** *adv.*

pre·di·gest (prē′dī jest′, -di-) *v.t.* to digest (food) partially or wholly by treating externally, as with enzymes, before taking into the stomach, as in the treatment of an illness or digestive disorder. —**pre′di·ges′tion,** *n.*

pre·di·lec·tion (pred′ə lek′shən, prē′də-) *n.* a preference or partiality (with *for*): *I have a predilection for jazz.* [French *prédilection,* going back to Latin *prae* before + *dīligere* to choose, love.]

pre·dis·pose (prē′dis pōz′) *v.t.,* **-posed, -pos·ing. 1.** to make susceptible, liable, or subject to. **2.** to give an inclination to; influence: *His openness predisposed her to like him.*

pre·dis·po·si·tion (prē′dis pə zish′ən) *n.* the state or condition of being predisposed; tendency; inclination: *I have a predisposition to worry during airplane flights.*

pred·ni·sone (pred′nə sōn′, -zōn′) *n.* a synthetic derivative of cortisone used to treat allergies and inflammatory diseases, as arthritis. Formula: $C_{21}H_{26}O_5$ [*Pre(gnane)* a steroid hydrocarbon (from *pregnant* + -ANE; because it is found in the urine of pregnant women) + *d(ie)n(e)* a compound with two bonds (from DI-[1] + -ENE) + (CORT)ISONE.]

pre·dom·i·nance (pri dom′ə nəns) *n.* the state or quality of being predominant. Also, **pre·dom′i·nan·cy.**

pre·dom·i·nant (pri dom′ə nənt) *adj.* **1.** having or using superior power, authority, or influence over others: *The military is predominant in that country.* **2.** more or most frequent, common, or noticeable: *Red is the predominant color in that painting.* —**pre·dom′i·nant·ly,** *adv.* —For Synonyms, see **dominant.**

pre·dom·i·nate (pri dom′ə nāt′) *v.i.,* **-nat·ed, -nat·ing. 1.** to exert power, authority, or influence; have control. **2.** to surpass others, as in power, influence, or amount; prevail: *Bright pink predominates in this printed fabric.* —**pre·dom′i·na′tion,** *n.*

pree·mie (prē′mē) *also,* **premie.** *n. Informal.* a prematurely born infant. [PREM(ATURE) + -IE.]

pre·em·i·nent (prē em′ə nənt) *also,* **pre-em·i·nent.** *adj.* superior to or surpassing others; outstanding: *the preeminent orator in the senate.* [Latin *praeēminēns,* present participle of *praeēminēre* to excel.] —**pre·em′i·nence;** *also,* **pre-em′i·nence,** *n.* —**pre·em′i·nent·ly;** *also,* **pre-em′i·nent·ly,** *adv.*

pre·empt (prē empt′) *also,* **pre-empt.** *v.t.* **1.** to get or take possession of before others. **2.** to settle on (land) with the right to purchase it before others. **3.** (of a radio or television program) to be presented in the place of (another): *The football game preempted the regularly scheduled program.* **4.** to cause (a radio or television program) to be canceled and present another in its place. **5.** to take priority over: *The victory celebration preempted all other activities.* [From PREEMPTION.] —**pre·emp′tor;** *also,* **pre-emp′tor,** *n.*

pre·emp·tion (pri emp′shən) *also,* **pre-emp·tion.** *n.* **1.** the right to buy something, such as public land, before others. **2.** the taking of something, such as power, rights, or responsibilities, before others. [PRE- + Latin *emptiō* a buying.]

pre·emp·tive (pri emp′tiv) *also,* **pre-emp·tive.** *adj.* **1.** of, relating to, or capable of preemption. **2.** of or relating to an offensive strategy taken against possible or expected aggression: *a preemptive military strike against an enemy.* **3.** *Bridge.* of or relating to a high defensive opening bid in any suit to keep opponents from scoring. —**pre·emp′tive·ly;** *also,* **pre-emp′tive·ly,** *adv.*

preen (prēn) *v.t.* **1.** (of birds) to clean and smooth (feathers) with the beak. **2.** to dress or adorn (oneself) carefully; primp. **3.** to take or display pride or satisfaction in: *to preen oneself for having won an award.* —*v.i.* to primp. [Possibly form of archaic *prune* to preen; of uncertain origin; influenced by dialectal *preen* to pierce, going back to Old English *prēon* pin (referring to a bird's use of its beak to preen its feathers).]

pre·ex·ist (prē′eg zist′, -ig-) *also,* **pre-ex·ist.** *v.t., v.i.* to exist beforehand.

pre·ex·ist·ent (prē′eg zis′tənt, -ig-) *also,* **pre-ex·ist·ent.** *adj.*

existing beforehand. —**pre′ex·ist′ence;** *also,* **pre′-ex·ist′ence,** *n.*

pref. 1. preface. **2.** preferred. **3.** prefix.

pre·fab (prē fab′, prē′fab′) *n.* a prefabricated building, esp. a house.

pre·fab·ri·cate (prē fab′ri kāt′) *v.t.,* **-cat·ed, -cat·ing. 1.** to construct or manufacture in standardized parts for easy and rapid assembly, and often, low cost. **2.** to make up beforehand: *to prefabricate an excuse for being late.* —**pre′fab·ri·ca′tion,** *n.*

pref·ace (pref′is) *n.* **1.** an introduction to a speech, book, or other literary work, often written by the author. **2.** anything introductory or preliminary. —*v.t.,* **-faced, -fac·ing. 1.** to introduce or furnish with a preface. **2.** to serve as a preface to: *A short documentary prefaced the featured movie.* [Old French *preface* introduction to a book, going back to Latin *praefatiō* introduction to a speech or to writing, a saying beforehand.] —For Synonyms *(n.),* see **introduction.**

pref·a·to·ry (pref′ə tôr′ē) *adj.* relating to, of the nature of, or serving as a preface; introductory: *prefatory remarks.*

pre·fect (prē′fekt) *also,* **praefect.** *n.* **1.** in ancient Rome, any of various high-ranking military or civil officials. **2.a.** the head administrative official of one of the departments of France. **b.** the police chief of Paris. [Latin *praefectus* commander, overseer, director.]

pre·fec·ture (prē′fek chər) *n.* **1.** the office, district, or authority of a prefect. **2.** the official residence of a prefect. **3.** an administrative district of Japan, headed by a governor. [Latin *praefectūra* office of an overseer.]

pre·fer (pri fûr′) *v.t.,* **-ferred, -fer·ring. 1.** to like better; choose above others: *I prefer tea to coffee.* **2.** to put forward for a decision before a court of law or other legal authority: *We didn't prefer charges, since the stolen articles were returned.* **3.** to advance or promote, as in rank or office. [Latin *praeferre* to carry in front, set before.] —**pre·fer′rer,** *n.*

pref·er·a·ble (pref′ər ə bəl, pref′rə-) *adj.* worthy of being chosen over another or others; more desirable. —**pref′er·a·bly,** *adv.*

pref·er·ence (pref′ər əns, pref′rəns) *n.* **1.** the act of choosing one over another or others or the state of being so chosen. **2.** the right or opportunity of so choosing. **3.** a person or thing that is preferred; first choice. **4.** the granting of rights or priorities to one over others, as to one country or group of countries with regard to international trade.

pref·er·en·tial (pref′ə ren′chəl) *adj.* **1.** of, giving, or receiving preference: *to give someone preferential treatment.* **2.** arising from or indicating preference: *a preferential tariff.* —**pref′er·en′tial·ly,** *adv.*

preferential shop, an establishment in which union members are given special privileges, as in hiring.

pre·fer·ment (pri fûr′mənt) *n.* **1.** advancement, as to higher rank; promotion. **2.** a position, rank, or office to which a person is advanced, esp. one having prestige, honor, or financial profit.

preferred stock, stock on which dividends must be paid before they can be paid on common stock. ➥ distinguished from **common stock.**

pre·fig·u·ra·tion (prē′fig yə rā′shən) *n.* **1.** the act of prefiguring. **2.** something that prefigures; prototype.

pre·fig·ure (prē fig′yər) *v.t.,* **-ured, -ur·ing. 1.** to show or suggest beforehand; foreshadow. **2.** to imagine to oneself beforehand. [Late Latin *praefigūrāre* to represent beforehand, from Latin *prae* before + *figūrāre* to form.] —**pre·fig′ure·ment,** *n.*

pre·fix (*n.,* prē′fiks′; *v.,* prē fiks′) *n.* a syllable or group of syllables attached to the beginning of a word, root, or stem so as to alter or modify its meaning or to form a new word. In the word *postwar, post-* is a prefix. —*v.t.* to put before or at the beginning: *to prefix a title to a name.* [Modern Latin *praefixum,* from Latin *praefixus,* past participle of *praefīgere* to fix in front.]

pre·flight (prē flīt′) *adj.* taking place before flight or flying: *preflight training of a student pilot, preflight inspection of an airplane.*

pre·fron·tal (prē frun′təl) *adj.* of or situated in the anterior portion of the frontal lobe of the brain: *prefrontal lobotomy.* [PRE- + FRONTAL.]

preg·na·ble (preg′nə bəl) *adj.* capable of being taken by force; open to attack. [Middle French *prenable,* from *prendre* to take, seize, from Latin *prehendere.*]

preg·nan·cy (preg′nən sē) *n., pl.* **-cies.** the condition, quality, or period of being pregnant.

preg·nant (preg′nənt) *adj.* **1.** (of a woman or female mammal) having one or more unborn offspring in the uterus; being with child or young. **2.** full of significance or importance; having meaning: *a pregnant statement.* **3.** filled; abounding: *a remark that is pregnant with meaning.* **4.** abounding with ideas; inventive;

imaginative: *a pregnant mind*. [Latin *praegnāns* being with child or with young.] —**preg′nant·ly**, *adv*.

pre·heat (prē hēt′) *v.t.* to heat before using, as an oven.

pre·hen·sile (prē hen′səl, -sīl) *adj*. adapted for grasping or holding, esp. by wrapping around: *Certain monkeys have prehensile tails*. [French *préhensile*, from Latin *prehēnsus*, past participle of *prehendere* to grasp, seize.]

pre·his·tor·ic (prē′his tôr′ik, -tor′ik) *adj*. of, relating to, or belonging to the period before recorded history: *prehistoric peoples*. Also, **pre′·his·tor′i·cal.** —**pre′his·tor′i·cal·ly**, *adv*.

pre·his·to·ry (prē his′tə rē) *n*. the events or conditions on earth before recorded history; prehistoric matters or times.

pre·ig·ni·tion (prē′ig·nish′ən) *n*. ignition in an internal-combustion engine that occurs prematurely, as while the intake valve is open.

pre·judge (prē juj′) *v.t.*, **-judged, -judg·ing.** to judge beforehand or without knowing all the facts. —**pre·judg′ment;** *also,* **pre·judge′ment,** *n*.

prehensile tail of an opposum

prej·u·dice (prej′ə dis) *n*. **1.a.** an unfavorable opinion or judgment formed beforehand or without proof or basis in fact. **b.** the act or state of holding such an opinion. **2.** a particular preference or preconceived notion either for or against something: *Don't let your prejudices interfere with your decision*. **3.** hatred or intolerance of a particular group, such as members of a race or religion. **4.** injury or damage resulting from a judgment or action by another or others. —*v.t.*, **-diced, -dic·ing. 1.** to cause to have a prejudice: *An unfavorable review can often prejudice the public against a movie*. **2.** to damage or injure, as by an unfair judgment or action. [Old French *prejudice* act of deciding beforehand, from Latin *praejūdicium* a preceding judgment, disadvantage.]

Synonyms *n*. **Prejudice** and **bias** mean an attitude or opinion formed without reasonable consideration. **Prejudice** is a preconceived judgment that is usually unfavorable and intolerant: *The organization is dedicated to overcoming prejudice against minority groups*. **Bias** indicates an inclination either to favor or to disapprove of something: *The movie critic had a bias in favor of comedies*.

prej·u·di·cial (prej′ə dish′əl) *adj*. causing prejudice or injury; detrimental: *prejudicial testimony during a trial*. —**prej′u·di′cial·ly**, *adv*.

prel·a·cy (prel′ə sē) *n., pl.* **-cies. 1.** the rank or dignity of a prelate. **2.** prelates collectively. **3.** the system of church government by prelates.

prel·ate (prel′it) *n*. a member of the clergy of high rank, esp. one with authority over other clerics. Bishops, archbishops, and cardinals are prelates. [Old French *prelat*, going back to Latin *praelātus*, past participle of *praeferre* to set before, carry in front.]

prelim., preliminary.

pre·lim·i·nar·y (pri lim′ə ner′ē) *adj*. coming before and leading up to or preparing for the main event, subject, or action: *preliminary arrangements, a preliminary statement, a preliminary boxing bout*. —*n., pl.* **-nar·ies. 1.** a preliminary step or action. **2.** a contest or match coming before the main one. [French *préliminaire*, going back to Latin *prae-* before + *līmen* threshold.] —**pre·lim′i·nar′i·ly**, *adv*.

pre·lit·er·ate (prē lit′ər it) *adj*. (of a society or culture) not having a written language.

prel·ude (prel′ūd, prā′lūd) *n*. **1.** a preliminary or introductory event, action, or performance. **2.a.** a musical composition or movement preceding or introducing another, such as that played before a religious service or before a fugue. **b.** a short, independent musical composition in a free style, often written for a keyboard instrument or an orchestra. —*v.*, **-ud·ed, -ud·ing.** —*v.t.* **1.** to serve as a prelude to. **2.** to introduce with a prelude. —*v.i.* to serve as a prelude. [French *prélude* introduction, introduction to a piece of music, going back to Latin *praelūdere* to play beforehand.]

pre·mar·i·tal (prē mar′i təl) *adj*. taking place before marriage: *premarital counseling*.

pre·ma·ture (prē′mə chùr′, -tyùr′, -tùr′) *adj*. arriving, occurring, or existing before the usual or proper time: *a premature baby, a premature decision*. [Latin *praemātūrus*, from *prae* before

+ *mātūrus* ripe.] —**pre′ma·ture′ly**, *adv*. —**pre′ma·ture′ness, pre′ma·tur′i·ty**, *n*.

pre·med (prē′med′) *Informal. adj*. premedical. —*n*. a premedical student.

pre·med·i·cal (prē med′i kəl) *adj*. of, relating to, or preparing for the study of medicine.

pre·med·i·tate (prē med′i tāt′) *v.t.*, **-tat·ed, -tat·ing.** to consider, think out, or plan beforehand: *to premeditate a crime*. [Latin *praemeditātus*, past participle of *praemeditārī* to think over beforehand.]

pre·med·i·ta·tion (prē′med i tā′shən) *n*. **1.** the act of premeditating. **2.** the planning and deliberation of a crime in advance, showing intent to commit the crime.

pre·men·stru·al syndrome (prē men′strü əl) various symptoms, such as bloating, irritability, and depression, that occur in some women before the menstrual period. Also, **PMS.**

pre·mie (prē′mē) preemie.

pre·mier (pri mîr′, -myîr′, prē′mē ər) *n*. the prime minister in certain European countries, such as France and Italy. —*adj*. **1.** first in position, rank, or authority; chief: *a premier reason*. **2.** first in order of time; earliest. [French *premier* first, from Latin *prīmārius* of the first rank, chief, from *prīmus* first.]

pre·miere (pri mîr′, -myâr′, prē′mē âr′, -ər) *also,* **pre·mière.** *n*. the first formal public performance or presentation, as of a play or motion picture. —*v.t., v.i.*, **-miered, -mier·ing.** to present or appear for the first time. —*adj*. being the first or foremost; chief. [French *première*, from *premier* first. See PREMIER.]

prem·ise (prem′is) *n*. **1.** a statement or principle accepted as true without proof; self-evident or universally accepted truth from which a conclusion is drawn. **2. premises. a.** a particular piece of land and the buildings on it. **b.** a building or part of a building. **3.** *Logic*. one of the initial statements in a syllogism, asserted as true, from which the conclusion is drawn. **4. premises.** *Law*. **a.** matters previously stated, such as a description of the property or the names of the parties concerned in a deed or contract. **b.** property that is the subject of a conveyance. —*v.t.*, **-ised, -is·ing. 1.** to mention beforehand as an introduction or explanation. **2.** to state or assume as a premise in an argument. [Medieval Latin *praemissa (propositio)* literally, (proposition) put before, from Latin *praemissus*, past participle of *praemittere* to send or put before.]

pre·mi·um (prē′mē əm) *n*. **1.** something offered free or at a lower price as an inducement to buy something else. **2.** the amount paid at regular intervals by a policyholder for insurance. **3.** a high or unusual value: *to put a premium on honesty*. **4.** an amount paid in addition to the regular or usual price, wage, or other fixed amount. **5.** *Economics*. the value of one form of money in excess of another of the same nominal value. —*adj*. valued as higher or better in quality: *a premium gasoline*. [Latin *praemium* reward, booty, profit.]

 ·**at a premium. a.** in great demand; valuable. **b.** at more than the normal or usual price or value: *to buy something at a premium*.

pre·mo·lar (prē mō′lər) *n*. any of eight permanent human teeth, having double-pointed crowns and situated between the molars and the cuspids; bicuspid. —*adj*. of or relating to the premolars.

pre·mo·ni·tion (prē′mə nish′ən, prem′ə-) *n*. **1.** a feeling that something is about to happen. **2.** a warning or sign of something to come. [Late Latin *praemonitiō* forewarning, from Latin *praemonēre* to forewarn.] —**pre·mon·i·to·ry** (prē·mon′i tôr′ē), *adj*. —**pre·mon′i·to′ri·ly**, *adv*.

First premolar (bicuspid)

Second premolar (bicuspid)

premolars

pre·na·tal (prē nā′təl) *adj*. of or relating to the period prior to birth: *prenatal medical care*. —**pre·na′tal·ly**, *adv*.

pren·tice (pren′tis) *n. Archaic*. apprentice.

pre·nup·tial (prē nup′shəl) *adj*. occurring before a marriage: *a prenuptial financial agreement*.

pre·oc·cu·pa·tion (prē ok′yə pā′shən, prē′ok-) *n*. **1.** the state

953

or condition of being preoccupied; engrossment; absorption. **2.** anything that occupies the mind or attention: *Reading is my main preoccupation.* **3.** the act of occupying beforehand or before others. Also, **pre·oc'cu·pan·cy.**

pre·oc·cu·pied (prē ok'yə pīd') *adj.* **1.** absorbed in thought; engrossed. **2.** previously occupied.

pre·oc·cu·py (prē ok'yə pī') *v.t.,* **-pied, -py·ing. 1.** to occupy the mind or attention of; engross: *Vacation plans preoccupied them.* **2.** to occupy or take possession of beforehand or before others.

pre·op·er·a·tive (prē op'ər ə tiv) *adj.* in or occurring during the period preceding a surgical operation. —**pre·op'er·a·tive·ly,** *adv.*

pre·or·dain (prē'ôr dān') *v.t.* to ordain or appoint beforehand; predestine. —**pre·or·di·na·tion** (prē'ôr də nā'shən, prē ôr'-), *n.*

prep (prep) *n.* preparation, as for an activity, contest, or the like. —*adj.* preparatory: *prep sessions before a history test.* —*v.,* **prepped, prep·ping.** —*v.i.* **1.** to prepare for something: *We prepped for the test by studying our class notes.* **2.** to attend preparatory school: *Where did you prep?* —*v.t.* to get ready; prepare: *The nurse prepped the patient for surgery.*

prep. 1. preparatory. **2.** preposition.

pre·pack·age (prē pak'ij) *v.t.,* **-aged, -ag·ing.** to put (food or other goods) into packages of a particular weight, number, size, or type, usually marked with the price, before offering for sale.

pre·paid (prē pād') *v.* the past tense and past participle of **prepay.** —*adj.* paid for beforehand.

prep·a·ra·tion (prep'ə rā'shən) *n.* **1.** the act or process of preparing. **2.** the state of being prepared or in readiness. **3.** a measure or provision needed or taken to prepare for something: *I will take care of the preparations for our party.* **4.** something prepared for a specific purpose, as a medicine or food.

pre·par·a·tive (pri par'ə tiv) *adj.* preparatory. —*n.* something preparatory.

pre·par·a·to·ry (pri par'ə tôr'ē, prep'ər ə-) *adj.* **1.** serving to prepare; preliminary: *a preparatory course.* **2.** undergoing preparation, as for college: *a preparatory student.*
·**preparatory to.** in preparation for.

preparatory school, a school, esp. one that is private, that prepares students for college. Also, **prep school.**

pre·pare (pri pâr') *v.,* **-pared, -par·ing.** —*v.t.* **1.** to make ready or fit, as for a particular purpose, event, or undertaking: *They prepared themselves for the race by practicing daily.* **2.** to put together by combining various ingredients or parts or according to a plan: *to prepare a meal, to prepare a medicine, to prepare a speech.* **3.** to provide with whatever is necessary for an event or undertaking. —*v.i.* to get ready: *to prepare for college, to prepare for a party.* [Latin *praeparāre* to make ready beforehand.] —**pre·par'er,** *n.*

pre·par·ed·ness (pri pâr'id nis) *n.* the state or condition of being prepared, esp. for war.

pre·pay (prē pā') *v.t.,* **-paid, -pay·ing.** to pay or pay for in advance. —**pre·pay'ment,** *n.*

pre·pense (pri pens') *adj.* planned or considered beforehand; premeditated. ➡ used chiefly in the phrase *malice prepense.* [Modification of earlier *purpensed,* from Old French *purpense,* past participle of *purpenser* to premeditate, going back to Latin *prō* before + *pēnsāre* to weigh, ponder.]

pre·pon·der·ance (pri pon'dər əns) *n.* **1.** superiority, as in quantity, weight, power, or influence. Also, **pre·pon'der·an·cy. 2.** something that is preponderant: *A preponderance of the evidence supports the plaintiff's claim.*

pre·pon·der·ant (pri pon'dər ənt) *adj.* superior, as in quantity, weight, power, or influence; predominant. —**pre·pon'der·ant·ly,** *adv.* —For Synonyms, see **dominant.**

pre·pon·der·ate (pri pon'də rāt') *v.i.,* **-at·ed, -at·ing. 1.** to be superior, as in quantity, power, influence, or importance; predominate: *Which party will preponderate in the new Congress?* **2.** to be greater in weight. **3.** to descend or incline downward, as one end of a balance. [Latin *praeponderātus,* past participle of *praeponderāre* to outweigh.] —**pre·pon'der·a'tion,** *n.*

prep·o·si·tion (prep'ə zish'ən) *n.* any of a class of words in many languages that show the relationship between a noun or pronoun and another word, such as a verb or another noun. *By, into,* and *on* are prepositions in English. [Latin *praepositiō* a putting before, preposition.]

prep·o·si·tion·al (prep'ə zish'ə nəl) *adj.* relating to, functioning as, or having a preposition: *a prepositional phrase.* —**prep'o·si'tion·al·ly,** *adv.*

pre·pos·sess (prē'pə zes') *v.t.* **1.** to preoccupy the mind of to the exclusion of other thoughts, feelings, or ideas. **2.** to prejudice or influence beforehand, esp. in a favorable manner. **3.** to impress favorably from the start.

pre·pos·sess·ing (prē'pə zes'ing) *adj.* making a favorable impression; pleasing: *a prepossessing manner.*

pre·pos·ses·sion (prē'pə zesh'ən) *n.* **1.** an opinion formed beforehand; prejudice. **2.** the state of being preoccupied, as with thoughts or feelings.

pre·pos·ter·ous (pri pos'tər əs, -trəs) *adj.* contrary to truth, reason, or common sense; absurd; ridiculous: *a preposterous idea.* [Latin *praeposterus* reversed, absurd; literally, before coming after.] —**pre·pos'ter·ous·ly,** *adv.* —**pre·pos'ter·ous·ness,** *n.*

pre·po·tent (prē pō'tənt) *adj. Biology.* (of an individual organism) having a greater capacity than some other organism to transmit genetically determined characteristics to its offspring. [Latin *praepotentis,* genitive of *praepotēns* very powerful, from *prae-* indicating intensification + *potēns* powerful. See POTENT.] —**pre·po'ten·cy,** *n.*

prep·py (prep'ē) *also,* **prep·pie.** *n., pl.* **-pies.** *Informal.* **1.** a student or graduate of a preparatory school. **2.** a person who dresses or behaves in a manner thought to be typical at preparatory schools. —*adj.* relating to or characteristic of preppies: *preppy clothes.*

prep school, preparatory school.

pre·puce (prē'pūs) *n.* the fold of skin that covers the end of the penis or clitoris. [Latin *praepūtium.*]

Pre-Raph·a·el·ite (prē raf'ē ə līt') *n.* **1.** any of a group of nineteenth-century English artists and poets organized by Dante Gabriel Rossetti, whose works attempted a return to the strong religious feelings, themes, and styles of the medieval and early Renaissance periods, with an emphasis on personal fantasy, medieval legend, and the exotic. **2.** any Italian painter who preceded Raphael. —*adj.* of, relating to, or characteristic of the Pre-Raphaelites, their principles, or their style.

pre·re·cord (prē'ri kôrd') *v.t.* to record beforehand for later broadcast or telecast.

pre·req·ui·site (prē rek'wə zit) *n.* something required or necessary beforehand for something that follows: *a prerequisite for college entrance.* —*adj.* required or necessary beforehand: *a prerequisite course.*

pre·rog·a·tive (pri rog'ə tiv) *n.* **1.** a right or privilege belonging to a particular person, group, or class, esp. a hereditary or official right. **2.** any distinguishing and exclusive right or privilege. —*adj.* of, relating to, or having a prerogative. [Latin *praerogātīva* privilege, preference, previous choice, from *praerogātīvus* asked for an opinion ahead of others.]

pres., present.

Pres., President.

pres·age (*n.,* pres'ij; *v.,* pres'ij, pri sāj') *n.* **1.** a sign or warning of a future event; omen; portent. **2.** a feeling that something is about to happen; premonition; presentiment. **3.** the prophetic significance of something. —*v.,* **-aged, -ag·ing.** —*v.t.* **1.** to give or be a sign or warning of; portend. **2.** to have a feeling about beforehand; have a presentiment of. **3.** to give a prophecy of; predict; foretell. —*v.i.* to make a prediction. [Latin *praesāgium* foreboding.]

pres·by·o·pi·a (prez'bē ō'pē ə) *n.* a type of farsightedness that develops in middle age, caused by a loss of elasticity of the crystalline lens. [Modern Latin *presbyopia,* from Greek *presbys* old + *ōps* eye.] —**pres·by·op·ic** (prez'bē op'ik), *adj.* —**pres'by·ope',** *n.*

pres·by·ter (prez'bə tər, pres'-) *n.* **1.** in the early Christian church, an elder who belonged to a council that governed a congregation. **2.** a minister in a Presbyterian church. **3.** a lay elder in a Presbyterian church who belongs to a board that rules a local church. **4.** a minister or priest in a church having a hierarchy. [Church Latin *presbyter* an elder, from Greek *presbyteros,* comparative of *presbys* old. Doublet of PRIEST.]

Pres·by·te·ri·an (prez'bə tîr'ē ən, pres'-) *adj.* of, relating to, or belonging to any of various Calvinistic Protestant denominations, esp. those of English or Scottish origin, in which church government is by ministers or elders of equal rank. —*n.* a person who believes in Presbyterianism, esp. a member of a Presbyterian church.

Pres·by·te·ri·an·ism (prez'bə tîr'ē ə niz'əm, pres'-) *n.* **1.** a system of church government by ministers or elders of equal rank. **2.** the doctrines, beliefs, and practices of the Presbyterian churches.

pres·by·ter·y (prez'bə ter'ē, pres'-) *n., pl.* **-ter·ies. 1.** in Presbyterianism, a church court having jurisdiction over the congregations in a certain area, composed of all the ministers and certain of the elders of the congregations. **2.** the congregations under the jurisdiction of such a court, collectively. **3.** that part of a church reserved for the clergy. [Church Latin *presbyterium* council of elders, from Greek *presbyterion,* from *presbyteros* elder. See PRESBYTER.]

pre·school (prē′skül′) *adj.* of, relating to, or for a child past infancy but younger than school age, usually between the ages of two and five. —*n.* a school for children too young to attend kindergarten. Also, **nursery school.** —**pre′school′er,** *n.*

pre·sci·ence (prē′shē əns, presh′ē-) *n.* knowledge of something before it exists or occurs; foreknowledge. [Church Latin *prae-scientia,* from Latin *praesciēns,* present participle of *praescīre* to foreknow.]

pre·sci·ent (prē′shē ənt, presh′ē-) *adj.* having knowledge of something before it exists or happens.

pre·scribe (pri skrīb′) *v.,* **-scribed, -scrib·ing.** —*v.t.* **1.** to set down or give as a rule or direction to be followed. **2.** to order or recommend for use as a remedy or treatment. —*v.i.* **1.** to set down or give rules or directions; dictate. **2.** to give medical advice or a prescription. [Latin *praescrībere* to write before, order, appoint.]

pre·script (*n.,* prē′skript′; *adj.,* pri skript′, prē′skript′) *n.* something prescribed; rule or direction. —*adj.* prescribed. [Latin *praescrīptum* order, rule, from *praescrībere* to write before, order, appoint.]

pre·scrip·tion (pri skrip′shən) *n.* **1.a.** a formula written by a physician for the preparation and use of a medicine or other remedy. **b.** the medicine or remedy prescribed. **2.** the act of prescribing. **3.** something prescribed; rule or direction. **4.a.** the process of acquiring right or title to property by virtue of having used or possessed it for a long period of time. **b.** a title or right so acquired. —*adj.* (of a drug) sold only if prescribed by a doctor. ➡ distinguished from **over-the-counter** *(def. 2).* [Latin *prae-scrīptiō* a writing before, order, rule, from *praescrībere.* See PRE-SCRIBE.]

pre·scrip·tive (pri skrip′tive) *adj.* **1.** giving or setting down strict rules, laws, or directions. **2.** arising from established use or custom. **3.** acquired by or based on legal prescription. —**pre·scrip′tive·ly,** *adv.* —**pre·scrip′tive·ness,** *n.*

pres·ence (prez′əns) *n.* **1.** the state or fact of being in a specific place at a given time: *The big dog's presence in the room made me uneasy.* **2.** the area immediately surrounding a person or thing; close proximity: *to sign a contract in the presence of witnesses.* **3.** the immediate vicinity of a person of very high rank, esp. a sovereign. **4.a.** the appearance, carriage, or bearing of a person: *a stately presence.* **b.** a dignified, impressive, or self-assured appearance or bearing: *The stage actor had a lot of presence.* **5.** a spiritual being or invisible influence felt to be present. [Old French *presence* a being at hand, bearing, from Latin *praesentia* a being at hand.]

presence chamber, a reception room in which a king, queen, or other person of rank receives guests.

presence of mind, the ability to maintain one's self-control and act intelligently in an emergency or other difficult situation.

pres·ent[1] (prez′ənt) *adj.* **1.** in a specific place at a given time; at hand: *We may not be present when you arrive.* **2.** existing or going on at this time: *the present generation, present circumstances.* **3.** being dealt with, written, discussed, or considered; in mind: *the present question.* **4.** to be found; existing: *Lead is present in some gasolines.* **5.** *Grammar.* indicating an action now taking place or a state now existing. —*n.* **1.** the present time; time now passing: *There is no time like the present for our meeting. We are not busy at present.* **2.** *Grammar.* the present tense of a verb in the present tense. **3. presents.** *Law.* documents at hand. [Latin *praesēns* that is before one or at hand.]

pre·sent[2] (*v.,* pri zent′; *n.,* prez′ənt) *v.t.* **1.** to introduce formally to another or others: *May I present my friend?* **2.** to bring into the presence of another or others or into a particular place: *The mayor presented the plan to the city council.* **3.** to make a gift, award, offer, or donation of; bestow: *The principal will present the diplomas. Please present my compliments to the chef.* **4.** to put in the possession of something (with *with*): *The author presented me with a copy of his latest book.* **5.** to suggest, put forward, or bring up for consideration: *This latest development presents a problem.* **6.** to expose to view or notice, esp. before the public; display; show: *The gallery will present the works of a new artist.* **7.** to hand or send in; submit; as a bill or petition. **8.** to point, aim, or turn in the direction of. —*n.* something presented; gift or donation. [Old French *presenter* to offer, from Latin *praesentāre* to place before, hold out.] —**pre·sent′er,** *n.* —For Synonyms *(v.t.),* see **give.**

  ·**to present arms.** to salute by bringing a weapon, such as a rifle, to a vertical position in front of the body with the muzzle up and the trigger facing out.

pre·sent·a·ble (pri zen′tə bəl) *adj.* **1.** suitable to be present in company, as in appearance or attire: *to make oneself presentable.* **2.** fit or suitable to be offered, given, or shown: *to put a report in a presentable form, to make a room presentable.* —**pre·sent′a·bil′i·ty,** *n.* —**pre·sent′a·bly,** *adv.*

pres·en·ta·tion (prez′ən tā′shən, prē′zən-) *n.* **1.** the act of presenting or the state of being presented. **2.** an exhibition or showing: *The museum had a special presentation of works by women artists.* **3.** something presented; gift or donation. —**pres′en·ta′tion·al,** *adj.*

pres·ent-day (prez′ənt dā′) *adj.* of, belonging to, or occurring at the present time; current.

pre·sen·ti·ment (pri zen′tə mənt) *n.* a feeling that something is about to happen, esp. something bad; premonition. [Obsolete French *presentement,* going back to Latin *praesentīre* to perceive beforehand.]

pres·ent·ly (prez′ənt lē) *adv.* **1.** in a little while; shortly: *They will arrive presently.* **2.** at the present time; currently: *We are presently working out a new filing system.* —For Synonyms, see **soon.**

pre·sent·ment (pri zent′mənt) *n.* **1.** the act of presenting. **2.** something presented; exhibition; showing. **3.** a written statement by a grand jury concerning an offense, based on the jury's own knowledge or observation and presented without an indictment. **4.** the presentation of a note, bill of exchange, or the like for acceptance or payment. [Old French *presentement* act of presenting, from *presenter* to offer. See PRESENT[2].]

present participle, a participle expressing a present action or state, formed with the suffix *-ing* and used esp. to form the progressive tenses and as an adjective or noun. In the sentence *I am awaiting your reply,* the word *awaiting* is a present participle.

present perfect **1.** a verb tense expressing action completed at the time of speaking. In the sentence *She has seen that science fiction movie three times,* the phrase *has seen* is in the present perfect. **2.** a verb in this tense.

present tense **1.** a verb tense expressing an action or state that is occurring or exists at the present time. In the sentence *He plays the bugle well,* the word *plays* is in the present tense. **2.** a verb in this tense.

pres·er·va·tion (prez′ər vā′shən) *n.* the act of preserving or the state of being preserved.

pre·serv·a·tive (pri zûr′və tiv) *n.* anything that preserves, esp. a chemical substance added to foods to prevent or retard spoilage. —*adj.* tending or serving to preserve.

pre·serve (pri zûrv′) *v.t.,* **-served, -serv·ing.** **1.** to maintain or keep intact; make lasting: *to diet in order to preserve one's youthful figure.* **2.** to prepare (food) for future use, as by salting, smoking, or pickling. **3.** to protect from harm or danger; keep in safety; save: *to preserve a building of historical importance.* **4.** to keep from spoiling or decomposing, as with chemical substances. —*n.* **1.** *usually,* **preserves.** fruit that has been boiled with sugar and stored in airtight containers to prevent spoilage or fermentation. **2.a.** an area set aside for the protection of plant and animal life or other natural resources. **b.** an area set aside for restricted or private hunting or fishing. [Medieval Latin *praeservāre* to guard, from Late Latin *praeservāre* to observe, from Latin *prae* before + *servāre* to keep, protect.] —**pre·serv′a·ble,** *adj.* —**pre·serv′er,** *n.*

pre·set (prē set′) *v.t.,* **-set, -set·ting.** to set beforehand, esp. to adjust or set (a device or mechanism) before operation: *to preset the controls on a microwave oven.* —*adj.* set or able to be set in advance: *The radio has preset buttons for tuning in stations quickly.*

pre·shrink (prē shringk′) *v.t.,* **-shrank** (-shrangk′) or **-shrunk** (-shrungk′), **-shrunk** or **-shrunk·en** (-shrung′kən), **-shrink·ing.** to shrink during manufacture to minimize later shrinking during washing or dry cleaning: *to preshrink cotton.*

pre·shrunk (prē′shrungk′) *v.* a past participle of **preshrink.** —*adj.* (of a fabric) shrunk during manufacture to minimize later shrinkage during washing or dry cleaning: *preshrunk blue jeans.*

pre·side (pri zīd′) *v.i.,* **-sid·ed, -sid·ing.** **1.** to act as president or chairperson, as at a meeting. **2.** to exercise authority, direction, or control: *to preside over a business.* [Latin *praesidēre* to sit before, watch, guard.] —**pre·sid′er,** *n.*

pres·i·den·cy (prez′i dən sē) *n., pl.* **-cies.** **1.** the office or function of president. **2.** the time during which a president holds office. **3.** *also,* **Presidency.** the office of President of the United States.

pres·i·dent (prez′i dənt) *n.* **1.** *also,* **President.** the chief executive of a republic, esp. of the United States. **2.** a chief officer, as of a company, college, or organization. [Latin *praesidēns* ruler, director, from *praesidēre* to sit before, watch, guard.] —**pres·i·den·tial** (prez′i den′shəl), *adj.*

a	at	e	end	o	hot	u	up	hw	white		about
ā	ape	ē	me	ō	old	ū	use	ng	song	ə {	taken
ä	far	i	it	ô	fork	ü	rule	th	thin		pencil
âr	care	ī	ice	oi	oil	u̇	pull	th	this		lemon
		îr	pierce	ou	out	ûr	turn	zh	measure		circus

pres·i·dent-e·lect (prez′i dənt i lekt′) *n.* a person who has been elected president but has not yet been inaugurated.

President's Day, the third Monday in February, observed as a legal holiday in most states of the United States in commemoration of the birthdays of George Washington and Abraham Lincoln.

pre·sid·i·o (pri sid′e o) *n., pl.* **-i·os.** a fortified military post, esp. one in the western or southwestern United States. [Mexican Spanish *presidio* military post, from European Spanish *presidio,* from Latin *praesidium,* from *praeses* military governor, from *praesidēre.* See PRESIDE.]

pre·sid·i·um (pri sid′ē əm) *n.* **1.** any of various political or governmental committees in the Soviet Union empowered to act for a larger governing body between its sessions. **2. Presidium.** such a committee empowered to act for the Supreme Soviet. [Russian *prezidium,* from Latin *praesidium.* See PRESIDIO.]

press[1] (pres) *v.t.* **1.** to act on or against with steady force or weight; exert continuous pressure on: *to press a button, to press one's nose against a window.* **2.a.** to extract by pressure; squeeze out: *to press juice from grapes.* **b.** to compress or exert pressure on to extract juice from: *to press grapes.* **3.** to give a particular shape, consistency, smoothness, or thickness to by means of pressure: *to press vinyl into a phonograph record, to press ceramic clay into a dish.* **4.** iron: *to press a suit.* **5.** to hold close; embrace; hug. **6.** to urge strongly and persistently; entreat: *They pressed me to go with them.* **7.** to cause difficulties for; harass: *We are being sorely pressed by our enemies.* **8.a.** to lay stress on; emphasize: *to press a point.* **b.** to insist on; urge strongly: *to press a claim, to press charges against someone.* **9.** to constrain; compel; force: *to press another person to obey.* **10.** to urge onward; cause to hasten: *We pressed the cab driver to go faster.* —*v.i.* **1.** to exert pressure: *You have to press down on the lever to make the machine work.* **2.** to push or strain forward; advance with force, haste, or eagerness: *to press through a crowd, to press on in spite of the storm.* **3.** to demand or seek something urgently: *to press for reforms.* **4.** to crowd; throng: *The fans pressed against the barricades to see the rock star.* **5.** to iron clothes. **6.** to be capable of taking or holding an ironing: *This dress presses well.* **7.** to weigh heavily or bear down, as upon the mind. —*n.* **1.** the act or fact of pressing; push. **2.** a crowding or thronging forward or together: *the press of the people in the square.* **3.** urgency; hurry; pressure: *the press of events.* **4.** any of various instruments or machines for exerting pressure, as to stamp or compress materials or to extract juice from fruits or vegetables. **5.** printing press. **6.** an establishment for printing or publishing. **7.** the business, process, or art of printing. **8.a.** the media used for the collection and dissemination of news, as newspapers and periodicals. **b.** people who collect, write, or distribute news, such as reporters or journalists: *The press attended the opening of the new play.* **9.** something that appears in newspapers or magazines, such as comment or criticism: *The candidate's campaign tactics got a bad press.* **10.** the condition of being ironed: *This fabric holds a press nicely.* **11.** a large, usually shelved cupboard, as for linen. [Old French *presser* to strain, crush, urge strongly, going back to Latin *premere* to bear down upon, burden, force.]

press[2] (pres) *v.t.* **1.** to force into military service; impress. **2.** to use in a manner different from the ordinary or intended: *The French government pressed taxicabs into service to take troops to the front lines.* —*n.* impressment into military service. [Modification of obsolete *prest* to enlist by giving earnest money, from obsolete *prest* earnest money, from Old French *prest,* from *prester* to lend, from Latin *praestāre* to become surety for, furnish; formerly, recruits in England were given *prest* or earnest money, but later the forcing of men into military service became associated with PRESS[1] in the sense of "force."]

press agent, a person who manages publicity or public relations for an individual or organization, such as an actor or motion-picture studio.

press box, an enclosed area set aside for reporters, as at a sports event.

press conference, an interview granted to an assembly of reporters, as by a public official or celebrity.

press gang, formerly, a group of men employed to impress others into military service.

press·ing (pres′ing) *adj.* demanding or calling for immediate action or attention: *pressing business, a pressing problem.* —**press′ing·ly,** *adv.* —For Synonyms, see **urgent.**

press·man (pres′mən) *n., pl.* **-men** (-mən). a person who operates or has charge of a printing press.

press release, a bulletin formally issued or released to the press with information for broadcast or publication after a specified time.

press·room (pres′rüm′, -rŏŏm′) *n.* **1.** a room containing print-

ing presses at a newspaper or printing plant. **2.** a room set aside for reporters, as in a public building.

press secretary, a person in charge of the press conferences and public relations of a public figure.

pres·sure (presh′ər) *n.* **1.** the force exerted by one body upon another with which it is in contact. **2.** a compelling or constraining force or influence: *social pressure, to put pressure on someone.* **3.** urgent and stressing demands on one's time or energy: *to work well under pressure.* **4.** a burden or oppression, as of something difficult to bear: *the pressure of grief.* **5.** *Physics.* the amount of force exerted on a unit of area: *tires inflated to a pressure of 27 pounds per square inch.* **6.** atmospheric pressure. **7.** blood pressure. **8.** electromotive force. —*v.t.,* **-sured, -sur·ing.** to apply compelling or constraining force or influence on. [Latin *pressūra* a pressing, burden, oppression.] —For Synonyms (*n.*), see **stress.**

pressure cooker, an airtight metal pot for quick cooking by steam pressure at a temperature above the boiling point of water.

pressure gauge, a device for measuring the pressure of a liquid or gas.

pressure group, an interest group that tries by lobbying and propaganda to influence legislators or other government officials, or the public, to promote and protect a special interest.

pressure point, any of various points on the body, close to major arteries, where pressure may be applied in order to stop the flow of blood from a wound.

pressure suit, an inflatable suit worn, as by an aviator or astronaut, to maintain normal atmospheric pressure while flying at high altitudes or in space.

pres·sur·ize (presh′ə rīz′) *v.t.,* **-ized, -iz·ing. 1.** to maintain a certain atmospheric pressure in the interior of (something, such as an airplane, spacecraft, or diving apparatus). **2.** to subject to or keep under high pressure, as the contents of an aerosol can. —**pres′sur·i·za′tion,** *n.*

press·work (pres′wûrk′) *n.* **1.** the working or management of a printing press. **2.** work done by a printing press.

Pres·ter John (pres′tər) in medieval legend, a rich and powerful Christian priest-king who was believed to rule a great kingdom somewhere in Asia.

pres·ti·dig·i·ta·tion (pres′ti dij′i tā′shən) *n.* sleight of hand; legerdemain. [French *prestidigitation,* going back to Latin *praestō* ready, at hand + *digitus* finger.] —**pres′ti·dig′i·ta′tor,** *n.*

pres·tige (pres tēzh′, -tēj′, pres′tij) *n.* **1.** power, influence, or authority based on prior success, reputation, or achievements. **2.** the power to command the respect or admiration of others. [French *prestige* influence, magic spell, illusion, from Latin *praestīgium* trick, illusion.]

pres·ti·gious (pre stij′əs, -stē′jəs) *adj.* having or giving prestige; highly honored or respected: *a prestigious award given to top scientists.* [Latin *praestigiosus* illusory, from *praestigium* trick, illusion.]

pres·tis·si·mo (pres tis′ə mō′) *Music. adv.* in a very rapid tempo. —*adj.* very rapid. —*n.* a prestissimo passage, movement, or piece. [Italian *prestissimo* very quickly, superlative of *presto* quickly. See PRESTO.]

pres·to (pres′tō) *adv.* **1.** at once; immediately. **2.** *Music.* in a rapid tempo. —*adj. Music.* rapid; quick. —*n. Music.* a presto passage, movement, or piece. [Italian *presto* quick, quickly, going back to Latin *praestō* ready, at hand.]

pre·stressed concrete (prē′strest′) concrete that is reinforced with embedded wire strands or rods under tension so as to give added strength.

pre·sum·a·ble (pri zü′mə bəl) *adj.* capable of being presumed or taken for granted; likely; probable. —**pre·sum′a·bly,** *adv.*

pre·sume (pri züm′) *v.,* **-sumed, -sum·ing.** —*v.t.* **1.** to accept as true until proven otherwise; consider as likely; take for granted: *I presume that you know what you're talking about. The jury must presume the defendant is innocent.* **2.** to take upon oneself without permission or authority; dare: *Do you presume to tell me how to do my job?* —*v.i.* **1.** to be presumptuous; take liberties. **2.** to take unfair advantage of something (with *on* or *upon*): *to presume on a person's good nature.* [Late Latin *praesūmere* to assume, from Latin *praesūmere* to take beforehand, anticipate.] —**pre·sum·ed·ly** (pri zü′mid lē), *adv.* —**pre·sum′er,** *n.* —**pre·sum′ing·ly,** *adv.*

pre·sump·tion (pri zump′shən) *n.* **1.** the act of presuming. **2.** something taken for granted; supposition; assumption: *I went to the party on the presumption that you would be there.* **3.** a cause or reason for presuming; evidence leading to a probability. **4.** excessive boldness or arrogance in thought or conduct; effrontery. **5.** *Law.* the inference of a fact, based on its connection with known or proven facts. [Late Latin *praesumptiō* boldness, from Latin *praesumptiō* a taking beforehand, supposition.]

pre·sump·tive (pri zump′tiv) *adj.* **1.** giving reasonable

grounds for acceptance or belief: *presumptive evidence.* **2.** based on presumption or inference; presumed. —**pre·sump′tive·ly,** *adv.*

pre·sump·tu·ous (pri zump′chü əs, -shəs) *adj.* too bold or arrogant; taking liberties; impertinent. [Late Latin *praesūmptuōsus,* from *praesūmptiō* boldness. See PRESUMPTION.] —**pre·sump′tu·ous·ly,** *adv.* —**pre·sump′tu·ous·ness,** *n.*

pre·sup·pose (prē′sə pōz′) *v.t.,* **-posed, -pos·ing. 1.** to take for granted; assume beforehand. **2.** to involve or imply as a necessary condition: *A good performance presupposes much rehearsal.*

pre·sup·po·si·tion (prē′sup ə zish′ən) *n.* **1.** the act of presupposing. **2.** something presupposed.

pret., preterit.

pre·teen (prē tēn′) *also,* **pre-teen.** *n.* a child who is not yet thirteen years old, esp. one nearing that age. —*adj.* of or relating to preteens: *preteen styles of clothing.* [PRE- + TEEN.]

pre·tence (prē′tens, pri tens′) pretense.

pre·tend (pri tend′) *v.t.* **1.** to claim, esp. falsely or insincerely: *I do not pretend to be an expert chess player.* **2.** to give a false show or appearance of; feign: *to pretend sleep.* **3.** to act out in play; make believe: *The child pretended to be a doctor.* **4.** to presume; venture; attempt. —*v.i.* **1.** to act out in play: *Children love to pretend.* **2.** to give a false appearance in order to deceive: *We all knew you weren't really ill, only pretending.* **3.** to lay claim (with *to*): *to pretend to a throne.* —*adj. Informal.* not real or genuine: *a pretend playmate, pretend money.* [Latin *praetendere* to stretch forth, allege, simulate.]

Synonyms *v.t.* **Pretend, feign,** and **simulate** mean to assume a false appearance. **Pretend** often suggests a relatively simple or innocent attempt to mislead: *I pretended to be asleep to avoid further conversation.* **Feign** implies a more elaborate, serious, or hypocritical pretense: *The suspect feigned ignorance of the crime.* **Simulate** emphasizes the outward appearance adopted: *Although disappointed in the birthday gift, the child simulated pleasure with gasps and squeals.*

pre·tend·ed (pri ten′did) *adj.* **1.** alleged or claimed, esp. falsely or insincerely: *pretended allegiance.* **2.** not genuine; false: *a pretended friend.* —**pre·tend′ed·ly,** *adv.*

pre·tend·er (pri ten′dər) *n.* **1.** a person who makes false or insincere claims or presents a false appearance. **2.** a person who lays claim to something, esp. to a throne.

pre·tense (prē′tens, pri tens′) *also,* **pretence.** *n.* **1.** a false show or appearance for the purpose of deceiving: *His behavior is totally without pretense.* **2.** a false reason or excuse; pretext: *The child used any pretense to avoid going to bed.* **3.** a claim made or implied, esp. one that is false or insincere. **4.** an affected or ostentatious show or display. **5.** an acting out in play; fantasy. [Anglo-Norman *pretensse* claim, affectation, going back to Late Latin *pratēnsus,* past participle of Latin *praetendere* to stretch forth, allege.]

pre·ten·sion (pri ten′shən) *n.* **1.** a claim or assertion of a claim (often with *to*): *pretensions to greatness.* **2.** a false show or display; affectation; ostentation. **3.** the act of laying claim to something; assertion. **4.** a false reason or excuse; pretext; allegation.

pre·ten·tious (pri ten′shəs) *adj.* **1.** making claims to, or presenting a false or exaggerated display of, some distinction or quality: *a talented but pretentious writer.* **2.** intended to show off or attract attention; ostentatious: *a pretentious house.* [French *prétentieux,* going back to Latin *praetentus,* past participle of *praetendere* to stretch forth, allege.] —**pre·ten′tious·ly,** *adv.* —**pre·ten′tious·ness,** *n.*

preter- *prefix* more than; beyond; past: *preternatural.*

pret·er·it (pret′ər it) *also,* **pret·er·ite.** *Grammar. n.* **1.** a past tense. **2.** a verb in the past tense. —*adj.* expressing past time or action: *the preterit tense.* [Latin *praeteritus* gone by, past participle of *praeterīre* to go by.]

pre·ter·mit (prē′tər mit′) *v.t.,* **-mit·ted, -mit·ting. 1.** to leave out or leave undone; omit. **2.** to interrupt or suspend: *to pretermit payments on a loan.* **3.** to let pass unnoticed; disregard. [Latin *praetermittere* to let pass, neglect, from *praeter* past + *mittere* to send.]

pre·ter·nat·u·ral (prē′tər nach′ər əl) *adj.* **1.** going beyond or differing from the natural or ordinary; extraordinary or abnormal. **2.** supernatural. [Medieval Latin *praeternaturalis* that is beyond nature, going back to Latin *praeter* beyond + *nātūra* nature, character, order of things, world.] —**pre′ter·nat′u·ral·ly,** *adv.*

pre·test (*n.,* prē′test′; *v.,* prē test′) *n.* **1.** a preliminary test designed to give practice in certain kinds of schoolwork or to determine readiness for this work: *a spelling pretest.* **2.** a test given to certain merchandise prior to public sale. —*v.t.* to give a pretest to.

pre·text (prē′tekst′) *n.* a false reason or excuse given to conceal a true reason or motive: *He returned to her house on the pretext of having forgotten something.* [Latin *praetextum,* from *praetexere* to allege; literally, to weave in front.]

pre·tor (prē′tər) praetor.

pre·to·ri·an (pri tôr′ē ən) praetorian.

pre·tri·al (prē trī′əl) *adj.* relating to, occurring, or presented before a trial actually begins in a court of law: *a pretrial hearing to limit issues to be argued in a lawsuit.* —*n.* a meeting held by a judge to clarify charges or procedure or to try to reach a settlement before a trial actually begins.

pret·ti·fy (prit′ə fī′) *v.t.,* **-fied, -fy·ing.** to make pretty. —**pret′ti·fi·ca′tion,** *n.*

pret·ty (prit′ē) *adj.,* **-ti·er, -ti·est. 1.** pleasing or attractive to the eye, esp. in a graceful or dainty way: *a pretty baby, a pretty flower.* **2.** giving pleasure; pleasant; charming: *a pretty poem, a pretty thought.* **3.** fine; nice. ➡ usually used ironically: *You certainly got us into a pretty mess this time.* **4.** *Informal.* fairly large in amount; considerable: *a pretty sum of money.* —*adv.* fairly; rather; quite: *It was raining pretty hard when we left.* —*n., pl.* **-ties.** a person or thing that is pleasing or attractive. —*v.t.,* **-tied, -ty·ing.** *Informal.* to make pretty, attractive, or pleasant (often with *up*): *to pretty up a room.* [Old English *praettig* crafty, tricky.] —**pret′ti·ly,** *adv.* —**pret′ti·ness,** *n.* —For Synonyms *(adj.),* see **beautiful.**

· **sitting pretty.** *Informal.* in a good or favorable condition or position; well-off.

pret·zel (pret′səl) *n.* a slender roll of dough that is baked in any of various forms, esp. a loose knot or a short stick, and usually salted on the outside. [German *Brezel,* going back to Latin *bracchium* arm; possibly because it resembles a pair of folded arms. See BRACE.]

pre·vail (pri vāl′) *v.i.* **1.** to prove superior in power or influence; be victorious; triumph: *to prevail over an enemy.* **2.** to prove successful; be effective; succeed: *If words do not prevail, we must use force.* **3.** to be widespread; persist: *Violence still prevails in our cities.* **4.** to be the most usual; be predominant: *Warm weather prevails in that region.* [Latin *praevalēre* to have greater power.]

· **to prevail on** (or **upon**). to be successful in persuading: *They prevailed on me to stay.*

pre·vail·ing (pri vā′ling) *adj.* **1.** most common or frequent: *prevailing winds.* **2.** having superior power or influence. —**pre·vail′ing·ly,** *adv.*

prev·a·lent (prev′ə lənt) *adj.* of common or general occurrence, use, or acceptance; widespread: *a prevalent belief.* [Latin *praevalēns,* present participle of *praevalēre* to have greater power.] —**prev′a·lence,** *n.* —**prev′a·lent·ly,** *adv.*

pre·var·i·cate (pri var′i kāt′) *v.i.,* **-cat·ed, -cat·ing.** to speak falsely or deceptively; evade the truth; lie. [Latin *praevāricātus,* present participle of *praevāricārī* to walk crookedly, collude.] —**pre·var′i·ca′tion,** *n.* —**pre·var′i·ca′tive,** *adj.* —**pre·var′i·ca′tor,** *n.*

pre·vent (pri vent′) *v.t.* **1.** to keep from happening or developing: *to prevent forest fires.* **2.** to keep from doing something (often with *from*): *We must prevent them from leaving.* —*v.i.* to occur as a hindrance or obstacle: *We will have the picnic Saturday if nothing prevents.* [Latin *praeventus,* past participle of *praevenīre* to go before, hinder.] —**pre·vent′a·ble;** *also,* **pre·vent′i·ble,** *adj.* —**pre·vent′er,** *n.*

pre·ven·tion (pri ven′shən) *n.* **1.** the act of preventing. **2.** something that prevents.

pre·ven·tive (pri ven′tiv) *adj.* serving or intended to prevent something; concerned with prevention: *to take preventive measures against disease.* —*n.* **1.** something that prevents; means of preventing. **2.** a drug or other agent used to prevent disease. Also, **pre·vent·a·tive** (pri ven′tə tiv). —**pre·ven′tive·ly,** *adv.* —**pre·ven′tive·ness,** *n.*

preventive medicine 1. the branch of medicine that studies the origins of disease, how disease spreads, and methods of preserving health. **2.** treatment or other measures designed to prevent the development of disease.

pre·view (prē′vū′) *also,* **prevue.** *n.* **1.** an advance presentation of a motion picture, play, or exhibition before its formal presentation to the public. **2.** an advance showing of scenes from a motion picture or television program for the purpose of advertisement. **3.** an advance view, indication, or survey: *The teacher gave a preview of the term's work.* —*v.t.* to present or view in advance.

a	at	e	end	o	hot	u	up	hw	white		about
ā	ape	ē	me	ō	old	ū	use	ng	song		taken
ä	far	i	it	ô	fork	ü	rule	th	thin	ə	pencil
âr	care	ī	ice	oi	oil	ů	pull	th	this		lemon
				îr	pierce	ou	out	ûr	turn	zh	measure		circus

P

pre·vi·ous (prē′vē əs) *adj.* **1.** coming or made before; earlier: *the previous day, a previous appointment.* **2.** *Informal.* occurring or done too soon; premature; hasty. [Latin *praevius* going before.] —**pre′vi·ous·ly,** *adv.*
•**previous to.** before: *They left previous to my arrival.*

previous question, a motion in a parliamentary body that the pending question be brought to a vote without further debate.

pre·vi·sion (pri vizh′ən) *n.* **1.** knowledge of the future; prescience; foreknowledge. **2.** a prophetic vision or perception. —**pre·vi′sion·al,** *adj.*

pre·vue (prē′vū′) *n.* preview. —*v.t.,* -**vued, -vu·ing.** preview.

pre·war (prē′wôr′) *adj.* occurring or existing before a war. [PRE- + WAR.]

prey (prā) *n.* **1.** any animal hunted or killed for food. **2.** a person or thing that is a victim: *The old man was the prey of a mugger.* **3.** the act or instinct of hunting or killing for food: *a beast of prey.* [Old French *preie* animal seized by carnivorous animals for food, booty, from Latin *praeda* booty.]
•**to prey on** (or **upon**). **a.** to hunt or kill for food: *Owls prey on rodents and other small mammals.* **b.** to take advantage of; victimize: *swindlers who prey on the public.* **c.** to have a harmful or wearing effect: *Feelings of guilt preyed on her mind.* **d.** to plunder; pillage.

Pri·am (prī′əm) *n.* in Greek legend, the king of Troy during the Trojan War and father of Hector, Paris, and Cassandra.

pri·ap·ic (prī ap′ik) *adj.* **1.** phallic. **2.** preoccupied with virility or masculinity. [From *Priapus,* the Greek and Roman god of virility + -IC.]

price (prīs) *n.* **1.** the amount of money or its equivalent for which something is bought or sold: *The price of milk has gone up.* **2.** the cost at which something is obtained: *victory at the price of many lives.* **3.** the amount of money or other consideration necessary or sufficient for a bribe: *The racketeers thought they knew the police chief's price.* **4.** a reward offered for the capture or killing of a person. **5.** the value or worth of something: *Freedom was of greater price to them than riches.* —*v.t.,* **priced, pric·ing. 1.** to set a price on; fix the price of: *These meats are priced much too high.* **2.** *Informal.* to find out the price of: *to price a new car.* [Old French *pris* value, from Latin *pretium* value, reward.] —**pric′er,** *n.*
•**at any price.** no matter what it may cost: *Our orders are to change the design at any price.*
•**beyond** (or **without**) **price.** invaluable; priceless.

price·less (prīs′lis) *adj.* **1.** of greater value than can be measured; invaluable: *a priceless antique chest.* **2.** wonderfully or uniquely memorable, endearing, or amusing: *That remark was priceless.*

price support 1. the maintaining by government or by a business group of the market price of a manufactured or farm product, esp. by contracting to buy large amounts at a fixed price: *a system of price supports.* **2.** the maintaining of the value of a country's currency by purchasing it on a financial exchange at a fixed, artificial rate.

pric·ey (prī′sē) *also,* **pricy.** *adj.,* **pric·i·er, pric·i·est.** *Informal.* costing much; expensive: *a pricey meal.* —**pric′ey·ness,** *n.*

prick (prik) *v.t.* **1.** to pierce slightly with a sharp point: *to prick one's finger with a pin.* **2.** to cause sharp mental or emotional pain to; sting: *My conscience pricks me if I lie.* **3.** to mark, trace, or outline with punctures. **4.** to urge on with or as with a spur or other sharp point. —*v.i.* **1.** to have a sensation of being pricked with a sharp point. **2.** *Archaic.* to ride fast. —*n.* **1.** an act or instance of piercing or pricking or the sensation produced by this: *I felt the prick of the needle in my arm.* **2.** sharp mental or emotional pain: *a sudden prick of sorrow.* **3.** a mark or opening made by a sharp point; puncture. **4.** a pointed object or instrument, as a thorn. [Old English *prica* point.]
•**to prick up.** to stand erect or rise to an erect position.
•**to prick up one's ears. a.** to raise the ears to an erect position: *The dog pricked up its ears at the noise.* **b.** to listen closely or

with sudden interest: *I pricked up my ears when I heard my name mentioned.*

prick·le (prik′əl) *n.* **1.** a small, sharp point, as a thorn. **2.** a stinging or tingling sensation, as of being pricked. —*v.,* -**led, -ling.** —*v.t.* to cause a stinging or tingling sensation in, as by pricking. —*v.i.* to sting or tingle. [Old English *pricel* a goad.]

prick·ly (prik′lē) *adj.,* -**li·er, -li·est. 1.** having prickles. **2.** caused by or as by being pricked; stinging; tingling. **3.** difficult; troublesome: *a prickly situation.* —**prick′li·ness,** *n.*

prickly heat, heat rash.

prickly pear 1. the edible, red or purple, pear-shaped fruit of any of a large group of cacti, genus *Opuntia,* found in North and South America. **2.** the spiny plant bearing this fruit. Also, **tuna.**

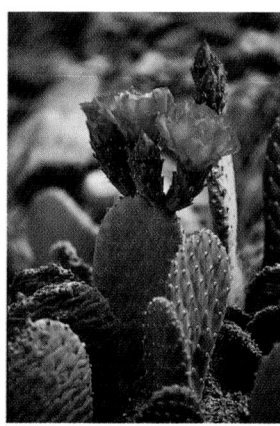

prickly pear

pric·y (prī′sē) *adj.,* **pric·i·er, pric·i·est.** pricey.

pride (prīd) *n.* **1.** a sense of one's personal worth or dignity; self-respect: *Despite years of poverty, the couple maintained their pride.* **2.** an exaggerated or unreasonable sense of one's worth or importance: *Ken knew he was wrong, but his foolish pride kept him from apologizing.* **3.** pleasure or satisfaction resulting as from an achievement or possession: *The woodcarver took great pride in her work.* **4.** a person or thing that causes such pleasure or satisfaction: *The sloop was the sailor's pride and joy.* **5.** the best or most flourishing part or time; prime. **6.** a family or group of lions. —*v.t.,* **prid·ed, prid·ing.** to take pride, pleasure, or satisfaction in (oneself) for (with *on* or *upon*): *They prided themselves on their financial success.* [Old English *prȳte* great self-esteem.]

pride·ful (prīd′fəl) *adj.* full of pride; haughty. —**pride′ful·ly,** *adv.*

pried (prīd) the past tense and past participle of **pry.**

prie-dieu (prē dyœ′) *n., pl.* **prie-dieus** or **prie-dieux** (prē-dyœz′). a piece of furniture having a shelf for a prayer book and a platform for kneeling in prayer. [French *prie-Dieu,* from *prier* to pray (from Latin *precārī* to ask) + *Dieu* God (from Latin *deus* a god).]

priest (prēst) *n.* **1.** in the Roman Catholic, Orthodox, and Anglican churches, a member of the clergy ranking next below a bishop, who has taken holy orders and is empowered to celebrate the Eucharist, administer sacraments, and pronounce absolution. **2.** any cleric of a Christian church. **3.** a person empowered to perform the duties of a deity or religion, esp. one who per-

prie-dieu

forms sacrificial rites or other public religious acts. [Old English *prēost* Christian priest, modification of Church Latin *presbyter* an elder, from Greek *presbyteros,* comparative of *presbys* old (referring to the respect for the elders of a community). Doublet of PRESBYTER.]

priest·ess (prē′stis) *n.* a woman who performs the rites of a deity or religion.

priest·hood (prēst′hùd) *n.* **1.** the office or dignity of a priest. **2.** priests collectively.

priest·ly (prēst′lē) *adj.,* -**li·er, -li·est. 1.** of or relating to a priest or the priesthood. **2.** like, characteristic of, or befitting a priest. —**priest′li·ness,** *n.*

prig (prig) *n.* a smug, self-righteous person whose rigid adherence to propriety or morality often annoys others. [Of uncertain origin.] —**prig′ger·y, prig′gish·ness,** *n.* —**prig′gish,** *adj.* —**prig′gish·ly,** *adv.*

prim (prim) *adj.,* **prim·mer, prim·mest.** stiffly or excessively formal, neat, or precise; proper. [Old French *prim* fine, delicate, from Latin *prīmus* first.] —**prim′ly,** *adv.* —**prim′ness,** *n.*

prim. 1. primary. **2.** primitive.

pri·ma ballerina (prē'mə) *pl.* **pri·ma ballerinas.** the leading female dancer in a ballet company. [Italian *prima ballerina,* from *prima* first (going back to Latin *prīmus*) + *ballerina.* See BALLERINA.]

pri·ma·cy (prī'mə sē) *n., pl.* **-cies. 1.** the state of being first, as in rank or importance. **2.** the rank or dignity of an ecclesiastical primate. **3.** in the Roman Catholic Church, the jurisdiction and supreme authority of the pope. [Medieval Latin *primatia* first place or rank, from Late Latin *prīmās* one of the first, chief. See PRIMATE.]

pri·ma don·na (prē'mə don'ə) *pl.* **pri·ma don·nas. 1.** the principal female singer in an opera company. **2.** a temperamental or vain person. [Italian *prima donna* literally, first lady, going back to Latin *prīmus* first + *domina* lady.]

pri·ma-fa·ci·e (prī'mə fā'shē ē', -shē) *adj. Law.* sufficient to establish a fact or legal claim unless the other side offers evidence to disprove it: *The prosecution laid out a prima-facie case of assault.*

pri·ma fa·ci·e (prī'mə fā'shē ē', fā'shē) at first sight; before further investigation. [Latin *prīmā faciē.*]

pri·mal (prī'məl) *adj.* **1.** of or from the earliest time; original; first; primitive. **2.** of first importance; fundamental. [Medieval Latin *primalis* principal, excellent, from Latin *prīmus* first.]

pri·ma·ri·ly (prī mer'ə lē) *adv.* **1.** most importantly; chiefly; principally. **2.** in the first place; originally.

pri·ma·ry (prī'mer ē, -mə rē) *adj.* **1.** first or greatest in importance or degree; principal: *Your safety is my primary concern.* **2.** first in order, as in a series, sequence, or grouping: *the primary grades in school.* **3.** first or earliest in time; primitive; elementary: *a primary phase of development.* **4.** forming a basic part of the basis of something; fundamental; elemental: *a primary structural unit.* **5.** not derived from something else; original; direct: *We consulted only primary sources in our research.* **6.** relating to the induction circuit, coil, or current in an electrical device: *the primary winding of a transformer.* —*n., pl.* **-ries. 1.** an election in which contenders from the same party oppose each other for the party's nomination or for the right to run for office with the party's support. Also, **primary election. 2.** one of the primary colors. **3.** an induction current, coil, or circuit. **4.** something that is first in order, importance, or degree. [Latin *prīmārius* of the first rank, chief, from *prīmus* first.]

primary accent 1. the principal stress in the pronunciation of a word. **2.** a mark (′) used to indicate this stress. Also, **primary stress.**

primary cell, a voltaic cell in which the chemical reaction that produces current cannot be reversed. Unlike a storage battery, a primary cell cannot be recharged by electrical means.

primary color 1. any one of three basic colors, red, yellow, or blue, which, when combined in pigments and dyes, produce all other colors. **2.** any of three colors of light, as red, green, or blue, from which light of all other colors can be produced.

primary election, primary *(n., def. 1).*

primary school, a school providing instruction for very young pupils, comprising the first three or four grades of elementary school.

pri·mate (prī'māt, -mit) *n.* **1.** in the Roman Catholic, Orthodox, and Anglican churches, an archbishop whose see ranks above all others in a country or church province. **2.** any member of the highly developed order of mammals, Primates, that includes human beings, apes, monkeys, lemurs, and tarsiers. [Late Latin *prīmāt-,* stem of *prīmās* of the first rank, archbishop, from Latin *prīmus* first.]

prime (prīm) *adj.* **1.** first in importance or value; main; chief: *Your welfare is my prime concern.* **2.** first in rank, dignity, influence, or authority: *the prime political figure of our time.* **3.** of the best quality; excellent: *a prime day for sailing.* **4.** first in order of time or development: *in the prime period of history.* **5.** *Mathematics.* **a.** relating to or designating a prime number. **b.** having no common divisor except 1. **6.** of the highest or best rating in a given series or scale: *prime beef.* —*n.* **1.** the best or most flourishing stage or condition: *The trees were cut down before they had reached their prime.* **2.a.** the time of early adulthood: *the prime of one's youth.* **b.** the most mature or flourishing time of a person's life: *to be in one's prime.* **3.** the best or most desirable part. **4.** the beginning or first part; earliest stage. **5.** the spring; springtime: *in the prime of the year.* **6.** the second of the seven canonical hours or the service for it. **7.** prime number. **8.a.** one of the parts, usually sixty, into which a degree, may be divided. **b.** a mark (′) indicating this. —*v.t.,* **primed, prim·ing. 1.** to make ready or prepare by filling or charging with something, as a car's carburetor with gasoline. **2.** to pour water into (a pump)

so as to make it ready for operation. **3.** to prepare for painting, as by applying a base coat: *to prime a wall, to prime a canvas for an oil painting.* **4.** to instruct or prepare (a person) beforehand as to what to say or do: *The lawyer primed the witness.* **5.** to prepare (a gun or mine) for firing by supplying a charge of gunpowder or a primer. [Partly from Latin *prīmus* first; partly from Old English *prīm* first hour of the day of the Church (originally beginning at 6 A.M.), from Latin *prīma (hōra)* first (hour).] —**prime'ness,** *n.*

prime meridian, the meridian that passes through Greenwich, England, designated as zero degrees longitude, and from which longitude east and west is measured. For illustration, see **longitude.**

prime minister, the highest-ranking member of a body of executive administrators or of a council of ministers, esp. in a parliamentary government, as that of Great Britain.

prime mover 1. the original or principal force in an undertaking. **2.** the initial force that puts a machine in motion. **3.** a machine that converts the energy of a natural force into work.

prime number, in the set of natural numbers, a number that can be divided without a remainder only by itself and by 1, as 2, 3, 7, 13, 29, or 41.

prim·er[1] (prim'ər) *n.* **1.** an elementary book for teaching children to read. **2.** an elementary or introductory book on any subject. [Medieval Latin *primarius (liber)* basic (book), from Latin *prīmārius* of the first rank, chief. See PRIMARY.]

prim·er[2] (prī'mər) *n.* **1.** a flat disk or other device that is filled with a small quantity of explosive and used to detonate the main charge in a cartridge, shell, or the like. **2.** a substance put on a surface in preparation for painting, esp. a first coat of paint applied as a base. **3.** a person or thing that primes. [PRIME + -ER[1].]

prime rate, the lowest rate of interest on loans offered by a bank at a particular time to its preferred customers.

prime time, the time period of television broadcasting that attracts the largest number of viewers, in the United States usually considered as from 7 P.M. to 11 P.M. —**prime'-time',** *adj.*

pri·me·val (prī mē'vəl) *adj.* of, relating to, or belonging to the first or earliest age or ages, esp. of the world; primitive. [Latin *prīmaevus* in the first period of life (from *prīmus* first + *aevum* age) + -AL[1].] —**pri·me'val·ly,** *adv.*

prim·ing (prī'ming) *n.* **1.** the powder or other material used to ignite an explosive charge. **2.** primer[2] *(def. 2).*

prim·i·tive (prim'i tiv) *adj.* **1.** of, relating to, or characteristic of an early or original stage, esp. in the development of something: *primitive life forms.* **2.** of, relating to, or characteristic of the earlier stages in the development of civilization or culture: *an exhibit of primitive artifacts.* **3.** crude or simple; unsophisticated: *primitive adobe huts, primitive manners.* **4.** not derived; original; basic. **5.a.** of, relating to, or characterized by naiveness, simplicity, and unsophistication and usually exhibiting a lack of formal technique: *to paint in a primitive style, a primitive portrait.* **b.** using a primitive style: *a primitive artist.* —*n.* **1.** a primitive artist, often self-taught. **2.** an artist active in the early stage of a movement or in an early artistic period. **3.** a work of art, esp. a painting, by such an artist. **4.** a member of a primitive people; person living in primitive times. [Latin *prīmitīvus* earliest of its kind, from *prīmus* first.] —**prim'i·tive·ly,** *adv.* —**prim'i·tive·ness,** *n.*

pri·mo·gen·i·tor (prī'mə jen'i tər) *n.* the earliest ancestor, as of a family. [Late Latin *prīmōgenitor,* going back to Latin *prīmus* first + *genitor* father.]

pri·mo·gen·i·ture (prī'mə jen'i chùr', -chər) *n.* **1.** the state or fact of being the first-born child of the same parents. **2.** a system of inheritance in which the eldest son has the right to inherit his father's entire estate. [Late Latin *prīmōgenitūra* a first birth, going back to Latin *prīmus* first + *genitūra* birth.]

pri·mor·di·al (prī môr'dē əl) *adj.* **1.** of, relating to, or existing at or from the very beginning; first in time or order. **2.** being the thing from which everything else derives; fundamental; basic. [Late Latin *prīmordiālis* original, from Latin *prīmordium* origin.] —**pri·mor'di·al·ly,** *adv.*

primp (primp) *v.t., v.i.* to dress, groom, or adorn, esp. with excessive or vain attention to detail. [Of uncertain origin.]

a	at	e	end	o	hot	u	up	hw	white		about
ā	ape	ē	me	ō	old	ū	use	ng	song		taken
ä	far	i	it	ô	fork	ü	rule	th	thin	ə	pencil
âr	care	ī	ice	oi	oil	ù	pull	th	this		lemon
				îr	pierce	ou	out	ûr	turn	zh	measure		circus

primrose plants

prim·rose (prim′rōz′) *n.* **1.** the trumpet-shaped flower of any of a large group of plants, genus *Primula,* cultivated as a garden flower. **2.** the plant bearing this flower. **3.** a pale greenish yellow color. —*adj.* **1.** designating a family, Primulaceae, of widely distributed plants growing mainly in the Northern Hemisphere, having flowers with petals united in a tube that flares out at the end, including the pimpernel, shooting star, and primrose. **2.** having the color primrose. [Medieval Latin *prima rosa* first rose, going back to Latin *prīmus* first + *rosa* rose (flower and bush).]
primrose path 1. a way of life characterized by ease, pleasure, and self-gratification: *the primrose path of dalliance* (Shakespeare, *Hamlet*). **2.** a course of action that appears easy but may prove disastrous.
prin. 1. principal. **2.** principle.
prince (prins) *n.* **1.** any male member of a royal family other than the sovereign, esp. a son or grandson in the paternal line of a British sovereign. **2.** a male sovereign; monarch. **3.** the ruler of a small state or territory. **4.** a high-ranking nobleman in certain countries. **5.** a person or thing that is preeminent in a group, class, or profession: *the prince of thieves, the prince of racing cars.* **6.** *Informal.* a fine, decent, or admirable person. [Old French *prince* sovereign, member of a royal house, the best of a group, from Latin *prīnceps* first man, leader.]
Prince Al·bert (al′bərt) a long, double-breasted frock coat. [Probably from *Prince Albert* (later Edward VII), who popularized it.]
prince consort, the husband of a female sovereign.
prince·dom (prins′dəm) *n.* **1.** the state or territory ruled by a prince; principality. **2.** the rank or dignity of a prince.
prince·ly (prins′lē) *adj.,* **-li·er, -li·est. 1.** of, relating to, or resembling a prince. **2.** suitable for a prince; lavish; sumptuous; magnificent: *a princely sum of money.* —**prince′li·ness,** *n.*
Prince of Darkness, the devil; Satan.
Prince of Wales (wālz) the male heir apparent to the British throne, a title usually given to the sovereign's eldest son.
prince royal, the eldest son and heir apparent of a sovereign.
prin·cess (prin′sis, -ses) *n.* **1.** any female member of a royal family other than the sovereign, esp. a daughter or granddaughter in the paternal line of a British sovereign. **2.** the wife of a prince. **3.** a female sovereign, esp. a female ruler of a principality. **4.** any woman considered as being like a princess, as in status or some quality. [French *princesse,* feminine of *prince.* See PRINCE.]
prin·cesse (prin ses′) *also,* **prin·cess.** *adj.* (of a woman's dress, coat, or similar garment) designed to fit closely and fall in an unbroken line from the shoulders to the hem. [French *princesse.* See PRINCESS.]
princess royal, the eldest daughter of a sovereign.
prin·ci·pal (prin′sə pəl) *adj.* greatest or first, as in importance, rank, or value; chief: *The striking workers made higher pay their principal demand.* —*n.* **1.** the administrative head of an elementary or secondary school, esp. a public school. **2.** a person who takes a leading part or plays the main role in some activity: *Who is the new principal in the play? She is one of the principals in the business.* **3.** an original sum of money borrowed or invested, exclusive of interest charged or income earned. **4.** the main body of an estate, as distinguished from income. **5.** *Law.* the person directly responsible for a crime. **6.** *Law.* a person or organization that authorizes another to act as agent. **7.** the person primarily responsible for legal obligations, as debts. [Latin *prīncipālis* chief,

first, from *prīnceps* first man, leader.] —For Synonyms *(adj.),* see main.
prin·ci·pal·i·ty (prin′sə pal′i tē) *n., pl.* **-ties. 1.** a state or territory ruled by a prince or from which a prince takes his title. **2.** the position or jurisdiction of a prince.
prin·ci·pal·ly (prin′sə pə lē, -si plē) *adv.* for the most part; mainly; chiefly.
principal parts, those forms of a verb from which all other inflected forms can be derived, consisting, in English, of the present infinitive, the past tense, and the past participle.
prin·ci·ple (prin′sə pəl) *n.* **1.** a fundamental truth, law, belief, or doctrine: *a government based on the principle that all people are created equal.* **2.** a rule of personal conduct: *It is my principle to answer letters promptly.* **3.** adherence to moral or ethical standards; sense of right or honorable action; integrity: *He is a man of principle.* **4.** ethical or moral standards or considerations collectively: *to act on principle.* **5.** a scientific rule or law concerned with or explaining the operation of a mechanical process or natural phenomenon: *to understand the principles of inertia.* **6.** a line of reasoning or mode of operation used as a basis for or guide to action: *the principles of formal debating.* [Modification of Latin *prīncipium* beginning, origin.]
prin·ci·pled (prin′sə pəld) *adj.* having, characterized by, or based on ethical or moral principles: *a principled decision.* ▶ often used in combination, as in *high-principled.*
prink (pringk) *v.t., v.i.* to dress, groom, or adorn in a showy manner; primp. [Possibly form of PRANK².]
print (print) *v.t.* **1.** to reproduce (a text, picture, or design) on a surface, as paper, by applying inked type, plates, or blocks. **2.** to reproduce a text, picture, or design on (a surface) by applying inked type, plates, or blocks. **3.** to cause to be printed; publish: *That newspaper printed the whole story.* **4.** to write in letters like those used in print: *Please print your name on the application.* **5.** to mark or indent by pressing or stamping: *to print butter with a trademark.* **6.** to produce, as a mark or indentation, by pressing or stamping: *The clerk printed the royal seal in the wax.* **7.** to impress or fix, as upon the mind or memory. **8.** to produce (a photograph) by transmission of light through a negative onto a sensitized surface. —*v.i.* **1.** to take an impression from or as from type, as in a printing press. **2.** to write in letters like those used in print. **3.** to produce something in print. **4.** to practice the trade of a printer. —*n.* **1.** printed lettering: *large print, clear print.* **2.** a mark or indentation made by pressing or stamping: *the print of a foot in the sand.* **3.** a device that produces a mark or figure by pressing or stamping, as a die, seal, or stamp. **4.** something that has been marked or formed by pressing or stamping: *a print of wax.* **5.** a picture or design printed from a block or plate. **6.** a photograph made from a negative. **7.** a printed publication, esp. a newspaper or periodical. **8.a.** a cloth with a design printed on it by means of dyes on engraved rollers, woodblocks, or screens. **b.** an article made of such cloth. [Old French *preinte* impression, stamp, from *preindre* to impress, stamp, from Latin *premere* to bear down upon.]
 • **in print. a.** in a printed form or state; published: *I finally saw my novel in print.* **b.** (of a book) still being printed and available for purchase from the publisher.
 • **out of print.** (of a book) no longer available for purchase from the publisher.
 • **to print out.** (of a computer) to produce (data, text, or graphics) in printed form.
print·a·ble (prin′tə bəl) *adj.* **1.** suitable for publication. **2.** capable of being printed or being printed from. —**print′a·bil′i·ty,** *n.*
printed circuit, an electric circuit consisting of a pattern of conducting material, such as copper, deposited on a flat plate or base of insulating material, widely used in electronic equipment.
print·er (prin′tər) *n.* **1.** a person or thing that prints, esp. a person or company whose business is printing. **2.** *Computers.* a device that delivers output data in printed form.
printer's devil, an apprentice or errand boy in a printing shop.
print·ing (prin′ting) *n.* **1.** the process, business, or art of producing printed matter, esp. by means of a printing press. **2.** something that is printed; printed matter. **3.** all the copies of a book or other matter printed at one time. **4.** writing that resembles that made by type.
printing press, a machine for producing copies by transferring ink from a metal plate, roller, or similar device to paper or other material. Also, **press¹.**
print·out (print′out′) *also,* **print-out.** *n.* the printed output of a computer, as on a sheet or continuous sheets of paper: *I will need a printout of the data for the afternoon meeting.*
pri·or¹ (prī′ər) *adj.* preceding in time, order, or importance: *a prior commitment.* [Latin *prior* sooner, former, superior.]
 • **prior to.** before.

pri·or² (prī′ər) *n.* a monk who ranks next below an abbot in a monastery or who is the superior of a priory. [Old English *prior* superior of a priory, from Late Latin *prior* administrator, superior, from Latin *prior* former, sooner, superior.]

pri·or·ess (prī′ər is) *n.* a nun who ranks next below an abbess in an abbey or who is the superior of a priory.

pri·or·i·tize (prī ôr′i tīz′, -or′-) *v.t.,* **-tized, -tiz·ing.** to rank or otherwise arrange in order of importance. —**pri·or′i·ti·za′tion,** *n.*

pri·or·i·ty (prī ôr′i tē, -or′-) *n., pl.* **-ties. 1.** the fact or condition of being first, as in order or importance. **2.** an acknowledged or established right to precedence or preferential treatment: *Emergency vehicles have priority on the road.* **3.** a matter or consideration deserving or receiving chief emphasis or attention: *Buying a new car was first on my list of priorities.*

priority mail, a class of mail for packages of more than 12 ounces, handled as first-class mail in the United States.

pri·o·ry (prī′ə rē) *n., pl.* **-ries.** a religious house ranking next below an abbey, governed by a prior or prioress. [Medieval Latin *prioria,* from Late Latin *prior* superior, administrator. See PRIOR².]

prise (prīz) *v.t.,* **prised, pris·ing.** prize⁴. —*n.* prize⁴.

prism (priz′əm) *n.* **1.** a polyhedron with two congruent and parallel faces, and whose other faces are parallelograms. **2.** a transparent solid having this shape, used for refracting or dispersing light or for breaking it up into its component colors. [Late Latin *prisma* the polyhedron, from Greek *prîsma* literally, something sawed, from *priein* to saw¹.]

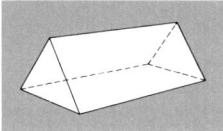

prism

pris·mat·ic (priz mat′ik) *adj.* **1.** of, relating to, or like a prism. **2.** formed by or as by a transparent prism. **3.** of varied colors; brilliant. Also, **pris·mat′i·cal.** —**pris·mat′i·cal·ly,** *adv.*

prismatic colors, the seven colors, red, orange, yellow, green, blue, indigo, and violet, that are produced when white light passes through a prism or water droplets; the colors of the visible spectrum.

pris·on (priz′ən) *n.* **1.** a building or institution in which persons convicted or accused of crimes are confined. **2.** any place of confinement. **3.** the state of being held against one's will; imprisonment. —*v.t.* imprison. [Old French *prison* building for the confinement of criminals, from Latin *prēnsiō,* form of *prehēnsiō* a seizing.]

pris·on·er (priz′ə nər) *n.* **1.** a person confined in a prison. **2.** a person who is arrested or taken into custody. **3.** a person or thing that is forcibly restrained, deprived of freedom, or held in captivity. **4.** prisoner of war.

prisoner of war, a person captured or held by the enemy in war.

pris·sy (pris′ē) *adj.,* **-si·er, -si·est.** very prim, fussy, or prudish. [Blend of PRIM and SISSY.] —**pris′si·ly,** *adv.* —**pris′si·ness,** *n.*

pris·tine (pris′tēn) *adj.* **1.** of or relating to the earliest time, period, or condition; original: *to restore an old house to its pristine state.* **2.** so new as to be untouched; uncorrupted; unspoiled: *the pristine beauty of freshly fallen snow.* [Latin *pristīnus* former, primitive.]

prith·ee (prith′ē) *interj. Archaic.* I pray thee; please.

pri·va·cy (prī′və sē; *British* priv′ə sē) *n., pl.* **-cies. 1.** the state or condition of being private, secluded, or isolated: *The writer needed privacy to finish the novel.* **2.** the right to be free from interference with one's private affairs: *Opening someone else's mail is an invasion of privacy.* **3.** the condition of not being generally known; secrecy: *I tell you this in privacy.*

pri·vate (prī′vit) *adj.* **1.** belonging or restricted to or reserved for a particular person or persons: *a private driveway, private property, a private club.* **2.** of or relating to one person; personal; individual: *private thoughts.* **3.** not intended for general or public knowledge; confidential: *a private conversation, a private matter.* **4.** not holding public office or having an official position: *a private citizen.* **5.** not supported or managed by or connected with the government: *an agency under private control.* **6.** away from the public; secluded; isolated: *We found a private spot for our picnic.* **7.** preferring to keep to oneself: *Our neighbor is a very private person.* —*n.* **1.** in the U.S. Army and Marine Corps, an enlisted person of the lowest rank. **2.** **privates.** private parts. [Latin *prīvātus* apart from the state, belonging to an individual. Doublet of PRIVY.] —**pri′vate·ly,** *adv.* —**pri′vate·ness,** *n.*

•**in private.** confidentially or secretly; privately.

private detective, a detective who is employed by a private person or group rather than a police force or government agency. Also, **private investigator.**

private enterprise, free enterprise.

pri·va·teer (prī′və tīr′) *n.* **1.** a privately owned armed ship commissioned by a government to attack enemy ships, esp. merchant ships. **2.** the commander or a member of the crew of such a ship. —*v.i.* to sail on or as a privateer.

private eye *Informal.* private detective.

private first class 1. in the U.S. Army, an enlisted person ranking below a corporal and above a private. **2.** in the U.S. Marine Corps, an enlisted person ranking below a lance corporal and above a private.

private investigator, private detective.

private parts, the external sexual organs; genitals. Also, **privates.**

private school, a school that is supported and managed by a private group rather than by the government.

pri·va·tion (prī vā′shən) *n.* **1.** the lack of the comforts or necessities of life or the condition resulting from such a lack. **2.** the act of depriving or the state of being deprived. [Latin *prīvātiō* a taking away.]

priv·a·tive (priv′ə tiv) *adj.* **1.** causing deprivation or loss. **2.** *Grammar.* altering the meaning of a word from positive to negative, as by means of a prefix. —*n. Grammar.* a privative prefix or suffix. [Latin *prīvātīvus* denoting privation, negative, from *prīvāre* to deprive, rob.] —**priv′a·tive·ly,** *adv.*

pri·va·tize (prī′və tīz′) *v.t.,* **-tized, -tiz·ing.** to transfer (an enterprise) from public or government control or ownership to private interests. [PRIVATE + -IZE.] —**pri′va·ti·za′tion,** *n.*

priv·et (priv′it) *n.* any of a group of shrubs or small trees, genus *Ligustrum,* of the olive family, widely used for hedges, usually having white flowers and black berries. [Of uncertain origin.]

priv·i·lege (priv′ə lij, priv′lij) *n.* **1.** a special right, advantage, benefit, or immunity granted to or enjoyed by a certain person, group, or class. **2.** a basic civil right: *the privileges or immunities of citizens of the United States.* —*v.t.,* **-leged, -leg·ing.** to grant a privilege to. [Latin *prīvilēgium* law for or against an individual, from *prīvus* one's own, individual + *lēx* law.]

priv·i·leged (priv′ə lijd, priv′lijd) *adj.* **1.** having or enjoying a privilege or privileges. **2.** for only certain specified persons; confidential; restricted: *privileged information.* **3.** *Law.* not required to be stated or exhibited in court or in a judicial hearing: *Conversations between doctor and patient relative to medical treatment are privileged.*

priv·i·ly (priv′ə lē) *adv.* in secret; privately; secretly.

priv·y (priv′ē) *adj.* **1.** participating in the knowledge of something secret or private (with *to*): *Only three people were privy to the plot.* **2.** *Archaic.* secret; concealed. **3.** *Archaic.* private; personal. —*n., pl.* **priv·ies.** outhouse (*def. 1*). [Old French *prive* intimate, private, from Latin *prīvātus* belonging to an individual. Doublet of PRIVATE.]

Privy Council, an honorary advisory body appointed by the British sovereign, having about 300 members. —**privy councilor;** *also,* **privy councillor.**

privy seal, in Great Britain, a seal affixed to certain documents.

prix fixe (prē′fiks′) *pl.* **prix fixes** (prē′fiks′). **1.** a complete meal served at a fixed price. **2.** the price charged for such a meal. [French *prix fixe* fixed price, going back to Latin *pretium* price, value and *fixus,* past participle of *figere* to fasten.]

prize¹ (prīz) *n.* **1.** something offered or won as a reward, esp. for winning in a competition or in a game of chance. **2.** anything

a	at	e	end	o	hot	u	up	hw	white		about
ā	ape	ē	me	ō	old	ū	use	ng	song	ə	taken
ä	far	i	it	ô	fork	ü	rule	th	thin		pencil
âr	care	ī	ice	oi	oil	u̇	pull	th	this		lemon
		îr	pierce	ou	out	ûr	turn	zh	measure		circus

worth striving for. —*adj.* **1.** that has won or is likely to win a prize: *a prize painting.* **2.** offered or given as a prize. **3.** worthy of a prize; outstanding: *a prize performance.* [Old French *pris* value, honor, from Latin *pretium* value, reward.]

Synonyms **Prize**, **reward**, and **award** mean something given to someone in recognition of service or achievement. **Prize** specifies something won in a competition: *Annette's project won a prize in the science fair.* **Reward** refers to something given in return for a specific service: *Michael received a reward for finding the lost briefcase.* **Award** indicates an honor given by a judge or organization for general merit or a specific accomplishment: *The group's first album received an award.*

prize² (prīz) *n.* something seized or taken, esp. an enemy ship captured at sea during wartime. [Old French *prise* seizure, booty, from *prendre* to take, from Latin *prehendere* to seize.]

prize³ (prīz) *v.t.,* **prized, priz·ing 1.** to value or esteem highly: *to prize a friend's advice.* **2.** to estimate the value of; appraise; evaluate. [Old French *pr(e)isier* to value, esteem, from Late Latin *pretiāre* to value, from Latin *pretium* value.] —For Synonyms *(v.t.),* see **cherish.**

prize⁴ (prīz) *also,* **prise.** *v.t.,* **prized, priz·ing.** to raise or force with a lever; pry. —*n.* **1.** an instrument used for prying; lever. **2.** leverage. [From PRIZE².]

prize·fight (prīz′fīt′) *n.* a boxing match between professional boxers. —**prize′fight′er,** *n.* —**prize′fight′ing,** *n.*

prize ring, a rope-enclosed area, usually on a raised platform, in which boxers fight.

prize·win·ner (prīz′win′ər) *n.* a person or thing that has been awarded a prize in a competition: *Our heifer was a prizewinner at the state fair last year.* —**prize′win′ning,** *adj.*

pro¹ (prō) *adv.* in favor of; for. —*n., pl.* **pros.** a reason, argument, or person in favor of something: *The speaker listed all the pros and cons of the proposal.* [Latin *prō* in favor of, for.]

pro² (prō) *Informal. n., pl.* **pros. 1.** a professional. **2. the pros.** a professional sports league or leagues: *Can this college star succeed in the pros?* —*adj.* professional: *a pro tennis tournament.* [Short for PROFESSIONAL.]

pro-¹ *prefix* **1.** in favor of; supporting; in behalf of: *proslavery.* **2.** forward; forth; out: *progress, project.* **3.** in place of; acting as; substituting for: *pronoun.* [Latin *prō* in favor of, for, before, instead of.]

pro-² *prefix* before in time or place: *prognosis, prologue.* [Greek *pro.*]

pro·a (prō′ə) *n.* a swift Malay boat having a triangular sail and a single outrigger. [Malay *prāu.*]

prob. 1. probable. **2.** probably. **3.** problem.

prob·a·bil·i·ty (prob′ə bil′i tē) *n., pl.* **-ties. 1.** the quality or state of being probable; likelihood: *A willingness to negotiate increased the probability of an early settlement.* **2.** something that is probable or likely. **3.** *Mathematics.* a measure of the likelihood that a certain event will occur, expressed as the ratio of the number of chances favoring the occurrence of the event to the total number of possible occurrences.

 ·**in all probability.** most probably; very likely.

prob·a·ble (prob′ə bəl) *adj.* **1.** more likely to occur than not; that can reasonably be expected: *The experts all agreed on the probable outcome of the boxing match.* **2.** likely to be true but not certain; plausible: *a probable answer.* [Latin *probābilis* provable, likely, from *probāre* to try, test, approve, demonstrate.]

probable cause *Law.* a standard by which various legal procedures may be justified. Probable cause to obtain a search warrant consists of reason to believe that a person or evidence pertinent to a case or investigation are to be found at the place named. Probable cause to proceed with a lawsuit or prosecution consists of a reasonable belief that the defendant is liable or guilty as charged.

prob·a·bly (prob′ə blē) *adv.* most likely; in all likelihood.

pro·bate (prō′bāt) *n.* the act or process of proving that a will is genuine and of distributing property according to its terms. —*adj.* of or relating to a probate court or to probate. —*v.t.,* **-bat·ed, -bat·ing.** to establish the authenticity or validity of (a will). [Latin *probātum* thing proved or approved, from *probāre* to test, demonstrate, approve.]

probate court, a court having jurisdiction over the probate of

proa

wills and over the administration of the property of deceased persons.

pro·ba·tion (prō bā′shən) *n.* **1.** a testing or trial of the ability, qualifications, or suitability of a person, as a new employee, usually for a specified period of time. **2.** *Law.* the action or practice of allowing a person convicted of a minor or first offense to go free under close supervision and on the condition that his or her behavior be exemplary. **3.** the period of being under such supervision or the status of someone under such supervision: *to be on probation.* [Latin *probātiō* a proving, approval.] —**pro·ba′tion·al, pro·ba′tion·ar′y,** *adj.*

pro·ba·tion·er (prō bā′shə nər) *n.* a person who is on probation.

probation officer, an officer appointed to supervise a probationer.

pro·ba·tive (prō′bə tiv) *adj.* **1.** affording proof or evidence. **2.** serving or designed to test. Also, **pro′ba·to′ry.**

probe (prōb) *n.* **1.** a thorough investigation or examination: *The court case led to a Senate probe into prison conditions.* **2.** a slender surgical instrument for exploring a body cavity, wound, or similar opening. **3.** a device, mechanism, or object used for investigation or exploration, esp. a space probe. —*v.,* **probed, prob·ing.** —*v.t.* **1.** to investigate, examine, or explore thoroughly: *The police probed all the details of the crime.* **2.** to examine or explore with a surgical probe. —*v.i.* to conduct a thorough investigation or examination: *Scientists probed into the nature of the substance.* [Medieval Latin *proba* examination, from Late Latin *proba* proof, from Latin *probāre* to test, demonstrate.] —**prob′er,** *n.* —For Synonyms *(n.),* see **inquiry.**

pro·bi·ty (prō′bi tē, prob′i-) *n.* the quality of being honest and upright; moral strength or excellence; integrity. [Latin *probitās* honesty, goodness.] —For Synonyms, see **honesty.**

prob·lem (prob′ləm) *n.* **1.** a question, situation, or condition that is difficult, perplexing, or unresolved: *Air pollution is a major problem facing our cities.* **2.** a person who is troublesome or causes difficulty: *The child was a problem to all the teachers.* **3.** a question proposed for consideration, discussion, or solution: *a physics problem.* —*adj.* **1.** being a problem; difficult to handle: *a problem child.* **2.** concerned with or presenting a moral or social problem, as a play or story. [Latin *problēma* question proposed for solution, from Greek *problēma* something put forward (as for discussion).]

prob·lem·at·ic (prob′lə mat′ik) *adj.* constituting, presenting, or involving a problem; uncertain. Also, **prob′lem·at′i·cal.** —**prob′lem·at′i·cal·ly,** *adv.*

pro bo·no (prō bō′nō) in reference to legal and other professional services, free of charge, so as to benefit the public, esp. less privileged sectors of the public: *to file a pro bono lawsuit, to work pro bono one day a week.* [Latin *pro bono* for the good.]

pro bo·no pu·bli·co (prō bō′nō pub′li kō′, pü′bli kō′) *Latin.* for the public good.

pro·bos·cis (prō bos′is) *n., pl.* **-bos·cis·es** or **-bos·ci·des** (-bos′i dēz′). **1.** the trunk of an elephant. **2.** a long, flexible snout, as of a tapir. **3.** the long, tubular mouthparts of certain insects, as mosquitoes and butterflies, adapted for sucking or piercing. **4.** the human nose. ➡ used humorously in def. 4. [Latin *proboscis* elephant's trunk, snout, from Greek *proboskis* elephant's trunk, from *pro-* before + *boskein* to feed.]

pro·caine (prō′kān) *n.* a synthetic drug widely used as a local anesthetic in dentistry and medicine. [PRO-¹ + (CO)CAINE.]

pro·cam·bi·um (prō kam′bē əm) *n. Botany.* the portion of the meristem that gives rise to the vascular bundles and, in most woody plants, the cambium. [Modern Latin *procambium.* See PRO-², CAMBIUM.] —**pro·cam′bi·al,** *adj.*

pro·car·y·ote (prō kar′ē ōt′) *n.* prokaryote. —**pro·car·y·ot·ic** (prō kar′ē ot′ik) *adj.*

pro·ce·dure (prə sē′jər) *n.* **1.** a particular accepted or prescribed course of action, esp. one that follows a definite order of steps: *What is the proper procedure for applying for a job here?* **2.** a customary or established way of conducting legal, parliamentary, or similar business. **3.** a manner of proceeding or acting. [French *procédure,* from *procéder* to come, go on, originate (from), from Latin *prōcēdere* to go forward.] —**pro·ce′du·ral,** *adj.* —**pro·ce′du·ral·ly,** *adv.* —For Synonyms, see **process.**

pro·ceed (prə sēd′) *v.i.* **1.** to continue, esp. after a stop or interruption: *The politician waited for the applause to die down and then proceeded with the speech.* **2.** to begin or undertake some action or process: *The mechanic jacked up the car and proceeded to change the tire.* **3.** to move on or forward: *The parade proceeded down Main Street.* **4.** to be carried on or put into action: *The experiment is proceeding as planned.* **5.** to come or originate (with *from*): *My ambition to become a nurse proceeded from a desire to help others.* **6.** to institute and carry on a legal action (often with

against). [Latin *prōcēdere* to go forward.] —For Synonyms, see **advance.**

pro·ceed·ing (prə sē′ding) *n.* **1.** an action or course of action; procedure. **2. proceedings.** a series of actions or events; happenings: *The police investigated the strange proceedings at the house.* **3. proceedings.** a record of business transacted at a meeting of a society or similar organization. **4.** *Law.* **a. proceedings.** legal action: *contempt proceedings.* **b.** the instituting and carrying on of legal action.

pro·ceeds (prō′sēdz) *pl. n.* the money or profit derived from a commercial undertaking, esp. money raised for a particular cause.

proc·ess (pros′es, prō′ses) *n.* **1.** a series of operations in the production of something: *the process of making butter.* **2.** a series of continuous changes or actions leading to a specified end: *the process of growth.* **3.** the course or lapse (of time): *In the process of time the job will be done.* **4.** the course of being done or going on: *The house is in the process of being built.* **5.** *Law.* **a.** a writ or summons by which a person is ordered to appear in court in a legal action. **b.** all of the proceedings in a legal action. **6.** *Biology.* an outgrowth of tissue or a protruding part: *a bony process.* —*v.t.* **1.** to handle by routine procedures: *to process applicants for a job.* **2.** to treat, make, or prepare, as by special method: *to process cheese.* **3.** *Law.* **a.** to institute legal action against. **b.** to serve a writ or summons on. —*adj.* made or prepared by some special series of operations: *process cheese.* [Old French *proces* legal proceedings, progress, from Latin *prōcessus* a going forward.]

Synonyms *n.* **Process, procedure,** and **method** mean a series of actions by which something is done. **Process** is used of an activity that involves distinct, connected steps or stages: *The biology teacher explained the digestive process.* **Procedure** emphasizes the steps of a process: *The flight instructor carefully outlined the procedure for takeoff.* **Method** suggests a systematic plan of the techniques to be followed: *The book describes special methods of teaching adults to play the piano.*

pro·ces·sion (prə sesh′ən) *n.* **1.** a continuous or steady forward movement or progression, esp. in a formal, orderly, or ceremonious manner. **2.** a group of persons or things moving along in this way, often in a long line: *The wedding procession moved slowly down the aisle.* **3.** any continuous course or succession: *the endless procession of day and night.* —*v.i. Archaic.* to move in procession. [Late Latin *prōcessiō* religious procession, from Latin *prōcessiō* a marching forward.]

pro·ces·sion·al (prə sesh′ə nəl) *adj.* of, relating to, or moving in a procession. —*n.* **1.** music accompanying or designed for a procession. **2.** a book containing the hymns, prayers, and rituals to be used in religious processions.

proc·es·sor (pros′es ər, prō′ses-) *n.* **1.** a person or thing that processes. **2.a.** central processing unit. **b.** microprocessor. **3.** food processor.

process server, a person who is authorized to deliver legal documents, such as writs, summonses, and subpoenas.

pro·choice (prō chois′) *adj.* favoring the right to obtain an abortion; supporting legalized abortion.

pro·claim (prə klām′) *v.t.* **1.** to announce officially; declare publicly: *to proclaim a truce.* **2.** to make clear; reveal: *The child's tears proclaimed great sadness.* [Latin *prōclāmāre* to cry out, call out.] —For Synonyms, see **declare.**

proc·la·ma·tion (prok′lə mā′shən) *n.* **1.** something that is proclaimed, esp. an official public announcement. **2.** the act of proclaiming.

pro·cliv·i·ty (prō kliv′i tē) *n., pl.* -ties. a tendency or inclination; propensity: *a proclivity to complain.* [Latin *prōclīvitās* tendency, steep descent.]

Proc·ne (prok′nē) *n.* see **Philomela.**

pro·con·sul (prō kon′səl) *n.* **1.** the governor or military commander of an ancient Roman province. **2.** the administrator of a colony, dependency, or occupied country, usually having extensive power. [Latin *prōcōnsul* the Roman governor, from *prō cōnsule* for the consul.] —**pro·con′su·lar,** *adj.* —**pro·con·su·late** (prō kon′sə lit), **pro·con′sul·ship′,** *n.*

pro·cras·ti·nate (prō kras′tə nāt′) *v.,* -nat·ed, -nat·ing. —*v.i.* to put off doing something until a future time, esp. to do this habitually. —*v.t.* to put off until a future time; postpone; defer. [Latin *prōcrāstinātus,* past participle of *prōcrāstināre* to delay, going back to *pro-* forward + *crās* tomorrow.] —**pro·cras′ti·na′tion,** *n.* —**pro·cras′ti·na′tor,** *n.*

pro·cre·ate (prō′krē āt′) *v.,* -at·ed, -at·ing. —*v.t.* to produce or beget (offspring). —*v.i.* to produce offspring. [Latin *prōcreātus,* past participle of *prōcreāre* to produce.] —**pro′cre·a′tion,** *n.* —**pro′cre·a′tor,** *n.*

pro·cre·a·tive (prō′krē ā′tiv) *adj.* **1.** capable of procreating. **2.** of or relating to procreation.

Pro·crus·te·an (prō krus′tē ən) *also,* **pro·crus·te·an.** *adj.*

1. of, relating to, or characteristic of Procrustes. **2.** forcing conformity by severe means.

Pro·crus·tes (prō krus′tēz) *n.* in Greek legend, a robber who stretched or mutilated his victims to make them fit the length of his bed.

proc·tol·o·gy (prok tol′ə jē) *n.* the branch of medicine dealing with the structure and diseases of the rectum and anus. [Greek *prōktos* anus + -LOGY.] —**proc·to·log·ic** (prok′tə loj′ik); *also,* **proc′to·log′i·cal,** *adj.* —**proc·tol′o·gist,** *n.*

proc·tor (prok′tər) *n.* **1.** a person appointed to maintain order and supervise students during an examination at a college or university. **2.** a person appointed to manage another's affairs or to represent another in a court of law. —*v.t.* to act as proctor for (an examination); supervise. [Contraction of PROCURATOR.] —**proc·to·ri·al** (prok tôr′ē əl), *adj.* —**proc′tor·ship′,** *n.*

pro·cum·bent (prō kum′bənt) *adj.* **1.** lying face down; prostrate; prone. **2.** *Botany.* (of a stem or plant) lying along the ground but not taking root. [Latin *prōcumbēns,* present participle of *prōcumbere* to fall forward.]

proc·u·ra·tor (prok′yə rā′tər) *n.* **1.** a person who manages the affairs of another or is authorized to act in another's behalf, as an agent or attorney. **2.** the chief financial agent or chief administrator of a province or district in the Roman Empire. [Latin *prōcūrātor.*] —**proc·u·ra·to·ri·al** (prok′yər ə tôr′ē əl), *adj.*

pro·cure (prə kyúr′) *v.,* -cured, -cur·ing. —*v.t.* **1.** to acquire or obtain, esp. with effort. **2.** to bring about; effect; cause. **3.** to obtain (women) for the purpose of prostitution. —*v.i.* to procure women. [Late Latin *prōcūrāre* to obtain, from Latin *prōcūrāre* to take care of, manage.] —**pro·cur′a·ble,** *adj.* —**pro·cure′ment,** *n.* —**pro·cur′er,** *n.*

Pro·cy·on (prō′sē on′) *n.* a double star, one of the brightest stars in the sky and the brightest in the constellation Canis Minor.

prod (prod) *v.t.,* prod·ded, prod·ding. **1.** to push or jab, as with a pointed instrument. **2.** to stir to action; rouse. —*n.* **1.** a push or jab, as with a pointed instrument. **2.** a pointed instrument used for prodding, as a goad. **3.** something that stirs to action. [Of uncertain origin.] —**prod′der,** *n.*

prod. **1.** produced. **2.** product.

prod·i·gal (prod′i gəl) *adj.* **1.** recklessly extravagant; wasteful: *The couple's prodigal spending habits brought them close to bankruptcy.* **2.** lavish or generous (often with *of*): *to be prodigal of hospitality.* **3.** existing in abundance; profuse: *prodigal talents.* —*n.* a person who is recklessly extravagant. [Late Latin *prōdigālis* wasteful, from Latin *prōdigus.*] —**prod·i·gal·i·ty** (prod′i gal′i tē), *n.* —**prod′i·gal·ly,** *adv.* —For Synonyms *(adj.),* see **wasteful.**

pro·di·gious (prə dij′əs) *adj.* **1.** huge or extraordinary in size, number, or degree; enormous: *The jagged peaks rose to a prodigious height.* **2.** causing amazement; marvelous: *a prodigious feat of strength.* [Latin *prōdigiōsus* strange, marvelous, from *prōdigium* portent, omen.] —**pro·di·gious·ly,** *adv.* —**pro·di·gious·ness,** *n.*

prod·i·gy (prod′i jē) *n., pl.* -gies. **1.** an extraordinarily gifted or talented person, esp. a child. **2.** something that causes wonder or amazement; marvel. **3.** *Archaic.* omen; portent. [Latin *prōdigium* portent, omen.]

pro·duce (*v.,* prə düs′, -dūs′; *n.,* prod′üs, -ūs, prō′düs, -dūs) *v.,* -duced, -duc·ing. —*v.t.* **1.** to make or bring into being, esp. by means of machinery and on a large scale; manufacture: *a company that produces steel.* **2.** to bring forth; yield; bear: *A cow produces milk. Our dog produced a litter of five puppies.* **3.** to bring into existence by mental or artistic effort; create: *a playwright who produced some of the greatest works of our time.* **4.** to give rise to; cause: *The startling news produced little reaction from those present.* **5.** to bring forward or present; show; furnish: *The prosecution could not produce any convincing evidence.* **6.** to prepare (a motion picture or similar form of entertainment) for public presentation, as by securing financial backing and hiring performers. **7.** *Geometry.* to lengthen or extend, as a line or plane. —*v.i.* to bring forth or make something: *These workers produce at a very fast rate.* —*n.* **1.** something that is produced. **2.** farm products, esp. fresh fruit and vegetables. [Latin *prōdūcere* to bring forward, bring forth.] —**pro·duc′i·ble,** *adj.*

pro·duc·er (prə dü′sər, -dū′-) *n.* **1.** a person or thing that produces. **2.** a person or organization that uses basic resources, as land or raw materials, to produce goods or services for consumer use. **3.** a person in charge of producing a play, motion picture, or

a	at	e	end	o	hot	u	up	hw	white		about
ā	ape	ē	me	ō	old	ū	use	ng	song		taken
ä	far	i	it	ô	fork	ü	rule	th	thin	ə	pencil
âr	care	ī	ice	oi	oil	ú	pull	th	this		lemon
		îr	pierce	ou	out	ûr	turn	zh	measure		circus

similar entertainment. **4.** an organism at the lowest level of the food chain, using inorganic substances to make its own food, as by photosynthesis.

producer gas, a mixture of carbon monoxide, nitrogen, and hydrogen prepared by the combustion of coke, used as a fuel in industrial processes.

producer goods, goods, such as machinery, tools, or raw materials, used to produce consumer goods, such as food and clothing. ➡ distinguished from **consumer goods.**

prod·uct (prod′ukt, -ǝkt) *n.* **1.** anything that is produced: *dairy products.* **2.** something brought about; result; consequence. **3.a.** a number or algebraic expression obtained by multiplication. **b.** a scalar product or vector product. [Latin *prōductum* something produced, from *prōdūcere* to bring forward, bring forth.]

pro·duc·tion (prǝ duk′shǝn) *n.* **1.** the act or process of producing. **2.** something that is produced, esp. a play, motion picture, or similar form of entertainment presented to the public. **3.** the amount of something produced: *Production of apples is up this year.*

production line, assembly line.

pro·duc·tive (prǝ duk′tiv) *adj.* **1.** producing abundantly; fertile or prolific: *productive land, a productive author.* **2.** having favorable, useful, or positive results; fruitful; effective: *Talks to end the strike have not been very productive.* **3.** yielding goods and services at a profit: *a productive business.* **4.** producing, tending to produce, or capable of producing (often with *of*): *The discussions seem productive only of more confusion.* —**pro·duc′tive·ly,** *adv.* —**pro·duc′tive·ness,** *n.*

pro·duc·tiv·i·ty (prō′dǝk tiv′i tē, prod′ǝk-) *n.* the state or quality of being productive.

pro·em (prō′em) *n.* an introductory statement or comment, as in a book; preface. [Latin *prooemium,* from Greek *prooimion,* from *pro* before + *oimos* way, path.]

prof (prof) *n. Informal.* professor.

Prof., professor.

prof·a·na·tion (prof′ǝ nā′shǝn, prō′fǝ-) *n.* an act or instance of profaning.

pro·fane (prō fān′, prǝ-) *adj.* **1.** showing or characterized by irreverence, disrespect, or contempt for God or sacred things; blasphemous. **2.** not concerned with or relating to religion or religious matters; secular. **3.** not consecrated to religious uses; not holy. **4.** vulgar; common; obscene. —*v.t.,* -**faned,** -**fan·ing.** **1.** to treat (something sacred) with irreverence, disrespect, or contempt; desecrate: *to profane an altar.* **2.** to put to wrong, degrading, or unworthy use; debase; abuse: *to profane one's talents.* [Latin *prōfānus* not sacred, unholy, from *prō* before (outside) + *fānum* temple.] —**pro·fan·a·to·ry** (prǝ fan′ǝ tôr′ē, prō-), *adj.* —**pro·fane′ly,** *adv.* —**pro·fane′ness,** *n.* —**pro·fan′er,** *n.*

pro·fan·i·ty (prō fan′i tē, prǝ-) *n., pl.* -**ties. 1.** profane language or a profane act. **2.** the use of profane or vulgar language. **3.** the quality or state of being profane.

pro·fess (prǝ fes′) *v.t.* **1.** to claim, esp. falsely or insincerely: *This writer professes to know everything about sculpture.* **2.** to declare openly; affirm: *We profess ourselves to be loyal citizens.* **3.** to affirm one's faith in: *to profess Judaism.* **4.** to have as one's profession; claim knowledge of or skill in: *to profess law.* —*v.i.* to make a declaration or affirmation. [From PROFESSED.]

pro·fessed (prǝ fest′) *adj.* **1.** declared insincerely or deceptively; pretended: *His professed ignorance is only a façade.* **2.** openly declared; affirmed: *a professed enemy.* **3.** having taken the vows of a religious order: *a professed nun.* [Latin *prōfessus* manifest, confessed, past participle of *prōfitērī* to declare publicly + -ED².] —**pro·fess·ed·ly** (prǝ fes′id lē), *adv.*

pro·fes·sion (prǝ fesh′ǝn) *n.* **1.** an occupation that requires special education and training, as law, medicine, or theology. **2.** the body of persons following such an occupation: *The young doctor was already a leading member of the medical profession.* **3.** any activity considered as a profession: *the acting profession.* **4.** an act or instance of professing or declaring: *a profession of loyalty.* **5.** an affirmation of faith in a religion. **6.** a professed or avowed religion or faith. **7.** the act of taking vows of a religious order following the period of novitiate. [Latin *professiō* declaration, a business.]

pro·fes·sion·al (prǝ fesh′ǝ nǝl) *adj.* **1.** of, relating to, characteristic of, or suitable for a profession or a person engaged in a profession: *a doctor's fee for professional services, professional training.* **2.** engaged in a profession: *professional people.* **3.** having as the source of one's livelihood an activity or occupation not usually pursued for gain, esp. a sport: *a professional golfer.* **4.** engaged in by professionals as opposed to amateurs: *professional basketball.* **5.** engaged in a certain activity as if it were a profession: *a professional revolutionary, a professional student.* —*n.* **1.** a person engaged in a profession. **2.** a person having as the source of livelihood an activity or occupation not usually pursued for gain, esp. a professional athlete. **3.** a person whose ability or professional approach to work or some undertaking is unquestionable or quite evident: *Their calm manner made it obvious that they were no novice firefighters, but professionals.* —**pro·fes′sion·al·ly,** *adv.*

pro·fes·sion·al·ism (prǝ fesh′ǝ nǝ liz′ǝm) *n.* professional methods, spirit, character, or status.

pro·fes·sor (prǝ fes′ǝr) *n.* **1.** a teacher of the highest rank in a college, university, or other institution of higher education. **2.** *Informal.* any teacher. **3.** a person who professes skill in or teaches some sport or art. ➡ sometimes used humorously. **4.** a person who professes, esp. one who affirms his or her faith in religion. [Latin *professor* teacher, from *prōfitērī* to declare publicly.]

pro·fes·sor·ate (prǝ fes′ǝr it) *n.* the office, position, or term of office of a professor.

pro·fes·so·ri·al (prō′fǝ sôr′ē ǝl, prof′ǝ-) *adj.* of, relating to, or characteristic of a professor. —**pro′fes·so′ri·al·ly,** *adv.*

pro·fes·sor·ship (prǝ fes′ǝr ship′) *n.* the position or duties of a professor.

prof·fer (prof′ǝr) *v.t.* to present for acceptance; offer. —*n.* something presented for acceptance; offer. [Anglo-Norman *profrer* to offer, going back to Latin *prō* before + *offerre* to bring before, present.]

pro·fi·cien·cy (prǝ fish′ǝn sē) *n., pl.* -**cies.** the state or quality of being proficient.

pro·fi·cient (prǝ fish′ǝnt) *adj.* highly skilled; expert; adept: *Years of practice have made the artist proficient in portraiture.* —*n. Archaic.* expert. [Latin *prōficiēns,* present participle of *prōficere* to advance, accomplish.] —**pro·fi′cient·ly,** *adv.* —For Synonyms, see **expert.**

pro·file (prō′fīl) *n.* **1.a.** a side view, esp. of a human face or head. **b.** an outline of this or a drawing or other representation of such an outline. **2.** any outline or representation of an outline: *The mountain's jagged profile stood out against the darkening sky.* **3.** a brief biographical sketch. **4.** an analysis, usually represented by means of a graph or diagram, of some person, process, or thing: *a personality profile, a voter profile.* **5.** a representation of a cutaway side view or vertical section of an architectural structure or land surface. **6.** soil profile. —*v.t.,* -**filed,** -**fil·ing,** to make, draw, or write a profile of: *The scout profiled each prospect for the coach.* [Italian *profilo* outline, side view, going back to Latin *prō* before + *fīlum* thread.] —For Synonyms *(n.),* see **outline.**

Renaissance **profiles** by Piero della Francesca

prof·it (prof′it) *n.* **1.** *also,* **profits.** the money remaining after all the costs of a business or business transaction, including the initial investment, have been paid. **2.** *also,* **profits.** financial gain, esp. the return or income received from investment or property. **3.** the difference between the initial cost of an item and its selling price. **4.** benefit or advantage; gain. —*v.i.* **1.** to derive benefit or profit; gain: *to profit from an experience.* **2.** to be of advantage, use, or benefit. —*v.t.* to be of advantage, use, or benefit to. [Old French *profit* advantage, gain from property, from Latin *prōfectus* advance, progress.] —For Synonyms *(n.),* see **benefit.**

prof·it·a·ble (prof′i tǝ bǝl) *adj.* **1.** yielding a financial profit: *a profitable business.* **2.** to one's advantage; beneficial; useful: *a profitable experience.* —**prof′it·a·bil′i·ty,** **prof′it·a·ble·ness,** *n.* —**prof′it·a·bly,** *adv.*

prof·it·eer (prof′i tîr′) *n.* a person who makes or seeks to make excessive profits, esp. by selling goods at exorbitant prices during a time of shortage. —*v.i.* to act as a profiteer.

profit sharing, a system by which employees are given a share of

the profits of a business in addition to their regular salary or wages. —**prof′it-shar′ing,** *adj.*

prof·li·gate (prof′li git) *adj.* **1.** totally corrupt with regard to one's morals; thoroughly immoral; dissolute. **2.** recklessly extravagant or wasteful. —*n.* a profligate person. [Latin *prōflīgātus* wretched, dissolute, past participle of *prōflīgāre* to dash to the ground, ruin.] —**prof·li·ga·cy** (prof′li gə sē), **prof′li·gate·ness,** *n.* —**prof′li·gate·ly,** *adv.*

pro for·ma (prō fôr′mə) *Latin.* as a matter of form; for the sake of form; as a formality. [Latin *pro forma* literally, for form.]

pro·found (prə found′) *adj.* **1.** showing or characterized by great understanding, knowledge, or insight: *a profound idea, a profound literary work.* **2.** coming from or penetrating to the depth of one's being; intensely felt: *We experienced profound sorrow upon hearing the news.* **3.** having a great or extensive effect; far-reaching: *The invention of the wheel has had a profound influence on the course of human history.* **4.** with no qualifications; absolute; complete; thorough: *a profound silence.* **5.** situated or extending far beneath the surface; of great depth: *the profound sea.* **6.** reaching far down; deep: *a profound obeisance.* [Old French *profond* deep, from Latin *prōfundus.*] —**pro·found′ly,** *adv.* —**pro·found′ness,** *n.*

pro·fun·di·ty (prə fun′di tē) *n., pl.* **-ties. 1.** the quality or state of being profound; depth. **2.** a profound or abstruse statement, idea, or matter. [Late Latin *prōfunditās* depth, from Latin *prōfundus* deep.]

pro·fuse (prə fūs′) *adj.* **1.** great or abundant in amount; plentiful: *profuse undergrowth, profuse bleeding.* **2.** given or giving freely, often to excess; lavish: *profuse expressions of praise.* [Latin *prōfūsus* spread out, lavish, past participle of *prōfundere* to pour out.] —**pro·fuse′ly,** *adv.* —**pro·fuse′ness,** *n.*

pro·fu·sion (prə fū′zhən) *n.* **1.** a plentiful amount; abundance. **2.** lavish or excessive spending; extravagance.

pro·gen·i·tor (prō jen′i tər) *n.* **1.** an ancestor from whom lineal descent is traced; forefather. **2.** a person or thing that comes before and is a source or model; precursor or originator: *a device that was the progenitor of later machines.* [Latin *prōgenitor* ancestor.]

prog·e·ny (proj′ə nē) *n., pl.* **-nies.** offspring, descendants, or children collectively. [Old French *progenie,* from Latin *prōgeniēs* lineage, descent, offspring.]

pro·ges·ta·tion·al (prō′jes tā′shə nəl) *adj.* of, relating to, or constituting the hormonal and uterine tissue changes that occur in a female mammal as ovulation begins and the corpus luteum forms: *progestational hormones.* [PRO-² + GESTATION + -AL¹.]

pro·ges·ter·one (prō jes′tə rōn′) *n.* a female sex hormone that functions with estrogen to prepare the uterus for receiving and nourishing a fertilized egg. It also helps maintain pregnancy by keeping the uterus in a suitable condition for the embryo. [PRO-¹ + GE(STATION) + STER(OL) + -ONE.]

prog·na·thous (prog′nə thəs) *adj.* having or characterized by jaws that project beyond the upper part of the face. Also, **prog·nath·ic** (prog nath′ik). [PRO-² + Greek *gnathos* jaw + -OUS.] —**prog·na·thism** (prog′nə thiz′əm), *n.*

prog·no·sis (prog nō′sis) *n., pl.* **-ses** (-sēz). **1.** a prediction of the probable course and outcome of a disease. **2.** any prediction or forecast. [Late Latin *prognōsis* foreknowledge, prediction of the course of a disease, from Greek *prognōsis.*]

prog·nos·tic (prog nos′tik) *adj.* **1.** of, relating to, or serving as a basis for a prognosis. **2.** predicting future events. —*n.* **1.** a sign or indication of some future occurrence. **2.** a prediction or forecast. [Latin *prognōsticon* sign of the future, from Greek *prognōstikon.*]

prog·nos·ti·cate (prog nos′ti kāt′) *v.t.,* **-cat·ed, -cat·ing. 1.** to predict on the basis of present indications; forecast. **2.** to give an advance indication of; foreshadow; presage. —**prog·nos′ti·ca′tion,** *n.* —**prog·nos′ti·ca′tor,** *n.* —For Synonyms, see **predict.**

pro·gram (prō′gram, -grəm) *also, British,* **programme.** *n.* **1.** a list or printed announcement, esp. for some public presentation, as a play or concert, usually indicating what is to be presented and in what order and who will participate. **2.** a presentation or performance, esp. a television or radio show. **3.** a particular course of action for dealing with some matter: *The Senate committee formulated a new crime-prevention program.* **4.** a set of organized activities or other offerings planned by or available at a particular place or institution: *Our school runs a weekend youth program. This university has an excellent English program.* **5.** the schedule of classes of an individual student or teacher in an educational institution. **6.** a sequence of coded instructions used to direct a computer in performing any of its operations or in solving a particular problem. **7.** material to be taught through programmed instruction, structured and presented according to a definite sequential method. —*v.t.,* **-grammed** or **-gramed,**

-**gram·ming** or -**gram·ing. 1.** to arrange or include in a program or schedule. **2.** to make up or work out a program for. **3.** to write a program for (a computer) or provide with such a program. **4.** to insert operating instructions in (a machine or other device): *to program a microwave oven to cook for ten minutes.* [Late Latin *programma* proclamation, from Greek *programma* public notice.]

Synonyms *n.* **Program** and **agenda** mean a list of things to be done in a certain order. **Program** refers to a schedule of events, as in an entertainment or ceremony: *The concert program featured works by Mozart.* **Agenda** is a formal order of business for a meeting: *The committee's agenda included the treasurer's report.*

pro·gram·er (prō′gram ər) programmer.

pro·gramme (prō′gram, -grəm) *British. n.* program. —*v.t.,* -**grammed, -gram·ming.** program.

programmed instruction, self-teaching with the aid of a textbook or teaching machine that presents material structured in a logical sequence. Programmed instruction allows the student to check an answer immediately for correctness.

programmed learning, learning by means of programmed instruction.

pro·gram·mer (prō′gram ər) *also,* **programer.** *n.* a person who programs, esp. one who programs computers.

prog·ress (*n.,* prog′rəs, -res; *British* prō′gres; *v.,* prə gres′) *n.* **1.** forward movement in space: *Heavy rains hindered the expedition's progress through the jungle.* **2.** movement toward a goal or toward completion: *Are you making any progress with your report?* **3.** development to a better or higher state; improvement: *a patient's progress toward recovery.* **4.** a journey, esp. a royal or official tour. —*v.i.* **1.** to move forward or onward; proceed: *The author's argument progresses logically from one step to the next.* **2.** to move toward a goal or toward completion: *Construction of the new hospital is progressing according to schedule.* **3.** to develop to a better or higher state; improve: *to progress in one's schoolwork.* [Latin *prōgressus* an advance, going forward.] —For Synonyms *(v.i.),* see **advance.**

·**in progress.** in the course of happening; going on: *The meeting was already in progress when I arrived.*

pro·gres·sion (prə gresh′ən) *n.* **1.** the act of progressing; advance. **2.** a sequence of numbers or algebraic expressions in which the same relation holds between each quantity and the one succeeding it; arithmetic progression or geometric progression. **3.** a sequence or succession, as of events. **4.** *Music.* **a.** a movement from one tone or chord to another. **b.** a succession of tones or chords.

pro·gres·sive (prə gres′iv) *adj.* **1.** moving forward; advancing. **2.** proceeding steadily or step by step. **3.** favoring, advocating, or characterized by progress, reform, or improvement, esp. in political or social matters. **4.** (of a disease) advancing steadily in severity or extent. **5.** designating or relating to a tax that increases in rate as the amount taxed increases. **6.** of or relating to a theory of education emphasizing each child's individual needs and capacities and favoring a more informal classroom situation. **7. Progressive.** of, relating to, or belonging to a Progressive Party. **8.** *Grammar.* denoting action in progress. —*n.* **1.** a person who favors or advocates progress or reform, as in political, social, or educational matters. **2. Progressive.** a member of a Progressive Party. —**pro·gres′sive·ly,** *adv.* —**pro·gres′sive·ness,** *n.*

Progressive Party 1. a political party formed by liberal Republicans in 1912 to back the candidacy of Theodore Roosevelt for president. It advocated direct election of senators, woman suffrage, and adoption of the initiative, referendum, and recall. **2.** a political party that was formed in 1924 and was supported by farm, labor, and socialist groups. **3.** a political party that was formed in 1948 and backed Henry A. Wallace for president.

pro·hib·it (prō hib′it) *v.t.* **1.** to forbid by authority: *Smoking is prohibited in this building.* **2.** to keep from doing something; prevent; hinder: *Poor health prohibits my grandparents from traveling.* [Latin *prōhibitus,* past participle of *prōhibēre* to forbid, prevent.] —For Synonyms, see **forbid.**

pro·hi·bi·tion (prō′ə bish′ən) *n.* **1.** the act of prohibiting. **2.** a law, order, or rule that forbids something. **3.a.** the forbidding by law of the manufacture, transportation, and sale of alcoholic beverages. **b. Prohibition.** the period from 1920 to 1933 during which alcoholic beverages were prohibited by federal law in the United States.

a	at	e	end	o	hot	u	up	hw	white		about
ā	ape	ē	me	ō	old	ū	use	ng	song	ə	taken
ä	far	i	it	ô	fork	ü	rule	th	thin		pencil
âr	care	ī	ice	oi	oil	u̇	pull	th	this		lemon
		îr	pierce	ou	out	ûr	turn	zh	measure		circus

pro·hi·bi·tion·ist (prō'ə bish'ə nist) *n.* **1.** a person who favors the prohibition of alcoholic beverages. **2.** a member of the Prohibition Party.

Prohibition Party, a U.S. political party organized in 1869 advocating the prohibition of the manufacture, sale, and consumption of alcoholic beverages.

pro·hib·i·tive (prō hib'i tiv) *adj.* **1.** such as to make difficult or impossible the purchase, use, or payment of something: *prohibitive prices, a prohibitive series of required procedures.* **2.** prohibiting or tending to prohibit. Also, **pro·hib·i·to·ry** (prō hib'ə tôr'ē). —**pro·hib'i·tive·ly,** *adv.* —**pro·hib'i·tive·ness,** *n.*

proj·ect (*n.,* proj'ekt; *v.,* prə jekt') *n.* **1.** a plan for action; scheme; proposal. **2.** a task or activity that is to be done; undertaking. **3.** a housing complex, usually made up of apartment buildings, esp. such a complex supported by the government to provide housing for low-income families. —*v.t.* **1.** to throw, shoot, or hurl forward: *The catapult projected stones into the air.* **2.** to cause (a shadow, light, or image) to fall on a surface: *The strange figure projected a frightening shadow on the wall.* **3.** to cause (one's voice) to be heard distinctly at a distance. **4.** to imagine in some situation or context: *to project oneself into the future.* **5.** to predict on the basis of certain given or known information: *to project the winner of an election.* **6.** *Psychoanalysis.* to attribute unconsciously (one's own feelings, thoughts, or qualities) to another. **7.** to plan; propose. **8.** to cause to stick out. **9.** *Geometry.* to represent (a given figure) on a plane or curved surface by means of a correspondence between the points of the given figure and those of the figure produced. —*v.i.* **1.** to stick out; protrude: *A narrow promontory projected into the sea.* **2.** to cause one's voice to be heard distinctly at a distance. **3.** *Psychoanalysis.* to attribute unconsciously one's own feelings, thoughts, or qualities to another. [Latin *prōjectus,* past participle of *prōicere* to throw forth.]

Synonyms *n.* Project, enterprise, and undertaking mean a systematically planned task or venture. **Project** suggests a complex, cooperative effort with a specific goal: *The project to computerize the company's operations required the services of three programmers for two months.* **Enterprise** emphasizes risk, individual effort, and competition: *Opening another video store in the same neighborhood seemed a risky enterprise.* **Undertaking** implies careful planning and an effort of great significance and seriousness: *The exploration of space is one of history's great undertakings.*

pro·jec·tile (prə jek'təl, -tīl) *n.* an object that is designed to be shot or otherwise projected, as a bullet. —*adj.* **1.** capable of being thrown, shot, or hurled forward. **2.** impelling or driving forward: *projectile vomiting, the projectile force of a weapon.*

pro·jec·tion (prə jek'shən) *n.* **1.** the act of projecting. **2.** something that sticks out or projects; protruding part. **3.a.** the process of projecting images, as from a film or printed page, onto a screen or other surface. **b.** an image so projected. **4.** a prediction based on certain given or known information: *a computer projection of an election's outcome.* **5.** *Psychoanalysis.* the act or process or an instance of unconsciously attributing one's own feelings, thoughts, or qualities to another. **6.** the forming of a plan. **7.** a representation on a plane surface, as in a map, of all or part of the earth's surface or of the celestial sphere. **8.** *Geometry.* the result or process of projecting a given figure on a plane or curved surface.

pro·jec·tion·ist (prə jek'shə nist) *n.* a person who operates a motion-picture or slide projector.

pro·jec·tive (prə jek'tiv) *adj.* **1.** relating to or being made by geometric projection. **2.** sticking out; projecting. **3.** of the nature of or made by projection: *projective election results.*

projective geometry, the study of those properties of geometric figures that do not vary under projection.

projective test, any of various psychological personality tests, as the Rorschach test.

pro·jec·tor (prə jek'tər) *n.* **1.** an apparatus that projects images, as from a film, transparent slide, or printed page, onto a screen or other surface. **2.** a person who devises projects or plans.

pro·kar·y·ote (prō kar'ē ōt') *also,* **procaryote.** *n.* any cell or unicellular organism lacking a membrane-bound nucleus and membrane-bound organelles, as bacteria and cyanobacteria. The monerans are all prokaryotes. ➡ distinguished from **eukaryote.** —**pro·kar·y·ot·ic** (prō kar'ē ot'ik), *adj.*

pro·lac·tin (prō lak'tin) *n.* a pituitary hormone that promotes lactation.

pro·lapse (*n.,* prō laps', prō'laps'; *v.,* prō laps') *Medicine. n.* the falling or slipping out of an internal structure or organ, as the uterus or a vertebral disk. —*v.i.,* -**lapsed,** -**laps·ing.** to fall or slip out of place. [Modern Latin *prolapsus,* from Late Latin *prolapsus* a falling forward, from Latin *prolapsus* past participle of *prolabi* to fall forward, from pro- forward + *labi* to fall.]

pro·late (prō'lāt) *adj.* lengthened in the direction of the polar

diameter, as a spheroid formed by the revolution of an ellipse about its longer axis. ➡ opposed to **oblate.** [Latin *prōlātus* extended, past participle of *prōferre* to bring forward, extend.]

pro·le·tar·i·an (prō'li târ'ē ən) *adj.* of, relating to, or characteristic of the proletariat. —*n.* a member of the proletariat. [Latin *prōlētārius* Roman citizen of the lowest class who was so poor that he was able to serve the state only by having children (from *prōlēs* offspring) + -AN.]

pro·le·tar·i·at (prō'li târ'ē ət) *n.* **1.a.** the working class, esp. the industrial working class. **b.** the lowest and poorest class, owning no means of production. **2.** in ancient Rome, the lowest class. [French *prolétariat* the working class, from Latin *prōlētārius* Roman citizen of the lowest class. See PROLETARIAN.]

pro·life (prō līf') *adj.* opposed to the right to have an abortion; against legalized abortion. —**pro·lif'er,** *n.*

pro·lif·er·ate (prə lif'ə rāt') *v.,* -**at·ed,** -**at·ing.** —*v.i.* to multiply, reproduce, or grow rapidly, as cells or microorganisms in a culture. —*v.t.* to cause to spread, increase, or reproduce: *to proliferate radical ideas.* [Medieval Latin *prolifer* bearing offspring (from Latin *prōlēs* offspring + *ferre* to bear) + -ATE.] —**pro·lif'er·a'tion,** *n.*

pro·lif·ic (prə lif'ik) *adj.* **1.** producing abundantly through creative or artistic effort; highly productive: *a prolific novelist.* **2.** producing offspring or fruit in abundance; fertile: *a prolific apple tree.* **3.** having an abundant supply of (with *in* or *of*): *a valley prolific in fruits and vegetables.* [Medieval Latin *prolificus* fertile, from Latin *prōlēs* offspring + *facere* to make.] —**pro·lif·i·ca·cy** (prə lif'i kə sē), **pro·lif'ic·ness,** *n.* —**pro·lif'i·cal·ly,** *adv.*

pro·line (prō'lēn, -lin) *n.* a nonessential amino acid that is synthesized in the body from a glutamate and is a major constituent of collagen. Formula: $C_5H_9NO_2$

pro·lix (prō liks', prō'liks') *adj.* **1.** so long and wordy as to be tedious: *a prolix sermon.* **2.** inclined to speak or write in a tediously long and wordy manner. [Latin *prōlixus* extended.] —**pro·lix'i·ty, pro·lix'ness,** *n.* —**pro·lix'ly,** *adv.*

pro·logue (prō'lôg', -log') *also,* **pro·log.** *n.* **1.** an introduction to a play, poem, discourse, or other literary work, esp. a speech by an actor directly to the audience. **2.** any introductory or preliminary act or event. [Latin *prōlogus* introduction to a play, from Greek *prologos* introduction to a play or speech.] —For Synonyms, see **introduction.**

pro·long (prə lông') *v.t.* to make longer, esp. in time or duration; extend: *They prolonged the suspense by not telling us what had happened until the next day.* [Late Latin *prōlongāre,* from Latin *prō* forward + *longus* not short, lengthy.]

pro·lon·gate (prə lông'gāt) *v.t.,* -**gat·ed,** -**gat·ing.** prolong.

pro·lon·ga·tion (prō'lông gā'shən) *n.* **1.** the act of prolonging or the state of being prolonged. **2.** something that prolongs or is prolonged.

prom (prom) *n. Informal.* a formal school or college dance. [Short for PROMENADE.]

prom·e·nade (prom'ə nād', -näd') *n.* **1.** a leisurely walk, esp. one taken in a public place for pleasure or to display oneself. **2.** a place or area for such walking. **3.a.** a formal dance; ball. **b.** a ceremonious march of the guests at the opening of a formal dance. **4.** a march of dancers as part of a square dance. —*v.,* -**nad·ed,** -**nad·ing.** —*v.i.* **1.** to go on a promenade or leisurely walk. **2.** to execute a promenade in a square dance. —*v.t.* **1.** to take a leisurely walk through or on. **2.** to display on or as if on a promenade; parade. [French *promenade* act of walking, place for walking, from Old French *promener* to walk, from Late Latin *prōminare* to drive forward, going back to Latin *prō* forward + *minārī* to threaten.] —**prom'e·nad'er,** *n.*

promenade deck, the upper deck of a passenger ship, or an open area of a deck, where passengers can walk.

Pro·me·the·an (prə mē'thē ən) *adj.* **1.** of, relating to, or like Prometheus. **2.** daringly creative or original. —*n.* a person who is Promethean in spirit or actions.

Pro·me·the·us (prə mē'thē əs, -thūs) *n.* in Greek mythology, a Titan who stole fire from the gods and brought it to humans. Zeus punished him by chaining him to a rock where an eagle ate away at his liver every day.

pro·me·thi·um (prə mē'thē əm) *n.* a radioactive, metallic element of the rare-earth group, produced by fission of uranium, thorium, or plutonium and used as a source of energy in batteries that power satellites and buoys. Symbol: **Pm** For tables, see **element.** [Modern Latin *promethium,* from PROMETHEUS.]

prom·i·nence (prom'ə nəns) *n.* **1.** the state or quality of being prominent. **2.** something prominent; projection. **3.** a cloud of glowing gas that arches across the upper levels of the sun's atmosphere. Also *(def. 3),* **solar prominence.** For illustration, see **sun.**

prom·i·nent (prom'ə nənt) *adj.* **1.** well-known or important;

notable: *a prominent member of the community.* **2.** very noticeable; conspicuous: *One decrepit shack was the landscape's only prominent feature.* **3.** sticking out from a surface; projecting: *The cliff had a prominent overhang.* [Latin *prōminēns,* present participle of *prōminēre* to project.] —**prom′i·nent·ly,** *adv.*

prom·is·cu·i·ty (prom′ə skū′i tē) *n., pl.* **-ties. 1.a.** the state or quality of being promiscuous. **b.** an instance of this; promiscuous sexual relations or behavior. **2.** an indiscriminate mixture.

pro·mis·cu·ous (prə mis′kū əs) *adj.* **1.** not discriminating, esp. engaging in sexual relations indiscriminately or with many persons. **2.** made up of varied and unrelated things, parts, or individuals. [Latin *prōmiscuus.*] —**pro·mis′cu·ous·ly,** *adv.* —**pro·mis′cu·ous·ness,** *n.*

prom·ise (prom′is) *n.* **1.a.** an assurance or pledge given that one will do or refrain from doing some act or that something will or will not occur: *Many people began to lose faith in the president's promises of prosperity.* **b.** something that is promised. **2.a.** an indication of or reasonable basis for expectation of future excellence, success, or progress: *a drug that shows promise in treating a disease.* **b.** an indication of something that may occur or develop: *There is a promise of spring in the air.* —*v.,* **-ised, -is·ing.** —*v.t.* **1.** to declare or guarantee with a promise. ➡ used with an infinitive or clause: *The boss promised to give everyone a raise.* **2.** to make a promise of (something): *Politicians often promise improvements that will never take place.* **3.** to give reason to expect or anticipate (something): *The clear skies promised a nice day.* ➡ often used with an infinitive: *This promises to be an interesting evening.* —*v.i.* **1.** to make a promise. **2.** to give reason for expectation. [Latin *prōmissum* assurance given regarding the future, expectation.] —**prom′is·er,** *n.*

Synonyms *v.t.* **Promise, pledge,** and **vow** mean to give one's word to act in a certain way. **Promise,** the most general of these terms, indicates an intention that may or may not be fulfilled: *The two friends promised to write to each other.* **Pledge** is used in reference to financial agreements and other formal guarantees involving honor or integrity: *The company pledged a large contribution to the charity's fundraising drive.* **Vow** indicates a solemn, intense, often religiously inspired declaration: *to vow obedience to the rules of a sect, to vow to be revenged for an insult.*

Promised Land 1. in the Bible, the land of Canaan, promised by God to Abraham and his descendants. **2. promised land.** any place where final happiness is hoped or expected to be found. **3.** heaven.

prom·is·ing (prom′ə sing) *adj.* giving promise or hope for the future: *The baseball season has had a promising start for our team.* —**prom′is·ing·ly,** *adv.*

prom·is·so·ry (prom′ə sôr′ē) *adj.* containing or conveying a promise: *a promissory agreement.*

promissory note, a written promise to pay a specified sum of money to a certain party at a future time or on demand.

prom·on·to·ry (prom′ən tôr′ē) *n., pl.* **-ries.** an elevated portion of land extending out into a body of water; headland. [Latin *prōmonturium.*]

pro·mote (prə mōt′) *v.t.,* **-mot·ed, -mot·ing. 1.** to raise in rank, position, or honor: *The university promoted several instructors to assistant professor this year.* **2.** to aid in or contribute to the growth, development, or progress of: *Certain foods promote tooth decay.* **3.** to work for; advocate: *to promote the passage of a bill.* **4.** to advance (a student) to the next higher grade. **5.** to try to sell, increase the popularity of, or obtain the necessary capital for (a product, business undertaking, or the like), as by advertising. [Latin *prōmōtus,* past participle of *prōmovēre* to move forward.]

pro·mot·er (prə mō′tər) *n.* **1.** a person or thing that promotes, advances, or furthers something. **2.** a person who organizes or promotes a business undertaking or commercial enterprise, esp. one who arranges for the presentation of a sports event.

pro·mo·tion (prə mō′shən) *n.* **1.** an advancement in rank, position, honor, or grade. **2.a.** the furthering of the growth or popularity of a product or enterprise. **b.** an instance of this: *The sale was a promotion for the new store.* **3.** the act of promoting. —**pro·mo′tion·al,** *adj.*

prompt (prompt) *adj.* **1.** acting or occurring at the proper time; on time; punctual: *The bus is usually prompt in arriving.* **2.** done or given without delay: *a repair shop known for its prompt service.* **3.** quick to act; ready: *Why are you always so prompt to criticize?* —*v.t.* **1.** to move to action; incite: *An odd sense of foreboding prompted me to return home.* **2.** to give rise to; inspire: *The scandal prompted a senate investigation.* **3.** to remind, advise, or direct, esp. to supply (a performer or speaker) with forgotten words or a missed cue. —*n.* a message or symbol displayed on a

computer screen that informs the operator of an error or provides instructions on how to proceed. [Latin *promptus* ready, at hand, past participle of *prōmere* to bring forth. Doublet of PRONTO.] —**prompt′ly,** *adv.* —**prompt′ness,** *n.*

prompt·er (promp′tər) *n.* a person or thing that prompts, esp. a person whose task is to prompt the actors in a theatrical production.

promp·ti·tude (promp′ti tüd′, -tūd′) *n.* the quality or habit of being prompt; promptness.

prom·ul·gate (prom′əl gāt′, prō mul′gāt) *v.t.,* **-gat·ed, -gat·ing. 1.** to make known or put into effect formally and officially, esp. by public declaration; proclaim: *to promulgate a law.* **2.** to make widespread; disseminate. [Latin *prōmulgātus,* past participle of *prōmulgāre* to make known, publish.] —**prom′ul·ga′tion,** *n.* —**prom′ul·ga′tor,** *n.*

pron. 1. pronoun. **2.** pronounced. **3.** pronunciation.

prone (prōn) *adj.* **1.** lying with the face or front downward; prostrate. **2.** naturally inclined; disposed (often with *to*): *Some people are prone to distrust strangers.* [Latin *prōnus* leaning forward, inclined.] —**prone′ly,** *adv.* —**prone′ness,** *n.*

prong (prông, prong) *n.* **1.** a sharply pointed end of a tool or implement, as of a fork. **2.** any sharply pointed projection, as of an antler. —*v.t.* to pierce or stab with or as with a prong. [Of uncertain origin.]

pronged (prôngd, prongd) *adj.* having prongs.

prong·horn (prông′hôrn′, prong′-) *n., pl.* **-horn** or **-horns.** a cud-chewing mammal, *Antilocapra americana,* resembling an antelope, found chiefly on the Rocky Mountain plains and having slender, pronged horns. Height: 3 feet (0.9 meter) at the shoulder. Also, **antelope, pronghorn antelope.**

pro·nom·i·nal (prō nom′ə nəl) *adj.* of, relating to, or having the nature or function of a pronoun. [Late Latin *prōnōmenālis,* from Latin *prōnōmen* pronoun.] —**pro·nom′i·nal·ly,** *adv.*

pro·noun (prō′noun′) *n.* a word used as a substitute for a noun, denoting a person, place, or thing without naming it, as *I, you, he, who, what, this.* [Latin *prōnōmen,* from *prō nōmine* instead of a noun.]

pronghorn

pro·nounce (prə nouns′) *v.,* **-nounced, -nounc·ing.** —*v.t.* **1.** to utter (a word or sound). **2.a.** to utter (a word or sound) in a particular way, esp. with a certain accent or according to an accepted standard: *to pronounce words correctly.* **b.** to indicate the correct manner of uttering (a word) with phonetic symbols. **3.** to declare or state, esp. officially, formally, or solemnly: *The jury pronounced the defendant not guilty.* —*v.i.* **1.** to state an opinion, judgment, or decision; make a pronouncement. **2.** to utter or pronounce words. [Old French *prononcier* to articulate, declare formally, from Latin *prōnūntiāre* to announce, recite, tell.] —**pro·nounce′a·ble,** *adj.* —**pro·nounc′er,** *n.*

pro·nounced (prə nounst′) *adj.* strongly defined; clearly recognizable; decided: *They spoke with a pronounced foreign accent.* —**pro·nounc·ed·ly** (prə noun′sid lē, -nounst′lē), *adv.*

pro·nounce·ment (prə nouns′mənt) *n.* **1.** a formal or authoritative declaration or statement. **2.** an opinion, judgment, or decision. **3.** the act of pronouncing.

pron·to (pron′tō) *adv. Informal.* at once; quickly; promptly; immediately. [Spanish *pronto* quick, quickly, from Latin *promptus* ready, at hand, past participle of *prōmere* to bring forth. Doublet of PROMPT.]

pro·nu·cle·us (prō nü′klē əs, -nū′-) *n., pl.* **-cle·i** (-klē ī′). either of the two haploid nuclei that join in the ovum after a sperm has penetrated it. Fusion of the pronuclei produces the diploid nucleus of the zygote. [Modern Latin *pronucleus,* from Greek *pro-* before + Modern Latin *nucleus* (see NUCLEUS).]

a	at	e	end	o	hot	u	up	hw	white		about
ā	ape	ē	me	ō	old	ū	use	ng	song		taken
ä	far	i	it	ô	fork	ü	rule	th	thin	ə	pencil
âr	care	ī	ice	oi	oil	u̇	pull	th	this		lemon
		îr	pierce	ou	out	ûr	turn	zh	measure		circus

pro·nun·ci·a·men·to (prə nun′sē ə men′tō) *n., pl.* **-tos.** a proclamation or manifesto, as by a government. [Spanish *pronunciamiento,* going back to Latin *prōnuntiāre* to announce, recite, tell.]

pro·nun·ci·a·tion (prə nun′sē ā′shən) *n.* **1.** the act or manner of pronouncing words: *to make one's pronunciation more distinct.* **2.a.** an accepted or standard way of pronouncing a word: *There are many words that have more than one pronunciation.* **b.** a phonetic transcription of a word indicating the way it is pronounced. [Latin *prōnūntiātiō* public declaration, delivery (of a speech).]

Synonyms Pronunciation, enunciation, and articulation mean a way of producing speech sounds. **Pronunciation** refers to patterns of accent, stress, and inflection, often as related to an accepted standard: *Her pronunciation of certain vowels indicated that the singer was British rather than American.* **Enunciation** concerns clarity of speech: *The actor's enunciation was so poor that many in the audience could not understand him.* **Articulation** emphasizes the physical process of speaking, esp. of producing distinct consonant sounds: *Articulation of the letter "t" involves putting the tongue against the palate.*

proof (prüf) *n.* **1.** evidence sufficient to establish a fact or induce belief. **2.** a test or trial, as of the truth, quality, or strength of something. **3.** establishment of the validity or truth of something; conclusive demonstration: *The philosopher used simple logic in the proof of the assertion.* **4.** *Law.* evidence serving to determine a judgment or verdict. **5.** a sequence of logical steps serving to demonstrate or establish a proposition. **6.a.** a measurement of the alcohol content of a liquor with reference to a standard, which is defined as being 100 proof. **b.** the standard itself, in the United States 50 percent ethyl alcohol by volume at 60 degrees Fahrenheit. **7.** *Printing.* a trial impression, as of type set from a manuscript, made for the purpose of checking and making corrections or changes before printing. **8.** *Etching and Engraving.* a trial impression taken from an engraved stone, plate, or block for the purpose of examination. **9.** *Photography.* a trial print from a photographic negative. —*adj.* **1.** firmly or successfully resistant to; impervious to (with *against*): *to be proof against temptation.* **2.** used in proving, testing, or correcting. **3.** of standard alcoholic strength. —*v.t.* **1.** to make resistant or impervious to. ➡ usually used in combination: *to shrinkproof a garment.* **2.** to make a proof of. **3.** proofread. [Old French *prueve* that which establishes the truth of something, from Late Latin *proba* test, evidence, from Latin *probāre* to test, demonstrate.] —For Synonyms *(n.),* see **evidence.**

-proof *combining form* **1.** impervious or resistant to: *waterproof, fireproof.* **2.** safe from; protected against: *foolproof.* [From PROOF.]

proof·read (prüf′rēd′) *v.t., v.i.,* **-read** (-red′), **-read·ing.** to read (written material, esp. printers' proofs) for the purpose of detecting and correcting errors. Also, **proof.** —**proof′read′er,** *n.*

prop[1] (prop) *v.t.,* **propped, prop·ping. 1.** to hold up, support, or hold in place by placing something under or against (often with *up*): *We propped up the sagging roof with some pieces of lumber.* **2.** to hold up, support, or hold in place by placing against something: *to prop a bicycle against a wall.* **3.** to sustain; give support or aid to; bolster (often with *up*): *to prop up a friend's spirits.* —*n.* **1.** something that serves to prop up something or hold something in place; support. **2.** a person or thing that props or sustains. [Possibly from Middle Dutch *proppe* a support.]

prop[2] (prop) *n.* property *(def. 6).*

prop[3] (prop) *n. Informal.* propeller.

prop. 1. property. **2.** proposition. **3.** proprietor.

prop·a·gan·da (prop′ə gan′də) *n.* **1.** a body of doctrines, ideas, or attitudes of a particular group promoted, often through public allegation and in a distorted or biased form, in order to influence the point of view of others, gain supporters, or damage an opposing group. **2.** the systematic promotion or dissemination of such doctrines, ideas, or attitudes. **3. Propaganda.** a congregation of the Roman Catholic Curia, composed of a committee of cardinals charged with the care of foreign missions and the training of missionaries. [Modern Latin *(congregatio de) propaganda (fide)* (congregation for) propagating (the faith).]

prop·a·gan·dism (prop′ə gan′diz əm) *n.* the act or practice of using propaganda. —**prop′a·gan′dist,** *n., adj.* —**prop′a·gan·dis′tic,** *adj.* —**prop′a·gan·dis′ti·cal·ly,** *adv.*

prop·a·gan·dize (prop′ə gan′dīz) *v.,* **-dized, -diz·ing.** —*v.t.* **1.** to spread by means of propaganda: *to propagandize a doctrine.* **2.** to subject to propaganda: *to propagandize a people.* —*v.i.* to spread or carry on propaganda.

prop·a·gate (prop′ə gāt′) *v.,* **-gat·ed, -gat·ing.** —*v.i.* to multiply by reproduction; breed. —*v.t.* **1.** to cause (animals or plants) to reproduce; breed or raise. **2.** (of an animal or plant) to reproduce (itself). **3.** to transmit (characteristics) to one's offspring. **4.** to spread or transmit from person to person, as information; disseminate: *to propagate false rumors.* **5.** to transmit (energy, as light or sound waves) through a medium or space: *to propagate radio waves over a great distance.* [Latin *prōpāgātus,* past participle of *prōpāgāre* to plant slips, beget, increase, extend.] —**prop′a·ga′tive,** *adj.* —**prop′a·ga′tor,** *n.*

prop·a·ga·tion (prop′ə gā′shən) *n.* **1.** multiplication by reproduction. **2.** a spreading, as of a belief; dissemination. **3.** the act or process of propagating or the state of being propagated: *the propagation of seismic waves through solid rock.*

pro·pane (prō′pān) *n.* a colorless gas found in petroleum and

---

Proofreader's Marks

∧ ⋏	Insert at this point or make subscript	⚇	Transpose	⊥ᴍ	Insert em dash	‖	Align vertically
∨ ⋎	Insert at this point or make superscript	ⓢⓟ	Spell out	#	Insert space	(/)	Insert parentheses	ⓛⓒ	Set lower case
⌃	Insert comma		Move to the right	⋁	Insert apostrophe	ⓒⓐⓟ	Set in CAPITALS
⊙	Insert period		Move to the left	⸌⸌ ⸍⸍	Insert quotation marks	ⓢⓒ	Set in SMALL CAPITALS
⌃	Insert semicolon		Center	ℐ	Delete	ⓘⓣⓐⓛ	Set in *italics*
⊙	Insert colon	∩	Move up	¶	Start new paragraph	ⓡⓞⓜ	Set in roman type
ⓢⓔⓣ ?	Insert question mark	∪	Move down	⌣	Close up space	ⓑⓕ	Set in **boldface**
⊨⊨	Insert hyphen	‗	Align horizontally	ⓢⓣⓔⓣ	Let copy stand without correction	ⓦⓕ	Wrong font; set in correct typeface
		⊥ɴ	Insert en dash			ⓧ	Reset broken letter

The sentence below has been corrected by a proofreader.

¶ teh Proofreader's ② basic tasks are to identify and   ⓟⓐⓡⓐⓖⓡⓐⓟⓗ / ⓒⓐⓟ / ⓣⓡ / ⓛⓒ / ⋎ / ⓢⓟ

correct any typographical spelling, or grammati cal   ⓘⓣⓐⓛ / ⌢⚬ / ⋌ / ⋋ / ⓒⓛⓞⓢⓔ ⓤⓟ

⌐errors their maybe in written material   ⓜⓞⓥⓔ ⓛⓔⓕⓣ / there / # / ⌢ā / ⊙

natural gas, widely used as a heating fuel. Formula: C_3H_8

pro·pa·nol (prō′pə nôl′) *n.* an isomer of propyl alcohol, used in making acetone. Formula: C_3H_7OH [PROPAN(E) + -OL.]

pro·pel (prə pel′) *v.t.,* **-pelled, -pel·ling. 1.** to cause to move forward or onward; put or sustain in motion: *to propel an aircraft by jet engines.* **2.** to urge onward: *A desire for fame propelled the actor.* [Latin *prōpellere* to drive forward.]

pro·pel·lant (prə pel′ənt) *also,* **propellent.** *n.* a propelling agent or substance, as a fuel for propelling a rocket or a gas for discharging the contents of an aerosol can.

pro·pel·lent (prə pel′ənt) *adj.* propelling or capable of propelling. —*n.* propellant.

pro·pel·ler (prə pel′ər) *n.* a device consisting of a hub having blades mounted at an angle. When the hub revolves, the action of the blades creates a driving force that can be used to propel a boat or aircraft. Also, **screw propeller, screw.**

pro·pen·si·ty (prə pen′si tē) *n., pl.* **-ties.** a natural tendency; inclination: *a propensity toward laziness.* [Latin *prōpēnsus* inclined, past participle of *prōpendēre* to be inclined + -ITY.]

prop·er (prop′ər) *adj.* **1.** suitable, appropriate, or correct for a given use or occasion: *To do good work, one must have the proper tools.* **2.** conforming to a particular or the accepted standard, as of procedure or behavior: *The visiting dignitary was given a proper welcome.* **3.** strictly formal, neat, or respectable; decorous; prim: *to be so proper that one is unwilling to defy the slightest convention.* **4.** understood or considered in a precise or strict sense: *The town is nearby, but it is not part of Boston proper.* **5.** belonging to or characteristic of (with *to*): *weather conditions proper to a particular region of the world.* **6.** *Grammar.* designating or derived from a particular person, place, or thing. **7.** *Archaic.* handsome; attractive. **8.** *Informal.* thorough; complete; out-and-out: *a proper rogue.* **9.** *Informal.* fine; excellent. [Old French *propre* suitable, characteristic of a person or thing, from Latin *proprius* one's own.]

> **Synonyms** **Proper, appropriate,** and **fitting** mean in accordance with a specific standard or criterion. **Proper** indicates that something conforms to an ethical or functional standard: *The principal set guidelines for proper attire for both students and teachers. This bulb is not the proper size for the light fixture.* **Appropriate** implies a relative standard that may vary with circumstances: *The guests weren't sure if it was appropriate to bring gifts to the retirement party.* **Fitting** emphasizes harmony between means and ends: *Community service was a fitting sentence for the official convicted of corruption.*

proper adjective, an adjective that is formed from a proper noun. For example, *Australian* is a proper adjective formed from *Australia.*

proper fraction, a fraction in which the numerator is less or of lower degree than the denominator, as $\frac{5}{8}$ or a/a^2.

prop·er·ly (prop′ər lē) *adv.* **1.** in a suitable, appropriate, or correct manner: *to be properly equipped for a fishing trip.* **2.** in accordance with a particular or the accepted standard, as of procedure or behavior: *to be properly married.* **3.** with precision or accuracy; exactly; strictly: *Properly speaking, a tomato is a fruit.* **4.** with good reason; justifiably. **5.** *Informal.* thoroughly; completely.

proper noun, a noun that denotes a particular person, place, or thing and, in English, is always capitalized when written. For example, *Elizabeth, Geneva,* and *Saturday* are proper nouns. ➤ distinguished from **common noun.**

proper subset, a set that contains fewer members than the set of which it is a subset. The proper subsets of the set [a,b] are [a], [b], and [0].

prop·er·tied (prop′ər tēd) *adj.* owning property, esp. much property: *the propertied class.*

prop·er·ty (prop′ər tē) *n., pl.* **-ties. 1.** something one has or may have as a possession: *The statue in the park is town property.* **2.** a piece of real estate: *expensive waterfront property.* **3.** anything, as a literary work, in which one has or may have a legal interest. **4.** the right to the possession, use, or disposal of a thing or things; ownership. **5.** a special attribute or quality belonging to a person or thing: *a metal with heat-resistant properties.* **6.** any movable article, except scenery and costumes, used on the set of a theatrical production. Also (*def. 6*), **prop.** [Old French *propriete* possession(s), special quality, from Latin *prōprietās* ownership, quality. Doublet of PROPRIETY.]

property man, a person who is in charge of theatrical properties. Also, **prop man.**

pro·phage (prō′fāj′) *n.* a bacteriophage that has become integrated into the chromosomes of its bacterial host, so that it reproduces when the host does.

pro·phase (prō′fāz′) *n.* an initial stage of cell division, which in

mitosis is marked by the condensing of the chromosomes and their movement towards the equatorial plate. In meiosis, homologous chromosomes pair up during prophase. For illustration, see **mitosis.** [PRO-^{2} + PHASE.]

proph·e·cy (prof′ə sē) *n., pl.* **-cies. 1.** the act of telling beforehand what is to come; foretelling of the future. **2.** something that is foretold; prediction. **3.** a divinely inspired utterance or revelation. **4.** the power or ability to foretell the future. [Old French *prophecie,* form of *prophetie* prediction, revelation of a prophet, from Late Latin *prophētīa* prediction, from Greek *prophēteiā.*]

proph·e·sy (prof′ə sī′) *v.,* **-sied, -sy·ing.** —*v.t.* to tell beforehand (what is to come); foretell; predict: *The oracle prophesied hard times for the city.* —*v.i.* **1.** to foretell the future; make predictions. **2.** to speak as a prophet. —**proph′e·si′er,** *n.* —For Synonyms, see **foretell.**

proph·et (prof′it) *n.* **1.** a person who speaks or claims to speak by divine inspiration or as the interpreter of divine will, esp. a religious teacher or leader professing or considered to be divinely inspired. **2.** a person who foretells the future. **3.** a spokesperson, as for a cause or movement. **4. the Prophet. a.** in Islam, Muhammad. **b.** in the Mormon Church, Joseph Smith. **5. the Prophets.** the second of the three divisions of the Jewish Scriptures, following the Law of Moses and preceding the Hagiographa, comprising those books either written by prophets or composed mainly of prophecies. [Late Latin *prophēta* person who predicts, soothsayer, from Greek *prophētēs* person who predicts, interpreter of divine will.]

pro·phet·ic (prə fet′ik) *adj.* **1.** containing or of the nature of prophecy. **2.** of, relating to, or belonging to a prophet. Also, **pro·phet′i·cal.** —**pro·phet′i·cal·ly,** *adv.*

pro·phy·lac·tic (prō′fə lak′tik, prof′ə-) *adj.* serving to protect against or prevent something, esp. disease. —*n.* **1.** a prophylactic device, medicine, or treatment. **2.** condom. [Greek *prophylaktikos* guarding from, going back to *pro* before + *phylassein* to guard.]

pro·phy·lax·is (prō′fə lak′sis, prof′ə-) *n., pl.* **-lax·es** (-lak′sēz). **1.** protection against or prevention of disease. **2.** drugs, treatment, or other measures used to prevent disease. [Modern Latin *prophylaxis,* from Greek *pro* before + *phylaxis* guarding.]

pro·pin·qui·ty (prō ping′kwi tē) *n.* **1.** nearness in time or place; proximity. **2.** nearness of relation; kinship. [Latin *propinquitās.*]

pro·pi·on·ic acid (prō′pē on′ik) a fatty acid that occurs naturally in perspiration, synthesized for use as a food preservative and as an intermediate in the manufacture of perfume. Formula: $C_3H_6O_2$ [PRO(TO)- + Greek *piōn* fat + -IC + ACID.]

pro·pi·ti·ate (prə pish′ē āt′) *v.t.,* **-at·ed, -at·ing.** to win over, as someone who has been offended; appease; conciliate: *The people thought they could propitiate the angry gods with a sacrifice.* [Latin *propitiātus,* past participle of *propitiāre* to render favorable.] —**pro·pi′ti·a′tion,** *n.* —**pro·pi′ti·a′tor,** *n.*

pro·pi·ti·a·to·ry (prə pish′ē ə tôr′ē) *adj.* serving, tending, or intended to propitiate: *a propitiatory gesture.*

pro·pi·tious (prə pish′əs) *adj.* **1.** of favorable import; boding well: *propitious omens.* **2.** presenting or attended by favorable or suitable conditions: *It seems to be a propitious time for our voyage.* **3.** favorably disposed; gracious: *a propitious judge.* [Latin *propitius* favorable; literally, falling or flying forward (possibly referring to the interpretation of the flight of birds in the ancient art of augury).] —**pro·pi′tious·ly,** *adv.* —**pro·pi′tious·ness,** *n.* —For Synonyms, see **favorable.**

prop·jet (prop′jet′) *n.* turboprop *(def. 2).* [Short for (TURBO)-PROP + JET.]

prop man, property man.

pro·po·nent (prə pō′nənt) *n.* **1.** a person who favors or supports something, as a cause; advocate: *The senator is a leading proponent of tax reform.* **2.** a person who proposes or propounds something. [Latin *prōpōnēns,* present participle of *prōpōnere* to set forth.]

pro·por·tion (prə pôr′shən) *n.* **1.** the relation of one thing to another with respect to size, number, amount, or degree; ratio: *the proportion of men to women in a profession.* **2.** a proper or balanced relation between parts; harmony; symmetry: *The length and height of the room were in proportion.* **3.** a part or share, esp. in relation to the whole: *A proportion of the profits was allotted to*

P

a	at	e	end	o	hot	u	up	hw	white		about
ā	ape	ē	me	ō	old	ū	use	ng	song		taken
ä	far	i	it	ô	fork	ü	rule	th	thin	ə	pencil
âr	care	ī	ice	oi	oil	u̇	pull	th	this		lemon
		îr	pierce	ou	out	ûr	turn	zh	measure		circus

each partner in the company. **4.** relative size, degree, or extent: *In proportion to Texas, Rhode Island is very small.* **5. proportions.** dimensions: *the proportions of a room.* **6.** the relation between two ratios in which the first of four quantities divided by the second is equal to the third divided by the fourth: *8 is to 4, as 6 is to 3.* —*v.t.* **1.** to cause to be in a proper or balanced relation to something else with respect to size or extent: *to proportion the width of a building to its height, to proportion expenditure to income.* **2.** to form the parts of (a whole) so as to be in harmonious or symmetrical relation. [Latin *prōportiō* analogy, comparative relation, from *prōportiōne* relatively.] —**pro·por′tion·ment,** *n.*

pro·por·tion·a·ble (prə pôr′shə nə bəl) *adj.* in proper proportion; proportional. —**pro·por′tion·a·bly,** *adv.*

pro·por·tion·al (prə pôr′shə nəl) *adj.* **1.** in or having proportion: *Achievement is usually proportional to effort expended.* **2.** of, relating to, or based on proportion; relative: *a proportional scale of values.* **3.** *Mathematics.* having the same or a constant ratio. —*n.* one of the terms of a mathematical proportion. —**pro·por′tion·al·i·ty,** *n.* —**pro·por′tion·al·ly,** *adv.*

proportional representation, a system of voting under which seats in the legislative body are distributed in proportion to the vote cast for the various parties.

pro·por·tion·ate (*adj.,* prə pôr′shə nit; *v.,* prə pôr′shə nāt′) *adj.* in proper proportion; proportional: *Our reward was proportionate to the time we spent.* —*v.t.,* **-at·ed, -at·ing.** to make proportionate. —**pro·por′tion·ate·ly,** *adv.*

pro·pos·al (prə pō′zəl) *n.* **1.** something put forward for consideration, discussion, or acceptance, as a plan or a course of action. **2.** an offer of marriage. **3.** the act of proposing.

pro·pose (prə pōz′) *v.,* **-posed, -pos·ing.** —*v.t.* **1.** to put forward for consideration, discussion, or acceptance: *The mayor proposed a new plan for settling the transit strike.* **2.** to suggest or present (someone), as for a position or office. **3.** to have in mind; intend; plan: *The general proposes to attack the city at dawn.* **4.** to offer or present (a toast). —*v.i.* to make an offer of marriage. [Old French *proposer* to put forth, make a formal proposal, modification (influenced by Old French *poser* to place, put) of Latin *prōpōnere* to set forth. See POSE¹.] —**pro·pos′er,** *n.*

prop·o·si·tion (prop′ə zish′ən) *n.* **1.** something proposed for consideration or acceptance; proposal, offer, or suggestion: *to reject a proposition as impractical.* **2.** *Informal.* a matter, undertaking, or situation: *Finding a buyer for this old car will not be an easy proposition.* **3.** a statement or subject to be discussed: *The two teams prepared to debate the proposition.* **4.** *Logic.* a statement in which something (the predicate) is affirmed or denied in relation to something else (the subject). **5.** *Mathematics.* a statement of a theorem to be demonstrated or a problem to be solved. **6.** *Informal.* a thought, idea, or possibility: *The proposition of working all night was quite depressing.* **7.** the act of proposing. —*v.t.* to make a proposal or offer to, esp. to suggest sexual intercourse to. [Latin *prōpositiō* a setting forth, statement.] —**prop′o·si′tion·al,** *adj.*

pro·pound (prə pound′) *v.t.* to put forward for consideration, as a theory; set forth; propose. [Earlier *propone,* from Latin *prōpōnere* to set forth.] —**pro·pound′er,** *n.*

pro·prae·tor (prō prē′tər) *also,* **pro·pre·tor.** *n.* an official sent to govern an ancient Roman province after having served as praetor in Rome. [Latin *prōpraetor,* from *prō praetōre* for the praetor.]

pro·pri·e·tar·y (prə prī′i ter′ē) *adj.* **1.** of, relating to, or characteristic of a proprietor or proprietors. **2.** made and sold by exclusive legal right, as a medicine. **3.** privately owned and operated: *a proprietary hospital.* —*n., pl.* **-tar·ies. 1.** proprietor. **2.** a group of proprietors. **3.** ownership; proprietorship. **4.** a proprietary medicine. [Late Latin *proprietārius* owner, belonging to someone as property, from Latin *proprietās* ownership, property.]

proprietary colony, any of certain early American colonies, such as Pennsylvania, granted by the British Crown to an individual or small group of individuals vested with full governing power.

pro·pri·e·tor (prə prī′i tər) *n.* **1.** a person who has legal title or right to something, esp. to property; owner. **2.** an owner or operator of a small business establishment. **3.** an individual granted a proprietary colony. [Modification of PROPRIETARY.] —**pro·pri′e·tor·ship′,** *n.*

pro·pri·e·ty (prə prī′i tē) *n., pl.* **-ties. 1.** the quality of being proper or appropriate; suitability. **2.** conformity with what is proper, esp. with socially accepted standards of manners and conduct. **3. the proprieties.** standards of manners and conduct approved by polite society: *to observe the proprieties.* [Latin *proprietās* proper signification of words, quality, ownership. Doublet of PROPERTY.]

pro·pri·o·cep·tive (prō′prē ə sep′tiv) *adj.* **1.** of, relating to, or designating stimuli that arise within an organism. **2.** of or relating to proprioceptors. [Latin *proprius* one's own + (RE)CEPTIVE.]

pro·pri·o·cep·tor (prō′prē ə sep′tər) *n.* a sensory receptor, as

in a muscle, tendon, or joint, that is responsive to stimuli arising from bodily movement. [Latin *proprius* one's own + (RE)CEPTOR.]

pro·pul·sion (prə pul′shən) *n.* **1.** the act or process of driving forward or propelling. **2.** something that propels; propelling force. [Latin *prōpulsus,* past participle of *prōpellere* to drive forward + -ION.]

pro·pul·sive (prə pul′siv) *adj.* serving to propel or capable of propelling: *a propulsive force.*

pro·pyl alcohol (prō′pəl) a colorless, volatile liquid used as a solvent, intermediate, and antiseptic. Formula: C_3H_7OH

pro·pyl·ene (prō′pə lēn′) *n.* a colorless, extremely flammable gas of the alkene, or olefin, series, used in the manufacture of artificial rubber. Formula: C_3H_6

propylene glycol, a colorless, viscous alcohol, used as a lubricant, antifreeze, and solvent. Formula: $C_3H_8O_2$

pro ra·ta (prō rā′tə, rä′-) in proportion; proportionately. [Latin *prō ratā (parte)* according to a calculated (portion), in proportion.]

pro·rate (prō rāt′, prō′rāt′) *v.t., v.i.,* **-rat·ed, -rat·ing.** to distribute, divide, or assess proportionately. [From PRO RATA.] —**pro·rat′a·ble,** *adj.* —**pro·ra′tion,** *n.*

pro·rogue (prō rōg′) *v.t.,* **-rogued, -rogu·ing.** to discontinue or suspend a session of (a lawmaking assembly), esp. by authority of a monarch. [Latin *prōrogāre* to extend, defer.] —**pro·ro·ga·tion** (prō′rə gā′shən), *n.*

pro·sa·ic (prō zā′ik) *adj.* **1.** lacking in uniqueness, freshness, or imagination; commonplace; ordinary. **2.** of or like prose; not poetic: *a prosaic verse style.* [Late Latin *prōsaicus* in prose (as opposed to verse), from Latin *prōsa (orātiō)* straightforward (speech).] —**pro·sa′i·cal·ly,** *adv.* —**pro·sa′ic·ness,** *n.*

pro·sce·ni·um (prə sē′nē əm) *n., pl.* **-ni·a** (-nē ə). **1.** the part of a theatrical stage in front of the curtain. **2.** the structure that frames the stage opening, usually arch-shaped. Also, **prosce·nium arch. 3.** the stage in an ancient theater. [Latin *proscēnium* stage, from Greek *proskēnion,* from *pro* before + *skēnē* tent, booth (in which actors dressed and before which they performed in the early Greek theater).]

pro·sciut·to (prə shü′tō) *n., pl.* **-tos** or **-ti** (-tē). a spiced Italian ham cured by drying and served in thin slices, often with melon. [Italian *prosciutto* this meat.]

pro·scribe (prō skrīb′) *v.t.,* **-scribed, -scrib·ing. 1.** to prohibit or condemn (something); interdict: *to proscribe smoking in an office.* **2.** to outlaw (someone); banish. [Latin *proscrībere* to publish in writing, outlaw.] —**pro·scrib′er,** *n.*

pro·scrip·tion (prō skrip′shən) *n.* **1.** the act of proscribing or the state of being proscribed. **2.** a law or order that proscribes; prohibition. —**pro·scrip′tive,** *adj.* —**pro·scrip′tive·ly,** *adv.*

prose (prōz) *n.* **1.** written or spoken language without metrical structure, as distinguished from poetry. **2.** a dull, commonplace discourse, expression, or quality. —*adj.* **1.** of, relating to, or written in prose: *a prose narrative.* **2.** commonplace; prosaic. —*v.t., v.i.,* **prosed, pros·ing.** to write or speak in prose. [Old French *prose* form of language without metrical structure (as opposed to poetry), from Latin *prōsa (orātiō)* straightforward (speech).]

pros·e·cute (pros′i kūt′) *v.,* **-cut·ed, -cut·ing.** —*v.t.* **1.** to begin and conduct legal proceedings against (a person, corporation, or institution) in a court of law. **2.** to seek to obtain or enforce by legal process: *to prosecute a claim for damages.* **3.** to follow up or pursue (something) to completion or conclusion: *to prosecute an investigation.* **4.** to engage in; carry on. —*v.i.* **1.** to begin and conduct legal proceedings in a court of law. **2.** to act as prosecutor. [Latin *prōsecūtus,* past participle of *prōsequī* to pursue.]

prosecuting attorney, a public official, as a district attorney, empowered to represent the government in instituting and conducting criminal prosecutions.

pros·e·cu·tion (pros′i kū′shən) *n.* **1.a.** the act or process of beginning and conducting legal proceedings, esp. criminal proceedings, in a court of law. **b.** the party or parties instituting and conducting such proceedings. **2.** the act or process of prosecuting.

pros·e·cu·tor (pros′i kū′tər) *n.* **1.** prosecuting attorney. **2.** the person who begins and conducts a legal action, esp. criminal proceedings. **3.** a person who prosecutes.

pros·e·lyte (pros′ə līt′) *n.* a person who has been brought over from one point of view, belief, or party to another, esp. a new convert to a religion. —*v.t., v.i.,* **-lyt·ed, -lyt·ing.** proselytize. [Late Latin *prosēlytus* stranger, religious convert, from Greek *prosēlytos.*]

pros·e·lyt·ism (pros′ə li tiz′əm, -lī-) *n.* **1.** the act or practice of proselytizing. **2.** the state of being or the fact of becoming a proselyte.

pros·e·lyt·ize (pros′ə li tīz′, -lī-) *v.t., v.i.,* **-ized, -iz·ing.** to

convert or attempt to convert, as from one religion or point of view to another.

Pro·ser·pi·na (prō sûr′pə nə) *also*, **Pro·ser·pi·ne** (prō sûr′pə-nē). *n.* in Roman mythology, the daughter of Jupiter and Ceres, whose uncle, Pluto, carried her off and made her queen of the underworld. She was allowed to revisit the earth for part of each year, and her return was accompanied by the coming of spring. Her Greek counterpart is Persephone.

pro·sim·i·an (prō sim′ē ən) *n.* any of a suborder, Prosimii, of mainly small, tree-climbing primates, including lemurs, lorises, pottos, and galagos. [PRO-² + SIMIAN.]

pro·sit (prō′sit, -zit) *interj.* to your health. ➡ used as a drinking toast, as in Germany. [Latin *prōsit* may it be profitable.]

pro·slav·er·y (prō slā′və rē) *adj.* favoring slavery, esp., in U.S. history, supporting the institution of slavery.

pros·o·dist (pros′ə dist) *n.* a person skilled in prosody.

pros·o·dy (pros′ə dē) *n.* **1.** the study or art of writing or composing verses. **2.** a particular system of versification. [Latin *prosōdia* tone or accent of a syllable, from Greek *prosōidiā* song sung to instrumental music, pronunciation, accent.] —**pro·sod·ic** (prə sod′ik); *also*, **pro·sod′i·cal**, *adj.* —**pro·sod′i·cal·ly**, *adv.*

pros·pect (pros′pekt) *n.* **1.** a mental vision of a future possibility or probability: *We were excited by the prospect of two weeks at the shore.* **2.** the act of looking forward to something; anticipation. **3.** *usually*, **prospects.** a chance for future success: *good prospects.* **4.** a person who shows promise of some kind, as a possible customer, potential political candidate, or athlete likely to be a star. **5.** a scene spread out before the eye; view. —*v.t.*, *v.i.* to search or explore: *to prospect an area for minerals, to prospect for gold.* [Latin *prōspectus* lookout, view.]

pro·spec·tive (prə spek′tiv) *adj.* **1.** probable or expected; future: *a prospective buyer, a prospective bride.* **2.** of, relating to, or in the future: *prospective laws.* —**pro·spec′tive·ly**, *adv.*

pros·pec·tor (pros′pek tər, prə spek′-) *n.* a person who explores an area for minerals or other resources, as gold or oil.

pro·spec·tus (prə spek′təs) *n.*, *pl.* **-tus·es.** a printed statement describing a proposed enterprise, undertaking, or work. [Latin *prōspectus* lookout, view.]

pros·per (pros′pər) *v.i.* to have success, wealth, or good fortune or health; flourish. [Latin *prosperāre* to make happy.]

> **Synonyms** **Prosper, thrive,** and **flourish** mean to achieve success or to grow or develop to a high level. **Prosper** is applied particularly to success marked by an increase in wealth and material possessions: *My parents came to America as poor immigrants but soon prospered.* **Thrive** usually refers to the vigorous physical growth of living things: *The cattle thrived on the new feed.* **Flourish** suggests reaching and sustaining a high level of development: *The arts flourished in Europe during the Renaissance.*

pros·per·i·ty (pros per′i tē) *n.* the state or condition of being prosperous, esp. economic well-being.

pros·per·ous (pros′pər əs) *adj.* **1.** having or characterized by success, wealth, or good fortune. **2.** conducive to success; favorable; propitious. [Latin *prosperus* favorable, from *prō* for + *spēs* hope.] —**pros′per·ous·ly**, *adv.* —**pros′per·ous·ness**, *n.*

pros·ta·glan·din (pros′tə glan′din) *n.* any of a group of fatty acids formed in animal tissue and involved in various functions, such as regulating blood pressure and body temperature and stimulating contraction of the smooth muscles.

pros·tate (pros′tāt) *n.* a chestnut-shaped organ present in male mammals, lying below the bladder and surrounding the urethra. It consists of glandular tissue that secretes an alkaline fluid discharged in semen, and muscle tissue that controls the flow of urine. Also, **prostate gland.** —*adj.* of, relating to, or affecting this organ. [Modern Latin *prostata*, from Greek *prostatēs* one who stands before, guardian.] —**pros·tat·ic** (pro stat′ik), *adj.*

pros·the·sis (pros thē′sis) *n.*, *pl.* **-ses** (-sēz). a mechanical or other artificial device used as a replacement for a missing part of the body, as a leg, arm, or eye. [Late Latin *prosthesis* prefixing a letter or syllable to a word, from Greek *prosthesis* addition.] —**pros·thet·ic** (pros thet′ik), *adj.*

pros·ti·tute (pros′ti tūt′, -tūt′) *n.* **1.** a person who engages in sexual acts for money. **2.** a person who puts personal qualities or abilities to an unworthy use, esp. for money. —*v.t.*, **-tut·ed,** **-tut·ing. 1.** to sell (oneself or another) for sexual purposes. **2.** to put (oneself or one's abilities) to an unworthy use, esp. for money. [Latin *prōstitūtus*, past participle of *prōstituere* to expose publicly, dishonor.]

pros·ti·tu·tion (pros′ti tū′shən, -tū′-) *n.* **1.** the act or practice of engaging in sexual acts for money. **2.** the act of putting (someone or something) to an unworthy use.

pros·trate (pros′trāt) *v.t.*, **-trat·ed, -trat·ing. 1.** to lay or throw (oneself) face downward on the ground in humility, adoration, or submission. **2.** to lay or throw down on the ground;

flatten: *With a single blow the intended victim prostrated the attacker.* **3.** to weaken or make helpless: *The flu prostrated me for days.* —*adj.* **1.** lying face downward on the ground in humility, adoration, or submission. **2.** lying or thrown down. **3.** completely exhausted, helpless, or overcome: *The country was left prostrate by war. The family was prostrate with grief.* [Latin *prōstrātus*, past participle of *prōsternere* to throw before one, throw down.]

pros·tra·tion (pros trā′shən) *n.* **1.** the act of prostrating or the state of being prostrated. **2.** extreme mental or physical exhaustion.

pros·y (prō′zē) *adj.*, **pros·i·er, pros·i·est. 1.** like prose; prosaic: *a poet with a prosy style.* **2.** lacking originality or interest; wearisome; tedious: *a prosy speaker.* —**pros′i·ly**, *adv.* —**pros′i·ness**, *n.*

Prot., Protestant.

prot·ac·tin·i·um (prō′tak tin′ē əm) *n.* a rare radioactive metallic element found in pitchblende and also produced artificially. Symbol: **Pa** For tables, see **element.** [PRO(TO)- + ACTINIUM.]

pro·tag·o·nist (prō tag′ə nist) *n.* **1.** the leading character in a novel, play, or other work of literature. **2.** the central figure, leader, or champion in an event, cause, or undertaking. [Greek *prōtagōnistēs* chief actor in a drama, going back to *prōtos* first + *agōn* contest.]

prot·a·mine (prō′tə mēn′) *n.* any of a group of simple proteins that are strongly basic, do not coagulate when heated, and yield only amino acids when they are decomposed. [PROT(O)- + AMINE.]

pro·te·an (prō′tē ən, prō tē′-) *adj.* readily assuming different shapes or aspects; variable: *a protean organism, a protean personality.* [PROTEUS + -AN.]

pro·te·ase (prō′tē ās′) *n.* any enzyme, as pepsin or trypsin, that breaks down or digests proteins by proteolysis. [PROTE(IN) + -ASE.]

pro·tect (prə tekt′) *v.t.* **1.** to defend or shield from harm; keep safe: *to protect oneself by wearing a seat belt.* **2.** to guard or promote the development of (a domestic industry) by means of a protective tariff. [Latin *prōtectus*, past participle of *prōtegere* to cover in front, shield from danger.] —**pro·tect′ing·ly**, *adv.* —For Synonyms, see **defend.**

pro·tec·tion (prə tek′shən) *n.* **1.** the act of protecting or the state of being protected. **2.** a person or thing that protects. **3.** a system of guarding or promoting the development of a domestic industry by means of a protective tariff. **4.** *Informal.* money paid to gangsters to keep them from committing violence against one.

pro·tec·tion·ism (prə tek′shə niz′əm) *n.* an economic system or the theory of guarding or promoting the development of domestic industries by means of protective tariffs. —**pro·tec′tion·ist**, *n.*, *adj.*

pro·tec·tive (prə tek′tiv) *adj.* serving or intended to protect: *a protective shell, protective measures.* —**pro·tec′tive·ly**, *adv.* —**pro·tec′tive·ness**, *n.*

protective coloration of a moth

protective coloration, any inherited coloration or pattern of coloration that helps to conceal an animal in its natural surroundings, enabling it to escape the notice of predators.

a	at	e	end	o	hot	u	up	hw	white		about
ā	ape	ē	me	ō	old	ū	use	ng	song		taken
ä	far	i	it	ô	fork	u̇	rule	th	thin	ə	pencil
âr	care	ī	ice	oi	oil	u̇	pull	th	this		lemon
		îr	pierce	ou	out	ûr	turn	zh	measure		circus

P

protective tariff, a tariff designed primarily to protect domestic industry against foreign competition rather than to raise revenue.
pro·tec·tor (prə tek′tər) *n.* **1.** a person or thing that protects; guardian; defender. **2.** in English history, a person who exercises control in place of a monarch who is too young, absent, or incapacitated.
pro·tec·tor·ate (prə tek′tər it) *n.* **1.** a relationship of protection and partial control assumed by a strong country over a weaker one. **2.** a country that surrenders part of its sovereignty to another country in such a relationship. **3.** the position or period of rule of a protector.
pro·té·gé (prō′tə zhā′, prō′tə zhā′) *n.* a person who is under the care, guidance, or patronage of someone influential or prominent. [French *protégé* favorite, dependent, from *protéger* to shield, guard, from Latin *protegere* to shield from danger.]
pro·té·gée (prō′tə zhā′) *n.* a woman or girl who is under the care, guidance, or patronage of someone influential or prominent.
pro·tein (prō′tēn, -tē in) *n.* **1.** any of a large group of organic compounds, containing nitrogen, carbon, hydrogen, and oxygen, whose complex molecules are formed of chains of amino acids. Proteins are present in all living cells and are the materials of cell growth and repair. **2.** plant or animal tissue that is rich in these molecules and eaten as a source of amino acids. Also, **pro·teid** (prō′tēd, -tē id). [German *Protein,* from Greek *prōteios* primary; because it is the *primary* material in the composition of animal and plant tissue.]
pro·tein·ase (prō′tē nās′ -tē i nās′) *n.* any of various proteases that hydrolyze proteins to form polypeptides. [PROTEIN + -ASE.]
pro tem (prō tem′) pro tempore.
pro tem·po·re (prō tem′pə rē) *Latin.* for the time being; temporarily: *the president pro tempore of the senate.*
pro·te·ol·y·sis (prō′tē ol′ə sis) *n.* the hydrolysis of proteins into peptones, proteoses, peptides, or other simpler substances, usually by enzymes, as in digestion. —**pro·te·o·lyt·ic** (prō′tē ə lit′ik), *adj.*
pro·te·ose (prō′tē ōs′) *n.* any of a group of water-soluble compounds that are formed during the initial stages of proteolysis, or protein digestion, and that after additional hydrolysis are converted to peptone. [PROTE(IN) + -OSE².]
Prot·er·o·zo·ic (prot′ər ə zō′ik, prō′tər-) *n.* the later of the two geologic divisions (Archean is the other) of the Precambrian era, during which a variety of invertebrate metazoan organisms evolved and fed upon the algae and bacteria in the seas. —*adj.* of, relating to, or characteristic of the Proterozoic. [Greek *proteros* former + *zōē* life + -IC.]
pro·test (*n.,* prō′test; *v.,* prə test′) *n.* **1.** a strong expression or declaration of disapproval or dissent: *They issued a protest against the proposed highway.* **2.** a solemn declaration or affirmation: *a suitor's protests of love.* **3.** a formal declaration in writing, prepared by a notary public, that a check, note, or other similar written order has been presented for payment or acceptance and has been refused. **4.** *Informal.* a public demonstration against something. —*v.i.* **1.** to express strong disapproval or dissent: *The group protested against the country's foreign policy.* **2.** to make a solemn declaration. —*v.t.* **1.** to express strong disapproval of; object to: *The committee protested the budget cuts.* **2.** to declare solemnly: *The youths, accused of the crime, protested their innocence.* **3.** to declare with a notarial certificate that (a check, note, or other similar written order) has been refused. [Middle French *protester* to declare in public, object, from Latin *prōtestārī* to declare in public, testify.] —**pro·test′er;** also, **pro·tes′tor,** *n.* —**pro·test′ing·ly,** *adv.*
Prot·es·tant (prot′ə stənt) *n.* **1.** a member of any of various Christian churches that originated in the repudiation of the pope's authority by certain churchmen, notably the German theologian Martin Luther, during the Reformation of the sixteenth century. **2.** a member of any Christian church other than the Roman Catholic Church or Orthodox churches. **3. protestant.** a person who protests. —*adj.* of or relating to Protestants or Protestantism. [Latin *prōtestāns,* present participle of *prōtestārī* to declare in public, testify.]
Protestant Episcopal Church, Episcopal Church.
Prot·es·tant·ism (prot′ə stən tiz′əm) *n.* **1.** the doctrines, beliefs, and practices of Protestants. **2.** Protestants or the Protestant churches collectively.
prot·es·ta·tion (prot′ə stā′shən, prō′tə-) *n.* **1.** the act of protesting. **2.** a solemn declaration or affirmation: *protestations of loyalty.* **3.** a strong expression of disapproval or dissent; protest.
Pro·te·us (prō′tē əs) *n.* in classical legend, a sea god who had the power of prophecy and of assuming many different shapes.
pro·thal·lus (prō thal′əs) *n., pl.* -thal·li (-thal′ī). a gametophyte of a fern or related plant. [Modern Latin *prothallus,* from Greek *pro-* before + *thallos* young shoot.] —**pro·thal·li·al** (prō-thal′ē əl), *adj.*

pro·tho·rax (prō thôr′aks) *n., pl.* -tho·rax·es or -tho·ra·ces (-thôr′ə sēz′). the frontmost of the three segments that compose an insect's thorax, bearing the first pair of legs. [Modern Latin *prothorax.* See PRO-², THORAX.] —**pro·thor·ac·ic** (prō′thô ras′-ik), *adj.*
pro·throm·bin (prō throm′bin) *n.* a protein in blood plasma that is produced by the liver and converted into thrombin, the enzyme that enables blood clotting.
pro·tist (prō′tist) *n.* any of a kingdom (Protista) of primitive nucleate organisms, some of which are plantlike, as the euglena and most algae, and others animallike protozoans, as the ameba and paramecium. For illustration, see **kingdom.** [Modern Latin *Protista,* from Greek *prōtistos* the very first, superlative of *protos* first.]
proto- *combining form* first in time; earliest; original: *protozoan, prototype.* [Greek *prōtos* first.]
pro·to·a·vis (prō′tō ā′vis) *n.* an extinct, birdlike animal that had a tail and hind legs like those of a dinosaur and bones and other features similar to those of birds. It flourished in the Triassic period, before archaeopteryx.
pro·to·col (prō′tə kôl′) *n.* **1.** polite behavior and order of rank observed by diplomats; customs and regulations of diplomatic etiquette. **2.** a first draft, original copy, or record of a document, as a treaty. **3.** the procedure followed in a medical treatment or scientific experiment. [Middle French *protocole* first draft or copy of a contract or deed, through Medieval Latin, from Late Greek *prōtokollon* first sheet glued to a manuscript containing its date and the author's name, from Greek *prōtos* first + *kolla* glue.]
Pro·to-In·do-Eu·ro·pe·an (prō′tō in′dō yŭr′ə pē′ən) *n.* the hypothetical prehistoric language from which Indo-European languages are thought to be derived. Also, **Indo-European.**
pro·ton (prō′ton) *n.* a subatomic particle found in the nucleus of all atoms, having a positive electric charge equal to the negative charge of an electron. The atomic number of an element is equal to the number of protons in the nucleus of its atom. For illustration, see **atom.** [Greek *prōton,* neuter of *prōtos* first.]
pro·to·plasm (prō′tə plaz′əm) *n.* the jellylike substance of which the cytoplasm and nucleus of every living cell of a plant, animal, or other organism is composed, consisting of water, proteins, sugars, fats, acids, and salts. [German *Protoplasma,* from Greek *prōtos* first + *plasma* something molded.] —**pro′to·plas′-mal, pro′to·plas·mat′ic, pro′to·plas′mic,** *adj.*
pro·to·type (prō′tə tīp′) *n.* **1.** an original or model from which something is derived or on which something is based. **2.** a typical or perfect example: *That character is the prototype of the romantic hero.* [Modern Latin *prototypon,* going back to Greek *prōtotypos* original, primitive, from *prōtos* first + *typos* model.] —**pro′to·typ′al, pro′to·typ′ic** (prō′tə tip′ik); *also,* **pro′to·typ′i·cal,** *adj.* —**pro′to·typ′i·cal·ly,** *adv.*
pro·to·zo·an (prō′tə zō′ən) *n., pl.* -zo·an or -zo·a (-zō′ə). any of a large group of single-celled, microscopic protists of the phylum Protozoa, as the ameba. —*adj.* of or relating to protozoans. [Modern Latin *Protozoa* (from Greek *prōtos* first + *zōia* animals) + -AN; because they were once considered to be the first animals of the earth.]
pro·tract (prō trakt′) *v.t.* **1.** to lengthen in time; prolong: *to protract a speech.* **2.** to draw (lines) with a scale and protractor. **3.** *Anatomy.* to extend or protrude. [Latin *prōtractus,* past participle of *prōtrahere* to draw forth, prolong.] —**pro·tract′ed·ly,** *adv.* —**pro·tract′ed·ness,** *n.* —**pro·tract′i·ble,** *adj.*
pro·trac·tile (prō trak′təl, -tīl) *adj.* capable of being extended or protruded: *a protractile tongue.*
pro·trac·tion (prō trak′shən) *n.* **1.** the act of protracting or the state of being protracted. **2.** something that has been protracted.
pro·trac·tor (prō trak′-tər) *n.* **1.** an instrument in the form of a semicircle marked off in degrees, used for measuring or drawing angles. **2.** a person or thing that protracts.

protractor
angle *AOB* = 65°

pro·trude (prō trüd′) *v.,* -trud·ed, -trud·ing. —*v.i.* to stick out; project: *Rocks protruded from the snow.* —*v.t.* to cause to stick out: *The snail protruded its horns from its shell.* [Latin *prōtrūdere* to thrust forward.]
pro·tru·sion (prō trü′zhən) *n.* **1.** the act of protruding or the state of being protruded. **2.** something that protrudes.
pro·tru·sive (prō trü′siv) *adj.* sticking out; protruding; projecting: *a protrusive chin.*

pro·tu·ber·ance (prō tü′bər əns, -tū′-) *n.* **1.** something that sticks out, as a swelling or bulge. **2.** the state or condition of being protuberant.

pro·tu·ber·ant (prō tü′bər ənt, -tū′-) *adj.* sticking out; bulging. —**pro·tu′ber·ant·ly,** *adv.*

proud (proud) *adj.* **1.** taking great personal satisfaction in someone or something: *the proud parents of a child, a father proud of his daughter's success.* **2.** having a sense of one's personal worth or dignity: *a person who is too proud to beg.* **3.** having an exaggerated or unreasonable sense of one's worth or dignity; haughty: *a proud, vain member of the nobility.* **4.** causing pleasure or satisfaction: *Winning the award was a proud moment for me.* **5.** noble or majestic; magnificent: *a proud ship.* **6.** arising from or caused by pride: *a proud, contemptuous look.* **7.** spirited: *a proud steed.* [Old English *prūd* valuing oneself highly, from Old French *prud, prod* valiant, brave, from Late Latin *prōde* useful, from Latin *prōdesse* to be useful or profitable.] —**proud′ly,** *adv.* —**proud′ness,** *n.*

Synonyms Proud, haughty, and arrogant mean having a strong or exaggerated sense of superiority. **Proud** suggests a sense of self-importance that may be misguided or contemptuous: *The proud man found few people worthy of his friendship. The reporter was too proud to admit she had made a mistake.* **Haughty** implies a contemptuous attitude based on real or imagined social superiority: *The wealthy parents encouraged their child's haughty disdain for poorer classmates.* **Arrogant** suggests a domineering, overbearing pride: *The arrogant official loved giving orders to subordinates.*

proud flesh, the swollen, irregular surface of flesh formed around the edges of a healing wound.

prov. **1.** province. **2.** provincial.

Prov. **1.** Provençal. **2.** Proverbs.

prove (prüv) *v.,* **proved, proved** or **prov·en, prov·ing.** —*v.t.* **1.** to show convincingly the truth or genuineness of: *The lawyer proved the innocence of the defendant.* **2.** to test or show the worth or qualities of: *to prove oneself as an athlete, to prove a new rifle.* **3.** to confirm the authenticity or validity of: *The probate judge proved the will.* **4.** *Mathematics.* to verify the correctness of: *to prove an equation.* —*v.i.* to turn out: *The play proved to be very good.* [Old French *prover* to try, approve, verify, from Latin *probāre* to test, try, approve, demonstrate.] —**prov′a·ble,** *adj.* —**prov′a·bly,** *adv.*

prov·e·nance (prov′ə nəns) *n.* the place or other source from which something comes, develops, or derives; origin. [French *provenance,* from *provenir* to originate, from Latin *provenire* to come forth, from *pro* before, for + *venire* to come.]

Pro·ven·çal (prov′ən säl′, prō′vən-) *adj.* of, relating to, or characteristic of Provence or its people, language, or culture. —*n.* **1.** a native or inhabitant of Provence. **2.** the Romance language of Provence.

prov·en·der (prov′ən dər) *n.* **1.** dry feed or fodder for livestock. **2.** *Informal.* food; provisions. [Old French *provend(r)e,* going back to Late Latin *praebenda* allowance. See PREBEND.]

prov·erb (prov′ərb) *n.* a short, pithy saying expressing popular wisdom. [Latin *prōverbium.*]

Synonyms Proverb, adage, maxim, and aphorism mean a concise expression of a commonly accepted truth. A **proverb** is a traditional saying in simple, concrete language, such as *no rose without a thorn.* An **adage** is a proverb that is widely circulated and often repeated, such as *A bird in the hand is worth two in the bush.* A **maxim** is a rule of behavior drawn from practical experience, such as *A good beginning makes a good ending.* An **aphorism,** which is often of known authorship, is of high literary quality and may state a profound idea, such as *Time flies over us but leaves its shadow behind* (Nathaniel Hawthorne).

pro·ver·bi·al (prə vûr′bē əl) *adj.* **1.** of, relating to, or characteristic of a proverb. **2.a.** expressed in a proverb: *proverbial wisdom.* **b.** mentioned in a proverb: *The proverbial early bird does not always get the worm.* **3.** commonly spoken of; well-known: *the proverbial ingenuity of American pioneers.* —**pro·ver′bi·al·ly,** *adv.*

Prov·erbs (prov′ərbz) *n.* a book of the Old Testament, containing practical advice and moral instruction. ➡ used as singular.

pro·vide (prə vīd′) *v.,* **-vid·ed, -vid·ing.** —*v.t.* **1.** to fit out with what is needed or desired; furnish: *The school provides the students with their books.* **2.** to give or produce: *Trees provide shelter from the sun.* **3.** to specify as a condition; stipulate: *The law provides that a person is innocent until proven guilty.* —*v.i.* **1.** to make adequate preparation for a future need (with *for* or *against*). **2.** to make provision for present need (with *for*): *They provided for their family by working in a mill.* [Latin *prōvidēre* to foresee, look after, act with foresight. Doublet of PURVEY.]

—**pro·vid′a·ble,** *adj.* —**pro·vid′er,** *n.* —For Synonyms (*v.t.*), see **furnish.**

pro·vid·ed (prə vī′did) *conj.* with the understanding that; on the condition that; if: *I'll lend you my saw, provided you return it by next week.* Also, **providing.**

prov·i·dence (prov′i dəns) *n.* **1.** God's care, control, or guidance, or an instance of it. **2.** prudent regard for the future; foresight. **3.** wise management, as of resources. **4. Providence.** God.

prov·i·dent (prov′i dənt) *adj.* **1.** having a prudent regard for the future. **2.** economical; frugal. [Latin *prōvidēns,* present participle of *prōvidēre* to foresee, look after.] —**prov′i·dent·ly,** *adv.*

prov·i·den·tial (prov′i den′shəl) *adj.* **1.** of, relating to, or proceeding from divine providence. **2.** coming about as if through divine intervention; fortunate: *A providential rain put out the fire.* —**prov′i·den′tial·ly,** *adv.*

pro·vid·ing (prə vī′ding) *conj.* provided.

prov·ince (prov′ins) *n.* **1.** a political division of a country: *Canada consists of ten provinces and two territories.* **2.** a sphere or range of activity or authority: *Judging the legality of the ordinance is within the province of the courts.* **3. the provinces.** the regions of a country outside the capital or cultural center. **4.** a territory outside Italy ruled by ancient Rome. **5.** the territory over which an archbishop or metropolitan has religious authority. [Old French *province* the political division, from Latin *prōvincia* such a Roman territory, official duty.]

pro·vin·cial (prə vin′shəl) *adj.* **1.** of or relating to a province: *a provincial government, a provincial dialect.* **2.** characteristic of the inhabitants of a certain province: *traditional provincial costumes.* **3.** characteristic of the inhabitants of the provinces; unsophisticated or unfashionable: *provincial manners.* **4.** having or showing a limited point of view; narrow-minded: *provincial attitudes.* —*n.* **1.** a native or inhabitant of a province. **2.** a person who is provincial, esp. in manner, speech, or point of view. —**pro·vin′cial·ly,** *adv.*

pro·vin·cial·ism (prə vin′shə liz′əm) *n.* **1.** the state or quality of being provincial, esp. in manner, speech, or point of view. **2.** something that is provincial, such as a particular word, expression, or pronunciation, or a habit or style of dress.

pro·vin·ci·al·i·ty (prə vin′shē al′i tē) *n., pl.* **-ties. 1.** the state or quality of being provincial. **2.** something that is provincial.

proving ground, a place for testing new devices or theories, esp. a tract of land for testing military weapons and equipment.

pro·vi·sion (prə vizh′ən) *n.* **1.** the act of giving or supplying: *The boss supervised the provision of equipment to the workers.* **2.** preparation made for a future or possible need: *They had made no provision for their retirement.* **3.** something that is given or supplied; stock: *We brought along a provision of gasoline.* **4.** something that is specified as a condition; stipulation: *A provision in the labor agreement called for a retroactive pay increase.* **5. provisions.** a supply of food: *The expedition had provisions for a month.* —*v.t.* to supply with provisions. [Latin *prōvīsiō* foresight.]

pro·vi·sion·al (prə vizh′ə nəl) *adj.* **1.** provided for a present or temporary need; for the time being: *The provisional government will serve until elections can be held.* **2.** agreed to or accepted on a conditional basis: *The provisional contract must be approved by the union members.* —**pro·vi′sion·al·ly,** *adv.*

pro·vi·so (prə vī′zō) *n., pl.* **-sos** or **-soes. 1.** a clause that specifies a condition: *a proviso in a contract.* **2.** a stipulation; condition: *The senator agreed to be interviewed with the proviso that certain questions would not be asked.* [Medieval Latin *proviso (quod)* it being provided (that), going back to Latin *prōvidēre* to foresee, look after.]

pro·vi·so·ry (prə vī′zə rē) *adj.* **1.** subject to or containing a proviso; conditional. **2.** provisional.

pro·vi·ta·min (prō vī′tə min) *n.* any of various substances that can be converted into a vitamin by the body, as carotene, which is converted into vitamin A.

prov·o·ca·tion (prov′ə kā′shən) *n.* **1.** the act of angering or inciting. **2.** something that angers or incites: *The country's large army was a provocation to its neighbors.* [Latin *prōvocātiō* summoning, challenging.]

pro·voc·a·tive (prə vok′ə tiv) *adj.* tending to provoke, esp. by arousing anger, interest, or desire: *a provocative glance, a provocative newspaper editorial.* —*n.* something that is provocative. —**pro·voc′a·tive·ly,** *adv.* —**pro·voc′a·tive·ness,** *n.*

P

a	at	e	end	o	hot	u	up	hw	white		about
ā	ape	ē	me	ō	old	ū	use	ng	song	ə	taken
ä	far	i	it	ô	fork	ü	rule	th	thin		pencil
âr	care	ī	ice	oi	oil	ů	pull	th	this		lemon
		îr	pierce	ou	out	ûr	turn	zh	measure		circus

pro·voke (prə vōk′) *v.t.,* **-voked, -vok·ing. 1.** to anger or enrage; irritate greatly. **2.** to stir up (a person) to some action or emotion; incite; arouse: *to provoke someone to anger.* **3.** to cause by inciting; bring about deliberately: *to provoke a fight, to provoke gossip.* **4.** to call forth or bring out; elicit: *to provoke interest.* [Latin *prōvocāre* to call forth, challenge.] —**pro·vok′er,** *n.* —**pro·vok′ing·ly,** *adv.* —For Synonyms, see **incite.**

pro·vost (prō′vōst, prov′əst) *n.* **1.** a high-ranking administrator in some colleges or universities. **2.** the chief magistrate of a Scottish town or city. **3.** the head of the clergy in some cathedrals or collegiate churches. [Old English *prōfost* ecclesiastical dignitary, one placed in charge, going back to Latin *praepositus* overseer.]

pro·vost marshal (prō′vō) **1.** an officer in the army in command of the military police, as at a base. **2.** an officer in the navy responsible for a prisoner who faces court-martial.

prow (prou) *n.* **1.** the forward part of a boat or ship; bow. **2.** something resembling the prow of a ship, such as the front end of an airplane. [Old French *prouë* forward part of a ship, through Italian and Latin, from Greek *prōira*.]

prow of a ship

prow·ess (prou′is) *n.* **1.** great valor, strength, or daring, esp. in battle. **2.** great ability or skill: *athletic prowess.* [Old French *proesce* bravery, from *prod* brave. See PROUD.]

prowl (proul) *v.i.* to rove about furtively, esp. in search of prey: *The tiger prowled through the jungle.* —*v.t.* to roam over or through furtively: *The thug prowled the streets at night.* —*n.* the act of prowling. [Of uncertain origin.] —**prowl′er,** *n.*
• **on the prowl,** prowling about or searching for something.

prowl car, squad car.

prox·i·mal (prok′sə məl) *adj.* **1.** located closest to the body or to the place or point of attachment, as of a limb or bone. ➡ distinguished from **distal. 2.** proximate *(def. 1).* [Latin *proximus* nearest + -AL¹.]

prox·i·mate (prok′sə mit) *adj.* **1.** nearest in sequence, space, time, or degree; next. **2.** approximate. [Latin *proximātus,* past participle of *proximāre* to approach.] —**prox′i·mate·ly,** *adv.* —**prox′i·mate·ness,** *n.*

prox·im·i·ty (prok sim′i tē) *n.* the state or condition of being near in sequence, space, time, or degree; nearness. [Latin *proximitās.*]

proximity fuse, a fuse designed to detonate an explosive projectile when it approaches within a certain distance of the target.

prox·i·mo (prok′sə mō′) *adv.* in or of the next month: *on the twelfth proximo.* [Latin *proximō (mense)* in the next (month).]

prox·y (prok′sē) *n., pl.* **prox·ies. 1.** a person authorized to act for another; substitute. **2.** the act or an instance of authorizing such a person: *to vote by proxy.* **3.** a document authorizing a person to act for another. **4.** a person or group acting or speaking in an ally's or associate's behalf: *Many regarded the guerrillas as the proxies of a foreign power.* [Modification of Middle English *procuracie* management or action for another, deputy, from Medieval Latin *procuratia* management, from Latin *prōcūrātiō.*]

prude (prüd) *n.* a person who is excessively modest or proper in behavior, dress, and speech. [French *prude,* short for *prudefemme* respectable woman, going back to Late Latin *prōde* useful + Latin *dē* from + *fēmina* woman. See PROUD.]

pru·dence (prü′dəns) *n.* **1.** the state or quality of being prudent; circumspection. **2.** careful or frugal management; economy.

pru·dent (prü′dənt) *adj.* **1.** having or exercising good judgment; wise: *a prudent leader.* **2.** proceeding with caution; circumspect: *a prudent investor.* **3.** marked by or resulting from good judgment or caution: *a prudent policy, a prudent act.* **4.** economical; frugal: *a prudent use of one's money.* [Latin *prūdēns* foreseeing, skilled.] —**pru′dent·ly,** *adv.*

pru·den·tial (prü den′shəl) *adj.* **1.** of, characterized by, or resulting from good judgment or caution. **2.** exercising good judgment or caution. —**pru·den′tial·ly,** *adv.*

prud·er·y (prü′də rē) *n., pl.* **-er·ies. 1.** excessive concern with modesty or propriety. **2.** an instance of prudish talk or behavior.

prud·ish (prü′dish) *adj.* characterized by an excessive concern with modesty or propriety: *a prudish attitude that resulted from an extremely strict upbringing.* —**prud′ish·ly,** *adv.* —**prud′ish·ness,** *n.*

prune¹ (prün) *n.* **1.** a dried fruit of certain varieties of plum. **2.** any of various kinds of plums that can be dried without spoiling. [Old French *prune* plum, going back to Latin *prūnum,* from Greek *proumnon.* Doublet of PLUM.]

prune² (prün) *v.,* **pruned, prun·ing.** —*v.t.* **1.** to cut off (branches, twigs, or roots). **2.** to cut off unwanted twigs, branches, or roots from (a plant), usually to improve growth or appearance. **3.** to remove unnecessary or unwanted parts from: *to prune a manuscript.* **4.** to remove (unnecessary or unwanted parts): *to prune scenes from an overly long movie.* —*v.i.* **1.** to cut off unwanted growth from a plant. **2.** to remove unnecessary or unwanted parts from something. [Old French *proignier* to trim (vines or trees); of uncertain origin.] —**prun′er,** *n.*

pru·ri·ent (prür′ē ənt) *adj.* characterized by, having, or arousing lewd or indecent thoughts. [Latin *prūriēns,* present participle of *prūrīre* to itch, be wanton.] —**pru′ri·ence,** *n.* —**pru′ri·ent·ly,** *adv.*

pru·ri·tus (prù rī′təs) *n.* an itching of the skin without a rash; itch. [Latin *prūrītus,* past participle of *prūrīre* to itch.] —**pru·rit·ic** (prù rit′ik), *adj.*

Prus·sian (prush′ən) *adj.* **1.** of, relating to, or characteristic of Prussia or its people. **2.** characteristic of or resembling the Prussian aristocracy; militaristic: *Prussian discipline.* —*n.* a native or inhabitant of Prussia.

Prussian blue, a dark blue pigment, used esp. in painting, consisting of cyanide and ferric iron.

prus·sic acid (prus′ik) hydrocyanic acid.

pry¹ (prī) *v.i.,* **pried, pry·ing.** to look closely or curiously; peer or search inquisitively: *to pry into another person's affairs.* —*n., pl.* **pries.** a person who is excessively curious. [Of uncertain origin.]

pry² (prī) *v.t.,* **pried, pry·ing. 1.** to move, raise, or pull by force of a lever: *to pry off the top of a box.* **2.** to get with much effort; extract: *to pry information from someone.* —*n., pl.* **pries.** anything used as a lever for prying, such as a crowbar. [From PRIZE⁴.]

pry·ing (prī′ing) *adj.* full of or characterized by excessive curiosity: *prying questions about private matters.* —**pry′ing·ly,** *adv.*

Ps., Psalm; Psalms.

P.S. 1. postscript. **2.** public school.

psalm (säm) *n.* **1.** a sacred poem, song, or hymn. **2.** Psalm. any of the sacred, lyric poems that form the book of Psalms in the Old Testament. [Old English *psalm, sealm* sacred song, esp. one of those in the Old Testament, from Late Latin *psalmus,* from Greek *psalmos* a plucking of the harp; hence, song accompanied by the harp.]

psalm·ist (sä′mist) *n.* **1.** a writer or composer of sacred poems, songs, or hymns. **2.** the Psalmist. King David of Israel, traditionally considered to be the composer of the Psalms.

psalm·o·dy (sä′mə dē, sal′mə-) *n., pl.* **-dies. 1.** the act, practice, or art of singing psalms, esp. in public worship. **2.** psalms collectively. [Late Latin *psalmōdia,* from Greek *psalmōidiā* singing to the harp, from *psalmos* song accompanied by the harp + *ōidē* song.]

Psalms (sämz) *n.* a book of the Old Testament, containing sacred lyric poetry, traditionally attributed to King David. ➡ used as singular.

Psal·ter (sôl′tər) *n.* **1.** Psalms. **2.** a version of all or part of the Psalms arranged for liturgical or devotional use. [Old English *(p)saltere,* from Church Latin *psaltērium* the Psalms of David in the Old Testament, from Latin *psaltērium* stringed instrument. See PSALTERY.]

psal·ter·y (sôl′tə rē, -trē) *n., pl.* **-ter·ies.** an ancient and medieval musical instrument having a flat sounding board and a variable number of strings, played by plucking. [Latin *psaltērium,* from Greek *psaltērion.*]

PSAT, Preliminary Scholastic Aptitude Test.

pseu·do (sü′dō) *adj.* false or pretended; spurious: *a pseudo intellectual.* [From PSEUDO-.]

pseudo- *combining form* **1.** false; pretended: *pseudonym.* **2.** closely or deceptively resembling: *pseudopod.* [Greek *pseudēs* false.]

pseu·do·carp (sü′də kärp′) *n.* a fruit consisting of other parts in addition to the ovary and its contents, as the apple. —**pseu′do·car′pous,** *adj.*

pseu·do·nym (süˈdə nim) *n.* a fictitious name, esp. one used by an author to conceal his or her true identity. [Greek *pseudōnymon*, from *pseudēs* false + (dialectal) *onyma* name, word.]

> **Synonyms** Pseudonym, pen name, and alias mean a name used in place of one's legal or true name. **Pseudonym** usually refers to a name assumed by a well-known person for anonymity or popular appeal: *The film star used a pseudonym and wore dark glasses while traveling.* **Pen name** is applied specifically to a pseudonym assumed by an author: *Many writers have published works under a pen name.* **Alias** is a name used by lawbreakers to conceal a criminal record or deceive an intended victim: *The swindler was known by many aliases.*

pseu·do·pod (süˈdə pod′) *n.* a temporary, tongue-shaped projection of protoplasm sent out by an ameba or other protozoan as a means of locomotion and to capture food. For illustration, see **ameba.**

pseu·do·po·di·um (süˈdə pōˈdē əm) *n., pl.* **-di·a** (-dē ə). pseudopod.

pshaw (shô) *interj.* used to express disdain, impatience, or disapproval.

psi (sī, psē) *n.* the twenty-third letter of the Greek alphabet (Ψ, ψ).

psi·lo·cy·bin (sīˈlə sīˈbin, silˈə-) *n.* a hallucinogenic drug obtained from the mushroom *Psilocybe mexicana.* Formula: $C_{12}H_{17}N_2O_4P$ [Modern Latin *psylocybe* (from Greek *psilos* bare + *kybē* head) + -IN[1].]

psit·ta·co·sis (sitˈə kōˈsis) *n.* an infectious disease of certain birds, esp. parrots, that can be transmitted to humans, in whom it produces a form of pneumonia. Also, **parrot fever.** [Modern Latin *psittacosis,* from Greek *psittakos* parrot + -OSIS.]

pso·ri·a·sis (sə rīˈə sis) *n.* a chronic skin disease characterized by dry, reddish patches covered with silvery scales. [Modern Latin *psoriasis,* going back to Greek *psōrā* itch, mange.] —**pso·ri·at·ic** (sôrˈē atˈik, sor′-), *adj.*

PST, Pacific Standard Time.

psych (sīk) *v.t. Informal.* **1.** to undermine the confidence or abilities of through psychological intimidation (often with *out*): *to psych out an opponent.* **2.** to get psychologically ready; prepare mentally (often with *up*): *The racers were psyched and anxious to start.* [Short for PSYCHOANALYZE.]

psych-, form of **psycho-** before certain vowels.

Psy·che (sīˈkē) *n.* **1.** in classical mythology, a beautiful princess who fell in love with Eros. She is considered the personification of the human soul. **2. psyche.** the human soul or mind. **3. psyche.** *Psychiatry.* the mind in its capacity to perform psychological functions or acts. [Latin *Psychē* the mythological character, from Greek *Psychē,* from *psychē* soul, mind.]

psy·che·del·ic (sīˈki delˈik) *adj.* **1.** of, characterized by, or promoting hallucinations, intensified perceptions, or a trancelike state. **2.** of or relating to psychedelic drugs. —*n.* a psychedelic drug. [Greek *psychē* soul, mind + *dēlos* clear + -IC.]

psy·chi·at·ric (sīˈkē atˈrik) *adj.* of or relating to psychiatry. Also, **psy·chi·at′ri·cal.** —**psy·chi·at′ri·cal·ly,** *adv.*

psy·chi·a·trist (si kīˈə trist, sī-) *n.* a physician who specializes in the diagnosis and treatment of emotional and mental disorders.

psy·chi·a·try (si kīˈə trē, sī-) *n.* the branch of medicine that deals with the diagnosis and treatment of emotional and mental disorders. [PSYCHO- + Greek *iātreiā* art of healing.]

psy·chic (sīˈkik) *adj.* **1.** of or relating to the human soul or mind; spiritual or mental. **2.** of, relating to, designating, or caused by extrasensory, nonphysical, or supernatural influences or forces. **3.** sensitive to such influences or forces. Also, **psyˈchi·cal.** —*n.* a person who is sensitive to extrasensory, nonphysical, or supernatural influences or forces. [Greek *psychikos* relating to the soul, from *psychē* soul, mind.] —**psyˈchi·cal·ly,** *adv.*

psycho- *combining form* mind or mental processes: *psychology, psychotherapy.* [Greek *psychē* soul, mind.]

psy·cho·ac·tive (sīˈkō akˈtiv) *adj.* of or relating to a substance, as a drug, that affects mental processes or behavior.

psy·cho·a·nal·y·sis (sīˈkō ə nalˈə sis) *n.* **1.** a theory of psychology, set forth by the Austrian physician Sigmund Freud, that seeks to explain the relationship of the unconscious mind to the conscious mind. **2.** a therapeutic procedure used to explore the unconscious mind and treat emotional and mental disorders. —**psy·cho·an·a·lyt·ic** (sīˈkō anˈə litˈik); *also,* **psy·cho·an·a·lytˈi·cal,** *adj.* —**psy·cho·an·a·lytˈi·cal·ly,** *adv.*

psy·cho·an·a·lyst (sīˈkō anˈə list) *n.* a person who practices psychoanalysis. Also, **analyst.**

psy·cho·an·a·lyze (sīˈkō anˈə līz′) *v.t.,* **-lyzed, -lyz·ing.** to treat by psychoanalysis.

psy·cho·dra·ma (sīˈkə dräˈmə, -dramˈə, sīˈkō dräˈmə, -dramˈə) *n.* a technique of group psychotherapy in which patients enact roles and incidents.

psy·cho·dy·nam·ics (sīˈkō dī namˈiks) *n.* the study of human behavior from the point of view of motivation and drives.
➡ used as singular. —**psyˈcho·dy·namˈic,** *adj.*

psy·cho·gen·ic (sīˈkə jenˈik) *adj.* of psychic origin, as a physical disorder that originates in the mind. —**psyˈcho·genˈi·cal·ly,** *adv.*

psy·cho·his·to·ry (sīˈkō hisˈtə rē, -hisˈtrē) *n.* **1.** the study of historical events or individual lives employing psychological and psychoanalytic theory and methods. **2.** an example of this, such as biography: *a psychohistory of a political leader.* —**psyˈcho·his·torˈi·cal,** *adj.*

psy·cho·ki·ne·sis (sīˈkō ki nēˈsis) *n.* the effect of the mind on objects or events without the aid of physical means, as in parapsychology. [PSYCHO- + Greek *kinēsis* motion (from *kinein* to move).] —**psyˈcho·ki·netˈic,** *adj.*

psy·cho·log·i·cal (sīˈkə lojˈi kəl) *adj.* **1.** of or relating to psychology. **2.** of or relating to the mind or mental processes. Also, **psyˈcho·logˈic.** —**psyˈcho·logˈi·cal·ly,** *adv.*

psychological moment, the most favorable or critical moment for producing a desired effect.

psychological warfare, the use of propaganda or other psychologically directed activities in an attempt to undermine an opponent's ability or will to fight or compete.

psy·chol·o·gist (sī kolˈə jist) *n.* a person who is trained or who specializes in psychology.

psy·chol·o·gy (sī kolˈə jē) *n., pl.* **-gies. 1.** the study of the mind and of mental and emotional processes and behavior. **2.** the mental, emotional, or behavioral processes characteristic of a person or group, or relating to an experience: *the psychology of the artist, the psychology of the criminal, the psychology of defeat.* [Modern Latin *psychologia,* from PSYCHO- + -LOGY.]

psy·cho·met·rics (sīˈkə metˈriks) *n.* the branch of psychology dealing with the measurement of mental abilities and processes.
➡ used as singular. Also, **psy·chom·e·try** (sī komˈi trē).

psy·cho·neu·ro·sis (sīˈkō nū rōˈsis, -nyū-) *n., pl.* **-ses** (-sēz). neurosis. —**psyˈcho·neu·rotˈic** (sīˈkō nū rotˈik, -nyū-), *adj.*

psy·cho·path (sīˈkə path′) *n.* a person afflicted with a serious mental disorder, esp. one who exhibits antisocial or criminal behavior. Also, **psychopathic personality.** —**psyˈcho·pathˈic,** *adj.*

psy·cho·pa·thol·o·gy (sīˈkō pə tholˈə jē) *n.* **1.** the science dealing with the origins of mental illness. **2.** disordered psychologic functioning, as in mental illness. —**psyˈcho·path·o·logˈi·cal** (sīˈkō path′ə lojˈi kəl), *adj.* —**psyˈcho·pa·tholˈo·gist,** *n.*

psy·chop·a·thy (sī kopˈə thē) *n.* **1.** any mental disorder. **2.** a serious personality disorder characterized by antisocial behavior, an inability to learn from experience, and a tendency to blame others.

psy·cho·phys·ics (sīˈkō fizˈiks) *n.* the branch of psychology that deals with the interrelation of mental phenomena and physical stimuli. ➡ used as singular.

psy·cho·sex·u·al (sīˈkō sekˈshü əl) *adj.* of or relating to the mental and emotional aspects of sexuality, rather than the strictly physical aspects. —**psyˈcho·sexˈu·alˈi·ty,** *n.*

psy·cho·sis (sī kōˈsis) *n., pl.* **-ses** (-sēz). a severe mental disorder involving loss of contact with reality. [Late Greek *psychōsis* animation, principle of life, from Greek *psychoun* to give life to.]

psy·cho·so·cial (sīˈkō sōˈshəl) *adj.* of or relating to psychological development or mental health as influenced by the social environment. —**psyˈcho·soˈcial·ly,** *adv.*

psy·cho·so·mat·ic (sīˈkō sə matˈik) *adj.* **1.** of or relating to the interrelation of mind and body. **2.** of or relating to physical symptoms and changes in the body that are the result of emotional or mental conditions: *a psychosomatic illness, psychosomatic medicine.*

psy·cho·sur·ger·y (sīˈkō sûrˈjə rē) *n.* the surgical interruption of neural pathways in the brain or removal of certain areas of brain tissue to treat chronic, severe mental disorders, as in lobotomy. —**psyˈcho·surˈgi·cal,** *adj.*

psy·cho·ther·a·py (sīˈkō therˈə pē) *n.* the treatment of emotional or mental disorders by psychological means, as by psychoanalysis and group therapy. —**psyˈcho·therˈa·pist,** *n.*

psy·chot·ic (sī kotˈik) *n.* a person afflicted with a psychosis. —*adj.* of, relating to, suffering from, or caused by a psychosis. —**psyˈchotˈi·cal·ly,** *adv.*

psy·chot·o·mi·met·ic (sī kotˈō mi metˈik) *adj.* of or relating to certain drugs, as LSD or mescaline, that induce a state resem-

a	at	e	end	o	hot	u	up	hw	white	⎰	about
ā	ape	ē	me	ō	old	ū	use	ng	song		taken
ä	far	i	it	ô	fork	ü	rule	th	thin	ə ⟨	pencil
âr	care	ī	ice	oi	oil	u̇	pull	th	this		lemon
		îr	pierce	ou	out	ûr	turn	zh	measure	⎱	circus

bling psychosis. —*n.* a psychotomimetic drug. [PSYCHOT(IC) + MIMETIC.]

psy·cho·trop·ic (sī′kə trop′ik, -trō′pik) *adj.* of or relating to a drug or other substance that acts on the mind. —*n.* such a drug, as a tranquilizer or hallucinogen.

psy·chrom·e·ter (sī krom′i tər) *n.* a meteorological instrument used to measure atmospheric humidity, consisting of a pair of thermometers, one of which is kept wet and subject to evaporative cooling. [Greek *psychros* cold + -METER.] —**psy·chro·met·ric** (sī′krə met′rik), *adj.*

Pt, the symbol for platinum.

pt *also,* **pt.** pint; pints.

pt. 1. part. 2. payment. 3. point; points. 4. port.

PTA, Parent-Teacher Association.

ptar·mi·gan (tär′mi gən) *n., pl.* **-gan** or **-gans.** any of various grouse, genus *Lagopus,* of arctic or subarctic regions, having white winter plumage, brownish summer plumage, and feathered legs and feet. [Modification of Scottish Gaelic *tarmachan.*]

PT boat, a small, fast, and highly maneuverable boat used extensively in the Pacific Ocean during World War II. [Abbreviation of *p(atrol) t(orpedo) boat.*]

pter·an·o·don (tə ran′ə don′) *n.* any of various extinct flying reptiles, genus *Pteranodon,* that lived during Cretaceous geologic time, and had a crestlike extension on the back of the head and a long, toothless beak. Wingspread: up to 25 feet (8 meters). [Modern Latin *pteranodon,* from Greek *pteron* feather, wing + *anodōn* toothless (from *an-* without + *odōn* tooth).]

pte·rid·o·phyte (tə rid′ə fīt′, ter′i dō-) *n.* any of a group of seedless, flowerless plants, such as club moss or ferns, that reproduce by means of spores. [Modern Latin *Pteridophyta,* from Greek *pteris* fern + *phyta* plants.] —**pte·rid·o·phyt·ic** (tə rid′ə fit′ik), *adj.*

pter·o·dac·tyl (ter′ə dak′təl) *n.* any of a group of extinct flying reptiles, order Pterosauria, having greatly enlarged fourth fingers supporting featherless, leathery wing membranes. Wingspan: to 20 feet (6.1 meters). [Greek *pteron* feather, wing + *daktylos* finger, toe; referring to the long finger to which the wing was attached.]

pter·o·saur (ter′ə sôr′) *n.* any of a group of flying reptiles of the extinct order Pterosauria, varying greatly in size and in the length of the tail. The pterodactyl was the largest pterosaur.

Ptol·e·ma·ic (tol′ə mā′ik) *adj.* 1. of or relating to the Greek astronomer Ptolemy or the Ptolemaic system. 2. of or relating to the Ptolemies or to their rule in Egypt from 323 B.C. to 30 B.C.

Ptolemaic system, a theory advanced by the Greek astronomer Ptolemy, maintaining that the earth was the center of the universe and that the sun, moon, and all the planets moved about it.

pto·maine (tō′mān, tō mān′) *also,* **pto·main.** *n.* 1. any of various smelly nitrogenous substances, some of which are poisonous, produced by bacteria during the decomposition of protein. 2. ptomaine poisoning. [Italian *ptomaina,* from Greek *ptōma* corpse.]

ptomaine poisoning, food poisoning, formerly thought to be caused by eating ptomaine.

pty·a·lin (tī′ə lin) *n.* an enzyme in the saliva that converts starch into dextrin and maltose. [Greek *ptyalon* saliva + -IN¹.]

Pu, the symbol for plutonium.

pub (pub) *n. Informal.* a tavern or inn. [Short for PUBLIC HOUSE.]

pu·ber·ty (pū′bər tē) *n.* the age at which a person becomes physically capable of producing offspring, occurring at about fourteen for boys and twelve for girls. [Latin *pūbertās* age of maturity.]

pu·bes (pū′bēz) the plural of **pubis.**

pu·bes·cence (pū bes′əns) *n.* 1. the state or quality of being pubescent. 2. a covering of soft down that grows on certain plants or insects.

pu·bes·cent (pū bes′ənt) *adj.* 1. attaining or having attained puberty. 2. covered with soft down: *a pubescent leaf.* [Latin *pūbēscēns,* present participle of *pūbēscere* to reach puberty.]

pu·bic (pū′bik) *adj.* of, relating to, or near the pubis.

pu·bis (pū′bis) *n., pl.* **-bes.** the portion of either hipbone that together with the other forms the front of the pelvis. For illustration, see **pelvis.** [Shortened from Modern Latin *os pubis* bone of the groin, from Latin *ōs* bone + *pūbis,* genitive of *pūbēs* groin.]

pub·lic (pub′lik) *adj.* 1. of, relating to, or affecting the people as a whole: *public welfare.* 2. for the use of all the people; open to all: *a public park, a public lecture.* 3. of, relating to, or engaged in the affairs or service of a community or country: *a question of public policy.* 4. existing, performed, or conducted in the open; generally known: *a public denial, a public disgrace.* 5. familiar to all or many of the people; well-known: *a public figure.* —*n.* 1. all the inhabitants of a community, state, or country; the people as a whole. 2. a group of people having similar interests or tastes: *the reading public, a movie star's public.* [Latin *pūblicus* relating to the people or state, going back to *populus* body of persons.]

·in public. not in private; openly: *to argue about personal matters in public.*

pub·lic-ad·dress system (pub′lik ə dres′) an electrical apparatus for amplifying sound out-of-doors or in an auditorium. *Also,* **PA system.**

pub·li·can (pub′li kən) *n.* 1. *British.* a keeper of a tavern or saloon. 2. a tax collector in ancient Rome. [Latin *pūblicānus* the tax collector, from *pūblicum* public revenue.]

pub·li·ca·tion (pub′li kā′shən) *n.* 1. the act of publishing or the state of being published: *The manuscript is ready for publication. The unpublished writer longed for publication.* 2. something that is published, such as a book, magazine, or newspaper. 3. public notification or announcement: *These comments are not for publication.* [Late Latin *pūblicātiō* a making known, publishing, going back to Latin *pūblicus.* See PUBLIC.]

public defender, an attorney employed at public expense to defend accused persons who cannot afford to hire their own attorneys.

public domain 1. lands owned by the government. 2. the condition of not or no longer being protected by a patent or copyright.

public enemy, a person who is a serious menace to the public, such as a criminal.

public health, the science and profession that combines medicine and social science to protect community health through preventive and sanitary measures, health education, communicable disease control, or the like.

public house 1. *British.* a tavern; saloon. 2. inn.

pub·li·cist (pub′lə sist) *n.* 1. a person who is skilled in or writes on law or public affairs. 2. press agent.

pub·lic·i·ty (pu blis′i tē) *n.* 1. information about someone or something brought to the public's attention. 2. public notice, attention, or notoriety resulting from such information. 3. the means, process, or work of achieving such public notice. 4. the state or condition of being public.

pub·li·cize (pub′lə sīz′) *v.t.,* **-cized, -ciz·ing.** to bring to the attention of the public; give publicity to: *to publicize a new motion picture.*

pub·lic·ly (pub′li klē) *adv.* 1. in a public manner or place. 2. by or in the name of the public, or with public consent: *a publicly owned beach.*

public opinion, the opinion of a majority of the people, esp. as a social or political force.

public relations, the act, process, methods, or work of promoting goodwill for an individual or organization.

public school 1. a free elementary or secondary school supported and administered by state and local officials. 2. in Great Britain, a private boarding school, esp. for boys, that prepares students for the university.

public servant, a person who serves the public by holding an elective or appointive government office.

public service 1. service to the community or public by a public servant; government employment. 2. something done to benefit the public: *The documentary was broadcast as a public service, with no commercials.* 3. the service provided by a public utility.

public speaking, the act or art of making a speech before an audience.

pub·lic-spir·it·ed (pub′lik spir′i tid) *adj.* showing a concern for or promoting the welfare of the community.

public television, television that broadcasts cultural and educational programs for the public. It is supported by donated private and public funds rather than by revenues from commercial advertising.

public utility, utility *(def. 2).*

public works, projects financed and constructed by a government for public use, such as roads, dams, or sewers.

pub·lish (pub′lish) *v.t.* 1.a. to produce and issue (printed material, as a book) for sale to the public. b. to produce and issue in printed form the works of (an author) for sale to the public. 2. to make known publicly; promulgate. —*v.i.* 1. to produce and issue printed material for sale to the public. 2. to have one's works issued in printed form: *The young writer hasn't published yet.* [Old French *publiss-,* a stem of *publier* to make public, from Latin *pūblicāre.*] —**pub′lish·a·ble,** *adj.*

pub·lish·er (pub′li shər) *n.* a person or company whose business is publishing printed material.

puce (pūs) *n.* a purplish or reddish brown color. —*adj.* having the color puce. [French *puce* flea, having the color of a flea, from Latin *pūlex* flea.]

puck¹ (puk) *n.* a black disk of rubber or other hard material used in playing ice hockey. [From dialectal English *puck* to strike, form of POKE¹.]

puck² (puk) *n.* 1. a mischievous spirit; elf. 2. **Puck.** a mischie-

vous fairy or sprite in English folklore. Also *(def. 2),* **Robin Goodfellow.** [Old English *pūca* goblin.]

puck·a (puk′ə) pukka.

puck·er (puk′ər) *v.t.* to gather into irregular folds or wrinkles: *to pucker a hem, to pucker the lips.* —*v.i.* to become gathered into wrinkles. —*n.* an irregular fold or wrinkle. [POKE² + -ER⁴.]

puck·ish (puk′ish) *adj.* mischievous; impish: *a child's puckish smile.* —**puck′ish·ly,** *adv.*

pud·ding (pùd′ing) *n.* **1.** a sweet dessert, usually having a soft consistency, that is cooked by being boiled, baked, or steamed. **2.** a similar preparation that is served as a main dish or as part of a main course: *corn pudding.* [Of uncertain origin.]

pud·dle (pud′əl) *n.* **1.** a small, shallow pool of water, esp. of muddy water. **2.** a small, shallow pool of any liquid: *a puddle of spilled milk.* **3.** a mixture of clay, sand, and water, used to make something watertight. —*v.t.,* **-dled, -dling. 1.** to make muddy. **2.** to make (clay, sand, and water) into a watertight mixture. **3.** to convert (pig iron) into wrought iron. [Middle English *podel* small pool of muddy water, diminutive of Old English *pudd* ditch.] —**pud′dly,** *adj.*

pud·dling (pud′ling) *n.* the process of converting pig iron into wrought iron by removing the impurities and excess carbon in a furnace.

pu·den·dum (pū den′dəm) *n., pl.* **-da** (-də). the external genital organs, esp. of the female. [Modern Latin *pudendum,* going back to Latin *pudendus* (something) to be ashamed of, from *pudēre* to make or feel ashamed.] —**pu·den′dal,** *adj.*

pudg·y (puj′ē) *adj.,* **pudg·i·er, pudg·i·est.** short and fat. [Of uncertain origin.] —**pudg′i·ly,** *adv.* —**pudg′i·ness,** *n.*

pueb·lo (pweb′lō) *n., pl.* **-los** or *(def. 2)* **-lo. 1.** an Indian village consisting of adobe and stone houses, found esp. in the southwestern United States. **2. Pueblo.** a member of any of several Indian tribes that live in such villages, such as the Hopi. [Spanish *pueblo* population, village, from Latin *populus* body of persons.]

pueblo in Taos, New Mexico

pu·er·ile (pū′ər əl, -ə rīl′, pyùr′əl, -īl) *adj.* **1.** childish; silly: *puerile pranks.* **2.** of or relating to childhood. [Latin *puerīlis* childish, from *puer* boy, child.] —**pu′er·ile·ly,** *adv.*

pu·er·il·i·ty (pū′ə ril′i tē, pyü ril′-) *n., pl.* **-ties. 1.** the state or quality of being puerile; childishness. **2.** a childish act, idea, or remark.

pu·er·per·al (pū ûr′pər əl) *adj.* of, relating to, or accompanying childbirth. [Latin *puerpera* woman in childbirth (from *puer* child + *parere* to bring forth) + -AL¹.]

puerperal fever, an infection of the lining of the uterus following childbirth, resulting from unhygienic delivery practices. Also, **childbed fever.**

puff (puf) *n.* **1.** a short, forceful emission or blast, as of breath, air, or smoke. **2.** the amount of air, smoke, or other material emitted at one time: *Large puffs of smoke rose from the fire.* **3.** the act of drawing in and blowing out smoke, as from a cigarette or pipe. **4.** something that looks soft and fluffy: *puffs of hair drawn back in a bow, puffs of clouds in the sky.* **5.** powder puff. **6.** a light pastry shell, usually having a filling, as of whipped cream. **7.** a portion of fabric that is gathered and held down at the edges but left full and fluffy in the middle, as on dresses and blouses. **8.** a slight swelling; protuberance. **9.** a quilted covering for a bed. **10.** excessive praise, as in a newspaper or advertisement. —*v.i.* **1.** to blow in or with a puff or puffs: *I puffed on the coals to get them burning.* **2.** to breathe hard, as from physical exertion. **3.** to be released in a puff or puffs: *Smoke puffed from the chimney.* **4.** to emit or give forth puffs, as of steam or smoke: *The locomo-*

tive *puffed.* **5.** to move while giving out puffs: *The car puffed up the hill.* **6.** to take puffs, as on a cigar, cigarette, or pipe. **7.** to swell or inflate, as with air or a liquid (usually with *up*): *Her sprained ankle puffed up.* **8.** to become filled with pride (usually with *up*). —*v.t.* **1.** to emit, blow, or send forth in a puff or puffs: *The engine puffed smoke.* **2.** to smoke (a cigar, cigarette, or pipe). **3.** to inflate, swell, or make fluffy: *The housekeeper puffed the pillows. The wind puffed out the ship's sails.* **4.** to swell with pride or conceit (usually with *up*): *His recent successes puffed him up.* **5.** to praise excessively. [Old English *pyffan* to blow.]

puff adder 1. a very poisonous snake, *Bitis arietans,* of Africa, that inflates its body and makes a hissing sound when startled. It has a brown or gray body with crescent-shaped yellow markings. Length: 3-5 feet (0.9-1.5 meters). **2.** hognose snake.

puff·ball (puf′bôl) *n.* any of a group of round, edible mushroomlike fungi, order Lycoperdales, that emit cloudlike mists of spores when mature.

puff·er (puf′ər) *n.* **1.** a person or thing that puffs. **2.** any of various spiny-finned fish, family Tetraodontidae, that can inflate their bodies with air or water.

puff·er·y (puf′ə rē) *n., pl.* **-er·ies.** an exaggerated claim or praise, esp. in advertising, publicity, or the like.

puf·fin (puf′in) *n.* any of various stout-bodied seabirds, genera *Fratercula* and *Lunda,* found chiefly around the edges of the Arctic Ocean and on the northern coasts of North America and Europe, having a large, brightly striped, triangular bill, webbed feet, and black plumage with white or grayish feathers on the cheeks, breast, and underparts. Length: 12-15 inches (30-38 centimeters). [Of uncertain origin.]

puff paste, a dough of flour, salt, and ice water, rolled into very thin sheets that puff up during baking, used to make very light, flaky pastries.

puffin

puff·y (puf′ē) *adj.,* **puff·i·er, puff·i·est. 1.** puffed up; swollen: *a puffy face.* **2.** blowing in puffs: *puffy smoke.* —**puff′i·ness,** *n.*

pug¹ (pug) *n.* **1.** a short-haired breed of dog resembling a small bulldog, having a black, silver, or fawn-colored glossy coat. Height: 11 inches (28 centimeters) at the shoulder. **2.** pug nose. [Of uncertain origin.]

pug² (pug) *n. Slang.* pugilist. [Short for PUGILIST.]

pu·gi·lism (pū′jə liz′əm) *n.* the art or practice of fighting with the fists; boxing. [Latin *pūgil* boxer + -ISM.]

pu·gi·list (pū′jə list) *n.* a person who fights with the fists, esp. a professional boxer. —**pu′gi·lis′tic,** *adj.*

pug·na·cious (pug nā′shəs) *adj.* disposed to fight or quarrel; combative or quarrelsome. [Latin *pūgnāci-,* stem of *pūgnāx* combative (from *pūgnāre* to fight) + -OUS.] —**pug·na′cious·ly,** *adv.* —**pug·na′cious·ness, pug·nac·i·ty** (pug nas′i tē), *n.*

pug nose, a short, broad, turned-up nose. —**pug′-nosed′,** *adj.*

puis·sance (pwis′əns, pū′i səns) *n.* power; strength; might.

puis·sant (pwis′ənt, pū′i sənt) *adj.* powerful; mighty. [Old French *puissant,* going back to Latin *posse* to be able.] —**puis′sant·ly,** *adv.*

puke (pūk) *Slang. v.t., v.i.,* **puked, puk·ing.** to vomit. —*n.* vomit. [Possibly imitative.]

puk·ka (puk′ə) *also,* **pucka.** *adj.* first-rate, genuine, or good. [Hindi *pakka* mature, from Sanskrit *pakva.*]

pu·la (pū′lä) *n., pl.* **-la.** the monetary unit of Botswana.

pul·chri·tude (pul′kri tüd′, -tūd′) *n.* physical beauty. [Latin *pulchritūdō.*]

pule (pūl) *v.i.,* **puled, pul·ing.** to cry in a weak voice; whimper; whine. [Probably imitative.] —**pul′er,** *n.*

Pu·litz·er Prize (pùl′it sər, pū′lit-) any of a group of annual prizes in journalism, literature, and music, established by Joseph Pulitzer, U.S. journalist and newspaper publisher.

pull (pùl) *v.t.* **1.** to exert force upon so as to cause or tend to cause motion toward the source of the force: *Two black horses pulled the wagon.* **2.** to exert a force upon as in snatching or grabbing: *She pulled his sleeve to get his attention.* **3.** to rip or tear by or as by exerting such a force: *The puppy pulled the blanket to*

a	at	e	end	o	hot	u	up	hw	white		about
ā	ape	ē	me	ō	old	ū	use	ng	song		taken
ä	far	i	it	ô	fork	ù	rule	th	thin	ə	pencil
âr	care	ī	ice	oi	oil	ù	pull	th	this		lemon
		îr	pierce	ou	out	ûr	turn	zh	measure		circus

P

pieces. **4.** to take, tear, or remove from a fixed position by exerting such a force: *to pull a tooth, to pull a branch from a tree.* **5.** to bring or cause to come into a particular state, condition, or position: *When I realized how late it was, I pulled my clothes on and ran out.* **6.** to injure or weaken by overexertion or excessive stretching; strain: *to pull a muscle in one's shoulder.* **7.** to exert an influence on; impel. **8.** to withdraw or remove (often with *out*): *to pull out troops, to pull a card from a deck.* **9.** *Informal.* to carry out or bring about; perform; accomplish (often with *off*): *He was suspected of pulling the holdup.* **10.** *Informal.* to draw or attract: *Her performances always pull a large crowd.* **11.** *Informal.* to draw (a weapon) out so as to use: *to pull a gun.* **12.** *Printing.* to take (an impression or proof) from or as if from type. **13.a.** to operate (an oar) in rowing. **b.** to be rowed with: *a boat that pulls four oars.* **14.** *Sports.* to hit (a ball) so that it moves to the left if one is right-handed or to the right if one is left-handed. —*v.i.* **1.** to perform the action of pulling: *Pull on the reins to slow the horse.* **2.** to move, go, or proceed: *The car pulled into the driveway. One runner pulled ahead of the others.* **3.** to move when pulled: *The sled pulls easily.* **4.** to exert a sucking or drawing force; drink or puff deeply (often with *on* or *at*): *to pull on a straw.* **5.** to row: *They pulled toward the bank of the river.* —*n.* **1.** an act or instance of pulling or exerting force in snatching, grabbing, or moving something toward one: *The toddler gave the tablecloth a pull and all the dishes went flying.* **2.** the force or effort expended in pulling. **3.** the effort expended in moving forward; arduous, continuous effort: *It was a long, hard pull for the professor to get tenure.* **4.** any instrument or device for pulling, such as a handle, knob, or rope. **5.** a force that draws or attracts: *the pull of a magnet.* **6.** *Informal.* a hold or claim on those who are powerful; means of gaining special consideration or treatment; influence: *I got the job through my pull with the manager.* **7.** *Informal.* the ability to draw or attract; appeal; allure: *a star with great box-office pull.* **8.** the act of exerting a sucking or drawing force; deep swallow or puff. **9.** *Sports.* an act or instance of pulling a ball. [Old English *pullian* to draw with force, pluck.] —**pull′er,** *n.*

• **to pull apart.** to criticize mercilessly or in detail.

• **to pull down. a.** to tear down, demolish, or overthrow: *to pull down a shack, to pull down a government.* **b.** to receive as a wage or salary; earn.

• **to pull for.** *Informal.* to hope for the success of; support, encourage, or root for: *to pull for the underdog.*

• **to pull in. a.** to arrive: *My train pulls in at noon.* **b.** *Slang.* to arrest and bring to police headquarters.

• **to pull off.** *Informal.* to accomplish in spite of difficulties.

• **to pull (oneself) together.** to regain one's self-control or self-possession; compose oneself.

• **to pull out. a.** to depart; leave: *The train pulls out in five minutes.* **b.** to retreat or withdraw, as from an undertaking: *to pull out from a deal.*

• **to pull out of. a.** to depart from; leave: *The car pulled out of the driveway.* **b.** to retreat or withdraw from: *The union pulled out of the negotiations.*

• **to pull over.** to drive to the side of the road and stop: *The police officer motioned the driver to pull over.*

• **to pull through.** to get through a serious or difficult situation or period successfully.

• **to pull together.** to work in harmony; cooperate.

• **to pull up. a.** to come or cause to come to a halt; stop: *The car pulled up in front of the store.* **b.** to move or cause to move closer, as in a race.

pull·back (pul′bak′) *n.* **1.** the act or process of pulling back, esp. an orderly military retreat. **2.** something that pulls back, as a device.

pul·let (pul′it) *n.* a young hen less than a year old. [Old French *poulette* young hen, diminutive of *poule* hen, going back to Latin *pullus* young fowl or animal.]

pul·ley (pul′ē) *n., pl.* **-leys. 1.** a grooved wheel on which a rope or chain is pulled, used to lift heavy loads or change the direction of an applied force. **2.** a simple machine consisting of such a wheel or set of such wheels mounted in a casing; block. [Old French *po(u)lie* the grooved wheel, going back to Greek *polos* pivot, axis.]

Pull·man (pul′mən) *n., pl.* **-mans. 1.** a railroad sleeping car or parlor car. **2.** a large suitcase. [From George M. *Pullman*, 1831-97, American industrialist who designed it.]

pull·out (pul′out′) *n.* **1.** the act or process of pulling out, esp. an orderly military retreat. **2.** something that is pulled out or intended to be pulled out, such as a special section of a newspaper. **3.** a maneuver in which an airplane is pulled out of a dive or spin and returned to level flight.

pulley

—*adj.* able or intended to be pulled out, as for use: *a pullout ad in a magazine.*

pull·o·ver (pul′ō′vər) *n.* a garment, such as a shirt or sweater, that is put on by being pulled over the head. —*adj.* put on by being pulled over the head.

pul·mo·nar·y (pul′mə ner′ē, pul′-) *adj.* **1.** of, relating to, or affecting the lungs: *the pulmonary organs, a pulmonary disease.* **2.** having lungs or lunglike organs; pulmonate. [Latin *pulmōnārius* relating to the lungs, from *pulmō* lung.]

pulmonary artery, an artery that carries blood from the heart to the lungs.

pulmonary vein, one of usually four veins that returns oxygenated blood from the lungs to the heart.

pul·mo·nate (pul′mə nāt′, -nit, pul′-) *adj.* **1.** having lungs or lunglike organs. **2.** of or belonging to a group of gastropod mollusks, subclass Pulmonata, such as land snails, slugs, and many freshwater snails, having a lunglike air sac. —*n.* any member of this mollusk group. [Modern Latin *pulmonatus,* from Latin *pulmō* lung + -ATE¹.]

Pul·mo·tor (pul′mō′tər, pul′-) *n. Trademark.* a machine for producing artificial respiration by forcing oxygen into the lungs of persons experiencing suffocation. [Latin *pul(mō)* lung + MOTOR.]

pulp (pulp) *n.* **1.** the soft, juicy part of certain fruits and vegetables. **2.** the inner part of a tooth containing soft tissue, blood vessels, and nerves. For illustration, see **tooth. 3.** any soft, moist, formless mass, such as the mixture of matted fibers of wood used in making paper. **4.** a magazine printed on a cheap grade of paper made from wood pulp, usually containing sensational stories or articles. —*v.t.* **1.** to make into pulp; reduce to pulp. **2.** to remove the pulp from. —*v.i.* to become pulp. [Latin *pulpa* fleshy part of animal bodies and fruit.] —**pulp′er,** *n.*

pul·pit (pul′pit, pul′-) *n.* **1.** a raised structure, often elaborately carved, from which a minister delivers a sermon or conducts a worship service. **2.** ministers collectively; the clergy. **3.** the profession of a minister. [Latin *pulpitum* scaffold, platform.]

pulp·wood (pulp′wud′) *n.* wood used to make paper, esp. softwood, as pine, fir, or spruce.

pulp·y (pul′pē) *adj.,* **pulp·i·er, pulp·i·est.** of or resembling pulp; soft or fleshy. —**pulp′i·ly,** *adv.* —**pulp′i·ness,** *n.*

pul·que (pul′kā, -kē) *n.* a drink of Mexico made from the fermented juice of the maguey plant.

pul·sar (pul′sär) *n.* any of a number of astronomical objects that emit intense pulses of radio waves at regular intervals, thought to be a rapidly spinning neutron star.

pul·sate (pul′sāt) *v.i.,* **-sat·ed, -sat·ing. 1.** to expand and contract rhythmically: *The heart pulsates.* **2.** to vibrate; quiver. **3.** to be animated or vibrant: *The city street pulsates with the bustle of holiday shoppers.* [Latin *pulsātus,* past participle of *pulsāre* to beat, strike.]

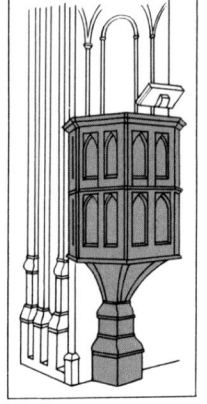

pulpit

pul·sa·tion (pul sā′shən) *n.* **1.** the act of pulsating. **2.** a single beat or vibration.

pulse¹ (puls) *n.* **1.** a rhythmic expansion and contraction of the arteries caused by the pulsation of the heart. **2.** any regular, rhythmical beating or vibrating. **3.** a single throb, beat, or vibration. **4.** the sentiment, feeling, or opinion of a group. —*v.,* **pulsed, puls·ing.** —*v.i.* to beat or vibrate; pulsate. —*v.t.* to cause to beat or vibrate. [Latin *pulsus* a beating.]

pulse² (puls) *n.* **1.** the edible seeds of such plants as peas, beans, or lentils. **2.** any plant yielding such seeds. [Latin *puls* thick pottage made of pulse.]

pulse-jet (puls′jet′) *n.* a type of jet engine, used for pilotless craft, in which air for combustion is emitted in bursts.

pul·ver·ize (pul′və rīz′) *v.,* **-ized, -iz·ing.** —*v.t.* **1.** to reduce to powder or dust, as by pounding or grinding. **2.** to smash or destroy completely. —*v.i.* to become powder or dust. [Late Latin *pulverizāre* to reduce to dust, from Latin *pulvis* dust.] —**pul′ver·iz′a·ble,** *adj.* —**pul′ver·i·za′tion,** *n.* —**pul′ver·iz′er,** *n.*

pu·ma (pū′mə) *n.* cougar. [Spanish *puma,* from Quechua *puma.*]

pum·ice (pum′is) *n.* a light, porous volcanic rock used for smoothing or polishing. Also, **pumice stone.** —*v.t.,* **-iced, -ic·ing.** to clean, smooth, or polish with pumice. [Old French *pomis* the rock, going back to Latin *pūmex.*]

pum·mel (pum′əl) *also,* **pommel.** *v.t.,* **-meled, -mel·ing;** *also, British,* **-melled, -mel·ling.** to strike repeatedly with the fists: *The two boxers pummeled one another.* [Form of POMMEL.]

pump¹ (pump) *n.* a device for moving fluids or gases from one place to another. —*v.t.* **1.** to make (a fluid) move from one place to another by means of a pump or something like a pump: *The heart pumps blood.* **2.** to remove fluid from (often with *out*): *to pump out a flooded basement.* **3.** to fill with a gas, esp. with air, by means of a pump (often with *up*): *to pump up a tire.* **4.** to move or operate by forcing up and down or back and forth repeatedly: *to pump an accelerator.* **5.** to shoot, eject, deliver, or inject as if by means of a pump: *to pump bullets into a target, to pump money into a project.* **6.a.** to obtain or attempt to obtain information from, esp. by persistent questioning. **b.** to obtain (information), esp. by persistent questioning. —*v.i.* **1.** to make a fluid move from place to place by means of a pump. **2.** to move up and down or back and forth repeatedly. **3.** to be moved by or as if by means of a pump: *The oil pumps through the pipe at a fast rate.* [Possibly from Middle Dutch *pompe* pipe of wood or metal, from Spanish *bomba* pumping device; imitative.]

pump² (pump) *n.* a low-cut shoe without laces or other fasteners. [Of uncertain origin.]

pump·er (pum′pər) *n.* **1.** a person or thing that pumps. **2.** a fire engine with pumping apparatus.

pum·per·nick·el (pum′pər nik′əl) *n.* a coarse black or dark brown bread made of unsifted rye flour. [German *Pumpernickel.*]

pump·kin (pump′kin, pum′-, pung′-) *n.* **1.** a large orange or yellow-orange fruit of a plant, genus *Cucurbita,* having a soft pulp containing many seeds and a firm outer rind. **2.** the trailing, coarse vine bearing this fruit. [Modification of earlier *pumpion,* from Middle French *pompon* pumpkin, melon, going back to Latin *pepō,* from Greek *pepōn* large melon.]

pump·kin·seed (pump′kin sēd′, pum′-, pung′-) *n.* **1.** a seed of a pumpkin. **2.** a freshwater sunfish, *Lepomis gibbosus,* found in lakes and ponds of eastern North America. Length: to 8 inches (20 centimeters).

pun (pun) *n.* a play on words in which a double meaning is applied to the same word or to two words having the same sound. —*v.i.,* **punned, pun·ning.** to make a pun or puns. [Possibly short for Italian *puntiglio* a fine point. See PUNCTILIO.]

punch¹ (punch) *v.t.* **1.** to hit (someone or something), esp. with the fist. **2.** to operate by pressing: *to punch an elevator button.* **3.** *Informal.* to herd or drive (cattle). —*v.i.* to hit, esp. with the fist. —*n.* **1.** a blow, esp. one made with the fist. **2.** the act of punching. **3.** *Informal.* force; vitality: *to put punch in one's words.* [Possibly from POUNCE¹.] —**punch′er,** *n.*
  • **to beat to the punch.** to best (one's opponent or competitor) by doing something first.
  • **to pull one's punches.** *Informal.* **a.** *Boxing.* to strike an opponent with intentionally ineffective punches. **b.** to refrain from speaking or acting frankly or bluntly.
  • **to punch in** (or **out**). to record one's arrival at (or departure from) work by use of a time clock.

punch² (punch) *n.* **1.** a tool for making holes in or stamping or impressing a design on a surface. **2.** a tool for driving a nail, bolt, or the like into or out of a hole. —*v.t.* **1.** to make holes in or stamp or impress a design on (a surface) with a punch. **2.** to drive (a nail or the like) with the aid of a punch. —*v.i.* to use a punch. [Short for PUNCHEON².]

punch³ (punch) *n.* a drink made from various ingredients, usually fruit juice and an alcoholic or carbonated beverage, often sweetened and spiced. [Hindi *pānch* five, from Sanskrit *pāñchan;* referring to the five ingredients originally used to make it.]

Punch (punch) *n.* the ill-tempered, humpbacked hero of a Punch-and-Judy show. [Short for PUNCHINELLO.]
  • **pleased as Punch.** extremely pleased; delighted.

Punch-and-Ju·dy show (punch′ən jü′dē) a puppet show noted for its broad humor and satirical dialogue, having as its main characters Punch and his wife Judy.

punch card, a card with holes punched in specific positions to provide instructions or information for a data-processing machine.

punch-drunk (punch′drungk′) *adj.* **1.** having a dazed mental condition brought about by repeated blows to the brain, as in boxing. **2.** *Informal.* dazed or confused.

pun·cheon¹ (pun′chən) *n.* **1.** a large cask of varying capacity, holding from 70 to 120 gallons (265 to 454 liters). **2.** the amount contained in a puncheon. [Old French *po(i)nchon* wine cask; of uncertain origin.]

pun·cheon² (pun′chən) *n.* **1.** a broad, heavy piece of timber roughly dressed on one side. **2.** a short upright piece of timber used as support in a wooden framing. [Old French *poinchon* pointed tool, from Latin *pūnctiō* a piercing.]

Pun·chi·nel·lo (pun′chə nel′ō) *n., pl.* -**los** or -**loes.** **1.** a humpbacked, doltish character in an Italian puppet show. **2.** *also,* **punchinello.** a person who resembles this puppet.

[Modification of Italian *Pulcinella,* diminutive of *pulcino* young chicken, going back to Latin *pullus* young fowl or animal.]

punching bag, an inflated or stuffed leather or canvas bag, usually suspended, punched for exercise or training in boxing.

punch line, the last sentence or phrase of a joke or story, which carries the humor or meaning.

punch press, a machine that uses pressure to cut, indent, or shape sheet metal.

punch·y (pun′chē) *adj.,* **punch·i·er, punch·i·est.** *Informal.* **1.** dizzy or groggy. **2.** having punch; forceful.

punc·til·i·o (pungk til′ē ō′) *n., pl.* -**i·os.** **1.** a fine point of proper or polite behavior. **2.** strict or careful observance of such fine points. [Italian *puntiglio* fine point, diminutive of *punto* point, from Latin *pūnctum.*]

punc·til·i·ous (pungk til′ē əs) *adj.* **1.** strictly attentive to the fine points of proper or polite behavior: *Our wonderful hosts were extremely punctilious.* **2.** very careful and exact: *punctilious bookkeeping.* —**punc·til′i·ous·ly,** *adv.* —**punc·til′i·ous·ness,** *n.* —For Synonyms, see **careful.**

punc·tu·al (pungk′chü əl) *adj.* **1.** acting or happening at the correct or appointed time; prompt. **2.** paid at the correct or appointed time: *a punctual payment.* [Medieval Latin *punctualis* relating to a point, from Latin *pūnctum* point.] —**punc·tu·al·i·ty** (pungk′chü al′i tē), *n.* —**punc′tu·al·ly,** *adv.* —**punc′tu·al·ness,** *n.*

punc·tu·ate (pungk′chü āt′) *v.,* -**at·ed, -at·ing.** —*v.t.* **1.** to mark (written material) with punctuation marks. **2.** to interrupt from time to time: *a speech punctuated by cheers.* **3.** to give emphasis to. —*v.i.* to use punctuation marks. [Medieval Latin *punctuatus,* past participle of *punctuare* to prick, mark by points, from Latin *pūnctum* point.] —**punc′tu·a′tor,** *n.*

punc·tu·a·tion (pungk′chü ā′shən) *n.* **1.** the act, practice, or system of marking written material with punctuation marks for clarity of meaning. **2.** a punctuation mark or marks.

punctuation mark, any of various marks, such as the comma, semicolon, or period, used to clarify the meaning of written material.

punc·ture (pungk′chər) *v.,* -**tured, -tur·ing.** —*v.t.* **1.** to make a hole in (something) with a sharp or pointed object. **2.** to make (a hole) by piercing. **3.** to lessen in importance; spoil or ruin as if by puncturing: *The critics' ridicule punctured the artist's ego.* —*v.i.* to become punctured. —*n.* **1.** a hole made by a sharp or pointed object. **2.** the act of puncturing. [Latin *pūnctūra* a pricking.] —**punc′tur·a·ble,** *adj.* —**punc′tur·er,** *n.* —For Synonyms *(v.t.),* see **pierce.**

pun·dit (pun′dit) *n.* **1.** a learned Brahmin, esp. one versed in the laws, language, or religion of India. **2.** a learned person. **3.** an authority, critic, or commentator: *a political pundit.* [Hindi *pandit* learned Brahmin, from Sanskrit *pandita* learned.]

pun·gent (pun′jənt) *adj.* **1.** sharply affecting the senses of taste or smell: *the pungent smell of ammonia.* **2.** sharply expressive, stinging, or severe: *a pungent wit, pungent criticism.* [Latin *pungēns,* present participle of *pungere* to prick.] —**pun′gen·cy,** *n.* —**pun′gent·ly,** *adv.*

Pu·nic (pū′nik) *adj.* of, relating to, or characteristic of ancient Carthage or its people, language, or culture. —*n.* the Semitic language of ancient Carthage.

pun·ish (pun′ish) *v.t.* **1.** to cause (someone) to suffer for an offense; subject to a penalty. **2.** to impose a penalty for (an offense). **3.** to treat or handle roughly or severely: *The sun's rays can punish the skin.* —*v.i.* to impose or inflict punishment. [Old French *puniss-,* a stem of *punir* to inflict punishment on, from Latin *pūnīre.*] —**pun′ish·a·bil′i·ty,** *n.* —**pun′ish·a·ble,** *adj.* —**pun′ish·er,** *n.*

pun·ish·ment (pun′ish mənt) *n.* **1.** the act of punishing or the state of being punished. **2.** a penalty imposed for a crime, offense, or fault. **3.** severe treatment; rough handling: *The car took a lot of punishment on the dirt road.*

pu·ni·tive (pū′ni tiv) *adj.* relating to, involving, or inflicting punishment: *a punitive law, a punitive action.* Also, **pu·ni·to·ry** (pū′ni tôr′ē). [French *punitif,* going back to Latin *pūnītus,* past participle of *pūnīre* to punish.] —**pu′ni·tive·ly,** *adv.* —**pu′ni·tive·ness,** *n.*

punk¹ (pungk) *n.* **1.** a dry substance that burns slowly without a flame, used esp. to light fireworks. **2.** dry, decayed wood, used esp. as tinder. [Possibly from Algonquian *punk* smoldering ashes.]

punk² (pungk) *Slang. n.* a young, contemptible, or inexperi-

a	at	e	end	o	hot	u	up	hw	white		about
ā	ape	ē	me	ō	old	ū	use	ng	song		taken
ä	far	i	it	ô	fork	ü	rule	th	thin	ə	pencil
âr	care	ī	ice	oi	oil	u̇	pull	th	this		lemon
		îr	pierce	ou	out	ûr	turn	zh	measure		circus

enced person, esp. a young hoodlum. —*adj.* **1.** of poor quality; worthless. **2.** of, relating to, or characteristic of punk rock music or musicians or their audience. [Of uncertain origin.]

pun·kah (pung′kə) *n.* a large fan that hangs from the ceiling and is kept in motion by a servant or by machinery, used esp. in India. [Hindi *pankhā*, from Sanskrit *pakshaka*.]

punk rock, a style of rock music characterized by loud, highly energetic music with fast tempos, crude instrumental techniques, and violent, often antiestablishment lyrics. [PUNK² + ROCK².]

pun·ster (pun′stər) *n.* a person who frequently makes puns.

punt¹ (punt) *n.* a flat-bottomed boat with square ends, usually propelled by a long pole. —*v.t.* **1.** to propel (a boat) with a long pole. **2.** to carry in a punt. —*v.i.* to go or travel in a punt. [Old English *punt* such a boat, from Latin *pontō*.] —**punt′er,** *n.*

punt² (punt) *n.* **1.** a kick in which a football is dropped from the hands and kicked before it reaches the ground. **2.** a football kicked in such a manner: *The punt rolled into the end zone.* —*v.t.* to kick (a football) before it reaches the ground. —*v.i.* to punt a football. [Of uncertain origin.] —**punt′er,** *n.*

punt³ (punt) *v.i.* **1.** to bet against the bank in a game of chance. **2.** *British.* to gamble. [French *ponter* to gamble, from *ponte* one who punts, ace in cards, from Spanish *punto* point, pip on cards, from Latin *pūnctum* point.]

pu·ny (pū′nē) *adj.,* **-ni·er, -ni·est.** inferior in size, strength, or importance; weak: *a puny child, a puny effort.* [Anglo-Norman *pune, puisne* born after, younger, going back to Latin *post nātus* born after.] —**pu′ni·ness,** *n.*

pup (pup) *n.* **1.** a young dog; puppy. **2.** a young animal of various other species, such as the fox, wolf, or seal. [From PUPPY.]

pu·pa (pū′pə) *n., pl.* **-pae** (-pē) or **-pas.** an insect in the intermediate stage of complete metamorphosis, coming after the larval stage and before the adult stage, as a caterpillar in a cocoon. For illustration, see **metamorphosis.** [Modern Latin *pupa*, from Latin *pūpa* girl, doll.] —**pu′pal,** *adj.*

pu·pate (pū′pāt) *v.i.,* **-pat·ed, -pat·ing.** to change into a pupa. —**pu·pa′tion,** *n.*

pu·pil¹ (pū′pəl) *n.* a person who studies under the direction of an instructor; student. [Latin *pūpillus* orphan, ward, diminutive of *pūpus* boy.]

pu·pil² (pū′pəl) *n.* the opening in the center of the iris that expands and contracts to admit light through the eye. For illustration, see **eye.** [Latin *pūpilla* little girl, pupil of the eye, diminutive of *pūpa* girl, doll; referring to the small images that can be seen reflected in the pupil of the eye.]

pup·pet (pup′it) *n.* **1.** a small, usually jointed, figure representing a person or animal and manipulated by the hand or by strings, wires, or rods. **2.** a small doll. **3.** someone or something that is under the complete domination of another, such as a government. [Old French *poupette* little doll, going back to Latin *pūpa* girl, doll.]

pup·pet·eer (pup′i tîr′) *n.* a person who operates puppets for the entertainment of others.

pup·pet·ry (pup′i trē) *n.* the art of making puppets or producing puppet shows.

pup·py (pup′ē) *n., pl.* **-pies. 1.** a young dog. **2.** a silly, conceited, or foppish young man. [Middle French *poupée* doll, toy, going back to Latin *pūpa* girl, doll.] —**pup′py·hood′,** *n.* —**pup′py·ish′,** *adj.*

puppy love, an infatuation of a girl or boy with another person.

pup tent, a small, portable tent for two people. Also, **shelter tent.**

pur·blind (pûr′blīnd′) *adj.* **1.** partially or almost blind. **2.** lacking in understanding; obtuse; dull. [Earlier *pure blind* completely blind. See PURE, BLIND.] —**pur′blind′ly,** *adv.* —**pur′blind′ness,** *n.*

pur·chas·a·ble (pûr′chə sə bəl) *adj.* **1.** capable of being purchased: *a purchasable commodity.* **2.** capable of being bribed or influenced by bribery: *The corrupt politician's support was purchasable.*

pur·chase (pûr′chəs) *v.t.,* **-chased, -chas·ing. 1.** to obtain by paying money or its equivalent; buy. **2.** to obtain by hardship, sacrifice, or suffering: *a military victory purchased at great cost of life.* **3.** to raise, move, or hold by mechanical power. —*n.* **1.** the act or an instance of purchasing. **2.** something purchased. **3.** a firm or secure hold, grasp, or footing on something: *My feet had no purchase on the icy pavement.* **4.** mechanical advantage or power; leverage. **5.** a device for obtaining such mechanical advantage or power. [Anglo-Norman *purchacer* to pursue, procure, going back to Latin *prō* before, for + *captāre* to try to catch, pursue.] —**pur′chas·er,** *n.* —For Synonyms *(v.t.),* see **buy.**

pur·dah (pûr′də) *n.* **1.** the practice among some Muslims and Hindus of concealing women from the gaze of men or strangers, esp. in India and neighboring countries. **2.** a curtain, screen, or garment used for the concealment of women. [Urdu *pardah* veil, from Persian *pardah*.]

pure (pyur) *adj.,* **pur·er, pur·est. 1.** having the same components or character throughout; not mixed with anything else; unadulterated: *a scarf of pure silk.* **2.** not stained, spotted, or contaminated; clean: *pure water.* **3.** free from moral corruption, evil intent, or guilt: *a pure heart.* **4.** virtuous; chaste. **5.** free from foreign or incongruous elements: *to speak pure Italian.* **6.a.** of unmixed descent: *That cat is pure Siamese.* **b.** possessed of a feature that has been passed on through many generations, as would a pureblood; homozygote. **7.** nothing but; sheer; utter: *Your explanation of what happened is pure speculation.* **8.** concerned with theory rather than practical application: *pure science.* [Old French *pur* unmixed, mere, from Latin *pūrus* clean, unmixed, chaste.] —**pure′ness,** *n.*

pure·blood (pyur′blud′) *n.* an individual of unmixed descent, esp. a purebred farm animal. —*adj.* of, relating to, or characteristic of a pureblood. Also *(adj.),* **pure′blood′ed.**

pure·bred (pyur′bred′) *adj.* descended from ancestors of unmixed stock: *a purebred Arabian stallion.* —*n.* a purebred animal.

pu·rée (pyu rā′, -rē′, pyur′ā) *also,* **pu·ree.** *n.* **1.** raw or cooked food that is put through a sieve, food mill, or blender and made into a thick, moist mass. **2.** a smooth, thick soup. —*v.t.,* **-réed, -rée·ing.** to make (food) into a puree. [French *purée* thick soup, from *purer* to strain, from Latin *pūrāre* to cleanse.]

pure·ly (pyur′lē) *adv.* **1.** merely; simply: *What happened is purely coincidental.* **2.** entirely; completely: *They are motivated purely by money.* **3.** in a pure manner. **4.** in a virtuous, innocent, or chaste manner.

pur·ga·tion (pûr gā′shən) *n.* the act of purging.

pur·ga·tive (pûr′gə tiv) *n.* a medicine that causes the bowels to empty; strong laxative; cathartic. —*adj.* tending to purge. [Late Latin *pūrgātivus* cathartic, from Latin *pūrgāre* to cleanse, purify.]

pur·ga·to·ri·al (pûr′gə tôr′ē əl) *adj.* **1.** of, relating to, or resembling purgatory. **2.** serving to purge from sin; expiatory.

pur·ga·to·ry (pûr′gə tôr′ē) *n., pl.* **-ries. 1.** in Roman Catholic doctrine, a temporary place or condition of purification, where souls are purged of unrepented minor sins or of major sins that have been forgiven but not wholly punished. **2.** any place or condition of temporary punishment or suffering. [Medieval Latin *purgatorium* a means of cleansing, going back to Latin *pūrgāre* to cleanse, purify.]

purge (pûrj) *v.,* **purged, purg·ing.** —*v.t.* **1.** to cleanse or rid of whatever is unclean or undesirable. **2.** to remove by or as if by cleansing. **3.** to eliminate persons from (a political party, government, or other organization). **4.** to eliminate (a person or persons) from a political party, government, or other organization. **5.** to free of sin or guilt. **6.** to induce expulsion of urine, feces, or stomach contents, as by vomiting or taking diuretics or laxatives. —*v.i.* **1.** to become clean or pure. **2.** to undergo a purging of the bowels. —*n.* **1.** the act or process of purging. **2.** the elimination, esp. by expulsion or death, of persons from a political party, government, or other organization. **3.** a purgative medicine; cathartic. [Old French *purg(i)er* to cleanse, purify, from Latin *pūrgāre*.] —**purg′er,** *n.*

pu·ri·fi·ca·tion (pyur′ə fi kā′shən) *n.* the act or process of purifying or the state of being purified.

pu·ri·fy (pyur′ə fī) *v.t., v.i.,* **-fied, -fy·ing.** to make or become pure or clean. [Old French *purifier* to make pure, from Latin *pūrificāre*.] —**pu′ri·fi′er,** *n.*

Pu·rim (pur′im) *n.* an annual Jewish holiday observed in February or March, commemorating the deliverance of the Persian Jews by Queen Esther from a massacre plotted by Haman. [Hebrew *pūrīm*, plural of *pūr* lot.]

pu·rine (pyur′ēn) *n.* **1.** a colorless, crystalline organic compound, the parent substance of a group of nitrogenous compounds, including guanine and adenine, that serve as the fundamental base of many biochemical substances. Formula: $C_5H_4N_4$ **2.** any of these compounds, such as uric acid.

pur·ism (pyur′iz əm) *n.* strict adherence to or insistence upon purity, as in language.

pur·ist (pyur′ist) *n.* a person who advocates, practices, or insists upon strict adherence to purity, as of language or artistic style. —**pu·ris′tic,** *adj.*

Pu·ri·tan (pyur′i tən) *n.* **1.** a member of a Protestant sect in England and New England in the sixteenth and seventeenth centuries who advocated simplified religious ceremonies and high standards of morality. **2. puritan.** a person who is scrupulously or excessively strict in matters of morality or religion. —*adj.* **1.** of, relating to, or characteristic of the Puritans or Puritanism. **2. puritan.** of, relating to, or characteristic of a puritan or puritanism. [Late Latin *pūritās* cleanliness + -AN. See PURITY.]

pu·ri·tan·i·cal (pyur′i tan′i kəl) *adj.* **1.** scrupulously or exces-

sively strict in matters of morality or religion: *a puritanical attitude.* **2. Puritanical.** of, relating to, or characteristic of the Puritans or Puritanism. Also, **pu'ri·tan'ic. —pu'ri·tan'i·cal·ly,** *adv.* **—pu'ri·tan'i·cal·ness,** *n.*

Pu·ri·tan·ism (pyŭr'i tə niz'əm) *n.* **1.** the beliefs and practices of the Puritans. **2. puritanism.** scrupulous or excessive strictness in matters of morality or religion.

pu·ri·ty (pyŭr'i tē) *n.* **1.** the state or quality of being pure; freedom from extraneous matter or contamination. **2.** freedom from moral corruption, evil intent, or guilt. **3.** freedom from foreign or incongruous elements: *purity of language.* [Late Latin *pūritās* cleanliness, from Latin *pūrus* clean, unmixed, chaste.]

purl¹ (pûrl) *v.i.* to flow, ripple, or swirl, esp. with a murmuring sound. —*n.* a murmuring sound made by a shallow stream or brook. [Possibly imitative.]

purl² (pûrl) *v.t., v.i.* **1.** to knit with reversed stitches. **2.** to decorate or finish (fabric) with small loops. —*n.* **1.** a reversed knitting stitch. **2.** a small loop, or chain of small loops, used to decorate or finish the edge of lace or other fabric; picot. **3.** a thread of twisted gold or silver wire, used in embroidery. [Of uncertain origin.]

pur·lieu (pûr'lü, pûrl'ū) *n.* **1.** a neighboring or outlying area. **2. purlieus.** **a.** outskirts. **b.** environs. **3.** an area that one knows well or frequents. [Modification (influenced by French *lieu* place) of Anglo-Norman *puralee* perambulation, from Old French *po(u)raler* to traverse, going back to Latin *prō* before, for + *ambulāre* to walk.]

pur·lin (pûr'lin) *also,* **pur·line.** *n.* one of the horizontal timbers supporting the rafters of a roof. [Of uncertain origin.]

pur·loin (pûr loin') *v.t., v.i.* to steal. [Anglo-Norman *purloigner* to delay, remove, going back to Latin *prō* before, forth + *longē* far.] **—pur·loin'er,** *n.*

pur·ple (pûr'pəl) *n.* **1.** a color between crimson and violet, formed by mixing red and blue. **2.** formerly, a deep crimson. **3.** a cloth or garment of this color, esp. as worn as a symbol of royalty or high rank. **4.** imperial, royal, or princely rank. —*adj.* **1.** having the color purple. **2.** full of exaggerated or florid literary devices or effects: *purple passages.* [Old English *purple* of the color purple, going back to Latin *purpura* a shellfish yielding a purple dye, this dye, from Greek *porphyrā*.]

Purple Heart, a U.S. military award given to a member of the armed forces who is wounded while in action against the enemy.

purple martin, a North American swallow, *Progne subis,* the male of which has glossy, blue-black plumage. Length: 8 inches (20 centimeters).

Purple Heart

pur·plish (pûr'plish) *adj.* somewhat purple.

pur·port (*v.,* pər pôrt'; *n.,* pûr'pôrt) *v.t.* **1.** to claim or profess, often falsely: *to purport to be an expert on automobiles.* **2.** to intend; mean. —*n.* meaning or substance: *The letter gives the purport of our conversation.* [Anglo-Norman *purporter* to intend, contain, going back to Latin *prō* forth + *portāre* to carry.]

pur·pose (pûr'pəs) *n.* **1.** the result or goal that is desired; object to which effort is directed; intention. **2.** the object or reason for which something is made or exists; function or use. **3.** the act or fact of having resolve; determination; resolution. —*v.t., -posed, -pos·ing.* to intend, resolve, or propose. [Old French *purpos* resolution, from *purposer* to intend, propose, modification (influenced by Old French *poser* to place, put) of Latin *prōpōnere* to set forth. See POSE¹.]

• **on purpose.** not by accident; intentionally.
• **to good purpose.** with good results or effects.
• **to little** (or **no**) **purpose.** with few (or no) results or effects.
• **to the purpose.** to the point; pertinent; relevant.

Synonyms *n.* **Purpose, aim,** and **intention** mean what a person hopes to achieve by doing something. **Purpose** implies the existence of a specific goal: *The students' primary purpose in visiting France was to improve their conversational French.* **Aim** suggests the seeking of a general goal: *The commissioner's aim was to improve the school system.* **Intention** is used to indicate a general personal inclination: *It is my intention to become a millionaire.*

pur·pose·ful (pûr'pəs fəl) *adj.* **1.** having a purpose or meaning; intentional. **2.** having or showing determination: *a purposeful*

attitude toward work. **—pur'pose·ful·ly,** *adv.* **—pur'pose·ful·ness,** *n.*

pur·pose·less (pûr'pəs lis) *adj.* without a purpose or meaning. **—pur'pose·less·ly,** *adv.* **—pur'pose·less·ness,** *n.*

pur·pose·ly (pûr'pəs lē) *adv.* with or for a certain purpose; intentionally; deliberately.

purr (pûr) *n.* **1.** the soft, murmuring sound made by a cat when pleased or contented. **2.** any similar sound: *the purr of a tuned-up engine.* —*v.i.* to make a soft, murmuring sound. —*v.t.* to express by making a soft, murmuring sound. [Imitative.] **—purr'ing·ly,** *adv.*

purse (pûrs) *n.* **1.** a woman's handbag. **2.** a small bag, pouch, or case for carrying money. **3.** anything resembling this, as in shape or use. **4.** available money; funds. **5.** a sum of money offered as a prize or given as a gift. —*v.t.,* **pursed, purs·ing. 1.** to draw together into wrinkles or folds; pucker: *to purse the lips.* **2.** to put into a purse. [Old English *purs* small bag for carrying money, from Late Latin *bursa* leather bag, wallet, from Greek *byrsā* hide², skin (used to make purses). Doublet of BOURSE, BURSA.]

purs·er (pûr'sər) *n.* the officer who has charge of financial matters on board a ship.

purs·lane (pûrs'lin, -lān) *n.* any of several plants, genus *Portulaca,* esp. *P. oleracea,* having bright yellow flowers and fleshy stems and leaves, sometimes used as a salad green. [Old French *porcelaine,* modification of Latin *porcilāca,* form of *portulāca.* See PORTULACA.]

pur·su·ance (pər sü'əns) *n.* the act of carrying out; execution: *In pursuance of their plan, the young couple bought the house.*

pur·su·ant (pər sü'ənt) *adj.* going in pursuit; pursuing. —*adv.* in accordance with (often with *to*): *I loaned them the money, pursuant to our agreement.*

pur·sue (pər sü') *v.,* **-sued, -su·ing.** —*v.t.* **1.** to follow in order to overtake, capture, or kill: *The police pursued the thieves.* **2.** to proceed along or hold to the course of; follow: *to pursue a plan of action.* **3.** to endeavor to attain; strive for; seek: *to pursue pleasure, to pursue a goal.* **4.** to continue or follow through: *to pursue the study of Spanish.* **5.** to continue to distress, disturb, or trouble; plague; harass: *Questions about their bravery pursued the defeated soldiers.* —*v.i.* **1.** to go in pursuit; follow. **2.** to go on; continue. [Anglo-Norman *pursuer* to follow up or closely, going back to Latin *prōsequī* to follow after.] **—pur·su'a·ble,** *adj.* **—pur·su'er,** *n.* —For Synonyms, see **hunt.**

pur·suit (pər süt') *n.* **1.** the act of following in order to overtake: *the pursuit of a bandit.* **2.** the act of seeking: *the pursuit of wealth.* **3.** any occupation, pastime, or interest.

pur·sui·vant (pûr'swi vənt) *n.* **1.** a heraldic official ranking below a herald. **2.** an attendant; follower. [Old French *pursivant* follower, from *pursivre* to pursue, going back to Latin *prōsequī.*]

pu·ru·lence (pyŭr'ə ləns, pyŭr'yə-) *n.* **1.** the condition of forming, containing, or discharging pus; suppuration. **2.** pus. Also, **pu'ru·len·cy.**

pu·ru·lent (pyŭr'ə lənt, pyŭr'yə-) *adj.* forming, containing, or discharging pus; suppurating. [Latin *pūrulentus* festering, from *pūs* pus.]

pur·vey (pûr vā') *v.t.* to supply (something, esp. food or provisions). [Anglo-Norman *purveier* to provide, from Latin *prōvidēre* to foresee, provide. Doublet of PROVIDE.] **—pur·vey'ance,** *n.*

pur·vey·or (pûr vā'ər) *n.* a person who supplies something, esp. food or provisions.

pur·view (pûr'vū) *n.* **1.** a range or scope of authority, activity, or concern. **2.** a range of vision or comprehension. **3.** *Law.* the body of a statute, containing its purpose, scope, or limit. [Anglo-Norman *purveu* provided (as in the phrases *purveu est* it is provided, and *purveu que* provided that), past participle of *purveier* to provide. See PURVEY.]

pus (pus) *n.* a thick, yellowish fluid that collects in abscesses and other infections in the body, and contains bacteria and dead white blood cells. [Latin *pūs.*]

push (pŭsh) *v.t.* **1.** to exert force upon or against so as to cause or tend to cause motion away from the source of the force: *I pushed the door with my shoulder but couldn't budge it.* **2.** to move by such exertion of force: *She pushed the wheelbarrow up the hill. He impatiently pushed the hair out of his eyes.* **3.** to urge with vigor and persistence the adoption or advancement of; recommend or advocate strongly: *a legislator who consistently pushes reform in government.* **4.** to make with effort or force, as against opposition or difficulty: *They pushed their way through the underbrush.* **5.** to

a	at	e	end	o	hot	u	up	hw	white		about
ā	ape	ē	me	ō	old	ū	use	ng	song		taken
ä	far	i	it	ô	fork	ü	rule	th	thin	ə	pencil
âr	care	ī	ice	oi	oil	u̇	pull	th	this		lemon
			îr	pierce	ou	out	ûr	turn	zh	measure		circus

P

put forcibly into some condition, situation, or position: *Increased demand has pushed prices up.* **6.** to advance or expand by or as if by persistent or diligent effort; extend: *The settlers pushed the frontier farther west.* **7.** to put under pressure or stress; bear hard upon; press: *The parents pushed their child to become a doctor.* **8.** to carry on, prosecute, or follow up with energy: *to push a claim.* **9.** *Informal.* to be close to, as in time; near; approach: *You may be pushing fifty, but you look younger.* **10.** to advertise persistently and otherwise make a determined effort to sell: *The company is really pushing its new brand of soap.* **11.** *Slang.* to sell (drugs) illegally. —*v.i.* **1.** to exert force upon or against something so as or as if to move it: *If you push against the fence, it will give way.* **2.** to move, advance, or proceed with effort or vigor or as against opposition: *to push through a crowd.* **3.** to put forth vigorous or persistent effort (often with *for*): *a group pushing for the adoption of a proposed law.* —*n.* **1.** the act of pushing or exerting force so as or as if to move something: *to give someone a push out of the way.* **2.** a vigorous or determined effort, attempt, or drive: *The troops made one last push to take the town.* **3.** something that stimulates or provokes; inducement or stimulus, as to action: *The economy has been lagging for months and needs a push of some kind.* **4.** a condition, instance, or time of stress or urgency; emergency. **5.** *Informal.* persevering energy or enterprise: *to have enough push to get ahead in a profession.* [Old French *pousser* to thrust, from Latin *pulsāre* to beat, strike, thrust.]

• **to push around.** *Informal.* to deal roughly or unfairly with; abuse; mistreat.

• **to push off.** *Informal.* to leave; depart.

• **to push on.** to continue advancing or pursuing; proceed: *to push on through the jungle, to push on with one's research.*

push·ball (push′bôl′) *n.* **1.** a game in which players of two opposing teams try to push a large, inflated ball, usually 6 feet (1.8 meters) in diameter, across a goal line. **2.** the ball used in this game.

push-but·ton (push′but′ən) *adj.* **1.** operated by a push button or push buttons: *a push-button telephone.* **2.** using or controlled by or as by automatic or remote-control mechanisms: *push-button warfare.*

push button, a small button or knob pushed to operate a device, esp. by opening or closing an electric circuit.

push·cart (push′kärt′) *n.* a small cart pushed by hand, used esp. by a peddler.

push·er (push′ər) *n.* **1.** a person or thing that pushes. **2.** an airplane with its propeller or propellers located behind the wings. **3.** *Slang.* a person who sells drugs illegally.

push·o·ver (push′ō′vər) *n. Slang.* **1.** a person who is easily defeated, influenced, or taken advantage of. **2.** anything easily done.

Push·tu (push′tü) Pashto.

push-up (push′up′) *n.* an exercise in which a person lies face down and, keeping the body straight, alternately raises and lowers the body by straightening and bending the arms.

push·y (push′ē) *adj.,* **push·i·er,** **push·i·est.** *Informal.* self-assertive or aggressive in an offensive manner. —**push′i·ly,** *adv.* —**push′i·ness,** *n.*

pu·sil·la·nim·i·ty (pū′sə lə nim′i tē) *n.* the state or quality of being cowardly; cowardliness; faintheartedness.

pu·sil·lan·i·mous (pū′sə lan′ə məs) *adj.* lacking courage; fainthearted; cowardly. [Late Latin *pūsillanimis* (from Latin *pūsillus* very small + *animus* mind, soul) + -OUS.] —**pu′sil·lan′i·mous·ly,** *adv.*

puss[1] (pus) *n.* **1.** a cat. **2.** a girl or young woman. [Possibly imitative of the spitting of a cat.]

puss[2] (pus) *n. Slang.* the face or mouth. [Irish *pus* lip, mouth.]

puss·y[1] (pus′ē) *n., pl.* **puss·ies.** **1.** a cat. Also, **pus·sy·cat** (pus′ē kat′). **2.** a catkin of a pussy willow. [PUSS[1] + -Y[2].]

pus·sy[2] (pus′ē) *adj.,* **-si·er, -si·est.** forming, containing, or resembling pus. [PUS + -Y[1].]

puss·y·foot (pus′ē füt′) *v.i. Informal.* **1.** to move quietly, cautiously, or stealthily. **2.** to act in a cautious or timid manner; be unwilling to commit oneself, as on a political issue. —**puss′y·foot′er,** *n.*

pussy willow, a shrub or small tree, *Salix discolor* or *S. caprea,* growing in moist regions of eastern North America, bearing furry silvery gray catkins.

pus·tu·lant (pus′chə lənt) *adj.* causing pustules to form. —*n.* a medicine or agent that causes pustules to form.

pus·tu·lar (pus′chə lər) *adj.* of, resembling, or characterized by pustules.

pus·tu·la·tion (pus′chə lā′shən) *n.* the formation of pustules.

pus·tule (pus′chül) *n.* **1.** a small, inflamed swelling of the skin containing pus. **2.** any similar swelling. [Latin *pustula* pimple, blister.]

put (put) *v.,* **put, put·ting.** —*v.t.* **1.** to cause to be in a specified place or position; place; set; lay: *Put the package on the table. He put another log on the fire.* **2.** to cause to be in a specified condition: *Her smile put us at ease.* **3.** to cause to go or move: *to put one's foot through the floor.* **4.** to cause or enable to do something: *to put an army to flight, to put an unemployed person to work.* **5.** to cause to undergo; subject: *to put a person to a great deal of trouble.* **6.** to set at a certain point or amount; estimate as being: *to put the value of an old car at five hundred dollars.* **7.** to assign; ascribe; attribute: *The report put the blame on the mayor.* **8.** to throw or cast with an overhand pushing motion: *to put the shot.* **9.** to propose for consideration or judgment: *to put a question to a person.* **10.** to express; state: *to put an idea in simple terms.* **11.** to render into another language or form of expression; translate. **12.** to adapt: *to put a poem to music.* **13.** to bring to bear; apply: *to put one's knowledge to use.* **14.** to impose: *to put a tax on gasoline.* **15.** to bet: *to put two dollars on a horse.* **16.** to invest: *to put all one's money into stocks.* —*v.i.* to direct one's course; go; proceed: *to put out to sea.* —*n.* **1.** an overhand, pushing throw, esp. the act of putting the shot. **2.** an option that gives its buyer the right to sell a specified amount of a stock or commodity at a specified price within a designated time period. [From an unrecorded Old English word parallel to Old English *potian* to thrust.]

• **to put about.** **a.** to put (a ship) on the opposite tack; cause to change direction. **b.** to change direction, as a ship.

• **to put across.** *Informal.* **a.** to cause to be understood or accepted. **b.** to carry out with success.

• **to put aside** (or **by**). to reserve for later use; save.

• **to put away.** **a.** to reserve for later use; save. **b.** *Informal.* to consume by eating or drinking. **c.** *Informal.* to confine in a mental institution or jail. **d.** to give up; discard; abandon: *to put away childish habits.* **e.** *Informal.* to kill for humane reasons.

• **to put down.** **a.** to land or cause to land: *to put an airplane down in a cornfield.* **b.** to make a down payment of: *to put $1,500 down on a car.* **c.** *Slang.* to treat in a disparaging or slighting manner; belittle, embarrass, or snub. **d.** *Informal.* to kill for humane reasons.

• **to put forth.** **a.** to send out; sprout; grow: *The tree put forth leaves.* **b.** to exert: *to put forth great effort.* **c.** to set out; start on one's way, as to sea.

• **to put in.** **a.** (of a ship) to enter port. **b.** *Informal.* to spend (time) in a specified manner: *to put in a day at the office.* **c.** to present or submit (a request, offer, claim, or the like). **d.** to interpose; insert: *He put in a good word for her.*

• **to put in for.** to make an application or request for: *The soldier put in for a transfer.*

• **to put off.** **a.** to cause (someone) to wait until a later time. **b.** to get rid of by delay or evasion. **c.** to disturb, upset, or repel: *Their strange behavior put me off.*

• **to put on.** **a.** to assume or adopt (an affectation): *to put on airs.* **b.** to pretend; feign: *to put on a display of concern.* **c.** to stage, present, or perform: *to put on a play.* **d.** to gain: *to put on twenty pounds.* **e.** *Slang.* to tease or fool (a person); deceive playfully; poke fun at: *Stop putting me on.*

• **to put one** (or **something**) **over on.** *Informal.* to deceive or trick.

• **to put out.** **a.** to disconcert; embarrass. **b.** to inconvenience: *Will it put you out to pick up the package for me?* **c.** to publish; issue: *to put out a new edition of a book.* **d.** to go out on the sea: *The boat put out at noon.*

• **to put over.** *Informal.* to complete or carry out (something) successfully.

• **to put through.** **a.** to cause to have a successful conclusion. **b.** to put into effect: *The new rates have not been put through yet.* **c.** to make a telephone call for: *Can you put me through to New York?* **d.** to make (a telephone call).

• **to put to it.** to place in a difficult situation: *I was put to it to keep up my grades.*

• **to put up.** **a.** to erect; build. **b.** to preserve (food). **c.** to provide or obtain lodgings: *We put up for the night at a farmhouse.* **d.** to make available; provide: *to put up money for a project.* **e.** to stake; wager: *to put up two dollars on a racehorse.* **f.** to propose or nominate: *to put up a candidate for office.* **g.** to offer, as for public sale: *to put up a struggle.* **i.** to show: *You put up a calm front when you were frightened.*

• **to put upon.** to take advantage of; treat unfairly.

• **to put up to.** *Informal.* to encourage (a person) to do: *Who put those students up to that prank?*

• **to put up with.** to bear patiently; tolerate; endure.

• **to stay put.** *Informal.* to stay in the same place or position: *The restless child would not stay put.*

v.t. **Put** and **place** mean to position in a particular location. **Put** is used informally and stresses the act of positioning an object: *Put your coat in the closet.* **Place** has a more formal connotation: *Place the ring on my finger.*

pu·ta·tive (pū′tə tiv) *adj.* generally considered or supposed; reputed: *the putative sculptor of an ancient statue.* [Late Latin *putātīvus* imaginary, from Latin *putāre* to think.]

put-down (pùt′doun′) *n. Slang.* a remark or action that belittles, embarrasses, or snubs another person, or one that is meant to do so.

put-on (*adj.*, pùt′ôn′, -on′; *n.*, pùt′ôn′, -on′) *adj.* pretended; assumed: *a put-on display of grief.* —*n. Slang.* **1.** the act or an instance of deceiving someone with a falsehood or practical joke. **2.** a falsehood or practical joke: *The whole story was an elaborate put-on.*

put-out (pùt′out′) *n. Baseball.* the act or an instance of putting out a batter or base runner.

pu·tre·fac·tion (pū′trə fak′shən) *n.* the act or process of rotting or the state of being rotten.

pu·tre·fac·tive (pū′trə fak′tiv) *adj.* **1.** causing putrefaction. **2.** of, relating to, or characterized by putrefaction.

pu·tre·fy (pū′trə fī′) *v.*, **-fied**, **-fy·ing.** —*v.t.* to cause to rot; make putrid. —*v.i.* to rot. [Latin *putrefacere* to make rotten, from *puter* rotten + *facere* to make.]

pu·tres·cent (pū tres′ənt) *adj.* **1.** becoming rotten; decaying. **2.** of or relating to putrefaction. [Latin *putrēscēns*, present participle of *putrēscēre* to grow rotten.] —**pu·tres′cence**, *n.*

pu·trid (pū′trid) *adj.* **1.** decayed and foul-smelling; rotten. **2.** characteristic of or produced by putrefaction. **3.** extremely bad; terrible; vile: *a putrid situation, a putrid place.* [Latin *putridus* rotten, corrupt.] —**pu·trid′i·ty**, **pu′trid·ness**, *n.* —**pu′trid·ly**, *adv.*

putsch (pùch) *also*, **Putsch.** *n.* an armed uprising or revolt. [German *Putsch.*]

putt (put) *n. Golf.* a rolling shot made on a putting green in an attempt to send the ball into the cup. —*v.t.*, *v.i.* to hit (a ball) gently so as to make such a shot. [Form of PUT.]

put·tee (put′ē, pu tē′) *n.* **1.** a long, narrow strip of cloth wound round the leg from ankle to knee, worn as a protection and support to the leg. **2.** a cloth or leather legging that similarly covers the lower leg. [Hindi *pattī* bandage, band[2].]

put·ter[1] (put′ər) *also*, **potter.** *v.i.* to work, act, or proceed in a trifling or aimless way. —*v.t.* to waste (time) in puttering (with *away*). [Form of POTTER[2].] —**put′ter·er**, *n.*

putt·er[2] (put′ər) *n.* **1.** a golf club with a short shaft and a metal head having little or no loft, used in putting. **2.** a person who putts. [PUTT + -ER[1].]

putting green, green *(def. 4).*

put·ty (put′ē) *n.*, *pl.* **-ties. 1.** a soft, doughlike mixture of whiting and linseed oil, used esp. for filling cracks or attaching panes of glass. **2.** any of various similar substances. —*v.t.*, **-tied**, **-ty·ing.** to fill, fasten, or cover with putty. [French *potée* loam for molding; originally, potful, from *pot* pot, jug; of Germanic origin.]

put-up (pùt′up′) *adj. Informal.* devised or arranged beforehand in a secret or underhanded manner: *The voters' so-called overwhelming approval of the dictator was a put-up job.*

put-up·on (pùt′ə pôn′, -pon′) *adj. Informal.* taken advantage of; imposed upon.

puz·zle (puz′əl) *n.* **1.** a problem, game, or toy designed to challenge one's skill and ingenuity. **2.** a person or thing that perplexes or confuses. **3.** a state of perplexity or difficulty; quandary; dilemma. —*v.*, **-zled**, **-zling.** —*v.t.* **1.** to perplex; bewilder: *Their recent actions puzzle me.* **2.** to solve or arrive at an understanding of, esp. by persistent effort: *to puzzle a problem out.* —*v.i.* **1.** to be perplexed: *I'm puzzled about this situation.* **2.** to endeavor to achieve an understanding or solution; ponder: *to puzzle over a cryptic note.* [Of uncertain origin.] —**puz′zler**, *n.*

v.t. **Puzzle, perplex,** and **bewilder** mean to cause mental confusion or disturbance. **Puzzle** indicates a mild distress caused by a problem that is difficult to solve or understand: *The satellite's momentary change of course puzzled the controllers.* **Perplex** suggests a deep and continuing confusion: *The detectives were perplexed after months of fruitless efforts to solve the case.* **Bewilder** implies a confusion profound enough to prevent coherent thought or action: *The victim was too bewildered to describe the robber.*

puz·zle·ment (puz′əl mənt) *n.* **1.** the state of being puzzled; perplexity; confusion. **2.** a person or thing that puzzles.

PVC, polyvinyl chloride.

Pvt., Private.

PWA, Public Works Administration.

pwt., pennyweight.

PX, Post Exchange.

pyc·nom·e·ter (pik nom′i tər) *n.* a graduated glass vessel used esp. for measuring the relative density of liquids. [Greek *pyknos* thick, tight + -METER.]

py·e·mi·a (pī ē′mē ə) *also*, **py·ae·mi·a.** *n.* a disease caused by certain bacteria releasing pus in the bloodstream, which creates abscesses in organs of the body. [Modern Latin *pyaemia*, from Greek *pyon* pus + *haima* blood.] —**py·e′mic**, *adj.*

py·gid·i·um (pī jid′ē əm) *n.*, *pl.* **-gid·i·a** (-jid′ē ə). the posterior or tail region of certain invertebrates, as trilobites, crustaceans, and insects. [Modern Latin *pygidium*, from Greek *pygidion*, diminutive of *pygē* rump.]

Pyg·ma·lion (pig māl′yən, -mā′lē ən) *n.* in Greek legend, a sculptor and king of Cyprus who fell in love with the statue of a maiden he had carved. Aphrodite brought the statue, called Galatea, to life in response to Pygmalion's prayers.

Pyg·my (pig′mē) *also*, **Pigmy.** *n.*, *pl.* **-mies. 1.a.** a member of a dark-skinned people of small stature living in the tropical rain forests of Africa. **b.** a member of a people of small stature living in Southeast Asia. **2. pygmy.** a very small or insignificant person or thing. —*adj.* **1.** of, relating to, or characteristic of the Pygmies. **2. pygmy.** very small or insignificant. [Latin *pygmaeus* dwarfish, from Greek *pygmaios* literally, as tall as a *pygmē*, from *pygmē* fist, cubit.]

py·ja·mas (pə jä′məz, -jam′əz) *British.* pajamas.

py·lon (pī′lon) *n.* **1.** a tall steel tower that supports high-tension wires. **2.** a tower for guiding aviators, esp. in a race. **3.** a monumental gateway, esp. to an Egyptian temple. [Greek *pylon* gateway.]

py·lo·rus (pī lôr′əs) *n.*, *pl.* **-lo·ri** (-lôr′ī). the opening between the stomach and the duodenum of the small intestine. [Late Latin *pylorus*, from Greek *pylōros* gatekeeper, pylorus; because it was thought of as the gatekeeper to the intestines.] —**py·lor′ic**, *adj.*

py·or·rhe·a (pī′ə rē′ə) *also*, **py·or·rhoe·a.** *n.* an inflammation of the gums and other soft tissues that surround the teeth, resulting, in some cases, in the loosening and loss of the teeth. [Modern Latin *pyorrhoea*, from Greek *pyon* pus + *rhoiā* flow, flux.] —**py′or·rhe′al, py′or·rhe′ic**, *adj.*

pyr-, form of **pyro-** before *h* and certain vowels.

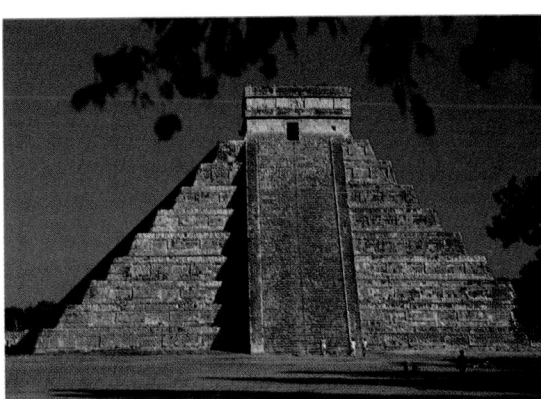

pyramid at Chichén Itzá, Mexico

pyr·a·mid (pir′ə mid′) *n.* **1.** *also*, **Pyramid.** a massive structure of masonry, usually having a square base and four triangular sides that slope upward to an apex or platform, built esp. in ancient Egypt as tombs. **2.** *Geometry.* a solid figure having a polygonal base and triangular sides intersecting at a point. **3.** anything resembling a pyramid in form or structure: *The acrobats formed a human pyramid.* —*v.t.* to arrange or raise in or as in the shape of a pyramid. —*v.i.* **1.** to assume the shape of a pyramid. **2.** to rise or increase, esp. on a progressively broader base, as prices or wages: *The cost of food has pyramided in recent years.* [Latin *pȳramis* the geometric figure, Egyptian tomb shaped like such a figure, from Greek *pȳramis*; possibly of Egyptian origin.]

py·ram·i·dal (pi ram′i dəl) *adj.* of, relating to, or resembling a pyramid. Also, **pyr·a·mid·ic** (pir′ə mid′ik), **pyr′a·mid′i·cal.** —**py·ram′i·dal·ly**, *adv.*

a	at	e	end	o	hot	u	up	hw	white		about
ā	ape	ē	me	ō	old	ū	use	ng	song		taken
ä	far	i	it	ô	fork	ü	rule	th	thin	ə	pencil
âr	care	ī	ice	oi	oil	u̇	pull	th	this		lemon
		îr	pierce	ou	out	ûr	turn	zh	measure		circus

Pyr·a·mus and Thisbe (pir'ə məs) in classical mythology, two young lovers of Babylon. Believing Thisbe slain by a lion, Pyramus took his own life, and Thisbe, upon finding his body, killed herself.

pyre (pīr) *n.* a pile of wood or other combustible material, used esp. for burning a dead body. [Latin *pyra* funeral pyre, from Greek *pyrā*.]

py·re·thrin (pī rē'thrin) *n.* either of two liquid compounds extracted from pyrethrum flowers, the active ingredient of the insecticide pyrethrum. Formula: $C_{21}H_{28}O_3$ or $C_{22}H_{28}O_5$ [PYRE-THRUM + -IN[1].]

py·re·thrum (pī rē'thrəm) *n.* **1.** any of several chrysanthemums, as *Chrysanthemum cinerariaefolium,* whose dried flowers are ground and used as an insecticide. **2.** an insecticide made from the dried flowers of these chrysanthemums. [Modern Latin *Pyrethrum,* going back to Greek *pyrethron* feverfew, possibly from *pyretos* fever.]

py·ret·ic (pī ret'ik) *adj.* relating to, causing, or affected with fever; febrile. [Modern Latin *pyreticus,* from Greek *pyretos* fever, from *pȳr* fire.]

Py·rex (pī'reks) *n. Trademark.* a heat-resistant glass used in ovenware, laboratory glassware, and telescope mirrors.

pyr·i·dine (pir'i dēn', -din) *n.* a liquid organic compound with a penetrating odor, used in the synthesis of vitamins and drugs, as a solvent, and formerly as an antiseptic. Formula: C_5H_5N [PYR- + -ID[2] + -INE[2].]

pyr·i·dox·ine (pir'i dok'sēn, -sin) *n.* a water-soluble vitamin of the vitamin B complex, important in the utilization of protein in the body, found esp. in whole-grain cereals, yeast, and liver. Formula: $C_8H_{11}NO_3$ Also, **vitamin B$_6$.**

py·rim·i·dine (pī rim'i dēn', pi-) *n.* **1.** a colorless, liquid or crystalline organic compound, the fundamental form of a group of nitrogenous bases that are constituents of nucleic acid and other biochemical substances. Formula: $C_4H_4N_2$ **2.** any of these bases, as cytosine, thymine, or uracil.

py·rite (pī'rīt) *n.* a hard, shiny, yellow mineral, iron disulfide, often mistaken for gold, used in the manufacture of sulfuric acid. Formula: FeS_2 Also, **fool's gold, iron pyrites.** [Latin *pyrītēs.* See PYRITES.] —**py·rit·ic** (pī rit'ik), *adj.*

py·ri·tes (pī rī'tēz, pi-, pī'rīts) *pl. n.* any of various mineral compounds of sulfur and a metal, as marcasite or chalcopyrite. [Latin *pyrītēs* flint, from Greek *pyrītēs* flint, relating to fire, from *pȳr* fire.]

pyro- *combining form* fire or heat, or resulting from fire or heat: *pyromania, pyrotechnic, pyroelectric.* [Greek *pȳr* fire.]

py·ro·clas·tic (pī'rō klas'tik) *adj.* of, relating to, or designating fragmentary rock material formed by explosive eruption, as volcanic ash or cinders, or a rock consisting of such material, as tuff. [Greek *pȳros,* genitive of *pȳr* fire + *klastos* broken + -IC.]

py·ro·e·lec·tric (pī'rō i lek'trik) *adj.* of, relating to, or exhibiting pyroelectricity. —*n.* a pyroelectric substance, as the mineral tourmaline.

py·ro·e·lec·tric·i·ty (pī'rō i lek tris'i tē) *n.* polarized electric charges that form on certain crystals when heated.

py·ro·gen·ic (pī'rō jen'ik) *adj.* producing or produced by fever or heat.

py·rog·ra·phy (pī rog'rə fē) *n.* the art or process of burning designs on material, as on wood or leather. —**py·ro·graph** (pī'rə graf'), *n.* —**py·rog'ra·pher,** *n.* —**py'ro·graph'ic,** *adj.*

py·ro·lu·site (pī'rō lü'sīt) *n.* a gray or black oxide mineral mined as an ore of manganese. Formula: MnO_2 [German *pyrolusit,* from Greek *pȳr* fire + *lousis* a washing (from *louein* to wash) + German *-it* -ite[1].]

py·rol·y·sis (pī rol'ə sis) *n.* chemical decomposition of a substance resulting from subjection to heat. —**py·ro·lyt·ic** (pī'rə-lit'ik), *adj.*

py·ro·ma·ni·a (pī'rə mā'nē ə) *n.* an uncontrollable desire to set fire to things. [PYRO- + -MANIA.] —**py'ro·ma'ni·ac,** *adj., n.* —**py·ro·ma·ni·a·cal** (pī'rō mə nī'ə kəl), *adj.*

py·rom·e·ter (pī rom'i tər) *n.* an electrical device designed to measure high temperature. —**py·ro·met·ric** (pī'rə met'rik), *adj.* —**py·rom'e·try,** *n.*

py·rope (pī'rōp) *n.* a deep red garnet containing magnesium and aluminum, transparent varieties of which are used as gems. [Middle English *pirope,* from Middle French *pirope,* from Latin *pyropus* red bronze, from Greek *pyrōpus* literally, fiery red.]

py·ro·tech·nic (pī'rə tek'nik) *adj.* **1.** of or relating to fireworks. **2.** resembling or suggesting fireworks; brilliant or exciting: *a pyrotechnic display of wit.* Also, **py'ro·tech'ni·cal.** [PYRO- + TECHNIC.] —**py'ro·tech'ni·cal·ly,** *adv.*

py·ro·tech·nics (pī'rə tek'niks) *n.* **1.** the manufacture or use of fireworks. ➤ used as singular. Also, **py'ro·tech'ny. 2.** a display of fireworks. **3.** a brilliant, dazzling, or sensational display, as of wit or musical ability. —**py'ro·tech'nist,** *n.*

py·rox·ene (pī rok'sēn) *n.* any of a group of common rock-forming minerals, such as augite, that are complex silicates, some of which contain iron and magnesium, and others, sodium and aluminum. [French *pyroxène,* from Greek *pȳr* fire + *xenos* stranger.]

py·rox·y·lin (pī rok'sə lin) *also,* **py·rox·y·line** (pī rok'sə lēn', -lin) *n.* a highly flammable nitrocellulose, used in the manufacture of such products as collodion and artificial leather. [PYRO- + Greek *xylon* wood + -IN[1]; referring to its very flammable nature.]

Pyr·rha (pir'ə) *n.* see **Deucalion and Pyrrha.**

Pyr·rhic victory (pir'ik) a victory won at an excessive or ruinous cost. [From *Pyrrhus,* 318?-272 B.C., king of Epirus who sustained extremely heavy losses in defeating the Romans in 279 B.C.]

py·ru·vic acid (pī rü'vik) a colorless, organic acid that is an important intermediate in the metabolism of carbohydrates and proteins. Formula: $C_3H_4O_3$ [PYRO- + Latin *ūva* grape + -IC + ACID.]

Py·thag·o·re·an (pi thag'ə rē'ən) *adj.* of or relating to the Greek mathematician Pythagoras, his doctrines, or his followers. —*n.* a follower of Pythagoras.

Pythagorean theorem, the theorem that in a right triangle, the square of the length of the hypotenuse is equal to the sum of the squares of the lengths of the other two sides.

Pythagorean theorem
$c^2 = a^2 + b^2$

Pyth·i·an (pith'ē ən) *adj.* **1.** of or relating to Apollo, Delphi, or the Delphic oracle. **2.** of or relating to the Pythian games. [Latin *Pȳthius* relating to Delphi or Apollo (from Greek *Pȳthios* relating to Delphi, from *Pȳthō* earlier name of Delphi) + -AN.]

Pythian games, in ancient Greece, a Panhellenic festival held every four years at Delphi in honor of Apollo.

Pyth·i·as (pith'ē əs) *n.* see **Damon and Pythias.**

py·thon (pī'thon, -thən) *n.* any of a small group of nonpoisonous snakes, genus *Python,* related to the boas, found in tropical regions of Asia, Africa, the East Indies, and Australia, that coil around and suffocate or crush their prey. Length: 3-30 feet (0.9-9.1 meters). [Latin *Pȳthōn* serpent killed by Apollo near Delphi, from Greek *Pȳthōn,* from *Pȳthō* earlier name of Delphi.]

py·tho·ness (pī'thə nis) *n.* **1.** a priestess of Apollo at Delphi. **2.** a female prophet or soothsayer. [Late Greek *pȳthōn* spirit of divination + -ESS.]

pyx (piks) *n.* **1.** a container made of precious metal in which the consecrated Host is kept, esp. a small, flat box for carrying the Host to the sick. **2.** a box or chest at a mint in which sample coins are deposited and held for testing. [Latin *pyxis* box[1], from Greek *pyxis* box[1] (originally made of boxwood), from *pyxos* boxwood.]

pyx·id·i·um (pik sid'ē əm) *n., pl.* **-i·a** (-ē ə). a seed vessel having an upper portion that acts as a lid by splitting open. [Modern Latin *pyxidium,* from Greek *pyxidion* little box, diminutive of *pyxis* box[1]. See PYX.]

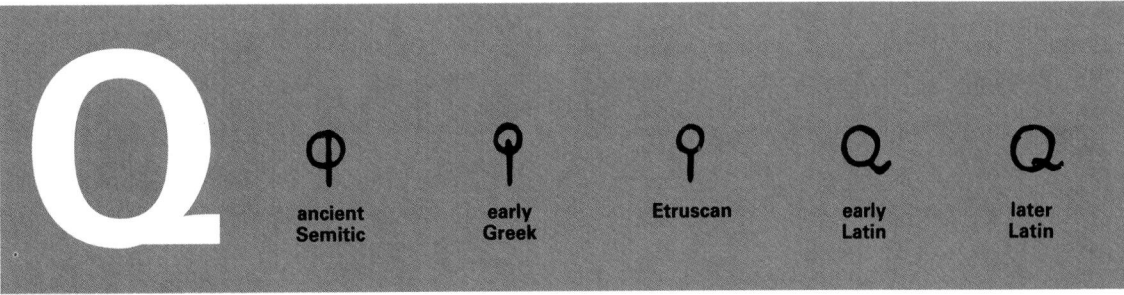

| ancient Semitic | early Greek | Etruscan | early Latin | later Latin |

Q The oldest form of the letter **Q** was the ancient Semitic letter *koph*, meaning "monkey." This letter, which was pronounced either as a hard **K** or as a guttural **K** produced in the back of the throat, was passed down to the early Greeks, who called it *koppa*. Because the Greeks eventually used another letter, *kappa*, to represent both the hard *k* sound and the guttural *k* sound, *koppa* was dropped from later Greek alphabets. When the Etruscans borrowed the early Greek alphabet, they inherited three letters, *gamma*, *kappa*, and *koppa*, to represent the same hard *k* sound. The only distinction they made in their use was in spelling. *Koppa*, for example, the forerunner of our letter **Q**, was used before **U**. In classical Latin, the letter **K** was dropped almost entirely and **Q** was used only in combination with the letter **U**, in order to produce a *kw* sound, which is just how we use it today. We also write the letter **Q** much as the Romans did some 2,000 years ago.

q, Q (kū) *n., pl.* **q's, Q's. 1.** the seventeenth letter of the English alphabet. **2.** the shape of this letter or something having this shape.

q *also,* **q.** quart; quarts.

q. 1. quarter. **2.** quarterly. **3.** quarto. **4.** query. **5.** question. **6.** quire[1].

Q *Chess.* queen.

Q., queen.

Q.E.D., which was to be proved or demonstrated. [Abbreviation of Latin *quod erat demonstrandum*.]

Q fever, an acute, flulike disease caused by the rickettsia *Coxiella burnetii*, transmitted by contact, by raw milk, and by ticks. [Abbreviation of *q(uery)*; referring to the many questions about undetermined aspects of the disease when it was initially identified.]

QM, quartermaster.

QMG, Quartermaster General.

qr. 1. quarter; quarterly. **2.** quire[1].

qt *also,* **qt.** quart; quarts.

qt. quantity.

q.t. *Informal.* quiet.
• **on the q.t.** in secret; secretly: *They exchanged notes on the q.t.*

qty., quantity.

qua (kwā, kwä) *adv.* in the capacity or role of; functioning as; as: *the historian qua social commentator.* [Latin *qua* which way, feminine ablative singular of *quis* who.]

Quaa·lude (kwā′lüd) *n. Trademark.* methaqualone. [Possibly form of *(metha)qual(one)* + arbitrary use of *-ude*, as in INTERLUDE.]

quack[1] (kwak) *n.* the harsh, flat sound made by a duck. —*v.i.* to make such a sound. [Imitative.]

quack[2] (kwak) *n.* **1.a.** an unqualified person who falsely practices as a doctor. **b.** an incompetent, poorly qualified doctor. **2.** a person with little knowledge or skill who poses as an expert in a field; charlatan. —*adj.* of, relating to, or characteristic of a quack or quackery; fake: *quack medicine, a quack solution.* [Short for earlier *quacksalver* charlatan, from obsolete Dutch *quacksalver* literally, one who prattles about his ointments, from *quacken* to prattle + *salf* ointment.] —**quack′ish,** *adj.*

quack·er·y (kwak′ə rē) *n., pl.* **-er·ies.** the practices or methods of a quack; fakery.

quack grass, a grassy weed, *Agropyron repens*, having a white creeping stem, that spreads easily in cultivated ground. Also, **couch grass.**

quad[1] (kwod) *n. Informal.* a quadrangle or courtyard, esp. one at a college. [Short for QUADRANGLE.]

quad[2] (kwod) *n. Informal.* a quadruplet. [Short for QUADRUPLET.]

quad[3] (kwod) *adj. Informal.* quadraphonic. [Short for *quadraphonic*.]

Quad·ra·ges·i·ma (kwod′rə jes′ə mə) *n.* **1.** the first Sunday in Lent. Also, **Quadragesima Sunday. 2.** formerly, the forty days of Lent. [Latin *quadrāgēsima (diēs)* literally, fortieth (day); reckoned approximately as the fortieth day before Easter and therefore applied to the forty days of Lent.]

quad·ran·gle (kwod′rang′gəl) *n.* **1.** a polygon having four angles and four sides; quadrilateral. **2.a.** a square or oblong space, esp. a courtyard, partially or totally surrounded by a building or buildings. **b.** the building or buildings surrounding such a space. [Late Latin *quadrangulum* square, going back to Latin *quadrus* square, fourfold + *angulus* corner, angle.] —**quad·ran′gu·lar,** *adj.*

quad·rant (kwod′rənt) *n.* **1.** a quarter of a circle, or an arc of 90 degrees. **2.** an instrument consisting of an arc divided into 90 degrees, used in navigation and astronomy for measuring altitude or angular distance above the horizon. **3.** any of the four parts into which a plane is divided by perpendicular coordinate axes. [Latin *quadrāns* a fourth part, quarter.] —**quad·ran·tal** (kwodran′təl), *adj.*

quad·ra·phon·ic (kwod′rəfon′ik) *adj.* of or relating to the transmission, recording, or reproduction of sound by the use of four different channels.

quad·rat (kwod′rit) *n.* a small quadrilateral area that has been fenced or otherwise

quadrant (def. 2)

marked off for ecological studies, as in analysis of plant and animal densities. [Form of QUADRATE.]

quad·rate (kwod′rāt, -rit) *n.* **1.** a square or rectangular object or area. **2.** one of a pair of bones or cartilaginous structures joining the upper and lower jaws in bony fish, amphibians, reptiles, and birds. —*adj.* **1.** square or rectangular. **2.** of or relating to the quadrate bone or cartilage. [Latin *quadrātus* squared, past participle of *quadrāre* to make square.]

quad·rat·ic (kwo drat′ik) *Algebra. adj.* of, relating to, or involving a quantity or quantities that are squared, with none that are raised to a higher power. $x^2 + 4x + 3 = 15$ is a quadratic equation. —*n.* a quadratic equation or expression. [QUADRATE + -IC.]

quad·rat·ics (kwo drat′iks) *n.* the branch of algebra dealing with quadratic equations. ➡ used as singular.

quad·ra·ture (kwod′rə chŭr′, -chər) *n.* **1.** *Mathematics.* the process of finding a square equal in area to the surface of a given geometrical figure. **2.** *Astronomy.* **a.** an angular distance of 90 degrees between two celestial bodies as measured from a third

a	at	e	end	o	hot	u	up	hw	white	⟨	about
ā	ape	ē	me	ō	old	ū	use	ng	song		taken
ä	far	i	it	ô	fork	ü	rule	th	thin	ə	pencil
âr	care	ī	ice	oi	oil	u̇	pull	th	this		lemon
		îr	pierce	ou	out	ûr	turn	zh	measure	⟨	circus

celestial body. **b.** the first or the third quarter of the moon. [Latin *quadrātūra* a squaring.]

quad·ren·ni·al (kwod ren′ē əl) *adj.* **1.** occurring every four years: *a quadrennial election.* **2.** lasting four years: *a quadrennial term of office.* —*n.* an event occurring every four years. [Latin *quadrennium* period of four years (from *quadrus* fourfold, square + *annus* year) + -AL¹.] —**quad·ren′ni·al·ly,** *adv.*

quadri- also, **quadr-, quadru-.** *combining form* having four; four: *quadrilateral, quadraphonic, quadruplet.*

quad·ri·ceps (kwod′rə seps′) *n., pl.* **-ceps** or **-ceps·es** (-sep′-siz). the large muscle located in the front of the thigh that extends the leg.

quad·ri·lat·er·al (kwod′rə lat′ər əl) *adj.* having four sides. —*n.* a polygon with four sides and four angles. [Latin *quadrilaterus* four-sided (from *quadrus* fourfold, square + *latus* side) + -AL¹.]

qua·drille (kwo dril′, kwə-) *n.* **1.** a square dance popular in the nineteenth century, performed by two to four couples and consisting of five series of steps or movements. **2.** the music for such a dance. [French *quadrille* square dance with four couples, small troop of cavalry, from Spanish *cuadrilla* troop, from *cuadra* a square, from Latin *quadra.*]

quad·ril·lion (kwo dril′yən) *n.* **1.** in the United States, the cardinal number that is represented by 1 followed by 15 zeros. **2.** in Great Britain, the cardinal number that is represented by 1 followed by 24 zeros. —*adj.* numbering one quadrillion. [Latin *quadrus* fourfold, square + (M)ILLION.] —**quad·ril′-lionth,** *adj., n.*

quad·ri·no·mi·al (kwod′rə nō′mē əl) *n.* an algebraic expression with four terms. [Latin *quadrus* fourfold, square + (BI)-NOMIAL.]

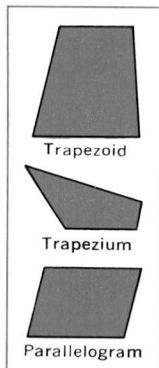

quadrilaterals

quad·ri·ple·gic (kwod′rə plē′jik) *adj.* paralyzed in both arms and legs. —*n.* a person who is quadriplegic.

quad·ri·va·lent (kwod′rə vā′lənt) *adj. Chemistry.* tetravalent.

quad·riv·i·um (kwo driv′ē əm) *n.* in medieval universities, four sciences, arithmetic, geometry, astronomy, and music, that composed the more advanced group of the seven liberal arts. ➡ distinguished from **trivium.** [Late Latin *quadrivium* from Latin *quadrivium* crossroads, from *quadrus* fourfold, square + *via* way, road.]

quad·roon (kwo drün′) *n.* a person who has one black and three white grandparents. ➡ often considered offensive. [Spanish *cuarterón,* from *cuarto* a fourth part, from Latin *quartus* fourth.]

quad·ru·ped (kwod′rə ped′) *n.* any animal, esp. a mammal, having four feet. —*adj.* having four feet. [Latin *quadrupēs* having four feet, from *quadrus* fourfold, square + *pēs* foot.] —**quad·ru·pe·dal** (kwo drü′pi dəl, kwod′rŭ ped′əl), *adj.*

quad·ru·ple (kwo drü′pəl, -drup′əl, kwod′rə pəl) *adj.* **1.** consisting of four parts or members: *a quadruple alliance.* **2.** four times as much or as many: *The value of the painting is quadruple what it was a hundred years ago.* **3.** *Music.* having four beats to each measure, with the first and third beats stressed: *quadruple meter, quadruple time.* —*v.,* **-pled, -pling.** —*v.i.* to become four times as great or as many: *The value of their farm quadrupled when the new road was built.* —*v.t.* to make four times as great or as many: *to quadruple one's income.* —*n.* a number or amount four times as great as another. [Latin *quadruplus* fourfold.]

quad·rup·let (kwo drup′lit, -drü′plit, kwod′rə plit) *n.* **1.a.** one of four offspring born at one birth. **b. quadruplets.** four offspring born at one birth. **2.** any set or group of four. [QUADRU-PLE + -ET.]

quad·ru·pli·cate (*adj., n.,* kwo drü′pli kit; *v.,* kwo drü′pli kāt′) *adj.* four times as much or as many; quadruple. —*n.* one of four identical things, esp. copies of printed material. —*v.t.,* **-cat·ed, -cat·ing.** to multiply by four; quadruple. [Latin *quadruplicātus,* past participle of *quadruplicāre* to multiply by four.] —**quad·ru′-pli·ca′tion,** *n.*

  · **in quadruplicate.** in four identical copies.

quaes·tor (kwes′tər, kwēs′-) *n.* in ancient Rome, any of various officials, esp. those who were in charge of public taxes and expenditures or prosecuting major criminal cases. [Latin *quaestor.*] —**quaes′tor·ship,** *n.*

quaff (kwof, kwaf) *v.t., v.i.* to drink heartily and with large swallows, as water. —*n.* **1.** the act of quaffing. **2.** a hearty drink. [Of uncertain origin.] —**quaff′er,** *n.*

quag (kwag, kwog) *n.* a quagmire; marsh. [Of uncertain origin.]

quag·ga (kwag′ə) *n.* an extinct southern African relative of the zebra, *Equus quagga,* that had a reddish brown coat with white stripes on the head, neck, and shoulders. [Probably of Bantu origin.]

quag·gy (kwag′ē, kwog′ē) *adj.,* **-gi·er, -gi·est.** **1.** soft and muddy; marshy. **2.** soft and flabby: *quaggy muscles.* [QUAG + -Y¹.]

quag·mire (kwag′mīr′, kwog′-) *n.* **1.** soft, muddy ground that yields under the foot. **2.** a difficult or burdensome situation: *to be caught in a quagmire of debts.* [QUAG + MIRE.]

quagga

qua·hog (kwô′hôg′, -hog′) *n.* a roundish hard-shelled clam, *Venus mercenaria,* found in shallow waters along the Atlantic coast of North America. [Short for Algonquian *poquaûhock,* from *pokhemi* closed + *hogki* shell.]

quail¹ (kwāl) *n., pl.* **quail** or **quails.** any of various game birds, family Phasianidae, usually having gray or brown plumage that is often speckled with white, as the **European quail,** *Coturnix coturnix.* Length: 7-12 inches (18-30 centimeters). [Old French *quaille,* from Medieval Latin *quaccula* quail; of imitative origin.]

quail² (kwāl) *v.i.* to recoil or shrink back in fear; lose heart; cower: *The child quailed when the dog growled.* [Of uncertain origin.]

quaint (kwānt) *adj.* **1.** charming or attractive in an old-fashioned way: *We enjoyed walking through the quaint, narrow streets of the old town.* **2.** pleasingly unusual or odd: *The class found the teacher's French accent quaint.* [Old French *queinte, cointe* neat, fine, from Latin *cognitus* known, past participle of *cognōscere* to know.] —**quaint′ly,** *adv.* —**quaint′ness,** *n.*

quake (kwāk) *v.i.,* **quaked, quak·ing.** **1.** to shake or tremble, as the surface of the earth during an earthquake. **2.** to shiver or shudder, as from fear or cold: *to quake at the sight of a snake.* —*n.* **1.** earthquake. **2.** a trembling or shuddering. [Old English *cwacian* to shake, tremble.] —**quak′er,** *n.* —**quak′ing·ly,** *adv.*

Quak·er (kwā′kər) *n.* a member of the Society of Friends. Also, **Friend.** [QUAKE + -ER¹; supposedly because the society's founder, George Fox, 1624-91, urged people to *quake* at the word of God.]

Quak·er·ism (kwā′kə riz′əm) *n.* the doctrines and practices of the Quakers.

Quak·er-la·dies (kwā′kər lā′dēz) *pl. n.* bluets.

qual·i·fi·ca·tion (kwol′ə fi kā′shən) *n.* **1.** the act of qualifying or the state of being qualified. **2.** any ability, accomplishment, knowledge, or condition that makes a person suitable for a certain job, task, or office: *His past teaching experience was a qualification for his position as principal of the school.* **3.** something that limits or restricts: *She is, without qualification, the most intelligent person I've ever known.*

qual·i·fied (kwol′ə fīd′) *adj.* **1.** having the necessary abilities, accomplishments, or requirements for a given position, privilege, or function: *a qualified teacher, a qualified voter.* **2.** limited; restricted: *The play was at best a qualified success.* —**qual′i·fied′ly,** *adv.* —**qual′i·fied·ness,** *n.*

qual·i·fi·er (kwol′ə fī′ər) *n.* **1.** a person or thing that qualifies. **2.** a word, such as an adjective or adverb, that modifies or limits the meaning of another word.

qual·i·fy (kwol′ə fī′) *v.,* **-fied, -fy·ing.** —*v.t.* **1.** to make capable or suitable, as for a certain job, position, or office. **2.** to make legally eligible; license. **3.** to limit or modify: *Qualify your statements with the phrase "in most cases."* **4.** to designate or characterize in a particular way: *The theologian's beliefs were qualified as heretical.* **5.** to alter or modify the flavor or strength of: *to qualify tea with a little honey.* **6.** *Grammar.* to limit or modify the meaning of (a word or phrase). —*v.i.* to meet the necessary standards or requirements: *to qualify for a job.* [Medieval Latin *qualificare* to provide with a quality, from Latin *quālis* of what sort + *facere* to make.] —**qual′i·fi′a·ble,** *adj.* —**qual′i·fi′er,** *n.* —**qual′i·fy′ing·ly,** *adv.*

qual·i·ta·tive (kwol′i tā′tiv) *adj.* of or relating to quality. ➡ distinguished from **quantitative.** —**qual′i·ta′tive·ly,** *adv.*

qualitative analysis, a procedure for identifying the constituents in a chemical substance by employing both physical and chemical tests. ➡ distinguished from **quantitative analysis.**

qual·i·ty (kwol′i tē) *n., pl.* **-ties.** **1.** a distinctive feature or characteristic that makes a person or thing what it is: *Lemons have a sour quality.* **2.** a basic or inherent feature: *The sound of the*

waves had a soothing quality. **3.** degree of excellence; grade: *beef of a very high quality.* **4.** excellence; superiority: *The restaurant prides itself on the quality of its food.* **5.** *Music.* the timbre or overtone of a sound that distinguishes one voice or musical instrument from another. **6.** high rank or social position: *people of quality.* —*adj.* of high or superior value or worth; excellent: *quality merchandise, quality work.* [Latin *quālitās* nature, property.] —For Synonyms *(n.)*, see **characteristic.**

quality control, a system or method for maintaining a desired level of excellence in a product, manufacturing process, or service, primarily through regular inspections.

qualm (kwäm) *n.* **1.** a twinge of conscience; compunction: *to have qualms about cheating.* **2.** a sudden feeling of apprehension or doubt; misgiving: *to have qualms about taking a test.* **3.** a sudden, but quickly passing, feeling of faintness, nausea, or illness. [Of uncertain origin.]

qualm·ish (kwä′mish) *adj.* **1.** having or feeling qualms. **2.** of the nature of or causing qualms. —**qualm′ish·ly,** *adv.*

quan·da·ry (kwon′də rē, -drē) *n., pl.* **-ries.** a state of difficulty or uncertainty; dilemma; predicament. [Of uncertain origin.]

quan·ta (kwon′tə) the plural of **quantum.**

quan·ti·fy (kwon′tə fī′) *v.t.,* **-fied, -fy·ing.** to calculate or express the quantity of. —**quan′ti·fi′a·ble,** *adj.* —**quan′ti·fi·ca′tion,** *n.* —**quan′ti·fi′er,** *n.*

quan·ti·ta·tive (kwon′ti tā′tiv) *adj.* **1.** of or relating to quantity. ➡ distinguished from **qualitative. 2.** capable of being measured: *a quantitative increase.* —**quan′ti·ta′tive·ly,** *adv.*

quantitative analysis, a procedure for determining the amounts of each constituent of a chemical substance, as by measuring weights and volumes. ➡ distinguished from **qualitative analysis.**

quan·ti·ty (kwon′ti tē) *n., pl.* **-ties. 1.** a specified or indefinite number or amount: *Add a small quantity of pepper to your food.* **2.** a large number or amount: *The restaurant buys supplies in quantity.* **3.** an exact number or amount: *What was the quantity of books ordered?* **4.** the property of a thing that can be determined by measurement, as of volume, length, or weight. **5.** an amount, number, or algebraic expression representing a mathematical value. **6.** the relative length of a vowel sound or syllable in pronunciation or prosody. **7.** *Music.* the relative duration of a note or tone. [Latin *quantitās* greatness, amount.]

quan·tize (kwon′tīz) *v.t.,* **-tized, -tiz·ing.** *Physics.* **1.** to restrict (a quantity, as energy) to discrete amounts, or quanta. **2.** to describe (a physical system or the like) in terms of quantum mechanics. [QUANT(UM) + -IZE.] —**quan′ti·za′tion,** *n.*

quan·tum (kwon′təm) *n., pl.* **-ta** (-tə). *Physics.* a small, separate amount, or packet, of energy. [Latin *quantum,* neuter of *quantus* how much.]

quantum leap 1. *Physics.* a sudden change in energy level, as of an electron, atom, or molecule. **2.** a sudden change or advance. Also, **quantum jump.**

quantum mechanics, a theory of the mechanics of atoms and molecules, developed from quantum theory, that incorporates the uncertainty principle in explaining how matter and radiation interact at the atomic level. —**quan′tum-me·chan′i·cal;** *also,* **quantum mechanical,** *adj.*

quantum number, in quantum mechanics, any of a set of integers or halves of odd integers that specify the state of an atom, subatomic particle, or quantum mechanical system.

quantum theory *Physics.* the theory, formulated by the German physicist Max Planck in 1900, stating that radiant energy is emitted and absorbed in quanta, rather than in a continuous manner.

quar·an·tine (kwôr′ən tēn′, kwor′-) *n.* **1.** the isolation of persons, animals, ships, or goods infected by or exposed to an infectious disease, to prevent the spread of that disease. **2.** the place or length of time of such isolation. **3.** any enforced isolation, as for political, social, or economic reasons. —*v.t.,* **-tined, -tin·ing. 1.** to keep away from others to prevent the spreading of a disease; put in quarantine. **2.** to isolate or exclude from normal relations, as for political, social, or economic reasons. [Italian *quarantina* isolation to prevent the spread of disease (referring to the period of forty days during which ships from regions noted for contagious diseases were formerly isolated), from *quaranta* forty, from Latin *quadrāginta.*] —**quar′an·tin′a·ble,** *adj.*

quark (kwôrk) *n. Physics.* one of the five hypothetical particles that are thought to be the basic constituents of all known atomic particles. [Named by Murray Gell-Mann, born 1929, American physicist, from a word coined by the Irish writer James Joyce, 1882-1941, in *Finnegans Wake.*]

quar·rel[1] (kwôr′əl, kwor′-) *n.* **1.** an angry conflict or difference of opinion, often creating resentment and an end of friendly relations. **2.** a cause for such a conflict or difference of opinion: *I have no quarrel with your work.* —*v.i.,* **-reled, -rel·ing;** *also, British,* **-relled, -rel·ling. 1.** to engage in a quarrel: *The children quarreled about who would ride the bicycle first.* **2.** to end or strain friendly relations as a result of a quarrel. **3.** to find fault; complain: *We quarreled with your methods, not with your goals.* [Old French *querele* dispute, from Latin *querēla* complaint.] —**quar′rel·er;** *also, British,* **quar′rel·ler,** *n.*

quar·rel[2] (kwôr′əl, kwor′-) *n.* **1.** formerly, a short arrow with a square iron head, that was shot with a crossbow. **2.** a small, diamond-shaped or square pane of glass, as used in a lattice window. [Old French *quarrel* square tile, bolt for a crossbow, from Medieval Latin *quadrellus,* diminutive of Latin *quadrus* square.]

quar·rel·some (kwôr′əl səm, kwor′-) *adj.* prone to starting arguments; inclined to quarrel: *to dislike a quarrelsome neighbor.* —**quar′rel·some·ly,** *adv.* —**quar′rel·some·ness,** *n.*

quar·ry[1] (kwôr′ē, kwor′ē) *n., pl.* **-ries.** a pit in the ground from which stone is cut or blasted out for use in building, road construction, and other purposes. —*v.t.,* **-ried, -ry·ing. 1.** to cut or blast from a quarry: *to quarry marble.* **2.** to make a quarry in: *to quarry a hillside.* [Old French *quarriere* quarry of stone, from Late Latin *quadrāria* quarry for squared stones, going back to Latin *quadrus* square.] —**quar′ri·er,** *n.*

quar·ry[2] (kwôr′ē, kwor′ē) *n., pl.* **-ries. 1.** an animal that is hunted or chased; prey. **2.** anything that is hunted or pursued: *The police kept their quarry under close watch.* [Modification of Old French *cuiree,* originally, parts of a slain animal wrapped in a skin and given to the hounds after a hunt, from *cuir* skin, from Latin *corium.*]

quart (kwôrt) *n.* **1.** a unit of liquid measure equal to 1/4 of a gallon, or 2 pints (0.946 liter). **2.** a unit of dry measure equal to 1/8 of a peck, or 2 pints (1.101 liters). **3.** a container for holding or measuring 1 quart. [Old French *quarte* measure of capacity, from Latin *quārta (pars)* a fourth (part).]

quar·tan (kwôr′tən) *adj.* (of an illness, esp. a fever) recurring approximately every seventy-two hours, or every fourth day, counting each recurrence as both the last day in one cycle and the first day in the following cycle. —*n.* a mild form of malarial fever that recurs every fourth day, with two nonfeverish days in between. [Old French *quartaine* fever recurring every fourth day, from Latin *quārtāna (febris)* (fever) occurring every fourth day, going back to *quārtus* fourth.]

quar·ter (kwôr′tər) *n.* **1.** one of four equal or corresponding parts into which anything is or may be divided; one fourth. **2.** a coin of the United States and Canada equal to twenty-five cents, or one quarter of a dollar. **3.a.** one fourth of an hour; fifteen minutes. **b.** the moment marking the beginning or end of such a period. **4.** one fourth of a year; three months. **5.** a part of a school or college year, usually lasting three months. **6.** *Astronomy.* **a.** a fourth part of the period of the moon's revolution around the earth, lasting approximately seven days: *The moon is in its second quarter.* **b.** either of the two phases of the moon when it appears half lighted as seen from earth; half-moon. For illustration, see **moon. 7.** *Sports.* one of the four equal time periods into which certain games, as football or basketball, are divided. **8.** one fourth of a yard; 9 inches; span. **9.** one fourth of a hundredweight, equal to 25 pounds in the United States and 28 pounds in Great Britain. **10.** one of the four principal divisions of the compass. **11.** the rear part of the side of a ship. **12.** one of the four parts into which an animal's carcass is divided; half of a side. **13.** *Heraldry.* **a.** one of four or more equal sections into which a shield is divided. **b.** an emblem or figure that occupies such a section, esp. one in the upper right fourth of a shield. **14.** the part of a boot or shoe above the heel that extends from the center of the back to the upper front part on both sides. **15.** a section or district, as of a city or town: *Sightseers are delighted with the quaint French quarter.* **16.** a person, place, or group, esp. one that is unspecified: *The ruling came from the highest quarters.* **17. a. quarters.** a place of residence; living accommodations. **b.** an assigned position or station, as on a warship. **18.** the forequarters or hindquarters of a four-footed animal, esp. a horse. **19.** mercy, esp. when granted to a defeated enemy: *The judges gave no quarter to the traitor.* —*v.t.* **1.** to divide into four equal parts: *to quarter an apple.* **2.** to divide into several parts or pieces. **3.** to provide

quarter
(n., def. 13)

Q

a	at	**e**	end	**o**	hot	**u**	up	**hw**	white		about
ā	ape	**ē**	me	**ō**	old	**ū**	use	**ng**	song		taken
ä	far	**i**	it	**ô**	fork	**ü**	rule	**th**	thin	ə	pencil
âr	care	**ī**	ice	**oi**	oil	**u̇**	pull	**th̲**	this		lemon
		îr	pierce	**ou**	out	**ûr**	turn	**zh**	measure		circus

with living accommodations; lodge: *to quarter troops for a night.*
4. formerly, to cut the body of (an executed person) into four parts. **5.** to place or bear (coats of arms) in the quarters of a shield. —*v.i.* **1.** to have or be assigned living accommodations; lodge. **2.** (of the wind) to blow upon a ship's quarter. —*adj.* **1.** being one of four equal parts: *The four partners each received a quarter part of the profits.* **2.** constituting one fourth of a standard unit of measure: *a quarter pound of butter.* [Old French *quartier* a fourth part, district, from Latin *quārtārius* a fourth part, from *quārtus* fourth.] —**quar′ter·er,** *n.*
 • **at close quarters.** at close range; very close together.

quar·ter·back (kwôr′tər bak′) *n. Football.* **1.** a player whose position is directly behind the center, and who directs the team and calls signals for the offense. **2.** the position played by such a player. —*v.t., v.i.* **1.** to act as a quarterback. **2.** to be in charge of; lead or direct: *to quarterback a fundraising drive.*

quarter day, any of the four days of the year regarded as the beginning of a new quarter, when quarterly payments are often due.

quar·ter·deck (kwôr′tər dek′) *n.* the part of the upper deck of a ship between the stern and mainmast, generally reserved for officers.

quarter horse, any of a western U.S. breed of light but muscular horses, used in range and rodeo work. [Because of its racing ability at a *quarter* mile.]

quar·ter·hour (kwôr′tər our′) *also,* **quarter hour.** *n.* **1.** fifteen minutes. **2.** the point on a clock fifteen minutes before or after an hour.

quar·ter·ly (kwôr′tər lē) *adj.* occurring at intervals of three months: *the quarterly interest on a savings account.* —*n., pl.* **-lies.** a publication issued four times a year, or once every three months. —*adv.* once every three months: *The payments were made quarterly.*

quar·ter·mas·ter (kwôr′tər mas′tər) *n.* **1.** in the U.S. Army, an officer responsible for providing quarters, clothing, food, equipment, and the like for troops. **2.** in the U.S. Navy, a petty officer on a ship who is in charge of navigation and certain equipment, as compasses and signals.

quar·tern (kwôr′tərn) *n.* a quarter, or fourth part, of certain weights and units of measure, as of a peck or a pound. [Old French *quarteron* quarter (of a pound), from *quartier* a fourth part. See QUARTER.]

quarter note *Music.* a note having one fourth the duration of a whole note. For illustration, see **note.**

quar·ter·saw (kwôr′tər sô′) *v.t.,* **-sawed, -sawed** or **-sawn, -saw·ing.** to saw (a log) lengthwise into quarters and then into planks so that the grain is at right angles to the broad face.

quarter section, a tract of land, usually square, containing 160 acres, or ¼ of a square mile (0.65 square kilometer).

quarter sessions, in Great Britain and certain states of the United States, any of various courts of law held quarterly.

quar·ter·staff (kwôr′tər staf′) *n., pl.* **-staves** (-stāvz′). a stout, iron-tipped pole, 6-8 feet (1.8-2.4 meters) long, formerly used in England as a weapon.

quar·tet (kwôr tet′) *also,* **quar·tette.** *n.* **1.** a musical composition for four voices or instruments. **2.** a musical group of four performers. **3.** any group or set of four. [Italian *quartetto,* from *quarto* fourth, from Latin *quārtus.*]

quar·tile (kwôr′tīl, -təl) *n. Statistics.* any of three values that divide a frequency distribution into four equal parts. The 25th, 50th, and 75th percentiles of a frequency distribution are the first, second, and third quartiles, dividing the total population into four parts, each containing one quarter of the population. [Modern Latin *quartilis,* from Latin *quārtus* fourth.]

quar·to (kwôr′tō) *n., pl.* **-tos.** **1.** the page size of a book composed of sheets of paper folded twice to form four leaves, each usually about 9 by 12 inches (23 by 30 centimeters). **2.** a book composed of pages of this size. [Short for Modern Latin *in quarto* in a fourth part (of a sheet of paper), going back to Latin *in* in + *quārtus* fourth.]

quartz (kwôrts) *n., pl.* **quartz·es.** a very hard form of silica that occurs in crystals or in a single mass and is colorless and transparent in its pure state. Certain colored varieties, as amethyst, are used as semiprecious stones. Quartz, the most common of minerals, is the principal constituent of sand. Formula: SiO_2 [German *Quarz;* of uncertain origin.] —**quartz·ose** (kwôrts′ōs), *adj.*

quartz clock, an electronic clock that uses a quartz crystal to control the frequency of the current supplied to the clock motor.

quartz glass, an amorphous form of clear silica composed of fused quartz, entirely transparent to the spectrum of radiation extending from the infrared to the ultraviolet and able to withstand extreme changes in temperature.

quartz·ite (kwôrts′īt) *n.* a granular metamorphic rock consisting primarily of quartz.

quartz lamp, a discharge tube consisting of a clear quartz bulb containing mercury vapor, used as a source of ultraviolet light.

qua·sar (kwā′zär, -sär) *n. Astronomy.* any of various starlike celestial bodies that are extremely powerful emitters of radio waves, light, and other electromagnetic radiation. [Short for *quas(i-stell)ar (radio source).* See QUASI, STELLAR.]

quash[1] (kwosh) *v.t.* to put down or suppress forcibly and quickly: *The army quickly quashed the uprising.* [Old French *quasser* to break, from Latin *quassāre* to shake.] —**quash′er,** *n.*

quash[2] (kwosh) *v.t.* to nullify or set aside, as a law, decision, election, or indictment: *The judge quashed the lower court's decision.* [Old French *quasser* to annul, from Latin *quassāre* to shake; influenced by Late Latin *cassāre* to annul, from Latin *cassus* empty.]

qua·si (kwā′zī, -sī, kwä′zē, -sē) *adj.* resembling or similar to, but not the same as: *a quasi compliment.* [Latin *quāsi* as if.]

quasi- *combining form* seemingly, but not exactly; almost or somewhat: *quasi-apologetic, quasi-fashionable, quasi-rural.*

quas·sia (kwosh′ə) *n.* **1.** a drug obtained from the wood of a tropical American tree, *Quassia amara,* used as a bitter tonic. **2.** any of a small group of shrubs and trees, genus *Quassia,* found in Central and South America, bearing clusters of scarlet flowers. [From Graman *Quassi,* a slave from Surinam who discovered the value of the Surinam quassia for medicinal purposes about 1730.]

Qua·ter·na·ry (kwä′tər ner′ē, kwə tûr′nə rē) *n., pl. (def. 2)* **-nar·ies.** **1.** the second geologic period of the Cenozoic era, including the Pleistocene and Recent epochs. **2. quaternary.** a group of four. —*adj.* **1.** of, relating to, or characteristic of the Quaternary period. **2. quaternary.** consisting of or arranged in groups of four. [Latin *quaternārius* consisting of four each, from *quaternī* four each.]

quat·rain (kwot′rān) *n.* a stanza or poem of four lines, often with alternately rhyming lines. [French *quatrain,* from *quatre* four, from Latin *quattuor.*]

quat·re·foil (kat′ər foil′, kat′rə-) *n.* **1.** a leaf having four leaflets, or a flower having four petals. **2.** an architectural ornament consisting of four lobes or arcs joined together. [Old French *quatre* four (from Latin *quattuor*) + *foil* leaf (from Latin *folium*).]

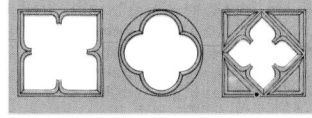
quatrefoil *(def. 2)*

qua·ver (kwā′vər) *v.i.* **1.** to tremble or shake: *The child's voice quavered with fright.* **2.** to perform trills in singing or in playing a musical instrument. —*n.* **1.** a shaking or trembling, esp. of the voice. **2.** a trill produced or performed in singing or in playing a musical instrument. **3.** *British.* eighth note. [Obsolete *quave* to tremble (possibly imitative) + -ER⁴.] —**qua′ver·er,** *n.* —**qua′ver·ing·ly,** *adv.* —**qua′ver·y** *adj.*

quay (kē) *n.* a landing place, usually constructed of concrete or stone, for loading and unloading ships. [Modification (influenced by French *quai*) of Old French *cai;* of Celtic origin.]

Que., Quebec.

quean (kwēn) *n.* **1.** a brazen, impudent, or disreputable girl or woman. **2.** prostitute. [Old English *cwene* woman, prostitute.]

quea·sy (kwē′zē) *adj.,* **-si·er, -si·est. 1.** sick to one's stomach; nauseated: *The rough boat trip made us queasy.* **2.** causing or tending to cause nausea. **3.** uneasy; uncomfortable: *I had a queasy feeling that something was wrong.* **4.** easily troubled, esp. as a result of a guilty conscience. [Of uncertain origin.] —**quea′si·ly,** *adv.* —**quea′si·ness,** *n.*

que·bra·cho (kā brä′chō) *n., pl.* **-chos. 1.** any of several tropical American trees of the cashew family, having very hard wood, esp. the **red quebracho,** *Schinopsis lorentzii.* **2.** the wood or bark of any of these trees, used in tanning and dyeing. [Spanish *quebracho* this tree; literally, ax-breaker, from *quebrar* to break (from Latin *crepitāre* to crack) + *hacha* ax (of Germanic origin); because of the hardness of the wood.]

Quech·u·a (kech′ü ə, kə chü′ə) *n., pl. (def. 1)* **-u·a** or **-u·as. 1.** one of a tribe of South American Indians that dominated the Incan empire before the Spanish conquest in the sixteenth century. **2.** a South American Indian language, formerly spoken by the Incas, now spoken mainly in Peru, Ecuador, and parts of Bolivia and Argentina. —**Quech′u·an,** *adj., n.*

queen (kwēn) *n.* **1.** the wife or widow of a king. **2.** a female sovereign of a kingdom who rules in her own right. **3.** a girl or woman honored for some outstanding attribute, as beauty. **4.** a place

queen *(def. 7)*

or thing considered to be outstanding or preeminent in some respect: *The new ocean liner is the queen of the seas.* **5.** a fully developed female in a colony of social insects, as bees, ants, or termites, whose main function is to lay eggs. **6.** a playing card bearing a picture of a queen, in most games higher in value than a jack but lower in value than a king. **7.** *Chess.* the most powerful piece, able to move any number of spaces in any straight or diagonal line. —*v.i.* to reign as or act like a queen. —*v.t.* to make (a girl or woman) a queen. [Old English *cwēn* king's wife, female sovereign of a kingdom, outstanding woman.] —**queen′like′,** *adj.*

Queen Anne's lace, a biennial plant, *Daucus carota,* of the parsley family, found in Eurasia, Africa, and North America, having a coarse, hairy stem and yellowish green leaves, and bearing a flat-topped, lacelike cluster of tiny, white flowers. Also, **wild carrot.**

queen consort, the wife of a reigning king, esp. one who does not share his sovereignty.

queen dowager, the widow of a king.

queen·ly (kwēn′lē) *adj.,* -li·er, -li·est. characteristic of, like, or suitable for a queen. —*adv.* in a queenly manner. —**queen′li·ness,** *n.*

Queen Mab, see **Mab, Queen.**

queen mother, a queen dowager who is also the mother of a reigning sovereign.

queen post, one of two vertical posts in a roof truss or the like, supporting the rafters above and resting on the tie beam below. For illustration, see **truss.**

queen regent 1. a queen ruling in place of a king who is absent, incapacitated, or too young to reign. **2.** queen regnant.

queen regnant, a queen ruling in her own right.

Queen's English, King's English.

queen-size (kwēn′sīz′) *adj.* **1.** larger than average in size. **2.** of or relating to a bed 60 inches wide by 80 inches (152 centimeters by 203 centimeters) long, a size larger than a standard double bed but smaller than a king-size bed: *queen-size sheets.* Also, **queen-sized** (kwēn′sīzd′).

queer (kwîr) *adj.* **1.** differing from what is normal or expected; strange; odd; peculiar: *a queer sense of humor.* **2.** of a questionable nature; suspicious: *a queer request.* **3.** slightly ill or faint: *to feel queer.* **4.** *Informal.* slightly unbalanced mentally. **5.** *Slang.* not genuine or authentic; counterfeit: *queer money.* **6.** *Slang.* homosexual. ➡ usually considered offensive. —*v.t. Slang.* to spoil; ruin: *to queer one's chances for a job.* —*n. Slang.* homosexual. ➡ usually considered offensive. [German *quer* perverse, cross, oblique.] —**queer′ish,** *adj.* —**queer′ly,** *adv.* —**queer′ness,** *n.*

quell (kwel) *v.t.* **1.** to put down; crush; suppress: *to quell a mutiny.* **2.** to put an end to; allay; ease: *Medicine quelled the pain.* [Old English *cwellan* to kill.] —**quell′er,** *n.*

quench (kwench) *v.t.* **1.** to satisfy; slake: *We quenched our thirst with a cold glass of lemonade.* **2.** to put out or extinguish: *The firefighters quenched the fire.* **3.** to put an end to; suppress: *to quench a rebellion.* **4.** to cool suddenly, as hot iron or steel, by plunging into a liquid. [Old English *ācwencan* to extinguish.] —**quench′a·ble,** *adj.* —**quench′er,** *n.* —**quench′less,** *adj.*

quern (kwûrn) *n.* a hand-operated mill for grinding grain, usually consisting of two circular stones. [Old English *cweorn.*]

quer·u·lous (kwer′ə ləs, kwer′yə-) *adj.* **1.** inclined to complain or find fault; complaining: *The sick child was querulous about everything.* **2.** characterized by complaining or faultfinding: *a querulous personality.* [Latin *querulus,* from *querī* to complain.] —**quer′u·lous·ly,** *adv.* —**quer′u·lous·ness,** *n.*

que·ry (kwîr′ē) *n., pl.* -ries. **1.** something asked; question. **2.** a mental reservation; doubt. **3.** a question mark (?), esp. when used to express doubt regarding the accuracy or validity of written or printed material: *The proofreader wrote a query next to the illegible word.* —*v.t.,* -ried, -ry·ing. **1.** to ask about; inquire into: *My friend queried my reasons for quitting my job.* **2.** to ask a question or questions of: *The author queried the editor about the changes in the manuscript.* **3.** to express doubt about the accuracy or validity of (written or printed material) by marking with a question mark. [Modification of Latin *quaere* inquire, imperative of *quaerere* to inquire, seek.] —For Synonyms *(v.t.),* see **ask.**

quest (kwest) *n.* **1.** a search or pursuit made in order to obtain an object or achieve a goal: *a quest for sunken treasures, a quest for eternal youth.* **2.** in the Middle Ages, an expedition or journey made by a knight or knights, either for adventure or to fulfill a special mission. **3.** the knight or knights on such an expedition or journey. —*v.i.* to go on a quest. [Old French *queste* search, going back to Latin *quaesīta* thing sought, from *quaerere* to seek, inquire.] —**quest′er,** *n.*

ques·tion (kwes′chən) *n.* **1.** something asked in order to receive a reply or obtain information: *I could not answer the teacher's*

question. **2.** a matter to be discussed or deliberated; issue: *The meeting dealt with the question of civil rights.* **3.** a matter of dispute or doubt; controversy: *A question arose as to who was the legal heir.* **4.** a possibility of being uncertain; uncertainty; doubt: *That student is, without question, the smartest person in the class.* **5.** a proposal to be debated or voted on, as in a legislative assembly or by the electorate: *to put the question to the voters.* —*v.t.* **1.** to ask a question or questions of; interrogate: *The police questioned the suspect.* **2.** to ask questions about: *Feel free to question anything you don't understand.* **3.** to feel or express doubts about; dispute; challenge: *The experts questioned the authenticity of the painting.* —*v.i.* to ask a question or questions: *The best way to learn is to question.* [Old French *question* that which is asked, from Latin *quaestiō* a seeking, inquiry.] —**ques′tion·er,** *n.* —**ques′tion·ing·ly,** *adv.* —For Synonyms *(v.t.),* see **ask.**

  • **beside the question.** not relevant to the subject under discussion; off the topic: *Your comments are beside the question.*
  • **beyond question.** without a doubt; beyond dispute: *You are, beyond question, the best athlete on the team.*
  • **in question.** under discussion or consideration: *Congress debated the matter in question.*
  • **out of the question.** not to be considered; not within the realm of possibilities: *Without a passport, your trip to Europe is out of the question.*

ques·tion·a·ble (kwes′chə nə bəl) *adj.* **1.** of doubtful character, propriety, honesty, respectability, or the like: *questionable motives.* **2.** open to doubt or dispute; uncertain: *a questionable theory.* —**ques′tion·a·ble·ness,** *n.* —**ques′tion·a·bly,** *adv.*

ques·tion·ing·ly (kwes′chə ning lē) *adv.* in the manner of one who questions: *He looked at her questioningly.*

question mark, a punctuation mark (?) placed after a sentence to indicate a direct question or used to question the accuracy of something written or printed. Also, **interrogation point.**

ques·tion·naire (kwes′chə nâr′) *n.* a written or printed form consisting of a series of questions, usually distributed to a number of persons to obtain statistically useful information. [French *questionnaire* list of questions, from *question* interrogation, query. See QUESTION.]

quet·zal (ket säl′) *n., pl.* -zals or -za·les (-sä′lās). **1.** a Central American bird, *Pharomachrus mocino,* having an iridescent green body and bright red underparts, and the male of which has a feathery chest and four long tail feathers. Length: to 4 feet (1.2 meters), including tail. **2.** the monetary unit of Guatemala. [Spanish *quetzal,* from Nahuatl *quetzaltototl* this bird, from *quetzalli* beautiful tail feather + *tototl* bird.]

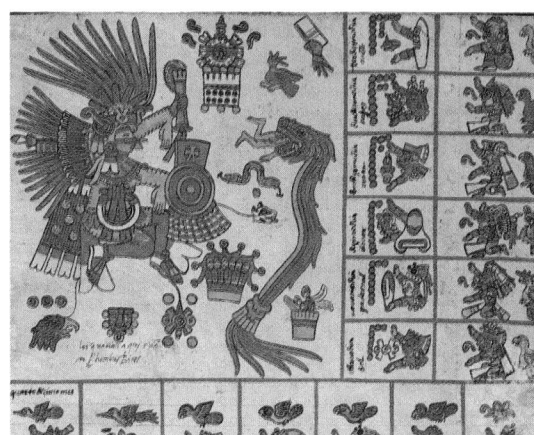

Aztec drawing of the gods **Quetzalcoatl** (right)
and Tezcatlipoca (left)

Quet·zal·co·a·tl (ket säl′kō ä′təl) *n.* a god of the Aztecs and Toltecs, depicted as a serpent with feathers.

queue (kū) *n.* **1.** a braid of hair hanging from the back of the head; pigtail. **2.** *also,* **cue.** a line of people, vehicles, or the like, waiting as for service. —*v.i.,* **queued, queu·ing.** to form, stand,

a	at	e	end	o	hot	u	up	hw	white		about
ā	ape	ē	me	ō	old	ū	use	ng	song		taken
ä	far	i	it	ô	fork	ü	rule	th	thin	ə	pencil
âr	care	ī	ice	oi	oil	u̇	pull	th	this		lemon
		îr	pierce	ou	out	ûr	turn	zh	measure		circus

or wait in a line (often with *up*): *People queued up to buy tickets for the play.* [French *queue* tail, going back to Latin *cauda.*] —**queu′er,** *n.*

quib·ble (kwib′əl) *v.i.,* **-bled, -bling.** to make petty objections or critical remarks, often to avoid the truth or main point: *The lawyers quibbled over a legal technicality in the contract.* —*n.* a petty objection or criticism. [Diminutive of obsolete *quib* quip, probably from Latin *quibus,* dative or ablative plural of *quī* who, which (much used in legal documents).] —**quib′bler,** *n.*

quiche (kēsh) *n.* a rich pie baked with a mixture of cheese, eggs, cream, and other ingredients, usually served hot: *a spinach quiche, a salmon quiche.* [French *quiche,* from German dialect *Küche* little cake, from *Küchen* cake.]

quick (kwik) *adj.* **1.a.** done or occurring with promptness or within a very short time: *a quick return of a loan, a quick response.* **b.** lasting for a very short time: *a quick conversation, a quick glance.* **2.** moving or acting with considerable speed: *a quick typist.* **3.** understanding, learning, responding, or thinking rapidly: *a quick learner, a quick mind.* **4.** easily provoked or stirred: *a quick temper.* **5.** keenly perceptive; sensitive: *a quick sense of hearing.* **6.** sharp or sharply curved: *a quick bend in the road.* **7.** readily convertible into cash: *quick assets.* **8.** *Archaic.* having life; living; alive. —*n.* **1.** tender, sensitive flesh, esp. that beneath a fingernail or toenail. **2.** the most tender, sensitive part of one's emotions: *Your criticism cut me to the quick.* **3.** living persons. ➡ used chiefly in the phrase *the quick and the dead.* —*adv.* quickly: *to run as quick as a deer.* [Old English *cwic* living, alive.] —**quick′ness,** *n.*

Synonyms *adj.* **Quick, fast**[1], and **rapid** mean moving with great speed. **Quick** describes an event that happens suddenly and lasts a short time: *A quick throw to first base ended the inning.* **Fast** stresses constant speed: *A fast runner can cover the distance in two hours.* **Rapid** may refer to fast movement that is not necessarily constant: *The growth of the microchip industry has been rapid in recent years.*

quick·en (kwik′ən) *v.t.* **1.** to cause to go or move more rapidly; hasten or accelerate: *He quickened his steps. Fear quickened her pulse.* **2.** to restore life to; revive: *to quicken the dying embers of a fire.* **3.** to stir up; excite; stimulate: *to quicken the spirits.* —*v.i.* **1.** to go or move more rapidly: *The runner's pace quickened after the second lap.* **2.** to return to life; revive. **3.** to begin to show signs of life: *The earth quickened when spring arrived.* **4.** to reach the stage of pregnancy at which movement of the fetus can be felt by the mother. —**quick′en·er,** *n.*

quick-freeze (kwik′frēz′) *v.t.,* **-froze** (-frōz′), **-fro·zen** (-frō′zən), **-freez·ing.** to freeze food so rapidly that it retains its flavor and can be stored for long periods of time at low temperatures.

quick·ie (kwik′ē) *Slang. n.* something, as a book or motion picture, done or produced cheaply or in haste. —*adj.* done in haste or in less time than is usual: *a quickie lunch.*

quick·lime (kwik′līm′) *n.* lime[1].

quick·ly (kwik′lē) *adv.* with speed or haste; rapidly.

quick·sand (kwik′sand′) *n.* a bed of loose, wet sand, usually of considerable depth, that readily engulfs any heavy object that rests or moves upon it.

quick·set (kwik′set′) *n.* **1.** cuttings of a plant, esp. hawthorn, set to grow in a hedge. **2.** a hedge grown from such cuttings.

quick·sil·ver (kwik′sil′vər) *n.* mercury *(def. 1).* [Old English *cwicseolfor* literally, living silver, translation of Latin *argentum vīvum;* because the silver-colored metal is liquid and moves about as if alive. See QUICK, SILVER.]

quick·step (kwik′step′) *n.* **1.** a spirited marching step. **2.** march music with a rapid tempo. **3.** a lively dance step.

quick-tem·pered (kwik′tem′pərd) *adj.* easily angered or irritated; irascible.

quick time, the normal military marching rate, consisting of 120 thirty-inch steps per minute.

quick-wit·ted (kwik′wit′id) *adj.* having or showing a lively or alert mind; mentally sharp or keen: *a quick-witted pupil.* —**quick′-wit′ted·ly,** *adv.* —**quick′-wit′ted·ness,** *n.*

quid[1] (kwid) *n.* a piece of something to be chewed, esp. tobacco. [Old English *cwidu* what is chewed, cud.]

quid[2] (kwid) *n., pl.* **quid.** *British. Slang.* one pound sterling. [Of uncertain origin.]

quid·nunc (kwid′nungk′) *n.* an inquisitive, nosy person; busybody. [Latin *quid nunc?* what now?]

quid pro quo (kwid′prō kwō′) *Latin.* one thing given or taken in return for something else; equal exchange; substitution.

qui·es·cent (kwī es′ənt) *adj.* in a state of inactivity or repose: *a quiescent frame of mind.* [Latin *quiēscēns,* present participle of *quiēscere* to rest.] —**qui·es′cence,** *n.* —**qui·es′cent·ly,** *adv.*

qui·et (kwī′it) *adj.* **1.** making little or no noise: *The children were quiet while I read them a story.* **2.** with or characterized by

little or no noise: *a quiet library.* **3.** having little or no motion; still: *a quiet pond.* **4.** free from disturbance or excessive activity; uneventful; peaceful: *a quiet evening, a quiet life.* **5.** not easily agitated or upset; calm: *a quiet mood, a quiet person.* **6.** not showy or pretentious: *a quiet gesture of charity.* **7.** restful or soothing, as to the eye: *quiet scenery, quiet colors.* **8.** private or secluded: *a quiet hideaway.* —*n.* the quality or state of being quiet. —*v.t.* to make quiet (often with *down*): *The nurse quieted the baby down.* —*v.i.* to become quiet (often with *down*): *The waves quieted down after the storm passed.* [Latin *quiētus* at rest, calm. Doublet of COY.] —**qui′et·er,** *n.* —**qui′et·ly,** *adv.* —**qui′et·ness,** *n.*

qui·e·tude (kwī′i tüd′, -tūd′) *n.* the state or condition of being calm or restful; tranquillity: *the quietude of the countryside.* [Late Latin *quiētūdō,* from Latin *quiētus* at rest, calm.]

qui·e·tus (kwī ē′təs) *n., pl.* **-tus·es. 1.** the final ending or settling of something, as a debt, obligation, or office. **2.** a release from life; death. **3.** a state or period of inactivity. [Short for Medieval Latin *quietus est* he is acquitted, from Latin *quiētus est* he is at rest.]

quill (kwil) *n.* **1.a.** a feather, esp. a large, stiff feather from the tail or wing. **b.** the hard, hollow stem of a feather. For illustration, see **feather. 2.** a pen made from the hollow stem of a feather. **3.** one of the sharp spines of the porcupine or hedgehog. **4.** anything made from or as from the hollow stem of a feather, as a toothpick. [Possibly of Low German origin.] —**quill′like′,** *adj.*

Micmac Indian box made of **quills**

quilt (kwilt) *n.* **1.** a bed cover consisting of two pieces of cloth filled with soft stuffing material, as feathers or cotton batting, and held together by lines of stitching, usually in a pattern, across the entire surface. **2.** anything used as or resembling a quilt. —*v.i.* to make a quilt or quilts. —*v.t.* **1.** to stitch together (two pieces of cloth) with a soft interlining. **2.** to stitch with lines or patterns resembling those of a quilt. [Old French *cuilte* mattress, from Latin *culcita* cushion, mattress.] —**quilt′er,** *n.*

quilt·ing (kwil′ting) *n.* **1.** the act or process of making quilts or quilted work. **2.** the material used in making quilts.

quilting bee, a social gathering to make quilts. Also, **quilting party.**

quince (kwins) *n.* **1.** the pear-shaped yellow fruit of a small Asian tree, *Cydonia oblonga,* of the rose family, used esp. for making preserves. **2.** the tree bearing this fruit, having round white or pale pink flowers. [Originally plural of obsolete *quine* this fruit, from Old French *coin,* through Latin, going back to Greek *kydōnion mēlon* literally, apple of Cydonia (ancient Cretan city).]

qui·nine (kwī′nīn) *n.* a bitter, colorless, crystalline drug obtained from the bark of the cinchona tree, used to treat malaria and other illnesses. [Spanish *quina* bark of cinchona (from Quechua *kina* bark) + -INE[2].]

qui·noa (kēn′wä) *also,* **qui·nua.** *n.* a goosefoot, *Chenopodium quinoa,* that is native to the Andes and is cultivated there for its edible seeds. [South American Spanish *quínua,* from Quechua *kínwa.*]

Quin·qua·ges·i·ma (kwing′kwə jes′i mə) *n.* the last Sunday before Lent, immediately preceding Shrove Tuesday and Ash Wednesday. Also, **Quinquagesima Sunday.** [Latin *quīnquāgēsima (diēs)* literally, fiftieth (day); reckoned approximately as the fiftieth day before Easter.]

quin·quen·ni·al (kwing kwen′ē əl) *adj.* **1.** of or lasting for five years: *a quinquennial course of study.* **2.** occurring every five years: *a quinquennial celebration.* —*n.* **1.** an event lasting for five years. **2.** an event occurring every five years. [Latin *quīnquennis* (from *quinque* five + *annus* year) + -AL[1].] —**quin·quen′ni·al·ly,** *adv.*

quin·sy (kwin′zē) *n.* an acute inflammation of the tonsils and throat, often followed by the formation of an abscess. [Old French *quinancie* very sore throat, from Late Latin *cynanchē,* from

Greek *kynanchē*, from *kyōn* dog + *anchein* to strangle; because a sensation of strangling accompanies this disease.]

quint (kwint) *n. Informal.* quintuplet.

quin·tal (kwin′tal) *n.* **1.** in the United States, a measure of weight equal to 100 pounds (45.4 kilograms); hundredweight. **2.** a metric measure of weight equal to 100 kilograms, or 220.46 pounds avoirdupois. [Old French *quintal* weight of one hundred pounds, from Arabic *qintār*, going back to Latin *centēnārius* consisting of one hundred.]

quin·tes·sence (kwin tes′əns) *n.* **1.** the purest part or form of something: *the quintessence of a philosopher's writings.* **2.** the most perfect example of something: *the quintessence of beauty.* [Middle English *quyntecense*, from Medieval French *quinte essence*, from Medieval Latin *quinta essentia*, translation of Greek *pemptē ousia* fifth essence (which Aristotle, the coiner of the term, thought to be ether).] —**quin·tes·sen·tial** (kwin′tə sen′shəl), *adj.*

quin·tet (kwin tet′) *also*, **quin·tette.** *n.* **1.** a musical composition for five voices or instruments. **2.** a musical group of five performers. **3.** any group or set of five. [Italian *quintetto*, from *quinto* fifth, from Latin *quīntus.*]

quin·til·lion (kwin til′yən) *n.* **1.** in the United States, the cardinal number represented by 1 followed by 18 zeros. **2.** in Great Britain, the cardinal number represented by 1 followed by 30 zeros. —*adj.* numbering one quintillion. [Latin *quīntus* fifth + (M)ILLION.] —**quin·til′lionth** (-yənth), *n.*

quin·tu·ple (kwin tü′pəl, -tū′-, kwin′tə-) *adj.* **1.** consisting of five parts or members. **2.** five times as great or as many. —*v.t., v.i.,* **-pled, -pling.** to make or become five times as great or as many. —*n.* a number or amount five times as great as another. [French *quintuple* fivefold, going back to Latin *quīntus* fifth.]

quin·tu·plet (kwin tup′lit, -tə plit) *n.* **1.a.** one of five offspring born at one birth. **b.** quintuplets. five offspring born at one birth. **2.** any set or group of five. [QUINTUPLE + -ET.]

quip (kwip) *n.* **1.** a clever or witty remark or saying, usually made on the spur of the moment. **2.** a sharp or sarcastic remark or retort; taunt; gibe. **3.** something strange or curious; oddity. —*v.i.,* **quipped, quip·ping.** to make a quip or quips. [Form of obsolete *quippy* clever or sarcastic remark, possibly from Latin *quippe* forsooth, indeed (used sarcastically).] —**quip′ster,** *n.*

quire[1] (kwīr) *n.* twenty-four or twenty-five sheets of paper of the same size and quality. [Old French *quaier* group of four sheets, going back to Latin *quāternī* four each, four at a time, from *quattuor* four.]

quire[2] (kwīr) *n. Archaic.* choir.

Quir·i·nal (kwir′ə nəl) *n.* **1.** one of the seven hills on which ancient Rome was built. **2.** a palace built on this hill, formerly the residence of popes and kings, but now the official residence of the president of Italy. Also, **Quirinal Palace. 3.** the civil or royal government of Italy, as distinguished from the Vatican.

quirk (kwûrk) *n.* **1.** a peculiar personal trait or mannerism; idiosyncrasy. **2.** a sudden or unexpected twist or turn: *a quirk of fate.* **3.** a showy curve or flourish in handwriting. [Of uncertain origin.]

quirk·y (kwûr′kē) *adj.,* **quirk·i·er, quirk·i·est.** having or full of quirks. —**quirk′i·ly,** *adv.* —**quirk′i·ness,** *n.*

quirt (kwûrt) *n.* a flexible riding whip made of braided strips of leather and having a short handle. —*v.t.* to strike with a quirt: *to quirt a horse.* [Possibly from Spanish *cuerda* rope, from Latin *c(h)orda* gut, rope, from Greek *chordē* gut, string of gut.]

quis·ling (kwiz′ling) *n.* a traitor, esp. one who collaborates with an invading enemy by serving in a puppet government. [From Major Vidkun *Quisling*, 1887-1945, Norwegian who collaborated with the Nazi invaders of Norway during World War II.]

quit (kwit) *v.,* **quit** or **quit·ted, quit·ting.** —*v.t.* **1.** to stop doing (something); cease; discontinue: *We quit studying to eat lunch.* **2.** to give up, abandon, or resign: *to quit a job.* **3.** to go away from; leave: *The guards quit their post at midnight.* **4.** to pay up; repay: *to quit a debt.* **5.** *Archaic.* to behave or conduct (oneself) in a specified manner. —*v.i.* **1.** to stop doing something. **2.** to resign from a job or position: *She quit because the pay was too low.* **3.** to give up or stop trying, as in defeat or discouragement: *He quit the race when he realized he was so far behind.* —*adj.* free, clear, or rid of, as an obligation: *quit of all debts.* [Old French *quite* discharged, freed, clear, going back to Latin *quiētus* at rest, calm.]

quit·claim (kwit′klām′) *Law. n.* **1.** the giving up of one's claim, title, or right of action. **2.** a deed transferring one's interest in property, but not guaranteeing that anyone else has a claim to it. Also *(def. 2),* **quitclaim deed.** —*v.t.* to give up one's claim or title to or right of action on. [Anglo-Norman *quiteclamer* to declare free, going back to Latin *quiētus* at rest + *clāmāre* to call, proclaim.]

quite (kwīt) *adv.* **1.** completely; entirely; wholly: *to be left quite*

alone, quite the opposite. **2.** actually; really: *quite an accomplishment.* **3.** to a considerable extent or degree; rather: *quite warm, quite sophisticated.* [Middle English *quite* completely, from *quite* free, clear, from Old French *quite* freed. See QUIT.]

quit·rent (kwit′rent′) *also*, **quit-rent.** *n.* formerly, rent paid to a feudal lord in place of services owed. [QUIT + RENT[1].]

quits (kwits) *adj.* on even terms by means of repayment or retaliation: *After we made the last payment on the equipment, we were quits with the store.* [Medieval Latin *quittus* at rest, free, from Latin *quiētus* at rest, calm.]
• **to call it quits.** to discontinue something, as an activity or relationship: *After we studied all morning, we decided to call it quits.*
• **to cry quits.** to agree that both sides are even and discontinue competition: *The chess game was taking too long, so we cried quits.*

quit·tance (kwit′əns) *n. Law.* **1.** a discharge or release, as from debt or obligation. **2.** a document or receipt certifying this. **3.** repayment; recompense: *We received money in quittance for the extra work.* [Old French *quitance* acquittance, from *quiter* to release, going back to Latin *quiētus* at rest.]

quit·ter (kwit′ər) *n.* a person who gives up easily.

quiv·er[1] (kwiv′ər) *v.i.* to shake slightly but rapidly; shiver; tremble: *to quiver from fright.* —*n.* the act or motion of quivering. [Possibly imitative.] —**quiv′er·er,** *n.* —**quiv′er·ing·ly,** *adv.*

quiv·er[2] (kwiv′ər) *n.* **1.** a case for holding arrows. **2.** the arrows in such a case. [Old French *quivre*; probably of Germanic origin.]

qui vive (kē vēv′) who goes there? ➡ used as a challenge by a guard. [French *Qui vive?* literally, (long) live who? (used as a sentinel's challenge), going back to Latin *quī* who + *vīvere* to live.]
• **on the qui vive.** on the alert; watchful: *The sentry was on the qui vive all night.*

Qui·xo·te, Don (ki hō′tē, kwik′sət) see **Don Quixote.**

quix·ot·ic (kwik sot′ik) *adj.* ridiculously chivalrous or romantic; idealistic to an impractical degree: *a quixotic young reformer.* Also, **quix·ot′i·cal.** [From Don *Quixote.*] —**quix·ot′i·cal·ly,** *adv.*

quix·o·tism (kwik′sə tiz′əm) *n.* quixotic character or behavior.

quiz (kwiz) *n., pl.* **quiz·zes.** a short, informal examination: *a history quiz.* —*v.t.,* **quizzed, quiz·zing. 1.** to question or examine: *The police quizzed the suspect.* **2.** to give a quiz to; test the knowledge of: *The teacher quizzed the students.* [Of uncertain origin.] —**quiz′zer,** *n.*

quiz show, a radio or television show in which contestants try to answer questions for money or prizes. Also, **quiz program.**

quiz·zi·cal (kwiz′i kəl) *adj.* **1.** questioning; uncertain; puzzled: *a quizzical expression.* **2.** teasing; mocking; bantering: *a quizzical remark.* **3.** odd or comical: *a quizzical sight.* —**quiz′zi·cal′i·ty, quiz′zi·cal·ness,** *n.* —**quiz′zi·cal·ly,** *adv.*

quoin (koin, kwoin) *n.* **1.** an external angle of a wall or building. **2.** one of the stones forming such an angle; cornerstone. **3.** a wedge or wedge-shaped piece of material used for various purposes, as to keep objects from rolling or to lock printing type in a galley. [Form of COIN.]

quoit (kwoit) *n.* **1. quoits.** a game played by throwing a flattened ring made of metal, rope, or another material in an attempt to encircle or come as close as possible to a peg stuck in the ground. ➡ used as singular. **2.** the flattened ring used in this game. [Of uncertain origin.]

quon·dam (kwon′dəm) *adj.* that once was; former; erstwhile: *a quondam friend.* [Latin *quondam* formerly.]

Quon·set hut (kwon′sit) *Trademark.* a prefabricated building made of corrugated metal and supported by steel trusses, having a semicircular roof whose sides curve down to form the walls. [From *Quonset* Point, Rhode Island, where it was first produced.]

quo·rum (kwôr′əm) *n.* the minimum number of members of a committee, organization, assembly, or other group who must be present before binding decisions can be made. [Latin *quōrum* of whom (word occurring in earlier designations of the number of justices of the peace whose presence was necessary at certain court sessions in England).]

quot., quotation.

quo·ta (kwō′tə) *n.* **1.** a fixed amount, or a share of a total, assigned to or required from each member of a given group: *Each*

Q

a	at	e	end	o	hot	u	up	hw	white		about
ā	ape	ē	me	ō	old	ū	use	ng	song		taken
ä	far	i	it	ô	fork	u̅	rule	th	thin	ə	pencil
âr	care	ī	ice	oi	oil	u̇	pull	th	this		lemon
				ir	pierce	ou	out	ûr	turn	zh	measure		circus

991

soldier received a daily quota of rations. The salesclerks failed to sell their quota of shoes. **2.** a fixed or maximum number or proportion of a certain group or category of people permitted to join or be admitted, as to a country or school. [Medieval Latin *quota* share, short for Latin *quota pars* how great a part.]

quot·a·ble (kwō′tə bəl) *adj.* suitable for or worth quoting: *The reporters found nothing quotable in the senator's speech.* —**quot′a·bil′i·ty,** *n.* —**quot′a·bly,** *adv.*

quo·ta·tion (kwō tā′shən) *n.* **1.** words quoted, esp. a passage from a book: *The book contained quotations from various authors.* **2.** the act or process of quoting. **3.a.** a statement of the current prices offered or bid for a particular stock, bond, or commodity. **b.** the price so stated.

quotation mark, one of a pair of punctuation marks (" ") used chiefly to indicate the beginning and end of a quotation. Single quotation marks (' ') are usually used to indicate a quotation within another quotation.

quote (kwōt) *v.,* **quot·ed, quot·ing.** *v.t.* **1.** to repeat or reproduce the exact words from or of: *to quote a speech, to quote Shakespeare.* **2.** to bring forward or refer to for proof or support: *The driving instructor quoted the statistics on automobile accidents to the class.* **3.** to state (a price) for something, as goods or services: *The painter quoted a price for painting the house.* **4.** to enclose in quotation marks. —*v.i.* to repeat or reproduce the exact words of another: *If you're going to quote, give credit to the author.* —*n. Informal.* **1.** quotation *(def. 1).* **2.** quotation mark. —*interj.* I am about to begin quoting. ➡ used by a speaker before the first word in a quotation. [Medieval Latin *quotare* to number, mark references by numbers, from Latin *quot* how many.] —**quot′er,** *n.*

quoth (kwōth) *v.t. Archaic.* said or spoke. ➡ used before a first-person or third-person subject: *Quoth I to the question: "Never."* [Past tense of obsolete *quethe* to speak, say, from Old English *cwethan.*]

quoth·a (kwō′thə) *interj. Archaic.* in truth; without doubt; indeed. ➡ usually used to express sarcasm or surprise in repeating the words of another. [Contraction of *quoth he.*]

quo·tid·i·an (kwō tid′ē ən) *adj.* **1.** recurring or occurring every day; daily. **2.** common or usual: *quotidian household chores.* —*n.* a fever, esp. malarial fever, that occurs daily. [Latin *quotīdiānus* daily.]

quo·tient (kwō′shənt) *n.* a number or algebraic expression obtained by dividing one number or algebraic expression by another. In $12 \div 4 = 3$, *3* is the quotient. [Latin *quotiēns* how many times.]

quo war·ran·to (kwō wə ran′tō) *pl.* **-tos.** **1.** a legal proceeding undertaken to prevent the continued exercise by a person of an office, franchise, privilege, or liberty. **2.** formerly, a writ in English law calling upon a person to show by what authority an office or franchise is maintained. [Medieval Latin *quo warranto* by what warrant, from *quo,* ablative of Latin *quod* what + *warranto,* ablative of *warrantum* warrant (of Germanic origin).]

q.v., which see; look in the place just mentioned. [Abbreviation of Latin *quod vide.*]

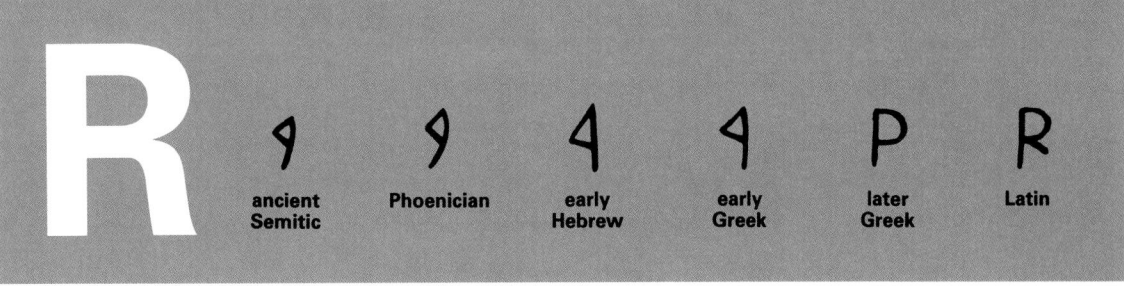

| | ancient Semitic | Phoenician | early Hebrew | early Greek | later Greek | Latin |

R The earliest ancestor of the English **R** was the letter *resh*, meaning "head," in the ancient Semitic alphabets. *Resh* continued to be written in much the same way in the Phoenician and early Hebrew alphabets. The early Greeks, who borrowed *resh* around 900 B.C. and called it *rho*, wrote either from right to left or in alternating rows of right to left and left to right. Later, when the Greeks began to write only from left to right, the shape of certain letters, including *rho*, was reversed. The reversed form of *rho*, which looked like our modern capital letter **P**, was adopted by the Romans. Later, a stroke was added to the Latin *rho*, making the shape of that letter the forerunner of our modern capital **R**.

r, R (är) *n., pl.* **r's, R's. 1.** the eighteenth letter of the English alphabet. **2.** the shape of this letter or something having this shape. **3. the three R's.** the basics of elementary education, esp. reading, writing, and arithmetic (humorously spelled *reading, 'riting,* and *'rithmetic*).
r 1. *Electricity.* resistance. **2.** roentgen. **3.** *also,* **r.** rod (measure of length).
r. 1. radius. **2.** railroad. **3.** railway. **4.** rare. **5.** received. **6.** residence. **7.** road. **8.** ruble. **9.** *Baseball.* run; runs. **10.** rupee.
R 1. *Chemistry.* radical. **2.** *Electricity.* resistance. **3.** *Chess.* rook.
R. 1. rabbi. **2.** railroad. **3.** railway. **4.** Republican. **5.** river. **6.** road. **7.** royal. **8.** *Baseball.* run; runs.
Ra (rä) *n.* in Egyptian mythology, the hawk-headed sun god, the chief official deity under the early dynasties. Also, **Re.**
Ra, the symbol for radium.
R.A. **1.** rear admiral. **2.** Royal Academy.
rab·bet (rab′it) *n.* **1.** a cut or groove made on the edge of a board to receive the edge of another, sometimes similarly cut or grooved board, as to form a joint. **2.** a joint formed using a rabbet or rabbets. Also *(def. 2),* **rabbet joint.** —*v.t.* **1.** to cut a rabbet in. **2.** to join with a rabbet or rabbets. [Old French *rabat* recess, from *rabattre* to beat down. See REBATE.]
rab·bi (rab′ī) *n.* **1.** the ordained leader of a Jewish congregation. **2.** a teacher of the Jewish religion who has completed a prescribed course of study. [Hebrew *rabbī* my master.]
rab·bin·ate (rab′ə nit, -nāt′) *n.* **1.** the position or term of office of a rabbi. **2.** rabbis collectively.
Rab·bin·ic (rə bin′ik) *n.* the Hebrew language as used in medieval rabbinical writings.
rab·bin·i·cal (rə bin′i kəl) *adj.* of or relating to rabbis, their language, views, or writings. Also, **rab·bin′ic.**
rab·bit (rab′it) *n.* **1.** any of various rodentlike mammals, family Leporidae, related to but usually smaller than the hare, having long ears and a short tail, as the cottontail. Length: 5-29 inches (13-74 centimeters). **2.** the fur of this animal. **3.** Welsh rabbit. [Middle English *rabet* the animal, possibly from Walloon *robete,* diminutive of Middle Dutch *robbe.*]
rabbit ears *Informal.* an indoor television antenna consisting of two movable and usually extendible rods attached to a base so that they form a V.
rabbit fever, tularemia.
rab·ble (rab′əl) *n.* **1.** a disorderly crowd; mob. **2. the rabble.** the common people; masses. ➡ used contemptuously in def. 2. [Of uncertain origin.]
rab·ble-rous·er (rab′əl rou′zər) *n.* a person who tries to stir up masses of people by exciting their emotions, prejudices, or passions.
Rab·e·lai·si·an (rab′ə lā′zē ən, -zhən) *adj.* of, relating to, or suggesting the French satirist François Rabelais or his broad, lusty humor.
rab·id (rab′id) *adj.* **1.** unreasonably zealous or enthusiastic in

beliefs or actions; fanatical: *a rabid racist, a rabid tennis fan.* **2.** violent; raging; furious: *rabid hunger.* **3.** of or affected with rabies; mad. [Latin *rabidus* raving.] —**rab′id·ly,** *adv.* —**rab′-id·ness,** *n.*
ra·bies (rā′bēz) *n.* a viral disease of mammals that attacks the central nervous system and can be transmitted to humans by the bite of a rabid animal. Symptoms in humans include fever, headache, and seizures; left untreated, the disease is fatal. Formerly, **hydrophobia.** [Latin *rabiēs* rage, madness.]
rac·coon (ra kün′) *also,* **racoon.** *n., pl.* **-coons** or **-coon. 1.** a small tree-dwelling mammal, *Procyon lotor,* of North and Central America, having brownish gray fur with black, masklike facial markings. Length: up to 42 inches (107 centimeters), including tail. **2.** the fur of this animal. Also, **coon.** [Algonquian *ärähkun* the animal.]
race¹ (rās) *n.* **1.**a. a contest of speed, as in running or riding. **b. races.** a series of such contests, esp. horse races, run at a fixed time over the same course. **2.** any contest or competition: *a race for political office.* **3.**a. a

raccoon

strong or swift current of water. **b.** a channel for such a current. **4.** an artificial channel transporting water to or from a point where its energy is utilized, as a millrace. Also, **raceway. 5.** a track or groove in a machine in which a part slides or rolls. Also, **race-way. 6.** an onward movement or course, as of time or life. —*v.,* **raced, rac·ing.** —*v.i.* **1.** to take part in a contest of speed: *We raced on our bicycles.* **2.** to run, move, or go rapidly: *I raced down the stairs because I was late.* **3.** (of machinery) to run too fast, as when the load is reduced while the power remains constant. —*v.t.* **1.** to try to go faster than; be in a contest of speed against: *I'll race you to the store.* **2.** to cause to race. [Old Norse *rās* running.]
race² (rās) *n.* **1.** a subdivision of the human species based on distinguishing physical characteristics that are passed on to succeeding generations. **2.** a group of persons sharing a common ancestry, history, nationality, or area of origin. **3.** lineage; ancestry. **4.** a group of people sharing similar characteristics, interests, or habits. **5.** a group of animals or plants having distinguishing characteristics that are passed on to succeeding generations; variety or subspecies. **6.** humanity. [French *race* lineage, family, breed, from Italian *razza* breed, kind², possibly from Arabic *rā′s* origin.]
race·course (rās′kôrs′) *n.* racetrack.
race·horse (rās′hôrs′) *n.* a horse bred and trained for racing.
ra·ceme (rā sēm′, rə-) *n.* a simple inflorescence in which the flowers are arranged on short stalks arising from the main stem. For illustration, see **inflorescence.** [Latin *racēmus* cluster of grapes. Doublet of RAISIN.]
rac·e·mose (ras′ə mōs′) *adj.* arranged in or having the form of a raceme. [Latin *racēmosus* full of clusters, clustering, from *racē-mus* cluster of grapes.]
rac·er (rā′sər) *n.* **1.** a person or thing that races or takes part in a race, or is capable of great speed. **2.** any of various swift American snakes, esp. the blacksnake.
race·track (rās′trak′) *n.* an area of ground, usually oval, laid out for racing, esp. for horse racing. Also, **racecourse.**

a	at	e	end	o	hot	u	up	hw	white		about
ā	ape	ē	me	ō	old	ū	use	ng	song		taken
ä	far	i	it	ô	fork	ü	rule	th	thin	ə	pencil
âr	care	ī	ice	oi	oil	u̇	pull	th	this		lemon
		îr	pierce	ou	out	ûr	turn	zh	measure		circus

R

993

race·way (rās′wā′) *n.* **1.** race[1] *(def. 4).* **2.** a conduit for electric cables in a building. **3.** a racetrack, esp. for harness racing or automobile racing. **4.** race[1] *(def. 5).*

ra·chis (rā′kis, rak′is) *n., pl.* **ra·chis·es** or **rach·i·des** (rak′i-dēz′, rā′ki-). **1.** the elongated axis of an inflorescence or of a compound leaf. **2.** the shaft of a feather, esp. the part bearing the barbs. **3.** the spinal column. [Modern Latin *rachis,* from Greek *rhachis* spine.]

ra·chi·tis (rə kī′tis) *n.* rickets. [Modern Latin *rachitis,* from Greek *rhachitis* disease of the spine, from *rhachis* spine + *-itis.* See -ITIS.] —**ra·chit·ic** (rə kit′ik), *adj.*

ra·cial (rā′shəl) *adj.* **1.** of, relating to, or characteristic of a race. **2.** of, relating to, or arising from relations between races: *racial prejudice, racial harmony.* —**ra′cial·ly,** *adv.*

rac·ism (rā′siz əm) *n.* **1.** a doctrine or belief that one race, esp. one's own, is superior to another. **2.** a political policy or social system based on such a doctrine or belief. Also, **ra′cial·ism.**

rac·ist (rā′sist) *n.* a person who believes in or supports racism. —*adj.* of or relating to racism.

rack[1] (rak) *n.* **1.** a framework or stand for hanging, displaying, or storing things. **2.** hayrack *(def. 2).* **3.** a former instrument of torture used to stretch or pull a victim's body in different directions. **4.** *Pool.* the triangular frame in which the balls are set before the opening shot. **5.** a bar with teeth on one surface that meshes with a toothed gear or wheel. **6.** the state or cause of acute mental or physical suffering. **7.** violent strain, as that caused by a storm: *a tree bent by the rack of storms.* —*v.t.* **1.** to cause to suffer mentally or physically; torment: *a body racked with pain.* **2.** to torture on a rack. **3.** *Pool.* to arrange (the balls) in the rack. [Possibly from Middle Dutch *rec* framework.]

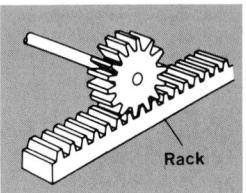

rack[1] *(def. 5)*

• **on the rack.** suffering acute pain, tension, or anxiety.

• **to rack one's brains.** to strain very hard to remember, understand, or think: *I racked my brains trying to remember where I put my keys.*

• **to rack up.** *Informal.* to score or achieve, esp. impressively: *Our team racked up points during the last five minutes of the game.*

rack[2] (rak) *n.* **to go to rack and ruin.** to fall apart; deteriorate: *They let the old farmhouse go to rack and ruin.* [Form of WRACK.]

rack[3] (rak) *n.* either of two gaits of a horse, pace or single-foot. —*v.i.* (of a horse) to move at either of these gaits. [Possibly form of ROCK[2].]

rack[4] (rak) *n.* a mass of thin or broken clouds driven by the wind. [Probably of Scandinavian origin.]

rack·et[1] (rak′it) *n.* **1.** a loud or confusing noise; clamor. **2.** *Informal.* a dishonest or illegal scheme or activity, esp. one for getting money by the use of bribery, extortion, fraud, or threats of violence. **3.** *Slang.* a profession or occupation. [Possibly imitative.]

rack·et[2] (rak′it) *also,* **racquet.** *n.* **1.a.** a round or oval frame strung with a network of gut, nylon, or other material, and having a handle of various lengths, used to strike a ball, as in tennis or squash. **b.** paddle[1] *(def. 2).* **2. rackets.** see racquet *(def. 1).* [French *raquette* the frame; earlier, *rachette* palm of the hand, going back to Arabic *rāha.*]

rack·et·eer (rak′ə tîr′) *n.* a person engaged in a dishonest or illegal scheme or activity for getting money. —*v.i.* to engage in a racket. —**rack′et·eer′ing,** *n.*

rac·on·teur (rak′on tûr′) *n.* a person skilled in telling stories. [French *raconteur,* from *raconter* to narrate. See RECOUNT[1].]

ra·coon (ra kün′) *n., pl.* **-coons** or **-coon.** raccoon.

rac·quet (rak′it) *n.* **1. racquets.** a game resembling tennis, played in a walled court. ➡ used as singular. **2.** racket[2] *(def. 1).*

rac·quet·ball (rak′it bôl′) *n.* a game similar to squash, played in a walled court with a strung racket that is shorter than a tennis racket.

rac·y (rā′sē) *adj.,* **rac·i·er, rac·i·est. 1.** somewhat indecent or improper; suggestive or risqué. **2.** full of spirit; lively; spirited: *a racy style of writing.* [From RACE[2] (referring to that which is characteristic or distinctive) + -Y[1].] —**rac′i·ly,** *adv.* —**rac′i·ness,** *n.*

rad (rad) *n.* a unit for measuring the amount of ionizing radiation absorbed in the body of a human or animal, equal to 100 ergs of energy per gram of the absorbing body. [Short for RADIATION.]

ra·dar (rā′där) *n.* a device or system for detecting the position and direction of movement of a distant object by sending out high-frequency radio waves and measuring the time taken for them to be reflected back from the object. [Short for *ra(dio) d(etecting) a(nd) r(anging)*.]

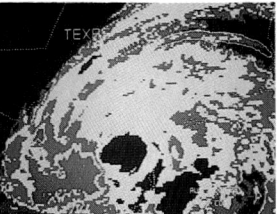

radar showing a hurricane over Texas

radar beacon, a radar system that receives and transmits radio waves in a narrow beam as a navigational aid to ships and aircraft.

radar detector, a microwave receiver installed in a motor vehicle in order to detect the radar transmissions used by police in monitoring the speed of vehicular traffic.

ra·dar·scope (rā′där skōp′) *n.* the viewing screen of a radar receiver.

ra·di·al (rā′dē əl) *adj.* **1.** of, relating to, or arranged like rays or radii. **2.** having parts extending from a common center. **3.** being or moving in the direction of a radius. **4.** displaying radial symmetry, as the arms of a starfish. **5.** of, relating to, or near the radius bone. —*n.* **1.** a radial thing or part. **2.** radial tire. —**ra′di·al·ly,** *adv.*

radial engine, an internal-combustion engine with radially arranged cylinders, used esp. in airplanes.

radial symmetry, the arrangement of similar body parts around a central point or axis, as in the starfish and sea anemone.

radial tire, an automobile tire having layers of material arranged at right angles to the direction in which the tire rolls, forming sidewalls with exceptional flexibility.

ra·di·an (rā′dē ən) *n.* a unit of angular measurement, equal to the angle at the center of a circle subtended by an arc of the circle equal in length to the radius, or approximately 57.2958 degrees. [RADIUS + -AN.]

ra·di·ance (rā′dē əns) *n.* **1.** the quality or state of being radiant. **2.** a bright light; brightness: *A radiance surrounded the Virgin Mary in the painting.* Also, **ra′di·an·cy.**

ra·di·ant (rā′dē ənt) *adj.* **1.** shining brightly; beaming. **2.** beaming, as with joy, contentment, or love: *a radiant smile.* **3.** emitting rays, as of light or heat. **4.** emitted or transmitted by radiation. —*n.* a point or object from which rays are emitted. [Latin *radiāns,* present participle of *radiāre* to emit beams.] —**ra′di·ant·ly,** *adv.* —For Synonyms, see **bright.**

radiant energy, energy transmitted by waves, esp. electromagnetic waves. X rays, visible light, and radio waves are forms of radiant energy.

radiant heating, a system of heating a room or building by wall, ceiling, or floor panels in which electric coils or hot-air or hot-water pipes are embedded.

ra·di·ate (rā′dē āt′) *v.,* **-at·ed, -at·ing.** —*v.i.* **1.** to emit rays, as of light or heat. **2.** to issue in rays: *Heat radiates from the sun.* **3.** to move or spread outward from a center: *Several narrow streets radiated from the town's main square.* —*v.t.* **1.** to emit in rays; irradiate: *The sun radiates light.* **2.** to show, as joy, contentment, pleasure, or love. **3.** to spread outward from a center. —*adj.* **1.** having rays spreading outward from a center: *a radiate flower.* **2.** radiating from a center. **3.** *Zoology.* displaying radial symmetry. [Latin *radiātus,* past participle of *radiāre* to emit beams.]

ra·di·a·tion (rā′dē ā′shən) *n.* **1.** the act, process, or state of radiating. **2.** *Physics.* **a.** the process of emitting nuclear or other subatomic particles or radiant energy. **b.** the particles or energy emitted. **3.** *Biology.* a process of evolutionary divergence whereby a group of organisms adapt to life in a variety of new environments.

radiation sickness, a reaction to overexposure to the ionizing radiation given off by X-ray machines and radioactive materials, characterized by nausea, diarrhea, internal bleeding, and damage to tissue structure.

radiation therapy, radiotherapy.

ra·di·a·tor (rā′dē ā′tər) *n.* **1.** a heating device consisting of a series of pipes or coils through which steam or hot water circulates. **2.** a cooling device through which water or other fluid circulates, as in an automobile engine. **3.** a person or thing that radiates.

rad·i·cal (rad′i kəl) *adj.* **1.** to the fullest extent; thoroughgoing; complete; extreme: *a radical change of attitude.* **2.** favoring or supporting basic or extreme change, esp. in political, social, or economic institutions. **3.** going to or coming from the root or origin; fundamental; basic. **4.** *Mathematics.* of or forming the root of a number or quantity, or relating to the radical sign: *a*

radical expression. **5.** *Botany.* pertaining to or arising from a root or roots. —*n.* **1.** a person who favors or supports basic or extreme change, esp. in political, social, or economic institutions. **2.** *Chemistry.* a group of atoms remaining connected and acting as a unit, often in the form of an ion, in chemical reactions. **3.** *Mathematics.* **a.** a root of a number or quantity. **b.** radical sign. **4.** *Linguistics.* root¹ (*def. 7*). [Late Latin *rādicālis* having roots, from Latin *rādix* root.] —**rad′i·cal·ly,** *adv.* —**rad′i·cal·ness,** *n.*

rad·i·cal·ism (rad′i kə liz′əm) *n.* **1.** the favoring or supporting of basic or extreme change, esp. in political, social, or economic institutions. **2.** radical principles or doctrines.

rad·i·cal·ize (rad′i kə līz′) *v.t., v.i.,* **-ized, -iz·ing.** to make or become radical or more radical, esp. in politics. —**rad′i·cal·i·za′tion,** *n.*

radical sign *Mathematics.* the sign ($\sqrt{}$) placed above a number or an algebraic expression to indicate that its root is to be extracted. Also, **radical.**

rad·i·cand (rad′i kand′) *n.* the quantity under a radical sign: *9 is the radicand of $\sqrt{9}$.*

rad·i·ces (rad′ə sēz′, rā′də-) a plural of **radix.**

rad·i·cle (rad′i kəl) *n.* **1.** the part of the embryo of a plant that develops into the root. **2.** *Anatomy.* a small, rootlike part, as the beginning of a nerve or vein. [Latin *rādīcula* small root, diminutive of *rādīx* root.]

rad·i·i (rā′dē ī′) a plural of **radius.**

ra·di·o (rā′dē ō′) *n., pl.* **-di·os. 1.** a form of telecommunication that uses electromagnetic waves transmitted through space, rather than electrical signals carried by wires. **2.** an apparatus for receiving radio broadcasts or for sending and receiving radio messages. **3.** radio broadcasting as an industry or entertainment form. **4.** a message sent by radio. —*adj.* **1.** of, relating to, used in, or sent by radio. **2.** of or relating to radio frequency. —*v.,* **-di·oed, -di·o·ing.** —*v.t.* **1.** to transmit (a message) by radio. **2.** to send a radio message to. —*v.i.* to transmit a message by radio. [Short for RADIOTELEGRAPHY.]

radio- *combining form* **1.** radio: *radiotelephone.* **2.** radioactive: *radiocarbon.* **3.** radiation: *radiometer.* [Latin *radius* ray¹.]

ra·di·o·ac·tive (rā′dē ō ak′tiv) *adj.* of, relating to, caused by, or exhibiting radioactivity. —**ra′di·o·ac′tive·ly,** *adv.*

radioactive disintegration series, a sequence of radioactive isotopes, each of which decays to form the next lighter one until a stable form, usually lead, is reached.

ra·di·o·ac·tiv·i·ty (rā′dē ō ak tiv′i tē) *n.* the emission of radiation in the form of alpha and beta particles and gamma rays from the nuclei of atoms during a process of decay, or disintegration, in which atoms of one element are transformed into atoms of another, more stable element.

radio astronomy, the branch of astronomy that studies celestial objects by means of the radio waves they emit. —**radio astronomer.**

radio beacon, a radio transmitter that sends out a special signal to assist ships and aircraft in determining their position and course.

ra·di·o·bi·ol·o·gy (rā′dē ō bī ol′ə jē) *n.* the branch of biology that deals with the effects of ionizing radiation on organisms and uses radioactive tracers to study metabolic processes. —**ra′di·o·bi′o·log′i·cal,** *adj.* —**ra′di·o·bi·ol′o·gist,** *n.*

ra·di·o·broad·cast (*n.,* rā′dē ō brôd′kast; *v.,* rā′dē ō brôd′kast′) *n.* a broadcast from a radio transmitting station. —*v.t., v.i.,* **-cast** or **-cast·ed, -cast·ing.** to broadcast by radio.

ra·di·o·car·bon (rā′dē ō kär′bən) *n.* radioactive carbon, esp. carbon 14.

radiocarbon dating, a technique for determining the age of organic materials, such as bone or fossils, by measuring the amount of radiocarbon they contain. Also, **carbon dating.**

ra·di·o·chem·is·try (rā′dē ō kem′ə strē) *n.* the branch of chemistry that is concerned with radioactive substances and with the chemical effects of ionizing radiation.

radio compass, a direction finder used for navigation, as in conjunction with a radio beacon.

ra·di·o·el·e·ment (rā′dē ō el′ə mənt) an element that is naturally radioactive, as any of the elements with an atomic number of 84 or higher.

radio frequency, an electromagnetic frequency from about 10 kilohertz to several thousand megahertz, used esp. in transmitting radio and television signals. —**ra′di·o-fre′quen·cy,** *adj.*

radio galaxy *Astronomy.* a galaxy that is a strong source of radio waves.

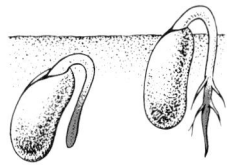

radicle

ra·di·o·gen·ic (rā′dē ō jen′ik) *adj.* resulting from radioactivity or formed by radioactive decay: *radiogenic lead.* [RADIO- + -GEN + -IC.]

ra·di·o·gram (rā′dē ō gram′) *n.* **1.** a message transmitted by radiotelegraphy. **2.** radiograph.

ra·di·o·graph (rā′dē ō graf′) *n.* a picture produced on a sensitive surface by radiation other than visible light, esp. by X rays. —*v.t.* to make a radiograph of.

ra·di·og·ra·phy (rā′dē og′rə fē) *n.* the process or technique of producing radiographs, widely used in radiology and in industry for detecting flaws in manufactured products. [RADIO- + -GRAPHY.] —**ra·di·o·graph′ic,** *adj.*

ra·di·o·i·so·tope (rā′dē ō ī′sə tōp′) *n.* a radioactive isotope, used in scientific research and certain forms of medical treatment.

ra·di·o·lar·i·an (rā′dē ō lâr′ē ən) *n.* any of a group of marine protozoans, order Radiolaria, one-celled plankton having skeletons made of silica and small spines radiating from their bodies. [Modern Latin *Radiolaria,* from Late Latin *radiolus,* diminutive of *radius* ray¹.]

ra·di·ol·o·gist (rā′dē ol′ə jist) *n.* a doctor who specializes in radiology.

ra·di·ol·o·gy (rā′dē ol′ə jē) *n.* the branch of medicine dealing with the use of X rays or nuclear radiation in the diagnosis and treatment of disease. [RADIO- + -LOGY.] —**ra·di·o·log·ic** (rā′dē ə loj′ik); *also,* **ra′di·o·log′i·cal,** *adj.*

ra·di·om·e·ter (rā′dē om′i tər) *n.* **1.** an instrument for demonstrating conversion of radiant energy into mechanical work, consisting of a glass bulb enclosing a partial vacuum and containing four thin pieces of metal that rotate when exposed to sunlight. **2.** an instrument for detecting and measuring various forms of radiant energy, as microwave radiation from the earth or heavenly bodies. [RADIO- + -METER.] —**ra·di·o·met·ric** (rā′dē ō met′rik), *adj.*

ra·di·o·nu·clide (rā′dē ō nū′klīd, -nū′-) *n. Physics.* a nuclide that undergoes radioactive decay.

ra·di·o·phone (rā′dē ō fōn′) *n.* radiotelephone.

ra·dio·pho·to (rā′dē ō fō′tō) *n.* a photograph or other illustration transmitted by radio. Also, **ra·di·o·pho·to·graph** (rā′dē ō fō′tə graf′).

ra·di·os·co·py (rā′dē os′kə pē) *n.* the process or technique of using radiation, esp. X rays, to examine the internal structure of objects that are not transparent. [RADIO- + Greek *skopia* a watching, seeing, from *skopein* to see.] —**ra·di·o·scop·ic** (rā′dē ō skop′ik), *adj.*

ra·di·o·sonde (rā′dē ō sond′) *n.* an instrument that is carried aloft by a balloon to radio back information about meteorological conditions at high altitudes. [RADIO- + French *sonde* sounding line (probably of Germanic origin).]

radio spectrum, the portion of the electromagnetic spectrum in which radiation consists of radio waves, used in radio and television broadcasting and radar.

ra·di·o·tel·e·graph (rā′dē ō tel′i graf′) *n.* the sending of messages by radiotelegraphy. —**ra′di·o·tel′e·graph′ic,** *adj.*

ra·di·o·te·leg·ra·phy (rā′dē ō tə leg′rə fē) *n.* wireless telegraphy. [RADIO- + TELEGRAPHY.]

ra·di·o·tel·e·phone (rā′dē ō tel′ə fōn′) *n.* a telephone that uses radio waves to transmit audible communication. Also, **radi·ophone.** —**ra·di·o·tel·e·phon·ic** (rā′dē ō tel′ə fon′ik), *adj.*

ra·di·o·tel·e·scope (rā′dē ō tel′ə skōp′) *n.* a telescope that detects radio waves that come from various cosmic sources, consisting of a reflector to focus the waves and a sensitive radio receiver.

ra·di·o·ther·a·py (rā′dē ō ther′ə pē) *n.* the use of X rays or radioactive substances to treat disease, esp. cancer. Also, **radiation therapy.**

radio tube, a vacuum tube used in radio sets.

radio wave, an electromagnetic wave within the radio spectrum.

rad·ish (rad′ish) *n.* **1.** the edible, fleshy root of a plant, *Raphanus sativus,* of the mustard family, usually white or red and having a pungent taste. **2.** the plant itself. [Old English *rædic,* from Latin *rādīx* root¹; influenced by French *radis* the plant, through Italian, from Latin *rādīx.* Doublet of RADIX.]

ra·di·um (rā′dē əm) *n.* a white, highly radioactive metallic element found in pitchblende and other uranium ores that is part of the radioactive disintegration series of uranium, used in radiotherapy and, formerly, in luminescent paint. Symbol: **Ra** For

a	at	e	end	o	hot	u	up	hw	white		about
ā	ape	ē	me	ō	old	ū	use	ng	song		taken
ä	far	i	it	ô	fork	ü	rule	th	thin	ə	pencil
âr	care	ī	ice	oi	oil	u̇	pull	th	this		lemon
		îr	pierce	ou	out	ûr	turn	zh	measure		circus

R

tables, see **element**. [Modern Latin *radium,* from Latin *radius* ray[1]; because it gives off radiation.]

ra·di·us (rā′dē əs) *n., pl.* **-di·i** (-dē ī′) or **-di·us·es. 1.a.** a line joining the center of a circle or sphere and any point on the circumference or surface. **b.** the length of such a line. **c.** the circular area defined by such a line of specified length from a specified or given center: *the population within a ten-mile radius of a volcano.* **2.** range or scope, as of activity or influence. **3.** a radial part, as the spoke of a wheel. **4.a.** the shorter and thicker of the two bones of the forearm, extending from the humerus to the wrist on the thumb side of the arm. For illustration, see **humerus. b.** a similar bone in the forelimb of other vertebrates. [Latin *radius* rod, ray[1]. Doublet of RAY[1].]

radius vector, a line segment that joins a variable point and the fixed point, or pole, in a system of polar coordinates.

ra·dix (rā′diks) *n., pl.* **rad·i·ces** (rad′ə sēz′, rā′də-) or **ra·dix·es. 1.** *Linguistics.* root[1] *(def. 7).* **2.** a root of a plant. **3.** *Mathematics.* a number taken as the base of a system of numbers. Two is the radix of the binary system, ten of the decimal. [Latin *rādīx* root[1]. Doublet of RADISH.]

ra·dome (rā′dōm′) *n.* a dome-shaped protective housing for a radar antenna. [RA(DAR) + DOME.]

ra·don (rā′don) *n.* an invisible, radioactive gaseous element belonging to the radioactive disintegration series of radium, used in radiotherapy but considered a health hazard when present in the air in high concentrations. Radon, the heaviest of the gaseous elements, is heavier atomically than lead. Symbol: **Rn** For tables, see **element**. [From RADIUM.]

rad·u·la (raj′ə lə) *n., pl.* **-lae** (-lē′) or **-las.** a flexible, filelike organ in most mollusks, bearing rows of small, horny teeth, used to tear up food. [Latin *rādula* scraper.] —**rad′u·lar,** *adj.*

rad·waste (rad′wāst′) *n.* radioactive waste material, as by-products from the operation of a nuclear reactor or from the reprocessing of depleted nuclear fuel. [Short for *rad(ioactive) waste.*]

RAF, Royal Air Force.

raf·fi·a (raf′ē ə) *n.* **1.** a strong fiber obtained from the leaves of an evergreen palm tree, *Rafia finifera,* used to make matting and baskets. **2.** the tree itself, native to Madagascar, having long featherlike leaves. [Of Malagasy origin.]

raf·fi·nose (raf′ə nōs′) *n.* a crystalline sugar occurring in sugar beets and cottonseed meal. Formula: $C_{18}H_{32}O_{16} \cdot 5H_2O$

raf·fish (raf′ish) *adj.* **1.** vulgar in a flashy way; tawdry. **2.** having or characterized by a showy or unconventional style or manner; jaunty; rakish. —**raf′fish·ly,** *adv.* —**raf′fish·ness,** *n.*

raf·fle (raf′əl) *n.* a lottery in which chances are sold for a prize. —*v.,* **-fled, -fling.** —*v.t.* to dispose of by a raffle (often with *off*): *to raffle off a turkey.* —*v.i.* to conduct or take part in a raffle. [Middle French *rafle* a gambling game with dice; of Germanic origin.]

raf·fle·sia (rə flē′zhə, -zhē ə) *n.* any of a group of parasitic plants, genus *Rafflesia,* esp. *R. arnoldii,* of the Malay Archipelago, bearing a single, huge, malodorous flower.

raft[1] (raft) *n.* **1.** a flat, floating platform, as of logs or planks fastened together, used for transportation on water. **2.** life raft. —*v.t.* **1.** to transport or carry on a raft. **2.** to make into a raft. —*v.i.* to travel on a raft: *to raft down a river.* [Old Norse *raptr* rafter.]

raft[2] (raft) *n. Informal.* a large collection or quantity. [Form of dialectal English *raff* abundance; of uncertain origin.]

raft·er (raf′tər) *n.* one of the sloping beams that supports a roof. [Old English *ræfter.*]

rag[1] (rag) *n.* **1.** a small piece of cloth, esp. a torn or worn one. **2. rags.** old, worn, tattered clothing: *to be dressed in rags.* **3.** any article of clothing: *I can't wear this old rag anymore.* **4.** a fragment or shred of something, as cloth: *to use rags for dusting.* **5.** cotton or linen cloth remnants used in making paper: *Paper of 100 percent rag is the best you can buy.* **6.** *Slang.* a

rafters

newspaper or other publication viewed with scorn: *I refuse to read that rag.* Also, **rag sheet.** [Middle English *ragge* small piece of cloth, going back to Old Norse *rögg* tuft of fur.]

rag[2] (rag) *v.t.,* **ragged, rag·ging.** *Slang.* **1.** to tease. **2.** to scold. **3.** *British.* to play practical jokes upon. [Of uncertain origin.]

ra·ga (rä′gə) *n.* **1.** any of the traditional melodic patterns of

Hindu music used as a source of improvisation, esp. on the sitar. **2.** such an improvisation. [Sanskrit *râga* color, tone.]

rag·a·muf·fin (rag′ə muf′in) *n.* a ragged, unkempt person, esp. a ragged, dirty child. [From *Ragamoffyn,* name of a demon in the medieval poem *Piers Plowman.*]

rage (rāj) *n.* **1.** violent or uncontrolled anger; fury: *eyes flashing with rage.* **2.** a fit of violent anger: *to be in a rage.* **3.** intense force or violence, as of a disease or storm. **4.** great enthusiasm or ardent desire. **5.** a fad; fashion; craze: *Blue knapsacks were the rage at school.* —*v.i.,* **raged, rag·ing. 1.** to feel or show violent anger; be in a rage. **2.** to act or move with great violence: *A hurricane raged from the south.* **3.** to spread or prevail without control: *The plague raged across the continent.* [Old French *rage* violent anger, madness, going back to Latin *rabiēs.*]

rag·ged (rag′id) *adj.* **1.** worn into rags; tattered; frayed: *a ragged coat.* **2.** wearing tattered clothing: *a ragged beggar.* **3.** having a rough, tousled, messy appearance; not trim or neat: *ragged fur, a ragged beard.* **4.** having rough or uneven projections; jagged: *ragged cliffs.* **5.** discordant, as a sound: *an opera singer with a ragged voice.* —**rag′ged·ly,** *adv.* —**rag′ged·ness,** *n.* **·to run ragged.** to cause to be extremely tired; exhaust the energy of.

rag·ged·y (rag′i dē) *adj.,* **-ged·i·er, -ged·i·est.** ragged.

rag·lan (rag′lən) *n.* **1.** a sleeve that extends over the shoulder to the collar. Also, **raglan sleeve.** **2.** a loose overcoat having such sleeves. —*adj.* of or having such sleeves. [From Lord *Raglan,* 1788-1855, British general, who is said to have designed such an overcoat.]

rag·man (rag′man′) *n., pl.* **-men** (-men′). a person who collects and deals in rags and junk. Also, **rag′pick′er.**

ra·gout (ra gü′) *n.* a highly seasoned meat and vegetable stew. [French *ragoût,* from *ragoûter* to restore the appetite, going back to Latin *re-* again, back + *ad* to + *gustus* taste.]

rag sheet *Slang.* rag[1] *(def. 6).*

rag·tag (rag′tag′) *adj.* **1.** consisting of varied elements or individuals; motley: *a ragtag group of people.* **2.** messy or unkempt; ragged. —*n.* low, disreputable people; riffraff. Also, **ragtag and bobtail.** [RAG[1] + TAG[1].]

rag·time (rag′tīm′) *n.* **1.** a kind of music originating in the United States in the nineteenth century, written primarily for the piano and characterized by a steady, marchlike rhythm in the bass and syncopation in the treble. **2.** the syncopated rhythm of such music. [Possibly from RAGGED + TIME; referring to the syncopated beat.]

rag·weed (rag′wēd′) *n.* **1.** any of several weeds, genus *Ambrosia,* of the composite family, whose pollen is one of the major causes of hay fever in the fall. **2.** *British.* ragwort. [RAG[1] + WEED[1]; referring to the ragged appearance of its leaves.]

rag·wort (rag′wûrt′) *n.* any of several plants, genus *Senecio,* of the composite family, usually having yellow flowers. [RAG[1] + WORT; referring to the ragged appearance of its leaves.]

rah (rä) *interj., n.* hurrah. [Short for HURRAH.]

raid (rād) *n.* **1.** a sudden, surprise invasion, as by police, for the purpose of seizing illegal or stolen goods and making arrests. **2.** a sudden attack, esp. by a small force for military purposes. **3.** an attack made on a competitor in an effort to lure away employees. **4.** an attempt made by speculators to cause stock market prices to drop. —*v.t.* to make a raid on. —*v.i.* to take part in or conduct a raid. [Scottish form of ROAD.] —**raid′er,** *n.* —For Synonyms *(n.),* see **invasion.**

rail[1] (rāl) *n.* **1.** a long, narrow bar, as of wood or metal, resting horizontally on posts, used as a guard or support. **2.** a fence or railing. **3.** one of a pair of metal bars that make up a railroad track. **4.** a railroad as a means of transportation: *to travel through Europe by rail.* —*v.t.* to furnish or enclose with a rail or rails. [Old French *reille* bar, from Latin *rēgula* bar, model. Doublet of RULE.]

rail[2] (rāl) *v.i.* to use abusive language; scold or complain bitterly (with *at* or *against*): *to rail against higher taxes.* [French *railler* to jest, mock, through Provençal, going back to Late Latin *ragere* to neigh; possibly imitative.] —**rail′er,** *n.*

rail[3] (rāl) *n.* any of numerous small birds, family Rallidae, that have short wings, strong legs, long toes, and a harsh cry and are found in marshy areas in most parts of the world. [Old French *raale,* from *raaler* to screech; probably of imitative origin.]

rail·ing (rā′ling) *n.* **1.** a fence or barrier made of a rail and its supports. **2.** rails collectively. **3.** the material for making rails.

rail·ler·y (rā′lə rē) *n., pl.* **-ler·ies.**

rail[3]

good-natured teasing or ridicule; banter. [French *raillerie* jesting, bantering, from *railler*. See RAIL².]

rail·road (rāl′rōd′) *n.* **1.** a permanent road laid with parallel steel rails fixed by ties and providing a track for trains and other rolling stock. **2.a.** an entire system of such roads, including stations, rolling stock, and right of way. **b.** a company that owns or manages such a system. —*v.t.* **1.** to transport by railroad. **2.** *Informal.* **a.** to rush or push through with great haste, esp. without proper consideration: *to railroad a bill through Congress.* **b.** to cause to be imprisoned on false charges or without a fair trial. —*v.i.* to work on a railroad. —**rail′road′er,** *n.*

rail·road·ing (rāl′rō′ding) *n.* the construction or operation of railroads.

rail·way (rāl′wā′) *n.* **1.** a railroad, esp. one operating lighter-weight rolling stock within a limited area, as within a city or between a mountain's base and summit. **2.** any line or set of rails for wheels, as in a mine or factory.

rai·ment (rā′mənt) *n. Archaic.* clothing; attire. [Short for obsolete *arrayment,* from Anglo-Norman *araiement,* from *arayer* to array. See ARRAY.]

rain (rān) *n.* **1.** water condensed from vapor in the atmosphere, falling in drops from the sky to the earth. **2.** a fall of rain; rainstorm or shower. **3.** rainy weather. **4.** a heavy or rapid fall of anything. **5. the rains.** the rainy season, as in tropical climates. —*v.i.* **1.** (of rain) to fall: ➡ used with *it*: *It's raining hard.* **2.** to fall like rain: *Rice rained down on the newlyweds.* —*v.t.* **1.** to pour or send down like rain: *to rain confetti.* **2.** to give abundantly: *to rain compliments on someone.* [Old English *regn* precipitation in the form of water.]

 • **to rain out.** to cause (an outdoor event) to be canceled or postponed because of rain.

rain·bow (rān′bō′) *n.* **1.** an arc of spectral colors seen in the sky opposite the sun and caused by the reflection and refraction of the sun's rays by water droplets in the air. **2.** any similar arc. [Old English *regnboga* the rainbow seen in the sky.]

rainbow trout, a mainly freshwater game fish, *Salmo gairdneri,* native to cool stream and coastal waters of the West and the upper Midwest, many having a long pink stripe along a cobalt and silver body. Weight: 2-5 pounds (0.9-2.3 kilograms).

rain check 1. a ticket stub on an outdoor event entitling the holder to admission at a future date if the original event is canceled or postponed because of rain. **2.** the postponement of an invitation until a future date: *We asked our friend for a rain check when she invited us to dinner.* **3.** a coupon given to a customer by a store having a sale entitling the customer to purchase at a later time an item that is sold out at its sale price.

rain·coat (rān′kōt′) *n.* a waterproof or water-resistant coat for use when it rains.

rain date, an alternate date set for an outdoor event in case the event must be postponed because of rain.

rain·drop (rān′drop′) *n.* a drop of rain.

rain·fall (rān′fôl′) *n.* **1.** a fall or shower of rain. **2.** the total amount of water falling in the form of rain, snow, sleet, or hail in a given area within a given time; precipitation.

rain forest, a dense, usually tropical forest in a region having a high annual rainfall.

rain gauge, an instrument for measuring the depth of rainfall. Also, **pluviometer.**

rain·mak·er (rān′mā′kər) *n.* **1.** (esp. among American Indians) a person who tries to cause rain by incantation or supernatural means. **2.** *Informal.* a person who tries to cause rain artificially by using scientific techniques.

rain·proof (rān′prüf′) *adj.* not letting rain in; shedding rain.

rain·storm (rān′stôrm′) *n.* a storm with rain.

rain·wa·ter (rān′wô′tər, -wot′ər) *n.* water that has fallen as rain.

rain·wear (rān′wâr′) *n.* raincoats, rubbers, boots, and other clothing made for wearing in the rain.

rain·y (rā′nē) *adj.,* **rain·i·er, rain·i·est. 1.** characterized by or full of rain: *rainy weather.* **2.** bringing rain: *rainy clouds.* **3.** wet with rain: *rainy streets.* —**rain′i·ness,** *n.*

rainy day, a time or possible time of need: *to save money for a rainy day.*

raise (rāz) *v.,* **raised, rais·ing.** —*v.t.* **1.** to move or cause to move to a higher level or position; lift: *Raise the blinds. Raise your hand.* **2.** to set upright or in a standing position. **3.** to build; construct: *to raise a barn.* **4.** to cause to rise or appear: *The bee sting raised a bump on my arm.* **5.** to move to a higher rank, position, or degree of worth: *The bank raised the teller to an administrative position.* **6.** to increase in amount, size, or value: *to raise taxes.* **7.** to increase in degree, intensity, strength, or pitch: *to raise one's voice.* **8.** to gather together; collect: *to raise money.* **9.a.** to breed or grow: *to raise wheat.* **b.** to bring up; rear: *to raise a family.* **10.** to bring up for consideration or discussion: *to raise a question.* **11.** to stir up; arouse: *to raise a commotion.* **12.** to

cause to come about; provoke: *The joke raised a laugh.* **13.** to bring back from or as if from death. **14.** to utter, esp. with a loud voice: *to raise a cry.* **15.** to make light: *to raise bread with yeast.* **16.** to bet more than (a preceding bet or better in poker). **17.** to increase the bid of (one's bridge partner). **18.** *Nautical.* to come into sight of (land, another ship, or the like) by proceeding toward. **19.** to make contact with by radio, or pick up radio signals from. **20.** to end (a siege) by withdrawing troops or by forcing the enemy to withdraw its troops. —*v.i.* to increase a bet in poker. —*n.* **1.** an act or instance of raising. **2.** an increase in amount. [Old Norse *reisa* to cause to rise.] —**rais′er,** *n.*

v.t. **Raise, lift,** and **elevate** mean to move or cause to move upward. **Raise** is the most general term: *to raise one's arms, to raise a flag, to raise an eyebrow.* **Lift** more strongly suggests effort: *to lift a suitcase, to lift a child up in the air.* **Elevate** is less common than *raise* and *lift,* and stresses the idea of height rather than that of effort: *We need to elevate the stage so the audience will have a better view.*

rai·sin (rā′zin) *n.* a sweet grape of any of various kinds, dried in the sun or artificially. [Old French *raisin* grape, from Latin *racēmus* cluster of grapes. Doublet of RACEME.]

rai·son d'ê·tre (Re zôN de′trə; rā′zôn det′rə) *French.* justification for existing.

raj (räj) *n.* (in India) rule; reign. [Hindi *rāj.*]

ra·jah (rä′jə) *also,* **ra·ja.** *n.* a ruler or prince in India and the East Indies. [Hindi *rājā,* from Sanskrit *rājan* king.]

Raj·put (räj′püt′) *also,* **Raj·poot.** *n.* a member of a Hindu ruling caste supposedly descended from ancient warriors.

rake¹ (rāk) *n.* **1.** a long-handled tool with teeth, used to gather such things as hay or fallen leaves or to smooth rough ground. **2.** any of various similar tools. —*v.,* **raked, rak·ing.** —*v.t.* **1.** to gather, scrape, loosen, or smooth with or as with a rake. **2.** to gather or collect in abundance; amass: *to rake in money.* **3.** to search carefully and thoroughly: *to rake files for a lost document.* **4.** to bring to renewed attention; uncover facts about (with *up*): *to rake up an old scandal.* **5.** to direct gunfire along the length of. —*v.i.* to use a rake. [Old English *raca* the long-handled tool with teeth.] —**rak′er,** *n.*

rake² (rāk) *n.* a dissolute person; roué; libertine. [Short for archaic *rakehell,* from RAKE¹ + HELL, from the idea that one would have to *rake* hell to find such a person.]

rake³ (rāk) *n.* a slope or inclination, as of the mast of a ship. —*v.i.,* **raked, rak·ing.** to slope or incline. [Of uncertain origin.]

rake·off (rāk′ôf′, -of′) *n. Slang.* a share or rebate, esp. one that is illegitimate.

rak·ish¹ (rā′kish) *adj.* **1.** showy or stylish; jaunty: *a rakish outfit.* **2.** having a streamlined appearance suggesting speed, as a boat. [RAKE³ + -ISH.] —**rak′ish·ly,** *adj.* —**rak′ish·ness,** *n.*

rak·ish² (rā′kish) *adj.* like a rake; dissolute. [RAKE² + -ISH.] —**rak′ish·ly,** *adj.* —**rak′ish·ness,** *n.*

rale (räl) *n. Medicine.* a crackling noise that accompanies the normal sounds of breathing, indicating a lung disorder. [French *râle,* from *râler* to rattle, from Middle French *raller* to screech, rattle.]

rall., rallentando.

ral·len·tan·do (rä′len tän′dō) *adj., adv. Music.* gradually slower. [Italian *rallentando,* present participle of *rallentare* to slow down, slacken, going back to Latin *re-* again + *ad* to + *lentus* slow.]

ral·ly¹ (ral′ē) *v.,* **-lied, -ly·ing.** —*v.t.* **1.** to bring together so as to restore order: *to rally scattered troops.* **2.** to bring together for a common purpose; assemble: *to rally club members for a special meeting.* **3.** to pull together; revive or arouse: *to rally one's strength.* —*v.i.* **1.** to come together and into order again: *The troops rallied.* **2.** to come together for a common purpose: *Fans rallied at the airport to welcome back their hometown hockey team.* **3.** to come to aid or support a cause or person: *Members of both political parties rallied behind the president during the crisis.* **4.** to recover normal strength, vigor, or energy: *The patient rallied briefly, then suffered a relapse.* **5.** (in tennis and similar games) to exchange a series of strokes before a point is made. —*n., pl.* **-lies. 1.** the act of rallying. **2.** a mass meeting for a common purpose: *a political rally.* **3.** (in tennis and similar games) a series of strokes exchanged before a point is made. **4.** a long-distance automobile race over public highways. [French *rallier* to assemble, going back to Latin *re-* again + *ad* to + *ligāre* to bind.]

a	at	e	end	o	hot	u	up	hw	white	⎧	about
ā	ape	ē	me	ō	old	ū	use	ng	song		taken
ä	far	i	it	ô	fork	ü	rule	th	thin	ə	pencil
âr	care	ī	ice	oi	oil	u̇	pull	th	this		lemon
		îr	pierce	ou	out	ûr	turn	zh	measure	⎩	circus

R

997

ral·ly² (ral′ē) *v.t.*, *v.i.*, **-lied**, **-ly·ing**. to tease good-naturedly; banter. [French *railler* to jest, mock. See RAIL².]

ram (ram) *n.* **1.** a male sheep. **2.** any of various devices used to batter, crush, or force something by impact, as a battering ram. **3.** the plunger or piston of a force pump. **4.** hydraulic ram. **5.a.** a projection on the bow of a warship, used to batter and crush an enemy ship. **b.** a warship with such a projection. —*v.*, **rammed**, **ram·ming**. —*v.t.* **1.** to batter or strike against with great force; butt against. **2.** to force or drive down or into place: *to ram a tent stake into the ground*. **3.** to force acceptance of: *to ram a proposal through a committee*. **4.** to stuff or cram: *We rammed all the junk into a box.* —*v.i.* to strike or hit with great force; collide: *The car skidded on the ice and rammed into the car ahead.* [Old English *ram(m)* male sheep, battering ram.] —**ram′mer**, *n.*

rams

RAM (ram) *n.* a type of computer memory that stores data temporarily. The time required to store or retrieve data in RAM does not depend on the position of the data in the memory. [Short for *r(andom)-a(ccess) m(emory)*.]

Ra·ma (rä′mə) *n.* in Hinduism, any of three incarnations of Vishnu who were heroes, esp. the hero of the Ramayana.

Ram·a·dan (ram′ə dän′) *n.* **1.** the ninth month of the Islamic year, observed as a fast from sunrise to sunset for thirty days. **2.** the daily fasting itself.

Ra·ma·ya·na (rä mä′yə nə) *n.* a Hindu epic, written in Sanskrit, recounting the adventures of Rama.

ram·ble (ram′bəl) *v.i.*, **-bled**, **-bling**. **1.** to go about or move about in an aimless, leisurely manner; roam. **2.** to talk or write aimlessly and at length: *The speaker rambled on and never came to the point.* **3.** to grow or spread without definite direction, as a vine. —*n.* an aimless, leisurely walk. [Possibly ROAM + -LE.] —For Synonyms *(v.i.)*, see **roam**.

ram·bler (ram′blər) *n.* **1.** a person or thing that rambles. **2.** any of various climbing roses.

ram·bunc·tious (ram bungk′shəs) *adj.* wild and boisterous. [Possibly modification of earlier *robustious* strong, boisterous, from ROBUST.] —**ram·bunc′tious·ly**, *adv.*

ram·e·kin (ram′i kin) *also*, **ram·e·quin.** *n.* **1.** an individual baking dish, esp. of earthenware. **2.** a portion of food, esp. a cheese mixture with bread crumbs and eggs, cooked or served in such a dish. [French *ramequin;* of Germanic origin.]

ram·ie (ram′ē, rä′mē) *n.* **1.** an Asian shrub, *Boehmeria nivea*, whose stems yield a fiber used to make fabrics and other products. **2.** the fiber itself. [Malay *rāmī* the plant.]

ram·i·fi·ca·tion (ram′ə fi kā′shən) *n.* **1.** the act or process of dividing or spreading into branches or branchlike parts. **2.** a branch, as of an artery. **3.** a result or consequence developing from a situation or statement: *We discussed the possible ramifications of the plan.*

ram·i·fy (ram′ə fī′) *v.i.*, **-fied**, **-fy·ing**. to divide or spread into or as into branches or branchlike parts. [Old French *ramifier* to branch, going back to Latin *rāmus* branch + *facere* to make.]

ram·jet (ram′jet′) *n.* a jet engine in which the fuel is ignited along with air compressed by the high forward speed of the aircraft or missile that the engine powers.

ra·mose (rä′mōs) *adj.* having many branches; branching. [Latin *rāmōsus,* from *rāmus* branch.]

ra·mous (rä′məs) *adj.* **1.** ramose. **2.** of or like a branch.

ramp¹ (ramp) *n.* **1.** a sloping passageway or roadway connecting different levels. **2.** a movable staircase for entering or leaving an airplane. [French *rampe* slope, from *ramper* to climb. See RAMP².]

ramp² (ramp) *v.i.* **1.** to act menacingly or violently; rampage. **2.** to stand in a rampant position, as a lion in heraldry. **3.** to leap or rush with fury. [Old French *ramper* to creep, climb; of Germanic origin.]

ram·page (*n.*, ram′pāj; *v.,* ram′pāj, ram pāj′) *n.* a fit of violent or reckless behavior or action: *The angry bear went on a rampage at the campsite.* —*v.i.*, **-paged**, **-pag·ing**. to behave in a violent or reckless manner; rage. [RAMP² + -AGE.] —**ram·pag′er**, *n.*

ramp·an·cy (ram′pən sē) *n.* the quality or state of being rampant.

ramp·ant (ram′pənt) *adj.* **1.** growing profusely; luxuriant: *a rampant growth of wildflowers.* **2.** going beyond usual limits; unchecked; unrestrained: *Flu was rampant in our county last winter.* **3.** *Heraldry.* (of an animal) rising on the left hind leg, with the other legs and tail raised and the head and body in profile. **4.** violent in behavior or action: *a rampant bull.* [Old French *rampant,* present participle of *ramper* to creep, climb. See RAMP².] —**ramp′ant·ly**, *adv.*

ram·part (ram′pärt′, -pərt) *n.* **1.** an embankment built for defense, esp. around a castle. **2.** anything that serves as a defense or protection. [French *rempart* from *remparer* to fortify, going back to Latin *re-* back + *ante* before + *parāre* to make ready.]

ram·rod (ram′rod′) *n.* **1.** a rod used for ramming the charge down the barrel of a muzzleloading firearm. **2.** a rod used to clean the barrel of a rifle or other firearm.

ram·shack·le (ram′shak′əl) *adj.* likely to collapse; dilapidated; rickety. [From earlier *ramshackled,* originally past participle of obsolete *rans(h)ackle* to ransack, from RANSACK + -LE.]

ra·mus (rä′məs) *n., pl.* **-mi** (-mī). *Biology.* a branch or branchlike projection, as of a bone or vein. [Modern Latin *ramus,* from Latin *rāmus,* branch.]

ran (ran) the past tense of **run.**

Ran (rän) *n.* in Norse mythology, a sea goddess.

ranch (ranch) *n.* **1.** a large farm, esp. in the western United States, used to raise large herds of livestock. **2.** any farm devoted to raising a particular crop or animal. **3.** persons employed or living on a ranch. **4.** ranch house. —*v.i.* to manage or work on a ranch. [Spanish *rancho* small farm, group of people who eat together, from Old High German *hring* circle.]

ranch·er (ran′chər) *n.* a person who owns or works on a ranch.

ranch house 1. the main building of a ranch, esp. the owner's house. **2.** a long, low house with all the rooms on one floor.

ranch·man (ranch′mən) *n., pl.* **-men** (-mən). rancher.

ran·cid (ran′sid) *adj.* having the unpleasant odor or taste of a spoiled oily substance: *rancid butter.* *rancid oil stinking.*] —**ran·cid′i·ty**, **ran′cid·ness**, *n.* —**ran′cid·ly**, *adv.*

ran·cor (rang′kər) *also*, *British,* **ran·cour.** *n.* bitter or rankling malice or resentment; hatred; spite. [Old French *rancour* hatred, from Latin *rancor* grudge, rancidity.]

ran·cor·ous (rang′kər əs) *adj.* bitterly resentful; spiteful. —**ran′cor·ous·ly**, *adv.* —**ran′cor·ous·ness**, *n.*

rand (rand) *n.* the monetary unit of South Africa. [Afrikaans *rand;* originally, shield, from Dutch *rand* edge.]

R and D *also*, **R&D.** research and development. [Abbreviation of *r(esearch)* and *d(evelopment)*.]

ran·dom (ran′dəm) *adj.* lacking definite aim, pattern, or purpose; haphazard: *a random choice.* [Old French *randon* impetuosity, from *randir* to run impetuously; of Germanic origin.] —**ran′dom·ly**, *adv.* —**ran′dom·ness**, *n.*

·at random. with no definite reason, plan, or purpose: *I selected a book at random from the shelf.*

Synonyms *adj.* **Random** and **haphazard** mean without plan or direction. **Random** is applied to something occurring by chance or through lack of guidance: *One theory about the beginnings of the universe is that it is the result of a series of random events.* **Haphazard** often implies a careless disregard for the potential results of an action: *The child applied paint in a haphazard way.*

ran·dom-ac·cess memory (ran′dəm ak′ses) see **RAM.**

ran·dom·ize (ran′də mīz′) *v.t.*, **-ized**, **-iz·ing**. *Statistics.* to put, take, or perform at random or by using random samples, esp. as a way of excluding irrelevant variables. [RANDOM + -IZE.]

random number, a number chosen as a random sample, as from a table of such numbers or by a computer.

random sample *Statistics.* a sample drawn from a group in which each individual has an equal chance of being drawn.

ra·nee (rä′nē) *also*, **rani.** *n.* **1.** the wife of a rajah. **2.** a reigning Hindu queen or princess. [Hindi *rānī* queen, from Sanskrit *rājñī.*]

rang (rang) the past tense of **ring².**

range (rānj) *n.* **1.** the limits between which something varies: *a wide range of prices.* **2.** the area of operation or action: *range of vision.* **3.a.** the maximum effective distance that a projectile, as a bullet, can be propelled. **b.** the distance of a weapon from a target: *to shoot at close range.* **4.** the maximum distance that an aircraft, ship, or vehicle can travel without refueling. **5.a.** a place or area set aside for shooting practice. **b.** an area set aside for

testing rockets and missiles. **6.** the extent of variation in pitch of a singing voice or musical instrument. **7.** a large area of open land over which livestock roam and graze. Also, **rangeland. 8.** a row, line, or series. **9.** mountain range. **10.** a large stove having burners and an oven. **11.** a region in which a certain kind of plant or animal normally lives or grows. **12.** rank, class, or order. **13.** *Mathematics.* a set of values that the dependent variable in a function may have. **14.** the act of wandering around. —*v.*, **ranged, rang·ing.** —*v.t.* **1.** to place in a particular order, esp. in rows or lines; arrange: *to range books on the shelf.* **2.** to place in a particular position, company, or category; classify. **3.** to move over or explore (an area): *My friend and I ranged the field looking for wildflowers.* **4.** to wander or roam over: *Herds of bison once ranged the prairie.* **5.** to put (livestock) to graze on a range. **6.** to align (a gun or telescope) with a target. **7.** to obtain the range of, as a target. —*v.i.* **1.** to vary within limits: *The quality of food ranges from good to excellent.* **2.** to move over or explore an area: *My eye ranged over the crowded room, seeking a familiar face.* **3.** to wander or roam: *to range through the woods.* **4.** to stretch out in or as in a line; extend: *Trees ranged along the road.* **5.** (of plants and animals) to extend throughout or occur in a given region. [Old French *ranger* to array, rank, from *reng* rank[1], row[1]. See RANK[1].] —For Synonyms *(n.)*, see **scope.**

range finder, any of various instruments, as on a gun or camera, for determining the distance to a given object.

range·land (rānj′land′) *n.* range *(def. 7).*

rang·er (rān′jər) *n.* **1.** a. forest ranger. b. park ranger. **2.** a member of a body of armed persons who patrol a region to maintain law and order. **3.** a member of the Texas state police. **4. Ranger.** a soldier in the U.S. Army specially trained to carry out raids on enemy positions; commando. **5.** a person or thing that ranges.

rang·y (rān′jē) *adj.,* **rang·i·er, rang·i·est. 1.** suited for ranging or running, as an animal. **2.** slender and long-limbed: *a rangy youth.* **3.** having or permitting a wide range.

ra·ni (rä′nē) ranee.

rank[1] (rangk) *n.* **1.a.** a relative position, standing, or class. **b.** an official position or grade: *the rank of captain.* **c.** a high position, standing, or class: *a doctor of rank.* **2.a.** a line of persons, animals, or things placed side by side. **b.** a row of soldiers standing side by side in close order. ➡ distinguished from **file[1]. 3. ranks.** a. common soldiers of an army, as opposed to the officers. b. army. **4.** *Chess.* any row of squares running across the board. For illustration, see **chessboard.** —*v.t.* **1.** to arrange in a row or rows: *to rank soldiers.* **2.** to assign a position to; classify: *to rank students according to their grades.* **3.** to take precedence over; outrank: *Lieutenants rank sergeants.* —*v.i.* **1.** to have a certain rank or position, esp. in relation to others: *a student who ranks high in class.* **2.** to form in a row or rows. [Old French *reng, renc* row[1], range; of Germanic origin.]

· **to break ranks. a.** to leave one's assigned place in a row or formation, as of soldiers. **b.** to break away from or refuse to give support to one's co-workers, political party, or group that shares one's ideology.

· **to close ranks. a.** to move together more closely, as soldiers in a row or formation: *The soldiers closed ranks to face the advancing enemy.* **b.** to give one's full support, as to one's co-workers or political party: *The workers closed ranks in the face of management's opposition to better working conditions.*

· **to pull (one's) rank** (often with **on**). *Informal.* to exert authority in order to get something done or overcome opposition: *The senator pulled rank to get the bureaucrat to approve a request. The office manager had to pull rank on an employee who was reluctant to complete an assignment.*

| **Synonyms** | *n.* **Rank[1], position, standing,** and **status** can |

all mean the place a person or group occupies in society: **Rank** is usually applied to hierarchical orders such as those of the military or the aristocracy: *The royal wedding united two families of the highest rank.* **Position** suggests a high but less clearly defined rank: *Some people attach more importance to social position than to wealth.* **Standing** emphasizes the requirements that must be met to achieve status in a particular group or profession: *Unethical behavior damaged the lawyer's professional standing.* **Status** is often used to denote the position of a particular group: *The economic status of women was the focus of the conference.*

rank[2] (rangk) *adj.* **1.** growing profusely or luxuriantly, as vegetation. **2.** producing profuse growth, as land. **3.** having a strong, foul smell or taste; rancid. **4.** utter or complete; extreme: *a rank liar.* **5.** vulgar, gross, or indecent. [Old English *ranc* strong.] —**rank′ly,** *adv.* —**rank′ness,** *n.*

rank and file 1. common soldiers of an army, as distinguished

from the officers. **2.** the people who make up a group, as distinguished from the leaders.

rank·ing (rang′king) *adj.* **1.** of a high rank, as in seniority: *a ranking member of a committee.* **2.** having distinction; outstanding; prominent; foremost: *That playwright is one of the ranking figures in American theater.* —*n.* **1.** an act or instance of indicating order, as of importance, rank, or quality. **2.** a list showing this. [RANK[1].]

ran·kle (rang′kəl) *v.t., v.i.,* **-kled, -kling.** to irritate or anger (someone) continuously. [Old French *rancler,* form of *draoncler* to fester, from *draoncle* ulcer, going back to Late Latin *dracunculus* literally, little dragon, diminutive of Latin *dracō* serpent, reptile monster. See DRAGON.]

ran·sack (ran′sak′) *v.t.* **1.** to search thoroughly: *to ransack a drawer for a missing glove.* **2.** to search through for plunder; pillage: *Thieves ransacked the house.* [Old Norse *rannsaka* to search a house.] —**ran′sack′er,** *n.*

ran·som (ran′səm) *n.* **1.** the release of a captive or captured property for a price. **2.** the price paid or demanded. **3.** redemption from sin and its consequences. —*v.t.* **1.** to obtain the release of by paying a certain price. **2.** to release upon receiving payment of ransom. **3.** to redeem from sin and its consequences. [Old French *raençon* price paid for the release of a captive, from Latin *redēmptiō* a buying back. Doublet of REDEMPTION.] —**ran′som·er,** *n.*

rant (rant) *v.i.* to speak in a wild, excited, or loud way; rave. —*n.* wild, excited, or loud speech or language. [Obsolete Dutch *ranten* to rave.] —**rant′er,** *n.*

rap[1] (rap) *n.* **1.** a quick, sharp, or light blow or knock. **2.** *Slang.* punishment or blame, esp. a prison sentence: *to take the rap for stealing.* —*v.*, **rapped, rap·ping.** —*v.i.* to knock or tap sharply: *to rap at a door.* —*v.t.* **1.** to knock or hit sharply: *to rap a table with a pencil.* **2.** to say sharply (with *out*): *to rap out a reply.* **3.** *Slang.* to be critical of; berate: *to rap the competition.* [Imitative.]

rap[2] (rap) *n. Informal.* the least bit: *I don't care a rap about sports.* [Of uncertain origin.]

rap[3] (rap) *v.i.,* **rapped, rap·ping.** *Slang.* to discuss openly and informally: *We rapped for a few hours about sports and music.* —*adj. Slang.* involving open, informal discussion: *The students had a rap session in the dormitory discussing politics.* —*n.* **1.** *Slang.* an open and informal conversation or discussion. **2.** a style of popular music in which rhyming lyrics are spoken in a rapid, rhythmical way, set to a simple, repetitive beat. Also *(def. 2),* **rap music.** [Perhaps short for *repartee.*] —**rap′per,** *n.*

ra·pa·cious (rə pā′shəs) *adj.* **1.** wanting more than one's share; very greedy. **2.** (of animals) living on live prey; predatory. **3.** given to taking by force; plundering. [Latin *rapāci-,* stem of *rapāx* grasping + -OUS.] —**ra·pa′cious·ly,** *adv.* —**ra·pa′cious·ness,** *n.*

ra·pac·i·ty (rə pas′i tē) *n.* the quality of being rapacious.

rape[1] (rāp) *n.* **1.a.** the crime of forcing a person to have sexual intercourse against his or her will. **b.** statutory rape. **2.** a seizing and carrying off by force. —*v.t.,* **raped, rap·ing. 1.** to force to have sexual intercourse. **2.** *Archaic.* to seize and carry off by force. **3.** to plunder, as a city. [Latin *rapere* to seize.]

rape[2] (rāp) *n.* a leafy branching plant, *Brassica napus,* whose leaves are used as fodder and whose seeds yield an oil; cole. [Latin *rāpa* turnip.]

rape[3] (rāp) *n.* the refuse of grapes after the juice has been extracted, used in making vinegar. [French *râpe* grape stalk; of Germanic origin.]

rape·seed (rāp′sēd′) *n.* the seed of the rape plant, used as birdseed and for a cooking oil that is also a lubricant. Also, **colza.**

Raph·a·el (raf′ē əl, rā′fē-, rä′fī el′) *n.* one of the archangels.

ra·phe (rā′fē) *n.* **1.** *Anatomy.* a seam uniting the lateral halves of an organ or structure, as the tongue or scrotum. **2.** *Botany.* a seamlike ridge on some seeds. [Modern Latin *raphe,* from Greek *raphē* seam, from *rhaptein* to stitch together.]

rap·id (rap′id) *adj.* moving, acting, or happening with speed; swift: *a rapid pace, a rapid worker, rapid development.* —*n.* usually, **rapids.** a part of a river where the current is swift, caused by a steep descent of the riverbed. [Latin *rapidus* swift.] —**rap′id·ly,** *adv.* —**rap′id·ness,** *n.* —For Synonyms *(adj.),* see **quick.**

rapid eye movement, see REM.

a	at	e	end	o	hot	u	up	hw	white		about
ā	ape	ē	me	ō	old	ū	use	ng	song		taken
ä	far	i	it	ô	fork	ü	rule	th	thin	ə	pencil
âr	care	ī	ice	oi	oil	u̇	pull	th	this		lemon
		îr	pierce	ou	out	ûr	turn	zh	measure		circus

R

rap·id-fire (rap′id fīr′) *adj.* **1.** (of guns) firing or capable of firing shots in quick succession. **2.** characterized by or occurring in quick succession: *rapid-fire questions.*

ra·pid·i·ty (rə pid′i tē) *n.* the state or quality of being rapid; quickness.

rapid transit, a system of fast urban public transportation using electric rail lines to move a great volume of riders, esp. during rush hour, such as a subway system.

ra·pi·er (rā′pē ər) *n.* **1.** a long, slender sword with a two-edged blade, used during the sixteenth and seventeenth centuries. **2.** a light sword of the eighteenth century, having a sharp point and no cutting edge, used only for thrusting. [French *rapière;* earlier, in phrase *espee rapiere* rapier sword; of uncertain origin.]

rap·ine (rap′in) *n.* the act of seizing and carrying off property belonging to another; plunder; pillage. [Latin *rapīna.*]

rap·ist (rā′pist) *n.* a person who has committed the crime of rape.

rap·port (ra pôr′) *n.* a relationship that is characterized by harmony or close agreement: *The professor had good rapport with the students.* [French *rapport,* from *rapporter* to bring back, going back to Latin *re-* back *+ ad* to *+ portāre* to carry.]

rap·proche·ment (ra prōsh män′) *n.* the establishment or reestablishment of friendly relations, as between nations. [French *rapprochement* a bringing together, from *rapprocher* to bring together, going back to Latin *re-* again *+ ad* to *+ prope* near.]

rap·scal·lion (rap skal′yən) *n.* a rascal; rogue; scamp. [Earlier *rascallion,* from RASCAL.]

rapt (rapt) *adj.* **1.** carried away with strong emotion, as with joy or delight; enraptured. **2.** deeply absorbed; engrossed: *rapt attention.* **3.** showing or caused by rapture: *a rapt smile.* [Latin *raptus,* past participle of *rapere* to seize.]

rap·to·ri·al (rap tôr′ē əl) *adj.* **1.** of or relating to birds of prey. **2.** adapted for seizing prey: *raptorial talons.* **3.** predatory. [Latin *raptor* one who seizes by force *+ -IAL.*]

rap·ture (rap′chər) *n.* **1.** the state of being carried away by strong emotion, as joy or love. **2.** *also,* **raptures.** an expression of great joy.

rap·tur·ous (rap′chər əs) *adj.* showing or feeling rapture. —**rap′tur·ous·ly,** *adv.*

ra·ra a·vis (râr′ə ā′vis) *pl.* **ra·ra a·vis·es** or **ra·rae a·ves** (râr′ē ā′vēz). a rare person or thing. [Latin *rāre avis* rare bird.]

rare¹ (râr) *adj.,* **rar·er, rar·est. 1.** seldom occurring, seen, or found; unusual; uncommon: *a rare species, a rare experience.* **2.** unusually excellent; remarkably good or fine: *a rare talent, a rare taste in art.* **3.** of thin consistency; not dense: *The air is rare at high altitudes.* [Latin *rārus* uncommon, thin.] —**rare′ness,** *n.* —For Synonyms, see **uncommon.**

rare² (râr) *adj.,* **rar·er, rar·est.** (of meat) cooked for a brief period of time. [Old English *hrēr* underdone.]

rare·bit (râr′bit) *n.* Welsh rabbit.

rare earth 1. an oxide of any of the rare-earth elements. **2.** any rare-earth element.

rare-earth element (râr′ûrth′) any of a group of silvery, reactive, metallic elements of atomic numbers 57 through 71; any element belonging to the lanthanide series. Also, **rare-earth metal.**

rar·e·fac·tion (râr′ə fak′shən) *n.* **1.** the act of rarefying. **2.** the state of being rarefied.

rar·e·fy (râr′ə fī′) *v.,* **-fied, -fy·ing.** —*v.t.* **1.** to make thinner or less dense: *to rarefy air.* **2.** to make more refined, pure, or lofty. —*v.i.* to become thinner or less dense. [Latin *rārēfacere* to make thin, from *rārus* thin *+ facere* to make.] —**rar′e·fi·a·ble,** *adj.*

rare gas, noble gas.

rare·ly (râr′lē) *adv.* **1.** not often; seldom; infrequently: *My friend rarely writes letters.* **2.** in an unusual degree; exceptionally. **3.** remarkably well; excellently: *a rarely written novel.*

rar·i·ty (râr′i tē) *n., pl.* **-ties. 1.** a rare person or thing: *Rain is a rarity in the desert.* **2.** the quality, state, or fact of being rare: *the rarity of the air at high altitudes.*

ras·cal (ras′kəl) *n.* **1.** a mischievous, playful person; scamp. **2.** a low, mean, dishonest person; scoundrel. [Old French *rascaille* outcasts, from *rasche* filth. See RASH².]

ras·cal·i·ty (ras kal′i tē) *n., pl.* **-ties. 1.** the character or behavior of a rascal. **2.** a mean dishonest act.

ras·cal·ly (ras′kə lē) *adj.* of or characteristic of a rascal. —*adv.* in a rascally manner.

rash¹ (rash) *adj.* **1.** acting too hastily or with lack of thought: *a rash person.* **2.** characterized by too great haste or lack of thought: *a rash decision.* [Probably from an unrecorded Old English word.] —**rash′ly,** *adv.* —**rash′ness,** *n.*

Synonyms **Rash¹** and **reckless** mean acting or speaking without forethought or preparation. **Rash** applies especially to immoderate behavior under stressful conditions: *In the heat of the debate the candidate made several rash statements.* **Reckless** emphasizes indifference to the dangerous consequences of an act: *The workers showed a reckless disregard for safety procedures.*

rash² (rash) *n.* **1.** an eruption of red spots on the skin. **2.** an outbreak of a number of related incidents occurring within a short time: *a rash of burglaries.* [Old French *rasche* scurf, filth, going back to Latin *rāsus,* past participle of *rādere* to scrape, scratch.]

rash·er (rash′ər) *n.* **1.** a slice of bacon for frying or broiling. **2.** a serving of such slices. [Of uncertain origin.]

rasp (rasp) *v.t.* **1.** to scrape or grate with or as with a rough instrument. **2.** to be an annoyance to; grate upon; irritate: *The loud noise rasped my nerves.* **3.** to utter in a rough, grating voice. —*v.i.* **1.** to scrape or grate. **2.** to make a rough, grating sound. —*n.* **1.** a rough, grating sound. **2.** a coarse file with raised, pointed projections, used esp. on wood. **3.** the act of rasping. [Old French *rasper* to scrape, scratch; of Germanic origin.]

rasp·ber·ry (raz′ber′ē, -bə rē) *n., pl.* **-ries. 1.** the edible, thimble-shaped fruit of any of several plants, genus *Rubus,* of the rose family, consisting of a cluster of red, black, or yellow drupelets. **2.** the often prickly plant that bears this fruit. **3.** *Slang.* a sound of disapproval or contempt made with the tongue vibrating between the lips. [Obsolete *raspis* the fruit and plant (of uncertain origin) *+* BERRY.]

rasp·y (ras′pē) *adj.,* **rasp·i·er, rasp·i·est.** rough; grating: *My sore throat left me with a raspy voice.* —**rasp′i·ness,** *n.*

Ras·ta·far·i·an (ras′tə fâr′ē ən) *n.* a member of a black religious group, originating in Jamaica, who believe Africa is the promised land and that the former emperor of Ethiopia, Haile Selassie I, is divine. [From *Ras Tafari,* name of Haile Selassie I (1892-1975) before becoming emperor of Ethiopia.] —**Ras·ta·far′i·an·ism,** *n.*

rat (rat) *n.* **1.** any of a great variety of rodents, genus *Rattus* and related genera, of the family Muridae, found throughout most of the world, resembling, but larger than, a mouse. Length: 5-12 inches (13-30 centimeters), without tail. **2.** *Slang.* a sneaky, contemptible person, esp. one who deserts or betrays associates or a cause. **3.** a pad worn under strands of hair to make the hair look thicker. —*v.i.,* **rat·ted, rat·ting. 1.** to hunt for rats. **2.** *Slang.* **a.** to betray one's associates by informing; act as an informer. **b.** to desert one's associates or a cause. [Old English *ræt* the rodent.]

•**to smell a rat.** to suspect something underhanded.

rat·a·ble (rā′tə bəl) *also,* **rateable.** *adj.* **1.** capable of being rated or estimated. **2.** *British.* taxable. —**rat′a·bil′i·ty,** *n.* —**rat′a·bly,** *adv.*

ra·tan (ra tan′) rattan.

ratch·et (rach′it) *n.* **1.** a mechanism consisting of a bar or wheel with slanted teeth that are caught by a pawl, allowing motion in one direction only, used in escapements and various other mechanical devices. **2.** the bar, wheel, or pawl of such a mechanism. [French *rochet,* earlier *rocquet* blunt head of a lance (referring to the resemblance between the head of a lance and the teeth of a ratchet); of Germanic origin.]

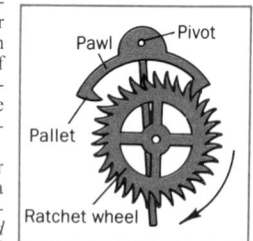

ratchet *(def. 1)*

rate¹ (rāt) *n.* **1.** an amount or number of one thing in relation to a certain amount or number of something else: *the rate of miles traveled per hour.* **2.** a price or charge fixed according to a standard, scale, or ratio: *telephone rates.* **3.** relative quality or rank: *a movie of the first rate.* **4.** the degree of speed of working, moving, or acting: *to build at a rapid rate.* **5.** *British.* a local tax on property. —*v.,* **rat·ed, rat·ing.** —*v.t.* **1.** to estimate the value of; appraise: *to rate a house for tax purposes.* **2.** to place in a certain class or rank: *to rate a ship.* **3.** to consider; regard: *Historians rate the general as one of the greatest in our nation's history.* **4.** to fix or set a rate for. **5.** *Informal.* to be deserving of; merit: *to rate a raise in salary.* —*v.i.* **1.** to have rank or class. **2.** to have value or standing: *That author rates among the best novelists.* [Old French *rate* price, value, from Medieval Latin *rata* fixed amount, from Latin *rata,* feminine past participle of *rērī* to reckon, think.] —For Synonyms *(v.t.),* see **estimate.**

•**at any rate. a.** in any case; regardless of what happens: *At any*

rate, the decision is up to us. **b.** at least: *The car is not in the best condition, but at any rate it was cheap.*

rate² (rāt) *v.t., v.i.,* **rat·ed, rat·ing.** to scold. [Possibly of Scandinavian origin.] —**rat′er,** *n.*

rate·a·ble (rā′tə bəl) ratable.

ra·tel (rā′təl, rä′-) *n.* a badgerlike mammal, genus *Mellivora,* of Africa and parts of Asia. Length: 2½ feet (0.8 meter), including tail.

rate of exchange, the ratio at which the currency of one country is converted into the currency of another country.

rath·er (rath′ər, rä′thər) *adv.* **1.** more readily or willingly: *I would rather stay home tonight than go out.* **2.** more properly; with better reason or ground: *They, rather than we, deserve the reward.* **3.** more correctly or precisely: *The airplane is arriving at noon or, rather, 12:15.* **4.** in some measure or degree; somewhat: *I rather thought you would agree. It is rather cold outside.* **5.** on the contrary: *It is not raining; rather, the sun has come out.* —*interj. British.* certainly. [Old English *hrathor* the more readily, comparative of *hræthe* quickly.]

raths·kel·ler (rät′skel′ər, rat′-, rath′-) *n.* **1.** the cellar of a German town hall, often used as a restaurant or beer hall. **2.** a restaurant or bar modeled after such a cellar. [German *Ratskeller,* from *Rat(haus)* town hall + *Keller* cellar.]

rat·i·fi·ca·tion (rat′ə fi kā′shən) *n.* the act of ratifying or the state of being ratified.

rat·i·fy (rat′ə fī′) *v.t.,* **-fied, -fy·ing.** to validate by giving formal consent, approval, or sanction; confirm. [Old French *ratifier* to confirm, going back to Latin *ratus* fixed, past participle of *rērī* to reckon, think + *facere* to make.] —**rat′i·fi′er,** *n.*

rat·ing (rā′ting) *n.* **1.** a classification according to a relative measure or standard, as of a member of the military; rank; grade. **2.** a particular position in a classification. **3.** an amount fixed as a rate. **4.** an estimate of the financial status of a person, business, or security. **5.** the operating capacity of a piece of electrical machinery, expressed as in horsepower or kilowatts. **6.** a percentage of the public who make up the audience of a television or radio program: *The special holiday concert boosted the television show's rating.*

ra·ti·o (rā′shē ō′, rā′shō) *n., pl.* **-ti·os. 1.** the comparison in quantity, amount, or size between two things. **2.** *Mathematics.* the proportional relationship between two numbers or algebraic expressions, expressed as a quotient. The ratio of 3 to 7 is written 3:7 or ³⁄₇. [Latin *ratiō* calculation, relation. Doublet of RATION, REASON.]

ra·ti·oc·i·nate (rash′ē os′ə nāt′) *v.i.,* **-nat·ed, -nat·ing.** to reason. [Latin *ratiōcinātus,* past participle of *ratiōcinārī* to calculate, consider.] —**ra′ti·oc′i·na′tion,** *n.*

ra·tion (rash′ən, rā′shən) *n.* **1.** a fixed portion or share. **2.** a fixed daily food allowance, as for a soldier. **3. rations.** food. —*v.t.* **1.** to distribute in fixed portions: *During the blizzard, meat was rationed until new deliveries could be made.* **2.** to supply with rations, as an army. **3.** to restrict to fixed portions: *People were rationed to a quart of milk a week during the war.* [French *ration,* allowance, from Latin *ratiō* calculation, relation. Doublet of RATIO, REASON.]

ra·tion·al (rash′ə nəl) *adj.* **1.** showing or conforming to reason; sensible: *Although the arguments are rational, we are not convinced.* **2.** of sound mind; sane. **3.** endowed with the ability to reason: *a rational being.* **4.** of, relating to, or based on reason. **5.** *Mathematics.* of or relating to a rational number or to an algebraic expression without radicals. [Latin *ratiōnālis* relating to reason, from *ratiō* reason, calculation, relation.] —**ra′tion·al·ly,** *adv.* —For Synonyms, see **reasonable.**

ra·tion·ale (rash′ə nal′) *n.* an underlying reason; rational or logical basis. [Latin *ratiōnāle* rational thing, neuter of *ratiōnālis* relating to reason. See RATIONAL.]

ra·tion·al·ism (rash′ə nə liz′əm) *n.* reliance on reason alone as the supreme authority in matters of opinion, belief, or conduct. —**ra′tion·al·ist,** *n., adj.* —**ra′tion·al·is′tic,** *adj.* —**ra′tion·al·is′ti·cal·ly,** *adv.*

ra·tion·al·i·ty (rash′ə nal′i tē) *n.* the quality or state of being rational.

ra·tion·al·ize (rash′ə nə līz′) *v.,* **-ized, -iz·ing.** —*v.t.* **1.** to explain or justify (one's behavior) in a way that seems reasonable or plausible but is probably untrue: *to rationalize cheating by saying that everyone cheats.* **2.** to explain or interpret in a rational way. **3.** to make rational. **4.** *Mathematics.* to remove radicals from (an expression) without changing its value: *to rationalize the denominator of a fraction.* —*v.i.* to devise plausible but inaccurate explanations for behavior. —**ra′tion·al·i·za′tion,** *n.* —**ra′tion·al·iz′er,** *n.*

rational number, a real number that can be expressed as a quotient of two integers or as an integer. ¾ and 5 are rational numbers.

rat·ite (rat′īt) *n.* any flightless bird with a flat breastbone, as the ostrich, emu, cassowary, kiwi, and rhea, formerly placed together in a group, Ratitae, but now classified in various orders. —*adj.* of or relating to such a bird. [Latin *ratitus* marked with the figure of a raft, from *ratis* raft; because its flat breastbone resembles a raft.]

rat·line (rat′lin) *also,* **rat·lin.** *n.* one of the small ropes stretching horizontally across the shrouds of a ship, used as a ladder for going aloft. [Of uncertain origin.]

rat race *Slang.* any frantic, tiring activity, esp. one that is highly competitive and stressful.

rat·tan (ra tan′) *also,* **ratan.** *n.* **1.** the long thin stems of any of several tropical climbing palm trees, genus *Calamus,* used for mats, baskets, chairs, and other products. **2.** the tree itself, found in southern Asia and the East Indies. **3.** a cane or switch made from the rattan stem. [Malay *rōtan* the plant.]

rat·ter (rat′ər) *n.* an animal, as a dog or cat, that catches rats.

rat·tle (rat′əl) *v.,* **-tled, -tling.** —*v.i.* **1.** to make a rapid succession of short, sharp sounds, as of small, hard objects colliding. **2.** to move with such sounds; clatter: *The old car rattled over the cobblestones.* **3.** to talk quickly and aimlessly; chatter (often with *on*): *The child rattled on about school.* —*v.t.* **1.** to cause to rattle. **2.** to say rapidly and fluently (usually with *off*): *The student rattled off the dates of the major battles.* **3.** to cause to be confused or embarrassed; disconcert: *The jeers from the audience rattled the speaker.* —*n.* **1.** a rapid succession of short, sharp sounds. **2.** a sealed container, esp. a baby's toy, with small pellets or stones inside that move around and rattle when the container is shaken. **3.** a rattling sound caused by mucus in the throat, supposedly heard just before death. **4.** the series of interlocking rings of horny tissue at the end of a rattlesnake's tail. [Imitative.]

rat·tle·brain (rat′əl brān′) *n.* an empty-headed, talkative person.

rat·tler (rat′lər) *n.* **1.** a person or thing that rattles. **2.** rattlesnake.

rat·tle·snake (rat′əl snāk′) *n.* any of a group of venomous New World snakes, genera *Crotalus* and *Sistrurus,* having a series of interlocking rings of horny tissue at the end of the tail that rattle when shaken. Length: from 15 inches (38 centimeters) to over 8 feet (2.4 meters).

rattlesnake

rat·tle·trap (rat′əl trap′) *n.* anything old and rattling, esp. an old car.

rat·ty (rat′ē) *adj.,* **-ti·er, -ti·est. 1.** of or relating to rats. **2.** infested with rats. **3.** *Slang.* disheveled or shabby: *You always wear the same ratty sweater around the house.*

rau·cous (rô′kəs) *adj.* **1.** harsh; grating: *a raucous voice.* **2.** disorderly; rowdy: *The raucous party left the house in a shambles.* [Latin *raucus* hoarse.] —**rau′cous·ly,** *adv.* —**rau′cous·ness,** *n.*

raun·chy (rôn′chē) *adj.,* **-chi·er, -chi·est.** *Slang.* **1.** crudely or openly sexual; obscene: *raunchy jokes.* **2.** shabby, dirty, or sloppy: *raunchy clothes.* [Of uncertain origin.]

rau·wol·fi·a (rô wŭl′fē ə) *n.* **1.** any of a genus, *Rauwolfia,* of tropical trees and shrubs, esp. *R. serpentina,* a southern Asian shrub, the source of a medicinal extract. **2.** the alkaloid extracted from this shrub, a source of reserpine and other tranquilizing drugs used in the treatment of mental disorders and hypertension. [Modern Latin *rauwolfia,* from Leonhard *Rauwolf,* died 1596, German botanist.]

rav·age (rav′ij) *v.,* **-aged, -ag·ing.** —*v.t.* to lay waste to; destroy: *The tornado ravaged the town.* —*v.i.* to lay waste; be destructive. —*n.* a destructive or ruinous action or its result: *The ravages of time left their marks on the old manor house.* [Old French *ravage* havoc, from *ravir* to carry away, seize, going back to Latin *rapere.*] —**rav′ag·er,** *n.*

rave (rāv) *v.i.,* **raved, rav·ing. 1.** to talk wildly or irrationally.

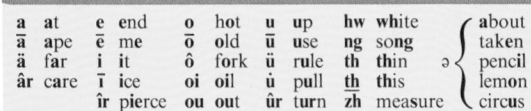

a	at	e	end	o	hot	u	up	hw	white		about
ā	ape	ē	me	ō	old	ū	use	ng	song		taken
ä	far	i	it	ô	fork	ü	rule	th	thin	ə	pencil
âr	care	ī	ice	oi	oil	u̇	pull	th	this		lemon
			ir	pierce	ou	out	ûr	turn	zh	measure		circus

R

2. to talk with much or too much enthusiasm: *The critics raved about the new movie.* **3.** to roar; rage: *The storm raved along the coast.* —*n.* **1.** the act of raving. **2.** very enthusiastic approval or recommendation. —*adj.* very enthusiastic or approving: *The new show received rave reviews.* [Old French *raver, resver* to wander, be delirious; of uncertain origin.] —**rav′er,** *n.* —**rav′ing·ly,** *adv.*

rav·el (rav′əl) *v.,* **-eled, -el·ing;** *also, British,* **-elled, -el·ling.** —*v.t.* **1.** to cause (cloth or rope) to separate into loose threads; fray. **2.** to make plain or clear; unravel. **3.** to entangle, confuse, or perplex. —*v.i.* **1.** to become raveled; fray. **2.** *Archaic.* to become entangled, confused, or perplexing. —*n.* a loose thread or raveled part. [Middle Dutch *ravelen* to entangle, fray.] —**rav′el·er,** *n.*

rav·el·ing (rav′ə ling) *also, British,* **rav·el·ling.** *n.* a loose thread; ravel.

ra·ven[1] (rā′vən) *n.* any of several large New and Old World birds, family Corvidae, having glossy black plumage and a loud, harsh cry. Length: to 27 inches (69 centimeters). —*adj.* having a glossy black color. [Old English *hræfn* the bird.]

rav·en[2] (rav′ən) *v.i.* **1.** to eat voraciously; feed greedily. **2.** to seek plunder or prey voraciously. —*v.t.* to devour voraciously. [Old French *raviner* to ravage, going back to Latin *rapīna* plunder.] —**rav′en·er,** *n.*

rav·en·ing (rav′ə ning) *adj.* greedy for plunder; rapacious. [RAVEN[2].]

rav·en·ous (rav′ə nəs) *adj.* **1.** very hungry; famished; voracious. **2.** greedy for plunder; rapacious: *The ravenous mob pillaged the town.* **3.** very eager, as for satisfaction or gratification: *to be ravenous for attention.* [Old French *ravineux* violent, from *raviner* to ravage. See RAVEN[2].] —**rav′en·ous·ly,** *adv.* —**rav′en·ous·ness,** *n.*

ra·vine (rə vēn′) *n.* a deep, narrow valley, esp. one eroded by running water. [French *ravine;* earlier, violent rush, as of water, from Latin *rapīna* violence, plunder.]

rav·ing (rā′ving) *adj.* **1.** wild; frenzied: *a raving lunatic.* **2.** *Informal.* outstanding; extraordinary: *a raving success, a raving beauty.* —*n.* wild, irrational talk.

rav·i·o·li (rav′ē ō′lē) *n.* small envelopes of dough containing various fillings, such as chopped meat or cheese, which are boiled and served with a sauce, as of tomato or broth. ➡ used as singular or plural. [Italian *ravioli,* plural of dialectal Italian *raviolo* little turnip, diminutive of *rava* turnip, from Latin *rāpa.*]

rav·ish (rav′ish) *v.t.* **1.** to seize and carry off by force. **2.** to rape. **3.** to carry away with joy; enrapture; enchant. [Old French *raviss-,* a stem of *ravir.* See RAVAGE.] —**rav′ish·er,** *n.* —**rav′ish·ment,** *n.*

rav·ish·ing (rav′i shing) *adj.* causing great joy; enchanting; delightful. —**rav′ish·ing·ly,** *adv.*

raw (rô) *adj.* **1.** uncooked. **2.** not refined, manufactured, or processed; in a natural state: *raw cotton, raw milk, raw sewage.* **3.** having the skin rubbed off, as a wound. **4.** having no experience or training: *a raw recruit.* **5.** piercingly damp and cold, as the weather. **6.** brutally frank or vulgar: *raw humor.* **7.** severe or unfair: *a raw deal.* [Old English *hrēaw* uncooked.] —**raw′ly,** *adv.* —**raw′ness,** *n.*

 ·in the raw. a. in the natural state; with no refinements or niceties: *We went camping for a week to experience nature in the raw.* **b.** in the nude; naked.

raw·boned (rô′bōnd′) *adj.* having little flesh; gaunt.

raw·hide (rô′hīd′) *n.* **1.** the untanned hide of cattle or other animals. **2.** a rope or whip made of such hide. —*v.t.,* **-hid·ed, -hid·ing.** to whip with or as with a rawhide.

raw material, material not yet refined, manufacturered, or processed: *Wood is the raw material of paper.*

ray[1] (rā) *n.* **1.** a narrow beam of light. **2.** a very small amount; hint; trace: *a ray of hope.* **3.** *Geometry.* **a.** a raylike line, esp. one of a group of lines emanating from a common center. **b.** a straight line that extends from a point. **4.** *Physics.* **a.** a narrow beam of radiant energy. **b.** a stream of particles moving in the same line. **5.** *Zoology.* **a.** one of the arms of a radiate animal, as a starfish. **b.** one of the bony rods supporting a fish's fin membrane. **6.** *Botany.* **a.** one of the flower stalks of an umbel. **b.** ray flower.

—*v.t.* to send forth in rays; radiate. [Old French *rai* beam of light, from Latin *radius* rod, beam of light. Doublet of RADIUS.] —For Synonyms (*n.*), see **beam.**

ray[2] (rā) *n.* any of a number of flat, saltwater fish, order Rajiformes, belonging to the group that includes the sharks and skates, having a skeleton of cartilage rather than bone. Length: 1-22 feet (0.3-6.7 meters). Weight: to 3,500 pounds (1,588 kilograms). [Old French *raie,* from Latin *raia.*]

ray[2]

ray flower, one of the marginal flowers around the flower head of certain composite plants, as the daisy. Also, **ray**[1], **ray floret.** For illustration, see **composite.**

ray·on (rā′on) *n.* any of a group of synthetic textile fibers made by pressing chemically treated cellulose through very fine holes and solidifying the resulting filaments. [From RAY[1]; referring to the fiber's shine.]

raze (rāz) *v.t.,* **razed, raz·ing.** to tear down; demolish. [Old French *raser* to shave, demolish, going back to Latin *rāsus,* past participle of *rādere* to scrape, scratch.] —For Synonyms, see **demolish.**

ra·zor (rā′zər) *n.* **1.** a sharp-edged instrument used for shaving off or cutting hair. **2.** an electrically driven clipper used for the same purpose. [Old French *rasor,* from *raser* to shave. See RAZE.]

ra·zor·back (rā′zər bak′) *n.* a wild or partly wild hog common in the southern United States, having a thin body, long legs, and a ridged back.

razor clam, any rapidly burrowing clam, family Solenidae, having an elongated shell with razor-sharp edges. Those with especially narrow shells, genera *Solen* and *Ensis,* are called **jackknife clams.**

razz (raz) *v.t. Slang.* to make fun of; ridicule. —*n.* raspberry *(def. 3).* [From RASPBERRY.]

raz·zle-daz·zle (raz′əl daz′əl) *n. Informal.* confusing, gaudy, or showy action or display.

razz·ma·tazz (raz′mə taz′) *n. Slang.* **1.** razzle-dazzle. **2.** liveliness; vitality; zest. [Probably from RAZZLE-DAZZLE.]

Rb, the symbol for rubidium.

rbi *also,* **r.b.i.** run batted in; runs batted in.

R.C. 1. Red Cross. **2.** Roman Catholic.

rd *also,* **rd.** rod; rods.

Rd. *also,* **rd.** road.

RD *also,* **R.D.** rural delivery.

RDA, the amount of a vitamin, mineral, or other nutrient that must be consumed daily to meet the nutritional needs of an average person. [Abbreviation of *r(ecommended) d(aily) a(llowance)* or *r(ecommended) d(ietary) a(llowance).*]

re[1] (rā) *n.* the second of the series of syllables used to name the eight tones of the diatonic scale. For illustration, see **do**[2]. [See GAMUT.]

re[2] (rē) *prep.* about; concerning. [Latin *rē* (n.) the matter, ablative of *rēs* thing, matter.]

Re (rā) Ra.

Re, the symbol for rhenium.

re- *prefix* **1.** again: *re-count.* **2.** back: *repel.* [Latin *re-* again, back; often through French *re-.*]

The following list contains a selection of compounds that can be formed with the prefix **re-**. The meaning of a word on the list can be understood by combining the appropriate sense of the prefix with the root word.

reabsorb	reacclimate	reacquaintance	readdict	readmission	readoption
reabsorption	reaccuse	reacquire	readdress	readmit	reaffirm
reaccept	reaccustom	reacquisition	readjourn	readmittance	reaffirmation
reacceptance	reacquaint	readapt	readjournment	readopt	reaffix

-'re *suffix* (used in contractions) are: *They're here.*

reach (rēch) *v.t.* **1.** to arrive at; get as far as; come to: *to reach a destination, to reach a conclusion.* **2.** to touch or grasp: *to reach a book on a shelf.* **3.** to stretch or extend: *We reached out our arms to greet each other.* **4.** *Informal.* to hold out and give by or as by the outstretched hand; pass: *Will you reach me the sugar?* **5.** to communicate with; contact: *I reached my friend by telephone.* **6.** to affect or influence: *to try to reach a troubled person with kindness and understanding.* **7.** to amount to: *The profit on our venture reached over a million dollars.* —*v.i.* **1.** to stretch, as with the arm or hand: *The gymnast reached toward the ceiling.* **2.** to try to grasp something: *to reach for a book.* **3.** to stretch or extend in space, time, or influence: *The fad reached to the furthest corners of the country.* **4.** to carry; penetrate: *How far can the actor's voice reach?* **5.** to sail with the wind just forward of, on, or just behind the beam. —*n.* **1.** the act of reaching or stretching out. **2.** the extent or distance covered in reaching: *One would need a long reach to be able to touch the ceiling.* **3.** the extent or amount that a person is able to understand or do; range: *Choose a goal within your reach.* **4.** a continuous stretch or course; expanse: *a reach of level ground, a reach of water.* **5.** a stretch of a river or channel between bends. **6.** a tack sailed with the wind forward of, on, or just behind the beam. [Old English *rǣcan* to stretch out, succeed in touching.] —**reach'a·bil'i·ty,** *n.* —**reach'able,** *adj.* —**reach'er,** *n.*

re·act (rē akt') *v.i.* **1.** to act in response to something, as to a stimulus: *The press reacted to the demand for censorship with angry editorials.* **2.** to act in opposition: *to react against a liberal political trend.* **3.** to act in return or reciprocally. **4.** to act in a reverse way, esp. as to return to a former condition. **5.** to undergo a chemical reaction.

re-act (rē akt') *v.t.* to act again.

re·ac·tance (rē ak'təns) *n. Electricity.* the opposition, measured in ohms, that a circuit offers to an alternating current because of its capacitance and inductance.

re·ac·tant (rē ak'tənt) *n.* any substance that undergoes change in a chemical reaction.

re·ac·tion (rē ak'shən) *n.* **1.** an action made in response to something, as to a stimulus: *What was the playwright's reaction to the reviews of the play?* **2.** a reversing or opposing action. **3.** a movement or a tendency to return to a former condition, esp. one of political and social conservatism. **4.** *Chemistry.* a process in which substances are changed chemically into new substances. **5.** *Physics.* **a.** a force equal to but opposing the force that produces it. **b.** a process that involves change in atomic nuclei, as fission in a nuclear reactor.

re·ac·tion·ar·y (rē ak'shə ner'ē) *adj.* of, relating to, or favoring a return to a former political or social condition. —*n., pl.* **-ar·ies.** a person who favors or tends toward political and social reaction.

reaction engine, an engine, usually on a rocket or jet plane, in which power is produced as a reaction to the momentum of its exhaust gases.

reaction time, the time interval between the application of a stimulus and the beginning of an individual's response to it.

re·ac·ti·vate (rē ak'tə vāt') *v.t.,* **-vat·ed, -vat·ing.** to make active again. —**re·ac'ti·va'tion,** *n.*

re·ac·tive (rē ak'tiv) *adj.* **1.** tending to react. **2.** relating to or characterized by reaction. **3.** *Electricity.* relating to or characterized by reactance.

re·ac·tor (rē ak'tər) *n.* **1.** nuclear reactor. **2.** a person who reacts, esp. positively, to a medical test, as for allergies.

read¹ (rēd) *v.,* **read** (red), **read·ing.** —*v.t.* **1.** to understand the meaning of (something written, printed, or stamped): *to read a magazine.* **2.** to utter aloud (something written or printed): *The baby-sitter read bedtime stories to the children.* **3.** to understand letters or symbols in (a foreign language): *to read French.* **4.** to understand, as by interpreting outward signs: *to read someone's thoughts.* **5.** to explain the meaning of; interpret: *There are two ways of reading their behavior.* **6.** to bring (to a certain state) by reading: *The mother read her son to sleep.* **7.** to have or give as the wording in a particular passage: *The book reads "effect" for "affect."* **8.** to indicate or register: *The speedometer read 60 miles per hour.* **9.** to foretell; predict: *to read the future.* **10.** lip-read. **11.** *British.* to study: *to read classics.* **12.** (of a computer) to convert (information) from the form supplied, as a floppy disk, and enter into memory for computation or storage. **13.** to be able to interpret or perform (a musical composition): *to read music.* —*v.i.* **1.** to understand something written, printed, or stamped. **2.** to utter aloud something written or printed. **3.** to learn by reading (with *of* or *about*): *I read about the incident in the newspaper.* **4.** to have or produce a particular impression when read: *The novelist's prose reads like poetry.* **5.** to have a specific wording: *The two editions read differently.* **6.** to allow or make possible interpretation: *The law reads two ways.* **7.** to give a public reading or recital. **8.** (of a computer) to read information. [Old English *rǣdan* to guess, interpret, understand writing; referring originally to the interpretation of magic runes scratched on pieces of wood.]

• **to read between the lines.** to find another meaning besides the one expressed in the written or spoken words.

• **to read in.** to place (information) in computer storage.

• **to read into.** to find (an additional meaning or meanings) in (written or spoken words); infer from: *You shouldn't try to read insults or threats into that person's harmless remarks.*

• **to read (someone) like a book.** to know (someone's character and motivations) very well: *You can't hide anything from me; I can read you like a book.*

• **to read out.** to provide a display of (information stored in or produced by a computer).

• **to read out of.** to expel from (a political party or other group).

• **to read the riot act to.** to rebuke severely.

• **to read up on.** to study; research.

read² (red) *adj.* informed by reading: *a well-read person.* [Past participle of READ¹.]

read·a·ble (rē'də bəl) *adj.* **1.** easy or interesting to read. **2.** capable of being read; legible. —**read'a·bil'i·ty, read'a·ble·ness,** *n.*

read·er (rē'dər) *n.* **1.** a person who reads. **2.** a schoolbook with exercises for learning and practicing reading. **3.** a person employed to read manuscripts submitted to a publisher and to judge their fitness for publication. **4.** a professor's assistant who reads and grades examinations and papers. **5.** proofreader. **6.** *British.* a lecturer or instructor in a university. **7.** a person authorized to read the lessons or other parts of the service in a church.

read·er·ship (rē'dər ship') *n.* **1.** the readers of a newspaper or magazine. **2.** *British.* the position or office of a reader.

read·i·ly (red'ə lē) *adv.* **1.** in a favorably disposed or cooperative manner; without opposition; willingly: *to readily follow a friend's advice.* **2.** without difficulty; easily: *The poem could not be readily understood.* **3.** in a prompt or speedy manner; quickly.

read·i·ness (red'ē nis) *n.* **1.** the quality or state of being ready. **2.** a favorable tendency or disposition to accept or do something; willingness. **3.** ease; facility.

read·ing (rē'ding) *n.* **1.** the act or practice of a person who reads. **2.** an act or instance of uttering aloud, esp. publicly, something written or printed. **3.** material read or to be read: *This book is good reading.* **4.** the extent to which a person has read; literary knowledge. **5.** the form in which a given word, sentence, or passage appears in a particular text. **6.** a personal or particular interpretation of a written work or musical composition: *a fine reading of Bach.* **7.** information indicated or registered, as on a meter, dial, or graduated instrument. —*adj.* **1.** inclined to read: *the reading public.* **2.** made or used for reading: *reading glasses.*

reading room, a room for reading, as in a library or club.

read·just (rē'ə just') *v.t.* to adjust again: *to readjust a tie.* —*v.i.* to become adapted to again: *The returning soldier had to readjust to civilian life.* —**re'ad·just'a·ble,** *adj.* —**re'ad·just'er,** *n.* —**re'ad·just'ment,** *n.*

read-on·ly memory (rēd'ōn'lē) see ROM.

read·out (rēd'out') *n.* **1.** a display of information stored in or produced by a computer. **2.a.** a device that displays numerical information in digital form. **b.** the information so displayed.

read·y (red'ē) *adj.,* **read·i·er, read·i·est. 1.** prepared or fit for use or action: *The car is ready for the trip. We are ready to go.* **2.** favorably disposed; mentally prepared; willing: *I was ready to take any job in order to pay my tuition.* **3.** having a tendency; apt; inclined: *to be too ready to criticize others.* **4.** immediately liable or likely: *The dynamite is ready to explode.* **5.** made or given without delay; prompt or quick: *a ready answer.* **6.** showing or characterized by cleverness or mental adroitness: *a ready mind.* **7.** immediately available: *ready cash.* —*v.t.,* **read·ied, read·y·ing.** to make ready; prepare: *to ready a runway for the takeoff of a jet.* [Old English *rǣde* prepared, prompt, swift.]

read·y-made (red'ē mād') *adj.* **1.** made in quantity and not to order: *a rack of ready-made dresses.* **2.** unoriginal or commonplace, as an idea.

read·y-to-wear (red'ē tə wâr') *n.* ready-made clothing: *ladies' ready-to-wear.* —*adj.* relating to, being, or dealing in ready-made clothing: *men's ready-to-wear suits.*

re·a·gent (rē ā'jənt) *n.* any substance used in a chemical reaction for the purpose of detecting, measuring, examining, or producing other substances.

a	at	e	end	o	hot	u	up	hw	white		about
ā	ape	ē	me	ō	old	ū	use	ng	song		taken
ä	far	i	it	ô	fork	ü	rule	th	thin	ə	pencil
âr	care	ī	ice	oi	oil	u̇	pull	th	this		lemon
		îr	pierce	ou	out	ûr	turn	zh	measure		circus

R

re·a·gin (rē ā′jin) *n.* a type of antibody that reacts with allergens, as of hay fever and asthma, to liberate histamines, causing allergic symptoms. [REAG(ENT) + -IN[1].]

re·al[1] (rē′əl, rēl) *adj.* **1.** occurring as a fact; actual or true; not imagined: *The novel is based on a real event.* **2.** not artificial; genuine; authentic: *real pearls.* **3.** not pretended or pretending: *real grief.* **4.** *Law.* relating to or designating permanent or immovable things, as lands or buildings: *real property.* ➡ distinguished from **personal. 5.** *Mathematics.* of or relating to a real number. —*adv. Informal.* very; extremely: *I was real sorry to hear the sad news.* [Late Latin *reālis* actual, relating to a thing, from Latin *rēs* thing, matter.] —**re′al·ness,** *n.*

> **Synonyms** *adj.* **Real**[1], **actual,** and **true** mean corresponding to fact. **Real** implies that something is what it seems to be in concrete, measurable terms: *The appraisal underestimated the real value of the property.* **Actual** emphasizes what is, as distinguished from what is possible or ideal: *The car's fuel consumption was tested in the laboratory and not under actual road conditions.* **True** often refers to a deeper reality that encompasses the existing facts but may go beyond them: *We'll never know which of the three versions of the event is the true one.*

re·al[2] (rā äl′) *n., pl.* **re·als** or **re·a·les** (rä ä′lās). a former coin and monetary unit of Spain and various Latin-American countries. [Spanish *real,* going back to Latin *rēgālis* royal, from *rēx* king.]

real estate, land together with the permanent buildings, trees, water, or mineral deposits on it.

real focus, focus *(def. 1a).*

re·al·gar (rē al′gär) *n.* a red or orange mineral that is a sulfide of arsenic, used as a pigment. Formula: AsS [Middle English *realgar,* from Medieval Latin, going back to Arabic *rahj al-ghār* literally, dust of the cave; because it was originally obtained by mining.]

real image, image *(def. 7a).*

re·al·ism (rē′ə liz′əm) *n.* **1.** concern with and preference for what is actual or practical, as opposed to what is imaginary or visionary. **2.** an artistic and literary style that shows people, things, and events as they appear, in as accurate and objective a manner as possible. ➡ opposed to **idealism. 3.** *Philosophy.* **a.** the view that ideas, esp. universal concepts, have a real existence independent of the material world and our consciousness of them. **b.** the view that the world of material objects has a real existence both independent of and proven by our consciousness of it.

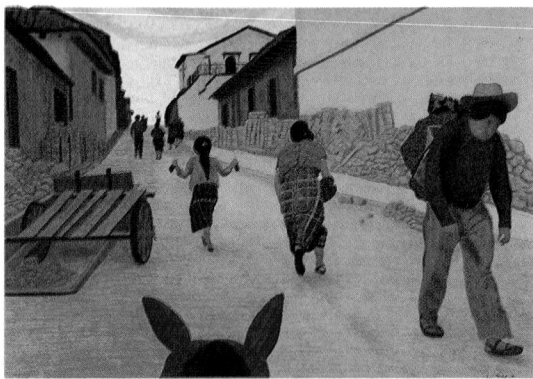

realism in a painting
by Guatemalan artist Eric Guttelewitz

re·al·ist (rē′ə list) *n.* **1.** a person who is concerned with and prefers what is actual or practical, as opposed to what is imaginary or visionary. **2.** an artist or writer whose work is characterized by realism. **3.** *Philosophy.* a person who believes in realism.

re·al·is·tic (rē′ə lis′tik) *adj.* **1.** showing people, things, or events as they actually appear in everyday life: *a realistic painting, a realistic play.* **2.** concerned with what is actual or practical; not visionary or idealistic: *a realistic appraisal of a situation.* **3.** *Philosophy.* of or relating to realists or realism. —**re′al·is′ti·cal·ly,** *adv.*

re·al·i·ty (rē al′i tē) *n., pl.* **-ties. 1.** the state or quality of being real. **2.** a real object, fact, or event. **3.** *Philosophy.* **a.** something that has real existence. **b.** the totality of real objects, facts, and events.

•**in reality.** actually; really: *You thought you were being helpful, but in reality you were in the way.*

re·al·i·za·tion (rē′ə lə zā′shən) *n.* **1.** the act of realizing or the state of being realized. **2.** something realized.

re·al·ize (rē′ə līz′) *v.t.,* **-ized, -iz·ing. 1.** to understand completely; comprehend clearly. **2.** to make real, as an idea or emotion: *My hopes were never realized.* **3.** to cause to seem real, as a character in a play. **4.** to gain (a sum of money), as by selling property or investing capital. **5.** to bring (a certain sum of money), as profit from a sale: *The auction realized over 10,000 dollars.*

re·al·life (rē′əl līf′, -līf′, rēl′-) *adj.* not imagined or artificial; real; genuine: *a real-life hero.*

re·al·ly (rē′ə lē, rē′lē) *adv.* **1.** according to the facts; actually: *The witness wrote an account of how the accident really happened.* **2.** without doubt; indeed: *Really, that was a terrible mistake.* ➡ used for emphasis. **3.** with no qualifications; truly; genuinely: *We spent a really pleasant day in the park.*

realm (relm) *n.* **1.** kingdom. **2.** a sphere or province, as of knowledge, power, or influence: *the realm of science, the realm of fantasy.* [Old French *realme* kingdom, going back to Latin *regimen* government; influenced by Old French *reial* royal, from Latin *rēgālis.*]

real number *Mathematics.* any rational or irrational number.

re·al·tor (rē′əl tər) *n.* a real estate agent or broker.

re·al·ty (rē′əl tē) *n.* real estate. [REAL[1] + -TY[2].]

ream[1] (rēm) *n.* **1.** a quantity of paper of uniform size and quality, varying from 480 to 500 sheets, depending on grade. **2.** *Informal.* a great amount: *to have reams of homework.* [Old French *raime,* from Arabic *rizmah* bundle.]

ream[2] (rēm) *v.t.* **1.** to create or enlarge (a hole). **2.** to remove with a reamer. [Old English *rēman* to open up.]

ream·er (rē′mər) *n.* **1.** a cylindrical steel tool with lengthwise blades or cutting edges, turned in a drilled hole to enlarge or shape it. **2.** a utensil used for extracting juice from oranges, lemons, and other fruit; juicer. **3.** a person or thing that reams.

reap (rēp) *v.t.* **1.** to cut down and gather (grain). **2.** to obtain or gather (a crop) by reaping. **3.** to cut down or harvest the crop or produce from: *to reap fields.* **4.** to receive, esp. as a reward: *The child's good behavior reaped praise.* —*v.i.* **1.** to harvest a crop. **2.** to receive in return for something done. [Old English *repan* to cut grain.]

reap·er (rē′pər) *n.* **1.** a person who reaps. **2.** a harvesting machine formerly used to cut and collect grain.

re·ap·pear (rē′ə pîr′) *v.i.* to appear again. —**re′ap·pear′ance,** *n.*

rear[1] (rîr) *n.* **1.** the part, position, or space that is behind or in the back; back. **2.** the part of a military force farthest from the fighting area; last elements in a column or line of march. **3.** the buttocks. —*adj.* relating to or situated at or in the back: *a rear seat in an airplane.* [Short for archaic *arrear* the back, behind, from Old French *arere* backward. See ARREARS.]

rear[2] (rîr) *v.t.* **1.** to help bring to maturity; raise, esp. a child. **2.** to construct; build: *The city government reared the building in 1841.* **3.** to bring to an upright position; lift up: *The dog reared its head from the pillow when we came in.* —*v.i.* (of an animal) to rise on the hind legs. [Old English *rǣran* to raise.]

rear admiral, an officer in the U.S. Navy ranking below a vice admiral and above a captain.

rear guard, a body of troops assigned to bring up the rear and guard it from attack, esp. during a retreat.

realign	reappointment	reassemble	reassort	reauthorize	rebill
realignment	reapportion	reassembly	reattach	reavow	rebind
reallocate	reapportionment	reassert	reattachment	reavowal	reboil
reallocation	reappraisal	reassertion	reattack	reawake	rebroaden
reanalyze	reappraise	reassess	reattain	reawaken	reburial
reannex	reapproval	reassessment	reattainment	rebalance	rebury
reannexation	reapprove	reassign	reattempt	rebaptism	rebutton
reapplication	reargue	reassignment	reauthenticate	rebaptize	recalculate
reapply	rearouse	reassociate	reauthentication	rebeautification	recalibrate
reappoint	rearrest	reassociation	reauthorization	rebeautify	recalibration

re·arm (rē ärm′) *v.t.* to arm again, esp. with new or better weapons. —**re·ar′ma·ment,** *n.*

rear·most (rîr′mōst′) *adj.* farthest in the rear; last.

re·ar·range (rē′ə rānj′) *v.t.,* **-ranged, -rang·ing.** to arrange again, esp. in a different way. —**re′ar·range′ment,** *n.*

rear·view mirror (rîr′vū′) a mirror on an automobile, motor-cycle, or other vehicle, placed so as to provide the driver with a view of the road behind.

rear·ward (rîr′wərd) *adj.* located in or moving toward the rear. —*adv.* also, **rear·wards.** in, at, or toward the rear.

rea·son (rē′zən) *n.* **1.** something that serves as a ground, motive, or cause: *There is no reason to doubt your word.* **2.** a statement used to justify, prove, or explain: *I could give no reason for my premonition of disaster.* **3.** the power or ability to think logically, draw conclusions, or make inferences. **4.** a sensible view; good judgment: *The prime minister's actions showed a lack of reason.* **5.** sanity: *I nearly lost all reason when I heard the news.* —*v.i.* **1.** to think logically and clearly: *The professor's aim was to teach students to reason.* **2.** to try to persuade or influence someone by logical argument (with *with*): *It was useless to try to reason with that mob.* **3.** to engage in discussion; dispute; argue: *Let us reason together.* —*v.t.* **1.** to think about logically and carefully (with *out*): *to reason a problem out and come to a rational conclusion.* **2.** to give reasons for; support by argument. [Old French *raison* understanding, act of reasoning, from Latin *ratiō* calculation, relation, understanding, cause. Doublet of RATIO, RATION.] —**rea′son·er,** *n.*

· **by reason of.** due to the fact that; because of.

· **in (or within) reason.** conforming to what is considered sensible, fair, or proper; reasonable: *I'll do anything to please them, within reason.*

· **to stand to reason.** to be logical or reasonable: *It stands to reason that the air is cleaner in the country than in the city.*

Synonyms *n.* **Reason** and **motive** mean factors that cause a person to act in a certain way. **Reason** stresses the use of a rational process to arrive at a course of action: *The study gave compelling reasons for overhauling the company.* **Motive** suggests an emotional basis for an act, such as a need or desire that may not be rational: *The murderer's motive appeared to be jealousy.*

rea·son·a·ble (rē′zə nə bəl, rēz′nə-) *adj.* **1.** showing or using good sense or judgment; not foolish; sensible: *a reasonable person, a reasonable assumption.* **2.** kept within sensible or proper limits; not excessive or extravagant; moderate: *a reasonable request.* **3.** worth the price asked for: *The used car was reasonable, so we bought it.* **4.** having the ability to reason. —**rea′son·a·ble·ness,** *n.* —**rea′son·a·bly,** *adv.*

Synonyms **Reasonable** and **rational** mean capable of using reason in making decisions or coming to conclusions. **Reasonable** applies to the ability to make practical decisions in everyday situations: *The manager had a reasonable approach to handling employees' problems.* **Rational** emphasizes a reliance on unemotional, systematic logic: *The judge's decisions, while always rational, were sometimes harsh.*

rea·son·ing (rē′zə ning, rēz′ning) *n.* **1.** the mental process employed to draw conclusions from facts. **2.** something that is used in this process, as arguments or evidence.

re·as·sure (rē′ə shûr′) *v.t.,* **-sured, -sur·ing.** **1.** to restore confidence or courage in: *to reassure a frightened child.* **2.** to assure again: *Please reassure them that we shall be there.* **3.** to insure again. —**re′as·sur′ance,** *n.* —**re′as·sur′er,** *n.* —**re′as·sur′ing·ly,** *adv.*

Ré·au·mur (rā′ə myūr′) *also,* **Re·au·mur.** *adj.* of, according to, or designating a temperature scale on which the boiling point of water is 80 degrees and the freezing point is 0 degrees, now virtually unused. [From René Antoine Ferchault de *Réaumur,* 1683-1757, French physicist who developed the temperature scale.]

reave (rēv) *v.t.,* **reaved** or **reft, reav·ing.** *Archaic.* to take or deprive of forcibly; carry away; rob. [Old English *rēafian.*]

re·bate (rē′bāt, ri bāt′) *n.* a sum of money that is deducted or returned from an amount paid, as a discount. —*v.t.,* **-bat·ed, -bat·ing.** to make a rebate of. [Old French *rebattre* to beat down again, from *re-* (see RE-) + *abat(t)re* to beat down. See ABATE.]

re·bec (rē′bek) *also,* **re·beck.** *n.* a medieval musical instrument resembling a violin and usually having three strings. [Old French *rebec,* form of *rebebe,* from Arabic *rabāb.*]

reb·el (*n., adj.,* reb′əl; *v.,* ri bel′) *n.* **1.** a person who joins in an armed resistance against the legal government of his or her own country. **2.** a person who resists or refuses to obey any law or authority. **3.** **Rebel.** a person who fought on the side of the Confederacy in the American Civil War. —*adj.* **1.** relating to or

engaged in a rebellion: *rebel forces.* **2.** of a rebel or rebels: *a rebel victory.* —*v.i.* **re·belled, re·bel·ling.** **1.** to join in an armed resistance against the legal government of one's own country. **2.** to resist or disobey any law or authority. **3.** to feel or show intense dislike or aversion: *My stomach rebelled against the bitter-tasting medicine.* [Old French *rebeller* to revolt, from Latin *rebel-lāre* from *re-* again + *bellāre* to make war. Doublet of REVEL.]

re·bel·lion (ri bel′yən) *n.* **1.** an organized armed resistance against a legal government; insurrection. **2.** a resistance or defi-ance against any control or authority. [Old French *rebellion* act of revolting, from Latin *rebelliō* revolt.] —For Synonyms, see **re·volt.**

re·bel·lious (ri bel′yəs) *adj.* **1.** behaving like a rebel. **2.** charac-teristic of or marked by rebels or rebellion: *a rebellious period in history.* **3.** relating to or engaged in a rebellion. **4.** hard to manage or treat; refractory. —**re·bel′lious·ly,** *adv.* —**re·bel′-lious·ness,** *n.*

re·birth (rē bûrth′, rē′bûrth′) *n.* **1.** a second birth; reincarna-tion. **2.** revival; renaissance: *There's been a rebirth of interest in art of that period.*

re·born (rē bôrn′) *adj.* experiencing new or renewed life or spirit; born again.

re·bound (*v.,* ri bound′; *n.,* rē′bound′, ri bound′) *v.i.* to bound back, as from force of impact; spring back. —*n.* **1.** an act or instance of springing back. **2.** *Basketball.* **a.** a ball that has bounced off the backboard or rim of the net and is still in play. **b.** the act or an instance of recovering control of such a ball: *The forward scored twenty points and had thirteen rebounds in last night's game.* [Old French *rebondir* to leap back, from *re-* (see RE-) + *bondir* to leap. See BOUND².]

· **on the rebound. a.** as it bounces back: *Our tallest player caught the ball on the rebound.* **b.** after being hurt by rejection: *to marry on the rebound.*

re·broad·cast (rē brôd′kast′) *v.t.,* **-cast** or **-cast·ed, -cast-ing.** **1.** to broadcast (a program) again at a later time from the same station. **2.** to broadcast (a program relayed from another station). —*n.* **1.** the act of rebroadcasting. **2.** a program that is or was rebroadcast.

re·buff (ri buf′) *n.* **1.** a blunt or sudden rejection, as of a person's offer to help, or a request for something; snub. **2.** a sudden check, as to further action or progress; repulse. —*v.t.* **1.** to reject bluntly or suddenly; snub. **2.** to check suddenly; repulse. [Italian *ribuffo* check, scolding, from *ri-* back (from Latin *re-*) + *buffo* puff (imitative).]

re·build (rē bild′) *v.,* **-built** (-bilt′), **-build·ing.** —*v.t.* **1.** to build (something) again. **2.** to make extensive changes in; repair or remodel. —*v.i.* to build again.

re·buke (ri būk′) *v.t.,* **-buked, -buk·ing.** to scold sharply; reprimand. —*n.* a sharp scolding; reprimand; reproof. [Anglo-Norman *rebuker* to repel, going back to Old French *re-* (see RE-) + *buschier* to strike, cut wood (from *busche* log; of Germanic origin).] —**re·buk′er,** *n.* —For Synonyms *(v.t.),* see **repri·mand.**

re·bus (rē′bəs) *n., pl.* **-bus·es.** the representation of a syllable, word, or phrase by pictures or symbols whose names sound like the intended syllable or words. A picture of an eye followed by one of a tin can is a rebus for "I can." [Latin *rēbus* by means of things (because things or pictures are used in a rebus), ablative plural of *rēs* thing.]

re·but (ri but′) *v.t.,* **-but·ted, -but·ting.** to disprove, as by counterargument; refute. [Old French *reboter* to repulse, from *re-* (see RE-) + *boter* to push (of Germanic origin).] —**re·but′ter,** *n.*

re·but·tal (ri but′əl) *n.* the act of rebutting, esp. in law; refuta-tion.

rec. 1. receipt. **2.** recipe. **3.** record. **4.** recorder.

re·cal·ci·trant (ri kal′si trənt) *adj.* stubborn and hard to man-age; obstinately defiant; unmanageable; refractory. —*n.* a recal-citrant person. [Latin *recalcitrāns,* present participle of *recalci-trāre* to kick back, going back to *re-* back + *calx* heel.] —**re·cal′ci·trance, re·cal′ci·tran·cy,** *n.*

re·call (*v.,* ri kôl′; *n.,* ri kôl′, rē′kôl′) *v.t.* **1.** to call back to mind; remember: *I don't recall your name.* **2.** to call back; summon back: *The diplomats were recalled home when war broke out.* **3.** to take back; revoke: *The chess player's careless move could not be recalled.* **4.** to bring back; restore. **5.** to remove (a public official)

a	at	e	end	o	hot	u	up	hw	white		about
ā	ape	ē	me	ō	old	ū	use	ng	song	ə	taken
ä	far	i	it	ô	fork	ů	rule	th	thin		pencil
âr	care	ī	ice	oi	oil	ú	pull	th	this		lemon
		îr	pierce	ou	out	ûr	turn	zh	measure		circus

R

1005

from office by popular vote before the end of his or her term. **6.** to ask for the return of a purchased product because it is defective or dangerous in some way. —*n.* **1.** a remembering of someone or something; remembrance: *to have total recall of something read.* **2.** a calling back; summoning back: *The recall of the ambassador was embarrassing for the country.* **3.** the act of recalling a defective or dangerous product. **4.** the taking back of something granted earlier. **5.** the process of removal, or right of removal, of a public official from office before his or her term is over, by direct popular vote. **6.** a signal, as a bugle call or flag, used to call back soldiers or ships. —For Synonyms *(v.t.),* see **remember.**

re·cant (ri kant′) *v.t.* to take back or deny formally or publicly, as a statement or opinion; renounce; retract. —*v.i.* to take back or deny a previously held opinion or allegiance. [Latin *recantāre* to sing again, revoke.] —**re·can·ta·tion** (rē′kan tā′shən), *n.*

re·cap[1] (*v.,* rē′kap′, rē kap′; *n.,* rē′kap′) *v.t.,* **-capped, -cap·ping. 1.** to put a cap back on: *to recap an opened bottle.* **2.** to cement and vulcanize a strip of rubber on the worn surface of the tread of a pneumatic tire; retread. —*n.* a recapped tire; retread. [RE- + CAP.]

re·cap[2] (rē′kap′) *Informal. v.t., v.i.,* **-capped, -cap·ping.** to recapitulate. —*n.* recapitulation. [Short for RECAPITULATE.]

re·ca·pit·u·late (rē′kə pich′ə lāt′) *v.t., v.i.,* **-lat·ed, -lat·ing.** to restate briefly; summarize. [Late Latin *recapitulātus,* past participle of *recapitulāre* to summarize, going back to Latin *re-* again + *capitulum* chapter of a book. See CHAPTER.]

re·ca·pit·u·la·tion (rē′kə pich′ə lā′shən) *n.* **1.** the act of recapitulating. **2.** a brief restatement; summary.

re·cap·ture (rē kap′chər) *v.t.,* **-tured, -tur·ing. 1.** to retake possession of; capture again. **2.** to bring back to mind: *to recapture one's youth.*

re·cast (*v.,* rē kast′; *n.,* rē′kast′) *v.t.,* **-cast, -cast·ing. 1.** to cast again or anew. **2.** to change the form or structure of; reconstruct: *to recast a statement.* **3.** to provide (a theatrical production) with a new cast. —*n.* something recast.

recd. *also,* **rec′d.** received.

re·cede (ri sēd′) *v.i.,* **-ced·ed, -ced·ing. 1.** to move back or away: *The waves receded.* **2.** to become, or seem to become, more distant: *The houses receded as we drove by.* **3.** to slope or appear to slope backward: *My cousin's hairline is receding.* **4.** to withdraw, as from a promise, position, or bargain. [Latin *recēdere* to retreat, go back.]

re·ceipt (ri sēt′) *n.* **1.** a written acknowledgment that something has been received. **2. receipts.** an amount or quantity received, esp. of money. **3.** the act of receiving or the state of being received. **4.** recipe. —*v.t.* **1.** to write a receipt for (money, goods, or mail). **2.** to mark (an account) as paid. [Anglo-Norman *receite* money or value received, going back to Latin *recepta* thing received, from *recipere* to take back, accept.]

re·ceiv·a·ble (ri sē′və bəl) *adj.* **1.** capable of being received; acceptable. **2.** awaiting payment; due. Accounts receivable are unpaid accounts held by a creditor, rather than a debtor. —*n.* **receivables.** accounts or bills that are awaiting payment.

re·ceive (ri sēv′) *v.,* **-ceived, -ceiv·ing.** —*v.t.* **1.** to take (something) into one's hands or possession; acquire; get: *to receive a letter.* **2.** to take in or acquire mentally; learn; comprehend: *to receive instructions.* **3.a.** to meet with; experience: *to receive a shock.* **b.** to be subjected to; suffer: *The fighter received a broken jaw.* **4.** to greet or welcome: *The host received guests at the door.* **5.** to allow to enter; admit: *The country club received the new member.* **6.** to listen to: *to receive a confession.* **7.** to take the impact or force of; bear: *My foot received the entire weight of the box when it fell.* **8.** to have capacity for; take in; hold: *The car was too little to receive all the passengers.* **9.** to accept as authentic or valid; believe: *The medical community received the results of the research with enthusiasm.* **10.** to have (something) bestowed or conferred, as a title, honor, or office: *to receive a knighthood.* —*v.i.* **1.** to take or get something; be a recipient: *Be grateful for what you receive.* **2.** to greet and entertain visitors. **3.** to convert incoming radio or television signals into sound or pictures. [Old French *receivre* to accept, going back to Latin *recipere.*]

Synonyms *v.t.* **Receive** and **accept** mean to come into possession of something. **Receive** does not necessarily imply the approval or consent of the recipient: *The principal was surprised to receive the history teacher's resignation.* **Accept** suggests open or implied consent or appreciation: *The president accepted the committee's suggestions.*

re·ceiv·er (ri sē′vər) *n.* **1.** a person or thing that receives. **2.** a person who knowingly receives or buys stolen goods; fence. **3.** a person who is appointed by a court of law to take charge of and administer the property or business of others pending the outcome of litigation, as when a company becomes bankrupt. **4.a.** a device that receives electrical impulses or radio waves and converts them into pictures or sound, as the part of a telephone held to the ear. **b.** a television or radio receiving set.

re·ceiv·er·ship (ri sē′vər ship′) *n.* **1.** the condition of being in the hands of a receiver. **2.** the position and functions of a receiver.

receiving set, an apparatus for receiving electromagnetic waves and converting them into pictures or sounds, as in radio or television reception; receiver.

re·cen·sion (ri sen′shən) *n.* **1.** a critical or careful revision or editing of a text. **2.** the text resulting from such revision.

re·cent (rē′sənt) *adj.* **1.** done, happening, or made just before the present: *What is the most recent news?* **2.** of or belonging to a period of time not far removed; modern: *a recent period in history.* **3. Recent.** of, relating to, or characteristic of the present geologic epoch. Also *(def. 3),* **Holocene.** —*n.* **Recent.** the present geologic epoch, the second of the Quaternary period, during which the climate has become warmer, glaciers have melted, and modern human beings have flourished. Also, **Holocene.** For table, see **geologic time.** [Latin *recēns* fresh, new.] —**re′cent·ly,** *adv.* —**re′cent·ness.** *n.*

re·cep·ta·cle (ri sep′tə kəl) *n.* **1.** an object or place that receives and holds something, as a box or bag. **2.** the swollen tip of the stem of a flower, which bears the sepals, the petals, the stamens, and the carpels. **3.** an electrical outlet or socket. [Latin *receptāculum* place to receive things.]

re·cep·tion (ri sep′shən) *n.* **1.** the act of receiving or fact of being received. **2.** the way in which someone or something is accepted or received: *a cordial reception.* **3.** a social gathering, esp. one at which guests are formally received: *a wedding reception.* **4.** the conversion of radio or television signals into sound or pictures, esp. with reference to quality. [Latin *receptiō* a receiving.]

re·cep·tion·ist (ri sep′shə nist) *n.* a person who is employed in an office to receive calls and visitors, make appointments, and give information.

re·cep·tive (ri sep′tiv) *adj.* able or willing to receive suggestions, new ideas, or impressions: *The committee was receptive to the plan.* —**re·cep′tive·ly,** *adv.* —**re·cep′tive·ness, re·cep·tiv·i·ty** (rē′sep tiv′i tē), *n.*

re·cep·tor (ri sep′tər) *n.* **1.** a cell or group of cells connected to one or more nerve cells, that, when stimulated, cause nerve impulses to be relayed to the brain. **2.** a molecular structure on the surface of a cell that can combine with complementary molecules, as of an enzyme or hormone, or with other cells. [Latin *receptor* receiver.]

re·cess (rē′ses, ri ses′) *n.* **1.** a period of time during which work or other activity is temporarily stopped. **2.** the part in a wall that is depressed or indented from the rest; niche. **3.** a remote or secret spot or part; quiet, hidden place: *the recesses of one's heart.* —*v.t.* **1.** to place in or as in a recess; set back or away. **2.** to make a recess in: *to recess a wall.* —*v.i.* to take a recess: *The court recessed at noon.* [Latin *recessus* a going back, retreat.]

re·ces·sion[1] (ri sesh′ən) *n.* **1.** the act of receding; withdrawal. **2.** a period of decline in business activity, less severe than a depression, occurring esp. after a period of relative economic prosperity. [Latin *recessiō* a going back, receding.] —**re·ces′sion·ar′y,** *adj.*

re·ces·sion[2] (ri sesh′ən) *n.* a ceding back of territory to the country or government previously owning it. [RE- + CESSION.]

re·ces·sion·al (ri sesh′ə nəl) *adj.* of, relating to, or occurring at the end of a church service. —*n.* **1.** a recessional hymn or music. **2.** the procession at the end of a ceremony, as of the clergy returning to the sacristy from the sanctuary.

re·ces·sive (ri ses′iv) *adj.* **1.** tending to go back; receding. **2.** *Genetics.* **a.** relating to or designating one of a pair of alleles for a gene whose effect is masked by the other allele when both are present in the same cell or organism: *The allele for shortness in sweet pea plants is recessive.* **b.** relating to or designating the trait or characteristic determined by such an allele. —*n.* *Genetics.* **1.** a recessive allele or characteristic. **2.** an organism having one or more recessive characteristics.

re·charge (*v.,* rē chärj′; *n.,* rē chärj′, rē′chärj′) *v.,* **-charged,**

recatalog	recertify	recharter	recirculate	reclassify	recolor
recelebrate	rechallenge	recheck	recirculation	reclean	recomb
recelebration	rechannel	rechristen	reclasp	recolonization	recombine
recertification	rechart	recircle	reclassification	recolonize	recommence

-charg·ing. —*v.t.* **1.** to charge with electricity or electrical energy again: *to recharge a battery.* **2.** to invigorate anew; revitalize; refresh. —*v.i.* to make a new charge or attack. —*n.* an act, process, or instance of recharging.

re·cher·ché (rə shâr′shā, -shâr shā′) *adj.* **1.** carefully sought out; choice. **2.** refined; elegant. **3.** overrefined; strained. [French *recherché,* from *rechercher* to seek. See RESEARCH.]

re·cid·i·vism (ri sid′ə viz′əm) *n.* the return to previous behavior or activity, esp. undesirable or criminal behavior. —**re·cid′i·vist,** *n.* —**re·cid′i·vis′tic, re·cid′i·vous,** *adj.*

rec·i·pe (res′ə pē′) *n.* **1.** a list of ingredients and directions for the preparation of food or drink. **2.** a method or formula for attaining an end: *a recipe for happiness.* **3.** formerly, a medical prescription. [Latin *recipe* take (imperative of *recipere* to take); originally, an order to the pharmacist to "take" certain drugs and fill a doctor's prescription.]

re·cip·i·ent (ri sip′ē ənt) *n.* a person or thing that receives. —*adj.* receiving or able to receive; receptive. [Latin *recipiēns,* present participle of *recipere* to take, receive.]

re·cip·ro·cal (ri sip′rə kəl) *adj.* **1.** existing on both sides: *reciprocal respect, reciprocal acts of hostility.* **2.** given, felt, or shown in return: *reciprocal aid.* **3.** denoting a pronoun that expresses mutual action or relation. *One another* is a reciprocal pronoun. **4.** *Mathematics.* of or relating to a reciprocal. —*n.* *Mathematics.* a number or algebraic expression by which a given number or an algebraic expression is multiplied to yield 1 as the product. The reciprocal of $^3/_5$ is $^5/_3$, since $^3/_5 \times ^5/_3 = 1$. [Latin *reciprocus* returning, alternating + -AL[1].] —**re·cip′ro·cal·ly,** *adv.* —For Synonyms *(adj.),* see **mutual.**

re·cip·ro·cate (ri sip′rə kāt′) *v.,* **-cat·ed, -cat·ing.** —*v.t.* **1.** to give, feel, or show in return: *to reciprocate love.* **2.** to give and return in exchange; interchange: *to reciprocate favors.* —*v.i.* to act or feel something in return: *to love someone who does not reciprocate.* [Latin *reciprocātus,* past participle of *reciprocāre* to move backward and forward.] —**re·cip′ro·ca′tion,** *n.* —**re·cip′ro·ca′tive, re·cip·ro·ca·to·ry** (ri sip′rə kə tôr′ē), *adj.* —**re·cip′ro·ca′tor,** *n.*

reciprocating engine, any engine in which mechanical power is produced by the backward and forward motion of pistons in cylinders.

rec·i·proc·i·ty (res′ə pros′i tē) *n.* **1.** the quality or state of being reciprocal. **2.** the mutual interchange between countries, states, or organizations, such as the exchange of trading privileges.

re·cit·al (ri sī′təl) *n.* **1.** a performance or concert of music or dance, often given by a single performer or devoted to the works of a single composer. **2.** the act of repeating or reading something aloud in public: *a poetry recital.* **3.** a detailed account, as of facts or events.

rec·i·ta·tion (res′i tā′shən) *n.* **1.** the act of repeating or reading something aloud in public; recital. **2.a.** the act of reciting a lesson. **b.** a class meeting in which students orally answer questions or recite or discuss a lesson. **3.** the material recited.

rec·i·ta·tive (res′i tə tēv′) *n.* **1.** a style of vocal music intermediate between speaking and singing, esp. found in the narrative parts and dialogue of operas and oratorios. **2.** a passage, part, or composition in this style. [Italian *recitativo,* from *recitare* to repeat, perform, from Latin *recitāre* to read aloud.]

re·cite (ri sīt′) *v.,* **-cit·ed, -cit·ing.** —*v.t.* **1.** to repeat from memory. **2.** to give an account of; narrate: *to recite one's life story.* **3.** to list one by one; enumerate. —*v.i.* **1.** to repeat something memorized, esp. before an audience. **2.** to repeat a lesson orally or answer questions in class. [Latin *recitāre* to read aloud, repeat from memory.] —**re·cit′er,** *n.*

reck (rek) *v.t., v.i. Archaic.* **1.** to take or have care; heed. **2.** to concern or interest (one); be important; matter. [Old English *reccan* to heed.]

reck·less (rek′lis) *adj.* **1.** careless or unmindful, as of danger; heedless. **2.** characterized or distinguished by such heedlessness; irresponsible: *reckless driving.* [Old English *recceléas* heedless.] —**reck′less·ly,** *adv.* —**reck′less·ness,** *n.* —For Synonyms, see **rash**[1].

reck·on (rek′ən) *v.t.* **1.** to count or figure; calculate: *Interest on my savings account is reckoned from day of deposit to day of withdrawal.* **2.** to suppose to be; consider: *They reckon that horse a winner.* **3.** *Informal.* to think; suppose: *I reckon that they will come.* —*v.i.* **1.** to count, depend, or rely (with *on*): *You can reckon on our support.* **2.** to make a calculation; count or figure. **3.** *Informal.* to suppose; guess. [Old English *(ge)recenian* to explain.] —**reck′on·er,** *n.* —For Synonyms, see **calculate.**

· **to reckon with. a.** to take into consideration: *I didn't reckon with any opposition to the plan.* **b.** to deal or contend with: *You'll have to reckon with them if there are any problems.*

reck·on·ing (rek′ə ning) *n.* **1.** the act of calculating; calcula-

tion. **2.** a settlement of accounts. **3.** a bill, as at an inn or hotel. **4.** dead reckoning.

re·claim (ri klām′) *v.t.* **1.** to render useful or restore to a useful state or condition: *to reclaim land.* **2.** to obtain or recover from old or waste products: *to reclaim copper from a copper alloy coin.* **3.** to bring back from error or improper behavior; reform. [Old French *reclamer* to call back, invoke, going back to Latin *re-* back + *clāmāre* to call.] —**re·claim′a·ble,** *adj.* —**re·claim′er,** *n.*

re-claim (rē klām′) *v.t.* to get or attempt to get back.

rec·la·ma·tion (rek′lə mā′shən) *n.* the act of reclaiming or the state of being reclaimed; restoration.

re·cline (ri klīn′) *v.t., v.i.,* **-clined, -clin·ing.** to lie or cause to lie back or down. [Latin *reclīnāre* to lean back.]

re·clin·er (ri klī′nər) *n.* an armchair with a back that can be adjusted to let the occupant lie back with the feet up on a footrest.

re·cluse (rek′lüs, ri klüs′) *n.* a person who lives alone, away from other people. —*adj.* away from other people; solitary. [Old French *reclus,* past participle of *reclure* to shut up, from Late Latin *reclūdere,* from Latin *reclūdere* to open.] —**re·clu′sion,** *n.* —**re·clu′sive,** *adj.*

rec·og·ni·tion (rek əg nish′ən) *n.* **1.** the act of recognizing or the state of being recognized. **2.** the acceptance of something as true or valid: *There was no recognition of their claim to ownership.* **3.** the formal acceptance of a person's right to speak, as in a legislature, club meeting, or the like: *recognition of a convention delegate.* **4.** the formal acceptance of one government's existence or legitimacy by another. **5.** favorable attention or notice; acceptance: *The doctors gained recognition for their work in cancer research.* [Latin *recognitiō* a recognizing, reviewing.]

re·cog·ni·zance (ri kog′nə zəns, -kon′ə-) *n. Law.* **1.** a bond or obligation by which a person promises to perform a particular act, such as to appear for a hearing or trial. **2.** the amount of such a bond, to be forfeited if the act is not performed. [Old French *recoignisance* a recognizing, acknowledgment, from *reconoistre* to recognize, from Latin *recognōscere.*]

rec·og·nize (rek′əg nīz′) *v.t.,* **-nized, -niz·ing. 1.** to perceive to be identical to something previously known; know again. **2.** to identify, as from a description or distinctive feature: *to recognize a bird by its coloring.* **3.** to perceive clearly; realize: *to recognize the extent of a problem.* **4.** to accept fully as true or valid; admit: *to recognize one's obligations.* **5.** to take notice of, esp. as a way of granting permission to speak. **6.** to indicate appreciation of: *The community recognized the volunteers' contributions at the annual dinner.* **7.** to formally accept the existence of (another nation) by a proclamation or diplomatic exchange. [RECOGN(ITION) + -IZE.] —**rec′og·niz·a·ble,** *adj.* —**rec′og·niz·a·bly,** *adv.* —For Synonyms, see **discern.**

re·coil (*v.,* ri koil′; *n.,* ri koil′, rē′koil′) *v.i.* **1.** to draw or shrink back, as in fear, horror, or surprise. **2.** to fly back, as from force of impact or discharge; spring back. **3.** to return to or as to or against a starting point or source; react: *Our treatment of others often recoils on us.* —*n.* **1.** the act of recoiling. **2.** the backward movement of a firearm when discharged. [Old French *reculer* to go back, retire, going back to Latin *re-* back + *cūlus* rump.]

rec·ol·lect (rek′ə lekt′) *v.t.* to call back into mind; remember. —*v.i.* to have a recollection; remember. [Medieval Latin *recollectus,* past participle of *recolligere* to recall, from Latin *recolligere* to gather again.] —For Synonyms, see **remember.**

re-col·lect (rē′kə lekt′) *v.t.* **1.** to collect or gather again, as things scattered. **2.** to recover control of (oneself); compose (oneself).

rec·ol·lec·tion (rek′ə lek′shən) *n.* **1.** the act or power of calling back into mind; remembrance. **2.** a thing or things remembered; memory. —For Synonyms, see **memory.**

re·com·bi·nant (rē kom′bə nənt) *n. Genetics.* an individual organism or cell in which recombination has occurred. —*adj.* **1.** formed by recombination: *recombinant chromosomes.* **2.** of, relating to, or formed from recombinant DNA.

recombinant DNA, DNA that results from gene-splicing, in which genetic material from one organism is inserted into the DNA of another organism. For illustration, see **gene-splicing.**

re·com·bi·na·tion (rē′kom bə nā′shən) *n.* **1.** a combining again. **2.** *Genetics.* the appearance in offspring of gene combinations that are different from those of their parents, produced during cell division by crossing-over or by random combination of chromosomes.

a	at	e	end	o	hot	u	up	hw	white		about
ā	ape	ē	me	ō	old	ū	use	ng	song		taken
ä	far	i	it	ô	fork	ü	rule	th	thin	ə	pencil
âr	care	ī	ice	oi	oil	ů	pull	th	this		lemon
		îr	pierce	ou	out	ûr	turn	zh	measure		circus

R

rec·om·mend (rek′ə mend′) *v.t.* **1.** to speak of or present favorably: *to recommend a movie.* **2.** to suggest as a sound or expedient course; advise: *to recommend going to the doctor.* **3.** to make acceptable, pleasing, or attractive: *Your speaking ability recommended you to the debating group.* **4.** to put or give into the charge or keeping of; commit; entrust (with *to*): *I recommend this matter to your care.* [Medieval Latin *recommendare* to entrust, obtain a favor for, from Latin *re-* again + *commendāre* to entrust.] —**rec′om·mend′a·ble**, *adj.*

rec·om·men·da·tion (rek′ə mən dā′shən, -men-) *n.* **1.** the act of recommending. **2.** any communication, such as a letter, that recommends. **3.** a quality or action that recommends: *Your summer job is a strong recommendation for this position.* **4.** anything recommended: *In this situation, what is your recommendation?*

rec·om·men·da·to·ry (rek′ə men′də tôr′ē) *adj.* recommending or serving to recommend.

re·com·mit (rē′kə mit′) *v.t.,* -**mit·ted,** -**mit·ting. 1.** to commit again. **2.** to refer again to a committee, as a legislative bill. —**re′com·mit′tal, re′com·mit′ment,** *n.*

rec·om·pense (rek′əm pens′) *v.t.,* -**pensed, -pens·ing. 1.** to pay or repay (someone), as for something done or given; reward. **2.** to make up for, as a loss; give compensation for. —*n.* **1.** payment, as for something done or given; reward. **2.** compensation, as for loss or injury. [Late Latin *recompēnsāre* to reward, make amends, from Latin *re-* back + *compēnsāre* to weigh together.]

rec·on·cile (rek′ən sīl′) *v.t.,* -**ciled, -cil·ing. 1.** to restore to friendship or good relations, as after an estrangement: *to reconcile quarreling friends.* **2.** to make (someone) accept or be content with something (with *to*): *The children could not reconcile themselves to having their trip canceled.* **3.** to settle, as a controversy, difference, or disagreement. **4.** to bring into agreement; make harmonious or congruous: *to reconcile the different accounts of an accident.* [Latin *reconciliāre* to bring together again.] —**rec′on·cil′a·bil′i·ty,** *n.* —**rec′on·cil′a·ble,** *adj.* —**rec′on·cile′ment,** *n.* —**rec′on·cil′er,** *n.*

rec·on·cil·i·a·tion (rek′ən sil′ē ā′shən) *n.* **1.** the act of reconciling or the state of being reconciled. **2.** the process of bringing into agreement; making harmonious or congruous. —**rec′on·cil′i·a·to′ry,** *adj.*

rec·on·dite (rek′ən dīt′, ri kon′dīt) *adj.* **1.** difficult to understand; profound; abstruse. **2.** dealing with difficult or abstruse matters. **3.** known to only a few; esoteric; obscure. [Latin *reconditus,* past participle of *recondere* to put away, hide.]

re·con·di·tion (rē′kən dish′ən) *v.t.* to restore to good condition, as by repairing or cleaning.

re·con·nais·sance (ri kon′ə səns) *n.* an examination or survey to obtain information, esp. military information about an enemy. [French *reconnaisance,* from *reconnaître* to recognize, from Latin *recognōscere.*]

re·con·noi·ter (rē′kə noi′tər, rek′ə-) *also, British,* **reconnoitre.** *v.t., v.i.* to make a reconnaissance of (something). [Obsolete French *reconnoître* to recognize, from Latin *recognōscere.*] —**re′con·noi′ter·er,** *n.*

re·con·noi·tre (rē′kə noi′tər, rek′ə-) *v.t., v.i.,* -**tred, -tring.** *British.* reconnoiter. —**re′con·noi′trer,** *n.*

re·con·sid·er (rē′kən sid′ər) *v.t.* to consider again, esp. with a view to revise or reverse an action or decision. —*v.i.* to consider an action or decision again. —**re′con·sid′er·a′tion,** *n.*

re·con·sti·tute (rē kon′sti tūt′, -tūt′) *v.t.,* -**tut·ed, -tut·ing. 1.** to constitute or form again. **2.** to restore to a former condition: *to reconstitute powdered milk by adding water.* —**re′con·sti·tu′tion,** *n.*

re·con·struct (rē′kən strukt′) *v.t.* **1.** to construct again; rebuild. **2.** to re-create (what happened or existed) in the mind from available evidence or information: *to reconstruct a series of events.*

re·con·struc·tion (rē′kən struk′shən) *n.* **1.** the act of reconstructing or the state of being reconstructed. **2.** something reconstructed. **3.** Reconstruction. **a.** the process for restoring the former Confederate states to the Union after the American Civil War. **b.** the period during which this process took place, from 1867 to 1877. —**re′con·struc′tive,** *adj.*

Re·con·struc·tion·ism (rē′kən struk′shə niz′əm) *n.* a twentieth-century movement in American Judaism that views Judaism as a religious civilization and preserves the traditional customs and observances but adapts them to modern-day living.

rec·ord (*n., adj.,* rek′ərd; *v.,* ri kôrd′) *n.* **1.** an account preserved in writing or other permanent form: *health records.* **2.** the known facts about someone or something's activity, performance, or achievement: *a candidate's political record, a truck's service record.* **3.** a performance surpassing all others of its kind, as in sports: *The racehorse set a track record.* **4.** a disk on which the conversion of sounds has been stored mechanically, to be played back on a phonograph. **5.** a history of criminal behavior. **6.** an official written account of public acts or proceedings: *a record of a town meeting.* —*adj.* surpassing all others of its kind: *a record attendance.* —*v.t.* **1.** to set down in permanent form, as in writing or statistically: *to record history, to record temperature throughout the day.* **2.** to show a temporary phenomenon; indicate; register: *The dial on the left records speed.* **3.a.** to convert (sound or images) by electrical or mechanical means into a form that can be registered permanently, as on a phonograph record or magnetic tape. **b.** to make a recording of: *to record a symphony.* —*v.i.* **1.** to make a record or recording of something: *The singer recorded in the morning.* **2.** to admit of being recorded or of being used to record: *Some kinds of folk music do not record easily. Does this machine record well?* [Old French *recorder* to call to mind, remember, from Latin *recordārī,* from *re-* back, again + *cor* mind, heart; referring to the fact that records were originally learned by heart or memorized before writing became common.] —**re·cord′a·ble,** *adj.*

 ·off the record. a. not for quotation, publication, or identification: *These remarks are off the record.* **b.** unofficial or unofficially: *The president spoke off the record.*

 ·on record. set down; recorded.

record changer, a device that holds a stack of phonograph records and automatically drops each one on a turntable after the preceding record has finished playing.

re·cord·er (ri kôr′dər) *n.* **1.** a person who is employed to take notes and keep records. **2.** a machine that records sounds, as on magnetic tape. **3.** in certain cities, a judge. **4.** any of several musical instruments of the woodwind family, having eight finger holes to regulate pitch, and producing a tone similar to a flute's.

re·cord·ing (ri kôr′ding) *n.* **1.** a phonograph record, magnetic tape, compact disc, or the like that contains stored sounds or images. **2.** the sound or images registered on a phonograph record, magnetic tape, or other medium. **3.** the process of putting sound or images onto magnetic tape or the like.

record player, phonograph.

re·count[1] (ri kount′) *v.t.* **1.** to tell in detail; narrate. **2.** to tell in order; enumerate. [Dialectal Old French *reconter* to narrate, from *re-* (see RE-) + *conter* to tell, reckon. See COUNT[1].]

re·count[2] (*v.,* rē kount′; *n.,* rē′kount′, rē kount′) *also,* **re-count.** *v.t.* to count again. —*n.* a second count, esp. of votes in an election. [RE- + COUNT[1].]

re·coup (ri küp′) *v.t.* **1.** to make up for; regain the equivalent of, as a loss. **2.** to reimburse; repay, as for a loss. **3.** to get back; recover: *to recoup prestige after a humiliating defeat.* —*v.i.* to get back or make up for something: *to recoup quickly after a setback.* [Old French *recouper* to cut back or again, from *re-* (see RE-) + *couper* to cut (from *coup* blow, stroke). See COUP.] —**re·coup′a·ble,** *adj.* —**re·coup′ment,** *n.*

re·course (rē′kôrs′, ri kôrs′) *n.* **1.** an appeal or resort to someone or something for help or protection. **2.** a person or thing that is appealed to; resort. **3.** the right to demand payment from the maker or endorser of a negotiable commercial paper. [Old French *recours* appeal, resort, from Latin *recursus* a running back, retreat.]

re·cov·er (ri kuv′ər) *v.t.* **1.** to get back (something lost or stolen); regain. **2.** to make up for, as a loss or damage. **3.** to restore (oneself) to a normal condition or position. **4.** to obtain by legal process: *to recover damages for an injury, to recover title to a piece of land.* **5.** to get back (a substance or material) in a form in which it may be used again: *to recover steel from junked cars.* —*v.i.* **1.** to get back to a normal or healthy position or condition. **2.** to be successful in a lawsuit. [Old French *recovrer* to get again, from Latin *recuperāre.*]

re·cov·er (rē kuv′ər) *v.t.* to cover again.

---

recommencement	reconcentration	reconnection	reconsolidate	reconvene	recopy
recommission	recondense	reconquer	reconsolidation	reconverge	recouple
recompilation	reconduct	reconquest	reconsult	reconvergence	recrate
recompile	reconfine	reconsecrate	reconsultation	reconvict	recriticize
recomputation	reconfirm	reconsecration	recontact	reconviction	recross
recompute	reconfirmation	reconsign	recontaminate	reconvince	recrown
reconcentrate	reconnect	reconsignment	recontamination	recook	recultivate

re·cov·er·y (ri kuv′ə rē) n., pl. **-er·ies. 1.** the act or an instance of recovering or being recovered. **2.** the return of a person to a healthy or normal condition.

recovery room, a hospital room, usually close to the operating room, where patients are temporarily placed after an operation for special care and observation while recovering from anesthesia.

rec·re·ant (rek′rē ənt) adj. **1.** not maintaining loyalty or adhering to an oath; unfaithful; disloyal. **2.** without the courage to maintain loyalty or a position; craven; cowardly. —n. **1.** an ally or supporter who deserts; traitor. **2.** coward. [Old French recreant, present participle of recroire to surrender, from Medieval Latin recredere, from Latin re- again + crēdere to believe.] —**rec′re·ance, rec′re·an·cy,** n.

rec·re·ate (rek′rē āt′) v., **-at·ed, -at·ing.** —v.t. to refresh or enliven, as with some form of amusement or relaxation, esp. after work; amuse; entertain. —v.i. to take recreation. [Latin recreātus, past participle of recreāre to restore, refresh.]

re·cre·ate (rē′krē āt′) v.t., **-at·ed, -at·ing.** to create anew. —**re·cre·a·tion** (rē′krē ā′shən), n.

rec·re·a·tion (rek′rē ā′shən) n. **1.** refreshment by means of some form of amusement or relaxation; diversion. **2.** any form of amusement or relaxation. —**rec′re·a′tion·al,** adj. —For Synonyms, see **amusement.**

recreational vehicle, a motor vehicle designed for recreational and vacation use, usually equipped with living and sleeping facilities. Also, **RV.**

re·crim·i·nate (ri krim′ə nāt′) v., **-nat·ed, -nat·ing.** —v.i. to accuse someone of something in return for being accused. —v.t. to accuse (someone) in return; make a counter accusation against. [Medieval Latin recriminatus, past participle of recriminare to make charges against, from Latin re- again + crīminārī to accuse of crime.] —**re·crim′i·na′tion,** n. —**re·crim′i·na′tive, re·crim·i·na·to·ry** (ri krim′ə nə tôr′ē), adj.

re·cru·desce (rē′krü des′) v.i., **-desced, -desc·ing.** to break out or appear again, as a disease. [Latin recrūdēscere.]

re·cru·des·cence (rē′krü des′əns) n. a new outbreak; reappearance. [Latin recrūdēscere to break out again + -ENCE.] —**re′cru·des′cent,** adj.

re·cruit (ri krüt′) n. **1.** a newly enlisted member of an armed force. **2.** a new member of any group or organization. —v.t. **1.** to get (someone) to join an armed force; enlist (someone) for military service. **2.** to raise, make up, or fill up the number of by getting new members: to recruit a new force of deputies. **3.** to hire or otherwise obtain the services of: to recruit teachers for a school system. **4.** to secure the support or allegiance of, as for some cause, organization, or position. —v.i. to persuade people to join; enlist new members or employees. [French recruter to levy troops, going back to recroître to grow again, from Latin recrēscere.] —**re·cruit′er,** n. —**re·cruit′ment,** n.

rect-, form of **recti-** before vowels, as in rectangle.

rect. 1. receipt. **2.** rectangle. **3.** rectangular. **4.** rectified. **5.** rector. **6.** rectory.

rec·ta (rek′tə) a plural of **rectum.**

rec·tal (rek′təl) adj. relating to, affecting, or near the rectum.

rec·tan·gle (rek′tang′gəl) n. a parallelogram having four right angles. [Medieval Latin rectangulus having a right angle, from Latin rēctus straight, right + angulus angle[1], corner.]

rec·tan·gu·lar (rek tang′gyə lər) adj. **1.** shaped like a rectangle. **2.** having a base or section in the form of a rectangle: a rectangular pyramid. **3.** having one or more right angles. —**rec·tan′gu·lar′i·ty,** n. —**rec·tan′gu·lar·ly,** adv.

rectangular coordinate, a Cartesian coordinate in a Cartesian coordinate system whose axes meet at right angles.

recti- combining form straight; right: rectilinear. [Latin rēctus.]

rectangles

rec·ti·fi·er (rek′tə fī′ər) n. **1.** a person or thing that rectifies. **2.** Electronics. a device for changing alternating current into direct current.

rec·ti·fy (rek′tə fī′) v.t., **-fied, -fy·ing. 1.** to set or make right; amend; correct: to rectify an error. **2.** to put or set right by adjustment or calculation; adjust. **3.** Electronics. to change (an alternating current) into a direct current. **4.** Geometry. to determine the length of (the arc of a curve). **5.** Chemistry. to refine or purify (liquids) by repeated distillation. [Late Latin rēctificāre to make right, from Latin rēctus right + facere to make.] —**rec′ti·fi′a·ble,** adj. —**rec′ti·fi·ca′tion,** n.

rec·ti·lin·e·ar (rek′tə lin′ē ər) adj. **1.** moving in or forming a straight line or lines. **2.** consisting of or bounded by a straight line or lines. Also, **rec′ti·lin′e·al.** [Late Latin rēctilīneus having

straight lines (from Latin rēctus straight + līnea linen thread, stroke[1]) + -AR[1].] —**rec′ti·lin′e·ar·ly,** adv.

rec·ti·tude (rek′ti tüd′, -tūd′) n. **1.** the quality of being moral and honest. **2.** conduct that reveals this quality. [Late Latin rēctitūdō straightness, uprightness, from Latin rēctus straight, right.]

rec·to (rek′tō) n., pl. **-tos. 1.** any right-hand page of a printed book. **2.** the front side of a page. ➡ opposed to **verso.**

rec·tor (rek′tər) n. **1.** a member of the Anglican or Episcopalian clergy who has charge of a parish, esp. in Britain, one who receives the parish income. **2.** a priest in the Roman Catholic Church, esp. in the Jesuit order, in charge of a seminary, college, or religious house. **3.** in certain schools, colleges, or universities, the chief administrator. [Latin rēctor ruler.]

rec·to·ry (rek′tə rē) n., pl. **-ries. 1.** a rector's dwelling. **2.** in Britain, the benefice held by a rector.

rec·tum (rek′təm) n., pl. **-tums** or **-ta.** the terminal part of the large intestine, connecting the colon to the anus, where feces are stored until discharge. [Modern Latin rectum, short for Latin intestīnum rēctum the straight intestine.]

rec·tus (rek′təs) n., pl. **-ti** (-tī). any of various straight muscles, as of the abdomen and thigh or any of four muscles of the eye. [Modern Latin rectus, from Latin rēctus (mūsculus) straight (muscle).]

re·cum·bent (ri kum′bənt) adj. lying down; reclining; leaning. [Latin recumbēns, present participle of recumbere to recline.] —**re·cum′bence, re·cum′ben·cy,** n. —**re·cum′bent·ly,** adv.

re·cu·per·ate (ri kü′pə rāt′, -kū′-) v., **-at·ed, -at·ing.** —v.i. to regain health or strength; recover. —v.t. to get (health or something lost) back. [Latin recuperātus, past participle of recuperāre to get again, regain.] —**re·cu′per·a′tion,** n.

re·cu·per·a·tive (ri kü′pə rā′tiv, -pər ə tiv, -kū′-) adj. relating to, assisting in, or promoting recovery, as from a disease or operation. Also, **re·cu·per·a·to·ry** (ri kü′pər ə tôr′ē, -kū′-).

re·cur (ri kûr′) v.i., **-curred, -cur·ring. 1.** to take place, come up, or appear again: The patient's fever recurred after two days. **2.** to come back or return to the mind or memory: Thoughts of home and family recurred to the traveler. **3.** to go back or return in thought or discourse: to recur to a subject. [Latin recurrere to run back, return.] —**re·cur′rence,** n.

re·cur·rent (ri kûr′ənt) adj. **1.** happening or appearing again, esp. repeatedly or periodically. **2.** Anatomy. turning back in the opposite direction, as a nerve. [Latin recurrēns, present participle of recurrere. See RECUR.] —**re·cur′rent·ly,** adv.

re·cy·cla·ble (rē sī′klə bəl) adj. able to be or designed to be recycled: recyclable containers. —n. something that can be recycled, esp. something designed to be recycled after being used: We store bottles and other recyclables in the shed.

re·cy·cle (rē sī′kəl) v.t., **-cy·cled, -cy·cling. 1.** to make (waste material) available or suitable for reuse. **2.** to use again or repeatedly. **3.** to set a new or different cycle in, as a machine or process. **4.** to reset a cycle in, as a machine or process. —**re·cy′cler,** n.

red (red) n. **1.** the color appearing at the lower end of the spectrum, opposite violet; the color of fresh blood. **2.a.** something that imparts this color, such as a dye or paint. **b.** something having this color, such as cloth or paper: to wrap a present in red. **3.** also, **Red.** Informal. **a.** a political leftist, radical, or revolutionary, esp. a communist. **b.** an inhabitant of a country governed or dominated by a Communist party, such as the People's Republic of China. —adj., **red·der, red·dest. 1.** having the color red. **2.** having one's complexion glow, as from a rush of blood to the surface; florid; blushing; flushed: to be red with embarrassment. **3.** inflamed or bloodshot, as the eyes. **4.** also, **Red.** Informal. **a.** politically leftist, radical, or revolutionary, esp. communist. **b.** of or relating to a country governed or dominated by a Communist party, such as the People's Republic of China. **5.** of or relating to American Indians. ➡ often considered offensive. [Old English rēad having the color red.]

•**in the red.** losing or owing money. ➡ opposed to **in the black.**

•**to see red.** Informal. to be or become extremely angry.

re·dact (ri dakt′) v.t. **1.** to draw up or frame, as a statement or a decree. **2.** to put into proper literary form; prepare for publication; edit. [Latin redāctus. See REDACTION.] —**re·dac′tor,** n.

re·dac·tion (ri dak′shən) n. **1.** the act or process of preparing literary matter for publication. **2.** the result of such a process, esp.

a	at	e	end	o	hot	u	up	hw	white		about
ā	ape	ē	me	ō	old	ū	use	ng	song	ə	taken
ä	far			ô	fork	ü	rule	th	thin		pencil
âr	care	ī	ice	oi	oil	u̇	pull	th	this		lemon
		îr	pierce	ou	out	ûr	turn	zh	measure		circus

R

a new edition; revision. [French *rédaction* editing, from Latin *redāctus,* past participle of *redigere* to bring back, reduce.]

red algae, any of a division, Rhodophyta, of primarily marine, multicellular algae, having red pigments in addition to chlorophyll. Red algae are usually attached to rocks or other algae or grow as part of coral reefs.

red·bird (red'bûrd') *n.* any of several birds, such as the cardinal, bullfinch, or scarlet tanager, having predominantly red plumage.

red blood cell, one of the cells of the blood of humans and other vertebrates, the most abundant type of blood cell, containing hemoglobin and functioning chiefly to carry oxygen to the cells and tissues and carbon dioxide back to the respiratory organs. Also, **erythrocyte, red blood corpuscle.**

red-blood·ed (red'blud'id) *adj.* full of vitality and will power; vigorous.

red·breast (red'brest') *n.* **1.** any of various birds having a red breast, esp. a robin. **2.** a freshwater sunfish, *Lepomis auritus,* of the eastern United States, having a reddish belly.

red·bud (red'bud') *n.* any of a group of shrubs or small trees, genus *Cercis,* of the pea family, having clusters of red, pink, or white budlike flowers and heart-shaped leaves. Also, **Judas tree.**

red·cap (red'kap') *n.* a porter who handles baggage, esp. at a railroad station. [From the *red cap* often worn by such a porter.]

red carpet, a display of elaborate or deferential courtesy, hospitality, or welcome. [From the traditional practice of laying down a strip of *red carpet* for a distinguished visitor to walk upon.]

red cedar 1. a juniper of northeastern North America, *Juniperus virginica.* **2.** the fragrant, durable, red wood of this tree, used esp. in making storage chests and in lining closets.

red cent *Informal.* a very small or insignificant amount; least bit: *That advice isn't worth a red cent.*

red clover, a type of clover, *Trifolium pratense,* having large, round, red flower heads, and cultivated for forage.

red·coat (red'kōt') *n.* a British soldier of a time when the British uniform included a red coat, as during the American Revolution and the War of 1812.

Red Cross 1. an international humanitarian organization founded in 1864, having as its main purpose the care and relief of victims of war and natural disasters, such as floods, fires, or earthquakes. **2.** any national branch of this organization. **3. red cross.** a red Greek cross on a white ground, the emblem of this organization.

red deer 1. a reddish brown deer, *Cervus elaphus,* native to the forests of Europe, Asia, and northern Africa, having a yellowish patch of fur on the rump. Height: 4 feet (1.2 meters) at the shoulder. **2.** the white-tailed deer, *Odocoileus virginianus,* in summer, when its coat turns reddish brown.

red·den (red'ən) *v.i.* **1.** to become red. **2.** to blush or flush, as from embarrassment or anger. —*v.t.* to make red.

red·dish (red'ish) *adj.* mixed or tinged with red; somewhat red.

re·deem (ri dēm') *v.t.* **1.** to recover ownership of, as something pawned or lost through foreclosure, by payment. **2.** to pay off, as a promissory note. **3.** to exchange, as trading stamps, for money or merchandise. **4.** to get or win back; regain; recover: *to redeem one's good name.* **5.** to make up for or offset; compensate for: *The play's*

red deer

witty dialogue does nothing to redeem the absurdity of its plot. **6.** to make good or fulfill (a pledge or promise). **7.** to set free, as from captivity; rescue; ransom. **8.** *Religion.* to deliver from a state of sinfulness and its penalties. [Latin *redimere* to buy back.] —**re·deem'a·ble,** *adj.*

re·deem·er (ri dē'mər) *n.* **1.** a person who redeems or rescues another. **2. Redeemer.** Jesus.

re·deem·ing (ri dē'ming) *adj.* offsetting or compensating for what is faulty, weak, or lacking: *a redeeming quality.*

re·demp·tion (ri demp'shən, -dem'-) *n.* **1.** the act or an instance of redeeming or the state of being redeemed. **2.** *Chris-*

tianity. deliverance or salvation from sin through the Atonement of Jesus. [Late Latin *redemptiō* deliverance from sin, from Latin *redemptiō* a buying back. Doublet of RANSOM.] —**re·demp'tive,** *adj.* —**re·demp'tive·ly,** *adv.*

red-faced (red'fāst') *adj.* having a red face, esp. as a result of anger or embarrassment; flushed or blushing.

red flag 1. a signal warning of danger ahead: *On seeing the red flag, the driver stopped the train.* **2.** *Informal.* something that provokes or is likely to provoke anger, hostility, or attention: *Talk about closing the factory was a red flag to the townspeople.* **3.** a symbol of revolution or of a revolutionary party.

red fox, any of various foxes, genus *Vulpes,* often having reddish fur, such as *V. fulva,* of the United States, Canada, and Iceland, and *V. vulpes,* of Europe, Asia, and northern Africa.

red giant *Astronomy.* a star that has burned most of its hydrogen, grown to a size many times that of the sun, and taken on a reddish hue as its surface temperature has decreased.

red grouse, a ptarmigan, *Lagopus scoticus,* whose plumage remains brown in winter, native to England and Ireland. Also, **moorfowl.**

red gum 1. any of several Australian eucalyptuses, as *Eucalyptus calophylla* or *E. camaldulensis,* having a hard, reddish wood. **2.** sweet gum.

red-hand·ed (red'han'did) *adj.* in the act of doing or having just done something, esp. something wrong.

red·head (red'hed') *n.* **1.** a person having red hair. **2.** a freshwater diving duck, *Aythya americana,* native to North America, the male of which has a reddish brown head. Length: 18-22 inches (46-56 centimeters).

red-head·ed (red'hed'id) *adj.* having red hair or a red head.

redheaded woodpecker, an eastern and central North American woodpecker, *Melanerpes erythrocephalus,* having a bright red head, neck, and throat, contrasting with a blue-black back and white underparts. Length: about 9 inches (23 centimeters).

red heat 1. the temperature at which a substance, such as a metal, turns red with heat. **2.** the state or condition of being red with heat.

red herring 1. a herring dried and smoked to a reddish color. **2.** something intended to divert attention from the problem at hand. [Def. 2 is derived from the custom of drawing a herring across an animal's track in hunting, in order to throw the hounds off the scent.]

red-hot (red'hot') *adj.* **1.** red or glowing with heat; very hot. **2.** marked by or showing great intensity, as of anger, enthusiasm, or violence. **3.** fresh from a source; new. **4.** very popular or exciting: *Computer games were red-hot gifts last year.*

re·did (rē did') the past tense of **redo.**

red·in·gote (red'ing gōt') *n.* **1.** a man's double-breasted, full-skirted overcoat, popular in the eighteenth and early nineteenth centuries. **2.** a belted dress or overcoat worn by women during this period, open down the front to show a dress or petticoat beneath. [French *redingote,* modification of English *riding coat.*]

re·di·rect (rē'di rekt', -dī rekt') *v.t.* **1.** to change the direction or course of: *to redirect traffic.* **2.** to direct again. —*n. Law.* the questioning or examination of a witness, after cross-examination, by the lawyer who originally questioned him or her. —*adj. Law.* of, relating to, or designating a redirect. —**re'di·rec'tion,** *n.*

re·dis·trict (rē dis'trikt) *v.t.* to revise or rearrange the boundaries of, esp. electoral or administrative districts.

red lead, a bright red, powdery oxide of lead, used chiefly in rust-preventive paints and as a pigment in red pencils and rubber. Formula: Pb_3O_4 Also, **minium.**

red-let·ter (red'let'ər) *adj.* especially significant or happy; memorable: *a red-letter day.* [From the practice of marking holidays with *red letters* on church calendars.]

red light 1. a red traffic signal indicating a directive to stop. **2.** a red warning or danger signal.

red·lin·ing (red'lī'ning) *n.* the practice of refusing to grant home loans, mortgages, or insurance to people living in neighborhoods considered to be poor financial risks.

red man, American Indians collectively. ➡ often considered offensive.

red maple, a common North American maple, *Acer rubrum,* having reddish twigs and leaves that turn red or orange in autumn.

red·neck (red'nek') *n. Informal.* **1.** a poor white farmer,

redecorate	redemonstrate	redesign	redigest	redistillation	redrive
redecoration	redeploy	redesignate	redigestion	redistribute	redry
rededicate	redeployment	redetermination	rediscount	redistribution	redust
rededication	redeposit	redetermine	rediscover	redivide	redye
redefine	redescend	redevelop	rediscovery	redock	reedit
redeliver	redescent	redeveloper	redissolve	redraft	reeducate
redelivery	redescribe	redevelopment	redistill	redraw	reeducation

sharecropper, or other resident of a rural area, esp. in the southern United States. **2.** an uneducated, esp. rural person regarded as having a narrow, bigoted view of the world. —*adj.* of, relating to, or characteristic of rednecks. ➡ considered offensive in all defs. [From the sunburned necks that laborers typically get while working in the fields.]

re·do (rē dü′) *v.t.*, **-did** (-did′), **-done** (-dun′), **-do·ing. 1.** to do over or again. **2.** to change the design or structure of; remodel; renovate.

red oak 1. any of several North American oaks, esp. *Quercus rubra,* having dark gray or brown to blackish bark, bristle-tipped leaves or leaf lobes, and acorns that mature in two years. **2.** the wood of such a tree.

red ocher, a red, earthy hematite, used as a pigment.

red·o·lent (red′ə lənt) *adj.* **1.** having or giving off a pleasant odor; fragrant. **2.** giving off a certain odor; smelling (with *of*): *a garden redolent of roses.* **3.** giving a very strong suggestion of, as though permeated with (with *of* or *with*): *a custom redolent of superstition.* [Latin *redolēns,* present participle of *redolēre* to emit a scent.] —**red′o·lence, red′o·len·cy,** *n.* —**red′o·lent·ly,** *adv.*

re·done (rē dun′) the past participle of **redo.**

re·dou·ble (rē dub′əl) *v.,* **-bled, -bling.** —*v.t.* **1.** to increase greatly or renew with great vigor; intensify: *We redoubled our efforts to finish the work on time.* **2.** to double again. —*v.i.* **1.** to be increased; become intensified: *The horse's pace redoubled entering the home stretch.* **2.** to turn back; double back (with *on*). **3.** *Bridge.* to double an opponent's bid of a double.

re·doubt (ri dout′) *n.* **1.** a small enclosed fortification, esp. one used for temporary defense. **2.** any refuge; retreat. [French *redoute* small fortification, through Italian, going back to Latin *reductus,* past participle of *redūcere* to bring back.]

re·doubt·a·ble (ri dou′tə bəl) *adj.* **1.** inspiring or causing fear; formidable; awesome. **2.** deserving or commanding respect, trust, or deference. [Old French *redoutable* formidable, from *redouter* to fear, going back to Latin *re-* back + *dubitāre* to be uncertain.] —**re·doubt′a·ble·ness,** *n.* —**re·doubt′a·bly,** *adv.*

re·dound (ri dound′) *v.i.* **1.** to have an effect or result on something; contribute (with *to*): *Your generous act redounds to your credit.* **2.** to come or be reflected back. [Old French *redonder* to overflow, abound, from Latin *redundāre,* going back to *re-* back, again + *unda* wave.]

re·dox (rē′doks) *n.* oxidation-reduction. [Shortened from *red(uction-)ox(idation).*]

red panda, panda *(def. 2).*

red pepper 1. the edible podlike fruit of any of a group of either hot or sweet pepper plants. **2.** cayenne.

red·poll (red′pōl′) *n.* either of two finches, genus *Carduelis,* having an orange-red cap and black chin: the **common redpoll,** *C. flammea,* or the **hoary** or **arctic redpoll,** *C. hornemanni.* Length: 5 ½ inches (14 centimeters). [RED + POLL; because it has a red crown.]

re·dress (*v.,* ri dres′; *n.,* re′dres, ri dres′) *v.t.* **1.** to correct and compensate for; set right; rectify; remedy: *to redress a grievance.* **2.** to make reparation or amends to; compensate. —*n.* **1.** compensation, as for injury suffered or wrong done; reparation; satisfaction. **2.** the act or an instance of redressing. [Middle French *redresser* to straighten, going back to Latin *re-* back, again + *dīrēctus* straight, just.] —**re·dress′a·ble,** *adj.*

re·dress (rē dres′) *v.t., v.i.* to dress again.

red salmon, sockeye.

red shift *also,* **red·shift** (red′shift′). the shift of starlight toward the longer wavelengths, or the red end, of the spectrum, interpreted as a Doppler effect that results from increasing distance between the star and the observer.

red·skin (red′skin′) *n. Informal.* a North American Indian. ➡ considered offensive.

red snapper 1. an important food fish, *Lutjanus campechanus,* of the snapper family, scarlet in color, of coastal Atlantic waters and the Gulf of Mexico. **2.** any of several other reddish fish, esp. a rockfish, *Sebastes ruberrimus,* of the Pacific coast of North America.

red spider, spider mite.

red spruce, a spruce, *Picea rubens,* of eastern North America, having a reddish-brown bark, used for timber and wood pulp.

red squirrel, a North American squirrel, genus *Tamiasciurus,* having reddish fur. Length: 12-14 inches (30-36 centimeters), including tail. Also, **chickaree.**

red·start (red′stärt′) *n.* **1.** a fly-catching warbler, *Setophaga ruticilla,* of eastern North America, the male of which is black with orange or red patches. Length: 5 inches (13 centimeters). **2.** a European thrush, genus *Phoenicurus,* having a reddish tail. Length: 6 inches (15 centimeters). [RED + obsolete *start* tail (from Old English *steort*).]

red tape 1. attention to or the following of official rules, forms,

and procedures, esp. when it results in inaction and delay. **2.** the rules, forms, and procedures themselves. [From the practice that began in the seventeenth century in England of using *red tape* to tie official documents.]

red tide, a discoloration of a body of salt or fresh water caused by a rapid increase, or bloom, of red dinoflagellates, one-celled organisms that produce a poison that kills fish and other aquatic animals.

red·top (red′top′) *n.* a grass, genus *Agrostis,* esp. *A. gigantea,* widely grown for pasture and as hay in northern North America.

re·duce (ri düs′, -dūs′) *v.,* **-duced, -duc·ing.** —*v.t.* **1.** to make less or smaller, as in size, number, or degree; decrease; diminish: *to reduce the speed of an automobile, to reduce the price of an item.* **2.** to bring from a higher to a lower position or condition; degrade: *The colonel reduced the sergeant to private.* **3.a.** to bring to a particular state, form, or condition: *The fire reduced the forest to ashes.* **b.** to compel or force, as by want or need, into some act or condition: *Hunger reduced them to stealing.* **4.** to bring under control or into submission; conquer; subdue: *to reduce a town by siege.* **5.** to break down or bring to a systematic or simpler form or character: *to reduce an argument to its basic propositions.* **6.** *Mathematics.* to change (an expression) to an equivalent but more elementary form: *to reduce* $^4/_8$ *to* $^1/_2$. **7.** *Chemistry.* **a.** to decrease the oxidation number of (the atoms of an element) by adding electrons. **b.** to remove oxygen from (a compound); deoxidize. **c.** to convert, as an ore mineral, to a metallic state by the removal of nonmetallic elements. **8.** *Medicine.* to restore (a fractured or displaced body part) to normal position or condition. —*v.i.* **1.** to lose weight, as by dieting. **2.** to become reduced. [Latin *redūcere* to bring back, withdraw.] —**re·duc′er,** *n.* —**re·duc′i·ble,** *adj.*

reducing agent, any chemical compound that decreases the oxidation number of or gives up electrons to a compound that reacts with it. Also, **re·duc·tant** (ri duk′tənt).

re·duc·tase (ri duk′tās) *n.* any enzyme that functions as a reducing agent or that catalyzes chemical reduction. [REDUCT-(ION) + -ASE.]

re·duc·ti·o ad ab·sur·dum (ri duk′shē ō′ ad ab sûr′dəm) a disproof of a proposition by showing that it leads to an absurd proposition when it is carried to its logical conclusion. [Latin *reductiō ad absurdum* literally, a bringing back or reduction to absurdity.]

re·duc·tion (ri duk′shən) *n.* **1.** the act or process of reducing or the state of being reduced. **2.** an amount by which something is reduced. **3.** something that results from reducing, such as a copy of something that is smaller than the original. [Latin *reductiō* a bringing back.] —**re·duc′tion·al, re·duc′tive,** *adj.*

reduction division, meiosis.

re·dun·dan·cy (ri dun′dən sē) *n., pl.* **-cies. 1.a.** the use of needlessly repeated words to convey an idea. **b.** an instance of this, for example: *The clock strikes on the hour every sixty minutes.* **2.** an excessive amount; superfluity. **3.** the quality or condition of being redundant. Also, **re·dun·dance.**

re·dun·dant (ri dun′dənt) *adj.* **1.** using more words than are necessary; characterized by wordiness or repetition. **2.** not necessary because enough exists already; superfluous. [Latin *redundāns,* present participle of *redundāre* to overflow, abound. See REDOUND.] —**re·dun′dant·ly,** *adv.*

re·du·pli·cate (*v.,* ri dü′pli kāt′, -dū′-; *adj.,* ri dü′pli kit, -kāt′, -dū′-) *v.,* **-cat·ed, -cat·ing.** —*v.t.* **1.** to double, repeat, or copy. **2.** to repeat (a letter, syllable, or word) in order to form a word, for example, in French the word *bon* is reduplicated to get the name of the confection *bonbon.* —*v.i.* to become doubled or repeated. —*adj.* doubled, repeated, or copied. —**re·du′pli·ca′-tion,** *n.*

red·wing (red′wing′) *n.* **1.** a Eurasian thrush, *Turdus iliacus,* having its flanks and the underside of its wings colored a deep chestnut red. Average length: 8 inches (20 centimeters). **2.** red-winged blackbird.

red-winged blackbird (red′wingd′) a North American blackbird, *Agelaius phoeniceus,* the male of which has a scarlet patch edged with yellow or white at the shoulder of each wing. Also, **redwing, redwing blackbird.**

red·wood (red′wud′) *n.* **1.** a tall evergreen tree, *Sequoia sempervirens,* having a thick, reddish brown bark, found only along the western coast of North America. Redwoods may grow from 300 to 340 feet (91.4 to 103.6 meters) tall and some are probably more

a	at	e	end	o	hot	u	up	hw	white		about
ā	ape	ē	me	ō	old	ū	use	ng	song		taken
ä	far	i	it	ô	fork	ū	rule	th	thin	ə	pencil
âr	care	ī	ice	oi	oil	u̇	pull	th	this		lemon
		îr	pierce	ou	out	ûr	turn	zh	measure		circus

R

than 2,000 years old. **2.** the soft, light wood of this tree, strong and highly resistant to decay.

re·ech·o (rē ek′ō) *also,* **re-ech·o.** *v.,* **-ech·oed, -ech·o·ing.** —*v.i.* to repeat or send back an echo; reverberate: *The voices reechoed through the vast cave.* —*v.t.* to repeat the echo of: *The hall reechoed the children's singing.* —*n., pl.* **-ech·oes.** something reechoed.

reed (rēd) *n.* **1.** any of a number of tall grasses, having long narrow leaves and slender, jointed, often hollow, stems, growing chiefly around marshes and other wet areas. **2.** the stem of such a grass. **3.** a musical pipe made from a reed or from some other hollow stalk or stem. **4.** *Music.* **a.** a thin tongue of wood, reed, or other flexible material, used in the mouthpiece of certain wind instruments and the pipes of certain organs, which, when caused to vibrate by a current of air, produces a musical sound. **b.** a musical wind instrument, as of the clarinet, saxophone, or oboe family, whose tone is produced by the vibration of a single or double reed. Also *(def. 4b),* **reed instrument.** [Old English *hrēod* stalk of such a grass.]

reed·buck (rēd′buk′) *n., pl.* **-buck** or **-bucks.** any of a group of small African antelopes, genus *Redunca,* having widely spread hooves adapted for walking on marshy ground. The male has prominently ringed horns. Height: 29-38 inches (71-97 centimeters) at the shoulder. [Translation of Dutch *rietbok.*]

reed organ, harmonium.

reed pipe, an organ pipe whose tone is produced by currents of air vibrating small metal reeds.

reed·y (rē′dē) *adj.,* **reed·i·er, reed·i·est.** **1.** having a sound like a reed instrument: *reedy voices.* **2.** resembling a reed or reeds; slender: *reedy grass, reedy legs.* **3.** full of reeds: *still, reedy waters along the lake's edge.* —**reed′i·ly,** *adv.* —**reed′i·ness,** *n.*

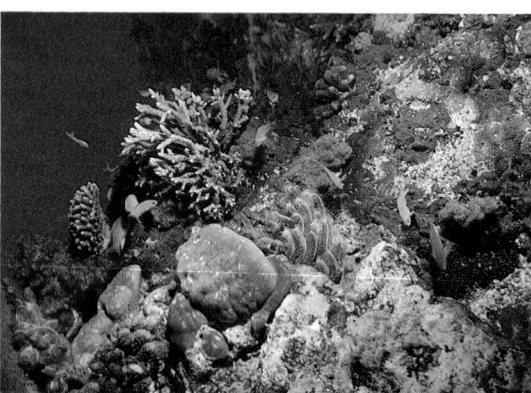

coral **reef**

reef[1] (rēf) *n.* **1.** a ridge of sand, rock, or coral, that lies at or near the surface of a sea or other body of water. **2.** *Mining.* an ore deposit; lode. [Dutch *rif* ridge, from Old Norse *rif* ridge, rib.]

reef[2] (rēf) *n.* **1.** a portion of a sail that can be rolled up or let out in order to regulate the area of the sail exposed to the wind. **2.** a reduction of sail area: *We took a reef in the mainsail when the wind increased.* —*v.t.* **1.** to reduce the area of (a sail) by rolling or folding up a portion and securing it. **2.** to reduce the length of, as a topmast or bowsprit. [Old Norse *rif* foldable portion of a sail, rib.]

reef·er[1] (rē′fər) *n.* **1.** a short, usually double-breasted coat or jacket of heavy fabric, often worn by sailors and fishermen. **2.** a person who reefs. [REEF[2] + -ER[1].]

reef·er[2] (rē′fər) *n. Slang.* a marijuana cigarette. [Probably from REEF[2], in the sense of "to roll up."]

reef knot, square knot.

reek (rēk) *v.i.* **1.** to give off or be permeated by a strong, offensive odor; smell strongly and unpleasantly: *The lot reeks from the*

garbage dumped there. **2.** to exhibit, give an impression of, or be pervaded with something offensive (often with *of* or *with*): *Those political appointments reek of corruption.* **3.** to give off smoke or vapor; steam; fume. —*v.t.* to give off or exude (fumes, an odor, or the like). —*n.* a strong, offensive odor. [Old English *rēc* vapor.] —**reek′ing·ly,** *adv.* —**reek′y,** *adj.*

reel[1] (rēl) *n.* **1.** a spool, cylindrical frame, or other device, usually turning on an axle, on which long strips or strands, as of rope, fishline, or magnetic tape, can be wound for convenient use and storage. **2.a.** this device and what is wound on it, such as wire. **b.** the quantity of material wound on a reel. —*v.t.* **1.** to draw or pull in by or as by winding a line on a reel

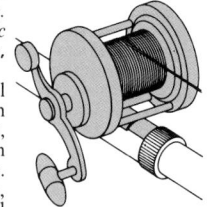

fishing **reel**

(often with *in*): *to reel in a fish.* **2.** to wind on a reel. [Old English *hrēol* device for winding thread or silk.]

· **to reel off.** to say or write quickly, easily, or fluently: *The students reeled off the answers without a pause.*

reel[2] (rēl) *v.i.* **1.** to fall back, recoil, or be thrown off balance, as from a blow; stagger. **2.** to walk or move unsteadily, as from drunkenness; totter; lurch. **3.** to be dizzy or in confusion, as from sickness or shock. **4.** to turn or seem to turn round and round; whirl. —*v.t.* to cause to reel. —*n.* a reeling movement. [Possibly from REEL[1].]

reel[3] (rēl) *n.* **1.** a lively folk dance, performed by two or more couples, in which the dancers form two lines facing each other. **2.** the music for such a dance. [From REEL[2].]

re·e·lect (rē′i lekt′) *also,* **re-e·lect.** *v.t.* to elect again. —**re′e·lec′tion,** *n.*

re·en·force (rē′en fôrs′) *also,* **re-en·force.** *v.t.,* **-forced, -for·cing.** reinforce. —**re′en·force′ment,** *n.*

re·en·list (rē′en list′) *also,* **re-en·list.** *v.t., v.i.* to enlist again. —**re′en·list′ment;** *also,* **re′-en·list′ment,** *n.*

re·en·ter (rē en′tər) *also,* **re-en·ter.** *v.t., v.i.* to enter again. —**re·en′trance,** *n.*

re·en·try (rē en′trē) *also,* **re-en·try.** *n., pl.* **-tries. 1.** the act or an instance of entering again. **2.** the passage of a missile, spacecraft, or the like back into the earth's atmosphere. **3.** the act of reclaiming possession of real property, as from a tenant, by entering or setting foot on it.

reeve[1] (rēv) *n. British.* **1.** formerly, the chief official of a town or district, who took authority from the crown. **2.** in the feudal system, the overseer of an estate; steward; bailiff. [Old English *(ge)rēfa* officer.]

reeve[2] (rēv) *v.t.,* **reeved** or **rove** (rōv), **reev·ing.** *Nautical.* **1.** to pass (a rope or line) through an opening or pulley block. **2.** to pass a rope or line through (an opening or pulley block). **3.** to fasten by reeving. [Of uncertain origin.]

re·ex·am·ine (rē′eg zam′in, -ig-) *also,* **re-ex·am·ine.** *v.t.,* **-ined, -in·ing. 1.** to examine again. **2.** *Law.* to question (a witness) again after cross-examination. —**re′ex·am′i·na′tion;** *also,* **re′-ex·am′i·na′tion,** *n.* —**re′ex·am′in·er;** *also,* **re′-ex·am′in·er,** *n.*

ref. 1. referee. **2.** reference. **3.** referred. **4.** reformed. **5.** refund.

re·fec·tion (ri fek′shən) *n.* **1.** refreshment, esp. with food or drink. **2.** a light meal; repast. [Latin *refectiō* a restoring.]

re·fec·to·ry (ri fek′tə rē) *n., pl.* **-ries.** a dining hall, as in a school, monastery, or other institution. [Late Latin *refectōrium* dining hall in a monastery, going back to Latin *reficere* to restore.]

re·fer (ri fûr′) *v.,* **-ferred, -fer·ring.** —*v.t.* **1.** to send or direct (someone), as for information or aid: *The doctor referred the patient to a specialist.* **2.** to submit or turn over, as a problem, for consideration or for a recommendation or decision: *The parties referred the dispute to arbitration.* **3.** to assign to a cause or source; attribute. —*v.i.* **1.** to call or direct attention; make reference; allude (with *to*): *The speaker referred to our mayor as an up-and-coming politician.* **2.** to use as a source, as of information or aid (with *to*): *to refer to notes while speaking.* **3.** to be restricted; pertain; relate; apply (with *to*). [Latin *referre* to carry back.] —**ref·er·a·ble** (ref′ər ə bəl, ri fûr′-), *adj.* —**re·fer′rer,** *n.*

ref·er·ee (ref′ə rē′) *n.* **1.** an official in certain sports and games, often the chief official, who interprets and enforces the rules and sometimes keeps score. **2.** a person to whom a matter or question in dispute is referred for decision or settlement. —*v.*, **-er·eed**, **-er·ee·ing.** —*v.t.* to act as referee in. —*v.i.* to act as referee.

ref·er·ence (ref′ər əns) *n.* **1.** the act of referring. **2.** a directing of attention; mention; allusion: *a disparaging reference to someone's past.* **3.** connection with some matter; relation; respect; regard (with *to*): *in reference to your letter of November 5.* **4.** a person or thing that is referred to; source, as of information or aid. **5.** a statement attesting to a person's character, ability, or record. **6.** a person to whom another is referred for such a statement. **7. a.** a note referring a reader to or acknowledging the use of another source or authority. **b.** a mark or sign, such as a number or asterisk, designating such a note. **c.** a source or authority so used: *The author cites many references.* —*adj.* used for or offering information or aid: *a reference desk in a library.*

reference book, a book, such as a dictionary, encyclopedia, atlas, or almanac, that contains information arranged in a systematic, convenient way for easy access.

ref·er·en·dum (ref′ə ren′dəm) *n., pl.* **-dums** or **-da** (-də). **1.** a direct popular vote on a public measure. **2.** the procedure by which public measures are submitted to such a vote. [Latin *referendum* that which must be carried back, neuter gerundive of *referre* to carry back.]

ref·er·ent (ref′ər ənt) *adj.* existing or acting as a reference; containing a reference. —*n.* **1.** a person referred to or consulted. **2.** a person or thing that a symbol stands for or a word refers to. [Latin *referens,* present participle of *referre* to carry back.]

re·fer·ral (ri fûr′əl) *n.* **1.** the act or an instance of referring: *a doctor's referral of a patient to a specialist, the referral of a problem to someone in charge.* **2.** a person who has been referred: *The job applicant was a referral from an employment agency.*

re·fill (*v.,* rē fil′; *n.,* rē′fil′) *v.t.* to fill again. —*n.* a supply of a product, such as lipstick or a medicine, replacing material that filled the original container and has been used up. —**re·fill′a·ble,** *adj.*

re·fine (ri fīn′) *v.,* **-fined, -fin·ing.** —*v.t.* **1. a.** to free from impurities or other unwanted matter; make fine or pure: *to refine sugar.* **b.** to subject (a mixture) to an extractive process, such as fractional distillation, in order to obtain useful substances: *to refine crude oil.* **2.** to free from imperfections or defects; perfect: *to refine a speech.* **3.** to free from coarseness; imbue with culture, polish, or delicate sensibilities. **4.** to take or remove by purifying (with *out* or *away*): *They refined the gold out of the ore.* —*v.i.* **1.** to become free of impurities or other unwanted matter. **2.** to use overly fine distinctions in thought or speech. [RE- + earlier *fine* to make fine, from FINE¹.] —**re·fin′er,** *n.*

• **to refine on** (or **upon**). to improve by adding subtleties or fine distinctions.

re·fined (ri fīnd′) *adj.* **1.** free from coarseness, commonness, or vulgarity: *refined manners.* **2.** free from impurities or other unwanted matter: *refined sugar.* **3.** precise or subtle to a fine degree.

re·fine·ment (ri fīn′mənt) *n.* **1.** freedom from coarseness, commonness, or vulgarity. **2.** the act or process of refining. **3.** a change or addition intended to improve or perfect; improvement. **4.** the result of any process of refining: *This book is a refinement of the earlier edition.*

re·fin·er·y (ri fī′nə rē) *n., pl.* **-er·ies.** a place or establishment where some raw substance, such as crude oil or sugar, is refined.

re·fit (rē fit′) *v.t., v.i.,* **-fit·ted, -fit·ting.** to make or be made fit for use again, as by the adjustment or repair of machinery or material or the provision of new supplies.

re·flect (ri flekt′) *v.t.* **1.** to turn or throw back (waves of light, heat, sound, or the like). **2.** to give back an image of; mirror. **3.** to be a truthful representation of: *That choice reflects your good taste.* **4.** to bring or give back as a result; cast (with *on* or *upon*): *Your efforts will reflect credit on you.* **5.** to ponder or realize: *He reflected that he hadn't seen her in some time.* —*v.i.* **1.** to return light, heat, or sound, or give back an image: *Matte surfaces do not reflect.* **2.** to think seriously or carefully; ponder: *to reflect on a question.* **3.** to bring blame or discredit (with *on* or *upon*): *One's acts reflect on one's character.* [Latin *reflectere* to turn or bend back.] —For Synonyms *(v.i.),* see **meditate.**

re·flec·tance (ri flek′təns) *n. Physics.* the ratio of radiant energy reflected from a given surface to the total energy falling on the surface.

reflecting telescope, a telescope that forms an image by reflecting light from the objective, a concave mirror, to the eyepiece, camera, or the like. Also, **reflector.**

re·flec·tion (ri flek′shən) *also, British,* **reflexion.** *n.* **1.** an image given back by a reflecting surface. **2.** something reflected or produced by reflection: *The reflection of the sun on the windshield was blinding.* **3.** serious or careful thinking; consideration. **4.** an

observation or statement that results from such thinking. **5.** *Physics.* the turning back of energy, such as waves of light, heat, or sound, upon striking the surface of a solid or liquid or a boundary within the medium through which the energy is traveling. **6.** something that represents or exhibits something else: *The child's smile was a reflection of happiness.* **7.** something that brings or incurs blame or discredit. **8.** the blame or discredit incurred. **9.** the act of reflecting or the state of being reflected.

re·flec·tive (ri flek′tiv) *adj.* **1.** given to or showing serious or careful thinking; thoughtful; pensive. **2.** causing or capable of causing waves of light, heat, sound, or the like to reflect: *Polished silver has a reflective surface.* **3.** of, relating to, or produced by reflection. —**re·flec′tive·ly,** *adv.* —**re·flec′tive·ness, re·flec·tiv·i·ty** (rē′flek tiv′i tē), *n.*

re·flec·tor (ri flek′tər) *n.* **1.** something that reflects. **2.** a surface or device designed to reflect or direct light, heat, sound, or the like. **3.** reflecting telescope.

re·flex (*n., adj.,* rē′fleks′; *v.,* ri fleks′) *n.* **1.** an involuntary response to a stimulus, for example, the contraction of a muscle or the secretion of a substance by a gland. **2. reflexes.** the capacity to react quickly and appropriately: *It takes good reflexes to hit a pitched ball.* **3.** *Archaic.* a reflection, or an image produced by reflection. —*adj.* **1.** relating to, produced by, or designating an involuntary response to a stimulus: *Pulling your hand away from a hot surface is a reflex response.* **2.** bent or turned back, as by reflection at a surface or boundary. **3.** *Geometry.* (of an angle) between 180 and 360 degrees. —*v.t.* to bend or turn back; reflect. [Latin *reflexus,* past participle of *reflectere* to bend or turn back.]

reflex arc *Physiology.* the path traveled by the neural impulses involved in a reflex action.

reflex camera, a single- or double-lens camera in which the image received through the lens is reflected by a mirror onto a ground-glass screen for viewing and focusing.

re·flex·ion (ri flek′shən) *British.* reflection.

re·flex·ive (ri flek′siv) *adj.* **1.** *Grammar.* relating to, expressing, or denoting an action directed back upon the subject or agent and having a subject or agent and an object that are identical. In the sentence *They taught themselves, themselves* is a reflexive pronoun and *taught* is a reflexive verb. **2.** of, relating to, or capable of a reflex. —*n.* a reflexive verb or pronoun. —**re·flex′ive·ly,** *adv.* —**re·flex′ive·ness, re·flex·iv·i·ty** (rē′flek siv′i tē), *n.*

ref·lu·ent (ref′lü ənt) *adj.* flowing back; ebbing. [Latin *refluēns,* present participle of *refluere* to flow back.] —**ref′lu·ence,** *n.*

re·flux (rē′fluks′) *n.* a flowing back; ebb. [RE- + FLUX.]

re·for·est (rē fôr′ist, -for′-) *v.t., v.i.* to reseed or replant (an area) with trees, esp. an area stripped of trees by fire or logging or in the course of mining operations. —**re′for·est·a′tion,** *n.*

re·form (ri fôrm′) *v.t.* **1.** to make a change for the better in; correct what is wrong with (something), esp. by removing defects or abuses: *an effort to reform the postal system.* **2.** to cause (someone) to change for the better; rehabilitate: *to reform a drunkard.* —*v.i.* to become changed for the better. —*n.* **1.** the act or process of reforming or the state of being reformed: *reform of a prison system.* **2.** a change for the better in conduct or character, esp. a giving up of wrongdoing or irresponsible ways. —*adj.* **1.** of or relating to reform or correction. **2. Reform.** of, relating to, or designating Reform Judaism. [Latin *reformāre* to shape again, change.] —**re·form′a·ble,** *adj.* —**re·form′a·tive,** *adj.* —**re·form′er, re·form′ist,** *n.*

re-form (rē fôrm′) *v.t., v.i.* to form again.

ref·or·ma·tion (ref′ər mā′shən) *n.* **1.** the act of reforming or the state of being reformed. **2. Reformation.** a religious movement in sixteenth-century Europe, led by the German theologian Martin Luther, that began as an attempt to reform the Catholic Church and resulted in the establishment of Protestantism.

re·form·a·to·ry (ri fôr′mə tôr′ē) *n., pl.* **-ries.** a penal institution to which youthful criminals and certain others convicted for the first time are sent and which emphasizes rehabilitation rather than punishment. Also, **reform school.** —*adj.* serving or intended to reform.

re·formed (ri fôrmd′) *adj.* **1.** improved in character, conduct, or morals: *a reformed gambler.* **2.** freed of defects or abuses; corrected: *a reformed text.* **3. Reformed.** of, relating to, or designating those Protestant churches deriving their beliefs and practices from the teachings of the theologians Huldreich Zwingli and John Calvin.

a	at	e	end	o	hot	u	up	hw	white	ə	about
ā	ape	ē	me	ō	old	ū	use	ng	song		taken
ä	far	i	it	ô	fork	ü	rule	th	thin		pencil
âr	care	ī	ice	oi	oil	u̇	pull	th	this		lemon
				ir	pierce	ou	out	ûr	turn	zh	measure		circus

R

Reform Judaism, a branch of Judaism that rejects the strict observance of traditional religious rituals, focuses on Jewish ethics, and accepts variations in religious practice.

reform school, reformatory.

re·fract (ri frakt′) *v.t.* to cause to undergo refraction. [Latin *refractus,* past participle of *refringere* to break up.]

refracting telescope, a telescope that forms an image by refracting light through a concave objective lens and directing it toward the eyepiece, camera, or the like. Also, **refractor.**

re·frac·tion (ri frak′shən) *n.* the bending of waves, esp. light waves, as they pass from a substance in which they travel at one velocity to a substance in which they travel at another, or as they pass through a substance whose density is not uniform.

re·frac·tive (ri frak′tiv) *adj.* **1.** of, relating to, or resulting from refraction. **2.** having the capacity to refract. —**re·frac′tive·ly,** *adv.* —**re·frac′tive·ness, re·frac·tiv·i·ty** (rē′frak tiv′i tē), *n.*

refractive index, index of refraction.

re·frac·tor (ri frak′tər) *n.* **1.** something that refracts. **2.** refracting telescope.

re·frac·to·ry (ri frak′tə rē) *adj.* **1.** difficult to control or manage; rebellious; obstinate. **2.** resisting treatment, as a disease. **3.** resistant to heat, fusion, or reduction, such as firebrick and certain ores or metals. —*n., pl.* **-ries.** a person or thing that is refractory, esp. a heat-resistant material, such as firebrick. [Earlier *refractary,* from Latin *refrāctārius* stubborn.] —**re·frac′to·ri·ly,** *adv.* —**re·frac′to·ri·ness,** *n.*

re·frain[1] (ri frān′) *v.i.* to hold oneself back; restrain oneself: *We could scarcely refrain from laughing.* [Old French *refrener* to bridle, from Latin *refrēnāre,* from *re-* back + *frēnum* a bridle, curb.] —**re·frain′ment,** *n.*

re·frain[2] (ri frān′) *n.* **1.** a phrase or verse in a song, poem, or the like, recurring regularly, esp. at the end of each stanza; chorus. **2.** a musical setting for this. **3.** a saying or utterance that is frequently repeated. [Old French *refrain* repeated phrase or verse (of a ballad), from *refraindre* to sing a refrain, break, going back to Latin *refringere* to break up; because it breaks the flow of the melody or poem.]

re·fran·gi·ble (ri fran′jə bəl) *adj.* capable of being refracted, as light waves. —**re·fran′gi·bil′i·ty, re·fran′gi·ble·ness,** *n.*

re·fresh (ri fresh′) *v.t.* **1.** to restore strength or vitality to, as through food or rest; revive. **2.** to cause to recollect; prompt (the memory). **3.** to fill again; replenish. **4.** to impart freshness to, as by wetting or cooling. —*v.i.* **1.** to become fresh again; be restored. **2.** to take refreshment; eat or drink. [Old French *refreschir* to restore, revive, from *re-* (see RE-) + *fresche,* feminine of *fres* fresh (of Germanic origin).]

re·fresh·er (ri fresh′ər) *n.* **1.** a person or thing that refreshes. **2.** refresher course.

refresher course, a course of instruction reviewing material previously studied, often providing instruction in recent developments in a professional field.

re·fresh·ing (ri fresh′ing) *adj.* **1.** pleasingly novel or unusual. **2.** that refreshes. —**re·fresh′ing·ly,** *adv.*

re·fresh·ment (ri fresh′mənt) *n.* **1. refreshments.** food or drink, such as snacks or a light meal. **2.** something that refreshes. **3.** the act of refreshing or the state of being refreshed.

re·fried beans (rē′frīd′) boiled and fried beans that are mashed, then seasoned and fried again in fat, used esp. in Mexican cooking.

re·frig·er·ant (ri frij′ər ənt) *n.* any substance, such as water or ammonia, capable of absorbing heat when changing from one form to another, as from a liquid to a gas, used as an agent in cooling or refrigeration. —*adj.* cooling or freezing; refrigerating.

re·frig·er·ate (ri frij′ə rāt′) *v.t.,* **-at·ed, -at·ing.** to make or keep cold, esp. to chill or freeze (food) to prevent spoilage. [Latin *refrīgerātus,* past participle of *refrīgerāre* to make cool.]

re·frig·er·a·tion (ri frij′ə rā′shən) *n.* **1.** a process or system of maintaining cool or freezing temperatures in an enclosed area, as through compression and expansion of a refrigerant. **2.** the state of being refrigerated.

re·frig·er·a·tor (ri frij′ə rā′tər) *n.* **1.** an insulated, boxlike appliance, esp. one equipped with a cooling apparatus, in which low temperatures are maintained, used for keeping food and other perishables cool. **2.** any enclosed area, such as a room or railroad car, that is kept cool by refrigeration.

reft (reft) a past tense and past participle of **reave.**

re·fu·el (rē fū′əl) *v.,* **-eled, -el·ing;** *also, British,* **-elled, -el-**

ling. —*v.t.* to replenish the fuel supply of. —*v.i.* to take on a fresh supply of fuel: *The jet refueled in flight.*

ref·uge (ref′ūj) *n.* **1.** shelter or protection, as from danger, trouble, or hardship. **2.** a place providing shelter, protection, or safety; haven. **3.** a source of safety, aid, or relief. [Old French *refuge,* from Latin *refugium.*] —For Synonyms, see **shelter.**

ref·u·gee (ref′yů jē′, ref′yů jē′) *n.* a person who flees to safety or refuge, esp. one who leaves home or a homeland because of persecution, war, or danger and seeks safety in another place. [French *réfugié,* going back to Latin *refugium* refuge.]

re·ful·gent (ri ful′jənt) *adj.* shining brightly; radiant. [Latin *refulgēns,* present participle of *refulgēre* to flash back, glitter.] —**re·ful′gence, re·ful′gen·cy,** *n.* —**re·ful′gent·ly,** *adv.*

re·fund[1] (*v.,* ri fund′; *n.,* rē′fund) *v.t.* to give or pay back: *We'll refund your deposit if you decide not to buy.* —*n.* **1.** a sum refunded. **2.** the act of refunding. [Latin *refundere* to pour back.] —**re·fund′a·ble,** *adj.*

re·fund[2] (rē fund′) *v.t.* **1.** to allocate funds for again or anew: *to refund a community program.* **2.** to replace (a security about to fall due) with a new security. [RE- + FUND.]

re·fur·bish (rē fûr′bish) *v.t.* to brighten or freshen up. —**re·fur′bish·ment,** *n.*

re·fus·al (ri fū′zəl) *n.* **1.** the act of refusing. **2.** an opportunity or the privilege of rejecting or accepting before others may; option: *to have first refusal.*

re·fuse[1] (ri fūz′) *v.,* **-fused, -fus·ing.** —*v.t.* **1.** to withhold acceptance of; turn down; reject: *to refuse a bribe.* **2.** to withhold the giving or granting of; deny: *to refuse permission.* **3.** to be determined not to (do something); be unwilling: *You always refuse to see my point of view.* **4.** (of a horse) to stop short at (a fence or other obstacle) instead of leaping. —*v.i.* to withhold acceptance, consent, or compliance: *They can't refuse if you ask politely.* [Old French *refuser* to push back, repudiate, recoil, possibly going back to Latin *recūsāre* to reject, be unwilling to do something; influenced by *refūtāre* to repel, rebut.]

> **Synonyms** *v.t.* **Refuse**[1], **reject,** and **decline** mean to deny a request or an offer. **Refuse** suggests an uncompromising decisiveness: *The angry squatters refused to move off the land.* **Reject,** the most strongly negative of these terms, implies abruptness or rudeness: *They rejected our offer of assistance.* **Decline,** the mildest of these terms, implies a concern for social form: *We declined the invitation with thanks.*

ref·use[2] (ref′ūs, -ūz) *n.* anything discarded as useless or worthless; waste; rubbish. —*adj.* discarded or rejected as useless or worthless. [Middle French *refus* rejection, remains, from Old French *refuser* to push back, repudiate, recoil. See REFUSE[1].]

re·fuse·nik (ri fūz′nik) *n.* a Jewish citizen of the Soviet Union denied governmental permission to emigrate. [Partial translation of Russian *otkaznik,* from *otkaz* refusal + *-nik* person.]

ref·u·ta·tion (ref′yů tā′shən) *n.* **1.** the act of refuting. **2.** something that refutes or disproves, such as evidence or an argument. Also, **re·fu·tal** (ri fū′ təl) *n.*

re·fute (ri fūt′) *v.t.,* **-fut·ed, -fut·ing.** **1.** to prove (a statement or argument) to be false or incorrect. **2.** to prove (someone) to be wrong. [Latin *refūtāre* to repel, rebut.] —**re·fut′a·bly,** *adv.* —**re·fut′er,** *n.*

reg. 1. regent. **2.** regiment. **3.** register. **4.** registered. **5.** registrar. **6.** registry. **7.** regular. **8.** regularly. **9.** regulation.

re·gain (rē gān′) *v.t.* **1.** to get possession of again; get back; recover. **2.** to reach again; get back to: *to regain the place one started from.*

re·gal (rē′gəl) *adj.* **1.** resembling, befitting, or characteristic of a king or other sovereign; stately; splendid; dignified: *a regal bearing.* **2.** of or belonging to a king or other sovereign; royal. [Latin *rēgālis* royal, from *rēx* king.] —**re·gal′i·ty** (ri gal′i tē), *n.* —**re′gal·ly,** *adv.* —For Synonyms, see **royal.**

re·gale (ri gāl′) *v.,* **-galed, -gal·ing.** —*v.t.* **1.** to delight or entertain; give great pleasure to: *They regaled us with wild stories.* **2.** to provide a feast for. —*v.i.* to feast. [French *régaler* to entertain; going back to Old French *gale* pleasure, from Middle Dutch *wale* wealth.] —**re·gale′ment,** *n.* —**re·gal′er,** *n.*

re·ga·li·a (ri gā′lē ə, -gāl′yə) *pl. n.* **1.** the insignia of royalty, including crowns, scepters, and ceremonial swords. **2.** the symbols, insignia, or decorations of any rank, office, society, or order. **3.** splendid or fancy clothes; finery. [Latin *rēgālia* literally, royal things, neuter plural of *rēgālis* royal. See REGAL.]

re·gard (ri gärd′) *v.t.* **1.** to look upon or think of; consider: *to*

regard a job as unpleasant but worth doing. **2.** to look at attentively; observe closely: *The sentry regarded us suspiciously.* **3.** to show respect or consideration for: *to regard the rights of others.* **4.** to have relation or pertinence to; have to do with; concern: *As it regards clean air, burning leaves is not helpful.* **5.** to pay attention to or take into account; heed: *I did not regard their warnings.* —n. **1.** careful thought, notice, or attention; heed; consideration: *No regard was given to the needs of the people.* **2.** an attitude or feeling of respect and warmth; esteem; affection: *I know no one for whom I have more regard.* **3.** reference; relation: *I'll write you later in regard to this matter.* **4. regards.** best wishes: *Give my regards to your family.* **5.** a particular respect or point being considered; matter: *I agree with you in that regard.* **6.** look; gaze. [French *regarder* to look at, see, from *re-* (see RE-) + *garder* to keep, watch over (of Germanic origin).] —For Synonyms *(n.)*, see **respect.**

re·gard·ful (ri gärd′fəl) *adj.* **1.** having a mind to; heedful; mindful (usually with *of*): *regardful of circumstances.* **2.** respectful. —**re·gard′ful·ly,** *adv.* —**re·gard′ful·ness.** *n.*

re·gard·ing (ri gär′ding) *prep.* with regard to; in reference to; concerning.

re·gard·less (ri gärd′lis) *adj.* having or showing no regard or consideration; heedless; unmindful. —*adv.* in spite of everything; anyway. —**re·gard′less·ly,** *adv.*

re·gat·ta (ri gat′ə, -gä′tə) *n.* a boat race or a series of boat races. [Dialectal Italian *regatta* gondola race; literally, contention for victory; of uncertain origin.]

regatta

re·gen·cy (rē′jən sē) *n., pl.* **-cies. 1.** the office, government, or power of a regent or body of regents. **2.** the period during which a regent or body of regents governs. **3.** a body of regents. **4.** the district or territory under the rule of a regent or body of regents. **5. Regency. a.** in English history, the period from 1811 to 1820. **b.** in French history, the period from 1715 to 1723. —*adj. also,* **Regency.** of, relating to, or characteristic of the Regency in French or English history, or to the styles of furniture prevalent during those periods.

re·gen·er·a·cy (ri jen′ər ə sē) *n.* the state of being regenerate or regenerated.

re·gen·er·ate (*v.,* ri jen′ə rāt′; *adj.,* ri jen′ər it) *v.,* **-at·ed, -at·ing.** —*v.t.* **1.** to cause to be morally or spiritually renewed. **2.** to form, produce, or create anew. **3.** to reproduce or grow anew, as a new limb or new tissue, in order to replace something lost or damaged: *The starfish regenerated its missing arm.* **4.** to restore (a reactant) to the original condition. The chemicals in home water softeners are regenerated by flushing them with salt water. —*v.i.* **1.** to become formed anew; be reproduced. **2.** to be spiritually renewed or morally improved. —*adj.* **1.** morally or spiritually renewed. **2.** restored to a better state; renewed. [Latin *regenerātus,* past participle of *regenerāre* to bring forth again.] —**re·gen′er·a′tion,** *n.* —**re·gen′er·a′tor,** *n.*

re·gen·er·a·tive (ri jen′ə rā′tiv, -ər ə tiv) *adj.* **1.** of or relating to regeneration: *regenerative power.* **2.** tending to regenerate: *a regenerative species.*

re·gent (rē′jənt) *n.* **1.** a person who exercises royal or ruling authority in place of a monarch who is absent, incapacitated, or too young. **2.** a member of a governing board, esp. of a state college or university or a state educational system. —*adj.* acting as a regent. ➡ usually follows the noun it modifies: *a prince regent.* [Latin *regēns* ruler, from *regere* to keep straight, guide, rule.] —**re′gent·ship′,** *n.*

reg·gae (reg′ā) *n.* a style of popular music of Jamaican origin that combines elements of rock 'n' roll, blues, and calypso. Reggae

is characterized by the use of syncopation and lilting rhythms, often with lyrics of social protest. [Of uncertain origin.]

reg·i·cide¹ (rej′ə sīd′) *n.* the act of killing a king or sovereign. [Latin *rēgi-,* stem of *rēx* king + -CIDE¹.] —**reg′i·cid′al,** *adj.*

reg·i·cide² (rej′ə sīd′) *n.* a person who kills or helps to kill a king or sovereign. [Latin *rēgi-,* stem of *rēx* king + -CIDE².]

re·gime (rə zhēm′, rā-) *also,* **ré·gime.** *n.* **1.** a prevailing administration or system or form of government: *a dictatorial regime.* **2.** a social pattern or system. **3.** the period during which a particular ruler or government is in power. **4.** regimen *(def. 1).* [French *régime,* from Latin *regimen* rule, government. Doublet of REGIMEN.]

reg·i·men (rej′ə mən, -men′) *n.* **1.** a systematic, regulated course or schedule, as for diet, exercise, sleep, or study, intended to improve health or to have some specific result. Also, **regime. 2.** government; control; rule. [Latin *regimen* rule, government. Doublet of REGIME.]

reg·i·ment (*n.,* rej′ə mənt; *v.,* rej′ə ment′) *n.* a military unit usually commanded by a colonel, composed of three battalions and a headquarters, and forming part of a division. —*v.t.* **1.** to force arbitrary or rigid uniformity upon; exert strict control over: *The company regiments its workers.* **2.** to form into an organized group. **3.** to organize or put into definite order or into a rigid pattern or system, esp. to achieve regulation and control: *to regiment one's thinking.* **4.** to assign to a regiment or group. [Late Latin *regimentum* rule, government, from Latin *regere* to rule.] —**reg′i·men′tal,** *adj.* —**reg′i·men·ta′tion,** *n.*

reg·i·men·tals (rej′ə men′təlz) *pl. n.* **1.** the uniform of a regiment. **2.** any military uniform.

re·gion (rē′jən) *n.* **1.a.** a geographic area having one or more unifying characteristics, such as particular topographic features, cultural factors, or economic activities, that set it apart from other areas: *an industrial region.* **b.** in some countries or states, an administrative division. **2.** an extensive or indefinite portion of territory, space, or a surface: *the upper regions of the atmosphere.* **3.** any indefinite space, area, or portion: *the dark unknown regions of the mind.* **4.** a division or part of the body: *the abdominal region.* **5.** a sphere of interest or activity; field; realm; domain: *the region of philosophy.* [Latin *regiō* line¹, direction, district.]

re·gion·al (rē′jə nəl) *adj.* **1.** of or relating to a particular region; local; sectional. **2.** of or relating to an entire region, esp. a geographic one. —**re′gion·al·ly,** *adv.*

re·gion·al·ism (rē′jə nə liz′əm) *n.* **1.** intense devotion or partiality to a particular region of a country or other locality. **2.** an emphasis on regional customs, characteristics, or speech in literature. **3.** a word, phrase, dialect, or custom distinctive of a particular region. —**re′gion·al·ist,** *n., adj.* —**re′gion·al·is′tic,** *adj.*

reg·is·ter (rej′ə stər) *n.* **1.a.** a formal or official record, as of names, data, or transactions: *a register of volunteers.* **b.** a book or system for such records, as for public or official purposes: *a hotel register.* **c.** a single entry in such a book or record. **2.** the fact of being entered in a formal record; registration; registry; enrollment. **3.** registrar. **4.** an automatic recording or counting device, such as a cash register. **5.** a device in a heating or ventilating system, esp. an adjustable grille over an opening in a wall or floor, used to regulate the passage of air into a room. **6.** *Music.* **a.** the range of a voice or instrument, esp. a particular portion of the range in which all the tones are produced in the same manner or are of similar timbre. **b.** the set of organ pipes controlled by one stop. **7.** *Printing.* the proper alignment of various plates, stones, or screens to assure clear and accurate reproduction, as of color: *in register, off register.* **8.** *Computers.* a memory location in a central processing unit. —*v.t.* **1.** to enter or have entered in or as in a register; record: *to register the names of absent students, to register a complaint.* **2.** to enroll formally or officially, as a voter or student. **3.** to indicate or record, as on a scale: *The thermometer registered 50 degrees.* **4.** to show or express: *The child's face and tone of voice registered disappointment.* **5.** to cause, as mail, to be officially recorded by payment of a fee, so as to insure against loss, theft, or damage. —*v.i.* **1.** to enter one's name or cause it to be entered in a register: *to register at a hotel.* **2.** to enroll formally or officially. **3.** *Informal.* to make an impression. [Medieval Latin *registrum,* form of *regestum* book for records, going back to Latin *regestus,* past participle of *regerere* to record, carry back.] —**reg′is·tra·ble,** *adj.*

reg·is·tered (rej′ə stərd) *adj.* **1.** recorded in a register, esp. officially recorded to insure against loss, theft, damage, or fraud.

a	at	e	end	o	hot	u	up	hw	white		about
ā	ape	ē	me	ō	old	ū	use	ng	song		taken
ä	far	i	it	ô	fork	ü	rule	th	thin	ə	pencil
âr	care	ī	ice	oi	oil	ü	pull	th	this		lemon
			ir	pierce	ou	out	ûr	turn	zh	measure	circus

R

1015

2. enrolled and certified as having met certain technical or legal qualifications: *a registered voter.*

reg·is·tered nurse, a nurse licensed by the state in which he or she practices after completing established training and education requirements.

reg·is·trar (rej′ə strär′, rej′ə strär′) *n.* an administrative official, esp. at a college or university, in charge of keeping records. [REGISTER + -AR³.]

reg·is·tra·tion (rej′ə strā′shən) *n.* **1.** the act or an instance of registering or the state of being registered. **2.** a document verifying this: *a car registration.* **3.** entry in a register. **4.** the number of people registered; total enrollment, esp. at a college or university.

reg·is·try (rej′ə strē) *n., pl.* **-tries. 1.** the act of registering. **2.** a place where a register is kept; office of registration. **3.** register *(def. 1).*

reg·nant (reg′nənt) *adj.* **1.** exercising rule; ruling; reigning. **2.** exercising authority, sway, or influence; predominant. **3.** occurring generally; prevalent; widespread. [Latin *regnāns,* present participle of *regnāre* to reign, rule.] —**reg′nan·cy,** *n.*

reg·o·lith (reg′ə lith′) *n. Geology.* the loose rock debris and soil that overlie bedrock. Also, **mantlerock.** [Greek *rhēgos* blanket + -LITH.]

re·gress (*v.,* ri gres′; *n.,* rē′gres′) *v.i.* **1.** to go back or return. **2.** to go back to an earlier or less advanced form or state; revert. —*n.* **1.** the act of going back; return. **2.** the power or right of returning. **3.** a backward movement; retrograde motion. [Latin *regressus,* past participle of *regredī* to go back, return.] —**re·gres′sor,** *n.*

re·gres·sion (ri gresh′ən) *n.* **1.** *Biology.* a reversion to a less advanced form. **2.** *Psychoanalysis.* a reversion to an earlier, less mature behavioral pattern. **3.** a lessening of the symptoms of a disease. **4.** a backward movement, such as a retreat of the sea from land; retrograde motion.

re·gres·sive (ri gres′iv) *adj.* **1.** regressing or tending to regress. **2.** of or characterized by regression. **3.** designating or relating to a tax that decreases in rate as the amount taxed increases. —**re·gres′sive·ly,** *adv.* —**re·gres′sive·ness,** *n.*

re·gret (ri gret′) *v.t.,* **-gret·ted, -gret·ting. 1.** to feel sorry or distressed about: *I regret the loss of my friend.* **2.** to remember with a sense of loss: *to regret one's lost youth.* —*n.* **1.** a feeling of distress, misgiving, or being sorry. **2.** a sense of loss or longing. **3. regrets.** an apology offered for one's absence, esp. a polite refusal of an invitation: *to send one's regrets.* [Old French *regreter* to bewail (the dead), probably from *re-* (see RE-) + Old Norse *grāta* to lament.] —**re·gret′ta·ble,** *adj.* —**re·gret′ta·bly,** *adv.* —**re·gret′ter,** *n.*

re·gret·ful (ri gret′fəl) *adj.* full of regret; feeling or expressing regret. —**re·gret′ful·ly,** *adv.* —**re·gret′ful·ness,** *n.*

Regt. **1.** regent. **2.** regiment.

reg·u·lar (reg′yə lər) *adj.* **1.a.** conforming to or fixed by the ordinary or customary course of events; normal; usual: *regular warm spring weather.* **b.** appearing or acting in the ordinary course of events: *Our regular teacher is absent today.* **2.** occurring at fixed or uniform intervals; unvarying; steady: *regular train departures.* **3.** conforming in form or arrangement to a type or standard; evenly or uniformly arranged: *regular teeth.* **4.** following a consistent pattern of behavior; habitual: *a regular customer.* **5.** conforming to some established or prescribed rule or usage. **6.** displaying order or discipline; methodical; well-ordered: *a regular life.* **7.** of, designating, or adhering to an official party leadership, organization, and program: *a regular Republican.* **8.** belonging to, designating, or constituting a permanent or standing armed force. **9.** *Grammar.* using the usual or most common inflectional endings in conjugations and declensions. **10.** *Geometry.* having all angles and sides equal or all faces congruent: *a regular polygon, a regular polyhedron.* **11.** *Religion.* belonging to a religious order or bound by its rule, as a monk or nun. **12.** (of a flower) having symmetrical parts that are identical in shape, size, or structure. **13.** *Informal.* **a.** unmitigated; thorough; out-and-out: *a regular nuisance.* **b.** nice; agreeable; pleasant. —*n.* **1.** a soldier belonging to a permanent or standing armed force. **2.** a member of a political party who can generally be relied upon to vote for and support its candidates or position. **3.** a person who belongs to a religious order bound by certain rules. **4.** *Informal.* a person or thing that is regular. [Late Latin *rēgulāris* usual, containing rules, from Latin *rēgulāris* relating to a rule or ruler, from *rēgula* rule, ruler, model.] —**reg·u·lar·i·ty** (reg′yə lar′i tē), **reg′u·lar·ness,** *n.* —**reg′u·lar·ly,** *adv.*

> **Synonyms** *adj.* **Regular, even, uniform,** and **constant** mean remaining the same, without variation. **Regular** implies a rule or schedule that is adhered to: *the regular reappearance of flowers each spring, the review of employees on a regular basis.* **Even** suggests steadiness in level: *to keep an even temperature, an even noise level.* **Uniform** connotes an absolute sameness, as in conforming to a standard: *a uniform procedure for registration, dancers of uniform height in a chorus line.* **Constant** suggests a regularity of character in any conditions: *a constant watchfulness through the night, the constant warmth of the tropics.*

reg·u·lar·ize (reg′yə lə rīz′) *v.t.,* **-ized, -iz·ing.** to make regular; standardize. —**reg′u·la·ri·za′tion,** *n.* —**reg′u·lar·iz′er,** *n.*

reg·u·late (reg′yə lāt′) *v.t.,* **-lat·ed, -lat·ing. 1.** to manage or control according to a rule, principle, or system: *to regulate the economy, to regulate one's habits.* **2.** to adjust for accurate functioning: *to regulate a clock.* **3.** to maintain in conformity with a certain standard or requirement, as of degree, rate, or amount; keep constant: *a valve that regulates the intake of air.* **4.** to put or keep in good or proper order. [Late Latin *rēgulātus,* past participle of *rēgulāre* to direct, from Latin *rēgula* rule, ruler, model.] —**reg′u·la′tive,** *adj.*

reg·u·la·tion (reg′yə lā′shən) *n.* **1.** an authoritative order or directive intended to control behavior or procedure; governing rule or law: *customs regulations.* **2.** the act or process of regulating or the state of being regulated. —*adj.* **1.** required by or in accordance with regulation: *a regulation uniform.* **2.** usual, as though required by regulation; ordinary: *Blue jeans are regulation dress for my friends.* —For Synonyms, see **law.**

reg·u·la·tor (reg′yə lā′tər) *n.* **1.** a person or thing that regulates. **2.** a device used to adjust the speed of the balance wheel of a clock or watch. **3.** a very precise clock used as a standard of time, by which other clocks are set or automatically controlled. **4.** any of several mechanical or electrical devices for controlling or keeping something constant under changing conditions, such as the flow of liquids, gases, or electric current or the speed of an engine.

reg·u·la·to·ry (reg′yə lə tôr′ē) *adj.* **1.** tending or serving to regulate or control: *Sweating is a regulatory mechanism that lowers body temperature.* **2.** providing or issuing regulations: *The practices of airlines are under the supervision of a government regulatory agency.* **3.** of or relating to the process of regulation: *regulatory hearings.*

Reg·u·lus (reg′yə ləs) *n.* a star system in the constellation Leo, appearing to the naked eye as a very bright star. [Modern Latin *Regulus,* from Latin *rēgulus,* diminutive of *rēx* king.]

re·gur·gi·tate (rē gûr′ji tāt′) *v.,* **-tat·ed, -tat·ing.** —*v.t.* **1.** to vomit. **2.** *Informal.* to give back or cast forth something that has not been assimilated: *to regurgitate names and dates without understanding history.* —*v.i.* to rush, surge, or flow back, as liquids, gases, or undigested food. [Medieval Latin *regurgitatus,* past participle of *regurgitare* to engulf, going back to Latin *re-* back, again + *gurges* whirlpool, gulf.] —**re·gur′gi·ta′tion,** *n.*

re·hab (rē′hab′) *n.* **1.** the act or fact of restoring something to

reglaze	rehearing	reincorporate	reinject	reinstitution	reinvestigation
reglue	reheat	reincorporation	reinjection	reinstruct	reinvigorate
regrade	reheel	reincur	reinjure	reinsulate	reinvigoration
regraft	rehem	reindict	reinoculate	reintegrate	reinvite
regrind	rehire	reindictment	reinoculation	reintegration	reinvoke
regroup	rehospitalization	reinfect	reinsert	reinter	rejudge
regrow	rehospitalize	reinfection	reinsertion	reinterment	rekeyboard
regrowth	rehouse	reinflame	reinspect	reinterpret	rekindle
rehammer	reignite	reinflammation	reinspection	reinterpretation	reknit
rehandle	reignition	reinflate	reinspire	reinterrogate	relabel
rehang	reimpose	reinflation	reinstall	reinterrogation	relace
reharden	reimposition	reinhabit	reinstallation	reintroduce	relacquer
reharness	reimprison	reinitiate	reinstallment	reintroduction	reland
rehear	reimprisonment	reinitiation	reinstitute	reinvestigate	relatch

good condition. **2.** a building, esp. an apartment building, that has been renovated. —*v.t.,* **-habbed, -hab·bing.** to restore to good condition; rehabilitate. [Short for *rehab(ilitation)*.]

re·ha·bil·i·tate (rē′hə bil′i tāt′) *v.t.,* **-tat·ed, -tat·ing. 1.** to restore or bring to a state of health or useful and purposeful activity, as through training or therapy. **2.** to restore to a good condition; renovate. **3.** to restore the former rank, privileges, or good name of; reinstate. [Medieval Latin *rehabilitatus,* past participle of *rehabilitare* to restore, going back to Latin *re-* again + *habilis* fit.] —**re′ha·bil′i·ta′tion,** *n.* —**re′ha·bil′i·ta′tive,** *adj.*

re·hash (*v.,* rē hash′; *n.,* rē′hash′) *v.t.* to review or rework (old material), sometimes in different form, without improving it. —*n.* **1.** a piece of work or thought that is not original or creative. **2.** the act of rehashing.

re·hears·al (ri hûr′səl) *n.* **1.** a practice session or performance in preparation for a public or official performance: *a dance rehearsal.* **2.** the act of rehearsing.

re·hearse (ri hûrs′) *v.,* **-hearsed, -hears·ing.** —*v.t.* **1.** to practice, as a play, song, or role, in preparation for a public or official performance. **2.** to instruct or prepare by repetition or practice: *The director rehearsed the cast thoroughly.* **3.** to tell in detail; enumerate. —*v.i.* to take part in or stage a rehearsal. [Old French *rehercier* to harrow over again, repeat, from *re-* (see RE-) + *hercer* to harrow (going back to Latin *hirpex* harrow, rake). See HEARSE.]

Reich (rīk; *German* RĪКН) *n.* **1.** *German.* empire. **2.** the German state in any of several historical periods.

reichs·mark (rīks′märk′) *n., pl.* **-marks** or **-mark.** the former monetary unit of Germany. [German *Reichsmark.*]

Reichs·tag (rīks′täg′; *German* RĪКНs′täk′) *n.* the elective legislative assembly of Germany during the time of the German Empire, from 1870 to 1918, and the Weimar Republic, from 1918 to 1934. [German *Reichstag,* from *Reichs* (genitive of *Reich*) + *-tag* meeting, assembly, from Middle High German *tagen* to gather, meet (on a certain day), from *tag* day.]

reign (rān) *n.* **1.** the period of rule of a monarch or ruler. **2.** supreme power or rule, as of a monarch; sovereignty. **3.** a pervasive or dominant influence: *the reign of reason.* —*v.i.* **1.** to hold or exercise the power of a monarch or other ruler. **2.** to have a pervasive influence; hold sway; prevail: *Famine reigns over the countryside.* [Old French *regne* kingdom, from Latin *rēgnum* kingdom, rule.] —For Synonyms *(v.i.),* see **rule.**

Reign of Terror, a period of the French Revolution, from about May 1793 to July 1794, during which thousands of persons were imprisoned or guillotined as counterrevolutionaries.

re·im·burse (rē′im bûrs′) *v.t.,* **-bursed, -burs·ing.** to pay back for what has been spent, used, or lost; recompense. [RE- + obsolete *imburse* to put into a purse, from Medieval Latin *imbursare,* from Latin *in* in + Late Latin *bursa* leather bag; influenced by French *rembourser* to repay. See PURSE.] —**re′im·burs′a·ble,** *adj.* —**re′im·burse′ment,** *n.*

rein (rān) *n.* **1.** one of two or more long, narrow straps attached to a bit at either side of the mouth and used to control a horse or other draft animal. **2.** any means of guidance, restraint, or control; check: *Keep a tight rein on your temper.* —*v.t.* to guide, control, or check with or as with reins. —*v.i.* to slow down or stop a horse or other animal by means of reins (with *in* or *up*). [Old French *rene* strap of a bridle, going back to Latin *retinēre* to hold back.]

  •**to give (free) rein to.** to give complete freedom to; free from restraint: *to give one's imagination free rein.*
  •**to take the reins.** to take control: *to take the reins of a business in trouble.*

re·in·car·nate (rē′in kär′nāt) *v.t.,* **-nat·ed, -nat·ing. 1.** to cause to undergo reincarnation. **2.** to bring back in a new form: *to reincarnate a play as a musical.*

re·in·car·na·tion (rē′in kär nā′shən) *n.* **1.** in some religions, the passage of a soul at death into another body; transmigration. **2.** the belief that the soul undergoes such a passage, as in Buddhism or Hinduism. **3.** a new incarnation or embodiment.

rein·deer (rān′dîr′) *n., pl.* **-deer.** a caribou, *Rangifer tarandus,* native to Lapland and Greenland, and introduced into other northern regions, having a white, gray, or brown coat, and branched antlers in both sexes, domesticated for use as a beast of burden and as a source of meat, milk, and hides. Height: 3½-4½ feet (1.1-1.4 meters) at the shoulder. [Old Norse *hreindȳri.*]

reindeer moss, any of several spongy lichens, genus *Cladonia,* esp. *C. rangiferina,* of northern and arctic regions, eaten by reindeer, caribou, and other animals.

re·in·force (rē′in fôrs′) *also,* **reenforce, re-enforce.** *v.t.,* **-forced, -forc·ing. 1.** to strengthen by repairing or refilling or by adding some extra support, part, or material: *to reinforce a dam with sandbags.* **2.** to strengthen, esp. a military or naval force,

with additional soldiers, supplies, or equipment. **3.** to make stronger or more forceful or effective. **4.** *Psychology.* to provide usually immediate and repeated reward or punishment for (behavior) in order to encourage the retention of learning or the reappearance of a particular response. [RE- + *inforce,* form of ENFORCE.] —**re′in·forc′er,** *n.*

reinforced concrete, concrete poured around or over metal, usually steel bars or mesh, and used where extra strength is needed to support heavy weight, as in buildings, bridges, and highways. Also, **ferroconcrete.**

re·in·force·ment (rē′in fôrs′mənt) *also,* **re·en·force·ment, re-en·force·ment.** *n.* **1.** the act or process of reinforcing or the state of being reinforced. **2.** something that reinforces. **3. reinforcements.** troops, vessels, or other supplies added to those originally committed to a military action.

re·in·state (rē′in stāt′) *v.t.,* **-stat·ed, -stat·ing.** to restore to a former position or condition. —**re′in·state′ment,** *n.*

re·in·sure (rē′in shûr′) *v.t.,* **-sured, -sur·ing.** to insure again, esp. by transferring the liability to another insurance company or by taking over liability from an insurance company now assuming the risk. —**re′in·sur′er,** *n.*

re·in·vest (rē′in vest′) *v.t.* to invest (money) again, esp. to invest income from previous investments. —**re′in·vest′ment,** *n.*

re·is·sue (rē ish′ū) *n.* a reprinting or subsequent issue, as of books or stamps. —*v.t.,* **-sued, -su·ing.** to issue or come forth again.

re·it·er·ate (rē it′ə rāt′) *v.t.,* **-at·ed, -at·ing.** to say or do again or repeatedly; repeat. [Late Latin *reiterātus,* past participle of *reiterāre* to repeat, going back to Latin *re-* again + *iterum* again.] —**re·it′er·a′tion,** *n.* —**re·it′er·a′tive,** *adj.*

re·ject (*v.,* ri jekt′; *n.,* rē′jekt) *v.t.* **1.** to refuse to accept, believe, grant, or approve: *The union rejected the company's offer.* **2.** to refuse (someone) acceptance, recognition, or consideration. **3.** to throw away, set aside, or discard as worthless or defective. **4.** (of the human body) to fail to accept (an organ or tissue transplant) because of an immune reaction: *The patient's body rejected the skin graft.* —*n.* a person or thing that is rejected. [Latin *rejectus,* past participle of *reicere* to throw back, scorn.] —**re·ject′er;** *also,* **re·jec′tor,** *n.* —**re·jec′tion,** *n.* —For Synonyms *(v.t.),* see **refuse**[1].

re·joice (ri jois′) *v.,* **-joiced, -joic·ing.** —*v.i.* to express joy or be filled with joy. —*v.t.* to fill with joy; gladden. [Old French *re(s)joiss-,* a stem of *re(s)joïr* to gladden, going back to Latin *re-* again + *gaudēre* to be glad.]

re·join[1] (rē join′) *v.t.* **1.** to join the company of again. **2.** to join together again. —*v.i.* to join or become joined together again. [RE- + JOIN.]

re·join[2] (ri join′) *v.t., v.i.* to answer; reply. [Old French *rejoindre* to join again, reunite, going back to Latin *re-* again + *jungere* to unite.]

re·join·der (ri join′dər) *n.* **1.** an answer to a reply. **2.** any response.

re·ju·ve·nate (ri jü′və nāt′) *v.t.,* **-nat·ed, -nat·ing.** to make young or vigorous again. [RE- + Latin *juvenis* young + -ATE[1].] —**re·ju′ve·na′tion,** *n.* —**re·ju′ve·na′tor,** *n.*

rel. 1. relating. **2.** relative. **3.** relatively. **4.** released. **5.** religion. **6.** religious.

re·lapse (*n.,* rē′laps′; *v.,* ri laps′) *n.* the act or an instance of falling or slipping back into a former condition, esp. the recurrence of an illness after partial recovery. —*v.i.,* **-lapsed, -laps·ing.** to fall or slip back into a former condition: *to relapse into a coma, to relapse into barbarism.* [Latin *relapsus,* past participle of *relābī* to slide back.]

relapsing fever, any of a group of acute infectious diseases characterized by recurrent attacks of fever and chills, caused by a spirochete transmitted by body lice and ticks.

re·late (ri lāt′) *v.,* **-lat·ed, -lat·ing.** —*v.t.* **1.** to report the events or details of; narrate; tell; *The witness related the facts.* **2.** to show as having to do with; bring into relation; link. —*v.i.* **1.** to have connection, reference, or relation; apply; pertain (with *to*): *How does that evidence relate to the case?* **2.** to establish rapport; feel empathy (often with *to*): *to relate well to children.* [Latin *relātus,* past participle of *referre* to carry back, report.] —**re·lat′er;** *also,* **re·la′tor,** *n.*

re·lat·ed (ri lā′tid) *adj.* **1.** having relation; connected: *related problems.* **2.** allied by blood, marriage, or common biological origin: *The zebra and horse are related.* —**re·lat′ed·ness,** *n.*

a	at	e	end	o	hot	u	up	hw	white		about
ā	ape	ē	me	ō	old	ū	use	ng	song		taken
ä	far	i	it	ô	fork	ü	rule	th	thin	ə	pencil
âr	care	ī	ice	oi	oil	ů	pull	<u>th</u>	this		lemon
		îr	pierce	ou	out	ûr	turn	zh	measure		circus

R

re·la·tion (ri lā′shən) *n.* **1.** the fact or condition of involving, affecting, or having to do with another thing or things; association between two or more things: *the relation of crime to poverty.* **2.** the position of one person or thing with respect to another: *the relation of the individual to society.* **3. relations. a.** conditions or associations that bring one person or thing in contact with another; affairs; dealings: *business relations, social relations.* **b.** sexual intercourse. **4.** kinship formed by blood, marriage, or common origin. **5.** a relative. **6.a.** the act or an instance of narrating or telling. **b.** something that is narrated or told; narrative; account. [Latin *relātiō* a carrying back, report.] —**re·la′tion·al,** *adj.*
  • **in** (or **with**) **relation to. a.** with regard to; speaking of: *With relation to supplies, the expedition is ready.* **b.** in proportion to: *to spend in relation to one's income.*

re·la·tion·ship (ri lā′shən ship′) *n.* **1.** the quality or state of being related; connection; link: *the relationship between supply and demand.* **2.a.** a state of emotional involvement or interaction. **b.** any state of interaction or involvement. **3.** the condition of being allied by blood, marriage, or common origin; kinship.

rel·a·tive (rel′ə tiv) *adj.* **1.** resulting from or determined by comparison; comparative: *They retired and lived in relative isolation.* **2.** existing or having significance only in relation to something else, as the terms *right* and *left.* **3.** *Grammar.* modifying or referring to an antecedent. —*n.* **1.a.** a person allied with another by blood or marriage. **b.** an animal or plant allied with another by common origin or descent. **2.** *Grammar.* a relative word or term, esp. a relative pronoun. [Late Latin *relātīvus* having reference to, from Latin *relātus,* past participle of *referre* to carry back, report.] —**rel′a·tive·ly,** *adv.* —**rel′a·tive·ness,** *n.*
  • **relative to. a.** regarding; as to: *Relative to our slow start, we've made up most of the time.* **b.** in relation to; considering: *Relative to its large size, the city has few museums.*

relative clause, a dependent clause introduced by a relative pronoun or adverb. In the sentence *He who laughs last laughs best,* the phrase *who laughs last* is a relative clause.

relative humidity, humidity *(def. 2).*

relative pronoun, a pronoun that connects a dependent clause to a main clause and refers to a substantive in the main clause. In the sentence *He who laughs last laughs best,* the word *who* is a relative pronoun.

rel·a·tiv·ism (rel′ə tə viz′əm) *n. Philosophy.* the theory that truth and standards of judgment are relative and may vary according to the individual, time, or place.

rel·a·tiv·ist (rel′ə tə vist) *n.* a person who adheres to or advocates either relativism or the theory of relativity.

rel·a·tiv·is·tic (rel′ə tə vis′tik) *adj.* **1.** of, relating to, or characterized by relativity. **2.** *Physics.* **a.** (of a body) moving at a velocity so close to the speed of light that its mass is appreciably greater than it would be at rest. **b.** subject to the theory of relativity. —**rel′a·tiv·is′ti·cal·ly,** *adv.*

rel·a·tiv·i·ty (rel′ə tiv′i tē) *n.* **1.** the quality, state, or fact of being relative. **2.** a theory of the interdependence of space, time, energy, and gravitation, developed by the German-American physicist Albert Einstein, who based it on the principle that all motion is relative but that the speed of light is the same with respect to all observers. The **special theory of relativity** discusses the behavior of matter, energy, and light as experienced by observers who are moving in a straight line at a constant speed. Among its conclusions are that nothing can move faster than the speed of light and that mass and energy are equivalent. The **general theory of relativity** extends this theory to explain the forces of gravity acting on the motion of celestial bodies.

re·lax (ri laks′) *v.t.* **1.** to make less rigid or tense; loosen: *to relax one's grip.* **2.** to make less strict, severe, or harsh: *to relax a law.* **3.** to reduce in intensity; lessen; slacken: *to relax one's attention.* **4.** to provide release from tension or strain: *I needed a swim to relax me.* —*v.i.* **1.** to become less rigid or tense. **2.** to become less strict, severe, or harsh. **3.** to become less formal, distant, or constrained; unwind. **4.** to avoid or be relieved from work, effort, or strain; rest. [Latin *relaxāre* to loosen. Doublet of RELEASE.] —**re·laxed′,** *adj.* —**re·lax′er,** *n.*

re·lax·ant (ri lak′sənt) *n.* a drug or procedure that relaxes, esp. one that relaxes muscles: *Massage can be an effective relaxant.*

re·lax·a·tion (rē′lak sā′shən) *n.* **1.** the act of relaxing or the state of being relaxed. **2.** anything that relaxes.

re·lax·in (ri lak′sin) *n.* a female sex hormone that relaxes the pelvic ligaments, facilitating childbirth. [RELAX + -IN¹.]

re·lay (*n.,* rē′lā′; *v.,* rē′lā′, ri lā′) *n.* **1.** a fresh set or team, as of persons or animals, prepared to replace or relieve another. **2. a.** relay race. **b.** one lap or portion of a relay race. **c.** the act or an instance of changing from one teammate to another in a relay race, esp. by passing a baton. **3.** an electric switch that opens or closes in response to changes in the condition of an electric current or to mechanical forces, used esp. in telecommunications equipment. —*v.t.,* **-layed, -lay·ing. 1.** to carry forward or pass along by or as by relays. **2.** to provide with relays. **3.** to transmit or redirect by an electrical relay. [Middle French *relais* set of fresh horses or dogs (as for a hunt), going back to Old French *re-* (see RE-) + *laier* to leave (going back to Latin *laxāre* to loosen).]

re·lay (rē lā′) *v.t.,* **-laid** (-lād′), **-lay·ing.** to lay again: *to re-lay rugs after cleaning.* [RE- + LAY¹.]

re·lay race (rē′lā′) a race between two or more teams in which each team member in turn covers a portion of the total course and is then relieved by a teammate.

re·lease (ri lēs′) *v.t.,* **-leased, -leas·ing. 1.** to set free or loose from restraint, confinement, or bondage: *to release pent-up emotions, to release a hostage.* **2.** to let go or cause to be free from something that holds or fastens: *to release a brake.* **3.** to relieve from obligation or from something that burdens or oppresses: *to release someone from a promise.* **4.** to authorize or permit the publication, circulation, sale, or use of: *to release a movie for distribution.* **5.** to surrender, as a right, privilege, or claim. —*n.* **1.** the act of releasing or the state of being released. **2.** something that offers deliverance or relief, as from work or tension. **3.** a written discharge or authorization: *You can't use those files without obtaining a release.* **4.** something that is formally issued or released to the public, such as a printed statement or a movie: *a news release.* **5.** a device, such as a catch or button, that activates or releases a mechanism. **6.** a surrender, as of a right, privilege, or claim, to another. [Old French *relaissier* to leave behind, abandon, from Latin *relaxāre* to loosen. Doublet of RELAX.]

re·lease (rē lēs′) *v.t.,* **-leased, -leas·ing.** to lease again.

rel·e·gate (rel′i gāt′) *v.t.,* **-gat·ed, -gat·ing. 1.** to send away or remove, esp. to an inferior position or obscure place: *to relegate old toys to the junk pile, to be relegated to exile.* **2.** to turn over or refer (a matter or task) to another. [Latin *relegātus,* past participle of *relegāre* to send away.] —**rel′e·ga′tion,** *n.*

re·lent (ri lent′) *v.i.* to become less harsh, severe, or persistent; soften; yield. [Possibly from RE- + Latin *lentus* flexible, slow.]

re·lent·less (ri lent′lis) *adj.* **1.** not lessening in severity; pitiless; unyielding; harsh. **2.** steady and persistent; unremitting; ceaseless. —**re·lent′less·ly,** *adv.* —**re·lent′less·ness,** *n.*

rel·e·vant (rel′ə vənt) *adj.* bearing upon or connected with the matter in hand; appropriate; pertinent: *a relevant question.* [French *relevant,* present participle of *relever* to raise up, help, from Latin *relevāre.*] —**rel′e·vance, rel′e·van·cy,** *n.* —**rel′e·vant·ly,** *adv.* —For Synonyms, see pertinent.

re·li·a·ble (ri lī′ə bəl) *adj.* able to be depended on with confidence; trustworthy: *a reliable firm.* —**re·li′a·bil′i·ty, re·li′a·ble·ness,** *n.* —**re·li′a·bly,** *adv.*

re·li·ance (ri lī′əns) *n.* **1.** the act of relying. **2.** the condition of trusting; confidence or dependence: *We must have the public's reliance if our business is to succeed.* **3.** a person or thing relied on; mainstay. —For Synonyms, see trust.

re·li·ant (ri lī′ənt) *adj.* having or showing reliance. —**re·li′ant·ly,** *adv.*

rel·ic (rel′ik) *n.* **1.** a remaining portion or fragment that has survived decay, destruction, or the passage of time; remnant: *relics of the ancient Roman civilization.* **2.** a surviving trace, as of some past or outmoded custom, institution, or belief. **3.** the body or part of the body of a saint, martyr, or other venerated person, or some object associated with him or her, often enshrined as a memorial. **4.** something that is cherished for its age or sentimental associations; memento; keepsake. **5.** *Informal.* any person or thing of great age. **6.** *Archaic.* corpse; remains. [Old French *reliques* remains of a saint after death, remains (as of a meal), from Latin *reliquiae* remains.]

rel·ict (rel′ikt) *n.* **1.** *Biology.* a species surviving in isolation as a remnant of a former period or of an almost extinct group. **2.** *Geology.* a persistent physical feature, as a ridge or pinnacle, remaining after a more extensive formation has been worn away. [Latin *relictus,* past participle of *relinquere* to leave behind.]

relaunch	relet	relicense	relink	relitigate	relubricate
relaunder	reletter	relight	reliquefy	reload	remagnetize
relearn	relevel	relimit	reliquidate	reloan	remagnify
relend	relevy	reline	reliquidation	relock	remail

re·lief¹ (ri lēf′) *n.* **1.** the freeing from or alleviating of physical or mental discomfort: *We sought relief from the heat in the shady garden. The audience longed for relief from the play's tension.* **2.** something that so frees or alleviates. **3.** financial assistance from government funds to those in poverty or need: *to go on relief.* **4.** aid or assistance, as to those in poverty or need: *relief for flood victims.* **5.** release from a post or duty, as by the substitution of a person or persons for another. **6.** a person or persons so substituting for another. [Old French *relief* reparation, act of restoring, from *relever.* See RELIEVE.]

re·lief² (ri lēf′) *n.* **1.** distinctness or prominence resulting from contrast: *The gnarled tree stood in bold relief against the clear sky.* **2.a.** the variation in elevation of an area of the earth's surface, esp. as depicted by a contour line on a topographic map. **b.** the difference in elevation between the highest and lowest parts of an area: *Rugged, mountainous areas have high relief.* **3.a.** the projection of a figure or design from a flat surface or ground, as in sculpture or architecture. **b.** the art or process of projecting a figure or design from such a surface, as by cutting, engraving, or sculpting. **c.** a work executed by this process. **4.** the illusion of depth created in a painting or drawing by the apparent projection of a figure or object from the surface, obtained by the use of line, shading, or color. [French *relief,* from Italian *rilievo* projection; literally, a raising, going back to Latin *relevāre* to raise again.]

architectural **relief**
on a temple in India

relief map, a map that shows the variations in elevation and other physical features of an area of the earth's surface by means of contour lines, shading, color, or molding.

relief pitcher, a pitcher who enters a baseball game to take the place of another pitcher. Also, **reliever.**

re·lieve (ri lēv′) *v.t.,* **-lieved, -liev·ing. 1.** to remove or make less or easier to bear; reduce: *This lotion relieves itching.* **2.** to free from pain, anxiety, discomfort, or the like. **3.** to free from a post or duty by providing or serving as a substitute: *The corporal will relieve the sentry in an hour. Our new pitcher relieved the starter in the sixth inning.* **4.** to furnish aid to. **5.** to break monotony through contrast or variety. [Old French *relever* to raise again, revive, restore, from Latin *relevāre* to raise again.]
 • **to relieve of.** to rid of or take from: *The bellhop relieved me of my packages.*

re·liev·er (ri lē′vər) *n.* **1.** relief pitcher. **2.** a person or thing that relieves.

re·lie·vo (ri lē′vō) *n., pl.* **-vos.** relief² *(def. 3).* [Italian *rilievo* projection, from *rilevare* to raise, protrude, from Latin *relevāre* to raise again.]

re·li·gion (ri lij′ən) *n.* **1.** belief in, reverence for, or worship of a divine or supernatural being or beings or power, often thought of as having created or as governing the universe. **2.a.** a system, esp. an institutionalized one, of such belief and worship, often involving the observance of particular doctrines and practices. **b.** the body of adherents to such a system, or the organization carrying on its observance: *to belong to a religion.* **3.** any object or principle attended to with devotion or conscientiousness. [Latin *religiō* reverence for the gods.]

re·li·gi·os·i·ty (ri lij′ē os′i tē) *n.* religious feeling or sentiment, esp. excessive or affected piety. —**re·li·gi·ose** (ri lij′ē ōs′, -lij′ē-ōs′), *adj.*

re·li·gious (ri lij′əs) *adj.* **1.** imbued with, adhering to, or showing devotion to a religion; pious. **2.** of, relating to, or involving religion: *religious instruction, religious beliefs.* **3.** scrupulously careful and exact; conscientious; strict: *to pay religious attention*

to details. **4.** of or relating to an order bound by monastic vows. —*n., pl.* **-gious. 1.** a person bound by monastic vows, such as a monk or nun. **2.** such persons collectively. [Latin *religiōsus* pious, from *religiō* reverence for the gods.] —**re·li′gious·ly,** *adv.* —**re·li′gious·ness,** *n.* —For Synonyms *(adj.),* see **pious.**

re·lin·quish (ri ling′kwish) *v.t.* **1.** to give over possession or control of; surrender; yield: *to relinquish territory, to relinquish a right.* **2.** to put aside or give up; abandon: *to relinquish a plan.* **3.** to let go, as a grasp; release: *to relinquish one's hold.* [Old French *relinquiss-,* a stem of *relinquir* to abandon, leave, from Latin *relinquere* to leave behind.] —**re·lin′quish·ment,** *n.*

rel·i·quar·y (rel′i kwer′ē) *n., pl.* **-quar·ies.** a receptacle, often of precious metal and richly decorated, for a religious relic or relics. [Old French *reliquaire,* going back to Latin *reliquiae* remains.]

rel·ish (rel′ish) *n.* **1.a.** a mixture of spices and chopped vegetables, such as pickles or other food, used chiefly as a condiment or as a side dish. **b.** a food, such as celery, olives, or pickles, to be eaten with other food as a garnish or appetizer or to add flavor. **2.** pleasurable enjoyment; eager appetite; zest: *to plan a trip with relish.* **3.** anything that lends pleasure, zest, or interest; attractive quality. **4.** a zestful, pleasing, or appetizing flavor. **5.** a trace or suggestion, as of a quality or characteristic. —*v.t.* **1.** to take pleasure in; savor; enjoy: *to relish a summer afternoon.* **2.** to give a pleasant flavor to. [Old French *reles* remainder, from *relaissier* to leave behind (referring to the good taste that is left behind). See RELEASE.]

re·live (rē liv′) *v.t.,* **-lived, -liv·ing.** to live over again, esp. in the mind: *to relive one's childhood.*

re·lo·cate (rē lō′kāt) *v.,* **-cat·ed, -cat·ing.** —*v.t.* to move (a business office, employee, or the like) to another place. —*v.i.* to move to another place.

re·luc·tance (ri luk′təns) *n.* **1.** the state of being reluctant; unwillingness. **2.** *Physics.* the resistance that magnetic flux encounters in passing through a closed circuit of magnetic material.

re·luc·tant (ri luk′tənt) *adj.* **1.** feeling hesitation; unwilling; averse: *I am reluctant to lend anyone my books.* **2.** marked by unwillingness or hesitation. [Latin *reluctāns,* present participle of *reluctārī* to struggle against, going back to *re-* back + *lucta* wrestling.] —**re·luc′tant·ly,** *adv.*

re·ly (ri lī′) *v.i.,* **-lied, -ly·ing. 1.** to have confidence; trust: *You can rely on me to be prompt.* **2.** to be dependent on; require: *We rely on the sun for heat.* [Old French *relier* to bind together, from Latin *religāre* to bind fast.]

rem (rem) *n.* a unit for measuring quantities of biologically absorbed ionizing radiation, equivalent to 1 roentgen of X rays.

REM (rem) *n.* the quick, frequent eye movements that occur during the dreaming period of sleep. [Short for *r(apid) e(ye) m(ovement).*]

re·main (ri mān′) *v.i.* **1.** to continue in the same place; stay; abide: *We should have remained at home.* **2.** to continue unchanged or in the same state; go on being: *We remained fast friends for years.* **3.** to be left, as after the removal, departure, or destruction of all else: *Only the walls of the old house remain.* **4.** to be left as still to be dealt with: *That remains to be seen.* [Old French *remaindre* to stay behind, from Latin *remanēre.*]

re·main·der (ri mān′dər) *n.* **1.** something that remains or is left; remaining part: *We played tennis for the remainder of the day.* **2.** *Mathematics.* **a.** the number found when one number is subtracted from another, for example: 10 subtracted from 12 leaves a remainder of 2. **b.** the number remaining when one number is divided by another, for example: 7 divided by 3 gives 2 and a remainder of 1. **3.** a copy of a book remaining with a publisher, esp. after the demand for it has fallen off. —*v.t.* to dispose of or sell, usually at a reduced price, as a book or clothing.

Synonyms *n.* **Remainder, rest**², **balance,** and **residue** denote something left over. **Remainder** is used generally of a thing or things left after a part or parts of the whole are removed: *the remainder of the audience, to take a slice of bread and pass the remainder.* **Rest** is used in much the same way, but sounds less formal: *We went to the movies, leaving the rest of our crowd to watch the game.* **Balance** is more formal, and is used chiefly in speaking of such matters as finances and parts of some formal structure: *After expenses were paid, a very small balance remained in our bank accounts. The first act was inspired, but the balance of the play did not live up to its promise.* **Residue** has a

a	at	e	end	o	hot	u	up	hw	white		about
ā	ape	ē	me	ō	old	ū	use	ng	song		taken
ä	far	i	it	ô	fork	ü	rule	th	thin	ə	pencil
âr	care	ī	ice	oi	oil	u̇	pull	t͟h	this		lemon
				îr	pierce	ou	out	ûr	turn	zh	measure		circus

more technical sound, connoting what is left over after some process: *When the fire went out, an ashy residue was left in the fireplace.*

re·mains (ri mānz′) *pl. n.* **1.** something that remains or is left: *the remains of ancient Rome.* **2.** a dead body; corpse. **3.** writings left unpublished when an author dies.

re·make (*n.,* rē′māk′; *v.,* rē māk′) *n.* **1.** something made again or anew: *a remake of an old motion picture.* **2.** the act of making something again or anew: *A remake is scheduled for tomorrow.* —*v.t.,* **-made, -mak·ing.** to make again or anew.

re·mand (ri mand′) *v.t.* **1.** to send, call, or order back: *to remand a soldier to a post.* **2.** *Law.* **a.** to return (a prisoner or an accused person) to custody. **b.** to send (a case) back to a lower court for further proceedings. —*n.* the act of remanding or the state of being remanded. [Late Latin *remandāre* to send back word, from Latin *re-* back + *mandāre* to order, consign.]

rem·a·nence (rem′ə nəns) *n. Physics.* the magnetization or magnetic flux remaining in a ferromagnetic substance after the magnetizing force or field has been withdrawn or reduced to zero. [Based on Latin *remanentis,* genitive of *remanens,* present participle of *remanere* to remain behind, stay.]

re·mark (ri märk′) *n.* **1.** an oral or written statement or observation, esp. a brief or casual comment. **2.** the act of taking notice or observing; notice: *a discovery worthy of remark.* —*v.t.* **1.** to express as an opinion or observation. **2.** to take notice of; observe; perceive. —*v.i.* to make remarks (with *on* or *upon*). [French *remarquer* to note, heed, from *re-* (see RE-) + *marquer* to mark (of Germanic origin).] —**re·mark′er,** *n.*

re·mark·a·ble (ri mär′kə bəl) *adj.* **1.** worthy of notice or likely to be noticed. **2.** having unusual qualities; extraordinary; uncommon. —**re·mark′a·ble·ness,** *n.* —**re·mark′a·bly,** *adv.*

re·mar·ry (rē mar′ē) *v.,* **-ried, -ry·ing.** —*v.i.* to marry again after being widowed or divorced. —*v.t.* to marry (a former spouse) again. —**re·mar·riage** (rē mar′ij), *n.*

re·me·di·a·ble (ri mē′dē ə bəl) *adj.* capable of being remedied or cured. —**re·me′di·a·ble·ness,** *n.* —**re·me′di·a·bly,** *adv.*

re·me·di·al (ri mē′dē əl) *adj.* **1.** providing or intended to provide a remedy. **2.** intended to overcome a deficiency or eliminate a difficulty: *a remedial reading program.* [Late Latin *remediālis* healing, from Latin *remedium.* See REMEDY.] —**re·me′di·al·ly,** *adv.*

rem·e·dy (rem′i dē) *n., pl.* **-dies. 1.** something, such as a medicine or treatment, that relieves or is intended to relieve a disease, disorder, or the like: *a headache remedy.* **2.** something that corrects, counteracts, or eliminates an evil: *a remedy for air pollution.* —*v.t.,* **-died, -dy·ing. 1.** to cause (a disease or disorder) to heal or improve, as by medicinal treatment. **2.** to set or make right; correct: *to remedy conditions in the slums.* [Latin *remedium* medicine, cure.] —For Synonyms *(v.t.),* see **cure.**

re·mem·ber (ri mem′bər) *v.t.* **1.** to bring back or recall to the mind or memory; recollect: *Try to remember where you put the keys.* **2.** to have come back into mind: *I just remembered a funny story.* **3.** to keep in mind carefully: *to remember an appointment.* **4.** to think of or keep in mind as worthy of affection, regard, or recognition: *I'll always remember you for your kindness.* **5.** to reward or present with a gift, such as a legacy or tip. **6.** to convey greetings from (with *to*): *Remember me to your parents.* —*v.i.* **1.** to have or use the faculty of memory. **2.** to keep something specific in mind or recall it to mind. [Old French *remembrer* to recall, from Late Latin *rememorārī,* going back to Latin *re-* again + *memor* mindful.]

> **Synonyms** **Remember, recollect,** and **recall** mean to bring to mind something from the past. **Remember** often implies an act that is effortless or involuntary: *I remember my European vacation fondly. She could remember people's faces, but not their names.* **Recollect** suggests a conscious effort to reconstruct past events: *Try as I may, I cannot recollect many details of my childhood.* **Recall** is often used to describe the bringing to mind of a specific fact or image: *As I recall, you were born in Chicago.*

re·mem·brance (ri mem′brəns) *n.* **1.** something that is remembered; recollection. **2.** the act or power of remembering or the state of being remembered. **3.** an object, such as a gift, serving to bring or keep in mind someone or something; memento; keepsake. **4.** the length of time over which one's memory extends: *It's the coldest winter in my remembrance.* —For Synonyms, see **keepsake, memory.**

re·mind (ri mīnd′) *v.t.* to make (a person) think of someone or something; to cause to remember. —**re·mind′er,** *n.*

rem·i·nisce (rem′ə nis′) *v.i.,* **-nisced, -nisc·ing.** to think or tell of past experiences or events: *We reminisced about home.*

rem·i·nis·cence (rem′ə nis′əns) *n.* **1.** the act of thinking or talking about past experiences or events. **2.** *also,* **reminiscences.** a narration or account of past experiences or events. **3.** something remembered; memory. **4.** something that recalls, suggests, or is a reminder of something else. [Late Latin *reminiscentia* remembrance, from Latin *reminiscī* to remember.]

rem·i·nis·cent (rem′ə nis′ənt) *adj.* **1.** reminding or suggestive of; calling up (with *of*): *This landscape is reminiscent of home.* **2.** marked by or given to reminiscence: *to become reminiscent about old times.*

re·miss (ri mis′) *adj.* **1.** failing to take proper care or make necessary efforts; careless or negligent; lax. **2.** characterized by a lack of earnestness, energy, or attention. [Latin *remissus,* past participle of *remittere* to send back, slacken.] —**re·miss′ly,** *adv.* —**re·miss′ness,** *n.*

re·mis·si·ble (ri mis′ə bəl) *adj.* capable of being remitted or pardoned, as a sin. —**re·mis′si·bil′i·ty,** *n.*

re·mis·sion (ri mish′ən) *n.* **1.** the act of remitting or the state of being remitted. **2.** release from penalty or guilt; pardon. **3.** an abatement, esp. a temporary one, of pain or the symptoms of a disease. **4.** a lessening of degree or intensity. **5.** cancellation, as of a debt.

re·mit (ri mit′) *v.,* **-mit·ted, -mit·ting.** —*v.t.* **1.** to send (money), as in payment. **2.** to release from the penalty or guilt of, as a sin or offense; pardon; forgive: *to remit sins.* **3.** to refrain from exacting or inflicting; cancel: *to remit punishment.* **4.** to allow to slacken or abate, as vigilance: *to remit one's efforts.* **5.** to submit or refer for consideration, decision, or action, esp. to one in authority. **6.** *Law.* to send (a case) back to a lower court for further proceedings. —*v.i.* **1.** to send money, as in payment. **2.** to become less; abate; diminish: *The child's fever remitted.* [Latin *remittere* to send back, slacken, forgive.] —**re·mit′ta·ble,** *adj.* —**re·mit′ter,** *n.*

re·mit·tal (ri mit′əl) *n.* remission.

re·mit·tance (ri mit′əns) *n.* **1.** the sending of money or its equivalent. **2.** the money or its equivalent sent.

re·mit·tent (ri mit′ənt) *adj.* characterized by abatements in severity: *a remittent heat wave.* —**re·mit′tent·ly,** *adv.*

rem·nant (rem′nənt) *n.* **1.a.** a remaining quantity, part, or piece; remainder; fragment: *remnants of a meal.* **b.** a surviving trace or vestige, as of a former time or condition. **2.** an odd piece of cloth, as at the end of a bolt, left over from the cutting of a larger piece, often sold at a reduced price. [Old French *remanant* residue, from *remanoir* to stay behind, from Latin *remanēre.*]

re·mod·el (rē mod′əl) *v.t.,* **-eled, -el·ing;** *also, British,* **-elled, -el·ling.** to make over or anew, as with a new structure; reconstruct; renovate.

re·mon·strance (ri mon′strəns) *n.* the act or an instance of remonstrating; protest.

re·mon·strant (ri mon′strənt) *adj.* that remonstrates. —*n.* a person who remonstrates.

re·mon·strate (ri mon′strāt) *v.,* **-strat·ed, -strat·ing.** —*v.t.* to say or plead in protest, opposition, or disapproval: *The neighborhood remonstrated that the new road would increase noise and pollution.* —*v.i.* to present reasons in complaint or objection; plead or argue in protest. [Medieval Latin *remonstratus,* past participle of *remonstrare* to demonstrate, going back to Latin *re-* again, back + *mōnstrāre* to show.] —**re·mon·stra·tion** (rē′mən strā′shən), *n.* —**re·mon·stra·tive** (ri mon′strə tiv), *adj.* —**re·mon′stra·tor,** *n.*

rem·o·ra (rem′ər ə) *n.* any of a group of fish of the family Echeneididae, found mainly in tropical seas, that attach themselves to sharks and other larger fish by means of a suction disk on the top of their heads. Remoras feed on parasitic crustaceans attached to their hosts or on food left over by their hosts.

re·morse (ri môrs′) *n.* a deep, painful feeling of guilt, sorrow, or distress for wrongdoing or past misdeeds. —**re·morse′ful,** *adj.* —**re·morse′ful·ly,** *adv.* —**re·morse′ful·ness,** *n.* —For Synonyms, see **penitence.**

re·morse·less (ri môrs′lis) *adj.* having no pity or compassion; merciless. —**re·morse′less·ly,** *adv.* —**re·morse′less·ness,** *n.*

re·mote (ri mōt′) *adj.,* **-mot·er, -mot·est. 1.** situated at a distance; not near; far away or off: *remote regions.* **2.** located out

remanufacture	rematch	rememorize	remix	remodify	remultiplication
remap	remeasure	remigrate	remobilization	remoisten	remultiply
remarket	remeet	remilitarization	remobilize	remold	rename
remarshal	remelt	remilitarize	remodification	remortgage	reneutralize

of the way; secluded: *a remote corner of the park.* **3.** far removed from the present; distant in time: *the remote past.* **4.** small in degree; slight; faint: *a remote possibility.* **5.** having no close or immediate connection or bearing: *a question remote from the topic under consideration.* **6.** not closely related by blood or marriage: *a remote ancestor.* **7.** lacking warmth and friendliness; aloof and cool; reserved. —*n.* remote control *(def. 2).* [Latin *remōtus* far off, past participle of *removēre* to move back.] —**re·mote′ly**, *adv.* —**re·mote′ness**, *n.*

remote control **1.** control from a distance of a machine or apparatus, such as a guided missile or television, esp. by means of radio signals. **2.** a device used for remote control. Also *(def. 2),* **remote.**

re·mount (*v.,* rē mount′; *n.,* rē′mount′) *v.t.* to mount (something) again: *The riders remounted their horses. The insect collector remounted several specimens.* —*v.i.* to mount again. —*n.* a fresh horse that takes the place of another.

re·mov·al (ri mū′vəl) *n.* **1.** the act or process of removing or the state of being removed. **2.** a changing of place or relocation, as of a business. **3.** dismissal, as from an office or position.

re·move (ri mūv′) *v.,* **-moved, -mov·ing.** —*v.t.* **1.** to take or move away, as from one place or position to another: *to remove dishes from a table.* **2.** to take off or shed, as an article of clothing. **3.** to do away with; eliminate: *to remove all cause for alarm.* **4.** to dismiss from an office or position. **5.** to take or withdraw; separate; extract (with *from*): *to remove a mineral from an ore.* **6.** to assassinate; murder. —*v.i.* **1.** to change one's place of residence or business; move. **2.** to be or be able to be removed: *Mud removes easily with warm water.* —*n.* **1.** a distance or interval separating one person or thing from another. **2.** a step, as in a graded scale. **3.** the act of removing; removal. [Old French *removoir* to take away, from Latin *removēre* to move back, take away.] —**re·mov′a·ble**, *adj.* —**re·mov′er**, *n.*

re·moved (ri mūvd′) *adj.* **1.** separated by a generation in relationship: *My parents' cousins are my cousins once removed.* **2.** distant; remote.

re·mu·ner·ate (ri mū′nə rāt′) *v.t.,* **-at·ed, -at·ing.** **1.** to pay an equivalent to (someone) for a service, loss, or expense; reward; repay. **2.** to compensate for: *I hope this will remunerate your efforts.* [Latin *remūnerātus,* past participle of *remūnerāre* to reward, repay.] —**re·mu′ner·a′tion,** *n.*

re·mu·ner·a·tive (ri mū′nə rā′tiv, -nər ə tiv) *adj.* **1.** tending to be well remunerated; lucrative; profitable: *a remunerative profession.* **2.** that remunerates. —**re·mu′ner·a′tive·ly,** *adv.* —**re·mu′ner·a′tive·ness,** *n.*

Re·mus (rē′məs) see **Romulus.**

Renaissance painting by Pesellino

ren·ais·sance (ren′ə säns′, -zäns′, ren′ə säns′, -zäns′, ri nā′səns) *also,* **renascence.** *n.* **1.** a renewal of activity, interest, or enthusiasm concerning something; rebirth; revival. **2. Renaissance. a.** a movement regarded as having originated in Italy in the fourteenth century, marked by a growth of interest in classical literature and art, the growth of individualism, and intellectual, scientific, and artistic activity. **b.** the period of European history during which this occurred, extending from the fourteenth through the sixteenth century. **c.** any of various styles of art, as in painting, sculpture, and architecture, developed during and characteristic of this period. **3.** *also,* **Renaissance.** any movement or period of flourishing artistic and intellectual activity. —*adj.* **Renaissance.** of, characteristic of, or in the style of the Renais-

sance. [French *renaissance* rebirth, renewal, from *renaître* to be born again, from Latin *renāscī.*]

re·nal (rē′nəl) *adj.* of, relating to, or near the kidneys: *a renal artery.* [Late Latin *rēnālis,* from Latin *rēn* kidney.]

re·nas·cence (ri nas′əns, -nā′səns) renaissance.

re·nas·cent (ri nas′ənt, -nā′sənt) *adj.* showing renewed growth or vigor; being born again; resurgent. [Latin *renāscēns,* present participle of *renāscī* to be born again.]

rend (rend) *v.,* **rent** (rent) *or* **rend·ed, rend·ing.** —*v.t.* **1.** to split or tear apart or into pieces forcibly or violently: *The gale rent the sails.* **2.** to divide or split into parts as if by tearing: *Racial strife rent the community.* **3.** to remove forcibly, as from a place or position; wrest. **4.** to pass through or disturb suddenly or sharply; pierce: *Screams rent the stillness.* **5.** to distress violently or painfully. —*v.i.* to become split or torn; come apart. [Old English *rendan* to tear.] —For Synonyms *(v.t.),* see **tear.**

ren·der (ren′dər) *v.t.* **1.** to cause to be or become; make: *to render someone speechless.* **2.** to give or pay as something owed or due: *to render an apology.* **3.** to give or make available; furnish; provide: *to render aid to the needy.* **4.** to give in return or requital. **5.** to perform; do; execute: *to render a service.* **6.** to represent or depict, as in painting. **7.** to present and interpret in performance, as a role or piece of music. **8.** to deliver or state formally: *The jury rendered a verdict of not guilty.* **9.** to reproduce or express in another language; translate. **10.** to offer or submit, as for consideration, approval, or payment: *to render a bill.* **11.** to give up; surrender; yield (often with *up*). **12.a.** to separate, clarify, or extract by melting: *to render lard from fat.* **b.** to melt down in order to do this: *to render fat.* [Old French *rendre* to give back, yield, going back to Latin *reddere;* influenced by Latin *prendere* to take.] —**ren′der·a·ble,** *adj.* —**ren′der·er,** *n.*

ren·dez·vous (rän′də vū′, -dā-) *n., pl.* **-vous** (-vūz′). **1.** an appointment to meet at a fixed place or time. **2.a.** the place appointed for such a meeting. **b.** the meeting itself. **3.** a meeting of a spacecraft with another object in outer space. **4.** any meeting or gathering place. —*v.t., v.i.,* **-voused** (-vūd′), **-vous·ing** (-vū′ing). to meet or cause to meet by arrangement. [French *rendez-vous* appointment, place of meeting, from *rendez-vous,* imperative of *se rendre* to betake oneself, yield. See **RENDER.**] —For Synonyms *(n.),* see **appointment.**

ren·di·tion (ren dish′ən) *n.* **1.a.** an interpretation given by a performer to an artistic, dramatic, or musical composition. **b.** a performance of such a composition. **2.** an interpretation or version of a text; translation. **3.** the act of rendering. [Obsolete French *rendition* a giving back, from Old French *rendre* to give back. See **RENDER.**]

ren·e·gade (ren′i gād′) *n.* **1.** a person who abandons, rejects, or turns against a group, religion, cause, or allegiance, often in favor of another; turncoat; apostate. **2.** outlaw. —*adj.* acting as or characteristic of a renegade; traitorous: *a renegade soldier.* [Spanish *renegado* apostate, from Medieval Latin *renegatus,* past participle of *renegare* to deny, from Latin *re-* again + *negāre* to deny.]

re·nege (ri nig′, -neg′, -nēg′, -nāg′) *v.i.,* **-neged, -neg·ing.** **1.** to fail to fulfill a promise or commitment: *to renege on a business deal.* **2.** *Card Games.* to fail to play a card of the suit led when the rules require such play and the player is able to make such a play. —*n. Card Games.* the act or an instance of reneging. [Medieval Latin *renegare* to deny. See **RENEGADE.**] —**re·neg′er,** *n.*

re·ne·go·ti·ate (rē′ni gō′shē āt′) *v.t., v.i.,* **-at·ed, -at·ing.** to negotiate again or anew, esp. to achieve more favorable conditions: *to renegotiate a contract.* —**re·ne·go′tia·ble** (rē′ni gō′-shə bəl, -shē ə bəl), *adj.* —**re′ne·go′ti·a′tion,** *n.* —**re′ne·go′-ti·a′tor,** *n.*

re·new (ri nū′, -nū′) *v.t.* **1.** to make new or as if new again; restore to a previous or sound condition; revive: *to renew one's energy by resting.* **2.** to begin again or start over; take up again; resume: *to renew a discussion.* **3.** to cause to continue in effect: *to renew a subscription, to renew a lease.* **4.** to say again, as if to reaffirm; repeat: *to renew an oath.* **5.** to bring back into use or existence; reestablish. **6.** to replace with something new of the same sort; fill again; replenish: *The ship renewed its provisions.* **7.** to make new spiritually; regenerate. —*v.i.* **1.** to become new or as if new again. **2.** to begin anew or start over; resume.

re·new·a·ble (ri nū′ə bəl, -nū′-) *adj.* **1.** able to be renewed or repeated: *This prescription is renewable three times.* **2.** able to be replaced or restored: *Lumber is a renewable natural resource.* —**re·new′a·bil′i·ty,** *n.*

a	at	e	end	o	hot	u	up	hw	white		about
ā	ape	ē	me	ō	old	ū	use	ng	song		taken
ä	far	i	it	ô	fork	ü	rule	th	thin	ə	pencil
âr	care	ī	ice	oi	oil	ú	pull	th	this		lemon
		îr	pierce	ou	out	ûr	turn	zh	measure		circus

R

re·new·al (ri nü′əl, -nū′-) *n.* **1.** the act or an instance of renewing or the state of being renewed. **2.** something renewed.

ren·i·form (ren′ə fôrm′, rē′nə-) *adj.* having the form of a kidney; kidney-shaped. [Latin *rēn* kidney + -FORM.]

ren·net (ren′it) *n.* a curdling agent containing rennin, obtained from the stomachs of young calves and added to milk to make cheese. [Possibly from an unrecorded Old English word.]

ren·nin (ren′in) *n.* an enzyme present in the gastric juice of certain mammals, esp. human infants and calves, that curdles milk into a pulpy mass. [RENNET + -IN[1].]

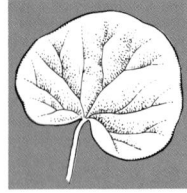

reniform leaf

re·nounce (ri nouns′) *v.t.,* **-nounced, -nounc·ing. 1.** to give up or abandon, esp. by formal declaration: *to renounce a claim.* **2.** to refuse to recognize or accept as one's own; repudiate; disown: *to renounce one's family.* [Old French *renoncer* to abandon entirely, from Latin *renūntiāre* to report, disclaim.] —**re·nounce′ment,** *n.* —**re·nounc′er,** *n.*

ren·o·vate (ren′ə vāt′) *v.,* **-vat·ed, -vat·ing.** —*v.t.* to make new or like new, esp. by extensive repair or alteration: *to renovate a building.* —*v.i.* to make changes or improvements; redecorate: *We renovated before moving into the house.* [Latin *renovātus,* past participle of *renovāre* to renew.] —**ren′o·va′tion,** *n.* —**ren′o·va′tive,** *adj.* —**ren′o·va′tor,** *n.*

re·nown (ri noun′) *n.* widespread reputation; fame. [Anglo-Norman *renoun,* going back to Latin *re-* again + *nōmen* name.]

re·nowned (ri nound′) *adj.* having renown; famous. —For Synonyms, see **famous.**

rent[1] (rent) *n.* **1.** a payment for the use or occupation of property, esp. such payment made periodically by a tenant to a landlord or owner. **2.** *Economics.* the income from the use or occupation of property. —*v.t.* **1.** to obtain the right to use or occupy (property) in return for the paying of rent: *to rent a car, to rent a house.* **2.** to grant the use or occupancy of (property) in return for the paying of rent (often with *out*): *to rent out a house, a store that rents bicycles.* —*v.i.* to be for rent: *The apartment rents by the month.* [Old French *rente* revenue, income, going back to Latin *reddita,* feminine past participle of *reddere* to give back.] —**rent′a·ble,** *adj.* —For Synonyms (*v.t.*), see **lease.**

·**for rent.** available for use or occupancy in return for the paying of rent.

rent[2] (rent) *v.* a past tense and past participle of **rend.** —*n.* **1.** an opening or hole made by rending or tearing; gap: *a rent in a dress, a rent in a wall.* **2.** a sharp division or split, as in a group or organization; schism: *a rent in a political party.* [From dialectal English *rent* to tear, form of REND.]

rent·al (ren′tal) *n.* **1.** an amount charged, paid, or collected as rent. **2.** the act of renting. **3.** property rented or available for renting. —*adj.* of, relating to, or for rent or renting: *a car rental agency, a rental car.*

rent·er (ren′tər) *n.* a person or organization that uses or occupies property through the payment of rent.

rent strike, an organized refusal by tenants to pay rent, usually in protest against increases in rent or against poor service.

re·nun·ci·a·tion (ri nun′sē ā′shən) *n.* the act or an instance of renouncing. [Latin *renūntiātiō.*] —**re·nun′ci·a′tive, re·nun·ci·a·to·ry** (ri nun′sē ə tôr′ē), *adj.*

re·o·pen (rē ō′pən) *v.t., v.i.* **1.** to open something again: *to reopen a container, to reopen for business.* **2.** to begin something again; resume: *to reopen discussion.*

re·or·der (rē ôr′dər) *v.t.* **1.** to order or organize in a new or different way; rearrange: *to reorder the books on a shelf.* **2.** to order again: *to reorder supplies.* **3.** to restore to proper or original order; put back in order. —*v.i.* to order something again. —*n.* a second or repeated order, as for goods or materials.

re·or·gan·i·za·tion (rē′ôr gə nə zā′shən) *n.* **1.** the act of reorganizing or the state of being reorganized. **2.** the thorough reconstruction of a business corporation, as after bankruptcy, involving a change in capital structure.

re·or·gan·ize (rē ôr′gə nīz′) *v.t., v.i.,* **-ized, -iz·ing.** to organize something again or anew. —**re·or′gan·iz′er,** *n.*

rep (rep) *also,* **repp.** *n.* a fabric made of cotton, wool, silk, or rayon, having alternating large and small ribs and often used for upholstery and drapes. [French *reps;* of uncertain origin.]

rep. 1. report. **2.** reporter. **3.** representative. **4.** republic.

Rep., Republican.

re·paid (ri pād′) the past tense and past participle of **repay.**

re·pair[1] (ri pâr′) *v.t.* **1.** to restore to a sound condition or working order, as by replacing parts or putting together what has broken; fix; mend: *to repair a toaster, to repair a highway.* **2.** to correct or eliminate by repairing: *The plumber repaired the leaks.* **3.** to bring back to a sound or healthy state; renew: *to repair damaged body tissues.* **4.** to make up for; set right; remedy: *to repair a wrong.* —*n.* **1.** the act or process of repairing: *The roof is beyond repair.* **2.** the result of repairing: *The repair in the rug is hardly noticeable.* **3.** condition with respect to soundness or the need for repair: *The barn is in good repair.* **4.** a state of being in good or sound condition: *Our car is out of repair.* [Latin *reparāre* to get back, restore.] —**re·pair′a·bil′i·ty,** *n.* —**re·pair′a·ble,** *adj.* —**re·pair′er,** *n.* —For Synonyms (*v.t.*), see **mend.**

re·pair[2] (ri pâr′) *v.i.* to go to a place: *to repair to bed.* —*n.* **1.** the act of repairing. **2.** the place to which one repairs, esp. frequently or habitually. [Old French *repair(i)er* to return, stay, from Late Latin *repatriāre* to return to one's country, from Latin *re-* back + *patria* native land.]

re·pair·man (ri pâr′man′, -mən) *n., pl.* **-men** (-men′, -mən). a person whose occupation is making repairs: *a television repairman.*

rep·a·ra·ble (rep′ər ə bəl) *adj.* capable of being repaired. —**rep′a·ra·bly,** *adv.*

rep·a·ra·tion (rep′ə rā′shən) *n.* **1.** the act of giving satisfaction or making amends, as for a wrong or injury. **2.** something done or given as satisfaction or to make amends. **3. reparations.** money or material given in compensation for damage or loss in war, esp. that given by a defeated nation to a victorious one. **4.** the act of repairing or the state of being repaired. [Late Latin *reparātiō* restoration, from Latin *reparāre.* See REPAIR[1].] —**re·par·a·tive** (ri par′ə tiv), *adj.*

rep·ar·tee (rep′ər tē′, -tā′, rep′är-) *n.* **1.** a spirited exchange of quick, witty replies. **2.** skill or quickness in making such replies. **3.** a quick, witty reply. [French *repartie* retort, reply, from *repartir* to reply, going back to Latin *re-* again, back + *pars* part.]

re·past (ri past′) *n.* a meal, or the food and drink eaten or provided at a meal. [Old French *repast,* going back to Late Latin *re-* again + *pāscere* to feed.]

re·pa·tri·ate (*v.,* rē pā′trē āt′, -pat′rē-; *n.,* rē pā′trē it, -pat′rē-) *v.t.,* **-at·ed, -at·ing.** to return (someone, such as a prisoner of war or refugee) to his or her country of origin or citizenship. —*n.* a person who has been repatriated. [Late Latin *repatriātus,* past participle of *repatriāre* to return to one's country, from Latin *re-* back + *patria* native land.] —**re·pa′tri·a′tion,** *n.*

re·pay (ri pā′) *v.t.,* **-paid, -pay·ing. 1.** to pay or give back, as money: *to repay a loan.* **2.** to give something back or make return to (someone): *I'll never be able to repay you for your help.* **3.** to give or make some return or recompense for: *They repaid our kindness with an invitation to dinner.* **4.** to give, make, or do (something equivalent) in return: *to repay a compliment.* —**re·pay′able,** *adj.* —**re·pay′ment,** *n.*

re·peal (ri pēl′) *v.t.* to withdraw or cancel formally or officially; annul; revoke: *to repeal a law.* —*n.* the act of repealing or the state of being repealed: *the repeal of a constitutional amendment.* [Anglo-Norman *repeler* to revoke, going back to Latin *re-* back + *appellāre* to call upon.] —**re·peal′a·ble,** *adj.* —**re·peal′er,** *n.* —For Synonyms (*v.t.*), see **revoke.**

re·peat (ri pēt′) *v.t.* **1.** to say or utter (something already said) again; reiterate: *to repeat a question.* **2.a.** to say (exactly what someone else has said): *Repeat each word after me.* **b.** to say again what has already been said by (oneself): *I don't like having to repeat myself.* **3.** to tell or divulge to another or others: *to repeat a secret.* **4.** to say again or recite from memory: *to repeat a joke.* **5.** to do, make, or perform again: *to repeat a mistake, to repeat a demonstration.* **6.** to undergo or go through again: *to repeat an experience.* —*v.i.* **1.** to say or do something again. **2.** to vote more than once in a single election. —*n.* **1.** the act of repeating. **2.** something repeated; repetition. **3.** a rebroadcast, esp. of a television program. **4.** *Music.* **a.** a passage, section, or movement that is to be repeated. **b.** any of several signs indicating this, esp. double bar lines with two dots, placed at the end (‖:), and usually also at the beginning (:‖), of such a passage. [Latin *repetere* to do again, say again.] —**re·peat′a·bil′i·ty,** *n.* —**re·peat′a·ble,** *adj.*

re·peat·ed (ri pē′tid) *adj.* said, done, or occurring again and again. —**re·peat′ed·ly**, *adv.*

re·peat·er (ri pē′tər) *n.* **1.** repeating firearm. **2.** a student who repeats a course, usually having previously failed it. **3.** a person who has been arrested or convicted more than once for violating the law. **4.** a person or thing that repeats. **5.** a timepiece, esp. a watch, having a spring or lever that, when pressed, causes it to strike again the hour or part of the hour last struck.

repeating decimal, a decimal in which a particular digit or series of digits is repeated indefinitely, for example: 0.666 . . . and 0.1232323 . . . Also, **periodic decimal.**

repeating firearm, a rifle or pistol that can be fired more than once without reloading.

re·pel (ri pel′) *v.,* **-pelled, -pel·ling.** —*v.t.* **1.** to drive back or away: *to repel an attack.* **2.** to cause to feel dislike or disgust: *Violence repels me.* **3.** to be resistant or impervious to: *Plastic repels water.* **4.** to refuse to accept or consider; reject: *to repel an offer.* **5.** to push away or force apart: *The negative poles of two magnets repel each other.* —*v.i.* **1.** to cause dislike, aversion, or disgust. **2.** to act so as to drive or push something away. [Latin *repellere* to drive back, from *re-* back + *pellere* to drive.] —**re·pel′ler,** *n.*

re·pel·lent (ri pel′ənt) *also,* **re·pel·lant.** *adj.* **1.** causing dislike or disgust; repugnant. **2.** resistant or impervious to something. ➡ usually used in combination: *a water-repellent coat.* **3.** serving or tending to drive away. —*n.* something that repels: *a mosquito repellent.* —**re·pel′lence, re·pel′len·cy,** *n.* —**re·pel′lent·ly,** *adv.*

re·pent (ri pent′) *v.i.* **1.** to feel such sorrow or contrition for one's sins or faults as to reject one's negative ways and reform one's life. **2.a.** to feel sorrow, deep regret, or compunction for something one has done or failed to do: *to repent for one's mistreatment of others.* **b.** to change one's mind regarding some past action or conduct. —*v.t.* **1.** to feel sorrow or deep regret for: *to repent one's mistakes.* **2.** to change one's mind about: *We repented our decision to sell the house.* [Old French *repentir,* going back to Latin *re-* again + *paenitēre* to cause to be sorry.] —**re·pent′er,** *n.*

re·pent·ance (ri pen′təns) *n.* **1.** sorrow, deep regret, or compunction, as for sin or wrongdoing. **2.** the act or process of repenting. —For Synonyms, see **penitence.**

re·pent·ant (ri pen′tənt) *adj.* feeling, showing, or characterized by repentance; penitent. —**re·pent′ant·ly,** *adv.*

re·per·cus·sion (rē′pər kush′ən) *n.* **1.** a result or effect, often indirect, of an action or event; consequence: *The firing of the coach caused repercussions throughout the league.* **2.** echo; reverberation: *the repercussions of a loud noise.* **3.** a recoil or rebound after impact: *the repercussion of a hammer after striking an anvil.* [Latin *repercussiō* a rebounding.] —**re′per·cus′sive,** *adj.*

rep·er·toire (rep′ər twär′) *n.* **1.** the stock of artistic works, such as plays, operas, or songs, that a performer or group of performers has learned and is prepared to perform. **2.** a list of such works. **3.** the range of skills, abilities, or devices possessed by a particular person or group in a particular field: *a chef's repertoire.* [French *répertoire* list, from Late Latin *repertōrium* inventory, from Latin *reperīre* to find again. Doublet of REPERTORY.]

rep·er·to·ry (rep′ər tôr′ē) *n., pl.* **-ries. 1.** repertoire. **2.** a store or collection. **3.** storehouse. **4.** repertory theater. [Late Latin *repertōrium* inventory, from Latin *reperīre* to find again. Doublet of REPERTOIRE.]

repertory theater, a theatrical organization in which a permanent acting company performs a set of several different plays, usually in rotation, during a season.

rep·e·tend (rep′i tend′, rep′i tend′) *n.* **1.** the number or numbers that repeat infinitely in a repeating decimal. **2.** a word, sound, or phrase that is repeated. [Latin *repetendus* to be repeated, gerund of *repetere* to repeat.]

rep·e·ti·tion (rep′i tish′ən) *n.* **1.** the act of repeating or the state of being repeated. **2.** something that is repeated. [Latin *repetitiō.*]

rep·e·ti·tious (rep′i tish′əs) *adj.* full of, characterized by, or containing repetition, esp. unnecessary or tiresome repetition: *a repetitious article, a repetitious speaker.* —**rep′e·ti′tious·ly,** *adv.* —**rep′e·ti′tious·ness,** *n.*

re·pet·i·tive (ri pet′i tiv) *adj.* characterized by or relating to repetition; repetitious. —**re·pet′i·tive·ly,** *adv.* —**re·pet′i·tive·ness,** *n.*

re·phrase (rē frāz′) *v.t.,* **-phrased, -phras·ing.** to phrase again, esp. to express in a different way: *to rephrase a question.*

re·pine (ri pīn′) *v.i.,* **-pined, -pin·ing.** to feel or express discontent or unhappiness; fret; complain. [RE- + PINE².] —**re·pin′er,** *n.*

re·place (ri plās′) *v.t.,* **-placed, -plac·ing. 1.** to take or fill the place of: *She will replace him as club president.* **2.** to provide or obtain a substitute or equivalent for: *The car battery is defective*

and should be replaced. **3.** to restore or return to the original or proper place; put back: *Please replace the magazine in the rack.* **4.** to repay or make good; return: *to replace money withdrawn from a savings account.* —**re·place′a·ble,** *adj.*

re·place·ment (ri plās′mənt) *n.* **1.** a person or thing that replaces. **2.** the act of replacing or the state of being replaced.

replacement set, domain *(def. 4).*

re·play (*v.,* rē plā′; *n.,* rē′plā′) *v.t.* to play again, as a game or phonograph record. —*n.* **1.** the act of replaying something: *The umpire ordered a replay of the point.* **2.** something replayed, esp. a recorded portion of a game: *In the replay, we could see the receiver drop the ball.* **3.** any repetition or recurrence: *a replay of an old argument.*

re·plen·ish (ri plen′ish) *v.t.* **1.** to bring back to a state of fullness or completeness, as by replacing what is lacking or has been used: *to replenish food supplies.* **2.** to provide a new supply for; fill again: *to replenish a linen closet.* [Old French *repleniss-,* a stem of *replenir* to fill up again, going back to Latin *re-* again + *plēnus* full.] —**re·plen′ish·er,** *n.* —**re·plen′ish·ment,** *n.*

re·plete (ri plēt′) *adj.* **1.** supplied or filled in abundance; overflowing; abounding (with *with*): *a garden replete with brightly colored flowers.* **2.** filled to satisfaction or capacity with food or drink; sated; gorged. [Latin *replētus* filled up, past participle of *replēre* to fill again.] —**re·plete′ness,** *n.*

re·ple·tion (ri plē′shən) *n.* **1.** the state or condition of being replete: *to eat to repletion.* **2.** satisfaction or fulfillment.

rep·li·ca (rep′li kə) *n.* **1.** a close or exact copy or reproduction, esp. one produced on a smaller scale than the original: *a replica of a battleship.* **2.** a copy or reproduction of a work of art, esp. one made by the original artist. [Italian *replica,* from *replicare* to duplicate, repeat, from Late Latin *replicāre.* See REPLY.] —For Synonyms, see **duplicate.**

rep·li·cate (rep′li kāt′) *v.,* **-cat·ed, -cat·ing.** —*v.t.* **1.** to make a replica of; reproduce. **2.** to repeat exactly: *to replicate an experiment.* **3.** to fold over or bend back. —*v.i.* to duplicate or reproduce exactly by genetic processes: *DNA divides and replicates in cell division.* [Late Latin *replicātus,* past participle of *replicāre.* See REPLY.]

rep·li·ca·tion (rep′li kā′shən) *n.* **1.** the act or process of replicating or reproducing. **2.** a copy or reproduction. **3.** a reply, esp. a reply to an answer; rejoinder. **4.** a duplication of a sound; reverberation or echo. **5.** *Law.* a plaintiff's reply to a defendant's counterclaim or defense. **6.** *Biology.* the process occurring during the division of cells, in which the DNA in a cell duplicates itself, thus ensuring that all new cells are exactly like the original. —**rep′li·ca′tive,** *adj.*

re·ply (ri plī′) *v.,* **-plied, -ply·ing.** —*v.i.* **1.** to respond in speech or in writing; answer. **2.** to respond by some action; react: *The teacher replied with only a smile.* **3.** to duplicate a sound; echo; resound. —*v.t.* to say in response; give as a response: *They replied that they would come.* —*n., pl.* **-plies.** something said, written, or done in response. [Old French *replier* to fold back, answer back, from Late Latin *replicāre* to repeat, from Latin *replicāre* to unfold.] —For Synonyms *(n.),* see **answer.**

re·port (ri pôrt′) *n.* **1.a.** an account, statement, or announcement: *We have heard only tentative reports on the outcome of the election.* **b.** a formal or official account, esp. an analysis or presentation based on investigation: *a monthly inflation report.* **2.** an explosive sound or noise, esp. that made by a rifle or pistol when fired. **3.** the record, often formal and detailed, of the proceedings of a meeting or legislative assembly. **4.** common talk; rumor; gossip: *Report has it that it will snow tonight.* **5.** reputation; repute: *a teacher of good report.* **6.** *also,* **reports.** a collection of volumes published periodically, containing accounts of state and federal court proceedings and their decisions. —*v.t.* **1.** to make or give an account, statement, or announcement of: *to report the findings of a study.* **2.** to make known; relate: *They reported that the job was done.* **3.** to bring back, repeat, or deliver, as a message; convey. **4.** to bring charges of wrongdoing or misconduct against or complain about: *to report a reckless driver to the police, to report a robbery.* **5.** (of a legislative committee) to send (a bill) to the entire legislative body, usually with a recommendation for passage (often with *out*): *The committee reported out the bill.* —*v.i.* **1.** to make a report: *to report on environmental conditions.* **2.** to work or act as a reporter: *to report for a local newspaper.* **3.** to present oneself: *to report for work at noon.* **4.** to be responsible or answerable: *They report to the president.* [Old French

a	at	e	end	o	hot	u	up	hw	white		about
ā	ape	ē	me	ō	old	ū	use	ng	song		taken
ä	far	i	it	ô	fork	ü	rule	th	thin	ə	pencil
âr	care	ī	ice	oi	oil	u̇	pull	th	this		lemon
		îr	pierce	ou	out	ûr	turn	zh	measure		circus

R

reporter to carry back, bring news, denounce, from Latin *reportāre* to carry back.] —**re·port'a·ble**, *adj.* —For Synonyms *(n.)*, see **account.**

report card, a periodic written report of a pupil's grades and conduct.

re·port·ed·ly (ri pôr'tid lē) *adv.* according to report: *The senator is reportedly going to retire.*

re·port·er (ri pôr'tər) *n.* **1.** a person employed to gather and report news, as for a newspaper or magazine or for television or radio. **2.** a person who transcribes or makes an official record of what is said during a court trial. **3.** any person who reports.

rep·or·to·ri·al (rep'ər tôr'ē əl) *adj.* **1.** of or relating to reporters: *reportorial skills.* **2.** of the nature of a report. —**rep'or·to'·ri·al·ly**, *adv.*

re·pose[1] (ri pōz') *n.* **1.** relaxation, as after exertion or activity; rest; sleep. **2.** peace and quiet; tranquillity: *the beauty and repose of the forest.* **3.** an absence of movement or activity; undisturbed condition: *a dancer in repose.* **4.** calmness or ease, as of manner; composure. —*v.,* **-posed, -pos·ing.** —*v.i.* **1.** to lie or be at rest; rest; sleep: *to repose on a sofa.* **2.** to be supported; rest; lie: *The book reposes on the table.* **3.** to lie buried or interred. **4.** *Archaic.* to depend or rely (with *on, upon,* or *in*). —*v.t.* to lay in a position of rest. ➡ often used reflexively: *to repose oneself on a sofa.* [Old French *reposer* to rest, going back to Latin *re-* again + Late Latin *pausāre* to cause to rest. See POSE[1].]

re·pose[2] (ri pōz') *v.t.* **-posed, -pos·ing.** to place, as confidence, hope, or power, in a person or thing: *to repose trust in the democratic system.* [RE- + POSE[1].]

re·pose·ful (ri pōz'fəl) *adj.* full of repose; calm; quiet. —**re·pose'ful·ly**, *adv.* —**re·pose'ful·ness**, *n.*

re·pos·i·to·ry (ri poz'i tôr'ē) *n., pl.* **-ries. 1.** a place or receptacle in which something is or may be stored or deposited. **2.** any rich or abundant source or supply: *The library is a repository of information.* **3.** a person to whom something is confided or entrusted. **4.** a burial vault; sepulcher. [Latin *repositōrium* storehouse.]

re·pos·sess (rē'pə zes') *v.t.* **1.** to possess again; regain possession of. **2.** to resume possession of (something bought on installments or credit) for failure of the buyer to make due payment. **3.** to put (someone) again in possession of something; return possession to. —**re'pos·ses'sion,** *n.* —**re'pos·ses'sor,** *n.*

re·pous·sé (rə pü sā') *adj.* **1.** raised in relief by hammering on the reverse side, as of a thin piece of metal: *a repoussé design.* **2.** ornamented or shaped with designs or figures formed in relief: *a repoussé box.* —*n.* the art or process of hammering repoussé designs. [French *repoussé,* from *repousser* to thrust back, from *re-* back (from Latin *re-*) + *pousser* to thrust. See PUSH.]

repp (rep) *n.* rep.

rep·re·hend (rep'ri hend') *v.t.* to criticize sharply; reprove; censure. [Latin *reprehendere* to hold back, blame.]

rep·re·hen·si·ble (rep'ri hen'sə bəl) *adj.* deserving sharp criticism or reproof. —**rep're·hen'si·bil'i·ty, rep're·hen'si·ble·ness,** *n.* —**rep're·hen'si·bly,** *adv.*

rep·re·hen·sion (rep'ri hen'shən) *n.* the act of reprehending; criticism; reproof. [Latin *reprehensiō.*] —**rep're·hen'sive,** *adj.* —**rep're·hen'sive·ly,** *adv.*

rep·re·sent (rep'ri zent') *v.t.* **1.** to serve as a symbol or expression of; stand for; signify; symbolize: *In the story the snake represents evil.* **2.** to express or designate by some symbol, character, sign, or the like: *to represent speech sounds by letters.* **3.** to speak or act for; serve as the delegate or agent of: *Two senators represent each state in the U.S. Congress.* **4.** to present an image or likeness of, as in painting or sculpture. **5.** to set forth or point out in words; describe; explain: *to represent one's ideas.* **6.** to be equivalent to; amount to; constitute: *Their actions represent a violation of the agreement.* **7.** to serve as an example, specimen, or instance of; exemplify; typify: *The works of Dickens represent the Victorian novel.* **8.** to claim to be; describe: *They represented themselves as experts.* **9.** to present or picture to the mind. **10.** to act the part or role of, as in a play. **11.** to perform or produce, as on the stage; present, as a play. [Latin *repraesentāre* to show, exhibit.] —**rep're·sent'a·ble,** *adj.*

rep·re·sen·ta·tion (rep'ri zen tā'shən, -zən-) *n.* **1.** the act of representing or the state of being represented. **2.** an account, statement, or description. **3.** something that represents, such as a picture or other likeness. **4.** the state, fact, or right of being represented in a legislative assembly. **5.** a body or number of representatives. **6.** a dramatic performance or presentation. **7.** a

statement of arguments, esp. one made in protest or intended to influence action or opinion. —**re'pre·sen·ta'tion·al,** *adj.*

rep·re·sent·a·tive (rep'ri zen'tə tiv) *n.* **1.** a person who is chosen or authorized to represent another or others; delegate; agent: *The company has a representative in Rome.* **2.** a person or thing serving to exemplify or typify a group, kind, or class. **3.** *also,* **Representative.** an elected member of a legislative assembly, esp. a member of the lower house of the U.S. Congress or of a state legislature. —*adj.* **1.** exemplifying or typifying a group, kind, or class: *a representative painting of the impressionist school.* **2.** acting for or authorized to act for another or others. **3.** composed of representatives or based on political representation: *a representative government.* **4.** serving to represent, portray, or symbolize: *literature that is representative of the times.* —**rep're·sen'ta·tive·ly,** *adv.* —**rep're·sen'ta·tive·ness,** *n.*

re·press (ri pres') *v.t.* **1.** to hold back or keep under control or in check; restrain: *to repress a smile.* **2.** to put down or put a stop to, esp. by force; subdue: *to repress an uprising.* **3.** to prevent the natural development or expression of: *The child's creative talents had been repressed for too long.* **4.** to prevent (painful memories or disturbing ideas or desires) from emerging from the unconscious mind. ➡ distinguished from **suppress.** [Latin *repressus,* past participle of *reprimere* to press back, check.] —**re·press'er;** *also,* **re·pres'sor,** *n.* —For Synonyms, see **oppress.**

re·pres·sion (ri presh'ən) *n.* **1.** the act or an instance of repressing or the state of being repressed. **2.** *Psychology.* an unconscious defense mechanism by which painful memories or disturbing ideas or desires are kept out of the conscious mind. ➡ distinguished from **suppression.**

re·pres·sive (ri pres'iv) *adj.* tending or serving to repress; capable of repressing. —**re·pres'sive·ly,** *adv.* —**re·pres'sive·ness,** *n.*

re·prieve (ri prēv') *n.* **1.** *Law.* **a.** an official postponement of the carrying out of a sentence, esp. a delay in the execution of a condemned person. **b.** the document ordering such a postponement. **2.** a respite or temporary relief or escape, as from something unpleasant or difficult. —*v.t.,* **-prieved, -priev·ing. 1.** to grant a reprieve to (someone), esp. to delay the execution of (a condemned person). **2.** to free temporarily, as from something unpleasant or difficult. [Middle English *repreven,* form of *reproven* to reprove; literally, to test again. See REPROVE.]

rep·ri·mand (rep'rə mand') *v.t.* to blame or criticize sharply or formally. —*n.* a sharp criticism, esp. one formally or officially given. [French *réprimande* reproof, check, from Latin *reprimenda* (thing) to be checked, feminine gerundive of *reprimere* to press back, check.]

Synonyms *v.t.* **Reprimand, reprove,** and **rebuke** mean to criticize or blame. **Reprimand** usually suggests sharp or formal criticism: *Their parents reprimanded them for staying out so late. The environmental organization reprimanded the company for polluting the river.* **Reprove** suggests a direct and sometimes kindly attempt to correct a fault: *The coach reproved the debating team for their poor performance.* **Rebuke,** the strongest of these terms, implies a severe warning or denunciation: *The principal rebuked the students for their dishonesty.*

re·print (*n.,* rē'print'; *v.,* rē print') *n.* **1.** a new edition of a work that has already been published. **2.** a separately printed excerpt, as of an article printed in a magazine. —*v.t.* to print a new edition or copy of; print again.

re·pris·al (ri prī'zəl) *n.* **1.** harm or injury done to an enemy in return for injuries or losses suffered; retaliation: *Military reprisals between the belligerent nations were common.* **2.** an act or instance of inflicting such harm. [Anglo-Norman *reprisaille* a seizing on, from Old French *repris,* past participle of *reprendre* to reprove, seize again, from Latin *reprehendere* to hold back.]

re·prise (ri prēz') *Music. n.* the repetition of part or all of a song or musical composition that has been played earlier. [Old French *reprise* a taking back, from *reprendre* to take back, seize again, from Latin *reprehendere* to hold back.] —*v.t.,* **-prised, -pris·ing.** to play a reprise.

re·pro (rē'prō) *n.* a sharp, clear proof, usually printed on glossy paper, of a quality suitable for reproduction by a photographic printing process, such as photo-offset or photolithography. [Short for *repro(duction proof).*]

re·proach (ri prōch') *v.t.* to charge with or blame for a fault or wrongdoing; chide; reprove: *The coach reproached the players for their poor performance.* —*n.* **1.** the act of reproaching; blame; reproof. **2.** an expression of this. **3.** a cause, object, or occasion

repost	repour	repressurize	reprocess	reprosecute	repurify
repostulate	repower	reprice	reprogram	reprotest	repursue
repostulation	repractice	reprioritize	reproject	republication	requalify
repot	represcribe	reprobe	repropose	republish	requestion

of blame or disgrace: *Litter in the street is a reproach to our city.* **4.** discredit; disgrace. [Old French *reprochier* to blame, accuse, going back to Latin *re-* again + *prope* near.] —**re·proach'a·ble,** *adj.* —For Synonyms *(v.t.),* see **blame.**

re·proach·ful (ri prōch'fəl) *adj.* full of or expressing reproach. —**re·proach'ful·ly,** *adv.* —**re·proach'ful·ness,** *n.*

rep·ro·bate (rep'rə bāt') *n.* **1.** an immoral, unprincipled, or wicked person. **2.** *Theology.* a person rejected and condemned by God. —*adj.* **1.** given to immorality or wickedness; depraved. **2.** *Theology.* rejected and condemned by God; damned. —*v.t.,* **-bat·ed, -bat·ing. 1.** to condemn or disapprove of strongly; censure. **2.** *Theology.* (of God) to reject and condemn (a person); damn. [Late Latin *reprobātus,* past participle of *reprobāre* to disapprove, condemn, from Latin *re-* again + *probāre* to test, try.]

rep·ro·ba·tion (rep'rə bā'shən) *n.* condemnation; censure. —**rep'ro·ba'tive,** *adj.*

re·pro·duce (rē'prə dūs', -dūs') *v.,* **-duced, -duc·ing.** —*v.t.* **1.** to produce, form, or bring about again or anew; re-create: *The architect hoped to reproduce the grandeur of the original building.* **2.** to make a duplicate or representation of: *to reproduce a picture.* **3.** to give rise to or produce (offspring or others of the same kind) by sexual or asexual means. **4.** to foster or bring about the generation of (plants or animals). —*v.i.* **1.** to give rise to or produce offspring or others of the same kind. **2.** to undergo reproduction. —**re'pro·duc'er,** *n.* —**re'pro·duc'i·bil'i·ty,** *n.* —**re'pro·duc'i·ble** *adj.*

re·pro·duc·tion (rē'prə duk'shən) *n.* **1.** the process by which living organisms give rise to or produce offspring or others of their kind. **2.** something that is reproduced. **3.** the act or process of reproducing or the state of being reproduced.

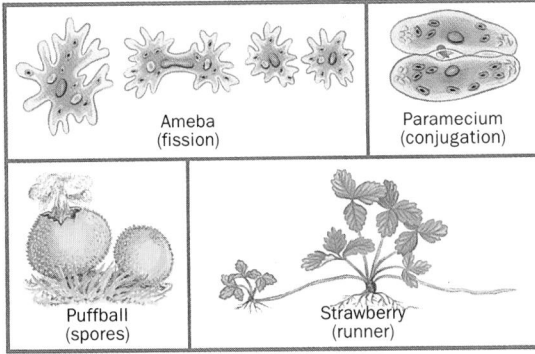

Ameba (fission)

Paramecium (conjugation)

Puffball (spores)

Strawberry (runner)

examples of asexual **reproduction**

re·pro·duc·tive (rē'prə duk'tiv) *adj.* **1.** of, relating to, or employed in reproduction. **2.** capable of reproduction; reproducing. —**re'pro·duc'tive·ly,** *adv.* —**re'pro·duc'tive·ness,** *n.*

reproductive system, the system of organs by which living things reproduce their own kind. In mammals, the reproductive system includes the penis and the testes in males and the uterus, the vagina, and the ovaries in females.

re·prog·ra·phy (ri prog'rə fē) *n.* the reproduction of documents or other written material by any electronic process or photographic means. [REPRO(DUCTION) + -GRAPHY.] —**re·pro·graph·ic** (rē'prə graf'ik), *adj.*

re·proof (ri prüf') *n.* **1.** the act of reproving. **2.** an expression of criticism; scolding or reprimand. Also, **re·prov·al** (ri prü'vəl). [Old French *reprove* reproach, from *reprover.* See REPROVE.]

re·prove (ri prüv') *v.t.,* **-proved, -prov·ing. 1.** to blame or scold, usually in an effort to correct; rebuke: *She reproved him for always being late.* **2.** to find fault with; disapprove of: *to reprove someone's behavior.* [Old French *reprover* to reproach, from Late Latin *reprobāre* to disapprove, condemn, from Latin *re-* again + *probāre* to test, try (suggesting testing again and condemning).] —**re·prov'a·ble,** *adj.* —For Synonyms, see **reprimand.**

rep·tile (rep'təl, -tīl) *n.* **1.** any of a group of cold-blooded vertebrates, class Reptilia, including lizards, snakes, crocodiles, turtles, and the tuatara, having dry, usually scaly skin and often reproducing by laying eggs. **2.** a groveling, treacherous, or despicable person. —*adj.* reptilian. [Late Latin *rēptile* creeping creature, neuter of *rēptilis* creeping, from Latin *rēpere* to creep, crawl.]

rep·til·i·an (rep til'ē ən, -til'yən) *adj.* **1.** of, relating to, or characteristic of a reptile or reptiles. **2.** resembling or suggesting a reptile: *reptilian features.* —*n.* reptile.

Repub. 1. Republic. **2.** Republican.

re·pub·lic (ri pub'lik) *n.* **1.** a form of government in which the

final authority of the state rests with voting citizens and is exercised by elected representatives of the people. **2.** a nation or state that has such a form of government. [Latin *rēspublica* state; literally, public thing.]

re·pub·li·can (ri pub'li kən) *adj.* **1.** of, characteristic of, or like a republic. **2. Republican.** of, relating to, or characteristic of the Republican Party. **3.** supporting or advocating a republic as a form of government. —*n.* **1. Republican.** a member of the Republican Party. **2.** a person who believes in or advocates a republic as a form of government.

re·pub·li·can·ism (ri pub'li kə niz'əm) *n.* **1.** the system or principles of government used by republics. **2.** a belief in or advocacy of such principles. **3. Republicanism.** the principles or policies of the Republican Party.

Republican Party, one of the two major political parties in the United States.

re·pu·di·ate (ri pū'dē āt') *v.t.,* **-at·ed, -at·ing. 1.** to reject as unjust or untrue: *to repudiate an accusation.* **2.** to refuse to have anything to do with; cast off; disown: *to repudiate a friend.* **3.** to refuse to acknowledge or pay: *to repudiate a debt.* [Latin *repudiātus,* past participle of *repudiāre* to put away, reject, from *repudium* divorce, a casting off.] —**re·pu'di·a'tion,** *n.* —**re·pu'di·a'tor,** *n.*

re·pug·nance (ri pug'nəns) *n.* extreme dislike or aversion; disgust. Also, **re·pug·nan·cy.** —For Synonyms, see **disgust.**

re·pug·nant (ri pug'nənt) *adj.* **1.** causing extreme dislike or aversion; highly distasteful; repulsive: *a repugnant odor.* **2.** contrary or opposed; antagonistic: *Censorship is repugnant to freedom of expression.* [Latin *repugnāns,* present participle of *repugnāre* to resist, oppose.] —**re·pug'nant·ly,** *adv.*

re·pulse (ri puls') *v.t.,* **-pulsed, -puls·ing. 1.** to beat or drive back; repel: *Our army repulsed the enemy's advance.* **2.** to refuse to accept; reject; rebuff: *to repulse an offer of assistance.* —*n.* **1.** the act of repulsing or the state of being repulsed. **2.** rejection; rebuff. [Latin *repulsus,* past participle of *repellere* to drive back.]

re·pul·sion (ri pul'shən) *n.* **1.** extreme dislike, aversion, or disgust. **2.** the act of repelling or the state of being repelled.

re·pul·sive (ri pul'siv) *adj.* **1.** causing extreme dislike, disgust, or aversion; highly distasteful or offensive. **2.** tending to repel. —**re·pul'sive·ly,** *adv.* —**re·pul'sive·ness,** *n.*

rep·u·ta·ble (rep'yə tə bəl) *adj.* having a good reputation; trustworthy; respectable: *a reputable company.* —**rep'u·ta·bil'i·ty,** *n.* —**rep'u·ta·bly,** *adv.*

rep·u·ta·tion (rep'yə tā'shən) *n.* **1.** general or public estimation of a person or thing: *to have a good reputation.* **2.** the state of being highly regarded or esteemed: *to ruin one's reputation.* **3.** a position of status, honesty, merit, or other favorable regard: *The doctor has built up a reputation for generosity.* [Latin *reputātiō* consideration, from *reputāre.* See REPUTE.]

re·pute (ri pūt') *n.* **1.** general or public estimation of a person or thing. **2.** the state of being highly regarded or esteemed: *a business of repute.* —*v.t.,* **-put·ed, -put·ing.** to consider to be; suppose. [Latin *reputāre* to think over, esteem.]

re·put·ed (ri pū'tid) *adj.* generally considered or supposed: *the reputed author of a poem.* —**re·put'ed·ly,** *adv.*

re·quest (ri kwest') *v.t.* **1.** to express a wish or desire for; ask for, esp. politely or formally: *He requested permission to leave.* **2.** to express a wish or desire to; ask: *She requested us to be on time.* —*n.* **1.** the act or an instance of requesting. **2.** something that is requested: *to grant a request.* **3.** the state of being sought after or in demand. [Old French *requeste* petition, probably from *request,* past participle of *requerre* to ask, ask for, going back to Latin *requīrere* to ask, seek again.] —**re·quest'er;** *also,* **re·ques'tor,** *n.*

· **by request.** in response to a request: *The band played that song by request.*

Req·ui·em (rek'wē əm, rē'kwē-, rā'-) *n.* **1.** a Roman Catholic Mass offered for the eternal rest of the soul of one or more deceased persons, esp. as part of a funeral. **2.** *also,* **requiem.** a musical setting for this. **3. requiem.** any musical composition, hymn, or service in honor of the dead. [Latin *requiem,* accusative of *requiēs* rest; the first word of the introit of the Mass for the dead.]

re·qui·es·cat (rek'wē es'kät, -kat) *n.* a wish or prayer for the repose of the dead. [Latin, first word of *requiescat in pace.*]

requiescat in pa·ce (pä'chā) *Latin.* may he or she rest in peace.

re·quire (ri kwīr') *v.,* **-quired, -quir·ing.** —*v.t.* **1.** to be in

a	at	e	end	o	hot	u	up	hw	white		about
ā	ape	ē	me	ō	old	ū	use	ng	song		taken
ä	far	i	it	ô	fork	ü	rule	th	thin	ə	pencil
âr	care	ī	ice	oi	oil	u̇	pull	th	this		lemon
		îr	pierce	ou	out	ûr	turn	zh	measure		circus

R

need of: *That injury requires medical attention.* **2.** to impose as an obligation or condition: *Knitting requires much patience.* **3.** to order or compel (someone) to do something: *The customs officer required us to open our luggage.* —*v.i.* to request or demand. [Latin *requīrere* to ask for, need.] —For Synonyms, see **demand.**

re·quire·ment (ri kwīr′mənt) *n.* **1.** something that is imposed as an obligation or condition: *Good grades are a requirement for getting into college.* **2.** something that is needed: *A proper diet is one requirement for good health.*

req·ui·site (rek′wə zit) *adj.* required; necessary; indispensable: *to have the requisite training for a job.* —*n.* something that cannot be done without; essential. [Latin *requīsītus,* past participle of *requīrere* to ask for, need.] —**req′ui·site·ly,** *adv.* —**req′ui·site·ness,** *n.*

req·ui·si·tion (rek′wə zish′ən) *n.* **1.a.** an official written request or application, as for new equipment. **b.** the act of putting through such a request. **c.** the form on which such a request is made. **2.** the act or an instance of taking or demanding, as by authority: *a military requisition of housing.* —*v.t.* **1.** to put through an official request for: *to requisition new supplies.* **2.** to take or demand, as by authority. **3.** to make a requisition of.

re·quit·al (ri kwī′təl) *n.* **1.** the act of requiting. **2.** something that is given or done in return: *a proper requital for generosity.*

re·quite (ri kwīt′) *v.t.,* **-quit·ed, -quit·ing. 1.** to give or pay back, often in kind; make return for: *He requited her love.* **2.** to repay or reward, as for a benefit or service or an injury or wrong. [RE- + obsolete *quite* to repay, form of QUIT.] —**re·quit′er,** *n.*

re·re·dos (rîr′dos, rîr′ə-, rãr′ə-) *n.* a screen or ornamental wall behind an altar. [Short for Old French *areredos,* going back to Latin *ad* to + *retrō* backward + *dorsum* back.]

re·route (rē rüt′, -rout′) *v.t.,* **-rout·ed, -rout·ing.** to send by a new or different route.

re·run (*n.,* rē′run′; *v.,* rē run′) *n.* **1.a.** the showing of a filmed or taped performance, such as a motion picture, after its original showing. **b.** the filmed or taped performance itself. **2.** the act or an instance of running again. —*v.t.,* **-ran, -run·ning. 1.** to show as a rerun. **2.** to run again: *to rerun a race.*

re·sale (rē′sāl′, rē sāl′) *n.* the act of selling what one has bought.

re·scind (ri sind′) *v.t.* to make void; annul; repeal: *to rescind a contract, to rescind a law.* [Latin *rescindere* to cut off, annul.] —**re·scind′a·ble,** *adj.* —**re·scind′er,** *n.* - For Synonyms, see **revoke.**

re·scis·sion (ri sizh′ən) *n.* the act of rescinding. [Late Latin *rescissiō,* from Latin *rescindere* to cut off, annul.]

re·script (rē′skript′) *n.* **1.** a formal written reply, as from a pope, to a written question or petition. **2.** any official edict, decree, or announcement. **3.** the act or product of rewriting. [Late Latin *rescriptum* emperor's decision, reply (to a letter), from Latin *rescrībere* to write in reply.]

res·cue (res′kū) *v.t.,* **-cued, -cu·ing. 1.** to save or free, as from danger: *to rescue a drowning swimmer.* **2.** *Law.* to remove (a person or thing) forcibly from legal custody. —*n.* the act of rescuing or the result of being rescued. [Old French *rescourre* to save, going back to Latin *re-* back, again + *excutere* to drive away (suggesting driving danger away).] —**res′cu·er,** *n.* —For Synonyms *(v.t.),* see **save.**

re·search (ri sûrch′, rē′sûrch′) *n.* systematic study or investigation in a particular field, usually for the purpose of learning new facts and making interpretations. —*v.t.* to make a systematic study or investigation of or for: *to research a topic, to research a term paper.* [Middle French *recerche* a diligent search, from *recercher* to seek, from Old French *re-* (see RE-) + *cerchier* to seek. See SEARCH.] —**re·search′er, re·search′ist,** *n.*

re·seat (rē sēt′) *v.t.* **1.** to seat again. **2.** to assign to a new or different seat. **3.** to install in office again; reelect. **4.** to provide with a new seat, as a chair or pair of pants.

re·sect (ri sekt′) *v.t. Medicine.* to cut out a portion of (an organ or bone); do resection on. [Latin *resectus,* past participle of *resecāre* to cut off, from *re-* back + *secāre* to cut.]

re·sec·tion (ri sek′shən) *n.* **1.** surgical removal of all or part of an organ or other part of the body. **2.** in surveying, the technique of determining the location of a point by taking observations from that point to several other points whose locations are shown on a map. [Latin *resectionis,* genitive of *resectio* a cutting, removal by cutting, from *resectus.* See RESECT.]

re·sem·blance (ri zem′bləns) *n.* **1.** the state or fact of resem-

bling; similarity, as of physical appearance; likeness: *a close resemblance between brother and sister.* **2.** a person or thing that is similar to another person or thing. [Anglo-Norman *resemblance* likeness, from Old French *resembler* to be like.]

re·sem·ble (ri zem′bəl) *v.t.,* **-bled, -bling.** to have the same appearance, characteristics, qualities, or nature as. [Old French *resembler,* going back to Latin *re-* again + *simulāre* to imitate, make like.]

re·sent (ri zent′) *v.t.* to feel resentment at or toward: *I resent your insulting comment.* [French *ressentir,* going back to Latin *re-* back, again + *sentīre* to feel.]

re·sent·ful (ri zent′fəl) *adj.* characterized by or tending to feel resentment: *a resentful loser.* —**re·sent′ful·ly,** *adv.* —**re·sent′ful·ness,** *n.*

re·sent·ment (ri zent′mənt) *n.* indignation, anger, or bitterness caused by a real or imagined offense or injury.

re·ser·pine (rə sûr′pin, -pēn) *n.* an alkaloid drug derived from the roots of certain rauwolfias, esp. *Rauwolfia serpentina,* used to treat hypertension and anxiety. Formula: $C_{33}H_{40}N_2O_9$ [German *reserpin,* probably contraction of Modern Latin *Rauwolfia serpentina* + German *-in* -ine[2].]

res·er·va·tion (rez′ər vā′shən) *n.* **1.a.** an arrangement whereby something, such as a theater seat or hotel room, is reserved. **b.** something that is reserved: *Our reservation for dinner is at 8:00.* **c.** a record of this, usually in writing: *Our hotel reservations arrived in the mail.* **2.** public land set aside, as by a government, for a special purpose, as for an Indian tribe to live on or for a wildlife preserve. **3.** doubt; misgiving: *Do you have reservations about traveling alone?* **4.** an expressed or tacit qualification or limiting factor; restriction: *They approved the plan without a single reservation.* **5.** the act or an instance of withholding or keeping for oneself.

re·serve (ri zûrv′) *v.t.,* **-served, -serv·ing. 1.** to set aside or have set aside for a particular person or purpose or for future use: *to reserve a table for two.* **2.** to withhold or save until a later time: *Reserve your strength for the race.* **3.** to keep for oneself: *I reserve the right to make my own decisions.* —*n.* **1.** something that is set aside, as for a special purpose or future use; store; supply: *to keep a reserve of firewood for cold weather.* **2.** public land set aside for a special purpose; preserve. **3.** self-control or restraint, as in speech or behavior: *to show reserve in the presence of adversity.* **4.** the tendency to keep silent, esp. with regard to one's feelings or thoughts. **5.** *Finance.* an amount of money or assets held back, as from investment, to meet emergencies or special demands. **6.** *also,* **reserves.** the part of the armed forces not on active duty but available for service in an emergency. **7. reserves.** that part of a fighting force withheld from action until needed. —*adj.* kept in reserve; constituting a reserve. [Latin *reservāre* to keep back, save up.] —For Synonyms *(n.),* see **stock.**

 • **in** (or **on**) **reserve.** set aside for a particular person or purpose or for future use: *to keep food in reserve for emergencies.*
 • **without reserve.** without restriction or limitation: *The offer is without reserve.*

reserve bank, Federal Reserve Bank.

re·served (ri zûrvd′) *adj.* **1.** set aside for a particular person or purpose or for future use. **2.** characterized by reserve in speech and behavior. —**re·serv·ed·ly** (ri zûr′vid lē) *adv.* —**re·serv′ed·ness,** *n.*

Reserve Officers' Training Corps, see ROTC.

re·serv·ist (ri zûr′vist) *n.* a member of a military reserve.

res·er·voir (rez′ər vwär′, -vôr′, rez′ə-) *n.* **1.** a natural or artificially constructed place used for the storage of water. **2.** a receptacle or part used for the storage of a liquid or gas. **3.** a place where anything is collected and stored: *Great literature is a reservoir of wisdom.* **4.** reserve; store; supply: *This book contains a reservoir of facts.* [French *réservoir,* going back to Latin *reservāre* to keep back, save up.]

re·set (*v.,* rē set′; *n.,* rē′set′) *v.t.,* **-set, -set·ting. 1.** to set again: *to reset the clock.* **2.** to set in a different place or position: *to reset shrubs behind a house.* —*n.* **1.** the act of resetting. **2.** something that is reset. —**re·set′ta·ble,** *adj.*

re·shape (rē shāp′) *v.t.,* **-shaped, -shap·ing.** to give a new or different shape to.

re·ship (rē ship′) *v.,* **-shipped, -ship·ping.** —*v.t.* **1.** to transport again, as by ship, rail, truck, or air; ship again. **2.** to transfer to another ship. —*v.i.* **1.** to sign up for another voyage as a crew

reread	resaddle	reseed	resentence	reshoot	resketch
rerecord	reschedule	resegregate	resettle	reshow	resoak
reregister	rescreen	resegregation	resettlement	reshuffle	resocialization
reregistration	reseal	reseize	resew	resilver	resocialize
reregulate	resealable	reseizure	resharpen	resituate	resolder
reroll	resecure	resell	reshine	resize	resolidify

member: *to reship on a merchant vessel.* **2.** to board a ship again; reembark. **—re·ship′per,** *n.*

re·ship·ment (rē ship′mənt) *n.* **1.** the act of transporting again, as by ship, rail, truck, or air. **2.** something that is transported again.

re·side (ri zīd′) *v.i.,* **-sid·ed, -sid·ing. 1.** to make one's home permanently or for a time. **2.** to be vested (with *in* or *with*): *The power of veto resides with the president.* **3.** to be present or inherent (with *in*): *Much benefit resides in regular exercise.* [Latin *residēre* to remain behind, abide.] **—re·sid′er,** *n.*

res·i·dence (rez′i dəns) *n.* **1.** a place where a person resides. **2.** the act or state of residing, esp. to satisfy legal requirements: *Residence in the town enabled me to vote there.* **3.** a period of time spent residing in a place: *ten years' residence in a community.* —For Synonyms, see **home.**

res·i·den·cy (rez′i dən sē) *n., pl.* **-cies. 1.** a period during which a physician receives advanced, specialized clinical training. **2.** residence.

res·i·dent (rez′i dənt) *n.* **1.** a person who resides in a particular place. **2.** a physician serving a residency. *—adj.* **1.** residing in a particular place. **2.** residing in a place in connection with work or duty: *a resident caretaker.*

res·i·den·tial (rez′i den′shəl) *adj.* **1.** of or relating to residence: *a residential requirement for voting.* **2.** characterized by, restricted to, or suitable for residences: *a residential neighborhood.*

re·sid·u·al (ri zij′ü əl) *adj.* of, relating to, or constituting a residue; remaining. *—n.* **1.** *also,* **residuals.** payments made to a performer for the repeated use of a recorded appearance, as in a television show. **2.** a remaining quantity or substance. **—re·sid′u·al·ly,** *adv.*

re·sid·u·ar·y (ri zij′ü er′ē) *adj.* of, relating to, or entitled to that part of an estate not otherwise disposed of by specific bequests.

res·i·due (rez′i dü′, -dū′) *n.* **1.** a substance remaining at the end of a separating process, such as evaporation, combustion, or filtration. **2.** anything that remains, as after a main part is taken away. **3.** *Law.* the part of a testator's estate that remains after all debts, claims, and bequests have been paid. [Middle French *residu* surplus, remainder, from Latin *residuum,* neuter of *residuus* remaining.] —For Synonyms, see **remainder.**

re·sid·u·um (ri zij′ü əm) *n., pl.* **-sid·u·a** (-zij′ü ə). residue.

re·sign (ri zīn′) *v.i.* to give up voluntarily, as a job, position, or office: *The president of the club resigned today.* *—v.t.* **1.** to give up (a position or responsibility) voluntarily: *to resign a job.* **2.** to make (oneself) accept without protest or complaint (with *to*): *to resign oneself to an unpleasant situation.* **3.** *Archaic.* to relinquish; surrender. [Old French *resigner* to give up, from Latin *resignāre* to unseal, annul.]

res·ig·na·tion (rez′ig nā′shən) *n.* **1.** the act of resigning. **2.** a formal, usually written, notice that a person is resigning. **3.** the acceptance of something without protest or complaint; acquiescence; submission: *to suffer a loss with resignation.*

re·signed (ri zīnd′) *adj.* characterized by or showing resignation; acquiescent; submissive: *a resigned attitude of acceptance.* **—re·sign·ed·ly** (ri zī′nid lē), *adv.* **—re·sign′ed·ness,** *n.*

re·sil·ience (ri zil′yəns, -zil′ē əns) *n.* the power or quality of being resilient. Also, **re·sil′ien·cy.**

re·sil·ient (ri zil′yənt, -zil′ē ənt) *adj.* **1.** capable of springing back to the original size, shape, or position after being bent, compressed, or stretched. **2.** capable of recovering quickly or easily, as from depression or adversity. [Latin *resiliēns,* present participle of *resilīre* to leap back, rebound.] **—re·sil′ient·ly,** *adv.*

res·in (rez′in) *n.* **1.** any of various translucent yellow or brown sticky substances, natural polymeric derivatives of organic acids, that are secreted by certain plants, such as pine or balsam fir trees, used esp. in the improvement of paints and plastics and in the manufacture of linoleum, adhesives, and rubber. **2.** any of various similar synthetic polymers that are the main constituents of plastics. **3.** rosin *(def. 1).* [Latin *rēsīna* resin from trees, from Greek *rhētínē* resin from the pine.]

res·in·ous (rez′ə nəs) *adj.* **1.** of, relating to, or resembling resin. **2.** obtained from or containing resin. **res′in·y.**

re·sist (ri zist′) *v.t.* **1.** to keep from yielding to; abstain from: *to resist telling a secret.* **2.** to fight or work against; repel or oppose: *to resist an invasion.* **3.** to withstand the action or effect of: *This metal resists corrosion.* *—v.i.* to act in opposition. *—n.* a coating that affords protection from corrosion, oxidation, or the like. [Latin *resistere* to withstand.] **—re·sist′er,** *n.*

re·sist·ance (ri zis′təns) *n.* **1.** the act of resisting. **2.** the capacity to resist something, esp. disease: *Low resistance may lead to a cold.* Also, **resistivity. 3.** an organized underground group that works against or opposes an occupying or oppressive army or government, esp. by guerrilla tactics. **4.** a force that opposes or hinders the motion of another: *Cars are streamlined to overcome air resistance.* **5.** the characteristic of a conductor that opposes

the flow of electric current and produces heat. A good conductor, such as silver, has low resistance; a superconductor, when cold enough, has no resistance. **6.** resistor.

re·sist·ant (ri zis′tənt) *adj.* offering resistance; resisting.

re·sist·i·ble (ri zis′tə bəl) *adj.* capable of being resisted. **—re·sist′i·bil′i·ty,** *n.* **—re·sist′i·bly,** *adv.*

re·sis·tive (ri zis′tiv) *adj.* **1.** inclined to resist; resisting. **2.** *Physics.* tending to oppose the flow of electric current and thereby produce heat; characterized by electrical resistance.

re·sis·tiv·i·ty (rē′zis tiv′i tē) *n.* **1.** resistance *(def. 2).* **2.** *Physics.* the degree of electrical resistance that is characteristic of a substance regardless of its size or shape; reciprocal of conductivity. Resistivity is highest in an insulator, lowest in a conductor, and intermediate in a semiconductor.

re·sist·less (ri zist′lis) *adj.* **1.** that cannot be resisted; irresistible. **2.** that does not or cannot resist.

re·sis·tor (ri zis′tər) *n.* an electric element or electronic component whose primary effect in a circuit is due to its resistance, often used to limit the flow of current or to produce heat, as in a toaster, electric stove, or broiler.

re·sole (rē sōl′) *v.t.,* **-soled, -sol·ing.** to put a new sole on.

re·sol·u·ble (ri zol′yə bəl) *adj.* capable of being resolved.

res·o·lute (rez′ə lüt′) *adj.* having or characterized by strong or steadfast determination. [Latin *resolūtus,* past participle of *resolvere* to untie, separate.] **—res′o·lute′ly,** *adv.* **—res′o·lute′ness,** *n.*

res·o·lu·tion (rez′ə lü′shən) *n.* **1.** the act or process of resolving or determining. **2.** something that is resolved upon; vow: *to make a New Year's resolution to get better grades.* **3.** a formal statement of a decision, opinion, or course of action, presented to or adopted by an assembly. **4.** the state or quality of being resolute. **5.** the act or result of settling, explaining, or solving: *the resolution of a problem.* **6.** the act or process of breaking or transforming into separate or simpler parts. **7.** *Optics.* the degree to which a system of lenses, as in a telescope or camera, enables discrimination of the fine details of an image. **8.** *Music.* **a.** the progression of a dissonant tone or chord to a consonant tone or chord. **b.** the tone or chord to which such progression is made.

re·solv·a·ble (ri zol′və bəl) *adj.* capable of being settled, explained, or solved.

re·solve (ri zolv′) *v.,* **-solved, -solv·ing.** *—v.t.* **1.** to decide (to do something); determine: *I resolved not to go to the party.* **2.** to settle, explain, or solve, as a mystery, problem, or dispute. **3.** to formally express a decision or opinion by vote, as in a legislative assembly. **4.** to dispel, as a doubt or fear. **5.** to break or transform into simpler or separate parts by or as by dissolution: *The prism resolved the light into the colors of the spectrum.* **6.** *Optics.* to separate (an image) into constituent parts and thereby make distinguishable: *A good telescope resolves this hazy patch of light into hundreds of stars.* **7.** *Music.* to progress from a dissonant tone or chord to a consonant tone or chord. *—v.i.* **1.** to come to a decision; decide (often with *on* or *upon*): *The board resolved on a budget for the project.* **2.** to be broken or transformed into simpler or separate parts, as by dissolution. *—n.* **1.** steadfast determination or firmness of purpose. **2.** something resolved upon; resolution. [Latin *resolvere* to untie, separate, disclose.] **—re·solv′er,** *n.* —For Synonyms *(v.t.),* see **decide.**

re·solved (ri zolvd′) *adj.* resolute; determined. **—re·solv·ed·ly** (ri zol′vid lē), *adv.*

resolving power, resolution *(def. 6).*

res·o·nance (rez′ə nəns) *n.* **1.** the quality or state of being resonant; fullness and richness of sound: *the resonance of a piano.* **2.** *Physics.* **a.** the state of a mechanical or electrical system characterized by a vibration or oscillation of large amplitude, occurring when an external force is applied at a frequency equal to or nearly equal to one of the natural frequencies of the system. Because of resonance, a swing will rise to a great height if it is given a regular series of pushes at the same frequency at which it swings. **b.** the vibration produced in such a state. **3.** the reinforcement and prolongation of sound by the sympathetic vibration of another object, as when the tone produced by the strings of a violin is enhanced by vibrations of the body of the instrument. **4.** *Chemistry.* the property of a molecule of being intermediate in structure between two or more theoretically possible forms that differ only in the distribution of their electrons. **5.** *Phonetics.* the intensification of a vocal sound caused by its vibration in a resonating cavity, such as the mouth or the nose.

a	at	e	end	o	hot	u	up	hw	white	⌠	about
ā	ape	ē	me	ō	old	ū	use	ng	song		taken
ä	far	i	it	ô	fork	ü	rule	th	thin	ə ⟨	pencil
âr	care	ī	ice	oi	oil	u̇	pull	th	this		lemon
				ou	out	ûr	turn	zh	measure	⌡	circus
		îr	pierce								

R

res·o·nant (rez′ə nənt) *adj.* **1.** continuing to sound; echoing. **2.** capable of increasing or prolonging sounds: *the resonant wood of a guitar.* **3.** having a full, rich sound: *a resonant voice.* [Latin *resonāns,* present participle of *resonāre* to sound again, reecho.] —**res′o·nant·ly,** *adv.*

res·o·nate (rez′ə nāt′) *v.i.,* **-nat·ed, -nat·ing.** to exhibit or produce resonance. [Latin *resonātus,* past participle of *resonāre* to sound again, reecho.]

res·o·na·tor (rez′ə nā′tər) *n.* a device that produces resonance or increases sound by means of resonance. [Modern Latin *resonator,* from Latin *resonāre* to sound again, reecho.]

re·sorb (ri sôrb′, -zôrb′) *v.t.* to break down and assimilate again, esp. a substance or structure previously produced by the body, as a fetus; reabsorb. —*v.i.* to undergo resorption. [Latin *resorbēre,* from *re-* again + *sorbēre* to suck.]

res·or·cin·ol (ri zôr′sə nôl′) *n.* a white crystalline substance made from benzene, used esp. in medicine and in making dyes. Formula: $C_6H_4(OH)_2$ Also, **res·or′cin.**

re·sorp·tion (ri sôrp′shən, -zôrp′-) *n.* the act or process of resorbing.

re·sort (ri zôrt′) *v.i.* **1.** to make use of or appeal to for aid, relief, protection, or support (with *to*): *to resort to lying when in trouble.* **2.** to go frequently or customarily, as for recreation. —*n.* **1.** a place where people go, esp. for recreation or relaxation: *a ski resort.* **2.** a person or thing that one makes use of or appeals to, as for protection or support: *Emergency shelters were the only resort for the tornado victims.* **3.** use of or appeal to, as for protection or support: *to have resort to friends in an emergency.* **4.** the act of gathering at a place frequently or regularly. [Old French *resortir* to go out again, repair[2], from RE- + *sortir* to go out (of uncertain origin).]

re·sort (rē sôrt′) *v.t., v.i.* to sort (something) again: *to re-sort index cards.*

re·sound (ri zound′) *v.i.* **1.** to be filled with sound: *The church resounded with music.* **2.** to produce a loud, echoing, or prolonged sound: *The brass band resounded as it marched down the street.* **3.** (of sounds) to be echoed; resonate; ring: *The shouts resounded in our ears.* **4.** *Archaic.* to be much talked about, esp. with praise; be extolled or celebrated: *Our leader's name will resound through the ages.* —*v.t.* **1.** to bounce back (sound); echo. **2.** *Archaic.* to extol or celebrate. [Old French *reson(n)er* to give back sound, give forth sound, from Latin *resonāre* to sound again, reecho.]

re·sound·ing (ri zoun′ding) *adj.* **1.** producing a loud, echoing, or prolonged sound: *a resounding thunderclap.* **2.** echoing or resonating with a deep or rich sound: *the resounding voice of an impassioned orator.* **3.** thoroughgoing; decisive; impressive: *a resounding achievement.* —**re·sound′ing·ly,** *adv.*

re·source (rē′sôrs′, -zôrs′, ri sôrs′, -zôrs′) *n.* **1.** a person or thing that is appealed to or made use of, as for aid or support. **2.** *usually,* **resources.** actual wealth or the means of producing wealth: *a country's resources.* **3.** skill and ingenuity in dealing with circumstances: *We must use all of our resources to solve the problem.* **4.** the action or means resorted to in an emergency or difficult situation; expedient: *In the desert, our only resource was to dig for water.* [French *ressource* resort, expedient, from Old French *resourdre* to rise again, from Latin *resurgere.*]

re·source·ful (ri sôrs′fəl, -zôrs′-) *adj.* capable of or skilled in dealing with new or difficult situations. —**re·source′ful·ly,** *adv.* —**re·source′ful·ness,** *n.*

re·spect (ri spekt′) *n.* **1.a.** a regard for or appreciation of the fundamental worth or value of a person or thing: *a respect for life.* **b.** recognition of superiority, worth, or excellence, as in force or wisdom: *The chief had the respect of everyone in the village.* **2.** the state or condition of being regarded with esteem: *The doctor is held in great respect in the community.* **3.** high or courteous regard or consideration: *to show respect for one's elders.* **4.** a specific aspect or manner; particular detail: *In some respects, I think you are right.* **5.** relation; reference: *an improvement with respect to grades.* **6. respects.** courteous expressions of regard and greeting: *Please send my respects to your family.* —*v.t.* **1.** to have or feel respect for; regard highly: *to respect honesty.* **2.** to show consideration for; act so as not to interfere with: *to respect a person's privacy.* **3.** to relate or refer to; concern: *The report is correct as it respects time and place.* [Latin *respectus* a looking about, regard.] —**re·spect′er,** *n.*

• **in respect of.** with reference to; regarding; concerning.

• **to pay one's last respects.** to attend a funeral or interment.

• **to pay one's respects.** to express courteous regard and esteem, as by a visit: *We must pay our respects to your parents tomorrow.*

Synonyms *n.* **Respect, regard,** and **consideration** mean a sympathetic or courteous attitude toward a person or thing. **Respect** suggests compliance with a social or moral code or set of values: *We are taught respect for the flag.* **Regard** indicates a general, formal goodwill: *Most people hold the medical profession in high regard.* **Consideration** implies sensitive, thoughtful awareness of the effects of one's actions: *The counselor treats all children with patient consideration.*

re·spect·a·bil·i·ty (ri spek′tə bil′i tē) *n.* the state, quality, or condition of being respectable.

re·spect·a·ble (ri spek′tə bəl) *adj.* **1.** having or showing proper or approved standards of conduct; worthy of respect: *a respectable leader.* **2.** well thought of; held in high esteem: *Respectable authorities differ on the question.* **3.** fit to be seen or used; presentable: *a respectable suit of clothes.* **4.** considerable in size or quantity; substantial: *There was a respectable turnout for the school play.* **5.** better than average; reasonably good: *a respectable performance.* —**re·spect′a·bly,** *adv.*

re·spect·ful (ri spekt′fəl) *adj.* full of, characterized by, or showing respect, esp. courteousness. —**re·spect′ful·ly,** *adv.* —**re·spect′ful·ness,** *n.*

re·spect·ing (ri spek′ting) *prep.* with respect to; concerning: *What are your views respecting the candidate?*

re·spec·tive (ri spek′tiv) *adj.* relating or belonging to each of two or more persons or things under consideration; particular: *We studied the respective advantages of each method.*

re·spec·tive·ly (ri spek′tiv lē) *adv.* with respect to each of two or more in the order considered: *Mr. Jones and Ms. Stein are, respectively, the producer and director of the film.*

res·pi·ra·tion (res′pə rā′shən) *n.* **1.** the act of breathing in and out. **2.** the metabolic processes by which living things obtain energy from food, including delivery of oxygen to tissues, oxidation of nutritive substances in the cells, and release of energy, along with carbon dioxide, water, and other oxidation products.

res·pi·ra·tor (res′pə rā′tər) *n.* **1.** a device with compressed air or oxygen, used in giving artificial respiration. Also, **ventilator.** **2.** a device worn over the mouth or the nose and mouth to prevent inhalation of fumes, dust, or the like.

res·pi·ra·to·ry (res′pər ə tôr′ē, ri spīr′ə-) *adj.* of or relating to respiration or to organs used in respiration: *a respiratory disease.*

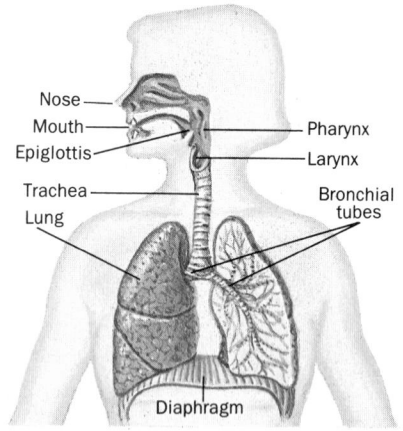

Nose — Mouth — Epiglottis — Trachea — Lung — Pharynx — Larynx — Bronchial tubes — Diaphragm

human **respiratory system**

respiratory system, the system of organs and passages by which living things take in and use oxygen. In mammals, the respiratory system includes the nasal passages, the mouth, the pharynx, the larynx, the trachea, and the lungs.

re·spire (ri spīr′) *v.t., v.i.,* **-spired, -spir·ing.** to inhale and exhale; breathe. [Latin *respīrāre.*]

res·pite (res′pit) *n.* **1.** a brief or temporary period of rest or relief, as from work or unpleasantness: *We took a short respite*

---

resow	resplice	resprinkle	restaff	restart	restipulation
respace	respray	resprout	restage	resterilize	restir
respecify	respread	restabilize	restamp	restimulate	restitch
respell	respring	restack	restandardize	restipulate	restock

from raking the leaves. **2.** a delay or postponement, as in carrying out a sentence of death. —*v.t.*, **-pit·ed, -pit·ing.** to give a respite to. [Old French *respit* delay, from Latin *respectus* a looking about.]

re·splend·ence (ri splen′dəns) *n.* the state or quality of being full of splendor; dazzling brightness. Also, **re·splen′den·cy.**

re·splend·ent (ri splen′dənt) *adj.* full of splendor; gleaming; brilliant. [Latin *resplendēns*, present participle of *resplendēre* to shine brightly.] —**re·splend′ent·ly,** *adv.*

re·spond (ri spond′) *v.i.* **1.** to give an answer: *to respond to a question.* **2.** to act in return; react: *to respond to bright light by blinking the eyes.* **3.** to be improved or positively affected by: *The patient responded to treatment.* —*v.t.* to answer by saying. [Latin *respondēre* to answer, promise in return.] —**re·spond′er,** *n.*

re·spond·ent (ri spon′dənt) *adj.* answering; responding. —*n.* **1.** *Law.* **a.** a person against whom a motion is filed or a case brought, esp. a defendant in a divorce case. **b.** a person against whom an appeal is brought. **2.** a person who responds.

re·sponse (ri spons′) *n.* **1.** the act of responding. **2.** something said in answer: *What is your response to the question?* **3.** *Biology.* behavior that is in reaction to an external influence or stimulus. **4.** words said or sung by a congregation or choir in answer to something said or sung by its leader. [Latin *respōnsum* answer, reply.] —For Synonyms, see **answer.**

re·spon·si·bil·i·ty (ri spon′sə bil′i tē) *n., pl.* **-ties. 1.** the state, quality, or condition of being responsible. **2.** a job, duty, or area of concern: *Opening the mail is your responsibility.*

re·spon·si·ble (ri spon′sə bəl) *adj.* **1.** accountable for the performance of duty or of a certain job or task: *Congress is responsible to the electorate for making laws.* **2.** faithful to one's obligations; trustworthy; reliable: *We need a responsible babysitter.* **3.** being the primary cause: *The freezing weather is responsible for the cracks in the pavement.* **4.a.** carefully and thoroughly considered, esp. as to consequences; prudent: *a responsible action.* **b.** kept within prescribed bounds; temperate: *responsible criticism.* **5.** involving obligations or duties: *a responsible position.* **6.** capable of making moral distinctions between right and wrong and thus to think and behave rationally and be held accountable for one's actions. **7.** under the supervision of; answerable to (with *to*): *The manager is responsible to the owner.* [Latin *responsus,* past participle of *respondēre* to answer + -IBLE.] —**re·spon′si·ble·ness,** *n.* —**re·spon′si·bly,** *adv.*

re·spon·sive (ri spon′siv) *adj.* **1.** readily reacting with sympathy, warmth, or understanding: *to be responsive to a friend's misery.* **2.** of, relating to, or conveying an answer: *a responsive gesture.* **3.** characterized by or made up of responses: *a responsive chant.* —**re·spon′sive·ly,** *adv.* —**re·spon′sive·ness,** *n.*

rest¹ (rest) *n.* **1.** a period of inactivity, relaxation, or refreshment, as after work or physical exertion: *The carpenter took a rest before finishing the job.* **2.** freedom from exertion, distress, or disturbance; quiet; ease: *a day of rest.* **3.** peace, quiet, and refreshment given by sleep: *One must get enough rest at night.* **4.** the state of being motionless: *Bodies at rest tend to remain at rest.*

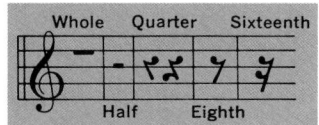

musical **rests**

5. something that serves as a stand or support: *a book rest.* **6.** a temporary lodging place: *a travelers' rest.* **7.** death. **8.** *Music.* **a.** an interval of silence between tones, corresponding in duration to a note of the same name: *half rest, whole rest.* **b.** any of the various symbols indicating such a pause. **9.** a pause or break in a line of verse; caesura. **10.** *Military.* a command to soldiers in formation, permitting them to relax and talk while keeping the right foot in place. —*v.i.* **1.** to relax or refresh oneself, esp. after work or physical exertion, as by sleeping or sitting down: *to rest in a hammock.* **2.** to be quiet or at ease: *They wouldn't rest until they knew their child was safe.* **3.** to come to rest; cease moving: *After skidding 90 feet, the car finally rested in a ditch.* **4.** to sleep: *I did not rest at all last night.* **5.** to be supported, as by leaning or lying: *My hands rested in my lap.* **6.** to be fixed or directed (with *on* or *upon*): *The audience's attention rested on the stage.* **7.** to remain without change or further action; stand: *to let a matter rest.* **8.** to be dependent; rely (with *on* or *upon*): *The outcome rests on your decision.* **9.** to be placed as a burden or responsibility: *The burden of proof rests on the accuser.* **10.** to be or lie in a specified place: *The trouble rests with them.* **11.** to lie in death: *May they rest in peace.* **12.** *Law.* to cease presenting evidence in a case voluntarily: *The defense rests.* —*v.t.* **1.** to give rest to: *We rested our horses after the long ride.* **2.** to put, lay, or lean (something), as for support: *I rested my arm on the table.* **3.** to direct or

fix, as the eyes. **4.** to make dependent; base; ground: *to rest a theory on years of research.* **5.** *Law.* to cease presenting evidence in (a case) voluntarily. [Old English *rest* quiet, repose, bed.]

• **at rest. a.** asleep. **b.** not moving; inactive. **c.** in a state of ease, as from worry. **d.** dead.

• **to lay to rest. a.** to bury. **b.** to put an end to: *Their safe return laid to rest all my fears.*

rest² (rest) *n.* **1.** something that remains; remainder. **2.** those remaining; others: *The rest are to wait for us.* ➡ used as plural in def. 2. —*v.i.* to continue to be; remain: *You may rest assured that I'll be there.* [Old French *reste* remainder, from *rester* to remain, from Latin *restāre* to stand still, remain.] —For Synonyms, see **remainder.**

re·state (rē stāt′) *v.t.*, **-stat·ed, -stat·ing.** to state again or in a new or different way. —**re·state′ment,** *n.*

res·tau·rant (res′tər ənt, -tə ränt′) *n.* an establishment where food is prepared and served to customers, often at tables by a waiter or waitress. [French *restaurant,* from *restaurer* to restore, refresh, from Latin *restaurāre* to restore, renew.]

res·tau·ra·teur (res′tər ə tûr′) *n.* a person who owns or manages a restaurant. [French *restaurateur,* from *restaurer.* See RESTAURANT.]

rest·ful (rest′fəl) *adj.* **1.** full of or giving rest: *a restful vacation, a restful sleep.* **2.** quiet; tranquil: *a restful landscape.* —**rest′ful·ly,** *adv.* —**rest′ful·ness,** *n.*

rest home, an establishment where housing and special care are provided for aged or convalescent patients.

rest·ing (res′ting) *adj.* **1.** in a state of rest or quiescence. **2.** *Biology.* **a.** dormant, as certain eggs or spores under unfavorable conditions. **b.** not undergoing division or preparing to divide, as cells or cell nuclei. [REST¹ + -ING².]

res·ti·tu·tion (res′ti tü′shən, -tū′-) *n.* **1.** the act of restoring something that has been lost or taken away. **2.** compensation for loss or damage; reparation. [Latin *restitūtiō* a restoring.] —**res′ti·tu′tive,** *adj.*

res·tive (res′tiv) *adj.* **1.** unable to rest; restless; fretful. **2.** stubborn and difficult to manage; unruly: *restive children.* **3.** refusing to move; balky: *a restive horse.* [Old French *restif* stubborn, refusing to go forward, from *rester* to remain. See REST².] —**res′tive·ly,** *adv.* —**res′tive·ness,** *n.*

rest·less (rest′lis) *adj.* **1.** nervous or agitated in mind or body; unable to rest. **2.** characterized by lack of rest; not restful: *a restless night.* **3.** constantly in motion; never still: *the restless sea.* **4.** constantly shifting or changing from one thing to another: *a restless mind.* —**rest′less·ly,** *adv.* —**rest′less·ness,** *n.*

rest mass, the mass of a body, as an atom or subatomic particle, that is not in motion, as measured by an observer who is also not in motion.

restoration at Plimoth Plantation, Massachusetts

res·to·ra·tion (res′tə rā′shən) *n.* **1.** the act of restoring or the state of being restored. **2.** something that is or has been restored. **3. Restoration. a.** the reestablishment of the English monarchy

a	at	e	end	o	hot	u	up	hw	white		about
ā	ape	ē	me	ō	old	ū	use	ng	song		taken
ä	far	i	it	ô	fork	ü	rule	th	thin	ə	pencil
âr	care	ī	ice	oi	oil	u̇	pull	th	this		lemon
		ir	pierce	ou	out	ûr	turn	zh	measure		circus

R

in 1660 under Charles II. **b.** the period following this, including the reign of Charles II, from 1660 to 1685, and sometimes also the reign of James II, from 1685 to 1688.

re·stor·a·tive (ri stôr′ə tiv) *adj.* **1.** capable of restoring: *a restorative medicine.* **2.** of or relating to restoration: *restorative work on a building.* —*n.* something that restores, esp. that which restores health or strength.

re·store (ri stôr′) *v.t.,* **-stored, -stor·ing. 1.** to bring back; reestablish: *The monarchy was restored.* **2.** to bring back to a former or original state or condition: *The cathedral was restored during the early eighteenth century.* **3.** to return (something lost, taken, or stolen): *to restore stolen jewels to the rightful owner.* **4.** to put back into a former job, rank, or position: *to restore a monarch to the throne.* [Old French *restorer,* from Latin *restaurāre* to repair[1], renew.] —**re·stor′er,** *n.*

re·strain (ri strān′) *v.t.* **1.** to hold in; keep in check: *Try to restrain your laughter.* **2.** to prevent from acting; hold back: *to restrain an excited dog.* **3.** to deprive of liberty, as by confinement in prison. [Old French *restraindre* to confine, bind, from Latin *restringere* to bind back, tighten.] —**re·strain′a·ble,** *adj.* —**re·strain′ed·ly** (ri strā′nid lē), *adv.* —**re·strain′er,** *n.*

re·straint (ri strānt′) *n.* **1.** the act of restraining or the state of being restrained. **2.** something that restrains. **3.** a holding back; reserve.

restraint of trade, interference with the free movement of goods or services or with free competition.

re·strict (ri strikt′) *v.t.* to keep within prescribed limits; confine: *The club restricted the use of the pool to adults on Monday nights.* [Latin *restrictus,* past participle of *restringere* to bind back, tighten.]

re·strict·ed (ri strik′tid) *adj.* **1.** confined or limited: *a restricted diet.* **2.** available exclusively to certain persons or groups: *The pool is restricted to club members.* **3.** intended for use only by authorized persons: *a restricted government document.*

re·stric·tion (ri strik′shən) *n.* **1.** something that restricts, such as a rule or limitation. **2.** the act of restricting or the state of being restricted.

re·stric·tive (ri strik′tiv) *adj.* **1.** serving or tending to restrict: *a restrictive policy.* **2.** *Grammar.* designating a word, clause, or phrase that limits the meaning of the word it modifies and is usually not set off by commas. In the sentence *Anyone who stands up to that bully will be a neighborhood hero,* the clause *who stands up to that bully* is restrictive. ➡ opposed to **nonrestrictive.** —**re·stric′tive·ly,** *adv.* —**re·stric′tive·ness,** *n.*

rest room, a public bathroom in a building; washroom.

re·sult (ri zult′) *n.* **1.** something that occurs or is brought about because of an earlier action, process, or condition; effect: *The accident was the result of careless driving.* **2.** the outcome of a mathematical operation: *If you divide 4 by 2, the result is 2.* —*v.i.* **1.** to be a result (often with *from*): *Low grades may result from poor study habits.* **2.** to have as a result; terminate (with *in*): *The contest resulted in a draw.* [Medieval Latin *resultare* to happen, proceed from, from Latin *resultāre* to spring back, rebound.] —For Synonyms *(n.),* see **outcome.**

re·sult·ant (ri zul′tənt) *adj.* occurring or brought about as a result. —*n.* **1.** result. **2.** *Physics.* a force, esp. as represented by a vector, that is the equivalent and result of, and has the same effect as, two or more forces acting together.

re·sume (ri züm′) *v.,* **-sumed, -sum·ing.** —*v.t.* **1.** to proceed after interruption: *The violinist resumed playing after intermission.* **2.** to take or occupy again: *to resume a former position with a company.* **3.** to take on or use again: *to resume one's maiden name.* —*v.i.* to begin again, as after an interruption: *The meeting resumed after a break for lunch.* [Latin *resūmere* to take up again.] —**re·sum′a·ble,** *adj.*

ré·su·mé (rez′ŭ mā′, rez′ŭ mā′) *also,* **re·su·me.** *n.* **1.** a statement of one's qualifications and work record, used in applying for employment. **2.** a summing up; summary: *a résumé of the major points of a lecture.* [French *résumé* summary, from *résumer* to sum up, from Latin *resūmere* to take up again.]

re·sump·tion (ri zump′shən) *n.* the act or an instance of resuming.

re·sur·gence (ri sûr′jəns) *n.* a rising again; revival.

re·sur·gent (ri sûr′jənt) *adj.* rising or tending to rise again: *a resurgent political party.* [Latin *resurgēns,* present participle of *resurgere* to rise again.]

res·ur·rect (rez′ə rekt′) *v.t.* **1.** to raise (a person) from the dead; restore to life. **2.** to bring back or restore (something) after disuse or neglect: *to resurrect the writings of a forgotten author.* —*v.i.* to rise from the dead. [From RESURRECTION.]

res·ur·rec·tion (rez′ə rek′shən) *n.* **1.** the act of rising from the dead. **2.** the state of having risen from the dead. **3.** the restoration of something after disuse or neglect; revival. **4. Resurrection.** in Christian belief, the rising of Jesus after his death and burial. [Late Latin *resurrēctiō* a rising again from the dead, from Latin *resurgere* to rise again.] —**res′ur·rec′tion·al,** *adj.*

re·sus·ci·tate (ri sus′i tāt′) *v.t., v.i.,* **-tat·ed, -tat·ing.** to bring up or come back to life or consciousness. [Latin *resuscitātus,* past participle of *resuscitāre* to raise up again.] —**re·sus′ci·ta′tion,** *n.* —**re·sus′ci·ta′tive,** *adj.*

re·sus·ci·ta·tor (ri sus′i tā′tər) *n.* **1.** a person or thing that resuscitates. **2.** a machine or other device that resuscitates by forcing oxygen into the lungs.

ret (ret) *v.t.,* **ret·ted, ret·ting.** to dampen, as flax or hemp, and cause partial rotting in order to soften and separate the fibers. [Middle Dutch *reten.*]

re·tail (rē′tāl′; *v.t., def. 2., also,* ri tāl′) *n.* the sale of goods or articles individually or in small quantities, directly to the consumer. ➡ distinguished from **wholesale.** —*adj.* of, relating to, or engaged in the selling of goods at retail: *a retail store.* —*adv.* in a retail quantity or at a retail price: *to buy furniture retail.* —*v.t.* **1.** to sell (goods or articles) individually or in small quantities directly to the consumer: *to retail clothing.* **2.** to repeat or retell: *to retail gossip.* —*v.i.* to be sold at retail: *This shirt retails for twelve dollars.* [Old French *retaille* a shred, paring, going back to Latin *re-* again + *tālea* rod, cutting; with reference to selling things in small amounts.]

re·tail·er (rē′tā lər) *n.* a merchant, dealer, or store that sells retail: *a retailer of children's clothing.*

re·tain (ri tān′) *v.t.* **1.** to continue to have or hold; maintain or preserve: *to retain ownership of land.* **2.** to hold back or contain: *The cracked jar would not retain water.* **3.** to keep in mind; remember: *to retain facts.* **4.** to employ by the payment of a fee: *to retain a lawyer.* [Old French *retenir* to hold back, keep, going back to Latin *retinēre* to hold back.]

re·tain·er[1] (ri tā′nər) *n.* **1.** an attendant or servant, esp. one who wears a uniform. **2.** a metal wire for holding teeth in place after they have been straightened with braces. [RETAIN + -ER[1].]

re·tain·er[2] (ri tā′nər) *n.* **1.** the act of employing in one's service. **2.a.** a written agreement by which a client hires an attorney. **b.** a fee paid by a client to an attorney in advance or for a specified period of time for legal services. [Middle French *retenir,* noun use of the infinitive *retenir* to hold back, retain. See RETAIN.]

retaining wall, a wall for securing a bank, as of earth or slag.

re·take (*v.,* rē tāk′, rē′tāk′; *n.,* rē′tāk′) *v.,* **-took, -tak·en, -tak·ing. 1.** to take again: *to retake a test.* **2.** to take back: *We retook possession of our property.* **3.** to capture again: *to retake a military position.* **4.** to film or photograph again. —*n.* **1.** the act of filming or photographing again. **2.** the result of this: *This retake was more in focus than the original photograph.*

re·tal·i·ate (ri tal′ē āt′) *v.,* **-at·ed, -at·ing.** —*v.i.* to return or repay in kind, esp. to return a wrong or injurious act with a similar one: *Belligerent nations are quick to retaliate against one another.* —*v.t.* to repay (an injury or wrong) in kind. [Latin *retāliātus,* past participle of *retāliāre* to requite.] —**re·tal′i·a·tive, re·tal′i·a·to′ry,** *adj.*

re·tal·i·a·tion (ri tal′ē ā′shən) *n.* the act of retaliating; reprisal. —For Synonyms, see **vengeance.**

re·tard (*v.,* ri tärd′; *n.,* ri tärd′) *v.t.* to delay the progress of (an action or process); slow; hinder: *A long and serious illness can retard growth.* —*v.i.* to be delayed. —*n. Slang.* retardate. ➡ considered offensive. [Latin *retardāre* to delay.] —**re·tard′er,** *n.*

re·tard·ant (ri tär′dənt) *n.* something that retards, esp. an agent that impedes the progress of a chemical reaction. —*adj.* tending to retard or hinder. ➡ usually used in combination: *fire-retardant wall insulation.* [RETARD + -ANT.]

re·tard·ate (ri tär′dāt) *n.* an individual who is mentally retarded. [Latin *retardātus* (past participle of *retardāre* to retard) + -ATE[1].]

restraighten	restyle	resurface	retape	retest	retitle
restrike	resubmission	resurvey	retarget	retestify	retrain
restring	resubmit	reswallow	retaste	rethink	retransfer
restructure	resubscribe	retabulate	reteach	rethought	retranslate
restudy	resummon	retabulation	retelevise	retie	retranslation
restuff	resupply	retag	retell	retighten	retransmit

re·tar·da·tion (rē′tär dā′shən) *n.* **1.** the act of retarding or the state of being retarded. **2.** something that retards; impediment; hindrance. **3.** mental retardation.

re·tard·ed (ri tär′did) *adj.* having or characterized by mental retardation.

retch (rech) *v.i.* to make an effort to vomit, often without regurgitating anything. [Old English *hrǣcan* to clear the throat.]

retd., returned.

re·te (rē′tē) *n., pl.* **-ti·a** (-tē ə, -shē ə, -shə). *Anatomy.* any interlacing network of vessels, fibers, or tubules, esp. capillary blood vessels; plexus. [Latin *rēte* net.]

re·ten·tion (ri ten′shən) *n.* **1.** the act of retaining or the state of being retained. **2.** the ability or capacity to retain. **3.** the ability to remember. [Latin *retentiō* a holding back.]

re·ten·tive (ri ten′tiv) *adj.* having the ability or capacity to retain: *a retentive mind.* —**re·ten′tive·ly,** *adv.* —**re·ten′tive·ness,** *n.*

re·ten·tiv·i·ty (rē′ten tiv′i tē) *n.* **1.** the ability or capacity to retain; retentiveness. **2.** *Physics.* the ability of a substance to remain magnetized after the force that induced the magnetization is withdrawn.

ret·i·cence (ret′ə səns) *n.* restraint or reserve, esp. in speech: *The child's reticence in class is due to shyness.*

ret·i·cent (ret′ə sənt) *adj.* restrained or reserved, esp. in speech. [Latin *reticēns* present participle of *reticēre* to be silent.] —**ret′i·cent·ly,** *adv.*

re·tic·u·lar (ri tik′yə lər) *adj.* **1.** of or resembling a net. **2.** entangled; intricate; complicated.

re·tic·u·late (*v.,* ri tik′yə lāt′; *adj.,* ri tik′yə lit, -lāt′) *v.,* **-lat·ed, -lat·ing.** —*v.t.* to form into, cover, or mark with a network. —*v.i.* to form a network. —*adj.* covered with or resembling a network. [Latin *rēticulātus* netlike, going back to *rēte* net.]

re·tic·u·la·tion (ri tik′yə lā′shən) *n.* a reticulated structure or arrangement; netlike formation. [RETICULATE + -ION.]

ret·i·cule (ret′i kūl′) *n.* a small handbag, esp. one made of woven material or net, formerly used by women. [French *réticule,* from Latin *rēticulum* little net, network bag, diminutive of *rēte* net. Doublet of RETICULUM.]

re·tic·u·lo·en·do·the·li·al system (ri tik′yə lō en′dō thē′lē əl) the system of macrophages, found esp. in bone marrow, the lymphatic system, liver, and spleen, whose function is to rid the body of foreign matter and germs.

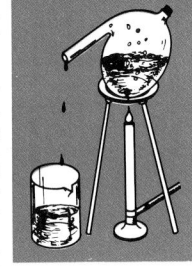

reticulate leaf

re·tic·u·lum (ri tik′yə ləm) *n., pl.* **-la** (-lə). **1.** any reticulated system or structure; network. **2.** the second stomach of cud-chewing animals. For illustration, see **ruminant.** [Latin *rēticulum* little net, network bag, diminutive of *rēte* net. Doublet of RETICULE.]

ret·i·na (ret′ə nə) *n., pl.* **-nas** or **-nae** (-nē′). the inner membrane of the eyeball, consisting of several layers of cells sensitive to light that transmit the images entering the eye to the optic nerve. For illustration, see **eye.** [Medieval Latin *retina,* probably from Latin *rēte* net; because it resembles a network.]

ret·i·nal[1] (ret′ə nəl) *adj.* of or relating to the retina. [RETIN(A) + -AL[1].]

ret·i·nal[2] (ret′ə nəl) *n.* retinene. [RETIN(A) + -al suffix used in names of chemicals having an aldehyde group.]

ret·i·nene (ret′ə nēn′) *n.* an orange-yellow carotenoid pigment, an aldehyde of vitamin A, produced when rhodopsin in the retina of the eye is exposed to light. Formula: $C_{20}H_{28}O$ Also, **retinal.** [RETIN(A) + -ENE.]

ret·i·no·ic acid (ret′ə nō′ik) a derivative of vitamin A, used in treating acne. Formula: $C_{20}H_{28}O_2$

ret·i·nol (ret′ə nôl′) *n.* vitamin A.

ret·i·nue (ret′ə nü′, -nū′) *n.* a group of people, such as servants or assistants, who accompany a person of rank or authority. [Old French *retenue,* from *retenir* to hold back, keep. See RETAIN.]

re·tire (ri tīr′) *v.,* **-tired, -tir·ing.** —*v.i.* **1.** to withdraw oneself from business, public life, or active service: *My grandparents both retired when they were sixty-five.* **2.** to go to bed. **3.** to go away, as for seclusion or rest: *to retire to the country.* **4.** to retreat, as from battle or danger; fall back. **5.** to move back or away, or appear to do so: *After serving the passengers dinner, the flight attendants retired to the rear of the plane.* —*v.t.* **1.** to remove from an office, position, or active service: *The board of directors retired the acting president.* **2.** to cause to withdraw from action. **3.a.** to pay off and cancel (an obligation, such as bonds or notes) before or on the date of maturity. **b.** to take (money) out of circulation. **4.** *Baseball.* to put out (a batter or side). [Old French

retirer to withdraw, from *re-* (see RE-) + *tirer* to draw, pull (of uncertain origin).]

re·tired (ri tīrd′) *adj.* **1.** no longer engaged in one's business or profession, usually because of age or poor health: *a retired baseball player.* **2.** secluded; withdrawn: *a retired cottage in the woods.*

re·tir·ee (ri tī rē′, -tīr′ē) *n.* a person who has retired from business, public life, or active service.

re·tire·ment (ri tīr′mənt) *n.* **1.** the act of retiring or the state of being retired. **2.** a place of seclusion or privacy.

re·tir·ing (ri tīr′ing) *adj.* tending to avoid people or publicity; reserved; shy.

re·took (rē tu̇k′) a past tense of **retake.**

re·tool (rē tül′) *v.t., v.i.* **1.** to change the machinery of (a factory) in order to adapt to the manufacture of new or different products. **2.** to reorganize to deal with new and different situations or conditions.

re·tort[1] (ri tôrt′) *v.i.* to make a reply, esp. in a quick, witty, or sharp manner. —*v.t.* **1.** to reply to in kind, esp. in a quick, witty, or sharp manner: *to retort an argument.* **2.** to return in kind, as an insult or injury; pay back. —*n.* **1.** a quick, witty, or sharp reply. **2.** the act of retorting. [Latin *retortus,* past participle of *retorquēre* to twist back.]

re·tort[2] (ri tôrt′, rē′tôrt) *n.* a container, usually consisting of a glass globe with a long tube extending downward, in which chemists distill or decompose substances by heat. [Medieval Latin *retorta* container with a bent neck; literally, twisted back, from Latin *retorta,* feminine past participle of *retorquēre* to twist back.]

re·touch (rē tuch′) *v.t.* **1.** to improve, as a painting, by additional touches or slight changes. **2.** to change (a photographic negative or print) by eliminating or adding details, often with an airbrush or brush and ink. —*n.* an additional touch, as to a painting or photograph, for improvement or change. —**re·touch′er,** *n.*

retort[2]

re·trace (rē trās′) *v.t.,* **-traced, -trac·ing. 1.** to go back over: *to retrace one's steps.* **2.** to trace back to a source or origin: *to retrace one's ancestors.* [French *retracer* to trace again, from *re-* (see RE-) + *tracer* to trace (going back to Latin *tractus,* past participle of *trahere* to draw).] —**re·trace′a·ble,** *adj.*

re-trace (rē trās′) *also,* **re·trace.** *v.t.,* **-traced, -trac·ing.** to trace over again, as in writing or drawing. [RE- + *trace.*]

re·tract (ri trakt′) *v.t.* **1.** to withdraw or recant (something); take back: *to retract a statement.* **2.** to draw (something) back or in: *The cat retracted its claws.* —*v.i.* **1.** to withdraw or recant something, such as an opinion or statement. **2.** to draw back or in: *Part of the roof retracts to allow the telescope to be extended.* [Latin *retractāre.*] —**re·tract′a·ble;** *also,* **re·tract′i·ble,** *adj.* —**re·tract′or,** *n.*

re·trac·tile (ri trak′təl) *adj.* capable of being drawn back or in, as the head of a turtle.

re·trac·tion (ri trak′shən) *n.* **1.** the act of retracting or the state of being retracted. **2.** a statement that retracts: *The newspaper printed a retraction of the story.*

re·trac·tor (ri trak′tər) *n.* **1.** a person or thing that retracts. **2.** a muscle that retracts an organ or protruded part. **3.** a surgical instrument for holding back the edges of a wound or incision.

re·tread (*v.,* rē tred′; *n.,* rē′tred′) *v.t.,* **-tread·ed, -tread·ing.** to put a new tread on (a tire casing). —*n.* **1.** a retreaded tire casing. **2.** *Slang.* a person who returns or is recalled to active duty or work, esp. in the military.

re-tread (rē tred′) *also,* **re·tread.** *v.t.,* **-trod, -trod·den, -tread·ing.** to tread again.

re·treat (ri trēt′) *v.i.* to withdraw, as from battle; draw back: *The defeated army retreated.* —*n.* **1.** the act of retreating. **2.** retirement to a quiet or private place: *a retreat from public life.* **3.** a place of retirement, rest, or relaxation: *a summer retreat.* **4.a.** retirement for religious study, contemplation, and prayer. **b.** a period of such retirement. **5.** a signal for a military retreat. **6.** *Military.* **a.** a flag-lowering ceremony at sunset. **b.** a signal, as on a bugle, played at this ceremony. [Old French *retraite* place of

a	at	e	end	o	hot	u	up	hw	white		about
ā	ape	ē	me	ō	old	ū	use	ng	song	ə	taken
ä	far	i	it	ô	fork	u̇	rule	th	thin		pencil
âr	care	ī	ice	oi	oil	u̇	pull	th	this		lemon
		îr	pierce	ou	out	ûr	turn	zh	measure		circus

R

refuge, from *retraire* to withdraw, from Latin *retrahere* to draw back.]

• **to beat a retreat.** to run away; flee.

re·trench (ri trench′) *v.t.* **1.** to cut back on (expenditures). **2.** to put an end to or remove: *The military regime gradually retrenched the people's freedoms.* —*v.i.* to reduce expenditures; economize. [Middle French *retrencher* to cut off, curtail, from *re-* (see RE-) + Old French *trencher* to cut (going back to Latin *truncāre* to cut off).] —**re·trench′ment**, *n.*

re·tri·al (rē trī′əl) *n.* a second trial, as of a judicial case.

re·tri·bu·tion (ret′rə bū′shən) *n.* **1.** the act of paying back for past deeds, esp. for evil committed. **2.** something that is done or given in repayment, such as punishment. [Latin *retribūtiō* repayment.] —For Synonyms, see **vengeance.**

re·trib·u·tive (ri trib′yə tiv) *adj.* serving as or characterized by retribution. Also, **re·trib′u·to·ry.** —**re·trib′u·tive·ly**, *adv.*

re·triev·al (ri trē′vəl) *n.* **1.** the act or process of retrieving or the state of being retrieved. **2.** the possibility of recovery or restoration: *The data is beyond retrieval.*

re·trieve (ri trēv′) *v.t.*, **-trieved, -triev·ing. 1.** to get back; recover; regain: *The golfer retrieved the ball from the lake.* **2.** to bring back to a former condition; restore: *Nothing could retrieve their spirits.* **3.** to make amends for; make good: *to retrieve a mistake.* **4.** to recall to mind: *to retrieve a name.* **5.** (of dogs) to locate and fetch (wounded or dead game). **6.** to get from storage, as in a computer. —*v.i.* (of dogs) to locate and fetch wounded or dead game. —*n.* the act of retrieving; recovery. [Old French *retreuv-*, a stem of *retrover* to find again, from *re-* (see RE-) + *trover* to find (of uncertain origin).] —**re·triev′a·ble**, *adj.*

re·triev·er (ri trē′vər) *n.* **1.** any of various hardy, medium-sized dogs with thick, coarse coats, originally bred to retrieve game for hunters. **2.** any dog trained or used for retrieving game.

retro- *prefix* backward, back, or behind: *retrograde; retrorocket.* [Latin *retrō.*]

ret·ro·ac·tive (ret′rō ak′tiv) *adj.* affecting something that has taken place prior to the time of enactment: *a retroactive law.* —**ret′ro·ac′tive·ly**, *adv.*

ret·ro·cede[1] (ret′rə sēd′) *v.i.*, **-ced·ed, -ced·ing.** to go back; recede. [Latin *retrōcēdere.*] —**ret·ro·ces·sion** (ret′rə sesh′ən), *n.*

ret·ro·cede[2] (ret′rə sēd′) *v.t.*, **-ced·ed, -ced·ing.** to cede back (territory). [RETRO- + CEDE.] —**ret·ro·ces·sion** (ret′rə sesh′ən), *n.*

ret·ro·fire (ret′rō fīr′) *n.* the firing of a retrorocket.

ret·ro·fit (ret′rə fit′) *v.t.*, **-fit·ted** or **-fit, -fit·ting.** to modernize (something) by incorporating improvements in design, construction, or equipment made in later models of the same type. —*n.* something, as an aircraft, that has been retrofitted.

ret·ro·flex (ret′rə fleks′) *also*, **ret·ro·flexed.** *adj.* **1.** bent backward. **2.** *Phonetics.* articulated with the tip of the tongue bent backward toward the soft palate. [Latin *retrōflexus*, past participle of *retrōflectere* to bend back.]

ret·ro·flex·ion (ret′rə flek′shən) *also*, **ret·ro·flec·tion.** *n.* the act of bending backward or the condition of being bent backward.

ret·ro·grade (ret′rə grād′) *adj.* **1.** moving backward; reversed: *Numbers in a countdown are given in retrograde order.* **2.** becoming worse; deteriorating: *There are retrograde conditions in the poorer section of the city.* **3.** moving from east to west, said esp. of the apparent motion of a planet relative to the motion of the earth or with respect to the stars. —*v.i.*, **-grad·ed, -grad·ing. 1.** to move backward; reverse. **2.** to become worse; deteriorate. [Latin *retrōgradus* going backward, going back to *retrō* backward + *gradī* to go.] —**ret′ro·gra·da′tion**, *n.*

ret·ro·gress (ret′rə gres′, ret′rə gres′) *v.i.* **1.** to move or go backward. **2.** to go to a worse or a less advanced condition. [Latin *retrōgressus*, past participle of *retrōgradī* to go backward.] —**ret′ro·gress′ion**, *n.*

ret·ro·gres·sive (ret′rə gres′iv) *adj.* of or characterized by retrogression. —**ret′ro·gres′sive·ly**, *adv.*

ret·ro·rock·et (ret′rō rok′it) *n.* a rocket engine that produces thrust opposite to the motion of a spacecraft in flight in order to reduce speed, to make mid-course corrections, or to separate a section of the spacecraft.

re·trorse (ri trôrs′) *adj. Biology.* bent backward or downward. [Latin *retrōrsus*, contraction of *retrōversus* bent backward, from *retrō* back + *versus*, past participle of *vertere* to turn.] —**re·trorse′ly**, *adv.*

ret·ro·spect (ret′rə spekt′) *n.* a contemplative view or survey of past events: *In retrospect, it seems we made a mistake.* [Latin *retrōspectus*, past participle of *retrōspicere* to look back.]

ret·ro·spec·tion (ret′rə spek′shən) *n.* the act of contemplating or surveying past events.

ret·ro·spec·tive (ret′rə spek′tiv) *adj.* **1.** looking back on or thinking about past events. **2.** applying to the past; retroactive. —*n.* an exhibition of works produced over a period of time by an artist or artists. —**ret′ro·spec′tive·ly**, *adv.*

ret·rous·sé (ret′rü sā′) *adj.* turned up at the tip: *a retroussé nose.* [French *retroussé*, past participle of *retrousser* to turn up, from *re-* (see RE-) + *trousser* to pack[1] (of uncertain origin).]

ret·ro·vi·rus (ret′rə vī′rəs) *n., pl.* **-rus·es.** any of a group of viruses that contain RNA and cause cancer in animals and AIDS in human beings.

re·try (rē trī′) *v.t.*, **-tried, -try·ing.** to try (a defendant or case) again.

re·turn (ri tûrn′) *v.i.* **1.** to come or go back, as to a former place or condition: *to return to consciousness, to return home.* **2.** to come or go back in thought or speech: *The speaker finally returned to the topic.* **3.** to happen or appear again; recur or reappear: *Winter returns every year.* **4.** to answer or reply. —*v.t.* **1.** to take, bring, send, give, or put back: *to return a book to the library.* **2.** to give or pay back in kind: *to return a phone call.* **3.** to give back as repayment for: *She returned his love with scorn.* **4.** to report officially; render: *The jury returned a verdict of guilty.* **5.** to elect or reelect: *The voters returned the senator to office.* **6.** to yield, as in income or profit: *The new tax returned only 50% of the estimated amount.* **7.** to carry (a football) in a runback. **8.** in certain games, such as tennis or badminton, to hit or throw (a ball or shuttlecock) back to an opponent. **9.** to say in response: *Questioned closely, the witness returned, "I don't remember."* —*n.* **1.** a coming or going back: *a slow return to health.* **2.** a recurrence or reappearance: *The return of winter brought hardship.* **3.** the act of taking, bringing, sending, giving, or putting back: *the return of a book to the library.* **4.** the act of giving or paying back in kind; reciprocation: *Thank you for your prompt return of my call.* **5.** an official or formal report: *a tax return, election returns.* **6.** *also*, **returns.** income or profit, as from land, labor, or an investment. **7.** answer. **8.** *Football.* runback. **9.a.** the act of returning a ball or shuttlecock. **b.** the ball or shuttlecock so returned. —*adj.* **1.** of, relating to, or for coming or going back: *a return ticket, a return route.* **2.** given or done in return for something: *a return visit.* **3.** played, performed, or presented again: *a return match.* [Old French *retourner* to turn back, give back, come back, from *re-* (see RE-) + *tourner* to cause to revolve, go around (from Latin *tornāre* to turn on a lathe). See TURN.] —**re·turn′er**, *n.*

re·turn·a·ble (ri tûr′nə bəl) *adj.* **1.** capable of being or meant to be returned: *returnable bottles.* **2.** required to be returned, as on a certain day. —*n.* a container or bottle that may be returned to a retailer when empty for a refund or deposit.

re·turn·ee (ri tûr nē′, -tûr′nē) *n.* a person who has returned, esp. to home from military service or duty abroad or to school after having dropped out.

re·tuse (ri tüs′, -tūs′) *adj.* (of a leaf) having a blunt, rounded end with a shallow notch or depression. [Latin *retūsus*, past participle of *retundere* to beat back.]

Reu·ben sandwich (rü′bən) a grilled sandwich of Swiss cheese, corned beef, and sauerkraut, usually spread with Russian dressing and served hot. [From the American restaurateur Arnold *Reuben*, 1883-1970, who created it.]

re·u·ni·fy (rē ū′nə fī′) *v.t., v.i.*, **-fied, -fy·ing.** to make or become one again after having been divided; restore unity to. —**re·u′ni·fi·ca′tion**, *n.*

re·un·ion (rē ūn′yən) *n.* **1.** the act of reuniting or the state of being reunited. **2.** a social gathering of friends, classmates, or relatives after separation or absence: *a high school reunion.*

re·u·nite (rē′ū nīt′) *v.t., v.i.*, **-nit·ed, -nit·ing.** to bring or come together again.

re·use (v., rē ūz′; n., rē ūs′) *v.t.*, **-used, -us·ing.** to use again, esp. after reprocessing or special treatment. —*n.* the act of using again. —**re·us′a·ble**, *adj.*

rev (rev) *Informal. n.* a revolution of a motor or engine. —*v.t.*, revved, rev·ving. **1.** to increase the speed of (an engine), esp.

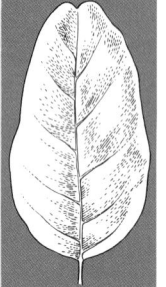

retuse leaf

while gears are not engaged: *The drivers revved their engines while waiting for the start of the race.* **2.** to excite or stimulate, as in anticipation of something (with *up*): *We were all revved up at the thought of vacation.*

rev. 1. revenue. **2.** reverse. **3.** review. **4.** revised. **5.** revision. **6.** revolution.

Rev. 1. Revelation. **2.** Reverend.

re·val·u·ate (rē val′ū āt′) *v.t.,* **-at·ed, -at·ing.** to set a new value for: *to revaluate currency.*

re·val·u·a·tion (rē val′ū ā′shən) *n.* **1.** the act or process of revaluating. **2.** the result of this.

re·vamp (rē vamp′) *v.t.* **1.** to repair or replace the vamp of (a shoe). **2.** to patch up, renovate, or revise: *The author revamped the novel.*

re·vanch·ism (ri van′chiz əm) *n.* a government policy that advocates or supports wars against other countries to regain lost territory. Also, **re·vanche** (ri vanch′, -vänsh′). [French *revanche* revenge (from Middle French *revancher* to avenge, from *re-* re- + *vencher,* variant of *vengier* to take vengeance, from Latin *vindicāre*) + -ISM.] —**re·vanch′ist,** *n., adj.*

re·veal (ri vēl′) *v.t.* **1.** to make known; divulge: *to reveal a secret.* **2.** to expose to view; display; show: *The clouds parted to reveal the full moon.* [Latin *revēlāre* to unveil, disclose.] —**re·veal′a·ble,** *adj.* —**re·veal′er,** *n.* —**re·veal′ment,** *n.*

> **Synonyms** Reveal, disclose, and divulge mean to make known something previously unknown or concealed. **Reveal** is the most general term, and connotes making something known either intentionally or accidentally: *Photographs transmitted by the Voyager spacecraft have revealed important new information about the solar system. I tried to appear calm before going on stage, but my shaking hands revealed my anxiety.* **Disclose** implies the deliberate uncovering of something previously kept hidden: *The couple disclosed that they had been secretly married for a year.* **Divulge** is similar to *disclose,* but may also imply a breach of trust: *Foreign agents persuaded the diplomat to divulge classified information.*

re·veil·le (rev′ə lē) *n. Military.* **1.** a signal, as on a bugle, to awaken military personnel and call them to formation. **2.** the first formation of the day, at which roll call is taken. [French *réveillez* wake up, imperative of *réveiller* to awaken, going back to Latin *re-* again + *vigilāre* to keep watch.]

rev·el (rev′əl) *v.i.,* **-eled, -el·ing;** *also, British,* **-elled, -el·ling. 1.** to take great pleasure; delight (with *in*): *The lottery winners reveled in their new wealth.* **2.** to participate in boisterous festivities; make merry: *The party guests reveled all night long.* —*n.* **1.** boisterous festivity; merrymaking. **2.** *also,* **revels.** an occasion of boisterous festivity; celebration. [Old French *reveler* to revolt, make merry noisily, from Latin *rēbellāre* to revolt, from *re-* again + *bellāre* to make war. Doublet of REBEL.] —**rev′el·er;** *also, British,* **rev′el·ler,** *n.*

rev·e·la·tion (rev′ə lā′shən) *n.* **1.** the act of revealing or disclosing; disclosure. **2.** something that is revealed or disclosed. **3.a.** a disclosure or communication of divine truth, esp. by supernatural means. **b.** something that has been so disclosed. **4. Revelation.** the last book of the New Testament, attributed to the Apostle John. Also, **Apocalypse, Revelations.** [Church Latin *revēlātio* uncovering, the Book of Revelation, from Latin *revēlāre* to unveil, disclose.] —**rev·e·la·to·ry** (rev′ə lə tôr′ē), *adj.*

rev·el·ry (rev′əl rē) *n., pl.* **-ries.** boisterous festivity; merrymaking.

re·venge (ri venj′) *n.* **1.** an opportunity to retaliate in return for an injury, wrong, or offense: *The victim's friends waited for their revenge.* **2.** a desire for vengeance; vindictiveness: *Revenge was their one consuming passion.* **3.** the act of retaliating in return for an injury, wrong, or offense. **4.** something that is done in return for an injury, wrong, or offense; vengeance. —*v.t.,* **-venged, -veng·ing. 1.** to inflict injury, harm, or punishment in return for: *to revenge an insult.* **2.** to take vengeance on behalf of (a person or oneself): *They vowed to revenge their parents.* [Old French *revengier* to take vengeance, going back to Latin *re-* again + *vindicāre* to avenge.] —**re·veng′er,** *n.*

> **Synonyms** *v.t.* **Revenge** and **avenge** mean to inflict damage or punishment in return for a wrong. **Revenge** suggests spite as a motive and an attempt to get even with someone: *The critic revenged himself on the actress who had spurned his advances by panning her performance.* **Avenge** implies an action, inspired by a sense of justice and an attempt to exact a deserved punishment, esp. for a wrong done to another: *They were determined to avenge the mistreatment of their comrade.*

re·venge·ful (ri venj′fəl) *adj.* full of or showing revenge; vindictive. —**re·venge′ful·ly,** *adv.* —**re·venge′ful·ness,** *n.*

rev·e·nue (rev′ə nü′, -nū′) *n.* **1.** the income from property or other investments or activities. **2.** the annual or current income of

a municipal, state, or federal government from taxation and other sources. **3.** an item or source of income. [Old French *revenue* rent, income, from *revenir* to return, from Latin *revenīre.*]

revenue sharing, the distribution of part of the taxes the federal government receives to state and city governments to help them pay their expenses.

revenue stamp, a stamp indicating that tax has been paid to the government, as for liquor, cigarettes, or hunting licenses.

re·ver·ber·ant (ri vûr′bər ənt) *adj.* reverberating; resonant. —**re·ver′ber·ant·ly,** *adv.*

re·ver·ber·ate (ri vûr′bə rāt′) *v.,* **-at·ed, -at·ing.** —*v.i.* **1.** to be echoed; resound: *The sound of footsteps reverberated through the empty house.* **2.** to be reflected, as light or heat. —*v.t.* **1.** to reecho (sound). **2.** to reflect, as light or heat. [Latin *reverberātus,* past participle of *reverberāre* to strike back, going back to *re-* back + *verber* whip, blow[1].] —**re·ver′ber·a′tive,** *adj.* —**re·ver′ber·a′tor,** *n.*

re·ver·ber·a·tion (ri vûr′bə rā′shən) *n.* **1.** the act or process of reverberating. **2.** something that is reverberated, as sound or heat.

re·ver·ber·a·to·ry (ri vûr′bər ə tôr′ē) *adj.* characterized or produced by reverberations. —*n., pl.* **-ries.** reverberatory furnace.

reverberatory furnace, a furnace or kiln that heats substances by means of a flame deflected downward from the ceiling.

re·vere (ri vîr′) *v.t.,* **-vered, -ver·ing.** to hold in deepest respect and affection; venerate. [Latin *reverērī* to stand in awe of, respect.] —**re·ver′er,** *n.* —For Synonyms, see **worship.**

rev·er·ence (rev′ər əns, rev′rəns) *n.* **1.** a feeling of deepest respect and affection; veneration. **2.** a gesture of respect, such as a bow or curtsy. **3.** the state of being revered. **4. Reverence.** a title used in addressing or referring to certain members of the clergy, usually preceded by *Your* or *His.* —*v.t.,* **-enced, -enc·ing.** to regard with reverence: *to reverence one's parents.* [Latin *reverentia* awe, respect.]

rev·er·end (rev′ər ənd, rev′rənd) *adj.* **1.** worthy of reverence. **2. Reverend.** a form of address used in referring to a member of the clergy, usually preceded by *the,* or used before the name, as in *Reverend Moore.* —*n. Informal.* a member of the clergy. [Latin *reverendus* to be respected, gerundive of *reverērī* to respect.]

rev·er·ent (rev′ər ənt, rev′rənt) *adj.* feeling or showing reverence: *to be reverent to one's elders.* [Latin *reverēns,* present participle of *reverērī* to respect.] —**rev′er·ent·ly,** *adv.*

rev·er·en·tial (rev′ə ren′shəl) *adj.* feeling or showing reverence; reverent. —**rev′er·en′tial·ly,** *adv.*

rev·er·ie (rev′ə rē) *also,* **revery.** *n.* **1.** fanciful musing, esp. on happy, pleasant things. **2.** an instance of this; daydream. [French *rêverie* dreaming, musing, from *rêver* to dream, muse, from Old French *resver* to be delirious, wander; of uncertain origin.]

re·ver·sal (ri vûr′səl) *n.* **1.** a change of fortune, esp. from good to bad. **2.** the act of reversing or the state of being reversed.

re·verse (ri vûrs′) *n.* **1.** something that is the direct opposite of something else; contrary: *Writing from right to left is the reverse of our usual practice.* **2.** a position of gears or mechanism in a machine that makes it transmit force or cause movement in a direction opposite to that which is usual. **3.** the back side of something: *the reverse of a fabric.* **4.** the side of a coin or medal that does not bear the principal design. ➡ opposed to **obverse. 5.** a change of fortune, esp. from good to bad; setback: *to suffer business reverses.* —*adj.* **1.** opposite, as in position, direction, or order. **2.** acting or moving in a direction opposite to that which is usual: *The reverse motion of the satellite was brought about by firing the retrorockets.* **3.** transmitting force or causing movement in a direction opposite to that which is usual: *in reverse gear.* —*v.,* **-versed, -vers·ing.** —*v.t.* **1.** to turn (something) around, upside down, or inside out: *to reverse a sock.* **2.** to exchange: *The debaters reversed positions.* **3.** to change to the opposite: *The government reversed its policy.* **4.** to turn or cause to turn or move in a direction opposite to that which is usual. **5.** to invert the order or sequence of: *to reverse a process.* **6.** to set aside, as a judgment; annul; revoke: *The judge reversed the original decision.* —*v.i.* to move or turn in the opposite direction, as in dancing. [Latin *reversus,* past participle of *revertere* to turn back, come back.] —**re·verse′ly,** *adv.* —**re·vers′er,** *n.*

re·vers·i·ble (ri vûr′sə bəl) *adj.* **1.** capable of reversing or of being reversed. **2.** made so as to be worn or used on either side: *a reversible jacket.* —*n.* a garment worn with either side out.

a	at	e	end	o	hot	u	up	hw	white		about
ā	ape	ē	me	ō	old	ū	use	ng	song		taken
ä	far	i	it	ô	fork	u̇	rule	th	thin	ə	pencil
âr	care	ī	ice	oi	oil	u̇	pull	th	this		lemon
		îr	pierce	ou	out	ûr	turn	zh	measure		circus

R

—re·vers′i·bil′i·ty, re·vers′i·ble·ness, *n.* —re·vers′i·bly, *adv.*

re·ver·sion (ri vûr′zhən, -shən) *n.* **1.** a return, as to a prior condition, practice, or belief. **2.** the act of reversing or the state of being reversed. **3.** atavism. **4.** *Law.* **a.** the return of an estate to the grantor or grantor's heirs after the period or term of the grant has expired. **b.** the estate so returned. **c.** the right of possession and future enjoyment of an estate presently in the possession of another. [Latin *reversiō* a turning back, returning.]

re·ver·sion·ar·y (ri vûr′zhə ner′ē, -shə-) *adj.* of, relating to, or involving reversion. Also, **re·ver′sion·al.**

re·vert (ri vûrt′) *v.i.* **1.** to return, as to a prior condition, practice, or belief: *Their thoughts reverted to the days of their youth.* **2.** to show, usually after many generations, an ancestral physical trait or characteristic. **3.** *Law.* to return to the grantor or grantor's heirs. [Latin *revertere* to turn back, come back.] —re·vert′er, *n.* —re·vert′i·ble, *adj.*

> **Usage** The phrase *revert back* is mistakenly used, as in *If all the money is not used, it will revert back to the general fund.* Since **revert** by itself means "return" or "go back," this phrase is redundant and should be avoided.

rev·er·y (rev′ə rē) *n., pl.* **-er·ies.** reverie.

re·vet (ri vet′) *v.t.,* **-vet·ted, -vet·ting.** to provide a revetment for (an embankment, rock, or other exposed surface). [French *revêtir,* going back to Latin *re-* again + *vestīre* to clothe.]

re·vet·ment (ri vet′mənt) *n.* any wall or covering, as of concrete or grass, that protects an exposed surface from erosion by the elements. [French *revêtement,* from *revêtir.* See REVET.]

re·view (ri vū′) *v.t.* **1.** to examine, study, or go over again: *to review notes in preparing for an exam.* **2.** to restate or present a summary of: *The speaker reviewed the key points for the audience.* **3.** to write or give a summary or critical evaluation of: *to review a book, to review a new restaurant.* **4.** to go over in one's mind; look back upon: *I reviewed the day's events with a smile.* **5.** to reconsider or reexamine (a court action) for constitutionality, legality, or points of law. **6.** to make a formal or official inspection of: *The general reviewed the troops.* **7.** *Archaic.* to view or see again. —*n.* **1.** the act of examining, studying, or going over again. **2.** a summary or survey: *The speaker presented a review of recent developments in the Middle East.* **3.** a summary or critical evaluation: *a review of a new motion picture.* **4.** a periodical containing articles of criticism, esp. relating to a particular field of interest: *a classics review, a literary review.* **5.** a reexamination by a higher court of an action of a lower court for constitutionality, legality, or points of law. **6.** a formal or official inspection, as of troops. **7.** revue. [French *revue* survey, critical article, magazine, from *revoir* to see again, going back to Latin *re-* again + *vidēre* to see.] —For Synonyms (*n.*), see **criticism.**

re·view·er (ri vū′ər) *n.* **1.** a person whose profession is to summarize or critically evaluate something, as books or plays. **2.** any person who reviews.

re·vile (ri vīl′) *v.,* **-viled, -vil·ing.** —*v.t.* to assail with insulting, contemptuous language; abuse verbally: *The defendant reviled the witness.* —*v.i.* to use abusive, contemptuous language. [Old French *reviler* to regard as vile, going back to Latin *re-* again + *vīlis* cheap, base².] —re·vile′ment, *n.* —re·vil′er, *n.*

re·vise (ri vīz′) *v.t.,* **-vised, -vis·ing. 1.** to change in order to correct, improve, or update: *to revise a manuscript.* **2.** to make different; alter: *to revise an opinion.* —*n.* a proof sheet embodying corrections made on a former proof sheet. [Latin *revīsere* to look back, revisit, going back to *re-* again + *vidēre* to see.] —re·vis′a·ble, *adj.* —re·vis′er, *n.*

Revised Standard Version, a modern edition of the Bible based on the King James Version and the American Standard Version. The New Testament was published in 1946 and the Old Testament in 1952.

Revised Version, a revised form of the King James Version of the Bible prepared by a commission of British and American scholars. The New Testament was published in 1881 and the Old Testament in 1885.

re·vi·sion (ri vizh′ən) *n.* **1.** the act or process of revising. **2.** something that is or has been revised.

re·vi·sion·ist (ri vizh′ə nist) *n.* a person who follows or advocates a revised or less vigorous version of a doctrine or creed, esp. one who revises Marxist doctrine by holding that socialism may be established by slow, peaceful means rather than by revolution. —re·vi′sion·ism, *n.*

re·vi·tal·ize (rē vīt′ə līz′) *v.t.,* **-ized, -iz·ing.** to give new life or vigor to after a period of decline: *The new office building revitalized that part of town.* —re·vi′tal·i·za′tion, *n.*

re·viv·al (ri vī′vəl) *n.* **1.** the act of reviving or the state of being revived. **2.** an awakening or return, as of a custom, style, or the like. **3.** an awakening or increase of interest in religion in a church, community, or denomination. **4.** a special service or series of services held to increase interest in religion.

re·viv·al·ist (ri vī′və list) *n.* a person who holds or promotes religious revivals. —re·viv′al·ism, *n.* —re·viv′al·is′tic, *adj.*

re·vive (ri vīv′) *v.,* **-vived, -viv·ing.** —*v.t.* **1.** to bring back to consciousness; resuscitate: *The firefighters revived the unconscious child.* **2.** to bring back into existence, use, currency, or awareness: *to revive an old movie.* **3.** to give new strength, vitality, or freshness to: *A good meal revived the weary hikers.* —*v.i.* **1.** to come back to consciousness; resuscitate. **2.** to show new strength, vitality, or freshness. [Latin *revīvere* to live again.] —re·viv′a·bil′i·ty, *n.* —re·viv′a·ble, *adj.* —re·viv′er, *n.*

re·viv·i·fy (rē viv′ə fī′) *v.t.,* **-fied, -fy·ing.** to restore to consciousness or give new strength, vitality, or freshness to; revive. —re·viv′i·fi·ca′tion, *n.*

rev·o·ca·ble (rev′ə kə bəl) *also,* **re·vok·a·ble** (ri vō′kə bəl). *adj.* capable of being revoked.

rev·o·ca·tion (rev′ə kā′shən) *n.* **1.** the act or fact of revoking: *the revocation of a driver's license.* **2.** the state of being revoked.

re·voke (ri vōk′) *v.,* **-voked, -vok·ing.** —*v.t.* to cancel or make no longer valid: *The city revoked the restaurant's license.* —*v.i.* renege *(def. 2).* —*n.* renege. [Latin *revocāre* to call back, recall.] —re·vok′er, *n.*

> **Synonyms** *v.t.* **Revoke, repeal,** and **rescind** mean to make something invalid by undoing it or setting it aside. **Revoke** implies the cancellation or annulling of something previously issued or declared: *The foundation revoked its earlier decision to give financial support to the research project.* **Repeal** is usually applied to the revoking of laws or governmental agreements: *Congress repealed the health insurance law it had passed the previous year.* **Rescind** often indicates the official voiding of an order or regulation: *The military commander rescinded the order to suspend all home leave.*

re·volt (ri vōlt′) *n.* **1.** an uprising or rebellion against existing governmental authority. **2.** any refusal to adhere or submit to authority or established practice. **3.** the state or condition of a person or persons who rebel: *to be in revolt.* —*v.i.* **1.** to rebel, esp. by beginning a revolution. **2.** to be disgusted or repelled. —*v.t.* to cause to feel disgust; repel. [French *révolter* to cause to rebel, disgust, from Italian *rivoltare* to overthrow, disgust, going back to Latin *revolvere* to roll back, revolve.] —re·volt′er, *n.*

> **Synonyms** *n.* **Revolt, rebellion, revolution, uprising, insurrection,** and **coup** mean an attempt, usually armed, to overthrow a government or ruling power. **Revolt** can be applied to a wide variety of attempts to cast off authority: *The shortage of food caused a revolt in the country's capital.* **Rebellion** describes a widespread, usually unsuccessful, defiance of authority: *The government called in the army to suppress the rebellion, which was spreading to different parts of the country.* **Revolution** is most often applied to a rebellion that is successful in overthrowing a government or system, and therefore implies great change: *The French Revolution did away with the monarchy.* **Uprising** denotes a limited, abortive attempt to seize power: *Several scattered uprisings preceded the revolution.* **Insurrection** is a more formal word applied to poorly organized military efforts to seize political power: *The general was imprisoned after leading the unsuccessful insurrection.* **Coup,** or *coup d'etat,* indicates an attempt by a small group to overthrow a government, often without bloodshed: *No one was injured in the overnight coup, which brought the army leaders to power.*

re·volt·ing (ri vōl′ting) *adj.* disgusting or repulsive; repellent: *a revolting smell.* —re·volt′ing·ly, *adv.*

rev·o·lute (rev′ə lüt′) *adj.* rolled backward, as the edges of a leaf. [Latin *revolūtus,* past participle of *revolvere* to roll back.]

rev·o·lu·tion (rev′ə lü′shən) *n.* **1.** the overthrow of an existing political system or form of government by those governed, usually by force, and the establishment of a new or different system or government. **2.** any sudden, far-reaching, or radical change: *Modern machines brought about a revolution in industry.* **3.** movement in a closed curve around a central point or object. **4.a.** a spinning or turning around an axis; rotation. **b.** one complete turn of a rotating body: *The crankshaft of this engine makes up to 5,000 revolutions per minute.* **5.a.** the movement of one celestial

reveto	revisualization	rewake	rewater	reweave	rewet
revindicate	revisualize	rewaken	rewax	rewed	rewind
revindication	revote	rewarm	reweaken	reweigh	rewrap
revisit	rewager	rewash	rewear	reweld	rezone

body in an orbit around another, esp. the movement of the planets about the sun. **b.** one complete course of such a body. **c.** the time it takes to complete this. **6.** a cycle of successive events: *the revolution of the seasons.* [Late Latin *revolūtiō* return, a rolling back, from Latin *revolvere* to roll back, revolve.] —For Synonyms, see **revolt.**

rev·o·lu·tion·ar·y (rev′ə lü′shə ner′ē) *adj.* **1.** relating to, of the nature of, or tending to promote a revolution. **2.** causing, involving, or constituting a complete or radical change: *a revolutionary new diet plan.* **3.** Revolutionary. of or relating to the American Revolution. —*n.,* *pl.* **-ar·ies.** a person who takes part in or supports a revolution.

Revolutionary War, American Revolution.

rev·o·lu·tion·ist (rev′ə lü′shə nist) *n.* revolutionary.

rev·o·lu·tion·ize (rev′ə lü′shə nīz′) *v.t.,* **-ized, -iz·ing.** to produce a far-reaching or radical change in: *The development of the airplane revolutionized transportation.*

re·volve (ri volv′) *v.,* **-volved, -volv·ing.** —*v.i.* **1.** to move in a closed curve around a central point or object; move in a circle: *The planets revolve around the sun.* **2.** to spin or turn around on an axis; rotate: *Wheels revolve when in motion.* **3.** to proceed or occur in a cycle; recur periodically, as the seasons. **4.** to have as a focus or central point; be concerned primarily (with *around*): *The doctor's whole life revolves around the hospital.* —*v.t.* **1.** to cause to move in a circle or orbit. **2.** to cause to rotate. **3.** to think about carefully; ponder; consider: *Revolve that thought around your mind.* [Latin *revolvere* to roll back.] —**re·volv′a·ble,** *adj.*

re·volv·er (ri volv′ər) *n.* a pistol fitted with a cylinder that holds the cartridges and revolves after each shot, thus enabling the weapon to be fired several times without reloading.

re·vue (ri vū′) *also,* **review.** *n.* a theatrical presentation usually consisting of songs, satirical skits, and jokes that parody people and recent events. [French *revue,* from *revoir* to see again. See REVIEW.]

re·vul·sion (ri vul′shən) *n.* **1.** an aversion aroused by something offensive; disgust; repugnance. **2.** the act of drawing back or away; withdrawal. [Latin *revulsiō* a tearing away.]

Rev. Ver., Revised Version.

re·ward (ri wôrd′) *n.* **1.** something given or received in return, as for service or merit; recompense: *The student received a certificate as a reward for high marks.* **2.** money offered or given, as for the recovery of lost property or the capture of criminals. —*v.t.* **1.** to give a reward to: *The judges rewarded each winner with a medal.* **2.** to give a reward for; recompense: *The city rewarded the firefighter's bravery.* **3.** to be a reward for: *Success rewarded their efforts.* [Anglo-Norman *rewarder,* form of Old French *regarder* to look at (suggesting looking at and judging to be worthy of reward). See REGARD.] —**re·ward′a·ble,** *adj.* —**re·ward′er,** *n.* —For Synonyms *(n.),* see **prize**[1].

re·wire (rē wīr′) *v.t.,* **-wired, -wir·ing.** to provide (a house, machine, or the like) with new electric wiring.

re·word (rē wûrd′) *v.t.* to write or say again in another way; put into other words: *to reword a question for clarity.*

re·work (rē wûrk′) *v.t.,* **-worked** or **-wrought** (-rôt), **-work·ing.** **1.** to process again for reuse: *to rework metal.* **2.** to rewrite or revise: *to rework parts of a musical composition.*

re·write (*v.,* rē rīt′; *n.,* rē′rīt′) *v.t.,* **-wrote** (-rōt′), **-writ·ten** (-rit′ən), **-writ·ing.** **1.** to write again, esp. in a different or improved form: *to rewrite an article.* **2.** *Journalism.* to write (a news story, based on a reporter's notes or description) in a form suitable for publication. —*n.* **1.** a revision of something that has been written: *a rewrite of a term paper.* **2.** a news story written from a reporter's notes or description. —**re·writ′er,** *n.*

Reye's syndrome (rīz, rāz) a rare, serious disease of the brain, occurring in children, usually following a viral disease such as influenza. [From the Australian pediatrician Ralph D. K. *Reye,* 1912-78, who first described it.]

Reyn·ard (ren′ərd, rā′nərd, -närd) *n.* in medieval fables, the clever fox who outwits other animals. [Old French *renard* fox; originally, the name of the fox in the medieval story of *Reynard the Fox,* from Old High German *Reginhart* literally, strong in counsel; referring to the wiliness of the fox.]

r.f. *also,* **R.F.** **1.** radio frequency. **2.** rapid-fire.

RFD *also,* **R.F.D.** Rural Free Delivery.

Rh, the symbol for rhodium.

R.H., Royal Highness.

rhap·sod·ic (rap sod′ik) *adj.* of, relating to, or characteristic of rhapsody; overly emotional or enthusiastic. Also, **rhap·sod′i·cal.** —**rhap·sod′i·cal·ly,** *adv.*

rhap·so·dist (rap′sə dist) *n.* **1.** a person who speaks or writes with intense emotion or excessive enthusiasm. **2.** a singer or reciter of poetry, esp. of epic poetry in ancient Greece.

rhap·so·dize (rap′sə dīz′) *v.,* **-dized, -diz·ing.** —*v.i.* **1.** to

speak or write with intense emotion or excessive enthusiasm. **2.** to write or recite rhapsodies. —*v.t.* to recite as a rhapsody.

rhap·so·dy (rap′sə dē) *n., pl.* **-dies.** **1.** speech or writing characterized by or expressing intense emotion or excessive enthusiasm: *to go into rhapsodies in describing a sunset.* **2.** an instrumental musical composition that is irregular in form and suggestive of improvisation. **3.** an epic poem or part of an epic poem, suitable for a single recitation. [Latin *rhapsōdia* part of an epic poem, from Greek *rhapsōidiā* epic poem, reciting of an epic poem.]

rhe·a (rē′ə) *n.* any of several flightless South American birds, genera *Rhea* and *Pterocnemia,* resembling, but smaller than, the ostrich and having predominantly brownish plumage. Height: 3½-4½ feet (1.1-1.4 meters). [Unexplained use of RHEA.]

rhea

Rhe·a (rē′ə) *n.* in Greek mythology, the wife and sister of Cronus and mother of Zeus, Hera, Poseidon, Hades, Demeter, and Hestia.

Rhein·gold (rīn′gōld′) *also,* **Rhinegold.** *n.* in Germanic legend, a hoard of gold kept at the bottom of the river Rhine, which gives its possessor magical powers.

Rhen·ish (ren′ish) *adj.* of or relating to the river Rhine or the regions bordering it. —*n.* Rhine wine. [Latin *Rhēn(us)* Rhine + -ISH.]

rhe·ni·um (rē′nē əm) *n.* a soft, heavy, silver-white element, with a very high melting point, used esp. in alloys for making electrical contacts. Symbol: **Re** For tables, see **element.** [Modern Latin *rhenium,* from Latin *Rhēnus* Rhine.]

rhe·ol·o·gy (rē ol′ə jē) *n.* the scientific study of the flow and deformation of matter. [Greek *rheos* current, stream + -LOGY.] —**rhe·o·log′i·cal** (rē′ə loj′i kəl), *adj.* —**rhe·ol′o·gist,** *n.*

rhe·o·stat (rē′ə stat′) *n.* an electrical device for varying the resistance of a circuit, used esp. in switches that dim lights gradually. [Greek *rheos* stream + *statos* standing.] —**rhe·o·stat′ic,** *adj.*

rhe·sus monkey (rē′səs) a yellowish brown monkey, *Macaca mulatta,* native to northern India, used extensively in biological experiments. [Unexplained use of the name *Rhesus,* a mythical king of Thrace.]

rhet·o·ric (ret′ər ik) *n.* **1.** the art or skill of speaking or writing effectively, esp. for the purpose of persuasion. **2.** the study of the rules and principles of literary composition and oratory. **3.** pretentious, inflated language in speech or writing; bombast; grandiloquence: *The politician's speech was mere rhetoric.* [Latin *rhētorica* art of oratory, from Greek *rhētorikē (technē)* rhetorical (art), from *rhētōr* orator.]

rhe·tor·i·cal (ri tôr′i kəl, -tor′-) *adj.* **1.** of, relating to, or like rhetoric. **2.** using rhetoric. —**rhe·tor′i·cal·ly,** *adv.* —**rhe·tor′i·cal·ness,** *n.*

rhetorical question, a question asked only for effect, with no answer expected: *The speaker asked the rhetorical question, "Don't we all want happiness?"*

rhet·o·ri·cian (ret′ə rish′ən) *n.* **1.** a person who is skilled in or teaches rhetoric. **2.** a person who writes or speaks in a grandiloquent manner.

rheum (rüm) *n.* **1.** a watery discharge from mucous membranes, as in the nose. **2.** *Archaic.* catarrh; cold. [Old French *reume* catarrh, from Late Latin *rheuma* flow, catarrh, from Greek *rheuma* stream, discharge from the body.] —**rheum′y,** *adj.*

rheu·mat·ic (rü mat′ik) *adj.* **1.** of, relating to, or caused by rheumatism. **2.** subject to or affected with rheumatism. —*n.* a person who is subject to or affected with rheumatism. [Latin *rheumaticus* troubled with rheum, from Greek *rheumatikos,* from *rheuma.* See RHEUM.] —**rheu·mat′i·cal·ly,** *adv.*

rheumatic fever, an inflammatory disease that sometimes follows a streptococcal infection, most frequently occurring in childhood, characterized esp. by inflammation in the connective tissues and often resulting in serious damage to the heart.

rheu·ma·tism (rü′mə tiz′əm) *n.* any of several diseases characterized by inflammation, swelling, and stiffness of the muscles and joints. [Latin *rheumatismus* catarrh, from Greek *rheumatismos* discharge from the body, going back to *rheuma.* See RHEUM.]

a	at	e	end	o	hot	u	up	hw	white		about
ā	ape	ē	me	ō	old	ū	use	ng	song		taken
ä	far	i	it	ô	fork	ü	rule	th	thin	ə	pencil
âr	care	ī	ice	oi	oil	u̇	pull	th	this		lemon
		îr	pierce	ou	out	ûr	turn	zh	measure		circus

R

rheu·ma·toid arthritis (rü′mə toid′) a chronic progressive disease involving an autoimmune reaction, affecting the joints and characterized by inflammation, swelling, and deformity of the affected joints.

Rh factor, a type of inherited antigen in the blood of most humans and higher mammals. Blood containing this antigen, **Rh positive,** often causes a severe antibody reaction when combined with blood lacking it, **Rh negative,** as in transfusions. [In reference to its discovery in the blood of the *rh*esus monkey.]

rhi·nal (rī′nəl) *adj.* of or relating to the nose; nasal. [Greek *rhīn-*, stem of *rhīs* nose + -AL[1].]

Rhine·gold (rīn′gōld′) Rheingold.

rhine·stone (rīn′stōn′) *n.* an artificial gem made of quartz or glass paste, used to imitate diamonds. [Translation of French *caillou du Rhin* literally, pebble of the Rhine; because first made at Strasbourg (located on the Rhine).]

Rhine wine (rīn) **1.** any of several light-bodied wines, usually white, produced in the vicinity of the Rhine Valley. **2.** any of various light white wines produced elsewhere.

rhi·ni·tis (rī nī′tis) *n.* an inflammation of the mucous membranes of the nose. [Greek *rhīn-*, stem of *rhīs* nose + -ITIS.]

rhi·no (rī′nō) *n., pl.* **-nos.** rhinoceros.

rhi·noc·er·os (rī nos′ər əs) *n., pl.* **-os·es** or **-os.** any of several thick-skinned herbivorous mammals, family Rhinocerotidae, native to Africa and Asia, having a large, rotund body, a massive head, and one or two horns rising from the snout. Height: 4½-6½ feet (1.4-1.9 meters) at the shoulder. [Latin *rhīnocerōs,* from Greek *rhīnokerōs,* from *rhīs* nose + *keras* horn; in reference to the horn(s) on its snout.]

rhinoceros

rhi·no·vi·rus (rī′nō vī′rəs, rī′nə vī′-) *n.* any of a large group of RNA-bearing viruses that cause the common cold. [Greek *rhīnos,* genitive of Greek *rhīs* nose + VIRUS.]

rhi·zoid (rī′zoid) *adj.* rootlike. —*n.* a rootlike filament of certain plants, such as liverwort and moss, that attaches the plant to the subsoil. [Greek *rhiza* root[1] + -OID.] —**rhi·zoi′dal,** *adj.*

rhi·zome (rī′zōm) *n.* a fleshy underground stem, usually growing parallel to the surface of the ground, containing stored food materials and bearing nodes that give rise to new plants. Also, **rootstock.** [Greek *rhizōma* mass of roots of a tree, going back to *rhiza* root[1].] —**rhi·zom·a·tous** (rī zom′ə təs, -zō′mə-), *adj.*

rhi·zo·pod (rī′zə pod′) *n.* any of a group of one-celled animals, class Rhizopoda, including amebas, that form temporary projections of protoplasm for locomotion and for taking in food. [Modern Latin *Rhizopoda* literally, having rootlike feet, from Greek *rhiza* root[1] + -POD.]

rho (rō) *n., pl.* **rhos.** the seventeenth letter of the Greek alphabet (P, ρ), corresponding to English *R, r.*

Rhode Island Red (rōd) any of an American breed of domestic fowl having dark red plumage marked with black on the wings and tail.

Rho·de·sian man (rō dē′zhən) an extinct Pleistocene hominid whose remains were first discovered in Northern Rhodesia (now Zambia).

rho·di·um (rō′dē əm) *n.* a heavy, silver-white, corrosion-resistant metallic element, often used in alloys with platinum for making high-temperature laboratory equipment. Symbol: **Rh** For tables, see **element.** [Modern Latin *rhodium,* from Greek *rhodon* rose[1]; because its salts are rose-colored.]

rho·do·den·dron (rō′də den′drən) *n.* any of a large group of shrubs and trees, usually evergreen, genus *Rhododendron,* bearing clusters of usually bell-shaped pink, white, or purple flowers. [Latin *rhododendron* oleander, from Greek *rhododendron* literally, rose tree, from *rhodon* rose[1] + *dendron* tree.]

rho·dop·sin (rō dop′sin) *n.* a deep red, photosensitive pigment in the rods of the retina whose conversion to retinene triggers nerve impulses to the brain. Rhodopsin plays an important part in night vision. Also, **visual purple.** [Greek *rhodon* rose[1] + *opsis* sight (from *ops* eye) + -IN[1].]

rhomb (rom, romb) *n.* rhombus.

rhom·bic (rom′bik) *adj.* relating to or having the form of a rhombus. Also, **rhom′bi·cal.**

rhom·bo·he·dron (rom′bə hē′drən) *n., pl.* **-drons** or **-dra** (-drə). a six-sided prism whose faces are rhombuses. [Modern Latin *rhombohedron,* from Greek *rhombos* magic wheel, lozenge + *hedra* base[1], side.]

rhom·boid (rom′boid) *n.* an oblique-angled parallelogram with unequal adjacent sides. —*adj.* **1.** having the shape of a rhomboid. **2.** having a shape similar to that of a rhombus. [Late Latin *rhomboīdēs* the geometric figure, from Greek *rhomboeidēs* shaped like a rhombus, from *rhombos.* See RHOMBUS.] —**rhom·boi′dal,** *adj.*

rhom·bus (rom′bəs) *n., pl.* **-bus·es** or **-bi** (-bī). an equilateral parallelogram having two obtuse angles and two acute angles. [Latin *rhombus,* from Greek *rhombos* magic wheel, lozenge.]

rhu·barb (rü′bärb) *n.* **1.** any of several Asian plants of the genus *Rheum,* cultivated in temperate areas. Some species, as *R. rhabarbarum,* have edible reddish leafstalks, which have a slight acidic taste; others have a medicinal rhizome from which a cathartic, astringent compound is obtained.

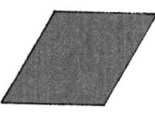
rhombus

Also, **pieplant. 2.** the leafstalks of the edible species of these plants, cooked in pies, sauces, and other dishes. **3.** *Slang.* a heated dispute or squabble. [Old French *reubarbe* this plant,. its stalks used as food, from Medieval Latin *rheubarbarum* the plant, going back to Greek *rhēon barbaron* literally, foreign rhubarb.]

rhum·ba (rum′bə) rumba.

rhumb line (rum, rumb) the path of a ship traveling in a constant direction, forming a line that intersects all meridians at the same angle when plotted on a map or globe. Also, **rhumb.**

rhyme (rīm) *also,* **rime.** *n.* **1.** the correspondence or repetition of sounds in words, esp. at the ends of lines of verse. **2.** a word having a sound that is similar to or the same as another. *Tide* is a rhyme for *side.* **3.** a verse or poetry whose lines have similar or the same terminal sounds. —*v.,* **rhymed, rhym·ing.** —*v.i.* **1.** to form or make a rhyme. *Stale* rhymes with *pail.* **2.** to compose rhyme or verse. —*v.t.* **1.** to put into rhyme: *to rhyme a fable.* **2.** to use (a word) as a rhyme. [Old French *rime* correspondence of the final sounds of words or lines of verse; of Germanic origin; confused with English *rhythm.*] —**rhym′er,** *n.*

•**rhyme or reason.** sense or logic: *Your scheme to find sunken treasures is without rhyme or reason.*

rhyme royal, in poetry, a stanza of seven lines in iambic pentameter in which the first and third lines rhyme, the second, fourth, and fifth lines rhyme, and the sixth and seventh lines rhyme: *ababbcc.* It was first used in English by the fourteenth-century English poet Geoffrey Chaucer.

rhyme scheme, the arrangement of rhymes in a poem, stanza, or verse. Rhyme scheme is usually indicated by letters, as *a, b, c,* which mark each corresponding rhyme, so that *ababbcc* indicates the pattern of rhyme royal.

rhyme·ster (rīm′stər) *also,* **rimester.** *n.* a writer of poor rhymes or verses; poetaster.

rhyn·cho·ce·pha·li·an (ring′kō sə fā′lē ən, -fāl′yən) *n.* any member of a group of lizardlike reptiles, order Rhynchocephalia, having two complete bony arches in the cheek region and a beaked upper jaw, of which the tuatara is the sole surviving representative. —*adj.* of or relating to this order of reptiles. [Greek *rhynchos* snout + *kephalē* head + -IAN.]

rhy·o·lite (rī′ə līt′) *n.* a light-colored volcanic rock with an acidic, silica-rich composition like that of granite. [German *rhyolit,* from Greek *rhyax* stream (of lava) + -LITE; because it commonly occurs as a lava flow.] —**rhy·o·lit·ic** (rī′ə lit′ik), *adj.*

rhythm (rith′əm) *n.* **1.** the regular repetition or orderly recurrence of elements, as sounds or movements: *the rhythm of drumbeats.* **2.** movement marked by such repetition or recurrence. **3.** *Poetry.* meter. **4.** *Music.* **a.** a repetition of beats, formed by the different lengths of tones and the way in which the tones are accented. **b.** a specific or characteristic form of this: *tango rhythm, disco rhythm.* [Latin *rhythmus* measure in music or speech, from Greek *rhythmos* measured motion, time, proportion.]

rhythm and blues, a style of American popular music based on the blues and characterized by a strong rhythm and steady beat. It formed the foundation for rock'n'roll.

rhyth·mi·cal (rith′mi kəl) *adj.* of, relating to, or characterized by rhythm. Also, **rhyth′mic.** —**rhyth′mi·cal·ly,** *adv.*

rhythm method, a method of birth control based on not having sexual intercourse during the time of month when ovulation is likely to occur.

RI, the postal abbreviation for Rhode Island.

R.I., Rhode Island.

ri·al (rī′əl) *n.* the monetary unit of Iran and Oman. [Persian *rial,* from Arabic *riyāl* Arab coin, from Spanish *real* royal, from Latin *rēgalis,* from *rēx* king.]

ri·al·to (rē al′tō, -äl′tō) *n., pl.* **-tos.** any bustling, centrally located district in a large city, esp. a commercial or a theater district.

ri·a·ta (rē ä′tə) *n.* lariat; lasso.

rib (rib) *n.* **1.** in most vertebrates, one of the series of curved bones attached in pairs to the backbone and enclosing the chest

cavity. For illustration, see **skeleton**. **2.** a cut of meat including one or more ribs. **3.** any long, stiff structural part, as an exposed timber in an arched roof or a thin rod in the fabric of an umbrella. **4.** a raised ridge, as in a knitted sweater or sock. **5.** a primary vein or any prominent vein of a leaf or leaflike organ. **6.** *Informal.* a remark made in jest; joke. —*v.t.,* **ribbed, rib·bing. 1.** *Informal.* to poke fun at; tease. **2.** to strengthen or support with ribs. **3.** to make raised ridges in. [Old English *ribb* the bone.] —**rib′ber,** *n.*
rib·ald (rib′əld) *adj.* characterized by vulgarity or coarseness; indecent: *ribald humor.* [Old French *ribaud* ruffian, from *riber* to be licentious; of Germanic origin.]
rib·ald·ry (rib′əl drē) *n.* ribald behavior or language.
rib·and (rib′ənd) *also,* **rib·band.** *n. Archaic.* ribbon.
ribbed (ribd) *adj.* marked with or having ribs: *a ribbed fabric.*
rib·bing (rib′ing) *n.* **1.** *Informal.* teasing. **2.** ribs collectively.
rib·bon (rib′ən) *n.* **1.** a band of fabric, paper, or other material used for decoration, as in trimming garments or tying packages. **2.** any similar band of a flexible material, as the inked strip of cloth used in a typewriter against which the characters are struck to print on the paper beneath. **3.** a narrow band or strip: *The road was a ribbon of concrete across the desert.* **4.** *Military.* a small strip of cloth of one or more colors worn on the left breast of a uniform or other garment to indicate the award of a particular medal or other honor. **5.** a strip of colored material awarded as a prize or symbol of honor or achievement. [Old French *riban, ruban* the band of fabric; of Germanic origin.] —**rib′bon·like′,** *adj.*
·to cut (or **tear**) **to ribbons.** to destroy or demolish.
rib·bon·fish (rib′ən fish′) *n., pl.* **-fish** or **-fish·es.** any of various snakelike fish, families Trachipteridae, Regalicidae, and Lophotidae, inhabiting deep seas throughout the world, having a single fin that begins at the head and runs the length of the body. Length: 8-20 feet (2.4-6.1 meters).
ribbon worm, any of a group of long, flat, unsegmented, marine worms, phylum Nemertinea, with no true body cavity and a retractible, hooked proboscis. Some species reach a length of 100 feet (30 meters). [Because its size and shape are reminiscent of a ribbon.]
rib cage, the protective bony framework of the chest, made up of the ribs, sternum, and upper part of the backbone.
ri·bo·fla·vin (rī′bə flā′vin) *n.* an orange-yellow, water-soluble vitamin of the B complex, required for growth and the utilization of carbohydrates, and found in liver, eggs, milk, and lean meats. Formula: $C_{17}H_{20}N_4O_6$ Also, **lactoflavin, vitamin B$_2$, vitamin G.**
ri·bo·nu·cle·ase (rī′bō nü′klē ās′, -nū′-) *n.* any of various enzymes that are instrumental in the hydrolysis of RNA. [RIBO(SE) + NUCLEASE.]
ri·bo·nu·cle·ic acid (rī′bō nü klē′ik, -nū-) see **RNA.**
ri·bo·nu·cle·o·tide (rī′bō nü′klē ə tīd′, -nū′-) *n.* a nucleotide containing ribose, one of the building blocks of RNA. [RIBO(SE) + NUCLEOTIDE.]
ri·bose (rī′bōs) *n.* a simple sugar that is a component of ribonucleic acid. Formula: $C_5H_{10}O_5$
ri·bo·some (rī′bə sōm′) *n.* a tiny structure in the cytoplasm of cells where protein is manufactured for cell growth and other activities. For illustration, see **cell.** —**ri′bo·so′mal,** *adj.*
rice (rīs) *n.* **1.** the edible grains of a cereal grass, *Oryza sativa,* grown in many warm regions, that is an important food in countries such as India and China. **2.** the plant itself. —*v.t.,* **riced, ric·ing.** to reduce to small grains resembling rice: *to rice potatoes.* [Old French *ris* the grain and the plant, from Italian *riso,* through Latin, from Greek *orȳza;* probably of Persian origin.]
rice·bird (rīs′bûrd′) *n.* any of several birds, as the bobolink, that are common in rice-growing areas.
rice paper 1. a thin paper made from the stems of rice plants. **2.** a fine, thin paper made from the pith of other plants.
ric·er (rī′sər) *n.* a kitchen utensil used to rice vegetables, such as potatoes, by forcing them through small perforations.
rich (rich) *adj.* **1.** having great wealth: *a rich industrialist.* **2.** well-supplied with something; abounding: *The old house was rich in memories.* **3.** productive; fertile: *a rich harvest, a rich imagination.* **4.** deep and full in tone or quality: *a rich brown color, a rich baritone voice.* **5.** (of foods) having a heavy, strong flavor or containing concentrated amounts of nutritious, sugary, or creamy ingredients: *a rich sauce.* **6.** not thin or diluted: *a rich mixture of fuel.* **7.** elegant; sumptuous; extravagant: *rich ornamentation.* **8.** *Informal.* amusing; ridiculous. —*n.* **the rich.** wealthy people collectively. [Middle English *rich,* from Old English *rīce* powerful, wealthy. Related to RICHES.] —**rich′ness,** *n.*
rich·es (rich′iz) *pl. n.* an abundance of money, land, or other valuable possessions; wealth. [Middle English *richess,* from Old French *richesse,* from *riche* rich. Related to RICH.]
rich·ly (rich′lē) *adv.* **1.** amply; fully: *rewards richly merited.* **2.** in a rich manner: *a richly decorated vase.*

Richter Scale

The Richter scale is used to measure the magnitude of earthquakes. Magnitude, in this case, is defined as the amount of energy released at a quake's epicenter, or focus. The distance felt is the distance (in miles or kilometers) over which tremors can be felt.

Magnitude	Distance Felt	Some Effects of Earthquakes
1.0–2.9	—	Usually detected only by seismometers
3.0–3.9	15.5 mi (25 km)	Vibration felt; suspended objects swing
4.0–4.9	31 mi (50 km)	Walls crack; dishes and windows may break
5.0–5.9	68.5 mi (110 km)	Heavy furniture moves; some damage to well-constructed buildings; considerable damage to poorly built buildings
6.0–6.9	124 mi (200 km)	Heavy furniture may overturn; considerable damage to ordinary buildings; walls and chimneys collapse
7.0–7.9	248.6 mi (400 km)	Considerable damage to specially constructed buildings; shift in foundations; many structures destroyed; underground pipes broken; ground cracks; landslides
8.0–9.0	450.6 mi (725 km)	Buildings and bridges destroyed; land movement; rails bend; broad fissures; total devastation (8.5 or higher)

Rich·ter scale (rik′tər) a logarithmic scale for measuring the magnitude of earthquakes, having graded steps from 1 upward, with each step representing approximately ten times the magnitude of the preceding step. Magnitude 1.5 stands for a very slight earthquake, 4.5 for an earthquake causing slight damage, and 8.5 for a devastating earthquake. [From Charles F. *Richter,* 1900-85, American seismologist who devised this scale.]
rick (rik) *n.* a stack of hay, straw, or grain often covered for protection from the weather. —*v.t.* to form into a rick or ricks. [Old English *hrēac* heap.]
rick·ets (rik′its) *n.* a disease occurring in infants and children, usually caused by lack of vitamin D, calcium, and often phosphorus, characterized by softening, and sometimes bending, of the bones and enlargement of the liver and spleen. Also, **rachitis.** [Of uncertain origin.]
rick·ett·si·a (ri ket′sē ə) *n., pl.* **-si·ae** (-sē ē′) or **si·as.** any of a genus, *Rickettsia,* of bacterialike parasitic microorganisms living in various insects, mites, and ticks, which can transmit them to animals and humans, causing diseases that include Rocky Mountain spotted fever and typhus. [From Harold T. *Ricketts,* 1871-1910, U.S. pathologist who discovered the bacterium that causes typhus.] —**rick·ett′si·al,** *adj.*
rick·et·y (rik′i tē) *adj.* **1.** liable to fall; tottering; shaky: *a rickety old fence.* **2.** affected with, subject to, or like rickets. **3.** weak in the joints; infirm. —**rick′et·i·ness,** *n.*
rick·rack (rik′rak′) *n.* a flat braid made in a zigzag pattern, used as a trimming on material. [From RACK¹.]
rick·sha (rik′shô′) *also,* **rick·shaw.** *n.* a two-wheeled carriage with a retractable top, drawn by one or two persons, originally used in the Orient. Also, **jin·rick′sha, jin·rik′i·sha.** [Short for JINRICKSHA.]
ric·o·chet (rik′ə shā′, rik′ə shā′; *British,* rik′ə shet′) *n.* **1.** the skipping or glancing of an object off a surface that it strikes at an

a	at	e	end	o	hot	u	up	hw	white		about
ā	ape	ē	me	ō	old	ū	use	ng	song		taken
ä	far	i	it	ô	fork	ü	rule	th	thin	ə	pencil
âr	care	ī	ice	oi	oil	u̇	pull	th	this		lemon
		îr	pierce	ou	out	ûr	turn	zh	measure		circus

R

angle. **2.** an object skipping or glancing in this way, as a bullet: *A bystander was hit by a ricochet during the gun battle.* —*v.i.,* **-cheted** (-shād′), **-chet·ing** (-shā′ing); *also, British,* **-chet·ted** (-shet′id), **-chet·ting** (-shet′ing). to skip or glance off a surface: *The ball ricocheted off the step.* [French *ricochet* rebound, succession; of uncertain origin.]

ri·cot·ta (ri kot′ə, -kô′tə) *n.* a soft, moist uncured cheese resembling cottage cheese, made from whole milk or whey. [Italian *ricotta,* from Latin *recocta,* feminine past participle of *recoquere* to cook again.]

rid¹ (rid) *v.t.,* **rid** or **rid·ded, rid·ding.** to clear or free, as from something unpleasant or undesirable. [Old Norse *rythja* to clear, empty.]
· **to be rid of.** to be free from: *to be rid of debts.*
· **to get rid of. a.** to get free from: *to get rid of a cold.* **b.** to kill or drive away: *Insect spray got rid of the ants in the house.*

rid² (rid) *Archaic.* a past tense and past participle of **ride.**

rid·dance (rid′əns) *n.* the act of ridding or the state of being rid.
· **good riddance.** a welcome relief, as from someone or something undesirable or unpleasant.

rid·den (rid′ən) a past participle of **ride.**

-ridden *combining form* overwhelmed by or obsessed with; burdened with: *guilt-ridden, debt-ridden.*

rid·dle¹ (rid′əl) *n.* **1.** a puzzling problem or question so worded as to test one's ingenuity in solving or answering it. **2.** a person or thing that is difficult to understand; enigma. —*v.,* **-dled, -dling.** —*v.i.* to speak in riddles. —*v.t.* to solve or explain (a riddle). [Old English *rǣdels* enigma.] —For Synonyms *(n.),* see **mystery.**

rid·dle² (rid′əl) *v.t.,* **-dled, -dling. 1.** to pierce in many places: *to riddle a target with arrows.* **2.** to penetrate throughout in a harmful manner: *The scientist's theory was riddled with inaccuracies.* **3.** to sift through a coarse sieve: *to riddle grain.* —*n.* a coarse sieve. [Old English *hriddel.*]

ride (rīd) *v.,* **rode** or *(archaic)* **rid, rid·den** or *(archaic)* **rid, rid·ing.** —*v.i.* **1.** to sit on and be carried by something in motion, such as a horse or vehicle, while controlling its movement: *to ride to school on a bicycle.* **2.** to travel or be carried on or in something, as a vehicle or other conveyance: *We rode through the countryside on the train.* **3.** to proceed or be carried along, as if riding. **4.** to be carried or supported while moving: *While making the turn, the car rode on two wheels.* **5.** to move or float or appear to move or float: *The ship rode over the waves.* **6.** to carry or support a rider in a certain manner: *The car rides smoothly.* **7.** to depend (with *on*): *The outcome will ride on their decision.* **8.** *Nautical.* to be moored: *The ship rode at anchor in the harbor.* **9.** *Informal.* to continue unchanged or without interruption: *Let the matter ride until further notice.* —*v.t.* **1.** to sit on and be carried by (something) in motion, while controlling its movement: *to ride a horse.* **2.** to travel or be carried on or in (something): *to ride a train.* **3.** to cause to proceed or be carried. **4.** to ride over or along: *The cowhand rode the range.* **5.** to accomplish or perform by riding: *to ride a race.* **6.** *Informal.* to harass or tease: *My friends rode me about my new haircut.* —*n.* **1.** a short trip by any means of conveyance: *We took a ride in the car.* **2.** any of various vehicles or devices, as a merry-go-round or Ferris wheel, that people can ride on or in for amusement. **3.** the manner in which something, esp. a vehicle, moves: *a smooth ride.* [Old English *rīdan* to be carried by a horse, to sail on the water.]
· **to ride down. a.** to collide with and knock down while riding. **b.** to overtake by riding.
· **to ride out.** to withstand and endure successfully: *to ride out a storm, to ride out a political scandal.*
· **to ride up.** to move or work upward out of place: *This sweater rides up in the back.*
· **to take for a ride.** *Slang.* **a.** to murder. **b.** to swindle or trick.

rid·er (rī′dər) *n.* **1.** a person or thing that rides. **2.** an amendment or addition, as to a contract or legislative bill. —**rid′er·less,** *adj.*

ridge (rij) *n.* **1.** the long and narrow upper part or crest of something: *the ridge of a hill.* **2.** any raised narrow strip, as on fabric: *Corduroy has ridges.* **3.** a long and narrow elevation of land, or a chain of hills or mountains. **4.** a horizontal line formed by the juncture of two sloping sides: *the ridge of a roof.* **5.** the back or backbone of an animal. —*v.,* **ridged, ridg·ing.** —*v.t.* **1.** to form or make into ridges. **2.** to mark or cover with ridges. —*v.i.* to form a ridge or ridges. [Old English *hrycg* back of a man or an animal, crest.]

ridge·pole (rij′pōl′) *n.* a horizontal timber or pole along the top of a roof or tent to which sloping beams or fabric are fastened.

ridg·y (rij′ē) *adj.,* **ridg·i·er, ridg·i·est.** rising in a ridge or ridges; ridged.

rid·i·cule (rid′i kūl′) *v.t.,* **-culed, -cul·ing.** to make (a person or thing) appear foolish; laugh at or expose to laughter; mock. —*n.* words or actions intended to ridicule a person or thing:

Their strange behavior exposed them to ridicule. [French *ridicule* something laughable, from Latin *rīdiculum.*] —**rid′i·cul′er,** *n.* —For Synonyms *(v.t.),* see **mock.**

ri·dic·u·lous (ri dik′yə ləs) *adj.* deserving or arousing ridicule; laughable; silly. [Latin *rīdiculus.*] —**ri·dic′u·lous·ly,** *adv.* —**ri·dic′u·lous·ness,** *n.*

rid·ing habit (rī′ding) any of various outfits designed to be worn while horseback riding, usually consisting of pants, a jacket, boots, and hat.

rid·ley (rid′lē) *n.* either of two species of small, marine turtles, genus *Lepidochelys,* having a wide, almost circular shell: the endangered **Atlantic** or **Kemp's ridley,** *L. kempi,* or the **Indo-Pacific ridley,** *L. olivacea.* Length: to 27 inches (69 centimeters). [Of uncertain origin.]

rife (rīf) *adj.* **1.** occurring commonly or frequently; widespread; rampant: *Discontent is rife throughout the land.* **2.** large in number or quantity; abundant; plentiful. **3.** filled; abounding (with *with*): *The report was rife with errors.* [Old English *rȳfe* abundant, probably from Old Norse *rīfr.*]

riff (rif) *Music. n.* in jazz, a melodic phrase played repeatedly, serving as the main theme or background. —*v.i.* to play a jazz riff. [Probably shortened and altered form of REFRAIN².]

rif·fle (rif′əl) *n.* **1.** a shallow place in the bed of a river or stream over which water moves swiftly so that the surface is broken into ripples; shallow rapids. **2.** ripple. **3.** the act or method of shuffling cards by separating them into two piles and bending and releasing the edges of the cards so that the two piles mix. **4.** *Mining.* a groove or indentation in the bottom of a trough or sluice to trap gold contained in sand or gravel. —*v.t.,* **-fled, -fling. 1.** to cause ripples on (the surface of water): *The breeze riffled the lake.* **2.** to leaf or thumb through (something) hurriedly: *The student riffled the pages of the book.* **3.** to shuffle (cards). [Possibly blend of RIPPLE and RUFFLE¹.]

riff·raff (rif′raf′) *n.* **1.** low, disreputable, or worthless persons; rabble. **2.** trash; rubbish. [Old French *rif et raf* one and all, completely, from *rifler* to plunder (of uncertain origin) + *et* and (from Latin *et*) + *raffler* to snatch away (of Germanic origin).]

ri·fle¹ (rī′fəl) *n.* **1.** a firearm, designed to be fired from the shoulder, having a spirally grooved bore that gives bullets a spinning motion and a predictable trajectory. **2. rifles.** formerly, a military unit equipped with rifles. —*v.t.,* **-fled, -fling.** to cut spiral grooves in (the bore of a firearm). [From earlier *rifle* to form spiral grooves in (from French *rifler* to file, plane²; of uncertain origin) + GUN.]

ri·fle² (rī′fəl) *v.,* **-fled, -fling.** —*v.t.* **1.** to search through (something) thoroughly and rob; ransack: *The thief rifled the safe.* **2.** to seize and carry off as plunder; steal. **3.** to strip (something) bare; despoil (often with *of*): *The thieves rifled the house of its contents.* —*v.i.* to search thoroughly and rob. [Old French *rif(f)ler* to plunder; of uncertain origin.] —**ri′fler,** *n.*

ri·fle·man (rī′fəl mən) *n., pl.* **-men** (-mən). **1.** a soldier armed with a rifle. **2.** a person skilled in the use of a rifle.

rifle range, an area set aside for target practice with a rifle or other firearms.

ri·fle·ry (rī′fəl rē) *n.* the art or practice of shooting at targets with a rifle.

ri·fling (rī′fling) *n.* **1.** the act or process of cutting spiral grooves in the bore of a firearm. **2.** the spiral grooves of a firearm collectively.

rift (rift) *n.* **1.** an opening made by splitting; break; fissure. **2.** *Geology.* a long, narrow section of the earth's crust, bounded by faults, that has sunk beneath the level of the surrounding land. **3.** a breach in a relationship, as between friends; quarrel. —*v.t., v.i.* to cleave; split. [Of Scandinavian origin.]

rig (rig) *v.t.,* **rigged, rigging. 1.** to fit (a boat or ship) with masts, sails, spars, lines, and the like. **2.** to fit (sails, spars, lines, and the like), as to their respective masts or yards. **3.** to fit out; equip: *We rigged the car to carry skis.* **4.** to make or build hurriedly or as a makeshift (often with *up*): *We rigged up a radio from spare parts.* **5.** to manipulate, control, or fix (something) fraudulently, as for personal gain: *to rig an election.* **6.** *Informal.* to dress, as with costumes (often with *out* or *up*): *to rig oneself up for Halloween.* —*n.* **1.** the arrangement of masts, sails, spars, lines, and the like on a boat or ship. **2.** the apparatus or equipment used for drilling an oil well. **3.** any apparatus or equipment used for a particular purpose: *fishing rig.* **4.** *Informal.* dress; costume. **5.** a truck that transports freight: *an eighteen-wheel rig carrying frozen food.* [Middle English *riggen;* of Scandinavian origin.]

rig·a·ma·role (rig′ə mə rōl′) *n.* rigmarole.

Ri·gel (rī′jəl, -gəl) *n.* a star system in the constellation Orion,

appearing to the naked eye as a very bright star. [Arabic *rijl* foot; because it is in the left foot of Orion.]

rig·ger (rig′ər) *n.* **1.** a person who rigs. **2.** a person who installs and repairs the rigging and hoisting gear of sailboats or ships.

rig·ging (rig′ing) *n.* **1.** all the lines of a boat or ship, as the ropes, chains, and wires, used for supporting the masts or working the sails. **2.** apparatus or equipment used for a special purpose; tackle.

right (rīt) *adj.* **1.** conforming to truth, fact, or reason; correct; accurate: *the right answer to an arithmetic problem.* **2.** just, moral, or good: *Telling the truth was the right thing to do.* **3.** of, on, or toward the side of the body that is to the east when one is facing north: *the right hand, a right turn on a highway.* **4.** appropriate; suitable; proper: *the right person for a job.* **5.** with, having, or exposing the surface meant to be seen: *the right side of a piece of cloth.* **6.** *also,* **Right.** relating to or characterized by political views ranging from conservative to reactionary. **7.** in a normal or proper state; in good order. **8.** healthy; sound: *not in one's right mind.* **9.** *Geometry.* having its axis perpendicular to the base: *a right cone.* **10.** straight: *a right line.* —*n.* **1.** something that is just, moral, or good: *the triumph of right over wrong.* **2.** *also,* **rights.** a just, legal, or moral claim: *the right to free speech.* **3.** the right side or direction: *to drive on the right.* **4.** *also,* **Right.** a party or group characterized by political views ranging from conservative to reactionary. Also, **right wing. 5.** a blow delivered with the right hand, as in boxing. **6.a.** the privilege held by a stockholder of subscribing for additional shares of stock, usually at a price lower than the market value. **b.** a negotiable certificate entitling a stockholder to such a privilege. —*adv.* **1.** according to truth, fact, or reason; correctly: *You didn't spell my name right.* **2.** according to that which is just, moral, or good: **3.** in a proper or suitable manner: *This telephone doesn't work right.* **4.** exactly; precisely: *Put the book right here on the table.* **5.** without delay or pause; immediately: *Let's leave right now.* **6.** satisfactorily; favorably. **7.** in a straight line; directly: *The arrow went right to the mark.* **8.** to or toward the right: *to lean right.* **9.** *Informal.* extremely; very: *We had a right good time at the party.* ➡ also used informally as part of certain titles: *the right honorable senator.* **10.** completely: *The rain washed the dust right off the plants.* —*v.t.* **1.** to make reparation for; redress or avenge: *to right a wrong.* **2.** to make right; correct: *to right a technical error.* **3.** to restore to an upright or normal position: *The crew righted the capsized boat.* **4.** to do justice to (someone). —*v.i.* to recover an upright or normal position. [Old English *riht* straight, good, true, correct, proper.]

- **by right** (or **rights**). if justice prevails; properly; rightly.
- **in one's own right**. through one's own ability or accomplishment; independently of others.
- **in the right**. not wrong, mistaken, or at fault.
- **right away** (or **off**). without delay; immediately: *I'll be there right away.*
- **to rights**. *Informal.* in or into a correct or proper condition: *to put a room to rights after a party.*

right angle, an angle of 90 degrees, formed by two lines perpendicular to each other. For illustration, see **angle**[1].

right-an·gled (rīt′ang′gəld) *adj.* containing one or more right angles.

right ascension, the angular distance east of the vernal equinox of a celestial body, measured along the celestial equator.

right·eous (rī′chəs) *adj.*
1. doing what is right; virtuous. **2.** proceeding from a sense of what is right; justifiable: *to show righteous indignation at an insult.* [Old English *rihtwīs,* from *riht* good + *wīs(e)* way, manner.]
—**right′eous·ly,** *adv.*
—**right′eous·ness,** *n.*

right field *Baseball.*
1. the right section of the outfield when viewed from home plate. **2.** the position of the player stationed in this area.
—**right fielder**.

right·ful (rīt′fəl) *adj.*
1. having a just, legal, or moral claim: *the rightful heir to a throne.* **2.** owned or held by such claim:

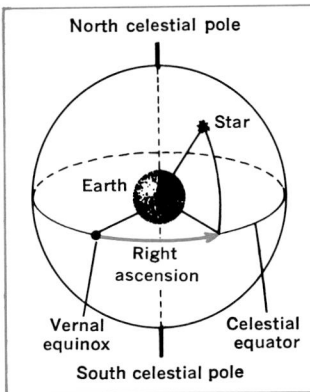

right ascension

rightful property. **3.** appropriate; proper: *rightful action.*
—**right′ful·ly,** *adv.* —**right′ful·ness,** *n.*

right-hand (rīt′hand′) *adj.* **1.** on or to the right: *She drove on the right-hand side of the street.* **2.** of, relating to, for, or with the right hand. **3.** most trusted and useful: *He is the boss's right-hand man.*

right-hand·ed (rīt′han′did) *adj.* **1.** using the right hand habitually and more easily than the left. **2.** done with the right hand: *a right-handed catch.* **3.** made to be held in or used by the right hand. **4.** turning or moving from left to right; clockwise: *a right-handed spiral.* —*adv.* with the right hand: *to pitch right-handed.* Also, **right′-hand′ed·ly.** —**right′-hand′ed·ness,** *n.*

right-hand·er (rīt′han′dər, -han′-) *n.* **1.** a person who is right-handed, esp. a right-handed baseball pitcher. **2.** *Informal.* a blow given with the right hand.

right·ist (rī′tist) *n.* a person who has political views ranging from conservative to reactionary. —*adj.* of, relating to, or characterized by conservative to reactionary political views.

right·ly (rīt′lē) *adv.* **1.** in a correct way; accurately: *to answer a question rightly.* **2.** properly; suitably. **3.** justly or honestly. [Old English *rihtlīce.*]

right-mind·ed (rīt′mīn′did) *adj.* having or characterized by correct or honest opinions or principles. —**right′-mind′ed·ly,** *adv.* —**right′-mind′ed·ness,** *n.*

right of way *pl.* **rights of way** or **right of ways. 1.** the right of a person or thing to proceed first or cross in front of another or others: *A pedestrian in a crosswalk has the right of way.* **2.a.** a legal right to go across property belonging to another. **b.** the path or route used in doing this. **3.** a strip of land set aside for a specific purpose, as for railroad tracks, public roads, or power lines.

right-on (rīt′ôn′, -on′) *adj. Slang.* exactly correct; perfectly right: *That weather forecast was right-on.*

right-to-die (rīt′tə dī′) *adj.* advocating the right to refuse the use of artificial means or extreme measures to prolong the life of a person who is terminally ill or in an irreversible coma.

right-to-life (rīt′tə līf′) *adj.* of or relating to any movement, group, or law that is against abortion, esp. legalized abortion. —**right′-to-lif′er,** *n.*

right triangle, a triangle with a right angle.

right whale, any of a group of baleen whales, family Balaenidae, distinguished by an enormous head, upwardly bowed mouth cleft, and long whalebone plates that fold on the floor of the closed mouth. Included are the **black right whale** (genus *Eubalaena*), the **pygmy right whale** (genus *Capera*), and the bowhead.

right-wing (rīt′wing′) *adj.* of, relating to, or belonging to the right wing. —**right′-wing′er,** *n.*

right wing 1. right *(n., def. 4)*. **2.** a portion of a political party or other group having a more conservative or reactionary outlook than the rest. [Because distinguished and noble members of the French National Assembly of 1789, who tended to be politically conservative, were seated to the right of the presiding officers; probably from the custom of seating honored guests on the host's right at formal gatherings. See LEFT WING.]

rig·id (rij′id) *adj.* **1.** not yielding or bending; stiff: *Rigid steel girders made up the frame of the building.* **2.** strict; rigorous: *a rigid disciplinarian.* **3.** unchanging and inflexible; fixed: *The requirements for club membership are rigid.* **4.** scrupulously exact, as in method or procedure; punctilious. [Latin *rigidus* stiff, stern.] —**ri·gid′i·ty, rig′id·ness,** *n.* —**rig′id·ly,** *adv.* —For Synonyms, see **stiff.**

rig·ma·role (rig′mə rōl′) *n.* **1.** a complicated and often foolish or unnecessary procedure: *We went through a lot of rigmarole to get a check cashed.* **2.** foolish and senseless talk; nonsense. Also, **rigamarole.** [Modification of obsolete *ragman roll* list, catalog, from *ragman* (of uncertain origin) + ROLL.]

rig·or (rig′ər) *also, British,* **rigour.** *n.* **1.** the state or quality of being strict; strictness; inflexibility: *the rigor of the law.* **2.** severity; inclemency: *the rigor of winter.* **3.** a harsh or oppressive act or policy: *the rigors of tyranny.* **4.** a condition of extreme hardship or oppressiveness. **5.** exactness or precision, as in an intellectual endeavor; exactitude: *the rigors of mathematics.* **6.a.** a chill preceding fever or caused by cold or shock. **b.** a rigidity of body

a	at	e	end	o	hot	u	up	hw	white		about
ā	ape	ē	me	ō	old	ū	use	ng	song		taken
ä	far	i	it	ô	fork	ŭ	rule	th	thin	ə	pencil
âr	care	ī	ice	oi	oil	ü	pull	th	this		lemon
		îr	pierce	ou	out	ûr	turn	zh	measure		circus

R

tissues or organs, as in rigor mortis. [Latin *rigor* stiffness, hardness.]

rigor mor·tis (môr′tis) the stiffening of the muscles that begins shortly after death and persists until the onset of decomposition. [Latin *rigor mortis* stiffness of death.]

rig·or·ous (rig′ər əs) *adj.* **1.** very strict or inflexible: *a rigorous interpretation of the law.* **2.** severe; inclement: *the rigorous climate of the far north.* **3.** very exact or precise. —**rig′or·ous·ly,** *adv.* —**rig′or·ous·ness,** *n.*

rig·our (rig′ər) *British.* rigor.

Rig-Ve·da (rig vā′də, -vē′də) *n.* the oldest and most important of the sacred Hindu books, written in Sanskrit.

rile (rīl) *v.t.,* **riled, ril·ing.** *Informal.* **1.** to irritate or annoy; provoke: *Your rudeness really riles me.* **2.** to roil (liquid). [Form of ROIL.]

rill[1] (ril) *n.* a tiny stream or brook. [Low German *rille.*]

rill[2] (ril) *also,* **rille.** *n.* any of a class of long, straight or winding lunar trenches visible through powerful telescopes and apparent on some photographs of the moon taken from spacecraft. [German *rille* groove, furrow.]

rim (rim) *n.* **1.** the outer edge or border of something: *the rim of a glass.* **2.** the outer edge of a wheel, as on a bicycle or automobile, to which a tire is fitted. —*v.t.,* **rimmed, rim·ming. 1.** to form a rim around: *The mountains rimmed the valley.* **2.** to roll around the rim of (something) without going in: *The basketball rimmed the basket and bounced out.* [Old English *rima* border, coast.] —For Synonyms (*n.*), see **edge.**

rime[1] (rīm) *n.* rhyme. —*v.,* **rimed, rim·ing.** rhyme.

rime[2] (rīm) *n.* hoarfrost. —*v.t.,* **rimed, rim·ing.** to cover with rime. [Old English *hrīm* hoarfrost.]

rime·ster (rīm′stər) *n.* rhymster.

rim·y (rī′mē) *adj.,* **rim·i·er, rim·i·est.** covered with rime; frosty.

rind (rīnd) *n.* the firm outer covering or skin, as of fruit or cheese: *grated orange rind, pickled watermelon rind.* [Old English *rind(e)* bark of a tree, crust.]

rin·der·pest (rin′dər pest′) *n.* an acute, usually fatal, infectious disease of cattle and sometimes sheep, goats, and other cud-chewing animals. [German *Rinderpest,* from *Rinder,* plural of *Rind* ox + *Pest* plague (from Latin *pestis*).]

color-enhanced **rings** of Saturn

ring[1] (ring) *n.* **1.** a continuous, closed curved line; circle: *The teacher drew a ring around the error.* **2.** a circular band, often of precious metal, worn on the finger. **3.** any circular band, as of metal, wood, or plastic, used esp. for holding or carrying something: *a napkin ring, curtain rings.* **4.** a circular course: *The children danced in a ring around the fire.* **5.** a group of persons or things forming a circle: *The president was surrounded by a ring of bodyguards.* **6.** a circular, usually enclosed, area used for circus performances or exhibitions. **7.a.** an enclosed, usually square, area used for boxing or wrestling matches. **b.** the sport of boxing: *a career in the ring.* **8.** a group of persons working together, esp. for an illicit or criminal purpose: *a ring of car thieves.* **9.** *Botany.* annual ring. **10.** *Chemistry.* a closed chain of atoms, as a benzene ring. **11.** *Astronomy.* a circular band of particulate matter in orbit around a planet, as around Saturn or Neptune. —*v.,* **ringed, ring·ing.** —*v.t.* **1.** to enclose with a ring; encircle. **2.** to form into a ring or rings. **3.** to provide with a ring. **4.** in certain games,

to throw a horseshoe, ring, or other object over (a stake or pin). **5.** to put a ring in the nose of (an animal): *to ring a bull.* —*v.i.* to move in a ring or spiral. [Old English *hring* circle of metal, circular group.] —**ring′like′,** *adj.*

• **to run rings around.** to surpass or be better than: *We ran rings around the other team.*

ring[2] (ring) *v.,* **rang** or **rung, rung, ring·ing.** —*v.i.* **1.** to make a clear, resonant sound, as that made by a bell when struck. **2.** to cause a bell or bells to sound, esp. as a signal or summons: *We rang for assistance.* **3.** to resound loudly and clearly; reverberate; echo: *The room rang with laughter.* **4.** to be filled with talk or rumor: *The school rang with praise for the team.* **5.** to appear to be of a certain quality: *Their promises rang false to me.* **6.** to have a sensation, as of an echoing sound or buzzing; *My ears rang from the shrill noise.* —*v.t.* **1.** to cause (something) to ring: *The visitor rang the doorbell.* **2.** to announce, signal, or proclaim by or as by the ringing of bells: *The chimes rang the hour.* **3.** to call on the telephone (often with *up*): *Ring me up when you get home.* **4.** to make (a sound) by or as by ringing. —*n.* **1.** the act of ringing something, esp. a bell. **2.** a clear, resonant sound, as that made by a bell when struck. **3.** a sound expressing a certain quality; tone: *a voice with a ring of sincerity.* **4.** *Informal.* a telephone call. [Old English *hringan* to clash, make a clear, resonant sound.]

• **to give (someone) a ring.** to telephone (someone).

• **to ring a bell.** to remind someone of something: *That story rings a bell.*

• **to ring down the curtain.** to signal for a theater curtain to be lowered.

• **to ring down the curtain on.** to conclude (something): *The scandal rang down the curtain on the politician's career.*

• **to ring up the curtain.** to signal for a theater curtain to be raised.

• **to ring up the curtain on.** to begin (something).

ring·bolt (ring′bōlt′) *n.* a bolt with a ring fitted into an eye in its head.

ringed (ringd) *adj.* **1.** having or wearing a ring or rings: *fingers ringed and bejeweled with diamonds.* **2.** marked with a ring or rings. **3.** enclosed by a ring or rings: *a ringed city of towers and walls.* **4.** formed of or with a ring or rings.

ring·er[1] (ring′ər) *n.* **1.** a person or thing that rings or encircles. **2.** a horseshoe or quoit thrown so as to encircle a stake or pin. [RING[1] + -ER[1].]

ring·er[2] (ring′ər) *n.* **1.** a person or thing that rings a bell, chime, or the like. **2.** *Slang.* a horse or athlete fraudulently entered in a contest, as by the falsification of name or age. **3.** *Slang.* a person or thing that closely resembles another: *You're a ringer for that new movie star.* [RING[2] + -ER[2].]

Ring·er's solution (ring′ərz) a liquid medium in physiological research, consisting of a solution of distilled water and various salts, that has the same osmotic pressure as blood and tissue fluids and can be used to keep animal tissues alive for several hours. [From Sydney *Ringer,* 1835-1910, English physiologist who first prepared it.]

ring finger, the finger next to the little finger, esp. of the left hand. [Because the wedding ring is traditionally worn on it.]

ring·git (ring′git) *n.* the monetary unit of Malaysia.

ring·lead·er (ring′lē′dər) *n.* a person who leads others, esp. in unlawful acts or enterprises. [From the earlier phrase *to lead the ring* to take the lead.]

ring·let (ring′lit) *n.* **1.** a coiled or curved lock of hair. **2.** *Archaic.* a small ring.

ring·mas·ter (ring′mas′tər) *n.* a person who introduces the acts in a circus.

ring-necked pheasant (ring′nekt′) a large, originally Asian, game fowl, *Phasianus colchicus,* introduced worldwide. It has a long, pointed tail, and the iridescent, bronze-colored male usually has a broad, white neck ring. Length: 21-33 inches (53-84 centimeters).

ring·side (ring′sīd′) *n.* **1.** the area just outside the ring, as that containing the first row of seats at a prizefight. **2.** any area affording a close view.

ring-tailed (ring′tāld′) *adj.* **1.** having dark or colored stripes or bands around the tail, as a raccoon. **2.** having a tail carried in a loop: *a ring-tailed breed of dog.*

ring·worm (ring′wûrm′) *n.* any of several contagious fungus infections of the skin, including athlete's foot, characterized by ring-shaped patches.

rink (ringk) *n.* **1.** a building, part of a building, or area containing a smooth, open surface, as for ice skating or roller skating. **2.** the surface itself. [Possibly from Old French *renc* range, row[1], circle; of Germanic origin.]

rink·y-dink (ring′kē dingk′) *Slang. adj.* **1.** of little or inferior quality or status; small-time: *a rinky-dink company.* **2.** old-fashioned or shoddy: *a rinky-dink ice-cream parlor.* —*n.* something that is rinky-dink. [Of uncertain origin.]

rinse (rins) *v.t.,* **rinsed, rins·ing. 1.** to remove (soap or impurities) by washing with clear water (often with *out* or *off*): *to rinse soap off one's hands.* **2.** to remove soap or impurities from (something) by washing with clear water: *to rinse clothes.* **3.** to cleanse or wash lightly (often with *out* or *off*): *to rinse one's mouth out with water.* —*n.* **1.** the act of rinsing. **2.** water or other liquid used for rinsing. **3.** a liquid preparation that is applied to the hair to tint or condition it. [Old French *raincier* to cleanse with water; of uncertain origin.] —**rins′er,** *n.*

ri·ot (rī′ət) *n.* **1.** a disorderly, often violent, disturbance or outbreak by a large crowd. **2.** *Law.* a disturbance of the peace by three or more persons acting together. **3.** a bright, lavish display: *The autumn leaves were a riot of color.* **4.** *Archaic.* wanton behavior; wild revelry. **5.** *Slang.* a person or thing that is extremely amusing. —*v.i.* **1.** to engage in a disorderly, often violent, disturbance. **2.** *Archaic.* to engage in debauchery or wild revelry. [Old French *riote* dispute, brawling, from *rihoter* to make a disturbance; of uncertain origin.] —**ri′ot·er,** *n.*
• **to run riot. a.** to behave or move wildly and without restraint. **b.** to grow profusely, uncontrollably, or luxuriantly.

Riot Act, an English law of 1715 providing for the dispersal or punishment of any group of twelve or more persons who disturb the peace.
• **to read the riot act to.** to scold harshly and warn against continuing offensive behavior or actions.

ri·ot·ous (rī′ə təs) *adj.* **1.** of, relating to, or engaging in a disorderly, often violent, disturbance. **2.** boisterous; uproarious: *riotous laughter.* **3.** loose; wanton: *riotous living.* —**ri′ot·ous·ly,** *adv.* —**ri′ot·ous·ness,** *n.*

rip¹ (rip) *v.,* **ripped, rip·ping** —*v.t.* **1.** to tear (something); rend: *I ripped my trousers on the fence.* **2.** to make by ripping: *The nail ripped a hole in the tent.* **3.** to tear or cut into pieces (with *up*): *to rip up a piece of paper.* **4.** to remove (something) by tearing or pulling (often with *off, out,* or *away*): *to rip out a seam.* **5.** to saw or split (wood) along the grain. —*v.i.* to become torn apart. —*n.* a torn place; tear. [Probably from Middle Dutch *rippen* to tear¹, rip¹.] —**rip′pa·ble,** *adj.* —**rip′per,** *n.* —For Synonyms *(v.t.),* see **tear¹.**
• **to let it** (or **her**) **rip.** *Slang.* to proceed with no restraints.
• **to rip into.** *Informal.* to set upon vigorously; attack.
• **to rip off.** *Slang.* **a.** to rob or steal. **b.** to cheat or swindle (someone).

rip² (rip) *n.* **1.** a stretch of rough water made turbulent by the meeting of opposing currents. **2.** riptide. [Possibly from RIP¹.]

R.I.P., requiescat in pace.

ri·par·i·an (ri pâr′ē ən, rī-) *adj.* of, relating to, or on the bank, as of a river. [Latin *rīpārius* (from *rīpa* bank¹, shore) + -AN.]

rip cord, a cord with a handle that opens a parachute when pulled.

rip current, riptide.

ripe (rīp) *adj.,* **rip·er, rip·est. 1.** fully grown and ready to be gathered and used as food: *The tomatoes are not ripe.* **2.** aged or developed to the best stage or fullest flavor for use; matured: *ripe cheese.* **3.** advanced in years: *a ripe old age.* **4.** fully prepared to do or undergo something; on the verge; ready: *The country was ripe for revolution.* **5.** (of time) favorable or suitable. **6.** healthy, ruddy, and full like ripe fruit: *ripe lips.* [Old English *rīpe* ready for reaping.] —**ripe′ly,** *adv.* —**ripe′ness,** *n.*

rip·en (rī′pən) *v.t., v.i.* to make or become ripe; mature.

rip·off (rip′ôf′, -of′) also, **rip-off.** *n. Slang.* **1.** a swindle, robbery, or other form of exploitation: *After waiting six weeks for my merchandise, I suspected a ripoff.* **2.** a copy or imitation, esp. one that is inferior: *This radio is a ripoff of the more expensive model.* [From *to rip off* to steal.]

ri·poste (ri pōst′) also, **ri·post.** *n.* **1.** *Fencing.* a quick thrust made after successfully parrying an opponent's lunge. **2.** a quick, witty, or sharp reply; retort. —*v.i.,* **-post·ed, -post·ing.** to make a riposte. [French *riposte* thrust in fencing, retort, from Italian *risposta* response, from *rispondere* to answer, from Latin *respondēre.*]

rip·ping (rip′ing) *British. Slang. adj.* excellent; splendid; first-rate. —*adv.* very.

rip·ple (rip′əl) *n.* **1.** a very small wave on the surface of a liquid, as water. **2.** anything resembling this: *ripples in a fabric.* **3.** a sound resembling that made by the flowing of very small waves: *a ripple of applause.* —*v.,* **-pled, -pling.** —*v.i.* **1.** to form or have very small waves on the surface. **2.** to flow with such waves.

3. to make a sound resembling that made by the flowing of very small waves. —*v.t.* to cause very small waves on. [Of uncertain origin.]

ripple effect, a gradually spreading effect caused by a single act or event: *A slowdown in construction had a ripple effect on the building trades.*

rip·ply (rip′lē) *adj.* marked or characterized by ripples.

rip·rap (rip′rap′) *n.* **1.** a layer of large stones or rocks used as a cover to protect earth or soft rock from being washed away or as the foundation for an artificial jetty or breakwater. —*v.t.,* **-rapped, -rap·ping.** to make a riprap in or on. [Repetition of RAP¹, with vowel change in the first syllable.]

rip·roar·ing (rip′rôr′ing) *adj. Informal.* noisy and lively; uproarious: *We had a riproaring good time at the festival.*

rip·saw (rip′sô′) *n.* a handsaw with squared, chisellike cutting edges on its teeth, designed to cut wood with the grain, not across it. [RIP¹ + SAW¹.]

rip·tide (rip′tīd′) *n.* a strong seaward movement of water that returns water brought shoreward by waves. Also, **rip, rip current.**

Rip Van Win·kle (rip′van wing′kəl) the hero of a story of the same name by the American author Washington Irving who slept for twenty years and awakened to find his home, life, village, and country completely changed.

rise (rīz) *v.i.,* **rose, ris·en, ris·ing. 1.** to assume an upright posture or position; get up; stand up. **2.** to move from a lower to a higher place or position; go upward: *Smoke rose from the chimney.* **3.** to get out of bed: *The farmer always rises early.* **4.** (of the sun and other heavenly bodies) to appear above the horizon. **5.** to incline or slope upward: *The hills rise beyond the fields.* **6.** to have elevation or altitude; extend upward: *The monument rises above the trees.* **7.** to increase, as in amount, value, degree, or intensity: *The cost of living rose last year.* **8.** to advance, as in rank, position, or influence: *to rise to the presidency.* **9.** to reach a higher level; increase in height: *The river rose two feet.* **10.** to be built or erected: *New apartment buildings rose on the site.* **11.** to expand and become lighter; swell up: *The cake will rise.* **12.** to increase in pitch or volume: *My voice rose with anger.* **13.** to become more animated and vigorous: *The army's morale rose with the ending of winter.* **14.** to engage in a revolt; rebel (often with *up*): *The oppressed people rose up against the tyrant.* **15.** to emanate or originate: *A loud roar rose from the crowd.* **16.** to come into being; emerge; appear: *A blister rose on my hand after raking leaves.* **17.** to come to pass; happen. **18.** to come back from death or the grave; return to life. —*n.* **1.** an upward movement; ascent: *the rise of water in a river.* **2.** an increase, as in amount, value, degree, or intensity: *a rise in prices.* **3.** an upward slope or direction. **4.** a piece of rising ground; hill. **5.** an elevation or advance, as in rank, fortune, power, or influence: *the rise of a politician.* **6.** an increase in loudness or pitch. **7.** the appearance of a heavenly body above the horizon. **8.** origin; beginning; source: *Where do these problems have their rise?* **9.** vertical height, as of a step, landing, or arch. [Old English *rīsan* to go up, ascend.]
• **to get a rise out of.** *Informal.* to get a response from, esp. one of anger or annoyance.
• **to give rise to.** to be the cause of; originate: *The depression gave rise to widespread unemployment.*
• **to rise above.** to free oneself from the limitations of.
• **to rise to.** to be or become equal to the demands of: *to rise to a challenge.*

ris·en (riz′ən) the past participle of **rise.**

ris·er (rī′zər) *n.* **1.** a person or thing that rises: *Because of the nature of their work, farmers have to be early risers.* **2.** the vertical part of a step.

risers

ris·i·ble (riz′ə bəl) *adj.* **1.** able or disposed to laugh. **2.** causing laughter; amusing; laughable: *the risible antics of a clown.* [Late Latin *rīsibilis* laughable, from Latin *rīdēre* to laugh.] —**ris′i·bil′i·ty,** *n.*

a	at	e	end	o	hot	u	up	hw	white	⎧	about
ā	ape	ē	me	ō	old	ū	use	ng	song	⎪	taken
ä	far	i	it	ô	fork	ü	rule	th	thin	⎨	pencil
âr	care	ī	ice	oi	oil	u̇	pull	th	this	⎪	lemon
		îr	pierce	ou	out	ûr	turn	zh	measure	⎩	circus

R

ris·ing (rī′zing) *n.* **1.** the act of a person or thing that rises. **2.** an uprising; insurrection. —*adj.* that rises; ascending.

risk (risk) *n.* **1.** exposure to loss or harm; danger: *There is great risk involved in that plan.* **2.** a person or thing with reference to the probability of loss from insuring or relying on him, her, or it: *a bad risk.* —*v.t.* **1.** to expose to loss or harm: *to risk one's life to save a drowning child.* **2.** to take the risk of: *to risk losing money in an investment.* [French *risque* peril, from Italian *risico,* from *risicare* to venture; of uncertain origin.] —**risk′er,** *n.* —For Synonyms *(n.),* see **danger;** *(v.t.),* see **venture.**

• **at risk.** in a dangerous or precarious situation.

• **to take (or run) a risk.** to expose oneself to the possibility of injury or loss: *to take a risk in the stock market.*

risk·y (ris′kē) *adj.,* **risk·i·er, risk·i·est.** attended with risk; dangerous. —**risk′i·ness,** *n.*

ri·sot·to (ri sô′tō) *n.* a dish of rice cooked in broth and flavored with cheese, vegetables, or the like.

ris·qué (ris kā′) *adj.* slightly improper; suggestive; indecent: *a risqué joke.* [French *risqué,* past participle of *risquer* to venture, from Italian *rischiare;* of uncertain origin.]

rit., ritardando. Also, **ritard.**

ri·tar·dan·do (rē′tär dän′dō) *Music. adj., adv.* becoming gradually slower. —*n., pl.* **-dan·dos. 1.** a gradual slowing of tempo. **2.** a passage in this tempo. [Italian *ritardando,* present participle of *ritardare* to be slow, delay, from Latin *retardāre* to hinder, delay.]

rite (rīt) *n.* **1.** a formal act or set of acts prescribed by ritual or tradition: *marriage rites.* **2.** the procedure or ceremony prescribed for this: *the rite of baptism.* **3.** *also,* **Rite.** a specific form of public worship, esp. the communion service; liturgy. [Latin *rītus* religious ceremony, custom.] —**rite′less,** *adj.* —For Synonyms, see **ceremony.**

rite of passage 1. a ceremony marking the important changes in a person's life, such as birth, puberty, and marriage. **2.** any event in a person's life regarded as marking a significant change in status.

rit·u·al (rich′ü əl) *n.* **1.** a set form or procedure governing the performance of a religious or solemn rite. **2.** a system or body of rites. **3.** the observance of such a system or body of rites. **4.** a routine faithfully followed, often in an excessive or elaborate manner: *to make a ritual of exercising every morning.* —*adj.* of, relating to, or performed as a ritual. [Latin *rītuālis* relating to religious ceremonies, from *rītus* religious ceremony, custom.] —**rit′u·al·ly,** *adv.* —For Synonyms, see **ceremony.**

rit·u·al·ism (rich′ü ə liz′əm) *n.* **1.** a strict observance of or adherence to ritual. **2.** a study of religious ritual.

rit·u·al·ist (rich′ü ə list) *n.* **1.** a person who practices or advocates ritualism. **2.** a person who studies religious ritual.

rit·u·al·is·tic (rich′ü ə lis′tik) *adj.* **1.** of or relating to ritual or ritualism. **2.** fond of or advocating ritual. —**rit′u·al·is′ti·cal·ly,** *adv.*

rit·u·al·ize (rich′ü ə līz′) *v.,* **-ized, -iz·ing.** —*v.t.* to make into a ritual. —*v.i.* to practice or advocate ritualism.

ritz·y (rit′sē) *adj.,* **ritz·i·er, ritz·i·est.** *Slang.* very elegant or luxurious; posh; swanky. [From the *Ritz* hotels known for their elegance, established by the Swiss entrepreneur César *Ritz,* 1850-1918.]

riv., river.

ri·val (rī′vəl) *n.* **1.** a person who competes with another to achieve the same thing or tries to equal or surpass another; competitor. **2.** a person or thing that compares favorably with or equals another: *Alaska has no rival for size among American states.* —*v.t.,* **-valed, -val·ing;** *also, British,* **-valled, -val·ling. 1.** to try to equal or surpass; compete with. **2.** to compare favorably with or be the equal of: *London rivals New York in population.* —*adj.* being a rival; competing: *rival football teams.* [Latin *rīvālis* competitor, neighbor, one getting water from the same brook as another, from *rīvus* brook.]

ri·val·ry (rī′vəl rē) *n., pl.* **-ries. 1.** the act of rivaling; competition. **2.** the state of being rivals: *There was great rivalry between the two schools.*

rive (rīv) *v.t.,* **rived, rived or riv·en** (riv′ən), **riv·ing. 1.** to split; cleave: *to rive a log with an ax.* **2.** to rend or distress (the heart, soul, or spirit). [Old Norse *rīfa* to tear, break.]

riv·er¹ (riv′ər) *n.* **1.** a large stream of water within a definite course or channel, usually larger than a creek. **2.** anything resembling a river, as in quantity or flow. [Anglo-Norman *rivere*

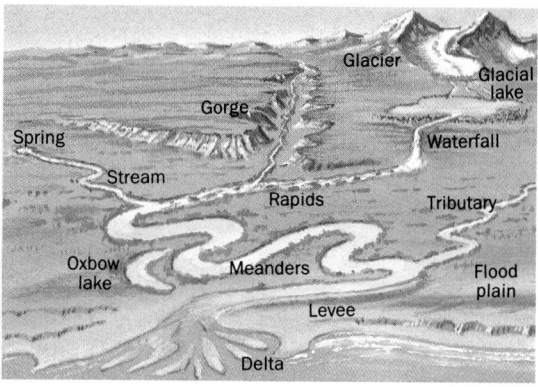

river¹
features of a river system

stream, going back to Latin *rīpārius* relating to the bank of a stream, from *rīpa* bank of a stream.]

• **to sell down the river.** to betray or deceive.

• **up the river.** *Slang.* to or in jail: *If you get caught, you'll be sent up the river.*

riv·er² (rī′vər) *n.* a person or thing that rives. [RIVE + -ER¹.]

riv·er·bank (riv′ər bangk′) *n.* the ground bordering a river.

river basin, the land area drained by a river and its tributaries.

riv·er·bed (riv′ər bed′) *n.* the bottom of the channel through which a river flows or formerly flowed.

riv·er·boat (riv′ər bōt′) *n.* a boat used for river travel, esp. a large paddle-wheel boat used on the southern and midwestern rivers of the United States during the nineteenth and early twentieth centuries.

riv·er·head (riv′ər hed′) *n.* the source of a river.

river horse, hippopotamus.

riv·er·ine (riv′ə rēn′, -rīn′) *adj.* **1.** of, like, or relating to a river. **2.** situated or living on the banks of a river.

riv·er·side (riv′ər sīd′) *n.* the area along the edge or the bank of a river.

riv·et (riv′it) *n.* a threadless metal bolt used to make permanent fastenings, esp. in metalwork and leather. The shaft of the rivet is put through aligned holes in materials to be joined, and then the headless end is flattened to make a tight connection. —*v.t.* **1.** to fasten with a rivet or rivets. **2.** to fasten or hold firmly: *The entire audience's attention was riveted on the tightrope walker.* **3.** to flatten the headless end of (a bolt, pin, or rod), esp. to secure it in place. [Old French *rivet* small bolt, from *river* to fasten, fix; of uncertain origin.] —**riv′et·er,** *n.*

riv·u·let (riv′yə lət) *n.* **1.** any tiny stream; trickle. **2.** a small brook. [Italian *rivoletto,* diminutive of *rivolo* brook, going back to Latin *rīvus.*]

rix-dol·lar (riks′dol′ər) *n.* any of several silver coins formerly used in the Netherlands, Denmark, Germany, Sweden, and Austria. [Obsolete Dutch *rijcksdaler,* from *rijck* realm + *daler* dollar. See DOLLAR.]

ri·yal (rē yäl′) *n.* the monetary unit of Qatar, Saudi Arabia, and the Yemen Arab Republic.

rm. 1. ream. **2.** room.

RM, reichsmark; reichsmarks.

Rn, the symbol for radon.

RN 1. registered nurse. **2.** Royal Navy.

RNA, any of various nucleic acids found in the cytoplasm and nucleus of all living cells, consisting of a long strand made up of alternating units of sugar and phosphate connected by a nitrogen base. One form of this acid, **messenger RNA,** carries the genetic information contained in DNA from the cell nucleus to the ribosomes in the cytoplasm. Another form, **transfer RNA,** transports amino acids to the ribosomes, which then read the information and arrange the amino acids so that protein is produced in the manner directed by DNA. [Abbreviation of *r(ibo)n(ucleic) a(cid).*]

roach¹ (rōch) *n.* cockroach.

roach² (rōch) *n., pl.* **roach or roach·es. 1.** a freshwater fish, *Rutilus rutilus,* related to the carp and found in lakes and rivers in northern Europe. **2.** any of several similar fish found in North America. [Old French *roche* the European fish; of uncertain origin.]

road (rōd) *n.* **1.** a strip of pavement or cleared, packed ground used for traveling between places; open way for the passage of

vehicles, persons, or animals. **2.** any means of advancing or progressing toward a specific end: *the road to power.* **3.** a protected area near the shore where ships can ride at anchor, less sheltered than a harbor. **4.** railroad. [Old English *rād* journey, a riding.]

•**down the road.** in the future.
•**on the road. a.** traveling, as a salesperson. **b.** performing on tour, as a theatrical troupe.
•**to hit the road.** *Slang.* to leave or begin traveling.
•**to take to the road.** to begin traveling, as on a tour.

road agent, formerly, a highwayman, esp. one who robbed stagecoaches in the western United States.

road·bed (rōd′bed′) *n.* **1.** a foundation or bed for the ties and rails of a railroad. **2.** the foundation or surface of a road.

road·block (rōd′blok′) *n.* **1.** a blockade to stop traffic on a road, as that used by the police to stop criminals. **2.** anything that hinders progress.

road hog *Informal.* a driver who obstructs traffic, esp. by occupying part of another driver's lane.

road·house (rōd′hous′) *n., pl.* **-hous·es** (-hou′ziz). a tavern, nightclub, or similar establishment located on a highway, usually outside city limits.

road map, a map showing the roads and highways of an area.

road metal, broken stone, cinders, and similar materials used in making and repairing roads and roadbeds.

road·run·ner (rōd′run′ər) *n.* a ground-dwelling cuckoo, *Geococcyx californianus,* native to flat, barren country from the southwestern United States to central Mexico, having brownish black streaked plumage, a long, white-tipped tail, and a shaggy crest. Length: 20-24 inches (51-61 centimeters).

road·side (rōd′sīd′) *n.* an area along the side of a road. —*adj.* along the side of a road: *a roadside vegetable stand.*

road·stead (rōd′sted′) *n.* road *(def. 3).*

roadrunner

road·ster (rōd′stər) *n.* an open automobile with a single seat for two or more people, often with a rumble seat or luggage compartment in the rear. Also, **runabout.**

road-test (rōd′test′) *v.t.* to give a road test to a vehicle.

road test 1. a test of a vehicle or any of its parts under actual driving conditions. **2.** a test of the driving skill of an applicant for a driver's license.

road·way (rōd′wā′) *n.* a road, esp. that part over which vehicles travel.

road·work (rōd′wûrk′) *n.* physical exercise or training consisting of long runs over a road or path.

roam (rōm) *v.i.* to go about without a specific purpose or destination, esp. over a large area; wander: *to roam through the woods.* —*v.t.* to wander over or through (a place): *Hungry wolves roamed the forest in search of food.* [Of uncertain origin.] —**roam′er,** *n.*

> **Synonyms** *v.i.* **Roam, ramble, rove[1],** and **wander** mean to travel about in a random, leisurely way. **Roam** implies a free and pleasurable journeying from place to place: *They roamed through southern France all summer, visiting Romanesque churches.* **Ramble** suggests walking in leisurely fashion, and more aimlessly than roaming: *I rambled through the fields without knowing where I would end up.* **Rove** is similar to *roam,* but can also denote a more energetic movement, sometimes with a specific purpose: *The police roved through the hills looking for the escaped prisoner.* **Wander** is often applied to the movements of a person or group with an itinerant way of life: *The tribe wandered freely in an area covering six states.*

roan (rōn) *n.* **1.** a reddish brown color mixed with gray or white. **2.** a horse of this color. —*adj.* having the color roan. [Old French *roan* the color, from Spanish *roano;* of uncertain origin.]

roar (rôr) *v.i.* **1.** to utter a loud, deep sound or cry. **2.** to resound loudly and deeply: *The motor roared.* **3.** to move with a loud, deep noise: *The plane roared up the runway.* **4.** to laugh loudly: *The audience roared at the comedian's jokes.* —*v.t.* to shout or express in a roar: *The crowd roared its approval of the speech.* —*n.* **1.** a loud, deep sound or cry, as of a human or animal. **2.** a loud, resounding noise: *the roar of ocean waves.* [Old English *rārian* to shout, yell.] —**roar′er,** *n.*

roast (rōst) *v.t.* **1.** to cook without liquid in an oven or over an open fire or hot coals: *to roast a chicken, to roast chestnuts.* **2.** to dry and brown by heat: *to roast coffee beans.* **3.** *Informal.* to criticize or ridicule severely: *The critics roasted the new play.* **4.** to make warm or excessively hot. **5.** *Metallurgy.* to heat (ore) with air in a furnace so as to purify, dehydrate, or oxidize. —*v.i.* **1.** to be cooked without liquid in an oven or over an open fire or hot coals. **2.** to be uncomfortably hot: *I'm roasting in this heavy coat.* —*n.* **1.** a cut of meat that has been roasted or is prepared to be roasted. **2.** an outdoor gathering at which food is cooked over an open fire or hot coals. **3.** an entertainment at which a series of speakers playfully mock a guest of honor, usually a celebrity. —*adj.* roasted: *a roast chicken.* [Old French *rostir* to cook before a fire; of Germanic origin.]

roast·er (rōs′tər) *n.* **1.** a pan or appliance used for roasting. **2.** an animal suitable for roasting, esp. a chicken or a young pig.

rob (rob) *v.,* **robbed, rob·bing.** —*v.t.* **1.** to take property from unlawfully, esp. with the threat or use of violence: *They robbed the jewelry store in broad daylight.* **2.** to deprive of something deserved or rightfully due, esp. by unjust or deceitful means: *to be robbed of an opportunity.* **3.** *Informal.* to take away (property) by unlawful means; steal. —*v.i.* to commit robbery. [Old French *rob(b)er* to steal; literally, to strip; of Germanic origin.]

rob·ber (rob′ər) *n.* a person who robs.

robber baron, a capitalist in the United States in the late nineteenth century who became very wealthy through exploitation, as of natural resources, and unethical business practices.

rob·ber·y (rob′ə rē) *n., pl.* **-ber·ies.** the act of unlawfully taking another's property, esp. with the threat or use of violence; theft. [French *roberie,* from *rober.* See ROB.] —For Synonyms, see **theft.**

robe (rōb) *n.* **1.** a long, loose outer garment, esp. one worn at home or on informal occasions: *a beach robe.* **2.** also, **robes.** such a garment worn to show office, profession, or rank: *a judge's robes, a cleric's robe.* **3.** a blanket or other covering, as for use by spectators at outdoor sporting events: *a lap robe.* —*v.,* **robed, rob·ing.** —*v.t.* to put on; dress. —*v.i.* to put on a robe; dress. [Old French *robe* garment, booty (because booty in medieval times often consisted of clothing); of Germanic origin.]

rob·in (rob′in) *n.* **1.** a North American thrush, *Turdus migratorius,* having a reddish orange breast and a black head and tail. Length: 10 inches (25 centimeters). **2.** a plump-bodied thrush, *Erithacus rubecula,* native to Europe and parts of Asia and Africa, having a brown back, a white underside, and a reddish brown breast and forehead. Length: 6 inches (15 centimeters). Also, **robin redbreast.** [Old French *Robin,* familiar form of *Robert,* man's proper name.]

Rob·in Good·fel·low (rob′in gŭd′fel′ō) See **puck**[2] *(def. 2).*

Robin Hood, in English legend, an outlaw who lived in Sherwood Forest with his band of followers and robbed the rich to give help to the poor.

rob·in's-egg blue (rob′inz eg′) a light greenish blue color.

Rob·in·son Cru·soe (rob′in sən krü′sō) the castaway hero of a novel of the same name by the English author Daniel Defoe.

ro·bot (rō′bot, -bət) *n.* **1.** a machine that somewhat resembles a human being and can perform some human functions. **2.** a person who performs or acts in a mechanical way; automaton. **3.** any device, as a chess-playing computer, that performs complex tasks either without human guidance or by remote control: *a submersible robot for exploring the ocean depths.* [Czech *robot* the machine, from *robota* compulsory labor, coined by Karel Čapek, 1890-1938, Czech playwright, for his play *R.U.R.*] —**ro·bot′ic,** *adj.*

robot bomb, buzz bomb.

ro·bot·ics (rō bot′iks) *n.* the science or technology of using automated or computer-controlled robots to perform routine tasks, as in a factory. ➡ used as singular.

ro·bust (rō bust′, rō′bust) *adj.* **1.** having or showing strength and vigor; in good health; hardy: *a robust young athlete, a robust appetite.* **2.** requiring strength and vigor: *the robust life of a forest ranger.* **3.** rich and full-bodied: *a robust flavor.* **4.** coarse; boisterous: *robust humor.* [Latin *rōbustus* oaken, strong, from *rōbur* oak, strength.] —**ro·bust′ly,** *adv.* —**ro·bust′ness,** *n.*

roc (rok) *n.* in Arabian legend, an enormous and fearsome bird of prey, able to carry off large animals. [Arabic *rukhkh;* of Persian origin.]

a	at	e	end	o	hot	u	up	hw	white		about
ā	ape	ē	me	ō	old	ū	use	ng	song		taken
ä	far	i	it	ô	fork	ü	rule	th	thin	ə	pencil
âr	care	ī	ice	oi	oil	ů	pull	th	this		lemon
		îr	pierce	ou	out	ûr	turn	zh	measure		circus

R

Ro·chelle salt (rō shel′) a salt of tartaric acid, the piezoelectric crystals of which are used in phonograph pickups and microphones, and the powder as a laxative; potassium sodium tartrate. Formula: $KNaC_4H_4O_6 \cdot 4H_2O$ [From *(La) Rochelle*, a French seaport.]

roch·et (roch′it) *n.* a knee-length vestment of white linen with close-fitting sleeves, worn by bishops and other church dignitaries. [Old French *rochet*; of Germanic origin.]

rock¹ (rok) *n.* **1.** a fragment or piece of stone. **2.** a large mass of stone forming a cliff, peak, or reef: *The ship was dashed violently against the rocks.* **3.** *Geology.* **a.** an extensive, naturally formed uniform mass of mineral matter that forms part of the crust of the earth. **b.** a particular kind of such matter, characterized by origin as igneous, sedimentary, or metamorphic, or by composition and texture as granite, limestone, marble, or the like. **4.** something resembling a rock in firmness, esp. a source of strength or support. **5.** *Informal.* a large gem, esp. a diamond. [Old French *rocque*, *roche* mass of hard stone; of uncertain origin.]

· **between a rock and a hard place.** confronted by two highly undesirable choices.

· **on the rocks.** *Informal.* **a.** (of a drink) served over ice cubes. **b.** in a state of destruction or ruin. **c.** without money; bankrupt.

rock² (rok) *v.t.* **1.** to move back and forth or from side to side gently: *to rock a baby in one's arms.* **2.** to move or shake violently: *The hurricane rocked the house.* **3.** to upset or unnerve: *The news of the mayor's death rocked the city.* —*v.i.* **1.** to be moved back and forth or from side to side gently: *The porch chair rocked in the breeze.* **2.** to be shaken violently: *The ship rocked in the squall.* —*n.* **1.** a rocking motion. **2.a.** rock 'n' roll. **b.** a form of popular music that evolved from rock 'n' roll, influenced by folk and country and western music and characterized by generally more complex lyrics and arrangements than rock 'n' roll. Also *(def. 2b)*, **rock music.** [Old English *roccian* to move to and fro.]

rock-and-roll (rok′ən rōl′) rock 'n' roll.

rock bottom, the lowest level; very bottom: *The stock market hit rock bottom.* —**rock′-bot′tom,** *adj.*

rock-bound (rok′bound′) *adj.* hemmed in or surrounded by rocks; rocky: *the rock-bound coast of Maine.*

rock candy, clear, hard crystals of pure sugar.

rock crystal, a clear, colorless variety of quartz, used to make optical devices, jewelry, vases, and other ornaments.

rock dove, a wild, Old World pigeon, *Columba livia,* the ancestor of domestic varieties and feral populations of pigeons now distributed worldwide. Average length: 12½ inches (32 centimeters).

rock·er (rok′ər) *n.* **1.** rocking chair. **2.** one of the two curved pieces on which a cradle, rocking chair, or other object rocks.

· **off one's rocker.** *Slang.* not in one's right mind; crazy.

rock·et (rok′it) *n.* **1.** a device that is propelled by a jet of hot gases ejected in a direction opposite to the direction of motion and does not require air from the outside for its operation. **2.** a vehicle, missile, or projectile propelled by such a device. —*v.i.* to move or rise swiftly: *The price of food is rocketing.* [Italian *rocchetta* a firework, bobbin, diminutive of *rocca* distaff; of Germanic origin; because the shape of this kind of firework resembles that of a bobbin or distaff.]

rock·et·eer (rok′i tîr′) *n.* a person who works with rockets, esp. an expert in rocketry.

rocket launcher, a tube or cluster of tubes from which rockets are launched.

rock·et·ry (rok′i trē) *n.* the science of rocket design, construction, and flight.

rock·fish (rok′fish′) *n., pl.* -fish or -fish·es. **1.** any of several food and game fish, genus *Sebastes,* of the scorpionfish family, having a number of sharp, strong spines projecting from the top and bottom fins. Length: 18 inches (46 centimeters). **2.** any of numerous fish, as striped bass, found around rocks.

rock garden, a garden arranged with flowers and plants on rocky ground or among rocks.

rocking chair, a chair mounted on rockers or springs, so that it can rock back and forth.

rocking horse, a toy horse mounted on rockers, large enough for a child to ride. Also, **hobbyhorse.**

rock lobster, spiny lobster.

rock music, rock² *(n., def. 2b).*

rock 'n' roll (rok′ən rōl′) *also,* **rock-and-roll.** *n.* a form of popular music derived from the blues, country and western music, and jazz, characterized esp. by a strong, persistent beat, electronically amplified instruments, and relatively simple lyrics and arrangements. —*adj.* of or relating to this music: *rock 'n' roll bands.* —*v.i.* to perform this music.

rock-ribbed (rok′ribd′) *adj.* **1.** marked by rows or ridges of

rock. **2.** unyielding in feeling, belief, or position: *a rock-ribbed skeptic.*

rock salt, a common salt occurring in solid form, esp. in large crystals; halite.

rock·weed (rok′wēd′) *n.* any of various brown algae seaweeds, esp. of the genus *Fucus* or *Ascophyllum,* that grow on rocks within the intertidal zone of the seashore. [ROCK + WEED¹.]

rock wool, mineral wool.

rock·y¹ (rok′ē) *adj.,* rock·i·er, rock·i·est. **1.** composed of or abounding in rocks: *rocky ground.* **2.** resembling rock; hard; unyielding. [ROCK¹ + -Y¹.] —**rock′i·ness,** *n.*

rock·y² (rok′ē) *adj.,* rock·i·er, rock·i·est. **1.** inclined to sway or totter; shaky. **2.** doubtful; uncertain: *a rocky future.* **3.** *Informal.* physically weak or unsteady: *The fever made me feel rocky.* [ROCK² + -Y¹.] —**rock′i·ness,** *n.*

Rocky Mountain goat, a goatlike, cud-chewing mammal, *Oreamnos americanus,* native to mountain ranges of western North America, having short black horns and a thick coat of long white hair. Height: 3½ feet (1.1 meters) at the shoulder. Also, **mountain goat.**

Rocky Mountain sheep, bighorn.

Rocky Mountain spotted fever, an infectious disease caused by a rickettsia and transmitted by the bite of a tick, characterized by high fever, headache, generalized pain, and a red or purple rash. [From the *Rocky Mountains,* where it was first discovered.]

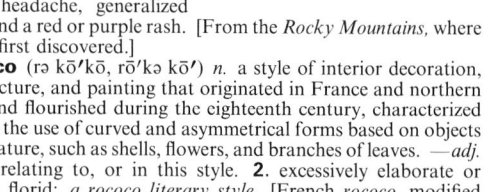

Rocky Mountain goat

ro·co·co (rə kō′kō, rō′kə kō′) *n.* a style of interior decoration, architecture, and painting that originated in France and northern Italy and flourished during the eighteenth century, characterized esp. by the use of curved and asymmetrical forms based on objects from nature, such as shells, flowers, and branches of leaves. —*adj.* **1.** of, relating to, or in this style. **2.** excessively elaborate or ornate; florid: *a rococo literary style.* [French *rococo,* modified form of *rocaille* shellwork, from *roc* rock¹; of uncertain origin; from the use of shell patterns in this style of decoration.]

rod (rod) *n.* **1.** a thin, straight, usually cylindrical piece of metal, wood, or other material: *a curtain rod.* **2.** a slender, straight stick cut from or growing on a tree or bush. **3.** fishing rod. **4.a.** a stick or bundle of sticks used to beat or punish. **b.** the rod. punishment; discipline: *Spare the rod and spoil the child* (Samuel Butler, 1664). **5.** a unit of linear measurement equal to 5½ yards or 16½ feet (5 meters). **6.** a stick or bar used for measuring. **7.** *Slang.* a pistol or revolver. **8.** one of the rod-shaped cells on the retina of the eye that are sensitive to dim light. **9.** a scepter, staff, or similar object carried or used as a symbol of power or authority. [Old English *rodd* thin, straight stick, pole¹.] —**rod′less,** *adj.* —**rod′like,** *adj.*

rode (rōd) a past tense of **ride.**

ro·dent (rōd′ənt) *n.* any of numerous mammals constituting the order Rodentia, having a pair of chisellike front teeth adapted for gnawing. Rats, mice, squirrels, guinea pigs, porcupines, and beavers are rodents. —*adj.* **1.** gnawing: *the rodent teeth of a beaver.* **2.** of, relating to, or characteristic of a rodent. [Latin *rōdēns,* present participle of *rōdere* to gnaw.]

ro·dent·i·cide (rō den′tə sīd′) *n.* any chemical or poison used to kill rodents, esp. rats and mice.

ro·de·o (rō′dē ō′, rō dā′ō) *n., pl.* -de·os. **1.** a show in which contestants compete in various events, such as horseback and bull riding, calf roping, and steer wrestling, often for cash prizes. **2.** a roundup of cattle. [Spanish *rodeo* roundup, from *rodear* to go around, from *rueda* wheel, from Latin *rota.*]

rod·o·mon·tade (rod′ə mon tād′ -täd′) *n.* vain boasting; bluster; gasconade. —*adj.* vainly boastful. —*v.i.,* -tad·ed, -tad·ing. boast; bluster. [French *rodomantade,* from Italian *rodomontata,* from *Rodomonte* boastful character in the epic poem *Orlando Furioso* by Ludovico Ariosto, 1474-1533.]

roe¹ (rō) *n.* the eggs of fish or crustaceans, some of which are eaten as a delicacy, either raw or cooked. [Possibly from Old Norse *hrogn.*]

roe² (rō) *n., pl.* **roes** or **roe.** a small deer, *Capreolus capreolus,* native to the forests of Europe and northern Asia, having a coarse, reddish brown coat with a white patch over the rump. Height: 30 inches (76 centimeters) at the shoulder. Also, **roe deer.** [Old English *rāha, rā.*]

roe·buck (rō′buk′) *n., pl.* **-bucks** or **-buck**. the male of the roe deer.

roent·gen (rent′gən, runt′-) *n.* a unit formerly used for measuring the intensity of exposure to X rays or gamma rays in terms of the ionization such radiation produces in dry air. [From Wilhelm Konrad *Roentgen,* 1845-1923, German physicist who discovered X rays.]

roent·gen·ol·o·gy (rent′gə nol′ə jē, runt′-) *n.* the branch of radiology that deals with the use, properties, and effects of X rays. **—roent′gen·ol′o·gist,** *n.*

Roentgen ray, X ray. [From Wilhelm Konrad *Roentgen,* 1845-1923, German physicist who discovered X rays.]

ro·ga·tion (rō gā shən) *n.* a solemn prayer of supplication, esp. the litanies chanted on the Monday, Tuesday, and Wednesday preceding Ascension Day. [Latin *rōgātiō* supplication.]

rog·er (roj′ər) *interj.* **1.** used in radio communications to indicate that a message has been received and understood. **2.** *Informal.* all right or okay. [From *Roger,* proper name used in communications for *r,* the first letter of *received.*]

rogue (rōg) *n.* **1.** a person who is dishonest and deceitful; scoundrel. **2.** a person who is mischievous and playful. **3.** a wild animal, esp. an elephant, of a dangerous or savage nature, driven away or living apart from the herd. [Of uncertain origin.]

ro·guer·y (rō′gə rē) *n., pl.* **-guer·ies. 1.** behavior or actions characterized by dishonesty and trickery. **2.** playfully mischievous actions or conduct.

rogues' gallery, a collection of photographs of known criminals and suspects kept by police to aid in making identifications.

ro·guish (rō′gish) *adj.* **1.** dishonest and deceitful; unscrupulous; unprincipled. **2.** playfully mischievous. **—ro′guish·ly,** *adv.* **—ro′guish·ness,** *n.*

roil (roil) *v.t.* **1.** to make (liquid) muddy or unsettled by stirring up sediment. **2.** to disturb or make angry; vex. **—v.i.** to be unsettled or agitated. [Of uncertain origin.]

rois·ter (roi′stər) *v.i.* **1.** to revel or frolic in a loud and riotous manner. **2.** swagger. [Old French *ru(i)stre* ruffian, form of *ruste* a rustic, from Latin *rūsticus* peasant, rustic.] **—rois′ter·er,** *n.*

Ro·land (rō′lənd) *n.* in French literature, a historical hero who fought under Charlemagne and, according to legend, was killed by the Saracens in 778. In Italian versions of the story, he is called Orlando.

role (rōl) *also,* **rôle.** *n.* **1.** a character or part played by an actor. **2.** a part played by a person or anything; position or function: *The article dealt with the role of the press in determining public opinion. I had the role of interpreter for the tour group.* [French *rôle* actor's part; originally, roll of paper containing such a part, going back to Latin *rotula* little wheel. See ROLL.]

role model, a person whose behavior sets an example, esp. for those who are young or impressionable: *Teachers and parents are important role models.*

role-play (rōl′plā′) *v.t., v.i.* to assume and act out the behavior and attitudes of (another person) in a situation based on real life in order to gain better understanding of other viewpoints, often done as part of a job training program or some form of psychotherapy. **—role′-play′ing,** *n.*

roll (rōl) *v.i.* **1.** to move by rotating on an axis or by turning over and over: *The ball rolled down the hill.* **2.** to move or be moved on rollers or wheels: *The wagon rolled down the driveway.* **3.** to turn over many times in succession: *The dog rolled in the mud.* **4.** to move in a smooth, rising and falling manner: *The fog rolled in from the water.* **5.** to extend in gentle rises and falls: *The hills rolled toward the horizon.* **6.** to pass or elapse (with *by* or *on*): *The years roll on.* **7.** to form a ball or cylinder when turned over and over: *Clay won't roll if you don't work it.* **8.** to turn around wholly or partially: *Their eyes rolled in amazement.* **9.** to rock or move from side to side; sway: *The ship rolled violently in the storm.* **10.** to walk with a swaying motion. **11.** to make a deep, continuous sound; rumble: *The drums rolled.* **12.** to become spread out or flattened under a roller: *This paint rolls on easily.* **13.** *Informal.* to make progress or start: *Let's get this project rolling.* **14.** (of a celestial body) to perform a periodical revolution. **15.** to recur periodically (with *around*): *Winter has rolled around again.* **—v.t. 1.** to cause to move by rotating on an axis or by turning over and over: *to roll a hoop.* **2.** to move (something) by means of rollers or wheels: *to roll a bed against a wall.* **3.** to wrap (something) around on itself or on something else; shape into a cylinder or a ball: *to roll a blanket.* **4.** to enfold or wrap, as in a covering: *to roll a wet swimsuit in a towel.* **5.** to drive or impel with a sweeping motion: *The wind rolled the waves onto the shore.* **6.** to spread out, flatten, or make smooth with a roller: *to roll metal into sheets, to roll out dough.* **7.** to cause to rock from side to side: *The strong wind rolled the boat.* **8.** to beat (a drum) with quick continuous blows. **9.** to pronounce (a speech sound) with a trill, esp. the sound of *r.* **10.** to emit a prolonged deep sound. **11.** to turn (the eyes) around, wholly or partially. **12.** to cast (dice), as in craps. **13.** *Slang.* to rob (an incapacitated or unconscious person). **—n. 1.** a ball or cylinder formed by winding something round and round; something rolled up: *a roll of string, a roll of stamps, a roll of wallpaper.* **2.** a quantity of something rolled up, usually considered as a standard measure. **3.** a list of names of people belonging to a group: *a class roll.* **4.** a catalog, list, or record. **5.** a mass of something that is somewhat rounded or cylindrical. **6.a.** a small cake of baked dough. **b.** any food, as meat or cake, that is rolled up. **7.** a rolling or swaying motion: *The roll of the boat was making us dizzy.* **8.** a rapid, continuous series of short sounds, as those made by beating on a drum. **9.** a deep, loud reverberation: *the roll of thunder.* **10.** a gentle rising and falling: *the roll of hilly terrain.* **11.** roller. **12.** an act or instance of rolling. **13.** *Slang.* money, esp. a wad of paper money. **14.** a change in the position of an aircraft around a front to back axis, so that one wing rises and the other drops. [Old French *roller, rouler* to move by turning over and over, wind on a cylinder, going back to Latin *rotula* little wheel, diminutive of *rota* wheel.] **—roll′a·ble,** *adj.*

- **to roll back.** to reduce to a previous lower level: *to roll back wages.*
- **to roll in. a.** to arrive, esp. in large numbers or amounts: *The train rolled in two hours late. Orders rolled in faster than they could be filled.* **b.** *Informal.* to luxuriate or abound in: *to be rolling in money.*
- **to roll over. a.** to automatically renew a loan, certificate of deposit, or the like. **b.** to transfer funds from one account that is qualified for tax-deferred status to another in such a way as to preserve the status of these funds.
- **to roll up. a.** to increase in quantity; accumulate; amass: *We rolled up a large score against the visiting team.* **b.** *Informal.* to arrive in a car or other form of transportation.
- **to strike off** (or **from**) **the rolls.** to deprive of membership.

roll·back (rōl′bak′) *n.* a reduction of prices or wages to a previous lower level, as by a governmental order.

roll bar, a heavy metal bar that extends overhead across the interior of a motor vehicle to protect the occupant in the event that the vehicle turns over.

roll call 1. the act of calling a list of names, as those registered in a class, to determine who is present. **2.** the time or signal at which this is done.

roll·er (rō′lər) *n.* **1.** a cylinder on which something is rolled or wound up: *the roller of a window shade.* **2.** a cylinder that smooths, spreads out, flattens, or crushes: *a paint roller.* **3.** a small wheel or caster on which something is rolled: *We had to put the piano on rollers to move it.* **4.** any of various cylindrical devices over which something is moved. **5.** a hollow cylinder of wire mesh or plastic on which hair is rolled up. **6.** a long, swelling wave breaking on a shoreline. **7.a.** any of various jaylike birds, family Coraciidae, native to Africa, Eurasia, the East Indies, and Australia, having brightly colored plumage and noted for the tumbling and rolling flight of the male during courtship.

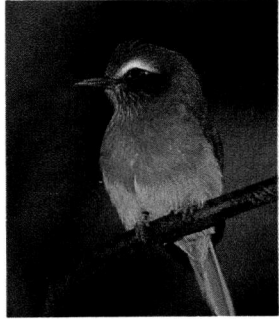

roller *(def. 7a)*

Length: 9½-18 inches (24-46 centimeters). **b.** a canary having a rolling, or trilling, song. **8.** a person or thing that rolls.

roller bearing, a bearing used esp. for heavy loads, in which the friction-reducing parts are cylindrical or cone-shaped rollers.

roller coaster, an amusement ride consisting of a series of open, attached cars that move at high speeds over a track having sharp turns and steep inclines and dips.

roll·er-skate (rō′lər skāt′) *v.i.,* **-skated, -skat·ing.** to skate on roller skates.

a	at	e	end	o	hot	u	up	hw	white		about
ā	ape	ē	me	ō	old	ū	use	ng	song		taken
ä	far	i	it	ô	fork	ü	rule	th	thin	ə	pencil
âr	care	ī	ice	oi	oil	u̇	pull	th	this		lemon
		îr	pierce	ou	out	ûr	turn	zh	measure		circus

R

roller skate, a skate having small wheels on the bottom instead of a runner, used for skating on a flat surface, as a floor or sidewalk.

rol·lick (rol′ik) *v.i.* to behave in a carefree, joyous manner; frolic; gambol; romp. [Possibly blend of ROMP and FROLIC.]

rol·lick·ing (rol′i king) *adj.* jovial and carefree; merry; frolicking.

roll·ing (rō′ling) *adj.* **1.** moving by turning over and over: *a rolling hoop.* **2.** moved by or moving on wheels: *a rolling teacart.* **3.** extending in gentle rises and falls: *rolling hills.* **4.** moving in swells or undulations: *the rolling sea.* **5.** moving from side to side; swaying: *a rolling gait.* **6.** deep and resounding; reverberating: *rolling thunder.* **7.** folded over as if on a cylinder: *a rolling collar.* —*n.* the action or motion of a person or thing that rolls or is rolled.

rolling mill 1. a steel mill where metal is made into sheets, bars, or plates by being passed between heavy rollers. **2.** a machine with rollers for doing this.

rolling pin, a smooth cylinder, usually wooden, with a handle at each end, used to roll out dough.

rolling stock, locomotives, cars, and other wheeled vehicles of a railroad.

roll·o·ver (rōl′ō′vər) *n.* **1.** the automatic renewal of a loan, certificate of deposit, or the like. **2.** the transfer of funds from one account that is qualified for tax-deferred status to another in such a way as to preserve the status of these funds.

roll-top desk (rōl′top′) a writing desk with a slatted movable top that can be rolled back.

ro·ly-po·ly (rō′lē pō′lē) *adj.* short and plump; pudgy: *a roly-poly child.* —*n., pl.* **-lies. 1.** a short, plump person or thing. **2.** *British.* a cakelike pudding made of seasoned jam or fruit spread on dough, rolled up, and cooked in any of various ways.

ROM (rom) *n.* a type of computer memory that holds permanent data that can usually be read at high speed but to which no new data can be added. [Short for *r(ead-)o(nly) m(emory).*]

Rom. 1. Roman. **2.** Romance (languages). **3.** Romans (New Testament).

Ro·ma·ic (rō mā′ik) *n.* the vernacular of modern Greece. —*adj.* of or relating to this speech or to those who use it.

ro·maine (rō mān′) *n.* **1.** the narrow crisp leaves of a lettuce plant, variety *longifolia,* forming a long loose head. **2.** the plant itself. [French *romaine,* from *romain* Roman (with reference to its having come from Avignon when Avignon was the papal residence), from Latin *Rōmānus* relating to Rome.]

Ro·man (rō′mən) *adj.* **1.** of, relating to, or characteristic of ancient or modern Rome or its people or culture. **2.** of or relating to the Roman Catholic Church or its members. **3.** *usually,* **roman.** of or designating the most widely used style of type or lettering, characterized by upright letters. This sentence is in roman type. **4.** of or designating a style of architecture used in ancient Rome, characterized esp. by the arch, vault, and dome and by the use of brick and concrete. —*n.* **1.** a native, inhabitant, or citizen of ancient or modern Rome. **2.** *usually,* **roman.** roman type or lettering. [Latin *Rōmānus* relating to Rome, from *Rōma* Rome.]

ro·man à clef (Rô mä nä klä′) *pl.* **ro·mans à clef** (Rô mänz ä-klä′). a novel in which real people and events are depicted in disguised form. [French *roman à clef* literally, novel with a key, going back to Latin *Rōmānus* (see ROMAN) + *ad* to, at + *clāvis* key. See ROMANCE.]

Roman candle, a firework consisting of a long tube that shoots out balls of fire and different kinds of sparks.

Roman Catholic 1. of, relating to, or characteristic of the Roman Catholic Church. **2.** a member of the Roman Catholic Church.

Roman Catholic Church, the Christian church that recognizes the pope as its supreme head.

Roman Catholicism, the beliefs, practices, and system of government of the Roman Catholic Church.

ro·mance (rō mans′, rō′mans) *n.* **1.** a love affair. **2.** a quality or appearance of love, excitement, mystery, or adventure: *the romance of the sea, the romance of a dimly lit restaurant.* **3.** an interest in or tendency toward that which is exciting, adventurous, mysterious, or amorous. **4.** a work of literature primarily concerned with a love story. **5.** a narrative in prose or verse dealing with heroes and their deeds, esp. one about knights and chivalry: *the romances of King Arthur and his knights of the Round Table.* **6.** any narrative, esp. a novel, emphasizing adventure, mysterious events, or exotic settings: *a Gothic romance.* **7.** a fanciful or exaggerated account. —*v.,* **-manced, -manc·ing.** —*v.i.* **1.** to

behave or speak in a romantic way. **2.** to compose or relate fanciful stories. —*v.t. Informal.* to make love to; court; woo. —*adj.* **Romance.** of or relating to a Romance language. [Old French *romanz* (later, *roman*) work written in a Romance language, from Late Latin *Rōmānicē* in a Romance language, from Latin *Rōmānus* relating to Rome.] —**ro·manc′er,** *n.*

Romance language, a language descended from Latin, such as French, Italian, Spanish, Portuguese, Romanian, Catalan, or Provençal.

Ro·man·esque (rō′mə nesk′) *adj.* **1.** of, relating to, or designating the style of architecture that flourished in western Europe during the eleventh and twelfth centuries, characterized by massive stone construction and rounded arches and vaults. **2.** of or designating a corresponding style of art or sculpture. —*n.* the Romanesque style of architecture, art, or sculpture.

Romanesque arch

Ro·ma·ni·an (rō mā′nē ən) *also,* **Roumanian, Rumanian.** *adj.* of, relating to, or characteristic of Romania or its people, language, or culture. —*n.* **1.** a native or citizen of Romania. **2.** a person of Romanian descent. **3.** a Romance language spoken in Romania and parts of the southwestern Soviet Union, containing words borrowed from Slavic and other languages.

Ro·man·ic (rō man′ik) *adj.* **1.** of, relating to, or derived from the ancient Romans. **2.** of or relating to the Romance languages.

Ro·man·ism (rō′mə niz′əm) *n.* Roman Catholicism. ➡ used derisively. —**Ro′man·ist,** *n.*

Roman nose, a nose with a jutting or prominent bridge.

Roman numeral, any of the numerals I, V, X, L, C, D, M or any combination of these, used in the ancient Roman system of notation. I = 1, V = 5, X = 10, L = 50, C = 100, D = 500, and M = 1,000. The value of any combination of numerals is their sum, except when one is preceded by another of smaller value, in which case the smaller is subtracted from the larger; thus, VI = 6, but IV = 4. A bar over the numeral indicates multiplication by 1,000; thus $\overline{X}$ = 10,000.

Ro·ma·no (rō mä′nō) *n.* a sharp, hard cheese made from sheep's, cow's, or goat's milk, often grated and served over food, esp. spaghetti and other pasta. [Italian *romano* Roman, from Latin *Rōmānus.*]

Ro·ma·nov (rō′mə nôf′, -nof′, rō mä′nəf) *also,* **Ro·ma·noff.** *n.* the imperial dynasty that ruled Russia from 1613 to 1917.

Ro·mans (rō′mənz) *n.* a book of the New Testament consisting of an Epistle written by the Apostle Paul to the Christians of Rome. ➡ used as singular.

Ro·mansh (rō mansh′, -mänsh′) *also,* **Ro·mansch.** *n.* a small group of Romance dialects spoken in eastern Switzerland. —*adj.* of or relating to Romansh.

ro·man·tic (rō man′tik) *adj.* **1.** relating to, characterized by, or having thoughts and feelings of love; amorous: *a romantic story, a romantic person.* **2.** having a quality of adventure, excitement, or mystery: *the romantic life of a spy.* **3.** suitable for or conducive to love or romance: *a romantic setting.* **4.** not practical or real; visionary; idealized: *romantic notions.* **5.** *also,* **Romantic.** of or relating to romanticism in art, literature, or music. —*n.* **1.** a romantic person. **2.** romanticist. [French *romantique* emotional, relating to romanticism, from Middle French *romant* tale in a Roman language, from Late Latin *Rōmānicē* in a Romance language. See ROMANCE.] —**ro·man′ti·cal·ly,** *adv.*

ro·man·ti·cism (rō man′tə siz′əm) *n.* **1.** *also,* **Romanticism.** a style in literature, music, and art during the last part of the eighteenth century and the first half of the nineteenth century, characterized by spontaneous feeling, appreciation of nature, and disregard of rules and forms. **2.** a spirit, quality, or feeling of romance.

ro·man·ti·cist (rō man'tə sist) *n.* an adherent of romanticism in literature, music, or art.

ro·man·ti·cize (rō man'tə sīz') *v.,* **-cized, -ciz·ing.** —*v.t.* to invest with a romantic spirit or character; make romantic: *to romanticize one's life.* —*v.i.* to act, talk, or think romantically. —**ro·man'ti·ci·za'tion,** *n.*

Romantic Movement, romanticism in literature, music, and art in the late eighteenth century and early nineteenth century in Europe and America.

Rom·a·ny (rom'ə nē, rō'mə-) *n., pl.* **-nies. 1.** Gypsy. **2.** the language of the Gypsies, belonging to the Indo-Iranian branch of the Indo-European language family. —*adj.* of or relating to the Gypsies or their language or culture.

Rome (rōm) *n.* **1.** the ancient Roman republic. **2.** the Roman Empire. **3.** the Roman Catholic Church: *Henry VIII of England broke with Rome in 1534.*

Ro·me·o (rō'mē ō') *n.* **1.** the love-stricken hero of Shakespeare's tragedy *Romeo and Juliet.* **2.** any man who is or is thought to be a great lover of women.

romp (romp) *v.i.* **1.** to play or frolic in a lively or boisterous way. **2.** to win easily, as in a race. —*n.* **1.** lively or boisterous play; frolic: *The children went for a romp in the woods.* **2.** an easy victory. [Form of RAMP².] —**romp'er,** *n.*

romp·ers (rom'pərz) *pl. n.* a loose one-piece garment combining trousers and a top, worn by young children.

Rom·u·lus and Remus (rom'yə ləs) in Roman mythology, the twin sons of Mars and the founders of the city of Rome, who were abandoned as infants and raised by wolves.

ron·deau (ron'dō, ron dō') *n., pl.* **-deaux** (-dōz, -dōz'). a poem consisting of ten or thirteen lines, using two rhymes, and repeating the opening words in the middle and at the end of the poem. [French *rondeau,* later form of Old French *rondel* form of lyric poetry (in which the first two lines are repeated or come *round*), from *rond* circular, from Latin *rotundus.*]

ron·do (ron'dō, ron dō') *n., pl.* **-dos.** a musical composition or movement having a principal theme that is repeated at least three times in the same key and is returned to after the introduction of each subordinate theme. [Italian *rondo,* from French *rondeau* rondeau. See RONDEAU.]

rood (rüd) *n.* **1.** a unit of land measure equal to 40 square rods (¹⁄₁₀ of a hectare); ¹⁄₄ acre. **2.** a cross or crucifix, esp. a large crucifix over an altar. [Old English *rōd* pole¹, cross, measure of land.]

roof (rüf, růf) *n.* **1.** the external covering of the top of a building. **2.** something resembling a roof in position or function: *the roof of the mouth, the roof of a car.* **3.** a house or home. —*v.t.* to provide or cover with a roof: *to roof a house.* [Old English *hrōf* external covering of the top of a building.] —**roof'like',** *adj.*

 •**to go through the roof. a.** to exceed all expectations; become excessive: *Taxes are going through the roof.* **b.** *Informal.* to become very angry or agitated.

 •**to hit the roof.** *Informal.* to become very angry or agitated.

 •**to raise the roof.** *Informal.* **a.** to be very noisy or boisterous. **b.** to complain in a loud, excited manner.

roof·er (rü'fər, růf'ər) *n.* a person who constructs or repairs roofs.

roof·ing (rü'fing, růf'ing) *n.* the material used to construct roofs.

roof·less (rüf'lis, růf'-) *adj.* **1.** having no roof. **2.** homeless.

roof·top (rüf'top', růf'-) *n.* the roof of a building.

roof·tree (rüf'trē', růf'-) *n.* the ridgepole of a roof.

rook¹ (růk) *n.* **1.** a Eurasian bird, *Corvus frugilegus,* closely related to and resembling the crow. Length: 18 inches (46 centimeters). **2.** a person who cheats, esp. at dice or cards. —*v.t. Informal.* to cheat; swindle. [Old English *hrōc* the bird.]

rook² (růk) *n. Chess.* any of the four pieces, two to each player, that may move any number of spaces parallel to the sides of the board. Also, **castle.** [Old French *roc,* from Persian *rukh.*]

rook·er·y (růk'ə rē) *n., pl.* **-er·ies. 1.** a breeding place or colony of rooks. **2.** a breeding place or colony of other birds or of animals, such as penguins and seals.

rook²

rook·ie (růk'ē) *n. Informal.* **1.** an inexperienced recruit, as on a police force. **2.** a first-year player in a major professional sport, as baseball, football, basketball, or tennis. **3.** any beginner; novice; tyro. [Modification (influenced by ROOK¹) of RECRUIT.]

room (rüm, rům) *n.* **1.** an area that is or may be occupied by something; space: *Is there enough room in the corner to put the*

desk? **2.** an area within a house or other structure that is separated or set off by walls or partitions: *a house with seven rooms.* **3.a.** the people in such an area: *The whole room applauded the singer.* **b.** the contents of such an area: *to rearrange a room.* **4.** a suitable chance or opportunity; possibility: *There is room for improvement in your work.* **5.** **rooms.** living quarters; lodging: *The student rented rooms near the campus.* —*v.i.* to live in a room or rooms; lodge. [Old English *rūm* space.]

room and board, lodging and meals.

room·er (rü'mər, rům'ər) *n.* a person who occupies a rented room or rooms in another's house; lodger.

room·ette (rü met', rů-) *n.* a small private compartment on a railroad sleeping car.

room·ful (rüm'fůl', rům'-) *n., pl.* **-fuls. 1.** as much or as many as a room will hold. **2.** the people or objects in a room.

rooming house, a house with furnished rooms for rent.

room·mate (rüm'māt', rům'-) *n.* a person, or one of the persons, with whom one shares a room or rooms.

room·y (rü'mē, rům'ē) *adj.,* **room·i·er, room·i·est.** having ample room; large; spacious. —**room'i·ness,** *n.*

roost (rüst) *n.* **1.** a perch on which birds, esp. domestic fowl, rest or sleep. **2.** a place for birds to rest or sleep for the night. **3.** a place in which people rest, stay, or congregate. —*v.i.* **1.** to rest or sleep on or as on a roost. **2.** to settle or lodge, esp. for the night. [Old English *hrōst* resting place for birds.]

 •**to come home to roost.** to have repercussions, esp. negative ones, on the doer or originator of an action, policy, or the like.

 •**to rule the roost.** to have complete control; dominate; reign.

roost·er (rüs'tər) *n.* the male of the domestic fowl. Also, **cock.**

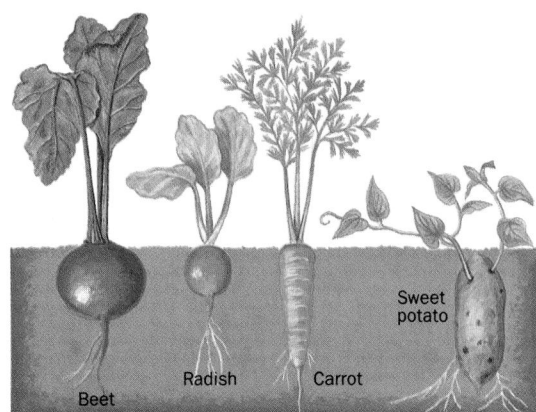

root¹
root vegetables

Sweet
potato

Beet   Radish   Carrot

root¹ (rüt, růt) *n.* **1.** the lower part of a plant that grows downward, serving to anchor the plant in the soil. Roots absorb water and dissolved nutrients from the soil and store food. **2.** any of various underground plant parts, as a tuber or rhizome. **3.** an attached or embedded part of an organ or structure: *the root of a tooth, the root of a hair.* **4.** that from which anything comes or develops; origin; source: *The teacher traced the roots of the Industrial Revolution.* **5.** the basic part; essence; core: *We must get to the root of the problem.* **6. roots. a.** ancestors or family background: *to have roots in a country.* **b.** a condition or feeling of being settled and having ties to a particular place, society, or tradition: *to move so often that one has no roots anywhere.* **7.** *Linguistics.* the fundamental form of a word to which affixes are added to form other words. *Faith* is the root of *faithful, faithless,* and *unfaithful.* **8.** *Mathematics.* **a.** a quantity that, when multiplied by itself a specified number of times, will produce a given quantity. The square root of 9 is 3, and the cube root of 27 is 3. Also, **radical, radix. b.** a quantity that, when substituted for

a	at	e	end	o	hot	u	up	hw	white	⟨	about
ā	ape	ē	me	ō	old	ū	use	ng	song		taken
ä	far	i	it	ô	fork	ü	rule	th	thin	ə	pencil
âr	care	ī	ice	oi	oil	ů	pull	th	this		lemon
		îr	pierce	ou	out	ûr	turn	zh	measure	⟨	circus

R

an unknown quantity in an equation, will satisfy the equation. **9.** *Music.* **a.** a tone from whose overtones a chord is constructed. **b.** the lowest tone of a chord. —*v.i.* **1.** to develop roots and begin to grow: *These plants will not root in such arid soil.* **2.** to be or become firmly settled or established. —*v.t.* **1.** to fix or establish firmly by or as by roots: *Fear rooted the child to the spot.* **2.** to pull, tear, or dig by or as by the roots; remove completely (with *up* or *out*): *to root up a weed, to root out an informer.* [Old Norse *rōt* underground part of a plant.] —**root′like′,** *adj.*

· **to take root. a.** to develop roots and begin to grow. **b.** to become firmly fixed or established.

root² (rüt, růt) *v.i.* **1.** to turn up or dig in the earth with or as with the snout or nose. **2.** to search for something; rummage: *I rooted through the closet for my missing shoe.* —*v.t.* to turn up or dig with or as with the snout or nose. [Old English *wrōtan* to turn up with the snout.] —**root′er,** *n.*

root³ (rüt, růt) *v.i.* **1.** to give encouragement to a contestant or team, as by applauding or shouting; cheer (with *for*): *Everyone was rooting for our side to win.* **2.** to lend support or wish success to someone or something: *We're all rooting for you to win the scholarship.* [Possibly a form of earlier *rout* to make a loud noise; probably of Scandinavian origin.] —**root′er,** *n.*

root beer, a nonalcoholic beverage made from or flavored with the extracted juice of the roots of various plants, as sarsaparilla.

root canal 1. a chamber in the pulp of the root of a tooth, containing blood vessels and nerves. **2.** a procedure for treating disease in the pulp of a tooth, esp. by removing the pulp and replacing it with filling. [ROOT¹ + CANAL.]

root cap *Botany.* a hoodlike mass of parenchyma that covers and protects the growing tip of a root.

root cellar, an underground storage area for root crops and other vegetables.

root crop, a crop, such as carrots or beets, grown for its edible roots.

root hair, a thin, hairlike projection of a plant root that absorbs water and dissolved minerals from the soil.

root·less (rüt′lis, růt′-) *adj.* **1.** without ties to a particular place, society, or tradition. **2.** having no roots. —**root′less·ness,** *n.*

root·let (rüt′lit, růt′-) *n.* small root.

root·stock (rüt′stok′, růt′-) *n.* **1.** rhizome. **2.** a root used as the stock for grafting a slip from another plant.

rope (rōp) *n.* **1.** a strong cord made of twisted or intertwined strands of fiber, wire, or similar material. **2.** a string of things joined together by twisting, twining, or threading: *a rope of pearls.* **3.** a hangman's noose. **4.** execution or death by hanging. **5.** lasso. **6.** a sticky, threadlike formation, as in a liquid. **7. ropes.** the details or procedures of an operation or activity: *I'll show the new employee the ropes.* —*v.,* **roped, rop·ing.** —*v.t.* **1.** to tie, bind, or fasten with or as with a rope. **2.** to separate or enclose with a rope: *to rope off a street for a parade.* **3.** to catch with a lasso. —*v.i.* to form threadlike, sticky strands. [Old English *rāp* strong, twisted cord.] —**rop′er,** *n.*

· **at the end of one's rope. a.** at the end of one's patience. **b.** having run out of resources.

· **to rope in.** *Informal.* to persuade or involve by deceit.

rope·danc·er (rōp′dan′sər) *n.* a person who dances, walks, or does stunts on the tightrope.

rope·walk (rōp′wôk′) *n.* a long, narrow area, as a covered path or building, where ropes are made.

rope·walk·er (rōp′wô′kər) *n.* ropedancer. —**rope′walk′ing,** *n.*

rop·y (rō′pē) *adj.,* **rop·i·er, rop·i·est. 1.** forming or having sticky, stringy threads: *a ropy syrup.* **2.** like a rope or cord. —**rop′i·ness,** *n.*

Roque·fort (rōk′fərt) *n. Trademark.* a pungent, often crumbly, cream-colored cheese veined with a blue mold. [From *Roquefort,* a town in France where it was originally made.]

ror·qual (rôr′kwəl) *n.* finback. [French *rorqual,* from Norwegian *röyrkval* literally, red whale (with reference to its red streaks).]

Ror·schach test (rôr′shäk) *n.* a psychological test of personality in which a subject interprets each of a series of inkblots. [From Hermann *Rorschach,* 1884-1922, Swiss psychiatrist who developed it.]

ro·sa·ceous (rō zā′shəs) *adj.* **1.** of or relating to the rose family. **2.** resembling a rose. [Latin *rosāceus,* from *rosa* rose¹.]

ro·sar·i·an (rō zâr′ē ən) *n.* a person who specializes in the cultivation of roses. [ROSE¹ + -ARIAN.]

ro·sa·ry (rō′zə rē) *n., pl.* **-ries. 1.a.** in the Roman Catholic Church, a string of beads used for counting in the recitation of prayers. **b.** a series of prayers said with these beads, commonly

consisting of fifteen decades of Ave Marias, each decade preceded by a paternoster and followed by a Gloria Patri. **2.** any string of beads used similarly in other religions. [Medieval Latin *rosarium,* from Latin *rosārium* rose garden, from *rosa* rose¹.]

rose¹ (rōz) *n.* **1.** the fragrant flower of any of a large group of plants, genus *Rosa,* usually having from three to nine toothed leaflets and growing in a variety of colors. Roses are among the most widely cultivated of all garden flowers. **2.** the woody plant bearing this flower, having thorny stems that are usually erect and stout, but which sometimes trail or climb. **3.** a pinkish red color. **4.** something resembling a rose in shape or form. **5.** rosette. **6.** a round, perforated nozzle on a pipe or watering can. **7.** compass card. **8.** a type of gem cut characterized by a flat base and a many-faceted top. —*adj.* **1.** designating a large family, Rosaceae, of flowering plants, shrubs, and trees that grow in temperate parts of the world. Many plants of the family are cultivated for their fruits and flowers, as apple and cherry trees and strawberry and rose bushes. **2.** having the color rose. [Old English *rose* the flower and plant, from Latin *rosa.*] —**rose′like′,** *adj.*

rose² (rōz) the past tense of **rise.**

ro·sé (rō zā′) *n.* a pink, usually dry, table wine made from red grapes whose skins are removed early in the fermentation process. [French *rosé* this wine, pink, from *rose* rose¹, from Latin *rosa.*]

ro·se·ate (rō′zē it, -āt′) *adj.* **1.** tinged or colored with rose; rosy. **2.** full of hope or optimism; promising: *a roseate outlook.*

rose·bay (rōz′bā′) *n.* any of several rhododendrons, esp. *Rhododendron maximum,* bearing rosy flowers spotted with green.

rose·bud (rōz′bud′) *n.* the bud of a rose.

rose·bush (rōz′bůsh′) *n.* a plant bearing roses.

rose-col·ored (rōz′kul′ərd) *adj.* **1.** tinted pinkish red, as eyeglasses. **2.** cheerful; optimistic, rosy: *to have a rose-colored outlook.*

rose fever, a seasonal form of hay fever usually caused by grass pollen, incorrectly attributed to rose pollen because roses are in bloom at the same time.

rose·fish (rōz′fish′) *n., pl.* **-fish** or **-fish·es.** an orange-red food fish, *Sebastes marinus,* found in the North Atlantic. Also, redfish.

rose geranium, any of several geraniums, genus *Pelargonium,* having fragrant, narrowly divided leaves and yielding an oil used in the manufacture of perfume and soap.

rose hip, hip².

rose mallow, any of a large group of plants, genus *Hibiscus,* of the mallow family, esp. *H. moscheutos,* a hairy marsh herb, widely cultivated for its pink or white flowers.

rose·mar·y (rōz′mâr′ē) *n., pl.* **-mar·ies. 1.** the fragrant lance-shaped leaves of an evergreen shrub, *Rosmarinus officinalis,* of the mint family, used as an herb. **2.** the shrub bearing these leaves, having pale blue tubular flowers borne in clusters. The leaves and flowers yield an oil that is used in the manufacture of perfume, soap, and other products. For illustration, see **herb.** [Modification (influenced by ROSE¹ and *Mary*) of obsolete *rosmarine,* from Latin *rōs marīnus* literally, dew of the sea.]

rose of Shar·on (shar′ən) a hardy Asian shrub, *Hibiscus syriacus,* of the mallow family, bearing oval or lobed leaves and cultivated for its bell-shaped flowers, which may be red, purple, violet, or white.

ro·se·o·la (rō′zē ō′lə) *n.* a rose-colored rash, esp. from German measles. [Modern Latin *roseola,* diminutive of Latin *roseus* rosy, from *rosa* rose.]

Ro·set·ta stone (rō zet′ə) a basalt slab inscribed with a decree written in 196 B.C., found in 1799 near Rosetta, Egypt. Written in hieroglyphics, demotic characters, and Greek, it provided the key to deciphering ancient Egyptian writing.

ro·sette (rō zet′) *n.* **1.** an ornament, usually made of gathered or pleated ribbon in the shape of a rose, used as a decoration or as a badge of honor or office. **2.** anything shaped like a rose, as a circular carved architectural ornament or a circlet of leaves. [French *rosette* rose-shaped object, small rose, diminutive of *rose* rose¹, from Latin *rosa.*]

rose water, a preparation usually made by mixing or distilling oil of roses with water, used in cosmetics and in cooking.

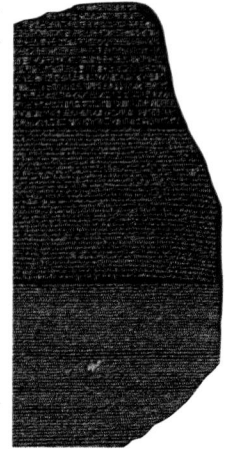

Rosetta stone
(detail)

rose window, a circular window, usually made up of stained glass sections that radiate from a center.

rose·wood (rōz′wud′) *n.* **1.** the hard, strongly grained, dark red wood of any of several tropical evergreen trees, genus *Dalbergia,* of the pea family, widely used to make furniture, sporting goods, and other products. **2.** a tree yielding such wood.

Rosh Ha·sha·nah (rōsh′hə shä′nə) the Jewish New Year, occurring in September or early October. [Hebrew *rōsh hashshānāh* literally, head of the year.]

Ro·si·cru·cian (rō′zi krü′shən) *n.* **1.** a member of an international secret society devoted to the improvement of the human race through the application of occult and religious doctrines. **2.** a member of any of several similar secret societies prominent in the seventeenth and eighteenth centuries. —*adj.* of, relating to, or characteristic of the Rosicrucians. [From the Latinized form (*rosa crucis* rose of the cross) of the German name of the alleged founder of this society, Christian *Rosenkranz* literally, rosy cross.] —**Ro′·si·cru′cian·ism,** *n.*

ros·in (roz′in) *n.* **1.** a hard, brittle substance obtained by heating crude turpentine from pine trees in copper stills and removing the surface oil. It is used in the manufacture of paints and other products and is rubbed on the surface of certain items, as violin bows and dancers' shoes, to make them less slippery. **2.** resin (*def. 1*). —*v.t.* to rub or cover with rosin. [Form of RESIN.]

ros·ter (ros′tər) *n.* **1.** a list of military officers and other personnel enrolled for duty. **2.** any list of names; roll; register. [Dutch *rooster* gridiron, list (referring to the resemblance of lined paper to a gridiron).]

ros·trum (ros′trəm) *n., pl.* **-trums** or **-tra** (-trə). **1.** a raised area, such as a platform or pulpit, used for public speaking. **2.** a projection on the bow of a ship, esp. one on an ancient Roman warship used for ramming. **3.** *Biology.* a beaklike part or projection. [Latin *rōstrum* beak; with reference to the platform for speakers (that was adorned with the *beaks* of captured ships) in the Roman forum.] —**ros′tral,** *adj.*

ros·y (rō′zē) *adj.,* **ros·i·er, ros·i·est. 1.** having the color rose; pinkish red; blushing: *The baby's cheeks were rosy from the cold.* **2.** full of hope or optimism; bright; promising: *a rosy outlook on life.* —**ros′i·ly,** *adv.* —**ros′i·ness,** *n.*

rot (rot) *v.,* **rot·ted, rot·ting.** —*v.i.* **1.** to become damaged or ruined by breaking down in composition, as through the action of bacteria or disease: *The apples rotted on the tree.* **2.** to deteriorate, as by decay or idleness. **3.** to become morally corrupt; degenerate. —*v.t.* to cause to become damaged or ruined by breaking down in composition. —*n.* **1.** the process of rotting. **2.** something that is rotting or rotted. **3.** a disease of plants caused by any of various fungi or bacteria, characterized by breakdown of tissue. **4.** any of various parasitic diseases of animals, characterized by tissue loss. **5.** *Informal.* nonsense; rubbish; trash. —*interj.* used to express disgust, disdain, or impatience. [Old English *rotian* to decay, putrefy.]

ro·ta·ry (rō′tə rē) *adj.* **1.** turning or designed to turn around an axis; rotating. **2.** characterized by or occurring with a rotating movement. **3.** having a part or parts that rotate: *a rotary plow.* —*n., pl.* **-ries. 1.** traffic circle. **2.** a rotary machine, device, or part. [Latin *rota* wheel + -ARY[1].]

Rotary Club, a local club belonging to **Rotary International,** an international organization of business and professional people dedicated to serving the community, founded in Chicago in 1905. —**Ro·tar·i·an** (rō târ′ē ən), *n.*

rotary engine 1. an internal-combustion engine in which circularly arranged cylinders revolve about a fixed crankshaft, used esp. in airplanes. **2.** any engine, as a turbine or Wankel engine, that produces rotation or torque directly rather than by back-and-forth movement.

rotary press, a high-speed printing press with a cylinder to which curved printing plates are attached, so that when revolving they will print on a continuous sheet of paper fed from a roll.

ro·tate (rō′tāt) *v.t., v.i.,* **-tat·ed, -tat·ing. 1.** to turn or cause to turn around on or as on an axis. **2.** to change or cause to change in sequence; alternate regularly: *The farmer rotates crops yearly. The guards rotate every four hours.* [Latin *rotātus,* past participle of *rotāre* to turn around, revolve.] —**ro′tat·a·ble,** *adj.*

ro·ta·tion (rō tā′shən) *n.* **1.** the act or process of turning on or as on an axis. **2.** one complete turn of such a movement: *The rotation of the earth takes twenty-four hours.* **3.** a change or alternation in sequence: *the rotation of assignments among the reporters on a newspaper.* —**ro·ta′tion·al,** *adj.*

rotation of crops, a systematic alternation of the crops grown in a given field from one year to the next, esp. to prevent the loss of soil fertility or to control plant disease.

ro·ta·tor (rō′tā tər) *n.* a person or thing that rotates, as a muscle that serves to rotate a part of the body. [Latin *rotātor.*]

ro·ta·to·ry (rō′tə tôr′ē) *adj.* **1.** of, relating to, or characterized by rotation. **2.** causing rotation.

ROTC, Reserve Officers' Training Corps, a U.S. military corps in which college and high school students are trained to become officers in the armed services.

rote (rōt) *n.* mechanical routine. —*adj.* characterized by mechanical routine: *rote learning.* [Of uncertain origin.]
  • **by rote,** in a mechanical way, without attention to meaning or thought: *to learn by rote, to recite by rote.*

ro·te·none (rō′tə nōn′) *n.* a poisonous, white compound obtained from the roots of several plants, widely used as an insecticide. Formula: $C_{23}H_{22}O_6$

ro·ti·fer (rō′tə fər) *n.* any of a group of multicellular, microscopic aquatic animals, phylum Rotifera, common in ponds and puddles, having a crown of cilia that is used for locomotion and feeding and which resembles a rotating wheel when in motion. [Modern Latin *Rotifera,* from Latin *rota* wheel + *ferre* to carry.] —**ro·tif·er·al** (rō tif′ər əl), *adj.*

ro·tis·se·rie (rō tis′ə rē) *n.* **1.** a cooking device or appliance having a rotating spit on which food is roasted. **2.** a restaurant or shop selling food thus produced.

ro·to·gra·vure (rō′tə grə vyur′, -grāv′yər) *n.* **1.** a printing process in which the image to be printed is reproduced on a copper surface in a pattern of depressions. These depressions are then filled with ink, and the pattern is transferred under pressure to the surface to be printed. **2.** a picture or print made by this process. **3.** a pictorial section of a newspaper, esp. one containing pictures printed by this process. [Latin *rota* wheel + GRAVURE.]

ro·tor (rō′tər) *n.* **1.** a rotating part of a motor or other machine. **2.** a set of large, revolving blades that lifts and moves an aircraft, as a helicopter. [Short for ROTATOR.]

ro·to·till (rō′tə til′) *v.t.* to dig up and cultivate with a rototiller. [From ROTOTILLER.]

ro·to·till·er (rō′tə til′ər) *n.* a motorized plow with rotating spokelike blades that dig up and cultivate the ground. [ROT(ARY) + TILLER[2].]

rot·ten (rot′ən) *adj.* **1.** damaged or ruined by having undergone a breakdown in composition; putrid: *a rotten apple, meat that smells as though it may be rotten.* **2.** unsound, as if from rotting; not safe; weak: *rotten timbers.* **3.** very bad; disagreeable: *a rotten cold, rotten weather.* **4.** worthy of contempt: *a rotten thing to say.* **5.** corrupt, dishonest, or depraved: *rotten politics.* [Old Norse *rotinn* putrid.] —**rot′ten·ly,** *adv.* —**rot′ten·ness,** *n.*

rotten borough 1. a borough in England having only a few voters, but still entitled to representation in Parliament, abolished by reform legislation in 1832. **2.** any election district having greater representation than is warranted by its population.

rot·ten·stone (rot′ən stōn′) *n.* a crumbly, siliceous limestone, used for polishing metal. [Because it is so decomposed that it is easily broken up.]

rott·weil·er (rot′wī′lər) *also,* **Rott·weil·er.** *n.* any of a German breed of large, muscular, short-haired, black dogs with tan markings, a short tail, and small drooping ears, originally used for herding cattle. [German *Rottweiler* literally, native or resident of Rottweil, a town in southern Germany where this breed was originally used for herding cattle.]

ro·tund (rō tund′) *adj.* **1.** rounded or plump: *A rotund little clown waddled into the ring.* **2.** suggesting roundness or fullness in sound; full-toned; sonorous: *a rotund delivery of a speech.* [Latin *rotundus* circular. Doublet of ROUND.] —**ro·tund′ly,** *adv.* —**ro·tund′ness,** *n.*

ro·tun·da (rō tun′də) *n.* **1.** a circular building or section of a building, esp. one having a dome. **2.** a large, circular, high-ceilinged room or hall, as a main room of a public building. [Latin *rotunda,* feminine of *rotundus* circular.]

ro·tun·di·ty (rō tun′di tē) *n., pl.* **-ties. 1.** the state or condition of being rotund; roundness; fullness. **2.** something that is round, as a part or protuberance.

rou·ble (rü′bəl) ruble.

rou·é (rü ā′, rü′ā) *n.* a dissipated, lecherous man; rake; profligate. [French *roué,* from *rouer* to break on the wheel, from *roue* wheel, from Latin *rota;* originally applied to a group of eighteenth-century French profligates, who it was felt deserved to be punished in this way.]

a	at	e	end	o	hot	u	up	hw	white		about
ā	ape	ē	me	ō	old	ū	use	ng	song		taken
ä	far	î	it	ô	fork	ū	rule	th	thin	ə	pencil
âr	care	ī	ice	oi	oil	u̇	pull	th	this		lemon
		îr	pierce	ou	out	ûr	turn	zh	measure		circus

R

rouge (rüzh) *n.* **1.** any of various red or pink cosmetics used to color the cheeks. **2.** a red, powdery pigment, composed chiefly of ferric oxide, used as an abrasive and polishing agent for metal, gems, and other materials. —*v.*, **rouged, roug·ing.** —*v.t.* to color with rouge. —*v.i.* to use cosmetic rouge. [French *rouge* red, from Latin *rubeus*.]

rough (ruf) *adj.* **1.** having an uneven surface; not smooth or level: *a rough road, rough stucco walls.* **2.** characterized by or showing force, violence, or boisterousness: *Ice hockey is a rough game. A rough bunch of rowdies interrupted the speech.* **3.** having or showing harshness of temperament; brutal: *a rough way of dealing with people.* **4.** not calm; stormy; tempestuous; turbulent: *rough weather, rough seas.* **5.** partially, inexactly, or hastily done: *a rough estimate, a rough sketch.* **6.** in a natural or crude state: *rough, unpolished gems.* **7.** lacking grace, culture, or refinement; uncouth: *a rough manner of talking, rough table manners.* **8.** characterized by strain or hardship; difficult: *a rough day on the job, a rough life.* **9.** having a shaggy or uneven texture; coarse: *rough wool.* **10.** (of sound) lacking harmony or beauty; harsh; discordant: *the rough squeal of a car's brakes.* **11.** *Phonetics.* pronounced with the sound of *h*, as in *heaven.* —*v.t.* **1.a.** to deal with or treat violently (with *up*): *The gang roughed up two passersby.* **b.** in football and certain other sports, to treat (an opponent) with unnecessary violence. **2.** to plan, shape, or sketch in an incomplete form (usually with *in* or *out*): *to rough out the layout of a house.* **3.** to make rough; roughen. —*adv.* in a rough manner; roughly. —*n.* **1.** any rough, uneven, or difficult object, state, or condition: *to take the rough along with the smooth in life.* **2.** the unmowed part of a golf course surrounding the fairways and greens. **3.** a crude, rough person; ruffian; rowdy. [Old English *rūh* not smooth, shaggy.] —**rough′ly,** *adv.* —**rough′ness,** *n.* —For Synonyms *(adj.),* see **uncouth.**

· **in the rough.** in a crude or unfinished condition.

· **to rough it.** to live without the usual comforts or conveniences: *to rough it on a canoe trip.*

rough·age (ruf′ij) *n.* **1.** coarse food material, as bran or lettuce, that has a relatively high percentage of fiber and serves to stimulate peristalsis in the digestive tract. **2.** any rough or coarse material.

rough-and-read·y (ruf′ən red′ē) *adj.* **1.** rough and crude, but effective in use or action: *a rough-and-ready approach to a problem.* **2.** having or showing rough vigor rather than subtlety or politeness: *rough-and-ready manners.*

rough-and-tum·ble (ruf′ən tum′bəl) *adj.* characterized by roughness, violence, and disregard for rules: *a rough-and-tumble fight.* —*n.* a rough fight or struggle.

rough·cast (ruf′kast′) *n.* **1.** a coarse plaster for covering an outside surface, as a wall. **2.** a rough or preliminary model or form. —*v.t.*, **-cast, -cast·ing. 1.** to cover with roughcast. **2.** to make or shape in a rough or preliminary form.

rough-dry (ruf′drī′) *also,* **rough-dry.** *v.t.*, **-dried, -dry·ing.** to dry (laundry) without smoothing or ironing. —*adj.* dried without smoothing or ironing.

rough·en (ruf′ən) *v.t.*, *v.i.* to make or become rough.

rough·hew (ruf′hū′) *v.t.*, **-hewed, -hewed** or **-hewn, -hew·ing. 1.** to hew (something, as timber or stone) without smoothing or finishing. **2.** to make or shape in rough or preliminary form; roughcast: *to roughhew the story for a play.* —**rough′hewn′;** *also,* **rough′-hewn′,** *adj.*

rough·house (*n.,* ruf′hous′; *v.,* ruf′hous′, -houz′) *n., pl.* **-hous·es** (-hou′siz, -hou′ziz). rough, boisterous play or conduct. —*v.*, **-housed** (-houst′, -houzd′), **-hous·ing** (-hou′sing, -hou′zing). —*v.i.* to behave or play in a rough, boisterous way. —*v.t.* to handle or treat in a rough, unrestrained manner, esp. in fun.

rough·neck (ruf′nek′) *n. Informal.* **1.** a rough, belligerent person; rowdy. **2.** a member of a crew on an oil-drilling rig.

rough·rid·er (ruf′rī′dər) *n.* **1.** a person who breaks in or rides wild, untrained horses. **2. Roughrider.** a member of a cavalry regiment recruited by Theodore Roosevelt and others to fight in the Spanish-American War. Also *(def. 2),* **Rough Rider.**

rough·shod (ruf′shod′) *adj.* having horseshoes with calks or other projections to prevent slipping.

· **to ride roughshod over.** to treat roughly and with arrogance; be inconsiderate of.

rou·lade (rü läd′) *n.* **1.** a musical embellishment consisting of a rapid succession of notes sung to one syllable. **2.** a thin slice of meat rolled around a filling and cooked. [French *roulade,* from *rouler* to roll, revolve, from Old French *rouler.* See ROLL.]

rou·lette (rü let′) *n.* **1.** a gambling game in which the players bet on which compartment of a wheel a ball will come to rest in after the wheel has been spun. **2.** a small wheel with a raised pattern used to make repeating marks or holes when rolled over a surface. —*v.t.*, **-let·ted, -let·ting.** to mark or perforate with a roulette. [French *roulette* gambling game, small wheel, going back to *roue* wheel, from Latin *rota.*]

Rou·ma·ni·an (rü mā′nē ən, -mān′yən) Romanian.

round (round) *adj.* **1.** shaped like a sphere or part of a sphere; spherical, as a globe or ball. **2.** shaped like a circle or part of a circle; circular, as a tire: *a round tablecloth.* **3.** having circular cross sections; cylindrical: *a round tower.* **4.** having a curved surface; not angular or flat: *round shoulders.* **5.** not lacking any of its elements; complete; entire: *a round dozen.* **6.** liberal, as in amount or volume; ample; large: *a round sum of money.* **7.** expressed in round numbers. **8.** involving or done with a circular motion: *a round dance.* **9.** quick and vigorous; brisk: *The horses proceeded at a good, round pace.* **10.** full and mellow; sonorous: *The tuba had a rich, round tone.* **11.a.** candid; outspoken; blunt: *round criticism.* **b.** without hesitation or qualification: *a round assertion.* **12.** *Phonetics.* pronounced with the lips assuming a nearly oval shape: *a round vowel.* —*n.* **1.** something round in shape; that which is spherical, circular, or cylindrical. **2. rounds.** a fixed or customary course, action, or duty: *a sentry's rounds, a doctor's rounds.* **3.** a complete movement in or as in a circle or around a fixed point; revolution: *the rounds of planets about the sun.* **4.** a recurring or successive series, as of actions or events: *a round of speaking engagements, a round of parties, the round of the seasons.* **5.** a single outburst, as of applause or cheering. **6.a.** any of various periods or sections into which certain sports and games are divided: *a boxing match of ten rounds.* **b.** *Golf.* a complete match or section of a tournament, usually consisting of eighteen holes. **7.** *Music.* a short song in which each section is the same length as, and can be harmonized with, any other section. It is sung by three or more voices, each voice beginning in turn at equal intervals. "Row, Row, Row Your Boat" is a round. **8.a.** a single discharge of a firearm. **b.** the ammunition for a single shot. **9.** one service of an alcoholic drink to each of the members of a group. **10.** a cut of beef just above the hind shank, between the leg and the rump. **11. round dance. 12.a.** a round rung of a ladder. **b.** a round crosspiece between the legs of a chair. **13.** the whole extent of something; range: *within the round of medical knowledge.* —*v.t.* **1.** to make round in shape: *The sculptor rounded the clay into a sphere.* **2.** to pass or travel to the other side of; go around: *to round a corner, to round the tip of a peninsula.* **3.** to make complete; finish or perfect (usually with *out* or *off*): *The violinist rounded out the concert with an encore.* **4.** to express as a round number (usually with *off*): *Round off 1,457 to the nearest hundred.* **5.** *Phonetics.* to pronounce with the lips nearly oval. —*v.i.* **1.** to become round in shape. **2.** to turn or spin around. **3.** to become complete, full, or finished (usually with *into* or *out*): *The row of lilacs rounded out nicely.* **4.** to take a circular or curved course. —*adv.* **1.** around: *The top went round and round.* **2.** through a recurring or complete period of time; from beginning to end: *We now live in Florida the whole year round.* —*prep.* **1.** around: *The crowd gathered round the speaker.* **2.** all during; throughout: *round the year.* [Old French *roont* circular, from Latin *rotundus.* Doublet of ROTUND.] —**round′ness,** *n.*

· **in the round. a.** performed on or having a central stage surrounded by seats. **b.** in full sculptured form, standing free from any background.

· **to go (or make) the rounds.** to be passed continually from one person or place to another; be in circulation.

· **to round up.** to gather or drive together; assemble: *to round up cattle, to round up all the children at a party.*

round·a·bout (*adj.,* round′ə bout′, round′ə bout′; *n.,* round′ə-bout′) *adj.* not direct or straightforward; circuitous; indirect: *a roundabout route, a roundabout way of saying something.* —*n.* **1.** formerly, a short, tight-fitting jacket for men or boys. **2.** *British.* **a.** merry-go-round. **b.** traffic circle.

round dance 1. any of several ballroom dances characterized by circular or revolving movements, as the waltz or the polka. **2.** a folk dance in which the dancers move in a circle.

roun·del (roun′dəl) *n.* **1.** a round form or figure, as a window or panel. **2.** rondeau. **3.** roundelay *(def. 2).* [Old French *roundel* form of lyric poetry.]

roun·de·lay (roun′də lā′) *n.* **1.** a song in which a section, phrase, or line, esp. the first verse, is continually repeated. **2.** a dance performed in a circle. [Old French *rondelet,* diminutive of *rondel* form of lyric poetry; confused with *lay⁴* song. See RONDEAU.]

round·er (roun′dər) *n.* **1.** a habitual drunkard, petty criminal, or dissolute drifter. **2. rounders.** an English game similar to

baseball. ➡ used as singular. **3.** a person or thing that rounds, esp. a tool for rounding the edges or surface of something.

Round·head (round′hed′) *n.* a member of the Puritan or Parliamentary party during the English Civil War from 1642 to 1652. [From the short-cropped hair of the members of this party, as distinguished from the long hair of their opponents, the Cavaliers.]

round·house (round′hous′) *n., pl.* **-hous·es** (-hou′ziz). **1.** a circular building with a turntable in the center, used for housing, repairing, and switching locomotives. **2.** a cabin on the rear part of the quarterdeck of a ship. **3.** a blow delivered with a wide swing of the arm. **4.** a pitch in baseball in which the ball makes a slow, wide curve.

round·ish (roun′dish) *adj.* somewhat round.

round·ly (round′le) *adv.* **1.** in a frank, straightforward manner; bluntly; candidly: *The next speaker denounced the proposal roundly.* **2.** fully; thoroughly: *to be beaten roundly.* **3.** in a round form.

round number, a number expressed to the nearest whole number or to a multiple of five or ten. The round number for 498 is 500, and the round number for 5⅞ is 6.

round robin 1. a tournament, as in tennis, in which each player or team plays every other player or team. **2.** a document, as a petition, circulated for signature or comment, esp. one in which the signatures are arranged in a circle so as to disguise the order of signing.

round-shoul·dered (round′shol′dərd) *adj.* having the shoulders bent forward so that the shoulders and upper back appear rounded.

round steak, a steak cut from a round of beef.

Round Table 1. in Arthurian legend, the table around which King Arthur and his knights sat. It was round to prevent quarrels about the order of seating. **2.** King Arthur and his knights collectively. **3. round table. a.** a group of persons gathered for a conference or discussion. **b.** such a conference or discussion. —**round′-ta′ble,** *adj.*

round-the-clock (round′thə klok′) *adj., adv.* around-the-clock.

round trip, a trip to a place and back to the starting point. —**round′-trip′,** *adj.*

round·up (round′up′) *n.* **1.** an act or instance of bringing scattered cattle together, as for counting, branding, or selling. **2.** the people and horses engaged in this. **3.** any gathering together, as of people, objects, or data: *a news roundup, a roundup of criminal suspects.*

round·worm (round′wûrm′) *n.* any nematode worm, esp. a species, *Ascaris lumbricoides,* that lives as a parasite in the intestines of humans and other animals.

rouse (rouz) *v.,* **roused, rous·ing.** —*v.t.* **1.** to cause to awaken from sleep, unconsciousness, or a similar resting condition: *Singing birds roused us at daybreak.* **2.** to stir up, as to action or strong emotion; excite: *The tirade roused the crowd to a frenzy.* —*v.i.* **1.** to awaken from sleep, unconsciousness, or a similar resting condition. **2.** to become active or excited. [Of uncertain origin.] —**rous′er,** *n.*

rous·ing (rou′zing) *adj.* **1.** able to inspire enthusiasm or excitement; stirring: *a rousing pep talk.* **2.** brisk; active; lively: *The store did a rousing business during the sale.* **3.** *Informal.* extraordinary; astonishing: *The conference was a rousing success.* —**rous′ing·ly,** *adv.*

roust·a·bout (roust′tə bout′) *n.* **1.** an unskilled, often transient laborer, esp. one who works on a ranch or at an oil-drilling site. **2.** a laborer on a dock or ship. **3.** a laborer at a circus who sets up and dismantles the tents. [Dialectal *roust* to rout out (possibly modification of ROUSE) + ABOUT.]

rout[1] (rout) *n.* **1.** an overwhelming defeat. **2.** a disorderly flight or retreat after a defeat. **3.** a disorderly crowd; rabble. —*v.t.* **1.** to defeat overwhelmingly: *to rout a team in football.* **2.** to put to disorderly flight. [Old French *route* defeat, going back to Latin *rupta,* feminine past participle of *rumpere* to break; because a defeat implies the breaking up of an army.]

rout[2] (rout) *v.t.* **1.** to uncover by searching; bring to view; discover (with *out*): *to rout out the traitors in an organization.* **2.** to drive or force out; expel: *The storm routed us from our homes.* **3.** to dig up with the snout: *The pigs routed roots from the mud.* —*v.i.* **1.** to dig with the snout. **2.** to search; rummage: *I routed through the drawers looking for the keys.* [Form of ROOT[2].]

route (rüt, rout) *n.* **1.** a course, road, or way for travel: *a trade route, an overland route, the most direct route.* **2.a.** the territory covered by a person selling or delivering something: *a milk route, a newspaper route.* **b.** the job of servicing or the right to service such a territory. —*v.t.,* **rout·ed, rout·ing. 1.** to arrange the

route or itinerary for: *Our travel agent routed us through Europe. The new subway line was routed through the financial district.* **2.** to send by a certain route; dispatch. [Old French *route* way, path, going back to Latin *rupta,* feminine past participle of *rumpere* to break; because a route was originally a path broken through a forest.]

rou·tine (rü tēn′) *n.* **1.** a fixed method of doing something; regular procedure: *a person's daily routine, a family's bedtime routine.* **2.** a habitual repetition of actions or procedures: *We were bored with the routine of camp life.* **3.** a theatrical act or part of an act, as a funny story or a dance number. **4.** a segment of a computer program containing coded instructions for performing an individual task. —*adj.* **1.** in accordance with or following routine; regular; habitual: *routine chores, routine complaints.* **2.** not creative or original; commonplace: *a routine performance.* [French *routine* regular procedure, diminutive of *route* way, path. See ROUTE.] —**rou·tine′ly,** *adv.* —**rou·tine′ness,** *n.*

rove[1] (rōv) *v.,* **roved, rov·ing.** —*v.i.* to move aimlessly from place to place; wander about. —*v.t.* to wander over or through. [Probably of Scandinavian origin.] —For Synonyms *(v.i.),* see **roam.**

rove[2] (rōv) a past tense and a past participle of **reeve**[2].

rov·er[1] (rō′vər) *n.* a person who roves; wanderer. [ROVE[1] + -ER[1].]

rov·er[2] (rō′vər) *n. Archaic.* **1.** a pirate. **2.** a pirate ship. [Middle Dutch *rover* robber.]

row[1] (rō) *n.* **1.a.** a series of people or things arranged in a line; line: *a row of trees, children standing in rows.* **b.** a line in or along which something is done or exists: *the rows of a cornfield.* **2.** a line of seats, as in a theater or classroom: *We were seated in the last row.* **3.a.** a line of houses on a street. **b.** a street lined with buildings on both sides. [Old English *rāw, rǣw* line[1].] • **a hard** (or **long**) **row to hoe.** a tiresome, difficult task.

row[2] (rō) *v.i.* to use oars to propel a boat. —*v.t.* **1.** to propel, as a boat, by the use of oars. **2.** to transport in a boat by rowing: *to row a person to shore.* **3.** to engage in (a race or contest) by using oars. **4.** (of a boat) to have or be propelled by (a specified number of oars). **5.** to use (oars, rowers, or a certain stroke) in rowing a race. **6.** to row against in a race. —*n.* **1.** an act or instance of using oars. **2.** a trip or outing in a rowboat. [Old English *rōwan* to use oars to propel a boat.] —**row′er,** *n.*

row[3] (rou) *n.* **1.** a noisy quarrel or fight. **2.** a disturbance; commotion; clamor: *The citizens' group raised a row over a threat to the environment.* —*v.i.* to engage in a noisy quarrel or disturbance. [Of uncertain origin.]

row·an (rō′ən, rou′-) *n.* **1.** a Eurasian mountain ash, *Sorbus aucuparia,* belonging to the rose family, raised for its hard wood. **2.** either of two closely related American trees. **3.** the reddish, berrylike fruit of these trees. Also *(def. 3),* **row·an·ber·ry** (rō′ən ber′ē). [Of Scandinavian origin.]

row·boat (rō′bōt′) *n.* a small boat propelled by oars.

row·dy (rou′dē) *n., pl.* **-dies.** a rude, boisterous, disorderly person. —*adj.,* **-di·er, -di·est.** rude; boisterous; disorderly. [Probably from ROW[3].] —**row′di·ly,** *adv.* —**row′di·ness,** *n.* —**row′dy·ism,** *n.* —**row′dy·ish,** *adj.*

row·el (rou′əl) *n.* a wheel with sharp radiating points, as on the end of a rider's spur. —*v.t.,* **-eled, -el·ing;** *also, British,* **-elled, -el·ling.** to urge on (a horse) with a rowel; spur. [Old French

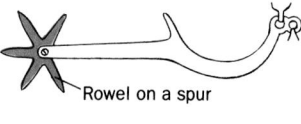

Rowel on a spur

rowel

roel(e) small wheel, diminutive of *roue* wheel, from Latin *rota.*]

row·en (rou′ən) *n.* a second crop or mowing of grass or hay in a season.

row house, a house attached to other similar houses in a row.

row·lock (rō′lok′) *n. British.* oarlock.

roy·al (roi′əl) *adj.* **1.** of, by, or relating to a king, queen, or other sovereign: *a royal command, royal blood, a royal palace.* **2.** belonging to or serving the government of a king, queen, or other sovereign: *the royal navy.* **3.** established or authorized by a king, queen, or other sovereign: *a royal society.* **4.** suitable for or

a	at	e	end	o	hot	u	up	hw	white		about
ā	ape	ē	me	ō	old	ū	use	ng	song		taken
ä	far	i	it	ô	fork	ü	rule	th	thin	ə	pencil
âr	care	ī	ice	oi	oil	u̇	pull	th	this		lemon
		îr	pierce	ou	out	ûr	turn	zh	measure		circus

R

characteristic of a king, queen, or other sovereign; magnificent; majestic; stately. **5.** first-rate; excellent: *We were in royal spirits.* —*n.* **1.** a small sail or mast above the topgallant. **2.** *Informal.* a member of the royalty. [Old French *roial* regal, kingly, from Latin *rēgālis,* from *rēx* king.] —**roy′al·ly,** *adv.*

Synonyms *adj.* **Royal, regal,** and **imperial** mean suitable for or characteristic of a queen, king, or other sovereign. **Royal** can be applied to aspects of sovereignty or to something befitting a sovereign: *Some members of Parliament criticized the large size of the royal budget. The astronauts were given a royal welcome.* **Regal** emphasizes the stateliness and dignity associated with a sovereign: *The coronation was an impressive display of regal splendor. The bride walked down the aisle with a regal bearing.* **Imperial** is used to describe an emperor or empress and implies exceptional grandeur. It also has the sense of dominant or overbearing: *the treasures of the imperial palace, an imperial manner that antagonized many people.*

royal blue, a vivid reddish or purplish blue color.
roy·al·ism (roi′ə liz′əm) *n.* adherence to a monarch or to the principles of a monarchy.
roy·al·ist (roi′ə list) *n.* **1.** a person who supports a monarch in power or wishes to restore or establish a royal government. **2. Royalist.** a supporter of King Charles I in his struggle with Parliament; Cavalier. **3. Royalist.** an American colonist who supported the British in the American Revolution; Tory.
royal jelly, a white, jellylike substance rich in proteins and vitamins, secreted by worker honeybees. It is fed to all young bee larvae for a few days after birth, and thereafter only to queen bee larvae.
royal palm, any of a group of tall ornamental palm trees, genus *Roystonea,* native to the Caribbean and northeastern South America, widely cultivated in tropical regions.
roy·al·ty (roi′əl tē) *n., pl.* **-ties. 1.** a royal person or royal persons collectively. **2.** the position or power of a king, queen, or other sovereign. **3.** royal quality or nature. **4.** a right or privilege enjoyed by or as by a person of royal blood. **5.a.** a share of the proceeds from the sale or performance of a work paid to the author, composer, or originator of the work, as by a publisher or producer. **b.** a payment made to the owner of a patent, property, or other right for the use of that right. [Old French *roialte* kingship, from *roial* regal, kingly. See ROYAL.]
rpm, revolutions per minute.
R.R. 1. *also,* **RR** Railroad. **2.** Right Reverend. **3.** *also,* **RR** rural route.
R.S.F.S.R., Russian Soviet Federated Socialist Republic.
R.S.V.P. *also,* **RSVP, r.s.v.p.** please reply. [Abbreviation of French *r(épondez) s(′il) v(ous) p(laît).*]
rt., right.
rte., route.
Rt. Hon., Right Honorable.
Ru, the symbol for ruthenium.
rub (rub) *v.,* **rubbed, rub·bing.** —*v.t.* **1.** to apply pressure in moving one's hand or hands over the surface of: *to rub one's leg to ease a cramp.* **2.** to apply or spread (something) with some degree of pressure: *to rub ointment on one's arm.* **3.** to move (an object or objects) with pressure against another or each other: *to rub two sticks together, to rub a cloth back and forth over a stain.* **4.** to subject (something) to pressure over its surface in order to clean, polish, or make smooth: *We rubbed the silverware until it gleamed.* **5.** to irritate or wear down by pressure and movement: *The elastic on this cuff is rubbing my wrist.* **6.** to remove or erase by pressure and movement (with *off* or *out*): *to rub off tarnish, to rub out ink stains.* —*v.i.* **1.** to exert pressure and move along a surface; press: *The cat rubbed gently against my leg.* **2.** to be able to be removed or erased by the application of pressure over its surface (with *out* or *off*): *This ink rubs out easily.* —*n.* **1.** an application of pressure over a surface; rubbing: *an alcohol rub.* **2.** an irritating or sarcastic remark. **3.** a difficulty; conflict; hindrance: *Aye, there's the rub* (Shakespeare, *Hamlet*). **4.** an uneven or rough spot caused by irritation or friction. [Of uncertain origin.]
  · **to rub down.** to massage: *to rub down an athlete after a game.*
  · **to rub it in.** *Informal.* to repeat or emphasize something unpleasant.
  · **to rub off on.** *Informal.* to be transmitted to by close or frequent contact or association: *Their love of camping rubbed off on their children.*
  · **to rub out.** *Slang.* to kill.
  · **to rub the wrong way.** to irritate; annoy; irk.
rub·ber¹ (rub′ər) *n.* **1.a.** a tough, elastic, waterproof substance obtained from the milky sap, or latex, of any of several tropical trees. **b.** any of various kinds of synthetic materials having the

same properties as this substance. **2.** an overshoe made of rubber. **3.** any of various other articles made of rubber, as a rubber band or a pencil eraser. **4.** the flat piece of rubber on which a baseball pitcher must place one foot while in the act of pitching. **5.** a person or thing that rubs. —*adj.* made of rubber. [RUB + -ER¹; because originally often used to rub out or erase pencil marks.]
rub·ber² (rub′ər) *n.* **1.** in bridge and other games and sports, a series of an odd number of games, usually three, in which the final winner is usually the side that takes the majority of games. **2.** the game that breaks a tie and determines the outcome of such a series. Also *(def. 2),* **rubber game.** [Of uncertain origin.]
rubber band, an elastic loop of rubber, used to hold things together.
rubber cement, an adhesive substance that hardens quickly when exposed to air, consisting of a solution of unvulcanized rubber in a chemical solvent.
rub·ber·ize (rub′ə rīz′) *v.t.,* **-ized, -iz·ing.** to coat or treat with rubber or a rubber preparation.
rub·ber·neck (rub′ər nek′) *Slang. n.* a person who gazes about with curiosity, in such a way as to strain the neck. Also, **rub′ber·neck′er.** —*v.i.* to gaze about with curiosity; gawk; stare: *Drivers rubbernecking at the accident caused traffic to slow down.*
rubber plant 1. a tropical evergreen plant, *Ficus elastica,* of the mulberry family, found growing wild as a tree in India and Malaya and widely raised as a houseplant, having a single woody stem and thick, leathery leaves. **2.** any of various plants yielding rubber.
rub·ber-stamp (rub′ər stamp′) *v.t.* **1.** to print or mark with a rubber stamp. **2.** *Informal.* to give approval or endorsement to as a matter of routine: *The executive committee merely rubber-stamps the owner's proposals.*
rubber stamp 1. a hand stamp with a raised message or design made of rubber, inked and used to mark articles. **2.** *Informal.* a person or group that gives approval or endorsement as a matter of routine.
rubber tree, any of several tropical trees yielding a latex used in making rubber, esp. *Hevea brasiliensis,* widely cultivated on plantations in Asia.
rub·ber·y (rub′ə rē) *adj.* resembling rubber, as in elasticity or appearance.
rubbing alcohol, denatured alcohol, used esp. for rubbing on the skin and as an antiseptic.
rub·bish (rub′ish) *n.* **1.** useless waste material; refuse; trash. **2.** worthless talk or thoughts; nonsense. [Of uncertain origin.] —**rub′bish·y,** *adj.*
rub·ble (rub′əl) *n.* **1.** rough fragments of solid material, such as stone or rock. **2.** this or similar material left after destruction of buildings by an earthquake, war, or the like. **3.** masonry made of rough, irregular stones. [Of uncertain origin.]
rub·down (rub′doun′) *n.* a massage, esp. a brief, brisk one after exercise.
rube (rüb) *n. Slang.* a naive, unsophisticated rural person; hick.
ru·bel·la (rü bel′ə) *n.* a contagious disease caused by a virus, usually producing a rose-colored rash and fever. Common in youth, it is esp. serious during pregnancy, when it may cause fetal birth defects. Also, **German measles.** [Modern Latin *rubella,* from Latin *rubellus* reddish, from *ruber* red.]
ru·be·o·la (rü bē′ə lə, rü′bē ō′-) *n.* measles *(def. 1).* [Modern Latin *rubeola,* from Latin *rubeus* red.]
Ru·bi·con (rü′bi kon′) *n.* **to cross the Rubicon.** to take an irrevocable step; make an unchangeable decision. [Referring to Julius Caesar's crossing of the *Rubicon,* a stream in Italy that formed part of the boundary between Gaul and the Roman Republic, which led to a civil war.]
ru·bi·cund (rü′bi kənd) *adj.* reddish; ruddy: *a rubicund complexion.* [Latin *rubicundus.*] —**ru′bi·cun′di·ty,** *n.*
ru·bid·i·um (rü bid′ē əm) *n.* a soft, light, silver-white metallic element with properties similar to potassium and sodium, used as a catalyst and in photoelectric cells and electron tubes. Symbol: **Rb** For tables, see **element.** [Modern Latin *rubidium,* from Latin *rubidus* reddish, red; from the red lines in its spectrum.]
ru·ble (rü′bəl) *also,* **rouble.** *n.* the monetary unit of the Soviet Union and of many of the countries that succeeded it. [Russian *rubl′.*]
ru·bric (rü′brik) *n.* **1.** a title, chapter heading, or other division in an early book or manuscript, printed in red or in a special color or design to distinguish it from the rest of the text. **2.** a direction or rule for the conduct of a religious ceremony, inserted in a prayer book, missal, or similar book. **3.** any established rule, guide, or custom. [Latin *rubrīca* red earth for coloring, title of law written in red, from *ruber* red.]
ru·bri·cal (rü′bri kəl) *adj.* of, relating to, or conducted according to religious rubrics.

ru·by (rü′bē) *n.* **1.** a highly prized gemstone, a transparent red variety of corundum, also used to make bearings for watches and scientific instruments. For illustration, see **semiprecious**. **2.** a deep red color. **3.** something made of or resembling a ruby. —*adj.* having the color ruby. [Old French *rubi(s)* the gem, going back to Latin *rubeus* red.]

ruck (ruk) *n.* the mass of ordinary undistinguished persons or things: *to rise above the ruck.* [Possibly of Scandinavian origin.]

ruck·sack (ruk′sak′, rùk′-) *n.* a kind of knapsack. [German *Rucksack* literally, back sack.]

ruck·us (ruk′əs) *n. Informal.* a loud commotion. [Possibly blend of RUCTION and RUMPUS.]

ruc·tion (ruk′shən) *n. Informal.* a noisy disturbance; uproar. [Possibly modification and shortening of INSURRECTION.]

rud·der (rud′ər) *n.* **1.** a broad, flat, movable attachment of wood, metal, or similar material, usually hinged to the stern of a boat or ship, used in steering. **2.** a similar structure at the tail of an aircraft, used to control the direction of flight to the left or right. [Old English *rōther* paddle.]

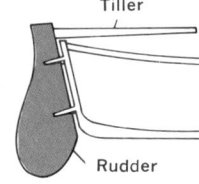
Tiller
Rudder
rudder

rud·dy (rud′ē) *adj.,* -di·er, -di·est. **1.** of or having a healthy redness: *a ruddy complexion.* **2.** tinged with red; reddish. [Old English *rudig* reddish.] —**rud′di·ness,** *n.*

rude (rüd) *adj.,* rud·er, rud·est. **1.** offensive in manner or actions; not polite or courteous; ill-mannered; uncivil: *a rude reply, a rude child.* **2.** roughly made or formed; showing a lack of skill or polish; crude: *the rude scrawls of a child just learning to write.* **3.** sudden and unpleasant; harsh: *a rude awakening.* **4.** in its early stages; primitive; undeveloped: *a rude culture, the rude outlines of a plan.* [Latin *rudis* rough, wild, unskilled.] —**rude′ly,** *adv.* —**rude′ness,** *n.*

ru·di·ment (rü′də mənt) *n.* **1.** a fact, rule, or element; first principle. ➡ usually used in the plural: *to learn the rudiments of chess.* **2.** the beginning or early stage of something. ➡ usually used in the plural: *the rudiments of civilization.* **3.** *Biology.* an organ or part that is not completely developed, esp. one that has no function in the adult individual, such as the appendix. [Latin *rudimentum.*]

ru·di·men·ta·ry (rü′də men′tə rē, -trē) *adj.* **1.** of or having the nature of a first principle; elementary: *rudimentary instruction.* **2.** in a beginning or early stage of development. **3.** *Biology.* incompletely or imperfectly developed: *A penguin has rudimentary wings.* Also, **ru′di·men′tal.** —**ru·di·men·ta·ri·ly** (rü′də men·ter′ə lē, -men′tər ə lē), *adv.*

rue[1] (rü) *v.t.,* rued, ru·ing. to feel sorrow or remorse for; regret: *to rue one's folly, to rue the day one left home.* —*n.* remorse or regret. [Old English *hrēowan* to cause regret or sorrow.]

rue[2] (rü) *n.* any of several aromatic Old World plants of the genus *Ruta,* of the same family as citrus trees, esp. the **common rue,** *R. graveolens,* an herb bearing dull yellow flowers once widely used in medicine. [Old French *rue,* from Latin *ruta,* from Greek *rhytē.*]

rue anemone, an American herb, *Anemonella thalictroides,* of the crowfoot family, having a slender stem and showy, white or pink flowers.

rue·ful (rü′fəl) *adj.* **1.** feeling, characterized by, expressing, or showing sorrow or regret: *a rueful mood, a rueful cry.* **2.** worthy of or causing sorrow or grief; pitiable: *a rueful situation.* —**rue′ful·ly,** *adv.* —**rue′ful·ness,** *n.*

ruff[1] (ruf) *n.* **1.** a collar of distinctively marked or projecting feathers or hairs along or around the neck of a bird or mammal. **2.** a stiff, circular frill, worn as a collar by men and women in the fifteenth, sixteenth, and seventeenth centuries. [Probably from RUFFLE[1].] —**ruffed,** *adj.*

ruff[2] (ruf) *v.t.* to trump (a card) in bridge and certain other card games. —*v.i.* to trump. —*n.* an act or instance of trumping. [Old French *roffle, ronfle* a card game, possibly modification of *triomphe* trump[1], card game, from Latin *triumphus* victory. See TRIUMPH.]

ruffed grouse, a North American game bird, *Bonasa umbellus,* having predominantly brownish plumage and a fan-shaped tail, the male of which has a tuft of black feathers on each side of the neck. Length: 16-19 inches (41-48 centimeters).

ruf·fi·an (ruf′ē ən, ruf′yən) *n.* a rough, brutal, or violent person. —*adj.* rough, brutal, and violent: *ruffian behavior.* [Middle French *rufien* pander, from Italian *ruffiano,* from *roffia* dirt, filth; of Germanic origin.] —**ruf′fi·an·ism,** *n.*

ruf·fle[1] (ruf′əl) *v.,* -fled, -fling. —*v.t.* **1.** to disturb the smoothness or order of: *The wind ruffled the water.* **2.** (of a bird) to stiffen (the feathers), as in anger or fright. **3.** to disturb or discompose; upset: *No emergency could ruffle the experienced pilot.* **4.** to gather together along one edge, forming a ruffle. —*v.i.* **1.** to lose composure or become upset. **2.** to become disordered or uneven. **3.** to rise or become stiff, as in anger or fright: *The bird's feathers ruffled at the sight of the cat.* —*n.* **1.** a strip of ribbon, lace, or other fabric gathered along one edge and used for trimming or as a border, as on garments or such items as curtains or bedspreads. **2.** something that disturbs or irritates. **3.** a disturbance of the evenness of a surface. [Of uncertain origin.]

ruf·fle[2] (ruf′əl) *n.* a steady drumbeat, not as loud as a roll. —*v.i., v.t.,* -fled, -fling. to make such a sound on (a drum). [From earlier *ruff* drumbeat; imitative.]

ru·fous (rü′fəs) *adj.* brownish red. [Latin *rufus* reddish.]

rug (rug) *n.* **1.** a piece of heavy, often woven fabric, used to cover part of a floor. **2.** an animal hide used as a floor covering: *a bearskin rug.* **3.** lap robe. [Of Scandinavian origin.]

Rug·by (rug′bē) *also,* **rug·by.** *n.* a form of football played with an oval ball by two teams of fifteen players each, in which the ball may be passed laterally or backward, carried, or kicked. The American form of football developed from this game. Also, **Rugby football.** [Short for earlier *Rugby football* and *Rugby's game;* referring to Rugby School (in Rugby, England), where the game was first played.]

rug·ged (rug′id) *adj.* **1.** having a sharply irregular outline or surface; rough and uneven: *rugged mountain peaks, a rugged coastline.* **2.** capable of enduring physical hardship; sturdy; robust: *a rugged miner.* **3.** (of the face or its features) strong, lined, and uneven in surface. **4.** difficult to do or endure; harsh; hard: *the rugged life of a sailor, a rugged test.* **5.** stormy; tempestuous: *The ship's passengers had a rugged crossing over the Atlantic.* [Of Scandinavian origin.] —**rug′ged·ly,** *adv.* —**rug′ged·ness,** *n.*

ru·in (rü′in) *n.* **1.** total destruction or decay; complete collapse: *the ruin of an empire.* **2.** *also,* **ruins.** a condition of destruction or decay: *The boat had gone to ruin through years of neglect. The former monastery is now in ruins.* **3.** **ruins.** the remains of something destroyed or decayed: *to visit the ruins of the Aztecs, to stand among the ruins of a bombed building.* **4.** a destroyed or decayed building or structure. **5.** a loss of position, power, honor, means, or health: *financial ruin.* **6.** something that causes destruction, decay, or collapse: *Fame is the ruin of some artists.* —*v.t.* **1.** to bring to ruin; devastate. **2.** to spoil or harm irrevocably: *My sprained ankle ruined my chances of winning the tournament.* **3.** to bring to moral or financial ruin. [Old French *ruine* downfall, remains of a building that has fallen down, from Latin *ruina.*] —For Synonyms *(n.),* see **destruction**.

Greek **ruins** at Delphi (370? B.C.)

ru·in·a·tion (rü′i nā′shən) *n.* **1.** the act of ruining or the state of being ruined. **2.** something that causes ruin: *Greed was the politician's ruination.*

ru·in·ous (rü′i nəs) *adj.* **1.** bringing or tending to bring ruin;

a	at	e	end	o	hot	u	up	hw	white		about
ā	ape	ē	me	ō	old	ū	use	ng	song		taken
ä	far	i	it	ô	fork	ü	rule	th	thin	ə	pencil
âr	care	ī	ice	oi	oil	ù	pull	th	this		lemon
		îr	pierce	ou	out	ûr	turn	zh	measure		circus

R

disastrous; destructive: *a ruinous war.* **2.** fallen to ruin; decayed; destroyed: *a building in a ruinous condition.* —**ru′in·ous·ly,** *adv.* —**ru′in·ous·ness,** *n.*

rule (rül) *n.* **1.** a fixed principle or direction regulating behavior, procedure, or action: *the rules of baseball, the rules of etiquette, the rules of logic.* **2.a.** controlling power or authority; government: *The rule of the many is better than the rule of the few.* **b.** a period of having control; reign: *The tyrant's rule lasted twenty years.* **3.** a code or body of regulations, esp. that observed by a religious order. **4.** *Law.* **a.** a regulation regarding the procedures of a court of law. **b.** an order made by a court of law with specific rather than general application. **5.** ruler *(def. 2).* **6.** *Printing.* **a.** a thin strip of metal, as brass or steel, that is used to print a line or lines. **b.** a line produced with such a device. **7.** something that usually or normally occurs or is done; that which is often the case: *Heavy rains are the rule on the island in August.* —*v.,* **ruled, rul·ing.** —*v.t.* **1.** to exercise authority over; govern; control: *to rule a country.* **2.** to have influence over; guide: *Fear ruled their actions.* **3.** to declare or determine with authority: *to rule someone out of order, to rule a law unconstitutional.* **4.** to keep in check; restrain: *to rule one's temper.* **5.** to mark with lines, esp. by using a ruler: *The student ruled the test paper carefully.* **6.** to form or mark (a line or lines) with or as with a ruler: *I ruled boxes on the page for a graph.* —*v.i.* **1.** to have authority or power; govern: *to rule with justice and mercy.* **2.** to make an authoritative decision or determination: *The club ruled against accepting new members.* **3.** to be current or prevalent. [Old French *riule* regulation, ruler, order, precept, from Latin *regula* bar, model. Doublet of RAIL[1].] —**rul′a·ble,** *adj.*

•**as a rule.** generally; usually.

•**to rule out.** to decide to reject or exclude.

Synonyms *v.i.* **Rule, govern,** and **reign** mean to exercise authority over a nation or other political unit. **Rule** implies an arbitrary power gained through means other than election: *The dictator ruled with an iron hand, allowing no opposition.* **Govern** suggests a system of control and guidance for the good of those governed: *The president governs with the help of the legislative and judicial branches.* **Reign** can mean to exercise supreme power as a sovereign, but also to hold the office of a sovereign with little power to govern: *Queen Elizabeth I reigned with autocratic power. Today in Britain, Parliament makes the laws, and the monarchs reign rather than rule.*

rule of thumb **1.** a general principle or guide that is widely useful although it is not derived scientifically. **2.** a rough measurement or procedure.

rul·er (rü′lər) *n.* **1.** a person who rules or governs. **2.** a straight-edged strip of wood, metal, or other material marked off into measuring units, used for drawing straight lines or measuring. Also *(def. 2),* **rule.**

rul·ing (rü′ling) *n.* **1.** an authoritative decision, as of a judge or regulatory commission. **2.** ruled lines, as on paper. —*adj.* **1.** having authority; governing: *the ruling political party.* **2.** having influence as if by authority; predominating; prevalent: *the ruling opinion in the community.*

rum[1] (rum) *n.* **1.** an alcoholic liquor distilled from fermented derivatives of sugarcane, such as juice, syrup, or molasses, or a combination of these derivatives. **2.** *also,* **Rum.** alcoholic liquor generally: *Rum caused their ruin.* [Short for earlier *rumbullion;* of uncertain origin.]

rum[2] (rum) *adj.* *British. Informal.* **1.** odd; queer: *a rum fellow.* **2.** posing danger or difficulty: *We have a rum bit of work ahead of us.* [Earlier *rome* good, possibly from Romany *rom* man, Gypsy; of Sanskrit origin.]

Ru·ma·ni·an (rü mā′nē ən, -mān′yən) Romanian.

rum·ba (rum′bə, rüm′-) *also,* **rhumba.** *n.* **1.** a Cuban dance of African origin. **2.** a modern ballroom adaptation of this dance. **3.** the music for this dance. —*v.i.* to dance the rumba. [Spanish *rumba* the dance, the music for this dance; of uncertain origin.]

rum·ble (rum′bəl) *v.,* **-bled, -bling.** —*v.i.* **1.** to make a heavy, deep, rolling sound, as thunder. **2.** to move or proceed with such a sound: *The tank rumbled along the road.* —*v.t.* to utter with a heavy, deep, rolling sound. —*n.* **1.** a heavy, deep, rolling sound. **2.** an indication or expression of discontent or uneasiness: *A rumble went through the crowd at the mention of the dictator's name.* **3.** *Slang.* a fight between gangs of youths. **4.** an area in the back of a carriage used for seating or as a luggage compartment. [Possibly of Low German origin.] —**rum′bler,** *n.* —**rum′bling·ly,** *adv.*

rumble seat, an open, folding seat in the back of an early automobile, as in a coupe or roadster.

ru·men (rü′mən) *n., pl.* **-mi·na** (-mə nə). **1.** the first stomach of

a ruminant, or cud-chewing animal. **2.** the cud of a ruminant. [Latin *rūmen* gullet.]

ru·mi·nant (rü′mə nənt) *n.* any of numerous cud-chewing, even-toed, hoofed mammals, constituting the suborder Ruminantia, that have a stomach consisting of four chambers. Cows, sheep, deer, antelope, giraffes, and camels are ruminants. —*adj.* **1.** of, relating to, or designating a ruminant. **2.** meditative; contemplative. [Latin *rūmināns,* present participle of *rūminārī* to chew the cud, from *rūmen* gullet.]

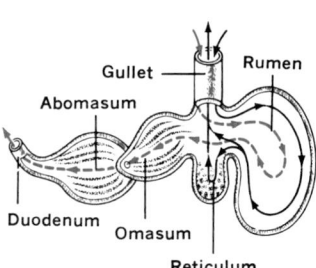

stomach of a **ruminant**

ru·mi·nate (rü′mə nāt′) *v.,* **-nat·ed, -nat·ing.** —*v.i.* **1.** to meditate or muse; ponder: *to ruminate on misfortunes.* **2.** to chew the cud. —*v.t.* **1.** to chew (food) again. **2.** to meditate upon; muse about. [Latin *rūminātus,* past participle of *rūminārī* to chew the cud. See RUMINANT.]

ru·mi·na·tion (rü′mə nā′shən) *n.* **1.a.** an act or instance of meditation; contemplation. **b.** a statement of such a meditation: *We read the author's ruminations on childhood.* **2.** the act or process of chewing the cud. —**ru′mi·na′tive,** *adj.*

rum·mage (rum′ij) *v.,* **-maged, -mag·ing.** —*v.t.* **1.** to search through (something) thoroughly, esp. by handling, moving about, and disarranging its contents: *I rummaged the entire attic for my old scrapbook.* **2.** to find or bring forth by searching (with *out, up,* or *from*): *to rummage an old suit out of a trunk.* —*v.i.* to search thoroughly and, usually, haphazardly: *The child rummaged in the toy box.* —*n.* **1.** a thorough search made by handling, and usually disarranging, things. **2.** miscellaneous items, esp. those on sale at a rummage sale. [Short for Middle French *arrumage* stowing cargo in a ship's hold, going back to Old French *a* to (from Latin *ad*) + *run* ship's hold (of Germanic origin); with reference to the disorder connected with disposing of a ship's cargo.] —**rum′mag·er,** *n.*

rummage sale **1.** a sale of miscellaneous donated items, as furniture or old clothing, usually held to raise money for some charitable purpose. **2.** a sale of merchandise for clearance, or of unclaimed items, as at a warehouse or dock.

rum·my[1] (rum′ē) *n.* a card game in which the players try to lay down all the cards in their hands by melding them in sets of three or four cards of the same rank, or in sets of three or more cards of the same suit in sequence. [Of uncertain origin.]

rum·my[2] (rum′ē) *n.* *Slang.* a drunkard. [RUM[1] + -Y[1].]

ru·mor (rü′mər) *n.* **1.** a report or statement circulating as truth without any evidence to support it; unverified story: *The stories you heard are mere rumors.* **2.** general talk; hearsay: *Rumor has it that the star will leave the play next week.* —*v.t.* to circulate or tell by rumor. [Old French *rumor* noise, quarrel, from Latin *rūmor* noise, report.]

ru·mor·mon·ger (rü′mər mung′gər, -mong′-) *n.* a person who spreads rumors, esp. with the knowledge that they are untrue.

rump (rump) *n.* **1.** that part of an animal's body where the trunk and hind legs are joined. **2.** a cut of beef from this part. **3.** the buttocks. **4.** the last, least important, or inferior part; remnant. **5.** a legislative body having, through expulsion or resignation, only a small part of its former membership and therefore regarded as unrepresentative and lacking authority. —*adj.* of or relating to an incomplete legislative body or committee: *a rump session.* [Probably of Scandinavian origin.]

rum·ple (rum′pəl) *v.t., v.i.,* **-pled, -pling.** to disarrange or become disarranged by wrinkling or creasing. —*n.* an irregular crease; wrinkle. [Middle Dutch *rompelen* to wrinkle.]

rum·pus (rum′pəs) *n.* *Informal.* a noisy disturbance; uproar. [Of uncertain origin.]

rumpus room, a room for play and informal parties.

rum·run·ner (rum′run′ər) *n.* a person or ship engaged in smuggling alcoholic liquor.

run (run) *v.,* **ran, run, run·ning.** —*v.i.* **1.** to move quickly by alternately bringing the legs off the ground so that both legs are in the air for an instant during each step; proceed at a pace faster than walking: *I had to run to catch the bus.* **2.** to go rapidly; rush; hasten: *We'll have to run to finish this job by five o'clock.* **3.** to leave or retreat rapidly; flee: *The dog broke loose and ran.* **4.** to make a short or quick trip: *to run to the store for a loaf of bread.*

5. to go or travel regularly; ply: *Is there a boat that runs between those ports?* **6.** to move about freely; go without restraint: *We always let our dog run in the yard.* **7.** to move, pass, or slide easily: *The wheelbarrow can run down this slope.* **8.** to pass or move quickly or lightly: *A wind ran through the tall grass. The days ran by.* **9.** to participate in a race: *Seven horses ran in the derby.* **10.** to compete for election: *to run for mayor.* **11.** to finish (in a specified position or condition) in a race, contest, or election: *Our candidate ran second.* **12.** to extend in space; lie in a certain direction: *The road runs due north. The street runs through the town.* **13.** (of plants) to grow over the ground or other surface (in a specified direction or area); creep; climb: *The ivy runs up the wall.* **14.** to be in operation; work; function: *The clock runs on batteries. The mills run night and day.* **15.** to be in effect; extend in time; last: *Our sale will run for one week.* **16.** to become or continue, as in a certain course or direction: *Feelings ran high against the newcomers.* **17.** to be or become current; circulate among the public: *An epidemic ran through the city. Gossip was running rampant.* **18.** to pass or get (into a specified state or condition): *to run into trouble.* **19.** to be, occur, or range in a specified character, size, quality, or price: *These shirts run small. Prices are running high.* **20.** to occur to the mind repeatedly: *The melody ran through my head.* **21.** to be persistent or common; recur: *A strange sense of humor runs in their family.* **22.** to tend or incline: *This designer's tastes run to the ornate.* **23.** to move in a stream; flow: *The water stopped running through the pipes.* **24.** to spread or mingle, esp. when exposed to water: *The colors in the fabric ran after the first washing.* **25.** to be wet with a flow: *The lost child's cheeks ran with tears.* **26.** to discharge serum, mucus, or pus: *The sore on my leg ran for three days.* **27.** to become liquid and flow. **28.** to have the stitches break at some point and unravel, esp. along the length of a line of stitches: *My stockings ran.* **29.** to be expressed (in a certain form or arrangement): *The refrain runs like this.* **30.** (of fish) to migrate, as upstream or from the sea toward the shore, for spawning, esp. in a school: *The salmon are running.* **31.** to be performed, published, or appear continually: *The musical ran for a year on Broadway. The advertisement ran for five days.* **32.** *Law.* **a.** to have legal validity or force, as in a certain area or for a specified period of time: *This contract runs for two years from today.* **b.** to accompany, go along with, or be attached to: *Water rights to use of the lake run with the lease.* **33.** to drive or be driven: *The driver ran off the road. The ship ran onto the rocks.* **34.** to continue to accrue or remain unpaid, as a debt. —*v.t.* **1.a.** to go along by running, as a path or route: *to run the length of the yard.* **b.** to cover (a distance) by running: *to run a mile.* **2.** to pass rapidly over or through: *We ran the rapids in a canoe.* **3.** to perform by or as by running: *to run a race, to run an errand.* **4.** to cause (an animal) to run or move rapidly: *to run a horse until it is exhausted, to run cattle through a valley.* **5.** to bring to a specified place, state, or condition by or as by running: *I ran myself ragged doing errands all morning.* **6.** to enter (a contestant, as a horse or dog) in a race. **7.** to enter as a candidate for election: *The party will run our mayor for governor.* **8.** to keep functioning; operate: *to run an engine.* **9.** to expose oneself to; incur: *to run a risk.* **10.** to cause to move, pass, or slide easily: *to run a flag up a pole.* **11.** to cause to proceed; direct; conduct; manage: *The new president ran the meeting well. The owner runs the store alone.* **12.** to cause (a conveyance) to go from place to place, esp. regularly: *to run a nightly express train from Boston to Washington.* **13.** to cause to flow or move in a stream: *to run water into a bathtub.* **14.** to cause to extend in a certain direction; lead: *to run a pipe underneath a building.* **15.** to cause to move quickly, as the eye or hand: *to run one's eyes down a page.* **16.** to publish, as in a newspaper or magazine: *to run an advertisement, to run a story in three issues.* **17.** to cause to be presented or shown: *to run a movie.* **18.** to perform, administer, or execute: *to run tests for allergies.* **19.** to search for and follow; trace: *to run a story back to its source.* **20.** to mark or draw, as a boundary line. **21.** to drive with force; thrust: *to run one's hand through a window.* **22.** to suffer from; have: *to run a fever.* **23.** to have moving through; flow with: *The streets ran muddy water.* **24.** to slip past or through: *to run a blockade, to run a stoplight.* **25.** to smuggle: *to run rifles.* **26.** to carry or transport, as in a vehicle: *Can you run me downtown?* **27.** to hunt or chase, as game. **28.** *Computers.* to execute or operate (a program). **29.** in billiards and some other games, to make (a series of plays, shots, or strokes) successfully. **30.** to cause (a vehicle) to come to a specified place or condition: *to run a car into a fence, to run a ship aground.* —*n.* **1.** an act or instance of running or moving rapidly: *to take a run around the block.* **2.** a pace faster than a walk: *to break into a run.* **3.** a distance covered or the time taken while moving at such a pace:

a mile run, a few minutes' run from the finish line. **4.** a short, quick trip or visit: *to make a run into the city.* **5.a.** a distance regularly traveled between two places, as by a train: *The run from Boston to New York is over 200 miles.* **b.** a journey or trip over this distance: *The train made four runs daily.* **6.** a regularly traveled route or course: *The milk truck driver finished the morning run early.* **7.** the freedom to move about; right to use: *We had the run of the hotel facilities. The dogs were given the run of the farm.* **8.** a continuous spell or unbroken series: *a run of rainy days.* **9.** a period of continuing performance or exhibition: *The movie had a long run.* **10.** a general type or class: *the usual run of weekend activities.* **11.** a general direction or tendency; trend: *Which way does the run of events seem to be heading?* **12.a.** a period of operation or functioning, as of a factory or machine. **b.** the amount produced during such a period; output. **13.** a continuous stretch or extent: *a run of iron pipe.* **14.** an extensive, esp. sudden, demand, as for money or commodities: *a run on a bank, a run on milk because of rumors of a strike.* **15.** a place where stitches have broken and unraveled, esp. along the length of a row of stitches: *a run in a stocking.* **16.** a flowing movement, as of a liquid. **17.** the amount or period of time of such a flow. **18.** a small swift stream or rush of water. **19.** a track or path made or frequented by animals. **20.** a number of animals, esp. a school of fish, moving together. **21.** an enclosed area where animals can exercise: *The kennel had a large run for the dogs.* **22.** a course, slope, or other area over which something can travel, as for skiing or bobsledding. **23.** a series of successful plays, shots, or strokes in any of various games. **24.** *Card Games.* a number of consecutive cards in one suit: *a run in spades.* **25.** *Baseball.* a score made by touching home plate after touching the three bases. **26.** *Football.* **a.** an attempt to advance the ball by carrying it around or through the opponent's line. **b.** a completed attempt: *a five-yard run.* **27.** *Cricket.* a score made when both batsmen run to the opposite wicket successfully. **28.** *Music.* a rapid succession of tones, as a roulade. **29.** *Military.* the approach of a plane or attacking vessel to its target. [Old English *rinnan* to move the legs quickly so as to proceed at a pace faster than walking, hasten, flow.]

• **a run for (one's) money.** **a.** serious competition: *We really gave our competitors a run for their money.* **b.** return or satisfaction for one's expenditure of effort.
• **in the long run.** when all the consequences are known; in the end.
• **on the run.** **a.** hurrying, as from one place to another: *I was on the run all day long.* **b.** in rapid retreat or flight.
• **to run across.** to meet or find by chance.
• **to run away with.** **a.** to win by excelling all others: *The favorite ran away with first prize.* **b.** to drive beyond self-control: *to let one's anger run away with one.*
• **to run down.** **a.** to lower or weaken, as in strength, worth, or health: *Office tensions ran the staff down.* **b.** to pursue until caught or killed: *to run down a stag, to run down a criminal.* **c.** to cease operating; stop functioning: *The clock ran down last week.* **d.** to knock down by colliding with: *to run down a traffic sign.* **e.** to speak of in a disparaging way. **f.** to find or trace by searching: *to run down the source of a malfunction.* **g.** *Baseball.* to catch and tag out (a base runner caught between bases).
• **to run for it.** to run in order to escape.
• **to run in.** **a.** *Slang.* to arrest: *The police ran our neighbor in for disturbing the peace.* **b.** to insert or include. **c.** *Printing.* to cause to be without breaks or paragraphs; make continuous.
• **to run into.** **a.** to meet or find by chance: *to run into an old friend.* **b.** to collide with: *The car ran into a telephone pole.*
• **to run off.** **a.** to print or make copies of. **b.** to cause (a contest, as an election) to be played or performed again to decide the outcome. **c.** to cause to leave; eject: *to run a trespasser off one's property.*
• **to run on.** to talk or write without stopping.
• **to run out.** to come to an end; be used up; expire: *Time ran out. My strength ran out.*
• **to run out of.** to exhaust a supply of; use up: *to run out of sugar.*
• **to run out on.** *Informal.* to abandon; desert.
• **to run over.** **a.** to ride or drive over: *We ran over a branch in the road.* **b.** to review or examine quickly: *I ran over my notes before the lecture.*

a	at	e	end	o	hot	u	up	hw	white		about
ā	ape	ē	me	ō	old	ū	use	ng	song		taken
ä	far	i	it	ô	fork	ü	rule	th	thin	ə	pencil
âr	care	ī	ice	oi	oil	u̇	pull	th	this		lemon
		îr	pierce	ou	out	ûr	turn	zh	measure		circus

R

• **to run through. a.** to use up or spend rapidly or wantonly: *to run through a fortune.* **b.** to drive into; pierce. **c.** to review or examine quickly.

• **to run up. a.** to construct or produce quickly: *to run up a costume, to run up a lean-to.* **b.** to allow to accumulate or mount up: *to run up a bill at a store.*

run·a·bout (run′ə bout′) *n.* **1.** a small motorboat. **2.** roadster. **3.** a light, open carriage or wagon. **4.** a person who wanders about from place to place.

run·a·round (run′ə round′) *n. Slang.* evasion or deception, esp. in the form of evasive answers or excuses in response to a request: *to give someone the runaround.*

run·a·way (run′ə wā′) *n.* **1.** a person, animal, or thing that runs away, as a fugitive or a horse that has broken free from a rider's control. **2.** an act or instance of running away. **3.** an easy victory. —*adj.* **1.** escaping from control; running away; fleeing: *a runaway horse.* **2.** easily won, as a race. **3.** brought about by running away or eloping: *a runaway marriage.* **4.** rising or expanding rapidly, as if out of control: *runaway prices, runaway inflation.*

run·back (run′bak′) *n.* **1.** a football play in which a player catches a punt or kickoff, intercepts a pass, or recovers a fumble, and carries it back toward the opposing team's goal. **2.** the distance covered by such a play.

run·ci·nate (run′sə nit, -nāt′) *adj.* (of a leaf) saw-toothed, usually with the lobes or notches pointing backward, as the leaves of some dandelions. [Latin *runcinātus,* past participle of *runcināre* to plane off, from *runcīna* plane[2] (formerly also understood to mean "saw"), from Greek *rhykanē.*]

run·down (run′doun′) *n.* **1.** a summary or brief report. **2.** *Baseball.* a play in which a base runner is caught between bases and tagged out after the ball is thrown back and forth between the bases.

run-down (run′doun′) *adj.* **1.** in poor health and tired out; exhausted. **2.** in disrepair; dilapidated: *a run-down old mansion.* **3.** not working for lack of power, such as a watch or batteries.

rune[1] (rün) *n.* **1.** a letter or character used in an ancient Germanic system of writing found mainly in Scandinavia and England. **2.** a similar letter or character that is supposed to have mysterious or magical power or meaning. [Old English *rūn* mystery, letter of an ancient Germanic system of writing; because writing was regarded as a mystery in earlier times when few could read and write.]

runes

rune[2] (rün) *n.* an ancient Scandinavian poem or song. [Finnish *runo,* from Old Norse *rūn* runic character.]

rung[1] (rung) the past participle and a past tense of **ring**[2].

rung[2] (rung) *n.* **1.** a crosspiece forming a step of a ladder. **2.** a supporting crosspiece placed between the legs or within the framework of the back of a chair. [Old English *hrung* pole[1], staff.]

ru·nic (rü′nik) *adj.* of, relating to, or consisting of runes.

run-in (run′in′) *n. Informal.* a disagreement; quarrel.

run·let (run′lit) *n.* a small stream or brook; runnel.

run·nel (run′əl) *n.* a small stream or brook; rivulet. [Old English *rynel,* from *rinnan* to run, flow.]

run·ner (run′ər) *n.* **1.** a person or animal that runs, as a contestant in a race. **2.a.** *Baseball.* base runner. **b.** *Football.* a player attempting to advance the ball by running. **3.a.** any of various devices that aid movement, as the support on which a sliding drawer moves. **b.** one of the long narrow parts on which a sled or ice skate glides. **4.** a person who runs errands or delivers messages. **5.** a person who solicits business, as for a store. **6.** a long, narrow rug or carpet, used for hallways and staircases.

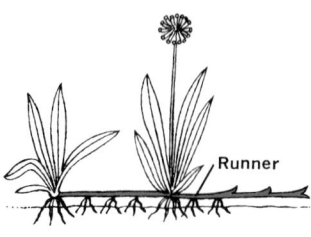

runner *(def. 9)*

7. a narrow strip of cloth used to cover table tops, dressers, and other furniture. **8.** a person or ship engaged in smuggling. **9.** *Botany.* **a.** a slender trailing stem of certain plants that gives rise to roots that produce new plants. **b.** a plant having such a stem, as the strawberry. **10.** a person who runs or operates something, as a machine.

run·ner-up (run′ər up′) *n., pl.* **run·ners-up. 1.** the contestant or team that finishes in second place in a race or other contest. **2.** any other competitor who finishes fairly near the winner: *Three runners-up finished within ten yards of the winner.*

run·ning (run′ing) *n.* **1.** the act of a person or thing that runs. **2.** an instance of running or being run: *the third running of a race.* —*adj.* **1.** moving rapidly; proceeding at a run. **2.** flowing: *running water.* **3.** going on continuously; proceeding without interruption: *a running battle.* **4.** started with, performed during, or accompanied by a run: *a running broad jump, a running catch of a fly ball.* **5.** in operation, as a machine; working: *the sound of a running dishwasher.* **6.** discharging serum, mucus, or pus: *a running sore.* **7.** (of measurements) in a straight line: *the cost of carpeting per running foot.* **8.** in progress; current: *the running favorite Broadway show.* **9.** of duration, operation, or performance: *the running time of a movie.* —*adv.* in succession; consecutively: *I had the same incredible dream for six nights running.*

• **in the running.** having a good chance for success.

• **out of the running.** having no chance for success.

running board, a footboard, mounted below the door, along the side of certain trucks and automobiles.

running gear, the working parts of an automobile or other vehicle, such as the wheels, transmission, and axle, excluding the body and engine.

running head, a title or heading placed at the top of each page or every other page, as in a book or magazine. Also, **running title.**

running knot, a knot made so as to form a noose that tightens as the line is pulled.

running light, any of the lights displayed while moving at night by a ship or aircraft.

running mate, a person who campaigns for office in association with another on the same ticket, esp. the candidate for the lesser of the two offices.

running rigging *Nautical.* the ropes or wires of a ship's rigging that run through blocks and pulleys, used in handling sails, yards, and the like, or in handling cargo. ➡ distinguished from **standing rigging.**

running stitch, a series of small, even stitches made by hand or machine.

running title, running head.

run·ny (run′ē) *adj.,* **-ni·er, -ni·est. 1.** tending to flow or drip; soft, melting, or watery: *runny paste, runny cheese.* **2.** discharging mucus: *a runny nose.*

run·off (run′ôf′, -of′) *n.* **1.** rain or melted snow that is not absorbed by the soil and forms surface streams. **2.** a final contest or election held to break a tie or to determine the outcome of a previous competition in which there was no decisive winner. **3.** something that runs off.

run-of-the-mill (run′əv thə mil′) *adj.* not special or outstanding in any way; ordinary; average.

run-on (run′ôn′, -on′) *adj.* added or appended without a break. —*n.* **1.** something that has been added in this way. **2.** run-on entry.

run-on entry, an undefined dictionary entry added at the end of a defined entry. It is formed by the addition of a suffix to the defined word, and its meaning can be derived from the meaning of the defined word and the meaning of the suffix. *Ruggedness* is a run-on entry under the word *rugged.*

run-on sentence, a sentence containing two or more independent clauses that are not separated by a semicolon or a coordinating conjunction, for example: *We missed the bus, we were late for school.*

runt (runt) *n.* **1.** a stunted or undersized animal or person. **2.** the smallest or weakest in a litter, esp. of puppies. [Of uncertain origin.]

run-through (run′thrü′) *n.* a quick rehearsal, review, or examination.

runt·y (run′tē) *adj.,* **runt·i·er, runt·i·est.** stunted; undersized. —**runt′i·ness,** *n.*

run·way (run′wā′) *n.* **1.** a long, narrow strip of ground where an airplane can take off and land, often surfaced with concrete. **2.** a ramp extending from a stage into the theater. **3.** a way, track, or path along, through, or over which something moves. **4.** a beaten track made and used by deer or other animals.

ru·pee (rü pē′) *n.* the monetary unit of India, Pakistan, Sri Lanka, and various other countries. [Hindustani *rūpiyah,* from Sanskrit *rūpya* silver.]

ru·pi·ah (rü pē′ə) *n.* the monetary unit of Indonesia. [Indonesian *rupiah,* from Hindustani *rūpiyah.* See RUPEE.]

rup·ture (rup′chər) *n.* **1.** an act or instance of breaking open or bursting: *a rupture in a water main.* **2.** a hernia, esp. one in or near

the groin. **3.** a break in friendly relations between people or countries. —*v.,* **-tured, -tur·ing.** —*v.t.* **1.** to break open or apart; burst: *to rupture a blood vessel, to rupture a tire.* **2.** to sever (diplomatic or friendly relations): *The incident ruptured relations between the two countries.* **3.** to affect with a hernia, esp. one in or near the groin. —*v.i.* **1.** to suffer a break; burst: *The patient's appendix ruptured. A gas pipe ruptured.* **2.** to suffer a hernia, esp. one in or near the groin. [Latin *ruptūra* fracture, breach.]

ru·ral (rŏŏr′əl) *adj.* **1.** of, relating to, or characteristic of the country, as distinguished from the city: *rural areas, a rural landscape, a rural population.* **2.** of or relating to agriculture: *a rural economy.* [Latin *rūrālis* relating to the country, from *rūs* the country.] —**ru′ral·ly,** *adv.*

> **Synonyms** Rural, rustic, and **bucolic** mean characteristic of the country as contrasted with the city. **Rural,** the most general of these terms, may be used to describe open country, a small country town or village, or a simple, agricultural way of life: *The candidate spoke of the enduring values of rural America.* **Rustic** implies the simplicity or lack of refinement of country life: *The cabin in the woods had few amenities, but the vacationers liked its unadorned, rustic architecture.* **Bucolic** denotes the pastoral charm of country living: *The poem extolled the bucolic pleasures of the shepherd's life.*

rural delivery, the delivery of mail in rural or farm areas by carriers employed by the government. Formerly, **rural free delivery.**

ruse (rŏŏz) *n.* an action or plan intended to deceive; stratagem; trick. [Middle French *ruse,* from *ruser* to use tricks, from Old French *reüser* to refuse, escape (as by using tricks), going back to Latin *recūsāre* to refuse.]

rush¹ (rŭsh) *v.i.* **1.** to move, go, or come with speed or haste: *He had to rush to catch the bus. Blood rushed to her head.* **2.** to act quickly and often rashly (with *into*): *I rushed into the agreement without examining every detail.* **3.** *Football.* to move or try to move the ball forward by running with it. —*v.t.* **1.a.** to cause to move with speed or haste: *to rush a bill through Congress.* **b.** to urge to act quickly, as by pestering: *Stop rushing me.* **2.** to perform or complete quickly or hastily: *I can't rush this work without making errors.* **3.** to attack or overcome swiftly and forcefully: *They planned to rush the fortress in the morning.* **4.** *Informal.* to lavish attention on, as when courting or seeking (someone's) membership: *The society is rushing twenty sophomores this semester.* **5.** *Football.* to move or carry (the ball) forward by carrying it. —*n.* **1.** an act or instance of rushing; sudden swift movement: *a rush of wind.* **2.** a sudden or hasty movement of many people to get to a place or to begin an activity: *the Monday morning rush of commuters to the city.* **3.** a state of bustling activity: *the rush of a crowded department store during the holidays.* **4.** a sudden, eager demand (with *for* or *on*): *a rush on new stock, a rush for tickets to a championship game.* **5.** a sudden outpouring or onset of activity: *a rush of questions, a rush of orders.* **6.** a hurried state: *to be in a rush.* **7.** *Football.* an attempt to advance the ball by running with it. **8. rushes.** in motion pictures, the first film prints of a scene, before they have been cut or edited. **9.** *Informal.* a lavishing of attention, as on someone being courted. **10.** *Informal.* a social gathering held by a fraternity or sorority to entertain and select new members. —*adj.* **1.** requiring haste; urgent: *a rush job.* **2.** characterized by great activity: *the rush season.* [Old French *reüser* to drive back, refuse, retreat, escape. See RUSE.] —**rush′er,** *n.*

rush² (rŭsh) *n.* **1.** any of several reedy or grasslike plants, genus *Juncus* or *Butomus,* found in marshy areas, having slender, often hollow stems, and clusters of small green or brown flowers. **2.** the stem of such a plant, often woven into mats, baskets, chair seats, and other products. [Old English *risc.*] —**rush′y,** *adj.*

rush hour, the period during a workday when traffic is heaviest and public transportation facilities are most crowded, as when many workers travel to or from work.

rusk (rŭsk) *n.* **1.** a sweet or plain bread or cake baked in the oven, sliced, and baked again to make it brown, dry, and crisp. **2.** a light, soft, sweetened biscuit. [Spanish *rosca* twist, roll (as of bread); of uncertain origin.]

Russ. 1. Russia. **2.** Russian.

rus·set (rŭs′it) *n.* **1.** a yellowish brown or reddish brown color. **2.** any of various kinds of apples or potatoes having russet-colored skin. **3.** a coarse, homespun, russet-colored woolen fabric formerly used for clothing, esp. in England. —*adj.* having the color russet. [Old French *rousset,* diminutive of *rous* reddish-brown, reddish, going back to Latin *russus* red.]

Rus·sian (rŭsh′ən) *adj.* of or relating to Russia or its people, language, or culture. —*n.* **1.a.** a native or inhabitant of Russia. **b.** a citizen of the former Soviet Union. **2.** a language belonging to the eastern division of the Slavic branch of the Indo-European

language family, spoken predominantly in Russia. For alphabet table, see **alphabet. 3.** a person of Russian descent.

Russian dressing, a dressing made of mayonnaise mixed with chili sauce or ketchup, and other ingredients, such as chopped pickles or olives.

Russian olive, a hardy Eurasian shrub, *Elaeagnus angustifolia,* bearing silvery leaves, fragrant yellow flowers, and yellow, olive-like fruit.

Russian Orthodox Church, the largest branch of the Orthodox Church, governed by a patriarch and a number of other prelates. It was the official church of imperial Russia. Also, **Russian Church.**

Russian Revolution, the revolution in Russia in 1917 that ended the czarist form of government and, after a brief period of parliamentary government, established the Soviet government under the leadership of the Bolsheviks and V. I. Lenin.

Russian roulette 1. a deadly game of chance in which one spins the cylinder of a revolver loaded with only one bullet, aims the gun at one's head, and pulls the trigger. **2.** any situation involving the risk of total destruction.

Russian thistle, a bushy weed, *Salsola kali* or *S. australis,* having threadlike prickly leaves and branches that break away in a tangled mass, forming a tumbleweed.

Russian wolfhound, borzoi.

rust (rŭst) *n.* **1.** a reddish brown or orange brittle mixture of iron compounds that forms on the surface of iron or steel when it is exposed to moisture and oxygen. **2.** a similar mixture of compounds, mainly metallic oxides, formed on other metals by oxidation or corrosion. **3.** any of various plant diseases caused by parasitic fungi, characterized by the appearance of reddish brown or orange blisterlike spots and streaks on the plants. **4.** any of several parasitic fungi causing such a disease, composed of tiny threadlike structures that obtain nourishment from the tissues of the host plant. **5.** a reddish brown or orange color. **6.** any harmful or deteriorating effect or influence, esp. one that is the result of inactivity: *an athlete affected by the rust of not having practiced for weeks.* —*v.i.* **1.a.** to become covered or affected with rust. **b.** to become corroded by the formation of rust. **2.** to deteriorate or lose usefulness, as through inactivity: *Without practice, your skills will rust.* **3.** (of a plant) to become infected with a rust. —*v.t.* **1.** to cause to rust. **2.** to cause deterioration through lack of use. —*adj.* having the color rust. [Old English *rūst* the reddish brown coating that forms on certain metals, corruption.]

rus·tic (rŭs′tik) *adj.* **1.** of, relating to, or characteristic of the country: *a rustic setting.* **2.** characteristic of country people or country life; simple and sometimes rough or awkward: *rustic innocence, rustic manners.* **3.** made of undressed wood: *rustic furniture.* —*n.* a person who lives in the country, esp. one who is unsophisticated, simple, or awkward. [Latin *rūsticus* relating to the country, from *rūs* the country.] —**rus′ti·cal·ly,** *adv.* —**rus·tic·i·ty** (rŭs tis′i tē), *n.* —For Synonyms, see **rural.**

rus·ti·cate (rŭs′ti kāt′) *v.,* **-cat·ed, -cat·ing.** —*v.i.* to go or retire to the country; stay in the country. —*v.t.* **1.** to send to the country. **2.** *British.* to suspend (a student) from a school or

a	at	e	end	o	hot	u	up	hw	white	(about
ā	ape	ē	me	ō	old	ū	use	ng	song	taken
ä	far	i	it	ô	fork	ü	rule	th	thin	ə pencil
âr	care	ī	ice	oi	oil	u̇	pull	th	this	lemon
		îr	pierce	ou	out	ûr	turn	zh	measure	(circus

R

college. [Latin *rūsticātus,* past participle of *rūsticārī* to live in the country.] —**rus′ti·ca′tion,** *n.* —**rus′ti·ca′tor,** *n.*

rus·tle (rus′əl) *v.,* **-tled, -tling.** —*v.i.* **1.** to make a series of soft sounds, as that of papers, silk, or leaves being stirred about. **2.** *Informal.* to steal cattle. —*v.t.* **1.** to cause to make a series of soft, fluttering sounds: *The wind rustled the leaves.* **2.** *Informal.* to make, get, or collect with much activity or energy (often with *up*): *to rustle up breakfast.* **3.** *Informal.* to steal (cattle). —*n.* a succession of soft, fluttering sounds. [Imitative.]

rus·tler (rus′lər) *n.* a cattle thief.

rust·proof (rust′prüf′) *adj.* not subject to rusting.

rust·y (rus′tē) *adj.,* **rust·i·er, rust·i·est. 1.** covered or affected with rust: *a rusty nail.* **2.** not working freely because of or as if because of rust: *a rusty window latch.* **3.** consisting of or made by rust: *rusty spots on an iron gate.* **4.** having the color rust. **5.** weakened or deteriorated through neglect or lack of practice: *My French is a bit rusty.* **6.** less skilled through disuse; out of practice: *I've gotten rusty in math.* **7.** shabby, worn, or faded. —**rust′i·ly,** *adv.* —**rust′i·ness,** *n.*

rut[1] (rut) *n.* **1.** a groove or other depression made in the ground by a wheel or by continuous wear. **2.** any groove or depression: *a rut in the surface of a wooden box.* **3.** a rigid way of living, thinking, or acting; boring routine. —*v.t.,* **rut·ted, rut·ting.** to make a rut in. [Middle French *route* way, track. See ROUTE.]

rut[2] (rut) *n.* **1.** the periodically recurring sexual excitement of various male animals, as deer, goats, and sheep. **2.** the period during which this lasts. —*v.i.* **rut·ted, rut·ting.** to be in such a state. [Old French *rut* the sexual excitement, its period, going back to Latin *rūgītus* roar (from the noise made by deer in rut).]

ru·ta·ba·ga (rü′tə bā′gə, rü′tə bā′-) *n.* a plant, *Brassica napobrassica,* of the mustard family, bearing thick yellow or white tubers that are used as food and livestock feed. [Dialectal Swedish *rotabagge.*]

ruth (rüth) *n. Archaic.* **1.** pity; compassion: *ruth for a sufferer.* **2.** sorrow; remorse: *to feel ruth at one's sins.* [Old Norse *hrygth* affliction, sorrow.]

Ruth (rüth) *n.* a book of the Old Testament, relating the story of Ruth.

ru·the·ni·um (rü thē′nē əm) *n.* a hard, silvery metallic element used as a hardener for platinum, for jewelry, and in alloys for electrical contacts. Symbol: **Ru** For tables, see **element.** [Modern Latin *ruthenium,* from Medieval Latin *Ruthenia* Russia; because it was discovered in Russia.]

ruth·er·for·di·um (ruth′ər fôr′dē əm) *n.* a proposed name for the artificially produced radioactive element with atomic number 104. Proposed symbol: **Rf** Also, **element 104, kurchatovium, unnilquadium.** For tables, see **element.** [From the English physicist Ernest *Rutherford,* 1871-1937.]

ruth·less (rüth′lis) *adj.* merciless and unrelenting in the pursuit of one's own ends: *a ruthless politician.* —**ruth′less·ly,** *adv.* —**ruth′less·ness,** *n.*

ru·tile (rü′tēl) *n.* a dark red oxide mineral mined as an ore of titanium. Formula: TiO_2 [Possibly from French *rutile,* from German *rutil,* or directly from German, going back to Latin *rutilus* red.]

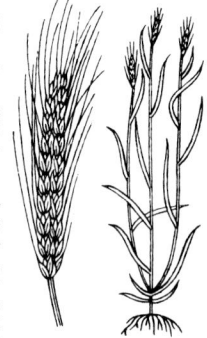

Grain head   Plant

rye

rut·ty (rut′ē) *adj.,* **-ti·er, -ti·est.** full of ruts. —**rut′ti·ness,** *n.*

RV 1. recreational vehicle. **2.** *also,* R.V. Revised Version (of the Bible).

Rx, prescription *(def. 1a).* [Form of R, symbol for Latin *recipe* take. See RECIPE.]

-ry, form of **-ery,** as in *baptistry, revelry, jewelry, ministry.* [Short for -ERY.]

Ry., railway.

rye (rī) *n.* **1.** the grain of a hardy, slender-stemmed plant, *Secale cereale,* of the grass family, used chiefly as feed for animals and for making flour, whiskey, gin, and alcohol. **2.** the plant itself, widely cultivated for its edible grain and also raised as a winter cover crop to prevent soil erosion. **3.** a whiskey distilled from fermented mash of rye grains or a mixture of rye and malt. [Old English *ryge* the grain.]

rye·grass (rī′gras′) *n.* any of a group of grasses, genus *Lolium,* having long, narrow, flat leaves, widely cultivated as forage grasses.

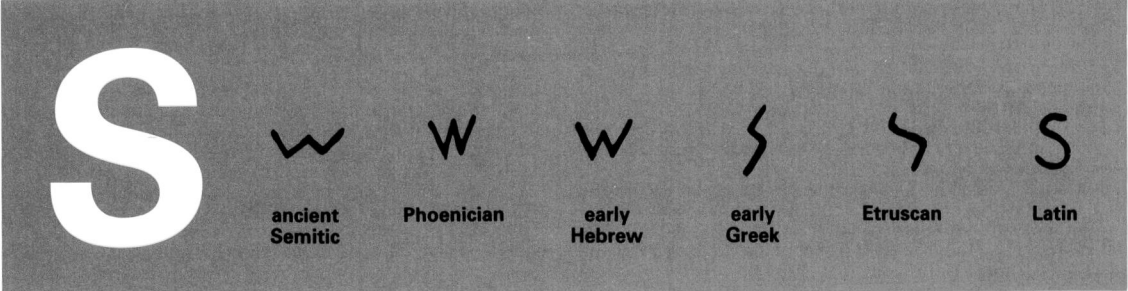

| ancient Semitic | Phoenician | early Hebrew | early Greek | Etruscan | Latin |

S The earliest form of **S** was the letter *shin*, meaning "tooth," and representing the *sh* sound in the ancient Semitic alphabets. The early Phoenician and early Hebrew versions of *shin* looked like our letter **W**. Sometime between 800 and 500 B.C., a new form of *shin*, closer in shape to our letter **S**, appeared in the earliest Greek alphabets. This letter, called *sigma* and used to represent the *s* sound, was later adopted by the Etruscans. When the Romans borrowed the Etruscan form of *sigma* for their Latin alphabet, they wrote it much as we write capital **S**.

s, S (es) *n., pl.* **s's, S's. 1.** the nineteenth letter of the English alphabet. **2.** the shape of this letter or something having this shape.

S, the symbol for sulfur.

-s *suffix* **1.** used to form the plural of most nouns: *horses.* **2.** used to form the third person singular of the present indicative of most verbs: *talks, runs, eats.* **3.** used to form certain adverbs: *always, sometimes.*

-'s[1] *suffix* used to form the possessive case of singular nouns, of plural nouns not ending in *s,* and of some pronouns: *a girl's dress, children's toys, anyone's hat.*

-'s[2] *suffix* (used in contractions) **1.** is: *She's three years old. He's away for the weekend.* **2.** has: *He's already been there.* **3.** us: *Let's go see her.*

s *also,* **s.** second; seconds.

s. 1. shilling. **2.** singular.

S *also,* **S. 1.** South. **2.** Southern.

S. 1. Saint. **2.** Saturday. **3.** School. **4.** September. **5.** Sunday.

S.A. 1. Salvation Army. **2.** South Africa. **3.** South America.

sab·a·dil·la (sab′ə dil′ə) *n.* a Mexican and Central American plant, *Schoenocaulon officinale,* of the lily family, whose seeds yield an alkaloid used esp. in insecticides. [Mexican Spanish *cebadilla,* diminutive of *cebada* barley, from Latin *cibare* to feed, from *cibus* food.]

Sab·ba·tar·i·an (sab′ə târ′ē ən) *n.* **1.** a person who observes Saturday as the Sabbath. **2.** a person who strictly observes Sunday as the Sabbath. —*adj.* of or relating to the Sabbath or to Sabbatarians. —**Sab′ba·tar′i·an·ism,** *n.*

Sab·bath (sab′əth) *n.* the day of the week reserved for rest and religious worship. Sunday is the Sabbath to most Christians; Saturday is observed as the Sabbath by the Jews and by some Christian denominations; Friday is the Muslim Sabbath. [Latin *sabbatum* the Jewish Sabbath, from Greek *sabbaton,* from Hebrew *sabbāth* rest, the Jewish Sabbath.]

sab·bat·i·cal (sə bat′i kəl) *n.* **1.** a period of leave from teaching duties, usually consisting of a year, granted at intervals to a professor or other teacher for travel, study, or rest. **2.** any similar period of leave from one's regular employment. Also, **sabbatical leave, sabbatical year.** —*adj. also,* **Sabbatical.** of, relating to, or appropriate for the Sabbath. Also, **sab·bat′ic.** [Greek *sabbatikos* relating to the Sabbath (from *sabbaton* the Jewish Sabbath) + -AL[1]; referring to the ancient Hebrew practice of resting the fields every seventh year by not cultivating them. See SAB-BATH.]

sa·ber (sā′bər) *also, British,* **sabre.** *n.* **1.** a heavy single-edged sword designed for cutting, having a long, slightly curved blade. **2.** a light, double-edged fencing sword, used for slashing and thrusting. —*v.t.* to strike, wound, or kill with a saber. [French *sabre* the heavy sword, through German, from Magyar *száblya,* from *szabni* to cut.]

saber rattling, a blatant show or threat of military force.

sa·ber-toothed tiger (sā′bər tütht′) any of various prehistoric members of the cat family, esp. of the extinct genus *Smilodon,* that had long, curved, upper canine teeth adapted for stabbing or slashing prey. Length: 6 feet (1.8 meters).

Sa·bine (sā′bīn) *n.* **1.** a member of a tribe that lived in hills northeast of ancient Rome and waged war against the Romans until 290 B.C. **2.** the extinct language of the Sabines, belonging to the Italic branch of the Indo-European language family. —*adj.* of or relating to the Sabines or their language.

saber-toothed tiger

sa·ble (sā′bəl) *n.* **1.** any of various martens, family Mustelidae, esp. the **Russian sable,** *Martes zibellina,* which is native to the northern pine forests of Siberia and Europe and has a bushy tail, round ears, and fur that is usually grayish brown in color. **2.** the valuable fur itself, used for making coats, stoles, and trimmings. **3.** the color black. **4. sables.** black mourning clothes. —*adj.* **1.** having the color black. **2.** made of sable: *a sable coat.* **3.** dark. [Old French *sable* the animal and the fur, through German, from Russian *sobol′.*]

sab·ot (sab′ō, sa bō′) *n.* **1.** a shoe carved from a single piece of wood, worn esp. in the Netherlands, Belgium, and France. **2.** a heavy leather sandal or shoe having a thick wooden sole. [French *sabot* wooden shoe; of uncertain origin.]

sab·o·tage (sab′ə täzh′) *n.* **1.** the deliberate damage or destruction of factory machinery, buildings, or other property, or interference with work or other activity, as by labor agitators during a strike or by enemy agents during a war. **2.** any deliberate, treacherous attempt to harm, destroy, or obstruct some activity or effort. —*v.t.,* **-taged, -tag·ing.** to commit sabotage against. [French *sabotage* deliberate destruction of property, from *saboter* to damage, bungle, from *sabot* wooden shoe; supposedly referring to the former practice of damaging an employer's machinery by throwing wooden shoes into it. See SABOT.]

sab·o·teur (sab′ə tûr′,-tûr′) *n.* a person who commits sabotage.

sa·bra (sä′brə) *n.* a native-born Israeli. [Hebrew *sābrāh.*]

sa·bre (sā′bər) *British. n.* saber. —*v.t.* **-bred, -bring.** saber.

sac (sak) *n.* a pouch or pouchlike structure or part in a plant or animal, often containing a liquid. [Latin *saccus* bag. See SACK[1].]

Sac (sak, sôk) *n., pl.* **Sacs** or **Sac.** Sauk.

SAC, Strategic Air Command.

sac·cha·ride (sak′ə rīd′) *n.* a sugar compound consisting of either a monosaccharide or a combination of monosaccharides, as a disaccharide or polysaccharide.

sac·cha·rin (sak′ər in) *also,* **saccharine.** *n.* a white crystalline powder that has a sweetening power several hundred times that of cane sugar, used chiefly as a calorie-free substitute for sugar. Formula: $C_7H_5NO_3S$.

sac·cha·rine (sak′ər in, -ə rīn′) *adj.* **1.** overly sweet: *a saccharine smile.* **2.** of, relating to, or of the nature of sugar. —*n.* saccharin. [Medieval Latin *saccharum* sugar (from Greek *sakcharon,* going back to Sanskrit *sharkarā* gravel, sugar) + -INE[1].] —**sac′cha·rine·ly,** *adv.*

sac·cule (sak′ūl) *n.* **1.** a small sac. **2.** the smaller of the two sacs

a	at	e	end	o	hot	u	up	hw	white		about
ā	ape	ē	me	ō	old	ū	use	ng	song		taken
ä	far	i	it	ô	fork	ü	rule	th	thin	ə	pencil
âr	care	ī	ice	oi	oil	u̇	pull	th	this		lemon
			îr pierce	ou	out	ûr	turn	zh	measure		circus

1059

in the membranous labyrinth of the inner ear. Also, **sac·cu·lus** (sak′yə ləs). [Latin *sacculus* little bag, diminutive of *saccus* bag. See SACK[1].]

sac·er·do·tal (sas′ər dō′təl) *adj.* of or relating to a priest or the priesthood; priestly. [Latin *sacerdōtālis,* from *sacerdōs* priest.] —**sac′er·do′tal·ly,** *adv.*

sac·er·do·tal·ism (sas′ər dō′tə liz′əm) *n.* the beliefs, practices, or character of the priesthood. —**sac′er·do′tal·ist,** *n.*

sac fungus, ascomycete.

sa·chem (sā′chəm) *n.* among certain North American Indians, the hereditary ruler or chief of a confederation of tribes. [Algonquian *sachem.*] —**sa·chem·ic** (sā chem′ik) *adj.*

sa·chet (sa shā′) *n.* **1.** a small bag or pad containing a fragrant substance, such as perfumed powder, used esp. to scent articles of clothing. **2.** a perfumed powder used in such a bag or pad. [French *sachet* small bag, diminutive of *sac* bag, from Latin *saccus.* See SACK[1].]

sack[1] (sak) *n.* **1.** a large bag made of coarse, strong material: *to put mail in sacks, a sack of potatoes.* **2.** any bag. **3.a.** a sack and what it contains. **b.** the quantity of material contained in a sack. **4.** *also,* **sacque.** a short, loose-fitting jacket for women and children. —*v.t.* **1.** to put into a sack or sacks. **2.** *Slang.* to dismiss from employment; fire. [Old English *sacc* bag, sackcloth, from Latin *saccus,* from Greek *sakkos,* from Hebrew *saq.*]
  • **the sack.** *Slang.* **a.** dismissal from one's job: *to get the sack.* **b.** bed: *to stay in the sack all morning.*
  • **to hit the sack.** *Slang.* to go to bed; go to sleep.
  • **to sack out.** *Slang.* to go to bed; go to sleep.

sack[2] (sak) *v.t.* to strip (a town or city) of possessions by force after capturing; plunder: *The soldiers sacked the great city.* —*n.* the act of sacking, esp. of sacking a captured city. [French *sac* plunder, from Italian *sacco,* going back to Latin *saccus* bag; referring to carrying off booty in a bag when plundering. See SACK[1].]

sack[3] (sak) *n.* **1.** a dry, light-colored sherry. **2.** any of several strong, dry white wines from southern Europe. [French *(vin) sec* dry (wine), from Latin *siccus* dry.]

sack·but (sak′but′) *n.* a musical instrument of medieval times, forerunner of the trombone. [French *saquebute* trombone, from Old French *saquer* to pull (of uncertain origin) + *bouter* to push (of Germanic origin); because it is played by pushing and pulling its sliding piece.]

sack·cloth (sak′klôth′) *n.* **1.** a coarse cloth for making sacks; sacking. **2.** a garment made from such cloth, worn as a sign of mourning, humility, or penitence.

sack coat, a man's loose-fitting jacket having a straight back.

sack·ful (sak′fʊl′) *n., pl.* **-fuls.** the amount that a sack holds.

sack·ing (sak′ing) *n.* any of various coarse woven cloths, used for making such items as bags and sacks.

sacque (sak) *n.* sack[1] *(def. 4).*

sa·cra (sā′krə, sak′rə) a plural of **sacrum.**

sa·cral (sā′krəl, sak′rəl) *adj.* of, relating to, or located in the area of the sacrum, or base of the spine. [Modern Latin *sacralis,* from *sacrum.* See SACRUM.]

sac·ra·ment (sak′rə mənt) *n.* **1.** any of several Christian rites. The Roman Catholic, Orthodox, and some Anglican churches recognize seven sacraments: baptism, penance, Holy Communion, confirmation, matrimony, holy orders, and anointing of the sick. **2.** *also,* **the Sacrament. a.** Holy Communion. **b.** the consecrated bread and wine used in Holy Communion, or the bread alone. **3.** something considered to have a sacred or mysterious character or significance. [Late Latin *sacrāmentum* religious rite, from Latin *sacrāmentum* oath, solemn obligation, going back to *sacer* holy.]

sac·ra·men·tal (sak′rə men′təl) *adj.* **1.** of, relating to, or used in a sacrament. **2.** of the nature of or having the force of a sacrament. —*n.* in some Christian churches, any object or ceremony, such as the use of holy water, that aids in devotion and in obtaining grace. —**sac′ra·men′tal·ly,** *adv.*

sa·cred (sā′krid) *adj.* **1.** set apart for, belonging to, or dedicated to a deity or religious use or purpose; commanding religious veneration or respect: *sacred ground, the sacred name of God.* **2.** of or relating to religion; not secular; religious: *sacred music.* **3.** regarded with or entitled to respect or reverence: *a philosopher whose memory is still sacred to disciples.* **4.** not to be broken or violated: *a sacred promise, a sacred duty.* [Middle English *sacred,* past participle of *sacren* to consecrate, from Latin *sacrāre.*] —**sa′cred·ly,** *adv.* —**sa′cred·ness,** *n.* —For Synonyms, see **holy.**

Sacred College, College of Cardinals. Also, **Sacred College of Cardinals.**

sacred cow, something or someone supposedly above reproach and not to be criticized.

sac·ri·fice (sak′rə fīs′) *n.* **1.** the act of making an offering, as of an animal or of a human life, to a god, in propitiation or worship.

2. an animal, person, or thing so offered. **3.a.** the act of giving up something that is valued or wanted, usually for the sake of something else: *My parents made many sacrifices to send me to college.* **b.** something given up. **4.** the loss of profit incurred in selling something below its presumed value. **5.** *Baseball.* sacrifice hit. —*v.,* **-ficed, -fic·ing.** —*v.t.* **1.** to offer as a sacrifice to a deity. **2.** to give up, forego, or suffer to be lost or destroyed for the sake of something else. **3.** to sell or part with at a loss. **4.** *Baseball.* to advance (a runner or runners) by making a sacrifice hit. —*v.i.* **1.** to offer or make a sacrifice. **2.** *Baseball.* to make a sacrifice hit. [Old French *sacrifice* offering to a god, from Latin *sacrificium,* from *sacer* holy + *facere* to make.] —**sac′ri·fic′er,** *n.*

sacrifice fly *Baseball.* a fly ball that enables a base runner to score after the ball is caught by an opposing player.

sacrifice hit *Baseball.* a bunt that advances the runner or runners on base but results in the batter being put out.

sac·ri·fi·cial (sak′rə fish′əl) *adj.* of, relating to, or used in a sacrifice. —**sac′ri·fi′cial·ly,** *adv.*

sacrificial lamb, a person or thing given up, often as a scapegoat, for some advantage or gain: *The candidate made her campaign manager the sacrificial lamb and fired him when the scandal broke.*

sac·ri·lege (sak′rə lij) *n.* **1.** a violation or desecration of anything sacred. **2.** outrageous disrespect toward or disregard for a cherished or revered person or thing. [Old French *sacrilege* desecration of a sacred thing, from Latin *sacrilegium* robbing of a temple, going back to *sacer* holy + *legere* to gather.]

sac·ri·le·gious (sak′rə lij′əs, -lē′jəs) *adj.* **1.** of, relating to, or being a sacrilege. **2.** guilty of sacrilege. —**sac′ri·le′gious·ly,** *adv.* —**sac′ri·le′gious·ness,** *n.*

sac·ris·tan (sak′rə stən) *n.* a person who is in charge of a sacristy.

sac·ris·ty (sak′rə stē) *n., pl.* **-ties.** a room or rooms in a church where the sacred vessels, robes, and other objects used in ceremonies are kept. [Medieval Latin *sacristia,* going back to Latin *sacer* holy.]

sac·ro·il·i·ac (sak′rō il′ē ak′) *n.* the area or joint at the base of the spine where the sacrum and ilium join. —*adj.* of or relating to this joint or the ligaments joining the sacrum and the ilium. [SACR(UM) + ILIAC.]

sac·ro·sanct (sak′rō sangkt′) *adj.* very sacred; inviolable. [Latin *sacrōsānctus,* from *sacer* holy + *sānctus* holy.] —**sac′ro·sanc′ti·ty,** *n.*

sac·rum (sak′rəm, sā′krəm) *n., pl.* **sac·ra** (sak′rə, sā′krə) or **sac·rums.** a triangular bone located near the base of the spine. In humans, it comprises five fused vertebrae and forms the back of the pelvis. For illustration, see **pelvis.** [Late Latin *(os) sacrum* holy (bone), going back to Latin *sacer* holy; referring to its use in sacrifice to the gods in ancient times.]

sad (sad) *adj.,* **sad·der, sad·dest. 1.** feeling or showing low spirits, unhappiness, or sorrow. **2.** causing or marked by low spirits, unhappiness, sorrow, or gloom. **3.** bad, unfortunate, or wretched; pitiful: *a sad state of affairs.* **4.** (of color) dark; dull; drab. [Old English *sæd* sated, weary.] —**sad′ly,** *adv.* —**sad′ness,** *n.*

sad·den (sad′ən) *v.t., v.i.* to make or become sad.

sad·dle (sad′əl) *n.* **1.** a seat for a rider, used on the back of a horse or similar animal, usually made of heavy leather over a well-padded frame and held to the animal's back by one or more girths that pass around the body. **2.** a similar padded seat, as on a motorcycle. **3.** something resembling a saddle. **4.** the padded part of a harness that fits over an animal's back and supports the shafts. **5.** a depression in a ridge joining two peaks or higher elevations, or the ridge itself. **6.** a cut of meat, esp. of mutton, veal, or lamb, consisting of the undivided back of an animal including the two loins. —*v.,* **-dled, -dling.** —*v.t.* **1.** to put a saddle on: *to saddle a horse.* **2.** to weigh down or load, as with a burden: *to be saddled with debts.* **3.** to place or impose on, as a responsibility (with *on* or *upon*): *to saddle the blame for one's bad behavior on one's peers.* —*v.i.* to put a saddle on a horse or similar animal.

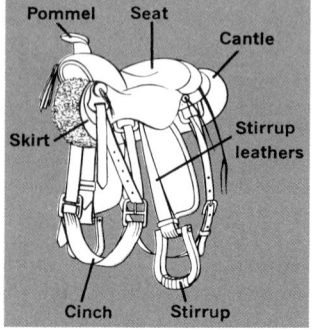

saddle

S

[Old English *sadol* seat for a rider put on the back of a horse or similar animal.]

• **in the saddle.** in a position of power or control.

sad·dle·bag (sad′əl bag′) *n.* a bag or pouch of leather or other material, usually one of a pair hung from a saddle.

saddle blanket, a blanket or pad put on an animal's back beneath the saddle to prevent chafing or irritation.

sad·dle·bow (sad′əl bō′) *n.* the arched front part of a saddle.

sad·dle·cloth (sad′əl klôth′) *n., pl.* **-cloths** (-klôthz′, -klôths′) **1.** a cloth bearing the number of a racehorse placed either under or over the saddle. **2.** saddle blanket.

saddle horse, a horse trained or suitable for riding.

sad·dler (sad′lər) *n.* a person who makes, repairs, or sells saddlery.

sad·dler·y (sad′lə rē) *n., pl.* **-dler·ies. 1.** saddles, harnesses, and other equipment, collectively, for horses, esp. equipment made of leather. **2.** the shop of a saddler. **3.** the craft, business, or work of a saddler.

saddle shoe, an oxford shoe, usually white in color, having a band of contrasting color across the instep.

saddle soap, a mild soap, usually containing neat's-foot oil, used to clean, soften, and preserve leather.

sad·dle·sore (sad′əl sôr′) *adj.* being sore or stiff from riding horseback.

saddle sore, a place on the body of a horse or rider where the skin is painful to the touch, caused by rubbing against a saddle.

sad·dle·tree (sad′əl trē′) *n.* the frame of a saddle.

Sad·du·cee (saj′ə sē′, sad′yə-) *n.* a member of a Jewish political and religious sect that believed in strict, literal interpretation of written Mosaic law, rejected oral law, and denied belief in fate, life after death, and resurrection. —**Sad′du·ce′an,** *adj.* —**Sad′du·cee′ism,** *n.*

sad·i·ron (sad′ī′ərn) *n.* a flatiron having two pointed ends and a removable handle. [SAD (in the dialectal sense of "heavy") + IRON.]

sa·dism (sā′diz əm, sad′iz-) *n.* **1.** an abnormal tendency to derive sexual pleasure from the infliction of physical or emotional pain on others. **2.** gratification of any sort derived from inflicting physical or emotional pain on others. [French *sadisme,* from the Marquis de *Sade,* 1740-1814, whose writings described and advocated behavior arising from such a tendency.] —**sa′dist,** *n.* —**sa·dis′tic,** *adj.*

sa·do·mas·o·chism (sā′dō mas′ə kiz′əm) *n.* the coexistence of sadism and masochism in an individual, characterized by a strong tendency to hurt others and to invite being hurt in social and sexual relationships. [SAD(ISM) + MASOCHISM.] —**sa′do·mas′o·chist,** *n.* —**sa′do·mas′o·chis′tic,** *adj.*

sad sack *Slang.* a person who is awkward, clumsy, and inept.

sa·fa·ri (sə fär′ē) *n., pl.* **-ris. 1.** a hunting expedition, esp. in Africa. **2.** any long or arduous trip, esp. one in search of something. [Swahili *safari* journey, from Arabic *safarī* relating to a journey, from *safar* journey.]

safe (sāf) *adj.,* **saf·er, saf·est. 1.** free from harm or danger: *It's not safe to walk there alone at night.* **2.** free from or having escaped hurt or injury; unharmed: *a safe flight, safe after crossing enemy lines in battle.* **3.** giving security, protection, or freedom from harm: *Find a safe place in which to put the papers.* **4.** involving no risk: *a safe bet, a safe investment.* **5.** unable to cause harm or injury: *The lion is safe in its cage.* **6.** avoiding risk or danger; prudent; cautious: *a safe player who sticks to a conservative style of play.* **7.** *Baseball.* having succeeded in reaching a base without being put out. —*n.* **1.** a strong container of metal or other material, capable of being locked, used for the safekeeping of valuables. **2.** any place used for storage and protection, such as a cooled box in which to keep perishable foods. [Old French *salf, sauf* free from danger or death, from Latin *salvus* unharmed, well¹.] —**safe′ly,** *adv.* —**safe′ness,** *n.*

Synonyms *adj.* **Safe** and **secure** mean free from danger or harm. **Safe** indicates having avoided or escaped from danger: *Their seat belts kept them safe in the collision.* **Secure** suggests not only physical safety but freedom from anxiety: *The passengers felt secure when the damaged ship entered the shelter of the harbor.*

safe·con·duct (sāf′kon′dukt) *n.* **1.** the privilege of being protected while passing through a hazardous region, such as enemy or occupied territory. **2.** an official document or escort assuring this privilege.

safe·crack·er (sāf′krak′ər) *n.* a thief who breaks into safes for the valuables they contain.

safe·de·pos·it (sāf′di poz′it) *adj.* of or relating to a metal drawer or other container, esp. in a bank, for the safekeeping of valuables. Also, **safe′ty·de·pos′it.**

safe-deposit box, a box for storing valuables, esp. one kept in a bank vault.

safe·guard (sāf′gärd′) *n.* **1.** something that protects: *The parents put a gate across the stairway as a safeguard for the baby.* **2.** a mechanical device or technical procedure designed to prevent accident or injury. —*v.t.* to guard; protect; defend.

safe house, an apartment, house, or other building that is secure from surveillance, used by the police or intelligence agents for meetings or for hiding a person.

safe·keep·ing (sāf′kē′ping) *n.* **1.** the act of keeping safe. **2.** care or protection; custody.

safe·light (sāf′līt′) *n. Photography.* a darkroom lamp with one or more color filters, used to provide light of a color that does not affect sensitive film or paper. [SAFE + LIGHT¹.]

safe·ty (sāf′tē) *n., pl.* **-ties. 1.** the quality or state of being safe; freedom from risk or harm. **2.** a device designed to prevent accident or injury or to reduce hazard, such as the catch on a firearm that prevents it from firing. **3.** *Football.* **a.** a score of two points for the defensive team, resulting from the ball being downed by the offensive team on or behind its own goal line, after that team caused the ball to cross the line. **b.** a play in which this occurs. **c.** a defensive player who takes the position, or one of the positions, nearest to his team's goal line. —*adj.* contributing to or giving safety.

safety belt 1. a belt, strap, or harness used to fasten a person working at great heights to a fixed object to prevent falling or injury. **2.** seat belt.

safety glass, a laminated glass that resists shattering, formed by inserting a layer of transparent plastic material between two sheets of glass.

safety lamp, a lamp designed for use in mines, having the flame enclosed to safeguard against explosion.

safety match, a match that will ignite only when struck against a friction surface coated with red phosphorus.

safety net 1. a net for catching a person who falls: *a safety net for circus acrobats.* **2.** something that guarantees financial security or protection, such as government insurance on bank deposits.

safety pin, a pin bent back on itself so as to form a spring, having a sheath at one end to cover and hold the point.

safety razor, a razor with a guard or guards around the blade to reduce skin cuts.

safety valve 1. a device on a container, as on a steam boiler, that opens automatically to allow steam or fluids to escape when the interior pressure reaches a danger point. **2.** anything serving as an outlet for the release of an excess, as of energy or emotion.

saf·flow·er (saf′lou′ər) *n.* a tall, thistlelike plant, *Carthamus tinctorius,* bearing yellowish orange flower heads and cultivated for an edible oil extracted from its seeds and a red dye made from its petals. [Middle French *saffleur,* through Italian, from Arabic *asfar* yellow, yellow plant; influenced by SAFFRON, FLOWER.]

saf·fron (saf′rən) *n.* **1.** a yellow coloring and flavoring agent made from the dried stigmas of a crocus, *Crocus sativus,* of the iris family. **2.** the plant itself, having fragrant purple or white flowers. **3.** an orange-yellow color. Also *(def. 3),* **saffron yellow.** —*adj.* **1.** flavored with saffron: *saffron rice.* **2.** having the color saffron: *the saffron robe of a Buddhist monk.* [Old French *safran,* going back to Arabic *za'farān* the plant.]

S. Afr. 1. South Africa. **2.** South African.

saf·ra·nine (saf′rə nēn′) *also,* **saf·ra·nin** (saf′rə nin). *n.* any of various red aniline dyes used for textiles and as stains in microscopy. [French *safran* (see SAFFRON) + -INE².]

sag (sag) *v.i.,* **sagged, sag·ging. 1.** to hang or curve down from or as if from weight or pressure: *This mattress sags so much that I get backaches when I sleep on it.* **2.** to bend or hang unevenly or loosely: *The rusty gate sagged on its hinges.* **3.** to lose firmness, strength, or elasticity; sink; weaken: *Their spirits sagged when they realized help wasn't on the way.* **4.** to slow up, decrease, or move unsteadily; decline: *Production has sagged during the recession.* **5.** (of a boat or ship) to drift, esp. to leeward. —*n.* **1.** the act, state, or extent of sagging. **2.** a place where something sags. [Probably of Scandinavian origin.] —For Synonyms *(v.i.),* see **droop.**

sa·ga (sä′gə) *n.* **1.** a prose narrative composed in Iceland during the Middle Ages, usually dealing with heroic figures and incidents from Scandinavian legend and history. **2.** any long, involved story or narrative, often one dealing with colorful or adventurous deeds. [Old Norse *saga* story.]

sa·ga·cious (sə gā′shəs) *adj.* having or showing wisdom and

a	at	e	end	o	hot	u	up	hw	white	⎧	about
ā	ape	ē	me	ō	old	ū	use	ng	song		taken
ä	far	i	it	ô	fork	ū	rule	th	thin	ə	pencil
âr	care	ī	ice	oi	oil	ů	pull	th	this		lemon
		îr	pierce	ou	out	ûr	turn	zh	measure	⎩	circus

good judgment: *a sagacious ruler.* [Latin *sagāci-*, stem of *sagāx* keen + -OUS.] —**sa·ga'cious·ly,** *adv.* —**sa·ga'cious·ness,** *n.*

sa·gac·i·ty (sə gas'i tē) *n.* the quality of being sagacious.

sag·a·more (sag'ə môr') *n.* among certain North American Indian tribes, an elective ruler or chief, esp. one subordinate to a sachem. [Algonquian *sagimo* literally, he prevails.]

sage[1] (sāj) *n.* a person of profound wisdom. —*adj.,* **sag·er, sag·est.** having or showing wisdom and good judgment; prudent; wise. [Old French *sage* wise, going back to Latin *sapere* to be wise.] —**sage'ly,** *adv.* —**sage'ness,** *n.*

sage[2] (sāj) *n.* **1.** the fragrant leaves of a plant, *Salvia officinalis,* of the mint family, widely used to flavor food. **2.** the plant itself, having fragrant, bell-shaped blue, purple, or white flowers. **3.** any plant of the genus *Salvia.* **4.** sagebrush. [Old French *sau(l)ge* the plant, from Latin *salvia* literally, the healing plant, from *salvus* unharmed, well [1]; because it was thought to have healing qualities.]

sage·brush (sāj'brush') *n.* any of several hardy shrubs, genus *Artemisia,* that grow on the dry plains of western North America, often in the form of dense bushes with silvery leaves and small yellow or whitish flower heads.

sage grouse, a grouse, *Centrocercus urophasianus,* native to the plains of western North America. It is the largest North American grouse.

sage hen, a sage grouse, esp. a female.

sag·it·tal (saj'i təl) *adj. Anatomy.* **1.** of or relating to the suture running lengthwise between the parietal bones on top of the skull. **2.** of or situated in the median plane of the body, dividing the body into right and left halves. [Modern Latin *sagittālis,* from Latin *sagitta* arrow.] —**sag'it·tal·ly,** *adv.*

Sag·it·tar·i·us (saj'ə târ'ē əs) *n.* **1.** a constellation located near the horizon in the northern sky, conventionally depicted as a centaur drawing a bow. **2.** the ninth sign of the zodiac. [Latin *sagittārius* archer.]

sag·it·tate (saj'i tāt') *adj.* shaped like an arrowhead, as certain leaves. [Modern Latin *sagittatus,* from Latin *sagitta* arrow.]

sa·go (sā'gō) *n., pl.* **-gos. 1.** a grainy or powdered starch extracted from the trunk and stems of various tropical palm trees and palmlike plants, used to thicken soups, sauces, and other foods. **2.** sago palm. [Malay *sāgū* the starch.]

sago palm, either of two trees, *Metroxlyn sagu* or *M. rumphi,* found in marshy areas of the East Indies, having long leaves made up of lance-shaped leaflets. They are the major source of sago.

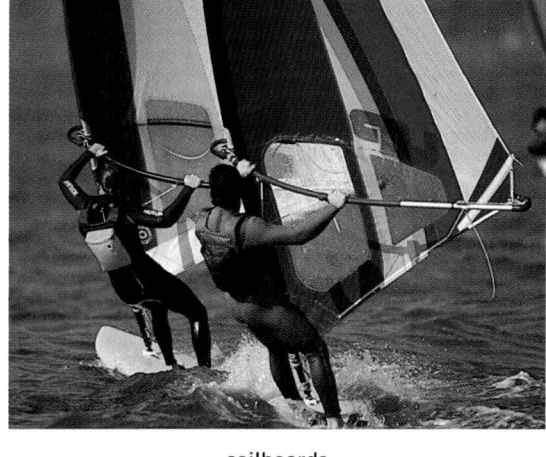
sailboards

sa·gua·ro (sə gwär'ō, -wär'ō) *also,* **sahuaro.** *n., pl.* **-ros.** a giant cactus, *Carnegiea gigantea,* found in southern Arizona and neighboring regions, having sparse branches covered with heavy spines, and bearing white flowers and edible fruit. [Spanish *saguaro;* of Mexican Indian origin.]

sagittate
leaf

sa·hib (sä'ib, -hib, -ēb, -hēb) *n.* sir; master. ➡ formerly used as a title of respect in India and Pakistan, esp. for Europeans. [Urdu *sāhib* lord, companion, from Arabic *sāhib.*]

sa·hua·ro (sə wär'ō) saguaro.

said (sed) *v.* the past tense and past participle of **say.** —*adj.* named or mentioned before; aforesaid. ➡ usually used only in legal or business contexts.

sail (sāl) *n., pl.* **sails** or *(def. 4)* **sail. 1.** a piece of canvas or other material attached to a vessel so as to catch the wind and cause the vessel to move through the water. **2.** such pieces collectively. **3.** something resembling a sail in shape, position, or function, such as an arm of a windmill. **4.** a trip or ride in a vessel, esp. in a sailboat. **5.** conning tower *(def. 2).* —*v.i.* **1.** (of a vessel) to move or be propelled over water by means of a sail or sails or by mechanical power. **2.** to travel over water in a vessel. **3.** to begin a voyage by boat, ship, or other vessel: *The ship will sail for Hawaii in two weeks.* **4.** to manage or operate a sailboat, esp. for sport. **5.** to move or proceed smoothly and effortlessly: *The volleyball sailed over the net.* —*v.t.* **1.** to move or travel over or across (a body of water): *This ship sailed the Mediterranean last year.* **2.** to steer, manage, or navigate (a vessel). [Old English *seg(e)l* piece of cloth attached to a vessel so as to catch the wind and cause the vessel to move through the water.] —For Synonyms *(v.i.),* see **fly**[2].

· **to make sail. a.** to spread out the sail or sails of a vessel. **b.** to begin a voyage by boat, ship, or other vessel.

· **to sail into. a.** to attack or criticize in a heated or violent manner. **b.** to begin or enter into with much energy or enthusiasm: *to sail into a new assignment.*

· **to set sail.** to begin a voyage by boat, ship, or other vessel.

· **under sail.** moving under the power of a sail or sails.

sail·board (sāl'bôrd') *n.* a large surfboard with a mast, sail, and centerboard, used in windsurfing.

sail·boat (sāl'bōt') *n.* a boat equipped with a sail or sails, by means of which it is propelled.

sail·cloth (sāl'klôth') *n.* canvas or other strong material used for making sails, tents, or the like.

sail·er (sā'lər) *n.* a boat or ship, esp. a sailing vessel, with reference to its sailing capability or power: *a fast sailer.*

sail·fish (sāl'fish') *n., pl.* **-fish** or **-fish·es.** any of several saltwater game fish, family Istiophoridae, found in warm coastal waters, and having a large, saillike dorsal fin and a long, spearlike snout. Length: up to 12 feet (3.7 meters).

sail·ing (sā'ling) *n.* **1.** the art or sport of managing, operating, or riding in sailboats. **2.** the art or skill of steering, managing, or navigating a vessel. **3.** the act of a person or thing that sails. **4.** the conditions under which a vessel sails: *smooth sailing.*

sail·mak·er (sāl'mā'kər) *n.* a person who makes or repairs sails.

sail·or (sā'lər) *n.* **1.** a person whose trade or occupation is handling, sailing, or navigating boats and ships; mariner. **2.** a member of a ship's crew whose rank is below that of officer. **3.** a member of a country's navy, esp. an enlisted person. **4.** a person traveling by boat, ship, or other vessel, with reference to his or her ability to avoid seasickness: *a poor sailor.* **5.** sailor hat.

sailor hat, a straw hat with a low, flat crown and a flat brim.

sail·plane (sāl'plān') *n.* a light glider having a streamlined fuselage and slender wings and tail.

saint (sānt) *n.* **1.** *Religion.* **a.** a person honored after death as being worthy of special reverence. In the Roman Catholic and Orthodox churches, a saint is a person who has been formally declared to be in heaven and worthy of veneration on earth. ➡ used as a title: *Saint Mark, Saint Mary.* **b.** a person who has died and whose spirit has gone to heaven. **c. Saint.** Latter-day Saint. **2.** a person who is noted for holiness, godliness, or virtue. **3.** a person who is very kind, patient, or unselfish. —*v.t.* to proclaim or venerate as a saint; canonize. [Old French *saint* holy, holy person, person canonized by the Roman Catholic Church, from Latin *sānctus* holy.]

Saint Ag·nes's Eve (ag'nə siz) the night of January 20, on which, according to tradition, a girl would see a vision of her future husband.

Saint Ber·nard (bər närd') a large, reddish brown and white dog having a massive head and a long, bushy tail, bred as a guide dog and used in rescuing people lost in the Alps. Height: to 30 inches (76 centimeters) at the shoulder. [From its use by monks of the hospice of *Saint Bernard* in the Swiss Alps.]

saint·ed (sān'tid) *adj.* **1.** declared to be saint; canonized. **2.** of or like a saint; pious; saintly. **3.** regarded as being among the saints in heaven; deceased.

Saint Bernard

saint·hood (sānt'húd') *n.* **1.** the character or condition of being a saint. **2.** saints collectively.

saint·ly (sānt'lē) *adj.*, **-li·er, -li·est.** relating to, resembling, or befitting a saint. —**saint'li·ness,** *n.*

Saint Pat·rick's Day (pat'riks) the day set aside to honor Saint Patrick, observed annually on March 17.

saint·ship (sānt'ship') *n.* sainthood *(def. 1).*

Saint Valentine's Day, Valentine's Day.

Saint Vi·tus' dance (vī'tə siz, vī'təs) *also,* **Saint Vitus's dance.** a form of chorea linked with rheumatic fever that affects all motor activities including speech and occurs esp. in children. [Because prayers for a cure of this disorder were addressed to *Saint Vitus,* the patron saint of actors and dancers.]

saith (seth, sā'ith) *Archaic.* the third person singular present indicative of **say.**

sake[1] (sāk) *n.* **1.** good or advantage; benefit; welfare: *You may not want to hear this, but I'm saying it for your own sake.* **2.** purpose; reason: *For the sake of argument, let's assume they're innocent.* [Old English *sacu* strife, lawsuit.]

sa·ke[2] (sä'kē) *also,* **sa·ki.** *n.* a fermented alcoholic beverage of Japanese origin, made from rice. [Japanese *sake.*]

sal (sal) *n.* salt. ➡ used chiefly in pharmaceutical and chemical contexts. [Latin *sāl.*]

sa·laam (sə läm') *n.* **1.** in certain Asian countries, a salutation or obeisance performed by bowing low, and usually clasping the hands together or touching the right hand to the forehead. **2.** a verbal greeting meaning "peace," used esp. among Muslims. —*v.i.* to make a salaam. —*v.t.* to greet with a salaam. [Arabic *salām* peace, salutation.]

sal·a·ble (sā'lə bəl) *also,* **saleable.** *adj.* capable of being sold; marketable. —**sal'a·bil'i·ty, sal'a·ble·ness,** *n.*

sa·la·cious (sə lā'shəs) *adj.* **1.** appealing to the sexual imagination; obscene. **2.** lustful; lecherous. [Latin *salaci-,* stem of *salāx* lustful (from *salīre* to leap) + -OUS.] —**sa·la'cious·ly,** *adv.* —**sa·la'cious·ness, sa·lac·i·ty** (sə las'i tē), *n.*

sal·ad (sal'əd) *n.* **1.** a usually cold dish consisting chiefly of raw, or sometimes cooked, chopped or sliced vegetables, such as lettuce, tomato, and cucumber, served with a dressing. **2.** a course consisting of such a dish. **3.** a usually cold dish consisting of chopped fruit, eggs, fish, or other food, often mixed with raw, chopped vegetables and prepared with mayonnaise or other dressing. **4.** any vegetable or herb used in or grown for salad. [Old French *salade* cold dish of seasoned vegetables, from Old Provençal *salada,* from *salar* to salt, from *sal* salt, from Latin *sāl.*]

salad bar, a self-service counter in a restaurant at which a variety of salads and dressings can be obtained.

salad days, the time of youthful innocence and inexperience. [From "my salad days, when I was green in judgment" (Shakespeare, *Antony and Cleopatra*).]

salad dressing, dressing *(def. 2).*

sal·a·man·der (sal'ə man'dər) *n.* **1.** any of a group of lizardlike amphibians, order Caudata, found in and near fresh water, having scaleless, usually smooth, moist skin. **2.** a mythical creature able to endure or live in fire. [Old French *salamandre* the mythical creature, through Latin, from Greek *salamandrā.*] —**sal·a·man·drine** (sal'ə man'drin), *adj.*

sa·la·mi (sə lä'mē) *n.* a sausage of seasoned pork or beef. [Italian *salami,* plural of *salame,* from *salar* to salt, going back to Latin *sāl* salt.]

sal ammoniac, ammonium chloride. [Latin *sāl ammoniācus* literally, salt of Ammon; because this salt supposedly was first prepared from camel dung near a temple of Ammon in Egypt.]

sal·a·ried (sal'ə rēd) *adj.* receiving or yielding a salary: *a salaried clerk, a salaried position.*

sal·a·ry (sal'ə rē) *n.*, *pl.* **-ries.** a fixed sum of money paid at regular intervals to someone employed, in return for work or service. [Latin *salārium* pay, allowance; originally, money given soldiers to buy salt, going back to *sāl* salt.] —For Synonyms, see **pay.**

sale (sāl) *n.* **1.** the transfer of ownership of something from one person or group to another in exchange for money: *the sale of a house.* **2.** the act or an instance of offering or selling off merchandise at a reduced price: *an end-of-the-season sale.* **3.** the public disposal of merchandise or property to the highest bidder; auction. **4. sales. a.** the quantity sold; gross receipt: *Sales are up at that store.* **b.** the activities, work, or department related to selling goods or services: *a job in sales.* [Old English *sala* act of selling.] •**for sale.** available for purchase. •**on sale.** offered at reduced price: *We bought sheets and towels on sale.*

sale·a·ble (sā'lə bəl) *adj.* salable. —**sale'a·bil'i·ty, sale'a·ble·ness,** *n.*

sales·clerk (sālz'klûrk') *n.* a person employed to sell merchandise in a store.

sales·girl (sālz'gûrl') *n.* a girl or woman employed to sell merchandise in a store.

sales·la·dy (salz'lā'dē) *n., pl.* **-dies.** saleswoman.

sales·man (sālz'mən) *n., pl.* **-men** (-mən). **1.** a man employed to sell merchandise in a store. **2.** a person employed to sell merchandise or services within a given area, as a traveling representative of a company. Also *(def. 2),* **sales representative.**

sales·man·ship (sālz'mən ship') *n.* ability, skill, or technique in selling.

sales·peo·ple (sālz'pē'pəl) *pl. n.* salespersons.

sales·per·son (sālz'pûr'sən) *n.* a person employed to sell merchandise or services.

sales representative, a salesperson employed to represent a manufacturing or wholesale company, usually in a specified territory or country: *the Los Angeles sales representative.*

sales talk, an argument or talk, sometimes accompanied by a demonstration, intended to persuade a prospective customer or customers to buy a product or service or to accept an idea or proposal. Also, **sales pitch.**

sales tax, a general tax placed on the sale of goods, usually levied as a percentage of the selling price of an item.

sales·wom·an (sālz'wûm'ən) *n., pl.* **-wom·en** (-wim'ən). a woman or girl employed to sell merchandise, esp. in a store. Also, **saleslady.**

Sa·li·an (sā'lē ən, sāl'yən) *adj.* of, relating to, or designating a tribe of Franks who settled in a region near the Zuider Zee in the fourth century A.D. —*n.* a Salian Frank.

Sal·ic (sal'ik, sā'lik) *also,* **Salique.** *adj.* of, relating to, or designating the Salian Franks.

sal·i·cin (sal'ə sin) *n.* a bitter, white glucoside, obtained chiefly from the bark of willow and poplar trees, and used in medicine. Formula: $C_{13}H_{18}O_7$ [French *salicine,* from Latin *salix* willow.]

Salic law, a law that excluded women from the right of succession to the throne, effective in France, Spain, and certain other European kingdoms and states. [Because the French established this law by broadly interpreting one provision of the old law code of the Salian Franks, which prohibited women from inheriting land.]

sa·lic·y·late (sə lis'ə lāt', -lit) *n.* a salt or ester of salicylic acid.

sal·i·cyl·ic acid (sal'ə sil'ik) a white, crystalline organic compound used esp. in the manufacture of aspirin. Formula: $C_7H_6O_3$

sa·lience (sāl'yəns, sā'lē əns) *n.* **1.** the state or quality of being salient. **2.** a salient object, part, or feature. Also, **sa'lien·cy.**

sa·lient (sāl'yənt, sā'lē ənt) *adj.* **1.** standing out from the rest; readily noticeable: *the salient traits of a personality.* **2.** projecting beyond a line or surface; jutting or protruding outward. **3.** leaping; bounding; jumping. —*n.* the part of a bastion, fortification, or battle line that most projects toward the enemy. [Latin *saliēns,* present participle of *salīre* to leap.] —**sa'lient·ly,** *adv.*

sa·li·en·tian (sā'lē en'shən) *n.* any of a group of tailless amphibians, order Salientia, including frogs and toads, having a broad body in which the head and trunk are fused and long, powerful hind legs. —*adj.* of, relating to, or belonging to this order. [Modern Latin *Salientia* literally, leaping ones (from Latin *saliēns*) + -AN. See SALIENT.]

sa·line (sā'lēn, -līn) *adj.* **1.** of, relating to, or resembling salt. **2.** consisting of or containing salt. —*n.* **1.** a saline solution, esp. as used in medicine, surgery, or biological experimentation. **2.** a metallic salt, esp. a salt of an alkali metal or of magnesium, often used in medicine as a cathartic. [French *salin* containing salt, salty, going back to Latin *sāl* salt.] —**sa·lin·i·ty** (sə lin'ə tē), *n.*

Sa·lique (sə lēk', sal'ik, sā'lik) Salic.

Salis·bur·y steak (sôlz'ber'ē, -bə rē, salz'-) ground beef, usually mixed with eggs or bread crumbs, formed into patties and either fried or broiled. [From J. H. *Salisbury,* 1823-1905, English physician interested in nutrition.]

Sa·lish (sā'lish) *n.* **1.** a member of a tribe of North American Indians living in northwestern Montana. **2.** the family of languages spoken by these and certain other North American Indians in the northwestern United States and in British Columbia. Also *(def. 2),* **Sa'lish·an.**

sa·li·va (sə lī'və) *n.* a colorless fluid that contains the enzyme ptyalin and is secreted by the salivary glands. Saliva keeps the

a	at	e	end	o	hot	u	up	hw	white		about
ā	ape	ē	me	ō	old	ū	use	ng	song		taken
ä	far	i	it	ô	fork	ü	rule	th	thin	ə	pencil
âr	care	ī	ice	oi	oil	ů	pull	th	this		lemon
		îr	pierce	ou	out	ûr	turn	zh	measure		circus

mouth moist, lubricates food during chewing, and starts the digestion of starches. [Latin *salīva*.]

sal·i·var·y (sal′ə ver′ē) *adj.* of, relating to, or secreting saliva.

salivary gland, any of the three pairs of glands that secrete saliva into the mouth.

sal·i·vate (sal′ə vāt′) *v.i.*, -vat·ed, -vat·ing. to secrete saliva; undergo a secretion of saliva. [Latin *salīvātus*, past participle of *salīvāre* to spit.] —**sal′i·va′tion,** *n.*

Salk vaccine (sôk) a sterile suspension of inactivated poliovirus, used to immunize children against poliomyelitis. [From Jonas Edward *Salk*, born 1914, U.S. physician and microbiologist.]

sal·low[1] (sal′ō) *adj.* of a sickly, yellowish color or complexion. [Old English *salo*.] —**sal′low·ness,** *n.*

sal·low[2] (sal′ō) *n.* any of various trees of the willow family, esp. *Salix caprea,* the wood of which is used as a source of charcoal. [Old English *sealh*.]

sal·ly (sal′ē) *v.i.,* -lied, -ly·ing. 1. to start or go out briskly: *The children sallied forth to play in the snow.* 2. to rush out suddenly: *The soldiers bravely sallied across the field to meet the enemy.* —*n., pl.* -lies. 1. a charge at an enemy. 2. a quick, witty, bold retort or quip. 3. a sudden rushing forth. 4. a short excursion. [French *saillie* an issuing forth, from *saillir* to issue forth, gush; earlier, leap, from *salīre* to leap.]

sal·ma·gun·di (sal′mə gun′dē) *n.* 1. a dish consisting of chopped ingredients, such as meat, anchovies, eggs, and onions, usually arranged in rows and served with a dressing. 2. any mixture or medley; hodgepodge. [French *salmigondis,* possibly from Middle French *salemine* viands (going back to Latin *sāl* salt) + *condir* to season (from Latin *condīre*).]

sal·mi (sal′mē) *also,* **sal·mis** (sal′mē). *n.* a highly spiced dish consisting of fowl or game partially roasted and stewed in wine. [French *salmis,* short for *salmigondis.* See SALMAGUNDI.]

salm·on (sam′ən) *n., pl.* -on or -ons. 1. any of a group of food and game fish, family Salmonidae, usually having a silver body with a dark back and yellowish pink flesh. Salmon return to spawn in the stream where they were hatched. Although some live and spawn in fresh water, most live in salt water and

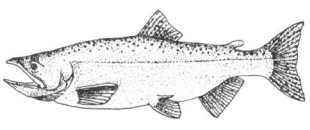

salmon

migrate to fresh water in order to spawn. 2. a yellowish pink color. Also *(def. 2),* **salmon pink.** —*adj.* having the color salmon; yellowish pink. [Old French *saumon* the fish, from Latin *salmō.*]

sal·mo·nel·la (sal′mə nel′ə) *n., pl.* -nel·lae (-nel′ē) or -nel·las or -nel·la. 1. any of a genus, *Salmonella,* of rod-shaped bacteria, some of which cause food poisoning and other diseases in humans. 2. *Informal.* salmonellosis.

sal·mo·nel·lo·sis (sal′mə nə lō′sis) *n., pl.* -ses (-sēz). an infection with or illness caused by salmonella bacteria, esp. a type of food poisoning.

salmon trout, any of several large trout that resemble salmon.

sa·lon (sə lon′) *n., pl.* -lons. 1. a reception hall or room, often elegantly furnished and large in size, for receiving or entertaining guests. 2. a gathering of guests in such a room, esp. a periodic gathering of renowned or fashionable people, such as literary figures, artists, or intellectuals. 3. a stylish shop or business establishment, esp. one specially equipped to provide a particular service or product: *a beauty salon, a dress salon.* 4. a place used for the exhibition of works of art. 5. an exhibition of works of art. [French *salon* drawing room, from Italian *salone* hall, drawing room, from *sala* hall; of Germanic origin.]

sa·loon (sə lün′) *n.* 1. a place where alcoholic drinks are served; bar; tavern. 2. a large room or hall for public gatherings or use, as for receptions, esp. the main social lounge on a passenger ship. [French *salon* drawing room. See SALON.]

sa·loon·keep·er (sə lün′kē′pər) *n.* a person who owns or operates a saloon where alcoholic drinks are served.

sal·sa (säl′sä) *n.* a Latin-American dance music similar to the mambo but with elements of jazz and rock music. [Spanish *salsa* literally, sauce; perhaps because it contains a mixture of elements.]

sal·si·fy (sal′sə fē′) *n., pl.* -fies. 1. the edible, carrot-shaped root of a plant, *Tragopogon porrifolius,* of the composite family. 2. the plant itself, having narrow, tapering leaves and bearing showy purple flower heads. Also, **oyster plant.** [French *salsifis* the plant, from obsolete Italian *salsifica;* of uncertain origin.]

sal soda, sodium carbonate *(def. 2).*

salt (sôlt) *n.* 1. a white crystalline compound of sodium and chlorine found in seawater and in mineral deposits, used as a food

seasoning and preservative and as a source of sodium and chlorine. Formula: NaCl Also, **sodium chloride.** 2. any compound formed, along with water, by the reaction of an acid with a base and composed of the positive ion of the base and the negative ion of the acid. 3. **salts. a.** any of various salts used as a laxative, such as Epsom salts. **b.** smelling salts. **c.** bath salts. 4. something that adds interest, liveliness, or humor to something else: *to add the salt of witty remarks to a conversation.* 5. *Informal.* a sailor, esp. an experienced one. —*adj.* 1. tasting of or containing salt: *salt tears.* 2. treated or preserved with salt: *salt butter.* 3. flooded with or growing in or near salt water: *a salt meadow, a salt plant.* —*v.t.* 1. to sprinkle or season with salt. 2. to cure or preserve with salt or a salt solution (often with *down* or *away*). 3. to enrich, as a mine or well, artificially and fraudulently, esp. by placing valuable material at the site. 4. to give (an animal) salt. 5. to add flavor or zest to; make lively or piquant; season. [Old English *sealt* the food seasoning.] —**salt′ness,** *n.*

•**salt of the earth.** any person or persons of good, sturdy character; extremely admirable individual or group.

•**to be worth one's salt.** to be so dependable or capable as to be deserving of wages or support.

•**to salt away.** *Informal.* to store away; save.

•**to salt out.** to cause (materials in solution or suspension) to precipitate by adding salt.

•**with a grain of salt.** with some reservation or skepticism regarding accuracy or truthfulness: *to accept an excuse with a grain of salt.*

salt-and-pep·per (sôlt′ən pep′ər) *adj.* pepper-and-salt.

salt·box (sôlt′boks′) *n.* a frame house of two stories in front and one at the rear, the latter of which is extended under a long, steeply sloping roof. [From its resemblance to the shape of boxes that formerly were used to hold salt.]

salt·cel·lar (sôlt′sel′ər) *n.* a shaker or dish used at the table for holding and dispensing salt. [SALT + obsolete *saler* saltcellar (from Old French *salier(e)* salt box, going back to Latin *sāl* salt).]

salt dome, a dome-shaped geologic structure formed by a large plug of rock salt forcing its way upward through a series of sedimentary strata, as in the Gulf Coast area of the southern United States. Many such structures contain oil and gas.

saltcellar

salt·er (sôl′tər) *n.* 1. a person who manufactures or sells salt. 2. a person who cures something, such as meat or fish, with salt.

salt flat, an expanse of level ground with deposits of salt on the surface, such as the bed of a former salt lake.

salt·ine (sôl tēn′) *n.* a thin, crisp, flat cracker sprinkled with salt.

salt lake, a lake, located in a dry region and lacking an outlet to the sea, that has a high concentration of salts in its waters, often saltier than seawater.

salt lick 1. an exposed natural salt deposit that animals can lick to obtain salt needed in their diet. 2. a preparation of salt with other mineral additives, set out, usually in the form of blocks, as a nutritive supplement for livestock and other animals.

salt marsh, a marsh that is periodically flooded by salt water because of the action of the wind or tide.

salt·pe·ter (sôlt′pē′tər) *also,* **salt·pe·tre.** *n.* potassium nitrate. [Old French *salpetre,* going back to Latin *sāl* salt + *petra* rock (from Greek *petra*); referring to the saltlike crust it forms on rocks.]

salt·shak·er (sôlt′shā′kər) *n.* a container with a perforated top for sprinkling salt.

salt·wa·ter (sôlt′wô′tər, -wot′ər) *adj.* of, relating to, or living in salt water or the sea.

salt·y (sôl′tē) *adj.,* salt·i·er, salt·i·est. 1. relating to, containing, or tasting of salt. 2. of or suggesting the sea or life at sea. 3. lively or witty, esp. in an earthy or coarse way: *salty remarks, salty humor.* —**salt′i·ly,** *adv.* —**salt′i·ness,** *n.*

sa·lu·bri·ous (sə lü′brē əs) *adj.* promoting or favorable to health or well-being; wholesome. [Latin *salūbris* (from *salūs* health) + -OUS.] —**sa·lu′bri·ous·ly,** *adv.* —**sa·lu′bri·ous·ness,** **sa·lu·bri·ty** (sə lü′bri tē), *n.*

sa·lu·ki (sə lü′kē) *also,* **Sa·lu·ki.** *n.* any of an ancient Middle Eastern breed of slender, fast hunting dogs, resembling a greyhound, with a silky coat and feathered ears, legs, and tail. [Arabic *salūgi* literally, native or resident of *Salūg,* an ancient city in southern Arabia.]

sal·u·tar·y (sal′yə ter′ē) *adj.* 1. promoting or favorable to health; healthful: *Hiking is a salutary exercise.* 2. having a bene-

S

ficial effect: *salutary advice.* [Latin *salūtāris* healthful, from *salūs* health.] —**sal·u·tar·i·ly** (sal′yə ter′ə lē, sal′yə ter′-), *adv.* —**sal′u·tar′i·ness,** *n.*

sal·u·ta·tion (sal′yə tā′shən) *n.* **1.** the act of greeting or saluting by gestures or words. **2.** a gesture or expression used in greeting or saluting. **3.** a word or phrase of greeting, such as "Dear Sir," opening a letter and preceding the body of the letter.

sa·lu·ta·to·ri·an (sə lü′tə tôr′ē ən) *n.* a student, usually ranking second in his or her class, who delivers the salutatory at a commencement exercise.

sa·lu·ta·to·ry (sə lü′tə tôr′ē) *adj.* of, relating to, or expressing a greeting or salutation. —*n., pl.* **-ries.** the opening address given at a commencement exercise.

sa·lute (sə lüt′) *v.,* **-lut·ed, -lut·ing.** —*v.t.* **1.** to recognize formally or pay respect to (a superior officer) in a prescribed manner, esp. by raising the right hand to the forehead. **2.** to honor or recognize (someone or something) ceremoniously: *They saluted the visiting ambassador by firing the ship's guns.* **3.** to greet or address with words or gestures of welcome, good wishes, or respect: *The president saluted the cheering crowds by smiling and waving.* **4.** to strike, as the senses. —*v.i.* to make a gesture of respect or formal or ceremonious recognition. —*n.* **1.** the act, gesture, or ceremony of saluting. **2.** a position or attitude assumed in saluting: *to stand at salute.* [Latin *salūtāre* to greet, wish health to, from *salūs* health.] —**sa·lut′er,** *n.*

Salv., Salvador.

sal·va·ble (sal′və bəl) *adj.* capable of being saved or salvaged. [Late Latin *salvāre* to save (from Latin *salvus* unharmed, well[1]) + -ABLE.] —**sal′va·bil′i·ty,** *n.*

Sal·va·do·ran (sal′və dôr′ən) *n.* a native or citizen of El Salvador. —*adj.* of, relating to, or characteristic of El Salvador or its people or culture. Also, **Sal′va·do′ri·an.**

sal·vage (sal′vij) *v.t.,* **-vaged, -vag·ing.** to save or rescue from loss or destruction: *The crew managed to salvage the cargo of the sinking ship.* —*n.* **1.** the act of saving a ship or its crew or cargo from loss or destruction. **2.** a ship, crew, or cargo so saved. **3.** the compensation given to those who aid in saving a ship or its crew or cargo from loss or destruction. **4.** the act of saving any endangered property from damage, loss, or destruction. **5.** property so saved. [Middle French *salvage* compensation to those who aid in saving a ship or its cargo, going back to Latin *salvus* unharmed, well[1].] —**sal′vage·a·bil′i·ty,** *n.* —**sal′vage·a·ble,** *adj.* —**sal′vag·er,** *n.*

sal·va·tion (sal vā′shən) *n.* **1.** deliverance from difficulty, danger, destruction, or evil. **2.** the source, cause, or means of such deliverance. **3.** *Religion.* deliverance of the soul from sin and from punishment for sin; redemption. [Late Latin *salvātiō* a saving, going back to Latin *salvus* unharmed, well[1].]

Salvation Army, an international Protestant evangelical and charitable organization founded in England in 1865 by William Booth.

salve[1] (sav, säv) *n.* **1.** a semisolid preparation, usually medicated, for external application, used esp. in the treatment of injuries and skin disorders; ointment. **2.** anything that soothes, remedies, or assuages: *a salve for one's conscience.* —*v.t.,* **salved, salv·ing. 1.** to soothe; assuage: *Kind words salved my hurt feelings.* **2.** to put salve on: *to salve a burn.* [Old English *sealf* the ointment.]

salve[2] (salv) *v.t.,* **salved, salv·ing.** to salvage. [From SALVAGE.]

sal·ver (sal′vər) *n.* a tray, usually made of metal, used esp. for serving food or drink. [Spanish *salva* tray, from *salvar* to taste food (placed on a tray) in order to detect poison, to save, from Late Latin *salvāre* to save. See SALVABLE.]

sal·vi·a (sal′vē ə) *n.* any of a large group of plants, genus *Salvia,* of the mint family, found in temperate and warm regions throughout the world, esp. those grown for their flowers, such as the scarlet sage, *S. splendens.* [Modern Latin *Salvia,* from Latin *salvia* the plant sage; literally, the healing plant. See SAGE[2].]

sal·vo (sal′vō) *n., pl.* **-vos** or **-voes. 1.** a simultaneous firing of several guns, often as a salute. **2.** the simultaneous release of all the bombs or missiles carried by an aircraft. **3.** the projectiles so fired or the bombs or missiles so released. **4.** a sudden outburst, as of cheers or applause. [Italian *salva* firing of guns as a salute, from Latin *salvē* hail, be well, imperative of *salvēre* to be well.]

sal vo·la·ti·le (sal′və lat′ə lē′) an aromatic solution of ammonium carbonate, used as smelling salts. [Modern Latin *sal volatile* literally, volatile salt; referring to the fact that it evaporates easily. See SAL, VOLATILE.]

SAM (sam) a missile that is capable of traveling from the earth to a target in space. [Short for *s(urface-to-)a(ir) m(issile).*]

Sam., Samuel.

S. Am. 1. South America. **2.** South American.

sam·a·ra (sam′ər ə, sə mâr′ə) *n.* a dry fruit, as of the maple or elm, whose seed or seeds are covered by a winglike structure that aids dispersal by the wind. Also, **key fruit.** [Latin *samara* seed of the elm; possibly of Celtic origin.]

Sa·mar·i·tan (sə mar′i tən) *n.* **1.** a member of the people who inhabited Samaria. **2.** Good Samaritan. —*adj.* of or relating to Samaria or its people.

sa·mar·i·um (sə mâr′ē əm) *n.* a silvery metallic element of the rare-earth group, used in the production of certain lasers and in nuclear reactors. Symbol: **Sm** For tables, see **element.** [Modern Latin *samarium,* from earlier *samarskite* a mineral in which it was discovered, from Colonel von *Samarski,* a nineteenth-century Russian mine inspector.]

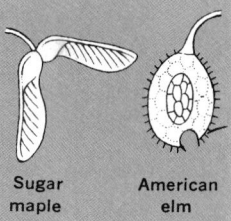

Sugar maple   American elm

samaras

sam·ba (sam′bə, säm′-) *n.* **1.** a dance of Brazilian origin characterized by a dipping movement of the knees. **2.** the music for this dance. —*v.i.* to dance the samba. [Portuguese *samba;* of African origin.]

Sam Browne belt (sam′broun′) a belt for a military or similar uniform, with a supporting strap running diagonally from the left of the waist and passing over the right shoulder, designed to carry the weight of a pistol or sword. [From Sir Samuel J. *Browne,* 1824-1901, British general who designed it.]

same (sām) *adj.* **1.** resembling another in every respect; exactly alike: *The twin sisters wore the same dress to the dance.* **2.** having a single or particular identity; being the very one; not another: *He's the same boy I sat next to in class last year.* **3.** unchanged, as in character: *You are the same generous person now as you were years ago.* **4.** just mentioned or indicated; aforesaid. —*n.* a person or thing that is the same. [Old English *same* similarly.]

• **all the same. a.** in spite of everything; nonetheless: *You may think the report is accurate, but I'd check it out all the same.* **b.** not a matter for concern; equally acceptable: *It's all the same to me whether you stay or go.*

• **just the same.** nevertheless.

• **the same.** in the same manner: *I feel the same as you about it.*

Synonyms *adj.* **Same, identical,** and **equivalent** mean having the characteristics of another or of a group of others. **Same** may indicate that the things compared are practically indistinguishable or that they do not differ significantly: *They appeared at the Halloween party wearing exactly the same costume. The applicants for the job had the same educational background.* **Identical** implies that two or more things are similar enough to be indistinguishable: *The two travelers had identical suitcases.* **Equivalent** suggests that things being compared are roughly alike and may be interchangeable in quality or quantity: *The generic form of this drug is the equivalent of the brand-name product.*

same·ness (sām′nis) *n.* **1.** the state or quality of being the same. **2.** the absence of variety; monotony.

S. Amer. 1. South America. **2.** South American.

sam·i·sen (sam′ə sen′) *n.* a musical instrument of Japanese origin, resembling a banjo but having three strings. [Japanese *samisen,* from Chinese (Mandarin) *san hsien* three strings.]

sam·ite (sam′īt, sā′mīt) *n.* a heavy, rich silk fabric, usually interwoven with gold or silver threads. [Old French *samit,* from Medieval Latin *examitum,* from Late Greek *hexamiton* fabric woven with six threads, from Greek *hex* six + *mitos* thread.]

Sam·nite (sam′nīt) *n.* **1.** a member of an ancient Italic tribe conquered by the Romans in the third century B.C. **2.** their extinct language, belonging to the Italic branch of the Indo-European language family.

Sa·mo·an (sə mō′ən) *n.* **1.** a member or close descendant of the people of Samoa. **2.** the language spoken by these people, belonging to the Polynesian branch of the Austronesian family of languages. —*adj.* of, relating to, or characteristic of Samoa or its people, language, or culture.

Sa·mo·a Standard Time (sə mō′ə) the local time used in American Samoa and the Midway Islands. It is 11 hours earlier than Greenwich Time.

a	at	e	end	o	hot	u	up	hw	white		about
ā	ape	ē	me	ō	old	ū	use	ng	song	ə	taken
ä	far	i	it	ô	fork	ü	rule	th	thin		pencil
âr	care	ī	ice	oi	oil	u̇	pull	th	this		lemon
		îr	pierce	ou	out	ûr	turn	zh	measure		circus

sam·o·var (sam′ə vär′, sam′ə vär′) *n.* a metal urn having a spigot and an internal heating tube, used esp. in Russia for boiling water for tea. [Russian *samover* literally, self-boiler.]

Sam·o·yed (sam′ə yed′) *n.* **1.** a member of a nomadic people speaking a Ural-Altaic language and living in northwestern Siberia and northeastern Russia. **2.** a dog of a breed originally developed in Siberia for pulling sleds and herding reindeer, having a thick, white coat that forms a ruff around the shoulders. Height: 24 inches (61 centimeters) at the shoulder.

Samoyed *(def. 2)*

samp (samp) *n.* **1.** coarsely ground hominy or Indian corn. **2.** a porridge made of this. [Algonquian *(na)saump* mush.]

sam·pan (sam′pan′) *n.* a small, flat-bottomed boat, as used in China and Japan, usually propelled by a scull at the stern and often having a single sail and a rounded shelter made of mats. [Chinese (Mandarin) *san pan* literally, three boards.]

sam·phire (sam′fīr) *n.* glasswort. [Earlier *sampire,* modification of French *(herbe de) Saint Pierre* Saint Peter's (herb).]

sam·ple (sam′pəl) *n.* **1.** a small part or piece of anything, or a single item of a group, that shows the quality, nature, or characteristics of the whole: *This drawing is a sample of the artist's work.* **2.** a number of individuals or items selected from a group for analysis: *a random sample of residents for an opinion poll.* Also *(def. 2),* **sampling.** *—v.t.,* **-pled, -pling.** to test or determine the quality of by taking a sample: *I sampled the soup, and it needs salt.* *—adj.* serving as a sample: *a sample piece of wallpaper.* [Short for Old French *essample* illustration, pattern. See EXAMPLE.] —For Synonyms *(n.),* see **example.**

sam·pler[1] (sam′plər) *n.* a cloth embroidered with designs or letters to show a person's ability in needlework. [Short for Old French *essemplaire* pattern, sample, going back to Latin *exemplum.*]

sam·pler[2] (sam′plər) *n.* a person who samples. [SAMPLE + -ER[1].]

sam·pling (sam′pling) *n.* **1.** sample *(def. 2).* **2.** the act or process of taking such a sample.

Sam·son (sam′sən) *n.* any man of great strength. [From *Samson,* a judge of Israel, famous for his great strength (Judges 13-16).]

Sam·u·el (sam′ū əl) *n.* either of two books, I Samuel and II Samuel, in the Old Testament, containing Hebrew history from the birth of the Hebrew prophet Samuel to the death of King David.

sam·u·rai (sam′ù rī′) *n., pl.* **-rai. 1.** in feudal Japan, a member of the warrior class, who were vassals of the daimyo or feudal nobility. **2.** the warrior class itself. [Japanese *samurai* warrior.]

samurai
a Japanese print depicting samurai in combat

San (sän) *n., pl.* **Sans** or **San. 1.** a member of a group of southern African people who speak a Khoisan language and live largely in the region of the Kalahari Desert. **2.** their language, belonging to the Khoisan language family. Also, **Bushman.**

san·a·tive (san′ə tiv) *adj.* having the power to heal or cure. [Medieval Latin *sanativus,* going back to Latin *sānus* healthy.]

san·a·to·ri·um (san′ə tôr′ē əm) *n., pl.* **-to·ri·ums** or **-to·ri·a** (-tôr′ē ə). **1.** an institution or establishment for the care and treatment of patients affected with chronic diseases, such as tuberculosis, that require long-term care. **2.** sanitarium *(def. 1).* [Modern Latin *sanatorium,* from Late Latin *sānātōrius* giving health, going back to Latin *sānus* healthy.]

San·cho Pan·za (san′chō pan′zə; *Spanish* sän′chō pän′thä) the peasant squire of Don Quixote, noted for his simple, practical nature.

sanc·ti·fy (sangk′tə fī′) *v.t.,* **-fied, -fy·ing. 1.** to set apart or designate as sacred or holy; consecrate. **2.** to make free from sin; purify. **3.** to give religious sanction to, so as to render legitimate or binding: *to sanctify a marriage with a religious ceremony.* **4.** to give moral, social, or intellectual approval to: *to sanctify a custom by long practice.* [Church Latin *sānctificāre* to make holy, from Latin *sānctus* holy + *facere* to make.] —**sanc′ti·fi·ca′tion,** *n.* —**sanc′ti·fi′er,** *n.*

sanc·ti·mo·ni·ous (sangk′tə mō′nē əs) *adj.* making a hypocritical, exaggerated, or smug show of piety or righteousness. —**sanc′ti·mo′ni·ous·ly,** *adv.* —**sanc′ti·mo′ni·ous·ness,** *n.*

sanc·ti·mo·ny (sangk′tə mō′nē) *n.* a hypocritical, exaggerated, or smug show of piety or righteousness. [Latin *sānctimōnia* piety.]

sanc·tion (sangk′shən) *v.t.* **1.** to give approval, support, or encouragement to; countenance: *The new owners do not sanction hunting on their land.* **2.** to permit, accept, or approve officially or authoritatively: *The court sanctioned the new law.* —*n.* **1.** official permission, acceptance, or approval. **2.** approval or encouragement that serves to render something acceptable or permissible. **3.** *usually,* **sanctions.** in international law, an action instituted by one or more countries to bring pressure on another country to force it to comply with legal obligations. **4.a.** a provision of a law requiring a penalty for disobedience to or violation of it. **b.** the penalty so provided. **5.** a binding force, or something that gives binding force. [Latin *sānctiō* a decreeing of something as inviolable, ordinance.] —**sanc′tion·er,** *n.* —For Synonyms *(v.t.),* see **approve.**

sanc·ti·ty (sangk′ti tē) *n., pl.* **-ties. 1.** piety, as of life or character; saintliness; godliness. **2.** the quality or state of being holy; sacredness. **3.** the quality or state of being regarded with respect or reverence: *the sanctity of individual rights.* **4.** *usually,* **sanctities.** something considered sacred. [Latin *sānctitās* holiness.]

sanc·tu·ar·y (sangk′chü er′ē) *n., pl.* **-ar·ies. 1.** any place of refuge or protection. **2.** the refuge or protection provided by such a place: *The ambassador who defected sought sanctuary in our country.* **3.a.** a holy or sacred place, such as a church, temple, or mosque. **b.** the most holy part of such a place. **4.** the area in a church around the main altar, including the area occupied by the clergy; chancel. **5.** any of the Temples in ancient Jerusalem, or its holy of holies. **6.** a wildlife preserve where animals are protected from hunters and can live unmolested. [Latin *sānctuārium* shrine.] —For Synonyms, see **shelter.**

sanc·tum (sangk′təm) *n., pl.* **-tums** or **-ta** (-tə). **1.** a holy or sacred place. **2.** a private retreat or room where one can be undisturbed. [Latin *sānctum* holy place.]

sanc·tum sanc·to·rum (sangk′təm sangk tôr′əm) **1.** holy of holies *(def. 1).* **2.** a place of privacy. [Latin *sānctum sānctorum* holy of holies.]

Sanc·tus (sangk′təs) *n.* a hymn coming just before the canon in the Mass and other Eucharistic services. [Latin *sānctus* holy; the first word of this hymn.]

sand (sand) *n.* **1.** loose, gritty material consisting of tiny, hard particles derived from rocks and minerals by the natural action of water or ice. **2.** *usually,* **sands.** a tract or region covered with or composed mainly of this material, such as a desert or beach. **3. sands.** moments or portions of life or time, as if measured by an hourglass. —*v.t.* **1.** to scrape, smooth, or polish with sand or sandpaper: *to sand a floor.* **2.** to sprinkle or cover with or as with sand. **3.** to add sand to. **4.** to fill up with sand. [Old English *sand* the loose, gritty material.]

san·dal (san′dəl) *n.* **1.** a shoe consisting of a sole that is held to the foot by one or more straps or thongs. **2.** a shoe having a top cut with openwork and usually fastened with a strap or straps, worn esp. by children. [Latin *sandalium* sole held to the foot by straps, going back to Greek *sandalon.*]

san·dal·wood (san′dəl wŭd′) *n.* **1.** the hard, yellowish, fine-grained wood of an evergreen tree, *Santalum album,* used for making ornamental boxes, chests, and fans and yielding a fragrant oil used in perfumes and soaps. **2.** the tree yielding this wood, cultivated throughout most of Asia, and bearing leathery oval leaves and trumpet-shaped flowers.

sand·bag (sand′bag′) *n.* **1.** a bag filled with or designed to hold sand, used as ballast, in military fortifications, and in strengthening levees during floods. **2.** a small, narrow bag filled with sand and used as a clublike weapon. —*v.t.,* **-bagged, -bag·ging. 1.** to place sandbags in or around; furnish with sandbags: *to*

sandbag *the banks of a river.* **2.** to hit or stun with a sandbag. **3.** *Informal.* to force to do something: *to be sandbagged into making a decision one hoped to avoid making.*

sand·bank (sand'bangk') *n.* a ridge or mass of sand, as on a hillside or shoal.

sand·bar (sand'bär') *also,* **sand bar.** *n.* a mass or ridge of sand, gravel, or other alluvial material deposited in a river or bay or along the shore, built up by the action of waves and currents and often obstructing navigation.

sand·blast (sand'blast') *v.t.* to clean, grind, or decorate (a hard surface, such as glass, metal, or the exterior of a building) by means of a high-speed stream of sand or other abrasive material. —*n.* a high-speed stream of such abrasive material, or the equipment used to provide it.

sand·box (sand'boks') *n.* a low, boxlike structure filled with sand for children to play in.

sand·bur (sand'bûr') *also,* **sand·burr.** *n.* any of several weedy plants, genus *Cenchrus,* found in tropical and temperate regions, whose seeds are covered by spiny burs.

sand·dab (sand'dab', san'-) *n., pl.* **-dab** or **-dabs.** any of various small to medium-sized, edible flounder of the genus *Citharichthys,* ranging from Alaska to Costa Rica.

sand dollar, any of a group of round, flat, spiny echinoderms, class Echinoidea, living on the sandy bottom of shallow ocean waters throughout the world.

sand·er (san'dər) *n.* **1.** a machine that sands, usually electric-powered and used esp. for floors or woodwork. **2.** a person who sands.

sand flea 1. a flea found in sandy places, such as the chigoe. **2.** any of various small crustaceans that are found on sandy beaches and that leap or hop like fleas.

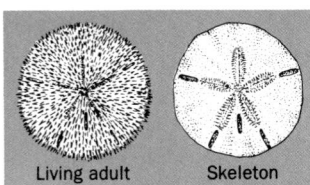

Living adult   Skeleton

sand dollars

sand·fly (sand'flī') *n., pl.* **-flies.** any of a group of tiny, mosquitolike, bloodsucking flies, order Diptera, found near the seashore and in damp areas, that cause several human diseases.

sand·glass (sand'glas') *n.* hourglass.

sand·hog (sand'hôg', -hog') *n.* a laborer who works on underground or underwater construction projects, as in a caisson.

S & L *also,* **S and L** savings and loan association.

sand·lot (sand'lot') *also,* **sand·lot.** *adj.* of or relating to games played by amateurs, often in organized leagues and traditionally in a vacant lot: *sandlot baseball.*

sand·man (sand'man') *n., pl.* **-men** (-men'). in folklore, a man who makes children sleepy by sprinkling sand on their eyes at bedtime.

sand·pa·per (sand'pā'pər) *n.* a strong, heavy paper with a coating of sand or other abrasive material bonded to it, used for smoothing, polishing, or cleaning surfaces. —*v.t.* to smooth, polish, or clean by rubbing with sandpaper.

sand·pip·er (sand'pī'pər) *n.* any of various shorebirds, family Scolopacidae, having a long, slender bill, long legs, and brown or grayish plumage. Length: 5-12 inches (13-30 centimeters).

sand·stone (sand'stōn') *n.* a sedimentary rock composed of sand grains, usually of the mineral quartz, cemented together by lime, silica, or the like, widely used as a building material.

sand·storm (sand'stôrm') *n.* a storm of high winds that carry sand through the air, commonly occurring in desert areas.

sandpiper

sand trap, a hazard on a golf course formed by a pit or other depression in the ground filled with sand.

sand·wich (sand'wich) *n.* **1.** two or more slices of bread with a filling of meat, cheese, or other food. **2.** something resembling a sandwich: *an ice-cream sandwich.* —*v.t.* to place, fit, or insert tightly: *The folder was sandwiched in between the two bulging files in the drawer.* [From the fourth Earl of *Sandwich,* 1718-92, who supposedly devised the sandwich so that he would not have to interrupt his card game and leave the gambling table to eat.]

sandwich board *also,* **sandwich boards.** a pair of signboards, each of which bears an advertisement or public notice, connected at the top by straps so as to hang from the wearer's shoulders.

sandwich man, a person who is hired to advertise by wearing a sandwich board.

sand·wort (sand'wûrt') *n.* any of a group of low-growing plants with small, white flower clusters, genus *Arenaria,* related to the carnation and the pink and found in temperate regions of the Northern Hemisphere.

sand·y (san'dē) *adj.,* **sand·i·er, sand·i·est. 1.** consisting of, covered with, or like sand. **2.** yellowish red in color: *a sandy moustache.* —**sand'i·ness,** *n.*

sane (sān) *adj.,* **san·er, san·est. 1.** sound and healthy in mind. **2.** having, showing, or proceeding from sound, clear judgment; sensible; rational: *sane advice, a sane approach to the problem.* [Latin *sānus* sound [2], healthy.] —**sane'ly,** *adv.* —**sane'ness,** *n.*

San·for·ize (san'fə rīz') *v.t.,* **-ized, -iz·ing.** to process (fabric) so as to be Sanforized.

San·for·ized (san'fə rīzd') *adj.* *Trademark.* (of fabric) preshrunk by a patented process before being made into clothing. [From *Sanford* L. Cluett, 1874-1968, American inventor of the process.]

sang (sang) the past tense of **sing.**

sang-froid (sän frwä') *n.* a calm and unemotional manner; cool composure: *sang-froid in the face of a mugger.* [French *sang froid* literally, cold blood, from Latin *sanguis* blood + *frīgidus* cold.]

san·gri·a (sang grē'ə, säng-) *n.* a drink usually consisting of red wine and citrus fruit.

san·gui·nar·y (sang'gwə ner'ē) *adj.* **1.** characterized by or involving much bloodshed; bloody. **2.** eager to shed blood; bloodthirsty. **3.** consisting of or stained with blood. [Latin *sanguinārius* relating to blood, from *sanguis* blood.] —**san'gui·nar'i·ly,** *adv.* —**san'gui·nar'i·ness,** *n.*

san·guine (sang'gwin) *adj.* **1.** cheerful and confident; hopeful; optimistic: *a sanguine personality, a sanguine outlook.* **2.** of a red color; ruddy: *a sanguine complexion.* [Latin *sanguineus* bloody, of blood, from *sanguis* blood, from the humor thought to cause cheerfulness. See HUMOR.] —**san'guine·ly,** *adv.* —**san'guine·ness, san·guin'i·ty,** *n.*

san·guin·e·ous (sang gwin'ē əs) *adj.* **1.** of, relating to, or containing blood. **2.** of the color of blood; red. **3.** of or involving bloodshed. **4.** hopeful; confident; sanguine.

San·he·drin (san hed'rin, -hē'drin, san'hi drin) *also,* **Sanhedrim** (san'hi drim). *n.* the highest religious and judicial tribunal of the Jewish people during the first century B.C. and several centuries thereafter.

san·i·tar·i·an (san'i târ'ē ən) *n.* a person who works or is an expert in the area of public health or sanitation. —*adj.* of or relating to health or sanitation; sanitary.

san·i·tar·i·um (san'i târ'ē əm) *n., pl.* **-i·ums** or **-i·a** (-ē ə). **1.** a health resort. **2.** sanatorium (*def. 2*). [Modern Latin *sanitarium,* from Latin *sānitās* health.]

san·i·tar·y (san'i ter'ē) *adj.* **1.** of or relating to health or to the preservation of health. **2.** free from dirt, bacteria, or conditions conducive to infection or disease. [French *sanitaire* relating to the preservation of health, from Latin *sānitās* health.] —**san·i·tar·i·ly** (san'i târ'ə lē), *adv.* —**san'i·tar'i·ness,** *n.*

sanitary belt, a belt, usually of elastic, for holding a sanitary napkin in place.

sanitary napkin, an absorbent pad, as of cotton, worn to absorb menstrual flow.

san·i·ta·tion (san'i tā'shən) *n.* **1.** the maintenance of sanitary conditions to protect public health, as by disposing of sewage and refuse, ensuring the purity of food, and controlling insects, rodents, and environmental pollution. **2.** the removal and disposal of sewage and refuse. [From SANITARY.]

san·i·tize (san'i tīz') *v.t.,* **-tized, -tiz·ing.** to make (something) clean and free of dirt or germs, as by sterilizing.

san·i·ty (san'i tē) *n.* **1.** a sound and healthy mental state or condition; state of being sane. **2.** soundness and clarity of judgment; sensibleness; reasonableness. [Latin *sānitās* health.]

San Jo·se scale (san'hō zā') a tiny scale insect, *Aspidiotus perniciosus,* found throughout North America, that is destructive to fruit, trees, and shrubs. [Because it first appeared in the United States in *San Jose,* California.]

sank (sangk) a past tense of **sink.**

sans (sanz; *French* säN) *prep.* without. [French *sans,* going back to Latin *sine;* influenced by Latin *absentīa* in the absence of.]

San·scrit (san'skrit) Sanskrit.

sans-cu·lotte (sanz'kyù lot', -kû-) *n.* **1.** a revolutionary in the French Revolution of 1789; Jacobin. **2.** any radical or revolution-

a	at	e	end	o	hot	u	up	hw	white		about
ā	ape	ē	me	ō	old	ū	use	ng	song		taken
ä	far	i	it	ô	fork	ü	rule	th	thin	ə	pencil
âr	care	ī	ice	oi	oil	ù	pull	th	this		lemon
				îr	pierce	ou	out	ûr	turn	zh	measure		circus

ary. [French *sans-culotte* literally, without knee breeches, from *sans* (see SANS) + *culotte* breeches, from *cul* (see CULOTTE); referring to lower-class Frenchmen, who wore trousers rather than the knee breeches associated with the upper classes at the time of the French Revolution.]

San·sei (sän'sā', sän sā') *also,* **san·sei.** *n., pl.* **-sei** or **-seis.** a third-generation Japanese-American. [Japanese *sansei,* from *san* third + *sei* generation.]

san·se·vie·ri·a (san'sə vîr'ē ə) *n.* any of several perennial plants, genus *Sansevieria,* native to dry areas of Africa and southern Asia, having tough, thick, striped or variegated leaves, commonly grown as houseplants. [Modern Latin *sansevieria,* from *San Seviero,* the principality of Raimondo di Sangro, 1710-71, a learned Neapolitan.]

San·skrit (san'skrit) *also,* **Sanscrit.** *n.* the literary and religious language of ancient India, belonging to the Indo-Iranian branch of the Indo-European language family. —**San·skrit'ic,** *adj.*

Words from Sanskrit

Sanskrit, a language from which Hindi, Urdu, Persian, and other Indic and Iranian languages have been derived, is in the Indo-Iranian branch of the Indo-European language family. Although no longer a spoken language, Sanskrit remains the sacred and literary language of Hinduism and Buddhism. Below are some loanwords that have come into English from Sanskrit. Those in the first column were borrowed directly from Sanskrit; the others came into English from Sanskrit through Hindi and various other languages.

ashram	bhang	lilac	pukka
avatar	cheetah	loot	pundit
karma	chintz	mahout	rajah
maharajah	cot¹	mandarin	ranee
maharishi	cowrie	musk	rupee
mahatma	deodar	opal	saccharine
nirvana	ghat	orange	sikh
raga	ginger	pal	sugar
swastika	guru	palanquin	swami
yoga	jungle	pepper	thug

---

sans ser·if (san ser'if) *also,* **sans-ser·if.** a letter or typeface without serifs. [SANS + SERIF.]

San·ta Claus (san'tə klôz') the legendary person who brings presents to children at Christmas, usually represented as a fat, jolly, white-bearded old man in a red suit. [Dialectal Dutch *Sante Klaas.*]

Santa Fe Trail (san'tə fā') an overland route between Independence, Missouri, and Santa Fe, New Mexico, widely used from approximately 1821 to 1880.

San·ta Ma·ri·a (san'tə mə rē'ə) the flagship of the Italian explorer Christopher Columbus on his first voyage to the New World, in 1492.

sap¹ (sap) *n.* **1.** a watery solution that circulates through a plant, carrying minerals, gases, and food materials from one part of the plant to another. **2.** any bodily fluid essential to life, health, or vitality. **3.** energy; vitality; vigor. **4.** *Slang.* a person who is foolish or easily deceived. [Old English *sæp* the watery solution in plants.]

sap² (sap) *v.,* **sapped, sap·ping.** —*v.t.* **1.** to weaken, exhaust, or destroy gradually and stealthily; undermine: *A long illness sapped all my strength.* **2.** to weaken by removing the underlying support of (a structure), as by digging under or wearing away the foundation. **3.** to approach (an enemy position under siege) by the use of one or more protected trenches. —*v.i.* to dig such a trench or trenches. —*n.* a protected trench dug for the purpose of approaching an enemy's position. [Middle French *sapper* to undermine, dig into, from Italian *zappare* to till the soil, from *zappa* spade¹, hoe; of uncertain origin.]

sa·pi·ence (sā'pē əns) *n.* wisdom. Also, **sa'pi·en·cy.**

sa·pi·ent (sā'pē ənt) *adj.* wise; sage. [Latin *sapiēns,* present participle of *sapere* to be wise.] —**sa'pi·ent·ly,** *adv.*

sap·less (sap'lis) *adj.* **1.** without sap; withered; dry. **2.** without energy, vitality, or vigor; dull; insipid.

sap·ling (sap'ling) *n.* **1.** a young tree. **2.** a young person; youth.

sap·o·dil·la (sap'ə dil'ə) *n.* **1.** a tall evergreen tree, *Achras zapota,* found in tropical America, having a heavy, fine-grained wood, bearing an edible fruit, and yielding chicle. **2.** the sweet, apple-shaped fruit of this tree, having brownish yellow flesh and rough, brown skin. [Spanish *zapotillo,* diminutive of *zapote,* from Nahuatl *tzapotl* this tree.]

sap·o·na·ceous (sap'ə nā'shəs) *adj.* resembling soap; soapy.

[Modern Latin *saponaceus,* from Latin *sāpō* soap; of Germanic origin.] —*n.*

sa·pon·i·fi·ca·tion (sə pon'ə fi kā' shən) *n.* the hydrolysis of a fat or oil, using an alkali, to form soap.

sa·pon·i·fy (sə pon'ə fī') *v.,* **-fied, -fy·ing.** —*v.t.* to convert (fat or oil) into soap by saponification. —*v.i.* to become converted into soap. [French *saponifier,* from Latin *sāpō* soap + *facere* to make.] —**sa·pon'i·fi'er,** *n.*

sap·per (sap'ər) *n.* **1.** a soldier employed in laying, locating, or disarming mines or in constructing fortifications and trenches. **2.** a person or thing that saps. [SAP² + -ER¹.]

Sap·phic (saf'ik) *adj.* **1.** of or relating to the Greek poet Sappho. **2.** of or relating to poetic forms used by Sappho. —*n.* a Sapphic line or stanza.

sap·phire (saf'īr) *n.* **1.** a highly prized precious stone, a transparent to translucent variety of corundum, esp. one with a deep blue color. **2.** a deep blue color. —*adj.* having the color sapphire; deep blue. [Old French *safir* the precious stone, from Latin *sapphīrus,* from Greek *sappheiros,* probably from Hebrew *sappīr,* possibly from Sanskrit *shanipriya* literally, dear to the planet Saturn (because gems were often associated with planets).]

sap·py (sap'ē) *adj.,* **-pi·er, -pi·est.** **1.** full of sap; juicy. **2.** *Slang.* **a.** overly or foolishly sentimental; mawkish; maudlin. **b.** silly; foolish. —**sap'pi·ness,** *n.*

sap·ro·phyte (sap'rə fīt') *n.* an organism, such as a fungus or a plant without chlorophyll, that obtains its food materials from dead or decaying plant or animal matter. [Greek *sapros* rotten, putrid + -PHYTE.] —**sap·ro·phyt·ic** (sap'rə fit'ik), *adj.*

sap·suck·er (sap'suk'ər) *n.* any of several North American woodpeckers, genus *Sphyrapicus,* that have predominantly black or brownish plumage and a yellow belly and drill into trees to feed on sap and insects. Length: 8-9 inches (20-23 centimeters).

sap·wood (sap'wud') *n.* the youngest portion of the wood of a tree or woody plant, containing the living cells that are a conduit for sap. Also, **alburnum.** For illustration, see **heartwood.**

sapsucker

Sar·a·cen (sar'ə sən) *n.* **1.** any Muslim, esp. of the time of the Crusades or during the Middle Ages. **2.** any Arab. **3.** a member of a nomadic desert tribe that lived between Egypt and Arabia as early as the fourth century A.D. —**Sar·a·cen·ic** (sar'ə sen'ik), *adj.*

sa·ran (sə ran') *n.* any of various thermoplastic resins used to make transparent wrappings and acid-resistant pipes.

sa·ra·pe (sə rä'pē, -pä) serape.

sar·casm (sär'kaz əm) *n.* **1.** the use of taunting or scornful language intended to mock, wound, or subject to contempt or ridicule: *He feels sarcasm is effective in intimidating people he finds obnoxious.* **2.** such a remark or language. **3.** the characteristic quality of such remarks or language: *The sarcasm in her voice was unmistakable.* [Late Latin *sarcasmos* taunt, bitter jest, from Late Greek *sarkasmos* sneer, mockery, from Greek *sarkazein* to tear flesh like dogs, speak sharply, sneer.]

sar·cas·tic (sär kas'tik) *adj.* **1.** characterized by or having the nature of sarcasm: *sarcastic comments.* **2.** given to the use of sarcasm: *a sarcastic critic.* —**sar·cas'ti·cal·ly,** *adv.*

sar·co·dine (sär'kə dīn', -dēn') *n.* any of a group of protozoans that use pseudopods to grasp food and for locomotion. Also, **sar·co·din·i·an** (sär'kə din'ē ən).

sar·co·ma (sär kō'mə) *n., pl.* **-mas** or **-ma·ta** (-mə tə). any of various highly malignant tumors originating in connective tissue. [Modern Latin *sarcoma,* from Greek *sarkōma* fleshy growth.]

sar·coph·a·gus (sär kof'ə gəs) *n., pl.* **-gi** (-jī') or **-gus·es.** a ceremonial coffin or burial casket placed above ground, usually of stone and often ornamented with sculpture or painting. [Latin *sarcophagus,* from Greek *sarkophagos* literally, flesh-eating, from *sarx* flesh + *phagein* to eat; referring to the making of coffins by the ancient Greeks from a kind of limestone thought to consume the flesh of corpses.]

sard (särd) *n.* a reddish brown chalcedony quartz, used esp. in jewelry. [Latin *sarda* a precious stone, probably carnelian, possibly from Greek *sardion* literally, stone from *Sardis.*]

sar·dine (sär dēn') *n., pl.* **-dines** or **-dine. 1.** a pilchard, esp. a young, small one, used for food and usually packed tightly in oil, in small, flat cans. **2.** any young herring or herringlike fish of the family Clupeidae similarly preserved and used for food. [French *sardine* pilchard, from Latin *sardīna.*]

sar·don·ic (sär don'ik) *adj.* sarcastically mocking or sneering, often in a nasty or bitter way: *a sardonic joker, a sardonic reply.* [French *sardonique,* from Latin *Sardonicus (rīsus),* translation of

Greek *Sardonios (gelōs)* Sardinian or bitter (laughter); referring to the fact that a certain poisonous plant of Sardinia, when eaten, was supposed to distort the face and cause convulsions resembling laughter.] —**sar·don′i·cal·ly,** *adv.* —**sar·don′i·cism,** *n.*

sar·don·yx (sär don′iks) *n.* a chalcedony quartz in which layers of white or black alternate with red or reddish brown, used esp. for cameos. [Latin *sardonyx,* from Greek *sardonyx* literally, onyx of Sardis, from *Sardeis* Sardis + *onyx* fingernail, onyx.]

sar·gas·so (sär gas′ō) *n., pl.* **-sos.** gulfweed. Also, **sargasso weed, sar·gas·sum** (sär gas′əm). [Portuguese *sargaço,* possibly from *sarga* grape; with reference to the resemblance of its sacs to grapes.]

sa·ri (sär′ē) *n., pl.* **-ris.** an outer garment worn chiefly by women in India and Pakistan, consisting of a long piece of cotton or silk wrapped around the body with the free end brought up in front and thrown over the left shoulder. [Hindi *sārī.*]

sa·rong (sə rông′, -rong′) *n.* a skirtlike outer garment consisting of a long, rectangular piece of printed cotton that is draped around the waist, worn chiefly in the Malay Archipelago and other islands of the Pacific by both men and women. [Malay *sārong* sheath, covering.]

sari

sar·sa·pa·ril·la (sas′pə ril′ə, sär′sə pə-) *n.* **1.** any of several climbing or trailing vines, genus *Smilax,* of the lily family, found in Mexico, Central America, and South America, having prickly stems and large, heart-shaped leaves with toothed edges. **2.** the dried, aromatic roots of one of these plants, used to flavor syrups and soft drinks. **3.** a flavoring extract obtained from these roots. **4.** a soft drink flavored with sarsaparilla. [Spanish *zarzaparrilla* the plant, from *zarza* bramble (from Arabic *sharas* thorny plant) + *parrilla,* diminutive of *parra* vine (of uncertain origin).]

sar·to·ri·al (sär tôr′ē əl) *adj.* **1.** of or relating to tailors or their work. **2.** of or relating to clothing or dress, esp. men's. [Latin *sartor* tailor + -IAL.] —**sar·to′ri·al·ly,** *adv.*

sar·to·ri·us (sär tôr′ē əs) *n.* a flat, narrow muscle of the thigh, the longest muscle in the human body, extending obliquely from the hip across the front of the thigh. [Modern Latin *sartorius,* from Latin *sartor* tailor; because it makes it possible to sit in the cross-legged position of a tailor at work.]

sash[1] (sash) *n.* a broad band of cloth or ribbon, often worn around the waist. or over one shoulder as part of a uniform. [Earlier *shash,* from Arabic *shāsh* turban.]

sash[2] (sash) *n.* a frame, esp. a sliding one, in which the panes of glass are set in a window or door. —*v.t.* to furnish with a sash or sashes. [Modification of CHASSIS.]

sa·shay (sa shā′) *v.i.* **1.** *Informal.* to walk, move, or go in a noticeably nonchalant or swaggering manner. **2.** to execute a chassé. [Modification of CHASSÉ.]

sa·shi·mi (sä shē′mē) *n.* a Japanese dish consisting of very thin slices of raw fish, usually served with horseradish paste and soy sauce. [Japanese *sashimi* this food.]

Sask., Saskatchewan.

Sas·quatch (sas′kwoch, -kwach) *also,* **sas·quatch.** *n.* Bigfoot. [Probably from a Salish word meaning wild men.]

sass (sas) *Informal.* n. back talk; impudence. —*v.t.* to talk back to; talk impudently or disrespectfully to. [From SASSY.]

sas·sa·fras (sas′ə fras′) *n.* **1.** any of a small group of aromatic trees, genus *Sassafras,* found in North America and Asia, esp. *S. albidum* of the eastern United States, the bark of whose roots is used as a flavoring. **2.** the bark itself, used to make a tea and to flavor various products, such as root beer, tobacco, and chewing gum. [Spanish *sasafrás* the tree; of uncertain origin.]

sas·sy (sas′ē) *adj.,* **-si·er, -si·est.** *Informal.* impudent; saucy. [Dialectal form of SAUCY.]

sat (sat) a past tense and past participle of **sit**.

Sat., Saturday.

Sa·tan (sā′tən) *n.* the devil. [Late Latin *Satan,* from Greek *Satan,* from Hebrew *sātān* enemy, adversary.]

sa·tan·ic (sā tan′ik, sə-) *adj.* **1.** of or relating to Satan. **2.** characteristic of or befitting Satan; extremely or fiendishly evil or cruel. Also, **sa·tan′i·cal.** —**sa·tan′i·cal·ly,** *adv.*

satch·el (sach′əl) *n.* a bag or valise for carrying clothing, instruments, books, or other articles, sometimes having a shoulder strap. [Old French *sachel* little bag, from Latin *sacellus,* diminutive of *saccus* bag. See SACK[1].]

sate[1] (sāt) *v.t.,* **sat·ed, sat·ing. 1.** to fill or satisfy completely: *to sate an appetite.* **2.** to furnish with more than enough; glut. [Probably blend of obsolete *sade* to satiate (from Old English *sadian*) and Latin *sat* enough.]

sate[2] (sat, sāt) *Archaic.* a past tense and past participle of **sit**.

sa·teen (sa tēn′) *n.* a strong cotton fabric woven with a smooth, lustrous finish so as to resemble satin, used for such items as linings and theatrical costumes. [Modification (influenced by VELVETEEN) of SATIN.]

sat·el·lite (sat′ə līt′) *n.* **1.** a celestial body that revolves in an orbit around another body larger than itself; moon. **2.** a device designed to be launched and placed in orbit around a body in space, such as the earth or the moon. **3.** a country dominated or controlled by another, more powerful country. **4.** a follower or attendant of a person of importance. **5.** any subservient follower. [Latin *satellit-,* stem of *satelles* attendant; possibly of Etruscan origin.]

sa·ti (su tē′, sut′ē) *n.* suttee.

sa·tia·ble (sā′shə bəl, sā′shē ə-) *adj.* able to be satiated. —**sa′tia·bil′i·ty, sa′tia·ble·ness,** *n.*

sa·ti·ate (sā′shē āt′) *v.t.,* **-at·ed, -at·ing. 1.** to furnish with more than enough; cloy; glut. **2.** to satisfy completely, as an appetite or desire. [Latin *satiātus,* past participle of *satiāre* to fill, satisfy, from *satis* enough.] —**sa′ti·a′tion,** *n.*

sa·ti·e·ty (sə tī′i tē) *n.* the state or condition of being satiated. [Latin *satietās* sufficiency.]

sat·in (sat′in) *n.* a fabric having a smooth, lustrous, glossy surface, made of silk or various synthetic fibers, and used for such items as evening clothes. —*adj.* resembling satin; smooth and glossy: *satin skin.* [Middle English *satyn(e),* from Middle French *satin,* from Spanish *setuni,* from Arabic *(atlas) zaytūnī* (satin) of Zaitun (now Quanzhou), Chinese city where it was manufactured.]

sat·in·wood (sat′in wŭd′) *n.* **1.** any of several woods having a satiny luster, esp. the wood of a small West Indian tree, *Zanthoxylum flavum,* or of a medium-sized tree, *Chloroxylon swietenia,* of India and Sri Lanka, used for veneers and furniture. **2.** any of the trees yielding such wood.

sat·in·y (sat′ə nē) *adj.* resembling satin in softness, smoothness, or glossiness.

sat·ire (sat′īr) *n.* **1.** a literary work that holds up to ridicule human vices or follies. **2.** the branch of literature composed of such works, or the art of writing them. **3.** any work, production, or presentation similar to such literary works in purpose, content, or technique: *That movie's a clever satire on the advertising industry.* **4.** the use of wit or irony to expose, attack, or ridicule human faults, vices, or follies. [Latin *satira,* form of *satura* medley, didactic poem on miscellaneous subjects.]

sa·tir·i·cal (sə tir′i kəl) *adj.* **1.** of, characterized by, or of the nature of satire. **2.** given to the use of satire. Also, **sa·tir′ic.** —**sa·tir′i·cal·ly,** *adv.*

sat·i·rist (sat′ər ist) *n.* a person who creates satirical works, esp. a writer of satires.

sat·i·rize (sat′ə rīz′) *v.t.,* **-rized, -riz·ing.** to criticize, attack, or ridicule by means of satire; subject to satire.

sat·is·fac·tion (sat′is fak′shən) *n.* **1.** the state or feeling of being satisfied, fulfilled, or contented. **2.** the act of satisfying or fulfilling. **3.** release from doubt or anxiety. **4.** reparation or compensation, as for a wrong or injury. **5.** an opportunity to repair a wrong, injury, or insult, as by fighting a duel. **6.** the cause or means of being satisfied; source of contentment or gratification: *A job well done can give a person much satisfaction.* [Latin *satisfactiō* amends, explanation.]

Synonyms **Satisfaction** and **contentment** mean the pleasurable condition that follows the fulfillment of a need or desire. **Satisfaction** implies the complete gratification of a need or requirement: *The leaders expressed total satisfaction with the terms of the agreement.* **Contentment** may fall short of total satisfaction, but implies acceptance of the degree of fulfillment one has: *Despite their poverty, the couple derived contentment from the affection they had for each other.*

sat·is·fac·to·ry (sat′is fak′tə rē) *adj.* good enough to meet a need, expectation, requirement, or demand. —**sat′is·fac′to·ri·ly,** *adv.* —**sat′is·fac′to·ri·ness,** *n.*

a	at	e	end	o	hot	u	up	hw	white		about
ā	ape	ē	me	ō	old	ū	use	ng	song		taken
ä	far	i	it	ô	fork	ü	rule	th	thin	ə	pencil
âr	care	ī	ice	oi	oil	ů	pull	th	this		lemon
		îr	pierce	ou	out	ûr	turn	zh	measure		circus

sat·is·fy (sat′is fī′) v., **-fied, -fy·ing.** —v.t. **1.** to meet the needs or desires of; make contented: *The team's performance didn't satisfy the coach.* **2.** to supply fully with what is desired or needed: *to satisfy one's curiosity, to satisfy one's thirst with water.* **3.** to release or set free from doubt or anxiety; assure; convince: *My friend's reassurance that everything was going well satisfied me.* **4.** to fulfill or answer the conditions or requirements of: *to satisfy an equation, to satisfy the requirements of a course.* **5.** to pay off fully, as a debt. **6.** to make reparation for; redress. **7.** to answer convincingly; dispel: *to satisfy objections.* **8.** to give what is due to: *to satisfy a creditor.* —v.i. to give satisfaction. [Old French *satisfier* to make amends, content, going back to Latin *satisfacere*.] —**sat′is·fi′er,** *n.* —**sat′is·fy′ing·ly,** *adv.*

sa·trap (sā′trap, sat′rap) *n.* **1.** the governor of a province in the ancient Persian Empire. **2.** any subordinate official or ruler, esp. a despotic one. [Latin *satrapēs* the Persian governor, from Greek *satrapēs,* from Old Persian *xshathrapāvan* protector of a province.]

sa·trap·y (sā′trə pē, sat′rə-) *n., pl.* **-trap·ies.** the territory or jurisdiction of a satrap.

sat·u·ra·ble (sach′ə bəl) *adj.* capable of being saturated.

sat·u·rate (sach′ə rāt′) v.t., **-rat·ed, -rat·ing. 1.** to fill, supply, or treat with something to the point where no more can be absorbed, esp., to soak thoroughly. **2.** to fill full or to excess: *a room saturated with the smell of perfume, to saturate a market with a product.* **3.** *Chemistry.* to supply (a solvent or solution) with as much of a particular solute as can be dissolved in it at a given temperature and pressure. [Latin *saturātus,* past participle of *saturāre* to fill.]

sat·u·rat·ed (sach′ə rā′tid) *adj.* **1.** *Chemistry.* **a.** (of solutions) containing the maximum amount of solute capable of being dissolved at a given temperature and pressure. **b.** (of organic compounds) having all the valence bonds of the atoms, esp. carbon atoms, attached to other atoms, as in some fatty acids. **2.** (of colors) of the highest intensity of hue; not diluted with white.

saturated fat, any of a class of fats that tend to be solid unless heated and consist largely of saturated fatty acids, such as butter, lard, or coconut oil.

sat·u·ra·tion (sach′ə rā′shən) *n.* **1.** the act or process of saturating. **2.** the state or condition of being saturated. **3.** the degree of intensity or vividness of a color. Also *(def. 3),* **chroma.**

saturation point 1. *Chemistry.* the point at which a chemical solution contains the maximum amount of solute that can be dissolved in it. **2.** the point or level at which the maximum capacity for something is reached; limit: *The market for the toy had reached the saturation point, and sales began to fall dramatically.*

Sat·ur·day (sat′ər dē, -dā′) *n.* the seventh day of the week. [Old English *Saeterdaeg,* translation of Latin *Sāturnī diēs* day of Saturn.]

Saturn

Sat·urn (sat′ərn) *n.* **1.** in Roman mythology, the god of agriculture. His Greek counterpart is Cronus. **2.** the second largest planet of the solar system (after Jupiter) and sixth in order of distance from the sun, having twenty-one satellites. It is surrounded by a system of rings composed of minute ice particles.

Sat·ur·na·li·a (sat′ər nā′lē ə, -nāl′yə) *n., pl.* **-li·a** or **-li·as.** **1.** the principal ancient Roman festival of Saturn, which began on December 17 and continued for seven days, characterized by great public celebration, feasting, and merrymaking. **2. saturnalia.** any period or occasion of unrestrained merrymaking and revelry. [Latin *Sāturnālia* the ancient Roman festival.]

sat·ur·na·li·an (sat′ər nā′lē ən, -nāl′yən) *adj.* **1.** characterized by or of the nature of unrestrained merrymaking and revelry. **2. Saturnalian.** of or relating to the Saturnalia.

Sa·tur·ni·an (sə tûr′nē ən) *adj.* **1.** of or relating to the god Saturn. **2.** of or relating to the planet Saturn.

sat·ur·nine (sat′ər nīn′) *adj.* having or showing a gloomy or moody nature. [SATURN + -INE[1]; referring to the supposedly gloomy disposition of those born under the sign of the planet Saturn.] —**sat′ur·nine′ly,** *adv.*

sat·yr (sat′ər, sā′tər) *n.* **1.** in Greek mythology, a minor deity of the woods and mountains, usually represented as a man having the horns, tail, and legs of a goat. **2.** a lecherous or lustful man. [Latin *satyrus* the woodland deity, from Greek *satyros.*]

sauce (sôs) *n.* **1.** any liquid or semisolid preparation, usually consisting of several ingredients, used in the making of food or served with food to add to or improve the flavor. **2.** fruit that has been stewed into a pulp and sweetened: *cranberry sauce.* **3.** something that adds zest, piquancy, or flavor to something else. **4.** *Informal.* impertinence. **5.** *Slang.* a distilled alcoholic beverage; liquor. ➡ often used with *the.* —v.t., **sauced, sauc·ing. 1.** to prepare or flavor with sauce. **2.** to add zest or flavor to. **3.** *Informal.* to be impertinent to. [Old French *sauce* the fluid preparation, from Latin *salsa,* feminine of *salsus* salted, going back to *sāl* salt.]

satyr

sauce·pan (sôs′pan′) *n.* a small enamel or metal pot with a projecting handle, used for cooking food.

sau·cer (sô′sər) *n.* **1.** a small, usually slightly concave dish, esp. one for holding a cup. **2.** something resembling a saucer in shape. [Old French *saussier* dish for holding sauces, from *sausse* sauce. See SAUCE.]

sau·cy (sô′sē) *adj.,* **-ci·er, -ci·est. 1.** bold or disrespectful in a flippant, brazen, or spirited way. **2.** piquant; roguish; sprightly: *a saucy smile.* **3.** boldly stylish; smart: *a saucy new hat.* [SAUCE + -Y[1].] —**sau′ci·ly,** *adv.* —**sau′ci·ness,** *n.*

Sa·u·di (sä ü′dē, sou′-, sô′-) *n.* a native or citizen of Saudi Arabia. —*adj.* of, relating to, or characteristic of Saudi Arabia or its people or culture.

sauer·bra·ten (sour′brä′tən, sou′ər-) *n.* beef marinated in vinegar, water, wine, onions, and spices, and then cooked like a pot roast. [German *Sauerbraten,* from *sauer* sour + *Braten* roast meat.]

sauer·kraut (sour′krout′, sou′ər-) *n.* finely shredded cabbage that has been salted and fermented in its own juice. [German *Sauerkraut,* from *sauer* sour + *Kraut* cabbage.]

sau·ger (sô′gər) *n., pl.* **-ger** or **-gers.** a small, North American pike perch, *Stizostedion canadense,* used as a food fish. Average length: 13 inches (33 centimeters).

Sauk (sôk) *also,* **Sac.** *n., pl.* **Sauk** or **Sauks.** a member of an Algonquian tribe of North American Indians who formerly lived in what is now Michigan and Wisconsin, now living in Oklahoma, Iowa, and Kansas.

sau·na (sou′nə, sô′-) *n.* **1.** a bath of a kind developed in Finland and resembling a steam bath, in which the bather is exposed to hot, relatively dry air, with steam being produced by water thrown on hot stones. **2.** a room or other enclosure in which to take such a bath. [Finnish *sauna* literally, bathroom.]

saun·ter (sôn′tər, sän′-) *v.i.* to walk in a leisurely, relaxed, or nonchalant way; stroll. —*n.* **1.** a leisurely, relaxed, or nonchalant way of walking: *to walk with a saunter.* **2.** a leisurely walk; idle stroll: *to take a saunter around the city.* [Of uncertain origin.] —**saun′ter·er,** *n.*

sau·ri·an (sôr′ē ən) *n.* a lizard or lizardlike reptile, such as a crocodile or dinosaur. —*adj.* of or relating to lizards or lizardlike reptiles. [Modern Latin *Sauria* (from Greek *sauros* lizard) + -AN.]

sau·ro·pod (sôr′ə pod′) *n.* any of a group of gigantic, plant-eating dinosaurs, suborder Sauropoda, characterized by four pillarlike legs and a long neck and tail, as the apatosaurus, or brontosaurus. —*adj.* of or relating to these dinosaurs. [Modern Latin *Sauropoda,* from Greek *sauros* lizard + Modern Latin *poda* feet (from Greek *podos,* genitive of foot).]

sau·sage (sô′sij) *n.* finely chopped, seasoned meat, such as pork, beef, or veal, made into patties or enclosed in a membranous casing. [Dialectal Old French *saussiche,* from Late Latin *salsīcia* literally, seasoned with salt, from Latin *salsus* salted.]

S

sau·té (sô tā′) *v.t.,* **-téed, -té·ing.** to cook or brown quickly in an open pan using a small amount of very hot fat. —*n.* food cooked in this manner. —*adj.* cooked or browned quickly in a small amount of very hot fat. [French *sauté* fried, tossed in a pan, from *sauter* to toss something occasionally while cooking it in a pan to prevent its sticking, leap, from Latin *saltāre* to dance.]

sau·terne (sô tûrn′) *also,* **Sau·ternes.** *n.* a sweet, white table wine. [From *Sauternes,* area in France producing this wine.]

sav·age (sav′ij) *adj.* **1.** mercilessly brutal; cruel; vicious: *savage fighting.* **2.** of a primitive or early stage of human social development; uncivilized: *a savage tribe that still uses stone tools.* **3.** not domesticated or tamed; wild; ferocious: *savage beasts.* **4.** not affected by people or human settlement; uncultivated; rugged: *a savage jungle.* —*n.* **1.** a person who belongs to an uncivilized people, group, or tribe, esp. one belonging to a people in the most primitive stage of development or civilization. **2.** a brutal, cruel, or vicious person. **3.** a rude, ill-mannered, boorish person. —*v.t.* **1.** to attack or assault violently or cruelly. **2.** to criticize mercilessly or devastatingly. [Old French *sauvage* wild, going back to Latin *silvāticus* relating to a forest, wild, from *silva* forest.] —**sav′age·ly,** *adv.* —**sav′age·ness,** *n.* —For Synonyms *(adj.),* see **barbarian, fierce.**

sav·age·ry (sav′ij rē) *n., pl.* **-ries. 1.** the state or quality of being savage. **2.** a savage disposition, behavior, or act.

sa·van·na (sə van′ə) *also,* **sa·van·nah.** *n.* **1.** a broad, treeless plain with grass or other low vegetation. **2.** a tropical region of grassland with some trees and shrubs. [Earlier Spanish *zavana* large, treeless plain; of Taino origin.]

sa·vant (sa vänt′, sə-, sav′ənt) *n.* a person of great learning. [French *savant,* from *savoir* to know, going back to Latin *sapere* to be wise.]

save¹ (sāv) *v.,* **saved, sav·ing.** —*v.t.* **1.** to deliver or to free from harm, danger, or destruction; make safe: *to save someone's life.* **2.** to set apart or aside for or as for future use (often with *up*): *I save part of my salary each week.* **3.** to keep from being lost, spent, or expended: *We omitted the last step to save time.* **4.** to prevent the need, use, or occurrence of: *to save wear and tear.* **5.** to keep intact or unhurt; safeguard; preserve: *to save one's reputation.* **6.** to treat carefully so as to avoid or lessen damage, wear, or fatigue: *Save your eyes by reading in good light.* **7.** to keep an opponent from winning (a game, match, or the like) or from scoring (a point or points). **8.** to deliver from sin and its consequences. —*v.i.* **1.** to set aside or accumulate money by way of economy. **2.** to avoid expense or waste; economize: *It's difficult to save on groceries.* —*n.* **1.** the act or an instance of keeping an opponent from winning or scoring. **2.** *Baseball.* a game in which a relief pitcher is credited with assuring a win by maintaining the winning team's lead. [Old French *sauver, salver* to deliver from harm, danger, or destruction, from Late Latin *salvāre* to make safe, from Latin *salvus* unharmed, well¹.] —**sav′a·ble;** *also,* **save′a·ble,** *adj.* —**sav′er,** *n.*

> **Synonyms** *v.t.* **Save¹** and **rescue** mean to free a person or thing from danger. **Save** indicates delivery from present danger or potential harm or disadvantage: *The job training program saved many young people from a life of poverty.* **Rescue** emphasizes the use of prompt and forceful action to save someone from current danger: *The police used a helicopter to rescue the drowning child.*

save² (sāv) *prep.* with the exception of; except; but: *No one save the immediate family attended the wedding.* —*conj.* **1.** except; but (often with *that*): *I would have come, save that I had no car.* **2.** *Archaic.* unless. [Form of SAFE with the obsolete meaning of reserving, excepting.]

sav·in (sav′in) *also,* **sav·ine.** *n.* **1.** a spreading shrub, *Juniperus sabina,* of the cypress family, whose tops yield a volatile oil formerly used in medicine. **2.** the oil itself, or a solution prepared from it. [Old English *safine, savine* the shrub, going back to Latin *Sabīna (herba)* literally, Sabine herb.]

sav·ing (sā′ving) *adj.* **1.** making up for something else; redeeming: *The old car's saving feature is its reliability.* **2.** thrifty; economical; frugal. **3.** making or containing a reservation; qualifying: *a saving clause.* —*n.* **1.** the act of a person or thing that saves something. **2.** something saved. **3.** a reduction in expenditure or cost. **4. savings.** money saved, esp. in a bank account. —*prep.* **1.** with the exception of; save. **2.** with respect to or for. —*conj.* except; save.

savings account, a bank account maintained for the purpose of saving money and on which interest is paid.

savings and loan association, an institution, owned by depositors, that offers savings accounts and invests in loans, esp. for home mortgages.

savings bank, a bank whose principal function is to accept deposits, invest its funds, and pay interest on the deposits.

savings bond, a bond issued by the United States government,

which a buyer may cash in for its value plus interest after a certain length of time.

sav·ior (sāv′yər) *also, British,* **sav·iour.** *n.* **1.** a person who saves from harm, danger, or destruction; person who brings salvation. **2. Savior.** Jesus. ➡ often used with *the.* [Old French *sauveor,* from Late Latin *salvātor,* going back to Latin *salvus* unharmed, well¹.]

sa·voir-faire (sav′wär fâr′) *n.* the faculty of knowing exactly what to do and the right or most charming way to do it; social tact. [French *savoir-faire* tact; literally, to know what to do, going back to Latin *sapere* to be wise + *facere* to do.]

sa·vor (sā′vər) *also, British,* **savour.** *n.* **1.** a particular flavor or aroma. **2.** the quality of a thing that affects the sense of taste or smell. **3.** a distinctive or characteristic quality. **4.** the power to arouse interest or excitement. —*v.t.* **1.** to taste or smell with pleasure or zest: *to savor a meal.* **2.** to take great delight in: *The team savored the news that their chief rival had lost also.* **3.** to give flavor to; season. —*v.i.* **1.** to have a particular flavor or aroma (with *of*): *The room savors of garlic.* **2.** to have or show a particular quality or trace; smack (with *of*): *The explosion savors of sabotage.* [Old French *savour* flavor, seasoning, from Latin *sapor* taste, flavor.] —**sa′vor·er,** *n.* —**sa′vor·ous,** *adj.*

sa·vor·y¹ (sā′və rē) *also, British,* **savoury.** *adj.,* **-vor·i·er, -vor·i·est. 1.** agreeable to the taste or smell; appetizing or fragrant. **2.** morally acceptable or respectable: *a savory reputation.* **3.** stimulating or sharp to the taste; pungent. —*n., pl.* **-vor·ies.** a small portion of highly seasoned food served as an appetizer or at the end of a meal. [Old French *savoure* tasty, fragrant, from *savour.* See SAVOR.] —**sa′vor·i·ness,** *n.*

sa·vor·y² (sā′və rē) *n., pl.* **-vor·ies.** any of several aromatic plants and small shrubs, genus *Satureja,* of the mint family, having narrow leaves and bearing clusters of white, pink, or purple flowers, esp. *S. hortensis* and *S. montana,* whose leaves are used to flavor food. [Old English *sætherīe,* from Latin *satureia.*]

sa·vour (sā′vər) *British.* savor.

sa·vour·y (sā′və rē) *British. adj.,* **-vour·i·er, -vour·i·est.** savory¹. —*n., pl.* **-vour·ies.** savory¹.

sa·voy (sə voi′) *n.* a cabbage of a variety having a compact head and wrinkled leaves. [From *Savoy,* France, where it originated.]

Sa·voy·ard (sə voi′ərd, sav′oi ärd′) *n.* a performer in, producer of, or admirer of Gilbert and Sullivan operas. [From the *Savoy Theatre* in London, England, where many Gilbert and Sullivan operas were first performed.]

sav·vy (sav′ē) *Informal. v.i.,* **-vied, -vy·ing.** to know; understand; comprehend. —*n.* understanding, esp. of a practical or shrewd nature; good sense. —*adj.* shrewd or knowledgeable: *a savvy defense lawyer who rarely loses a case.* [Modification of Spanish *¿sabe (Usted)?* do (you) know? from *saber* to know, going back to Latin *sapere* to be wise.]

saw¹ (sô) *n.* **1.** any of various hand or power tools having a metal blade or plate whose edge is notched with pointed teeth, used for cutting wood, metal, or other hard materials. **2.** a machine having such a tool or tools. —*v.,* **sawed, sawed** *or* **sawn, saw·ing.** —*v.t.* **1.** to cut with or as if with a saw: *to saw a log in half.* **2.** to shape or form by cutting with a saw: *They sawed a hole in the ice so that they could fish.* **3.** to cleave or cut through as if using a saw: *to saw the air with a pencil while talking.* **4.** to cause to move with a to-and-fro motion, as if using a saw: *to saw a knife through meat.* —*v.i.* **1.** to use or cut with a saw: *to saw along the grain of wood.* **2.** to be cut with a saw: *This pine saws more easily than hardwood.* **3.** (of a saw) to cut. **4.** to make motions as if using a saw: *The fiddler sawed at the strings.* [Old English *saga* cutting tool with a toothed edge.] —**saw′er,** *n.* —**saw′like′,** *adj.*

saw² (sô) the past tense of **see¹.**

saw³ (sô) *n.* a traditional and familiar saying, esp. one hackneyed from frequent use or repetition, such as *Too many cooks spoil the broth.* [Old English *sagu* a saying.]

saw·buck¹ (sô′buk′) *n.* a sawhorse, esp. one having X-shaped ends that extend above the crossbar. [Translation of Dutch *zaagbok.*]

saw·buck² (sô′buk′) *n. Slang.* a ten-dollar bill. [From SAWBUCK¹ (supposedly from the resemblance of X, the Roman numeral ten, to the ends of a sawbuck); possibly influenced by BUCK².]

saw·dust (sô′dust′) *n.* the fine particles that fall from wood or other material as it is being sawed.

a	at	e	end	o	hot	u	up	hw	white		about
ā	ape	ē	me	ō	old	ū	use	ng	song		taken
ä	far	i	it	ô	fork	ü	rule	th	thin	ə	pencil
âr	care	ī	ice	oi	oil	u̇	pull	<u>th</u>	this		lemon
		îr	pierce	ou	out	ûr	turn	zh	measure		circus

sawed-off (sôd′ôf′, -of′) *adj.* **1.** having one end sawed off: *a sawed-off shotgun.* **2.** *Slang.* of less than average height; short.

saw·fish (sô′fish′) *n., pl.* **-fish** or **-fish·es.** any of a group of large, elongated rays, family Pristidae, having a long, flat snout with sharp teeth along both edges. Length: to 35 feet (10.7 meters).

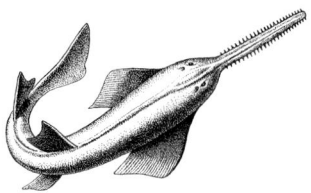

sawfish

saw·fly (sô′flī′) *n., pl.* **-flies.** any of a group of bluish black, flylike insects, suborder Tenthredinoidea, whose larvae feed on the leaves of fruit and shade trees and on the stems of wheat plants. The female has a sawlike organ that she uses to cut holes into plants and insert her eggs.

saw·horse (sô′hôrs′) *n.* a frame on which to rest boards or other objects while they are being sawed, usually consisting of a crossbar supported by a pair of legs at each end. Also, **buck.**

saw·mill (sô′mil′) *n.* a factory or other place where logs are sawed into lumber by machinery.

sawn (sôn) a past participle of **saw**[1].

saw-whet owl (sô′hwet′, -wet′) a small, North American woodland owl, *Aegolius acadicus,* reddish brown with white spots above, and white with red streaks below. Average length: 8 inches (20 centimeters). [Possibly because its call imitates that of a saw being whetted, or sharpened.]

saw·yer (sô′yər) *n.* a person whose work is sawing wood, as in a sawmill. [Middle English *sawier,* from SAW[1] + -IER.]

sax (saks) *n. Informal.* saxophone.

sax·horn (saks′hôrn′) *n.* any of various valved brass wind instruments resembling trumpets or tubas, having a full, mellow tone and a wide range of notes. It is most frequently used in marching bands. [From Antoine Joseph *Sax,* 1814-94, Belgian instrument maker who invented it + HORN.]

sax·i·frage (sak′sə frij) *n.* any of a large group of low-growing or trailing plants, genus *Saxifraga,* native to cool and temperate regions, bearing clusters of white, pink, purple, or yellow flowers, and often cultivated in rock gardens. [Late Latin *saxifraga (herba)* literally, rock-breaking (plant), from Latin *saxum* rock + *frangere* to break; probably because it grows among rocks.]

Sax·on (sak′sən) *n.* **1.** a member or descendant of a Germanic tribe that inhabited parts of northwestern Germany. A portion of this tribe, along with the Angles and Jutes, conquered Britain in the fifth and sixth centuries A.D. and founded the kingdoms of Essex, Sussex, and Wessex. **2.** Anglo-Saxon *(n., def. 1).* **3.** the language of the Saxons. **4.** a person of English nationality or descent. **5.** a native, inhabitant, or citizen of Saxony. *—adj.* **1.** of, relating to, or characteristic of the early Saxons or Anglo-Saxons or their languages or cultures. **2.** English. **3.** of, relating to, or characteristic of Saxony or its people or culture.

sax·o·phone (sak′sə fōn′) *n.* a single-reed wind instrument having a curving conical body made of metal and a series of keys for regulating the pitch of the tones. [From Antoine Joseph *Sax,* 1814-94, its inventor (see SAXHORN) + Greek *phōnē* sound, voice.] —**sax′o·phon′ist,** *n.*

sax·tu·ba (saks′tü′bə, -tū′-) *n.* a large bass or contrabass saxhorn. [SAX(HORN) + TUBA.]

say (sā) *v.,* **said, say·ing.** —*v.t.* **1.** to utter or pronounce the sound or sounds of; speak aloud: *I can't hear a word you're saying.* **2.** to make known or express in words; verbalize; state: *He said he'd call you soon.* **3.** to state as an opinion or with assurance: *No one can say how much longer the strike will last.* **4.** to take for or suppose as a fact; estimate; assume: *Let's say that we'll need two hundred dollars to make the purchase.* **5.** to repeat, as from memory; recite: *to say one's prayers.* **6.** to communicate, as by signs or symbols; indicate; show: *Her actions said more than a thousand words.* **7.** to report or allege; maintain: *Rugby is said to be the roughest of all sports.* —*v.i.* to express oneself; speak; declare: *He saw her an hour ago, or so he says.* —*n.* **1.** the right or chance to express an opinion: *Give him his say before you condemn him.* **2.** the right or power to influence or decide; voice; authority: *to have the final say.* **3.** what one says or has to say: *She said her say and then sat down.* —*adv.* **1.** as an estimate; approximately: *an industrialist who's worth, say, four million dollars.* **2.** for example: *Let's take a*

saxophone

trip, say, along the coast. —*interj.* used to attract attention or to express surprise, pleasure, annoyance, or the like. [Old English *secgan* to tell, declare, utter.] —**say′er,** *n.*

• **that is to say.** in other words.

• **to go without saying.** to be so obvious as not to require that it be stated.

Synonyms *v.t.* **Say, utter**[1], and **state** mean to put into words. **Say** is a broad term indicating the expression of something general or specific in speech or writing: *What did you say to your parents in your letter?* **Utter** emphasizes the act rather than the content of speech: *I was too surprised to utter a word.* **State** is a formal term stressing clarity of expression: *The judge stated the opinion clearly and concisely.*

say·ing (sā′ing) *n.* **1.** a pithy, familiar, commonly repeated statement believed to contain truth, wisdom, or common sense. *A stitch in time saves nine* is a saying. **2.** a commonly repeated phrase, expression, or statement: *He's mad as a hatter, as the saying goes.* **3.** something said; statement: *She collected sayings of her favorite authors in a notebook.*

sa·yo·na·ra (sī′ə när′ə) *Japanese. interj., n.* good-bye; farewell. [Japanese *sayō-nara,* from *sayō* thus, so + *nara* if it be.]

says (sez) the third person singular present indicative of **say.**

say-so (sā′sō′) *n., pl.* **-sos.** *Informal.* **1.** the authority to decide something: *Who gave you the say-so in this matter?* **2.** an authoritative statement or decision: *The architect went ahead with the building plans on the owner's say-so.* **3.** an unsupported statement or assertion: *No one's going to blame me on just your say-so.*

Sb, the symbol for antimony. [Latin *stibium.*]

sb., substantive.

S.B., Bachelor of Science. Also, **B.S.**

Sc, the symbol for scandium.

sc. 1. namely. **2.** scale. **3.** scene. **4.** science. **5.** scientific. **6.** *Sculpture.* he or she carved or engraved it.

s.c. *Printing.* small capitals.

Sc. 1. Scotch. **2.** Scotland. **3.** Scottish.

SC 1. the postal abbreviation for South Carolina. **2.** Security Council (of the United Nations). **3.** Signal Corps. **4.** Supreme Court.

S.C., South Carolina.

scab (skab) *n.* **1.** a crust of dried blood and lymph that forms a protective cover over a wound or sore during healing. **2.** a worker who refuses to join a labor union or who works under conditions contrary to those established by a labor union, esp. one who works when the union workers are on strike. ➡ considered offensive. **3.** scabies *(def. 2).* **4.** any of several plant diseases caused by bacteria and fungi in which crusty or scablike spots form on the leaves, fruits, stems, and roots. —*v.i.,* **scabbed, scab·bing. 1.** to become covered with or form a scab. **2.** to act as a scab.

scab·bard (skab′ərd) *n.* a case or sheath for the blade of a sword, bayonet, or other similar weapon. [Short for Anglo-Norman *escaubers* sheaths; of Germanic origin.]

scab·by (skab′ē) *adj.,* **-bi·er, -bi·est. 1.** consisting of, covered with, or resembling a scab or scabs. **2.** afflicted with scab. **3.** *Informal.* contemptible; low; mean. —**scab′bi·ly,** *adv.* —**scab′bi·ness,** *n.*

sca·bies (skā′bēz, -bē ēz′) *n.* **1.** a contagious skin disease in human beings characterized by intense itching, caused by parasitic mites that burrow under the skin and deposit eggs and irritating wastes. Also, **the itch. 2.** a similar disease in animals, esp. sheep. ➡ used as singular in both defs. [Latin *scabiēs* roughness, itch.]

sca·bi·ous[1] (skā′bē əs) *adj.* **1.** of, relating to, or resembling scabies. **2.** having or resembling a scab or scabs. [Latin *scabiōsus* scabby, scurfy, from *scabiēs.* See SCABIES.]

sca·bi·ous[2] (skā′bē əs) *n.* any of a group of plants, genus *Scabiosa,* of the teasel family, native to Eurasia and Africa, bearing showy blue, rose, yellowish, or white flower heads. [Medieval Latin *scabiosa (herba)* plant believed to heal some skin diseases, going back to Latin *scabiēs.* See SCABIES.]

scab·rous (skab′rəs, skā′brəs) *adj.* **1.** having a prickly or scabby surface; rough to the touch. **2.** difficult to solve or handle; knotty: *a scabrous problem.* **3.** obscene, scandalous, or risqué. [Late Latin *scabrōsus* rough, from Latin *scaber.*] —**scab′rous·ly,** *adv.* —**scab′rous·ness,** *n.*

scad (skad) *n., pl.* **scad** or **scads.** any of various flattened, edible fish with deeply forked tails, family Carangidae, esp. the silvery colored **mackerel scad,** *Decapterus macarellus,* of the western Atlantic. [Possibly modeled on SHAD.]

scads (skadz) *pl. n. Informal.* large quantities or amounts: *There are scads of fish in that lake.* [Of uncertain origin.]

scaf·fold (skaf′əld) *n.* **1.** a temporary wooden or metal platform, often suspended from a roof, used to support workers and materials, as in the repairing or cleaning of a building. **2.** an elevated platform on which criminals are executed. **3.** any raised framework, as for drying tobacco or fish. **4.** a raised stage or

S

stand, as for exhibition purposes. —*v.t.* to furnish or support with a scaffold or scaffolding. [Old French *eschafaud* (earlier *escadafaut*) pieces of wood supporting a platform, possibly going back to Latin *ex* out of + *cata* by (from Greek *kata* down) + *fala* scaffolding (of Etruscan origin).]

scaf·fold·ing (skaf′əl ding) *n.* **1.** a scaffold or a connected series of scaffolds. **2.** materials used to construct a scaffolding.

sca·lar (skā′lər) *adj.* **1.** having only magnitude, as a number used to represent length, mass, time, or temperature. **2.** arranged in or involving a scale or scales; graduated; progressive. —*n.* a scalar quantity. [Latin *scalaris* of a ladder, from *scalae* steps, ladder.]

sca·la·re (skə lär′ē, -lär′ē) *n., pl.* **-la·re** or **-lar·es.** any of a group of South American cichlid fish, genus *Pterophyllum*, with a flattened body and transparent pectoral fins, esp. the angelfish, *P. scalare*, popular as an aquarium fish. [Modern Latin *scalare*, from Latin *scalare* neuter of *scalaris* ladderlike.]

scalar product, a real number that is the product of the lengths of two vectors and the cosine of the angle between them.

scal·a·wag (skal′ə wag′) *also,* **scallawag, scallywag.** *n.* **1.** a white Southerner who aided in carrying out the program of Reconstruction following the American Civil War. ➡ usually used derisively. **2.** a worthless person; rascal. [Of uncertain origin.]

scald[1] (skôld) *v.t.* **1.** to burn with or as if with hot liquid or steam: *The coffee spilled and scalded my hand.* **2.** to clean or treat with steam or boiling liquid: *to scald medical instruments.* **3.** to heat to a temperature just below the boiling point: *to scald milk.* —*v.i.* to be or become scalded. —*n.* a burn caused by hot liquid or by a hot moist vapor, as steam. [Dialectal Old French *escalder* to burn with hot water, heat, from Late Latin *excaldāre* to wash in hot water, from *ex* out, very + *calidus* hot.]

scald[2] (skôld, skäld) *n.* skald. —**scald′ic,** *adj.*

scale[1] (skāl) *n.* **1.** any device or machine for determining the weight of something, as by balancing it against another weight or against the force of a spring. **2. scales.** balance *(def. 7).* **3.** the dish, pan, or platform of a balance. **4. the Scales.** Libra. —*v.,* **scaled, scal·ing.** —*v.i.* to amount to in weight; weigh. —*v.t.* to weigh (something) in or as if in a scale or scales. [Old Norse *skál* bowl, dish of a balance.]

· **to tip the scales** (or **scale**). to have a decisive influence or effect: *The prosecutor's perceptive questions tipped the scales against the defendant.*

· **to tip the scales** (or **scale**) **at.** to have a specified weight of; weigh.

scale[2] (skāl) *n.* **1.a.** one of the horny, flattened, platelike structures forming part or all of the external covering of certain animals, as many snakes, lizards, and fish. **b.** any structure resembling this, as on the wings of some insects or the legs of most birds. **2.** a thin, flat, flaky piece or plate, as of skin. **3.** a flattened, platelike structure or modified leaf that protects developing buds on certain plants. **4.** scale insect. **5.** a crust of metallic oxide that forms on hot metals as they cool. **6.** a crust formed on the inside of steam boilers by the evaporation of water containing minerals. —*v.,* **scaled, scal·ing.** —*v.t.* **1.** to remove the scales or scale from, esp. by scraping: *to scale a fish.* **2.** to remove in thin layers or scales: *to scale the bark off a branch.* **3.** to throw (something flat) so that it moves edgewise through the air or skips across water. —*v.i.* **1.** to peel or come off in scales, flakes, or thin layers; flake. **2.** to become covered with a scale or scales. [Old French *escale* shell, husk; of Germanic origin.]

scale[3] (skāl) *n.* **1.** a graduated or progressive classification, grouping, or order; series or scheme of steps or degrees: *the social scale.* **2.a.** the proportion that a plan, map, model, or other representation bears to what it represents; the ratio of the dimensions represented to the actual dimensions: *The scale of this map is 1 inch to 200 miles.* **b.** a divided line, as on a map, representing or indicating this proportion. **3.** a series of marks made along a line at regularly spaced distances or graduated intervals, used in measuring or calculating: *the scale on a slide rule, the scale on a protractor.* **4.** any instrument marked in this way, used esp. for measuring. **5.** relative extent or size: *The project was undertaken on a grand scale.* **6.** *Music.* a series of tones ascending or descending in pitch according to fixed intervals, esp. such a series contained within an octave. **7.** *Mathematics.* the numbers of a particular numeration system, collectively: *the decimal scale.* —*v.,* **scaled, scal·ing.** —*v.t.* **1.** to climb up or ascend: *to scale*

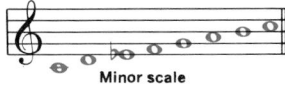

Minor scale

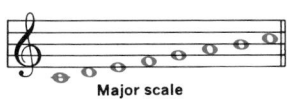

Major scale

music **scales**

a mountain. **2.** to adjust or regulate by or as if by a fixed proportion or scale: *to scale down the level of fighting.* **3.** to make according to a scale: *to scale a drawing.* **4.** to measure by or as if by a scale. —*v.i.* **1.** to climb; ascend. **2.** to rise, as in steps or stages. [Latin *scāla* ladder.] —For Synonyms *(v.t.),* see **climb.**

scale insect, any of various tiny, plant-sucking insects, superfamily Coccoidea, the female of which secretes tough, waxy scales that protect her body.

sca·lene (skā lēn′, skā′lēn) *adj.* (of a triangle) having three unequal sides. [Late Latin *scalēnus* of unequal sides, from Greek *skalēnos* uneven, unequal.]

scal·la·wag (skal′ə wag′) scalawag.

scal·lion (skal′yən) *n.* **1.** a young green onion whose bulb is just beginning to form. Also, **green onion.** **2.** shallot. **3.** leek. [Anglo-Norman *scal(o)un,* going back to Latin *(caepa) Ascalōnia* (onion) of Ashkelon, a city in Philistia (now in Israel).]

scal·lop (skol′əp, skal′-) *also,* **scollop, escallop.** *n.* **1.** any of a group of bivalve mollusks, family Pectinidae, found on the shallow ocean floor, having circular hinged shells, often ridged and with wavy edges. **2.** the edible muscle of certain species of this mollusk, used as food. **3.** one of a series of semicircles or curves resembling the edge of a scallop shell, made as an ornamental border on clothing and other articles. **4.** a thin, boneless slice of meat, esp. of veal. **5.** a shell of a scallop, or a similarly shaped fish, in which food, esp. seafood, is baked or served. —*v.t.* **1.** to shape or ornament with scallops, esp. by cutting: *The edges of the tablecloth were scalloped.* **2.** to bake in a casserole with a sauce, often with a topping of bread crumbs; escallop: *to scallop potatoes.* —*v.i.* to catch or dredge for scallops. [Old French *escalope* shell; of Germanic origin.] —**scal′lop·er,** *n.*

scal·ly·wag (skal′i wag′) scalawag.

scal·lo·pi·ne (skä′lə pē′nē, skal′ə-) *also,* **scal·lo·pi·ni, scalop·pi·ni.** *n.* a dish consisting of small, thin slices of meat, esp. veal, that are sautéed and served in a wine or tomato sauce. [Modification of Italian *scaloppine,* plural of *scaloppina* thin, boneless slice of meat, going back to Old French *escalope* shell; because often served curled like a shell. See SCALLOP.]

scalp (skalp) *n.* **1.** the skin that covers the human skull, usually covered with hair. **2.** part of this skin and attached hair, such as that cut or torn from the head of an enemy as a trophy or symbol of victory. **3.** the skin covering the skull of certain animals, esp. a wolf. **4.** any trophy or symbol of victory. —*v.t.* **1.** to cut or tear the scalp from. **2.** *Informal.* to buy and resell (tickets) at an excessive profit. **3.** *Informal.* to buy and sell (a stock or commodity) quickly in order to make a small profit. —*v.i. Informal.* to scalp tickets, stocks, or commodities. [Probably of Scandinavian origin.] —**scalp′er,** *n.*

scal·pel (skal′pəl) *n.* a small, pointed knife with a straight handle and curved cutting edge, used in surgery and dissections. [Latin *scalpellum,* diminutive of *scalprum* knife.]

scalp lock, a long lock or tuft of hair left on the crown of the shaven head by certain North American Indians as a challenge to their enemies.

scal·y (skā′lē) *adj.,* **scal·i·er, scal·i·est. 1.** covered with or consisting of scales. **2.** resembling scales. **3.** peeling or coming off in scales or flakes; flaking. —**scal′i·ness,** *n.*

scaly anteater, pangolin.

scam (skam) *Slang. n.* a scheme to trick or cheat someone; swindle. —*v.t.,* **scammed, scam·ming.** to defraud or cheat; swindle. [Of uncertain origin.]

scamp[1] (skamp) *n.* **1.** a worthless, dishonest, or unprincipled person; rogue. **2.** a mischievous or playful person, esp. a youngster. [From obsolete *scamp* to roam, from Middle Dutch *schampen* to run away, from Old French *escamper,* going back to Latin *ex* out of + *campus* field.]

scamp[2] (skamp) *v.t.* to do or perform carelessly or hastily. [Probably a blend of SCANT and SKIMP.]

scam·per (skam′pər) *v.i.* **1.** to run or flee quickly or hastily: *The rabbit scampered off into the woods.* **2.** to move about playfully or nimbly: *children scampering about.* —*n.* the act of scampering. [Obsolete *scamp* to roam + -ER[4]. See SCAMP[1].]

scam·pi (skam′pē, skäm′-) *n., pl.* **-pi** or **-pis** or **-pies. 1.** a large shrimp. **2.** a dish consisting of large shrimp cooked in garlic and butter or oil. [Italian *scampi,* plural of *scampo* a type of prawn or lobster.]

scan (skan) *v.,* **scanned, scan·ning.** —*v.t.* **1.** to look at closely and carefully; examine intensively: *She scanned his face for some*

a	at	e	end	o	hot	u	up	hw	white		about
ā	ape	ē	me	ō	old	ū	use	ng	song		taken
ä	far	i	it	ô	fork	ü	rule	th	thin	ə	pencil
âr	care	ī	ice	oi	oil	u̇	pull	t͟h	this		lemon
		îr	pierce	ou	out	ûr	turn	zh	measure		circus

sign of recognition. **2.** to search, pass, or look over (a wide area) thoroughly, esp. by a slow, sweeping movement: *to scan the horizon for a ship.* **3.** to glance over or go through quickly or hastily; skim: *to scan a manuscript for errors.* **4.** to mark off or analyze (verse) according to a metrical pattern. **5.** to sweep or cover (an area) with an electronic detecting device, such as radar. **6.** to trace out closely spaced parallel lines on, as the inside of the large end of a cathode-ray tube. **7.** to cover systematically with a scanner, as in certain types of medical examination. —*v.i.* **1.** to scan verse. **2.** (of verse) to conform to the form of a metrical pattern. **3.** (of the beam from an electron gun) to trace out closely spaced parallel lines that cover a target, as the screen of a television or radar or some other cathode-ray tube. —*n.* **1.** the act of scanning. **2.** the result or product of scanning. **3.** the scope of vision or knowledge; perception. [Late Latin *scandere* to measure verses, from Latin *scandere* to climb, rise.]

Scand. 1. Scandinavia. **2.** Scandinavian.

scan·dal (skan′dəl) *n.* **1.** any action, circumstance, or occurrence that shocks or offends public morality and disgraces those associated with it: *Housing conditions in the slums of this city are a scandal.* **2.** a reaction of indignation, outrage, or strong disapproval produced by such an action, circumstance, or occurrence: *Disclosure of the senator's underworld ties gave rise to a nationwide scandal.* **3.** defamatory talk; malicious gossip: *a family whose name has never been touched by scandal.* **4.** a person whose conduct is a cause of disgrace or dishonor: *The doctor uses unorthodox methods and is a scandal to the medical profession.* **5.** damage to reputation; disgrace; dishonor: *One traitor brought scandal to the whole battalion.* [Late Latin *scandalum* cause of offense, stumbling block, from Greek *skandalon* originally, trap. Doublet of SLANDER.]

scan·dal·ize (skan′də līz′) *v.t.,* **-ized, -iz·ing.** to shock or offend by something considered immoral or improper; outrage. —**scan′dal·i·za′tion,** *n.* —**scan′dal·iz′er,** *n.*

scan·dal·mon·ger (skan′dəl mung′gər, -mong′-) *n.* a person who spreads scandal or malicious gossip.

scan·dal·ous (skan′də ləs) *adj.* **1.** causing scandal; disgraceful; shocking. **2.** consisting of or spreading scandal; defamatory. —**scan′dal·ous·ly,** *adv.* —**scan′dal·ous·ness,** *n.*

scandal sheet, a newspaper or periodical that deals primarily in news of a scandalous or sensational nature.

Scan·di·na·vi·an (skan′də nā′vē ən) *adj.* of, relating to, or characteristic of Scandinavia or its peoples, languages, or cultures. —*n.* **1.** a native or citizen of a Scandinavian country. **2.** a person of Scandinavian ancestry. **3.** the languages of Scandinavia and Iceland collectively, a division of the Germanic branch of the Indo-European language family.

Words from Scandinavian

The Scandinavian languages (Danish, Swedish, Norwegian, and Icelandic) belong to the Germanic branch of the Indo-European language family. Many of the words that English has borrowed from Scandinavian languages originally came from Old Norse, the earliest recorded form of Scandinavian spoken in the Middle Ages. Below are some of the loanwords that have come into English from or through Scandinavian languages.

anger	gaunt	narwhal	skull
axle	geyser	odd	sky
bank	glimmer	ombudsman	slant
blink	gloss	outlaw	slaughter
boulder	gruesome	ransack	smile
brake	haggle	rift	smorgasbord
cake	harpoon	rotten	squall
call	harsh	rug	stumble
cower	hug	rugged	tangle
dandruff	husband	scare	tern
dawn	kitten	schooner	tight
dirt	law	scoff	trust
doze	leg	scour²	ugly
egg²	lemming	scowl	wail
encroach	link	scrawny	waive
fidget	loose	seat	walrus
fjord	lumber	shrivel	weak
fling	meek	sister	whirlwind
flounce	mink	ski	wicker
fluster	muggy	skin	window
freckle	nag¹	skip	wreck

---

scan·di·um (skan′dē əm) *n.* a rare, very light, silver-white metallic element. Symbol: **Sc** For tables, see **element.** [Modern Latin *scandium,* from Medieval Latin *Scandia* Scandinavia; because it was discovered there.]

scan·ner (skan′ər) *n.* **1.** a person or thing that scans. **2.** a device that examines or records by scanning, such as the machine used in performing a CAT scan.

scanning electron microscope, an electron microscope that scans the object being viewed with a beam of electrons. Electrons reflected by the object are collected and used to produce three-dimensional views magnified as much as 10,000 times on a television monitor.

scanning tunneling microscope, a device that uses a tiny electric current flowing between a moving needle and a sample in order to trace the contours of the atoms on the surface of the sample and produce an image of the sample's atomic structure magnified as much as 30 million times.

scan·sion (skan′shən) *n.* the analysis of verse according to one of several metrical patterns, using either long and short syllables, as in Latin poetry, or accented and unaccented syllables, as in English poetry. [Late Latin *scānsiō,* from Latin *scānsiō* a climbing.]

scant (skant) *adj.* **1.** lacking or inadequate in amount or quantity; scarcely enough: meager: *scant provisions for our journey.* **2.** not quite amounting to a specified measure. ➡ often used with the indefinite article, even when modifying a plural noun: *a scant 6 miles, a scant half-hour.* **3.** having an insufficient supply (with *of*): *to be scant of breath.* —*v.t.* **1.** to furnish a scant amount of; skimp on. **2.** to treat in an inadequate or careless manner. [Old Norse *skamt,* neuter of *skammr* short, brief.] —**scant′ly,** *adv.* —**scant′ness,** *n.*

scant·ling (skant′ling) *n.* **1.** a small piece of lumber, used esp. as a vertical member in the frame of a building. **2.** such lumber collectively. [Modification of Old French *escantillon* sample, standard (of weights and measures), going back to Latin *scandere* to climb (probably referring to gradations on a scale).]

scant·y (skan′tē) *adj.,* **scant·i·er, scant·i·est. 1.** scarcely sufficient or inadequate in amount or quantity; meager. **2.** limited or insufficient in extent or size: *a scanty meal.* [SCANT + -Y¹.] —**scant′i·ly,** *adv.* —**scant′i·ness,** *n.* —For Synonyms, see meager.

scape¹ (skāp) *n.* **1.** a leafless flower stalk rising from the ground, as that of the dandelion. **2.** something similar to a stalk, as the shaft of a feather or the shaft of a column. [Latin *scāpus* shaft, stalk¹.]

scape² (skāp) *also,* 'scape. *Archaic. v.i., v.t.,* **scap·ed, scap·ing.** escape. —*n.* escape.

-scape *combining form* view or scene, or a picture or representation of such: *seascape, moonscape.* [From LANDSCAPE.]

scape·goat (skāp′gōt′) *n.* a person or thing made to suffer for or bear the blame for the shortcomings, misfortunes, or mistakes of another or others or against which the irrational hostility or aggression of another or others is directed. [SCAPE² + GOAT; referring to the goat upon whose head Aaron symbolically placed the sins of the people and which was then allowed to escape into the wilderness (Leviticus 16:8, 10).]

scape·grace (skāp′grās′) *n.* an incorrigible, mischievous, or unprincipled person; scamp; rascal. [Short for *escape grace* (suggesting one who has escaped divine grace).]

scaph·o·pod (skaf′ə pod′) *n.* tooth shell. [Greek *skaphos* boat, hollow shell + *podos,* genitive of *pous* foot.]

scap·u·la (skap′yə lə) *n., pl.* **-lae** (-lē′) or **-las.** shoulder blade. [Latin *scapula* shoulder, shoulder blade.]

scap·u·lar (skap′yə lər) *n.* **1.** in the Roman Catholic Church, an outer garment consisting of two long, narrow pieces of cloth hanging from the shoulders in front and behind and reaching almost to the feet, worn by certain religious orders. **2.** two small squares of cloth joined by string, worn under the clothing about the shoulders by Roman Catholics as a mark of religious devotion. **3.** one of the shoulder feathers of a bird. —*adj. also,* **scap·u·lar·y** (skap′yə ler′ē). of or relating to the shoulder or shoulder blade. [Medieval Latin *scapulare* garment covering the shoulders, from Latin *scapula* shoulder, shoulder blade.]

scar (skär) *n.* **1.** any mark, discolored area, or similar trace left, esp. on the skin, by the replacement of tissue that has been destroyed by injury or disease. **2.** any mark or blemish resembling this. **3.** a lasting impression or injurious effect of a distressing or traumatic experience. **4.** *Botany.* a mark indicating a former point of attachment, as where a leaf has fallen from a stem. —*v.,* **scarred, scar·ring.** —*v.t.* to mark with a scar or scars; leave a scar or scars upon. —*v.i.* to form or become marked with a scar. [Old French *escare* scab, from Late Latin *eschara* scab, mark left by a burn, from Greek *eschara* scab, hearth.]

scar·ab (skar′əb) *n.* **1.** any of a large group of beetles, family Scarabaeidae, having stocky, oval bodies, esp. one of a species regarded as sacred by the ancient Egyptians. **2.** a representation of this beetle, such as a gem cut in its shape or a piece of jewelry bearing its image. [Latin *scarabaeus* beetle.]

scar·a·mouch (skar′ə müsh′, -müch′) *also,* **scar·a·mouche.** *n.* **1.** a cowardly, boastful person. **2.** a rascal or scamp. [French *Scaramouche* name of a cowardly braggart in comic plays, from Italian *Scaramuccia,* from *scaramuccia* skirmish; of Germanic origin.]

scarce (skârs) *adj.,* **scarc·er, scarc·est. 1.** insufficient for a need, demand, or requirement: *Provisions were growing scarce aboard ship.* **2.** difficult to acquire or find; rare: *Corn on the cob is scarce at this time of year.* —*adv.* scarcely. [Dialectal Old French *escars* scanty, going back to Latin *excerptus,* past participle of *excerpere* to select, pick out.] —**scarce′ness,** *n.*
• **to make (oneself) scarce.** to go or stay away.

scarce·ly (skârs′lē) *adv.* **1.** by a narrow margin; just; barely: *I had scarcely come in when the phone rang.* **2.** almost not: *There was scarcely a person on the street.* **3.** certainly or most probably not: *A better carpenter was scarcely to be found.*

scar·ci·ty (skâr′si tē) *n., pl.* **-ties. 1.** an insufficient amount or supply. **2.** the quality or state of being scarce.

> **Synonyms** Scarcity and dearth mean a shortage of something. **Scarcity** is used to indicate that a supply is not large enough for a demand: *The scarcity of food was the result of a drought.* **Dearth** suggests the mere absence or lack of something: *There is a dearth of talented musicians in this small town.*

scare (skâr) *v.,* **scared, scar·ing.** —*v.t.* **1.** to cause to be afraid or alarmed, esp. to strike with sudden fear; frighten: *The thunder scared the children.* **2.a.** to drive or force by frightening: *to scare away a thief.* **b.** to cause to be in a specified condition by frightening: *to scare someone speechless.* —*v.i.* to become scared: *I don't scare easily.* —*n.* **1.** a sudden fear or alarm, often with little or no ground; fright: *The sound of the explosion gave me quite a scare.* **2.** a state of widespread or public fear or alarm: *a bomb scare.* [Old Norse *skirra* to frighten.] —**scar′er,** *n.* —**scar′ing·ly,** *adv.*
• **to scare up.** *Informal.* to find, gather together, or prepare hastily: *I'll scare up some lunch for our visitors.*

scare·crow (skâr′krō′) *n.* **1.** a crude representation of a human figure, esp. of a person dressed in old clothes, set in a field to frighten crows and other birds away from crops. **2.** a person resembling a scarecrow, esp. a skinny or ragged person. **3.** something frightening but not really harmful.

scarf[1] (skärf) *n., pl.* **scarves** or **scarfs. 1.** a piece of cloth, usually rectangular, oblong, or triangular, worn for warmth, protection, or adornment, as about the neck or head. **2.** a strip of cloth used to cover the top of a piece of furniture, as a dresser or table; runner. [Probably from dialectal Old French *escarpe* sash, sling; of Germanic origin.]

scarf[2] (skärf) *n., pl.* **scarfs. 1.** a joint in which the ends of two timbers are notched or cut so that they lap over and interlock to form one continuous piece, often secured by bolts or straps. Also, **scarf joint. 2.** the notched or cut end of a timber, used to make such a joint. —*v.t.* **1.** to join by means of a scarf joint. **2.** to cut or notch the end of (a timber). [Probably of Scandinavian origin.]

scarf·skin (skärf′skin′) *n.* the outermost layer of skin; epidermis.

scar·i·fi·ca·tion (skar′ə fi kā′shən) *n.* **1.** the act or process of scarifying. **2.** a mark or marks made by scarifying; superficial incision or scratch.

scar·i·fy (skar′ə fī′) *v.t.,* **-fied, -fy·ing. 1.** to make a number of superficial incisions or scratches in, as in the skin during surgery. **2.** to criticize harshly or severely; wound with cutting remarks. **3.** to loosen, as topsoil, by scratching or breaking up the surface. **4.** to slit or soften the coating of (a seed) to hasten

sprouting. [Late Latin *scarīficāre* to scratch open, going back to Greek *skarīphāsthai* to sketch, scratch an outline.] —**scar′i·fi·er,** *n.*

scar·la·ti·na (skär′lə tē′nə) *n.* **1.** scarlet fever. **2.** *Informal.* a mild type of scarlet fever. [Modern Latin *scarlatina,* from Italian *scarlattina,* from *scarlatto* scarlet, probably from Persian *saqalāt.* See SCARLET.]

scar·let (skär′lit) *n.* **1.** a bright red color, tending toward orange. **2.** cloth or clothing having this color. —*adj.* **1.** having the color scarlet. **2.** offensive in a flagrant way. **3.** sinful or unchaste. [Modification of Old French *escarlate* rich cloth, usually red in color, probably from Persian *saqalāt,* through Arabic and Greek, from Latin *sigillātus* decorated with little figures.]

scarlet fever, a highly contagious disease occurring most often in children, caused by a streptococcus and characterized by a scarlet rash, high fever, and a sore throat. Also, **scarlatina.**

scarlet pimpernel, see pimpernel.

scarlet runner, a tall climbing bean plant, *Phaseolus coccineus,* of the American tropics, bearing clusters of bright red flowers and cultivated as an ornamental.

scarlet sage, either of two salvias, *Salvia coccinea* or *S. splendens,* bearing scarlet flowers, grown as garden annuals.

scarlet tanager, a North American tanager, *Piranga olivacea,* the male of which is bright red with black wings and tail, and the female greenish above and yellow below; redbird.

scarp (skärp) *n.* **1.** a cliff or steep slope. **2.** a wall or steep slope at the outer part of a fortification. —*v.t.* to cut or make into a steep slope; form into a scarp. [Italian *scarpa* slope (of land); of Germanic origin.]

scar tissue, the tough, fibrous connective tissue that replaces any body tissue damaged or destroyed by disease or injury.

scarves (skärvz) a plural of **scarf**[1].

scar·y (skâr′ē) *adj.,* **scar·i·er, scar·i·est.** *Informal.* **1.** causing fear, alarm, or uneasiness; frightening: *a scary movie.* **2.** characterized by fear: *a scary feeling.* **3.** easily scared; timid. —**scar′i·ness,** *n.*

scat[1] (skat) *v.i.,* **scat·ted, scat·ting.** *Informal.* to go away quickly. ➡ usually used in the imperative. [Possibly short for SCATTER.]

scat[2] (skat) *n.* jazz singing consisting of improvisation using nonsense syllables. Also, **scat singing.** —*v.i.,* **scat·ted, scat·ting.** to sing scat. [Possibly imitative.]

scat[3] (skat) *n.* fecal droppings of a wild animal. [Greek *skatos,* genitive of *skōr* excrement.]

scathe (skāth) *v.t.,* **scathed, scath·ing. 1.** to injure or hurt, esp. by burning. **2.** to criticize severely. —*n.* harm or injury. [Of Scandinavian origin.]

scath·ing (skā′thing) *adj.* **1.** bitterly severe; unsparingly harsh: *scathing sarcasm, a scathing rebuke.* **2.** severely injurious or painful. —**scath′ing·ly,** *adv.*

scat·o·log·i·cal (skat′ə loj′i kəl) *adj.* of, relating to, or characterized by scatology. Also, **scat·o·log′ic.**

sca·tol·o·gy (skə tol′ə jē) *n.* **1.** a preoccupation or concern with excrement or excretory functions, as in literature. **2.** the study of excrement, as in paleontology or medicine. [Greek *skat-,* stem of *skōr* dung + -LOGY.]

scat singing, scat[2].

scat·ter (skat′ər) *v.t.* **1.** to spread or throw about randomly or in various places; strew: *A gust of wind scattered leaves all over the yard.* **2.** to cause to separate and go off in various directions; disperse: *The gunshot scattered the herd.* **3.** to drive away or cause to vanish; dispel: *This final setback scattered all hopes for victory.* **4.** *Physics.* to deflect (particles or waves) in a random, unfocused way by collisions or other interactions. —*v.i.* to separate and go off in various directions: *The crowd scattered when the police arrived.* —*n.* **1.** a small, scattered amount: *a scatter of raindrops on the windshield.* **2.** the act of scattering. **3.** *Statistics.* the degree to which related data, as a series of repeated measurements, vary; dispersion. [Probably a form of SHATTER.] —**scat′ter·er,** *n.*

> **Synonyms** *v.t.* Scatter and disperse mean to cause a group of persons or things to break up. **Scatter** suggests the work of a random element or force: *The rough seas scattered the fleet.* **Disperse** suggests the breaking up of a group as the result of an intentional effort: *Police were brought in to disperse the unruly crowd.*

a	at	e	end	o	hot	u	up	hw	white		about
ā	ape	ē	me	ō	old	ū	use	ng	song	ə	taken
ä	far	i	it	ô	fork	ū	rule	th	thin		pencil
âr	care	ī	ice	oi	oil	u̇	pull	th	this		lemon
			ir	pierce	ou	out	ûr	turn	zh	measure	circus

scat·ter·brain (skat′ər brān′) *n.* a person lacking in powers of mental concentration; flighty, forgetful, or unthinking person.

scat·ter·brained (skat′ər brānd′) *adj.* **1.** flighty, forgetful, or unthinking. **2.** contrary to reason or common sense; ridiculous: *a scatterbrained idea.*

scat·ter·ing (skat′ər ing) *n.* **1.** a small, scattered number or amount: *Only a scattering of celebrities was in the audience.* **2.** the act of scattering. **3.** *Physics.* the random deflection of particles or waves, produced by collisions or other interactions.

scatter rug, a small rug used to cover part of a floor. Also, **throw rug.**

scaup (skôp) *n., pl.* **scaup** or **scaups.** any of several broad-billed diving ducks, genus *Aythya,* related to the canvasback and native to cold and temperate regions of the Northern Hemisphere. Also, **scaup duck.** [From Scottish *scaup,* form of dialectal English *scalp* bank of sand serving as a bed for shellfish (on which these ducks feed); of uncertain origin.]

scaup

scav·enge (skav′ənj) *v.,* **-enged, -eng·ing.** —*v.i.* to search, as for food or something salvageable: *Divers scavenged through the ship's wreckage.* —*v.t.* **1.** to find or collect (something) by searching: *They scavenged what food they could to keep alive.* **2.** to search (something) for salvageable material. **3.** to remove dirt or refuse from; clean up. [From SCAVENGER.]

scav·en·ger (skav′ən jər) *n.* **1.** an animal, as the hyena or vulture, that feeds on decaying plant or animal matter. **2.** a person or thing that scavenges, esp. a person who searches through refuse or discarded material for salvageable or useful things. [Modification of obsolete *scavager* officer who supervised street cleaning and, in earlier times, collected a toll on foreign merchants, going back to Anglo-Norman *scawage* the toll itself, inspection, going back to dialectal Old French *escauwer* to inspect; of Germanic origin.]

sce·nar·i·o (si när′ē ō′, -när′-) *n., pl.* **-nar·i·os. 1.a.** a rough script of a planned motion picture, giving an outline of the plot, short sketches of the characters, and other information. **b.** the finished script used during the actual filming of the picture; screenplay. **2.** a plot outline or synopsis of any dramatic work. **3.** an outline, esp. a hypothetical one, for an action or a series of events. [Italian *scenario* scenery, outline of a play, from Late Latin *scēnārius* relating to the stage, dramatic, from Latin *scēna* stage. See SCENE.]

sce·nar·ist (si när′ist, -när′-) *n.* a person who writes scenarios, esp. for motion pictures.

scene (sēn) *n.* **1.** the place where an event or action occurs or has occurred: *the scene of a robbery.* **2.** the place and time in which the action or part of the action of a dramatic, theatrical, or literary work is supposed to occur; setting: *The scene of this story is Germany during World War I.* **3.** a subdivision of an act of a dramatic or theatrical work: *The first scene in the second act contains a lengthy soliloquy.* **4.** an episode, situation, or sequence in a dramatic, theatrical, or literary work, esp. as containing a particular feature: *a murder scene.* **5.** set *(def. 8).* **6.** something presented to the eye; view; picture: *Taxis and buses were part of the street scene.* **7.** a real or imaginary incident, event, or set of circumstances, esp. when described: *The parting of the lovers was a very moving scene.* **8.** a display of strong or excited feeling or unseemly behavior, often resulting in embarrassment or public disturbance: *The angry child made a scene in the restaurant.* **9.** a particular area or field of activity or interest: *the political scene.* [Latin *scēna* stage, background of a stage, from Greek *skēnē* stage; originally, booth or tent in which actors dressed.]
• **behind the scenes.** in private; secretly.

scen·er·y (sē′nə rē) *n., pl.* **-er·ies. 1.** the general appearance or visible features of a locality, esp. the striking or picturesque natural features of a place. **2.** backdrops, hangings, or other structures used to create the setting of a dramatic or theatrical production.

sce·nic (sē′nik, sen′ik) *adj.* **1.** of, relating to, or abounding in natural scenery; picturesque: *a scenic route through the mountains.* **2.** of or relating to the stage or to stage scenery or effects. **3.** representing an action, event, or situation, as in a painting. —**sce′ni·cal·ly,** *adv.*

scent (sent) *n.* **1.** a distinctive smell, esp. an agreeable or delicate one: *the scent of lilacs, the scent of spices.* **2.** a characteristic smell left behind by an animal or person, used as a means of tracking. **3.** the trail or track by which someone or something can be traced or pursued: *Some deceptive clues threw the detectives off the scent of the gang.* **4.** the sense of smell: *a foxhound with a keen scent.* **5.** perfume *(def. 1).* **6.** an inkling; suggestion; trace: *a scent of danger.* —*v.t.* **1.** to perceive, recognize, or identify by the sense of smell. **2.** to perceive as if by smell; get an inkling or hint of: *to scent trouble.* **3.** to make fragrant; perfume: *to put a sachet in a closet to scent the clothes.* —*v.i.* (of a hound or other animal) to hunt by the sense of smell. [Old French *sentir* to feel, smell, from Latin *sentīre* to feel, perceive.] —**scent′ed,** *adj.* —**scent′less,** *adj.* —For Synonyms *(n.),* see **smell.**

scep·ter (sep′tər) *also, British,* **sceptre.** *n.* **1.** a rod or staff serving as a symbol of royal office or power, carried by a sovereign, esp. on ceremonial occasions. **2.** royal office or power. [Old French *sceptre* royal staff, from Latin *scēptrum,* from Greek *skēptron* staff, royal staff.]

scep·tic (skep′tik) skeptic.

scep·ti·cal (skep′ti kəl) *adj.* skeptical. —**scep′ti·cal·ly,** *adv.*

scep·ti·cism (skep′tə siz′əm) skepticism.

scep·tre (sep′tər) *British.* scepter.

sched·ule (skej′ül, -ŭl; *British* shed′ül, shej′ül) *n.* **1.** a list of the times at which certain events are to take place: *a television schedule, a schedule of train departures.* **2.** a plan or group of items to be handled or of events to occur at or during a particular time: *a busy social schedule.* **3.** a detailed plan or program of action, as for a proposed objective, esp. with regard to the time allotted for each item or phase included: *The factory was put on a new production schedule.* **4.** the time planned, indicated, or agreed upon, as in a schedule: *The planes are running behind schedule because of the strike.* **5.** a written or printed table or list, as of rates or prices: *a schedule of postal rates.* —*v.t.,* **-uled, -ul·ing. 1.** to place in or on a schedule: *The airline scheduled additional flights because of the holidays.* **2.** to plan or arrange for a specified time: *I scheduled an appointment with my dentist for Friday.* [Late Latin *schedula* small sheet of paper, diminutive of Latin *scheda* strip of papyrus.]

scheel·ite (shā′līt, shē′-) *n.* a brown, fluorescent mineral mined as an ore of tungsten. Formula: $CaWO_4$ [German *scheelit,* from Karl Wilhelm *Scheele,* 1742-1886, Swedish chemist.]

Sche·her·a·za·de (shə her′ə zä′də, -zäd′, -hir′-) *n.* in Arabic folklore, the bride of a sultan who had resolved to kill each of his wives on the morning after their marriage. She tricked him into sparing her life by relating tales to him nightly for 1,001 nights, in such a clever way that he remained interested in hearing them.

sche·ma (skē′mə) *n., pl.* **-ma·ta** (-mə tə). a diagrammatic or generalized representation, outline, or plan. [Greek *schēma* form.]

sche·mat·ic (skē mat′ik) *adj.* of, relating to, or in the form of a schema or scheme; diagrammatic: *a schematic drawing.* —*n.* a structural or generalized diagram or plan, esp. of an electrical or mechanical system. —**sche·mat′i·cal·ly,** *adv.*

sche·ma·tize (skē′mə tīz′) *v.t.,* **-tized, -tiz·ing. 1.** to form or arrange according to a scheme. **2.** to reduce to a schema or scheme; express or show schematically. —**sche′ma·ti·za′tion,** *n.*

scheme (skēm) *n.* **1.** a program or course of action for accomplishing some objective; plan: *a scheme for building a new community center.* **2.** an underhanded, devious, or secret plan; plot: *That so-called sale is a scheme to swindle the consumer.* **3.** a connected and orderly arrangement of related parts or things; system; design: *a striking color scheme for a room.* **4.** a chart, diagram, or outline; sketch: *a scheme of a control system for a rocket.* —*v.t., v.i.,* **schemed, schem·ing.** to plan or contrive, esp. in a devious manner; plot. [Latin *schēma* shape, figure, form, from Greek *schēma.*] —**schem′er,** *n.* —For Synonyms *(n.),* see **plot.**

scher·zan·do (sker tsän′dō, -tsan′-) *adj. Music.* playful; sportive. [Italian *scherzando,* gerund of *scherzare* to play, sport, from *scherzo.* See SCHERZO.]

scher·zo (sker′tsō) *n., pl.* **-zos** or **-zi** (-tsē). a playful, lively, or humorous movement or passage, esp. in a sonata or symphony. [Italian *scherzo* play, sport, lively movement (in music), from German *Scherz* fun, jest.]

Schick test (shik) a test used to determine immunity to diphtheria, consisting of the injection of a dilute diphtheria toxin just beneath the skin. Reddening of the area indicates susceptibility to the disease. [From Béla *Schick,* 1877-1967, U.S. pediatrician born in Hungary, who developed the test.]

schil·ling (shil′ing) *n.* the monetary unit of Austria. [German *Schilling.*]

schism (siz′əm, skiz′-) *n.* **1.a.** a division within a church or other religious body, usually over matters of discipline or jurisdiction. **b.** the offense of causing or contributing to such a division. **c.** a sect or group formed by such a division. **2.** any separation or breach of unity, esp. a division into mutually opposed factions or

groups. [Late Latin *schisma* split, separation, from Greek *schisma* split, division.]

schis·mat·ic (siz mat′ik, skiz-) *adj.* relating to, promoting, or guilty of schism. Also, **schis·mat′i·cal.** —*n.* a person who promotes or takes part in a schism. —**schis·mat′i·cal·ly**, *adv.*

schist (shist) *n.* a mica-rich metamorphic rock that is easily split because of its layered structure. [French *schiste*, through Latin, from Greek *schistos* easily split.]

schis·tose (shis′tōs) *adj.* relating to, resembling, or characteristic of schist. Also, **schis·tous** (shis′təs).

schis·to·some (shis′tə sōm′) *n.* any of a genus, *Schistosoma*, of disease-producing parasitic flukes that inhabit the blood vessels of birds and mammals, including humans. Also, **blood fluke.** [Modern Latin *schistosoma*, from Greek *schistos* cleft + *sōma* body.]

schis·to·so·mi·a·sis (shis′tə sō mī′ə sis) *n.* a prevalent, chronic disease of tropical and subtropical areas caused by parasitic schistosomes that inhabit the circulatory system, injuring the liver, bladder, lungs, and central nervous system.

schiz·o (skit′sō) *Informal. n., pl.* **schiz·os.** a schizophrenic. —*adj.* schizophrenic.

schizo- *combining form* split; cleft; divided: *schizophrenia.* [Greek *schizein* to split.]

schiz·o·carp (skiz′ə kärp′) *n. Botany.* a dry fruit, separating at maturity into two or more usually one-seeded vessels that remain closed. [Schizo- + *karpos* fruit.]

schiz·oid (skit′soid, skiz′oid) *adj.* relating to, characterized by, resembling, or showing a tendency toward schizophrenia. —*n.* a schizoid person.

schiz·o·my·cete (skiz′ō mī′sēt, -mī sēt′, skit′sō-) *n.* bacterium. [Schizo- + Modern Latin *-mycetes* class of fungi (from Greek *mykētes*, plural of *mykēs* fungus).]

schiz·o·phre·ni·a (skit′sə frē′nē ə, skiz′ə-) *n.* any of a group of psychoses characterized by a severe withdrawal from reality, illogical thought, inappropriate moods, hallucinations, and delusions. [Modern Latin *schizophrenia*, from Schizo- + Greek *phrēn* mind.]

schiz·o·phren·ic (skit′sə fren′ik, skiz′ə-) *adj.* of, relating to, characteristic of, or having schizophrenia. —*n.* a person who suffers from schizophrenia.

schle·miel (shlə mēl′) *also,* **shlemiel.** *n. Slang.* a person who is clumsy, dull, and easily duped by others; bungler. [Yiddish *shlumiel*, possibly from Hebrew *Shelūmīel*, biblical figure (Numbers) who, according to the Jewish tradition, lost battles constantly and thus became a symbol of bad luck.]

schlep (shlep) *also,* **schlepp.** *Slang. v.t.,* **schlepped, schlepping.** to carry, esp. clumsily or with difficulty; drag; lug. —*n.* **1.** a long and tiresome distance or journey: *It's such a schlep from here to the movie theater.* **2.** a dull, insignificant, or stupid person. [Yiddish *shleppen* to drag, from Middle Low German *slēpen.*]

schmaltz (shmôlts, shmälts) *also,* **schmalz.** *n.* **1.** *Informal.* extreme or maudlin sentimentality, as in music or drama. **2.** fat or grease used in cooking, esp. chicken fat. [German *Schmalz* melted fat, lard.] —**schmaltz′y;** *also,* **schmalz′y,** *adj.*

schmo (shmō) *also,* **schmoe.** *n., pl.* **schmoes.** *Slang.* a person who is foolish, dull, or naive. [Probably modification of Yiddish *shmok,* from Slovene *šmok.*]

schmuck (shmuk) *n. Slang.* a stupid or despicable person. [Yiddish *schmuck* penis, from German *Schmuck* ornament.]

schnapps (shnäps) *also,* **schnaps.** *n., pl.* **schnapps** or **schnaps.** any strong liquor. [German *Schnapps,* from Dutch *snaps* dram, mouthful.]

schnau·zer (shnou′zər) *n.* a wirehaired dog having a rectangular head, small, pointed ears, and a bearded muzzle. There are three distinct breeds, which differ only in size: the **miniature schnauzer,** to 14 inches (36 centimeters) at the shoulder; the **standard schnauzer,** to 20 inches (51 centimeters); and the **giant schnauzer,** to 25 inches (64 centimeters). [German *Schnauzer,* from *Schnauze* snout.]

schnit·zel (shnit′səl) *n.* a cutlet, usually of veal. [German *Schnitzel* literally, snippet, shaving, from Middle High German *snitzel,* diminutive of *sniz* a slice.]

schnook (shnук) *n. Slang.* a person who is easily fooled or taken advantage of by others. [Yiddish *shnok,* form of *shmok* fool. See SCHMO.]

schol·ar (skol′ər) *n.* **1.** a person who has thorough knowledge of, and is considered to be an authority in, a particular field, esp. one of the humanities: *a noted Shakespearean scholar.* **2.** a person having much knowledge and a serious interest in learning and study; learned or erudite person: *A judge who is a politician but also a scholar.* **3.** a person holding a scholarship. **4.** a person who learns from a teacher or attends school; pupil: *an apt scholar.*

[Late Latin *scholāris* relating to a school, from Latin *schola.* See SCHOOL[1].]

schol·ar·ly (skol′ər lē) *adj.* **1.** of, characteristic of, or befitting a scholar: *a scholarly life.* **2.** of, characteristic of, or based on scholarship: *a scholarly and illuminating book on the economics of the Depression.* **3.** having the qualities of a scholar: *a scholarly teenager.* —**schol′ar·li·ness,** *n.*

schol·ar·ship (skol′ər ship′) *n.* **1.** a grant of financial aid awarded to a student, as by a private foundation or an educational institution and usually in recognition of both need and academic merit, to help defray the cost of studies. **2.** academic or scholarly achievement: *to excel in scholarship in school.* **3.** knowledge acquired by study; learning; erudition: *a book that displays the considerable scholarship of its author.* **4.** the body of existing knowledge or study and research contributing to it: *the advanced state of scholarship in classical studies.*

scho·las·tic (skə las′tik) *adj.* **1.** of or relating to schools, scholars, or education: *scholastic standing, a scholastic meet.* **2.** *also,* **Scholastic.** of or relating to scholasticism or its teachings and methods. **3.** overly refined and restrictive; pedantic. Also, **scho·las′ti·cal.** —*n.* **1.** *also,* **Scholastic.** a theologian or philosopher in the Middle Ages who adhered to or taught the doctrines of scholasticism. **2.** a student; pupil. **3.** a pedant. [Latin *scholasticus* relating to a school, from Greek *scholastikos* learned, having leisure, going back to *scholē.* See SCHOOL[1].] —**scho·las′ti·cal·ly,** *adv.*

scho·las·ti·cism (skə las′tə siz′əm) *also,* **Scho·las·ti·cism.** *n.* **1.** a philosophical and theological system dominant in western Europe during the Middle Ages that sought to reconcile faith and reason by harmonizing the teachings of the Fathers of the Church with Greek philosophy, esp. that of Aristotle. **2.** adherence to traditional methods and doctrines, as of a school or sect.

scho·li·ast (skō′lē ast′) *n.* a commentator, esp. an ancient grammarian who annotated the Greek or Latin classics. [Late Greek *scholiastēs,* going back to Greek *scholion* comment, note.]

scho·li·um (skō′lē əm) *n., pl.* **-li·a** (-lē ə) or **-li·ums. 1.** an explanatory marginal note or comment, esp. one made by a scholiast in Greek or Latin classical texts. **2.** a note that illustrates or develops a point, as in a mathematical or scientific text. [Modern Latin *scholium,* from Greek *scholion.*]

school[1] (skül) *n.* **1.** an institution for academic instruction: *She got her bachelor's degree at one of the finest schools in the country.* **2.** an institution for instruction in a particular field or skill: *a dancing school.* **3.** a department or division of a college or university for instruction in a specialized field: *the school of medicine.* **4.** the classrooms, offices, building, or group of buildings of an educational institution: *The students helped build the new school.* **5.** a session, period, or set time of instruction at an educational institution: *There's no school today because of the snowstorm.* **6.** the process of being educated, esp. in a formal program of studies; attendance at school: *He finished school at sixteen and went to work.* **7.** the student body or the students, faculty, and other staff members of an educational institution: *The whole school was talking about the new library.* **8.a.** a group of people adhering to or influenced by the same teacher, beliefs, method, or style: *the Epicurean school of Greek philosophy.* **b.** the beliefs, method, or style of such a group: *a painting of the impressionist school.* **9.** a group of people sharing common traditions, opinions, or a general style of life: *My cousin is of the school that believes in doing as little work as possible.* **10.** any means or source of learning or instruction: *the school of experience.* —*v.t.* **1.** to teach in or as if in a school; educate. **2.** to bring under control; train; discipline: *Doctors must school themselves to be calm during emergencies.* —*adj.* of or relating to a school or schools. [Old English *scōl* place of learning, from Latin *schola* place of learning, leisure devoted to learning, sect, from Greek *scholē* leisure, esp. that devoted to learning, place of learning.]

school[2] (skül) *n.* a large group of fish or aquatic animals of the same kind swimming together: *a school of tuna.* —*v.i.* to swim together in a school. [Dutch *school* troop, crowd.]

school age 1. the age at which a child first goes to school. **2.** the years of age in which attending school is customary or required by law. —**school′·age′,** *adj.*

school board, a group of people, usually elected by a district or

a	at	e	end	o	hot	u	up	hw	white		(about
ā	ape	ē	me	ō	old	ū	use	ng	song		taken
ä	far	i	it	ô	fork	ü	rule	th	thin	ə {	pencil
âr	care	ī	ice	oi	oil	ù	pull	th	this		lemon
		îr	pierce	ou	out	ûr	turn	zh	measure		(circus

community, responsible for overseeing the operations of the public schools in an area.

school·book (skül′bŭk′) *n.* a book used for study in schools; textbook.

school·boy (skül′boi′) *n.* a boy attending school.

school bus, a bus or other vehicle used to carry children to and from school or school activities.

school·child (skül′chīld′) *n., pl.* **-chil·dren** (-chil′dren). a child attending school.

school day 1. a day when school is in session: *Election day is not a school day in most states.* **2.** the part of a day during which school is in session: *Our school day ends at 3 P.M.*

school·fel·low (skül′fel′ō) *n.* schoolmate.

school·girl (skül′gûrl′) *n.* a girl attending school.

school·house (skül′hous′) *n., pl.* **-hous·es** (-hou′ziz). a building used as a school.

school·ing (skü′ling) *n.* **1.** the process of being educated or instructed, esp. in a formal program of studies; education; instruction; training. **2.** the cost of attending a school: *The philanthropist paid the children's schooling.*

school·man (skül′mən, -man′) *also,* **School·man.** *n., pl.* **-men** (-mən, -men′). a scholastic of the Middle Ages.

school·marm (skül′märm′) *also,* **school·ma'am** (skül′mam′). *n. Informal.* a female schoolteacher, esp. one in a rural school or one considered to be strict, old-fashioned, or prudish.

school·mas·ter (skül′mas′tər) *n.* **1.** a male schoolteacher. **2.** a headmaster of a school.

school·mate (skül′māt′) *n.* a companion at school.

school·mis·tress (skül′mis′tris) *n.* **1.** a female schoolteacher. **2.** the headmistress of a school.

school·room (skül′rüm′, -rûm′) *n.* classroom.

school·teach·er (skül′tē′chər) *n.* a person who teaches in a school below the college level.

school·work (skül′wûrk′) *n.* lessons or assignments given to a student.

school·yard (skül′yärd′) *n.* the yard or playground of a school.

school year, that part of the year during which schools are in session, usually from September to June in the United States.

schooner

schoon·er (skü′nər) *n.* **1.** a fore-and-aft-rigged ship having two or more masts. **2.** a large, tall beer glass. **3.** prairie schooner. [Possibly from dialectal English *scoon* to skim along, from Scottish *scon* to make a stone skip across water; probably of Scandinavian origin.]

schot·tische (shot′ish) *n.* **1.** a round dance resembling the polka, marked by hopping and gliding steps. **2.** music for this dance. [German *schottische (Tanz)* Scottish (dance), going back to Late Latin *Scottus* Scot; of Celtic origin.]

schuss (shús, shüs) *v.i.* to ski down a straight, steep course without decreasing speed. —*v.t.* to ski down (a course) in this manner. —*n.* **1.** a straight, downhill run on skis, made without decreasing speed. **2.** a straight, steep course on which such a run is made. [German *Schuss* shot[1], swoop.]

schwa (shwä) *n.* **1.** an unstressed vowel sound occurring in many unstressed syllables in English, as the *a* in *ago* or the *o* in *lemon.* **2.** the symbol (ə) representing this sound. Also, **neutral vowel.** [Hebrew *sh'wā* sign indicating a faint vowel sound or the absence of a vowel sound.]

sci. **1.** science. **2.** scientific.

sci·at·ic (sī at′ik) *adj.* **1.** of, relating to, or affecting the ischium. **2.** affecting the hip or the sciatic nerve. [Late Latin *sciaticus* relating to pains in the hip, modification of Latin *ischiadicus,* from Greek *ischiadikos,* going back to *ischion* hip joint.]

sci·at·i·ca (sī at′i kə) *n.* pain in the area of the sciatic nerve and its branches, commonly caused by a slipped disk and felt in the hips, thighs, and legs. [Medieval Latin *sciatica,* from Late Latin *sciaticus.* See SCIATIC.]

sciatic nerve, the largest nerve of the body, originating in the lower back and extending along the back part of the thigh and leg.

sci·ence (sī′əns) *n.* **1.** the body of knowledge and theory on the nature and operation of natural phenomena and of the universe and all things in it, in which facts are organized into a systematic and meaningful pattern developed as a result of experimentation, observation, and insight. **2.** any branch of such knowledge, as physics, chemistry, or biology. **3.** any branch of systematized knowledge, esp. one in which the techniques and principles of the scientific method are followed: *the science of philology.* **4.** any activity, skill, or field of interest that may be studied like a science and to which systematic methods or principles may be applied: *an essay maintaining that chess is a science, not just a game.* **5. Science.** Christian Science. [Old French *science* knowledge, from Latin *scientia.*]

science fiction, fiction based on actual or imaginary developments or discoveries in science, often futuristic or fantastic.

sci·en·tif·ic (sī′ən tif′ik) *adj.* **1.** of, relating to, derived from, or used in science: *a scientific theory.* **2.** based on, using, or conforming to the principles and methods of science; systematic; exact: *to take a scientific approach to a problem.* —**sci·en·tif·i·cal·ly** (sī′ən tif′i kə lē, -i klē), *adv.*

scientific method, the method of research used by scientists, in which a problem is stated, a hypothesis is formed, data are collected through observation or experimentation, and the hypothesis is proved or disproved by analysis of the data.

sci·en·tist (sī′ən tist) *n.* a person who is highly skilled or knowledgeable in science, esp. in the area of natural science, and is engaged in it as a profession.

sci-fi (sī′fī′) *Informal. n.* science fiction. —*adj.* of or relating to science fiction.

scil·i·cet (sil′ə set′) *adv.* that is to say; namely. [Latin *scilicet* it is evident, from *scīre* to know + *licet* it is permitted.]

scim·i·tar (sim′i tər) *also,* **scim·i·ter, sim·i·tar.** *n.* a curved, single-edged sword, used esp. in the Middle East. [Italian *scimitarra,* from Persian *shimshīr.*]

scin·til·la (sin til′ə) *n.* a very small amount; trace: *There was not a scintilla of truth in that story.* [Latin *scintilla* spark.]

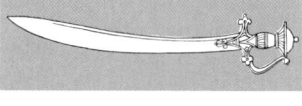

scimitar

scin·til·late (sin′tə lāt′) *v.,* **-lat·ed, -lat·ing.** —*v.i.* **1.** to be vibrant, animated, or brilliant: *an author whose short stories scintillate with wit.* **2.** to give off sparks or flashes of light; sparkle: *a rushing stream that scintillated in the morning sun.* **3.** to twinkle, as a star. —*v.t.* to give off as a flash or flashes. [Latin *scintillātus,* past participle of *scintillāre* to sparkle.]

scin·til·lat·ing (sin′tə lā′ting) *adj.* vibrant, animated, or brilliant: *a scintillating conversation.* —**scin′til·lat′ing·ly,** *adv.*

scin·til·la·tion (sin′tə lā′shən) *n.* **1.** the act of scintillating. **2.** a spark or flash of light. **3.** the twinkling of the stars.

scintillation counter, an instrument that detects ionizing radiation and measures its energy and intensity, consisting of a fluorescent material that gives off flashes of light when struck by radiation and an electron tube that converts this light into electric pulses.

sci·o·lism (sī′ə liz′əm) *n.* superficial or pretended knowledge; charlatanism. [Late Latin *sciolus* one who knows little (diminutive of Latin *scius* knowing) + -ISM.] —**sci′o·list,** *n.* —**sci·o·lis′tic,** *adj.*

sci·on (sī′ən) *n.* **1.** *also,* **cion.** a bud, or a branch having one or more buds, cut from a plant and used for grafting onto the stock of another plant. For illustration, see graft[1]. **2.** a descendant; heir: *the wealthy scion of a noble family.* [Old French *scion;* of Germanic origin.]

scis·sion (sizh′ən, sish′-) *n.* the act of cutting or dividing; division; separation. [Late Latin *scissiō* a dividing, from Latin *scindere* to cut, split.]

scis·sor (siz′ər) *v.t.* to cut with scissors. —*n.* scissors.

scis·sors (siz′ərz) *n.* **1.** a cutting implement having two blades that are fastened together by a bolt and form a double cutting edge

S

when they are closed over each other. ➡ used as singular or plural: *The scissors is in the left-hand drawer of my desk. The scissors are in the drawer.* However, the phrase *pair of scissors* is used only as singular: *This pair of scissors isn't very sharp.* **2.** a wrestling hold in which the legs are placed around a part of the opponent's body and locked in place by crossing the ankles. **3.** a gymnastic exercise in which the movement of the legs suggests the opening and closing of scissors. ➡ used as singular in defs. 2 and 3. [Old French *cisoires* shears, going back to Late Latin *cīsōrium* cutting implement, going back to Latin *caedere* to cut; Modern English spelling due to confusion with Latin *scissor* carver.]

scissors kick, a swimming kick, used chiefly with the sidestroke, in which the legs are moved apart, one forward and one backward, and then brought quickly together.

scis·sor·tail (siz′ər tāl′) *n.* a pearl-gray and pink flycatcher, *Tyrannus forficatus,* having extremely long tail feathers, often spread in flight, breeding in the south-central United States. Length: 13 inches (33 centimeters). [SCISSOR + TAIL; so called because its spread tail feathers resemble an open pair of scissors.]

scle·ra (sklir′ə) *n.* a tough, white, fibrous membrane covering the surface of the eye, and continuous with the cornea. For illustration, see **eye.** [Modern Latin *sclera,* from Greek *sklēros* hard.]

scle·ren·chy·ma (sklə reng′kə mə) *n.* a strengthening tissue of plants, composed of dead cells with thick, often lignified, cell walls. [Modern Latin *sclerenchyma,* from Greek *sklēros* hard + *enchyma* infusion.]

scle·rite (sklir′īt) *n.* any of the hard, chitinous, or calcareous plates or other parts forming the outer skeleton of arthropods. [Greek *sklēros* hard + -ITE[1].]

scle·rom·e·ter (skli rom′i tər) *n.* an instrument for determining the degree of hardness of a substance, esp. of a mineral. [Greek *sklēros* hard + -METER.]

scle·ro·sis (skli rō′sis) *n., pl.* **-ses** (-sēz). **1.** an abnormal hardening of a tissue or part of the body, as the wall of an artery. **2.** a hardening of a cell wall or tissue of a plant, as by the formation of wood. [Medieval Latin *sclerosis* callosity, from Greek *sklērōsis* hardening.]

scle·rot·ic (skli rot′ik) *adj.* **1.** of or relating to the sclera. **2.** of, relating to, or affected by sclerosis. [Modern Latin *scleroticus* hard, going back to Greek *sklēros.*]

scoff (skof, skôf) *v.i.* to express ridicule or contempt; mock; jeer (often with *at*): *to scoff at a foolish suggestion.* —*n.* an expression of ridicule, contempt, or mockery. [Probably of Scandinavian origin.] —**scoff′er,** *n.* —**scoff′ing·ly,** *adv.* —For Synonyms (*v.i.*), see **jeer.**

scoff·law (skof′lô′, skôf′-) *n.* a person who flouts the law, esp. one who habitually fails to pay fines incurred for traffic violations.

scold (skōld) *v.t.* to find fault with; speak sharply to; reprimand. —*v.i.* to find fault or express dissatisfaction sharply or continuously. —*n.* a person who scolds, esp. a shrewish woman. [Probably from Old Norse *skáld* poet (probably with reference to satirical poems).] —**scold′er,** *n.* —**scold′ing·ly,** *adv.*

> **Synonyms** *v.t.* **Scold, upbraid,** and **berate** mean to speak to someone harshly and critically. **Scold** suggests a verbal reproach, often growing out of irritation or anger: *The exhausted parent scolded the child for screaming.* **Upbraid** suggests a vehement rebuke by a superior: *The coach upbraided the team for playing poorly.* **Berate** usually connotes heaping angry reproaches on someone, often in a long-drawn-out fashion: *Several shareholders berated the chief executive officer for mismanaging the company.*

sco·lex (skō′leks) *n., pl.* **sco·le·ces** (skə lē′sēz). the head of a tapeworm, bearing hooks and suckers that are attached to the intestinal wall of the host. [Modern Latin *scolex,* from Greek *skōlēx* grub, worm.]

sco·li·o·sis (skō′lē ō′sis) *n., pl.* **-ses** (-sēz). an abnormal sideways curving of the spine. [Formed from Greek *skoliōsis* a bending, curvature of the body, from *skolios* crooked.]

scol·lop (skol′əp) scallop.

sconce[1] (skons) *n.* a projecting wall bracket or fixture used esp. for holding a candle or other light. [Old French *esconse* hiding place, screened lantern, going back to Latin *absconsa,* feminine past participle of *abscondere* to hide.]

sconce[2] (skons) *n.* the head or skull. [Of uncertain origin.]

scone (skōn, skon) *n.* a small biscuit, often round, traditionally served with butter. [Possibly short for Middle Dutch *schoonbrot* fine bread.]

scoop (skü p) *n.* **1.** any of various implements resembling a small shovel, consisting of a usually deep-sided, often curved, container attached to a handle, used chiefly for taking up loose material or powdery substances, such as flour or sugar. **2.** a utensil usually consisting of a deep circular bowl attached to a handle, used for forming and dispensing ball-shaped portions of food, such as ice cream. **3.** a large bucket of a dredge or steam shovel, used for taking up and depositing a load, as of dirt. **4.** the amount taken up in a scoop, esp. a ball-shaped portion: *a scoop of ice cream.* **5.** a dipping or sweeping movement: *The baby picked up the pebbles with a scoop of the hand.* **6.** a bowl-shaped hole or cavity. **7.** *Informal.* a news story reported first or exclusively, as by a newspaper or television network. —*v.t.* **1.** to take up or out with or as with a scoop (often with *out*): *Scoop out the center of the melon before you serve it.* **2.** to form by or as if by scooping: *The glacier scooped the valley out of the mountains.* **3.** to gather or put quickly or with a sweeping motion: *I scooped up my books and left the house.* **4.** *Informal.* to get the better of (a competitor) by reporting a news story first or exclusively. [Partly from Middle Dutch *schōpe* bucket; partly from Middle Dutch *schoppe* shovel.] —**scoop′er,** *n.*

scoop·ful (skü p′fu l′) *n., pl.* **-fuls.** the amount that a scoop holds: *to eat three scoopfuls of ice cream.*

scoot (skü t) *Informal. v.i.* to go hurriedly; dart: *The rabbit scooted off into the woods.* —*n.* the act of scooting. [Probably of Scandinavian origin.]

scoot·er (skü′tər) *n.* **1.** a toy vehicle consisting of a narrow footboard mounted on two aligned wheels and having a long upright steering post, propelled by pushing one foot against the ground while resting the other foot on the board. **2.** motor scooter. **3.** a wide, flat-bottomed sailboat with runners, capable of sailing on water or on ice. —*v.i.* to go or sail in or on a scooter. [From SCOOT.]

scope[1] (skōp) *n.* **1.** the range within which something operates or applies; area dealt with or taken in: *Relocating tenants falls within the scope of this agency.* **2.** the extent of perception, outlook, or ability; grasp: *an intellect rather limited in its scope.* **3.** opportunity or room for expression, development, or action: *to give a group full scope to air its views.* [Italian *scopo* target, aim, from Greek *skopos.*]

> **Synonyms** **Scope[1], compass,** and **range** mean the limits of knowledge, capacity, or possibility, and may be used to define what is included and what is excluded. **Scope** is usually applied to a field of activity: *Hiring new personnel fell within the scope of the manager's responsibilities.* **Compass,** which may be applied to knowledge as well as activity, often emphasizes restricted limits: *Advanced principles of algebra fell outside the narrow compass of the course.* **Range** describes the extent of power or possibility: *Serious roles were beyond the comedian's range.*

scope[2] (skōp) *n. Informal.* any of various magnifying viewing instruments, as a telescope, microscope, or the like. [From -SCOPE.]

-scope *combining form* instrument for viewing or examining: *kaleidoscope, fluoroscope.* [Modern Latin *-scopium,* from Greek *-skopion,* from *skopein* to view, examine.]

sco·pol·a·mine (skō pol′ə mēn′, -min) *n.* a drug used as a sedative and painkiller, esp. during childbirth, to prevent motion sickness, and as a truth serum. Formula: $C_{17}H_{21}NO_4$ Also, **hyoscine.** [Modern Latin *Scopolia* a genus of plants from which the drug is obtained (from G. A. *Scopoli,* 1723-88, Italian naturalist) + AMINE.]

scor·bu·tic (skôr bū′tik) *adj.* relating to, characteristic of, or affected with scurvy. Also, **scor·bu′ti·cal.** [Modern Latin *scorbuticus,* from *scorbutus* scurvy; probably of Germanic origin.]

scorch (skôrch) *v.t.* **1.** to burn so as to change in appearance, taste, or texture: *The hot iron scorched the tablecloth.* **2.** to dry up or wither with or as if with heat; parch: *The grass was scorched by the summer sun.* **3.** to criticize sharply or severely. —*v.i.* to become scorched. —*n.* a slight burn. [Possibly from Old Norse *skorpna* to shrivel.]

> **Synonyms** *v.t.* **Scorch, sear,** and **singe** mean to injure or damage by burning. **Scorch** describes a surface burning that changes color or texture: *Although scorched by the flames, the document was still readable.* **Sear** usually applies to the burning of animal tissue by fire or intense heat: *The branding iron seared the cow's hide.* **Singe** suggests a slight burning, as of the tips of hair: *I bent too close to the flame and singed my eyebrows.*

a	at	e	end	o	hot	u	up	hw	white		about
ā	ape	ē	me	ō	old	ū	use	ng	song		taken
ä	far	i	it	ô	fork	ü	rule	th	thin	ə	pencil
âr	care	ī	ice	oi	oil	u	pull	th	this		lemon
		îr	pierce	ou	out	ûr	turn	zh	measure		circus

scorched-earth (skôrcht'ûrth') *adj.* of, relating to, or involving scorched-earth policy: *a scorched-earth campaign.*

scorched-earth policy, a policy or strategy of destroying whatever lies in the path of an advancing or retreating army, such as crops or industrial equipment, so that it is not useful to the enemy.

scorch·er (skôr'chər) *n.* **1.** *Informal.* a very hot day. **2.** a person or thing that scorches. **3.** *Informal.* something that is sharply or severely critical, such as a remark or review.

score (skôr) *n.* **1.a.** a record of points made in a game or contest: *The score after six innings was 5 to 4.* **b.** the number of points made by one side or individual in such a competition: *The skier's brilliant performance earned her the highest score of the day.* **c.** the act or an instance of making a point or points: *The score came on a last-minute touchdown.* **2.** a grade or rating on a test or examination. **3.** a set or group of twenty; twenty: *a score of years.* **4. scores.** an indefinitely large number; very many: *Scores of people flock to the beach every summer.* **5.** basis, account, reason, or cause: *He had no right to brag on that score.* **6.a.** an account or reckoning, as of grievances, kept as if by a tally: *to even up the score.* **b.** a wrong or other grievance that requires revenge or other redress: *to settle an old score.* **7.** a notch, line, or other mark. **8.** an amount due; debt. **9.** the music for a motion picture, theatrical production, or television program. **10.** a written or printed notation for a musical composition, having all the instrumental and vocal parts arranged on two or more staffs aligned vertically. **11.** *Informal.* the reality of a situation; truth: *to learn the score.* —*v.*, **scored, scor·ing.** —*v.t.* **1.** to make or gain (points) in a game or contest. **2.** to keep a record of points made in (a game or contest). **3.** to count for or be worth (a specified number of points): *A touchdown scores 6 points.* **4.** to record or set down, with or as if with a notch or line; note: *Score 3 points on your list for our side.* **5.** to evaluate and give a grade or rating to: *to score an examination.* **6.** to make a specified grade or rating of: *Several students scored 100% on the spelling test.* **7.** to achieve; win: *to score a victory.* **8.** to cancel, eliminate, or strike out by or as if by drawing a line through (often with *out*): *Several passages in the manuscript had been scored out.* **9.** to make a mark or marks in or upon: *to score a piece of wood with a knife.* **10.** to criticize or denounce severely: *Union leaders scored the mayor for the city's refusal to raise wages.* **11.** to make superficial cuts in (meat or other food). **12.a.** to arrange or adapt (music) for a particular instrument or voice. **b.** to orchestrate. **c.** to write or provide music for (a motion picture, theatrical production, or television program). **13.** *Baseball.* to cause or enable (a runner) to make a run: *My hit scored the runner from first base.* —*v.i.* **1.** to make or gain a point or points in a game or contest. **2.** to keep the score in a game or contest. **3.** to make a specified grade or rating: *to score in the top third of the class.* **4.** to achieve a success or advantage: *to score in an argument.* [Old Norse *skor* notch, tally, twenty.] —**scor'er,** *n.*

score·board (skôr'bôrd') *n.* a large board or other surface on which the score of a game or contest, and often other pertinent information, is shown.

score·card (skôr'kärd') *n.* a card on which the scores of participants in a game or contest are recorded.

score·keep·er (skôr'kē'pər) *n.* a person, esp. an official, who keeps the score during a game or contest.

sco·ri·a (skôr'ē ə) *n., pl.* **sco·ri·ae** (skôr'ē ē'). **1.** a rough, irregular, cinderlike lava. **2.** the refuse remaining after metal has been smelted; slag. [Latin *scōria* dross, from Greek *skōriā,* from *skōr* dung.] —**sco·ri·a·ceous** (skôr'ē ā'shəs), *adj.*

scorn (skôrn) *n.* **1.** a feeling of contempt and repugnance for someone or something considered vile or inferior: *to regard political deception with scorn.* **2.** someone or something regarded as contemptible, low, or vile. —*v.t.* **1.** to treat or regard as contemptible, low, or vile; despise: *to scorn insincerity in one's friends.* **2.** to refuse or reject with contempt: *to scorn an offer of help.* [Modification of Old French *esc(h)arnir* to deride; of Germanic origin.] —**scorn'er,** *n.* —**scorn'ing·ly,** *adv.*

scorn·ful (skôrn'fəl) *adj.* showing or feeling scorn; contemptuous. —**scorn'ful·ly,** *adv.* —**scorn'ful·ness,** *n.*

Scor·pi·o (skôr'pē ō') *also,* **Scor·pi·us** (skôr'pē əs). *n.* **1.** a constellation in the southern sky, conventionally depicted as a scorpion. **2.** the eighth sign of the zodiac. [Latin *scorpiō.* See SCORPION.]

scor·pi·on (skôr'pē ən) *n.* **1.** any of a group of arachnids, order Scorpionida, found in temperate and tropical regions, having a long, segmented tail that ends

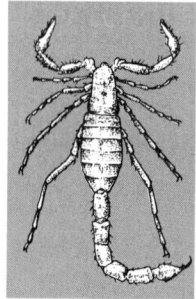

scorpion

in a venomous stinger. Length: to 8 inches (20 centimeters). **2. Scorpion.** Scorpio. [Latin *scorpiō,* going back to Greek *skorpios.*]

scor·pi·on·fish (skôr'pē ən fish') *n., pl.* **-fish** or **-fish·es.** any of a group of marine fish, family Scorpaenidae, having armored heads and thick spines in their fins, esp. fish of the genus *Scorpaena,* whose fins have poisonous spines. [Because it has a poisonous sting like that of the scorpion.]

Scot (skot) *n.* **1.** a native or citizen of Scotland. **2.** a person of Scottish ancestry. **3.** a member of an ancient Celtic people who migrated from northern Ireland to the northwestern part of Great Britain in the sixth century.

Scot. 1. Scotch. **2.** Scotland. **3.** Scottish.

scotch (skoch) *v.t.* **1.** to put an end to; crush or suppress: *to scotch a rebellion.* **2.** to injure so as to make harmless: *to scotch a snake.* [Of uncertain origin.]

Scotch (skoch) *n.* **1. the Scotch.** the Scottish people. **2.** *also,* **scotch.** a whiskey distilled, originally in Scotland, from malted barley, and having a smoky flavor. Also, **Scotch whisky.** —*adj.* Scottish.

Scotch-I·rish (skoch'ī'rish) *n.* **1.** a native or inhabitant of Northern Ireland who is descended from Scottish settlers. **2.** a person of such ancestry. —*adj.* of or relating to these people.

Scotch·man (skoch'mən) *n., pl.* **-men** (-mən). Scotsman. —For Usage Note, see **Scotch.**

Scotch plaid 1. a plaid pattern, esp. one that is predominantly bright red or blue combined with yellow, black, and white. **2.** fabric woven in such a pattern.

Scotch tape, a cellulose tape, usually transparent and with adhesive on only one side. *Trademark:* **Scotch.**

Scotch terrier, Scottish terrier.

Scotch whisky, Scotch *(n.,* def. 2).

Scotch·wom·an (skoch'wŭm'ən) *n., pl.* **-wom·en** (-wim'ən). Scotswoman. —For Usage Note, see **Scotch.**

sco·ter (skō'tər) *n.* any of various large diving ducks, genera *Oidemia* and *Melanitta,* native to northern regions of Europe and North America. Also, **coot.** [Of uncertain origin.]

scot-free (skot'frē') *adj.* free from injury, loss, punishment, or other penalty: *The defendant got off scot-free.* [Middle English *scot* payment, tax (from Old Norse *skot* contribution) + FREE.]

Scot·land Yard (skot'lənd) **1.** the metropolitan police of London, esp. the branch that investigates crime. **2.** its headquarters. Officially, **New Scotland Yard.** [From *Scotland Yard,* the location of its original headquarters in London, formerly the site of a medieval palace at which kings of Scotland stayed when visiting the city.]

Scots (skots) *adj.* Scottish. —*n.* Scottish *(def. 2).*

Scots Gaelic, Scottish Gaelic.

Scots·man (skots'mən) *n., pl.* **-men** (-mən). **1.** a person, esp. a man, who is a native or citizen of Scotland. **2.** a person, esp. a man, of Scottish ancestry. —For Usage Note, see **Scotch.**

Scots·wom·an (skots'wŭm'ən) *n., pl.* **-wom·en** (-wim'ən). **1.** a woman who is a native or citizen of Scotland. **2.** a woman of Scottish ancestry. —For Usage Note, see **Scotch.**

Scot·ti·cism (skot'ə siz'əm) *n.* a word, phrase, or usage originating in Scotland or peculiar to Scottish.

Scot·tie (skot'ē) *n.* Scottish terrier.

Scot·tish (skot'ish) *adj.* of, relating to, or characteristic of Scotland, its people, or their language. —*n.* **1. the Scottish.** the people historically inhabiting Scotland and those descended from them. **2.** any of the dialects of English spoken in Scotland.

Scottish Gaelic, the Gaelic spoken by inhabitants of the Scottish Highlands. Also, **Scots Gaelic.** For table of words borrowed from Scottish Gaelic, see **Gaelic.**

Scottish terrier, a small, short-legged terrier, believed to be the oldest breed native to Britain, having a large head, pointed ears,

Scottish terrier

and a rough coat of black, gray, or light tan hair. Height: 10 inches (25 centimeters) at the shoulder. Also, **Scotch terrier, Scottie.**

scoun·drel (skoun'drəl) *n.* an unprincipled, base, or dishonest

person; villain; rogue. [Of uncertain origin.] —**scoun′drel·ly,** *adj.*

scour¹ (skour) *v.t.* **1.** to rub (something) vigorously, often with an abrasive, in order to clean, wash, or brighten it: *to scour a pot.* **2.** to remove by rubbing in this manner: *to scour the rust off an old stove.* **3.** to remove dirt and grease from, as by washing with a detergent: *to scour wool.* **4.** to clear or wear, as a channel, by the flowing of water. **5.** to remove or wear away, as by water: *The flood had scoured the soil from under the foundation of the house.* **6.** to clear or rid of something undesirable: *to scour the sea of pirates.* —*v.i.* to rub something vigorously in order to clean, wash, or brighten. —*n.* **1.** the act of scouring. **2.** a place cleared or made by scouring, as of water. [Middle Dutch *schüren* to clean, from Old French *escurer,* going back to Latin *ex* utterly + *cūrāre* to take care of.] —**scour′er,** *n.*

scour² (skour) *v.t.* to move over or through, esp. in making a thorough search: *Police scoured the countryside for the fugitive.* —*v.i.* to move swiftly, as in making a search. [Possibly of Scandinavian origin.] —**scour′er,** *n.*

scourge (skûrj) *n.* **1.** a whip; lash. **2.** any means of inflicting punishment, vengeance, or suffering. **3.** a cause of great, usually widespread, affliction or destruction: *War has always been a scourge of humankind.* —*v.t.,* **scourged, scourg·ing. 1.** to whip; lash; flog. **2.** to punish or criticize severely. **3.** to cause suffering or destruction to; afflict or devastate: *the numerous wars that have scourged Europe.* [Old French *escorge* leather strap of a whip, from *escorgier* to whip, going back to Latin *ex* out of + *corrigia* strap.] —**scourg′er,** *n.*

scouring rush, any of several horsetails, esp. *Equisetum hyemale,* whose stems were once used to scour pots and pans.

scout¹ (skout) *n.* **1.** a person or thing sent out to gather and bring back information, such as a soldier, airplane, or ship sent out during wartime to gather information about the enemy. **2.** a person employed in finding or recruiting new talent, esp. in sports or entertainment. **3.** *also,* **Scout.** a member of the Boy Scouts or Girl Scouts. **4.** *Sports.* a person employed in observing opposing teams and obtaining information about their players and techniques. **5.** the act or an instance of scouting. **6.** *Informal.* a fellow; person: *a good old scout.* —*v.i.* **1.** to make a search; hunt: *Scout around and see what you can find.* **2.** to gather and bring back information as a scout; be employed for reconnaissance: *an Indian who scouts for the cavalry.* **3.** to search for new talent, esp. in sports or entertainment. —*v.t.* **1.** to observe, examine, or survey in order to obtain information: *Two soldiers went ahead and scouted the pass.* **2.** to find by searching (usually with *out* or *up*): *to scout up some wood for a campfire.* [Old French *escoute* spy, listener, from *escouter* to listen, going back to Latin *auscultāre* to listen to.]

scout² (skout) *v.t.* to reject with scorn or derision: *to scout a suggestion.* —*v.i.* to scoff: *to scout at a notion as foolish and impractical.* [Of Scandinavian origin.]

scout·ing (skou′ting) *n.* **1.** *also,* **Scouting.** the activities of the Boy Scouts or Girl Scouts, collectively. **2.** the act of a person or thing that scouts.

scout·mas·ter (skout′mas′tər) *n.* an adult leader of a troop of Boy Scouts.

scow (skou) *n.* a large, flat-bottomed boat with square ends that is usually pushed or towed, used chiefly for transporting bulk freight; barge. [Dutch *schouw* ferryboat.]

scowl (skoul) *n.* a facial expression of anger, sullenness, or disapproval; angry frown. —*v.i.* to wrinkle the forehead and contract the eyebrows in anger, sullenness, or disapproval; frown angrily. —*v.t.* to express with a scowl: *to scowl an objection to a plan.* [Probably of Scandinavian origin.] —**scowl′er,** *n.* —For Synonyms *(v.i.),* see **frown.**

scrab·ble (skrab′əl) *v.i.,* **-bled, -bling. 1.a.** to scratch, scrape, or paw about with hands, feet, or claws. **b.** to scramble, climb, or crawl. **2.** to struggle; strive: *to scrabble for a living.* **3.** to scribble, as on a wall. —*n.* the act or an instance of scrabbling. [Dutch *schrabbelen* to scratch, from *schrabben* to scrape.] —**scrab′bler,** *n.*

scrag (skrag) *n.* **1.** a thin, scrawny person or animal. **2.** a lean, bony piece of meat, esp. of mutton or veal. **3.** *Slang.* the human neck. —*v.t.,* **scragged, scrag·ging.** *Slang.* to kill by strangling; wring the neck of. [Possibly modification of obsolete *crag* throat, neck, from Middle Dutch *crāghe* neck, collar.]

scrag·gly (skrag′lē) *adj.,* **-gli·er, -gli·est.** having a ragged, sparse, or untended appearance: *a scraggly beard, a scraggly lawn.* —**scrag′gli·ness,** *n.*

scrag·gy (skrag′ē) *adj.,* **-gi·er, -gi·est. 1.** scrawny. **2.** scraggly. —**scrag′gi·ly,** *adv.* —**scrag′gi·ness,** *n.*

scram (skram) *v.i.,* **scrammed, scram·ming.** *Slang.* to leave quickly or immediately. ➡ usually used in the imperative. [Short for SCRAMBLE.]

scram·ble (skram′bəl) *v.,* **-bled, -bling.** —*v.t.* **1.** to mix together haphazardly; mix up: *to scramble the pieces of a puzzle.* **2.** to fry (eggs) with the whites and yolks mixed together. **3.** to gather or collect quickly and haphazardly: *The lawyer scrambled the papers together and raced out of the courtroom.* **4.** to alter (telecommunications signals) so that only a receiver that reverses the alterations can make transmissions intelligible. —*v.i.* **1.** to make one's way quickly by using the hands or feet to gain a hold; climb: *The hikers scrambled down the rocks along the stream.* **2.** to move or act hurriedly or frantically; rush: *I had to scramble into my clothes to be on time for work.* **3.** to struggle or compete with others: *Many countries were scrambling for control of the territory.* **4.** to get airplanes into the air on short notice to intercept enemy aircraft. —*n.* **1.** a confused, disorderly struggle or competition: *a scramble for the best seats in the arena.* **2.** the act of moving or climbing quickly or frantically: *I broke my leg in my scramble down the mountainside.* **3.** a difficult climb or walk, as over rough or rocky ground: *It's quite a scramble to reach the top of the cliff.* [Form of SCRABBLE.] —**scram′bler,** *n.*

scrap¹ (skrap) *n.* **1.** a small piece or fragment; bit: *a scrap of paper, not a scrap of evidence.* **2. scraps.** leftover or discarded bits of food. **3.** used or discarded metal that may be recycled by melting and refining: *to sell an old car for scrap.* **4.** any material that is left over or discarded as refuse or can be reprocessed for reuse. **5. scraps.** cracklings. —*v.t.,* **scrapped, scrap·ping. 1.** to discard or abandon as useless, worthless, or ineffective: *to scrap an idea.* **2.** to break up into parts for reprocessing or disposal; make scrap of: *to scrap an old battleship.* —*adj.* **1.** consisting of small or discarded pieces: *scrap lumber.* **2.** consisting of recyclable scrap: *a pile of scrap metal at a steel mill.* [Old Norse *skrap* trifles, scrapings.]

scrap² (skrap) *Informal. n.* a quarrel or disagreement, often involving a fist fight or scuffle. —*v.i.,* **scrapped, scrap·ping.** to take part in a scrap; fight. [Possibly from SCRAPE.] —**scrap′per,** *n.*

scrap·book (skrap′bŭk′) *n.* a book with blank pages in which pictures, clippings, or other items may be mounted or inserted for preservation.

scrape (skrāp) *v.,* **scraped, scrap·ing.** —*v.t.* **1.** to injure or damage the surface of by rubbing against something sharp or rough: *to scrape one's knee, to scrape the fender of a car.* **2.** to draw, move, or rub (something) roughly or forcefully or with a harsh, grating sound: *The student scraped the chalk against the blackboard.* **3.** to move or rub roughly or with a harsh, grating sound on or across (something): *The boat's keel scraped the bottom of the lake.* **4.** to rub (a surface), as with something sharp or abrasive, in order to remove an outer layer or make smooth or clean: *Scrape the dinner plates before you put them in the sink.* **5.** to remove by or as if by rubbing in this manner (often with *off*): *to scrape old paint off a wall.* **6.** to make or form by digging or rubbing, as with a sharp object: *to scrape one's name on a rock.* **7.** to collect, gather, or produce, esp. with difficulty or serious effort (with *up* or *together*): *to scrape up some money for a trip.* —*v.i.* **1.** to move or rub roughly or with a harsh, grating sound: *The broken tail pipe scraped along the ground.* **2.** to manage or make one's way barely or with difficulty (with *through, along,* or *by*): *The couple scraped by on their small income.* **3.** to save or economize by being extremely frugal: *I had to scrape while I was out of work.* **4.** to draw the foot back along the ground in making a bow. —*n.* **1.** a mark or abrasion made on a surface by scraping. **2.** a harsh, grating sound produced by scraping. **3.** the act of moving or rubbing roughly or with a harsh, grating sound. **4.a.** a difficult, troublesome, or unpleasant situation. **b.** a fight or quarrel; scrap. [Old Norse *skrapa* to scratch.]

scrap·er (skrā′pər) *n.* **1.** any of various tools or devices for cleaning or smoothing a surface or removing paint or other matter. **2.** a person or thing that scrapes.

scrap·ing (skrā′ping) *n.* **1.** the act of a person or thing that scrapes. **2.** a sound produced by scraping. **3.** *also,* **scrapings.** something that is removed or collected by scraping.

scrap·ple (skrap′əl) *n.* a boiled mixture of ground pork, cornmeal or flour, and seasonings, chilled until firm and then sliced and fried. [Diminutive of SCRAP¹.]

scrap·py¹ (skrap′ē) *adj.,* **-pi·er, -pi·est.** composed of scraps or fragments; fragmentary: *scrappy evidence.* [SCRAP¹ + -Y¹.] —**scrap′pi·ness,** *n.*

scrap·py² (skrap′ē) *adj.,* **-pi·er, -pi·est.** *Informal.* **1.** full of

a	at	e	end	o	hot	u	up	hw	white		about
ā	ape	ē	me	ō	old	ū	use	ng	song		taken
ä	far	i	it	ô	fork	ü	rule	th	thin	ə	pencil
âr	care	ī	ice	oi	oil	u̇	pull	th	this		lemon
		îr	pierce	ou	out	ûr	turn	zh	measure		circus

fighting spirit; vigorous and aggressive. **2.** given to fighting; quarrelsome. [SCRAP[2] + -Y[1].] —**scrap′pi·ly,** *adv.* —**scrap′pi·ness,** *n.*

scratch (skrach) *v.t.* **1.a.** to cut, mark, or mar the surface of with something rough, sharp, or pointed. **b.** to scrape, tear, or wound with or as with the nails or claws: *The brambles scratched my legs.* **2.** to rub or scrape (a part of the body), esp. to relieve itching: *Please scratch my back where I can't reach.* **3.** to cause to feel itchy or irritated: *The starched collar scratched my neck.* **4.** to strike out, withdraw, or cancel by or as if by drawing a line through (often with *out* or *off*): *The laboratory scratched that experiment for this year. The last sentence was scratched out.* **5.** to write or draw by or as if by scraping or cutting into a surface: *She scratched her initials on the freshly painted wall.* **6.** to write or draw hurriedly or carelessly. **7.** to drag or rub (something) over a surface with a harsh, grating sound. **8.** to amass or acquire with effort or difficulty (with *up* or *together*). **9.** *Sports.* to withdraw (an entry) from a race or other competition. —*v.i.* **1.** to dig, scrape, or wound, as with the nails or claws: *The chickens scratched in the dirt for corn.* **2.** to rub or scrape a part of the body to relieve itching: *My dog's been scratching so much I think it's got fleas.* **3.** to rub with a harsh, grating sound: *We could hear the puppy whimpering and scratching at the door.* **4.** to become cut, marked, or scraped: *a plastic that scratches easily.* **5.** to itch or irritate: *This sweater scratches.* **6.** to manage or survive with difficulty. **7.** to make a miss or a shot that incurs a penalty in billiards or pool. —*n.* **1.** a slight flesh wound or cut. **2.** any mark made by scratching: *a scratch on a finished surface.* **3.** a harsh, grating sound: *the scratch of a branch against a windowpane.* **4.** the act of scratching. **5.** a hasty or rough mark or scribble, as made by a pencil. **6.** a shot in billiards or pool that results in a penalty. **7.** a line or mark indicating the starting place of a race or contest. **8.** *Slang.* money. —*adj.* **1.** used for quick, rough, or informal writing or sketching: *scratch paper.* **2.** put together quickly and haphazardly: *a scratch basketball team.* [Blend of obsolete *scrat* to tear or scrape with the nails, and obsolete *cratch* to tear or scrape with the nails; both of uncertain origin.] —**scratch′er,** *n.*
·**from scratch.** from the beginning or from nothing: *to make a cake from scratch, to build a new business from scratch.*
·**up to scratch.** *Informal.* meeting a certain level or standard; in a fit or proper condition: *His clumsy efforts weren't up to scratch.*

scratch test, a test for a specific allergy, made by rubbing the suspected allergen into small scratches made in the skin.

scratch·y (skrach′ē) *adj.,* **scratch·i·er, scratch·i·est.** **1.** irritating to the skin; causing itching: *scratchy wool.* **2.** making a harsh, grating sound: *a scratchy recording.* **3.** covered with scratches: *a scratchy counter.* **4.** as if made with scratches; not smooth, regular, or even: *scratchy handwriting.* —**scratch′i·ly,** *adv.* —**scratch′i·ness,** *n.*

scrawl (skrôl) *v.t., v.i.* to write or draw (something) hastily or carelessly in a sprawling, irregular manner. —*n.* **1.** irregular, sprawling, almost illegible handwriting. **2.** something scrawled, such as a hastily written note. [Of uncertain origin.] —**scrawl′er,** *n.*

scraw·ny (skrô′nē) *adj.,* **-ni·er, -ni·est.** thin, bony, or undersized; skinny: *a scrawny old nag.* [Possibly of Scandinavian origin.] —**scraw′ni·ness,** *n.*

scream (skrēm) *v.i.* **1.a.** to utter a loud, shrill, piercing cry, esp. from fright or pain. **b.** to move with or make a loud, shrill, piercing sound. **2.** to shout or speak loudly or shrilly, esp. to express anger or displeasure: *Don't scream; I can hear what you're saying.* **3.** to laugh loudly and wildly: *The clown's antics left us screaming.* **4.** to have a startling or arresting effect, as if making a shrill sound: *The headlines about the earthquake screamed from the front page.* **5.** to make an urgent demand or request: *The schools are screaming for federal aid.* —*v.t.* to utter or express with or as if with a loud, shrill, piercing cry: *The boss screamed the instructions above the noise of the machinery.* —*n.* **1.** a loud, shrill, piercing cry or sound: *a scream of terror, the scream of a train whistle.* **2.** *Informal.* a hilariously funny person or thing. [Of uncertain origin.]

scream·er (skrē′mər) *n.* **1.** a person or thing that screams. **2.** any of various long-toed birds, family Anhimidae, native to South and Central America, having a loud, shrill cry.

scream·ing (skrē′ming) *adj.* **1.** startling in effect; boldly striking: *a screaming headline.* **2.** uttering screams: *a screaming child.* **3.** hilariously funny: *a screaming comedy.* **4.** *Informal.* extreme; absolute; unmitigated: *a screaming lunatic.*

scream·ing·ly (skrē′ming lē) *adv. Informal.* extremely: *a screamingly funny joke.*

screech (skrēch) *v.i.* **1.a.** to utter a shrill, high-pitched cry. **b.** to move with or make a shrill, piercing, or grating sound: *Metal screeched against metal. The car screeched to a halt.* **2.** to speak in

shrill, high-pitched tones: *As they argued, they screeched at each other.* —*v.t.* to utter or express with or as with a shrill, high-pitched cry. —*n.* a shrill, high-pitched cry or sound: *the screech of brakes.* [Modification of earlier *scritch;* of imitative origin.] —**screech′er,** *n.*

screech owl, a brown or gray North American owl, *Otus asio,* having earlike tufts of feathers on its forehead and a melodious, whistling call. Length: 10 inches (25 centimeters).

screech·y (skrē′chē) *adj.,* **screech·i·er, screech·i·est.** resembling a screech; shrill: *a screechy voice.*

screed (skrēd) *n.* **1.** a long, tiresome harangue or piece of writing. **2.** a strip of plaster, metal, or other material placed on a wall or other surface as a guide for applying or laying something, such as plaster, concrete, or sand. [Form of SHRED.]

18th-century Japanese **screen**

screen (skrēn) *n.* **1.** a tough mesh or netting, usually of wire and enclosed in a frame: *a window screen, a screen in front of a fireplace.* **2.** a portable device or structure consisting of a frame or a series of frames hinged together, often used as a room divider or as an ornament. **3.** anything that serves to separate, conceal, or protect: *The hedge forms a screen for our patio.* **4.** a surface, usually of light-reflecting material, on which motion pictures or slides may be projected. **5.** the surface on which the image is displayed in a cathode-ray tube, as that of a television, computer monitor, or radar set. **6.** the motion-picture medium or industry; motion pictures collectively: *star of stage, screen, and television, a play adapted for the screen.* **7.** a sieve, perforated plate, or similar device used for sifting or grading gravel, sand, or ore. —*v.t.* **1.** to provide with a screen or screening: *to screen a porch to keep out insects.* **2.** to shield, conceal, or protect with or as if with a screen: *The dense forest screened the enemy's movements. We screened our eyes from the sun with our hands.* **3.** to sift or grade by passing through a screen: *to screen gravel.* **4.** to block, remove, or filter as if by a screen (with *out*): *The earth's atmosphere screens out much of the sun's radiation.* **5.** to examine carefully or systematically, esp. so as to determine suitability or to make a selection: *to screen job applicants.* **6.** to show (a motion picture) on a screen. [Old French *escren* device used to protect from the heat of a fire, from Middle Dutch *scherm* shield, protection.] —**screen′a·ble,** *adj.* —**screen′er,** *n.*

screen·ing (skrē′ning) *n.* **1.** the act of a person or thing that screens. **2.** the act of showing a motion picture. **3.** fine mesh or wire netting, used to cover a window or to sift or grade gravel, sand, or the like. **4.** **screenings.** pebbles, hulls from grain, or other matter sifted out through a screen or sieve. ➡ used as singular or plural in def. 4.

screen·play (skrēn′plā′) *n.* a script for a motion picture or a television show.

screen test, a short scene filmed to appraise a person's ability as a motion-picture actor.

screen·writ·er (skrēn′rī′tər) *n.* a writer of screenplays.

screw (skrü) *n.* **1.** any of various fastening devices, consisting of a metal rod ridged with a spiraling thread and having a head, usually slotted, at one end. It is driven into place by being twisted or turned, as with a screwdriver. **2.** a simple machine, as used in a load-lifting device, consisting of a threaded cylinder that turns in a hole or socket cut with a matching thread. **3.** something resembling a screw in shape or function. **4.** a twist or turn of or as of a screw. **5.** propeller. **6.** thumbscrew (*def. 2*). —*v.t.* **1.** to attach or fasten with a screw or screws. **2.** to insert, attach, or fix (a screw or other threaded or grooved object) in place by a twisting or turning motion: *to screw a bulb into a socket, to screw the cap back on a tube of toothpaste.* **3.** to twist out of shape; contort (often with *up*): *She screwed up her mouth with displeasure.* **4.** to twist or turn: *He screwed his head around to see if they had arrived.* **5.** to

call forth or summon with difficulty; muster (often with *up*): *to screw up the courage to speak.* **6.** *Slang.* to take advantage of or cheat: *That company really screwed you on this deal. They screwed me out of a job.* —*v.i.* **1.** to be attached or fastened by means of a screw or screws: *The towel rack screws to the wall.* **2.** to become inserted, attached, or fixed in place by a twisting or turning motion: *The fuse screws into the socket.* **3.** to twist or turn as or like a screw: *The lid screws to the left to be closed.* [Old French *escroue* the hole in which a screw turns, nut for a bolt[1], going back to Latin *scrōfa* sow[2]; possibly because the threads of a screw resemble the coiling of a sow's tail.] —**screw′er,** *n.* —**screw′like′,** *adj.*

  ·**to screw up.** *Slang.* to make a mess of; botch: *to screw up a question on an exam, to screw up one's life.*

screw·ball (skrü′bôl′) *n.* **1.** *Slang.* an odd, eccentric, or crazy person. **2.** *Baseball.* a pitch made by snapping the wrist in a backward direction so that the ball curves to the side from which it was thrown as it passes the batter. —*adj.* *Slang.* contrary to reason or common sense; ludicrous: *a screwball notion.*

screw·driv·er (skrü′drī′vər) *n.* **1.** a tool for turning screws, consisting of a handle attached to a rod, usually of metal, having a beveled or grooved end that fits into the corresponding slot or slots of a screw. **2.** a cocktail consisting of vodka and orange juice.

screw propeller, propeller.

screw thread, thread *(def. 4).*

screw·worm (skrü′wûrm′) *n.* the larva of an American blowfly, *Callitroga hominivorax,* which develops in fresh wounds or nostrils of warm-blooded mammals, including humans.

screw·y (skrü′ē) *adj.,* **screw·i·er, screw·i·est.** *Informal.* **1.** odd, eccentric, or crazy: *a screwy person.* **2.** markedly absurd, strange, or unlikely: *a screwy idea.* —**screw′i·ness,** *n.*

scrib·al (skrī′bəl) *adj.* **1.** of or relating to a scribe. **2.** caused by or made in copying, as by a scribe: *scribal errors in a manuscript.*

scrib·ble (skrib′əl) *v.,* **-bled, -bling.** —*v.t.* **1.** to write or draw (something) carelessly or hastily: *I scribbled down the names of all who volunteered.* **2.** to cover with careless, illegible, or meaningless writing or marks. —*v.i.* to write or draw in a careless or hasty manner; make random or meaningless marks: *to scribble on a pad.* —*n.* writing, drawing, or a mark made by scribbling: *margins covered with messy scribbles.* [Medieval Latin *scribillare* to write hastily, from Latin *scrībere* to write.]

scrib·bler (skrib′lər) *n.* **1.** a person who scribbles. **2.** an inferior or unimportant writer; author of little or no reputation.

scribe[1] (skrīb) *n.* **1.** a person whose profession was writing down or copying letters, manuscripts, contracts, or other documents before the invention of printing. **2.** a public clerk or secretary. **3.** a writer, esp. a journalist. **4.** a teacher who interpreted the Mosaic law among the ancient Hebrews. [Latin *scrība* public writer, secretary.]

scribe[2] (skrīb) *n.* scriber. —*v.t.,* **scribed, scrib·ing.** to mark with a scriber or other pointed instrument. [Probably short for INSCRIBE or DESCRIBE.]

scrib·er (skrī′bər) *n.* a pointed steel tool for incising a mark on material, as wood or metal, that is to be cut. [SCRIBE[2] + -ER[1].]

scrim (skrim) *n.* **1.** loosely woven cotton or linen fabric used for such items as curtains or bunting. **2.** a piece of such fabric used as a backdrop or nearly transparent curtain in a theater. [Of uncertain origin.]

scrim·mage (skrim′ij) *n.* **1.** a rough and confused struggle or fight; tussle; scuffle. **2.** *Football.* **a.** the play that occurs from the time the ball is snapped back until it is called dead. **b.** a practice session, often taking the form of a full game. —*v.i., v.t.,* **-maged, -mag·ing.** to participate or oppose in a scrimmage. [Modification of obsolete *scrimish,* form of SKIRMISH.] —**scrim′mag·er,** *n.*

scrimp (skrimp) *v.i.* to be very sparing or frugal, esp. with money; economize (often with *on*): *to scrimp and save for a new dress, to scrimp on movies and other expenses in order to pay for a vacation.* —*v.t.* to be excessively sparing of or with. [Of uncertain origin.] —**scrimp′er,** *n.*

scrimp·y (skrim′pē) *adj.,* **scrimp·i·er, scrimp·i·est.** scarcely adequate in amount or quantity; skimpy; meager. —**scrimp′i·ly,** *adv.* —**scrimp′i·ness,** *n.*

scrim·shaw (skrim′shô′) *n.* **1.** a carved or engraved article made of bone, ivory, shell, or the like, often decorated with nautical scenes or motifs. **2.** such articles collectively, esp. as made by sailors during long whaling or other voyages. **3.** the art of carving or engraving scrimshaw. —*v.t.* to carve or engrave into scrimshaw. —*v.i.* to make or produce scrimshaw. [Of uncertain origin.]

scrip[1] (skrip) *n.* **1.** any temporary money equivalent or substitute, such as a certificate or token, usually issued by a government or business concern, to be exchanged for goods or services. **2.** paper money issued for temporary use in times of emergency, such

as that in amounts of less than a dollar issued in the United States during the Civil War. **3.** a temporary certificate representing a fractional share of stock, or such certificates collectively. [Short for obsolete *(sub)scrip(tion) (receipt)* receipt for part of a loan.]

scrip[2] (skrip) *n.* a small scrap of paper, esp. with something written on it, as a list or schedule. [Form of SCRIPT.]

scrip[3] (skrip) *n.* *Archaic.* a small bag or satchel. [Possibly from Old Norse *skreppa* bag.]

script (skript) *n.* **1.** writing in which the letters are joined together; cursive handwriting. **2.** any of various styles of type resembling this. **3.** a writing system or style: *Babylonian script, Gothic script.* **4.** a typed or written text of a theatrical presentation, motion picture, or radio or television program. —*v.t.* to write a script for: *to script a television show.* [Latin *scrīptum* something written.]

scrip·to·ri·um (skrip tôr′ē əm) *n., pl.* **-to·ri·a** (-tôr′ē ə) or **-to·ri·ums.** a room, esp. one in a monastery, set apart for writing, copying, or illuminating manuscripts. [Medieval Latin *scriptorium,* going back to Latin *scrīptus,* past participle of *scrībere* to write.]

scrip·tur·al (skrip′chər əl) *also,* **Scrip·tur·al.** *adj.* of, based on, or according to Scripture or any sacred writings.

Scrip·ture (skrip′chər) *n.* **1.** *also,* **the Scriptures. a.** the books of the Old and New Testaments, and often the Apocrypha, collectively; the Christian Bible. **b.** the Jewish Bible, equivalent to the Christian Old Testament. **2.** a passage from the Bible. **3.** *also,* **scripture.** a book or writings sacred to a religion. **4. scripture.** a writing or body of writings regarded as authoritative or absolutely true. [Latin *scrīptūra* a writing.]

script·writ·er (skript′rī′tər) *n.* a person who writes scripts, as for a motion picture or television program. —**script′writ′ing,** *n.*

scriv·en·er (skriv′nər) *n.* *Archaic.* a clerk or scribe. [From obsolete *scriven,* from Old French *escrivein,* from Late Latin *scrībānus* notary, from Latin *scrība* public writer.]

scrod (skrod) *n.* a young cod or haddock prepared for cooking. [Probably from Dutch origin.]

scrof·u·la (skrof′yə lə) *n.* a rare form of tuberculosis involving the lymph glands, esp. those in the neck. [Late Latin *scrōfulae* swellings of the neck glands, diminutive of Latin *scrōfa* sow[2]; possibly because the swellings were thought to resemble small pigs.]

scrof·u·lous (skrof′yə ləs) *adj.* **1.** relating to, affected with, or resembling scrofula. **2.** morally corrupt; degenerate.

scroll (skrōl) *n.* **1.** a roll of parchment, paper, silk, or other material containing or used for writings or paintings, often wound around one or a pair of rods so as to be conveniently used or stored. **2.** a figure or ornamental device resembling a partly unrolled scroll, such as the curved head on a violin. —*v.i. Computers.* to move characters displayed on a computer screen horizontally or vertically, as in locating specific information: *to scroll slowly through an alphabetical file.* [Modification (influenced by ROLL) of obsolete *scrow* roll of parchment or paper, from Anglo-Norman *escrowe* scrap[1], strip[2] (as of parchment); of Germanic origin.]

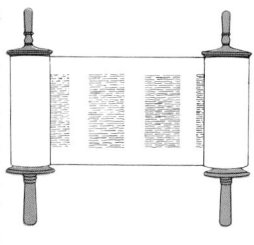

scroll *(def. 1)*

scroll saw, a hand or power saw having a narrow blade with fine teeth, used to cut curved or intricate patterns in thin wood.

scroll·work (skrōl′wûrk′) *n.* ornamental work consisting chiefly of scroll-like patterns, esp. such work cut with a scroll saw.

Scrooge (skrüj) *also,* **scrooge.** *n.* a nasty, mean-tempered miser. [From Ebenezer *Scrooge,* a mean-tempered, miserly old man in *A Christmas Carol,* a story by Charles Dickens, 1812-70, English novelist.]

scro·tum (skrō′təm) *n., pl.* **-ta** (-tə) or **-tums.** an external sac of skin and muscle that in most male mammals contains the testicles. [Latin *scrōtum.*] —**scro′tal,** *adj.*

scrounge (skrounj) *Informal.* *v.,* **scrounged, scroung·ing.** —*v.t.* **1.** to obtain, collect, or gather with effort or difficulty or as by foraging (often with *up*): *We scrounged some rusty tools out of*

a	at	e	end	o	hot	u	up	hw	white		about
ā	ape	ē	me	ō	old	ū	use	ng	song	ə	taken
ä	far	i	it	ô	fork	ü	rule	th	thin		pencil
âr	care	ī	ice	oi	oil	ů	pull	th	this		lemon
		îr	pierce	ou	out	ûr	turn	zh	measure		circus

that decrepit shack. They managed to scrounge up enough money for the rent. **2.** to borrow (something) without intending to return or repay; grub: *to scrounge a meal.* —*v.i.* **1.** to search; forage (often with *around*): *Can you scrounge around in that mess and dig up my book?* **2.** to grub; mooch. [Form of dialectal English *scrunge* to steal; of uncertain origin.] —**scroung′er,** *n.*

scrub¹ (skrub) *v.,* **scrubbed, scrub·bing.** —*v.t.* **1.** to rub vigorously in order to wash or clean: *to scrub a floor.* **2.** to remove by such rubbing: *I scrubbed the ink stains off my hands.* **3.** to cleanse (a gas or vapor) of impurities. **4.** *Informal.* to postpone or cancel (a planned event or activity): *NASA scrubbed the missile launch.* —*v.i.* to wash or clean something by hard rubbing. —*n.* the act of scrubbing. [Middle Dutch *schrobben* to scrape, rub.]

scrub² (skrub) *n.* **1.** vegetation consisting chiefly of low, stunted trees or shrubs. **2.** land or a tract or region that can support only such vegetation. **3.** a domestic animal of undersized growth or inferior or mixed stock. **4.** an undersized or insignificant person. **5.** *Sports.* a player who is not a member of the first or regular team. —*adj.* **1.** undersized, stunted, or inferior: *a scrub tree, scrub cows.* **2.** *Sports.* of, composed of, or played by players not on the first or regular team: *a scrub team, a scrub game.* [Form of SHRUB¹.]

scrub·ber (skrub′ər) *n.* **1.** a device used for scrubbing, esp. an apparatus for cleansing exhaust gas or smoke of chemical pollutants. **2.** a person who scrubs.

scrub·by (skrub′ē) *adj.,* **-bi·er, -bi·est. 1.** of inferior growth or stock; undersized; stunted: *a scrubby bush.* **2.** covered with or consisting of scrub. **3.** shabby, mean, or paltry: *a scrubby old coat.* —**scrub′bi·ly,** *adv.* —**scrub′bi·ness,** *n.*

scrub typhus, an infectious typhuslike disease occurring in Japan, Taiwan, and the South Pacific, characterized by headache, high fever, and a rash and caused by a rickettsia transmitted by larval mites.

scrub·wom·an (skrub′wum′ən) *n., pl.* **-wom·en** (-wim′ən). a woman hired to clean; charwoman.

scruff (skruf) *n.* the back of the neck or the skin covering it. [Modification of obsolete *scuff;* of uncertain origin.]

scruff·y (skruf′ē) *adj.,* **scruff·i·er, scruff·i·est.** worn or dirty; shabby. —**scruf′fi·ly,** *adv.* —**scruff′i·ness,** *n.*

scrump·tious (skrump′shəs) *adj. Informal.* extremely pleasing or delightful, esp. to the taste: *a scrumptious meal.* —**scrump′tious·ly,** *adv.* —**scrump′tious·ness,** *n.*

scrunch (skrunch) *v.t.* **1.a.** to press or squeeze into irregular folds or creases; crumple. **b.** to twist out of shape or draw into a more compact mass; squeeze, as if crumpling (often with *up*): *The child scrunched up her face in distaste. He scrunched himself up in the chair.* **2.** to crunch; crush: *The bear scrunched the ants beneath its paws.* —*v.i.* **1.** to make or move with a crunching sound: *The gravel scrunched under our feet. The car scrunched over the snow.* **2.** to assume or draw into a more compact shape; crouch: *He scrunched down in his seat so that she wouldn't see him.* —*n.* a crunching sound. [Modification of CRUNCH.]

scru·ple (skrü′pəl) *n.* **1.** a moral or ethical principle, consideration, or objection that restrains action or gives rise to doubt, hesitancy, or uneasiness of mind: *She has no scruples about telling people exactly what she thinks of them.* **2.** a very small amount or portion. **3.** an apothecaries' weight equal to 20 grains (1.3 grams), or ¹/₂₄ of an ounce. Three scruples are equal to 1 dram. —*v.i.,* **-pled, -pling.** to hesitate because of scruples; have scruples: *He doesn't scruple about lying when it serves his purpose.* [Latin *scrīpulus* small sharp stone, uneasiness (as that felt when having a stone in one's shoe), small weight, diminutive of *scrūpus* sharp stone, uneasiness.]

scru·pu·lous (skrü′pyə ləs) *adj.* **1.** having or showing a strict regard for what is right; unswervingly attentive to moral or ethical standards. **2.** thoroughly attentive to or careful of even the smallest details; painstaking: *scrupulous neatness, to follow directions with scrupulous care.* —**scru·pu·los·i·ty** (skrü′pyə los′ə tē), **scru′pu·lous·ness,** *n.* —**scru′pu·lous·ly,** *adv.*

scru·ti·nize (skrü′tə nīz′) *v.t.,* **-nized, -niz·ing.** to look at or examine closely or critically; inspect carefully or minutely: *He scrutinized her face for a sign of recognition.* —**scru′ti·niz′er,** *n.* —For Synonyms, see **examine.**

scru·ti·ny (skrü′tə nē) *n., pl.* **-nies. 1.** a close, critical study, examination, or inquiry; careful inspection. **2.** close observation or watch; surveillance: *The suspect's movements were under the scrutiny of the police.* [Late Latin *scrūtinium* search, inquiry, from Latin *scrūtārī* to search, examine.]

scu·ba (skü′bə) *n.* a portable underwater breathing device consisting of one or more cylinders of compressed air that are fastened on a diver's back and a hose or hoses for transmitting the air to a mouthpiece. —*adj.* of or relating to scuba or to scuba

diving: *a scuba tank, scuba equipment.* [Short for *s(elf)-c(ontained) u(nderwater) b(reathing) a(pparatus).*]

scuba diving, the activity of swimming underwater for extended periods of time using scuba gear. —**scuba diver.**

scuba diving

scud (skud) *v.i.,* **scud·ded, scud·ding. 1.** to run or move swiftly: *The clouds scudded across the sky.* **2.** *Nautical.* to run before a gale with little or no sail set. —*n.* **1.** the act of scudding. **2.** light clouds, spray, or rain driven swiftly before the wind. [Probably of Scandinavian origin.]

scuff (skuf) *v.t.* **1.** to scratch, mar, or roughen the surface of by scraping or wear. **2.** to move (the feet) with a scraping or dragging movement. —*v.i.* **1.** to walk by dragging the feet; shuffle. **2.** to become scratched, marred, or roughened by scraping or wear: *This linoleum scuffs easily.* —*n.* **1.** the act or sound of scuffing. **2.** a mar, scratch, or the like made by scuffing. **3.** a light, flat-heeled house slipper, esp. one having no covering for the heel. [Of Scandinavian origin.]

scuf·fle (skuf′əl) *n.* **1.** a confused, often rough, struggle or fight: *The pitcher hit the batter with a pitch, and a scuffle ensued.* **2.** the sound of feet shuffling. —*v.i.,* **-fled, -fling. 1.** to struggle or fight at close quarters in a rough, confused manner. **2.** to drag the feet or move with a shuffle. [Probably of Scandinavian origin.] —**scuf′fler,** *n.*

scull (skul) *n.* **1.** an oar used to propel a boat by working it from side to side over the stern. **2.** one of a pair of light oars used together, one on each side of a boat, by a single rower. **3.** a small boat propelled by sculls, esp. a light racing boat propelled by one or more rowers. —*v.t., v.i.* to propel (a boat) by a scull or sculls, esp. by a single oar worked from side to side over the stern. [Of uncertain origin.] —**scull′er,** *n.*

scul·ler·y (skul′ə rē) *n., pl.* **-ler·ies.** a place, often a small room adjoining a kitchen, where cooking utensils are cleaned and stored and other rough, messy kitchen chores are done. [Old French *escuelerie,* from *escuelle* dish, going back to Latin *scutella* salver, diminutive of *scutra* tray, dish.]

scul·lion (skul′yən) *n. Archaic.* **1.** a servant employed to wash cooking utensils and do dirty, messy, menial work in a kitchen. **2.** a low, contemptible person; wretch. [Of uncertain origin.]

scul·pin (skul′pin) *n., pl.* **-pin** or **-pins.** any of a group of inedible, spiny-finned fish, family Cottidae, found in fresh and salt waters of North America, Europe, and Asia, having a large head, broad mouth, and sharp spines in front of the gills. Also, **miller's-thumb.** [Of uncertain origin.]

sculpt (skulpt) *v.t.* **1.** to carve or otherwise form (a figure or design) by means of sculpture: *to sculpt a statue.* **2.** sculpture (*v.t.,* defs. 2, 3, 4). —*v.i.* to work as a sculptor; produce sculpture: *to sculpt in marble.*

sculp·tor (skulp′tər) *n.* a person who produces sculpture. [Latin *sculptor.*]

sculp·tress (skulp′tris) *n.* a woman who produces sculpture.

sculp·tur·al (skulp′chər əl) *adj.* of, relating to, or like sculpture. —**sculp′tur·al·ly,** *adv.*

sculp·ture (skulp′chər) *n.* **1.** the art or process of producing three-dimensional figures or designs, as by carving or chiseling wood or marble, modeling in clay or wax, or casting in bronze or a similar metal. **2.** a figure or design so produced, or such figures or designs collectively. —*v.,* **-tured, -tur·ing.** —*v.t.* **1.** to

produce (sculpture); sculpt. **2.** to make a sculpture of. **3.** to ornament or cover with sculpture. **4.** to form or shape by or as if by sculpture. —*v.i.* sculpt. [Latin *sculptūra* a carving.]

scum (skum) *n.* **1.** a filmy layer, as of foul or extraneous matter, that forms on or rises to the surface of a liquid or body of water. **2.** a low, vile, despicable person or persons: *The traitors were the scum of the earth.* —*v.i.,* **scummed, scum·ming.** to become covered with or form scum. [Middle Dutch *schūm(e)* foam.]

scum·my (skum′ē) *adj.,* **-mi·er, -mi·est. 1.** covered with, containing, or resembling scum. **2.** low; vile; despicable.

scup (skup) *n., pl.* **scup** or **scups.** a commercially important food fish, *Stenotomus chrysops,* found along the eastern coast of the United States. [Short for Algonquian *mishcup,* from *mishe* large + *kuppe* close together; referring to its scales.]

scup·per (skup′ər) *n.* a hole in the side of a ship that allows water to drain off the deck. [Of uncertain origin.]

scup·per·nong (skup′ər nông′, -nong′) *n.* **1.** a pale green muscadine grape with a plumlike taste, cultivated in the southeastern United States. **2.** a sweet white wine made from this grape. [From *Scuppernong,* a river and lake in North Carolina, where this grape was found in the eighteenth century.]

scurf (skûrf) *n.* **1.** dead, flaky skin, esp. dandruff. **2.** any scaly or flaky matter sticking to a surface. [Of Scandinavian origin.]

scurf·y (skûr′fē) *adj.,* **scurf·i·er, scurf·i·est.** covered with, resembling, or consisting of scurf. —**scurf′i·ness,** *n.*

scur·ril·i·ty (skə ril′i tē) *n., pl.* **-ties. 1.** the quality of being scurrilous. **2.** something that is scurrilous.

scur·ri·lous (skûr′ə ləs) *adj.* **1.** marked by obscenities and coarse abuse; offensively gross: *scurrilous language, a scurrilous attack on a person's character.* **2.** given to using coarse, obscene, or abusive language: *a scurrilous writer.* [Latin *scurrīlis* like a buffoon, jeering (from *scurra* buffoon) + -ous.] —**scur′ri·lous·ly,** *adv.* —**scur′ri·lous·ness,** *n.*

scur·ry (skûr′ē, skur′ē) *v.,* **-ried, -ry·ing.** —*v.i.* to go or move hurriedly: *The deer scurried off into the woods. We scurried from store to store in the rain.* —*v.t.* to cause to go or move hurriedly: *to scurry a fussy child out of a store.* —*n., pl.* **-ries.** the act or sound of scurrying: *the scurry of mice in the walls.* [Short for HURRY-SCURRY.]

scur·vy (skûr′vē) *n.* a disease caused by lack of vitamin C in the diet, characterized by spongy and bleeding gums, bleeding under the skin from hemorrhaging blood vessels, and extreme weakness. —*adj.,* **-vi·er, -vi·est.** mean and vile; contemptible; base: *a scurvy crew of thieves, a scurvy trick.* [SCURF + -Y[1].] —**scur′vi·ly,** *adv.* —**scur′vi·ness,** *n.*

scut (skut) *n.* a short tail, as of a rabbit or deer. [Possibly of Scandinavian origin.]

scu·tage (skū′tij) *n.* a money payment given to a feudal lord by a vassal in lieu of military service. [Medieval Latin *scutagium* literally, shield money, from Latin *scūtum* shield.]

scu·tate (skū′tāt) *adj.* **1.** *Botany.* shaped like a small shield, as a nasturtium leaf. **2.** *Zoology.* covered with bony or horny plates or large scales. [Latin *scūtātus* armed with a shield, from *scūtum* shield.]

scutch (skuch) *v.t.* to separate (flax or other plant fibers) from woody tissue or foreign particles. —*n.* a device or machine for scutching. Also *(n.),* **scutch′er.** [Obsolete French *escoucher* to beat flax, going back to Latin *excutare* to shake out.]

scutch·eon (skuch′ən) escutcheon.

scute (skūt) *n. Zoology.* **1.** any external, bony, horny, or chitinous plate, as in certain fish, reptiles, and arthropods. **2.** any large scale. Also, **scutum.** [Modification of Latin *scūtum* shield.]

scu·tel·late (skū tel′it, skū′tə lāt′) *adj. Zoology.* covered with a scutellum.

scu·tel·lum (skū tel′əm) *n., pl.* **-tel·la** (-tel′ə). a small plate, scale, or other shieldlike part, as on the body of an insect or the foot of a bird. [Modern Latin *scutellum,* diminutive of Latin *scūtum* shield.]

scut·tle[1] (skut′əl) *v.t.,* **-tled, -tling. 1.** to cause (a boat or ship) to sink by cutting, boring, or uncovering an opening in the bottom, deck, or sides. **2.** to abandon or destroy, as hopes or plans. —*n.* **1.** an opening, esp. in the deck, side, or compartment of a ship, usually having a movable cover. **2.** a lid or cover for such an opening. [Possibly from obsolete French *escoutille* hatch[2], from Spanish *escotilla,* diminutive of *escote* opening for the neck in a garment; of Germanic origin.]

scut·tle[2] (skut′əl) *n.* coal scuttle. [Latin *scutella* salver, diminutive of *scutra* dish.]

scut·tle[3] (skut′əl) *v.i.,* **-tled, -tling.** to go or move with short, rapid steps: *crabs scuttling across the ocean bottom.* —*n.* **1.** a rapid pace. **2.** a short, hurried run. [Form of dialectal English *scuddle* to run away, from SCUD.]

scut·tle·butt (skut′əl but′) *n. Informal.* rumor or gossip. [SCUTTLE[1] + BUTT[5].]

scu·tum (skū′təm) *n., pl.* **-ta** (-tə). scute. [Latin *scūtum* shield.]

Scyl·la (sil′ə) *n.* in Greek mythology, a monster having six heads and twelve feet, who lived in a cave on the Strait of Messina, opposite the monster Charybdis. Sailors who were not drowned by Charybdis were snatched from their ships and devoured by Scylla.
 ·**between Scylla and Charybdis.** caught between two dangers, neither of which can be avoided without confronting the other.

scy·pho·zo·an (sī′fə zō′ən) *n.* any of a group of swimming, umbrella-shaped coelenterates, class Scyphozoa, consisting of most of the larger jellyfish, as distinguished from the smaller, hydrozoan varieties. —*adj.* of or relating to scyphozoans. [Modern Latin *Scyphozoa,* from Greek *skyphos* cup + *zōon* animal + -AN.]

scythe (sīth) *n.* a hand implement consisting of a long curved blade attached at an angle to a long bent handle, used for mowing, cutting, or reaping. —*v.t.,* **scythed, scyth·ing.** to mow or cut with or as if with a scythe. [Old English *sīthe* the implement; Modern English spelling influenced by Latin *scindere* to cut.]

Scyth·i·an (sith′ē ən) *adj.* of, relating to, or characteristic of Scythia or its people, language, or culture. —*n.* **1.** a member of an ancient people in central Asia and southwestern Russia who founded a powerful empire. **2.** the language of the ancient Scythians, thought to belong to the Indo-European family of languages.

SD, the postal abbreviation for South Dakota.

S. Dak., South Dakota. Also, **S.D.**

Se the symbol for selenium.

SE 1. southeast. **2.** southeastern.

sea (sē) *n.* **1.** the continuous body of salt water that covers nearly three fourths of the earth's surface; the ocean. **2.** a large portion of this, partly or almost entirely enclosed by land, such as the Caribbean Sea or the Aegean Sea. **3.** a large inland body of water, salt or fresh, such as the Sea of Galilee or the Dead Sea. **4.** the condition of the ocean's surface, esp. with regard to the motion of the waves: *a calm sea, a stormy sea.* **5.** a large, heavy swell or wave: *The ship foundered in rough seas.* **6.** anything suggesting the sea in vastness or extent: *the sea of time, a sea of troubles, a sea of faces.* **7.** the sea considered as affording an occupation or way of life: *The sea has been my life for many years.* —*adj.* of or relating to the sea: *a sea animal.* [Old English *sǣ.*]
 ·**at sea. a.** out on the ocean. **b.** at a loss; bewildered.
 ·**to go to sea. a.** to become a sailor. **b.** to set out on an ocean voyage.
 ·**to put (out) to sea.** to embark on an ocean voyage; sail from land.

sea anchor, a conical, canvas-covered frame or other anchor that is dragged along behind a vessel in order to reduce drift or help keep the vessel heading into the wind. Also, **drogue.**

sea anemone, any of a group of sessile coelenterates, class Anthozoa, related to jellyfish, that attach themselves to rocks, wharves, and other objects, having numerous tentacles that bear stinging cells used to stun prey. For anatomical illustration, see **anthozoan.**

sea bass (bas) any of a group of saltwater bass, family Serranidae, that have a single notched dorsal fin and a large mouth, and that are important food and game fish.

sea·bed (sē′bed′) *n.* the ground at the bottom of the sea; ocean bed.

Sea·bee (sē′bē′) *n.* a member of a U.S. Navy construction battalion that is composed of skilled workers of all trades who build and maintain various installations, such as shipyards and ammunition depots. [Modification of *C.B.,* abbreviation of *C(onstruction) B(attalion).*]

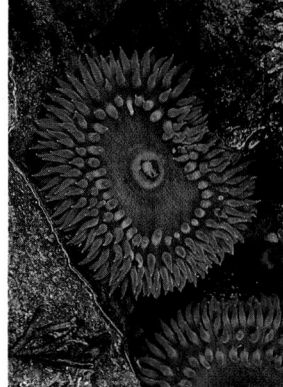

sea anemone

sea·bird (sē′bûrd′) *n.* any water bird whose chief habitat is the open ocean, such as an albatross or petrel.

sea biscuit, hardtack. Also, **sea bread.**

a	at	e	end	o	hot	u	up	hw	white		about
ā	ape	ē	me	ō	old	ū	use	ng	song		taken
ä	far	i	it	ô	fork	ü	rule	th	thin	ə	pencil
âr	care	ī	ice	oi	oil	u̇	pull	th	this		lemon
		îr	pierce	ou	out	ûr	turn	zh	measure		circus

sea·board (sē′bôrd′) *n.* the land near or bordering on the sea; seacoast.

sea·borne (sē′bôrn′) *adj.* **1.** carried on or over the sea. **2.** transported by ship: *seaborne freight.*

sea bream, any of several food and game fish, family Sparidae, found chiefly along the Atlantic coast of North America.

sea breeze, a breeze blowing inland from the sea.

sea·coast (sē′kōst′) *n.* the land near or bordering on the sea.

sea cow 1. dugong. **2.** manatee.

sea cucumber, any of a class (Holothuroidea) of cucumber-shaped echinoderms found in coastal waters and having a flexible body with several tentacles around the mouth; holothurian. Length: ¼ inch-20 inches (0.6-51 centimeters).

sea dog, a sailor, esp. an old or experienced one.

sea duck, any of various diving ducks, such as the scoter.

sea eagle, any of various eagles that feed chiefly on fish.

sea elephant, elephant seal.

sea fan, any of various purple or yellow corals, order Gorgonacea, consisting of colonial polyps that build flat, lacy, branching structures.

sea·far·er (sē′fâr′ər) *n.* a person engaged in seafaring, esp. a sailor.

sea·far·ing (sē′fâr′ing) *adj.* **1.** following the sea as a business or calling: *a seafaring merchant.* **2.** of or relating to the sea or to life or work as a sailor: *The old sailors recalled their seafaring days.* **3.** traveling on the sea: *a seafaring ship.* —*n.* **1.** the business or calling of a sailor. **2.** travel by sea.

sea·food (sē′fo͞od′) *also,* **sea food.** *n.* **1.** saltwater fish or shellfish used for food. **2.** any fish used for food.

sea·fowl (sē′foul′) *n.* a seabird, or seabirds collectively.

sea front, the land bordering on the sea.

sea·girt (sē′gûrt′) *adj.* surrounded by the sea: *Iceland is a seagirt nation.*

sea·go·ing (sē′gō′ing) *adj.* **1.** designed, suitable, or used for sea travel. **2.** seafaring.

sea green, medium bluish green.

sea gull, gull¹.

sea horse 1. any of various slender fish, genus *Hippocampus,* found in warm and temperate seas, having a head and neck resembling that of a horse and a prehensile tail with which it clings to underwater plants. Length: 2-8 inches (5-20 centimeters). **2.** a walrus. **3.** a mythical sea creature, half fish and half horse.

seal¹ (sēl) *n., pl.* **seals** or **seal. 1.** any of various aquatic mammals, order Pinnipedia, usually living in coastal waters, having a streamlined body, a muscular neck, and limbs that are modified to form flippers, and comprising the earless seals, such as the elephant seal, and the eared seals, such as the sea lion. **2.** the pelt or fur of a seal, esp. of a fur seal. **3.** leather made from the hide of a seal. —*v.i.* to hunt seals, esp. for their fur. [Old English *seolh* the marine mammal.]

seal² (sēl) *n.* **1.** an impression in relief of a design, figure, or word stamped on wax, paper, or other soft material to show owner-

sea horse

ship or authenticity, intended to officially represent a person, institution, or governing body. **2.** the representation of such an impression, or a disk or wafer of wax, paper, or other material bearing such an impression, affixed to a document to prove authenticity or to fasten it shut. **3.** a stamp, die, ring, or other object engraved with a design, figure, or word, used to impart such impressions. **4.** something that fastens firmly, closes completely, or makes airtight or watertight: *the seal on an envelope, the seal on a jar.* **5.** a decorative gummed stamp or sticker. **6.** something that serves to authenticate, confirm, or secure; pledge; assurance. **7.** *Archaic.* a mark or sign indicating ownership or serving as visible evidence of something. —*v.t.* **1.** to fasten or shut firmly, as to make airtight or watertight: *to seal an envelope, to seal a tomb.* **2.** to fill or stop up: *The painter sealed the cracks in the wall.* **3.** to shut in or confine; enclose tightly: *They sealed the documents in a strongbox.* **4.** to prevent or restrict access to (often with *off*): *The police sealed off the area of the accident.* **5.** to confirm, conclude, or assure as if by affixing a seal: *to seal a bargain with a handshake.* **6.** to put beyond doubt, question, or reversal; decide irrevocably: *The arrival of reinforcements sealed the army's victory.* **7.** to place a seal on, as to prove authenticity: *The notary sealed the application.* **8.** to mark or stamp with a seal in order to certify the size, weight, accuracy, or quality of: *to seal a grocer's scale.* [Old French *seel* engraved signet for stamping documents in order to authenticate them, going back to Latin *sigillum* little mark, small figure, diminutive of *signum* sign, mark¹.]

sea lamprey, a lamprey, *Petromyzon marinus,* of Atlantic coast

and Great Lakes waters. Those landlocked in the Great Lakes have parasitized and destroyed large numbers of lake trout.

seal·ant (sē′lənt) *n.* a substance used to seal pores, joints, cracks, or the like; sealer. [SEAL² + -ANT.]

sea lavender, any of a group of plants, genus *Limonium,* found in marshy seaside regions of the Northern Hemisphere, bearing small, usually blue or purple flowers.

sea legs *Informal.* the ability to walk steadily aboard ship, esp. on rough seas.

seal·er¹ (sē′lər) *n.* **1.** a person or thing that fastens, closes, or makes airtight or watertight. **2.** a substance applied to a porous or unfinished surface in preparation for painting or varnishing. **3.** an official who inspects weights, measures, or materials to ensure that they have met certain standards. [SEAL² + -ER¹.]

seal·er² (sē′lər) *n.* a person or ship engaged in seal hunting. [SEAL¹ + -ER¹.]

seal·er·y (sē′lə rē) *n., pl.* **-er·ies. 1.** the occupation of hunting for seals; seal hunting. **2.** any place where seals are hunted.

sea lettuce, any of a genus, *Ulva,* of green algal seaweed common along shores in temperate regions, sometimes eaten as greens.

sea level, the mean level of the surface of the sea, esp. halfway between mean high and low water, used as a standard above and below which land elevations and sea depths are measured.

sea lily, crinoid.

sealing wax, a mixture usually consisting of shellac and turpentine, that softens when heated but quickly hardens as it cools, used for sealing letters, packages, jars, and other items.

sea lion, any of various large eared seals, found chiefly in the Pacific Ocean, esp. the **California sea lion,** *Zalophus californianus.*

seal ring, signet ring.

seal·skin (sēl′skin′) *n.* the pelt or fur of a fur seal.

Sea·ly·ham terrier (sē′lē ham′, -lē əm) a small, short-legged breed of terrier having a long head, round-tipped ears, and a rough, wiry coat of white hair. Height: 10 inches (25 centimeters) at the shoulder.

seam (sēm) *n.* **1.** a line formed by sewing together the edges of two or more pieces of cloth, leather, or similar material: *a seam of a dress.* **2.** a similar line, groove, or ridge formed by adjoining edges, as of planks or layers of bricks. **3.** any mark resembling a seam, such as a scar or crack. **4.** a stratum or thin layer, as of coal or rock. —*v.t.* **1.** to join together by or as by sewing. **2.** to mark with a seam or seams; furrow; wrinkle: *Time had seamed the old sailor's face.* —*v.i.* to become furrowed, cracked, or fissured. [Old English *sēam* line formed by sewing or joining two edges.] —**seam′er,** *n.*

sea·man (sē′mən) *n., pl.* **-men** (-mən). **1.** a sailor; mariner. **2.** a person excelling in seamanship. **3.** in the U.S. Navy and Coast Guard, an enlisted person of any of the three lowest grades.

sea·man·ship (sē′mən ship′) *n.* skill in and knowledge of managing, maneuvering, or maintaining a boat or ship.

sea·mark (sē′märk′) *n.* any landmark visible from the sea, such as a lighthouse or beacon, that serves as a navigational aid.

sea mew, mew².

sea mile, nautical mile.

sea·mount (sē′mount′) *n.* a peak or flat-topped mountain that rises from the floor of the ocean, but not high enough to breach the surface; undersea prominence. [SEA + MOUNT².]

seam·stress (sēm′stris) *n.* a woman who is skilled at sewing, esp. one whose occupation is sewing. Also, **sempstress.**

seam·y (sē′mē) *adj.,* **seam·i·er, seam·i·est. 1.** dismal, squalid, or degraded; sordid: *the seamy side of life.* **2.** having or showing seams. —**seam′i·ness,** *n.*

sé·ance (sā′äns) *n.* **1.** a meeting in which a group of people attempt to communicate with the spirits of the dead through the help of a medium. **2.** a session or sitting, as for a secretive meeting. [French *séance* session, from Old French *seoir* to sit, from Latin *sedēre.*]

sea otter, a dark-brown otter, *Enhydra lutris,* that inhabits the coastal waters of western North America and other northern Pacific shores, having broad, flipperlike hind feet. It is the largest of all otters and the only one that lives in salt water. Length: 50-64 inches (127-163 centimeters), including tail.

sea·plane (sē′plān′) *n.* an airplane, esp. one equipped with floats, that is designed to take off from and land on water. Also, **hydroplane.**

sea·port (sē′pôrt′) *n.* **1.** a port or harbor for seagoing vessels. **2.** a city or town having such a port or harbor.

sea power 1. a nation that possesses formidable naval strength. **2.** naval strength.

sea purse, the tough, protective case or pouch encasing the eggs of skates and certain sharks.

sear (sîr) *v.t.* **1.** to burn the surface of; char; scorch: *to sear a steak.* **2.** to dry up or wither: *The prairie sun seared the tall grass.*

S

3. to harden or make callous: *The war seared the young soldier's feelings.* —*n.* a mark made by searing or burning. —*adj.* *Archaic.* dried; sere. [Old English *sēarian* to become withered, from *sēar* dry, withered.] —For Synonyms *(v.t.),* see **scorch.**

search (sûrch) *v.t.* **1.** to look through or explore carefully and thoroughly in order to find something: *The police searched the suspect for concealed weapons. I've searched all my drawers for the missing notebook.* **2.** to look into or examine carefully and closely; probe: *to search one's heart.* **3.** to find, uncover, or come to know through exploration or investigation (with *out*): *to search out the truth.* —*v.i.* to look carefully and thoroughly; make an examination or investigation: *to search through one's pockets, to search for a lost cat.* —*n.* the act of searching: *They found the missing child after a long search.* [Old French *cerchier* to seek, from Late Latin *circāre* to go round, explore, from Latin *circum* around, about.] —**search′er,** *n.*
• **in search of.** looking to find, uncover, or come to know: *to go in search of food, in search of truth.*

search·ing (sûr′ching) *adj.* **1.** keenly observant and penetrating: *a searching glance.* **2.** investigating and probing carefully: *a searching inquiry, searching questions.* —**search′ing·ly,** *adv.*

search·light (sûrch′līt′) *n.* **1.** a device that projects a strong beam of light in any chosen direction by means of a concave reflector or a lens that focuses the light in a concentrated stream of rays. **2.** the beam of light so projected. **3.** flashlight *(def. 1).*

search warrant, a court order authorizing law officers to search a specified place and to seize specified persons or things. It is issued by a court when there is probable cause to believe that the place or persons involved are connected with a crime.

sea robin, any of a group of reddish brown gurnards, esp. genus *Prionotus,* having a bony, often spiny head, winglike side fins, and several slender, fingerlike feelers under the fins. Length: to 3 feet (0.9 meter).

sea room, sufficient unobstructed space at sea for maneuvering a boat or ship easily and safely.

sea rover 1. a buccaneer; pirate. **2.** a pirate ship.

sea·scape (sē′skāp′) *n.* **1.** a picture depicting a sea scene. Also, **marine. 2.** a view of the sea. [SEA + (LAND)SCAPE.]

seascape
a painting by Arthur Dove

sea serpent, any of various legendary marine monsters, usually represented as a snakelike or dragonlike creature of enormous size and strength.

sea·shell (sē′shel′) *n.* the shell of any marine mollusk, such as an oyster or clam.

sea·shore (sē′shôr′) *n.* the land near or bordering on the sea.

sea·sick (sē′sik′) *adj.* nauseated and dizzy as a result of the rolling motion of a vessel at sea. —**sea′sick′ness,** *n.*

sea·side (sē′sīd′) *n.* the land near or bordering on the sea; seashore.

sea slug, nudibranch.

sea snake 1. any of a group of venomous snakes, family Hydrophidae, having a finlike tail, found in the warm inshore seas of Asia. **2.** *Archaic.* sea serpent.

sea·son (sē′zən) *n.* **1.** one of the divisions of the year, as determined by the tilt of the earth's axis in its orbit around the sun. The four seasons, spring, summer, autumn, and winter, are characterized chiefly by differences in weather, average temperature, and number of hours of daylight. **2.** a period or time of the year with reference to the weather conditions that characterize it: *the*

rainy season, the monsoon season. **3.** any period or time of the year associated with a particular activity or thing: *the football season, the opera season.* **4.** the period or time of the year during which something flourishes or is best or is available or permitted: *the peach season, the oyster season, fishing season.* **5.** the time of the year during which a particular place is most frequently visited for social activities, amusement, or recreation: *We went to Bermuda during the height of the season.* **6.** an appropriate, natural, or appointed time: *This is the season for shorts and bathing suits.* **7.** any period of time: *I worked hard during the season of my apprenticeship.* —*v.t.* **1.** to add seasoning to (food) in order to bring out or improve its flavor. **2.** to add zest or interest to: *to season a dry lecture with anecdotes.* **3.** to cure or render more suitable for use, as by drying or aging: *to season wood.* **4.** to condition or make fit through experience: *to season an athlete.* **5.** to make accustomed or inured; harden; acclimate: *to season troops to battle.* **6.** to make less severe; moderate; temper. —*v.i.* to become more suitable for use. —*adj.* valid for a specified period of time and often sold at a reduced rate: *a season subscription to the ballet.* [Old French *saison, seson* period of the year, from Medieval Latin *satio* time of sowing, from Latin *satiō* a sowing, planting.]
• **in season. a.** available or in the best condition for eating: *Peaches are now in season.* **b.** in or at the most appropriate time, as for social activities: *to go to the Riviera in season.* **c.** legally permitted to be hunted or caught: *Deer are now in season.* **d.** (of animals) ready to mate or breed; in heat.
• **out of season.** not in season.

sea·son·a·ble (sē′zə nə bəl) *adj.* **1.** usual for or in keeping with the time of year: *Seasonable temperatures are expected through Friday.* **2.** occurring at the right or proper time; opportune; timely. —**sea′son·a·ble·ness,** *n.* —**sea′son·a·bly,** *adv.*

sea·son·al (sē′zə nəl) *adj.* affected by, characteristic of, or occurring at a certain season or seasons: *seasonal storms, seasonal unemployment.* —**sea′son·al·ly,** *adv.*

sea·son·ing (sē′zə ning) *n.* **1.** something used to bring out or improve the flavor of food, such as a spice, herb, or condiment. **2.** something that adds zest or interest.

season ticket, a ticket for an entire season or series of scheduled performances, as of sporting events or concerts, or for transportation between two locations for a certain period of time.

sea spider, any of a group of long-legged, narrow-bodied, marine arthropods, class Pycnogonida, related to arachnids. The four pairs of heavy walking legs contain branches from the digestive and reproductive systems.

sea squirt, any of a small group of small, saclike marine chordates or tunicates, that live attached to the ocean bottom as adults and that, when disturbed, contract their bodies and squirt water.

sea star, starfish.

seat (sēt) *n.* **1.** something to sit on, such as a chair, stool, or bench. **2.** a place to sit: *Those who arrive late will have to find seats on the floor.* **3.** that part of an object on which one sits: *the seat of a chair.* **4.a.** that part of the body on which one sits; buttocks. **b.** that part of a garment that covers this: *the seat of one's pants.* **5.** membership or an official position, as in a legal, commercial, or legislative body: *a seat in the Senate, a seat on the stock exchange.* **6.** a reserved accommodation for sitting: *We have two seats for the afternoon performance.* **7.** the part on which something rests; base. **8.** a center or source: *a seat of learning, the seat of the emotions.* **9.** a manner of sitting, as on horseback. **10.** a place of residence, esp. a country estate. —*v.t.* **1.** to place on or conduct to a seat; assign a seat to: *The ushers seated the wedding guests.* **2.** to have the capacity or seats for: *The auditorium seats 300 people.* **3.** to establish in a particular place; settle; locate: *The government was seated in a rural town.* **4.** to put a seat in or on. **5.** to fit in place firmly or properly: *to seat a post in the ground.* [Old Norse *sæti* chair, position.] —**seat′ed,** *adj.* —**seat′er,** *n.*
• **to be seated.** to sit down.
• **to take a seat.** to sit down.

seat belt, a strap or set of straps that may be buckled to hold a person in a seat, as in a vehicle or aircraft. Also, **safety belt.**

seat·ing (sē′ting) *n.* **1.** the arrangement of seats: *The seating is excellent for viewing the stage.* **2.** the assignment of seats: *Our host took care of the seating of guests at the table.* **3.** the act of conducting to or providing with a seat or seats. **4.** material used for upholstering seats.

sea trout 1. any of various trout, such as the salmon trout, that

a	at	e	end	o	hot	u	up	hw	white	about
ā	ape	ē	me	ō	old	ū	use	ng	song	taken
ä	far	i	it	ô	fork	ü	rule	th	thin	ə pencil
âr	care	ī	ice	oi	oil	u̇	pull	th	this	lemon
		îr	pierce	ou	out	ûr	turn	zh	measure	circus

migrate to salt water and later return to fresh water to spawn. **2.** any of various weakfish that resemble trout.

sea urchin, any of a group of echinoderms, class Echinoidea, having a thin skeleton of limy plates under the skin and, usually, hard, movable spines. Also, **echinus, urchin.**

sea wall, a strong wall or embankment made to prevent erosion of a shoreline or to act as a breakwater.

sea·ward (sē′wərd) *adj.* **1.** toward the sea: *a seaward course.* **2.** from the sea: *a seaward wind.* —*adv.* also, **sea·wards.** in the direction of the sea: *The explorers walked seaward.*

sea·wa·ter (sē′wô′tər, -wot′ər) *n.* the salt water of a sea or ocean.

sea·way (sē′wā′) *n.* **1.** a route over the sea; shipping lane. **2.** an inland waterway deep and wide enough for ocean shipping. **3.** the headway of a ship or boat. **4.** a moderately rough sea.

sea·weed (sē′wēd′) *n.* any of various plants or algae living in the sea, esp. as found floating along the shore.

sea·wor·thy (sē′wûr′thē) *adj.* (of a ship or boat) fit or safe to sail under all conditions. —**sea′wor′thi·ness,** *n.*

se·ba·ceous (si bā′shəs) *adj.* **1.** of or relating to oil or fat; oily; greasy. **2.** secreting oil or fat. [Latin *sēbāceus* made of tallow, from *sēbum* tallow, grease.]

sebaceous gland, any of the glands of the skin that secrete an oily lubricating fluid to the skin and hair.

seb·or·rhe·a (seb′ə rē′ə) *n.* a disorder of the sebaceous glands, characterized by excessive secretion of sebum, resulting in an oily coating or crust on the skin. —**seb′or·rhe′ic,** *adj.*

se·bum (sē′bəm) *n.* the greasy secretion of the sebaceous glands, composed primarily of fat, that helps protect and lubricate the skin and hair. [Latin *sēbum* tallow, grease.]

sec 1. secant. **2.** *also,* **sec.** second.

sec. 1. secretary. **2.** section.

SEC, Securities and Exchange Commission.

se·cant (sē′kant, -kənt) *n.* **1.** *Trigonometry.* (of either acute angle of a right triangle) the trigonometric function that is the ratio of the length of the hypotenuse to the length of the side adjacent to the angle. **2.** *Geometry.* a straight line intersecting a curve at two or more points. —*adj.* intersecting. [Latin *secāns,* present participle of *secāre* to cut; because the line intersects or *cuts* the curve.]

se·cede (si sēd′) *v.i.,* **-ced·ed, -ced·ing.** to withdraw formally, esp. as a group, from a larger organization, usually to form an alternative organization. [Latin *sēcēdere* to go away, withdraw.] —**se·ced′er,** *n.*

se·ces·sion (si sesh′ən) *n.* **1.** the act or an instance of seceding. **2.** *also,* **Secession.** the withdrawal of eleven Southern states from the Union in 1860 and 1861 that led to the American Civil War. [Latin *sēcessiō* withdrawal, separation.]

se·ces·sion·ism (si sesh′ə niz′əm) *n.* the theory or principles of those who advocate secession.

se·ces·sion·ist (si sesh′ə nist) *n.* **1.** a person who favors or advocates secession. **2.** a member of a group that secedes. —*adj.* relating to or advocating secession or secessionism.

Seck·el (sek′əl, sik′-) *n.* a pear of a small, yellowish brown variety. [From *Seckel,* the surname of the Pennsylvania farmer who first grew it.]

se·clude (si klüd′) *v.t.,* **-clud·ed, -clud·ing.** to keep apart or remove from the company of others; isolate; sequester: *I secluded myself in my room to study.* [Latin *sēclūdere* to shut off.] —For Synonyms, see **isolate.**

se·clud·ed (si klü′did) *adj.* **1.** shut off or screened from view: *a secluded courtyard.* **2.** kept apart or removed from others; solitary: *a secluded life.* —**se·clud′ed·ly,** *adv.* —**se·clud′ed·ness,** *n.*

se·clu·sion (si klü′zhən) *n.* the act of secluding or the state of being secluded. [Medieval Latin *seclusio* a setting aside, from Latin *sēclūsus,* past participle of *sēclūdere* to shut off.] —For Synonyms, see **solitude.**

se·clu·sive (si klü′siv) *adj.* fond of or inclined toward seclusion. —**se·clus′ive·ly,** *adv.* —**se·clu′sive·ness,** *n.*

sec·o·bar·bi·tal (sek′ō bär′bi tôl′) *n.* a fast-acting, potentially addictive barbiturate used as a sleep-inducing drug and sedative, usually administered in the form of its bitter, powdery sodium salt. Formula: $C_{12}H_{18}N_2O_3$

Sec·o·nal (sek′ə nôl′) *n. Trademark.* secobarbital.

sec·ond[1] (sek′ənd) *adj.* **1.** (the ordinal of the number two) next after the first: *the second house from the corner.* **2.** additional or other; another: *a second visit to the dentist, a second helping of potatoes.* **3.** alternate: *to receive a magazine every second month.* **4.** below the first or best; subordinate; inferior: *my second favorite.* **5.** *Music.* of, relating to, or designating a part performed lower in pitch than or subordinate to another of the same category: *second violin, second soprano.* **6.** *Mechanics.* relating to or designating the forward gear next above first or low in the trans-

mission of a motor vehicle. —*adv.* in the group or position next after the first: *to finish second in a race.* —*n.* **1.** a person or thing that is next after the first: *I was the second to arrive.* **2.** an endorsement of an initial proposal or motion; formal approval or support: *The chairperson asked for a second.* **3.** a person who assists and supports another, as in a duel or boxing match. **4.** *also,* **seconds.** goods below the first or best quality, often having visible defects. **5.** *Mechanics.* the forward gear next above first or low in the transmission of a motor vehicle. **6.** *Music.* **a.** an interval between two notes or tones separated by one degree on the diatonic scale. D is the second of C. **b.** a note or tone separated by this interval from another. **c.** the harmonic combination of two such notes or tones. **7.** second base. —*v.t.* **1.** to formally approve or support; endorse: *to second a motion to adjourn.* **2.** to give support, encouragement, or assistance to: *The city council seconded the mayor's campaign against crime.* [Old French *second* the next to the first, from Latin *secundus* following, the next to the first, from *sequī* to follow; because it *follows* what is first.] —**sec′ond·er,** *n.*

sec·ond[2] (sek′ənd) *n.* **1.** a unit of time equal to $1/60$ of a minute or $1/3600$ of an hour. **2.** any very short interval of time: *It will take me only a second to put on my coat.* **3.** a unit of angular measurement equal to $1/60$ of a minute or $1/3600$ of a degree. [Medieval Latin *secunda (minuta)* second (minute) (referring to the *second* division of the hour into 3,600 seconds, as distinguished from the first division into 60 minutes), from Latin *secunda,* feminine of *secundus* the next to the first.]

Second Advent, Second Coming.

sec·ond·ar·y (sek′ən der′ē) *adj.* **1.** not principal or chief; less important; subordinate: *a secondary consideration.* **2.** coming from or based on that which is original or primary; derived: *They got all their information from secondary sources.* **3.** coming below or after the first as in order, place, or time: *a secondary consequence.* **4.** of or relating to an electrical coil or winding in which a current is produced by induction when the current in another, primary, coil or winding changes. —*n.* **1.** a person or thing that is secondary. **2.** an electrical coil or winding in which a current is produced by induction. **3.** *Football.* the defensive backfield. —**sec′ond·ar′i·ly,** *adv.*

secondary accent **1.** the weaker of the two stresses in any word that has two syllables accented or stressed. The third syllable of *sec′ond·ar′y* has a secondary accent. **2.** the mark (′) indicating this accent. Also, **secondary stress.**

secondary color, any color, such as orange, that results from the mixing of two primary colors.

secondary emission, the emission of electrons from the surface of a metal or other conducting substance that is bombarded by electrons or ions.

secondary school, a school providing instruction after elementary or grade school, comprising grades seven, eight, or nine through twelve.

secondary sex characteristic, any of the physical features not related to reproduction that are characteristic of each sex and usually appear at puberty, such as breast development or beard growth.

second base *Baseball.* **1.** the base that must be touched second by a base runner. **2.** the position of the player stationed near this base, on the side toward first base.

sec·ond-best (sek′ənd best′) *adj.* next or inferior to the best.

second best, something that is next or inferior to the best.

second childhood, senility; dotage.

sec·ond-class (sek′ənd klas′) *adj.* **1.** less than the highest or best; inferior: *a second-class intellect.* **2.** of or relating to a class of mail consisting primarily of newspapers and magazines. **3.** of or relating to a form of travel ranking next in price or luxury below first class. —*adv.* by or in second class: *to travel second-class.*

second class **1.** second-class travel accommodations. **2.** second-class mail.

Second Coming, in Christian theology, the return of Jesus on Judgment Day to judge the living and the dead. Also, **Second Advent.**

sec·ond-de·gree burn (sek′ənd di grē′) a burn of the outer and second layers of the skin; burn that causes blistering.

second fiddle, a minor or subordinate role or position: *to play second fiddle to a friend who is more popular.*

second growth, the tree growth that replaces virgin forest after an area has been logged or burned.

sec·ond-guess (sek′ənd ges′) *v.t., v.i.* **1.** to make judgments about (some decision or the person who made it) after the results of that decision are known. **2.** to outguess (someone) or anticipate (something): *It is very difficult to second-guess what the coach will do in tomorrow's game.* —**sec′ond-guess′er,** *n.*

sec·ond·hand (sek′ənd hand′) *also,* **sec·ond-hand.** *adj.* **1.** that has already been owned, used, or worn by someone else;

S

not new: *a secondhand car.* **2.** not obtained from the original source; derivative; borrowed: *secondhand knowledge of a subject.* **3.** dealing in previously used merchandise: *a secondhand furniture store.* —*adv.* in a secondhand manner; indirectly.

second hand, the hand or pointer of a timepiece that indicates the passage of seconds.

second lieutenant, a commissioned officer of the lowest level in the U.S. Army, Air Force, and Marine Corps, ranking below a first lieutenant.

sec·ond·ly (sek′ənd lē) *adv.* in the second place; second.

second nature, an acquired tendency or quality that is so deeply fixed in one's character as to appear innate.

second person, the form of a pronoun or verb that indicates the person or thing addressed. In the sentence *You were out when I called, you* and *were* are in the second person.

sec·ond-rate (sek′ənd rāt′) *adj.* not best in some quality or degree; mediocre or inferior: *The team played second-rate defense and lost the game.* —**sec′ond-rate′ness,** *n.* —**sec′ond-rat′er,** *n.*

second sight, the supposed power of seeing things that are not physically present, such as distant or future events; clairvoyance.

sec·ond-sto·ry man (sek′ənd stôr′ē) *Informal.* a burglar who enters buildings through upstairs windows.

sec·ond-string (sek′ənd string′) *adj.* **1.** *Sports.* of or relating to any of the generally less able members of a team who do not play at the start of a game but may appear later as substitutes. **2.** not preferred or best; mediocre; second-rate. —**sec′ond-string′er,** *n.*

second thought *also,* **second thoughts.** a reservation or doubt about an earlier decision, idea, or course of action.
•**on second thought.** after reconsideration: *On second thought, I think I'll accept your invitation.*

second wind 1. the return of relative ease in breathing following a period of labored breathing, as in running. **2.** renewed energy for or interest in any endeavor.

se·cre·cy (sē′krə sē) *n.* **1.** the state of being secret or being kept secret. **2.** the ability or practice of keeping secrets.

se·cret (sē′krit) *adj.* **1.** known only to oneself or a few; kept from general knowledge: *a secret password, a secret plan.* **2.** having goals, methods, or ceremonies known only to a few; acting in a hidden way: *a secret organization.* **3.** built or made to escape notice: *a secret panel in a wall.* **4.** beyond ordinary understanding; not readily apparent; mysterious: *secret knowledge.* **5.** dependable in keeping what one knows to oneself; close-mouthed; discreet: *a secret confidant.* **6.** providing privacy; secluded. —*n.* **1.** something that is known only to oneself or a few and kept from general knowledge: *to keep a secret.* **2.** a hidden reason or explanation: *the secret of one's success.* **3.** a true method or way of attaining something; key: *the secret of happiness.* **4.** a cause or process not readily understood or explained; mystery: *the secrets of nature.* [Old French *secret* hidden, discreet, from Latin *sēcrētus* hidden, past participle of *sēcernere* to put apart, separate.] —**se′cret·ly,** *adv.*
•**in secret.** not openly or in public; in private: *to meet in secret.*

> **Synonyms** *adj.* **Secret, covert,** and **clandestine** mean known to one person or to a small group. **Secret,** the broadest of these terms, is applied to anything that is purposely concealed: *The secret documents were kept in a safe.* **Covert** also implies concealing something, often through disguise or indirection: *a covert operation, a covert signal from the leader that started the demonstration.* **Clandestine** implies the hiding of something illicit or evil: *The burglars held clandestine meetings to plan the robbery.*

secret agent 1. an agent of a secret service whose identity is known only to a few. **2.** spy.

sec·re·tar·i·al (sek′rə târ′ē əl) *adj.* of or relating to a secretary or a secretary's duties.

sec·re·tar·i·at (sek′rə târ′ē it) *n.* **1.** the administrative department of an organization: *the secretariat of the United Nations.* **2.** officials who keep records or perform secretarial duties. **3.** the office or position of a secretary, esp. of a government department. [French *secrétariat,* from Medieval Latin *secretariatus* office of a secretary, from Late Latin *sēcrētārius.* See SECRETARY.]

sec·re·tar·y (sek′rə ter′ē) *n., pl.* **-tar·ies. 1.** a person employed to handle correspondence, do routine work, and keep records for an individual or company. **2.** an officer of an organization or company responsible for important records and correspondence. **3.** *also,* **Secretary.** the person who heads an executive department of a government: *the Secretary of State.* **4.** a piece of furniture having a fold-up writing surface, bookshelves, and drawers or compartments below. [Late Latin *sēcrētārius* confidential officer, going back to Latin *sēcrētus.* See SECRET.]

secretary bird, a long-legged bird, *Sagittarius serpentarius,* native to the plains of southern Africa, having a crest of feathers that resemble quill pens at the back of its head. Height: to 4 feet (1.2 meters).

sec·re·tar·y-gen·er·al (sek′rə ter′ē jen′ər əl) *n., pl.* **sec·re·taries-gen·er·al.** the chief administrative officer of a secretariat.

se·crete[1] (si krēt′) *v.t.,* **-cret·ed, -cret·ing.** to produce or discharge by means of secretion: *Some glands secrete hormones.* [From SECRETION[1].]

se·crete[2] (si krēt′) *v.t.,* **-cret·ed, -cret·ing.** to put in a hiding place; hide

secretary bird

away. [Modification of obsolete *secret* to hide, from SECRET.]

se·cre·tin (si krē′tin) *n.* a hormone that triggers secretion of pancreatic juice, produced in the small intestine. [SECRET(ION[1]) + -IN[1].]

se·cre·tion[1] (si krē′shən) *n.* **1.** the process by which a substance with a specific function, such as a hormone, is produced by a cell or gland and released within an organism or excreted. **2.** any substance so produced. [Latin *sēcrētiō* separation.]

se·cre·tion[2] (si krē′shən) the act of secreting; hiding.

se·cre·tive (sē′kri tiv, si krē′-) *adj.* **1.** of, characterized by, or indicating secrecy or concealment: *a secretive smile.* **2.** secretory. —**se′cre·tive·ly,** *adv.* —**se′cre·tive·ness,** *n.*

se·cre·to·ry (si krē′tə rē) *adj.* relating to, producing, or causing secretion.

secret police, a police force that operates mainly in secret, often using surveillance, intimidation, and violence to suppress opposition to its government's political policies.

Secret Service 1. the division of the U.S. Treasury Department that protects the president and other important people and enforces federal laws against counterfeiting U.S. currency and bonds. **2.** *also,* **secret service.** a government department or bureau that engages in such secret operations as espionage and counterespionage.

secs *also,* **secs.** seconds.

secs., sections.

sect (sekt) *n.* **1.** a religious body, esp. a small group separated from a larger, established denomination. **2.** any relatively small group sharing the same philosophical or political principles, beliefs, or opinions. [Latin *secta* following, faction, school (of philosophy).]

sect., section.

sec·tar·i·an (sek târ′ē ən) *adj.* **1.** of, relating to, or limited to one small and narrow group; partisan: *sectarian political beliefs.* **2.** of or relating to a religious sect; denominational: *a sectarian college.* —*n.* a person who belongs to a religious sect.

sec·tar·i·an·ism (sek târ′ē ə niz′əm) *n.* the practice of being sectarian.

sec·ta·ry (sek′tə rē) *n., pl.* **-ries. 1.** a dissenter from an established church, esp. a Protestant nonconformist. **2.** a person who is sectarian; dissenter; partisan. [Medieval Latin *sectarius* adherent, partisan, from Latin *secta.* See SECT.]

sec·tile (sek′təl) *adj.* capable of being cut or severed smoothly with a knife, as certain metallic minerals. —**sec·til·i·ty** (sek til′i tē), *n.*

sec·tion (sek′shən) *n.* **1.** a part of something separated or distinct from the rest; portion: *to plant vegetables in one section of a garden.* **2.** a division of something written, such as a book or document: *the sports section of a newspaper.* **3.** a part, piece, or unit that fits together with others: *The plumber replaced several sections of pipe.* **4.** a group of musicians who all play the same kind of instrument: *the violin section of an orchestra.* **5.** a piece or segment within certain kinds of fruit, such as grapefruit. **6.** a region or area, as of a nation or city, having characteristics that distinguish it from the rest: *the financial section of a city.* **7.** a drawing or other representation of something as it would appear if cut through to show its internal structure. **8.** a thin slice of

a	at	e	end	o	hot	u	up	hw	white		about
ā	ape	ē	me	ō	old	ū	use	ng	song		taken
ä	far	i	it	ô	fork	ü	rule	th	thin	ə	pencil
âr	care	ī	ice	oi	oil	u̇	pull	th	this		lemon
		îr	pierce	ou	out	ûr	turn	zh	measure		circus

matter used for study with a microscope. Also, **thin section.**
9. the act of cutting. **10.** a special office or division, as of a bureau: *The message was sent to the decoding section.* **11.** a measure of public land equal to 1 square mile (2.59 square kilometers) or 640 acres and making up 1/36 of a township. **12.** the portion of a railroad line maintained by one crew of workers. —*v.t.* to divide, as by separating or cutting into parts (often with *off*): *We sectioned off the pasture from the rest of the farm.* [Latin *sectiō* a cutting, from Latin *secāre* to cut.]

Synonyms *n.* **Section, division,** and **segment** mean a part of the whole. **Section** is the general term for a part that is distinguished from other parts by either physical characteristics or considerations of logic: *the newspaper's financial section, the brass section of the orchestra.* **Division** is similar to *section,* but is usually applied to something larger: *the museum's division of African-American art, the company's marketing division.* **Segment** suggests a part set off from the whole by natural dividing lines: *The fruit salad contained tangerine segments.*

sec·tion·al (sek′shə nəl) *adj.* **1.** of, arising from, or characteristic of different regions or areas: *sectional interests.* **2.** made up of several sections or parts fitting into one another: *a sectional cabinet.* —*n.* a sectional piece of furniture. —**sec′tion·al·ly,** *adv.*

sec·tion·al·ism (sek′shə nə liz′əm) *n.* excessive concern for the interests of a particular region or area.

sec·tor (sek′tər) *n.* **1.** a particular division or part, as of a population or economy: *the industrial sector of a country.* **2.** one of the parts into which an area, such as a city, is divided; zone. **3.** *Geometry.* a plane figure bounded by two radii of a circle and the intercepted arc. **4.** *Military.* a distinct area within which a unit operates and for which it is responsible. **5.** *Computers.* a part of one of the circular tracks on a floppy disk or a hard disk. [Late Latin *sector* the geometric figure, going back to Latin *secāre* to cut.]

sec·u·lar (sek′yə lər) *adj.* **1.** of or relating to matters apart from church or religion; worldly; temporal: *secular art, secular education.* **2.** (of clergy) living in an outside community, such as a parish, rather than in a monastery or other religious community: *a secular nun, a secular priest.* **3.** occurring or observed once in a century or more: *the secular games of ancient Rome.* **4.** continuing from age to age; long lasting: *secular changes of the earth's surface.* —*n.* **1.** a layperson. **2.** a member of the secular clergy. [Late Latin *saeculāris* worldly, profane, from Latin *saeculāris* relating to an age, from Latin *saeculum* age, generation.] —**sec′u·lar·ly,** *adv.*

sec·u·lar·ism (sek′yə lə riz′əm) *n.* the belief that civil affairs, such as public education, should be conducted without control or influence from religion. —**sec′u·lar·ist,** *n., adj.* —**sec′u·lar·is′tic,** *adj.*

sec·u·lar·i·ty (sek′yə lar′i tē) *n.* the quality or condition of being secular.

sec·u·lar·ize (sek′yə lə rīz′) *v.t.,* **-ized, -iz·ing. 1.** to separate from religion or religious institutions; make secular. **2.** to transfer (church property) to secular ownership. —**sec′u·lar·i·za′tion,** *n.* —**sec′u·lar·iz′er,** *n.*

se·cure (si kyŏŏr′) *adj.* **1.** not likely to be taken away; certain or guaranteed: *a secure job.* **2.** safe from danger or harm, as of loss or attack: *The cellar was a secure place to be during the tornado.* **3.** free from worry, care, or fear: *to feel secure about one's future.* **4.** not likely to give way; stable: *The house stands on a secure foundation.* —*v.t.,* **-cured, -cur·ing. 1.** to obtain or acquire possession or use of; get: *to secure a hall for a meeting.* **2.** to put or fasten firmly in place: *to secure the hatches of a ship.* **3.** to bring about; effect: *to secure a desired result, to secure the release of a prisoner.* **4.** to make safe; guard; protect: *The gold shipments were secured against theft by armed guards.* **5.** to make sure or certain; guarantee: *The large contract secured the company's continuing success.* **6.** to pledge property for repayment of (a loan) or fulfillment of (a contract). [Latin *sēcūrus* free from care. Doublet of SURE.] —**se·cure′ly,** *adv.* —**se·cure′ment,** *n.* —For Synonyms *(adj.),* see **safe**; *(v.t.),* see **gain.**

se·cu·ri·ty (si kyŏŏr′i tē) *n., pl.* **-ties. 1.** protection from danger, as of loss or attack: *the security of a fortress.* **2.** freedom from worry, care, or fear: *Their savings account gave the couple a feeling of security.* **3.** the state or condition of being certain or guaranteed: *The workers have job security and cannot be fired.* **4.a.** measures taken to guard against something, such as crime: *The building's security is good.* **b.** those persons assigned to carry out such measures: *We called security when we saw the broken window.* **5.** a stock or bond certificate. ➧ usually used in the plural: *to sell securities through a broker.* **6.** property given as a pledge, as for repayment of a loan or fulfillment of a contract. **7.** a person who agrees to be financially responsible for another; surety. [Latin *sēcūritās* freedom from care or danger.]

security blanket 1. a blanket or other familiar object carried around, esp. by a child, to give a feeling of security and reassurance. **2.** any person or thing that provides a sense of comfort or security.

Security Council, the body of the United Nations responsible for maintaining international peace, composed of five permanent members (the United States, Russia, Britain, France, and China) and ten rotating members elected by the General Assembly.

secy. *also,* **sec′y.** secretary.

se·dan (si dan′) *n.* an automobile with two or four doors, a solid roof, and seats in front and in back. [Of uncertain origin.]

sedan chair, a conveyance for one person, consisting of an enclosed chair attached to two horizontal poles carried by servants, used in the seventeenth and eighteenth centuries.

se·date (si dāt′) *adj.* quiet and restrained in style or manner; not excited or disturbed; calm; tranquil. —*v.t.,* **-dat·ed, -dat·ing.** to calm down with or as with a sedative: *to sedate a patient.* [Latin *sēdātus* quiet, calm, past participle of *sēdāre* to settle, assuage.] —**se·date′ly,** *adv.* —**se·date′ness,** *n.*

se·da·tion (si dā′shən) *n.* **1.** the state of being sedated: *The patient is under sedation.* **2.** the act or process of sedating.

sed·a·tive (sed′ə tiv) *n.* **1.** a drug or other agent that lessens nervous excitement. **2.** anything that lessens excitement, distress, or awareness. —*adj.* lessening nervousness, excitement, or distress; soothing; calming.

sed·en·tar·y (sed′ən ter′ē) *adj.* **1.** engaging in little or no physical exercise, activity, or movement: *a sedentary person.* **2.** involving or requiring little or no physical activity: *a sedentary job, a sedentary life.* **3.** (of certain marine invertebrates, such as barnacles) attached to one place or surface; not free-swimming. **4.** remaining in one area; not migratory: *sedentary birds.* [Latin *sedentārius* relating to sitting, going back to *sedēre* to sit.] —**sed′-en·tar′i·ly,** *adv.* —**sed′en·tar′i·ness,** *n.*

Se·der (sā′dər) *n.* in Judaism, a religious service and ceremonial feast held during Passover to commemorate the Exodus from Egypt. [Hebrew *sēdher* order, arrangement, division.]

sedge (sej) *n.* any of a large group of grassy plants, genus *Carex,* growing in marshes and other wet areas, bearing spikelike clusters of tiny greenish flowers. [Old English *secg.*]

sed·i·ment (sed′ə mənt) *n.* **1.** matter that settles to the bottom of a liquid; dregs; lees. **2.** *Geology.* solid matter, esp. particles of rock or earth, carried in suspension from one place and deposited in another by water, ice, or wind. **3.** anything left behind or deposited. [Latin *sedimentum* a settling.] —**sed·i·men·tal** (sed′-ə men′təl), *adj.*

sed·i·men·tar·y (sed′ə men′tə rē) *adj.* **1.** of, relating to, or containing sediment. **2.** *Geology.* formed from or by the deposit of sediment: *sedimentary rock.* —**sed′i·men′ta·ri·ly,** *adv.*

sedimentary rock of the Grand Canyon

sed·i·men·ta·tion (sed′ə mən tā′shən) *n.* the act or process of depositing or accumulating sediment.

se·di·tion (si dish′ən) *n.* speech or action causing discontent or inciting rebellion against an existing government. [Latin *sēditiō* dissension, insurrection.]

se·di·tious (si dish′əs) *adj.* **1.** taking part in, promoting, or guilty of sedition. **2.** of, relating to, or containing sedition: *a seditious document, a seditious speech.* —**se·di′tious·ly,** *adv.* —**se·di′tious·ness,** *n.*

se·duce (si dūs′, -dōōs′) *v.t.,* **-duced, -duc·ing. 1.** to persuade to engage in sexual intercourse. **2.** to tempt or persuade to do wrong, as with trickery or deceit; corrupt or lead astray: *Bribes*

seduced the witness to give false evidence. **3.** to win over; entice: *The candidate seduced the voters with false promises.* [Late Latin *sēdūcere* to lead astray, from Latin *sēdūcere* to lead apart.] —**se·duce′a·ble**; *also,* **se·duc′i·ble,** *adj.* —**se·duc′er,** *n.*

se·duc·tion (si duk′shən) *n.* **1.** the act of seducing or the state of being seduced. **2.** something that seduces. Also, **se·duce·ment** (si düs′mənt).

se·duc·tive (si duk′tiv) *adj.* tending or helping to seduce; alluring: *seductive behavior, seductive clothing.* —**se·duc′tive·ly,** *adv.* —**se·duc′tive·ness,** *n.*

sed·u·lous (sej′ə ləs) *adj.* working hard and diligently; assiduous; studious: *a sedulous employee.* [Latin *sēdulus* diligent, zealous, going back to *sē dolō* without deception.] —**se·du·li·ty** (si dü′li tē, -dū′-), **sed′u·lous·ness,** *n.* —**sed′u·lous·ly,** *adv.*

se·dum (sē′dəm) *n.* stonecrop. [Latin *sedum* houseleek.]

see[1] (sē) *v.,* **saw, seen, see·ing.** —*v.t.* **1.** to perceive with the eyes; succeed in getting a view of: *Can you see the sign?* **2.a.** to perceive with the mind; understand: *I don't see why you have to leave so soon.* **b.** to have as a mental image; picture in the mind: *I can still see my first day in school.* **3.** to attend as a spectator: *to see a movie.* **4.a.** to think of or look upon; regard; judge; view: *My friend and I see things the same way.* **b.** to think possible or suitable: *I can't see myself as company president.* **5.** to find out; ascertain: *I'll see what they want.* **6.** to make sure: *We'll see that you leave on time.* **7.** to go with; accompany; escort: *to see someone to the door.* **8.a.** to visit, encounter, or meet: *to see friends.* **b.** to have a consultation or meeting with: *to see a doctor.* **9.** to receive or admit, as for a visit, interview, or examination: *The doctor does not see patients on Monday.* **10.** to experience or undergo: *to see service in the army.* **11.** to have as a characteristic feature: *That intersection has seen many car accidents.* **12.** to predict or foresee: *I see many years of trouble ahead.* **13.** to look at for reference; refer to: *See the glossary for further information.* **14.** to prefer to have: *The government would see its citizens suffer before accepting foreign aid.* **15.** *Cards.* **a.** to match the bet of (a player). **b.** to match (a bet). **16.** *Informal.* to be romantically involved with; date: *They have been seeing each other for a year.* —*v.i.* **1.** to have or use the power of sight. **2.** to understand; comprehend: *I was confused at first, but now I see.* **3.** to judge or discover: *See for yourself.* [Old English *sēon* to perceive with the eyes, to perceive mentally.] —**see′a·ble,** *adj.*

• **to see about. a.** to take care of: *I'll see about getting tickets to the play.* **b.** to look into; investigate.

• **to see fit.** to judge or consider to be right: *Do as you see fit.*

• **to see off.** to go with (someone leaving, as on a trip) to the departure point.

• **to see out.** to continue with to the end; finish.

• **to see things.** to seem to see something, although it isn't really there: *I thought I saw a ghost, but I must have been seeing things.*

• **to see through. a.** to continue with to the end. **c.** to aid or watch over in time of difficulty. **c.** to understand the true meaning or nature of: *I see through your objections.*

• **to see to.** to attend to; take care of.

see[2] (sē) *n.* the office or jurisdiction of a bishop. [Old French *sed, sied* seat, throne, from Latin *sēdēs* seat, abode.]

seed (sēd) *n., pl.* **seeds** or **seed. 1.** the part of a plant that develops from a usually fertilized ovule and contains the developing embryo of a new plant. **2.** seeds collectively. **3.** any small, roundish, grainlike part or fruit, such as a kernel of corn or a grain of wheat. **4.** any part of a plant that serves to reproduce it, such as a tuber, bulb, or spore. **5.** sperm; semen. **6.** the origin or beginning from which something larger will grow or develop: *the seeds of dissent.* **7.** *Sports.* a tournament contestant or team placed, because of superior record or ranking, so as not to meet other strong competitors in the early rounds. **8.** *Archaic.* children, descendants, or offspring collectively. ➡ used as singular or plural. —*v.t.* **1.** to sow (land) with seed. **2.** to sow (seeds). **3.** to remove the seeds from: *to seed a watermelon.* **4.** *Sports.* **a.** to place (a tournament contestant or team) as a seed. **b.** to arrange (drawings for positions in a tournament) in this way. **5.** to spray (clouds) with dry ice, silver iodide crystals, or other substances in order to produce rain. —*v.i.* to produce seed. [Old English *sǣd* that which is sown, offspring.] —**seed′less,** *adj.* —**seed′like′,** *adj.*

• **to go to seed. a.** to become useless or run-down; deteriorate. **b.** to reach the stage of developing and shedding seeds.

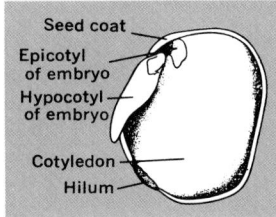

Seed coat
Epicotyl of embryo
Hypocotyl of embryo
Cotyledon
Hilum

seed

seed·bed (sēd′bed′) *n.* soil or a bed of soil prepared for planting seeds.

seed·case (sēd′kās′) *n.* the part of a flowering plant, such as a pod or capsule, that contains the seeds; pericarp.

seed coat, the protective covering of a seed.

seed·ed (sē′did) *adj.* **1.** having the seeds removed: *seeded raisins.* **2.a.** (of a tournament contestant or team) placed so as not to meet a stronger competitor in the early rounds. **b.** (of a tournament) having seeded contestants or teams.

seed·er (sē′dər) *n.* **1.** a person who sows or plants seeds. **2.** a device for sowing seeds. **3.** a device for removing seeds, as from fruit.

seed leaf, cotyledon.

seed·ling (sēd′ling) *n.* **1.** any young plant grown from a seed. **2.** a young tree less than 3 feet (0.9 meter) high.

seed money, money designated to start a new project or business and to help it grow.

seed oyster, in oyster cultivation, any young oyster that has settled and become attached to the bottom, esp. one suitable for transplanting. Also, **spat.**

seed pearl, a very small pearl.

seed plant, any plant that bears seeds, esp. a spermatophyte.

seeds·man (sēdz′mən) *n., pl.* **-men** (-mən). **1.** a person who scatters seed; sower of seed. **2.** a dealer in seed.

seed·y (sē′dē) *adj.,* **seed·i·er, seed·i·est. 1.** looking shabby or run-down: *a seedy restaurant, a seedy old coat.* **2.** having many seeds. —**seed′i·ness,** *n.*

see·ing (sē′ing) *conj.* in view of the fact; considering: *Seeing that it is late, we should go home.* —*n.* the ability to see; sight.

Seeing Eye dog, guide dog. *Trademark:* **Seeing Eye.** [From the *Seeing Eye,* Inc., a philanthropic organization founded near Morristown, New Jersey, in 1929, to breed and train such dogs.]

seek (sēk) *v.,* **sought, seek·ing.** —*v.t.* **1.** to go in search of; try to find; look for: *The company is seeking new employees.* **2.** to make an attempt; try: *Every candidate seeks to win.* **3.** to desire or try to obtain; ask for: *to seek aid.* —*v.i.* to search; make inquiry: *Seek and ye shall find* (Matthew 7:7). [Old English *sēcan* to look for, ask for.] —**seek′er,** *n.*

seem (sēm) *v.i.* **1.** to present the outward appearance of being; appear to be: *You seem much younger than you are.* **2.** to be or appear true, so far as one can tell: *The puppy seems happy in its new home. It seems that you disagree.* **3.** to appear to exist: *There seems no need in arguing the point.* **4.** to appear to oneself: *I seem to be mistaken.* [Old Norse *sœma* to honor, conform to.]

seem·ing (sē′ming) *adj.* appearing to be real or true, so far as one can tell: *The city has made seeming improvements in garbage collection.* —*n.* outward appearance. —**seem′ing·ly,** *adv.*

seem·ly (sēm′lē) *adj.,* **-li·er, -li·est. 1.** suitable, as to a purpose or occasion; decorous; proper: *It is not seemly to speak loudly in a library.* **2.** *Archaic.* pleasant to look at; handsome. [Old Norse *sœmiligr* becoming.] —**seem′li·ness,** *n.*

seen (sēn) the past participle of **see**[1].

seep (sēp) *v.i.* to spread or flow slowly, as through openings or pores: *Water seeped from the cracked pipe.* [Possibly form of dialectal English *sipe* to ooze, drip, from Old English *sipian.*]

seep·age (sē′pij) *n.* **1.** the act or process of seeping. **2.** something that seeps.

seer (sîr) *n.* a person who is believed to have the power of foreseeing future events or of knowing hidden or profound things; prophet.

seer·ess (sîr′is) *n.* a woman who is believed to have the power of foreseeing future events or of knowing hidden or profound things; prophetess.

seer·suck·er (sîr′suk′ər) *n.* a lightweight fabric with a creped effect, usually woven with alternating plain and crinkled stripes, used chiefly for summer clothing and children's wear. [Hindi *sīrsakar,* from Persian *shīr o shakkar* striped linen garment; literally, milk and sugar (phrase used to describe the alternating stripes of the fabric).]

see·saw (sē′sô′) *n.* **1.** a playground device consisting of a plank supported in the middle so that when a person is seated on each end, one end goes up as the other goes down. Also, **teeter-totter, teeter board. 2.** any up-and-down or back-and-forth action or movement: *the seesaw of political power.* —*v.i.* **1.** to move up and down on a seesaw. **2.** to move, act, or proceed in a

a	at	e	end	o	hot	u	up	hw	white	⎧	about
ā	ape	ē	me	ō	old	ū	use	ng	song		taken
ä	far	i	it	ô	fork	ü	rule	th	thin	ə	pencil
âr	care	ī	ice	oi	oil	u̇	pull	th	this		lemon
		îr	pierce	ou	out	ûr	turn	zh	measure	⎩	circus

way similar to the action of a seesaw: *The battle seesawed back and forth, with neither side gaining an advantage.* [Repetition of SAW[1], with vowel change in the first syllable; from the motion of persons sawing wood or stone.]

seethe (sēth) *v.,* **seethed, seeth·ing.** —*v.i.* **1.** to be in a state of intense, inward agitation, as from anger or frustration: *to seethe with rage.* **2.** to rise, surge, or form bubbles, as if boiling: *The waves seethed around the rocks.* —*v.t. Archaic.* **1.** to soak or steep. **2.** to boil. [Old English *sēothan* to boil.]

see-through (sē'thrü') *adj.* that allows a person to see what is underneath or inside; transparent or translucent: *see-through plastic wrap, a see-through fabric.* —*n.* a garment made of see-through fabric.

seg·ment (seg'mənt) *n.* **1.** each of the parts into which a thing is or may be divided; division; section: *the segments of an orange.* **2.** *Geometry.* **a.** a part of a plane figure cut off by a line, such as a part of a circle bounded by an arc and a chord. **b.** a part of a sphere cut off by a plane or by parallel planes. **c.** line segment. —*v.t., v.i.* to divide or become divided into segments. [Latin *segmentum* a piece cut off, from *secāre* to cut.] —**seg'ment·ed,** *adj.* —For Synonyms *(n.),* see **section.**

seg·men·tal (seg men'təl) *adj.* **1.** of, relating to, or composed of segments. **2.** having the shape of a segment of a circle. Also, **seg·men·tar·y** (seg'mən ter'ē). —**seg·men'tal·ly,** *adv.*

seg·men·ta·tion (seg'mən tā'shən) *n.* **1.** the act or process of dividing into segments or the state of being divided into segments. **2.** *Biology.* the division of a cell into many cells, as in a fertilized egg; cleavage.

segmentation cavity, blastocoele.

se·go (sē'gō) *n., pl.* **se·gos. 1.** a lilylike, bell-shaped flower of the deserts of the western United States, usually white with pink, purple, or greenish yellow markings. **2.** the plant, *Calochortus nuttallii,* of the lily family, that bears this flower, having edible underground corms. Also, **sego lily.** [Of Paiute origin.]

seg·re·gate (seg'ri gāt') *v.,* **-gat·ed, -gat·ing.** —*v.t.* **1.** to set apart from others or the rest; isolate: *to segregate a patient with a contagious disease.* **2.** to impose racial segregation on (racial groups, social facilities, or institutions): *to segregate schools.* —*v.i.* **1.** to become separate or separated; go apart. **2.** to have or practice racial segregation; be segregated. [Latin *sēgregātus,* past participle of *sēgregāre* to set apart, set apart from the flock, from *sē* apart + *grex* flock.] —**seg're·ga'tive,** *adj.* —For Synonyms *(v.t.),* see **isolate.**

seg·re·ga·tion (seg'ri gā'shən) *n.* **1.** the practice of separating one racial group, esp. blacks, from another or from the rest of society by making them live in certain areas or use different schools and social facilities. **2.** the act or process of segregating or the state of being segregated.

seg·re·ga·tion·ist (seg'ri gā'shə nist) *n.* a person who practices or supports racial segregation.

seiche (sāsh) *n.* a standing wave in a lake, bay, estuary, or the like, caused by changes in atmospheric pressure, an earthquake, the tide, or other forces.

Seid·litz powders (sed'lits) a mild, effervescent laxative. [From *Seidlitz,* the German name of Sedlčany, a village in Czechoslovakia with a spring whose water is said to have a laxative effect.]

sei·gneur (sēn yûr', sān-) *also,* **sei·gnior.** *n.* a feudal nobleman, esp. the lord of a manor. [Middle French *seigneur* lord, sir, going back to Latin *senior* elder, older person.] —**sei·gneur'i·al,** *adj.*

sei·gneur·y (sēn'yə rē, sān'-) *n., pl.* **-gneur·ies. 1.** the authority or jurisdiction of a seigneur. **2.** the domain of a seigneur. **3.** a group of lords.

seine (sān) *n.* a fishing net, esp. a long one that hangs vertically in the water, supported by floats on its upper edge and kept taut by weights on the bottom edge. —*v.t., v.i.,* **seined, sein·ing.** to catch (fish) with a seine. [Old English *segne* fishing net that hangs vertically, from Latin *sagēna* large fishing net, from Greek *sagēnē.*] —**sein'er,** *n.*

seis·mic (sīz'mik, sīs'-) *adj.* of, relating to, caused by, or subject to earthquakes. [Greek *seismos* earthquake + -IC.] —**seis'mi·cal·ly,** *adv.*

seismo- *also,* **seism-.** *combining form* of or relating to earthquakes: *seismology.* [Greek *seismos* earthquake.]

seis·mo·gram (sīz'mə gram', sīs'-) *n.* a record made by a seismograph.

seis·mo·graph (sīz'mə graf', sīs'-) *n.* an instrument that records seismic waves, from which the direction, intensity, and duration of earthquakes and other earth vibrations can be determined. [SEISMO- + -GRAPH.]

seis·mog·ra·phy (sīz mog'rə fē, sīs-) *n.* the art or science of using a seismograph in recording earthquakes or other earth vibrations. —**seis·mo·graph·ic** (sīz'mə graf'ik, sīs'-), *adj.*

seis·mol·o·gy (sīz mol'ə jē, sīs-) *n.* the study of earthquakes and related phenomena. [SEISMO- + -LOGY.] —**seis·mo·log·i·cal** (sīz'mə loj'i kəl, sīs'-), *adj.* —**seis·mol'o·gist,** *n.*

seis·mom·e·ter (sīz mom'i tər, sīs-) *n.* an electronic receiver, such as a geophone, designed to detect seismic waves and convert them into electrical signals.

sei whale (sā) *also,* **Sei whale.** a finback whale, or rorqual, *Balaenoptera borealis,* having a grayish blue back. Length: to 60 feet (18.3 meters). Weight: to 50 tons (45 metric tons). [Norwegian *seihval,* from *sei* coalfish + *hval* whale; because it arrives at fishing grounds with these fish.]

seize (sēz) *v.,* **seized, seiz·ing.** —*v.t.* **1.** to take hold of suddenly and forcibly; grab on to: *The dog seized the bone.* **2.** to take away or gain control or possession of by force or authority: *The health authorities seized the shipment of tainted food.* **3.** to capture or arrest: *The police seized the criminal.* **4.** to take advantage of; make immediate use of: *to seize an opportunity.* **5.** to have a sudden and powerful effect on; possess; afflict: *Panic seized the crowd when the fire broke out.* **6.** to bind or lash (ropes) together. **7.** *Archaic.* to put in possession of a property. ➡ used in the passive: *to be seized of property.* —*v.i.* (of a moving machine part) to bind or jam because of friction, heat, cold, or the like: *When the main bearing seized, the engine stopped.* [Old French *seisir* to take possession of, from Medieval Latin *sacīre;* of Germanic origin.] —**seiz'a·ble,** *adj.* —**seiz'er,** *n.* —For Synonyms *(v.t.),* see **take.**

· **to seize on** (or **upon**). to take hold of suddenly: *to seize on an idea.*

seiz·ing (sē'zing) *n. Nautical.* **1.** the act of fastening together two ropes or objects with turns of small rope, cord, or a similar material. **2.** the material used for such a fastening, or the fastening itself.

sei·zure (sē'zhər) *n.* **1.** the act of seizing. **2.** a sudden onset of a disease or symptom; attack: *an epileptic seizure.*

seizing

se·lah (sē'lə) *n.* a word of unknown meaning frequently occurring at the end of a verse in the Psalms, believed to be a musical direction or an indication to the reader. [Hebrew *selāh.*]

sel·dom (sel'dəm) *adv.* on few occasions; rarely: *We seldom go to the theater.* [Old English *seldan, seldum.*]

se·lect (si lekt') *v.t.* to take or pick out from among many; choose: *to select a book from a shelf.* —*v.i.* to make a selection; choose: *Don't select until you have seen what is available.* —*adj.* **1.** picked or chosen because of special ability or fitness: *to coach a select group of athletes.* **2.** of high quality; choice: *select apples.* **3.** careful in selecting; fastidious; discriminating. **4.** carefully or specially chosen, as based on social or economic considerations: *a club with a select membership.* [Latin *sēlectus* chosen, past participle of *sēligere* to choose, pick out.] —**se·lect'ness,** *n.* —For Synonyms *(v.t.),* see **choose.**

se·lect·ee (si lek tē') *n.* a person who is selected, esp. a draftee.

se·lec·tion (si lek'shən) *n.* **1.** the act of selecting or the state of being selected. **2.** a person or thing that is selected: *to read selections from a novel.* **3.a.** a person or thing that may be selected: *the selections on a menu.* **b.** a group or variety of such selections: *a large selection to choose from.* **4.** *Biology.* natural selection.

se·lec·tive (si lek'tiv) *adj.* **1.** of, relating to, or characterized by selection. **2.** careful in selecting. **3.** responding to or admitting electromagnetic radiations of a certain frequency only. —**se·lec'tive·ly,** *adv.* —**se·lec'tive·ness,** *n.*

selective breeding, the process or technique of choosing and mating animals that have desired characteristics, used esp. with horses, dogs, and cattle.

selective service, compulsory military service of persons selected according to age, physical fitness, and other criteria.

se·lec·tiv·i·ty (si lek tiv'i tē) *n.* **1.** the state or quality of being selective. **2.** the ability of a circuit or receiver to respond to electromagnetic waves of a particular frequency and exclude others.

se·lect·man (si lekt'mən) *n., pl.* **-men** (-mən). a member of a board that governs a town in most New England states.

se·lec·tor (si lek'tər) *n.* **1.** a person or thing that selects. **2.** a dial, switch, or lever used to control or select different operations of a machine or device.

Se·le·ne (si lē'nē) *n.* in Greek mythology, the goddess of the moon, often identified with Artemis. Her Roman counterpart is Luna.

sel·e·nite (sel'ə nīt') *n.* a clear, colorless variety of gypsum that

S

often splits into large, thin plates. [Latin *selēnītēs,* from Greek *selēnītēs (lithos)* (stone) of the moon, from *selēnē* moon; because its brightness supposedly was affected by the phases of the moon.]

se·le·ni·um (si lē′nē əm) *n.* a metalloid element resembling sulfur in chemical properties and in having several allotropic forms, one of which, a photosensitive semiconductor, is used in photoelectric cells. Symbol: **Se** For tables, see **element.** [Modern Latin *selenium,* from Greek *selēnē* moon; by analogy with *tellurium,* similar element named after earth (Latin *tellūs*).]

sel·e·nog·ra·phy (sel′ə nog′rə fē) *n.* the branch of astronomy devoted to studying and mapping the physical features of the moon. —**se·le·no·graph·ic** (sə lē′nə graf′ik), *adj.* —**sel′e·nog′ra·pher,** *n.* [Modern Latin *selenographia,* from Greek *selēnē* moon + *-graphia* (see -GRAPHY).]

self (self) *n., pl.* **selves. 1.** one's own person as distinguished from all others. **2.** the qualities or characteristics of a person or thing: *to appeal to one's better self.* **3.** personal interests, welfare, advantage, or the like. —*adj.* **1.** being the same throughout, as in color or texture; uniform. **2.** of the same material as a garment or article itself: *curtains with a self lining.* —*pron.* myself, himself, herself, or yourself: *accommodations for self and family.* [Old English *self* own, very, same.]

self- *prefix* **1.** of oneself or itself: *self-confidence, self-expression, self-contradiction.* **2.** by oneself or itself: *self-educated, self-contained, self-sustaining.* **3.** in or within oneself: *self-centered, self-absorbed.* **4.** to oneself: *self-addressed.* **5.** automatic: *self-starting.* **6.** of the same material: *self-lined, self-belted.* [From SELF.]

self-a·base·ment (self′ə bās′mənt) *n.* humiliation and degradation of oneself.

self-ab·ne·ga·tion (self′ab ni gā′shən) *n.* lack of regard for oneself or one's own interest; self-denial; self-sacrifice. —**self′-ab′ne·gat′ing,** *adj.*

self-ab·sorbed (self′ab sôrbd′, -zôrbd′) *adj.* preoccupied with one's own thoughts, interests, or activities. —**self-ab·sorp·tion** (self′ab sôrp′shən, -zôrp′-), *n.*

self-act·ing (self′ak′ting) *adj.* working or moving independently without external influence or manipulation; automatic.

self-ad·dressed (self′ə drest′) *adj.* addressed to oneself: *a self-addressed envelope.*

self-ad·vance·ment (self′ad vans′mənt) *n.* the act or process of promoting oneself or one's own interests.

self-ap·point·ed (self′ə poin′tid) *adj.* appointed by oneself alone without the consent or support of others: *a self-appointed spokesperson.*

self-as·ser·tion (self′ə sûr′shən) *n.* the act or practice of insisting upon one's own ideas, claims, or superiority. —**self′-as·sert′ing, self′-as·ser′tive,** *adj.*

self-as·sured (self′ə shûrd′) *adj.* having confidence in oneself or being sure of one's ability, position, or worth; self-confident. —**self-as·sur·ance, self-as·sur·ed·ness** (self′ə shûr′id nis), *n.*

self-cen·tered (self′sen′tərd) *also, British,* **self-cen·tred.** *adj.* preoccupied or engrossed in one's own thoughts, interests, or activities to the point of selfishness; egocentric; egotistical. —**self′-cen′tered·ness,** *n.*

self-clean·ing (self′klē′ning) *adj.* cleaning itself automatically or semiautomatically, as by mechanical means: *a self-cleaning oven.*

self-clos·ing (self′klō′zing) *adj.* closing automatically: *a self-closing refrigerator door.*

self-com·mand (self′kə mand′) *n.* control of one's own actions or feelings; self-control; composure.

self-com·pla·cent (self′kəm plā′sənt) *adj.* overly pleased or satisfied with oneself or itself; complacent about itself: *a self-complacent bureaucracy.* —**self′-com·pla′cence, self′-com·pla′cen·cy,** *n.* —**self′-com·pla′cent·ly,** *adv.*

self-com·posed (self′kəm pōzd′) *adj.* having or showing composure; calm; tranquil. —**self-com·pos·ed·ly** (self′kəm-pō′zid lē), *adv.*

self-con·ceit (self′kən sēt′) *n.* an unusually high opinion of oneself or one's worth; vanity. —**self′-con·ceit′ed,** *adj.*

self-con·cept (self′kon′sept) *n.* the view one has of oneself; self-image. Also, **self-con·cep·tion** (self′kən sep′shən).

self-con·fessed (self′kən fest′) *adj.* openly admitting oneself to be something: *a self-confessed liar.*

self-con·fi·dent (self′kon′fi dənt) *adj.* having confidence or faith in one's own ability or worth. —**self′-con′fi·dence,** *n.* —**self′-con′fi·dent·ly,** *adv.*

self-con·scious (self′kon′shəs) *adj.* **1.** uncomfortably aware of one's own actions, words, or thoughts, esp. in the presence of others; shy and embarrassed; timorous. **2.** showing such awareness or sensitivity: *a self-conscious laugh.* **3.** aware of oneself as a separate being. —**self′-con′scious·ly,** *adv.* —**self′-con′-scious·ness,** *n.*

self-con·sist·ent (self′kən sis′tənt) *adj.* in agreement with oneself or itself. —**self′-con·sist′en·cy,** *n.* —**self′-con·sist′ent·ly,** *adv.*

self-con·tained (self′kən tānd′) *adj.* **1.** reserved or restrained in behavior. **2.** having all that is necessary in oneself or itself; complete: *a self-contained machine.* **3.** having or showing self-control.

self-con·tra·dic·tion (self′kon′trə dik′shən) *n.* **1.** the fact of contradicting or being inconsistent with oneself or itself. **2.** a statement or concept that contains elements that contradict one another.

self-con·tra·dic·to·ry (self′kon′trə dik′tə rē) *adj.* inconsistent with or contradicting oneself or itself.

self-con·trol (self′kən trōl′) *n.* control over one's own actions or emotions.

self-crit·i·cal (self′krit′i kəl) *adj.* critical of oneself. —**self-crit·i·cism** (self′krit′ə siz′əm), *n.*

self-de·cep·tion (self′di sep′shən) *n.* the act of deceiving or deluding oneself. Also, **self-de·ceit** (self′di sēt′). —**self′-de·cep′tive,** *adj.*

self-de·feat·ing (self′di fē′ting) *adj.* having actions or consequences that defeat or work against the original purpose.

self-de·fense (self′di fens′) *also, British,* **self-de·fence.** *n.* **1.** the act or art of defending oneself: *to learn self-defense, a national policy of self-defense.* **2.** *Law.* the act, practice, or right of using physical force in defending and protecting oneself against a person or persons who are committing a felony, using physical force, or threatening to use physical force against one.

self-de·ni·al (self′di nī′əl) *n.* the practice of refusing to satisfy one's own immediate desires and interests for the sake of others or for a goal or ideal. —**self′-de·ny′ing,** *adj.*

self-dep·re·cat·ing (self′dep′ri kā′ting) *adj.* belittling or expressing disapproval of oneself: *a self-deprecating remark.* —**self′-dep′re·cat′ing·ly,** *adv.* —**self′-dep′re·ca′tion,** *n.*

self-de·struct (self′di strukt′) *v.i.* to destroy oneself or itself: *The missile is designed to self-destruct if it veers off course.*

self-de·struc·tion (self′di struk′shən) *n.* the destruction of oneself, esp. by suicide. —**self′-de·struc′tive,** *adj.*

self-de·ter·mi·na·tion (self′di tûr′mə nā′shən) *n.* **1.** the act of making one's own decisions without external influence. **2.** the right of a people to determine the form of government they shall have. —**self′-de·ter′min·ing,** *adj.*

self-dis·ci·pline (self′dis′ə plin) *n.* control or disciplining of one's own actions, responses, or emotions.

self-ed·u·cat·ed (self′ej′ə kā′tid) *adj.* educated by reading books or studying on one's own, without any formal classroom schooling or teachers. —**self′-ed′u·ca′tion,** *n.*

self-ef·fac·ing (self′i fā′sing) *adj.* tending to stay in the background; modest or shy. —**self′-ef·face′ment,** *n.* —**self′-ef·fac′ing·ly,** *adv.*

self-em·ployed (self′em ploid′) *adj.* earning income from one's own business or profession rather than being paid by an employer. —**self′-em·ploy′ment,** *n.*

self-es·teem (self′e stēm′) *n.* proper regard for or awareness of one's own worth and abilities as a person; self-respect.

self-ev·i·dent (self′ev′i dənt) *adj.* needing no proof or explanation; evident in itself.

self-ex·am·i·na·tion (self′eg zam′ə nā′shən) **1.** *n.* an examination into or reconsideration of one's own beliefs, motives, or interests; introspection. **2.** *Medicine.* an examination of one's own body for signs of injury or disease.

self-ex·ist·ent (self′eg zis′tənt) *adj.* having an existence that does not depend on anything else. —**self′-ex·ist′ence,** *n.*

self-ex·plan·a·to·ry (self′ek splan′ə tôr′ē) *adj.* needing no extra explanation or details; containing or being its own explanation: *The instructions are self-explanatory.*

self-ex·pres·sion (self′ek spresh′ən) *n.* expression of one's own thoughts, feelings, or true personality. —**self′-ex·press′ive,** *adj.*

self-fer·ti·li·za·tion (self′fûr′tə lə zā′shən) *n.* fertilization of a flower by its own pollen or of a hermaphroditic animal by its own sperm. Also, **autogamy.**

self-ful·fill·ing (self′fŭl fil′ing) *adj.* **1.** characterized by or achieving self-fulfillment. **2.** happening or realized as a result of being predicted or expected to happen: *a self-fulfilling prophecy.*

self-ful·fill·ment (self′fŭl fil′mənt) *n.* the achievement or realization of one's potentiality or ambitions.

a	at	e	end	o	hot	u	up	hw	white		about
ā	ape	ē	me	ō	old	ū	use	ng	song		taken
ä	far	i	it	ô	fork	ü	rule	th	thin	ə	pencil
âr	care	ī	ice	oi	oil	ů	pull	th	this		lemon
		îr	pierce	ou	out	ûr	turn	zh	measure		circus

self-gov·ern·ing (self′guv′ər ning) *adj.* **1.** ruled by its own people rather than by outside authority; having or exercising self-government. **2.** that controls or regulates itself.

self-gov·ern·ment (self′guv′ərn mənt, -guv′ər-) *n.* government or rule of a group by its own members rather than by external authority: *Many former colonies have achieved self-government.*

self-hard·en·ing (self′här′də ning) *adj.* of or relating to any steel that hardens after heating without being quenched.

self-heal (self′hēl′) *n.* a low-growing weed, *Prunella vulgaris,* found widely distributed in temperate regions, bearing clusters of small, purple flowers, and formerly used medicinally.

self-help (self′help′) *n.* the practice or process of helping oneself, esp. in solving personal problems without the help of professional counseling, as by reading or meeting with other people seeking to solve the same problem. —*adj.* of, relating to, or furthering self-help: *a self-help book, a self-help group.*

self-hyp·no·sis (self′hip nō′sis) *n.* the act of hypnotizing oneself, as with special mental exercises. Also, **autohypnosis.** —**self-hyp·not·ic** (self′hip not′ik), *adj.*

self-i·den·ti·ty (self′ī den′ti tē) *n.* **1.** awareness of oneself as an individual being. **2.** the identity of a thing with itself.

self-im·age (self′im′ij) *n.* the mental concept or picture one has of oneself, esp. an opinion of one's own abilities and of the kind of person one is or wants to be.

self-im·mo·la·tion (self′im′ə lā′shən) *n.* the intentional sacrificing of oneself by burning, esp. as a protest against a social or political injustice.

self-im·por·tant (self′im pôr′tənt) *adj.* having an exaggerated opinion of one's own importance; pompous and conceited. —**self′-im·por′tance,** *n.* —**self′-im·por′tant·ly,** *adv.*

self-im·posed (self′im pōzd′) *adj.* imposed by oneself: *a self-imposed restriction on eating sweets.*

self-im·prove·ment (self′im prüv′mənt) *n.* improvement of oneself through one's own efforts. —**self′-im·prov′er,** *n.*

self-in·crim·i·na·tion (self′in krim′ə nā′shən) *n.* the act of giving evidence that would incriminate oneself or make one liable to criminal prosecution. —**self′-in·crim′i·nat′ing,** *adj.*

self-in·duced (self′in düst′, -dūst′) *adj.* **1.** brought about or produced through one's own efforts: *self-induced hypnosis, a self-induced illness.* **2.** produced by self-induction.

self-in·duc·tion (self′in duk′shən) *n.* the induction of an electromotive force in a circuit when the current in the circuit changes.

self-in·dul·gence (self′in dul′jəns) *n.* giving in to one's own feelings, weaknesses, or desires. —**self′-in·dul′gent,** *adj.* —**self′-in·dul′gent·ly,** *adv.*

self-in·flict·ed (self′in flik′tid) *adj.* inflicted by oneself on oneself: *a self-inflicted cut.*

self-in·ter·est (self′in′trist, -tər ist) *n.* **1.** individual interest or advantage: *Preventing a war is in the self-interest of both countries.* **2.** the principle or practice of regarding one's own welfare as more important than the welfare of others. —**self′-in′ter·est·ed,** *adj.*

self·ish (sel′fish) *adj.* concerned for or serving one's own desires and interests above all others: *a selfish person, a selfish outlook.* [SELF + -ISH.] —**self′ish·ly,** *adv.* —**self′ish·ness,** *n.*

self-knowl·edge (self′nol′ij) *n.* knowledge and awareness of oneself and of one's abilities, character, and shortcomings.

self·less (self′lis) *adj.* having little thought for oneself; unselfish. —**self′less·ly,** *adv.* —**self′less·ness,** *n.*

self-load·ing (self′lō′ding) *adj.* (of firearms) automatic or semiautomatic.

self-love (self′luv′) *n.* **1.** high regard for or love of oneself. **2.** pride or conceit.

self-lu·bri·cat·ing (self′lü′bri kā′ting) *adj.* lubricating itself: *a self-lubricating motor.*

self-made (self′mād′) *adj.* **1.** made by oneself or itself. **2.** rising to wealth or success through one's own efforts: *a self-made millionaire.*

self-o·pin·ion·at·ed (self′ə pin′yə nā′tid) *adj.* **1.** having an excessively high regard for oneself; conceited. **2.** holding stubbornly to one's own opinions; obstinate.

self-per·pet·u·at·ing (self′pər pech′ü ā′ting) *adj.* continuing as it is regardless of efforts or demands to change: *a self-perpetuating political machine.*

self-pit·y (self′pit′ē) *n.* a feeling of pity for oneself.

self-pol·li·nate (self′pol′ə nāt′) *v.i., v.t.,* **-nat·ed, -nat·ing.** to undergo or cause to undergo self-pollination.

self-pol·li·na·tion (self′pol′ə nā′shən) *n.* the transfer of pollen from the anthers to the stigmas of the same flower, another flower on the same plant, or another flower on a different plant that is genetically alike. In some plants, this is accomplished by insects, and in others by gravity.

self-por·trait (self′pôr′trit, -trāt) *n.* a portrait of oneself made by oneself.

self-pos·sessed (self′pə zest′) *adj.* in control of oneself; composed; restrained. —**self-pos·ses·sion** (self′pə zesh′ən), *n.*

self-praise (self′prāz′) *n.* praise of oneself.

self-pres·er·va·tion (self′prez′ər vā′shən) *n.* **1.** protection of oneself or itself from injury, death, or danger. **2.** the instinctive desire or drive to protect oneself.

self-pro·claimed (self′prə klāmd′) *adj.* said or announced to be so by oneself, without proof or corroboration from others: *a self-proclaimed prophet.*

self-pro·pelled (self′prə peld′) *adj.* containing its own means of propulsion, as a missile.

self-pro·tec·tion (self′prə tek′shən) *n.* self-defense. —**self′-pro·tec′tive,** *adj.*

self-re·cord·ing (self′ri kôr′ding) *adj.* recording automatically.

self-re·gard (self′ri gärd′) *n.* **1.** regard or consideration for one's own interests or concerns. **2.** self-respect.

self-reg·u·lat·ing (self′reg′yə lā′ting) *adj.* regulating oneself or itself without need for further external control: *Research in cybernetics focuses upon self-regulating systems of control. Electronic timepieces are self-regulating.* —**self′-reg′u·la′tion,** *n.*

self-re·li·ance (self′ri lī′əns) *n.* reliance on one's own resources or abilities. —**self′-re·li′ant,** *adj.*

self-re·proach (self′ri prōch′) *n.* condemnation or censure of oneself by one's own conscience. —**self′-re·proach′ful,** *adj.* —**self′-re·proach′ing,** *adj.*

self-re·spect (self′ri spekt′) *n.* proper regard for or awareness of one's own worth and capabilities as a person. —**self′-re·spect′ing,** *adj.*

self-re·straint (self′ri strānt′) *n.* restraint imposed by oneself upon one's own actions or behavior; self-control: *You showed great self-restraint by not losing your temper.* —**self′-re·strained′,** *adj.*

self-re·veal·ing (self′ri vē′ling) *adj.* revealing one's inner thoughts or feelings, esp. when not intentional: *a self-revealing comment.* —**self′-rev′e·la′tion,** *n.*

self-right·eous (self′rī′chəs) *adj.* acting as if or thinking that one's own actions and beliefs are more moral or right than those of others. —**self′-right′eous·ly,** *adv.* —**self′-right′eous·ness,** *n.*

self-ris·ing (self′rī′zing) *adj.* rising by itself, esp. without the addition of leaven: *self-rising bread.*

self-sac·ri·fice (self′sak′rə f īs′) *n.* the giving up or ignoring of one's own interests and desires for the sake of duty or the welfare of another. —**self′-sac′ri·fic′ing,** *adj.* —**self′-sac′ri·fic′ing·ly,** *adv.*

self·same (self′sām′, -sām′) *adj.* exactly the same; identical.

self-sat·is·fied (self′sat′is f īd′) *adj.* feeling or showing satisfaction with oneself or one's achievements; complacent. —**self′-sat′is·fac′tion,** *n.*

self-seal·ing (self′sē′ling) *adj.* **1.** able to seal itself: *a self-sealing tire.* **2.** able to be sealed without moisture: *a self-sealing envelope.*

self-seek·ing (self′sē′king) *adj.* concerned mainly with furthering one's own personal interests; selfish. —*n.* selfishness. —**self′-seek′er,** *n.*

self-serve (self′sûrv′) *adj.* intended for or allowing self-service: *a self-serve pump at a gas station.*

self-serv·ice (self′sûr′vis) *n.* the act or process of serving oneself. —*adj.* requiring or allowing the users to serve themselves: *a self-service gas station, a self-service elevator.*

self-serv·ing (self′sûr′ving) *adj.* serving one's own ends and interests, often in disregard of others or of the truth: *self-serving testimony.*

self-start·er (self′stär′tər) *n.* **1.** starter *(def. 4).* **2.** *Informal.* a person who begins and carries out a project or other endeavor without requiring help or encouragement from others. —**self′-start′ing,** *adj.*

self-stick (self′stik′) *adj.* able to stick to a surface without the addition of glue, paste, or moisture; having its own adhesive: *self-stick mailing labels.*

self-styled (self′stīld′) *adj.* called or designated so by oneself alone, without the agreement of others: *a self-styled expert.*

self-suf·fi·cient (self′sə fish′ənt) *adj.* capable of fulfilling one's own needs without help from others; independent. —**self′-suf·fi′cien·cy,** *n.*

self-sup·port (self′sə pôrt′) *n.* support or providing for oneself or itself without outside assistance. —**self′-sup·port′ed,** *adj.* —**self′-sup·port′ing,** *adj.*

self-sus·tain·ing (self′sə stā′ning) *adj.* that sustains or keeps oneself or itself in existence without outside aid; self-supporting:

The program is self-sustaining because the trainees eventually become teachers.

self-taught (self′tôt′) *adj.* taught by oneself without aid from others: *a self-taught musician.*

self-will (self′wil′) *n.* insistence on having one's own way; stubbornness; obstinacy. —**self′-willed′,** *adj.*

self-wind·ing (self′wīn′ding) *adj.* (of a clock or watch) not needing to be wound by hand; wound automatically.

Sel·juk (sel′jŭk, sel jŭk′) *n.* any member of several Turkish dynasties who ruled much of western Asia during the eleventh and twelfth centuries. —*adj.* of or relating to the Seljuks. Also, **Sel·juk′i·an.**

sell (sel) *v.,* **sold, sell·ing.** —*v.t.* **1.** to give in return for money; accept money in payment for: *to sell a car, to sell time on a radio station.* **2.** to offer for sale; deal in: *Does this store sell shoes?* **3.** to bring about or promote the sale of: *Advertising sells new products.* **4.** to convince (someone) by vigorous, persuasive methods to do, approve, or accept something (with *on*): *Did you sell the bank on giving you a loan to open a new store?* **5.** to convince someone to do, approve, or accept (something) by such methods: *to sell a political candidate to the public.* —*v.i.* **1.** to sell goods, property, or the like, esp. to engage in selling things for a living. **2.** to be offered for sale or be sold: *This coat sells for $150.* **3.** to gain acceptance or approval: *That idea will never sell.* [Old English *sellan* to hand over (for money), give.]
  • **to sell off.** to dispose of by selling: *to sell off property.*
  • **to sell out. a.** to dispose of completely by selling: *The store sold out its stock of summer sweaters.* **b.** *Informal.* to betray, esp. for personal or material gain: *The spy sold out to the other side by providing secret information.*

sell·er (sel′ər) *n.* **1.** a person who sells or desires to sell. **2.** something that is sold, esp. that which is in great demand: *This new model is the best seller we've ever had.*

seller's market, a market in which goods are scarce in relation to demand, leading to high prices. ➡ opposed to **buyer's market.**

sell·out (sel′out′) *n.* **1.** the act of selling out. **2.** a performance or event for which all tickets have sold: *Friday night's movie was a sellout.* **3.** *Informal.* a person who betrays a country, organization, philosophy, or the like.

selt·zer (selt′sər) *n.* **1.** soda water. **2.** naturally effervescent spring water containing various minerals and having a slightly salty taste. [Modification of German *Selterser (Wasser)* (water) of Nieder*selters,* German village (near Wiesbaden) where this kind of mineral water was found.]

sel·va (sel′və) *n.* a rain forest of the tropics, esp. in South America. [American Spanish and Portuguese *selva* forest, from Latin *silva.*]

sel·vage (sel′vij) *also,* **sel·vedge.** *n.* the narrow, tightly woven edge on a fabric that prevents unraveling. [SELF + EDGE.]

selves (selvz) the plural of **self.**

se·man·tic (si man′tik) *adj.* **1.** of, based on, or concerned with the meanings of words. **2.** of or having to do with semantics. —**se·man′ti·cal·ly,** *adv.*

se·man·tics (si man′tiks) *n.* **1.** the branch of linguistics that deals with word meanings, esp. with regard to their historical development and change. **2.** the meaning of words or the interpretation of their meaning: *an argument over semantics.* ➡ used as singular in both defs. [French *sémantique,* from Greek *sēmantikos* significant, going back to *sēma* sign.]

sem·a·phore (sem′ə fôr′) *n.* **1.** a method of signaling using two flags, one held in each hand, the different positions of the arms representing the letters of the alphabet. **2.** any apparatus for signaling, as by a post with movable arms or an arrangement of lights or flags. —*v.i., v.t.,* **-phored, -phor·ing.** to signal by semaphore. [Greek *sēma* sign, signal + *-phoros* carrying.]

sem·blance (sem′bləns) *n.* **1.** an outward appearance, esp. one that is suspicious or false: *The defendant's alibi had a semblance of truth, but was shown to be a lie.* **2.** a likeness, image, or copy. [Old French *semblance* resemblance, appearance, from *sembler* to seem, resemble, from Latin *simulāre* to make like, represent.]

Sem·e·le (sem′ə lē′) *n.* in Greek mythology, a beautiful young woman who was stricken dead by thunderbolts when Zeus, at her request, dropped his disguise as a mortal and appeared as a god. Zeus rescued their unborn son Dionysus from her ashes.

se·men (sē′mən) *n.* a fluid secreted by the testes, containing sperm cells. [Latin *sēmen* seed.]

se·mes·ter (si mes′tər) *n.* one of two terms into which a school or college year is divided, usually about eighteen weeks. [German *Semester,* from Latin *sēmēstris* relating to six months, semiannual, from *sex* six + *mēnsis* month.]

sem·i (sem′ē, sem′ī) *n. Informal.* semitrailer. [Short for SEMI-TRAILER.]

semi- *prefix* **1.** half: *semitone, semicircle.* **2.** in part; not completely; partly: *semiconscious, semiofficial.* **3.** happening twice within a specified time period: *semimonthly, semiweekly.* [Latin *sēmi-* half.]

sem·i·an·nu·al (sem′ē an′ū əl) *adj.* occurring twice a year, esp. at six-month intervals. —**sem′i·an′nu·al·ly,** *adv.*

sem·i·a·quat·ic (sem′ē ə kwat′ik, -kwot′-) *adj.* living near and often entering water, but not inhabiting it: *A beaver is a semiaquatic animal.*

sem·i·ar·id (sem′ē ar′id) *adj.* of or relating to an area having an annual average of less than 20 inches (51 centimeters) of precipitation and characterized by grasslands, such as the Great Plains of the United States.

sem·i·au·to·mat·ic (sem′ē ô′tə mat′ik) *adj.* **1.** partly automatic. **2.** (of firearms) firing one shot each time the trigger is pulled, without reloading or cocking. —*n.* a semiautomatic firearm. —**sem′i·au′to·mat′i·cal·ly,** *adv.*

sem·i·breve (sem′ē brēv′, -brev′) *n. Music.* a whole note.

sem·i·cir·cle (sem′ē sûr′kəl) *n.* half a circle, or something arranged in or resembling half a circle. —**sem′i·cir′cu·lar,** *adj.*

semicircular canal, any of three curved tubes of membrane opening into the vestibule of the inner ear that help the body maintain equilibrium. For illustration, see **ear**[1].

sem·i·civ·i·lized (sem′ē siv′ə līzd′) *adj.* partly civilized.

sem·i·clas·si·cal (sem′ē klas′i kəl) *adj.* partly classical in form, as music intermediate in style between classical music and popular music.

sem·i·co·lon (sem′ē kō′lən) *n.* a mark of punctuation (;) that indicates a grammatical separation stronger than that indicated by a comma, but not as strong as that indicated by a period.

sem·i·con·duc·tor (sem′ē kən duk′tər) *n.* **1.** a crystalline nonmetal that is more conductive than an insulator but less so than a metal. This characteristic, imparted to elements such as silicon and germanium by adding other elements to the crystal lattice, is the basis of all solid-state electronics, from the transistor to the integrated circuit. **2.** an electronic component made from such a substance. —**sem′i·con·duct′ing,** *adj.*

sem·i·con·scious (sem′ē kon′shəs) *adj.* not completely conscious. —**sem′i·con′scious·ly,** *adv.* —**sem′i·con′scious-ness,** *n.*

sem·i·des·ert (sem′ē dez′ərt) *n.* an arid area with very sparse vegetation, often located between a desert and grassland.

sem·i·de·tached (sem′ē di tacht′) *adj.* **1.** (of a building) sharing one side wall with another building. **2.** partially detached or separate.

sem·i·di·vine (sem′ē di vīn′) *adj.* partly mortal and partly divine.

sem·i·fi·nal (sem′ē fī′nəl) *adj.* in the round before the final match, as in a tournament. —*n.* a semifinal match.

sem·i·fi·nal·ist (sem′ē fī′nə list) *n.* a person who takes part in a semifinal match.

sem·i·flu·id (sem′ē flü′id) *adj.* having fluid and solid characteristics. —*n.* a semifluid substance. Also, **semiliquid.**

sem·i·for·mal (sem′ē fôr′məl) *adj.* not completely formal; somewhat less than formal: *semiformal dress, a semiformal dance.*

sem·i·liq·uid (sem′ē lik′wid) *adj., n.* semifluid.

sem·i·lit·er·ate (sem′ē lit′ər it) *adj.* **1.** able to read and write only a little. **2.** able to read but not write.

sem·i·log·a·rith·mic (sem′ē lô′gə rith′mik, -log′ə-) *adj.* having a logarithmic scale on one axis and an arithmetic scale on the other: *semilogarithmic graph paper.*

sem·i·lu·nar (sem′ē lü′nər) *adj.* shaped like a half moon or crescent.

semilunar valve, either of two heart valves consisting of three crescent-shaped flaps, located at the opening of the aorta and at the opening of the pulmonary artery, that allow blood to flow out of the ventricles and keep it from flowing back into the heart.

sem·i·met·al (sem′ē met′əl) *n.* metalloid. —**sem′i·me·tal′-lic,** *adj.*

sem·i·month·ly (sem′ē munth′lē) *adj.* appearing or occurring two times a month. —*n., pl.* **-lies.** something that appears or takes place two times a month, such as a periodical. —*adv.* twice a month.

sem·i·nal (sem′ə nəl) *adj.* **1.** of, relating to, or containing semen or seed. **2.** of, belonging to, or promoting early growth or development. **3.** influential as a source of ideas; imaginative: *a seminal theory, a seminal thinker.* [Latin *sēminālis* relating to seed, from *sēmen* seed.] —**sem′i·nal·ly,** *adv.*

a	at	e	end	o	hot	u	up	hw	white		about
ā	ape	ē	me	ō	old	ū	use	ng	song		taken
ä	far	i	it	ô	fork	ü	rule	th	thin	ə	pencil
âr	care	ī	ice	oi	oil	ů	pull	th	this		lemon
		îr	pierce	ou	out	ûr	turn	zh	measure		circus

seminal vesicle, either of a pair of small glandular pouches that function in the male reproductive system to produce the thick, fluid part of the semen that protects and nourishes the sperm cells.

sem·i·nar (sem′ə när′) *n.* **1.** a group of advanced students, as at a university, doing independent study or research under supervision. **2.** a meeting or course of study in which such a group reports and discusses a specialized topic. [German *Seminar* class for advanced, supervised research, from Latin *sēminārium* nursery garden, seed plot, from *sēmen* seed. Doublet of SEMINARY.]

sem·i·nar·y (sem′ə ner′ē) *n., pl.* **-nar·ies. 1.** an institution that trains students for the priesthood, ministry, or rabbinate. **2.** a school or academy at or beyond the high school level, esp. a boarding school for young women. [Latin *sēminārium* nursery garden, seed plot, from *sēmen* seed. Doublet of SEMINAR.] **—sem·i·nar·i·an** (sem′ə när′ē ən), *n.*

sem·i·na·tion (sem′ə nā′shən) *n.* the act or process of sowing or disseminating seed; insemination.

sem·i·nif·er·ous (sem′ə nif′ər əs) *adj.* **1.** *Botany.* bearing or producing seed. **2.** containing or conveying semen. [Latin *sēmin-,* stem of *sēmen* seed + -FEROUS.]

sem·i·niv·o·rous (sem′ə niv′ər əs) *adj.* feeding on seeds. [Latin *sēmin-,* stem of *sēmen* seed + -*vorus* devouring.]

Sem·i·nole (sem′ə nōl′) *n., pl.* **-nole** or **-noles.** a member of a tribe of Muskogean North American Indians closely related to the Creeks, who originally lived in Florida, but now reside mostly in Oklahoma.

sem·i·of·fi·cial (sem′ē ə fish′əl) *adj.* having some degree of authority; partly official. **—sem′i·of·fi′cial·ly,** *adv.*

sem·i·per·me·a·ble (sem′ē pûr′mē ə bəl) *adj.* (of a membrane) permitting the passage of solvent molecules but not solute molecules, or the passage of liquids but not the colloidal particles dispersed in them. **—sem′i·per′me·a·bil′i·ty,** *n.*

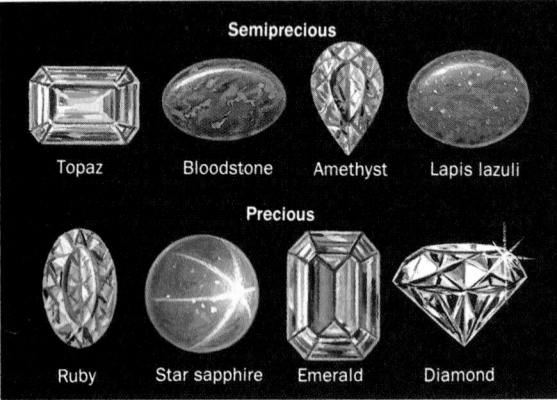

semiprecious and precious stones

sem·i·pre·cious (sem′ē presh′əs) *adj.* (of gems and minerals) having some commercial value, but less than that of precious stones.

sem·i·pri·vate (sem′ē prī′vit) *adj.* partly private, as a hospital room shared by two or four patients.

sem·i·pro (sem′ē prō′) *n.* semiprofessional.

sem·i·pro·fes·sion·al (sem′ē prə fesh′ə nəl) *adj.* **1.** working part-time at a job and receiving a salary or expenses: *a semiprofessional athlete.* **2.** of, relating to, or engaged in by part-time workers who receive a salary or expenses: *semiprofessional football.* **—***n.* a person engaged as a semiprofessional worker. **—sem′i·pro·fes′sion·al·ly,** *adv.*

sem·i·qua·ver (sem′ē kwā′vər) *n. Music.* a sixteenth note.

Se·mir·a·mis (sə mir′ə mis) *n.* the legendary queen of Assyria who ruled the city of Nineveh after her husband's death and founded Babylon in the early ninth century B.C.

sem·i·rig·id (sem′ē rij′id) *adj.* designating a type of airship that is partly rigid, having an inflatable envelope and a rigid keel to which the engine is attached.

sem·i·skilled (sem′ē skild′) *adj.* possessing or requiring limited skill, training, or ability: *semiskilled workers, a semiskilled job.*

sem·i·soft (sem′ē sôft′) *adj.* firm but soft and easily sliced: *semisoft cheese.*

sem·i·sol·id (sem′ē sol′id) *adj.* of moderate rigidity; not totally rigid, as stiff dough. **—***n.* a semisolid substance.

sem·i·sweet (sem′ē swēt′) *adj.* slightly sweetened, as chocolate.

Sem·ite (sem′ īt) *n.* **1.** a member of a group of peoples speaking related languages, living predominantly in the Middle East and parts of Africa, and including in modern times Hebrews, Arabs, Syrians, and a number of Ethiopians. Also, **Shemite. 2.** Jew.

Se·mit·ic (sə mit′ik) *adj.* of or relating to Semites, esp. Jews. **—***n.* a subdivision of the Semito-Hamitic language family, including Hebrew, Arabic, Syrian, and such ancient languages as Aramaic, Phoenician, and Assyrian.

Sem·i·tism (sem′i tiz′əm) *n.* **1.** Semitic customs or characteristics, esp. those of the Jewish people. **2.** a word or idiom of a Semitic language.

Sem·i·to-Ha·mit·ic (sem′i tō ha mit′ik) *adj.* of or belonging to a family of languages of various parts of Africa and the Middle East, including Arabic, Hebrew, and Berber.

sem·i·tone (sem′ē tōn′) *n. Music.* half step *(def. 1).*

sem·i·trail·er (sem′ē trā′lər) *n.* **1.** a trailer with no front wheels, designed to be attached to a tractor. **2.** a truck consisting of a tractor and a semitrailer.

sem·i·trans·par·ent (sem′ē trans pâr′ənt, -par′-) *adj.* partly or imperfectly transparent. **—sem′i·trans·par′en·cy,** *n.* **—sem′i·trans·par′ent·ly,** *adv.*

sem·i·trop·i·cal (sem′ē trop′i kəl) *adj.* subtropical.

sem·i·vow·el (sem′ē vou′əl) *n. Phonetics.* a letter or sound that has the vocal quality of a vowel but is used as a consonant, for example: *w* in *water* and *y* in *yard.*

sem·i·week·ly (sem′ē wēk′lē) *adj.* issued or occurring twice a week: *a semiweekly newspaper.* **—***n., pl.* **-lies.** a semiweekly publication. **—***adv.* twice a week.

sem·i·year·ly (sem′ē yîr′lē) *adj.* issued or occurring twice a year or once every six months; semiannual: *semiyearly business reports.* **—***n., pl.* **-lies.** something that is issued or occurs twice a year. **—***adv.* twice a year.

sem·o·li·na (sem′ə lē′nə) *n.* the hard, coarsely ground kernels of wheat that are left after flour has been ground and sifted, used in making soup, pudding, and pasta. [Italian *semolino,* diminutive of *semola* bran, fine flour, from Latin *simila* fine flour.]

sem·pi·ter·nal (sem′pi tûr′nəl) *adj.* having no end; lasting forever; eternal. [Late Latin *sempiternālis,* going back to Latin *semper* always + *aeternus* everlasting.] **—sem′pi·ter′nal·ly,** *adv.*

semp·stress (semp′stris, sem′-) *n.* seamstress.

sen (sen) *n., pl.* **sen.** ¹⁄₁₀₀ of any of various monetary units, such as the Japanese yen and the Indonesian rupiah. [Japanese *sen,* from Chinese (Mandarin) *ch'ien* coin, money.]

Sen. 1. Senate. **2.** Senator. **3.** *also,* **sen.** senior.

sen·ate (sen′it) *n.* **1.** a governing or lawmaking council or assembly. **2. Senate. a.** the upper chamber of the legislature of the United States or of most states of the United States. **b.** a similar chamber in other countries. **c.** in ancient Rome, the ruling body of citizens selected from the patricians and wealthy plebeians. [Latin *senātus* the council of elders of ancient Rome, from *senex* old, old man.]

sen·a·tor (sen′ə tər) *also,* **Sen·a·tor.** *n.* a member of a senate. **—sen′a·tor·ship′,** *n.*

sen·a·to·ri·al (sen′ə tôr′ē əl) *also,* **Sen·a·to·ri·al.** *adj.* **1.** of, relating to, or befitting a senator or a senate: *a senatorial debate.* **2.** consisting of senators.

send (send) *v.,* **sent, send·ing. —v.t. 1.** to cause to go to a certain place or from one place to another: *to send news by telegraph, to send a spacecraft into orbit.* **2.** to cause to go into a certain state or condition: *to send a person into a rage.* **3.** to cause to occur: *The scary movie sent chills up my spine.* **4.** to enable to go, as by providing financial support: *I sent my children through college.* **5.** *Slang.* to fill with delight or excitement: *That saxophone solo really sends me.* **—v.i.** to send messages or a signal, as on a radio. [Old English *sendan* to dispatch, cause to go, cause to happen.] **—send′er,** *n.*

  ·to send for. a. to ask (someone) to come; summon: *Did you send for a porter?* **b.** to ask that (something) be brought or sent; make a request for: *We sent for a free booklet.*

  ·to send out for. to ask someone to get or bring (someone or something): *to send out for a pizza.*

  ·to send up. *Informal.* to send to jail.

Synonyms *v.t.* **Send, dispatch,** and **transmit** mean to forward something from one place to another. **Send,** the broadest of these terms, often stresses the person or thing initiating an action: *Many friends and relatives sent congratulations.* **Dispatch** implies urgency and speed: *The police dispatched an ambulance to the scene of the accident.* **Transmit** often emphasizes the means by which something is sent or passed on: *The satellite transmits a signal every hour.*

send-off (send′ôf′, -of′) *n. Informal.* a demonstration of good will in honor of the start of a journey, new career, or the like.

Sen·e·ca (sen′i kə) *n.* a member of the largest tribe of the Iroquois Confederacy of North American Indians, formerly living

in western New York State. [Dutch *Sennecaas* name for a confederation of Iroquois tribes (including the Seneca tribe); probably of Algonquian origin.]

se·nes·cent (si nes'ənt) *adj.* growing old; aging. [Latin *senēscēns,* present participle of *senēscere* to grow old, going back to *senex* old, old man.] **—se·nes'cence,** *n.*

sen·es·chal (sen'ə shəl) *n.* in medieval times, an official in charge of a royal or noble household. [Old French *seneschal;* of Germanic origin.]

se·nile (sē'nīl, sen'īl) *adj.* **1.** suffering the weakness or deterioration that often occurs in old age, esp. mental deterioration, such as short-term memory loss. **2.** of, relating to, or caused by old age. [Latin *senīlis* relating to old people, aged, from *senex* old, old man.] **—se'nile·ly,** *adv.*

se·nil·i·ty (si nil'i tē) *n.* **1.** the mental and, sometimes, physical infirmities of old age. **2.** the state of being old.

sen·ior (sēn'yər) *adj.* **1.** being the older of two. ➡ distinguished from **junior;** often used after the name of a father whose son has the same name: *John Smith, Senior.* **2.** of relatively old age or long experience: *a senior member of the legal profession.* **3.** of higher position or rank, esp. after long service: *senior officers of the army.* **4.** (of a U.S. senator) having occupied a senatorial seat longer than the other senator from the same state. **5.** relating to, enrolled in, or designating the final year of high school or college. —*n.* **1.** a person who is older than another: *My cousin is my senior by three years.* **2.** a student in the final year of high school or college. **3.** a person of higher position or rank. [Latin *senior* older, comparative of *senex* old. Doublet of SIRE.]

senior citizen, an older person, esp. one who is over 65 years, retired, and eligible for a variety of special benefits.

senior high school, a school attended after junior high school, usually including grades nine or ten through twelve.

sen·ior·i·ty (sēn yôr'i tē, -yor'-) *n.* **1.** the state of being more advanced than another or others in age, position, or period of service. **2.** special consideration or privileges given a person in a job or office because of age, position, or length of service.

sen·na (sen'ə) *n.* **1.** a laxative made from the dried leaves of any of various plants, genus *Cassia.* **2.** the dried leaves themselves. [Modern Latin *senna,* from Arabic *sanā.*]

sen·nit (sen'it) *n.* **1.** a flat, plaited cordage made by braiding strands of rope yarn or similar fiber. **2.** plaited grass or a similar material, used esp. for making hats. [Of uncertain origin.]

se·ñor (sen yôr') *n., pl.* **se·ño·res** (sen-yôr'ās). sir; mister. ➡ the Spanish form of polite or respectful address for a man. [Spanish *señor,* from Latin *senior* older, comparative of *senex* old, old man.]

se·ño·ra (sen yôr'ə) *n.* madam. ➡ the Spanish form of respectful or polite address for a married woman. [Spanish *señora,* feminine of *señor.* See SEÑOR.]

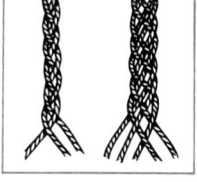

sennit

se·ño·ri·ta (sen'yə rē'tə) *n.* miss. ➡ the Spanish form of respectful or polite address for an unmarried girl or woman. [Spanish *señorita,* diminutive of *señora.* See SEÑORA.]

sen·sate (sen'sāt) *adj.* capable of feeling and perceiving; having consciousness or sensibility. [Late Latin *sēnsātus* gifted with sense, from Latin *sēnsus.* See SENSE.]

sen·sa·tion (sen sā'shən) *n.* **1.** a conscious impression resulting from the effect of a stimulus on a sense organ: *the sensation of touch.* **2.** the action or power of the senses collectively. **3.** a vague feeling or impression arising from some particular condition or set of circumstances: *a sensation of fear, a sensation of something being wrong.* **4.a.** a state of excitement or intense interest: *The political scandal caused a nationwide sensation.* **b.** a person or thing that causes such excitement or interest: *The author's latest novel became an instant sensation.*

sen·sa·tion·al (sen sā'shə nəl) *adj.* **1.** arousing or intended to arouse excitement or intense interest: *a sensational newspaper story.* **2.** of or having to do with the senses. **3.** *Informal.* exceptionally good; spectacular; great: *The play was sensational.* **—sen·sa'tion·al·ly,** *adv.*

sen·sa·tion·al·ism (sen sā'shə nə liz'əm) *n.* **1.** sensational language or writing intended to excite or stimulate an audience or the public. **2.** the use of such language or writing. **3.** *Philosophy.* an extreme form of empiricism, holding that knowledge is derived only from sensation. **—sen·sa'tion·al·ist,** *n., adj.* **—sen·sa'tion·al·is'tic,** *adj.*

sense (sens) *n.* **1.** in humans and other animals, any of the special modes or types of perceiving external and internal stimuli, such as sight, hearing, smell, taste, and touch. **2.** speech, thought,

or action that is reasonable or logical. **3.** wisdom or usefulness: *What is the sense of worrying about something that cannot be changed?* **4.** meaning or signification: *a word with many senses.* **5.** a vague feeling or awareness; impression: *a sense of well-being.* **6.** the mental capacity to perceive, understand, and appreciate (with *of*): *a sense of humor.* **7.** sound judgment or intelligence: *a person of good sense.* **8.** *also,* **senses.** normal, sound mental faculties: *They finally came to their senses.* **9.** a final, briefly summarized opinion or judgment: *The sense of the meeting was that we need a new leader.* —*v.t.,* **sensed, sens·ing. 1.** to be aware or conscious of; feel: *We sensed the tension in the conference room.* **2.** to grasp or understand; comprehend. [Latin *sēnsus* perception, feeling, understanding.]

• **in a sense.** from one aspect; in one way.

• **to make sense.** to be reasonable or logical; have an understandable meaning: *Your argument makes sense.*

sense·less (sens'lis) *adj.* **1.** lacking wisdom, usefulness, or logic; foolish; stupid: *a senseless action.* **2.** unconscious: *The blow knocked me senseless.* **3.** lacking signification; meaningless: *senseless babble.* **—sense'less·ly,** *adv.* **—sense'less·ness,** *n.*

sense organ, any of the organs that receive and respond to stimuli from the internal or external environment, including the eyes, ears, nose, and taste buds.

sen·si·bil·i·ty (sen'sə bil'i tē) *n., pl.* **-ties. 1.** the capacity to receive and respond to sensory stimuli; perception. **2.** *also,* **sensibilities.** refined or delicate feeling: *The vulgar language offended their sensibilities.* **3.** sensitivity in feeling or perception.

sen·si·ble (sen'sə bəl) *adj.* **1.** having, exhibiting, or characterized by good sense or sound judgment; wise; judicious: *a sensible person, a sensible decision.* **2.** easily perceived, noticed, or detected by the mind or senses. **3.** taking notice; conscious; aware (with *of*): *to be sensible of another's feelings.* [Late Latin *sēnsibilis* able to perceive, that can be perceived, from Latin *sēnsus,* past participle of *sentīre* to perceive, feel.] **—sen'si·ble·ness,** *n.* **—sen'si·bly,** *adv.*

sen·si·tive (sen'si tiv) *adj.* **1.** easily or readily affected by (with *to*): *sensitive to cold.* **2.** easily damaged, hurt, or irritated: *A baby's skin is very sensitive.* **3.** responsive to outside stimuli: *The film is sensitive to light.* **4.** painful to the touch: *My sprained finger is very tender and sensitive.* **5.** quick to take offense or be hurt; touchy: *They were sensitive about their failure to make the team.* **6.** keenly attuned and responsive to the feelings of others. **7.** involving highly secret or delicate matters; precarious; ticklish: *a sensitive post in the government.* **8.** requiring care, tact, or delicacy: *Religion and politics are sensitive topics.* **9.** of, relating to, or affecting the senses or sensation. —*n.* a person who is unusually receptive to occult or psychic powers; psychic. [Medieval Latin *sensitivus* relating to sensation, from Latin *sēnsus,* past participle of *sentīre* to perceive, feel.] **—sen'si·tive·ly,** *adv.* **—sen'si·tive·ness,** *n.*

sensitive plant 1. a shrubby tropical American plant, *Mimosa pudica,* whose leaflets fold up when touched. **2.** any of various other plants sensitive to touch.

sen·si·tiv·i·ty (sen'si tiv'i tē) *n.* **1.** the state or condition of being sensitive; sensitiveness. **2.** the degree to which a radio or television receiver responds to incoming signals.

sen·si·tize (sen'si tīz') *v.t.,* **-tized, -tiz·ing.** to make sensitive. **—sen'si·ti·za'tion,** *n.* **—sen'si·tiz'er,** *n.*

sen·si·tom·e·ter (sen'si tom'i tər) *n. Photography.* a device for measuring the sensitivity of photographic film or paper to light. [SENSIT(IVE) + -METER.] **—sen·si·to·met'ric** (sen'si tə met'rik), *adj.*

sen·sor (sen'sər, -sôr) *n.* any of various devices used to measure or detect light, radiation, heat, or other stimuli and to transmit a resulting electrical impulse, as for operating a control.

sen·so·ri·mo·tor (sen'sə rē mō'tər) *adj. Physiology.* of, relating to, or functioning in both the sensory and motor impulses: *sensorimotor disturbance.* [SENSORY + MOTOR.]

sen·so·ri·um (sen sôr'ē əm) *n., pl.* **-so·ri·ums** or **-so·ri·a** (-sôr'ē ə). **1.** the supposed seat or locale of receiving sensations in the gray matter of the brain. **2.** the entire apparatus of the brain responsible for interpreting various sensory stimuli. [Late Latin *sēnsōrium* the seat or organ of sensation, from Latin *sēnsus,* past participle of *sentīre* to perceive, feel.]

sen·so·ry (sen'sə rē) *adj.* of, relating to, or conveying sensation: *sensory stimulation, a sensory nerve.*

sen·su·al (sen'shü əl) *adj.* **1.** enjoying and seeking the pleasures

of the body or senses, esp. sexual pleasures. **2.** physically pleasing or alluring. **3.** of or relating to stimulation of the body or senses rather than the spirit or intellect: *sensual delights.* [Late Latin *sensuālis* endowed with feeling, from Latin *sēnsus* perception, feeling.] —**sen′su·al·ly,** *adv.*

sen·su·al·ist (sen′shü ə list) *n.* a person who is given to or has sensuality. —**sen′su·al·ism,** *n.* —**sen′su·al·is′tic,** *adj.*

sen·su·al·i·ty (sen′shü al′i tē) *n.* **1.** the state or quality of being sensual. **2.** indulgence in sensual pleasures; lewdness.

sen·su·al·ize (sen′shü ə līz′) *v.t.,* **-ized, -iz·ing.** to make sensual. —**sen′su·al·i·za′tion,** *n.*

sen·su·ous (sen′shü əs) *adj.* **1.** of, relating to, or affecting the senses: *Listening to music is a sensuous experience.* **2.** enjoying the pleasures of the senses; sensual. —**sen′su·ous·ly,** *adv.* —**sen′su·ous·ness,** *n.*

sent (sent) the past tense and past participle of **send.**

sen·tence (sen′təns) *n.* **1.** an independent unit of spoken or written language that consists of a word or words that make a statement, ask a question, or otherwise express a complete thought. A sentence usually contains a subject and predicate. *The musician and artist is not a sentence. The musician and artist are talented individuals is a sentence.* **2.** *Law.* **a.** the judgment by a court or judge setting the punishment of a defendant after conviction. **b.** the punishment itself. **3.** *Archaic.* a saying; maxim. **4.** *Mathematics.* any statement that expresses a relationship between numbers. A sentence may be true, as $5 + 3 = 8$, false, as $6 - 2 = 3$, or neither true nor false, as $x + 4 > 7$. A **closed sentence** has no unknown quantities, as $3 + 2 = 5$; an **open sentence** contains at least one variable, as $3a + 6 = 15$. —*v.t.,* **-tenced, -tenc·ing.** to set the punishment of: *The judge sentenced the defendant to three months in jail.* [Old French *sentence* opinion, decision given by judges, punishment, from Latin *sententia* opinion, way of thinking.] —**sen·ten·tial** (sen ten′shəl), *adj.* —**sen·ten′tial·ly,** *adv.*

sen·ten·tious (sen ten′shəs) *adj.* **1.** short and meaningful; pithy: *a book of sententious sayings.* **2.** inclined to sermonize; moralistic; pompous. **3.** tending to use trite phrases or maxims. [Latin *sententiōsus* full of meaning, pithy, from *sententia* opinion, way of thinking.] —**sen·ten′tious·ly,** *adv.* —**sen·ten′tious·ness,** *n.*

sen·tience (sen′shəns) *n.* the ability to receive sensory impressions or sensory stimuli; capacity for feeling; consciousness.

sen·tient (sen′shənt) *adj.* capable of experiencing sensation; having the power of feeling; conscious. [Latin *sentiēns,* present participle of *sentīre* to perceive, feel.] —**sen′tient·ly,** *adv.*

sen·ti·ment (sen′tə mənt) *n.* **1.** a mental attitude or point of view, esp. one arrived at after deliberation; opinion: *Popular sentiment is against the war.* **2.** an expression of feeling or emotion: *I appreciate the sentiment, but you didn't have to buy me a gift.* **3.** refined or tender emotion. **4.** an emotion that is exaggerated, overdone, or foolish; mawkishness. **5.** a thought or attitude based on or reflecting an emotion. [Medieval Latin *sentimentum* opinion, feeling, from Latin *sentīre* to perceive, feel.]

sen·ti·men·tal (sen′tə men′təl) *adj.* **1.** characterized by or showing emotion or feeling: *a sentimental love song.* **2.** influenced by or apt to be swayed by feeling rather than reason: *to be sentimental when one should be logical.* **3.** appealing to the emotions: *The candidate made a sentimental plea for support.* **4.** relating to or based on sentiment: *I save all my old letters for sentimental reasons.* **5.** characterized by exaggerated and mawkish emotion. —**sen′ti·men′tal·ly,** *adv.*

sen·ti·men·tal·ism (sen′tə men′tə liz′əm) *n.* **1.** the quality or state of being sentimental. **2.** the tendency to be influenced by feeling rather than by reason. **3.** an instance of either of these. —**sen′ti·men′tal·ist,** *n.*

sen·ti·men·tal·i·ty (sen′tə men tal′i tē, -mən-) *n., pl.* **-ties.** **1.** the quality or state of being sentimental. **2.** the tendency to be influenced by feeling rather than by reason. **3.** an expression of exaggerated or excessive emotion; mawkishness.

sen·ti·men·tal·ize (sen′tə men′tə līz′) *v.,* **-ized, -iz·ing.** —*v.i.* to be sentimental; indulge in sentiment. —*v.t.* **1.** to make (someone or something) an object of sentiment. **2.** to make sentimental. —**sen′ti·men′ta·li·za′tion,** *n.*

sen·ti·nel (sen′tə nəl) *n.* a person, animal, or thing that is stationed to keep watch and alert others of danger; guard; sentry. —*v.t.,* **-neled, -nel·ing;** *also, British,* **-nelled, -nel·ling.** to guard or watch over as a sentinel. [French *sentinelle* sentry, from Italian *sentinella* sentry, probably going back to Latin *sentīre* to perceive, feel.]

sen·try (sen′trē) *n., pl.* **-tries. 1.** a person, esp. a soldier, stationed to keep watch and alert others of danger. **2.** the watch kept by a sentry. [Possibly abbreviation of obsolete *centrinel,* form of SENTINEL.]

sentry box, a small building or booth intended to shelter a sentry on duty.

Sep. 1. September. **2.** Septuagint.

se·pal (sē′pəl) *n.* one of the leaflike divisions of the calyx of a flower, usually green but sometimes, as in the tulip, the same color as the petals. [Modern Latin *sepalum,* from modification of Greek *skepē* covering + Modern Latin *petalum.* See PETAL.]

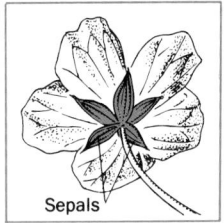
sepals of a geranium

sep·a·ra·ble (sep′ər ə bal, sep′rə-) *adj.* able to be separated. —**sep′a·ra·bil′i·ty,** *n.* —**sep′a·ra·bly,** *adv.*

sep·a·rate (*v.,* sep′ə rāt′; *adj., n.,* sep′ər it, sep′rit) *v.,* **-rat·ed, -rat·ing.** —*v.t.* **1.** to keep apart, esp. by acting as or placing a barrier between: *A fence separates the garden from the sidewalk.* **2.** to set apart: *to separate apples from oranges.* **3.** to recognize as different; distinguish: *to separate fact from fantasy.* **4.** to remove from a mass or mixture: *to separate cream from milk.* **5.** to divide or sort into individual parts or elements: *to separate a tangle of thread.* **6.** to release from the armed forces, employment, or the like. **7.** *Law.* to cause (a married couple) to live apart by court order. —*v.i.* **1.** to become disconnected or detached; come apart. **2.** to become set apart from a mass or mixture: *In a threshing machine, wheat kernels separate from chaff.* **3.** to go in different directions; part company: *The two friends separated at the corner.* **4.** (of a married couple) to live apart but without a divorce. —*adj.* **1.** set apart or divided from each other or others: *two separate rooms.* **2.** not the same; different: *Those are separate problems and cannot be handled in the same manner.* **3.** being one unit; single and distinct; individual: *each separate item on a list.* —*n.* **separates.** coordinated articles of clothing designed to be worn in various combinations. [Latin *sēparātus,* past participle of *sēparāre* to part, divide.] —**sep′a·rate·ly,** *adv.* —**sep′a·rate·ness,** *n.*

sep·a·ra·tion (sep′ə rā′shən) *n.* **1.** the act or process of separating or the state of being separated. **2.** the point at which two or more objects or parts are divided from each other; division. **3.** a condition in which a husband and wife live apart. **4.** the release of a person from the armed forces, employment, or the like.

sep·a·ra·tism (sep′ər ə tiz′əm, sep′rə-) *n.* the principle of advocating or wanting separation, esp. political or religious separation.

sep·a·ra·tist (sep′ər ə tist, sep′rə-) *n.* a person who supports or favors separation, esp. from a political or religious body.

sep·a·ra·tive (sep′ə rā′tiv, sep′ər ə-, sep′rə-) *adj.* tending or causing to separate.

sep·a·ra·tor (sep′ə rā′tər) *n.* **1.** a person or thing that separates. **2.** an apparatus for separating liquids, as cream from milk.

Se·phar·di (sə fär′dē) *n., pl.* **-dim** (-dim) a member or descendant of the group of Jewish people who settled in Spain and Portugal. ➡ distinguished from **Ashkenazi.** —**Se·phar′dic,** *adj.*

se·pi·a (sē′pē ə) *n.* **1.** a dark brown pigment originally made from the inky fluid secreted by the cuttlefish. **2.** a dark brown color. **3.** a drawing, photograph, or the like in this color. —*adj.* having the color sepia. [Latin *sēpia* cuttlefish, ink of the cuttlefish, from Greek *sēpiā.*]

se·poy (sē′poi) *n.* formerly, a native of India serving as a soldier in a European army, esp. in the British army. [Portuguese *sipai(a)* native soldier of India in the service of the British, from Hindustani *sipāhī* soldier, from Persian *sipāhī,* from *sipāh* army.]

sep·pu·ku (se pü′kü) *n.* hara-kiri. [Japanese *seppuku.*]

sep·sis (sep′sis) *n.* the presence of infective microorganisms or their toxins in the blood or other body tissues. [Modern Latin *sepsis,* from Greek *sēpsis* putrefaction.]

Sept. 1. September. **2.** Septuagint.

sep·tate (sep′tāt) *adj.* having or being divided by one or more septa. [Modern Latin *septatus,* from Latin *saeptum* fence.]

Sep·tem·ber (sep tem′bər) *n.* the ninth month of the year, containing thirty days. [Latin *September,* name of the seventh month in the early Roman calendar, in which March was the first month, from *septem* seven.]

sep·te·nar·y (sep′tə ner′ē) *adj.* **1.** of or relating to the number seven. **2.** forming into or containing seven things. **3.** septennial. —*n.* a group or set of seven persons or things. [Latin *septēnārius* consisting of seven, going back to *septem* seven.]

sep·ten·ni·al (sep ten′ē əl) *adj.* **1.** consisting of or lasting seven years. **2.** occurring once in every seven years. [Latin *septennium*

period of seven years (going back to *septem* seven + *annus* year) + -AL[1].] —**sep·ten′ni·al·ly,** *adv.*

sep·tet (sep tet′) *also,* **sep·tette.** *n.* **1.a.** a musical composition for seven voices or instruments. **b.** a musical ensemble of seven performers. **2.** a group or set of seven persons or things. [German *Septett* musical composition for seven instruments or voices, from Latin *septem* seven.]

sep·tic (sep′tik) *adj.* **1.** causing sepsis or infection. **2.** caused by sepsis or infection. [Latin *sēpticus* causing putrefaction, from Greek *sēptikos,* from *sēpein* to make rotten.]

sep·ti·ce·mi·a (sep′tə sē′mē ə) *also,* **sep·ti·cae·mi·a.** *n.* a disease caused by the absorption of certain bacteria and their toxins into the bloodstream; blood poisoning. [Modern Latin *septicaemia,* from Greek *sēptikos* causing putrefaction + *haima* blood.]

septic tank, an underground tank in which sewage is decomposed by the action of bacteria.

sep·til·lion (sep til′yən) *n.* **1.** in the United States, the cardinal number that is represented by 1 followed by 24 zeros. **2.** in Great Britain, the cardinal number that is represented by 1 followed by 42 zeros. —*adj.* numbering one septillion. [French *septillion* 1 followed by 24 zeros, from Latin *septem* seven, on the model of *million.* See MILLION.] —**sep·til′lionth,** *adj., n.*

sep·tu·a·ge·nar·i·an (sep′tü ə jə när′ē ən, -tü ə-, -chü ə-) *n.* a person who is seventy or between seventy and eighty years old. —*adj.* being seventy or between seventy and eighty years old. [Latin *septuāgēnārius* containing seventy (going back to *septuāgintā* seventy) + -AN.]

Sep·tu·a·ges·i·ma (sep′tü ə jes′ə mə, -tü-, -chü-) *n.* the third Sunday before Lent. [Latin *septuāgēsima (diēs)* literally, seventieth (day); day that was reckoned approximately as the seventieth day before Easter.]

Sep·tu·a·gint (sep′tü ə jint, -tü-, -chü-) *n.* the Greek translation of the Old Testament compiled by Jewish scholars before the time of Jesus. [Latin *septuāgintā* seventy; because this translation was supposedly done by seventy Jewish scholars.]

sep·tum (sep′təm) *n., pl.* **-ta** (-tə). a dividing wall, membrane, or partition in an animal or plant structure. [Latin *saeptum* fence.] —**sep′tal,** *adj.*

sep·tu·ple (sep′tə pəl, sep tü′-, -tū′-, -tup′əl) *adj.* **1.** consisting of seven parts or members. **2.** seven times as great or as many. —*v.t., v.i.,* **-pled, -pling.** to make or become seven times as great or as many; multiply by seven. [Late Latin *septuplus* sevenfold, from Latin *septem* seven + *-plus* -fold.]

sep·ul·cher (sep′əl kər) *also, British,* **sep·ul·chre.** *n.* **1.** a burial place, esp. a vault or tomb. **2.** a receptacle for relics, esp. in an altar. —*v.t.* to bury in or as in a sepulcher; entomb; inter. [Old French *sepulcre* tomb, from Latin *sepulcrum,* from *sepelīre* to bury.]

se·pul·chral (si pul′krəl) *adj.* **1.** of or relating to a sepulcher or tomb. **2.** of or having to do with burial or the dead. **3.** deep, dark, and dismal; funereal.

sep·ul·ture (sep′əl chər) *n.* burial; interment. [Old French *sepulture* a burying, from Latin *sepultūra* burial.]

seq., the following. [Latin *sequēns,* present participle of *sequī* to follow.]

se·quel (sē′kwəl) *n.* **1.** a literary or other work, complete in itself, that continues or completes a previous work: *a movie sequel.* **2.** something that follows. **3.** something that comes as a result; consequence. [Latin *sequēla* result, that which follows, from *sequī* to follow.]

se·que·la (si kwē′lə) *n., pl.* **-lae** (-lē). **1.** an abnormal condition resulting directly or indirectly from a previous disease. **2.** something that follows or comes as a result; sequel. [Latin *sequēla* result, that which follows. See SEQUEL.]

se·quence (sē′kwəns) *n.* **1.a.** the following of one thing after another; succession: *A strange sequence of events led to the incident.* **b.** the order in which things occur or are arranged: *alphabetical sequence.* **2.** a section of a film, confined to one time and place without any break or interruption, or edited to appear this way: *It took a week to film the fight sequence.* **3.** *Mathematics.* an ordered set of numbers such that there is a first term, second term, and so on. For example, 1, $\frac{1}{3}$, $\frac{1}{5}$, $\frac{1}{7}$ . . . is a sequence. **4.** a group or collection of connected things: *a sonnet sequence.* **5.** something that results; consequence. [Late Latin *sequentia* that which follows, from Latin *sequēns,* present participle of *sequī* to follow.]

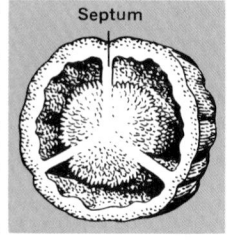

Septum

septum of a pepper

Synonyms **Sequence** and **series** mean a number of things arranged in a definite order. **Sequence** usually indicates an order that has a strong logic and regularity: *The mechanic adjusted the firing sequence of the engine's pistons.* **Series** connotes a set of similar or related things that together form a whole: *The championship was preceded by a series of play-off games. The foreign film series was always well attended.*

se·quent (sē′kwənt) *adj.* **1.** coming or happening after; subsequent: *sequent events.* **2.** following in a continuous order: *sequent images of a motion-picture film.* **3.** following as a result; consequent: *sequent effects.* [Latin *sequēns,* present participle of *sequī* to follow.]

se·quen·tial (si kwen′shəl) *adj.* **1.** characterized by or arranged in a sequence; following one after the other: *sequential numbers.* **2.** sequent.

se·ques·ter (si kwes′tər) *v.t.* **1.** to withdraw from or take out of the world at large; hide safely away: *money sequestered in a safe, to sequester a jury.* **2.** *Law.* to take and hold, as property, until a debt or claim is settled. **3.** to confiscate (enemy property). [Late Latin *sequestrāre* to separate, give up for safekeeping, from Latin *sequester* mediator, trustee.]

se·ques·trate (si kwes′trāt) *v.t.* **-trat·ed, -trat·ing.** sequester.

se·ques·tra·tion (sē′kwes trā′shən, si kwes trā′-) *n.* **1.** the act of sequestering or the state of being sequestered. **2.** the process of taking property into custody until a debt or claim is settled. **3.** the confiscation of the property of an enemy national.

se·quin (sē′kwin) *n.* **1.** a small, thin, usually disk-shaped ornament of metal or glass, esp. one sewn in large numbers onto a fabric. **2.** a former gold coin of Turkey and Italy. [French *sequin* small Italian coin, from Italian *zecchino* gold coin, from *zecca* mint[2], from Arabic *sikkah* die[2] (for coining).]

se·quined (sē′kwind) *adj.* ornamented with sequins.

se·quoi·a (si kwoi′ə) *n.* **1.** a giant evergreen tree, *Sequoiadendron giganteum,* native to central California and Oregon, having thick, spongy, reddish brown bark and sharply pointed leaves. Sequoias are among the oldest and largest of trees. **2.** redwood *(def. 1).* [Modern Latin *sequoia,* from *Sequoya,* died 1843, Cherokee Indian who devised a system of writing for the Cherokee language.]

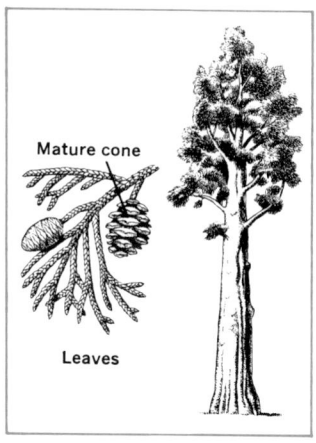

Mature cone

Leaves

sequoia

se·ra (sîr′ə) a plural of **serum.**

se·ragl·io (si ral′yō, -räl′-) *n., pl.* **-ragl·ios.** **1.** a portion of a Muslim house reserved for women; harem. **2.** a Turkish palace, esp. of a sultan. [Italian *serraglio* enclosure, harem, palace, from *serrare* to enclose, lock, going back to Latin *sera* bolt[1], bar; influenced by Turkish *serāī* palace.]

se·ra·pe (sə rä′pē) *also,* **sarape.** *n.* a blanketlike outer garment resembling a cloak or poncho, often made with bright colors and patterns, worn chiefly by men in Mexico and other Latin-American countries. [Spanish *serape;* of uncertain origin.]

ser·aph (ser′əf) *n., pl.* **-aphs** or **-a·phim** (-ə fim′). a member of the highest order of angels, who are said to stand before the throne of God. [Hebrew *serāphīm,* plural of *sārāph,* celestial being described in Isaiah 6:2; literally, the burning one.] —**se·raph·ic** (si raf′ik) *adj.* —**se·raph′i·cal·ly,** *adv.*

Se·ra·pis (sə rā′pis) *n.* a god of the dead, first worshiped in Egypt and later identified by the Greeks with their gods of the underworld, the heavens, and medicine.

Serb (sûrb) *n.* **1.** a native or inhabitant of Serbia. **2.** Serbian *(def. 1).* —*adj.* Serbian.

Ser·bi·an (sûr′bē ən) *adj.* of, relating to, or characteristic of

a	at	e	end	o	hot	u	up	hw	white		about
ā	ape	ē	me	ō	old	ū	use	ng	song		taken
ä	far	i	it	ô	fork	ü	rule	th	thin	ə	pencil
âr	care	ī	ice	oi	oil	u̇	pull	th	this		lemon
		îr	pierce	ou	out	ûr	turn	zh	measure		circus

Serbia or its people, language, or culture. —*n.* **1.** the language of the Serbs; Serbo-Croatian. **2.** Serb *(def. 1).*

Ser·bo-Cro·a·tian (sûr′bō krō ā′shən) *n.* a language belonging to the southern branch of the Slavic languages, spoken by Serbs and Croats. Serbo-Croatian is written in the Cyrillic alphabet by the Serbs and in the Roman alphabet by the Croats. —*adj.* of or relating to this language.

sere[1] (sîr) *adj.* withered; dry. [Form of SEAR.]

sere[2] (sîr) *n.* the entire series of ecological communities that succeed one another in the course of development of the biota of an area from the earliest stage to climax. [From SERIES.]

ser·e·nade (ser′ə nād′) *n.* **1.** a pleasant, melodious song or other musical performance played and sung personally for someone as an expression of love or admiration. **2.** an instrumental composition, usually written for a small orchestra or ensemble, typically consisting of a series of varied movements. —*v.,* -nad·ed, -nad·ing. —*v.t.* to perform a serenade to or for. —*v.i.* to perform a serenade. —**ser′e·nad′er,** *n.*

ser·en·dip·i·ty (ser′ən dip′i tē) *n.* the act or ability of making fortunate discoveries by accident. [From characters who had this ability in a fairy tale, *The Three Princes of Serendip,* by the English writer Horace Walpole, 1717-97.] —**ser′en·dip′i·tous,** *adj.* —**ser′en·dip′i·tous·ly,** *adv.*

se·rene (sə rēn′) *adj.* **1.** peaceful; calm; tranquil: *a serene look.* **2.** clear and bright: *a serene sky.* [Latin *serēnus.*] —**se·rene′ly,** *adv.* —For Synonyms, see **calm.**

se·ren·i·ty (sə ren′i tē) *n.* the state or quality of being serene.

serf (sûrf) *n.* a feudal peasant bound legally or by custom to the land or to the service of the landlord. A serf could neither leave at will nor be forced off the land. [French *serf* servant, thrall, from Latin *servus* slave.]

serf·dom (sûrf′dəm) *n.* **1.** the state or condition of being a serf. **2.** the practice of working the land with serfs, esp. during the feudal periods of the Muslims, Chinese, Japanese, western Europeans, and Russians.

serf·hood (sûrf′hŭd′) *n.* the state or condition of being a serf. Also, **serf·age** (sûr′fij).

serge (sûrj) *n.* any of a group of fabrics characterized by a flat twill weave, esp. a durable worsted used for suits. [French *serge,* going back to Latin *sērica,* feminine of *sēricus* silken, from Greek *sērikos,* from *Sēres* the Chinese, who were famous for their silken fabrics.]

ser·geant (sär′jənt) *n.* **1.** in the U.S. Army and Marine Corps, a noncommissioned officer in one of five grades above a corporal. **2.** in the U.S. Air Force, a noncommissioned officer in one of six grades above an airman first class. **3.** a police officer ranking above an officer assigned to patrol and below a captain or lieutenant. [Old French *sergent* officer, going back to Latin *serviēns,* present participle of *servīre* to be a servant, be of service to.] —**ser′gean·cy,** *n.*

sergeant at arms *pl.* **sergeants at arms.** an official charged with preserving order at meetings, as of a legislative assembly or court of law.

sergeant first class, in the U.S. Army, a noncommissioned officer ranking below a master sergeant and above a staff sergeant.

sergeant major **1.** in the U.S. Army, Air Force, and Marine Corps, a sergeant, usually a master sergeant, who acts as an assistant to a headquarters commander, esp. on a regimental level. **2.** in the U.S. Army and Marine Corps, a noncommissioned officer of the highest grade. **3.** in the U.S. Army, a master sergeant appointed to serve as a personal assistant to the Chief of Staff for matters relating to enlisted personnel.

se·ri·al (sîr′ē əl) *n.* a long story broken up into segments that are televised, broadcast, or published at regular intervals, usually with the end of each segment leading on to the next so that the audience or reader is eager to know what will happen. —*adj.* **1.** of, relating to, or appearing as a serial: *a serial novel.* **2.** of, relating to, or arranged in a series: *serial order.* **3.** bringing about or occurring in a series: *a serial murderer, a serial crime.* **4.** *Music.* of, relating to, or composed in the twelve-tone scale. [SERIES + -AL[1].] —**se′ri·al·ly,** *adv.*

se·ri·al·ize (sîr′ē ə līz′) *v.t.,* -ized, -iz·ing. to televise, broadcast, or publish as a serial. —**se′ri·a·li·za′tion,** *n.*

serial number, a number assigned to a person or thing for identification.

se·ri·a·tim (sîr′ē ā′tim, ser′-) *adv.* one after the other; in a series. [Medieval Latin *seriatim* in order, in succession, from Latin *seriēs* row[1], succession.]

ser·i·cul·ture (ser′i kul′chər) *n.* the breeding of silkworms for the production of raw silk. [French *sériculture,* going back to Latin *sēricus* silken + *cultūra* cultivation. See SERGE.]

se·ries (sîr′ēz) *n., pl.* -ries. **1.** a group of similar or related things arranged one coming after another: *a series of announcements, a series of rosebushes along a path.* **2.** a set of things that go

together to make a whole, often in a certain order: *a series of exercises.* **3.** a television program, esp. a dramatic one, seen each day or each week, rather than only once, and usually having a fixed set of characters but a different story from program to program. **4.** *Mathematics.* the sum of the numbers of a sequence. For example, $1 + \frac{1}{3} + \frac{1}{5} + \frac{1}{7} + \ldots$ is an infinite series. **5.** *Geology.* in stratigraphy, a subdivision of a system. **6.** *Chemistry.* a period, or part of one. [Latin *seriēs* row[1], succession.] —For Synonyms, see **sequence.**

·in series. (of electrical devices or circuits) arranged with the positive electrode of one connected to the negative electrode of the next, so that the same current flows through all devices or circuits. ➡ opposed to **in parallel.**

series winding, in an electric motor or generator, a winding in which the field winding is in series with the armature and therefore carries the same current.

ser·if (ser′if) *n. Printing.* any of the extra crosswise lines or triangles on the main strokes of certain typefaces, such as Roman. [Possibly from Dutch *schreef* dash, line[1].]

ser·i·graph (ser′i graf′) *n.* a print made by the silk-screen process. —**se·rig′ra·phy** (sə rig′rə fē), *n.*

ser·ine (ser′ēn, -in, sîr′-) *n.* a nonessential amino acid that is present in proteins such as casein and is synthesized in the body from glycine. Formula: $C_3H_7NO_3$

se·ri·o·com·ic (sîr′ē ō kom′ik) *adj.* combining serious and comic elements.

se·ri·ous (sîr′ē əs) *adj.* **1.** of, characterized by, or showing deep and earnest thought; grave; solemn: *a serious manner, a serious person.* **2.** not joking; in earnest; sincere: *Were you serious about not going to the picnic?* **3.** requiring thought, consideration, or effort: *a serious problem.* **4.** relating to or concerned with important matters or issues: *a serious literary work.* **5.** of a threatening nature; dangerous: *a serious illness.* [Late Latin *seriōsus* weighty, earnest, from Latin *sērius* earnest.] —**se′ri·ous·ly,** *adv.* —**se′ri·ous·ness,** *n.*

> **Synonyms** **Serious, grave**[2]**, solemn,** and **somber** mean not light or superficial but filled with or expressing thought and care. **Serious** is the most neutral of these terms, connoting a thoughtful attention to something: *to be serious about one's work.* **Grave** suggests concern with something weighty: *Following the disaster, the president addressed the nation in a grave voice.* **Solemn** suggests the dignity of ceremony: *a solemn funeral address.* **Somber** connotes melancholy as well as seriousness: *They talked in somber tones about their dying parent.*

se·ri·ous-mind·ed (sîr′ē əs mīn′did) *adj.* characterized by or having a serious disposition or intention. —**se′ri·ous-mind′ed·ly,** *adv.* —**se′ri·ous-mind′ed·ness,** *n.*

ser·mon (sûr′mən) *n.* **1.** a discourse delivered in public by a member of the clergy for the purpose of giving religious or moral instruction. **2.** any long speech concerning morals, correct behavior, or the like. [Latin *sermō* speech, discourse.]

ser·mon·ize (sûr′mə nīz′) *v.i.,* -ized, -iz·ing. **1.** to deliver a sermon, as in a church. **2.** to go on at great length in a dogmatic or moralizing way. —**ser′mon·iz′er,** *n.*

Sermon on the Mount, a major discourse of Jesus to his disciples, containing important principles of Christianity, including the Beatitudes.

se·rol·o·gy (si rol′ə jē) *n.* a branch of medical research that deals with serums, esp. their use in curing or preventing disease. —**se·ro·log·i·cal** (sîr′ə loj′i kəl), *adj.*

se·ro·sa (si rō′sə, -zə) *n., pl.* -sas or -sae (-sē, -zē). serous membrane. [Modern Latin *serosa,* from *serosus.* See SEROUS.] —**se·ro′sal,** *adj.*

ser·o·to·nin (ser′ə tō′nin) *n.* an organic compound derived from tryptophan that is present in the brain, spinal cord, blood serum, and other tissues. Serotonin is an important neurotransmitter and causes blood vessels to constrict, raising blood pressure. Formula: $C_{10}H_{12}N_2O$

se·rous (sîr′əs) *adj.* **1.** of, relating to, or secreting serum. **2.** like serum: *Tears are a serous fluid.* [Modern Latin *serosus,* from Latin *serum* whey.]

serous membrane, a thin membrane that lines certain cavities of the body not open to the outside, such as the peritoneum, and secretes a serous fluid.

ser·pent (sûr′pənt) *n.* **1.** a snake, esp. an extremely large or venomous one. **2.** a snakelike monster or creature, esp. a sea serpent. **3.** a sly or wicked person. [Latin *serpēns* snake; literally, creeping thing, from *serpere* to creep.]

ser·pen·tine (sûr′pən tēn′, -tīn′) *adj.* **1.** winding about like a snake's body: *a serpentine path through a garden.* **2.** sly or wicked. **3.** of or resembling a snake or serpent. —*n.* a hydrated silicate mineral, usually green with a greasy texture, used as a source of magnesium compounds. Its fibrous form, chrysotile, is the most

important source of asbestos. Formula: $3MgO\cdot2SiO_2\cdot2H_2O$ [Late Latin *serpentīnus* relating to snakes, snakelike, from Latin *serpēns* snake. See SERPENT.]

ser·rat·ed (ser′ā tid) *adj.* jagged or saw-toothed, as the edges of a saw or certain leaves, Also, **ser′rate.** [Latin *serrātus* notched like a saw, from *serra* saw[1].]

ser·ra·tion (se rā′shən) *n.* **1.** the state or condition of being serrated. **2.** a notch or jagged point on a serrated edge. **3.** a series of such notches.

ser·ried (ser′ēd) *adj.* packed closely together, as ranks of marching soldiers.

ser·ru·late (ser′yə lit, -lāt′, ser′ə-) *adj.* having very small serrations. Also, **ser′ru·lat·ed.** [Modern Latin *serrulatus*, from Latin *serrula* little saw, diminutive of *serra* saw[1].]

serrulate leaf

se·rum (sîr′əm) *n., pl.* **se·rums** or **se·ra** (sîr′ə). **1.** an antitoxin used to prevent or cure a disease, esp. an antitoxin obtained from the blood of an animal that has been made immune to the disease. **2.** a clear, thin, amber-colored fluid that separates from the blood when a clot forms, consisting of water, albumin, hormones, salts, and other substances. Also, **blood serum. 3.** any clear body fluid, such as lymph. **4.** any liquid medicine or potion: *a cough serum.* [Latin *serum* whey, watery part of something.]

serum albumin, the principal protein in blood serum, used as a plasma substitute in transfusions for shock and burn victims. It regulates osmotic pressure and helps transport fatty acids throughout the body.

ser·val (sûr′vəl) *n.* a large, nocturnal wildcat, *Felis serval,* native to Africa, having large erect ears, a short tail, and usually yellowish fur with black markings. Height: 20 inches (51 centimeters) at the shoulder. [French *serval,* from Spanish *(gato) cerval* lynx; literally, deerlike (cat), going back to Latin *cervus* deer.]

serval

serv·ant (sûr′vənt) *n.* **1.** a person who is employed in a household to perform certain duties, such as cooking or cleaning. **2.a.** civil servant. **b.** public servant. **3.** a person who is dedicated to the service of someone or something, such as a religion or cause: *a servant of God.* [Old French *servant,* noun use of present participle of *servir* to wait upon, be useful, serve (God), from Latin *servīre.* See SERVE.]

serve (sûrv) *v.,* **served, serv·ing.** —*v.t.* **1.a.** to prepare and set (food or drink) on a table or before a person or persons: *to serve dinner.* **b.** to set food or drink before (a person or persons): *The waiter served us tea.* **2.a.** to supply (customers) regularly, as with a service or product: *The bakery serves us with fresh bread daily.* **b.** to supply (a service or product) regularly. **3.** to act as a servant to; attend or wait upon; work for: *The cook served the same family for years.* **4.** to come to the aid of; give assistance to: *The salesperson offered to serve us.* **5.** to give homage or obedience to: *to serve God.* **6.** to pass (a specified period of time), as in military service, public office, or imprisonment: *The senator served two terms in the state legislature.* **7.** to be of use or service to; meet the requirements of: *The library serves the community. The agreement no longer serves our needs.* **8.** to treat in a specified manner: *The reporter served the mayor fairly in the news story.* **9.** in tennis, badminton, volleyball, and other games, to put (the ball or shuttlecock) in play. **10.** *Law.* **a.** to present (a court order or writ) to a person. **b.** to present with a court order or writ: *to serve a potential witness with a subpoena.* —*v.i.* **1.** to set food or drink before a person or persons. **2.** to perform a duty or duties, as of an office: *to serve on a jury, to serve as mayor.* **3.** to be of use; suffice: *The sofa served as a bed.* **4.** to be a servant. **5.** to be favorable or suitable. **6.** in tennis, badminton, volleyball, and other games, to put the ball or shuttlecock in play. **7.** to be a server for a priest during Mass. —*n.* **1.** the act or manner of serving a ball or shuttlecock. **2.** a turn at serving. [Latin *servīre* to be a slave or servant, be of use or service to, be fit for.]

• **to serve one right.** to be just what one deserves.

serv·er (sûr′vər) *n.* **1.** a person who serves. **2.** something used in serving, such as a tray. **3.** an attendant who helps the priest during Mass. **4.** in tennis, badminton, or other games, the player who serves the ball or shuttlecock.

serv·ice (sûr′vis) *n.* **1.** the act, process, or means of serving or helping: *to do someone a great service.* **2.** the supplying of something useful or necessary: *Telephone service was interrupted by the storm.* **3.** a system or means of supplying something useful or necessary: *the postal service.* **4.** an enterprise or agency that provides useful or necessary work, esp. as distinguished from goods: *a research service, a catering service.* **5.** *usually,* **services.** useful or necessary work or activity: *to pay for the services of a plumber, to provide a service to the community.* **6.** the repair, maintenance, or replacement of goods that have been sold to customers: *to take a hair dryer back to the store for service.* **7.** the state of being employed, esp. as a domestic servant. **8.** the manner of serving food and drink: *The service in that restaurant is very good.* **9.** a religious ceremony or ritual: *a burial service.* **10.a.** one of the branches of the armed forces: *to spend three years in the service.* **b.** duty in any such branch: *to see active service in the navy.* **11.a.** a branch or department of public employment: *the foreign service.* **b.** the persons employed in this. **12.** a set of things required for table use, such as silver or dishes: *a service for eight.* **13.** the act or manner of putting the ball or shuttlecock in play in tennis, badminton, volleyball, and other games. **14.** *Law.* the presentation or delivery of a court order or writ to the person or persons named therein. —*v.t.,* **-iced, -ic·ing. 1.** to make fit for use; keep conditioned or repaired: *to service an automobile.* **2.** to supply service to. —*adj.* **1.** of, relating to, or used by those in service: *a service entrance.* **2.** of or relating to the armed forces. **3.** of or relating to the repair, maintenance, or replacement of goods: *a service department in a store.* **4.** of or relating to useful economic activity other than the production of goods: *a service industry.* [Latin *servītium* slavery, servitude.]

• **at someone's service.** ready or available to serve or help someone: *The wealthy family placed their entire staff at our service.*

• **in service.** in use or operation: *All the copying machines are in service at the moment.*

• **of service.** useful; helpful: *Can I be of service to you?*

• **out of service.** not working; broken or defective: *The telephone has been out of service all morning.*

serv·ice·a·ble (sûr′və sə bəl) *adj.* **1.** capable of giving useful service; helpful; beneficial. **2.** wearing well in long or hard use; durable. —**serv′ice·a·bil′i·ty, serv′ice·a·ble·ness,** *n.* —**serv′ice·a·bly,** *adv.*

serv·ice·ber·ry (sûr′vis ber′ē) *n., pl.* **-ries. 1.** the fruit of a service tree. **2.** the shadbush or its fruit.

service club 1. an organization dedicated to working for the good of the community while also serving its members. **2.** a recreational facility for members of the armed forces.

service line 1. a line parallel to the net across a tennis court behind which the ball cannot fall when served. **2.** a line in a handball, racquets, or other court behind which a player must stand when serving.

serv·ice·man (sûr′vis man′) *n., pl.* **-men** (-men′). **1.** a member of one of the branches of the armed forces. **2.** a person whose work is maintaining or repairing something.

service mark, a symbol, word, or device used to identify a firm that supplies a service to the public, such as an airline, laundry, or insurance company.

service station 1. gas station. **2.** a place where repairs and adjustments can be made and parts are supplied for any of various mechanical or electrical devices.

service stripe, a stripe worn on the left sleeve of the uniform by a member of the armed forces to indicate a certain period of active service.

service tree, a tree of either of two European species, genus *Sorbus,* related to the mountain ash and having edible berries. [Earlier *serves* (thought incorrectly to be a singular), plural of obsolete *serve* this tree, from Old English *syrfe,* going back to Latin *sorbus.*]

serv·ice·wom·an (sûr′vis wum′ən) *n., pl.* **-wom·en** (-wim′ən). a female member of the armed forces.

ser·vi·ette (sûr′vē et′) *n. British.* table napkin. [French *serviette,* from *servir* to wait upon. See SERVANT.]

ser·vile (sûr′vəl, -vīl) *adj.* **1.** having or showing the character of a slave; lacking self-respect or independence; slavish: *servile behavior.* **2.** of, relating to, or appropriate for a slave: *servile duties.* [Latin *servīlis,* from *servus* slave.] —**ser′vile·ly,** *adv.* —**ser′vile·ness,** *n.*

a	at	e	end	o	hot	u	up	hw	white		about
ā	ape	ē	me	ō	old	ū	use	ng	song	ə	taken
ä	far	i	it	ô	fork	ü	rule	th	thin		pencil
âr	care	ī	ice	oi	oil	u̇	pull	th	this		lemon
		îr	pierce	ou	out	ûr	turn	zh	measure		circus

ser·vil·i·ty (sər vil′i tē) *n.* the quality or condition of being servile.

serv·ing (sûr′ving) *n.* **1.** a portion of food; helping. **2.** the act of a person or thing that serves. —*adj.* used in serving food: *a serving spoon.*

ser·vi·tor (sûr′vi tər) *n.* a person who serves another; servant; attendant. [Old French *servitor,* from Late Latin *servītor,* from Latin *servīre* to be a servant.]

ser·vi·tude (sûr′vi tüd′, -tūd′) *n.* **1.** the condition of being a slave; slavery; bondage. **2.** compulsory labor as a punishment. [Latin *servitūdō* slavery.]

ser·vo·mech·a·nism (sûr′vō mek′ə niz′əm) *n.* an automatic feedback control system in which one or more of the operations involves mechanical motion, used for various assembly line processes and for automatic pilot systems. [Servo(motor) + mecha-nism.]

ser·vo·mo·tor (sûr′vō mō′tər) *n.* a motor used in a servomechanism. [French *servo-moteur,* from Latin *servus* slave (see serf) + French *moteur* motor.]

ses·a·me (ses′ə mē) *n.* **1.** the small, oval, aromatic seed of a tropical plant, *Sesamum indicum,* native to India, used mainly in baked goods and candies. **2.** the plant itself. **3.** see **open sesame**. [Greek *sēsamē* this plant; of Semitic origin.]

ses·qui·cen·ten·ni·al (ses′kwi sen ten′ē əl) *n.* a 150th anniversary or its celebration. —*adj.* of or relating to a period of a century and a half. [Latin *sesqui-* one and a half + centennial.]

ses·qui·pe·da·li·an (ses′kwi pi dā′lē ən) *adj.* **1.** having many syllables; very long. **2.** given to using long words. —*n.* a very long word. [Latin *sesquipedālis* one foot and a half in length (from *sesqui-* one and a half + *pedālis* relating to the foot) + -an.]

ses·sile (ses′əl, -īl) *adj.* **1.** *Botany.* attached directly at the base rather than by a stem or stalk: *sessile leaves.* **2.** *Zoology.* permanently attached; not moving or swimming about; fixed; sedentary: *Sea anemones are sessile organisms.* [Latin *sessilis* relating to sitting, from *sessus,* past participle of *sedēre* to sit.]

ses·sion (sesh′ən) *n.* **1.a.** a meeting, as of a court, council, or legislature, for the transaction of business. **b.** a series of such meetings. **c.** the term of such a meeting or meetings. **2.a.** a period into which a school year is divided; term: *the summer session.* **b.** a time during which classes are conducted in a school or college: *The evening session begins at six o'clock.* **3.** a meeting held for any purpose or activity: *a recording session.* [Latin *sessiō* a sitting, a meeting, from *sedēre* to sit.] —**ses′sion·al,** *adj.*

  ·in session. in the process of meeting or being conducted: *Court is now in session.*

ses·terce (ses′tûrs) *n.* an ancient Roman coin, originally of silver, but later of copper or bronze. [Latin *sestertius.*]

ses·tet (ses tet′) *n.* **1.a.** the last six lines of a Petrarchan sonnet. ➡ distinguished from **octave**. **b.** any six-line unit of verse. **2.** *Music.* sextet. [Italian *sestetto* sextet in music, from *sesto* sixth, from Latin *sextus.*]

set (set) *v.,* **set, set·ting.** —*v.t.* **1.** to place in some location or position; put: *to set a lamp on a table.* **2.** to put in the correct, proper, or desired place, position, or condition: *to set a broken bone.* **3.** to arrange (the hair), as with rollers or clips. **4.** to prepare or arrange for use: *to set a trap, to set the table for a meal.* **5.** to arrange scenery and properties on (a stage) for a presentation. **6.** to adjust or regulate, esp. in accordance with a standard: *to set one's watch.* **7.** to cause to be in a certain condition: *to set a prisoner free, to set a log on fire, to set a boat adrift.* **8.** to cause to be in a firm, settled, or fixed position or condition: *to set cement, to set one's jaw, to set one's mind on doing something.* **9.** to determine or fix firmly; establish: *to set a date for a wedding.* **10.** to fix or determine (a price, value, or rate): *to set a mortgage rate of 7¹/₂%.* **11.** to place in a certain category or rank: *Many critics set Shakespeare above all other English writers.* **12.** to establish as the highest or greatest level or achievement: *The athlete set a record in the high jump.* **13.** to assign or allot: *to set a guard at a gate.* **14.** to present or provide for others to follow: *to set a pace, to set a poor example for others.* **15.** to cause to take a particular direction; direct: *to set a ship's course toward land.* **16.** to cause to sit. **17.** to place in a frame or mounting: *to set a diamond.* **18.** to adorn or ornament: *to set a crown with jewels.* **19.** *Printing.* **a.** to arrange (type) for printing. **b.** to put into type: *to set a manuscript.* **20.** *Music.* **a.** to write, adapt, or fit (words) to music. **b.** to compose or arrange (music) for words. **c.** to compose or arrange (music) for certain voices or instruments. **21.a.** to put (a hen) on eggs to hatch them. **b.** to put (eggs) under a hen or in an incubator to hatch them. **22.** (of a hunting dog) to point (game). **23.** *Bridge.* to defeat (one's opponents) by causing them to fall short of their contract by one or more tricks. —*v.i.* **1.a.** to

go down below the horizon: *At what time will the sun set today?* **b.** to draw to a close; decline; wane: *The power of Great Britain began to set after World War I.* **2.** to become firm or hard: *The cement set after a few hours.* **3.** (of a broken bone) to mend properly. **4.** to become fast or permanent, as a dye or color. **5.** to hang or fit in a particular way: *That jacket sets well on you.* **6.** to make a beginning, as in a task; apply oneself: *to set to work.* **7.** (of a hen) to sit on eggs. **8.** (of a hunting dog) to point game. **9.** to have a specified direction; tend. **10.** (of a young plant) to begin to develop, esp. as a result of pollination. —*adj.* **1.** fixed or prescribed beforehand; established: *a set procedure, a set fee.* **2.** fixed in a certain position; rigid: *a set smile.* **3.** stubbornly fixed, as in opinion or disposition; obstinate: *to be set in one's ways.* **4.** determined; resolute; intent: *They are set on leaving today.* **5.** customary or conventional; stereotyped: *a set phrase.* **6.** deliberately composed, arranged, or conceived; intentional: *a set purpose.* **7.** formed, built, or made in a certain way. ➡ used with a specifying adverb: *deep-set eyes, a heavy-set person.* **8.** ready; prepared: *We are all set to leave on our trip.* —*n.* **1.** the act or manner of setting or the state of being set. **2.** the position or attitude of a part of the body: *the set of one's shoulders.* **3.** the way something fits or hangs: *the set of a jacket.* **4.** an inclination or tendency: *the set of one's mind.* **5.** the direction or course of a current or wind. **6.** a group of persons associated in some way: *a set of clients, the younger set.* **7.a.** a group or collection of things that belong together: *a set of furniture, a chess set.* **b.** a group or collection of printed works, as books or magazines, written by the same author or dealing with the same subject. **8.** a complete unit of scenery, props, and structures used for a scene in a play, opera, motion picture, or television program. Also, **scene**. **9.** *Mathematics.* a collection of numbers, points, objects, or other things grouped together or having a certain property in common that distinguishes them from all other things not within the collection. The set of positive integers less than 5 is {1, 2, 3, 4}. **10.** a sending or receiving apparatus assembled as a unit for radio, television, telephone, or other communication. **11.** a group of six or more games making up a unit of a match in tennis. One player or side must win at least two more games than the other, or must win a tiebreaker after the game score has reached 6-6. **12.** the sinking of a heavenly body below the horizon. **13.** a permanent change of form, as of a metal, caused esp. by strain, pressure, or chemical action. **14.** a young plant or a plant part, such as a slip or shoot, suitable for planting. **15.a.** the number of couples required to perform a square dance. **b.** a series of movements or figures that compose a square dance. [Old English *settan* to cause to sit, place, plant, establish, found, subside.] —For Synonyms *(v.t.),* see **fix**.

  ·to set about. to begin to do; start.

  ·to set against. a. to cause to be hostile or unfriendly toward. **b.** to balance or compare: *to set one point of view against another.*

  ·to set aside. a. to place apart or to one side, as for later use; reserve; save. **b.** to discard, dismiss, or reject. **c.** to declare null and void: *to set aside a verdict.*

  ·to set back. a. to reverse, hinder, or check: *The costly war set back the country's economy.* **b.** *Informal.* to cost (a person) a certain sum of money: *That coat set me back ninety dollars.*

  ·to set down. a. to place on a surface. **b.** to record, esp. in writing or printing: *to set down one's thoughts.* **c.** to consider or attribute: *We set down the mistake to an error in judgment.*

  ·to set forth. a. to make known; state; declare. **b.** to start out on a journey.

  ·to set in. a. to begin to take place or prevail: *Winter set in early this year.* **b.** (of wind or water) to blow or flow toward shore.

  ·to set off. a. to make prominent by contrast; show to best advantage: *Dark hair sets off a fair complexion.* **b.** to start out or begin, as on a course or journey. **c.** to cause to explode; discharge: *to set off fireworks.* **d.** to cause to begin; touch off: *The senator's statement set off a lively debate.* **e.** to place apart from others; put by itself.

  ·to set on (or upon). to attack or urge to attack.

  ·to set out. a. to start out on a journey or course. **b.** to begin with a certain intention; undertake; attempt: *The detective set out to establish a motive for the crime.* **c.** to arrange or display: *to set out items for sale.* **d.** to plan or lay out, as a room, garden, or town. **e.** to establish the limits or boundaries of. **f.** to place in the ground to root and grow; plant.

  ·to set to. a. to make a beginning; start working: *to set to on a project.* **b.** to start fighting.

  ·to set up. a. to put in an upright position. **b.** to raise or

elevate. **c.** to raise to a position of authority or power. **d.** to assemble, erect, or prepare for use: *to set up a tent.* **e.** to bring into being; establish; found: *to set up an organization.* **f.** to provide (a person) with the means for something: *The wealthy woman set up her son in business.* **g.** to put forward; propose, as a theory. **h.** to lay claim for (oneself) as being something: *to set oneself up as an expert on politics.* **i.** to plan (something, esp. a crime) carefully: *to set up a burglary.*

Set (set) *also,* **Seth.** *n.* in Egyptian mythology, the god of evil, often portrayed with a doglike head and associated with darkness and drought.

se·ta (sē′tə) *n., pl.* **-tae** (-tē) any stiff hairlike structure or organ, as on certain plants, earthworms, or insects. [Latin *saeta* bristle.]

se·ta·ceous (si tā′shəs) *adj.* having or resembling bristles or setae.

set·back (set′bak′) *n.* **1.** a defeat or other check to progress, esp. one that is temporary or unexpected; reversal. **2.** any recessed upper section of a tall building that allows maximum light and ventilation in the street below. **3.** offset *(def. 5).*

Seth (seth) Set.

set·off (set′ôf′, -of′) *n.* **1.** anything that counterbalances or compensates, as for a loss. **2.a.** a counterclaim, esp. by a debtor against a creditor. **b.** the settlement of a debt by such a claim. **3.** something that adorns by providing contrast. **4.** offset *(def. 5).*

se·tose (sē′tōs) *adj.* bristly; setaceous.

set·screw (set′skrü′) *n.* a screw used to fasten parts of a machine together, as gears to a shaft.

set·tee (se tē′) *n.* a bench or small sofa with a high back and, usually, arms. [Possibly form of SETTLE².]

set·ter (set′ər) *n.* **1.** any of several breeds of long-haired bird dogs having drooping ears and a soft, silky coat, originally trained to crouch, or set, upon finding game, but now trained to point. Height: to 26 inches (66 centimeters) at the shoulder. **2.** a person or thing that sets.

set theory, a branch of mathematics dealing with sets and their properties and relationships.

set·ting (set′ing) *n.* **1.** a structure or the like in which something, such as a jewel, is set. **2.** the place and time of a dramatic or literary work:

setter

The setting of the novel is London during World War II. **3.** scenery and other properties for a theatrical performance. **4.** that which surrounds a person or thing; background; environment. **5.** china, silverware, and other articles for setting a place at a table. **6.** music composed for a particular text: *a setting for the twenty-third Psalm.* **7.** the number of eggs that a hen sets on or that are placed in an incubator for hatching at one time. **8.** the act of a person or thing that sets. **9.** the position of or regulation specified by a control, dial, or other instrument.

set·tle¹ (set′əl) *v.,* **-tled, -tling.** —*v.t.* **1.** to determine or decide; come to agreement about; resolve: *to settle an argument.* **2.** to arrange (something) in an orderly manner, esp. permanently: *I must settle all my affairs before leaving.* **3.** to make final disposition of by or as by paying: *to settle an account.* **4.a.** to establish inhabitants in; colonize. **b.** to cause to take up residence: *to settle one's family in a new home.* **5.** to establish or fix, as in a profession or way of life. **6.** to place in a proper or desired position; adjust: *to settle oneself on a couch, to settle one's feet in stirrups.* **7.** to make tranquil or calm; compose: *He took some medicine to settle his stomach.* **8.** to cause (a liquid) to change from an agitated or muddy condition to one of clearness; clarify. **9.** to cause to become compact, firm, or solid. **10.** *Law.* to give (property or the income from it) to a person or persons by legal means (with *on* or *upon*). —*v.i.* **1.** to decide, select, or agree, esp. beforehand: *Laura finally settled on the red dress.* **2.** to establish a residence, esp. permanently: *to settle in a small town after retirement.* **3.** to come to rest; alight: *The butterfly settled on the flower.* **4.** to sink gradually, as the foundations of a building. **5.** to sink to the bottom, as sediment. **6.** to become compact, firm, or solid: *The fresh concrete settled in one hour.* [Old English *setlan* to fix, place, from *setl* seat.] —For Synonyms *(v.t.),* see **decide.**

•**to settle down. a.** to become or make calm or composed: *After the excitement of the fire drill, it took the class a long time to settle down.* **b.** to direct one's effort and attention: *to settle down to studying.* **c.** to be established in a more regular life, esp. as a result of marriage.

set·tle² (set′əl) *n.* a long bench or seat for two or more people, with a high back, arms, and, sometimes, drawers under the seat. [Old English *setl* seat.]

set·tle·ment (set′əl mənt) *n.* **1.** the act of settling or the state of being settled. **2.** the deciding or determining of something in doubt or debate: *The two sides in the strike finally reached a settlement.* **3.** an orderly arrangement of affairs. **4.** a small village or group of houses. **5.a.** the establishment of inhabitants in a new country; colonization. **b.** a colony, esp. in its earlier stages. **6.** the establishment of a person in life, marriage, a profession, or business. **7.** an adjustment or payment, as

high-backed settle

of claims. **8.** *Law.* **a.** the act of settling property upon a person or persons. **b.** property so given. **9.** settlement house. **10.** a sinking down of all or part of a structure.

settlement house, a neighborhood institution with a staff of social workers that provides counseling, recreation, food, and other services to poor residents of the area.

set·tler (set′lər) *n.* **1.** a person who settles in a new country or territory. **2.** any person or thing that settles.

set·tlings (set′lingz) *pl. n.* sediment; dregs.

set-to (set′tü′) *n., pl.* **-tos.** *Informal.* a fight; conflict.

set·up (set′up′) *n.* **1.** the way in which a thing is arranged or organized; plan or structure: *the setup of a business.* **2.** a contest or task deliberately made easy. **3.** everything, except the liquor, needed in making alcoholic drinks, such as glasses, ice, soda water, or other mixers.

sev·en (sev′ən) *n.* **1.** the cardinal number that is one more than six. **2.** a symbol representing this number, such as 7 or VII. **3.** something having this many units or members, such as a playing card. —*adj.* numbering one more than six. [Old English *seofon.*]

seven deadly sins, the sins of anger, avarice (or covetousness), envy, gluttony, lust, pride, and sloth, regarded as the source of all other sins. Also, **cardinal sins, deadly sins.**

sev·en·fold (sev′ən fōld′) *adj.* **1.** seven times as great or as numerous. **2.** having or consisting of seven parts. —*adv.* so as to be seven times greater or more numerous.

seven seas, all the oceans and seas of the world, now considered to be the North Atlantic, South Atlantic, North Pacific, South Pacific, Arctic, Antarctic, and Indian oceans.

Seven Sisters, Pleiades.

sev·en·teen (sev′ən tēn′) *n.* **1.** the cardinal number that is seven more than ten. **2.** a symbol representing this number, such as 17 or XVII. **3.** something having this many units or members. —*adj.* numbering seven more than ten. [Old English *seofontīene.*]

sev·en·teenth (sev′ən tēnth′) *adj.* **1.** (the ordinal of seventeen) next after the sixteenth. **2.** being one of seventeen equal parts. —*n.* **1.** something that is next after the sixteenth. **2.** one of seventeen equal parts; 1/17.

sev·en·teen-year locust (sev′ən tēn′yîr′) a North American cicada, *Magicicada septendecim,* that has an underground larval stage lasting 17 years or, esp. in the southern United States, 13 years. It then emerges from the soil, usually in large numbers, to live a short time as an adult.

sev·enth (sev′ənth) *adj.* **1.** (the ordinal of seven) next after the sixth. **2.** being one of seven equal parts. —*n.* **1.** something that is next after the sixth. **2.** one of seven equal parts; 1/7. **3.** *Music.* **a.** a tone six diatonic degrees from a given tone, esp. the subdominant in any given key. **b.** an interval of six degrees between two tones of the diatonic scale. **c.** a harmonic combination of two tones separated by this interval. —*adv.* in the seventh place.

Sev·enth-Day Adventist (sev′ənth dā′) a member of a Protestant sect that stresses belief in the imminent second coming of Christ and observes the Sabbath on Saturday.

seventh heaven 1. a condition of great joy and happiness. **2.** according to certain theologies, the highest and most exalted part of heaven.

sev·en·ti·eth (sev′ən tē ith) *adj.* **1.** (the ordinal of seventy) next

a	at	e	end	o	hot	u	up	hw	white		about
ā	ape	ē	me	ō	old	ū	use	ng	song		taken
ä	far	i	it	ô	fork	ü	rule	th	thin	ə	pencil
âr	care	ī	ice	oi	oil	u̇	pull	th	this		lemon
		îr	pierce	ou	out	ûr	turn	zh	measure		circus

after the sixty-ninth. **2.** being one of seventy equal parts. —*n.* **1.** something that is next after the sixty-ninth. **2.** one of seventy equal parts; 1/70.

sev·en·ty (sev′ən tē) *n., pl.* **-ties. 1.** the cardinal number that is seven times ten. **2.** a symbol representing this number, such as 70 or LXX. **3. seventies.** the number series from seventy through seventy-nine ➡ used esp. in reference to the eighth decade of a century or of a person's life. —*adj.* numbering seven times ten. [Old English *seofontig*.]

Seven Wonders of the World, the seven most remarkable structures of ancient times: the pyramids of Egypt, the hanging gardens of Babylon, the Colossus of Rhodes, the mausoleum at Halicarnassus, the temple of Diana (Artemis) at Ephesus, the statue of Zeus by Phidias at Olympia, and the Pharos (lighthouse) of Alexandria.

sev·er (sev′ər) *v.t.* **1.** to separate by cutting or breaking apart or off: *to sever a branch from a tree.* **2.** to put an end to; break off; dissolve: *to sever diplomatic relations with another country.* —*v.i.* to become separated or be divided into parts. [Old French *severer* to separate, going back to Latin *sēparāre*.] —**sev′er·a·ble,** *adj.*

sev·er·al (sev′ər əl, sev′rəl) *adj.* **1.** more than two but not many: *to stay for several hours.* **2.** individual; different: *After the party, the guests went their several ways.* **3.** existing or considered individually; single; separate: *the several degrees on a scale.* —*n.* more than two but not many; a few: *The police managed to recover several of the stolen articles.* [Anglo-Norman *several* separate, distinct, going back to Latin *sēpar* different.]

sev·er·al·ly (sev′ər ə lē, sev′rə-) *adv.* **1.** separately; individually. **2.** respectively.

sev·er·al·ty (sev′ər əl tē, sev′rəl-) *n., pl.* **-ties. 1.** a being separate. **2.** an estate that a person holds in his or her own right, without being joined by any other person. **3.** the condition of an estate so held.

sev·er·ance (sev′ər əns, sev′rəns) *n.* **1.** the act of severing or the state of being severed; separation. **2.** severance pay.

severance pay, a sum of money paid in addition to salary to an employee upon termination of employment.

se·vere (sə vîr′) *adj.,* **-ver·er, -ver·est. 1.** very strict or exacting; inflexible: *severe laws, a severe disciplinarian.* **2.** difficult to endure; extremely cruel: *severe punishment.* **3.** causing great discomfort or suffering: *a severe winter, severe pain.* **4.** of a threatening nature; dangerous or critical: *a severe illness, a severe wound.* **5.** forbidding or grim in manner or appearance: *a severe look on someone's face.* **6.** austerely plain or simple; without ornament: *a severe style of dressing.* **7.** rigidly exact, accurate, or methodical: *a severe conformity to rules.* **8.** requiring great exertion or endurance: *a severe test of one's willpower.* [Latin *sevērus* serious, strict.] —**se·vere′ly,** *adv.* —**se·vere′ness,** *n.*

> **Synonyms** Severe, stern[1], and **austere** are used to describe behavior or appearance characterized by restraint or harshness. **Severe** implies an exacting adherence to high standards: *The teacher's severe manner inspires both fear and respect.* **Stern** suggests a lack of compassion: *The parents were stern, frequently punishing their children.* **Austere** indicates stark simplicity and reserve: *The settlers' austere way of life allowed them few pleasures.*

se·ver·i·ty (sə ver′i tē) *n., pl.* **-ties. 1.** the quality or condition of being very strict or exacting: *the severity of a law.* **2.** extreme cruelty: *the severity of a punishment.* **3.** the quality of causing great discomfort, grief, or suffering: *the severity of cold weather, the severity of a storm.* **4.** the quality of causing deep concern or anxiety; seriousness: *the severity of an illness, the severity of a wound.* **5.** a forbidding or grim manner or appearance: *severity of expression.* **6.** austere simplicity of style or taste: *severity of dress.* **7.** difficulty: *the severity of an assignment.* **8.** rigid accuracy or exactness.

Sè·vres (sev′rə) *n.* French porcelain of a kind originally made in the French city of Sèvres, distinguished by its excellent workmanship and fine design. Also, **Sèvres ware.**

sew (sō) *v.,* **sewed, sewed** or **sewn, sew·ing.** —*v.i.* to work with needle and thread or with a sewing machine. —*v.t.* **1.** to fasten, join, or attach with stitches: *to sew a button on a jacket.* **2.** to make or mend by means of a needle and thread or a sewing machine: *to sew a dress.* [Old English *siw(i)an* to fasten together with thread.]

• **to sew up. a.** to close with stitches: *to sew up a ripped sleeve.* **b.** *Informal.* to get or have complete control of: *to sew up stockholders' votes before a company's annual meeting.* **c.** *Informal.* to bring to a successful conclusion: *to sew up a business*

deal. **d.** to make certain of success in obtaining: *The last touchdown sewed up the championship for our team.*

sew·age (sü′ij) *n.* the waste matter carried off by sewers and drains.

sew·er[1] (sü′ər) *n.* an underground pipe or conduit used for carrying off wastewater and refuse. [Old French *sewiere* channel to drain a pond, going back to Latin *ex* out of + *aqua* water.]

sew·er[2] (sō′ər) *n.* a person or thing that sews. [SEW + -ER[1].]

sew·er·age (sü′ər ij) *n.* **1.** the removal of waste matter by means of sewers. **2.** a system of sewers. **3.** sewage.

sew·ing (sō′ing) *n.* **1.** work done with a needle and thread or with a sewing machine. **2.** something to be sewed. **3.** the act of a person who sews.

sewing circle, a group of women who meet regularly to sew.

sewing machine, a mechanical device for sewing fabric and other materials, usually powered by a small electric motor.

sewn (sōn) a past participle of **sew.**

sex (seks) *n.* **1.** either of the two divisions, male or female, into which human beings and most other organisms are divided according to their functions in the process of reproduction. **2.a.** the sum of the characteristics that determine whether an organism is male or female. **b.** the character or condition of being male or female. **3.** the instincts and urges attracting one sex to another, esp. as manifested in behavior. **4.** sexual activity, esp. sexual intercourse. **5.** sexuality. [Latin *sexus* either of the divisions male or female.]

sex·a·ge·nar·i·an (sek′sə jə när′ē ən) *n.* a person who is sixty or between sixty and seventy years old. —*adj.* being sixty or between sixty and seventy years old. [Latin *sexāgēnārius* containing sixty (going back to *sexāgintā* sixty) + -AN.]

Sex·a·ges·i·ma (sek′sə jes′ə mə) *n.* the second Sunday before Lent. [Latin *sexāgēsima (dies)* literally, sixtieth (day); reckoned approximately as the sixtieth day before Easter.]

sex·a·ges·i·mal (sek′sə jes′ə məl) *adj.* relating to or based on the number sixty.

sex appeal, the quality in a person that arouses sexual interest in others.

sex cell, gamete.

sex chromosome, either of the two types of chromosomes that contain the genes that determine the sex of an offspring; X chromosome or Y chromosome. A female germ cell always has an X chromosome; a male germ cell may have either an X chromosome or a Y chromosome. A fusion of germ cells resulting in a fertilized cell with two X chromosomes produces a female organism; a male results from an XY chromosome combination.

sex gland, gonad.

sex hormone, any of several hormones, such as estrogen or testosterone, that affect the growth and functioning of the reproductive system, the development of secondary sex characteristics, or the secretion of milk.

sex·ism (sek′siz əm) *n.* discrimination based on a person's sex, as in employment or politics.

sex·ist (sek′sist) *adj.* of, relating to, or exhibiting sexism: *sexist behavior.* —*n.* a person who is sexist.

sex·less (seks′lis) *adj.* **1.** lacking sexual characteristics; neuter. **2.** lacking sexual desire or sex appeal. —**sex′less·ness,** *n.*

sex·link·age (seks′ling′kij) *n.* the tendency for certain inherited traits or characteristics to be sex-linked and thus to appear more frequently in one sex than the other.

sex-linked (seks′lingkt′) *adj.* **1.** (of an inherited trait) determined by a gene carried by a sex chromosome, esp. one present in an X chromosome but not in a Y chromosome: *Color blindness is a sex-linked trait.* **2.** (of a gene) carried by a sex chromosome.

sex object, a person considered only as the focus of sexual interest.

sext (sekst) *n.* the fourth of the seven canonical hours. [Latin *sexta (hōra)* sixth (hour); because it was originally the sixth or noon hour of the day.]

sex·tant (sek′stənt) *n.* an instrument, used mainly in navigation, for measuring the altitude of the sun or a star as an aid in determining the position of the observer. [Latin *sextant-,* stem of *sextāns* sixth part; because it has the shape of a sixth of a circle.]

sex·tet (sek stet′) *also,* **sex·tette.** *n.* **1.a.** a musical composition for six

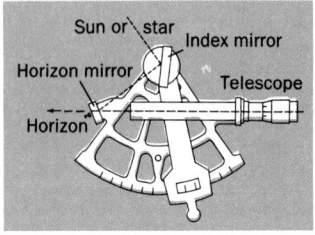

sextant

voices or instruments. **b.** a musical ensemble of six performers. **2.** a group of six persons or things. [Modification (influenced by Latin *sex* six) of SESTET.]

sex·til·lion (sek stil'yən) *n.* **1.** in the United States, the cardinal number that is represented by 1 followed by 21 zeros. **2.** in Great Britain, the cardinal number that is represented by 1 followed by 36 zeros. —*adj.* numbering one sextillion. [French *sextillion* 1 followed by 21 zeros (from Latin *sextus* sixth), on the model of *million.* see MILLION.] —**sex·til′lionth,** *adj., n.*

sex·ton (sek'stən) *n.* a person employed by a parish to take care of church property. The sexton's duties sometimes include ringing the church bell and digging graves for churchyard burials. [Old French *secrestein,* from Medieval Latin *sacristanus* keeper of sacred objects, going back to Latin *sacer* holy.]

sex·tu·ple (seks tü'pəl, -tū'-, -tup'əl, seks'tə pəl) *adj.* **1.** consisting of six parts or members. **2.** six times as great or as many. —*v.t., v.i.,* **-pled, -pling.** to make or become six times as great or as many; multiply by six. —*n.* a number or amount six times as great as another. [Latin *sextus* sixth, on the model of QUADRUPLE.]

sex·tu·plet (seks tup'lit, -tü'plit, -tū'-, seks'tə-) *n.* **1.a.** one of six offspring born at one birth. **b. sextuplets.** six offspring born at one birth. **2.** any set or combination of six. [SEXTUPLE + -ET.]

sex·u·al (sek'shü əl) *adj.* **1.** of or relating to sex or the sexes: *sexual instincts, sexual relations, sexual behavior.* **2.a.** characteristically male or female, rather than asexual; distinguished by sex. **b.** involving the union of male and female germ cells: *sexual reproduction.* [Late Latin *sexuālis* relating to sex, from Latin *sexus.* See SEX.] —**sex′u·al·ly,** *adv.*

sexual harassment, the act or practice of making sexually suggestive overtures or harassing with sexist behavior, esp. such acts or practices committed by an employer or co-worker toward an employee.

sexual intercourse, human sexual activity in which the genital organs are joined. Also, **coitus, copulation.**

sex·u·al·i·ty (sek'shü al'i tē) *n.* **1.** the condition of being distinguished by sex; sexual quality. **2.** the possession and expression of sexual feelings.

sexually transmitted disease, a disease passed from one person to another by sexual activity; venereal disease.

sex·y (sek'sē) *adj.,* **sex·i·er, sex·i·est.** *Informal.* arousing or intended to arouse sexual desire. —**sex′i·ly,** *adv.* —**sex′i·ness,** *n.*

SF, science fiction.

sfer·ics (sfer'iks) *pl. n.* atmospherics. ➡ used as singular.

sfor·zan·do (sfôrt sän'dō) *Music. adj.* heavily accented, as a single note or chord. —*adv.* in a sforzando manner. [Italian *sforzando* forcing, gerund of *sforzare* to force, going back to Latin *ex* out of + *fortis* strong.]

sg, specific gravity.

Sgt., Sergeant.

shab·by (shab'ē) *adj.,* **-bi·er, -bi·est. 1.** faded and dingy from wear or exposure: *a shabby coat, a shabby house.* **2.** wearing worn and faded clothes; seedy: *a shabby tramp.* **3.** unkind, ungenerous, or unfair: *shabby treatment.* **4.** decaying from neglect; run-down: *a shabby part of town.* [From obsolete *shab* scab, low fellow, from Old English *sceabb* scab, itch.] —**shab′bi·ly,** *adv.* —**shab′bi·ness,** *n.*

Sha·bu·oth (shə vü'əs, shä vü ōt') Shavuoth.

shack (shak) *n.* a small, roughly built hut or cabin; shanty.

shack·le (shak'əl) *n.* **1.** a metal band fastened around the ankle or wrist of a prisoner, usually one of a pair connected by a chain; fetter. **2.** *usually,* **shackles.** anything that hinders or restrains freedom of action or thought: *the shackles of censorship.* **3.** any of various devices for fastening or coupling. —*v.t.* **1.** to put a shackle or shackles on; fetter. **2.** to hinder or restrain (a person or thing) from freedom of action or action: *to shackle the mind.* [Old English *sceacul* fetter.] —**shack′ler,** *n.*

shad (shad) *n., pl.* **shad** or **shads.** any of several commercially important food and game fish of the herring family, found in the coastal waters of Europe and North America, esp. *Alosa sapidissima,* the **American shad,** which swims up coastal rivers in the spring to spawn, and whose roe is considered a delicacy. Weight: 1-8 pounds (0.5-3.6 kilograms). [Old English *sceadd.*]

shad·ber·ry (shad'ber'ē, -bə rē) *n., pl.* **-ries. 1.** the berry of the shadbush. **2.** shadbush.

shad·bush (shad'büsh') *n.* any of a group of North American shrubs and small trees, genus *Amelanchier,* of the rose family, bearing clusters of showy white flowers and round, juicy berries of dark purple. Also, **shad·blow** (shad'blō'), **serviceberry.** [Be-

cause it blooms about the same time in the spring that *shad* appear in the rivers.]

shad·dock (shad'ək) *n.* **1.** a large, pale yellow, usually pear-shaped citrus fruit of a tropical tree, *Citrus maxima.* It resembles the closely related grapefruit but is larger, coarser, and drier. **2.** the tree that bears this fruit, native to southern Asia. Also *(defs. 1, 2),* **pomelo.** [From Captain *Shaddock,* an English sailor who introduced this tree into the West Indies in the late seventeenth century.]

shade (shād) *n.* **1.** relative or partial darkness caused by something intercepting rays of light, as from the sun. **2.** a place or spot sheltered from light, esp. from the rays of the sun: *to rest in the shade.* **3.** window shade. **4.** a device fitted over a lamp to reduce the amount of light it casts. **5.** anything that shuts out or reduces light or heat. **6.a.** the level or degree of darkness of a color, determined by the amount of black mixed with the pure hue. **b.** a dark or grayish color: *a deep shade of violet.* **7.** the representation of a dark surface, as in a painting. **8.** a small degree; trace: *a shade of doubt.* **9.** a small difference; nuance: *a shade of meaning.* **10.** a disembodied spirit; ghost. **11. (the) shades. a.** growing darkness, as after sunset. **b.** the abode of the dead; Hades. **12. shades.** *Slang.* sunglasses. —*v.,* **shad·ed, shad·ing.** —*v.t.* **1.** to shelter, screen, or protect from glare, heat, or light: *The umbrella shaded us from the hot sun.* **2.** to mark (a drawing, painting, or the like) with gradations of darkness. **3.** to cover with shadow or make gloomy. **4.** to cause to change or vary by slight degrees. —*v.i.* to change or vary slightly or by degrees: *The colors in the painting shaded from deep green to bright yellow.* [Old English *sceadu* shadow.] —**shad′er,** *n.* —For Synonyms *(n.),* see **hue**[1].

shad·ing (shā'ding) *n.* **1.** the representing of different degrees of light and dark in a painting, drawing, or the like, as by using lines, dots, or varying tones of color. **2.** a small degree of change or variation; slight gradation. **3.** a shelter or screening, as from light or heat.

sha·doof (shä düf') *n.* an irrigation device used in Egypt and adjacent regions since ancient times, consisting of a long pole on a pivot with a bucket on one end and a weight on the other, used for lifting water. [Arabic *shādūf.*]

shad·ow (shad'ō) *n.* **1.a.** a relatively dark region produced when rays from a source of light are blocked by an opaque object. **b.** a representation of this, as in a painting or photograph: *The artist painted the shadows in a bluish gray shade.* **2.** any dark area: *to have deep shadows under the eyes.* **3. the shadows.** the darkness following sunset: *the shadows of twilight.* **4.** a faint image, representation, or indication; hint: *a shadow of former authority, a shadow of things to come.* **5.** a slight degree or suggestion; faintest trace: *a shadow of a doubt, a shadow of a smile.* **6.a.** a constant companion; close friend; follower. **b.** a person who follows another closely and secretly, such as a private detective or spy. **7.** a feeling or atmosphere of sadness or gloom: *The bad news cast a shadow over the holidays.* **8.** ghost; phantom. **9.** something unreal or imaginary. —*v.t.* **1.** to cast a shadow on or over; cover or obscure with a shadow. **2.** to represent or indicate faintly or vaguely. **3.** to follow closely, esp. to watch secretly. **4.** to make gloomy; sadden. [Old English *sceaduwe,* dative of *sceadu* shade.] —**shad′ow·er,** *n.*

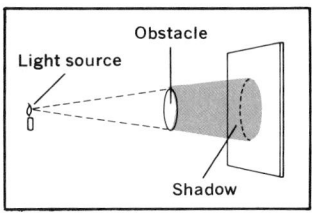

shadow

·in (or **under**) **the shadow of.** under the influence, domination, or threat of.

shad·ow·box (shad'ō boks') *v.i.* to make the motions of boxing with an imaginary opponent, esp. for practice or exercise. —**shad′ow·box′ing,** *n.*

shadow box, a small, shallow case with shelves and usually having a glass front, hung on a wall to display small objects.

shad·ow·graph (shad'ō graf') *n.* **1.** an image produced by

a	at	e	end	o	hot	u	up	hw	white		about
ā	ape	ē	me	ō	old	ū	use	ng	song		taken
ä	far	i	it	ô	fork	ü	rule	th	thin	ə	pencil
âr	care	ī	ice	oi	oil	u̇	pull	th	this		lemon
		îr	pierce	ou	out	ûr	turn	zh	measure		circus

throwing a shadow, usually made by the hands, on a lighted surface. **2.** an X-ray photograph; radiograph.

shadow play, a theatrical presentation performed by projecting the shadows of actors or puppets onto a lighted screen.

Indonesian **shadow play** with puppets

shad·ow·y (shad′ō ē) *adj.* **1.** full of shadow or shade; shady: *a shadowy corner of the yard.* **2.** like a shadow; dim; indistinct: *a shadowy figure.* **3.** without reality; imaginary.

shad·y (shā′dē) *adj.,* **shad·i·er, shad·i·est. 1.a.** sheltered from the sun; full of shade; shaded. **b.** shadowy or dark like shade. **2.** providing shade. **3.** *Informal.* of doubtful legality or honesty; disreputable: *a shady business deal.* —**shad′i·ly,** *adv.* —**shad′-i·ness,** *n.*

shaft (shaft) *n.* **1.** a long, slender body connected to the head of an arrow or spear. **2.** an arrow or spear. **3.** something like an arrow or missile in effect: *barbed shafts of wit.* **4.** a long line or columnlike stream, as of light; beam: *bright shafts of morning light.* **5.** either of the two wooden poles between which a horse or other draft animal is harnessed to pull a vehicle. **6.** the long, straight handle of any of various tools or implements, such as a hammer, golf club, or hockey stick. **7.** any long, straight cylindrical object or part, such as a pole. **8.** a bar in a machine that serves to support a rotating part, as does a camshaft, or to convey motion to other parts, as does a drive shaft. **9.a.** a deep passage, usually vertical, from ground level to an underground excavation, as in a mine. **b.** any similar vertical passage, as for an elevator or ventilation. **10.a.** the portion of a column between the base and capital. **b.** a slender column, such as those used to support vaulting. **c.** an obelisk, column, or the like serving as a memorial. **11.** the rodlike, stiff, central part of a feather from which the vane extends to either side. For illustration, see **feather.** [Old English *sceaft* long, slender part of a spear or arrow.] —For Synonyms, see **beam.**

shag[1] (shag) *n.* **1.** rough, matted hair, wool, or the like. **2.** a mass of this. **3.** a long, coarse nap, esp. on wool, cotton, or other fabrics used for rugs. **4.** a fabric or article, as a rug, having such a nap. **5.** a strong pipe tobacco cut into fine shreds. [Old English *sceacga* rough hair or wool.]

shag[2] (shag) *v.t.,* **shagged, shag·ging.** to chase after and retrieve (a baseball or golf ball) during practice. [Of uncertain origin.]

shag·bark (shag′bärk′) *n.* **1.** a hickory tree, *Carya ovata,* native to Canada and the eastern United States, having shaggy gray bark that peels off in long strips, grown for its timber and edible nuts. **2.** the wood of this tree, the most widely used hickory timber. **3.** the nut of this tree. Also, **shellbark.**

shag·gy (shag′ē) *adj.,* **-gi·er, -gi·est. 1.** covered with or having long, rough hair or wool. **2.** long, bushy, and rough, as eyebrows. **3.** poorly groomed; unkempt: *a shaggy tramp.* **4.** having a long, coarse nap, as a rug. **5.** covered with rough, tangled growth: *a shaggy hillside.* [SHAG[1] + -Y[1].] —**shag′gi·ly,** *adv.* —**shag′gi·ness,** *n.*

sha·green (shə grēn′) *n.* **1.** untanned leather having a rough surface, often dyed green, and used esp. for ornamental objects. It is made from the skins of various animals, such as the horse, camel, and shark. **2.** the rough skin of certain sharks. [French *chagrin,* from Turkish *sagry* the back of a horse, skin of the back of a horse (from which such leather was originally made).]

shah (shä) *n.* the title of the former hereditary sovereign of Iran. [Persian *shāh.*]

shake (shāk) *v.,* **shook, shak·en, shak·ing.** —*v.t.* **1.a.** to cause to move quickly to and fro, up and down, or from side to side: *Shake the bottle to mix the ingredients.* **b.** to cause to become mixed, stirred, or rearranged by moving in this way: *Shake the dressing well before pouring it on the salad.* **2.** to cause to tremble, vibrate, or quiver: *The earthquake shook the building.* **3.** to dislodge, scatter, or cause to fall by or as by such movement: *The dog shook the snow from its back. We shook apples down from the tree.* **4.** to weaken or impair; make less firm: *The district attorney's cross-examination shook the witness's testimony.* **5.** to move or stir the feelings of; upset; disturb: *The news of the accident shook us all.* **6.** *Informal.* to get rid of: *to shake one's pursuers.* **7.** *Music.* to trill. —*v.i.* **1.** to move quickly to and fro, up and down, or from side to side; vibrate: *The house shakes when the trains go by.* **2.** to move the body or a part of the body involuntarily, as from cold, fear, or anger: *to shake with fright.* **3.** to grasp hands, as in greeting or agreement: *We shook on the deal.* **4.** *Music.* to trill. —*n.* **1.** the act of shaking: *One shake of the stick scared the dog away.* **2.** something, esp. a beverage, made by shaking ingredients together. **3.** a crack or fissure produced during formation or growth, as in the earth or timber. **4.** *Informal.* earthquake. **5.** *Informal.* a brief time; moment; instant: *I'll be done in three shakes.* **6.** *Music.* trill. **7. (the) shakes.** *Informal.* a physical state or condition characterized by trembling or shivering, esp. one involving fever and chills. [Old English *sceacan* to move quickly, vibrate, cause to vibrate.] —**shak′a·ble;** *also,* **shake′a·ble,** *adj.*

·**a fair shake.** *Informal.* just or fair treatment.

·**no great shakes.** *Informal.* not unusual or outstanding; average.

·**to shake a leg.** *Informal.* to move or go quickly; hurry.

·**to shake down. a.** to cause to settle or become compact: *to shake down flour.* **b.** *Slang.* to get money from dishonestly.

·**to shake hands.** to grasp (another's or each other's hand), as in greeting or agreement.

·**to shake off.** to get rid of or away from: *to shake off a bad habit.*

·**to shake up. a.** to shake with force. **b.** to disturb mentally or physically: *The car accident shook them up.* **c.** to change (something) radically and thoroughly: *The new owner announced plans to shake up the company.*

shake·down (shāk′doun′) *n.* **1.** the act or process of shaking down. **2.** *Slang.* extortion. **3.** a makeshift bed, as of straw or blankets. —*adj.* designed to test the performance of a ship or aircraft under actual operating conditions: *a shakedown cruise.*

shak·en (shā′kən) the past participle of **shake.**

shake·out (shāk′out′) *n.* **1.a.** the failure of companies within an industry because of intense competition, poor management, or declining demand for a particular product or service. **b.** the failure of a product or similar products because of competition, limited demand, or the like. **2.** a downward movement, esp. sudden or unexpected, in market prices of stocks, bonds, or other securities that forces speculators and small investors to sell their holdings.

shak·er (shā′kər) *n.* **1.** a container having a perforated top, as for salt or pepper. **2.** any of various devices or machines used for shaking: *a cocktail shaker.* **3.** a person who shakes.

Shak·er (shā′kər) *n.* a member of an American religious sect practicing celibacy and communal living and holding all property in common. [Because they used to sing and dance with *shaking* movements at their prayer meetings.]

Shake·spear·e·an (shāk spir′ē ən) *also,* **Shake·spear·i·an.** *adj.* of, relating to, or like the English poet and dramatist William Shakespeare or his works. —*n.* a scholar of Shakespeare or his works.

Shakespearean sonnet, a sonnet form made famous by William Shakespeare, consisting of three quatrains and a concluding couplet. The rhyme scheme is usually *abab cdcd efef gg.* Also, **Elizabethan sonnet, English sonnet.**

shake·up (shāk′up′) *n.* a radical change in organization, as of a business or department of government.

shak·o (shak′ō) *n., pl.* **shak·os.** a high, stiff military hat with a visor and, usually, a plume attached in front. [French *s(c)hako,* from Hungarian *csákó (süveg)* peaked (cap), going back to German *Zacke* point, peak.]

shak·y (shā′kē) *adj.,* **shak·i·er, shak·i·est. 1.a.** trembling; shaking: *a scared and shaky child.* **b.** showing or suggesting the result of shaking or trembling: *shaky writing.* **2.** liable to break down or give way; unsound: *a shaky bridge.* **3.** not to be depended on: *shaky information.* —**shak′i·ly,** *adv.* —**shak′i·ness,** *n.*

shale (shāl) *n.* a fine-grained sedimentary rock, composed pre-

dominantly of hardened clay or mud in very thin layers that separate easily. [Probably from Old English *scealu* shell.]

shale oil, any of the liquid hydrocarbons extracted by distillation from oil shale.

shall (shal) *auxiliary verb* Present: **shall** or *(archaic second-person sing.)* **shalt.** Past: **should** or *(archaic second person sing.)* **shouldest** or **shouldst. 1.** used to express simple futurity: *I shall be in your town next week.* **2.** used to express determination, obligation, or compulsion: *She shall do as she is told.* **3.** used in direct questions, as in the form of suggestions or invitations: *Shall I call him tomorrow? Shall we dance? How shall we handle this problem?* **4.** used in conditional clauses to express future time: *If he shall die, his niece shall succeed him.* [Old English *sceal*, first and third person singular of *sculan* to owe, be under obligation.]

Usage Traditionally, to express the simple future tense, **shall** was generally used with the first person and **will** with the second and third persons: *I shall see you tomorrow. The receptionist will direct you to my office.* To show determination or obligation, **will** was used with the first person and **shall** with the second and third persons: *We will win the battle! You shall do as I say!* In current American usage **shall** and **will** are used interchangeably in these senses, with **will** being much more common, especially in speech. **Shall** is common in British English.

shal·loon (sha lün′) *n.* a lightweight woolen fabric woven with a twill, used esp. for linings. [From *Châlons,* French town where it was first made.]

shal·lop (shal′əp) *n.* a small open boat propelled by sails or oars. [French *chaloupe,* from Dutch *sloep* sloop. Doublet of SLOOP.]

shal·lot (shə lot′, shal′ət) *n.* **1.** a small bulb or clove of a plant, *Allium ascalonicum,* closely related to the onion, used to flavor foods. **2.** the small plant that grows from this bulb. [From obsolete *eschalot,* from French *échalote,* diminutive of Middle French *eschaloigne,* going back to Latin *Ascalōnia (caepa)* (onion) of Ashkelon, a city in Philistia (now in Israel).]

shal·low (shal′ō) *adj.* **1.** of little depth; not deep: *a shallow pond.* **2.** lacking depth of thought, reasoning, knowledge, or feeling: *a shallow mind.* —*n. usually,* **shallows.** a shallow area in a body of water. —*v.t., v.i.* to make or become shallow. [Probably from an unrecorded Old English word.] —**shal′low·ly,** *adv.* —**shal′low·ness,** *n.* —For Synonyms *(adj.),* see **superficial.**

sha·lom (shə lōm′) *interj.* a Jewish expression of greeting or farewell. [Hebrew *shālōm* peace.]

shalt (shalt) *Archaic.* a second person singular present tense of **shall.** ➡ used with *thou.*

shal·y (shā′lē) *adj.,* **shal·i·er, shal·i·est.** of, like, or containing shale.

sham (sham) *n.* **1.** something false intended to appear genuine or true; fraud; counterfeit. **2.** a person who falsely assumes a certain character for the purpose of deception. **3.** a decorative cover made to simulate an article of household linen and used in its place or over it: *a pillow sham.* —*adj.* not genuine or real; pretended or false: *a sham battle, sham diamonds.* —*v.,* **shammed, sham·ming.** —*v.t.* **1.** to assume the appearance of; feign: *to sham illness.* **2.** to produce a deceptive imitation of. —*v.i.* to make false pretenses; pretend. [Possibly dialectal form of SHAME.] —**sham′mer,** *n.*

sha·man (shā′mən, shä′-) *n.* in certain tribal religions, a person believed to have magical powers and to be able to influence good and evil spirits to cure illness, bring rain, and the like; medicine man. [Russian *shaman,* from Tungus *saman,* possibly going back to Sanskrit *shramana* Buddhist monk, ascetic.] —**sha′man·ism,** *n.* —**sha′man·ist,** *n.* —**sha′man·is′tic,** *adj.*

sham·ble (sham′bəl) *v.i.,* **-bled, -bling.** to walk awkwardly or unsteadily; shuffle. —*n.* a shambling walk or gait. [From earlier *shamble* ungainly, from *shamble* table for the sale of meat (with reference to its straddling trestles). See SHAMBLES.]

sham·bles (sham′bəlz) *n.* **1.** a place or condition of great disorder or confusion: *The burglars left the room a shambles.* **2.** a scene of wholesale slaughter or of great bloodshed. **3.** a slaughterhouse. ➡ used as singular or plural. [Plural of earlier *shamble* table for the sale of meat (associated with the blood of the slaughtered animals), from Old English *scamel* table, bench, from Latin *scamellum* little bench, stool.]

shame (shām) *n.* **1.** a painful feeling of guilt or embarrassment caused by having done something wrong, indecent, or foolish. **2.** an understanding of what is improper or disgraceful: *Have you no shame?* **3.** a loss of honor or reputation; ignominy: *Your actions brought shame to your entire family.* **4.** a person or thing that brings or causes disgrace: *Widespread corruption was the shame of that mayor's administration.* **5.** something to be sorry about: *What a shame that our team didn't win.* —*v.t.,* **shamed, sham·ing. 1.** to cause to feel shame; make ashamed; embarrass.

2. to bring shame upon; dishonor. **3.** to force or drive through shame or fear of shame: *They shamed me into volunteering to help.* [Old English *sceamu* feeling of being disgraced, disgrace.]
•**for shame.** shame on you; how shameful.
•**to put to shame. a.** to bring disgrace or dishonor upon; cause to feel ashamed. **b.** to surpass another or others in accomplishment or ability; outdo.

shame·faced (shām′fāst′) *adj.* **1.** bashful; shy. **2.** showing shame; ashamed. [Modification (influenced by FACE) of archaic *shamefast,* from Old English *sc(e)amfæst* literally, restrained by shame, from *sceamu* shame + *fæst* firm.] —**shame·fac·ed·ly** (shām′fā′sid lē, shām′fāst′-), *adv.*

shame·ful (shām′fəl) *adj.* **1.** causing shame; disgraceful. **2.** morally offensive; indecent. —**shame′ful·ly,** *adv.* —**shame′ful·ness,** *n.*

shame·less (shām′lis) *adj.* **1.** having no sense of shame; immodest; brazen. **2.** done without shame: *a shameless disregard for honesty.* —**shame′less·ly,** *adv.* —**shame′less·ness,** *n.*

sham·my (sham′ē) *n., pl.* **-mies.** chamois *(def. 2).*

sham·poo (sham pü′) *v.t.,* **-pooed, -poo·ing. 1.** to wash (the hair or scalp) with soap and water or a special preparation. **2.** to wash the hair and scalp of. **3.** to clean (upholstery or rugs) with any of various cleaning preparations. —*n.* **1.** the act or an instance of washing the hair or scalp. **2.** any of various preparations for use in shampooing. [Hindi *chāmpo,* imperative of *chāmpnā* to press, massage.] —**sham·poo′er,** *n.*

sham·rock (sham′rok′) *n.* **1.** a leaf consisting of three oval leaflets, such as the wood sorrel or the three-leaf clover. The shamrock is the national emblem of Ireland. **2.** any of several plants having such leaves, esp. the clover. [Irish *seamrōg* trefoil, clover, diminutive of *seamar.*]

Wood sorrel   White clover

shamrocks

sha·mus (shä′məs, shā′-) *n. Slang.* **1.** police officer. **2.** private detective. [Possibly blend of Irish *Séamus* James, and Yiddish *shames* sexton in a synagogue (from Hebrew *shammāsh* servant).]

shan·dy·gaff (shan′dē gaf′) *n.* a drink made of ale or beer mixed usually with ginger beer, ginger ale, or lemonade. Also, **shan′dy.** [Of uncertain origin.]

shang·hai (shang′hī′, shang hī′) *v.t.,* **-haied, -hai·ing. 1.** to make (someone) unconscious by drugs, liquor, or violence in order to force the person on a ship to serve as a sailor. **2.** to make (someone) do something unwillingly, esp. by fraud or force. [From the earlier practice of acquiring sailors against their will for voyages to *Shanghai.*] —**shang′hai′er,** *n.*

Shan·gri-La (shang′grə lä′, shang′grə lä′) *n.* an imaginary earthly paradise. [From *Shangri-La,* an imaginary ideal land described in the novel *Lost Horizon* by James Hilton, 1900-54, English writer.]

shank (shangk) *n.* **1.** the part of the leg in the human being that extends from the knee to the ankle. **2.** a corresponding part in certain animals and birds. **3.** the entire leg. **4.** a cut of meat from the leg of an animal. **5.** the part of an instrument, tool, or the like that connects the acting part with a handle or the part by which it is held or moved, such as the straight part of a nail. **6.** *Printing.* the body of a piece of type. **7.** the narrow part of a shoe under the arch of the foot, connecting the sole and the heel. **8.a.** the latter part of a period of time. **b.** the early or best part of a period of time: *the shank of the evening.* **9.** the part of an anchor between the stock and the flukes. —*v.t.* to hit (a golf ball) with the heel of the club. [Old English *sceanca* shinbone, leg.]
•**on shank's mare.** on foot.
•**to ride shank's mare.** to walk.

shan't (shant, shänt) *contr.* shall not.

shan·tey (shan′tē) *n., pl.* **-teys.** chantey.

shan·tung (shan′tung′, shan′tung′) *n.* a medium-weight soft fabric, esp. one of silk, having a textured surface. [From *Shantung* (now *Shandong*), a province in northeastern China where it is manufactured.]

shan·ty[1] (shan′tē) *n., pl.* **-ties.** a crude, flimsily built hut or cabin. [Possibly from Irish *sean toigh* literally, old house.]

a	at	e	end	o	hot	u	up	hw	white	{	about
ā	ape	ē	me	ō	old	ū	use	ng	song		taken
ä	far	i	it	ô	fork	ù	pull	th	thin	ə	pencil
âr	care	ī	ice	oi	oil	u	pull	th	this		lemon
		îr	pierce	ou	out	ûr	turn	zh	measure	{	circus

shan·ty² (shan′tē) *also*, **shantey**. *n., pl.* **-ties.** chantey.

shan·ty·town (shan′tē toun′) *n.* a poor section of a town where people live mainly in shanties.

shape (shāp) *n.* **1.** a characteristic outward surface of an object formed by following along its outer edges: *All circles have the same shape.* **2.** any of the forms in which a thing may exist or be represented; kind; sort. **3.** something that has or gives form; mold; pattern. **4.** outward appearance; guise. **5.** an imaginary or supernatural form; phantom. **6.a.** a particular state of being; condition: *They were in bad shape after the accident. That company is in good shape financially.* **b.** good physical condition: *to keep in shape by exercising.* **7.** the human body or its appearance; figure. **8.** a definite, regular, or proper form or arrangement; order: *Let's get things in shape before the others arrive.* —*v.*, **shaped, shap·ing.** —*v.t.* **1.** to give form to; fashion; mold: *to shape dough into loaves.* **2.** to adapt in form; adjust; modify. **3.** to give definite direction or character to: *to shape one's life.* **4.** to form mentally; plan; devise. **5.** to express verbally: *to shape one's answers carefully.* —*v.i.* to take on a definite form, order, or plan; develop: *Plans for the party are shaping up nicely.* [Old English *(ge)sceap* a form, creation.]

• **to take shape.** to assume or have a definite form, order, or plan: *Our plans for a vacation are beginning to take shape.*

> **Synonyms** **Shape, form,** and **figure** mean the visible aspects of something, as its contour or outline, as distinguished from the material from which it is made. Both **shape** and **form** may suggest three-dimensional qualities of bulk or mass: *The meteorite has an irregular shape. The sculptor worked the clay into the form of an animal.* In addition, *form* often suggests the intrinsic quality of a thing: *The magnified photograph revealed the snowflake's complex form.* **Figure** is applied either to lines that define an object or to the human shape: *The children drew geometric figures in their notebooks. A shadowy figure was seen running from the scene of the crime.*

shape·less (shāp′lis) *adj.* **1.** without definite or regular shape. **2.** having no beauty or elegance of form; unshapely: *a shapeless dress.* —**shape′less·ly,** *adv.* —**shape′less·ness,** *n.*

shape·ly (shāp′lē) *adj.*, **-li·er, -li·est.** having a beautiful or elegant shape; well-formed. —**shape′li·ness,** *n.*

shape-up (shāp′up′) *n.* a system of selecting work crews, esp. of longshoremen, by having the workers assemble at a certain place, with the foreman choosing among them.

shard (shärd) *also*, **sherd.** *n.* **1.** a fragment of some brittle material, as of glass. **2.** potsherd. [Old English *sceard* fragment.]

share¹ (shâr) *n.* **1.** a part that is allotted or belongs to or is contributed by one individual. **2.** a part of anything jointly owned by several parties: *I own a share in the airplane.* **3.** one of the equal portions into which the capital of a company or corporation is divided: *to own fifty shares of stock.* —*v.*, **shared, shar·ing.** —*v.t.* **1.** to use, enjoy, or take part in together or in common: *to share an apartment, to share someone's happiness.* **2.** to divide into portions and give to others as well as oneself: *to share one's dinner with friends.* —*v.i.* to have a share; take part: *to share in the profits of a company.* [Old English *scearu* division, cutting.] —**shar′er,** *n.*

• **to go shares.** to participate in or contribute toward jointly, as an enterprise.

share² (shâr) *n.* plowshare. [Old English *scear.*]

share·crop·per (shâr′krop′ər) *n.* a tenant farmer who farms land for the owner in return for a share of the crops.

share·hold·er (shâr′hōl′dər) *n.* stockholder.

shark¹

shark¹ (shärk) *n.* any of numerous medium to large, mostly saltwater predatory fish, order Squaliformes, having skeletons of cartilage rather than bone, with usually gray rough skin, a deeply forked tail, and a large mouth on the underside of the head with several rows of sharp teeth. [Of uncertain origin.]

shark² (shärk) *n.* **1.** a dishonest person who preys on others; swindler. **2.** *Slang.* a person who has exceptional ability in some special area: *a card shark.* [German *Schurke* rogue.]

shark·skin (shärk′skin′) *n.* **1.** a durable, tightly woven, crisp fabric of worsted or synthetic fibers. **2.** the skin of a shark, esp. as used for making leather.

sharp (shärp) *adj.* **1.** having a fine cutting edge or point; well suited for cutting or piercing: *a sharp blade.* **2.** having a pointed end; not rounded or blunt: *a sharp peak.* **3.** involving an abrupt or sudden change in direction: *a sharp turn.* **4.** highly critical or scornful; acrid: *sharp words, a sharp rebuke.* **5.** keenly affecting the senses or emotions; intensely felt: *sharp pangs of hunger.* **6.** (of food) having a biting or penetrating smell or taste: *sharp cheese.* **7.** high-pitched; shrill: *a sharp cry of pain.* **8.** distinct, as in outline or contour; not blurred: *That camera takes sharp pictures.* **9.** having or showing the ability to perceive quickly and keenly: *a sharp eye for detail, a sharp sense of smell.* **10.** showing skill or mental keenness; shrewd or clever: *to be sharp at cards.* **11.** closely observant; watchful; alert; vigilant: *Keep a sharp lookout.* **12.** full of vigor; rapid; brisk; energetic: *to walk at a sharp pace.* **13.** easily seen; clearly evident: *There were sharp differences between the two political platforms.* **14.** *Slang.* strikingly attractive; stylish; classy: *You really look sharp in that new outfit.* **15.** *Music.* **a.** raised a half step in pitch. **b.** above the true or proper pitch; too high. **c.** (of a key) having sharps in the signature. **16.** (of a consonant) articulated with the breath only; voiceless. —*adv.* **1.** at the moment specified; promptly; exactly: *to leave at 1:30 sharp.* **2.** in a sharp manner. —*n.* **1.** *Music.* **a.** a note or tone one half step above a given note or tone. **b.** the symbol (♯) which, when placed before a note or on a degree of the staff, indicates that the pitch will be raised by a half step. **2.** *Informal.* sharper. **3.** *Informal.* expert. [Old English *scearp* having a fine cutting edge or point, keen, severe.] —**sharp′ly,** *adv.* —**sharp′ness,** *n.*

sharp·en (shär′pən) *v.t., v.i.* to make or become sharp or sharper. —**sharp′en·er,** *n.*

sharp·er (shär′pər) *n.* a shrewd, dishonest person, esp. one who cheats at cards; cheat.

sharp·ie (shär′pē) *n.* **1.** a long, narrow, flat-bottomed sailboat having one or two masts. **2.** *Slang.* a shrewd, quick-witted, and often dishonest person.

sharp·shoot·er (shärp′shü′tər) *n.* **1.** anyone skilled in shooting, esp. with a rifle. **2.a.** the second category of proficiency in target shooting. **b.** a person who has qualified in this category. —**sharp′shoot′ing,** *n.*

sharp-sight·ed (shärp′sī′təd) *adj.* **1.** having acute eyesight. **2.** having or showing quickness and keenness of mind.

sharp-tongued (shärp′tungd′) *adj.* using or tending to use harsh, critical, or sarcastic language.

sharp-wit·ted (shärp′wit′id) *adj.* having or showing a quick, keen mind.

Shas·ta daisy (shas′tə) **1.** the showy white and yellow daisylike flower of any of several varieties of a plant, *Chrysanthemum superbum,* of the composite family. **2.** the plant bearing this flower head. [From Mount *Shasta,* California.]

shat·ter (shat′ər) *v.t.* **1.** to break (something, esp. a hard or brittle object) into pieces, as by a sudden blow. **2.** to destroy completely or damage greatly: *The defeat in the primary shattered the candidate's hopes.* —*v.i.* to break suddenly or fall into pieces. —*n.* **1.** the act or sound of shattering: *We were awakened by the shatter of glass.* **2.** shatters. *Archaic.* fragments: *a sea which dashed the ship to shatters against the rock* (Edward Dorrington, 1727). [Of uncertain origin.] —**shat′ter·er,** *n.*

shat·ter·proof (shat′ər prüf′) *adj.* made so as not to shatter, esp. so that fragments will not scatter or fly off: *The window was made of shatterproof glass.*

shave (shāv) *v.*, **shaved, shaved** *or* **shav·en, shav·ing.** —*v.t.* **1.** to remove hair from (a part of the body) with a razor: *to shave one's legs.* **2.** to cut (hair, esp. the beard) down close to the skin with a razor. **3.** to cut down the surface of by removing thin shavings or parings: *The carpenter shaved the edge of the board.* **4.** to cut off in thin slices or parings, as ice. **5.** to cut very closely, as a lawn. **6.** to touch slightly, as in passing, or come very near touching; graze. **7.** to reduce or lower by a slight margin: *The store shaved prices on last season's clothes.* —*v.i.* to remove hair with a razor. —*n.* **1.** the act or an instance of cutting off hair with a razor: *a quick shave.* **2.** a thin slice; shaving; paring. **3.** a tool for shaving or for removing thin slices, such as a spokeshave. [Old English *sceafan* to scrape, scrape away.]

shave·ling (shāv′ling) *n.* **1.** a tonsured monk or priest. ➡ usually considered offensive. **2.** youth.

shav·en (shā'vən) *v.* a past participle of **shave**. —*adj.* **1.** shaved. **2.** closely cut or trimmed, as grass. **3.** tonsured.

shav·er (shā'vər) *n.* **1.** a person who shaves. **2.** any device for shaving. **3.** *Informal.* young boy.

shave·tail (shāv'tāl') *n. Slang.* a second lieutenant.

Sha·vi·an (shā'vē ən) *adj.* of, relating to, or characteristic of the British author George Bernard Shaw or his works. —*n.* a scholar or admirer of Shaw or his works.

shav·ing (shā'ving) *n.* **1.** a very thin piece or slice, esp. a thin slice of wood cut off by a plane. **2.** the act or process of removing hair or trimming a surface with or as with a razor.

shaving cream, a soapy cream or foam for softening the beard before shaving.

Sha·vu·oth (shə vü'əs, shä vü ōt') *also,* **Sha·bu·oth, Sha·vu·ot.** *n.* a Jewish holiday, originally a harvest festival, observed fifty days after the first day of Passover and commemorating the giving of the law to Moses. Also, **Pentecost.** [Hebrew *shābhū'oth,* plural of *shabhūa'* week.]

shawl (shôl) *n.* a large scarf or wrap consisting of a square or oblong piece of fabric, often embroidered, usually worn over the shoulders. [Persian *shāl* shawl made of a superior wool, probably from *Shaliat,* a town in India where supposedly it was first made.]

shawm (shôm) *n.* a medieval double-reed wind instrument, the forerunner of the oboe. [Old French *chalemie,* form of *chalemel* reed pipe, going back to Latin *calamus* reed, from Greek *kalamos.*]

Shaw·nee (shô nē') *n., pl.* **-nee** or **-nees. 1.** a member of a tribe of Algonquian Indians, formerly living at various times in the East, South, and Midwest, now living mainly in Oklahoma. **2.** the language of this people.

shay (shā) *n.* chaise. [From CHAISE, mistaken for a plural.]

Shays' Rebellion (shāz) a series of tax revolts by western Massachusetts farmers against the Massachusetts legislature in 1786-87.

she (shē) *pron., sing.* nominative, **she**; possessive, **her, hers**; objective, **her**; *pl.* nominative, **they**; possessive, **their, theirs**; objective, **them. 1.** a female person or animal, or an object personified as female, that has been previously mentioned. **2.** any woman or girl. —*n., pl.* **shes.** a female person or animal. [Old English *sēo, sīo,* feminine of *se* the; originally, that.]

sheaf (shēf) *n., pl.* **sheaves. 1.** one of the bundles in which stalks of cereal plants, such as wheat, are bound after reaping. **2.** any bundle of things all of a kind put or tied together: *a sheaf of papers, a sheaf of arrows.* —*v.t.* to bind into a sheaf; sheave. [Old English *scēaf* bundle of stalks, esp. of grain.]

shear (shîr) *v.,* **sheared** or *(archaic)* **shore, sheared** or **shorn, shear·ing.** —*v.t.* **1.** to clip or cut with shears, scissors, or a similar sharp instrument. **2.** to cut the wool or hair from: *to shear sheep.* **3.** to cut off; remove by clipping: *to shear fleece.* **4.a.** to subject (a solid body) to shearing stress. **b.** to cause to break by shearing stress (usually with *off*): *to shear off a bolt.* —*v.i.* **1.** to come apart or break because of shearing stress. —*n.* **1.** the act or process of shearing. **2.** one blade of a pair of shears. **3.** a pair of shears. **4.a.** the deformation of a material body in the direction of a shearing stress. **b.** shearing stress. [Old English *sceran* to cut, shave.] —**shear'er,** *n.*

shearing stress, a stress applied to a material body in a direction parallel to its surface. Also, **shear stress.**

shears (shîrz) *pl. n.* **1.** any of various usually large, scissorlike instruments. **2.** large scissors. **3.** a device for lifting heavy loads, having two legs spread at the bottom and fastened together at the top to support a block and tackle. [Old English *scēara* (plural) scissors.]

shear·wa·ter (shîr'wô'tər, -wot'ər) *n.* any of several web-footed seabirds, esp. of the genus *Puffinus,* having slender, hooked bills, long wings, and plumage that is gray, black, or brown above and often whitish below. Length: 12-25 inches (30-64 centimeters). [From its habit of skimming the water as it flies, appearing to cut the crests of the waves.]

sheath (shēth) *n., pl.* **sheaths** (shēthz). **1.** a case for the blade of a cutting weapon, such as a sword or knife. **2.** any similar covering, such as a membrane covering a muscle. **3.** a tight, close-fitting dress. —*v.t.* sheathe. [Old English *scǣth* case for a blade.]

sheathe (shēth) *v.t.,* **sheathed, sheath·ing. 1.** to put into a sheath or scabbard: *to sheathe a sword.* **2.** to enclose or protect in a case or covering: *to sheathe a roof with metal.* **3.** to draw in (claws).

sheath·ing (shē'thing) *n.* **1.** something that covers or protects, such as the first covering of boards on a house or one of the metal plates on the bottom of a ship. **2.** the act of a person who sheathes.

sheath knife, a knife made to be carried in a sheath, usually having a fixed blade.

sheave¹ (shēv) *v.t.,* **sheaved, sheav·ing.** to gather and bind into a sheaf or sheaves. [From SHEAF.]

sheave² (shēv) *n.* a grooved wheel, such as the wheel of a pulley. [Form of dialectal English *shive* slice, probably from an unrecorded Old English word.]

sheaves (shēvz) the plural of **sheaf.**

she·bang (shi bang') *n. Informal.* **1.** a structure, esp. one that lacks permanence or solidity: *It rained, and the whole shebang caved in.* **2.** a thing, affair, or business: *The owners of the company sold the whole shebang and left town.* [Of uncertain origin.]

shed¹ (shed) *n.* **1.** a slight structure used for shelter or storage. **2.** a large, strongly built structure, often with open ends or sides, used for storage. [Old English *sced, scead* shade, shelter.]

shed² (shed) *v.,* **shed, shed·ding.** —*v.t.* **1.** to cause to flow; let fall or pour, as blood or tears. **2.a.** to throw off or lose by natural process, as skin, antlers, or leaves. **b.** to get rid of; remove: *I need to shed ten pounds.* **3.** to send forth; radiate; exude: *The lilacs shed their gentle fragrance throughout the room.* **4.** to cause to flow off without penetrating: *a coat that sheds rain.* —*v.i.* **1.** to throw off or lose a covering, esp. hair, by natural process. **2.** to fall off or drop, as leaves or seed. [Old English *scēadan* to separate, divide, scatter.]

• **to shed blood.** to cause death or severe injury.

she'd (shēd) *contr.* **1.** she had. **2.** she would.

shed·der (shed'ər) *n.* **1.** a person or thing that sheds. **2.** an animal, such as a crab, lobster, or snake, that is about to shed its shell or skin, or has just done so.

sheen (shēn) *n.* lustrous brightness; shininess: *the sheen of a waxed floor.* [From earlier *sheen* beautiful, bright, from Old English *scēne.*] —**sheen'y,** *adj.* —For Synonyms, see **luster.**

sheep (shēp) *n., pl.* **sheep. 1.** a cud-chewing, cloven-hoofed mammal, genus *Ovis,* related to the goat, esp. any of numerous domesticated breeds of the species *O. aries,* widely raised for their fleece and for meat, milk, and sheepskin. Height: 1½-4 feet (0.5-1.2 meters) at the shoulder. **2.** a person who is timid, meek, or easily led. **3.** sheepskin *(defs. 1, 2).* [Old English *scēap* this animal.] —**sheep'like',** *adj.*

sheep

sheep·cote (shēp'kōt') *n.* a shed or similar shelter for sheep.

sheep-dip (shēp'dip') *n.* any chemical used for bathing sheep to rid them of external parasites or to clean the fleece and skin before shearing.

sheep·dog (shēp'dôg') *also,* **sheep dog.** *n.* **1.** Old English sheepdog. **2.** any dog trained to guard, drive, or tend sheep, such as a collie. Also *(def. 2),* **shepherd dog.**

sheep·fold (shēp'fōld') *n.* an enclosure for sheep, such as a pen.

sheep·herd·er (shēp'hûr'dər) *n.* a person who raises or tends a large number of sheep, esp. on the open range. —**sheep'herd'-ing,** *n.*

sheep·ish (shē'pish) *adj.* **1.** awkwardly bashful or embarrassed: *a sheepish grin.* **2.** like a sheep; timid, meek, or easily led. —**sheep'ish·ly,** *adv.* —**sheep'ish·ness,** *n.*

sheeps·head (shēps'hed') *n.* a gray or yellow saltwater food fish, *Archosargus probatocephalus,* related to the porgy, found along the Atlantic and Gulf coasts of the United States. Length: to 30 inches (76 centimeters).

sheepshead

sheep·skin (shēp'skin') *n.* **1.** the skin of a sheep, esp. one prepared with the wool on it, used for such items as gloves and coats. **2.** leather or parchment made from this skin. **3.** *Informal.* diploma.

a	at	e	end	o	hot	u	up	hw	white		about
ā	ape	ē	me	ō	old	ū	use	ng	song		taken
ä	far	i	it	ô	fork	ü	rule	th	thin	ə	pencil
âr	care	ī	ice	oi	oil	u̇	pull	th	this		lemon
				îr	pierce	ou	out	ûr	turn	zh	measure		circus

sheep sorrel, a common weed, *Rumex acetosella,* related to buckwheat, having sour-tasting leaves and growing in dry or sandy soil.

sheep·walk (shēp′wôk′) *n. British.* a pasture or range for sheep.

sheer[1] (shîr) *adj.* **1.** very thin and fine; nearly transparent: *sheer fabric.* **2.** unmixed with anything else: *The driveway was sheer mud.* **3.** complete or total; utter; downright: *sheer nonsense, sheer stupidity.* **4.** straight up or straight down; steep: *a sheer drop.* —*adv.* **1.** completely; quite; altogether. **2.** very steeply up or down. —*n.* a very thin and fine material, or something made of it. [Possibly modification of dialectal English *shire* bright, thin, complete, clear, from Old English *scīr* bright, pure.] —**sheer′ly**, *adv.* —**sheer′ness,** *n.*

sheer[2] (shîr) *v.i.* to deviate from a course; turn aside or away; swerve: *The ship sheered off from the rocks.* —*v.t.* to cause to sheer. —*n.* **1.** a moving away of a ship or boat from its course. **2.** the upward curve of the deck from the middle of a boat or ship to the bow or stern. [Dutch *scheren* to cut, go away, move aside.]

sheet[1] (shēt) *n.* **1.** a large piece of fabric, usually cotton, used as a bed covering. **2.** any broad, usually flat and thin piece or object: *a sheet of clear plastic.* **3.** an oblong or square piece of paper or parchment, esp. for writing or printing on. **4.** *Informal.* a newspaper. **5.** a broad expanse or surface: *sheets of flame, a sheet of water.* —*v.t.* **1.** to furnish with a sheet or sheets. **2.** to cover with a sheet: *Snow sheeted the ground.* [Old English *scēte* large piece of cloth.]

sheet[2] (shēt) *n.* **1.** a rope or chain attached to one or both of the lower ends of a sail, used to adjust or control the sail. **2.** **sheets.** the space at both the bow and stern of an open boat, esp. in front of and behind the cross seats of a rowboat. [Old English *scēata* piece of cloth, lower corner of a sail.]

sheet anchor 1. a large anchor usually carried in the middle of a ship and used only in emergencies. **2.** a person or thing to be used as a final reliance or resort when everything else has failed. [Of uncertain origin.]

sheet·ing (shē′ting) *n.* **1.** a fabric used for bed sheets. **2.** a lining or covering of timber or metal, used on a surface for protection.

sheet lightning, lightning appearing as bright, broad flashes, as from within a cloud or beyond the horizon.

sheet metal, metal in thin, flat-rolled pieces.

sheet music, music printed on unbound sheets of paper.

sheik (shēk, shāk) *also,* **sheikh.** *n.* **1.** a leader of an Arab clan, tribe, or other large group. **2.** a Muslim religious leader, esp. the superior of a religious community. [Arabic *shaikh* elder, chief.] —**sheik′dom;** *also,* **sheikh′dom,** *n.*

shek·el (shek′əl) *n.* **1.** the monetary unit of Israel. **2.** any of various ancient units of weight, esp. one of the Babylonians, Phoenicians, Hebrews, and Assyrians, equal to about half an ounce. **3.** an ancient silver coin of the Hebrews weighing one shekel. **4. shekels.** *Slang.* coins; money. [Hebrew *sheqel* ancient Hebrew coin and unit of weight.]

shel·drake (shel′drāk′) *n., pl.* **-drakes** or **-drake. 1.** any of several large, gooselike ducks, family Anatidae, of Europe, North Africa, and Asia, esp. the **common sheldrake,** *Tadorna tadorna,* the male of which has a red bill with a prominent knob on top. Length: to 25 inches (64 centimeters). Also, **shelduck** (shel′duk′). **2.** any of various similar ducks, esp. the merganser. [Probably from dialectal English *sheld* pied (from Middle Dutch *schillede* variegated) + DRAKE.]

sheldrake

shelf (shelf) *n., pl.* **shelves. 1.** a thin, flat piece of wood, metal, stone, or other material, fastened horizontally to a wall or frame to hold things, such as books or dishes. **2.** the contents of a shelf. **3.** anything like a shelf, such as a projecting ledge of rock. **4.** a sandbar or reef. [Old English *scylfe* plank, ledge.] —**shelf′like′,** *adj.*

• **on the shelf.** put away or aside temporarily or permanently as not new or no longer wanted, needed, or useful: *The plan to build a new community center is on the shelf until additional funds are available.*

shelf life, the length of time that a product remains fresh or suitable for sale and use: *Milk has a short shelf life compared with dry cereal.*

shell (shel) *n.* **1.a.** the hard or tough outer covering of any of various animals, such as the turtle, lobster, and most mollusks. **b.** the material of which such a covering is composed. **2.** any similar outer covering, as of a seed, fruit, or egg. **3.** something like a shell in shape or structure. **4.** reluctance, refusal, or inability to communicate with others; air of reserve: *Your friendship has brought me out of my shell.* **5.a.** the framework or outer walls and roof of a building. **b.** a rounded or dome-shaped structure, such as a band shell. **6.** a hollow, rounded piece of pastry for holding filling. **7.a.** an artillery projectile that is designed to explode at or in a target or in the air. **b.** a piece of small-arms ammunition, esp. for a shotgun. **c.** that part of a cartridge or similar piece of ammunition that encases the charge and remains after the projectile has been fired off. **8.** a long, light racing boat propelled by oars. **9.** *Physics.* any of several energy levels that the electrons of an atom occupy as they orbit the nucleus. —*v.t.* **1.** to remove the shell, husk, or pod of: *to shell peanuts.* **2.** to remove grains from the ear or cob of: *to shell corn.* **3.** to subject to artillery fire; bombard with explosive shells. —*v.i.* **1.** to undergo separation between the shell or covering and the contents: *These peas shell easily.* **2.** to look for and gather seashells: *We went shelling on the beach.* [Old English *sciell* hard outer covering of an animal, fruit, or egg.] —**shell′like′,** *adj.*

• **to shell out.** *Informal.* to spend (money), esp. with reluctance or under pressure: *We shelled out fifty dollars for these tickets.*

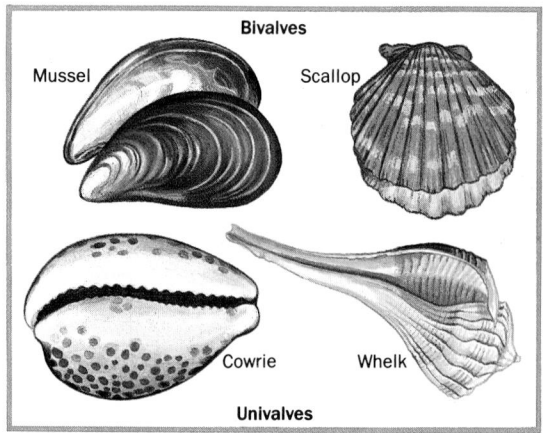

Bivalves

Mussel

Scallop

Cowrie

Whelk

Univalves

mollusk **shells**

she'll (shēl) *contr.* **1.** she shall. **2.** she will.

shel·lac (shə lak′) *also,* **shel·lack.** *n.* **1.** a solution of purified lac in alcohol, used as a varnish on floors, furniture, or similar surfaces. **2.** the lac itself when not dissolved, used in making certain insulating materials and phonograph records. —*v.t.,* **-lacked, -lack·ing. 1.** to coat or treat with shellac: *to shellac a piece of furniture.* **2.** *Slang.* **a.** to defeat decisively: *Our football team shellacked the visitors.* **b.** to beat; thrash. [SHELL + LAC[1].]

shell·bark (shel′bärk′) *n.* **1.** a hickory, *Carya laciniosa,* similar to the shagbark but with thick-shelled nuts. **2.** shagbark.

shell bean 1. any of various beans, as the lima bean, whose full-sized, immature seeds are removed from the pod and cooked and eaten as a vegetable. **2.** the seed of such a bean.

shell·fire (shel′fīr′) *n.* the firing or bursting of artillery shells.

shell·fish (shel′fish′) *n., pl.* **-fish** or **-fish·es.** any invertebrate having a shell and living in water, esp. a mollusk or crustacean. [Old English *scilfisc.*]

shell game 1. a dishonest game of chance in which the player bets on the location of a small object that supposedly is under one of three walnut shells or small cups. **2.** any dishonest scheme; swindle.

shell·proof (shel′prüf′) *adj.* able to resist shells or bombs.

shell shock, a nervous or mental disorder resulting from combat in war.

shell·shocked (shel′shokt′) *adj.* suffering from shell shock.

shell·y (shel′ē) *adj.,* **shell·i·er, shell·i·est. 1.** abounding in or covered with shells, esp. seashells. **2.** consisting of a shell or shells. **3.** forming or resembling a shell.

shel·ter (shel′tər) *n.* **1.** something that covers or protects, as

from weather, danger, or attack. **2.** the state of being protected; protection; refuge: *We sought shelter from the rain.* —*v.t.* **1.** to provide cover or protection for; shield. **2.** to take under one's protection: *to shelter an orphan.* —*v.i.* to find or take shelter. [Possibly modification of obsolete *sheltron* phalanx, from Old English *scildtruma* literally, shield troop.] —**shel′ter·er,** *n.*

Synonyms *n.* **Shelter, sanctuary,** and **refuge** mean a place of safety. **Shelter** is usually applied to an enclosed area that provides temporary cover or protection: *The city provides shelters for homeless people.* **Sanctuary** often denotes a structure or area that is set aside for a particular use and is considered inviolable or sacred: *The property is protected as a wildlife sanctuary.* **Refuge** denotes a place that provides an escape from danger or from a pursuer: *Many victims of political persecution have found refuge in the United States.*

shel·ter·belt (shel′tər belt′) *n.* a barrier of trees or shrubs that protects agricultural soils against erosion by winds and storms.

shelter tent, pup tent.

shel·tie (shel′tē) *also,* **shel·ty.** *n., pl.* **-ties. 1.** Shetland sheepdog. **2.** Shetland pony. [Probably from Old Norse *hjalti* inhabitant of the Shetland Islands.]

shelve[1] (shelv) *v.t.,* **shelved, shelv·ing. 1.** to place on a shelf: *to shelve books.* **2.** to put away or aside as done with or not needed: *to shelve a plan.* **3.** to remove from active service. **4.** to furnish with shelves. [From SHELVES.]

shelve[2] (shelv) *v.i.,* **shelved, shelv·ing.** to slope gradually. [Of uncertain origin.]

shelves (shelvz) the plural of **shelf.**

shelv·ing (shel′ving) *n.* **1.** material for shelves, such as wood or metal. **2.** shelves collectively.

Shem·ite (shem′īt) *n.* Semite.

she·nan·i·gan (shə nan′i gən) *usually,* **shenanigans.** *n. Informal.* nonsense or trickery. [Of uncertain origin.]

She·ol (shē′ōl) *n.* **1.** in the Old Testament, the abode of the spirits of the dead; underworld. **2.** *also,* **sheol.** hell. [Hebrew *she′ōl* the underworld.]

shep·herd (shep′ərd) *n.* **1.** a person who takes care of a flock of sheep. **2.** a spiritual leader; pastor. —*v.t.* **1.** to tend as a shepherd. **2.** to watch over or guide like a shepherd. *The teacher shepherded the children to the museum.* [Old English *scēaphyrde* one who herds sheep, from *scēap* sheep + *hyrde* herdsman.]

shepherd dog, sheepdog *(def. 2).*

shep·herd·ess (shep′ər dis) *n.* a woman or girl who takes care of a flock of sheep.

shepherd's pie, a casserole consisting of cubed meat cooked in gravy, with a top crust or ring of mashed potatoes.

shepherd's purse *also,* **shep·herd's-purse** (shep′ərdz pûrs′). a common weedy plant, *Capsella bursa-pastoris,* of the mustard family, having small triangular seed pods resembling purses or pouches.

Sher·a·ton (sher′ə tən) *adj.* in, of, or relating to a style of furniture characterized by simplicity of line, graceful, sweeping curves, and rich ornamentation, such as wood inlay. [From Thomas *Sheraton,* 1751-1806, English furniture designer.]

sher·bet (shûr′bit) *n.* **1.** a frozen dessert made of fruit juice, water, sweeteners, and small amounts of egg whites or milk. **2.** *British.* a beverage of sweetened fruit juice diluted with water. [Turkish and Persian *sherbet* drink made of sweetened fruit juice, from Arabic *sharbah* a drink.]

sherd (shûrd) shard.

she·rif (she rēf′) *n.* **1.** a descendant of Muhammad, founder of Islam, through his daughter and only child, Fatima. **2.** an Arab ruler, esp. the chief magistrate of Mecca or, formerly, the sovereign of Morocco. [Arabic *sharīf* noble.]

sher·iff (sher′if) *n.* the chief law enforcement officer of a county, who is in charge of keeping the peace, serving court orders, maintaining the jails, and other administrative functions. [Old English *scīrgerēfa* high officer representing the king in a shire, from *scīr* shire + *gerēfa* officer.]

Sher·lock Holmes (shûr′lok hōmz′) **1.** a fictional detective, noted for his remarkable powers of observation, analysis, and deduction, the main character in mystery stories by the British author Sir Arthur Conan Doyle. **2.** any remarkably shrewd, observant, or gifted detective.

Sher·pa (shûr′pə) *n., pl.* **-pa** or **-pas.** a member of a people of Tibetan origin living in the Himalaya Mountains of Nepal, best known as guides or porters for mountain-climbing expeditions.

sher·ry (sher′ē) *n., pl.* **-ries.** a strong wine of a kind that

originated in Spain, having a characteristic nutlike flavor and varying in color and taste from pale amber and somewhat dry to dark brown and quite sweet. [From earlier *sherris* (mistaken for a plural), a modification of *Xeres* (now *Jerez*), the town that is the center of the sherry-producing region of southern Spain.]

she's (shēz) *contr.* **1.** she is. **2.** she has.

Shet·land (shet′lənd) *n.* **1.** Shetland pony. **2.** Shetland wool.

Shetland pony, a small, hardy, rough-coated pony of a breed that originated in the Shetland Islands, having a long mane and tail. Height: 36-46 inches (91-117 centimeters) at the shoulder. Also, **sheltie.**

Shetland sheepdog, a thick-coated dog of a breed closely resembling the collie but approximately 10 inches (25 centimeters) shorter. Height: to 16 inches (41 centimeters) at the shoulder. Also, **sheltie.**

Shetland wool, a soft, lustrous wool obtained from the undercoats of

Shetland pony

sheep of a breed that originated in the Shetland Islands.

shew (shō) *Archaic. v.,* **shewed, shewn, shew·ing.** show. —*n.* show.

shew·bread (shō′bred′) *also,* **showbread.** *n.* in the ancient Jewish religion, unleavened bread placed near the altar by the priest on the Sabbath as an offering to God.

SHF, superhigh frequency.

Shi·a (shē′ə) *n.* the smaller of the two principal sects of Islam. The Shia sect considers Ali, Muhammad's son-in-law, as the true successor of Muhammad.

shib·bo·leth (shib′ə lith, -leth′) *n.* **1.** a catchword or slogan of a certain group or class of people or political party. **2.** any characteristic, such as of speech or usage, that distinguishes a group. [Hebrew *shibbōleth* stream. According to the story in Judges 12:6, this word was used to identify members of an enemy tribe, who were unable to pronounce the *sh,* saying *sibbōleth* instead.]

shied (shīd) the past tense and past participle of **shy**[2].

shield (shēld) *n.* **1.** a piece of defensive armor carried on the arm. **2.** a person or thing that serves as a defense against danger, injury, or distress. **3.** something shaped like a shield, such as a police officer's badge. **4.** escutcheon. **5.** a protective cover or barrier, such as the sheets of lead surrounding a nuclear reactor. **6.** a piece of some moisture-repellent fabric worn inside a garment, usually under the arms, as a protection from soiling by perspiration. —*v.t.* to give protection to; guard or defend: *The plastic glasses shielded the woodcutter's eyes.* —*v.i.* to act or serve as a shield. [Old English *sceld* the piece of armor.] —**shield′er,** *n.* —For Synonyms *(v.t.),* see **defend.**

shi·er (shī′ər) the comparative of **shy**[1].

shi·est (shī′ist) the superlative of **shy**[1].

shift (shift) *v.t.* **1.** to move or transfer from one person, place, or position to another: *to shift furniture around, to shift blame.* **2.** to replace with another or others; switch or change: *The candidate was constantly shifting his position on the issues.* **3.** to change (gears) from one arrangement to another, as in an automobile. —*v.i.* **1.** to move or change, as from one place or position to another: *She shifted in her chair to see better.* **2.** to change gears from one arrangement to another, as in driving an automobile. —*n.* **1.** a switch or change: *a shift in policy.* **2.** the act of moving or transferring, as from one place or position to another: *The shift in weight caused the rowboat to capsize.* **3.a.** a group of workers who alternate with another group or groups in carrying on some work or operation: *The day shift begins work at eight A.M.* **b.** the working time of such a group. **4.** a gearshift, esp. in an automobile. **5.** a loosely fitting dress designed to fall with straight lines from the shoulders to the hips. **6.** a scheme or trick for doing something or bringing something about. [Old English *sciftan* to divide, arrange.] —**shift′a·ble,** *adj.* —**shift′er,** *n.*

·to shift for oneself. to provide for one's own needs; get along

a	at	e	end	o	hot	u	up	hw	white		about
ā	ape	ē	me	ō	old	ū	use	ng	song		taken
ä	far	i	it	ô	fork	ü	rule	th	thin	ə	pencil
âr	care	ī	ice	oi	oil	u̇	pull	th̲	this		lemon
		îr	pierce	ou	out	ûr	turn	zh	measure		circus

by oneself: *As a stranger in the city, I soon learned to shift for myself.*

shift·less (shift'lis) *adj.* **1.** lacking in ambition; good-for-nothing; lazy. **2.** showing a lack of energy, efficiency, or resourcefulness. —**shift'less·ly,** *adv.* —**shift'less·ness,** *n.*

shift·y (shif'tē) *adj.,* **shift·i·er, shift·i·est. 1.** not to be trusted or believed; dishonest; tricky. **2.** showing slyness, trickery, or dishonesty: *shifty eyes.* **3.** capable of shifting for oneself; resourceful. —**shift'i·ly,** *adv.* —**shift'i·ness,** *n.*

Shi·ite (shē'īt) *n.* a follower of the Shia sect of Islam. —*adj.* of or relating to the Shia sect of Islam. [Arabic *shī 'ah* sect + -ITE[1].]

shill (shil) *Slang. n.* a person who acts as a decoy, as for a peddler or gambler, by pretending to buy or bet on something. —*v.i.* to act as a shill. [Of uncertain origin.]

shil·le·lagh (shə lā'lē, -lə) *also,* **shil·la·lah.** *n.* a cudgel, usually of oak or blackthorn. [From *Shillelagh,* village in Ireland noted for its oak trees and blackthorns.]

shil·ling (shil'ing) *n.* **1.** a coin of the United Kingdom equal to five pence or ¹/₂₀ of a pound, formerly equal to twelve pence. **2.** any of various coins used in several other countries, esp. those that were or are members of the Commonwealth of Nations. **3.** the monetary unit of Kenya, Somalia, Tanzania, and Uganda. [Old English *scilling* the British coin.]

shil·ly-shal·ly (shil'ē shal'ē) *v.i.,* **-lied, -ly·ing. 1.** to be undecided or hesitant. **2.** to waste time; dawdle. [Repetition, with modifications, of *shall I?*]

shim (shim) *n.* a thin, often wedge-shaped piece of metal or wood used to fill in a gap, as in a machine, or to align or secure adjoining sections in a construction. —*v.t.,* **shimmed, shimming.** to fit with a shim or shims. [Of uncertain origin.]

shim·mer (shim'ər) *v.i.* to shine with a faint, wavering light; glimmer. —*n.* a faint, wavering light; glimmer; gleam. [Old English *scimrian* to shine faintly.] —**shim'mer·y,** *adj.*

shim·my (shim'ē) *n., pl.* **-mies. 1.** an unusual shaking or vibration. **2.** a dance characterized by much shaking of the body, popular in the 1920s. **3.** *Informal.* chemise *(def. 1).* —*v.i.* **-mied, -my·ing. 1.** to shake; vibrate. **2.** to shake the body in or as in dancing the shimmy. [Modification of CHEMISE (mistaken for a plural).]

shin (shin) *n.* **1.** the front part of the lower leg, extending from the knee to the ankle. **2.** a corresponding part in certain animals and birds. —*v.t., v.i.,* **shinned, shin·ning.** to climb (something) by shinnying. [Old English *scinu* this part of the leg.]

shin·bone (shin'bōn') *n.* tibia *(def. 1).*

shin·dig (shin'dig') *n. Slang.* a festive or noisy social gathering, such as a dance or party. [Possibly SHIN + DIG.]

shine (shīn) *v., (v.i.)* **shone** or *(v.t.)* **shined, shin·ing.** —*v.i.* **1.** to give or send out light or brightness, as the sun. **2.** to be bright or gleam with reflected light; glow: *The newly waxed floor shone.* **3.** to be eminent or distinguished; excel: *to shine in one's profession.* **4.** to be clearly evident: *Happiness shone on the child's face.* —*v.t.* **1.** to put a gloss or polish on: *to shine shoes.* **2.** to cause to shine: *to shine a flashlight.* —*n.* **1.** light or brightness; radiance. **2.** luster or sheen, as of an object reflecting light. **3.** fair weather; sunshine: *Let's go on a hike, come rain or shine.* **4.** a polish given to shoes. **5.** trick; prank. ➡ usually used in the plural. [Old English *scīnan* to give out light, gleam, to excel.]

 ·**to shine up to.** *Informal.* to try to make oneself pleasing to or liked by.

 ·**to take a shine to.** *Informal.* to like very much, esp. on first meeting.

shin·er (shī'nər) *n.* **1.** a person or thing that shines. **2.a.** any of various small, silvery freshwater fish, genus *Notropis,* related to the minnow. **b.** any of various other silvery fish. **3.** *Informal.* black eye.

shin·gle[1] (shing'gəl) *n.* **1.** a thin piece of wood or other material applied to roofs and outside walls in overlapping rows. **2.** *Informal.* a small signboard, esp. that of a doctor or lawyer. **3.** a woman's close-cropped haircut. —*v.t.,* **-gled, -gling. 1.** to cover with shingles. **2.** to cut (the hair) very close. [Latin *scindula* split piece of wood.] —**shin'gler,** *n.*

shin·gle[2] (shing'gəl) *n.* loose, water-worn beach gravel composed of flattened pebbles and stones. [Of uncertain origin.]

shin·gles (shing'gəlz) *n.* a virus infection characterized by painful irritation of a group of nerves and the eruption of blisters. Also, **herpes zoster.** ➡ used as singular. [Medieval Latin *cingulus,* from Latin *cingulum* belt; because the eruption is often like a belt around the body.]

shin·ing (shī'ning) *adj.* **1.** sending out or reflecting light; bright. **2.** outstanding or distinguished: *a shining example of honesty.* —**shin'ing·ly,** *adv.*

shin·ny[1] (shin'ē) *v.i.,* **-nied, -ny·ing.** to climb by alternating the use of the hands or arms and the feet or legs in grasping or pulling (often with *up*): *to shinny up a tree.* [From SHIN.]

shin·ny[2] (shin'ē) *n.* a game resembling hockey, played with a curved stick and a ball or block of wood. [Possibly from *shin ye,* a cry used in the game.]

shin·plas·ter (shin'plas'tər) *n.* **1.** a medicated plaster applied to a sore leg. **2.** *Informal.* currency of little value.

shin·splints (shin'splints') *pl. n.* tiny rips in the muscles of the front of the lower leg, sometimes caused by persistent running or jumping on hard surfaces.

Shin·to (shin'tō) *n.* **1.** a religion native to Japan, emphasizing worship of nature, reverence of ancestors and ancient heroes, and, in some forms, the divinity of the emperor. **2.** an adherent of or believer in this religion. [Japanese *shintō* the religion, from Chinese (Mandarin) *shên tao* way of the gods.]

Shin·to·ism (shin'tō iz'əm) *n.* the Shinto religion. —**Shin'to·ist,** *n., adj.*

shin·y (shī'nē) *adj.,* **shin·i·er, shin·i·est. 1.** shining; bright. **2.** worn to a glossy smoothness. —**shin'i·ness,** *n.*

ship (ship) *n.* **1.a.** any large seagoing vessel. **b.** the crew of such a vessel. **2.** an airplane, airship, or spacecraft. **3.** formerly, a square-rigged sailing vessel having three or more masts and a bowsprit from which various jibs were rigged. —*v.,* **shipped, ship·ping.** —*v.t.* **1.** to send or transport, as by ship, air, rail, or truck. **2.** (of a boat or ship) to take in (water or some other substance, such as fuel) over the side. **3.** to engage for service on a ship. **4.** to put (an object) in its proper place for use on a boat or ship: *to ship a mast.* —*v.i.* **1.** to go on board a ship; embark. **2.** to depart on a ship, esp. as a member of the crew (often with *out*): *to ship out as a deckhand.* **3.** (of certain perishable foods) to withstand shipment: *Some fruit doesn't ship well.* [Old English *scip* large seagoing vessel.]

 ·**when one's ship comes home** (or **in**). when (or if) one's fortune is made.

-ship *suffix* (used to form nouns) **1.** the quality, state, or condition of being: *relationship, friendship.* **2.** the office, status, or rank of: *ambassadorship.* **3.** the art or skill of being: *horsemanship.* [Old English *-scipe,* suffix denoting state or condition.]

ship biscuit, hardtack.

ship·board (ship'bôrd') *adj.* happening on board a ship: *a shipboard romance.*

 ·**on shipboard.** aboard a ship.

ship·build·er (ship'bil'dər) *n.* a person who builds or designs ships.

ship·build·ing (ship'bil'ding) *n.* **1.** the act of building ships. **2.** the art or business of building ships.

ship canal, a canal wide and deep enough to allow the passage of ships.

ship·load (ship'lōd') *n.* all that a ship can hold or carry.

ship·man (ship'mən) *n., pl.* **-men** (-mən). *Archaic.* **1.** a sailor. **2.** the master of a ship.

ship·mas·ter (ship'mas'tər) *n.* the person in command of a ship other than a military ship.

ship·mate (ship'māt') *n.* a fellow sailor on the same ship.

ship·ment (ship'mənt) *n.* **1.** the act of shipping goods. **2.** something that is shipped. **3.** an amount shipped.

ship money, an English tax, abolished in 1640, that required coastal towns to provide ships, or money for ships.

ship of the line, formerly, a warship large enough to take a position in the line of battle.

ship·own·er (ship'ō'nər) *n.* the owner of a ship or ships.

ship·per (ship'ər) *n.* a person or company that ships goods.

ship·ping (ship'ing) *n.* **1.** the act or business of sending or transporting goods, as by ship. **2.** ships collectively, esp. those belonging to a particular port, country, or company. **3.** the total tonnage of such ships.

shipping clerk, a person whose job is the shipping and receiving of goods.

shipping room, a room or area in a business establishment from which goods are shipped.

ship·rigged (ship'rigd') *adj.* having three or more square-rigged masts; full-rigged.

ship·shape (ship'shāp') *adj.* in good or proper order; neat. —*adv.* in a shipshape manner.

ship·worm (ship'wûrm') *n.* any of a group of wormlike marine mollusks, genus *Teredo,* having long, slender bodies and two limy shells. Shipworms cause damage by burrowing into wharves, ship bottoms, or other waterlogged wood. Also, **teredo.**

ship·wreck (ship'rek') *n.* **1.** the destruction or loss of a ship. **2.** the remains of a wrecked ship; wreckage. **3.** a total failure, destruction, or loss. —*v.t.* **1.** to cause (a ship or its passengers) to

S

undergo shipwreck. **2.** to ruin; destroy. —*v.i.* to suffer shipwreck: *The tanker shipwrecked off the coast of England.*

ship·wright (ship′rīt′) *n.* a person, esp. a carpenter, whose work is building or repairing ships.

ship·yard (ship′yärd′) *n.* a place containing docks, workshops, and warehouses where ships can be built, equipped, and repaired.

shire (shīr) *n.* in Great Britain, a county. [Old English *scīr.*]

shirk (shûrk) *v.t.* to avoid or neglect doing (something that should be done): *to shirk one's duties.* —*v.i.* to avoid or neglect doing something that should be done. [Possibly from German *Schurke* rogue.] —**shirk′er,** *n.*

shirr (shûr) *v.t.* **1.** to gather (fabric) by means of a series of parallel threads. **2.** to bake (eggs) in a shallow dish with butter. [Of uncertain origin.]

shirr·ing (shûr′ing) *n.* a shirred arrangement of fabric.

shirt (shûrt) *n.* **1.** any of various garments for the upper part of the body, esp. one having a collar, sleeves, and buttons down the front. **2.** undershirt. [Old English *scyrte* tunic, short garment.]
   • **to give (someone) the shirt off one's back.** to give (someone) everything one owns or possesses.
   • **to keep one's shirt on.** *Slang.* to remain calm or patient.
   • **to lose one's shirt.** *Slang.* to lose everything one owns or possesses.

shirt·ing (shûr′ting) *n.* fabric used for making shirts or blouses.

shirt·sleeve (shûrt′slēv′) *n.* the sleeve of a shirt.
   • **in one's shirtsleeves.** without a coat or jacket over one's shirt.

shirt·tail (shûrt′tāl′) *n.* the part of a shirt extending below the waist, esp. in the back.

shirt·waist (shûrt′wāst′) *n.* **1.** a tailored dress having a bodice that resembles a shirt. Also, **shirtwaist dress. 2.** a tailored blouse.

shish ke·bab (shish′kə bob′) *also,* **shish ka·bob, shish ke·bob.** a dish consisting of cubes of meat, such as lamb or beef, and usually vegetables, such as onions, tomatoes, or green peppers, threaded on skewers and broiled. [Of Turkish origin.]

Shi·va (shē′və) *n.* the Hindu god who personifies the destructive forces of the universe and, with Brahma and Vishnu, forms the Hindu trinity. Also, **Siva.** [Hindu *Shiva,* from Sanskrit *Shiva* literally, the auspicious (one).]

shiv·a·ree (shiv′ə rē′, shiv′ə rē′) *n.* a mock serenade, as for a newly married couple, made by beating on kettles or other household utensils or by playing musical instruments out of tune. Also, **charivari, chivaree.** [Earlier *charivari,* from French *charivari,* from Late Latin *caribaria* headache, from Greek *karēbaria,* from *kara* head + *barys* heavy; referring to the effect of such a serenade on the head.]

shiv·er[1] (shiv′ər) *v.i.* to shake, as with cold or fear; tremble. —*n.* **1.** the act of shivering. **2.** a shivering sensation: *The tale of horror sent shivers up my spine.* [Of uncertain origin.]

shiv·er[2] (shiv′ər) *v.t., v.i.* to break into fragments or splinters; shatter. —*n.* a small broken bit; fragment: *a shiver of glass.* [Of uncertain origin.]

shiv·er·y (shiv′ə rē) *adj.* **1.** shivering, as from cold or fear; trembling. **2.** causing shivers: *a shivery ghost story.* **3.** inclined to shiver, as from cold.

shle·miel (shlə mēl′) schlemiel.

shoal[1] (shōl) *n.* **1.** a sandbank or sandbar visible at low tide. **2.** any area, as in a river or the ocean, where the water is shallow. —*v.i.* to become shallow: *The lake shoals near the shore.* —*v.t.* to make shallow. —*adj.* of little depth; shallow: *shoal water.* [Old English *sceald* shallow.]

shoal[2] (shōl) *n.* a school of fish. —*v.i.* (of fish) to collect in a shoal. [Old English *scolu* crowd, multitude.]

shoal·y (shō′lē) *adj.,* **shoal·i·er, shoal·i·est.** full of shoals or shallows.

shoat (shōt) *also,* **shote.** *n.* a young pig that has been weaned. [Of uncertain origin.]

shock[1] (shok) *n.* **1.a.** a sudden, violent disturbance of the mind or emotions: *the shock caused by a friend's death.* **b.** the cause of this: *The news was a shock to us.* **2.** a physical sensation, sometimes accompanied by muscular convulsions, produced by the passage of an electric current through the body. **3.** a sudden, violent shake, blow, or impact, as of an explosion or earthquake. **4.** a serious, abnormal physical state in which vital body functions, such as circulation and respiration, are severely depressed as a result of injury, blood loss, burn, or major surgery. It is characterized by a weak pulse, below normal body temperature, shallow breathing, and a great drop in blood pressure. —*v.t.* **1.** to disturb the mind or emotions of, as by surprising, horrifying, or disgusting. **2.** to give an electric shock to. **3.** to cause a physical shock

to. [French *choc* collision, clash, from Old French *choquer* to strike against, clash; probably of Germanic origin.] —**shock′er,** *n.*

shock[2] (shok) *n.* a bundle, as of wheat or corn, set upright in a field. —*v.t.* to gather into a shock or shocks. [Possibly from Middle Dutch *schocke* heap, shock of grain.]

shock[3] (shok) *n.* a thick, bushy mass, as of hair. [Possibly from SHOCK[2] (from its resemblance to a shock of wheat).]

shock absorber, any of various devices, as in automobiles, airplanes, or machines, that reduce the jarring or shaking effect of sudden impacts or bumps.

shock·ing (shok′ing) *adj.* **1.** causing offense, as to taste or decorum; revolting: *a shocking display of vulgarity.* **2.** causing horror or surprise: *shocking news.* —**shock′ing·ly,** *adv.*

shock·proof (shok′prüf′) *adj.* protected against damage from a sudden, violent blow or impact: *The watch is shockproof.* —*v.t.* to provide with protection against damage from a sudden, violent blow or impact.

shock therapy, a form of psychotherapy in which convulsions or coma are produced by electric current or chemicals, used esp. with severely depressed or psychotic patients. Also, **shock treatment.**

shock troops, troops specially chosen and trained to make sudden devastating or paralyzing attacks, esp. in leading a larger attack or invasion.

shock wave 1. a disturbance of the atmosphere created by a body, such as an airplane or rocket, traveling at supersonic speed, causing an abrupt increase in the pressure, density, and temperature of the air ahead of it. **2.** a similar disturbance caused by an explosion.

shod (shod) the past tense and past participle of **shoe.**

shod·dy (shod′ē) *adj.,* **-di·er, -di·est. 1.** inferior, as in quality; poorly made or done: *a shoddy piece of work.* **2.** lacking attentiveness and courtesy: *We resented the hotel's shoddy treatment of us.* **3.** worn out; shabby; seedy: *The old carpet looks pretty shoddy.* **4.** made or consisting of wool fibers reclaimed from woolen waste or other remnants: *shoddy cloth.* **5.** made of shoddy cloth. —*n., pl.* **-dies. 1.** wool fibers reclaimed from woolen waste or other remnants. **2.** cloth made of such fibers. [Of uncertain origin.] —**shod′di·ly,** *adv.* —**shod′di·ness,** *n.*

shoe (shü) *n.* **1.** any of various outer coverings, usually of leather, that serve to protect and support the human foot. **2.** something resembling a shoe in shape, position, or function. **3.** horseshoe. **4.** a protective metal covering, as on the end of a shaft or post. **5.** a curved metal piece in a brake that presses against the wheel, creating the friction that slows or stops the wheel. **6.** the outer casing of an automobile tire. **7.** a sliding contact plate by which an electric car receives current from the third rail. —*v.t.,* **shod, shoe·ing. 1.** to provide with a shoe or shoes. **2.** to provide or protect the end or edge of something with a metal covering. [Old English *scōh* the outer covering for the foot.]
   • **in another's shoes.** in another person's position or place.
   • **the shoe is on the other foot.** the situation is completely reversed: *I was winning, but now the shoe is on the other foot.*
   • **to fill someone's shoes.** to take another person's place and assume his or her responsibilities.

shoe·horn (shü′hôrn′) *n.* a curved device inserted at the back of a shoe to aid the foot in slipping into the shoe. —*v.t.* to force or fit into a small space.

shoe·lace (shü′lās′) *n.* a cord, usually of cloth or leather, for fastening a shoe.

shoe·mak·er (shü′mā′kər) *n.* a person who makes or repairs shoes and other footwear. —**shoe′mak′ing,** *n.*

shoe·shine (shü′shīn′) *n.* **1.** the act of cleaning and polishing a pair of shoes. **2.** the shine resulting from this.

shoe·string (shü′string′) *n.* **1.** shoelace. **2.** a very small amount of money or other resources: *The young artist was living on a shoestring.* —*adj.* at or near the shoestrings or ankles: *to make a shoestring catch of a baseball.*

shoe tree, a device inserted in a shoe to maintain its shape when it is not being worn.

sho·far (shō′fär, -fər) *n.* a ram's horn blown like a trumpet in various Jewish religious services, esp. during Rosh Hashanah and Yom Kippur. [Hebrew *shōphār* this horn.]

a	at	e	end	o	hot	u	up	hw	white		about
ā	ape	ē	me	ō	old	ū	use	ng	song		taken
ä	far	i	it	ô	fork	ü	rule	th	thin	ə	pencil
âr	care	ī	ice	oi	oil	u̇	pull	th	this		lemon
		îr	pierce	ou	out	ûr	turn	zh	measure		circus

a **shogun** in an 18th-century painting

sho·gun (shō′gən, -gun′) *n.* any of the hereditary administrative and political rulers of Japan from 1192 to 1867. [Japanese *shōgun* general (short for *Sei-i-tai-Shogun* literally, great general who subdues barbarians), from Chinese (Mandarin) *chiang chün* general.]

sho·gun·ate (shō′gə nit, -nāt′) *n.* the government or rule of a shogun.

sho·ji (shō′jē) *n., pl.* -**ji** or -**jis.** a screen or partition covered with rice paper or some other translucent material, used esp. in Japanese homes. Also, **shoji screen.** [Japanese *shōji;* of Chinese origin.]

shone (shōn) a past tense and past participle of **shine.**

shoo (shü) *interj.* an exclamation used to frighten or drive away a person or animal. —*v.,* **shooed, shoo·ing.** —*v.t.* to frighten or drive away by or as by crying or calling "shoo." —*v.i.* to cry or call "shoo."

shoo-in (shü′in′) *n. Informal.* a person or thing that seems certain to win something, such as a race or election.

shook (shůk) the past tense of **shake.**

shoot (shüt) *v.,* **shot, shoot·ing.** —*v.t.* **1.** to wound or kill (a person or animal) with a bullet, arrow, or other missile discharged from a weapon. **2.a.** to propel or discharge (a missile) from a weapon, such as a gun or bow. **b.** to make or remove in this way: *to shoot holes in a bucket.* **3.** to cause to discharge or explode (often with *off*): *to shoot a gun, to shoot off fireworks.* **4.** to send forth or direct rapidly or suddenly: *I shot a nasty look at them. The fire shot sparks at our feet.* **5.** to pass rapidly down, through, or over: *to shoot the rapids of a river.* **6.a.** to propel (a ball, puck, or other object) toward an objective, such as a goal. **b.** to score, as points or a goal, in this way. **7.** to measure the altitude of (a heavenly body), as with a sextant: *to shoot the sun.* **8.a.** to film (something) for television or a motion picture. **b.** to take a photograph of. **9.** to variegate, esp. with streaks of color. **10.** to empty out or discharge down or as down a chute; dump. **11.** to slide (a door bolt or similar device) into or out of a fastening. **12.** to play, as pool or craps. —*v.i.* **1.** to propel or discharge a bullet, arrow, or other missile from a weapon: *Don't shoot until the target shows.* **2.** (of a weapon) to propel a missile, such as a bullet or arrow, in a certain way: *This rifle shoots high.* **3.** to go or move suddenly or rapidly; dart: *My feet shot out from under me. A fish shot from under the edge of the rock.* **4.** to propel a ball, puck, or other object toward a goal or in a certain manner. **5.** to extend in a particular direction; project. **6.** to film something for television or a motion picture. **7.** to take a picture; photograph. —*n.* **1.** a new or young growth, as from a bud; sprout. **2.** that part of a plant that bears leaves and buds. **3.** a trip, expedition, or contest for shooting. **4.** chute. **5.** *Informal.* an occasion at which photographs or a film are made: *The crew is on a shoot in Florida.* [Old English *scēotan* to dart, rush, send forth, let fly.] —**shoot′er,** *n.*

· **to shoot at** (or **for**). *Informal.* to try to attain; strive for.

· **to shoot down. a.** to knock or bring down by hitting with a shot or shots: *to shoot down an enemy plane.* **b.** *Informal.* to reject (a person, idea, or proposal).

· **to shoot up. a.** to grow or rise suddenly or rapidly. **b.** *Informal.* to injure, damage, or harass by shooting or by letting off firearms in: *The outlaws shot up the town.* **c.** *Slang.* to inject a drug.

shooting gallery, a room or structure, such as an enclosed booth, for shooting at targets.

shooting star 1. meteor. **2.** any of a group of North American

plants, genus *Dodecatheon,* of the primrose family, having showy pink, purplish, or white flowers.

shoot·out (shüt′out′) *also,* **shoot-out.** *n.* a battle between two people or groups armed with handguns, rifles, or other firearms.

shop (shop) *n.* **1.** a small retail store: *a dress shop, a pet shop.* **2.** a department in a large store that specializes in a particular type of merchandise: *a kitchen shop.* **3.** a place where a specified type of work is done or where a specified service is provided: *a beauty shop.* **4.** a place where things are produced or repaired: *The TV is in the shop.* **5.a.** a specially equipped schoolroom where skills in working with wood, metal, and other materials are taught. **b.** a course of study in these skills: *Are you taking shop?* —*v.,* **shopped, shop·ping.** —*v.i.* **1.** to visit stores to look at, price, or purchase merchandise. **2.** to look; search (often with *for* or *around*): *We're shopping around for an apartment.* —*v.t.* to visit (a particular store) to look at, price, or purchase merchandise. [Old English *sceoppa* stall[1], booth.]

· **to close** (or **shut up**) **shop.** to stop work.

· **to set up shop.** to begin work or start a business.

· **to talk shop.** to talk about matters relating to one's work.

shop·keep·er (shop′kē′pər) *n.* a person who owns or operates a shop.

shop·lift (shop′lift′) *v.t., v.i.* to steal (merchandise) from a store while pretending to be a customer. —**shop′lift′ing,** *n.*

shop·lift·er (shop′lif′tər) *n.* a person who steals merchandise from a store while pretending to be a customer.

shoppe (shop) *n.* shop *(defs. 1, 2).*

shop·per (shop′ər) *n.* **1.** a person who visits stores to look at, price, or purchase merchandise; customer. **2.** comparison shopper.

shopping bag, a bag used to carry purchases, esp. a strong bag with handles.

shop·ping-bag lady (shop′ing bag′) bag lady.

shopping center, a complex of buildings, esp. in the suburbs, that houses various kinds of stores, shops, and other facilities.

shopping mall, mall *(def. 3).*

shop steward, a worker in a factory or other business establishment who has been elected by a union to represent its members in dealing with management and to enforce union rules.

shop·talk (shop′tôk′) *n.* **1.** discussion of matters relating to one's work, esp. after working hours. **2.** the jargon of an occupation.

shop·worn (shop′wôrn′) *adj.* **1.** soiled, frayed, or otherwise defective as a result of having been displayed or handled in a store. **2.** worn out, as from overuse; no longer fresh or new: *a shopworn phrase.*

shor·an (shôr′an) *n.* a short-range navigation system using radar that enables a ship or airplane to determine its position relative to two ground stations of known location. [Short for *sho(rt) ra(nge) n(avigation).*]

shore[1] (shôr) *n.* **1.** the land along the edge of a body of water, such as an ocean or lake. **2.** land, as opposed to a body of water: *The sailors are stationed on shore.* **3.** *also,* **shores.** a country: *one's native shore.* **4.** *Law.* the land lying between the usual high-water and low-water marks in a tidal area. [Middle Dutch *schōre* coast, strand, beach.]

Synonyms **Shore**[1] and **coast** denote land next to or surrounding a large body of water. **Shore** generally connotes the land right beside the water and may be used in reference to water other than a sea: *the shores of a lake, the shores of the Mississippi, the Pacific shore.* **Coast** may be used to describe land farther back from the *shore,* but is applied only to seas or oceans: *the Atlantic coast of the United States, to live on the coast about two miles from the water.*

shore[2] (shôr) *v.t.,* **shored, shor·ing.** to support with or as with a timber or beam (often with *up*). —*n.* a prop, esp. a timber or beam, placed against the side of a structure as a temporary support. [Middle Dutch *schoor* prop.]

shore[3] (shôr) *Archaic.* a past tense of **shear.**

shore·bird (shôr′bûrd′) *n.* any of various birds that frequent shores and riverbanks, such as plovers, sandpipers, and gulls.

shore dinner, a meal consisting of several different types of seafood.

shore leave, leave to go ashore granted to a crew on board a ship.

shore·line (shôr′līn′) *n.* the outline or contour of a shore.

Shore Patrol, a detail of the U.S. Navy, Coast Guard, or Marine Corps, assigned to military police duties on shore.

shore[2]

shore·ward (shôr′wərd) *adv., adj.* toward the shore.
shor·ing (shôr′ing) *n.* **1.** the act of supporting with or as with shores. **2.** a system of shores used as a support.
shorn (shôrn) a past participle of **shear.**
short (shôrt) *adj.* **1.** having little linear extension; not long: *short hair, a short jacket.* **2.** having relatively little height; not tall: *I'm short compared to those basketball players.* **3.** not long in time; of brief duration: *You will have a short wait. We took a short trip to the mountains.* **4.** using few words; concise; brief: *Give a short explanation of what is to be done.* **5.** having an insufficient amount or supply of; lacking (often with *of* or *on*): *We were short of funds. My laundry was short a pair of socks.* **6.** inadequate in amount or quantity: *We had a short supply of towels.* **7.** rudely brief or abrupt: *an unfriendly, short response.* **8.** not reaching far back: *to have a short memory, the short history of a town.* **9.** (of dough or pastry) rich and flaky due to the addition of shortening. **10.** (of vowels) relatively brief in duration, as the *i* in *bit.* **11.** *Finance.* **a.** not owning the securities or commodities one is selling. The short seller borrows the securities through a broker and contracts to repurchase and return them at a later date. **b.** of or relating to the sale of securities or commodities that the seller does not own at the time of sale. —*adv.* **1.** without warning; abruptly; suddenly: *We almost hit the car ahead of us when it stopped short.* **2.** not quite up to; on the near side of: *The ball stopped short of the goal line.* **3.** curtly; rudely. —*n.* **1.** something short. **2.** short circuit. **3.** short subject. **4. shorts. a.** short pants that extend to the knee or above. **b.** men's underpants. **5.** *Baseball.* shortstop. —*v.t.* to make a short circuit in. —*v.i.* to have a short circuit. [Old English *sceort* having little linear extension, brief.] —**short′ness,** *n.* —For Synonyms *(adj.),* see **abrupt.**
  · **for short.** by way of abbreviation: *The United States is called the U.S. for short.*
  · **in short.** in summary; briefly.
  · **short for.** an abbreviation of or shortened form for: *"Plane" is short for "airplane."*
  · **short of.** less than: *Nothing short of a disaster will prevent our accomplishing this.*
  · **to fall short.** to be or prove deficient; give out: *The water supply fell short during the drought.*
  · **to fall short of.** to fail to meet (a goal, requirement, or standard): *Contributions fell short of expectations.*
  · **to sell short. a.** to sell securities or commodities without owning them at the time of their sale. **b.** to underestimate the ability, determination, power, or chances of success of (someone or something).
short·age (shôr′tij) *n.* **1.** too small an amount or supply; deficiency in quantity; lack: *a shortage of funds.* **2.** the amount by which anything is deficient: *a shortage of twenty dollars.*
short·bread (shôrt′bred′) *n.* a crumbly, rich cake or cookie made of flour, sugar, and shortening.
short·cake (shôrt′kāk′) *n.* a dessert consisting of a rich biscuit or cake covered or filled with fruit, such as strawberries, and usually topped with whipped cream.
short·change (shôrt′chānj′) *v.t.,* **-changed, -chang·ing.** *Informal.* **1.** to give less than the proper change to. **2.** to deprive of something, as if to cheat: *to shortchange children of proper education.* —**short′chang′er,** *n.*
short·cir·cuit (shôrt′sûr′kit) *v.t.* to bring about a short circuit in. —*v.i.* to be affected with a short circuit.
short circuit, an electric circuit, usually formed accidentally, that has abnormally low resistance, resulting in an excessive flow of current that may blow a fuse or cause a fire. Also, **short.**
short·com·ing (shôrt′kum′ing) *n.* a failure to come up to some standard or expectation; deficiency; fault.
short·cut (shôrt′kut′) also, **short cut.** *n.* **1.** a way that is shorter than the ordinary way. **2.** any way or means that saves time or effort.
short division, a method of dividing one number by another, in which each step of the division is performed without writing out the remainders.
short·en (shôr′tən) *v.t.* **1.** to make short or shorter. **2.** to make rich or flaky by adding shortening. **3.** *Nautical.* reef² *(def. 1).* —*v.i.* to become short or shorter. —**short′en·er,** *n.*
short·en·ing (shôr′tə ning, shôrt′ning) *n.* **1.** any of various fats, such as butter, lard, or solidified vegetable oils, used in cooking. **2.** the act of making or becoming short or shorter.
short·fall (shôrt′fôl′) *n.* **1.** a failure to reach an amount that is needed or wanted; a falling short: *a shortfall in a grain harvest.* **2.** the amount by which something falls short; deficit; shortage: *a fifty-dollar shortfall in a budget.*
short·hand (shôrt′hand′) *n.* **1.** a method of rapid handwriting in which the words are replaced by symbols, characters, or letters,

➡ opposed to **longhand. 2.** writing done using such a method. —*adj.* **1.** using shorthand. **2.** written in shorthand.
short-hand·ed (shôrt′han′did) *adj.* lacking the necessary or usual number of workers, team members, or assistants.
short·horn (shôrt′hôrn′) *n.* one of a breed of beef cattle with short horns, originally bred in northern England. Weight: to 2,500 pounds (1,134 kilograms).
short·ish (shôr′tish) *adj.* somewhat short.
short·lived (shôrt′līvd′, -livd′) *adj.* living or lasting only a short time.
short·ly (shôrt′lē) *adv.* **1.** in a short time; presently; soon. **2.** in a few words; briefly. **3.** in a short manner; abruptly; curtly; sharply. —For Synonyms, see **soon.**
short-or·der (shôrt′ôr′dər) *adj.* relating to or specializing in food that is cooked quickly to order: *a short-order restaurant, a short-order cook.*
short order, an order of food requiring a short time to prepare, usually served at a lunch counter or diner.
short-range (shôrt′rānj′) *adj.* **1.** not reaching far into the future: *short-range plans.* **2.** capable of traveling or covering only a relatively short distance: *short-range guns.*
short rib, a cut of beef consisting of the ends of the ribs.
short shrift 1. abrupt treatment, as of a person, showing little interest, concern, or mercy: *The tourists gave short shrift to the beggar.* **2.** confession and absolution given in a short period of time, as to a condemned person before execution.
  · **to make short shrift of.** to take care of quickly.
short·sight·ed (shôrt′sī′tid) *adj.* **1.** not having or showing foresight: *a shortsighted plan.* **2.** nearsighted; myopic. —**short′sight′ed·ly,** *adv.* —**short′sight′ed·ness,** *n.*
short·stop (shôrt′stop′) *n.* *Baseball.* **1.** the infield position between second and third base. **2.** a player playing this position.
short story, a fictional prose work with a single theme, full plot, limited number of characters, and shorter length than a novel.
short subject, a short film, as a documentary or cartoon, usually shown with a main feature. Also, **short.**
short-tem·pered (shôrt′tem′pərd) *adj.* easily or quickly angered; quick-tempered; irascible.
short-term (shôrt′tûrm′) *adj.* **1.** planned for or involving a short period of time. **2.** requiring repayment within a short period of time, as a loan.
short ton, ton *(def. 1a).*
short·wave (shôrt′wāv′) *n.* a radio wave with a wavelength of 60 meters or less.
short-wind·ed (shôrt′win′did) *adj.* **1.** suffering from shortness of breath. **2.** concise or brief: *a short-winded speech.*
Sho·sho·ne (shə shō′nē) also, **Shoshoni.** *n., pl.* **-ne** or **-nes. 1.** a member of a tribe of North American Indians living in Idaho, Montana, Nevada, Oregon, Wyoming, and Utah. **2.** the language of this tribe, belonging to the Shoshonean group of the Uto-Aztecan language family.
Sho·sho·ne·an (shə shō′nē ən, shō-) *adj.* of or relating to a group of North American Indian languages of the Uto-Aztecan language family.
Sho·sho·ni (shə shō′nē, shō-) *n., pl.* **-ni** or **-nis.** Shoshone.
shot¹ (shot) *n., pl.* **shots** or *(def. 5)* **shot. 1.** a discharge of a firearm or other weapon: *We heard two shots.* **2.** an attempt to hit something with a firearm or similar weapon: *The second shot missed.* **3.** the act of shooting: *A noise interrupted my second shot.* **4.** a person who shoots: *to be a good shot.* **5.a.** a tiny pellet of lead or steel, a quantity of which are contained in a cartridge and discharged by a shotgun. **b.** such pellets collectively. **6.** a single ball of lead used as ammunition for a gun or cannon. **7.** the launching of a rocket or missile toward a particular target: *a moon shot.* **8.** an injection given with a needle or syringe; hypodermic. **9.** the distance over which something, such as a missile or sound, can travel; reach; range: *We are out of cannon shot.* **10.** a throw, kick, or stroke, esp. in a game: *to take a practice shot at the basket.* **11.** an attempt or guess. **12.a.** a photograph. **b.** the act or process of taking a photograph. **c.** a single piece of motion-picture film or videotape recording a continuous action, taken by one camera from one angle. **13.** *Sports.* the heavy metal ball used in the shot put. **14.** a blast, as in mining. **15.** *Informal.* a small amount of liquor, often consumed in one gulp. [Old English *sceot* a shooting, missile, rapid movement, contribution.]
  · **a shot in the arm.** something that gives help or encouragement: *The new contract is a shot in the arm for the company.*

a	at	e	end	o	hot	u	up	hw	white		about
ā	ape	ē	me	ō	old	ū	use	ng	song	ə	taken
ä	far	i	it	ô	fork	ü	rule	th	thin		pencil
âr	care	ī	ice	oi	oil	u̇	pull	th	this		lemon
		îr	pierce	ou	out	ûr	turn	zh	measure		circus

• **a shot in the dark.** a guess with no information behind it; wild guess.

• **like a shot.** very quickly: *The bird flew out of the bush like a shot.*

• **to call the shots.** to be in control or giving the orders.

• **to take** (or **have**) **a shot at.** to make an attempt; try: *I'll take a shot at answering the question.*

shot² (shot) *v.* the past tense and past participle of **shoot.** —*adj.* **1.** streaked, mixed, or woven so as to have variegated color: *a scarf of red silk shot with blue.* **2.** *Informal.* completely worn-out or ruined: *These shoes are shot.* **3.** having a particular element or note throughout (often with *through*): *a story shot through with irony.*

shote (shōt) *n.* shoat.

shot·gun (shot'gun') *n.* a smoothbore gun designed to fire cartridges that release a quantity of shot when discharged. —*adj.* scattered or spread widely, like shot from a shotgun: *a shotgun pattern of houses on a landscape.*

shot put (pút) *n.* a field event in which a shot is thrown for distance. —**shot'-put'ter,** *n.* —**shot'-put'ting,** *n.*

should (shùd) *auxiliary verb* a past tense of **shall. 1.** used to express an obligation or duty: *You should write a note thanking your host.* **2.** used to express the future from a point of view in the past: *I should have come if you had invited me.* **3.** used to express a condition: *If anyone should call, say I'll be back soon.* **4.** used to express probability or expectation: *They should be here soon.* **5.** used to express advice: *You should bandage that cut.* **6.** used to lessen the bluntness or directness of a statement: *I should not do that if I were you.* —For Synonyms, see **must¹.**

Usage Traditionally, **should** was used with the first person to express the future from a point of view in the past or to lessen the bluntness or directness of a statement: *We knew that we should encounter obstacles to our plan. I should imagine that you are disappointed.* In current American usage, however, **would** is much more commonly used in these senses. **Should** is common in British English.

shoul·der (shōl'dər) *n.* **1.** the part on either side of the body extending from the base of the neck to the upper arm or forelimb. **2. shoulders.** both shoulders and the part of the back connecting them. **3.** the portion of a garment covering the shoulders. **4.** the upper front leg and attached parts of an animal, cut as meat. **5.** the edge or border on either side of a road or highway. **6.** any projecting part or slope: *the shoulder of a hill.* **7.** *Printing.* the flat upper surface on a type body that extends beyond the base of the letter. —*v.t.* **1.** to force by pushing with the shoulder or shoulders: *to shoulder one's way through a crowd.* **2.** to take upon oneself, as a burden; assume: *to shoulder the blame for a mistake, to shoulder responsibility.* **3.** to place on and support or carry with the shoulder or shoulders. —*v.i.* to push forward or force one's way with the shoulder or shoulders. [Old English *sculder* the part of the body.]

• **shoulder to shoulder.** working or taking a position together: *to stand shoulder to shoulder on an issue.*

• **straight from the shoulder.** without evasion or deceit; honestly; frankly.

• **to put one's shoulder to the wheel.** to start work on something and exert great effort.

• **to rub shoulders with.** to mix with, as at work or in a social setting: *to rub shoulders with all kinds of people.*

• **to shoulder arms.** to bring a rifle to an upright position with the barrel resting against the shoulder and the butt resting in the hand on the same side.

shoulder blade, either of two flat, triangular bones in the upper part of the back. Also, **scapula.**

shoulder knot, an ornamental knot of ribbon or lace worn on the shoulder.

shoulder patch, a cloth insignia indicating one's branch or unit in the armed forces or some other organization, worn on the upper part of the sleeve of a uniform.

shoulder strap 1. a strap worn over the shoulder to support a garment or an accessory item, such as a purse, bag, or the like. **2.** an ornamental cloth strip fastened on each shoulder of a commissioned or warrant officer's uniform, often holding a metallic insignia to indicate rank.

Shoulder blade (back view)

Vertebrae

should·n't (shùd'ənt) *contr.* should not.

shouldst (shùdst) *also,* **should·est** (shùd'ist). *Archaic.* a second person singular past tense of **shall.** ➡ used with *thou.*

shout (shout) *n.* a loud cry made to express emotion or attract attention. —*v.i.* to cry out loudly; yell. —*v.t.* to utter with a shout; express by a shout: *to shout someone's name.* [Of uncertain origin.] —**shout'er,** *n.*

• **to shout down.** to silence or drown out by shouting: *The crowd shouted the speaker down.*

shove (shuv) *v.,* **shoved, shov·ing.** —*v.t.* **1.** to move along by the application of strength from behind; push: *Shove the chair closer to the table.* **2.** to push or press roughly: *The two children shoved each other in the hallway.* —*v.i.* to push or press roughly. —*n.* a strong push. [Old English *scūfan* to thrust, push.] —**shov'er,** *n.*

• **to shove off. a.** to push a boat away from the shore. **b.** *Informal.* to leave.

shov·el (shuv'əl) *n.* **1.** a tool consisting of a broad blade attached to a long handle, used for taking up and moving loose material, such as soil, snow, or gravel. **2.** any large, power-driven machine for taking up and moving loose material. **3.** shovelful. —*v.,* **-eled, -el·ing;** *also, British,* **-elled, -el·ling.** —*v.t.* **1.** to take up and move with a shovel: *to shovel snow.* **2.** to dig or clear with a shovel, as a path. **3.** to move or throw in large quantities as if with a shovel: *to shovel food into one's mouth.* —*v.i.* to use a shovel. [Old English *scofl* spadelike tool.]

shov·el·er (shuv'ə lər) *also, British,* **shov·el·ler.** *n.* **1.** a person or thing that shovels. **2.** any of several freshwater ducks, esp. *Spatula clypeata,* having a broad, flat bill; spoonbill.

shov·el·ful (shuv'əl fúl') *n., pl.* **-fuls.** the quantity that a shovel can hold.

show (shō) *v.,* **showed, shown** or **showed, show·ing.** —*v.t.* **1.** to expose to view; display: *Please show your tickets at the door.* **2.** to bring to public view; present; exhibit: *The theater showed the movie last week. The gallery is showing new paintings.* **3.** to make known or manifest, esp. by one's behavior; reveal: *He showed his anger by throwing a book. The company has shown itself to be reliable over the years.* **4.** to point out or lead to: *Show them the way to the bus station.* **5.** to act as an escort to; conduct; guide: *She showed the prospective buyers through the house.* **6.** to register, as on a scale: *The thermometer shows that it is freezing.* **7.** to demonstrate, prove, or explain: *Show me how to change a tire. I'll show that it can be done.* **8.** to give or grant; bestow: *The judge showed little mercy to the defendants.* —*v.i.* **1.** to become exposed to view; be displayed; appear. **2.** to be exhibited. **3.** to finish third in a horse race. ➡ distinguished from **place** and **win. 4.** *Informal.* to make one's appearance; be present: *Do you think they'll show?* —*n.* **1.** something that is shown; exhibition or demonstration. **2.** any entertainment, esp. a theatrical, radio, or television presentation. **3.** any public presentation: *a dog show, an art show.* **4.** elaborate or ostentatious display: *The gambler wears a jeweled stickpin for show.* **5.** the act or an instance of revealing something; appearance; sign: *There was little show of recognition when we met.* **6.** a feigned or misleading appearance; pretense: *I drove them away with a great show of anger.* **7.** the act or an instance of showing: *The cat's show of readiness to fight kept the dog at a distance.* **8.** the third finishing position in a horse race. [Old English *scēawian* to look at, see, display.]

• **to show off. a.** to behave so as to draw attention to oneself; be an exhibitionist. **b.** to display (something) in a proud or ostentatious manner: *to show off a new suit.*

• **to show up. a.** to make one's appearance: *to show up for a meeting.* **b.** to be conspicuous or prominent: *Will the rip in my shirt show up in the photograph?* **c.** to expose; reveal: *The investigation showed the club up for what it really was.* **d.** *Informal.* to easily be superior to; outclass: *We really showed the other team up.*

Synonyms *n.* Show, display, exhibition, and exhibit mean a presentation of something for public viewing. **Show** is a broad term that may be applied to presentations related to varied fields of activity, such as fashion, agriculture, or commerce: *The city sponsors a boat show every spring.* **Display** is a small presentation, usually designed to promote the sale of something: *There is a display of diamond rings in the jewelry store's window.* **Exhibition** denotes a large, wide-ranging show often designed to inform and entertain people as well as to demonstrate new products: *The international industrial exhibition will be held in Japan.* **Exhibit** specifies a display by one person or organization, often as part of a large show or exhibition: *About fifty publishers presented exhibits at the booksellers' convention.*

show bill, a poster advertising an entertainment.

show·boat (shō'bōt') *n.* **1.** a boat having a theater and troupe of performers on board for providing entertainment. **2.** *Informal.* show-off. —*v.i. Informal.* to show off in a particularly obvious manner.

show·bread (shō'bred') shewbread.

show business, the entertainment industry, including television, motion pictures, theater, circuses, and concerts.

S

show·case (shō′kās′) *n.* **1.** a glass case for displaying and protecting articles, as in a store or museum. **2.** a place or means for displaying or focusing attention on something: *The club is a showcase for new bands.* —*v.t.* to put on display or show attractively: *to showcase a performer.*
show·down (shō′doun′) *n.* a confrontation that brings a matter to a climax or conclusion.
show·er (shou′ər) *n.* **1.a.** a fall of rain of brief duration. **b.** a fall of hail, sleet, or snow of brief duration. **2.** a fall of anything in large number, as of tears, sparks, or meteors. **3.a.** a bath in which water is sprayed on a person from an overhead nozzle. **b.** a room or the apparatus for such a bath. Also, **shower bath. 4.** an abundant quantity or supply: *a shower of criticism.* **5.** a party for someone, such as a future bride or mother, to which gifts are brought. —*v.i.* **1.** to rain or fall in a shower. **2.** to take a shower. —*v.t.* **1.** to wet with water or other liquid; sprinkle; spray. **2.** to cause or appear to cause to fall in a shower: *to shower confetti on a parade.* **3.** to give or grant lavishly: *to shower compliments on a person.* [Old English *scūr* a fall of rain of brief duration.] —**show′er·y,** *adj.*
show·ing (shō′ing) *n.* **1.** the act or an instance of bringing to public view; presentation: *The showing of the art works caused great excitement.* **2.** something that is so presented; exhibition; display. **3.** a performance, as in a contest or test: *to make a poor showing in a race.*
show·man (shō′mən) *n., pl.* **-men** (-mən). **1.** a person who produces, presents, or manages a theatrical presentation. **2.** a person who presents something or habitually acts in a dramatic or theatrical manner. —**show′man·ship′,** *n.*
shown (shōn) a past participle of **show.**
show-off (shō′ôf′, -of′) *n.* **1.** a person who shows off; exhibitionist. **2.** the act of showing off.
show·piece (shō′pēs′) *n.* something displayed, esp. as a fine example of its kind.
show·place (shō′plās′) *n.* **1.** a place exhibited to the public because of its beauty, fame, or historical interest. **2.** any place that is beautifully and tastefully decorated.
show·room (shō′rüm′, -ru̇m′) *n.* a room used for the display of merchandise.
show·y (shō′ē) *adj.,* **show·i·er, show·i·est. 1.** making a striking display: *showy flowers.* **2.** bright or loud in a tasteless way; ostentatious or gaudy: *a showy dresser.* —**show′i·ly,** *adv.* —**show′i·ness,** *n.*
shrank (shrangk) the past tense of **shrink.**
shrap·nel (shrap′nəl) *n.* **1.** a thin-walled artillery shell filled with small lead fragments or balls that are scattered over a large area when the shell explodes. **2.** scattered fragments from an exploding shell or bomb. [From General Henry *Shrapnel,* 1761-1842, its British inventor.]

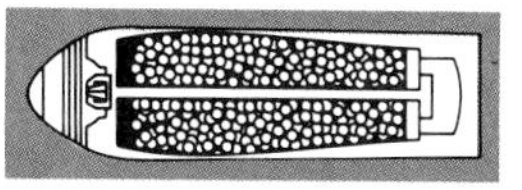

shrapnel

shred (shred) *n.* **1.** a very small piece or narrow strip torn or cut off something. **2.** a small amount; particle; scrap; bit: *There is not a shred of truth in that story.* —*v.t.,* **shred·ded** or **shred, shred·ding.** to tear or cut into shreds. [Old English *scrēade* fragment, strip, scrap.]
shred·der (shred′ər) *n.* **1.** a machine that shreds documents or other papers into small scraps, esp. to keep their contents secret. **2.** a person or thing that shreds.
shrew (shrü) *n.* **1.** any of numerous very small mammals, family Soricidae, related to the mole, found in nearly all parts of the world, having a long, pointed snout, short, rounded ears, and usually brownish fur. Also, **shrewmouse. 2.** a bad-tempered, nagging woman. [Middle English *schrewe* evil person, from Old English *scrēawa* shrewmouse; of Germanic origin.]

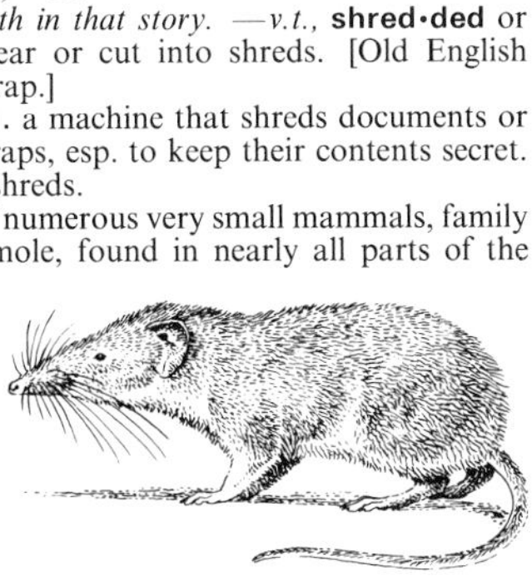

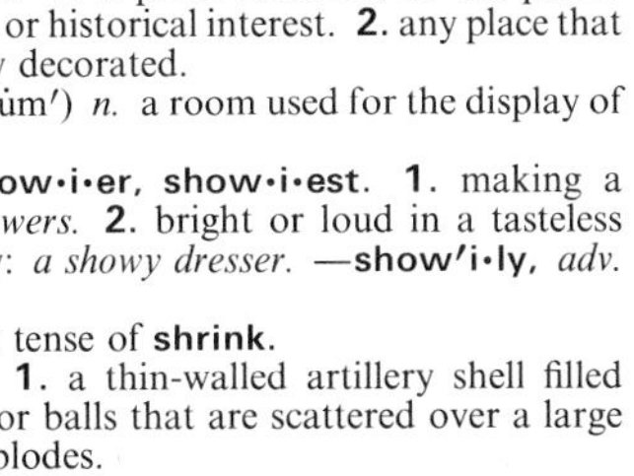

shrew

shrewd (shrüd) *adj.* **1.** clever or keen in practical matters or in dealing with others; astute: *a shrewd politician, a shrewd judge of character.* **2.** *Archaic.* sharp: *a sting of shrewdest pain* (Alfred, Lord Tennyson, 1842). [From SHREW.] —**shrewd′ly,** *adv.* —**shrewd′ness,** *n.*
shrew·ish (shrü′ish) *adj.* like a shrew; bad-tempered. —**shrew′ish·ly,** *adv.* —**shrew′ish·ness,** *n.*
shrew·mouse (shrü′mous′) *n., pl.* **-mice** (-mīs′). shrew (*def. 1*).
shriek (shrēk) *n.* a loud, shrill cry or sound: *shrieks of dismay, the shriek of a whistle.* —*v.i.* to make a loud, shrill cry or sound. —*v.t.* to utter with a shriek. [Possibly from Old Norse *skrækja* to screech.] —**shriek′er,** *n.*
shrift (shrift) *n. Archaic.* **1.** confession to a priest or the absolution given by a priest. **2.** the act of shriving. [Old English *scrift* penance, from *scrīfan* to impose penance, shrive. See SHRIVE.]
shrike (shrīk) *n.* any of various predatory birds, family Laniidae, having a strong, hooked beak, and feeding on insects and sometimes small birds, frogs, or mice. Length: 7-10 inches (18-25 centimeters). [Old English *scrīc* thrush.]
shrill (shril) *adj.* **1.** sharp and high-pitched in sound. **2.** emitting or producing such a sound: *a shrill jungle bird.* —*v.i.* to make or emit a shrill sound: *The bagpipes shrilled.* —*v.t.* to utter in a shrill manner: *The crowd shrilled its protests.* —*n.* a shrill sound. [Imitative.] —**shril′ly,** *adv.* —**shrill′ness,** *n.*
shrimp (shrimp) *n., pl.* **shrimp** or **shrimps. 1.** any of numerous long-tailed aquatic crustaceans, orders Decapoda, Stomatopoda, and Anostraca, usually found in salt water and often used as food. **2.** *Slang.* a person who is of small stature or size. —*v.i.* to fish for shrimp. [Of uncertain origin.] —**shrimp′er,** *n.*
shrine (shrīn) *n.* **1.** a case or other receptacle for sacred relics; reliquary. **2.** the tomb of a saint. **3.** a place consecrated to a deity, saint, or other sacred being. **4.** a place or thing hallowed by its history or past association: *The battlefield is a national shrine.* —*v.t.* enshrine. [Old English *scrīn* Ark of the Covenant, box containing a saint's relics, from Latin *scrīnium* case, chest.]
shrink[1] (shringk) *v.,* **shrank** or **shrunk, shrunk** or **shrunk·en, shrink·ing.** —*v.i.* **1.** to contract or become smaller because of exposure to heat, cold, or moisture: *Woolen cloth shrinks in hot water.* **2.** to draw back, as in fear, horror, or disgust. **3.** to become reduced; diminish: *The population of the town has shrunk in recent years.* —*v.t.* to cause to contract or be reduced: *The laundry shrank my new blouse.* —*n.* the act or an instance of shrinking. [Old English *scrincan* to contract, shrivel up.] —**shrink′a·ble,** *adj.* —**shrink′er,** *n.*
shrink[2] (shringk) *n. Slang.* a psychiatrist. [Short for HEADSHRINKER.]
shrink·age (shring′kij) *n.* **1.** the act or process of shrinking. **2.** the amount or proportion by which something shrinks. **3.** a reduction, as in quantity or value; depreciation: *the shrinkage of the dollar in times of inflation.*
shrink-wrap (shringk′rap′) *v.t.,* **-wrapped, -wrap·ping.** to wrap or package (an article) in a plastic film that, when heated, shrinks to fit tightly. —*n. also,* **shrink wrap.** the plastic film used in this process.
shrive (shrīv) *v.,* **shrove** or **shrived, shriv·en** or **shrived, shriv·ing.** —*v.t.* **1.** to hear the confession of and grant absolution to. **2.** to rid (oneself) of sin by confessing and doing penance. —*v.i.* **1.** to make confession, as to a priest. **2.** to hear confessions. [Old English *scrīfan* to hear the confession of, impose penance, going back to Latin *scrībere* to write.]
shriv·el (shriv′əl) *v.,* **-eled, -el·ing;** *also, British* **-elled, -el·ling.** —*v.i.* **1.** to shrink and become wrinkled or curled up: *The flowers shriveled and died after a week.* **2.** to become useless, helpless, or ineffectual. —*v.t.* to cause to shrivel. [Possibly of Scandinavian origin.]
shriv·en (shriv′ən) a past participle of **shrive.**
shroud (shroud) *n.* **1.** a cloth or garment used to wrap a dead body for burial. **2.** something that covers, conceals, or obscures. **3.** *Nautical.* a rope or wire giving lateral support to a mast. **4.** one of the lines from the canopy to the harness of a parachute. —*v.t.* **1.** to clothe for burial. **2.** to cover so as to conceal; obscure; veil: *Mist shrouded the mountaintop. The whole affair was shrouded in secrecy.* [Old English *scrūd* garment, clothing.]
shrove (shrōv) a past tense of **shrive.**
Shrove·tide (shrōv′tīd′) *n.* the three days preceding Ash Wednesday.
Shrove Tuesday, the day preceding Ash Wednesday.
shrub[1] (shrub) *n.* a woody plant smaller than a tree and having many stems that branch at or near the ground rather than one distinct trunk. [Old English *scrybb.*]
shrub[2] (shrub) *n.* a beverage made from fruit juice, sugar, and often liquor. [Arabic *shurb* beverage.]
shrub·ber·y (shrub′ə rē) *n., pl.* **-ber·ies. 1.** shrubs collectively. **2.** a plot planted with shrubs, as in a garden.
shrub·by (shrub′ē) *adj.,* **-bi·er, -bi·est. 1.** of or resembling a

a	at	e	end	o	hot	u	up	hw	white			ə	about, taken, pencil, lemon, circus
ā	ape	ē	me	ō	old	ū	use	ng	song				
ä	far	i	it	ô	fork	ü	rule	th	thin				
âr	care	ī	ice	oi	oil	u̇	pull	t͟h	this				
		îr	pierce	ou	out	ûr	turn	zh	measure				

shrub. **2.** consisting of or covered with shrubs. —**shrub′bi·ness,** *n.*

shrug (shrug) *v.t., v.i.,* **shrugged, shrug·ging.** to raise or draw up (the shoulders) to express doubt, indifference, or displeasure. —*n.* **1.** the act or an instance of shrugging. **2.** a short jacket or sweater with wide sleeves, worn by women. [Of uncertain origin.]
·**to shrug off.** to dismiss as being unimportant.

shrunk (shrungk) a past participle and past tense of **shrink.**

shrunk·en (shrung′kən) *v.* a past participle of **shrink.** —*adj.* shriveled up; made smaller; contracted.

shuck (shuk) *n.* **1.** the outer covering of corn or certain nuts. **2.** the shell of an oyster or clam. **3. shucks.** *Informal.* something having little value: *Their advice is not worth shucks.* —*v.t.* **1.** to remove the shucks from. **2.** to get rid of or remove (often with *off*): *to shuck one's friends, to shuck off one's clothes.* [Of uncertain origin.] —**shuck′er,** *n.*

shucks (shuks) *interj.* an exclamation of disappointment, annoyance, or embarrassment.

shud·der (shud′ər) *v.i.* to tremble suddenly, as from horror, fear, disgust, or cold. —*n.* the act or an instance of shuddering. [Middle English *shoddren* to tremble with fear, going back to Old English *scūdan* to shake, tremble.] —**shud′der·ing·ly,** *adv.*

shuf·fle (shuf′əl) *v.,* **-fled, -fling.** —*v.t.* **1.** to drag (the feet) along the ground or floor. **2.** to mix (playing cards) so as to rearrange them. **3.** to move (things) from one place to another: *to shuffle papers on one's desk.* —*v.i.* **1.** to walk by dragging the feet: *to shuffle down the street.* **2.** to mix playing cards so as to rearrange them. **3.** to move things about from one place to another. **4.** to move, act, or do something in a clumsy, haphazard, or hasty manner: *to shuffle through one's homework.* **5.** to perform a dance in which one shuffles the feet. —*n.* **1.** the act or an instance of shuffling the feet. **2.a.** the act or an instance of shuffling playing cards. **b.** the right or turn to shuffle playing cards: *Whose shuffle is it?* **3.** an instance of underhanded or evasive behavior; subterfuge; trick: *They gave us a fast shuffle.* **4.** a dance characterized by a series of shuffling steps. [Probably from Low German *schuffeln* to walk awkwardly.] —**shuf′fler,** *n.*
·**to shuffle off.** to get rid of or evade; thrust aside.

shuf·fle·board (shuf′əl bôrd′) *n.* **1.** a game played by pushing disks with a cue on a smooth level surface marked off in scoring areas. **2.** the marked surface on which this game is played. [Modification of obsolete *shove-board* this game, from SHOVE + BOARD.]

shul (shül, shúl) *n.* synagogue. [Yiddish *shul* literally, school, from Middle High German *schuol* school, from Latin *schola.*]

shun (shun) *v.t.,* **shunned, shun·ning.** to keep away from, esp. persistently or habitually; avoid: *The actor shunned publicity.* [Old English *scunian.*] —**shun′ner,** *n.* —For Synonyms, see avoid.

shunt (shunt) *v.t.* **1.** to move or turn aside or away. **2.** to switch (a train) from one track to another. **3.** to carry or divert (part of an electric current) by means of a conductor that acts as a bypass. **4.** to divert (blood) from one circulatory path to another. —*v.i.* to move or turn aside or away. —*n.* **1.** the act of shunting. **2.** a railroad switch. **3.** a conductor joining two points in an electric circuit that provides an electrical bypass for part of the current. **4.** a diversion of blood from its natural circulatory path, resulting from a congenital abnormality or surgical procedure. [Possibly from SHUN.] —**shunt′er,** *n.*

shush (shush) *interj.* be quiet; hush. —*v.t.* to quiet or silence.

shut (shut) *v.,* **shut, shut·ting.** —*v.t.* **1.** to move (something) into a closed position so as to obstruct or eliminate an entrance, passageway, or opening: *to shut a window.* **2.** to bring together the parts of so as to form a whole or eliminate openings: *to shut an umbrella, to shut a book.* **3.** to prevent access to (often with *off* or *up*): *to shut off several rooms of a house, to shut up a house.* **4.** to confine or enclose (often with *up*): *to shut an animal into a cage, to shut oneself up in a room.* **5.** to prevent from entering; keep out (with *out*): *to shut someone out of a meeting.* **6.** to suspend or stop the operation or operations of (often with *down*): *to shut a store, to shut down a mine.* **7.** to prevent the passage or flow of (with *off*): *to shut off water.* **8.** to make unresponsive or impervious: *to shut one's mind to reason.* —*v.i.* to become shut. [Old English *scyttan* to bolt¹, as a door.]
·**to shut out.** to prevent (the opposing team) from scoring in a contest, such as a baseball game.
·**to shut up.** *Informal.* to make or become silent.

shut·down (shut′doun′) *n.* a stopping of work, as in a factory.

shut-eye (shut′ī′) *n.* *Slang.* sleep.

shut-in (shut′in′) *adj.* confined to one's house or a hospital. —*n.* a person who is confined to the house or a hospital, as by illness.

shut-out (shut′out′) *n.* **1.** *Sports.* **a.** the preventing of the opposing team from scoring. **b.** a game in which one team does not score. **2.** lockout.

shut·ter (shut′ər) *n.* **1.** a movable panel or screen for a door or window, used to shut out light or to provide protection and privacy. **2.** a device that opens and closes the lens aperture of a camera. **3.** a person or thing that shuts. —*v.t.* to provide or cover with shutters. [SHUT + -ER¹.]

shut·ter·bug (shut′ər bug′) *n.* *Slang.* an amateur photographer.

shut·tle (shut′əl) *n.* **1.** a device on a loom that carries the weft yarn back and forth across or through the warp yarn. **2.** any of various devices that hold and carry thread, as in a sewing machine. **3.** a passenger vehicle, such as a bus, train, or airplane, that makes frequent trips back and forth between two points. **4.** space shuttle. —*v.i., v.t.,* **-tled, -tling.** to move or cause to move back and forth in or as in a shuttle. [Old English *scytel* dart, arrow.]

shut·tle·cock (shut′əl kok′) *n.* a cone-shaped object with feathers inserted into a rounded cork base, used in the game of badminton. Also, **bird.**

shy¹ (shī) *adj.,* **shy·er** or **shi·er, shy·est** or **shi·est. 1.** uncomfortable in the presence of others; bashful; retiring. **2.** exhibiting a lack of courage; easily frightened; timid: *Many animals are shy of humans.* **3.** cautious or distrustful; wary. **4.** *Informal.* lacking; short: *shy of money, a few dollars shy.* —*v.i.,* **shied, shy·ing. 1.** to move suddenly back or aside, as in fear; start: *The horse shied at the loud noise.* **2.** to draw back, as because of caution, distaste, or doubt (often with *away*). —*n., pl.* **shies.** a sudden movement back or aside, as in fear. [Old English *scēoh* timid.] —**shy′ly,** *adv.* —**shy′ness,** *n.*

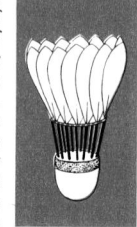
shuttlecock

shy² (shī) *v.t., v.i.,* **shied, shy·ing.** to throw (something), esp. with a jerk; fling; toss. —*n., pl.* **shies.** a quick, jerking throw. [Possibly from the former sport of *shying* or throwing sticks at cocks that had been taught to be *shy* or wary of missiles hurled at them.]

Shy·lock (shī′lok′) *n.* **1.** the exacting and merciless moneylender in William Shakespeare's play *The Merchant of Venice.* **2.** any exacting creditor.

shy·ster (shī′stər) *n.* *Slang.* a lawyer or other person whose professional methods and ethics are questionable. [Of uncertain origin.]

si (sē) *n.* *Music.* ti. [See GAMUT.]

Si, the symbol for silicon.

SI, International System of Units. [Abbreviation of French *Système International.*]

Si·a·mese (sī′ə mēz′, -mēs′) *n., pl.* **-mese.** Thai. —*adj.* Thai.

Siamese cat, a breed of cat, originally from Siam (now Thailand), having a slender body with light tan or grayish short hair and dark ears, nose, tail, and limbs.

Siamese twins, identical twins who are born joined together in some manner. [From the twins Eng and Chang, 1811-74, who were born in Siam (now Thailand) joined together.]

sib (sib) *adj.* ·related by blood; akin. —*n.* **1.** a kinsman or kinswoman; blood relative. **2.** blood relatives collectively; kindred. [Old English *sibb.*]

Si·be·ri·an husky (sī bîr′ē ən) a sturdy dog of a breed having a brushlike tail and a soft coat that may be gray, tan, white, black, or a combination of these. Height: 20-23 inches (51-58 centimeters) at the shoulder.

Siamese cat

sib·i·lant (sib′ə lənt) *adj.* having a hissing sound. —*n.* a consonant pronounced with a hissing sound, such as *s* or *sh.* [Latin *sībilāns,* present participle of *sībilāre* to hiss.] —**sib′i·lance, sib′i·lan·cy,** *n.* —**sib′i·lant·ly,** *adv.*

sib·ling (sib′ling) *n.* a brother or sister. [Old English *sibling* kinsman.]

sib·yl (sib′əl) *n.* **1.** in Greek and Roman mythology, any of various women who had powers of prophecy. **2.** any female prophet or fortuneteller.

si·byl·ic (si bil′ik) *also,* **si·byl·lic.** *adj.* sibylline.

sib·yl·line (sib′ə lēn′, -līn′, -lin) *adj.* **1.** of, like, or coming from a sibyl. **2.** prophetic or mysterious.

sic¹ (sik) *adv.* *Latin.* thus; so. ➡ used to indicate that an erroneous word or phrase in a quotation is an exact reproduction of the original.

sic² (sik) *also,* **sick.** *v.t.,* **sicked** or **sicced, sick·ing** or **sic·cing. 1.** to set upon; attack. ➡ used as a command, esp. to a

dog. **2.** to incite to make an attack: *They sicked their dog on us.* [Form of SEEK.]

sic·ca·tive (sik′ə tiv) *adj.* causing to dry; drying. —*n.* a siccative substance, esp. one used in painting. [Late Latin *siccātīvus* drying, from Latin *siccāre* to dry.]

Si·cil·ian (si sil′yən) *adj.* of, relating to, or characteristic of Sicily or its people, culture, or dialect. —*n.* **1.** a native or inhabitant of Sicily. **2.** a person of Sicilian descent. **3.** the dialect of Italian spoken predominantly in Sicily.

sick[1] (sik) *adj.* **1.** suffering from some disease; having poor health; ill. **2.** affected with nausea; nauseated. **3.** of or for sick people: *The company has very good sick benefits.* **4.** indicating sickness: *a sick look, a sick cough.* **5.** thoroughly weary: *I'm sick of this job.* **6.** annoyed or disgusted; chagrined: *Petty gossip makes me sick.* **7.** deeply affected with some strong feeling: *sick with envy, sick with the desire to travel.* **8.** emotionally or mentally disturbed. **9.** spiritually ailing; corrupt: *a sick society.* **10.** having an unsound condition; broken or impaired: *That old car looks sick.* **11.** sadistic or unwholesome in some way; morbid: *a sick joke.* —*n.* **the sick.** sick persons collectively. [Old English *sēoc* ill.]

sick[2] (sik) *sic*[2].

sick bay, a hospital or dispensary, esp. on a ship.

sick·bed (sik′bed′) *n.* the bed on which a sick person lies.

sick call 1. a gathering of soldiers, students, or campers who need to see a doctor, usually at a specific time of the day. **2.** a signal given to soldiers, campers, or the like, announcing that it is the time when medical attention is available.

sick·en (sik′ən) *v.t., v.i.* to make or become sick.

sick·en·ing (sik′ə ning) *adj.* affecting with or causing nausea or disgust. —**sick′en·ing·ly,** *adv.*

sick headache, migraine.

sick·ish (sik′ish) *adj.* **1.** somewhat sick. **2.** sickening. —**sick′-ish·ly,** *adv.* —**sick′ish·ness,** *n.*

sick·le (sik′əl) *n.* a hand tool consisting of a sharp crescent-shaped blade attached to a short handle, used for cutting grass, grain, or weeds. [Old English *sicol,* going back to Latin *secula.*]

sick leave 1. permission for absence from work or duty given to a soldier or worker because of illness or injury. **2.** the number of days permitted for absence from work or duty, usually given on an annual basis with pay.

sickle cell, a dysfunctional, sickle-shaped red blood cell, produced by chemical changes in hemoglobin and characteristic of sickle cell anemia. [Referring to the shape of the cell.]

sickle cell anemia, a hereditary, often fatal blood disease that occurs mainly in blacks, in which abnormal hemoglobin causes red blood cells to become sickle-shaped and unable to function.

sick·ly (sik′lē) *adj.,* **-li·er, -li·est. 1.** habitually sick; in poor health. **2.** of or characteristic of sickness: *a sickly complexion.* **3.** characterized by the presence of sickness. **4.** causing nausea; sickening: *sickly smells.* **5.** faint or weak; feeble: *a sickly winter sun.* **6.** insipid or weakly sentimental: *a sickly smile.* —*adv.* in a sick manner. —**sick′li·ness,** *n.*

sick·ness (sik′nis) *n.* **1.** the state of being sick. **2.** a particular disease or illness. **3.** nausea.

sic tran·sit glo·ri·a mun·di (sik tran′sit glôr′ē ə mun′dī) *Latin.* thus passes away the glory of the world.

sid·dur (sid′ər, -ùr; *Hebrew* sē dùr′) *n., pl.* **sid·durs;** *Hebrew* **sid·du·rim** (sē dù Rēm′). a book containing the Jewish prayers for daily, Sabbath, and festival worship. [Hebrew *siddūr* literally, arrangement.]

side (sīd) *n.* **1.** one of the surfaces or lines bounding an object or figure. **2.** any of the surfaces or lines of an object or figure that do not constitute its front or back, or its top or bottom: *The chair fell on its side. I scraped the paint on the side of the car against the guardrail.* **3.** either of the two surfaces of a two-dimensional or practically two-dimensional object, such as a piece of cloth, paper, or wood: *One side of the cloth is rough.* **4.a.** either of the two parts of a place lying to the right or left of a central line or point: *Put the chairs on the left side of the room.* **b.** any of various parts of a region or place in reference to a particular, usually central, line or point: *We live on the west side of town.* **5.** either the right or left part of the body of a person or animal. **6.** the area or space next to one, as distinguished from that in front of or behind one: *Come stand at my side.* **7.** a region or area separated from another region or area by an object, space, or line: *They have lived on both sides of the Atlantic.* **8.** a slope of a hill or bank. **9.** any one of two or more opposing groups or persons: *There were losses on all sides. Neither side scored in the game.* **10.** a position, attitude, or point of view: *There are always at least two sides to an argument.* **11.** an aspect of a person or thing: *I've never seen your humorous side before. Look at all sides of the question.* **12.** line of descent: *to have teachers on both one's mother's and one's father's side.* —*adj.* **1.** situated at or lying near one side. **2.** coming from or

directed toward one side. **3.** other than central; secondary; subordinate: *There were too many distracting side issues.* **4.** in addition to the main part. —*v.t.,* **sid·ed, sid·ing.** to provide with sides or siding. [Old English *sīde* lateral surface, place with reference to a central point.]

• **on the side.** *Informal.* **a.** in addition to the usual or principal job or duties: *The janitor repairs cars on the side.* **b.** in additon to the main part or course: *I ordered turnips on the side.*

• **side by side.** next to one another.

• **to side with.** to support, as in a dispute.

• **to take sides. a.** to support the position of one of two or more opposing groups or persons. **b.** (of two or more persons) to take positions supporting the sides in a dispute.

side·arm (sīd′ärm′) *adj.* of or designating a motion of the arm almost parallel to the ground, as in throwing a ball: *a sidearm pitch.* —*adv.* with a sidearm motion: *to throw sidearm.*

side arm, a weapon carried at the side, such as a sword or revolver.

side·board (sīd′bôrd′) *n.* a piece of dining room furniture, on which dishes may be placed before being brought to the table, and used esp. for storing tableware and linen.

side·burns (sīd′bûrnz′) *pl. n.* hair growing in front of a man's ears, esp. when worn as short whiskers with the rest of the beard shaved off. [Modification of BURNSIDES.]

sideburns (left) and burnsides (right)

side·car (sīd′kär′) *n.* a small, usually one-wheeled car attached to the side of a motorcycle for carrying a passenger.

sid·ed (sī′did) *adj.* having a particular kind or number of sides.
➤ used in combination: *one-sided, wood-sided.*

side dish, a portion of food served in addition to the main course, usually in a separate dish.

side effect, a secondary and often harmful effect, as of a medication or drug: *Sleepiness is a side effect of many antihistamines.*

side·kick (sīd′kik′) *n. Slang.* **1.** a close friend; companion; pal. **2.** a subordinate; confederate: *The leader arrived with a number of sidekicks.*

side·light (sīd′līt′) *n.* **1.** light coming from the side. **2.** a piece of incidental information or knowledge concerning some subject: *The speaker added interesting sidelights to what would otherwise have been a dry, factual presentation.* **3.** one of two lights, a red one on the port side and a green one on the starboard side, carried by a ship moving at night.

side·line (sīd′līn′) *n.* **1.** either of two lines that mark the limits of a playing area in certain sports, such as football or basketball. **2. sidelines.** the area just beyond these lines: *to stand on the sidelines.* **3.** work in addition to one's usual job or duties: *to paint signs as a sideline.* **4.** a line of goods additional to that regularly sold. —*v.t.,* **-lined, -lin·ing.** to keep from participating, as in a sport: *to be sidelined by an injury.*

side·ling (sīd′ling) *adj.* **1.** directed to the side; oblique: *a sideling motion.* **2.** inclined; sloping. —*adv.* sideways; sidelong.

side·long (sīd′lông′) *adj.* **1.** directed to the side: *to give a sidelong glance.* **2.** not straightforward; devious; indirect. —*adv.* toward the side.

side·piece (sīd′pēs′) *n.* a piece forming the side or a portion of the side of something.

si·de·re·al (sī dir′ē əl) *adj.* **1.** of or relating to the stars. **2.** determined or measured by means of the stars: *sidereal time, a*

a	at	e	end	o	hot	u	up	hw	white		about
ā	ape	ē	me	ō	old	ū	use	ng	song		taken
ä	far	i	it	ô	fork	ü	rule	th	thin	ə	pencil
âr	care	ī	ice	oi	oil	ù	pull	th	this		lemon
			ir	pierce	ou	out	ûr	turn	zh	measure		circus

sidereal day. [Latin *sīdereus* relating to the stars (from *sīdus* star, group of stars) + -AL[1].]

sidereal month, see month *(def. 4).*

sidereal year, year *(def. 2b).*

sid·er·ite (sid′ə rīt′) *n.* **1.** a brown iron carbonate mineral mined as an ore of iron. Formula: $FeCO_3$ **2.** a meteorite consisting mainly of iron. [Latin *sidērītēs* lodestone, from Greek *sidēros,* from *sideros* iron.]

side·sad·dle (sīd′sad′əl) *n.* a woman's saddle so constructed that the rider sits with both legs on the same side of the horse. —*adv.* on or as if on a sidesaddle: *to ride sidesaddle, to sit sidesaddle.*

side·show (sīd′shō′) *n.* **1.** a minor show connected to or forming part of a larger entertainment or exhibition. **2.** a minor incident or issue; subordinate matter or affair.

side·slip (sīd′slip′) *n.* **1.** the act or an instance of slipping or skidding to one side. **2.** (of an airplane) the act or an instance of sliding sideward, esp. downward toward the center of the curve made while turning. —*v.i.* **-slipped, -slip·ping.** to slip or skid to one side.

side·split·ting (sīd′split′ing) *adj.* **1.** (of laughter) boisterous or unrestrained. **2.** causing boisterous or unrestrained laughter: *a sidesplitting joke.*

side·step (sīd′step′) *v.,* **-stepped, -step·ping.** —*v.t.* to avoid by or as by stepping aside: *to sidestep a decision.* —*v.i.* **1.** to step to one side. **2.** to avoid a responsibility, decision, or difficulty. —**side′step′per,** *n.*

side step, a step or movement to one side, as in boxing.

side·stroke (sīd′strōk′) *n.* a swimming stroke performed while the swimmer is on one side and in which the forward arm reaches ahead while the rear arm pushes back, the arms then returning to meet in front of the chest, accompanied by a scissors kick with the feet.

side·swipe (sīd′swīp′) *v.t.,* **-swiped, -swip·ing.** to strike with a blow along the side, as in passing. —*n.* a blow made on or along the side.

side·track (sīd′trak′) *v.t.* **1.** to turn aside from the main concern, purpose, or course: *It's hard to get work done if you are easily sidetracked.* **2.** to shift (a train) to a siding. —*n.* a railroad siding.

side·walk (sīd′wôk′) *n.* a walk along the side of a street or road for pedestrians.

side·wall (sīd′wôl′) *n.* the side of an automobile tire, extending from the edge of the tread to the rim of the wheel.

side·ward (sīd′wərd) *adj.* moving or directed toward one side. —*adv. also,* **side·wards.** toward one side.

side·ways (sīd′wāz′) *also,* **side·way.** *adv.* **1.** toward or from one side. **2.** with one side foremost. —*adj.* moving or directed toward one side. Also *(adv., adj.),* **side·wise** (sīd′wīz′).

side·wheel (sīd′hwēl′, -wēl′) *adj.* (of a steamboat) having a paddle wheel on each side. —**side′-wheel′er,** *n.*

side whiskers, whiskers on the side of the face.

side·wind·er (sīd′wīn′dər) *n.* a rattlesnake, *Crotalus cerastes,* found in the southwestern United States and Mexico, that moves sideways and has hornlike knobs over each eye. [SIDE + WIND[2] + -ER[1]; from its form of locomotion.]

sid·ing (sī′ding) *n.* **1.** a short railroad track connected by a switch to a main track. **2.** wood, metal, or other material forming the outside covering of a frame building.

si·dle (sī′dəl) *v.i.,* **-dled, -dling.** to move sideways, esp. in a furtive or unobtrusive manner. —*n.* a sideways movement. [From SIDELING.]

SIDS, sudden infant death syndrome.

siege (sēj) *n.* **1.** the act or process of surrounding an enemy position in order to capture it by constant attack and by cutting off its supplies over a long period of time. **2.** any long or persistent attempt to overcome resistance. **3.** a long, distressing or tiring period, as of illness. —*v.t.,* **sieged, sieg·ing.** to subject to a siege; besiege. [Old French *s(i)ege* seat, act of sitting, act of settling, going back to Latin *sedēre* to sit.]

• **to lay siege to. a.** to subject to a siege; besiege. **b.** to try to capture or gain by long and persistent effort.

Siege Perilous, a place at King Arthur's Round Table, reserved for the knight destined to find the Holy Grail and fatal to any other knight. [See SIEGE, PERILOUS.]

Sieg·fried (sig′frēd′, sēg′-) *n.* in Germanic legend, a hero who killed a dragon and gained the treasure of the Nibelungs. His adventures are described in the *Nibelungenlied.*

sie·mens (sē′mənz) *n., pl.* **-mens.** the International System unit of conductance, equal to a mho. [From Sir William *Siemens,* 1823-83, British engineer and inventor.]

si·en·na (sē en′ə) *n.* **1.** a brown earth containing ferric oxide and manganese, used as a yellowish brown pigment, **raw sienna,** in its natural state or, after being roasted, as a reddish brown

pigment, **burnt sienna. 2.** a yellowish brown or reddish brown color. —*adj.* having the color sienna. [Short for Italian *terra di Sienna* literally, earth of Siena, where it was first obtained.]

si·er·ra (sē er′ə) *n.* a chain of rugged hills or mountains with sharp, jagged peaks that suggest the teeth of a saw. [Spanish *sierra* saw[1], chain of hills, from Latin *serra* saw[1].]

si·es·ta (sē es′tə) *n.* an afternoon nap or rest, esp. that taken during the hottest part of day in Spain and certain other hot countries. [Spanish *siesta,* from Latin *sexta (hōra)* sixth (hour), noon.]

sieve (siv) *n.* a utensil or instrument having a perforated or meshed bottom, used for sifting or draining substances. —*v.t., v.i.,* **sieved, siev·ing.** to pass through a sieve. [Old English *sife* strainer.]

sieve tube *Botany.* a tube formed of a series of cells connected end-to-end so as to form a conduit for conducting food materials through a plant, forming an essential element of the phloem in vascular plants.

sift (sift) *v.t.* **1.a.** to separate by passing through a sieve: *to sift sand from gravel.* **b.** to remove lumps from or make lighter by passing through a sieve: *to sift flour.* **2.** to sprinkle by shaking through a sieve: *to sift sugar over doughnuts.* **3.** to separate as if with a sieve; select: *to sift truth from fiction.* **4.** to examine with close scrutiny: *to sift evidence.* —*v.i.* **1.** to sift something. **2.** to fall loosely as if through a sieve: *Dust sifted through the cracks.* [Old English *siftan* to strain.] —**sift′er,** *n.*

sigh (sī) *v.i.* **1.** to emit a long, deep audible breath, as from grief, relief, or weariness. **2.** to make a sound suggestive of a sigh: *The wind sighed through the trees.* **3.** to wish earnestly; yearn; long: *They sighed for the good old days.* —*v.t.* to express with a sigh: *I sighed my relief.* —*n.* the act or sound of sighing. [Middle English *sighen* to emit a deep breath, going back to Old English *sīcan.*] —**sigh′er,** *n.*

sight (sīt) *n.* **1.** the faculty or power of seeing; vision. **2.** the act or an instance of seeing. **3.** the range of one's vision: *Keep the present out of their sight.* **4.** something seen; view: *The sunset was a beautiful sight.* **5.** *usually,* **sights.** something striking or worth seeing: *the sights of Paris.* **6.** personal estimation; judgment; mental regard: *In her sight, he can do nothing wrong.* **7.** any of various devices used as an aid in observing or aiming, as on a surveying instrument or firearm. **8.** an observation or aim taken with such a device. **9.** *Informal.* a person or thing messy or unpleasant to look at: *The room was a sight after the party.* —*v.t.* **1.** to perceive with the eyes; see: *After hiking for hours, we finally sighted a clearing in the forest.* **2.** to take sight of with an instrument. **3.** to aim by means of a sight or sights. **4.** to adjust the sight or sights of (a rifle or other weapon or optical device). [Old English *(ge)siht* a thing seen.]

• **at (or on) sight. a.** as soon as seen; immediately: *We bought the car on sight.* **b.** *Commerce.* on presentation.

• **by sight.** upon seeing; when seen: *to know someone by sight.*

• **sight unseen.** without having previously seen (the thing in question): *to buy a car sight unseen.*

• **to catch sight of.** to see briefly; glimpse.

• **to lose sight of. a.** to be no longer able to see: *to lose sight of something in the distance.* **b.** to fail to remember or take into account; overlook: *to lose sight of an important factor.*

sight draft *Commerce.* a draft payable on presentation.

sight·ed (sī′tid) *adj.* having sight; able to see; not blind: *The library is designed to be used by both blind and sighted students.*

sight·less (sīt′lis) *adj.* **1.** unable to see; blind. **2.** invisible. —**sight′less·ness,** *n.*

sight·ly (sīt′lē) *adj.,* **-li·er, -li·est. 1.** pleasing to the eye; comely. **2.** affording a fine view. —**sight′li·ness,** *n.*

sight-read (sīt′rēd′) *v.t., v.i.,* **-read** (-red′) **, -read·ing.** to read or be able to perform (a text or sheet music) without having previously seen or studied it.

sight·see (sīt′sē′) *v.i., v.t.,* **-saw** (-sô′) **, -seen** (-sēn′) **, -see·ing.** to visit or tour places of interest in (a place): *We plan to sightsee in the English countryside.* [From the phrase *to see the sights.*] —**sight′se′er,** *n.*

sight·see·ing (sīt′sē′ing) *n.* the act or an instance of visiting places of interest. —*adj.* used for or engaged in visiting places of interest.

sig·ma (sig′mə) *n.* **1.** the eighteenth letter of the Greek alphabet (Σ, σ, ς), corresponding to the English letter *S, s.* **2.** *Physics.* any of three subatomic particles of the baryon group.

sig·moid (sig′moid) *adj.* **1.** shaped like the letter S. **2.** of, relating to, affecting, or near the sigmoid flexure of the colon. Also, **sig·moi′dal.** [Greek *sigmoeidēs* shaped like a sigma, from *sigma* sigma + *eidos* form, shape.]

sigmoid flexure, the last curving portion of the colon, before the rectum.

sign (sīn) *n.* **1.** something that serves to represent, indicate, or

suggest some state, quality, condition, or feeling: *There were signs of wear on the carpet. Their failure to write is no sign that they have forgotten you.* **2.** a motion, gesture, or action that expresses an idea or issues a command or warning: *The photographer gave us the sign to hold still.* **3.** an inscribed plate or board that serves to convey information or issue a command or warning: *The sign on the door said they were closed for the day.* **4.** a conventional device or symbol that serves to represent an object, process, relationship, idea, or the like: *An ellipsis is the sign that something has been left out.* **5.** *Mathematics.* a symbol used to indicate an operation, such as division (÷) or multiplication (×), or to identify a term as positive (+) or negative (−). **6.** a warning or indication of what is to come; portent; omen: *Failure of the business may be a sign of hard times for the town.* **7.** a hint or trace: *There is no sign of them anywhere.* **8.** one of the twelve divisions of the zodiac. —*v.t.* **1.a.** to affix one's signature to: *to sign a receipt.* **b.** to attest to or confirm by affixing one's signature to: *If the artist signed the painting, it must be genuine.* **2.** to inscribe as a signature: *They signed their names to the document.* **3.** to engage or hire by means of a contract or other written agreement: *The team signed the pitcher for the year.* **4.** to communicate or express by a sign or signs or sign language: *to sign a story to an audience of the deaf.* **5.** to ratify or accept formally: *The two countries signed a peace treaty.* —*v.i.* **1.** to write one's signature. **2.** to accept employment or be hired by means of a contract or other written agreement. [Old French *signe* mark, token, from Latin *signum*.] —**sign′er,** *n.*

• **to sign away** (or **over**). to dispose of or transfer by or as by affixing one's signature to a document.
• **to sign in.** to sign a register upon arrival.
• **to sign off.** to cease television or radio transmission for the day.
• **to sign on.** to accept employment: *to sign on as a deckhand.*
• **to sign out.** to sign a register upon departure.
• **to sign up.** to enlist in or join an organization or group, esp. a branch of the military service.
• **to sign up for.** to enroll, as in a course of study.

Synonyms *n.* **Sign** and **signal** mean an action, event, or visible symbol that conveys information. **Sign,** the broader term, often signifies communication through physical gesture: *The sky was clear, with no sign of rain. A clenched fist is often a sign of anger.* **Signal** implies a generally accepted symbol that serves as a warning or command: *The official blew the whistle as a signal that a foul had been committed.*

sig·nal (sig′nəl) *n.* **1.** something, such as a gesture, sound, or light, that serves to warn, direct, inform, or instruct: *The flashing light was a signal that a train was coming.* **2.** an action or occurrence that serves to bring about or stir up something: *The dictator's barbaric decree was a signal for insurrection.* **3.** an electromagnetic wave or electric current that transmits sounds, pictures, or data to receiving equipment. —*v.,* **-naled, -nal·ing;** *also, British,* **-nalled, -nal·ling.** —*v.t.* **1.** to make a signal or signals to: *We signaled a passing ship for help.* **2.** to communicate or make known by a signal or signals: *The bugler signaled a retreat.* —*v.i.* to make a signal or signals. —*adj.* **1.** used as a signal: *a signal light.* **2.** standing out; remarkable; striking; notable: *a signal event.* [Medieval Latin *signale* something intended as a sign, going back to Latin *signum* mark, token.] —**sig′nal·er;** *also, British,* **sig′nal·ler,** *n.* —For Synonyms *(n.),* see **sign.**

Signal Corps, the part of the U.S. Army in charge of communications.

sig·nal·ize (sig′nə līz′) *v.t.,* **-ized, -iz·ing.** **1.** to make notable or striking: *Early fame signalized the artist's career.* **2.** to point out distinctly. —**sig′nal·i·za′tion,** *n.*

sig·nal·ly (sig′nə lē) *adv.* in a signal manner; remarkably.

sig·nal·man (sig′nəl mən, -man′) *n., pl.* **-men** (-mən, -men′). a person whose job is sending signals, as on a railroad or ship or in the armed forces.

sig·na·to·ry (sig′nə tôr′ē) *n., pl.* **-ries.** a person, party, or country that signs a document, such as a treaty. —*adj.* that has signed a document.

sig·na·ture (sig′nə chər) *n.* **1.** the name of a person, or a mark representing the person's name, written in his or her own hand. **2.** a melody, sound effect, or visual effect that identifies a radio or television program. **3.** *Printing.* **a.** a folded sheet ready for binding on which thirty-two pages, or any multiple of four, have been printed, forming one section of a book. **b.** a letter or number printed at the foot of the first page of such a sheet, serving as a guide for collating. **4.** that part of a medical prescription giving the amount and frequency of dosage. **5.** *Music.* a symbol or group of symbols at the beginning of a staff to indicate pitch or meter. **6.** a feature or characteristic that is typical of a person or thing. [Medieval Latin *signatura* a signing, going back to Latin *signum* mark, token.]

sign·board (sīn′bôrd′) *n.* a board bearing a notice or advertisement.

sig·net (sig′nit) *n.* **1.** a small seal, esp. one used to indicate that a document has authority. **2.** an impression made by or as by a signet. —*v.t.* to stamp or mark with a signet. [Old French *signet* seal², stamp, diminutive of *signe* mark, token. See SIGN.]

signet ring, a finger ring containing a signet.

sig·nif·i·cance (sig nif′i kəns) *n.* **1.** the state or quality of having special value or relevance; importance: *This fact has little significance for us.* **2.** that which is intended to be or actually is signified; meaning; import: *What is the significance of their actions?* **3.** the state or quality of having meaning; expressiveness; suggestiveness. Also, **sig·nif′i·can·cy.**

sig·nif·i·cant (sig nif′i kənt) *adj.* **1.** having special value or relevance; important; weighty: *a significant event.* **2.** signifying something; having a meaning. **3.** having or expressing a special or hidden meaning; suggestive: *to give a fellow conspirator a significant look.* [Latin *significāns* full of meaning, present participle of *significāre* to show by signs.] —**sig·nif′i·cant·ly,** *adv.*

significant digits, the digits of a number beginning with the first nonzero digit to the left of the decimal point or, if there is none, with the first nonzero digit after the decimal point and ending with the last digit to the right, signifying the degree of accuracy of a measurement. Also, **significant figures.**

sig·ni·fi·ca·tion (sig′nə fi kā′shən) *n.* **1.** that which is meant; meaning; import: *the signification of a word.* **2.** the act of signifying; communication.

sig·nif·i·ca·tive (sig nif′i kā′tiv) *adj.* **1.** signifying something. **2.** having meaning; significant; suggestive.

sig·ni·fy (sig′nə fī′) *v.,* **-fied, -fy·ing.** —*v.t.* **1.** to be a sign, symbol, or indication of; represent; mean: *Her smile signified her happiness.* **2.** to convey by signs, speech, or actions: *He signified his disapproval by frowning.* —*v.i.* to be of importance; matter. [Latin *significāre* to show by signs, from *signum* mark, token + *facere* to do, make.] —**sig′ni·fi′a·ble,** *adj.* —**sig′ni·fi′er,** *n.*

si·gnior (sēn yôr′, sin-) signor.

sign language, a system of communication in which gestures are substituted for speech, used esp. by the deaf. For illustration, see **manual alphabet.**

sign manual *pl.* **signs manual.** a person's signature, esp. that of a sovereign serving to authenticate a document.

sign of the cross, a sign made in the outline of a cross by touching one's forehead, chest, and shoulders with the fingers of the right hand as an act of religious devotion.

si·gnor (sēn yôr′, sin-) *also,* **signior.** *n., pl.* **si·gno·ri** (sēn yôr′ē, sin-) or **si·gnors.** mister; sir. ➡ an Italian form of respectful or polite address for a man, usually used before the name. [Italian *signor,* form of *signore.* See SIGNORE¹.]

si·gno·ra (sēn yôr′ə, sin-) *n., pl.* **si·gno·re** (sēn yôr′ā, sin-) or **si·gno·ras.** mistress; lady. ➡ an Italian form of respectful or polite address for a married woman. [Italian *signora,* feminine of *signore.* See SIGNORE¹.]

si·gno·re¹ (sēn yôr′ā, sin-) *n., pl.* **si·gno·ri** (sēn yôr′ē, sin-). mister; sir. ➡ an Italian form of respectful or polite address for a man, used in direct address without the name. [Italian *signore,* from Latin *senior* older, comparative of *senex* old, old man.]

si·gno·re² (sēn yôr′ā, sin-) a plural of **signora.**

si·gno·ri (sēn yôr′ē, sin-) a plural of **signor.**

si·gno·ri·na (sēn′yô rē′nə) *n., pl.* **-ne** (-nā) or **-nas.** miss. ➡ an Italian form of respectful or polite address for an unmarried girl or woman. [Italian *signorina,* diminutive of *signora.* See SIGNORA.]

sign·post (sīn′pōst′) *n.* **1.** a post bearing a sign. **2.** an indication, guide, or clue.

Si·gurd (sig′ərd) *n.* in Norse legend, the warrior who slew the dragon Fafnir and captured the treasure it was guarding.

Sikh (sēk) *n.* a follower of a monotheistic religion developed about A.D. 1500 that combines elements of both Hinduism and Islam. [Hindi *sikh* disciple, from Sanskrit *sishya.*] —**Sikh′ism,** *n.*

si·lage (sī′lij) *n.* green fodder preserved by packing it into an airtight silo or pit and allowing it to ferment. Also, **ensilage.**

sild (sild) *n., pl.* **sild** or **silds.** any of various small or immature herrings sold commercially as Norwegian sardines. [Norwegian *sild.*]

si·lence (sī′ləns) *n.* **1.** the absence of sound; complete quiet; stillness. **2.** the state of being or keeping silent: *to listen in silence.*

a	at	e	end	o	hot	u	up	hw	white		about
ā	ape	ē	me	ō	old	ū	use	ng	song		taken
ä	far	i	it	ô	fork	ü	rule	th	thin	ə	pencil
âr	care	ī	ice	oi	oil	u̇	pull	th	this		lemon
		îr	pierce	ou	out	ûr	turn	zh	measure		circus

3. the absence or omission of mention or notice: *to pass over a fact in silence.* **4.** a failure to communicate, as by writing or telephoning: *I wondered about my friend's silence after my letter.* —*v.t.,* **-lenced, -lenc·ing. 1.** to cause to be or keep silent: *to silence a noisy classroom.* **2.** to put a stop to or suppress: *Harsh measures were used to silence the critics of the government.* **3.** to put to rest: *to silence a child's fears.* **4.** to disable (enemy guns) by superior fire. —*interj.* be silent.

si·lenc·er (sī′lən sər) *n.* **1.** a person or thing that silences. **2.** a tubelike device attached to the front of a gun barrel to deaden the sound of firing.

si·lent (sī′lənt) *adj.* **1.** characterized by the absence of sound; completely quiet; still: *The old house was silent.* **2.** refraining from noise or speech: *The spectators at the trial were silent during the testimony.* **3.** not given to speaking; taciturn; reticent: *a shy, silent child.* **4.** not uttered or expressed; unspoken: *There was much silent opposition to our proposal.* **5.** free from activity or disturbance; inactive: *The theater, once so popular, is silent now.* **6.** characterized by the absence or omission of mention or notice; omitting all reference: *The book was silent on that subject.* **7.** (of a motion picture) having no soundtrack. **8.** *Linguistics.* (of a letter) not pronounced, as the *b* in *debtor.* [Latin *silēns,* present participle of *silēre* to be noiseless or still.] —**si′lent·ly,** *adv.* —**si′lent·ness,** *n.*

silent partner, a partner who has a financial investment in a business but does not participate actively in its management.

Si·le·nus (sī lē′nəs) *n., pl. (def. 2)* **-ni** (-nī). **1.** in Greek mythology, a nature spirit who was foster father, tutor, and companion of Dionysus. **2. silenus.** any of the older satyrs.

si·le·sia (si lē′zhə, -shə, -sī-) *n.* a cotton fabric having a glossy finish, used for linings. [From *Silesia,* region in eastern Europe where it was first made.]

sil·hou·ette (sil′ü et′) *n.* **1.** an outline of a figure or object filled in with a solid color, usually black. **2.** a dark outline seen against a lighter background. **3.** the outline or contour of anything. —*v.t.,* **-et·ted, -et·ting.** to cause to appear in or as in a silhouette. [From Étienne de *Silhouette,* 1709-67, French minister of finance noted for his petty economic policies; probably because silhouettes were far less expensive than painted portraits.] —For Synonyms *(n.),* see **outline.**

sil·i·ca (sil′i kə) *n.* a hard, glasslike, transparent compound occurring naturally as quartz, used in the manufacture of glass and ceramics. Formula: SiO_2 Also, **silicon dioxide.** [Modern Latin *silica,* from Latin *silex* flint.]

silica gel, a porous, adsorbent form of silica, used as a drying agent and for deodorizing and cleaning air.

sil·i·cate (sil′i kit, -kāt′) *n.* any of a wide variety of compounds consisting of either silica or a combination of silicon, oxygen, various metals, and sometimes hydrogen. Window glass and building bricks consist of silicates, as do many of the most abundant rocks and minerals.

si·li·ceous (si lish′əs) *adj.* of, resembling, or containing silica. [Latin *siliceus* relating to flint, from *silex* flint.]

si·lic·ic (si lis′ik) *adj.* of or relating to silica or silicon.

silicic acid, any of various weak, silicon-based acids in the form of gelatinous masses that decompose to silica and water, as H_4SiO_4.

si·lic·i·fy (sə lis′ə fī′) *v.,* **-fied, -fy·ing.** —*v.t.* to convert into or replace with silica. —*v.i.* to become converted into or replaced with silica, as wood when it becomes petrified. [SILICA + -FY.] —**si·lic·i·fi·ca·tion** (sə lis′ə fi kā′shən), *n.*

sil·i·con (sil′i kən, -kon′) *n.* a metalloid element that, in a purified state, forms either a brown powder or dark gray or black crystals, the latter used as a semiconductor. Silicon, the second most abundant element in the earth's crust, is everywhere found combined with oxygen. Symbol: **Si** For tables, see **element.** [From SILICA.]

silicon carbide, an extremely hard, bluish black, crystalline substance, used as an abrasive. Formula: SiC

silicon dioxide, silica.

sil·i·cone (sil′i kōn′) *n.* any of a class of polymeric compounds composed of chains of silicon and oxygen atoms to which organic radicals are attached. Silicones are used as oils, plastics, and synthetic rubbers and in various industrial processes because they are unaffected by extremes of temperature.

sil·i·co·sis (sil′i kō′sis) *n.* a chronic disease of the lungs caused by long-term inhalation of dust containing silicate particles, as by workers in some mines, foundries, and glass factories. [Modern Latin *silicosis,* from SILICA + -OSIS.]

silk (silk) *n.* **1.** a soft, lustrous, resilient fiber spun by silkworms. **2.** a strong, lustrous fabric made from these fibers, woven in various weights and used for such items as scarves, ties, and blouses. **3.** a filament or material resembling silk: *the silk of a butterfly's wing.* **4. silks.** a cap and blouse having distinctive colors, worn by a jockey or harness driver to identify the owner of the horse. —*adj.* of, relating to, or resembling silk. [Old English *seolc* the fiber, the fabric, going back to Greek *sērikon* the fabric, from *Sēres* the Chinese (who were famous for their silken fabrics).]

silk cotton, kapok.

silk-cot·ton tree (silk′kot′ən) any of various tropical trees found in South America, Java, Sri Lanka, and the Philippines, esp. *Ceiba pentandra,* from whose seed pods kapok is obtained. Also, **ceiba.**

silk·en (sil′kən) *adj.* **1.** made of silk. **2.** like silk in appearance or texture; silky. **3.** dressed in silk. **4.** luxurious or elegant.

silk·screen process (silk′skrēn′) a method or process of printing in which pigment or ink is forced through a screen of silk or other fine fabric on which a design, usually in the form of a cut stencil, has been imposed.

silk-stock·ing (silk′stok′ing) *adj.* aristocratic or wealthy: *the silk-stocking district of a city.* —*n.* an aristocratic or wealthy person.

silk·worm (silk′wûrm′) *n.* the caterpillar of a moth, *Bombyx mori,* originally domesticated in China. The cocoon it spins is processed to make silk thread and fabric.

silk·y (sil′kē) *adj.,* **silk·i·er, silk·i·est. 1.** like silk in appearance or texture; smooth, soft, and lustrous. **2.** made of silk. **3.** *Botany.* covered with fine soft hairs, as a leaf. —**silk′i·ly,** *adv.* —**silk′i·ness,** *n.*

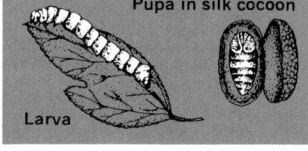

Pupa in silk cocoon / Larva

silkworm

sill (sil) *n.* **1.** a horizontal member across the bottom of a door or window. **2.** a horizontal beam that either rests on or forms the foundation of a structure. **3.** *Geology.* a tubular body of igneous rock intruded between horizontal strata. [Old English *syll* base [1], support.]

sil·la·bub (sil′ə bub′) syllabub.

sil·ly (sil′ē) *adj.,* **-li·er, -li·est. 1.a.** lacking in judgment or common sense; stupid: *a silly person.* **b.** suggesting a lack of judgment or common sense; absurd; ridiculous: *a silly notion.* **2.** *Informal.* dazed, as by a blow. **3.** *Archaic.* innocent. [Old English *(ge)sǣlig* happy, fortunate.] —**sil′li·ness,** *n.*

si·lo (sī′lō) *n., pl.* **-los. 1.** a structure, usually a tall, cylindrical tower of metal, concrete, or other material, for the storage and fermentation of green fodder. **2.** a structure built into a deep hole in the ground, used for storing and launching missiles. —*v.t.,* **-loed, -lo·ing.** to store in a silo. [Spanish *silo* underground granary, from Latin *sīrus,* from Greek *sīros.*]

silt (silt) *n.* very small particles of sand, soil, or the like, carried by water and deposited as sediment. —*v.t., v.i.* to fill or be filled with silt (with *up*). [Possibly of Scandinavian origin.] —**silt′y,** *adj.*

silt·stone (silt′stōn′) *n.* a sedimentary rock similar to shale but lacking its platy texture and containing a greater proportion of silt than is found in a mudstone. [SILT + STONE.]

Si·lu·ri·an (si lûr′ē ən, sī-) *n.* the third geologic period of the Paleozoic era, during which the first land plants appeared. For table, see **geologic time.** —*adj.* of, relating to, or characteristic of this period. [Latin *Silures* ancient people who once lived in Wales + -IAN; because rocks of this period were mainly studied in Wales.]

sil·van (sil′vən) sylvan.

sil·ver (sil′vər) *n.* **1.** a lustrous, white metallic element that is soft and easily shaped and is the best conductor of heat and electricity of any metal, used esp. in the manufacture of mirrors and as a catalyst in certain chemical processes. Symbol: **Ag** For tables, see **element. 2.** this metal used as a commodity or as a standard of currency. **3.** coins, esp. those made from silver; change. **4.** articles, such as tableware, made of silver or coated with a thin layer of silver. **5.** the color of silver; lustrous, grayish white or whitish gray. **6.** silverware *(def. 2).* —*adj.* **1.** made of or coated with a thin layer of silver. **2.** of or relating to silver: *silver mining.* **3.** resembling silver, as in color or luster. **4.** having a clear, bell-like tone; melodious: *silver laughter.* **5.** smooth and convincing; eloquent: *a silver tongue.* **6.** of or advocating the use or adoption of silver as a standard of currency. **7.** of or marking the twenty-fifth year or event in a series: *a silver wedding anniversary.* —*v.t.* **1.** to coat with a thin layer of silver or something resembling silver. **2.** to give (something) the color or luster of silver: *Age had silvered their hair.* —*v.i.* to become silver or silvery in color. [Old English *siolfor, seolfor* white precious metal, money.]

silver bell, any of several trees, genus *Halesia,* esp. *H. carolina,*

native to eastern North America and bearing showy clusters of white bell-shaped flowers.

silver bromide, a photosensitive, yellow compound used in photographic emulsions. Formula: AgBr

silver certificate, a certificate issued by the U.S. government, formerly circulated as money, stating that a certain amount of silver, specified on the face of the certificate, has been deposited in the Treasury for redemption on demand.

silver chloride, a photosensitive, white compound used in photographic emulsions. Formula: AgCl

sil·ver·fish (sil′vər fish′) *n., pl.* **-fish** or **-fish·es. 1.** a small, white, or gray, wingless insect, *Lepisma saccharina*, a common household pest that feeds on wallpaper, bookbindings, and other starchy materials. Length: to ½ inch (1 centimeter). **2.** a silvery goldfish, *Carassius auratus.* **3.** any of various silvery fish, such as the tarpon.

silver fox 1. a red fox whose fur is black, tipped with gray or white. **2.** the fur of this animal.

silver iodide, a photosensitive, yellow compound used in medicine and photography and for cloud seeding. Formula: AgI

silver lining, something good or positive that may come out of an unfortunate or apparently hopeless situation or condition.

sil·vern (sil′vərn) *adj. Archaic.* of or resembling silver.

silver nitrate, a white crystalline compound used in preparing photographic emulsions, in silver-plating, in making hair dyes, and as an antiseptic. Formula: AgNO₃

sil·ver-plate (sil′vər plāt′) *v.t.,* **-plat·ed, -plat·ing.** to coat with a thin layer of silver, as by electroplating.

silver plate, articles made of or coated with a thin layer of silver, such as table utensils.

sil·ver·sides (sil′vər sīdz′) *n., pl.* **-sides.** any of a group of small, spiny rayed, mostly marine fish, family Atherinidae, having a silvery stripe on the side, such as the grunion.

sil·ver·smith (sil′vər smith′) *n.* an artisan who makes or repairs articles of silver.

sil·ver-tongued (sil′vər tungd′) *adj.* having smooth, agreeable, and convincing speech; eloquent.

sil·ver·ware (sil′vər wâr′) *n.* **1.** articles, esp. tableware, made of or coated with a thin layer of silver. **2.** any metal table utensils.

sil·ver·y (sil′və rē) *adj.* **1.** having the lustrous color of silver. **2.** having a soft and clear musical sound. **3.** made of or coated with a thin layer of silver. —**sil′ver·i·ness,** *n.*

sil·vi·cul·ture (sil′vi kul′chər) *n.* forestry. [French *sylviculture,* from Latin *silva* wood, forest + *cultūra* cultivation, cure.] —**sil′-vi·cul′tur·al,** *adj.* —**sil′vi·cul′tur·ist,** *n.*

sim·i·an (sim′ē ən) *adj.* of, relating to, or resembling an ape or monkey. —*n.* an ape or monkey. [Latin *sīmia* ape (probably from *sīmus* snub-nosed, from Greek *sīmos*) + -AN.]

sim·i·lar (sim′ə lər) *adj.* **1.** having or bearing a marked resemblance; alike: *The general features of the two landscapes were similar. This car is similar to the one we used to have.* **2.** *Geometry.* having corresponding angles that are equal, and corresponding sides that are proportional: *similar triangles.* [French *similaire* like, from Latin *similis.*] —**sim′i·lar·ly,** *adv.* —For Synonyms, see **like**[1].

sim·i·lar·i·ty (sim′ə lar′i tē) *n., pl.* **-ties. 1.** the quality or state of being similar; likeness. **2.** an instance or point of likeness: *There are many similarities between the twins.*

sim·i·le (sim′ə lē) *n.* a figure of speech in which one object or idea is explicitly compared with another by the word *like* or *as* in order to suggest a similarity between the two; for example: *The sea was like glass.* [Latin *simile* comparison, likeness.]

si·mil·i·tude (si mil′i tüd′, -tūd′) *n.* **1.** the state of being similar; likeness. **2.** a person or thing that is similar to another. [Latin *similitūdō* likeness.]

sim·i·tar (sim′i tər) scimitar.

sim·mer (sim′ər) *v.i.* **1.** (of a liquid or something in a liquid) to cook at, or just below, the boiling point. **2.** to make a murmuring sound, as a liquid when just beginning to boil. **3.** to be on the verge of breaking into action: *to simmer with anger.* —*v.t.* to cook (something) at, or just below, the boiling point. —*n.* the state or process of simmering. [Earlier *simper;* possibly imitative.]

· **to simmer down. a.** to reduce (a liquid) in volume by simmering. **b.** *Informal.* to become calm: *When you simmer down, I'll explain what happened.*

si·mo·ni·ac (si mō′nē ak′) *n.* a person who practices simony. —**si·mo·ni·a·cal** (sī′mə nī′ə kəl, sim′ə-), *adj.*

si·mon-pure (sī′mən pyŭr′) *adj.* genuine; authentic. [From *Simon Pure,* a Quaker in the comedy *A Bold Stroke for a Wife* by the English playwright Susanna Centlivre, 1667?-1723, who is impersonated and must prove he is the real Simon Pure.]

si·mo·ny (sī′mə nē, sim′ə-) *n.* the act or practice of buying or selling sacred things, such as promotions or positions in the church. [Late Latin *sīmōnia* sale of sacred things, from *Simon Magus,* who tried to buy the gift of the Holy Ghost (Acts 8:18-19).]

si·moom (si müm′) *also,* **si·moon** (si mün′). *n.* a hot, dry, sand-laden wind of the Arabian and North African deserts. [Arabic *samūm,* from *samm* to poison; because of its effect on people.]

simp (simp) *n. Slang.* simpleton; fool. [Short for SIMPLETON.]

sim·per (sim′pər) *v.i.* to smile in a silly, self-conscious, affected way. —*v.t.* to say with a silly, self-conscious smile. —*n.* a silly, self-conscious smile. [Possibly of Scandinavian origin.] —**sim′-per·er,** *n.* —**sim′per·ing·ly,** *adv.*

sim·ple (sim′pəl) *adj.,* **-pler, -plest. 1.** easily done, used, or understood: *a simple task, a simple math problem.* **2.** consisting of only one part or one unit; uncompounded or undivided; unmixed: *a simple substance, a simple leaf.* **3.** with nothing added; mere; pure: *the simple truth.* **4.** without elaboration or ornament; unadorned; plain: *a simple style of writing, a simple design.* **5.a.** without sophistication, vanity, or pretense; unsophisticated or unpretentious; artless: *a simple and unaffected person.* **b.** without duplicity or guile; straightforward; honest; sincere: *a simple heart, simple motives.* **6.** without rank; humble or common: *a simple laborer, a simple citizen.* **7.** lacking in judgment or common sense; foolish. —*n.* **1.** something that is uncompounded; simple substance or element. **2.** a person who lacks judgment or common sense. **3.** *Archaic.* a person of humble birth or position; rustic. **4.** *Archaic.* an herb or other plant from which a medicine is made. [Old French *simple* plain[1], artless, going back to Latin *simplex.*] —**sim′ple·ness,** *n.* —For Synonyms *(adj.),* see **easy.**

simple fraction, common fraction.

simple fracture, a bone fracture in which the broken ends do not pierce the flesh.

sim·ple-heart·ed (sim′pəl här′tid) *adj.* without guile or deceit; straightforward; sincere.

simple machine, machine *(def. 2).*

sim·ple·mind·ed (sim′pəl mīn′did) *adj.* **1.** without sophistication; artless. **2.** lacking in common sense; foolish or stupid. **3.** mentally deficient; weak-minded. —**sim′ple·mind′ed·ly,** *adv.* —**sim′ple·mind′ed·ness,** *n.*

simple sentence, a sentence that consists of one independent clause without a dependent clause; for example: *A fox can move quickly.*

simple sugar, monosaccharide.

sim·ple·ton (sim′pəl tən) *n.* an unwise or silly person; fool. [From SIMPLE.]

sim·plic·i·ty (sim plis′i tē) *n., pl.* **-ties. 1.** the state or quality of being simple; freedom from difficulty or complexity. **2.** freedom from elaboration or ornament; plainness: *Their clothes were characterized by simplicity and good taste.* **3.** lack of duplicity or guile; sincerity. **4.** lack of common sense; foolishness or stupidity. [Latin *simplicitās* plainness, frankness.]

sim·pli·fi·ca·tion (sim′plə fi kā′shən) *n.* **1.** the act of simplifying or the state of being simplified. **2.** a result of simplifying.

sim·pli·fy (sim′plə fī′) *v.t.,* **-fied, -fy·ing.** to make less difficult, complex, or elaborate; make simple. [French *simplifier,* from Medieval Latin *simplificare,* from Latin *simplus* not complex, plain[1] + *facere* to make.] —**sim′pli·fi′er,** *n.*

sim·plis·tic (sim plis′tik) *adj.* characterized by oversimplification or by a tendency to oversimplify a problem or issue: *a simplistic statement, a simplistic thinker.* —**sim·plis′ti·cal·ly,** *adj.*

sim·ply (sim′plē) *adv.* **1.** in a clear, unpretentious, or straightforward manner. **2.** without elaboration or ornament; plainly: *The room was decorated simply.* **3.** without other aspects; merely; only: *It is simply a question of convenience.* **4.** to the fullest or highest degree; without qualification; absolutely: *The mountain is simply spectacular.*

sim·u·la·crum (sim′yə lā′krəm) *n., pl.* **-cra (-krə)** or **-crums. 1.** a shadowy or unreal likeness of something. **2.** a representation of something; image. [Latin *simulacrum.*]

sim·u·late (*v.,* sim′yə lāt′; *adj.,* sim′yə lit, -lāt′) *v.t.,* **-lat·ed, -lat·ing. 1.** to make a pretense of; pretend: *to simulate grief.* **2.** to have or take on the appearance or form of; imitate: *That painted panel simulates marble.* —*adj.* pretended; feigned. [Latin *simulātus,* past participle of *simulāre* to pretend, make like.] —**sim′u·la′tive,** *adj.* —**sim·u·la·to·ry** (sim′ye lə tôr′ē) *adj.* —**sim′-u·la′tor,** *n.* —For Synonyms *(v.t.),* see **pretend.**

sim·u·la·tion (sim′yə lā′shən) *n.* **1.** the act or process of simulating. **2.** something that simulates; imitation: *The art collec-*

a	at	e	end	o	hot	u	up	hw	white		about
ā	ape	ē	me	ō	old	ū	use	ng	song		taken
ä	far	i	it	ô	fork	ü	rule	th	thin	ə	pencil
âr	care	ī	ice	oi	oil	ù	pull	th	this		lemon
				ir	pierce	ou	out	ûr	turn	zh	measure		circus

tion included both genuine ivory carvings and simulations. **3.** the use of programs and data that enable a computer to represent a dynamic model of an actual or hypothetical physical system, such as an aircraft in flight or the evolution of the universe.

si·mul·cast (sī′məl kast′, sim′əl-) *v.t.,* **-cast** or **-cast·ed, -cast·ing.** to broadcast (a program) simultaneously over radio and television or on two or more stations or channels. *—n.* a program broadcast in this way. [SIMUL(TANEOUS) + (BROAD)-CAST.]

si·mul·ta·ne·ous (sī′məl tā′nē əs, sim′əl-) *adj.* existing, occurring, or accomplished at the same time: *simultaneous events.* [Medieval Latin *simultaneus,* from *simultas* simultaneousness, from Latin *simultas* competition, rivalry, from *simul* at the same time.] **—si·mul·ta·ne·i·ty** (sī′məl tə nē′i tē, sim′əl-), **si′mul·ta′ne·ous·ness,** *n.* **—si′mul·ta′ne·ous·ly,** *adv.*

simultaneous equations, two or more equations having variables that are satisfied by the same set of values. The equations $x + y = 2$ and $3x + 2y = 5$ are simultaneous equations because both are satisfied by $x = 1, y = 1.$

sin (sin) *n.* **1.** the willful violation of divine law or some religious principle. **2.** an instance of this. **3.** any violation of a standard, as of taste or propriety. *—v.i.,* **sinned, sin·ning. 1.** to violate a divine law or religious principle; commit sin. **2.** to commit an offense or wrong of any kind. [Old English *synn* violation of divine law, wrongdoing.]

sin, sine[1].

since (sins) *adv.* **1.** from then till now: *She left last week and has been away ever since.* **2.** at some time between then and now: *He was sick last month but has since recovered.* **3.** before now; ago: *She's been long since gone. —prep.* **1.** continuously after the time of: *He has been gone since five o'clock.* **2.** during the time following: *There have been many changes since the founding of this town. —conj.* **1.** during the period following the time when: *I haven't seen my roommate since we graduated.* **2.** continuously from the time when: *She has lived abroad since she was a young girl.* **3.** in view of the fact that; because: *Since he can't do the job, I'll do it.* [Middle English *sinnes,* contraction of *sithenes* then, from that time, going back to Old English *siththan* after that, later.]

sin·cere (sin sîr′) *adj.,* **-cer·er, -cer·est.** without affectation, hypocrisy, or pretense: *a sincere wish, a sincere friend.* [Latin *sincērus* pure, genuine.] **—sin·cere′ly,** *adv.*

sin·cer·i·ty (sin ser′i tē) *n.* the state or quality of being sincere.

sine[1] (sīn) *n.* (of either acute angle of a right triangle) the trigonometric function that is the ratio of the length of the side opposite the angle to the length of the hypotenuse. [Medieval Latin *sinus* (translation of Arabic *jaib* sine[1], bosom), from Latin *sinus* fold[1], bosom.]

si·ne[2] (sī′nē, sē′nā) *prep. Latin.* without.

si·ne·cure (sī′ni kyŭr′, sin′i-) *n.* an office or position that demands little or no work or responsibility, esp. one with a good salary. [Church Latin *(beneficium) sine cūrā* (benefice) without care (of souls).]

si·ne di·e (sī′nē dī′ē, sin′ā dē′ā) without fixing a day for a future meeting: *to adjourn sine die.* [Latin *sine diē* without a day (being set).]

si·ne qua non (sī′nē kwä non′, kwä, sin′ā) something absolutely necessary or essential. [Latin *sine quā nōn* literally, without which not.]

sin·ew (sin′ū) *n.* **1.** a tendon. **2.** muscular power or strength. **3.** *also,* **sinews.** a source of power or strength: *The sinews of a nation are its youth. —v.t.* to strengthen as with sinews: *The team was sinewed with experienced players.* [Old English *sinu* tendon.]

sine wave (sīn) *Physics.* the symmetrical waveform produced by a vibrating or oscillating body undergoing harmonic motion that repeats itself at a regular, unvarying rate; waveform characteristic of a single frequency. Such a wave may characterize an alternating current, the motion of a pendulum, sound, or electromagnetic radiation.

sin·ew·y (sin′ū ē) *adj.* **1.** characteristic of or containing sinews; tough; stringy: *a sinewy cut of meat.* **2.** physically strong or powerful; muscular. **3.** vigorous; robust.

sin·ful (sin′fəl) *adj.* full of or marked by sin; wicked; corrupt. **—sin′ful·ly,** *adv.* **—sin′ful·ness,** *n.*

sing (sing) *v.,* **sang** or **sung, sung, sing·ing.** *—v.i.* **1.** to utter words or sounds in musical succession or with musical tones; perform a song: *to sing well.* **2.** to produce melodious sounds: *The birds sang in the trees.* **3.** to relate or praise something in song or verse (with *of*): *The poet sang of the people's victory over tyranny.* **4.** to make a whistling, ringing, or humming sound: *The steam sang as it escaped from the teakettle.* **5.** to have a whistling, ringing, or humming sensation, as in the ears. **6.** to be adaptable for singing: *Rhyming poetry sings easily.* **7.** *Slang.* to confess to or give information about a crime: *to sing to the authorities. —v.t.* **1.** to utter or perform with musical tones; perform by singing: *to*

sing a song. **2.** to bring to a particular state or condition by or with singing: *to sing a child to sleep.* **3.** to recite in a singing voice; intone: *to sing a prayer during a religious service.* **4.** to proclaim enthusiastically: *to sing someone's virtues. —n.* a group gathering for the purpose of singing together: *We went to the community sing.* [Old English *singan* to make vocal sounds musically, chant, recount in song or verse.] **—sing′a·ble,** *adj.*

·to sing out. *Informal.* to call or cry out loudly.

sing., singular.

singe (sinj) *v.t.,* **singed, singe·ing. 1.** to burn superficially or lightly; scorch: *The hot iron singed the shirt.* **2.** to burn the ends or tips of (hair). **3.** to remove feathers or bristles from by subjecting briefly to a flame: *The cook singed the turkey before roasting it. —n.* **1.** the act of singeing. **2.** a superficial burn. [Old English *sengan* to burn superficially.] —For Synonyms *(v.t.),* see **scorch.**

sing·er (sing′ər) *n.* **1.** a person who sings, esp. a trained or professional vocalist. **2.** a bird that sings.

Sin·gha·lese (sing′gə lēz′, -lēs′) *adj.* Sinhalese. *—n., pl.* **-lese.** Sinhalese.

sin·gle (sing′gəl) *adj.* **1.** being a solitary object, unit, or individual; only one: *A single chair stood against the wall.* **2.** making up a separate distinct part or unit from others of its kind: *I think of you every single day.* **3.** of or designed for the use of one person only: *I requested a single room at the hotel.* **4.**a. unmarried: *a single person.* b. of, relating to, or characteristic of the unmarried state or unmarried persons. **5.** without another or others; unaccompanied: *There was a single customer in the store.* **6.** involving only two persons: *The two adversaries decided the matter by single combat.* **7.** honest; sincere: *I have a single devotion to my work.* **8.** (of a flower) having only one row or set of petals. *—n.* **1.** a solitary person or thing; individual. **2.** something that is for one person only, as a hotel room or a ticket: *I've reserved a single for you.* **3.** *Golf.* a game for two people only. **4.** *Baseball.* a hit that allows the batter to reach first base safely. **5. singles.** a match between two persons, as in tennis. ➡ used as singular. **6.** *Informal.* a one-dollar bill. *—v.,* **-gled, -gling.** *—v.t.* **1.** to select or separate from others (with *out*): *I singled out the white kitten as my favorite.* **2.** *Baseball.* a. to cause (a base runner) to advance by making a single: *I singled the runner to third.* b. to cause (a run) to score by making a single (often with *in*). *—v.i. Baseball.* to make a hit that allows the batter to advance to first base. [Old French *single* each, alone, not multiple, from Late Latin *singulus* separate, one only, from Latin *singulī* one to each, separate.] **—sin′gle·ness,** *n.* —For Synonyms *(adj.),* see **sole**[2].

single bond, a chemical bond in which a pair of electrons is shared between two atoms, as in saturated organic compounds.

sin·gle-breast·ed (sing′gəl bres′tid) *adj.* (of garments, esp. coats or jackets) having a row of buttons or other fastenings on one side only.

single file, a line of persons or things one behind another.

sin·gle-foot (sing′gəl fŭt′) *n.* the gait of a horse in which each foot is put down separately. *—v.i.* to go at such a gait.

sin·gle-hand·ed (sing′gəl han′did) *adj.* **1.** without the aid or support of another or others; unassisted: *a single-handed victory.* **2.** having, using, or needing only one hand. **—sin′gle-hand′ed·ly,** *adv.* **—sin′gle-hand′ed·ness,** *n.*

sin·gle-heart·ed (sing′gəl här′tid) *adj.* sincere and honest; straightforward: *a single-hearted desire to help the poor.* **—sin′-gle-heart′ed·ly,** *adv.* **—sin′gle-heart′ed·ness,** *n.*

sin·gle-lens reflex (sing′gəl lenz′) a camera in which the image received through the lens is reflected by a mirror to both an opaque glass screen for viewing and focusing and to the film.

sin·gle-mind·ed (sing′gəl mīn′did) *adj.* **1.** having only one aim or purpose. **2.** honest; sincere. **—sin′gle-mind′ed·ly,** *adv.* **—sin′gle-mind′ed·ness,** *n.*

sin·gle·stick (sing′gəl stik′) *n.* **1.** formerly, a swordlike stick used instead of a sword in fencing. **2.** fencing with such a stick.

single tax, a tax levied on land as the sole source of public revenue.

sin·gle·ton (sing′gəl tən) *n.* **1.** a playing card that is the only one of a particular suit held in the hand. **2.** a single person or thing, as distinct from a pair or group.

sin·gle-track (sing′gəl trak′) *adj.* having a limited range; narrow; one-track: *a single-track mind.*

sin·gle-tree (sing′gəl trē′) *n.* whiffletree. [Modification of SWINGLE TREE.]

sin·gly (sing′glē) *adv.* **1.** one at a time; individually; separately: *to consider each item on a list singly.* **2.** without the aid of another or others; single-handedly.

sing·song (sing′sông′) *n.* **1.** a monotonous, rhythmical cadence or tone, as in speaking. **2.** a verse, song, or speech characterized by this. *—adj.* having a monotonous, rhythmical cadence or tone.

sin·gu·lar (sing′gyə lər) *adj.* **1.** out of the ordinary; unusual or

remarkable; extraordinary: *a singular diamond ring.* **2.** strange or peculiar; odd: *singular behavior.* **3.** being the only one of its kind; unique: *a singular example of courage.* **4.** of or relating to a grammatical form that denotes a single person or thing: *"Am" is a singular verb.* —*n.* the form of a word denoting a single person or thing. [Latin *singulāris* single, separate, extraordinary, from *singulī* one to each, separate.] —**sin′gu·lar·ly,** *adv.*

sin·gu·lar·i·ty (sing′gyə lar′i tē) *n., pl.* **-ties. 1.** the state or quality of being singular. **2.** something that is singular.

Sin·ha·lese (sin′hə lēz′, -lēs′) *also,* **Singhalese.** *n., pl.* **-lese. 1.** a member of the people who constitute the majority of the population of Sri Lanka. **2.** the language spoken by the Sinhalese. —*adj.* of, relating to, or characteristic of Sri Lanka, the Sinhalese, or their language.

sin·is·ter (sin′ə stər) *adj.* **1.** threatening or suggesting evil; ominous: *The dark old house looked sinister at night.* **2.** malicious or evil: *a sinister plot.* **3.** *Heraldry.* situated on the bearer's left and thus to the right of the viewer. ➡ distinguished from **dex·ter. 4.** *Archaic.* of, relating to, or on the left. [Latin *sinister* left; referring to the belief of augurs in ancient times that the *left* side was unlucky.] —**sin′is·ter·ly,** *adv.* —**sin′is·ter·ness,** *n.*

sin·is·tral (sin′ə strəl) *adj.* **1.** of or on the left side. **2.** left-handed. ➡ distinguished from **dextral.** —**sin′is·tral·ly,** *adv.*

sink (singk) *v.,* **sank** or **sunk, sunk** or **sunk·en, sink·ing.** —*v.i.* **1.** to become partly or completely submerged in or as in water: *The wheels of the car sank into the mud. The ship sank after the collision.* **2.** to descend or appear to descend to a lower level, esp. gradually: *The water in the pond sank three feet last summer. The sun sank behind the mountain.* **3.** to slope downward: *The road sinks into a ditch.* **4.** to diminish or decrease, as in volume, force, degree, or intensity: *The commentator's voice sank to a whisper as the tennis match began.* **5.** to become less in value or estimation; decline: *The value of money sank during the inflationary period.* **6.** to pass or fall gradually into a certain state or condition: *to sink into a deep sleep.* **7.** to decline or fail rapidly in health; come near death. **8.** to penetrate deeply: *The stain sank into the cloth.* **9.** to become or seem hollow, as the eyes. —*v.t.* **1.** to cause to become partly or completely submerged in or as in water; cause to go down below a surface: *A violent storm sank the boat.* **2.** to cause to descend to a lower level. **3.** to reduce, as in volume, force, degree, or intensity. **4.** to excavate or dig: *We sank a well behind the house.* **5.** to force, lay, or bury in the ground: *The workers sank the pipeline.* **6.a.** to invest (money): *I sank much money into the business.* **b.** to lose (money) by investing unwisely. **7.** to pass over silently; conceal; suppress. **8.** *Basketball.* to toss (the ball) into the basket. **9.** *Golf.* to putt (the ball) into the hole. —*n.* **1.** a basin of metal or porcelain usually connected to a water supply, used for washing. **2.a.** a depression in a land surface where water collects. **b.** sinkhole. **3.** a place where vice or corruption prevail. [Old English *sincan* to become submerged in water, descend to a lower level.] —**sink′a·ble,** *adj.*

·**to sink in.** *Informal.* to be or become completely understood: *The meaning of what they said finally sank in.*

sink·er (sing′kər) *n.* **1.** a person or thing that sinks. **2.** a weight used to sink a fishing line. **3.** *Baseball.* a pitched ball that drops sharply as it reaches home plate. **4.** *Slang.* doughnut.

sink·hole (singk′hōl′) *n.* a vertical cavity worn in rock, esp. limestone, by water dripping downward. Also, **sink.**

sinking fund, a fund set aside in order to pay off a debt.

sin·less (sin′lis) *adj.* free from or without sin. —**sin′less·ly,** *adv.* —**sin′less·ness,** *n.*

sin·ner (sin′ər) *n.* a person who sins.

Sinn Fein (shin′ fān′) an Irish political party, founded about 1905, that demanded Irish independence from Great Britain. [Irish *sinn féin* we ourselves.]

Sino- *combining form* **1.** Chinese: *Sinology.* **2.** Chinese and: *Sino-Russian.* [Late Latin *Sinae* the Chinese, from Greek *Sinai,* going back to Chinese (Mandarin) *Ch'in* name of a Chinese dynasty of the third century B.C.]

Si·nol·o·gy (sī nol′ə jē, si-) *n.* the study of the Chinese people, their history, language, literature, or culture. [Sino- + -LOGY.] —**Si·no·log·i·cal** (sī′nə loj′i kəl), *adj.* —**Si·nol′o·gist,** *n.*

Si·no-Ti·bet·an (sī′nō ti bet′ən) *n.* a language family including Burmese, Chinese, and Thai, and other languages spoken predominantly in Burma, China, Thailand, Tibet, and certain other Far Eastern countries. —*adj.* of or relating to this language family.

sin·ter (sin′tər) *n.* a mixture of metallic or ceramic particles fired so that it is a coherent mass but is not completely fused. —*v.t., v.i.* to form into or become a sinter. [German *sinter,* from Old High German *sintar* dross, slag. See CINDER.]

sin·u·ate (sin′ū it, -āt′) *adj.* **1.** irregularly turning or curving; sinuous. **2.** (of a leaf) having a wavy margin. [Latin *sinuātus,* past participle of *sinuāre* to wind[2], bend.] —**sin′u·a′tion,** *n.*

sin·u·os·i·ty (sin′ū os′i tē) *n., pl.* **-ties. 1.** the state or quality of being sinuous. **2.** a curve or bend.

sin·u·ous (sin′ū əs) *adj.* full of bends, curves, or winds: *the sinuous course of a brook.* [Latin *sinuōsus* full of folds or curves, from *sinus* fold[1], curve.] —**sin′u·ous·ly,** *adv.* —**sin′u·ous·ness,** *n.*

si·nus (sī′nəs) *n., pl.* **-nus·es. 1.a.** any of the air-filled cavities connected with the nostrils in the bones of the face. **b.** a channel for the passage of venous blood. **2.** a narrow passage leading to an abscess. **3.** a curving part or hollow. **4.** a rounded indentation between two projecting lobes, as of a leaf. [Latin *sinus* fold[1], bay, curve.]

si·nus·i·tis (sī′nə sī′tis) *n.* inflammation of a sinus or sinuses, esp. in the skull.

Si·on (sī′ən) Zion.

Siou·an (sü′ən) *n.* **1.** a family of North American Indian languages, including the Sioux, Osage, and Crow. **2.** Sioux *(def. 1).* —*adj.* of or relating to the Siouan language family.

Sioux (sü) *n., pl.* **Sioux** (sü, süz). **1.** a member of any of various tribes of North American Indians speaking a Siouan language, formerly living in Minnesota, North and South Dakota, and Wyoming. **2.** Dakota *(def. 1).* **3.** the Siouan language spoken by these tribes.

sip (sip) *v.,* **sipped, sip·ping.** —*v.t.* to drink a very small quantity of (a liquid) at a time; drink little by little: *to sip a hot drink.* —*v.i.* to drink a very small quantity of a liquid at a time. —*n.* **1.** a quantity of liquid drunk at one time. **2.** the act of sipping. [Old English *sypian* to absorb moisture.]

si·phon (sī′fən) *also,* **syphon.** *n.* **1.** a bent tube with legs of unequal length, used to transfer a liquid from one container to another one at a lower level by atmospheric pressure. **2.** a tubelike organ of certain aquatic animals, as the clam or octopus, used for drawing in and expelling liquids. For illustration, see **octopus.** —*v.t.* to draw off through or as through a siphon. —*v.i.* to pass through a siphon. [Latin *sīphō* pipe, tube, from Greek *siphōn.*] —**si′phon·al,** *adj.*

sir (sûr) *n.* **1.** mister. ➡ a form of respectful or polite address for a man, used in direct address without the name: *May I help you, sir?* **2. Sir.** the title and form of address for a knight or baronet: *Sir Gawain.* **3.** *Archaic.* a title of respect used before a noun indicating a man's rank or profession: *sir Knight, sir Judge.* [Form of SIRE.]

siphon

sir·dar (sûr′där, sər där′) *n.* a dignitary, military chief, or other person of a high rank or importance in India, Pakistan, or Afghanistan. [Hindi *sardār* chief, from Persian *sardār.*]

sire (sīr) *n.* **1.** the male parent of a horse or other four-legged animal. **2.** a father or forefather. **3. Sire.** a form of address used in speaking to a king or nobleman. —*v.t.,* **sired, sir·ing.** to be the male parent of: *Our neighbor's dog sired a litter of puppies.* [Old French *sire* sir, master, lord, going back to Latin *senior* older, comparative of *senex* old. Doublet of SENIOR.]

si·ren (sī′rən) *n.* **1.** a device that produces a loud, shrill sound by the periodic escape of compressed air through a rotating shutter. **2. Siren.** in Greek mythology, one of several sea nymphs, part bird and part woman, whose singing lured sailors to their destruction. **3.** a charming but dangerous woman, esp. one who beguiles, seduces, or tempts men. —*adj.* of or like a Siren; charming, dangerously alluring, or enticing. [Latin *Sīrēn* this sea nymph, from Greek *Seirēn.*]

si·re·ni·an (sī rē′nē ən) *n.* any herbivorous, aquatic mammal of the order Sirenia, including the manatee and dugong. [Modern Latin *Sirenia* (from Latin *Sīrēn* Siren) + -AN. See SIREN.]

Sir·i·us (sir′ē əs) *n.* the Dog Star, a double star, the brightest star in the heavens, located in the constellation Canis Major. [Latin *Sīrius,* from Greek *Seirios;* named after *Sirius,* the hunting dog of the Greek hero Orion.]

sir·loin (sûr′loin′) *n.* a cut of beef from the upper part of the loin. [Earlier *surloyn,* from Old French *surlonge,* from *sur* above (from Latin *super* over, above) + *longe* loin (going back to Latin *lumbus*).]

si·roc·co (si rok′ō) *n., pl.* **-cos. 1.** a hot, dry wind blowing

a	at	e	end	o	hot	u	up	hw	white		about
ā	ape	ē	me	ō	old	ū	use	ng	song		taken
ä	far	i	it	ô	fork	ü	rule	th	thin	ə	pencil
âr	care	ī	ice	oi	oil	u̇	pull	th	this		lemon
		îr	pierce	ou	out	ûr	turn	zh	measure		circus

northward from North Africa across the Mediterranean Sea and into southern Europe, where it becomes warm and humid. **2.** any hot, oppressive wind. [Italian *s(c)irocco* the southeast wind, from Arabic *sharq* east.]

sir·rah (sir′ə) *n. Archaic.* fellow. ➠ used as a contemptuous form of address to men or boys. [Modification of SIR.]

sir·up (sir′əp, sûr′-) syrup.

sis (sis) *n. Informal.* sister.

sis·al (sī′səl, sis′əl) *n.* **1.** a coarse, strong fiber obtained from the leaves of a tropical American plant, *Agave sisalana,* used to make rope and bags. Also, **sisal hemp. 2.** the plant yielding this fiber. **3.** any of several fibers resembling this fiber. [From *Sisal,* Mexican town.]

sis·kin (sis′kin) *n.* **1.** a sharp-billed Eurasian finch, *Carduelis spinus,* colored yellow-green with black markings. Length: 5 inches (13 centimeters). **2.** any of several similar finches, genus *Carduelis,* esp. the North American **pine siskin,** *C. pinus,* colored tan with black streaks, and yellow at the base of the tail and flight feathers. [Earlier *sysken,* from Middle Dutch *sijsken,* from German *zeischen,* diminutive of *zeizig,* from Czech *čížek,* diminutive of *číž;* imitative.]

sis·sy (sis′ē) *n., pl.* **-sies. 1.** a boy or man whose behavior is considered to be effeminate. **2.** a coward. [SIS + -Y².]

sis·ter (sis′tər) *n.* **1.** a girl or woman having the same parents as another person of either sex. **2.** a girl or woman having one parent in common with another person of either sex; half sister. **3.** stepsister. **4.** a close female friend thought of as a sister. **5.** a woman who is a fellow member, as of a church, club, or sorority. **6.** a woman who is a member of a religious order for women; nun. **7.** something that resembles or corresponds in some way to another and is thought of as feminine: *Those two ships are sisters.* **8.** *British.* a nurse, esp. a head nurse in charge of a hospital ward. [Of Scandinavian origin.]

sis·ter·hood (sis′tər hŏŏd′) *n.* **1.** the state or quality of being a sister or sisters; relationship between sisters. **2.** a group of women united by some common aim or who are bound by vows to a religious organization.

sis·ter-in-law (sis′tər in lô′) *n., pl.* **sis·ters-in-law. 1.** the sister of one's husband or wife. **2.** the wife of one's brother. **3.** the wife of the brother of one's husband or wife.

sis·ter·ly (sis′tər lē) *adj.* relating to, characteristic of, or befitting a sister; kind; affectionate. —*adv.* in the manner of a sister. —**sis′ter·li·ness,** *n.*

Sis·tine Chapel (sis′tēn, -tin) a chapel (built 1473-81) in the Vatican in Rome, noted for its frescoes by Michelangelo painted in the sixteenth century.

sis·trum (sis′trəm) *n., pl.* **-trums** or **-tra** (-trə). a musical instrument consisting of a metal frame fitted with metal bars that rattle when shaken, used esp. in ancient Egypt in the worship of Isis. [Latin *sīstrum,* from Greek *seistron,* from *seiein* to shake.]

Sis·y·phe·an (sis′ə fē′ən) *adj.* **1.** of or relating to Sisyphus. **2.** endless and futile; unceasing; eternal: *a Sisyphean task.*

Sis·y·phus (sis′ə fəs) *n.* in Greek mythology, a king of Corinth, noted for his craftiness, punished in the Underworld by having to push a huge rock to the top of a hill, from which it would roll back down, thus forcing him to begin again.

sit (sit) *v.,* **sat** or *(archaic)* **sate, sit·ting.** —*v.i.* **1.** to be in a position in which the weight of the body rests on the buttocks, while the rest of the body bends at the hips and, usually, the knees. **2.** to rest on a perch; roost: *The bird sat on a branch.* **3.** (of a chicken) to cover eggs in order to hatch them; brood. **4.** to be situated, placed, or positioned: *The cabin sits in the middle of a forest.* **5.** to assume or hold a particular pose for an artist or photographer; model: *to sit for a portrait.* **6.** to be or remain unused or inactive: *The store sat empty for a year.* **7.** to be a member of a council, jury, assembly, or legislative body: *to sit in a state legislature.* **8.** to hold a session; be convened: *The legislature sits in the fall.* **9.** to bear down as a burden; weigh: *Old age sits lightly upon my grandparents.* **10.** to fit or hang on the body in a certain way: *The coat sits well on you.* **11.** to baby-sit. —*v.t.* **1.** to cause to sit; seat: *The guests sat themselves around the table.* **2.** to ride (a horse). [Old English *sittan* to be seated, perch, be situated, take a seat.]

· **to sit down.** to take a seat; assume a sitting position.

· **to sit in on.** to attend or take part in: *The newspaper reporter sat in on the committee meeting.*

· **to sit on. a.** to keep from acting; squelch. **b.** to prevent the publication or expression of: *The newspaper editor sat on the story.*

· **to sit out. a.** to endure to the end of: *to sit out a bad performance.* **b.** to remain seated and take no part in: *to sit out a dance.*

· **to sit up. a.** to delay retiring until after one's usual bedtime. **b.** to become attentive or alert: *to sit up in surprise.*

si·tar (si tär′) *n.* a stringed musical instrument of India, having a long, fretted neck and a rounded body, made from a gourd or hollowed-out wood, played with a plectrum. [Hindi *sitār.*]

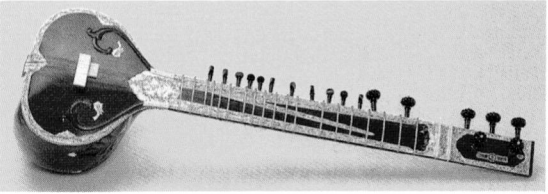

sitar

sit·com (sit′kom′) *n. Informal.* situation comedy. [Short for *sit(uation) com(edy).*]

sit-down strike (sit′doun′) a strike in which the strikers remain at their place of employment until an agreement is reached.

site (sīt) *n.* **1.** the position, as of a town, city, or building, esp. with reference to the surrounding region: *The village occupied a mountain site.* **2.** the location in which anything is, has been, or is to be located: *the site of an ancient city.* —*v.t.,* **sit·ed, sit·ing.** to give a position to; place; locate: *Where should we site our tent?* [Latin *situs* position, situation.]

sith (sith) *adv., prep., conj. Archaic.* since. [Old English *siththa* then, after.]

sit-in (sit′in′) *n.* a protest demonstration in which persons sit in a public place and refuse to leave, often until their demands are met or acknowledged or until they are forcibly evicted. —*v.i.* **sat-in, sit·ting-in.** to participate in a sit-in.

si·tol·o·gy (sī tol′ə jē) *n.* dietetics. [Greek *sītos* food, grain + -LOGY.]

sit·ter (sit′ər) *n.* **1.** a person who sits. **2.** a baby-sitter. **3.** a brooding hen.

sit·ting (sit′ing) *n.* **1.** the act of a person or thing that sits. **2.** the period of time that a person sits for or is occupied with a particular purpose: *I read the entire book in one sitting.* **3.** the session or term of a court or meeting. **4.** the number of eggs on which a hen sits at one time. —*adj.* relating to or used for sitting.

sitting duck *Informal.* a person or thing that is an easy target or victim.

sitting room, a room used for sitting, as in a home, hotel, or club.

sit·u·ate (*v.,* sich′ŏŏ āt′; *adj.,* sich′ŏŏ it, -āt′) *v.t.,* **-at·ed, -at·ing.** to give a position to; place: *to situate a house on top of a hill.* —*adj. Archaic.* situated. [Late Latin *situātus,* past participle of *situāre* to locate, place, from Latin *situs* position.]

sit·u·at·ed (sich′ŏŏ ā′tid) *adj.* **1.** placed in relation to surroundings: *The house is poorly situated.* **2.** placed in relation to circumstances, esp. financial circumstances: *to be well situated in a job.*

sit·u·a·tion (sich′ŏŏ ā′shən) *n.* **1.** a condition or state of affairs: *The lack of sales at the store created a difficult financial situation. What is the political situation in that country?* **2.** a place in relation to surroundings; location; position: *The situation of the barn is to the left of the house.* **3.** the work in which a person is engaged or employed; post of employment. —**sit′u·a′tion·al,** *adj.* —For Synonyms, see **circumstance.**

situation comedy, a comedy series, esp. on television, in which the same characters appear in different situations in successive episodes.

sit-up (sit′up′) *n.* an exercise in which a person lies with the back flat, bends at the waist into a sitting position without shifting the position of the legs, and then returns to a lying position.

si·tus (sī′təs) *n., pl.* **-tus.** position or location, esp. the proper or usual position, as of a part or organ. [Latin *situs.*]

sitz bath (sits, zits) **1.** a bath taken while sitting with only the lower trunk of the body submerged, usually for therapeutic reasons. **2.** a chairlike bathtub or a basin for taking such a bath. [Partial translation of German *Sitzbad* sitz bath, from *Sitz* sitting + *Bad* bath.]

Si·va (sē′və, shē′və) Shiva.

six (siks) *n.* **1.** the cardinal number that is one more than five. **2.** a symbol representing this number, such as 6 or VI. **3.** something having this many units or members, such as a playing card. —*adj.* numbering one more than five. [Old English *six.*]

· **at sixes and sevens. a.** in confusion. **b.** at odds; in disagreement.

six·fold (siks′fōld′) *adj.* **1.** six times as great or as numerous. **2.** having or consisting of six parts. —*adv.* so as to be six times greater or more numerous: *The company's sales increased sixfold.*

six-gun (siks′gun′) *n.* six-shooter.

Six Nations, Iroquois.

six-pack (siks′pak′) *n.* a container or package of six cans, bottles, or other merchandise, sold as a unit.

six·pence (siks′pəns) *n.* a former coin of the United Kingdom, equal to six pennies.

six·pen·ny (siks′pen′ē, -pə nē) *adj.* **1.** of the worth or value of six British pennies. **2.** of little value or worth; cheap; meager. **3.** designating a nail 2 inches (5 centimeters) in length.

six-shoot·er (siks′shü′tər) *n. Informal.* a revolver that can be fired six times without being reloaded. Also, **six-gun.**

six·teen (siks′tēn′) *n.* **1.** the cardinal number that is six more than ten. **2.** a symbol representing this number, such as 16 or XVI. **3.** something having this many units or members. —*adj.* numbering six more than ten. [Old English *sixtŷne.*]

six·teenth (siks′tēnth′) *adj.* **1.** (the ordinal of sixteen) next after the fifteenth. **2.** being one of sixteen equal parts. —*n.* **1.** something that is next after the fifteenth. **2.** one of sixteen equal parts; ¹⁄₁₆.

sixteenth note *Music.* a note having one sixteenth the time value of a whole note. For illustration, see **note.**

sixth (siksth) *adj.* **1.** (the ordinal of six) next after the fifth. **2.** being one of six equal parts. —*n.* **1.** something that is next after the fifth. **2.** one of six equal parts; ¹⁄₆. **3.** *Music.* **a.** a tone that is a total of four whole steps and one half step above a given note. *A* is the sixth of *C.* **b.** an interval of four whole steps and one half step. **c.** two tones separated by this interval. —*adv.* in the sixth place.

sixth sense, a seeming ability to know or sense things that could not be known or sensed with the five senses; intuition.

six·ti·eth (siks′tē ith) *adj.* **1.** (the ordinal of sixty) next after the fifty-ninth. **2.** being one of sixty equal parts. —*n.* **1.** something that is next after the fifty-ninth. **2.** one of sixty equal parts; ¹⁄₆₀.

six·ty (siks′tē) *n., pl.* **-ties. 1.** the cardinal number that is six times ten. **2.** a symbol representing this number, such as 60 or LX. **3. sixties.** the number series from sixty through sixty-nine. ➡ used esp. in reference to the seventh decade of a century or of a person's life. —*adj.* numbering six times ten. [Old English *sixtig.*]

six·ty-fourth note (siks′tē fôrth′) *Music.* a note having one sixty-fourth the time value of a whole note.

siz·a·ble (sī′zə bəl) *also,* **sizeable.** *adj.* somewhat large: *a sizable two-story house, a sizable donation.*

size¹ (sīz) *n.* **1.** the degree of length, breadth, or height that something has: *the size of a room, the size of a tree.* **2.** greatness of extent; bigness: *There is no house of any size in that neighborhood.* **3.** amount or number: *the size of an inheritance, the size of a town.* **4.** a measurement by which manufactured articles are classified, arranged, or sorted: *the size of a hat.* **5.** the mental or moral qualities with reference to the ability to meet requirements: *The position needs an arbiter of larger size.* **6.** *Informal.* the true state of affairs; actual circumstances: *That's the size of it.* —*v.t.,* **sized, siz·ing. 1.** to classify, arrange, or sort according to size: *to size eggs.* **2.** to make of a certain or required size: *The jeweler sized the ring to fit my finger.* [Short for ASSIZE (mistaken for *a size*) in the earlier sense of "a fixed quantity."]
    • **of a size.** of the same or nearly the same size: *The two ships are of a size.*
    • **to size up.** *Informal.* to make an estimate of; form an opinion of: *The mayor sized up the political situation before running for governor.*

size² (sīz) *n.* any of various glues or pastes used to coat or glaze a porous surface, as of fabric or paper. Also, **sizing.** —*v.t.,* **sized, siz·ing.** to treat or coat with size. [Of uncertain origin.]

size·a·ble (sī′zə bəl) sizable.

sized (sīzd) *adj.* having a specified size. ➡ used in combination: *mid-sized, full-sized.*

siz·ing (sī′zing) *n.* **1.** size². **2.** the act or process of treating with or applying size.

siz·zle (siz′əl) *v.i.,* **-zled, -zling. 1.** to make a hissing sound, esp. while burning or frying. **2.** to be very hot, as a summer day: *It's sizzling outside.* **3.** *Informal.* to be simmering with rage: *I was sizzling as I listened to the lies and accusations.* —*n.* a hissing sound. [Imitative.]

SK, the postal abbreviation for Saskatchewan.

skald (skôld, skäld) *also,* **scald.** *n.* an ancient Scandinavian poet; bard. [Old Norse *skald.*] —**skald′ic,** *adj.*

skate¹ (skāt) *n.* **1.** ice skate. **2.** roller skate. —*v.i.,* **skat·ed, skat·ing.** to glide or move along on or as on skates. [Dutch *schaats* an ice skate, from Old French *eschace* stilt; of Germanic origin.] —**skat′er,** *n.*

skate² (skāt) *n., pl.* **skates** or **skate.** any of a group of rays,

family Rajidae, found in warm and temperate seas, having two broad, winglike side fins. Length: 2-8 feet (0.6-2.4 meters). [Old Norse *skata.*]

skate³ (skāt) *n. Slang.* **1.** an old, worn-out horse; nag. **2.** a fellow; guy. [Of uncertain origin.]

skate·board (skāt′bôrd′) *n.* a short, flat, oblong board having wheels attached to the bottom, ridden usually with the rider balancing in a standing position. —**skate′board′er,** *n.* —**skate′board′ing,** *n.*

skat·ing (skā′ting) *n.* the act or sport of moving over a surface on ice skates or roller skates.

ske·dad·dle (ski dad′əl) *Informal. v.i.,* **-dled, -dling.** to run away; flee in haste. —*n.* the act of running away hastily. [Of uncertain origin.] —**ske·dad′dler,** *n.*

skeet shooting (skēt) trapshooting in which clay pigeons, or disks, are launched to simulate the flight of birds and are fired at from various positions along the range. Also, **skeet.**

skein (skān) *n.* **1.** a continuous strand of yarn or thread coiled in a bundle. **2.** something resembling this: *a skein of hair.* **3.** a flock of geese or similar birds in flight. [Old French *escaigne* hank of yarn; of uncertain origin.]

skel·e·tal (skel′i təl) *adj.* of, relating to, forming, or resembling a skeleton. —**skel′e·tal·ly,** *adv.*

skel·e·ton (skel′i tən) *n.* **1.** the framework of bones supporting the muscles, organs, and other soft parts of the body of a vertebrate. **2.** a supporting framework or structure, as of a building. **3.** an outline, as of a literary work; sketch. **4.** *Informal.* a very thin or emaciated person or animal. —*adj.* **1.** of, relating to, or resembling a skeleton. **2.** consisting of or reduced to the mere outline or essential number required for something: *a skeleton staff.* [Modern Latin *skeleton,* from Greek *skeleton,* from *skeletos* dried up.]
    • **skeleton in the closet.** a secret, usually about one's past, kept hidden because of fear, shame, or possible dishonor.

skel·e·ton·ize (skel′i tə nīz′) *v.t.,* **-ized, -iz·ing.** to reduce to or construct in skeleton form. —**skel′e·ton·i·za′tion,** *n.*

skeleton key, a key with a large part of the bit filed away to enable it to open a number of different locks.

skep·tic (skep′tik) *also,* **sceptic.** *n.* **1.** a person who habitually doubts or questions the truth of generally accepted beliefs or conclusions. **2.** a person who tends to be doubtful or suspicious, esp. concerning the assertions of others. **3.** a person who doubts religious principles or doctrines. **4.** *also,* **Skeptic.** an adherent of any philosophical school of skepticism. [Greek *skeptikos* thoughtful.]

skep·ti·cal (skep′ti kəl) *also,* **sceptical.** *adj.* **1.** characterized by or showing doubt or suspicion; questioning; disbelieving: *a skeptical attitude.* **2.** of, relating to, or characteristic of skeptics or skepticism. —**skep′ti·cal·ly,** *adv.*

skep·ti·cism (skep′tə siz′əm) *also,* **scepticism.** *n.* **1.** a doubt-

Cranium (skull)
Clavicle (collarbone)
Sternum (breastbone)
Scapula (shoulder blade)
Humerus
Ribs
Spinal column
Radius
Ulna
Pelvis (hips)
Femur
Patella (kneecap)
Fibula
Tibia

human **skeleton**

ing or questioning disposition or state of mind. **2.** doubt concerning religious principles or doctrines. **3.** *also,* **Skepticism.** the philosophical view that certain knowledge is unattainable.

sker·ry (sker′ē) *n.* a small, rocky island or reef in the sea. [Scottish dialect *skerri* rock in the sea, from Old Norse *sker* reef.]

sketch (skech) *n.* **1.** a rough, unfinished, or rapidly executed drawing, esp. one intended to serve as the basis of a more finished work: *The artist made several sketches of the model before starting the painting.* **2.** a short description, presentation, or plan giving the essential features of something; outline. **3.** a brief, informal literary composition. **4.** a short scene or play, as in a revue, musical comedy, or other theatrical program. —*v.t.* to make a sketch or outline of: *The painter sketched the old barn.* —*v.i.* to make a sketch or sketches. [Dutch *schets* model, draft, through Italian, from Latin *schedium* extemporaneous poem, going back to Greek *schedios* offhand, extemporaneous.] —**sketch′er,** *n.*

sketch·book (skech′bŏŏk′) *n.* **1.** a pad or book used for sketching or drawing. **2.** a book of literary sketches.

sketch·y (skech′ē) *adj.,* **sketch·i·er, sketch·i·est. 1.** not detailed or finished: *a sketchy outline of a speech.* **2.** incomplete or fragmentary; imperfect; slight: *The dazed driver could give only a sketchy account of the accident.* —**sketch′i·ly,** *adv.* —**sketch′i·ness,** *n.*

skew (skū) *v.i.* **1.** to veer away from a straight line; swerve; twist: *The railroad tracks skew to the left after crossing the river.* **2.** to look obliquely; squint. —*v.t.* **1.** to cause to turn aside from a straight line; set at an angle. **2.** to slant or twist the meaning or significance of; distort: *The witnesses skewed their testimony to favor the defendant.* —*adj.* **1.** having an oblique position or direction; turned to one side. **2.** having a part that deviates from a straight line, right angle, or the like. **3.** *Geometry.* lying in different planes; neither intersecting nor parallel. **4.** *Statistics.* asymmetrical in frequency. —*n.* an oblique movement, position, or direction; deviation from a straight line. [Dialectal Old French *eskiuwer,* form of *eschiver* to shun; of Germanic origin.] —**skew′ness,** *n.*

skew·back (skū′bak′) *n.* **1.** a slanting surface supporting the end of an arch. **2.** a stone, course of masonry, or other supporting member having such a surface.

skew·er (skū′ər) *n.* **1.** a long pin of wood or metal used to hold meat, fish, or other food together while cooking. **2.** any of various items having a similar shape or use. —*v.t.* to fasten or pierce with or as with a skewer or skewers. [Form of dialectal English *skiver;* of uncertain origin.]

ski (skē; *British* shē) *n.* **1.** one of a pair of long, narrow runners, usually of wood or metal, curving upward at the front and designed to be fastened to a boot for gliding over snow. **2.** water ski. —*v.,* **skied, ski·ing.** —*v.i.* to glide or travel on skis, esp. as a sport. —*v.t.* to glide or travel over on skis: *to ski a steep slope.* [Norwegian *ski* billet of wood, ski for traveling over snow, from Old Norse *skīth* snowshoe.] —**ski′er,** *n.*

skid (skid) *n.* **1.** the act of sliding or slipping, usually sideways, as over an icy or wet surface. **2.** a device, as a wedge of wood or metal, placed against the wheel of a vehicle to prevent the vehicle from moving. **3.** a plank or frame used as a track on which something heavy may be slid or pushed along. **4.** a runner that is part of the landing gear of certain aircraft. —*v.,* **skid·ded, skid·ding.** —*v.i.* **1.** to slide or slip, usually sideways, esp. because of loss of traction: *The airplane skidded on the wet runway.* **2.** (of a wheel of a moving vehicle) to slide without rotating. —*v.t.* **1.** to prevent (a wheel) from moving by applying a skid. **2.** to haul, slide, move, or place on a skid or skids. [Possibly of Scandinavian origin.] —**skid′der,** *n.*

· **to be on** (or **hit**) **the skids.** *Slang.* to rapidly decline in prestige, power, value, or quality: *The entertainer's career was on the skids.*

skid row *Slang.* a rundown section of a city inhabited and frequented by the homeless and those with little or no money, such as indigent alcoholics and heavy drug users.

skies (skīz) the plural of **sky.**

skiff (skif) *n.* a small, light boat propelled by motor, sail, or oars. [French *esquif* little boat, from Italian *scifo;* of Germanic origin.]

ski·ing (skē′ing) *n.* the act or sport of gliding or traveling on skis.

ski jump 1. a steep snow-covered ramp, track, or course ending abruptly above a long, gentle slope, designed for long-distance jumping by skiers. **2.** a jump made by a skier over such a course.

skil·ful (skil′fəl) *British.* skillful.

ski lift, an apparatus for transporting skiers up a slope, usually consisting of a motor-operated cable to which seats are attached.

skill (skil) *n.* **1.** the power or capacity to do something, resulting

from knowledge, training, practice, or experience; proficiency: *to show great skill in playing the violin.* **2.** a particular power: *reading skills.* **3.** an art, trade, or occupation requiring special knowledge and dexterity, esp. manual dexterity: *Carpentry is a skill.* [Old Norse *skil* distinction, knowledge.] —For Synonyms, see **ability.**

skilled (skild) *adj.* **1.** having or showing skill or competence; proficient: *a skilled musician.* **2.** having or requiring specialized ability or training: *skilled labor.* —For Synonyms, see **expert.**

skil·let (skil′it) *n.* **1.** a shallow pan with a handle, used for frying; frying pan. **2.** *British.* a saucepan with a long handle. [Possibly from Old French *escuellete* small dish, diminutive of *escuelle* dish, going back to Latin *scutella* salver.]

skill·ful (skil′fəl) *also, British,* **skilful.** *adj.* having, showing, or involving skill: *a skillful chess player, a skillful maneuver.* —**skill′ful·ly,** *adv.* —**skill′ful·ness,** *n.*

skim (skim) *v.,* **skimmed, skim·ming.** —*v.t.* **1.** to clear (a liquid) of floating matter: *to skim soup.* **2.** to remove (floating matter) from a liquid: *to skim fat from soup.* **3.** to glance over or read hastily or superficially: *to skim a newspaper.* **4.** to move or glide lightly and swiftly over or across: *The duck skimmed the water.* **5.** to throw so as to pass or bounce lightly over or along a surface: *to skim a stone across a lake.* **6.** to cover with a thin film or layer, as of ice. —*v.i.* **1.** to move or glide lightly and swiftly over or across a surface: *The little sailboat skimmed across the pond.* **2.** to make a hasty or superficial examination of something (with *over* or *through*): *to skim through a newspaper.* **3.** to become covered with a thin film or layer. —*n.* **1.** the act or process of skimming. **2.** something that has been skimmed. **3.** a thin film or layer. —*adj.* that has been skimmed. [Probably from Old French *escumer* to clear (a liquid) of floating matter, from *escume* foam, scum; of Germanic origin.]

skim·mer (skim′ər) *n.* **1.** a person or thing that skims. **2.** a utensil, esp. a shallow ladle having a flat, perforated bowl, used to skim liquids. **3.** any of various gull-like seabirds, family Rynchopidae, that skim the water with the long, lower beak while in flight, searching for food. Length: 16-19 inches (41-48 centimeters). **4.** a wide-brimmed hat, usually of straw, with a flat crown.

skimmer *(def. 3)*

skim milk *also,* **skimmed milk.** milk from which the cream has been removed.

skimp (skimp) *v.i.* to be very sparing or thrifty: *The cook skimped on the meat in the stew.* —*v.t.* **1.** to perform (a task) carelessly, hastily, or with poor material. **2.** to be very sparing or thrifty with: *Don't skimp the gravy with the mashed potatoes.* [Of uncertain origin.]

skimp·y (skim′pē) *adj.,* **skimp·i·er, skimp·i·est. 1.** less than what is needed; scanty; insufficient; meager: *a skimpy dinner.* **2.** very sparing or thrifty: *a skimpy person.* —**skimp′i·ly,** *adv.* —**skimp′i·ness,** *n.* —For Synonyms, see **meager.**

skin (skin) *n.* **1.** the outer body covering of an animal. **2.** such an outer covering removed from the body of an animal; pelt or hide. **3.** anything resembling skin in appearance, nature, or function: *the skin of an apple.* **4.** a vessel or container made of animal skin, used for holding liquids, esp. wine. **5.** a person's life or personal safety: *to save one's skin.* —*v.,* **skinned, skinning.** —*v.t.* **1.** to remove the skin from: *to skin a rabbit.* **2.** to injure the surface of or remove a portion of skin from, esp. by scraping: *to skin one's knee.* **3.** to cover with or as with skin. **4.** *Slang.* to swindle; cheat. —*v.i.* **1.** to become covered with skin. **2.** to climb: *to skin up a rope.* [Old Norse *skinn* hide².] —**skin′less,** *adj.* —**skin′like′,** *adj.*

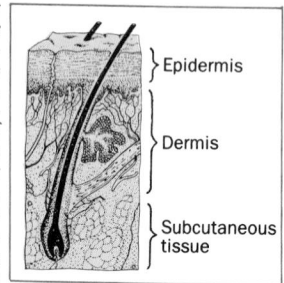

human skin

· **by the skin of one's teeth.** by a very narrow margin; barely: *I passed the test by the skin of my teeth.*

· **no skin off one's nose** (or **back**). *Informal.* not having any effect on one: *It's no skin off my nose if you don't study for the test.*

• **to get under one's skin.** to be or become annoying or irritating.

• **to have a thick skin.** to be insensitive, esp. to criticism or insult.

• **to have a thin skin.** to be very sensitive, esp. to criticism.

skin-deep (skin′dēp′) *adj.* only on the surface; superficial; shallow: *Beauty is only skin-deep.* —*adv.* superficially; shallowly.

skin-dive (skin′dīv′) *v.i.*, **-dived** or **-dove** (-dōv′), **-dived, -div-ing.** to engage in skin diving.

skin diving, underwater swimming for extended periods of time, usually with a face mask and flippers, and sometimes with oxygen tanks or a snorkel to enable the swimmer to remain submerged longer. —**skin diver.**

skin·flint (skin′flint′) *n.* an extremely stingy person; miser; niggard.

skin·ful (skin′fŭl′) *n., pl.* **-fuls. 1.** the amount of liquid that a skin container can hold. **2.** *Informal.* as much as a person can eat or drink.

skin game *Informal.* a dishonest or fraudulent game, scheme, or business operation.

skin graft, a piece of skin taken from an undamaged area of the body and surgically transplanted to an area where tissue has been destroyed, as by severe burns.

skink (skingk) *n.* any of a large group of lizards, family Scincidae, having an elongated, shiny body with smooth scales and short or vestigial legs. [Latin *scincus*, from Greek *skinkos*.]

skin·ner (skin′ər) *n.* **1.** a person who deals in animal skins, esp. one who removes and processes animal skins and furs. **2.** a driver of draft animals, esp. a mule driver.

skin·ny (skin′ē) *adj.*, **-ni·er, -ni·est. 1.** very thin; lean; emaciated; gaunt. **2.** of or like the skin. —*n. Slang.* secret or inside information. —**skin′ni·ness,** *n.*

skin test, any diagnostic test made on the skin, as a patch test or scratch test.

skin·tight (skin′tīt′) *adj.* fitting tightly: *skintight pants.*

skip (skip) *v.*, **skipped, skip·ping.** —*v.i.* **1.** to spring or bound along, hopping lightly on one foot and then the other: *The children skipped down the path.* **2.** to pass from one point to another, omitting or paying little or no attention to what lies between: *to skip over a chapter.* **3.** to bounce along or across a surface; skim. **4.** to be promoted in school beyond the next regular grade. **5.** *Informal.* to leave hurriedly or in secret: *The cashier skipped with the day's profits.* —*v.t.* **1.** to jump or spring lightly over: *to skip rope.* **2.** to omit or pass over or by: *I skipped the problems I couldn't do.* **3.** to cause to bounce along or across a surface; skim. **4.** to be promoted in school beyond (the next regular grade). **5.** *Informal.* to leave (a place) hurriedly or in secret: *The embezzler skipped town.* —*n.* **1.** a light springing, bounding, or jumping step. **2.** a gait consisting of such steps. **3.** the act of passing over or omitting. [Probably of Scandinavian origin.]

skip·jack (skip′jak′) *n., pl.* **-jacks** or **-jack.** any of various fish that often leap above the surface of the water, as some varieties of tuna or bluefish.

ski pole, a long, slender pole with a metal point on the bottom and an encircling disk just above the point, used as an aid by skiers.

skip·per[1] (skip′ər) *n.* **1.** the captain of a ship, esp. of a small trading, fishing, or pleasure boat. **2.** a person in a position of leadership, as the captain of a sports team. [Middle Dutch *schipper* sailor, from *schip* ship.]

skip·per[2] (skip′ər) *n.* **1.** a person or thing that skips. **2.** any of a group of butterflylike insects, family Hesperiidae, that fly with quick, darting movements. [SKIP + -ER[1].]

skirl (skûrl) *v.i.* (of a bagpipe) to sound loudly and shrilly. —*v.t.* to play (music) on a bagpipe. —*n.* the loud, shrill sound of a bagpipe. [Of Scandinavian origin.]

skir·mish (skûr′mish) *n.* **1.** a minor encounter or conflict between small groups of people or small bodies of troops. **2.** any brief or minor encounter or conflict. —*v.i.* to take part in a skirmish. [Old French *eskirmiss-*, a stem of *eskirmir* to fight with a sword; of Germanic origin.] —**skir′mish·er,** *n.*

skirt (skûrt) *n.* **1.** a woman's or girl's garment that is fastened around the waist or hips and hangs down to varying lengths. **2.** that part of a dress or similar garment that hangs from the waist down. **3. skirts.** outlying or bordering parts, esp. of a town or city; outskirts. **4.** a rim, edge, or outer margin: *Deer came to the skirts of the field.* **5.** one of the flaps hanging from the side of a saddle. **6.** *Slang.* a girl or woman. ➡ considered offensive. —*v.t.* **1.** to lie along or form the border or edge of: *Trees skirted the country estate.* **2.** to move along the border or edge of; pass around rather than go through: *The highway skirted the town.* **3.** to avoid, as by refusing to discuss or deal with: *The speaker skirted the controversial issue of new taxes.* **4.** to border or edge

with. —*v.i.* to move along or be near the border or edge of something. [Old Norse *skyrta* shirt.]

ski run, a slope or course used for skiing.

skit (skit) *n.* a short, often humorous dramatic presentation or literary piece. [Probably of Scandinavian origin.]

ski tow, a continuous, motor-operated moving rope or cable for pulling skiers up a slope.

skit·ter (skit′ər) *v.i.* to glide or skim lightly and quickly over a surface. —*v.t.* to cause to skitter. [Dialectal English *skite* to dart swiftly (probably of Scandinavian origin) + -ER[4].]

skit·tish (skit′ish) *adj.* **1.** easily frightened or excited; jumpy: *a skittish horse.* **2.** not dependable; fickle; capricious. **3.** bashful; coy. [Dialectal English *skit* to move rapidly (probably of Scandinavian origin) + -ISH.] —**skit′tish·ly,** *adv.* —**skit′tish·ness,** *n.*

skit·tle (skit′əl) *n.* **1. skittles.** ninepins in which a wooden disk or ball is used to knock down the pins. ➡ used as singular. **2.** a pin used in this game. [Possibly of Scandinavian origin.]

skiv·vy (skiv′ē) *n., pl.* **-vies.** *Slang.* **1.** a man's short-sleeved undershirt. Also, **skivvy shirt. 2. skivvies.** a man's underwear, consisting of a T-shirt and briefs or shorts. [Of uncertain origin.]

skoal (skōl) *interj.* to your health. ➡ used as a toast. [Danish and Norwegian *skaal* cup, from Old Norse *skāl* bowl[1].]

Skt., Sanskrit.

sku·a (skū′ə) *n.* a predatory, gull-like seabird, *Catharacta skua,* of the cold regions of the Pacific and Atlantic oceans, having dark brown plumage. Length: 20-23 inches (51-58 centimeters). [Of Scandinavian origin.]

skul·dug·ger·y (skul′dug′ə rē) *also,* **skullduggery.** *n.* underhanded or deceitful actions; trickery. [Of uncertain origin.]

skulk (skulk) *v.i.* **1.** to move in a furtive or stealthy manner; slink: *The burglar skulked from house to house.* **2.** to hide or conceal oneself; stay out of sight, esp. in order to avoid work or danger; malinger. —*n.* a person who skulks. [Of Scandinavian origin.] —**skulk′er,** *n.*

skull (skul) *n.* **1.** the framework of bones of the head of a vertebrate, consisting of the bones that enclose the brain and support the face. **2.** the head, esp. regarded as the seat of thought, intelligence, or understanding: *Can't you get it through your skull that you are wrong?* **3.** death's-head. [Of Scandinavian origin.]

skull and crossbones, a representation of a human skull above two crossed bones, a symbol of death once used on the flags of pirate ships, now used chiefly as a warning sign, as on poisons.

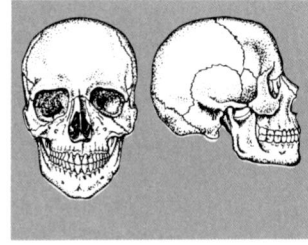

human **skull**

skull·cap (skul′kap′) *n.* a close-fitting, brimless cap covering only a small portion of the crown of the head, often worn indoors, and usually having religious significance.

skull·dug·ger·y (skul′dug′ə rē) skulduggery.

skunk (skungk) *n.* **1.** any of several black-and-white mammals of the weasel family, Mustelidae, native to North, Central, and South America, that discharge a rank-smelling liquid when frightened or attacked. The most common species in North America is the **striped skunk,** *Mephitis mephitis,* having two white bands extending down its back. Length: 2½ feet (0.8 meter), including tail. **2.** the fur of this animal. **3.** *Informal.* a despicable or contemptible person. —*v.t. Slang.* to defeat decisively or overwhelmingly in a game or contest, esp. without allowing an opponent to score. [Of Algonquian origin.]

skunk cabbage, a weedy marsh plant, *Symplocarpus foetidus,* found in eastern North America, noted for the foul smell emitted by its leaves, esp. when crushed.

sky (skī) *n., pl.* **skies. 1.** the upper atmosphere, appearing as a great hemisphere over the earth and having a light blue color on clear days. **2.** the area or expanse of the heavens; firmament: *Sirius is the brightest star in the sky.* **3.** *also,* **skies.** the condition or appearance of the upper atmosphere: *a cloudy sky, sunny skies.* **4.** climate. **5.** the celestial heaven. —*v.t.,* **skyed, sky·ing.** to throw or hit into the air. [Old Norse *skȳ* cloud.]

a	at	e	end	o	hot	u	up	hw	white	‍	about
ā	ape	ē	me	ō	old	ū	use	ng	song	ə	taken
ä	far	i	it	ô	fork	ü	rule	th	thin		pencil
âr	care	ī	ice	oi	oil	u̇	pull	th	this		lemon
		îr	pierce	ou	out	ûr	turn	zh	measure		circus

• **out of a clear (blue) sky.** without warning; suddenly; unexpectedly: *Out of a clear blue sky, my grade school buddy called me.*

• **to the skies.** to the highest point, level, or degree; enthusiastically; lavishly: *to praise someone to the skies.*

sky-blue (skī′blü′) *n.* a warm, light blue, like the color of the clear sky. —*adj.* having the color sky-blue.

sky·cap (skī′kap′) *n.* a porter at an airport or air terminal. [SKY + (RED)CAP.]

sky·dive (skī′dīv′) *v.i.,* -dived or -dove (-dōv′), -dived, -diving. to engage in skydiving.

sky·div·ing (skī′dī′ving) *n.* the act or sport of parachuting from an airplane and falling unrestrained as far as safely possible before opening the parachute, sometimes including the execution of certain intricate maneuvers. —**sky′div′er**, *n.*

Skye terrier (skī) a small terrier of a breed originally developed on the Isle of Skye, having a long body, short legs, and a coat of long, straight hair. Height: 10 inches (25 centimeters) at the shoulder.

Skye terrier

sky·ey (skī′ē) *adj.* **1.** of, relating to, from, or resembling the sky. **2.** of great height; lofty.

sky-high (skī′hī′) *adv.* **1.** to an extremely high point, level, or degree: *The cost of living rose sky-high.* **2.** into pieces; to bits; apart: *The explosion blew the building sky-high.* —*adj.* extremely high: *sky-high prices.*

sky·jack (skī′jak′) *v.t.* Informal. to hijack (an airplane), esp. a commercial airliner. [SKY + (HI)JACK.] —**sky′jack′er**, *n.* —**sky′jack′ing**, *n.*

Sky·lab (skī′lab′) *n.* a U.S. space station used for scientific experiments, in earth orbit from 1973 to 1979.

sky·lark (skī′lärk′) *n.* an Old-World lark, *Alauda arvensis,* having dull brown plumage with black and whitish markings, noted for the rippling, flutelike song produced by the male during the breeding season. —*v.i.* to frolic about; play; rollick.

sky·light (skī′līt′) *n.* a window in a roof or ceiling for admitting daylight.

sky·line (skī′līn′) *n.* **1.** the outline of buildings, mountains, or other objects seen against the sky. **2.** the line at which the earth and sky appear to come together; horizon.

sky pilot Slang. a member of the clergy, esp. a military chaplain.

sky·rock·et (skī′rok′it) *n.* a small rocket used chiefly in fireworks displays, designed to explode high in the air, giving off a shower of colored sparks and lights. —*v.i.* to rise rapidly, suddenly, or greatly: *Rents in the city skyrocketed.* —*v.t.* to cause to rise rapidly, suddenly, or greatly: *Higher wages skyrocketed construction costs.*

sky·sail (skī′sāl′, -səl) *n.* a light sail above the royal on a square-rigged ship.

sky·scrap·er (skī′skrā′pər) *n.* a very tall building.

sky·ward (skī′wərd) *adv.* also, **sky·wards.** toward or in the direction of the sky. —*adj.* directed toward the sky: *a skyward glance.*

sky wave, a radio wave that is propagated upward from earth and may or may not be reflected by the ionosphere. ➡ distinguished from **ground wave.**

sky·way (skī′wā′) *n.* **1.** air lane. **2.** an elevated highway.

sky·writ·ing (skī′rī′ting) *n.* **1.** the act or process of forming words, symbols, or the like in the sky by releasing a trail of smoke or other visible substance from an airplane. **2.** the words or symbols so formed. —**sky′writ′er**, *n.*

slab (slab) *n.* **1.** a broad, flat, and usually thick piece of something: *a slab of stone, a slab of bacon.* **2.** a rough outside piece cut from a log.

slack¹ (slak) *adj.* **1.** not tight, taut, or firm; loose: *a slack rope, a slack grip.* **2.** slow in motion; unhurried; sluggish: *a slack pace.* **3.** lacking in activity; not busy or lively: *The department store's business was slack after the big sale.* **4.** negligent, careless, or inefficient: *a slack worker.* **5.** (of the wind or tide) moving with little force or speed. —*n.* **1.** the part that is slack or hangs loose: *to take up the slack in a rope.* **2.** a lack of tightness or firmness; looseness. **3.** a period of little or no activity; lull: *a slack in business.* **4.** a cessation of movement, as in a current of water. —*v.t.* **1.** to slacken: *The sailor slacked the rope.* **2.** to slake (lime). —*v.i.* to be or become slack: *The wind slacked.* —*adv.* in a slack or loose manner. [Old English *slæc* slow, lazy, careless.] —**slack′ly,** *adv.* —**slack′ness,** *n.*

• **to slack off. a.** to decrease in activity or intensity: *Business at*

the store slacked off after Christmas. **b.** to become less tight or firm; loosen. **c.** to become less diligent, careful, or efficient: *to slack off in one's work.*

• **to slack up.** to slow down; proceed more slowly.

slack² (slak) *n.* small bits of coal remaining after coal is screened. [Probably from Middle Dutch *slacke* slag, dross.]

slack·en (slak′ən) *v.t.* **1.** to make slower: *to slacken one's pace.* **2.** to make less tight, taut, or firm: *to slacken a tense wire.* **3.** to reduce the intensity, forcefulness, or severity of: *to slacken production at a factory.* —*v.i.* **1.** to become slower. **2.** to become less tight, taut, or firm. **3.** to become less active, intense, forceful, or severe: *My interest in poetry slackened after I left school.*

slack·er (slak′ər) *n.* a person who avoids or attempts to avoid work or an obligation or responsibility; shirker; malingerer.

slacks (slaks) *pl. n.* trousers, esp. for casual wear.

slack water, the period at the turn of the tide when there is no visible tidal current. Also, **slack tide.**

slag (slag) *n.* **1.** fused waste material remaining after metallic ore is smelted. Also, **cinder. 2.** volcanic scoria. [Middle Low German *slagge* metal dross.] —**slag′gy,** *adv.*

slain (slān) the past participle of **slay.**

slake (slāk) *v.,* **slaked, slak·ing.** —*v.t.* **1.** to relieve or satisfy; quench: *The cool water slaked the runner's thirst.* **2.** to make less active or intense. **3.** to cause a chemical change in (lime) by treatment with water. —*v.i.* **1.** (of lime) to undergo a chemical change through treatment with water. **2.** Archaic. to become less active or intense. [Old English *slacian* to grow slack.]

slaked lime, a white compound formed by treating lime with water, used in mortar, plaster, and cement. Also, **calcium hydroxide.**

sla·lom (slä′ləm) *n.* **1.** a downhill skiing race over a zigzag course marked by flag-topped poles. **2.** water skiing on one ski designed to hold both feet, often through a zigzag course marked by buoys. —*v.i.* **1.** to ski in a slalom. **2.** to water-ski a slalom course. [Norwegian *slalom* ski course having an even slope, from *slad* sloping + *lom* path.]

slalom *(def. 2)*

slam¹ (slam) *v.,* **slammed, slam·ming.** —*v.t.* **1.** to close forcefully and with a loud noise: *to slam a car door.* **2.** to strike, throw, put, or move (something) with force and a loud noise: *The batter slammed the ball into right field.* **3.** Informal. to criticize harshly or severely. —*v.i.* **1.** to close with force and a loud noise: *The wind made the door slam.* **2.** to strike or move forcefully and noisily: *The shutters slammed against the side of the house.* —*n.* **1.** a forceful and noisy closing or striking. **2.** the noise made by this. **3.** Informal. harsh or severe criticism. [Probably of Scandinavian origin.]

slam² (slam) *n.* the winning of twelve or all thirteen tricks in a round of bridge; grand slam or little slam. [Of uncertain origin.]

slam-bang (slam′bang′) Informal. *adv.* **1.** with a great deal of loud noise; clamorously. **2.** swiftly and recklessly: *to drive a car slam-bang through country roads.* —*adj.* **1.** very noisy; clamorous. **2.** swift and reckless. —*v.i.* to go or happen noisily and recklessly.

slan·der (slan′dər) *n.* **1.** Law. the act or crime of damaging a person's reputation by making a false and malicious oral statement about him or her. ➡ distinguished from **libel. 2.** any false or malicious statement that damages a person's reputation: *The magazine's slander destroyed the senator's chance of reelection.* —*v.t.* to utter false and malicious statements about; injure by spreading slander against. —*v.i.* to utter or spread slander. [Old French *esclandre* offense, disgrace, noise, from Late Latin *scan-*

dalum cause of offense, from Greek *skandalon;* originally, trap. Doublet of SCANDAL.] —**slan′der·er,** *n.*

slan·der·ous (slan′dər əs) *adj.* **1.** containing or constituting slander: *slanderous statements.* **2.** uttering or spreading slander. —**slan′der·ous·ly,** *adv.*

slang (slang) *n.* **1.** colloquial, nonstandard speech that expresses ideas in an unconventional and often playful and colorful manner. Much slang is popular for only a short time, but many words that were originally considered slang are now in standard usage. **2.** the vocabulary peculiar to a particular group, class, or profession; jargon; argot: *military slang.* [Of uncertain origin.]

slang·y (slang′ē) *adj.,* **slang·i·er, slang·i·est. 1.** of the nature of, characterized by, or containing slang. **2.** given to the use of slang: *a slangy writer.* —**slang′i·ly,** *adv.* —**slang′i·ness,** *n.*

slank (slangk) *Archaic.* a past tense of **slink.**

slant (slant) *v.i.* to have or take a direction that deviates from the horizontal or vertical, or from a straight line or course: *The barn roof slants toward the ground.* —*v.t.* **1.** to cause to slant; give an oblique direction to: *to slant a ladder against a wall.* **2.** to present in a way that supports a particular opinion or bias, or appeals to a particular interest: *to slant a magazine toward the young.* —*n.* **1.** a slanting or oblique direction, line, surface, or plane; inclination; angle: *The picture hung on a slant.* **2.** a point of view; attitude; opinion: *The theory offered a new slant on an old problem.* —*adj.* having or being on a slant; oblique. [Of Scandinavian origin.]

Synonyms *v.i.* **Slant, slope,** and **incline** mean to diverge from a horizontal or vertical line or course. **Slant** is applicable to any such type of divergence: *Your handwriting slants to the right.* **Slope** implies a gradual downward change of level: *The path slopes gently down into the valley.* **Incline** often designates a divergence upward from the horizontal: *The road inclines steeply toward the mountaintop.*

slant·wise (slant′wīz′) *adv.* in a slanting direction or position; at a slant; obliquely. Also, **slant·ways** (slant′wāz′). —*adj.* not straight up and down; slanting; oblique.

slap (slap) *n.* **1.** a sharp, quick blow, esp. with the open hand or with something flat. **2.** the sound made by such a blow. **3.** a sharp or insulting reproof or remark. —*v.,* **slapped, slap·ping.** —*v.t.* **1.** to strike with a sharp, quick blow, esp. with the open hand or with something flat: *to slap a fly with a swatter.* **2.** to put, place, or throw forcefully, noisily, or carelessly: *to slap a book down on a table.* **3.** *Informal.* to impose; administer (often with *on*): *The judge slapped a stiff fine on the defendant for contempt of court.* —*v.i.* to strike or beat with or as with a slap: *The waves slapped against the side of the boat.* —*adv. Informal.* directly and suddenly: *The wagon rolled slap into the tree.* [Low German *slapp* sound made by a blow; of imitative origin.]
·**to slap down.** *Informal.* **a.** to subdue, as by a blow or force; quash. **b.** to restrain or reprove sharply.

slap·dash (slap′dash′) *adj.* hasty and careless: *a slapdash piece of work.* —*adv.* in a hasty and careless manner. —*n.* hasty and careless work or action.

slap·hap·py (slap′hap′ē) *adj. Informal.* **1.** dazed or silly from or as from repeated blows to the head; punch-drunk. **2.** cheerfully silly or giddy.

slap·jack (slap′jak′) *n.* **1.** a pancake; griddlecake; flapjack. **2.** a card game played chiefly by children, the object being to slap one's hand on any jack that is turned face up.

slap·stick (slap′stik′) *n.* **1.** a type of comedy characterized by loud, exaggerated, and boisterous action. **2.** a paddle usually consisting of two long, narrow, flat pieces of wood fastened together so as to slap against each other loudly when struck against something, occasionally used by clowns or comedians. —*adj.* resembling, characterized by, or relating to slapstick: *slapstick humor.*

slash (slash) *v.t.* **1.** to cut or wound with a forceful, sweeping stroke or strokes, as with a knife or other sharp instrument. **2.** to strike with a whip; lash. **3.** to cut slits in (a garment), as to show underlying material of a different color. **4.** to reduce sharply or drastically: *to slash production costs.* **5.** to criticize severely. —*v.i.* to make a forceful, sweeping stroke or strokes with or as with a knife or other sharp instrument. —*n.* **1.** a forceful, sweeping stroke: *the slash of a whip.* **2.** a cut or wound made by or as by such a stroke. **3.** an ornamental slit in a garment. **4.** a sharp or drastic reduction: *a slash in prices.* **5.a.** a clearing in a forest, produced as by logging operations, usually littered with wood chips, broken branches, and other debris. **b.** the debris found in such a clearing. **6.** a low, swampy area, usually overgrown with bushes or trees. **7.** virgule. [Possibly from Old French *esclachier* ·to break; of imitative origin.] —**slash′er,** *n.*

slat (slat) *n.* a thin, narrow, flat strip of wood, metal, or other material: *the slats of a Venetian blind.* —*v.t.,* **slat·ted, slat·ting.**

to provide or make with slats. [Short for Old French *esclat* splinter, from *esclater* to split; of Germanic origin.]

slate (slāt) *n.* **1.** a fine-grained, usually bluish gray metamorphic rock that splits easily into thin sheets or layers. **2.** a thin piece of this rock, used esp. to make roofing tiles and blackboards. **3.** a small blackboard, usually held in the hand. **4.** the record of a person's past actions or performance: *The candidate has a clean slate.* **5.** a list of candidates proposed for nomination or election. **6.** a dull, dark, bluish gray color. —*v.t.,* **slat·ed, slat·ing. 1.** to cover with slate or a substance like slate. **2.** to put on a list of candidates. **3.** to schedule or designate: *The conference was slated for early June.* —*adj.* having the color slate. [Old French *esclate,* form of *esclat* splinter, from *esclater* to split. See SLAT.] —**slate′-like′,** *adj.*

slat·er (slā′tər) *n.* a person employed to lay slates, as for roofing.

slath·er (slath′ər) *Informal. v.t.* to spread thickly: *to slather jam on bread.* —*n. usually,* **slathers.** a large or generous amount. [Of uncertain origin.]

slat·tern (slat′ərn) *n.* **1.** an untidy, slovenly woman or girl. **2.** a disreputable or promiscuous woman. [Possibly from dialectal English *slatter* to spill, slop, from *slat* to flap, dash; possibly of Scandinavian origin.]

slat·tern·ly (slat′ərn lē) *adj.* **1.** relating to or characteristic of a slattern. **2.** slovenly; untidy. —*adv.* in a slovenly manner. —**slat′tern·li·ness,** *n.*

slat·y (slā′tē) *adj.,* **slat·i·er, slat·i·est. 1.** of, relating to, containing, or resembling slate: *a slaty ridge of rock.* **2.** having the color of slate; bluish gray.

slaugh·ter (slô′tər) *n.* **1.** the act of killing an animal or animals for food. **2.** the brutal or violent killing of a person. **3.** the brutal and indiscriminate killing of a large number of persons; massacre. **4.** *Informal.* a complete or overwhelming defeat, esp. in an athletic contest. —*v.t.* **1.** to kill (an animal or animals) for food; butcher. **2.** to kill in a brutal or violent manner. **3.** to kill (persons) indiscriminately and in large numbers; massacre. **4.** *Informal.* to defeat completely or overwhelmingly, esp. in an athletic contest; trounce. [Old Norse *slātr* butcher's meat.] —**slaugh′ter·er,** *n.*

slaugh·ter·house (slô′tər hous′) *n., pl.* **-hous·es** (-hou′ziz). a place where animals are butchered for food; abattoir.

slaugh·ter·ous (slô′tər əs) *adj.* brutally destructive; murderous. —**slaugh′ter·ous·ly,** *adv.*

Slav (släv, slav) *n.* a member or close descendant of a group of culturally and linguistically related peoples living predominantly in eastern, southeastern, and central Europe, usually divided into **Western Slavs,** composed chiefly of Poles, Czechs, and Slovaks, **Southern Slavs,** composed chiefly of Serbs, Croats, Slovenes, and Bulgarians, and **Eastern Slavs,** composed of Russians, Ukrainians, and Byelorussians (now of Belarus).

slave (slāv) *n.* **1.** a person who is the property of another and is under that person's complete domination. **2.** a person who is under the control of some influence or person: *a slave to a habit.* **3.** a person who works or is compelled to work hard and long: *I felt like a slave at my job.* —*v.i.,* **slaved, slav·ing.** to work hard and long: *The editor had been slaving away on the novel for weeks.* [Medieval Latin *Sclavus* one of the Slavic people, bond servant of Slavic descent, bond servant, from Late Greek *Sklabos,* going back to *(hoi) Sklabēnoi* (the) Slavic people (of Slavic origin); referring to the enslavement of many Slavs by the Germans in the early Middle Ages.]

Slave Coast, a region on the western coast of Africa, between Ghana and Nigeria, that served as a center of the slave trade from the sixteenth to nineteenth centuries.

slave driver 1. a person charged with overseeing slaves at work. **2.** a harsh or exacting employer or taskmaster; martinet.

slave·hold·er (slāv′hōl′dər) *n.* a person who owns slaves. —**slave′hold′ing,** *adj., n.*

slav·er[1] (slā′vər) *n.* **1.** a person who deals in slaves. **2.** a ship used to transport slaves. [SLAVE + -ER[1].]

slav·er[2] (slav′ər) *v.i.* to let saliva run out from the mouth; drool; slobber. —*v.t. Archaic.* to wet or cover with saliva. —*n.* saliva running out from the mouth. Also *(n.),* **slobber.** [Of Scandinavian origin.]

slav·er·y (slā′və rē) *n.* **1.** the institution or practice of owning slaves. **2.** the condition of being a slave; bondage; thralldom. **3.** the condition of being under the control of some influence or person. **4.** hard or exhausting work; drudgery.

a	at	e	end	o	hot	u	up	hw	white		about
ā	ape	ē	me	ō	old	ū	use	ng	song		taken
ä	far	i	it	ô	fork	ü	rule	th	thin	ə	pencil
âr	care	ī	ice	oi	oil	u̇	pull	th	this		lemon
		îr	pierce	ou	out	ûr	turn	zh	measure		circus

Slave State, any state of the United States in which slavery was legal before the American Civil War.

slave trade, the business of acquiring, transporting, and selling slaves, esp. the former transportation of black Africans to America for sale as slaves.

slav·ey (slā′vē) *n., pl.* **-eys**. *British. Informal.* a female domestic servant, esp. one who does all kinds of housework.

Slav·ic (slä′vik, slav′ik) *adj.* of or relating to the Slavs or their languages. —*n.* the group of languages spoken by the Slavs, belonging to the Indo-European language family, and including such languages as Polish, Russian, and Serbo-Croatian.

slav·ish (slā′vish) *adj.* **1.** of, like, characteristic of, or befitting a slave or slaves: *slavish work, a slavish habit.* **2.** not original or independent; imitative: *a slavish copy of a great painting.* —**slav′ish·ly,** *adv.* —**slav′ish·ness,** *n.*

Sla·von·ic (slə von′ik) *adj.* Slavic. —*n.* any Slavic language, or the Slavic language group.

slaw (slô) *n.* coleslaw. [Dutch *sla*, short for *salade* salad, from French *salade*. See SALAD.]

slay (slā) *v.t.*, **slew** or *(def. 2)* **slayed, slain, slay·ing. 1.** to kill by violent means. **2.** *Slang.* to overcome completely, as with laughter; overwhelm: *The comedian slayed the audience with a barrage of hilarious jokes.* [Old English *slēan* to strike, kill.] —**slay′er,** *n.* —For Synonyms, see **kill**[1].

sleaze (slēz) *n. Informal.* **1.** the quality or condition of being sleazy. **2.** a sleazy person.

slea·zy (slē′zē) *adj.*, **-zi·er, -zi·est. 1.** (of fabric) thin or flimsy in texture or substance. **2.** of poor quality; shoddy; cheap: *a sleazy hotel.* **3.** mean or disreputable: *a sleazy politician.* [Of uncertain origin.] —**slea′zi·ly,** *adv.* —**slea′zi·ness,** *n.*

sled (sled) *n.* **1.** a vehicle on runners, used to carry people or loads over snow and ice. **2.** a small, similarly constructed vehicle having a wooden frame, used for sliding down snow-covered slopes, as by children. —*v.*, **sled·ded, sled·ding.** —*v.i.* to ride or be carried on a sled. —*v.t.* to carry on a sled. [Middle Dutch *sledde* sledge[1].] —**sled′der,** *n.*

sled·ding (sled′ing) *n.* **1.** the act of riding on or using a sled. **2.** the condition of the ground for the use of sleds: *The heavy snow made for good sledding.*
   • **hard sledding.** difficult conditions affecting the course or progress of any action: *It looks like hard sledding until business picks up.*

sledge[1] (slej) *n.* a sled or sleigh. —*v.*, **sledged, sledg·ing.** —*v.i.* to ride or be carried on a sled or sleigh. —*v.t.* to carry on a sled or sleigh. [Middle Dutch *sleedse* sled.]

sledge[2] (slej) *n.* sledgehammer. —*v.t.*, **sledged, sledg·ing.** sledgehammer. [Old English *slecg* heavy hammer.]

sledge·hammer (slej′ham′ər) *n.* a heavy hammer with a long handle, usually held with both hands. —*v.t.* to strike with or as with such a hammer. —*adj.* like a sledgehammer; powerful; smashing: *a sledgehammer punch.*

sleek (slēk) *adj.* **1.** smooth and glossy, as if polished: *The cat has sleek black fur.* **2.** having a healthy, well-groomed, or well-fed appearance: *a sleek horse.* **3.** having a trim, uncluttered design. **4.** polished in manner or speech, esp. in a specious or insincere way: *a sleek orator.* —*v.t.* to make smooth and glossy; polish. [Form of SLICK.] —**sleek′ly,** *adv.* —**sleek′ness,** *n.*

sleep (slēp) *n.* **1.** a naturally recurring state of relatively suspended sensory and motor activity, characterized by total or partial unconsciousness and the inactivity of nearly all voluntary muscles. **2.** a period of sleep: *I had a good sleep last night.* **3.** any condition of inactivity or reduced consciousness that resembles sleep, as death or a hypnotic trance. —*v.*, **slept, sleep·ing.** —*v.i.* **1.** to be or fall asleep: *The baby slept peacefully.* **2.** to be in a condition resembling or likened to sleep. —*v.t.* **1.** to repose in (a particular kind of sleep): *to sleep the peaceful sleep of the young.* **2.** to provide or be able to provide with accommodations for sleeping: *This cabin sleeps six people.* [Old English *slǣpan* to slumber, be dead, be numb, be inert.] —**sleep′ful,** *adj.* —**sleep′like′,** *adj.*
   • **to sleep away. a.** to spend in sleeping: *to sleep away the afternoon.* **b.** to get rid of by sleeping.
   • **to sleep in. a.** (of domestic help) to sleep at the place of one's employment. **b.** to sleep later than usual in the morning.
   • **to sleep off.** to get rid of by sleeping: *to sleep off a headache.*
   • **to sleep on.** to postpone a decision on, esp. overnight, to allow more time for consideration.
   • **to sleep over.** to spend the night.

sleep·er (slē′pər) *n.* **1.** a person or thing that sleeps: *a light sleeper.* **2.** someone or something previously unknown or unimportant that unexpectedly or suddenly attains success, fame, or importance: *That movie is the sleeper of the year.* **3.** sleeping car. **4.** a strong horizontal beam used as a support, esp. a railroad tie.

sleeping bag, a long, warmly lined or padded bag, often waterproof, used to sleep in, esp. out-of-doors.

sleeping car, a railroad car having sleeping accommodations for passengers. Also, **sleeper.**

sleeping pill, a pill or capsule containing a sleep-inducing drug, esp. a barbiturate.

sleeping sickness 1. an infectious disease, often fatal, caused by a parasite transmitted by the tsetse fly and characterized by headaches, high fever, convulsions, and coma. It is most common in tropical Africa. **2.** a viral encephalitis that causes weakness and sleepiness.

sleep·less (slēp′lis) *adj.* **1.** unable to sleep. **2.** marked by the absence of sleep; affording no sleep: *a sleepless night.* **3.** constantly in motion or action. **4.** always alert and watchful; vigilant. —**sleep′less·ly,** *adv.* —**sleep′less·ness,** *n.*

sleep·walk·ing (slēp′wô′king) *n.* the act or practice of walking about while asleep; somnambulism. —**sleep′walk′er,** *n.*

sleep·y (slē′pē) *adj.*, **sleep·i·er, sleep·i·est. 1.** ready for, in need of, or inclined to sleep; drowsy. **2.** of, showing, or characterized by drowsiness: *sleepy eyes.* **3.** characterized by lack of activity; dull; quiet: *a sleepy little village.* —**sleep′i·ly,** *adv.* —**sleep′i·ness,** *n.*

sleep·y·head (slē′pē hed′) *n. Informal.* a sleepy person.

sleet (slēt) *n.* **1.** precipitation consisting of ice pellets, smaller than hail, formed by the freezing or partial freezing of rain. **2.** a mixture of rain and snow or hail. —*v.i.* to shower sleet. [From an unrecorded Old English word.] —**sleet′y,** *adj.*

sleeve (slēv) *n.* **1.** the part of a garment that covers and usually encloses all or part of the arm. **2.** a paper or plastic cover or envelope, as for protecting a phonograph record or computer disk. **3.** a tubelike part of a machine that fits over a rod, shaft, or the like. [Old English *slīef* part of a garment that covers the arm.] —**sleeved,** *adj.* —**sleeve′less,** *adj.*
   • **up one's sleeve.** secretly in reserve for use when needed; hidden: *to have a trick up one's sleeve.*

sleigh (slā) *n.* a vehicle on runners, usually horse-drawn, used for traveling over snow or ice. —*v.i.* to ride or travel in a sleigh. [Dutch *slee*, form of *slede* sled.]

sleight (slīt) *n.* **1.** skill or dexterity in doing or making something. **2.** craftiness; cunning. **3.** a clever trick or deception. [Old Norse *slægth* slyness.]

sleight of hand 1. skill and dexterity in using the hands, esp. in performing tricks or to deceive; legerdemain. **2.** tricks or feats requiring such skill, as those performed

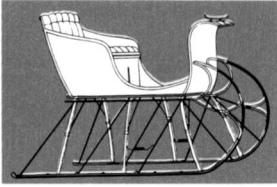

sleigh

by a magician or juggler. **3.** the performance of such tricks or feats.

slen·der (slen′dər) *adj.* **1.** thin, esp. in an attractive or graceful way: *slender fingers.* **2.** having a small circumference in proportion to height or length: *a slender pole.* **3.** small in size, amount, extent, or degree: *The candidate won the election by a slender margin.* [Of uncertain origin.] —**slen′der·ly,** *adv.* —**slen′der·ness,** *n.*

slen·der·ize (slen′də rīz′) *v.*, **-ized, -iz·ing.** —*v.t.* **1.** to make slender. **2.** to cause to appear slender. —*v.i.* to become slender.

slept (slept) the past tense and past participle of **sleep.**

sleuth (slüth) *n.* **1.** *Informal.* a detective. **2.** sleuthhound. —*v.i. Informal.* to act as a detective. [Old Norse *slōth* track.]

sleuth·hound (slüth′hound′) *n.* bloodhound.

slew[1] (slü) the past tense of **slay.**

slew[2] (slü) **slue**[1].

slew[3] (slü) *n.* slough[1] *(def. 2).*

slew[4] (slü) *n. Informal.* a large number or group; great amount: *A whole slew of people came to the party.* [Irish Gaelic *sluagh* multitude.]

slice (slīs) *n.* **1.** a thin, flat piece cut from a larger object: *a slice of bread.* **2.** a part, portion, or share: *I spent a large slice of my savings on a new car.* **3.** any of various implements having a thin, broad blade, as a spatula. **4.** *Sports.* **a.** a stroke, as in baseball or golf, that causes a ball to curve off to the right if the player is right-handed, or to the left if the player is left-handed. **b.** the course followed by such a ball. —*v.*, **sliced, slic·ing.** —*v.t.* **1.** to cut into slices or pieces: *to slice a cake.* **2.** to remove in the form of a slice or slices (often with *off*): *to slice off a piece of cheese.* **3.** to divide into parts, portions, or shares. **4.** to move through or across like a knife: *The bow of the boat sliced the waves.* **5.** *Sports.* to hit (a ball) so that it makes a slice. —*v.i.* **1.** to move or cut like a knife: *The speeding boat sliced through the waves.* **2.** *Sports.*

a. to hit a ball with a slice. **b.** (of a ball) to curve in a slice. [Old French *esclice* splinter, from *esclicier* to split; of Germanic origin.] —**slic′er,** *n.*

slick (slik) *adj.* **1.** smooth and glossy; sleek: *slick, wet hair.* **2.** smooth and slippery: *The roads were slick with ice.* **3.** cleverly or skillfully devised, done, or said: *a slick solution to a problem.* **4.** shrewd or sly in thought, action, or speech: *a slick gambler.* **5.** having or showing skill that is only superficial or that lacks any real significance: *a slick style of writing.* **6.** *Slang.* excellent; great. —*n.* **1.** a smooth or slippery area on a surface. **2.** an oily film, esp. on the surface of water. **3.** *Informal.* a magazine printed on glazed or coated paper. —*v.t.* **1.** *Informal.* to make sleek, smooth, or glossy. **2.** to make neat, trim, or tidy (often with *up*): *to slick up a messy room.* [Old English *slīcian* to make smooth.] —**slick′ly,** *adv.* —**slick′ness,** *n.*

slick·er (slik′ər) *n.* **1.** a raincoat made of oilskin, plastic, or a similar material. **2.** *Informal.* a clever, sly, or deceptive person.

slide (slīd) *v.,* **slid** (slid), **slid** or **slid·den** (slid′ən), **slid·ing.** —*v.i.* **1.** to pass or move along a surface with a smooth, continuous movement: *The wet bar of soap slid across the floor.* **2.** to shift, fall, or move suddenly from a position, as by a loss of balance or traction: *As I crossed the icy walk, my feet slid out from under me.* **3.** to pass or move smoothly, quietly, or gradually: *My friend slid into the seat next to me.* **4.** to continue or go by without intervention or interference: *We let the matter slide for the moment.* **5.** to pass or fall into a specified state or condition: *to slide into oblivion.* **6.** *Baseball.* to throw oneself along the ground toward a base, usually feet first, in order to avoid being tagged by a fielder. —*v.t.* **1.** to cause to move along a surface with a smooth, continuous movement: *to slide a heavy box along the floor.* **2.** to put or move smoothly, quietly, or imperceptibly: *to slide a note under a door.* —*n.* **1.** an act or instance of sliding: *to take a slide down a hill on a sled.* **2.** a smooth, usually inclined track, channel, or surface for sliding: *The children played on the slide in the playground.* **3.** a small plate of glass on which an object is mounted for examination under a microscope. **4.** a small, transparent, usually color photograph to be magnified and projected on a screen; transparency. **5.a.** a fall of a mass of rock, snow, or other matter down a slope. **b.** such a mass of matter. **6.** a part that operates by sliding, esp. the U-shaped section of tubing of a trombone that is pushed in or out to alter the pitch of the tones. [Old English *slīdan* to glide.]
  • **to let slide.** to let go by; neglect: *to let one's homework slide, to let an insult slide.*

slide projector, a projector designed to accommodate photographic slides.

slid·er (slī′dər) *n.* **1.** a person or thing that slides. **2.** *Baseball.* a fast pitch that curves sharply for a short distance.

slide rule, a device used to perform the mathematical operations now usually done with a calculator, consisting of a ruler and a central sliding piece that are both marked with logarithmic scales.

sliding scale, a scale of wages, prices, tariffs, or the like that varies or can be adjusted in accordance with certain conditions or factors, as the cost of living or the selling price of goods.

sli·er (slī′ər) a comparative of **sly.**

sli·est (slī′ist) a superlative of **sly.**

slight (slīt) *adj.* **1.** small in quantity, degree, or intensity: *There is a slight possibility that we will be late.* **2.** of small importance: *a slight problem.* **3.** slender or thin in build or form; delicate: *a person with a slight build.* **4.** lacking in substance or strength; flimsy. —*v.t.* **1.** to treat with disrespect or indifference or with a marked lack of consideration; snub or insult: *They slighted their neighbors when they didn't invite them to the party.* **2.** to do or perform carelessly or negligently: *to slight one's duty.* **3.** to treat as unimportant: *to slight someone's advice.* —*n.* a show of disrespect or indifference, esp. when contemptuous and deliberate. [Middle Dutch *slicht, schlecht* even¹, simple.] —**slight′ly,** *adv.* —**slight′ness,** *n.*

slight·ing (slī′ting) *adj.* constituting or conveying a slight; disparaging; insulting: *a slighting remark.* —**slight′ing·ly,** *adv.*

slim (slim) *adj.,* **slim·mer, slim·mest. 1.** small in thickness in proportion to height or length; slender; thin: *The fashion model had a very slim build.* **2.** small in amount, degree, or extent: *a slim chance of victory.* —*v.t., v.i.,* **slimmed, slim·ming.** to make or become slim or slender. [Dutch *slim* awry, bad.] —**slim′ly,** *adv.* —**slim′ness,** *n.*

slime (slīm) *n.* **1.** wet, soft, often sticky mud. **2.** any substance resembling this, esp. when regarded as disgusting or filthy. **3.** a thin, sticky mucuslike substance given off by certain animals, as snails. [Old English *slīm* sticky mud.]

slime mold, any of a group of funguslike protists, class Myxomycetes, that alternate between a stage during which they release spores as a fungus does and a stage during which they look like a small mass of jelly. Slime molds live on dead wood or other decay-ing matter and sometimes as parasites on potato, cabbage, or other plants; myxomycete.

slim·y (slī′mē) *adj.,* **slim·i·er, slim·i·est. 1.** covered with slime. **2.** of or like slime. **3.** disgusting or filthy; foul. —**slim′i·ly,** *adv.* —**slim′i·ness,** *n.*

sling (sling) *n.* **1.** a device for hurling stones, usually consisting of a piece of leather with a string fastened to each end. **2.** slingshot. **3.** a loop of cloth suspended from the neck to support an injured arm or hand. **4.** a strap for carrying a rifle or other object over the shoulder. **5.** a device, as a chain or rope formed into a loop, used for raising, lowering, carrying, or suspending heavy objects. **6.** the act of slinging or hurling; throw. —*v.t.,* **slung, sling·ing. 1.** to hurl with or as with a sling; throw; fling: *to sling a rock.* **2.** to suspend with a sling or strap: *A guitar was slung over the singer's shoulder.* **3.** to hang or throw loosely: *to sling a hammock between two trees.* **4.** to raise, lower, carry, or suspend by means of a sling. [Probably from Old Norse *slyngva* to fling, throw.] —**sling′er,** *n.*

sling chair, any of various lightweight chairs having a seat and back made of a single piece of canvas, leather, or similar material that is attached loosely to a frame.

sling·shot (sling′shot′) *n.* a Y-shaped piece of wood or metal, with an elastic band fastened to the prongs, used to shoot small stones or other small objects.

slink (slingk) *v.i.,* **slunk** or *(archaic)* **slank, slunk, slink·ing.** to move in a quiet, stealthy, or sneaking manner: *The fox slunk closer to its prey.* [Old English *slincan* to creep, crawl.]

slink·y (sling′kē) *adj.,* **slink·i·er, slink·i·est. 1.** stealthy; sneaking. **2.** *Informal.* sleek and sinuous in form, appearance, or movement: *a slinky evening dress.*

slip¹ (slip) *v.,* **slipped** or *(archaic)* **slipt, slip·ping.** —*v.i.* **1.** to lose one's balance or footing; slide suddenly or accidentally: *to slip on a banana peel.* **2.** to move or slide out of place or out of control: *The bottle slipped out of my hands.* **3.** to move or pass smoothly, or with an easy, gliding motion: *The young child slipped into bed and went right to sleep.* **4.** to move or go quietly, stealthily, or unnoticed: *The thief slipped out of the apartment without a sound.* **5.** (of time) to pass imperceptibly: *Another month slipped by.* **6.** to escape (often with *by* or *away*): *You let the chance of a lifetime slip by!* **7.** to be lost from memory: *The appointment had completely slipped from my mind.* **8.** to be said, divulged, or made known unintentionally (often with *out*): *The name of the winner slipped out.* **9.** to decline or fall, as from an accustomed or desired level: *Sales slipped sharply last year.* **10.** to decline or deteriorate in physical or mental condition or ability: *The elderly couple feared their health was slipping.* **11.** to put on or take off clothing, esp. quickly or easily (with *into* or *out of*): *to slip into one's pajamas.* **12.** to pass or fall into a specified state, condition, or activity: *to slip into unconsciousness.* **13.** to make a mistake (often with *up*): *I sometimes slip up when I'm under pressure. I almost slipped and told them about the surprise party.* —*v.t.* **1.** to cause to move with a smooth, sliding motion: *to slip a ring off one's finger.* **2.** to put or give quietly, quickly, or stealthily: *to slip someone a note.* **3.** to fail to be remembered or noticed by: *The name of the new student had slipped my mind.* **4.** to put on or take off (clothing), esp. quickly or easily (with *on* or *off*): *I slipped a sweater on and dashed out the door.* **5.** to free oneself or itself from: *The horse slipped its bridle.* **6.** to release or free, as a dog from a leash; let loose. **7.** to dislocate, as a bone. **8.** to transfer (a stitch) from one needle to another without knitting it. —*n.* **1.** the act of slipping or sliding. **2.** a mistake or error, as in speech, judgment, or conduct. **3.** a mishap; accident. **4.** a decline or fall, as from an accustomed level: *a slip in prices.* **5.** a woman's undergarment, usually of a light material, as nylon. **6.** a pillowcase. **7.a.** a space between wharves or piers where ships can dock. **b.** a sloping pier leading into the water and serving as a landing place. [Middle Dutch *slippen* to glide, slide.]
  • **to give (someone) the slip.** *Slang.* to escape from; elude: *The prowler gave the police the slip.*
  • **to let slip.** to say or divulge unintentionally: *to let the truth slip.*
  • **to slip one** (or **something**) **over on.** *Informal.* to take advantage of; trick.

slip² (slip) *n.* **1.** a small shoot or twig cut from a plant, used for grafting or planting. **2.** a long, thin piece or strip of some material, as cloth. **3.** a small piece of paper, esp. one designed or used for a specific purpose: *a bank deposit slip.* **4.** a slender or slight

a	at	e	end	o	hot	u	up	hw	white		about
ā	ape	ē	me	ō	old	ū	use	ng	song	ə	taken
ä	far	i	it	ô	fork	ü	rule	th	thin		pencil
âr	care	ī	ice	oi	oil	u̇	pull	th	this		lemon
			pierce	ou	out	ûr	turn	zh	measure		circus

person, esp. a young one: *a mere slip of a child.* —*v.t.*, **slipped,
slip·ping.** to cut a shoot or twig from (a plant) for grafting or
planting. [Middle Dutch *slippe* strip, slit.]

slip·case (slip′kās′) *n.* a protective box for a book or set of
books, open at one end.

slip·cov·er (slip′kuv′ər) *n.* a removable
cover, usually of cloth, for a piece of furniture, as a sofa. —*v.t.* to put a slipcover on:
to slipcover a sofa.

slip·knot (slip′not′) *n.* **1.** a knot made so
that it will slip along the rope or line around
which it is tied. **2.** a knot made so that it can
be easily undone by pulling on either of the
free ends.

slip noose *also,* **slip·noose** (slip′nüs′). a
noose made with a slipknot.

slipknot
(def. 1)

slip-on (slip′ôn′, -on′) *adj.* (of an article of
clothing) easily put on or removed: *slip-on shoes.* —*n.* a slip-on
article of clothing.

slip·o·ver (slip′ō′vər) *adj.* (of a garment) designed to be put on
or removed by drawing over the head; pullover. —*n.* a slipover
garment.

slip·page (slip′ij) *n.* **1.** an act or instance of slipping: *a slippage
in popularity.* **2.** the amount or extent of slipping.

slipped disk, a disorder caused by the protrusion of one of the
spongy plates of cartilage that serve as cushions between the vertebrae of the spine, characterized by severe back pain.

slip·per (slip′ər) *n.* a light, low shoe that is easily slipped on or
off the foot, worn chiefly indoors. —**slip′pered,** *adj.*

slip·per·y (slip′ə rē) *adj.,* **-per·i·er, -per·i·est. 1.** causing or
likely to cause slipping or sliding: *Freezing rain made the roads
slippery.* **2.** tending to slip or slide, as from the grasp: *The wet fish
was too slippery to hold.* **3.** not to be relied or depended on; tricky.
4. able to slip away or escape easily; elusive: *a slippery thief.*
[Middle English *sliper* (from Old English *slipor*) + -Y¹.] —**slip′-
per·i·ness,** *n.*

slippery elm 1. a North American elm tree, *Ulmus fulva,* having
gray or dark reddish brown outer bark and white, sticky inner
bark. **2.** the dried, powdered inner bark of this tree, used medicinally in a demulcent.

slip ring, one of two or more metal rings in an electric motor or
machine that serves to conduct a current through contact with
stationary brushes.

slip·shod (slip′shod′) *adj.* **1.** carelessly made or done: *The
mechanic did a slipshod job in repairing the car.* **2.** untidy or
slovenly in appearance.

slip·stream (slip′strēm′) *n.* **1.** a current of air driven back by
the revolving propeller of an aircraft. **2.** a region of reduced air
pressure and forward suction directly behind a race car or other
vehicle traveling at a high speed.

slipt (slipt) *Archaic.* a past tense of **slip¹.**

slip-up (slip′up′) *n. Informal.* a mistake; error; oversight.

slit (slit) *n.* a long, narrow, usually straight cut or opening:
Sunlight came through the slits in the Venetian blinds. —*v.t.,* **slit,
slit·ting.** to cut or make a slit or slits in. [Middle English *slitten*
to cut, divide, possibly going back to Old English *slītan* to tear,
divide.]

slith·er (slith′ər) *v.i.* **1.** to move along with a sliding or gliding
motion: *The snake slithered under a rock.* **2.** to slip or slide, as on
a loose or slippery surface. —*v.t.* to cause to slither or slide. —*n.*
a slithering movement. [Old English *sliderian* to slip.]

slith·er·y (slith′ə rē) *adj.* slippery; slick.

sliv·er (sliv′ər) *n.* **1.** a slender, often pointed piece that has been
broken, cut, or torn off; splinter: *a sliver of wood, a sliver of glass.*
2. a continuous strand of loose, untwisted textile fiber after it has
been carded. —*v.t., v.i.* to cut or break into slivers. [From
dialectal English *slive* to cleave, slice off, from Old English *slīfan*
to cleave.]

slob (slob) *n. Informal.* a sloppy, dirty, or crude person. [Irish
slab mud; probably of Scandinavian origin.]

slob·ber (slob′ər) *v.i.* **1.** to let saliva, food, or liquid run or spill
from the mouth; slaver. **2.** to express oneself in an overly sentimental manner; speak or write effusively; gush. —*v.t.* to wet or
smear with saliva, food, or liquid running from the mouth. —*n.*
1. slaver². **2.** overly sentimental speech or writing. [Probably
imitative.] —**slob′ber·er,** *n.* —**slob′ber·y,** *adj.*

sloe (slō) *n.* **1.** blackthorn *(def. 1).* **2.** the tart, plumlike,
blue-black fruit of the blackthorn. [Old English *slāh* fruit of the
blackthorn.]

slog (slog) *v.,* **slogged, slog·ging.** —*v.i.* **1.** to move with great
effort; plod: *The weary soldiers slogged through the mud.* **2.** to
work hard: *to slog through a long homework assignment.* —*v.t.* to
make (one's way) with great effort. [Form of SLUG².]

slo·gan (slō′gən) *n.* **1.** a distinctive phrase, statement, or motto

used by a particular group, as a club or political party, or by an
individual, as a candidate for political office. **2.** a catch phrase
used in advertising or in promoting a particular product, business,
or service. **3.** formerly, a rallying or battle cry used by the Highland clans. [Gaelic *sluagh-ghairm* the signal for battle among the
Highland clans, from *sluagh* army + *gairm* outcry.]

sloop (slüp) *n.* a fore-and-aft-rigged sailboat with a single mast,
a mainsail, and a jib. [Dutch *sloep.* Doublet of SHALLOP.]

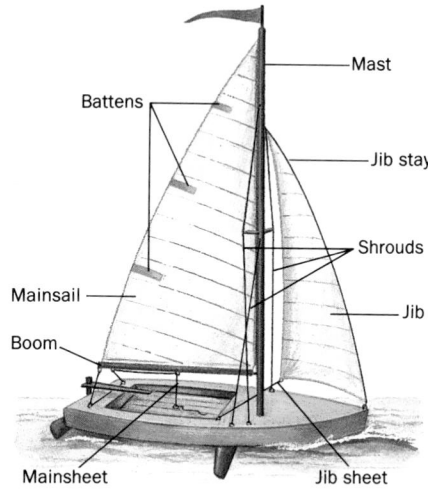

Mast
Battens
Jib stay
Shrouds
Mainsail
Jib
Boom
Mainsheet
Jib sheet

sloop

sloop of war, formerly, a small warship having guns mounted
on only one deck.

slop (slop) *n.* **1.** liquid that has been spilled or splashed. **2.** soft,
watery mud or snow; slush. **3.** unappetizing or distasteful food or
liquid. **4.** *also,* **slops.** wet feed made from grains and refuse
food, used to feed pigs; swill. **5.** any liquid or semiliquid waste.
—*v.,* **slopped, slop·ping.** —*v.i.* **1.** (of liquid) to spill or splash
(often with *over*): *The water in the pail slopped all over the floor.*
2. to walk or move with splashes through mud, slush, or water.
3. *Informal.* to talk or act with excessive sentiment or emotion
(with *over*). —*v.t.* **1.** to cause (a liquid) to spill or splash. **2.** to
spill or splash liquid upon. **3.** to feed slop to: *to slop the pigs and
feed the chickens.* [Old English *-sloppe* dung (in *cūsloppe* cowslip;
literally, cow dung).]

slope (slōp) *v.,* **sloped, slop·ing.** —*v.i.* to lie or move at an
angle from the horizontal or vertical; take a slanting direction:
The road slopes toward the river. —*v.t.* to cause to slope; make
with a slope: *The builders sloped the roof of the house.* —*n.* **1.** a
stretch of ground that is not flat or level; natural or artificial
incline: *The house was built on a slope.* **2.** any slanting line,
surface, position, or direction. **3.a.** any deviation from the horizontal. **b.** the degree or amount of such deviation. **4.** *Mathematics.* **a.** the degree of inclination measured by the tangent of an
angle formed by a line and the *x*-axis in a Cartesian coordinate
system. **b.** (of a point of a plane curve) the slope of the line that
is tangent to a curve at a point. [Short for earlier *aslope* sloping,
possibly from Old English *āslopen,* past participle of *āslūpan* to
slip away.] —For Synonyms *(v.i.),* see **slant.**

slop·py (slop′ē) *adj.,* **-pi·er, -pi·est. 1.** very wet, muddy, or
slushy: *The sidewalk was wet and sloppy.* **2.** spotted or splashed
with liquid or slop: *a sloppy floor.* **3.** careless; slipshod: *a sloppy
job.* **4.** very untidy; messy: *a sloppy room.* **5.** *Informal.* excessively sentimental; gushy; maudlin. —**slop′pi·ly,** *adv.* —**slop′-
pi·ness,** *n.*

slosh (slosh) *v.i.* **1.** to move clumsily or splash about, as in water
or mud: *to slosh through a bog.* **2.** (of a liquid) to splash about.
—*v.t.* to stir or splash about (a liquid or something in a liquid):
The child sloshed the milk around in the glass. —*n.* **1.** slush. **2.** the
sound of splashing liquid. [Form of SLUSH.]

slot¹ (slot) *n.* **1.** a narrow, usually straight opening or groove:
A mailbox has a slot for letters. **2.** *Informal.* a place or position,
as in a schedule or sequence: *That television program will appear
in the ten o'clock time slot.* —*v.t.,* **slot·ted, slot·ting. 1.** to
make or cut a slot in. **2.** to place or position, as in a schedule or
sequence. [Old French *esclot* the depression between the breasts;
of uncertain origin.]

slot² (slot) *n.* the track or trail of an animal, esp. a deer; spoor.

[Old French *esclot* print of a horse's hoof, from Old Norse *slōth* track, trail.]

sloth (slôth, slōth, sloth) *n.* **1.** a disinclination to work or exertion; laziness; indolence. **2.** any of several slow-moving, tree-dwelling mammals, family Bradypodidae, native to the tropical forests of Central and South America, having long limbs with curved claws, and coarse, shaggy hair. Length: 2 feet (0.6 meter). [From SLOW.]

sloth (def. 2)

sloth bear, a long-haired black bear, *Melursus ursinus,* native to India and Sri Lanka. Height: 2½ feet (0.8 meter) at the shoulder.

sloth·ful (slôth′fəl, slōth′-, sloth′-) *adj.* characterized by sloth; lazy; indolent. —**sloth′ful·ly,** *adv.* —**sloth′ful·ness,** *n.*

slot machine 1. a gambling machine that is operated by inserting a coin through a slot and pulling a lever that actuates a set of spinning disks with symbols on them, various combinations of which provide a payoff to the player. **2.** vending machine.

slouch (slouch) *v.i.* **1.** to sit, stand, or walk with an awkward, drooping posture, or in an overly loose or relaxed manner; slump; hunch. **2.** to hang down, as the brim of a hat; droop. —*n.* **1.** a drooping of the head and shoulders in sitting, standing, or walking; awkward or drooping posture. **2.** a hanging down, as of the brim of a hat. **3.** *Informal.* an awkward, lazy, or incompetent person. ➡ used chiefly with a negative: *He is no slouch at chess. She is not a slouch when it comes to a hard game of tennis.* [Of uncertain origin.]

slouch hat, a soft, usually felt hat, with a broad, flexible brim.

slouch·y (slou′chē) *adj.,* **slouch·i·er, slouch·i·est.** slouching, esp. in posture. —**slouch′i·ly,** *adv.* —**slouch′i·ness,** *n.*

slough[1] (*defs. 1, 3,* slou; *def. 2,* slü) *n.* **1.** a place full of soft, deep mud. **2.** *also,* **slew, slue.** a swamp, marsh, or bog, esp. one that is part of a backwater. **3.** a state of dejection, discouragement, or degradation. [Old English *slōh* piece of muddy ground.] —**slough′y,** *adj.*

slough[2] (sluf) *n.* **1.** the outer skin shed by a snake. **2.** a layer of dead skin or tissue that separates from the surrounding tissue, as of a healing wound. **3.** anything that has been shed or cast off. —*v.t.* **1.** to cast off or get rid of (often with *off*): *to slough off a tight sweater.* —*v.i.* **2.** to be shed or cast off. **2.** to shed an outer skin. **3.** to separate from the surrounding tissue (often with *off*). [Of uncertain origin.] —**slough′y,** *adj.*

Slo·vak (slō′vak, -väk) *n.* **1.** a member or close descendant of a Slavic people living predominantly in Slovakia and closely related to the Czechs and the Moravians. **2.** the language of these people, belonging to the western branch of the Slavic languages and closely related to Czech. —*adj.* of, relating to, or characteristic of Slovakia or its people, language, or culture. Also, **Slo·va′ki·an.**

slov·en (sluv′ən) *n.* a person who is untidy or careless, esp. in appearance or dress. [Possibly from Middle Dutch *slof* careless, lax.]

Slo·vene (slō′vēn) *n.* **1.** a member or close descendant of a Slavic people living in Slovenia and closely related to the Serbs and Croats. **2.** the language of these people, belonging to the southern branch of the Slavic group of languages, which also include the closely related Serbo-Croatian. —*adj.* of, relating to, or characteristic of Slovenia or its people, language, or culture. Also, **Slo·ve′ni·an.**

slov·en·ly (sluv′ən lē) *adj.,* **-li·er, -li·est. 1.** untidy or careless, esp. in appearance or dress; unkempt. **2.** characteristic of a sloven; slipshod. —*adv.* in a slovenly manner. —**slov′en·li·ness,** *n.*

slow (slō) *adj.* **1.** acting, moving, or occurring with little speed; not fast or quick: *a slow reader, slow progress.* **2.** taking or requiring a relatively long time to be completed or performed: *a slow trip, a slow game.* **3.** (of a timepiece) indicating a time behind the true time: *My watch is always slow.* **4.** not quick to learn or understand; mentally dull; obtuse: *a slow student.* **5.** unsuitable for or not conducive to rapid movement: *a slow track.* **6.** not active; sluggish: *Business is slow this season.* **7.** not prompt, hasty, or easily moved: *slow to answer letters, slow to anger.* **8.** lacking in liveliness; uninteresting; dull; boring: *Shy guests make for a slow party.* **9.** burning at moderate intensity; low: *a slow fire.* **10.** *Photography.* requiring a long exposure time: *slow film.* —*adv.* in a slow manner; slowly: *Drive slow through town.* —*v.t., v.i.* to make or become slow or slower (often with *down* or *up*): *The driver slowed down the car. Please slow up on your pace.* [Old English *slāw* dull, sluggish.] —**slow′ly,** *adv.* —**slow′ness,** *n.*

slow·down (slō′doun′) *n.* a reduction in pace, esp. a deliberate slowing down of the rate of production by workers or management.

slow·ish (slō′ish) *adj.* somewhat slow.

slow-mo·tion (slō′mō′shən) *adj.* **1.** of or relating to a motion-picture or videotape sequence in which the action appears to be taking place at a much slower than normal speed. **2.** moving, operating, or proceeding at less than normal speed: *slow-motion traffic, a slow-motion waltz.*

slow·poke (slō′pōk′) *n. Informal.* a person who moves, works, or acts at a very slow pace.

slow-wit·ted (slō′wit′id) *adj.* slow to understand; mentally dull; dense. —**slow′-wit′ted·ly,** *adv.*

slow·worm (slō′wûrm′) *n.* blindworm *(def. 1).*

SLR, single-lens reflex.

sludge (sluj) *n.* **1.** mud or mire, esp. a muddy deposit at the bottom of a body of water. **2.** any mudlike or slushy mass or mixture, as the deposit formed in a boiler or the sediment produced in the treatment of sewage. **3.** broken or half-formed ice, as on the sea. [Of uncertain origin.] —**sludg′y,** *adj.*

slue[1] (slü) *also,* **slew.** *v.,* **slued, slu·ing.** —*v.t.* to turn or twist about, esp. on a pivot or fixed point: *to slue a steering wheel sharply to the left.* —*v.i.* to turn or twist about; swing around. —*n.* **1.** the act of sluing. **2.** the position attained by sluing. [Of uncertain origin.]

slue[2] (slü) *n.* slough[1] *(def. 2).*

slug[1] (slug) *n.* **1.** any of several terrestrial mollusks, class Gastropoda, closely resembling a snail but either lacking a shell or having only a rudimentary shell. A slug moves by sliding on a thin layer of slime. **2.** the larva of certain moths and other insects that resembles a slug. **3.** sluggard. **4.a.** a small piece or lump of

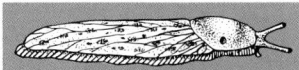

slug[1] *(def. 1)*

metal, esp. a piece of lead or other metal for firing from a gun. **b.** *Slang.* bullet. **5.** a piece of metal shaped like and used in place of a coin, esp. one used illegally, as in a vending machine. **6.** *Printing.* **a.** a strip of metal, thicker than a lead, used to space lines of type. **b.** a line of type cast in one piece, as by a Linotype machine. **7.** *Physics.* a unit of mass that acquires an acceleration of 1 foot per second when acted upon by a force of 1 pound. It is equal to about 32.2 pounds (15 kilograms). **8.** *Slang.* a single drink of alcoholic liquor; shot. [Probably of Scandinavian origin.]

slug[2] (slug) *Informal. v.t.,* **slugged, slug·ging.** to strike heavily, as with the fist or a blunt instrument: *The batter slugged the ball over the fence.* —*n.* a heavy blow, as with the fist. [Possibly from SLUG[1].]

slug·fest (slug′fest′) *n. Informal.* **1.** a fight or boxing match in which many hard blows are exchanged. **2.** a baseball game in which many hits and runs are made.

slug·gard (slug′ərd) *n.* a person who is habitually lazy or idle; slouch; loafer. —*adj. also,* **slug′gard·ly.** lazy or idle; slothful. [Possibly from obsolete *sluggy* lazy (probably of Scandinavian origin) + -ARD.]

slug·ger (slug′ər) *n.* a person who slugs, esp. a hard-hitting baseball player or a prizefighter able to throw hard punches.

slug·gish (slug′ish) *adj.* **1.** having or marked by little motion, speed, or activity: *Trading was sluggish on the stock market today.* **2.** characterized by or showing a lack of vigor, energy, or alertness: *a sluggish mind.* **3.** disinclined to action or exertion; slothful; lazy. **4.** not acting or functioning with full or usual energy or efficiency: *My car engine is sluggish on cold mornings.* [SLUG[1] + -ISH.] —**slug′gish·ly,** *adv.* —**slug′gish·ness,** *n.*

sluice (slüs) *n.* **1.** an artificial channel for conducting water, equipped with a gate or valve for controlling the flow. **2.** the gate or valve of such a channel, usually a sliding vertical plate. Also, **sluice gate. 3.** the water controlled by such a gate. **4.** any artificial channel, esp. one for draining off excess water. **5.** a long, sloping trough through which water is run, as for separating placer gold from sand or gravel or for floating logs. —*v.,* **sluiced, sluic·ing.** —*v.t.* **1.** to draw off by or through a sluice: *to sluice water.* **2.a.** to wash with water running through or from a sluice. **b.** to wash with a rush of water: *to sluice the decks of an aircraft carrier.* **3.** to float (logs) in a sluice. **4.** to wash (gold) from sand or gravel with water in a sluice. —*v.i.* to flow out from or as from

a	at	e	end	o	hot	u	up	hw	white		about
ā	ape	ē	me	ō	old	ū	use	ng	song	ə	taken
ä	far	i	it	ô	fork	ü	rule	th	thin		pencil
âr	care	ī	ice	oi	oil	ů	pull	th	this		lemon
		îr	pierce	ou	out	ûr	turn	zh	measure		circus

a sluice. [Old French *escluse* floodgate, going back to Latin *exclūsa* feminine past participle of *exclūdere* to shut out.]

sluice·way (slūs'wā') *n.* an artificial channel for the passage of water; sluice.

slum (slum) *n. also,* **slums.** a heavily populated section of a city, characterized by poverty, deteriorated housing, and squalid living conditions. —*v.i.,* **slummed, slum·ming. 1.** to visit a slum out of curiosity or for amusement: *to go slumming.* **2.** to visit a place regarded as socially inferior or disreputable, as for amusement. [Of uncertain origin.] —**slum'mer,** *n.*

slum·ber (slum'bər) *v.i.* **1.** to sleep or doze: *The baby slumbered peacefully.* **2.** to be quiet, calm, or inactive: *The town slumbered under the afternoon sun.* —*v.t.* to pass or spend in sleeping (often with *away*): *to slumber away the day.* —*n.* **1.** a light sleep or doze. **2.** a quiet, calm, or inactive state. [Middle English *slumeren* to doze, be inactive, going back to Old English *slūma* light sleep.] —**slum'ber·er,** *n.*

slum·ber·ous (slum'bər əs) *also,* **slum·brous** (slum'brəs). *adj.* **1.** sleepy or drowsy; somnolent. **2.** causing sleep; soporific; somniferous. **3.** like or characteristic of sleep. **4.** calm; quiet; peaceful.

slum·lord (slum'lôrd') *n.* a landlord of slum housing, esp. one who charges high rents and is negligent in caring for the property.

slump (slump) *v.i.* **1.** to fall or sink suddenly or heavily: *The dazed boxer staggered, then slumped to the floor.* **2.** to decline or deteriorate sharply, as in activity, performance, or value: *The football team slumped badly after its star quarterback was injured.* **3.** to assume a drooping posture; slouch: *to slump in one's seat.* —*n.* **1.** a sharp or prolonged decline or deterioration, as in business activity or performing ability: *a slump in sales, a slump in batting average.* **2.** an act or instance of slumping. [Imitative.]

slung (slung) the past tense and past participle of **sling.**

slunk (slungk) the past tense and past participle of **slink.**

slur (slûr) *n.* **1.** a disparaging statement or remark; aspersion; calumny. **2.** an indistinct pronunciation. **3.** *Music.* **a.** a combination of two or more tones of different pitch played or sung in a smooth, connected manner. **b.** the curved mark indicating this. —*v.t.,* **slurred, slur·ring. 1.** to pass over hurriedly or carelessly without giving due attention or consideration (often with *over*): *The author slurred over many details in order to get the book finished by summer.* **2.** to speak slightingly of; disparage: *to slur a person's reputation.* **3.** to pronounce indistinctly, as by running sounds together: *to slur one's words.* **4.** *Music.* **a.** to play or sing (two or more tones of different pitch) in a smooth, connected manner. **b.** to mark with a slur. [Possibly from Middle Dutch *sleuren* to trail in mud.]

slur *(n., def. 3b)*

slurp (slûrp) *Slang. v.t., v.i.* to drink, sip, or eat (something) with a pronounced sucking sound. —*n.* the noise made by slurping. [Dutch *slurpen* to lap³.]

slur·ry (slûr'ē) *n., pl.* **-ries.** a thin mixture of water or other liquid and some fine, insoluble substance, as clay, cement, or plaster of Paris.

slush (slush) *n.* **1.** partially melted snow or ice. **2.** soft mud; mire. **3.** any of various greasy materials used as lubricants. **4.** maudlin or silly, sentimental speech or writing; drivel. [Of uncertain origin.] —**slush'i·ness,** *n.* —**slush'y,** *adj.*

slush fund, money set aside for bribery, graft, or other corrupt political practices.

slut (slut) *n.* **1.** a disreputable or promiscuous woman. **2.** a dirty, slovenly woman; slattern. [Of uncertain origin.] —**slut'tish, slut'ty,** *adj.* —**slut'tish·ly,** *adv.* —**slut'tish·ness,** *n.*

sly (slī) *adj.,* **sli·er** or **sly·er, sli·est** or **sly·est. 1.** displaying or characterized by cleverness, shrewdness, or craftiness: *a sly trick.* **2.** clever or skillful in avoiding notice or detection; cunning; wily: *The sly thief eluded the police for months.* **3.** mischievous in a playful way; puckish; impish: *a sly glance.* [Old Norse *slœgr* cunning.] —**sly'ly;** *also,* **sli'ly,** *adv.* —**sly'ness,** *n.*

• **on the sly.** in a stealthy way; secretly; furtively: *Our friends met on the sly to plan the surprise party.*

Synonyms Sly, cunning, crafty, and wily mean characterized by devious, secretive actions or attitudes. **Sly** emphasizes evasiveness and lack of openness: *The candidate for mayor leaked rumors to the press in a sly attempt to discredit the incumbent.* **Cunning** suggests an instinctively devious intelligence: *The fox was cunning enough to evade the pursuing hounds.* **Crafty** implies a sophisticated, practiced deception: *The embezzler developed a crafty system to defraud investors.* **Wily** is similar to **crafty,** but may also suggest the intention to entrap or ensnare: *The wily thief tried to have an innocent person blamed for the crime.*

Sm, the symbol for samarium.

S.M. 1. Master of Science. Also, **M.S. 2.** Soldier's Medal.

smack¹ (smak) *v.t.* **1.** to press together and open (the lips) rapidly so as to make a sharp sound. **2.** to strike or slap sharply, as with the open hand: *to smack someone's face.* **3.** to kiss noisily. —*v.i.* **1.** to smack the lips. **2.** to strike something forcibly and noisily: *The car skidded and smacked into the side of the barn.* —*n.* **1.** a sharp sound made by smacking the lips. **2.** a sharp blow or slap, as with the open hand. **3.** a noisy kiss. —*adv. Informal.* **1.** in a sudden, violent manner: *to fall smack into the pool.* **2.** precisely; directly: *I ran smack into the very person I was trying to avoid.* [Imitative.]

smack² (smak) *n.* **1.a.** a distinctive or characteristic taste or flavor, esp. one that is only slightly perceptible: *The pudding had a smack of cinnamon.* **b.** a suggestion or trace. **2.** a small quantity or amount. —*v.i.* **1.** to have a taste or flavor (with *of*): *The meat smacks of garlic.* **2.** to have a suggestion or trace (with *of*): *That statement smacks of dishonesty.* [Old English *smæc* taste.]

smack³ (smak) *n.* a small sailboat, usually fore-and-aft-rigged, used chiefly for fishing. [Dutch *smak.*]

smack·er (smak'ər) *n.* **1.** a person or thing that smacks. **2.** *Informal.* a noisy kiss; smack. **3.** *Slang.* a dollar.

smack·ing (smak'ing) *adj.* brisk or vigorous; lively: *a smacking breeze.*

small (smôl) *adj.* **1.** not large or great in size, amount, degree, or number, esp. in comparison to others of the same kind: *a small car, a small town, a small crowd.* **2.** limited in degree, duration, intensity, or value: *a small possibility.* **3.** of limited importance; trivial: *a small problem.* **4.** carrying on or involved in business in a limited way: *a small retailer, a small investor.* **5.** of low or inferior social position or rank. **6.** modest; humble: *Everyone contributed in a small way.* **7.** young: *When I was a small child, I loved to visit the zoo.* **8.** soft or weak; not loud; low: *a small voice.* **9.** mean, petty, or selfish; small-minded: *It was small of them not to pay their share of the cost.* —*adv.* **1.** in or into small pieces. **2.** in low tones; softly. **3.** in a small manner. —*n.* a small or narrow part: *the small of the back.* [Old English *smæl* thin, narrow, of limited size.] —**small'ness,** *n.*

• **to feel small.** to feel humiliated or ashamed: *Their kindness made me feel small after my rudeness.*

small arms, firearms, as pistols or rifles, that can be carried easily and can be held in the hands when fired ➡ distinguished from **artillery.**

small calorie, calorie *(def. 1).*

small capital, a capital letter of slightly smaller size than the regular letter of the same font. THIS SENTENCE IS IN SMALL CAPITALS.

small change 1. coins of small denomination, such as dimes or nickels. **2.** something of little value or importance.

small circle, on the surface of a sphere, a circle whose plane, unlike that of a great circle, does not pass through the center of the sphere.

small-claims court (smôl'klāmz') a special court established by a state or municipality to hear and decide lawsuits, usually without the presence of lawyers, involving amounts of money smaller than a specified sum.

small·clothes (smôl'klōz', -klōthz') *pl. n.* close-fitting knee breeches worn in the eighteenth century.

small fry 1. a young or small child or children. **2.** people or things of little or no importance.

small game, small wild animals and birds sought by hunters for sport.

small hours, the hours between midnight and dawn: *We talked into the small hours.*

small intestine, that part of the digestive tract extending from the stomach to the large intestine, in which food broken up in the stomach is digested and absorbed. It consists of the duodenum, the jejunum, and the ileum, about 20 feet (6.1 meters) long in the adult human.

small·ish (smô'lish) *adj.* somewhat small.

small letter, a letter that is not a capital letter.

small-mind·ed (smôl'mīn'did) *adj.* having or showing a narrow, selfish, or petty outlook or nature; prejudiced. —**small'-mind'ed·ly,** *adv.* —**small'-mind'ed·ness,** *n.*

small potatoes *Informal.* unimportant or insignificant persons or things: *They are strictly small potatoes in the union.*

small·pox (smôl'poks') *n.* an acute, highly contagious disease caused by a virus and characterized by fever and pustular skin eruptions that often leave small, pit-shaped, permanent scars, now eradicated worldwide by vaccination. Also, **variola.**

small-scale (smôl'skāl') *adj.* **1.** of small or limited scope; not extensive: *a small-scale undertaking, a small-scale attack.*

2. drawn or made on a small scale and permitting little detail to be shown: *a small-scale map.*

small talk, light conversation about common or unimportant matters; chitchat.

small-time (smôl′tīm′) *adj. Informal.* of no real importance; minor; petty: *a small-time lawyer.*

smart (smärt) *adj.* **1.** clever or intelligent; bright: *a smart student, a smart investment.* **2.** *Informal.* flippantly or disrespectfully witty: *Don't give me any smart answers!* **3.** neat and trim; spruce; sharp: *The musicians looked very smart in their uniforms.* **4.** fashionable; stylish: *a smart outfit, a smart restaurant.* **5.** brisk or vigorous; lively: *The soldiers marched at a smart pace.* **6.** causing sharp or stinging pain. **7.** equipped with or employing microprocessors, sensors, or the like, as for monitoring operating conditions and responding to changes in them. **8.** *Informal.* considerable; large: *a smart sum of money.* —*v.i.* **1.a.** to cause a sharp or stinging pain: *The antiseptic smarted as it was applied to the wound.* **b.** to feel or experience such pain: *My face smarted from the cold wind.* **2.** to experience mental pain, suffering, or distress: *to smart from criticism.* **3.** to suffer a penalty (with *for*): *to smart for a wrongdoing.* —*v.t.* to cause to smart or feel pain. —*n.* **1.** a sharp or stinging physical or mental pain. **2. smarts.** *Slang.* intelligence or common sense. —*adv.* in a smart manner; smartly: *to dress smart.* [Old English *smeortan* to be painful.] —**smart′ly,** *adv.* —**smart′ness,** *n.*

smart al·eck (al′ik) *Informal.* a person who is obnoxiously or arrogantly conceited and assertive. —**smart′-al′eck·y,** *adj.*

smart·en (smär′tən) *v.t.* **1.** to improve in appearance; spruce up (often with *up*): *The theatrical troupe smartened up their costumes before the performance.* **2.** to make more brisk or lively. **3.** to make more aware, clever, or knowing (often with *up*): *Smarten up your friends before they get into trouble.* —*v.i.* to become more aware, clever, or knowing (often with *up*).

smart set, fashionable, sophisticated people considered as a social group.

smart·weed (smärt′wēd′) *n.* any of several kinds of knotgrass having a bitter juice that can cause skin irritation.

smash (smash) *v.t.* **1.** to break (something), esp. into pieces, suddenly and often with noise and violence: *The ball smashed the window.* **2.** to strike with a hard blow: *The batter smashed the ball over the fence.* **3.** to accomplish or produce by striking forcefully: *Firefighters smashed the door down.* **4.** to destroy, crush, or defeat completely or decisively: *to smash a crime operation, to smash a theory.* **5.** to hit with a racket, as a tennis ball, with a hard, swift overhand stroke. —*v.i.* **1.** to break into pieces, esp. as the result of impact: *The plate slipped out of my hand and smashed on the floor.* **2.** to move or be propelled with force or violence (often with *against, into,* or *through*): *The cart smashed into the side of the house.* —*n.* **1.** an act or instance of smashing. **2.** the noise produced by smashing: *the smash of glass.* **3.** a hard blow. **4.** a collision or crash; smashup. **5.** a complete or crushing defeat or disaster: *the smash of one's hopes.* **6.** a hard, swift overhand stroke made with a racket, as in tennis. **7.** a beverage made of water, sugar, mint, and an alcoholic liquor, as brandy. **8.** *Informal.* a tremendous success: *The show was an immediate smash.* —*adj. Informal.* tremendously successful: *The new play is a smash hit.* [Probably blend of SMACK¹ and MASH.] —**smash′er,** *n.*

smash·ing (smash′ing) *adj. Informal.* **1.** extremely good or impressive; outstanding: *Their debut as a comedy act was a smashing success.* **2.** devastating; ruinous: *a smashing defeat.* —**smash′ing·ly,** *adv.*

smash·up (smash′up′) *n.* **1.** a violent collision, as of automobiles. **2.** a complete collapse, failure, or defeat.

smat·ter (smat′ər) *v.t.* **1.** to speak with little knowledge or with very limited understanding, as a foreign language. **2.** to study or learn superficially; dabble in. —*n.* a shallow or superficial knowledge; smattering. [Possibly of Scandinavian origin.]

smat·ter·ing (smat′ər ing) *n.* **1.** a superficial or very limited knowledge: *to have only a smattering of French.* **2.** a small number or amount: *Only a smattering of the students knew the answer.*

smaze (smāz) *n.* a mixture of smoke and haze in the lower atmosphere, less damp than smog. [Blend of SMOKE and HAZE¹.]

smear (smîr) *v.t.* **1.** to cover, spread, or stain with paint, grease, dirt, or another substance: *The child smeared her face with mud.* **2.** to spread or apply (paint, grease, dirt, or other substance): *The boy smeared dirt all over his clothes.* **3.** to cause to become indistinct, untidy, or disordered, as by rubbing with the hand: *to smear a signature.* **4.** to damage the reputation of, as by making slanderous statements: *The candidate smeared his opponent by accusing him of corruption.* **5.** *Slang.* to defeat completely or overwhelmingly, as in an athletic contest. —*v.i.* to be or become smeared or spread: *The wet paint smeared when I touched it.* —*n.* **1.** a mark or stain made by smearing: *There was an ink smear on the letter.* **2.** a small quantity of a substance, as blood, placed on a slide for

microscopic examination. **3.** a substance to be smeared on a surface. **4.** an attack on a person's reputation, as with slanderous statements: *The politician was subjected to vicious smears by her opponent's supporters.* [Old English *smerian* to anoint or rub with a greasy substance.] —**smear′er,** *n.*

smear·y (smîr′ē) *adj.,* **smear·i·er, smear·i·est. 1.** marked or characterized by smears; smeared. **2.** tending or likely to smear or smudge. —**smear′i·ness,** *n.*

smell (smel) *v.,* **smelled** or **smelt, smell·ing.** —*v.t.* **1.** to perceive by means of the nose and its olfactory nerves; detect the odor of: *Do you smell something burning?* **2.** to test or sample by smelling: *to smell food to see if it's fresh.* **3.** to sense the presence or existence of: *to smell danger.* —*v.i.* **1.** to have or give off an odor: *The kitchen smells of freshly baked bread.* **2.** to have or give off an unpleasant or offensive odor: *Rotten meat smells.* **3.** to use the sense of smell; sniff: *The dog smelled at the meat and then gulped it down.* **4.** to give or exhibit an indication; be suggestive (with *of*): *Your actions smell of cowardice.* **5.** *Informal.* to have the appearance of being evil, dishonest, or corrupt: *The senator's chummy relationship with the indicted banker smells.* —*n.* **1.** the sense by means of which odors are perceived. **2.** that property of a thing or substance that makes it perceptible to the sense of smell; odor: *the smell of the sea.* **3.** the act of smelling: *One smell of this awful brew could make you sick.* **4.** a suggestion, hint, or feeling of something: *The smell of victory was in the air long before the game was over.* [Of uncertain origin.] —**smell′er,** *n.*

·**to smell up.** to cause to have an unpleasant or offensive odor: *That awful cheese is smelling up the refrigerator.*

Synonyms *n.* **Smell, odor, aroma,** and **scent** mean the property of something perceived by means of the nose. **Smell** is the most general of these terms, and may be applied to both pleasant and unpleasant odors: *the smell of fresh bread, the smell of rotting fish.* **Odor** implies a penetrating and not necessarily pleasant quality: *The corridor bore the unmistakable odor of disinfectant.* **Aroma** also suggests a pervasive and pungent quality, but usually one that is pleasing: *The aroma of baking pizza filled the kitchen.* **Scent** emphasizes not only the pleasantness but often the delicacy of a smell: *The scent of roses was just perceptible on the summer breeze.*

smelling salts, an ammonium salt in an aromatic liquid solution that evaporates on contact with air, emitting an odor that acts as a stimulant or restorative, inhaled to relieve headaches or faintness.

smell·y (smel′ē) *adj.,* **smell·i·er, smell·i·est. *Informal.* having or giving off an unpleasant or offensive smell. —**smell′i·ness,** *n.*

smelt¹ (smelt) *v.t.* **1.** to melt (ore) to separate the metal from it. **2.** to obtain or refine (metal) in this manner. [Middle Dutch *smelten* to melt, make liquid, found³.]

smelt² (smelt) *n., pl.* **smelts** or **smelt.** any of a group of slender, silvery food fish, family Osmeridae, found in cold and temperate waters of the Northern Hemisphere. [Old English *smelt.*]

smelt³ (smelt) a past tense and past participle of **smell.**

smelt·er (smel′tər) *n.* **1.** a person whose work or business is smelting. **2.** an establishment for smelting. **3.** a furnace for smelting.

smid·gen (smij′ən) *also,* **smid·geon, smid·gin.** *n. Informal.* a very small amount; bit. [Of uncertain origin.]

smi·lax (smī′laks) *n.* **1.** a climbing African vine, *Asparagus asparagoides,* having stiff, shiny branches and tiny greenish white flowers that ripen into small purple berries, often grown indoors as an ornamental. **2.** greenbrier. [Latin *smīlax* bindweed, from Greek *smīlax.*]

smile (smīl) *n.* **1.** a facial expression characterized by an upward turning of the corners of the mouth, showing any of a wide range of feelings or attitudes, as happiness, amusement, friendliness, sympathy, or contempt. **2.** a favorable or pleasant appearance, aspect, or disposition. —*v.,* **smiled, smil·ing.** —*v.i.* **1.** to have, show, or give a smile. **2.** to show or seem to show approval or favor (often with *on, upon,* or *at*): *Fortune smiled upon our plans.* —*v.t.* **1.** to express with a smile: *to smile one's gratitude.* **2.** to have or give (a smile, esp. of a specified type): *The happy child smiled a big smile at the new bike.* **3.** to affect, change, or accomplish by or as by smiling: *to smile away one's fears.* [Possibly of Scandinavian origin.] —**smil′er,** *n.* —**smil′ing·ly,** *adv.*

a	at	e	end	o	hot	u	up	hw	white		about
ā	ape	ē	me	ō	old	ū	use	ng	song	ə	taken
ä	far	i	it	ô	fork	ü	rule	th	thin		pencil
âr	care	ī	ice	oi	oil	u̇	pull	th	this		lemon
		îr	pierce	ou	out	ûr	turn	zh	measure		circus

smirch (smûrch) v.t. **1.** to stain, soil, or discolor with dirt, grime, or a similar substance. **2.** to bring dishonor or disgrace upon: *to smirch a person's reputation.* —n. **1.** a dirty spot or stain; smudge. **2.** a blot or stain on reputation or honor. [Of uncertain origin.]

smirk (smûrk) v.i. to smile in an affected, self-satisfied, or silly manner. —n. an affected, self-satisfied, or silly smile. [Old English *smearcian* to smile.] —smirk′er, n. —smirk′ing·ly, adv.

smite (smīt) v., smote, smit·ten or smit (smit) or smote, smit·ing. —v.t. **1.** to strike hard, esp. with the hand or with a weapon. **2.** to destroy, kill, or defeat by or as by striking in this manner. **3.** to afflict or attack, esp. suddenly and with a disastrous effect: *to be smitten by disease.* **4.** to affect suddenly or strongly with some powerful or distressing feeling, as love, fear, or remorse. **5.** to make a favorable impression on: *We were smitten by the child's grace.* —v.i. to strike with or as if with a hard blow. [Old English *smītan* to smear, pollute.] —smit′er, n.

smith (smith) n. **1.** a person who makes or repairs metal objects. ➡ usually used in combination, as in *gunsmith.* **2.** blacksmith. [Old English *smith.*]

smith·er·eens (smith′ə rēnz′) pl. n. *Informal.* little pieces or fragments; bits: *The explosion blew the old shack to smithereens.* [Irish Gaelic *smidirīn,* diminutive of *smiodar* fragment.]

smith·son·ite (smith′sə nīt′) n. a variously colored carbonate mineral mined as an ore of zinc. Formula: $ZnCO_3$ [From James *Smithson,* 1765?-1829, English scientist + -ITE[1].]

smith·y (smith′ē, smith′ē) n., pl. smith·ies. **1.** the workshop of a smith, esp. a blacksmith's shop; forge. **2.** blacksmith. [Old Norse *smithja* forge, from *smithr* smith.]

smit·ten (smit′ən) a past participle of **smite.**

smock (smok) n. a loose outer garment, usually resembling a long shirt, worn to protect clothing. —v.t. to ornament with smocking. [Old English *smoc* woman's undergarment.]

smock·ing (smok′ing) n. a decorative pattern formed by gathering fabric with rows of stitches, often with a honeycomb design.

smog (smog, smôg) n. a combination of smoke and fog, found esp. over urban or industrial and manufacturing areas. [Blend of SMOKE and FOG.] —smog′gy, adj.

smoke (smōk) n. **1.a.** a suspension of solid particles, esp. of carbon, in a gas, produced by combustion of organic matter, such as wood or coal. **b.** a cloud or column of this. **2.** anything resembling this, such as steam or mist. **3.** something lacking substance, value, or permanence. **4.** something that obscures or deceives. **5.** the act or a period of smoking tobacco: *to take time out for a smoke.* **6.** a cigarette, cigar, or the like. **7.** a pale bluish gray color. —v., smoked, smok·ing. —v.i. **1.** to emit or produce smoke: *We could see a chimney smoking in the distance.* **2.** to emit smoke excessively or improperly: *The fireplace is smoking.* **3.a.** to draw the smoke of a cigarette, cigar, or the like into the mouth, and often the lungs, and exhale it. **b.** to smoke habitually. —v.t. **1.** to draw in and exhale the smoke of (a cigarette, cigar, or the like). **2.** to cure or preserve (food) by exposure to smoke: *to smoke fish.* **3.** to subject or expose to smoke. **4.** to fumigate. **5.** to force with or as if with smoke: *to smoke an animal from its burrow.* [Old English *smoca* visible vapor given off by burning substances.]

· to smoke out. **a.** to force into the open with smoke: *to smoke out a skunk from under a house.* **b.** to drive or bring out of hiding or secrecy: *to smoke out a plot against the government.*

smoke detector, an electronic device that sounds an alarm when it detects smoke, used to warn of fire. Also, **smoke alarm.**

smoke·house (smōk′hous′) n., pl. -hous·es (-hou′ziz) a building where food, as meat or fish, is exposed to smoke to preserve and flavor it.

smoke·jump·er (smōk′jum′pər) also, smoke jumper. n. a firefighter who parachutes into an area near or in a forest fire.

smoke·less (smōk′lis) adj. having or giving off little or no smoke.

smokeless powder, a gunpowder substitute that consists chiefly of nitrocellulose and gives off little or no smoke.

smok·er (smō′kər) n. **1.** a person or thing that smokes, esp. a person who habitually smokes tobacco. **2.** smoking car. **3.** an informal social gathering for men.

smoke screen **1.** a thick cloud of smoke used to hinder or prevent observation, as of a military force or movement. **2.** anything used or intended to conceal or deceive.

smoke·stack (smōk′stak′) n. a pipe or funnel for the escape of smoke or gases, as on a factory, ship, or locomotive.

smoke tree, any of several shrubs and small trees, genus *Cotinus,* of the cashew family, having flower clusters resembling puffs of smoke.

smoking car, a railroad car or compartment where smoking is permitted. Also, **smoker.**

smoking gun *Informal.* something that provides indisputable evidence or conclusive proof, esp. of wrongdoing.

smoking jacket, a man's loose jacket for wear at home.

smok·y (smō′kē) adj., smok·i·er, smok·i·est. **1.** giving off smoke, esp. an excessive or undesirable amount of smoke: *a smoky fire, a smoky chimney.* **2.** filled with or containing smoke: *a smoky room, smoky air.* **3.** like or suggestive of smoke, as in color or taste: *a smoky haze, a smoky taste, a smoky blue.* **4.** darkened or discolored by smoke. —smok′i·ly, adv. —smok′i·ness, n.

smoky quartz, a transparent or semitransparent variety of quartz crystal colored smoky brown by mineral impurities.

smol·der (smōl′dər) also, smoulder. v.i. **1.** to burn and smoke with little or no flame. **2.** to exist or continue in a suppressed state: *All seemed calm, but resentment smoldered among the people.* **3.** to display repressed emotion: *Her eyes smoldered with rage at his accusation.* —n. a smoldering fire or the smoke produced by or as by such a fire. [Of uncertain origin.]

smolt (smōlt) n. a young salmon, bright silver in color, when it first descends to the sea. [Of uncertain origin.]

smooch (smūch) *Slang.* v.i., v.t. to kiss or pet. —n. kiss. [Possibly imitative.]

smooth (smūth) adj. **1.a.** having a surface that is free or relatively free from perceptible projections or irregularities: *a smooth road, smooth skin.* **b.** having projections worn down or away by use: *a smooth tire.* **2.** even, easy, or gentle in movement: *a smooth ride, smooth sailing.* **3.** having an even consistency; free from lumps: *a smooth batter.* **4.** free from difficulties or obstacles: *a smooth transition, smooth progress.* **5.** emotionally calm or even; serene: *a smooth disposition.* **6.a.** able, skillful, or polished: *a smooth dancer.* **b.** characterized by insincere friendliness or politeness: *a smooth, glib politician.* **7.** characterized by gentle or flowing sounds or rhythms: *a smooth voice, a smooth style of writing.* **8.** pleasing to the taste; not harsh or biting: *a smooth sauce.* —v.t. **1.** to make smooth, even, or level: *to smooth a wrinkled tablecloth.* **2.** to remove or eliminate (often with *away* or *out*): *Please smooth out the wrinkles. Do you think we can smooth out our differences?* **3.** to free from difficulties or obstacles; make easy: *to smooth the way.* **4.** to calm; soothe: *to smooth someone's temper.* **5.** to make more polished or flowing, as a writing style; refine. —v.i. to become smooth. —adv. in a smooth manner; smoothly. —n. **1.** a smooth part or surface. **2.** the act of smoothing. [Old English *smōth* not uneven or rough.] —smooth′er, n. —smooth′ly, adv. —smooth′ness, n.

· to smooth over. to make less unpleasant or serious; minimize: *to smooth over a problem.*

smooth·bore (smūth′bôr′) adj. (of a firearm) not rifled. —n. a firearm having a bore that is not rifled.

smooth·en (smū′thən) v.t., v.i. to make or become smooth.

smooth muscle, muscle that forms the walls of such internal organs as the esophagus, stomach, and bladder, controlled by the autonomic nervous system.

smooth-tongued (smūth′tungd′) adj. able to speak smoothly, convincingly, or ingratiatingly.

smor·gas·bord (smôr′gəs bôrd′) also, smör·gås·bord. n. **1.** a large assortment of food, such as hors d'oeuvres, meats, fish, and cheese, usually arranged on a table so that people can serve themselves. **2.** a meal consisting of such an assortment. **3.** a restaurant offering a smorgasbord. **4.** any large and varied assortment or group: *The new curriculum offers a smorgasbord of classes.* [Swedish *smörgåsbord* assortment of hors d'oeuvres served before a meal, from *smörgås* sandwich + *bord* table.]

smote (smōt) the past tense and a past participle of **smite.**

smoth·er (smuth′ər) v.t. **1.a.** to prevent from breathing in air. **b.** to kill in this way. **2.** to cause (a fire) to go out or die down by covering it so as to cut off oxygen: *to smother flames with a blanket.* **3.** to cover thickly: *to smother a steak with onions.* **4.** to conceal or suppress: *to smother a yawn, to smother feelings of resentment.* **5.** to provide (someone) with an excessive or stifling amount of something: *Some parents smother their children with love.* —v.i. **1.a.** to be prevented from breathing in air. **b.** to die in this way. **2.** to be concealed or suppressed. —n. something that smothers, such as a dense cloud of smoke or dust. [Middle English *smorther* dense stifling smoke, going back to Old English *smorian* to suffocate.] —smoth′er·er, n. —smoth′er·y, adj.

smoul·der (smōl′dər) smolder.

smudge (smuj) v., smudged, smudg·ing. —v.t. **1.** to make dirty; soil or smear: *to smudge a white shirt with grimy hands.* **2.** to fill (a planted area) with dense smoke to repel insects or protect against frost. —v.i. **1.** to be or become smudged or smeared: *A charcoal drawing smudges easily.* **2.** to make a smear; blur or smear. —n. **1.** a mark or stain made by smearing or smudging: *The child's dirty hand left a smudge on the wall.* **2.a.** a smoky fire built to repel insects or protect against frost. **b.** the dense smoke

produced by such a fire. [Of uncertain origin.] —**smudg′i‑ly**, *adv.* —**smudg′i‑ness**, *n.* —**smudg′y**, *adj.*

smudge pot, a pot or similar vessel for burning a fuel to produce smudge.

smug (smug) *adj.,* **smug‑ger, smug‑gest.** having, showing, or characterized by great or excessive self-satisfaction; overly pleased with oneself; complacent: *a smug person, a smug attitude.* [Probably from Low German *smuck* neat, trim.] —**smug′ly**, *adv.* —**smug′ness**, *n.*

smug‑gle (smug′əl) *v.,* **-gled, -gling.** —*v.t.* **1.** to take into or out of a country secretly and unlawfully, as goods on which the required duties have not been paid, or whose importation or exportation is prohibited by law: *to smuggle heroin into a country.* **2.** to bring, take, or transport secretly or stealthily: *to smuggle a weapon to a prisoner in jail.* —*v.i.* to engage in smuggling. [Low German *smuggeln.*] —**smug′gler**, *n.*

smut (smut) *n.* **1.a.** sooty matter; soot; dirt. **b.** a particle of such matter. **2.** a spot or stain made by soot or dirt; smudge. **3.a.** obscene material or writing; pornography. **b.** indecent or obscene language. **4.a.** any of several fungus diseases of plants, commonly affecting cereal grains, as corn and wheat, and characterized by the appearance of black, powdery masses or spores. **b.** any of several parasitic fungi that cause such a disease. —*v.,* **smut‑ted, smut‑ting.** —*v.t.* to mark, stain, or affect with smut. —*v.i.* to become affected by smut. [Possibly of Low German origin.]

smutch (smuch) *v.t.* to make dirty; soil; smudge. —*n.* a smudge; stain. [Possibly from Middle High German *smutzen* to smear.] —**smutch′y**, *adj.*

smut‑ty (smut′ē) *adj.,* **-ti‑er, -ti‑est. 1.** soiled with smut; dirty. **2.** obscene, indecent, or pornographic: *smutty language, a smutty film.* **3.** (of plants) affected with smut. —**smut′ti‑ly**, *adv.* —**smut′ti‑ness**, *n.*

Sn, the symbol for tin. [Latin *stannum.*]

snack (snak) *n.* a small quantity of food or drink, esp. a light meal eaten between regular meals. —*v.i.* to eat a snack: *to snack on fruit.* [Probably from Middle Dutch *snacken* to snap at, bite, snatch.]

snack bar, an eating place where snacks are served, esp. at a counter.

snaf‑fle (snaf′əl) *n.* a slender, jointed horse's bit. Also, **snaf‑fle·bit** (snaf′əl bit′). —*v.t.,* **-fled, -fling.** to provide or control with a snaffle. [Probably from Dutch *snavel* beak, horse's muzzle.]

sna‑fu (sna fü′) *Slang. adj.* in a state of great or total confusion or disorder. —*v.t.* to throw into confusion or disorder. —*n.* a confused or chaotic situation. [Short for *s(itua‑tion) n(ormal) a(ll) f(ouled) u(p).*]

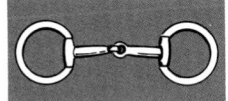

snaffle

snag (snag) *n.* **1.** a sharp, jagged, or rough projecting part, as one of the points on barbed wire. **2.** a branch, stump, or trunk of a tree embedded in the bottom of a lake, river, or the like and constituting a hazard to navigation. **3.** a tear or hole made by or as by a sharp projection. **4.** an unexpected or concealed obstacle or difficulty. —*v.,* **snagged, snag‑ging.** —*v.t.* **1.** to catch, tear, or damage on or as on a snag. **2.** to impede by or as by a snag; hinder; block. **3.** *Informal.* to catch or obtain, esp. by quick action: *The outfielder leaped and snagged the fly ball.* —*v.i.* **1.** to be or become caught on or impeded by a snag: *The fishing line snagged on an overhanging branch.* **2.** to develop a snag or snags: *My sweater snags very easily.* [Probably of Scandinavian origin.] —**snag′gy**, *adj.*

snag‑gle·tooth (snag′əl tüth′) *n., pl.* **-teeth** (-tēth′). a tooth that sticks out or is broken or irregular. —**snag‑gle·toothed** (snag′əl tütht′, -tüthd′), *adj.*

snail (snāl) *n.* **1.** any of a large group of soft-bodied mollusks, class Gastropoda, found in water and on land and having a spirally coiled shell. **2.** a slow-moving or lazy person: *You're such a snail that you never get anywhere on time.* [Old English *snegel* the mollusk.]

snail darter, a small, perchlike, North American freshwater fish, *Percina tanasi,* that is nearly extinct. Average length: 2 inches (5 centimeters).

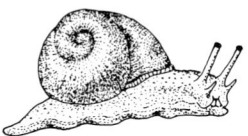

snail

snake (snāk) *n.* **1.** any of a group of limbless reptiles, suborder Serpentes, having long, scaly bodies. Some snakes have a venomous bite. **2.** a treacherous, deceitful, or despicable person. **3.** a plumbing tool used to clear clogged drains, consisting of a long, very flexible metal wire or rod.

—*v.,* **snaked, snak‑ing.** —*v.i.* **1.** to move or crawl like a snake. **2.** to follow a winding or curving course: *The road snaked up the mountain.* —*v.t.* to drag or pull lengthwise, esp. with a chain or rope: *to snake logs through a forest, to snake new wiring through a wall.* [Old English *snaca* the reptile.] —**snake′like′**, *adj.*

snake·bird (snāk′bûrd′) *n.* any of various large, fish-eating birds, family Anhingidae, having a long neck, a small head, and a sharp-pointed bill. Also, **darter.**

snake·bite (snāk′bīt′) *n.* **1.** the bite of a snake, esp. a venomous snake. **2.** painful poisoning caused by such a bite.

snake charmer, an entertainer who appears to charm or control snakes by means of music and rhythmic body movements.

snake dance 1. a ceremonial dance in which snakes are handled or imitated by the dancers, esp. a Hopi Indian dance in which live rattlesnakes are held in the mouths of the participants. **2.** an informal parade or procession of persons moving single file in a winding or zigzag course.

snake fence, worm fence.

snake in the grass 1. a sly, evil, or unreliable person who is seemingly friendly. **2.** a hidden or unforeseen danger.

snake oil, any of various preparations supposedly able to cure a wide variety of ailments, as sold by hucksters at a carnival.

snake pit 1. a pit or hole full of snakes. **2.** *Informal.* a place or situation of frightening confusion or oppressiveness, such as a badly neglected institution for the mentally ill.

snake·root (snāk′rüt′, -rút′) *n.* **1.** any of several plants whose roots were once believed to be a cure for snakebite. **2.** the root of such a plant.

snake·skin (snāk′skin′) *n.* the skin of a snake, or leather made from such a skin.

snak·y (snā′kē) *adj.,* **snak·i·er, snak·i·est. 1.** of or relating to a snake or snakes. **2.** having a form or movement like that of a snake; winding; twisting: *a snaky road.* **3.** treacherous; deceitful. **4.** infested with snakes: *a snaky swamp.* —**snak′i·ly**, *adv.* —**snak′i·ness**, *n.*

snap (snap) *v.,* **snapped, snap·ping.** —*v.i.* **1.** to make or emit a sudden, sharp sound: *The dry wood snapped and crackled as it burned.* **2.** to break or be released suddenly, usually with a sharp sound: *The twig snapped when she stepped on it.* **3.** to give way suddenly, esp. under mental strain or tension: *This final misfortune caused his mind to snap.* **4.** to close or move into place with a swift movement and often with a sharp sound: *The lid snapped shut.* **5.** to attempt to bite or seize something by closing the jaws with a sudden, swift motion (often with *at*): *The fish snapped at the bait.* **6.** to seize or snatch suddenly or eagerly (often with *at*): *to snap at an opportunity.* **7.** to speak harshly, abruptly, or angrily (often with *at*). **8.** to move or act quickly and smartly: *to snap to attention.* —*v.t.* **1.** to seize or snatch with or as if with a swift biting motion (often with *up*): *The puppy snapped the cookie out of my hand.* **2.** to break or sever suddenly, usually with a sharp sound: *The enormous fish snapped the line.* **3.** to utter harshly, abruptly, or angrily: *The witness snapped a furious reply to the attorney's question.* **4.** to cause to make or emit a sudden, sharp sound: *to snap one's fingers.* **5.** to close, fasten, or move into place, often with a sharp sound: *to snap a padlock closed.* **6.a.** to take (a photograph): *The reporter snapped two pictures without anyone knowing it.* **b.** to take a snapshot of (someone or something): *I snapped the passing scenery as we drove along.* **7.** to cause to move quickly, suddenly, or smartly. **8.** *Football.* to put (the ball) into play by sending it back from the line of scrimmage to a member of the backfield: *The center snapped the ball to the quarterback.* —*n.* **1.** a sharp sound made by or as if by snapping or breaking. **2.** the act of snapping or breaking. **3.** any of several fastening devices that operate with a snapping or clicking sound. **4.** a sudden attempt to seize or snatch with or as if with a swift biting motion. **5.** a brief spell or period, esp. of cold weather. **6.** a thin, crisp cookie. **7.** snapshot. **8.** *Informal.* something of little or no difficulty; task requiring little effort: *That spelling test was a snap.* **9.** *Informal.* vigor; energy; liveliness: *Put some snap in your step!* **10.** *Football.* the act of snapping the ball. Also (*def. 10*), **snapback.** —*adj.* **1.** made or done hastily or without due deliberation: *a snap decision.* **2.** fastening with a snap. **3.** *Informal.* of little or no difficulty; requiring little work or effort: *Astronomy is no snap course.* [Middle Dutch *snappen* to seize, speak quickly.]

·**to snap back.** to recover suddenly or quickly: *to snap back after a disappointment.*

·**to snap out of.** to recover or change from a specified state, or

a	at	e	end	o	hot	u	up	hw	white	about
ā	ape	ē	me	ō	old	ū	use	ng	song	taken
ä	far	i	it	ô	fork	ú	rule	th	thin	pencil
âr	care	ī	ice	oi	oil	ú	pull	th	this	lemon
		îr	pierce	ou	out	ûr	turn	zh	measure	circus

cause to do so: *The arrival of spring has snapped me out of the doldrums.*

snap·back (snap′bak′) *n.* snap *(def. 10).*

snap bean, string bean.

snap·dra·gon (snap′drag′ən) *n.* **1.** the sac-shaped flower of any of a group of erect or climbing plants, genus *Antirrhinum,* esp. *A. majus,* the common snapdragon, usually red, purple, or white, widely cultivated as a garden flower. **2.** the plant bearing these flowers. [Because the flower is thought to resemble a dragon's mouth.]

snap·per (snap′ər) *n.* **1.** a person or thing that snaps. **2.** snapping turtle. **3.** any of a large group of brightly colored food and game fish, family Lutjanidae, found in warm seas, esp. the red snapper.

snapping beetle, click beetle.

snapping turtle, any of several freshwater turtles, family Chelydridae, found in North and Central America, having powerful jaws. Also, **snapper.**

snapping turtle

snap·pish (snap′ish) *adj.* **1.** abrupt and sharp in speech or manner; irritable: *a cranky, snappish boss.* **2.** characterized by or resulting from being easily annoyed: *a snappish mood, a snappish reply.* **3.** inclined to snap or bite, as a dog. —**snap′pish·ly,** *adv.* —**snap′pish·ness,** *n.*

snap·py (snap′ē) *adj.,* -**pi·er,** -**pi·est. 1.** *Informal.* lively; brisk: *to walk at a snappy pace.* **2.** *Informal.* smart in appearance; stylish: *a snappy dresser.* **3.** *Informal.* briskly cool or chilly: *a snappy breeze.* **4.** snappish. —**snap′pi·ly,** *adv.* —**snap′pi·ness,** *n.*
  ·**to make it snappy.** *Slang.* to do something quickly; hurry up. ➡ used chiefly in the imperative.

snap·shot (snap′shot′) *n.* an informal photograph.

snare[1] (snâr) *n.* **1.** a trap for catching small animals, usually consisting of a noose that jerks tightly closed when triggered. **2.** anything that entangles or entraps. —*v.t.,* **snared, snar·ing. 1.** to catch with a snare or similar device. **2.** to catch, acquire, or accomplish, esp. by means of skill, cleverness, or trickery: *The detectives snared the jewel thief.* [Old English *sneare* noose, from Old Norse *snara.*] —**snar′er,** *n.*

snare[2] (snâr) *n.* one of the wires or strings of gut or rawhide stretched across the bottom of a snare drum. [Probably from Middle Low German *snāre* cord, string.]

snare drum, a small, double-headed drum having wires or strings of gut or rawhide that are stretched across the lower head and produce a rattling sound when the drum is struck.

snarl[1] (snärl) *v.i.* **1.** to growl viciously or angrily while baring the teeth, as a dog or wolf. **2.** to speak angrily or harshly: *The angry customer snarled at the salesclerk.* —*v.t.* to utter or express with a snarl. —*n.* **1.** a vicious or angry growl. **2.** an angry or harsh utterance. [Modification of obsolete *snar* to growl, from Middle Low German *snarren* to rattle.] —**snarl′er,** *n.* —**snarl′ing·ly,** *adv.*

snarl[2] (snärl) *n.* **1.** a tangled or knotted mass, as of hair. **2.** a confused, tangled, or chaotic state or situation: *The bankrupt company's records were in a complete snarl.* —*v.t.* **1.** to make tangled or knotted: *The wind and rain had snarled my hair.* **2.** to make confused, disordered, or chaotic: *The fierce storm snarled traffic for hours.* —*v.i.* to become snarled: *The yarn snarled and was hard to untangle.* [From SNARE[1].]

snarl·y[1] (snär′lē) *adj.,* **snarl·i·er, snarl·i·est.** inclined to snarl; irritable; cross. [SNARL[1] + -Y[1].]

snarl·y[2] (snär′lē) *adj.,* **snarl·i·er, snarl·i·est.** full of snarls or tangles. [SNARL[2] + -Y[1].]

snatch (snach) *v.t.* **1.** to seize or grasp suddenly, quickly, or eagerly: *The thief snatched the purse and ran.* **2.** to take, remove, or get suddenly or hastily: *to snatch a hat from someone's head, to snatch a nap in the afternoon.* **3.** *Slang.* to kidnap. —*v.i.* **1.** to attempt to seize or grasp something suddenly or quickly (with *at*): *to snatch at a life preserver.* **2.** to accept or take advantage of something eagerly (with *at*): *to snatch at an opportunity.* —*n.* **1.** the act of snatching. **2.** a brief period of time: *to sleep in snatches.* **3.** a small amount, part, or portion; bit: *to overhear snatches of a conversation.* **4.** *Slang.* the act of kidnapping. [Of uncertain origin.] —**snatch′er,** *n.*

snatch·y (snach′ē) *adj.,* **snatch·i·er, snatch·i·est.** occurring or done in snatches; not continuous; irregular.

snath (snath) *also,* **snathe** (snāth). *n.* the long handle of a scythe. [Form of dialectal English *snead,* from Old English *snæd.*]

snaz·zy (snaz′ē) *adj.,* -**zi·er,** -**zi·est.** *Slang.* attractive or stylish, esp. in a showy way; smart; flashy. [Possibly a blend of SN(APPY) and (J)AZZY.] —**snaz′zi·ly,** *adv.* —**snaz′zi·ness,** *n.*

sneak (snēk) *v.,* **sneaked** or **snuck, sneak·ing.** —*v.i.* **1.** to move or go in a stealthy or furtive manner to avoid being detected: *to sneak into a theater without paying.* **2.** to behave in a sly, secret, or cowardly manner. —*v.t.* to move, take, get, or put in a stealthy or secret manner: *The shoplifter sneaked a watch into the bag.* —*n.* **1.** a person who sneaks, esp. a sly, dishonest person. **2.** the act of sneaking. **3.** *Informal.* sneaker *(def. 1).* —*adj.* done, planned, or acting in a stealthy or secret manner: *a sneak attack.* [Possibly form of Middle English *sniken* to creep, crawl, from Old English *snīcan.*]

sneak·er (snē′kər) *n.* **1.** a canvas shoe with a soft rubber sole, worn chiefly for sports. **2.** a person who sneaks; sneak.

sneak·ing (snē′king) *adj.* **1.** furtive; stealthy; underhanded. **2.a.** not admitted or made known; secret. **b.** nagging; persistent: *I have a sneaking suspicion that somebody stole the letter from my desk.* —**sneak′ing·ly,** *adv.*

sneak preview, an advance showing of a motion picture before its release to the general public, as to observe audience reaction.

sneak thief, a person who steals without employing violent or forceful means, as by sneaking into buildings through unlocked doors or windows rather than breaking into them.

sneak·y (snē′kē) *adj.,* **sneak·i·er, sneak·i·est. 1.** like or having the characteristics of a sneak: *to be too sneaky to be trusted.* **2.** characteristic of a sneak; sly, dishonest, or underhanded: *That was a pretty sneaky trick you pulled!* —**sneak′i·ly,** *adv.* —**sneak′i·ness,** *n.*

sneer (snîr) *n.* **1.** a facial expression showing contempt or derision, usually characterized by a slight curling of the upper lip. **2.** a contemptuous, derisive, or disparaging remark or statement. —*v.i.* **1.** to have or show a sneer. **2.** to speak or write in a contemptuous, derisive, or disparaging manner. —*v.t.* to utter or express with a sneer or in a sneering manner: *to sneer a reply to an insult.* [Possibly of Low German origin.] —**sneer′er,** *n.* —**sneer′ing·ly,** *adv.* —For Synonyms *(v.i.),* see jeer.

sneeze (snēz) *v.i.,* **sneezed, sneez·ing.** to expel air suddenly and violently through the nose and mouth by an involuntary spasm, as a result of irritation of the nasal mucous membrane. —*n.* the act or an instance of sneezing. [Modification of Middle English *fnesen* to sneeze, from Old English *fnēosan.*] —**sneez′er,** *n.* —**sneez′y,** *adj.*
  ·**to sneeze at.** *Informal.* to show insufficient regard, consideration, or respect for. ➡ used chiefly in the phrase *not to be sneezed at: Such a large sum of money is not to be sneezed at.*

sneeze·weed (snēz′wēd′) *n.* any of several coarse North American plants, genus *Helenium,* esp. the **common sneezeweed,** *H. autumnale,* having toothed leaves and showy yellow or reddish flowers. [Because its odor is thought to cause sneezing.]

snell (snel) *n.* a short piece of material, as nylon or gut, by which a fishhook is fastened to a longer line. [Of uncertain origin.]

snick (snik) *v.t.* to make a small cut in; cut slightly. —*n.* a small or slight cut; nick. [From obsolete *snick and snee* to thrust and cut (with knives), modification of *stick and snee,* from Dutch *steken en snijen.*]

snick·er (snik′ər) *n.* a sly or partly suppressed laugh, usually expressing derision or disrespect. —*v.i.* to laugh in such a manner. Also, **snigger.** [Imitative.] —**snick′er·er,** *n.* —**snick′er·ing·ly,** *adv.*

snide (snīd) *adj.,* **snid·er, snid·est.** unkind or critical in a sly or sarcastic way: *a snide remark.* [Of uncertain origin.] —**snide′ly,** *adv.* —**snide′ness,** *n.*

sniff (snif) *v.i.* **1.** to inhale through the nose in short, quick, audible breaths, as in smelling something. **2.** to express disdain or contempt by or as by sniffing (often with *at*): *They sniffed at our offer of help.* —*v.t.* **1.** to inhale (something) through the nose: *The dog sniffed the mountain air.* **2.** to smell by sniffing: *to sniff a flower.* **3.** to detect or discover by or as by sniffing (often with *out*): *to sniff out danger.* —*n.* **1.** the act or sound of sniffing. **2.** something sniffed; scent; smell. [Imitative.] —**sniff′er,** *n.*

snif·fle (snif′əl) *v.i.,* -**fled,** -**fling.** to breathe noisily through the nose, as when holding back tears or when the nose is congested; sniff repeatedly. —*n.* **1.** the act or sound of sniffling. **2. the sniffles,** a condition accompanied by sniffling, as a head cold. Also *(def. 2),* **the snuffles.** [SNIFF + -LE.] —**snif′fler,** *n.*

sniff·y (snif′ē) *adj.,* **sniff·i·er, sniff·i·est.** *Informal.* inclined to sniff, as in contempt; disdainful. —**sniff′i·ly,** *adv.* —**sniff′i·ness,** *n.*

snift·er (snif′tər) *n.* a pear-shaped glass that narrows at the top to concentrate the aroma of its contents, as of brandy.

snig·ger (snig′ər) *n., v.i.* snicker. —**snig′ger·er,** *n.* —**snig′ger·ing·ly,** *adv.*

snip (snip) *v.*, **snipped, snip·ping.** —*v.t.* **1.** to cut or clip with scissors or shears in a short, quick stroke or strokes. **2.** to remove (something) by or as by cutting in this way (often with *off*): *to snip off dead flowers from a plant.* —*v.i.* to cut or clip with short, quick strokes. —*n.* **1.** the act or sound of snipping. **2.** a small cut made by snipping. **3.** a small piece that is snipped off. **4.** any small amount, piece, or portion; bit. **5.** **snips.** heavy hand shears used for cutting sheet metal and wire mesh. **6.** *Informal.* a young, small, or insignificant person, esp. a rude or impertinent one. Also *(def. 6),* **snippet.** [Dutch *snippen* to clip, snap.] —**snip'per,** *n.*

snipe (snīp) *n., pl.* **snipes** or **snipe.** any of several long-billed wading birds, family Scolopacidae, native to marshes and bogs in most parts of the world, usually having a striped head and brownish plumage mottled with black and white. Length: 10-16 inches (25-41 centimeters). —*v.i.*, **sniped, snip·ing. 1.** to shoot at a person or persons from a concealed place. **2.** to attack with criticism, esp. in a snide manner (often with *at*). **3.** to hunt or shoot snipe. [Probably of Scandinavian origin.]

snip·er (snī'pər) *n.* a person who shoots at a person or persons from a concealed place.

snip·pet (snip'it) *n.* **1.** a small piece or part; bit; scrap. **2.** *Informal.* snip *(def. 6).*

snip·py (snip'ē) *adj.*, **-pi·er, -pi·est. 1.** *Informal.* curt or sharp, esp. in an impertinent or disdainful way. **2.** composed of bits or scraps; fragmentary. Also, **snip·pet·y** (snip'i tē). —**snip'pi·ly,** *adv.* —**snip'pi·ness,** *n.*

snipe

snit (snit) *n. Informal.* a state of irritation, anger, or agitation. ➡ used chiefly in the phrase *in a snit.* [Of uncertain origin.]

snitch (snich) *Slang. v.i.* to be an informer; tattle (often with *on*). —*v.t.* to steal; swipe; pilfer. —*n.* a person who snitches; informer. Also, **snitch'er.** [Of uncertain origin.]

sniv·el (sniv'əl) *v.i.*, **-eled** or **-elled, -el·ing** or **-el·ling. 1.** to cry with sniffling. **2.** to have mucus running from the nose. **3.** to draw mucus up through the nose noisily; sniffle. **4.** to complain in a whining or tearful manner. —*n.* **1.** the act of sniveling. **2.** nasal mucus. [Possibly from an unrecorded Old English word.] —**sniv'el·er;** *also,* **sniv'el·ler,** *n.*

snob (snob) *n.* **1.** a person who places great value on wealth and social position, and looks with contempt on those he or she considers to be inferior in social status. **2.** a person who has little regard or respect for people who are supposedly inferior in intelligence, achievement, or taste: *an intellectual snob.* [Of uncertain origin.]

snob·ber·y (snob'ə rē) *n., pl.* **-ber·ies.** snobbish character or conduct. Also, **snob·bism** (snob'iz əm).

snob·bish (snob'ish) *adj.* of, relating to, or characteristic of a snob. —**snob'bish·ly,** *adv.* —**snob'bish·ness,** *n.*

snood (snüd) *n.* **1.** a small net or netlike bag, sometimes forming part of a hat, worn by women to keep the hair in place. **2.** a band or ribbon for a woman's hair; fillet. —*v.t.* to bind or secure (the hair) with a snood. [Old English *snōd* band for the hair.]

snook (snuk, snūk) *n., pl.* **snook** or **snooks.** any of a group of food and game fish, family Centropomidae, that inhabit warm waters of the Atlantic and Pacific oceans, esp. the common snook, *Centropomus undecimalis,* of the southern Atlantic. [Dutch *snoek* pike.]

snook·er (snuk'ər) *n.* a variety of pool in which fifteen red balls and six other balls are used. —*v.t. Slang.* to deceive or cheat. [Of uncertain origin.]

snoop (snüp) *Informal. v.i.* to look or go about in a sneaking, sly way; prowl or pry: *Someone was seen snooping around the warehouse.* —*n.* **1.** a person who snoops. Also, **snoop'er. 2.** the act of snooping. [Dutch *snoepen* to eat secretly.]

snoop·y (snü'pē) *adj.*, **snoop·i·er, snoop·i·est.** *Informal.* given or inclined to snooping.

snoot (snüt) *n. Slang.* **1.** the nose or snout. **2.** snob. [Form of SNOUT.]

snoot·y (snü'tē) *adj.*, **snoot·i·er, snoot·i·est.** *Slang.* **1.** snobbish. **2.** for snobs or the wealthy; exclusive: *a snooty restaurant.* —**snoot'i·ly,** *adv.* —**snoot'i·ness,** *n.*

snooze (snüz) *Informal. v.i.*, **snoozed, snooz·ing.** to take a nap; doze. —*n.* a nap; doze. —**snooz'er,** *n.*

snore (snôr) *v.i.*, **snored, snor·ing.** to make harsh or noisy sounds in sleep by breathing through the open mouth or through the mouth and nose, causing the soft palate to vibrate. —*n.* the act or noise of snoring. [Possibly imitative.] —**snor'er,** *n.*

snor·kel (snôr'kəl) *n.* **1.** a device in a submarine that permits it to remain submerged for long periods, consisting of retractable tubes that extend above the surface of the water to take in fresh air and discharge foul air and exhaust gases. **2.** a J-shaped tube permitting a person to breathe while swimming on or just below the surface with the face under the water. —*v.i.* to swim using a snorkel. [German *Schnorchel* snorkel of a submarine, air inlet.] —**snor'kel·er,** *n.*

snorkeling

snort (snôrt) *v.i.* **1.** to force air violently and noisily through the nostrils. **2.** to make any similar sound. **3.** to express contempt, indignation, or anger by snorting. **4.** *Informal.* to laugh loudly or boisterously. —*v.t.* **1.** to utter while, or express by, snorting. **2.** to expel or discharge by or as if by snorting: *The elephant snorted water over its back.* **3.** *Slang.* to take (a drug) by inhaling into the nose. —*n.* **1.** the act or sound of snorting. **2.** *Slang.* a small drink of alcoholic liquor taken quickly. [Possibly imitative.] —**snort'er,** *n.*

snout (snout) *n.* **1.** the part of an animal's head that projects forward, including the nose, mouth, and jaws, as in a pig. **2.** a similar extension of the anterior part of the head in certain insects, as weevils. **3.** something similar to an animal's snout in shape or use. **4.** *Informal.* the human nose, esp. when large. [Probably of Low German origin.] —**snout'ed,** *adj.*

snout beetle, weevil *(def. 1).*

snow (snō) *n.* **1.** solid precipitation in the form of soft, white, crystalline flakes of widely varying shape, formed by the freezing of water vapor in the atmosphere. **2.** a fall of snow; snowstorm. **3.** an accumulation or expanse of snow. **4.** something that resembles snow, as in color. **5.** a pattern of small white spots on a television screen that results from weak reception. —*v.i.* (of snow) to fall. ➡ used with *it: It snowed all night.* —*v.t.* **1.** to cause to fall or scatter as or like snow. **2.** to cover, obstruct, or shut in with or as with snow (often with *in* or *under*). ➡ usually used in the passive: *The hunters were snowed in at the lodge for three days.* **3.** *Slang.* to overpower with insincere flattery, esp. in order to deceive. [Old English *snāw* the frozen vapor of the atmosphere that falls in flakes, snowstorm.]

·to snow under, to overwhelm: *The store was snowed under with requests for the new recording.*

snow·ball (snō'bôl') *n.* **1.** a roundish mass of snow pressed or rolled together, as for throwing. **2.** any of several shrubs, genus *Viburnum,* of the honeysuckle family, having large clusters of white flowers resembling snowballs. —*v.t.* to throw snowballs at. —*v.i.* to grow rapidly in importance, size, or number: *That small business has snowballed into a huge corporation.*

snow·bank (snō'bangk') *n.* a large mound or drift of snow.

snow·ber·ry (snō'ber'ē, -bə rē) *n., pl.* **-ries.** any of a number of shrubs of the honeysuckle family, genus *Symphoricarpos,* esp. *S. albus,* bearing clusters of pink flowers and small, white berries. Also, **waxberry.**

snow·bird (snō'bûrd') *n.* **1.** a grayish North American junco, *Junco hyemalis,* that breeds in cold northern regions and winters throughout the United States, having white plumage on its underside. Length: 6 inches (15 centimeters). **2.** snow bunting. **3.** *Informal.* a person from a region with a cold winter climate who vacations in or moves to a warmer locale during the winter.

a	at	e	end	o	hot	u	up	hw	white		about
ā	ape	ē	me	ō	old	ū	use	ng	song	ə	taken
ä	far	i	it	ô	rule	ü	rule	th	thin		pencil
âr	care	ī	ice	oi	oil	u̇	pull	th	this		lemon
		îr	pierce	ou	out	ûr	turn	zh	measure		circus

snow-blind (snō′blīnd′) *adj.* affected with snow blindness.

snow blindness, a temporary or partial blindness caused by the reflection of ultraviolet rays from snow.

snow blower, a motor-driven machine on wheels, used to remove snow from sidewalks and streets.

snow·bound (snō′bound′) *adj.* shut in or confined to a place by a heavy fall of snow.

snow bunting, a small bird, *Plectrophenax nivalis,* of cold northern regions, having predominantly black-and-white plumage. Length: 6 inches (15 centimeters). Also, **snowbird.**

snow·cap (snō′kap′) *n.* a cap or crest of snow, as on a mountain peak. —**snow′capped′,** *adj.*

snow·drift (snō′drift′) *n.* a heap or mass of snow piled up by the wind.

snow·drop (snō′drop′) *n.* any of a small group of Eurasian plants, genus *Galanthus,* that bloom in the early spring, esp. a common garden species, *G. nivalis,* bearing a single, drooping, white flower.

snow·fall (snō′fôl′) *n.* **1.** a fall of snow. **2.** the amount of snow that falls during a given period or in a particular area.

snow·field (snō′fēld′) *n.* an expanse of permanent snow, esp. at the head of a glacier.

snow·flake (snō′flāk′) *n.* one of the small, feathery masses or crystals in which snow falls.

snow leopard, a large cat, *Panthera uncia,* of the mountains of central Asia, having gray or buff fur marked with black broken rings. Length: 6½ feet (1.9 meters), including tail. Also, **ounce.**

snow line, a line on a mountain slope above which the ground is perpetually snow covered.

snow·man (snō′man′) *n., pl.* **-men** (-men′). a figure roughly resembling that of a person, made by shaping a mass of snow.

snow·mo·bile (snō′mō bēl′) *n.* a motorized vehicle adapted for travel on snow.

snow-on-the-moun·tain (snō′ôn thə moun′tən, -on-) *n.* a North American spurge, *Euphorbia marginata,* grown in gardens for its decorative white bracts and white-edged leaves.

snow·plow (snō′plou′) *n.* **1.** any of various devices or vehicles for clearing away snow, as from a road or sidewalk. **2.** in skiing, a maneuver used for stopping or slowing down in which the heels of both skis are forced outward.

snow·shed (snō′shed′) *n.* a long shed or shelter for protection against snow, as over a railroad track on a mountain slope.

snow·shoe (snō′shü′) *n.* a light, racket-shaped wooden frame strung with a webbing of rawhide or other material, attached to the foot to enable a person to walk over deep snow without sinking in. —*v.i.,* **-shoed, -shoe·ing.** to walk or travel by means of snowshoes. —**snow′sho′er,** *n.*

snowshoe hare, a North American hare, *Lepus americanus,* having white fur in winter and brown fur in summer and large hind feet covered with long hairs that enable it to travel over deep snow. Also, **snowshoe rabbit.**

snow·slide (snō′slīd′) *n.* an avalanche of snow.

snow·storm (snō′stôrm′) *n.* a heavy fall of snow accompanied by strong winds.

snow·suit (snō′süt′) *n.* a child's one-piece or two-piece heavily lined outer garment for cold weather.

snow tire, a tire with a deeply grooved tread for extra traction on snow or ice.

snow train, a special train that carries passengers to and from a place for winter sports, esp. skiing.

snow-white (snō′hwīt′, -wīt′) *adj.* white as snow.

snow·y (snō′ē) *adj.,* **snow·i·er, snow·i·est. 1.** covered with snow: *snowy mountain peaks.* **2.** bringing or including snow: *snowy weather.* **3.** resembling snow; white or unblemished. —**snow′i·ly,** *adv.* —**snow′i·ness,** *n.*

snub (snub) *v.t.,* **snubbed, snub·bing. 1.** to treat with disrespect, scorn, or contempt: *to snub former friends by ignoring them.* **2.** to rebuke in a sharp or sarcastic manner. **3.** to control or stop (an animal or thing) suddenly by winding an attached rope or line around a post: *to snub a boat to a dock.* **4.** to stop the movement of (a rope or cable that is running out) suddenly by winding it around a post. —*n.* **1.** disrespectful or scornful treatment; deliberate slight. **2.** a sudden stop, as of a rope or cable that is running out. —*adj.* (of the nose) short and slightly turned up. [Old Norse *snubba* to rebuke.] —**snub′ber,** *n.* —**snub′bing·ly,** *adv.*

snub·by (snub′ē) *adj.,* **-bi·er, -bi·est.** somewhat snub.

snub-nosed (snub′nōzd′) *adj.* having a snub nose.

snuck (snuk) a past tense and past participle of **sneak.**

snuff[1] (snuf) *v.t.* **1.** to inhale through the nose. **2.** to detect by smelling. **3.** (of an animal) to examine by smelling; sniff at. —*v.i.* **1.** to sniff, esp. curiously. **2.** to inhale powdered tobacco into the nose. —*n.* a preparation of powdered tobacco taken into the

nose by inhalation. [Middle Dutch *snuffen* to snuffle, sniff.]

· **up to snuff.** *Informal.* in good or usual order or condition: *sloppy work that isn't up to snuff.*

snuff[2] (snuf) *v.t.* **1.** to cut or pinch off the charred end of (a candlewick). **2.** to put out or extinguish (often with *out*): *to snuff the lights, to snuff out a candle.* —*n.* the charred part of a candlewick. [Of uncertain origin.]

· **to snuff out. a.** to put an end to suddenly and completely: *The loss of the game snuffed out our team's chance to win the championship.* **b.** to kill.

snuff·box (snuf′boks′) *n.* a box for holding snuff.

snuff·ers (snuf′ərz) *pl. n.* an instrument resembling scissors, used for removing the burnt wick or putting out the flame of a candle.

snuf·fle (snuf′əl) *v.,* **-fled, -fling.** —*v.i.* **1.** to breathe noisily because of partly congested nasal passages. **2.** to snuff or smell. **3.** to speak through the nose; talk in a nasal tone. —*v.t.* to utter or say in a nasal tone. —*n.* **1.** the act of snuffling or the sound made by it. **2.** a nasal tone of voice. **3. the snuffles.** see **sniffle** *(def. 2).* [Dutch *snuffelen* to smell out.] —**snuf′fler,** *n.*

snuff·y (snuf′ē) *adj.,* **snuff·i·er, snuff·i·est. 1.** resembling snuff, as in color or smell. **2.** soiled with or smelling of snuff.

snug (snug) *adj.,* **snug·ger, snug·gest. 1.** comfortable and warm; cozy: *a snug bed.* **2.** fitting closely or tightly, as a garment. **3.** enabling a person to live comfortably: *a snug income.* **4.** out of sight; hidden. **5.** (of a ship or its parts). **a.** neat; trim; compact. **b.** seaworthy. —*v.,* **snugged, snug·ging.** —*v.t.* to make snug. —*v.i.* to lie or nestle closely; snuggle. —*adv.* in a snug manner. [Probably of Scandinavian origin.] —**snug′ly,** *adv.* —**snug′ness,** *n.*

snug·ger·y (snug′ə rē) *n., pl.* **-ger·ies.** a cozy or comfortable place, as a room.

snug·gle (snug′əl) *v.,* **-gled, -gling.** —*v.i.* to lie closely and comfortably, as for warmth or comfort or to show affection; cuddle: *The bear cubs snuggled together in the cave.* —*v.t.* to draw close, as for warmth or comfort, or to show affection: *to snuggle a baby.* [SNUG + -LE.]

so[1] (sō) *adv.* **1.** as shown, described, or indicated; in such a manner: *Write the words so.* **2.** in this or that way; as follows; thus: *So the story goes.* **3.** of or in that condition, state, or description: *The lock was worn and had been so for three months.* **4.** to such an extent or degree: *It was so cold that we stayed indoors.* **5.** in a high degree; very; extremely: *I am so tired.* **6.** very much: *He loved her so.* **7.** for this or that reason; accordingly; therefore: *We were tired, so we went home early.* **8.** too; also: *I sing in the choir and so does my cousin.* **9.** *Informal.* such being the case; as it seems: *So, you don't like the cake I baked.* —*adj.* in accordance with fact; true: *Is it so you're thinking of leaving the club?* —*conj.* **1.** with the reason or purpose that; in order that: *Please turn out the light so I can sleep.* **2.** with the result that: *Everyone stood up, so I did also.* —*pron.* **1.** the same: *That is a lazy dog and will always be so.* **2.** more or less: *a month or so.* —*interj.* used to express surprise, awareness, or displeasure: *So! We meet again.* [Old English *swā* in such a manner, to that extent, thus.]

· **so as.** in order to: *to run so as not to be late.*

· **so that.** in order that: *We left early so that we would be home before dark.*

so[2] (sō) *n.* sol[1]. [See GAMUT.]

So. 1. South. **2.** Southern.

soak (sōk) *v.t.* **1.** to make very wet; wet thoroughly; drench: *The rain soaked me to the skin.* **2.** to take in; absorb (with *in* or *up*): *The ground soaked up the heavy rainfall.* **3.** to cause (something) to remain immersed in water or another liquid, as for cleansing: *to soak a sprained ankle to reduce the swelling.* **4.** *Slang.* to make pay too heavily; overcharge: *The mechanic soaked us for the car repairs.* —*v.i.* **1.** to become thoroughly wet. **2.** to remain immersed in a liquid: *Leave the dishes in the sink to soak.* **3.** to penetrate into or through something, as a liquid does: *The gravy soaked through the tablecloth.* **4.** to become absorbed in the mind, as an idea. —*n.* **1.** the act of soaking or the state of being soaked. **2.** *Slang.* a heavy drinker; drunkard. [Old English *socian* to remain in liquid until saturated.] —**soak′er,** *n.* —**soak′ing·ly,** *adv.*

soak·age (sō′kij) *n.* **1.** the act of soaking or the state of being soaked. **2.** the amount of liquid that soaks into or seeps out of something.

so-and-so (sō′ən sō′) *n., pl.* **-sos. 1.** a person or thing not named or specified. **2.** *Informal.* an offensive or disagreeable person. ➡ used as a euphemism for a more offensive term.

soap (sōp) *n.* **1.** any of various substances used for washing and cleansing, usually consisting of a mixture of the sodium or potas-

sium salts of various animal fats, and made by treating such a fat with alkali. **2.** *Chemistry.* any metallic salt of a fatty acid. **3.** *Informal.* soap opera. —*v.t.* to rub, cover, or treat with soap. [Old English *sāpe* substance used for washing and cleansing.]
• **no soap.** *Slang.* absolutely not.

soap·bark (sōp′bärk′) *n.* **1.** a Chilean tree, *Quillaja saponaria,* having shiny leaves and white flowers. **2.** the bark of this tree, used as a substitute for soap.

soap·ber·ry (sōp′ber′ē) *n., pl.* **-ries. 1.** the pulpy fruit of any of various chiefly tropical trees, genus *Sapindus,* used as a substitute for soap. **2.** any of these trees.

soap·box (sōp′boks′) *n.* **1.** a container in which soap is packed, as a box or crate. **2.** an empty box used as a platform for making a speech, esp. on a public street. —*adj.* speaking or spoken in an impassioned, eccentric, or demagogic manner: *soapbox oratory.*

soapbox derby, a race in which homemade children's racing cars without power coast down a hill.

soap bubble 1. a bubble formed from soapy water. **2.** anything unsubstantial or impermanent.

soap opera, a television or radio serial drama, characterized by emotional, sentimental, and melodramatic situations, usually presented in the daytime. [Because many such programs were originally sponsored by *soap* manufacturers.]

soap plant, any plant having a part that may be used as a substitute for soap, esp. *Chlorogalum pomeridianum,* whose bulb California Indians used as soap.

soap·stone (sōp′stōn′) *n.* a variety of talc used for hearths, laboratory table tops, and carvings. Also, **steatite.**

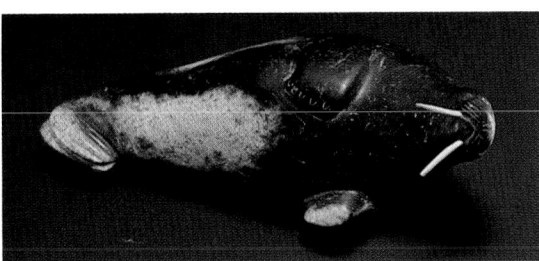

soapstone
an Inuit carving of a walrus

soap·suds (sōp′sudz′) *pl. n.* suds from soapy water.

soap·wort (sōp′wûrt′) *n.* an herb, *Saponaria officinalis,* related to the pink, native to Europe and growing wild in the United States, having clusters of pink or white flowers and leaves that yield a soapy substance. Also, **bouncing Bet.**

soap·y (sō′pē) *adj.,* **soap·i·er, soap·i·est. 1.** containing or combined with soap: *soapy water.* **2.** covered with soap: *soapy dishes.* **3.a.** resembling soap; smooth or greasy. **b.** *Informal.* overly smooth and charming; suave; oily: *soapy manners.* —**soap′i·ly,** *adv.* —**soap′i·ness,** *n.*

soar (sôr) *v.i.* **1.** to fly upward or rise high into the air. **2.** (of a bird) to fly or glide high in the air without visibly moving the wings. **3.** (of an aircraft) to glide along without losing altitude. **4.** to rise to a great height, as a mountain or building. **5.a.** to go or move upward in position or status; rise sharply: *The price of meat soared.* **b.** to rise above the common or everyday: *The poet's imagination soared.* —*n.* **1.** the act of soaring. **2.** the height attained in soaring. [Middle French *essorer* to throw up in the air, fly up, going back to Latin *ex* out of + *aura* breeze (from Greek *aura*).] —**soar′er,** *n.* —For Synonyms, see **fly².**

sob (sob) *v.,* **sobbed, sob·bing.** —*v.i.* **1.** to cry while catching the breath in short gasps. **2.** to make a sound resembling this. —*v.t.* **1.** to utter with a sob or sobs: *to sob out a sad story.* **2.** to put, bring, or send by sobbing: *to sob oneself to sleep.* —*n.* **1.** the act or sound of sobbing. **2.** a sound resembling a sob: *the sob of the wind on a cold, wintry night.* [Probably imitative.]

so·ber (sō′bər) *adj.* **1.** not drunk. **2.** moderate or temperate, esp. in the use of alcoholic drink. **3.** grave or sedate in character or nature; serious: *a sober life.* **4.** not bold or gaudy: *a dark, sober suit.* **5.** showing no exaggeration or excess: *sober facts.* **6.** showing good sense; sensible: *sober judgment.* —*v.t., v.i.* to make or become sober (often with *up*). [Old French *sobre* temperate, moderate, from Latin *sōbrius* not drunk, temperate.] —**so′ber·ly,** *adv.* —**so′ber·ness,** *n.*

so·bri·e·ty (sə brī′i tē) *n., pl.* **-ties. 1.** the state or quality of being sober. **2.** temperance or moderation, esp. in the use of

alcoholic drink. **3.** a serious or solemn nature; gravity; solemnity. [Latin *sōbrietās* temperance, moderation.]

so·bri·quet (sō′bri kā′, -ket′, sō′bri kā′, -ket′) *also,* **soubri·quet.** *n.* nickname. [French *sobriquet;* of uncertain origin.]

sob sister, a journalist who writes overly sentimental stories about human misfortune.

sob story, an overly sentimental story of personal hardship or misfortune told to gain sympathy.

soc., society.

so-called (sō′kôld′) *adj.* called thus, esp. incorrectly or improperly: *a so-called expert.*

soc·cer (sok′ər) *n.* a game in which two teams of eleven players each attempt to move a round ball into a goal by kicking it or by striking it with any part of the body except the hands and arms. Also, **association football.** [Short for *(as)soc(iation football)* + -ER¹.]

soccer

so·cia·bil·i·ty (sō′shə bil′i tē) *n., pl.* **-ties.** the quality, state, or instance of being sociable.

so·cia·ble (sō′shə bəl) *adj.* **1.** liking to associate with others; fond of company; friendly; affable. **2.** characterized by or giving opportunity for companionship and friendly conversation: *a sociable atmosphere.* —*n.* a social. [Latin *sociābilis* easily united, going back to *socius* companion, ally.] —**so′cia·bly,** *adv.*

> **Synonyms** *adj.* **Sociable** and **social** mean involved in the company of other people. **Sociable** implies a liking for the company of others: *They are a sociable couple who go out of their way to meet new people.* **Social** suggests a not necessarily pleasurable involvement in society: *People in high office are obliged to attend many social functions, leaving them little time to relax at home.*

so·cial (sō′shəl) *adj.* **1.** of or relating to human beings as a group; having to do with society: *The family is a social unit.* **2.** relating to the life, welfare, and relations of human beings: *social behavior, social unrest.* **3.** relating to or based on rank or status within a particular society: *one's social position.* **4.** of or relating to fashionable or polite society: *a social event.* **5.** relating to, characterized by, or furthering companionship or friendly relations: *a social visit, a social engagement.* **6.** enjoying the company of others; friendly; sociable: *a social person.* **7.a.** (of animals) habitually living in organized communities, as ants, bees, or baboons. **b.** (of plants) growing in clumps or patches. —*n.* an informal social gathering, as for members of a church. [Latin *sociālis* allied, companionable, from *socius* companion, ally.] —For Synonyms *(adj.),* see **sociable.**

social climber, a person who attempts to gain acceptance in fashionable society.

social contract, the theory that society came into being from the voluntary association of individuals for mutual protection and that government therefore rests on the consent of the governed.

social democracy, the principles of a social democrat.

social democrat, a member of a political party that favors a gradual, peaceful, and democratic change from capitalism to socialism.

social democratic, relating to a social democrat or social democracy.

social disease, venereal disease.

so·cial·ism (sō′shə liz′əm) *n.* **1.** the theory or system of social organization based on collective or government ownership and control of the basic means of production, distribution, and exchange. **2.** the policies or practices of those who favor or support such a system. **3.** in Marxist theory, the stage of society following capitalism in the transition to communism.

so·cial·ist (sō′shə list) *n.* **1.** a person who favors or supports socialism. **2.** *also,* **Socialist.** a member of a Socialist Party. —*adj.* socialistic.

a	at	e	end	o	hot	u	up	hw	white	⎧	about
ā	ape	ē	me	ō	old	ū	use	ng	song		taken
ä	far	i	it	ô	fork	ü	rule	th	thin	ə	pencil
âr	care	ī	ice	oi	oil	u̇	pull	th	this		lemon
				ir	pierce	ou	out	ûr	turn	zh	measure	⎭	circus

so·cial·is·tic (sō′shə lis′tik) *adj.* **1.** of, relating to, or resembling socialism. **2.** favoring or supporting socialism. —**so′cial·is′ti·cal·ly,** *adv.*

Socialist Party, a political party that favors socialism, as the U.S. party founded in 1901 under the leadership of Eugene V. Debs.

so·cial·ite (sō′shə līt′) *n.* a member of fashionable society; socially prominent person.

so·ci·al·i·ty (sō′shē al′i tē) *n.* **1.** the state or quality of being social; sociability. **2.** the tendency of persons to form social groups or communities.

so·cial·ize (sō′shə līz′) *v.*, **-ized, -iz·ing.** —*v.t.* **1.** to establish or regulate according to the theories of socialism; make socialistic: *to socialize medicine.* **2.** to make fit for companionship with others; cause to become sociable. **3.** to adapt or make conform to the needs of a social group. —*v.i.* to take part in social activities; associate with others. —**so′cial·i·za′tion,** *n.* —**so′cial·iz′er,** *n.*

socialized medicine, a system for providing complete medical care for an entire nation at nominal cost by means of government regulation and subsidization of medical and health services.

so·cial·ly (sō′shə lē) *adv.* **1.** in a social manner: *Are you acquainted with them professionally or socially?* **2.** as a part of society; with regard to society: *socially prominent.* **3.** by or from society: *socially imposed standards of behavior.*

social register, a directory listing people who are socially prominent.

social science 1. the study of society and the activities and relationship of persons and groups within society. **2.** a particular field of study dealing with society, such as sociology, psychology, history, political science, or economics.

social security 1. any system that provides assistance for a person or a family through government programs financed by taxation. **2.** *also,* **Social Security.** a system of old-age, retirement, or disability insurance maintained by the U.S. government and financed by special taxes.

social service, social work.

social studies, a course of instruction in an elementary or secondary school that includes geography, history, and political science.

social work, any activity or service designed to improve the conditions of a community, as by providing help and health and recreation facilities for those who are old, poor, or handicapped.

social worker, a person who does social work, esp. as a profession.

so·ci·e·tal (sə sī′i təl) *adj.* of or relating to society: *societal development, societal unrest.* —**so·ci′e·tal·ly,** *adv.*

so·ci·e·ty (sə sī′i tē) *n., pl.* **-ties. 1.** human beings as a group; all people: *to act for the good of society.* **2.** a group of people forming a community and having common interests, traditions, and culture: *French society.* **3.** a system or condition of individuals living together in such a community: *an agricultural society.* **4.** a portion of a community regarded as forming a class with certain distinguishing standards or characteristics: *middle-class society.* **5.** a group of persons associated for a common purpose or interest, as a club or fraternity: *a literary society.* **6.** the wealthy or aristocratic members of a community; fashionable people as a group. **7.** the state of being associated, as in a casual or close relationship; companionship; company; fellowship: *to enjoy the society of other people.* **8.** a group of plants or animals, esp. of the same species, living together under the same conditions and influences. —*adj.* of or relating to fashionable society: *a society column.* [Latin *societās* fellowship, alliance, community, association.]

Society of Friends, a religious group founded by George Fox in England about 1650, having no ritual, ordained clergy, or formal sacraments, and opposed to all forms of violence, including war. Its members are commonly called Quakers.

Society of Jesus, the religious order of the Jesuits.

so·ci·o·ec·o·nom·ic (sō′sē ō ek′ə nom′ik, -ē′kə-, sō′shē ō-) *adj.* of, relating to, or involving both social and economic factors.

so·ci·o·log·i·cal (sō′sē ə loj′i kəl, sō′shē-) *adj.* **1.** of or relating to sociology. **2.** of or relating to society: *Hunger is a sociological problem.* —**so′ci·o·log′i·cal·ly,** *adv.*

so·ci·ol·o·gy (sō′sē ol′ə jē, sō′shē-) *n.* the science or study of human society, including its origin, history, organization, and institutions; study of social behavior and relationships. [French *sociologie,* from Latin *socius* companion, sharing + Greek *-logiā.* See -LOGY.] —**so′ci·ol′o·gist,** *n.*

so·ci·o·path (sō′sē ə path′, sō′shē-) *n.* an individual suffering from a personality disorder manifesting itself chiefly as extreme, antisocial behavior. —**so′ci·o·path′ic,** *adj.*

so·ci·o·po·lit·i·cal (sō′sē ō pə lit′i kəl, sō′shē-) *adj.* of, relating to, or involving both social and political factors.

sock[1] (sok) *n.* **1.** a short stocking, esp. one reaching above the ankle but below the knee. **2.** a light, low shoe worn by comic actors in ancient Greek and Roman plays. **3.** a comic drama; comedy. [Old English *socc* slipper, from Latin *soccus* low-heeled light shoe.]

sock[2] (sok) *Slang. v.t.* to hit or strike hard, esp. with the fist. —*n.* a hard blow or punch. [Of uncertain origin.]

sock·et (sok′it) *n.* **1.** the hollow part or place into which something fits. **2.** an opening that forms a holder for an electric bulb or plug. **3.** a hollow part of the body into which another part fits. [Anglo-Norman *soket* spearhead shaped like a small plowshare, diminutive of Old French *soc* plowshare; probably of Celtic origin.]

sock·eye (sok′ī′) *n.* a salmon, *Onorhynchus nerka,* of northern Pacific coastal waters, that in spring ascends rivers to spawn and is a commercial food fish. [Modification of Salish *suk-kegh.*]

So·crat·ic (sə krat′ik, sō-) *adj.* of or relating to the Greek philosopher Socrates, his philosophy, or his followers.

Socratic method, the method of teaching used by Socrates, in which the instructor, by means of a successive series of questions, guides the person who answers from an unproved supposition or hypothesis to its logical conclusion; method of inductive reasoning.

sod (sod) *n.* **1.** the surface of the ground, esp. when covered with grass. **2.** a layer or piece of soil covered with grass and held together by roots. —*v.t.,* **sod·ded, sod·ding.** to cover with sod. [Middle Low German or Middle Dutch *sode* turf.]

so·da (sō′də) *n.* **1.** any of a group of compounds that contain sodium, esp. sodium carbonate, sodium bicarbonate, or sodium hydroxide. **2.a.** soda water. **b.** a soft drink made with soda water and flavoring. Also, **soda pop, pop. c.** a beverage containing soda water, flavoring, and often ice cream. [Medieval Latin *soda* a plant from which the chemical soda is produced; of uncertain origin.]

soda ash, an impure form of anhydrous sodium carbonate, used commercially.

soda biscuit 1. a biscuit made with sodium bicarbonate and sour milk or buttermilk. **2.** soda cracker.

soda cracker, a light, crisp cracker made from yeast dough containing sodium bicarbonate.

soda fountain 1. a counter having equipment for preparing and serving soft drinks, sodas, sundaes, ice cream, and the like. **2.** an apparatus for drawing off soda water through faucets.

soda jerk *Slang.* a person who works at a soda fountain.

soda lime, a mixture of sodium hydroxide and slaked lime, used as a reagent and to absorb moisture and gases.

so·dal·i·ty (sō dal′i tē) *n., pl.* **-ties. 1.** fellowship; companionship; brotherhood. **2.** a society of the Roman Catholic Church having religious or charitable aims. **3.** any association or society. [Latin *sodālitās* companionship; association.]

soda pop, soda *(def. 2b).*

soda water, a bubbling drink consisting of water charged under pressure with carbon dioxide gas. Also, **seltzer.**

sod·den (sod′ən) *adj.* **1.** filled with water or moisture; soaked through; saturated. **2.** (of food) heavy and moist because of improper cooking. **3.** expressionless, dull, or stupid, as from drunkenness. —*v.t., v.i.* to make or become sodden. [Obsolete past participle of SEETHE.] —**sod′den·ly,** *adv.* —**sod′den·ness,** *n.*

so·dic (sō′dik) *adj.* of, like, or containing sodium: *sodic feldspar.* [SOD(IUM) + -IC.]

so·di·um (sō′dē əm) *n.* a very light, soft, silver-white metallic element similar to potassium that is highly reactive and ignites in water. Symbol: **Na** For tables, see **element.** [Modern Latin *sodium,* from SODA; because first obtained from caustic soda.]

sodium benzoate, a white, odorless powder, the sodium salt of benzoic acid, used chiefly as a food preservative. Formula: $C_7H_5O_2Na$ Also, **benzoate of soda.**

sodium bicarbonate, a white, crystalline compound with a slightly salty taste, used esp. in baking powder and fire extinguishers and in medicine as an antacid. Formula: $NaHCO_3$ Also, **baking soda, bicarbonate of soda.**

sodium borate, borax.

sodium carbonate 1. a white, powdery, anhydrous compound used as in the manufacture of glass, soap, and paper. Formula: Na_2CO_3 **2.** either of two hydrated forms of this compound, white, crystalline substances that are used for bleaching and cleansing and in photography. Also *(def. 2),* **sal soda, washing soda.**

sodium chloride, salt *(def. 1).*

sodium cyanide, an extremely poisonous, white, powdery compound used in electroplating metals, in extracting gold and silver from ores, and as an insecticide. Formula: $NaCN$

sodium fluoride, a poisonous, solid compound, used chiefly in

the fluoridation of water, as an insecticide, and in rat poisons. Formula: NaF

sodium hydroxide, a white, solid compound that is a strong, caustic base, used as in making rayon, soap, and detergents. Formula: NaOH Also, **caustic soda.**

sodium hypochlorite, an unstable, green salt used to bleach paper and textiles and as a water purifier and fungicide. Formula: NaOCl

sodium hyposulfite 1. a colorless, crystalline salt used as a bleaching agent. Formula: $Na_2S_2O_4$ **2.** sodium thiosulfate.

sodium nitrate, a colorless, crystalline compound used as an oxidizer in solid rocket propellants and in making explosives and fertilizer. Formula: $NaNO_3$ Also, **Chile saltpeter.**

sodium nitrite, a yellow, crystalline compound from which nitrous acid is made, used to inhibit corrosion and to fix dyes and added to processed meat as a preservative. Formula: $NaNO_2$

sodium pentothal, Pentothal.

sodium silicate, water glass *(def. 2).*

sodium sulfate, a white, crystalline salt, the anhydrous precursor of Glauber's salt, occurring naturally in a variety of minerals and produced from sodium chloride for use in dyeing and in the manufacture of glass, glazes, and detergents. Formula: Na_2SO_4

sodium thi·o·sul·fate (thī′ō sul′fāt) a colorless or white crystalline salt, used as in dyeing and as a fixing agent in photography. Formula: $Na_2S_2O_3 \cdot 5H_2O$ Also, **hypo, hyposulfite, sodium hyposulfite.**

so·di·um-va·por lamp (sō′dē əm vā′pər) an electric lamp in which a current passing between two electrodes causes sodium vapor in the lamp to glow with a yellow, glareless light, used on streets and highways.

sod·om·ize (sod′ə mīz′) *v.t.,* **-ized, -iz·ing.** to perform the act of sodomy with. **—sod′om·ist, sod′om·ite,** *n.*

sod·om·y (sod′ə mē) *n.* sexual intercourse that is not vaginal, esp. anal intercourse between males or intercourse with an animal. [Middle English *sodomie,* from *Sodome* Sodom, in the Old Testament, a city destroyed by God for the wickedness of its inhabitants.]

so·ev·er (sō ev′ər) *adv.* **1.** in any way; to any extent or degree. ➡ usually used with an adjective preceded by *how* or a superlative preceded by *the: how hard soever the task may be.* **2.** of any or every kind. ➡ usually used with a noun modified by *any, no,* or *what: all who wish to help in any way soever.*

-soever *combining form* soever: *whatsoever, howsoever, whosoever.*

so·fa (sō′fə) *n.* a long, upholstered seat with a back and arms. [Arabic *suffah.*]

sofa bed, a sofa having a concealed section that pulls out to form a bed.

sof·fit (sof′it) *n.* the underside of a structural part, as a beam or arch. [Italian *soffitto* ceiling, going back to Latin *suffixus,* past participle of *suffigere* to fasten below.]

soffit

soft (sôft, soft) *adj.* **1.** readily yielding to touch or pressure; easily shaped or worked; not hard: *soft clay, a soft bed.* **2.** not hard for its kind; not as hard as is normal or desirable: *soft wood.* **3.** smooth or fine to the touch; having a delicate texture; not rough or coarse: *soft skin.* **4.** not loud or harsh; quiet and melodious; gentle: *a soft tone of voice.* **5.** not glaring, sharp, or harsh to the sight; subdued: *soft lighting.* **6.** mild and agreeable; gentle; temperate: *a soft breeze.* **7.a.** showing or expressing sympathy or kindness; tender: *soft words.* **b.** yielding easily or too easily to emotion; sympathetic; compassionate: *a soft heart.* **8.a.** lacking strength; not robust; flabby; weak: *soft muscles.* **b.** having a weak or delicate character. **c.** *Informal.* stupid or silly. ➡ usually used in the phrase *soft in the head.* **d.** easily influenced, imposed upon, or impressed; compliant. **9.** not harsh or severe; lenient: *The sergeant is too soft on the recruits.* **10.** *Informal.* requiring little work or effort; easy: *a soft job.* **11.** (of water) relatively free of mineral salts that interfere with the lathering and cleansing action of soap. **12.** *Phonetics.* **a.** (of *c* and *g*) pronounced with the sound of *s,* as in *city,* and *j,* as in *gem.* **b.** (of consonants) pronounced with vibration of the vocal cords; voiced. —*adv.* in a soft manner; softly. —*n.* anything that is soft. [Old English *sōfte* gentle.] **—soft′ly,** *adv.* **—soft′ness,** *n.*

soft·ball (sôft′bôl′, soft′-) *n.* **1.** a game very similar to baseball but played on a smaller field with a larger and softer ball that must be pitched underhand. **2.** the ball used in this game.

soft-boiled (sôft′boild′, soft′-) *adj.* (of eggs) boiled for only a short time, so that the yolk is still soft.

soft coal, bituminous coal.

soft-cov·er (sôft′kuv′ər, soft′-) *adj.* (of a book) having a soft, flexible cover; paperback. Also, **soft·bound** (sôft′bound′, soft′-). —*n.* a book having such a cover.

soft drink, a beverage that contains no alcohol, esp. one that is carbonated.

soft·en (sô′fən, sof′ən) *v.t., v.i.* to make or become soft or softer.

· **to soften up.** to weaken the resistance or opposition of.

soft·en·er (sô′fə nər, sof′ə-) *n.* **1.** a person or thing that softens. **2.** water softener.

soft-finned (sôft′find′, soft′-) *adj.* (of fish) having fins supported by soft or flexible rays rather than by spines. ➡ opposed to **spiny-finned.**

soft-head·ed (sôft′hed′id, soft′-) *adj.* having a weak mind; stupid; foolish; silly. **—soft′-head′ed·ness,** *n.*

soft-heart·ed (sôft′här′tid, soft′-) *adj.* kind and sympathetic. **—soft′-heart′ed·ness,** *n.*

soft·ies (sôf′tēz, sof′-) the plural of **softy.**

soft landing, a landing, as of a spacecraft on the moon or another celestial body, at a slow speed in order to avoid damaging the vehicle or its contents.

soft palate, the fold of soft tissue at the back of the roof of the mouth, behind the hard palate, partially dividing the mouth and the pharynx; velum.

soft-ped·al (sôft′ped′əl, soft′-) *v.t.,* **-aled, -al·ing;** *also, British,* **-alled, -al·ling. 1.** to soften the tone of by means of the soft pedal. **2.** to make less conspicuous or emphatic: *to soft-pedal criticism.*

soft pedal, the pedal of a piano that is pressed with the foot to soften the tone.

soft rock, rock music with a subdued beat and instrumentation and an emphasis on melody and lyrics.

soft sell, a subtle, indirect, and quietly persuasive method of selling or advertising a product. ➡ distinguished from **hard sell.**

soft-shell (sôft′shel′, soft′-) *also,* **soft-shelled.** *adj.* (of certain shellfish) having a soft shell, as a crab that has recently molted.

soft-shell clam, a common edible clam, *Mya arenaria,* of the coastal waters of North America, having a thin, elongated shell; steamer.

soft-shoe (sôft′shü′, soft′-) *adj.* of or relating to a kind of tap dancing done without metal taps on the shoes.

soft shoulder, the soft earth along the edge of a paved road.

soft-soap (sôft′sōp′, soft′-) *v.t. Informal.* to flatter: *Don't try to soft-soap me into lending you money.* **—soft′-soap′er,** *n.*

soft soap 1. a fluid or semifluid soap. **2.** *Informal.* flattery.

soft-spo·ken (sôft′spō′kən, soft′-) *adj.* **1.** (of persons) speaking with a soft, low voice. **2.** (of words) spoken softly or mildly.

soft spot 1. a weak, sensitive, or vulnerable part: *an economic soft spot, a soft spot in a defense system.* **2.** a particular fondness; tender regard: *a soft spot for puppies.*

soft·ware (sôft′wâr′, soft′-) *n.* written or printed programs, information, or the like, used in the operation of a computer, as distinguished from its physical equipment.

soft wheat, a type of wheat having soft, starchy grains, used esp. in making pastry flour.

soft·wood (sôft′wud′, soft′-) *n.* **1.** any of a large group of trees bearing cones and having needlelike leaves, as pines, firs, and spruces. **2.** the wood of such a tree, used chiefly for construction. **3.** any soft, light, easily cut wood.

soft·y (sôf′tē, sof′-) *n., pl.* **soft·ies.** *Informal.* **1.** a person who is easily imposed upon or moved to emotion. **2.** a weak person.

sog·gy (sog′ē) *adj.,* **-gi·er, -gi·est. 1.** saturated with water or moisture; soaked. **2.** damp and heavy, as poorly baked bread or cake. **3.** lacking life or spirit; dull. [Dialectal English *sog* bog (of uncertain origin) + -Y¹.] **—sog′gi·ness,** *n.*

soi-di·sant (swä dē zäN′) *adj. French.* so-called; self-styled. ➡ usually used disparagingly: *a soi-disant intellectual.*

soil¹ (soil) *n.* **1.** the part of the earth's surface in which plants grow, a loose material made up of small rock particles, decayed organic matter, and living organisms. **2.** a particular kind of soil: *sandy soil.* **3.** a land, country, or region: *to land on foreign soil.* **4.** any place or condition favorable to growth or development. [Anglo-Norman *soil* land, possibly going back to Latin *solium* seat; influenced in meaning by Latin *solum* ground.]

a	at	e	end	o	hot	u	up	hw	white		about
ā	ape	ē	me	ō	old	ū	use	ng	song		taken
ä	far	i	it	ô	fork	ü	rule	th	thin	ə	pencil
âr	care	ī	ice	oi	oil	ù	pull	th	this		lemon
		îr	pierce	ou	out	ûr	turn	zh	measure		circus

soil² (soil) *v.t.* **1.** to make dirty, esp. on the surface. **2.** to bring disgrace or dishonor to; sully: *Malicious gossip can soil a person's reputation.* —*v.i.* to become soiled or dirty: *White clothes soil easily.* —*n.* **1.** a dirty mark or place; spot; stain. **2.** filthy matter, as refuse or sewage. **3.** manure that is used as fertilizer; night soil. **4.** the act of soiling or the state of being soiled. [Old French *soillier* to dirty, going back to Latin *suculus* little boar, diminutive of *sūs* pig, boar.]

soil·age (soi′lij) *n.* green crops cut for feeding to penned livestock.

soil bank, a Federal program that pays farmers to cultivate less of certain surplus crops and to enrich land thereby made idle, as by planting soil-enriching crops.

soil profile, the vertical zonation of soil into layers, or horizons, as revealed in the face of a cliff or gully wall or by a hole dug in the ground.

soi·ree (swä rā′) *also,* **soi·rée.** *n.* a party, reception, or other social gathering taking place in the evening. [French *soirée*, from *soir* evening, going back to Latin *sērus* late.]

so·journ (sō′jûrn, sō jûrn′) *v.i.* to live in a place for a brief time, as on a visit. —*n.* a brief stay. [Old French *sojorner* to rest, stay, going back to Latin *sub* under + *diurnus* relating to the day, daily.] —**so′journ·er,** *n.*

sol¹ (sōl) *n. Music.* the fifth of the series of syllables used to name the eight tones of the diatonic scale. Also, **so.** For illustration, see **do².** [See GAMUT.]

sol² (sol, sôl) *n.* the former monetary unit of Peru. [Spanish *sol* sun, from Latin *sōl;* because of the design of the sun on the coin.]

sol³ (sol, sôl) *n.* a colloidal system in a liquid state. [From SOLUTION.]

Sol (sol) *n.* **1.** in Roman mythology, the god of the sun. His Greek counterpart is Helios. **2.** the sun. [Latin *sōl.*]

sol. 1. soluble. **2.** solution.

Sol. 1. Solicitor. **2.** Solomon.

sol·ace (sol′is) *n.* **1.** relief from sorrow or disappointment; comfort; consolation: *The widow found solace in the companionship of her friends.* **2.** a person or thing that gives relief from sorrow or disappointment: *His friends were a solace during his time of grief.* —*v.t.,* **-aced, -ac·ing. 1.** to relieve from sorrow or disappointment; comfort; console. **2.** to alleviate or soothe, as sorrow. [Old French *solaz* consolation, from Latin *sōlācium.*]

so·la·num (sə lā′nəm) *n.* any of a large group of herbs and shrubs, genus *Solanum,* of the nightshade family, including the potato and eggplant. [Latin *sōlānum* nightshade; literally, sunflower, from *sōl* sun.]

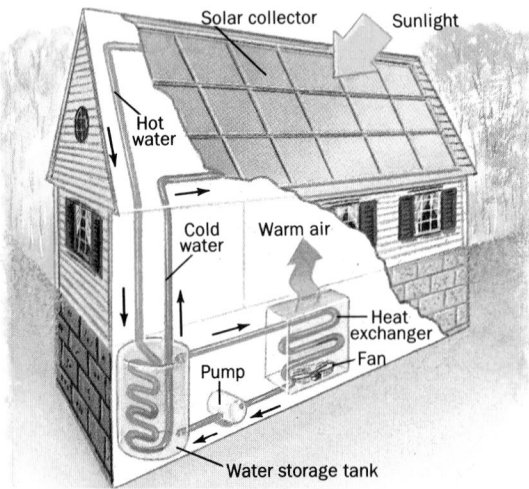

Solar collector Sunlight Hot water Cold water Warm air Heat exchanger Fan Pump Water storage tank

solar heating system

so·lar (sō′lər) *adj.* **1.** of or relating to the sun: *solar phenomena.* **2.** produced by or proceeding from the sun: *solar energy.* **3.** measured by the earth's course in relation to the sun: *solar time.* **4.** (of a mechanism) operating by means of or with the aid of the light or heat of the sun; using solar energy: *a solar furnace, a solar telegraph.* [Latin *sōlāris* relating to the sun, from *sōl* sun.]

solar battery, an array of solar cells used as a source of direct current.

solar cell, a photovoltaic device consisting of a thin slice of silicon or other semiconductor material that converts sunlight directly into electrical energy.

solar collector, a device that collects heat from the sun's rays and transmits it to a liquid, as water or a chemical solution, that is circulated to heat a building, make hot water, or make steam to generate electricity.

solar day, day *(def. 3a).*

solar eclipse, see eclipse *(def. 1).*

solar flare, a sudden eruption of gases from the surface of the sun. The bursts of radiation accompanying this cause disturbances in the earth's magnetic field that interfere with telecommunications.

so·lar·i·um (sə lâr′ē əm) *n., pl.* **-lar·i·a** (-lâr′ē ə). a glass-enclosed room, porch, or balcony exposed to the rays of the sun, as in a hospital or sanitarium.

so·lar·ize (sō′lə rīz′) *v.t.,* **-ized, -iz·ing.** (in photography) to overexpose (a film or plate) to light. —**so′lar·i·za′tion,** *n.*

solar month, month *(def. 5).*

solar panel, a broad, thin solar battery, used chiefly to supply electrical power for satellites, space stations, and space probes.

solar plex·us (plek′səs) **1.** a large network of nerves located in the upper part of the abdomen, just behind the stomach. **2.** *Informal.* the pit of the stomach.

solar prominence, prominence *(def. 3).*

solar system, the sun and all the celestial bodies that revolve around it, including the planets, their satellites, asteroids, comets, and meteors. For illustration, see **planet.**

solar wind, a constant stream of electrically charged particles that flows outward from the sun's corona in all directions, interacting with the earth's magnetic field to produce such phenomena as the aurora. For illustration, see **magnetosphere.**

solar year, year *(def. 2a).*

sold (sōld) the past tense and past participle of **sell.**

sol·der (sod′ər) *n.* **1.** any metal or metallic alloy used when melted for joining metal surfaces or parts. **2.** anything that joins or unites. —*v.t.* **1.** to join, fasten, or repair with solder. **2.** to unite firmly or closely. —*v.i.* **1.** to work with solder. **2.** to become joined or united with or as with solder. [Old French *soldure* this metal, from *sou(l)der* to fasten together, going back to Latin *solidus* firm.] —**sol′der·er,** *n.*

sol·der·ing iron (sod′ər ing) a metal tool that uses heat to melt and apply solder.

sol·dier (sōl′jər) *n.* **1.** a person who serves in an army. **2.** an enlisted person in an army, as distinguished from a commissioned officer. **3.** a brave, skilled, or experienced warrior. **4.** a person who works for any cause: *a soldier of Christ.* **5.** an ant or termite having a large head and powerful jaws adapted for fighting in defense of the colony. —*v.i.* to be a soldier; serve in an army. [Old French *soldier* one who fights for pay, from *soulde* pay, from Late Latin *solidus* a Roman gold coin. See SOLIDUS.]

sol·dier·ly (sōl′jər lē) *adj.* relating to or characteristic of a soldier: *a soldierly bearing.*

soldier of fortune. 1. a person who will serve in any army for money, adventure, or pleasure. **2.** any restless, adventurous person.

Soldier's Medal, a U.S. military decoration awarded for heroic action not involving combat with an enemy.

sol·dier·y (sōl′jə rē) *n., pl.* **-dier·ies. 1.** soldiers as a group. **2.** a body of soldiers. **3.** military knowledge or training; military science.

sol·do (sōl′dō) *n., pl.* **-di** (-dē). a former copper coin of Italy, equal to 1/20 of a lira. [Italian *soldo,* from Late Latin *solidus* a Roman gold coin. See SOLIDUS.]

sole¹ (sōl) *n.* **1.** the bottom surface of the foot. **2.** the corresponding part of a shoe, boot, sock, or other article of footwear. **3.** the lower part or bottom surface of anything, as the bottom of the head of a golf club. —*v.t.,* **soled, sol·ing.** to furnish with a sole. [Old English *sole* sandal, going back to Latin *solea* sole of a sandal, sandal, from *solum* ground, bottom.]

sole² (sōl) *adj.* **1.** being the only one; without another or others; only; individual; single: *the sole heir to a fortune.* **2.** limited or belonging to a single person or group; exclusive: *The film company bought sole rights to two popular novels.* **3.** *Archaic.* having no companion; alone; solitary. [Latin *sōlus* alone.]

Synonyms *adj.* Sole², single, and only mean one and no more. Sole stresses being the only one that exists: *The bird in the zoo is thought to be the sole remaining member of its species.* Single is applied to an unaccompanied or unattached person or thing: *The vase contains a single flower.* Only is used to designate a specific person or thing: *This is the only copy of the book in the library.*

sole³ (sōl) *n., pl.* **soles** or **sole. 1.** any of a group of small flatfish, family Soleidae, having small eyes and a small mouth and found in warm and temperate seas. The **European sole,** *Solea*

solea, is highly valued as a food fish. **2.** any of various other edible flatfish, as the flounder. [Old French *sole,* from Latin *solea* sandal, sole[3]; with reference to its being as flat as a sandal.]

sol·e·cism (sol′ə siz′əm, sō′lə-) *n.* **1.** an error in grammar or in choice of words. **2.** an error in social behavior; violation of etiquette. **3.** any error, impropriety, or incongruity. [Latin *soloecismus* grammatical error, from Greek *soloikismos,* going back to *Soloi,* a Greek colony in Asia Minor, where Greek was spoken incorrectly.] —**sol′e·cist,** *n.* —**sol′e·cis′tic,** *adj.*

sole custody, custody of a child by only one parent after a divorce or separation. ➡ distinguished from **joint custody.**

sole·ly (sōl′lē) *adv.* **1.** excluding all other persons or things; without any other; alone: *to be solely to blame for an accident.* **2.** for no other reason than; merely: *to live solely for pleasure, to take a job solely for the money.*

sol·emn (sol′əm) *adj.* **1.** having or showing a grave, serious, or earnest character; sober: *a solemn mood.* **2.** inspiring serious thoughts or reflections; causing awe: *a solemn occasion.* **3.** having to do with religion or religious observances; sacred. **4.** performed with or accompanied by formality or ceremony. [Latin *sōllemnis* established, religious, from *sollus* whole + *annus* year.] —**sol′emn·ly,** *adv.* —**sol′emn·ness,** *n.* —For Synonyms, see **serious.**

so·lem·ni·ty (sə lem′ni tē) *n., pl.* **-ties. 1.** the state or quality of being solemn; seriousness; gravity; impressiveness. **2.** *also,* **solemnities.** a solemn ceremony, proceeding, or observance.

sol·em·nize (sol′əm nīz′) *v.t.,* **-nized, -niz·ing. 1.** to celebrate with formal ceremony or by a ritual, as a religious holiday. **2.** to perform (a ceremony): *to solemnize a marriage.* **3.** to cause to have a solemn character; make serious. —**sol′em·ni·za′tion,** *n.*

so·le·noid (sō′lə noid′) *n.* a cylindrical coil of wire that produces a magnetic field when an electric current is passed through it. The solenoid is the basis for all electromagnets. [French *solénoïde,* from Greek *sōlēnoeidēs* shaped like a pipe, from *sōlēn* pipe, channel.] —**so′le·noi′dal,** *adj.*

sol-fa (sōl′fä′, sōl′fä′) *Music. n.* **1.** sol-fa syllables. **2.** the system or practice of singing tones to the sol-fa syllables. —*v.,* **-faed, -fa·ing.** —*v.i.* to use the sol-fa syllables in singing. —*v.t.* to sing (a melody or exercise) to the sol-fa syllables. [SOL[1] + FA. See GAMUT.]

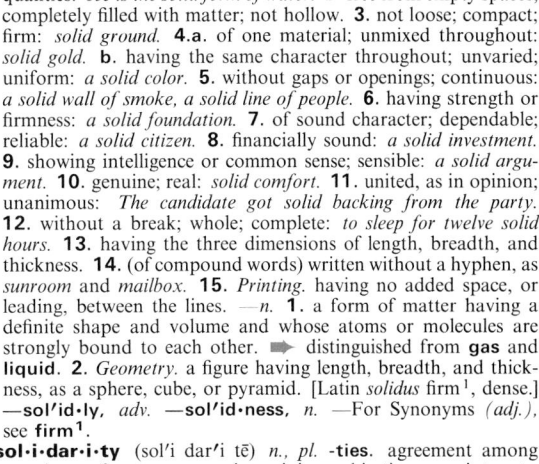

Direction of current

Magnetic field

solenoid

sol-fa syllables *Music.* the syllables *do, re, mi, fa, sol, la,* and *ti,* used in singing or naming the tones of the scale.

sol·feg·gio (sol fej′ō, -fej′ē ō′) *n., pl.* **-gios.** *Music.* **1.** a singing exercise in which scales, arpeggios, or similar runs are sung to the sol-fa syllables. **2.** solmization. [Italian *solfeggio* sol-fa, from *solfa* gamut, scale[3], from *sol* SOL[1] + *fa* FA. See GAMUT.]

so·lic·it (sə lis′it) *v.t.* **1.** to ask for earnestly; seek: *to solicit help, to solicit business.* **2.** to entreat or petition (a person) for something or to do something; urge; importune: *to solicit people for charitable contributions.* **3.** to tempt to do wrong. **4.** to accost or lure for an immoral purpose. —*v.i.* to solicit someone or something. [Latin *sollicitāre* to incite, urge to wrongdoing.]

so·lic·i·ta·tion (sə lis′i tā′shən) *n.* **1.** the act of soliciting; earnest plea or request; entreaty. **2.** a temptation to do wrong.

so·lic·i·tor (sə lis′i tər) *n.* **1.** a person who solicits, esp. a person who seeks business or trade. **2.** a British lawyer who advises clients and prepares cases for presentation in court but who may plead cases only in the lower court. ➡ distinguished from **barrister. 3.** a lawyer for a city, county, or other division of government.

solicitor general *pl.,* **solicitors general. 1.** a law officer ranking next below an attorney general. **2.** the chief law officer in some states of the United States.

so·lic·i·tous (sə lis′i təs) *adj.* **1.** full of concern or anxiety; concerned: *to be solicitous about a person's health.* **2.** full of desire or eagerness; anxious: *to be solicitous to please.* [Latin *sollicitus* anxious, agitated.] —**so·lic′i·tous·ly,** *adv.* —**so·lic′i·tous·ness,** *n.*

so·lic·i·tude (sə lis′i tüd′, -tūd′) *n.* **1.** the state of being solicitous; care; concern, esp. excessive concern. **2.** *usually,* **solicitudes.** something that causes care or concern. —For Synonyms, see **care.**

sol·id (sol′id) *adj.* **1.a.** having a definite shape and volume; not liquid or gaseous. **b.** characterized by the possession of such qualities: *Ice is the solid form of water.* **2.** free from empty spaces; completely filled with matter; not hollow. **3.** not loose; compact; firm: *solid ground.* **4.a.** of one material; unmixed throughout: *solid gold.* **b.** having the same character throughout; unvaried: *a solid color.* **5.** without gaps or openings; continuous: *a solid wall of smoke, a solid line of people.* **6.** having strength or firmness: *a solid foundation.* **7.** of sound character; dependable; reliable: *a solid citizen.* **8.** financially sound: *a solid investment.* **9.** showing intelligence or common sense; sensible: *a solid argument.* **10.** genuine; real: *solid comfort.* **11.** united, as in opinion; unanimous: *The candidate got solid backing from the party.* **12.** without a break; whole; complete: *to sleep for twelve solid hours.* **13.** having the three dimensions of length, breadth, and thickness. **14.** (of compound words) written without a hyphen, as *sunroom* and *mailbox.* **15.** *Printing.* having no added space, or leading, between the lines. —*n.* **1.** a form of matter having a definite shape and volume and whose atoms or molecules are strongly bound to each other. ➡ distinguished from **gas** and **liquid. 2.** *Geometry.* a figure having length, breadth, and thickness, as a sphere, cube, or pyramid. [Latin *solidus* firm[1], dense.] —**sol′id·ly,** *adv.* —**sol′id·ness,** *n.* —For Synonyms *(adj.),* see **firm[1].**

sol·i·dar·i·ty (sol′i dar′i tē) *n., pl.* **-ties.** agreement among members of a group, as in opinion, objectives, or interests. [French *solidarité,* from *solidaire* interdependent, from Latin *(in) solidum* (for) the whole.] —For Synonyms, see **union.**

solid geometry, the branch of geometry dealing with three-dimensional figures.

so·lid·i·fy (sə lid′i fī′) *v.,* **-fied, -fy·ing.** —*v.t.* **1.** to make solid, firm, or compact. **2.** to cause to be firmly united. —*v.i.* to become solid, firm, or compact: *The water solidified into ice.* —**so·lid′i·fi·ca′tion,** *n.*

so·lid·i·ty (sə lid′i tē) *n.* **1.** the state or quality of being solid. **2.** soundness or stability of mind, moral character, or finances.

sol·id-state (sol′id stāt′) *adj.* **1.** of or relating to the branch of physics that deals with the structure and properties of solids, esp. crystals. **2.** of or relating to electronic devices made with semiconductors, as transistors, rather than with thermionic devices, as electron tubes.

sol·i·dus (sol′i dəs) *n., pl.* **-di** (-dī′). **1.** a Roman gold coin introduced by Constantine and used until the fall of the Byzantine Empire, commonly called a bezant during medieval times. **2.** a sign (/) used to separate shillings from pence and in writing fractions or dates. [Late Latin *solidus* a Roman gold coin, from Latin *solidus* firm[1].]

so·lil·o·quist (sə lil′ə kwist′) *n.* a person who soliloquizes.

so·lil·o·quize (sə lil′ə kwīz′) *v.i.,* **-quized, -quiz·ing.** to talk to oneself; utter a soliloquy. —**so·lil′o·quiz′er,** *n.*

so·lil·o·quy (sə lil′ə kwē) *n., pl.* **-quies. 1.** an act or instance of talking to oneself. **2.** a dramatic speech in which a character reveals his or her thoughts to the audience but not to the other characters. [Late Latin *sōliloquim* talking to oneself, from Latin *sōlus* alone + *loquī* to speak.]

sol·ip·sism (sol′ip siz′əm) *n. Philosophy.* the theory that the self cannot know anything but its own experiences or that nothing but the self exists. [Latin *sōlus* alone + *ipse* self + -ISM.]

sol·i·taire (sol′i târ′) *n.* **1.** any of a number of card games for one person. Also, **patience. 2.** a single gem, esp. a diamond set by itself in a ring. [Old French *solitaire* alone, lonely, from Latin *sōlitārius.* Doublet of SOLITARY.]

sol·i·tar·y (sol′i ter′ē) *adj.* **1.** living, being, or going alone: *a solitary traveler.* **2.** made, done, or spent alone: *a solitary life.* **3.** not frequented; secluded; desolate; lonely: *a solitary cabin high in the mountains.* **4.** having no companions; lonesome; lonely. **5.** being the only one; only; sole. —*n., pl.* **-tar·ies. 1.** a person who lives alone, away from others; hermit; recluse. **2.** *Informal.* solitary confinement. [Latin *sōlitārius* alone, lonely. Doublet of SOLITAIRE.] —**sol′i·tar′i·ly,** *adv.* —**sol′i·tar′i·ness,** *n.* —For Synonyms, see **alone.**

solitary confinement, the confinement of a prisoner in a cell or other place completely isolated from all other prisoners.

sol·i·tude (sol′i tüd′, -tūd′) *n.* **1.** the state of being or living alone; isolation; remoteness; seclusion. **2.** a lonely, secluded, or unfrequented place. [Latin *sōlitūdō,* from *sōlus* alone.]

a	at	e	end	o	hot	u	up	hw	white	(	about
ā	ape	ē	me	ō	old	ū	use	ng	song	ə ⟨	taken
ä	far	i	it	ô	fork	ü	rule	th	thin		pencil
âr	care	ī	ice	oi	oil	u̇	pull	th	this		lemon
		îr	pierce	ou	out	ûr	turn	zh	measure	(	circus

1147

Solitude and **seclusion** mean the state of being alone. **Solitude** suggests tranquillity and the mental as well as physical aspects of isolation: *The monks were given frequent periods of solitude for prayer and meditation.* **Seclusion** implies separation from society to escape unwanted conditions or influences: *Although acquitted of the crime, the defendant went into seclusion after the trial.*

sol·ler·et (sol′ə ret′) *n.* a flexible steel shoe made of overlapping plates, forming part of a medieval suit of armor. For illustration, see **armor.**

sol·mi·za·tion (sol′mə zā′shən) *n. Music.* the act, practice, or system of using certain syllables, esp. the sol-fa syllables, in naming the tones of the scale. [French *solmisation,* going back to *sol* (see SOL[1]) + *mi* (see MI). See GAMUT.]

so·lo (sō′lō) *n., pl.* -**los. 1.** a musical composition or passage for a single voice or instrument, with or without accompaniment. **2.** any performance or action done by one person alone, as an airplane flight. —*adj.* **1.** composed or arranged for or performed by a single voice or instrument. **2.** playing a solo, as a musician or instrument: *a solo trumpet.* **3.** made or done by one person alone: *a solo flight.* —*v.i.* -**loed,** -**lo·ing. 1.** to make a flight alone in an airplane, esp. for the first time. **2.** to perform alone. [Italian *solo* alone, from Latin *sōlus.*]

so·lo·ist (sō′lō ist) *n.* a person who performs a solo, esp. a musical solo.

Sol·o·mon (sol′ə mən) *n.* a very wise man. [From *Solomon,* king of Israel in the tenth century B.C., renowned for his wisdom.]

Sol·o·mon's-seal (sol′ə mənz sēl′) *n.* any of a small group of erect leafy plants of the lily family, genus *Polygonatum,* having greenish or yellowish drooping flowers and scarred rhizomes.

Solomon's seal, a figure consisting of two triangles placed one upon the other to form a six-pointed star, formerly believed to possess magical powers and used as an amulet.

So·lon (sō′lən, -lon) *n. also,* **solon.** a wise man, esp. a wise lawmaker. [From *Solon,* 638?-559? B.C., Athenian statesman and lawgiver.]

so long *Informal.* good-bye.

sol·stice (sol′stis, sōl′-) *n.* **1.** either of the two times during the year when the sun appears farthest from the equator. In the Northern Hemisphere, the **summer solstice** occurs when the sun reaches the northernmost point on its path, on or about June 21, and the **winter solstice** occurs when the sun reaches its southernmost point, on or about December 22. The summer solstice is the longest period of daylight during the year, and the winter solstice is the shortest. **2.** either of the two diametrically opposite points on the apparent annual path of the sun that is farthest from the celestial equator. [Old French *solstice,* from Latin *sōlstitium,* going back to *sōl* sun + *sistere* to cause to stand.]

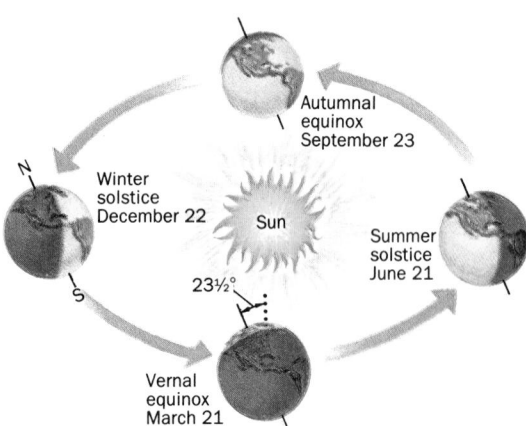

solstices and equinoxes marking the earth's seasons

sol·sti·tial (sol stish′əl, sōl-) *adj.* of or relating to a solstice.

sol·u·bil·i·ty (sol′yə bil′i tē) *n., pl.* -**ties. 1.** the quality or condition of being soluble; ability of a substance to be dissolved in another substance. **2.** the amount of a substance that can be dissolved in a given solvent at a given temperature.

sol·u·ble (sol′yə bəl) *adj.* **1.** capable of being dissolved in another substance. **2.** capable of being solved: *a soluble problem.* [Late Latin *solūbilis* dissolvable, from Latin *solvere* to loosen, dissolve.] —**sol′u·ble·ness,** *n.* —**sol′u·bly,** *adv.*

soluble glass, water glass *(def. 2).*

sol·ute (sol′ūt, sō′lūt) *n.* a substance that is dissolved by another substance to form a solution. ➡ distinguished from **solvent.** [Latin *solūtus,* past participle of *solvere* to loosen, dissolve.]

so·lu·tion (sə lü′shən) *n.* **1.** the act, process, or method of solving a problem. **2.** the answer to a problem; explanation. **3.a.** a homogeneous mixture of atoms, molecules, or ions of two or more substances. Solutions are usually formed by solids, liquids, or gases dissolved in liquids but may also consist of gases dissolved in gases or solids dissolved in solids. **b.** the act or process of forming such a mixture: *the solution of sugar in water.* **c.** the state of being dissolved: *Seawater contains salts in solution.* **4.** a separation or breaking up. [Latin *solūtiō* a loosening, explanation.]

solution set *Mathematics.* the set of all values that satisfy an equation. Also, **truth set.**

solv·a·ble (sol′və bəl) *adj.* capable of being solved: *a solvable problem.* —**solv′a·bil′i·ty,** *n.*

Sol·vay process (sol′vā) a process for making sodium carbonate from common salt. Carbon dioxide is passed through a solution of salt and ammonia to produce sodium bicarbonate, which is then heated to produce sodium carbonate. [From Ernest *Solvay,* 1838-1922, Belgian chemist who invented it.]

solve (solv) *v.t.,* **solved, solv·ing.** to find the solution to; provide an answer or explanation for: *to solve a problem.* [Latin *solvere* to loosen, explain, dissolve.] —**solv′er,** *n.*

sol·ven·cy (sol′vən sē) *n.* the quality or state of being solvent.

sol·vent (sol′vənt) *adj.* **1.** able to pay all debts, as a business establishment whose assets exceed its liabilities. **2.** having the power to dissolve; causing solution. —*n.* **1.** a substance that dissolves another substance or substances to form a solution. Solvents are usually liquids but can be solids or gases. ➡ distinguished from **solute. 2.** something that solves; explanation. [Latin *solvēns,* present participle of *solvere* to loosen, dissolve.]

so·ma (sō′mə) *n., pl.* **so·ma·ta** (sō′mə tə). the body of a living organism, as opposed to its germ cells. [Greek *sōma* body.]

So·ma·li (sə mä′lē) *n., pl.* -**li** or -**lis. 1.** a member of a group of Hamitic people living in parts of Somalia, Kenya, and Ethiopia. **2.** the Hamitic language of these people.

so·mat·ic (sō mat′ik, sə-) *adj.* **1.** of or relating to the body, as distinguished from the mind, soul, or psyche; physical; corporeal. **2.** of or relating to the walls of the body cavity. **3.** of or relating to the soma. [Greek *sōmatikos* relating to the body, from *sōma* body.]

somatic cell, any cell of the body other than a germ cell.

so·ma·to·plasm (sō′mə tə plaz′əm, sə mat′ə-) *n.* the protoplasm of a somatic cell, as distinguished from that of a germ cell. [Greek *sōmat-,* stem of *sōma* body + -PLASM.]

so·ma·to·type (sō′mə tə tīp′, sō mat′ə-) *n.* a classification that describes a person's body build. The primary types are ectomorph, endomorph, and mesomorph. [Greek *sōmat-,* stem of *sōma* + TYPE.]

som·ber (som′bər) *also,* **som·bre.** *adj.* **1.** dark and gloomy; dark and dull: *a somber sky, a somber shade of gray.* **2.** melancholy, dismal, or depressing: *a somber mood.* [French *sombre* dark, gloomy, going back to Latin *sub* under + *umbra* shade.] —**som′ber·ly;** *also,* **som′bre·ly,** *adv.* —**som′ber·ness;** *also,* **som′bre·ness,** *n.* —For Synonyms, see **serious.**

som·brer·o (som brâr′ō, səm-) *n., pl.* -**brer·os.** a hat with a broad brim and high crown, worn esp. in Mexico and the southwestern United States. [Spanish *sombrero* hat, from *sombra* shade, going back to Latin *sub* under + *umbra* shade.]

some (sum; *unstressed* səm) *adj.* **1.** being a certain one or ones not specified or known: *Some people are offended by sarcasm. Some birds cannot fly.* **2.** being of a certain unspecified number, quantity, or amount: *It happened some weeks ago. Please have some potatoes.* **3.** *Informal.* worthy of consideration; remarkable; striking; unusual: *That was some game yesterday.* —*pron.* **1.** certain ones not specified or known: *Some still believe the defendant is innocent of the crime.* **2.** a certain unspecified number, quantity, or amount: *I kept some and gave the rest away.* —*adv.* **1.** approximately; about: *The club has some forty members.* **2.** *Informal.* somewhat: *The patient's condition has improved some.* [Old English *sum.*]

-some[1] *suffix* (used to form adjectives) characterized by, tending to, or tending to be (what is indicated by the stem): *handsome, wholesome, gruesome.* [Old English *-sum.*]

-some[2] *suffix* used to form nouns indicating a group of a specified number: *threesome, foursome.* [Old English *sum* some.]

-some[3] *combining form* body: *chromosome.* [Greek *sōma* body.]

some·bod·y (sum′bod′ē, -bə dē) *pron.* an unknown or unspecified person; someone: *Somebody has taken my raincoat.* —*n., pl.* -**bod·ies.** a person who is important or famous. —For Usage Note, see **anybody.**

some·day (sum′dā′) *adv.* at some future time: *That species may someday become extinct.*

some·how (sum′hou′) *adv.* in a way or by a method not known, stated, or understood: *We must get this fixed somehow.*

some·one (sum′wun′, -wən) *pron.* somebody: *Someone will have to mail these letters.* —For Usage Note, see **anybody.**

some·place (sum′plās′) *adv. Informal.* in, at, or to some place not specified or known; somewhere: *We'll have dinner someplace near the theater.*

som·er·sault (sum′ər sôlt′) *also,* **summersault.** *n.* an acrobatic leap, roll, or dive in which the body turns heels over head, making a complete revolution. —*v.i.* to perform a somersault. [Old French *sombresau(l)t* leap, through Provençal, from Latin *suprā* above + *saltus* leap.]

som·er·set (sum′ər set′) *n.* somersault. —*v.i.*, **-set·ted, -set·ting.** somersault.

some·thing (sum′thing′) *pron.* a certain thing not specified or known; some thing: *Something is wrong with the car.* —*n.* an important person or thing: *You think you are something since you won the contest.* —*adv.* **1.** to some extent; somewhat. ➡ used in the phrase *something like: Your house is something like ours.* **2.** *Informal.* to an extreme degree; quite: *It rained something awful all day.*

some·time (sum′tīm′) *adv.* **1.** at some time not specified or known: *I bought the car sometime last spring.* **2.** at some unspecified time in the future: *I'll finish this work sometime.* —*adj.* having been formerly; former: *a sometime actor.*

some·times (sum′tīmz′) *adv.* now and then; at times; occasionally: *Sometimes we spend the weekend in the country.*

some·way (sum′wā′) *also,* **some·ways.** *adv.* in some way; somehow.

some·what (sum′hwut′, -hwot′, -wut′, -wot′) *adv.* in some measure or degree; to some extent; rather: *to be somewhat upset.* —*n.* some part, portion, amount, or degree: *That movie was somewhat of a disappointment.*

some·where (sum′hwâr′, -wâr′) *adv.* **1.** in, at, or to some place not specified or known: *I left my jacket somewhere in the park.* **2.** at some time, amount, degree, age, or figure: *Let's meet somewhere about five o'clock. It costs somewhere around ten dollars.* —*n.* a place that is not known or specified.

som·me·lier (sum′əl yā′) *n.* a person who is responsible for selecting and serving wine in a restaurant or club. Also, **wine steward.** [French *sommelier,* from Old French *sommelier* person in charge of supplies, driver of pack animals, going back to Late Latin *sagma* packsaddle, from Greek *sagma.*]

som·nam·bu·lant (som nam′byə lənt) *adj.* walking while asleep or having the habit of walking while asleep.

som·nam·bu·late (som nam′byə lāt′) *v.i.*, **-lat·ed, -lat·ing.** to walk while asleep. [Latin *somnus* sleep + AMBULATE.] —**som·nam′bu·la′tion,** *n.* —**som·nam′bu·la′tor,** *n.*

som·nam·bu·lism (som nam′byə liz′əm) *n.* the act or habit of walking about while asleep; sleepwalking.

som·nam·bu·list (som nam′byə list) *n.* a person who walks about while sleeping; sleepwalker. —**som·nam′bu·lis′tic,** *adj.*

som·nif·er·ous (som nif′ər əs) *adj.* causing or inducing sleep; soporific. [Latin *somnifer* + -OUS.]

som·no·lence (som′nə ləns) *n.* sleepiness; drowsiness.

som·no·lent (som′nə lənt) *adj.* **1.** sleepy; drowsy. **2.** tending to cause sleep. [Latin *somnolentus* sleepy, from *somnus* sleep.] —**som′no·lent·ly,** *adv.*

Som·nus (som′nəs) *n.* in Roman mythology, the god of sleep. His Greek counterpart is Hypnos.

son (sun) *n.* **1.** a male child considered in relation to one or both of his parents. **2.** a male child adopted as a son. **3.** a male descendant: *the sons of Adam.* **4.** a male person regarded as the product or offspring of a certain country, place, or influence: *a son of the soil, sons of the Depression.* **5.** a familiar term of address to a boy or man from an older person. **6. the Son.** Jesus. [Old English *sunu.*]

so·nance (sō′nəns) *n.* the condition or quality of being sonant.

so·nant (sō′nənt) *adj.* **1.** having sound; sounding. **2.** *Phonetics.* voiced. —*n. Phonetics.* a voiced sound. [Latin *sonāns,* present participle of *sonāre* to make a noise.]

so·nar (sō′när) *n.* a device that detects the presence and determines the location of submerged objects, as submarines, by means of sound waves reflected from or produced by the objects. [Short for *so(und) na(vigation) r(anging).*]

so·na·ta (sə nä′tə) *n.* an instrumental composition, often written for the piano, typically having three or four movements in contrasting forms and rhythms but related keys. [Italian *sonata* literally, a sounding, from *sonare* to sound, from Latin *sonāre* to make a noise.]

son·a·ti·na (son′ə tē′nə) *n.* a short or simplified sonata. [Italian *sonatina,* diminutive of *sonata.* See SONATA.]

song (sông) *n.* **1.** a musical composition for one or more voices. **2.a.** a poem that can be set to music. **b.** poetry; verse. **3.** the act or art of singing. **4.** any melodious sound or series of sounds, as the call of a bird. [Old English *sang.*]
· **for a song.** at a very low price; very cheaply: *I bought this painting for a song.*

song and dance *Informal.* a statement, esp. one offered as an excuse, that is evasive, confusing, or misleading.

song·bird (sông′bûrd′) *n.* a bird that utters a musical call.

song·fest (sông′fest′) *n.* an informal gathering at which there is group singing.

song·ful (sông′fəl) *adj.* full of song; melodious; tuneful.

song·less (sông′lis) *adj.* having no song; unable to sing: *a songless bird.*

Song of Solomon, a book of the Old Testament, traditionally attributed to King Solomon, containing lyric and mystical hymns of love. Also, **Song of Songs, Canticles.**

song sparrow, a common North American sparrow, *Melospiza melodia,* having predominantly brownish plumage marked with dark brown streaks, noted for its song.

song·ster (sông′stər) *n.* **1.** a person who sings. **2.** a writer of songs or poems. **3.** songbird. [Old English *sangestre* singer.]

song·stress (sông′stris) *n.* a female singer, esp. of popular songs.

song thrush, a European thrush, *Turdus philomelos,* having predominantly brown plumage with a yellow-and-white breast marked with brown spots. Length: 9 inches (23 centimeters). Also, **mavis.**

song·writ·er (sông′rī′tər) *n.* a person who composes lyrics or music or both for songs, esp. popular songs.

son·ic (son′ik) *adj.* **1.** of, relating to, or utilizing sound, esp. at audible frequencies: *sonic vibrations.* **2.** relating to or denoting the speed at which sound travels through the air at sea level, about 1,088 feet (331.6 meters) per second, or 740 miles (1,191 kilometers) per hour. [Latin *sonus* noise + -IC.] —**son′i·cal·ly,** *adv.*

sonic barrier, sound barrier.

sonic boom, a loud, explosive noise caused by the shock wave that emanates from an object, as an aircraft, traveling at or above the speed of sound.

son-in-law (sun′in lô′) *n., pl.* **sons-in-law.** the husband of one's daughter.

son·net (son′it) *n.* a poem containing fourteen lines, usually in iambic pentameter, having a fixed pattern of rhyme and usually dealing with a single theme, idea, or sentiment. The two basic forms are the Shakespearean sonnet and the Petrarchan sonnet. [Italian *sonetto,* diminutive of *suono* sound¹, from Latin *sonus* noise.]

son·net·eer (son′ə tîr′) *n.* a person who writes sonnets.

sonnet sequence, a series of sonnets written by one poet and usually having a single theme or subject.

son·ny (sun′ē) *n., pl.* **-nies.** a young boy. ➡ used as a familiar form of address.

son·o·gram (son′ə gram′, sō′nə-) *n. Medicine.* a record of ultrasonic waves as they are reflected in passing through the body. A sonogram provides an image of the shape, location, and movement of organs and other kinds of tissue.

so·nor·i·ty (sə nôr′i tē, -nor′-) *n.* the quality or state of being sonorous.

so·no·rous (sə nôr′əs, son′ər-) *adj.* **1.** producing or capable of producing sound, esp. deep, full, or rich sound. **2.** (of sound) loud, deep, or resonant. **3.** rich and full in sound, as language or the voice. **4.** having an imposing or impressive quality, effect, or style: *sonorous phrases.* [Latin *sonōrus* resounding, noisy, from *sonor* noise.] —**so·no′rous·ly,** *adv.* —**so·no′rous·ness,** *n.*

son·ship (sun′ship′) *n.* the fact, condition, or relation of being a son.

soon (sün) *adv.* **1.** in the near future; before long; shortly: *Visit us again soon.* **2.** ahead of the normal or appointed time; early: *We arrived too soon for the meeting.* **3.** without delay; promptly; quickly: *I'll come as soon as I can.* **4.** readily; willingly: *I would as soon do it now as later.* [Old English *sōna* within a short time.]

Synonyms **Soon, presently,** and **shortly** mean in the near future. **Soon,** the broadest of these terms, can be applied to anything happening with a minimum of delay: *Dinner will be ready soon.* **Presently,** a more formal term, often implies an indefiniteness, esp. concerning a person's immediate inten-

a	at	e	end	o	hot	u	up	hw	white		about
ā	ape	ē	me	ō	old	ū	use	ng	song		taken
ä	far	i	it	ô	fork	ü	rule	th	thin	ə	pencil
âr	care	ī	ice	oi	oil	u̇	pull	th	this		lemon
		îr	pierce	ou	out	ûr	turn	zh	measure		circus

tions: *I'll be home presently.* **Shortly** is usually more specific than **soon** or **presently** about when something will happen: *They planned to sail shortly after dawn.*

soot (sut, süt) *n.* a black, powdery substance, composed mostly of particles of carbon, produced during the incomplete burning of such fuels as wood, coal, or oil. —*v.t.* to soil or cover with soot. [Old English *sōt* the black, powdery substance.]

sooth (süth) *Archaic. n.* truth; reality. —*adj.* **1.** true; real. **2.** soft; soothing; sweet. [Old English *sōth.*]

soothe (süth) *v.,* **soothed, sooth·ing.** —*v.t.* **1.** to bring to a quiet or composed condition; give solace to; calm; comfort: *The soft music soothed his nerves.* **2.** to make less painful or severe; relieve; alleviate: *The medicine soothed her headache.* —*v.i.* to have a soothing effect. [Old English *sōthian* to prove to be true.] —**sooth′er,** *n.* —For Synonyms, see **appease.**

sooth·ing (sü′thing) *adj.* capable of calming or quieting: *soothing words, a soothing medicine.* —**sooth′ing·ly,** *adv.*

sooth·ly (süth′lē) *adv. Archaic.* in truth; truly.

sooth·say·er (süth′sā′ər) *n.* a person who claims to be able to foretell future events. [SOOTH + SAY + -ER[1].]

sooth·say·ing (süth′sā′ing) *n.* **1.** the act or practice of foretelling future events. **2.** an instance of this; prediction; prophecy.

soot·y (sut′ē, sü′tē) *adj.,* **soot·i·er, soot·i·est. 1.** covered or soiled with soot: *sooty buildings.* **2.** relating to, consisting of, or producing soot: *sooty deposits.* **3.** having the color of soot: *sooty black.* —**soot′i·ly,** *adv.* —**soot′i·ness,** *n.*

sop (sop) *n.* **1.** a piece of food soaked or dipped in a liquid, as bread in milk or gravy. **2.** anything that is thoroughly soaked. **3.** anything given to pacify or quiet, or as a bribe: *That law is merely a sop to those who have been calling for reform.* —*v.,* **sopped, sop·ping.** —*v.t.* **1.** to soak or dip in a liquid: *to sop bread in milk.* **2.** to take up (water or other liquid) by absorption (usually with *up*): *to sop up gravy with a biscuit.* **3.** to wet thoroughly; drench. —*v.i.* **1.** to be or become thoroughly wet. **2.** (of a liquid) to be absorbed; soak in. [Old English *sopp* piece of bread soaked in liquid.]

sop., soprano.

soph., sophomore.

soph·ism (sof′iz əm) *n.* a clever argument that has the appearance of truth or reason but is actually logically unsound or misleading; false or deceptive argument. [Latin *sophisma* fallacy, from Greek *sophisma* clever device, captious argument, going back to *sophos* wise, clever.]

soph·ist (sof′ist) *n.* **1.** *usually,* **Sophist.** one of a class of teachers of philosophy, rhetoric, and ethics in Greece in the fifth century B.C., some of whom were criticized for relying on eloquence, subtlety, or ingenuity rather than sound reasoning in their arguments. **2.** a learned person. **3.** a person who argues in a clever but logically unsound or misleading way; false or deceptive reasoner.

so·phis·tic (sə fis′tik) *adj.* **1.** relating to or characteristic of Sophists or sophistry: *sophistic tricks, sophistic subtlety.* **2.** clever but logically unsound or misleading: *a sophistic argument.* Also, **so·phis′ti·cal.** —**so·phis′ti·cal·ly,** *adv.*

so·phis·ti·cate (*v.,* sə fis′ti kāt′; *n.,* sə fis′ti kit, -kāt′) *v.,* **-cat·ed, -cat·ing.** —*v.t.* **1.** to cause to have worldly knowledge and experience; make less natural, simple, or artless. **2.** to make complex; complicate. **3.** to make impure; adulterate. **4.** *Archaic.* to mislead or corrupt (a person). —*v.i.* to use sophistry. —*n.* a sophisticated person. [Medieval Latin *sophisticatus,* past participle of *sophisticare* to adulterate, tamper with, disguise, going back to Greek *sophistikos* sophistic, from *sophistēs* Sophist.]

so·phis·ti·cat·ed (sə fis′ti kā′tid) *adj.* **1.a.** having worldly knowledge and experience; lacking natural simplicity; not naive; worldly-wise. **b.** able to make subtle distinctions; perceptive; knowledgeable; cultured: *a sophisticated novelist.* **2.** suitable for or appealing to sophisticated people: *sophisticated entertainment.* **3.** developed to a highly complex level: *sophisticated electronic equipment.* —**so·phis′ti·cat′ed·ly,** *adv.*

so·phis·ti·ca·tion (sə fis′ti kā′shən) *n.* **1.** the quality or character of being sophisticated; sophisticated ideas, tastes, or ways. **2.** the act of sophisticating.

soph·ist·ry (sof′ə strē) *n., pl.* **-ries. 1.** a method of reasoning that is clever and superficially plausible but fundamentally unsound. **2.** a clever but logically unsound or misleading argument; sophism. **3.** the methods or teachings of the Sophists.

soph·o·more (sof′ə môr′) *n.* **1.** a student in the second year of a four-year high school or college. **2.** a person who is in the second year of any endeavor. [Earlier *sophumer,* from *sophom,* obsolete form of SOPHISM; with reference to the earlier use of sophistic arguments for intellectual training.]

soph·o·mor·ic (sof′ə môr′ik, -mor′-) *adj.* **1.** of or relating to a sophomore or sophomores. **2.** overconfident of knowledge and intelligence though immature, shallow, and uninformed.

sop·o·rif·er·ous (sop′ə rif′ər əs, sō′pə-) *adj.* bringing sleep; soporific. [Latin *soporifer* + -OUS.] —**sop′o·rif′er·ous·ly,** *adv.* —**sop′o·rif′er·ous·ness,** *n.*

sop·o·rif·ic (sop′ə rif′ik, sō′pə-) *adj.* **1.** causing or tending to cause sleep. **2.** sleepy; drowsy. —*n.* something that causes sleep, esp. a drug. [Latin *sopor* deep sleep + -FIC.]

sop·ping (sop′ing) *adj.* thoroughly wet; soaked; drenched.

sop·py (sop′ē) *adj.,* **-pi·er, -pi·est. 1.** soaked through with water or other liquid; saturated: *soppy land.* **2.** rainy: *soppy weather.*

so·pran·o (sə pran′ō, -prä′nō) *n., pl.* **-pran·os. 1.** the highest singing voice of women and boys. **2.** a singer having such a voice. **3.** an instrument having the highest range in a family of musical instruments. **4.** a part composed for a soprano voice or instrument. —*adj.* **1.** able to sing soprano: *a soprano voice.* **2.** for a soprano: *a soprano score.* **3.** having the highest range in a family of musical instruments: *a soprano saxophone.* [Italian *soprano* highest, treble in music, from *sopra* above, from Latin *suprā.*]

so·ra (sôr′ə) *n.* a small, short-billed wading bird, *Porzana carolina,* of the rail family, common in the marshes of North America. [Probably of American Indian origin.]

sorb[1] (sôrb) *n.* **1.** any of several trees of the apple family, as the service tree or rowan tree. **2.** the fruit of any of these trees. [Latin *sorbum* the fruit of this tree, from *sorbus* this tree.]

sorb[2] (sôrb) *v.t.* to absorb or adsorb. [From ABSORB and ADSORB.]

sor·bet (sôr′bit, sôr bā′) *n.* a frozen dessert similar to sherbet but made without egg whites or milk. [French *sorbet,* from Italian *sorbetto,* from Turkish *sherbet* a drink made from sweetened fruit juice, going back to Arabic *sharbah* a drink.]

sor·bi·tol (sôr′bi tôl′) *n.* a sweet, odorless alcohol present in fruits and berries that is used as a sugar substitute and in the manufacture of vitamin C. Formula: $C_6H_{14}O_6$ [SORB[1] + -ITE[1] + -OL.]

Sor·bonne (sôr bon′) *n.* the seat of the faculties of literature and science of the University of Paris.

sor·cer·er (sôr′sər ər) *n.* a person who practices sorcery.

sorceress (sôr′sər is) *n.* a woman who practices sorcery.

sor·cer·y (sôr′sə rē) *n., pl.* **-cer·ies.** the use of supernatural powers gained through the aid of evil spirits, esp. to do harm to another person; witchcraft. [Old French *sorcerie* casting of lots, magic, going back to Latin *sors* lot.] —**sor′cer·ous,** *adj.* —For Synonyms, see **magic.**

sor·did (sôr′did) *adj.* **1.** dirty or filthy; squalid; foul: *sordid surroundings.* **2.** having a base or degraded character; low; mean; vile: *the sordid details of a crime.* **3.** meanly selfish; mercenary; avaricious. [Latin *sordidus* dirty, vile.] —**sor′did·ly,** *adv.* —**sor′did·ness,** *n.*

sore (sôr) *adj.,* **sor·er, sor·est. 1.** painful or sensitive to the touch; causing physical pain, as an injured or diseased part of the body: *sore muscles.* **2.** feeling physical pain, as from wounds or bruises: *to be sore from a fall.* **3.** filled with sadness, grief, or misery; distressed: *a sore heart, a sore conscience.* **4.** causing sadness, grief, or misery; distressing: *to be in sore need.* **5.** causing irritation or anger; annoying; vexing: *Their failure on the test is a sore point with them.* **6.** *Informal.* annoyed; angry; offended: *Are you still sore at me for not inviting your friends to the party?* —*n.* **1.** an area of the body where the skin is broken, bruised, or inflamed, causing pain. **2.** any source of pain, anger, sorrow, or distress. —*adv. Archaic.* sorely. [Old English *sār* painful.] —**sore′ness,** *n.*

sore·head (sôr′hed′) *n. Informal.* a person who is easily angered, annoyed, or offended.

sore·ly (sôr′lē) *adv.* **1.** painfully; grievously; severely: *sorely troubled.* **2.** to a great extent; extremely: *Those people are sorely in need of money.*

sore throat, a painful throat due to an inflammation of the tissues that line the pharynx, usually caused by a bacterial or viral infection.

sor·ghum (sôr′gəm) *n.* **1.** any of a group of tall, tropical grasses, *Sorghum vulgare,* widely cultivated for grain, fodder, syrup, and broom fiber. **2.** a syrup made from the sweet juice of certain varieties of sorghum. [Modern Latin *sorghum,* from Italian *sorgo* this grass, possibly going back to Latin *Syricum (grāmen)* (grass) of Syria.]

sor·go (sôr′gō) *n., pl.* **-gos.** any of several varieties of sorghum cultivated chiefly for their sweet, watery juice, from which syrup is made, and also used for fodder. Also, **sweet sorghum.** [Italian *sorgo.* See SORGHUM.]

so·ri (sôr′ī) the plural of **sorus.**

so·ror·i·cide[1] (sə rôr′ə sīd′, -ror′-) *n.* the act of killing one's sister. [Late Latin *sorōricīdium,* from Latin *soror* sister + -cīdium. See -CIDE[1].]

so·ror·i·cide² (sə rôr′ə sīd′, -ror′-) *n.* a person who kills his or her sister. [Latin *sorōricīda,* from *soror* sister + *-cīda.* See -CIDE².]
so·ror·i·ty (sə rôr′i tē, -ror′-) *n., pl.* **-ties.** a social organization of girls or women, esp. a society of female students in a college. [Medieval Latin *sororitas* sisterhood, from Latin *soror* sister.]
sorp·tion (sôrp′shən) *n.* absorption or adsorption. [From ABSORPTION and ADSORPTION.]
sor·rel¹ (sôr′əl, sor′-) *n.* **1.** any of several weedy plants, genus *Rumex,* bearing long, branching clusters of small, greenish or reddish flowers and sour, heart-shaped leaves; dock. The leaves of certain species are sometimes used as salad greens or to make a soup. **2.** wood sorrel. [Old French *surele,* from *sur* sour; of Germanic origin.]
sor·rel² (sôr′əl, sor′) *n.* **1.** a reddish brown color. **2.** a horse of this color. —*adj.* having the color sorrel. [Old French *sorel* reddish brown horse, from *sor;* of Germanic origin.]
sorrel tree, a small North American tree, *Oxydendrum arboreum,* of the heath family, having large drooping clusters of white flowers and sour leaves. Also, **sourwood.**
sor·row (sôr′ō, sor′ō) *n.*
1. mental suffering or distress caused by loss, injury, disappointment, or trouble. **2.** a cause of grief or regret: *Your illness is a sorrow to us all.* **3.** the expression of grief, regret, sadness, or disappointment. —*v.i.* to feel or express sorrow; be sad. [Old English *sorg* grief, anxiety.]
—**sor′row·er,** *n.*

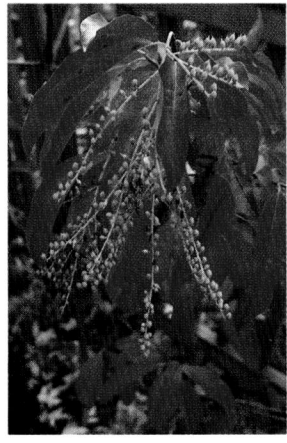
sorrel tree
branch in autumn

sor·row·ful (sôr′ō fəl, sor′ə-, sôr′-) *adj.* **1.** feeling sorrow; sad: *A sorrowful crowd watched the funeral procession pass by.* **2.** expressing sorrow: *a sorrowful look.* **3.** causing sorrow: *a sorrowful occasion.* —**sor′row·ful·ly,** *adv.* —**sor′row·ful·ness,** *n.*
sor·ry (sor′ē, sôr′ē) *adj.,* **-ri·er, -ri·est. 1.** full of or feeling sorrow, pity, sympathy, or remorse: *I was sorry to hear of your illness.* **2.** inferior in value or quality; poor; worthless: *a sorry attempt.* **3.** causing or inspiring sadness or pity; wretched; miserable: *The once beautiful village was a sorry sight after the war.* [Old English *sārig* sad.] —**sor′ri·ly,** *adv.* —**sor′ri·ness,** *n.*
sort (sôrt) *n.* **1.** a group of persons or things that are alike or similar; class; kind; type: *This sort of plant usually grows in swampy soil.* **2.** quality; character; nature: *Sarcastic remarks of that sort will only make him angrier.* **3.** a particular kind of person: *She's not a bad sort.* **4. sorts.** one of the characters in a font of type. —*v.t.* **1.** to place, arrange, or separate according to class or type: *to sort mail, to sort socks by color.* **2.** to separate from others (often with *out*): *Sort out the magazines you want to keep and throw the others away.* —*v.i. Archaic.* to be alike; agree; harmonize. [Old French *sorte* manner, kind, from Medieval Latin *sors,* from Latin *sors* lot, condition, destiny.] —**sort′er,** *n.*
• **of sorts. a.** of a poor or mediocre kind or quality: *a musician of sorts.* **b.** of different or various kinds.
• **out of sorts. a.** ill-tempered; cross. **b.** slightly ill.
• **sort of.** *Informal.* to some extent; somewhat: *to act sort of strange.*
sor·tie (sôr′tē, sôr tē′) *n.* **1.** a sudden attack by troops who are surrounded or besieged; sally. **2.** a single round trip of an aircraft on a combat mission. [French *sortie* a going out, departure, from *sortir* to go out; of uncertain origin.]
so·rus (sôr′əs) *n., pl.* **so·ri** (sôr′ī). a dotlike cluster of sporangia usually on the underside of the frond of a fern. [Modern Latin *sorus,* from Greek *sōros* heap.]
SOS (es′ō′es′) **1.** a radio signal of distress, used esp. by ships and airplanes. In the international code used in telegraphy, it is represented by (. . . --- . . .). **2.** any call or signal for help.
so-so (sō′sō′) *adj.* neither very good nor very bad; mediocre: *Skiing conditions were only so-so after the rain.* —*adv.* in a mediocre manner; passably.
sos·te·nu·to (sos′tə nü′tō) *Music. adj.* with the time value of the tones sustained or prolonged. —*n., pl.* **-tos** or **-ti** (-tē). a movement or passage performed in this manner. —*adv.* in a

sostenuto manner. [Italian *sostenuto,* past participle of *sostenere* to maintain, uphold, from Latin *sustinēre.*]
sot (sot) *n.* a person who habitually drinks to excess; chronic drunkard. [Old English *sott* fool, from Medieval Latin *sottus* stupid.]
sot·tish (sot′ish) *adj.* **1.** stupefied from or as from excessive drinking; stupid. **2.** given to excessive drinking; drunken. —**sot′tish·ly,** *adv.* —**sot′tish·ness,** *n.*
sot·to vo·ce (sot′ō vō′chē) in a low tone of voice, esp. so as not to be overheard. [Italian *sotto voce* literally, under the voice, from Latin *subtus* below + *vōx* sound¹, tone, voice.]
sou (sü) *n.* a former French coin of little value. [French *sou,* going back to Late Latin *solidus* ancient Roman gold coin. See SOLIDUS.]
sou·bise (sü bēz′) *n.* a white or brown sauce containing onions. [From Prince Charles *Soubise,* 1715-87, French general.]
sou·brette (sü bret′) *n.* **1.** in light opera or comedy, the role of a pert, scheming lady's maid or of any coquettish young woman. **2.** a singer or actress playing such a part. [French *soubrette,* from Provençal *soubreto,* feminine of *soubret* affected, from *soubra* to pass over, exceed, from Latin *superāre* to surpass.]
sou·bri·quet (sō′bri kā′, -ket′, sō′bri kā′, -ket′) sobriquet.
sou·chong (sü′shong′, -chong′) *n.* a variety of black tea, originally from China. [Chinese (Mandarin) *hsiao chung* small kind.]
souf·flé (sü flā′) *n.* a baked dish made with egg yolks, white sauce, and other ingredients, such as cheese or chocolate, made light and fluffy by adding beaten egg whites before baking. —*adj.* made light and fluffy in cooking. [French *soufflé,* from *souffler* to blow, from Latin *sufflāre* to blow up, puff out.]
sough (sou, suf) *v.i.* to make a rushing, rustling, or sighing sound: *The wind soughed through the branches overhead.* —*n.* a rushing, rustling, or sighing sound. [Old English *swōgan* to sound¹.]
sought (sôt) the past tense and past participle of **seek.**
soul (sōl) *n.* **1.** the nonphysical aspect of human life including thought, emotion, and will and regarded as distinct from the body; spiritual part of human beings. **2.** *Theology.* the moral or spiritual part of a person that is believed to be immortal and to separate from the body at death. **3.** the spirit of a dead person, thought of as having an existence of its own. **4.** the emotional part of human nature, as distinguished from the intellect. **5.** spiritual or emotional warmth or energy: *a clever novel that lacks soul.* **6.** the most essential, fundamental, or animating part; vital element: *Discipline is the soul of an army.* **7.** a person who leads or inspires: *Churchill was the soul of British resistance to Germany in World War II.* **8.** a person considered to embody a certain quality; personification: *She is the soul of integrity.* **9.** person: *I didn't see a soul on my walk.* **10.** a feeling of ethnic pride among American blacks. **11.** a deeply felt and strongly conveyed emotion, esp. of a performer or artist. —*adj. Informal.* relating to, characteristic of, or derived from American blacks or black culture. [Old English *sāwol* principle of life in the human being, spiritual part of people, disembodied spirit of a dead person.]
soul food, food traditionally eaten by American blacks, esp. in the South, such as chitterlings, pigs' knuckles, corn bread, and turnip greens.
soul·ful (sōl′fəl) *adj.* full of or expressing deep feeling: *a soulful gaze, soulful poetry.* —**soul′ful·ly,** *adv.* —**soul′ful·ness,** *n.*
soul·less (sōl′lis) *adj.* having no soul; lacking deep feelings; insensitive. —**soul′less·ly,** *adv.* —**soul′less·ness,** *n.*
soul music, a popular music developed by American blacks, fusing gospel music with rhythm and blues and elements of jazz, and thought of as authentic in expressing emotions, esp. passion.
soul-search·ing (sōl′sûr′ching) *n.* a deep and serious examination of one's own beliefs, motives, and values.
sound¹ (sound) *n.* **1.** vibrations that are transmitted through air, water, or another medium and produce sensation in the ear. **2.** a sensation produced in the organs of hearing by such vibrations. **3.** a particular instance of this sensation; something that is heard: *the sound of music.* **4.** the distance over which a sound may be heard: *We were within sound of the cannon.* **5.** one of the noises made by the vocal organs: *a consonant sound.* **6.** the mental effect produced by what is heard or read; implication: *The patient didn't*

a	at	e	end	o	hot	u	up	hw	white		about
ā	ape	ē	me	ō	old	ū	use	ng	song		taken
ä	far	i	it	ô	fork	ü	rule	th	thin	ə	pencil
âr	care	ī	ice	oi	oil	u̇	pull	th	this		lemon
		îr	pierce	ou	out	ûr	turn	zh	measure		circus

like the sound of the doctor's report. **7.** meaningless noise. —*v.i.* **1.** to make or give forth a sound: *The bell sounded from the tower.* **2.** to convey a certain impression; seem: *Your explanation sounds reasonable.* —*v.t.* **1.** to cause to make a sound: *The driver sounded the horn.* **2.** to give an order or signal for by a sound; announce by a sound: *to sound a retreat, to sound a warning.* **3.** to make known; proclaim: *Each speaker sounded the praises of the party's candidate.* **4.** to utter audibly; pronounce: *to sound a syllable.* **5.** to examine by causing to give forth sounds; auscultate: *The doctor sounded the patient's chest for signs of pneumonia.* [Old French *son* sensation produced on the organ of hearing by vibrations, from Latin *sonus* noise.] —**sound′a·ble,** *adj.*
·**to sound off.** *Informal.* **a.** to call out one's name or serial number in a military formation. **b.** to speak in a loud, annoying way, as to boast or complain: *She was tired of hearing him sound off about the mayor's policies.*

sound² (sound) *adj.* **1.** free from damage, defect, or decay: *a house with a sound foundation.* **2.** free from injury or illness; healthy: *a sound mind in a sound body.* **3.** stable or safe; secure; reliable: *a sound investment.* **4.** in accordance with truth, fact, or reason; sensible: *sound reasoning.* **5.** legally valid. **6.** morally good; honest; upright: *a person of sound character.* **7.** compatible with an established or accepted point of view; conservative; orthodox: *sound doctrine.* **8.** thorough; forceful; complete: *a sound thrashing.* **9.** (of sleep) deep and unbroken. —*adv.* in a sound manner: *sound asleep.* [Old English *(ge)sund* healthy, unhurt.] —**sound′ly,** *adv.* —**sound′ness,** *n.*

sound³ (sound) *v.t.* **1.** to measure the depth of (water), as by letting down a calibrated line with a weight on the end or by echoing sound off the bottom. **2.** to measure (depth) in this way, esp. at sea. **3.** to explore or examine (the bottom of the sea or another body of water) by means of a line adapted to bring up adhering particles of matter. **4.** to seek to determine or ascertain; investigate; examine: *to sound a person's opinions on an issue.* **5.** to try to learn the opinions and attitudes of (usually with *out*): *The president sounded out the other members of the club about the proposal.* —*v.i.* **1.** to measure the depth of water or of a body of water. **2.** (of a whale or fish) to go deep under water; dive swiftly downward. **3.** to make an inquiry or investigation, esp. by indirect methods. [Old French *sonder* to try, test, search the depth of, going back to Latin *sub* under + *unda* wave.]

sound⁴ (sound) *n.* **1.** a relatively long, narrow passage of water between larger bodies of water or between the mainland and an island. **2.** a long inlet or arm of the sea. **3.** the air bladder of a fish. [Old English *sund* swimming, strait (that one can swim across).]

sound barrier, a sudden sharp increase in resistance that the air presents to an aircraft as its speed nears the speed of sound. Also, **sonic barrier.**

sound·board (sound′bôrd′) *n.* sounding board *(def. 1).*

sound box *also,* **sound·box** (sound′boks′). a hollow chamber in a stringed musical instrument, such as a violin or acoustical guitar, in which the sound resonates. For illustration, see **violin.**

sound effects, artificially produced sounds, as of rain or hoofbeats, used to imitate the sounds called for in a play, motion picture, or radio or television program.

sound·er¹ (soun′dər) *n.* **1.** a person or thing that makes a sound. **2.** a device in a telegraph that converts electromagnetic code impulses into sound. [SOUND¹ + -ER¹.]

sound·er² (soun′dər) *n.* a person or thing that measures the depth of water. [SOUND³ + -ER¹.]

sound·ing¹ (soun′ding) *adj.* **1.** causing or making a sound. **2.** giving forth a deep, full sound; resounding; resonant. **3.** having an imposing sound but little significance; high-sounding. [SOUND¹ + -ING².]

sound·ing² (soun′ding) *n.* **1.** the act or process of measuring the depth of water, as by letting down a weighted line. **2.** *also,* **soundings.** the depth of water so measured. **3.** **soundings.** a place where the water is shallow enough to allow a sounding line to reach bottom. **4.** an investigation of conditions in space or in the atmosphere at a given altitude, esp. with a rocket. **5.** an examination, investigation, or sampling, as of public opinion. [SOUND³ + -ING¹.]

sounding board 1. a thin, resonant board of wood in a musical instrument, such as a piano or violin, for increasing the fullness and richness of its tone. Also, **soundboard. 2.** a structure suspended behind or over a stage, platform, pulpit, or the like to reflect sound toward the audience. **3.** a means of spreading or publicizing ideas or opinions: *a newspaper column that is a sounding board for the editor.* **4.** a person or group on whom one tests one's opinions, ideas, or plans: *The executive used the secretary as a sounding board.*

sounding lead (led) a lead or other weight at the end of a sounding line.

sounding line, a line weighted at one end and marked at intervals of a fathom, used in determining the depth of water. Also, **lead line.**

sound·less¹ (sound′lis) *adj.* having or making no sound; silent. [SOUND¹ + -LESS.] —**sound′less·ly,** *adv.* —**sound′less·ness,** *n.*

sound·less² (sound′lis) *adj.* too deep to be sounded; unfathomable: *the soundless depths of the ocean.* [SOUND³ + -LESS.] —**sound′less·ly,** *adv.* —**sound′less·ness,** *n.*

sound·proof (sound′prüf′) *adj.* not letting sound pass in or out; deadening or absorbing sound: *a soundproof room.* —*v.t.* to make soundproof: *to soundproof a building.*

sound·track (sound′trak′) *also,* **sound track. 1.** a narrow strip along the edge of a motion-picture film that carries the sound recording. **2.** a recording of the musical score of a play or motion picture.

sound truck, a truck carrying one or more loudspeakers, used for broadcasting public announcements, such as political speeches.

sound wave, a longitudinal pressure wave in a material medium, such as air or water, esp. one that is audible to the human ear.

soup (süp) *n.* **1.** a liquid food, usually made by cooking meat, fish, vegetables, or other ingredients in water, broth, milk, or the like. **2.** *Slang.* thick fog. [French *soupe* sop, broth; of Germanic origin.]
·**in the soup.** *Slang.* in trouble or difficulty.
·**to soup up.** *Slang.* to increase the power or capacity for speed of (a motor, engine, or motor vehicle).

soup·çon (süp sôN′, süp′sôN′) *n.* a slight trace or flavor; minute quantity: *Add a soupçon of salt to the sauce.* [French *soupçon* suspicion, hint, going back to Late Latin *suspectio* awe, suspicion, from Latin *suspicere* to regard with awe, mistrust.]

soup kitchen, a place that serves food free or at very low cost to needy people.

soup·spoon (süp′spün) *n.* a spoon used in eating soup, somewhat larger than a teaspoon.

soup·y (sü′pē) *adj.,* **soup·i·er, soup·i·est.** having the consistency or appearance of soup; thick and liquid.

sour (sour, sou′ər) *adj.* **1.** having a sharp, acid taste, as lemon or lime juice. **2.** having an acid taste because of fermentation; fermented: *sour milk.* **3.** having a foul odor, as of decay: *sour breath.* **4.a.** distasteful or disagreeable; unpleasant. **b.** having or showing an irritable or sullen nature; bad-tempered; peevish: *a sour expression.* **5.a.** below the desired or usual standard or quality; poor: *Their business turned sour during the recession.* **b.** *Music.* off pitch, esp. in a noticeable way: *The inexperienced trumpeter played several sour notes.* **6.** (of soil) containing excessive acid and damaging to crops. **7.** (of crude oil or natural gas) containing excessive sulfur. —*n.* **1.** something sour. **2.** a cocktail made with lemon or lime juice: *a whiskey sour.* —*v.i., v.t.* **1.** to become or make sour: *The milk soured in the hot sun. Lack of refrigeration soured the cream.* **2.** to make or become bad-tempered, disillusioned, or bitter: *Her attitude toward the project soured after her suggestion was ignored. The rejection soured him on romance.* [Old English *sūr* having a tart or acid taste, fermented.] —**sour′ly,** *adv.* —**sour′ness,** *n.*

sour·ball (sour′bôl′, sou′ər-) *n.* a hard, round piece of candy with a mildly sour taste.

source (sôrs) *n.* **1.** a spring, lake, or other body of water that is the point of origin of a river or stream. **2.** a place or thing from which something comes, develops, or derives: *The dam is a source of electrical power.* **3.** a person or thing that supplies information or evidence: *That almanac is a reliable source.* [Old French *sourse* point of origin of a river or stream, from *sourdre* to rise, going back to Latin *surgere*.] —For Synonyms, see **origin.**

sour cherry 1. a small cherry tree, *Prunus cerasus,* having gray bark, stiff, pointed leaves, and clusters of small white flowers. **2.** the tart, red fruit of this tree, used as in baking.

sour cream, thick cream made sour by the natural action of lactic acid bacteria or by artificial processes, used in cooking and as an ingredient in dips, salads, and other dishes.

sour·dough (sour′dō′, sou′ər-) *n.* **1.** fermented dough used as leaven in making bread. **2.** a prospector or pioneer in western Canada or Alaska, esp. in the Yukon.

sour grapes, an attitude of scorn or disparagement toward something because one cannot have it. [From the fable by Aesop, 620?-560 B.C., about a fox that calls some grapes sour because he is unable to reach them.]

sour gum, a tree, *Nyssa sylvatica,* of eastern North America, having close-grained wood and blue-black fruit.

sour·ish (sour′ish, sou′ər-) *adj.* somewhat sour.

sour mash, grain mash used in distilling some whiskeys, consisting of a mixture of new mash with some mash from a previous distillation.

sour·puss (sour′pus′, sou′ər-) *n. Slang.* a person who has a gloomy or disagreeable expression or disposition; grouch.

sour·sop (sour′sop′, sou′ər-) *n.* **1.** a small evergreen tree, *Annona muricata,* of tropical America, belonging to the same family as the custard apple. **2.** the juicy, edible fruit of this tree, having a greenish skin and a slightly acid pulp.

sour·wood (sour′wûd′, sou′ər-) *n.* sorrel tree.

sou·sa·phone (sü′zə fōn′) *n.* a large circular tuba with a wide flaring bell that faces forward, used chiefly in marching bands. [From John Philip *Sousa,* 1854-1932, American musical composer and bandmaster.]

souse (sous) *v.,* **soused, sous·ing.** —*v.t.* **1.** to plunge into water or other liquid; immerse. **2.** to make soaking wet; drench. **3.** to steep or soak in vinegar or brine; pickle. **4.** *Slang.* to make drunk; intoxicate. —*v.i.* **1.** to be or become immersed or soaked in water or other liquid. **2.** to become drunk. —*n.* **1.a.** a pickled food, esp. the feet, ears, and head of a pig. **b.** a liquid used in pickling; brine. **2.** the act of plunging into water or another liquid. **3.** *Slang.* a drunkard. [Old French *sous* something pickled; of Germanic origin.]

sou·tache (sü tash′) *n.* a narrow, flat cloth braid, used for trimming and decoration. [French *soutache* galloon, from Hungarian *sujtás.*]

sou·tane (sü tän′, -tan′) *n.* a cassock worn by priests of the Roman Catholic Church. [French *soutane,* from Italian *sottana* literally, undergarment (because worn under vestments), from *sotto* under, from Latin *subtus* beneath.]

south (south) *n.* **1.** the general direction to one's left as one faces the sunset. **2.** one of the four cardinal points of the compass, lying directly opposite north and at 180 degrees. **3.** *also,* **South.** any region situated toward this direction in relation to a specified point of reference. —*adj.* **1.** toward or in the south; southern: *on the south side of the street.* **2.** coming from the south: *a south wind.* —*adv.* toward the south: *Many birds fly south in the winter.* [Old English *sūth* in the direction opposite to the north.]

South African **1.** of or relating to southern Africa. **2.** of or relating to the Republic of South Africa. **3.** a person who was born in or is a citizen of the Republic of South Africa.

south·bound (south′bound′) *adj.* going southward: *a southbound train.*

South·down (south′doun′) *n.* one of a breed of small, hornless sheep of English origin, having short wool and raised esp. for food. [From the *South Downs,* a range of low grassy hills in southeastern England, where the breed was developed.]

south·east (south′ēst′; *Nautical* sou′ēst′) *n.* **1.** the direction halfway between south and east. **2.** the point of the compass indicating this direction. **3.** *also,* **Southeast.** any region situated toward this direction in relation to a specified point of reference. —*adj.* **1.** toward or in the southeast; southeastern. **2.** from the southeast: *a southeast wind.* —*adv.* toward the southeast.

south·east·er (south′ēs′tər; *Nautical* sou′ēs′tər) *n.* a storm or heavy wind from the southeast.

south·east·er·ly (south′ēs′tər lē; *Nautical* sou′ēs′tər lē) *adj., adv.* toward or from the southeast.

south·east·ern (south′ēs′tərn; *Nautical* sou′ēs′tərn) *adj.* **1.** toward or in the southeast. **2.** *also,* **Southeastern.** of, relating to, or characteristic of the southeast or Southeast. **3.** from the southeast: *a southeastern wind.*

south·east·ward (south′ēst′wərd; *Nautical* sou′ēst′wərd) *adv. also,* **south·east·wards.** toward the southeast. —*adj.* toward or in the southeast. —*n.* a southeastern direction, point, or place.

south·east·ward·ly (south′ēst′wərd lē; *Nautical* sou′ēst′wərd lē) *adj., adv.* toward or from the southeast.

south·er (sou′thər) *n.* a strong wind or storm from the south.

south·er·ly (suth′ər lē) *adj., adv.* **1.** toward the south: *a southerly direction, to travel southerly.* **2.** from the south: *a southerly breeze.* —*n., pl.* **-lies.** a wind blowing from the south.

south·ern (suth′ərn) *adj.* **1.** toward or in the south: *a room with a southern exposure.* **2.** *also,* **Southern.** of, relating to, or characteristic of the south or South. **3.** from the south: *a southern wind.* [Old English *sūtherne* from the south, relating to the south.]

Southern Cross, a constellation visible in the Southern Hemisphere, having four bright stars in the form of a cross. Also, **Crux.**

south·ern·er (suth′ər nər) *n.* **1.** a person who was born or lives in the south. **2.** *usually,* **Southerner.** a person who was born or lives in the South of the United States.

Southern Hemisphere, the half of the earth south of the equator.

southern lights, aurora australis.

south·ern·most (suth′ərn mōst′) *adj.* farthest south.

south·land (south′lənd, -land′) *also,* **Southland.** *n.* land in the south, such as the southern region of a country.

south·paw (south′pô′) *Informal. n.* **1.** *Sports.* a player who is left-handed, esp. a left-handed baseball pitcher. **2.** any left-handed person. —*adj.* left-handed. [Presumably coined by humorist Finley Peter Dunne in the 1880s, when he was a Chicago sports journalist and the Chicago baseball field was oriented with home plate to the west, so that the pitcher's left arm was toward the south.]

South Pole **1.** the southernmost point on the earth; southern end of the earth's axis. **2.** **south pole.** the pole of a magnet that points to the south when the magnet swings freely.

south-south·east (south′south′ēst′; *Nautical* sou′sou′ēst′) *n.* the point of the compass halfway between south and southeast. —*adj., adv.* toward the south-southeast.

south-south·west (south′south′west′; *Nautical* sou′sou′west′) *n.* the point of the compass halfway between south and southwest. —*adj., adv.* toward the south-southwest.

south·ward (south′wərd; *Nautical* suth′ərd) *adv. also,* **southwards.** toward the south: *to travel southward.* —*adj.* toward or in the south. —*n.* a southern direction, point, or place: *The river flows to the southward.*

south·west (south′west′; *Nautical* sou′west′) *n.* **1.** the direction halfway between south and west. **2.** the point of the compass indicating this direction. **3.** *also,* **Southwest.** any region situated toward this direction in relation to a specified point of reference. —*adj.* **1.** toward or in the southwest; southwestern. **2.** from the southwest: *a southwest wind.* —*adv.* toward the southwest: *to sail southwest.*

south·west·er (south′wes′tər; *Nautical* sou′wes′tər) *also,* **sou′wester.** *n.* **1.** a storm or heavy wind from the southwest. **2.** a waterproof hat with a broad brim that widens in the back to protect the neck in stormy weather, worn esp. by sailors.

south·west·er·ly (south′wes′tər lē; *Nautical* sou′wes′tər lē) *adj., adv.* toward or from the southwest.

south·west·ern (south′wes′tərn; *Nautical* sou′wes′tərn) *adj.* **1.** toward or in the southwest. **2.** *also,* **Southwestern.** of, relating to, or characteristic of the southwest or Southwest. **3.** from the southwest: *a southwest wind.*

southwester
(def. 2)

south·west·ward (south′west′wərd; *Nautical* sou′west′wərd) *adv. also,* **south·west·wards.** toward the southwest. —*adj.* toward or in the southwest. —*n.* a southwestern direction, point, or place.

south·west·ward·ly (south′west′wərd lē; *Nautical* sou′west′wərd lē) *adj., adv.* toward or from the southwest.

sou·ve·nir (sü′və nîr′, sü′və nîr′) *n.* something kept as a reminder of a person, place, or event; keepsake; memento: *to save a ticket stub from the circus as a souvenir.* [French *souvenir,* from *souvenir* to remember, from Latin *subvenīre* to come up, come to mind.] —For Synonyms, see **keepsake.**

sou·vla·ki (sü vlä′kē) *n.* a Greek dish consisting of lamb that has been broiled on a skewer. Also, **sou·vla·ki·a** (sü vlä′kē ə). [Modern Greek *souvlákia* a little spit², from *souvla* a skewer.]

sou′west·er (sou′wes′tər) southwester.

sov·er·eign (sov′rən, sov′ər ən) *n.* **1.** the supreme ruler of a monarchy, such as a king or queen. **2.** an individual or group having supreme authority. **3.** a former British gold coin worth one pound. —*adj.* **1.** having supreme power, rank, or authority: *a sovereign ruler.* **2.** not controlled by others; having independent authority: *a sovereign state.* **3.** superior to all others; supreme: *a sovereign right.* **4.** effective or powerful, as a cure or remedy. [Old French *soverain* supreme ruler, supreme, going back to Latin *super* above.] —**sov′er·eign·ly,** *adv.*

sov·er·eign·ty (sov′rən tē, sov′ər ən-) *n., pl.* **-ties.** **1.** supreme authority: *The king or queen holds sovereignty in a monarchy.* **2.** independence from the political control of other states; power of self-government. **3.** a state, community, or other political unit that is sovereign. **4.** the rank, dominion, or authority of a sovereign.

so·vi·et (sō′vē et′, -it, sov′ē-) *n.* **1.** in the Soviet Union, the basic legislative and executive unit at all levels of government. **2.** **Soviets.** the government officials or people of the Soviet Union. —*adj.* **1.** of or relating to a soviet or government by soviets. **2.** **Soviet.** of or relating to the Soviet Union. [Russian *sovet* council.]

a	at	e	end	o	hot	u	up	hw	white		about
ā	ape	ē	me	ō	old	ū	use	ng	song		taken
ä	far	i	it	ô	fork	ü	rule	th	thin	ə	pencil
âr	care	ī	ice	oi	oil	u̇	pull	th	this		lemon
		îr	pierce	ou	out	ûr	turn	zh	measure		circus

so·vi·et·ism (sō′vē i tiz′əm, sŏv′ē-) *n.* a system of government by soviets.
so·vi·et·ize (sō′vē i tīz′, sŏv′ē-) *v.t.,* **-ized, -iz·ing.** to change to a soviet system of government. —**so′vi·et·i·za′tion,** *n.*
sov·ran (sŏv′rən) *n., adj. Archaic.* sovereign.
sow[1] (sō) *v.,* **sowed, sown** (sōn) or **sowed, sow·ing.** —*v.t.*
1. to spread or scatter (seed) over the ground for growth: *to sow corn.* **2.** to spread or scatter seed on or upon (land): *to sow a field with corn.* **3.** to introduce, implant, or encourage: *to sow dissension, to sow suspicion.* **4.** to spread or cover with anything. —*v.i.* to spread or scatter seed over the ground for growth. [Old English *sāwan* to scatter seed over the ground for growth.] —**sow′er,** *n.*
sow[2] (sou) *n.* an adult female pig. [Old English *sugu.*]
sow bug (sou) wood louse *(def. 1).*
sow thistle (sou) any plant of the genus *Sonchus,* esp. *S. oleraceus,* a coarse, spiny weed with yellow flowers that is a common garden pest.
sox (soks) *pl. n. Informal.* socks.
soy (soi) *n.* **1.** soy sauce. **2.** soybean. [Japanese *shōyu* the sauce, from Chinese (Mandarin) *chiang yu.*]
soy·a (soi′ə) *n.* **1.** soybean. **2.** soy sauce. [Dutch *soja* this bean, from Japanese *shōyu.* See SOY.]
soy·bean (soi′bēn′) *n.* **1.** the seed of a bushy Asian plant, *Glycine max,* of the pea family, widely cultivated, esp. in the United States. It is rich in oil and protein, and is used for fodder and soil improvement. Oil and meal from the seeds are also used in making many food and chemical products. **2.** the plant itself. Also, **soy, soya.**
soy sauce, a salty, dark brown sauce made from soybeans fermented and steeped in brine, used esp. in Chinese and Japanese cooking. Also, **soy, soya.**
sp. 1. special. **2.** species. **3.** specific. **4.** specimen. **5.** spelling. **6.** spirit.
Sp. 1. Spain. **2.** Spanish.
SP, Shore Patrol.
spa (spä) *n.* **1.** a mineral spring. **2.** a place where such springs exist, esp. a resort. [From *Spa,* Belgian town famous as a resort with mineral springs.]
space (spās) *n.* **1.a.** an unlimited expanse extending in all directions that includes the entire universe, within which all material objects are contained and all events take place. **b.** the region beyond the earth's atmosphere; outer space: *to launch a rocket into space.* **2.** the distance or area between or within points or objects: *a space between buildings.* **3.** a particular area set apart or available for some purpose: *a parking space, to need more shelf space.* **4.** a particular extent of time: *the space of an hour.* **5.** reserved or available accommodations on a train, bus, airplane, or other means of transportation. **6.** an area or time available for or used by advertising, as in a magazine or newspaper or on a television or radio program. **7.** any blank or empty place, as between lines in a book. **8.** *Printing.* a small, blank piece of type metal used to separate words or characters. **9.** *Music.* one of the degrees or intervals between the lines of the staff. **10.** an interval during the transmission of a telegraph message when the key is open or not in contact. **11.** *Mathematics.* a set of points or elements among which a metrical or other relationship exists or that can be represented in a coordinate system by real numbers. **12.** *Informal.* freedom or privacy to follow one's own interests, goals, or needs: *My friend always knows when to give me space.* —*adj.* of, relating to, or for use in outer space, esp. as a field of exploration: *space research, space food.* —*v.t.,* **spaced, spac·ing. 1.** to arrange with spaces in between; separate by spaces: *The builder spaced the houses far apart.* **2.** to divide into spaces. [Old French *espace* extent of place or time, from Latin *spatium* room, extent, interval.] —**spac′er,** *n.*
space capsule, capsule *(def. 2).*
space charge *Physics.* an electrical charge arising from a collection of electrons occupying a particular volume of empty space, as the vicinity of a heated cathode.
space·craft (spās′kraft′) *n., pl.* **-craft.** any vehicle, occupied or unoccupied, designed to be orbited around the earth or launched into outer space. Also, **spaceship.**
spaced-out (spāst′out′) *adj. Slang.* **1.** having or showing a lack of awareness of one's surroundings; dazed or stupefied by or as if by drugs: *a spaced-out addict, a spaced-out look.* **2.** unconventional; eccentric: *a spaced-out wardrobe.* Also, **spaced.**
space·flight (spās′flīt′) *n.* the act or an instance of traveling into or in outer space.
space heater, a small heating unit, often portable, for warming an enclosed area, such as a room or tent.
space·less (spās′lis) *adj.* **1.** having no limits in space; infinite; boundless. **2.** occupying no space.
space·man (spās′man′, -mən) *n., pl.* **-men** (-men′, -mən). astronaut.

space medicine, the branch of medicine that deals with the medical, physiological, and psychological problems encountered in spaceflight.
space platform, space station.
space·port (spās′pôrt′) *n.* an installation at which spacecraft are tested, launched, or maintained.
space probe, an artificial satellite or other spacecraft equipped with instruments designed to obtain and record information about outer space.
space·ship (spās′ship′) *n.* spacecraft.
space shuttle, a reusable spacecraft, used to carry astronauts and equipment, that is launched into orbit like a rocket but lands like an airplane when returning to earth. Also, **shuttle.**
space station, an earth-orbiting satellite designed to support a crew, used for observation and experimentation and as a launch pad for further space travel. Also, **space platform.**
space·suit (spās′süt′) *n.* a pressurized suit that offers protection against low pressure and temperatures, for use in spaceflight.
space-time (spās′tīm′) *n.* a four-dimensional frame of reference within which any event may be precisely located. Three of these dimensions are the ordinary space coordinates, length, breadth, and thickness, and the fourth is time. Also, **space-time continuum.**
space·walk (spās′wôk′) *n.* an excursion by an astronaut who, in the weightlessness of spaceflight, exits the spacecraft, as to repair or assemble something while in orbit.

space shuttle blasting off

space writer, a journalist or other writer who is paid according to the amount of space in print filled by his or her writing.
spac·ing (spā′sing) *n.* **1.** the act of a person or thing that spaces. **2.** an arrangement of spaces, as in printing: *open spacing, wide spacing.* **3.** a space or spaces, as between printed words.
spa·cious (spā′shəs) *adj.* **1.** having or providing much space; roomy: *a spacious house.* **2.** having a broad scope or range; of great extent; vast: *spacious skies.* [Latin *spatiōsus* roomy, of great extent, from *spatium* room, extent, interval.] —**spa′cious·ly,** *adv.* —**spa′cious·ness,** *n.*
Spack·le (spak′əl) *n. Trademark.* a plasterlike substance, in either paste or powder form, that hardens upon drying, used to fill holes or cracks in plaster or plasterboard, esp. before painting or papering. —*v.t.,* **-led, -ling.** to apply Spackle to (a wall, holes, or cracks).
spade[1] (spād) *n.* **1.** a tool used for digging, having a heavy, flat iron blade that can be pressed into the ground with the foot, and a long handle with a grip at the top. **2.** any of various tools or implements resembling a spade. —*v.t.* to dig or cut with a spade: *to spade a garden.* [Old English *spadu* tool for digging.] —**spad′er,** *n.*
 • **to call a spade a spade.** to call something by its right name; speak frankly and truthfully.
spade[2] (spād) *n.* **1.** a playing card marked with one or more black figures shaped like this: ♠ **2. spades.** the suit of such playing cards. [Italian *spada* sword, figure on a playing card, from Latin *spatha* broadsword, from Greek *spathē* broad blade.]
 • **in spades.** *Informal.* to a high or extreme degree; emphatically: *I expressed my opposition in spades.*
spade·work (spād′wûrk′) *n.* **1.** work done with a spade. **2.** preliminary work necessary to a project or activity.
spa·dix (spā′diks) *n., pl.* **spa·di·ces** (spā dī′sēz, spā′də sēz′). a thick or fleshy spike of tiny flowers, usually enclosed in a spathe, as in the calla. [Latin *spādix* palm branch broken off, from Greek *spādix.*]
spa·ghet·ti (spə get′ē) *n.* a food consisting of a mixture of wheat flour and water shaped into long strings, thinner than macaroni and not hollow. It is cooked by boiling and is usually served

with a sauce. [Italian *spaghetti,* plural of *spaghetto* string, diminutive of *spago* string, cord; of uncertain origin.]

spake (spāk) *Archaic.* a past tense of **speak.**

span[1] (span) *n.* **1.** the distance from the tip of the thumb to the tip of the little finger when the hand is fully spread out, considered as 9 inches (23 centimeters) when used as a unit of measure. **2.** the full extent, amount, or reach of anything: *the span of a person's life, a short attention span.* **3.a.** the distance between two supports, as of an arch, beam, or bridge. For illustration, see **arch**[1]. **b.** a part or section between two supports. **4.** the distance between the wing tips of an airplane; wingspan. **5.** a short space of time. —*v.t.,* **spanned, span·ning. 1.** to measure by or as by the hand with the thumb and little finger extended. **2.** to encircle or encompass with a hand or hands, as the waist or wrist. **3.** to extend over or across: *That highway spans the state.* **4.** to provide with something that extends over or across: *to span a river with a bridge.* [Old English *span(n)* such a distance measured from the thumb.]

span[2] (span) *n.* a pair of mules or other draft animals driven together in harness. [Dutch *span.*]

span[3] (span) *Archaic.* a past tense of **spin.**

Span., Spanish.

span·drel (span′drəl) *n.* **1.** the triangular space between the outer

spandrels

curve of an arch and the rectangular framework surrounding it. **2.** the space between two adjoining arches and the horizontal molding or cornice running above them. [Diminutive of Anglo-Norman *spaundre,* from Old French *espandre* to spread out, expand, from Latin *expandere.*]

span·gle (spang′gəl) *n.* **1.** a small, thin, often circular piece of glittering metal or plastic used for decoration, esp. on clothing. **2.** any small glittering object. —*v.,* **-gled, -gling.** —*v.t.* to decorate with or as with spangles; cause to glitter. —*v.i.* to sparkle with or as with spangles; glitter. [Diminutive of obsolete *spang* small glittering ornament, from Middle Dutch *spange* clasp, buckle.]

Span·iard (span′yərd) *n.* **1.** a native or citizen of Spain. **2.** a person of Spanish ancestry.

span·iel (span′yəl) *n.* a small or medium-sized dog of any of various breeds, such as the cocker spaniel or water spaniel, usually having long, drooping ears and a silky, wavy coat. [Old French *espaignol* literally, Spanish, from Spanish *español* Spanish, from *España* Spain, from Latin *Hispānia.*]

Span·ish (span′ish) *adj.* of, relating to, or characteristic of Spain or its people, language, or culture. —*n.* **1.** the people of Spain collectively. **2.** a Romance language spoken in Spain and Spanish America.

Span·ish-A·mer·i·can (span′ish ə mer′i kən) *adj.* **1.** of or relating to Spain and America or to Spain and the United States. **2.** of, relating to, or characteristic of Spanish America or its people or culture. —*n.* **1.** a native or resident of Spanish America. **2.** a resident of the United States who is of Spanish or Spanish-American descent.

Spanish-American War, the war between the United States and Spain in 1898.

Spanish Armada, a fleet sent to invade England in 1588 by Philip II of Spain. It was defeated by the English and later mostly destroyed by storms. Also, **the Armada.**

Spanish bayonet, any of several tall, treelike species of yucca, esp. *Yucca aloifolia,* native to the southern United States, Mexico, and the West Indies, bearing stiff, sword-shaped leaves and large, showy flowers.

Spanish fly 1. a bright green blister beetle, *Cantharis vesicatoria,* native to southern Europe. **2.** a poisonous substance prepared from these beetles, formerly used to treat a variety of diseases and as an aphrodisiac.

Spanish Inquisition, the form of the Inquisition practiced in Spain from 1478 to 1820, notorious for its cruelty.

Spanish mackerel, any of several edible saltwater fish of the genus *Scomberomorus,* esp. *S. maculatus,* a commercially important species found in warm Atlantic waters.

Spanish moss, a grayish green epiphyte, *Tillandsia usneoides,* that grows in long, slender, hanging strands on the branches of certain trees in the southern United States and tropical America.

Spanish onion, a large onion with a mild flavor.

spank (spangk) *v.t.* to strike with the open hand or a flat object, esp. on the buttocks, as punishment. —*n.* a blow with the open hand or a flat object. [Possibly imitative.]

spank·er (spang′kər) *n.* **1.** a fore-and-aft sail, attached to a gaff and boom, on the mast nearest the stern of a square-rigged ship. **2.** the

Spanish moss

mast nearest the stern in a ship having four or more masts.

spank·ing[1] (spang′king) *n.* a series of slaps with the open hand or a flat object, given as punishment to a child.

spank·ing[2] (spang′king) *adj.* **1.** *Informal.* exceptional of its kind; very large, great, or fine. **2.** (of a breeze) brisk and fresh. **3.** moving with or characterized by a quick, vigorous pace: *a spanking trot.* —*adv. Informal.* completely or strikingly; very: *a spanking new car.* [Of uncertain origin.]

span·ner (span′ər) *n.* **1.** a person or thing that spans. **2.** *British.* wrench.

span·worm (span′wûrm′) *n.* inchworm.

spar[1] (spär) *n.* **1.** a pole, such as a yard, gaff, or boom, supporting or extending the rigging of a ship or boat. **2.** one of the principal lateral members of the framework of an airplane wing. —*v.t.,* **sparred, spar·ring.** to furnish (a ship) with spars. [Possibly from Old Norse *sperra* beam, rafter.]

spar[2] (spär) *v.i.,* **sparred, spar·ring. 1.** to box, esp. for practice. **2.** to argue or dispute cautiously or in a restrained way, as if to test one's opponent. **3.** (of a gamecock) to fight or strike with the feet or spurs. [Old English *sperran* to strike.]

spar[3] (spär) *n.* any of various crystalline, lustrous minerals that split easily into flakes or chips, such as fluorite or calcite. [Middle Low German *spar* gypsum.]

SPAR (spär) *also,* **Spar.** *n.* a member of the women's reserve of the U.S. Coast Guard. [Short for Latin *s(emper) par(ātus)* always ready (motto of the U.S. Coast Guard).]

spare (spâr) *v.,* **spared, spar·ing.** —*v.t.* **1.** to refrain from killing, destroying, or harming; show mercy to: *to spare a defeated enemy, to spare someone's life.* **2.** to deal with gently or leniently; show consideration for: *to spare a person's feelings.* **3.** to save or free (someone) from something unpleasant or burdensome: *Their call spared me much anxiety. Spare me the details of the accident.* **4.** to manage or do without; part with, esp. without inconvenience: *Can you spare a cup of sugar? Could you spare a few minutes to help me with this problem?* **5.** to use or dispense with restraint.

a	at	e	end	o	hot	u	up	hw	white		about
ā	ape	ē	me	ō	old	ū	use	ng	song		taken
ä	far	i	it	ô	fork	ü	rule	th	thin	ə	pencil
âr	care	ī	ice	oi	oil	ů	pull	th	this		lemon
		îr	pierce	ou	out	ûr	turn	zh	measure		circus

➡ used chiefly with a negative: *Give me some more meat, and don't spare the gravy.* —*v.i.* **1.** to refrain from inflicting harm or punishment; be merciful or forbearing. **2.** to use or practice economy; be frugal. —*adj.,* **spar·er, spar·est. 1.** in excess of what is needed; held in reserve: *a spare tire, a spare room, spare cash.* **2.** (of time) not taken up by usual or ordinary duties; free: *a few spare minutes.* **3.** not fat; thin; lean: *a spare figure.* **4.** containing or consisting of little; scanty; meager: *a spare meal, a spare diet.* —*n.* **1.** something extra or held in reserve, such as a spare tire. **2.** *Bowling.* **a.** the act or an instance of knocking down all the pins with two rolls of the ball in one frame. **b.** a score so made. [Old English *sparian* to leave unhurt, abstain from using.] —**spare′a·ble,** *adj.* —**spare′ly,** *adv.* —**spare′ness,** *n.* —**spar′er,** *n.*
• **to spare.** beyond what is needed; left over; in excess: *I finished the test with time to spare.*

spare·ribs (spâr′ribz′) *pl. n.* a cut of pork consisting of the thin end of the ribs with most of the meat trimmed off. [Inverted form of earlier *ribspare,* from Middle Low German *ribbespēr* rib cut, from *ribbe* rib + *spēr* spit².]

spar·ing (spâr′ing) *adj.* **1.** careful in spending or using; frugal: *to be sparing with one's savings.* **2.** small in amount, quantity, or extent; scanty; meager. **3.** merciful or forbearing. —**spar′ing·ly,** *adv.* —**spar′ing·ness,** *n.*

spark¹ (spärk) *n.* **1.** a small, hot, glowing particle, esp. one thrown off from something burning or produced by one hard object striking another, as steel against flint. **2.a.** a short, brilliant flash of light produced by a discharge of electricity through air or another insulating material. **b.** the discharge itself. **c.** the electrical discharge produced by a spark plug. **d.** the mechanism controlling such a discharge. **3.** any sparkle or flash of light. **4.** a vital or animating factor; motivating force: *The assassination was the spark that touched off the war.* **5.** a small amount of something active; trace: *a spark of interest.* **6.** a trace of life or vitality: *a personality with no spark.* —*v.i.* **1.** to throw off or produce sparks. **2.** to flash or fall as or like sparks. —*v.t.* to be the motivating force or reason for; stir to activity; incite: *The new tax sparked a revolt. The captain's enthusiasm sparked the team to victory.* [Old English *spearca* small particle of fire, small amount.]

spark² (spärk) *n.* **1.** a dashing, foppish young man. **2.** a beau, lover, or suitor. —*v.t., v.i. Informal.* to court; woo. [Possibly from Old Norse *sparkr* lively.]

spark arrester, a device that prevents sparks from escaping, such as a piece of mesh on top of a chimney.

spark coil, an induction coil used to produce an electric spark, as in an internal-combustion engine.

spark gap, an open space between two electrodes, as in a spark plug, through which a discharge of electricity may pass. Also, **gap.**

spar·kle (spär′kəl) *v.,* **-kled, -kling.** —*v.i.* **1.** to shine intermittently, as if giving off sparks; reflect or emit flashes of light: *The jewels sparkled. Her eyes sparkled with merriment.* **2.** to give off sparks. **3.** to be brilliant, lively, or vivacious: *His conversation sparkled with wit.* **4.** to bubble, as champagne or soda water; effervesce. —*v.t.* to cause to sparkle. —*n.* **1.** a sparkling appearance or quality: *the sparkle of clear blue ocean waters.* **2.** brilliance, liveliness, or vivacity. **3.** a small spark or glowing particle. [SPARK¹ + -LE.]

spar·kler (spär′klər) *n.* **1.** a person or thing that sparkles. **2.** a combustible device that burns slowly and throws off a brilliant shower of sparks. **3.** *Informal.* a gem that sparkles, esp. a diamond.

spar·kling (spär′kling) *adj.* **1.** giving off sparks: *sparkling coals.* **2.** reflecting or emitting light; shining or glittering: *a sparkling diamond.* **3.** brilliant or lively: *sparkling conversation.* **4.** bubbling; effervescent: *sparkling water.* —**spar′kling·ly,** *adv.*

sparkling wine, wine that is naturally carbonated by a second fermentation within the bottle, such as champagne.

spark plug 1. a device that is fitted into the cylinder of an internal-combustion engine and ignites the mixture of fuel and air by means of an electric spark. **2.** *Informal.* a person who activates, inspires, or leads some activity or undertaking: *The captain is the spark plug of the team.*

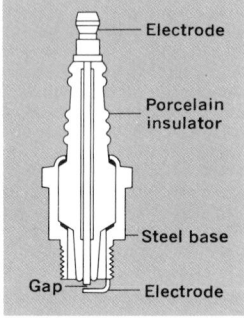

spark plug

Electrode
Porcelain insulator
Steel base
Gap — Electrode

sparring partner, a person with whom a boxer spars for practice.

spar·row (spar′ō) *n.* any of numerous small seed-eating birds, families Fringillidae, Prunellidae, and Ploceidae, having a stout, conical bill, a medium-length tail, and predominantly brown plumage with a white, gray, or buff underside, such as the house sparrow or song sparrow. Length: 5-7 inches (13-18 centimeters). [Old English *spearwa.*]

sparrow hawk 1. kestrel. **2.** a bird-eating hawk, *Accipiter nisus,* native to Europe and Asia. Length: 11-15 inches (28-38 centimeters).

sparse (spärs) *adj.,* **spars·er, spars·est.** thinly spread or distributed; not crowded or dense: *a sparse population, a desert with sparse vegetation.* [Latin *sparsus,* past participle of *spargere* to scatter.] —**sparse′ly,** *adv.* —**sparse′ness, spar′si·ty,** *n.*

Spar·tan (spär′tən) *adj.* **1.** of or relating to Sparta or its people or culture. **2.** resembling or characteristic of the people of Sparta as in being militaristic, stoical, highly disciplined, courageous, or austere. —*n.* **1.** a native or citizen of Sparta. **2.** a person who has Spartan characteristics. —**Spar′tan·ism,** *n.*

spasm (spaz′əm) *n.* **1.** a sudden, involuntary, often convulsive contraction of a muscle or group of muscles. **2.** any sudden, brief burst of energy, activity, or feeling: *a spasm of laughter, a spasm of fear.* [Latin *spasmus* convulsion, from Greek *spasmos,* from *spaein* to draw, tear.]

spas·mod·ic (spaz mod′ik) *adj.* **1.** relating to or characterized by a spasm or spasms: *a spasmodic disease.* **2.a.** resembling a spasm; sudden, violent, and temporary: *spasmodic anger.* **b.** happening irregularly; intermittent; fitful: *to make spasmodic attempts to break a bad habit.* **3.** highly emotional or excitable. [Modern Latin *spasmodicus,* from Greek *spasmōdēs* convulsive, from *spasmos* convulsion.] —**spas·mod′i·cal·ly,** *adv.*

spas·tic (spas′tik) *adj.* **1.** relating to, characterized by, or suffering from a spasm or spasms. **2.** suffering from spastic paralysis. —*n.* a person who suffers from spastic paralysis. [Latin *spasticus* afflicted with spasms, from Greek *spastikos* drawing in, from *span* to draw, pull.] —**spas′ti·cal·ly,** *adv.*

spastic paralysis, a form of paralysis, caused by damage to the central nervous system, in which the affected muscles are tense and somewhat rigid and the reflexes are abnormally active.

spat¹ (spat) *n.* **1.** a petty quarrel; slight argument. **2.** *Informal.* a slap. **3.** a slapping or splashing sound. —*v.,* **spat·ted, spat·ting.** —*v.i.* **1.** to engage in a petty quarrel. **2.** to strike with a slapping or splashing sound. —*v.t. Informal.* to slap. [Probably imitative.]

spat² (spat) a past tense and past participle of **spit¹.**

spat³ (spat) *n.* a short covering of cloth or leather worn over the instep of a shoe and the ankle, usually fastened under the shoe with a strap. [From earlier *spatterdash* a long legging, from SPATTER + DASH.]

spat⁴ (spat) *n.* **1.** the spawn of an oyster or similar shellfish. **2.a.** a young oyster. **b.** young oysters collectively. **c.** seed oyster. —*v.i.,* **spat·ted, spat·ting.** (of oysters) to spawn. [Of uncertain origin.]

spate (spāt) *n.* **1.** a sudden or strong outpouring, as of words or emotion: *The scandal produced a spate of proposals for reform.* **2.** *British.* **a.** a sudden flood. **b.** a sudden heavy fall of rain. [Of uncertain origin.]

spathe (spāth) *n.* a leaf or leaflike part, often large, enclosing a flower cluster or spadix, as in the calla. [Latin *spatha* broad, flat, wooden instrument, from Greek *spathē* broad blade.]

spa·tial (spā′shəl) *adj.* **1.** relating to space. **2.** existing or occurring in space. [Latin *spatium* room, extent + -AL¹.] —**spa·ti·al·i·ty** (spā′shē al′i tē), *n.* —**spa′tial·ly,** *adv.*

spa·ti·o·tem·po·ral (spā′shē ō tem′pər əl) *adj.* **1.** of, relating to, or existing in both space and time. **2.** of or relating to space-time.

spat·ter (spat′ər) *v.t.* **1.** to scatter in drops or small particles: *to spatter paint on a canvas.* **2.** to splash with drops or small particles, esp. so as to soil or stain: *The mud spattered their shoes.* **3.** to stain with slander or disgrace; defame. —*v.i.* **1.** to send out or throw off drops or small particles. **2.** to fall or strike in or as in a shower: *Bullets spattered around the target.* —*n.* **1.a.** the act or an instance of spattering. **b.** the sound made by this: *the spatter of raindrops on a roof.* **2.** a splash or spot of something spattered: *There were spatters of grease on the stove.* [Possibly imitative.]

spat·ter·dock (spat′ər dok′) *n.* any of a group of water plants, genus *Nuphar,* of the water lily family, found in stagnant waters of eastern North America and having globular yellow flowers.

spat·u·la (spach′ə lə) *n.* a small implement with a flat, flexible blade, used for spreading, stirring, or mixing thick, soft substances, such as paint, plaster, and foods, and for lifting or scraping, as in cooking. [Latin *spatula* broad piece, diminutive of

spatha broad, flat, wooden instrument for stirring, broadsword, from Greek *spathē* broad blade.]

spat·u·late (spach′ə lit, -lāt′) *adj.* shaped like a spatula or spoon: *a spatulate leaf.*

spav·in (spav′in) *n.* a disease of the hock joint of horses, causing stiffness and lameness. [Shortened from Old French *espavin;* of uncertain origin.] —**spav′ined,** *adj.*

spawn (spôn) *n.* **1.** the eggs of certain aquatic animals, such as fish, shellfish, or amphibians, deposited in masses. **2.** numerous offspring. **3.** something produced; product; result. **4.** the mycelium of fungi. —*v.i.* **1.** to deposit eggs or sperm into the water, as fish do. **2.** to produce; engender. —*v.t.* **1.** to produce (eggs or offspring). **2.** to bring forth or give rise to; engender: *The successful product spawned many imitators.* [Anglo-Norman *espaundre* to shed roe, going back to Latin *expandere* to spread out. Doublet of EXPAND.]

spay (spā) *v.t.* to remove the ovaries of (an animal), usually to prevent reproduction. [Anglo-Norman *espeier* to pierce with a sword, from Old French *espee* sword, from Latin *spatha.* See SPADE[2].]

SPCA, Society for the Prevention of Cruelty to Animals.

SPCC, Society for the Prevention of Cruelty to Children.

speak (spēk) *v.,* **spoke** or *(archaic)* **spake, spo·ken** or *(archaic)* **spoke, speak·ing.** —*v.i.* **1.** to utter words; talk: *to speak with a slight French accent.* **2.** to make known or convey an idea, fact, or feeling: *Will you speak to them about their behavior? Actions speak louder than words.* **3.** to have a conversation; converse: *We spoke on the telephone yesterday.* **4.** to deliver a speech: *The author spoke before a large audience.* **5.** to produce a sound: *The guns spoke.* **6.** (of dogs) to bark when ordered. —*v.t.* **1.** to give voice to; utter: *to speak words of sympathy.* **2.** to use or be able to use in speaking: *to speak Gaelic fluently.* **3.** to make known or convey; reveal; express: *to speak the truth.* [Old English *specan* to utter words.]

•**so to speak.** speaking figuratively: *The company's red ink is finally turning black, so to speak.*

•**to speak for. a.** to express the views of; represent: *The captain spoke for the entire team.* **b.** to ask for; reserve: *The biggest puppy in the litter is already spoken for.*

•**to speak of.** deserving mention. ➡ used with a negative: *The applicant had no work experience to speak of.*

•**to speak out** (or **up**). to speak freely, publicly, or forcefully: *a politician who speaks out against corruption.*

•**to speak well for.** to give a good impression of: *Your manners speak well for your parents.*

speak·eas·y (spēk′ē′zē) *n., pl.* **-eas·ies.** *Slang.* a place where alcoholic beverages are sold illegally, as during Prohibition.

speak·er (spē′kər) *n.* **1.** a person who speaks, esp. one who makes speeches. **2.** *usually,* **Speaker.** the presiding officer of a legislative assembly: *Speaker of the House.* **3.** loudspeaker.

speak·er·ship (spē′kər ship′) *n.* the position of presiding officer in a legislative assembly.

speak·ing (spē′king) *adj.* **1.** using or involving speech: *a speaking part in a play, a speaking engagement.* **2.** expressive, suggestive, or striking: *a speaking gesture, a speaking likeness.* —*n.* the act or utterance of a person who speaks.

speaking in tongues, glossolalia *(def. 1).*

spear (spîr) *n.* **1.** a weapon consisting of a sharp-pointed head attached to a long shaft, used for thrusting or throwing. **2.** a shoot or slender stalk, as of grass: *asparagus spears.* —*v.t.* to stab, penetrate, or take hold of with or as with a spear. —*v.i.* (of a plant) to send forth shoots or stems; sprout. [Old English *spere* this weapon.] —**spear′er,** *n.*

spear·fish (spîr′fish′) *n., pl.* **-fish** or **-fish·es.** any large marine fish, family Istiophoridae, with a long bill-like extension on the upper jaw, esp. any marlin of the genus *Tetrapturus.* [Because its bill-like extension resembles a spear.]

spear·head (spîr′hed′) *n.* **1.** the sharp-pointed head of a spear. **2.** a person or group that leads: *The paratroopers were the spearhead of the invasion.* —*v.t.* to be in the forefront of; lead: *to spearhead an attack.*

spear·man (spîr′mən) *n., pl.* **-men** (-mən). a person who is armed with a spear.

spear·mint (spîr′mint′) *n.* **1.** a fragrant plant, *Mentha spicata,* of the mint family, bearing sharply toothed, lance-shaped leaves. **2.** the aromatic oil obtained from this plant, used as a flavoring.

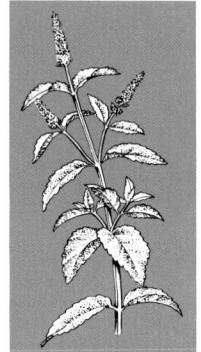

spearmint

spear side, the paternal branch or male side of a family. ➡ distinguished from **distaff side.**

spec., special.

spe·cial (spesh′əl) *adj.* **1.** out of the ordinary; unusual; exceptional: *a special talent.* **2.** marked off from others by some distinguishing quality or character: *a special day.* **3.** made, arranged, or designed for a particular occasion, purpose, or person: *a special performance to benefit cancer research, to get special permission to do something.* —*n.* **1.** something made, designed, or used for a particular occasion or purpose: *a television special on the French Revolution.* **2.a.** a special offer or price reduction; sale: *a special on winter coats.* **b.** something offered for sale at a reduced price or on special terms. [Latin *speciālis* individual, particular, from *speciēs* appearance, kind[2].] —**spe′cial·ly,** *adv.*

special delivery, delivery of mail by a special messenger, in advance of regular delivery, for an additional fee.

special education, the teaching or training of students with special learning needs, such as handicapped and gifted children.

special interest group, a group of people who promote a single cause or interest, as by seeking to enact or change laws that affect the cause or interest.

spe·cial·ist (spesh′ə list) *n.* a person who concentrates on a particular branch of a profession or field of study, esp. a doctor who practices a particular branch of medicine.

spe·cial·i·za·tion (spesh′ə lə zā′shən) *n.* the act of specializing or the state of being specialized.

spe·cial·ize (spesh′ə līz′) *v.,* **-ized, -iz·ing.** —*v.i.* **1.** to concentrate on a particular product, activity, branch of a profession, or field of study. **2.** *Biology.* to become adapted to a special function or environment. —*v.t.* **1.** to adapt or limit to a specific purpose, use, or function. **2.** to mention specifically; itemize.

special prosecutor, independent counsel.

spe·cial·ty (spesh′əl tē) *n., pl.* **-ties. 1.** a particular branch of a profession or field of study that a person concentrates on. **2.** a particular product or service that a store or other business sells or excels in: *a restaurant whose specialty is fish.* **3.** the state of being special or of having a special character or quality. Also, *British,* **spe·ci·al·i·ty** (spesh′ē al′i tē).

spe·ci·a·tion (spē′shē ā′shən, -sē ā′shən) *n.* the development by evolution of new species from existing ones. [SPECI(ES) + -ATION.]

spe·cie (spē′shē) *n.* coined money; coin. [Latin *(in) speciē* (in) kind (ablative singular of *speciēs* kind[2]).]

spe·cies (spē′shēz, -sēz) *n., pl.* **-cies. 1.a.** a subdivision of a genus in the classification of living things, containing members having certain permanent characteristics in common and able to breed with each other but not with members of other species. **b.** an organism belonging to such a subdivision. **2.** a distinct kind or type; sort. **3.** the consecrated bread or wine used in the Mass. **4. the species.** the human race. [Latin *speciēs* appearance, kind[2]. Doublet of SPICE.]

specif., specifically.

spe·cif·ic (spi sif′ik) *adj.* **1.** distinctly or explicitly named or defined; definite; precise: *a specific offer, a specific amount.* **2.** belonging exclusively to; peculiar to: *the specific characteristics of a region.* **3.** of or relating to a species, as of a plant or animal. **4.** (of a remedy) effective in the prevention or treatment of a particular disease. **5.** (of a disease) produced by a particular condition or microorganism. —*n.* **1.** something that has or is intended to have a specific effect or result, such as a medicine used to prevent or treat a particular disease. **2.** an explicitly named or defined detail or fact; particular: *the specifics of a contract.* [Late Latin *specificus* constituting a species, particular, from Latin *speciēs* kind[2], appearance + *facere* to make.] —**spec·i·fic·i·ty** (spes′ə fis′ə tē), *n.*

spe·cif·i·cal·ly (spi sif′i kə lē, -i klē) *adv.* in a specific manner; definitely; explicitly: *The invitation specifically said to dress casually.*

spec·i·fi·ca·tion (spes′ə fi kā′shən) *n.* **1.** the act of specifying. **2.** an item or article specified, as in a plan or contract. **3.** *usually,* **specifications.** a detailed list and description of the dimensions, methods, and materials of a projected work, such as a building.

specific gravity, the ratio of the density of a given substance to the density of a substance used as a standard. Water is used as the standard for solids and liquids, and air or hydrogen is used for gases.

specific heat, the amount of heat necessary to raise the temperature of 1 gram of a given substance by 1 degree Celsius.

a	at	e	end	o	hot	u	up	hw	white		about
ā	ape	ē	me	ō	old	ū	use	ng	song		taken
ä	far	i	it	ô	fork	ü	rule	th	thin	ə	pencil
âr	care	ī	ice	oi	oil	u̇	pull	th	this		lemon
				îr	pierce	ou	out	ûr	turn	zh	measure		circus

spec·i·fy (spes′ə fī′) *v.t.,* **-fied, -fy·ing 1.** to mention specifically; state or describe in detail: *to specify a place for a meeting.* **2.** to set down as a specification: *The architect specified oak for the floors.* [Old French *specifer* to particularize, from Late Latin *specificare* to endow with form, from *specificus* particular. See SPECIFIC.]

spec·i·men (spes′ə mən) *n.* **1.** a single person or thing considered to be representative or typical of its class or group; example. **2.** a sample, as of tissue or urine, for medical analysis and diagnosis. **3.** *Informal.* a peculiar person; sort. [Latin *specimen* example, indication.] —For Synonyms, see **example**.

spe·cious (spē′shəs) *adj.* **1.** seemingly true, probable, or reasonable, but actually false; plausible: *specious arguments.* **2.** attractive but deceptive: *specious advertising.* [Latin *speciōsus* beautiful, from *speciēs* appearance, form.] —**spe′cious·ly,** *adv.* —**spe′cious·ness,** *n.*

speck (spek) *n.* **1.** a very small bit; particle: *There was not a speck of dirt anywhere after we finished cleaning.* **2.** a small spot, stain, or mark. —*v.t.* to mark with specks; speckle. [Old English *specca* spot, mark.]

speck·le (spek′əl) *n.* a spot or mark, as on fur or skin. —*v.t.,* **-led, -ling.** to mark or cover with speckles.

speckled trout, brook trout.

specs (speks) *pl. n. Informal.* **1.** spectacles. **2.** specifications.

spec·ta·cle (spek′tə kəl) *n.* **1.** something seen, esp. an impressive or unusual sight. **2.** a public display, exhibition, or performance, esp. on a grand scale. **3. spectacles.** eyeglasses. [Latin *spectāculum* show, sight.]
  • **to make a spectacle of oneself.** to behave badly or improperly in public.

spec·ta·cled (spek′tə kəld) *adj.* **1.** wearing spectacles. **2.** (of an animal) having a marking or markings that suggest spectacles.

spec·tac·u·lar (spek tak′yə lər) *adj.* of, relating to, or resembling a spectacle. —*n.* an elaborate or lavish show, such as a movie or television program. —**spec·tac′u·lar·ly,** *adv.*

spec·ta·tor (spek′tā′tər, spek tā′-) *n.* a person who watches something without participating; observer. [Latin *spectātor.*]

Synonyms Spectator, onlooker, and **observer** mean someone who watches an event or activity without taking part in it. **Spectator** is usually applied to a member of a gathering, esp. at an outdoor event such as a sports contest: *The spectators gave the winning team a standing ovation.* **Onlooker** denotes a person who casually or accidentally views an event: *A crowd of onlookers watched the demolition of the building.* **Observer** often describes a person who watches with thoughtful attention: *They went to the conference as observers, not participants.*

spec·ter (spek′tər) *also, British,* **spectre.** *n.* **1.** the visible spirit of a dead person; ghost. **2.** something that threatens or causes fear: *The treaty banished the specter of war.* [Latin *spectrum* appearance, apparition.] —For Synonyms, see **ghost**.

spec·tra (spek′trə) a plural of **spectrum**.

spec·tral (spek′trəl) *adj.* **1.** of or resembling a specter; ghostly: *The trees cast spectral shadows on the lawn.* **2.** of, relating to, or produced by a spectrum. —**spec′tral·ly,** *adv.*

spec·tre (spek′tər) *British.* specter.

spectro- *combining form* of or concerning a spectrum: *spectroscope.* [From SPECTRUM.]

spec·tro·gram (spek′trə gram′) *n.* a photograph of a spectrum.

spec·tro·graph (spek′trə graf′) *n.* an instrument used for photographing a spectrum, esp. the spectrum of a celestial object. —**spec′tro·graph′ic,** *adj.* —**spec′tro·graph′i·cal·ly,** *adv.*

spec·tro·he·li·o·graph (spek′trō hē′lē ə graf′) *n.* an instrument used for studying and photographing the spectrum of the sun.

spec·trom·e·ter (spek trom′i tər) *n.* an instrument for measuring spectral wavelengths or indexes of refraction. —**spec·tro·met·ric** (spek′trə met′rik), *adj.* —**spec·trom′e·try,** *n.*

spec·tro·pho·tom·e·ter (spek′trō fə tom′i tər) *n.* a type of spectrometer that incorporates a photoelectric cell in order to reproduce the spectra of invisible radiation or to compare the intensity of different spectra of visible light. [SPECTRO- + PHOTOMETER.]

spec·tro·scope (spek′trə skōp′) *n.* an instrument that separates white light into a spectrum by causing the light to pass through a series of lenses and a prism or diffraction grating. [SPECTRO- + -SCOPE.] —**spec·tro·scop·ic** (spek′trə skop′ik); *also,* **spec′tro·scop′i·cal,** *adj.* —**spec′tro·scop′i·cal·ly,** *adv.*

spec·tros·co·py (spek tros′kə pē) *n.* the study of spectra with a spectroscope. —**spec·tros′co·pist,** *n.*

spectrum

spec·trum (spek′trəm) *n., pl.* **-tra** (-trə) *or* **-trums. 1.** a band of colors into which white light is separated according to wavelength by being passed through a prism or diffraction grating. The colors of the spectrum are red, orange, yellow, green, blue, indigo, and violet. **2.a.** a range of electromagnetic radiation, from the shortest to the longest waves. **b.** electromagnetic spectrum. **3.** a range or scope of related ideas, activities, or qualities: *the spectrum of opinion on an issue.* [Latin *spectrum* appearance.]

spec·u·lar (spek′yə lər) *adj.* of, relating to, or resembling a mirror. [Latin *speculāris,* from *speculum* mirror.]

spec·u·late (spek′yə lāt′) *v.,* **-lat·ed, -lat·ing.** —*v.i.* **1.** to think carefully or seriously in order to form a tentative conclusion; conjecture; reflect: *to speculate on the origins of the universe, to speculate about someone's motives.* **2.** to take risks in business, esp. to buy or sell securities, commodities, land, or the like in the hope of profiting by the rise or fall of prices. —*v.t.* to conclude tentatively; conjecture; guess: *The police speculated that the thief was someone familiar with the building.* [Latin *speculātus,* past participle of *speculārī* to watch, examine, from *specula* watchtower.]

spec·u·la·tion (spek′yə lā′shən) *n.* **1.** the act or an instance of speculating; conjecture. **2.** a conclusion or opinion reached by speculating. **3.** the act or practice of speculating in business.

spec·u·la·tive (spek′yə lā′tiv, -lə tiv) *adj.* **1.** given to serious thinking or inquiry; reflective; thoughtful: *a speculative scholar, a speculative mind.* **2.** of, characterized by, or based upon speculation; theoretical rather than practical: *speculative ideas.* **3.** involving financial risk: *speculative investments.* **4.** of, relating to, or involved in financial speculation: *a speculative investor.* —**spec′u·la′tive·ly,** *adv.* —**spec′u·la′tive·ness,** *n.*

spec·u·la·tor (spek′yə lā′tər) *n.* a person who speculates, esp. in business. [Latin *speculātor* explorer, spy.]

spec·u·lum (spek′yə ləm) *n., pl.* **-la** (-lə) *or* **-lums. 1.** a mirror, esp. of polished metal, used as a reflector in telescopes. **2.** a surgical instrument used to enlarge an opening for the purpose of examination. [Latin *speculum* mirror.]

sped (sped) a past tense and past participle of **speed**.

speech (spēch) *n.* **1.** the ability to express ideas or feelings by the use of spoken words; power of speaking. **2.** the act of speaking: *to express one's thoughts in speech.* **3.** something spoken, esp. before an audience: *an acceptance speech.* **4.** a manner of speaking, esp. a habitual or characteristic one: *slurred speech.* **5.** a particular idiom, dialect, or language: *Southern speech.* **6.** the study of oral communication. [Old English *spǣc* act of speaking, talk, language.] —For Synonyms, see **talk**.

speech community, a group of people who use the same idiom, dialect, or language: *Americans form a speech community of English.*

speech·i·fy (spē′chə fī′) *v.i.,* **-fied, -fy·ing.** to make a speech, esp. a long, wordy, or pompous speech; harangue. —**speech′i·fi′er,** *n.*

speech·less (spēch′lis) *adj.* **1.** temporarily unable to speak, esp. because of emotion or shock: *We were speechless with anger.* **2.** not expressed or capable of being expressed in words: *speechless anxiety.* **3.** lacking the power of speech; mute; dumb. —**speech′less·ly,** *adv.* —**speech′less·ness,** *n.*

speed (spēd) *n.* **1.** rapidity or quickness of motion; swiftness: *a game that emphasizes speed and coordination.* **2.** rate of motion, without regard to the direction of the motion; velocity. **3.** a gear or combination of gears, as in the transmission of a motor vehicle. **4.a.** the sensitivity of a photographic film, paper, or plate to light,

expressed in any of several number systems. **b.** the amount of light that a fully open lens permits to pass through, indicated by its f-number. **5.** *Archaic.* prosperity; success. **6.** *Slang.* amphetamine. —*v.,* **sped** or **speed·ed, speed·ing.** —*v.i.* **1.** to move or act rapidly or quickly; hasten: *to speed through one's chores.* **2.** to drive a motor vehicle faster than is safe or legally permitted. **3.** *Archaic.* to prosper or succeed. —*v.t.* **1.** to cause to move rapidly; give speed to: *The driver sped the ambulance to the hospital.* **2.** to send rapidly: *to speed food shipments to starving refugees.* **3.** to promote or ease the progress of; expedite; further: *The lawyer helped speed the processing of the will.* **4.** *Archaic.* to cause or help to prosper or succeed. [Old English *spēd* quickness, swiftness, success.]
 · **to speed up.** to move or cause to move faster; accelerate.

speed·boat (spēd′bōt′) *n.* a motorboat built to travel at high speeds.

speed·er (spē′dər) *n.* a person or thing that speeds, esp. a person who drives a motor vehicle faster than is safe or legally permitted.

speed limit, the maximum or minimum speed that is legally permitted on a given road.

speed·om·e·ter (spē dom′i tər, spi-) *n.* a device for measuring the speed of a vehicle, in miles per hour or kilometers per hour.

speed-read·ing (spēd′rē′ding) *n.* the practice of reading, with understanding, at a speed much faster than average by controlling one's eye movements, skimming, concentrating on the text, and other methods.

speed skating, the act or sport of ice-skating for speed, esp. in competition.

speed·ster (spēd′stər) *n.* a person who speeds, esp. a person who drives a motor vehicle at very high speeds.

speed trap, a town or section of road that is closely monitored by police, often from concealed vehicles or by radar, for violations of traffic laws.

speed·up (spēd′up′) *n.* an increase in speed, output, or work, esp. a forced increase in the speed of work without an increase in pay.

speed·way (spēd′wā′) *n.* **1.** a road designed or reserved for driving at high speeds. **2.** a track for motorcycle or automobile races.

speed·well (spēd′wel′) *n.* any of various herbs, genus *Veronica,* found in cool and temperate regions, having small pink, blue, or white flowers. Also, **veronica.**

speed·y (spē′dē) *adj.,* **speed·i·er, speed·i·est. 1.** moving rapidly; swift: *speedy runners.* **2.** without delay; prompt: *a speedy reply.* —**speed′i·ly,** *adv.* —**speed′i·ness,** *n.*

spe·le·ol·o·gist (spē′lē ol′ə jist) *n.* an expert in the study and exploration of caves.

spe·le·ol·o·gy (spē′lē ol′ə jē) *n.* the exploration and scientific study of caves. —**spe·le·o·log·i·cal** (spē′lē ə loj′i kəl), *adj.*

spell¹ (spel) *v.,* **spelled** or **spelt, spell·ing.** —*v.t.* **1.** to write or name the letters of (a word), esp. in their proper or correct order. **2.** (of letters) to form (a word): *D-o-g spells dog.* **3.** to amount to; signify: *The drought spelled ruin for many farmers.* —*v.i.* to form a word or words by letters. [Old French *espeller* to explain; of Germanic origin.]
 · **to spell out. a.** to explain clearly or in detail; make explicit: *The memorandum spelled out the procedure for a fire drill.* **b.** to read slowly or with difficulty: *to spell out a barely legible note.*

spell² (spel) *n.* **1.** a word or group of words believed to have magic power. **2.** a state or condition of enchantment; trance. **3.** irresistible influence or attraction; fascination; charm: *to fall under the spell of beautiful music.* [Old English *spell* story, saying.]

spell³ (spel) *n.* **1.** a brief, indefinite period of time: *We sat outside for a spell.* **2.** a period of weather of a specified sort: *a hot spell, a dry spell.* **3.** an attack, bout, or fit of something, such as an illness: *a dizzy spell.* **4.** a period or term of work or other activity: *a three-year spell as a deckhand.* **5.** a turn of work taken to relieve another: *to take a spell at the oars.* —*v.t.,* **spelled, spell·ing.** to relieve by taking a turn: *The two friends spelled each other driving during the trip.* [Old English *spelian* to take the place of.]

spell·bind (spel′bīnd′) *v.t.,* **-bound, -bind·ing.** to hold under or as if under a spell; enchant.

spell·bind·er (spel′bīn′dər) *n.* a speaker who holds another or others spellbound, esp. a political speaker.

spell·bound (spel′bound′) *adj.* held as by a spell; entranced; rapt: *a spellbound audience.*

spell·er (spel′ər) *n.* **1.** a person who spells words. **2.** a textbook used to teach spelling. Also *(def. 2),* **spelling book.**

Spelling

Some words in English are difficult to learn how to spell for some of the reasons shown below.

The following words are not spelled the way they are pronounced:

eight	piece	sophomore
guard	precede	technique
height	psychology	thorough
license	quest	villain
marriage	rhythm	weather
physical	sergeant	xylophone

Some words that sound the same are spelled differently:

altar, alter	dual, duel	plain, plane
ascent, assent	fair, fare	principal, principle
bare, bear	hear, here	right, rite, write
berth, birth	its, it's	sole, soul
capital, capitol	know, no	their, there, they're
cite, sight, site	peace, piece	your, you're

In some words the same letters represent different sounds:

rough, though, through	physical, phylum
good, food	weak, weather
beau, beauty	who, whole

---

spell·ing (spel′ing) *n.* **1.** the way a word is spelled; orthography. **2.** the act of a person who spells.

spelling bee, a spelling competition, esp. an oral one in which contestants are eliminated when they spell a word incorrectly.

spelt¹ (spelt) a past tense and past participle of **spell¹.**

spelt² (spelt) *n.* a variety of wheat, *Triticum aestivum spelta,* cultivated in southern Europe, used mainly for livestock feed. [Old English *spelt,* from Late Latin *spelta;* of Germanic origin.]

spel·ter (spel′tər) *n.* zinc, esp. in the form of slabs, plates, or ingots. [Possibly a modification (influenced by Italian *peltro* pewter) of Dutch *spiauter* pewter.]

spe·lunk·er (spi lung′kər) *n.* a person who explores caves. [Obsolete *spelunk* cave (from Latin *spēlunca,* from Greek *spēlynx*) + -ER¹.]

spe·lunk·ing (spi lung′king) *n.* the act or process of exploring caves.

spen·cer (spen′sər) *n.* a short, tailless jacket worn by men and women in the late eighteenth and early nineteenth centuries, usually having a collar that turned down and long, tight sleeves. [From George John *Spencer,* English politician, 1758-1834.]

Spen·ce·ri·an¹ (spen sîr′ē ən) *adj.* of or relating to the English philosopher Herbert Spencer or his philosophy. —*n.* a follower of Herbert Spencer or his philosophy.

Spen·ce·ri·an² (spen sîr′ē ən) *adj.* of or relating to a system of penmanship characterized by clearly formed, rounded, and slanted letters. [From Platt Rogers *Spencer,* 1800-64, U.S. teacher who developed the Spencerian system of penmanship.]

spend (spend) *v.,* **spent, spend·ing.** —*v.t.* **1.** to pay out (money); disburse: *to spend ten dollars on a scarf.* **2.** to pass (time) in a specified manner or place: *to spend two years traveling through Europe.* **3.** to give or devote: *to spend one's energy on community activities.* **4.** to use up or wear out; exhaust: *The storm spent itself at sea.* —*v.i.* to pay out or use up money or other possessions. [Old English *spendan* to pay out, from Latin *expendere* to weigh out (money), pay. Doublet of EXPEND.] —**spend′er,** *n.*

Synonyms *v.t.* Spend, expend, and disburse mean to pay money or other legal tender for goods or services. **Spend,** although it can be applied broadly, often indicates payments made by individuals: *They spend one third of their income on rent. They spend a lot of money on clothes.* **Expend** is a more formal term that usually refers to large sums allotted, as by business or government, for some purpose: *The sales department expends millions each year on travel.* **Disburse** usually describes the allocation of large amounts from public or private funds: *The federal, state, and local governments disburse funds to the city's Board of Education.*

---

a	at	e	end	o	hot	u	up	hw	white	about
ā	ape	ē	me	ō	old	ū	use	ng	song	taken
ä	far	i	it	ô	fork	ü	rule	th	thin	ə pencil
âr	care	ī	ice	oi	oil	ů	pull	th	this	lemon
		îr	pierce	ou	out	ûr	turn	zh	measure	circus

spending money, money reserved or used for personal expenses.

spend·thrift (spend′thrift′) *n.* a person who spends money foolishly, extravagantly, or wastefully. —*adj.* lavish or wasteful; extravagant.

Spen·se·ri·an (spen sîr′ē ən) *adj.* of, relating to, or characteristic of Edmund Spenser or his poetry.

Spenserian stanza, a stanza consisting of eight lines in iambic pentameter followed by a final Alexandrine, and rhyming *ababbcbcc.* [From the English poet Edmund *Spenser,* 1552-99, who used it in his allegorical poem *The Faerie Queene.*]

spent (spent) *v.* the past tense and past participle of **spend.** —*adj.* deprived of strength or energy; worn-out; exhausted: *a spent athlete, a spent volcano.*

sperm[1] (spûrm) *n., pl.* **sperm** or **sperms. 1.** sperm cell. **2.** the fluid secreted by the testes, containing the male reproductive cells; semen. [Late Latin *sperma* seed, from Greek *sperma.*]

sperm[2] (spûrm) *n.* **1.** spermaceti. **2.** sperm whale. [Short for SPERMACETI, SPERM OIL, and SPERM WHALE.]

sper·ma·cet·i (spûr′mə set′ē, -sē′tē) *n.* a white, waxy substance derived from sperm oil, used to make cosmetics and to waterproof paper and fabrics. [Medieval Latin *sperma ceti* sperm of a whale, from Late Latin *sperma* seed (see SPERM[1]) + Latin *cētī,* genitive of *cētus* whale[1] (from Greek *kētos*).]

sper·ma·ry (spûr′mə rē) *n., pl.* **-ries.** an organ or gland in which male reproductive cells are generated; testis.

spermat-, form of **spermato-** before vowels, as in *spermatid.*

sper·ma·the·ca (spûr′mə thē′kə) *n., pl.* **-cae** (-sē) a saclike structure connected to the female reproductive system of many invertebrates, esp. insects and amphibians, for the storage of sperm until actual fertilization later. [Modern Latin *spermatheca.* See SPERM, THECA.]

sper·mat·ic (spûr mat′ik) *adj.* of or relating to sperm or to a spermary.

sperm·a·tid (spûr′mə tid) *n.* any of the four haploid cells that result from the meiotic divisions of a spermatocyte and become differentiated into motile, mature spermatozoa. [SPERMAT- + -ID[2].]

spermato- *combining form* seed or sperm: *spermatogenesis.* [Greek *spermatos,* genitive of *sperma* seed.]

sper·mat·o·cyte (spûr mat′ə sīt′, spûr′mə tə-) *n.* **1.** *Biology.* any of the diploid male germ cells that form by mitotic division of spermatogonia and then divide into haploid spermatids by meiosis. **2.** *Botany.* a cell that develops into the flagellate male gamete of certain mosses and ferns. [SPERMATO- + Greek *kytos* hollow vessel.]

sper·ma·to·gen·e·sis (spûr′mə tə jen′ə sis, spûr mat′ə-) *n.* the entire sequence of cell divisions that results in formation of sperm cells, beginning with the spermatogonium and ending with the spermatozoan. [Modern Latin *spermatogenesis.* See SPERMATO-, GENESIS.]

sper·ma·to·go·ni·um (spûr′mə tə gō′nē əm, spûr mat′ə-) *n., pl.* **-ni·a** (-nē ə). any of the unspecialized, diploid cells in the testes that develop first into spermatocytes and then into spermatids. [SPERMATO- + Modern Latin *gonium* cell, seed (from Greek *gonos* seed, procreation).]

sper·mat·o·phyte (spûr mat′ə fīt′, spûr′mə tə-) *n.* any of the seed-producing plants of the division Spermatophyta, including the angiosperms and gymnosperms. [SPERMATO- + -PHYTE.]

sper·ma·to·zo·id (spûr′mə tə zō′id, spûr mat′ə-) *n. Botany.* a ciliated, motile male gamete of a plant, usually produced in an antheridium. [From SPERMATOZOON.]

sper·ma·to·zo·on (spûr′mə tə zō′ən, spûr mat′ə-) *n., pl.* **-zo·a** (-zō′ə). sperm cell. [SPERMATO- + *zōion* animal.]

sperm cell, a male gamete or germ cell, usually motile and smaller than the egg cell, or female gamete, with which it unites at the moment of fertilization. Also, **sperm, spermatozoon.**

sperm oil, a yellow oil obtained from the head of the sperm whale, used as a lubricant.

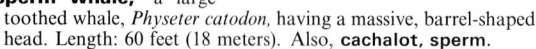
sperm whale

sperm whale, a large toothed whale, *Physeter catodon,* having a massive, barrel-shaped head. Length: 60 feet (18 meters). Also, **cachalot, sperm.**

spew (spū) *also,* **spue.** *v.t.* **1.** to throw out or produce in a gush or flood: *The chimney spewed smoke.* **2.** to cast up; vomit. —*v.i.*

1. to flow or gush out forcefully or in large quantities: *Water spewed from the hose.* **2.** to vomit. —*n.* something that is spewed. [Old English *spīwan, spēowan* to cast out, vomit.]

sp gr, specific gravity.

sphag·num (sfag′nəm) *n.* any of a group of pale green mosses, genus *Sphagnum,* found growing in bogs and marshes, where their decomposed remains accumulate and form peat. [Modern Latin *sphagnum,* from Greek *sphagnos.*]

sphal·er·ite (sfal′ə rīt′, sfā′lə-) *n.* a zinc sulfide mineral, usually containing iron and cadmium, an important ore of zinc. Formula: ZnS Also, **zinc blende.** [Greek *sphaleros* slippery, deceptive + -ITE[1]; because commonly mistaken for lead ore.]

sphe·no·don (sfē′nə don′, sfen′ə-) *n.* tuatara.

sphe·noid (sfē′noid) *adj.* **1.** wedge-shaped, as the crystals of some minerals. **2.** of, relating to, or designating a wedge-shaped compound bone of the skull located below the frontal bone and to the front of the temporal bone. Also, **sphe·noi′dal.** —*n.* the sphenoid bone. [Modern Latin *sphenoides,* from Greek *sphēnoeidēs* wedge-shaped, from *sphēn* wedge + *eidos* form, shape.]

sphere (sf îr) *n.* **1.** a three-dimensional figure having all the points of its surface at an equal distance from the center. **2.** a body having this shape; ball; globe. **3.** range, field, or extent, as of interest, influence, knowledge, or activity: *That task is outside my sphere of responsibility.* **4.** social class, rank, or position: *They associate only with people in their own sphere.* **5.** any of various celestial bodies, such as stars or planets. **6.** celestial sphere. **7.** any of a series of ten concentric globes believed by ancient astronomers to revolve around the earth and to carry the planets and stars. [Late Latin *sphēra* ball, globe, going back to Greek *sphaira.*]

spher·i·cal (sfer′i kəl, sf îr′-) *adj.* **1.** shaped like a sphere; globular. **2.** of or relating to a sphere or spheres. Also, **spher′ic.** —**spher′i·cal·ly,** *adv.*

spherical aberration, the failure of a spherically shaped lens or mirror to bring rays of light from an object to a single focus, resulting in a blurred or fuzzy image.

spherical angle, an angle on a sphere, formed by the intersection of the arcs of two great circles; any of the vertices of a spherical triangle.

spherical triangle, a closed figure on a sphere, formed by the intersecting arcs of three great circles.

sphe·ric·i·ty (sfi ris′i tē) *n.* the state of being spherical; roundness.

sphe·roid (sf îr′oid) *n.* a round three-dimensional figure that approaches a sphere in shape. —**sphe·roi′dal,** *adj.* —**spheroi′dal·ly,** *adv.*

spher·ule (sfer′ül, -ūl, sf îr′-) *n.* a little sphere or spherical body; globule.

spher·u·lite (sfer′ū līt′, -yū-, sf îr′-) *n.* a spherical or rounded mass of needlelike crystals found in some igneous rocks. [SPHERULE + -ITE[1].] —**spher·u·lit·ic** (sfer′ū lit′ik, -yū-, sf îr′-), *adj.*

sphinc·ter (sfingk′tər) *n.* a circular band of muscle that surrounds a passage or opening in the body and contracts or expands to close or open it. [Late Latin *sphinctēr,* from Greek *sphinktēr* band[2], muscle closing an opening.]

sphinx (sfingks) *n., pl.* **sphinx·es** or **sphin·ges** (sfin′jēz). **1.** in Egyptian mythology, a creature with the head of a human or animal and the body of a lion. **2. the Sphinx.** a large statue of such a creature with a human head, at Giza in Egypt. **3. Sphinx.** in Greek mythology, a winged monster having the head and breasts of a woman and the body of a lion, who posed a riddle to passersby and strangled all who could not answer it. **4.** a person who is mysterious or hard to understand. [Latin *Sphinx* Sphinx of Greek mythology, from Greek *Sphinx,* from *sphingein* to bind tight, strangle.]

sphyg·mo·graph (sfig′mə graf′) *n.* an instrument that records the rate, strength, and variations of the pulse. [Greek *sphygmos* pulse + -GRAPH.]

sphyg·mo·ma·nom·e·ter (sfig′mō mə nom′i tər) *n.* an instrument that measures blood pressure in the arteries. [Greek *sphygmos* pulse + MANOMETER.]

Spi·ca (spī′kə) *n.* a bright, bluish white star in the constellation Virgo. [Latin *spīca* point, ear of grain.]

spic-and-span (spik′ən span′) spick-and-span.

spi·cate (spī′kāt) *adj. Botany.* having or forming a spike or spikes; arranged in spikes. [Latin *spīcātus,* past participle of *spīcāre* to furnish with ears of grain, from *spīca* point, ear of grain.]

spice (spīs) *n.* **1.** any of various plant substances that have a distinctive smell or taste and are used to season food. **2.** such

substances collectively. **3.** that which adds zest or interest: *Variety is the spice of life.* **4.** a pungent or fragrant odor, as of perfume. —*v.t.,* **spiced, spic·ing. 1.** to season with a spice or spices. **2.** to add zest or interest to: *to spice one's conversation with jokes.* [Old French *espice* substance used to season food, from Late Latin *speciēs,* from Latin *speciēs* kind[2], appearance. Doublet of SPECIES.]

spice·ber·ry (spīs′ber′ē) *n., pl.* **-ries.** wintergreen *(def. 1).*

spice·bush (spīs′bŭsh′) *n.* **1.** an aromatic shrub, *Lindera benzoin,* found in swamps in eastern North America, bearing clusters of small, yellowish flowers. **2.** a shrub, *Calycanthus occidentalis,* found in California, sometimes cultivated for its fragrant, pale brown flowers.

spic·er·y (spī′sə rē) *n.* **1.** spices. **2.** a spicy quality, flavor, or fragrance.

spick-and-span (spik′ən span′) *also,* **spic-and-span.** *adj.* **1.** thoroughly neat and clean: *a spick-and-span house.* **2.** new or fresh. [Short for obsolete *spick-and-span-new: spick,* form of SPIKE[1] (referring to a newly made nail) + AND + *span-new* entirely new, from Old Norse *spānnȳr* new as a chip just shaved off (from *spānn* chip + *-nȳr* new).]

spic·u·late (spik′yə lāt′, -lit) *adj.* **1.** having or forming a spicule or spicules. **2.** resembling a spicule; needlelike. Also, **spic′u·lar.**

spic·ule (spik′ūl) *n.* a small, needlelike part, esp. one of the siliceous or calcareous projections that form the skeleton of a sponge. [Latin *spīculum* small, sharp point, arrow, diminutive of *spīca* point, ear of grain.]

spic·y (spī′sē) *adj.,* **spic·i·er, spic·i·est. 1.** seasoned with spice; containing spice: *spicy food.* **2.** resembling or suggesting spice; pungent or fragrant: *a spicy aroma.* **3.** full of zest or spirit; lively: *a spicy debate.* **4.** slightly improper; risqué; racy: *a spicy story.* —**spic′i·ly,** *adv.* —**spic′i·ness,** *n.*

spi·der (spī′dər) *n.* **1.** any of a group of small arthropods, order Araneida, characterized by a body divided into two parts, four pairs of legs, and several pairs of spinnerets that spin silken threads for making cocoons and webs. **2.** a person or thing that resembles or suggests a spider, as in appearance or movement. **3.** a cast-iron frying pan, originally one having a long handle and legs for use on a hearth. [Old English *spīthra* invertebrate of the order Araneida; literally, spinner, going back to *spinnan* to spin.]

spider crab, any of various crabs, family Majidae, characterized by long, slender legs and a relatively small, triangular body.

spider mite, any of a group of small mites, family Tetranychidae, that infest and defoliate various crops. All have silk glands opening near the mouth and make loose webs among leaves. Also, **red spider.**

spider monkey, any of a group of monkeys of tropical America, genus *Ateles,* having long, slender limbs and a long, prehensile tail.

spi·der·web (spī′dər web′) *n.* a web of silken threads spun by a spider, used to trap small prey.

spi·der·wort (spī′dər wûrt′) *n.* any of a group of often trailing plants, genus *Tradescantia,* bearing small white, blue, rose, or purple flowers.

spi·der·y (spī′də rē) *adj.* **1.** resembling or suggesting a spider or spiderweb, esp. in being thin and delicate: *spidery handwriting, spidery legs.* **2.** infested with spiders: *a spidery attic.*

spied (spīd) the past tense and past participle of **spy.**

spiel (spēl, shpēl) *n. Slang.* a speech, often long or extravagant, intended to persuade or sell; pitch. [Dialectal German *spiel* talk.] —**spiel′er,** *n.*

•**to spiel off.** *Slang.* to list or describe at length.

spiff·y (spif′ē) *adj.,* **spiff·i·er, spiff·i·est.** *Slang.* smart in dress or appearance; dapper; neat: *a spiffy dresser, a spiffy suit.* [Of uncertain origin.]

spig·ot (spig′ət) *n.* **1.** faucet. **2.** a plug or valve in a faucet for regulating the flow of liquid. **3.** a small wooden plug or peg for stopping the vent of a barrel or cask. [Of uncertain origin.]

spike[1] (spīk) *n.* **1.** a large, heavy nail. **2.** any sharp-pointed object or projection, as along the top of a wall or fence. **3.a.** one of several sharp-pointed metal projections attached to the sole and heel of a shoe to prevent slipping, worn in certain sports, such as golf or baseball. **b. spikes.** a pair of shoes having such projections. **4.a.** a long, narrow high heel attached to a woman's shoe. Also, **spike heel. b. spikes.** a pair of shoes having such heels. Also, **spike heels.** —*v.t.,* **spiked, spik·ing. 1.** to fasten or provide with spikes. **2.** to pierce with or impale on a sharp-pointed object. **3.** to stand in the way of or put an end to; block; thwart: *to spike a plan.* **4.** *Slang.* to add an alcoholic beverage to: *to spike punch.* **5.** *Baseball.* to injure with spikes. **6.** to hit (a volleyball) hard and almost straight down into the opponents'

court while jumping into the air from a position close to the net. [Possibly from Middle Dutch *spike* nail.]

spike[2] (spīk) *n.* **1.** an ear of grain. **2.** a flower cluster in which the flowers arise directly from an elongated, unbranched stalk. [Latin *spīca* point, ear of grain.]

spike·let (spīk′lit) *n.* a small spike, esp. a small cluster of flowers that make up part of the spike of a grass.

spike·nard (spīk′nərd, -närd) *n.* **1.** an aromatic ointment made in ancient times from the fragrant roots and stems of an East Indian plant, *Nardostachys jatamansi.* **2.** the plant itself, having spoon-shaped leaves and bearing clusters of reddish purple flowers. **3.** a woodland herb, *Aralia racemosa,* of eastern North America, having spicy, aromatic roots and bearing clusters of small, greenish flowers. [Medieval Latin *spica nardi* ear of nard, from Latin *spīca* (see SPIKE[2]) + *nardus* (see NARD).]

spik·y (spī′kē) *adj.,* **spik·i·er, spik·i·est. 1.** having a spike or spikes: *a spiky fence.* **2.** resembling a spike or spikes: *spiky thorns.*

spile (spīl) *n.* **1.** a wooden plug for stopping the opening of a barrel or cask. **2.** a small spout for taking sap from a sugar maple. **3.** a beam or post driven vertically into the ground as a support; pile. —*v.t.,* **spiled, spil·ing. 1.** to furnish (a barrel, cask, or tree) with a spile. **2.** to plug (a hole) with a spile. **3.** to support with beams or posts. [Middle Low German *spile* splinter, peg.]

spike of wheat

spil·ing (spī′ling) *n.* spiles collectively; piling.

spill[1] (spil) *v.,* **spilled** or **spilt, spill·ing.** —*v.t.* **1.** to cause or allow (a substance) to fall, flow, or run out of a container, esp. unintentionally. **2.** to shed (blood). **3.a.** to empty (a sail) of wind. **b.** to reduce the force of (wind) on a sail. **4.** *Informal.* to make known; reveal; divulge: *to spill a secret.* **5.** *Informal.* to cause to tumble or fall off: *The horse spilled its rider.* —*v.i.* **1.** to flow or run out: *The water spilled all over the floor. The crowd spilled into the street.* —*n.* **1.** the act or an instance of spilling. **2.** something spilled: *The oil spill covered much of the bay.* **3.** *Informal.* a tumble or fall, as from a horse. [Old English *spillan* to destroy, waste.]

spill[2] (spil) *n.* a thin strip of wood or folded piece of paper, used to light a fire. [Probably from Middle Low German *spil(l)e* splinter, peg.]

spill·age (spil′ij) *n.* **1.** the act or an instance of spilling: *Tighten the lid to prevent spillage.* **2.** an amount spilled: *The flour mill sold spillage at half price.*

spil·li·kin (spil′i kin) *n.* jackstraw. [SPILL[2] + -KIN.]

spill·way (spil′wā′) *n.* a channel that allows the escape of surplus water, as from a reservoir.

spilt (spilt) a past tense and past participle of **spill**[1].

spin (spin) *v.,* **spun** or *(archaic)* **span, spun, spin·ning.** —*v.t.* **1.** to draw out and twist (fibers) into thread. **2.** to form or make (thread) in this way. **3.** (of a spider or silkworm) to form (a silken thread, web, or cocoon) from a liquid, gumlike substance extruded from the body. **4.** to cause to turn or revolve quickly or rapidly; twirl: *to spin a top.* **5.** to extend in time; prolong; draw out (often with *out*): *They spun out the debate.* **6.** tell: *to spin ghost stories.* —*v.i.* **1.** to turn or revolve rapidly; whirl. **2.** to make by spinning, as thread. **3.** to have a sensation of revolving rapidly; feel dizzy: *All that noise made my head spin.* **4.** to go or move rapidly: *The excited crowd spun past our window.* —*n.* **1.** the act of spinning or the state of being spun. **2.** a short ride in a motor vehicle, esp. for pleasure. **3.** tailspin *(def. 1).* **4.** *Physics.* the portion of the angular momentum of a subatomic particle that exists independently of the motion of the particle, expressed as a quantum number. Leptons have a spin of $\frac{1}{2}$; mesons, 0, 1, 2, etc. [Old English *spinnan* to draw out and twist into thread.]

spi·na bi·fi·da (spī′nə bif′i də) a congenital defect in which the membranes surrounding the spinal cord protrude through an incomplete area of the backbone, often leading to paralysis. [Mod-

a	at	e	end	o	hot	u	up	hw	white		about
ā	ape	ē	me	ō	old	ū	use	ng	song		taken
ä	far	i	it	ô	fork	ü	rule	th	thin	ə	pencil
âr	care	ī	ice	oi	oil	ů	pull	th	this		lemon
		îr	pierce	ou	out	ûr	turn	zh	measure		circus

ern Latin *spina bifida,* from Latin *spīna* spine + *bifida* divided, cloven.]

spin·ach (spin'ich) *n.* **1.** the dark green, oblong leaves of a plant, *Spinacia oleracea,* eaten as a vegetable either cooked or raw. **2.** the plant itself, related to the goosefoot, cultivated in many temperate regions. [Old French *espinache,* from Spanish *espinaca,* from Arabic *isfināj,* from Persian *aspanākh.*]

spi·nal (spī'nəl) *adj.* of, relating to, or affecting the spinal column or the spinal cord. —*n.* an anesthetic injected into the spinal column, producing anesthesia in part of the body without inducing unconsciousness. [Late Latin *spīnālis* relating to the spine, from Latin *spīna* backbone.] —**spi'nal·ly,** *adv.*

spinal column, a series of vertebrae joined in a column that encloses the spinal cord and forms the central supporting structure of the body in all vertebrates. Also, **backbone, spine, vertebral column.**

spinal cord, a thick, tubular mass of nerve tissue extending down from the brain through the spinal column. The spinal cord conducts impulses to and from the brain and acts as a center for simple reflexes. For illustration, see **nervous system.**

spin·dle (spin'dəl) *n.* **1.** a round, tapered stick weighted at one end and revolved by hand, used to twist fibers into thread. **2.** a pin or rod on a spinning machine, used to hold a bobbin. **3.** any rod that turns or serves as an axis on which something, such as a shaft or axle, turns. **4.** a spike set upright in a base, on which papers, such as business receipts, are impaled. **5.** *Biology.* a mass of nuclear fibers formed between the centrioles, along which the chromosomes move during cell division. —*v.,* **-dled, -dling.**

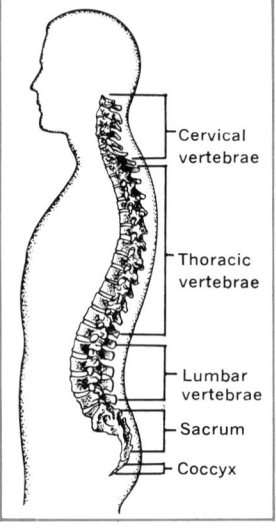

Cervical vertebrae

Thoracic vertebrae

Lumbar vertebrae

Sacrum

Coccyx

spinal column

—*v.i.* to grow into a long, slender stalk, shape, or body. —*v.t.* **1.** to form into a spindle. **2.** to impale (paper) on a spindle. [Old English *spinel* rod used in spinning thread.]

spin·dle·leg·ged (spin'dəl leg'id, -legd') *adj.* having spindle-legs. Also, **spin·dle-shanked** (spin'dəl shangkt').

spin·dle·legs (spin'dəl legz') *n.* **1.** long, slim legs. **2.** *Informal.* a person with long, thin legs. ➡ used as plural in def. 1, as singular in def. 2. Also, **spin·dle-shanks** (spin'dəl shangks').

spin·dling (spind'ling) *adj.* tall and slender, esp. disproportionately thin in relation to height: *spindling pines.*

spin·dly (spind'lē) *adj.,* **-dli·er, -dli·est.** having a tall, slender shape; spindling.

spin·drift (spin'drift') *n.* spray blown from the sea by heavy winds. Also, **spoondrift.** [Form of SPOONDRIFT.]

spine (spīn) *n.* **1.** spinal column. **2.** anything resembling or functioning as a backbone, such as the back of a book. **3.** any stiff, pointed projection on an animal or plant, such as a quill of a porcupine or one of the hard, thin leaves of a cactus. [Latin *spīna* thorn, prickle (of certain animals), backbone.]

spi·nel (spi nel', spin'əl) *n.* a crystalline mineral most commonly composed of oxides of magnesium and aluminum, sometimes used as a gem. [French *spinella,* from Italian *spinella,* going back to Latin *spīna* thorn; referring to its pointed crystals.]

spine·less (spīn'lis) *adj.* **1.** lacking a spinal column; invertebrate. **2.** lacking stiff, pointed projections: *a spineless variety of cactus.* **3.** lacking or showing a lack of courage or willpower: *a spineless coward, spineless indecision.* —**spine'less·ly,** *adv.* —**spine'less·ness,** *n.*

spin·et (spin'it) *n.* **1.** a stringed keyboard instrument resembling a small harpsichord, having a single keyboard and one string for each musical tone. **2.** a small upright piano. [Middle French *espinette* small harpsichord, from Italian *spinetta.*]

spin·na·ker (spin'ə kər) *n.* a large sail that swells or billows out before the mast when filled, used on a yacht or other racing boat when sailing before the wind. [Possibly a modification of *Sphinx,* name of the first yacht to use this sail regularly (in 1866).]

spin·ner (spin'ər) *n.* a person or thing that spins.

spin·ner·et (spin'ə ret') *n.* **1.** an organ by which various arthropods, such as spiders and certain caterpillars, spin silken threads. **2.** a plate with numerous small openings through which synthetic fibers are spun. [SPINNER + -ET.]

spin·ney (spin'ē) *n., pl.* **-neys.** *British.* a small wood or thicket; grove. [Old French *espinei* place full of thorny shrubs, from Latin *spīnētum,* from *spīna* thorn.]

spin·ning (spin'ing) *n.* **1.** the act or process of twisting fibers into thread. **2.** a method of fishing using a fixed spool, a light line, and light lures. —*adj.* that spins or is used for spinning.

spinning jenny, a hand-operated spinning machine having more than one spindle so that a number of threads can be spun at once.

spinning wheel, a hand-operated spinning machine consisting of a large wheel and single spindle, used to spin fibers into thread.

spin-off (spin'ôf', -of') *also,* **spin·off.** *n.* **1.** a distribution of the stock that a parent corporation holds in a subsidiary among the shareholders of the parent corporation. **2.** a work derived from an earlier one, such as a television series based on a character or situation that originated in a successful earlier series. **3.** a product or enterprise derived from another field: *a plastic used in eyeglass lenses that is a spin-off of technology developed for the aerospace industry.*

spi·nose (spī'nōs) *adj.* full of or covered with sharp, thornlike projections; thorny. [Latin *spīnōsus,* from *spīna* thorn.]

spi·nous (spī'nəs) *adj.* **1.** resembling a thorn; sharp. **2.** spinose; thorny.

spin·ster (spin'stər) *n.* **1.** an unmarried woman, esp. an elderly woman who has never been married; old maid. **2.** a woman who spins fibers into thread. [SPIN + -STER; referring to the fact that unmarried women formerly spent much of their time spinning.] —**spin'ster·hood',** *n.* —**spin'ster·ish,** *adj.*

spi·nule (spī'nūl, spin'ūl) *n.* a small, sharp, thornlike projection.

spin·y (spī'nē) *adj.,* **spin·i·er, spin·i·est.** **1.** having or covered with sharp, thornlike projections; thorny. **2.** resembling a thorn; sharp. **3.** troublesome; difficult: *a spiny predicament.* —**spin'i·ness,** *n.*

spiny anteater, echidna.

spin·y-finned (spī'nē find') *adj.* having fins supported by spiny rays. ➡ opposed to **soft-finned.**

spiny lobster, any of several edible crustaceans, genus *Palinurus,* having sharp spines on the body and lacking the large pincer claws of the true lobster. Also, **langouste, rock lobster.**

spi·ra·cle (spī'rə kəl, spir'ə-) *n.* an opening for breathing, such as one of the paired openings in the abdomen of an insect or spider or the opening behind the eye of a shark. [Latin *spīrāculum,* from *spīrāre* to breathe.]

spi·rae·a (spī rē'ə) *n.* spirea.

spi·ral (spī'rəl) *n.* **1.** a plane curve traced by a point moving around and continuously increasing or diminishing its distance from a fixed point. **2.** the three-dimensional curve that winds around the surface of a cylinder or cone; helix. **3.** something having the shape or form of a spiral. **4.** a continuous, accelerating increase or decrease: *the upward spiral of prices.* —*adj.* having the shape or form of a spiral; circling; winding: *a spiral staircase.* —*v.,* **-raled, -ral·ing;** *also, British,* **-ralled, -ral·ling.** —*v.i.* **1.** to take a spiral form or course; wind in a spiral: *Smoke spiraled from the chimney.* **2.** to move steadily up or down: *Prices spiraled*

spinnaker

higher. —*v.t.* to cause to take a spiral course or form: *to spiral clay into the shape of a vase.* [Medieval Latin *spiralis* winding, Latin *spīra* coil, from Greek *speira.*] —**spi′ral·ly,** *adv.*

spiral galaxy, a galaxy having a central nucleus of closely packed stars and two or more arms consisting of stars and interstellar material spiraling out from it. Also, **spiral nebula.**

spi·rant (spī′rənt) *n.* fricative. [Latin *spīrāns,* present participle of *spīrāre* to breathe.]

spire[1] (spīr) *n.* **1.** a tall, tapering structure on the top of a tower. **2.** any tapering and pointed object or formation; pinnacle. —*v.i.* **spired, spir·ing.** to rise up in the form of a spire. [Old English *spīr* stalk of a plant.]

spire[2] (spīr) *n.* **1.** a spiral or single twist of a spiral. **2.** the upper portion of a spiral shell. [Latin *spīra* coil, from Greek *speira.*]

spi·re·a (spī rē′ə) *also,* **spiraea.** *n.* any of a group of shrubs, genus *Spiraea,* of the rose family, bearing loose clusters of small white or pink flowers, found throughout the Northern Hemisphere, often cultivated as an ornamental. [Latin *spīraea,* from Greek *speiraiā.*]

spi·ril·lum (spī ril′əm) *n., pl.* **-ril·la** (-ril′ə). any of a genus of spiral-shaped, flagellate bacteria, some of which cause a fever and are spread by rats. For illustration, see **bacteria.** [Modern Latin *spirillum* little coil, from Latin *spīra* coil. See SPIRE[2].]

spir·it (spir′it) *n.* **1.** the moral or spiritual part of a person, believed to be immortal and to separate from the body at death; soul. **2.** the religious, mental, or emotional part of human nature or life: *to be concerned with the things of the spirit.* **3.a.** a supernatural, disembodied being, often thought to haunt the living; specter; ghost. **b.** a small, often mischievous supernatural being having magical powers; fairy; elf: *woodland spirits.* **4. the Spirit.** *Theology.* the third person of the Trinity; Holy Ghost. **5.** a person considered to have a specified character or temperament: *a noble spirit, a brave spirit.* **6.** a principle or attitude that inspires or animates: *the spirit of cooperation.* **7.** a pervading quality, mood, or tendency: *The novel captured the spirit of the times.* **8.** essence, real meaning, or intent: *the spirit of the law.* **9.** liveliness; vivacity; animation: *to dance with spirit.* **10.** enthusiasm, devotion, and loyalty: *school spirit.* **11. spirits.** mental state or attitude; disposition: *to be in high spirits.* **12.** *usually,* **spirits. a.** any of various solutions produced by distillation. **b.** a distilled alcoholic beverage. —*v.t.* **1.** to remove or carry off secretly or mysteriously (with *off* or *away*): *Someone spirited the dog away during the night.* **2.** to give liveliness or vigor to; enliven; animate; stimulate (usually with *up*). [Latin *spīritus* breath, life, soul. Doublet of ESPRIT, SPRITE.] —For Synonyms (*n.*), see **ghost.**

spir·it·ed (spir′i tid) *adj.* **1.** full of animation; lively; vigorous: *a spirited dancer, spirited exercise, a spirited refusal.* **2.** having (a specified kind of) character or temperament. ➡ used in combination: *a mean-spirited person, a high-spirited horse.* —**spir′it·ed·ly,** *adv.* —**spir′it·ed·ness,** *n.*

spir·it·ism (spir′i tiz′əm) *n.* spiritualism.

spir·it·less (spir′it lis) *adj.* lacking animation, enthusiasm, or energy; dejected; listless.

spirit level, a level consisting of a glass tube that is filled with alcohol containing an air bubble. The bubble rests in the center when the tube is exactly horizontal.

spir·i·to·so (spir′i tō′sō) *adj. Music.* spirited; animated. [Italian *spiritoso* jocular, witty, from *spirito* spirit, soul, wit, from Latin *spīritus* breath, life, soul.]

spirits of turpentine, turpentine (*def. 2*).

spir·i·tu·al (spir′i chü əl) *adj.* **1.** of or relating to the human soul. **2.** of, relating to, or consisting of spirit; not material. **3.** of, relating to, or concerned with things of the spirit. **4.** of, relating to, or concerned with religious or ecclesiastical matters; sacred. —*n.* a religious folk song of a type originated by blacks in the southern United States. —**spir′i·tu·al·ly,** *adv.* —**spir′it·u·al·ness,** *n.*

spir·i·tu·al·ism (spir′i chü ə liz′əm) *n.* **1.** the belief that the dead communicate with the living, esp. through mediums. **2.** any of various philosophical or religious theories that reality is essentially spiritual rather than material. —**spir′i·tu·al·is′tic,** *adj.*

spir·i·tu·al·ist (spir′i chü ə list) *n.* a person who believes in or supports spiritualism.

spir·i·tu·al·i·ty (spir′i chü al′i tē) *n., pl.* **-ties. 1.** devotion to or concern with things of the spirit. **2.** the state or quality of being spiritual.

spir·i·tu·al·ize (spir′i chü ə līz′) *v.t.,* **-ized, -iz·ing. 1.** to make spiritual. **2.** to invest with a spiritual sense or meaning. —**spir′i·tu·al·i·za′tion,** *n.*

spire[1]

spir·i·tu·el (spir′i chü el′) *also,* **spir·i·tu·elle.** *adj.* marked by or demonstrating grace, refinement, or wit. [French *spirituel,* going back to Latin *spīritus* breath, mind, soul.]

spir·i·tu·ous (spir′i chü əs) *adj.* **1.** containing alcohol; alcoholic: *a spirituous punch.* **2.** produced by distillation rather than fermentation. —**spir·i·tu·os·i·ty** (spir′i chü os′i tē), *n.*

spi·ro·chete (spī′rə kēt′) *n.* any of a large group of bacteria, order Spirochaetales, having a slender, spiral shape, including the bacteria that cause syphilis. [Modern Latin *Spirochaeta,* from Latin *spīra* coil + Greek *chaitē* long hair. See SPIRE[2].] —**spi′ro·chet′al,** *adj.*

spi·ro·gy·ra (spī′rə jī′rə) *n.* any of a genus of freshwater green algae having spiral chloroplasts, sometimes visible as a scum on the surface of ponds. [Modern Latin *spirogyra,* from Latin *spīra* coil + Greek *gȳros* circle. See SPIRE[2].]

spi·rom·e·ter (spī rom′i tər) *n.* an instrument for measuring the volume of air inhaled and exhaled by the lungs. [Latin *spīrāre* to breathe + -METER.]

spirt (spûrt) spurt.

spir·y (spīr′ē) *adj.* having the form of a spire.

spit[1] (spit) *v.,* **spit** or **spat, spit·ting.** —*v.i.* **1.** to eject saliva from the mouth. **2.** to express scorn or contempt by or as by spitting: *I spit at your accusation.* **3.** to make a hissing or popping noise, as hot oil; sputter. **4.** to rain or snow lightly in scattered drops or flakes. —*v.t.* **1.** to eject from the mouth: *to spit out a seed.* **2.** to eject or utter in a violent, noisy, or explosive manner: *a machine that spits out tickets, to spit insults.* —*n.* **1.** saliva. **2.** the act of spitting. **3.** a frothy mass secreted by certain insects. Also (*defs. 1, 3*), **spittle.** [Old English *spittan* to eject saliva from the mouth.] —**spit′ter,** *n.*

·**to spit up. a.** to vomit. **b.** to cough up.

spit[2] (spit) *n.* **1.** a slender, pointed rod on which meat is roasted over a fire. **2.** a narrow point of land extending into the sea. —*v.t.,* **spit·ted, spit·ting.** to pierce or thrust through with or as with a spit. [Old English *spitu* the pointed rod.]

spit·ball (spit′bôl′) *n.* **1.** a wad of folded and chewed paper used as a missile. **2.** an illegal pitch in baseball in which the ball is moistened, as with saliva, to cause it to curve more sharply when thrown.

spite (spīt) *n.* a feeling of ill will toward another; desire to irritate, hurt, or humiliate; malice: *to spread rumors out of spite.* —*v.t.,* **spit·ed, spit·ing.** to irritate, hurt, or humiliate out of spite: *neighbors who make noise just to spite each other.* [Short for DESPITE.]

·**in spite of.** without regard for; despite.

·**to cut off one's nose to spite one's face.** to damage one's own interests in the course of doing something spiteful to another or others.

spite·ful (spīt′fəl) *adj.* filled with or characterized by spite; malicious: *a spiteful person, a spiteful remark.* —**spite′ful·ly,** *adv.* —**spite′ful·ness,** *n.*

spit·fire (spit′fīr′) *n.* a quick-tempered, fiery person.

spitting image, an exact likeness: *a child that is the spitting image of a parent.*

spit·tle (spit′əl) *n.* **1.** saliva. **2.** spit[1] (*def. 3*). [Old English *spātl* saliva; influenced by SPIT[1].]

spit·tle·bug (spit′əl bug′) *n.* any of a group of small, hopping, homopterous insects, family Cercopidae, the nymphs of which produce white frothy masses on plants. Also, **cuckoo spit.**

spit·toon (spi tün′) *n.* a receptacle for spit and objects such as chewed tobacco; cuspidor.

spitz (spits) *n.* any of several breeds of small, stocky dogs having a pointed muzzle, small, erect ears, and a fluffy tail that curls over the back, such as the chow or Pomeranian. [German *Spitz,* from *spitz* pointed; referring to its pointed muzzle.]

splanch·nic (splangk′nik) *adj.* visceral (*def. 1*). [Modern Latin *splanchnicus,* from Greek *splanchnikos,* from *splanchnon* gut.]

splash (splash) *v.t.* **1.** to scatter or throw (a liquid) about: *to splash paint on the floor.* **2.** to wet, soil, or stain by scattering or throwing with a liquid or other substance: *He splashed his face with water. A passing car splashed her dress with mud.* **3.** to mark or decorate by or as by splashing: *The wallpaper was splashed with bright colors.* **4.** to make (one's) way by splashing. **5.** to display in a prominent or showy way: *The newspaper splashed the story across the front page.* —*v.i.* **1.** to cause a liquid to scatter about. **2.** to fall or strike in scattered drops or masses: *The milk splashed*

a	at	e	end	o	hot	u	up	hw	white		about
ā	ape	ē	me	ō	old	ū	use	ng	song		taken
ä	far	i	it	ô	fork	ü	rule	th	thin	ə	pencil
âr	care	ī	ice	oi	oil	u̇	pull	th	this		lemon
				îr	pierce	ou	out	ûr	turn	zh	measure		circus

out of the glass. **3.** to move with a splash or splashes: *The car splashed through the flooded streets.* —*n.* **1.** the act or sound of splashing. **2.** a spot or patch: *The horse had a splash of white on its forehead. There are splashes of mud on my shoes.* **3.** a sensation or stir: *The play made quite a splash on Broadway.* [Modification of PLASH.] —**splash′er,** *n.*

• **to splash down. a.** (of a spacecraft or missile) to land in a body of water. **b.** to land in a body of water in a spacecraft: *The astronauts splashed down in the Pacific.*

splash·down (splash′doun′) *n.* the landing of a spacecraft on a body of water.

splash guard, a flap, as of rubber, hung so as to deflect mud or other material thrown up by a wheel, as of a truck. Also, **mudguard.**

splash·y (splash′ē) *adj.,* **splash·i·er, splash·i·est. 1.** making a splash or splashes. **2.** full of irregular spots or patches; blotchy; spotty: *a splashy pattern.* **3.** creating a sensation or stir; ostentatious; showy: *a splashy party.*

splat (splat) *n.* a flat piece of wood, used esp. to form the central part of a chair back. [Of uncertain origin.]

splat·ter (splat′ər) *v.i., v.t.* spatter. —*n.* spatter. [Blend of SPATTER and SPLASH.]

splay (splā) *adj.* **1.** spread or spreading out; broad. **2.** awkward or awkwardly formed; clumsy. —*n.* a sloping surface, esp. in the opening of a window or door. —*v.t.* **1.** to spread out; extend. **2.** to make slanting; bevel. —*v.i.* **1.** to be spread out. **2.** to slant. [Short for DISPLAY.]

splay·foot (splā′fŏot′) *n., pl.* **-feet** (-fēt′). **1.** a flatfoot that turns outward. **2.** an abnormal condition in which the foot is flat and turns outward. —**splay′-foot′ed,** *adj.*

spleen (splēn) *n.* **1.** a large, oval, ductless organ near the stomach that serves to produce white blood cells, break down old red blood cells, and filter the blood. **2.** ill temper; malice; spite: *to vent one's spleen.* **3.** *Archaic.* low spirits; melancholy. [Latin *splēn* the organ, from Greek *splēn.*]

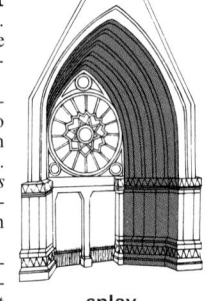
splay

splen·dent (splen′dənt) *adj.* **1.** reflecting light; gleaming; lustrous. **2.** impressive; illustrious. [Latin *splendēns,* present participle of *splendēre* to shine.]

splen·did (splen′did) *adj.* **1.** impressive to the eye because of beauty or richness; brilliant; magnificent: *a splendid array of colors, a splendid interior.* **2.** impressive; illustrious; glorious: *a splendid achievement.* **3.** very good; excellent: *a splendid idea.* [Latin *splendidus* bright, magnificent.] —**splen′did·ly,** *adv.* —**splen′did·ness,** *n.* —For Synonyms, see **magnificent.**

splen·dif·er·ous (splen dif′ər əs) *adj. Informal.* splendid; magnificent.

splen·dor (splen′dər) *also, British,* **splen·dour.** *n.* **1.** a great or stately display, as of riches or beautiful objects; magnificence; pomp: *the splendor of a palace.* **2.** an impressive or commanding quality or character; illustriousness; glory. **3.** great brightness; brilliance; luster: *the splendor of the setting sun.* [Latin *splendor* brightness, brilliance.]

sple·net·ic (spli net′ik) *adj.* **1.** of or relating to the spleen; splenic. **2.** ill-tempered; malicious; spiteful. Also, **sple·net′i·cal.** —**sple·net′i·cal·ly,** *adv.*

splen·ic (splē′nik, splen′ik) *adj.* of, relating to, or contained within the spleen. [Latin *splēnicus,* from Greek *splēnikos,* from *splēn.* See SPLEEN.]

splice (splīs) *v.t.,* **spliced, splic·ing. 1.** to join together, as ropes, by interweaving the strands of the ends. **2.** to join together (film or magnetic tape) at the ends, as where sections have been cut out. **3.** to join together (pieces of timber) by overlapping. **4.** to join (genes of DNA segments from different organisms) to form new genetic combinations. —*n.* a joint or union made by splicing. [Middle Dutch *splissen* to join ropes together by interweaving the strands of the ends.] —**splic′er,** *n.*

spline (splīn) *n.* **1.** a narrow, thin strip of wood, metal, or other material; slat. **2.** a flexible strip of wood, metal, or other material used in drawing curves. **3.** a rectangular key projecting from a mechanical part, such as a shaft, that fits into a groove or slot in another mechanical part. —*v.t.,* **splined, splin·ing.** to fit or provide with a spline. [Of uncertain origin.]

splint (splint) *n.* **1.** a device made of wood, metal, or other material, used to immobilize and protect a fractured, dislocated, or broken bone. **2.** a thin, flexible strip of wood used in weaving baskets or caning chairs. **3.** splinter. **4.** a bony growth on the

splint bone of a horse. [Middle Low German *splinte* metal plate or pin.]

splint bone, one of the two small bones on either side of the cannon bone between the hock or knee and the fetlock in hoofed animals, esp. horses.

splin·ter (splin′tər) *n.* **1.** a thin, sharp, usually small piece chipped or broken off from something hard or brittle, such as wood, glass, or metal. **2.** a smaller group that breaks off from a larger one, such as a political party or religious sect. Also *(def. 2),* **splinter group.** —*v.t., v.i.* **1.** to break or split into splinters. **2.** to split into factions or smaller groups. [Middle Dutch *splinter* shaving, chip.] —**splin′ter·y,** *adj.*

split (split) *v.,* **split, split·ting.** —*v.t.* **1.** to break apart or divide lengthwise or in layers: *to split logs.* **2.** to divide or break up into parts (often with *up*): *to split up an art collection.* **3.** to divide into shares; share: *to split the cost of dinner.* **4.** to burst or tear open or apart: *to split one's pants at the seams.* **5.** to divide or separate into sides or factions: *The controversy split the political party.* **6.** to divide (the stock of a company) into a larger number of shares, usually without any increase in their total value. **7.** *Physics.* to divide (a heavy atomic nucleus) into two nuclei of approximately equal mass by bombardment with neutrons. —*v.i.* **1.** to break apart lengthwise or in layers: *This wood splits easily.* **2.** to become divided; separate: *The search party split into two groups.* **3.** to burst or tear open or apart. **4.** (of stock) to be or become split. **5.** *Slang.* to leave: *Everyone split when it was time to clean up.* —*n.* **1.** the act of splitting or the state of being split. **2.** a result of splitting; break or crack. **3.** a division or rupture in a group. **4.** a dish of sliced bananas or other fruit, ice cream, whipped cream, and a topping of syrup and nuts. **5.** *Informal.* a bottle of an alcoholic or carbonated drink that is half the usual size, or about 6 ounces (180 milliliters). **6.** *also,* **splits.** a movement or exercise in dancing or calisthenics in which a person slides to the floor or leaps into the air with the legs spread apart and parallel to the floor. **7.** the act or result of splitting stock. Also *(def. 7),* **stock split.** —*adj.* **1.** divided lengthwise or in layers. **2.** broken up; separated. [Middle Dutch *splitten* to cleave.] —**split′ter,** *n.*

split decision 1. a majority decision in a boxing match in which the judges and referee do not agree on the winner. **2.** any judgment or conclusion that is not unanimous.

split infinitive, an infinitive having a word or phrase, such as an adverb, placed between *to* and the verb: *to really love, to hardly know.*

split-lev·el (split′lev′əl) *adj.* having two or more floor levels each about a half story above or below the adjoining level or levels and connected by short flights of stairs: *a split-level house.* —*n.* a split-level house or condominium.

split personality, multiple personality. ➡ popular term for **multiple personality;** split personality should not be confused with **schizophrenia.**

split second, an extremely brief period of time; instant; flash. —**split′-sec′ond,** *adj.*

split ticket 1. a ballot cast for candidates of more than one political party. **2.** a slate of candidates from more than one political party.

split·ting (split′ing) *adj.* **1.** (of the head) aching severely. **2.** acute; severe: *a splitting headache.*

splotch (sploch) *n.* a large, irregular spot; blot; stain. —*v.t.* to soil or cover with splotches. [Possibly blend of SPOT and BLOTCH.] —**splotch′y,** *adj.*

splurge (splûrj) *v.i.,* **splurged, splurg·ing. 1.** to spend money without attention to cost; indulge oneself by spending too much money: *to splurge on clothes.* **2.** to make a gaudy or flashy display; show off. —*n.* an act or period of spending too much money: *to go on a splurge.* [Possibly blend of SPLASH and SURGE.]

splut·ter (splut′ər) *v.i.* **1.** to speak in a rapid, unclear way, as when confused, angry, or excited. **2.** to make popping, spitting, or hissing sounds, as food being fried; sputter. —*v.t.* to say in a rapid, unclear way, as from anger or excitement: *to splutter a demand for an apology.* —*n.* a spluttering noise or disturbance. [Modification (influenced by SPLASH) of SPUTTER.] —**splut′ter·er,** *n.*

spoil (spoil) *v.,* **spoiled** or **spoilt, spoil·ing.** —*v.t.* **1.** to cause damage or harm to (something), esp. with regard to its excellence, quality, value, or efficacy: *The beetles spoiled most of our roses. The loud noise spoiled the golfer's swing.* **2.** to weaken or damage the character of, as by too much praise or indulgence: *to spoil a child.* **3.** to put an end to; destroy: *The scandal spoiled the senator's chances for reelection.* —*v.i.* to become unfit for use: *The meat spoiled when we left it out overnight.* —*n. usually,* **spoils. 1.** goods or property seized by force, esp. in time of war; booty; plunder. **2.** appointive public offices or other favors given

to supporters of a victorious political party. [Old French *espoillier* to strip, plunder, from Latin *spoliāre*, from *spolium* booty.]

· **to be spoiling for,** to be eager or anxious for: *to be spoiling for a fight.*

spoil·age (spoi′lij) *n.* **1.** the act or process of spoiling or the state of being spoiled. **2.** something that has spoiled. **3.** the amount that has spoiled.

spoil·er (spoi′lər) *n.* **1.** a person or thing that causes spoilage. **2.** a person or group that competes in a contest with little chance of winning but does well enough to keep another from winning. **3.** a device on the upper surface of an airplane wing that can be raised to increase drag and decrease lift. **4.** a similar device on an automobile, designed to alter the flow of air around the vehicle at high speeds.

spoils·man (spoilz′mən) *n., pl.* **-men** (-mən). a person who supports a political party or candidate for a share of political spoils.

spoil·sport (spoil′spôrt′) *n.* a person who spoils the pleasure of others by his or her behavior or attitude.

spoils system, the system or practice of distributing appointive public offices or other favors to supporters of a victorious political party.

spoilt (spoilt) a past tense and past participle of **spoil.**

spoke[1] (spōk) the past tense and archaic past participle of **speak.**

spoke[2] (spōk) *n.* **1.** one of the bars or rods radiating from the hub to the rim of a wheel. **2.** a rung of a ladder. —*v.t.,* **spoked, spok·ing.** to fit or provide with a spoke or spokes. [Old English *spāca* bar or rod of a wheel.]

spo·ken (spō′kən) *v.* the past participle of **speak.** —*adj.* **1.** uttered or expressed in speech; oral. **2.** speaking or using (a specified kind of) speech. ➡ used in combination: *a plain-spoken person.*

spoke·shave (spōk′shāv′) *n.* a type of drawknife used by carpenters to plane curved surfaces.

spokes·man (spōks′mən) *n., pl.* **-men** (-mən). a person who speaks on behalf of another or others.

spokes·per·son (spōks′pûr′sən) *n.* a person who speaks on behalf of another or others: *a company spokesperson.*

spokes·wom·an (spōks′wŭm′ən) *n., pl.* **-wom·en** (-wim′ən). a woman who speaks on behalf of another or others.

spo·li·a·tion (spō′lē ā′shən) *n.* an act or instance of plundering, esp. in time of war. [Latin *spoliātiō.*]

spon·da·ic (spon dā′ik) *adj.* of, relating to, or consisting of spondees.

spon·dee (spon′dē) *n.* in poetry, a metrical foot consisting of two accented or long syllables, for example: *Baa, baa, / black sheep.* [Latin *spondēus,* from Greek *spondeios,* from *spondē* libation; because solemn songs were sung in this meter at libations.]

sponges

sponge (spunj) *n.* **1.** any of a large group of chiefly marine invertebrates, phylum Porifera, that live in colonies attached to rocks or other solid objects and have porous bodies supported by a fibrous skeleton. Sponges are of various sizes, shapes, and colors. **2.** a light, fibrous, absorbent network forming the skeleton of certain sponges, used for washing or other purposes. **3.** an article made from any of various substances, as cellulose or rubber, resembling this skeleton in structure or use. **4.** an absorbent pad, as of gauze or prepared cotton, used in surgery. **5.** a soft, light-textured, raised dough. **6.** *Informal.* a person who makes a practice of living at the expense of another or others. —*v.,* **sponged, spong·ing.** —*v.t.* **1.** to cleanse or rub with or as with a wet sponge. **2.** to remove with a sponge (with *out* or *off*): *The teacher sponged the crayon marks off the wall.* **3.** to absorb with or as with a sponge: *to sponge up spilled milk.* **4.** *Informal.* to get without

paying: *to sponge a meal.* —*v.i.* **1.** to absorb liquid, as a sponge. **2.** to gather sponges from the sea. **3.** *Informal.* to live at the expense of another or others (with *on* or *off*): *to sponge off a rich relative.*

· **to throw (or toss) in the sponge.** *Informal.* to admit defeat.

sponge bath, a bath taken by washing with a wet sponge or damp cloth without the use of a shower or bathtub.

sponge cake, a light cake made without shortening, containing eggs, sugar, flour, and flavoring.

spong·er (spun′jər) *n.* **1.** *Informal.* a person who makes a practice of living at the expense of another or others. **2.a.** a person who gathers sponges from the sea. **b.** a boat used for gathering sponges.

sponge rubber, foam rubber.

spon·gy (spun′jē) *adj.,* **-gi·er, -gi·est.** of or resembling a sponge; elastic, porous, or absorbent. —**spon′gi·ness,** *n.*

spongy parenchyma, the usually lower layer in the mesophyll of some leaves, containing cells with large intercellular spaces that facilitate the exchange of gases with the atmosphere during photosynthesis and respiration. Also, **spongy mesophyll.** [Because the intercellular spaces resemble the pores of a sponge.]

spon·son (spon′sən) *n.* **1.** a structure projecting from the side of a boat or ship, used to support or protect something, as a gun or searchlight. **2.** an air-filled structure attached to either side of a canoe or seaplane to increase stability and prevent sinking. [Possibly form of EXPANSION.]

spon·sor (spon′sər) *n.* **1.** a person who assumes responsibility or support for another person or a thing. **2.** a person or organization, as a business firm, that finances some event or entertainment. **3.** a person who answers for an infant at baptism, making the required promises and professions of faith; godfather or godmother. —*v.t.* to act as sponsor for. [Latin *spōnsor* surety.] —**spon·so·ri·al** (spon sôr′ē əl), *adj.* —For Synonyms *(n.),* see **patron.**

spon·sor·ship (spon′sər ship′) *n.* the act of sponsoring.

spon·ta·ne·i·ty (spon′tə nē′i tē, -nā′-) *n., pl.* **-ties. 1.** the fact, quality, or condition of being spontaneous. **2.** spontaneous action, impulse, or behavior.

spon·ta·ne·ous (spon tā′nē əs) *adj.* **1.** arising from or caused by a natural impulse or desire; not planned: *spontaneous laughter.* **2.** arising or occurring without external cause; having an internal cause or origin: *spontaneous motion.* **3.** (of plants) growing naturally without cultivation. [Late Latin *spontāneus* voluntary, from Latin *sponte* voluntarily.] —**spon·ta′ne·ous·ly,** *adv.* —**spon·ta′ne·ous·ness,** *n.* —For Synonyms, see **automatic.**

spontaneous combustion, the catching fire of a substance, as oily rags, because of an accumulation of heat from slow oxidation.

spontaneous generation, the theory, now discredited, that organisms can originate from nonliving matter, independently of previously existing life forms. A form of spontaneous generation may have occurred several billion years ago, when life first evolved from organic molecules. Also, **abiogenesis.**

spoof (spüf) *Informal. n.* **1.** a light parody. **2.** a trick or deception; hoax. —*v.t.* **1.** to make a parody of; satirize lightly. **2.** to trick or deceive. [From *Spoof* (probably blend of SPORT and GOOF), a card game involving trickery and tomfoolery devised by Arthur Roberts, 1852-1933, English comedian.] —**spoof′er,** *n.*

spook (spük) *Informal. n.* a ghost; specter. —*v.t.* **1.** to haunt (a person or place). **2.** to frighten or make uneasy: *The sudden noise spooked the horse.* —*v.i.* to become frightened or uneasy. [Dutch *spook* ghost.]

spook·y (spü′kē) *adj.,* **spook·i·er, spook·i·est.** *Informal.* causing fear, alarm, or uneasiness; scary: *a spooky old house, a spooky visitor.* —**spook′i·ly,** *adv.* —**spook′i·ness,** *n.*

spool (spül) *n.* **1.** a small, cylindrical piece of wood, plastic, or other material around which thread, wire, or tape may be wound. **2.** an amount of thread, wire, or tape wound on a spool. —*v.t.* to wind on a spool. [Middle Dutch *spoele* bobbin.]

spoon (spün) *n.* **1.** a utensil of wood, metal, or plastic, consisting of a handle with a small, shallow bowl at the end, used in preparing, serving, or eating food. **2.** something resembling this in shape or function. **3.** a golf club having a wooden head, used for long shots; number three wood. —*v.t.* to lift up or transfer with a spoon: *to spoon soup into one's mouth.* —*v.i. Informal.* to make love, as by kissing or caressing. [Old English *spōn* chip, splinter.]

spoon·bill (spün′bil′) *n.* **1.** any of several long-legged wading birds, family Threskiornithidae, native to most temperate and

a	at	e	end	o	hot	u	up	hw	white		about
ā	ape	ē	me	ō	old	ū	use	ng	song		taken
ä	far	i	it	ô	fork	ü	rule	th	thin	ə	pencil
âr	care	ī	ice	oi	oil	u̇	pull	th	this		lemon
		îr	pierce	ou	out	ûr	turn	zh	measure		circus

tropical regions of the world, having a long, flat bill with a tip shaped like a spoon. Length: 3 feet (0.9 meter). **2.** any of various birds having a similar bill, as the shoveler.

spoon bread, a moist bread made of cornmeal, eggs, milk, and shortening, baked to a consistency that is soft enough to be served with a spoon.

spoon·drift (spün′drift′) *n.* spindrift. [Obsolete *spoon* to scud (of uncertain origin) + DRIFT.]

spoon·er·ism (spü′nə riz′əm) *n.* the unintentional transposition of initial or other sounds of two or more words, as in *seeping slickness* for *sleeping sickness.* [From W. A. *Spooner,* 1844-1930, English member of the clergy, who was famous for such expressions.]

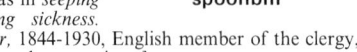

spoonbill

spoon-feed (spün′fēd′) *v.t.* **-fed** (-fed′), **-feed·ing. 1.** to feed (someone) with a spoon: *to spoon-feed a baby.* **2.** to spoil by indulging too much; coddle; pamper. **3.** to teach or treat in such a way as to not allow independent thought or action: *to spoon-feed students.*

spoon·ful (spün′fül′) *n., pl.* **-fuls.** the amount that a spoon can or does hold.

spoor (spür, spôr) *n.* a track or trail, esp. of a wild animal. —*v.t., v.i.* to trace by or follow a spoor. [Dutch *spoor* trail, track.]

spo·rad·ic (spə rad′ik) *adj.* **1.** occurring at irregular intervals; occasional: *The repair work caused sporadic interruption of telephone service.* **2.** occurring or appearing singly or in widely separate localities. **3.** (of a disease) occurring in isolated instances or cases; not epidemic. Also, **spo·rad′i·cal.** [Medieval Latin *sporadicus* scattered, from Greek *sporadikos* scattered (like seeds), going back to *sporā* seed, a sowing.] —**spo·rad′i·cal·ly,** *adv.* —For Synonyms, see **periodic.**

spo·ran·gi·um (spə ran′jē əm) *n., pl.* **-gi·a** (-jē ə). in certain plants, fungi, algae, and bacteria, a sac in which spores are produced. Also, **spore case.** [Modern Latin *sporangium,* from Greek *sporā* seed + *angeion* receptacle.] —**spo·ran·gial,** *adj.*

spore (spôr) *n.* **1.** a tiny reproductive body formed by a plant or microscopic animal and distributed by air or water currents to a place suitable for germination. **2.** a microorganism, as a bacterium, that has grown a tough outer wall that is highly resistant to chemical and physical conditions. [Modern Latin *spora,* from Greek *sporā* seed.]

spo·ro·phore (spôr′ə fôr′) *n.* the fruiting body of a fungus.

spo·ro·phyll (spôr′ə fil′) *also,* **spo·ro·phyl.** *n.* a leaf or modified leaf, such as a stamen, that bears spores or sporangia. [Greek *sporā* seed + *phyllon* leaf.]

spo·ro·phyte (spôr′ə fīt′) *n.* a stage in the life cycle of plants that undergo alternation of generations, during which asexual spores are produced. ➡ distinguished from **gametophyte.** [Greek *sporā* seed + -PHYTE.]

spo·ro·zo·an (spôr′ə zō′ən) *n.* any parasitic protozoan of the phylum or class Sporozoa, which produces spores to reproduce, such as the plasmodium that causes malaria. —*adj.* of, relating to, or designating this phylum or class. [Modern Latin *Sporozoa,* from *spora* (see SPORE) + Greek *zōia,* plural of *zōion* animal.]

spor·ran (spôr′ən, spor′-) *n.* a large pouch or purse worn from the belt in front of a kilt. [Scottish Gaelic *sporan.*]

sport (spôrt) *n.* **1.** an athletic game or contest that requires physical activity and some skill, as tennis, fishing, basketball, soccer, bowling, or golf. **2.** any pastime or activity that provides pleasure or recreation; amusement; diversion. **3.** playfulness or jest; fun: *to tease someone in sport.* **4.** *Informal.* **a.** a person who is a fair or obliging companion. **b.** a person with regard to his or her ability to accept teasing, criticism, or defeat: *a good sport.* **5.** *Informal.* a person who is interested in sports for purposes of gambling. **6.** *Biology.* a plant or animal that exhibits a sudden or marked variation from the normal type; mutation. —*v.i.* **1.** to engage in physical exercise or activity for pleasure or recreation; play. **2.** to make fun; treat lightly; joke;

Sporran

trifle. **3.** *Biology.* to mutate. —*v.t. Informal.* to wear or display, esp. in a showy way: *to sport a new suit, to sport a mustache.* —*adj. also,* **sports.** fitted or suitable for informal wear: *sport clothes.* [Short for DISPORT.] —**sport′ful,** *adj.* —**sport′ful·ly,** *adv.* —**sport′ful·ness,** *n.*

• **to make sport of.** to ridicule; deride.

sport car, sports car.

sport·ing (spôr′ting) *adj.* **1.** of, relating to, suitable for, used in, or engaged in sports: *a sporting event, sporting goods, sporting dogs.* **2.** characteristic of a sportsman or sportswoman; fair or obliging: *That was very sporting of you.* **3.** of or relating to gambling, esp. on sports. —**sport′ing·ly,** *adv.*

sporting chance *Informal.* an even or fair chance for a successful outcome.

spor·tive (spôr′tiv) *adj.* **1.** frolicsome; playful; lively. **2.** of, relating to, or characterized by sport. —**spor′tive·ly,** *adv.* —**spor′tive·ness,** *n.*

sports (spôrts) *adj.* **1.** of, relating to, or suitable for a sport or sports: *a sports enthusiast, sports equipment.* **2.** sport.

sports car *also,* **sport car.** a small, low automobile designed to maneuver easily and achieve high speeds, usually seating two passengers.

sports·cast (spôrts′kast′) *n.* a radio or television broadcast of a sports event or of sports commentary. —**sports′cast·er,** *n.*

sports·man (spôrts′mən) *n., pl.* **-men** (-mən). **1.** a person who is interested or engages in sports, esp. outdoor sports, as hunting or fishing. **2.** a person who plays fair and accepts defeat graciously. —**sports′man·like′, sports′man·ly,** *adj.*

sports·man·ship (spôrts′mən ship′) *n.* **1.** conduct characteristic or worthy of a sportsman or sportswoman, as fair play or the ability to accept defeat graciously. **2.** skill in sports.

sports·wear (spôrts′wâr′) *n.* clothing designed for informal wear.

sports·wom·an (spôrts′wüm′ən) *n., pl.* **-wom·en** (-wim′ən). **1.** a woman who is interested or engages in sports, esp. outdoor sports. **2.** a woman who plays fair and accepts defeat graciously.

sports·writ·er (spôrts′rī′tər) *n.* a person who writes about sports events, esp. for a newspaper or magazine.

sport·y (spôr′tē) *adj.,* **sport·i·er, sport·i·est.** *Informal.* **1.** characteristic of a sportsman or sportswoman; sporting. **2.** loud or flashy, as clothes: *a sporty outfit.* —**sport′i·ly,** *adv.* —**sport′i·ness,** *n.*

spor·u·late (spôr′yə lāt′) *v.i.,* **-lat·ed, -lat·ing.** to form spores. [Modern Latin *sporula* little spore, from *spora* (see SPORE) + -ATE¹.] —**spor′u·la′tion,** *n.*

spot (spot) *n.* **1.** a difference in color or texture produced by dirt or other foreign matter: *a spot of grease.* **2.** a flaw or blemish: *a spot on one's reputation.* **3.** a small mark or part differing from the surrounding area, as in color or material: *a dog with brown spots.* **4.** a place where something is, has been, or is to be located; site: *an interesting spot for a picnic, the spot where an accident took place.* **5.** a position or situation: *the third spot in line, to have a good spot in a company.* **6.a.** one of the marks on dominoes, dice, or playing cards. **b.** a playing card having (a specified number of) such marks. **7.** *Informal.* a small quantity; little bit: *a spot of tea.* **8.** *Informal.* spotlight *(defs. 1, 2).* **9.** *Slang.* a piece of paper currency having a specified value: *a ten spot.* —*v.,* **spot·ted, spot·ting.** —*v.t.* **1.** to mark with a spot or spots: *The mud spotted the rug.* **2.** to locate or pick out with the eyes; recognize: *We spotted them easily in the crowd.* **3.** to blemish; disgrace. **4.** to place or scatter in various locations: *Guards were spotted throughout the store.* **5.** to place in a specific position: *The jewelry store spotted a guard at the door.* —*v.i.* **1.** to become spotted: *The fabric will spot easily.* **2.** to cause a stain; make a spot: *The ink spots permanently.* —*adj.* paid or requiring payment on delivery: *spot cash, a spot transaction.* [Possibly from Middle Dutch *spotte* stain, speck.]

• **in a spot.** in a difficult, disagreeable, or embarrassing situation.

• **on the spot. a.** at the place indicated: *The reporters were on the spot when the celebrities arrived.* **b.** at once; immediately: *to demand payment on the spot.* **c.** in an awkward position: *to put someone on the spot by asking a personal question.*

• **to hit the spot.** *Informal.* to be exactly right or exactly what is needed: *A cold drink hits the spot on a warm day.*

spot-check (spot′chek′) *v.t.* to make a quick examination by selecting samples at random.

spot check, a quick examination made by selecting samples at random.

spot·less (spot′lis) *adj.* **1.** absolutely clean; immaculate: *a spotless kitchen.* **2.** having no flaws or blemishes; unsullied: *a spotless reputation.* —**spot′less·ly,** *adv.* —**spot′less·ness,** *n.*

spot·light (spot′līt′) *n.* **1.** a strong beam of light projected on a particular person, place, or object, esp. for dramatic or theatrical effect. **2.** a lamp projecting such a light. **3.** public attention or

notoriety: *The scientists were in the spotlight after their discovery.* —*v.t.* **1.** to project a spotlight on: *to spotlight a stage.* **2.** to call attention to.

spot·ted (spot′id) *adj.* **1.** marked or covered with spots: *a spotted pony.* **2.** blemished; sullied: *a spotted public image.*

spotted fever, any of several diseases characterized by fever and spots on the skin, as typhus.

spot·ter (spot′ər) *n.* **1.** a person who removes spots from garments in dry cleaning. **2.** a person who watches for enemy planes, usually over a populated area. **3.** *Informal.* a detective who keeps watch for dishonesty among employees, as in a store.

spot·ty (spot′ē) *adj.*, **-ti·er, -ti·est. 1.** marked or covered with spots; spotted. **2.** not consistent or uniform; uneven: *spotty attendance, a spotty performance.* —**spot′ti·ly,** *adv.* —**spot′ti·ness,** *n.*

spous·al (spou′zəl) *adj.* of or relating to a spouse or marriage.

spouse (spous, spouz) *n.* a married person; husband or wife. [Old French *espous* bridegroom, husband, and *espouse* bride, wife; respectively from Latin *spōnsus* betrothed man, and *spōnsa* betrothed woman.]

spout (spout) *v.t.* **1.** to pour out (a liquid or other substance) forcibly in a stream or spray; spurt: *An elephant spouts water from its trunk.* **2.** *Informal.* to say in a wordy, pompous, or conceited manner: *The visitor went about the house spouting unwanted advice.* —*v.i.* **1.** to pour out forcibly: *Water spouted from the burst pipe.* **2.** to discharge a liquid or other substance continuously or in spurts. **3.** *Informal.* to speak in a wordy, pompous, or conceited manner (often with *off*): *to spout off about one's success in business.* —*n.* **1.** a tube or lip projecting from a vessel that channels the liquid being poured. **2.** a pipe or other channel, as a faucet or spigot, through which liquid flows or is discharged. **3.** a jet or column, as of water. [Possibly from Middle Dutch *spouten* to spurt.] —**spout′er,** *n.*

S.P.Q.R., Roman Senate and People. [Abbreviation of Latin *S(enatus) P(opulus)q(ue) R(omanus).*]

sprain (sprān) *n.* an injury caused by a violent or sudden wrenching or twisting of the ligaments or tendons around a joint. —*v.t.* to subject to a sprain. [Old French *espreindre* to press, wring, from Latin *exprimere* to press out.]

sprang (sprang) a past tense of **spring.**

sprat (sprat) *n.* **1.** a bluish green saltwater fish, *Clupea sprattus,* found off the Atlantic coast of Europe, used for food. **2.** any of various related fish, as a young herring. [Old English *sprott.*]

sprawl (sprôl) *v.i.* **1.** to lie or sit with the body and limbs stretched out in an awkward or careless manner: *The child sprawled on the sofa.* **2.** to spread out in an irregular or straggling manner: *The housing development sprawled across the countryside.* —*v.t.* to cause to spread out in an awkward, careless, or straggling manner. —*n.* an act, instance, or position of sprawling: *to lay in a sprawl across a bed.* [Old English *sprēawlian* to move the limbs convulsively.]

spray[1] (sprā) *n.* **1.** water or other liquid in the form of fine particles or droplets: *the spray from a waterfall.* **2.** anything resembling this, such as fine particles or small objects discharged through the air: *a spray of dust.* **3.** any of various liquids emitted in a stream of fine particles by a device, as an atomizer or aerosol can: *a spray for bugs.* **4.** the device itself: *a paint spray.* —*v.t.* **1.** to apply spray to (a surface): *to spray a bookcase with paint.* **2.** to apply a spray of: *to spray perfume on one's wrist.* **3.** to discharge a spray in: *to spray a room with disinfectant.* —*v.i.* **1.** to scatter or emit spray. **2.** to be emitted as spray. [Possibly from Middle Dutch *spra(e)yen* to sprinkle.] —**spray′a·ble,** *adj.* —**spray′er,** *n.*

spray[2] (sprā) *n.* **1.** a slender twig or branch of a plant with its leaves, flowers, or fruit; sprig. **2.** an ornament, pattern, or design resembling this. [Probably from an unrecorded Old English word.]

spray can, aerosol can.

spray gun, a device that emits a spray of liquid, as paint or insecticide, under pressure applied by a pump.

spread (spred) *v.,* **spread, spread·ing.** —*v.t.* **1.** to unfold or open up so as to cover a larger area: *to spread a blanket over a bed, to spread a map on a table.* **2.** to push or move further apart: *to spread one's fingers.* **3.** to cover with a thin layer of something: *to spread a canvas with paint, to spread a roll with jam.* **4.** to put as a thin covering: *to spread butter on toast.* **5.** to distribute or disperse over an area: *to spread fertilizer on the ground, to spread furniture around a room.* **6.** to extend over a period of time: *to spread work over three days, to spread a payment over a year.* **7.** to cause to become more widely known: *to spread rumors.* **8.** to extend the incidence of something, esp. a disease. **9.a.** to set (a table) for a meal; place food on. **b.** to set (food) on a table. —*v.i.* **1.** to be situated, distributed, or dispersed over an area: *The forest spread out across the landscape. The rash spread on my arm. The fire*

spread through the house. **2.** to be put as a thin covering: *The butter spreads easily.* **3.** to become more widely known; circulate: *Word spread quickly about the accident.* **4.** to be pushed apart; become more separated. —*n.* **1.** the act of spreading. **2.** the amount of spreading or capacity for spreading. **3.** something that is spread out: *the spread of gravel in a driveway, the spread of branches overhead.* **4.** a cloth covering, esp. for a bed. **5.** printed material, as an advertisement, that covers two facing pages or several columns in a periodical or newspaper. **6.** soft food that can be spread, such as butter or cheese. **7.** *Informal.* a lavish display of food; feast. **8.** *Informal.* a ranch or farm. [Old English *sprǣdan* to extend.] —**spread′a·ble,** *adj.*

·**to spread oneself thin.** to try to do too many things at the same time: *I spread myself thin this semester by taking two extra classes.*

> **Synonyms** *v.t.* **Spread, circulate,** and **disseminate** mean to make known over a wide area. **Spread** denotes a rapid dispersal of information, esp. by word of mouth: *News of the disaster spread with remarkable speed.* **Circulate** implies an organized activity that occurs within a specific or limited circle: *The personnel department circulated details of the new benefits plan.* **Disseminate** also applies to the organized distribution of information, but usually on a large scale and not directed toward individuals: *The society disseminates information to the media on the subject of good nutrition.*

spread-ea·gle (spred′ē′gəl) *adj.* **1.** having or suggesting the form or appearance of an eagle with legs and wings spread out. **2.** *Informal.* boastful, esp. in patriotic expression. —*v.t., v.i.,* **-gled, -gling.** to stretch out or cause to stretch out in a spread-eagle position.

spread eagle, the representation of an eagle with legs and wings spread out, used as an emblem of the United States.

spread·er (spred′ər) *n.* **1.** a person or thing that spreads. **2.** a small knife used to spread butter, cheese, or other soft food. **3.** a device or machine used to spread seed, hay, or fertilizer.

spread·sheet (spred′shēt′) *n.* a type of microcomputer software designed for organizing financial data into columns and rows in such a way that sets of data can be processed and analyzed in relation to each other. [SPREAD + SHEET.]

spree (sprē) *n.* **1.** unrestrained or excessive indulgence in an activity: *a shopping spree.* **2.** a lively frolic. [Of uncertain origin.]

spri·er (sprī′ər) a comparative of **spry.**

spri·est (sprī′ist) a superlative of **spry.**

sprig (sprig) *n.* **1.** a shoot, twig, or branch of a plant with its leaves, flowers, or fruit: *a sprig of parsley.* **2.** a pattern or ornament resembling this. **3.** a small brad without a head. **4.** a young man; youth. —*v.t.,* **sprigged, sprig·ging.** to fasten with brads. [Of uncertain origin.]

spright·ly (sprīt′lē) *adj.,* **-li·er, -li·est.** full of animation and light-heartedness; merry; gay: *a sprightly tune.* [*Spright,* form of SPRITE + -LY[2].] —**spright′li·ness,** *n.*

spring (spring) *v.,* **sprang** or **sprung, sprung, spring·ing.** —*v.i.* **1.** to move forward or jump up quickly: *The soldiers sprang to attention. John sprang from his seat. The gazelle sprang gracefully into the air.* **2.** to appear or arise suddenly: *The words sprang to her lips.* **3.** to shift or move by or as by elastic force: *The rubber band sprang back into shape. The bear trap sprang shut. The door suddenly sprang open from the force of the wind.* **4.** to come into existence or grow suddenly or rapidly (often with *up*): *Houses in the development sprang up overnight. The weeds sprang up everywhere.* **5.** to be descended: *to spring from an illustrious old family.* **6.** to become warped, cracked, or split: *The window sprang from the humidity.* —*v.t.* **1.** to cause to spring. **2.** to cause (a mechanism) to work suddenly: *to spring a trap.* **3.** to present or produce suddenly or unexpectedly: *to spring a surprise.* **4.** to leap over; clear: *to spring a fence.* **5.** to cause to warp, crack, or split: *The wind sprang the tree.* **6.** to develop: *The radiator sprang a*

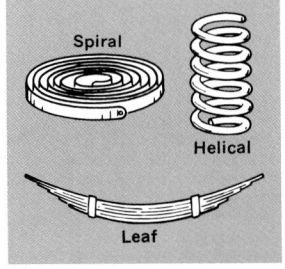

springs

a	at	e	end	o	hot	u	up	hw	white	⎧	about
ā	ape	ē	me	ō	old	ū	use	ng	song		taken
ä	far	i	it	ô	fork	ü	rule	th	thin	ə	pencil
âr	care	ī	ice	oi	oil	u̇	pull	th	this		lemon
				ir	pierce	ou	out	ûr	turn	zh	measure	⎭	circus

1167

leak. **7.** *Slang.* to free (someone), as from prison. —*n.* **1.** the act of springing; leap. **2.** an elastic device, as a spiral-shaped piece of metal, that recovers its original shape when released after being bent, compressed, or stretched, used to transmit motion, check motion, or maintain a separation between two objects. **3.** elasticity or buoyancy: *There was little spring in the old dog's muscles. There was no spring in the depressed person's walk.* **4.** a place where underground water flows out of the earth. **5.** the season of the year coming between winter and summer. In the Northern Hemisphere it extends from the vernal equinox, about March 21, to the summer solstice, about June 21. **6.** the first or early stage: *the spring of life.* **7.** the source or origin: *the springs of thought.* —*adj.* **1.** of, relating to, characteristic of, or suitable for the season of spring: *spring wheat, spring rain, a spring outfit.* **2.** having, acting like, or suspended on a spring or springs: *a spring mattress, a spring watch, a spring valve.* [Old English *springan* to grow, come forth, move with a sudden jerk.] —**spring′like′,** *adj.* —For Synonyms *(v.i.),* see **jump.**

spring beauty 1. a delicate pink or white flower of any of a group of plants, genus *Claytonia,* found in meadows and fields of North America. **2.** the plant bearing this flower, having fleshy leaves.

spring·board (spring′bôrd′) *n.* **1.** a flexible board fastened at one end and extending out over water, esp. at a swimming pool. **2.** a flexible board used in tumbling. **3.** something that provides a starting or moving force: *A good education can be the springboard to success.*

spring·bok (spring′bok′) *also,* **springbuck.** *n., pl.* **-bok** or **-boks.** a small antelope, *Antidorcas marsupialis,* native to the plains of southern Africa, having horns and a predominantly tan-and-white coat. Height: 30 inches (76 centimeters) at the shoulder. [Afrikaans *springbok,* from Dutch *springen* to spring + *bok* buck[1]; because it springs into the air when startled.]

spring·buck (spring′buk′) *n., pl.* **-buck** or **-bucks.** springbok.

springbok

spring chicken 1. a young chicken, esp. a broiler or fryer. **2.** *Slang.* a young person.

spring-clean·ing (spring′klē′ning) *n.* a thorough cleaning, as of a house, commonly done in the spring.

springe (sprinj) *n.* a snare consisting of a noose attached to a branch, used to catch small game. —*v.t.,* **springed, spring·ing.** to catch in a spring. [Probably from an unrecorded Old English word.]

spring·er (spring′ər) *n.* **1.** a person or thing that springs. **2.** the first or lowest wedge-shaped block of an arch. For illustration, see **arch**[1].

springer spaniel, a spaniel of either of two breeds, Welsh or English, having a predominantly white coat and often used for flushing and retrieving game. Height: to 18 inches (46 centimeters) at the shoulder.

spring fever, a feeling of laziness or listlessness that is commonly associated with the coming of spring.

spring·halt (spring′hôlt′) stringhalt.

spring·house (spring′hous′) *n., pl.* **-hous·es** (-hou′ziz). a small building constructed over a spring, used to keep perishable foods cool.

spring·let (spring′lit) *n.* a small spring or stream.

spring peeper, a small, brown or gray tree frog, *Hyla crucifer,* of the eastern United States, having a dark cross on its back, and known for its high-pitched, peeping calls in early spring. Average length: 1 inch (3 centimeters).

spring·tail (spring′tāl′) *n.* any of a group of small, wingless insects, order Collembola, having a powerful appendage on the abdomen that enables them to make springlike jumps.

spring·tide (spring′tīd′) *n.* springtime.

spring tide 1. the tide that has the greatest rise and ebb, occurring at or soon after the new or full moon. **2.** any great rush, flood, or swell: *in the spring tide of prosperity.*

spring·time (spring′tīm′) *n.* the spring season.

spring·y (spring′ē) *adj.,* **spring·i·er, spring·i·est.** having a light, bouncing, or flexible quality: *a springy step, a springy mattress.* —**spring′i·ly,** *adv.* —**spring′i·ness,** *n.*

sprin·kle (spring′kəl) *v.,* **-kled, -kling.** —*v.t.* **1.** to scatter (a liquid or other substance) in small drops or particles: *to sprinkle powdered sugar on cake.* **2.** to scatter small drops or particles of a liquid or other substance on: *to sprinkle clothes with water.* **3.** to scatter at random: *to sprinkle grass seed over an area.* —*v.i.* **1.** to rain lightly: *It sprinkled this morning.* **2.** to scatter a liquid or other substance in drops or small particles. —*n.* **1.** a light rain. **2.** a small quantity of something; sprinkling. **3.** the act of sprinkling. [Possibly from Dutch *sprenkelen* to sprinkle (with water), from Middle Dutch *sprenkel* small spot.]

sprin·kler (spring′klər) *n.* **1.** any of various devices for sprinkling a lawn, as a perforated nozzle attached to a hose. **2.** an outlet of a sprinkler system.

sprinkler system 1. an automatic system for extinguishing fires in buildings. **2.** a system of pipes or hoses, usually underground, for sprinkling a lawn, garden, or other area.

sprin·kling (spring′kling) *n.* a small or limited quantity, esp. one falling or scattered at random: *a sprinkling of rain, a sprinkling of humor in a speech.*

sprint (sprint) *n.* a short race at full speed. —*v.i.* to run at full speed, esp. for a short distance. [Of Scandinavian origin.] —**sprint′er,** *n.*

sprit (sprit) *n.* a small spar extending diagonally from the mast to the upper corner of a fore-and-aft sail. [Old English *sprēot* pole[1].]

sprite (sprīt) *n.* a small, often mischievous supernatural being; elf. [Old French *esprit* soul, mind, from Latin *spīritus* breath, mind, soul. Doublet of ESPRIT, SPIRIT.]

sprit·sail (sprit′sāl′, -səl) *n.* a sail spread and supported by a sprit.

sprock·et (sprok′it) *n.* **1.** any of the toothlike projections on the rim of a wheel that are arranged to engage the links of a chain. **2.** a wheel with sprockets. Also *(def. 2),* **sprocket wheel.** [Of uncertain origin.]

sprout (sprout) *v.i.* **1.** to put forth young growth or buds; begin to grow: *The seeds we planted finally sprouted.* **2.** to develop or grow suddenly or rapidly: *Stores have sprouted up near the new housing development.* —*v.t.* to cause to sprout: *The plant sprouted new leaves.* —*n.* **1.** a new or young growth on a plant, developed from a seed, bud, or root. **2. sprouts. a.** young shoots of mung beans, alfalfa, or the like, eaten as a vegetable. **b.** Brussels sprouts. [Old English *sprūtan* to shoot forth, grow.]

spruce[1] (sprüs) *n.* **1.** any of a group of cone-bearing evergreen trees, genus *Picea,* of the pine family, having short, needlelike leaves and drooping cones, found in cold and temperate regions of the Northern Hemisphere. **2.** its wood, used for construction and paper pulp. [From obsolete *Spruce* Prussia, modification of *Pruce,* from Medieval Latin *Prussia;* probably because the tree came from Prussia.]

spruce[2] (sprüs) *v.t., v.i.,* **spruced, spruc·ing.** to make or become neat or trim (usually with *up*): *to spruce up a room, to spruce up before dinner.* —*adj.* **spruc·er, spruc·est.** having a neat or trim appearance; dapper. [Possibly from obsolete *Spruce* Prussia, brought from Prussia (hence, considered neat or smart). See SPRUCE[1].] —**spruce′ly,** *adv.* —**spruce′ness,** *n.*

sprue (sprü) *n.* a chronic, mainly tropical, gastrointestinal disease characterized by impaired absorption of foods, minerals, and water by the small intestine, and resulting in anemia, fatigue, and weight loss. [Dutch *spruw.*]

sprung (sprung) a past tense and past participle of **spring.**

spry (sprī) *adj.,* **spry·er** or **spri·er, spry·est** or **spri·est.** lively and nimble: *My grandparents are still spry at eighty.* [Of uncertain origin.] —**spry′ly,** *adv.* —**spry′ness,** *n.*

spt., seaport.

spud (spud) *n.* **1.** a narrow, sharp, spadelike tool for digging up weeds or removing bark from trees. **2.** *Informal.* a potato. —*v.t.,* **spud·ded, spud·ding.** to dig or remove with a spud. [Of uncertain origin.]

spue (spū) *v.t., v.i.,* **spued, spu·ing.** spew. —*n.* spew.

spume (spūm) *n.* foam; froth. —*v.i.,* **spumed, spum·ing.** to foam; froth. [Latin *spūma* foam.]

spu·mo·ni (spù mō′nē) *also,* **spu·mo·ne.** *n.* Italian ice cream having various layers of different flavors and colors, sometimes containing fruit or nuts. [Italian *spumone,* from *spuma* foam, from Latin *spūma.*]

spun (spun) a past tense and the past participle of **spin.**

spun glass, fiberglass.

spunk (spungk) *n. Informal.* courage, spirit, and determination; pluck: *You have a lot of spunk.* [Of uncertain origin.]

spunk·y (spung′kē) *adj.,* **spunk·i·er, spunk·i·est.** *Informal.* characterized by or having courage, spirit, and determination; plucky. —**spunk′i·ly,** *adv.* —**spunk′i·ness,** *n.*

spun silk, silk made from the short fibers of silk waste.

spun sugar, cotton candy.

spur (spûr) *n.* **1.** a device worn on the heel of the boot of the rider of a horse, used to urge a horse forward. **2.** something that goads, impels, or urges to action: *Your encouragement was the spur I needed to continue writing my book.* **3.** something that resembles a spur, as the sharp, hard projection on the leg of a rooster. **4.** a short, stunted branch, as of a fruit tree. **5.** a ridge or mountain projecting from the main mountain range. **6.** spur track. **7.** *Botany.* a hollow, tubular projection from some part of a flower, as from the calyx of a columbine. —*v.*, **spurred, spur-ring.** —*v.t.* **1.** to urge forward with a spur or spurs. **2.** to move or urge on; stimulate; incite: *The cheers spurred the team to victory.* —*v.i.* to ride quickly by urging one's horse with spurs. [Old English *spura* the device on the heel of a boot.]
  ·**on the spur of the moment.** without preparation; on impulse: *to change plans on the spur of the moment.*
spurge (spûrj) *n.* any of a family of plants, Euphorbiaceae, esp. of the genus *Euphorbia,* including poinsettias, that have a milky, acrid sap. [Old French *espurge,* from *espurgier* to purge, from Latin *expurgāre;* because some of these plants were once used as laxatives.]
spur gear 1. a cogwheel with teeth parallel to its axis. **2.** a gear mechanism having such cogwheels, used to transfer motion from one shaft to a parallel shaft.
spu-ri-ous (spyur′ē əs) *adj.* not being what it appears or is claimed to be; not genuine or authentic; false: *a spurious Rembrandt painting, a spurious claim.* [Latin *spurius.*] —**spu′ri-ous-ly,** *adv.* —**spu′ri-ous-ness,** *n.*
spurn (spûrn) *v.t.* **1.** to reject with contempt or disdain; scorn: *to spurn the offer of a bribe.* **2.** *Archaic.* to strike or push away with the foot. —*v.i.* to exhibit contempt or disdain. —*n.* **1.** a contemptuous or disdainful rejection. **2.** *Archaic.* a kick. [Old English *spurnan* to reject with disdain.] —**spurn′er,** *n.*
spurred (spûrd) *adj.* fitted with or having spurs.
spurt (spûrt) *also,* **spirt.** *v.i.* **1.** to gush or pour out suddenly or forcibly in a stream; spout: *The water spurted from the broken pipe.* **2.** to make or show a sudden, brief effort: *The horse spurted ahead of the others as it neared the finish line.* —*v.t.* to throw or force out suddenly in a stream. —*n.* **1.** a sudden gush, esp. of liquid. **2.** a sudden, brief spell, as of activity, effort, or emotion: *to work in spurts.* [Of uncertain origin.]
spur track, a short sidetrack of a railroad connected at one end with the main track.
sput-nik (sput′nik, spût′-) *n.* any of several satellites launched into earth orbit by the Soviet Union; the first, *Sputnik I,* on October 4, 1957. [Russian *sputnik* satellite; literally, traveling companion, from *s* with + *put′* way + -NIK.]
sput-ter (sput′ər) *v.i.* **1.** to make popping, spitting, or hissing noises: *The motor sputtered and then stopped.* **2.** to utter words or sounds in a confused or hasty manner: *to sputter in anger.* **3.** to throw out or spit small particles of food or saliva, as when speaking excitedly. —*v.t.* **1.** to throw out or spit small particles (food or saliva), as when speaking excitedly. **2.** to utter (words or sounds) in a confused or hasty manner. —*n.* **1.** the act or noise of sputtering. **2.** a confused or hasty speech. [Probably imitative.] —**sput′ter-er,** *n.*
spu-tum (spū′təm) *n., pl.* **-ta** (-tə). saliva mixed with mucus or pus coughed up or spit out from the lungs or windpipe. [Latin *spūtum.*]
spy (spī) *n., pl.* **spies. 1.** an undercover agent who is employed by a government to discover the military, political, or other secrets about another government. **2.** a person hired by a company to obtain secret information about the business dealings of another company. **3.** a person who watches others secretly or who gathers secret information about others. —*v.*, **spied, spy-ing.** —*v.i.* **1.** to act as a spy: *to spy on enemy troop movements, to spy on a neighbor.* **2.** to make a search or investigation; pry (usually with *into*): *to spy into someone's past.* —*v.t.* **1.** to catch sight of; observe; notice: *to spy a ship on the horizon.* **2.** to discover or observe secretly (with *out*): *The detective spied out the suspected thief.* [Old French *espier* to watch attentively; of Germanic origin.]
spy-glass (spī′glas′) *n.* a small telescope.
sq *also,* **sq.** square; squares.
sq., the following.
sq ft *also,* **sq. ft.** square foot; square feet.
sq in. *also,* **sq. in.** square inch; square inches.
sq mi *also,* **sq. mi.** square mile; square miles.
squab (skwob) *n., pl.* **squabs** or **squab.** a young pigeon, esp.

while still an unfledged nestling. [Probably of Scandinavian origin.]
squab-ble (skwob′əl) *v.t.,* **-bled, -bling.** to argue noisily, esp. over something of little importance; bicker; wrangle: *The children squabbled over who would ride the bicycle first.* —*n.* a petty argument or dispute. [Probably imitative.] —**squab′bler,** *n.*
squad (skwod) *n.* **1.** a military unit usually composed of ten people and forming part of a platoon, usually commanded by a noncommissioned officer. **2.** a small group of persons organized as a team or for a particular purpose or function: *a patrol squad, a baseball squad.* [Obsolete French *esquade* small party (of soldiers), from Italian *squadra* group, square, going back to Latin *ex-* (see EX-¹) + *quadra* square; with reference to the arranging of soldiers into square formations.]
squad car, a police car assigned to a particular area and equipped with a radiotelephone for communication with headquarters. Also, **patrol car, prowl car.**
squad-ron (skwod′rən) *n.* **1.** in the U.S. Air Force, a basic combat unit consisting of twelve or more planes divided into three or more flights of three to five planes each. **2.** in the U.S. Navy, a unit of a fleet, including eight amphibious ships of varying types and four minesweepers. **3.** formerly, a unit of cavalry usually having from 120 to 200 soldiers. **4.** any large organized body or group. [Italian *squadrone* troop of men, from *squadra* group, square. See SQUAD.]
squal-id (skwol′id) *adj.* **1.** having a gloomy, wretched, poverty-stricken appearance: *a squalid beggar, squalid tenements.* **2.** morally bad; sordid: *the squalid details of a scandal.* [Latin *squālidus* filthy.] —**squa-lid′i-ty, squal′id-ness,** *n.* —**squal′id-ly,** *adv.*
squall¹ (skwôl) *n.* **1.** a sudden, violent storm or wind, often accompanied by rain, snow, or sleet. **2.** *Informal.* a sudden, short disturbance or commotion. —*v.i.* to blow a squall; storm. [Probably of Scandinavian origin.]
squall² (skwôl) *v.i.* to cry or scream loudly or harshly: *The child fell and began to squall.* —*n.* a loud, harsh cry or scream. [Possibly imitative.] —**squall′er,** *n.*
squall-y (skwô′lē) *adj.,* **squall-i-er, squall-i-est. 1.** marked by squalls; stormy; gusty: *squally seas, squally winds.* **2.** *Informal.* marked by or threatening trouble.
squal-or (skwol′ər) *n.* the state or condition of being squalid; wretchedness or sordidness: *to live in squalor.* [Latin *squālor* filth.]
squa-ma (skwā′mə) *n., pl.* **-mae** (-mē). a scale or scalelike structure. [Latin *squāma* scale².]
squa-mate (skwā′māt) *adj.* having or covered with scales.
squa-mous (skwā′məs) *also,* **squa-mose** (skwā′mōs). *adj.* like, covered with, or formed of scales. [Latin *squāmōsus,* from *squāma* scale².]
squan-der (skwon′dər) *v.t.* to spend, use, or expend in a wasteful or extravagant manner: *to squander an inheritance, to squander one's affections.* [Of uncertain origin.] —**squan′der-er,** *n.*
square (skwâr) *n.* **1.** a plane figure having four sides of equal length and four right angles. **2.** an object, part, or the like having this shape: *I moved the piece to the next square on the checkerboard.* **3.** an open space in a city or town bounded by streets on all sides, often planted with grass, trees, or flowers, and usually used as a park. **4.** any similar open space, esp. one formed by the intersection of several streets. **5.a.** a space or section in a city or town, bounded by streets on four sides: *The shopping area took up ten squares in the center of town.* **b.** the distance between one of these streets and the next; block. **6.a.** T square. **b.** try square. **7.** *Mathematics.* the product of a number or algebraic expression multiplied by itself. The square of 5 is 25. **8.** *Slang.* a person who is conventional and conservative and does not know or follow the latest trends, fashions, or facts. —*adj.,* **squar-er, squar-est. 1.** having four sides of equal length and four right angles. **2.** resembling a square in form: *a square suitcase, a square jaw.* **3.** designating a unit of measure expressing area in the form of a square having sides of a specified length: *square foot, square meters, square mile.* **4.** of a specified length on each of four sides of a square: *a piece of land 100 feet square.* **5.** forming a right angle. **6.** just; fair; honest: *a merchant who was always square with customers.* **7.** on equal terms; even: *The teams were square as they went into the fifth inning. When you pay me back, we'll be square.* **8.** straightforward or direct; absolute: *a square denial.* **9.** being the square of an integer. The numbers 1, 4, 9, and 16 are square numbers. **10.** solid and strong, esp. having a broad, stocky build.

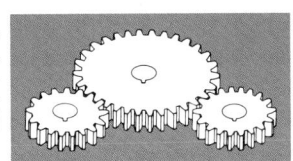

spur gears

a	at	e	end	o	hot	u	up	hw	white		about
ā	ape	ē	me	ō	old	ū	use	ng	song		taken
ä	far	i	it	ô	fork	ü	rule	th	thin	ə	pencil
âr	care	ī	ice	oi	oil	u̇	pull	<u>th</u>	this		lemon
				îr	pierce	ou	out	ûr	turn	zh	measure		circus

11. *Slang.* having or showing little knowledge of or interest in fads or fashions; conventional or conservative. —*v.,* **squared, squaring.** —*v.t.* **1.** to form with four equal sides and four right angles; make or form like a square. **2.** to bring to or as to the form of a right angle or a straight line: *to square one's shoulders.* **3.** to mark out or divide into squares. **4.** to arrange to fit some given measure or standard; regulate; adjust: *to square facts with a person's story, to square one's opinion with that of the majority.* **5.** to adjust so as to leave no balance; settle: *to square business accounts.* **6.** to make equal, level, or even, as a score. **7.** *Mathematics.* **a.** to multiply (a number or algebraic expression) times itself. **b.** to find the square measure of (an area). —*v.i.* **1.** to agree; conform; fit: *Their opinions don't square with mine.* —*adv.* **1.** so as to be at or form right angles: *The building doesn't sit square on the lot. The driveway lies square to the right.* **2.** so as to be in a square form: *The carpet was cut square to fit the room.* **3.** directly: *to look someone square in the face.* **4.** *Informal.* fairly or honestly. [Old French *esquarre,* past participle of *esquarrer* to make quadrangular, going back to Latin *ex-* (see EX-[1]) + *quadrāre* to make quadrangular, put in proper order, agree.] —**square′ly,** *adv.* —**square′ness,** *n.*

• **on the square. a.** at right angles. **b.** *Informal.* in a just or fair way; honestly.

• **out of square. a.** not at right angles. **b.** not in order or agreement; at variance: *The news report is out of square with what we heard yesterday.*

• **to square away. a.** *Nautical.* to place the yards at right angles to the keel, so the ship sails before the wind. **b.** *Informal.* to get ready.

• **to square off.** *Informal.* to prepare to fight.

• **to square up.** *Informal.* to pay what is owed: *I squared up with my friend, who had lent me five dollars the week before.*

square-dance (skwâr′dans′) *v.i.,* **-danced, -danc·ing.** to perform or take part in a square dance.

square dance 1. a folk or social dance, developed in America and performed by groups of four or more couples who are arranged in a square at the beginning of the dance. **2.** an event or social gathering featuring square dances.

square deal *Informal.* fair and honest treatment or transaction.

square knot, a knot formed by two interlaced loops going in opposite directions.

square meal, a complete or substantial meal: *to eat three square meals a day.*

square measure, a unit or system of units for measuring area. For Weights and Measures table, see **weight.**

square one *Informal.* the very beginning; the starting point: *Our plan didn't work out, so we're back to square one.*

square-rigged (skwâr′rigd′) *adj.* having square sails as the principal sails.

square-rig·ger (skwâr′rig′ər) *n.* a square-rigged ship.

square root, a number that when squared produces a given number. The square root of 9 is 3.

square sail, a four-sided sail, as used on a schooner when sailing before the wind.

square shooter *Informal.* a person who is honest and straightforward in dealing with others.

squar·ish (skwâr′ish) *adj.* almost or somewhat square.

squash[1] (skwosh) *v.t.* **1.** to beat or press into a soft or flat mass; crush: *You squashed my hat when you sat on it.* **2.** to force or squeeze into a small area; cram; crowd: *We squashed all the clothes into one suitcase.* **3.** to put down or suppress completely and forcibly: *to squash a revolt.* —*v.i.* **1.** to be or become crushed: *The fallen leaves squashed underfoot.* **2.** to make or move with a squashing sound. **3.** to squeeze into a small space; crowd: *I squashed into the back seat of the car between my friends.* —*n.* **1.** a crushed or crowded mass, esp. of people. **2.** the act of squashing or the state of being squashed. **3.** the sound of squashing. **4.** either of two games, **squash racquets** or **squash tennis,** in which a rubber ball is hit with a racket against a wall in a concrete court. **5.** *British.* a soft drink, usually containing fruit juice and soda water. [Old French *esquasser* to break in pieces, going back to Latin *ex-* (see EX-[1]) + *quassāre* to shake, shatter.] —**squash′er,** *n.*

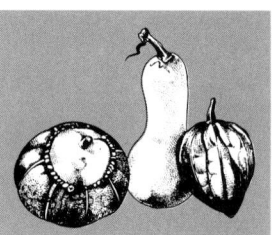

squash[2]

squash[2] (skwosh) *n.* **1.** the round or oblong fruit of any of a group of plants, genus *Cucurbita,* of the gourd family, cooked and eaten as a vegetable, or used as food for livestock. **2.** the plant bearing this fruit, having broad leaves and threadlike tendrils,

cultivated in most parts of the world. [Shortened from Algonquian *askutasquash* literally, vegetables eaten green.]

squash bug, a dark brown insect, *Anasa tristis,* found in North America, destructive to squash plants.

squash·y (skwosh′ē) *adj.,* **squash·i·er, squash·i·est. 1.** easily squashed: *squashy tomatoes.* **2.** soft and wet: *squashy mud.* —**squash′i·ly,** *adv.* —**squash′i·ness,** *n.*

squat (skwot) *v.,* **squat·ted** or **squat, squat·ting.** —*v.i.* **1.** to sit or crouch with the knees bent and drawn close to the body: *We squatted around the campfire. I squatted down to pet the cat.* **2.** to settle on land without having right or title to it, but often in order to gain title or right. **3.** to occupy abandoned property without right, title, or payment of rent. —*v.t.* to put (oneself) in a squatting position. —*adj.* **1.** short and thick; low and broad: *a squat person waddling down the street.* **2.** sitting or being in a crouching position. [Old French *esquatir* to crush, going back to Latin *ex-* (see EX-[1]) + *coāctus* forced, past participle of *cogere* to drive together, force.] —**squat′ly,** *adv.* —**squat′ness,** *n.*

squat·ter (skwot′ər) *n.* **1.** a person or thing that squats. **2.** a person who settles on land without having any right or title to it. Squatters are sometimes given title to land after having lived on it for a certain period of time. **3.** a person who occupies abandoned property without right, title, or payment of rent.

squat·ty (skwot′ē) *adj.,* **-ti·er, -ti·est.** squat.

squaw (skwô) *n.* **1.** a North American Indian woman or wife. **2.** *Slang.* a woman or wife. ➡ considered offensive in both defs. [Algonquian *squaws* woman.]

squaw·fish (skwô′fish′) *n., pl.* **-fish** or **-fish·es.** any of a group of long, slender, carplike fish, genus *Ptychocheilus,* of western North American rivers.

squawk (skwôk) *v.i.* **1.** to utter a shrill, harsh cry, as a gull or parrot. **2.** *Informal.* to complain or protest loudly or raucously: *The child squawked at having to take a nap.* —*n.* **1.** a shrill, harsh cry. **2.** *Informal.* a loud complaint or protest. [Imitative.] —**squawk′er,** *n.*

squeak (skwēk) *n.* a short, thin high-pitched cry or sound. —*v.i.* **1.** to make or utter a squeak: *The rusty gate squeaked when it opened.* **2.** to accomplish, pass, survive, or win something by a narrow margin or with difficulty (with *through* or *by*): *to squeak through an exam, to squeak by on a small allowance.* —*v.t.* to utter or produce with a squeak. [Probably imitative.] —**squeak′er,** *n.*

squeak·y (skwē′kē) *adj.,* **squeak·i·er, squeak·i·est.** tending to squeak; squeaking: *squeaky floors.* —**squeak′i·ly,** *adv.* —**squeak′i·ness,** *n.*

squeal (skwēl) *v.i.* **1.** to make or utter a loud, shrill cry or sound: *to squeal with delight.* **2.** *Slang.* to betray a confidence; turn informer: *The accomplice squealed to the police.* —*v.t.* to utter or produce with a squeal. —*n.* a loud, shrill cry or sound. [Imitative.] —**squeal′er,** *n.*

squeam·ish (skwē′mish) *adj.* **1.** easily sickened or nauseated: *to be squeamish about the sight of blood.* **2.** feeling sick; nauseated: *The boat trip made me squeamish.* **3.** readily offended or shocked; overly modest; prudish: *a squeamish attitude toward sex.* **4.** overly scrupulous, fastidious, or sensitive, as in standards of action or belief: *trifles magnified into importance by a squeamish conscience* (Thomas Babington Macaulay, 1855). [Modification of earlier *squeymous, scoymus,* from Anglo-Norman *escoymous* fastidious; of uncertain origin.] —**squeam′ish·ly,** *adv.* —**squeam′ish·ness,** *n.*

squee·gee (skwē′jē) *n.* **1.** a T-shaped implement with a rubber or leather edge, used in wiping off or spreading liquid on flat, smooth surfaces, as in washing windows. **2.** a device with a rubber roller or brush, used in photography for pressing excess water from a negative or print. —*v.t.,* **-geed, -gee·ing.** to wipe, spread, or press with a squeegee. [From *squeege,* form of SQUEEZE.]

squeeze (skwēz) *v.,* **squeezed, squeez·ing.** —*v.t.* **1.** to apply strong pressure to, esp. by pressing from opposing sides: *to squeeze a tube of toothpaste, to squeeze one's eyes shut.* **2.** to obtain (something) by the application of pressure; extract: *to squeeze juice from an orange, to squeeze water from a mop.* **3.** to get by unfair or dishonest means, esp. money; extort: *to squeeze a contribution from someone.* **4.** to press or hug, as in sympathy or affection: *to squeeze someone's hand.* **5.** to force by pressure; thrust forcibly: *to squeeze a book onto a crowded shelf.* **6.** to oppress. —*v.i.* **1.** to apply or exert pressure. **2.** to be capable of being squeezed; yield to pressure. **3.** to pass or force one's way by squeezing: *to squeeze into a seat, to squeeze between parked cars.* —*n.* **1.** the act of squeezing; application of pressure. **2.** a close embrace; hug. **3.** the pressure of a crowd of people; crush: *There is always a squeeze in the subway during rush hours.* **4.** an impression of some object, as a coin, made by pressing a substance around or over it. **5.** a position of difficulty; time of need: *a tight squeeze from lack of funds, a financial squeeze.* **6.** *Informal.* force

or pressure exerted by means of coercion or threats: *Thugs hired by gangsters put the squeeze on the small storekeepers to pay protection.* [Possibly modification of obsolete *quease* to press, from Old English *cwȳsan* to bruise, crush.] —**squeez'a·ble,** *adj.* —**squeez'a·bly,** *adv.* —**squeez'er,** *n.*

squeeze play, a play in baseball in which a runner on third base runs toward home plate as the ball is pitched, and the batter attempts to bunt the ball so that the runner can score.

squelch (skwelch) *v.t.* **1.** to stamp out or eliminate forcibly and completely; crush; squash: *to squelch political opposition.* **2.** to put down or subdue, as with a crushing or sarcastic remark. —*v.i.* to make or move with a sucking or splashing sound, as when walking on wet ground. —*n.* **1.** *Informal.* a crushing remark or response. **2.** a sucking or splashing sound. [Imitative.] —**squelch'er,** *n.* —**squelch'ing·ly,** *adv.*

squib (skwib) *n.* **1.** a short, written or spoken attack of a witty or satiric nature. **2.** a small combustible device that burns with a hissing noise and then explodes. **3.** a broken firecracker that burns but does not explode. [Of uncertain origin.]

squid (skwid) *n., pl.* **squids** or **squid.** any of a group of saltwater invertebrates, order Dibranchia, related to the cuttlefish and octopus, having a cylindrical body, a pair of fins that aid in swimming, and ten arms with suckers, used for catching prey. Length: 2 inches to 50 feet (5 centimeters to 15.2 meters). [Of uncertain origin.]

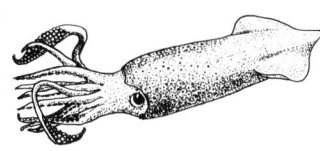

squid

squig·gle (skwig'əl) *n.* a wavy or twisting line; wriggly mark or twist: *I drew a few squiggles in my notebook as I listened to the long, boring lecture.* —*v.,* -**gled,** -**gling.** —*v.t.* **1.** to write or draw carelessly or hastily; scribble. **2.** to make into squiggles. —*v.i.* **1.** to scribble. **2.** to move with a wavy or twisting motion; wriggle. [Blend of SQUIRM and WIGGLE.]

squill (skwil) *n.* any of several plants of the lily family, native to Europe, Asia, and Africa, esp. *Urginea maritima,* bearing clusters of small white flowers, or plants of the genus *Scilla,* having blue, purple, or white flowers. [Latin *squilla, scilla,* from Greek *skilla.*]

squint (skwint) *v.i.* **1.** to look with partly closed eyes: *We squinted in the bright sunlight.* **2.** to look sideways; look askance. **3.** to be cross-eyed. —*v.t.* **1.** to hold (the eyes) partly closed: *The smoke made me squint my eyes.* **2.** to cause to squint. —*n.* **1.** the act or habit of squinting. **2.** the condition of being cross-eyed. —*adj.* looking askance. [Shortened from earlier *asquint* obliquely, askance; of uncertain origin.] —**squint'er,** *n.* —**squint'ing·ly,** *adv.* —**squint'y,** *adj.*

squire (skwīr) *n.* **1.** an English country gentleman or landowner. ➡ often used as a title and form of address. **2.** in feudal society, a young nobleman who, in preparation for his own knighthood, attended a knight. **3.** a man who escorts a woman. **4.** a local U.S. judicial official, as a justice of the peace or magistrate. —*v.t.,* **squired, squir·ing.** to attend (someone) as a squire or escort. [Short for ESQUIRE.]

squirm (skwûrm) *v.i.* **1.** to turn or twist the body: *to squirm in one's seat.* **2.** to show or feel discomfort, uneasiness, or mental distress: *to blush and squirm with embarrassment.* —*n.* the act or motion of squirming. [Possibly imitative.] —**squirm'y,** *adj.*

squir·rel (skwûr'əl) *n.* **1.** any of various tree-dwelling rodents, family Sciuridae, native to most regions of the world, usually having a slender body and a long, bushy tail, and feeding chiefly on nuts. Length: up to 3 feet (0.9 meter), including tail. **2.** its short, soft gray, reddish, or dark brown fur. **3.** any of various burrowing or ground-dwelling members of the squirrel family, as the ground squirrel, chipmunk, and prairie dog. —*v.t.,* -**reled** or -**relled,** -**rel·ing** or -**rel·ling.** to save and store or hide (usually with *away*): *to squirrel away money for the future.* [Old French *escurel* the tree-dwelling rodent, going back to Latin *sciūrus,* from Greek *skiouros* literally, shadow-tail, from *skiā* shade + *ourā* tail; with reference to its bushy tail.]

squirt (skwûrt) *v.t.* **1.** to eject or force out (liquid) through a narrow opening in a thin jet or stream: *to squirt oil on a rusty hinge.* **2.** to wet with liquid so ejected: *to squirt someone with a hose.* —*v.i.* **1.** to come out in a thin jet or stream: *The ink squirted from the fountain pen.* **2.** to eject or force out a thin jetlike stream of liquid. —*n.* **1.** the act of squirting. **2.** a thin, usually short, jet or stream. **3.** something used for squirting liquid, as a syringe or small pump. **4.** *Informal.* a rude, brash young person full of self-importance. [Form of dialectal English *swirt,* possibly from Low German *swirtjen* to eject liquid in a stream.] —**squirt'er,** *n.*

squirting cucumber, a trailing vine, *Ecballium elaterium,* of the

gourd family, native to the Mediterranean region, bearing small, prickly, oblong fruits that squirt their seeds and juicy pulp when ripe.

squish (skwish) *v.i.* to make a splashing or gushing sound when pressed or walked on. —*v.t.* *Informal.* to press or squeeze into a soft or flat mass. —**squish'y,** *adj.*

sq yd *also,* **sq. yd.** square yard; square yards.

Sr, the symbol for strontium.

Sr. 1. senior. **2.** señor. **3.** sister.

Sra., señora.

SRO *also,* **S.R.O.** standing room only.

SS, the corps of black-uniformed German troops organized by Adolf Hitler in the 1920s as his personal bodyguard and later put in charge of exterminations and massacres in conquered countries, such as Poland, during World War II. [Abbreviation of German *Schutzstaffel* literally, protection staff.]

SS 1. *also,* **S/S** steamship. **2.** *also,* **S.S.** Sunday school.

SSE, south-southeast.

SSW, south-southwest.

st. 1. stanza. **2.** stone (weight). **3.** street.

St. 1. Saint. **2.** Strait. **3.** Street.

stab (stab) *v.,* **stabbed, stab·bing.** —*v.t.* **1.** to pierce with or as with a pointed weapon: *to stab one's finger on a thorn.* **2.** to thrust or drive (a pointed instrument or weapon) into something: *to stab a fork into meat.* —*v.i.* to thrust with or as with a pointed weapon. —*n.* **1.** a thrust made with or as with a pointed weapon. **2.** a wound or puncture made by stabbing. **3.** a sharp but momentary sensation or feeling; pang: *a stab of pain, a stab of regret.* **4.** *Informal.* an attempt; effort; try: *to make a stab at a hard job.* [Possibly form of dialectal English *stob* to pierce, from *stob* nail, stick, form of STUB.] —**stab'ber,** *n.*

·**to stab (someone) in the back.** to do harm or injury to (someone) in a treacherous manner; betray.

sta·bile (*adj.* stā'bəl; *n.* stā'bēl) *adj.* not likely to fall or be overturned; firm; stable. —*n.* a sculpture of metal, plastic, cardboard, or other material hung on wires that hold the sculpture in a fixed position. [Latin *stabilis* firm, steady. See STABLE².]

sta·bil·i·ty (stə bil'i tē) *n., pl.* -**ties. 1.** the condition of being stable. **2.** consistency or steadiness, as of character or purpose. **3.** a lasting or enduring nature or quality; permanence.

sta·bi·lize (stā'bə līz') *v.t.,* -**lized,** -**liz·ing. 1.** to make fixed, firm, or steady. **2.** to prevent from fluctuating: *to stabilize stock prices.* —**sta'bi·li·za'tion,** *n.*

sta·bi·liz·er (stā'bə lī'zər) *n.* **1.** a person or thing that makes something stable. **2.** a gyroscopic device in a ship, airplane, or the like that keeps it steady in rough water or turbulent air. **3.** the vertical fin or either of the horizontal surfaces of the tail of an airplane.

sta·ble¹ (stā'bəl) *n.* **1.** a building, esp. one with stalls, where horses or cattle are kept and fed. **2.** the animals housed in such a building. **3.** *also,* **stables. a.** racehorses belonging to a particular establishment or owner. **b.** personnel, grounds, and equipment of such an establishment. **4.** a group of persons engaged in the same activity and under the same management: *a publisher's stable of authors, a manager's stable of boxers.* —*v.,* -**bled,** -**bling.** —*v.t.* to put or keep in a stable. —*v.i.* to live in or as in a stable: *The horses stable in the barn.* [Old French *estable* covered place where one lodges animals, from Latin *stabulum* abode, stall.]

sta·ble² (stā'bəl) *adj.* **1.** not easily moved, shaken, or overthrown; fixed in position; firm: *a stable platform, a stable government.* **2.** reliable, consistent, or steady, as in character or purpose. **3.** continuing without much change; lasting or enduring; permanent: *a stable language.* **4.** *Chemistry.* (of chemical compounds) resistant to chemical change; not easily decomposed. **5.** *Physics.* **a.** (of a substance) not subject to radioactive decay; not radioactive. **b.** (of a body) resistant to mechanical forces that disturb equilibrium, shape, or form: *A car with a low center of gravity is more stable than one with a high center of gravity.* [Old French *(e)stable* firm, upright, from Latin *stabilis* firm, steady, from *stāre* to stand.] —**sta'bly,** *adv.*

sta·ble·boy (stā'bəl boi') *n.* a man or boy who works in a stable.

stab·lish (stab'lish) *v.t., v.i. Archaic.* establish.

stacc., staccato.

stac·ca·to (stə kä'tō) *adj.* **1.** *Music.* produced with or having breaks between the successive tones; disconnected; abrupt.

a	at	e	end	o	hot	u	up	hw	white		about
ā	ape	ē	me	ō	old	ū	use	ng	song		taken
ä	far	i	it	ô	fork	ü	rule	th	thin	ə	pencil
âr	care	ī	ice	oi	oil	u̇	pull	th	this		lemon
		îr	pierce	ou	out	ûr	turn	zh	measure		circus

2. composed of or characterized by abrupt, sharp emphasis, sound, or movement: *staccato gunfire.* —*adv.* in a staccato manner. —*n.* an abrupt, sharp manner or sound: *to speak in a staccato.* [Italian *staccato* literally, detached, past participle of *staccare* to detach, separate, going back to Latin *dis-* apart + Low German *takk* pointed thing.]

stack (stak) *n.* **1.** a large, rectangular or cone-shaped pile of hay, straw, or unthreshed grain left in the field, often thatched or otherwise arranged to protect it from the weather. **2.** an orderly or systematically arranged pile: *a stack of plates, postcards arranged in small stacks on a table.* **3.** a number of rifles standing muzzle upward against each other and forming a cone. **4.** a pipe or series of pipes carrying off smoke, waste, or poisonous flames. **5.a.** *also,* **stacks.** a rack in which books are arranged above one another on shelves. **b. stacks.** a library area in which most of the books are shelved. **6.** *Informal.* a large quantity: *a stack of work to do.* —*v.t.* **1.** to gather or arrange in a stack: *to stack papers, to stack corn up in a barn.* **2.** to load

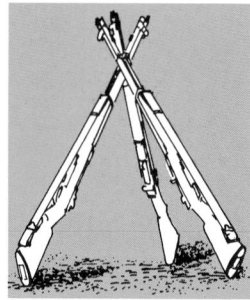

stack of rifles

with stacks of material: *to stack shelves in a grocery store.* **3.** to arrange (playing cards or a deck) beforehand so that the cards will come up in a certain order. **4.** to arrange, as facts, circumstances, or events, ahead of time to one's advantage or another person's disadvantage: *The odds are stacked against our winning.* [Old Norse *stakkr* haystack.]

• **to stack up. a.** to fulfill or meet (expectations); compare: *How does your latest novel stack up against your first two?* **b.** to be true or seemingly true according to what is already known: *That news account doesn't stack up with the true facts of the matter.*

sta·di·a[1] (stā′dē ə) *n.* a surveying method using a long graduated rod, or **stadia rod**, the number of whose divisions when sighted between the cross hairs of a transit is multiplied by a constant to give the distance between the transit and the rod. [Of uncertain origin.]

sta·di·a[2] (stā′dē ə) a plural of **stadium.**

sta·di·um (stā′dē əm) *n., pl.* **-di·ums** or **-di·a. 1.** a large, usually roofless, oval or U-shaped structure surrounding an open area, used for athletic events and other purposes, as rallies or concerts, and equipped with rows of seats for spectators. **2.** in ancient Greece and Rome, a U-shaped track for foot races and other athletic events, about 607 feet (185 meters) long with rows of seats for spectators except at the open end. [Latin *stadium* measure of length of about 607 feet (185 meters), course for racing, from Greek *stadion.*]

staff (staf) *n., pl.* **staffs** or *(defs. 1, 4)* **staves. 1.a.** a stick, rod, or pole, often used as an aid in walking and as a weapon or symbol of authority. **b.** flagpole. **2.** a body of permanent employees working in an institution or business or making up a specialized group within such a body: *the hospital staff, a nursing staff.* **3.** military personnel with administrative duties who do not take part in combat. **4.** *Music.* the five horizontal lines and four spaces on which musical notation is made, used to represent the pitches of tones. —*v.t.* to provide (an office, establishment, military

staff
(n., def. 4)

unit, or the like) with officers or employees: *to staff a new store.* [Old English *stæf* stick, pole[1].]

staff·er (staf′ər) *n.* a member of a staff.

staff officer, an officer who is a member of a staff. ➡ distinguished from **line officer.**

staff of life, any staple food, esp. bread, regarded as the mainstay of a diet.

staff sergeant *U.S. Military.* a noncommissioned officer ranking in the Army below a sergeant first class, in the Air Force below a technical sergeant, and in the Marine Corps below a gunnery sergeant.

stag (stag) *n.* **1.** a full-grown male of various deer, esp. of the red deer. **2.** the male of various other animals, esp. when castrated after reaching maturity. **3.** a man who goes to a social gathering unaccompanied by a woman. **4.** a social gathering attended by men only. —*adj.* for or attended by men only: *a stag party.* —*adv.* (of a man) not accompanied by a woman: *to go to a dance stag.* [From an unrecorded Old English word.]

stage (stāj) *n.* **1.** a raised platform in a theater or hall, on which

a performance takes place. **2.** the theater as a profession: *to write for the stage.* **3.** a place where some important event takes place; scene of action: *Europe has been the stage for many wars.* **4.** a step, period, or degree in a process, progression, or development: *an early stage of childhood, in the last stage of a disease.* **5.** the distance traveled between two places of rest on a road or journey; definite portion of a journey: *The first stage of our trip took us across the Atlantic Ocean.* **6.** a regular stopping place on a journey. **7.** stagecoach. **8.** the small shelf on a microscope on which the object to be examined is placed. **9.** one of the self-propelling sections of a rocket vehicle that can be separated from the rest of the vehicle. **10.** a platform or scaffold, as for painters, carpenters, or other workers. —*v.t.,* **staged, stag·ing. 1.** to put, arrange, or exhibit on or as on a stage: *to stage a play.* **2.** to take part in, manage, or direct: *The protesters staged a demonstration in front of the embassy.* [Old French *estage* dwelling, story[2], floor, condition, going back to Latin *stāre* to stand.]

• **by** (or **in**) **easy stages.** with many stops, as for rest; gradually; slowly.

stage·coach (stāj′kōch′) *n.* a horse-drawn coach traveling on a regular schedule over a fixed route, carrying passengers, mail, and baggage. Also, **stage.**

stage·craft (stāj′kraft′) *n.* skill in the writing, directing, and producing of a theatrical work or similar entertainment.

stagecoach

stage fright, nervousness experienced by a performer or speaker before an audience.

stage·hand (stāj′hand′) *n.* in the theater, a person who moves scenery, sets props, controls lighting, and performs certain other duties.

stage manager, a person who is in charge of the stage and its arrangement before and during a performance, as of a play or concert.

stag·er (stā′jər) *n.* a person experienced in a profession or way of life; veteran. [Possibly from Old French *estagier* resident, from *estage.* See STAGE.]

stage·struck (stāj′struk′) *adj.* fascinated by the theater, esp. with the hopes of becoming an actor.

stage whisper 1. in the theater, a whisper meant to be heard by the audience and supposedly unheard by some or all of the other players on the stage. **2.** a whisper intended to be overheard by persons other than the person addressed.

stag·ey (stā′jē) *adj.,* **stag·i·er, stag·i·est.** stagy.

stag·ger (stag′ər) *v.i.* **1.** to move unsteadily or with a swaying motion; totter; reel: *to stagger under a heavy load.* **2.** to become confused or overwhelmed; falter in purpose or action; waver: *I staggered at the amount of work still to be done.* —*v.t.* **1.** to cause to totter or reel: *The punch staggered the fighter.* **2.** to confuse or overwhelm, as with grief or surprise: *an act of bravery that staggers the imagination.* **3.** to schedule, arrange, or distribute in a continuous or overlapping order, as to relieve congestion: *to stagger traffic lights, to stagger work shifts.* **4.** to arrange in a zigzag or alternating pattern or manner: *to stagger pictures on a wall.* —*n.* **1.** the act or motion of staggering. **2.** a staggered pattern or arrangement. **3. staggers.** any of several diseases of the central nervous system in cattle and other domestic animals, causing sudden falls and a staggering gait. ➡ used as singular or plural. [Old Norse *stakra* to push, cause to reel.] —**stag′ger·er,** *n.* —**stag′ger·ing·ly,** *adv.*

stag·horn coral (stag′hôrn′) a coral, *Acropora cervicornis,* whose colonies develop in a branchlike arrangement that resembles a stag's horn.

staghorn fern, any epiphytic fern of the genus *Platycerium* that bears two forms of leaves, one of which grows as long, forked fronds that resemble a stag's horn in shape.

stag·ing (stā′jing) *n.* **1.** a temporary wooden or metal platform; scaffolding. **2.** the directing and presenting of a theatrical or similar entertainment.

staging area, an area where military personnel or supplies are assembled, usually in preparation for a battle.

stag·nant (stag′nənt) *adj.* **1.** still, as air or water; motionless. **2.** foul from standing still: *stagnant water in a swamp.* **3.** not growing, changing, or developing; inactive; dull: *stagnant trade, a stagnant life.* [Latin *stāgnāns,* present participle of *stāgnāre* to form a pool of standing water, from *stāgnum* pool.] —**stag′nan·cy,** *n.* —**stag′nant·ly,** *adv.*

stag·nate (stag′nāt) *v.i.,* **-nat·ed, -nat·ing. 1.** to stop grow-

ing, changing, or developing; be or become inactive or dull: *to allow the mind to stagnate.* **2.** to be or become stagnant: *The water in the pond stagnated.* [Latin *stāgnātus,* past participle of *stāgnāre.* See STAGNANT.] —**stag·na′tion,** *n.*

stag·y (stā′jē) *also,* **stagey.** *adj.,* **stag·i·er, stag·i·est.** of, suited to, or suggestive of the stage, esp. having or characterized by a theatrical or affected manner. —**stag′i·ly,** *adv.* —**stag′i·ness,** *n.*

staid (stād) *v. Archaic.* a past tense and past participle of **stay**[1]. —*adj.* conservative or sober in character or style; sedate. —**staid′ly,** *adv.* —**staid′ness,** *n.*

stain (stān) *n.* **1.** a spot or streak produced on or in something by another substance; discoloration: *an ink stain, grass stains.* **2.** a liquid dye or thin pigment, used esp. in coloring wood. **3.** a colored solution used to treat a microscopic specimen so as to render structures visible. **4.** a moral taint or blemish: *a stain on one's reputation.* —*v.t.* **1.** to spot, streak, or discolor with foreign matter: *Spilled coffee stained the carpet.* **2.** to color or treat with a dye, pigment, or other colored solution: *to stain a bookcase, to stain a slide.* **3.** to bring dishonor upon; taint or blemish. —*v.i.* **1.** to become or be capable of being stained: *This synthetic material stains easily.* **2.** to cause or be capable of causing a stain. [Short for DISTAIN.] —**stain′a·ble,** *adj.* —**stain′er,** *n.*

stained glass, glass that has been colored by fusing metal oxides or by having pigments burned into the surface, widely used in pieces held together by strips of lead. —**stained′-glass′,** *adj.*

Tiffany **stained glass**

stain·less (stān′lis) *adj.* having no stains or blemishes: *a stainless reputation.* —*n.* tableware made of stainless steel. —**stain′less·ly,** *adv.* —**stain′less·ness,** *n.*

stainless steel, an alloy of steel with large amounts of chromium, and often of nickel, that is highly resistant to corrosion and heat and is strong, durable, and easy to shape. It is used for cutlery, cooking utensils, instruments, appliances, and structural parts.

stair (stâr) *n.* **1.** *usually,* **stairs.** a series or flight of steps for passing from one level or floor of a building to another. **2.** a step or one of a series of steps. [Old English *stǣger* flight of steps.]

stair·case (stâr′kās′) *n.* a flight or a series of flights of stairs with its supporting framework.

stair·way (stâr′wā′) *n.* staircase.

stair·well (stâr′wel′) *n.* a vertical shaft enclosing a staircase.

stake (stāk) *n.* **1.** a stick or post sharpened at one end for driving into the ground, esp. one used as a support or boundary. **2.a.** a post to which a person was bound for execution by burning: *Joan of Arc was burned at the stake.* **b.** an execution performed in this manner. **3.** *also,* **stakes.** something that is risked in a wager or gambling game, as money. **4.** an interest, share, or involvement in any project, esp. a financial interest: *As the star of the play, the actor has a stake in its success.* **5.** *also,* **stakes.** a sum of money offered the winner of a contest or race; prize; purse. —*v.t.,* **staked, stak·ing. 1.** to mark the boundaries of with or as with stakes; claim or reserve (often with *off* and *out*): *to stake out a campsite, to stake out one's area of responsibility.* **2.** to fasten or tie to a stake; support with a stake: *to stake tomato plants.* **3.** to gamble or risk: *to stake all one's savings on a business venture.*

4. to provide what is needed, as money: *to stake someone to dinner.* [Old English *staca* strong stick, post[1].]

·**at stake.** in question or danger; at issue: *The firefighters acted quickly because many lives were at stake.*

·**to pull up stakes.** to move on or away; leave.

·**to stake out. a.** to assign (a police officer, detective, or the like) to conduct a surveillance, as of a suspect or place. **b.** to maintain a surveillance of: *to stake out a warehouse.*

stake·out (stāk′out′) *n.* **1.** a surveillance of a person or place, as by the police. **2.** a place that is under surveillance, esp. by the police.

Sta·kha·no·vism (stə kä′nə viz′əm) *n.* in the Soviet Union, a system of speeding up industrial production by increasing wage rates for more productive workers. [From Alexei *Stakhanov,* Russian miner who developed such a system in 1935.] —**Sta·kha′no·vite′,** *n.*

sta·lac·tite (stə lak′tīt, stal′ək tīt′) *n.* an iciclelike formation on the ceiling of a cave, usually composed of calcium carbonate deposited by water seeping through the rock above. ➡ distinguished from **stalagmite.** [Modern Latin *stalactites,* from Greek *stalaktos* trickling, dripping; because it is formed by the dripping of water.] —**stal·ac·tit·ic** (stal′ək tit′ik), *adj.*

sta·lag·mite (stə lag′mīt, stal′əg mīt′) *n.* a formation resembling a cone, built up on the floor of a cave by calcium carbonate in water dripping from the ceiling. ➡ distinguished from stalactite. [Modern Latin *stalagmites,* from Greek *stalagmos* a dripping.] —**stal·ag·mit·ic** (stal′əg mit′ik), *adj.*

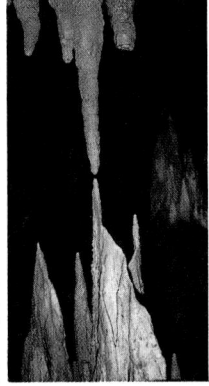

stalactites and **stalagmites**

stale (stāl) *adj.,* **stal·er, stal·est. 1.** having lost freshness: *stale cake.* **2.** having lost novelty or interest; hackneyed: *stale news.* **3.** out of condition: *The athlete was stale from lack of exercise.* —*v.t., v.i.,* **staled, stal·ing.** to make or become stale. [Of uncertain origin.] —**stale′ly,** *adv.* —**stale′ness,** *n.*

stale·mate (stāl′māt′) *n.* **1.** a situation in chess in which the player whose turn it is to move cannot move without putting the king in check. Such a move is against the rules, therefore the game is counted as a draw. **2.** any position or situation in which no further action is possible; impasse; standstill. —*v.t.,* -**mat·ed,** -**mat·ing. 1.** to bring to a stalemate. **2.** to place in an impasse. [Middle English *stale* stalemate (in chess), probably from Anglo-Norman *estale* position (from *estaler* to stop, set in place; of Germanic origin) + MATE[2].]

stalk[1] (stôk) *n.* **1.** the main stem or axis of a plant. **2.** the stem of any plant part, as the petiole of a leaf, or the peduncle of a flower cluster. **3.** a similar part supporting part of an animal, as the eyes of some crustaceans, or the whole animal, as a crinoid. [Middle English *stalke* main stem of a plant, possibly diminutive of *stale* handle, from Old English *stalu* side of a ladder.]

stalk[2] (stôk) *v.t.* **1.** to hunt, track, or pursue stealthily: *The lion stalked its prey.* **2.** to move or walk menacingly or stealthily through; haunt: *The fugitive stalked the streets. Pestilence and famine stalk the countryside.* —*v.i.* **1.** to walk or stride in a stiff, determined, or angry manner: *The furious child stalked out of the room.* **2.** to hunt or track game. **3.** to move in a menacing or stealthy manner: *Fear of crime stalked across the city.* [Old English *bestealcian* to go stealthily.] —**stalk′er,** *n.*

stalk·ing-horse (stô′king hôrs′) *n.* **1.** anything used to conceal real motives or actual plans; pretext. **2.** a horse or figure of a horse, behind which a hunter hides while stalking game.

stall (stôl) *n.* **1.** a compartment in a barn or stable for one horse, cow, or other animal. **2.** a booth or counter for setting up wares for sale, as at a fair. **3.** an enclosed seat in the chancel of a church, usually reserved for the clergy. **4.** *British.* an orchestra seat in the front of a theater. **5.** *Informal.* evasion, pretense, or other delaying tactic. **6.** a condition in which an aircraft lacks the required speed necessary to generate lift, causing the aircraft to drop. **7.** a space marked off for parking a car or other vehicle, as in a garage.

a	at	e	end	o	hot	u	up	hw	white
ā	ape	ē	me	ō	old	ū	use	ng	song
ä	far	i	it	ô	fork	ü	rule	th	thin
âr	care	ī	ice	oi	oil	u̇	pull	th	this
		îr	pierce	ou	out	ûr	turn	zh	measure

ə { about, taken, pencil, lemon, circus }

8. a small, enclosed space or compartment. —*v.t.* **1.** to delay or prevent from acting: *The store owner stalled the robber until the police arrived.* **2.** to block the motion or progress of; bring to a standstill: *The disabled locomotive stalled the train for an hour.* **3.** to cause (an engine, automobile, or the like) to stop running. **4.** to put or lodge (an animal) in a stall. —*v.i.* **1.** to make delays; be evasive: *to stall for time.* **2.** to come to a standstill: *Traffic stalled at the entrance to the stadium.* **3.** to stop running: *The car often stalls on cold mornings.* **4.** (of an aircraft) to stop generating lift as a result of the lack of the speed required to do so; go into a stall. [Old English *steall* place, station, division in a stable.]

stal·lion (stal′yən) *n.* a male horse, esp. one used as a stud horse. [Old French *estalon*; of Germanic origin.]

stal·wart (stôl′wərt) *adj.* **1.** physically strong; robust: *a stalwart gymnast.* **2.** having or showing much courage; brave; valiant: *a stalwart warrior.* **3.** faithful and unwavering; firm; resolute: *a stalwart ally.* —*n.* **1.** a person who is stalwart. **2.** an unwavering supporter, as of a political party or cause; partisan. [Old English *stælwierthe* serviceable, from *stathol* foundation + *wierthe* worth.] —**stal′wart·ly,** *adv.* —**stal′wart·ness,** *n.*

sta·men (stā′mən) *n., pl.* **stamens** or **stam·i·na.** the pollen-bearing organ of a flowering plant, consisting of a slender stalk, or filament, and the anther, which consists of two sacs containing the pollen grains. [Latin *stāmen* thread.]

stam·i·na[1] (stam′ə nə) *n.* the moral or physical capacity to withstand fatigue, disease, or hardship; endurance. [Latin *stāmina,* plural of *stāmen* thread; with reference to the thread supposedly spun by the Fates at birth that determined by its length the duration of one's life.] —For Synonyms, see **endurance.**

stam·i·na[2] (stam′ə nə) a plural of **stamen.**

stam·i·nate (stam′ə nit, -nāt′) *adj.* **1.** having a stamen or stamens. **2.** having stamens but no pistils.

stam·mer (stam′ər) *v.i.* to speak haltingly, esp. by repeating a letter or sound. —*v.t.* to say or utter with a stammer: *to stammer a refusal.* —*n.* the habit or instance of stammering. [Old English *stamerian* to stutter.] —**stam′mer·er,** *n.*

stamp (stamp) *v.t.* **1.** to bring down (the foot or feet) forcefully and heavily: *to stamp one's foot in anger and frustration.* **2.** to strike forcefully with the sole of the foot: *to stamp the ground in time to music.* **3.** to mark (an impression, design, or the like): *to stamp an initial on stationery.* **4.** to mark (an object, surface, or the like) with a device that cuts or imprints a design, letters, or the like: *to stamp butter, to stamp an invoice as paid.* **5.** to impress deeply; fix: *an event stamped on one's memory.* **6.** to show to be of a certain quality or nature; characterize: *Their actions stamped them as true patriots.* **7.** to affix a postage stamp or other official mark on: *to stamp a letter, to stamp a passport.* **8.** to pound, crush, or pulverize (something, as ore). —*v.i.* **1.** to strike the foot forcefully downward upon the ground, as in walking: *to stamp on the floor.* **2.** to walk forcefully with heavy steps: *to stamp out of a room in anger.* —*n.* **1.** a device or tool for cutting or impressing a design, letters, or the like on paper, wax, metal, or other surface. **2.** an impression or design made with such a device. **3.a.** postage stamp. **b.** any similar stamped or printed paper, usually issued by a government and placed on something to show that a tax or other charge has been paid. **4.** an impressed mark or seal used to certify or assure validity: *a royal stamp.* **5.** a distinguishing mark or impression: *The author's work bears the stamp of a vivid imagination.* **6.** quality or nature; type; sort; kind: *to be of the same stamp as one's parents.* **7.** a machine to crush rock, ore, or the like: *The mine had a mill with five stamps.* **8.** the act of stamping. [Probably from an unrecorded Old English word.]

　· **to stamp out. a.** to put out or extinguish by stamping with the foot or feet: *to stamp out a campfire.* **b.** to put an end to; eliminate: *to stamp out crime.*

stam·pede (stam pēd′) *n.* **1.** a sudden scattering or headlong flight of frightened animals, as a herd of cattle or horses. **2.** a sudden scattering or headlong flight of a mob or crowd. **3.** a mass movement set off by a common impulse: *a stampede of resignations.* —*v.,* **-ped·ed, -ped·ing.** —*v.i.* to be part of a stampede. —*v.t.* to cause to stampede: *The rustlers stampeded the cattle.* [Spanish *estampida* uproar, rush, from *estampar* to stamp; of Germanic origin.]

stamp·er (stam′pər) *n.* **1.** a person who stamps or operates a machine that stamps. **2.** a machine or instrument used for stamping.

stamping ground *Informal.* a person's favorite or frequent gathering place or haunt.

stance (stans) *n.* **1.** a manner or mode of standing, esp. the particular position assumed by an athlete while playing. **2.** a moral or intellectual attitude; viewpoint: *to take a conservative*

stance on an issue. [French *stance* stay[1] (obsolete), stanza from Italian *stanza* station, dwelling, stanza. See STANZA.]

stanch[1] (stônch, stänch) *also,* **staunch.** *v.t.* **1.** to stop or check the flow of (blood or other fluid). **2.** to stop or check the flow of blood or other liquid from (a wound or other opening). [Old French *estanchier* to stop the flow of blood, slake thirst; of uncertain origin.] —**stanch′er,** *n.*

stanch[2] (stônch, stänch) *adj.* staunch[1]. —**stanch′ly,** *adv.* —**stanch′ness,** *n.*

stan·chion (stan′shən) *n.* **1.** an upright pillar or bar used as a support. **2.** a device for restricting the movements of animals, as dairy cows, usually consisting of a pair of bars loosely fitting around the neck. —*v.t.* **1.** to provide with or support by stanchions. **2.** to fasten (animals) to or enclose with stanchions. [Old French *estanchon* prop, diminutive of *estance,* going back to Latin *stāre* to stand.]

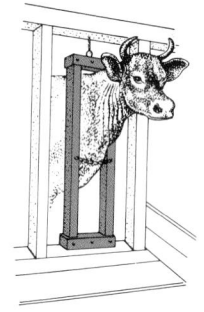

stanchion *(def. 2)*

stand (stand) *v.,* **stood, stand·ing.** —*v.i.* **1.** to be in an upright position supported by one's feet: *We had to stand because there were no seats available.* **2.** to rise to one's feet: *The congregation was asked to stand for the singing of a hymn.* **3.** to be of a specified height when upright or vertical: *My cousin stands 6 feet 3 inches. The skyscraper stands more than 1,000 feet high.* **4.** to be or remain upright: *A ladder stood against the side of the barn.* **5.** to have location or position; be situated; lie: *The village stands at the foot of the hill.* **6.** to hold a particular place, as of degree, rank, or class: *to stand in first place.* **7.** to be in a specified state or condition: *to stand prepared, to stand corrected.* **8.** to remain unchanged or in force; hold good: *The judge's decision stands and cannot be appealed.* **9.** to endure; last: *The building stood for many years.* **10.** to assume or maintain a specific position: *to stand aside, to stand at attention.* **11.** to assume a particular attitude; adopt a certain course: *to stand and fight for one's rights.* **12.** to collect and remain: *Water stood in the gutter.* **13.** to come to a stop; halt: *The traffic laws prohibit cars from standing here.* **14.** to be a candidate, esp. for election to public office. **15.** (of a dog) to point. **16.** *Nautical.* to hold a specified course; take a direction: *The ship stood into the gale.* —*v.t.* **1.** to set in an upright position: *Stand the barrel on its end.* **2.** to put up with; endure; tolerate: *I can't stand all this noise.* **3.** to undergo without damage; withstand: *to stand the test of time.* **4.** to be subjected to; undergo: *to stand trial.* **5.** *Informal.* to bear the expense of: *to stand a round of drinks.* —*n.* **1.** a position, attitude, or opinion: *What is the president's stand on disarmament?* **2.** a determined effort for or against something: *to take a stand against discrimination.* **3.** a stop or halt, esp. for battle: *The soldiers dug in to make a stand.* **4.** a place where or in which someone or something stands: *The guards' stand was at the gate.* **5.** a rack or similar structure for placing things: *an umbrella stand.* **6.** a booth, counter, or stall for carrying on a business: *a newspaper stand.* **7.** *also,* **stands.** a raised platform or similar structure, usually consisting of several tiers on which one can sit or stand: *We watched the baseball game from the stands. The parade passed the reviewing stand.* **8.** witness stand. **9.** a place or station from which vehicles may be hired: *a taxi stand.* **10.** one of a series of performances made on a theatrical tour. **11.** a group of trees or plants, growing in a particular area. [Old English *standan* to be in or assume an upright position.] —For Synonyms *(v.t.),* see **bear**[1].

　· **to stand a chance.** to have a particular place or likelihood: *Our team stands a chance of winning.*

　· **to stand by. a.** to be present without interfering, as a spectator: *to refuse to stand by and watch a dog be mistreated.* **b.** to take the side of; support; defend: *to stand by a friend during a crisis.* **c.** to abide by; maintain: *to stand by one's promise.* **d.** to be or become ready, as for use or action: *Please stand by and wait for further instructions.*

　· **to stand for. a.** to represent; mean. **b.** *Informal.* to put up with; tolerate: *The teacher wouldn't stand for such behavior.*

　· **to stand in for.** to be a substitute for.

　· **to stand off.** to repel or keep at a distance: *A small troop of brave soldiers stood the enemy off.*

　· **to stand on. a.** to be based or grounded on. **b.** to insist upon; make much of; demand: *to stand on ceremony.*

　· **to stand out. a.** to jut out; project; protrude. **b.** to be prominent or noticeable: *to stand out in a crowd.* **c.** to refuse to yield or comply.

S

• **to stand pat. a.** in poker, to play one's hand as dealt, without drawing new cards. **b.** to resist or oppose change or reform.

• **to stand to reason.** to be consistent with or conform to reason; be logical: *It stands to reason that with that much popular support the candidate can't lose the election.*

• **to stand up. a.** to rise to or be on one's feet. **b.** to withstand wear, hardship, pressure, or the like; endure; last. **c.** *Informal.* to fail to keep an appointment with: *The person I was to meet at the restaurant stood me up.*

• **to stand up for.** to take the part of; defend; support.

• **to stand up to.** to confront fearlessly; encounter boldly.

stand·ard (stan′dərd) *n.* **1.** anything accepted as a rule and used to serve as a model or measure, as of value, quality, or extent. **2.a.** *usually,* **standards.** a rule or requirement set by authority, custom, or an individual as acceptable or desirable: *a school with a strict dress standard, to live up to someone's standards.* **b.** a level of achievement, attainment, or excellence regarded as acceptable or desirable: *Your work is not up to standard.* **3.** an established unit of weight or measure. **4.** a commodity, as gold or silver, used to set the basic value of a unit of currency in a monetary system. **5.** a flag, figure, or other object used as an emblem: *the standard of a regiment.* **6.** an upright support or part: *the standard of a lamp.* **7.** a tree or shrub with a single, vertical stem. **8.** a large, upper petal of a flower. —*adj.* **1.** serving or fitted to serve as a standard. **2.** having recognized and lasting excellence, reliability, or authority: *a standard book on English literature.* **3.** widely used; typical; usual: *a standard medical practice.* **4.** conforming to usage in speech or writing that is generally accepted as correct or preferred: *standard spelling.* [Old French *estandart, estandard* flag, banner; probably of Germanic origin.]

| **Synonyms** | *n.* **Standard, criterion,** and **gauge** mean some- |

thing used in making evaluations, comparisons, or judgments. **Standard** is applied to rules that are established through authority or custom: *The school has strict standards of dress and conduct.* A **criterion** is not so much a rule as an ideal for making judgments: *Organizational skill is a criterion that should be taken into account in choosing a manager.* **Gauge** denotes a scale used to measure something that varies: *The poll serves as a gauge of public opinion.*

stand·ard·bear·er (stan′dərd bâr′ər) *n.* **1.** a person who is assigned to carry the flag or standard of a unit or group. **2.** a person who is the leader or representative of a movement, organization, or the like.

stand·ard·bred (stan′dərd bred′) *n.* a horse of a breed developed in America for harness racing.

Standard English, the English language as written and spoken by educated people and clearly understood by the majority of speakers of English. It follows generally conservative conventions of spelling, grammar, and vocabulary as used in major dictionaries and other publications.

stand·ard·ize (stan′dər dīz′) *v.t.,* **-ized, -iz·ing.** to cause to conform to or regulate by a standard. —**stand′ard·i·za′tion,** *n.*

standard of living, the average level of goods, services, luxuries, and the like available to and enjoyed by a person, group, or country.

standard time, civil time for any region based on its longitudinal distance from the meridian of Greenwich, England. The earth is divided into twenty-four time zones. In North America and U.S. territories in the Pacific Ocean, the standard time zones are Atlantic, Eastern, Central, Mountain, Pacific, Alaska, Hawaii-Aleutian, and Samoa.

stand·by (stand′bī′) *n., pl.* **-bys. 1.** a person or thing that can be depended upon in an emergency. **2.** a person or thing kept ready to be used as a replacement or substitute. **3.** a person waiting for a seat on an airplane to become available through a cancellation.

• **on standby.** in a state or condition of readiness for action or use: *All military personnel were put on standby during the crisis.*

stand·ee (stan dē′) *n. Informal.* a person who stands, esp. when there are no vacant seats, as in a theater, train, or the like.

stand-in (stand′in′) *n.* **1.** a person who takes the place of a motion-picture or television actor while lights, cameras, and other technical equipment are being set up and adjusted. **2.** any person who substitutes for another.

stand·ing (stan′ding) *adj.* **1.** remaining upright or on end; straight; erect: *standing corn, a standing collar, a standing screen.* **2.** done from or in an upright position: *a standing start, a standing ovation.* **3.** continuing in existence, operation, or effect: *a standing rule, a standing joke, a standing committee.* **4.** (of water) stagnant; still. —*n.* **1.** status, grade, or rank in a profession or

society; repute: *amateur standing, scholastic standing.* **2.** good reputation, credit, or position: *The scandal may affect your standing in the community.* **3.** the length or period of time for which something goes on; duration: *a friendship of long standing.* **4.** the act or condition of standing; erectness. —For Synonyms *(n.),* see **rank.**

standing rigging *Nautical.* the ropes or wires of a ship's rigging that are fastened down. Stays and shrouds are part of the standing rigging. ➡ distinguished from **running rigging.**

standing room, space in which to stand, as in a theater, when there are no vacant seats.

standing wave *Physics.* a waveform that contains nodes, or points at which there is no movement, separated by points of maximum movement, a characteristic of energy being reflected back upon itself.

stand-off (stand′ôf′, -of′) *n.* **1.** a tie or draw, as in a game or contest. **2.** a counterbalancing effect.

stand-off·ish (stand′ô′fish, -of′ish) *adj.* lacking warmth or friendliness; reserved; aloof. —**stand′off′ish·ly,** *adv.* —**stand′off′ish·ness,** *n.*

stand·out (stand′out′) *n.* a person or thing that is noticeable or prominent, as for its excellence or superiority: *The new television news program is a standout.* —*adj.* excellent; outstanding: *a standout performance.*

stand·pipe (stand′pīp′) *n.* a large vertical pipe or tower used to store water, usually located on high ground or in a high place so as to provide pressure in a water system.

stand·point (stand′point′) *n.* a position from which things are viewed and judged; point of view.

stand·still (stand′stil′) *n.* a state or condition in which there is no movement or activity; halt: *The accident brought highway traffic to a standstill.*

stand-up (stand′up′) *adj.* **1.** in a standing or erect position: *a stand-up collar.* **2.** performed or accomplished in a standing position: *a stand-up comic routine, a stand-up meal.* **3.** (of a comedian) performing something, as a monologue, while standing alone on a stage: *a stand-up comic.* **4.** *Slang.* loyal to friends, associates, co-workers, and the like: *a stand-up person.*

stan·hope (stan′hōp′, stan′əp) *n.* a light, open, two-wheeled or four-wheeled carriage, usually seating one or two passengers. [From Fitzroy *Stanhope,* 1787-1864, English member of the clergy, for whom the first one was made.]

stank (stangk) a past tense of **stink.**

stan·nic (stan′ik) *adj.* of, relating to, or containing tin, esp. in its higher oxidation state of +4. [Latin *stannum* tin + -IC.]

stan·nous (stan′əs) *adj.* of, relating to, or containing tin, esp. in its lower oxidation state of +2.

St. An·tho·ny's fire (an′thə nēz) erysipelas.

stan·za (stan′zə) *n.* in poetry, a group of lines arranged in any of various patterns according to meter, rhyme, and the like. [Italian *stanza* dwelling, room, stanza, going back to Latin *stāre* to stand.]

sta·pes (stā′pēz) *n., pl.* **sta·pes** or **sta·pe·des** (stə pē′dēz, stā′pi dēz′). the innermost of the three small bones in the middle ear. Also, **stirrup, stirrup bone.** For illustration, see **ear¹.** [Medieval Latin *stapes* stirrup, probably going back to Latin *stāre* to stand + *pēs* foot.]

staph (staf) *n.* staphylococcus.

staph·y·lo·coc·cus (staf′ə lə kok′əs) *n., pl.* **-coc·ci** (-kok′sī). **1.** any of various spherical bacteria, genus *Staphylococcus,* often occurring in irregular clusters and including a number of pathogenic organisms. Pneumonia and impetigo are caused by staphylococci. **2.** an infection caused by these bacteria. [Modern Latin *Staphylococcus,* from Greek *staphylos* bunch of grapes + COC-CUS.] —**staph′y·lo·coc′cal,** *adj.*

sta·ple¹ (stā′pəl) *n.* **1.** a small bent piece of thin wire used for fastening together papers, fabrics, or other thin materials. **2.** a U-shaped piece of metal with pointed ends, driven into something for fastening, as to support a hook or hold wire fencing to a post. —*v.t.,* **-pled, -pling.** to secure or fasten with or as with a staple or staples. [Old English *stapol* post¹, pillar.]

sta·ple² (stā′pəl) *n.* **1.** a basic commodity or other item in widespread use or demand, as flour, salt, or cotton. **2.** a major product grown or manufactured in a country or region: *Wine is a staple of France.* **3.** a basic or major element; substance; bulk.

a	at	e	end	o	hot	u	up	hw	white		about
ā	ape	ē	me	ō	old	ū	use	ng	song	ə	taken
ä	far	i	it	ô	fork	ü	rule	th	thin		pencil
âr	care	ī	ice	oi	oil	u̇	pull	th	this		lemon
				îr	pierce	ou	out	ûr	turn	zh	measure		circus

4. raw material. **5.a.** a textile fiber of a given length and quality for spinning in the manufacture of yarn. **b.** the length of such a fiber. —*adj.* **1.** major or basic: *staple industries, a staple reference book found in every library.* **2.** regularly produced, used, or sold in large quantities for the market: *a staple crop.* —*v.t.,* **-pled, -pling.** to sort according to fiber or fiber length. [Old French *estaple* mart, from Middle Dutch *stapel* pillar, mart.]

sta·pler¹ (stā′plər) *n.* a small device for fastening paper and other thin materials together with wire staples. [STAPLE¹ + -ER¹.]

sta·pler² (stā′plər) *n.* a person who sorts and grades fibers according to staple. [STAPLE² + -ER¹.]

star (stär) *n.* **1.** any celestial body that appears as a bright point of light in the night sky. **2.** *Astronomy.* a large, roughly spherical celestial body that produces its own light, as distinguished from planets with their satellites and comets and meteors. **3.a.** a geometric figure usually having five or more points radiating from a center. **b.** something resembling or suggesting this shape: *The horse had a white star on its forehead.* **4.** asterisk. **5.** a person who is outstanding in some field: *a baseball star.* **6.** an actor, singer, or other performer who plays the lead in a play, motion picture, opera, television program, or the like. **7.** a heavenly body regarded as influencing human destiny. **8.** *also,* **stars.** fate; destiny. —*v.,* **starred, star·ring.** —*v.t.* **1.** to set or ornament with stars or spangles. **2.** to mark with an asterisk: *to star a favorite passage in a book.* **3.** to present (a performer) in a leading role: *The movie starred my favorite actor.* —*v.i.* **1.** to perform a leading part: *to star in a play.* **2.** to perform outstandingly: *The pitcher starred in the game.* —*adj.* **1.** most prominent; best; leading: *a star performer, a star basketball player.* **2.** of or relating to a star or stars. [Old English *steorra* celestial body.]

• **to see stars.** *Informal.* to have the sensation of seeing flashes of light, as from a hard blow on the head.

• **to thank one's (lucky) stars.** to be thankful for one's good fortune.

star·board (stär′bərd) *n.* the right side of a boat or ship, as one faces forward. ➡ opposed to **port².** —*v.t., v.i.* to turn (the helm or rudder) of a boat or ship to the right so that the vessel will move to the right. —*adj.* of, relating to, or on the right side of a boat or ship. [Old English *stēorbord* side on which a ship was steered, from *stēor* steering paddle + *bord* board, side of a ship; because early Teutonic ships were steered by a paddle on the *right* side.]

starch (stärch) *n.* **1.** a white, granular carbohydrate manufactured and stored in all green plants. Starch is used in the food, paper, and textile industries. **2.** any food rich in starch, as rice, corn, and wheat products. **3.** any of various substances, including natural starch, used for stiffening or finishing linen and for industrial purposes. **4.** an overly formal or pompous manner or conduct. **5.** *Informal.* vigor or spirit. —*v.t.* to stiffen with or as with starch: *The laundry starched all my shirts.* [From Middle English *sterchen* to stiffen, going back to Old English *stearc* stiff.]

Star Chamber 1. formerly, a secret English court that heard many kinds of criminal cases without a jury, often using torture, and that was able to impose any punishment except death. It was abolished by Parliament in 1641. **2.** *also,* **star chamber.** any court or group that proceeds by secret or unfair methods. [Probably with reference to the ceiling of the room of the original Star Chamber, which was supposedly decorated with gilt *stars.*]

star chart, a map of the night sky showing the location of major stars and constellations.

starch·y (stär′chē) *adj.,* **starch·i·er, starch·i·est. 1.** of, resembling, or containing starch: *a starchy liquid, a starchy diet.* **2.** stiffened with starch. **3.** overly formal or pompous; stiff: *The reception was a starchy affair.* —**starch′i·ness,** *n.*

star-crossed (stär′krôst′) *adj.* threatened by or destined for misfortune; doomed from the start: *a star-crossed love.*

star·dom (stär′dəm) *n.* the status of a star performer: *to achieve stardom after a long career.*

stare (stâr) *v.,* **stared, star·ing.** —*v.i.* to look intently with eyes wide open, as in surprise, admiration, or fear. —*v.t.* **1.** to look intently at: *to stare someone up and down.* **2.** to affect by staring in a particular way: *to stare someone into keeping quiet.* —*n.* an act or instance of staring: *the stares of an audience, a vacant stare.* [Old English *starian* to look intently.] —**star′er,** *n.*

• **to stare down.** to make uneasy, embarrassed, or fearful by or as by staring: *The speaker stared down the heckler.*

• **to stare one** (or **someone**) **in the face. a.** to confront directly and boldly: *I don't think you are brave enough to stare him in the face and make such an accusation.* **b.** to be obvious or imminent to: *The missing glove was staring her in the face and she didn't see it. Bankruptcy and ruin stared the family in the face.*

starfish

star·fish (stär′fish′) *n., pl.* **-fish** or **-fish·es.** any of a group of flattened, star-shaped echinoderms, found on or near the sea bottom, having five or more tapering arms.

star·gaze (stär′gāz′) *v.i.,* **-gazed, -gaz·ing. 1.** to gaze at or study the stars. **2.** to daydream. —**star′gaz·er,** *n.*

stark (stärk) *adj.* **1.** absolute or unqualified; complete: *stark tyranny, stark misery.* **2.** strictly and distinctly expressed; plain: *the stark truth.* **3.** harsh, grim, or severe: *stark weather, a stark look.* **4.** barren or desolate; bare: *a stark room, a stark landscape.* **5.** rigid or stiff. —*adv.* **1.** absolutely; completely: *to go stark raving mad, stark naked.* **2.** in a stark manner. [Old English *stearc* hard, stiff, severe.] —**stark′ly,** *adv.* —**stark′ness,** *n.*

star·let (stär′lit) *n.* in motion pictures, a young actress who is being given publicity as a future star.

star·light (stär′līt′) *n.* light from a star or stars. —*adj.* starlit.

star·ling (stär′ling) *n.* any of various birds, family Sturnidae, found in most parts of the world, usually having a stout body, pointed wings, and a short tail, as the **common starling,** *Sturnus vulgaris,* having black plumage with purplish markings. Length: 7-13 inches (18-33 centimeters). [Old English *stærlinc.*]

star·lit (stär′lit′) *adj.* lighted by the stars: *the starlit sky.* Also, **starlight.**

star-of-Beth·le·hem (stär′əv beth′lə hem′, -lē əm) *n.* any of several low plants, esp. *Ornithogalum umbellatum,* of the lily family, bearing small, green-and-white, star-shaped flowers, growing wild in eastern North America and the Mediterranean area.

Star of Bethlehem, in the New Testament, the star that heralded the birth of Jesus and guided the Magi to Bethlehem.

Star of Da·vid (dā′vid) a six-pointed star, a symbol of Judaism and now of Israel. Also, **Magen David, Mogen David.**

star·ry (stär′ē) *adj.,* **-ri·er, -ri·est. 1.** studded with or lighted by stars: *a starry night.* **2.** shining like a star; bright. **3.** shaped or arranged in the form of a star. **4.** of, relating to, or proceeding from the stars. —**star′ri·ness,** *n.*

star·ry-eyed (stär′ē īd′) *adj.* given to wishful, impractical, or naive thinking.

Star of David

Stars and Bars, the first official flag of the Confederacy, during the American Civil War.

Stars and Stripes, the flag of the United States, consisting of alternating red and white stripes representing the thirteen original colonies and, in the upper left corner, a blue field with fifty stars representing the states.

star sapphire, a precious variety of blue-gray corundum that exhibits asterism when cut as a gem in cabochon form. For illustration, see **semiprecious.**

star-span·gled (stär′spang′gəld) *adj.* spangled or studded with stars.

Star-Spangled Banner 1. the U.S. national anthem, the words of which were written by the American lawyer Francis Scott Key during the War of 1812. **2.** the flag of the United States.

star-stud·ded (stär′stud′id) *adj.* **1.** scattered or spread over with stars: *a star-studded winter sky.* **2.** filled with stars and other celebrities: *a star-studded production, a star-studded audience.*

start (start) *v.i.* **1.** to make a beginning; set out: *We started on our trip Monday. Classes started yesterday.* **2.** to begin; commence: *The movie starts at ten o'clock.* **3.** to make a sudden, flinching or jumping movement, as from fear or surprise: *She started when he walked up behind her. A deer started from the bushes*

as we walked by. The horse started and threw its rider. **4.** to issue forth suddenly: *Blood started from the cut.* **5.** to appear to burst or protrude. **6.** to break away; become loose. **7.** to be one of the entrants in a race or one of the first participants in a game or contest: *I'm going to start at second base in tonight's game.* —*v.t.* **1.** to begin (something): *to start a lecture with a quote.* **2.** to cause to move; set in action or motion: *to start an engine.* **3.** to put in operation; establish; initiate: *to start a business, to start a controversy.* **4.** to cause or enable to begin or enter upon some course, as a business: *Their parents started them in business.* **5.** to rouse: *to start birds from a bush.* **6.** to cause to loosen: *The water started a crack in the molding.* **7.** to cause to be one of the entrants in a race or one of the first participants in a game or contest: *The coach is starting a freshman at quarterback.* —*n.* **1.** a beginning, as of a course of action, movement, or journey. **2.** a sudden movement, as a jerk: *I gave a start when my friend tapped me on the shoulder.* **3.** an opportunity for beginning something, as a career: *to give someone a good start.* **4.** the first movement in some course or direction: *to get a running start.* **5.** a sudden burst of activity. **6.** the advantage gained by beginning first, as in a race: *to have a 20-foot start.* **7.a.** the point or line at which a race begins. **b.** a signal to start something, as a race. [Probably from an unrecorded Old English word.] —For Synonyms *(v.i.),* see **begin.**
 • **to start in.** **a.** to begin: *They started in eating before the food got cold.* **b.** *Slang.* to confront in an unfriendly or belligerent way: *Don't start in on me with your insults.*
 • **to start something.** *Informal.* to begin an argument or fight: *The school bully tried to start something with the new student.*
 • **to start up.** **a.** to begin operating or put into operation, as a machine: *to start up an engine.* **b.** to begin organizing or working on: *We started up the club last winter.* *The scientists started up the research project as soon as they received the grant.*
start·er (stär′tər) *n.* **1.** a person or thing that begins something. **2.** the first element or beginning of a process, activity, or series: *You might try to be helpful, as a starter.* **3.** a culture used to start fermentation of a substance. **4.** a device that starts an internal-combustion engine automatically. Also, **self-starter. 5.** a person whose work is supervising the departure of public conveyances: *a bus starter.* **6.** a person who gives the signal for starting a race. **7.** any of the persons or things starting in a race, contest, or game.
star·tle (stär′təl) *v.,* **-tled, -tling.** —*v.t.* to arouse or excite suddenly, as with surprise, fear, or astonishment; shock. —*v.i.* to become startled. —*n.* sudden surprise, fright, or astonishment; shock. [Old English *steartlian* to struggle.]
star·tling (stärt′ling) *adj.* causing sudden surprise, fear, or astonishment: *startling news.* —**star′tling·ly,** *adv.*
star·va·tion (stär vā′shən) *n.* an act or instance of starving or the state of being starved.
starve (stärv) *v.,* **starved, starv·ing.** —*v.i.* **1.** to suffer from or die of hunger. **2.** to need or desire greatly; feel deprived of (with *for*): *a child who starved for affection.* **3.** *Informal.* to feel hungry. —*v.t.* **1.** to deprive of adequate food or nourishment; cause to suffer or die because of hunger. **2.** to bring to a specified condition by starving: *to starve a besieged enemy into surrendering.* [Old English *steorfan* to die.]
starve·ling (stärv′ling) *n.* a starving person, animal, or plant. —*adj.* weak from a lack of food; starving; hungry: *starveling pines.*
Star Wars *Informal.* Strategic Defense Initiative. [From *Star Wars,* an American science-fiction film.]
stash (stash) *Informal. v.t.* to store or hide for safekeeping or future use. —*n.* something that is stored or concealed. [Of uncertain origin.]
sta·sis (stā′sis) *n., pl.* **-ses** (-sēz). **1.** a state of equilibrium or stagnancy. **2.** a cessation of the flow of fluid in the body, as of blood or a reduction in peristaltic movement of intestinal contents. [Modern Latin *stasis,* from Greek *stasis* a standing still, from *histanai* to stand.]
stat. 1. stationary. **2.** statistics. **3.** statuary. **4.** statute.
state (stāt) *n.* **1.** a particular mental, emotional, or physical condition or temperament: *a state of anxiety, a state of disrepair.* **2.** position, rank, or standing, as in the world or community; station: *The wealthy family lived in a manner suitable to their state in life.* **3.** also, **State.** a sovereign political community that has authority over its own members; nation: *The continent of Africa has many new, independent states.* **4.** one of the subdivisions of a nation that has a federal system. **5.** the territory of a state or nation. **6.** also, **State. a.** secular civil government, authority, or organization: *the separation of church and state.* **b.** the business of government: *Senators and representatives are frequently involved in important matters of state.* **7.** one of the three conditions, solid, liquid, or gaseous, of matter. **8.** *Informal.* a condition of disarray, confusion, or agitation: *The two roommates ran out, leaving their*

room in a state. **9.** *Archaic.* dignity and pomp. **10. the States.** the United States. For History of the U.S. State Names, see table on following page. —*v.t.,* **stat·ed, stat·ing. 1.** to express or explain fully in words; declare; represent: *to state an opinion, to state a problem.* **2.** to establish or set; fix: *to state a time for the meeting.* —*adj.* **1.** also, **State.** of or relating to a state: *a state tax, a state highway.* **2.** of or relating to national or state government: *state policy, state affairs.* **3.** of, relating to, or for ceremonious or official occasions; formal: *a state reception.* [Latin *status* condition, position, from *stāre* to stand.]
 • **to lie in state.** (of a dead person) to be exhibited publicly with honor and ceremony prior to burial: *The diplomat's body lay in state for three days.*

> **Synonyms** *n.* **State, nation,** and **country** may all denote a political unit that has sovereignty over its land and possessions and authority over its own people. **State** is the broadest term, implying little beyond independent existence: *The states of Africa have many different political systems.* **State** is also used of entities that are theoretically independent but that are part of a federal system: *the United States of America, the states that make up Australia.* **Nation** is often used in the same contexts as *state,* but more strongly suggests the people who make up a state: *We traveled with several Swedes and met people from other nations.* **Country,** which can often be substituted for *nation,* is used in less formal contexts. It may also suggest the land that makes up a state: *In my country most people live on farms. Spain is a country I dream about visiting.* For other Synonyms *(v.t.),* see **say.**

state bank, a bank operating under a state charter.
state·craft (stāt′kraft′) *n.* the art of conducting state affairs; statesmanship.
stat·ed (stā′tid) *adj.* **1.** explicitly set forth; announced; declared: *The stated facts conflict with what actually happened.* **2.** fixed; established; regular: *The worker was hired at the stated salary.*
State Department, the department of the executive branch of the U.S. government responsible for establishing and maintaining diplomatic relations of the United States with other countries.
state·hood (stāt′húd′) *n.* the condition or status of a state, esp. a state of the United States.
state·house (stāt′hous′) *also,* **State House.** *n., pl.* **-hous·es** (-hou′ziz). the building in which the legislature of a state of the United States meets.
state·less (stāt′lis) *adj.* having no citizenship or nationality: *stateless refugees.* —**state′less·ness,** *n.*
state·ly (stāt′lē) *adj.,* **-li·er, -li·est.** formal or dignified; majestic: *a stately mansion, a stately procession.* —**state′li·ness,** *n.* —For Synonyms, see **grand.**
state·ment (stāt′mənt) *n.* **1.** the act or manner of stating something: *Accurate statement of the facts is essential.* **2.** something stated; declaration; assertion: *a false statement.* **3.** a written or oral communication setting forth facts, arguments, or the like: *The president issued a statement on tax reform.* **4.** a report or summary of the financial condition of a business or individual: *a bank statement, a corporation's statement of profit and loss.*
state-of-the-art (stāt′əv thē ärt′) *adj.* using or incorporating the latest technology; being at the most advanced or up-to-date stage of development: *a state-of-the-art computer system.*
state prison, a prison maintained by a state for the confinement of prisoners, esp. those convicted of felonies.
state·room (stāt′rüm′, -rùm′) *n.* a private, often luxurious cabin on a ship or compartment on a railroad train.
state's attorney, an attorney elected or appointed to represent the state in court.
state's evidence, testimony for the prosecution in a criminal trial, esp. that given against associates by a participant in a crime.
 • **to turn state's evidence.** to testify against one's associates in a crime, usually in return for some consideration, as a lesser sentence or immunity from prosecution.
States-Gen·er·al (stāts′jen′ər əl) *n.* **1.** the legislative body in France before the revolution of 1789, made up of representatives of the Church, the nobles, and the common people. Also, **Estates-General. 2.** the parliament of the Netherlands, made up of an upper chamber and a lower chamber.
state·side (stāt′sīd′) *also,* **State·side.** *adj.* of or in the continental United States. —*adv.* to, toward, or in the continental United States.
states·man (stāts′mən) *n., pl.* **-men** (-mən). a person engaged

a	at	e	end	o	hot	u	up	hw	white		about
ā	ape	ē	me	ō	old	ū	use	ng	song		taken
ä	far	i	it	ô	fork	ü	rule	th	thin	ə	pencil
âr	care	ī	ice	oi	oil	ù	pull	th	this		lemon
		îr	pierce	ou	out	ûr	turn	zh	measure		circus

Alabama   From *Alibamu,* the name of a tribe of Creek Indians that lived near the Alabama River.

Alaska   From the word meaning "mainland" in the language of the inhabitants of the Aleutian Islands, used to distinguish the Alaskan peninsula from the islands.

Arizona   From an Indian phrase meaning "little spring" or "place of the small spring."

Arkansas   From an Indian name for a tribe that lived near the Arkansas River.

California   From the name of a fictitious island rich in gold and jewels. Named by Spanish explorers who landed on the southern tip of the Baja California peninsula and thought it was an island.

Colorado   From a Spanish word meaning "reddish colored," named after a river with a reddish appearance (Colorado River).

Connecticut   From an Algonquian word meaning "beside the long tidal river" (Connecticut River).

Delaware   Named after Thomas West, Lord De la Warr, who was first governor of the colony of Virginia. Later, English settlers transferred the name to the area that became the state of Delaware.

Florida   From a Spanish word meaning "flowery." So named by the Spanish explorer Ponce de León, who landed there during the Spanish festival of flowers.

Georgia   Named after King George II of England, who authorized the establishment of a colony there.

Hawaii   From the Polynesians' traditional name for the mythical homeland of their ancestors.

Idaho   Probably from an Apache name for the Comanche Indians.

Illinois   From the French form of an Algonquian word meaning "men" or "tribe of great men," used as the name of an American Indian tribe that lived there.

Indiana   From a Modern Latin word meaning "Indian."

Iowa   From a Dakota Indian name for a tribe that lived in what is now Iowa.

Kansas   From a Siouan name for an Indian tribe that lived in what is now northeastern Kansas.

Kentucky   From an Iroquois word probably meaning "meadow" or "level land."

Louisiana   Named after King Louis XIV of France by the French explorer Sieur de La Salle.

Maine   From the term "the main" (also spelled "the maine"), meaning "the mainland," used by explorers of the coast of northern New England to distinguish the mainland from coastal islands.

Maryland   Named for Queen Henrietta Maria, wife of King Charles I of England.

Massachusetts   From an Algonquian word meaning "at the big hill," referring to the hills near Boston.

Michigan   French version of an Algonquian phrase for "big water" or "great lake" (Lake Michigan).

Minnesota   A Siouan name meaning "water the color of the sky" or "cloudy water," first applied to a river in the southern part of what is now Minnesota.

Mississippi   From two Algonquian words meaning "big river," "great water," or "father of the waters."

Missouri   From an Algonquian word meaning "people of the big canoes," a reference to a Sioux tribe living near the mouth of the Missouri River.

Montana   From a word meaning "mountainous" in Spanish and Latin.

Nebraska   From a Siouan name for the Platte River, meaning "flat water."

Nevada   A Spanish word meaning "snowy" or "snow-covered," from the name given by Spanish explorers to the Sierra Nevada mountains.

New Hampshire   Name given to an area of land granted to John Mason, an English settler whose home county in England was Hampshire.

New Jersey   Named after the British island of Jersey in the English Channel, from which one of the colony's original proprietors came.

New Mexico   Translation of a name given by a Spanish explorer wanting to imply that the land would be as rich as that of Mexico. (The name *Mexico* is derived from the name of an Aztec god.)

New York   Called New Amsterdam when first settled by the Dutch. Later taken by the English and renamed New York by James, Duke of York and Albany, who combined *New* from "New Amsterdam" with *York,* his title.

North Carolina   The northern part of the English colony of Carolina, named for King Charles I. The colony was originally called *Carolana,* meaning "from Charles."

North Dakota   The northern part of the Dakota territory, named after the Dakota Indians, from a Siouan word meaning "allied tribes."

Ohio   An Iroquoian name meaning "fine, great, beautiful river" (Ohio River).

Oklahoma   From a Choctaw word meaning "red people," used in an 1886 Indian treaty to designate Choctaw lands.

Oregon   Possibly from *Ouariconsint,* a misspelling of the Indian name for the Wisconsin River and a name that changed several times before it became *Oregon.*

Pennsylvania   The name coined by King Charles II for the land he granted to William Penn to found a colony. The name is a combination of Penn's family name and the Latin *silva,* meaning forest or woods.

Rhode Island   From the name given to Block Island because of its resemblance to Rhodes, an island in the Aegean Sea. Later, Rhode Island became the name of the state.

South Carolina   The southern part of the English colony of Carolina, named for King Charles I. The colony was originally called *Carolana,* meaning "from Charles."

South Dakota   The southern part of the Dakota territory, named after the Dakota Indians, from a Siouan word meaning "allied tribes."

Tennessee   From a Cherokee name for the tribe's ancient capital.

Texas   From an American Indian word meaning "friends," which the Spanish applied to the Indians living in the eastern part of Texas.

Utah   From the Spanish pronunciation of *Ute,* the name of a Shoshone tribe that lived in what is now Colorado and Utah. *Ute* may have meant "the people" in Shoshone.

Vermont   Probably from *Vert Mont,* the French translation of "Green Mountain," the area's English name.

Virginia   From the title "The Virgin Queen," given to Queen Elizabeth I because she never married. The colony of Virginia was founded during her reign.

Washington   Named by Congress after George Washington.

West Virginia   The name chosen by the people in western Virginia who formed their own government during the Civil War.

Wisconsin   From the French form of an Algonquian word meaning "at the big (or long) river" or, perhaps, "gathering of the waters," referring to a river in central Wisconsin.

Wyoming   From the Algonquian word meaning "at the big plains" or "flat area between mountains."

in public or national affairs, esp. a political leader who shows wisdom and distinction in promoting the public good. —**states'-man·like'**, **states'man·ly**, *adj.*

states·man·ship (stāts'mən ship') *n.* the qualities or characteristics of a statesman or stateswoman; skill and wisdom in conducting public or national affairs.

States of the Church, Papal States.

states' rights 1. rights or powers not delegated to the U.S. federal government or prohibited to the states under the Constitution. **2.** the doctrine that the powers of the U.S. federal government should not encroach upon the powers of the various state governments.

states·wom·an (stāts'wùm'ən) *n., pl.* **-wom·en** (-wim'ən). a woman engaged in public or national affairs, esp. a political leader who shows wisdom and distinction in promoting the public good.

state·wide (stāt'wīd') *also,* **state-wide.** *adj.* extending throughout or applying to all of a state: *a statewide building boom, statewide elections.*

stat·ic (stat'ik) *adj.* **1.** characterized by little or no growth, change, or progress; that remains the same: *a static population.* **2.** showing no movement; stationary. **3.** *Physics.* **a.** of or relating to bodies at rest or to forces in equilibrium. **b.** acting by weight without producing motion: *static pressure.* **4.** of, relating to, or designating charges of electricity that have accumulated on a body and do not move about. Static electricity can be produced by combing dry hair with a dry comb. —*n.* **1.** random electrical charges in the atmosphere, as produced by lightning, power stations, or cosmic radiation, that may be picked up by a radio or television receiver and heard as crackling or hissing sounds. **2.** *Slang.* **a.** any interference, esp. verbal, with the expression or accomplishment of something: *Do you expect your teacher to give you any static when you ask for an extension on your term paper?* **b.** criticism: *I got a lot of static for being late.* [Modern Latin *staticus,* from Greek *statikos* causing to stand.] —**stat'i·cal·ly,** *adv.*

stat·ics (stat'iks) *n. Physics.* the branch of mechanics that deals with bodies at rest or in equilibrium under the action of several forces. ➡ used as singular.

sta·tion (stā'shən) *n.* **1.** a place, building, or establishment set up as a headquarters for a business, public service, or the like: *a first-aid station, a ranger station.* **2.** a regular stopping place along a route, as of a bus or train line, for the transfer of freight or passengers; terminal; depot. **3.** the place or position in which one stands or is assigned to stand in the performance of some duty; assigned post: *a sentry station, to report to a station for duty.* **4.** the social position of an individual; standing; rank: *The judge has a high station in life.* **5.a.** a place where radio or television programs originate. **b.** a specific channel or frequency used for making broadcasts. —*v.t.* to assign to a station; place in a post or position: *The bank stationed a guard at the door.* [Latin *statiō* a standing still, place, position.]

sta·tion·ar·y (stā'shə ner'ē) *adj.* **1.** having a fixed place or position; permanent: *The desks in the classroom are stationary.* **2.** not moving; stopped: *The train was stationary when I fell.* **3.** unchanging in character, condition, or quantity. [Latin *statiōnārius* relating to a post² or station, from *statiō* a standing still, place, position.]

station break, an interruption or pause in a television or radio program to identify a network or station or to make an announcement.

sta·tion·er (stā'shə nər) *n.* a person or business that sells stationery. [Medieval Latin *stationarius* shopkeeper (with reference to having a fixed, as opposed to a traveling, shop), from *statio* shop, from Latin *statiō* a standing still, place, position.]

sta·tion·er·y (stā'shə ner'ē) *n.* **1.** writing paper and envelopes. **2.** materials used in writing, such as pens, pencils, or paper, and office supplies, such as typewriter ribbons and paper clips.

station house 1. police station. **2.** firehouse.

sta·tion·mas·ter (stā'shən mas'tər) *n.* a person in charge of a railroad station or bus station.

stations of the cross *also,* **Stations of the Cross.** in the Roman Catholic Church, a series of fourteen representations of the last events of Jesus' life from his condemnation to his Crucifixion and burial, before which devotions are performed.

station wagon, an automobile having one or more folding or removable rear seats and a door across the back that can be used as for loading and unloading passengers or luggage.

stat·ism (stā'tiz əm) *n.* the advocacy of or tendency toward the centralization of all forms of economic and political power in the government or state, often at the expense of personal freedoms. —**stat'ist,** *n.*

sta·tis·tic (stə tis'tik) *n.* a single numerical fact or element that is collected, along with many other such facts, and used as information about a particular subject.

sta·tis·ti·cal (stə tis'ti kəl) *adj.* of, relating to, consisting of, or based on statistics: *a statistical problem, a statistical analysis.* —**sta·tis'ti·cal·ly,** *adv.*

stat·is·ti·cian (stat'ə stish'ən) *n.* a person who is expert in compiling and interpreting statistics.

sta·tis·tics (stə tis'tiks) *n.* **1.** the science of collecting, classifying, and using numerical data as they relate to a particular subject. **2.** the data themselves. ➡ used as singular in def. 1, as plural in def. 2. [German *Statistik* science of collecting, classifying, and using numerical data, from Modern Latin *statisticus* relating to state affairs, from Latin *status* condition, position, state.]

sta·tor (stā'tər) *n.* a stationary part of a motor, dynamo, or similar machine, about or within which a rotor rotates. For illustration, see **capacitor.** [Modern Latin *stator,* from Latin *stator* one that stands.]

stat·u·ar·y (stach'ü er'ē) *n., pl.* **-ar·ies. 1.** statues collectively. **2.** the art of carving statues. —*adj.* of, relating to, or suitable for statues.

stat·ue (stach'ü) *n.* a representation, often life-size or larger, of a human or animal figure that has been carved, cast, or modeled in stone, bronze, clay, or another material. [Old French *statue* from Latin *statua* image, statue, going back to *stāre* to stand.]

Statue of Liberty, a monumental statue situated on an island in New York Harbor that depicts liberty as a crowned woman holding a torch aloft. The Statue of Liberty was given to the United States by France in 1884.

stat·u·esque (stach'ü esk') *adj.* resembling or suggestive of a statue, as in proportion, grace, or dignity; stately; majestic; imposing. —**stat'u·esque'ly,** *adv.* —**stat'u·esque'ness,** *n.*

stat·u·ette (stach'ü et') *n.* a small statue. [French *statuette,* diminutive of *statue.* See STATUE.]

stat·ure (stach'ər) *n.* **1.** the height of a person or animal in a normal standing position: *an athlete of average stature.* **2.** a degree or level, as of achievement or mental growth; standing: *moral stature, a writer of great stature.* [Old French *stature* height or position of a body, from Latin *statūra* upright posture, height.]

sta·tus (stā'təs, stat'əs) *n.* **1.** a particular manner of being or existence; state: *the status of a nation's economy.* **2.** relative place or rank, esp. social or professional standing: *student status, low status in an organization.* **3.** the character or condition of a person or thing in relation to some aspect of the law: *marital status.* [Latin *status* condition, position.] —For Synonyms, see **rank.**

status quo (kwō) the existing or present state of affairs. [Latin *status quō* the condition in which (things are).]

status symbol, something a person possesses or does, regarded as being associated with high social or economic position in life.

stat·ute (stach'üt) *n.* **1.** a law enacted by a legislative body. **2.** a written rule or law regulating an organization, such as a university or corporation. [Old French *statut* decree, law, from Late Latin *statūtum,* from Latin *statuere* to establish.] —For Synonyms, see **law.**

statute law, law as established by statutes; written law.

statute mile, mile.

statute of limitations, a law limiting the time in which legal action may be taken in certain cases.

stat·u·to·ry (stach'ə tôr'ē) *adj.* of, relating to, set by, or punishable under statute: *a statutory fine, a statutory offense.* —**stat'u·to'ri·ly,** *adv.*

statutory rape, sexual intercourse with a girl who is under the legal age of consent, with or without her actual consent.

staunch¹ (stônch, stänch) *also,* **stanch.** *adj.* **1.** loyal and dependable; steadfast: *a staunch ally.* **2.** soundly built or constructed: *a staunch bridge, a staunch argument.* **3.** watertight: *a staunch ship.* [Old French *estanche* reliable, watertight, from *estanchier.* See STANCH¹.] —**staunch'ly,** *adv.* —**staunch'ness,** *n.*

staunch² (stônch) *v.t.* stanch¹. —**staunch'er,** *n.*

stave (stāv) *n.* **1.** any long, narrow, flexible strip of wood, such as one used on the sides of a barrel, cask, or bucket. **2.** a rod, pole, or staff. **3.** a rung, as of a ladder or chair. **4.** a verse or stanza, as of a poem or song. **5.** *Music.* staff. —*v.,* **staved** or **stove, stav·ing.** —*v.t.* **1.** to smash or break in, as the staves

staves
of a barrel

a	at	e	end	o	hot	u	up	hw	white		about
ā	ape	ē	me	ō	old	ū	use	ng	song	ə	taken
ä	far	i	it	ô	fork	ü	rule	th	thin		pencil
âr	care	ī	ice	oi	oil	ù	pull	th	this		lemon
		ir	pierce	ou	out	ûr	turn	zh	measure		circus

of a cask or barrel. **2.** to puncture a hole in (usually with *in*): *An iceberg stove in the hull of the ship.* **3.** to furnish with a stave or staves: *to stave a barrel.* —*v.i.* to be punctured or smashed in. [From *staves,* plural of STAFF.]
 • **to stave off.** to ward off or prevent: *to stave off a blow, to stave off an unpleasant discussion.*

staves (stāvz) a plural of **staff.**

stay[1] (stā) *v.,* **stayed** or *(archaic)* **staid, stay·ing.** —*v.i.* **1.** to continue in a place or condition: *to stay seated, to stay young.* **2.** to reside in a place, esp. for a short or indefinite period of time; lodge; sojourn: *They stayed at a hotel while visiting the city.* **3.** to cease movement or activity; stop; halt: *We drove through the city, but could not stay to sightsee. I can only stay for a minute.* **4.** to delay going; linger: *Will you stay for coffee? We could not stay at the theater for the last act.* **5.** *Informal.* to last or persevere, as in a race or contest. —*v.t.* **1.** to remain for the duration of: *to stay the night in a motel.* **2.** to put off; defer: *The judge stayed the proceedings until the following day.* **3.** to check or stop, esp. temporarily; abate: *The poor family had barely enough food to stay their hunger.* —*n.* **1.** the act or an instance of staying or remaining; stopover; sojourn: *Our stay in town was cut short after two days.* **2.** a break or delay of action, motion, or progression; stop; halt: *The governor requested a stay on raises for all state employees.* **3.** *Law.* a temporary delay in carrying out an order of a court of law: *a stay of execution.* **4.** *Informal.* power of endurance or resistance; staying power. [Probably from Old French *estai-,* a stem of *ester* to stand, from Latin *stāre.*]

stay[2] (stā) *n.* **1.** something used to support, strengthen, or sustain; prop; brace. **2.** a piece of plastic, metal, or other stiff material, inserted in corsets, bathing suits, shirt collars, and other garments to give shape and support. **3. stays.** corset. —*v.t.,* **stayed, stay·ing.** to support, strengthen, or sustain. [Old French *estayer* to prop, support, from *estaye* a prop, support; of Germanic origin.]

stay[3] (stā) *n.* **1.** a strong rope, usually of wire, used to support a mast on a boat or ship. **2.** any rope or chain used for a similar purpose. —*v.,* **stayed, stay·ing.** —*v.t.* **1.** to secure or steady with a stay or stays. **2.** to cause (a boat or ship) to change from one tack to another. —*v.i.* (of a boat or ship) to change from one tack to another. [Old English *stæg* large rope used to support a mast.]
 • **in stays.** (of a boat or ship) heading toward the wind in the process of changing from one tack to another.

staying power, the ability to endure; stamina: *It takes a lot of staying power to run a marathon.*

stay·sail (stā′sāl′, -səl) *n.* a sail, usually triangular, that is attached to a stay.

STD, sexually transmitted disease.

S.T.D., Doctor of Sacred Theology.

Ste., abbreviation of *Sainte,* the feminine form of French *Saint.*

stead (sted) *n.* a place or position usually or previously occupied by another: *My associate went to the meeting in my stead.* —*v.t. Archaic.* to be of use or service to; benefit; help. [Old English *stede* place.]
 • **to stand in good stead.** to be of use or service to; be advantageous to: *Your experience will stand you in good stead.*

stead·fast (sted′fast′, -fəst) *also,* **stedfast.** *adj.* **1.** consistent in adhering to a principle, action, or association; unwavering; faithful: *steadfast loyalty to a cause, a steadfast friend.* **2.** firmly fixed; direct; steady: *a steadfast gaze.* [Old English *stedefæst* firmly fixed, from *stede* place + *fæst* firm.] —**stead′fast′ly,** *adv.* —**stead′fast′ness,** *n.* —For Synonyms, see **faithful.**

stead·y (sted′ē) *adj.,* **stead·i·er, stead·i·est. 1.** maintained at an even rate; regular or uniform in operation or intensity: *a steady pace, a steady rise in unemployment.* **2.** firm or sure in movement or position; not tottering or faltering: *The artist had a steady hand.* **3.** regular or permanent: *a steady customer, a steady job.* **4.** reliable; dependable: *a steady worker.* **5.** not easily upset; calm: *steady nerves.* **6.** unwavering in principle or action; steadfast. **7.** (of a boat or ship) remaining upright, as in a turbulent sea. —*v.,* **stead·ied, stead·y·ing.** —*v.t.* to make or keep steady: *to steady a ladder.* —*v.i.* to become steady. —*interj.* **1.** take it easy; keep calm. **2.** *Nautical.* keep the ship headed in the same direction. ➡ used as a command to the sailor at the helm. —*adv.* in a steady manner; steadily. —*n., pl.* **stead·ies.** *Informal.* a person one dates regularly and exclusively. [STEAD + -Y[1].] —**stead′i·ly,** *adv.* —**stead′i·ness,** *n.*
 • **to go steady.** to date regularly and exclusively.

steady state *Physics.* a condition in which all the forces acting upon or within a physical system cancel each other out, in which case the system either does not change with time or maintains a state of equilibrium.

steady state theory, the theory that the average properties of the universe as a whole do not change with time. According to this theory, although the universe is constantly expanding, new matter is being created continuously at a rate that balances the thinning-out effect of the expansion.

steak (stāk) *n.* **1.a.** a slice of meat. esp. beef, cut for cooking by broiling or frying. **b.** a boneless slice of large fish, such as salmon or swordfish. **2.** chopped or ground beef, usually formed into patties for cooking: *hamburger steak.* [Old Norse *steik* slice of meat roasted on a spit.]

steal (stēl) *v.,* **stole, sto·len, steal·ing.** —*v.t.* **1.** to take from another secretly and without right or permission: *Thieves stole several paintings from the exhibition.* **2.** to take by surprise, stealth, or trick: *to steal a kiss, to steal an hour off from work.* **3.** to take and claim as one's own work, idea, or the like: *The movie producer stole the plot for the new film from the young author's book.* **4.** to move, carry, or place secretly or unobserved: *I stole the surprise birthday cake into the office.* **5.** *Baseball.* to gain (the next base) without any assistance from the batter or error by any fielder. —*v.i.* **1.** to commit or practice theft. **2.** to move or pass secretly, gradually, or unseen: *I stole off to be alone.* **3.** *Baseball.* to steal a base. —*n.* **1.** the act or an instance of stealing; theft. **2.** *Baseball.* the act or an instance of stealing a base. **3.** *Informal.* a bargain: *The ten-speed bike was a steal at $100.* [Old English *stelan* to take dishonestly or secretly.] —**steal′er,** *n.*

Synonyms	*v.t.* **Steal, pilfer,** and **filch** mean to take something that rightfully or legally belongs to someone

else. **Steal,** the broadest of these terms, can be applied to the taking of any possession: *The pickpocket stole my wallet while I was standing on the bus.* **Pilfer** suggests a series of unnoticed thefts, of small items or in small quantities: *The clerk pilfered merchandise for weeks before being caught.* **Filch** is applied to the taking of something of little value: *The child filched a handful of cookies when the baby-sitter left the room.*

stealth (stelth) *n.* a secret action, procedure, or manner of behavior; furtiveness: *The store obtained the information about its competitors by stealth.* —*adj.* **Stealth.** relating to, used in, or designating aircraft designed esp. to evade detection, as by radar or infrared sensors. [From STEAL.]

stealth·y (stel′thē) *adj.,* **stealth·i·er, stealth·i·est.** moving, proceeding, or acting in a secret manner; furtive. —**stealth′i·ly,** *adv.* —**stealth′i·ness,** *n.*

steam (stēm) *n.* **1.** water in the form of a gas. It is used to provide heat for buildings and for industrial processes, and to power engines and other mechanical devices. **2.** mechanical power, heat, or other energy generated by steam: *to turn the steam up.* **3.** mist formed by condensed vapor. **4.** any vapor or fume given off by a heated substance. **5.** *Informal.* driving power; energy; initiative: *I ran out of steam before I finished the project.* —*v.t.* to treat with or expose to the action of steam, as in cooking or cleaning: *to steam clams, to steam out the wrinkles from a suit.* —*v.i.* **1.** to give off steam or vapor: *The fabric steamed from the heat of the iron.* **2.** to become or rise in the form of steam. **3.** to be covered by condensed vapor or mist (often with *up*): *My glasses steamed up in the locker room.* **4.** to move or travel by steam: *The vessel steamed into port.* **5.** *Informal.* to be angry; seethe. **6.** *Informal.* to be uncomfortably warm. [Old English *stēam* vapor, smoke.]
 • **to let (or blow) off steam.** *Informal.* to give vent to one's pent-up emotions, energy, or tensions.

steam bath 1. a type of therapeutic bathing involving exposure to steam, which induces excessive perspiration. **2.** a special room or enclosure for bathing in steam.

steam·boat (stēm′bōt′) *n.* any of various steam-driven boats, used esp. in lake and river navigation.

steam boiler, a closed vessel in which water is boiled in order to generate steam.

steam chest, in a steam engine, the chamber from which steam is admitted to the cylinder from the boiler by the action of a valve. Also, **steam box.**

steam engine, an engine using the energy of steam to do mechanical work, as by the expansion of the steam within a cylinder to drive a piston in a back and forth motion.

steam·er (stē′mər) *n.* **1.** something driven or powered by steam, such as a steamship. **2.** a soft-shell clam, usually cooked by steaming. **3.** a special container in which something is steamed, esp. a large pot for steaming clams.

steamer trunk, a traveling trunk, originally designed to fit under the berth in a ship.

steam fitter, a person who installs and repairs steam pipes, fittings, and other steam heating equipment.

steam heat, heat given off by a steam heating system.

steam heating, a system of heating buildings and other facilities with steam produced by a boiler and piped through radiators.

steam iron, an electric iron with a compartment for water, the

S

steam of which is given off from the bottom onto the fabric being pressed, to aid in ironing.

steam·roll (stēm′rōl′) *v.i., v.t.* steamroller.

steam·roll·er (stēm′rō′lər) *also,* **steam roller.** *n.* **1.** a vehicle, esp. a steam-driven one, moving on heavy rollers, used in work on roads, as for leveling freshly laid pavement or smoothing earth. **2.** any large and powerful force or influence that can overwhelm, suppress, or defeat opposition. —*v.i. Informal.* to move or proceed with overwhelming force or organization: *The presidential campaign steamrollered through the South.* —*v.t.* **1.** to overwhelm or suppress ruthlessly; defeat: *to steamroller all opposition.* **2.** to level or smooth with a steamroller.

steam·ship (stēm′ship′) *n.* a large, oceangoing vessel propelled by steam power. ➡ distinguished from **motorship.**

steam shovel, a power-driven, esp. steam-driven, digging machine having a single large bucket or scoop at the end of a long beam.

steam table, a table or counter used in restaurants, having openings to hold trays or containers of cooked food that are kept heated by warm water or steam circulating beneath them.

steam turbine, a turbine using steam as a source of energy.

steam·y (stē′mē) *adj.,* **steam·i·er, steam·i·est. 1.** giving off, covered by, or filled with steam: *a steamy window.* **2.** uncomfortably warm and humid: *steamy weather.* —**steam′i·ly,** *adv.* —**steam′i·ness,** *n.*

ste·ap·sin (stē ap′sin) *n.* a digestive enzyme, the lipase of pancreatic juice. [Greek *steār* fat + (PE)PSIN.]

ste·a·rate (stē′ə rāt′, stîr′āt) *n.* a salt or ester of stearic acid. Soaps are stearates.

ste·ar·ic (stē ar′ik, stîr′ik) *adj.* of or relating to stearin. [Greek *steār* fat + -IC.]

stearic acid, a colorless waxy compound found in animal and vegetable fats and used to make lubricants, soaps, and shoe polish. It is the most common fatty acid. Formula: $C_{18}H_{36}O_2$

ste·a·rin (stē′ər in, stîr′in) *n.* a colorless crystalline or powdery compound consisting of an ester of stearic acid, found in most fats and used to make candles, synthetic ivory and stone, and soap. [French *stéarine,* from Greek *steār* fat.]

ste·a·tite (stē′ə tīt′) *n.* soapstone. [Latin *steātitis,* from Greek *steāt-,* stem of *steār* fat.] —**ste·a·tit·ic** (stē′ə tit′ik), *adj.*

sted·fast (sted′fast′, -fəst) *adj.* steadfast. —**sted′fast′ly,** *adv.* —**sted′fast′ness,** *n.*

steed (stēd) *n.* a horse, esp. a high-spirited riding horse. [Old English *stēda* stallion.]

steel (stēl) *n.* **1.** any alloy of iron mixed with a small amount of carbon, often with other elements added to improve certain properties, such as strength or malleability. **2.** something made from steel, such as a sword. **3.** a quality or characteristic of steel, esp. hardness, strength, or durability: *muscles of steel.* —*adj.* **1.** made or consisting of steel. **2.** of or relating to the production of steel. **3.** resembling steel: *steel nerves.* —*v.t.* **1.** to cover with steel, as by edging or plating. **2.** to cause to be unflinching or unyielding; strengthen; harden: *to steel oneself for bad news.* [Old English *stēli, stȳle* artificially produced variety of iron.]

steel band, a musical band that uses percussion instruments made from steel oil drums. Steel bands originated in Trinidad.

steel blue, a dark grayish blue color, as of tempered steel. —**steel′-blue′,** *adj.*

steel gray, a bluish gray color. —**steel′-gray′,** *adj.*

steel·head (stēl′hed′) *n., pl.* **-head** or **-heads.** a large, silvery rainbow trout that moves between rivers and the ocean.

steel mill, a plant or facilities where steel is made. Also, **steel·works.**

steel wool, fine threads of steel matted together, as in a pad, used for polishing or cleaning surfaces, as of wood or metal.

steel·work·er (stēl′wûr′kər) *n.* a person who works in a steel mill.

steel·works (stēl′wûrks′) *n.* steel mill. ➡ used as singular or plural.

steel·y (stē′lē) *adj.,* **steel·i·er, steel·i·est. 1.** made or consisting of steel. **2.** resembling or suggestive of steel: *steely eyes.* —**steel′i·ness,** *n.*

steel·yard (stēl′yärd′, stil′yərd) *n.* a weighing device consisting of a horizontal bar suspended off center, with the object to be weighed at the shorter end and a movable weight on the longer end. The weight is slid along the bar until a balance is reached and the correct weight is registered on a scale marked off on the bar. [STEEL + YARD[1], owing to the incorrect translation of Middle Low German *stālhof* sample courtyard (Middle Low German *stāl* sample, confused with Middle Low German *stāl* steel); so called because a scale was hung in the *Stalhof* of the Hanseatic merchants in London in the thirteenth century.]

steen·bok (stēn′bok′, stān′-) *also,* **steinbok.** *n., pl.* **-boks** or **-bok.** a small light brown or gray antelope, *Raphicerus campes-*

tris, native to southeastern Africa. Height: 22 inches (56 centimeters) at the shoulder. [Dutch *steenbok,* from *steen* stone + *bok* buck[1]; because it is found in rocky places.]

steep[1] (stēp) *adj.* **1.** having an almost perpendicular face or slope: *a steep stairway, to climb the steeper side of a mountain.* **2.** *Informal.* too much or too high; excessive or extreme; unreasonable: *a steep fee.* —*n.* a steep slope or place. [Old English *stēap* high.] —**steep′ly,** *adv.* —**steep′ness,** *n.*

steep[2] (stēp) *v.t.* **1.** to soak in liquid, so as to soften, cleanse, or extract some element, such as flavor: *to steep tea leaves.* **2.** to involve or absorb deeply or thoroughly; saturate: *a mind steeped in classical literature, a house steeped in mystery.* —*v.i.* to undergo soaking in liquid. —*n.* **1.** the process of soaking or the state of being soaked. **2.** a liquid used for soaking. [Possibly from Old Norse *steypa* to pour out liquids, cast metals.] —**steep′er,** *n.*

steenbok

steep·en (stē′pən) *v.t., v.i.* to make or become steeper.

stee·ple (stē′pəl) *n.* **1.** a lofty tower with a spire or similar superstructure at the top, esp. on a church. **2.** the spire on the top of the tower of a church or similar building. [Old English *stēpel, stȳpel* high tower.]

stee·ple·bush (stē′pəl bùsh′) *n.* hardhack.

stee·ple·chase (stē′pəl chās′) *n.* **1.** a horse race on a course furnished with hedges, ditches, and other obstacles over which the horses must jump. **2.** a footrace furnished with similar obstacles over which runners must hurdle. [STEEPLE + CHASE[1]; supposedly from the eighteenth-century English practice of selecting a church *steeple* as the goal of a race.] —**stee′ple·chas′er,** *n.*

stee·ple·jack (stē′pəl jak′) *n.* a person whose work is climbing steeples, towers, and other tall structures to paint them or to make repairs.

steer[1] (stîr) *v.t.* **1.** to guide the course of (a vessel or vehicle) as with a wheel, handle, or the like. **2.** to set and follow (a course): *The ship steered a course for the West Indies.* **3.** to direct or guide the movement or course of: *The police steered the presidential candidate through the crowd.* —*v.i.* **1.** to guide a vessel or vehicle. **2.** to follow or direct one's course: *The captain is steering for the island.* **3.** to be guided, as by a wheel or person: *The truck does not steer easily.* —*n. Informal.* a piece of advice; suggestion; tip: *a bum steer.* [Old English *stīeran, stēoran* to direct, guide.]
•**to steer clear of.** to avoid completely; shun; eschew.

steer[2] (stîr) *n.* a bull that has been castrated, esp. one raised for beef. [Old English *stēor* young ox.]

steer·age (stîr′ij) *n.* **1.** formerly, the portion of a passenger ship occupied by those passengers paying the cheapest fare. **2.** the act of steering.

steer·age·way (stîr′ij wā′) *n.* sufficient speed for a boat or ship to be steered effectively.

steering committee, a committee that draws up an agenda and recommends proposals to be considered by a larger committee, legislature, or other deliberative body.

steering gear, a mechanism used for steering, as in an automobile or a ship.

steering wheel, a wheel turned by a driver or pilot to direct the course of a vehicle or vessel.

steers·man (stîrz′mən) *n., pl.* **-men** (-mən). helmsman.

steg·o·sau·rus (steg′ə-sôr′əs) *also,* **steg·o·saur** (steg′ə sôr′) *n., pl.* **-sau·ri** (-sôr′ī) or **-sau·rus·es.** any of a group

stegosaurus

of herbivorous dinosaurs, genus *Stegosaurus,* living in North America during the Jurassic period, having a spiked tail and bony plates on its back along the spine. Length: to 20 feet (6.1 meters). [Modern Latin *Stegosaurus,* from Greek *stegos* roof + *sauros*

a	at	e	end	o	hot	u	up	hw	white		about
ā	ape	ē	me	ō	old	ū	use	ng	song	ə	taken
ä	far	i	it	ô	fork	ü	rule	th	thin		pencil
âr	care	ī	ice	oi	oil	ù	pull	th	this		lemon
		îr	pierce	ou	out	ûr	turn	zh	measure		circus

lizard; with reference to the earlier belief that certain bones of this creature were arranged like a roof's slates.]

stein (stīn) *n.* **1.** a beer mug, usually made of earthenware. **2.** the quantity of liquid that a stein holds, usually about a pint (0.48 liter). [Possibly from German *Steingut* earthenware, pottery.]

stein·bok (stīn′bok′) steenbok.

ste·le (stē′lē, stēl) *n., pl.* **-les** or *(defs. 1, 2)* **-lae** (-lē). **1.** a vertical stone slab or pillar, engraved as with an inscription or sculptural design, usually serving as a memorial. **2.** a prepared surface, as on the face of a building, engraved as with an inscription or sculptural design. **3.** the central cylinder, within the cortex, of stems and roots of vascular plants. [Greek *stēlē* gravestone.]

Maya **stelae** in western Honduras

stel·lar (stel′ər) *adj.* **1.** of, relating to, or resembling a star or stars; astral; sidereal: *stellar light.* **2.** of or relating to a star performer: *a stellar part in a play.* **3.** very important or outstanding: *a stellar achievement.* [Late Latin *stēllāris* starry, from Latin *stēlla* star.]

stel·late (stel′āt, -it) *adj.* radiating from a center like the points of a star; star-shaped: *a stellate leaf.* Also, **stel′lat·ed.** [Latin *stēllātus* starry, set with stars, star-shaped, from *stēlla* star.]

St. El·mo's fire (el′mōz) *n.* a discharge of electricity, often during a thunderstorm, that appears as a bright glow around objects, as on the masts of a ship or the wings of an aircraft. [From *Saint Elmo*, died 303, patron saint of sailors.]

stem[1] (stem) *n.* **1.** the main axis of a plant, which supports leaves or flowers and may bear buds. **2.** a stalk that joins a leaf, flower, or fruit to the plant it grows on, such as a petiole, peduncle, or pedicel. **3.** something resembling this in shape or function: *the stem of a wine glass, the stem of a pipe.* **4.** the main line of descent in a family. **5.** the part of a word to which affixes and inflectional endings are added to change the meaning of the word. *Swim* is the stem of *swimming, swims,* and *swimmer.* **6.** an upright member extending from the keel of a boat or ship, to which the sides are joined at the bow. **7.** the bow of a boat or ship. —*v.,* **stemmed, stem·ming.** —*v.t.* **1.** to remove the stem of or from: *to stem a cluster of grapes.* **2.** to fit with a stem or stems. —*v.i.* to have as a source; originate, develop, or be descended: *Many health problems stem from poor eating habits.* [Old English *stemn* trunk of a tree, stalk of a plant, prow of a ship.] —**stem′less,** *adj.* —**stem′mer,** *n.*

• **from stem to stern.** from one end to the other; thoroughly: *The house had to be cleaned from stem to stern.*

stem[2] (stem) *v.,* **stemmed, stem·ming.** —*v.t.* **1.** to stop, check, or restrain by or as if by damming; stanch: *to stem the flow of water from a broken pipe, to stem the tide of rebellion.* **2.** to make progress or headway against (something): *When tacking a sailboat, you must stem the wind.* **3.** to point (a ski or skis) inward and shift one's weight in order to turn, stop, or slow down. —*v.i.* to slow down, stop, or turn by stemming one's skis. —*n.* the act or an instance of stemming on skis. [Old Norse *stemma* to dam up, restrain.]

stemmed (stemd) *adj.* **1.** having a stem. ➡ used chiefly in combination: *long-stemmed roses.* **2.** having the stem removed: *stemmed and pitted cherries.*

stem·ware (stem′wâr′) *n.* drinking or dessert vessels, usually of glass, that have stems.

stem·wind·ing (stem′wīn′ding) *adj.* (of a watch) wound by turning a ridged knob attached to a stem.

stench (stench) *n.* a disagreeable or offensive odor; stink. [Old English *stenc* odor.]

sten·cil (sten′səl) *n.* **1.** a thin sheet, as of metal or paper, in which a pattern is cut so that when paint or ink is applied it passes through the openings to form a design on the surface against which the sheet has been pressed. **2.** a printing or design produced by using a stencil. —*v.t.,* **-ciled, -cil·ing;** *also, British,* **-cilled, -cil·ling.** to mark or paint with a stencil. [Old French *estenceler* to sparkle, cover with stars, adorn with colors, from *estencelle* spark, going back to Latin *scintilla.*]

stencil

sten·o·graph (sten′ə graf′) *n.* **1.** writing in shorthand. **2.** a keyboard machine for writing in shorthand. —*v.t.* to write in shorthand.

ste·nog·ra·pher (stə nog′rə fər) *n.* a person who is skilled at recording and transcribing dictated material in shorthand.

sten·o·graph·ic (sten′ə graf′ik) *adj.* of, relating to, or using stenography. Also, **sten′o·graph′i·cal.** —**sten′o·graph′i·cal·ly,** *adv.*

ste·nog·ra·phy (stə nog′rə fē) *n.* the act or skill or a method of taking or typing in shorthand, esp. when recorded from another's spoken words. [Greek *stenos* narrow + -GRAPHY.]

ste·no·sis (stə nō′sis) *n. Medicine.* a narrowing or constriction of a passage or opening. [Modern Latin *stenosis,* from Greek *stenōsis,* from *stenos* narrow + *-ōsis* used to form nouns.] —**ste·not·ic** (sti not′ik), *adj.*

sten·o·type (sten′ə tīp′) *n.* **1.** a keyboard machine used in stenotypy. Trademark: **Stenotype.** **2.** a letter or group of letters representing a sound, word, or phrase in stenotypy. [Greek *stenos* narrow + TYPE.]

sten·o·typ·y (sten′ə tī′pē) *n.* a method of shorthand in which letters of the alphabet represent sounds, words, and phrases.

Sten·tor (sten′tôr) *n.* in Greek legend, a herald who had a voice as loud as fifty men.

sten·to·ri·an (sten tôr′ē ən) *adj.* extremely loud; roaring; booming: *to speak in stentorian tones, a stentorian voice.* [From STENTOR (from Greek *stenein* to moan, groan) + -IAN.]

step (step) *n.* **1.** the movement of raising the foot and putting it down in a new position, as in walking, climbing, or the like. **2.** the distance covered in one such movement: *I was two steps from the door when it swung open.* **3.** any short distance; little way: *The store is only a few steps from our house.* **4.** any place or rest for the foot in going up or coming down, such as a stair or rung of a ladder. **5. steps.** a flight of stairs: *to trip and fall down the steps.* **6.** an action or one of a series of actions leading to a particular goal or result: *The signing of the agreement was a step toward peace.* **7.** a degree, grade, or stage in a progression or series: *to bring a project one step nearer to completion.* **8.** the sound made by putting the foot down; footfall: *The deer heard my step and ran away.* **9.** footprint: *The new snow covered our steps.* **10.** *also,* **steps.** course; path; example: *Children often follow in the steps of their parents.* **11.** a manner of walking: *a light, graceful step.* **12.** a combination of foot and body movements in dancing which form a basic pattern: *Some say that the waltz step is the hardest to learn.* **13.** the rhythm or pace of another or a group, esp. in marching: *to be out of step.* **14.** something resembling a step, such as the socket or supporting frame holding the lower end of a ship's mast. **15.** *Music.* an interval corresponding to one degree on the staff or in a scale. —*v.,* **stepped, stepping.** —*v.i.* **1.** to move by taking a step or steps: *to step to the rear of a bus.* **2.** to walk a short distance: *I have to step to the next building.* **3.** to put or press the foot: *to step on a piece of broken glass.* **4.** to move into a new situation, condition, or the like as if in a single step: *The new employee stepped into the job without sufficient preparation.* **5.** *Informal.* to move or act quickly. —*v.t.* **1.** to put or move (the foot) in taking a step: *Who was the first person to step foot on the moon?* **2.** to measure by taking steps (usually with *off*): *to step off twenty paces.* **3.** to cut steps in; furnish with steps. **4.** *Nautical.* to fix or place (a mast) in a socket or supporting framework. [Old English *steppan* to tread, go on foot, advance.] —**step′less,** *adj.* —**step′like′,** *adj.*

• **in step. a.** stepping in rhythm with: *marchers in step with each other, dancers in step with the music.* **b.** following or reflecting the latest in fashions or ideas: *in step with the newest fads.*

• **out of step**. not in step.
• **step by step**. little by little; by degrees; gradually.
• **to step down**. **a**. to resign from a position or office. **b**. to decrease, as in rate of speed: *to step down production*.
• **to step in**. to enter into another's or others' affairs or disputes; intervene.
• **to step on it**. *Informal*. to go faster; hurry up.
• **to step out**. **a**. to go outside briefly. **b**. *Informal*. to go out for fun or entertainment: *We used to step out every Saturday night to go dancing*. **c**. to walk with brisk, long strides.
• **to step up**. to increase, as in rate of speed: *to step up production*.
• **to take steps**. to begin to do whatever is necessary to advance, prevent, or change something: *to take steps to prevent a landmark from being demolished, to take steps to have an employee promoted*.
• **to watch one's step**. to act or proceed carefully and cautiously: *Watch your step when you meet the new manager*.

step- *combining form* related by the remarriage of a parent rather than by blood: *stepsister, stepbrother*. [Old English *stēop-* originally, orphaned.]

step·broth·er (step'bruth̵'ər) *n*. a son of one's stepparent by a former marriage.

step·child (step'chīld') *n., pl.* **-chil·dren** (-chil'drən). a child of one's husband or wife by a former marriage; stepdaughter or stepson.

step·daugh·ter (step'dô'tər) *n*. a daughter of one's husband or wife by a former marriage.

step-down (step'doun') *adj*. **1**. decreasing or reducing by degrees or stages. **2**. *Electricity*. reducing voltage, usually in fixed increments: *a step-down transformer*. —*n*. a decrease or reduction, as in amount.

step·fa·ther (step'fä'th̵ər) *n*. the husband of one's mother after the death or divorce of one's father.

step-in (step'in') *adj*. (of a garment or shoes) put on by being stepped into. —*n*. a step-in garment or shoe.

step·lad·der (step'lad'ər) *n*. a ladder that stands by itself on four legs and has flat steps instead of rungs.

step·moth·er (step'muth̵'ər) *n*. the wife of one's father after the death or divorce of one's mother.

step·par·ent (step'pâr'ənt) *n*. a stepfather or stepmother.

steppe (step) *n*. **1**. any of the vast, grassy plains extending from southeastern Europe into central Siberia. **2**. any extensive, treeless plain. [Russian *step'* wasteland.]

stepped-up (stept'up') *adj*. increased, as in activity or intensity; accelerated: *a stepped-up political campaign*.

step·per (step'ər) *n*. a person or thing that steps, esp. in a lively manner, such as a horse or a dancer.

step·ping·stone (step'ing stōn') *also*, **stepping stone**. *n*. **1**. a stone or one of a series of stones on which to step, as in crossing a stream. **2**. an opportunity or means of progressing toward some goal: *The Senate has often been a steppingstone to the presidency*.

step·sis·ter (step'sis'tər) *n*. a daughter of one's stepparent by a former marriage.

step·son (step'sun') *n*. a son of one's husband or wife by a former marriage.

step-up (step'up') *n*. an increase or escalation in intensity, amount, or activity: *a step-up in a war, a step-up in sales*. —*adj*. **1**. increasing by degrees or stages. **2**. *Electricity*. increasing voltage, usually in fixed increments: *a step-up transformer*.

step·wise (step'wīz') *adv*. in the manner or arrangement of a series of steps; gradually.

-ster *suffix* (used to form nouns) **1**. a person who makes, uses, or is occupied with: *punster, prankster*. **2**. a person who is: *youngster*. **3**. a person who is related or belongs to: *gangster*. [Old English *-estre, -istre*.]

stere (stîr) *n*. a metric measure of capacity equal to 1 cubic meter. [French *stère*, from Greek *stereos* solid, firm [1].]

ster·e·o (ster'ē ō', stîr'-) *n., pl.* **-os**. **1**. a high-fidelity system designed for stereophonic sound reproduction. **2**. stereophonic sound. —*adj*. stereophonic.

stereo- *combining form* three-dimensional; solid: *stereoscope, stereochemistry*. [Greek *stereos* solid, firm [1].]

ster·e·o·chem·is·try (ster'ē ō kem'ə strē, stîr'-) *n*. the study of the spatial arrangement of atoms and molecules in chemical compounds.

ster·e·o·mi·cro·scope (ster'ē ō mī'krə skōp', stîr'ē-) *n*. stereoscopic microscope. [STEREO- + MICROSCOPE.]

ster·e·o·phon·ic (ster'ē ə fon'ik, stîr'-) *adj*. **1**. of or relating to a system of sound reproduction in which the sound is heard from two or more sources. In stereophonic recording, sound is picked up by two or more microphones and reproduced through two or more loudspeakers, thus creating a more natural effect. ➡ distin-

guished from **monaural**. **2**. of, relating to, characterized by, or designating sound as it is heard naturally by both ears.

ster·e·op·ti·con (ster'ē op'ti kən, stîr'-) *n*. a compound slide projector that can project two overlapping pictures simultaneously or in quick succession, so as to produce a fading of one picture into the other. [STEREO- + Greek *optikon*, neuter of *optikos* relating to vision.]

ster·e·o·scope (ster'ē ə skōp', stîr'-) *n*. an optical instrument consisting of two lenses through which the eyes separately view a given scene from different angles, giving the illusion of seeing the image in three dimensions. [STEREO- + -SCOPE.]

ster·e·o·scop·ic (ster'ē ə skop'ik, stîr'-) *adj*. **1**. designating or adapted for three-dimensional vision or viewing. **2**. characterized by a three-dimensional appearance. **3**. of or relating to a stereoscope. Also, **ster'e·o·scop'i·cal**. —**ster'e·o·scop'i·cal·ly**, *adv*.

stereoscopic microscope, a binocular microscope having two parallel systems of compound lenses, providing a three-dimensional image. Also, **stereomicroscope**.

ster·e·os·co·py (ster'ē os'kə pē, stîr'ē-) *n*. **1**. the phenomenon of three-dimensional vision. **2**. the science or study of stereoscopic optical effects. [STEREO- + Greek *skopia* a watching, seeing.]

ster·e·o·type (ster'ē ə tīp', stîr'-) *n*. **1**. a method or process of making metal plates by taking a mold of the raised surface of the original composed type, in or as in papier-mâché, and making a cast in type metal from the mold. **2**. a printing plate of type metal cast by this process. **3**. an oversimplified or conventional image, opinion, or conception of a certain person, group, issue, or the like, usually held in common by some segment of society. **4**. a person or thing that embodies such an image or conception. —*v.t.*, **-typed, -typ·ing**. **1**. to make a stereotype of. **2**. to develop a fixed, conventional view of. —**ster'e·o·typ'er**, *n*. —**ster·e·o·typ·ic** (ster'ē ə tip'ik, stîr'-); *also*, **ster'e·o·typ'i·cal**, *adj*.

ster·e·o·typed (ster'ē ə tīpt', stîr'-) *adj*. **1**. characteristic of a stereotype; lacking originality or individuality; conventional; commonplace. **2**. printed from stereotype plates.

ster·e·o·typ·y (ster'ē ə tī'pē, stîr'-) *n*. **1**. the process or art of making stereotype plates. **2**. the act of printing from such plates.

ster·ile (ster'əl) *adj*. **1**. incapable of reproducing; not producing offspring; barren. **2**. producing little or no vegetation; not fertile; arid: *a dry and sterile desert region*. **3**. free from bacteria or microorganisms: *sterile surgical instruments, sterile milk bottles*. **4**. lacking imagination or vitality; conventional; stale: *sterile writing*. [Latin *sterilis* barren.] —**ster'ile·ly**, *adv*. —For Synonyms, see **barren**.

ste·ril·i·ty (stə ril'i tē) *n*. the condition or quality of being sterile.

ster·i·li·za·tion (ster'ə lə zā'shən) *n*. the act or process of sterilizing or the state of being sterilized.

ster·i·lize (ster'ə līz') *v.t.*, **-lized, -liz·ing**. to make sterile. —**ster'i·liz'er**, *n*.

ster·ling (stûr'ling) *adj*. **1**. designating a silver alloy containing 92.5% pure silver. **2**. made of sterling silver. **3**. consisting of, relating to, or payable in British money. **4**. of accepted or proven worth; excellent: *a sterling reputation*. —*n*. **1.a**. a silver alloy containing 92.5% pure silver; sterling silver. **b**. an article or articles made of sterling silver, such as flatware. **2**. British money. **3**. the British standard of fineness for gold and silver coinage. [Middle English *sterling* English silver penny of the medieval period, going back to Old English *steorra* star + -LING [1] (with reference to the star on early coins).] —**ster'ling·ly**, *adv*. —**ster'ling·ness**, *n*.

stern[1] (stûrn) *adj*. **1**. severe in disposition or conduct; strict; inflexible; uncompromising: *a stern moralist, a stern policy*. **2**. characterized by or expressing extreme displeasure; harsh: *to speak in a stern voice*. **3**. grim or forbidding in manner or appearance; austere; gloomy: *a stern look*. **4**. not easily shaken or swayed; resolute; unwavering: *a stern resolve*. **5**. impossible to escape or avoid; compelling; relentless: *stern reality*. [Old English *stirne* severe, hard.] —**stern'ly**, *adv*. —**stern'ness**, *n*. —For Synonyms, see **severe**.

stern[2] (stûrn) *n*. the rear of a boat or ship. [Probably from Old Norse *stjōrn* a steering.]

ster·nal (stûr'nəl) *adj*. of, near, or relating to the breastbone, or sternum.

a	at	e	end	o	hot	u	up	hw	white		about
ā	ape	ē	me	ō	old	ū	use	ng	song		taken
ä	far	i	it	ô	fork	ü	rule	th	thin	ə	pencil
âr	care	ī	ice	oi	oil	u̇	pull	th̵	this		lemon
		îr	pierce	ou	out	ûr	turn	zh	measure		circus

stern·most (stûrn′mōst′) *adj.* **1.** nearest astern. **2.** farthest in the rear, as of a line of ships.

stern·post (stûrn′pōst′) *n.* the principal upright member at the stern of a ship, extending from the keel and usually supporting the rudder.

ster·num (stûr′nəm) *n., pl.* **-nums** or **-na** (-nə). breastbone. For illustration, see **skeleton**. [Modern Latin *sternum,* from Greek *sternon* chest.]

ster·nu·ta·to·ry (stər nü′tə tôr′ē, -nū′-) *adj.* causing or tending to cause sneezing. Also, **ster·nu′ta·tive.**

stern·ward (stûrn′wərd) *adj.* toward or at the stern. —*adv. also,* **stern·wards.** toward the stern.

stern·way (stûrn′wā′) *n.* the backward movement of a boat or ship.

stern·wheel·er (stûrn′hwē′lər, -wē′-) *n.* a steamboat propelled by a single paddle wheel at the stern.

ster·oid (ster′oid, stîr′-) *n.* any of a group of lipid compounds secreted by animals and plants and important in metabolism, sexual development, and synthesis of vitamins and other useful substances. Hormones, digitalis, and sterols are steroids. Some steroids, such as cortisone, are made synthetically and used to treat inflammation. [STER(OL) + -OID.]

ster·ol (ster′ôl, stîr′-) *n.* any of a group of solid alcohols found in the tissues of animals and plants, as cholesterol. Also, **steroid alcohol.** [From CHOLESTEROL.]

ster·to·rous (stûr′tər əs) *adj.* characterized or accompanied by a deep snoring or rasping sound: *stertorous sleep.* [Modern Latin *stertor* snoring (from Latin *stertere* to snore) + -OUS.] —**ster′to·rous·ly,** *adv.* —**ster′to·rous·ness,** *n.*

stet (stet) *n.* a proofreading mark indicating that canceled or corrected matter should be printed as it appeared originally. —*v.t.,* **stet·ted, stet·ting.** to cancel a correction or deletion, as by writing *stet* in the margin and underscoring the correction or deletion with a row of dots. [Latin *stet* let it stand.]

steth·o·scope (steth′ə skōp′) *n.* an instrument used to listen to sounds made by the internal organs of the body, esp. the lungs and heart. [Greek *stēthos* chest + -SCOPE.]

steth·o·scop·ic (steth′ə skop′ik) *adj.* **1.** observed or made by means of a stethoscope: *a stethoscopic examination.* **2.** of or relating to a stethoscope or its use. Also, **steth′o·scop′i·cal.** —**steth′o·scop′i·cal·ly,** *adv.*

ste·ve·dore (stē′və dôr′) *n.* a person whose work is loading and unloading cargo from ships. —*v.,* **-dored, -dor·ing.** —*v.t.* to load or unload the cargo of (a ship). —*v.i.* to load or unload a ship. [Spanish *estivador,* from *estivar* to stow cargo, from Latin *stīpāre* to press together.]

stew (stü, stū) *v.t.* to cook (food) slowly by simmering. —*v.i.* **1.** to be cooked by slow simmering; undergo stewing: *The cook let the meat stew for several hours.* **2.** *Informal.* to be angry, disturbed, or agitated; fret; worry: *to stew over a problem.* —*n.* **1.** food cooked by stewing, esp. a mixture of meats and vegetables cooked together. **2.** *Informal.* a state of anxiety, anger, or worry: *The child was in a stew over the lost dog.* [Old French *estuver* to bathe in hot water, going back to Latin *ex-* out + Greek *tȳphos* smoke, vapor.] —**stew′a·ble,** *adj.*

　•**to stew in one's own juice.** to remain disturbed or suffer, esp. from one's own actions.

stew·ard (stü′ərd, stū′-) *n.* **1.** a person who manages the property, finances, or affairs of another. **2.a.** a person in charge of food and other passenger services, as on a ship, airplane, or train. **b.** any member of a staff or crew who provides passenger services on a ship, airplane, or train. **3.** a person employed in an institution, club, or resort as the manager of household affairs. **4.** shop steward. [Old English *stigweard* official directing a household, from *stig* house, hall + *weard* keeper.]

stew·ard·ess (stü′ər dis, stū′-) *n.* a woman employed to provide passenger services on a ship, airplane, or train.

stew·ard·ship (stü′ərd ship′, stū′-) *n.* **1.** the position or duties of a steward. **2.** responsibility for wise use or protection: *The speaker talked about the stewardship of our natural resources.*

stew·pan (stü′pan′, stū′-) *n.* a heavy pot used for stewing.

stib·nite (stib′nīt) *n.* a lustrous, gray sulfide mineral mined as an ore of antimony. Formula: Sb_2S_3

stick[1] (stik) *n.* **1.** a small branch or shoot that has broken or been cut off a tree or shrub. **2.** a long, slender piece of wood used for any of various purposes, such as a walking stick, baton, or staff. **3.** anything resembling a stick, esp. in shape: *a stick of dynamite, carrot and celery sticks.* **4.** an implement used to propel a ball or puck in any of various games: *a hockey stick.* **5.a.** the lever that controls the up-and-down and side-to-side movement of an airplane. **b.** stickshift. **6.** *Printing.* **a.** composing stick. **b.** the amount of type that a composing stick can hold. **7.** *Informal.* a dull, stiff, unresponsive person. **8. the sticks.** *Informal.* an area that is far from a city or town, esp. one regarded as being provin-cial or culturally backward. —*v.t.* to provide a stick or sticks for support. [Old English *sticca* short piece of wood, slender branch of a tree or shrub.]

stick[2] (stik) *v.,* **stuck, stick·ing.** —*v.t.* **1.** to stab, pierce, or puncture (something) with a pointed object: *The child stuck the balloon with a pin.* **2.** to push, thrust, or drive the point or end of (something) into something else: *to stick a tack in a bulletin board.* **3.** to fasten or attach with a pin, nail, or other pointed object: *The student stuck a notice on the bulletin board.* **4.** to fasten or attach by means of an adhesive substance or material: *to stick a stamp on an envelope.* **5.** to put or thrust into a specified place or position: *to stick one's tongue out, to stick one's arm out a window.* **6.** to keep from proceeding or moving; delay or obstruct: *Our car was stuck in traffic for an hour.* **7.** to kill by piercing. **8.** *Informal.* to puzzle; confuse: *You stuck me on that question.* **9.** *Informal.* to cause to bear the responsibility or blame for (with *with*): *They stuck us with the bill.* **10.** *Slang.* to cheat or take advantage of. —*v.i.* **1.** to be or become fixed in place by having the end, edge, or point embedded in something: *The piece of glass stuck in my foot.* **2.** to continue in the performance or pursuit of something, such as a course of action: *to stick to a job until it's finished.* **3.** to remain faithful or loyal: *to stick to a bargain, to stick by one's friends.* **4.** to become or remain closely attached or associated: *If we don't stick together, we'll get lost in this crowd.* **5.** to be or become immovable or unworkable: *The drawer stuck when I tried to open it.* **6.** to hold fast, as if glued; cling; adhere: *The wet shirt stuck to my back.* **7.** to follow closely (with *to*): *We should stick to the main road since we're not sure of the way.* **8.** to be unable to resolve something; be puzzled: *Can you solve the riddle, or are you stuck?* —*n.* **1.** a poke, thrust, or stab with or as with a pointed object: *Someone in the crowd gave me a stick in the ribs with an elbow.* **2.** the state or condition of adhering or of causing to adhere. [Old English *stician* to stab, pierce, remain fixed.]

　•**to be stuck on.** *Informal.* to be in love or infatuated with.

　•**to stick around.** *Informal.* to remain or wait nearby: *I'm going to stick around until my friend returns.*

　•**to stick by** (or **to**). to stay loyal to: *to stick by a friend in trouble.*

　•**to stick it out.** to put up with or endure something.

　•**to stick out. a.** to extend; protrude: *A white handkerchief stuck out from my pocket.* **b.** *Informal.* to be obvious or conspicuous.

　•**to stick up.** *Slang.* to rob, esp. at gunpoint.

　•**to stick up for.** *Informal.* to support or defend: *to stick up for a friend who is in trouble.*

stick·ball (stik′bôl′) *n.* a form of baseball played with a rubber ball and a broomstick or similar object for a bat.

stick·er (stik′ər) *n.* **1.** a label, promotional device, or other printed paper with glue on the back. **2.** a burr, bramble, or the like.

sticking plaster, adhesive tape.

sticking point 1. a point beyond which a person or thing cannot be pushed or will not proceed. **2.** something that causes an impasse, as in negotiations: *The issue of tenure was a sticking point in the contract talks.*

stick insect, walking stick *(def. 2).*

stick-in-the-mud (stik′in thə mud′) *n.* *Informal.* an old-fashioned or conventional person who resists new ideas, attitudes, or activities.

stick·le (stik′əl) *v.i.,* **-led, -ling. 1.** to argue or insist stubbornly, esp. about trifles. **2.** to hesitate or raise objections over trifles; scruple. [Modification of obsolete *stightle* to arrange, control, strive, going back to Old English *stihtan* to arrange.]

stick·le·back (stik′əl bak′) *n., pl.* **-backs** or **-back.** any of a group of small fish, family Gasterosteidae, having sharp, bony spines on the back and bony plates on the sides in place of scales. The male stickleback builds and guards the nest. [Middle English *stykylbak,* from Old English *sticel* prickle, sting + *bæc* back[1]; referring to the spines on its back.]

stick·ler (stik′lər) *n.* **1.** a person who stubbornly insists that something be done in an exact, strict way (often with *for*): *to be a stickler for neatness.* **2.** *Informal.* something puzzling or difficult.

stick·pin (stik′pin′) *n.* a long ornamental pin, usually with a jeweled head, worn esp. in a necktie or ascot.

stick·shift (stik′shift′) *also,* **stick shift.** *n.* a manually operated transmission in a motor vehicle, esp. one with the gearshift lever mounted on the floor.

stick·tight (stik′tīt′) *n.* any of several weedy plants, genus *Bidens,* of the composite family, usually having yellow flower heads, and bearing small barbed fruits that stick to clothing and animal fur.

stick-to-it·ive (stik′tü′i tiv) *adj.* *Informal.* not giving up easily; persistent; persevering: *a stick-to-it-ive person.* —**stick′-to′-it·ive·ness,** *n.*

stick·um (stik′əm) *n. Informal.* any sticky or gummy substance, esp. a glue or other adhesive matter: *stickum on the flap of an envelope.* [STICK² + -*um,* a form of 'EM.]

stick·up (stik′up′) *n. Slang.* a robbery, esp. at gunpoint.

stick·y (stik′ē) *adj.,* **stick·i·er, stick·i·est. 1.** tending to stick or hold fast: *a sticky piece of gum.* **2.** coated or covered with glue or other adhesive: *a sticky poster.* **3.** hot and humid; muggy. **4.** difficult to deal with tactfully; touchy: *a sticky problem.* —**stick′i·ly,** *adv.* —**stick′i·ness,** *n.*

sties (stīz) the plural of **sty¹** and **sty².**

stiff (stif) *adj.* **1.** not easily bent; not pliant: *The new leather belt was very stiff.* **2.** unable to move easily without pain or difficulty: *My back was stiff after sitting for so many hours.* **3.** not natural, easy, or graceful in manner or movement; formal: *a stiff bow, a stiff writing style.* **4.** harsh; severe: *The judge handed down a stiff sentence.* **5.** unusually high, as in amount or degree; excessive: *a stiff price.* **6.** requiring great effort to succeed in or overcome; difficult: *stiff competition, a stiff examination in mathematics.* **7.** not liquid or fluid; thick: *Beat the egg whites until they are stiff.* **8.** not working or moving smoothly or easily, as parts of machinery. **9.** having a strong, steady movement or force: *a stiff breeze.* **10.** tightly drawn; taut. **11.** strong or potent: *a stiff dose of medicine.* —*n. Slang.* **1.** a dead body; corpse. **2.** a very formal and staid person; prig. **3.** a rough, awkward person. **4.** a fellow; chap: *a lucky stiff.* —*adv.* **1.** so as to be rigid or unmovable: *The handle was frozen stiff.* **2.** so as to feel or seem unable to move: *scared stiff, bored stiff.* —*v.t. Slang.* **1.** to cheat out of money. **2.** to refuse to tip: *to stiff a waiter for unsatisfactory service.* [Old English *stíf* rigid.] —**stiff′ly,** *adv.* —**stiff′ness,** *n.*

> **Synonyms** *adj.* **Stiff, inflexible,** and **rigid** mean difficult to bend. **Stiff** is a general term applied to anything that is in some degree resistant to bending: *a stiff new toothbrush, a stiff fabric that is hard to pleat.* **Inflexible** implies a high degree of resistance to bending: *a glass rod that remains inflexible unless it is heated.* **Rigid** is often used to describe a thing that cannot be bent without being broken: *a rigid plastic case that protects the typewriter.*

stiff·en (stif′ən) *v.t., v.i.* to make or become stiff or stiffer. —**stiff′en·er,** *n.*

stiff-necked (stif′nekt′) *adj.* **1.** having a stiff neck or wryneck. **2.** unyielding; stubborn: *a stiff-necked refusal to agree.*

sti·fle (stī′fəl) *v.,* -**fled, -fling.** —*v.t.* **1.** to prevent or inhibit the growth, development, or progress of: *to stifle someone's creative talent.* **2.** to prevent the emission; hold back: *to stifle a yawn, to stifle a laugh.* **3.** to kill by depriving of air; suffocate; smother. —*v.i.* **1.** to feel smothered because of a lack of air, as in a stuffy room. **2.** to die of suffocation. [Possibly modification of Old French *estouffer* to suffocate; of uncertain origin.] —**sti′fler,** *n.*

stig·ma (stig′mə) *n., pl.* **stig·ma·ta** (stig mä′tə, stig′mə-) or **stig·mas. 1.** a mark or token of shame, infamy, or disgrace: *to suffer the stigma of a humiliating defeat.* **2.** a distinguishing mark or characteristic, esp. one indicating a defect or abnormality. **3.** a mark or spot on the skin that bleeds, usually as a result of nervous tension. **4.** the part of the pistil of a plant on which pollen is deposited in pollination. For illustration, see **flower. 5. stigmata.** marks or wounds corresponding to or resembling the five wounds on the crucified body of Jesus, said to appear supernaturally on the bodies of certain mystics. **6.** *Archaic.* a mark burned into the skin of a slave or criminal; brand. [Latin *stigma* mark¹, brand, from Greek *stigma.*] —**stig′mal,** *adj.*

stig·mat·ic (stig mat′ik) *adj.* of, relating to, or marked by a stigma or stigmata. Also, **stig·mat′i·cal.** —*n.* a person who is marked with religious stigmata. Also, **stig′ma·tist.**

stig·ma·tize (stig′mə tīz′) *v.t.,* -**tized, -tiz·ing. 1.** to characterize or brand as shameful, infamous, or disgraceful: *to be stigmatized by an association with criminals.* **2.** to mark with a stigma; brand. **3.** to cause stigmata to appear on. —**stig′ma·ti·za′tion,** *n.*

stile¹ (stīl) *n.* **1.** a step or series of steps permitting passage over a wall or fence. **2.** turnstile. [Old English *stigel* the series of steps.]

stile² (stīl) *n.* one of the vertical members of a frame or panel, as in a door or window. [Dutch *stijl* doorpost, probably going back to Latin *stilus* post¹, stake.]

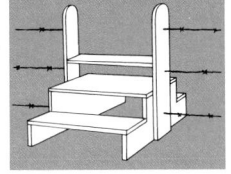

stile¹

sti·let·to (stə let′ō) *n., pl.* -**tos** or -**toes. 1.** a dagger with a very narrow tapering blade. **2.** a small, pointed instrument used for making eyelets in embroidery. [Italian *stiletto,* diminutive of *stilo* dagger, from Latin *stílus* pointed instrument.]

still¹ (stil) *adj.* **1.** without movement; motionless: *The water was still after the storm.* **2.** without sound; noiseless; silent; quiet: *Be still and listen.* **3.** free from agitation or excitement; tranquil; peaceful: *The night is still.* **4.** not loud; subdued; soft: *a still voice.* **5.** having little or no effervescence; not carbonated or sparkling: *a still beverage.* **6.** of, relating to, or designating a photograph, as distinguished from a motion picture. —*v.t.* **1.** to make silent; quiet: *to still a barking dog.* **2.** to make less intense or severe; assuage; allay: *to still one's thirst, to still a child's fears.* **3.** to make peaceful or tranquil. —*v.i.* to become still or calm. —*n.* **1.** the quality or state of being still; quiet; silence; calm: *in the still of the night.* **2.** a photograph, esp. one made from a single frame of a motion picture and used for publicity purposes. —*adv.* **1.** without movement; motionless: *Sit still.* **2.** at or up to the time indicated; as before: *Our family still lives in this neighborhood.* **3.** in increasing amount or degree; beyond this: *Still greater things are expected from you.* **4.** even then; all the same; nevertheless: *Though I dieted, I still could not lose weight.* **5.** *Archaic.* constantly; always. —*conj.* despite that; yet: *It's raining; still, I'd like to go.* [Old English *stille* motionless, silent.] —**still′ness,** *n.*

still² (stil) *n.* **1.** an apparatus for distilling liquids, esp. alcoholic liquors, in which a mixture of liquid substances is heated until the most volatile liquid vaporizes. **2.** distillery. [From obsolete *still* to distill, short for DISTILL.]

still alarm, a burglar alarm or fire alarm given by telephone or other means without sounding a signal apparatus at the site.

still·birth (stil′bûrth′) *n.* **1.** the birth of a stillborn fetus. **2.** a stillborn fetus.

still·born (stil′bôrn′) *adj.* dead at birth.

still life *pl.* **still lifes. 1.** a painting or photograph of inanimate objects, such as bottles, vases, fruit, or flowers. **2.** inanimate objects or an arrangement of them as a category of subject matter in painting or photography. —**still′-life′,** *adj.*

still life by Haitian artist Seneque Obin

stil·ly (*adj.,* stil′ē; *adv.,* stil′lē) *adj.,* -**li·er, -li·est.** quiet; still; calm. —*adv.* calmly; quietly.

stilt (stilt) *n., pl.* **stilts** or *(def. 3)* **stilt. 1.** one of a pair of long poles, each having a footrest attached at some distance from the bottom end, used to enable a person, such as a clown in a circus, to walk with the feet above the ground. **2.** one of the posts used to support a building, pier, or other structure above ground or water. **3.** any of several water birds, family Recurvirostridae, native to most temperate and tropical regions of the world, having a slender bill, long, thin legs, and usually predominantly white plumage. Length: 13-16 inches (33-41 centimeters). [Middle English *stilte;* probably of Middle Dutch or Middle Low German origin.]

stilt·ed (stil′tid) *adj.* **1.** artificially or stiffly dignified or formal; turgid: *a stilted style of writing.* **2.** elevated or supported by or as by stilts so as to be above ground or water. **3.** (of an arch) having

a	at	e	end	o	hot	u	up	hw	white		about
ā	ape	ē	me	ō	old	ū	use	ng	song		taken
ä	far	i	it	ô	fork	ü	rule	th	thin	ə	pencil
âr	care	ī	ice	oi	oil	ů	pull	th	this		lemon
		îr	pierce	ou	out	ûr	turn	zh	measure		circus

its arc heightened by an extended vertical support. —**stilt′ed·ly,** *adv.* —**stilt′ed·ness,** *n.*

Stil·ton (stil′tən) a rich white cheese, resembling Roquefort, made of whole milk and cream and marbled with blue-green mold. [From *Stilton,* a village in England where it supposedly was first sold.]

stim·u·lant (stim′yə lənt) *n.* **1.** a drug or other substance that increases, heightens, or arouses the activity of an organism or bodily function or part: *The caffeine in tea and coffee acts as a stimulant.* **2.** anything that rouses or incites to action; stimulus: *Reading is a stimulant to the imagination.* **3.** an alcoholic beverage. ➡ Alcohol is popularly regarded as a stimulant, but it is actually a depressant. —*adj.* stimulating. [Latin *stimulāns,* present participle of *stimulāre* to prick with a goad, urge on, from *stimulus* goad, incentive.]

stim·u·late (stim′yə lāt′) *v.,* -**lat·ed,** -**lat·ing.** —*v.t.* **1.** to rouse to increased action or effort; have an animating effect on: *The warm spring days stimulated us to work in the garden.* **2.** to act as a stimulus or stimulant to (an organism or bodily function or part). **3.** to affect with an alcoholic beverage. —*v.i.* to act as a stimulus or stimulant to an organism or bodily function or part. [Latin *stimulātus,* past participle of *stimulāre* to prick with a goad, urge on. See STIMULANT.] —**stim′u·la′tion,** *n.* —**stim′u·la′tor;** *also,* **stim′u·lat′er,** *n.*

stim·u·la·tive (stim′yə lā′tiv) *adj.* tending or serving to stimulate. —*n.* something that stimulates; stimulus.

stim·u·lus (stim′yə ləs) *n., pl.* -**li** (-lī′). **1.** something that rouses or incites to action or effort; impetus: *Reduced tariffs were a stimulus to foreign trade.* **2.** anything that produces a response in or influences the activity of an organism or bodily function or part. [Latin *stimulus* goad, incentive.] —For Synonyms, see **incentive.**

sti·my (stī′mē) *n., pl.* -**mies.** stymie. —*v.t.,* -**mied,** -**my·ing.** stymie.

sting (sting) *v.,* **stung, sting·ing.** —*v.t.* **1.** to prick painfully with a sharp, usually pointed, organ or object: *The bee stung me on the foot.* **2.** to cause to feel a sharp, smarting pain: *The iodine stung my cut finger.* **3.** to cause to suffer sharp mental or emotional pain: *The harsh criticism stung the young artist.* **4.** to goad or incite suddenly and sharply; provoke: *Insults stung the child into making an angry reply.* **5.** *Slang.* to take advantage of by overcharging. —*v.i.* **1.** to have, use, or wound with a stinger, as certain insects. **2.** to cause or feel sharp physical or mental pain: *The soap will sting if it gets in your eyes.* —*n.* **1.** the act or an instance of stinging. **2.** a wound or smarting, burning sensation resulting from this. **3.** something that causes sharp mental or physical pain: *a sting of regret.* **4.** stinger *(def. 1).* **5.** goad; spur. **6.** *Slang.* a confidence game, esp. one carried out by police to entrap a criminal or criminals. [Old English *stingan* to pierce with a pointed organ or object.]

sting·a·ree (sting′ə rē′) *n.* stingray.

sting·er (sting′ər) *n.* **1.** a sharp, usually pointed organ with which an insect or animal stings. Also, **sting. 2.** *Informal.* a stinging remark, criticism, blow, or the like.

sting·ray (sting′rā′) *n.* any of a group of rays, family Dasyatidae, having a whiplike tail with two sharp, poisonous spines that can inflict a painful wound. Length: to 14 feet (4.3 meters), including tail.

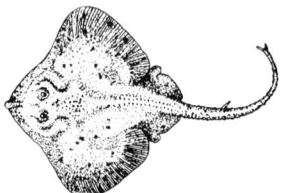
stingray

stin·gy (stin′jē) *adj.,* -**gi·er,** -**gi·est.** **1.** reluctant or unwilling to give or share something, esp. money; niggardly; penurious. **2.** scarcely sufficient in amount or quantity; scanty; meager: *a stingy portion of food.* [Possibly from *stinge,* dialectal form of STING + -Y¹.] —**stin′gi·ly,** *adv.* —**stin′gi·ness,** *n.*

stink (stingk) *n.* **1.** a strong, offensive smell; disgusting odor; stench. **2.** *Slang.* a great fuss, disturbance, or outcry: *There was quite a stink over who was to blame for the accident.* —*v.,* **stank** or **stunk, stunk, stink·ing.** —*v.i.* **1.** to give off or be permeated by a strong, offensive smell: *That dead fish stinks.* **2.** to be extremely offensive or abhorrent: *Your negative attitude stinks.* **3.** *Slang.* to have or possess something to an extreme or offensive degree (often with *of* or *with*): *to stink of wealth.* **4.** *Slang.* to be of an extremely low or inferior character or quality: *That play stinks.* —*v.t.* to cause to stink (often with *up*). [Old English *stincan* to have an odor.] —**stink′y,** *adj.*

• **to stink out,** to drive or force out with a strong, offensive, or suffocating odor or fumes.

stink·bug (stingk′bug′) *n.* any of a group of bugs, family Pentatomidae, that emit a foul-smelling liquid when disturbed.

stink·er (sting′kər) *n.* **1.** a person or thing that stinks. **2.** *Informal.* an offensive, untrustworthy, or disagreeable person. **3.** *Informal.* something difficult or troublesome: *The exam was a real stinker.*

stink·weed (stingk′wēd′) *n.* any of various plants having a strong, offensive odor, such as jimsonweed.

stint (stint) *v.t.* **1.** to limit or restrict, as in amount or degree; be stingy or sparing with: *to stint one's praise.* **2.** *Archaic.* to cease; stop. —*v.i.* to be stingy or sparing. —*n.* **1.** an allotted amount or share of work or duty to be carried out within a specified period of time: *to serve a two-year stint in the army.* **2.** limitation; restriction: *to strive for perfection without stint.* [Old English *styntan* to make dull, blunt.] —**stint′er,** *n.* —**stint′ing·ly,** *adv.*

stipe (stīp) *n. Botany.* a stalk or stemlike support, such as that supporting the cap of a mushroom. [French *stipe,* from Latin *stīpes* tree trunk, log.]

sti·pel (stī′pəl) *n.* a stipule of a leaflet in a compound leaf. [Modern Latin *stipella,* diminutive of Latin *stipula* stem.]

sti·pend (stī′pend, -pənd) *n.* **1.** a fixed or regular payment or allowance, such as one given to a student on a scholarship or fellowship. **2.** a payment for services; salary. [Latin *stīpendium* tax, tribute, pay, from *stips* contribution, wages + *pendere* to weigh out, pay.]

sti·pen·di·ar·y (stī pen′dē er′ē) *adj.* **1.** receiving or performing services for a stipend. **2.** paid for by a stipend: *stipendiary services.* **3.** of or having the nature of a stipend. —*n., pl.* -**ar·ies.** a person who receives a stipend, such as a member of the clergy.

stip·ple (stip′əl) *v.t.,* -**pled,** -**pling.** **1.** to paint, draw, or engrave by using dots or light, short touches instead of strokes or lines. **2.** to produce gradations in shade or color by painting, drawing, or engraving in this way. —*n. also,* **stip′pling. 1.** the art or technique of producing a painting, drawing, or engraving by using dots or light, short touches. **2.** the effect produced by this technique. **3.** a painting, drawing, or engraving produced by this technique. [Dutch *stippelen* to speckle, going back to *stip* point.] —**stip′pler,** *n.*

stip·u·lar (stip′yə lər) *adj.* **1.** of, relating to, or resembling a stipule or stipules. **2.** growing on a stipule or stipules.

stip·u·late¹ (stip′yə lāt′) *v.,* -**lat·ed,** -**lat·ing.** —*v.t.* **1.** to demand or specify as an essential condition of agreement: *The two stars stipulated their approval of the film's script.* **2.** to guarantee, as in a contract or agreement. —*v.i.* **1.** to make an express demand for something as a condition of agreement (with *for*). **2.** to make an agreement or contract. [Latin *stipulātus,* past participle of *stipulārī* to bargain.] —**stip′u·la′tor,** *n.* —**stip·u·la·to·ry** (stip′yə lə tôr′ē), *adj.*

stip·u·late² (stip′yə lit, -lāt′) *adj.* having stipules. [Latin *stipula* stem + -ATE¹.]

stip·u·la·tion (stip′yə lā′shən) *n.* **1.** the act of stipulating. **2.** a term or condition of an agreement or contract; something stipulated: *a contract complicated by many stipulations.*

stip·ule (stip′ūl) *n.* one of a pair of small leaflike structures occurring at the base of certain leaves. [Latin *stipula* stem.]

stir¹ (stûr) *v.,* **stirred, stir·ring.** **1.** to agitate (something, such as a liquid) in order to change the relative position of its parts, esp. by a continuous circular movement: *to stir paint.* **2.** to urge on or instigate; incite; provoke (often with *up*): *to stir someone to action, to stir up trouble.* **3.** to excite to deep feeling or emotion; affect strongly; move: *The lawyer's plea for mercy stirred the jury.* **4.** to call forth; work (often with *up*): *That song stirs up old memories.* **5.** to rouse, as from sleep. **6.** to cause to move, esp. slightly: *The breeze stirred the fallen leaves.* —*v.i.* **1.** to make a slight movement: *We didn't stir, so as not to scare the bird away.* **2.** to be active; move about: *No one was stirring in the darkened house.* **3.** to begin to show signs of activity. **4.** to be roused or excited. **5.** to be capable of being stirred: *The paste hardened too much to stir.* **6.** to be in circulation; be current: *Rumors were stirring through the town.* —*n.* **1.** commotion or excitement; disturbance; tumult: *The movie star's appearance created quite a stir.* **2.** a slight or momentary movement: *A gust of wind made a stir in the curtains.* **3.** the act or an instance of stirring, as with a spoon. [Old English *styrian* to move, agitate.] —**stir′rer,** *n.* —For Synonyms *(v.t.),* see **mix.**

stir² (stûr) *n. Slang.* prison: *The convict had been in stir for nine years.* [Of uncertain origin.]

stir-crazy (stûr′krā′zē) *adj. Slang.* extremely restless or irritable as a result of confinement.

stir-fry (stûr′frī′) *v.t.,* -**fried,** -**fry·ing.** to fry (food) quickly in very little oil over high heat while stirring rapidly.

stirps (stûrps) *n., pl.* **stir·pes** (stûr′pēz). **1.** a family or branch of a family; line of descendants; stock. **2.** *Law.* the person from whom a family is descended. [Latin *stirps* stock, stem.]

stir·ring (stûr′ing) *adj.* **1.** inspiring or exciting; thrilling: *The flutist played a stirring tune.* **2.** active; lively. —**stir′ring·ly,** *adv.*

stir·rup (stûr′əp, stir′-) *n.* **1.** one of a pair of metal, wooden, or leather loops or rings, flattened at the bottom and suspended from a saddle, used to support a rider's foot in mounting and riding. **2.** any of various similarly shaped devices, used esp. as a support. **3.** stapes. Also *(def. 3),* **stirrup bone.** [Old English *stígráp* loop suspended from a saddle to support a rider's foot, from *stígan* to climb + *ráp* rope.]

stirrup cup 1. a farewell drink, originally one given to a rider mounted for departure. **2.** a cup or bowl used for such a drink.

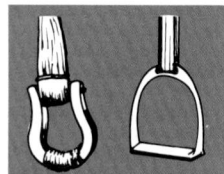

stirrups

stitch (stich) *n.* **1.** one complete movement of a threaded needle in and out of fabric, as in sewing, or through skin and flesh, as in surgery. **2.** a similar movement made to knot or loop yarn or thread on needles, as in knitting. **3.** a single loop or knot of thread or yarn made by a stitch. **4.** a particular method of arranging the thread, as in sewing or knitting. **5.** a sudden, sharp pain, esp. in the side or back. **6.** *Informal.* an article of clothing. **7.** *Informal.* slightest bit: *I didn't do a stitch of work all day.* —*v.t.* **1.** to make, fasten, join, or mend with stitches (often with *up*): *to stitch up a tear in fabric.* **2.** to fasten by means of staples. —*v.i.* **1.** to make stitches; sew. [Old English *stice* sudden, sharp pain, puncture.] —**stitch′er,** *n.*

·**in stitches.** *Informal.* laughing hilariously: *The comedian's imitation of a seal had us in stitches.*

stith·y (stith′ē, stith′ē) *n., pl.* **stith·ies. 1.** an anvil. **2.** a smithy or forge. [Old Norse *stethi* anvil.]

sti·ver (stī′vər) *n.* **1.** a coin of the Netherlands, equal to 1/20 of a guilder. **2.** anything of little or no value: *not worth a stiver.* [Dutch *stuiver* the coin.]

St. John's bread (jonz′bred′) the flat, leathery pod of the carob tree, containing many seeds and surrounded by an edible pulp.

St.-John's-wort (sānt jonz′wûrt′) *n.* any of a large group of plants and shrubs, genus *Hypericum,* having abundant yellow flowers.

sto·a (stō′ə) *n., pl.* **sto·as.** a portico or covered colonnade, often detached, having columns on one side and a wall on the other. [Greek *stoā.*]

stoat (stōt) *n.* an ermine, esp. when in its brown summer coat. [Of uncertain origin.]

sto·chas·tic (stə kas′tik) *adj.* relating to, involving, or resulting from chance or probability; random. [Greek *stochastikos* proceeding by guesswork; literally, skillful in aiming, from *stochazesthai* to guess at, to aim at, from *stochos* guess, aim.]

stock (stok) *n.* **1.** the total amount of goods that a merchant or commercial establishment keeps on hand for sale: *This store has a large stock of fishing equipment.* **2.** a quantity of something accumulated or held in reserve, esp. for future use; store: *The squirrel was putting away a stock of nuts for the winter.* **3.** domestic animals raised or kept on a farm or ranch, such as cattle, sheep, or pigs; livestock. **4.** ancestry or descent: *a person of Scandinavian stock.* **5.** the source of a line of descent; ancestor, as of a family. **6.** a group of related languages; language family: *the Indo-European stock.* **7.** the original type from which a group of plants or animals has descended. **8.** a family or other related group of plants or animals. **9.** an ethnic group or race. **10.** a liquid in which meat, poultry, or fish has been boiled, used as a base for gravies, soups, or sauces. **11.** *Finance.* **a.** ownership or partial ownership of a company or corporation as represented by the total number of shares that it is authorized to issue. **b.** the number of such shares held by an individual or group. **c.** stock certificate. **12.** the raw material from which something is made. **13.** **stocks.** a wooden frame with holes for confining a person's ankles and sometimes wrists, formerly used as a punishment for minor crimes. **14.** the wooden or metal support or handle of a gun, to which the barrel and mechanism are attached. **15.a.** the stem of a plant onto which a graft is made. For illustration, see **graft**[1]. **b.** a tree, plant, or plant part that furnishes cuttings for grafting. **16.** the trunk or main stem of a tree or other plant. **17.** an underground stem; rhizome. **18.** the crosspiece below the ring of an anchor. For illustration, see **anchor. 19. stocks.** a timber framework that is used to support a boat or ship during construction. **20.a.** a stock company *(def. 2).* **b.** the repertoire of a stock company. **21.** a close-fitting, stiff neckcloth worn in the eighteenth and nineteenth centuries. **22.** any of a group of downy plants, genus *Matthiola,* of the mustard family, such as the gillyflower, bearing stiff showy spikes of purple to white flowers. —*v.t.* **1.** to supply or furnish with stock or a stock: *The campers stocked the cabin with enough food for the weekend.* **2.** to have or keep a supply of, esp. for future use or sale: *That hardware store stocks*

all kinds of tools. **3.** to supply with livestock: *to stock a farm.* **4.** to provide with wild animals, fish, or other game, esp. for private or restricted hunting or fishing: *to stock a lake.* **5.** to fasten to or fit with a stock. —*v.i.* **1.** to lay in a stock or supply (often with *up*): *to stock up for a party.* **2.** (of a plant) to send out new shoots. —*adj.* **1.** regularly kept in stock: *a stock size.* **2.** commonly or constantly used or brought forward; commonplace: *a stock phrase.* **3.** employed in handling goods or merchandise: *a stock clerk.* [Old English *stocc* log, post[1], trunk of a tree.]

·**in stock.** available for sale or use: *The store does not have any air conditioners in stock during the winter.*

·**out of stock.** not available for sale or use.

·**to put** (or **take**) **stock in.** to have faith, trust, or confidence in.

·**to take stock. a.** to make an inventory of the goods one has on hand for use or sale. **b.** to make an estimate or appraisal: *Near the end of high school, many students take stock of their accomplishments.*

Synonyms *n.* **Stock, store,** and **reserve** mean a supply of something. **Stock** usually denotes a permanent collection of items kept for sale or for occasional use: *a boutique with a stock of expensive sweaters, a desk drawer with a large stock of envelopes.* **Store** is applied to accumulated necessities, particularly those for use in emergencies: *Because of the threat of hurricanes, they have a store of water, canned food, and candles on hand.* **Reserve** suggests something that is set aside for special use from a regular supply: *The couple used most of their cash reserve for a European vacation.*

stock·ade (sto kād′) *n.* **1.** a defensive barrier made of strong, usually tall, posts set upright in the ground, usually forming an enclosure. **2.** any similar barrier or enclosure. **3.** a military prison. —*v.t.,* **-ad·ed, -ad·ing.** to surround or fortify with a stockade. [French *estacade* bulwark made with stakes, from Spanish *estacada,* from *estaca* stake; of Germanic origin.]

stock·bro·ker (stok′brō′kər) *n.* a person who buys and sells stocks or other securities for others.

stock·bro·ker·age (stok′brō′kər ij) *n.* the work or business of a stockbroker.

stock car 1. a standard automobile modified for racing. **2.** a railroad car used for transporting livestock.

stock certificate, a certificate issued by a company or corporation to a stockholder as evidence of ownership of a particular number of shares.

stock company 1. a company or corporation whose capital is divided into shares. **2.** a theatrical troupe playing regularly at a particular theater in a variety of productions.

stock exchange 1. a place where stocks and bonds are bought and sold. Also, **stock market. 2.** an association of stockbrokers who engage in the business of buying and selling stocks and bonds according to fixed regulations.

stock farm, a farm on which livestock is raised. —**stock farmer.** —**stock farming.**

stock·fish (stok′fish′) *n., pl.* **-fish** or **-fish·es.** a fish, such as cod, that is split and dried in the open air without salt.

stock·hold·er (stok′hōl′dər) *n.* a person who owns stock in a company or corporation; shareholder.

stock·i·net (stok′ə net′) *also,* **stock·i·nette.** *n.* an elastic knitted fabric, often of wool or cotton, used for making such items as underwear or stockings.

stock·ing (stok′ing) *n.* **1.** a close-fitting, knitted covering for the foot and leg, esp. one made of nylon or other artificial fiber and worn by women. **2.** anything resembling this. [Obsolete *stock* this covering for the leg (from Old English *stocc* log, tree trunk) + -ING[1].]

·**in one's stocking feet.** wearing socks or stockings but no shoes.

stocking cap, a knitted cap, usually having a pointed end that is worn flopped over toward the back.

stock in trade 1. the goods in which a store or shop deals. **2.** the tools and equipment of a particular profession or trade. **3.** a quality or ability that is characteristic of a particular person, group, or profession.

stock·man (stok′mən) *n., pl.* **-men** (-mən). **1.** a person who raises livestock. **2.** a person in charge of the stock of goods in a company.

stock market 1. stock exchange. **2.** the business carried on in a stock exchange.

stock·pile (stok′pīl′) *n.* a supply of foodstuffs, raw materials, or

a	at	e	end	o	hot	u	up	hw	white		about
ā	ape	ē	me	ō	old	ū	use	ng	song		taken
ä	far	i	it	ô	fork	ü	rule	th	thin	ə	pencil
âr	care	ī	ice	oi	oil	u̇	pull	th	this		lemon
		îr	pierce	ou	out	ûr	turn	zh	measure		circus

other items accumulated and held in reserve for future use, as during an emergency or shortage: *a stockpile of medical supplies.* —*v.,* **-piled, -pil·ing.** —*v.t.* to accumulate a stockpile of: *to stockpile canned goods.* —*v.i.* to accumulate a stockpile.

stock·room (stok'rüm', -rüm') *n.* a room in which stocks of goods or supplies are stored.

stock split, split *(n., def. 7).*

stock·still (stok'stil') *adj.* without moving; motionless: *to stand stock-still.*

stock·y (stok'ē) *adj.,* **stock·i·er, stock·i·est.** having a solid, sturdy, and compact build; thickset. —**stock'i·ly,** *adv.* —**stock'i·ness,** *n.*

stock·yard (stok'yärd') *n.* an enclosure consisting of pens and sheds where livestock is kept before being slaughtered or shipped to market.

stodg·y (stoj'ē) *adj.,* **stodg·i·er, stodg·i·est. 1.** extremely old-fashioned and stuffy. **2.** lacking freshness or interest; commonplace; dull: *a stodgy speech.* **3.** (of food) heavy and thick; indigestible. **4.** thickset; stocky. [Earlier *stodge* to fill full of (uncertain origin) + -Y[1].] —**stodg'i·ly,** *adv.* —**stodg'i·ness,** *n.*

sto·gy (stō'gē) *also,* **sto·gie.** *n., pl.* **-gies.** a long, slender, inexpensive cigar. [From *(Cone)stog(a),* town in Pennsylvania.]

Sto·ic (stō'ik) *n.* **1.** an adherent of a school of philosophy founded by Zeno of Citium about 300 B.C., that stressed that people should be free from passion, indifferent to pain and pleasure, and calmly accept all life's happenings as manifestations of divine will. **2. stoic.** a person who is apparently indifferent to or unaffected by pain or pleasure. —*adj.* **1.** of or relating to the Stoics or Stoicism. **2. stoic.** indifferent to or unaffected by pain or pleasure, esp. accepting or resigned to suffering. Also *(def. 2),* **sto'i·cal.** [Latin *Stōicus* relating to the Stoics, from Greek *Stōikos* literally, relating to a stoa, from *stoa* stoa (because Zeno taught at a stoa in Athens).] —**sto'i·cal·ly,** *adv.*

Sto·i·cism (stō'ə siz'əm) *n.* **1.** the philosophy of the Stoics. **2. stoicism.** indifference to pleasure or pain; impassivity; dispassion.

stoke (stōk) *v.t., v.i.,* **stoked, stok·ing. 1.** to stir up and feed fuel to (a fire or a furnace). **2.** to tend (a fire or furnace). [From STOKER.]

stoke·hold (stōk'hōld') *n.* a room or compartment on a steamship containing the furnaces or boilers.

stoke·hole (stōk'hōl') *n.* **1.** a hole through which fuel is fed into a furnace. **2.** stokehold.

stok·er (stō'kər) *n.* **1.** a person who tends and supplies fuel to a furnace or boiler, as on a steamship or locomotive. **2.** a mechanical device that supplies fuel to a furnace. [Dutch *stoker* one who kindles a fire, from *stoken* to make a fire, stir up.]

STOL (stōl) an airplane that needs only a short distance to take off and land. [Short for *s(hort) t(ake) o(ff and) l(anding)*.]

stole[1] (stōl) the past tense of **steal.**

stole[2] (stōl) *n.* **1.** a woman's long scarf, usually of fur, worn around the shoulders with the ends hanging down in front. **2.** a vestment consisting of a long narrow strip of silk or other material, worn around the neck by a member of the clergy during certain religious services. **3.** a long outer garment or robe worn by matrons in ancient Rome. [Old English *stole* long robe, from Latin *stola* robe, garment, from Greek *stolē.*]

sto·len (stō'lən) the past participle of **steal.**

stol·id (stol'id) *adj.* having or showing little or no emotion; not easily moved or stirred; impassive; dispassionate. [Latin *stolidus* firm[1], dull.] —**sto·lid·i·ty** (stə lid'i tē), *n.* —**stol'id·ly,** *adv.*

sto·lon (stō'lən) *n.* **1.** *Botany.* a stem that trails along the ground and takes root at the nodes or the tip to form a new plant; runner. **2.** *Zoology.* a stemlike growth on the body of certain animals, such as the coral, that gives rise to buds from which new organisms develop. [Latin *stolon-,* stem of *stolō* shoot, branch, sucker of a plant.]

sto·ma (stō'mə) *n., pl.* **sto·ma·ta** or **sto·mas. 1.** a small opening or pore, esp. on a plant leaf, through which gases and water vapor pass in or out. **2.** a tiny, mouthlike opening in the body of a lower animal, such as a nematode. [Modern Latin *stoma,* from Greek *stoma* mouth.]

stom·ach (stum'ək) *n.* **1.** in humans and other vertebrates, a muscular, saclike organ of the alimentary canal that receives ingested food from the esophagus, lubricates it, mixes it, and begins the digestion of proteins and fats. **2.** the corresponding part in certain invertebrates, such as lobsters and insects. **3.** the part of the body containing the stomach; abdomen; belly. **4.** an inclination or liking; desire: *to have no stomach for violent movies.* **5.** desire for food; appetite. —*v.t.* **1.** to put up with; tolerate; endure: *I can't stomach their inconsiderate behavior.* **2.** to take into and retain in the stomach. [Old French *estomac* this organ, from Latin *stomachus,* from Greek *stomachos.*]

stom·ach·ache (stum'ək āk') *n.* a pain in or near the region of the stomach.

stom·ach·er (stum'ə kər) *n.* a former ornamental garment covering the stomach and chest, often extending in a V-shape to below the waistline, worn esp. by women in the sixteenth and seventeenth centuries.

sto·mach·ic (stō mak'ik) *adj.* **1.** of or relating to the stomach; gastric. **2.** beneficial to or stimulating digestion in the stomach. Also, **stom·ach·al** (stum'ə kəl), **sto·mach'i·cal.** —*n.* a medicine that stimulates the functioning of the stomach.

stomach pump, a suction pump with a long, flexible tube, used to empty the contents of the stomach, as in a case of poisoning.

sto·ma·ta (stō'mə tə, stom'ə-) a plural of **stoma.**

sto·ma·tal (stom'ə təl, stō'mə-) *adj.* of, relating to, or having a stoma or stomata.

stomp (stomp) *v.t.* **1.** to tread heavily or violently on or upon: *to stomp the floor in anger.* **2.** to bring down (the foot or feet) forcefully and heavily; stamp. —*v.i.* to tread heavily or violently: *to stomp angrily out of a room.* —*n.* **1.** an early form of jazz music having a heavy beat and lively rhythm. **2.** a dance to this music. [Form of STAMP.]

stone (stōn) *n., pl.* **stones** or *(def. 8)* **stone. 1.** a hard, naturally formed mass of mineral matter; rock. **2.** a small fragment or piece of this. **3.** a piece of such hard matter that has been shaped or cut for a particular purpose, as for building, marking a grave, or paving a road. **4.** a precious stone; gem. **5.** anything resembling a stone, as in shape or hardness. **6.** a hardened mass found in certain organs of the body, such as the gallbladder or kidney. **7.** the hard inner layer that encloses the seed of a drupaceous fruit, such as the cherry, peach, or avocado. **8.** a unit of weight of varying value. In Great Britain it is equal to 14 pounds avoirdupois (6.4 kilograms). —*adj.* **1.** made or built of stone: *a stone house, a stone wall.* **2.** made of stoneware. —*v.t.,* **stoned, ston·ing. 1.** to pelt or kill with stones. **2.** to furnish, fit, pave, or line with stones: *to stone a road.* **3.** to remove the stones from (fruit): *to stone peaches for canning.* [Old English *stān* rock, hard mineral matter, piece of rock, piece of hard mineral matter.]

  • **to cast the first stone.** to be the first to condemn, accuse, or criticize.

  • **to leave no stone unturned.** to pursue every possibility in seeking to find a solution: *We will leave no stone unturned in our search for the missing child.*

Stone Age, the earliest known stage in the development of civilization, characterized by the use of stone tools and weapons.

stone-blind (stōn'blīnd') *adj.* completely blind.

stone-broke (stōn'brōk') *adj. Informal.* without funds; penniless.

stone·chat (stōn'chat') *n.* a small, thrushlike bird, *Saxicola torquata,* native to Europe, Africa, and Asia, having predominantly brown plumage and a reddish breast. Length: 5 inches (13 centimeters).

stone·crop (stōn'krop') *n.* any of a large group of fleshy, low-growing plants, genus *Sedum,* found in cool regions of the Northern Hemisphere, bearing clusters of white, yellow, pink, or blue flowers. Also, **sedum.** [Old English *stāncrop.*]

stonecutter

stone·cut·ter (stōn'kut'ər) *n.* a person or machine that cuts or carves stone. —**stone'cut'ting,** *n.*

stoned (stōnd) *adj. Slang.* intoxicated, as by drugs or liquor.

stone-deaf (stōn'def') *adj.* completely deaf.

stone·fly (stōn'flī') *n., pl.* **-flies.** any of a group of insects, order Plecoptera, having two pairs of transparent, veined wings held

folded over the body. The nymph lives for several years in streams under stones and has a pair of pincerlike tail appendages.

stone fruit, drupe.

Stone·henge (stōn′henj′) *n.* a structure in southern England erected by a prehistoric people, consisting mainly of a circular arrangement of giant stone blocks, now in ruins.

stone marten 1. a marten, *Martes foina,* native to Europe and Asia, having gray-brown fur with a patch of white on the throat and breast. **2.** the fur of this animal.

stone·ma·son (stōn′mā′sən) *n.* a person who cuts stone or builds structures in stone. —**stone′ma′son·ry,** *n.*

stone's throw, a short distance: *Their house is just a stone's throw from here.*

stone·wall (stōn′wôl′) *v.t. Informal.* to obstruct or prevent by evasive or delaying action: *to stonewall investigators, to stonewall legislation.* —*v.i.* to use evasive or delaying actions in obstructing or preventing something from happening. —**stone′wall′er,** *n.*

stone·ware (stōn′wâr′) *n.* hard, dense pottery made of clay and stone that has been ground into a fine powder and baked at a very high temperature.

stone·work (stōn′wûrk′) *n.* **1.** work or a construction made of stone. **2.** the art, process, or technique of working in stone. **3. stoneworks.** a place where stone is cut and prepared. ➡ used as singular or plural. —**stone′work′er,** *n.*

ston·y (stō′nē) *adj.,* **ston·i·er, ston·i·est. 1.** without expression; fixed; motionless: *a stony stare.* **2.** having or feeling no emotion; cold; unfeeling: *a stony heart.* **3.** abounding in or covered with stones. **4.** hard as stone. —**ston′i·ly,** *adv.* —**ston′i·ness,** *n.*

stood (stŏŏd) the past tense and past participle of **stand.**

stooge (stūj) *n. Informal.* **1.** an entertainer who assists a comedian, as by feeding lines, heckling from the audience, or serving as the butt of jokes. **2.** anyone who is used or taken advantage of by another; dupe. [Of uncertain origin.]

stool (stūl) *n.* **1.** an individual seat supported on legs or a pedestal, usually having no back or arms. **2.** a low, backless and armless bench, used as a support for the feet or legs when sitting, or for the knees when kneeling. **3.** toilet *(def. 2).* **4.** waste matter evacuated from the bowels at each movement. **5.a.** a stump from which sprouts shoot up. **b.** the shoots growing from such a stump. —*v.i.* to send out shoots; sprout. [Old English *stōl* seat.]

stool pigeon 1. a pigeon used as a decoy to trap other pigeons. **2.** *Slang.* any person acting as an informer or decoy, esp. for the police. Also *(def. 2),* **stool′ie.**

stoop[1] (stūp) *v.i.* **1.** to bend the body forward and downward, often with the knees bent: *She stooped to pick up the paper she had dropped.* **2.** to stand or walk with the head and shoulders bent forward: *The old man stoops when he walks.* **3.** to lower or degrade oneself to do or employ something: *Don't stoop to cheating in order to pass the examination.* **4.** to pounce or swoop down, as a bird on prey. —*v.t.* to bend (one's head or other part of the body) forward. —*n.* **1.** a forward bending, esp. habitual, of the head and shoulders: *to walk with a stoop.* **2.** the act of bending forward and downward. **3.** the act of swooping down, as a bird on prey. [Old English *stūpian* to bend down, bow down.] —**stoop′er,** *n.* —**stoop′ing·ly,** *adv.*

stoop[2] (stūp) *n.* a structure at the entrance of a building or house, consisting of a number of steps leading up to a raised platform. [Dutch *stoep* flight of steps.]

stop (stop) *v.,* **stopped, stop·ping.** —*v.t.* **1.** to check or arrest the movement, action, or progress of: *to stop a car, to stop a clock, to stop traffic.* **2.** to prevent from continuing; end: *to stop the spread of a fire, to stop an enemy's advance.* **3.** to prevent (a person) from carrying out an action; restrain: *We couldn't stop our friend from taking the dangerous trip. Stop me if you've heard this joke before.* **4.** to put a temporary halt to (an action); interrupt: *Please stop your talking for a minute and listen to the news report.* **5.** to obstruct or close up (a hole, passage, or cavity), as by stuffing something into it or placing something over it (often with *up*): *to stop up a drain.* **6.** to close (a receptacle or vessel) by blocking its mouth with a plug or other stopper (often with *up*): *to stop up a bottle.* **7.** to prevent the passage or flow of: *to stop a leak.* **8.** to cease from doing (something): *Please stop making so much noise.* **9.** to keep back or withhold: *to stop payment on a check.* **10.** to instruct a bank to withhold payment on: *to stop a check.* **11.** *Music.* to close (a finger hole) or press down on (a string) in order to produce a desired tone. **12.** *Sports.* to defeat. —*v.i.* **1.** to come to an end; discontinue: *The music stopped at midnight.* **2.** to come to a standstill or halt: *to stop in the middle of a speech to answer a question.* **3.** to halt during one's course or journey: *We stopped in a small town to buy additional supplies.* —*n.* **1.** the act of stopping or the state of being stopped: *to come to a stop at the light.* **2.** a place at which a stop is made: *a bus stop.* **3.** something that stops or hinders, such as an obstacle or impediment. **4.** a

device or part of a device that serves to check or control movement or action in a mechanism. **5.** a punctuation mark. **6.** *Photography.* the aperture of a camera lens. **7.** *Music.* **a.** a graduated set of organ pipes operated by one lever. **b.** a lever operating such a set of pipes. **c.** any mechanical part or device used to stop a string or finger hole. **8.** *Phonetics.* **a.** a complete stopping of the outgoing breath stream, followed by its sudden release. **b.** a consonant formed by such a stopping, such as *p, t, k, b,* or *d;* plosive. [Old English *-stoppian* (found only in the compound *forstoppian* to stop up, close), from Late Latin *stuppāre* to stop up with tow, cram, from Latin *stūppa* tow[2], from Greek *styppē*.] —**stop′pa·ble,** *adj.*

·**to pull out all the stops.** to use every means possible; to pursue without reservation.

·**to put a stop to.** to cause to stop; end.

·**to stop by** (or **off** or **over**). to stop for a brief visit or stay during the course of a journey or on the way to somewhere else.

·**to stop down.** *Photography.* to decrease the size of the aperture of a camera lens, thereby reducing the amount of light to which the film is exposed.

·**to stop in.** to make a brief, casual visit.

> **Synonyms** *v.i.* **Stop, cease,** and **desist** mean to come to an end. **Stop,** the most general of these terms, suggests an abrupt or complete conclusion: *The rain stopped suddenly.* **Cease** is a more formal word that is often used in an official context: *The general predicted that enemy attacks would cease within a week.* **Desist** (usually with *from*) is another formal word, which implies a temporary end to an action, often as a result of restraint: *The rebel leaders agreed to desist from military action during the peace negotiations.*

stop·cock (stop′kok′) *n.* a valve for controlling the flow of a liquid or gas.

stope (stōp) *n.* an excavation in a mine from which ore has been removed in a series of steps after shafts have been sunk. —*v.t., v.i.* to mine from or excavate a stope. [Possibly from Low German *stope* literally, step of a building.]

stop·gap (stop′gap′) *n.* something devised or used to supply a need temporarily; makeshift. —*adj.* used as a stopgap; makeshift: *stopgap measures to furnish supplies to flood victims.*

stop·light (stop′līt′) *n.* **1.** traffic light. **2.** a light at the rear of a vehicle that lights up when the brakes are applied.

stop·o·ver (stop′ō′vər) *n.* a brief visit or stay, esp. overnight, at a place during the course of a journey. Also, **stop·off** (stop′ôf′, -of′).

stop·page (stop′ij) *n.* the act of stopping or the state of being stopped.

stop·per (stop′ər) *n.* **1.** something, such as a cork or plug, used to close or stop up an opening in a receptacle or vessel. **2.** a person or thing that stops or arrests the movement, action, or progress of something. —*v.t.* to close with a stopper. —**stop′per·less,** *adj.*

stop·ple (stop′əl) *n.* stopper. —*v.t.,* **-pled, -pling.** to close with a stopper. [Probably from STOP.]

stop·watch (stop′woch′) *n.* a watch having a button that can be pressed to stop the hands or the display instantly, used for making precise timings of races and contests.

stor·age (stôr′ij) *n.* **1.** the act of storing goods or other items, as in a warehouse. **2.** the state of being stored. **3.** a place for storing goods or other items: *That sofa has been in storage for over a year.* **4.** the charge for storing, as in a warehouse. **5.** *Computers.* **a.** the process of storing data, as on a disk. **b.** the device or location where data are stored.

storage battery, a battery that produces an electric current by a chemical reaction and can be recharged by an electric current.

sto·rax (stôr′aks) *n.* **1.** any of several trees or shrubs, genus *Styrax,* that produce a fragrant resin. **2.** the resin itself, formerly used in perfume. **3.** a balsam obtained from several trees of the genus *Liquidambar.* [Late Latin *storax,* form of Latin *styrax.* See STYRENE.]

store (stôr) *n.* **1.** a place or establishment in which a variety of goods are kept for sale: *a grocery store, a hardware store, a clothing store.* **2.** a quantity of something laid up or held in reserve for future use: *a store of medical supplies, a store of energy.* **3. stores.** supplies, as of food or equipment. **4.** storehouse. **5.** a quantity of supply, esp. when large or abundant. —*v.t.,* **stored, stor·ing. 1.** to put away or hold in reserve for future use: *The squirrel is storing nuts for the winter.* **2.** to put in a warehouse or other place for safekeeping: *to store furniture.* **3.** to provide or

a	at	e	end	o	hot	u	up	hw	white		about
ā	ape	ē	me	ō	old	ū	use	ng	song		taken
ä	far	i	it	ô	fork	ü	rule	th	thin	ə	pencil
âr	care	ī	ice	oi	oil	u̇	pull	th	this		lemon
		îr	pierce	ou	out	ûr	turn	zh	measure		circus

furnish; supply. **4.** *Computers.* to put or hold (data) in a computer memory or on a device, such as a hard disk. [Old French *estor* provision, from *estorer* to establish, restore, going back to Latin *instaurāre* to construct, restore.] —**stor′a·ble,** *adj.* —**stor′er,** *n.* —For Synonyms (*n.*), see **stock.**

• **in store.** in reserve; forthcoming: *There's a surprise in store for you when you get home.*

• **to set** (or **put**) **store by.** to have regard for; value; esteem: *The doctor sets little store by home remedies.*

store·front (stôr′frunt′) *n.* **1.** the front side of a store facing a street, often having windows for the display of merchandise. **2.** a room or rooms behind a storefront, esp. when used for a special purpose: *The campaign headquarters are set up in a storefront.* —*adj.* established in or operating from a storefront: *a storefront church, a storefront clinic.*

store·house (stôr′hous′) *n., pl.* **-hous·es** (-hou′ziz). **1.** a place or building where things are stored. **2.** an abundant supply or source: *My history teacher was a storehouse of information.*

store·keep·er (stôr′kē′pər) *n.* **1.** a person who owns or runs a retail store. **2.** a person who is in charge of receiving and distributing stores or supplies, as on a ship.

store·room (stôr′rüm′, -rum′) *n.* a room in which things are stored.

sto·rey (stôr′ē) *n., pl.* **-reys.** story².

sto·ried¹ (stôr′ēd) *adj.* **1.** celebrated or recorded in story, history, or legend: *Daniel Boone is a storied hero.* **2.** ornamented with designs representing scenes from history or legend: *a storied mural.* [STORY¹ + -ED².]

sto·ried² (stôr′ēd) *adj.* having or divided into stories or floors. ➡ usually used in combination: *a six-storied building.* [STORY² + -ED².]

stork (stôrk) *n., pl.* **storks** or **stork.** **1.** any of various long-legged wading birds, family Ciconiidae, having a long neck, a large, strong bill, and, typically, black, white, and gray plumage. Height: 3-6 feet (0.9-1.8 meters). **2. the stork.** this bird as the legendary conveyor of newborn babies. [Old English *storc.*]

stork

storm (stôrm) *n.* **1.** any disturbed state of the atmosphere, usually accompanied by strong winds and some form of precipitation, such as rain or snow. **2.** any wind whose speed is from 64 to 72 miles (102.9 to 115.8 kilometers) per hour on the Beaufort scale. **3.** a sudden or violent outburst, as of emotion or excitement: *a storm of tears.* **4.** a violent disturbance or upheaval, as in political, civil, or domestic affairs: *The scandal over school funds caused a storm of protest in town.* **5.** a sudden, violent attack, esp. on a fortified position: *The enemy took the hill by storm.* **6.** a heavy discharge or shower of objects, such as missiles. —*v.i.* **1.** to blow or precipitate with great force: *It stormed all day Friday.* **2.** to move or rush violently or angrily: *The frustrated customer stormed out of the store.* **3.** to be extremely angry; rage. —*v.t.* to make a sudden, violent attack on; take or attempt to take by storm: *The rebels stormed the palace.* [Old English *storm* tempest, disturbance, tumult, violent attack.]

storm·bound (stôrm′bound′) *adj.* isolated, delayed, or confined by the effects of a storm: *a stormbound resort area, stormbound travelers.*

storm cellar, an underground shelter for use during cyclones, tornadoes, or the like.

storm center 1. the center of a cyclonic storm, an area of low atmospheric pressure and relative calm. **2.** any focal point or center of trouble, commotion, or controversy.

storm door, an additional door outside of an ordinary door, installed for protection against drafts or storms or other severe weather.

storm petrel, any of various small petrels, family Hydrobatidae, usually having black or brownish plumage and white markings, whose presence, according to superstition, indicates an approaching storm. Also, **Mother Carey's chicken, stormy petrel.**

storm surge, a sudden rise in sea level along a coast, caused by the approach of a cyclonic storm, as a hurricane.

storm trooper, a member of a military organization in Nazi Germany noted for terrorism and brutality. Also, **brown shirt.**

storm window, an additional window outside of an ordinary window, installed for protection against drafts or storms or other severe weather.

storm·y (stôr′mē) *adj.,* **storm·i·er, storm·i·est. 1.** affected by, characterized by, or subject to storms: *stormy weather, stormy seas.* **2.** characterized by violent or intense emotion or activity: *a stormy life, a stormy session of Congress.* —**storm′i·ly,** *adj.* —**storm′i·ness,** *n.*

stormy petrel, storm petrel.

sto·ry¹ (stôr′ē) *n., pl.* **-ries. 1.** a narration or recital of an event or series of events that have happened or are alleged to have happened. **2.** a prose or verse narrative, often fictional, intended to entertain the reader or hearer. **3.** an account, allegation, or statement of the facts of a matter or case: *According to their story, you started the argument.* **4.** short story. **5.** a joke; anecdote. **6.a.** a news account, as in a newspaper or on television: *The story of the fire was on the evening news.* **b.** the event or material used for such an account. **7.** the succession or order of events in a play, novel, or the like. **8.** a romantic or traditional legend or history: *The pioneers live on in song and story.* **9.** *Informal.* a falsehood; lie. [Anglo-Norman *storie* history, tale, from Latin *historia* narrative of past events, tale, from Greek *historia* inquiry, information, account. Doublet of HISTORY.] —For Synonyms, see **account.**

sto·ry² (stôr′ē) *also,* **storey.** *n., pl.* **-ries. 1.** one of the horizontal structural divisions of a building, extending from the floor to the ceiling or roof directly above. **2.** a set of rooms on the same floor level of a building. **3.** any of a series of horizontal divisions, stages, or levels. —*adj.* having or divided with stories or floors. ➡ used in combination: *a ten-story building.* [Possibly from Medieval Latin *historia* picture, section of a building decorated with pictures, story of a building, from Latin *historia* narrative of past events. See STORY¹.] —For Synonyms, see **floor.**

sto·ry·book (stôr′ē būk′) *n.* a book containing a story or stories, esp. for children. —*adj.* occurring in or resembling things occurring in a storybook; romantic: *a storybook marriage.*

sto·ry·tell·er (stôr′ē tel′ər) *n.* **1.** a person who tells or writes stories. **2.** *Informal.* a liar; fibber. —**sto′ry·tell′ing,** *adj., n.*

stoup (stüp) *n.* **1.** a basin containing holy water at or near the entrance of a church; font. **2.** *Archaic.* a drinking vessel, such as a cup, flagon, or tankard. [Old Norse *staup* cup.]

stout (stout) *adj.* **1.** having a thick, bulky figure; thickset; fat. **2.** having courage; valiant; brave: *stout warriors.* **3.** having strength and vigor; physically strong; robust: *stout laborers.* **4.** firm or stubborn; resolute: *stout determination.* **5.** solid in structure, substance, or material: *a stout ship, a stout meal.* —*n.* a strong, very dark, heavy ale. [Old French *estout* bold, fierce, insolent; of Germanic origin.] —**stout′ly,** *adv.* —**stout′ness,** *n.*

stout-heart·ed (stout′här′tid) *adj.* valiant; brave; courageous. —**stout′-heart′ed·ly,** *adv.* —**stout′-heart′ed·ness,** *n.*

stove¹ (stōv) *n.* **1.** a kitchen appliance used for cooking that operates on gas or electricity and consists of burners, an oven, and sometimes a storage compartment. **2.** any of various heating or cooking devices that use wood, coal, gas, oil, or electricity. **3.** a heated room or box used for some special purpose, such as a hothouse or kiln. [Middle Dutch *stove* heated chamber.]

stove² (stōv) a past tense and past participle of **stave.**

stove·pipe (stōv′pīp′) *n.* **1.** a pipe, usually of sheet metal, used to convey smoke, fumes, and noxious gases from a stove. **2.** *Informal.* a tall silk hat. Also *(def. 2),* **stovepipe hat.**

stow (stō) *v.t.* **1.** to put or pack away, esp. in a neat, compact manner. **2.** to fill by packing; load. **3.** (of a space or receptacle) to have room or space for; accommodate: *The hold of the ship stows cargo.* **4.** *Slang.* to put an end to; stop; cease. [Middle English *stowen* to place, from *stowe* a place, from Old English *stōw.*]

• **to stow away.** to be a stowaway.

stow·age (stō′ij) *n.* **1.** the act or manner of stowing or the state of being stowed. **2.** a space or room for stowing goods or other items. **3.** something stowed or to be stowed. **4.** the charge for stowing goods.

stow·a·way (stō′ə wā′) *n.* a person who hides on a ship or airplane, esp. in order to obtain free passage.

str. 1. steamer. **2.** strait.

stra·bis·mus (strə biz′məs) *n.* an abnormality of vision in which both eyes cannot be focused on the same point at the same time. [Modern Latin *strabismus,* from Greek *strabismos* squinting.] —**stra·bis′mal, stra·bis′mic,** *adj.*

strad·dle (strad′əl) *v.,* **-dled, -dling.** —*v.t.* **1.** to sit, stand, or walk with one leg on each side of: *to straddle a fence, to straddle a horse.* **2.** to appear to favor both sides of (an issue). **3.** to spread (the legs) wide apart. —*v.i.* **1.** to sit, stand, or walk with the legs wide apart. **2.** to appear to favor both sides of an issue. **3.** (of the legs) to be wide apart. —*n.* **1.** the act of straddling. **2.** the distance between the legs of a person who straddles. **3.** a refusal

or failure to commit oneself on an issue. [STRIDE + -LE.] —**strad′dler,** *n.*

Strad·i·var·i·us (strad′ə vâr′ē əs) *n.* a violin, viola, or cello made by Antonio Stradivari, Italian musical instrument maker.

strafe (strāf) *v.t., v.i.,* **strafed, straf·ing.** to attack (troops, ships, or the like) with machine-gun or rocket fire from low-flying aircraft. [From the German expression (used in World War I) *Gott strafe England* God punish England.] —**straf′er,** *n.*

strag·gle (strag′əl) *v.i.,* **-gled, -gling. 1.** to wander or be spread about in an irregular, rambling manner: *The exhausted hikers straggled through the woods.* **2.** to stray from or lag behind the main course or body. **3.** to arrive or depart separately or at irregular intervals: *Election returns straggled in all evening.* [Of uncertain origin.] —**strag′gler,** *n.*

strag·gly (strag′lē) *adj.,* **-gli·er, -gli·est.** spread out or scattered in an irregular, rambling manner: *a straggly group of hikers, straggly hair.*

straight (strāt) *adj.* **1.** proceeding in the same direction without deviating, changing, or turning: *a straight line.* **2.** not curly, wavy, or kinky: *straight hair.* **3.** not crooked or stooping; erect: *straight posture, to stand with a straight back.* **4.** in proper arrangement, order, or condition: *Try to keep your room straight. I couldn't keep the twins' names straight.* **5.** honest and to the point; frank; candid: *a straight answer.* **6.** uninterrupted; unbroken; continuous: *The politician spoke for three straight hours.* **7.** marked by adherence to truth, fairness, and honesty; upright: *a straight dealer.* **8.** strictly adhering to or supporting the platform, policy, and candidates of a particular political party: *to vote a straight Democratic slate.* **9.** having no irregularities; even or smooth: *a straight hemline.* **10.** not mixed, altered, or diluted, as an alcoholic liquor. **11.** *Slang.* following convention, as in thinking or behavior. **12.** *Slang.* heterosexual. **13.** *Slang.* not using drugs. —*adv.* **1.** in a straight line or course: *Go straight down Main Street.* **2.** all the way to the end; continuously: *Read straight through chapter 2.* **3.** without delay; immediately: *I went straight home after the movie.* **4.** in an upright manner: *Please stop leaning on the wall and stand straight.* **5.** honestly and directly: *Talk straight with us.* —*n.* **1.** something straight, such as a line or part. **2.** a straight part of a racetrack, such as that between the last turn and the finish line. **3.** *Poker.* a hand consisting of five cards in sequence. **4.** *Slang.* a heterosexual person. [Middle English *streiht* not crooked, direct, past participle of *strecchen* to extend, from Old English *streccan.*] —**straight′ly,** *adv.* —**straight′ness,** *n.*
 • **straight off** (or **away**). without delay; immediately.
 • **to go straight.** to reform after having engaged in criminal activities.

straight angle, an angle of 180 degrees.

straight-arm (strāt′ärm′) *Football. v.t.* to ward off (a potential tackler) with one's arm held out straight. —*n.* the act of straight-arming.

straight·a·way (strāt′ə wā′) *adv.* at once; immediately. —*adj.* extending in a straight line or course. —*n.* a straight course or part, esp. of a racetrack.

straight·edge (strāt′ej′) *n.* a strip of wood, metal, or other material having a straight edge, used for drawing straight lines or testing straight lines or plane surfaces, such as a ruler.

straight·en (strā′tən) *v.t., v.i.* **1.** to make or become straight (often with *up* or *out*). **2.** to restore or be restored to the proper order, arrangement, or condition (usually with *up* or *out*). **3.** to make or become honest or respectable (usually with *out*). —**straight′en·er,** *n.*

straight face, a face that shows or betrays no emotion: *The comedian told the joke with a straight face.*

straight-faced (strāt′fāst′) *adj.* showing no emotion.

straight flush, a hand in poker consisting of a sequence of five cards in the same suit.

straight·for·ward (strāt′fôr′wərd) *adj.* **1.** having or showing no guile; honest; frank; sincere. **2.** clear and to the point: *The directions are straightforward.* **3.** proceeding or directed straight ahead. —*adv. also,* **straight′for′wards.** in a straightforward manner or course. —**straight′for′ward·ly,** *adv.* —**straight′- for′ward·ness,** *n.*

straight·jack·et (strāt′jak′it) straitjacket.

straight man, an entertainer who assists a comedian, as by feeding lines or serving as the butt of jokes.

straight ticket **1.** a ballot cast for candidates of one political party. **2.** a slate of candidates from one political party.

straight·way (strāt′wā′) *adv.* at once; immediately.

strain[1] (strān) *v.t.* **1.** to draw or pull tight; stretch: *The wind strained the ropes of the tent.* **2.** to injure or weaken by excessive stretching or overexertion: *to strain a muscle, to strain one's eyes.* **3.** to use or push to the utmost: *I strained my voice to be heard above the noise of the engine.* **4.** to stretch beyond proper, normal, or legitimate limits: *The judge strained the law in deciding the case.*

5.a. to press or pour through a strainer, sieve, or other filtering device. **b.** to separate or remove by filtration: *to strain lumps from a sauce.* **6.** *Physics.* to change (a material body or structure) in size or shape by applying stress. —*v.i.* **1.** to make continued, serious, sometimes painful or violent efforts to do or achieve something; exert oneself to the utmost: *The child strained to reach the top shelf.* **2.** to pull forcibly (with *at*): *The horse strained at the rope.* **3.** to be subjected to great pressure or force: *The awning strained under the heavy snow.* **4.** to be capable of being strained, as a liquid: *Honey strains slowly.* —*n.* **1.** extreme physical force or pressure. **2.** an injury or impairment caused by excessive stretching or overexertion: *muscle strain.* **3.** extreme mental or emotional pressure or tension: *to break under the strain of combat.* **4.** the act of straining or the state of being strained. **5.** *Physics.* a change in the size and shape of a material body or structure resulting from the application of stress. [Old French *estraindre* to grip, wring, press tightly, from Latin *stringere* to draw tight.] —For Synonyms *(n.),* see **stress.**

strain[2] (strān) *n.* **1.a.** a line of descent; ancestry; stock. **b.** the descendants of a common ancestor collectively. **2.** a group of animals or plants having distinguishing characteristics and forming a small part or subdivision of a larger group: *a new strain of yellow-and-white roses.* **3.** an inherited or characteristic quality or tendency: *a strain of nobility.* **4.** a manner, style, or tone of expression: *The speaker went on in the same strain for a while.* **5.** a musical passage; tune. ➡ often used in the plural: *We heard the first strains of the national anthem.* [Old English *strēon* gain, product.]

strained (strānd) *adj.* not natural; forced: *a strained smile.*

strain·er (strā′nər) *n.* **1.** any of various utensils or devices, such as a colander or sieve, used to separate liquids from solids or solids of different sizes from one another. **2.** a person or thing that strains.

strait (strāt) *n. also,* **straits. 1.** a narrow waterway or channel connecting two larger bodies of water. **2.** a position or circumstance of difficulty, distress, or need: *to be in desperate financial straits.* —*adj. Archaic.* **1.** narrow or confining. **2.** righteous or strict. [Anglo-Norman *estreit* narrow, strict, from Latin *strictus* tight, severe, past participle of *stringere* to draw tight. Doublet of STRICT.]

strait·en (strā′tən) *v.t.* **1.** to cause to be in need or difficulty, esp. financially. **2.** to make narrow or confining.

strait·jack·et (strāt′jak′it) *also,* **straightjacket.** *n.* a jacket-like canvas garment with elongated sleeves that wrap around the body, used to confine the arms of a violent patient or prisoner.

strait-laced (strāt′lāst′) *adj.* excessively strict or rigid in morals or manners; prudish.

straits (strāts) *n.* strait.

strake (strāk) *n.* a continuous line of planking or plating extending along the side of a ship from the bow to the stern.

stra·mo·ni·um (strə mō′nē əm) *n.* a drug prepared from the dried leaves and seeds of jimsonweed, used as a sedative and to treat asthma. [Modern Latin *stramonium;* of uncertain origin.]

strand[1] (strand) *v.t., v.i.* **1.** to drive, run, or leave (a boat, whale, or the like) aground. **2.** to leave or be left in a difficult or helpless position, esp. in a strange or isolated place. —*n.* land bordering a body of water; shore or beach. [Old English *strand* land bordering a body of water.]

strand[2] (strand) *n.* **1.** one of the threads, wires, or fibers twisted together to form a rope, cord, or other line. **2.** any single thread, hair, or other stringlike structure: *a strand of spaghetti, strands of hair.* **3.** a string of things joined together by twisting, twining, or threading: *a strand of pearls.* —*v.t.* to twist or thread together to form a rope or the like. [Of uncertain origin.]

strange (strānj) *adj.,* **strang·er, strang·est. 1.** differing from the usual or ordinary; remarkable or odd: *That was a strange thing to do.* **2.** not previously known, seen, or experienced; unfamiliar: *That part of town is strange to me.* **3.** ill at ease; uncomfortable: *I would feel strange asking such a favor.* **4.** unaccustomed to or inexperienced in (with *to*): *I'm strange to this work.* [Old French *estrange* foreign, from Latin *extrāneus* external, foreign, from *extrā* outside. Doublet of EXTRANEOUS.] —**strange′ly,** *adv.* —**strange′ness,** *n.*

> **Synonyms** Strange, odd, peculiar, and weird mean differing from what is usual or anticipated. **Strange,** the most widely applied of these terms, is applied to what is new or foreign and may imply fear: *The music was played on a strange instrument. My new roommate gave me a strange look, which*

a	at	e	end	o	hot	u	up	hw	white		about
ā	ape	ē	me	ō	old	ū	use	ng	song	ə	taken
ä	far	i	it	ô	off	ü	rule	th	thin		pencil
âr	care	ī	ice	oi	oil	u̇	pull	th	this		lemon
		îr	pierce	ou	out	ûr	turn	zh	measure		circus

made me feel ill at ease. **Odd** describes something that is inconsistent, irregular, or otherwise markedly different from others of its type: *an apple with an odd, elongated shape.* **Peculiar** is often used in describing distinctive qualities: *The peculiar odor of a new car's interior.* **Weird** suggests mysterious, supernatural qualities: *the weird call of the loon at sunset.*

stran·ger (strān′jər) *n.* **1.** a person with whom one is not acquainted or familiar. **2.** a foreigner, outsider, or newcomer. **3.** a person who is ignorant of, unacquainted with, or unaccustomed to something specified (with *to*): *to be a stranger to political intrigue.* [Middle English *stranger,* from Middle French *estranger* foreign, foreigner and Old French *estrange* strange, foreign. See STRANGE.]

stran·gle (strang′gəl) *v.,* **-gled, -gling.** —*v.t.* **1.a.** to kill or attempt to kill by squeezing the throat to prevent breathing; throttle. **b.** to suffocate or choke in any manner. **2.** to prevent or inhibit the growth, development, or functioning of: *a bill intended to strangle foreign trade.* —*v.i.* to become strangled. [Old French *estrangler* to choke, from Latin *strangulāre,* from Greek *strangalān.*] —**stran′gler,** *n.*

stran·gle·hold (strang′gəl hōld′) *n.* **1.** an illegal wrestling hold that chokes an opponent. **2.** any force or influence that hinders, restricts, or stifles the freedom or progress of something.

stran·gu·late (strang′gyə lāt′) *v.t.,* **-lat·ed, -lat·ing. 1.** strangle. **2.** to obstruct, compress, or constrict (a bodily part) so as to prevent circulation or the passage of fluid. [Latin *strangulātus,* past participle of *strangulāre* to choke. See STRANGLE.]

stran·gu·la·tion (strang′gyə lā′shən) *n.* **1.** the act of strangling or the state of being strangled. **2.** the obstruction, compression, or constriction of a bodily part so as to prevent circulation or the passage of fluid.

strap (strap) *n.* **1.** a long, narrow, flexible strip of leather, cloth, or other material, often having a buckle or other fastener, for securing or holding things together or in position. **2.** a loop of metal, leather, or other material, grasped by the hand, used as in pulling on boots or in steadying oneself in a moving vehicle. **3.** shoulder strap. **4.** a narrow metal band used to fasten or hold things together or in position. **5.** strop. —*v.t.,* **strapped, strapping. 1.** to fasten, secure, or support with a strap. **2.** to beat with a strap, as punishment. **3.** to sharpen on a strop. [Form of STROP.]

strap·hang·er (strap′hang′ər) *n. Informal.* a standing passenger on a bus or subway who holds onto an overhead strap or other support.

strapped (strapt) *adj. Informal.* having little or no money; broke.

strap·ping (strap′ing) *adj. Informal.* tall and sturdy; robust: *a strapping youth.*

stra·ta (strā′tə, strat′ə) a plural of **stratum.**

strat·a·gem (strat′ə jəm) *n.* **1.** a scheme or maneuver designed to outwit, deceive, or surprise an enemy. **2.** a scheme or trick used to achieve a goal or obtain an advantage. [French *stratagème,* from Latin *stratēgēma,* from Greek *stratēgēma,* from *stratēgos* general. See STRATEGY.]

stra·te·gic (strə tē′jik) *adj.* **1.** of or relating to strategy. **2.** important or essential to strategy, esp. military strategy. **3.** trained or intended to destroy the communications, industry, and transportation, and thus the ability to fight, of an enemy: *a strategic raid.* **4.** essential to the effective waging of war: *strategic materials.* Also, **stra·te′gi·cal.** —**stra·te′gi·cal·ly,** *adv.*

Strategic Defense Initiative, a U.S. Defense Department research program designed to develop weapons based in space for destroying missiles and warheads in flight.

strat·e·gist (strat′i jist) *n.* a person who is trained or skilled in strategy, esp. military strategy.

strat·e·gy (strat′i jē) *n., pl.* **-gies. 1.** the art or science of planning and directing large-scale military operations and campaigns. ➡ distinguished from **tactics. 2.** the skillful use of planning, as in business, politics, or social relations. **3.** a plan or device designed to achieve a specific goal or advantage. [Greek *strategiā* generalship, command, from *stratēgos* general, from *stratos* army + *agein* to lead.]

strat·i·fi·ca·tion (strat′ə fi kā′shən) *n.* **1.** the act or process or an instance of stratifying. **2.** the state of being stratified. **3.** a stratified structure or formation, as of rock.

strat·i·fy (strat′ə fī′) *v.,* **-fied, -fy·ing.** —*v.t.* **1.** to form or arrange in layers or strata. **2.** to divide into social groups or classes, as according to common social or economic characteristics. —*v.i.* to form strata. [French *stratifier* to arrange in layers or strata, from Medieval Latin *stratificare* to form strata, from Latin *strātum* covering + *facere* to make.]

stra·tig·ra·phy (strə tig′rə fē) *n.* the branch of geology dealing with the formation, composition, and age of rock strata. [STRATUM + -GRAPHY.] —**strat·i·graph·ic** (strat′i graf′ik); *also,* **strat′i·graph′i·cal,** *adj.*

stra·to·cu·mu·lus (strā′tō kū′myə ləs, strat′ō-) *n., pl.* **-li** (-lī′) or **-lus.** a mass of low-lying clouds spread out against the sky in a layer of puffy rolls. For illustration, see **cloud.** [STRAT(US) + CUMULUS.]

strat·o·sphere (strat′ə sf îr′) *n.* a layer of the atmosphere, above the troposphere and below the mesosphere, extending from an average of 8 miles (13 kilometers) to about 30 miles (50 kilometers) above the earth's surface. Ozone formed in the upper part of this region protects the earth from ultraviolet solar radiation. For illustration, see **atmosphere.** [STRAT(UM) + (ATM)OSPHERE.] —**strat·o·spher·ic** (strat′ə sfer′ik); *also,* **strat′o·spher′i·cal,** *adj.*

stra·tum (strā′təm, strat′əm) *n., pl.* **stra·ta** (strā′tə, strat′ə) or **stra·tums. 1.** a horizontal layer of material, esp. one of several parallel layers placed or lying one on top of the other. **2.** a social group or class distinguished by certain common social or economic characteristics. **3.** *Geology.* **a.** a rock formation consisting of a number of originally horizontal layers of rock of approximately the same material. **b.** a single layer of sedimentary rock, whether in its original horizontal position or tilted at an angle. **4.** *Biology.* a layer of tissue or bone; lamella. [Modern Latin *stratum,* from Latin *strātum* covering; literally, something spread out, from *sternere* to spread out.]

stra·tus (strā′təs, strat′əs) *n., pl.* **stra·ti** (strā′tī, strat′ī) or **stra·tus.** a low-lying, grayish cloud having a uniform horizontal base and foglike appearance. For illustration, see **cloud.** [Modern Latin *stratus,* from Latin *strātus,* past participle of *sternere* to spread out.]

straw (strô) *n.* **1.** the dry stalks or stems of any of various grains, such as rye, oats, wheat, or barley, after they have been threshed. Straw is used esp. as bedding for livestock and for making hats, baskets, and other woven products. **2.** a single such stalk or stem. **3.** a long slender tube, as of paper or plastic, used for sucking up a liquid. **4.** something of little value or significance; trifle. —*adj.* **1.** made of straw: *a straw hat.* **2.** of or resembling straw. **3.** of little value or significance; trifling. **4.** yellowish in color. [Old English *strēaw* stalks of certain grains.]

·**to clutch** (or **catch** or **grasp**) **at a straw** (or **straws**). to use any means that offers even the slightest possibility of being helpful or successful.

straw·ber·ry (strô′ber′ē, -bə rē) *n., pl.* **-ries. 1.** the edible, sweet, usually red fruit of any of a group of plants, genus *Fragaria,* of the rose family. **2.** the low-growing plant bearing this fruit, having many slender stalks and grown in temperate regions of the world.

strawberry blond *also,* **strawberry blonde.** a person having reddish blond hair.

straw·board (strô′bôrd′) *n.* a coarse cardboard made of straw, used for boxes, book covers, and the like.

straw boss *Informal.* an assistant foreman, esp. of a work crew.

straw·flow·er (strô′flou′ər) *n.* any of several flowers that retain their form and color when dried, as *Helichrysum bracteatum,* an Australian

strawberries

annual of the daisy family that has orange, red, yellow, or white flower heads.

straw man 1. a bundle of straw made to resemble the figure of a person. **2.** a weak argument deliberately set up so that it may easily be refuted. **3.** a person who is weak or unimportant. **4.** a person who disguises the activities of another, esp. one who serves as a front in a fraudulent activity.

straw vote, an unofficial vote taken to estimate a consensus or a division of opinion on some issue. Also, **straw poll.**

stray (strā) *v.i.* **1.** to wander from a given course or group or beyond proper limits: *The puppy strayed from the yard.* **2.** to wander or move about idly or without direction; rove: *The grazing sheep strayed over the mountainside.* **3.** to turn from a course that is considered morally right or good; err. **4.** to digress or become easily distracted from the matter at hand: *The student's thoughts strayed.* —*adj.* **1.** wandering, lost, or homeless: *a stray sheep.* **2.** found or occurring randomly or occasionally; scattered or isolated: *There were a few stray hairs on the coat.* **3.** deviating

from the proper or intended course: *A bystander was hit by a stray bullet.* —*n.* a lost or homeless animal or person. [Old French *estraier* to rove, go astray, going back to Latin *extrā* beyond + *vagārī* to wander.] —**stray′er,** *n.*

streak (strēk) *n.* **1.** a long, thin irregularly shaped mark, line, or band differing in color or texture from the material or surface of which it forms a part: *to have streaks of gray in one's hair.* **2.** a trace or tendency that contrasts with the predominant character of a person or thing: *a streak of genius, a streak of madness.* **3.** a temporary run or spell; brief period: *a streak of bad luck.* **4.** an unbroken series: *a winning streak of ten games.* **5.** a flash, as of lightning. —*v.t.* to mark with a streak or streaks; form streaks on or in. —*v.i.* **1.** to form a streak or streaks: *Lightning streaked across the sky.* **2.** to become streaked. **3.** to move, run, or go at great speed. [Old English *strica* mark, line[1].]
· **like a streak.** very quickly.

streak·y (strē′kē) *adj.,* **streak·i·er, streak·i·est. 1.** marked with, characterized by, or occurring in streaks. **2.** of variable or uneven quality or character; inconsistent: *a streaky performer, a streaky run of luck.* —**streak′i·ly,** *adv.* —**streak′i·ness,** *n.*

stream (strēm) *n.* **1.** a body of running water, esp. a small river. **2.** the force, volume, or direction of the current in a body of water. **3.** a steady flow or current of any fluid: *a stream of air.* **4.** any continuous, uninterrupted movement, emission, or succession: *a stream of people, a stream of words.* **5.** a prevalent tendency or course: *the stream of public opinion.* **6.** a ray or beam of light. —*v.i.* **1.** to flow or issue in a stream: *Tears streamed down the child's face. Light streamed into the room when I parted the curtains.* **2.** to pour forth or emit a stream (often with *with*): *He came out of the sauna streaming with perspiration.* **3.** to move along steadily or smoothly; flow: *The audience streamed out of the auditorium.* **4.** to wave, float, or extend outward: *Banners streamed in the wind.* **5.** to hang or fall loosely: *Her hair streamed over her shoulders.* —*v.t.* to pour out, discharge, or emit in a stream. [Old English *strēam* current, flowing water, river.]

stream·bed (strēm′bed′) *n.* the channel in which a stream flows or has flowed. [STREAM + BED.]

stream·er (strē′mər) *n.* **1.** a long, narrow flag or banner. **2.** any long, narrow strip of material. **3.** a newspaper headline that extends across the entire page. **4.** a stream of light, such as one in an aurora.

stream·let (strēm′lit) *n.* a little stream.

stream·line (strēm′līn′) *v.t.,* **-lined, -lin·ing. 1.** to design or construct so that there is the least possible resistance to air or water: *to streamline an automobile.* **2.** to make more modern or efficient: *to streamline the administration of government.* —*adj.* streamlined.

stream·lined (strēm′līnd′) *adj.* **1.** designed or constructed so as to offer the least possible resistance to air or water. **2.** efficient and smooth-running: *streamlined procedures.* **3.** neat, trim, and having few nonessential parts; compact and simple in design.

stream-of-con·scious·ness (strēm′əv kon′shəs nis) *adj.* of, relating to, or using a literary device that presents the dramatic action of a fictional work through the spontaneous flow of the thoughts, feelings, and emotions of a character: *a stream-of-consciousness monologue.*

stream of consciousness *Psychology. n.* the conscious experience of an individual regarded as a series of events or experiences flowing continuously onward, rather than as separate, disconnected occurrences.

street (strēt) *n.* **1.** a public way in a city or town, usually with sidewalks and buildings on one or both sides: *a tree-lined street, a street of shops.* **2.** that part of such a roadway for vehicles, excluding the sidewalks and buildings: *Be careful crossing the street.* **3.** the people who live, work, or gather in a street: *The whole street went to the meeting.* [Old English *strǣt* paved way, road, from Late Latin *strāta (via)* paved (way), from Latin *sternere* to spread out, pave.]

street Arab, a homeless person, esp. a child who wanders about the streets.

street·car (strēt′kär′) *n.* a public passenger vehicle that operates on rails in city streets, powered by electricity. Also, **trolley, trolley car.**

street people 1. homeless or socially alienated people who live on the streets or in other public areas of a city. **2.** people involved in petty criminal activities, such as illicit drug traffic, that take place on the street.

street-smart (strēt′smärt′) *adj. Informal.* streetwise.

street·wise (strēt′wīz′) *adj.* knowledgeable about the ways of urban life and esp. about how to avoid trouble on the streets.

strength (strengkth, strength, strenth) *n.* **1.** the state or quality of being strong; physical power or energy: *to lift heavy weights to build up one's strength.* **2.a.** the power to sustain or resist force, strain, or stress without breaking or yielding: *to test the strength*

of a rope. **b.** the power to resist attack: *the strength of a fort.* **3.** the power or ability to act, command, enforce obedience, or make decisions: *My boss's strength is based on an ability to think quickly.* **4.** firmness of mind, character, will, or purpose; moral courage: *It sometimes takes great strength to resist peer pressure.* **5.** legal, moral, or intellectual power, influence, or effectiveness: *the strength of an argument.* **6.** vigor or intensity, as of feeling: *the strength of one's devotion.* **7.** degree of intensity, as of light, sound, or color: *the strength of an electric current.* **8.** degree of concentration or effectiveness: *the strength of a wine, the differing strengths of a drug.* **9.** strongest point or aspect; place where available force or backing is concentrated: *The strength of the party is among farmers and rural voters. Our opponents' main strength is their speed.* **10.** military power derived from numbers of armed personnel, equipment, or resources. **11.** a person or thing that strengthens; source of power or force. [Old English *strengthu* quality of being strong, power.]
· **on the strength of.** based or depending on: *We'll eat there on the strength of your recommendation.*

strength·en (strengk′thən, streng′-, stren′-) *v.t., v.i.* to make or become strong or stronger. —**strength′en·er,** *n.*

stren·u·ous (stren′ū əs) *adj.* **1.** requiring or characterized by great effort or exertion: *a strenuous task, strenuous exercise.* **2.** very active or ardent; vigorous; energetic: *strenuous opposition.* [Latin *strēnuus* vigorous, active.] —**stren′u·ous·ly,** *adv.* —**stren′u·ous·ness,** *n.*

strep (strep) *adj. Informal.* streptococcal: *a strep infection.*

strep throat, a serious infection of the throat caused by a streptococcus and characterized by fever and the presence of pus in the throat.

strep·to·coc·cal (strep′tə kok′əl) *adj.* of, relating to, or caused by streptococci: *a streptococcal bacterium.* Also, **strep·to·coc·cic** (strep′tə kok′sik).

strep·to·coc·cus (strep′tə kok′əs) *n., pl.* **-coc·ci** (-kok′sī). any of a genus of spherical or oval bacteria that multiply by dividing in one direction only, forming chains. Such diseases as scarlet fever, rheumatic fever, and strep throat are caused by various species of streptococci. [Modern Latin *streptococcus,* from Greek *streptos* twisted chain + *kokkos* berry, seed.]

strep·to·my·cin (strep′tə mī′sin) *n.* a powerful antibiotic prepared from an actinomycete, effective against tuberculosis, typhoid fever, certain types of meningitis, and other bacterial infections. Formula: $C_{21}H_{39}N_7O_{12}$ [Greek *streptos* twisted + *mykēs* fungus + -IN[1].]

stress (stres) *n.* **1.a.** mental or physical tension or pressure. **b.** a problem or situation causing this; constraining influence. **2.** special significance, emphasis, or importance attached to something (with *on* or *upon*): *My family puts much stress on education.* **3.** relative emphasis given to a particular sound, syllable, or word in speech. In the word *employ,* the stress is on the second syllable. **4.** relative emphasis given to a particular word or syllable marking the rhythm of verse, usually occurring at fixed intervals. **5.** *Music.* the accent given to certain notes or chords. **6.** *Physics.* **a.** an externally applied force or pressure that tends to strain or deform a material body or structure. **b.** the internal resistance of a material body or structure to such force or pressure. **c.** the intensity of such force or pressure, measured either in pounds per square inch or in pascals. —*v.t.* **1.** to place special significance, emphasis, or importance on: *The article stressed the need for conservation of natural resources.* **2.** to pronounce (a syllable, word, or words) with particular emphasis. **3.** to subject (a material body or structure) to stress. [Partly shortened from DISTRESS; partly from Old French *estrece* narrowness, oppression, going back to Latin *strictus,* past participle of *stringere* to draw tight.] —**stress′ful,** *adj.* —**stress′ful·ly,** *adv.*

Synonyms *n.* Stress, strain[1], pressure, and tension are factors that produce discomfort or emotional disturbance. **Stress** and **strain** are used interchangeably to suggest strong forces that may be specific, general, intermittent, or continuous: *The discharged workers were under a lot of stress because they were unable to pay all their bills. Many people cannot tolerate the strains of city life.* **Pressure** suggests a pervasive, unrelenting influence: *The pressure to keep up with co-workers left many employees with little time for leisure.* **Tension** implies the pressure of two contending forces: *The attempt to please teachers as well as parents can create tension in students.* For other Synonyms *(n.),* see **emphasis.**

a	at	e	end	o	hot	u	up	hw	white		about
ā	ape	ē	me	ō	old	ū	use	ng	song		taken
ä	far	i	it	ô	fork	ü	rule	th	thin	ə	pencil
âr	care	ī	ice	oi	oil	u̇	pull	th	this		lemon
		îr	pierce	ou	out	ûr	turn	zh	measure		circus

stress mark, accent *(def. 2)*.

stress test, a medical procedure that tests the health of the heart and circulatory system by monitoring blood pressure, pulse, and the like while the patient exercises.

stretch (strech) *v.t.* **1.** to straighten or spread out to full length or width (often with *out*): *She stretched her legs out. The cat stretched itself on the sofa.* **2.** to hold out; put forth (often with *out*): *He stretched his hand out to shake mine.* **3.** to cause to extend from one place to another or across a given area: *to stretch a clothesline across a yard.* **4.** to draw or pull tight: *to stretch a canvas over a frame.* **5.** to straighten or spread out beyond normal, so as to injure; strain; pull: *to stretch a muscle.* **6.** to extend beyond proper, natural, or legitimate limits: *to stretch a point in an argument, to stretch the rules.* **7.** to widen, lengthen, or pull out of shape: *to stretch a sweater.* **8.** to extend in time; prolong (often with *out*): *to stretch a visit out for two weeks.* **9.** to use or exert to the utmost: *to stretch one's abilities.* —*v.i.* **1.** to lie down and extend the body to full length (often with *out*): *She stretched out on the bed.* **2.** to straighten or spread out one's body or limbs to full length: *He stretches when he gets up in the morning. The outfielder stretched to catch the ball.* **3.** to extend from one place to another or across a given area: *The road stretches for another thirty miles.* **4.** to become widened, lengthened, or pulled out of shape: *The pants stretched at the knees.* **5.** to extend over a period of time: *The experiment stretched over a period of two years.* —*n.* **1.** an unbroken space or area: *We flew over a stretch of desert.* **2.** an unbroken period of time: *She was out of the country for a stretch of two years.* **3.** the act of stretching or the state of being stretched. **4.** the extent to which something is or must be stretched: *It's a five-foot stretch from here to the shelf.* **5.** a straight part of a racetrack, esp. the part between the last turn and the finish line. **6.** *Informal.* the last part of any contest or activity: *The election campaign is now coming into the stretch.* **7.** *Slang.* a period or term of imprisonment. —*adj.* **1.** made of material having elastic qualities: *stretch gloves, stretch pants.* **2.** longer than usual for its type: *a stretch limousine, a stretch jet.* [Old English *streccan* to extend.]

stretch·er (strech'ər) *n.* **1.** a bedlike structure consisting of a piece of canvas or similar material stretched across a frame, used for carrying a sick, injured, or dead person. **2.** any of various devices used to widen, lengthen, or shape a material or garment, such as the wooden frame on which an artist's canvas is spread. **3.** a person or thing that stretches. **4.** a bar, rod, or beam placed horizontally in a frame to brace other members. **5.** a brick or piece of stone placed horizontally in a wall.

strew (strü) *v.t.* **strewed, strewed** or **strewn, strew·ing. 1.** to spread or throw about at random or in various places: *to strew hay on a barn floor.* **2.** to cover with something spread or thrown about in this way: *The streets were strewn with scraps of paper and other litter.* **3.** to be scattered over (a surface): *Confetti strewed the floor.* [Old English *strēowian* to scatter.]

stri·a (strī'ə) *n., pl.* **stri·ae** (strī'ē). a narrow groove, band, streak, or stripe of distinctive color, texture, or structure, esp. one of a number of that are parallel in arrangement. [Latin *stria* furrow, channel, groove.]

stri·at·ed (strī'ā tid) *adj.* marked or characterized by striae: *striated rock.* Also, **stri'ate.**

striated muscle, muscle that has fibers consisting of alternate light and dark bands, and that can be controlled at will, such as all the muscles attached to the skeleton. The heart is the only involuntary striated muscle.

stri·a·tion (strī ā'shən) *n.* **1.** the state or condition of being striated: *the striation of muscle.* **2.** one of a set or system of striae; stria. **3.** a pattern of striae: *the striation in a fabric.*

striae
of a column

strick·en (strik'ən) *v.* a past participle of **strike.** —*adj.* **1.** strongly affected or overwhelmed, as by sorrow, disease, or catastrophe. **2.** struck or wounded: *a stricken animal.*

strict (strikt) *adj.* **1.** demanding or observing rigid conformity to rules or regulations: *a strict disciplinarian.* **2.** rigorously or closely maintained, enforced, or adhered to: *strict visiting hours, to keep a strict watch on supplies.* **3.** based on or following something exactly; literal: *a strict interpretation of the rules.* **4.** without variation or exception; complete; absolute: *They told me the plan in strict confidence.* [Latin *strictus* tight, severe, past participle of *stringere* to draw tight. Doublet of STRAIT.] —**strict'ly,** *adv.* —**strict'ness,** *n.*

stric·ture (strik'chər) *n.* **1.** an unfavorable or severe criticism; censure. **2.** something that limits, confines, or restrains. **3.** an abnormal contraction or narrowing of some duct or tube of the body. [Latin *strictūra* contraction, pressure.]

stride (strīd) *v.,* **strode, strid·den** (strid'ən), **strid·ing.** —*v.i.* **1.** to walk with long, sweeping steps, esp. in a vigorous or imposing manner. **2.** to take a single long step, as in passing over or across an obstacle. —*v.t.* **1.** to move over, along, or through with long, sweeping steps. **2.** to pass over or across in a single long step. **3.** to straddle; bestride. —*n.* **1.** a long, sweeping step or steps. **2.** the distance covered by such a step or steps. **3.** a forward progressive movement of an animal, esp. a horse, completed when all the feet are returned to the same relative positions that they occupied at the beginning. **4.** a movement forward; advancement, progress, or improvement. **—** usually used in the plural: *Great strides have been made in medical research.* **5.** the manner in which one runs or walks: *a runner with an uneven stride.* [Old English *strīdan* to straddle.]

· **to hit one's stride.** to reach one's normal speed or level of activity.

· **to take in one's stride.** to adjust to, accept, or deal with without undue difficulty, effort, or hesitation.

stri·dent (strī'dənt) *adj.* **1.** making or having a harsh, shrill, grating sound. **2.** forceful and combative: *strident objections.* [Latin *strīdēns,* present participle of *strīdēre* to make a harsh sound.] —**stri'dence, stri'den·cy,** *n.* —**strid'ent·ly,** *adv.*

strid·u·late (strij'ə lāt') *v.i.,* **-lat·ed, -lat·ing.** to make a harsh, shrill, grating sound, as a cricket does by rubbing certain body parts together. [Latin *strīdulus* creaking, rattling + -ATE[1].] —**strid'u·la'tion,** *n.*

strid·u·lous (strij'ə ləs) *adj.* making a harsh or grating sound; shrill; strident: *the stridulous cries of gulls.* Also, **strid'u·lant.** [Latin *strīdulus* creaking, shrill, from *strīdēre* to make a harsh sound.] —**strid'u·lous·ly,** *adv.*

strife (strīf) *n.* **1.** bitter dissension, discord, or conflict. **2.** a state of conflict or struggle between rivals to gain superiority: *armed strife.* [Old French *estrif* debate, contention; of uncertain origin.]

strike (strīk) *v.,* **struck, struck** or **strick·en, strik·ing.** —*v.t.* **1.** to give a physical blow to: *to strike someone in anger.* **2.** to give, as a blow; inflict. **3.** to come against forcibly; meet with physical impact: *The car skidded and struck a tree.* **4.a.** to cause to make forceful contact with; hit: *She struck her head against the shelf when she fell.* **b.** to cause to move, as by a blow: *to strike an insect from one's shoulder.* **c.** to make by or as by blows: *to strike a trail through the forest.* **5.a.** to cause to ignite by friction: *to strike a match.* **b.** to produce (a fire, spark, or light) by friction. **6.** to erase, cancel, or otherwise remove (often with *off, from,* or *out*): *The testimony was struck from the record.* **7.** to come upon physically; attack; assault: *Our troops struck the enemy camp at dawn. The flu struck the town at the beginning of winter.* **8.** to give the impression of being; appear to: *The idea struck me as being impractical.* **9.** to come into the mind of; occur to: *The solution struck me immediately.* **10.** to take on; assume: *to strike a pose.* **11.** to give or announce by ringing or otherwise sounding: *The clock struck the hour.* **12.** to come upon suddenly or unexpectedly; discover; find: *They were hoping to strike oil.* **13.** to cause to be overwhelmed or seized (with *with*): *The storm struck us with apprehension.* **14.** to cause (a feeling or emotion) to penetrate deeply: *The tiger's sudden appearance struck terror into their hearts.* **15.** to impress strongly or appeal to: *The idea struck my fancy.* **16.a.** to participate in a work stoppage against (an industry, employer, factory, or other source of employment). **b.** to participate in a stoppage of study, consuming, or other activity against, in order to make a protest or gain certain ends: *Students struck the college to call for changes in the admissions policy.* **17.** to arrive at or determine, esp. by computation: *to strike a balance between two fluids in a solution.* **18.** to make or conclude: *to strike a bargain.* **19.** to come to, as if touching; reach: *The strains of music struck our ears. An amazing sight struck our eyes.* **20.** to fall upon: *Sunlight struck the leaves.* **21.** to bring suddenly and completely into some specified state: *The news struck them dumb.* **22.** to make or form by pressing or stamping: *to strike a medal.* **23.** to lower or take down: *The ship struck its sails. The stagehands will strike the sets when the play ends.* —*v.i.* **1.** to give or aim a blow or blows. **2.** to come into forcible contact; hit. **3.** to make an attack: *We will strike at dawn. The wolf struck again last night.* **4.** to participate in a stoppage of work or other activity. **5.** to make a sound, as by ringing: *The chimes strike on the hour.* **6.** to be announced, as by ringing: *The hour struck.* **7.** to come suddenly or as if with force: *The solution struck as we were talking about something else. The big day struck before we were ready.* **8.** (of fish) to seize the bait. **9.** to ignite: *This match will strike only on the box.* —*n.* **1.** the act or an instance of striking; blow: *a military strike.* **2.** a stoppage of work or other activities: *a consumer strike.* **3.** a sudden or unexpected discovery, as of a rich vein of ore: *a gold strike.* **4.** an unexpected or unusual stroke of success or good luck. **5.** *Baseball.* **a.** a pitched ball that a batter swings at and misses. **b.** a pitched ball that is not swung at but is

judged by the umpire to be within the strike zone. **c.** a foul bunt, a foul tip with less than two strikes against the batter that is not caught by the catcher, or a foul tip with two strikes against the batter that is caught by the catcher. **d.** any other foul ball not caught by a fielder, unless there are already two strikes against the batter. **6.** *Bowling.* **a.** the act or an instance of knocking down all the pins with the first ball in a frame. **b.** a score made in this way. **7.** a seizing of the bait by a fish. [Old English *strícan* to go, move, rub, stroke, smooth.]
• **on strike.** engaged in a labor or other strike.
• **to have two strikes against one.** *Informal.* to be at a great disadvantage because of a handicap or liability.
• **to strike it rich.** to come into sudden wealth or success.
• **to strike out. a.** *Baseball.* to put out or be put out by a strikeout. **b.** to begin, as on an undertaking or journey: *We struck out for California.* **c.** *Informal.* to be a failure in some undertaking.
• **to strike up. a.** to start; begin: *to strike up a conversation, to strike up an acquaintance.* **b.** to cause to begin: *Strike up the music.*
strike·bound (strīk′bound′) *adj.* closed down or out of operation because of a strike: *a strikebound steel plant.*
strike·break·er (strīk′brā′kər) *n.* a person who continues to work during a strike, takes the place of a worker on strike, supplies workers to take the place of strikers, or otherwise works to end a strike to the benefit of the employer. —**strike′break′ing,** *n.*
strike·out (strīk′out′) *n. Baseball.* an out resulting from three strikes charged against a batter.
strik·er (strī′kər) *n.* **1.** a worker who participates in a strike. **2.** a person or thing that strikes. **3.** an enlisted person in the U.S. Navy training for a petty officer's rating. **4.** the striking mechanism of a clock that sounds the hours or rings an alarm; hammer. **5.** *Soccer.* a player in an attacking forward position.
strike zone *Baseball.* the area directly over home plate and between the batter's knees and armpits, through which a pitched ball must pass in order to be judged a strike if it is not swung at.
strik·ing (strī′king) *adj.* **1.** making a vivid impression on the mind or senses; impressive: *There was a striking contrast between the two paintings.* **2.** engaged in a strike: *striking workers.* —**strik′ing·ly,** *adv.* —**strik′ing·ness,** *n.*
string (string) *n.* **1.** a slender line consisting of twisted or intertwined strands of fiber, wire, or similar material. **2.** anything resembling this, such as a strip of cloth used for tying parts together: *the strings of an apron.* **3.** a set or number of things joined together in a line by twisting, twining, or arranging on a string or by attaching them to each other: *a string of pearls, a string of daisies.* **4.** a series or succession, as of persons, things, or events: *a string of small towns along a highway, a string of robberies.* **5.** a group of things owned or managed together: *a string of shops.* **6.** *usually,* **strings.** *Informal.* a limitation or condition connected with something: *There were no strings attached to the offer.* **7.** a thin strand of wire, gut, nylon, or other material used to produce tones in certain musical instruments. **8.a.** a musical instrument played on strings, such as the violin, viola, and cello. **b. strings.** such instruments collectively in an orchestra or ensemble. **c. strings.** players of such instruments, collectively. **9.** a group of players on an athletic team who are ranked together as a unit, esp. according to ability: *The injured player was replaced by a member of the second string.* **10.** a stringlike organ, part, or formation, such as the fiber or fibers of certain plants. **11.** *Computers.* a sequence of letters, numerals, or other characters treated as a unit. **12.** *Physics.* a mathematical representation of a subatomic particle that, in the space-time frame of reference, has a stringlike character. In the theories employing this representation, what was formerly considered a particle occupying a point in space is treated as a wave traveling along a string. —*v.,* **strung, string·ing.** —*v.t.* **1.** to put on or as on a string: *to string beads.* **2.** to furnish with a string or strings: *to string a bow, to string a tennis racket.* **3.** to extend (something like a string) from one place to another or across a given area: *to string a clothesline across a yard.* **4.** to arrange in or as in a row: *We strung the lights on the Christmas tree.* **5.** to remove fibers or strings from: *to string beans.* —*v.i.* to form into or proceed in a string or series. [Old English *streng* line[1], cord, thread.] —**string′like′,** *adj.*
• **to pull strings.** to use one's power or influence to obtain what one wants.
• **to string along.** *Informal.* to agree or cooperate: *We'll string along with you if you keep your part of the bargain.*
• **to string out.** *Informal.* to extend beyond the usual or proper limits; prolong.
• **to string (someone) along.** *Informal.* to fool or deceive (someone).
• **to string up.** *Slang.* to kill by hanging.

string bean 1. a long, green immature pod of a bean plant, *Phaseolus vulgaris,* eaten as a vegetable. **2.** the plant itself, closely related to the kidney bean. Also *(defs. 1, 2),* **green bean, snap bean. 3.** *Informal.* a very skinny, tall person.
string·course (string′kôrs′) *n.* a horizontal band, as of stone or brick, often ornamented, projecting from or flush with a building.
stringed instrument, a musical instrument, such as a cello, violin, harp, or guitar, that has strings which produce tones when they are played with a bow or plucked.
strin·gen·cy (strin′jən sē) *n., pl.* **-cies.** the quality or condition of being stringent.
strin·gent (strin′jənt) *adj.* **1.** rigorously maintained, enforced, or adhered to; rigid: *stringent requirements.* **2.** persuasive because of force and logic; convincing: *a stringent argument.* **3.** characterized by or proceeding from a scarcity or lack of available funds: *a stringent economic situation.* [Latin *stringēns,* present participle of *stringere* to draw tight.] —**strin′gent·ly,** *adv.*
string·er (string′ər) *n.* **1.** a person or thing that strings. **2.a.** a long horizontal member supporting the vertical members or crosspieces of a framework or structure. **b.** a structural member that supports the skin or shell of something, such as the wings or fuselage of an aircraft. **3.** a member of a particular string on an athletic team. ➡ usually used in combination: *second-stringer.* **4.** a part-time or local correspondent for a news publication or news service.
string·halt (string′hôlt′) *n.* a disease of horses causing involuntary spasms of the hind legs when walking or trotting. Also, **springhalt.** [Probably STRING + HALT[2].]
string·piece (string′pēs′) *n.* a long horizontal beam used for strengthening, supporting, or connecting parts of a framework.
string tie, a narrow necktie, usually worn tied in a bow.
string·y (string′ē) *adj.,* **string·i·er, string·i·est. 1.** having or consisting of tough fibers or strings: *stringy celery.* **2.** resembling string; thin: *stringy hair.* **3.** forming strings: *stringy glue.* —**string′i·ness,** *n.*
strip[1] (strip) *v.,* **stripped** or **stript, strip·ping.** —*v.t.* **1.** to remove or pull off the clothing or other covering from: *to strip beds to wash the sheets.* **2.** to remove or pull off, as clothing (often with *off*): *to strip bark from a tree, to strip off one's clothes.* **3.** to remove all the details, accessories, working parts, or essentials from; make bare or empty: *to strip an automobile body.* **4.** to deprive, as of rights, honors, or possessions; divest: *The disgraced politician was stripped of several honorary offices.* **5.** to rob or plunder: *The burglars stripped the museum of its most famous treasures.* **6.** to damage or break the threads or teeth of (a bolt, gear, screw, or the like). —*v.i.* **1.** to undress. **2.** to come or be taken off, as a covering: *This wallpaper strips easily.* [Old English *strīepan* (in the compound *bestrīepan* to rob, plunder).] —**strip′per,** *n.*
strip[2] (strip) *n.* **1.** a long, narrow piece of something: *a strip of paper, a strip of land.* **2.** airstrip. **3.** comic strip. [Middle English *strip,* possibly from Middle Low German *strippe* strap.]
stripe[1] (strīp) *n.* **1.** a long, narrow band differing, as in color or texture, from the material or surface of which it forms a part: *The material had white stripes on a red background.* **2.** any of various strips of cloth worn on the sleeve of a military uniform to indicate rank, length of service, or some other distinction. **3.** a particular kind or character; sort: *The members of the assembly are of many different political stripes.* —*v.t.,* **striped, strip·ing.** to mark with a stripe or stripes. [Middle Dutch or Middle Low German *strīpe* strip[2], streak.]
stripe[2] (strīp) *n.* a stroke or lash, as with a rod or whip. [Of uncertain origin.]
striped (strīpt, strī′pid) *adj.* having or marked with a stripe or stripes: *a striped material.*
striped bass (bas) a large sport and food fish, *Morone saxatilis,* of fresh and coastal waters of the eastern United States, bearing six to nine dark stripes along its upper sides. Length: 6 feet (1.8 meters).
strip·ling (strip′ling) *n.* a youth; lad. [STRIP[2] + -LING[1]; in the sense of "slender as a strip."]

string bean

Pod
Seed

a	at	e	end	o	hot	u	up	hw	white		about
ā	ape	ē	me	ō	old	ū	use	ng	song		taken
ä	far	i	it	ô	fork	ü	rule	th	thin	ə	pencil
âr	care	ī	ice	oi	oil	ů	pull	th	this		lemon
		îr	pierce	ou	out	ûr	turn	zh	measure		circus

strip-mine (strip′mīn′) *v.t., v.i.,* **-mined, -min·ing.** to mine (a mineral deposit) from a strip mine.

strip mine, a mine worked on the surface, rather than underground, by removing overlying material in successive strips to expose a mineral deposit, esp. coal or ore. [STRIP¹ + MINE².]

strip mine

stript (stript) a past tense and past participle of **strip¹.**

strive (strīv) *v.i.,* **strove** or **strived, striv·en** (striv′ən), **striv·ing. 1.** to make a strenuous effort: *to strive to succeed, to strive for accuracy in one's work.* **2.** to engage in conflict; fight; contend. [Old French *estriver* to contend, from *estrif* contention. See STRIFE.]

strobe (strōb) *n.* **1.** a device that emits a very brief, intense flash of light, used as a light source in photography and as a warning signal. Also, **strobe light. 2.** stroboscope. [From STROBOSCOPE.]

stro·bi·lus (strō bī′ləs) *n., pl.* **-li** (-lī). **1.** a seed-bearing cone, as of a pine tree. **2.** a cone-shaped structure consisting of a mass of compactly arranged scalelike leaves. Also, **stro·bile** (strō′bīl, -bəl). [Late Latin *strobilus* cone of a pine tree, from Greek *strobīlos* round ball, whirlwind, from *strobos* a whirling around.]

stro·bo·scope (strō′bə skōp′) *n.* a strobe that flashes at set intervals, thereby allowing moving objects to be seen as if they were standing still. [Greek *strobos* a whirling around + -SCOPE.] —**stro·bo·scop·ic** (strō′bə skop′ik), **stro′bo·scop′i·cal,** *adj.*

strode (strōd) the past tense of **stride.**

stro·ga·noff (strō′gə nôf′, strô′-) *n.* a dish usually of beef sliced and cooked with chopped onions, mushrooms, seasoning, and sour cream, often served over rice or noodles. [From Count Pavel (Paul) *Stroganov,* 1774-1817, Russian diplomat.]

stroke¹ (strōk) *n.* **1.** the act or an instance of striking, as with the hand. **2.** an action or event having a specified effect: *a stroke of misfortune.* **3.** a brilliant, inspired, or forceful act, achievement, or idea: *a stroke of genius.* **4.** a sound produced by striking. **5.** the time indicated by a striking, as of a clock: *They left at the stroke of three.* **6.** a single unbroken or complete movement, as of the hand, an instrument, or something held in the hand. **7.** one of a series of repetitive, reciprocating movements of a mechanical part, such as a piston in an internal-combustion engine. **8.** a mark made by a pen, pencil, brush, or other implement. **9.** a sudden weakness or paralysis caused by rupture, spasm, or blockage of blood vessels in the brain; apoplexy. **10.** a combination of repeated arm and leg movements for propelling the body through water in swimming. **11.a.** the act or an instance of striking the ball in certain sports, such as golf or tennis. **b.** the manner in which this is done. **12.** a pulsation, as of the heart. **13.** stroke oar *(def. 2).* —*v.t.,* **stroked, strok·ing. 1.** to act as stroke oar for. **2.** to mark or cancel with a stroke, as of a pen (usually with *out* or *through*): *to stroke through a line of print.* [Probably from an unrecorded Old English word.]

stroke² (strōk) *v.t.,* **stroked, strok·ing. 1.** to rub gently or caressingly with the hand, usually in the same direction and repeatedly. **2.** *Informal.* to flatter or reassure with kind or praiseful words. —*n.* a light, caressing movement of the hand. [Old English *strācian* to rub gently with the hand.]

stroke oar 1. the oar at the stern of a boat, esp. a racing shell. **2.** the rower who pulls this oar and sets the rhythm for the other rowers. Also *(def. 2),* **stroke.**

stroll (strōl) *v.i.* to walk in a leisurely or idle manner. —*v.t.* to walk along or through in a leisurely or idle manner. —*n.* a leisurely walk. [Possibly from dialectal German *strollen* to rove about.]

stroll·er (strō′lər) *n.* **1.** a small, chairlike, wheeled vehicle in which a small child sits and is wheeled about. **2.** a person who strolls.

strong (strông) *adj.* **1.** having great muscular power; physically powerful: *strong arms, a strong athlete.* **2.** having or showing good health, vigor, or robustness: *The patient may not be strong enough to undergo the operation. A strong heart is a great asset.* **3.** capable of withstanding strain, stress, or force: *a strong chain, a strong chair.* **4.** firm in mind, character, will, or purpose; morally powerful or courageous: *to be strong enough to resist a temptation.* **5.** having or showing the power to be persuasive; convincing: *a strong argument, a strong debater.* **6.** having or showing marked mental or intellectual ability: *a strong mind, to be strong in mathematics.* **7.** exceeding that which is usual, moderate, or reasonable; extreme: *strong measures.* **8.** having a noticeably ripe, sharp, bitter, or offensive taste or odor: *a strong cheese, a strong tobacco.* **9.** clearly perceptible; marked; distinct: *to bear a strong resemblance to a grandparent.* **10.** marked or characterized by forcefulness or vehemence: *The senator took a strong stand on the issue.* **11.** having or showing much ability, power, or authority: *Our next opponent is the strongest team we will play this year.* **12.** critical, abusive, or harsh in nature: *That is strong language to use in talking about a friend.* **13.** moving with or having great force or speed: *strong winds, a strong undertow.* **14.** having a great degree of intensity or power: *a strong smell, a strong heartbeat, a strong light.* **15.** securely fixed; firm: *I took a strong hold on the rope.* **16.** containing much alcohol: *a strong drink.* **17.** having a large amount of the proper or essential ingredients: *strong tea.* **18.** *Chemistry.* (of an acid or base) ionizing readily in solution. **19.** *Optics.* (of a lens or instrument) having great power of magnification or refraction. **20.** having a specified numerical force. ➡ used after the noun and the number: *an army 10,000 strong.* **21.** *Phonetics.* stressed; accented. **22.** *Grammar.* (of a verb) forming the past tense and past participle by changing a vowel within the stem of the word, as in *ring, rang, rung.* —*adv.* in a strong manner; vigorously; powerfully. [Old English *strang* physically powerful, resolute, forceful, able, severe, rigorous.] —**strong′ly,** *adv.*

strong·arm (strông′ärm′) *Informal. adj.* using or depending on physical power, force, or coercion: *strong-arm tactics.* —*v.t.* to use physical power, force, or coercion against.

strong·box (strông′boks′) *n.* a strongly made chest or safe for storing money, documents, and other valuables.

strong force *Nuclear Physics.* the force that binds protons and neutrons together and gives the atomic nucleus its stability. Also, **strong interaction.**

strong·hold (strông′hōld′) *n.* **1.** a place fortified against attack or danger. **2.** a place noted for the predominance or concentration of a particular idea or way of thinking: *That part of the state is a stronghold of conservatism.*

strong-mind·ed (strông′mīn′did) *adj.* having or showing firmness or determination of mind, will, or purpose. —**strong′-mind′ed·ly,** *adv.* —**strong′-mind′ed·ness,** *n.*

strong suit 1. something at which a person is very good; long suit: *Athletics is my strong suit.* **2.** in some card games, the suit of playing cards in which a person holds the highest cards.

stron·ti·um (stron′shē əm, -tē-) *n.* a soft, silvery metallic element, used in fireworks and alloys and in the manufacture of television picture tubes. Strontium is one of the alkaline-earth metals, with chemical properties similar to those of calcium. Symbol: **Sr** For tables, see **element.** [Modern Latin *strontium,* from *Strontian,* village in Scotland, where it was discovered.]

strontium 90 *also,* **strontium-90.** a radioactive isotope of strontium with a half-life of twenty-eight years, used in radiology and nuclear batteries. It is found in dangerous amounts in nuclear fallout.

strop (strop) *n.* a flexible strip of material, such as leather or canvas, used to sharpen razors. —*v.t.,* **stropped, strop·ping.** to sharpen on a strop. [Old English *stropp* thong, from Latin *stroppus* thong, strap, from Greek *strophos* twisted cord.] —**strop′per,** *n.*

stro·phe (strō′fē) *n.* **1.** *Poetry.* a stanza, esp. one of irregular length or structure. **2.** in ancient Greek drama, that part of an ode sung by the chorus while moving from right to left. [Greek *strophē* stanza of a choral ode; literally, a turning (referring to the turning of the chorus after singing such a stanza).] —**stroph·ic** (strof′ik, strō′fik), *adj.*

strove (strōv) a past tense of **strive.**

struck (struk) *v.* the past tense and a past participle of **strike.** —*adj.* closed or affected by a labor or other strike.

struc·tur·al (struk′chər əl) *adj.* **1.** of, relating to, having, or characterized by structure: *a structural fault in a building, the structural unity of a novel.* **2.** used in or necessary to building or construction: *a structural beam.* **3.** *Biology.* of or relating to the

S

organic structure of animals or plants; morphological. **4.** *Geology.* relating to the structure of rocks and other parts of the earth's crust: *structural geology.* —**struc′tur·al·ly,** *adv.*

structural formula *Chemistry.* see **formula** *(def. 3).*

struc·tur·al·ize (struk′chər ə līz′) *v.t.,* **-ized, -iz·ing.** to form into or include as part of a structure. —**struc′tur·al·i·za′tion,** *n.*

structural linguistics, a type of language study that emphasizes concrete, observable features such as word endings, the position of words in sentences, and sentence patterns.

struc·ture (struk′chər) *n.* **1.** anything that is built or constructed, such as a building. **2.** the way in which something is constructed, arranged, or organized: *the structure of a society, the structure of a language.* **3.** the arrangement or interrelation of the constituent parts or elements that make up a thing: *to study the structure of a cell.* **4.** an organized body or combination of mutually connected and dependent parts or elements: *The brain is a complex structure.* —*v.t.,* **-tured, -tur·ing. 1.** to arrange in an orderly, systematic manner: *to structure an argument.* **2.** to build or construct: *to structure a bridge.* [Latin *structūra* a fitting together, construction.]

stru·del (strü′dəl, shtrü′-) *n.* a pastry consisting of a filling, as of fruit, wrapped in a thin sheet of dough and baked: *cheese strudel, apple strudel.* [German *Strudel* literally, whirlpool.]

strug·gle (strug′əl) *v.i.,* **-gled, -gling. 1.** to make strenuous effort; strive: *I had to struggle to pass my final examinations.* **2.** to progress or make one's way with great effort: *The children struggled through the heavy snowdrifts.* **3.** to engage in physical combat, as with an adversary: *They struggled for the knife.* —*n.* **1.** a very great or strenuous effort: *It was a struggle for me to make them understand.* **2.** a fight, combat, or other physical opposition: *The thief gave up without a struggle. The treaty ended years of struggle between the two nations.* [Of uncertain origin.] —**strug′gler,** *n.* —For Synonyms *(n.),* see **fight.**

strum (strum) *v.,* **strummed, strum·ming.** —*v.t.* to play, esp. in an idle, monotonous, or unskillful manner: *to strum a banjo, to strum a tune.* —*v.i.* to play a stringed musical instrument, esp. in an idle, monotonous, or unskillful manner. —*n.* the act or sound of strumming. [Possibly blend of STRING and THRUM[1].] —**strum′mer,** *n.*

stru·ma (strü′mə) *n., pl.* **-mae** (-mē). **1.** goiter. **2.** *Botany.* a cushionlike swelling on an organ, as at the base of certain moss capsules. [Latin *strūma* scrofulous tumor.]

strum·pet (strum′pit) *n.* a prostitute; whore. [Of uncertain origin.]

strung (strung) the past tense and past participle of **string.**

strut[1] (strut) *v.i.,* **strut·ted, strut·ting.** to walk in a vain, pompous, or arrogant manner. —*n.* a vain, pompous, or arrogant manner of walking. [Old English *strūtian* to stand out stiffly.] —**strut′ter,** *n.*
 • **to strut one's stuff.** *Slang.* to behave, dress, or display one's possessions in a showy manner; show off.

strut[2] (strut) *n.* a bar, brace, or other supporting piece that is designed to resist pressure or thrust, as in an architectural framework. [Probably from STRUT[1] (referring to a stiff piece of wood).]

strych·nine (strik′nin, -nēn, -nīn) *also,* **strych·nin** (strik′nin). *n.* a very poisonous alkaloid obtained from nux vomica and related plants, formerly used in medicine to stimulate the nervous system. Formula: $C_{21}H_{22}N_2O_2$ [French *strychnine,* from Latin *strychnos* nightshade, from Greek *strychnos.*]

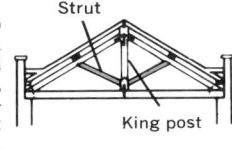

Strut

King post

strut[2]

stub (stub) *n.* **1.** a short piece that remains after something has been worn away, removed, cut, or broken off: *a cigar stub, the stub of a pencil.* **2.** a remaining or detachable portion, as of a check, ticket, or bill, that provides a record or receipt of payment. **3.** a short, thick, projecting piece or part. **4.** a stump of a tree trunk or plant stem. —*v.t.,* **stubbed, stub·bing. 1.** to strike (one's toe or foot) accidentally against something. **2.** to dig up by the roots. **3.** to clear (land) of stumps. **4.** to extinguish (a cigarette or cigar) by crushing (usually with *out*). [Old English *stub(b)* stump of a tree or shrub.]

stub·ble (stub′əl) *n.* **1.** short stalks of grain and certain other plants left standing in the ground after a crop has been harvested. **2.** anything resembling this, such as a short, bristly beard. [Old French *estouble* straw, from Late Latin *stupula,* form of Latin *stipula* stem, straw.] —**stub′bly,** *adj.*

stub·born (stub′ərn) *adj.* **1.** not yielding or receptive to argument, persuasion, or reason; obstinate. **2.** done, carried on, or maintained in an unyielding, obstinate manner: *a stubborn refusal to cooperate.* **3.** difficult to overcome, treat, or cure: *a stubborn*

illness. [Middle English *stibourne* obstinate, possibly from Old English *stubb* stub or stump of a tree or shrub (as if meaning "unyielding like a stub").] —**stub′born·ly,** *adv.* —**stub′born·ness,** *n.*

stub·by (stub′ē) *adj.,* **-bi·er, -bi·est. 1.** short and thick: *a stubby tail, stubby toes.* **2.** short, thick, and bristly: *a stubby beard.* **3.** covered with or consisting of stubs or stubble: *a stubby field.* —**stub′bi·ness,** *n.*

stuc·co (stuk′ō) *n., pl.* **-coes** or **-cos. 1.** plaster or cement, of varying degrees of fineness, used for coating walls or for making ornamental reliefs and other decorations. **2.** ornamental work made of stucco. Also *(def. 2),* **stuc·co·work** (stuk′ō wûrk′). —*v.t.,* **-coed, -co·ing.** to cover or ornament with stucco. [Italian *stucco* plaster; of Germanic origin.]

stucco buildings in Greece

stuck (stuk) the past tense and past participle of **stick**[2].

stuck-up (stuk′up′) *adj. Informal.* conceited or snobbish.

stud[1] (stud) *n.* **1.** a nail head, knob, or similar object, usually of metal, fixed to and protruding from a surface, used. esp. as an ornament. **2.** an ornamental buttonlike fastener used on men's formal shirts. **3.** a vertical post, as in the framework of a wall, to which horizontal boards, plasterboard, laths, and the like are nailed. **4.** any of various short, projecting pins, as on a machine. —*v.t.,* **stud·ded, stud·ding. 1.** to set or ornament with or as with studs: *to stud a bracelet with diamonds.* **2.** to lie scattered over or be spread about in: *Stars studded the sky.* **3.** to furnish with or support by a vertical post or posts. [Old English *studu* post[1], support.]

stud[2] (stud) *n.* **1.** a male animal, esp. a horse, kept for breeding. **2.** a group of animals, esp. horses, selected and raised for breeding. **3.** a place where horses are kept for breeding. **4.** a collection of horses kept for hunting, riding, or racing. [Old English *stōd* place where horses are kept for breeding, group of such horses.]

stud·book (stud′buk′) *n.* an official registry of the pedigrees of thoroughbred animals, esp. horses or dogs.

stud·ding (stud′ing) *n.* **1.** studs collectively, such as those in the framework of a wall. **2.** material from which such studs are made.

stu·dent (stü′dənt, stū′-) *n.* **1.** a person enrolled in or attending a school, college, or university. **2.** a person devoted to or engaged in the study or investigation of a particular subject: *a student of language.* [Latin *studēns,* present participle of *studēre* to be eager or diligent, apply oneself to learning.]

student teacher, a person who is studying to be a teacher and practices teaching in an elementary or secondary school under professional supervision. —**student teaching.**

student union 1. an organization at a college or university, providing social, recreational, cultural, and, often, dining services. **2.** the building in which such an organization is located.

stud·horse (stud′hôrs′) *n.* a male horse used for breeding; stallion.

stud·ied (stud′ēd) *adj.* characterized by or showing deliberate effort, intention, or preparation: *a studied reply.* —**stud′ied·ly,** *adv.* —**stud′ied·ness,** *n.*

stu·di·o (stü′dē ō′, stū′-) *n., pl.* **-di·os. 1.** a place where an artist or photographer works. **2.** a place for instruction in and practice of one of the performing arts: *The new studio offers classes in modern dance.* **3.**a. a place where motion pictures are filmed. **b.** an organization engaged in the business of making motion pictures: *The star signed a contract with a different studio.*

a	at	e	end	o	hot	u	up	hw	white		about
ā	ape	ē	me	ō	old	ū	use	ng	song		taken
ä	far	i	it	ô	fork	ü	rule	th	thin	ə	pencil
âr	care	ī	ice	oi	oil	u̇	pull	th	this		lemon
				îr	pierce	ou	out	ûr	turn	zh	measure		circus

c. a place where radio or television programs are performed or recorded. d. a place where music is recorded. 4. studio apartment. [Italian *studio* workroom, office, study, from Latin *studium* zeal, application to learning.]

studio apartment, a one-room apartment with kitchen and bathroom facilities.

studio couch, a couch, usually without arms, that can be used as a bed.

stu·di·ous (stü′dē əs, stū′-) *adj.* 1. given to or fond of study or learning. 2. showing or characterized by careful or earnest consideration or attention: *a studious effort, to be studious of one's health.* —**stu′di·ous·ly,** *adv.* —**stu′di·ous·ness,** *n.*

stud·y (stud′ē) *v.,* **stud·ied, stud·y·ing.** —*v.t.* 1. to apply the mind in order to acquire a knowledge of (something): *to study medicine, to study history.* 2. to look at closely or critically; examine; scrutinize: *The expert studied the painting and decided it was a forgery.* 3. to look or inquire into; investigate: *to study the geology of a region.* 4. to give careful thought and consideration to: *I will study the matter and give you my opinion.* 5.a. to seek to learn by memorizing: *The actor studied the part before the audition.* b. to seek to become familiar with the contents of: *I studied my notes for the exam.* —*v.i.* 1. to apply the mind in order to acquire knowledge: *to study for a test.* 2. to pursue a regular course of instruction; be a student: *to study for a career in nursing, to study at a state university.* —*n., pl.* **stud·ies.** 1. the act or process of studying: *For me, study requires a quiet place.* 2. the act or process of acquiring knowledge of something: *the study of human nature.* 3. a careful or critical examination or investigation: *to make a study of local traffic patterns.* 4. the product of such examination or investigation: *The crime commission's study will be published next week.* 5. something that is studied or to be studied; branch of learning: *the study of medicine.* 6. **studies.** the process of being educated; schooling: *to complete one's studies at a university.* 7. a room in a house used or set apart for study, reading, writing, or meditation. 8. a preliminary sketch, design, or plan for an artistic work or for some detail or portion of it. 9. an artistic work, esp. a painting, devoted to the detailed consideration of a particular aspect or subject: *a study in black and white.* 10. the state of being absorbed in deep thought or meditation. 11. *Informal.* a perfect example, as if conceived by an artist: *The look on the child's face was a study in disappointment.* 12. a person, such as an actor, with reference to his or her ability to memorize: *to be a quick study.* [Latin *studium* zeal, application to learning.] —For Synonyms *(v.t.),* see **consider.**

study hall 1. a room in a school reserved for studying. 2. a period of a school day set aside for studying.

stuff (stuf) *n.* 1. the substance or material of which a thing is made or can be made: *What kind of stuff is in this pillow?* 2. any indefinite, vague substance or matter: *What is this stuff in the bowl?* 3.a. inward character or capabilities: *Those explorers were made of hardy stuff.* b. character or nature in general: *This movie is strong stuff for children.* 4. personal belongings; possessions: *We packed all our stuff in the back of the car.* 5. a fabric, esp. one made of wool. 6. worthless or useless matter or things; rubbish; junk: *There is stuff scattered all over the vacant lot.* 7. foolish, irrational, or worthless ideas, speech, or writing; nonsense. 8. something to be consumed: *Try some of this stuff and tell me if you like the taste.* —*v.t.* 1. to fill by loading to excess; cram full: *to stuff a closet with dresses.* 2. to force or thrust (something) tightly, as into a container: *to stuff papers into an envelope.* 3. to fill with suitable material, as for padding: *to stuff a pillow with foam rubber.* 4. to block or stop up (an opening or cavity) by thrusting something tightly in; plug: *I stuffed my ears with cotton to shut out the noise.* 5. to fill with too much food: *Stop stuffing yourself.* 6. *Cooking.* to fill (poultry or other food) with stuffing. 7. to fill the skin of (a dead animal) to restore and preserve its natural appearance. 8. to put fraudulent votes into (a ballot box). [Old French *estoffe* material, matter, going back to Latin *stup(p)a* tow[2], from Greek *styppē.*]

stuffed shirt *Informal.* a person who is extremely pompous or formal and has an inflated concept of his or her own importance.

stuff·ing (stuf′ing) *n.* 1. material used for filling, packing, enlarging, or stuffing something. 2. a food mixture, as of seasoned bread crumbs or rice, used to fill poultry or other food. 3. the act of stuffing something.

stuff·y (stuf′ē) *adj.,* **stuff·i·er, stuff·i·est.** 1. having inadequate ventilation; close: *a stuffy room.* 2. lacking freshness; uninteresting; boring: *a stuffy speech.* 3. extremely strait-laced; formal; pompous: *a stuffy person, a stuffy manner.* 4. affected with the sensation of obstruction in the respiratory passages: *The cold made my nose stuffy.* —**stuff′i·ly,** *adv.* —**stuff′i·ness,** *n.*

stul·ti·fy (stul′tə fī′) *v.t.,* **-fied, -fy·ing.** 1. to make ineffectual, futile, or worthless: *to stultify ambition.* 2. to cause to be or appear foolish, dull-witted, or illogical. 3. to make dull or slug-

gish: *This inactivity will stultify your mind.* [Late Latin *stultificāre* to render foolish, from Latin *stultus* foolish + *facere* to make.] —**stul′ti·fi·ca′tion,** *n.* —**stul′ti·fi′er,** *n.*

stum·ble (stum′bəl) *v.,* **-bled, -bling.** —*v.i.* 1. to lose one's balance, as by missing one's footing, stubbing one's toe, or tripping over an obstacle. 2. to move or walk unsteadily or awkwardly: *I stumbled around the dark room until I found the light switch.* 3. to behave, act, or speak in a clumsy, awkward manner, as from confusion or nervousness: *to stumble over a difficult word, to stumble through a performance.* 4. to make a mistake or blunder, esp. one that is sinful. 5. to discover accidentally or unexpectedly (with *on* or *across*): *to stumble on a solution to a problem.* —*v.t.* to cause to stumble or fall; trip. —*n.* 1. the act or an instance of stumbling. 2. a mistake; blunder; slip. [Probably of Scandinavian origin.] —**stum′bler,** *n.* —**stum′bling·ly,** *adv.*

stum·ble·bum (stum′bəl bum′) *n. Slang.* a blundering or incompetent person. [STUMBLE + BUM; originally referred to an inept boxer.]

stumbling block, something that stands in the way of or prevents progress; hindrance; obstruction.

stump (stump) *n.* 1. the part of a tree trunk or plant stem remaining in the ground after the main part is cut or breaks off. 2. that part of anything which remains after the main or more important part has been removed or worn away, esp. the remaining part of an amputated limb or damaged tooth. 3. a place or occasion for a political speech. 4. a wooden leg. 5.a. a heavy step or gait, such as that of a person with a wooden leg. b. the heavy, blunted sound made by such a step or gait; thud; clomp. 6. **stumps.** *Slang.* legs. 7. a small, pointed roll of paper or leather or piece of soft rubber, used to shade the tones in pencil or charcoal drawings. —*v.t.* 1. to cause to be at a loss; perplex; baffle: *They tried to stump the panel of experts. This problem has really got me stumped.* 2. to reduce to a stump; truncate; lop off. 3. to remove stumps from (land). 4. *Informal.* to travel through, as a state or section, making political speeches. 5. *Informal.* to stub: *I stumped my toe on the rock.* —*v.i.* 1. to walk stiffly, heavily, or noisily, as if with a wooden or lame leg: *The old sailor stumped down the street.* 2. *Informal.* to travel about making political speeches. [Middle Dutch *stomp* stub, stem.] —**stump′-er,** *n.*

•**up a stump.** *Informal.* in a difficult or perplexing situation, esp. in conversation or in an intellectual effort; baffled.

stump·y (stum′pē) *adj.,* **stump·i·er, stump·i·est.** 1. short and thick like a stump. 2. (of land) abounding with tree stumps. —**stump′i·ness,** *n.*

stun (stun) *v.t.,* **stunned, stun·ning.** 1. to make unconscious or semiconscious, as by a blow. 2. to overwhelm with some strong emotion or impression: *The country was stunned by the president's resignation.* 3. to daze or bewilder, as with some loud noise: *They were stunned by the explosion.* —*n.* the act or result of stunning. [Old French *estoner* to astonish, resound, going back to Latin *ex-out* + *tonāre* to thunder.]

stung (stung) the past tense and past participle of **sting.**

stunk (stungk) a past tense and the past participle of **stink.**

stun·ner (stun′ər) *n.* 1. a person or thing that stuns. 2. *Informal.* an extraordinarily attractive person or thing.

stun·ning (stun′ing) *adj.* 1. *Informal.* extremely attractive or good-looking: *a stunning figure, a stunning person.* 2. that stuns, as a blow. —**stun′ning·ly,** *adv.*

stunt[1] (stunt) *v.t.* 1. to stop or hinder the growth or development of: *You will stunt that tree by planting it in deep shade.* 2. to check or hinder (growth, development, or progress). —*n.* the act or an instance of stunting. [From dialectal English *stunt* dwarfed in growth, going back to Old English *stunt* foolish.]

stunt[2] (stunt) *Informal. n.* any act that is done to attract attention, esp. one requiring or exhibiting extraordinary strength, skill, or daring: *spectacular stunts on the high trapeze.* —*v.i.* to perform a stunt or stunts. [Of uncertain origin.]

stunt man, a person skilled in performing physical feats or stunts, who substitutes for an actor in scenes requiring such skill, esp. in dangerous scenes involving aerial acrobatics, crashes, leaps, falls, or high-speed riding or driving.

stu·pa (stü′pə) *n.* a Buddhist shrine consisting of a dome-shaped mound of masonry or the like, often containing a sacred relic. [Sanskrit *stūpa* dome.]

stupe (stüp, stūp) *n.* a cloth immersed in hot water, wrung out, and applied to a part of the body as a compress. [Latin *stup(p)a* tow[2], from Greek *styppē.*]

stu·pe·fa·cient (stü′pə fā′shənt, stū′-) *adj.* producing stupor; stupefying. —*n.* a narcotic drug. [Latin *stupefaciēns,* present participle of *stupefacere* to benumb, stun. See STUPEFY.]

stu·pe·fac·tion (stü′pə fak′shən, stū′-) *n.* 1. the act of stupefying or the state of being stupefied. 2. overwhelming astonishment; amazement.

stu·pe·fy (stü′pə fī′, stū′-) *v.t.,* **-fied, -fy·ing. 1.** to cause to become stupid, senseless, or torpid; blunt the faculties or senses of. **2.** to cause to be amazed; astound: *The daring stunt stupefied the audience.* [Latin *stupefacere* to benumb, stun, from *stupēre* to be amazed + *facere* to make.] —**stu′pe·fi′er,** *n.* —**stu′pe·fy′-ing·ly,** *adv.*

stu·pen·dous (stü pen′dəs, stū-) *adj.* **1.** causing astonishment; overwhelming; astounding. **2.** astoundingly large or great: *a stupendous mountain of earth, a stupendous achievement.* [Latin *stupendus* to be wondered at, gerundive of *stupēre* to be amazed.] —**stu·pen′dous·ly,** *adv.* —**stu·pen′dous·ness,** *n.*

stu·pid (stü′pid, stū′-) *adj.* **1.** lacking ordinary intelligence; slow-witted; dumb. **2.** dull in ideas or expression; inane; uninteresting; boring: *I'm tired of this stupid game.* **3.** having one's faculties deadened or blunted; in a stupor; stunned; dazed: *I felt stupid in the intense heat.* **4.** of, resulting from, or characterized by a lack of intelligence: *a stupid answer, a stupid attempt.* —*n. Informal.* a stupid person. [Latin *stupidus* senseless, dull.] —**stu′pid·ly,** *adv.* —**stu′pid·ness,** *n.*

stu·pid·i·ty (stü pid′i tē, stū-) *n., pl.* **-ties. 1.** the state or quality of being stupid: *The answer revealed the speaker's stupidity. The stupidity of their plan was obvious.* **2.** a statement, act, or the like that reveals a lack of intelligence or understanding.

stu·por (stü′pər, stū′-) *n.* **1.** a partly conscious condition; lessening of the power to use one's senses. **2.** mental or moral numbness; apathy. [Latin *stupor* numbness, stupidity.]

stur·dy (stûr′dē) *adj.,* **-di·er, -di·est. 1.** having a strong, hardy constitution: *sturdy recruits.* **2.** solidly built or constructed: *a sturdy fortress.* **3.** hard to overcome; unyielding; resolute: *The enemy put up a sturdy defense.* [Old French *estourdi* reckless, dazed, past participle of *estourdir* to daze, possibly going back to Latin *ex-* (see EX-[1]) + *turdus* thrush (thought of as drunk or foolish).] —**stur′di·ly,** *adv.* —**stur′di·ness,** *n.*

stur·geon (stûr′jən) *n., pl.* **-geons** or **-geon.** any of a group of fish, family Acipenseridae, found in fresh and salt waters in temperate regions, having rows of bony, pointed scales, and valued as food and as a source of caviar and isinglass. Length: 7-10 feet (2.1-3 meters). [Anglo-Norman *sturgeon;* of Germanic origin.]

Sturm und Drang (shtûrm′ ûnt drāng′) *German.* **1.** confused agitation or commotion; violent disturbance or change; turmoil: *the Sturm und Drang of war.* **2.** a movement in German literature of the late eighteenth century, marked by themes of romantic adventure and emotional conflict. [German *Sturm und Drang* literally, storm and stress, from the drama *Der Wirrwarr, oder Sturm und Drang* by Friedrich von Klinger, 1752-1831, German writer.]

stut·ter (stut′ər) *v.i.* to speak with frequent, involuntary repetition of sounds or syllables, often caused by a nervous defect, fear, or excitement: *The child has stuttered ever since the shock of the accident.* —*v.t.* to utter (a word or the like) by stuttering: *to stutter an apology.* —*n.* the act or habit of stuttering or an instance of this. [Dialectal English *stut* to stutter (of Germanic origin) + -ER[4].] —**stut′ter·er,** *n.* —**stut′ter·ing·ly** *adv.*

St. Vi·tus′ dance (vī′təs) see **Saint Vitus′ dance.**

sty[1] (stī) *n., pl.* **sties. 1.** a pen or enclosure where pigs are kept; pigpen; pigsty. **2.** any filthy place; hovel. [Old English *stig* hall, pen[2].]

sty[2] (stī) *also,* **stye.** *n., pl.* **sties.** a small, inflamed swelling on the edge of the eyelid, caused by a bacterial infection. [From earlier *styany* (thought to mean "sty on the eye"), going back to Old English *stīgend* literally, rising (in the sense of "swelling") + *ēage* eye.]

Styg·i·an (stij′ē ən) *adj.* **1.** of, relating to, or characteristic of the mythological river Styx or the lower world in which it flows. **2.** resembling the river Styx or its atmosphere; black; gloomy.

style (stīl) *n.* **1.a.** a particular mode or fashion, esp. of apparel: *to dress in the style of the nineteenth century.* **b.** something in such a mode: *We looked at the spring styles in the boutique.* **2.a.** a luxurious or elegant way of doing something: *to live in style, to travel in style.* **b.** a tasteful, intelligent, and appropriate way of doing something: *to handle a difficult situation with style.* **3.** a distinctive mode of doing or making something; way: *a terse style of speaking, a forceful style of writing.* **4.** a mode of expression in the arts: *a building in the baroque style, a style of music popular long ago.* **5.a.** a pointed instrument used by the ancients to write on wax tablets. **b.** something pointed or used like a style, such as the pointer on a compass. Also *(def. 5),* **stylus. 6.** *Botany.* a stalklike structure of the pistil of a flower, extending from the ovary to the stigma. For illustration, see **flower. 7.** *Printing.* special rules, as of spelling, punctuation, or capitalization, followed by a particular author, publisher, or printer. **8.** *Archaic.* a formal or official name or title. —*v.t.,* **styled, styl·ing 1.** to design in accordance with a particular mode; fashion: *She commissioned him to style her entire fall wardrobe.* **2.** to change in

order to conform to a particular style of printing or writing: *The editor had to style the entire manuscript.* **3.** to give a title or name to; call: *The newspaper article styled the restaurant "the finest in the city."* [Old French *style* pointed writing instrument, manner of expressing oneself, from Latin *stilus.*] —**styl′er,** *n.* —For Synonyms, see **fashion.**

style·book (stīl′bùk′) *n.* **1.** a book containing rules, as of punctuation, capitalization, or spelling, observed or employed by a particular author, printer, or publisher, or in producing a particular book or series of books. **2.** a book showing styles in dress and when they were in fashion.

styl·ish (stī′lish) *adj.* conforming to current or approved style; fashionable; chic. —**styl′ish·ly,** *adv.* —**styl′ish·ness,** *n.*

styl·ist (stī′list) *n.* **1.** a writer or speaker who is distinguished for excellence or individuality of style. **2.** a person who designs or advises on styles, as in clothing or furnishings.

sty·lis·tic (stī lis′tik) *adj.* of or relating to style; characteristic of a particular style or current styles. —**sty·lis′ti·cal·ly,** *adv.*

styl·ize (stī′līz) *v.t.,* **-ized, -iz·ing.** to make (something, such as an artistic representation) conform to the rules of a particular style or convention. —**styl′i·za′tion,** *n.* —**styl′i·zer,** *n.*

sty·lo·bate (stī′lə bāt′) *n. Architecture.* a continuous base or substructure supporting a colonnade.

sty·lus (stī′ləs) *n., pl.* **-li** (-lī) or **-lus·es. 1.** an instrument with a pointed or rounded head used to make stencils or impressions on soft materials, or for similar purposes. **2.a.** needle *(def. 5).* **b.** a needle used to cut the grooves on a phonograph record. **3.** a pen that records impulses on a graph or chart, as in a seismograph or chronograph. **4.** style *(def. 5).* [Incorrect spelling of Latin *stilus* pointed writing instrument.]

sty·mie (stī′mē) *v.t.,* **-mied, -mie·ing.** to bring to or keep at a standstill or in a state of inaction; frustrate; hinder; block: *Lack of money stymied us in our efforts to expand the business.* —*n.* formerly, a situation in golf in which one player's ball lies on the putting green in a direct line between another player's ball and the cup. [Of uncertain origin.]

styp·tic (stip′tik) *adj.* able to stop bleeding by contracting body tissues; astringent. —*n.* a styptic agent or substance, such as alum. [Latin *stypticus* astringent, from Greek *styptikos,* from *styphein* to contract.]

styptic pencil, a small stick of alum or other styptic agent, used to stop bleeding from small cuts, as in shaving.

sty·rene (stī′rēn, stir′ēn) *n.* a colorless, aromatic, liquid hydrocarbon, used esp. in making plastics and the most widely used type of synthetic rubber. Formula: C_8H_8 [Latin *styrax* storax (from Greek *styrax*) + -ENE; because obtained from storax.]

Sty·ro·foam (stī′rə fōm′) *n. Trademark.* a rigid polystyrene foam used as a lightweight insulating material. [STYR(ENE) + FOAM.]

Styx (stiks) *n.* in Greek mythology, the chief river surrounding Hades, the land of the dead, over which the souls of the dead were ferried by Charon.

su·a·ble (sü′ə bəl) *adj.* capable of being or liable to be sued. —**su′a·bil′i·ty,** *n.*

sua·sion (swā′zhən) *n.* the act or an instance of exhorting or urging; persuasion. [Latin *suāsiō,* from *suādēre* to persuade.]

sua·sive (swā′siv) *adj. Archaic.* having the ability to influence or persuade; persuasive.

suave (swäv) *adj.* having a smooth, agreeable, urbane manner. [Latin *suāvis* sweet, agreeable.] —**suave′ly,** *adv.* —**suave′ness, suav′i·ty,** *n.*

sub (sub) *Informal. n., adj.* **1.** substitute. **2.** submarine. —*v.i.,* **subbed, sub·bing.** to act as a substitute.

sub- *prefix* **1.** under; below; beneath: *substrata, substandard.* **2.** used to express a further division or distinction: *subcontract, subdivide.* **3.** partially or slightly; less than: *subhuman.* **4.** used to designate a person who is in a lower position: *subdeacon.* **5.** nearly; almost: *subtropical.* [Latin *sub* under.]

sub. 1. subscription. **2.** substitute. **3.** suburban.

sub·ac·id (sub as′id) *adj.* **1.** slightly acid. **2.** slightly tart or biting: *a subacid comment.*

sub·aer·i·al (sub âr′ē əl) *adj.* existing, situated, or taking place on the surface of the earth in the open air, rather than underground: *subaerial erosion.* —**sub·aer′i·al·ly,** *adj.*

sub·a·gent (sub ā′jənt) *n.* a person who is employed to work for or under an agent; agent of an agent. —**sub·a′gen·cy,** *n.*

sub·al·tern (sub ôl′tərn, sub′əl-) *n.* **1.** a person of subordinate

a	at	e	end	o	hot	u	up	hw	white	{	about
ā	ape	ē	me	ō	old	ū	use	ng	song		taken
ä	far	i	it	ô	fork	ü	rule	th	thin	ə	pencil
âr	care	ī	ice	oi	oil	ù	pull	th	this		lemon
		îr	pierce	ou	out	ûr	turn	zh	measure		circus

rank or position; aide. **2.** an officer in the British army, ranking below a captain. —*adj.* **1.** having a subordinate rank or position. **2.** of or relating to a subaltern. [Late Latin *subalternus* subordinate, going back to Latin *sub* under + *alter* other.]

sub·a·quat·ic (sub′ə kwat′ik, -ə kwot′-) *adj. Biology.* partly aquatic and partly terrestrial.

sub·a·que·ous (sub ā′kwē əs, -ak′wē-) *adj.* existing, performed, constructed, or used underwater.

sub·arc·tic (sub ärk′tik, -är′tik) *adj.* of or relating to those regions just outside the Arctic Circle.

sub·ar·id (sub ar′id) *adj.* moderately dry; partially arid.

sub·a·tom·ic (sub′ə tom′ik) *adj.* of or relating to an entity smaller than an atom or to a phenomenon occurring within an atom.

subatomic particle, any of a number of particles smaller than an atom that are the most fundamental constituents of nature as yet known. For each particle there exists a corresponding particle called an antiparticle. Also, **elementary particle, fundamental particle.**

sub·base·ment (sub′bās′mənt) *n.* a basement that is below a main basement.

sub·cel·lar (sub′sel′ər) *n.* a cellar below another or main cellar.

sub·chas·er (sub′chā′sər) *n.* a small, fast patrol boat designed for pursuing and attacking submarines.

sub·class (sub′klas′) *n. Biology.* a major subdivision of a class, esp. a taxonomic category ranking below a class but above an order.

sub·cla·vi·an (sub klā′vē ən) *adj.* located under the clavicle. —*n.* a subclavian structure, as an artery or muscle. [Modern Latin *subclavius* small muscle of the shoulder.]

sub·clin·i·cal (sub klin′i kəl) *adj.* of or relating to a disease, or the beginning stages of a disease, in which the symptoms are not detected by clinical observation: *subclinical cancer.*

sub·com·mit·tee (sub′kə mit′ē) *n.* a committee formed from and acting under a main committee for some special purpose.

sub·com·pact (sub kom′pakt) *n.* an automobile that is smaller than a compact model.

sub·con·scious (sub kon′shəs) *adj.* **1.** existing in the mind but not perceived in consciousness: *a subconscious wish.* **2.** not completely conscious; involving feeble or vague perception. —*n.* the aspects and processes of the mind that exist or take place below the threshold of consciousness. —**sub·con′scious·ly,** *adv.* —**sub·con′scious·ness,** *n.*

sub·con·ti·nent (sub kon′tə nənt, sub′kon′-) *n.* a large landmass that is smaller than a continent, esp. a large section of a continent regarded as a distinct geographical or political unit: *the Indian subcontinent.*

sub·con·tract (*n.,* sub kon′trakt, sub′kon′-; *v.,* sub′kən trakt′) *n.* a contract made to carry out all or part of another, original contract: *The lumber company had a subcontract with the builder to provide all of the lumber needed for the new house.* —*v.t.* to contract to carry out all or part of a previous contract for: *to subcontract plumbing.* —*v.i.* to make a subcontract.

sub·con·trac·tor (sub kon′trak tər, sub′kon′-, sub′kən trak′-) *n.* a person or company that contracts to carry out all or part of a previous contract.

sub·crit·i·cal (sub krit′i kəl) *adj. Nuclear Physics.* having or designating a mass of fissionable material that is less than the minimum needed for an ongoing chain reaction.

sub·cul·ture (sub′kul′chər) *n.* **1.** a bacterial culture made from another culture. **2.** a group within a larger culture having particular elements distinguishing it from others in the same society. —**sub·cul′tur·al,** *adj.*

sub·cu·ta·ne·ous (sub′kū tā′nē əs) *adj.* **1.** situated under the skin. **2.** (of certain parasites) living under the skin of the host. **3.** injected or performed under the skin; hypodermic. —**sub′cu·ta′ne·ous·ly,** *adv.*

sub·dea·con (sub dē′kən, sub′dē′-) *n.* in the Roman Catholic and Orthodox churches, a cleric next below a deacon in rank.

sub·deb (sub′deb′) *n. Informal.* subdebutante.

sub·deb·u·tante (sub deb′yu tänt′, -yə-) *n.* a young woman soon to become a debutante.

sub·di·vide (sub′di vīd′, sub′di vīd′) *v.,* -**vid·ed,** -**vid·ing.** —*v.t.* to divide or separate further (a part of a whole) after a previous division: *to subdivide a tract of land into building lots.* —*v.i.* to become divided further.

sub·di·vi·sion (sub′di vizh′ən, sub′di vizh′-) *n.* **1.** the act or an instance of dividing further (a part of a whole) into still smaller parts, or the state of being so divided. **2.** one of the parts into which a larger part has been divided; part of a part. **3.** an area of land divided into lots for building homes.

sub·dom·i·nant (sub dom′ə nənt) *Music. n.* the fourth tone of the diatonic scale; tone next below the dominant. —*adj.* of, based on, or relating to the subdominant.

sub·due (səb dü′, -dū′) *v.t.,* -**dued,** -**du·ing.** **1.** to bring under control; overcome, as by force or persuasion: *The speaker subdued the angry crowd.* **2.** to bring into subjection; conquer; vanquish: *to subdue an enemy.* **3.** to reduce the intensity, strength, or force of; tone down; soften: *The screens subdued the light in the room.* **4.** to hold down; keep back; repress: *to subdue one's urge to laugh.* [Old French *suduire* to seduce, from Latin *subdūcere* to draw away; influenced in meaning by Latin *subdere* to subjugate, bring under.] —**sub·du′a·ble,** *adj.* —**sub·du′er,** *n.*

su·ber·in (sü ber′in) *n.* a hard, waxy substance present in the walls of cork cells. [French *subérine,* from Latin *suber* cork + French -*ine* -ine².]

su·ber·ize (sü′bə rīz′) *v.i., v.t.,* -**ized,** -**iz·ing.** to become or cause to become impregnated with suberin, forming cork tissue. —**su′ber·i·za′tion,** *n.*

sub·fam·i·ly (sub fam′ə lē, sub′fam′-) *n., pl.* -**lies.** *Biology.* a major subdivision of a family, esp. a taxonomic category ranking below a family but above a genus.

sub·freez·ing (sub′frē′zing) *adj.* below freezing: *subfreezing weather.*

sub·ge·nus (sub jē′nəs, sub′jē′-) *n., pl.* -**gen·er·a** (-jen′ər ə, -jen′ər ə). *Biology.* a major subdivison of a genus, esp. a taxonomic category ranking below a genus but above a species.

sub·group (sub′grüp′) *n.* a group composed from and subordinate to a larger group.

sub·head (sub′hed′) *n.* **1.** a subordinate heading or title, as in a book, chapter, or article. **2.** one of the subdivisions into which a main head or title is broken up. Also, **sub′head′ing.**

sub·hu·man (sub hū′mən, sub ū′-) *adj.* **1.** having some characteristics of human beings, but not quite human. **2.** not fit for humans. **3.** infrahuman *(def. 1).*

subj. **1.** subject. **2.** subjective. **3.** subjunctive.

sub·ja·cent (sub jā′sənt) *adj.* **1.** situated directly underneath; underlying. **2.** situated at a lower level, but not directly beneath. [Latin *subjacēns,* present participle of *subjacēre* to lie under.]

sub·ject (*n., adj.,* sub′jikt; *v.,* səb jekt′) *n.* **1.a.** something that is the basis of thought, discussion, or investigation; topic: *The subject under discussion today is politics.* **b.** a range or sphere, as of study; field: *English was my best subject in school.* **2.** a theme, esp. the main theme, of a work of art or literary composition. **3.** *Music.* theme *(def. 3a).* **4.** in a sentence, a word, phrase, or clause that performs the action of the verb or, if the verb is in the passive voice, receives the action of the verb. In the sentence *The dog ran fast,* the word *dog* is the subject. **5.** a person or thing that is under the authority, control, or influence of another, esp. a citizen of a country that is in theory or reality ruled by a monarch, or a citizen of a country dominated by another: *The people were loyal subjects of the crown.* **6.** a person or thing that is the recipient of certain treatment: *They used mice as subjects in the experiments. The plan was the subject of much criticism.* **7.** the term of a proposition in logic about which a statement is made. In the proposition *A tree is a plant,* the word *tree* is the subject. **8.** *Philosophy.* the mind; self; ego. —*adj.* **1.** under the control, rule, or influence of (with *to*): *Employees are subject to the rules and regulations of the company.* **2.** easily affected by; susceptible (with *to*): *subject to all kinds of allergies.* **3.** dependent or conditional upon (with *to*): *subject to my approval.* —*v.t.* **1.** to bring under domination, influence, or control; subjugate. **2.** to cause to undergo or experience; expose (with *to*): *to subject someone to ridicule, to subject clay to great heat in a kiln.* [Latin *subjectus* past participle of *subicere* to place under, throw under.]

Synonyms *n.* **Subject** and **object** may both refer to a focus of interest or discussion. **Subject,** in this usage, more clearly suggests that the thing in question has interest, complexity, or value: *The subject of the lecture was Italian painting. The subject of the conference is the reorganization of our business procedures.* **Object,** on the other hand, suggests something more specific to which attention is directed, which may be a goal: *The object of the meeting was to inform the employees about the new business procedures.* For other Synonyms *(n.),* see **citizen.**

sub·jec·tion (səb jek′shən) *n.* **1.** the act of bringing under the control or domination of another; subjugation. **2.** the state or condition of being under the control or domination of another.

sub·jec·tive (səb jek′tiv) *adj.* **1.** of, existing in, or proceeding from the individual who is thinking, based on his or her own feelings, thoughts, or experiences; personal and not objective. **2.** in literature and art, based on or expressing the feelings, thoughts, and experiences of the artist or author. **3.** designating the case of the subject of a verb. —**sub·jec′tive·ly,** *adv.* —**sub·jec′tive·ness,** *n.*

sub·jec·tiv·i·ty (sub′jek tiv′i tē) *n.* **1.** the tendency to view things solely in relation to one's own feelings, thoughts, or experiences. **2.** the quality or condition of being subjective.

subject matter 1. the main body of facts or ideas with which something is concerned; that with which a discussion, project, or the like is concerned. **2.** the body of ideas presented in a book, speech, or the like, as distinguished from form or style.

sub·join (səb join′) *v.t.* to add at the end; append. [Middle French *subjoindre* to add (to), from Latin *subjungere* to join to.]

sub·ju·gate (sub′jə gāt′) *v.t.*, **-gat·ed, -gat·ing.** to bring or have under one's control or dominance; subdue. [Late Latin *subjugātus,* past participle of *subjugāre* to bring under the yoke, subject, from Latin *sub* under + *jugum* yoke; with reference to the Roman custom of forcing defeated soldiers to crawl under a yoke to symbolize their defeat.] —**sub′ju·ga′tion,** *n.* —**sub′ju·ga′tor,** *n.*

sub·junc·tive (səb jungk′tiv) *n.* **1.** the mood of a verb that indicates action or state of being as possible, conditional, contrary to fact, or dependent, rather than as actual. In the sentence *If I were you, I wouldn't go,* the word *were* is in the subjunctive. **2.** a verb form in this mood. —*adj.* of, relating to, or constituting this mood. [Late Latin *subjūnctīvus* subordinate, connecting, from Latin *subjūnctus,* past participle of *subjungere* to join to.]

sub·king·dom (sub king′dəm, sub′king′-) *n. Biology.* a major subdivision of a kingdom, esp. a taxonomic category ranking next below a kingdom but above a phylum of animals or a division of plants.

sub·lease (*n.,* sub′lēs′; *v.,* sub lēs′) *n.* a lease granted by a tenant transferring all or part of the rights under the original lease to another person. —*v.t.,* **-leased, -leas·ing.** to grant or obtain a sublease for.

sub·let (sub let′, sub′let′) *v.t.,* **-let, -let·ting. 1.** to grant or obtain a sublease for (some property or business); sublease. **2.** to give to another a part of (a contract held by oneself); subcontract: *The company sublet the contract for the electrical work to a smaller company.*

sub·li·mate (*v.,* sub′lə māt′; *n., adj.,* sub′lə mit, -māt′) *v.t.,* **-mat·ed, -mat·ing. 1.** to act upon (something) so as to produce a refined product; refine; purify. **2.** *Psychology.* to subject (thoughts or impulses) to sublimation. **3.** *Chemistry.* to sublime (a substance). —*n.* any solid, crystalline material resulting when a substance is sublimed. Mercuric chloride is a poisonous sublimate of mercuric sulfate and salt. [Latin *sublīmātus,* past participle of *sublīmāre* to lift up, from *sublīmis* lofty.]

sub·li·ma·tion (sub′lə mā′shən) *n.* **1.** the act of sublimating or subliming or the state of being sublimated or sublimed. **2.** something that has been sublimated or sublimed. **3.** *Psychology.* the process by which painful or socially unacceptable thoughts and impulses that have been repressed in the subconscious emerge in a new, socially acceptable form.

sub·lime (sə blīm′) *adj.* **1.** elevated or exalted in manner, expression, or appearance; grand; lofty; noble: *sublime scenery, a sublime poem.* **2.** *Informal.* outstanding; splendid. —*n.* **the sublime.** that which is elevated or exalted in manner, expression, or appearance; sublimity. —*v.,* **-limed, -lim·ing.** —*v.t. Chemistry.* to cause (a substance) to pass directly from a solid to a gaseous state, or from a gaseous to a solid state, without becoming liquid; sublimate. —*v.i. Chemistry.* to change directly from a solid to a vapor, or from a vapor to a solid, without first becoming a liquid. Mothballs and dry ice sublime. [Latin *sublīmis* lofty.] —**sub·lim′er,** *n.*

sub·lim·i·nal (sub lim′ə nəl) *adj. Psychology.* existing below the threshold of sensation or consciousness; too low or slight to be consciously recognized: *a subliminal impression, subliminal motivation.* [SUB- + Latin *līmin-,* stem of *līmen* threshold + -AL¹.] —**sub·lim′i·nal·ly,** *adv.*

sub·lim·i·ty (sə blim′i tē) *n., pl.* **-ties. 1.** the state or quality of being sublime; loftiness; grandeur. **2.** a person or thing that is sublime.

sub·lit·to·ral (sub lit′ər əl) *adj.* of or relating to that part of the offshore ocean environment that extends from below the water level at low tide downward to depths of about 300 feet (90 meters).

sub·lu·nar·y (sub′lü ner′ē, sub lü′nə rē) *adj.* **1.** of, existing, or situated beneath the moon, that is, either between the moon and the earth or on the earth. **2.** lacking anything of the sublime; earthbound; mundane. Also, **sub·lu·nar** (sub lü′nər). [Late Latin *sublūnāris* under the moon, from Latin *sub* under + *lūna* moon.]

sub·ma·chine gun (sub′mə shēn′) a portable, lightweight, automatic or semiautomatic gun that fires pistol ammunition and is designed for shooting from the hip or shoulder.

sub·mar·gin·al (sub mär′jə nəl) *adj.* **1.** *Biology.* near the margin, as of a wing. **2.** below established or reasonable standards: *submarginal living conditions.* **3.** not productive enough to be profitable: *submarginal farmland, submarginal ore deposits.*

sub·ma·rine (*n.,* sub′mə rēn′, sub′mə rēn′; *adj.,* sub′mə rēn′) *n.* **1.** a vessel that can operate underwater, esp. one used as an attack

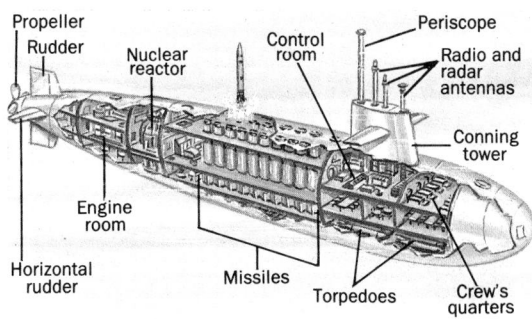

nuclear **submarine**

Propeller / Rudder / Nuclear reactor / Control room / Periscope / Radio and radar antennas / Conning tower / Engine room / Horizontal rudder / Missiles / Torpedoes / Crew's quarters

or reconnaissance vessel. **2.** a hero sandwich. —*adj.* **1.** situated, existing, occurring, relating to, or used below the surface of the sea. **2.** of, relating to, or involving submarines.

sub·ma·rin·er (sub′mə rē′nər, sub′mə rē′-, sub mar′ə-) *n.* a member of the crew on a submarine, or a person whose profession is working on submarines.

sub·max·il·lar·y (sub mak′sə ler′ē) *n., pl.* **-lar·ies. 1.** the lower jawbone; mandible. **2.** submaxillary gland. —*adj.* **1.** of or relating to the lower jaw or jawbone. **2.** of or relating to the submaxillary glands.

submaxillary gland, one of a pair of salivary glands that lie on either side of the mouth beneath the mandible.

sub·merge (səb mûrj′) *v.,* **-merged, -merg·ing.** —*v.t.* **1.** to place under or cover with some liquid, esp. water. **2.** to overshadow so as to make unnoticeable; cover; hide; obscure. —*v.i.* to sink out of sight by or as by passing beneath the surface of a liquid: *The submarine submerged.* [Latin *submergere* to plunge under.] —**sub·mer′gence,** *n.* —For Synonyms *(v.t.),* see **dip.**

sub·merse (səb mûrs′) *v.t.,* **-mersed, -mers·ing.** submerge. [Latin *submersus,* past participle of *submergere* to plunge under.] —**sub·mer·sion** (səb mur′zhən, -shən), *n.*

sub·mers·i·ble (səb mûr′sə bəl) *adj.* able or designed to be submerged. —*n.* any of certain vessels designed to operate underwater, as for research or exploration.

sub·mi·cro·scop·ic (sub′mī krə skop′ik) *adj.* too small to be seen through an ordinary compound microscope.

sub·mis·sion (səb mish′ən) *n.* **1.** the act of yielding to some power or authority. **2.** the state or quality of being submissive or deferential; submissiveness; acquiescence; humility. **3.** the referral of a dispute to the decision or judgment of a third party or parties. **4.a.** the act of presenting something for consideration by another or others. **b.** something thus presented: *This drawing was my submission to the contest.* [Latin *submissiō* a lowering.]

sub·mis·sive (səb mis′iv) *adj.* inclined to yield to power or authority; exhibiting ready compliance; meek; humble. —**sub·mis′sive·ly,** *adv.* —**sub·mis′sive·ness,** *n.* —For Synonyms, see **obedient.**

sub·mit (səb mit′) *v.,* **-mit·ted, -mit·ting.** —*v.i.* **1.** to yield oneself to some power or authority; give up; surrender: *The rebels swore never to submit.* **2.** to subject oneself; expose oneself (with *to*): *Why are you willing to submit to such rude treatment?* —*v.t.* **1.** to present for consideration, decision, or examination by another or others: *I submitted my term paper three weeks late.* **2.** to put forward as an opinion or proposition; urge in a respectful manner; propose: *I submit that the defendant is not guilty.* **3.** to yield or subject (oneself) to some power or authority. [Latin *submittere* to let down, lower, put below.] —For Synonyms, see **yield.**

sub·mu·co·sa (sub′mū kō′sə, -zə) *n., pl.* **-sae** (-sē, -zē) or **-sas.** the layer of fibrous connective tissue that attaches a mucous membrane to the surface that it lines. [SUB- + MUCOSA.] —**sub′mu·co′sal,** *adj.*

sub·nor·mal (sub nôr′məl) *adj.* less than usual, average, or normal, esp. in intelligence. —*n.* a person of less than normal intelligence. —**sub·nor·mal·i·ty** (sub′nôr mal′i tē), *n.* —**sub·nor′mal·ly,** *adv.*

sub·or·bit·al (sub ôr′bi təl) *adj.* **1.** (of a missile, spacecraft, space flight, or the like) not attaining an orbit; making less than

a	at	e	end	o	hot	u	up	hw	white		about
ā	ape	ē	me	ō	old	ū	use	ng	song	ə	taken
ä	far	i	it	ô	fork	ü	rule	th	thin		pencil
âr	care	ī	ice	oi	oil	u̇	pull	th	this		lemon
				ou	out	ûr	turn	zh	measure		circus
		îr	pierce								

one complete orbit. **2.** *Anatomy.* below or under the eye or its orbit.

sub·or·der (sub'ôr'dər) *n. Biology.* a major subdivision of an order, esp. a taxonomic category ranking below an order but above a family.

sub·or·di·nate (*adj., n.,* sə bôr'də nit; *v.,* sə bôr'də nāt') *adj.* **1.** belonging to a lower rank, grade, class, or the like: *a subordinate officer.* **2.** having less importance; not principal or predominant; minor. **3.** dependent upon the main or principal thing; secondary. —*n.* a person or thing that is subordinate. —*v.t.,* **-nat·ed, -nat·ing.** to cause to be, or treat as, secondary or inferior; render dependent, subservient, or of less importance. [Medieval Latin *subordinatus,* past participle of *subordinare* to place in a lower order, going back to Latin *sub* under + *ordō* row[1], rank[1].] —**sub·or'di·na'tion,** *n.*

subordinate clause, dependent clause.

subordinating conjunction, a conjunction that introduces dependent clauses, such as *if* or *when.*

sub·orn (sə bôrn') *v.t.* **1.a.** to cause (a witness) to give false testimony in a court of law, as by bribery. **b.** to obtain (perjured testimony). **2.** to influence (a person) to commit a misdeed, esp. by bribery. [Latin *subōrnāre* to provide, incite secretly.] —**sub·or·na·tion** (sub'ôr nā'shən), *n.* —**sub·orn'er,** *n.*

sub·phy·lum (sub fī'ləm, sub'fī'-) *n., pl.* **-la** (-lə). *Biology.* a major subdivision of a phylum, esp. a taxonomic category below a phylum but above a class.

sub·plot (sub'plot') *n.* a minor or secondary story line in a literary work, such as a play or novel.

sub·poe·na (sə pē'nə) *also,* **sub·pe·na.** *n.* an official document ordering a person to appear in a court of law or before a legislative committee, grand jury, or other governmental body or to present specified documents; summons. —*v.t.,* **-naed, -na·ing.** to summon (someone or something) by presenting with a subpoena: *to subpoena a potential witness, to subpoena evidence.* [Latin *sub poenā* under a penalty (the first words of this writ).]

sub·po·lar (sub pō'lər) *adj.* of, relating to, or designating regions just outside the Arctic or Antarctic circles.

sub ro·sa (sub rō'zə) confidentially; privately. [Latin *sub rosā* under the rose; the rose was associated with the ancient Greek god of silence.]

sub·rou·tine (sub'rü tēn') *n. Computers.* a set of computer instructions that is used to perform a specific task and that may be returned to and repeated as often as needed while a program is being run.

sub·scribe (səb skrīb') *v.,* **-scribed, -scrib·ing.** —*v.i.* **1.** to pay a specified amount in order to receive a newspaper, magazine, or other periodical or similar material for a specified period of time (with *to*). **2.** to promise to pay or contribute a definite amount of money for some special purpose or service (with *to*): *They subscribe to the same charities every year.* **3.a.** to sign one's name at the end of something to signify one's assent or concurrence (with *to*). **b.** to express agreement, concurrence, or acquiescence; give one's assent or approval: *I have read your statement, and I heartily subscribe.* —*v.t.* **1.** to promise to give or pay, esp. by writing one's name under an agreement: *Each member subscribed ten dollars for the charity.* **2.** to sign (one's name) beneath, as if to signify assent or concurrence. **3.** to sign one's name to (something) to express agreement or consent: *to subscribe an appeal for support.* [Latin *subscrībere* to write under, sign, agree to.] —**sub·scrib'er,** *n.*

sub·script (sub'skript') *n.* a character, such as a number, letter, or symbol, usually of relatively small size, printed or written beneath or on the lower half of a line of print. In the formula H_2O, the number *2* is a subscript. —*adj.* printed or written beneath or on the lower half of the line. [Latin *subscrīptus,* past participle of *subscrībere* to write under, sign.]

sub·scrip·tion (səb skrip'shən) *n.* **1.** the right to receive a newspaper, magazine, or other periodical or similar material for a certain period of time in return for a specified payment. **2.** a sum of money pledged, as to a charity; donation; contribution. **3.** a fund raised through the contributions of a number of persons. **4.** something added at the end of a document, esp. a signature. **5.** the act of subscribing.

sub·sec·tion (sub'sek'shən) *n.* a part or division of a section.

sub·se·quence (sub'si kwəns) *n.* **1.** the state or condition of being subsequent. **2.** something that is subsequent; sequel; result.

sub·se·quent (sub'si kwənt) *adj.* coming or occurring later or after, or as a result: *Subsequent investigations discovered new evidence.* [Latin *subsequēns,* present participle of *subsequī* to follow.] —**sub'se·quent·ly,** *adv.*

· **subsequent to.** after; following: *Subsequent to the meeting there will be a break for lunch.*

sub·serve (səb sûrv') *v.t.,* **-served, -serv·ing.** to be instrumen-

tal in promoting or furthering (someone or something); assist; aid. [Latin *subservīre* to serve, comply with.]

sub·ser·vi·ence (səb sûr'vē əns) *n.* **1.** obsequious, servile behavior or a similar attitude; fawning servility; slavish obedience. **2.** the state or an instance of being instrumental in furthering an end. Also, **sub·ser'vi·en·cy.**

sub·ser·vi·ent (səb sûr'vē ənt) *adj.* **1.** slavishly submissive in behavior or attitude; obsequious. **2.** useful as an instrument or means to further an end; instrumental; serviceable. [Latin *subserviēns,* present participle of *subservīre* to serve, comply with.] —**sub·ser'vi·ent·ly,** *adv.*

sub·set (sub'set') *n. Mathematics.* a set whose members are all contained within another given set. The subsets of the set {a,b} are {a,b}, {a}, {b}, and {0}.

sub·side (səb sīd') *v.i.,* **-sid·ed, -sid·ing.** **1.** to sink to a low or lower level, esp. to the normal or usual level: *The floodwaters subsided.* **2.** to decrease in volume, activity, or intensity; be calmed; abate: *The fury of the storm subsided.* **3.** to sink down or fall to the bottom, as sediment; settle; precipitate. [Latin *subsīdere* to settle down.] —**sub·sid·ence** (səb sī'dəns, sub'si dəns), *n.*

sub·sid·i·ar·y (səb sid'ē er'ē) *adj.* **1.** serving to help, assist, or supplement; supplementary: *a subsidiary source of income.* **2.** subordinate, as in importance or position; secondary: *Cost is only a subsidiary consideration.* **3.** of, relating to, consisting of, or depending on a subsidy or subsidies. —*n., pl.* **-ar·ies.** **1.** a company owned or controlled by another company, usually resulting from the parent company's ownership of all or a majority of the other company's stock. Also, **subsidiary company.** **2.** any subsidiary person or thing. [Latin *subsīdiārius* relating to a reserve, from *subsīdium* reserve troops, aid.]

sub·si·dize (sub'si dīz') *v.t.,* **-dized, -diz·ing.** **1.** to aid or support with a subsidy: *The government subsidizes some farmers when they agree not to produce certain crops.* **2.** to purchase the aid or assistance of by the payment of a subsidy. **3.** to secure the cooperation of by bribery. —**sub'si·di·za'tion,** *n.* —**sub'si·diz'er,** *n.*

sub·si·dy (sub'si dē) *n., pl.* **-dies.** a contribution, esp. of money, given as a supplement or assistance. [Latin *subsīdium* reserve troops, aid.]

sub·sist (səb sist') *v.i.* **1.** to maintain existence; support life; exist (usually with *on*): *The lost explorers barely managed to subsist on the fruits and berries they could find.* **2.** to have existence or continue to exist; remain; abide: *traditions that have subsisted through the ages.* [Latin *subsistere* to stand still, stay[1].]

sub·sist·ence (səb sis'təns) *n.* **1.a.** the state or condition of remaining alive; continued existence. **b.** the means of supporting life; support; livelihood. **2.** actual existence; real being. —**sub·sist'ent,** *adj.*

subsistence farming **1.** the raising of crops and livestock sufficient for the needs of the farmer, without surplus for the marketplace. **2.** the raising of crops and livestock in such quantities as to produce only enough income to maintain the farm without profit.

sub·soil (sub'soil') *n.* the layer of soil lying immediately beneath the surface soil.

sub·son·ic (sub son'ik) *adj.* of, relating to, or characterized by a speed, or a body moving at a speed, less than that of sound.

sub·spe·cies (sub'spē'shēz, -sēz, sub spē'-) *n., pl.* **-cies.** *Biology.* a subdivision of a species, esp. a taxonomic grouping of plants or animals within a species, usually distinguished by geographical distribution and physical type, such as a race or variety.

subst. **1.** substantive. **2.** substitute.

sub·stance (sub'stəns) *n.* **1.a.** that which a physical thing consists of; underlying matter; basic material. **b.** material or matter of a particular type: *a radioactive substance.* **2.** the real or essential thing or part, esp. of something written or spoken; essence. **3.a.** ample or solid quality; density; body: *These cheap, light plastics have no substance to them.* **b.** the quality of being real and substantial, rather than apparent; reality: *There is substance to the accusation.* **4.** material possessions; wealth; means: *a person of substance.* [Latin *substantia* essence, material; literally, that which stands beneath, going back to *sub* beneath + *stāre* to stand.] —For Synonyms, see **material.**

· **in substance.** **a.** as relates to essentials; in the main. **b.** actually; really.

sub·stand·ard (sub stan'dərd, sub'stan'-) *adj.* below or deviating from the established standard.

sub·stan·tial (səb stan'shəl) *adj.* **1.** of considerable amount, worth, or importance; ample: *to show a substantial profit, to enjoy substantial success.* **2.** having a solid base or basis; firmly or strongly established or constructed: *a substantial building.* **3.** possessing abundant wealth; well-to-do; wealthy. **4.** having actual existence or corporeal form; not imaginary or visionary; real. [Late Latin *substantiālis* relating to the essence, from Latin *sub-*

stantia essence. See SUBSTANCE.] —**sub·stan·ti·al·i·ty** (səb-stan′shē al′i tē), *n.*

sub·stan·tial·ly (səb stan′shə lē) *adv.* **1.** in the main; essentially. **2.** in reality; actually. **3.** strongly; solidly.

sub·stan·ti·ate (səb stan′shē āt′) *v.t.,* **-at·ed, -at·ing. 1.** to furnish factual evidence in order to prove; verify: *Can you substantiate your claim?* **2.** to give actual form to; embody. —**sub·stan′ti·a′tion,** *n.* —For Synonyms, see **confirm.**

sub·stan·ti·val (sub′stən tī′vəl) *adj.* of, relating to, or characteristic of a substantive or substantives.

sub·stan·tive (sub′stən tiv) *n.* a noun or pronoun, or an adjective, phrase, or clause used as a noun substitute. —*adj.* **1.a.** used as a noun or noun substitute. **b.** denoting the verb of existence, *to be.* **2.** standing of or by itself; independent. **3.** having substance; solid; real. **4.** of considerable amount; substantial. **5.** of or relating to essentials; essential. [Late Latin *substantīvus* self-existent, from Latin *substantia* essence. See SUBSTANCE.] —**sub′stan·tive·ly,** *adv.*

sub·sta·tion (sub′stā′shən) *n.* a subsidiary station, esp. a post office branch or an auxiliary power station where electricity is transformed in some way.

sub·sti·tute (sub′sti tüt′, -tūt′) *n.* a person or thing that acts or is used in place of another. —*v.,* **-tut·ed, -tut·ing.** —*v.t.* to put (someone or something) in place of another: *We substituted broccoli for cauliflower in the recipe.* —*v.i.* to act as a substitute. —*adj.* taking the place of or performing the function of another: *a substitute teacher.* [Latin *substitūtus,* past participle of *substituere* to put instead of.]

sub·sti·tu·tion (sub′sti tü′shən, -tū′-) *n.* **1.** the act of substituting or the state of being substituted. **2.** a substitute. —**sub′sti·tu′tion·al, sub′sti·tu′tion·ar′y,** *adj.*

sub·sti·tu·tive (sub′sti tü′tiv, -tū′-) *adj.* **1.** of, relating to, or tending to carry out substitution. **2.** being a substitute or capable of being one.

sub·strate (sub′strāt) *n.* **1.** substratum. **2.** a substance on which an enzyme acts.

sub·stra·tum (sub′strā′təm, -strat′əm) *n., pl.* **-stra·ta** (-strā′tə, -strat′ə) or **-stra·tums. 1.** a substance that lies under another, esp. a layer of earth, the subsoil, that lies beneath the surface layer. **2.** a basis or foundation. [Modern Latin *substrātum* spread underneath, from Latin *substrātum,* neuter past participle of *substernere* to spread under.]

sub·struc·ture (sub′struk′chər) *n.* an underlying part that supports a main structure; foundation. —**sub·struc′tur·al,** *adj.*

sub·sume (səb süm′) *v.t.,* **-sumed, -sum·ing.** to include in some larger, higher, or more general classification or category (with *under*): *Suppose we subsume our insurance costs under "overhead."* [Modern Latin *subsūmere* to take under, from Latin *sub* under + *sūmere* to take.]

sub·tem·per·ate (sub tem′pər it) *adj.* **1.** of or relating to colder parts or areas of a temperate zone. **2.** barely temperate in climate.

sub·ten·an·cy (sub ten′ən sē) *n., pl.* **-cies.** the status, right, or holding of a subtenant.

sub·ten·ant (sub ten′ənt, sub′ten′-) *n.* a person or organization that occupies a place by renting or subleasing from a tenant.

sub·tend (səb tend′) *v.t.* **1.** *Geometry.* (of a line) to extend under or be positioned opposite to or across from so as to mark the extent of. A chord subtends its arc. **2.** *Botany.* (of a leaf or bract) to extend beneath so as to enclose or enfold, as a bud. [Latin *subtendere* to stretch beneath.]

sub·ter·fuge (sub′tər fūj′) *n.* a device or expedient used to escape a situation or conceal an aim or purpose; evasion; ruse. [Late Latin *subterfugium,* going back to Latin *subter* secretly, underneath + *fugere* to flee.]

sub·ter·ra·ne·an (sub′tə rā′nē ən) *adj.* **1.** existing, situated, or taking place below the surface of the earth; underground: *a subterranean tunnel, subterranean life.* **2.** existing or occurring out of sight; done secretly. Also, **sub′ter·ra′ne·ous.** [Latin *subterrāneus* underground (from *sub* under + *terra* earth) + -AN.] —**sub′ter·ra′ne·an·ly;** also, **sub′ter·ra′ne·ous·ly,** *adv.*

sub·text (sub′tekst′) *n.* a meaning or theme of a literary work, film, or play that is not expressed directly but is implicit or presented metaphorically.

sub·tile (sut′əl, sub′təl) *adj. Archaic.* subtle. —**sub′tile·ly,** *adv.*

sub·til·i·ty (sub til′i tē) *n., pl.* **-ties.** *Archaic.* subtlety.

sub·til·ty (sut′əl tē, sub′təl-) *n., pl.* **-ties.** *Archaic.* subtlety.

sub·ti·tle (sub′tī′təl) *n.* **1.** a secondary or additional title, as of a book or article, usually of an explanatory nature. **2.** a translation of foreign-language dialogue in a motion picture, superimposed on the screen, usually near the bottom. —*v.t.,* **-tled, -tling.** to provide with a subtitle or subtitles.

sub·tle (sut′əl) *adj.* **1.** having a faint, delicate quality, so as to be

nearly imperceptible; elusive; tenuous: *a subtle aroma.* **2.** suggesting something, such as a secret; provocative; mysterious: *The subject in the painting is famous for her subtle smile.* **3.** capable of discerning or understanding fine distinctions in meaning; perceptive: *a subtle mind.* **4.** treacherously or deceitfully cunning; crafty; sly: *a subtle plan to cheat someone.* **5.** characterized by cleverness or ingenuity; artful; ingenious. **6.** difficult to solve or understand; ambiguous; abstruse: *a subtle problem.* **7.** working so as not to be easily detected: *a subtle influence.* [Old French *soutil* thin, keen, crafty, from Latin *subtīlis* thin, keen, precise; originally, finely woven, from *sub* under + *tēla* web.] —**sub′tly,** *adv.* —**sub′tle·ness,** *n.*

sub·tle·ty (sut′əl tē) *n., pl.* **-ties. 1.** the quality or an instance of being subtle. **2.** something that is subtle, esp. a fine distinction.

sub·ton·ic (sub ton′ik) *n. Music.* the seventh tone of the diatonic scale; tone next below the upper tonic.

sub·top·ic (sub′top′ik) *n.* a secondary topic that is a subdivision of the main topic, as of an article or lecture.

sub·to·tal (sub′tō′təl, sub tō′-) *n.* the sum of part of a group of numbers or quantities being added, esp. such a sum arrived at in the process of determining the final, complete total for the whole group —*v.t., v.i.,* **-taled, -tal·ing;** also, *British,* **-talled, -tal·ling.** to determine the sum of part of a group of numbers or quantities being added. —*adj.* less than complete: *the subtotal removal of a tumor.*

sub·tract (səb trakt′) *v.t.* **1.** to take away or deduct (a number) from a given number in order to determine the number remaining: *If you subtract 3 from 7, that leaves 4.* **2.** to withdraw or take away (any element) from a whole; deduct. —*v.i.* to perform the operation or process of subtraction: *Do you know how to subtract with negative numbers?* [Latin *subtractus,* past participle of *subtrahere* to draw off, remove.] —**sub·tract′er,** *n.*

sub·trac·tion (səb trak′shən) *n.* **1.** the operation or process of determining the difference between two numbers. **2.** the act or an instance of subtracting.

sub·trac·tive (səb trak′tiv) *adj.* **1.** of or relating to subtraction. **2.** inclined to or having the ability to subtract; detracting. **3.** that is to be subtracted; having the minus sign (−); being subtracted.

sub·tra·hend (sub′trə hend′) *n.* a number or quantity that is to be subtracted from another. In the equation $11 - 4 = 7$, the number 4 is the subtrahend. ➡ distinguished from **minuend.** [Latin *subtrahendus* to be subtracted, gerundive of *subtrahere* to draw off, remove.]

sub·treas·ur·y (sub trezh′ə rē, sub′trezh′-) *n., pl.* **-ur·ies.** a subordinate or branch treasury.

sub·trop·i·cal (sub trop′i kəl) *adj.* **1.** of or relating to regions bordering on the tropics. **2.** having a nearly tropical climate.

sub·trop·ics (sub trop′iks, sub′trop′-) *pl. n.* subtropical regions.

sub·urb (sub′ûrb) *n.* **1.** a residential district close to or on the outer edge of a city: *We live in a suburb of Detroit.* **2. the suburbs.** an area consisting of such districts: *to move to the suburbs.* [Latin *suburbium,* from *sub* under + *urbs* city.]

sub·ur·ban (sə bûr′bən) *adj.* of, relating to, or characteristic of a suburb or of suburbanites: *suburban housing, suburban habits.*

sub·ur·ban·ite (sə bûr′bə nīt′) *n.* a person who lives in the suburbs.

sub·ur·bi·a (sə bûr′bē ə) *n.* **1.** the suburbs or suburbanites collectively. **2.** the interests, activities, or viewpoints regarded as characteristic of the suburbs or suburbanites.

sub·ven·tion (səb ven′shən) *n.* **1.** a grant of money for aid or support, esp. a government subsidy. **2.** the act or an instance of giving such aid. [Late Latin *subventiō* assistance, from Latin *subvenīre* to assist, come to one's aid.]

sub·ver·sion (səb vûr′zhən, -shən) *n.* **1.** the act of undermining or bringing about the destruction of a government or other established institution. **2.** something that causes such undermining or destruction. [Late Latin *subversiō* an overthrow, from Latin *subvertere* to turn upside down, overthrow.]

sub·ver·sive (səb vûr′siv) *adj.* attempting, advocating, or tending to overthrow, undermine, or destroy: *a subversive speech, subversive activities.* —*n.* a person who advocates or attempts the overthrow or undermining of a government or other established institution. —**sub·ver′sive·ly,** *adv.* —**sub·ver′sive·ness,** *n.*

sub·vert (səb vûrt′) *v.t.* **1.** to bring about the destruction of; overthrow; destroy: *to subvert a dictatorship.* **2.** to undermine, as the loyalty, faith, or principles of; corrupt: *to subvert someone with*

a	at	e	end	o	hot	u	up	hw	white		about
ā	ape	ē	me	ō	old	ū	use	ng	song		taken
ä	far	i	it	ô	fork	ü	rule	th	thin	ə	pencil
âr	care	ī	ice	oi	oil	u̇	pull	th	this		lemon
		îr	pierce	ou	out	ûr	turn	zh	measure		circus

a bribe. [Latin *subvertere* to turn upside down, overthrow.] —**sub·vert′er**, *n.*

sub·way (sub′wā′) *n.* **1.** a railway that runs wholly or partly underground, esp. one in a large urban area providing passenger and commuting service. **2.** *British.* an underground passage, as for a water main, electric cables, or pedestrians.

suc·ceed (sək sēd′) *v.i.* **1.** to have the desired result or conclusion: turn out successfully: *The venture succeeded even better than they had expected.* **2.** to accomplish what is attempted or intended; obtain the desired object or outcome: *The researchers succeeded in discovering a new vaccine.* **3.** to come next in the place of another or that which has preceded, esp. to ascend to a position after the removal or death of the occupant (with *to*): *After the death of the king, his daughter succeeded to the throne.* **4.** to have success, as in one's career: *The young actor dreamed of succeeding on Broadway.* —*v.t.* to take the place of; be heir or successor to, as in some occupation or position: *He succeeded her as treasurer of the club.* [Latin *succēdere* to go beneath, follow.] —**suc·ceed′er**, *n.* —For Synonyms *(v.i.)*, see **follow.**

suc·cess (sək ses′) *n.* **1.** a favorable result or conclusion; attainment of a desired end. **2.** the attainment or acquisition of wealth, status, or other desirable condition. **3.** a person or thing that succeeds or is successful: *The young actor was an overnight success.* [Latin *successus* good result, from *succēdere* to follow.]

suc·cess·ful (sək ses′fəl) *adj.* **1.** having, attaining, or resulting in success; fortunate. **2.** having attained success, esp. by becoming wealthy: *a successful investor.* —**suc·cess′ful·ly**, *adv.* —**suc·cess′ful·ness**, *n.*

suc·ces·sion (sək sesh′ən) *n.* **1.** a group of people or things following one after another in time or place; sequence; series: *The business had a succession of problems. A succession of children followed the parade.* **2.** the act of one person or thing following another in time or place. **3.a.** the right of being next in line for an office, rank, or the like held by another: *The princess challenged the prince's succession to the throne.* **b.** the order or line of persons having such a right.

· **in succession.** one after another; in orderly sequence.

suc·ces·sive (sək ses′iv) *adj.* coming one after another in an uninterrupted sequence. —**suc·ces′sive·ly**, *adv.* —**suc·ces′-sive·ness**, *n.*

Synonyms Successive and consecutive mean following one another in sequence, but consecutive also denotes a sequence in which there is no interruption: *They drilled through successive layers of sand, clay, and rock. The team won six consecutive games. The numbers 1, 2, and 3, are consecutive.*

suc·ces·sor (sək ses′ər) *n.* a person or thing that follows or takes the place of another, esp. a person who succeeds or is in line to succeed another in some office, rank, or the like. [Latin *successor* follower.]

suc·cinct (sək singkt′) *adj.* **1.** written or spoken in few words; brief and concise; terse. **2.** characterized by verbal brevity and conciseness: *a succinct style of writing.* [Latin *succinctus* prepared, short, past participle of *succingere* to tuck up, gird below.] —**suc·cinct′ly**, *adv.* —**suc·cinct′ness**, *n.* —For Synonyms, see **concise.**

suc·cor (suk′ər) *also, British,* **succour.** *n.* **1.** help; assistance; relief. **2.** a person or thing that helps or gives relief. —*v.t.* to give help, assistance, or relief to. [Old French *sucurre* to aid, assist, from Latin *succurrere* to run up to, aid.]

suc·co·ry (suk′ə rē) *n., pl.* **-ries.** chicory.

suc·co·tash (suk′ə tash′) *n.* corn kernels and beans, usually lima beans, cooked together. [Modification of Algonquian *msiquatash* ear of corn; literally, the grains are unbroken.]

Suc·coth (sŭk′əs; *Hebrew* sü kôt′) *also,* **Suc·cot.** *n.* Sukkoth.

suc·cour (suk′ər) *British.* succor.

suc·cu·bus (suk′yə bəs) *n., pl.* **-bi** (-bī′). a female demon or evil spirit, esp. in medieval legend, that supposedly appeared to men while they were sleeping and had sexual intercourse with them. [Medieval Latin *succubus* strumpet, from Late Latin *succuba*, from Latin *succubāre* to lie under.]

suc·cu·lence (suk′yə ləns) *n.* the state or quality of being succulent. Also, **suc′cu·len·cy.**

suc·cu·lent (suk′yə lənt) *adj.* **1.** full of juice; juicy. **2.** rich and delicious: *a succulent morsel.* **3.** providing mental stimulation; provoking interest. **4.** having thick, fleshy tissues, such as stems and leaves, that can store large quantities of water. —*n.* a succulent plant, such as a cactus. [Latin *succulentus* full of juice, from *succus* juice.]

suc·cumb (sə kum′) *v.i.* **1.** to give way, as under pressure or force; submit; yield (often with *to*): *to succumb to temptation.* **2.** to die from a disease, wound, or the like (often with *to*): *to*

succumb to a bullet wound. [Latin *succumbere* to lie under, surrender.]

such (such) *adj.* **1.** of the same kind or degree as that or those mentioned or indicated: *Have you ever heard such a story?* **2.** of that particular kind or degree: *Such an old car is next to useless.* **3.** of a similar kind or degree; like: *We bought lettuce, tomatoes, and such items for a salad.* **4.** of an extreme degree, quantity, or kind: *Winning the contest was such a surprise.* —*pron.* **1.** a person or thing of the same kind or degree as that or those previously mentioned or indicated: *pens, pencils, and such.* **2.** a person or thing mentioned, indicated, or exemplified: *Such was their fate.* —*adv.* to a great degree; so: *such good friends.* [Old English *swylc, swelc, swilc* of the kind mentioned or implied.]

· **as such. a.** as a person or thing of the same or a similar kind as previously mentioned or indicated: *A lawyer, as such, should have a good knowledge of the law.* **b.** in itself; intrinsically: *Success, as such, does not always bring happiness.*

· **such and such.** of indefinite name, location, or the like; some: *The play opened on such and such a day.*

· **such as. a.** of the same or a particular kind or degree: *A person such as that will surely succeed.* **b.** by way of illustration: *dogs, such as dachshunds and poodles.*

such·like (such′līk′) *adj.* of the same or a similar kind. —*pron.* persons or things of such a kind: *magazines, newspapers, and suchlike.*

suck (suk) *v.t.* **1.** to draw (something) into the mouth by creating a partial vacuum with the lips and tongue: *to suck milk through a straw.* **2.** to draw liquid from (something) by applying the mouth: *to suck an orange.* **3.** to hold in the mouth and absorb by the action of the tongue and the muscles of the cheeks: *I sucked a lozenge for my sore throat.* **4.** to draw in or absorb by or as by the use of suction: *The vacuum cleaner sucked the dust up out of the crevices. The plants sucked up all the water.* **5.** to put in the mouth and exert a sucking force on: *to suck one's thumb.* —*v.i.* **1.** to draw by sucking or suction. **2.** to draw milk from a breast or a bottle; suckle. **3.** (of a pump) to draw air instead of water. —*n.* **1.** the act or an instance of sucking. **2.** the sound made when sucking. [Old English *sūcan* to draw liquid with the mouth.]

· **to suck in. a.** to pull in and flatten: *to suck in one's stomach.* **b.** *Slang.* to deceive or cheat.

suck·er (suk′ər) *n.* **1.** a person or thing that sucks. **2.** any of a group of toothless freshwater fish, family Catostomidae, native to North America and Asia, having fleshy, sucking lips on the underside of the head. Length: from 2 inches to 3 feet (5 centimeters to 0.9 meter). **3.** an organ of any of certain animals, such as octopuses, barnacles, or certain parasites, used for sucking or for attaching to something by suction. **4.** a shoot growing from the underground stem or root of a plant. **5.** *Slang.* a person who can easily be deceived, cheated, or imposed upon. **6.** *Informal.* a piece of candy that is licked or held in the mouth and absorbed, such as a lollipop. —*v.i.* (of a plant) to produce suckers. —*v.t.* to remove suckers or young shoots from (corn, tobacco, or other plants).

suck·le (suk′əl) *v.,* **-led, -ling.** —*v.t.* **1.** to give milk to (a person or animal) from a breast, udder, or the like. **2.** to bring up; nurture. —*v.i.* to drink milk from a breast, udder, or the like. [SUCK + -LE.]

suck·ling (suk′ling) *n.* an infant or young animal that is not yet weaned. —*adj.* **1.** young and inexperienced. **2.** not yet weaned.

su·crase (sü′krās) *n.* invertase.

su·cre (sü′krā) *n.* the monetary unit of Ecuador. [From Antonio José de *Sucre*, 1795-1830, South American military leader and liberator.]

su·crose (sü′krōs) *n.* common sugar, a crystalline disaccharide, obtained esp. from sugar beets and sugarcane and used for sweetening foods. Formula: $C_{12}H_{22}O_{11}$ [French *sucre* (see SUGAR) + -OSE².]

suc·tion (suk′shən) *n.* **1.** a force created by a complete or partial vacuum that draws a gas or liquid into a space from which all or part of the air or liquid has been removed. **2.** the act or an instance of drawing a liquid or gas into a space where a partial vacuum has been created. —*adj.* causing, relating to, or done by suction. [Late Latin *sūctiō* a sucking, from Latin *sūctus*, past participle of *sūgere* to suck.]

suction cup, a device that is cup-shaped so that it creates a partial vacuum when it is applied to a surface.

suction stop, click *(n., def. 3).*

suc·to·ri·al (suk tôr′ē əl) *adj. Biology.* relating to, adapted for, or characterized by sucking or suction.

Su·dan grass (sü dan′) sorghum of a variety native to the Sudan, suited to semiarid conditions and cultivated in many places as hay and fodder for livestock.

su·da·to·ri·um (süˈdə tôrˈē əm) *n., pl.* **-to·ri·a** (-tôrˈē ə). a room in which a steam bath or hot-air bath is taken to produce sweating. [Latin *sūdātōrium* a sweating bath, going back to *sūdor* sweat.]

sud·den (sudˈən) *adj.* **1.** done or occurring without warning; unexpected: *The sudden arrival of guests forced us to change our plans.* **2.** done, made, or happening swiftly or abruptly; hasty: *a sudden decision, a sudden stop.* [Middle French *soudain* immediate, quick, going back to Latin *subitāneus* unexpected, hasty.] —**sudˈden·ness,** *n.*

  • **all of a sudden.** without notice; all at once; unexpectedly.

sudden death *Sports.* extra time played to break a tie, the winner being the first person or side to go ahead, as by scoring in hockey or by winning a hole in golf.

sudden infant death syndrome, the sudden death, without known cause or warning symptoms, of an apparently healthy infant, usually occurring during sleep between the ages of one month and four months. Also, **crib death.**

sud·den·ly (sudˈən lē) *adv.* without warning, preparation, or premeditation.

su·dor·if·er·ous (süˈdə rifˈər əs) *adj. Physiology.* secreting or producing sweat: *a sudoriferous gland.*

su·dor·if·ic (süˈdə rifˈik) *adj.* of, relating to, or causing sweat. —*n.* a medicine or remedy that causes sweating. [Modern Latin *sudorificus,* going back to Latin *sūdor* sweat + *facere* to make.]

suds (sudz) *pl. n.* **1.** a frothy mass of bubbles that forms on the top of water containing soap or detergent. **2.** such a frothy mass together with its water. **3.** any foam or froth. **4.** *Slang.* beer. —*v.i.* (of a soap or detergent) to produce suds. —*v.t.* to wash (something) with water containing suds. [Probably from Middle Dutch *sudse* marsh, bog.]

sud·sy (sudˈzē) *adj.,* **-si·er, -si·est.** full of or like suds.

sue (sü) *v.,* **sued, su·ing.** —*v.t.* **1.** to start a suit against in a court of law, esp. in order to obtain a certain amount in damages. **2.** *Archaic.* to pay court to; woo. —*v.i.* **1.** to take legal action: *to sue for damages.* **2.** to appeal or plead (with *for*): *to sue for forgiveness.* [Old French *suir,* form of *sivre* to follow, going back to Latin *sequī* to follow.] —**suˈer,** *n.*

suede (swād) *also,* **suède.** *n.* **1.** a soft leather that has a velvety nap, usually on the flesh side of the skin. **2.** a fabric made with a short nap on one side to resemble this leather. Also *(def. 2),* **suede cloth.** —*adj. also,* **sueded.** of, resembling, or characteristic of suede. [French *Suède* Sweden, as in the phrase *gants de Suède* (leather) gloves of Sweden.]

su·et (süˈit) *n.* the hard fat from around the kidneys and loins of cattle and sheep, used in cooking or to make tallow. [From an unrecorded diminutive of Anglo-Norman *sue, seu* suet, from Latin *sēbum.*] —**suˈet·y,** *adj.*

suf-, form of **sub-** before *f,* as in *suffix, suffuse.*

suf·fer (sufˈər) *v.i.* **1.** to experience or be subject to intense physical, emotional, or mental discomfort or stress: *I suffer from various allergies. The child suffered under the cruel teasing.* **2.** to undergo loss or damage; be hurt: *My schoolwork suffered because of my social activities.* —*v.t.* **1.** to feel or be subject to; undergo: *to suffer acute embarrassment when speaking before a group.* **2.** to allow to do something; permit: *Suffer the little children to come unto me* (Mark 10:14). **3.** to put up with; tolerate; endure: *I cannot suffer rude behavior.* [Latin *sufferre* to undergo, endure.] —**sufˈfer·er,** *n.*

suf·fer·a·ble (sufˈər ə bəl, sufˈrə-) *adj.* capable of being endured, tolerated, or permitted. —**sufˈfer·a·bly,** *adv.*

suf·fer·ance (sufˈər əns, sufˈrəns) *n.* **1.** sanction, consent, or acquiescence given or implied by the absence of intervention or prevention. ➡ usually used in the phrase *on sufferance,* and implying bare tolerance. **2.** *Archaic.* the capacity to undergo suffering; patient endurance; submission.

suf·fer·ing (sufˈər ing, sufˈring) *n.* **1.** the act or an instance of undergoing extreme pain, distress, or hardship. **2.** the condition of a person who suffers.

suf·fice (sə fīsˈ) *v.,* **-ficed, -fic·ing.** —*v.i.* to be sufficient or adequate; be enough: *One jacket will suffice for the weekend. A simple answer will suffice.* —*v.t.* to meet the desires, needs, or requirements of; be enough for; satisfy: *A light lunch will suffice me.* [Latin *sufficere* to provide, be enough.]

suf·fi·cien·cy (sə fishˈən sē) *n., pl.* **-cies. 1.** an adequate amount or quantity. **2.** the state or quality of being adequate or sufficient; adequacy.

suf·fi·cient (sə fishˈənt) *adj.* **1.** as much as is necessary or needed; adequate; enough: *One blanket will provide sufficient warmth.* **2.** *Archaic.* competent; capable. [Latin *sufficiēns,* present

participle of *sufficere* to provide, be enough.] —**suf·fiˈcient·ly,** *adv.* —For Synonyms, see **enough.**

suf·fix (*n.,* sufˈiks; *v.,* sufˈiks, sə fiksˈ) *n.* a word element added as an inflection at the end of a word to form another word of different meaning or function, such as *-ness* in bad*ness* and *-ly* in good*ly.* —*v.t.* to add or attach at the end, esp. as a suffix. [Modern Latin *suffixum,* from Latin *suffixum,* neuter past participle of *suffigere* to fasten to or beneath.]

suf·fix·al (sufˈik səl) *adj.* of, relating to, or characteristic of a suffix or suffixes.

suf·fo·cate (sufˈə kātˈ) *v.,* **-cat·ed, -cat·ing.** —*v.t.* **1.** to kill by preventing breathing; stifle. **2.** to interrupt or impede the breathing of: *The crowded room was suffocating us.* **3.** to smother or suppress by or as by depriving of oxygen; extinguish: *to suffocate a fire.* —*v.i.* **1.** to die from an interrupted or insufficient supply of air. **2.** to experience difficulty in breathing; choke. [Latin *suffocātus,* past participle of *suffocāre* to choke.] —**sufˈfo·cat·ing·ly,** *adv.* —**sufˈfo·caˈtion,** *n.* —**sufˈfo·caˈtive,** *adj.*

suf·fra·gan (sufˈrə gən) *n.* **1.** in the Anglican Church, a bishop who assists another bishop but who does not have the right of succession. **2.** any bishop subordinate to an archbishop or metropolitan. —*adj.* of, relating to, or acting as a suffragan. [Old French *suffragant* subordinate, bishop subordinate to an archbishop, going back to Latin *suffrāgārī* to vote for, support.]

suf·frage (sufˈrij) *n.* **1.** the right or privilege of voting, esp. the exercise of voting power in political affairs; franchise. **2.** the act of casting a vote; voting. **3.** a vote, esp. in favor of an issue or a candidate for office. **4.** a short prayer or petition. [Latin *suffrāgium* a vote, the right of voting.]

suf·fra·gette (sufˈrə jetˈ) *n.* a woman who militantly advocates the right of women to vote and hold office.

suf·fra·gist (sufˈrə jist) *n.* a person who favors extending the right to vote, esp. to women.

suf·fuse (sə fūzˈ) *v.t.,* **-fused, -fus·ing.** to spread through or over, as with a light, color, or emotion. ➡ usually used in the passive: *a room suffused with sunshine, eyes suffused with tears, a face suffused with happiness.* [Latin *suffūsus,* past participle of *suffundere* to pour beneath, fill, tinge.] —**suf·fuˈsion,** *n.*

Su·fi (süˈfē) *n.* a member of a mystical Islamic sect. [Arabic *sūfī* literally, man of wool (probably a reference to the woolen garments of the Sufis), from *sūf* wool.] —**Suˈfism** (süˈfiz əm), *n.*

sug-, form of **sub-** before *g,* as in *suggest.*

sug·ar (shoogˈər) *n.* **1.** any of several white or brown crystalline forms of the organic compound sucrose, obtained mainly from sugarcane and sugar beets and used esp. for sweetening foods. Formula: $C_{12}H_{22}O_{11}$ **2.** any of a class of water-soluble, sweet-tasting carbohydrates having a relatively simple molecular structure, including sucrose, glucose, fructose, maltose, and lactose. —*v.t.* **1.** to mix, cover, sprinkle, or sweeten with sugar: *to sugar grapefruit.* **2.** sugarcoat. —*v.i.* **1.** to form sugar. **2.** to boil down maple syrup to make maple sugar (usually with *off*). [Old French *sucre* sweet substance extracted from various plants, through Italian, Arabic, and Persian, from Sanskrit *śharkarā* gravel, grit, granule, candied sugar.]

sugar beet, a leafy plant, *Beta vulgaris crassa,* whose long, thick, yellow or white roots are a major source of sugar.

sug·ar·bush (shoogˈər booshˈ) *n.* a grove of sugar maples.

sug·ar·cane (shoogˈər kānˈ) *n.* a high-growing plant, *Saccharum officinarum,* of the grass family, containing sweet, dark gray juice and having jointed stems, or canes, and downy white flowers, grown in warm climates as a source of sugar.

sug·ar·coat (shoogˈər kōtˈ) *v.t.* **1.** to cover with sugar: *to sugarcoat a cookie.* **2.** to disguise or soften (something unpleasant) in order to make it more pleasant or acceptable: *to sugarcoat bad news.*

sugar corn, sweet corn.

sugar daddy *Slang.* a well-to-do, usually older man who gives expensive gifts or money to a young woman in return for her sexual favors and companionship.

sug·ar-free (shoogˈər frēˈ) *adj.* containing no sugar: *a sugar-free soft drink.*

sug·ar·loaf (shoogˈər lōfˈ) *n., pl.* **-loaves** (-lōvzˈ). **1.** a conical hard mass of refined sugar. **2.** something having the shape of a sugarloaf, such as a conical hill. —*adj.* having the shape of a sugarloaf.

a	at	e	end	o	hot	u	up	hw	white	⎰	about
ā	ape	ē	me	ō	old	ū	use	ng	song		taken
ä	far	i	it	ô	fork	ü	rule	th	thin		pencil
âr	care	ī	ice	oi	oil	u̇	pull	th	this		lemon
		îr	pierce	ou	out	ûr	turn	zh	measure	⎱	circus

1205

sugar maple, a maple tree of eastern North America, *Acer saccharum,* whose sap is the major source of maple syrup.

sugar pine, a tall pine, *Pinus lambertiana,* found from Oregon to lower California, having deep green needles and large cones.

sug·ar·plum (shŭg′ər-plum′) *n.* a small, usually round piece of candy; bonbon.

sug·ar·y (shŭg′ə rē) *adj.* **1.** of, consisting of, or like sugar. **2.** excessively sweet or insincerely flattering, esp. in order to disguise deceit; cloying: *a sugary smile, a sugary compliment.* —**sug′ar·i·ness,** *n.*

sugar maple

sug·gest (səg jest′, sə jest′) *v.t.* **1.** to offer or mention for consideration or action: *I suggest we meet again at a later date.* **2.** to bring or call to mind, as through association or connection: *This perfume suggests roses.* **3.** to express or indicate indirectly; intimate; hint: *The heavy sigh suggested sadness.* **4.** to provide a motive for; prompt: *The committee's report would suggest a further investigation.* [Latin *suggestus,* past participle of *suggerere* to carry under, supply, advise.]

sug·gest·i·ble (səg jes′tə bəl, sə jes′-) *adj.* **1.** highly susceptible to suggestion; easily influenced or manipulated. **2.** able to be suggested. —**sug·ges′ti·bil′i·ty,** *n.*

sug·ges·tion (səg jes′chən, sə jes′-) *n.* **1.** the act or an instance of suggesting: *We left at their suggestion.* **2.** something that is suggested: *The suggestion was acceptable to everyone.* **3.** the process by which something is brought to mind through an association or connection with something else: *The cold wind carried a suggestion of the winter to come.* **4.** a very small indication; trace; hint: *the slightest suggestion of garlic in a sauce.*

sug·ges·tive (səg jes′tiv, sə jes′-) *adj.* **1.** giving a suggestion or hint (with *of*): *The architecture of the building is suggestive of the Gothic style.* **2.** tending to bring to mind ideas or courses of action; full of suggestions. **3.** tending to suggest something improper or indecent; provocative. —**sug·ges′tive·ness,** *n.*

su·i·cid·al (sū′ə sī′dəl) *adj.* **1.** of, relating to, or causing suicide: *suicidal tendencies.* **2.** apt to cause disaster to oneself; dangerously rash; ruinous: *a suicidal business policy.* **3.** having a definite inclination to suicide: *a suicidal person.* —**su′i·cid′al·ly,** *adv.*

su·i·cide¹ (sū′ə sīd′) *n.* **1.** the act or an instance of intentionally taking one's own life. **2.** the destruction of one's own interests or aims, as in business or politics: *The company committed financial suicide.* [Modern Latin *suicidium,* from Latin *suī* of oneself + *-cidium.* See -CIDE¹.]

su·i·cide² (sū′ə sīd′) *n.* a person who has intentionally taken his or her own life. [Modern Latin *suicidium,* from Latin *suī* of oneself + *-cīda.* See -CIDE².]

su·i ge·ne·ris (sū′ī jen′ər is, sū′ē) *Latin.* of his, her, its, or their own kind; singular; unique.

suit (sūt) *n.* **1.** a set of garments designed to be worn together, esp. a jacket with a skirt or matching pair of trousers. **2.** an act, process, or proceeding in a court of law for the redress of a wrong or the enforcement of a claim. **3.** any of the four sets of playing cards in a deck; spades, hearts, diamonds, or clubs. **4.** the act or an instance of suing or petitioning, esp. for a woman's hand in marriage. **5.** a set of similar or matched things used or intended to be used together. —*v.t.* **1.** to meet the requirements of; be correct or adapted to: *The house suits our needs.* **2.** to make right for; adapt: *The orchestra suited the music to the occasion.* **3.** to be flattering to: *That color suits you well.* **4.** to be agreeable to; please; satisfy: *to suit one's tastes.* **5.** *Archaic.* to furnish with clothes; dress. —*v.i.* to be suitable, fitting, or convenient. [Old French *suite* pursuit, retinue, going back to Latin *sequī* to follow.]
 • **to follow suit. a.** to play a card of the same suit as the card led. **b.** to do the same thing as another.
 • **to suit oneself.** to act in the manner one wishes.
 • **to suit up.** to put on a uniform or other special outfit: *The astronauts suited up.*

suit·a·ble (sū′tə bəl) *adj.* that suits a particular purpose, object, or occasion; proper. —**suit′a·bil′i·ty, suit′a·ble·ness,** *n.* —**suit′a·bly,** *adv.* —For Synonyms, see **fit¹.**

suit·case (sūt′kās′) *n.* a flat, usually rectangular bag used for carrying clothes and other articles when traveling; valise.

suite (swēt; *def. 2, also,* sūt) *n.* **1.** a group of connected rooms considered as a unit, as in a hotel. **2.** a set of matching furniture: *a living room suite.* **3.** any set of similar or matched things, used or intended to be used together. **4.** a group of attendants or followers; retinue. **5.** *Music.* **a.** an early form of instrumental composition consisting of a series of dance tunes in the same or related key. **b.** an instrumental composition consisting of a series of short movements, often adapted from a longer work. [French *suite* retinue, set, modification of Old French *suite* pursuit, retinue. See SUIT.]

suit·ing (sū′ting) *n.* fabric used chiefly for making suits.

suit·or (sū′tər) *n.* **1.** a man who courts or woos a woman. **2.** a person who institutes a lawsuit. **3.** a person who pleads or petitions; suppliant.

su·ki·ya·ki (sū′kē yä′kē, skē yä′-) *n.* a Japanese dish consisting chiefly of thin strips of meat and vegetables sautéed quickly, usually at the dining table. [Japanese *sukiyaki* slices of beef.]

Suk·koth (sŭk′əs; *Hebrew* sü kôt′) *also,* **Suk·kot, Suc·coth, Suc·cot.** *n.* a Jewish holiday that begins five days after Yom Kippur, giving thanks for the harvest and commemorating the wandering of the Hebrews in the wilderness after the Exodus from Egypt. [Hebrew *sukkōth* booths, tabernacles; referring to the temporary shelters used by the Hebrews while wandering in the wilderness.]

sul·cus (sul′kəs) *n., pl.* **-ci** (-sī). any of various anatomical furrows, grooves, or linear depressions, as in a bone or on the surface of the cerebrum. [Latin *sulcus* furrow.]

sul·fa·di·a·zine (sul′fə dī′ə zēn′, -zin) *n.* a sulfa drug derived from sulfanilamide, used in treating urinary tract infections, malaria, and meningitis. Formula: $C_{10}H_{10}N_4O_2S$

sul·fa drug (sul′fə) any of a group of synthetic drugs used, often with antibiotics, to treat many infectious diseases such as pneumonia, meningitis, and cholera. Sulfa drugs do not kill bacteria but inhibit their growth. Also, **sulfa.**

sul·fa·nil·a·mide (sul′fə nil′ə mīd′, -mid) *n.* an early sulfa drug, now used esp. in the manufacture of other, less toxic sulfa drugs.

sul·fa·pyr·i·dine (sul′fə pîr′ə dēn′, -din) *n.* a sulfa drug now used chiefly to treat certain skin inflammations. Formula: $C_{11}H_{11}N_3O_2S$

sul·fate (sul′fāt) *also,* **sulphate.** *n.* a salt of sulfuric acid. [Modern Latin *sulphatum,* from Latin *sulphur, sulfur* sulfur.]

sul·fa·thi·a·zole (sul′fə thī′ə zōl′) *n.* a sulfa drug, formerly used esp. in treating pneumonia.

sul·fide (sul′fīd) *also,* **sulphide.** *n.* a compound resulting when sulfur is heated with another element. [SULF(UR) + -IDE.]

sul·fite (sul′fīt) *also,* **sulphite.** *n.* a salt of sulfurous acid. [SULF(UR) + -ITE².]

sul·fon·a·mide (sul fon′ə mīd′) *n.* **1.** any of a variety of organic sulfur compounds containing the group $SO_2·NH_2$. **2.** sulfa drug.

sul·fur (sul′fər) *also,* **sulphur.** *n.* a yellow, nonmetallic element with three common allotropic forms, two crystalline and one amorphous. Sulfur is abundant in nature and is used to make sulfuric acid, in the vulcanization of rubber, and to manufacture fungicides, fertilizers, and gunpowder. Symbol: **S** For tables, see **element.** [Latin *sulphur, sulfur.*]

sul·fu·rate (sul′fə rāt′, -fyə-) *v.t.* **-rat·ed, -rat·ing.** to combine or treat (something) with sulfur or a sulfur compound. Also, **sulfurize.**

sulfur dioxide, a colorless gas with a sharp, irritating odor, used to make sulfuric acid and as a bleaching agent, refrigerant, and food preservative. Formula: SO_2

sul·fu·re·ous (sul fyûr′ē əs) *adj.* sulfurous.

sul·fu·ric (sul fyûr′ik) *also,* **sulphuric.** *adj.* **1.** of or relating to sulfur. **2.** containing sulfur in its higher valence.

sulfuric acid, a strong, corrosive, oily liquid whose powerful dehydrating and oxidizing properties make it useful in the manufacture of a wide variety of chemical products as well as in many industrial processes. Formula: H_2SO_4 Also, **oil of vitriol.**

sul·fu·rize (sul′fə rīz′, -fyə-) *v.t.,* **-rized, -riz·ing.** sulfurate.

sul·fur·ous (sul′fər əs, sul fyûr′-) *also,* **sulphurous.** *adj.* **1.** of or relating to sulfur. **2.** containing sulfur in its lower valence. **3.** like burning sulfur, as in odor. **4.** of or resembling the fires of hell; infernal. Also, **sulfureous.**

sulfurous acid, a colorless, unstable solution of sulfur dioxide in water, used esp. in synthesizing organic compounds and as a food preservative. Formula: H_2SO_3

sulfur trioxide, a colorless, solid compound used as an intermediate in the preparation of sulfuric acid. An increasingly common atmospheric pollutant produced by combustion of fossil fuels, it is one of the reactants responsible for acid rain. Formula: SO_3

sul·fur·y (sul′fə rē) *adj.* of or resembling sulfur.

sulk (sulk) *v.i.* to be silent or withdrawn as a sign of bad humor

or resentfulness. —*n.* **1.** the state of sulking: *to be in a sulk.* **2. the sulks.** a sulking mood: *to have the sulks.* [Possibly from SULKY.]

sulk·y (sul′kē) *adj.,* **sulk·i·er, sulk·i·est. 1.** obstinately silent or withdrawn as a display of bad humor or resentfulness. **2.** gloomy or dismal: *sulky weather.* —*n., pl.* **sulk·ies.** a light two-wheeled, one-horse carriage seating one passenger, used esp. for racing. [Possibly from obsolete *sulke* slow (possibly going back to Old English *āsolcen* slothful) + -Y[1].] —**sulk′i·ly,** *adv.* —**sulk′i·ness,** *n.*

sul·len (sul′ən) *adj.* **1.** obstinately withdrawn or gloomy because of bad humor; sulky; morose. **2.** dismal or depressing: *low, sullen clouds.* [Old French *solain* solitary, going back to Latin *sōlus* alone.] —**sul′len·ly,** *adv.* —**sul′len·ness,** *n.*

sul·ly (sul′ē) *v.t.,* **-lied, -ly·ing. 1.** to stain the honor or purity of; defile or disgrace: *The scandal sullied the family name.* **2.** to stain the cleanness of; soil. —*n., pl.* **-lies.** *Archaic.* something that sullies; stain; blemish. [French *souiller* to soil, dirty. See SOIL[2].]

sul·phate (sul′fāt) sulfate.

sul·phide (sul′fīd) sulfide.

sul·phite (sul′fīt) sulfite.

sul·phur (sul′fər) *n.* **1.** sulfur. **2.** any of several yellow or orange butterflies, family Pieridae.

sul·phu·ric (sul fyŭr′ik) sulfuric.

sul·phur·ous (sul′fər əs, sul fyŭr′əs) sulfurous.

sul·tan (sul′tən) *n.* in a Muslim country, a sovereign or ruling monarch. Turkey and Morocco were formerly ruled by sultans. [French *sultan,* from Arabic *sultān* power, ruler, from Aramaic *shultānā* power.]

sul·tan·a (sul tan′ə, -tä′nə) *n.* **1.** a female member of a sultan's court, such as a wife, mother, or sister of a sultan. **2.** the Thompson seedless grape, used to make raisins. [Italian *sultana,* feminine of *sultano* sultan, from Arabic *sultān.* See SULTAN.]

sul·tan·ate (sul′tə nāt′) *n.* **1.** a country or area under a sultan's rule. **2.** the office or reign of a sultan.

sul·try (sul′trē) *adj.,* **-tri·er, -tri·est. 1.** oppressively hot and humid; sweltering: *the sultry tropics.* **2.** producing or emitting excessive heat. **3.** suggesting, expressing, or eliciting the heat of passion; sensual. [From obsolete *sulter* to be very hot, form of SWELTER.] —**sul′tri·ness,** *n.*

Su·lu (sū′lü) *n.* **1.** a member of the chief tribe of Moros, living in the Sulu Archipelago. **2.** the language of the Malay Moro tribes of the Sulu Archipelago, belonging to the Austronesian language family.

sum (sum) *n.* **1.** a result obtained from addition. **2.** the whole quantity; entirety: *the sum of all our efforts.* **3.** an amount of money: *Untold sums were spent on repairs.* **4.** *Informal.* an arithmetic problem, esp. a list of numbers to be added. **5.** summary; substance; gist: *That's the sum of what happened.* —*v.,* **summed, sum·ming.** —*v.t.* **1.** to find the numerical sum of; total (often with *up*): *to sum up a column of numbers.* **2.** to give a summary of (with *up*): *to sum up a meeting.* —*v.i.* to come to a total; amount: *Our business losses summed into the hundreds.* [Latin *summa* top, summit, amount, total; originally feminine of *summus* highest; referring to the Roman practice of reckoning upward and placing the sum at the top.]

sum-, form of sub- before *m,* as in *summon.*

su·mac (sū′mak, shū′-) *also,* **su·mach.** *n.* **1.** any of a large group of trees, shrubs, and vines, genus *Rhus,* of the cashew family, having milky or resinous juice that is capable of causing a severe itching skin rash. Poison sumac and poison ivy are sumacs. **2.** the dried leaves of some of these trees, shrubs, or vines, esp. *R. coriaria,* which yield tannin, used in processing leather. [Old French *sumac* sumac tree, from Arabic *summāq,* probably from Syriac *summāq* red.]

Su·me·ri·an (sū mîr′ē ən, -mer′-) *adj.* of, relating to, or characteristic of Sumer or its people, language, or culture. —*n.* **1.** a member of an ancient people whose civilization existed in Sumer from about 4000 B.C. to 2000 B.C. **2.** the extinct language of these people, of unknown origin, preserved in cuneiform inscriptions.

sum·ma cum lau·de (sŭm′ə kŭm lou′dē, sum′ə kum lô′də) with highest praise. ➡ used to signify graduation with highest honors from a college or university. [Modern Latin *summa cum laude.*]

sum·ma·rize (sum′ə rīz′) *v.t.,* **-rized, -riz·ing.** to state briefly or succinctly; make a summary of; sum up. —**sum′mar·ist,** *n.,* **sum′ma·riz′er,** *n.* —**sum′ma·ri·za′tion,** *n.*

sum·ma·ry (sum′ə rē) *n., pl.* **-ries.** a condensed statement or brief account containing the main points of something: *The theater program had a summary of the play.* —*adj.* **1.** containing the main points; concise; brief: *to give a summary statement of one's job experience.* **2.** performed rapidly without hesitation or formality: *a summary procedure, a summary dismissal.* [Latin *sum-*

mārium abstract, epitome, from *summa* amount, principal part, total.] —**sum·mar·i·ly** (sə mer′ə lē, sum′ər ə-), *adv.*

sum·ma·tion (sə mā′shən) *n.* **1.** the act or process of finding the total; addition. **2.** a result of addition; total. **3.** the final part of an argument in which the facts are reviewed and a conclusion presented, as in a trial.

sum·mer (sum′ər) *n.* the season of the year coming between spring and autumn. In the Northern Hemisphere it extends from about June 21 to about September 22. —*adj.* of, like, characteristic of, or occurring in summer: *summer vacation.* —*v.i.* to pass the summer: *We summered in the south of France.* —*v.t.* to keep or maintain during the summer: *The farmer summers the livestock in the high pasture.* [Old English *sumor* this season.]

sum·mer·house (sum′ər hous′) *n., pl.* **-hous·es** (-hou′ziz). a small, roofed, often rustic structure situated in a garden or park, used as a shady retreat in summer.

sum·mer·sault (sum′ər sôlt′) somersault.

summer school, a school session held in summertime for students to improve their skills or take extra or remedial courses.

summer solstice, see solstice *(def. 1).*

summer squash, any of a group of squash having relatively thin skins and light-colored flesh, grown in the summer and eaten before ripening. ➡ distinguished from **winter squash.**

sum·mer·time (sum′ər tīm′) *n.* the summer season.

sum·mer·y (sum′ə rē) *adj.* characteristic of or suitable for summer.

sum·mit (sum′it) *n.* **1.** the highest part or degree; acme. **2.** the highest level, as of government or political authority: *to have a meeting at the summit.* —*adj.* of, relating to, or concerned with the highest level of government or political authority, esp. heads of state: *a summit conference on nuclear disarmament.* [Old French *somete* the top, highest point, diminutive of *som* the top (esp. of a hill), from Latin *summum* the top, highest place.] —For Synonyms, see peak.

sum·mon (sum′ən) *v.t.* **1.** to send for or request the presence of, esp. with authority: *to summon a porter.* **2.** to order to appear in court by means of a summons; issue a summons to. **3.** to cause to assemble; convene; convoke: *to summon a council.* **4.** to request or command to do some specified act: *to summon someone to wait, to summon a garrison to surrender.* **5.** to bring or urge to action; rouse (often with *up*): *to summon up one's courage, to summon all one's strength.* [Latin *summonēre* to remind, suggest, warn.] —**sum′mon·er,** *n.* —For Synonyms, see call.

sum·mons (sum′ənz) *n., pl.* **-mons·es. 1.** a notice, signal, or command to appear somewhere or to do something. **2.** *Law.* a document notifying someone to appear in court. [Old French *somonse* act of calling together, warning, from *somondre* to remind, warn, bid, going back to Latin *summonēre* to remind, warn, suggest.]

sum·mum bo·num (sum′əm bō′nəm) *Latin.* the highest or supreme good.

su·mo wrestling (sū′mō) a Japanese form of wrestling in which a contestant loses a match if he steps out of a ring or is forced to touch the mat with any part of his body except the feet. [Japanese *sumô* this style of wrestling, from *sumafu* to wrestle.]

sump (sump) *n.* **1.** a pit or reservoir for collecting liquid, such as water, oil, or sewage. **2.** a drainage pit or well at the bottom of a mine shaft. [Middle Dutch *sump* pool, swamp.]

sump·ter (sump′tər) *n.* an animal, such as a horse or mule, for carrying loads; pack animal. [Old French *sommetier* driver of a pack animal, going back to Late Latin *sagma* packsaddle, from Greek *sagma.*]

sump·tu·ar·y (sump′chü er′ē) *adj.* **1.** relating to or concerned with regulating expenditures, esp. to prevent extravagance. **2.** concerned with or designed to regulate personal behavior on

a	at	e	end	o	hot	u	up	hw	white	⎧	about
ā	ape	ē	me	ō	old	ū	use	ng	song	⎪	taken
ä	far	i	it	ô	fork	ü	rule	th	thin	ə	pencil
âr	care	ī	ice	oi	oil	u̇	pull	th	this	⎪	lemon
		îr	pierce	ou	out	ûr	turn	zh	measure	⎩	circus

moral or religious grounds. [Latin *sūmptuārius* relating to expenses, from *sumptus* expense.]

sump·tu·ous (sump′chü əs) *adj.* involving or produced at great expense; costly and magnificent; lavish: *a sumptuous apartment, a sumptuous dinner.* [Latin *sūmptuōsus,* from *sūmptus* expense.] —**sump′tu·ous·ly,** *adv.* —**sump′tu·ous·ness,** *n.*

Sum·ter, Fort (sum′tər) a fort in the harbor of Charleston, South Carolina. On April 12, 1861, the American Civil War began when Confederate forces attacked this fort.

sum total 1. a whole numerical quantity or amount: *This is the sum total of the week's receipts from all sources.* **2.** that which includes everything: *That is the sum total of what I know about the project.*

sun (sun) *n.* **1.** the star that is the central body of the solar system, around which the earth and other planets revolve and from which they receive light and heat. The sun has a mean distance from earth of about 93 million miles (150 million kilometers), a diameter of about 865,000 miles (1.4 million kilometers), and a mass of about 330,000 times that of the earth. **2.** light and heat from the sun; sunshine: *Too much sun can produce a painful burn.* **3.** any star that is the center of a planetary system. —*v.,* sunned, sun·ning. —*v.t.* **1.** to expose to the rays of the sun. **2.** to warm or dry in the sun. —*v.i.* to expose oneself to the rays of the sun: *We sunned on the terrace.* [Old English *sunne* the brightest of the heavenly bodies as seen from earth.]
  • **a place in the sun.** a prominent position or condition.
  • **under the sun.** on earth; anywhere: *The immigrants' letters described the United States as the greatest country under the sun.*

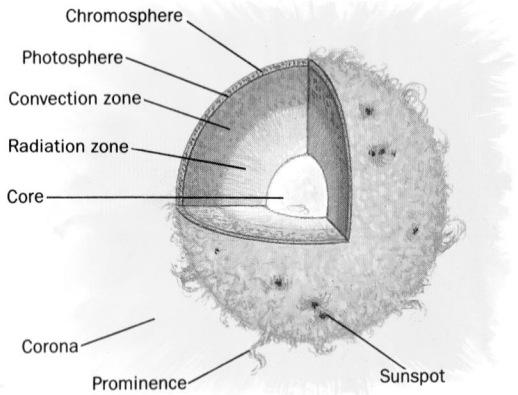

Chromosphere
Photosphere
Convection zone
Radiation zone
Core
Corona
Prominence
Sunspot

structure of the **sun**

Sun., Sunday.

sun·bath (sun′bath′) *n., pl.* **-baths** (-bathz′, -baths′). exposure of the body to the rays of the sun or a sunlamp.

sun·bathe (sun′bāth′) *v.i.,* -bathed, -bath·ing. to bask in the sun; take a sunbath. —**sun′bath′er,** *n.*

sun·beam (sun′bēm′) *n.* a beam of sunlight.

Sun·belt (sun′belt′) *also,* **Sun Belt.** *n.* the southern and southwestern United States.

sun·bird (sun′bûrd′) *n.* any of several small songbirds, family Nectariniidae, found in tropical regions of Africa, Asia, and Australia and having brightly colored, iridescent plumage. Length: to 8 inches (20 centimeters).

sun·block (sun′blok′) *n.* a substance applied to the skin to prevent sunburn by filtering out the sun's ultraviolet rays.

sun·bon·net (sun′bon′it) *n.* a woman's bonnet that has a broad brim to protect the face and a flap to protect the neck.

sun·burn (sun′bûrn′) *n.* an inflammation of the skin caused by overexposure to sunlight or a sunlamp. —*v.,* -burned *or* -burnt, -burn·ing. —*v.t.* to overexpose to the sun or a sunlamp; affect with sunburn: *to sunburn one's back.* —*v.i.* to become affected with sunburn: *Some people sunburn easily.*

sun·burst (sun′bûrst′) *n.* **1.** a sudden burst of sunlight, as through a break in the clouds. **2.** an ornamental design or object, such as a piece of jewelry, with a central disk and rays emanating from it.

sun·dae (sun′dē, -dā) *n.* ice cream served with a topping, such as syrup, nuts, fruit, or whipped cream. [Possibly modification of SUNDAY; supposedly because it was originally sold only on Sunday as a special treat since it was more expensive than plain ice cream.]

Sun·day (sun′dē, -dā) *n.* the first day of the week and the Sabbath for most Christians. [Old English *sunnandæg* literally, sun's day, translation of Latin *diēs sōlis.*]

Sunday best *Informal.* a person's best clothes.

Sunday school 1. a school usually affiliated with a church and held on Sunday for religious instruction. **2.** the pupils and teachers of such a school.

sun deck, any area used for sunbathing, such as a terrace or ship's deck.

sun·der (sun′dər) *v.t.* to separate or divide; sever: *Distance sundered the two friends. War sundered the nation.* —*v.i.* to become divided; separate. [Old English *sundrian.*] —**sun′der·a·ble,** *adj.* —**sun′der·ance,** *n.*

sun·dew (sun′dü′, -dū′) *n.* any of a group of plants, genus *Drosera,* having leaves covered with sticky, hairlike structures that trap insects.

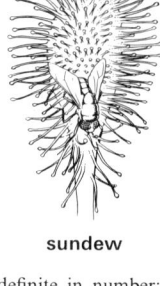

sun·di·al (sun′dī′əl, -dīl′) *n.* a device that indicates the time of the day by the position and length of the shadow cast by a gnomon on a flat, usually round surface, or dial, marked with numbers.

sun·dog (sun′dôg′) *n.* **1.** parhelion. **2.** a small or incomplete rainbow.

sun·down (sun′doun′) *n.* sunset.

sun·dries (sun′drēz) *pl. n.* miscellaneous small items.

sundew

sun·dry (sun′drē) *adj.* more than one; indefinite in number; several; various: *sundry persons, sundry parts.* [Old English *syndrig* separate.]

sun·fast (sun′fast′) *adj.* that will not fade when exposed to sunlight, as a fabric or color.

sun·fish (sun′fish′) *n., pl.* **-fish** *or* **-fish·es. 1.** any of several small freshwater fish, family Centrarchidae, found in North America. Length: 1-15 inches (2.5-38 centimeters). **2.** any of a group of large ocean fish, family Molidae, having a flattened, oval body and weighing up to 2,000 pounds (907 kilograms).

sun·flow·er (sun′flou′ər) *n.* **1.** the large flower of any of several tall plants, genus *Helianthus,* of the composite family, having petallike rays surrounding a yellowish or purplish brown disk. **2.** the plant bearing such a flower, the seeds of which are edible and used as a source of oil.

sung (sung) a past tense and the past participle of **sing.**

Sung (sùng) *n.* the Chinese dynasty that ruled from A.D. 960 to 1279, a period noted for high artistic achievement, esp. in painting and ceramics.

sun·glass·es (sun′glas′iz) *pl. n.* eyeglasses having shaded or tinted lenses to protect the eyes from the sun's glare.

sun god, any god identified with the sun, such as Apollo or Ra.

sunk (sungk) a past tense and a past participle of **sink.**

sunk·en (sung′kən) *v.* a past participle of **sink.** —*adj.* **1.** having sunk below the surface of the water or ground: *sunken treasure, sunken rock.* **2.** situated below the surrounding area: *a sunken living room.* **3.** abnormally depressed; hollow: *sunken cheeks.*

sun·lamp (sun′lamp′) *n.* a lamp that gives off ultraviolet radiation, used for tanning the skin.

sun·less (sun′lis) *adj.* without sunlight; dark or gloomy.

sun·light (sun′līt′) *n.* the light of the sun.

sun·lit (sun′lit′) *adj.* lighted by the sun: *a cheery, sunlit room.*

Sun·ni (sùn′ē) *n., pl.* **-ni. 1.** the larger of the two principal sects of Islam. It regards the traditional sayings and practices of Muhammad as part of Muslim law and considers the first four caliphs as the true successors of Muhammad. **2.** a member or follower of this sect. Also *(def. 2),* **Sunnite.** —*adj.* of or relating to this sect. —**Sun′nism,** *n.*

Sun·nite (sùn′īt) *n.* Sunni *(def. 2).* —*adj.* of or relating to the Sunni sect of Islam.

sun·ny (sun′ē) *adj.,* -ni·er, -ni·est. **1.** full of or warmed by sunlight: *a sunny room.* **2.** cheerful; happy; bright: *a sunny disposition, a sunny smile.* —**sun′ni·ly,** *adv.* —**sun′ni·ness,** *n.*

sun parlor, a room or porch with glass walls or large windows for admitting sunlight. Also, **sun porch, sunroom.**

sun·rise (sun′rīz′) *n.* **1.** the apparent rising of the sun above the horizon at the beginning of the day. **2.** the time when the sun rises: *Farmers begin their chores before sunrise.* Also, **sunup.**

sun·roof (sun′rüf′, -rùf′) *n.* a section in the roof of an automobile that can be slid back or lifted up to admit light and air.

sun·set (sun′set′) *n.* **1.** the apparent descent of the sun below the horizon at the end of the day. **2.** the time when the sun sets. Also, **sundown.**

sun·shade (sun′shād′) *n.* something used to provide protection from the sun, such as an awning, parasol, or broad hat.

sun·shine (sun′shīn′) *n.* **1.** the shining of the sun; direct sunlight. **2.** cheerfulness; happiness; brightness. —**sun′shin′y,** *adj.*

sun·spot (sun′spot′) *n.* one of the groups of dark spots that appear periodically on the surface of the sun, giving rise to magnetic storms in the earth's atmosphere. For illustration, see **sun.**

sun·stroke (sun′strōk′) *n.* heatstroke brought on by overexposure to solar radiation.

sun·struck (sun′struk′) *adj.* suffering from sunstroke.

sun·tan (sun′tan′) *n.* a brown color of the skin resulting from exposure to sunlight or a sunlamp; tan. —**sun′tanned′,** *adj.*

sun·up (sun′up′) *n.* sunrise.

sun·ward (sun′wərd) *adv. also,* **sun·wards.** toward the sun. —*adj.* directed toward or facing the sun.

sup¹ (sup) *v.i.,* **supped, sup·ping.** to eat the evening meal; have supper. [Old French *super;* of Germanic origin.]

sup² (sup) *v.t.,* **supped, sup·ping.** to take (liquid) in small quantities; sip, as from a cup or spoon. —*n.* a sip of a liquid. [Old English *sūpan* to take liquid in small quantities.]

sup. 1. superior. **2.** superlative. **3.** supine. **4.** supplement. **5.** supplementary. **6.** supra.

su·per (sū′pər) *n.* **1.** *Informal.* a superintendent in an apartment house. **2.** *Informal.* a performer having a minor, nonspeaking part; supernumerary; extra. **3.** the section of a beekeeper's hive in which the honey is stored. For illustration, see **hive.** —*adj. Slang.* very good; first-rate; excellent.

super- *prefix* **1.** over; above: *superstructure, supersede.* **2.** higher or greater; superior: *superfamily, superpower.* **3.** to an excessive extent or degree: *superfine, supersensitive.* [Latin *super* over, above, beyond.]

su·per·a·ble (sū′pər ə bəl) *adj.* capable of being overcome or conquered; surmountable. [Latin *superābilis,* from *superāre* to overcome, from *super* over.] —**su′per·a·bly,** *adv.*

su·per·a·bound (sū′pər ə bound′) *v.i.* to abound greatly or excessively: *The stream superabounds in trout.* [Late Latin *superabundāre.* See SUPERABUNDANT.]

su·per·a·bun·dant (sū′pər ə bun′dənt) *adj.* being more than is necessary or desirable; too abundant; excessive. [Late Latin *superabundāns,* present participle of *superabundāre* to be very abundant, from Latin *super* over, above + *abundāre* to overflow. See ABOUND.] —**su′per·a·bun′dance,** *n.* —**su′per·a·bun′dant·ly,** *adv.*

su·per·add (sū′pər ad′) *v.t.* to add over and above. [Latin *superaddere.*] —**su′per·ad·di′tion,** *n.*

su·per·an·nu·ate (sū′pər an′ū āt′) *v.,* **-at·ed, -at·ing.** —*v.t.* **1.** to retire (an employee) with a pension because of age or infirmity. **2.** to set aside as too old or obsolete. —*v.i.* to become too old or obsolete. [From SUPERANNUATED.]

su·per·an·nu·at·ed (sū′pər an′ū ā′tid) *adj.* **1.** retired from service with a pension because of age or infirmity. **2.** too old for use or work. **3.** out-of-date; obsolete. [Modification (influenced by ANNUAL) of Medieval Latin *superannuatus* more than a year old (from Latin *super* above, beyond + *annus* year) + -ED².] —**su′per·an′nu·a′tion,** *n.*

su·perb (sū pûrb′, sů-) *adj.* **1.** of superior quality; very fine; first-rate: *a superb performance.* **2.** having nobility or grandeur; magnificent; majestic: *a superb building.* **3.** sumptuous; elegant; rich: *superb jewels.* [Latin *superbus* proud, superior.] —**su·perb′ly,** *adv.* —**su·perb′ness,** *n.*

su·per·car·go (sū′pər kär′gō) *n., pl.* **-goes** or **-gos.** an officer on board a merchant ship who is in charge of the cargo and the commercial transactions of the voyage. [Modification of earlier *supracargo,* from Spanish *sobrecargo,* from *sobre* over, above (from Latin *super*) + *cargo* load. See CARGO.]

su·per·charge (sū′pər chärj′) *v.t.,* **-charged, -charg·ing.** to increase the power of (an engine) with or as with a supercharger.

su·per·charg·er (sū′pər chär′jər) *n.* a device for increasing the power of an internal-combustion engine by compressing air or a mixture of fuel and air and forcing it into the cylinder at a pressure greater than that of the surrounding atmosphere.

su·per·cil·i·ar·y (sū′pər sil′ē er′ē) *adj. Anatomy.* of, relating to, or situated near the eyebrow. [Modern Latin *superciliaris,* from Latin *supercilium* eyebrow.]

su·per·cil·i·ous (sū′pər sil′ē əs) *adj.* having or showing excessive pride or scorn; haughty; disdainful; arrogant: *a supercilious expression on a person's face.* [Latin *superciliōsus,* from *supercilium* eyebrow, pride (with reference to showing pride by raising the eyebrows) from *super* above, over + *cilium* eyelid.] —**su′per·cil′i·ous·ly,** *adv.* —**su′per·cil′i·ous·ness,** *n.*

su·per·class (sū′pər klas′) *n.* a category of taxonomic classification that comprises several related classes of organisms within a phylum or division.

su·per·col·li·der (sū′pər kə lī′dər) *n.* a particle accelerator of exceptional size, tens of miles in circumference, in which positively and negatively charged particles travel an oval track in opposite directions and collide head-on, generating energy measured in trillion electron volts.

su·per·com·put·er (sū′pər kəm pū′tər) *n.* a type of mainframe computer capable of extremely rapid calculation for solving complex mathematical problems.

su·per·con·duc·tiv·i·ty (sū′pər kon′duk tiv′i tē) *n. Physics.* the loss of all resistance to the passage of an electric current in certain metals and alloys at temperatures near absolute zero and in new classes of ceramic compounds at somewhat higher temperatures. —**su′per·con·duc′tive,** *adj.*

su·per·con·duc·tor (sū′pər kən duk′tər) *n.* a metal, alloy, or ceramic material that at very low temperatures displays superconductivity.

su·per·cool (sū′pər kül′) *v.t.* to cool (a liquid) below its freezing point without causing solidification.

su·per·dom·i·nant (sū′pər dom′ə nənt) *n. Music.* the sixth tone of the diatonic scale; tone next above the dominant.

su·per·e·go (sū′pər ē′go, -eg′ō) *n., pl.* **-gos.** *Psychoanalysis.* the part of the psyche formed in childhood by internalizing the standards of role models. It acts as a moral censor and creates guilt or anxiety when its instructions are ignored.

su·per·em·i·nent (sū′pər em′ə nənt) *adj.* supremely eminent. —**su′per·em′i·nence,** *n.* —**su′per·em′i·nent·ly,** *adv.*

su·per·er·o·gate (sū′pər er′ə gāt′) *v.i.,* **-gat·ed, -gat·ing.** to do more than is requested or required. [Late Latin *superērogātus,* past participle of *superērogāre* to pay out more, from Latin *super* over, above + *ērogāre* to pay out.]

su·per·er·o·ga·tion (sū′pər er′ə gā′shən) *n.* the act or an instance of doing more than is requested or required.

su·per·e·rog·a·to·ry (sū′pər i rog′i tôr′ē) *adj.* **1.** going beyond what is requested or required. **2.** not necessary; excessive; superfluous: *supererogatory embellishments.*

su·per·fam·i·ly (sū′pər fam′ə lē, -fam′lē) *n., pl.* **-lies.** *Biology.* a category in the classification of plants and animals, ranking below an order and above a family.

su·per·fi·cial (sū′pər fish′əl) *adj.* **1.** of, relating to, or located on the surface: *a superficial resemblance, a superficial wound.* **2.** lacking depth or thoroughness; shallow: *a superficial person, superficial research.* [Late Latin *superficiālis* relating to the surface, from Latin *superficiēs* surface.] —**su′per·fi′cial·ly,** *adv.* —**su′per·fi′cial·ness,** *n.*

> **Synonyms** **Superficial** and **shallow** mean lacking in depth. **Superficial** denotes that a person is either unable or disinclined to go beyond the surface of things: *This writer is amusing but very superficial, with ideas that are obvious.* **Shallow** is usually used pejoratively, suggesting that a person is incapable of deep thought or feeling: *The director thought the actor was too shallow to play a character of such psychological complexity.*

su·per·fi·ci·al·i·ty (sū′pər fish′ē al′i tē) *n., pl.* **-ties. 1.** the quality or condition of being superficial. **2.** something superficial.

su·per·fi·ci·es (sū′pər fish′ē ēz′, -fish′ēz) *n., pl.* **-ci·es. 1.** the surface of a body or area. **2.** the outward appearance or aspect. [Latin *superficiēs* surface.]

su·per·fine (sū′pər f īn′) *adj.* **1.** extremely fine in quality; of the best kind: *superfine cloth.* **2.** excessively refined or subtle; fastidious: *superfine distinctions.* **3.** consisting of extremely fine particles or parts: *superfine sugar.*

su·per·flu·i·ty (sū′pər flü′i tē) *n., pl.* **-ties. 1.** the state of being superfluous. **2.** a greater quantity than is needed or desired; excess: *a superfluity of luxuries.* **3.** something that is superfluous: *They wasted their money on expensive superfluities.*

su·per·flu·ous (sů pûr′flü əs) *adj.* **1.** more than is needed or desired: *superfluous words, superfluous ornamentation.* **2.** not required or essential; needless; unnecessary: *a superfluous warning.* [Latin *superfluus* overflowing, unnecessary.] —**su·per′flu·ous·ly,** *adv.* —**su·per′flu·ous·ness,** *n.*

su·per·gi·ant (sū′pər jī′ənt) *n.* an extremely large, bright star.

su·per·heat (sū′pər hēt′) *v.t.* **1.** to heat to an extremely high temperature; overheat. **2.** to raise the temperature of (a liquid) above the normal boiling point without causing vaporization. **3.** to raise the temperature of (vapor or steam) to increase the pressure. —**su′per·heat′er,** *n.*

a	at	e	end	o	hot	u	up	hw	white	⎰	about
ā	ape	ē	me	ō	old	ū	use	ng	song		taken
ä	far	i	it	ô	fork	ů	rule	th	thin	ə	pencil
âr	care	ī	ice	oi	oil	ủ	pull	<u>th</u>	this		lemon
		îr	pierce	ou	out	ûr	turn	zh	measure	⎱	circus

su·per·het·er·o·dyne (sü′pər het′ə ə dīn′) *adj.* of or relating to a method of radio reception in which the received carrier wave is changed by the heterodyne process into a new, lower frequency, which is amplified and rectified to reproduce sound. —*n.* a superheterodyne radio receiver. [Super(sonic) + heterodyne.]

su·per·high frequency (sü′pər hī′) a radio frequency between 3,000 and 30,000 megahertz.

su·per·high·way (sü′pər hī′wā′, sü′pər hī′wā) *n.* a high-speed highway, usually having four or more lanes, with opposing lanes of traffic separated by a median strip.

su·per·hu·man (sü′pər hū′mən, -ū′mən) *adj.* **1.** beyond what is human; divine: *of superhuman origin.* **2.** beyond ordinary human capacity or power: *a superhuman effort, superhuman strength.* —**su′per·hu′man·ly,** *adv.*

su·per·im·pose (sü′pər im pōz′) *v.t.,* -posed, -pos·ing. to place (something) on, above, or over something else: *to superimpose tracing paper over a picture.* —**su′per·im·pos′a·ble,** *adj.* —**su·per·im·po·si·tion** (sü′pər im′pə zish′ən), *n.*

su·per·in·cum·bent (sü′pər in kum′bənt) *adj.* **1.** lying or resting on or above something else. **2.** exerted from above, as pressure. —**su′per·in·cum′bence, su′per·in·cum′ben·cy,** *n.* —**su′per·in·cum′bent·ly,** *adv.*

su·per·in·duce (sü′pər in düs′, -dūs′) *v.t.,* -duced, -duc·ing. to bring in over and above something else; introduce in addition. —**su′per·in·duc′tion,** *n.*

su·per·in·tend (sü′pər in tend′, sü′prin-) *v.t.* to direct or control the work or operation of; oversee; manage: *to superintend the renovation of a building.* [Late Latin *superintendere,* from Latin *super* over, above + *intendere* to direct.] —**su′per·in·tend′ence,** *n.*

su·per·in·tend·en·cy (sü′pər in ten′dən sē, sü′prin-) *n., pl.* -cies. the position, duty, or authority of a superintendent.

su·per·in·tend·ent (sü′pər in ten′dənt, sü′prin-) *n.* **1.** a person who directs the work or operation of something, such as a group of workers, an institution, or a business: *a superintendent of the police, a superintendent of schools.* **2.** a person who manages and is responsible for the maintenance of an apartment or office building.

su·pe·ri·or (sə pîr′ē ər, sü-) *adj.* **1.** higher or greater than the ordinary or average in degree or quality; surpassing others; exceptional: *superior talent, a superior dancer, a superior piece of writing.* **2.** higher in status, rank, or office: *a superior officer.* **3.** greater in amount or quantity: *a superior force.* **4.** characterized by or showing disdain or arrogance; supercilious; haughty: *a superior attitude.* **5.** not influenced or affected by; indifferent to (with *to*): *to be superior to one's surroundings.* **6.** *Biology.* **a.** higher in place or position, as an organ or part; above in relation to another organ or structure. **b.** in the direction of the head: *The lungs are superior to the intestines.* —*n.* **1.** a person who is higher than others, as in status, rank, or office: *The mayor is the police commissioner's superior.* **2.** the head of an abbey, monastery, or other religious community. [Latin *superior* higher, comparative of *superus* upper, that is above, from *super* over, above.] —**su·pe′ri·or·ly,** *adv.*

superior court, in most U.S. states, a court of general jurisdiction in which cases are tried. It is distinguished from the lower courts, such as traffic or domestic relations courts, and in some states has some appellate jurisdiction.

su·pe·ri·or·i·ty (sə pîr′ē ôr′i tē, -or′-, sü-) *n.* the state or quality of being superior: *The horse demonstrated its superiority by winning the race.*

superiority complex, an attitude of conceit characterized by arrogant and overly assertive behavior as compensation for feelings of inferiority.

superl., superlative.

su·per·la·tive (sə pûr′lə tiv, sü-) *adj.* **1.** of the highest degree or quality; surpassing all others; supreme. **2.** *Grammar.* denoting the third or highest degree of quality, quantity, or relation that can be expressed by an adjective or adverb. *Fastest* is the superlative degree of the adjective *fast.* ➡ distinguished from **positive** and **comparative.** —*n.* **1.** a person or thing that surpasses all others; highest example. **2.a.** *Grammar.* the superlative degree. **b.** a word or group of words that expresses this degree. *Best* is the superlative of *good.* [Late Latin *superlātīvus* exaggerated, in the superlative degree, going back to Latin *super* above, beyond + *lātus,* past participle of *ferre* to carry, bear[1].] —**su·per′la·tive·ly,** *adv.* —**su·per′la·tive·ness,** *n.*

su·per·man (sü′pər man′) *n., pl.* -men (-men′). a man who has strength or intelligence beyond what is normal.

su·per·mar·ket (sü′pər mär′kit) *n.* a self-service retail store, usually large, carrying a wide selection of food and other household items.

su·per·nal (sü pûr′nəl) *adj.* **1.** of or relating to a higher world; celestial; heavenly. **2.** of, relating to, or existing in the sky: *a supernal phenomenon.* [Old French *supernal* higher, supreme, from Latin *supernus* upper, celestial, from *super* over, above.] —**su·per′nal·ly,** *adv.*

su·per·na·tant (sü′pər nā′tənt) *adj.* **1.** floating on the surface. **2.** *Chemistry.* of or relating to a liquid remaining after precipitation or centrifugation.

su·per·nat·u·ral (sü′pər nach′ər əl) *adj.* **1.** of or relating to a realm or existence beyond or exceeding the power of the natural world: *supernatural forces.* **2.** of or relating to ghosts or spirits. —*n.* a person or thing that exists beyond the natural world. —**su′per·nat′u·ral·ly,** *adv.* —**su′per·nat′u·ral·ness,** *n.*

su·per·nat·u·ral·ism (sü′pər nach′ər ə liz′əm) *n.* **1.** the quality or state of being supernatural. **2.** a belief in supernatural forces or beings. —**su′per·nat′u·ral·ist,** *n., adj.* —**su′per·nat′u·ral·is′tic,** *adj.*

su·per·no·va (sü′pər nō′və) *n., pl.* -vas or -vae (-vē). **1.** a stellar explosion in which the center of the star collapses, the outer layers are blown away, and the brightness increases by many orders of magnitude. **2.** a star that explodes in this manner.

su·per·nu·mer·ar·y (sü′pər nü′mə rer′ē, -nū′-) *adj.* exceeding in number what is usual, expected, or needed; additional; extra. —*n., pl.* -ar·ies. **1.** a person or thing that is extra. **2.** a performer in a play or film who has a minor, nonspeaking part. [Late Latin *supernumerārius* excessive in number, from Latin *super* beyond + *numerus* unit (in counting), quantity.]

su·per·phos·phate (sü′pər fos′fāt) *n.* a widely used fertilizer made by the action of sulfuric acid on rock that contains insoluble phosphates.

su·per·pose (sü′pər pōz′) *v.t.,* -posed, -pos·ing. **1.** superimpose. **2.** *Geometry.* to place (a figure) on top of another so that all parts coincide. [French *superposer* to place above something else, modification (influenced by French *poser* to place) of Latin *superpōnere* to place over.] —**su′per·pos′a·ble,** *adj.* —**su·per·po·si·tion** (sü′pər pə zish′ən), *n.*

su·per·pow·er (sü′pər pou′ər) *n.* one of the powerful nations that dominates world affairs, esp. through the possession of nuclear weapons.

su·per·sat·u·rate (sü′pər sach′ə rāt′) *v.t.,* -rat·ed, -rat·ing. to add to or concentrate in (a solution) more solute than can normally be held at a given pressure and temperature. If a solution is supersaturated, it becomes very unstable, and the excess solute readily forms a precipitate. —**su′per·sat′u·ra′tion,** *n.*

su·per·scribe (sü′pər skrīb′, sü′pər skrīb′) *v.t.,* -scribed, -scrib·ing. **1.** to write or engrave on the top or outside of something, esp. to write (a name or address) on a letter or package. **2.** to write or engrave on the top or outside of. [Latin *superscrībere* to write over.]

su·per·script (sü′pər skript′) *adj.* written above. —*n.* a character or symbol written, printed, or set above and to one side of another. In *a[2],* the symbol [2] is the superscript. [Latin *superscriptus,* past participle of *superscrībere* to write over.]

su·per·scrip·tion (sü′pər skrip′shən) *n.* writing or an inscription on the top or outside of something, esp. an address on a letter or package.

su·per·sede (sü′pər sēd′) *v.t.,* -sed·ed, -sed·ing **1.** to force out of use as inferior, obsolete, or useless; replace: *This rule supersedes all previous policy statements. Jets have superseded prop planes on most transatlantic flights.* **2.** to take the position, function, or office of; succeed: *You may eventually supersede your boss as manager of the project.* **3.** to remove or cause to be removed in favor of another; displace: *The town council voted to have the mayor superseded immediately.* [Latin *supersedēre* to be superior to, refrain; literally, to sit above.] —**su′per·sed′er,** *n.*

su·per·sen·si·tive (sü′pər sen′si tiv) *adj.* too sensitive; hypersensitive: *The child is supersensitive and cries easily.* —**su′per·sen′si·tive·ly,** *adv.* —**su′per·sen′si·tive·ness,** *n.*

su·per·ses·sion (sü′pər sesh′ən) *n.* the act of superseding or the state of being superseded. [Medieval Latin *supersessio,* from Latin *supersessus,* past participle of *supersedēre* to be superior to, refrain, sit above.] —**su′per·ses′sive,** *adj.*

su·per·son·ic (sü′pər son′ik) *adj.* **1.** relating to or designating a speed, or a body moving at a speed, greater than that of sound in air, approximately 740 miles (1,190 kilometers) per hour at sea level, or a speed greater than Mach 1. **2.** capable of traveling at a speed greater than the speed of sound: *a supersonic aircraft.* **3.** ultrasonic. —**su′per·son′i·cal·ly,** *adv.*

su·per·son·ics (sü′pər son′iks) *n.* **1.** ultrasonics. **2.** the scientific study of supersonic phenomena. ➡ used as singular in both defs.

su·per·star (sü′pər stär′) *n.* **1.** a person who is thought to surpass the most outstanding people in a field or profession, such as acting, sports, or popular music; exceptionally successful star: *a television superstar.* **2.** any exceptionally successful or outstanding person or thing: *a superstar among cars, a superstar of racehorses.*

su·per·sti·tion (sü′pər stish′ən) *n.* **1.** an irrational belief or set of beliefs based on assumptions that are inconsistent with scientific fact or religious doctrine, often resulting from fear of the unknown combined with a trust in the power of magical forces. **2.** a particular rite or practice based on such a belief or set of beliefs. Throwing spilled salt over one's shoulder to avoid bad luck is a superstition. **3.** such beliefs or practices collectively. [Latin *superstitiō* wonder, unreasonable religious belief; literally, a standing over.]

su·per·sti·tious (sü′pər stish′əs) *adj.* **1.** having or given to believing in superstitions: *a superstitious person.* **2.** of, relating to, or characterized by superstition: *superstitious fears, superstitious beliefs.* —**su′per·sti′tious·ly,** *adv.* —**su′per·sti′tious·ness,** *n.*

su·per·struc·ture (sü′pər struk′chər) *n.* **1.** the part of a building above the foundation. **2.** the part of a ship, esp. a warship, above the main deck. **3.** any structure perceived in relation to a more basic foundation: *the symbolic superstructure of a novel.*

su·per·tank·er (sü′pər tang′kər) *n.* a very large cargo ship equipped with tanks for carrying enormous quantities of liquid, usually oil, in excess of 500,000 tons capacity.

su·per·tax (sü′pər taks′) *n.* surtax.

su·per·ton·ic (sü′pər ton′ik) *n. Music.* the second tone of the diatonic scale; tone next above the tonic.

su·per·vene (sü′pər vēn′) *v.i.,* **-vened, -ven·ing.** to take place as something additional or unexpected and often as an interruption or a cause of change: *Bad health supervened and kept me from making the trip.* [Latin *supervenīre* to come upon, be added to.] —**su·per·ven·tion** (sü′pər ven′shən), *n.*

su·per·vise (sü′pər vīz′) *v.t.,* **-vised, -vis·ing.** to watch over in order to guide, direct, or control; oversee: *to supervise a cleaning staff, to supervise a fundraising campaign.* [Medieval Latin *supervisus,* past participle of *supervidere* to look over, oversee, from Latin *super* over + *vidēre* to see.]

su·per·vi·sion (sü′pər vizh′ən) *n.* **1.** the act or process of supervising. **2.** care or management: *We left the children under the supervision of their grandparents.*

su·per·vi·sor (sü′pər vī′zər) *n.* a person who supervises, esp. one who is in charge of a business, government, or educational department.

su·per·vi·so·ry (sü′pər vī′zə rē) *adj.* of or relating to a supervisor or supervision: *supervisory personnel, supervisory decisions.*

su·per·wom·an (sü′pər wüm′ən) *n., pl.* **-wom·en** (-wim′ən). **1.** a woman who has strength or intelligence beyond what is normal. **2.** a woman who successfully manages a career, marriage, and motherhood.

su·pine (*adj.,* sü pīn′; *n.,* sü′pīn) *adj.* **1.** lying on the back with the face turned upward. **2.** having or showing moral or mental indifference; apathetic: *supine neglect, supine slaves of authority.* —*n. Grammar.* in Latin, a verbal noun formed from the stem of the past participle and occurring only in the accusative and ablative cases. [Latin *supīnus* lying on the back, indolent.] —**su·pine′ly,** *adv.* —**su·pine′ness,** *n.*

supp. *also,* **suppl. 1.** supplement. **2.** supplementary.

sup·per (sup′ər) *n.* **1.** the last meal of the day, eaten in the evening. **2.** a social or community event where such a meal is served: *a church supper.* [Old French *soper* evening meal, from *soper* to eat one's supper; of Germanic origin.]

sup·plant (sə plant′) *v.t.* **1.** to take the place of: *The automobile has supplanted the horse as the main means of transportation.* **2.** to take the place of (someone) by scheming, treachery, or other devious means. **3.** to remove or get rid of in order to replace with something else. [Latin *supplantāre* to overthrow, trip up one's heels, from *sub* under + *planta* sole of the foot, plant.] —**sup·plant′er,** *n.*

sup·ple (sup′əl) *adj.,* **-pler, -plest. 1.** easily bent or folded without breaking or cracking; flexible: *supple leather, a supple fishing rod.* **2.** exhibiting or characterized by agility, as in bending, twisting, or other movement: *the supple limbs of a dancer.* **3.** readily yielding to persuasion or influence, esp. to the point of being compliant or servile. **4.** showing or having the ability to adapt to changes in people, ideas, or surroundings; adaptable: *a supple mind.* [Old French *souple* agile, flexible, from Latin *supplex* submissive; literally, bending under.] —**sup′ple·ly,** *adv.* —**sup′ple·ness,** *n.*

sup·ple·ment (*n.,* sup′lə mənt; *v.,* sup′lə ment′) *n.* **1.** something added to make up for a deficiency or to extend or complete something: *an annual supplement to an encyclopedia, a vitamin supplement.* **2.** *Geometry.* the measure of an angle or arc that must be added to the measure of a given angle or arc to produce a sum equal to 180 degrees. —*v.t.* to add or form a supplement to: *to supplement a diet with vitamins, two books that supplement one another.* [Latin *supplēmentum* a filling up, supply.]

sup·ple·men·ta·ry (sup′lə men′tə rē) *adj.* serving as a supplement; additional. Also, **sup′ple·men′tal.**

supplementary angle, an angle that is added to a given angle to make the sum of the two angles 180 degrees.

sup·pli·ance (sup′lē əns) *n.* supplication.

sup·pli·ant (sup′lē ənt) *n.* a person who supplicates. —*adj.* **1.** asking or entreating humbly and earnestly; imploring; beseeching: *suppliant beggars.* **2.** expressing supplication: *suppliant words.* [French *suppliant,* present participle of *supplier* to supplicate, from Latin *supplicāre.*] —**sup′pli·ant·ly,** *adv.*

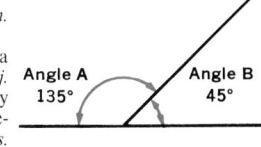

supplementary angles

sup·pli·cant (sup′li kənt) *n.* a person who supplicates; suppliant. —*adj.* asking or entreating humbly and earnestly; beseeching. [Latin *supplicāns,* present participle of *supplicāre* to supplicate.]

sup·pli·cate (sup′li kāt′) *v.,* **-cat·ed, -cat·ing.** —*v.t.* **1.** to make a humble and earnest request for: *to supplicate forgiveness.* **2.** to ask humbly and earnestly of; beseech: *to supplicate a judge for mercy.* —*v.i.* to make a humble and earnest request, as by prayer. [Latin *supplicātus,* past participle of *supplicāre* to beg humbly, implore.] —**sup′pli·ca′tor,** *n.*

sup·pli·ca·tion (sup′li kā′shən) *n.* **1.** the act of supplicating. **2.** an earnest request or humble prayer. Also, **suppliance.**

sup·pli·ca·to·ry (sup′li kə tôr′ē) *adj.* making or expressing supplication.

sup·pli·er (sə plī′ər) *n.* a person or thing that supplies.

sup·ply[1] (sə plī′) *v.t.,* **-plied, -ply·ing. 1.** to make (what is wanted, needed, or desirable) available for use: *to supply information, a reservoir that supplies water to a community.* **2.** to provide (someone) with what is wanted, needed, or desired: *The librarian supplied me with a number of reference books. Our company supplies wholesalers.* **3.** to meet or comply with (a need or want); satisfy: *Too few shares were issued to supply the demand for the stock.* **4.** to make good or compensate for (a loss or deficiency). —*n., pl.* **-plies. 1.** the amount necessary or available for a given use; stock; store: *a new supply of pencils, a week's supply of linens and towels.* **2.** *usually,* **supplies.** necessary items, such as food, clothing, or equipment, that are set aside and held for distribution and use: *The army was cut off from its supplies.* **3.** *Economics.* the quantity of a commodity available for sale at a certain price at a given time. **4.** the act of supplying. [Old French *soupleier* to fill up, make up, from Latin *supplēre* to fill up.] —For Synonyms (*v.t.*), see FURNISH.

sup·ply[2] (sup′lē) *adv.* in a supple manner. [SUPPLE + -LY[1].]

sup·port (sə pôrt′) *v.t.* **1.** to bear or hold up; keep from falling: *Brackets supported the shelves. That small chair won't support your weight.* **2.** to provide for or maintain, as with money or the necessary means of living: *to support a family, a planet that can support life.* **3.** to strengthen the cause or position of by one's assistance or approval; back; uphold: *The senator did not support the new tax reform. I can't support either of the candidates.* **4.** to comfort or strengthen, as in time of need: *My friends supported me in my grief.* **5.** to show to be valid or true; verify; substantiate: *There is no evidence to support your theory.* **6.** to be able to withstand; undergo; endure: *The country could not support another attack.* **7.** to act in a lesser part or as an added attraction with (a leading actor). —*n.* **1.** the act of supporting or the state of being supported: *to undertake the support of a foster child.* **2.** a person or thing that supports. [Old French *supporter* to endure, from Late Latin *supportāre,* from Latin *supportāre* to bring to.]

sup·port·a·ble (sə pôr′tə bəl) *adj.* able to be supported; bearable; endurable. —**sup·port′a·bly,** *adv.*

a	at	e	end	o	hot	u	up	hw	white		about
ā	ape	ē	me	ō	old	ū	use	ng	song		taken
ä	far	i	it	ô	fork	ü	rule	th	thin	ə	pencil
âr	care	ī	ice	oi	oil	ú	pull	th	this		lemon
		îr	pierce	ou	out	ûr	turn	zh	measure		circus

sup·port·er (sə pôr′tər) n. **1.** a person who supports, esp. one who aids or approves: *an ardent supporter of the current administration's foreign policy.* **2.** something that supports, such as a garter.

sup·por·tive (sə pôr′tiv) adj. **1.** providing support or reinforcement: *a supportive arch, supportive testimony.* **2.** providing approval, aid, or encouragement: *supportive parents, to be supportive of one's friends.*

sup·pose (sə pōz′) v.t., **-posed, -pos·ing. 1.** to imagine or consider as possible, esp. for the sake of argument: *Just suppose that you were a millionaire.* **2.** to hold as an opinion; believe to be probable: *I suppose that I have enough money to make the trip. I suppose the company will expand in the near future, depending on the economy.* **3.** to consider as a possibility or suggestion. ⇒ used in the imperative: *Suppose you let me finish before you interrupt.* **4.** to expect or require; obligate. ⇒ used in the passive: *The plane is supposed to arrive at nine o'clock.* **5.** to require as a condition; imply; presuppose: *Their plan supposes a universal desire for peace.* [Old French *supposer* to set under, imagine, modification (influenced by French *poser* to place, put) of Latin *suppōnere* to put under.]

sup·posed (sə pōzd′) adj. considered to be true, real, or possible, often wrongly: *The supposed explanation proved not to be true.* —**sup·pos·ed·ly** (sə pō′zid lē), adv.

sup·po·si·tion (sup′ə zish′ən) n. **1.** something that is supposed; hypothesis: *On the supposition that the weather would be warm, we wore no jackets.* **2.** the act of supposing. [Medieval Latin *suppositio* hypothesis, from Latin *suppositiō* substitution.] —**sup′po·si′tion·al,** adj. —**sup′po·si′tion·al·ly,** adv.

sup·pos·i·ti·tious (sə poz′i tish′əs) adj. **1.** substituted in order to deceive or defraud; spurious; counterfeit. **2.** supposed; hypothetical. [Latin *supposītītius* substituted, false.] —**sup·pos′i·ti′-tious·ly,** adv.

sup·pos·i·to·ry (sə poz′i tôr′ē) n., pl. **-ries.** a solid medicinal substance, usually in the form of a cone or cylinder, made to be inserted into the rectum or vagina, where body heat causes it to melt and the medicine is absorbed into the tissue. [Late Latin *suppositōrium* (something) placed underneath, going back to Latin *suppōnere* to put under.]

sup·press (sə pres′) v.t. **1.** to put an end to or put down forcibly; crush: *to suppress a revolt.* **2.** to hold or keep in; restrain: *to suppress a laugh.* **3.** to prevent or prohibit the publication, circulation, or expression of; keep secret; censor: *to suppress evidence, to suppress a news story.* **4.** to stop or arrest the flow or course of, as a hemorrhage. **5.** to dismiss from conscious consideration, as painful thoughts or disturbing ideas. ⇒ distinguished from **repress.** [Latin *suppressus,* past participle of *supprimere* to press under, restrain.] —**sup·press′i·ble, sup·pres′sive,** adj. —**sup·pres′sor;** also, **sup·press′er,** n. —For Synonyms, see **oppress.**

sup·pres·sant (sə pres′ənt) n. something that reduces, checks, or stifles an action or condition: *a cough suppressant, carpeting that is a noise suppressant.*

sup·pres·sion (sə presh′ən) n. **1.** the act of suppressing or the state of being suppressed. **2.** a psychological process by which a memory, thought, or action is deliberately excluded from consciousness. ⇒ distinguished from **repression.**

sup·pu·rate (sup′yə rāt′) v.i., **-rat·ed, -rat·ing.** to form or discharge pus. [Latin *suppūrātus* past participle of *suppūrāre* to form pus.]

sup·pu·ra·tion (sup′yə rā′shən) n. **1.** the formation or discharge of pus. **2.** pus.

sup·pu·ra·tive (sup′yə rā′tiv) adj. **1.** relating to or causing suppuration. **2.** discharging pus. —n. a medicine, salve, or other agent that causes or induces suppuration.

su·pra (sü′prə) adv. above. ⇒ used esp. as a reference to an earlier part of a text. [Latin *suprā.*]

supra- prefix above; over; beyond: *suprarenal, supranational.* [Latin *suprā.*]

su·pra·na·tion·al (sü′prə nash′ə nəl) adj. extending beyond the boundaries or limitations of a state or nation: *supranational ethics of war.* [SUPRA- + NATIONAL.]

su·pra·or·bit·al (sü′prə ôr′bi təl) adj. located above the orbit of the eye. [SUPRA- + ORBITAL.]

su·pra·re·nal (sü′prə rē′nəl) adj. situated on or above the kidneys; adrenal. —n. a suprarenal organ, such as an adrenal gland. [SUPRA- + RENAL.]

suprarenal gland, adrenal gland.

su·prem·a·cist (sə prem′ə sist, sù-) n. a person who believes in or advocates the supremacy of a particular group, esp. a racial group.

su·prem·a·cy (sə prem′ə sē, sù-) n. **1.** the quality or condition of being supreme. **2.** supreme power or authority: *naval supremacy.*

su·preme (sə prēm′, sù-) adj. **1.** highest in rank, authority, or power: *The president is the supreme executive officer of the United States.* **2.** greatest in significance, degree, or quality; utmost: *supreme artistry, supreme wisdom.* **3.** ultimate; final; last: *the supreme goal.* [Latin *suprēmus* highest, superlative of *superus* upper, that is from *super* above.] —**su·preme′ly,** adv.

Supreme Being, God.

Supreme Court 1. the highest court of the United States, with the power to hear appeals from lower courts and to declare laws unconstitutional. The chief justice presides over the Supreme Court. **2.** the highest court in most U.S. states.

supreme sacrifice, the sacrifice of one's own life.

Supreme Soviet, the legislature of the Soviet Union, which consisted of two equal houses, one elected according to population and the other elected by the various national groups.

Supt., superintendent.

sur-¹ prefix over; above; beyond: *surcharge, surpass.* [Old French *s(o)ur* on, over, above, from Latin *super.*]

sur-², form of sub- before r, as in *surrogate.*

su·rah (sùr′ə) n. a soft twilled fabric made of silk or rayon fibers. [From *Surat,* India, where it was first made.]

sur·cease (sûr sēs′) *Archaic.* n. a cessation; end: *a surcease of pain.* —v.t., v.i., **-ceased, -ceas·ing.** to cease; stop. [Old French *sursis,* past participle of *surseoir* to refrain, from Latin *supersedēre* literally, to sit above.]

sur·charge (n., sûr′chärj′; v., sûr chärj′, sûr′chärj′) n. **1.** an additional charge added to the usual amount, fare, or fee: *a tax surcharge.* **2.** an additional mark officially printed over a postage stamp to raise its value. —v.t., **-charged, -charg·ing. 1.** to charge an extra amount, fare, or fee. **2.** to overcharge (a person). **3.** to weigh down; overburden; overload. **4.** to print an additional mark on (postage stamps) to raise their value, instead of issuing new stamps. [French *surcharger* to overload, from *sur* (see SUR-¹) + *charger* to load. See CHARGE.]

sur·cin·gle (sûr′sing′gəl) n. a belt or band around the body of a horse or pack animal to hold down a saddle, blanket, or pack. [Old French *surcengle,* from *sur* (see SUR-¹) + *cengle* a girth (from Latin *cingula* belt).]

sur·coat (sûr′kōt′) n. an outer coat, esp. a short garment worn over armor during the Middle Ages. [Old French *surcote,* from *sur* (see SUR-¹) + *cote* (see COAT).]

surd (sûrd) n. **1.** a consonant sound articulated without vibration of the vocal cords, such as f, k, p, s, and t. **2.** an irrational number that is a root of a positive integer or quotient of positive integers. The numbers $\sqrt{3}$ and $\sqrt{3/5}$ are surds. —adj. **1.** articulated without vibration of the vocal cords; voiceless. **2.** *Mathematics.* irrational. [Latin *surdus* deaf, silent.]

sure (shùr) adj., **sur·er, sur·est. 1.** firmly believing in the existence, inevitability, or truth of something; having or showing no doubt; confident: *to be sure of someone's approval, to be sure an answer is correct.* **2.** incapable of being doubted or questioned; completely true; indisputable: *to have sure proof of someone's guilt.* **3.** bound to be or happen; destined; inevitable: *a sure winner, a problem sure to be worked out.* **4.** not liable to miss or fail; unerring; infallible: *a sure sign of a storm, the surest way to get to a place on time.* **5.** not liable to give way; steady; firm: *a sure grip, on sure ground.* **6.** worthy of being relied upon or trusted; dependable: *a sure friend.* —adv. *Informal.* surely. [Old French *sur* certain, safe, from Latin *sēcūrus* free from care. Doublet of SECURE.] —**sure′ness,** n.

surcoat

•**for sure.** without doubt; unquestionably.

•**to be sure.** undoubtedly; indeed.

•**to make sure.** to be certain: *Make sure that all your facts are correct before you present your report.*

Synonyms *adj.* **Sure, positive,** and **certain** mean free from doubt and are generally interchangeable. **Sure,** the least formal of these terms, is applied broadly to indicate the absence of doubt: *I'm sure we'll have a good time.* **Positive** may suggest an inflexible inner conviction: *I'm positive I'm the best person for the job.* **Certain** often indicates a conviction that is supported by evidence: *You can be certain the earthquake will be followed by aftershocks.*

S

sure·fire (shŏor′fīr′) *adj. Informal.* bound to be successful; that cannot fail; foolproof: *a surefire scheme.*

sure·foot·ed (shŏor′fŏŏt′id) *adj.* not liable to stumble or fall: *The gymnast was surefooted on the balance beam.* —**sure′foot′ed·ly,** *adv.* —**sure′foot′ed·ness,** *n.*

sure·ly (shŏor′lē) *adv.* **1.** without doubt; truly; positively: *Surely I can't have been sleeping for two hours.* **2.** without hesitation; firmly; steadily: *The driver guided the car surely around the curves.* **3.** without fail; inevitably; infallibly. ➡ usually used in the phrase *slowly but surely: We're getting the work done slowly but surely.*

sure·ty (shŏor′i tē) *n., pl.* **-ties. 1.** security, as against loss or damage, or for the fulfillment of an obligation. **2.** *Law.* a person who is responsible for the obligations of another, as for debts or for the failure to perform a duty. **3.** the state of being sure, esp. of oneself; assurance; certainty. **4.** a basis for confidence or certainty: *the surety of one's faith.* **5.** *Archaic.* something that is beyond doubt.

surf (sûrf) *n.* **1.** the swell of the sea or the splash of its waves breaking on the shore or upon a reef. **2.** the foam or sound caused by this. —*v.i.* to ride the crest of a wave, usually on a surfboard. [Of uncertain origin.] —**surf′er,** *n.*

sur·face (sûr′fis) *n.* **1.a.** the outer face or exterior extent of a thing: *the earth's surface.* **b.** a particular aspect or portion of a thing's exterior: *The smoothest surface in the whole rink is in this corner. How many surfaces does this gem have?* **2.** external appearance or aspect; appearance: *The problem seemed simple on the surface but proved to be complex.* **3.** *Mathematics.* a straight or curved set of points that has the dimensions of length and width but lacks the dimension of thickness. —*adj.* **1.** of, on, or relating to a surface: *a surface scratch on a table.* **2.** without much depth; superficial; apparent: *a surface explanation.* —*v.,* **-faced, -fac·ing.** —*v.i.* **1.** to come or rise to the surface: *The submarine surfaced. My anger finally surfaced after that last insult.* **2.** to come into notice or view, esp. after being hidden: *My lost glove finally surfaced. The fugitive surfaced in another country.* —*v.t.* **1.** to cover or finish the surface of, esp. to make smooth or level: *to surface tennis courts with clay, to surface roads with asphalt.* **2.** to bring or cause to rise to the surface. [French *surface* exterior of something, from *sur* (see SUR-¹) + *face* (see FACE).]

surface mail, mail that is sent by land or sea.

surface tension, a property of a liquid that causes its surface to behave like an elastic film, resulting from forces that tend to draw the surface molecules together.

sur·face-to-air (sûr′fis tə âr′) *adj.* (of a guided missile) launched from the surface of the earth to intercept and destroy an airborne target, as an aircraft or another missile.

surf·board (sûrf′bôrd′) *n.* a long, narrow, flat board used to ride the crest of a wave. —*v.i.* to engage in surfing. —**surf′board′er,** *n.* —**surf′board′ing,** *n.*

surf·boat (sûrf′bōt′) *n.* a strong, buoyant boat used esp. in heavy surf.

surf·cast·ing (sûrf′kas′ting) *n.* the sport of fishing by casting a line into the surf from the shore. —**surf′cast′er,** *n.*

sur·feit (sûr′fit) *v.t.* to feed or supply to excess; sate; satiate. —*v.i. Archaic.* to indulge to excess; overindulge. —*n.* **1.** an excessive amount or supply; excess: *a surfeit of food.* **2.** the act or an instance of overindulging oneself, esp. with food or drink. **3.** the disgust or discomfort caused by overindulgence. [Old French *sorfait* excess; originally, past participle of *sorfaire* to overdo, going back to Latin *super* above + *facere* to do, make.]

surf·fish (sûrf′fish′) *n., pl.* **-fish** or **-fish·es.** any of a group of saltwater fish, family Embiotocidae, found in temperate coastal waters of the Pacific Ocean, having oval bodies and spiny fins. Length: 5-18 inches (13-46 centimeters). Also, **surf·perch** (sûrf′pûrch′).

surf·ing (sûr′fing) *n.* a sport in which a person rides the crest of a breaking wave into the shore, usually on a surfboard.

surge (sûrj) *v.i.,* **surged, surg·ing. 1.** to move with a violent, heaving, swelling motion like that of waves: *The crowd surged forward to catch a glimpse of the celebrity. The lava surged over the ridge.* **2.** to increase or rise suddenly: *The stock market surged today.* —*n.* **1.** a heaving or swelling motion like that of waves: *the surge of an angry mob.* **2.** a sudden increase or onset: *a surge of electric current, a surge of public opinion.* **3.** a rolling swell, wave, or billow of water; storm surge. [Old French *sorgir* to rise, going back to Latin *surgere.*]

sur·geon (sûr′jən) *n.* a doctor of medicine who specializes in surgery. [Anglo-Norman *surgien,* short for Old French *cirurgien,* from *cirurgie* surgery, through Latin, going back to Greek *cheirourgiā.* See SURGERY.]

Surgeon General *pl.* **Surgeons General. 1.** the chief medical officer of one of the armed services of the United States. **2.** the chief medical officer of the U.S. Public Health Service.

sur·ger·y (sûr′jə rē) *n., pl.* **-ger·ies. 1.** the branch of medicine that deals with the treatment of diseases, injuries, and the like by the removal or repair of the affected parts of the body. **2.** a room or suite of rooms, esp. in a hospital, where such treatment is performed. **3.** the treatment itself: *to undergo surgery.* [Old French *surgerie, cirurgie* the art of performing surgical operations, through Latin, going back to Greek *cheirourgiā,* from *cheir* hand + *ergon* work.]

sur·gi·cal (sûr′ji kəl) *adj.* of, relating to, used in, or done by means of surgery: *surgical procedures, surgical instruments, surgical complications.* —**sur′gi·cal·ly,** *adv.*

sur·ly (sûr′lē) *adj.,* **-li·er, -li·est.** expressing or characterized by bad-tempered rudeness or hostility; gruff: *a surly salesclerk, a surly demand.* [Earlier *sirly* literally, like a ''sir'' or lord in arrogance, from SIR + -LY².] —**sur′li·ness,** *n.*

sur·mise (*v.,* sər mīz′; *n.,* sər mīz′, sûr′mīz) *v.,* **-mised, -mis·ing.** *v.t.* to infer (something) from little or no evidence; guess: *When we didn't see your coat, we surmised that you had already left.* —*v.i.* to guess; conjecture. —*n.* **1.** an idea or opinion based on little or no evidence; guess. **2.** the act or process of surmising. [Old French *surmise* accusation, from *surmettre* to accuse, from Medieval Latin *supermittere,* from Latin *super* above + *mittere* to send.] —For Synonyms *(v.t.),* see **guess.**

sur·mount (sər mount′) *v.t.* **1.** to prevail over; conquer; overcome: *to surmount financial difficulties.* **2.** to climb up or get over physically: *to surmount a wall.* **3.** to stand, lie, or be above; top; crown: *A dome surmounts the building.* [Old French *surmonter* to surpass, rise above, going back to Latin *super* above + *mōns* mountain.] —**sur·mount′a·ble,** *adj.*

sur·name (*n.,* sûr′nām; *v.,* sûr′nām′, sûr nām′) *n.* **1.** a last name or family name. ➡ distinguished from **given name. 2.** an added name or nickname; epithet: *Abraham Lincoln was given the surname ''the Great Emancipator.''* —*v.t.,* **-named, -nam·ing.** to give a surname to; call by a surname. [Partial translation of Old French *surnom* epithet or additional name, from *sur* (see SUR-¹) + *nom* name (from Latin *nōmen*).]

sur·pass (sər pas′) *v.t.* **1.** to go beyond, as in degree, amount, or quality; excel: *to surpass the other members of a team in ability.* **2.** to be beyond the range, reach, or capacity of; exceed: *Love surpasses understanding.* [French *surpasser* to excel, from *sur* (see SUR-¹) + *passer.* See PASS.] —**sur·pass′a·ble,** *adj.* —For Synonyms, see **excel.**

sur·pass·ing (sər pas′ing) *adj.* excelling others in degree, amount, or quality; excessive: *a dancer of surpassing beauty and grace.* —**sur·pass′ing·ly,** *adv.*

sur·plice (sûr′plis) *n.* a loose-fitting white vestment with wide sleeves, worn by members of the clergy, choir singers, and those assisting at the altar in the Roman Catholic and certain other churches. [Anglo-Norman *surplis,* from Medieval Latin *superpelliceum,* going back to Latin *super* above + *pellis* pelt², skin; because it was originally worn over a garment of fur.]

sur·plus (sûr′plus′, -pləs) *n.* **1.** an amount or quantity over and above what is used or needed; excess: *a crop surplus, a surplus of dishes at a banquet.* **2.a.** the assets remaining after all costs, expenses, and debts have been paid; profit. **b.** the excess of the net worth of a business establishment over the stated value of its stock. —*adj.* over and above what is used or needed: *surplus army goods.* [Anglo-Norman *surplus* overplus, going back to Latin *super* over + *plūs* more.]

sur·plus·age (sûr′plus′ij) *n.* **1.** a surplus; excess. **2.** unnecessary or irrelevant words or matter.

sur·prise (sər prīz′) *v.t.,* **-prised, -pris·ing. 1.** to cause to feel sudden wonder or astonishment: *to surprise someone with an unexpected gift.* **2.** to come upon suddenly or unexpectedly; take or catch unawares: *to surprise someone in the act of stealing.* **3.** to attack or capture suddenly and without warning: *We surprised the enemy with a night attack.* **4.a.** to cause (someone) to do or say something unintended (with *into*): *to surprise a suspect into a confession.* **b.** to bring out (something) in such a manner: *to surprise an admission of guilt from a culprit.* —*n.* **1.** the state or feeling of being surprised; sudden feeling of wonder: *I could*

a	at	e	end	o	hot	u	up	hw	white		about
ā	ape	ē	me	ō	old	ū	use	ng	song		taken
ä	far	i	it	ô	fork	ü	rule	th	thin	ə	pencil
âr	care	ī	ice	oi	oil	u̇	pull	th	this		lemon
		îr	pierce	ou	out	ûr	turn	zh	measure		circus

1213

hardly contain my surprise when they arrived. **2.** something that causes this feeling: *The news came as a surprise.* **3.** the act of surprising; taking or catching unawares. [Middle French *surprise* a taking unawares, from *surprendre* to take unawares, overtake, going back to Latin *super* over + *prehendere* to seize.]

· **to take by surprise. a.** to come upon suddenly and unexpectedly; take or catch unawares. **b.** to astound or amaze: *The cost of the trip took me by surprise.*

sur·pris·ing (sər prī′zing) *adj.* causing surprise or wonder; unexpected: *a surprising defeat.* —**sur·pris′ing·ly,** *adv.*

sur·re·al (sə rē′əl) *adj.* **1.** having the qualities of surrealism; surrealistic: *surreal art, surreal writing.* **2.** having some of the qualities of a dream; unreal; bizarre; eerie: *surreal fantasies, a surreal world.*

sur·re·al·ism (sə rē′ə liz′əm) *n.* a movement in twentieth-century art and literature characterized by dreamlike distortions and unexpected arrangements of subject matter, often intended to reflect the subconscious. [French *surréalisme,* from *sur* (see SUR-[1]) + *réalisme* realism (going back to Latin *rēs* thing).]

surrealism
a painting by René Magritte

sur·re·al·ist (sə rē′ə list) *n.* an artist or writer whose work is characterized by surrealism. —*adj.* of, relating to, or characteristic of surrealism; surrealistic.

sur·re·al·is·tic (sə rē′ə lis′tik) *adj.* **1.** of, relating to, or characteristic of surrealism. **2.** having some of the qualities of a dream; bizarre; surreal. —**sur·re′al·is′ti·cal·ly,** *adv.*

sur·ren·der (sə ren′dər) *v.t.* **1.** to give over possession or control of because of force or demand: *to surrender a fort, to surrender stolen goods to the police.* **2.** to yield claim to (an office, position, or the like) in favor of another: *The chairwoman will surrender her post next month.* **3.** to put aside as hopeless or useless; abandon: *He surrendered all thoughts of winning.* **4.** to yield (oneself) to an emotion, influence, or course of action. —*v.i.* to give oneself up to someone or something; yield: *The troops surrendered.* —*n.* the act or an instance of surrendering. [Old French *surrendre* to hand over, from *sur* (see SUR-[1]) + *rendre* to yield. See RENDER.] —For Synonyms, see **yield.**

sur·rep·ti·tious (sûr′əp tish′əs) *adj.* **1.** done or accomplished by stealthy means: *a surreptitious meeting.* **2.** acting in a secret, sly manner: *a surreptitious investigator.* [Latin *surreptītius* stolen, concealed, going back to *sub* under, secretly + *rapere* to seize.] —**sur′rep·ti′tious·ly,** *adv.* —**sur′rep·ti′tious·ness,** *n.*

sur·rey (sûr′ē, sur′ē) *n., pl.* **-reys.** a light, four-wheeled carriage with two seats, usually with a flat top. [From *Surrey,* England, where it was first made.]

sur·ro·gate (sûr′ə gāt′, -git, sur′-) *n.* **1.** a person who acts in place of another; substitute: *The guardian was the orphan's surrogate parent.* **2.** in some states, a judge or judicial officer having charge of certain matters, such as the administration of estates, guardianships, and the probate of wills. **3.** a woman who, by artificial insemination or surgical implantation of a fertilized egg, carries a child until birth for another family. Also *(def. 3),* **surrogate mother.** [Latin *surrogātus,* past participle of *surrogāre* to substitute.]

sur·round (sə round′) *v.t.* **1.** to stand, lie, or be situated on all sides of; form a circle around: *A crowd surrounded the celebrity's car.* **2.** to cause to be encircled: *to surround a pool with a fence.* **3.** to enclose or confine (a place, body of troops, or the like) so as to prevent escape or communication. —*n.* something that encir-

cles or surrounds. [Old French *s(o)uronder* to overflow, surpass, going back to Latin *super* above + *unda* wave; influenced in form and meaning by association with ROUND.]

sur·round·ings (sə round′dingz) *pl. n.* the objects, circumstances, influences, or conditions characteristic of a place or in which a person exists: *to enjoy the peaceful surroundings of the countryside.*

sur·tax (sûr′taks′) *n.* an additional or extra tax, esp. one added to the normal income tax. Also, **supertax.** [French *surtaxe,* from *sur* (see SUR-[1]) + *taxe* tax (going back to Latin *taxāre* to rate[1], value).]

sur·tout (sər tü′, -tüt′; *French* SYR tü′) *n., pl.* **-touts** (-tüz′, -tüts′; *French* -tü′). a man's long, close-fitting overcoat; frock coat. [French *surtout,* from *sur* (see SUR-[1]) + *tout* all (from Latin *tōtus*).]

sur·veil·lance (sər vā′ləns, -vāl′yəns) *n.* **1.** a close watch kept over a person, group, or place in order to gather information: *The police have the suspect under constant surveillance.* **2.** observation for the purpose of supervision and control: *New staff members work under the manager's surveillance.* [French *surveillance* supervision, from *surveiller* to watch, going back to Latin *super* above, over + *vigilāre* to watch.]

sur·vey (*v.,* sər vā′; *n.,* sûr′vā, sər vā′) *v.t.* **1.** to view or consider generally; examine as a whole: *to survey the panorama of a city, a course that surveys nineteenth-century English literature.* **2.** to examine or inspect in detail: *The authorities surveyed the damage after the flood.* **3.** to determine the shape, area, and boundaries of (a region or tract of land) by taking measurements of lines and angles with various instruments and applying the principles of geometry and trigonometry. —*v.i.* to survey land. —*n., pl.* **-veys. 1.** a detailed study or examination, such as one made by taking a sampling of opinions: *a telephone survey, a statistical survey.* **2.** a general or comprehensive view: *The exhibition is a survey of modern art.* **3.a.** the act or process of surveying land. **b.** a plan, map, or written statement of the results of this. [Anglo-Norman *surveier* to look over, going back to Latin *super* above, over + *vidēre* to see.]

sur·vey·ing (sər vā′ing) *n.* the act, science, or occupation of making land surveys.

sur·vey·or (sər vā′ər) *n.* a person who surveys, esp. a person whose work is surveying land.

surveyor's measure, a system of linear measurement used by surveyors, having the chain as its unit.

sur·viv·al (sər vī′vəl) *n.* **1.** the act of surviving or the state of having survived. **2.** a person or thing that survives, such as a custom or ritual from the past.

sur·viv·al·ist (sər vī′və list) *n.* a person who has a strong desire to survive, esp. one who prepares for a supposedly approaching catastrophic event, such as nuclear war or economic anarchy, by hoarding supplies and preparing living quarters to exist without the services and benefits of organized society.

survival of the fittest *Biology.* natural selection.

sur·vive (sər vīv′) *v.,* **-vived, -viv·ing.** —*v.t.* **1.** to live longer than; remain alive after the death of; outlive: *to survive other members of one's family.* **2.** to live, exist, or be active through and after: *Two people survived the automobile accident. The politician survived the official purges and continued in power for many years.* —*v.i.* to continue to live, exist, or remain active; endure: *These plants won't survive without sunlight. The music of Bach has survived through the years.* [Middle French *survivre* to outlive, from Latin *supervīvere.*]

sur·vi·vor (sər vī′vər) *n.* **1.** a person or thing that survives. **2.** a person who manages to get along in spite of adverse conditions or misfortune.

sus-, form of **sub-** before *c, p, t,* as in *susceptible, suspect, sustain.*

Su·san·na (sü zan′ə) *n.* a book of the Protestant and Catholic Apocrypha.

sus·cep·ti·bil·i·ty (sə sep′tə bil′i tē) *n., pl.* **-ties. 1.** the quality or condition of being susceptible. **2. susceptibilities.** strong and sensitive feelings: *The critic's remarks wounded the author's susceptibilities.*

sus·cep·ti·ble (sə sep′tə bəl) *adj.* **1.** easily affected or influenced by; readily yielding; open (often with *to*): *a child susceptible to colds, an argument susceptible to criticism.* **2.** capable of undergoing or experiencing; admitting (with *of*): *a good paper susceptible of improvements.* **3.** highly emotional or sensitive; impressionable. [Late Latin *susceptibilis* capable of receiving, from Latin *suscipere* to receive.] —**sus·cep′ti·ble·ness,** *n.* —**sus·cep′ti·bly,** *adv.*

sus·cep·tive (sə sep′tiv) *adj.* **1.** receptive. **2.** susceptible. —**sus·cep′tive·ness, sus·cep·tiv·i·ty** (sus′ep tiv′i tē), *n.*

su·shi (sü′shē) *n.* a Japanese dish of cold, cooked rice topped or

wrapped with garnishes, as of raw fish or seaweed. [Japanese *sushi.*]

sus·pect (*v.,* sə spekt′; *n.,* sus′pekt; *adj.,* sus′pekt′, sə spekt′) *v.t.* **1.** to consider true, likely, or possible: *I suspect they have already left for the airport. I suspect trouble.* **2.** to think (someone) guilty with little or no proof: *The police suspected them of the robbery.* **3.** to have doubts about; lack confidence in; distrust: *I suspect their sincerity.* —*v.i.* to have suspicions. —*n.* a person who is suspected, esp. of having committed a crime. —*adj.* open to or viewed with suspicion; suspected: *Their motives are suspect.* [Latin *suspectus,* past participle of *suspicere* to look up to, mistrust.]

sus·pend (sə spend′) *v.t.* **1.** to attach from above so as to allow free movement; hang: *to suspend a swing from a tree branch.* **2.** to keep from falling or sinking with no apparent support: *to suspend particles in a liquid.* **3.** to make ineffective, invalid, or inoperative, esp. on a temporary basis: *to suspend a driver's license.* **4.** to cause to stop for a time; interrupt: *to suspend payments on a car, to suspend service during a strike, to suspend a hearing until a later date.* **5.** to exclude for a time from some privilege, function, or rank, usually as a punishment: *to suspend a student from school.* **6.** to refrain from forming or concluding definitely; hold in abeyance: *I'll suspend judgment for now.* —*v.i.* **1.** to stop for a time: *The rain suspended long enough for us to walk home.* **2.** to fail to meet one's financial obligations; stop payment. [Latin *suspendere* to hang up.]

suspended animation, a state of unconsciousness with no apparent signs of life.

sus·pend·ers (sə spen′dərz) *pl. n.* a pair of straps worn over the shoulders and attached to the waistband of a garment, such as trousers or a skirt, usually worn instead of a belt to hold up the garment.

sus·pense (sə spens′) *n.* **1.** a state of being undecided or in doubt: *We were all in suspense, wondering who had won the contest.* **2.** the worry, tension, or excitement resulting from this: *The novel was full of suspense.* [Old French *suspens* abeyance, delay, going back to Latin *suspēnsus,* past participle of *suspendere* to hang up.] —**sus·pense′ful,** *adj.*

sus·pen·sion (sə spen′shən) *n.* **1.** the act of suspending or the state of being suspended. **2.** *Chemistry.* **a.** a mixture consisting of small solid particles or liquid droplets dispersed in a liquid. The particles will separate out if the suspension is allowed to stand. **b.** the state or condition of the particles or droplets in such a mixture. **3.** a device from which something is suspended. **4.** a system of springs, torsion bars, absorbers, and other parts, used to support the body of a vehicle in order to maintain a smooth ride. **5.** a stopping of payment of one's financial obligations.

suspension bridge, a bridge suspended from cables or chains that are hung between towers.

suspension bridge over Tampa Bay, Florida

sus·pen·sive (sə spen′siv) *adj.* **1.** having the power or serving to suspend operation or activity: *suspensive conditions, a suspensive veto.* **2.** of, relating to, or characterized by suspense or indecision.

sus·pen·sor (səs pen′sər) *n.* **1.** a cell or chain of cells at the base of the embryo of many seed plants that pushes the embryo deep into the endosperm, which is its food supply. **2.** suspensory. [Modern Latin *suspensor,* from Latin *suspensus* suspended (past participle of *suspendere* to suspend) + *-or* -OR.]

sus·pen·so·ry (sə spen′sə rē) *adj.* **1.** serving to hold up or support: *a suspensory bandage.* **2.** causing a delay in the completion of something: *a suspensory proposal.* —*n., pl.* **-ries.** something that supports a part of the body, such as a ligament, muscle, truss, bandage, or athletic support. Also *(n.),* **sus·pen·sor.**

suspensory ligament, a muscle or ligament that supports an organ or bodily part, esp. the ligament supporting the lens of the eye.

sus·pi·cion (sə spish′ən) *n.* **1.** the act or an instance of suspecting something wrong or bad with little or no proof; feeling of distrust or uncertainty: *Suspicions were aroused by the witness's hesitant answer.* **2.** a feeling or impression that is based on little or no proof: *I have a suspicion that you're right.* **3.** the state or condition of being suspected: *Such an honest person is above suspicion.* **4.** a slight trace or suggestion: *a suspicion of smoke.* [Latin *suspīciō* mistrust.]

· **under suspicion.** suspected of being wrong, bad, or guilty.

sus·pi·cious (sə spish′əs) *adj.* **1.** tending to arouse suspicion; questionable: *the suspicious circumstances of a fire.* **2.** inclined to suspect; distrustful: *to be suspicious of strangers.* **3.** expressing or indicating suspicion: *a suspicious glance.* —**sus·pi′cious·ly,** *adv.* —**sus·pi′cious·ness,** *n.*

sus·pire (sə spīr′) *v.i.,* **-pired, -pir·ing. 1.** to sigh. **2.** to take a breath; breathe. [Latin *suspīrāre* to draw a deep breath, sigh.] —**sus·pi·ra′tion,** *n.*

sus·tain (sə stān′) *v.t.* **1.** to keep up or in effect; keep going: *to sustain interest in a story.* **2.** to keep up the spirits or courage of; keep from despair; comfort: *Your faith will sustain you in times of challenge.* **3.** to supply with food, clothing, or other necessities of life; support: *These provisions will sustain us for a week.* **4.** to keep from sinking or falling; support from below: *More posts were needed to sustain the platform.* **5.** to bear up under or against; be able to endure: *a metal that can sustain the pressure of supersonic speed, a book that can sustain comparison with the classics.* **6.** to undergo or experience, as loss or injury: *to sustain a broken arm in an accident.* **7.** to accept or uphold as valid, true, or just: *The judge sustained the objection.* **8.** to bear out the truth or validity of; prove; confirm: *The new information sustains our earlier findings.* [Old French *so(u)stein-,* a stem of *so(u)stenir* to hold up, going back to Latin *sustinēre.*] —**sus·tain′a·ble,** *adj.* —**sus·tain′er,** *n.*

sustaining program, a radio or television program without a commercial sponsor, presented by a station or network at its own expense.

sus·te·nance (sus′tə nəns) *n.* **1.** something that sustains or supports life, esp. food. **2.** a means of support; livelihood. **3.** the act or process of sustaining or the state of being sustained. [Old French *so(u)stenance* maintenance, support, from *so(u)stenir* to hold up. See SUSTAIN.]

sut·ler (sut′lər) *n.* formerly, a person who followed an army or established a store on an army post to sell food and provisions to the soldiers. [Obsolete Dutch *soeteler* one who does menial work.]

sut·tee (su tē′, sut′ē) *n.* **1.** a former Hindu funeral practice or custom in which the surviving wife of a deceased man burned herself to death on the man's funeral pyre. **2.** a widow cremated by suttee. Also, **sati.** [Sanskrit *satī* faithful wife.]

su·ture (sü′chər) *n.* **1.** the act or method of joining together the edges of a cut or wound by or as by stitching. **2.** one of the stitches or fastenings of thread, wire, or other material so used. **3.** a line or seam formed in joining two surfaces, such as that of a wound sewed together. **4.** the act of sewing together or joining together as if by sewing. **5.** a line where two bones are joined by having grown together, found esp. in the skull. **6.** a line along which plant parts meet, such as that between the parts that can be split in a pea pod. —*v.t.,* **-tured, -tur·ing.** to secure or join together with a suture. [Latin *sūtūra* a sewing together, seam.]

Sutures

sutures in the skull

su·ze·rain (sü′zər in, -zə rān′) *n.* **1.** a feudal lord. **2.** a state or government having control of another state that has its own government. [French *suzerain* feudal lord, from *sus* above (from Latin *sursum*); influenced by French *souverain* sovereign.]

a	at	e	end	o	hot	u	up	hw	white		about
ā	ape	ē	me	ō	old	ū	use	ng	song		taken
ä	far	i	it	ô	fork	u̇	rule	th	thin	ə	pencil
âr	care	ī	ice	oi	oil	u̇	pull	th	this		lemon
		îr	pierce	ou	out	ûr	turn	zh	measure		circus

su·ze·rain·ty (sü′zər in tē, -zə rān′tē) *n., pl.* **-ties.** the position or power of a suzerain.

svelte (svelt, sfelt) *adj.* slender and graceful; willowy. [French *svelte,* from Italian *svelto,* from *svellere* to pluck or pull out, going back to Latin *ex* out + *vellere* to pluck, pull.]

SW **1.** southwest. **2.** southwestern.

swab (swob) *also,* **swob.** *n.* **1.** a small piece of cotton, sponge, or other material, usually at the tip of a small stick, used esp. to apply medication or cosmetics and to clean certain parts of the body, such as the ears. **2.** a mop used on ships to clean decks or other surfaces. **3.** a long brush for cleaning the bore of a firearm. **4.a.** *Slang.* a clumsy, awkward fellow; lout. **b.** sailor. Also *(def. 4b),* **swabby.** —*v.t.,* **swabbed, swab·bing.** to clean, treat, or apply with or as with a swab: *to swab decks, to swab a cut with ointment.* [From SWABBER.]

swab·ber (swob′ər) *n.* **1.** a person who uses a swab, esp. on a ship. **2.** swab *(def. 2).* [Dutch *zwabber.*]

swab·by (swob′ē) *also,* **swab·bie.** *n., pl.* **-bies.** *Slang.* sailor.

swad·dle (swod′əl) *v.t.,* **-dled, -dling. 1.** to wrap or bind with or as with bandages. **2.** to wrap (an infant) in swaddling clothes. —*n.* a band of cloth or bandage used for swaddling. [Old English *swæthel* band used for swaddling, bandage.]

swaddling clothes 1. long, narrow bands of cloth formerly wrapped around newborn infants to prevent free movement of the limbs. **2.** rigid controls or restrictions, such as ones placed on the young or inexperienced. Also, **swaddling bands.**

swag (swag) *n.* **1.** an ornamental drapery, fabric, or garland hung in a loop between two points. **2.** *Slang.* stolen or illegally obtained goods or profits; booty: *The burglar escaped with the swag.* [Probably of Scandinavian origin.]

swage (swāj) *n.* a tool, die, or stamp, often one of a pair, for bending metal or for shaping or impressing it by hammering. —*v.t.* **swaged, swag·ing.** to bend, shape, or impress (metal) by using a swage. [French *suage* decorative molding; of uncertain origin.]

swag·ger (swag′ər) *v.i.* **1.** to walk or behave in a bold, rude, or arrogant manner: *The winning team swaggered off the field.* **2.** to boast; brag. —*n.* a swaggering movement, expression, or manner. [SWAG + -ER[4].] —**swag′ger·er,** *n.*

swagger stick, a short, light cane with metal at each end, carried esp. by army officers.

Swa·hi·li (swä hē′lē) *n., pl.* **-lis** or **-li. 1.** a member of a Bantu people of Zanzibar and the adjacent coast of Africa. **2.** the Bantu language of the Swahilis, used as the lingua franca of eastern Africa and Zaire. Also, **Kiswahili, Ki-Swahili.**

swain (swān) *n.* **1.** a lover; suitor. **2.** a country youth, esp. a shepherd. [Old Norse *sveinn* lad, servant.]

swale (swāl) *n.* wet or marshy lowland. [Probably of Scandinavian origin.]

swal·low[1] (swol′ō) *v.t.* **1.** to cause (a food or other substance) to pass through the mouth and the esophagus into the stomach. **2.** to take in or engulf by or as by swallowing; devour; envelop (often with *up*): *The earthquake swallowed up the whole city.* **3.** to utter indistinctly; mumble: *to swallow one's words.* **4.** to keep from expressing or giving vent to; suppress: *to swallow one's pride and ask for a favor.* **5.** to put up with; accept without protest; tolerate: *to swallow an insult.* **6.** to take back (something said); retract. **7.** *Informal.* to accept too readily or without question: *They swallowed my excuse for being late.* —*v.i.* to perform the act or motion of swallowing: *The speaker swallowed nervously and went on with the lecture.* —*n.* **1.** the act or an instance of swallowing: *to drink water in one swallow.* **2.** a quantity swallowed at one time: *to take a swallow of soup.* [Old English *swelgan* to take into the stomach through the throat.] —**swal′low·er,** *n.*

swal·low[2] (swol′ō) *n.* any of various small perching birds, family Hirundinidae, having a slender body and, often, a deeply forked tail. It is noted for the extent and regularity of its migrations. Length: 4-9 inches (10-23 centimeters). [Old English *swealwe.*]

swal·low·tail (swol′ō tāl′) *n.* **1.** a deeply forked tail, such as that of certain kites or butterflies, resembling the tail of a barn swallow. **2.** any of a genus of butterflies, *Papilio,* having such a tail. **3.** swallow-tailed coat.

swal·low-tailed (swol′ō tāld′) *adj.* having a deeply forked tail resembling that of a barn swallow.

swallow-tailed coat, a man's coat with tails, used for formal wear. Also, **tails.**

swam (swam) a past tense of **swim.**

swa·mi (swä′mē) *n., pl.* **-mis.** a Hindu mystic or religious teacher. [Hindi *svāmī* master, lord, from Sanskrit *svāmin.*]

swamp (swomp, swômp) *n.* an area of low-lying, wet land that is usually covered with dense vegetation, such as grasses, trees, and shrubs. —*v.t.* **1.** to overwhelm, as with difficulties or work; burden: *to swamp someone with work, to be swamped with requests for one's autograph.* **2.** to drench or cover with water: *The spring floods swamped the coastal areas.* **3.** to sink or fill (a boat or ship) with water. —*v.i.* **1.** to be overwhelmed or burdened. **2.** (of a boat or ship) to sink or become filled with water. [Possibly of Low German origin.]

swamp fever, malaria.

swamp·land (swomp′land′, swômp′-) *n.* land covered with swamps.

swamp·y (swom′pē, swôm′-) *adj.,* **swamp·i·er, swamp·i·est.** of, consisting of, or resembling a swamp or swamps.

swan

swan (swon) *n.* **1.** any of several large, graceful, long-necked water birds, family Anatidae, having a broad, flat bill, a plump body, and webbed feet, the adult of which has, in most species, white plumage. Length: 3½-6 feet (1.1-1.8 meters). **2. Swan.** *Astronomy.* Cygnus. [Old English *swan.*]

swan dive, a forward dive in which the arms are extended straight out to the side, with the back arched, the arms being brought together in front of the head just before entering the water.

swank·y (swang′kē) *adj.,* **swank·i·er, swank·i·est.** *Informal.* having or characterized by elegance or luxury; stylish; posh: *a swanky outfit, a swanky hotel.* Also, **swank.** —**swank′i·ly,** *adv.* —**swank′i·ness,** *n.*

swans·down (swonz′doun′) *n.* **1.** the soft down of a swan. **2.** a fine, thick, soft fabric made from wool or cotton, used for such items as infants' wear and underwear.

swan song 1. a song that, according to legend, a swan sings just before it dies. **2.** a farewell appearance or final work or expression, as at the end of a career, life, or period of time.

swap (swop) *also,* **swop.** *Informal.* —*v.t., v.i.,* **swapped, swap·ping.** to exchange (one thing for another); trade. —*n.* an exchange; trade. [Middle English *swappen* to strike (referring to the custom of striking the hands to signify that a bargain has been made); probably imitative.] —**swap′per,** *n.*

sward (swôrd) *also,* **swarth.** *n.* land covered with grass; lawn; meadow. [Old English *sweard* skin.]

swarm[1] (swôrm) *n.* **1.** a large group of insects or other small animals flying or moving about together. **2.a.** a group of bees, led by the queen of a hive, that flies off together to start a new colony. **b.** such a group of bees newly settled in a hive. **3.** a great number of people, animals, or the like, esp. when in motion: *Swarms of shoppers filled the store during the big sale.* —*v.i.* **1.** (of bees) to fly off together to start a new colony. **2.** to come together, occur, or move in a large mass or group: *The fans swarmed out of the stadium.* **3.** to be filled, crowded, or overrun; teem: *a river swarming with alligators.* —*v.t.* to fill with a throng or multitude; crowd. [Old English *swearm* group of bees that leaves the old hive to start a new one.]

swarm[2] (swôrm) *v.t., v.i.* to climb (a pole, tree, or the like) by grasping with the arms and legs; shin. [Of uncertain origin.]

swarth (swôrth) sward.

swarth·y (swôr′thē, -thē) *adj.,* **swarth·i·er, swarth·i·est.** having a dark or sunburned color or complexion: *swarthy skin.* Also *(archaic),* **swart, swarth.** [Modification of obsolete *swarty,* going back to Old English *sweart* black, dark + -Y[1].] —**swarth′i·ly,** *adv.* —**swarth′i·ness,** *n.*

swash (swosh, swôsh) *v.t.* **1.** to dash (water or other liquid) about; splash. **2.** to splash water or other liquid upon or against. —*v.i.* **1.** to strike, move, or wash noisily or with a splash, as waves do. **2.** to swagger. —*n.* **1.** a swashing action or sound, esp. of water. **2.** swagger. **3.** the rush of water up onto a beach after a wave has broken. **4.** a channel running through or behind a sandbank. [Imitative.]

swash·buck·ler (swosh′buk′lər, swôsh′-) *n.* a flamboyant or boastful adventurer or soldier. [SWASH + BUCKLER; referring to the swaggering behavior of a swordsman who showed off by repeatedly hitting his adversary's buckler with a sword.]

swash·buck·ling (swosh′buk′ling, swôsh′-) *adj.* acting like or characteristic of a swashbuckler; flamboyant; boastful.

swas·ti·ka (swos′ti kə) *n.* **1.** a symbol or ornament, used widely in both ancient and modern times, in the shape of an

S

equal-armed cross, the spars bent in the center at right angles. **2.** this symbol having the spars bent clockwise, used as an emblem of the Nazi Party. [Sanskrit *svastika* a good luck sign, from *svasti* good luck, well-being.]

swat (swot) *v.t., v.i.,* **swat·ted, swat·ting.** to hit (someone or something) with a short, sharp blow: *to swat a mosquito, to swat at a fly.* —*n.* a short, sharp blow. [Form of SQUAT.] —**swat'ter,** *n.*

SWAT (swot) *n.* a special unit of a law enforcement agency armed and trained to handle unusual and dangerous situations such as terrorist attacks or the holding of hostages. Also, **SWAT team.** [Short for *s(pecial) w(eapons) a(nd) t(actics).*]

swatch (swoch) *n.* a small sample of a particular cloth or other material. [Of uncertain origin.]

swath (swoth, swôth) *also,* **swathe.** *n.* **1.** the area covered by a single sweep of a scythe or other mowing implement or machine. **2.** a width or strip of grass or other grain cut in one such sweep. **3.** a long, broad belt, strip, or path: *a swath of color encircling the hem of a dress.* **4.** an area or extent destroyed as if by a scythe. [Old English *swæth* track, trace.]
• **to cut a wide swath.** to make a big impression or display; have a great influence: *The candidate's style cut a wide swath with the audience.*

swathe¹ (swoth, swāth) *v.t.,* **swathed, swath·ing. 1.** to bind or wrap: *to swathe an arm with bandages.* **2.** to surround; enclose: *The coast was swathed in fog.* —*n.* a wrapping or binding; bandage. [Old English *swathian* to wrap.]

swathe² (swoth, swāth) swath.

sway (swā) *v.i.* **1.** to move or swing back and forth or from side to side: *to sway in time to music, branches swaying in the wind.* **2.** to bend, lean, or turn to one side, as from excess weight or pressure: *The car swayed off the road after taking a sharp turn.* —*v.t.* **1.** to cause to move back and forth or from side to side: *The heavy winds swayed the palm trees.* **2.** to cause to bend, lean, or turn to one side. **3.** to turn aside or divert, as from a course of action; deter: *Nothing could sway me from my convictions.* **4.** to cause to be directed or biased in a particular way; have or exert pressure, power, or control over: *The lawyer's argument visibly swayed the jurors.* —*n.* **1.** the act or an instance of swaying; back-and-forth or side-to-side motion: *the sway of a ladder, to walk with a sway.* **2.** a prevailing or overpowering influence, power, or control; domination: *Your best friend has too great a sway in your life.* **3.** sovereign power or authority; dominion; rule: *The dictator held sway over the entire country.* [Old Norse *sveigja* to bend.]

sway·back (swā'bak') *n.* an extreme concave or sagging condition of the back, as of a horse.

sway·backed (swā'bakt') *adj.* having the back concave or sagging to an unusual degree.

swear (swâr) *v.,* **swore, sworn, swear·ing.** —*v.i.* **1.** to make a solemn declaration with an appeal to God or to some other sacred being or object: *The witnesses in the trial had to swear before they could testify.* **2.** to make a solemn promise. **3.** to use profane language. —*v.t.* **1.** to declare (something) solemnly with an appeal to God or some other sacred being or object: *The witnesses swore that they had seen no one.* **2.** to promise (something) in a solemn manner: *I swear that I'm telling the truth.* **3.** to cause to take an oath; bind by an oath: *to be sworn to defend one's country.* **4.** to take or utter (an oath). [Old English *swerian* to take an oath, make a solemn promise.]
• **to swear by. a.** to appeal to or name (someone or something) as when taking an oath. **b.** to place great confidence in; consider infallible.
• **to swear in.** to induct into office by administering an oath: *A judge swore in the new mayor.*
• **to swear off.** *Informal.* to promise to give up; vow to abstain from: *to swear off a bad habit.*
• **to swear out.** to get (a warrant for arrest) by making a charge on oath.

swear·word (swâr'wûrd') *n.* a profane or obscene word used in cursing or swearing.

sweat (swet) *n.* **1.** a clear, salty fluid produced by glands beneath the skin and secreted through the pores; perspiration. **2.** a similar moisture either exuded by something or gathered on its surface: *a cold pipe covered with sweat.* **3.** the act or state of emitting sweat through the pores of the skin, esp. as a result of heat, exertion, or emotion. **4.** *Informal.* an emotional state, such as stress, irritation, or anxiety, that may induce sweat: *You needn't get into a sweat over the problem.* —*v.,* **sweat** or **sweat·ed, sweat·ing.** —*v.i.* **1.** to secrete sweat through the pores of the skin; perspire. **2.** to exude moisture. **3.** to gather moisture from

the surrounding air by condensation: *The glass of ice water sweated in the hot, humid air.* **4.** to be exuded in drops; ooze. **5.** *Informal.* to work hard; drudge; toil: *to sweat over a project for science class.* **6.** to feel great anxiety or stress: *to sweat over unpaid bills, to sweat off a difficult decision.* —*v.t.* **1.** to emit (moisture) in drops, as from the pores. **2.** to wet, soak, or stain with sweat. **3.** to cause to sweat. **4.** to force moisture out of, esp. in the process of curing or preparing for use: *to sweat hides.* **5.** to get rid of or decrease by or as by sweating: *to sweat off several pounds by working in the yard.* **6.** to join (metal parts) by heating, usually with another substance, such as solder, to which they adhere. **7.** to cause to work hard; overwork. **8.** *Informal.* to force (someone, such as an employee) to work under poor conditions, for low wages, or for long hours: *The factory supervisor sweated the workers.* **9.** *Slang.* **a.** to extract (information or the like) from a person, as by intense interrogation: *The interrogator sweated a confession out of the prisoner.* **b.** to extract information from, as by intense interrogation. [Old English *swætan* to perspire, work hard.]
• **to sweat blood. a.** to work too hard. **b.** to feel great anxiety or worry: *to sweat blood over a job interview.*
• **to sweat out.** *Slang.* to wait anxiously or impatiently for: *to sweat out the results of a test.*

sweat·band (swet'band') *n.* **1.** a narrow band of leather or other material, sewn into the edge of the crown of a hat to absorb sweat. **2.** a narrow band of terry or similar material worn around the forehead or wrists to absorb sweat.

sweat·er (swet'ər) *n.* a knitted garment, often of wool or cotton, for the upper part of the body.

sweat gland, a small gland beneath the skin that secretes sweat.

sweat·pants (swet'pants') *pl. n.* loose-fitting pants made of an absorbent material and elasticized or drawn in at the ankles and waist, used when exercising to prevent chill and to induce sweating.

sweat·shirt (swet'shûrt') *n.* a loose-fitting, absorbent shirt, worn esp. during athletic exercise.

sweat·shop (swet'shop') *n.* a factory or workshop where workers are employed for long hours, at low wages, or under poor conditions.

sweat suit, a suit worn when exercising, consisting of a sweatshirt and sweatpants.

sweat·y (swet'ē) *adj.,* **sweat·i·er, sweat·i·est. 1.** covered with, stained with, or smelling of sweat: *sweaty hands, sweaty sneakers.* **2.** causing sweat; laborious: *hard, sweaty labor.* —**sweat'i·ly,** *adv.* —**sweat'i·ness,** *n.*

Swed. 1. Sweden. **2.** Swedish.

Swede (swēd) *n.* **1.** a native or citizen of Sweden. **2.** a person of Swedish ancestry.

Swe·den·bor·gi·an (swē'dən bôr'jē ən, -gē-) *n.* a person who believes in or practices the religious doctrines of the Swedish mystic Emanuel Swedenborg. —*adj.* of or relating to Swedenborg, his doctrines, or his followers.

Swed·ish (swē'dish) *n.* **1.** the people of Sweden, collectively. **2.** the language of Sweden, belonging to the northern group of the Germanic branch of the Indo-European language family. —*adj.* of, relating to, or characteristic of Sweden or its people, language, or culture.

sweep (swēp) *v.,* **swept, sweep·ing.** —*v.t.* **1.** to clear or cleanse with or as if with a broom, brush, or the like: *to sweep a floor.* **2.** to remove, collect, or clear away with or as if with a broom, brush, or the like: *to sweep dust from under a sofa.* **3.** to touch or pass over the surface of with a sweeping motion: *The train of her gown swept the floor.* **4.** to pass over or through with a swift, continuous movement: *His eyes swept the newspaper for reports of the incident.* **5.** to move, bring, or carry with a swift, surging movement: *The flood swept away everything in its path.* **6.** to pass over (a place or surface) in order to remove something that occupies; clear: *The minesweepers swept the channel of mines. The agents swept the room of hidden microphones.* **7.** to win (an election) by an overwhelming majority. **8.** to win every game of a series. —*v.i.* **1.** to clear or clean a surface with or as if with a broom, brush, or the like. **2.** to move or pass along with a swift, surging movement: *The wind swept through the trees. Cars swept past the house.* **3.** to move with dignity or stateliness: *The king*

a	at	e	end	o	hot	u	up	hw	white		about
ā	ape	ē	me	ō	old	ū	use	ng	song		taken
ä	far	i	it	ô	fork	ü	rule	th	thin	ə	pencil
âr	care	ī	ice	oi	oil	ů	pull	th	this		lemon
		îr	pierce	ou	out	ûr	turn	zh	measure		circus

1217

swept into the room. **4.** to extend continuously for a long distance: *The highway sweeps along the coast.* —*n.* **1.** the act of sweeping. **2.** any swift, surging, or continuous force, movement, or process: *the sweep of the tides, a sweep of the hand.* **3.** a search of a room, building, or area, as for hidden microphones or other listening devices or for trespassers. **4.** a turn, bend, or curve: *the sweep of her hair as it fell over her eye.* **5.** the reach or range of a continuous motion: *the sweep of an ax, the sweep of a telescope as it scans the sky.* **6.** an extent, range, stretch, or expanse: *a sweep of desert.* **7.** a person who sweeps, esp. a chimney sweep. **8.** a long oar used to steer or propel a boat or ship. **9.** a device consisting of a long pole mounted on a post, used as a lever to raise and lower a bucket in a well. **10.** an overwhelming election victory. **11.** the winning of every game in a series. **12. sweeps.** sweepstakes. [Of uncertain origin.]

sweep·back (swēp′bak′) *n.* the backward slant of the leading edge of an airplane wing toward the wing tip.

sweep·er (swē′pər) *n.* a person or thing that sweeps floors or other surfaces, esp. a mechanical device used to sweep carpets.

sweep hand, a second hand that is mounted in the center of a clock or watch and extends to the edge of the dial. Also, **sweep second hand.**

sweep·ing (swē′ping) *adj.* **1.** moving, passing, or curving continuously over a surface or wide area: *a sweeping arc.* **2.** extending over or affecting a wide area; comprehensive; complete: *sweeping reforms, a sweeping generalization.* —*n.* **1. sweepings.** things swept out or up; trash; rubbish. **2.** the act of a person or thing that sweeps. —**sweep′ing·ly,** *adv.*

sweep·stakes (swēp′stāks′) *also,* **sweep·stake.** *n.* **1.** a lottery in which the winners are determined by the running of a horse race. **2.** a horse race run for this purpose. **3.** any lottery or contest. **4.** any of the prizes awarded in a lottery or similar contest. ➡ used as singular or plural in all defs.

sweet (swēt) *adj.* **1.** having a taste or flavor like that of sugar or honey. **2.** pleasing to the mind or senses: *a sweet fragrance, a sweet melody.* **3.** not sour or salted: *sweet cream, sweet butter.* **4.** having or marked by pleasing, agreeable, or kindly characteristics: *a sweet disposition, a sweet and thoughtful gesture.* **5.** greatly loved or cared for; dear; beloved. **6.** (of soil) free from acid and thus good for farming. —*n.* **1.** a person or thing that is sweet. **2.** *British.* a sweet dish, esp. a dessert. **3. sweets.** sweet edible things, such as cake or candy. **4.** a person who is dear or beloved; darling. ➡ usually used as a term of endearment. **5.** something that is pleasing or agreeable. —*adv.* in a sweet manner; sweetly. [Old English *swēte* pleasing to the senses of taste, smell, and hearing, pleasant, dear, kindly.] —**sweet′ly,** *adv.* —**sweet′ness,** *n.*

· **to be sweet on.** *Informal.* to have a special fondness for; be enamored of.

sweet alyssum, a low-growing plant, *Lobularia maritima,* of the mustard family, native to the Mediterranean region, widely cultivated for its clusters of tiny, fragrant white or purple flowers.

sweet basil, a widely grown basil, *Ocimum basilicum,* having fragrant leaves used as a seasoning in salads and in cooking.

sweet bay 1. a North American tree or shrub, *Magnolia virginiana,* raised for its fragrant white flowers. **2.** laurel *(def. 1).*

sweet·bread (swēt′bred′) *also,* **sweet·breads.** *n.* the pancreas or thymus gland of an animal, esp. a calf or lamb, when used as food.

sweet·bri·er (swēt′brī′ər) *also,* **sweet·bri·ar.** *n.* a rosebush, *Rosa eglanteria,* bearing pink flowers and small scarlet fruit. Also, eglantine.

sweet cherry 1. a Eurasian cherry, *Prunus avium,* bearing white flowers, widely cultivated in North America for its edible fruit. **2.** the sweet, red fruit of this tree.

sweet cider, freshly made, unfermented cider.

sweet clover, any of a number of cloverlike herbs, genus *Melilotus,* of the pea family, having small, fragrant white or yellow flowers that attract bees, widely grown as forage and green manure.

sweet corn, a variety of corn with kernels that have a high sugar content and are shriveled when fully mature, grown chiefly for human consumption.

sweet·en (swē′tən) *v.t.* **1.** to make sweet with or as with sugar: *to sweeten lemonade.* **2.** to make less painful or trying; lighten: *They sweetened the task with their good humor.* **3.** *Informal.* to increase the value or attractiveness of by adding to, as a pot in poker. —*v.i.* to become sweet or sweeter.

sweet·en·er (swē′tə nər) *n.* **1.** a substance that sweetens, esp. a noncaloric or low-calorie sugar substitute, such as saccharin. **2.** a person or thing that sweetens.

sweet·en·ing (swē′tə ning, swēt′ning) *n.* **1.** a person or thing that sweetens; sweetener. **2.** the act or process of making something sweet.

sweet fern, an aromatic shrub, *Comptonia peregrina,* of eastern North America, having fernlike leaves.

sweet flag, a fragrant marsh plant, *Acorus calamus,* of the arum family, whose root yields an aromatic oil used in liqueurs and perfumes. Also, **calamus.**

sweet gale, an aromatic shrub, *Myrica gale,* growing along streams in cool regions of the Northern Hemisphere, bearing brown male flowers in catkins and female flowers in small conelike clusters. Also, **gale.**

sweet gum, a tall North American tree, *Liquidambar styraciflua,* bearing glossy star-shaped leaves, and having a reddish brown bark that yields a fragrant yellow resin sometimes used medicinally. Also, **red gum.**

sweet·heart (swēt′härt′) *n.* a person who is loved by and loves another: *They've been sweethearts for years.*

sweet·ie (swē′tē) *n. Informal.* sweetheart. Also, **sweetie pie.**

sweet·ing (swē′ting) *n.* **1.** a sweet apple. **2.** *Archaic.* darling; sweetheart.

sweet·ish (swē′tish) *adj.* somewhat or rather sweet.

sweet marjoram, marjoram.

sweet·meat (swēt′mēt′) *n.* any sweet food, esp. candy, cake, or candied or preserved fruit.

sweet pea 1. the fragrant flower of a plant of the pea family, *Lathyrus odoratus,* growing singly or in short-stalked clusters in a variety of colors. **2.** the plant itself, having a rough hairy stem, and bearing pairs of short oval or oblong leaflets.

sweet pepper 1. the mild-flavored, podlike, edible fruit of a pepper plant, esp. *Capsicum annuum grossum,* eaten in its ripe (red) or unripe (green) state. **2.** the plant bearing this fruit. Also, **bell pepper.**

sweet potato 1. the fleshy, edible root of a long, trailing vine, *Ipomoea batatus,* of the morning glory family, having yellow, brown, or reddish skin and white to orange flesh, cooked and eaten as a vegetable. **2.** the vine itself, widely cultivated in warm areas throughout the world, bearing violet or pink funnel-shaped flowers.

sweet·sop (swēt′sop′) *n.* **1.** a tropical American tree, *Annona squamosa,* bearing sweet, yellowish green edible fruits and thin, bluish gray leaves. **2.** the fruit of this tree, sometimes used for making sherbets, jams, and jellies.

sweet sorghum, sorgo.

sweet-talk (swēt′tôk′) *v.t.* to flatter or use charm and pleasant talk to try to get (someone) to do something; cajole. —*v.i.* to use flattery.

sweet talk, flattery, charm, or pleasant talk, esp. when used to try to get someone to do something; cajolery.

sweet tooth, a fondness or craving for sweets.

sweet william *also,* **sweet William.** a plant of the pink family, *Dianthus barbatus,* native to Eurasia, widely cultivated for its dense, rounded clusters of variously colored flowers with fringed petals.

swell (swel) *v.,* **swelled, swelled** or **swol·len, swell·ing.** —*v.i.* **1.** to increase in size or extent, esp. by absorption of moisture or inflation with air: *The sponge swelled as it absorbed the water.* **2.** to be distended; bulge out; protrude: *The sails swelled in the breeze.* **3.** to increase in amount, degree, intensity, or force: *Attendance swelled at the evening concerts.* **4.** to rise above the ordinary or surrounding level: *The*

sweet william

heavy rains made the river swell. **5.** to become greater in volume; grow louder: *The baby's whimper soon swelled to a howl.* **6.** *Informal.* **a.** to become filled with pride, arrogance, or other emotion: *The victorious athlete's head swelled with pride.* **b.** to arise and increase; well up: *Hope swelled in my breast.* —*v.t.* **1.** to cause to increase in size; enlarge: *The infection swelled my hand.* **2.** to cause to distend: *The wind swelled the sails.* **3.** to cause to increase in amount, degree, intensity, or force: *New members swelled the rolls of the club.* **4.** *Informal.* to fill, as with pride, arrogance, or other emotion: *Happiness swelled their hearts.* —*n.* **1.** the act of swelling or the state of being swollen. **2.** a part that is swollen or distended; protuberance; swelling: *The ice reduced the swell on my head.* **3.** a piece of land that rises gradually and evenly above the surrounding level; rounded elevation. **4.a.** a tall, unbroken wave or waves; billow; surge. **b.** waves coming from a direction other

than that from which the wind is blowing. **c.** ground swell *(def. 1).* **5.** (of sound) a gradual increase in loudness or force. **6.** *Music.* **a.** a gradual crescendo immediately followed by a gradual diminuendo. **b.** a sign (< >) indicating this. **c.** a device, as in a pipe organ, by which the volume of a tone may be varied. **7.** *Informal.* a person of high social position, esp. one who is fashionably or stylishly dressed: *We watched the swells coming out of the opera house.* —*adj. Slang.* **1.** excellent; fine. **2.** elegant; stylish. [Old English *swellan* to increase in size, become distended.] —For Synonyms *(v.i.),* see **expand.**

swelled head, an excessively high opinion of oneself.

swell·head (swel′hed′) *n.* a person who thinks too highly of himself or herself. —**swell′head′ed,** *adj.*

swell·ing (swel′ing) *n.* **1.** the act or process of increasing, as in size or extent: *the swelling of a river after heavy rains.* **2.** an abnormal enlargement of some part of the body.

swel·ter (swel′tər) *v.i.* to suffer or sweat from heat. —*v.t.* to oppress with heat. —*n.* a sweltering condition. [From dialectal *swelt* to be overcome (by heat), from Old English *sweltan* to die.]

swel·ter·ing (swel′tər ing) *adj.* suffering from or characterized by excessive heat; very hot: *a sweltering summer day.* —**swel′ter·ing·ly,** *adv.*

swept (swept) the past tense and past participle of **sweep.**

swept·back (swept′bak′) *adj.* (of the wing of an airplane) having the leading edge extending backward to form an acute angle with the fuselage.

swept·wing (swept′wing′) *adj.* (of an aircraft) having swept-back wings.

swerve (swûrv) *v.i., v.t.,* **swerved, swerv·ing.** to turn or cause to turn aside from a straight course or aim: *The car swerved to avoid hitting the motorcycle. The driver swerved the truck.* —*n.* the act or process of swerving. [Old English *sweorfan* to rub, polish.]

swift (swift) *adj.* **1.** moving or capable of moving with great speed; fleet: *a swift runner.* **2.** happening, passing, or accomplished quickly or without delay: *a swift rebuttal, a swift kick.* **3.** acting or responding readily; prompt: *swift to make excuses.* —*adv.* fast: *to run swift and hard.* —*n.* any of various swallow-like birds related to the hummingbird, family Apodidae, having narrow, crescent-shaped wings and predominantly dark gray, brown, or bluish plumage. Length: 3½-9 inches (9-23 centimeters). [Old English *swift* rapid, prompt.] —**swift′ly,** *adv.* —**swift′ness,** *n.*

swift-foot·ed (swift′fút′id) *adj.* able to run fast or to cover great distances quickly.

swig (swig) *Informal. n.* a large swallow or gulp. —*v.t.,* **swigged, swig·ging.** to drink in large swallows or gulps. [Of uncertain origin.] —**swig′ger,** *n.*

swill (swil) *n.* **1.a.** a liquid or semiliquid mixture used to feed animals, esp. slops fed to swine. **b.** kitchen refuse; garbage. **c.** any dirty liquid or semiliquid mess. **2.** a large swallow; swig. —*v.t.* **1.** to drink freely, thirstily, or to excess; guzzle. **2.** to feed or supply (hogs or the like) with swill. —*v.i.* to guzzle, esp. liquor. [Old English *swilian* to wash.]

swim (swim) *v.,* **swam** or *(archaic)* **swum, swim·ming.** —*v.i.* **1.** to move along on or in the water by means of movements of the body or parts of the body. **2.** to move with a gliding, flowing motion, as if swimming through water: *Small clouds swam across the sky.* **3.** to float on water or other liquid: *peaches swimming in cream.* **4.** to be covered or flooded with or immersed in water or other liquid: *The child's eyes swam with tears.* **5.** to have a dizzy or giddy sensation; reel; whirl: *All this confusion makes my head swim.* —*v.t.* **1.** to swim across or through: *to swim the English Channel.* **2.** to cause to swim. —*n.* the act or an instance, period, or distance of swimming: *to take a quick swim before lunch.* [Old English *swimman* to move in water by movements of parts of the body, float.] —**swim′mer,** *n.*

  ·in the swim. in the current trend of affairs, esp. aware of or participating in what is fashionable.

swim bladder, air bladder.

swim·mer·et (swim′ə ret′) *n.* one of the abdominal appendages of lobsters, shrimp, and other crustaceans, adapted for swimming, aiding in respiration, and, in the female, serving as a place for attaching fertilized eggs. [SWIM + -ER¹ + -ET.]

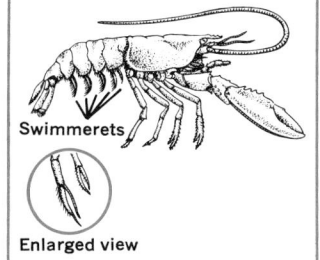

Swimmerets

Enlarged view

swimmerets

swim·ming (swim′ing) *n.* the act of a person or thing that swims. —*adj.* **1.** of, relating to, or used for swimming or swimmers. **2.** habitually moving in or on the water: *a swimming insect.* **3.** dizzy or lightheaded: *a swimming feeling.*

swimming bladder, air bladder.

swim·ming·ly (swim′ing lē) *adv.* very well; successfully; smoothly: *Those two get-along swimmingly.*

swimming pool, pool¹ *(def. 2).*

swim·suit (swim′süt′) *n.* bathing suit.

swin·dle (swin′dəl) *v.,* **-dled, -dling.** —*v.t.* **1.** to deprive by fraud of money or property rightfully due. **2.** to obtain (something, such as money or property) by this means. —*v.i.* to practice fraud; cheat. —*n.* the act or an instance of swindling; fraud. —**swin′dler,** *n.* —For Synonyms *(v.t.),* see **cheat.**

swine (swīn) *n., pl.* **swine.** **1.** any of various stout-bodied mammals, family Suidae, such as the pig or boar, having a long, mobile snout, cloven hoofs, and thick, bristly skin. **2.** a stupid, brutal, or contemptible person. [Old English *swīn* this animal.]

swine flu, an influenza caused by a highly contagious virus that was first identified in infected swine. The flu epidemic of 1918, which killed millions of people, was caused by a closely related virus.

swine·herd (swīn′hûrd′) *n.* a person who tends swine.

swing (swing) *v.,* **swung, swing·ing.** —*v.t.* **1.** to cause to move backward and forward, esp. with a steady movement, as below or about a fixed point. **2.** to cause to turn as if on a hinge or pivot; move in an arc: *to swing a door shut.* **3.** to move or lift in a sweeping motion: *to swing a bat at a ball.* **4.** to change the course or direction of by turning: *to swing a car off the highway.* **5.** to attach from above so as to hang freely; suspend: *to swing a lantern on a hook, to swing a hammock from two posts.* **6.** *Informal.* to influence or control to one's advantage; bring about successfully: *to swing an election, to swing a contract.* **7.** to play (music) in a style of jazz characterized by generally legato melody and relatively simple harmonies: *to swing a popular tune.* —*v.i.* **1.** to move backward and forward, esp. with a steady movement, as below or about a fixed point. **2.** to turn on a hinge or pivot: *The gate swung open.* **3.** to ride on a swing: *The little girl swung higher and higher when her brother pushed her.* **4.** to strike or attempt to strike with a swinging motion: *The batter swung at the ball and missed.* **5.** to act or move freely, smoothly, and easily: *The acrobats swung into their routine.* **6.** to turn: *The car swung into the driveway.* **7.** *Informal.* to be hanged. **8.** to play music in a style of jazz characterized by generally legato melody and relatively simple harmonies: *This band really swings.* **9.** *Slang.* to be lively, esp. in an up-to-date manner: *This town swings in the summer.* —*n.* **1.** the act of swinging: *the swing of a pendulum, the swing of public opinion.* **2.** the distance covered by the arc or curve made by swinging: *a wide swing.* **3.** a recreational device consisting of some form of seat suspended by ropes, chains, or the like, on which one may swing back and forth. **4.** a free, swinging, rhythmic movement or gait: *There is a swing in the dancer's step.* **5.** a sweeping blow or stroke: *a swing of an ax.* **6.** freedom of action; license. **7.** a continuous, vigorous, and forceful movement or progress. **8.** a rhythmic property essential to jazz, that combines a constant forward drive with a sense of freedom, or suspension, within the basic meter. **9.** a style of jazz first prominent in the 1930s, characterized by generally legato melody and relatively simple harmonies, performed most notably by large bands playing written arrangements. Also *(def. 9),* **swing music.** —*adj.* of, relating to, or characteristic of music in the style of swing: *a swing arrangement, a swing band.* [Old English *swingan* to scourge, rush¹.] —**swing′er,** *n.*

  ·in full swing. operating to the greatest extent; proceeding without hindrance or reservation: *Ten weeks before the election, the campaign was in full swing.*

swin·gle (swing′gəl) *n.* a large, knifelike wooden instrument used for beating flax or hemp to remove the woody or coarse portions. —*v.t.,* **-gled, -gling.** to clean (flax or hemp) with such an instrument. [Middle Dutch *swinghel* instrument for beating flax.]

swin·gle·tree (swing′gəl trē′) *n.* whiffletree.

swing music, swing *(n., def. 9).*

swing shift, a work shift between the day and night shifts, usually between 3 P.M. and 11 P.M.

a	at	e	end	o	hot	u	up	hw	white		about
ā	ape	ē	me	ō	old	ū	use	ng	song		taken
ä	far	i	it	ô	fork	ü	rule	th	thin	ə	pencil
âr	care	ī	ice	oi	oil	ú	pull	th	this		lemon
		îr	pierce	ou	out	ûr	turn	zh	measure		circus

swin·ish (swī′nish) *adj.* like or befitting swine; brutish; beastly: *rude, swinish behavior.* —**swin′ish·ly**, *adv.* —**swin′ish·ness**, *n.*

swipe (swīp) *n. Informal.* a sweeping stroke, glancing blow, or punch: *The cat took a swipe at the ball of yarn.* —*v.t.,* **swiped**, **swip·ing. 1.** *Informal.* to hit with a sweeping or glancing blow. **2.** *Slang.* to steal; pilfer; snatch. [Possibly modification of SWEEP.]

swirl (swûrl) *v.i.* to move with a twisting or eddying motion; whirl: *A gust of wind made the leaves swirl.* —*v.t.* to cause to whirl; twist; curl. —*n.* **1.** a whirling motion; eddy. **2.** something having a twisted shape; curl; spiral: *We decorated the cake with chocolate swirls.* [Possibly imitative.]

swish (swish) *v.i.* **1.** to move with or make a soft, muffled sound; rustle: *The silk banners swished in the breeze.* **2.** to move with or make a thin, hissing or whistling sound, as a slender rod or scythe cutting through the air. —*v.t.* to cause to swish: *The cow stood silently swishing its tail.* —*n.* a swishing movement or sound: *the swish of a cat's tail.* [Imitative.]

Swiss (swis) *adj.* of, relating to, or characteristic of Switzerland or its people or culture. —*n., pl.* **Swiss. 1.** a native or citizen of Switzerland. **2.** a person of Swiss ancestry.

Swiss chard, a beet, *Beta vulgaris cicla,* often cultivated for its yellowish to reddish green leaves and long, thick, white to greenish or red leafstalks, both of which are cooked and eaten as a vegetable. Also, **chard.**

Swiss cheese, a firm, pale yellow or whitish cheese having many large holes.

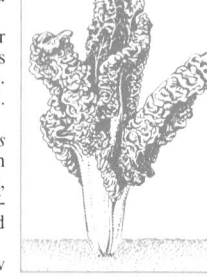

Swiss chard

Swiss Guards, a corps of soldiers, recruited from Switzerland, employed as bodyguards of the pope since the sixteenth century.

switch (swich) *n.* **1.** a slender, flexible rod, twig, or stick used for whipping. **2.** a stroke, lash, or other sudden, whisking movement: *a switch across the back.* **3.** the act or an instance of changing; shift, as of opinion or approach: *a switch from one political party to another.* **4.** a device used to open or close an electric circuit or to transfer current from one conductor to another: *Flip the switch to turn on the lights.* **5.** an apparatus for transferring trains or train cars from one track to another. **6.** a woman's hairpiece consisting of a thick bunch or braid of real or synthetic hair. **7.** the bushy end of the tail of certain animals, as cows. —*v.t.* **1.** to turn aside, divert, or convert: *to switch a conversation to a less controversial topic.* **2.** to exchange: *The friends switched coats.* **3.** to connect or disconnect by means of a switch (with *on* or *off*): *to switch on the lights.* **4.** to beat, strike, or whip with or as with a switch: *to switch a horse.* **5.** to move or swing sharply or suddenly; whisk: *The cat switched its tail in anger.* **6.** to move (a train or train cars) from one track to another; shunt. —*v.i.* **1.** to turn aside, shift, or change: *The senator switched to another political party.* **2.** to be turned aside or changed. **3.** to change from one railroad track to another. [Possibly from Middle Dutch *swijch* twig, branch, whip.] —**switch′er**, *n.*

switch·back (swich′bak′) *n.* a railroad, road, path, or the like that ascends a steep incline in a series of sharp turns or zigzags.

switch·blade (swich′blād′) *n.* a pocketknife with a blade operated by a spring and released by a catch when a button on the side of the handle is pressed. Also, **switchblade knife.**

switch·board (swich′bôrd′) *n.* a control panel with switches, dials, buttons, or receptacles for plugs, that connects, disconnects, combines, or adjusts electric circuits, as for telephone lines.

switch hitter, a baseball player who can bat both left-handed and right-handed.

switch·man (swich′mən) *n., pl.* -**men** (-mən). a person in charge of one or more switches on a railroad.

switch·yard (swich′yärd′) *n.* a railroad yard where trains are assembled and switched from one track to another.

swiv·el (swiv′əl) *n.* **1.** a link or other fastening device that allows attached parts of a mechanism to turn freely. **2.** a pivoted support on which something, such as a chair or stool, may be turned in a horizontal plane. —*v.,* -**eled**, -**el·ing**; *also, British,* -**elled**, -**el·ling.** —*v.i.* to turn on or as on a piano stool: *to swivel around on a piano stool.* **1.** to turn or swing sharply or as on a swivel: *to swivel one's chair around.* **2.** to secure with or fasten by means of a swivel. [Middle English *swyvel* the fastening device, from Old English *swīfan* to revolve.]

swivel chair, a chair whose seat turns horizontally on a swivel.

swiz·zle stick (swiz′əl) a short rod or stick, as of wood or plastic, used to stir drinks, esp. alcoholic beverages.

swob (swob) *n.* swab. —*v.t.,* **swobbed**, **swob·bing.** swab.

swol·len (swō′lən) *v.* a past participle of **swell.** —*adj.* enlarged by or as by swelling: *swollen eyes, a swollen river.*

swoon (swoon) *v.i.* to lose consciousness briefly; faint. —*n.* the act of swooning; fainting fit. [Middle English *swownen* to faint, going back to Old English *geswōgen* in a faint.]

swoop (swoop) *v.i.* to rush or descend with a sudden sweeping movement, as a bird diving on its prey (often with *down*): *Outlaws swooped down from the hills to attack the stagecoach.* —*v.t.* to seize or remove suddenly; scoop (often with *up*): *The infielder swooped up the ball and threw.* —*n.* the act or an instance of swooping; sudden sweeping descent, blow, or stroke. [Old English *swāpan* to sweep, rush[1].]

· **in** (or **at**) **one fell swoop.** all at one time or all together: *My bonus helped me pay all of my bills in one fell swoop.*

swoosh (swoosh) *Informal. v.t., v.i.* to move or cause to move with a sweeping motion that tends to stir up the air and make a blowing sound. —*n.* the act or sound of swooshing. [Imitative.]

swop (swop) *n.* swap. —*v.t.,* *v.i.,* **swopped**, **swop·ping.** swap.

sword (sôrd) *n.* **1.** a weapon, such as a saber, scimitar, or broadsword, usually of metal, consisting of a hilt and a straight or curved pointed blade, used for thrusting or cutting. **2.** sovereign power or authority. **3.** force or the use of force, as in war: *The pen is mightier than the sword.* **4.** any instrument or cause of death, destruction, or ruin. [Old English *sweord* this weapon, military force, a destroying agency.] —**sword′like′**, *adj.*

· **at swords′ points.** ready to fight; mutually antagonistic; hostile.

· **to cross** (or **measure**) **swords. a.** to fight. **b.** to disagree or argue violently.

· **to put to the sword.** to kill or slay with a sword, esp. in battle.

sword·fish (sôrd′fish′) *n., pl.* -**fish** or -**fish·es.** a large saltwater food and game fish, *Xiphias gladius,* found in temperate and tropical seas, having a scaleless, streamlined body and a long, flattened, swordlike snout. Length: to 15 feet (4.6 meters).

sword grass, any of various grasses or plants with swordlike leaves.

sword knot, a ribbon or tassel attached to the hilt of a sword for ornament.

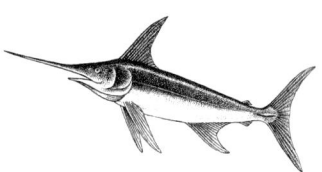

swordfish

sword·play (sôrd′plā′) *n.* the action, art, or technique of using a sword, esp. in fencing.

swords·man (sôrdz′mən) *also,* **sword·man.** *n., pl.* -**men** (-mən). **1.** a person who is armed with a sword, such as a soldier or fencer. **2.** a person who is skilled in the use of a sword. —**swords′man·ship′**, *n.*

sword·tail (sôrd′tāl′) *n.* platy[2]. [Because the male has a swordlike lower tail fin.]

swore (swôr) the past tense of **swear.**

sworn (swôrn) the past participle of **swear.**

'swounds (zwoundz, zoundz) zounds.

swum (swum) the past participle and archaic past tense of **swim.**

swung (swung) the past tense and past participle of **swing.**

sy-, form of **syn-** before *s* plus a consonant, as in *systole.*

syb·a·rite (sib′ə rīt′) *n.* a person who is devoted to luxury and pleasure; epicure. [Latin *Sybarīta* inhabitant of Sybaris, from Greek *Sybarītēs,* from *Sybaris,* an ancient city in southern Italy notorious for luxurious living.] —**syb·a·rit·ic** (sib′ə rit′ik); *also,* **syb′a·rit′i·cal,** *adj.*

syc·a·more (sik′ə môr′) *n.* **1.** a plane tree, *Platanus occidentalis,* of eastern North America, sometimes planted as an ornamental. Also, **buttonwood. 2.** a fig tree, *Ficus sycomorus,* of Egypt and Asia Minor, bearing sweet edible fruit. [Late Latin *sȳcomorus* mulberry tree, from Greek *sȳkomoros* fig tree; probably of Semitic origin.]

syc·o·phan·cy (sik′ə fən sē) *n., pl.* -**cies.** the behavior or character of a sycophant; fawning or self-seeking servility.

syc·o·phant (sik′ə fənt) *n.* a person who fawns over or flatters powerful or important people as a means of gaining favor or influence. [Latin *sȳcophanta* informer, flatterer, from Greek *sȳkophantēs* informer.] —**syc·o·phan·tic** (sik′ə fan′tik); *also,* **syc′o·phan′ti·cal,** *adj.*

sy·e·nite (sī′ə nīt′) *n.* a granular, plutonic igneous rock composed of feldspar, hornblende, or biotite, and little or no quartz.

[Latin *Syēnītēs (lapis)* (stone) of Syene, syenite, from *Syene,* a town in ancient Egypt where this stone was quarried.] —**sy·e·nit·ic** (sī′ə nit′ik), *adj.*

syl-, form of **syn-** before *l,* as in *syllable.*

syl·lab·ic (si lab′ik) *adj.* **1.** of, relating to, or consisting of a syllable or syllables. **2.** relating to a consonant sound that forms a separate syllable by itself without the help of a vowel sound, as the *l* in *rattle.* **3.** pronounced with each syllable distinctly enunciated. **4.** designating a type of poetry based on the number of syllables in a line rather than on stress or rhythm. —*n.* a syllabic sound. —**syl·lab′i·cal·ly,** *adv.*

syl·lab·i·cate (si lab′i kāt′) *v.t.,* -**cat·ed, -cat·ing.** to form or divide into syllables. —**syl·lab′i·ca′tion,** *n.*

syl·lab·i·fy (si lab′ə fī′) *v.t.,* -**fied, -fy·ing.** syllabicate. —**syl·lab′i·fi·ca′tion,** *n.*

syl·la·ble (sil′ə bəl) *n.* **1.** a unit of spoken language pronounced with a single uninterrupted sounding of the voice, consisting of a single vowel sound or of a vowel sound grouped with one or more consonants or of a single consonant pronounced alone. The words *bit* and *break* have one syllable; the word *amazement* has three. **2.** a letter or group of letters used in writing and printing to represent such a spoken unit, serving to indicate where a word may be hyphenated at the end of a line. **3.** a slightest bit, mention, or expression: *There was not a syllable of doubt as to the defendant's guilt.* —*v.t.,* -**bled, -bling.** to pronounce in syllables. [Old French *sillabe* part of a word forming only one sound, through Latin, from Greek *syllabē* literally, that which holds together.]

syl·la·bub (sil′ə bub′) *also,* **sillabub.** *n.* a whipped drink or topping, usually made with cream and liquor and sometimes thickened with gelatin, eaten as a chilled dessert. [Of uncertain origin.]

syl·la·bus (sil′ə bəs) *n., pl.* -**bus·es** or -**bi** (-bī′). a brief statement, summary, or plan listing main points to be covered and requirements to be met, as in a course of study. [Modern Latin *syllabus,* from a printer's mistaken rendering of Latin *sittybas,* accusative plural of *sittyba* label (from Greek *sittybā*).]

syl·lo·gism (sil′ə jiz′əm) *n.* **1.** a form of argument or reasoning consisting of a major premise, a minor premise, and a conclusion that is logically drawn from them. If the premises are accepted as true, it must follow that the conclusion is true. For example: All men are mortal (major premise); Socrates is a man (minor premise); therefore, Socrates is mortal (conclusion). **2.** reasoning based on deduction; deductive reasoning. [Latin *syllogismus,* from Greek *syllogismos* calculation, reasoning, deductive argument.]

syl·lo·gis·tic (sil′ə jis′tik) *adj.* of, relating to, or consisting of a syllogism or syllogisms. Also, **syl′lo·gis′ti·cal.** —**syl′lo·gis′ti·cal·ly,** *adv.*

syl·lo·gize (sil′ə jīz′) *v.t., v.i.,* -**gized, -giz·ing.** to argue, reason, or deduce (something) by means of syllogisms.

sylph (silf) *n.* **1.** a slender, graceful girl or young woman. **2.** an imaginary being supposed to inhabit the air. [Modern Latin *sylphes* (plural), possibly coined by Paracelsus from Latin *sylva* (form of *silva* a wood, forest) and *nympha.* See NYMPH.]

syl·van (sil′vən) *also,* **silvan.** *adj.* **1.** of, situated in, or inhabiting a wood or woods: *a sylvan deity.* **2.** formed by or abounding in trees; wooded; woody: *a sylvan grove.* **3.** relating to or characteristic of a wood or woods; rustic. [Latin *silvānus* relating to a wood, from *silva* a wood, forest.]

sym-, form of **syn-** before *b, m,* and *p,* as in *symbiosis, symmetry, symptom.*

sym·bi·ont (sim′bī ont′, -bē-) *n.* an organism that lives in a symbiotic relationship with another, dissimilar organism.

sym·bi·o·sis (sim′bī ō′sis, -bē-) *n., pl.* -**ses** (-sēz). **1.** the living together in close association of two unlike organisms, esp. in a relationship that is mutually beneficial. The association between termites and the protozoans living in their stomachs and intestines is an example of symbiosis. The protozoans break down the cellulose eaten by the termite so that it can be digested, and in turn all the protozoans' nourishment is provided by the termite. **2.** any association of mutual interdependence, as between persons or groups. [Modern Latin *symbiosis,* from Greek *symbiōsis* a living together.]

sym·bi·ot·ic (sim′bī ot′ik, -bē-) *adj.* relating to, living in, or characterized by symbiosis. Also, **sym′bi·ot′i·cal.** —**sym′bi·ot′i·cal·ly,** *adv.*

sym·bol (sim′bəl) *n.* **1.** something that stands for or represents something else, esp. a material object considered to typify some abstract or invisible quality, condition, or idea: *The dove is a symbol of peace. A gold band is a symbol of marriage.* **2.** a letter, figure, or other printed or written device used to express or represent an object, quantity, process, relation, or the like, as in mathematics, music, or chemistry: *C is the symbol for carbon.* —*v.t.,*

-**boled, -bol·ing;** *also, British,* -**bolled, -bol·ling.** symbolize. [Latin *symbolum* token, sign, from Greek *symbolon.*]

sym·bol·ic (sim bol′ik) *adj.* **1.** serving as a symbol: *The owl is symbolic of wisdom and learning.* **2.** relating to or expressed by a symbol or symbols. **3.** characterized by or involving the use of symbols, esp. in art or literature: *symbolic poetry.* Also, **symbol′i·cal.** —**sym·bol′i·cal·ly,** *adv.*

sym·bol·ism (sim′bə liz′əm) *n.* **1.** the practice or convention of representing things by symbols or of investing objects, acts, or relations with symbolic meaning or significance, esp. in art or literature. **2.** a category or system of symbols: *pictorial symbolism, pagan symbolism.* **3.** a symbolic quality, character, or meaning. **4.** the theories and practices of symbolists in art or literature.

sym·bol·ist (sim′bə list) *n.* **1.** a person who uses symbols. **2.** a person who is skilled in the interpretation of symbols. **3.** a person who uses or is skilled in the use of symbolism, esp. an artist or writer. **4.** any of a group of chiefly French artists and writers of the late nineteenth century who rejected realism and attempted to express ideas and emotions through the use of symbolic sounds, words, and objects. —**sym′bol·is′tic;** *also,* **sym′bol·is′ti·cal,** *adj.*

sym·bol·ize (sim′bə līz′) *v.,* -**ized, -iz·ing.** —*v.t.* **1.** to be or serve as a symbol of; represent or stand for: *A white lily symbolizes purity.* **2.** to represent by a symbol or symbols: *Writing symbolizes the sounds made in speaking.* —*v.i.* to use symbols. —**sym′bol·i·za′tion,** *n.*

sym·bol·o·gy (sim bol′ə jē) *n.* the study or use of symbols or symbolism.

sym·met·ri·cal (si met′ri kəl) *adj.* having or exhibiting symmetry. Also, **sym·met′ric.** —**sym·met′ri·cal·ly,** *adv.*

sym·me·trize (sim′ə trīz′) *v.t.,* -**trized, -triz·ing.** to make symmetrical.

sym·me·try (sim′ə trē) *n., pl.* -**tries.** **1.** an exact correspondence in size, form, and arrangement of the parts of something, either on opposite sides of a median line or plane, as in bilateral symmetry, or around a central point or axis, as in radial symmetry. Leaves, starfish, and human beings display one form of symmetry or another. **2.** beauty, proportion, and harmony of form. [Latin *symmetria* proportion, from Greek *symmetriā.*]

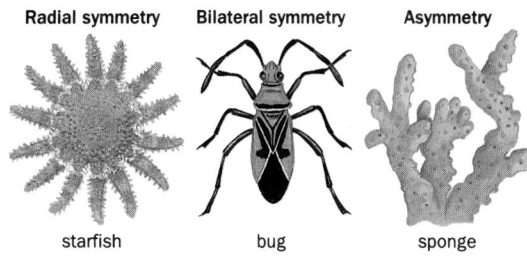

Radial symmetry   Bilateral symmetry   Asymmetry

starfish   bug   sponge

symmetry and asymmetry

sym·pa·thet·ic (sim′pə thet′ik) *adj.* **1.** expressing, feeling, or resulting from sympathy: *a sympathetic friend, a sympathetic statement.* **2.** favorably inclined toward; in agreement with (with *to*): *to be sympathetic to someone's plans.* **3.** being in accord or harmony; congenial. **4.** of or relating to the sympathetic nervous system. **5.** *Physics.* produced by or designating responsive vibrations caused by the transmission of vibrations from one body to another: *sympathetic sound, sympathetic tone, sympathetic vibrations.* —**sym′pa·thet′i·cal·ly,** *adv.*

sympathetic nervous system, the part of the autonomic nervous system consisting of nerves that originate in the lumbar and thoracic regions of the spinal cord and mediate involuntary responses to stress by speeding the heart rate, raising blood pressure, or the like. ➡ distinguished from **parasympathetic nervous system.**

sym·pa·thize (sim′pə thīz′) *v.i.,* -**thized, -thiz·ing.** **1.** to feel or express compassion: *to sympathize with another's hurt feelings.* **2.** to share in or agree with the feelings or ideas of; be in accord:

a	at	e	end	o	hot	u	up	hw	white	⎧	about
ā	ape	ē	me	ō	old	ū	use	ng	song		taken
ä	far	i	it	ô	fork	ū	rule	th	thin	ə	pencil
âr	care	ī	ice	oi	oil	u̇	pull	th	this		lemon
		îr	pierce	ou	out	ûr	turn	zh	measure	⎩	circus

I sympathize with the candidate's efforts for reform. [French *sympathiser* to feel alike, from *sympathie* feeling in common, from Latin *sympathīa.* See SYMPATHY.] **—sym′pa·thiz′ing·ly,** *adv.*

sym·pa·thiz·er (sim′pə thī′zər) *n.* a person who sympathizes, esp. a person who is favorably inclined toward a particular party or cause without being fully committed to it.

sym·pa·thy (sim′pə thē) *n., pl.* **-thies. 1.** the act or capacity of entering into or sharing the feelings of another or others. **2.** a feeling or expression of pity or compassion; commiseration: *The newspaper article aroused a great deal of sympathy for the victims of the hurricane.* **3.** a relationship between two things whereby whatever affects one affects the other in the same way. **4.** agreement in personality, disposition, or point of view; affinity: *Those two friends get along so well because they are in complete sympathy.* **5.** a favorable attitude or leaning toward some cause or party; accord, allegiance, or commitment: *I am in sympathy with the striking workers.* [Latin *sympathīa* feeling in common, from Greek *sympatheia,* going back to *syn* together + *pathos* feeling.]

Synonyms Sympathy, empathy, compassion, and pity mean a sharing in the feelings of others. **Sympathy,** the broadest of these terms, ranges in its implications from a simple sharing of another's views to a deep concern over another's misfortunes: *The state's governor was in sympathy with the goals of the conservationists. Many friends came to visit the bereaved husband and express their sympathy.* **Empathy** emphasizes emotional identification with someone else's feelings, as if experiencing those feelings oneself: *I felt empathy with the steelworkers who had lost their jobs, having been out of work for several months myself.* **Compassion** implies sharing another's distress and also feeling a desire to alleviate it: *Their compassion toward the homeless led them to volunteer at the local soup kitchen.* **Pity** suggests sympathy from an emotional distance and is often accompanied by feelings of condescension: *The battle-scarred veteran needed job retraining, not pity.*

sympathy strike, a strike by a body of workers to give support to a strike by another group.

sym·pet·al·ous (sim pet′ə ləs) *adj. Botany.* gamopetalous.

sym·phon·ic (sim fon′ik) *adj.* **1.** of, relating to, or having the character of a symphony or symphony orchestra. **2.** agreeing in sound; harmonious. **—sym·phon′i·cal·ly,** *adv.*

sym·pho·ni·ous (sim fō′nē əs) *adj.* in harmony; harmonious.

sym·pho·ny (sim′fə nē) *n., pl.* **-nies. 1.** an extended orchestral composition usually having three or four movements written in varied forms, tempos, and keys. **2.** symphony orchestra. **3.** harmony, esp. of sounds. **4.** anything characterized by an agreeable or harmonious blending of elements. [Latin *symphōnia* harmony, concord, agreement of sounds, from Greek *symphōnia,* going back to *syn* together + *phōnē* sound.]

symphony orchestra, a large orchestra organized to play symphonies and other similar compositions, usually consisting of string, brass, woodwind, and percussion sections.

sym·po·si·um (sim pō′zē əm) *n., pl.* **-si·ums** or **-si·a** (-zē ə). **1.** a meeting or conference for the discussion of a particular subject, esp. a meeting at which several speakers give short addresses before an audience on a single topic. **2.** a collection of comments or opinions on a particular subject, esp. a published group of essays or articles. [Latin *symposium* banquet, from Greek *symposion* banquet, drinking party, from *syn* together + *posis* drinking; referring to the ancient Greek custom of having intellectual discussions at a drinking party.]

symp·tom (simp′təm, sim′-) *n.* **1.** a noticeable change in the normal condition or functions of the body or any of its parts that indicates or accompanies a disease or other disorder: *Vomiting and muscular cramps are symptoms of cholera.* **2.** anything serving as a sign or indication of something: *The disappearance of fish in a river is often a symptom of water pollution.* [Late Latin *symptōma* indication of disease, from Greek *symptōma* happening, accident.]

symp·to·mat·ic (simp′tə mat′ik, sim′-) *adj.* **1.** indicating or accompanying a disease or other abnormal condition of the body (usually followed by *of*): *Fever, chills, and repeated coughing may be symptomatic of pneumonia.* **2.** of or relating to the symptoms of a disease: *symptomatic treatment.* **3.** serving as a sign or indication: *A falling barometer is symptomatic of bad weather.* **—symp′to·mat′i·cal·ly,** *adv.*

syn- *prefix* at the same time or in conjunction; together; with: *synod, synchronize.* [Greek *syn* together, with.]

syn. 1. synonym. **2.** synonymous.

syn·a·gogue (sin′ə gog′, -gôg′) *n.* **1.** a congregation of Jews assembled for religious instruction and worship. **2.** a building used for such instruction and worship. [Late Latin *synagōga,* from Greek *synagōgē* a bringing together, assembly.]

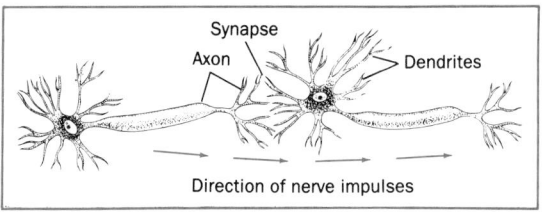

synapse

syn·apse (sin′aps, si naps′) *n.* the site at which a nerve impulse is transmitted between two nerve cells or between a nerve cell and a muscle or gland. *—v.i.* to form a synapse or join in synapsis. [Greek *synapsis* contact, junction.]

syn·ap·sis (si nap′sis) *n., pl.* **-ses** (-sēz). *Biology.* **1.** during the first stage of meiosis, the association, side by side, of homologous maternal and paternal paired chromosomes. **2.** synapse. [Modern Latin *synapsis,* from Greek *synapsis* contact, junction.]

syn·ap·tic (si nap′tik) *adj.* of or relating to a synapsis or synapse. **—syn·ap′ti·cal·ly,** *adv.*

sync (singk) also, **synch.** *n. Informal.* **1.** the act or process of synchronizing. **2.** the condition of being synchronized; synchronism: *My plans were in sync with theirs.* [Short for SYNC(HRO-NIZE).]

syn·chro·cy·clo·tron (sing′krō sī′klə tron′, -sik′lə-) *n.* a cyclotron in which the frequency of the voltage of the electrical field is synchronized to compensate for increases in mass as particles approach the speed of light, enabling the particles to acquire higher energies.

syn·chro·mesh (sing′krə mesh′, -krō-) *n.* a device in an automobile transmission that synchronizes the speeds of the gears so that they will mesh smoothly when shifted. *—adj.* relating to or using such a device: *a synchromesh transmission, synchromesh shifting.*

syn·chro·nism (sing′krə niz′əm) *n.* **1.** the condition or quality of being synchronous; simultaneous occurrence; coincidence. **2.** a chronological listing or arrangement of historical events or persons to indicate their simultaneous occurrence or existence.

syn·chro·nize (sing′krə nīz′) *v., -nized, -niz·ing. —v.i.* **1.** to happen at the same time; agree in time; coincide: *The closing of the old store synchronized with the opening of the new shopping plaza.* **2.** to move or operate at the same rate and exactly together. *—v.t.* **1.** to cause to happen or operate at the same rate and exactly together: *to synchronize the sound and the action of a motion picture.* **2.** to make (timepieces) agree in keeping or indicating time: *The referees synchronized their watches before the game.* **3.** to list or arrange (historical events or persons) to indicate simultaneous occurrence or existence. [Greek *synchronizein* to be contemporary with, going back to *syn* together + *chronos* time.] **—syn′chro·ni·za′tion,** *n.* **—syn′chro·niz′er,** *n.*

syn·chro·nous (sing′krə nəs) *adj.* **1.** occurring at the same time; simultaneous; coincident: *synchronous events.* **2.** happening or operating at the same rate of speed: *synchronous gears.* **3.** *Physics.* having the same period and phase, as vibrations. [Late Latin *synchronus* contemporary, from Greek *synchronos,* from *syn* together + *chronos* time.] **—syn′chro·nous·ly,** *adv.* **—syn′chro·nous·ness,** *n.*

syn·chro·tron (sing′krə tron′) *n.* a cyclotron in which subatomic particles are accelerated along a fixed, circular path by increasing the intensity of a magnetic field.

synchrotron radiation, radiation in the ultraviolet to X-ray range produced by charged particles moving in a magnetic field at velocities close to the speed of light, as in a synchrotron or certain regions of outer space.

syn·cline (sing′klīn′, sin′-) *n.* a fold of rocks in which the strata dip inward from both sides toward the axis. ➡ opposed to **anticline.** For illustration, see **anticline.** [Greek *synklīnein* to lean together, from *syn-* together + *klīnein* to lean.] **—syn·cli′-nal,** *adj.*

syn·co·pate (sing′kə pāt′, sin′-) *v.t., -pat·ed, -pat·ing.* **1.** *Music.* to treat or modify (a tone or passage) by syncopation. **2.** to shorten (a word) by omitting one or more sounds or letters, as *sou'wester* for *southwester.* [Late Latin *syncopātus,* past participle of *syncopāre* to swoon, shorten by syncope, from *syncopē* a swooning, contraction. See SYNCOPE.]

syn·co·pa·tion (sing′kə pā′shən, sin′-) *n.* **1.a.** *Music.* a metric pattern created by stressing one or more normally unaccented beats in a measure, used esp. in ragtime music. **b.** syncopated music, rhythm, dance steps, or the like. **2.** syncope *(def. 1).*

syn·co·pe (sing′kə pē′, sin′-) *n.* **1.** a contraction of a word by

S

the omission of one or more sounds or letters from the middle, as *Lester* for *Leicester*. **2.** a loss of consciousness caused by a temporary inadequate supply of blood to the brain; faint. [Late Latin *syncopē* a swooning, contraction, from Greek *synkopē* a cutting short.]

syn·dic (sin′dik) *n.* **1.** a person who represents and manages the affairs of a community, corporation, or institution, esp. a university. **2.** a civil magistrate or other government official. [Late Latin *syndicus* delegate, advocate, from Greek *syndikos* advocate, from *syn* with + *dikē* lawsuit, judgment.] —**syn′di·cal**, *adj.*

syn·di·cal·ism (sin′di kə liz′əm) *n.* a political and economic theory advocating that all means of production and distribution be brought under the control of groups of workers by means of direct action, such as industrial sabotage, boycotts, demonstrations, and esp. a general strike. —**syn′di·cal·ist**, *n.*

syn·di·cate (*n.,* sin′di kit; *v.,* sin′di kāt′) *n.* **1. a.** an association of individuals or companies formed to carry out a business enterprise, esp. one requiring a large amount of capital. **b.** a group of persons combined to carry out any enterprise. **2.** an organization that sells material, such as special articles and photographs, for simultaneous publication in a number of newspapers or periodicals. **3.** a council or body of syndics. **4.** *Informal.* an association of racketeers or gangsters controlling organized crime. —*v.,* -**cat·ed**, -**cat·ing**. —*v.t.* **1.** to manage as or combine into a syndicate. **2.** to sell (an article, column, comic strip, or the like) for simultaneous publication in a number of newspapers or periodicals. —*v.i.* to form a syndicate. [French *syndicat* trusteeship, from *syndic* trustee, from Late Latin *syndicus* delegate, advocate. See SYNDIC.] —**syn′di·ca′tion**, *n.* —**syn′di·ca′tor**, *n.*

syn·drome (sin′drōm) *n.* **1.** a group of symptoms that together are characteristic of a particular disease or disorder. **2.** any group of characteristics that indicate or identify a particular condition or quality, esp. a social condition. [Modern Latin *syndrome,* from Greek *syndromē* a running together, combination.]

syn·ec·do·che (si nek′də kē′) *n.* a figure of speech in which a part is substituted for the whole, or the whole for a part, for example: many *mouths* (people) to feed; starting a *car* (the car's engine). [Late Latin *synecdochē,* from Greek *synekdochē* literally, a receiving together.]

syn·er·gism (sin′ər jiz′əm) *n.* the action of separate substances, agents, or organs that produces a greater effect than the sum of their individual actions, as in a medicine composed of several different drugs. [Modern Latin *synergismus,* from Greek *synergos* working together.] —**syn′er·gis′tic**, *adj.*

syn·es·the·sia (sin′əs thē′zhə, -zē ə) *n.* a phenomenon in which the stimulation of one of the senses produces a secondary, subjective sensation associated with a different sense, as when the hearing of a particular sound gives someone a mental impression of a certain color. —**syn·es·thet·ic** (sin′əs thet′ik), *adj.*

syn·fu·el (sin′fū′əl) *n.* a gaseous or liquid fuel manufactured from coal or extracted from other mineral resources, such as oil shale or tar sand.

syn·od (sin′əd) *n.* **1.** a council or assembly of ecclesiastical officials. **2.** any council or assembly. **3.** in the Presbyterian Church, a governing body ranking next above the presbytery. [Late Latin *synodus* ecclesiastical council, from Greek *synodos* meeting, assembly, from *syn* together + *hodos* way.] —**syn′od·al**, *adj.*

syn·od·i·cal (si nod′i kəl) *adj.* **1.** of or relating to the conjunctions of celestial bodies, esp. the period between two successive conjunctions of a planet with the sun. **2.** relating to or of the nature of a synod. Also, **syn′od′ic**.

syn·o·nym (sin′ə nim) *n.* **1.** a word that has the same or nearly the same meaning as another word in the same language. *Large* is a synonym of *big; leap* is a synonym of *jump.* ➡ opposed to **antonym**. **2.** a word or phrase accepted as a substitute for another; symbolic or figurative name; metonym: *Broadway has become a synonym for the American commercial theater.* **3.** *Biology.* **a.** a scientific name that has been rejected as incorrect or out-of-date. **b.** one of two or more scientific names that have been given to the same organism. [Latin *synōnymum* word having the same meaning as another word, from Greek *synōnymon.*]

syn·on·y·mize (si non′ə mīz′) *v.t.,* -**mized**, -**miz·ing**. to give a synonym or synonyms for (a word).

syn·on·y·mous (si non′ə məs) *adj.* **1.** equivalent or very similar in meaning; bearing a synonym or synonyms. The words *bravery, valor, gallantry,* and *courage* are synonymous. **2.** expressing or implying the same idea; having the same significance: *Lack of education is not synonymous with lack of intelligence.* —**syn·on′y·mous·ly**, *adv.*

syn·on·y·my (si non′ə mē) *n., pl.* -**mies**. **1.** the state or quality of being synonymous. **2.** the study or classification of synonyms.

3. a list or collection of synonyms, esp. one in which synonyms are discriminated from one another according to their implications, connotations, and uses.

syn·op·sis (si nop′sis) *n., pl.* -**ses** (-sēz). a brief statement giving a review, outline, or condensation of a book, speech, play, or similar work; summary: *a synopsis of the plot of a novel.* [Late Latin *synopsis* general view, plan, from Greek *synopsis* general view.] —For Synonyms, see **summary**.

syn·op·size (si nop′sīz) *v.t.,* -**sized**, -**siz·ing**. to make a synopsis of; summarize.

syn·op·tic (si nop′tik) *adj.* **1.** of, relating to, or forming a synopsis; providing a general view. **2.** presented from or taking a common point of view. **3.** *usually,* **Synoptic.** relating to or designating the first three Gospels of the New Testament. Also, **syn·op′ti·cal**. —**syn·op′ti·cal·ly**, *adv.*

syn·o·vi·a (si nō′vē ə) *n.* a clear, viscid lubricating fluid secreted by certain membranes, such as those lining the joints. [Modern Latin *synovia;* coined by Paracelsus, 1493-1541, Swiss physician and alchemist.] —**syn·o′vi·al**, *adj.*

syn·tac·tic (sin tak′tik) *adj.* of, relating to, or according to the rules of syntax. Also, **syn·tac′ti·cal**. —**syn·tac′ti·cal·ly**, *adv.*

syn·tax (sin′taks) *n.* **1.** the way in which words are put together to form sentences and phrases; relationship and arrangement of words in a sentence. **2.** the branch of grammar that deals with this. [Late Latin *syntaxis* the connection of words, from Greek *syntaxis* arrangement, a putting together of words.]

syn·the·sis (sin′thə sis) *n., pl.* -**ses** (-sēz). **1.** the assembling or combining of separate parts or subordinate elements into a complex or systematic whole. ➡ distinguished from **analysis. 2.** a complex whole or entity formed in this manner: *The book is a synthesis of the professor's research in three different fields.* **3.** the act or process of producing a chemical compound by combining two or more compounds, elements, or radicals. **4.** a conclusion reached by dialectic reasoning; result of the interplay of one idea (thesis) with its opposite (antithesis). [Latin *synthesis* mixture, compound, from Greek *synthesis* a putting together.]

syn·the·size (sin′thə sīz′) *v.t.,* -**sized**, -**siz·ing**. **1.** to combine so as to form a complex or systematic whole: *an effort to synthesize Asian and Western philosophies.* **2.** to produce by chemical synthesis: *to synthesize rubber.*

syn·the·siz·er (sin′thə sī′zər) *n.* **1.** a person or thing that synthesizes. **2.** an electronic device consisting of solid-state circuitry that can simulate the sounds made by a wide variety of musical instruments and also produce sounds not obtainable from ordinary instruments, played or operated using a keyboard, knobs, or other devices.

syn·thet·ic (sin thet′ik) *adj.* **1.** produced artificially; not occurring naturally: *Nylon is a synthetic fiber.* **2.** lacking genuine emotion or sincerity; artificial: *a synthetic smile.* **3.** relating to, of the nature of, or proceeding by synthesis. Also *(def. 3),* **synthet′i·cal**. —*n.* something synthetic, esp. a product made by chemical synthesis: *This fabric is a synthetic.* —**syn·thet′i·cal·ly**, *adv.* —For Synonyms *(adj.),* see **artificial**.

synthetic fuel, synfuel.

syph·i·lis (sif′ə lis) *n.* an infectious, chronic disease caused by a spirochete, usually transmitted by sexual intercourse or acquired congenitally. If untreated, the disease progresses in severity and can damage the heart, blood vessels, spinal cord, eyes, or brain. [Modern Latin *syphilis,* from *Syphilus,* the hero of a poem about the disease by Girolamo Fracastoro, 1483-1553, Italian physician and poet.]

syph·i·lit·ic (sif′ə lit′ik) *adj.* of, relating to, or affected with syphilis. —*n.* a person who is affected with syphilis.

sy·phon (sī′fən) siphon.

Syr·i·ac (sir′ē ak′) *n.* a Semitic language based on ancient Aramaic, spoken in Syria from the third to the thirteenth century A.D., surviving chiefly as the liturgical and literary language of several Eastern Christian churches.

sy·rin·ga (sə ring′gə) *n.* mock orange.

sy·ringe (sə rinj′, sir′inj) *n.* a device consisting of a nozzle and a rubber bulb or piston, by means of which a liquid may be drawn in and then forced out in a thin stream. It is used esp. for injecting fluids into the body and cleansing wounds. —*v.t.,* -**ringed**, -**ring·ing**. to cleanse, inject, or the like, with or as with a syringe. [Medieval Latin *syringa* the device, going back to Greek *syrinx* pipe, tube.]

syr·inx (sir′ingks) *n., pl.* **sy·rin·ges** (sə rin′jēz) or **syr·inx·es**.

a	at	e	end	o	hot	u	up	hw	white	ə	about
ā	ape	ē	me	ō	old	ū	use	ng	song		taken
ä	far	i	it	ô	fork	ü	rule	th	thin		pencil
âr	care	ī	ice	oi	oil	u̇	pull	th	this		lemon
		îr	pierce	ou	out	ûr	turn	zh	measure		circus

1. panpipe. **2.** the vocal organ of birds, located at the lower end of the trachea at its junction with the bronchi. [Greek *sȳrinx* shepherd's pipe, tube.] —**sy·rin·ge·al** (sə rin′jē əl), *adj.*

syr·up (sir′əp, sûr′-) *also,* **sirup.** *n.* a sweet, thick liquid, esp. one obtained by boiling sugar with water or fruit juice, often with the addition of flavoring or medication: *cough syrup.* [Old French *sirop,* going back to Arabic *sharāb* beverage.]

syr·up·y (sir′ə pē, sûr′-) *also,* **sirupy.** *adj.* **1.** of or like syrup, esp. in appearance or consistency. **2.** excessively sentimental; mawkish: *syrupy dialogue.*

sys·tem (sis′təm) *n.* **1.** a group of things or parts related or combined in such a way as to form a unified or complex whole: *a heating system, a system of roads, a public school system, a loudspeaker system.* **2.** any group of related parts or members: *a system of weights and measures.* **3.a.** a set of organs or parts of the body that act together to perform a specific function: *the digestive system.* **b.** the entire body considered as a functioning organism: *The patient's system was greatly weakened by the long illness.* **4.** a related group or series of natural objects, such as rivers or mountains. **5.** an organized and comprehensive set of facts, rules, laws, doctrines, or principles: *a system of philosophy, a system of government.* **6.a.** any particular form of political, economic, or social organization or practice: *an oligarchic system, a communist system.* **b.** *usually,* **the system.** the established structure of society or government, esp. when regarded as hindering, restrictive, or repressive. **7.** any method or form of classification, arrangement, or notation: *a taxonomic system.* **8.** a plan or method of operation or procedure: *to have a system for studying for an examination.* **9.** a condition of orderliness or regularity. **10.** a group of

bodies moving or existing in relation to one another in accordance with certain natural laws, such as the solar system. **11.** *Geology.* a major division of rocks, composed of all the rocks formed during a geologic period. [Late Latin *systēma* a whole consisting of several parts, from Greek *systēma.*]

sys·tem·at·ic (sis′tə mat′ik) *adj.* **1.** of, constituting, or relating to a system: *a systematic statement of foreign policy, a systematic philosophy of life.* **2.** carried out or done by or as by a system: *a systematic course of study, a systematic attack on a person's reputation.* **3.** characterized by orderliness and careful planning; methodical: *a systematic person.* Also, **sys′tem·at′i·cal.** —**sys′-tem·at′i·cal·ly,** *adv.* —For Synonyms, see **orderly.**

sys·tem·a·ti·za·tion (sis′tə mə tə zā′shən) *n.* **1.** the act or process of systematizing. **2.** something systematized.

sys·tem·a·tize (sis′tə mə tīz′) *v.t.,* **-tized, -tiz·ing.** to form into or arrange according to a system. —**sys′tem·a·tiz′er,** *n.*

sys·tem·ic (sis tem′ik) *adj.* **1.** of or relating to a system or systems. **2.** of, relating to, or affecting the body as a whole.

sys·tem·ize (sis′tə mīz′) *v.t.,* **-ized, -iz·ing.** systematize. —**sys′tem·i·za′tion,** *n.* —**sys′tem·iz′er,** *n.*

systems analysis 1. the evaluation of an activity, such as data processing, to identify the objectives of the persons engaged in it and to determine procedures for attaining these objectives more efficiently. **2.** the profession of making such evaluations. —**systems analyst.**

sys·to·le (sis′tə lē) *n.* a normal contraction of the heart, alternating rhythmically with the period of dilation, or diastole. During systole the blood is forced outward from the heart. [Greek *systolē* contraction.] —**sys·tol·ic** (sis tol′ik), *adj.*

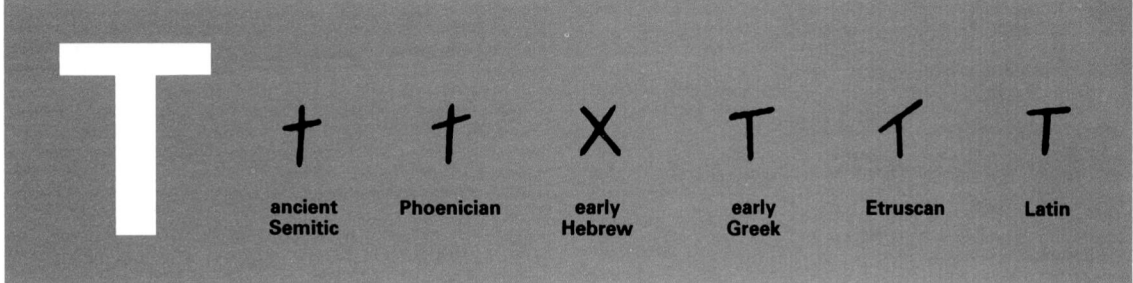

| ancient Semitic | Phoenician | early Hebrew | early Greek | Etruscan | Latin |

T The earliest ancestor of **T** was the letter *taw*, meaning "mark" in the ancient Semitic alphabets. The ancient Semitic *taw* and the later Phoenician version of it resembled our lower case *t*, but the early Hebrew version was closer in shape to the modern lower case *x*. *Taw* was the last letter of these early alphabets. The early Greeks borrowed *taw* and called it *tau*, a letter that was adopted, with only minor changes, by the Etruscans, and later by the Romans for their Latin alphabet. The shape of our capital letter **T** has come down almost unchanged from the Latin form of *tau*.

t, T (tē) *n., pl.* **t's, T's. 1.** the twentieth letter of the English alphabet. **2.** the shape of this letter or something having this shape.
• **to a T.** to perfection; exactly: *That suit fits you to a T.*
T, a symbol for tritium.
t *also,* **t. 1.** teaspoon; teaspoons. **2.** ton; tons.
t. 1. temperature. **2.** tenor. **3.** tense. **4.** time. **5.** transitive.
T *also,* **T. 1.** tablespoon; tablespoons. **2.** ton; tons. **3.** temperature.
T. 1. Territory. **2.** Testament. **3.** Tuesday.
Ta, the symbol for tantalum.
tab (tab) *n.* **1.** a small flap, strip, or other attachment projecting from an object, used esp. to make opening, fastening, or handling easier: *Pull the tab on the soda can to open it.* **2.** a small extension on a card or the edge of a paper, used as an aid in filing or indexing. **3.** a small ornamental flap or loop on a garment, as on the back or pocket of a shirt. **4.** a small auxiliary airfoil attached or set into a control surface of an airplane. **5.** tabulator *(def. 1).* **6.** *Informal.* a bill to be paid; check: *to pick up the tab for a meal.* —*v.,* **tabbed, tab·bing.** —*v.t.* **1.** to provide with a tab. **2.** to pick out or designate: *The coach has tabbed those players to start the game.* —*v.i.* to operate a tabulator on a computer or typewriter. [Of uncertain origin.]
• **to keep tabs** (or **a tab**) **on.** *Informal.* to watch closely; check up on: *The police kept tabs on the suspect's activities.*
tab·ard (tab'ərd) *n.* **1.** a short, loose outer garment resembling a coat, worn by knights over their armor. **2.** a coarse, heavy, short jacket worn outdoors, as by peasants during the Middle Ages. [Old French *tabart;* of uncertain origin.]
Ta·bas·co (tə bas'kō) *n. Trademark.* a hot, pungent sauce made from the fruit of a variety of red pepper. [From *Tabasco,* a Mexican state and river.]
tab·by (tab'ē) *n., pl.* **-bies. 1.** a domestic cat having a tawny or gray coat with darker stripes. **2.** any domestic cat, esp. a female. **3.** a fabric with a plain weave, esp. silk or taffeta with a moiré or watered finish. —*adj.* **1.** tawny or gray with darker stripes; brindled. **2.** made of or resembling tabby. [Old French *tabis* striped taffeta, from Arabic *'attābīy* watered silk, a district of Baghdad where this silk was first made.]
tab·er·nac·le (tab'ər nak'əl) *n.* **1.** a place of worship, esp. one for a large body of worshipers. **2. Tabernacle. a.** a portable tent containing the Ark of the Covenant, which served as a place of worship for the Israelites during their exodus from Egypt to Palestine. **b.** a Jewish temple; synagogue. **3.** in the Roman Catholic and some Anglican churches, a container for the consecrated host, usually placed in the center of the altar. **4.** a canopied niche or recess, esp. one containing a tomb or shrine. [Latin *tabernāculum* tent, diminutive of *taberna* hut.]
ta·bes dor·sal·is (tā'bēz dôr sal'is) a chronic degeneration of the nerves of the spinal cord that usually develops fifteen to twenty years after untreated syphilitic infection, characterized by shoot-

ing pains, difficulty in walking, and other disorders. [Modern Latin *tabes dorsalis* literally, a wasting away of the back.]
ta·ble (tā'bəl) *n.* **1.** a piece of furniture consisting of a flat, horizontal surface supported by one or more legs: *a coffee table, a billiard table.* **2.** such a table upon which food is served: *The child left the table before the meal was over.* **3.** the food served at a table or a particular place: *a lavish table.* **4.** the people seated at a table: *The table next to us was very noisy.* **5.** a concise, ordered list or guide; synopsis: *a table of contents.* **6.** an orderly arrangement of facts or information, usually in a series of columns to facilitate comparison of data: *a table of measurements, a statistical table.* **7.** the information presented in such an arrangement: *to learn the multiplication tables.* **8.** a gambling table, as for poker or roulette. **9.** tableland; plateau. **10.** any flat, horizontal surface. **11.** *Architecture.* **a.** a vertical member, usually rectangular and often ornamented, set into or projecting from a wall. **b.** a horizontal projecting course or molding, as a cornice. **12.** a thin, flat slab, as of stone or metal, used esp. for writing; tablet. —*v.t.,* **-bled, -bling. 1.** to postpone discussion or decision of indefinitely: *to table a motion.* **2.** to put on a table. **3.** to form into a list; tabulate: *to table population statistics.* —*adj.* **1.** of, for, or used with a table: *table saw, table lamp.* **2.** of, relating to, or for meals or eating: *table etiquette.* [Old English *tabule* board, tablet, from Latin *tabula.*]
• **at table.** having a meal; dining.
• **on the table.** postponed for discussion or decision for an indefinite period of time.
• **to turn the tables.** to reverse the situation completely, as between two opponents.
• **under the table.** secretly and illegally: *to pay money under the table in return for a politician's support.*
tab·leau (ta blō') *n., pl.* **-leaux** (-blōz') or **-leaus. 1.** a vivid and picturesque description or representation: *The movie was a tableau of life in Russia.* **2.** a group of persons or objects forming a picturesque scene. **3.** a silent and motionless representation of a scene, painting, or incident, enacted by a person or persons appropriately costumed and posed: *a tableau of Washington crossing the Delaware.* [French *tableau* picture, scene, diminutive of *table* table, slab, from Latin *tabula* board, tablet, picture.]
ta·ble·cloth (tā'bəl klôth') *n., pl.* **-cloths** (-klôthz', -klôths'). a cloth for covering a dining table, esp. at meals.
ta·ble d'hôte (tā'bəl dōt', tab'əl) *pl.* **ta·bles d'hôte** (tā'bəlz-dōt', tab'əlz). a complete meal consisting of several specified courses served at a fixed price. ➡ distinguished from **a la carte.** [French *table d'hôte* literally, table of the host, going back to Latin *tabula* board + *dē* from + *hospes* host[1], guest.]
ta·ble·land (tā'bəl land') *n.* an elevated, relatively flat land area; plateau.
table linen, tablecloths, napkins, doilies, and other items made of linen or similar material, used in setting a table.
table salt, salt *(def. 1).*
ta·ble·spoon (tā'bəl spün') *n.* **1.** a spoon larger than a teaspoon or dessert spoon, used esp. for serving and measuring. **2.** the amount one tablespoon holds, a standard cooking measurement equivalent to 3 teaspoons or ½ fluid ounce (14.8 milliliters).
ta·ble·spoon·ful (tā'bəl spün fûl') *n., pl.* **-fuls.** tablespoon *(def. 2).*
tab·let (tab'lit) *n.* **1.** a number of sheets of paper fastened

a	at	e	end	o	hot	u	up	hw	white		about
ā	ape	ē	me	ō	old	ū	use	ng	song		taken
ä	far	i	it	ô	fork	ü	rule	th	thin	ə	pencil
âr	care	ī	ice	oi	oil	ů	pull	th	this		lemon
		îr	pierce	ou	out	ûr	turn	zh	measure		circus

together at one edge, used esp. for writing; pad. **2.** a small, compressed piece of material, as medicine, soap, or candy. **3.** a thin, flat slab, as of wood or stone, used for writing or drawing. **4.** a slab of stone or metal bearing an inscription, esp. a commemorative or explanatory one; plaque. [Old French *tablete* something flat used for writing, small table, diminutive of *table* table, from Latin *tabula* board, tablet, picture.]

table talk, informal conversation at or as if at meals.

table tennis, a game similar to tennis, played on a table with a small plastic ball and wooden paddles. Also, **Ping-Pong.**

ta·ble·ware (tā′bəl wâr′) *n.* articles placed on a table for use at meals, as dishes, glasses, and silverware.

table wine, wine that contains less than 14% alcohol, usually served with meals.

tab·loid (tab′loid) *n.* a newspaper with pages half the size of an ordinary newspaper page, having brief news articles and many pictures, esp. one having items of a sensational nature. —*adj.* **1.** condensed; shortened. **2.** luridly sensational: *tabloid journalism* [TABL(ET) + -OID.]

ta·boo (tə bü′, ta-) *also,* **tabu.** *n., pl.* **-boos. 1.** among certain Polynesian peoples, a sacred prohibition or restriction observed out of fear that grave danger, misfortune, or death will come directly to anyone who breaks it. **2.** any prohibition or ban, esp. one imposed by social custom or convention. —*adj.* **1.** prohibited or restricted under a taboo. **2.** prohibited or forbidden for any reason: *During Prohibition the sale of alcoholic beverages was taboo.* —*v.t.,* **-boo·ed, -boo·ing.** to put under a taboo; ban; prohibit. [Polynesian *tabu,* sacred, set apart.]

ta·bor (tā′bər) *n.* a small drum, esp. one formerly used to accompany oneself on a pipe or fife. [Old French *tabour* drum, possibly going back to Persian *tabīr.*]

tab·o·ret (tab′ə ret′, -rā′) *also,* **tab·ou·ret.** *n.* **1.** a small, low seat or stool without a back or arms. **2.** a frame for embroidery. **3.** a small tabor. [French *tabouret* stool, diminutive of Old French *tabour* drum. See TABOR.]

ta·bu (tə bü′, ta-) taboo.

tab·u·lar (tab′yə lər) *adj.* **1.** having a broad, flat surface. **2.** of or arranged in lists or tables. **3.** computed or calculated by means of tables. [Latin *tabulāris* relating to a board, from *tabula* board, tablet.] —**tab′u·lar·ly,** *adv.*

tabor

ta·bu·la ra·sa (tab′yə lə rä′sə, -zə, rā′-)
1. a slate that is blank or has been erased; clean slate. **2.** the mind before it has received any impressions from experience, as in a newborn baby. [Latin *tabula rāsa* erased tablet, clean slate.]

tab·u·late (*v.,* tab′yə lāt′; *adj.,* tab′yə lit, -lāt′) *v.t.,* **-lat·ed, -lat·ing.** to arrange in lists or columns; put into a table: *to tabulate statistics.* —*adj.* having a broad, flat surface; tabular. —**tab′u·la′tion,** *n.*

tab·u·la·tor (tab′yə lā′tər) *n.* **1.** a key on a typewriter or computer used for arranging material in columns. Also, **tab. 2.** a person or machine that tabulates.

tac·a·ma·hac (tak′ə mə hak′) *n.* **1.** a gum resin with a strong odor, used in incenses, ointments, and formerly in medicines. **2.** any of various trees yielding this resin, esp. a North American poplar, *Populus balsamifera.* [Obsolete Spanish *tacamahaca* the tree; of Nahuatl origin.]

ta·chom·e·ter (ta kom′i tər, tə-) *n.* an instrument that measures speed of rotation, as of the crankshaft of an engine. [Greek *tachos* speed + -METER.]

tach·y·on (tak′ē on′) *n.* any of a class of hypothetical subatomic particles that travel faster than the speed of light. [Greek *tachys* swift + -ON.]

tac·it (tas′it) *adj.* **1.** not openly expressed but understood or implied; implicit: *The conductor's smile was tacit approval of the orchestra's performance.* **2.** without words; unspoken; silent: *a tacit prayer.* [Latin *tacitus,* past participle of *tacēre* to be silent.] —**tac′it·ly,** *adv.* —**tac′it·ness,** *n.*

tac·i·turn (tas′i tûrn′) *adj.* not inclined to speak very much; silent or extremely reserved. [Latin *taciturnus* quiet.] —**tac′i·tur′ni·ty,** *n.* —**tac′i·turn′ly,** *adv.*

tack (tak) *n.* **1.** a small nail with a sharp point and a broad, flat head. **2.** a stitch that can be easily removed, used in fastening. **3.** a course of action or method: *We decided to take a new tack in dealing with the problem.* **4.** *Nautical.* **a.** the direction of a boat or ship's fore-and-aft line with respect to the wind. When the wind is on a ship's starboard or right side, the ship is sailing on a star-

board tack. **b.** a change of direction to take advantage of side winds. **c.** one of a series of movements to starboard and port alternately in a zigzag against the wind. **5.** *Nautical.* **a.** a rope holding in place a corner of some sails, as the lower forward corner of a fore-and-aft sail. **b.** a corner thus held in place. **6.** the equipment used in outfitting a horse, as saddles, bridles, and harnesses. —*v.t.* **1.** to fasten with or as with a tack or tacks: *The teacher tacked the poster to the bulletin board.* **2.** to sew or fasten with temporary stitches: *to tack a bow on a dress.* **3.** to attach as a supplement; add: *to tack an amendment onto a bill.* **4.** *Nautical.* **a.** to change the course (of a vessel) by turning the head to the wind. **b.** to sail (a vessel) against the wind by a series of tacks. —*v.i.* **1.** *Nautical.* to tack a vessel. **2.** *Nautical.* (of a vessel) to go on an opposite tack or change course by going on opposite tacks. **3.** to change one's course of action. [Dialectal Old French *taque* nail; of Germanic origin.] —**tack′er,** *n.*

tack·le (tak′əl) *n.* **1.** the equipment or gear used for an activity, as fishing. **2.** a system of ropes and pulleys for hoisting, lowering, or pulling heavy loads, as those used on a ship to raise, lower, and move the sails. **3.** *Football.* **a.** either of the two players who line up between the guard and the end. **b.** the position played by either of these players. **c.** the act of stopping and bringing a ball carrier to the ground. **4.** the act of seizing, stopping, and bringing to the ground. —*v.,* **-led, -ling.** —*v.t.* **1.** to deal with; work on: *How do you think we should tackle this problem?* **2.** to seize and jump on in order to stop: *The police officer tackled the fleeing thief.* **3.** *Football.* to bring (a ball carrier) to the ground by seizing or by using one's weight against the player. **4.** to harness (a horse). —*v.i.* to make a football tackle. [Middle Low German *takel* equipment, ship's rigging, from *taken* to lay hold of.] —**tack′ler,** *n.*

tack·y¹ (tak′ē) *adj.,* **tack·i·er, tack·i·est.** sticky, as partially dried paint or glue. [TACK + -Y¹; with reference to the use of a tack in attaching things.] —**tack′i·ness,** *n.*

tack·y² (tak′ē) *adj.,* **tack·i·er, tack·i·est.** *Informal.* **1.** lacking taste or style; dowdy or shabby: *a tacky suit.* **2.** in poor taste; cheap or vulgar: *a tacky comment.* [Of uncertain origin.] —**tack′i·ness,** *n.*

ta·co (tä′kō) *n., pl.* **-cos.** a Mexican dish consisting of a fried tortilla wrapped around a filling, as of cheese, ground beef, or chicken. [Spanish *taco* wad, light meal; probably of Germanic origin.]

tac·o·nite (tak′ə nīt′) *n.* a low-grade iron ore, consisting of a flintlike rock containing silica and iron minerals, occurring esp. in the areas of Michigan, Wisconsin, and Minnesota around Lake Superior. [From the *Taconic* mountain range in New England and New York + -ITE¹.]

tact (takt) *n.* the ability to deal with people or situations without offending anyone. [Latin *tāctus* touch.]

tact·ful (takt′fəl) *adj.* having or showing tact; diplomatic: *a tactful supervisor, tactful criticism.* —**tact′ful·ly,** *adv.* —**tact′ful·ness,** *n.*

tac·tic (tak′tik) *n.* **1.** a plan of action or device used to achieve a goal. **2.** a method of arranging and using military forces in action. [Modern Latin *tacticus,* from Greek *taktikos* fit for arranging, from *tassein* to arrange.]

tac·ti·cal (tak′ti kəl) *adj.* **1.** of or relating to tactics, esp. military tactics. **2.** showing skill in tactics; characterized by clever planning and maneuvering. —**tac′ti·cal·ly,** *adv.*

tactical unit, a unit of troops, aircraft, or naval forces that can operate independently in battle, usually including support elements, as artillery.

tac·ti·cian (tak tish′ən) *n.* **1.** a person who is skilled in military tactics. **2.** anyone who is skilled in planning and executing a means to an end; clever maneuverer: *a political tactician.*

tac·tics (tak′tiks) *n.* **1.** the art or science of using and maneuvering military forces and equipment in actual combat. ➡ distinguished from **strategy;** used as singular. **2.** such use or maneuvering of military forces. **3.** any methods or devices employed to achieve a goal: *campaign tactics.* ➡ used as plural in defs. 2 and 3. [Plural of TACTIC.]

tac·tile (tak′təl, -tīl) *adj.* **1.** of or relating to touch: *The skin receives tactile sensations.* Also, **tactual. 2.** endowed with the sense of touch: *The whiskers of a cat are tactile organs.* **3.** capable of being felt by touch; tangible. [Latin *tāctilis* tangible, from *tāctus,* past participle of *tangere* to touch.] —**tac·til·i·ty** (tak til′i tē), *n.*

tact·less (takt′lis) *adj.* having or showing no tact; lacking diplomacy: *a tactless comment.* —**tact′less·ly,** *adv.* —**tact′less·ness,** *n.*

tac·tu·al (tak′chü əl) *adj.* **1.** tactile *(def. 1).* **2.** caused by the

touch; producing a feeling of touch. [Latin *tāctus* touch + -AL[1].] —**tac′tu·al·ly,** *adv.*

tad (tad) *n. Informal.* **1.** a small child, esp. a boy. **2.** a little bit; small amount: *Just a tad of sugar sweetens grapefruit.* [Probably from the dialect word *tad,* a form of TOAD.]

tad·pole (tad′pōl′) *n.* the aquatic larva of a frog or toad, having external gills, an egg-shaped body, and a slender tail. Also, **polli·wog.** [Middle English *taddepol* literally, toad (that is all) head, from *tadde* toad + *pol* head. See TOAD, POLL.]

ta′en (tān) *v.t., v.i. Archaic.* taken.

taf·fe·ta (taf′i tə) *n.* a shiny, somewhat stiff fabric, usually made of silk or rayon. [Old French *taffetas* smooth, shiny cloth of silk, going back to Persian *tāftah* silken or linen cloth.]

taff·rail (taf′rāl′) *n.* **1.** a rail around the stern of a ship. **2.** the upper part of the stern of a ship. [Dutch *taffereel* panel, diminutive of *tafel* table, going back to Latin *tabula* board, tablet.]

taf·fy (taf′ē) *n., pl.* **-fies.** a chewy candy made of brown sugar or molasses mixed with butter, boiled down and then pulled until it holds its shape. [Form of TOFFEE.]

tag[1] (tag) *n.* **1.** a piece of paper, plastic, or other material attached to or hanging loosely from something for the purpose of labeling or identifying it: *a name tag, a price tag.* **2.** a part or piece hanging from or loosely attached to something else. **3.** a hard tip or binding on a string or cord, as at the end of a shoelace. **4.** *Informal.* an automobile license plate. **5.** an identifying epithet. **6.** a saying or quotation used in speech or writing, for emphasis, ornament, or effect. **7.** the last line or lines ending a speech, as in a play. **8.** *Medicine.* a radioisotope that is ingested so that its path through the body can be traced; tracer. —*v.,* **tagged, tag·ging.** —*v.t.* **1.** to fasten an identifying tag to: *to tag a suitcase.* **2.** to label or designate with an epithet. **3.** to add as an appendage: *to tag superfluous comments onto a report.* **4.** to follow closely. **5.** *Informal.* to put a ticket on (a vehicle) for a traffic violation. **6.** *Informal.* to charge with breaking the law. —*v.i.* to follow closely; trail: *The dog tagged along wherever they went.* [Probably of Scandinavian origin.] —**tag′ger,** *n.*

tag[2] (tag) *n.* **1.** a game in which one player, usually called "it," chases the other players until he or she touches one who then, in turn, becomes "it" and must chase the others. **2.** in baseball and similar games, the act of putting out a runner by touching him or her with the ball or with the hand holding the ball. —*v.,* **tagged, tag·ging.** —*v.t.* **1.** to touch or tap, as in the game of tag. **2.** in baseball and similar games, to put out (a base runner) by touching with the ball or with the hand holding the ball. **3.** to hit with great force: *to tag a baseball into the outfield, to tag an opponent with an uppercut.* —*v.i.* in baseball and similar games, to make a tag. [Of uncertain origin.]
  • **to tag up.** in baseball and similar games, to return to and touch a base before running to the next base after a fly ball has been caught.

Ta·ga·log (tä gä′ləg, -lôg) *n., pl.* **-log** or **-logs. 1.** a member of a people of Malayan stock who make up part of the native population of the Philippines. **2.** their language, belonging to the Indonesian branch of the Austronesian language family, now the official national language of the Philippines.

tag end, the last or final part of anything; remnant.

tag line 1. the last line of a joke, phrase, speech, play, or the like. **2.** a phrase associated through repetition with a particular person, group, or thing.

tag sale, a sale of used, unwanted household items, each priced with a tag, and usually held in a garage or yard; garage sale.

Ta·hi·tian (tə hē′shən, -hē′tē ən) *adj.* of or relating to Tahiti or its people, language, or culture. —*n.* **1.** a native or inhabitant of Tahiti. **2.** the language of Tahiti, belonging to the Polynesian branch of the Austronesian language family.

t'ai chi (tī′jē′) *also,* **tai chi.** a Chinese system of exercise, originally a martial art, employing measured, deliberate movements and emphasizing balance and self-control. Also, **t'ai chi ch'uan** (tī′jē′chwän′), **tai chi chuan.**

tai·ga (tī′gə) *n.* any of the coniferous, swampy forests of subarctic North America, Europe, and Asia.

tail (tāl) *n.* **1.** the hindmost part of an animal's body, which in vertebrates consists of a number of vertebrae forming a flexible attachment at the end of the spine. **2.** anything resembling a tail in shape. **3.** a stream of luminous gases and solid matter trailing from a comet. **4.** the rear portion of an aircraft. **5.** the rear, bottom, or last part of anything: *the tail of a bicycle.* **6.** a long lock of hair banded or braided together. **7.** tails. the side of a coin not bearing a figure or inscription; reverse side of a coin. ➡ opposed to **heads;** used as singular. **8.** one of the two panels in the back of a man's formal coat. **9. tails. a.** a swallow-tailed coat. **b.** a man's full-dress formal evening wear. ➡ usually used as plural. **10.** *Informal.* a person or thing that follows closely, as a spy or detective: *The police put a tail on the suspect.* —*v.t.* **1.** to furnish with or as with a tail. **2.** to cut the tail from. **3.** to be the end or tail of. **4.** to join end to end: *to tail two ropes together.* **5.** to fasten the end of (a beam, brick, or similar part) into a wall or other support. **6.** *Informal.* to follow closely and secretly for the purpose of observing: *The secret agent tailed the spy.* —*v.i.* **1.** to form or move in a line suggesting a tail. **2.** to lessen gradually; diminish (usually with *off*): *Protests tailed off after the new policies were put in effect.* —*adj.* located at or coming from the rear: *the tail feathers of a bird.* [Old English *tægel* hindmost part of an animal's body.] —**tail′less,** *adj.* —**tail′like′,** *adj.*
  • **on someone's tail.** following closely: *The police were on the suspect's tail.*
  • **to turn tail.** to flee from danger, trouble, or something unpleasant.

tail·back (tāl′bak′) *n. Football.* an offensive halfback whose position is farthest behind the line of scrimmage.

tail·board (tāl′bôrd′) *n.* tailgate.

tail·bone (tāl′bōn′) *n.* coccyx.

tail end 1. a rear or hindmost part: *the tail end of a line.* **2.** a concluding part or end: *the tail end of a meeting.*

tail·gate (tāl′gāt′) *n.* a board, gate, or other closure at the rear of a station wagon or other vehicle that can be let down or removed for loading or unloading. Also, **tailboard.** —*v.i., v.t.,* **-gat·ed, -gat·ing.** *Informal.* to drive too closely behind another vehicle.

tail·ing (tā′ling) *n.* **1.** the part of a projecting stone or brick fastened into a wall. **2. tailings.** the part of a material separated as refuse, as in mining or grain milling.

tail·light (tāl′līt′) *n.* a warning light, usually red, at the rear of a vehicle.

tai·lor (tā′lər) *n.* a person who makes, alters, or mends clothing, esp. outer garments. —*v.t.* **1.** to make or fashion as a tailor: *to tailor a suit to fit properly.* **2.** to make, alter, or adapt to meet a special requirement or need: *The reading program was tailored to the needs of young children.* **3.** to fit or furnish with clothing. —*v.i.* to work as a tailor. [Old French *tailleur* cutter, from *taillier* to cut, from Late Latin *tāliāre,* from Latin *tālea* rod, cutting.]

tai·lor·bird (tā′lər bûrd′) *n.* any of several warblers, genus *Orthotomus,* native to Asia and Africa, that sew a nest of broad leaves together, using their needlelike bills and vegetable fibers. Length: 5 inches (13 centimeters).

tai·lored (tā′lərd) *adj.* **1.** well-finished with neat, simple lines and a trim fit, as some women's clothing. **2.** made by a tailor; custom-made.

tai·lor·ing (tā′lər ing) *n.* **1.** the workmanship or skill of a tailor. **2.** the business or occupation of a tailor.

tai·lor·made (tā′lər mād′) *adj.* **1.** made by a tailor or with the workmanship characteristic of a tailor. **2.** meeting specific needs or requirements; well-suited; made-to-order: *That role was tailor-made for the actor.*

tail·piece (tāl′pēs′) *n.* **1.** a part or piece that is the end or that is added on at the end. **2.** *Printing.* a small, ornamental mark placed at the bottom of a page, esp. at the end of a chapter. **3.** a triangular piece of wood at the lower end of violins and similar instruments to which the strings are attached. **4.** a short beam or rafter inserted in a wall and supported by a header.

tail·pipe (tāl′pīp′) *n.* a pipe that carries exhaust gases from an engine to the rear of a vehicle.

tail·race (tāl′rās′) *n.* the section of a millrace downstream from a waterwheel.

tail·spin (tāl′spin′) *n.* **1.** the rapid descent of an airplane in a spiral path, with the nose pointing downward and moving in a smaller circle than the tail. **2.** a sudden or worsening state of confusion, anxiety, or depression.

tail·stock (tāl′stok′) *n.* a movable support at one end of a lathe, used to hold the material being shaped.

tail·wind (tāl′wind′) *n.* a wind blowing in the same direction that something, as an aircraft or ship, is moving.

Tai·no (tī′no) *n., pl.* **-nos. 1.** a member of an extinct tribe of South American Indians formerly inhabiting parts of the West Indies. **2.** their language.

taint (tānt) *v.t.* **1.** to touch or affect with something that blemishes, spoils, or sullies: *The charges of corruption tainted the*

a	at	e	end	o	hot	u	up	hw	white	⎧	about
ā	ape	ē	me	ō	old	ū	use	ng	song		taken
ä	far	i	it	ô	fork	u̇	rule	th	thin	ə	pencil
âr	care	ī	ice	oi	oil	u̇	pull	th	this		lemon
		îr	pierce	ou	out	ûr	turn	zh	measure	⎩	circus

police department. **2.** to corrupt or weaken morally: *to be tainted by association with criminals.* **3.** to contaminate; pollute; spoil. —*v.i.* to become tainted. —*n.* a trace or hint of something undesirable, as a blemish or mark of decay; corruption. [Partly from French *teint,* past participle of *teindre* to dye, stain, from Latin *tingere* to moisten, dye; partly short for ATTAINT.] —**taint′less,** *adj.*

Taj Ma·hal (täzh′ mə häl′, täj′) a mausoleum of white marble in Agra, India, considered to be one of the most beautiful examples of Islamic architecture, built in the seventeenth century.

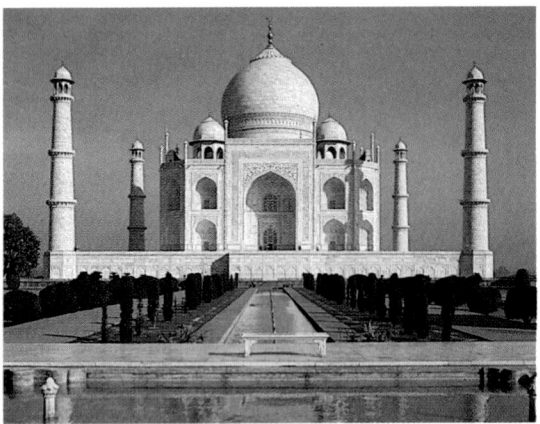

the **Taj Mahal**

take (tāk) *v.,* **took, tak·en, tak·ing.** —*v.t.* **1.** to lay hold of, as with the hand; grasp: *to take a person's arm, to take a book from a shelf.* **2.** to get possession of: *to take control of a business.* **3.** to bring into one's possession by force; catch; capture: *The invading army took many prisoners.* **4.** to win or earn, as in a contest: *This painting takes first prize.* **5.** to rent or hire: *to take an apartment.* **6.** to buy: *I'll take both suits.* **7.** to receive regularly for payment; subscribe to: *to take a newspaper.* **8.** to choose; select: *Take the road on the left.* **9.** to occupy: *to take a seat.* **10.** to carry with one; bring: *We took two suitcases on the trip.* **11.** to move away; remove: *We took the trash to the town dump.* **12.** to remove by death: *The harsh winter took many of the settlers.* **13.** to subtract; deduct: *to take 15 from 35.* **14.** to conduct; lead: *This staircase will take you to an exit.* **15.** to use as a means of transportation: *We took the train home.* **16.** to escort: *to take one's date to a party.* **17.** to resort to; make use of: *The fleeing deer took refuge in the forest.* **18.** to come down with; be infected with: *to take a cold.* **19.** to receive into the body, as by swallowing or inhaling: *to take a breath of fresh air, to take medicine.* **20.** to avail oneself of, esp. as an indulgence: *to take a bath, to take a lunch break.* **21.** to do, perform, or accomplish: *Let's take a walk.* **22.** to undertake or participate in: *to take a test, to take dancing lessons.* **23.** to assume, as an office, duty, or task: *to take charge, to take credit for the success of a project.* **24.** to receive; accept: *Please take my advice.* **25.** to endure; withstand: *Over the years this suitcase has taken a lot of punishment.* **26.** to be subjected to; undergo; suffer: *to take a beating.* **27.** to react to: *to take bad news calmly.* **28.** to have a sense of; feel: *We take pride in our work.* **29.** to be guided by; follow: *to take a hint, to take directions.* **30.** to need; require: *It takes practice to learn how to play the guitar. I usually take a size seven shoe.* **31.** to please or charm; captivate: *to take one's fancy.* **32.** to record by writing: *The secretary took notes at the meeting.* **33.** to make (an image or likeness) by photography: *to take a picture of a group.* **34.** to determine by some special procedure or method: *to take inventory, to take a person's temperature.* **35.** to be able to acquire or absorb: *This material takes dye easily.* **36.** *Baseball.* (of a batter) to let (a pitched ball) pass without swinging at it. **37.** *Grammar.* to be used with in a construction: *A transitive verb takes a direct object.* **38.** *Slang.* to swindle; cheat. —*v.i.* **1.** to be effective; work: *The dye took immediately.* **2.** to detract (with *from*): *The smokestacks take from the beauty of the city.* **3.** to become: *to take sick.* **4.** (of a seed, plant, or the like) to begin to grow. —*n.* **1.** the act of taking. **2.** something that is taken. **3.** the amount or quantity taken: *a meager take of fish.* **4.** *Informal.* profit or receipts, as from a show or sporting event. **5.a.** a portion of a movie, television program, or recording that is photographed or recorded without interruption. **b.** an act or instance of photo-

graphing or recording such a portion. [Old Norse *taka* to seize, grasp.] —**tak′a·ble,** *also,* **take′a·ble,** *adj.* —**tak′er,** *n.*

• **to be on the take.** *Slang.* to be looking for or receiving graft or illegal money.

• **to take after.** to resemble in appearance, character, or actions: *Do you take after your mother or your father?*

• **to take back. a.** to regain possession or ownership of: *I took back my records yesterday.* **b.** to return (a good or product), as to a store: *I took back the defective radio.* **c.** to retract: *I take back what I just said.*

• **to take down. a.** to remove from a high place. **b.** to disassemble; dismantle. **c.** to record in writing: *The reporter took down everything that was said.* **d.** to lower the pride or position of; humble.

• **to take for.** to suppose to be, esp. mistakenly: *I was always taken for my older cousin.*

• **to take in. a.** to receive; admit: *to take in boarders.* **b.** to reduce in size; make smaller: *I had to take in all my clothes after I lost weight.* **c.** to comprehend; understand: *to take in the facts.* **d.** *Informal.* to deceive; cheat; dupe: *to be taken in by misleading advertising.* **e.** to include; comprise: *The article takes in all aspects of the problem.* **f.** *Informal.* to go to see; view or attend: *to take in a movie.*

• **to take it. a.** to assume; believe: *I take it you're ready.* **b.** to withstand or endure hardship or adversity.

• **to take it out on.** *Informal.* to use (another person or object) to relieve one's anger or frustration.

• **to take off. a.** to remove, as a garment: *Take off your hat.* **b.** to deduct; subtract. **c.** *Informal.* to imitate, esp. in ridicule; mimic. **d.** to rise up in flight. **e.** *Informal.* to achieve sudden or accelerated growth or success: *My career has finally taken off.* **f.** *Informal.* to depart; leave.

• **to take on. a.** to hire; employ: *Retail stores often take on extra help during the holiday season.* **b.** to begin to deal with or handle; undertake: *to take on a new responsibility.* **c.** to adopt or acquire: *to take on the characteristics of a parent.* **d.** to face as an opponent.

• **to take out. a.** to remove. **b.** to obtain from the proper agency or authority: *to take out a loan.* **c.** *Informal.* to escort, as on a date.

• **to take over.** to assume ownership, control, or management of: *to take over a business.*

• **to take to. a.** to go to, as for escape: *to take to the hills, to take to one's bed.* **b.** to form a liking for: *We took to each other immediately.*

• **to take up. a.** to fold or pull up so as to make shorter or smaller: *to take up a hem.* **b.** to engage in; undertake; learn: *to take up stamp collecting.* **c.** to occupy or consume: *This couch takes up too much room. This project takes up too much time.* **d.** to accept or agree to. **e.** to pick up; raise; lift.

• **to take up with.** *Informal.* to become friendly with.

Synonyms *v.t.* **Take, grasp,** and **seize** mean to get hold of something physically, esp. with the hand. **Take** is applied broadly to this type of action: *We took some candy from the bowl.* **Grasp** implies the holding of something firmly with a clasping action: *The cat grasped the toy with its claws.* **Seize** denotes a sudden, forcible action: *The police officer seized the assailant's gun.*

take-home pay (tāk′hōm′) the actual salary or wages a person receives after all deductions, as for taxes or insurance, have been made.

tak·en (tā′ken) the past participle of **take.**

take·off (tāk′ôf′, -of′) *n.* **1.** the act of leaving the ground, esp. in the beginning of an airplane flight: *Despite the storm, we had a smooth takeoff.* **2.** the spot from which one takes off. **3.** *Informal.* an imitation, esp. one that is humorous or satirical; parody: *Their comedy routine was a takeoff on self-righteous politicians.*

take-out (tāk′out′) *adj.* relating to, providing, or being food that is to be taken away from the place of sale and eaten elsewhere: *a restaurant with take-out service, take-out Chinese food.* Also, **carry-out.**

take·o·ver (tāk′ō′vər) *n.* assumption or seizure of ownership, control, responsibility, or authority: *The new management executed a smooth takeover.*

tak·ing (tā′king) *adj.* attractive; captivating: *a taking smile.* —*n.* **1.** the act of a person who takes. **2.** *also,* **takings.** something that is taken, esp. receipts, as money.

talc (talk) *n.* **1.** a soft, translucent magnesium silicate mineral, green, white, or dark gray in color, used in making powders and other cosmetic preparations and as an ingredient in ceramics, electrical insulators, paints, and rubber. Formula: $Mg_3(Si_4O_{10})(OH)_2$ **2.** talcum powder. [French *talc,* from Arabic *talq.*]

tal·cum powder (tal′kəm) a fine powder made of white

talc, often perfumed or medicated, used esp. on the face and body. Also, **talc, talcum.**

tale (tāl) *n.* **1.** a story or account of an event or series of events; narrative: *a tale of life at sea.* **2.** a malicious or scandalous story; piece of gossip. **3.** a story that is untrue; falsehood; lie: *No one believes your tale of what happened.* **4.** *Archaic.* a count; tally; enumeration. [Old English *talu* narrative.]

tale·bear·er (tāl′bâr′ər) *n.* a person who deliberately spreads secrets or rumors; telltale. —**tale′bear′ing,** *n.*

tal·ent (tal′ənt) *n.* **1.** a special natural aptitude or ability, usually in a particular area: *musical talent.* **2.** a person or persons having talent: *The director was always looking for new acting talent.* **3.** *Informal.* a tendency or knack: *to have a talent for saying the right thing.* **4.** any of various ancient units of weight and money. [Old French *talent* will, desire, sum of money, from Latin *talentum* weight, sum of money, from Greek *talanton.*] —For Synonyms, see ability.

tal·ent·ed (tal′ən tid) *adj.* having, exhibiting, or characterized by talent: *a talented performer.*

talent scout, a person whose business is to discover unknown talented people for motion pictures, professional sports, or other fields of activity.

ta·ler (tä′lər) *also,* **thaler.** *n., pl.* **-ler.** any of several former coins of Germany. [German *Taler*, earlier *Thaler*. See DOLLAR.]

tales·man (tālz′mən, tā′lēz-) *n., pl.* **-men** (-mən). a person chosen from the onlookers in a court to act as a juror when there are not enough of those summoned to fill the jury. [Medieval Latin *tales (de circumstantibus)* such (of the bystanders), plural of Latin *tālis* such + MAN.]

tale·tell·er (tāl′tel′ər) *n.* **1.** a person who relates stories; narrator; storyteller. **2.** talebearer. —**tale′tell′ing,** *n.*

ta·li (tā′lī) the plural of **talus**[1].

tal·i·pes (tal′ə pēz′) *n.* clubfoot.

tal·is·man (tal′is mən, -iz-) *n., pl.* **-mans. 1.** an engraved stone, ring, or other object believed to have power to keep away evil and bring good fortune; charm; amulet. **2.** anything regarded as having magical or supernatural power. [French *talisman*, from Arabic *tilsam, tilasm* magical image, from Late Greek *telesma* consecrated object, mystery, from Greek *telesma* payment, from *telein* to pay, initiate into the mysteries.]

tal·is·man·ic (tal′is man′ik, -iz-) *adj.* of, relating to, or like a talisman; magical. Also, **tal′is·man′i·cal.**

talk (tôk) *v.i.* **1.** to express ideas or information by means of speech; speak; converse: *Can I talk to you about my career?* **2.** to express ideas or information by some other means; discuss: *to talk in sign language.* **3.** to make sounds suggestive of speech, as some birds. **4.** to consult or confer, esp. for the purpose of negotiating: *Labor refused to talk with management.* **5.** to speak trivially; chatter; prate. **6.** to spread rumors; gossip. **7.** *Informal.* to reveal confidential or incriminating information, esp. under duress: *The prisoner refused to talk.* —*v.t.* **1.** to express in words: *You're talking nonsense.* **2.** to make the subject of one's speech; discuss: *to talk politics.* **3.** to use in speaking; express oneself orally in: *to talk Spanish.* —*n.* **1.** an expression of ideas in speech; conversation: *The talk at our table centered upon the two candidates.* **2.** a speech or lecture, esp. one that is informal or impromptu: *The professor gave a talk about Africa.* **3.** a formal discussion; conference; negotiation: *The two superpowers engaged in disarmament talks.* **4.** rumor; gossip. **5.** the subject of conversation or gossip: *The new show is the talk of New York.* **6.** empty or meaningless speech: *That's just talk.* **7.** *Informal.* a particular way of speaking of a given group; argot; lingo; dialect: *Southern talk.* [Middle English *talken* to converse, speak, possibly based on Old English *talian* to reckon, account.]

· **to talk back.** to give a rude or disrespectful reply.

· **to talk down.** to silence or overpower by speaking longer, louder, or more effectively; outtalk.

· **to talk down to.** to speak to in a condescending or patronizing manner.

· **to talk into.** to persuade (someone) to do something.

· **to talk out.** to discuss thoroughly so as to reach an understanding: *We talked out our different approaches to solving the problem.*

· **to talk out of.** to dissuade (someone) from doing something.

· **to talk over.** to go over in conversation; discuss.

· **to talk up. a.** to speak in a loud, clear voice. **b.** to speak in favor of; advocate enthusiastically: *If you believe in this issue, please talk up now.*

Synonyms *n.* **Talk, speech,** and **discourse** mean thoughts expressed in spoken words. **Talk** may be applied generally either to conversation or to someone's informal remarks to an audience: *There was much talk about our new neighbors at the dinner party. The coach delivered a talk to the team*

about the dangers of using drugs. **Speech** is a more formal term in its general application, but is the most commonly used word for an address delivered to an audience: *Freedom of speech is an invaluable privilege. The candidate was preparing a campaign speech.* **Discourse** suggests a formal exchange or presentation of thoughts or ideas: *The panel of professors conducted a discourse on the history of U.S. foreign policy. The speaker's comments turned into a lengthy discourse.*

talk·a·tive (tô′kə tiv) *adj.* given to talking a great deal. —**talk′a·tive·ly,** *adv.* —**talk′a·tive·ness,** *n.*

Synonyms **Talkative, loquacious,** and **garrulous** mean inclined to express oneself verbally often or at length. **Talkative** indicates a general fondness for expressing oneself in words and can have both positive and negative connotations: *The presence of many talkative children in the class made for lively discussions. The report card stated that the child was too talkative and constantly interrupted the teachers.* **Loquacious** is a mildly disapproving word that implies excessive or compulsive talking: *The meeting ran late because two of the committee members were so loquacious.* **Garrulous** is more disapproving than *loquacious* and is applied to speakers who are inconsiderately long-winded, often about trivial matters: *Our garrulous neighbor has an endless supply of boring anecdotes.*

talk·er (tô′kər) *n.* **1.** a person who talks. **2.** a talkative person.

talk·ie (tô′kē) *n. Informal.* a motion picture with sound synchronized to the action.

talking book, a recording of a reading of printed material for use by blind persons.

talking point, an idea, argument, or topic that is suitable for discussion or can be used to support a point of view.

talk·ing-to (tô′king tü′) *n., pl.* **-tos.** *Informal.* a sharp scolding; reprimand.

talk show, a television or radio program in which guests are interviewed and often engage in discussions with the host or members of the audience.

talk·y (tô′kē) *adj.,* **talk·i·er, talk·i·est. 1.** talkative. **2.** containing too much talk or dialogue: *The first speech on the program was so talky that the audience became restless.* —**talk′i·ness,** *n.*

tall (tôl) *adj.* **1.** of more than average height; not low or short: *a tall youngster, a tall tree.* **2.** having a specified height: *five feet tall.* **3.** unusually large in amount or degree; considerable; substantial: *a tall price, a tall order.* **4.** *Informal.* exaggerated so as to be improbable; unbelievable: *a tall story.* —*adv.* in a confident, erect, and proud manner: *to walk tall.* [Old English *(ge)tæl* swift, prompt.] —**tall′ness,** *n.* —For Synonyms, see high.

tal·lit (tä′lis, tä lēt′) *n., pl.* **tal·lits** or **tal·li·tim** (tä lē′sim, tä′lē tēm′). tallith.

tal·lith (tä′lis, tä lēt′) *also,* **tallit.** *n., pl.* **tal·liths** or **tal·li·thim** (tä lē′sim, tä′lē tēm′). *Judaism.* a shawl worn by Jewish men during morning prayer services, having fringes at the four corners. [Hebrew *tallīth* literally, cloak, cover.]

tal·low (tal′ō) *n.* fat extracted from the suet of cattle and sheep, used chiefly for making candles, soap, and margarine. —*v.t.* to smear with tallow. [Probably of Low German origin.] —**tal′low·like′, tal′low·y,** *adj.*

tal·ly (tal′ē) *n., pl.* **-lies. 1.** an account or reckoning; score: *The first tally of the vote was incorrect.* **2.** formerly, a piece of wood with notches that indicated an amount, as of a debt or payment. **3.** anything on which a record or account is kept. **4.** a mark representing a certain number or quantity, used in keeping a record. **5.** anything that corresponds exactly with another; counterpart. **6.** agreement; correspondence. —*v.,* **-lied, -ly·ing.** —*v.t.* **1.** to keep or make a count or record (often with *up*): *The grocer tallied up our bill.* **2.** to cause to correspond or agree; match. —*v.i.* **1.** to correspond; agree: *The witness's account of the accident does not tally with the facts.* **2.** to make a point or points in a game; score. [Anglo-Norman *tallie* notch, score kept on a piece of wood, going back to Latin *tālea* rod, cutting.]

tal·ly-ho (*interj.,* tal′ē hō′; *n.,* tal′ē hō′) *interj.* a hunter's shout signifying the sighting of a fox. —*n., pl.* **-hos. 1.** the act of shouting "tallyho." **2.** a coach drawn by four horses. [Probably modification of French *taïaut*, an interjection used in deer hunting; of imitative origin.]

Tal·mud (tal′məd, täl′mud) *n.* the collection of Jewish civil and

a	at	e	end	o	hot	u	up	hw	white		about
ā	ape	ē	me	ō	old	ū	use	ng	song		taken
ä	far	i	it	ô	fork	ü	rule	th	thin	ə	pencil
âr	care	ī	ice	oi	oil	u̇	pull	th	this		lemon
		îr	pierce	ou	out	ûr	turn	zh	measure		circus

canonical law, consisting of a compilation of oral tradition comprising the Mishna and the Gemara. [Hebrew *talmūd* instruction.]

Tal·mud·ic (tal mü′dik, -mü′-) *adj.* of, relating to, or characteristic of the Talmud: *a Talmudic scholar.* Also, **Tal·mud′i·cal.**

Tal·mud·ist (tal′mə dist, täl′mü-) *n.* **1.** one of the authors of the Talmud. **2.** a student of the Talmud; Talmudic scholar. **3.** a person who accepts or follows the doctrines of the Talmud.

tal·on (tal′ən) *n.* **1.** the claw of a bird or other animal, esp. of a bird of prey. **2.** anything that resembles a claw in appearance or action. [Old French *talon* heel, going back to Latin *tālus* heel, ankle.]

ta·lus¹ (tā′ləs) *n., pl.* **-li** (-lī). **1.** anklebone. **2.** ankle *(def. 1).* [Latin *tālus* ankle, anklebone, heel.]

ta·lus² (tā′ləs, tal′əs) *n., pl.* **-lus·es. 1.** a slope. **2.** a sloping heap of coarse rock at the base of a cliff or covering a slope below a cliff. [French *talus* slope, probably from Latin *talūtium* slope that gives evidence of the existence of gold under the earth; of Celtic origin.]

tam (tam) *n.* tam-o′-shanter.

ta·ma·le (tə mä′lē) *n.* a Mexican dish made of cornmeal, minced meat, and red peppers, rolled up and tied in cornhusks, and cooked by steaming or roasting. [Spanish *tamales,* plural of *tamal* tamale, from Nahuatl *tamalli.*]

tam·a·rack (tam′ə rak′) *n.* **1.** a larch tree, *Larix laricina,* of the pine family, found in swampy regions of northern North America and valued for its wood. Also, **American larch, hackmatack. 2.** the wood of this tree, used esp. for fence posts, telephone poles, and railroad ties. [Of Algonquian origin.]

tam·a·rind (tam′ə rind′) *n.* **1.** a tropical evergreen tree, *Tamarindus indica,* of the pea family, bearing clusters of small, yellow flowers and edible fruit. **2.** the acid-flavored fruit itself, which is eaten raw, cooked with rice, or used to make cool drinks. [Spanish *tamarindo,* from Arabic *tamr hindī* date of India.]

tam·a·risk (tam′ə risk′) *n.* any of a group of shrubs and small trees, genus *Tamarix,* of western Europe, Africa, and Asia, having pink or white flowers borne in clusters and branches covered with tiny, scalelike leaves. [Late Latin *tamariscus,* form of Latin *tamarīx.*]

tam·bour (tam′bûr) *n.* **1.** a drum. **2.** a pair of embroidery hoops that fit together to form a frame that holds the fabric to be embroidered. **3.** embroidery done on such a frame. [French *tambour* drum, from Old French *tabour.* See TABOR.]

tam·bou·rine (tam′bə rēn′) *n.* a shallow, one-headed drum having metal disks loosely mounted in the rim, usually played by shaking or by striking with the knuckles. [French *tambourin* tabor, diminutive of *tambour* drum. See TAMBOUR.]

tame (tām) *adj.,* **tam·er, tam·est. 1.** taken by humans from a state of native wildness and domesticated: *a tame elephant.* **2.** showing no ferocity, fear, or shyness, as if domesticated; gentle: *The deer was tame enough to let us photograph it.* **3.** made submissive or meek; docile; tractable: *a person with a tame spirit.*

tambourine

4. without force or effect; dull; insipid: *a tame reprimand, a tame description.* —*v.,* **tamed, tam·ing.** —*v.t.* **1.** to remove from a wild state and make domestic: *to tame a wild stallion.* **2.** to take the spirit or courage from; make submissive or subdued: *to tame an unruly crowd.* **3.** to tone down; soften. —*v.i.* to become tame. [Old English *tam* domesticated, docile.] —**tame′a·ble;** *also,* **tam′a·ble,** *adj.* —**tame′ly,** *adv.* —**tame′ness,** *n.* —**tam′er,** *n.*

tame·less (tām′lis) *adj.* not tamed or able to be tamed. —**tame′less·ly,** *adv.* —**tame′less·ness,** *n.*

Tam·il (tam′əl) *n., pl.* **-il** or **-ils. 1.** a member of a Dravidian people living in parts of southern India, northern Sri Lanka, and Malaysia. **2.** their language, belonging to the Dravidian language family. —*adj.* of, relating to, or characteristic of the Tamil or their language.

Tam·ma·ny Hall (tam′ə nē) a fraternal Democratic political organization founded in New York City in 1789, associated with bossism and corruption in the late 1800s and early 1900s. Also, **Tam′ma·ny.** [From *Tammany Hall,* the headquarters of this organization, from *Tammany,* the name of a seventeenth-century Indian chief who was friendly to settlers.]

tam-o′-shan·ter (tam′ə shan′tər) *n.* a soft, woolen cap of Scottish origin, with a wide, flat, circular crown and a fitted head-

band, often having a pompom in the center. Also, **tam.** [From the hero of the poem *Tam o' Shanter,* by Robert Burns, 1759-96, Scottish poet.]

tamp (tamp) *v.t.* **1.** to force or pound down by a series of light blows or taps; pack down: *to tamp dirt around a new fence post.* **2.** to pack (a drilled hole) with sand or dirt after an explosive charge has been placed in the hole. [From TAMPION.]

tam·per¹ (tam′pər) *v.i.* **1.** to interfere or meddle, usually with a harmful effect (with *with*): *Someone has been tampering with the radio.* **2.** to deal or negotiate with clandestinely so as to influence or corrupt (with *with*): *to tamper with a jury.* **3.** to alter so as to be misleading (with *with*): *to tamper with a document.* [Form of TEMPER.] —**tam′per·er,** *n.*

tam·per² (tam′pər) *n.* **1.** an implement for tamping. **2.** a person who tamps. [TAMP + -ER¹.]

tam·pi·on (tam′pē ən) *n.* a plug or cover put in the muzzle of a gun or cannon when not in use to keep out dust and moisture. [French *tampon* stopper, plug, form of *tapon;* of Germanic origin.]

tam·pon (tam′pon) *n.* a cylinder of cotton or other absorbent material, esp. one used to absorb menstrual flow. —*v.t.* to fill or stop with or as with a tampon. [French *tampon* stopper. See TAMPION.]

tan (tan) *v.,* **tanned, tan·ning.** —*v.t.* **1.** to make (a hide or skin) into leather by soaking it in tannin or a similar solution. **2.** to make brown or tawny by exposure to the sun or a sunlamp. **3.** *Informal.* to beat severely; thrash. —*v.i.* to become brown or tawny by exposure to the sun or a sunlamp: *My skin tans slowly.* —*n.* **1.** a yellowish brown color. **2.** a brown or tawny tint imparted to a person's skin by exposure to the sun or a sunlamp. **3.** tannin or a similar tanning agent. **4.** tanbark. —*adj.,* **tan·ner, tan·nest.** having the color tan. [Medieval Latin *tannare* to make a hide into leather, from *tannum* oak bark (used for tanning hides); possibly of Celtic origin.]

tan, tangent.

tan·a·ger (tan′ə jər) *n.* any of various New World songbirds, family Thraupidae, the males of which have brightly colored plumage. Length: 4-8 inches (10-20 centimeters). [Modern Latin *tanagra;* of Tupi-Guarani origin.]

tan·bark (tan′bärk′) *n.* any bark, as of oak or hemlock, yielding tannin. It is used as a covering after the tannin has been removed, as for circus rings. Also, **tan.**

tanager

tan·dem (tan′dəm) *adv.* one behind the other; in single file: *to march tandem.* —*adj.* arranged or having parts or participants arranged one behind the other: *a tandem bicycle, tandem seats.* —*n.* **1.** a bicycle having two or more seats, handlebars, and sets of pedals, one behind the other. **2.** a team, esp. of horses, harnessed one behind the other. **3.** a two-wheeled carriage drawn by two or more horses so harnessed. [Latin *tandem* at length; the modern meanings are a pun on the Latin, which actually meant "at length in time."]

•**in tandem. a.** one behind the other: *They rode their bicycles in tandem along the trail.* **b.** in close association: *The federal project works in tandem with local programs.*

tang¹ (tang) *n.* **1.** a sharp taste, flavor, or odor: *the tang of a crisp, red apple.* **2.** a slight trace or suggestion; hint: *a tang of remorse.* **3.** a distinctive characteristic or quality. **4.** a pronglike extension of a blade or metal tool, as of a chisel, file, or sword, to which the handle is fitted. [Of Scandinavian origin.]

tang² (tang) *n.* a loud, ringing sound; ring; clang. —*v.i., v.t.* to make or cause to make such a sound. [Imitative.]

tan·ge·lo (tan′jə lō′) *n., pl.* **-los.** any of a variety of hybrid citrus fruits produced by crossing a tangerine with a grapefruit, usually resembling an orange in appearance and flavor. [Modification of TANGERINE.]

tan·gen·cy (tan′jən sē) *n.* the state of being tangent.

tan·gent (tan′jənt) *adj.* **1.** in contact; touching. **2.** *Geometry.* touching a curve or curved surface at only one point without passing through it. —*n.* **1.** *Geometry.* a tangent line, curve, or surface. **2.** *Trigonometry.* (of an acute angle of a right triangle) the trigonometric function that is the ratio of the length of the side opposite the acute angle to the length of the side adjacent to the angle. **3.** an abrupt and often irrelevant change in thought, discussion, or course of action; digression: *The speaker went off on a tangent.* [Latin *tangēns* touching, present participle of *tangere* to touch.]

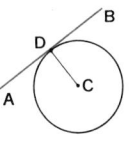

AB is **tangent** at *D*

tan·gen·tial (tan jen′chəl) *adj.* **1.** *Mathematics.* of, relating to, or in the direction of a tangent. **2.** not relevant; divergent; digressive: *The profes-*

sor's talk was filled with *tangential but interesting comments.* **3.** only slightly connected: *Your answer is tangential to the question asked.* —**tan·gen′tial·ly,** *adv.*

tan·ge·rine (tan′jə rēn′) *n.* **1.** the sweet, juicy, orange or reddish orange citrus fruit of a small, Asian evergreen tree, *Citrus reticulata,* containing small, pointed seeds and having a skin that is easily peeled. **2.** the tree bearing this fruit, closely related to the mandarin orange, widely cultivated in warm regions of the United States and southern Europe. **3.** a reddish orange color. —*adj.* having the color tangerine. [From *Tangier,* Moroccan city from which this fruit was originally obtained.]

tan·gi·ble (tan′jə bəl) *adj.* **1.** capable of being touched; perceptible by touch; material: *The medals were tangible reminders of the war.* **2.** capable of being measured or appraised for value: *A house and its land are tangible assets.* **3.** capable of being grasped by the mind; definite; real: *tangible proof.* —*n.* **tangibles.** property that can be appraised for value; material assets. [Late Latin *tangibilis* touchable, from Latin *tangere* to touch.] —**tan′gi·bil′i·ty, tan′gi·ble·ness,** *n.* —**tan′gi·bly,** *adv.*

tan·gle (tang′gəl) *v.,* **-gled, -gling.** —*v.t.* **1.** to intertwine or unite in a disordered mass; snarl: *The wind tangled my hair.* **2.** to catch or involve in something that hampers, obstructs, or confuses: *The fly was tangled in the spider's web. The power failure tangled traffic in the city.* —*v.i.* **1.** to be or become entangled: *The branches tangled as they grew.* **2.** *Informal.* to fight, quarrel, or argue: *The children tangled over the bicycle.* —*n.* **1.** a jumbled, knotted, or twisted mass: *a tangle of yarn.* **2.** a confused or jumbled condition. **3.** *Informal.* a dispute; argument: *We got into a tangle over the rules of the game.* [Of Scandinavian origin.]

tan·gly (tang′glē) *adj.* full of or consisting of tangles; knotted; snarled.

tan·go (tang′gō) *n., pl.* **-gos. 1.** a ballroom dance of Latin-American origin, characterized by long, gliding steps. **2.** the music for such a dance. —*v.i.* **-goed, -go·ing.** to dance the tango. [Spanish *tango* the dance; of uncertain origin.]

tan·gram (tang′grəm) *n.* a Chinese puzzle consisting of a square cut into five triangles, a square, and a rhomboid, which can be assembled to form a large number of different shapes. [Possibly Chinese (Cantonese) *t'ang* Chinese + -GRAM¹, on the model of words like *cryptogram.*]

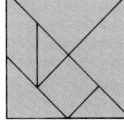
tangram

tang·y (tang′ē) *adj.,* **tang·i·er, tang·i·est.** having a tang. —**tang′i·ness,** *n.*

tank (tangk) *n.* **1.** a large container for holding a liquid or gas: *an oxygen tank, an oil tank.* **2.** the amount that a tank can hold; tankful: *a tank of gasoline.* **3.** *Military.* a fully enclosed, armored combat vehicle equipped with machine guns and cannon, and moving on caterpillar tracks. **4.** *Slang.* a jail cell or enclosure, esp. for prisoners awaiting a hearing. —*v.t.* to place or store in a tank. [Gujarati *tānkh* cistern, reservoir, possibly from Sanskrit *tadāga* pond.]

tank·age (tang′kij) *n.* **1.** the amount that a tank can hold. **2.** the act or process of putting or storing in tanks. **3.** the amount charged or paid for storage in tanks. **4.** rendered waste matter from tanks in a slaughterhouse, used as fertilizer or animal feed.

tank·ard (tang′kərd) *n.* a large, one-handled drinking cup, often having a hinged lid. [Of uncertain origin.]

tank car, a railroad car with a long, cylindrical tank for transporting liquids or gases.

tank·er (tang′kər) *n.* **1.** a cargo ship equipped with tanks for carrying oil or other liquids. **2.** an airplane, truck, or other vehicle similarly equipped for carrying liquids.

tank farm, an area of land containing tanks for the storage of fuel oil.

tank farming, hydroponics.

tank·ful (tangk′fŏŏl′) *n., pl.* **-fuls.** the amount that a tank can hold.

tank top, a sleeveless upper garment with a wide opening at the neck and wide shoulder straps, similar to the top of a one-piece bathing suit.

tan·nate (tan′āt) *n.* a salt of tannic acid.

tan·ner (tan′ər) *n.* a person whose work or business is the tanning of hides.

tan·ner·y (tan′ə rē) *n., pl.* **-ner·ies.** a place where hides and skins are tanned and finished as leather.

Tann·häu·ser (tän′hoi′zər) *n.* in medieval German legend, a knight and poet who, after leaving the earth to live a life of pleasure with Venus, returns and seeks absolution, is rejected by the pope, and returns to Venus.

tan·nic acid (tan′ik) a white or yellow organic compound found in nutgalls and oak bark, used esp. in tanning hides and in the preparation of ink, rubber, and medicine.

tan·nin (tan′in) *n.* **1.** tannic acid. **2.** any of various acid substances found in leaves, bark, and red wine, used in tanning and dyeing and as an astringent. [French *tanin,* from *tan* tanbark; possibly of Celtic origin.]

tan·ning (tan′ing) *n.* **1.** the art or process of converting hide or skins into leather by soaking in tannin or a similar solution. **2.** the act or process of making the skin brown or tawny, as by exposure to the sun or a sunlamp. **3.** *Informal.* a severe beating; whipping; thrashing.

tan·sy (tan′zē) *n., pl.* **-sies.** any of a group of strong-smelling plants, genus *Tanacetum,* of the composite family, growing throughout the Northern Hemisphere, esp. *T. vulgare,* having yellow flower heads and feathery leaves, formerly used in cooking and medicine. [Old French *tanesie,* possibly short for Medieval Latin *athanasia,* from Greek *athanasia* immortality.]

tan·ta·lite (tan′tə līt′) *n.* a heavy, black, crystalline mineral that is the principal ore of tantalum. Formula: $(Fe, Mn)(Ta, Nb)_2)O_6$

tan·ta·lize (tan′tə līz′) *v.t.,* **-lized, -liz·ing.** to torment or tease by tempting with something that is not attainable. [*Tantalus* + -IZE; from the teasing nature of the punishment of Tantalus.] —**tan′ta·li·za′tion,** *n.* —**tan′ta·liz′er,** *n.* —**tan′ta·liz′ing·ly,** *adv.*

tan·ta·lum (tan′tə ləm) *n.* a heavy, very hard, metallic element that has a very high melting point and resists corrosion by most acids, used in alloys for missile and aircraft parts and surgical instruments and in filaments for incandescent lamps. Symbol: **Ta** For tables, see **element.** [From *Tantalus.*]

Tan·ta·lus (tan′tə ləs) *n.* in Greek mythology, a son of Zeus who served up his own son as a meal to the gods. He was punished in Hades by being immersed in water that receded as he bent down to drink it, and being surrounded by delicious fruit that rose up beyond his grasp as he reached to eat it.

tan·ta·mount (tan′tə mount′) *adj.* having as much importance, value, force, or effect; equivalent (with *to*): *Your lack of enthusiasm for our project is tantamount to rejecting it.* [Anglo-Norman *tant amunter* to amount to as much, from Old French *tant* so much (from Latin *tantus*) + *amonter* to amount to. See AMOUNT.]

tan·tar·a (tan tar′ə, tan′tər ə) *n.* **1.** a flourish blown on a trumpet or horn; fanfare. **2.** any similar sound. [Imitative.]

tan·trum (tan′trəm) *n.* an outburst of bad temper or anger; violent fit of rage. [Of uncertain origin.]

Tao·ism (tou′iz əm) *n.* one of the principal religions of China, based on the doctrines of its founder, Lao-tsu, and characterized by an emphasis on living in harmony with nature and with one's fellow human beings. [Chinese (Mandarin) *tao* way, truth, reason + -ISM.] —**Tao′ist,** *adj., n.*

tap¹ (tap) *v.,* **tapped, tap·ping.** —*v.t.* **1.** to strike (someone or something) lightly: *to tap someone on the shoulder.* **2.** to strike lightly and usually repeatedly with: *The conductor tapped the baton for attention.* **3.** to make, do, or produce by striking lightly and repeatedly: *to tap a beat with one's foot.* **4.** to attach a piece of metal or leather to (the tip of the sole or heel of a shoe or boot). **5.** to select or designate, as for membership in a club. —*v.i.* to strike with a light blow or blows: *to tap on a desk with a ruler.* —*n.* **1.** a light or gentle blow: *I felt a tap on my shoulder.* **2.** the sound made by such a blow: *the taps of raindrops against a window.* **3.** a piece of metal or leather placed on the tip of the sole or heel of a shoe or boot. [Old French *taper* to strike; of imitative origin.]

tap² (tap) *n.* **1.** a device consisting of a valve and a hand-operated part that opens or closes it, used to turn on or off a flow of liquid, as from a pipe or keg. **2.** a long peg or plug used to close a hole in a cask or other vessel containing liquid. **3.** liquor of a particular quality, brew, or cask. **4.** *Medicine.* the removal of fluid from a body cavity: *a spinal tap.* **5.** a place for connecting electrical devices or additional wires to a flow of current. **6.** a tool screwed into a hole to cut internal screw threads. **7.** wiretap. —*v.t.,* **tapped, tap·ping. 1.** to pierce (something) in order to draw liquid from: *to tap the trunk of a maple tree for sap.* **2.** to pull out the tap from (a barrel, cask, or other container). **3.** to draw off (liquid) from a source: *to tap cider in a keg.* **4.** to furnish with a tap or spigot. **5.** *Medicine.* to draw fluid from (a cavity of the body) by using a long hollow needle. **6.** to draw upon or begin to use: *We have just begun to tap the vast resources of the oceans.* **7.** to make a connection with (a water, gas, or electric line) in order to draw from. **8.** to cut into and connect with secretly, so as to obtain information; wiretap: *to tap a telephone.* **9.** to cut an

a	at	e	end	o	hot	u	up	hw	white		about
ā	ape	ē	me	ō	old	ū	use	ng	song		taken
ä	far	i	it	ô	fork	ü	rule	th	thin	ə	pencil
âr	care	ī	ice	oi	oil	ŭ	pull	th	this		lemon
		îr	pierce	ou	out	ûr	turn	zh	measure		circus

internal screw thread. [Old English *taeppa* stopper, plug, faucet.] —**tap′per,** *n.*
• **on tap. a.** (of beer or liquor) in a tapped keg or cask and ready to be drawn off and served. **b.** *Informal.* ready for use; available.

ta·pa (tä′pə) *n.* **1.** an unwoven cloth made in the Pacific islands by steeping and beating the fibrous inner bark of any of several native trees. **2.** this bark. [Of Polynesian origin.]

tapa drying in the sun

tap-dance (tap′dans′) *v.i.,* **-danced, -danc·ing.** to perform a tap dance. —**tap′-danc′er,** *n.*

tap dance, a dance in which the steps and the rhythm are emphasized by sounds made by taps on the dancer's shoes.

tape (tāp) *n.* **1.** a long, narrow strip of woven fabric, as that used to bind books or seams. **2.** a long, narrow strip of plastic, paper, or other material coated with a sticky substance, used for fastening, binding, or repairing. **3.** any long, narrow strip of metal, plastic, or other material. **4.a.** magnetic tape. **b.** a magnetic tape on which sound, images, or data have been recorded: *The reviewers saw a tape of the show before it was actually broadcast.* **5.** a thin strip of string, cloth, or other material stretched across the finish line of a footrace. **6.** tape measure. —*v.t.,* **taped, tap·ing. 1.** to fasten, bind, or wrap with tape: *to tape a sprained ankle.* **2.** to record on magnetic tape: *to tape an interview, to tape a television program.* **3.** to measure with a tape measure. [Old English *tæppe* strip of cloth.]

tape deck, an audio tape recorder made for use with other components, lacking its own speakers and power amplifier.

tape measure, a long, flexible strip of cloth, plastic, or flexible steel marked with a scale for measuring, often coiled up in a case.

tape player, a device, as in an automobile stereo system, for playing recordings made on magnetic tape.

ta·per (tā′pər) *v.t.* to make gradually narrower toward one end: *The tailor tapered the trousers.* —*v.i.* **1.** to become gradually narrower toward one end: *The candle tapers to a point.* **2.** to decrease gradually, as in volume or intensity; diminish (usually with *off*): *Sales tapered off after the holiday rush.* —*n.* **1.** a small, slender candle. **2.** a long, wax-coated wick, as that used to light candles or fires. **3.** a gradual decrease of thickness or width: *the taper of a spire.* [Old English *tapor* wax candle; with reference to the fact that a candle is often narrower at one end than the other.]

tape-re·cord (tāp′ri kôrd′) *v.t.* to record (as music or a television program) on magnetic tape.

tape recorder, a device for recording sound, images, or data on a tape coated with magnetically sensitive material. Most tape recorders also have a reproduction system for playing back what they have recorded.

tape recording 1. the act or process of recording sound, images, or data on magnetic tape. **2.** the tape on which sound, images, or data have been recorded.

tap·es·try (tap′ə strē) *n., pl.* **-tries. 1.** a heavy fabric, traditionally handwoven, decorated with designs or pictures often depicting historical or mythological events. Tapestries are used as wall hangings, floor coverings, and on furniture. **2.** any of various fabrics made to resemble tapestry, used for such items as upholstery and garments. —*v.t.,* **-tried, -try·ing.** to cover with or as with tapestry: *The garden walls were tapestried with ivy.* [French *tapisserie* the heavy decorated fabric, going back to *tapis* carpet, going back to Greek *tapētion,* diminutive of *tapēs* carpet.]

tape·worm (tāp′wûrm′) *n.* any of a group of flatworms, class Cestoda, that in the adult stage are parasites in the intestines of humans and other vertebrates. Length: to 20 feet (6.1 meters).

tap·i·o·ca (tap′ē ō′kə) *n.* a granular starch obtained from the root of the cassava plant, used in cooking to make pudding and as a thickening agent. [Portuguese *tapioca,* from Tupi-Guarani *tipioca* juice obtained from the cassava plant, from *tipi* dregs + *ok* to squeeze out.]

ta·pir (tā′pər) *n., pl.* **-pirs** or **-pir.** any of several hoofed, piglike mammals, genus *Tapirus,* native to the tropical regions of Latin America and Southeast Asia, having a heavy, rounded body and a short, flexible snout. Height: to 4 feet (1.2 meters) at the shoulder. [Tupi-Guarani *tapīra.*]

tap·pet (tap′it) *n.* an arm, cam, or other projection attached to a movable part so that it can receive intermittent motion and transmit it to another part of the machine. [TAP[1] + -ET.]

tap·room (tap′rüm′, -rŭm′) *n.* a barroom; tavern.

tap·root (tap′rüt′, -rŭt′) *n.* the primary downward-growing root of a plant, from which lateral roots may develop.

taps (taps) *n.* a military signal, usually played on a bugle at the end of the day to indicate that all lights must be turned off, and also sounded at military funerals and memorial services. ➡ used as singular.

tap·ster (tap′stər) *n.* a bartender or barkeeper. [Old English *tæppestre* woman who taps liquors, from *tæppa* tap[2].]

tar[1] (tär) *n.* **1.** a dark, sticky, semifluid mixture of hydrocarbons obtained chiefly by the destructive distillation of soft coal and pine wood, used widely as road-paving and waterproofing material. **2.** any of the brownish, solid or liquid components of tobacco smoke. **3.** coal tar. —*v.t.,* **tarred, tar·ring.** to smear, coat, or cover with or as with tar: *to tar a highway.* —*adj.* of, containing, or covered with tar. [Old English *teoru* the dark, sticky, semifluid substance.] —**tar′like′,** *adj.*
• **to tar and feather. a.** to pour heated tar over (someone) and then cover with feathers as a punishment. **b.** *Informal.* to punish or criticize harshly.

tar[2] (tär) *n. Informal.* a sailor. [Short for TARPAULIN; from the tarpaulin hats formerly worn by sailors in the British navy.]

tar·an·tel·la (tar′ən tel′ə) *n.* **1.** a lively, whirling southern Italian dance in ⁶/₈ time, usually performed by a single couple. **2.** the music for this dance. [Italian *tarantella* the dance, from *Taranto* a lively Italian city; also influenced by the belief that this dance was a cure for a disease that was supposedly caused by a *tarantula* bite.]

ta·ran·tu·la (tə ran′chə lə) *n., pl.* **-las** or **-lae** (-lē′). **1.** any of a group of large, hairy spiders, family Theraphosidae, as *Aphonopelma chalcodes,* of the southwestern United States, whose bite is painful but generally harmless. **2.** a wolf spider, *Lycosa tarentula,* of the Mediterranean region, whose bite was once thought to cause uncontrollable dancing. [Medieval Latin *tarantula,* from Italian *tarantola,* from *Taranto,* Italian city where it is frequently found.]

tar·boosh (tär büsh′) *n.* a brimless cap of cloth or felt, worn by Muslim men. [Arabic *tarbūsh.*]

tar·dy (tär′dē) *adj.,* **-di·er, -di·est. 1.** coming or happening after the specified or appropriate time; late: *The student was punished for being tardy so frequently.* **2.** moving, acting, or happening slowly: *We were tardy in making preparations for the trip.* [Old French *tardif,* going back to Latin *tardus.*] —**tar′di·ly,** *adv.* —**tar′di·ness,** *n.* —For Synonyms, see **late.**

tare[1] (târ) *n.* **1.** any of several mostly climbing varieties of vetch, esp. *Vicia sativa,* cultivated in the United States as a forage or cover crop. **2.** the seed of this plant. **3.** in the New Testament, a weed harmful to crops, possibly the darnel. [Of uncertain origin.]

tare[2] (târ) *n.* a deduction made from gross weight to allow for the weight of the container. [French *tare* waste, loss, going back to Arabic *tarhah* deduction; literally, that which is thrown away.]

targe (tärj) *n. Archaic.* a light shield or buckler. [Old French *targe;* of Germanic origin.]

tar·get (tär′git) *n.* **1.** an object that is aimed at in shooting practice and competitions, as a padded disk marked with concentric circles used in archery. **2.** anything that is shot at or is the object of a military attack: *a bombing target.* **3.** a person or thing that is the object of ridicule, criticism, or abuse: *The inexperienced candidate was an easy target for the opposition.* **4.** a person or thing that is the object of an action or effort: *The target of this advertising campaign is high-income couples without children.* —*v.i.* to have, use, or designate as a target. [Old French *targuete,* form of *targete* small shield, diminutive of *targe* shield. See TARGE.]

target date, the date designated for the undertaking or completion of a project.

tarantula

tar·iff (tar′if) *n.* **1.** a list or system of duties imposed by a government on imports or exports. **2.** a duty or rate of duty so imposed: *a low tariff on cameras.* **3.** any list of rates or prices, as for a railroad, bus line, or hotel. —*v.t.* to impose a tariff on. [French *tarif* rate, list of prices, through Spanish, from Arabic *ta'rīf* information.]

tar·la·tan (tär′lə tən) *n.* a thin, transparent muslin with an open weave and a stiff finish, used chiefly for theater costumes, drapes, and women's hats. [French *tarlatane,* earlier *tarnatane;* of uncertain origin.]

tar·mac (tär′mak) *n.* **1.** a road, airport runway, or other surface covered with macadam or blacktop. **2. Tarmac.** *Trademark.* a bituminous material used for paving roads.

tarn (tärn) *n.* a small mountain lake or pool, esp. one of glacial origin. [Old Norse *tjörn.*]

tar·nish (tär′nish) *v.t.* **1.** to dull the luster of or discolor, as a metallic surface by oxidation. **2.** to mar the purity of; disgrace; sully: *The scandal tarnished the family name.* —*v.i.* to become dull or discolored by exposure to air: *The silver will tarnish if left uncovered.* —*n.* **1.** a coating or surface resulting from tarnishing. **2.** a loss of luster; discoloration. [French *terniss-,* a stem of *ternir* to dull, stain; probably of Germanic origin.]

ta·ro (tär′ō, tar′ō) *n., pl.* **-ros. 1.** a tropical plant, *Colocasia esculenta,* of the arum family, widely grown in Hawaii and other Pacific islands for its edible tuber. **2.** the fleshy round tuber itself, used to make poi or cooked and eaten like a potato. [Of Polynesian origin.]

tar·ot (tar′ō) *n.* one of a set of twenty-two cards, similar to playing cards, each bearing a picture of a figure in costume, such as Harlequin, used in fortunetelling or added to a deck of playing cards as trumps. [French *tarot,* from Italian *tarocchi,* plural; of uncertain origin.]

tarp (tärp) *n. Informal.* tarpaulin.

tar paper *also,* **tar·pa·per** (tär′pā′pər). a heavy paper coated with tar, used esp. as a building and waterproofing material.

tar·pau·lin (tär pô′lin, tär′pə-) *n.* a waterproofed canvas or other material, as nylon, used as a protective covering for boats, athletic fields, or other objects exposed to the weather. [Earlier *tarpauling,* from TAR¹ + PALL¹ + -ING¹.]

tar·pon (tär′pon) *n., pl.* **-pon** or **-pons.** a large, silvery game fish, *Megalops cyprinoides,* found in coastal waters of the Atlantic Ocean and sometimes in fresh water, weighing up to 350 pounds (158.8 kilograms). Length: to more than 8 feet (2.4 meters). [Of uncertain origin.]

tar·ra·gon (tar′ə gon′, -gən) *n.* **1.** a bushy European plant, *Artemisia dracunculus,* of the composite family, whose fragrant leaves are used to season food. **2.** the leaves themselves.

tar·ry¹ (tar′ē) *v.i.,* **-ried, -ry·ing. 1.** to delay in doing something, esp. in coming or going; linger; dawdle: *We must not tarry if we are to arrive on time.* **2.** to remain in a place, esp. longer than expected; sojourn: *The tourists tarried for an hour in Copenhagen before going on to their next stop.* [Of uncertain origin.] —**tar′ri·er,** *n.*

tar·ry² (tär′ē) *adj.,* **-ri·er, -ri·est.** of, like, or covered with tar. [TAR¹ + -Y¹.]

tar·sal (tär′səl) *adj.* of or relating to the tarsus, or ankle. —*n.* any bone or cartilage in the ankle.

tar sand *also,* **tar sands.** a bed of sand or sandstone saturated or impregnated with heavy hydrocarbons, esp. asphalt. The tar sands of Alberta, Canada, are among the world's largest petroleum resources.

tar·si·er (tär′sē ā′, -sē ər) *n.* any of various tree-dwelling mammals, family Tarsiidae, native to the East Indies, having prominent eyes and ears, elongated digits, and a long, thin tail. Length: 16 inches (41 centimeters), including tail. [French *tarsier,* from *tarse* ankle, from Modern Latin *tarsus;* because it has long ankles. See TARSUS.]

tar·sus (tär′səs) *n., pl.* **-si** (-sī). **1.** the ankle or the seven small bones of which it is composed. **2.** the shank of a bird's leg. **3.** the terminal segment of the leg in insects and certain other arthropods, corresponding to the foot. **4.** a small plate of connective tissue that supports the edge of the eyelid. [Modern Latin *tarsus,* from Greek *tarsos* ankle, sole of the foot, flat basket.]

tart¹ (tärt) *adj.* **1.** sharp in taste; not sweet; sour: *The unripe apple has a tart flavor.* **2.** sharp in tone or meaning; caustic: *a tart remark.* [Old English *teart* sharp, severe.] —**tart′ly,** *adv.* —**tart′ness,** *n.*

tart² (tärt) *n.* **1.** an individual piece of pastry having a filling, as custard or fruit, with or without a top crust. **2.** *British.* any fruit pie. **3.** *Slang.* a promiscuous woman or prostitute. [Old French *tarte;* of uncertain origin.]

tar·tan¹ (tär′tən) *n.* **1.** a plaid woolen fabric woven with one of the distinctive patterns of the Scottish Highland clans. **2.** the plaid pattern itself. **3.** any fabric with a similar design. —*adj.* of, like, or made of tartan. [Old French *tertaine,* form of *tiretaine* linsey-woolsey; of uncertain origin.]

tar·tan² (tär′tən) *n.* a small, single-masted boat with a lateen sail, jib, and bowsprit, used esp. in the Mediterranean. [French *tartane,* from Italian *tartana,* possibly from Arabic *tarīdah* small boat.]

tar·tar (tär′tər) *n.* **1.** the sediment or residue that collects in wine casks, consisting mainly of cream of tartar and calcium tartrate, used to make tartaric acid. **2.** a hard, brownish deposit on the teeth, formed by the action of various salts on the dead bacteria in dental plaque. [Medieval Latin *tartarum* the sediment, from Middle Greek *tartaron;* of uncertain origin.]

Tar·tar (tär′tər) *n.* **1.** Tatar. **2. tartar.** a person who has a violent temper or savage disposition. —*adj.* Tatar.

• **to catch a tartar.** to attack or confront someone or something that proves too formidable or difficult to handle.

tartar emetic, a poisonous, white compound with a sweet taste, containing antimony, used as a mordant for cloth and leather and in medicine as an expectorant and to treat amebiasis.

tar·tar·ic acid (tär tar′ik) a colorless crystalline compound with an acid taste, used in baking powder, plastics, and effervescent drinks, in photography, and in several industrial processes, including dyeing and tanning. It occurs in fruits and vegetables, esp. grapes. Formula: $C_4H_6O_6$

tar·tar·ous (tär′tər əs) *adj.* of, like, containing, or derived from tartar.

tartar sauce *also,* **tar·tare sauce.** a sauce made of mayonnaise and chopped condiments, as pickles, capers, onions, and olives, served esp. with seafood.

Tar·ta·rus (tär′tər əs) *n. Greek Mythology.* **1.** a region deep in the underworld where wicked people were punished for their crimes after death. **2.** the land of the dead; Hades; underworld.

tart·let (tärt′lit) *n.* a small pastry tart.

tar·trate (tär′trāt) *n.* a salt of tartaric acid.

tar·trat·ed (tär′trā tid) *adj.* containing, derived from, or combined with tartaric acid.

task (task) *n.* **1.** a piece of work to be done, esp. one assigned by one person to another. **2.** a tiring or burdensome job or duty: *Writing that long report was quite a task.* —*v.t.* **1.** to assign a task to. **2.** to burden with excessive work; put a strain upon: *The difficult drawing tasked the artist's skills.* [Medieval Latin *tasca,* form of *taxa* a taxation, rating, from *taxare* to impose a tax. See TAX.] —For Synonyms, see **job.**

• **to take to task.** to call to account; reprimand; scold: *The manager took the workers to task for not getting the job done on time.*

task force 1. a number of military units, esp. naval units, brought together under one commander for a specific mission. **2.** any group that is formed or brought together to deal with a specific problem: *a task force on poverty.*

task·mas·ter (task′mas′tər) *n.* a person, esp. a strict and uncompromising individual, who assigns tasks to others.

Tas·ma·ni·an devil (taz mā′nē ən) a bearlike marsupial, *Sarcophilus harrisii,* native to Tasmania, having a coarse brown or black coat. Length: 3 feet (0.9 meter), including tail.

tas·sel (tas′əl) *n.* **1.** a hanging ornament consisting of a group of threads, cords, or similar materials bound together at one end. **2.** anything resembling this in shape, as the branched male flower at the top of a

tartan¹ *(def. 2)*

—Tassel

tassels
on a corn plant

a	at	e	end	o	hot	u	up	hw	white	⌠	about
ā	ape	ē	me	ō	old	ū	use	ng	song		taken
ä	far	i	it	ô	fork	ü	rule	th	thin	ə	pencil
âr	care	ī	ice	oi	oil	u̇	pull	th	this		lemon
		îr	pierce	ou	out	ûr	turn	zh	measure	⌡	circus

stalk of corn. —*v.*, **-seled, -sel·ing**; *also, British*, **-selled, -sel·ling.** —*v.t.* to attach a tassel or tassels to. —*v.i.* (of corn) to put forth a tassel. [Old French *tassel* fastening, clasp; of uncertain origin.]

taste (tāst) *n.* **1.** the sense by which the flavor of a thing is perceived. **2.** a particular sensation as perceived by this sense. The four basic tastes are sweet, bitter, sour, and salty. **3.** a small amount to be eaten or sampled: *May I have a taste of your dessert?* **4.** a brief experience of anything; sample: *The preview gave a taste of what the television series would be like.* **5.** a preference or liking: *That house is not to my taste.* **6.** the ability to recognize and appreciate that which is excellent, beautiful, or appropriate, as in art or decorum: *to have good taste in music.* **7.** the manner in which the quality of such ability is reflected: *Your remarks are in poor taste.* —*v.*, **tast·ed, tast·ing.** —*v.t.* **1.** to perceive or distinguish the flavor of (something) through the sense of taste: *I can taste the garlic in this stew.* **2.** to take (something) into the mouth in order to test the flavor: *to taste soup for salt.* **3.** to take a small quantity of (a food or drink) into the mouth: *May I taste the soup?* **4.** to experience, esp. briefly or for the first time: *to taste power.* —*v.i.* **1.** to have a particular flavor: *The sauce tastes too sweet. The soup tastes of onion.* **2.** to have the sense of taste; perceive flavor. **3.** to take a small quantity of something into the mouth, as in testing the flavor. **4.** to have experience or knowledge; partake (usually *of*): *to taste of freedom.* [Old French *taster* to feel, try, handle, possibly going back to a blend of Latin *tangere* to touch, and *gustāre* to eat a little, partake of.]

taste bud, any of a cluster of cells located chiefly in the lining of the tongue and mouth and containing receptors that are sensitive to taste.

taste·ful (tāst′fəl) *adj.* having or exhibiting a good sense of what is beautiful, excellent, or appropriate: *a tasteful outfit.* —**taste′ful·ly,** *adv.* —**taste′ful·ness,** *n.*

taste·less (tāst′lis) *adj.* **1.** without flavor; bland: *a tasteless sauce.* **2.** having or exhibiting poor judgment as to what is excellent, beautiful, or appropriate: *a tasteless remark.* —**taste′less·ly,** *adv.* —**taste′less·ness,** *n.*

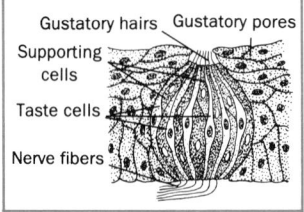

Gustatory hairs Gustatory pores
Supporting cells
Taste cells
Nerve fibers

taste bud

tast·er (tās′tər) *n.* a person who tastes, esp. one who is employed to judge the quality of such beverages as wine, tea, or coffee by tasting.

tast·y (tās′tē) *adj.*, **tast·i·er, tast·i·est. 1.** pleasing to the sense of taste; flavorful; savory. **2.** tasteful. —**tast′i·ly,** *adv.* —**tast′i·ness,** *n.*

tat (tat) *v.*, **tat·ted, tat·ting.** —*v.t.* to make by tatting. —*v.i.* to make tatting. [From TATTING.]

Ta·tar (tä′tər) *n.* **1.** a member of the tribes of Mongols and Turks who overran parts of Asia and Europe during the Middle Ages. **2.** a member of a Turkic people descended from them, now living chiefly in parts of the Soviet Union in central and western Asia. **3.** the language of these people, belonging to the Turkic branch of the Ural-Altaic language family. —*adj.* of, relating to, or characteristic of the Tatars or their language or culture. Also, **Tartar.**

tat·ter (tat′ər) *n.* **1.** an irregularly torn and often hanging piece or shred of something: *The sail was ripped to tatters by the wind.* **2. tatters.** worn or ragged clothing; rags. —*v.t.* to tear into pieces or shreds; make ragged. —*v.i.* to become ragged. [Of Scandinavian origin.]

tat·ter·de·mal·ion (tat′ər di māl′yən, -mal′-) *n.* a person dressed in worn or ragged clothing; ragamuffin. [TATTER + -demalion (word element of uncertain meaning and origin).]

tat·tered (tat′ərd) *adj.* **1.** hanging or torn in shreds: *a tattered shirt.* **2.** dressed in worn or ragged clothes: *a tattered waif.*

tat·ter·sall (tat′ər sôl′) *n.* **1.** a pattern of dark lines on a light background forming checks or squares. **2.** a fabric having such a pattern. —*adj.* having or made of such a pattern: *a tattersall shirt.* [From the pattern commonly found on blankets at *Tattersall's* horse market in London.]

tat·ting (tat′ing) *n.* **1.** the art or process of making a delicate lace by looping and knotting cotton or linen thread with a special shuttle. **2.** lace made in this way, used for such items as doilies, collars, and trimmings. [Of uncertain origin.]

tat·tle (tat′əl) *v.*, **-tled, -tling.** —*v.i.* **1.** to reveal the secrets, activities, or private affairs of another. **2.** to talk idly; prate; chatter. —*v.t.* to tell or reveal by gossiping: *to tattle a secret.*

—*n.* idle talk or chatter; gossip. [Middle Dutch *tatelen* to stutter; of imitative origin.] —**tat′tler,** *n.*

tat·tle·tale (tat′əl tāl′) *n. Informal.* a person who deliberately reveals secrets; talebearer; telltale.

tat·too¹ (ta tü′) *n., pl.* **-toos. 1.** a military signal, as on a bugle, given at night to call soldiers or sailors to return to their quarters. **2.** military exercises given as entertainment. **3.** a rapid, continuous beating or tapping: *the tattoo of rain on a roof.* [Dutch *taptoe* this signal, from *tap* tap² + *toe* to shut; possibly referring to the earlier custom of giving a signal in the evening to shut off the taps of casks in bars.]

tat·too² (ta tü′) *v.t.*, **-tooed, -too·ing. 1.** to mark (the skin) permanently with colored figures or designs, usually by pricking it with a pointed instrument that has been dipped in pigment. **2.** to mark (figures or designs) on the skin in this way. —*n., pl.* **-toos.** a pattern, figure, or design made by tattooing. [Polynesian *tatau* a tattoo mark.] —**tat·too′er,** *n.*

tat·ty (tat′ē) *adj.*, **-ti·er, -ti·est.** shabby or worn; frayed. [Possibly from TATTER.] —**tat′ti·ly,** *adv.* —**tat′ti·ness,** *n.*

tau (tou, tô) *n.* **1.** the nineteenth letter (T, τ) of the Greek alphabet, corresponding to the English letter *T, t.* **2.** *Physics.* an unstable lepton thousands of times more massive than the electron.

taught (tôt) the past tense and past participle of **teach.**

taunt (tônt, tänt) *v.t.* **1.** to mock or reproach with insults or scornful language: *The crowd taunted the team for its poor performance.* **2.** to get or provoke by taunting: *The children taunted the dog into a fit of barking.* —*n.* an insulting, often provocative remark. [Of uncertain origin.] —**taunt′er,** *n.* —**taunt′ing·ly,** *adv.*

taupe (tōp) *n.* a dark gray color, tinged with brown, purple, or yellow. —*adj.* having the color taupe.

Tau·rus (tôr′əs) *n.* **1.** a constellation in the northern sky containing Aldebaran, the Hyades, and the Pleiades, conventionally depicted as a bull. **2.** the second sign of the zodiac. [Latin *taurus* bull.]

taut (tôt) *adj.* **1.** tightly drawn or stretched; not slack or loose: *a taut wire.* **2.** showing tension or strain; tight: *My nerves are taut.* **3.** in good condition; orderly; tidy: *The captain kept a taut ship.* [Middle English *toght* tense; of uncertain origin.] —**taut′ly,** *adv.* —**taut′ness,** *n.*

tau·tog (tô tog′, -tôg′) *n.* a food fish, *Tautoga onitis,* found in Atlantic coastal waters of the United States. Also, **blackfish.** [Narragansett *tautauog,* plural of *tautau* sheepshead.]

tau·tol·o·gy (tô tol′ə jē) *n., pl.* **-gies. 1.a.** the useless repetition of an idea in different words, for example: *We left simultaneously at the same time.* **b.** an instance of this. **2.** a statement that is necessarily true because it includes all possibilities, for example: *Either it will rain tomorrow or it will not.* [Late Latin *tautologia,* from Greek *tautologiā* going back to *to auto* the same (thing) + *legein* to speak.] —**tau·to·log·i·cal** (tô′tə loj′i kəl), **tau·tol·o·gous** (tô tol′ə gəs), *adj.* —**tau·to·log′i·cal·ly,** *adv.*

tav·ern (tav′ərn) *n.* **1.** a place where alcoholic beverages are sold to be drunk on the premises; bar. **2.** a public place providing food and lodging, esp. for travelers. [Old French *taverne,* from Latin *taberna* hut.]

taw (tô) *n.* **1.** a fancy marble with which a player shoots in a game of marbles. **2.** the line from which the players shoot in this game. [Of uncertain origin.]

taw·dry (tô′drē) *adj.*, **-dri·er, -dri·est.** cheap and gaudy; tasteless; showy: *a tawdry display of wealth.* [Modification of *Saint Audrey* (referring to the gaudy laces sold at Saint Audrey's annual fair, formerly held in Ely, England).] —**taw′dri·ly,** *adj.* —**taw′dri·ness,** *n.*

taw·ny (tô′nē) *adj.*, **-ni·er, -ni·est.** brownish yellow: *The lion has a tawny mane.* [Old French *tan(n)e,* past participle of *tan(n)er* to tan hides, from Medieval Latin *tannare.* See TAN.] —**taw′ni·ness,** *n.*

tax (taks) *n.* **1.** money that must be paid by persons and businesses for the support of a government. **2.** an oppressive burden or heavy demand; strain: *The long hike was a tax on my strength.* —*v.t.* **1.** to place or impose a tax on, as income, property, or sale of goods. **2.** to require to pay a tax: *The government taxes all citizens.* **3.** to make a heavy demand on; burden; strain: *to tax one's brain for a solution to a problem.* **4.** to accuse or reprove; take to task: *to tax someone for being constantly late.* [Medieval Latin *taxare* to impose a financial tax, from Latin *taxāre* to rate¹, value, handle.] —**tax′er,** *n.*

tax·a·ble (tak′sə bəl) *adj.* subject or liable to taxation: *Certain purchases are not taxable.* —**tax′a·bil′i·ty,** *n.* —**tax′a·bly,** *adv.*

tax·a·tion (tak sā′shən) *n.* **1.** the act or system of imposing and collecting taxes. **2.** a tax or assessment imposed. **3.** the revenue raised by taxes.

T

tax base, wealth, in the form of income, real estate, or investments, that is subject to taxation.

tax-ex·empt (taks'eg zempt') *adj.* not subject to taxes.

tax·i (tak'sē) *n., pl.* **tax·is** or **tax·ies.** taxicab. —*v.*, **tax·ied, tax·i·ing** or **tax·y·ing. 1.** to ride in a taxicab: *We taxied to the theater.* **2.** (of an airplane) to move slowly along the ground or on the surface of water. —*v.t.* to cause (an airplane) to taxi.

tax·i·cab (tak'sē kab') *n.* an automobile for public hire, usually having a meter that records the fare to be paid. [TAXI(METER) + CAB.]

tax·i·der·mist (tak'si dûr'mist) *n.* a person whose work or business is taxidermy.

tax·i·der·my (tak'si dûr'mē) *n.* the art of preparing and stuffing the skins of dead animals and mounting them in lifelike positions for study or display. [Greek *taxis* arrangement + *derma* skin.] —**tax'i·der'mic,** *adj.*

tax·i·me·ter (tak'sē mē'tər, tak sim'i-) *n.* the meter in a taxicab that automatically computes and displays the fare due. [French *taximètre,* from *taxe* rate[1], charge (going back to Medieval Latin *taxare* to impose a tax) + *-mètre* -meter. See TAX, -METER.]

tax·is (tak'sis) *n., pl.* **tax·es** (tak'sēz). an involuntary movement made by an animal, microorganism, or cell in response to a specific stimulus, as light or heat. [Greek *taxis* arrangement.]

tax·on (tak'son) *n., pl.* **tax·a** (tak'sə). a taxonomic group or entity, as a species, genus, or family. [German *Taxon,* from *Taxonomie* taxonomy.]

Taxonomic Classification			
Taxonomic level	**Human**	**Dog**	**Corn**
Kingdom	Animalia	Animalia	Plantae
Phylum* Division	Chordata	Chordata	Anthophyta
Class	Mammalia	Mammalia	Monocotyledones
Order	Primates	Carnivora	Commelinales
Family	Hominidae	Canidae	Poaceae
Genus	*Homo*	*Canis*	*Zea*
Species	*sapiens*	*familiaris*	*mays*

*Phylum and division are equivalent taxonomic levels: phylum describes animals, division describes plants.

tax·o·nom·ic (tak'sə nom'ik) *adj.* of, relating to, or according to taxonomy. Also, **tax'o·nom'i·cal.** —**tax'o·nom'i·cal·ly,** *adv.*

tax·on·o·my (tak son'ə mē) *n.* **1.** *Biology.* the classification of organisms into categories on the basis of their structural and evolutionary relationships, the categories ranging from the broadest to the most specific, chiefly: kingdom, phylum or division, class, order, family, genus, species. **2.** the study of the general principles of scientific classification. [French *taxonomie* science of the laws of classification, from Greek *taxis* arrangement + *-nomiā* arrangement, law.] —**tax·on'o·mist,** *n.*

tax·pay·er (taks'pā'ər) *n.* a person who pays or is subject to a tax.

tax shelter, a financial arrangement, such as an investment or a depreciation allowance, whereby a person or corporation can reduce or eliminate income taxes.

Tay-Sachs disease (tā'saks') a fatal genetic disease in which the body is unable to make an enzyme that is needed to break down fat. [From the English physician Warren *Tay,* 1843-1927, and the American neurologist Bernard *Sachs,* 1858-1944, who discovered this disease.]

Tb, the symbol for terbium.

TB, tuberculosis.

T-bill (tē'bil') *n.* Treasury bill.

T-bone steak (tē'bōn') a loin steak containing some tenderloin and a T-shaped bone. Also, **T-bone.**

tbs *also,* **tbs., tbsp** tablespoon; tablespoons.

Tc, the symbol for technetium.

T cell, any of the lymphocytes, largely differentiated in the thymus, that are mainly responsible for killing foreign or invading cells as well as activating B cells to secrete antibodies. [Abbreviation of *t(hymus)* + CELL.]

Te, the symbol for tellurium.

tea (tē) *n.* **1.** a beverage made from the dried and prepared leaves of a shrub or small tree, *Thea sinensis,* of Asia. **2.** the dried leaves used to make this beverage. **3.** the plant bearing these leaves, having mildly fragrant, drooping white flowers. **4.** any of various beverages made by soaking the leaves or other parts of certain other plants or substances: *camomile tea, beef tea.* **5.** *British.* a late afternoon refreshment or light meal, usually consisting of bread and butter, cakes, and similar food served with tea. **6.** a reception or other social gathering, usually small in size and occurring in the afternoon, at which tea and other refreshments are served. [Dialectal Chinese *t'e* the tea plant, beverage made from its leaves.]

tea bag, a small, porous bag of thin paper or cloth containing shredded or ground tea leaves for immersing in hot water to make tea.

tea ball, a small, perforated metal ball for immersing tea leaves in hot water to make tea.

tea·ber·ry (tē'ber'ē, -bə rē) *n.* the bright red berry of the wintergreen; checkerberry.

tea·cart (tē'kärt') *n.* a tray or small table set on wheels, used in serving tea and other refreshments; serving cart. Also, **tea wagon.**

teach (tēch) *v.*, **taught, teach·ing.** —*v.t.* **1.** to impart knowledge to, esp. through lessons or formal schooling: *to teach a class of students, to teach someone to play the piano.* **2.** to give instruction or lessons in; impart a knowledge of: *to teach English literature, to teach swimming.* **3.** to cause or help to learn: *The accident taught me to drive more carefully.* —*v.i.* to act or be employed as a teacher; give instruction: *My cousin teaches at an elementary school.* [Old English *tǣcan* to show, instruct.]

Synonyms *v.t.* **Teach, instruct, educate,** and **train** mean to impart knowledge or to help others develop skills. **Teach** is a general term applied to informal as well as formal instruction: *Most parents teach their children good manners. Trained educators know both how and what to teach.* **Instruct** implies formal or institutionalized teaching of a specialized subject: *There was a shortage of teachers qualified to instruct students in advanced mathematics.* **Educate** stresses the process rather than the content of instruction: *Some wealthy families educate their children abroad.* **Train** denotes the development of a skill, often in connection with a particular occupation: *The institute trains computer programmers and technicians.*

teach·a·ble (tē'chə bəl) *adj.* **1.** capable of being taught: *I do not think common sense is teachable.* **2.** capable of or interested in learning: *Porpoises are very bright and teachable.* —**teach'a·bil'i·ty, teach'a·ble·ness,** *n.*

teach·er (tē'chər) *n.* a person who teaches, esp. as an occupation.

teacher's aide, a person hired to assist a teacher in a school, esp. in the classroom.

teachers college *also,* **teachers' college.** a four-year college specializing in the training of teachers.

teach-in (tēch'in') *n., pl.* **teach-ins.** an extended, informal gathering, as at a college or university, for the purpose of discussing and debating a particular public issue, often held as an expression of social protest.

teach·ing (tē'ching) *n.* **1.** the act, work, or occupation of a teacher. **2.** *also,* **teachings.** something that is taught, esp. a doctrine or precept: *the teachings of Plato.*

teaching machine, any of various devices that present a course of programmed instruction and that are operated by the user, providing questions and immediate responses to the user's answers.

tea·cup (tē'kup') *n.* **1.** a cup in which tea is served. **2.** teacupful.

tea·cup·ful (tē'kup fŭl') *n., pl.* **-fuls.** the amount that a teacup will hold, usually 4 fluid ounces (118 milliliters).

tea dance, a dance held in the late afternoon.

tea·house (tē'hous') *n., pl.* **-hous·es** (-hou'ziz). a public place, esp. in China and Japan, where tea and other light refreshments are served.

teak (tēk) *n.* **1.** the hard, fragrant, yellowish brown wood of a tree, *Tectona grandis,* used in shipbuilding, furniture, and flooring. Also, **teakwood. 2.** the tree bearing this wood, a member of the verbena family, cultivated in Asia, western Africa, and tropical

a	at	e	end	o	hot	u	up	hw	white		about
ā	ape	ē	me	ō	old	ū	use	ng	song	ə	taken
ä	far	i	it	ô	fork	ü	rule	th	thin		pencil
âr	care	ī	ice	oi	oil	ù	pull	th	this		lemon
		îr	pierce	ou	out	ûr	turn	zh	measure		circus

America, having large, oval leaves and small, white or bluish flowers. [Portuguese *teca,* from Malayalam *tēkka.*]

tea·ket·tle (tē′ket′əl) *n.* a kettle, usually with a lid, spout, and handle, in which water is boiled.

teak·wood (tēk′wŭd′) *n.* teak *(def. 1).*

teal (tēl) *n., pl.* **teal** or **teals.** **1.** any of several small, short-necked ducks, family Anatidae, having predominantly gray, brown, green, and white plumage and inhabiting rivers, ponds, and marshes. Length: 14-17 inches (36-43 centimeters). **2.** a dark, dull blue or greenish blue color. —*adj.* having the color teal. [Of uncertain origin.]

teal

team (tēm) *n.* **1.** a group making up one side in an athletic contest or other competition: *a debating team, a hockey team.* **2.** any group working together in some joint action: *a comedy team, a team of engineers.* **3.** two or more horses, oxen, or other animals harnessed together, as to pull a wagon or plow. **4.** a vehicle, as a wagon or plow, together with the animal or animals harnessed to it. —*v.t.* **1.** to bring or join together in a team: *to team horses.* **2.** to haul or transport by means of a team: *to team logs.* —*v.i.* **1.** to work together; form a team (often with *up*): *The children teamed up to distribute the newspapers.* **2.** to drive a team. [Old English *tēam,* brood, two or more animals harnessed together for work.]

team·mate (tēm′māt′) *n.* a fellow member of a team.

team·ster (tēm′stər) *n.* **1.** a person whose work or occupation is driving a truck. **2.** a person whose work or occupation is driving a team of horses, oxen, or other animals.

team·work (tēm′wûrk′) *n.* a cooperative and coordinated effort or action on the part of a number of people working together, as to achieve a common goal: *The winners attributed their victory to great teamwork.*

tea·pot (tē′pot′) *n.* a pot with a lid, spout, and handle, for making and serving tea.

tear[1] (târ) *v.,* **tore, torn, tear·ing.** —*v.t.* **1.** to pull apart or split into pieces, as by force or with a sharp edge; rip; rend: *to tear a paper in half, to tear one's jacket on a nail.* **2.** to make by tearing: *I accidentally tore a hole in my coat.* **3.** to wound by tearing; lacerate: *The thorns tore my skin.* **4.** to pull, pluck, or remove forcibly, as from an attachment or fixed place: *The storm tore many leaves and twigs off the tree.* **5.** to force as if by pulling: *We couldn't tear our eyes away from the movie screen.* **6.** to disrupt, divide, or split into sides or factions: *The country was torn by civil war.* **7.** to distress violently or painfully; torment: *My mind was torn by doubt.* **8.** to disarrange or damage, as by violence (often with *apart* or *up*): *We tore the place apart looking for the missing papers.* —*v.i.* **1.** to become torn: *The coat tore on the nail.* **2.** to move with great haste or energy; rush headlong: *The tenants tore out of the house when they heard the fire alarm.* **3.** to move, touch, or distress (with *at*): *That sad movie tears at your heartstrings.* —*n.* **1.** a torn part or place, as a split or hole: *Let me sew the tear in your sleeve.* **2.** the act or process of tearing. **3.** a headlong rush. **4.** *Informal.* spree: *to go on a tear.* [Old English *teran* to rend, lacerate.]

•**to tear at.** to make pulling, snatching, or tearing motions at; pluck at: *to tear at an annoying bandage.*

•**to tear down.** to destroy by taking apart or knocking down; raze: *to tear down a building.*

•**to tear into.** *Informal.* to set upon or attack vigorously; castigate: *The manager tore into the employee for the error.*

•**to tear up. a.** to tear into small pieces. **b.** to cancel; nullify; abrogate: *I think you should tear up that contract.*

Synonyms	*v.t.* **Tear**[1], **rip**[1], and **rend** mean to pull or split apart. **Tear** is usually interchangeable with *rip,* but is more likely to be used when the pulling apart leaves ragged edges: *The nail tore a hole in his coat. She tore the letter to shreds.* **Rip** sometimes suggests the use of a stronger force, esp. along a straight edge or seam: *The saw ripped the plywood panel in half.* **Rend,** a term with a formal, literary quality, implies a violent splitting or wrenching apart: *The earthquake's vast power rent the massive walls that surrounded the castle.*

tear[2] (tîr) *n.* **1.** a drop of the clear, slightly salty fluid secreted by the lacrimal glands, which lubricates the eyeballs, keeping them free of foreign matter, and which in weeping or crying flows from the eye. **2.** something resembling a tear. **3. tears.** the act of weeping or crying: *to burst into tears.* —*v.i.* to shed tears. [Old English *tēar* drop of fluid secreted by the eye.]

tear·drop (tîr′drop′) *n.* **1.** a single tear. **2.** something resembling a tear in shape, as a pendant gem.

tear·ful (tîr′fəl) *adj.* **1.** full of or covered with tears; weeping:

tearful eyes. **2.** causing tears; woeful; sad: *a tearful story.* —**tear′ful·ly,** *adv.* —**tear′ful·ness,** *n.*

tear-gas (tîr′gas′) *v.t.,* **-gassed, -gas·sing.** to direct tear gas against; use tear gas on.

tear gas (tîr) any of various gases that irritate the eyes, causing a flow of tears and temporary blindness, used chiefly in dispersing riotous crowds and driving armed individuals from cover.

tear-jerk·er (tîr′jûr′kər) *n. Slang.* an extremely sad or poignant film, play, or other presentation, often intended to arouse great sorrow or sympathy.

tea·room (tē′rüm′, -rum′) *n.* a small room or restaurant where beverages and light meals are served.

tea rose **1.** any of various large roses descended chiefly from a rose of Chinese origin, *Rosa odorata,* having a delicate scent thought to resemble that of tea. **2.** the spreading shrub bearing such a rose, cultivated esp. in warmer regions of the United States.

tear·y (tîr′ē) *adj.,* **tear·i·er, tear·i·est.** full of or wet with tears; marked by weeping. —**tear′i·ly,** *adv.* —**tear′i·ness,** *n.*

tease (tēz) *v.,* **teased, teas·ing.** —*v.t.* **1.** to provoke, vex, or harass, as with mischievous or playful gibes or taunts. **2.** to fluff (hair) by combing or brushing in strokes from the end of a strand toward the scalp. **3.** to raise a nap on (cloth), esp. by means of a teasel. **4.** to separate the fibers of in preparation for spinning; card; comb: *to tease wool.* —*v.i.* to engage in teasing; provoke, harass, or playfully make fun of someone. —*n.* **1.** a person given to teasing others. **2.** a flirtatious person, esp. a coquettish girl or woman. **3.** the act of teasing. [Old English *tæsan* to pluck, pull, card (as wool).]

tea·sel (tē′zəl) *also,* **teazel, teazle.** *n.* **1.a.** any of an Old World group of coarse thistlelike plants, genus *Dipsacus,* esp. **fuller's teasel,** *D. sativus,* raised for its dense, bristly flower heads, which are dried and used for brushing wool fabrics to raise a nap on them. **b.** the flower head of this plant. **2.** any device used for raising a nap on cloth. —*v.t.,* **-seled, -sel·ing;** *also, British,* **-selled, -sel·ling.** to raise a nap on (cloth) with a teasel or teasels. [Old English *tæsel* the plant.]

teas·er (tē′zər) *n.* **1.** a person or thing that teases. **2.** *Informal.* something difficult, perplexing, or annoying; puzzler.

tea service, a set of articles, as of silver or china, used in serving tea or other hot beverages, consisting of such items as a matching teapot, sugar bowl, and creamer.

tea·spoon (tē′spün′) *n.* **1.** a spoon, smaller than a tablespoon or soup spoon, used esp. to stir beverages in a cup and to eat desserts. **2.** the amount one teaspoon will hold, a standard cooking measurement equivalent to $1/3$ of a tablespoon, or $1\frac{1}{3}$ fluid drams (4.9 milliliters).

tea·spoon·ful (tē′spün fùl′) *n., pl.* **-fuls.** teaspoon *(def. 2).*

teat (tēt, tit) *n.* a small projection on the breast or udder in most female mammals, through which milk is drawn; nipple. [Old French *tete;* of Germanic origin.]

tea wagon, teacart.

tea·zel (tē′zəl) *n.* teasel. —*v.t.,* **-zeled, -zel·ing;** *also, British,* **-zelled, -zel·ling.** teasel.

tea·zle (tē′zəl) *n.* teasel. —*v.t.,* **-zled, -zling.** teasel.

tech. **1.** technical. **2.** technology.

tech·ne·ti·um (tek nē′shē əm) *n.* a silver-gray, radioactive metallic element that is a fission product of uranium, discovered in 1937 by bombarding molybdenum in an atomic accelerator and since detected in the spectra of certain stars. Symbol: **Tc** For tables, see **element.** [Modern Latin *technetium,* from Greek *technētos* artificial.]

tech·nic (tek′nik, tek nēk′) *n.* technique. [Greek *technikos* relating to art, skillful. See TECHNIQUE.]

tech·ni·cal (tek′ni kəl) *adj.* **1.** relating to, involving, or characteristic of some science, art, profession, or other field, or the particulars peculiar to it: *technical experts, technical training, technical language.* **2.** of or relating to engineering, applied science, or the mechanical or industrial arts: *a technical school that offers few courses in liberal arts.* **3.** of, relating to, or showing technique: *The musician has technical ability but little imagination.* **4.** according to strict interpretation or application of specific rules and principles: *If you really want to be technical, the team should have been disqualified, not just penalized.* [Greek *technikos* relating to art, skillful (from *technē* art, skill, craft) + -AL[1].] —**tech′ni·cal·ly,** *adv.* —**tech′ni·cal·ness,** *n.*

technical foul, in certain sports, esp. basketball, a foul that does not involve bodily contact, such as unsportsmanlike conduct or language.

tech·ni·cal·i·ty (tek′ni kal′i tē) *n., pl.* **-ties. 1.** the state or quality of being technical. **2.** a detail, point, method, or other factor peculiar to a particular science, art, profession, or other field. **3.** a point or detail so minute or specialized as to seem petty or a matter of form only: *a legal technicality.*

technical knockout *Boxing.* a decision determined in favor of

a fighter when the opponent, although not actually knocked out, is hurt so badly that the referee stops the fight.

technical sergeant, a noncommissioned officer in the U.S. Air Force ranking above a staff sergeant and below a master sergeant.

tech·ni·cian (tek nish′ən) *n.* **1.** a person who is skilled in a particular science, art, profession, or other field, esp. a person trained to deal with specialized equipment or processes: *a medical technician, a lighting technician.* **2.** a person who is skilled in technique, as a writer, artist, or musician.

tech·ni·col·or (tek′ni kul′ər) *n.* **1. Technicolor.** *Trademark.* a process of making color motion pictures, in which three single-color films, one in red, one in yellow, and one in blue, are exposed and then processed and combined into a single developed film that reproduces the filmed sequence in the colors of the original scene. **2.** bright, vivid color, as that resulting from or reproduced by this process. —*adj.* strikingly colorful; brilliant; intense: *technicolor dreams.*

tech·nique (tek nēk′) *n.* **1.** a method or manner of achieving a desired result in a science, art, sport, or other field: *teaching techniques, bicycling techniques.* **2.** any method or manner used to perform an operation or achieve a goal. [French *technique* procedures and methods of an art or profession, from Greek *technikos* relating to art, skillful, from *technē* art, skill, craft.]

tech·noc·ra·cy (tek nok′rə sē) *n., pl.* **-cies. 1.** the theory that government and society should be controlled by a selected group especially trained to solve technical problems, as scientists, engineers, and other technicians. **2.** government or rule by such a group. [Greek *technē* art, skill, craft + -*kratiā* power, rule.] —**tech·no·crat** (tek′nə krat′), *n.* —**tech′no·crat′ic,** *adj.*

tech·no·log·i·cal (tek′nə loj′i kəl) *adj.* **1.** of, relating to, or involving technology: *technological advances, a technological era.* **2.** resulting from technical progress: *technological unemployment.* Also, **tech′no·log′ic.** —**tech′no·log′i·cal·ly,** *adv.*

tech·nol·o·gy (tek nol′ə jē) *n.* **1.** the application of scientific knowledge and advances to practical purposes, esp. in the field of industry. **2.** the body of methods, processes, and devices derived or resulting from such application. **3.** any use of materials or objects, as tools, to serve human needs. [Greek *technologiā* systematic treatment, from *technē* art, skill, craft + -*logiā.* See -LOGY.] —**tech·nol′o·gist,** *n.*

tech·y (tech′ē) *adj.,* **tech·i·er, tech·i·est.** tetchy.

tec·ton·ic (tek ton′ik) *adj.* of, relating to, or designating the internal forces that operate to reshape the earth's crust, or the geologic structures they create. A tectonic map displays the geologic structure of a region by emphasizing individual faults and folds and tilted strata. [Late Latin *tectonicus,* from Greek *tektonikos* relating to construction, from *tektōn* carpenter, builder.]

tec·ton·ics (tek ton′iks) *n.* the branch of geology that studies tectonic forces. ➡ used as singular.

ted (ted) *v.t.,* **ted·ded, ted·ding.** to spread out or scatter for drying, as newly mown hay. [Old Norse *tethja* to spread manure.] —**ted′der,** *n.*

ted·dy bear (ted′ē) *also,* **Ted·dy bear.** a toy resembling a small bear, usually stuffed with soft material and covered with plush to imitate fur. [From *Teddy,* nickname of U.S. President Theodore Roosevelt, 1858-1919; because of a cartoon in which he was represented as having spared the life of a bear cub while hunting.]

Te De·um (tā dā′əm, tē dē′əm) **1.** in the Roman Catholic and Anglican churches, a hymn of praise and thanksgiving sung at morning service or on special occasions. **2.** the musical setting for this hymn. [Latin *Tē Deum (laudāmus)* Thee, God (we praise), the opening words of this hymn.]

te·di·ous (tē′dē əs, tē′jəs) *adj.* causing weariness and boredom, as from length or dullness; boring; tiresome: *a tedious job, a tedious lecture.* [Late Latin *taediōsus,* wearisome, irksome, from Latin *taedium* weariness, disgust.] —**te′di·ous·ly,** *adv.* —**te′di·ous·ness,** *n.*

te·di·um (tē′dē əm) *n.* the state or quality of being tedious.

tee¹ (tē) *n.* *Golf.* **1.** a small peg of wood, plastic, or other material, having a concave head on which a golf ball is placed to be driven at the start of play for each hole. **2.** a small mound of earth or sand used for the same purpose. **3.** a usually raised area from which a player starts play for each hole. —*v.t., v.i.,* **teed, tee·ing.** to place (a golf ball) on a tee (often with *up*). [Of uncertain origin.]

•**to tee off. a.** to drive a golf ball from a tee in starting play. **b.** to begin; start: *to tee off a new advertising campaign.* **c.** *Slang.* to make angry, annoyed, or disgusted.

tee² (tē) *n.* a target aimed at in certain games, as curling or quoits. [Possibly because such targets were once shaped like the letter *T.*]

•**to a tee.** perfectly; exactly: *We followed the directions to a tee and still got lost.*

teem¹ (tēm) *v.i.* to be at or as if at the point of overflowing; be

full; abound; swarm (with *with*): *The creek teemed with trout. By noon the beach was teeming with people.* [Old English *tēman* to bring forth.]

teem² (tēm) *v.i.* to flow heavily, as rain; pour: *The rain teemed down all night. Water teemed out of the broken pipe.* [Of Scandinavian origin.]

teen (tēn) *adj.* teenage. —*n.* teenager.

-teen *suffix* (used to form cardinal numbers from thirteen to nineteen) ten plus the base number: *sixteen.* [Old English -*tēne,* -*tȳne,* inflected form of ten.]

teen·age (tēn′āj′) *also,* **teen-age, teen·aged, teen-aged.** *adj.* relating to or characteristic of people in their teens.

teen·ag·er (tēn′ā′jər) *also,* **teen-ag·er.** *n.* a person who is older than twelve and younger than twenty years of age.

teens (tēnz) *pl. n.* **1.** the years from thirteen to nineteen, as of a person's life or a century: *to be barely out of one's teens.* **2.** the numbers thirteen to nineteen inclusive. [See -TEEN.]

tee·ny (tē′nē) *adj.,* **-ni·er, -ni·est.** *Informal.* extremely small; tiny. Also, **teen·sy** (tēn′sē).

tee·pee (tē′pē) tepee.

tee shirt, T-shirt.

tee·ter (tē′tər) *v.i.* **1.** to walk or move unsteadily and uncertainly, often with a swaying motion, as if about to fall; stagger; totter: *The acrobat teetered on the tightrope.* **2.** to move back and forth in an uncertain, unpredictable way; waver: *The country teetered on the brink of war.* —*n.* **1.** a teetering movement. **2.** seesaw *(def. 1).* [Form of earlier *titter* to totter, sway, possibly from Old Norse *titra* to tremble.]

tee·ter-tot·ter (tē′tər tot′ər) *n.* seesaw *(def. 1).* Also, **teeter board.**

teeth (tēth) the plural of **tooth.**

teethe (tēth) *v.i.,* **teethed, teeth·ing.** to grow or develop teeth; cut one's teeth.

teeth·ing ring (tē′thing) a ring of plastic, rubber, or other material upon which a teething infant may bite.

tee·to·tal (tē′tōt′əl) *v.i.,* **-taled, -tal·ing;** *also, British,* **-talled, -tal·ling.** to abstain totally from alcoholic liquor. —*adj.* **1.** of or relating to total abstinence from alcoholic liquor. **2.** *Informal.* total; complete. [From TOTAL, with repetition of the first letter *t* for emphasis.]

tee·to·tal·er (tē′tōt′ə lər) *also, British,* **tee·to·tal·ler.** *n.* a person who totally abstains from drinking alcoholic liquor.

tee·to·tal·ism (tē′tōt′ə liz′əm) *n.* the principle or practice of totally abstaining from alcoholic liquor. —**tee′to′tal·ist,** *n.*

Tef·lon (tef′lon) *n.* *Trademark.* a chemical polymer that is somewhat slippery and has a surface that most substances will not adhere to, commonly used as a coating for cooking utensils.

teg·men (teg′mən) *n., pl.* **-mi·na** (-mə nə). **1.** integument. **2.** *Botany.* the inner coat of a seed. **3.** *Zoology.* the hardened or thickened forewing of certain insects, esp. beetles; elytron. [Latin *tegmen,* from *tegere* to cover.]

teg·u·ment (teg′yə mənt) *n.* integument. [Latin *tegumentum* covering.]

tek·tite (tek′tīt) *n.* any of numerous small, dark, glassy objects of various shapes found strewn over large areas of the earth's surface, as in Australia, Indonesia, and Czechoslovakia, thought to have been created by cataclysmic meteorite impacts. [Greek *tēktos* molten + -ITE¹.]

tel. 1. telegram. **2.** telegraph. **3.** telephone.

tele- *combining form* **1.** at a distance; far: *telepathy.* **2.** of or relating to television: *telethon.* [Greek *tēle* far off, afar.]

tel·e·cast (tel′i kast′) *v.t., v.i.,* **-cast** or **-cast·ed, -cast·ing.** to broadcast (a program) by television; televise. —*n.* a program broadcast over television. [TELE(VISION) + (BROAD)CAST.] —**tel′e·cast′er,** *n.*

tel·e·com·mu·ni·ca·tion (tel′i kə mū′ni kā′shən) *n.* **1.** the sending of messages or data over long distances by electronic means, as by telegraph, television, or telephone. **2.** a message or data sent by such means. **3. telecommunications.** the science and technology of telecommunication. ➡ used as singular.

tel·e·con·fer·ence (tel′i kon′fər əns, -kon′frəns) *n.* a conference in which persons in different locations are brought together by means of telephone or television. —*v.i.,* **-enced, -enc·ing.** to take part in such a conference. [TELE- + CONFERENCE.]

tel·e·gen·ic (tel′i jen′ik) *adj.* having or likely to have an attractive appearance on television. [TELE- + (PHOTO)GENIC.] —**tel′e·gen′i·cal·ly,** *adv.*

a	at	e	end	o	hot	u	up	hw	white		about
ā	ape	ē	me	ō	old	ū	use	ng	song		taken
ä	far	i	it	ô	fork	ü	rule	th	thin	ə	pencil
âr	care	ī	ice	oi	oil	u̇	pull	th	this		lemon
		îr	pierce	ou	out	ûr	turn	zh	measure		circus

tel·e·gram (tel′i gram′) *n.* a message sent by telegraph.

tel·e·graph (tel′i graf′) *n.* the system, process, or equipment used for sending messages over a distance by means of coded electrical impulses. —*v.t.* **1.** to send (a message) by telegraph. **2.** to send a message to by telegraph. **3.** to reveal or indicate unintentionally to another, as by a look or gesture. —*v.i.* to send a message by telegraph. [TELE- + -GRAPH.]

te·leg·ra·pher (tə leg′rə fər) *n.* a person whose work is sending and receiving messages by telegraph; telegraph operator. Also, **te·leg′ra·phist.**

tel·e·graph·ic (tel′i graf′ik) *adj.* **1.** relating to, resembling, or sent by telegraph. **2.** like a telegram in style; brief or concise. Also, **tel′e·graph′i·cal.** —**tel′e·graph′i·cal·ly,** *adv.*

te·leg·ra·phy (tə leg′rə fē) *n.* the operation or use of telegraphs to send messages; communications by means of a telegraph.

tel·e·ki·ne·sis (tel′i ki nē′sis) *n.* the apparent production of motion in an object, as by a spiritualist medium, without physical contact, application of force, or other explicable means. [TELE- + Greek *kinēsis* movement.] —**tel·e·ki·net·ic** (tel′i ki net′ik), *adj.*

Te·lem·a·chus (tə lem′ə kəs) *n.* in Greek legend, the son of Ulysses and Penelope, who after many years is reunited with his father and helps him slay Penelope's suitors.

tel·e·mar·ket·ing (tel′ə mär′ki ting) *n.* the selling of products or services by telephone or television.

te·lem·e·ter (tə lem′i tər, tel′ə mē′-) *n.* an electronic instrument, as on a spacecraft, for measuring a physical quantity, as speed, temperature, pressure, or radiation, and transmitting the data to a distant receiving station. —*v.t., v.i.* to measure or transmit (data) by telemeter.

te·lem·e·try (tə lem′i trē) *n.* **1.** the branch of engineering, esp. relating to space studies, dealing with the measurement at a distance of various physical quantities, as temperature, pressure, or radiation. **2.** the process of making physical measurements and relaying the data to a distant receiving station. [TELE- + -METRY.] —**tel·e·met·ric** (tel′ə met′rik); *also,* **tel′e·met′ri·cal,** *adj.*

tel·e·ol·o·gy (tel′ē ol′ə jē, tē′lē-) *n., pl.* **-gies. 1.** the fact or quality of having or being directed toward a definite end or purpose. **2.a.** the doctrine that natural processes or events are not entirely determined by mechanical forces, but are directed toward an ultimate goal. **b.** the study of the evidence for this doctrine. **3.** an explanation or evaluation of a thing according to its purpose, aim, or end. [Modern Latin *teleologia,* from Greek *telos* end + -LOGY.] —**tel·e·o·log·ic** (tel′ē ə loj′ik, tē′lē-); *also,* **tel′e·o·log′i·cal,** *adj.* —**tel′e·ol′o·gist,** *n.*

tel·e·ost (tel′ē ost′, tē′lē-) *n.* any of a large group of advanced bony fishes, subclass Teleostei, having an entirely bony skeleton, highly developed jaws, a symmetrical tail, and rounded, overlapping, smooth scales. Most living fish are teleosts. —*adj.* of or relating to the teleosts. Also *(adj.),* **tel·e·os·te·an** (tel′ē os′tē ən, tē′lē-). [Greek *teleos* complete, from *telos* end, completion + *osteon* bone.]

te·lep·a·thy (tə lep′ə thē) *n.* the apparent communication of one mind with another by means other than ordinary speaking, writing, or gesturing. [TELE- + -PATHY.] —**tel·e·path·ic** (tel′ə path′ik), *adj.* —**tel′e·path′i·cal·ly,** *adv.* —**te·lep′a·thist,** *n.*

tel·e·phone (tel′ə fōn′) *n.* **1.** a system for sending messages over distances by converting sound into electrical impulses that are transmitted over wires or optical fibers or by microwaves and turned back into sound by a receiver. **2.** an instrument in such a system, equipped with a transmitter, a receiver, and often a dial or buttons for directing calls. —*v.,* **-phoned, -phon·ing.** —*v.t.* **1.** to communicate with by telephone. **2.** to send by telephone: *to telephone a message.* —*v.i.* to communicate or attempt to communicate by telephone: *Did you telephone ahead for reservations? I telephoned, but no one answered.* [TELE- + Greek *phōnē* voice, sound.] —**tel′e·phon′er,** *n.*

telephone book, a book containing an alphabetical listing of those persons or businesses in a given area who have telephones, together with their phone numbers and usually their addresses. Also, **telephone directory.**

tel·e·phon·ic (tel′ə fon′ik) *adj.* of, relating to, or transmitted by or as by a telephone.

te·leph·o·ny (tə lef′ə nē) *n.* the science or technology of communication by telephone.

tel·e·pho·to·graph (tel′ə fō′tə graf′) *n.* **1.** a photograph taken with a telephoto lens. **2.** a photograph or picture sent by telephotography.

tel·e·pho·to·graph·ic (tel′ə fō′tə graf′ik) *adj.* of, relating to, or characteristic of telephotography. Also, **tel′e·pho′to.**

tel·e·pho·tog·ra·phy (tel′ə fə tog′rə fē) *n.* **1.** photography with a telephoto lens. **2.** the production and transmission of facsimiles of photographs or pictures by wire, as in Wirephoto, or by radio.

tel·e·pho·to lens (tel′ə fō′tō) a camera lens that magnifies the image of a distant object.

tel·e·print·er (tel′ə prin′tər) *n.* teletypewriter.

Tel·e·Promp·Ter (tel′ə promp′tər) *n. Trademark.* a television monitor on which a magnified script is displayed line by line for a television performer or speaker.

tel·e·ran (tel′ə ran′) *n.* a navigation system in which radar information and maps are transmitted to airplanes over television. [Short for *tele(vision) r(adar) a(ir) n(avigation).*]

tel·e·scope (tel′ə skōp′) *n.* **1.** an optical instrument for making distant objects, as heavenly bodies, appear nearer and larger, consisting of one or more tubes. A **refracting telescope** has a concave lens at the upper or far end that refracts light toward an eyepiece, camera, or other device. A **reflecting telescope** has a concave mirror at its base that reflects light toward an eyepiece, camera, or other device. **2.** any of various electronic devices analogous to such an instrument, as a radio telescope, that focus radiation from parts of the electromagnetic spectrum outside the visible light range. —*v.t.,* **-scoped, -scop·ing. 1.** to compress or drive together or into one another, as the sliding tubes of certain telescopes: *The impact of the collision telescoped the two cars.* **2.** to make shorter or smaller; condense; abridge: *to telescope a three-volume book into one.* [Modern Latin *telescopium,* going back to Greek *tēle* afar + *-skopion.* See -SCOPE.]

reflecting **telescope**

tel·e·scop·ic (tel′ə skop′ik) *adj.* **1.** of, relating to, or characteristic of a telescope. **2.** seen or obtained by means of a telescope: *telescopic images.* **3.** visible only through a telescope. **4.** able to see over a great distance; far-seeing: *a telescopic lens.* **5.** consisting of parts that can slide into one another, as the tubes of certain telescopes. —**tel′e·scop′i·cal·ly,** *adv.*

tel·e·thon (tel′ə thon′) *n.* a long television program during which callers pledge money, as to a charity. [TELE(VISION) + (MARA)THON.]

Tel·e·type (tel′i tīp′) *n. Trademark.* communications equipment by which a message typed on one teletypewriter is transmitted over telephone lines to another teletypewriter. —*v.t., v.i.,* **-typed, -typ·ing.** to transmit (a message) by teletypewriter. —**tel′e·typ′er, tel′e·typ′ist,** *n.*

tel·e·type·writ·er (tel′i tīp′rī′tər) *n.* a keyboard machine that looks like an electric typewriter, used for receiving and sending messages over telephone lines. Also, **teleprinter.**

tel·e·van·gel·ism (tel′i van′jə liz′əm) *n.* the use of television to preach Christian theology, usually of a fundamentalist nature, and to convert viewers to the following of a television minister. —**tel′e·van′gel·ist,** *n.* [Blend of TELEVISION and EVANGELISM.]

tel·e·view (tel′ə vū′) *v.t., v.i.* to watch or observe by means of television. —**tel′e·view′er,** *n.*

tel·e·vise (tel′ə vīz′) *v.t., v.i.,* **-vised, -vis·ing.** to transmit or receive by television.

tel·e·vi·sion (tel′ə vizh′ən) *n.* **1.** a system of sending and receiving images and sound by transforming them into electrical signals, then into waves, and then back into signals, which are converted back to images and sound by a receiver. **2.** a set in which such images are received and reproduced. **3.** the industry, medium, or art of television broadcasting. —*adj.* of or relating to television. [TELE- + VISION.]

tel·ex (tel′eks) *n.* **1.** a system for sending and receiving messages using a teletypewriter. **2.** the equipment used in such a system. **3.** a message sent or received by such a system. —*v.t.* **1.** to send

(a message) by this system. **2.** to send a telex to (someone). [Tel(ETYPEWRITER) + EX(CHANGE).]

tell (tel) *v.,* **told, tell·ing.** — *v.t.* **1.** to give a detailed account of; narrate: *to tell a fairy tale to a child.* **2.** to put or express in written or spoken words: *to tell a lie.* **3.** to give information to; let know: *Tell us about your vacation.* **4.** to make known, esp. something that is confidential; reveal; disclose: *to tell a secret.* **5.** to give an order, command, or direction to: *I told you to be quiet.* **6.** to distinguish, as one thing from another; discern; determine: *A jeweler can tell a real diamond from an imitation.* **7.** to assure emphatically: *It won't work, I tell you!* **8.** to name or count one by one, as the beads of a rosary. — *v.i.* **1.** to give an account: *The old sailors told of their many great adventures.* **2.** to disclose something secret; report; inform: *If you misbehave, I'll tell.* **3.** to serve as evidence; be an indication: *Only time will tell if we have been successful.* **4.** to have or produce an effect: *The strain is beginning to tell.* [Old English *tellan* to reckon, narrate.] — **tell'a·ble,** *adj.*
• **to tell off. a.** to count off and detach, as for some special duty: *to tell off recruits for a special mission.* **b.** *Informal.* to reprimand severely; scold; chastise.
• **to tell on.** *Informal.* to inform on; tattle; snitch.

tell·a·ble (tel′ə bəl) *adj.* capable of or suitable for being told.

tell·er (tel′ər) *n.* **1.** a person who relates, narrates, or informs: *a teller of tall stories.* **2.** a person who counts or enumerates. **3.** a person who is employed in a bank and receives or gives out money over a counter.

tell·ing (tel′ing) *adj.* having the intended or desired effect; striking; forceful: *a telling blow, a telling style.* — **tell′ing·ly,** *adv.*

tell·tale (tel′tāl′) *n.* **1.** tattletale. **2.** any of various devices that indicate or register something or serve as a warning. — *adj.* revealing what is not intended to be known or seen: *There were telltale spots of blood on the suspect's coat.*

tel·lu·ride (tel′yə rīd′) *n.* a compound of tellurium with a metallic element. Lead telluride is used as a semiconductor.

tel·lu·ri·um (te lûr′ē əm) *n.* a lustrous, silver-white, semimetallic element that is a semiconductor and is also used in stainless steel and lead alloys. Symbol: **Te** For tables, see **element.** [Modern Latin *tellurium,* from Latin *tellūr-,* stem of *tellūs* earth.]

tel·o·phase (tel′ə fāz′) *n.* in cell division, the stage during which the new nuclear membranes form, each surrounding an identical set of chromosomes. For illustration, see **mitosis.** [Greek *télos* end + PHASE.]

Tel·u·gu (tel′i gü′) *n., pl.* **-gu** or **-gus. 1.** a member or close descendant of a Dravidian people living predominantly in southern India. **2.** their language, belonging to the Dravidian language family. — *adj.* of, relating to, or characteristic of the Telugu or their language or culture.

tem·blor (tem′blər, -blôr; *Spanish* tem blôr′) *n., pl.* **-blors** or *(Spanish)* **-blo·res** (-blôr′ās). an earthquake or tremor. [Spanish *temblor* a trembling, going back to Latin *tremulus* trembling.]

te·mer·i·ty (tə mer′i tē) *n.* foolish or reckless boldness, as in speech or behavior; rashness. [Latin *temeritās.*]

temp. 1. temperature. **2.** temporary.

tem·per (tem′pər) *n.* **1.a.** an inclination to become angry or irritated. **b.** an angry state of mind; rage: *to be in a temper after a trying day.* **2.** a habitual or usual frame of mind; temperament: *an even temper.* **3.** command over the emotions; self-control; composure; equanimity: *to lose one's temper.* **4.** hardness, elasticity, or other quality of a material, esp. a metal, imparted by special treatment. **5.** a substance added to another to modify, neutralize, or subdue its properties. — *v.t.* **1.** to restrain the severity or harshness of; moderate; soften: *to temper justice with mercy.* **2.** to bring (metal or glass) to a proper or desired condition by controlled heating and cooling: *to temper steel with heat.* **3.** to adjust the pitch of (a note or instrument) by temperament; tune. [Old English *temprian* to mingle, regulate, from Latin *temperāre.*]

tem·per·a (tem′pər ə) *n.* **1.** a painting medium usually consisting of egg yolk, ground pigment, and water. **2.** the art or technique of painting with such a medium. [Italian *tempera,* from *temperare* to mix colors, moderate, from Latin *temperāre* to mingle, regulate.]

tem·per·a·ment (tem′pər ə mənt, -prə mənt) *n.* **1.** a combination of qualities that make up the natural disposition of a person and affect actions, thinking, and emotions: *a calm temperament.* **2.** a natural inclination to assert one's individuality, esp. a tendency to be extremely moody, sensitive, or irritable. **3.** *Music.* **a.** the tuning of an instrument, esp. a keyboard instrument, so that the intervals of all twelve half tones are equal, making it possible to play in all keys. **b.** the system according to which this is done. [Latin *temperāmentum* mixing in due proportion, disposition; with reference to the earlier belief that one's temperament resulted from

the relative proportions of the four humors in one's system. See HUMOR.] — For Synonyms, see **disposition.**

tem·per·a·men·tal (tem′pər ə men′təl, -prə men′təl) *adj.* **1.** having or exhibiting extreme moodiness, sensitivity, or irritability: *a temperamental actor.* **2.** relating to or caused by temperament: *a temperamental outburst.* **3.** not dependable; unpredictable: *a temperamental machine.* — **tem′per·a·men′tal·ly,** *adv.* — For Synonyms, see **moody.**

tem·per·ance (tem′pər əns, -prəns) *n.* **1.** the observance of moderation or self-restraint in behavior of any kind, esp. in regard to the drinking of alcoholic beverages. **2.** total abstinence from alcoholic beverages. [Latin *temperantia* moderation.]

tem·per·ate (tem′pər it, -prit) *adj.* **1.** characterized by temperance in behavior. **2.** generally free from extremes of temperature: *a temperate climate.* [Latin *temperātus* moderate, past participle of *temperāre* to mingle, moderate, regulate.] — **tem′per·ate·ly,** *adv.* — **tem′per·ate·ness,** *n.*

Temperate Zone, either of the two climatic zones of the earth characterized by a temperate climate with four distinct seasons. One zone lies north of the equator between the Arctic Circle and the Tropic of Cancer, the other south of the equator between the Tropic of Capricorn and the Antarctic Circle. For illustration, see **zone.**

tem·per·a·ture (tem′pər ə chər, -prə chər) *n.* **1.** the degree of heat or coldness of a body or substance as measured by a thermometer or other graduated scale. **2.** *Informal.* an abnormally high body temperature; fever: *I have a temperature, so I'm staying home today.* [Latin *temperātūra* due measure, proportion.]

tem·per·a·ture-hu·mid·i·ty index (tem′pər ə chər hū mid′i·tē, -ū mid′-, tem′prə chər-) a value computed from measurements of atmospheric temperature and humidity, used by the U.S. Weather Bureau to express the relative comfort or discomfort caused by the combination of the two.

tem·pered (tem′pərd) *adj.* **1.** having a specified disposition.
➡ used in combination: *an even-tempered person.* **2.** modified or moderated by the addition of some other substance or quality; lessened; softened. **3.** treated so as to have the desired degree of hardness and elasticity: *tempered glass.* **4.** *Music.* adjusted or tuned to a temperament.

tem·pest (tem′pist) *n.* **1.** a violent windstorm, usually accompanied by rain, hail, snow, or thunder. **2.** any violent commotion or disturbance; tumult. [Old French *tempest(e)* storm, going back to Latin *tempestās* season, weather, storm, from *tempus* time, season.]

tem·pes·tu·ous (tem pes′chü əs) *adj.* **1.** characteristic of a tempest; turbulent; stormy: *tempestuous winds.* **2.** subject to or characterized by strong or violent emotion: *a tempestuous mob.* — **tem·pes′tu·ous·ly,** *adv.* — **tem·pes′tu·ous·ness,** *n.*

Tem·plar (tem′plər) *n.* **1.** a member of a medieval religious and military order of knights that protected the pilgrims on their crusades to the Holy Land. **2.** Knight Templar *(def. 2).* [Medieval Latin *templarius* member of a religious and military order of knights in the Middle Ages, from Latin *templum* sanctuary, consecrated place.]

tem·plate (tem′plit) *also,* **templet.** *n.* **1.** a pattern or gauge used as a guide in bringing a piece of a work to a desired shape. **2.** *Genetics.* a macromolecule, such as DNA, upon which synthesis of another macromolecule, such as RNA, is patterned. **3.** a short piece of stone or timber used to receive and distribute pressure, as of a beam or girder.

tem·ple¹ (tem′pəl) *n.* **1.** a building dedicated to the worship of a god or gods. **2.** **Temple.** any of three buildings erected successively in Jerusalem as the center of Jewish worship. **3.** synagogue *(def. 2).* **4.** Christian church. **5.** a place or object in which God is considered to dwell, as in the body of a person who is sanctified. **6.** any Mormon house of worship. **7.** **Temple.** either of two buildings in London, the **Inner Temple** and the **Middle Temple,** formerly the dwelling place of the Knights Templar, now belonging to English legal societies. [Old English *temp(e)l* building dedicated to divine worship, from Latin *templum* sanctuary, consecrated place.]

tem·ple² (tem′pəl) *n.* the flattened part on either side of the forehead, above the cheekbone and in front of the ear. [Old French *temple,* going back to Latin *tempus.*]

tem·plet (tem′plit) template.

tem·po (tem′pō) *n., pl.* **-pos** or **-pi** (-pē). **1.** *Music.* the relative speed at which a musical composition, movement, or passage is or

a	at	e	end	o	hot	u	up	hw	white		about
ā	ape	ē	me	ō	old	ū	use	ng	song	ə	taken
ä	far	i	it	ô	fork	ů	rule	th	thin		pencil
âr	care	ī	ice	oi	oil	ů	pull	th	this		lemon
		îr	pierce	ou	out	ûr	turn	zh	measure		circus

should be played. **2.** a characteristic pace or speed: *the fast tempo of life in a modern city.* [Italian *tempo* time, from Latin *tempus.* Doublet of TENSE².]

tem·po·ral¹ (tem′pər əl, -prəl) *adj.* **1.** of or relating to time. **2.** of short duration; temporary. **3.** of or relating to this life on earth; material; worldly: *temporal pleasures.* **4.** not religious; secular; civil; lay: *a religious leader with temporal powers.* [Late Latin *temporālis* worldly, from Latin *temporālis* relating to time, from *tempus* time, season.] —**tem′po·ral·ly,** *adv.* —**tem′po·ral·ness,** *n.*

tem·po·ral² (tem′pər əl, -prəl) *adj.* of, relating to, or situated near one or both temples. —*n.* temporal bone. [Late Latin *temporālis* relating to the temples (of the head), from Latin *tempus* temple².]

temporal bone, in humans and certain other mammals, either of a pair of bones that form the sides and part of the base of the skull and enclose the middle and inner ear.

tem·po·ral·i·ty (tem′pə ral′i tē) *n., pl.* **-ties. 1.** the state or quality of being temporal; temporariness. **2.** *also,* **temporalities.** something that is temporal or secular, esp. material possessions of a church.

tem·po·rar·y (tem′pə rer′ē) *adj.* lasting, existing, or occurring for a limited time only; not permanent: *a temporary shelter, a temporary job.* —*n.* an employee hired for a limited period of time, esp. to work in an office. [Latin *temporārius,* from *tempus* time.] —**tem′po·rar′i·ly,** *adv.* —**tem′po·rar′i·ness,** *n.*

tem·po·rize (tem′pə rīz′) *v.i.,* **-rized, -riz·ing. 1.** to delay or postpone immediate action or decision, so as to avoid arguments, disapproval, or other difficulty or to gain time. **2.** to adapt one's acts or opinions in order to conform to the time or circumstances; comply. **3.** to effect a settlement, esp. through compromise; negotiate. [French *temporiser* to delay, through Medieval Latin, from Latin *tempus* time.] —**tem′po·ri·za′tion,** *n.* —**tem′po·riz′er,** *n.*

tempt (tempt) *v.t.* **1.** to attempt to persuade (someone) to do something that is sinful, illegal, or foolish. **2.** to cause (someone) to think of doing or to want to do something; incline strongly: *Hunger tempted the refugee to steal food.* **3.** to attract strongly; lure: *The unappetizing food didn't tempt us.* **4.** to act presumptuously or recklessly toward; provoke; defy: *to tempt fate.* [Latin *temptāre* to handle, test, try.] —**tempt′a·ble,** *adj.*

temp·ta·tion (temp tā′shən) *n.* **1.** the act of tempting or the state of being tempted. **2.** something that tempts: *The cake was a temptation that we couldn't resist.*

tempt·er (temp′tər) *n.* a person or thing that tempts or entices.

tempt·ing (temp′ting) *adj.* producing temptation; enticing; attractive; seductive: *a tempting offer.* —**tempt′ing·ly,** *adv.*

tempt·ress (temp′tris) *n.* a woman who tempts, esp. a seductive, alluring woman.

tem·pu·ra (tem pŏŏr′ə) *n.* a Japanese dish made with shrimp, other seafood, vegetables, or combinations of these ingredients, dipped in batter and fried in deep fat. [Japanese *tenpura* this dish.]

tem·pus fu·git (tem′pəs fū′jit) *Latin.* time flies.

ten (ten) *n.* **1.** the cardinal number that is one more than nine. **2.** a symbol representing this number, such as 10 or X. **3.** something having this many units or members, such as a playing card. —*adj.* numbering one more than nine. [Old English *tēn, tien.*]

ten·a·ble (ten′ə bəl) *adj.* capable of being held, maintained, or defended: *a tenable fortress, a tenable situation, a tenable theory.* [Old French *tenable* holdable, from *tenir* to hold, from Latin *tenēre.*] —**ten′a·bil′i·ty, ten′a·ble·ness,** *n.* —**ten′a·bly,** *adv.*

te·na·cious (tə nā′shəs) *adj.* **1.** holding or inclined to hold firmly: *a tenacious grip.* **2.** tending to adhere to another substance; adhesive; sticky: *Tar is a tenacious substance.* **3.** not easily pulled or broken apart; tough: *a tenacious alloy.* **4.** stubborn or persistent; resolute; obstinate: *a tenacious will, a tenacious resistance to change.* **5.** tending to retain; retentive: *a tenacious memory.* [Latin *tenāci-,* stem of *tenāx* holding fast + -OUS.] —**te·na′cious·ly,** *adv.* —**te·na′cious·ness,** *n.*

te·nac·i·ty (tə nas′i tē) *n.* the quality or state of being tenacious.

ten·an·cy (ten′ən sē) *n., pl.* **-cies. 1.** the occupancy of property for which rent is paid; state of being a tenant. **2.** the period of time during which a tenant occupies property. **3.** the property occupied by a tenant.

ten·ant (ten′ənt) *n.* **1.** a person who pays rent to occupy or use the property of another, such as land, a house, apartment, or office. **2.** an occupant or inhabitant of any place: *the present tenant of the White House.* **3.** a person who possesses land or property by any kind of title. —*v.t.* to hold or occupy as a tenant;

inhabit. [Old French *tenant* one who holds or possesses, from *tenir* to hold, from Latin *tenēre.*]

tenant farmer, a farmer who works land owned by another and pays rent either in cash or a share of the crops.

ten·ant·ry (ten′ən trē) *n., pl.* **-ries. 1.** tenants collectively, as of an estate. **2.** the state of being a tenant; tenancy.

tench (tench) *n., pl.* **tench** or **tench·es.** a freshwater fish, *Tinca tinca,* of the carp family, found in Europe and Asia. It is capable of living out of water for fairly long periods. [Old French *tench,* from Late Latin *tinca;* possibly of Celtic origin.]

Ten Commandments, the ten rules for living and for worship that, according to the Old Testament, God presented to Moses on Mount Sinai, engraved on tablets of stone.

tend¹ (tend) *v.i.* **1.** to be disposed in action or thought; be likely or apt: *My cat is fat because it tends to overeat. They tend to be optimistic.* **2.** to lead to some state or condition; have a specified result: *The difficult negotiations seem to be tending toward collapse.* **3.** to move, extend, or be directed in a particular direction: *The path tends toward the left at the river.* [Old French *tendre* to stretch, bend, aspire to, offer, from Latin *tendere* to stretch, direct, aim.]

tend² (tend) *v.t.* **1.** to attend to the needs or requirements of; care for; watch over; minister to: *to tend a sick person, to tend a plant, to tend a child.* **2.** to be in charge of or work at; manage or operate: *to tend a machine, to tend a store.* **3.** to serve or wait (with *on* or *upon*). —*v.i. Informal.* to take care of; pay attention (with *to*): *Tend to your own affairs.* [Short for ATTEND.]

tend·ance (ten′dəns) *n.* attention or care, as to the sick.

tend·en·cy (ten′dən sē) *n., pl.* **-cies. 1.** a natural or habitual disposition to move or act in a particular manner: *They have a tendency to make friends easily. My car's engine has a tendency to stall in cold weather.* **2.** the meaning or purpose of something written or said; purport. [Medieval Latin *tendentia* direction, going back to Latin *tendere* to stretch, direct, aim.]

ten·den·tious (ten den′shəs) *adj.* written or spoken in behalf of some particular cause or point of view; biased: *a tendentious account of a political campaign.* [Medieval Latin *tendentia* direction + -OUS. See TENDENCY.] —**ten·den′tious·ly,** *adv.* —**ten·den′tious·ness,** *n.*

ten·der¹ (ten′dər) *adj.* **1.** soft or delicate in substance; not tough or hard: *tender beef.* **2.** easily injured or bruised; not hardy, robust, or strong; fragile: *the tender petals of a flower.* **3.** having the delicacy of youth; fresh; immature: *a tender age, tender years.* **4.** not forcible or rough; light; gentle: *a tender touch.* **5.** expressing or characterized by warmth of feeling; kind or loving; affectionate: *a tender look, a tender tone of voice, tender memories.* **6.** acutely or painfully sensitive; easily hurt; sore: *My arm was still tender after the cut healed.* **7.** (of plants) unable to survive exposure to freezing temperatures. **8.** sensitive to the feelings of others; sympathetic; compassionate: *a tender heart.* **9.** requiring cautious, delicate, or tactful handling or treatment; ticklish: *a tender subject.* **10.** easily injured, distressed, or offended: *a tender conscience, tender sensibilities.* **11.** delicate or soft in quality or effect, as light or a color. [Old French *tendre* delicate, gentle, from Latin *tener* delicate, soft.] —**ten′der·ly,** *adv.* —**ten′der·ness,** *n.*

ten·der² (ten′dər) *v.t.* **1.** to present for acceptance, esp. in a formal manner: *to tender one's resignation from a job.* **2.** *Law.* to offer in payment of a debt, claim, demand, or other obligation. —*n.* **1.** a formal offer presented for acceptance: *a tender of marriage, a tender to purchase shares of a company's stock.* **2.** something that is tendered, esp. money offered in payment. **3.** *Law.* an offer of money, goods, or services in payment of a debt or other obligation. [Old French *tendre* to offer, from Latin *tendere* to stretch, direct, aim.] —**ten′der·er,** *n.*

tend·er³ (ten′dər) *n.* **1.** a person who cares for, attends to, or manages someone or something. **2.** a small boat or ship used to attend a large vessel, as by carrying supplies or passengers between the vessel and the shore. **3.** a railroad car attached to the rear of a steam locomotive, used to carry fuel and water. [TEND² + -ER¹.]

ten·der·foot (ten′dər fŏŏt′) *n., pl.* **-foots** or **-feet** (-fēt′). **1.** a newcomer to ranch or mining life of the American West, who is unused to the hardships or rough conditions of such life. **2.** any inexperienced person; novice. **3. Tenderfoot.** a boy who is in the lowest rank of the Boy Scouts.

ten·der-heart·ed (ten′dər här′tid) *adj.* easily moved to pity, love, or sorrow; compassionate; sympathetic. —**ten′der-heart′ed·ly,** *adv.* —**ten′der-heart′ed·ness,** *n.*

ten·der·ize (ten′də rīz′) *v.t.,* **-ized, -iz·ing.** to make (meat) tender, as by pounding, marinating, or applying a tenderizer.

ten·der·iz·er (ten′də rī′zər) *n.* any substance applied to meat to make it tender, esp. one containing an enzyme from papaya juice. —**ten′der·i·za′tion,** *n.*

ten·der·loin (ten′dər loin′) *n.* **1.** the tenderest part of the loin of beef or pork, located under the short ribs and running parallel to the backbone. **2.a. Tenderloin.** formerly, a district of New York City below 42nd Street west of Broadway, in which there was much vice and graft, and which was regarded as a choice assignment for a corrupt police officer. **b.** any district of a city notorious for vice and graft.

ten·di·nous (ten′də nəs) *adj.* **1.** of, relating to, or resembling a tendon. **2.** consisting of tendons.

ten·don (ten′dən) *n.* a strong cord or band of fibrous connective tissue that attaches a muscle to a bone or other part of the body; sinew. [French *tendon,* from Latin *tendere* to stretch.]

ten·do·ni·tis (ten′də nī′tis) *also,* **ten·di·ni·tis.** *n.* an inflammation of a tendon, usually where it attaches to a bone. [TENDON + -ITIS.]

ten·dril (ten′drəl) *n.* **1.** a threadlike, leafless, often spirally coiling part of a climbing plant, as the grape, that serves to support the plant by twining around or clinging to a tree trunk, wall, or other object. **2.** something resembling this: *wispy tendrils of hair.* [Modification of obsolete French *tendrillon* tender shoot, diminutive of Old French *tendron,* going back to Latin *tener* delicate, soft.]

ten·e·brous (ten′ə brəs) *adj.* characterized by darkness; gloomy. [Latin *tenebrōsus,* from *tenebrae* darkness.] —**ten′e·brous·ness,** *n.*

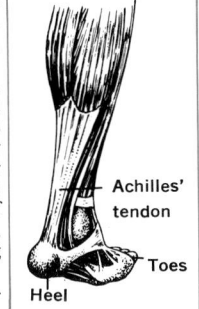

Achilles' tendon
Toes
Heel

tendon

ten·e·ment (ten′ə mənt) *n.* **1.** an apartment building or rooming house that is poorly built or maintained and usually overcrowded, esp. one that is located in a slum and inhabited by poor people. Also, **tenement house. 2.** any house or building to live in, esp. one that is rented or intended for rent. **3.** a room or set of rooms occupied by a tenant as a separate dwelling. **4.** *Law.* any permanent property that one person may hold for another, as land or buildings. **5.** *Archaic.* any residence or dwelling place; abode. [Medieval Latin *tenementum* a holding, fief, house, from Latin *tenēre* to hold.]

ten·et (ten′it) *n.* a doctrine, principle, or belief held to be true by an individual or group. [Latin *tenet* he holds.]

ten·fold (ten′fōld′) *adj.* **1.** ten times as great or numerous. **2.** having or consisting of ten parts. —*adv.* so as to be ten times greater or more numerous.

ten-gal·lon hat (ten′gal′ən) a wide-brimmed felt hat with a high crown, worn esp. in the southwestern United States.

Tenn., Tennessee.

ten·nis (ten′is) *n.* **1.** a racket game in which two or four players hit a light, fabric-covered rubber ball back and forth over a low net stretched across the center of a level, rectangular court of grass, clay, concrete, or other material. Also, **lawn tennis. 2.** any of several similar and related games, as court tennis. [Old French *tenez* hold (supposedly referring to the call of the player serving the ball), imperative of *tenir* to hold, from Latin *tenēre.*]

tennis shoe, a low sneaker worn in playing tennis.

ten·on (ten′ən) *n.* a projecting part cut on the end of a timber or other piece of wood for insertion into a corresponding hole, or mortise, in another piece to form a joint. —*v.t.* **1.** to cut such a projecting part in (a piece of wood). **2.** to join (two pieces of wood) with a tenon and mortise joint. [Old French *tenon* the end of a piece of wood put into a mortise, from *tenir* to hold, from Latin *tenēre.*]

ten·or (ten′ər) *n.* **1.** a general or usual tendency, course, or direction: *the quiet tenor of country life.* **2.** a general meaning or effect of something spoken or written; drift: *The sad tenor of your letter worried me.* **3.** *Music.* **a.** a male singing voice, intermediate between baritone and countertenor. **b.** a singer who has such a voice. **c.** an instrument corresponding in range to this voice. **d.** a part composed for such a voice or instrument. —*adj. Music.* **1.** able to sing tenor: *a tenor voice.* **2.** for a tenor: *a tenor score.* **3.** having a range corresponding to that of a tenor voice: *a tenor saxophone.* [Latin *tenor* a holding on, course, sense of a law, tone.]

ten pence, a coin of the United Kingdom equal to ten pennies or $1/10$ of a pound.

ten·pen·ny (ten′pen′ē, -pə nē) *adj.* **1.** worth or costing ten pennies, esp. ten British pennies. **2.** designating a nail 3 inches (8 centimeters) in length.

ten·pin (ten′pin′) *n.* **1. tenpins.** a bowling game using ten bottle-shaped wooden pins and a large ball, and allowing a player

to bowl two balls in each frame. ➡ used as singular. **2.** a pin used in this game.

tense¹ (tens) *adj.,* **tens·er, tens·est. 1.** stretched or drawn tight; strained; taut: *tense muscles.* **2.** undergoing or showing mental or emotional strain: *a tense person, a tense expression.* **3.** characterized by or causing strain or suspense: *a tense moment, a tense situation, a tense drama.* —*v.t., v.i.,* **tensed, tensing.** to make or become tense. [Latin *tensus,* past participle of *tendere* to stretch.] —**tense′ly,** *adv.* —**tense′ness,** *n.*

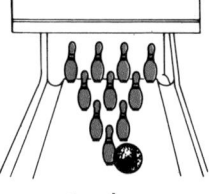

tenpins

tense² (tens) *n.* **1.** a form of a verb that shows the time of its action or state of being. *We sit* is in the present tense. *We sat* is in the past tense. *We will sit* is in the future tense. **2.** a set of such forms for a particular tense. The present tense of the verb *go* is *I go; you go; he, she, or it goes; we go; you go; they go.* [Old French *tens* time, from Latin *tempus.* Doublet of TEMPO.]

ten·sile (ten′səl, -sīl) *adj.* **1.** of or relating to tension: *tensile strain.* **2.** capable of being elongated or stretched; ductile: *a tensile metal.* [Modern Latin *tensilis,* from Latin *tendere* to stretch.] —**ten·sil·i·ty** (ten sil′i tē), *n.*

tensile strength, the resistance that a material offers to lengthwise stress, measured by the greatest amount of stretching force that can be applied without tearing the material apart.

ten·sion (ten′shən) *n.* **1.** the act of stretching or making taut or the state of being stretched. **2.** mental or emotional strain; feeling of anxiety, fear, excitement, or suspense. **3.** any strained state or relationship: *tension between rival nations.* **4.** *Physics.* **a.** a force or combination of forces tending to cause extension or elongation of the parts of a material or object, as a line or cord; stress caused by pulling. **b.** the condition of a body when acted upon by such a force or forces. **5.** voltage. **6.** a device for regulating tautness, as of thread in a sewing machine. [Latin *tēnsiō* a stretching.] —For Synonyms, see **stress.**

ten·sion·al (ten′shə nəl) *adj.* relating to tension.

ten·si·ty (ten′si tē) *n.* the state of being tense; tension.

ten·sive (ten′siv) *adj.* relating to or causing tension.

ten·sor (ten′sər, -sôr) *n.* any muscle that stretches or tenses a part of the body. [Modern Latin *tensor,* from Latin *tensus,* past participle of *tendere* to stretch.]

ten-speed (ten′spēd′) *n.* a bicycle with a derailleur and a system of gears having ten forward gear ratios. [Short for *ten-speed bicycle.*]

ten-strike (ten′strīk′) *n.* **1.** a strike in the game of tenpins. **2.** *Informal.* any entirely successful action or undertaking.

tent (tent) *n.* **1.** a collapsible, portable shelter, usually of canvas, supported by one or more poles and fastened by cords attached to pegs in the ground. **2.** anything that resembles this in form or use, as an oxygen tent. —*v.i.* to live or camp in a tent; encamp: *We tented by the stream for the night.* —*v.t.* **1.** to cover with or as if with a tent. **2.** to provide with or lodge in tents. [Old French *tente* pavilion, going back to Latin *tendere* to stretch.]

ten·ta·cle (ten′tə kəl) *n.* **1.** any of various long, slender, flexible processes or appendages of animals, esp. invertebrates, usually growing on the head or about the mouth, used esp. for feeling, grasping, and moving. **2.** anything resembling this, as a grasping, far-reaching power or influence: *a city held in the tentacles of organized crime.* **3.** a sensitive, hairlike growth on the leaves of some plants, as sundews. [Modern Latin *tentaculum,* from Latin *tentāre* to feel, try.] —**ten·tac·u·lar** (ten tak′yə lər), *adj.*

ten·ta·tive (ten′tə tiv) *adj.* **1.** made, done, or proposed as a trial or experiment; not definite or final; provisional: *tentative plans, a tentative agreement, a tentative outline for a novel.* **2.** showing hesitancy or uncertainty: *a tentative smile.* [Medieval Latin *tentativus* trying, from Latin *tentāre* to feel, try.] —**ten′ta·tive·ly,** *adv.* —**ten′ta·tive·ness,** *n.*

tent caterpillar, any of a group of destructive caterpillars, genus *Malacosoma,* that spin large, tentlike, silken webs on the branches of trees.

ten·ter (ten′tər) *n.* a framework or machine on which cloth is stretched so as to dry evenly without shrinkage. —*v.t.* to stretch (cloth) on a tenter. [Middle English *tentour,* from Latin *tentus,* past participle of *tendere* to stretch.]

a	at	e	end	o	hot	u	up	hw	white		about
ā	ape	ē	me	ō	old	ū	use	ng	song		taken
ä	far	i	it	ô	fork	ü	rule	th	thin	ə	pencil
âr	care	ī	ice	oi	oil	u̇	pull	th	this		lemon
		îr	pierce	ou	out	ûr	turn	zh	measure		circus

T

ten·ter·hook (ten'tər hŭk') *n.* a sharp hooked nail used for fastening cloth on a tenter.
• **on tenterhooks.** in a state of suspense or anxiety: *The candidate's followers were on tenterhooks as they awaited the results of the election.*

tenth (tenth) *adj.* **1.** (the ordinal of ten) next after the ninth. **2.** being one of ten equal parts. —*n.* **1.** something that is next after the ninth. **2.** one of ten equal parts; 1/10. —*adv.* in the tenth place.

ten·u·ity (tə nü'i tē, -nū'-, te-) *n.* the state of being thin, insubstantial, or rarefied; tenuous condition.

ten·u·ous (ten'ū əs) *adj.* **1.** having a thin, slender, or delicate form, as a thread. **2.** having little strength, substance, or significance; weak; flimsy: *a tenuous argument, a tenuous claim to an inheritance.* **3.** not dense, as air at high altitudes; rare. [Latin *tenuis* thin, fine + -OUS.] —**ten'u·ous·ly,** *adv.* —**ten'u·ous·ness,** *n.*

ten·ure (ten'yər) *n.* **1.** the act or right of holding or possessing something, as property, a title, or office. **2.a.** a length of time during which something is held: *The tenure of the presidency is four years.* **b.** the conditions or terms under which something is held. **3.** the status of permanent position that is granted to an employee, as a teacher or civil servant, after specified requirements are fulfilled. [Old French *tenure* a holding, possession, condition under which one holds a fief, going back to Latin *tenēre* to hold.]

ten·ured (ten'yərd) *adj.* **1.** having tenure, esp. at a college or university: *a tenured professor.* **2.** offering or leading to tenure: *to apply for a tenured position.*

te·nu·to (tə nü'tō) *adj. Music.* held or sustained for its full time value. [Italian *tenuto* held, past participle of *tenere* to hold, from Latin *tenēre*.]

te·o·sin·te (tē'ə sin'tē) *n.* a tall annual grass of Mexico and Central America, *Zea mexicana,* that is related to corn and is planted as forage. [Mexican Spanish *teosinte,* from Nahuatl *teo:sinλi, teo:senλi* literally, divine maize, from *teo:λ* god + *sinλi, senλi* maize.]

te·pee (tē'pē) *also,* **teepee.** *n.* a cone-shaped tent, usually of animal skins, used by North American Indians, esp. the Plains Indians. [Dakota *tīpī,* from *ti* to dwell + *pi* for use.]

tep·id (tep'id) *adj.* **1.** moderately or slightly warm; lukewarm: *tepid water.* **2.** characterized by a lack of interest, warmth, or enthusiasm: *a tepid writing style, a tepid welcome.* [Latin *tepidus.*] —**te·pid·i·ty** (te pid'i tē), **tep'id·ness,** *n.* —**tep'id·ly,** *adv.*

te·qui·la (tə kē'lə) *n.* a strong alcoholic beverage produced in Mexico from the sap of an agave plant. [From *Tequila,* district in Mexico where it was first produced.]

ter. **1.** terrace. **2.** territory.

tera- *combining form* trillion. [Greek *teras* marvel, monster.]

te·rat·o·gen (tə rat'ə jən ter'ə tə-) *n.* an agent, as a drug, pollutant, or disease, that can trigger a birth defect. —**te·rat·o·gen·ic** (tə rat'ə jen'ik, ter'ə tə-), *adj.*

ter·a·tol·o·gy (ter'ə tol'ə jē) *n. Biology.* the study of monstrosities or abnormal formations in animals or plants. [Greek *terat-,* stem of *teras* marvel, monster + -LOGY.] —**ter·a·to·log·i·cal** (ter'ə tə loj'i kəl), *adj.*

ter·bi·um (tûr'bē əm) *n.* a very soft, silver-gray, metallic element of the rare-earth group, used as a laser material. Symbol: **Tb** For tables, see **element.** [From *(Yt)terb(y),* Swedish town where it was discovered.]

ter·cel (tûr'səl) *n.* a male falcon, esp. the male of the peregrine falcon. [Old French *tercel,* going back to Latin *tertius* third; with reference to the belief that every third egg laid by a hawk produced a male.]

ter·cen·te·nar·y (tûr'sen ten'ə rē, tər sen'tə ner'ē) *n., pl.* -**nar·ies.** a 300th anniversary or its celebration. —*adj.* of or relating to a period of 300 years. Also, **ter'cen·ten'ni·al.** [Latin *ter* three times + CENTENARY.]

ter·cet (tûr'sit) *n.* a group of three lines of verse that rhyme together or are connected by rhyme with the adjacent group or groups of lines. [French *tercet,* from Italian *terzetto,* diminutive of *terzo* third, from Latin *tertius.*]

ter·e·binth (ter'ə binth') *n.* a large Mediterranean shrub, *Pistacia terebinthus,* yielding a turpentinelike oleoresin. [Middle English *terebint,* from Middle French *therebinthe,* from Latin *terebinthus,* from Greek *terebinthos.*]

te·re·do (tə rē'dō) *n., pl.* -**dos.** shipworm.

ter·gal (tûr'gəl) *adj.* of or relating to the tergum; dorsal.

ter·gi·ver·sate (tûr'jə vər sāt') *v.i.,* -**sat·ed,** -**sat·ing.** **1.** to change one's beliefs about or become a renegade to a cause or political party. **2.** to be evasive; use subterfuge; equivocate. [Latin *tergiversātus,* past participle of *tergiversārī* to turn one's

back, shift, evade, going back to *tergum* back + *vertere* to turn.] —**ter'gi·ver·sa'tion,** *n.* —**ter'gi·ver·sa'tor,** *n.*

ter·gum (tûr'gəm) *n., pl.* -**ga** (-gə). the back of an animal, esp. the dorsal surface of the body of an arthropod. [Latin *tergum* the back.]

ter·i·ya·ki (ter'ē yä'kē) *n.* a Japanese dish consisting of cubes of meat or fish marinated or dipped in soy sauce and then broiled, grilled, or barbecued, usually on skewers. [Japanese *teriyaki,* from *teri* sunshine + *yaki* broiling.]

term (tûrm) *n.* **1.** a word or phrase having a precise meaning in some particular field: *legal terms, scientific terms.* **2.** any word or phrase used in a precise sense: *"Darling" is a term of endearment.* **3. terms.** a particular manner of speaking or type of language used: *to speak in loving terms, to answer a question in vague terms.* **4.** a definite or limited period of time; time during which a thing lasts: *the term of a lease, a term of office.* **5.** a division of a school year: *the spring term.* **6.** *Law.* a period of time during which a court of law is in session. **7. terms.** a relationship between or among people: *to be on good terms with someone.* **8. terms.** conditions or stipulations according to which something is to be done: *the terms of a treaty.* **9.** *Mathematics.* **a.** each of the quantities that composes a fraction or ratio or forms a series or progression. **b.** each of the quantities connected by plus or minus signs in an algebraic expression. **10.** *Logic.* **a.** either the subject or predicate of a proposition. **b.** one of the three elements of a syllogism, each of which appears twice. **11.** *Archaic.* boundary; limit; end. —*v.t.* to apply a particular term to; name; designate: *The governor can be termed a conservative in economic matters.* [Old French *terme* limit, date, word, going back to Latin *terminus* boundary line, end. Doublet of TERMINUS.]
• **to bring to terms.** to cause to agree, esp. by force.
• **to come to terms.** to reach an agreement: *The two sides came to terms and the strike ended.*
• **in terms of.** with regard to; in relation to; considering: *Applicants for the keyboarder's job will be judged in terms of accuracy as well as speed.*

ter·ma·gant (tûr'mə gənt) *n.* a boisterous, quarrelsome, scolding woman; shrew. —*adj.* having the characteristics of a termagant; quarrelsome; shrewish. [From Old French *Tervagan* a supposed Muslim divinity who was represented in medieval plays as violent; of uncertain origin.]

ter·mi·na·ble (tûr'mə nə bəl) *adj.* **1.** capable of being terminated; not perpetual: *a terminable contract.* **2.** terminating after a certain time: *a terminable annuity.* —**ter'mi·na·bil'i·ty, ter'mi·na·ble·ness,** *n.* —**ter'mi·na·bly,** *adv.*

ter·mi·nal (tûr'mə nəl) *adj.* **1.** at or forming the end, end part, or boundary of something: *a terminal post marking the border of the property.* **2.** *Botany.* growing at the end of a stem or branch: *a terminal bud.* **3.** coming or occurring at the end of a series; concluding; closing: *the terminal name on a list.* **4.** of or relating to a term; occurring in each term: *terminal examinations.* **5.** relating to or in the final state of a fatal disease: *terminal cancer, a terminal patient.* **6.** relating to, situated at, or forming the end of a railroad or other transportation line. —*n.* **1.** something that terminates; terminal part or structure; extremity; end. **2.a.** a point on an electric circuit where a connection can be made. **b.** a device making such a connection. **3.a.** either end of a railroad, bus, air, or other transportation line. **b.** the station or city located at such a point. **c.** any station on a transportation line, esp. one that is centrally located or serves as a junction with other lines. **4.** *Computers.* a keyboard and monitor combined in one unit and used for input and output of data. **5.** an ornamental figure or object, as a carving, situated at the end of a structure. [Latin *terminālis* relating to a boundary or end, from *terminus* boundary line, end.] —**ter'mi·nal·ly,** *adv.*

terminal leave, a leave of absence granted to a member of the armed forces immediately before being discharged, equal to the amount of unused leave time that has been accumulated.

ter·mi·nate (tûr'mə nāt') *v.,* -**nat·ed,** -**nat·ing.** —*v.t.* **1.** to bring to an end; put an end to: *to terminate a marriage by divorce.* **2.** to come at the end of; form the conclusion of: *A song terminated the ceremony.* **3.** to form or be situated at the boundary of; bound; limit: *The river terminates the property.* **4.** to dismiss from a position of employment; fire. —*v.i.* **1.** to come to an end: *The show terminated at eleven o'clock.* **2.** to have a specified end or result (usually with *in*): *The game terminated in a victory for the home team.* [Latin *terminātus,* past participle of *termināre* to limit.] —**ter'mi·na'tive,** *adj.* —**ter'mi·na'tive·ly,** *adv.* —For Synonyms *(v.t.),* see **end.**

ter·mi·na·tion (tûr'mə nā'shən) *n.* **1.** the act of terminating or the state of being terminated. **2.** the end of something in space or

life-size **terra cotta** figures
excavated near Xian, China

time; limit or conclusion. **3.** an outcome or result. **4.** the end of a word, as a suffix or inflectional ending. —**ter′mi·na′tion·al,** *adj.*

ter·mi·na·tor (tûr′mə nā′tər) *n.* **1.** a person or thing that terminates. **2.** the line separating the illuminated and dark portions of the disk of a moon or planet.

ter·mi·nol·o·gy (tûr′mə nol′ə jē) *n., pl.* **-gies.** the terms or system of terms used in an art, science, trade, or other specialized subject: *legal terminology, the terminology of chemistry.* [German *Terminologie,* from Medieval Latin *terminus* definition, expression (from Latin *terminus* end) + Greek *-logiā* (see -LOGY). See TERM.] —**ter·mi·no·log·i·cal** (tûr′mə nə loj′i kəl), *adj.* —**ter′mi·no·log′i·cal·ly,** *adv.* —**ter′mi·nol′o·gist,** *n.*

term insurance, insurance that expires at the end of a specified period of time.

ter·mi·nus (tûr′mə nəs) *n., pl.* **-nus·es** or **-ni** (-nī′). **1.** a point or place at which something comes to an end; end or goal. **2.a.** either end of a railroad, bus, air, or other transportation line. **b.** the city or station at such a point. **3.a.** a boundary, border, or limit. **b.** a stone, post, or other object used to indicate a boundary or limit. [Latin *terminus* boundary line, end. Doublet of TERM.]

Ter·mi·nus (tûr′mə nəs) *n.* in Roman mythology, the god who presided over boundaries and landmarks.

ter·mite (tûr′mīt) *n.* any of a group of social insects, order Isoptera, found in temperate and tropical regions, having a whitish body and dark head and feeding on wood, paper, and other organic material. Termites cause great damage to buildings, furniture, and some crops. Also, **white ant.** [Modern Latin *termit-,* stem of *termes,* from Latin *termes* wood worm.]

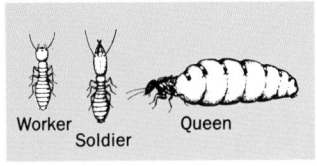

Worker   Soldier   Queen

termites

term paper, a long report, essay, or other written assignment required of a student during a school or college term.

tern (tûrn) *n.* any of various web-footed seabirds, family Laridae, esp. of the genus *Sterna,* closely related to gulls but having a more slender body, narrow wings, a deeply forked tail, and, usually, white and gray plumage with a black patch on the head. Length: 8-23 inches (20-58 centimeters). Wingspread: to 2½ feet (0.8 meter). [Of Scandinavian origin.]

ter·na·ry (tûr′nə rē) *adj.* **1.** consisting of or relating to three; grouped in threes. **2.** *Chemistry.* relating to or containing three different elements, atoms, radicals, or groups: *a ternary acid.* **3.** third in rank, order, or position. [Latin *ternārius* consisting of three, going back to *ter* three times.]

ter·nate (tûr′nāt, -nit) *adj.* consisting of or arranged in groups of three, as a compound leaf composed of three leaflets. [Modern Latin *ternatus,* going back to Latin *ter* three times.] —**ter′nate·ly,** *adv.*

ter·pene (tûr′pēn) *n.* any of a group of unsaturated hydrocarbons that are the principal constituents of essential oils, from which they are extracted, used as solvents and in organic synthesis. Formula: $C_{10}H_{16}$ [German *terpen,* from *terpentin* turpentine + *-en* -ene.]

Terp·sich·o·re (tûrp sik′ə rē) *n.* in Greek mythology, the Muse of dancing and choral song.

terp·si·cho·re·an (tûrp′si kə rē′ən, -si kôr′ē ən) *adj.* relating to dancing.

terr. **1.** terrace. **2.** territory.

ter·race (ter′is) *n.* **1.** a balcony extending from a floor of a house or apartment building. **2.** an open, usually paved or tiled area adjacent to a house, used esp. for lounging, outdoor cooking or dining, and parties. **3.** a raised, level platform of earth with a vertical or sloping front or side, esp. one of a series of such levels placed one above the other and built for the cultivation of certain crops or to conserve moisture and retard erosion. **4.** *Geology.* a relatively level strip of land extending along the margin of a sea, lake, or river and descending abruptly on the side toward the water. **5.a.** a group of houses or apartments built on a raised or sloping area of land. **b.** a street on which such a row of houses or apartments faces. **6.** a parklike strip of land in the middle of a street. **7.** a flat roof of a house, esp. of a house built in an Eastern or Spanish style. —*v.t.,* **-raced, -rac·ing.** to form into or provide with a terrace or terraces: *to terrace a hillside.* [Middle French *terrace* platform, pile of earth, going back to Latin *terra* earth.]

ter·ra cot·ta (ter′ə kot′ə) **1.** a hard, durable, brownish orange

earthenware used esp. for vases, statuettes, or as a facing for buildings. **2.** an object made of this substance: *an exhibition of terra cottas.* **3.** a brownish orange color. —*adj.* **1.** made of terra cotta: *a terra cotta figurine.* **2.** having the color terra cotta. [Italian *terra cotta* earthenware; literally, baked earth, from Latin *terra* earth + *cocta,* feminine past participle of *coquere* to cook.]

ter·ra fir·ma (ter′ə fûr′mə) solid ground; dry land. [Latin *terra firma* solid land.]

ter·rain (tə rān′, te-) *n.* **1.** a region or tract of land, esp. with regard to its natural features or suitability for some special purpose, as farming: *hilly terrain, rocky terrain.* **2.** *Geology.* terrane. [French *terrain* ground, earth, site, going back to Latin *terrēnum* land, from *terra* land, earth.]

ter·ra in·cog·ni·ta (ter′ə in′kog nē′tə, in kog′ni tə) an unknown or unexplored region or field of knowledge. [Latin *terra incognita* unknown land.]

Ter·ra·my·cin (ter′ə mī′sin) *n. Trademark.* an antibiotic derived from a microorganism found in the soil, effective against a large number of disease-causing organisms. Formula: $C_{22}H_{24}N_2O_9$ [Latin *terra* earth + Greek *mykēs* fungus + -IN[1].]

ter·rane (tə rān′, te-) *also,* **terrain.** *n. Geology.* a rock formation or series of related formations. [Form of TERRAIN.]

ter·ra·pin (ter′ə pin′) *n.* any of a group of edible North American turtles, family Emydidae, found in fresh and brackish waters, esp. the diamondback. [Modification of Algonquian *torope* little turtle.]

ter·rar·i·um (tə râr′ē əm) *n., pl.* **-rar·i·ums** or **-rar·i·a** (-râr′ē ə). a small enclosure or container, esp. a glass case, for growing plants or raising small land-dwelling animals, as snakes, turtles, or lizards. [Modern Latin *terrarium,* from Latin *terra* land (on the model of AQUARIUM).]

ter·raz·zo (te raz′ō, -rät′sō) *n.* a mosaic flooring usually consisting of small chips of marble or colored stone set in plain or colored cement. [Italian *terrazzo* mosaic floor, balcony, going back to Latin *terra* earth.]

ter·res·tri·al (tə res′trē əl) *adj.* **1.** of, relating to, or representing the earth: *a terrestrial globe, terrestrial magnetism.* **2.** relating to or consisting of land, as distinct from water or air. **3.** growing in the ground or on land: *a terrestrial plant.* **4.** living on land, rather than in the air, water, or trees: *Most mammals are terrestrial.* **5.** of or relating to this world; worldly; earthly; mundane. —*n.* an inhabitant of the earth. [Latin *terrestris* earthly, relating to the earth (from *terra* earth) + -AL[1].] —**ter·res′tri·al·ly,** *adv.*

ter·ret (ter′it) *n.* one of the rings on a harness through which the reins pass. [Old French *toret* small wheel, diminutive of *tour* a turn, circuit, lathe, from Latin *tornus* lathe. See TOUR.]

ter·ri·ble (ter′ə bəl) *adj.* **1.** causing terror or awe; dreadful; awful: *The volcano erupted with a terrible roar.* **2.** extremely violent or severe; causing great distress or pain: *a terrible automobile accident.* **3.** *Informal.* inferior or poor in quality; very bad or unpleasant: *a terrible performance, terrible food.* **4.** *Informal.* very

a	at	e	end	o	hot	u	up	hw	white		about
ā	ape	ē	me	ō	old	ū	use	ng	song		taken
ä	far	i	it	ô	fork	ü	rule	th	thin	ə	pencil
âr	care	ī	ice	oi	oil	u̇	pull	th	this		lemon
		îr	pierce	ou	out	ûr	turn	zh	measure		circus

great; excessive: *a terrible bore.* [Latin *terribilis* frightful, from *terrēre* to frighten.] —**ter′ri·ble·ness,** *n.* —**ter′ri·bly,** *adv.*

ter·ri·er (ter′ē ər) *n.* any of various breeds of lively, rugged, usually small dogs with a coat that ranges from smooth and short to wiry and fairly long, as the fox terrier or Scottish terrier. Terriers were originally used to hunt burrowing animals. Height: 9-23 inches (23-58 centimeters) at the shoulder. [French *terrier,* from *terrier* burrow, from *terre* earth, from Latin *terra.*]

ter·rif·ic (tə rif′ik) *adj.* **1.** *Informal.* unusually great, intense, or severe: *a terrific pain, a terrific hardship.* **2.** *Informal.* extremely good; excellent; wonderful: *a terrific singer, a terrific idea.* **3.** causing great fear or dread; terrifying; dreadful. [Latin *terrificus* frightful, from *terrēre* to frighten + *ficus.* See -FIC.] —**ter·rif′i·cal·ly,** *adv.*

fox **terrier**

ter·ri·fy (ter′ə fī′) *v.t.,* -**fied,** -**fy·ing.** to fill with terror; frighten or alarm greatly. [Latin *terrificāre* to frighten.] —**ter′ri·fy′ing·ly,** *adv.*

ter·ri·to·ri·al (ter′i tôr′ē əl) *adj.* **1.** of, relating to, or belonging to land or territory: *territorial acquisitions, territorial laws.* **2.** relating to or restricted to a particular district or region: *a territorial government.* **3.** *also,* **Territorial.** relating to a territory of the United States. **4.** *Zoology.* exhibiting territoriality: *a territorial species.* **5.** *also,* **Territorial.** organized in regional groups for home defense: *the British Territorial Army.* —*n. also,* **Territorial.** a member of a territorial military force. —**ter′ri·to·ri·al·ly,** *adv.*

ter·ri·to·ri·al·ism (ter′i tôr′ē ə liz′əm) *n.* a social system giving predominance in a state to the landowners. —**ter′ri·to·ri·al·ist,** *n.*

ter·ri·to·ri·al·i·ty (ter′i tôr′ē al′i tē) *n.* **1.** the quality, condition, or status of being a territory. **2.** *Zoology.* a pattern of behavior that animals exhibit with regard to their territory, characterized by establishing boundaries, vocalization, and repelling intruders.

ter·ri·to·ri·al·ize (ter′i tôr′ē ə līz′) *v.t.,* -**ized,** -**iz·ing.** **1.** to reduce to the status of a territory; establish as a territory; make territorial. **2.** to enlarge by adding territory to. —**ter′ri·to′ri·al·i·za′tion,** *n.*

territorial waters, the coastal and inland waters under the jurisdiction of a state or nation, traditionally ocean waters within 3 miles (4.8 kilometers) of shore but now generally ocean waters within 12 miles (19.3 kilometers) or 200 miles (322 kilometers) of shore.

ter·ri·to·ry (ter′i tôr′ē) *n., pl.* -**ries. 1.** any large tract of land of unspecified boundaries; region; area: *unexplored territory, territory held by an enemy.* **2.** land and waters under the jurisdiction of a state, nation, or ruler: *Hudson Bay is part of the territory of Canada.* **3.a.** formerly, a part of the United States not having the status of a state and usually administered by an appointed governor, but having its own legislature. **b.** any region with a similar status, as in Canada or Australia. **4.** an assigned district or area, as of a traveling sales representative or agent. **5.** a field or sphere of action, thought, or interest: *Agriculture and horticulture cover some of the same territory.* **6.** *Zoology.* a particular area inhabited by an animal or pair or group of animals, usually used for nesting, breeding, and foraging and defended against intruders, esp. of the same species. [Latin *territōrium* domain, district, from *terra* land.]

ter·ror (ter′ər) *n.* **1.** an overpowering or intense fear. **2.** a person or thing that causes intense fear: *The cruel dictator was a terror to the oppressed citizens.* **3.** a party, group, or program employing terrorism. **4.** *Informal.* an annoying or troublesome person or thing, esp. a mischievous child. ➡ used esp. in the phrase *a holy terror.* [Latin *terror* dread, great fear, from *terrēre* to frighten.]

Synonyms **Terror** and **panic** mean extreme fear. **Terror** implies a fear growing out of imminent danger, sometimes so intense as to be paralyzing: *The villagers stared in terror at the approaching tornado.* **Panic** is a sudden fear that leads to irrational action, esp. by a group of people: *When the fire broke out, the crowd rushed toward the exits in panic.*

ter·ror·ism (ter′ə riz′əm) *n.* **1.** the act of terrorizing; use of terror, violence, or threats of violence to intimidate or frighten into submission, esp. when used for political purposes, as by a government to intimidate the population or by an insurgent group to oppose the government in power. **2.** a state of fear and subjugation produced by this.

ter·ror·ist (ter′ər ist) *n.* a person who advocates or uses terrorism. —*adj.* relating to or characteristic of terrorism or terrorists: *terrorist methods.* Also, **ter′ror·is′tic.**

ter·ror·ize (ter′ə rīz′) *v.t.,* -**ized,** -**iz·ing. 1.** to fill with extreme fear; overcome with terror; terrify. **2.** to control, dominate, or coerce through the use of terror: *to terrorize hostages into submission.* —**ter′ror·i·za′tion,** *n.*

ter·ry (ter′ē) *n., pl.* -**ries. 1.** an uncut loop forming the pile of a fabric. **2.** terry cloth. [Of uncertain origin.]

terry cloth, a fabric having uncut loops on both sides, esp. a highly absorbent cotton cloth used chiefly for towels and robes. Also, **terry.**

terse (tûrs) *adj.,* **ters·er, ters·est.** having no superfluous words; brief and to the point; concise; succinct: *a terse summary, a terse reply.* [Latin *tersus* clean, neat, past participle of *tergēre* to wipe, polish.] —**terse′ly,** *adv.* —**terse′ness,** *n.* —For Synonyms, see **concise.**

ter·tial (tûr′shəl) *adj.* relating to or designating the flight feathers on the basal part of a bird's wing. —*n.* a tertial feather. [Latin *tertius* third + -AL[1]; because these feathers form the *third* row of a bird's flight feathers.]

ter·tian (tûr′shən) *adj.* recurring every other day, or every three days when counting from each day of occurrence. A tertian fever occurs once in 48 hours. —*n.* a tertian fever or ague, esp. a tertian malaria. [Latin *tertiāna* the fever, from *tertius* third.]

ter·ti·ar·y (tûr′shē er′ē) *n., pl.* -**ar·ies. 1. Tertiary.** the earlier of the two geologic periods of the Cenozoic era, during which high mountain systems, as the Alps, Rockies, and Himalayas, were formed and modern mammals and plants appeared. **2.** a tertial feather. **3.** a member of the Third Order of a religious body. —*adj.* **1.** third in rank, order, degree, importance, or value. **2. Tertiary.** of, relating to, or characteristic of the Tertiary period. **3.** tertial. **4.** relating to the Third Order of a religious body. **5.** relating to or designating an accent that is weaker than a secondary accent. **6.** *Chemistry.* resulting from the substitution of three atoms or groups: *tertiary alcohol.* [Latin *tertiārius* containing a third part, from *tertius* third.]

ter·za ri·ma (ter′tsə rē′mə) a form of iambic verse in which each line has ten or eleven syllables. The lines are arranged in tercets and the middle line of each tercet rhymes with the first and third lines of the following tercet. The form was first used by medieval Italian poets. [Italian *terza rima,* from *terza,* feminine of *terzo* third (from Latin *tertius*) + *rima* verse, rhyme (of Germanic origin).]

tes·la (tes′lə) *n.* the International System unit of magnetic flux density, equal to 1 weber of flux per square meter. [From Nikola *Tesla,* 1856-1943, U.S. electrical engineer and inventor.]

tes·sel·late (*v.,* tes′ə lāt′; *adj.,* tes′ə lit, -lāt′) *v.t.,* -**lat·ed,** -**lat·ing.** to form or make with small squares or cubes; form or arrange in a mosaic or checkered pattern, as a floor. —*adj.* arranged in a mosaic or checkered pattern; tessellated. [Latin *tessellātus* of small square stones, checkered, going back to *tessera* square piece of stone or wood. See TESSERA.] —**tes′sel·la′tion,** *n.*

tessellate table top

tes·ser·a (tes′ər ə) *n., pl.* **tes·ser·ae** (tes′ə rē). **1.** a small, usually square piece of marble, stone, glass, or similar material, used in mosaic work. **2.** a small tablet, esp. of bone, wood, or ivory, used in ancient Rome as a token, tally, label, or ticket. [Latin *tessera* square piece of stone or wood, possibly from dialectal Greek *tessera,* neuter of *tesseres* four.]

test[1] (test) *n.* **1.** a set of questions, problems, or exercises intended to determine a person's knowledge, aptitude, skill, or intelligence: *a spelling test.* **2.** any method, process, or means of determining or examining the nature or quality of something: *a hearing test, a blood test, a swimming test.* **3.** that by which the genuineness or quality of something is determined: *Their friendship has withstood the test of time.* **4.** a particular means of evaluation or judgment; standard; criterion. **5.** *Chemistry.* a procedure for detecting the presence of an ingredient in a substance or determining the nature of a substance: *a test for carbon dioxide.* **b.** a substance employed in such a procedure: *Litmus is the test for the presence of acid.* —*v.t.* **1.** to subject to a test of any kind; administer a test to; try: *to test a class, to test a car, to test a person's loyalty.* **2.** to subject to a chemical test. —*v.i.* **1.** to undergo or give a test (usually with *for*): *to test for a job, to test for acidity.* **2.** to exhibit specified tendencies or qualities under testing (often with *out*): *That child tests out as almost a genius.* [Middle English *test* vessel used to assay metals, from Old French

test pot, from Latin *testum* pot, earthen vessel.] —**test′a·ble,** *adj.*

test² (test) *n.* a hard outer covering of certain invertebrate animals, as the shell of a clam or oyster. [Latin *testa* shell.]

Test., Testament.

tes·ta (tes′tə) *n., pl.* **-tae** (-tē). the hard outer covering of a seed. [Latin *testa* covering, shell.]

tes·ta·ceous (tes tā′shəs) *adj.* **1.** of the nature or substance of a shell or shells. **2.** having a shell, esp. a hard shell: *a testaceous animal.* **3.** having a dull reddish brown or yellowish brown color. [Latin *testāceus* covered with a shell, from *testa* shell.]

tes·ta·cy (tes′tə sē) *n.* the condition of being testate.

tes·ta·ment (tes′tə mənt) *n.* **1.** a will, esp. one disposing of personal property. ➡ now used chiefly in the phrase *last will and testament.* **2.** in the Bible, a covenant between God and human beings. **3. Testament. a.** either of the two main divisions of the Christian Bible; Old Testament or New Testament. **b.** the New Testament or a volume containing it. **4.** a statement of beliefs or principles; creed. **5.** evidence or proof of the existence, validity, or quality of something: *Your success is a testament to your hard work.* [Church Latin *testāmentum* Scripture, from Latin *testāmentum* last will, from *testārī* to be a witness, make a will.]

tes·ta·men·ta·ry (tes′tə men′tə rē, -men′trē) *adj.* **1.** relating to a will or the administration or settlement of a will. **2.** given by or contained in a will: *The estate was disposed of according to the deceased's testamentary instructions.* **3.** done in accordance with a will.

tes·tate (tes′tāt) *adj.* having made and left a legally valid will before death. [Latin *testātus,* past participle of *testārī* to make a will, be a witness.]

tes·ta·tor (tes′tā′tər, tes tā′-) *n.* a person who has died and left a legally valid will.

tes·ta·trix (tes tā′triks) *n., pl.* **tes·ta·tri·ces** (tes tā′trə sēz, tes′tə trī′-). a woman who has died and left a legally valid will.

test ban, an agreement among nations not to engage in the testing of nuclear weapons, esp. in the atmosphere.

test case 1. a legal case whose outcome is likely to be used as a precedent. **2.** a case entered into for the purpose of testing the constitutionality of a particular law.

test-drive (test′drīv′) *v.t.,* **-drove** (-drōv′), **-driv·en** (-driv′ən), **-driv·ing.** to test the performance of (a vehicle) by driving it.

test·er¹ (tes′tər) *n.* a person or thing that tests. [TEST + -ER¹.]

tes·ter² (tes′tər) *n.* a canopy, esp. one over a bed or pulpit. [Medieval Latin *testrum* canopy of a bed, going back to Latin *testa* shell, covering.]

tes·tes (tes′tēz) the plural of **testis.**

tes·ti·cle (tes′ti kəl) *n.* one of the pair of male reproductive glands in human beings and most other animals, producing sperm and male sex hormones and enclosed in a scrotum in most mammals. Also, **testis.** [Latin *testiculus,* diminutive of *testis* testicle, witness (as of virility).] —**tes·tic·u·lar** (tes tik′yə lər), *adj.*

tes·ti·fy (tes′tə fī′) *v.,* **-fied,** **-fy·ing.** —*v.i.* **1.** to give evidence under oath in a court of law: *to testify for the defense.* **2.** to serve as evidence; be proof: *Possession of the stolen goods testified to the defendant's guilt.* **3.** to bear witness, esp. for the purpose of establishing some truth or fact: *I can testify to their honesty.* **4.** to express a personal belief, esp. the belief that one has been saved through the grace of God. —*v.t.* **1.** to declare under oath in a court of law: *The witness testified that the defendant was home the night of the crime.* **2.** to affirm as fact or truth; declare solemnly. **3.** to give or be evidence of; demonstrate; show. **4.** to make known publicly; declare openly. [Latin *testificārī* to bear witness, from *testis* witness + *facere* to make.] —**tes′ti·fi′er,** *n.*

tes·ti·mo·ni·al (tes′tə mō′nē əl) *n.* **1.** an affirmation of the superior character or quality of someone or something; letter or statement of recommendation: *A satisfied customer gave a testimonial for the product.* **2.** something given or done to express respect, admiration, or appreciation: *The retiring employee was given a watch as a testimonial for many years of service.* —*adj.* relating to or constituting a testimonial: *a testimonial dinner, a testimonial gift.*

tes·ti·mo·ny (tes′tə mō′nē) *n., pl.* **-nies. 1.** a statement or declaration made under oath by a witness in a court of law, usually in response to questioning by a lawyer. **2.** proof or demonstration; evidence: *The farmer's rugged hands were testimony of years of hard work.* **3.** an open declaration or attestation, esp. of one's faith or of a religious experience. **4.** in the Christian Bible, the Ten Commandments, esp. in their original form on two stone tablets. **5. testimonies.** the precepts or laws of God, esp. the Scriptures. [Latin *testimōnium* evidence, from *testis* witness.] —For Synonyms, see **evidence.**

tes·tis (tes′tis) *n., pl.* **-tes.** testicle. [Latin *testis* testicle, witness (as of virility).]

tes·tos·ter·one (tes tos′tə rōn′) *n.* **1.** a sex hormone produced

by the testes that controls the growth of the male reproductive system and stimulates the development of male secondary sexual characteristics, such as the growth of the beard, muscular development, and deepening of the voice. **2.** this hormone obtained from bulls' testicles or produced synthetically, used in medicine to treat certain deficiencies and diseases.

test paper 1. a paper on which a person taking a test has written his or her answers. **2.** paper saturated with a reagent, esp. litmus, and used in making chemical tests.

test pattern, a fixed picture, usually a special design of lines and circles, broadcast by a television station for testing purposes or for a set time before regular programming begins.

test pilot, a pilot who tests new or experimental aircraft.

test tube, a thin, transparent glass tube closed and rounded at the bottom, used esp. in chemical and biological experiments.

test-tube baby (test′tūb′, -tūb′) a baby conceived by the union of an ovum and sperm outside the womb, as in a laboratory. The fertilized ovum is later implanted in a uterus, where it develops normally.

tes·tu·do (tes tü′dō, -tū′-) *n., pl.* **-di·nes** (-də nēz′). **1.** a portable shelter with a strong, arched roof, used by the ancient Romans to protect a force besieging a stronghold. **2.** a shelter formed by a body of troops locking their shields together above their heads. [Latin *testūdō* tortoise, tortoise shell, ancient Roman military shelter.]

tes·ty (tes′tē) *adj.,* **-ti·er, -ti·est.** showing or characterized by irritability, impatience, or crossness; peevish; touchy: *a testy answer, a testy patient.* [Anglo-Norman *testif* headstrong, from Old French *teste* head, from Late Latin *testa* skull, from Latin *testa* shell.] —**tes′ti·ly,** *adv.* —**tes′ti·ness,** *n.*

Tet (tet) *n.* a Vietnamese holiday, celebrating the lunar new year. [Vietnamese *tet;* of Chinese origin.]

te·tan·ic (te tan′ik) *adj.* **1.** relating to or characterized by tetanus. **2.** of or relating to a substance, such as a poison, that causes tetanic muscle spasms.

tet·a·nize (tet′ə nīz′) *v.t.,* **-nized, -niz·ing.** to cause (a muscle) to have tetanic spasms; produce tetanus in.

tet·a·nus (tet′ə nəs) *n.* **1.** an acute, often fatal, infectious disease caused by the toxin of a certain bacillus that usually enters the body through a wound, such as a nail puncture. Tetanus is characterized by violent spasms and stiffness of the voluntary muscles, esp. those of the neck and jaw. Also, **lockjaw. 2.** a prolonged state of muscle contraction during which a muscle does not return to its normal range or tension. [Latin *tetanus* spasm of the neck, from Greek *tetanos* convulsive spasm.]

tet·a·ny (tet′ə nē) *n.* a disorder characterized by periodic painful spasms of the muscles, usually caused by a deficiency in calcium salts. [From TETANUS.]

tetch·y (tech′ē) *also,* **techy.** *adj.,* **tetch·i·er, tetch·i·est.** tending to become irritable; peevish; touchy. [Possibly from obsolete *teche* blemish, fault (from Old French *teche;* probably of Germanic origin) + -Y¹.] —**tetch′i·ly,** *adv.* —**tetch′i·ness,** *n.*

tête-à-tête (tāt′ə tāt′, tet′ə tet′) *n.* **1.** a private or intimate conversation between two people. **2.** an S-shaped sofa or seat on which two people can sit facing each other. —*adv.* (of two people) face to face; together in private: *to dine tête-à-tête.* —*adj.* for or between two people only; private; intimate: *Their dinner was a tête-à-tête affair.* [French *tête-à-tête* private conversation between two people; literally, head to head, from *tête* head, from Old French *teste.* See TESTY.]

teth·er (teth′ər) *n.* **1.** a rope or chain used to fasten a horse, donkey, or other animal so that it is confined within certain limits. **2.** the range of one's strength, ability, or resources. —*v.t.* to fasten or confine with or as with a tether: *to tether a horse to a tree.* [Probably from Old Norse *tjothr* fetter for an animal.]
  · at the end of one's tether. at the extreme end or limit of one's resources, patience, or endurance.

teth·er·ball (teth′ər bôl′) *n.* **1.** a game played by two people with a ball hanging from a cord fastened to the top of a pole. The object of each player is to strike the ball so as to wind the cord completely around the pole. **2.** the ball used in this game.

tet·ra (tet′rə) *n., pl.* **-ras** or **-ra.** any of several small, brightly colored tropical fish of the family Characidae, often kept in aquariums.

tetra- *combining form* four: *tetrachord.* [Greek *tetra-,* combining form of *tettares* four.]

a	at	e	end	o	hot	u	up	hw	white		about
ā	ape	ē	me	ō	old	ū	use	ng	song		taken
ä	far	i	it	ô	fork	ü	rule	th	thin	ə	pencil
âr	care	ī	ice	oi	oil	u̇	pull	th	this		lemon
		îr	pierce	ou	out	ûr	turn	zh	measure		circus

tet·ra·chlo·ride (tet′rə klôr′īd) *n.* a chloride containing four atoms of chlorine in each molecule.

tet·ra·chord (tet′rə kôrd′) *n. Music.* a series of four consecutive tones of the diatonic scale, having an interval of a fourth between the first and the last. [Greek *tetrachordon* scale of four notes, from *tetra-* (see TETRA-) + *chordē* string.]

tet·ra·cy·cline (tet′rə sī′klēn, -klin) *n.* a yellow, crystalline antibiotic used in treating a wide variety of infectious diseases. Formula: $C_{22}H_{24}N_2O_8$

tet·rad (tet′rad) *n.* **1.** a group or set of four. **2.** *Biology.* a group of four haploid cells formed by division of a pair of chromosomes during meiosis. **3.** *Chemistry.* an atom, element, or radical having a valence of four. [Greek *tetrad-*, stem of *tetras* group of four.]

tet·ra·eth·yl lead (tet′rə eth′əl) *also,* **tet·ra·eth·yl·lead** (tet′-rə eth′əl led′). a heavy, colorless, poisonous, flammable liquid added to gasoline to reduce engine knock. Formula: $Pb(C_2H_5)_4$

tet·ra·gon (tet′rə gon′) *n.* a four-sided polygon, as a square or rhombus; quadrilateral. [Late Latin *tetragonum,* from Greek *tetragōnon,* from *tetra-* (see TETRA-) + *gōnia* angle.] —**te·trag·o·nal** (te trag′ə nəl) *adj.*

tet·ra·he·dral (tet′rə hē′drəl) *adj.* relating to or having the form of a tetrahedron; having plane faces. [Late Latin *tetragonum,* from Greek *tetragōnon,* from *tetra-* (see TETRA-) + *gōnia* angle.]

tet·ra·he·dron (tet′rə hē′drən) *n., pl.* **-drons** or **-dra** (-drə). a solid figure with four faces, esp. one with four plane triangular faces. [TETRA- + Greek *hedra* seat, base; on the model of Late Greek *tetraedron,* neuter of *tetraedros* having four sides.]

tet·ra·hy·dro·can·nab·i·nol (tet′rə-hī′drō kə nab′ə nôl′, -nōl′) *n.* the principal psychoactive ingredient in marijuana. Formula: $C_{21}H_{30}O_2$

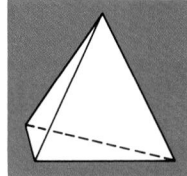

tetrahedron

te·tral·o·gy (te tral′ə jē, -trol′-) *n., pl.* **-gies.** a series of four related artistic works, as plays, operas, or novels. [Greek *tetralogiā* group of four dramas, from *tetra-* (see TETRA-) + *-logiā.* See -LOGY.]

te·tram·e·ter (te tram′i tər) *n.* **1.** a line of verse containing four metrical feet. **2.** a verse consisting of such lines. —*adj.* consisting of four metrical feet. [Latin *tetrametrus,* from Greek *tetrametros* having four measures.]

tet·ra·ploid (tet′rə ploid′) *adj.* having four complementary sets of chromosomes, four times the haploid number. —*n.* an organism or cell having four sets of chromosomes. [TETRA- + -*ploid,* on the model of DIPLOID, HAPLOID.] —**tet′ra·ploi′dy,** *n.*

tet·ra·pod (tet′rə pod′) *n.* any vertebrate animal with four legs or limbs, including amphibians, reptiles, birds, and mammals. [TETRA- + -POD.]

tet·rarch (tet′rärk′, tē′trärk′) *n.* **1.** a governor of a part, esp. a fourth part, of a province in the ancient Roman Empire. **2.** a subordinate ruler, esp. a ruler of a fourth part. [Late Latin *tetrarcha,* from Greek *tetrarchēs,* from *tetra-* (see TETRA-) + *archos* ruler.]

tet·rar·chy (tet′rär′kē, tē′trär′-) *n., pl.* **-chies.** **1.** the government, territory, or jurisdiction of a tetrarch. **2.** government by a group of four. **3.** a group of four rulers.

tet·ra·va·lent (tet′rə vā′lənt) *adj. Chemistry.* having a valence of four.

...ode (tet′rōd) *n.* an electron tube containing four electrodes.

te·trox·ide (tet rok′sīd, -sid) *n.* an oxide containing four atoms of oxygen in each molecule.

tet·ter (tet′ər) *n.* any of several skin diseases characterized by itching and eruptions, as eczema, psoriasis, and shingles. [Old English *teter.*]

Teu·ton (tü′tən, tū′-) *n.* **1.** a member of an ancient tribe, probably of Germanic stock, that inhabited parts of what is now northern Germany. **2.** a member of any of several groups of northern European peoples, including the Germans, Dutch, Scandinavians, and English. **3.** a native of Germany or person of German ancestry; German.

Teu·ton·ic (tü ton′ik, tū-) *adj.* **1.** of or relating to the ancient Teutons. **2.** of or relating to any of the Teutons, their languages, or their cultures. **3.** of, relating to, or characteristic of Germany or the Germans; German. **4.** of, relating to, or characteristic of the Germanic family of languages. —*n.* Germanic. —**Teu·ton′i·cal·ly,** *adv.*

Tex., Texas.

tex·as (tek′səs) *n.* a structure on the upper deck of a river steamboat, where the pilothouse and officers' cabins are located. [From *Texas;* because the cabins on Mississippi steamboats were named after the different states, and the officers' cabins were the largest.]

Texas fever, an infectious disease of cattle caused by a protozoan parasite in the red blood cells and transmitted by ticks.

Texas leaguer *Baseball.* a short fly ball that falls beyond the infielders and in front of the outfielders for a base hit. [From *Texas League,* a minor baseball league.]

Texas Ranger, a member of a mounted police force of the state of Texas, originally a small band of mounted riflemen organized to fight Indians and maintain order on the frontier.

Texas tower, an offshore platform supported by pilings sunk into the ocean floor, used esp. as a radar station. [From its resemblance to structures used for drilling oil off the coast of *Texas.*]

text (tekst) *n.* **1.a.** the main body of matter on a written or printed page, as distinguished from headings, illustrations, or notes. **b.** the main part of a book, exclusive of front and back matter. **2.** any of the various forms or versions in which a written work exists. **3.** the original or actual words of a writer or speaker, as opposed to a revision, condensation, or translation. **4.** a short passage or verse of Scripture, quoted in support of a doctrine or used as the subject of a sermon. **5.** any subject on which one writes or speaks; theme; topic. **6.** textbook. [Medieval Latin *textus* Gospel, passage, wording, from Latin *textus* texture, tissue, style (of an author), context, from *texere* to weave.]

text·book (tekst′bŭk′) *n.* a book used in the study of a particular subject, esp. one used as a basis of instruction in an academic course: *a history textbook, an algebra textbook.*

tex·tile (teks′tīl, -təl) *n.* **1.** a fabric made by weaving, knitting, or otherwise arranging yarn, thread, or other fibers. **2.** any material that can be made into such a fabric, as cotton, wool, or nylon. —*adj.* relating to textiles or their manufacture: *the textile industry.* [Latin *textilis* woven, from *texere* to weave.]

tex·tu·al (teks′chü əl) *adj.* relating to, based on, or contained in a text: *textual notes, textual inaccuracies.* —**tex′tu·al·ly,** *adv.*

tex·ture (teks′chər) *n.* **1.** the character of a woven fabric resulting from the arrangement, feel, quality, or size of its threads: *Silk has a smooth texture.* **2.** the characteristic arrangement of the parts or particles of any body or material; composition; structure: *the rough texture of sandpaper.* **3.** the essential or distinctive nature or quality of anything: *the texture of modern life, a long novel of uneven texture.* **4.** the character of the surface of a painting or other work of art, or the surface structure of an object or part in such a work. **5.** anything produced by weaving; woven fabric. —*v.t.,* **-tured, -tur·ing.** to cause to have a particular texture. [Latin *textūra* web, fabric, structure, from *texere* to weave.] —**tex′tur·al,** *adj.* —**tex′tur·al·ly,** *adv.*

Th, the symbol for thorium.

-th *suffix* used to form ordinal numbers: *fifth, seventeenth, hundredth.* [Old English -(*o*)*tha,* -(*o*)*the.*]

Th. 1. Thursday. **2.** theology.

Thai (tī) *adj.* of, relating to, or characteristic of Thailand or its people, language, or culture. —*n.* **1.** a native or citizen of Thailand. **2.** a person of Thai ancestry. **3.** the official language of Thailand. **4.** a group of languages spoken in parts of southeastern Asia, a branch of the Sino-Tibetan language family. Also, **Siamese.**

thal·a·mus (thal′ə məs) *n., pl.* **-mi** (-mī′). **1.** a large, oblong mass in the diencephalon of the forebrain, composed largely of gray matter, from which nerve fibers extend to the cerebellum, spinal cord, cranial nerves, and cerebral cortex. The major function of the thalamus is to relay sensory information between the cerebral cortex and other parts of the brain, head, trunk, and limbs. For illustration, see **brain. 2.** *Botany.* the receptacle of a flower; torus. [Latin *thalamus* inner chamber, from Greek *thalamos.*] —**tha·lam·ic** (thə lam′ik), *adj.*

tha·las·sic (thə las′ik) *adj.* **1.** of or relating to the ocean or the sea. **2.** of, relating to, or located next to a small arm of the sea or an inland sea. [French *thalassique,* from Greek *thalassa* sea + French *-ique* -ic.]

tha·ler (tä′lər) *n., pl.* **-ler.** taler.

Tha·li·a (thə lī′ə, thal′yə) *n. Greek Mythology.* **1.** the Muse of comedy and pastoral poetry. **2.** one of the three Graces.

tha·lid·o·mide (thə lid′ə mīd′) *n.* a drug formerly prescribed as a sedative and hypnotic. Its use during pregnancy causes abnormalities in the fetus, esp. malformed limbs. Formula: $C_{13}H_{10}N_2O_4$

thal·li·um (thal′ē əm) *n.* a soft, bluish gray, poisonous metallic element that looks like lead, used in alloys, in ant and rat poisons, and in the manufacture of optical glass and infrared equipment. Symbol: **Tl** For tables, see **element.** [Modern Latin *thallium* from Greek *thallos* green shoot; because there is a green line in its spectrum.]

thal·lo·phyte (thal′ə fīt′) *n.* any of a large group of plantlike organisms, formerly considered a division of the plant kingdom,

lacking roots, stems, or leaves, including algae, fungi, slime molds, and bacteria. [Modern Latin *Thallophyta,* from Greek *thallos* green shoot + -PHYTE.] —**thal·lo·phyt·ic** (thal′ə fit′ik), *adj.*

thal·lus (thal′əs) *n., pl.* **thal·li** (thal′ī) or **thal·lus·es.** the undifferentiated, vegetative body of a thallophyte. [Modern Latin *thallus,* from Greek *thallos* green shoot.]

than (than; *unstressed* thən) *conj.* **1.** used after an adjective or adverb to introduce the second part of a comparison: *A cow is bigger than a rabbit. I would rather listen to music than study.* **2.** used after an adjective or adverb such as *other* or *else* to express exception or difference: *to respect no opinion other than one's own.* —*prep.* used in such phrases as *than whom* and *than which* to express comparison: *a city than which there is none more beautiful.* [Old English *thanne, thonne.*]

> **Usage** Than can be used as a preposition, as in *More than fifty people came to the party,* or as a conjunction when it introduces the second part of a comparison. When **than** is used as a conjunction, the pronoun that follows it may take the nominative or objective case depending on the verb that is understood: *He is taller than she (is). The movie amused me more than (it amused) her.* Although it is incorrect, in informal speech, the objective form of the pronoun is sometimes used regardless of the implied verb. *She is older than him (he is). He spent more money than me (I did).*

thane (thān) *also,* **thegn.** *n.* **1.** in English history, a man who held lands from the king in return for military service, esp. a member of a class ranking above ordinary freemen but below the nobility. **2.** in Scottish history, a lord or baron, esp. the chief of a clan. [Old English *theg(e)n* man who held lands from the king in return for military service.]

thank (thangk) *v.t.* **1.** to express gratitude or appreciation to, as for something given or done; give thanks to: *to thank a person for a gift.* ➡ often used in the conventional polite phrase *thank you,* with the subject *I* understood: *Thank you for the flowers.* **2.** to consider or hold responsible; credit or blame: *You have only yourself to thank for failing the test.* [Old English *thancian* to give thanks.]

thank·ful (thangk′fəl) *adj.* feeling or expressing thanks; grateful. —**thank′ful·ly,** *adv.* —**thank′ful·ness,** *n.* —For Synonyms, see **grateful.**

thank·less (thangk′lis) *adj.* **1.** not likely to be rewarded or appreciated: *a thankless task.* **2.** not feeling or showing gratitude; ungrateful: *a spoiled, thankless child.* —**thank′less·ly,** *adv.* —**thank′less·ness,** *n.*

thanks (thangks) *interj.* I thank you: *Thanks very much for the ride.* —*pl. n.* **1.** an expression of gratitude: *to give thanks.* **2.** a feeling of gratitude: *to show one's thanks.*

• **thanks to. a.** as a result or consequence of; owing to; because of: *Thanks to your efforts, the project will be a success.* **b.** thanks be given to.

thanks·giv·ing (thangks′giv′ing) *n.* **1.** the act of giving thanks. **2.** an expression of thanks, esp. a prayer of thanks to God. **3.** a day set apart to give thanks for God's favor, esp. in a public celebration. **4. Thanksgiving. a.** a legal holiday in the United States, observed on the fourth Thursday in November as a day of thanksgiving and feasting. It commemorates the harvest feast celebrated by the Pilgrims in 1621. **b.** a similar holiday celebrated in Canada on the second Monday of October. Also *(defs. 4a, 4b),* **Thanksgiving Day.**

thank-you (thangk′ū′) *n.* an expression of gratitude: *We sent our thank-yous for the presents.*

that (that) *adj., pl.* **those. 1.** used to indicate a person or thing previously mentioned, pointed out, or understood: *Who wrote that book? Who sent those flowers?* **2.** used to indicate something more distant than or contrasted with another thing: *I prefer that coat to this one. This problem is more difficult than that one.* —*pron., pl.* **those. 1.** used to indicate a person or thing previously mentioned, pointed out, or understood: *That is the person who did it. That was the best movie I've seen this year.* **2.** used to indicate something more distant than or contrasted with another thing: *I prefer this dress to that.* **3.** used in restrictive clauses in place of *who, whom,* or *which: the family that lives next door, the animals that are native to Africa.* **4.** used to designate a point in time: *the year that they were married.* —*conj.* **1.** used to introduce a subordinate clause, esp. one serving as the subject or object of the main verb: *I think that my friend will accept the job.* **2.** used to show reason or cause: *I'm sorry that you can't come to the party.* **3.** used to show result: *to eat so much that one becomes ill.* **4.** used to show purpose: *Our soldiers went to war that we might remain free.* ➡ often used with *so: Open the door so that the dog can come in.* **5.** used to introduce an expression of desire: *Oh, that she were with us today!* **6.** used to introduce an expression of surprise or indignation: *That he should act so rudely toward you!* —*adv.* to

such an extent or degree; to that extent; so: *How could you sing that well after only one lesson?* [Old English *thæt.*]

• **that's that.** that is settled or resolved.

> **Usage** Traditionally, **who** and **whom** were used to refer to people and **that** to things. However, **that** is commonly used for people as well as things, as in *the trip that I took* or *the friend that I spoke about.* Often the pronouns "that," "who," or "whom" are omitted completely: *the trip I took* or *the friend I spoke about.* For another Usage Note, see **which.**

thatch (thach) *n.* **1.** straw, reeds, rushes, or similar material used to cover a roof. **2.** a roof or roofing of such material. **3.** anything resembling such a covering: *a thick thatch of hair.* —*v.t.* to cover with or as with thatch. [Old English *theccan* to cover.]

thatch
thatching a roof in India

that'll (that′əl) *contr.* **1.** that will. **2.** that shall.

that's (thats) *contr.* that is.

thau·ma·tur·gy (thô′mə tûr′jē) *n.* the working of miracles or wonders; magic. [Greek *thaumatourgiā* literally, wonder working, going back to *thauma* wonder + *ergon* work.] —**thau′ma·tur′-gic;** *also,* **thau′ma·tur′gi·cal,** *adj.*

thaw (thô) *v.i.* **1.** to pass from a frozen state to a liquid or unfrozen state; become free of frost or ice; melt: *The ice on the road thawed from the heat of the sun.* **2.** to become free of the physical effects of cold (often with *out*): *The ice skaters thawed out before a large fire.* **3.** (of the weather or temperature) to become warm enough to melt ice or snow; rise above the freezing point. **4.** to grow less stiff and reserved in manner; become friendlier: *The new student's chilly manner thawed after we became friends.* —*v.t.* to cause to thaw: *The sun thawed the snow on the roof.* —*n.* **1.** the act of thawing. **2.** a period of weather warm enough to melt ice and snow: *a spring thaw.* **3.** a becoming less cold, formal, or reserved; lessening of tension or hostility: *The meeting of the heads of state marked a thaw in relations between the two countries.* [Old English *thāwian* to cause to melt.]

THC, tetrahydrocannabinol.

the[1] (*before a consonant,* thə; *before a vowel,* thē) *definite article. The* refers to a particular person, thing, or group. Some specific uses of *the* are: **1.** to indicate a particular one or ones previously mentioned, pointed out, or understood: *Close the door. Give me the book.* **2.** to show that a noun designates something unique: *the sun, the wind, the past, the Amazon.* **3.** to indicate a particular one regarded as best known, most important, or greatest: *the place to go for a winter vacation.* ➡ usually emphasized by italics in writing or by stress in speech. **4.** to make a singular noun general: *The lion is found in Africa.* **5.** in place of a possessive pronoun: *A stone hit me on the arm.* **6.** before an adjective to make it function as a noun: *a home for the aged.* **7.** as part of a title: *the Duke of Edinburgh, the Queen of Sweden.* **8.** to refer to each individual of a group separately, equivalent in meaning to *per, each,* or *every: 50 cents the dozen.* [Old English *thē, the.*]

the[2] (*before a consonant,* thə; *before a vowel,* thē) *adv.* to that degree; by that much: *The sooner you finish it the better.* [Old English *thē, thȳ, thon.*]

the·a·ter (thē′ə tər) *also,* **theatre.** *n.* **1.** a building, part of a building, or outdoor structure for the presentation of plays, op-

a	at	e	end	o	hot	u	up	hw	white		about
ā	ape	ē	me	ō	old	ū	use	ng	song		taken
ä	far	i	it	ô	fork	u̇	rule	th	thin	ə	pencil
âr	care	ī	ice	oi	oil	u̇	pull	<u>th</u>	this		lemon
			ir	pierce	ou	out	ûr	turn	zh	measure		circus

eras, motion pictures, ballets, or other similar performances. **2.** a place resembling a theater, esp. a room or hall having tiers of seats rising like steps, used esp. for lectures and surgical demonstrations. **3.** the writing and performing of plays; dramatic art or literature; the drama: *French theater, modern theater.* **4.** the world of the theater and those involved in theatrical productions: *to write about the theater.* **5.** the quality or effectiveness of a dramatic presentation: *That new play is excellent theater.* **6.** a place where some action takes place; field of operations: *a theater of war.* [Latin *theātrum* playhouse, stage, from Greek *theātron* place for seeing (esp. plays).]

the·a·ter·go·er (thē′ə tər gō′ər) *also*, **theatregoer.** *n.* a person who attends the theater, esp. a person who goes frequently or regularly.

the·a·ter-in-the-round (thē′ə tər in thə round′) *n.* a theater in which the stage is at the center of the auditorium, surrounded by seats on all sides. Also, **arena theater.**

theater of the absurd, a twentieth-century dramatic movement based on a belief in the irrationality of human beings and the absurdity of life. Theater of the absurd uses incongruous or meaningless dialogue and unconventional plot structure and characterization to express a feeling of alienation and futility.

the·a·tre (thē′ə tər) theater.

the·a·tre·go·er (thē′ə tər gō′ər) theatergoer.

the·at·ri·cal (thē at′ri kəl) *adj.* **1.** relating to or characteristic of the theater, actors, or dramatic presentations: *a theatrical performance.* **2.** suggestive of a dramatic performance; artificial or affected; showy; overdone: *a theatrical display of grief.* —*n.* **theatricals.** theatrical performances, esp. by amateurs. —**the·at·ri·cal·i·ty** (thē at′ri kal′i tē), *n.* —**the·at′ri·cal·ly,** *adv.*

the·at·rics (thē at′riks) *n.* **1.** the art of staging plays. **2.** dramatic or artificial effects or behavior; histrionics. ➡ used as singular in def. 1, as plural in def. 2.

the·ca (thē′kə) *n., pl.* **-cae** (-sē). a case, sac, sheath, or capsule covering an organism or one of its parts. [Latin *thēca* case², cover, from Greek *thēkē.*] —**the′cal,** *adj.*

the·co·dont (thē′kə dont) *n.* any of an order, Thecodontia, of extinct reptiles of Triassic geologic time, consisting of medium to large, four-legged and two-legged creatures having teeth rooted in sockets. They are believed to be the ancestors of dinosaurs, crocodiles, pterosaurs, and birds. [Modern Latin *Thecodontia,* taxonomic name of the order, from Greek *thēkē* case + *odont-,* stem of *odōn* tooth.]

thé dan·sant (tā′ däɴ säɴ′) *pl.* **thés dan·sants** (tā′ däɴ säɴ′). *French.* tea dance.

thee (thē) *pron. Archaic.* the objective case of **thou.** ➡ used in place of *thou* by members of the Society of Friends: *Thee speaks the truth.* [Old English *thē.*]

theft (theft) *n.* an act or instance of stealing; larceny. [Old English *thēofth.*]

| **Synonyms** | **Theft, larceny, robbery,** and **burglary** mean |

the act of taking what rightfully belongs to someone else. **Theft,** the most general of these words, can be applied to any type of stealing: *The police department's annual report showed an increase in the number of thefts.* **Larceny** is the broad legal term for the act of taking someone's property with the intention of keeping it: *The shoplifter was charged with petty larceny.* **Robbery,** although sometimes used generally, more specifically refers to the taking of a person's property in the victim's presence by the use of threats or violence: *The bank robbery was committed by three masked people armed with pistols.* **Burglary** denotes theft that involves breaking into a building: *The burglary took place when the family had left the house empty for the weekend.*

thegn (thān) thane.

the·ine (thē′ēn, -in) *n.* caffeine, esp. as found in tea. [Modern Latin *thea* tea (from dialectal Chinese *t'e*) + -INE².]

their (thâr) *adj.* **1.** (the possessive form of **they**) of, relating to, or belonging to them: *their house, their class, their efforts.* **2.** *Informal.* his or her: *Somebody left their umbrella on the bus.* [Old Norse *their(r)a.*] —For Usage Note, see **they.**

theirs (thârz) *pron.* **1.** of, relating to, or belonging to them: *The money is theirs.* ➡ used with *of* after a noun or pronoun: *We are friends of theirs.* **2.** the one or ones that relate or belong to them: *Our car is new; theirs is old.* ➡ *Theirs* is the absolute form of the possessive adjective **their,** used when no noun follows. It is used as singular or plural depending on the noun to which it refers. **3.** *Informal.* his or hers: *I'll bring my bathing suit if everyone else brings theirs.* —For Usage Note, see **they.**

the·ism (thē′iz əm) *n.* **1.** a belief in one personal God as creator and ruler of the universe. **2.** a belief in the existence of a god or gods. [Greek *theos* god + ISM.]

the·ist (thē′ist) *n.* a person who adheres to theism. —**the·is′-tic,** *adj.*

them (them; *unstressed* thəm) *pl. pron.* **1.** the objective case of **they:** *We met them at the station.* **2.** *Informal.* him or her: *Nobody followed the advice I had given them.* [Old Norse *theim.*] —For Usage Notes, see **me, they.**

the·mat·ic (thē mat′ik) *adj.* of or relating to a theme or themes.

theme (thēm) *n.* **1.** a main subject or train of thought, as in a speech, conversation, or written composition; topic: *The theme of the book was courage.* **2.** a brief essay or written composition: *We were assigned five themes in our English literature course.* **3.** *Music.* **a.** the principal melody in a composition, movement, or passage; subject. **b.** a melody on which variations are constructed. **4.** theme song *(def. 2).* [Latin *thema* subject, topic, from Greek *thema* proposition, subject; literally, something laid down.]

theme park, an amusement park with attractions, designs, marketing, and the like based on a central theme.

theme song 1. a melody recurring throughout a film, musical, or dramatic presentation, often intended to convey a mood, that becomes identified with the production. **2.** a melody that is used to identify or is identified with a particular performer, group, or radio or television program.

them·selves (them selvz′, thəm-) *pl. pron.* **1.** the emphatic form of **they** or **them:** *They had to do the job themselves.* **2.** the reflexive form of **them:** *They blamed themselves for the tragedy.* **3.** their normal or average selves: *The players on the losing team were certainly not themselves today.* **4.** *Informal.* himself or herself: *Anybody could support themselves on that income.* —For Usage Note, see **they.**

then (then) *adv.* **1.** at that time: *I was much thinner then.* **2.** immediately or soon afterward; next in time, order, or space: *The overture ended and then the curtain went up.* **3.** at another time: *Sometimes the car will run smoothly; then it will stall at every corner.* **4.** in that case; if that is so; consequently; therefore: *If you don't want that book, then give it to me.* **5.** in addition; besides: *The price is right, and then I really need a new coat.* —*adj.* being or acting as such at that time; of that time: *The then ambassador was present at the conference.* —*n.* that time: *I hope to have it finished before then.* [Old English *thaenne* at that time, in that case.]

• **now and then.** once in a while; occasionally: *Now and then we spend an evening together.*

• **then and there.** at that very time; immediately: *Our friends decided to stop smoking then and there.*

thence (thens) *adv.* **1.** from that place; from there: *The bank is two blocks thence.* **2.** from that time; after that: *We saw them again a few weeks thence.* **3.** from that fact, circumstance, or reason; consequently; therefore: *They stole the money; thence they should be punished.* [Middle English *thannes* from that place, going back to Old English *thanon.*]

thence·forth (thens′fôrth′) *adv.* from that time on; after that; thereafter. Also, **thence·for·ward** (thens′fôr′wərd).

the·oc·ra·cy (thē ok′rə sē) *n., pl.* **-cies. 1.** a government in which God or a god is considered the supreme ruling power. **2.** government by a priesthood or other religious authority claiming to rule by divine sanction. **3.** a country or group ruled in such a way. [Greek *theokratiā* rule of God, from *theos* a god + *-kratiā* rule.]

the·o·crat (thē′ə krat′) *n.* **1.** a person who rules or is a member of the ruling group in a theocracy. **2.** a person who advocates or supports theocracy.

the·o·crat·ic (thē′ə krat′ik) *adj.* of or relating to a theocracy. Also, **the′o·crat′i·cal.** —**the′o·crat′i·cal·ly,** *adv.*

the·od·o·lite (thē od′ə līt′) *n.* an instrument used in surveying for measuring horizontal and vertical angles. [Of uncertain origin.] —**the·od·o·lit·ic** (thē od′ə lit′ik), *adj.*

the·o·lo·gian (thē′ə lō′jən, -jē ən) *n.* an expert in theology.

the·o·log·i·cal (thē′ə loj′i kəl) *adj.* of, relating to, or concerned with theology: *a theological seminary.* Also, **the′o·log′ic.** —**the′o·log′i·cal·ly,** *adv.*

theological virtues, faith, hope, and charity, considered by Saint Paul and other early Christian moralists to be necessary for a good Christian life. ➡ often distinguished from **cardinal virtues.**

the·ol·o·gize (thē ol′ə jīz′) *v.,* **-gized, -giz·ing.** —*v.i.* to theorize or speculate on theological subjects; reason theologically. —*v.t.* to make theological; treat theologically. —**the·ol′o·giz′-er,** *n.*

the·ol·o·gy (thē ol′ə jē) *n., pl.* **-gies. 1.** the study of the nature and being of God and God's relations to humanity and the universe, esp. in connection with an organized system of religion. **2.** a particular system of religion or religious beliefs, esp. of a Christian church. [Latin *theologia* science of divine things, from Greek *theologiā,* going back to *theos* a god + *-logiā.* See -LOGY.]

the·o·rem (thē′ər əm) *n.* **1.** any statement or proposition that is not self-evident but can be proved to be true or is accepted as such.

2. a statement in mathematics that has been proved or can be proved from certain assumptions and definitions. **3.** a rule or statement of relations expressed in an equation or formula. [Late Latin *theōrēma* proposition to be proved, from Greek *theōrēma* spectacle, principle, speculation, from *theōrein* to look at.]

the·o·ret·i·cal (thē′ə ret′i kəl) *adj.* **1.** of, relating to, or consisting of theory, rather than that which is practical or applied: *theoretical physics.* **2.** limited to or derived from theory; hypothetical: *a novel based on the theoretical triumph of the South in the American Civil War.* **3.** given to theorizing; speculative: *a theoretical mind.* Also, **the′o·ret′ic.**

the·o·ret·i·cal·ly (thē′ə ret′i kə lē, -i klē) *adv.* **1.** in a theoretical way: *Human beings are theoretically incapable of flight.* **2.** in accordance with an anticipated or ideal outcome: *I've just had my car repaired, so theoretically it should run well.*

the·o·re·ti·cian (thē′ər i tish′ən) *n.* a person who theorizes, esp. someone who specializes in the theory of a particular subject rather than in its practical application.

the·o·rist (thē′ər ist) *n.* a person who theorizes.

the·o·rize (thē′ə rīz′) *v.i.,* **-rized, -riz·ing.** to form a theory or theories; speculate: *to theorize about life on other planets.* **—the′o·ri·za′tion,** *n.* **—the′o·riz′er,** *n.*

the·o·ry (thē′ə rē) *n., pl.* **-ries. 1.** an idea or ideas that explain a group of facts or phenomena; hypothesis that has been confirmed or proved by observation, experiment, or reasoning: *the theory of relativity.* **2.** a formulation assumed to be true but based on certain principles not completely verified. **3.** the branch of a science or art that deals with its principles, methods, or abstract applications rather than its practice: *Not all politicians have a good understanding of political theory.* **4.** abstract reasoning; speculation. **5.** an assumption or guess based on some evidence but not proved: *Have you any theories as to what caused the sudden rise in prices?* [Late Latin *theōria* philosophical speculation, from Greek *theōriā* a beholding, consideration, speculation.]

the·os·o·phy (thē os′ə fē) *n.* **1.** any of several philosophical or religious systems that claim to have a special knowledge of the nature of God and the world through mystical insight. **2.** *often,* **Theosophy.** the doctrines and beliefs of the Theosophical Society, a modern sect founded in the United States in 1875, incorporating aspects of Buddhism and Brahmanism, esp. a belief in reincarnation. [Medieval Latin *theosophia* knowledge of divine things, from Late Greek *theosophiā*, going back to Greek *theos* a god + *sophiā* wisdom.] **—the·o·soph·ic** (thē′ə sof′ik), **the′o·soph′i·cal,** *adj.* **—the′o·soph′i·cal·ly,** *adv.* **—the·os′o·phist,** *n.*

ther·a·peu·tic (ther′ə pū′tik) *adj.* of or relating to the treatment or curing of diseases or disorders; curative: *therapeutic medicine, the therapeutic effects of a warm, dry climate.* Also, **ther′a·peu′ti·cal.** [Greek *therapeutikos* inclined to serve, inclined to take care of (medically), from *therapeuein* to serve, treat medically.] **—ther′a·peu′ti·cal·ly,** *adv.*

ther·a·peu·tics (ther′ə pū′tiks) *n.* the branch of medical science dealing with the treatment of disease. ➡ used as singular.

ther·a·peu·tist (ther′ə pū′tist) *n.* therapist.

ther·a·pist (ther′ə pist) *n.* a person who gives therapy, esp. a doctor or other person who specializes in a particular kind of therapy.

the·rap·sid (thə rap′sid) *n.* any of an order, Therapsida, of extinct, mammallike reptiles of Permian and Triassic geologic time, including a variety of plant-eating and flesh-eating creatures with characteristics intermediate between those of reptiles and mammals. [Modern Latin *Therapsida,* taxonomic name of the order, from Greek *thēr* beast + *apsidis,* genitive of *apsis* arch.]

ther·a·py (ther′ə pē) *n., pl.* **-pies. 1.** the treatment of a disease or physical or mental disorder by any of various methods: *speech therapy.* ➡ often used in combination: *hydrotherapy.* **2.** psychotherapy. [Modern Latin *therapia,* from Greek *therapeiā* service, medical treatment.]

there (thâr) *adv.* **1.** at or in that place: *Stay there. Put the box down there.* ➡ also used to indicate or emphasize a specific person or thing being referred to: *My friend's house there is the most beautiful in our neighborhood.* **2.** to, toward, or into that place: *We walked there after lunch.* **3.** at that point, as in time, action, or thought: *There the speaker paused.* **4.** on or concerning that matter or issue: *I agree with you there.* **—pron.** used as a function word: **1.** used to introduce a sentence or clause in which the verb precedes the subject: *There is no more milk.* **2.** used as the equivalent of a pronoun in expressions of encouragement or approval: *There's a good dog.* **3.** used as a vague substitute for a name in addressing a person: *Hey, there! Well, hello there.* **4.** used to call attention to someone or something: *There is the noon whistle.* **—n.** that place: *Do you know the way home from there?* **—interj.** used to express various emotions, as triumph,

satisfaction, encouragement, or sympathy: *There, there! Don't worry.* [Old English *thær.*]

> **Usage** When **there** is used to introduce a sentence or clause in which the verb precedes the subject, or to call attention to someone or something, the verb that follows **there** may be either singular or plural depending on the subject: *There is one cracker left in the box. There are the shoes I want to buy.*

there·a·bouts (thâr′ə bouts′) *also,* **there·a·bout.** *adv.* near that place, time, number, amount, or degree: *They live in Chicago or thereabouts.*

there·af·ter (thâr af′tər) *adv.* **1.** from then on; after that; afterward: *The sun shone the first day of their vacation, but it rained every day thereafter.* **2.** *Archaic.* according to that; accordingly.

there·at (thâr at′) *adv.* **1.** at that place or time; there. **2.** because of that; on that account.

there·by (thâr bī′, thâr′bī′) *adv.* **1.** by that means: *That driver finished first in the race, thereby winning the championship.* **2.** in that connection: *The shipwrecked crew barely made it to shore, and thereby hangs a tale.*

there·for (thâr fôr′) *adv.* for or in return for this, that, or it: *The bank agreed to lend me the money and issued a check therefor.*

there·fore (thâr′fôr′) *adv.* for this or that reason; as a result; consequently: *The runner sprained an ankle and therefore could not run the race.*

there·from (thâr from′, -frum′) *adv.* from this, that, or it.

there·in (thâr in′) *adv.* **1.** in or into that place, time, or thing: *The fire destroyed the warehouse and all the property therein.* **2.** in that particular point or respect; in that matter: *There are no maps of that region; therein lies the danger of the expedition.*

there·in·af·ter (thâr′in af′tər) *adv.* in a later or subsequent part, as of a legal document, speech, or book.

there·in·to (thâr in′tü) *adv. Archaic.* into that place or thing.

there·of (thâr uv′, -ov′) *adv.* **1.** of that or it: *The new law applies to the town and the residents thereof.* **2.** from that or it; therefrom.

there·on (thâr ôn′, -on′) *adv.* **1.** on or upon that or it. **2.** immediately after that; thereupon.

there's (thârz) *contr.* **1.** there is. **2.** there has.

there·to (thâr tü′) *adv.* **1.** to that place or thing. **2.** *Archaic.* in addition to that; besides; also.

there·to·fore (thâr′tə fôr′) *adv.* before or until that time; up to then.

there·un·der (thâr un′dər) *adv.* under or beneath this, that, or it.

there·un·to (thâr un′tü, thâr′un tü′) *adv.* thereto.

there·up·on (thâr′ə pôn′, -pon′) *adv.* **1.** immediately after that; at once. **2.** as a consequence of that; therefore. **3.** with reference to that; upon that.

there·with (thâr with′, -with′) *adv.* **1.** with this, that, or it. **2.** immediately after that; thereupon.

there·with·al (thâr′with ôl′) *adv.* **1.** in addition to that; besides. **2.** *Archaic.* with that; therewith.

therm-, form of **thermo-** before vowels, as in *thermion.*

ther·mal (thûr′məl) *adj.* of, relating to, or causing heat or warmth: *a thermal unit, thermal baths.* Also, **thermic.** **—n.** a rising current of warm air: *The glider pilot used a thermal to gain altitude.* [Greek *thermē* heat + -AL¹.] **—ther′mal·ly,** *adv.*

thermal barrier, a limit to the speed of a rocket, spacecraft, or other vehicle in the atmosphere that is imposed by the effect of aerodynamic heat. Also, **heat barrier.**

thermal spring, a spring having a higher temperature than local ground water.

ther·mic (thûr′mik) *adj.* thermal.

therm·i·on (thûrm′ī′ən, thûrm′ē-) *n.* an electrically charged particle emitted by a body that is heated to incandescence. [THERM(O)- + ION.]

therm·i·on·ic (thûrm′ī on′ik, thûrm′ē-) *adj.* relating to thermions: *thermionic current, a thermionic tube.*

ther·mis·tor (thər mis′tər) *n.* a component of an electric circuit whose resistance decreases as its temperature increases, usually made of a semiconductor and used to regulate temperature and voltage. [THERM(AL) + (RES)ISTOR.]

Ther·mit (thûr′mit) *n. Trademark.* thermite.

ther·mite (thûr′mīt) *n.* a mixture of powdered oxide of iron or another metal and powdered aluminum that yields an intense heat when ignited, used in incendiary bombs and welding.

a	at	e	end	o	hot	u	up	hw	white		about
ā	ape	ē	me	ō	old	ū	use	ng	song	ə	taken
ä	far	i	it	ô	fork	ü	rule	th	thin		pencil
âr	care	ī	ice	oi	oil	ù	pull	<u>th</u>	this		lemon
				ou	out	ûr	turn	zh	measure		circus
		îr	pierce								

thermo- *combining form* heat: *thermoelectricity.* [Greek *thermē* heat.]

ther·mo·chem·is·try (thûr′mō kem′ə strē) *n.* the branch of chemistry dealing with the relationship between chemical action and heat.

ther·mo·cline (thûr′mə klīn′) *n.* in a lake or the sea, a layer of water in which temperature decreases relatively rapidly as depth increases, separating warmer water near the surface from colder water of the depths. [THERMO- + *-cline,* as in ANTICLINE.]

ther·mo·cou·ple (thûr′mə kup′əl) *n.* a device used for measuring temperature, consisting of two dissimilar metallic conductors joined together at their ends. When one of these junctions is heated to a higher temperature than the other, an electric current flows around the circuit. The difference in temperature of the two junctions can be determined by measuring the voltage of the current. Also, **thermoelectric couple.**

ther·mo·dy·nam·ic (thûr′mō dī nam′ik) *adj.* of or relating to thermodynamics.

ther·mo·dy·nam·ics (thûr′mō dī nam′iks) *n.* the branch of physics that deals with the relationship between heat and other forms of energy, esp. mechanical energy, and the conversion of one of these forms into another. ➧ used as singular.

ther·mo·e·lec·tric (thûr′mō i lek′trik) *adj.* of or relating to thermoelectricity. Also, **ther′mo·e·lec′tri·cal.**

thermoelectric couple, thermocouple.

ther·mo·e·lec·tric·i·ty (thûr′mō i lek tris′i tē, -ē′lek-) *n.* electricity produced by the direct action of heat, esp. that produced in a circuit composed of two wires of dissimilar metal when one junction of the wires is at a higher temperature than the other.

thermogram of a house showing areas of greatest heat loss (white and orange) and least heat loss (green)

ther·mo·gram (thûr′mə gram′) *n.* a visual image produced by thermography, showing variations in temperature surrounding a body or object.

ther·mog·ra·phy (thər mog′rə fē) *n.* **1.** a process through which variations in temperature surrounding a body or object are measured and represented visually, as on a computer screen or in a photograph. **2.** a medical test that uses this method to detect variations in surface temperature between normal and abnormal tissue. —**ther·mo·graph·ic** (thûr′mə graf′ik) *adj.*

ther·mom·e·ter (thər mom′i tər) *n.* a device for measuring temperature, usually by the expansion or contraction of a fluid substance according to changes in temperature. The most common type is a thin glass tube containing mercury or colored alcohol and marked with a numbered scale, in which the height of the liquid in the tube indicates the temperature. [French *thermomètre,* from Greek *thermē* heat + *metron* measure.] —**ther·mo·met·ric** (thûr′mō met′rik) *adj.*

ther·mo·nu·cle·ar (thûr′mō nü′klē ər, -nū′-) *adj.* **1.** of or relating to the fusion of atomic nuclei at temperatures of millions of degrees, as in the sun or a hydrogen bomb. **2.** of or relating to thermonuclear weapons: *thermonuclear warfare.*

ther·mo·pile (thûr′mə pīl′) *n.* a device that detects and measures radiant energy or that generates thermoelectricity, consisting of a number of interconnected thermocouples, used in a variety of applications in industry and science. [THERMO- + PILE[1].]

ther·mo·plas·tic (thûr′mə plas′tik) *adj.* becoming soft and pliable when subjected to heat, without any change in its original properties, as certain plastics or resins. —*n.* a thermoplastic substance.

ther·mos (thûr′məs) *n.* a container in which liquids can be kept hot or cold for many hours, usually consisting of an outer container of metal enclosing a bottle that has another bottle within it, with a vacuum between the two bottles to inhibit the passage of heat. Also, **thermos bottle, vacuum bottle.** [Greek *thermos* hot + BOTTLE.]

ther·mo·set·ting (thûr′mō set′ing) *adj.* hardening into a permanent shape when subjected to heat, as certain plastics or resins.

ther·mo·sphere (thûr′mə sf îr′) *n.* the region of the atmosphere where air temperature increases with altitude, extending upward from the mesopause to outer space. For illustration, see **atmosphere.** [THERMO- + *-sphere,* as in ATMOSPHERE.]

ther·mo·stat (thûr′mə stat′) *n.* an instrument that automatically regulates temperature, as in a furnace, oven, refrigerator, or room. [THERMO- + Greek *statos* standing.] —**ther′mo·stat′ic,** *adj.* —**ther′mo·stat′i·cal·ly,** *adv.*

ther·mot·ro·pism (thər mot′rə piz′əm) *n.* the tendency of a plant or other organism to turn toward or away from a source of heat, esp. the sun. [THERMO- + TROPISM.] —**ther·mo·trop·ic** (thûr′mə trop′ik, -trō′pik) *adj.*

the·sau·rus (thə sôr′əs) *n., pl.* **-sau·ri** (-sôr′ī) or **-sau·rus·es.** **1.** a book containing a store of words or information, esp. a book of synonyms and antonyms arranged in categories. **2.** a treasury or storehouse. [Latin *thēsaurus* treasure, storehouse, from Greek *thēsauros.* Doublet of TREASURE.]

these (thēz) the plural of **this.**

The·se·us (thē′sē əs, -süs) *n.* in Greek legend, a hero and king of Athens, who killed the Minotaur and escaped from the Labyrinth with the help of Ariadne.

the·sis (thē′sis) *n., pl.* **-ses** (-sēz). **1.** a statement or proposition that is presented and then defended or maintained, esp. in argument or debate. **2.** an extended formal treatise or discourse based on original research and relating to a specific topic or theme, esp. one presented by a candidate for an academic degree. [Latin *thesis* proposition, from Greek *thesis* a placing, position, a setting down.]

thes·pi·an (thes′pē ən) *also,* **Thes·pi·an.** *adj.* **1.** of or relating to drama; dramatic. **2.** of or relating to Thespis, ancient Greek dramatist. —*n.* an actor. [From *Thespis,* sixth-century B.C. Greek dramatist, supposed founder of ancient Greek tragedy + -AN.]

Thess., Thessalonians.

Thes·sa·lo·ni·an (thes′ə lō′nē ən) *adj.* of, relating to, or characteristic of Thessalonica or its people. —*n.* **1.** a native or inhabitant of Thessalonica. **2. Thessalonians.** either of two books, I Thessalonians and II Thessalonians, of the New Testament, consisting of Epistles written by the Apostle Paul to the people of Thessalonica. ➧ used as singular.

the·ta (thā′tə, thē′-) *n.* the eighth letter of the Greek alphabet (Θ, θ), corresponding to the English *th.*

The·tis (thē′tis) *n.* in Greek legend, a sea nymph who was the mother of Achilles. She made him invulnerable, except for his heel, by dipping him in the river Styx when he was a baby.

thews (thüz, thūz) *pl. n.* **1.** muscles; sinews. **2.** bodily strength. [Old English *thēaw* habit, custom.]

they (thā) *pl. pron.* nominative, **they;** possessive, **their, theirs;** objective, **them. 1.** the persons or things previously or last mentioned or implied. **2.** people in general; any persons: *You know what they always say.* **3.** *Informal.* he or she: *A person has to do what they think is right.* [Old Norse *their* those.]

Usage The plural pronouns **they, them,** and **their** are sometimes used to refer to an antecedent that is grammatically singular: *If anyone wants to speak, they should do so at once.* This usage is generally considered unacceptable in formal speech and writing unless the antecedent clearly refers to more than one person and is in a different clause: *Everybody jumped when they heard the noise.* However, this usage is sometimes employed to avoid sexist language without resorting to the phrase "he or she": *Everyone should leave their books on the table* is less clumsy than *Everyone should leave his or her books on the table.*

they'd (thād) *contr.* **1.** they had. **2.** they would.

they'll (thāl) *contr.* **1.** they will. **2.** they shall.

they're (thâr) *contr.* they are.

they've (thāv) *contr.* they have.

T.H.I., temperature-humidity index.

thi·a·mine (thī′ə min, -mēn′) *also,* **thi·a·min** (thī′ə min). *n.* a vitamin necessary for normal carbohydrate metabolism, found in lean pork, dry beans, peas, and liver. A lack of thiamine causes beriberi. Also, **vitamin B₁.**

Thi·bet·an (ti bet′ən) Tibetan.

thick (thik) *adj.* **1.** having relatively great extent or depth from one surface or side to its opposite; not thin: *a thick piece of wood.*

T

2. having a specified measurement between opposite surfaces or sides: *That stone wall is three feet thick.* **3.** not pouring or flowing easily; viscous: *thick soup.* **4.** having its constituent parts closely packed together: *thick underbrush, a thick beard.* **5.** abounding, filled, or covered (with *with*): *a field thick with wheat.* **6.** considerable or pronounced: *to speak with a thick German accent.* **7.** *Informal.* mentally dull; stupid. **8.** indistinct and husky in sound: *a thick voice.* **9.** difficult to penetrate; dense: *thick smog.* **10.** humid and oppressive: *The air is thick today.* **11.** broad or fat: *thick ankles.* **12.** *Informal.* very close or friendly; intimate. —*adv.* so as to be thick; thickly: *Cut the steak thick.* —*n.* **1.** the thickest part of anything. **2.** a part, place, or stage of greatest intensity or activity: *in the thick of a fight.* [Old English *thicce* not thin, plentiful, dense.] —**thick′ish**, *adj.* —**thick′ly**, *adv.*
· **through thick and thin.** through the good times and the bad; under any circumstances.
· **to lay it on thick.** *Informal.* to exaggerate or be excessive, as in one's praise or flattery.

thick·en (thik′ən) *v.t., v.i.* **1.** to make or become thick or thicker. **2.** to make or become more intense, intricate, or complex, as the plot of a story. —**thick′en·er**, *n.*

thick·en·ing (thik′ə ning) *n.* **1.** something added to a liquid to thicken it. **2.** the act or process of making or becoming thick. **3.** a thickened place or part.

thick·et (thik′it) *n.* a dense growth, as of shrubs or bushes. [Old English *thiccet.*]

thick·head·ed (thik′hed′id) *adj.* slow to learn or understand; stupid; dull. —**thick′head′ed·ness**, *n.*

thick·ness (thik′nis) *n.* **1.** the state or quality of being thick. **2.** the dimension of a solid between its two opposite surfaces, as distinguished from its length or width. **3.** a layer or sheet, as of paper.

thick·set (thik′set′) *adj.* **1.** having a short, stocky build. **2.** planted, placed, or growing close together: *thickset trees.*

thick-skinned (thik′skind′) *adj.* **1.** having a thick skin, as certain fruit. **2.** insensitive or oblivious, esp. to criticism, ridicule, or reproach: *Politicians often have to be thick-skinned.*

thick-wit·ted (thik′wit′id) *adj.* dull; stupid.

thief (thēf) *n., pl.* **thieves.** a person who steals, esp. secretly and without the use of force. [Old English *thēof.*]

thieve (thēv) *v.t., v.i.,* **thieved, thiev·ing.** to steal, esp. secretly and without the use of force. [Old English *thēofian.*]

thiev·er·y (thē′və rē) *n., pl.* **-er·ies.** **1.** the act or practice of stealing. **2.** an instance of this.

thieves (thēvz) the plural of **thief.**

thiev·ish (thē′vish) *adj.* **1.** inclined to stealing. **2.** characteristic of or resembling a thief; stealthy; furtive; sly: *a thievish manner.* —**thiev′ish·ly**, *adv.* —**thiev′ish·ness**, *n.*

thigh (thī) *n.* the part of the leg that extends from the hip to the knee. [Old English *thēoh.*]

thigh·bone (thī′bōn′) *n.* femur.

thig·mot·ro·pism (thig mot′rə piz′əm) *n.* the tendency of a plant or other organism to turn toward or away from physical contact. [Greek *thigma* touch + TROPISM.] —**thig·mo·trop·ic** (thig′mə trop′ik, -trō′pik), *adj.*

thill (thil) *n.* either of the shafts between which an animal is hitched to the vehicle it is drawing. [Possibly from Old English *thille* plank.]

thim·ble (thim′bəl) *n.* **1.** a small metal cap designed to be worn on the fingertip to protect it when pushing a needle through material in sewing. **2.** a metal ring in a rope or in the rope hole of a sail to prevent wear. **3.** a short length of pipe used in forming a joint. [Old English *thȳmel* covering worn to protect a finger, from *thūma* thumb.]

thim·ble·ber·ry (thim′bəl ber′ē) *n., pl.* **-ries.** any of various North American raspberries with a thimble-shaped fruit, esp. the black raspberry.

thim·ble·ful (thim′bəl fŏŏl′) *n., pl.* **-fuls.** as much as a thimble can hold; very small quantity.

thim·ble·rig (thim′bəl rig′) *n.* a type of shell game using thimblelike cups rather than shells. —**thim′ble·rig′ger**, *n.*

thin (thin) *adj.,* **thin·ner, thin·nest.** **1.** having relatively little distance from one surface or side to its opposite; having little thickness or depth: *a thin piece of wood, thin paper.* **2.** not plump or fat; lean: *a long, thin face.* **3.** having little density, substance, or consistency; watery: *a thin gravy.* **4.** easily seen through; not convincing or adequate; flimsy: *a thin excuse.* **5.** not dense or less dense than is usual: *thin air.* **6.** having a faint, often shrill sound; lacking fullness, volume, or depth; weak: *a small thin voice.* **7.** few in number; scanty: *There was a thin showing of hands when volunteers were called for.* **8.** having little or no depth or intensity of color; pale: *a thin shade of blue.* —*adv.* so as to be thin; thinly: *Slice the ham thin.* —*v.t., v.i.,* **thinned, thin·ning.** to make or become thin or thinner (often with *out* or *down*). [Old English

thynne not thick or dense, lean [2], scanty, of little worth.] —**thin′ly**, *adv.* —**thin′ness**, *n.*

thine (thīn) *Archaic. pron.* the possessive case of **thou.** **1.** belonging to thee, or you. **2.** the one or ones belonging to thee, or you. —*adj.* thy. ➡ used before a vowel or *h:* Drink to me only with thine eyes (Ben Jonson, 1616). [Old English *thīn* of thee.]

thing (thing) *n.* **1.** that which has existence; any matter, substance, object, or being: *A thing of beauty is a joy forever* (John Keats, 1818). The small child was curious about all the wondrous things of the world. **2.** that which is the subject of discussion, concern, feeling, or action: *We have to go over these things before we make a final decision.* **3.** an inanimate object, as distinguished from a living organism: *A stone is a thing.* **4.** an organic being: *I wish no living thing to suffer pain* (Percy Bysshe Shelley, 1819). **5.** an object that is not or cannot be described or named: *What in the world is that thing?* **6.** any act or deed: *That was a terrible thing to do!* **7.** any detail or item: *The hosts didn't overlook a thing in planning the party.* **8.** any idea or notion: *Say the first thing that comes into your mind.* **9.** any statement or utterance: *Don't say things like that.* **10.** an article of clothing: *I haven't got a thing to wear.* **11. things.** the general state of affairs: *Things changed while you were gone.* **12.** a piece of information: *Don't tell me a thing about the movie.* **13. things. a.** possessions; belongings: *I put all my things in a box.* **b.** equipment or implements needed for some special activity or purpose: *I can't find my tennis things.* **14.** a person or animal regarded as an object of pity, affection, or contempt: *The lost child was a sad little thing.* **15.** a desired end or result: *The thing is to get ahead.* **16.** *Informal.* an idea, desire, or fear that obsesses: *to have a thing about heights.* **17.** the latest style or fashion. **18.** a work of art, music, or literature: *I've seen a few things written by that playwright.* [Old English *thing* a being, entity, matter, act, meeting.]
· **sure thing.** *Informal.* **a.** something certain; certainty. **b.** certainly; surely.
· **to do one's (own) thing.** *Slang.* to act, speak, or think according to one's beliefs or inclinations.
· **to make a good thing of.** *Informal.* to derive profit or gain from.
· **to see (or hear) things.** to have hallucinations.

thing·a·ma·bob (thing′ə mə bob′) *also,* **thing·u·ma·bob.** *n. Informal.* thingamajig. Also, **thing·um·bob** (thing′əm bob′)

thing·a·ma·jig (thing′ə mə jig′) *also,* **thing·u·ma·jig.** *n. Informal.* something whose name is not known or has been forgotten.

think (thingk) *v.,* **thought, think·ing.** —*v.i.* **1.** to exercise the mind, as in forming opinions, drawing inferences, or using judgment: *A person should think carefully before speaking.* **2.** to have in the mind as an impression, opinion, belief, or attitude (often with *of*): *to think of someone as clever.* **3.** to occupy one's thoughts with something or someone; reflect (often with *about, of,* or *on*): *Let's think about what we will give them for Christmas. I'm always thinking of you.* **4.** to conceive or entertain the idea or notion of doing something: *We're thinking of going to Europe this summer.* **5.** to call to mind or remember (often with *of*): *I could not think of the incident without smiling.* **6.** to have care or consideration (with *of*): *You shouldn't always think of yourself first.* **7.** to form an image or idea in the mind (with *of*): *Who thought of the first alphabet?* **8.** to be of a particular opinion: *If you think so, don't come.* —*v.t.* **1.** to form or have in the mind, as an impression, opinion, belief, or attitude: *to think good thoughts.* **2.** to hold the opinion that: *My friend thinks we should go home. I think you are right.* **3.** to examine by reasoning in order to arrive at a decision, conclusion, or answer (with *over, out,* or *through*): *Think it through carefully before you give me your final decision.* **4.** to regard as certain or probable; anticipate; expect: *We did not think to meet him there.* **5.** to have in mind as a purpose; intend; mean: *They think to influence the voters.* **6.** to regard as; consider: *I think it only proper that you thank the hosts.* **7.** to recall (something) to the mind or memory; remember: *I can't think what your old house looks like.* **8.** to have one's mind full of or focused on: *Think happy thoughts and you'll feel better.* —*n.* **1.** *Informal.* the act of thinking: *You have another think coming if you expect me to go.* **2.** a product of this; thought: *A thing must be a think before it be a thing* (George MacDonald, 1887). [Old English *thencan* to exercise the mind, be of the opinion, consider, meditate.]
· **to think a lot (or highly or well) of.** to hold a favorable

a	at	e	end	o	hot	u	up	hw	white		about
ā	ape	ē	me	ō	old	ū	use	ng	song	ə	taken
ä	far	i	it	ô	fork	ū	rule	th	thin		pencil
âr	care	ī	ice	oi	oil	ŏŏ	pull	th	this		lemon
		îr	pierce	ou	out	ûr	turn	zh	measure		circus

1251

opinion of (someone or something): *We think a lot of you and believe you have a bright future.*

• **to think back on.** to remember: *I often think back on my school days and the good teachers I had.*

• **to think better of.** to decide against after reconsidering.

• **to think nothing of.** **a.** to treat in an offhand manner: *My friend thinks nothing of spending $100 for a pair of shoes.* **b.** to treat as having little or no importance or relevance: *That person thinks nothing of lying or cheating in order to achieve a goal.*

• **to think twice.** to consider very carefully before acting.

• **to think up.** to devise or conceive: *to think up a plan.*

think·a·ble (thing′kə bəl) *adj.* capable or worthy of being considered; conceivable; possible.

think·er (thing′kər) *n.* **1.** a person who thinks. **2.** a person who has developed and exercised mental powers to an exceptional degree.

think·ing (thing′king) *adj.* having the ability to think or reason. —*n.* **1.** the act of one who thinks. **2.** the product of this.

think tank, a center for the study of contemporary culture and society and for research and problem solving in economics, politics, science, and other important areas.

thin·ner (thin′ər) *n.* a liquid, as turpentine, used to thin a substance, esp. paint.

thin section, section *(def. 8).*

thin-skinned (thin′skind′) *adj.* **1.** having a thin skin: *a thin-skinned fruit.* **2.** acutely and unduly sensitive to criticism, ridicule, or reproach; easily hurt or offended.

thi·o·u·re·a (thī′ō yü rē′ə) *n.* a colorless, bitter compound used in photography and in vulcanizing rubber. Formula: CH_4N_2S

third (thûrd) *adj.* **1.** (the ordinal of three) next after the second. **2.** being one of three equal parts. —*n.* **1.** something that is next after the second. **2.** one of three equal parts; $\frac{1}{3}$. **3.** the third forward gear, as of an automobile. **4.** *Music.* **a.** an interval of three degrees between two tones of the diatonic scale. **b.** a tone separated from another tone by this interval, esp. the third tone of the diatonic scale. **c.** a harmonic combination of two tones separated by this interval. **5.** third base. —*adv.* in the third place. [Old English *thridda* (the ordinal of three) next after the second.]

third base *Baseball.* **1.** the third base that a player must try to reach. **2.** the position played by the player stationed in this area of the field.

third-class (thûrd′klas′) *adj.* **1.** of, relating to, or belonging to a class that is next below or inferior to second class, as in order, quality, or importance. **2.** designating a class of mail that includes all printed matter except newspapers and magazines and meets certain governmental limits, as of weight. **3.** designating a class of travel accommodations on a ship or other conveyance, usually the least expensive and luxurious, ranking next below second class. —*adv.* by third-class mail or conveyance.

third class **1.** third-class travel accommodations. **2.** third-class mail.

third degree *Informal.* an intensive and often brutal interrogation of a prisoner to obtain information or a confession.

third-de·gree burn (thûrd′di grē′) a severe burn in which all layers of the skin are destroyed and possibly underlying tissues as well.

third dimension **1.** the dimension of depth or thickness, as possessed by a three-dimensional object, or the appearance or effect of this dimension, as displayed by a three-dimensional image. **2.** a quality of being lifelike or seeming real: *flat fictional characters that lack a third dimension.* —**third-di·men·sion·al** (thûrd′di men′shə nəl), *adj.*

third estate, the third and lowest organized political group of a kingdom, esp. in France before the revolution of 1789, comprising the common people, as distinguished from the nobility or clergy.

third·ly (thûrd′lē) *adv.* in the third place.

Third Order, an organization of lay members affiliated with a certain religious order.

third party **1.** a political party organized to oppose the two principal parties in a country or state with a tradition of a two-party system. **2.** a party or person who is not a principal in a case or matter, esp. one involving a legal proceeding: *a third party in a damage suit.*

third person, the form of a pronoun or verb that indicates the person or thing spoken of. In the sentence *Whenever he sees her, she is nice to him,* the words *he, sees, her, she, is,* and *him* are in the third person.

third rail, a rail that runs beside the tracks of an electric railroad and carries the current.

third-rate (thûrd′rāt′) *adj.* **1.** third in class, order, quality, or importance; third-class. **2.** distinctly inferior; very poor: *a third-rate movie.* —**third′-rat′er,** *n.*

Third Reich, Germany under the Nazis, from 1933 to 1945.

Third World, the developing or emerging countries of the world.

thirst (thûrst) *n.* **1.** an uncomfortable feeling of dryness in the mouth and throat caused by a desire or need to drink fluids. **2.** a desire or need to drink: *to have an insatiable thirst.* **3.** a strong or powerful desire; craving: *a thirst for power, a thirst for learning.* —*v.i.* **1.** to want something to drink; be thirsty. **2.** to have a strong desire; yearn: *to thirst for knowledge.* [Old English *thurst* uncomfortable feeling caused by lack of drink.]

thirst·y (thûrs′tē) *adj.,* **thirst·i·er, thirst·i·est.** **1.** having the sensation of wanting something to drink. **2.** lacking water; arid; parched: *thirsty farmland.* **3.** having a strong desire (with *for*). —**thirst′i·ly,** *adv.* —**thirst′i·ness,** *n.*

thir·teen (thûr′tēn′) *n.* **1.** the cardinal number that is three more than ten. **2.** a symbol representing this number, such as 13 or XIII. **3.** something having this many units or members. —*adj.* numbering three more than ten. [Old English *thrēotēne.*]

thir·teenth (thûr′tēnth′) *adj.* **1.** (the ordinal of thirteen) next after the twelfth. **2.** being one of thirteen equal parts. —*n.* **1.** something that is next after twelve. **2.** one of thirteen equal parts; $\frac{1}{13}$.

thir·ti·eth (thûr′tē ith) *adj.* **1.** (the ordinal of thirty) next after the twenty-ninth. **2.** being one of thirty equal parts. —*n.* **1.** something that is next after twenty-nine. **2.** one of thirty equal parts; $\frac{1}{30}$.

thir·ty (thûr′tē) *n., pl.* **-ties.** **1.** the cardinal number that is three times ten. **2.** a symbol representing this number, such as 30 or XXX. **3.** **thirties.** the number series from thirty to thirty-nine. ➡ used esp. in reference to the fourth decade of a century or of a person's life. —*adj.* numbering three times ten. [Old English *thrītig.*]

thir·ty-sec·ond note (thûr′tē sek′ənd) *Music.* a note having a time value equal to one thirty second of a whole note. Also, **demisemiquaver.**

Thirty Years' War, a series of religious and territorial wars among various European countries between 1618 and 1648.

this (this) *adj., pl.* **these.** **1.** used to indicate a person or thing that is present or near at hand: *This house is ten years old.* **2.** used to indicate a person or thing that is understood or has just been mentioned or pointed out: *This news is most distressing.* **3.** indicating a person or thing that is nearer than or contrasted with another: *This dress is nicer than that one.* —*pron., pl.* **these.** **1.** used to indicate a person or thing that is present or near at hand: *Is this your coat?* **2.** used to indicate a person or thing that is understood or has just been mentioned or pointed out: *This is a serious matter.* **3.** a person or thing that is nearer than or contrasted with another: *This is mine; that is yours.* **4.** something that is about to be said or explained: *This is what I mean.* —*adv.* to this extent or degree; so: *Is it this hot every day?* [Old English *thes* (masculine), *thēos* (feminine), *this* (neuter).]

This·be (thiz′bē) *n.* see **Pyramus and Thisbe.**

this·tle (this′əl) *n.* any of several prickly leaved plants of the composite family, as the common thistle, *Cirsium vulgare,* which bears reddish or purplish flower heads. [Old English *thistel.*]

this·tle·down (this′əl doun′) *n.* the silky down on the flower head of a thistle.

this·tly (this′lē) *adj.* resembling a thistle or thistles; prickly.

thith·er (thith′ər) *adv.* to or toward that place. —*adj.* located on the farthest side. [Old English *thider* to that place.]

thith·er·ward (thith′ər wərd) *also,* **thith·er·wards.** *adv.* to or toward that place; thither.

tho (thō) *also,* **tho′.** *conj., adv.* though.

thole (thōl) *n.* a peg or pair of pegs, as of wood or metal, on the upper edge of either side of a boat, serving as fulcrum for an oar in rowing. Also, **thole′pin′.** [Old English *thol.*]

Tho·mism (tō′miz əm, thō′-) *n.* the philosophy of Saint Thomas Aquinas and his followers that emphasized application of the powers of both faith and reason to phenomena of the natural world to attain knowledge of the universe. —**Tho′mist,** *adj., n.*

Thomp·son seedless (tomp′sən) a pale green, oval-shaped grape that is the major source of seedless raisins.

Thompson submachine gun *Trademark.* a .45-caliber, air-cooled, gas-operated automatic weapon designed to be carried and operated by one person. Also, **Tommy gun.** [From John T. Thompson, 1860-1940, U.S. army officer who was one of its inventors.]

thong (thông, thong) *n.* **1.** a narrow strip of leather or similar material, used esp. as a fastening. **2.** a sandal that is held to the foot by a pair of thongs that fits between the first two toes. **3.** the lash of a whip. [Old English *thwang* narrow strip of leather.]

thistle

Thor (thôr) *n.* in Norse mythology, the god of thunder.

tho·rac·ic (thô ras′ik) *adj.* of, relating to, or situated in or near the thorax.

tho·rax (thôr′aks) *n., pl.* **tho·rax·es** or **tho·ra·ces** (thôr′ə sēz′). **1.** in humans and certain other vertebrates, that part of the body extending from the base of the neck to the diaphragm, containing the heart, lungs, and ribs; chest. **2.** the section of an arthropod's body that contains the legs and, if present, the wings, extending from the head to the abdomen. [Latin *thōrax* chest, breastplate, from Greek *thōrāx*.]

Tho·ra·zine (thôr′ə zēn′) *n. Trademark.* chlorpromazine. [Shortening and rearrangement of *(2-chl)or(o-N,N-dimethyl-10-H-pheno)th(i)azine(-10-propanamine)*.]

tho·ri·a (thôr′ē ə) *n.* the oxide of thorium, a white powder used as a catalyst and in gas mantles and other refractory materials. Formula: ThO_2 [Modern Latin *thoria,* from Swedish *Thorjord* literally, Thor-earth; so named by Jöns Jakob Berzelius, 1779-1848, Swedish chemist. See THORIUM.]

tho·rite (thôr′īt) *n.* a rare, highly radioactive, black or yellow silicate ore of thorium. Formula: $ThSiO_4$

tho·ri·um (thôr′ē əm) *n.* a heavy, silver-white, radioactive metallic element used in photoelectric cells and as a nuclear fuel in breeder reactors. Symbol: **Th** For tables, see **element**. [Modern Latin *thorium,* from *Thor;* so named by Jöns Jakob Berzelius, 1779-1848, Swedish chemist who discovered it.]

thorn (thôrn) *n.* **1.** a short, sharp-pointed growth on a stem or branch. **2.** any of various trees or shrubs bearing thorns. [Old English *thorn.*]
 • **a thorn in one's side.** a cause of annoyance or worry.

thorn apple 1. the fruit of the hawthorn; haw. **2.** jimsonweed.

thorn·y (thôr′nē) *adj.,* **thorn·i·er, thorn·i·est. 1.** full of thorns; spiny; prickly. **2.** difficult or irritating: *a thorny problem.*

tho·ron (thôr′on) *n.* a gaseous radioisotope with an atomic weight of 220, one of the twenty isotopes of radon, produced by the radioactive decay of thorium. [Modern Latin *thoron,* from *thorium* (see THORIUM) + *-on,* as in Greek *argon* (see ARGON).]

thor·ough (thûr′ō) *adj.* **1.** done or carried out to the fullest extent; omitting nothing: *a thorough search, a thorough cleaning.* **2.** painstakingly accurate and conscientious, esp. with regard to details: *Those scientists were very thorough in their research.* **3.** not limited or restricted in any way; utter; absolute; unqualified: *a thorough bore.* [Old English *thuruh,* form of *thurh.* See THROUGH.] **—thor′ough·ly,** *adv.* **—thor′ough·ness,** *n.*

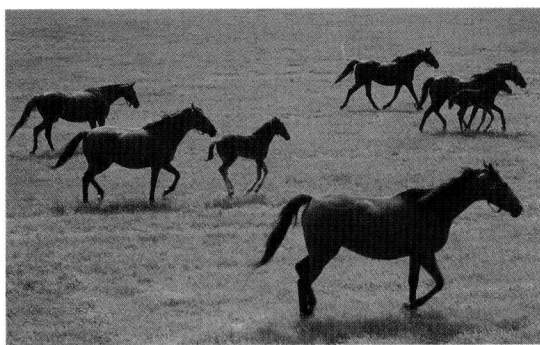

thoroughbreds

thor·ough·bred (thûr′ə bred′) *n.* **1.** an animal, as a horse or dog, that is of pure or unmixed breed or stock. **2. Thoroughbred.** a horse descended from a breed originally developed at the end of the eighteenth century by crossing English mares with any one of three specific Arabian stallions. Thoroughbreds are bred and trained chiefly for horse racing. **3.** a person of good breeding and education. **—adj. 1.** of pure or unmixed breed or stock. **2. Thoroughbred.** relating to or designating a Thoroughbred. **3.** having good breeding and education.

thor·ough·fare (thûr′ə fâr′) *n.* **1.** a public road that is a major route of travel. **2.** a passage that is open at both ends, esp. one connecting two streets.

thor·ough·go·ing (thûr′ə gō′ing) *adj.* **1.** characterized by thoroughness, esp. with regard to details. **2.** utter; unqualified; thorough: *a thoroughgoing liar.*

those (thōz) the plural of **that.**

Thoth (thōth, tōt) *n.* in Egyptian mythology, the god of the moon, wisdom, and learning, the scribe of the gods, usually represented as an ibis or as a man with the head of either an ibis or dog.

thou (thou) *pron.* nominative, **thou;** possessive, **thy, thine;** objective, **thee;** *pl.,* nominative, **you, ye;** possessive, **your, yours;** objective, **you, ye.** *Archaic.* the one spoken to; you. [Old English *thū.*]

though (thō) *conj.* **1.** in spite of the fact that: *I was late for work, though I got up early.* **2.** but; yet; nevertheless; however: *The meal was good, though it could have been better.* **3.** granting or supposing that; even if: *Though we were poor, we were still happy.* **—adv.** nonetheless; however: *They won't help you; you can count on us, though.* [Of Scandinavian origin.]

thought (thôt) *v.* the past tense and past participle of **think.** **—n. 1.** the act or process of thinking: *lost in thought.* **2.** something that one thinks; idea: *What are your thoughts on the subject?* **3.** the intellectual activity or ideas characteristic of a particular group, time, or place: *modern thought, scientific thought.* **4.** careful notice, attention, or consideration; heed: *Please give some thought to the problem.* **5.** something that is intended; aim: *Our only thought was to put out the fire.* **6.** expectation; anticipation: *I had no thought of meeting them.* **7.** a little bit; trifle: *to be a thought more polite.* [Old English *thôht* act of thinking, idea.] —For Synonyms *(n.),* see **idea.**

thought·ful (thôt′fəl) *adj.* **1.** expressing, showing, or characterized by a regard for others and their feelings; considerate: *a thoughtful person, a thoughtful gift.* **2.** engaged in or full of thought; meditative: *a thoughtful mood.* **3.** showing or characterized by thought; serious: *a thoughtful question.* **—thought′ful·ly,** *adv.* **—thought′ful·ness,** *n.*

thought·less (thôt′lis) *adj.* **1.** having, showing, or characterized by little or no regard for others and their feelings; inconsiderate: *His thoughtless remark hurt her feelings.* **2.** showing or characterized by a lack of thought; careless; heedless: *a thoughtless error.* **—thought′less·ly,** *adv.* **—thought′less·ness,** *n.*

thou·sand (thou′zənd) *n.* **1.** the cardinal number that is ten times one hundred. **2.** a symbol representing this number, such as 1,000 or M. **—adj.** numbering one thousand. [Old English *thūsend.*]

thou·sand·fold (thou′zənd fōld′) *adj.* **1.** one thousand times as great or as numerous. **2.** having or consisting of one thousand parts. **—adv.** so as to be one thousand times greater or more numerous.

thou·sandth (thou′zəndth, -zənth) *adj.* **1.** (the ordinal of thousand) next after the 999th. **2.** being one of a thousand equal parts. **—n. 1.** something that is next after the 999th. **2.** one of a thousand equal parts; $1/1,000$.

thrall (thrôl) *n.* **1.** a person who is in bondage; slave; serf. **2.** a person who is enslaved by some moral or mental power or influence. **3.** the condition of being enslaved or like a slave. [Old Norse *thrǣll* serf, slave.]

thrall·dom (thrôl′dəm) *also,* **thral·dom.** *n.* the state or condition of being a thrall.

thrash (thrash) *v.t.* **1.** to administer repeated, forceful blows to; give a beating to. **2.** to move, swing, or strike in a wild or violent manner: *to thrash one's arms.* **3.** to defeat completely; overwhelm. **4.** thresh. **—v.i. 1.** to make wild, flailing movements; toss violently. **2.** to move or proceed by thrashing: *We thrashed our way through the underbrush.* **3.** thresh. [Form of THRESH.]
 • **to thrash out.** to discuss thoroughly and bring to a conclusion: *The company and the union thrashed out a new contract.*
 • **to thrash over.** to go over repeatedly, as in one's mind.

thrash·er (thrash′ər) *n.* **1.** a person or thing that thrashes. **2.** thresher *(def. 3).* **3.** any of various North American songbirds, family Mimidae, closely related to the mockingbird, having a curved bill, a long tail, short wings, and predominantly brownish plumage. Length: 8-13 inches (20-33 centimeters).

thrasher

thrash·ing (thrash′ing) *n.* a severe beating.

thread (thred) *n.* **1.a.** very fine, thin cord made of two or more fibers, as of cotton, wool, or silk, twisted together, used in sewing and in weaving cloth. **b.** a piece of this. **2.** anything resembling thread, as in slenderness, length, or composition: *A thread of paint trickled down the wall.* **3.** anything that runs through the whole of something and connects its parts: *the thread of a story.* **4.** a spiral

a	at	e	end	o	hot	u	up	hw	white		about
ā	ape	ē	me	ō	old	ū	use	ng	song		taken
ä	far	i	it	ô	fork	ü	rule	th	thin	ə	pencil
âr	care	ī	ice	oi	oil	u̇	pull	<u>th</u>	this		lemon
				îr	pierce	ou	out	ûr	turn	zh	measure		circus

ridge running continuously around a screw, bolt, or nut. Also *(def. 4),* **screw thread.** —*v.t.* **1.** to pass a thread through, esp. in order to sew: *to thread a needle.* **2.** to string together on or as if on a thread: *to thread beads.* **3.** to pass or proceed through in a winding or twisting manner: *hair threaded with a string of pearls.* **4.** to make (one's way) in this manner: *to thread one's way through a crowd.* **5.** to cut a thread on, in, or around (a screw, bolt, or nut). —*v.i.* **1.** to pass or proceed in a winding or twisting manner: *The river threads between the mountains.* **2.** to form a fine thread when dropped from a spoon, such as boiling syrup that has reached a certain consistency. [Old English *thrǣd* fine long cord.] —**thread′like′,** *adj.*

thread·bare (thred′bâr′) *adj.* **1.** having the nap worn off so as to expose the threads; worn; shabby: *threadbare upholstery.* **2.** wearing threadbare clothes; seedy. **3.** no longer fresh or current; hackneyed; stale: *a threadbare joke.*

thread·worm (thred′wûrm′) *n.* any of various threadlike roundworms, esp. a pinworm.

thread·y (thred′ē) *adj.,* **thread·i·er, thread·i·est. 1.** composed of, covered with, or resembling thread. **2.** forming threads: *a thready liquid.* **3.** weak and thin: *a thready voice.* —**thread′i·ness,** *n.*

threat (thret) *n.* **1.** an expression of the intention to inflict punishment, harm, or pain. **2.** a person or thing that is a source of misfortune, danger, or harm: *The murderer was a threat to society.* **3.** an indication or possibility, as of impending misfortune, danger, or harm: *The citizens lived under the threat of war.* [Old English *thrēat* danger, menace.]

threat·en (thret′ən) *v.t.* **1.** to utter or make a threat against: *The terrorist threatened the hostage.* **2.** to be a threat to; endanger: *The drought threatened the whole crop.* **3.** to be an indication of: *The dark clouds threaten rain.* **4.** to make a threat of: *to threaten to go to the police.* —*v.i.* **1.** to use or utter threats. **2.** to be or pose a threat; menace. [Old English *thrēatnian* to force.] —**threat′en·er,** *n.* —**threat′en·ing·ly,** *adv.*

three (thrē) *n.* **1.** the cardinal number that is one more than two. **2.** a symbol representing this number, such as 3 or III. **3.** something having this many units or members, such as a playing card. —*adj.* numbering one more than two. [Old English *thrēo.*]

3-D (thrē′dē′) *also,* **three-D.** *n.* a three-dimensional motion picture, representation, or the like. —*adj.* three-dimensional.

three-deck·er (thrē′dek′ər) *n.* **1.** a ship having three decks or gun decks. **2.** anything having three stories, layers, or levels, esp. a sandwich made with three slices of bread.

three-di·men·sion·al (thrē′di men′shə nəl) *adj.* **1.** of, relating to, or having three dimensions. **2.** having or giving the illusion of depth, as a 3-D movie or a stereoscopic display.

three·fold (thrē′fōld′) *adj.* **1.** three times as great or numerous. **2.** having or consisting of three parts. —*adv.* so as to be three times greater or more numerous.

three-mile limit (thrē′mīl′) an area of water extending 3 miles (4.8 kilometers) out from the shore of a nation and formerly regarded, under international law, as the outer bound of that nation's jurisdiction.

three·pence (thrip′əns, threp′-, thrup′-) *n.* **1.** a sum of three British pennies; three pence. ➡ used as singular or plural. **2.** a coin having this value.

three·pen·ny (thrip′ə nē, threp′-, thrup′-, thrē′pen′ē) *adj.* **1.** having the value of or costing threepence. **2.** of little worth; cheap; worthless.

three-ply (thrē′plī′) *adj.* consisting of three thicknesses, strands, layers, or folds.

three-point landing (thrē′point′) an airplane landing in which the two main wheels of the landing gear and the tail wheel or the nose wheel touch down simultaneously.

three R's, reading, writing, and arithmetic, considered as the three basic elements of elementary education. [From the jocular spelling *r(eading), ′r(iting),* and *′r(ithmetic).*]

three·score (thrē′skôr′) *adj., n.* three times twenty; sixty.

three·some (thrē′səm) *n.* a group of three persons.

three-toed sloth (thrē′tōd′) any of a group of tree-dwelling Central and South American sloths, genus *Bradypus,* that have three curved claws on their forelimbs and four on their hind limbs, and may appear greenish because of algae growing on their gray-brown fur. Length: 20-24 inches (51-61 centimeters).

Three Wise Men, in the New Testament, the Magi.

thren·o·dy (thren′ə dē) *n., pl.* **-dies.** a song or poem of lamentation, esp. one composed for the funeral of an important person. [Greek *thrēnōidiā* lamentation, from *thrēnos* lament + *ōidē* song.]

thre·o·nine (thrē′ə nīn′) *n.* an essential amino acid important for the growth of infants and for nitrogen balance in adults. Formula: $C_4H_9NO_3$ [*Threon-* (modification of Greek *erythron,* neuter of *erythros* red) + -INE².]

thresh (thresh) *v.t.* **1.a.** to separate the grain from (a cereal grass) with a threshing machine or by beating with a flail. **b.** to separate (grain) from straw or chaff in this manner. **2.** to give a beating to; thrash. —*v.i.* **1.** to thresh grain. **2.** to toss violently; thrash. [Old English *therscan* to separate the grains of a cereal from the husks, esp. by beating with a flail, flog.]

·**to thresh out.** to thrash out.

·**to thresh over.** to thrash over.

thresh·er (thresh′ər) *n.* **1.** a person or thing that threshes. **2.** threshing machine. **3.** a large shark, genus *Alopias,* having a very long tail that it uses to drive together the schools of small fish on which it feeds. Also *(def. 3),* **thrasher.**

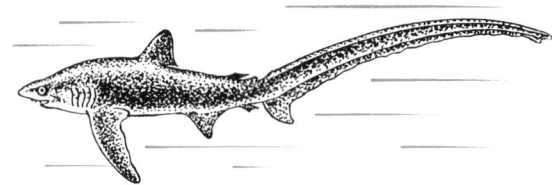

thresher *(def. 3)*

threshing machine, a machine that separates grain from the stalk, straw, or chaff. Also, **thresher.**

thresh·old (thresh′ōld, -hōld′) *n.* **1.** a piece of wood, stone, metal, or the like forming the lower horizontal member of a door frame. **2.** a point of entering or beginning: *to be on the threshold of a new job.* **3.** the limit or point below which a stimulus cannot produce a response or be perceived: *to have a high threshold for pain.* [Old English *therscold* piece of stone or wood beneath a doorway, line crossed in entering.]

threw (thrü) the past tense of **throw.**

thrice (thrīs) *adv.* **1.** three times. **2.** three times as great or numerous as; threefold. **3.** greatly; extremely. [Old English *thrīga, thrīwa* three times.]

thrift (thrift) *n.* **1.** careful or frugal management of money and other material resources; frugality. **2.** any of a group of summer-flowering plants, genus *Armeria,* usually having white or pink flowers, often used in rock gardens. [Old Norse *thrift* prosperity.]

thrift·less (thrift′lis) *adj.* not exercising frugality; wasteful; extravagant; improvident. —**thrift′less·ly,** *adv.* —**thrift′less·ness,** *n.*

thrift shop, a store selling secondhand items, esp. clothing, at low prices and often for a charity.

thrift·y (thrif′tē) *adj.,* **thrift·i·er, thrift·i·est. 1.** prudent in the use and management of money and other resources; avoiding waste or extravagance; frugal. **2.** successful; thriving; flourishing. —**thrift′i·ly,** *adv.* —**thrift′i·ness,** *n.*

Synonyms Thrifty, frugal, and economical mean avoiding the waste of money or material resources. **Thrifty** stresses the prudent management of assets and the building up of savings: *It is possible to be thrifty and still indulge in an occasional luxury.* **Frugal** suggests a simple, modest way of life in which spending is restricted to necessities: *My parents are well-to-do, but because they grew up poor, they live a frugal life and spend very little on themselves.* **Economical** stresses efficiency and the lack of waste in the use of resources: *It is economical to buy fruit and vegetables when they are in season and preserve them for future use.*

thrill (thril) *n.* **1.** a pleasurable or exciting feeling or sensation: *the thrill of owning one's own car.* **2.** something that produces such a feeling or sensation: *My first airplane trip was a thrill for me.* —*v.t.* to fill with a sudden wave of pleasure or excitement: *The speech thrilled the crowd.* —*v.i.* **1.** to experience a sudden wave of pleasure or excitement. **2.** to move tremulously; quiver; tremble. [Earlier *thirl* to pierce, from Old English *thȳrlian.*] —**thrill′ing·ly,** *adv.*

thrill·er (thril′ər) *n.* **1.** a play, story, book, or the like that arouses feelings of excitement or suspense. **2.** a person or thing that thrills.

thrips (thrips) *n.* any of a group of minute, destructive insects, order Thysanoptera, that suck the juices from fruit, vegetables, cotton plants, and other crops. [Latin *thrips* wood worm, from Greek *thrīps.*]

thrive (thrīv) *v.i.,* **throve** or **thrived, thrived** or **thriv·en** (thriv′ən), **thriv·ing. 1.** to be successful or fortunate: *I hope your parents' new business will thrive.* **2.** to grow vigorously: *The plant throve in the sunlight.* [Old Norse *thrīfask* to prosper; literally, to grasp for oneself, from *thrīfa* to grasp.] —**thriv′ing·ly,** *adv.* —For Synonyms, see **prosper.**

throat (thrōt) *n.* **1.** the area behind and below the mouth,

containing the pharynx, upper part of the esophagus, larynx, and upper part of the trachea. **2.** the front surface of the neck, extending from below the chin to the collarbones. **3.** any narrow opening or passage resembling the throat: *the throat of a bottle.* [Old English *throte.*]

throat·ed (thrō′tid) *adj. Zoology.* having or marked by a particular kind of throat. ➡ used in combination: *a white-throated sparrow.*

throat·y (thrō′tē) *adj.,* **throat·i·er, throat·i·est.** produced or modified deep in the throat; husky; guttural: *a throaty laugh.* —**throat′i·ness,** *n.*

throb (throb) *v.i.,* **throbbed, throb·bing. 1.** to pulsate or pound heavily and with increasing rapidity, as the heart when one is afraid or excited. **2.** to have or experience a throbbing sensation: *The noise made my head throb.* **3.** to vibrate or sound with a strong, steady rhythm: *The drums throbbed.* —*n.* **1.** the act of throbbing. **2.** a beat or vibration; pulsation: *a heart throb.* [Probably imitative.] —**throb′bing·ly,** *adv.*

throe (thrō) *n.* **1. throes.** a condition of extreme pain, anguish, or struggle: *the throes of battle, in the throes of death.* **2.** *also,* **throes.** a violent spasm or pang, esp. of pain. [Earlier *throwe,* possibly going back to Old English *thrawu* threat, affliction, pang.]

throm·bin (throm′bin) *n.* an enzyme in the blood that combines with fibrinogen to form fibrin, enabling blood to clot.

throm·bo·cyte (throm′bə sīt′) *n.* blood platelet. [Greek *thrombos* clot + *kytos* hollow vessel.]

throm·bo·sis (throm bō′sis) *n., pl.* **-ses** (-sēz). the formation of a clot of blood in a blood vessel or chamber of the heart, causing a complete or partial obstruction to the flow of blood. [Modern Latin *thrombosis,* from Greek *thrombōsis* blocked vein, going back to *thrombos* clot.] —**throm·bot·ic** (throm bot′ik), *adj.*

throm·bus (throm′bəs) *n., pl.* **-bi** (-bī). a clot of blood that forms in the circulatory system, sometimes obstructing the flow of blood.

throne (thrōn) *n.* **1.** a chair occupied by a sovereign, pope, bishop, or other dignitary during state or ceremonial occasions. **2.** royal power or authority; sovereignty. —*v.t.,* **throned, throning.** to place on or as on a throne; enthrone. [Latin *thronus* elevated seat, from Greek *thronos* chair, chair of state.]

throng (thrông, throng) *n.* **1.** a large number of people assembled or crowded together. **2.** any large number of things assembled or crowded together. —*v.i.* to move or assemble in a group or large numbers; crowd: *The people thronged to the county fair.* —*v.t.* **1.** to fill (a place) to capacity; crowd into: *Spectators thronged the courtroom.* **2.** to crowd around; press in on: *Fans thronged the rock group wherever they went.* [Old English *(ge)-thrang* crowd.]

throt·tle (throt′əl) *n.* **1.** a valve that controls or regulates the supply of steam in a steam engine or turbine or the supply of fuel vapor in an internal-combustion engine. Also, **throttle valve. 2.** a lever or pedal that operates such a valve. —*v.t.,* **-tled, -tling. 1.** to kill by choking; strangle; suffocate. **2.** to check the flow or action of; suppress: *The army throttled the rebellion by cutting the lines of supply.* **3.a.** to reduce or shut off the flow of (steam or fuel vapor) in an engine. **b.** to reduce the speed of (an engine) in this way (often with *down*). [Possibly THROAT + -LE.] —**throt′tler,** *n.*

through (thrü) *prep.* **1.** from the beginning to the end of: *to read through a book in one day.* **2.** into one side or end and out the opposite or other side or end: *to drive a nail through a board.* **3.** in or to various parts or places in: *We plan to travel through Europe this summer.* **4.** in the midst of; among: *to wander through the trees.* **5.** by reason of; on account of; because of: *to lose one's job through constant tardiness.* **6.** by means of: *We got the news through our friend.* **7.** having finished or done with: *Is your cousin through college yet?* —*adv.* **1.** from one side or end to the opposite or other side or end: *The farmer opened the gate and the cattle passed through.* **2.** from beginning to end: *to read a letter through.* **3.** to a conclusion or termination: *to carry a project through.* **4.** along the whole distance; all the way: *The river runs through to the mill.* **5.** throughout; completely: *to be soaked through.* ➡ often used emphatically in the phrase *through and through.* —*adj.* **1.a.** going the whole distance with few or no stops and no changes: *a through train.* **b.** relating to or allowing travel to the end of the line with few or no stops and no changes: *a through ticket.* **2.** passing or extending from one end or side to the other. **3.** allowing free or unobstructed passage: *a through street.* **4.** having arrived at a point of completion or termination; finished: *Are you through with your homework?* **5.** no longer having relations, dealings, or connections: *I'm through with those people!* [Old English *thurh* from one side to the other, from end to end, everywhere, in, by means of, because of.]

through·out (thrü out′) *prep.* **1.** in every part of; everywhere in: *That author is famous throughout Europe.* **2.** during the whole

time or course of: *Close friends visited me throughout my illness.* —*adv.* **1.** in or to every place or part; everywhere: *Are your facts correct throughout?* **2.** from beginning to end.

through·way (thrü′wā′) thruway.

throve (thrōv) a past tense of **thrive.**

throw (thrō) *v.,* **threw, thrown, throw·ing.** —*v.t.* **1.** to propel up into or through the air with or as with the hand or hands: *to throw a ball, to throw a pebble into the water.* **2.** to cause to fall to the ground: *The horse threw its rider.* **3.** to place or remove carelessly or hurriedly, as an article of clothing: *I threw a coat on and ran out the door.* **4.** to put or place in a specified position, state, or condition: *to throw a crowd into confusion.* **5.** to direct, turn, or project; cast: *to throw someone a nasty look.* **6.** to move (a lever or switch) so as to connect or disconnect parts of a mechanism or to complete or break an electric circuit. **7.** to lose or shed: *The horse threw a shoe.* **8.** to play or put aside (a card or cards). **9.** to shape on a potter's wheel. **10.a.** to roll (dice). **b.** to roll (a specified number) with dice: *to throw a ten.* **11.** (of certain domestic animals) to bring forth (young). **12.** to twist (silk or other filaments) into threads or yarn. **13.** *Informal.* to lose (a game, race, or other contest) intentionally and often for a payoff. **14.** *Informal.* to surprise, confuse, or disconcert: *The reporter's question threw the candidate.* **15.** *Informal.* to mislead; deceive: *Don't let a big smile throw you.* **16.** to give (a party, dance, or the like). —*v.i.* to propel something up into or through the air, esp. with the hand or hands. —*n.* **1.** the act of throwing; toss. **2.** the distance that something is or may be thrown: *a long throw.* **3.** a scarf, shawl, or similar covering worn draped over the shoulders. **4.** a spread, coverlet, or similar covering draped over something, such as a sofa or bed. **5.** a roll of dice or the number rolled. [Old English *thrāwan* to twist, turn, hurl.] —**throw′er,** *n.*

• **to throw away. a.** to dispose of; discard. **b.** to spend or use in a wasteful or extravagant manner; squander: *to throw away a fortune by gambling.* **c.** to neglect to take advantage of: *to throw away an opportunity.*

• **to throw cold water on.** to discourage by being indifferent, pessimistic, or disparaging.

• **to throw in.** to add or include as a bonus: *My boss threw in an extra week's vacation.*

• **to throw off. a.** to rid or free oneself of. **b.** to give off; emit. **c.** to do or say in a rapid, haphazard manner: *The comedian threw off a few jokes before we even got seated.*

• **to throw oneself at.** to strive to win the attention, love, or friendship of.

• **to throw oneself into.** to enter into or engage in rigorously or completely: *to throw oneself into one's work.*

• **to throw oneself on** (or **upon**). to ask for or depend on (another's mercy, support, goodwill, or the like): *to throw oneself on the mercy of the court.*

• **to throw open. a.** to open suddenly or widely, as a door or window. **b.** to remove all restrictions or barriers from.

• **to throw out. a.** to reject; discard: *They threw out all of our suggestions.* **b.** to utter or offer, as a hint or suggestion. **c.** *Baseball.* to put out (a base runner) by throwing the ball to the fielder on the base toward which the base runner is running.

• **to throw over.** to forsake; abandon; jilt.

• **to throw the book at.** *Slang.* to penalize or punish severely.

• **to throw together.** to make, put together, or assemble hurriedly or haphazardly: *to throw together a meal.*

• **to throw up. a.** *Informal.* to vomit. **b.** to erect or build rapidly: *to throw up a dike against a flood.* **c.** to give up; abandon.

Synonyms *v.t.* **Throw, toss, hurl,** and **pitch**[1] mean to propel an object through the air by releasing it from the hand. **Throw** is the most general of these terms and can be applied to a variety of such actions: *The children threw bread to the ducks. Don't throw the empty cans on the ground.* **Toss** denotes a casual, leisurely throw: *I tossed the ball in the air and the dog fetched it.* **Hurl** implies the throwing of something swiftly for a long distance: *The soldiers hurled the hand grenades toward the enemy lines.* **Pitch** suggests careful aim at a definite target and is generally used in specific expressions: *They were learning to pitch horseshoes.*

throw·a·way (thrō′ə wā′) *n.* **1.** a leaflet or handbill distributed free and meant to be thrown away after reading. **2.** anything meant to be thrown away after use, such as a disposable bottle,

a	at	e	end	o	hot	u	up	hw	white		about
ā	ape	ē	me	ō	old	ū	use	ng	song	ə	taken
ä	far	i	it	ô	fork	ü	rule	th	thin		pencil
âr	care	ī	ice	oi	oil	u̇	pull	th	this		lemon
		îr	pierce	ou	out	ûr	turn	zh	measure		circus

can, or other container. —*adj.* designed or meant to be thrown away after use; disposable: *throwaway containers.*

throw·back (thrō′bak′) *n.* **1.** a reversion to an earlier or ancestral type or character. **2.** an instance of this.

thrown (thrōn) the past participle of **throw.**

throw rug, scatter rug.

thru (thrü) through.

thrum[1] (thrum) *v.,* **thrummed, thrum·ming.** —*v.t.* to play (a stringed instrument), esp. in an idle, monotonous, or unskillful manner; strum. —*v.i.* **1.** to drum or tap idly or repeatedly with the fingers: *to thrum on a desk top.* **2.** to thrum a stringed instrument. —*n.* a monotonous sound produced by thrumming. [Imitative.]

thrum[2] (thrum) *n.* **1.a.** a fringe of warp threads left on a loom after the fabric has been cut off. **b.** one of these threads. **2.** any short tuft or fringe of threads or fibers, as on the end of a piece of cloth. [Old English *-thrum* ligament (found in *tungethrum* ligament of the tongue).]

thrush[1] (thrush) *n.* any of numerous songbirds, family Turdidae, including the robin, bluebird, wood thrush, and nightingale, usually having a chunky body, long legs, a slender bill, and solid or mottled black, brown, or gray plumage. Length: 4-13 inches (10-33 centimeters). [Old English *thrysce.*]

thrush[2] (thrush) *n.* **1.** a disease, esp. of infants and debilitated patients, caused by a fungus, *Candida albicans,* producing small whitish spots on the tongue and mouth. **2.** a diseased condition of the bottom pad of a horse's foot, characterized by a foul discharge. [Akin to Danish *trøske* and Swedish *torsk,* probably going back to unrecorded Old Norse *thruskr.*]

thrust (thrust) *v.,* **thrust, thrust·ing.** —*v.t.* **1.** to push or shove forcibly or suddenly: *I thrust the money into my pocket.* **2.** to drive or force (a pointed instrument or weapon) into something or someone: *to thrust a fork into a piece of meat.* **3.** to put forcibly into some condition, position, or situation: *to thrust oneself into an argument.* —*v.i.* **1.** to make a stab or lunge, as with a pointed instrument or weapon: *to thrust with a knife.* **2.** to make or force one's way, as through a crowd. —*n.* **1.** a sudden, forceful push, shove, or drive: *The army made a thrust into enemy territory.* **2.** a stab. **3.** *Architecture.* the outward and downward pressure exerted by one part on another, as the pressure exerted by one stone on another in an arch. **4.** the driving force exerted by a rotating propeller. **5.** the force pushing a rocket or jet engine forward, created when hot gases, formed by the combustion of propellants, rush out through a rear nozzle. **6.** the main point or purpose: *What is the thrust of your argument?* [Old Norse *thrȳsta* to press, force.]

thrust·er (thrus′tər) *n.* a small rocket attached to and used to control a spacecraft after it is in orbit or has entered space.

thru·way (thrü′wā′) *also,* **throughway.** *n.* a wide, usually divided highway with limited points of access or exit, providing rapid and direct transit between distant points.

thud (thud) *n.* **1.** a dull, heavy sound. **2.** a heavy stroke or blow producing such a sound. —*v.i.,* **thud·ded, thud·ding.** to make a thud when falling or striking against something. [Probably from Old English *thyddan* to strike, push.]

thug (thug) *n.* **1.** a rough, brutal, and often violent person; ruffian. **2. Thug.** a member of a secret and violent religious society in northern India that robbed and strangled its victims, suppressed by the British in the 1830s. [Hindi *thag* cheat, robber who strangles travelers, from Sanskrit *sthaga* rogue.]

Thu·le (thü′lē) *n.* ultima Thule *(def. 1).*

thu·li·um (thü′lē əm) *n.* a soft, lustrous rare-earth element, an isotope of which is used in radiography. Symbol: **Tm** For tables, see **element.** [Modern Latin *thulium,* from THULE.]

thumb (thum) *n.* **1.** the short, thick finger of the human hand, next to the index finger. **2.** a corresponding digit in other primates. **3.** that part of a glove or mitten that covers the thumb. —*v.t.* **1.** to turn and glance at the pages of; leaf (with *through*): *to thumb through a magazine.* **2.** to soil or wear out by handling carelessly or frequently with or as with the thumb. **3.** *Informal.* to obtain or make by hitchhiking: *to thumb a ride, to thumb one's way to New York.* —*v.i. Informal.* to hitchhike. [Old English *thūma* the short, thick finger of the human hand.] —**thumb′like′,** *adj.*
• **all thumbs.** clumsy, as when using the hands.
• **thumbs down.** a sign or gesture expressing disapproval or rejection.
• **thumbs up.** a sign or gesture expressing approval or acceptance.
• **under the thumb of.** completely under the power, control, or influence of.

thumb-in·dex (thum′in′deks) *v.t.* to provide (a book) with a thumb index.

thumb index, a series of labeled, graduated indentations cut into the outside edges of the pages of a book that mark off and provide easy access to specific parts of the book.

thumb·nail (thum′nāl′) *n.* the nail of the thumb. —*adj.* very brief or concise: *a thumbnail sketch.*

thumb·print (thum′print′) *n.* **1.** an impression of the markings on the inner surface of the tip of a thumb, usually made with ink for purposes of identification. **2.** a distinguishing mark or characteristic; stamp: *The author's latest novel bears the thumbprint of an experienced storyteller.*

thumb·screw (thum′skrü′) *n.* **1.** a screw, often having a flat, upright head, designed to be turned by the thumb and a finger. **2.** formerly, an instrument of torture used to crush or squeeze the thumbs. Also *(def. 2),* **screw.**

thumb·tack (thum′tak′) *n.* a tack with a round, flat head, designed to be pressed into a wall, board, or the like by the thumb.

thump (thump) *n.* **1.** a heavy blow, as with a blunt object. **2.** the heavy, hollow sound made

thumbscrew
(def. 1)

by such a blow. —*v.t.* to beat or hit so as to produce a heavy, hollow sound: *I thumped my head on the floor when I fell.* —*v.i.* **1.** to produce a thump when falling or striking against something. **2.** to beat or pound heavily and with increasing rapidity; throb; pulsate: *My heart thumped when they announced the winner.* [Imitative.] —**thump′er,** *n.*

thump·ing (thum′ping) *adj.* **1.** that thumps. **2.** *Informal.* very great or impressive; large or excellent: *The play was a thumping success.* —**thump′ing·ly,** *adv.*

thun·der (thun′dər) *n.* **1.** a loud, rumbling sound produced by a lightning discharge as the result of rapid heating and expansion of the air along the path of the lightning. **2.** any noise resembling thunder: *the thunder of applause, the thunder of cannons.* **3.** a threatening, terrifying, or vehement utterance. —*v.i.* **1.** to give forth or produce thunder. **2.** to make a noise resembling thunder: *The train thundered into the station.* **3.** to make loud or strong denunciations or threats. —*v.t.* to express loudly or strongly, esp. in a threatening manner; roar. [Old English *thunor* the sound accompanying lightning.] —**thun′der·er,** *n.*
• **to steal someone's thunder.** to anticipate and use another's idea or methods without permission and without giving credit.

thun·der·bolt (thun′dər bōlt′) *n.* **1.** a flash of lightning accompanied by a clap of thunder. **2.** something that is sudden, unexpected, and terrible. **3.** a person who acts with sudden and furious energy.

thun·der·clap (thun′dər klap′) *n.* **1.** a loud crash or burst of thunder. **2.** something that is loud, sudden, and unexpected.

thun·der·cloud (thun′dər kloud′) *n.* a dark, billowing, electrically charged cloud that produces thunder and lightning.

thun·der·head (thun′dər hed′) *n.* one of the round, swelling cloud masses that often develops into a thundercloud.

thun·der·ous (thun′dər əs) *adj.* **1.** full of or producing thunder. **2.** producing a noise like thunder: *thunderous applause.* —**thun′der·ous·ly,** *adv.*

thun·der·show·er (thun′dər shou′ər) *n.* a rain shower accompanied by thunder and lightning.

thun·der·storm (thun′dər stôrm′) *n.* a storm accompanied by thunder and lightning, and usually rain.

thun·der·struck (thun′dər struk′) *adj.* stunned or shocked, as with disbelief or surprise; astonished; amazed. Also, **thun·der·strik·en** (thun′dər strik′ən).

thu·ri·ble (thŭr′ə bəl) *n.* censer. [Latin *t(h)uribulum,* from *t(h)ūs* incense, from Greek *thyos* burnt sacrifice.]

Thurs. *also,* **Thur.** Thursday.

Thurs·day (thûrz′dē, -dā) *n.* the fifth day of the week. [Old English *Thūres dæg* literally, Thor's day; influenced by Old Norse *Thōrsdagr* literally, Thor's day. See THOR.]

thus (thus) *adv.* **1.** in this, that, or the following way: *Written thus, the directions are easy to understand.* **2.** as a result; consequently; therefore: *I didn't study and thus failed the test.* **3.** to this extent or degree: *We have not heard from them thus far.* **4.** for example. [Old English *thus* in this way, to this extent.]

thwack (thwak) *v.t.* to strike vigorously with something flat; whack. —*n.* a sharp, vigorous blow with something flat. [Probably imitative.] —**thwack′er,** *n.*

thwart (thwôrt) *v.t.* **1.** to prevent from doing or achieving something; oppose successfully: *Nothing will thwart the team's quest for the championship.* **2.** to prevent (something, as a plan) from being accomplished or achieved. —*n.* a transverse seat in a boat, on which a rower or passenger sits. —*adj.* lying or extending across something; transverse. —*adv., prep. Archaic.* across; athwart. [Old Norse *thvert* across, originally neuter of *thverr* transverse.] —For Synonyms *(v.t.),* see **frustrate.**

thy (<u>th</u>ī) *Archaic. pron.* possessive case of **thou.** of or belonging to you; your. [Short for THINE.]

thyme (tīm) *n.* any of a group of erect or trailing plants, genus *Thymus,* of the mint family, whose leaves have a strong mintlike odor and are often used as a seasoning. [Latin *thymum,* from Greek *thymon.*]

thy·mine (thī′mēn, -min) *n.* a pyrimidine base that is an essential constituent of DNA. Formula: $C_5H_6N_2O_2$ For illustration, see **double helix.**

thy·mol (thī′môl) *n.* a crystalline compound made synthetically or obtained from an oil found in thyme and certain other plants, used esp. as an antiseptic. Formula: $C_{10}H_{14}O$

thy·mus (thī′məs) *n., pl.* **-mus·es** or **-mi** (-mī). an endocrine gland, located in the neck or chest, that is the primary gland of the lymphatic system, producing a hormone that plays a critical role in immunity. It grows from childhood to adolescence and then shrinks or disappears in adulthood. Also, **thymus gland.** [Modern Latin *thymus,* from Greek *thymos.*] —**thy·mic** (thī′mik), *adj.*

thy·roid (thī′roid) *n.* **1.** thyroid gland. **2.** thyroid cartilage. **3.** a medicine obtained from the dried and powdered thyroid glands of certain domestic animals, used in the treatment of disorders that result from the malfunctioning of the thyroid gland. —*adj.* of, relating to, or characteristic of the thyroid gland or thyroid cartilage. [Modern Latin *thyroides,* from Greek *thyreoeidēs* shield-shaped, from *thyreos* oblong shield (from *thyrā* door) + *eidos* form, shape.] —**thy·roi′dal,** *adj.*

thyroid cartilage, the largest cartilage of the larynx, which covers and protects the thyroid gland and forms the Adam's apple. Also, **thyroid.**

thyroid gland, an endocrine gland that secretes thyroxin, located in front of and on either side of the trachea. Also, **thyroid.**

thy·rox·in (thī rok′sin) *also,* **thy·rox·ine** (thī rok′sēn, -sin). *n.* a hormone obtained from the thyroid gland or made synthetically, important in regulating the growth and rate of metabolism of body cells, used in treating thyroid disorders, such as goiter and cretinism.

thyr·sus (thûr′səs) *n., pl.* **-si** (-sī). in Greek mythology, a staff topped with a pine cone and entwined with ivy and vine branches, carried by Dionysus and his attendants.

thy·self (thī self′) *pron. Archaic.* yourself. ➡ used as the reflexive or emphatic form of *thee* or *thou.*

ti (tē) *n. Music.* **1.** the seventh of the series of syllables used to name the eight tones of the diatonic scale. For illustration, see **do². 2.** the note B. [Modification of SI.]

Ti, the symbol for titanium.

ti·ar·a (tē ar′ə, -är′ə) *n.* **1.** a crownlike ornament, often made with jewels or precious metals, worn esp. by women. **2.** the triple crown worn by the pope, symbolic of the papal office. **3.** a raised headdress or high cap worn by the ancient Persians. [Latin *tiāra* ancient Oriental headdress, from Greek *tiārā* ancient Persian headdress.]

Ti·bet·an (ti bet′ən) *also,* **Thibetan.** *adj.* of, relating to, or characteristic of Tibet or its people, language, or culture. —*n.* **1.** a member or recent descendant of the Mongoloid people of Tibet. **2.** the language of Tibet, belonging to the Sino-Tibetan language family.

Tibetan Buddhism, the form of Buddhism that developed in Tibet and recognizes the Dalai Lama as its spiritual and political leader.

tiara

tib·i·a (tib′ē ə) *n., pl.* **tib·i·ae** (tib′ē ē′) or **tib·i·as. 1.** the inner and thicker of the two bones of the leg, extending from the knee to the ankle; shinbone. **2.** the corresponding bone in the legs of birds and certain other animals. **3.** in insects, the fourth joint of the leg, between the femur and the tarsus. **4.** an ancient flute, originally made from an animal's leg bone. [Latin *tībia* shinbone, flute.]

tib·i·al (tib′ē əl) *adj.* of or relating to the tibia.

tic (tik) *n.* a habitual, involuntary twitching of a muscle, esp. in the face or the extremities. [French *tic;* probably of imitative origin.]

tick¹ (tik) *n.* **1.** a light, rhythmic, clicking sound, as that made by a watch or a clock. **2.** a dot, slash, or other mark, often used in checking off items in a series. **3.** *British. Informal.* a very short

period of time, as between two ticks of a clock; instant. —*v.i.* **1.** to make a light, rhythmic, clicking sound, as that of a clock. **2.** (of time) to pass: *The minutes ticked away as we waited.* **3.** *Informal.* to work, function, or go: *What makes that person tick?* —*v.t.* to mark or indicate with or as with a tick (with *off*): *to tick names off a list.* [Probably imitative.]

   •**to tick off.** *Slang.* to cause to become angry, annoyed, or irritated.

tick² (tik) *n.* **1.** any of a group of wingless, insectlike arachnids, order Acarina, that are parasites of humans and animals, attaching themselves to the skin of the host and sucking its blood. Some ticks transmit diseases, such as Rocky Mountain spotted fever and Lyme disease. Length: to ½ inch (1 centimeter). **2.** any of various louselike insects, family Hippoboscidae, that are parasites of horses, sheep, and birds. [Old English *ticia.*]

tick³ (tik) *n.* **1.** the cloth covering or case of a mattress or pillow. **2.** *Informal.* ticking. [Middle Dutch *tīke* case², cover, going back to Latin *t(h)ēca,* from Greek *thēkē.*]

tick·er (tik′ər) *n.* **1.** a person or thing that ticks. **2.** a telegraphic receiving instrument that prints stock market reports or news on a paper tape. **3.** a similar device that displays such information electronically. **4.** *Slang.* the heart. **5.** *Slang.* a watch.

ticker tape, the paper tape or ribbon on which a ticker prints.

tick·et (tik′it) *n.* **1.** a card or piece of paper indicating that the bearer is entitled to specified rights, privileges, or services: *We have to buy our tickets before boarding the train. You must present your ticket when picking up your laundry.* **2.** a card, tag, or other piece of paper attached to something, esp. to indicate its contents, price, or owner. **3.** a list or group of candidates belonging to a particular political party, to be voted on in an election. **4.** a legal summons ordering a person to pay a fine or appear in court, esp. for a traffic violation. —*v.t.* **1.** to attach a ticket to: *They ticketed our baggage at the airport.* **2.** to serve with a legal summons, esp. for a traffic violation. **3.** to provide with a ticket or tickets: *to ticket airline passengers.* [Middle French *etiquet* a little note or bill¹, from Old French *estiquier* to attach. See ETIQUETTE.]

   •**to write one's own ticket.** to state and obtain one's own terms in an arrangement or agreement, esp. with respect to a fee or a salary.

tick·ing (tik′ing) *n.* a strong, durable fabric of closely woven cotton or linen twill, used esp. to make covers for mattresses and pillows.

tick·le (tik′əl) *v.,* **-led, -ling.** —*v.t.* **1.** to touch or stroke (a person or a part of the body) so as to produce a chilling or tingling sensation, often resulting in laughter. **2.** to please, amuse, or excite agreeably; delight: *The aroma from the kitchen tickled our taste buds. The children were tickled by the clown's antics.* —*v.i.* to feel or produce a chilling or tingling sensation. —*n.* **1.** the act of tickling or the state of being tickled. **2.** a tickling sensation: *A tickle in my throat made me cough.* [Of uncertain origin.]

   •**to be tickled pink.** *Informal.* to be extremely pleased or delighted.

tick·ler (tik′lər) *n.* **1.** a person or thing that tickles. **2.** a memorandum book, card index, or other device used to aid the memory.

tick·lish (tik′lish) *adj.* **1.** sensitive to tickling: *a ticklish person.* **2.** requiring caution, tact, and careful handling; delicate: *a ticklish situation.* **3.** easily offended; sensitive; touchy. —**tick′lish·ly,** *adv.* —**tick′lish·ness,** *n.*

tick·seed (tik′sēd′) *n.* **1.** coreopsis. **2.** beggar's-ticks.

tick·tock (tik′tok′) *n.* the sound made by a clock or watch. —*v.i.* to make this sound.

tick trefoil, any of a group of mostly weedy plants of the pea family, found worldwide and usually having pink or purple flowers.

tick·y-tack·y (tik′ē tak′ē) *Informal. adj.* **-tack·i·er, -tack·i·est.** lacking taste or style; cheap and unimaginative: *a development of ticky-tacky houses.* —*n., pl.* **-tack·ies.** something that is ticky-tacky: *a bargain counter full of ticky-tackies.* [From TACKY².]

tic-tac-toe (tik′tak tō′) *also,* **tick-tack-toe.** *n.* a game played with a diagram having nine squares, in which two players alternately put X's or O's in the squares. The winner is the first person to complete a row of three X's or O's.

a	at	e	end	o	hot	u	up	hw	white		about
ā	ape	ē	me	ō	old	ū	use	ng	song		taken
ä	far	i	it	ô	fork	ü	rule	th	thin	ə	pencil
âr	care	ī	ice	oi	oil	u̇	pull	<u>th</u>	this		lemon
		îr	pierce	ou	out	ûr	turn	zh	measure		circus

tid·al (tī′dəl) *adj.* **1.** of, relating to, or affected by tides: *a tidal basin, tidal action.* **2.** dependent on the state of the tide, as a ship whose time of arrival and departure is regulated by the time of the tides: *a tidal steamer.* —**tid′al·ly,** *adv.*

tidal bore, a high wave or wall of tidal water that forms in a funnel-shaped, shallow bay or estuary and moves upstream at high tide with great force. Also, **bore, eagre.**

tidal wave 1.a. tsunami. **b.** storm surge. **2.** any great movement or display of strong feeling, opinion, or sentiment: *A tidal wave of political unrest swept across the country.*

tid·bit (tid′bit′) *also,* **titbit.** *n.* a small, choice piece, as of food or gossip. [Dialectal English *tid* nice (of uncertain origin) + BIT².]

tid·dly·winks (tid′lē wingks′) *n.* a game in which the players attempt to propel small colored disks into a little cup by snapping them on the edge with a larger disk. ➡ used as singular. Also, **tid·dle·dy·winks** (tid′əl dē wingks′).

tide¹ (tīd) *n.* **1.** the regular rise and fall of the oceans and bodies of water connected to them, caused by the gravitational pull of the moon and the sun. High tide occurs at a given spot about every twelve hours and twenty-five minutes, with low tide occurring halfway between each high tide. **2.** flood tide. **3.** a general or dominant trend, tendency, or direction: *The tide of public opinion turned against the administration.* **4.** anything that tends to rise and fall or increase and decrease: *A tide of tourists swept through the town every summer.* **5.** time or season. ➡ used in combination: *wintertide.* —*v.,* **tid·ed, tid·ing.** —*v.t.* to carry, as with the tide. —*v.i.* to flow or surge like a tide. [Old English *tīd* time, season, opportunity.]

• **to tide over.** to aid in getting along during a difficult period or until a specific time: *This money should tide you over until payday.*

• **to turn the tide.** to reverse a condition or situation, esp. to a more favorable one.

tide² (tīd) *v.i.,* **tid·ed, tid·ing.** *Archaic.* to betide; befall; happen. [Old English *tīdan* to happen, from *tīd* time.]

tide·land (tīd′land′) *n.* **1.** land alternately covered and uncovered by tides. **2. tidelands.** an area of submerged land, often yielding oil, within the historical boundaries of a coastal state of the United States and regarded as belonging to it.

tide pool, a pool of water that remains on the shore or a reef after the tide recedes.

tide·wa·ter (tīd′wô′tər, -wot′ər) *n.* **1.** a body of water affected by tides. **2.** low-lying coastal land whose waters are affected by tides. **3.** water that inundates land at high tide. —*adj.* of, relating to, or situated along a tidewater.

tide·way (tīd′wā′) *n.* a channel in which a tidal current runs.

ti·dings (tī′dingz) *pl. n.* news; information: *The messenger brought good tidings.* [Old English *tīdung,* probably from Old Norse (plural) *tīthendi.*]

ti·dy (tī′dē) *adj.,* **-di·er, -di·est. 1.** arranged in a clean and orderly manner; well-organized: *a tidy kitchen.* **2.** inclined to keep oneself or one's things in a clean and orderly manner: *a tidy person.* **3.** *Informal.* relatively large; considerable: *We managed to save a tidy sum of money.* **4.** *Informal.* rather good; acceptable: *a tidy business arrangement.* —*v.,* **-died, -dy·ing.** —*v.t.* to arrange in a clean and orderly manner; make tidy (often with *up*): *to tidy up a room, to tidy the drawers in a desk.* —*v.i.* to arrange things or oneself in a clean and orderly manner (with *up*): *We tidied up after the guests left.* —*n., pl.* **-dies.** a small decorative covering placed over the back or arms of a chair or sofa to keep it from becoming soiled or worn; antimacassar. [Middle English *tidy* timely, in good condition, from *tid* time (from Old English *tīd*) + -Y¹.] —**ti′di·ly,** *adv.* —**ti′di·ness,** *n.*

tie (tī) *v.,* **tied, ty·ing.** —*v.t.* **1.** to fasten with a rope, string, or similar material: *to tie a price tag to a suit.* **2.** to fasten together, as with a rope or cord: *to tie a bundle of newspapers with string.* **3.a.** to make a knot or bow in: *to tie one's shoelaces.* **b.** to make a knot or bow with the strings or laces of: *to tie one's shoes.* **4.** to make (a knot or bow). **5.** to draw together or join closely or firmly: *Mutual interests tied us together.* **6.** to restrain or restrict; confine: *Family obligations tied me to my hometown.* **7.** to equal the record, score, or achievement of (an opponent). **8.** to equal (a record, score, or achievement). **9.** *Music.* to unite (notes) by a curved line written above or below two notes of the same pitch. —*v.i.* **1.** to be secured with a rope, string, or similar material: *This smock ties in the front.* **2.** to make the same record, score, or achievement; be equal: *The candidates tied in the preelection poll.* —*n.* **1.** a cord, string, or similar material used to tie things. **2.** anything that unites or joins together: *The business partners have long been bound by ties of friendship.* **3.** necktie. **4.a.** equality between opponents or competitors, as in scores, records, or

achievement: *The game ended in a tie.* **b.** competition where such equality occurs; draw: *The game was a tie.* **5.** a structural member, such as a beam or rod, that holds together or strengthens other members. **6.** one of the transverse pieces, usually of wood, to which railroad rails are fastened. **7. ties.** low shoes fastened with laces. **8.** *Music.* a curved line written above or below notes of the same pitch, indicating that the tone is to be held for the combined time values of the two notes. [Old English *tīgan* to secure, as with a rope, from *tēag* rope.] —For Synonyms *(n.),* see **bond.**

• **to tie down.** to restrict the action or movement of; confine: *Holding two jobs tied me down most days.*

• **to tie in.** to connect or be connected, esp. by being relevant or consistent: *This book ties in with the lecture series.*

• **to tie off.** to close off or constrict, as with a rope or cord: *We tied off the water hose so it would not leak.*

• **to tie up. a.** to secure with a rope, string, or similar material. **b.** to restrict the movement or action of; block: *The accident tied up traffic for hours.* **c.** to be in use, committed, or busy in such a way as to be unavailable for anything else: *We've tied up our cash in the stock market. The campaign had our staff tied up for weeks.* **d.** to bring to an end; finish, esp. successfully: *to tie up a business deal.* **e.** to make interrelated.

tie beam, a timber or piece serving as a tie, esp. the lowest horizontal member of a roof truss connecting the lower ends of the two principal rafters.

tie·break·er (tī′brā′kər) *n.* **1.** a period of additional play or any other method used to decide the winner when the players or teams are tied at the end of a contest. **2.** in tennis, a period of play used to decide a set tied at 6-6.

tie-dye (tī′dī′) *v.t.,* **-dyed, -dye-ing.** to dye (cloth) by the process of tie-dyeing.

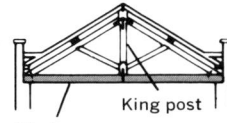

King post
Tie beam

tie beam

tie-dye·ing (tī′dī′ing) *n.* a process of dyeing cloth in which parts of the cloth are folded and tied so that they will not be exposed to the dye, thereby producing a mottled appearance.

tie-in (tī′in′) *n.* **1.** a relation or connection; link: *This report has no tie-in with our previous work.* **2.a.** a sale in which two articles are offered together so that the buyer must purchase both articles in order to get the desired one. **b.** one of the two articles sold in this manner, esp. the less desirable one.

tier¹ (tîr) *n.* one of a series of layers or rows, as of seats, arranged one above another: *The bleachers are arranged in two tiers.* —*v.t.* to arrange in tiers. [Old French *tire* rank¹, row¹, series, order; possibly of Germanic origin.] —**tiered,** *adj.*

ti·er² (tī′ər) *n.* a person or thing that ties. [TIE + -ER¹.]

tierce (tîrs) *n.* **1.** a sequence of three playing cards of the same suit. **2.** *Fencing.* the third guard position. **3.** *Music.* an interval of a third. **4.** the third of the seven canonical hours, or the service for it. [Old French *tierce,* feminine of *tiers* third, from Latin *tertius.*]

tie-up (tī′up′) *n.* **1.** a stoppage or slowdown of work, action, or progress: *The accident caused a tie-up at the intersection.* **2.** *Informal.* a connection or association; link: *I don't see the tie-up between those two events.*

tiff (tif) *n.* **1.** a slight, usually petty, quarrel; spat. **2.** a slight fit of bad temper or peevishness; huff. —*v.i.* to be in or have a tiff. [Of uncertain origin.]

ti·ger (tī′gər) *n.* **1.** a carnivorous Asian mammal, *Panthera tigris,* having a yellowish coat marked with black or brownish stripes. Length: 10 feet (4 meters), including tail. **2.** an energetic, aggressive person. [Old French *tigre,* from Latin *tigris,* from Greek *tigris.*] —**ti′ger·like′,** *adj.*

tiger beetle, any of a group of brightly colored beetles, family Cicindelidae, that prey on other insects and whose larvae live in burrows in sandy soil.

tiger cat 1. any of several small, tigerlike wildcats, such as the ocelot and serval. **2.** a domestic cat having striped markings, esp. a tabby.

ti·ger·eye (tī′gər ī′) tiger's-eye.

ti·ger·ish (tī′gər ish) *adj.* resembling a tiger in manner or appearance; fierce. Also, **tigrish.**

tiger lily, a lily, *Lilium lancifolium,* having reddish orange flowers spotted with black.

tiger moth, any of a large group of moths, family Arctiidae, found in temperate and tropical regions. [Because the wings of certain species which are banded in black and orange or yellow resemble a tiger's markings.]

ti·ger's-eye (tī′gərz ī′) *also,* **tigereye.** *n.* a semiprecious stone, usually yellowish brown and containing iron oxide, that has a variable luster and is a silicified form of an asbestos mineral.

tiger shark, a large shark, *Galeocerdo cuvieri,* with faint striping along the sides, inhabiting warm ocean waters. Length: to over 14 feet (4.3 meters). [Because it is so voracious.]

tight (tīt) *adj.* **1.** fastened or held firmly; secure: *These windows are too tight to open.* **2.** having its component parts close together; closely arranged or packed; compact; compressed: *That fabric has a tight weave.* **3.** of such close construction as to be impervious to liquid or gas: *a tight boat.* **4.** pulled or drawn to the fullest extent; taut: *Keep the volleyball net tight between the posts.* **5.** fitting the body closely, esp. too closely: *a tight belt.* **6.** having or allowing little time or space to spare: *a tight schedule.* **7.** difficult to deal with or manage: *to be in a tight spot financially.* **8.** strict; severe: *The government keeps tight controls on public utilities.* **9.** concisely worded or reasoned; terse; succinct: *a tight writing style.* **10.** allowing little room for dispute; well-organized: *The prosecution built a tight case around the evidence.* **11.** constricted, as from tension: *a tight feeling in the pit of one's stomach.* **12.** *Informal.* not generous, esp. with money; close-fisted; stingy. **13.** *Informal.* evenly matched; close: *a tight pennant race.* **14.** *Slang.* intoxicated; drunk. **15.** difficult to obtain; scarce: *Jobs are tight right now.* **16.** characterized by a scarcity, as of goods or money: *a tight market.* **17.** *Archaic.* well-made; trim; tidy. —*adv.* in a tight manner; firmly; securely: *to close a jar tight.* [Old Norse *thēttr* watertight, close.] —**tight′ly,** *adv.* —**tight′ness,** *n.*
• **to sit tight.** to hold onto one's position or opinion; take no action.
• **to sleep tight.** to sleep soundly.

tight·en (tī′tən) *v.t., v.i.* to make or become tight or tighter.

tight-fist·ed (tīt′fis′tid) *adj.* not generous, esp. with money; stingy; miserly.

tight-knit (tīt′nit′) *adj.* **1.** tightly knit. **2.** closely united or unified by common purpose, mutual interest, friendship, or the like: *a tightknit group of old school friends.*

tight-lipped (tīt′lipt′) *adj.* **1.** having the lips closed tightly. **2.** disinclined or reluctant to speak; quiet or secretive.

tight·rope (tīt′rōp′) *n.* a tightly stretched wire, cable, or rope, usually high above the ground, on which acrobats perform balancing feats.

tights (tīts) *pl. n.* a skin-tight garment covering the lower part of the body and the feet or extending from the waist to the ankles.

tight·wad (tīt′wod′) *n. Slang.* a stingy person; miser.

ti·gress (tī′gris) *n.* a female tiger.

ti·grish (tī′grish) tigerish.

tike (tīk) tyke.

til·bu·ry (til′ber′ē, -bə rē) *n., pl.* **-ries.** a light, open, two-wheeled carriage. [From *Tilbury,* the Englishman who designed it in the nineteenth century.]

til·de (til′də) *n.* **1.** in Spanish, a diacritical mark (˜) used over *n* to indicate the pronunciation *ny,* as in *señor* (sen yôr′). **2.** in Portuguese, the same mark, used over the vowels *a* and *o* to indicate nasal pronunciation, as in *João* (zhwouɴ). [Spanish *tilde* the diacritical mark, from Latin *titulus* superscription, label.]

tile (tīl) *n.* **1.** a thin, often decorated slab, as of baked clay, cement, porcelain, or linoleum, used for covering roofs, floors, or walls. **2.** tiles collectively; tiling. **3.** a piece used in playing various games, such as dominoes, mah jongg, or anagrams. **4.** a short pipe, as of baked clay or concrete, used as a drain. —*v.t.,* **tiled,** **til·ing.** to cover with tiles. [Old English *tigele* tile used for covering roofs, from Latin *tēgula* literally, that which covers, from *tegere* to cover.]

til·er (tī′lər) *n.* a person who makes or lays tile.

til·ing (tī′ling) *n.* **1.** tiles collectively. **2.** the act of covering with tiles. **3.** something covered with or consisting of tiles.

till[1] (til) *prep.* **1.** up to the time of: *Wait till tomorrow before calling.* **2.** before (a specified time): *Our friends won't arrive till Sunday.* —*conj.* **1.** up to the time when or that: *Wait till you hear from me before writing.* **2.** before: *We didn't see the manager till the meeting was over.* [Old English *til* to.]

till[2] (til) *v.t.* to prepare and use (land) for raising crops. [Old English *tilian* to labor, cultivate.] —**till′a·ble,** *adj.*

till[3] (til) *n.* a drawer or other receptacle in which money is kept, as in a store. [Of uncertain origin.]

till[4] (til) *n.* glacial drift that is unsorted and shows no signs of being stratified. Such material is deposited by being dropped directly from the ice of a glacier and consists of a jumbled mix of sand, gravel, boulders, and clay. [Possibly a form of Middle English *thill* thin layer of clay, possibly from *thille* board, flooring.]

till·age (til′ij) *n.* **1.** the cultivation of land. **2.** land that is under cultivation. Also, **tilth.**

till·er[1] (til′ər) *n.* a bar or handle used to turn the rudder of certain boats. [Old French *telier* weaver's beam, going back to Latin *tēla* web.]

till·er[2] (til′ər) *n.* a person or thing that tills land. [TILL[2] + -ER[1].]

till·er[3] (til′ər) *n.* a shoot that develops from the base of a stem, esp. characteristic of grasses. —*v.i.* to sprout tillers. [Old English *telgor, telga* branch, bough, shoot.]

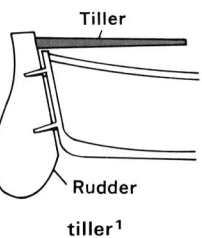

Tiller

Rudder

tiller[1]

tilt (tilt) *v.t.* **1.** to raise one end or side of; put at an angle; tip: *Don't tilt your chair or you will fall.* **2.a.** to point or thrust (a lance) in a joust. **b.** to charge (an opponent) in or as in a joust. —*v.i.* **1.** to be in or assume a sloping position or direction; incline. **2.** to engage in a joust. **3.** to charge or attack in or as in a joust (with *at*): *The young lawyer tilted at injustice.* —*n.* **1.** a sloping position; inclination: *The tilt of the table made everything roll off.* **2.** in medieval times, a contest between two mounted knights or other individuals armed with lances and other weapons; joust. **3.** any combat, confrontation, or struggle resembling this. [Middle English *tilten* to totter, fall, cause to fall, probably going back to Old English *tealt* unsteady.]
• **(at) full tilt.** (at) full speed or with full force: *The horse ran at full tilt. The cart crashed full tilt against the shed.*
• **to tilt at windmills.** to attack imaginary enemies or injustices.

tilth (tilth) *n.* **1.** tillage. **2.** the texture or composition of soil under cultivation. [Old English *tilth* tillage, crop.]

Tim., Timothy.

tim·bal (tim′bəl) also, **tymbal.** *n.* kettledrum. [French *timbale,* through Spanish, going back to Arabic *attabl* the drum.]

tim·bale (tim′bəl, tim bäl′) *n.* **1.a.** a dish made of finely minced meat, fish, vegetables, or cheese, cooked in a cream sauce in a mold. **b.** the mold, usually drum-shaped, in which such a dish is cooked. **2.** a small cup-shaped mold made of fried pastry and often filled with a minced meat mixture. [French *timbale* dish, as of meat or fish, prepared in a mold, kettledrum; referring to the resemblance of the mold to a drum. See TIMBAL.]

tim·ber (tim′bər) *n.* **1.** wood suitable for building, carpentry, or similar forms of construction. **2.** a single piece of wood used in construction; beam. **3.** one of the curved pieces leading from the keel and forming part of the framework of a ship. **4.** trees collectively. **5.** timberland; forest. —*interj.* a cry to warn others that a tree is being felled. —*v.t.* to cover, support, or provide with timber: *to timber an underground passage.* [Old English *timber* building, material for building.]

tim·bered (tim′bərd) *adj.* **1.** covered with growing trees; wooded: *a heavily timbered region.* **2.** built or made of timber.

timber hitch, a knot used to fasten a line around a spar, post, or the like. For illustration, see **knot.**

tim·ber·ing (tim′bər ing) *n.* **1.** timbers collectively. **2.** work made of timbers.

tim·ber·land (tim′bər land′) *n.* land covered with trees to be used commercially, esp. for lumber.

tim·ber·line (tim′bər līn′) *n.* tree line.

timber wolf, gray wolf.

tim·bre (tim′bər, tam′-) *n.* the characteristic property of sound, independent of pitch and volume, that distinguishes one voice or musical instrument from another. [French *timbre,* from Old French *timbre* bell that is struck by a hammer, drum, timbrel, going back to Greek *tympanon* kettledrum.]

tim·brel (tim′brəl) *n.* a tambourine or similar instrument. [Diminutive of Middle English *timbre,* from Old French *timbre.* See TIMBRE.]

time (tīm) *n.* **1.** the past, present, and future considered in terms of duration; every second there has ever been or will ever be. **2.** an indefinite extent during which events, conditions, and actions occur, exist, or continue in uninterrupted succession: *The changing seasons show the passing of time.* **3.** an exact point in time as shown by a clock or calendar: *What time is it?* **4.** a definite or specific point in time: *The senator has no comment at this time. I can only answer one question at a time.* **5.** a favorable, appropriate, customary, or appointed point in time: *Tomorrow between two and three o'clock is the time you should speak with your boss.* **6.** a particular point in time in which something has occurred, is occurring, or will occur: *At the time of their marriage,*

a	at	e	end	o	hot	u	up	hw	white		about
ā	ape	ē	me	ō	old	ū	use	ng	song		taken
ä	far	i	it	ô	fork	ü	rule	th	thin	ə	pencil
âr	care	ī	ice	oi	oil	u̇	pull	th	this		lemon
		îr	pierce	ou	out	ûr	turn	zh	measure		circus

they were living in Iowa. **7.** a definite or specific part or portion of time: *Summer is the warmest time of the year.* **8.** a portion of time available or necessary for some purpose: *I have no time to argue with you.* **9.** an amount of time: *There's very little time left before we have to go.* **10.** a specific amount of time taken or needed for the completion of a given action or process: *The runner's time for the mile was four minutes.* **11.** a system of measuring or computing time: *solar time.* **12.** *also,* **times. a.** a portion or extent of time in history: *the time of Julius Caesar, medieval times.* **b.** the present time, often considered with reference to prevailing conditions: *Are the times changing for the better or for the worse?* **13.** a portion or extent of time considered with reference to someone's personal experience: *I had a hard time finding a job.* **14.** lifetime: *Do you think science will discover a cure for this disease in our time?* **15.** one of a number of repeated or recurring actions or instances: *We have visited the library many times.* **16. times.** instances of being multiplied: *After four months, the rabbit was three times larger in size.* **17.a.** a period worked or to be worked by an employee. **b.** the pay received for this period. **18.** death: *The elderly couple felt their time was drawing near.* **19.** *Informal.* a period of imprisonment: *to serve time for robbery.* **20.** a rate of speed or movement, as in marching. **21.** *Music.* the rhythm, meter, or tempo, esp. of a particular kind of musical composition: *waltz time.* **22.** *Sports.* time-out. —*interj. Sports.* an indication that play has ended or is to be temporarily halted, as for substitutions or a discussion of strategy. —*v.t.,* **timed, tim·ing. 1.** to regulate, adjust, or arrange according to time: *The VCR was timed to come on at eight o'clock.* **2.** to measure or ascertain the time, duration, or rate of: *to time a runner, to time a cake while it is baking.* **3.** to choose the time or occasion for: *The mayor's announcement was timed to maximize its effect on the coming election.* —*adj.* **1.** of or relating to time. **2.** regulated, adjusted, or devised to operate at a certain time: *a time lock on a bank vault.* **3.** payable at a future date or in installments over a period of time. [Old English *tīma* period of existence or duration, point in such a period, era, age, opportunity.]

- **·against time.** in an effort to finish within or before a certain time: *The rescuers were working against time in their search for the survivors of the shipwreck.*
- **·ahead of time.** before the time due or expected; early: *We arrived at the appointed place ahead of time.*
- **·at the same time.** however; nevertheless.
- **·at times.** sometimes; occasionally.
- **·behind the times.** no longer in fashion or fashionable; old-fashioned; out-of-date.
- **·for the time being.** for the present; temporarily.
- **·from time to time.** now and then; occasionally.
- **·in good time. a.** at the proper time; within reasonable time: *You will be advised of your mission in good time.* **b.** when or sooner than expected; quickly: *We finished our work in good time.*
- **·in no time.** almost instantly; very rapidly.
- **·in time. a.** before it is too late: *Do you think we can get to the theater in time for the first act?* **b.** in the course of time; eventually: *In time, all this will be forgotten.* **c.** in the correct or corresponding rhythm or tempo: *to clap in time to music.*
- **·on time. a.** at the correct or appointed time; punctual or punctually: *Did you arrive at your job on time?.* **b.** payable in installments over a period of time: *to buy a car on time.*
- **·time after time** or **time and again.** again and again; repeatedly.
- **·time out of mind.** longer than can be remembered.
- **·to keep time. a.** to record time, as a clock. **b.** to heed, follow, or maintain the tempo of a passage or work of music.
- **·to make time. a.** to move rapidly, as in attempting to recover lost time. **b.** *Slang.* to progress in gaining favor or acceptance, as in carrying on a flirtation.

time and a half, a rate of payment equal to one and one half times the regular rate, as for overtime.

time bomb, a bomb that can be set to explode at a specific time.

time capsule, a receptacle containing records and objects of current culture, deposited in a secure place for discovery by some future age.

time·card (tīm′kärd′) *n.* a card for recording the number of hours that an employee has worked.

time clock, a clock with a mechanism for automatically recording the arrival and departure times of an employee on a timecard.

time-con·sum·ing (tīm′kən sü′ming) *adj.* taking up or wasting a great deal of time.

time deposit, a bank deposit that cannot be withdrawn without advance notice or until a specified future date.

time draft, a draft payable after a specified number of days stated in the draft.

time exposure 1. the exposure of a photographic film for a

relatively long period of time, as for several seconds. **2.** a photograph made by such an exposure.

time frame, a particular period of time during which something occurs or is scheduled to occur: *The time frame for production is six months.*

time fuse, a fuse set to detonate an explosive device at a specific time.

time-hon·ored (tīm′on′ərd) *adj.* revered, respected, or observed because of age or long usage: *a time-honored custom.*

time immemorial, time so long past as to be beyond memory or record.

time·keep·er (tīm′kē′pər) *n.* a person or thing that keeps, measures, or records time.

time·less (tīm′lis) *adj.* **1.** unaffected by the passage of time; eternal. **2.** referring to or characteristic of no particular time. —**time′less·ly,** *adv.* —**time′less·ness,** *n.*

time line, a representation of times or dates as points on a line, used to show the chronological relationship of events.

time lock, a lock having a mechanism that can be set to open at a specific time.

time·ly (tīm′lē) *adj.,* -li·er, -li·est. occurring at a suitable or appropriate time; well-timed. —**time′li·ness,** *n.*

time-out (tīm′out′) *n.* **1.** *Sports.* a short period of time during which play is stopped, as for substitutions or a discussion of strategy. **2.** any brief cessation of work or activity; break; respite.

time·piece (tīm′pēs′) *n.* any apparatus that records, measures, or keeps time, esp. a watch or clock.

tim·er (tī′mər) *n.* **1.** a person or thing that measures, records, or keeps time; timekeeper. **2.** a device for measuring intervals of time, such as a stopwatch. **3.** a device that indicates, as by a buzzer or bell, the lapse of a preset interval of time, or automatically starts or stops, at preset times, another mechanism, such as a light. **4.** a device in the ignition system of an internal-combustion engine that causes the spark to be produced in the cylinder at the right instant.

times (tīmz) *prep.* multiplied by: *Two times two equals four.*

time·sav·ing (tīm′sā′ving) *adj.* lessening the amount of time spent on or needed for doing something: *The microwave oven is a timesaving kitchen appliance.* —**time′sav′er,** *n.*

time·serv·er (tīm′sûr′vər) *n.* a person who conforms to the current or popular standards of conduct or thinking in order to achieve personal gain or win approval. —**time′serv′ing,** *adj., n.*

time-shar·ing (tīm′shâr′ing) *also,* **time sharing.** *n.* **1.** *Computers.* an arrangement by which a mainframe computer can simultaneously serve several users at different terminals. **2.** an arrangement by which two or more people share in the ownership or rental of a house or other dwelling and occupy it at different times of the year, as for vacations. Also *(def. 2),* **time share.**

time signature, a sign, usually expressed as a fraction, placed on a staff to indicate the meter of the music that follows.

time·ta·ble (tīm′tā′bəl) *n.* a list showing the times at which successive events are to be done or happen, esp. a schedule showing the arrival and departure times of trains, buses, boats, or airplanes.

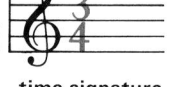

time signature
for three-quarter
time

time warp, a discontinuation, distortion, or reversal in the regular passage of time, used esp. as a literary device by writers of science fiction.

time·worn (tīm′wôrn′) *adj.* **1.** showing the effects of time or long use; worn; weathered. **2.** used too frequently; trite; stale: *a timeworn joke.*

time zone, any of the 24 longitudinal regions, of 15 degrees each, into which the earth is divided for measuring standard time from the prime meridian at Greenwich, England.

tim·id (tim′id) *adj.* characterized by or exhibiting a lack of courage, boldness, or self-confidence; shy: *The timid child hid whenever a visitor came to the house.* [Latin *timidus.*] —**ti·mid′i·ty,** **tim′id·ness,** *n.* —**tim′id·ly,** *adv.*

tim·ing (tī′ming) *n.* the act of determining and using the opportune moment or appropriate speed for some action or occurrence in order to produce the desired effect: *the timing of a batter's swing, the timing of a news release.*

tim·or·ous (tim′ər əs) *adj.* characterized by or exhibiting a lack of courage, boldness, or self-confidence; timid. [Medieval Latin *timorosus,* from Latin *timor* fear.] —**tim′or·ous·ly,** *adv.* —**tim′or·ous·ness,** *n.*

tim·o·thy (tim′ə thē) *n.* a tall, stout grass, *Phleum pratense,* having smooth, hollow stems with dense spikelike clusters of tiny flowers at the tips, cultivated for hay and sometimes for grazing. [From *Timothy* Hanson, U.S. farmer who supposedly brought it from New York to the Carolinas about 1720.]

Tim·o·thy (tim′ə thē) *n.* either of two books of the New Testa-

ment, I Timothy and II Timothy, consisting of epistles written to Timothy by the Apostle Paul.

tim·pa·ni (tim′pə nē) *also,* **tympani.** *pl. n., sing.,* **-no** (-nō′). kettledrums, esp. those played in an orchestra. [Italian *timpani,* plural of *timpano* kettledrum, from Latin *tympanum* drum. See TYMPANUM.] —**tim′pa·nist,** *n.*

tin (tin) *n.* **1.** a lustrous, silver-white, metallic element that resists rusting and corrosion, used esp. as a coating on sheet steel for cans and alloyed with copper to make bronze. Symbol: Sn For tables, see **element. 2.** tin plate. **3.** any object made of tin, such as a baking sheet. **4.** *British.* can² *(def. 2).* —*adj.* made or consisting of tin. —*v.t.,* **tinned, tin·ning. 1.** to cover, coat, or plate with tin. **2.** *British.* to preserve or pack in tin cans; can: *to tin peaches.* [Old English *tin* the metal.]

tin·a·mou (tin′ə mü′) *n.* any of various game birds, family Tinamidae, native to Central and South America, resembling the partridge. Length: 15 inches (38 centimeters). [French *tinamou,* from Carib *tinamu.*]

tinc·ture (tingk′chər) *n.* **1.** a solution, usually with alcohol as a solvent, containing a drug or other medicinal agent. **2.** a small amount; trace; hint: *a tincture of sadness in one's voice.* **3.** a tinge of color; tint: *a tincture of blue in the night sky.* —*v.t.,* **-tured, -tur·ing. 1.** to give a tinge of a peculiar quality or character to. **2.** to tint; stain. [Latin *tinctūra* a dyeing.]

tin·der (tin′dər) *n.* any substance that burns easily, esp. something used to kindle a fire from a spark, such as dry twigs. [Old English *tynder.*]

tin·der·box (tin′dər boks′) *n.* **1.** a box used for holding the materials necessary for kindling a fire, as flint or coal. **2.** any place or situation that is a potential source of strife or trouble.

tine (tīn) *n.* a sharp projecting point or prong, as of a fork. [Old English *tind.*]

tin·e·a (tin′ē ə) *n.* any of various skin eruptions due to a fungal infection, as ringworm or barber's itch. [Going back to Latin *tinea* gnawing worm, moth.]

tin·foil (tin′foil′) *n.* a very thin sheet of tin or other metal, such as aluminum, used as a wrapping, esp. for food.

ting (ting) *n.* a clear, high-pitched, metallic sound, as that made by a small bell. —*v.t., v.i.* to make or cause to make a ting. [Imitative.]

tinge (tinj) *v.t.,* **tinged, tinge·ing** or **ting·ing. 1.** to color slightly; tint; stain. **2.** to affect with a slight trace, touch, or flavor of some other quality or characteristic. —*n.* **1.** a faint trace of color. **2.** a small amount; touch; trace: *There was a tinge of autumn in the air.* [Latin *tingere* to moisten, dye.]

tin·gle (ting′gəl) *v.,* **-gled, -gling.** —*v.i.* **1.** to have a slight prickling or stinging sensation, as from sudden excitement, cold, or a sharp blow. **2.** to cause such a sensation. —*v.t.* to cause to tingle. —*n.* a tingling sensation. [Probably form of TINKLE.] —**tin′gly,** *adj.*

tin·horn (tin′hôrn′) *Slang. adj.* pretending to have qualities that one does not possess, such as influence, wealth, or skill: *a tinhorn gambler.* —*n.* a person who has tinhorn ways, esp. a gambler.

tink·er (ting′kər) *n.* **1.** a person, usually itinerant, who mends pots, pans, and other metal household utensils. **2.** a person who can do many different kinds of repair work; jack-of-all-trades. **3.** an unskillful or clumsy worker; bungler. —*v.i.* **1.** to busy oneself in a trifling or aimless way; putter: *to tinker with an old clock.* **2.** to work in an unskilled or clumsy manner. **3.** to work as a tinker; mend household utensils. [Possibly from obsolete *tink* to tinkle, ring (of imitative origin) + -ER¹; referring to the tinkling sound made in working on pots and pans.] —**tin′ker·er,** *n.*

tinker's damn *also,* **tinker's dam.** *Slang.* the slightest bit. ➡ *Your advice isn't worth a tinker's damn.*

tin·kle (ting′kəl) *v.,* **-kled, -kling.** —*v.i.* to produce or emit clear, light, ringing sounds, as those made by a tiny bell. —*v.t.* **1.** to cause to tinkle. **2.** to summon or call by tinkling. —*n.* a clear, light, ringing sound. [Obsolete *tink* to ring (of imitative origin) + -LE.]

tin·ner (tin′ər) *n.* a person who works with or deals in tin; tinsmith.

tin·ny (tin′ē) *adj.,* **-ni·er, -ni·est. 1.** of, relating to, or containing tin. **2.** having a metallic flavor, sound, or quality: *The canned juice had a tinny taste.* —**tin′ni·ness,** *n.*

Tin Pan Alley 1. a district, esp. one in New York City, associated with composers, performers, and publishers of popular music. **2.** these people collectively.

tin plate, thin sheets of metal, esp. iron or steel, coated with tin.

tin·sel (tin′səl) *n.* **1.** very thin strips of glittering metallic material, used for ornamentation, esp. on Christmas trees. **2.** anything showy or attractive but having little or no intrinsic worth. **3.** a fabric woven with metallic threads, as of silver or gold. —*v.t.,* **-seled, -sel·ing;** *also, British,* **-selled, -sel·ling.** to trim with or as with tinsel. —*adj.* **1.** made of, resembling, or decorated with

tinsel. **2.** showy or attractive but having little or no intrinsic worth. [Shortened from Middle French *estincelle* spark, flash, going back to Latin *scintilla* spark.] —**tin′sel·ly,** *adj.*

tin·smith (tin′smith′) *n.* a person who works with, repairs, or deals in tin, tinware, or other light articles made of metal.

tin·stone (tin′stōn′) *n.* cassiterite. [TIN + STONE.]

tint (tint) *n.* **1.** a trace of a color: *There are tints of gold in your hair.* **2.a.** the level or degree of lightness of a color, determined by the amount of white mixed with the pure hue: *The painter mixed a tint of red to suggest rosy cheeks in the portrait.* **b.** a delicate, pale color. **3.** a dye for the hair. —*v.t.* to add or give a slight color to: *The children tinted the Easter eggs with vegetable dye.* [Earlier *tinct,* from Latin *tinctus* a dyeing, from *tingere* to moisten, dye.] —**tint′er,** *n.* —For Synonyms *(n.),* see **hue¹.**

tin·tin·nab·u·la·tion (tin′tə nab′yə lā′shən) *n.* **1.** the ringing of bells. **2.** a sound produced by or as by bells. [Latin *tintinnābulum* bell + -ATION.]

tin·type (tin′tīp′) *n.* a photograph made on a tin-coated iron plate treated with a light-sensitive substance.

tin·ware (tin′wâr′) *n.* articles made of tin plate.

ti·ny (tī′nē) *adj.,* **-ni·er, -ni·est.** very small or slight; wee. [Obsolete *tine* (of uncertain origin) + -Y¹.]

-tion *suffix* (used to form nouns) **1.** the action or process of: *adoption.* **2.** the state or condition of being: *relaxation.* **3.** the result of: *contamination.* [Latin *-tiō,* often through French *-tion.*]

tip¹ (tip) *n.* **1.** the extreme or outermost point or end of anything: *to scuff the tip of one's shoe.* **2.** a small piece or part attached to or forming the end of something: *the tip of a pen.* —*v.t.,* **tipped, tip·ping. 1.** to furnish with a tip. **2.** to cover, decorate, or serve as the tip of. [Of uncertain origin.]

tip² (tip) *v.,* **tipped, tip·ping.** —*v.t.* **1.** to raise one end or side of. **2.** to cause to fall or tumble; overturn (often with *over*): *I accidentally tipped over the chair.* **3.** to raise or touch (one's hat) in greeting. —*v.i.* **1.** to be in or assume a sloping position or direction; tilt. **2.** to fall or topple (with *over*): *The table tipped over.* —*n.* an inclined position; tilt. [Of uncertain origin.]

tip³ (tip) *n.* **1.** a gift of money given in return for services rendered; gratuity: *I gave the bellhop a tip for carrying my suitcase.* **2.a.** an item of useful information, given privately or secretly, esp. by an expert: *a tip from a stockbroker.* **b.** any useful or helpful hint or suggestion: *My friends gave me some tips about buying a used car.* —*v.,* **tipped, tip·ping.** —*v.t.* to give a gratuity to. —*v.i.* to give a tip or tips. [Of uncertain origin.] —**tip′per,** *n.*

• **to tip off.** *Informal.* **a.** to give private or secret information to: *An informer tipped off the police about the whereabouts of the gang.* **b.** to warn of possible danger; caution: *Someone tipped off the criminals, and they got away before the police arrived.*

tip⁴ (tip) *v.t.,* **tipped, tip·ping. 1.** to strike or hit lightly; tap. **2.** *Baseball.* to hit (the ball) with a glancing blow. —*n.* **1.** a light, sharp blow; tap. **2.** *Baseball.* **a.** the act of hitting a ball with a glancing blow. **b.** a ball hit in this way. [Possibly of Low German origin.]

tip-off (tip′ôf′, -of′) *n. Informal.* **1.** an item of private or secret information providing useful data about a person, event, or situation. **2.** a warning of possible danger; caution.

tip·pet (tip′it) *n.* **1.** a scarflike covering worn about the neck and shoulders with loose ends hanging down in front. **2.** in the Anglican Church, a long black scarf worn over the robe of a member of the clergy. **3.** formerly, a long, narrow hanging part, as of a hood or sleeve. [Of uncertain origin.]

tip·ple¹ (tip′əl) *v.t., v.i.,* **-pled, -pling.** to drink (alcoholic beverages) habitually and frequently in small quantities. —*n.* alcoholic liquor. [Of uncertain origin.] —**tip′pler,** *n.*

tip·ple² (tip′əl) *n.* **1.** a device that empties loaded coal cars and the like by tipping them. **2.** the place where cars are emptied in this way. [Dialectal English *tipple* to tumble.]

tip·ster (tip′stər) *n. Informal.* a person who gives or sells private or secret information, esp. to bettors or speculators. [TIP³ + -STER.]

tip·sy (tip′sē) *adj.,* **-si·er, -si·est. 1.** slightly intoxicated. **2.** inclined to tip; unsteady; shaky. [From TIP².] —**tip′si·ly,** *adv.* —**tip′si·ness,** *n.*

tip·toe (tip′tō′) *v.i.,* **-toed, -toe·ing.** to move or walk on or as if on the tips of one's toes; walk quietly or stealthily. —*n.* the tip of a toe. —*adj.* **1.** standing or walking on or as if on the tips of one's toes. **2.** cautious; stealthy. —*adv.* cautiously; stealthily.

a	at	e	end	o	hot	u	up	hw	white		about
ā	ape	ē	me	ō	old	ū	use	ng	song		taken
ä	far	i	it	ô	fork	ü	rule	th	thin	ə	pencil
âr	care	ī	ice	oi	oil	u̇	pull	th	this		lemon
		îr	pierce	ou	out	ûr	turn	zh	measure		circus

• **on tiptoe. a.** standing or walking on the tips of one's toes. **b.** full of expectation or eagerness. **c.** quietly; stealthily.

tip·top (tip'top') *Informal. n.* the highest point or part. —*adj.* **1.** situated at the highest point. **2.** of the highest quality; first-rate; excellent.

ti·rade (tī rād', tī'rād') *n.* a long, vehement speech, esp. one containing abuse, criticism, or censure. [French *tirade* long speech, from Italian *tirata* literally, a pulling, from *tirare* to pull; of uncertain origin.]

tire[1] (tīr) *v.,* **tired, tir·ing.** —*v.t.* **1.** to weaken or exhaust the strength or energy of; make weary; fatigue: *Reading in the dim light tired my eyes.* **2.** to exhaust the attention, interest, or patience of; bore: *The speaker's monotonous voice tired the audience.* —*v.i.* **1.** to become fatigued or weary: *to tire easily.* **2.** to become bored with (with *of*): *The children tired of the new game quickly.* [Old English *tēorian* to weary or become weary.] • **to tire out.** to weary to the point of exhaustion.

tire[2] (tīr) *also, British,* **tyre.** *n.* a doughnut-shaped band, usually of rubber, either solid or filled with air under pressure, mounted on the rim of a wheel and usually having a tread. Tires absorb shock and provide traction for a wide variety of wheeled vehicles. [Possibly from TIRE[3]; because thought of as the wheel's *attire*.]

tire[3] (tīr) *Archaic. n.* **1.** attire. **2.** headdress. —*v.t.,* **tired, tir·ing.** to dress. [Short for ATTIRE.]

tired (tīrd) *adj.* fatigued; weary; exhausted. [TIRE[1] + -ED[2].] —**tired'ly,** *adv.* —**tired'ness,** *n.*

tire·less (tīr'lis) *adj.* never wearying; untiring: *a tireless worker.* —**tire'less·ly,** *adv.* —**tire'less·ness,** *n.*

tire·some (tīr'səm) *adj.* tedious; boring; tiring: *tiresome details.* —**tire'some·ly,** *adv.* —**tire'some·ness,** *n.*

ti·ro (tī'rō) *n., pl.* **-ros.** tyro.

'tis (tiz) *contr.* it is.

tis·sue (tish'ü) *n.* **1.** in animals and plants, a group of similar cells performing the same function. In the human body there are four basic types of tissue: epithelium, connective tissue, muscle, and the tissue forming the nervous system. **2.** a soft, thin, absorbent piece of paper, usually consisting of two layers, used esp. as a handkerchief. **3.** tissue paper. **4.** a woven fabric, usually having a light, gauzy texture. **5.** an interwoven series or sequence; network; web: *a tissue of lies.* [Old French *tissue* woven, woven cloth, from *tistre* to weave, from Latin *texere.*]

tissue paper, a very thin, nearly transparent paper, used esp. for wrapping or packing.

tit[1] (tit) *n.* **1.** titmouse. **2.** any of various small birds, such as the pipit. [From TITMOUSE.]

tit[2] (tit) *n.* a teat or breast. [Old English *tit.*]

Ti·tan (tī'tən) *n.* **1.** in Greek mythology, any of a race of giants who were the offspring or descendants of Uranus and Gaea and who ruled the world until overthrown by the Olympian gods. **2. titan.** a person who has extraordinary size, strength, or power. **3.** the largest of Saturn's moons, the only moon in the solar system with its own atmosphere. —*adj.* Titanic.

ti·ta·nate (tī'tə nāt') *n.* any of the various salts formed when an oxide of titanium reacts with an alkali compound. [TITAN(IUM) + -ATE[2].]

Ti·ta·ni·a (ti tā'nē ə, tī-) *n.* in medieval folklore, the wife of Oberon and queen of the fairies.

ti·tan·ic (tī tan'ik) *adj.* **1.** having great size, strength, or power. **2.** Titanic. of, relating to, or characteristic of the Titans. —**ti·tan'i·cal·ly,** *adv.*

ti·ta·ni·um (tī tā'nē əm, ti-) *n.* a light, strong, silver-white, metallic element, used esp. to make steel and other alloys for structural parts and engines of aircraft and spacecraft. Symbol: Ti For tables, see **element.** [From TITAN.]

titanium dioxide, a white, powdery compound identical in chemical composition to rutile, used as a pigment and as a filler for plastics and rubber. Formula: TiO₂

ti·tan·o·there (tī tan'ə thir') *n.* any of a family, Brontotheriidae, of extinct, rhinoceroslike mammals of Eocene and Oligocene geologic time, related to the horse.

tit·bit (tit'bit') *n.* tidbit.

tit for tat, retaliation in kind; blow for blow.

tithe (tīth) *n.* **1.** one tenth of a person's annual income, paid in either labor or money, esp. for the support of a church and its clergy. **2.** one tenth of anything. **3.** any small tax, tribute, or levy. **4.** a very small part. —*v.t.,* **tithed, tith·ing. 1.** to impose a tax of a tenth on. **2.** to give one tenth of (one's annual income), esp. for the support of a church and its clergy. [Old English *tēotha,* contraction of *teogotha* tenth.] —**tith'a·ble,** *adj.* —**tith'er,** *n.*

Ti·tho·nus (ti thō'nəs) *n.* in Greek Mythology, the beloved of Eos, who secured immortality for him but not eternal youth, so that he became old and shriveled and was finally changed into a grasshopper.

ti·tian (tish'ən) *n.* a reddish or golden brown color. —*adj.* having the color titian. [From *Titian,* 1477?-1576, Venetian painter who often used this color in painting hair.]

tit·il·late (tit'ə lāt') *v.t.,* **-lat·ed, -lat·ing. 1.** to excite or stimulate agreeably: *to titillate the imagination.* **2.** to produce a tickling sensation in. [Latin *tītillātus,* past participle of *tītillāre* to tickle.] —**tit'il·lat'er,** *n.* —**tit'il·la'tion,** *n.*

tit·i·vate (tit'ə vāt') *v.t., v.i.,* **-vat·ed, -vat·ing.** *Informal.* to add finishing touches to; dress up; spruce up. [Possibly from TIDY, on the model of CULTIVATE.] —**tit'i·va'tion,** *n.*

tit·lark (tit'lärk') *n.* pipit. [TIT[1] + LARK[1].]

ti·tle (tī'təl) *n.* **1.** the name by which a particular thing, such as a book, painting, statue, poem, song, or play, is identified, known, or referred to. **2.** a general or descriptive heading, as of a chapter or section of a book. **3.** a word or group of words attached to the proper name of a person or family, used as an expression of respect or to indicate office, rank, occupation, status, or the like. *Madam, Lord, Lady, Professor, Doctor,* and *Sergeant* may be used as titles. **4.** in certain sports, the championship: *the heavyweight boxing title.* **5.** *Law.* **a.** a right that a person has to the ownership of property: *to have title to a house.* **b.** something that serves as evidence of such a right, such as a deed. **c.** the means by which one acquires such a right. **6.** a section of a bill or law, usually given a roman numeral. **7.** an established or recognized right; just claim. —*v.t.,* **-tled, -tling.** to give a title to; call; entitle: *to title an essay.* [Old French *title* name indicating rank, designation of a subject treated in a book, from Latin *titulus* label, superscription. Doublet of TITTLE.]

ti·tled (tī'təld) *adj.* having a title, esp. one of rank: *titled nobility.*

title deed, a deed that constitutes or is evidence of title to property.

ti·tle·hold·er (tī'təl hōl'dər) *n.* the holder of a title, esp. a championship title in a sport.

title page, a page at the beginning of a book, usually containing the title of the book and the names of the author and publisher.

title role, the role or character in a play, motion picture, or other theatrical presentation for which the presentation is named. *Macbeth* is the title role of Shakespeare's play *Macbeth.*

ti·tlist (tī'tə list, tīt'list) *n.* a titleholder of a championship.

tit·mouse (tit'mous') *n., pl.* **-mice** (-mīs'). any of various small, plump songbirds, family Paridae, having soft, thick, predominantly gray and brown plumage. Length: 3-8 inches (8-20 centimeters). Also, **tit.** [Middle English *titemose,* from *tit* something small (of imitative origin) + Old English *māse* titmouse.]

Ti·to·ism (tē'tō iz'əm) *n.* a system of national communism based on independence from the Soviet Union, nonalignment in foreign policy, and decentralized economic development, established by Marshal Tito in Yugoslavia in the late 1940s.

ti·trate (tī'trāt) *v.t., v.i.,* **-trat·ed, -trat·ing.** *Chemistry.* to determine the concentration of (a solution) by titration. [French *titrer* (from *titre* standard, qualification, heading, going back to Latin *titulus* label) + -ATE[1].]

ti·tra·tion (tī trā'shən) *n. Chemistry.* a method of determining the concentration of a solute in a solution by noting the amount of a solution of known strength that must be added to produce a completed chemical reaction, as shown by a certain effect, such as a change in the color of the solution.

ti·tri·met·ric (tī'trə met'rik) *adj.* measured or determined by titration: *a titrimetric analysis.* —**tit'ri·met'ri·cal·ly,** *adj.*

tit·ter (tit'ər) *v.i.* to laugh in a restrained or nervous manner. —*n.* a restrained or nervous laugh. —**tit'ter·er,** *n.*

tit·tle (tit'əl) *n.* **1.** a very small part or amount; minute quantity. **2.** a small diacritical mark, as over a letter, in writing or printing. The dot over a *j* is a tittle. [Medieval Latin *titulus* mark over a word, accent, from Latin *titulus* label, superscription. Doublet of TITLE.]

tit·tle-tat·tle (tit'əl tat'əl) *v.i.,* **-tled, -tling.** to talk idly or foolishly; chatter. —*n.* idle or foolish talk; chatter. [Repetition of TATTLE, with a change of vowel in the first syllable.]

tit·u·lar (tich'ə lər) *adj.* **1.** having the title or name of an office without having or exercising the powers or duties associated with it; nominal: *The former president was the titular leader of the political party.* **2.** having a title, esp. of nobility; titled. **3.** of or designating a title role: *the titular character in a play.* [Latin *titulus* label, superscription + -AR[1].] —**tit'u·lar·ly,** *adv.*

Ti·tus (tī'təs) *n.* a book of the New Testament, consisting of an Epistle written to Titus by the Apostle Paul.

tiz·zy (tiz'ē) *n., pl.* **-zies.** *Slang.* a state of extreme excitement, agitation, or confusion; dither. ➡ used chiefly in the phrase *to be in a tizzy.* [Of uncertain origin.]

Tl, the symbol for thallium.

Tlin·git (tling'git) *n., pl.* **-git** or **-gits. 1.** a member of a North American Indian tribe living along the coast of the southernmost

T

part of Alaska and portions of the coast of British Columbia. **2.** the language of this tribe.

Tm, the symbol for thulium.

TM, transcendental meditation.

tme·sis (tə mē′sis, mē′sis) *n.* the insertion into a compound word of another word or words, as in *what might be soever* for *whatsoever might be.* [Greek *tmēsis* a cutting.]

tn *also,* **tn.** ton; tons.

TN, the postal abbreviation for Tennessee.

TNT, a yellow, crystalline compound, made from toluene, widely used as a high explosive. Formula: $C_7H_5N_3O_6$ [Abbreviation of T(RI)N(ITRO)T (OLUENE).]

to (tü; *unstressed* tů, tə) *prep.* **1.a.** in the direction of; toward: *Turn to the left. His back was to the audience. She pointed to a clump of trees.* **b.** in the direction of and reaching: *We took the train to London. The tree fell to the ground.* **2.** as far as: *wet to the skin, generous to a fault.* **3.** near or in contact with; on, upon, or against: *Tack the carpet to the floor.* **4.** toward or into a condition of: *The glass was smashed to bits. They worked to exhaustion.* **5.** so as to cause or result in: *To our surprise, they agreed with our plan.* **6.** for the purpose of; for: *The coast guard came to our aid.* **7.** until: *The store is open from nine to six.* **8.** before: *It's five minutes to three.* **9.** as compared with: *Our team won by a score of three to one.* **10.** comprising; constituting: *There are two pints to a quart.* **11.** accompanied by; along with; with: *We danced to the music.* **12.** belonging with or used with: *the vest to a suit.* **13.** in agreement or accord with: *a plan drawn to scale.* **14.** in honor of: *They drank a toast to their success.* **15.** regarding; about; concerning: *That's all there was to it.* **16.** also used: **a.** for indicating the application of an adjective: *hostile to strangers, unknown to us, a portrait that is true to life.* **b.** for indicating the application of a noun: *a newcomer to the city, a pretender to the throne.* **c.** for indicating the recipient of an action: *The mail carrier gave the letter to me.* **d.** for introducing the infinitive form of a verb: *I learned to swim last summer.* ➡ In this sense *to* is often used alone when the verb is understood from the context: *You may go home whenever you want to.* —*adv.* **1.** forward: *The boat turned to.* **2.** into a shut or closed position: *Please push the door to.* **3.** to the matter at hand; to action or work. [Old English *tō* toward, until, in order to, so as to result in.]

toad (tōd) *n.* **1.** any of a group of froglike amphibians, family Bufonidae, found in most temperate regions of the world, having dry, warty skin and relatively short legs, and living most of its

toad

life on land rather than in water. **2.** any of various toadlike reptiles, such as the horned toad. **3.** a person or thing regarded as repugnant, hideous, or contemptible. [Old English *tāde,* short for *tādige.*]

toad·fish (tōd′fish′) *n., pl.* **-fish** or **-fish·es.** any of a group of stout, scaleless fish, family Batrachoididae, found in temperate and tropical waters along the Atlantic coast of the Americas, having a large, sharp-toothed mouth and often poisonous spines on the back. Length: to 18 inches (46 centimeters).

toad·flax (tōd′flaks′) *n.* butter-and-eggs.

toad·stool (tōd′stül′) *n.* any of various umbrella-shaped mushrooms, esp. one regarded as inedible or poisonous.

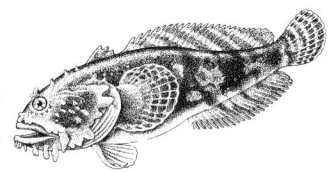

toadfish

toad·y (tō′dē) *n., pl.* **toad·ies.** a person who flatters another for personal gain; obsequious, fawning person. —*v.,* **toad·ied, toad·y·ing.** —*v.i.* to be or behave like a toady (with *to*): *to toady to one's superiors.* —*v.t.* to fawn upon in an obsequious manner. [From earlier *toadeater* assistant of a charlatan who pretended to eat a *toad* (once considered poisonous) so that the charlatan might appear to save the assistant's life with his quack medicines.] —**toad′y·ism,** *n.*

to-and-fro (tü′ən frō′) *adj.* moving forward and backward; back-and-forth: *to-and-fro movement.* —*n., pl.* **-fros.** a regular forward and backward movement: *the to-and-fro of a pendulum.*

to and fro, alternately in opposite directions; forwards and backwards: *to swing to and fro.*

toast¹ (tōst) *n.* sliced bread browned by heat. —*v.t.* **1.** to brown by heating, as in a toaster or over a fire. **2.** to warm thoroughly, as before a fire or heater: *to toast one's feet.* —*v.i.*

to become toasted: *Bread toasts more evenly in the new toaster.* [Old French *toster* to roast, going back to Latin *tostus,* past participle of *torrēre* to parch.]

toast² (tōst) *n.* **1.** the act of drinking in honor of or to the health of a person or thing: *There were several toasts to the bride and groom.* **2.** a person or thing that is honored in this way: *The senator was the toast of the banquet.* —*v.t.* to drink in honor of or to the health of: *At midnight, we toasted the New Year.* —*v.i.* to propose or drink a toast or toasts. [From TOAST¹; supposedly from the former practice of flavoring liquor by putting spiced *toast* in it.]

toast·er¹ (tōs′tər) *n.* a device, usually electrical, for toasting bread. [TOAST¹ + -ER¹.]

toast·er² (tōs′tər) *n.* a person who proposes a toast. [TOAST² + -ER¹.]

toaster oven, an electric oven that fits on a kitchen counter and is used for toasting, broiling, or baking small amounts of food.

toast·mas·ter (tōst′mas′tər) *n.* a person who proposes the toasts and introduces the guests and speakers at a formal dinner or other gathering.

toast·mis·tress (tōst′mis′tris) *n.* a woman who proposes the toasts and introduces the guests and speakers at a formal dinner or other gathering.

toast·y (tōs′tē) *adj.,* **toast·i·er, toast·i·est.** **1.** of or like toast. **2.** warm and cozy: *a toasty fire, a toasty sweater.*

Tob., Tobit.

to·bac·co (tə bak′ō) *n., pl.* **-cos.** **1.** the prepared leaves of any of various plants, genus *Nicotiana,* of the nightshade family, used for smoking, chewing, and as snuff. **2.** any of these plants, esp. *N. tabacum,* having large, lance-shaped leaves covered with hairs and pink, white, or red, funnel-shaped flowers. **3.** products prepared from the leaves of these plants, such as cigars, cigarettes, or snuff. [Spanish *tabaco* the plant, its leaves, from Taino *tabaco* pipe in which the plant was smoked, roll of tobacco leaves for smoking.]

tobacco mosaic virus, a viral disease of tobacco, tomato, and other plants of the nightshade family, characterized by mottled leaves.

to·bac·co·nist (tə bak′ə nist) *n.* a dealer in tobacco.

to-be (tə bē′) *adj.* expected to be the thing indicated in the immediate or foreseeable future. ➡ usually used after a noun and in combination: *a party for the husband-and-wife-to-be.*

To·bi·as (tə bī′əs) *n.* in the Douay Bible, Tobit.

To·bit (tō′bit) *n.* a book of the Protestant Apocrypha.

to·bog·gan (tə bog′ən) *n.* a long, flat-bottomed sled without runners and having a curled-up front end, used for coasting on snow or for transporting goods. —*v.i.* **1.** to coast or ride on a toboggan. **2.** to decline or decrease rapidly, as in value. [Micmac *tobāgun* type of Algonquian Indian sled.] —**to·bog′gan·er, to·bog′gan·ist,** *n.*

to·by (tō′bē) *n., pl.* **-bies.** a small jug or mug, usually in the form of a fat man wearing a long coat and a three-cornered hat. Also, **toby jug.** [From *Toby,* familiar form of *Tobias,* masculine proper name.]

toc·ca·ta (tə kä′tə) *n.* a musical composition for a keyboard instrument, written in the style of an improvisation, intended to exhibit the performer's technique. [Italian *toccata,* from *toccare* to touch, play (a keyboard instrument), from an assumed Vulgar Latin word based on an imitation of the sound of striking.]

to·coph·er·ol (tō kof′ə rôl′) *n.* vitamin E. [Greek *tokos* childbirth + *pherein* to bear¹ + -OL.]

toc·sin (tok′sin) *n.* **1.** a signal or alarm sounded on a bell. **2.** a bell or other signal used to sound an alarm. [French *tocsin* alarm bell, going back to Provençal *tocar* to strike, touch (from an assumed Vulgar Latin word based on an imitation of the sound of striking) + *senh* bell, mark (from Latin *signum* mark).]

to·day (tə dā′) *also,* **to-day.** *n.* the present day, time, or age. —*adv.* **1.** on or during the present day. **2.** at the present time; nowadays; currently: *Fashions today are different from what they were ten years ago.* [Old English *tōdæg(e)* on this day.]

tod·dle (tod′əl) *v.i.,* **-dled, -dling.** to walk or move with short, unsteady steps, as a child who is just learning to walk. —*n.* the act of toddling. [Of uncertain origin.]

tod·dler (tod′lər) *n.* a small child, esp. one who is just learning to walk.

tod·dy (tod′ē) *n., pl.* **-dies.** **1.** a drink made with brandy or other liquor, hot water, spices, sugar, and sometimes a slice of

a	at	e	end	o	hot	u	up	hw	white		about
ā	ape	ē	me	ō	old	ū	use	ng	song		taken
ä	far	i	it	ô	fork	ü	rule	th	thin	ə	pencil
âr	care	ī	ice	oi	oil	ů	pull	th	this		lemon
		îr	pierce	ou	out	ûr	turn	zh	measure		circus

lemon. Also, **hot toddy. 2.a.** a drink made from the fermented sap of certain East Indian palm trees. **b.** the sap of such trees. [Hindi *tārī* sap of the palm tree, from *tār* palm tree, from Sanskrit *tāla;* probably of Dravidian origin.]

to-do (tə dü′) *n., pl.* **-dos.** *Informal.* bustle or fuss; commotion.

toe (tō) *n.* **1.** any of the five separate parts at the end of the foot. **2.** the part of a stocking, shoe, or other piece of footwear that covers the toes. **3.** the forward part of a foot or hoof. **4.** anything resembling a toe in shape, position, or function. —*v.,* **toed, toe·ing.** —*v.t.* **1.** to furnish with a toe or toes. **2.a.** to drive (a nail) obliquely. **b.** to fasten or attach by nails driven in this way; toenail. —*v.i.* to turn the toes in a specific direction: *to toe out.* [Old English *tā* any of the five digits of the human foot.]
  • **on one's toes.** mentally or physically prepared for action; alert; ready.
  • **to step** (or **tread**) **on someone's toes.** to offend or irritate someone, esp. by intruding on that person's authority, responsibility, or rights.
  • **to toe the line** (or **mark**). **a.** to act in accordance with an established rule, standard, or code of behavior; conform. **b.** to stand with the tips of one's toes touching a starting line or mark, as in a race.

toed (tōd) *adj.* having toes, esp. a specific number or kind of toes. ➡ usually used in combination: *a three-toed sloth, square-toed shoes.*

toe·hold (tō′hōld′) *n.* **1.** a small ledge, ridge, or niche from which one may secure just enough support for a toe or some part of the foot, esp. in climbing. **2.** a means by which to enter, advance, or gain an advantage: *Once the infection gained a toehold, it spread rapidly.* **3.** a hold in which one wrestler twists the foot of the other.

toe·nail (tō′nāl′) *n.* **1.** a nail that grows on a toe. **2.** a carpenter's nail driven obliquely. —*v.t.* to fasten or attach with obliquely driven nails.

tof·fee (tô′fē, tof′ē) *also,* **toffy.** *n., pl.* **-fees.** a hard, chewy candy made of butter, sugar, and often nuts. [Of uncertain origin.]

tof·fy (tô′fē, tof′ē) *n., pl.* **-fies.** toffee.

to·fu (tō′fü) *n.* a soft, white food made from mashed soybeans, formed into a cake, widely used in Asian and vegetarian cooking. Also, **bean curd.** [Japanese *tōfu.*]

tog (tog) *Informal. n.* **togs.** clothes, esp. those worn for a particular activity: *tennis togs, riding togs.* —*v.t.,* **togged, tog·ging.** to dress or array (often with *out* or *up*). [Possibly short for obsolete *togemans* cloak, from Latin *toga* man's outer garment worn in ancient Rome.]

to·ga (tō′gə) *n.* **1.** a loose outer garment draped over the entire body, covering the left arm and leaving the right arm exposed, worn by citizens of ancient Rome. The approximate social position of a person could be determined by the color and ornamentation of the toga worn. **2.** a robe or similar garment characteristic of an office or profession. [Latin *toga* man's outer garment worn in ancient Rome.] —**to′gaed,** *adj.*

to·geth·er (tə geth′ər) *adv.* **1.** one with the other; with one another; in company: *The bride and her father walked down the aisle together.* **2.** in or into one gathering, company, mass, or body: *The staff will meet together next week.* **3.** in or into union, contact, combination, or association with each other: *The streets come together at the intersection. Mix the flour and water together.* **4.** in or into agreement, harmony, or cooperation: *Let's try to get together on this problem.* **5.** considered as a whole: *The coach is wiser than all of us together.* **6.** at the same time; simultaneously: *The three sirens went off together.* **7.** without intermission; continuously: *It rained for three days together.* **8.** *Slang.* in a stable, well-organized condition: *If you want to graduate, you better get yourself together.* [Old English *tōgædere* into one company or gathering, into union.]

to·geth·er·ness (tə geth′ər nis) *n.* **1.** the state or condition of being in the company of one another. **2.** a feeling or sense of fellowship or of belonging together, as that of members of a family.

tog·ger·y (tog′ə rē) *n., pl.* **-ger·ies.** *Informal.* clothes; togs.

tog·gle (tog′əl) *n.* **1.** a pin, bolt, or rod put through the eye of a rope or the link of a chain to prevent slipping, to tighten, or to secure an attachment. **2.** an ornamental, oblong button sewn on clothing or other items and serving as a fastening when inserted through a loop or similar opening. **3.** a toggle joint, or a device having one. **4.** toggle switch. —*v.t.,* **-gled, -gling.** to fasten or furnish with a toggle or toggles. [Of uncertain origin.]

toggle bolt, a bolt designed to anchor something heavy to a hollow wall, having two hinged wings that close for passage through a hole drilled in the wall and then spring open to hold the bolt in place.

toggle joint, a joint consisting of two bars pivoted together end to end and bent at an angle so that when a force is applied to the

joint to straighten it, pressure is transmitted to the outer ends.

toggle switch, a switch consisting of a projecting lever whose movement, as up or down, opens or closes an electric circuit. Also, **toggle.**

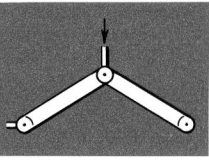
toggle joint

toil¹ (toil) *n.* hard and exhausting work or effort. —*v.i.* **1.** to engage in hard and exhausting work, esp. for a considerable length of time: *The workers toiled to build the railroad.* **2.** to move with difficulty, weariness, or pain. [Anglo-Norman *toiller* to dispute, strive, from Old French *toeillier* to make dirty, drag about, stir, from Latin *tudiculāre* to stir up, from *tudicula* machine for bruising olives, from *tundere* to beat.] —**toil′er,** *n.*

toil² (toil) *n.* **1.** *usually,* **toils.** something that ensnares or entangles as a net: *The drug smugglers were caught in the toils of the law.* **2.** *Archaic.* a net for trapping game. [French *toile* cloth, web, from Latin *tēla* web.]

toi·let (toi′lit) *n.* **1.** a fixture consisting of a water-filled basin usually having a lid, a hinged seat, and a flushing device connected to a water tank, used for the elimination and disposal of human waste products. **2.** a room containing such a fixture; bathroom. **3.** the act or process of washing, dressing, and grooming oneself; toilette. **4.** *Archaic.* a dressing table. **5.** a person's dress; attire. —*adj.* of, relating to, or for the toilet. [French *toilette* doily, dressing table, lavatory, dress, diminutive of *toile* cloth. See TOIL².]

toilet paper, thin, absorbent paper, usually in a roll, used for cleaning oneself after using a toilet.

toi·let·ry (toi′li trē) *n., pl.* **-ries.** any of various articles, such as soap or cologne, used in grooming oneself.

toi·lette (toi let′, twä-) *n.* **1.** the act or process of washing, dressing, and grooming oneself. **2.** a person's dress or manner of dress. [French *toilette.* See TOILET.]

toilet water, a scented liquid serving as a light perfume, as for use after a bath; cologne.

toil·some (toil′səm) *adj.* requiring hard work; tiresome; laborious. —**toil′some·ly,** *adv.* —**toil′some·ness,** *n.*

toil·worn (toil′wôrn′) *adj.* exhausted or worn out by toil or hard work.

to·ka·mak (tō′kə mak′) *n.* an experimental prototype of a thermonuclear reactor that uses a chamber shaped like a torus or doughnut to confine a plasma, with strong magnetic fields to guide the charged particles of the plasma so that they do not touch the chamber walls.

To·kay (tō kā′) *n.* **1.** a rich, golden wine varying from dry to very sweet. **2.** any similar wine. **3.** the whitish or purplish grape from which this wine is made. [From *Tokay,* a town in Hungary, where this wine was first made.]

to·ken (tō′kən) *n.* **1.** something that serves to indicate or represent some fact, event, object, or feeling; sign; symbol: *This gift is a token of our appreciation.* **2.** something given as an expression of affection or as a memento; keepsake. **3.** something, as a printed card or badge, that serves to indicate authenticity, authority, or identity. **4.** a piece of metal resembling a coin, used as a substitute for money, as in paying for transportation fares or in operating a telephone. **5.** in various board games, a playing piece. —*adj.* **1.** having little or no value, force, or effect: *a token fee, token resistance.* **2.** being the only one of its kind; serving merely for show: *to be the token female representative on a committee.* [Old English *tāc(e)n* sign, symbol.]
  • **by the same token.** in an equivalent manner; likewise; similarly.
  • **in token of.** as evidence, proof, or indication of.

tol·bu·ta·mide (tol bū′tə mīd′) *n.* an oral drug used to treat diabetes by stimulating release of insulin from the pancreas. Formula: $C_{12}H_{18}N_2O_3S$

told (tōld) *v.* the past tense and past participle of **tell.**
  • **all told.** counting all; in all: *They invited fifty people all told.*

To·le·do (tə lē′dō) *n., pl.* **-dos.** a fine-tempered sword blade or sword, as formerly made in Toledo, Spain.

tol·er·a·ble (tol′ər ə bəl) *adj.* **1.** capable of being endured; bearable: *a tolerable pain.* **2.** moderately good; passable: *a tolerable performance.* [Latin *tolerābilis* bearable, endurable, from *tolerāre* to bear¹, endure.] —**tol′er·a·ble·ness,** *n.* —**tol′er·a·bly,** *adv.*

tol·er·ance (tol′ər əns) *n.* **1.** the ability or willingness to accept or respect the behavior, customs, opinions, or beliefs of others. **2.** the act of tolerating or the state or quality of being tolerant. **3.** the ability to take, resist, or endure increasing amounts of something, such as a drug or poison, without being affected. **4.** the power or ability to endure something, such as pain. **5.** a permissible deviation from a specified standard, as in the weight of coins or in the size of a machine part.

Synonyms Tolerance and toleration mean a willingness to accept or respect behavior, actions, or beliefs that differ from one's own. **Tolerance** suggests a liberal or humane attitude: *Although the couple disagreed radically on social issues, each showed great tolerance for the other's belief.* **Toleration** often implies sufferance rather than acceptance: *a toleration of eccentric behavior, a toleration of extremist political positions.*

tol·er·ant (tol′ər ənt) *adj.* **1.** inclined to accept or respect the behavior, opinions, customs, or beliefs of others. **2.** capable of resisting or enduring the effects of something, such as a drug or poison. —**tol′er·ant·ly,** *adv.*

tol·er·ate (tol′ə rāt′) *v.t.,* **-at·ed, -at·ing. 1.** to allow to exist or be done without prohibiting or interfering: *to tolerate the practice of different religions.* **2.** to suffer or endure; put up with; bear: *How can you tolerate all that noise while you're working?* **3.** to develop or have tolerance for (a drug, poison, or the like). [Latin *tolerātus,* past participle of *tolerāre* to bear[1], endure.]

tol·er·a·tion (tol′ə rā′shən) *n.* **1.** the act or practice of tolerating. **2.** recognition of an individual's right to certain freedoms and privileges, esp. freedom of worship. —For Synonyms, see **tolerance.**

toll[1] (tōl) *v.i.* (of a bell) to sound with slow, regular strokes; peal. —*v.t.* **1.** to cause (a bell) to sound with slow, regular strokes. **2.** to announce or summon by tolling: *The bells tolled the hour.* —*n.* **1.** the act of tolling a bell. **2.** the sound made by a bell being tolled. [Middle English *tollen* to pull, draw (referring to pulling a bell to make a sound); of uncertain origin.]

toll[2] (tōl) *n.* **1.** a tax or fixed fee paid for the right or privilege to use something, such as a bridge, highway, or tunnel. **2.** a charge for a particular service rendered, as the transmission of a long-distance telephone call. **3.** a number of people or things lost, destroyed, or damaged: *The earthquake took a heavy toll of lives.* [Old English *toll* payment, tax, duty, going back to Late Latin *telōnium* custom house, from Greek *telōnion,* from *telos* tax.]

toll bar, a gate or other barrier, as across a road, used to obstruct passage until a toll is paid.

toll·booth (tōl′büth′) *n., pl.* **-booths** (-büthz′, -büths′). a booth, as at a toll bridge, where a toll is collected.

toll bridge, a bridge at which a toll is charged for passage.

toll call, a telephone call costing more than a local call, such as a long-distance call.

toll collector, a person employed to collect tolls at a tollbooth or tollgate. Also, **toll·keep·er** (tōl′kē′pər).

toll·gate (tōl′gāt′) *n.* a gate or other barrier used to obstruct passage until a toll is paid.

toll road, a road on which a toll is collected for the privilege of using it.

Tol·tec (tol′tek) *n.* a member of a group of Nahuatl-speaking Indian tribes dominant in central and southern Mexico from the eleventh to the thirteenth centuries. —*adj.* of, relating to, or characteristic of the Toltecs or their culture or civilization. Also *(adj.),* **Tol·tec′an.**

to·lu (tə lü′) *n.* a fragrant balsam obtained from a tropical tree, genus *Myroxylon,* of the pea family, used in cough drops, candies, and chewing gum and in making perfumes. [From Santiago de *Tolú,* city in Colombia where it is found.]

tol·u·ene (tol′ū ēn′) *n.* a flammable, aromatic hydrocarbon compound that smells like benzene, made from petroleum, used as a solvent and for making explosives and dyes. Formula: C_7H_8 [TOLU (from which it was first obtained) + -ENE.]

tom (tom) *n.* the male of certain animals, esp. cats. —*adj.* male: *a tom turkey.* [From *Tom,* familiar form of the masculine proper name *Thomas.*]

tom·a·hawk (tom′ə hôk′) *n.* a light ax used as a weapon or tool by North American Indians. —*v.t.* to attack, strike, or kill with a tomahawk. [Algonquian *tämähāk,* short for *tämähākan* cutting implement.]

to·ma·to (tə mā′tō, -mä′-) *n., pl.* **-toes. 1.** the juicy red, green, or yellow fruit of one of two plants, *Lycopersicon lycopersicum* or *L. pimpinellifolium,* of the nightshade family, eaten as a vegetable either raw or cooked. **2.** the plant itself, bearing yellow, bell-shaped flowers. [Spanish *tomate,* from Nahuatl *tomatl.*]

tomb (tüm) *n.* **1.** a vault or chamber in which a dead body is placed. **2.** any place of burial; grave. [Old French *tombe* grave, from Late Latin *tumba,* from Greek *tymbos.*] —**tomb′like′,** *adj.*

tom·boy (tom′boi) *n.* a young girl who enjoys those activities and interests that are traditionally considered to be preferred by boys. —**tom′boy′ish,** *adj.* —**tom′boy′ish·ness,** *n.*

tomb·stone (tüm′stōn′) *n.* a stone placed at the head of a grave, usually inscribed with the dead person's name and dates of birth and death.

tom·cat (tom′kat′) *n.* a male cat.

tom·cod (tom′kod′) *n.* either of two small cod, *Microgradus*

tomcod of the North Atlantic, or *M. proximus* of the North Pacific. Length: to 14 inches (36 centimeters).

Tom, Dick, and Harry, any people taken at random. ➡ often used disparagingly and preceded by *every: They seem to know every Tom, Dick, and Harry in town.*

tome (tōm) *n.* **1.** a book, esp. a large, heavy, scholarly one. **2.** one of a set of books containing several volumes. [French *tome* volume, from Latin *tomus,* from Greek *tomos.*]

tom·fool (tom′fül′) *adj.* extremely stupid or foolish: *a tomfool thing to do.* —*n.* a person who acts in a stupid or foolish manner.

tom·fool·er·y (tom′fü′lə rē) *n., pl.* **-er·ies.** foolish or absurd behavior; nonsense.

Tom·my gun (tom′ē) *Informal.* Thompson submachine gun.

tom·my·rot (tom′ē rot′) *n. Informal.* utter nonsense; foolishness.

to·mog·ra·phy (tə mog′rə fē) *n.* an X-ray technique, used in medical diagnosis, that produces detailed images of body tissues in a series of different planes. The data thus acquired are then processed by computer to obtain a three-dimensional image of the interior of the body or of selected parts. [From Greek *tomos* section + -GRAPHY.] —**to·mo·graph·ic** (tō′mə graf′ik), *adj.* —**to′mo·graph′i·cal·ly,** *adv.*

to·mor·row (tə mor′ō, -môr′ō) *n.* **1.** the day after today: *Tomorrow is my birthday.* **2.** some indefinite time in the future: *The world of tomorrow will be very different.* —*adv.* **1.** on the day after today: *We are going away tomorrow.* **2.** in the future, esp. the near future. [Middle English *to morwe,* going back to Old English *tō* to + *morgen* morning, morrow.]

Tom Thumb 1. in English folklore, a dwarf no larger than a thumb. **2.** any diminutive person or thing.

tom·tit (tom′tit′) *n.* any of various small birds, such as the titmouse and wren.

tom-tom (tom′tom′) *n.* **1.** any of various small drums, usually beaten with the hands. **2.** a dull, repetitious sound, as that made by a tom-tom. [Hindi *tam-tam* drum; of imitative origin.]

ton (tun) *n.* **1.a.** a unit of weight equal to 2,000 pounds avoirdupois (907.2 kilograms) in the United States and Canada. Also, **short ton. b.** a unit of weight equal to 2,240 pounds avoirdupois (1,016 kilograms) in Great Britain. Also, **long ton. 2.** a unit for measuring the carrying capacity of a ship, equal to 100 cubic feet (2.8 cubic meters). **3.** a unit for measuring the freight-carrying capacity of a ship, equal to 40 cubic feet (1.1 cubic meters). **4.** a unit for measuring the weight of water displaced by a ship, equal to 35 cubic feet (1 cubic meter) of seawater weighing approximately 1 long ton. **5.** metric ton. **6.** *Informal.* an extremely large quantity of anything: *I have a ton of work to do before I leave.* [Old English *tunne* barrel, large cask (referring to its weight when full). See TUN.]

ton·al (tō′nəl) *adj.* of or relating to tone or tonality. —**ton′al·ly,** *adv.*

to·nal·i·ty (tō nal′i tē) *n., pl.* **-ties. 1.** *Music.* **a.** the melodic and harmonic relation existing between the tones of a scale or musical system. **b.** a particular scale or system of tones; key. **2.** the arrangement of tones or colors, as in a painting or photograph.

tone (tōn) *n.* **1.** any sound considered with reference to its pitch, quality, duration, or volume. **2.** the quality of sound: *This stereo has good tone.* **3.** *Music.* **a.** a sound having definite pitch and character. **b.** a whole step. **4.** a particular style or manner of speaking or writing: *an angry tone of voice.* **5.** a general or prevailing character, style, or tendency, as of thought or behavior: *The tone of the meeting was serious.* **6.** a degree of tension or firmness, as of muscle; tonicity. **7.** the effect of the combination of light, shade, and color, as in a painting: *a silvery tone.* **8.** a tint or shade of a particular color: *The painter used various tones of blue.* —*v.,* **toned, ton·ing.** —*v.t.* **1.** to give a particular tone or quality to, as in sound or color. **2.** to alter or correct the color of. —*v.i.* **1.** to harmonize in color. **2.** to assume a particular color or tint. [Latin *tonus* sound, a stretching, from Greek *tonos* musical note, a stretching, thing stretched.] —**tone′less,** *adj.* —**tone′-less·ly,** *adv.*

• **to tone down.** to soften or lessen, as in volume, intensity, or severity.

• **to tone up.** to increase or gain, as in strength, intensity, or vitality.

tone arm, the device on a phonograph that holds the cartridge.

tone-deaf (tōn′def′) *adj.* unable to distinguish differences in musical pitch. —**tone′-deaf′ness,** *n.*

a	at	e	end	o	hot	u	up	hw	white		about
ā	ape	ē	me	ō	old	ū	use	ng	song	ə	taken
ä	far	i	it	ô	fork	ü	rule	th	thin		pencil
âr	care	ī	ice	oi	oil	u̇	pull	<u>th</u>	this		lemon
		îr	pierce	ou	out	ûr	turn	zh	measure		circus

1265

tone language, a language, such as Thai or Chinese, in which different pitches of the voice distinguish words that would otherwise sound identical.

tong (tong, tông) *v.t.* to grasp, hold, or handle with tongs. [From TONGS.]

tongs (tongz, tôngz) *pl. n.* any of various devices for grasping objects, usually having two curved arms connected by a pivot. [Old English *tange.*]

tongue (tung) *n.* **1.** the movable organ attached to the floor of the mouth, used in tasting, swallowing, and, in human beings, for talking. **2.** an animal's tongue prepared and used as food. **3.** a spoken language or dialect: *My native tongue is English.* **4.** a manner of speaking, esp. in regard to meaning or intent: *a biting tongue.* **5.** the ability to speak; power of speech: *I knew the subject, but when I got up in front of the class I couldn't find my tongue.* **6.** anything resembling the

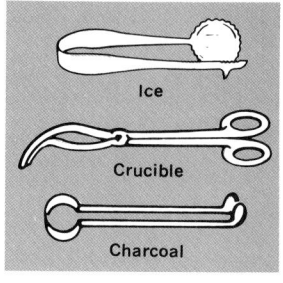

tongs

human tongue in shape, position, or function, as a tapering jet of flame. **7.** a narrow strip of land projecting into a body of water. **8.** a strip of leather or other material lying under the laces or fastenings of a shoe or boot. **9.** the clapper of a bell. **10.** a pole of a wagon, carriage, or similar vehicle to which horses are yoked. **11.** a free or vibrating end of a reed in a musical wind instrument. **12.** *Carpentry.* a projecting strip on the edge of a board that fits into a groove on the edge of another board, thereby forming a **tongue-and-groove joint.** —*v.,* **tongued, tongu·ing.** —*v.t.* **1.** to articulate or interrupt the tones of (a flute or certain other wind instruments) with the tongue. **2.** to touch or lick with the tongue. **3.** *Carpentry.* to cut a tongue on (a board). **4.** *Archaic.* to scold or reprimand. —*v.i.* to use the tongue in playing the flute and certain other wind instruments. [Old English *tunge* the movable organ in the mouth, power of speech, language.] —**tongue'-less,** *adj.* —**tongue'like',** *adj.*

• **on the tip of one's tongue.** on the verge of being remembered or spoken.
• **to hold one's tongue.** to refrain from speech; be silent.
• **(with) tongue in cheek.** with sarcasm or irony; insincerely.

tongue-in-cheek (tung'in chēk') *adj.* sarcastic or ironic; insincere: *a tongue-in-cheek remark.*

tongue-tied (tung'tīd') *adj.* **1.** unable to speak or express oneself, as from fear, shyness, or embarrassment. **2.** unable to speak distinctly because of an abnormally short frenum.

tongue twister, a word, phrase, or sentence that is difficult to pronounce distinctly and rapidly, usually because of the repetition of a sound or sounds. *Round the ragged rock the ragged rascal ran* and *Peter Piper picked a peck of pickled peppers* are tongue twisters.

ton·ic (ton'ik) *n.* **1.** anything that refreshes, invigorates, or strengthens: *The cool weather was a tonic after the heat spell.* **2.** a medicine or drug that invigorates or strengthens. **3.** *Music.* a note on which a scale or system of tones is based. **4.** a carbonated beverage containing quinine, used for mixing with liquor, such as gin or vodka. **5.** a liquid preparation for the hair or scalp. —*adj.* **1.** refreshing; bracing; invigorating. **2.** *Physiology.* denoting or characterized by continuous contraction, esp. of the muscles: *tonic spasm.* **3.** of or relating to tone or tones. **4.** *Music.* of, relating to, or based on a tonic: *a tonic chord.* **5.** of, relating to, or characterized by tone or pitch, as certain languages: *the tonic changes of the Chinese language.* [Greek *tonikos* relating to stretching, relating to tones, from *tonos* musical note, a stretching.] —**ton'i·cal·ly,** *adv.*

to·nic·i·ty (tō nis'i tē) *n.* the normal elastic tension or tone of living muscles, arteries, and other parts of the body. Also, **tonus.**

to·night (tə nīt') *n.* **1.** the night of this day: *The weather report says tonight will be rainy.* **2.** the present night; this night: *Tonight has been rather cool so far.* —*adv.* on or during the present or coming night. [Old English *tōniht* on the night of this day. See TO, NIGHT.]

ton·nage (tun'ij) *n.* **1.** the carrying capacity of a ship, expressed in tons. **2.** the total amount of shipping, as of a port or nation, with reference to carrying capacity. **3.** a duty, tax, or similar charge levied on ships at so much per ton of cargo. **4.** weight measured in tons, as of goods shipped or produced.

tonne (tun) *n.* metric ton.

ton·neau (tə nō') *n.* **1.** a rear compartment in an early type of automobile, containing seats for passengers. **2.** the body of an

automobile having such a compartment. [French *tonneau* cask, diminutive of *tonne* cask. See TUNNEL.]

ton·sil (ton'səl) *n.* **1.** either of a pair of oval masses of spongy lymphoid tissue located on each side of the tongue at the back of the mouth in human beings, which produce lymphocytes and thereby protect against infection. **2.** any of several similar masses of tissue located in the mouth or throat of amphibians, birds, reptiles, and mammals. [Latin *tōnsillae* (plural) tonsils, diminutive of *tōlēs* (plural) goiter.] —**ton'sil·lar;** *also,* **ton'sil·ar,** *adj.*

ton·sil·lec·to·my (ton'sə lek'tə mē) *n., pl.* -**mies.** the surgical removal of a tonsil or tonsils. [Latin *tōnsillae* tonsils + Greek *ektomē* a cutting out.]

ton·sil·li·tis (ton'sə lī'tis) *n.* inflammation of a tonsil or tonsils. [Latin *tōnsillae* tonsils + -ITIS.]

ton·so·ri·al (ton sôr'ē əl) *adj.* of or relating to a barber or a barber's work. ➡ often used humorously. [Latin *tōnsōrius* relating to shaving (from *tōnsor* barber) + -AL[1].]

ton·sure (ton'shər) *n.* **1.** in the Roman Catholic and Orthodox churches, a shaving of a part or all of the head of a person entering the priesthood of a monastic order. **2.** that part of the head so shaven. —*v.t.,* -**sured,** -**sur·ing.** to shave the head of. [Latin *tōnsūra* a shearing, clipping.]

ton·tine (ton'tēn, ton tēn') *n.* **1.** an annuity shared by a group of subscribers, with the share of the survivors increasing as various subscribers die, until a specified time or until the last survivor receives the total amount that is left. **2.** the share that each subscriber contributes. **3.** the share that each surviving subscriber receives. **4.** the subscribers to such an annuity, collectively. **5.** any of various similar insurance plans. [French *tontine* the annuity, the share, from Lorenzo *Tonti,* seventeenth-century Italian banker who devised the system.]

to·nus (tō'nəs) *n.* tonicity.

ton·y (tō'nē) *adj.,* **ton·i·er, ton·i·est.** *Informal.* fashionable or stylish, often pretentiously so: *a tony neighborhood.* [TONE + -Y[1].]

too (tü) *adv.* **1.** in addition; besides; also: *Your friend is very bright and a good worker too.* **2.** more than enough: *There were too many people in the room.* **3.** exceedingly; very: *I was not too sorry to see them go.* **4.** *Informal.* indeed. ➡ used for emphasis: *You will too come!* [Form of TO.]

took (tůk) the past tense of **take.**

tool (tül) *n.* **1.** any of various devices held in the hand and used in doing work, such as a hammer, wrench, or saw. **2.a.** a power-driven instrument or machine used to cut and shape machinery parts. **b.** the cutting or shaping part of such an instrument or machine. **3.** a person who is manipulated or used by another; dupe. **4.** anything used in or necessary to the carrying out of an action, profession, or trade: *A good library is an invaluable tool for doing research projects.* —*v.t.* **1.** to work, shape, or mark with a tool. **2.** to provide (a factory or plant) with machinery or tools for production (often with *up*). **3.** to impress or ornament (something, such as leather) with special hand tools. **4.** to drive (a vehicle). —*v.i.* **1.** to work with a tool or tools. **2.** to drive a vehicle: *They tooled along the country road.* [Old English *tōl* implement for manual work, means.] —**tool'er,** *n.*

tool·box (tül'boks') *n.* a box or chest for storing or carrying tools.

tool·ing (tü'ling) *n.* **1.** work or ornamentation done with special tools, esp. stamped or gilded designs on leather. **2.** the process of providing a factory or plant with machinery or tools in preparation for production.

toot (tüt) *v.t.* to cause (a horn, whistle, or the like) to sound with a short, quick blast or blasts. —*v.i.* to produce a short, quick blast or blasts: *The factory whistle tooted every day at noon.* —*n.* **1.** a short, quick blast, as that produced by a horn. **2.** the act of producing such a sound. [Imitative.]

tooth (tüth) *n., pl.* **teeth. 1.** in humans and certain other vertebrates, one of the hard, calcified structures set in the jaws and supported by the gums, used esp. for biting and chewing. A human adult has thirty-two permanent teeth. **2.** a similar structure in certain invertebrates. **3.** something resembling a tooth in shape or function, as one of the projecting pieces on a comb. **4. teeth.** denture. **5.** a taste or palate for something: *a sweet tooth.* **6. teeth.** that part of something that is most ravaging or destructive. —*v.t.* **1.** to

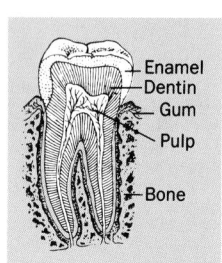

tooth

furnish or supply with teeth or toothlike projections: *to tooth a saw.* **2.** to make jagged, as an edge. [Old English *tōth* one of the bonelike structures set in the jaws.] —**tooth′like′,** *adj.*

•**in the teeth of.** in the face of; in opposition to.
•**long in the tooth.** old; elderly.
•**to fight tooth and nail.** to fight with all one's strength.
•**to get** (or **sink**) **one's teeth into.** to become completely involved in; get a firm grasp on.
•**to put teeth into.** to give force or effect to: *to put teeth into a law.*
•**to the teeth.** to the utmost degree; completely; fully: *armed to the teeth, dressed to the teeth.*

tooth·ache (tüth′āk′) *n.* a pain in a tooth, the teeth, or the surrounding area.

tooth·brush (tüth′brush′) *n.* a small, narrow brush with a long handle, used for cleaning the teeth.

toothed (tütht) *adj.* **1.** having teeth, esp. of a specific kind or number. ➡ usually used in combination: *a saber-toothed tiger.* **2.** having notches; serrated; jagged: *a toothed leaf.*

toothed whale, any member of the cetacean suborder Odontocetes, having cone-shaped teeth and a single blowhole, such as the sperm whale, dolphin, and porpoise.

tooth·less (tüth′lis) *adj.* **1.** having no teeth. **2.** without force or effect; ineffectual: *a toothless law.*

tooth·paste (tüth′pāst′) *n.* a paste dentifrice used for cleaning the teeth.

tooth·pick (tüth′pik′) *n.* a small, narrow sliver of wood, plastic, or similar material, used to remove food or other matter from between the teeth.

tooth powder, a powdered dentifrice.

tooth shell, any of a class, Scaphopoda, of bottom-dwelling, marine mollusks having a slightly curved, tusk-shaped shell open at both ends, with an extensible foot at the larger end. Also, **scaphopod.**

tooth·some (tüth′səm) *adj.* **1.** pleasing to the taste; palatable; tasty. **2.** attractive; pleasant. —**tooth′some·ly,** *adv.* —**tooth′some·ness,** *n.*

top¹ (top) *n.* **1.** the highest or uppermost point, part, surface, or end of something: *the top of a flagpole, the top of a page, the top of the stairs, the top of a hill.* **2.** the cover or lid of something, or a part forming a cover: *a box top.* **3.** a garment for the upper half of the body, usually part of a two-piece outfit: *a pajama top.* **4.** the head, esp. the crown of the head. **5.** the part of certain plants that grows above ground; stalk and leaves of a plant. **6.a.** the highest or leading position or rank: *to graduate at the top of one's class.* **b.** a person or thing that occupies this position or rank. **7.** the highest pitch or degree: *to scream at the top of one's voice.* **8.** the best or choicest part. **9.** the beginning or first part: *to read from the top.* **10.** a platform around the head of a lower mast of a ship, used as a place to stand when extending the rigging of the topmast. —*adj.* **1.** of or at the top: *the top drawer, the top floor of a building.* **2.** first or highest in rank, position, or quality; foremost: *the top person in a field.* **3.** greatest or maximum in degree or amount: *to drive at top speed.* —*v.,* **topped, top·ping.** —*v.t.* **1.** to provide with a top or cover; put a top on. **2.** to serve as, be at, or form the top of. **3.** to reach the top of. **4.** to go above or beyond the top of: *The small airplane barely topped the mountain peak.* **5.** to be greater than or superior to, as in quality, amount, or degree; surpass; exceed. **6.** to cut off or remove the top of: *to top a tree before cutting it down.* **7.** to hit (a ball) above its center, as in golf or tennis. —*v.i.* to top someone or something. [Old English *top* highest point or part.]
•**off the top of one's head.** without careful thought or advance preparation.
•**on top. a.** at the highest point or level. **b.** in a dominant or successful position.
•**on top of. a.** on or at the top of. **b.** resting or lying upon. **c.** in addition to: *On top of everything else, I lost my wallet.* **d.** closely or immediately following: *one problem on top of another.* **e.** *Informal.* in control of: *to be on top of a situation.*
•**over the top. a.** over the front of a trench, as in attacking. **b.** beyond a goal or quota.
•**to top off.** to complete, esp. by adding a finishing touch.

top² (top) *n.* a toy usually having a rounded body that tapers to a point on which it is spun. [Old English *top.*]

to·paz (tō′paz) *n.* a lustrous aluminum silicate mineral, occurring in a variety of colors, used as a gem, esp. in the yellow variety. For illustration, see **semiprecious.** [Latin *topazus,* from Greek *topazos.*]

top boot, a high boot, usually having the upper part trimmed with a different material or color.

top·coat (top′kōt′) *n.* a lightweight overcoat.

top dog *Informal.* a person or group holding a position of power or authority, esp. as a result of winning in a competition.

top-drawer (top′drôr′) *adj. Informal.* of the highest quality, rank, importance, or merit.

tope (tōp) *v.t., v.i.,* **toped, top·ing.** to drink (alcoholic liquor) often and to excess. [Of uncertain origin.]

top·er (tō′pər) *n.* a person who topes; drunkard.

top·flight (top′flīt′) *adj. Informal.* of the highest quality, rank, or merit; excellent; superior.

top·gal·lant (tə gal′ənt, top′gal′-) *n.* a mast, sail, rigging, or the like above the topmast. —*adj.* of or relating to the topgallant.

top hat, a man's hat, usually made of silk, having a high, cylindrical crown and a small brim, worn on formal occasions.

top-heav·y (top′hev′ē) *adj.* too heavy at the top and often unstable and liable to topple.

to·pi·ar·y (tō′pē er′ē) *n., pl.* **-ar·ies. 1.** the art or result of trimming and training trees or shrubs into ornamental shapes. **2.** a garden of ornamentally trimmed trees or shrubs. —*adj.* **1.** (of trees or shrubs) ornamentally trimmed. **2.** of or relating to topiary. [Latin *topiarius* of ornamental gardening, from *topia* ornamental gardening, going back to Greek *topos* a place.]

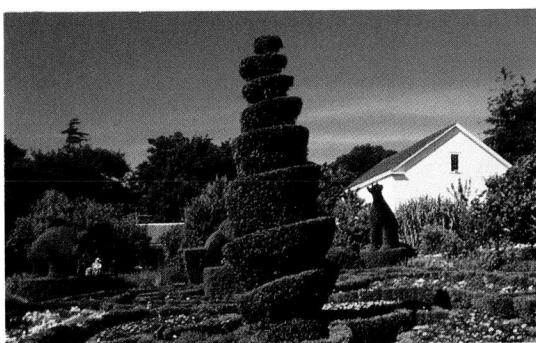

topiary in a garden

top·ic (top′ik) *n.* a subject, as of a speech, discussion, or written composition. [Latin *Topica* title of a rhetorical treatise by Aristotle, 384-322 B.C., Greek philosopher, from Greek *(Ta) Topika* literally, things relating to commonplaces, from Greek *topos* place.]

top·i·cal (top′i kəl) *adj.* **1.** relating to or dealing with matters of current or local interest: *a topical speech, a topical book.* **2.** of, relating to, or belonging to a specific area or place; local. **3.** of or relating to a topic or topics. **4.** *Medicine.* relating to, applied externally to, or affecting a particular part or organ of the body: *a topical antibiotic ointment.* —**top′i·cal·ly,** *adv.*

top·knot (top′not′) *n.* **1.** a knot, tuft, or crest of hair or feathers on the top of the head. **2.** a bow or other ornament worn on the top of the head.

top·less (top′lis) *adj.* **1.** appearing to have no top: *topless skyscrapers in the fog.* **2.a.** (of clothing) lacking a top piece: *a topless swimsuit.* **b.** wearing a garment without a top part: *a topless waitress.* **c.** having waitresses or dancers who wear topless clothing: *a topless bar.* —**top′less·ness,** *n.*

top·loft·y (top′lôf′tē, -lof′-) *adj. Informal.* haughty or pompous in manner or character.

top·mast (top′məst, -mast′) *n.* the second section of a mast, above the lower mast.

top·min·now (top′min′ō) *n.* **1.** livebearer. **2.** killifish. [TOP + MINNOW; because they swim near the surface of the water.]

top·most (top′mōst′) *adj.* at the very top; uppermost; highest.

top·notch (top′noch′) *also,* **top-notch.** *adj. Informal.* first-rate; superior.

to·pog·ra·pher (tə pog′rə fər) *n.* a person who is skilled at or expert in topography.

top·o·graph·i·cal (top′ə graf′i kəl) *adj.* of, relating to, or involving topography: *a topographical map, a topographical survey.* Also, **top′o·graph′ic.** —**top′o·graph′i·cal·ly,** *adv.*

to·pog·ra·phy (tə pog′rə fē) *n., pl.* **-phies. 1.** the detailed description or drawing, as on a map, of the natural and artificial surface features of a place or area. **2.** all the natural and artificial

a	at	e	end	o	hot	u	up	hw	white		about
ā	ape	ē	me	ō	old	ū	use	ng	song	ə	taken
ä	far	i	it	ô	fork	ü	rule	th	thin		pencil
âr	care	ī	ice	oi	oil	u̇	pull	th	this		lemon
		îr	pierce	ou	out	ûr	turn	zh	measure		circus

surface features of a place or area, such as hills, depressions, lakes, roads, and bridges. [Late Latin *topographia* description of a place, from Greek *topographiā*.]

to·pol·o·gy (tə pol′ə jē) *n.* **1.** the branch of mathematics dealing with those properties of figures that are not changed when the figures are stretched, twisted, or otherwise distorted. **2.** the branch of anatomy that deals with regions or specific parts of the body, esp. with respect to diagnosis or treatment. **3.** the topography of an area studied from the perspective of how it has affected the area's history. [Greek *topos* place + -LOGY.] —**top·o·log·i·cal** (top′ə loj′i kəl), *adj.* —**to·pol′o·gist,** *n.*

top·per (top′ər) *n.* **1.** a short, lightweight overcoat for a woman. **2.** *Informal.* a top hat. **3.** *Slang.* a person or thing that surpasses or tries to surpass that which has come before: *Your story was the topper of the evening.*

top·ping (top′ing) *n.* a sauce, frosting, or other garnish put on food: *a dessert topping.*

top·ple (top′əl) *v.,* **-pled, -pling.** —*v.i.* **1.** to fall forward; tumble (often with *over*): *The bookcase toppled over.* **2.** to lean or hang over, as if about to fall. —*v.t.* **1.** to cause to fall or tumble; overturn. **2.** to remove from power or authority; overthrow: *to topple a government.* [TOP¹ + -LE.]

tops (tops) *adj. Informal.* the very best; first-rate.

top·sail (top′səl, -sāl′) *n.* **1.** on a square-rigged ship, the square sail next above the lowest sail on a mast. **2.** on a fore-and-aft-rigged ship, the square or triangular sail above the gaff of a lower sail.

top-se·cret (top′sē′krit) *adj.* of, relating to, or containing highly confidential information.

top sergeant *Informal.* first sergeant.

top·side (top′sīd′) *n.* the upper part of a ship's side, esp. above the water line. —*adv.* also, **top·sides.** to or on the upper portions of a ship; on deck.

top·soil (top′soil′) *n.* the top or upper part of the soil, which contains most of the materials, including minerals and humus, essential to plant growth, and which is the part turned over by the plow in cultivation.

top·sy-tur·vy (top′sē tûr′vē) *adv.* **1.** in reverse of the usual or natural order; upside down. **2.** in or into a state of utter confusion or disorder. —*adj.* **1.** utterly confused or disorderly. **2.** turned upside down. —*n.* the state of utter confusion or disorder. [Possibly from TOP¹ + modification of so¹ (in the sense of "as") + obsolete *tirve* to turn, overturn (of uncertain origin); literally, top as if overturned.] —**top′sy-tur′vi·ly,** *adv.* —**top′sy-tur′vi·ness,** *n.*

toque (tōk) *n.* **1.** a small, close-fitting woman's hat with a soft crown and either a small, rolled brim or no brim at all. **2.** a small plumed hat with a brim, worn by men and women in the sixteenth century. [French *toque,* from Spanish *toca;* of uncertain origin.]

tor (tôr) *n.* a high, rocky hill.

To·rah (tôr′ə) *also,* **To·ra.** *n. Judaism.* **1.** the Pentateuch. **2.** handwritten scrolls containing the Pentateuch, used in a synagogue during services. **3.** *also,* **torah.** the whole body of Jewish teaching, thought, and literature. **4.** torah. instruction, doctrine, or law. [Hebrew *tōrāh* instruction, doctrine, law.]

toque *(def. 2)*

torch (tôrch) *n.* **1.** a flaming light consisting of a stick of resinous wood or some inflammable substance wound around the end of a stick. **2.** any of various hand-held, gas-burning devices producing a very hot flame, such as a blowtorch, used esp. in welding. **3.** something considered to be a source or symbol of enlightenment, inspiration, or guidance: *the torch of liberty.* **4.** *British.* flashlight. —*v.t. Slang.* to set fire to, esp. to commit arson. [Old French *torche* light made of a bundle of twisted straw covered with wax, link², going back to Latin *torquēs* twisted neck chain, wreath.]

  ·to carry a (or **the**) **torch for.** *Informal.* to be in love with (someone), esp. when it is unrequited.

torch·bear·er (tôrch′bâr′ər) *n.* **1.** a person who carries a torch. **2.** a person who is a source of enlightenment, truth, or inspiration.

torch·light (tôrch′līt′) *n.* the light given off by a torch or torches.

tor·chon lace (tôr′shon) **1.** a handmade bobbin lace made of loosely twisted cotton or linen threads in simple open patterns. **2.** a machine-made imitation of this. [French *torchon* dishcloth (from *torche* torch) + LACE. See TORCH.]

torch singer, a person who sings torch songs.

torch song, a sentimental popular song of unrequited love and yearning. [From the phrase *to carry a torch for.* See TORCH.]

tore (tôr) the past tense of **tear**¹.

tor·e·a·dor (tôr′ē ə dôr′) *n.* matador. [Spanish *toreador,* going back to *toro* bull, from Latin *taurus.*]

to·re·ro (tə râr′ō) *n., pl.* **-ros.** a bullfighter, esp. one who fights on foot.

to·ri (tôr′ī) the plural of **torus.**

to·ri·i (tôr′ē ē′) *n., pl.* **to·ri·i.** a gateway at the entrance of a Shinto shrine, consisting of two uprights supporting two horizontal crosspieces, the upper of which may be slightly concave. [Japanese *torii.*]

torii

tor·ment (*v.,* tôr ment′; *n.,* tôr′ment) *v.t.* **1.** to afflict with extreme mental or physical pain or suffering. **2.** to worry, annoy, or aggravate excessively. —*n.* **1.** extreme mental or physical pain or suffering; agony. **2.** the source of such pain or suffering. [Old French *torment* torture, from Latin *tormentum.*]

tor·men·tor (tôr men′tər) *also,* **tor·ment·er.** *n.* a person or thing that torments.

torn (tôrn) the past participle of **tear**¹.

tor·na·do (tôr nā′dō) *n., pl.* **-does** or **-dos.** a violent cyclonic storm, usually over land, producing a dark, funnel-shaped column of air rotating around a low-pressure center at speeds of over 300 miles (483 kilometers) per hour. Because of the powerful suction of the relative vacuum at its center, objects are drawn up into the storm and almost everything along its narrow path is destroyed. [Modification of Spanish *tronada* thunderstorm, going back to Latin *tornāre* to thunder.] —**tor·nad′ic** (tôr nad′ik, -nā′dik), *adj.*

tor·pe·do (tôr pē′dō) *n., pl.* **-does. 1.a.** a large, self-propelled, cigar-shaped underwater missile that can be launched from ships, submarines, or airplanes, used for underwater attack against enemy vessels. **b.** an underwater mine. **2.** a small explosive charge placed on a railroad track, serving as a signal when detonated by the weight of the train passing over it. **3.** a type of firework that explodes when thrown against a hard surface. **4.** any of several electric rays, genus *Torpedo.* —*v.t.,* **-doed, -do·ing.** to damage, destroy, or sink with or as with a torpedo. [Latin *torpēdō* electric ray (whose electrical discharges stun its victims), numbness, from *torpēre* to be numb.]

torpedo boat, PT boat.

tor·pid (tôr′pid) *adj.* **1.** without strength or energy; lethargic; sluggish; dull. **2.** dormant, as an animal in hibernation. **3.** lacking the power of motion or feeling; numb. [Latin *torpidus* benumbed.] —**tor·pid′i·ty, tor′pid·ness,** *n.* —**tor′pid·ly,** *adv.*

tor·por (tôr′pər) *n.* the state or quality of being torpid. [Latin *torpor* numbness.]

torque (tôrk) *n.* **1.a.** *Physics.* the turning effect, or moment, of a force about a pivot point, measured as the product of the force and the distance between the point where the force is applied and the pivot point. **b.** a force that causes something either to rotate or twist. **2.** an ornamental necklace, bracelet, or armband, usually made of twisted metal, worn esp. by the ancient Gauls and Britons. [Latin *torquēs* twisted neck chain, wreath.]

tor·rent (tôr′ənt, tor′-) *n.* **1.** a violent, swiftly flowing stream, esp. of water. **2.** a violent, overwhelming flow of anything: *a torrent of insults.* [Latin *torrēns* a rushing stream (of water), boiling, impetuous.]

tor·ren·tial (tô ren′chəl, tə-) *adj.* of, resembling, or caused by a torrent: *a torrential rainfall.*

tor·rid (tôr′id, tor′-) *adj.* **1.** subjected to or parched by the intense heat of the sun: *the torrid regions of the world.* **2.** intensely hot or burning; scorching: *a torrid climate.* **3.** full of passion; passionate; ardent: *a torrid love story.* [Latin *torridus* parched.] —**tor·rid′i·ty, tor′rid·ness,** *n.* —**tor′rid·ly,** *adv.*

Torrid Zone, a warm region between the Tropic of Cancer and the Tropic of Capricorn; tropics. For illustration, see **zone.**

tor·sion (tôr′shən) *n.* **1.** the act of twisting or the state of being twisted. **2.** the strain exerted on a body when one end is twisted in one direction while the other end is held firm or twisted in the opposite direction. [Late Latin *torsiō* torture, a wringing, from Latin *torquēre* to twist.] —**tor′sion·al,** *adj.* —**tor′sion·al·ly,** *adv.*

tor·so (tôr′sō) *n., pl.* **-sos. 1.** the trunk of the human body. **2.** a sculptural representation of this. [Italian *torso* stalk¹, stump, trunk of a statue, through Latin, from Greek *thyrsos* stalk¹, rod, thyrsus.]

tort (tôrt) *n. Law.* any private or civil wrong or injury not involving breach of contract, for which the wronged party may bring civil suit. [Old French *tort* wrong, offense, from Medieval Latin *tortum* wrong, going back to Latin *torquēre* to twist.]

torte (tôrt) *n.* a rich cake made of eggs, sugar, bread crumbs or a little flour, and usually ground nuts. [German *Torte* flat cake, tart², probably going back to Late Latin *tōrta.* See TORTILLA.]

tor·ti·col·lis (tôr′ti kol′is) *n.* wryneck *(def. 1).* [Modern Latin *torticollis,* from Latin *tortus,* past participle of *torquēre* to twist + *collum* neck.]

tor·til·la (tôr tē′yə) *n.* a thin, round, unleavened bread made from water and cornmeal and baked on a griddle. [Spanish *tortilla* little cake, diminutive of *torta* round cake, from Late Latin *tōrta* round loaf of bread; of uncertain origin.]

tor·toise (tôr′təs) *n.* a slow-moving land turtle, family Testudinidae, found on every continent except Australia. [Earlier *tortuce,* from Late Latin *tortūca* tortoise, turtle, possibly from Latin *tortus,* past participle of *torquēre* to twist; supposedly with reference to its crooked feet.]

tortoise beetle, a small, turtle-shaped beetle, resembling the ladybug, that is destructive to crops.

tor·toise-shell (tôr′təs shel′) *adj.* **1.** made of tortoise shell. **2.** having the mottled yellow-and-brown colors of tortoise shell.

tortoise shell 1. the hard, mottled, yellow-and-brown material making up the outer shell of certain turtles, used esp. to make combs, small decorative objects, and furniture inlay. **2.** any of a group of butterflies, genus *Nymphalis,* with mottled yellow, brown, and black coloration.

tor·to·ni (tôr tō′nē) *n.* a rich Italian ice cream, often having minced almonds and cherries. [Perhaps from Italian *Tortoni* literally, of Tortona, an Italian community.]

tor·tu·ous (tôr′chū əs) *adj.* **1.** having many twists, turns, or bends; winding: *a tortuous road.* **2.** not direct, straightforward, or frank; devious: *long and tortuous excuses.* [Latin *tortuōsus* full of turns, entangled, from *tortus,* past participle of *torquēre* to twist.] —**tor′tu·ous·ly,** *adv.* —**tor′tu·ous·ness,** *n.*

tor·ture (tôr′chər) *v.t.,* **-tured, -tur·ing. 1.** to subject to severe physical abuse or cruelty: *The enemy tortured the prisoners.* **2.** to cause to suffer extreme mental or physical pain or suffering: *The knowledge of what I had done tortured me.* **3.** to distort, as in shape or meaning; twist. —*n.* **1.** extreme mental or physical pain or suffering; agony. **2.** the act of inflicting or subjecting to extreme physical abuse or cruelty. **3.** a source or cause of mental or physical pain or suffering. [Late Latin *tortūra* twisting, torment, from Latin *tortus,* past participle of *torquēre* to twist.] —**tor′tur·er,** *n.*

tor·tur·ous (tôr′chər əs) *adj.* relating to, characterized by, or causing torture: *a torturous toothache.*

to·rus (tôr′əs) *n., pl.* **to·ri** (tôr′ī). **1.** a large convex molding, usually forming part of the base of a column. **2.** *Anatomy.* any rounded ridge or protruding part. **3.** *Botany.* the receptacle of a flower. **4.** *Geometry.* a doughnut-shaped figure generated by rotating a circle about any line in its plane that does not intersect it. [Latin *torus* bulge, cushion, round molding.]

torus

To·ry (tôr′ē) *n., pl.* **-ries. 1.** a member of a political party in Great Britain that favored royal power and the preservation of existing institutions, such as the Anglican Church. Since 1832, it has been known as the Conservative Party. **2.** any colonial American who remained loyal to England at the time of the American Revolution. **3.** *also,* **tory.** any person who is very conservative in politics. —*adj.* of, relating to, or characteristic of a Tory or Tories. [Irish *tōraidhe* pursued person, robber; originally referring to Irishmen who, persecuted by the English in the seventeenth century, became outlaws.] —**To′ry·ish,** *adj.* —**To′ry·ism,** *n.*

toss (tôs, tos) *v.t.* **1.** to propel lightly up into or through the air, esp. with the hand or hands: *Please toss me a towel.* **2.** to fling or move back and forth: *The waves tossed the little boat.* **3.** to lift quickly or suddenly: *The horse tossed its head.* **4.** to mix (a salad) lightly, esp. so as to coat with a dressing. **5.** to cause to fall to the ground: *The horse tossed its rider.* **6.a.** to throw (a coin) into the air so as to decide something on the basis of which side lands upward. **b.** to toss a coin with (someone): *I'll toss you to see who goes first.* **7.** *Informal.* to discuss (something) freely or casually, as in a group. —*v.i.* **1.** to move about restlessly, esp. in one's sleep: *to toss and turn all night.* **2.** to be flung or moved back and forth. **3.** to throw a coin into the air so as to decide something on the basis of which side lands upward. —*n.* **1.** the act of tossing. **2.** the distance over which something is or can be tossed. [Possibly of Scandinavian origin.] —**toss′er,** *n.* —For Synonyms *(v.t.),* see **throw.**

 • **to toss off. a.** to do quickly, casually, and easily: *to toss off a note to a friend.* **b.** to drink the whole of: *to toss off three glasses of water.*

toss-up (tôs′up′, tos′-) *also,* **toss·up.** *n.* **1.** an even chance or possibility. **2.** the act of tossing a coin in order to decide something.

tos·ta·da (tō stä′də) *n.* a tortilla fried in deep fat, usually

topped with a mixture of meat, beans, and raw vegetables. [Mexican Spanish *tostada* this food, from *tostado,* past participle of *tostar* to toast, fry, going back to Latin *tostus,* past participle of *torrēre* to make dry.]

tot[1] (tot) *n.* **1.** a small child. **2.** a small amount of something, such as an alcoholic beverage. [Of uncertain origin.]

tot[2] (tot) *v.i., v.t.,* **tot·ted, tot·ting.** to total (usually with *up*).

to·tal (tō′təl) *adj.* **1.** relating to, making up, or including the entire quantity, number, or extent of something: *I paid the total amount of the bill.* **2.** realized to the fullest extent possible; with no qualifications; absolute: *a total disaster, a total absence of respect.* —*n.* the whole amount; sum. —*v.,* **-taled, -tal·ing;** *also,* British, **-talled, -tal·ling.** —*v.t.* **1.** to compute or find the sum of; add up: *to total a bill.* Also, **totalize. 2.** to reach to the sum of: *The damage totaled $4,000.* **3.** *Slang.* to destroy completely; wreck: *The fire totaled the old shed.* —*v.i.* to amount (often with *to*): *The bill totals to ten dollars.* [Medieval Latin *totalis* whole, entire, from Latin *tōtus.*] —For Synonyms *(adj.),* see **complete.**

total eclipse *Astronomy.* an eclipse of a celestial body, esp. the sun or moon, in which the face of the body is thrown into complete darkness.

to·tal·i·tar·i·an (tō tal′i târ′ē ən) *adj.* characteristic of or tending toward totalitarianism. —*n.* a person who favors or supports totalitarianism.

to·tal·i·tar·i·an·ism (tō tal′i târ′ē ə niz′əm) *n.* a system of government in which one political party aims at total control over the lives of people, as by employing a powerful secret police, restricting meetings and assemblies, and censoring publications.

to·tal·i·ty (tō tal′i tē) *n., pl.* **-ties. 1.** the total amount; whole. **2.** the state of being whole or complete.

to·tal·i·za·tor (tō′tə lə zā′tər) *n.* pari-mutuel *(def. 2).*

to·tal·ize (tō′tə līz′) *v.t.,* **-ized, -iz·ing.** total *(def. 1).* —**to′tal·iz′er,** *n.*

to·tal·ly (tō′tə lē) *adv.* to the fullest extent; completely; entirely; wholly.

tote (tōt) *Informal. v.t.,* **tot·ed, tot·ing. 1.** to haul or carry, esp. on one's back or in one's arms. **2.** to have on one's person habitually: *The Texas Ranger totes a gun.* —*n.* **1.** something carried; load. **2.** tote bag. [Of uncertain origin.] —**tot′er,** *n.*

tote bag, a large handbag used esp. to carry small packages and other items.

to·tem (tō′təm) *n.* **1.** among North American Indians and certain other peoples, an animal, plant, or other natural object taken as the ancestral emblem of a clan or other family group related by blood. **2.** a representation of this, esp. one carved and painted on poles. [Ojibwa *ototeman* his brother-sister kin.] —**to·tem·ic** (tō tem′-ik), *adj.*

to·tem·ism (tō′tə miz′əm) *n.* **1.** belief in totems and the customs and practices associated with them. **2.** a social system in which tribes are divided into clans or families according to their totems.

totem pole, a pole consisting of carved and painted representations of totems, erected in front of a dwelling, esp. by the American Indians of the northwestern Pacific coast.

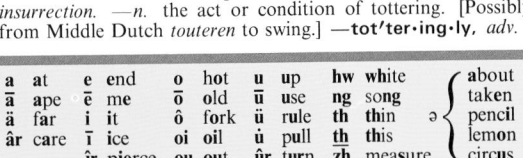

totem poles of the Tlingit tribe

toth·er (tuth′ər) *also,* **t′oth·er.** *Informal. pron., adj.* the other. [Middle English *the tother,* incorrect division of *thet other* the other, from Old English *thæt* that + OTHER.]

tot·ter (tot′ər) *v.i.* **1.** to walk or move with weak, unsteady steps. **2.** to shake or sway as if about to fall; be unbalanced or unsteady: *The glass tottered on the edge of the table.* **3.** to be unstable and about to collapse: *The government tottered after the insurrection.* —*n.* the act or condition of tottering. [Possibly from Middle Dutch *touteren* to swing.] —**tot′ter·ing·ly,** *adv.*

a	at	e	end	o	hot	u	up	hw	white		about
ā	ape	ē	me	ō	old	ū	use	ng	song		taken
ä	far	i	it	ô	fork	ü	rule	th	thin	ə	pencil
âr	care	ī	ice	oi	oil	u̇	pull	th	this		lemon
		îr	pierce	ou	out	ûr	turn	zh	measure		circus

tot·ter·y (tot′ə rē) *adj.* unsteady; shaky.

tou·can (tü′kan, tü kan′) *n.* any of various fruit-eating tropical American birds, family Ramphastidae, having a heavy body, a very large beak, and, typically, brightly colored plumage. Length: 7-25 inches (18-64 centimeters), including beak. [Tupi-Guarani *tucana, tucā;* referring to the sound of its cry.]

toucan

touch (tuch) *v.t.* **1.** to bring a hand, finger, or other part of the body in contact with: *Don't touch the hot stove or you'll burn yourself.* **2.** to bring (something) into contact with something else: *He touched his nose to the window.* **3.** to be in or come into contact with: *Her hand touched mine.* **4.** to affect the emotions or feelings of: *The sentimental card really touched me.* **5.** to have an effect or bearing on; affect: *The new taxes will not touch the very rich.* **6.** to use or partake of: *She didn't touch any of her food.* **7.** to color slightly; tinge: *hair touched with gray.* **8.** to compare with; equal: *No one can touch him in his field.* **9.** to lay a hand or hands on, esp. so as to harm or molest: *If you touch me, I'll scream!* **10.** to be next to; border on. **11.** to arrive at or visit in passing: *I'm going to go ashore when the ship touches port.* **12.** to impair slightly; blemish: *The plants were touched by the frost.* **13.** *Slang.* to succeed in getting or borrowing money from: *to touch a friend for a loan.* —*v.i.* **1.** to come into or be in contact: *Their hands touched.* **2.** to make a brief stop in passing (often with *at*): *The freighter touched at every port in France.* —*n.* **1.** the sense by which external objects are perceived through direct contact with a part of the body. **2.** the quality of an object as perceived by touching or coming into contact with it: *the soft touch of silk.* **3.** the act or an instance of touching or coming into contact. **4.** a subtle sign or indication, as of a quality or attribute: *a touch of genius.* **5.** a small amount; little bit: *a touch of salt.* **6.** a slight attack; twinge: *a touch of rheumatism.* **7.** a slight change or addition made to modify or improve something, such as a painting or literary work. **8.** the state of being in close communication or contact: *Have you kept in touch with them?* **9.** a distinctive manner or way of doing something: *The room showed the touch of a decorator.* **10.** a light stroke or dab, as with a pen, pencil, or brush. **11.a.** the manner of striking or touching the keys of a keyboard instrument, such as a piano or typewriter. **b.** the manner in which the keys of a keyboard instrument respond to the pressure exerted on them by the fingers. **12.** an official stamp on gold, silver, or other metal indicating that it has been tested and testifying to its fineness. **13.** *Slang.* a person from whom money is obtained. [Old French *touchier* to strike, affect, from an assumed Vulgar Latin word based on an imitation of the sound of striking.] —**touch′a·ble,** *adj.*

· **to put the touch on.** *Slang.* to obtain or attempt to obtain money from.

· **to touch down.** (of an aircraft or spacecraft) to land.

· **to touch off. a.** to cause to explode or ignite. **b.** to cause to occur; initiate: *to touch off an argument.*

· **to touch on.** to deal with or mention, esp. in passing: *The politician's speech touched on many issues.*

· **to touch up.** to improve by making slight changes: *to touch up a painting.*

touch-and-go (tuch′ən gō′) *adj.* of uncertain outcome: *The baseball game was touch-and-go up to the last few minutes.*

touch and go, an uncertain or risky situation or state of affairs.

touch·back (tuch′bak′) *n. Football.* a play in which the ball is declared dead beyond a team's goal line after it has been impelled there by the opposing team. No points are awarded for a touchback.

touch·down (tuch′doun′) *n.* **1.** *Football.* **a.** a scoring play worth six points, made by being in possession of the ball on or beyond the opponent's goal line. **b.** the score so made. **2.** the act of landing an aircraft or spacecraft. **3.** the moment of contact with the ground of a landing aircraft or spacecraft.

tou·ché (tü shā′) *interj.* touched. ➡ used in fencing to acknowledge that one's opponent has scored a hit; also used figuratively to acknowledge a point well made in an argument or a witty reply made in a conversation. [French *touché,* past participle of *toucher* to touch, from Old French *tuchier* to touch. See TOUCH.]

touched (tucht) *adj.* **1.** moved, as to feelings of pity, tenderness, or compassion; emotionally stirred: *We were touched by the child's tears.* **2.** *Informal.* slightly disturbed mentally.

touch football, a form of football in which a ball carrier is stopped by being touched with one or both hands rather than tackled.

touch·hole (tuch′hōl′) *n.* in early cannons and firearms, a vent in the breech through which the charge was ignited.

touch·ing (tuch′ing) *adj.* stirring or appealing to the emotions or feelings. —*prep.* with respect to; as to; concerning. —**touch′ing·ly,** *adv.*

Synonyms *adj.* **Touching, moving, poignant,** and **affecting** mean appealing to or exciting the emotions. **Touching** suggests the arousal of tender but not necessarily deep feelings: *The children's devotion to their elderly grandparents was touching to watch.* **Moving** is associated with a broad range of strong emotional responses: *The minister delivered a moving eulogy.* **Poignant** implies a piercing, often melancholy quality: *It was a poignant moment when the lovers said good-bye for the last time.* **Affecting** is applied to something that causes a display of emotion, such as tears: *The play's final scene was so affecting that it often left the audience weeping openly.*

touch-me-not (tuch′mē not′) *n.* any of several species of the genus *Impatiens,* esp. *I. noli-tangere,* whose seed pods burst open when ripe.

touch·stone (tuch′stōn′) *n.* **1.** a hard, black stone, such as basalt or jasper, used to test the fineness of an alloy of gold or silver by comparing the color of the streak made on the stone by the alloy with the streak made by an alloy of known fineness. **2.** anything by which the quality, value, or genuineness of something is tested; test.

touch system, a method of typewriting without looking at the keyboard, each finger being trained to touch a particular key or keys.

touch terminal, a computer terminal with a pressure-sensitive screen that enables the user to input commands by touching the screen.

touch-tone (tuch′tōn′) *adj.* of, relating to, or designating a telephone apparatus with which calls are made by pushing buttons rather than by turning a rotary dial. The buttons activate production of electronic tones that correspond to the digits of the number being called.

touch-type (tuch′tīp′) *v.t., v.i.,* -**typed,** -**typ·ing.** to type using the touch system.

touch·wood (tuch′wùd′) *n.* dry, decayed wood used as tinder; punk.

touch·y (tuch′ē) *adj.,* **touch·i·er, touch·i·est. 1.** easily offended; very sensitive. **2.** requiring caution, tact, and careful handling: *a touchy situation.* —**touch′i·ly,** *adv.* —**touch′i·ness,** *n.*

tough (tuf) *adj.* **1.** able to withstand great pressure or strain without breaking; strong but pliable. **2.** difficult to cut or chew: *a tough piece of meat.* **3.** capable of enduring great strain, hardship, or adversity: *a tough constitution.* **4.** characterized by or showing harshness or inflexibility of temperament; stern: *The traffic laws are tough on offenders.* **5.** difficult to do, deal with, or accomplish; requiring a great deal of effort: *a tough job, a tough question.* **6.** difficult to manage, influence, or intimidate: *a tough customer.* **7.** having or characterized by a rough, brutal, and often violent atmosphere: *a tough neighborhood.* **8.** *Informal.* unhappy or unfortunate: *a tough life.* —*n.* a rough, brutal, and often violent person; ruffian; thug. [Old English *tōh* not easily broken, not tender, sticky.] —**tough′ly,** *adv.* —**tough′ness,** *n.*

tough·en (tuf′ən) *v.t., v.i.* to make or become tough or tougher.

tou·pee (tü pā′) *n.* a small wig worn by men to cover baldness. [French *toupet* tuft of hair, from Old French *to(u)p;* of Germanic origin.]

tour (tùr) *n.* **1.** a journey in which many places are visited, usually for short periods of time: *They took a tour of the Greek isles.* **2.a.** a brief journey, often organized for a group of people, to or through a place for the purpose of seeing or inspecting it: *The real estate agent took us on a tour of the house.* **b.** a group of people organized for or making such a journey: *I joined the tour*

in Paris. **3.** a circuit or journey, as of a theatrical or musical company, made to a number of places in order to give performances. **4.** a period of time in which some obligatory or assigned task or service is fulfilled in one place, esp. in the military service. —*v.t.* to make a tour of or through. —*v.i.* to go on a tour. [Old French *to(u)r* a turn, circuit, lathe, from Latin *tornus* lathe, from Greek *tornos.*]

tour de force (tŭr′də fôrs′) a feat of extraordinary strength, skill, or ingenuity, esp. one that is not likely to be repeated or equaled. [French *tour de force* feat of strength or skill. See TOUR, FORCE.]

touring car, a large, open antique automobile seating five or more passengers.

tour·ism (tŭr′iz əm) *n.* **1.** the business of providing services for tourists: *Tourism is the basis of that country's economy.* **2.** travel for pleasure.

tour·ist (tŭr′ist) *n.* a person who travels for pleasure. —*adj.* of or for tourists. —*adv.* in or by means of tourist class: *to travel tourist.*

tourist class **1.** on a passenger ship, a class of accommodations next below cabin class. **2.** on an airplane, a class of accommodations below first class.

tour·ma·line (tŭr′mə lin, -lēn) *also,* **tour·ma·lin** (tŭr′mə lin) *n.* a glassy or lustrous silicate of boron and aluminum, occurring in a variety of colors, esp. black. Transparent red or green varieties are used as gems. [French *tourmaline,* going back to Singhalese *tōramalli* carnelian.]

tour·na·ment (tŭr′nə mənt, tûr′-) *n.* **1.** a series of contests involving two or more persons or teams: *a bridge tournament.* **2.a.** a formal combat between two or more mounted knights or other individuals armed with lances and other weapons. **b.** a series of such combats. [Old French *torneiement,* from *torneier* to joust, turn round. See TOURNEY.]

tour·ney (tŭr′nē, tûr′-) *n., pl.* **-neys.** tournament. —*v.i.,* **-neyed, -ney·ing.** to take part in a tournament. [Old French *tornei* tournament, from *torneier* to joust, turn round, going back to Latin *tornāre* to turn in a lathe. See TURN.]

tour·ni·quet (tŭr′ni kit, tûr′-) *n.* a device, such as a rubber tube or a tight bandage, used to stop bleeding by pressing on a blood vessel. [French *tourniquet,* from *tourner* to turn, from Latin *tornāre* to turn in a lathe. See TURN.]

tou·sle (tou′zəl) *v.t.,* **-sled, -sling.** to put into disorder; dishevel: *The wind tousled my hair.* —*n.* an untidy, disheveled mass, esp. of hair. [Dialectal *touse* to pull roughly, tear (of uncertain origin) + -LE.]

tout (tout) *Informal. v.i.* to try to get customers, employment, patronage, or the like, esp. in a persistent or brazen way: *The campaign manager touted for votes.* —*v.t.* **1.** to solicit, as for business or support; importune. **2.** to praise or publicize in an exaggerated manner: *The publicity department touted the new movie as a future classic.* **3.** to give or sell information about (a racehorse) to a bettor. —*n.* a person who touts. [Probably from an unrecorded Old English word.] —**tout′er,** *n.*

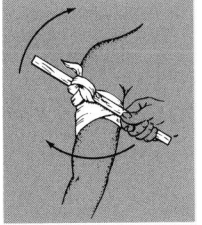

tourniquet

tout à fait (tü tä fe′) *French.* completely; entirely; quite.

tout de suite (tüt swēt′) *French.* at once; immediately.

tout en·sem·ble (tü tän sän′blə) *French.* all the parts considered as or forming a whole; general effect.

tow[1] (tō) *v.t.* to pull, drag, or draw behind, esp. by means of a rope, chain, or the like: *The truck towed the car to the service station.* —*n.* **1.** the act or an instance of towing, or the state of being towed. **2.** something that is being towed. **3.** towline. [Old English *togian* to draw, pull.]
  • **in tow. a.** being towed or pulled along: *a small child with a wagon in tow.* **b.** under one's protection, guidance, or influence: *to take a new employee in tow.*

tow[2] (tō) *n.* coarse, shorter fibers of flax or hemp used to make yarn and twine. [Old English *tow-* a spinning.]

tow·age (tō′ij) *n.* **1.** the act of towing or the state of being towed. **2.** a charge made for towing.

to·ward (tôrd, tō′ərd, tə wôrd′) *also,* **towards.** *prep.* **1.** in the direction of: *The puppy ran toward the house.* **2.** with respect to; concerning; regarding: *What are your feelings toward them?* **3.** near in time; shortly before: *The snow stopped toward morning.* **4.** as a contribution or an aid to; in order to obtain: *to save one's allowance toward a new bicycle, to take courses toward a master's degree.* [Old English *tōweard* in the direction of, from *tō* to + -*weard* -ward.]

tow·boat (tō′bōt′) *n.* **1.** tugboat. **2.** a boat designed to push a barge or barges, used in inland waterways.

tow·el (tou′əl) *n.* a piece of absorbent material, esp. paper or terry cloth, used for wiping or drying. —*v.t.,* **-eled, -el·ing;** *also, British,* **-elled, -el·ling.** to wipe or dry with a towel: *to towel oneself after swimming.* [Old French *toaille* cloth for wiping or drying; of Germanic origin.]
  • **to throw** (or **toss**) **in the towel.** *Informal.* to give up; admit defeat; quit.

tow·el·ing (tou′ə ling) *also, British,* **tow·el·ling.** *n.* any of various absorbent, relatively coarse fabrics, such as cotton or linen, used for making towels.

tow·er (tou′ər) *n.* **1.** a tall but relatively narrow structure, often forming a part of and rising above a building or other structure. **2.** such a structure designed for a special purpose, such as an airport control tower or a water tower. —*v.i.* to rise or extend to a great height: *The skyscraper towered above the other buildings.* [Old French *tour* tall structure, from Latin *turris* citadel, high structure, from Greek *tyrsis.*] —**tow′er·y,** *adj.*

tow·er·ing (tou′ər ing) *adj.* **1.** very tall; lofty: *Towering palm trees lined the beach.* **2.** very great; outstanding: *a composer of towering musical genius.* **3.** very violent or intense: *a towering rage.*

Tower of London, a historic fortress and prison on the north bank of the Thames, in London, England.

tow·head (tō′hed′) *n.* **1.** a head of very pale blond hair. **2.** a person having such hair. —**tow′head′ed,** *adj.*

tow·hee (tou′hē′, tō′-) *n.* any of several North American songbirds, family Fringillidae, resembling a large sparrow. Length: 6-10 inches (15-25 centimeters). Also, **chewink.** [Imitative of its cry.]

tow·line (tō′līn′) *n.* a rope, chain, or the like used for towing.

town (toun) *n.* **1.** a group of houses and public and private buildings, larger than a village but smaller than a city. **2.** any densely populated place: *Boston is a very old town.* **3.** the inhabitants of a town. **4.** the commercial or industrial part of a town or city: *The farmer went into town to buy feed and supplies.* **5.** a geographical and political division, smaller than a county, that governs itself. **6.** in New England, a basic governmental unit that may include both rural and densely settled areas. [Old English *tūn* enclosure, village; referring to the protection of settlements in earlier times by enclosures.]
  • **to go to town.** *Informal.* to act or do something with much speed, ability, and efficiency.
  • **to paint the town (red).** *Informal.* to go on a spree; celebrate wildly.

town clerk, the official in charge of the records of a town.

town crier, formerly, a person employed to make public proclamations or announcements in the streets of a town.

town hall, a building that houses the offices of officials of a town or is used for town meetings.

town house **1.** a house in a town or city, esp. one owned by a person who has a house in the country. **2.** one of a row of houses, usually connected by common side walls and located in a city.

town·ie (tou′nē) *also,* **town·y.** *n. Informal.* **1.** a person who lives in a town or city. **2.** a person who lives permanently in a college town, as distinguished from a student or teacher at the college.

town meeting **1.** a meeting of all the voters of a town, esp. in New England, to express their opinions and decide directly on local matters. **2.** any general meeting of the inhabitants of a town.

towns·folk (tounz′fōk′) *pl. n.* townspeople.

town·ship (toun′ship′) *n.* **1.** a geographical and political division of a county, having certain limited powers of municipal government. **2.** in surveys of public land, an area containing thirty-six sections of one square mile each. [Old English *tūnscipe* village community, from *tūn* village + -*scipe* -ship.]

towns·man (tounz′mən) *n., pl.* **-men** (-mən). **1.** an inhabitant of a town. **2.** a fellow inhabitant of one's town.

towns·peo·ple (tounz′pē′pəl) *pl. n.* the inhabitants of a town collectively.

towns·wom·an (tounz′wùm′ən) *n., pl.* **-wom·en** (-wim′ən). **1.** a female inhabitant of a town. **2.** a fellow female inhabitant of one's town.

tow·path (tō′path′) *n.* a path along the bank of a canal or river used, as by draft animals, in towing boats.

tow·rope (tō′rōp′) *n.* a rope used in towing, esp. a hawser or cable used for towing boats.

a	at	e	end	o	hot	u	up	hw	white		about
ā	ape	ē	me	ō	old	ū	use	ng	song	ə	taken
ä	far	i	it	ô	fork	ü	rule	th	thin		pencil
âr	care	ī	ice	oi	oil	ù	pull	th	this		lemon
				îr	pierce	ou	out	ûr	turn	zh	measure		circus

tow truck, a truck with towing equipment for moving disabled or wrecked vehicles. Also, **wrecker.**

tox·e·mi·a (tok sē′mē ə) *also,* **tox·ae·mi·a.** *n.* blood poisoning caused by toxins. [Modern Latin *toxaemia,* going back to Greek *toxikon (pharmakon)* (poison) for arrows + *haima* blood. See TOXIC.]

tox·e·mic (tok sē′mik) *also,* **tox·ae·mic.** *adj.* **1.** of, relating to, or caused by toxemia. **2.** affected with or having toxemia.

tox·ic (tok′sik) *adj.* **1.** of, relating to, or caused by poison. **2.** affected with poison; poisoned. **3.** containing or acting as a poison; poisonous: *a toxic chemical.* [Medieval Latin *toxicus* poisonous, from Latin *toxicum* poison, from Greek *toxikon (pharmakon)* (poison) for arrows, from *toxon* bow[2].]

tox·ic·i·ty (tok sis′i tē) *n., pl.* **-ties. 1.** the state or quality of being toxic. **2.** the degree to which something is toxic.

tox·i·col·o·gy (tok′si kol′ə jē) *n.* the science that deals with the nature and effects of poisons and the treatment of poisoning. [TOXIC + -LOGY.] —**tox′i·co·log′i·cal,** *adj.* —**tox′i·col′o·gist,** *n.*

toxic shock syndrome, a rare bacterial disease that causes a high fever, a sunburnlike rash, stomach upset, and a sudden drop in blood pressure and is sometimes fatal.

tox·in (tok′sin) *n.* any poisonous product of animal or vegetable cells. The toxins produced by harmful bacteria cause the symptoms of many diseases. [TOX(IC) + -IN[1].]

tox·oid (tok′soid) *n.* a toxin that has been detoxified by heat or chemical treatment but still retains its antigenic properties and can thus be used for immunization. [TOX(IN) + -OID.]

toy (toi) *n.* **1.** an object for a child to play with. **2.** something of little or no value or importance. —*v.i.* to treat someone or something as having little importance; trifle: *to toy with someone's feelings, to toy with an idea.* —*adj.* **1.** of, like, or used as a toy. **2.** smaller than the usual or standard, as certain breeds of dog. [Of uncertain origin.]

to·yon (toi′ən, tō′yən) *n.* a tall evergreen shrub, *Heteromeles arbutifolia,* of the rose family, native to California, bearing red or yellow fruits and shiny deep green leaves that resemble holly. [Spanish *tollon;* probably of Nahuatl origin.]

tp., township.

TPN, a coenzyme that is involved in the oxidation of glucose and in numerous oxidation-reduction reactions within living cells. Formula: $C_{21}H_{28}N_7O_{17}P_3$ [Abbreviation of *t(ri)p(hosphopyridine) n(ucleotide).*]

tr. 1. transitive. **2.** translation. **3.** translator. **4.** transpose. **5.** treasurer.

trace[1] (trās) *n.* **1.** something left behind as evidence that some person, thing, or event has existed or taken place: *The earthquake left its traces on the city. The archaeologist found traces of an ancient temple.* **2.** a track made by the passage of someone or something, such as a footprint or tire mark. **3.** a small, almost indiscernible amount or indication: *a trace of mint in a sauce, a trace of sarcasm in a person's tone.* **4.** a line drawn, esp. one made by a self-recording instrument, such as an electrocardiograph; tracing. —*v.,* **traced, trac·ing.** —*v.t.* **1.** to follow the track, trail, or path of; pursue: *to trace a missing person.* **2.** to follow the course, development, or history of: *to trace a system of government back to the ancient Romans.* **3.** to discover by research or investigation: *to trace the origins of a word.* **4.** to mark out; delineate: *to trace a figure in the sand, to trace an outline of a plan, to trace a route on a map.* **5.** to copy (something, such as a drawing) by following lines as seen through a transparent sheet placed over it. **6.** to ornament with tracery. **7.** to mark by means of a curved or broken line: *A machine traced the patient's respiration rate.* —*v.i.* to have its origin; go back in time: *Our friendship traces back to childhood.* [Old French *tracier* to follow a trail, going back to Latin *tractus,* past participle of *trahere* to draw, drag.] —**trace′a·bil′i·ty,** *n.* —**trace′a·ble,** *adj.* —**trace′a·bly,** *adv.*

> **Synonyms** *n.* **Trace[1]** and **vestige** mean evidence that something has existed or occurred. **Trace** is applied particularly to a physical clue such as a footprint or stain: *Traces of blood were found on the suspect's clothing.* **Vestige** usually indicates fragmentary remains of something that no longer exists: *The cave contains vestiges of ancient drawings.*

trace[2] (trās) *n.* either of the two straps, ropes, or chains by which the harness of a draft animal is attached to the vehicle it pulls. [Old French *trais,* plural of *trait* a pulling, harness strap, from Latin *tractus* a pulling, dragging.]

· **to kick over the traces.** to free oneself from control or influence; show independence; rebel.

trace element, an element present in amounts too small to measure, esp. various metallic elements that a plant or animal needs very small amounts of in order to function.

trac·er (trā′sər) *n.* **1.** a person or thing that traces. **2.** any of various devices for making tracings of drawings. **3.** an inquiry sent from place to place to locate someone or something that is missing, esp. mail lost in transit. **4.** an easily detected and located substance, usually a radioisotope, that is introduced internally in some system, such as a gas pipeline or a human body, to keep track of the movements and changes inside. **5.** a projectile, such as a bullet or shell, treated with a chemical compound so that its trajectory can be traced by the trail of fire or smoke that it leaves in its path.

trac·er·y (trā′sə rē) *n., pl.* **-er·ies. 1.** ornamental stonework forming geometric or curved patterns, used esp. in Gothic windows and arches. **2.** any similar ornamentation, as in a screen, paneling, or embroidery.

tracery

tra·che·a (trā′kē ə) *n., pl.* **-che·ae** (-kē ē′). the tube extending from the larynx to the bronchi. Also, **windpipe.** For illustration, see **respiratory system.** [Medieval Latin *trachea,* going back to Greek *trācheia (artēriā)* literally, rough (windpipe); because of its roughness.] —**tra′che·al,** *adj.*

tra·che·id (trā′kə id) *n.* an elongated, thick-walled cell of the xylem of nearly all vascular plants that serves as a conduit for the movement of water and nutrients and provides support.

tra·che·ot·o·my (trā′kē ot′ə mē) *n., pl.* **-mies.** a surgical operation in which an opening is made through the neck into the trachea, usually to remove an obstruction in the throat.

tra·cho·ma (trə kō′mə) *n.* a chronic, contagious bacterial disease of the eye, common in tropical regions, characterized by inflammation and granulation of the eyelids. If not treated, it can lead to blindness. [Modern Latin *trachoma,* from Greek *trāchōma* roughness; because of the symptomatic roughness of the eyelids.]

tra·chom·a·tous (trə kom′ə təs, -kō′mə-) *adj.* of, relating to, or caused by trachoma.

trac·ing (trā′sing) *n.* **1.** the act of a person or thing that traces. **2.** a copy of something made by tracing its lines through transparent paper. **3.** a line or similar record made by a self-recording instrument; trace.

track (trak) *n.* **1.** a mark or set of marks made by a person, animal, or object in passage: *tire tracks in the snow.* **2.** a course along which anything moves; path; route: *the track of a comet, the track of a storm, a track through the woods.* **3.** a course of action or way of proceeding: *Your answer isn't correct, but you are on the right track.* **4.** a rail or set of parallel rails on which a vehicle, such as a railroad car, travels. **5.** a course laid out for racing. **6.a.** a sport consisting of running events, such as high hurdles or relay races. **b.** track and field. **7.** one of the two continuous metal belts on which a crawler tractor or similar vehicle runs tread. **8.a.** a band on a magnetic tape, on which sounds, images, or data are stored or recorded. **b.** a separate, individual segment of a recording, such as one song on a compact disc. **9.** *Computers.* a data-recording path on a magnetic disk. —*v.t.* **1.** to follow the tracks or scent of: *to track wild game through the forest.* **2.** to discover, pursue, or find by following tracks or investigating evidence (often with *down*): *to track the source of a problem, to track down the address of an old friend.* **3.** to observe and record the path of: *to track a hurricane, to track a space vehicle.* **4.** to make a track of footprints or other marks on (often with *up*): *The children tracked up the freshly waxed floor.* **5.** to make marks with (something) carried on one's feet: *to track snow on a carpet.* [Old French *trac*[1], beaten path, course; probably of Germanic origin.] —**track′er,** *n.*

· **in one's tracks.** *Informal.* exactly where one is at the moment; then and there: *The explosion made me stop in my tracks.*

· **to keep track of.** to maintain contact with or keep informed about.

· **to lose track of.** to fail to maintain contact with or keep informed about.

· **to make tracks.** *Informal.* to depart or move quickly.

track·age (trak′ij) *n.* **1.** the tracks of a railway system, collectively. **2.a.** the right of one railroad company to use the tracks of another. **b.** a charge for this right.

track and field, a group of sports events involving the basic physical activities of walking, running, jumping, and throwing.

tracking station, a facility equipped with instruments and an-

T

tennas for following or recording data from an object in the atmosphere or in space, as a meteoroid or a spacecraft.

track·less (trak′lis) *adj.* **1.** without or unmarked by paths or trails: *a trackless wilderness.* **2.** not running on tracks or rails: *Trolley buses are trackless vehicles.*

track meet, an athletic contest consisting of track and field events.

track record, a record of performance or achievement of a person or thing: *The senator has a good track record on civil rights issues.*

tract[1] (trakt) *n.* **1.** a stretch or expanse of land; area; region: *a tract of woodland.* **2.** a group of parts or organs in the body that together have a specific function: *the digestive tract, the urinary tract.* **3.** *Archaic.* a period or lapse of time. [Latin *tractus* region, course, a drawing out. Doublet of TRAIT.]

tract[2] (trakt) *n.* a booklet or pamphlet, esp. one on a religious or moral subject. [Modification of Latin *tractātus* handling, treatise.]

trac·ta·ble (trak′tə bəl) *adj.* **1.** easily controlled, dominated, or influenced; compliant; docile: *a tractable personality, a tractable horse.* **2.** easily worked or handled; malleable: *a tractable metal.* [Latin *tractābilis* manageable, from *tractāre* to handle. See TREAT.] —**trac′ta·bil′i·ty, trac′ta·ble·ness,** *n.* —**trac′ta·bly,** *adv.*

trac·tile (trak′təl) *adj.* capable of being drawn out in length; ductile.

trac·tion (trak′shən) *n.* **1.** the act of drawing or pulling something, such as a vehicle or load, along a road or other surface. **2.** the state or condition of being drawn or pulled. **3.** the power used for drawing or pulling: *steam traction.* **4.** the adhesive friction of a body on a surface: *A deep tread in tires provides better traction on snow-covered roads.* **5.** *Medicine.* **a.** the act of pulling a muscle, as of the leg, by means of some apparatus, so as to relieve pressure or bring fractured or dislocated bones into place. **b.** a state of tension maintained by a constant pull of this kind: *The victim was hospitalized and placed in traction.* [Medieval Latin *tractiō* act of drawing, from Latin *tractus,* past participle of *trahere* to draw, drag.]

traction engine, a locomotive for pulling heavy loads on roads or fields rather than on tracks.

trac·tive (trak′tiv) *adj.* capable of or used in drawing or pulling.

trac·tor (trak′tər) *n.* **1.** a motor vehicle having rubber tire wheels or treads, used esp. on farms for pulling harvesting machinery and plows and for hauling heavy loads. **2.** a truck with a short chassis, a powerful motor, and a driver's cab, used in combination with a trailer for transporting freight. [Modern Latin *tractor* literally, that which drags, from Latin *tractus,* past participle of *trahere* to drag, draw.]

trade (trād) *n.* **1.** the business of buying and selling; exchange of goods; commerce: *foreign trade, domestic trade.* **2.** a particular kind of business, including the people and firms engaged in it: *the building trade, a newspaper for the grocery trade.* **3.** the customers of a particular kind of business: *the theater trade.* **4.** something that a person does to earn a living, esp. an occupation requiring manual or mechanical skill: *to be a carpenter by trade, to learn the trade of an electrician.* **5.** the exchange of one thing for another; swap: *to make a trade of a pair of skates for a catcher's mitt.* **6. trades.** trade winds. —*adj.* **1.** for the general public: *a trade book, a trade edition.* **2.** of or for a particular kind of business: *a trade association, a trade magazine.* —*v.,* **trad·ed, trad·ing.** —*v.i.* **1.** to engage in buying and selling; be in commerce. **2.** to exchange one thing for another. **3.** to do business; shop: *I refuse to trade with that company again. We trade at the local shops.* —*v.t.* **1.** to exchange or swap: *to trade places, to trade blows.* **2.** to buy and sell. [Middle Low German *trade* track, course.]

• **to trade in.** to give in exchange as payment or part payment for something else: *to trade in an old car when buying a new one.*

• **to trade off.** to dispose of by sale or exchange.

• **to trade on.** to take advantage of or profit from; exploit: *to trade on someone's goodwill, to trade on one's political connections to get a good job.*

• **to trade up.** to give or sell something of less worth or value for something of greater worth or value.

trade-in (trād′in′) *n.* **1.** something given or received as payment or partial payment for something else, esp. a used item given to a dealer as partial payment for a similar, new item. **2.** a transaction involving a trade-in.

trade·mark (trād′märk′) *n.* **1.** a distinctive mark, such as a word, symbol, or device, used to identify and distinguish the goods or services of a particular merchant or manufacturer from those of another. A trademark is registered officially and cannot be used by anyone else. **2.** any distinctive sign, characteristic, or the like by which a person or thing comes to be known: *That tune has become*

the singer's trademark. —*v.t.* **1.** to place a trademark on. **2.** to register as a trademark.

trade name **1.** a name, often registered as a trademark, used to identify and distinguish the goods or services of a particular merchant or manufacturer. **2.** the name by which an article, service, or the like is commonly referred to in trade. **3.** the name under which a firm carries on business.

trade-off (trād′ôf′, -of′) *also,* **trade-off.** *n.* the exchange of one thing for another, esp. to gain a balance or compromise: *The company's offer was a trade-off between lower wages and higher benefits.*

trad·er (trā′dər) *n.* **1.** a person whose business is buying and selling. **2.** a ship used in trading.

trade school, vocational school.

trades·man (trādz′mən) *n., pl.* **-men** (-mən). shopkeeper.

trades·peo·ple (trādz′pē′pəl) *pl. n.* people who carry on a trade; shopkeepers.

trade union *also, British,* **trades union. 1.** a labor union in which the members are made up of workers engaged in a particular trade or craft. **2.** any labor union.

trade unionism, unionism *(def. 1).*

trade unionist **1.** a member of a trade union. **2.** a person who favors or supports trade unionism.

trade wind, either of two winds blowing steadily toward the equator from about 30 degrees north latitude to about 30 degrees south latitude, coming from the northeast north of the equator and from the southeast south of the equator. For illustration, see **wind.**

trading post, a store or station established by a trader or trading company in a sparsely settled or frontier region, where the local people can obtain goods, often in exchange for local products.

trading stamp, a stamp given as a premium to a customer, esp. in a retail establishment, to be exchanged in specified quantities for merchandise.

tra·di·tion (trə dish′ən) *n.* **1.** the handing down of knowledge, beliefs, customs, or the like from one generation to another. **2.** knowledge, beliefs, customs, or the like handed down in this manner. **3.** a long-established and generally accepted custom, practice, or the like: *It is a tradition in my family to celebrate birthdays by going out for dinner.* **4.a.** among the Jews, the body of unwritten laws and doctrines said to have been handed down by Moses. **b.** among certain Christians, the written precepts and doctrines handed down by Christ and the Apostles to the Church and preserved by its theologians. [Latin *trāditiō* surrender, delivery. Doublet of TREASON.]

Synonyms **Tradition, heritage,** and **legacy** can all denote something handed down from previous generations. **Tradition** is the general term for the knowledge, customs, attitudes, and history that have been passed on: *Thanksgiving is a holiday steeped in American tradition.* **Heritage** puts more emphasis on the inheriting of such things: *The principles embodied in the Constitution are part of every American's heritage.* **Legacy** connotes something specific derived from the past: *The American Civil War left the South with a legacy of economic depression.*

tra·di·tion·al (trə dish′ə nəl) *adj.* of, derived from, or in accordance with tradition: *Thanksgiving is a traditional American holiday.* Also, **tra·di·tion·ar·y** (trə dish′ə ner′ē). —**tra·di′tion·al·ly,** *adv.*

tra·di·tion·al·ism (trə dish′ə nə liz′əm) *n.* firm, often strict, attachment to tradition, esp. in religious practices. —**tra·di′tion·al·ist,** *n.*

tra·duce (trə düs′, -dūs′) *v.t.,* **-duced, -duc·ing.** to speak falsely or maliciously of; slander. [Latin *trādūcere* to lead across, dishonor.] —**tra·duc′er,** *n.*

traf·fic (traf′ik) *n.* **1.** vehicles, vessels, people, or the like moving along or through an area or route: *There was little traffic on the highway in the early morning hours.* **2.** the passage or flow of vehicles, vessels, people, or the like along or through an area or route: *The stop sign has made traffic safer on that road.* **3.** the exchange of goods, esp. for profit; buying and selling; trade. **4.** the dealing or bargaining in something illegal or improper: *The police attempted to stop narcotics traffic in the city.* **5.a.** the business done by a railroad, steamship, or other transportation line. **b.** the

a	at	e	end	o	hot	u	up	hw	white		about
ā	ape	ē	me	ō	old	ū	use	ng	song		taken
ä	far	i	it	ô	fork	ü	rule	th	thin	ə	pencil
âr	care	ī	ice	oi	oil	u̇	pull	th	this		lemon
		îr	pierce	ou	out	ûr	turn	zh	measure		circus

passengers or freight transported by such a line. **6.** communications, connections, or dealings between persons or groups: *In the story, they were accused of having traffic with the devil.* —*v.i.,* **-ficked, -fick·ing. 1.** to carry on commerce, esp. illegally; deal: *to traffic in stolen goods.* **2.** to have dealings or trade: *to traffic with known criminals.* [Middle French *trafique* commerce, from Italian *traffico;* of uncertain origin.] —**traf′fick·er,** *n.*

traffic circle, a circular intersection around which traffic moves in one direction, designed to allow vehicles to enter or leave any of the converging roads without disturbing the flow of traffic. Also, **rotary.**

traffic court, a local court that administers the laws relating to driving on public roads.

traffic island, a marked or raised area, such as a median strip, used to separate opposing lanes of traffic or to provide pedestrians with protection from the flow of traffic.

traffic light, a signal, usually with red and green and sometimes amber or yellow lights, that by changing color or blinking on or off controls the flow of traffic, esp. at an intersection. Also, **stoplight, traffic signal.**

trag·a·canth (trag′ə kanth′) *n.* a dull white gum obtained from any of several western Asian plants, esp. a shrub, *Astragalus gummifer,* used as a thickening and emulsifying agent in ice cream and candy, and in the making of printing inks and cosmetics. Also, **gum tragacanth.** [Latin *tragacantha* plant from which this gum is obtained, from Greek *tragakantha,* from *tragos* goat + *akantha* thorn.]

tra·ge·di·an (trə jē′dē ən) *n.* **1.** an actor who specializes in playing tragic roles. **2.** a writer of tragedies.

tra·ge·di·enne (trə jē′dē en′) *n.* an actress who specializes in playing tragic roles.

trag·e·dy (traj′i dē) *n., pl.* **-dies. 1.** a drama in which life is viewed or treated seriously, usually having a sad ending, esp. one involving the downfall or destruction of the main character through his or her actions or failings. **2.** the branch of drama composed of such plays. ➡ distinguished from **comedy. 3.** any work of literature having the characteristics of a dramatic tragedy. **4.** the art of writing, acting, or producing a tragedy or tragedies: *Shakespeare was a master of tragedy.* **5.** a dreadful or disastrous event: *The mine explosion was a tragedy that claimed seventeen lives.* **6.** a sad or unfortunate quality or element. [Old French *tragedie* serious play that usually has an unhappy ending, from Latin *tragoedia,* from Greek *tragōdiā* literally, goat song, from *tragos* goat + *ōidē* song; the reason for the name "goat song" is still disputed.]

trag·ic (traj′ik) *adj.* **1.** of, relating to, or characteristic of tragedy, esp. dramatic tragedy: *The play had a tragic ending.* **2.** very sad, unfortunate, or disastrous: *a tragic accident, a tragic decision.* **3.** writing or acting in tragedy: *a tragic actor.* Also, **trag′i·cal.** [Latin *tragicus,* from Greek *tragikos* relating to tragedy, relating to a goat, from *tragos* goat. See TRAGEDY.] —**trag′i·cal·ly,** *adv.*

tragic flaw, a flaw in the character of the protagonist of a tragedy that brings about his or her downfall.

trag·i·com·e·dy (traj′i kom′i dē) *n., pl.* **-dies. 1.** a drama containing both tragic and comic elements, usually having a happy ending. **2.** an event or set of circumstances combining tragic and comic elements. [French *tragicomédie,* going back to Latin *tragicocōmoedia* drama containing both tragic and comic elements, from *tragicus* (see TRAGIC) + *cōmoedia* (see COMEDY.)] —**trag′i·com′ic;** *also,* **trag′i·com′i·cal,** *adj.*

trail (trāl) *n.* **1.** a passage or track, as through a wild or uninhabited region: *The hikers followed the trail through the woods.* **2.** a mark, scent, or path made by an animal or person in passage: *The snail left a slimy trail on the glass of the tank. The posse lost the escaped convict's trail at the river edge.* **3.** something that follows or is drawn along behind: *a trail of smoke, a trail of destruction.* —*v.t.* **1.** to follow behind, esp. in a haphazard or lagging manner: *The children trailed the parade down the street.* **2.** to drag or draw along or behind: *The children trailed their kites on the ground.* **3.** to follow the track or scent of. **4.** to be behind or losing, as in a competition: *Our product trailed the others in sales.* —*v.i.* **1.** to hang down or be drawn behind, as the train of a dress. **2.** to move or flow slowly; drift: *The audience trailed in after the intermission.* **3.** to extend or grow over or along the ground or other surface: *The vines trailed along the side of the building.* **4.** to be losing, as in a contest or game; lag: *Our team trailed in the fifth inning, but went on to win.* **5.** to lessen gradually (with *off* or *away*): *Conversation trailed off as the evening wore on.* [Old French *traïller* to tow a boat, going back to Latin *trāgula* dragnet.]

trail·blaz·er (trāl′blā′zər) *n.* **1.** pathfinder. **2.** a pioneer in any field: *a painter who was a trailblazer in abstract art.*

trail·er (trā′lər) *n.* **1.** a person or thing that trails. **2.** a vehicle without its own motive power, designed to be pulled by a car,

truck, or similar vehicle, used as for transporting goods or the like. **3.** a similar vehicle, used esp. as a dwelling place. **4.** a plant or vine that extends or grows over or along the ground or other surface. **5.** a short film or videotape used to advertise a motion picture or program that will be shown in the future.

trailer court, a large area, usually equipped with plumbing and electrical facilities, where trailers can be parked and lived in. Also, **trailer camp, trailer park.**

trailing arbutus, an evergreen vine, *Epigaea repens,* of the heath family, growing along the ground in shady areas, bearing clusters of small, very fragrant pink or white blossoms.

trailing edge, the rear edge of an airfoil or propeller blade.

train (trān) *n.* **1.** a connected line of railroad cars. **2.** a group of people, animals, or vehicles traveling together, esp. in a long line or procession: *a mule train.* **3.** a connected series or succession, as of events or ideas: *to follow a train of thought.* **4.** a series of events, circumstances, or conditions resulting from or following something: *The play involved a train of comic episodes following an initial case of mistaken identity.* **5.** a part of a dress or robe that hangs down from the skirt and trails behind the wearer. **6.** something that is drawn along behind, such as the tail feathers of a peacock or the tail of a comet. **7.** a group of attendants; following; retinue: *a train of courtiers.* **8.** a group of vehicles and people following and attending an army, esp. to carry its supplies. **9.** a series of interconnected mechanical parts for transmitting motion, such as the wheels and pinions of a watch. —*v.t.* **1.** to develop or mold the character, thoughts, and behavior of; bring up; rear: *to train a child to respect the feelings of others.* **2.** to make able or skilled by instruction and practice, as in a particular trade or profession: *to train a new salesperson.* **3.** to prepare physically, as with regular drill, diet, and exercise: *to train an athlete.* **4.** to instruct (an animal) so as to make it obedient or capable of performing certain tasks or tricks. **5.** to cause to grow or lie in a desired form or direction: *to train one's hair to curl, to train ivy to grow up a wall.* **6.** to focus or direct; aim: *to train one's eyes on a distant object, to train a gun on a target.* —*v.i.* to undergo and follow a course of instruction or discipline: *to train for a big race, to train for a job.* [Old French *traïner* to drag, draw, going back to Latin *trahere.*] —For Synonyms *(v.t.),* see **teach.**

train·ee (trā nē′) *n.* a person who is undergoing training, esp. vocational or military training.

train·er (trā′nər) *n.* **1.** a person who trains, esp. a person responsible for the physical training and conditioning of an athlete, racehorse, or the like. **2.** a device used in training.

train·ing (trā′ning) *n.* **1.** the act, process, or method of a person who trains. **2.** the state or process of being trained.

train·load (trān′lōd′) *n.* the amount that a freight train or passenger train can carry.

train·man (trān′mən) *n., pl.* **-men** (-mən). a person who is employed on a railroad, esp. one who assists a conductor.

traipse (trāps) *v.i.,* **traipsed, traips·ing.** *Informal.* to walk about idly or aimlessly.

trait (trāt) *n.* a distinguishing aspect or quality, as of a person's character: *bravery, honesty, and other noble traits.* [French *trait,* from Latin *tractus* a drawing out, region, course. Doublet of TRACT[1].] —For Synonyms, see **characteristic.**

trai·tor (trā′tər) *n.* **1.** a person who commits treason. **2.** a person who betrays any trust. [Old French *traïtor,* from Latin *trāditor.*]

trai·tor·ous (trā′tər əs) *adj.* **1.** of, relating to, or characteristic of a traitor. **2.** of, relating to, or of the nature of treason. —**trai′tor·ous·ly,** *adv.*

tra·jec·to·ry (trə jek′tə rē) *n., pl.* **-ries.** the curved path described by a vehicle or projectile body, such as a bullet or ballistic missile, or by a meteor, moving through space or the atmosphere. [Medieval Latin *trajectorius* throwing across, from Latin *trājectus,* past participle of *trā(j)icere* to throw across.]

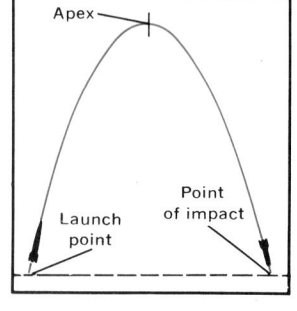

trajectory

tram (tram) *n.* **1.** *British.* streetcar. Also, **tram′car′. 2.** *British.* tramway *(def. 1).* **3.** a four-wheeled vehicle that runs on tracks, used to convey coal in a mine. **4.** an overhead cable car. [Middle Low German *trame* beam.]

tram·mel (tram′əl) *also,* **tram·el, tram·ell.** *n.* **1.** anything that confines, restrains, or hinders freedom, action, or progress. ➡ usually used in the plural: *to shake off the trammels of despair.* **2.** a shackle for hobbling a horse and training it to amble. **3.** a hook in a fireplace for suspending pots over the fire. **4.** a net for catching fish, consisting of two taut outside nets with large mesh and a slack middle net with a fine mesh. Also *(def. 4),* **trammel net.** *—v.t.,* **-meled, -mel·ing;** *also, British,* **-melled, -mel·ling. 1.** to hinder the freedom, action, or progress of; impede. **2.** to entangle in or as in a net; ensnare. [Middle French *tremail* dragnet, from Late Latin *trēmāclum* net with meshes for catching fish, possibly from Latin *trēs* three + *macula* mesh.] —**tram′mel·er;** *also, British,* **tram′mel·ler,** *n.*

tramp (tramp) *v.i.* **1.** to walk with a firm, heavy step: *The children tramped into the house in their boots.* **2.** to travel on foot; walk: *to tramp through the woods.* **3.** to step heavily (with *on* or *upon*): *to tramp on flowers.* **4.** to travel or wander as a tramp or vagabond. *—v.t.* **1.** to press or compress by stepping heavily upon; trample: *to tramp the grass.* **2.** to travel over or through on foot: *The hikers tramped the countryside.* *—n.* **1.** a person who wanders or travels from place to place, has no permanent residence or means of support, and usually begs for food, money, or temporary employment. **2.** a heavy footstep or series of footsteps. **3.** the sound made by such a step or steps: *We could hear the tramp of the marching soldiers.* **4.** a long walk; hike. **5.** a cargo ship, esp. a steamship, that does not trade regularly between fixed ports, but takes cargo wherever obtainable and for any port. [Probably of Germanic origin.] —**tramp′er,** *n.*

tram·ple (tram′pəl) *v.,* **-pled, -pling.** *—v.t.* **1.** to injure, crush, or destroy by or as by treading on heavily: *Don't trample the flowers.* **2.** to treat cruelly, harshly, or contemptuously: *to trample the opposition.* *—v.i.* to tread heavily. *—n.* the act or sound of trampling. [TRAMP + -LE.] —**tram′pler,** *n.*

tram·po·line (tram′pə lēn′, tram′pə lēn′) *n.* a piece of gymnastic equipment consisting of a sheet of canvas or other elastic material anchored by springs to a metal frame on legs, used for acrobatic tumbling. [Italian *trampolino* springboard, from *trampoli* stilts; of Germanic origin.] —**tram′po·lin′er, tram′po·lin′ist,** *n.*

tram·road (tram′rōd′) *n.* a railway in a coal mine.

tram·way (tram′wā′) *n.* **1.** *British.* streetcar track. **2.** tramroad. **3.** an overhead cable car line or system.

trance (trans) *n.* **1.** a semiconscious state resembling sleep, such as that produced by hypnotism. **2.** a dazed or stunned state; stupor. **3.** a state of deep mental absorption or concentration. **4.** a state of intense rapture, esp. one produced by a religious or spiritual experience. *—v.t.,* **tranced, tranc·ing.** *Archaic.* to put into or as into a trance. [Old French *transe* great fear, swoon, going back to Latin *trānsīre* to go across, die.]

tran·quil (trang′kwəl) *adj.* **-quil·er, -quil·est;** *also,* **-quil·ler, -quil·lest. 1.** free from agitation, esp. mental or emotional disturbance; calm: *a tranquil temperament, a tranquil childhood.* **2.** quiet and motionless: *a tranquil lake.* [Latin *tranquillus.*] —**tran′quil·ly,** *adv.* —For Synonyms, see **calm.**

tran·quil·ize (trang′kwə līz′) *also,* **tran·quil·lize.** *v.t., v.i.,* **-ized, -iz·ing.** to make or become tranquil, esp. by the use of tranquilizers.

tran·quil·iz·er (trang′kwə lī′zər) *also,* **tran·quil·liz·er.** *n.* any of certain drugs, other than barbiturates, that produce a calming effect by reducing nervous tension, anxiety, or the like.

tran·quil·li·ty (trang kwil′i tē) *also,* **tran·quil·i·ty.** *n.* the state or quality of being tranquil.

trans- *prefix* **1.** across; through; over: *transatlantic, transept.* **2.** so as to change completely: *transmute.* [Latin *trāns* across, beyond, over, through.]

trans. 1. transactions. **2.** transitive. **3.** transportation.

trans·act (tran sakt′, -zakt′) *v.t.* to conduct and carry through, esp. business affairs. *—v.i.* to do business. [Latin *trānsāctus,* past participle of *trānsigere* to drive through, accomplish.] —**trans·ac′tor,** *n.*

trans·ac·tion (tran sak′shən, -zak′-) *n.* **1.** the act of transacting or the state of being transacted. **2.** something that is or has been transacted, esp. a business dealing. **3. transactions.** a record, usually published, of the proceedings of a society, club, or the like.

trans·al·pine (trans al′pīn, -pin, tranz-) *adj.* beyond the Alps, esp. in relation to Rome.

trans·at·lan·tic (trans′ət lan′tik, tranz′-) *adj.* **1.** crossing or spanning the Atlantic: *a transatlantic telephone call.* **2.** on the opposite side of the Atlantic.

trans·ceiv·er (tran sē′vər) *n.* a combined radio transmitting and receiving unit, some components of which are used for both transmission and reception. [TRANS(MITTER) + (RE)CEIVER.]

tran·scend (tran send′) *v.t.* **1.** to pass or go beyond the limits or powers of; exceed: *The concept of infinity transcends human understanding.* **2.** to be greater or better than in some respect, quality, or attribute; be superior to; surpass: *This painting transcends the artist's earlier works.* **3.** in theology and philosophy, to exist above, beyond, or independent of (the universe, material existence, experience, or the like). [Latin *trānscendere* to climb over, surpass.]

tran·scend·ence (tran sen′dəns) *n.* the act of transcending or the state of being transcendent.

tran·scend·ent (tran sen′dənt) *adj.* **1.** surpassing or excelling others; superior; preeminent. **2.** *Religion.* (of God) existing above or independently of the universe. —**tran·scend′ent·ly,** *adv.*

tran·scen·den·tal (tran′sen den′təl) *adj.* **1.** superior; transcendent. **2.** beyond human experience or what is natural; supernatural. **3.** in Kantian philosophy, not derived from experience but based on the a priori elements of experience; transcending experience but not knowledge. **4.** *Mathematics.* not capable of being a solution of a rational algebraic equation. π is a transcendental number. —**tran′scen·den′tal·ly,** *adv.*

tran·scen·den·tal·ism (tran′sen den′tə ləm) *n.* **1.** the state or quality of being transcendental. **2.** the religious and philosophical ideas of a group of New England thinkers active from about 1835 to 1860, including Ralph Waldo Emerson and Henry David Thoreau, who held that God is inherent in nature and in human beings and that each person must use conscience and intuition to discover moral and spiritual truths. **3.** the doctrine, as in the philosophy of the German Immanuel Kant, that reality transcends human experience, and that knowledge of it can be obtained by a priori or intuitive, rather than empirical, principles. —**tran′scen·den′tal·ist,** *adj., n.*

transcendental meditation, a Hindu system of meditation that is supposed to lead to a state of consciousness somewhere between sleep and wakefulness.

trans·con·ti·nen·tal (trans′kon tə nen′təl) *adj.* **1.** crossing or spanning a continent: *a transcontinental communications network.* **2.** on the opposite side of a continent.

tran·scribe (tran skrīb′) *v.t.,* **-scribed, -scrib·ing. 1.** to make a written or typewritten copy of; rewrite or type: *to transcribe the recording of a meeting.* **2.** to write out or type out from one written form to another: *to transcribe shorthand notes.* **3.** to translate or transliterate. **4.** to represent (speech sounds) by phonetic symbols. **5.a.** to arrange or adapt (a musical composition) for a different voice or instrument. **b.** to reduce (music) to notation: *to transcribe a saxophone improvisation.* **6.** to make a recording of (a radio program or the like) to be broadcast later. **7.** *Biology.* to form a strand of RNA using the genetic information in a strand of DNA as a template. [Latin *trānscrībere* to copy off, transfer in writing.] —**tran·scrib′er,** *n.*

tran·script (tran′skript′) *n.* **1.** a written, typewritten, or printed copy: *The judge reviewed the transcript of the trial.* **2.** any reproduction or copy, esp. an official one, such as that of a student's cumulative academic record in a school or college. [Latin *trānscrīptum,* neuter past participle of *trānscrībere* to copy off, transfer in writing.]

tran·scrip·tion (tran skrip′shən) *n.* **1.** the act of transcribing. **2.** a transcript; copy. **3.a.** an adaptation or arrangement of a musical composition for another voice or instrument. **b.** a reduction of a piece of music, such as an improvisation, to notation. **4.** a recording, as on magnetic tape, of a radio program or the like to be broadcast later. **5.** a representation of speech sounds by phonetic symbols. **6.** *Biology.* the process of forming a strand of RNA using the genetic information in a strand of DNA as a template.

trans·du·cer (trans dü′sər, -dū′-, tranz-) *n.* a device that converts energy from one form into another, esp. one that converts sound or light into an electrical signal or vice versa. A microphone, one type of transducer, converts sound into an electrical signal, while a loudspeaker, another type, converts an electrical signal into sound. [Latin *transducere* to lead across (from *trans-* over + *ducere* to lead) + -ER¹.]

tran·sect (tran sekt′) *v.t.* to cut across; divide transversely. *—n.* a line marked out across an area along which the distribution of plant species can be studied. —**tran·sec′tion,** *n.*

a	at	e	end	o	hot	u	up	hw	white		about
ā	ape	ē	me	ō	old	ū	use	ng	song		taken
ä	far	i	it	ô	fork	ü	rule	th	thin	ə	pencil
âr	care	ī	ice	oi	oil	u̇	pull	th	this		lemon
		îr	pierce	ou	out	ûr	turn	zh	measure		circus

tran·sept (tran′sept) *n.* **1.** the transverse portion of a cruciform church. **2.** one of the two parts of this transverse portion, on either side of the main section of the church. [Modern Latin *transeptum,* going back to Latin *trāns* across + *sēptum* fence, enclosure.]

trans·fer (*v.,* trans fûr′, trans′fər; *n.,* trans′fər) *v.,* -**ferred,** -**fer·ring.** —*v.t.* **1.** to move or remove from one person, place, or the like to another: *to transfer money from one pocket to another.* **2.** to make over title or possession of to another: *to transfer land.* **3.** to convey (a drawing, design, pattern, or the like) from one surface to another. —*v.i.* **1.** to transfer oneself: *to transfer to a new job.* **2.** to be transferred: *The office will transfer to new quarters.* **3.** to withdraw from one school, course, class, or the like to enter another. **4.** to switch from one vehicle or transportation line to another, usually with little or no extra charge: *All passengers for Denver must transfer in Chicago.* —*n.* **1.** the act of transferring or the state of being transferred. Also, **trans·fer′al, trans·fer′ral. 2.** something that is transferred, esp. a drawing,

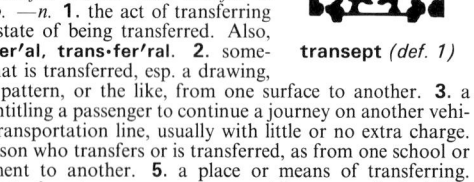

transept *(def. 1)*

design, pattern, or the like, from one surface to another. **3.** a ticket entitling a passenger to continue a journey on another vehicle or transportation line, usually with little or no extra charge. **4.** a person who transfers or is transferred, as from one school or department to another. **5.** a place or means of transferring. [Latin *trānsferre* to carry over, transport.] —**trans·fer′a·bil′i·ty,** *n.* —**trans·fer′a·ble,** *adj.*

trans·fer·ence (trans fûr′əns, trans′fər əns) *n.* **1.** the act of transferring or the state of being transferred. **2.** *Psychoanalysis.* the reproduction of emotions relating to forgotten or repressed experiences, esp. of childhood, and the shift of the focus of them to another person or object, esp. one's psychoanalyst.

transfer RNA, see RNA.

trans·fig·u·ra·tion (trans fig′yə rā′shən) *n.* **1.** the act of transfiguring or the state of being transfigured. **2. the Transfiguration. a.** in the New Testament, the miraculous change in the appearance of Jesus on a mountain in the presence of the Apostles Peter, James, and John. **b.** the church festival commemorating this event, observed on August 6.

trans·fig·ure (trans fig′yər) *v.t.,* -**ured,** -**ur·ing. 1.** to change the outward appearance of; alter in form or figure. **2.** to give an idealized appearance to; glorify. [Latin *trānsfigūrāre* to change in shape, transform.]

trans·fix (trans fiks′) *v.t.* **1.** to make motionless, as from awe or fear. **2.** to pierce through with or as with a sharpened instrument; impale. **3.** to fix or fasten by piercing. [Latin *trānsfīxus,* past participle of *trānsfīgere* to pierce through.]

trans·form (*v.,* trans fôrm′; *n.,* trans′fôrm′) *v.t.* **1.** to change the shape, form, or appearance of: *A little paint will soon transform this old car.* **2.** to change the character, condition, or nature of. **3.** to change (one form of energy) into another, as mechanical energy into electricity, or electric energy into light or heat. **4.** to change (an electric current) to a higher or lower voltage or to direct or alternating current. **5.** *Mathematics.* to change the form but not the value of (an algebraic expression or the like). —*n. Mathematics.* an expression derived from another by replacing variables without affecting the value of the expression. [Latin *trānsfōrmāre* to change the form of.]

trans·for·ma·tion (trans′fər mā′shən) *n.* **1.** the act of transforming or the state of being transformed. **2.** *Mathematics.* the process of deriving one expression, set, or space from another by means of specified mathematical operations.

trans·for·ma·tion·al grammar (trans′fər mā′shə nəl) a grammatical system that considers all sentences in a language either basic, or kernel, sentences or variations (transformations) of them developed as a speaker applies certain standard operations, or rules, to the basic sentences.

trans·form·er (trans fôr′mər) *n.* **1.** a person or thing that transforms. **2.** a device for transferring electric energy from one alternating current circuit to another by induction, usually with a change in voltage and current.

trans·fuse (trans fūz′) *v.t.,* -**fused,** -**fus·ing. 1.** to pour (a liquid) from one receptacle into another; transfer by pouring. **2.** to transfer (blood) intravenously from one individual to another. **3.** to inject (a saline solution or the like) into a blood vessel. **4.** to cause to be imparted or instilled: *The team members transfused their enthusiasm into the crowd.* [Latin *trānsfūsus,* past parti-

ciple of *trānsfundere* to pour from one receptacle into another, transfer.] —**trans·fus′a·ble,** *adj.*

trans·fu·sion (trans fū′zhən) *n.* the act of transfusing, esp. the intravenous transfer of blood from one individual to another.

trans·gen·ic (trans jen′ik, tranz-) *adj.* of or relating to an organism possessing a gene that has been transferred from another organism, as by means of a technique whereby foreign genetic material is injected into the nucleus of a fertilized egg. [TRANS- + GENE + -IC.]

trans·gress (trans gres′, tranz-) *v.i.* to break or violate a law, commandment, or the like; sin. —*v.t.* **1.** to break or violate (a law, commandment, or the like). **2.** to exceed or go beyond (a limit or bound). [Latin *trānsgressus,* past participle of *trānsgredī* to step across.] —**trans·gres′sor,** *n.*

trans·gres·sion (trans gresh′ən, tranz-) *n.* the act or an instance of transgressing, esp. the breaking of a law or commandment.

tran·ship (tran ship′) *v.t., v.i.* -**shipped,** -**ship·ping.** transship. —**tran·ship′ment,** *n.*

tran·sience (tran′shəns, -zhəns, -zē əns) *n.* the state or quality of being transient. Also, **tran′sien·cy.**

tran·sient (tran′shənt, -zhənt, -zē ənt) *adj.* **1.** of temporary or brief duration; not lasting or durable; transitory: *transient fame, transient beauty.* **2.** stopping only for a short time; passing through: *a transient house guest.* —*n.* **1.** a person or thing that is transient, esp. a person who passes through a place or stays in it only for a short time: *This boarding house caters mainly to transients.* **2.** *Physics.* a transient phenomenon, such as a surge in voltage. [Latin *trānsiēns,* present participle of *trānsīre* to go across, pass over.] —**tran′sient·ly,** *adv.*

tran·sis·tor (tran zis′tər) *n.* **1.** a miniature electronic device made of crystals of semiconductors, used instead of electron tubes to control and amplify electric current in television sets, computers, and other electronic equipment. **2.** transistor radio. [TRANS(FER) + (RE)SISTOR; because it transfers an electronic signal across a resistor.]

tran·sis·tor·ize (tran zis′tə rīz′) *v.t.,* -**ized,** -**iz·ing.** to equip with or make using transistors.

transistor radio, a radio, usually portable and battery-operated, whose components include printed circuits and transistors instead of electron tubes.

trans·it (tran′sit, -zit) *n.* **1.** the act or an instance of passing across or through; movement from one place or point to another: *We were delayed in transit by traffic.* **2.** the act of carrying or the state of being carried from one place or point to another; conveyance: *The transit of fresh fruit to markets must be done quickly.* **3.** a transition or change. **4.** a telescopic instrument used in surveying to measure horizontal and vertical angles. **5.** *Astronomy.* **a.** the passage of a planet directly between the earth and the sun so that it can be seen as a black dot moving across the disk of the sun. **b.** the passage of a celestial body across the celestial meridian. —*v.t.* to pass across or through. [Latin *trānsitus* a going over.]

tran·si·tion (tran zish′ən) *n.* **1.** a passage from one state, position, condition, or activity to another: *the transition from childhood to adolescence.* **2.** the period of such a passage. **3.** *Music.* **a.** a change of key. **b.** a passage connecting two parts, themes, or the like. [Latin *trānsitiō* a going across.] —**tran·si′tion·al,** *adj.* —**tran·si′tion·al·ly,** *adv.*

transition element, an element of any of the eight groups of metallic elements, IIIB through IIB of the periodic table, that are good conductors of heat and electricity, have high melting points, and have an atomic structure characterized by an incomplete complement of electrons in an inner shell. Also, **transition metal.**

tran·si·tive (tran′si tiv, -zi-) *adj.* (of verbs) taking a direct object to complete the action of the sentence. —*n.* a transitive verb. [Late Latin *trānsitīvus* passing over, from Latin *trānsitus,* past participle of *trānsīre* to go across.] —**tran′si·tive·ly,** *adv.*

tran·si·to·ry (tran′si tôr′ē, -zi-) *adj.* of brief duration; momentary. —**tran′si·to′ri·ly,** *adv.* —**tran′si·to′ri·ness,** *n.*

trans·late (trans lāt′, tranz-) *v.,* -**lat·ed,** -**lat·ing.** —*v.t.* **1.** to express in or change into another language: *to translate an American play into German.* **2.** to explain by using other words, terms, or signs: *The mathematician's theorem cannot be translated into simpler terms.* **3.** to change from one place, form, or condition to another: *to translate dreams into reality.* **4.** to remove bodily to heaven before death: *The prophet Elijah was translated in a fiery chariot by angels.* **5.** *Computers.* to convert (a program, data files, or the like) from one computer language to another. —*v.i.* **1.** to act as translator: *The guide translated for the tourists.* **2.** to be capable of being translated, as into another language: *an idiomatic style that doesn't translate well.* [Latin *trānslātus,* past parti-

ciple of *trānsferre* to carry over, transfer.] —**trans·lat'a·ble,** *adj.*

trans·la·tion (trans lā′shən, tranz-) *n.* **1.** the act of translating or the state of being translated. **2.** something that is produced as a result of translating, esp. a literary work in a different language from the original. **3.** *Biology.* the stage in the natural synthesis of protein in which the genetic code in messenger RNA establishes the sequence of amino acids in a polypeptide. **4.** *Mathematics.* the replacement of the coordinates of a point with coordinates that refer to a different pair of *x*- and *y*-axes.

trans·la·tor (trans lā′tər, tranz-) *n.* a person who translates from one language into another.

trans·lit·er·ate (trans lit′ə rāt′, tranz-) *v.t.,* -**at·ed, -at·ing.** to change (letters or words of one alphabet) into characters of another alphabet that have corresponding sounds. [TRANS- + Latin *littera* letter + -ATE[1].] —**trans·lit·er·a′tion,** *n.*

> **Usage** There may be several different systems for transliterating words into English from a language that does not use the Latin alphabet. Because of this, a word borrowed from such languages as Arabic, Chinese, Greek, Hebrew, or Russian may have more than one spelling. Although sometimes one of the spellings becomes the preferred or even the only one, often more than one spelling remains common. For example, when reading texts on Russian history, one can find the word **czar** spelled *czar, tzar,* or *tsar,* all of which are correct. Since **czar** is now the spelling most frequently used, dictionaries enter it as the main entry and enter the other spellings as variants. Some common transliterated words include (with the most frequent spelling shown in boldface) **ketchup,** catchup, catsup (from Malay); **sheik,** sheikh (from Arabic); **hallelujah,** halleluiah, alleluia (from Hebrew); **veranda,** verandah (from Hindi); **yogurt,** yoghurt, yoghourt (from Turkish prior to its conversion to a modified Roman alphabet). Some transliterated geographic terms include: **Beijing,** Peking, Peiping (China); **Giza,** Gizeh (Egypt); **Jakarta,** Djakarta (Indonesia); **Tehran,** Teheran (Iran). To determine the currently preferred form, one should check a recently published dictionary (an older dictionary will show the preferred spelling when that dictionary was compiled).

trans·lu·cence (trans lü′səns, tranz-) *n.* the state or quality of being translucent. Also, **trans·lu′cen·cy.**

trans·lu·cent (trans lü′sənt, tranz-) *adj.* allowing light to pass, but diffusing it so that objects on the other side cannot be clearly distinguished, such as frosted glass. [Latin *trānslūcēns,* present participle of *trānslūcēre* to shine through.] —**trans·lu′cent·ly,** *adv.* —For Synonyms, see **clear.**

trans·ma·rine (trans′mə rēn′, tranz′-) *adj.* **1.** crossing or spanning a sea. **2.** on the opposite side of a sea.

trans·mi·grate (trans mī′grāt, tranz-) *v.i.,* -**grat·ed, -grat·ing. 1.** (of a soul) to pass to another body at death. **2.** to migrate from one place of abode to another, esp. from one country to another. [Latin *trānsmigrātus,* past participle of *trānsmigrāre* to migrate from one place to another.] —**trans′mi·gra′tion,** *n.*

trans·mis·si·ble (trans mis′ə bəl, tranz-) *adj.* capable of being transmitted.

trans·mis·sion (trans mish′ən, tranz-) *n.* **1.** the act of transmitting or the state of being transmitted. Also, **transmittal. 2.** something that is transmitted, such as a television picture or telegraphic message. **3.** in an automobile, a series of gears and mechanical devices for transmitting power from the engine to the driving wheels. **4.a.** the sending out of signals, such as the electromagnetic waves used in radio and television communication. **b.** the passage of such signals through the air or space. [Latin *trānsmissiō* a sending across.]

trans·mit (trans mit′, tranz-) *v.t.,* -**mit·ted, -mit·ting. 1.** to send or cause to go from one person or place to another: *to transmit freight, to transmit a virus.* **2.** to communicate or convey: *to transmit greetings, to transmit one's feelings by facial expressions.* **3.** to pass on by or as by inheritance or heredity; hand down: *Genes are transmitted from one generation to another by chromosomes.* **4.a.** to cause (something, such as light, heat, or sound) to pass through a medium: *A tuning fork transmits sound waves through the air.* **b.** (of a medium) to allow (something, such as light, heat, or sound) to pass through: *Water transmits sound.* **5.** to send out (signals, a radio or television program, or the like) on electromagnetic waves or by wire. [Latin *trānsmittere* to send across, dispatch.] —For Synonyms, see **send.**

trans·mit·tal (trans mit′əl, tranz-) *n.* transmission *(def. 1).*

trans·mit·ter (trans mit′ər, tranz-) *n.* **1.** a person or thing that transmits. **2.** an apparatus that produces radio or television frequency signals for sending from an antenna. **3.** a device in a

telephone or telegraph that changes sound waves or movement into electrical impulses that can be carried over wires.

trans·mog·ri·fy (trans mog′ri fī′, tranz-) *v.t.,* -**fied, -fy·ing.** to change into another form or shape, esp. one that is fantastic or grotesque. [Of uncertain origin.] —**trans·mog′ri·fi·ca′tion,** *n.*

trans·mu·ta·tion (trans′mū tā′shən, tranz′-) *n.* **1.** the act of transmuting or the state of being transmuted. **2.** *Physics.* the conversion of one element into another by a natural or artificially produced change in its nuclear structure. —**trans′mu·ta′tion·al, trans·mut·a·tive** (trans mū′tə tiv, tranz-) *adj.*

trans·mute (trans mūt′, tranz-) *v.t.,* -**mut·ed, -mut·ing. 1.** to change in form, nature, or quality: *Alchemists tried to transmute metal into gold.* **2.** *Physics.* to subject (an element) to transmutation. [Latin *trānsmūtāre* to change, from *trans-* (see TRANS-) + *mūtāre* to change.] —**trans·mut′a·bil′i·ty, trans·mut′a·ble·ness,** *n.* —**trans·mut′a·ble,** *adj.* —**trans·mut′er,** *n.*

trans·o·ce·an·ic (trans′ō shē an′ik, tranz′-) *adj.* **1.** crossing or spanning an ocean. **2.** on the opposite side of the ocean.

tran·som (tran′səm) *n.* **1.** a window above a door or other window, usually hinged to a horizontal bar. **2.** a horizontal bar that divides a window or separates a door or window from a window above. [Probably a modification of Latin *trānstrum* crossbeam, from *trāns* across.]

tran·son·ic (tran son′ik) *also,* **trans·sonic.** *adj.* of, relating to, or moving at speeds close to the speed of sound, 700-780 miles (1,135-1,265 kilometers) per hour: *a transonic jetliner.*

trans·pa·cif·ic (trans′pə sif′ik) *adj.* **1.** crossing or spanning the Pacific. **2.** on the opposite side of the Pacific.

trans·par·en·cy (trans pâr′ən sē, -par′-) *n., pl.* -**cies. 1.** the state or quality of being transparent. Also, **trans·par′ence. 2.** something transparent, esp. a photographic slide.

trans·par·ent (trans pâr′ənt, -par′-) *adj.* **1.** transmitting light so that objects

transom

on the other side can be seen distinctly, as the lenses in a pair of glasses or the panes of a window. **2.** easily perceived or seen through; evident; obvious: *a transparent lie.* **3.** so fine or loosely woven as to be easily seen through: *transparent fabric.* **4.** honest and open; frank; candid. [Medieval Latin *transparens,* present participle of *transparere* to show through, from Latin *trāns* through, across + *pārēre* to appear.] —**trans·par′ent·ly,** *adv.* —**trans·par′ent·ness,** *n.* —For Synonyms, see **clear.**

tran·spi·ra·tion (tran′spə rā′shən) *n.* the act or process of transpiring, esp. the giving off of vaporous waste products by a living organism.

tran·spire (tran spīr′) *v.,* -**spired, -spir·ing.** —*v.i.* **1.** to take place; happen; occur: *It was impossible to predict what would transpire once the game started.* **2.** to become known; come to light: *It finally transpired that the fire was deliberately set.* **3.** *Biology.* to give off waste products in the form of vapor, as through the pores of the skin. —*v.t.* **1.** *Biology.* to give off (waste products) in the form of vapor. [French *transpirer* to exhale, perspire, become known, from Latin *trāns* through, across + *spīrāre* to breathe.]

> **Usage** **Transpire** is commonly used to mean "take place" or "happen," as in *The delegates will give a report on what transpires at the conference.* Although this usage is widespread, some think it unacceptable.

trans·plant (trans plant′) *v.t.* **1.** to remove (a plant) from one site and plant it again in another. **2.** to move from one place to another; transport: *The farmer transplanted the entire herd to a new pasture.* **3.** *Medicine.* to transfer (skin, an organ, or the like) from one person or animal to another or from one part of the body to another. —*v.i.* to be capable of being moved or removed, as from one place to another. —*n.* **1.** something that is transplanted: *The transplant flourished in new soil. The patient received a kidney transplant.* **2.** the act or process of transplanting. [Late Latin *trānsplantāre* to remove, transport, from *trāns* across + *plantāre* to plant, fix in place.] —**trans·plant′a·ble,** *adj.*

a	at	e	end	o	hot	u	up	hw	white		about
ā	ape	ē	me	ō	old	ū	use	ng	song		taken
ä	far	i	it	ô	fork	ü	rule	th	thin	ə	pencil
âr	care	ī	ice	oi	oil	u̇	pull	th	this		lemon
		îr	pierce	ou	out	ûr	turn	zh	measure		circus

—**trans·plan·ta·tion** (trans'plan tā'shən), *n.* —**trans·plant'-er,** *n.*

trans·po·lar (trans pō'lər, tranz-) *adj.* lying, extending, or traveling across either the North or South Pole or polar region: *a transpolar expedition.*

tran·spond·er (tran spon'dər) *n.* a radio transmitter-receiver that upon receiving a certain signal automatically transmits a signal of its own, used in navigating a plane or controlling the flight of a rocket. [TRAN(SMITTER) + (RE)SPONDER.]

trans·port (*v.,* trans pôrt'; *n.,* trans'pôrt') *v.t.* **1.** to bring or convey from one place or person to another: *to transport freight by rail.* **2.** to carry away by strong emotion; enrapture: *The beautiful music transported us.* **3.** to punish (a criminal) by sending him or her abroad to a penal colony. **4.** *Archaic.* to kill. —*n.* **1.** the act of transporting. **2.** a ship used to carry military personnel. **3.** an airplane used to transport passengers, mail, or freight. **4.** the state or condition of being transported; rapture. **5.** a convict who is sentenced to exile. [Latin *trānsportāre* to carry across.] —**trans·port'a·bil'i·ty,** *n.* —**trans·port'a·ble,** *adj.* —**trans·port'er,** *n.* —For Synonyms (*v.t.*), see carry.

trans·por·ta·tion (trans'pər tā'shən) *n.* **1.** the act of transporting or the state of being transported. **2.** a means of transporting, such as a vehicle. **3.** the cost of transporting, esp. for traveling by a public conveyance: *Transportation to and from work was two dollars per day.*

trans·pose (trans pōz') *v.t.,* -posed, -pos·ing. **1.** to put each of (two or more things) in the place of the other or others; reverse the order of; interchange: *The typesetter accidentally transposed the initials J and K, so that JFK read KFJ.* **2.** to move (something) from one place or time to another: *a medieval story transposed by the author to the twentieth century.* **3.** to write or perform (music) in other than the original or given key. **4.** *Mathematics.* to transfer (an algebraic term) from one side of an equation to the other, changing the plus or minus sign to maintain equality. [Middle French *transposer* to transfer, move from one place to another, modification (influenced by French *poser* to place, put) of Latin *trānspōnere* to place across, remove, transfer.] —**trans·pos'a·ble,** *adj.* —**trans·pos'er,** *n.*

trans·po·si·tion (trans'pə zish'ən) *n.* **1.** the act of transposing or the state of being transposed. **2.** something that has been transposed. Also, **trans·pos·al** (trans pō'zəl). —**trans'po·si'-tion·al,** *adj.*

trans·sex·u·al (trans sek'shü əl) *n.* an individual who is extremely uncomfortable with his or her own anatomical sex and identifies strongly with the opposite sex, sometimes to the extent of seeking to change sex through surgery and hormone injections. —**trans·sex'u·al·ism,** *n.*

trans·ship (trans ship') *also,* **tranship.** *v.t., v.i.,* -shipped, -ship·ping. to transfer (cargo) from one ship, train, truck, or other conveyance to another for further transit. —**trans·ship'-ment,** *n.*

trans·son·ic (trans son'ik, tran-) transonic.

tran·sub·stan·ti·a·tion (tran'səb stan'shē ā'shən) *n.* **1.** the transformation of one substance into another. **2.** the doctrine that the bread and wine of the Eucharist becomes the body and blood of Jesus, although the appearance and taste are unchanged. [Medieval Latin *transubstantiatio* transmutation, going back to Latin *trāns* across, over + *substantia* essence, material.]

trans·u·ran·ic (trans'yů ran'ik, tranz'-) *adj.* of, relating to, or designating those elements having an atomic number greater than 92, the atomic number of uranium, comprising the series of actinides from neptunium through lawrencium, which are all subject to radioactive decay and thus relatively rare in nature.

trans·ver·sal (trans vûr'səl, tranz-) *adj.* transverse. —*n.* a line that intersects two or more lines.

trans·verse (trans vûrs', tranz-) *adj.* situated or lying across or in a crosswise direction. —*n.* something that is transverse. [Latin *trānsversus* turned across, athwart.] —**trans·verse'ly,** *adv.*

transverse wave *Physics.* a wave, as of water or of certain kinds of seismic vibrations in the earth, in which the disturbance of the medium through which the wave is traveling takes place in a direction perpendicular to the direction of travel.

trans·ves·tite (trans ves'tīt, tranz-) *n.* a person, esp. a male, who dresses in clothing usually worn by the opposite sex. —**trans·ves'tism, trans·ves·ti·tism** (trans ves'ti tiz'əm, tranz-), *n.*

trap[1] (trap) *n.* **1.** a contrivance, such as a falsely covered pit or mechanical device that springs shut suddenly, used for catching game or other animals. **2.** any trick or stratagem used to catch a person unawares: *The district attorney's question was a trap that caused the defendant to admit guilt.* **3.** a bend in a pipe, usually

U-shaped or S-shaped, that fills with liquid to form a seal, as to keep air in the pipe or to prevent the return flow of a gas. **4.** a device used to hurl clay pigeons or the like into the air for target shooting. **5.** a light, two-wheeled carriage with springs. **6.** in certain games, an obstacle or hazard, esp. a sand trap in a golf course. **7.** trapdoor. **8.** *Slang.* mouth: *Shut your trap!* —*v.,* **trapped, trap·ping.** —*v.t.* **1.** to catch in a trap; entrap; ensnare: *Hunters trapped the bear.* **2.** to catch by a trick or stratagem: *They trapped me into admitting I knew about the surprise party.* **3.** to furnish or provide

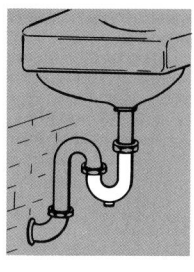

trap[1] *(def. 3)*

with a trap or traps. **4.** to stop and hold (gas, liquid, or the like) as with a trap. —*v.i.* **1.** to set traps for game: *The forest ranger arrested the poacher for trapping in the game preserve.* **2.** to be a trapper. [Old English *træppe* device for catching animals.]

trap[2] (trap) *v.t.,* **trapped, trap·ping.** to furnish or adorn with trappings. —*n.* **traps.** *Informal.* personal belongings, esp. luggage or baggage. [Probably from Old French *drap* cloth. See DRAPE.]

trap[3] (trap) *n.* any dark, igneous rock with a fine-grained texture, as basalt or diabase, crushed and used in making and repairing roads. [Swedish *trapp,* from *trappa* stair; because its outcrops look like stairs.]

trap·door (trap'dôr') *n.* a hinged or sliding door in a floor, ceiling, or roof.

tra·peze (tra pēz', trə-) *n.* a short, swinging horizontal bar suspended from two ropes, used in gymnastics and acrobatics. [French *trapèze,* from Late Latin *trapezium* trapezium, from Greek *trapezion* small table, trapezium.]

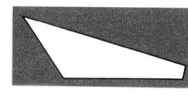

trapezium

tra·pe·zi·um (trə pē'zē əm) *n., pl.* -zi·ums or -zi·a (-zē ə). **1.** a quadrilateral with no two sides parallel. **2.** *British.* trapezoid *(def. 1).* [Late Latin *trapezium,* from Greek *trapezion* trapezium, small table, diminutive of *trapeza* table.]

tra·pe·zi·us (trə pē'zē əs) *n., pl.* -us·es or -zi·i (-zē ī'). a wide, flat muscle located on each side of the neck, shoulders, and back. A trapezius moves a shoulder and the head.

trap·e·zoid (trap'ə zoid') *n.* **1.** a quadrilateral with only two sides parallel. **2.** *British.* trapezium *(def. 1).* [Modern Latin *trapezoides,* from Greek *trapezoeidēs* shaped like a table or trapezium, from *trapeza* table + *eidos* form.] —**trap'e·zoi'dal,** *adj.*

trap·per (trap'ər) *n.* a person who traps wild animals, esp. one who traps fur-bearing animals for their pelts.

trap·pings (trap'ingz) *pl. n.* **1.** an ornamented cloth or covering spread over the harness or saddle

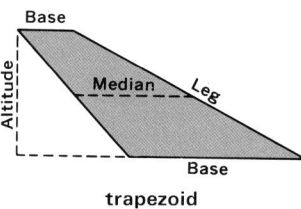

trapezoid

of a horse. **2.** external or superficial adornments: *crowns and other trappings of royalty.* **3.** outward signs regarded as characteristic or indicative of something: *multiple houses, a private plane, and other trappings of great wealth.* [TRAP[2] + -ING[1] + -S[1].]

Trap·pist (trap'ist) *n.* a member of a Roman Catholic order of monks established in 1664 as a branch of the Cistercians, noted for observing strict silence and many other austere rules. —*adj.* of or relating to the Trappists. [French *Trappiste,* from *La Trappe,* a monastery of this order in Normandy, France.]

trap·shoot·ing (trap'shü'ting) *n.* a recreational and competitive sport in which shooters fire shotguns at clay pigeons hurled into the air singly or in pairs at an angle like that of a game bird taking flight. —**trap'shoot'er,** *n.*

trash (trash) *n.* **1.** worthless or discarded objects or matter. **2.** worthless or foolish talk, writing, ideas, or the like: *How can a book that's such trash be so popular?* **3.** a low, contemptible person or persons. **4.** something that is broken or cut off, esp. trimmings from a plant or tree. —*v.t. Slang.* **1.** to damage or destroy (property) completely: *The vandals trashed the building.* **2.** to criticize severely. [Of uncertain origin.]

trash·y (trash'ē) *adj.,* trash·i·er, trash·i·est. **1.** of or like trash; worthless; inferior: *a trashy movie.* **2.** containing trash: *a trashy yard.* —**trash'i·ly,** *adv.* —**trash'i·ness,** *n.*

trau·ma (trô′mə, trou′-) *n., pl.* **-mas** or **-ma·ta** (-mə tə). **1.** a severe and painful emotional shock, usually having a lasting effect on the personality. **2.** a bodily wound or injury. [Greek *trauma* wound.]

trau·mat·ic (trô mat′ik, trou-) *adj.* of, relating to, of the nature of, or caused by a trauma. —**trau·mat′i·cal·ly,** *adv.*

trau·ma·tize (trô′mə tīz′, trou′-) *v.t.,* **-tized, -tiz·ing. 1.** to wound or injure. **2.** to subject (an individual) to a severe and painful emotional shock.

trav·ail (trə vāl′, trav′āl) *n.* **1.** difficult, exhausting mental or physical labor. **2.** intense anguish or suffering, esp. when caused by extreme hardship. **3.** the pains of childbirth; labor. —*v.i.* **1.** to exert oneself; toil. **2.** to suffer the pains of childbirth; be in labor. [Old French *travail* toil, labor, torment, going back to Medieval Latin *trepalium* instrument of torture (possibly made of three stakes), from Latin *trēs* three + *pālus* stake.]

trav·el (trav′əl) *v.,* **-eled, -el·ing;** *also, British,* **-elled, -el·ling.** —*v.i.* **1.** to go from one place to another; make a journey: *to travel through Ireland.* **2.** to go from place to place as a traveling salesman. **3.** to pass or be transmitted from one point to another: *Sound waves travel through water.* **4.** to be habitually in the company of; associate with (with *with*): *to travel with a bad crowd.* **5.** *Basketball.* to walk or run more than the allowed number of steps, usually two, while holding the ball instead of dribbling it. **6.** *Informal.* to move with speed: *We'll have to travel in order to make the train in time.* —*v.t.* to move or journey over or through; make a tour of: *to travel the country making speeches.* —*n.* **1.** the act of traveling from one place to another. **2.** movement or progress in general; advancement. **3.a.** the motion of a mechanical part, esp. a reciprocating one. **b.** the length of mechanical stroke, as of a piston. **4. travels. a.** a long trip to many different places; journeys: *We met many interesting people in our travels.* **b.** a written account of one's experiences and observations while traveling. [Form of TRAVAIL; probably originally referring to the discomforts and dangers of travel in earlier times.]

travel agency, a business establishment that makes travel arrangements for travelers, as by arranging transportation or securing hotel reservations.

trav·eled (trav′əld) *also, British,* **trav·elled.** *adj.* **1.** having done extensive traveling, esp. to foreign countries. **2.** (of a road, route, or the like) frequented by many travelers.

trav·el·er (trav′ə lər, trav′lər) *also, British,* **trav·el·ler.** *n.* **1.** a person who travels. **2.** *British.* traveling salesman.

traveler's check, a check or draft for a fixed amount of money that is bought for use in place of cash, esp. by travelers. It is payable when countersigned by the bearer in the presence of the person cashing it.

traveling salesman, a person who travels from place to place selling or taking orders for goods from the company he or she represents.

trav·e·logue (trav′ə lôg′, -log′) *also,* **trav·e·log.** *n.* **1.** a lecture, usually illustrated with films, describing travel. **2.** a motion picture about a particular country or region. [TRAVEL + *-logue,* as in MONOLOGUE or DIALOGUE.]

trav·erse (trə vûrs′, trav′ərs) *v.,* **-ersed, -ers·ing.** —*v.t.* **1.** to pass or move across, over, or through: *The climbers traversed the mountain range.* **2.** to go back and forth over or along; cross and recross: *The airline traverses the country from coast to coast.* **3.** to extend over or across; span: *The bridge traverses the deep gorge.* **4.** to go up, down, or across on a diagonal: *to traverse a hill.* **5.** to go against; oppose; thwart. **6.** to examine carefully; scrutinize: *to traverse a book for a particular passage.* —*v.i.* **1.** to move or go along, across, or back and forth: *You can traverse to the other side where there is an overpass.* **2.** to go down a slope on a diagonal: *The skier traversed down the slope.* —*n.* **1.a.** the act of traversing or crossing. **b.** the distance traversed or crossed. **2.** something, such as a part or structure, put or lying across. **3.** a bank or wall of earth protecting a trench or an exposed place in a fortification. **4.** a gallery or loft going from one side of a building, esp. a church, to the other. **5.** transversal. **6.** sideways motion or zigzag course, such as that of a ship, piece of artillery, part in a machine, or skier. **7.** *Nautical.* a tack taken by a ship because of contrary winds or currents. **8.** something that hinders or opposes; obstacle. **9.** in surveying, a surveyed line or interconnected system of such lines. —*adj.* lying or being across. —*adv. Archaic.* across; crosswise. [Old French *traverser* to cross, thwart, from Late Latin *trānsversāre* to cross, from Latin *trānsversus* turned across, athwart.] —**tra·vers′a·ble,** *adj.* —**tra·vers′al,** *n.* —**tra·vers′er,** *n.*

trav·er·tine (trav′ər tēn′, -tin) *also,* **trav·er·tin** (trav′ər tin). *n.* a freshwater limestone deposited, esp. in caves, by water from springs. A compact form of this rock is cut and polished for use as a decorative building stone. [Italian *travertino,* modification of earlier *tivertino,* from Latin *(lapis) Tīburtīnus* (stone) from Tibur, an ancient town in Latium.]

trav·es·ty (trav′ə stē) *n., pl.* **-ties. 1.** a grotesque or absurd imitation: *The jury's biased verdict was a travesty of justice.* **2.** in literature, a grotesque or burlesque treatment of a serious work or a serious subject. —*v.t.,* **-tied, -ty·ing.** to ridicule by grotesque parody or imitation. [French *travesti,* past participle of *travestir* to disguise, burlesque, going back to Latin *trāns* across + *vestīre* to dress.]

tra·vois (trə voi′, trav′oi) *n., pl.* **-vois.** a V-shaped sled, used esp. by Indians of the Great Plains, consisting of a platform or net supported by two long poles, the front ends of the poles harnessed to a horse, dog, or other draft animal, the rear ends dragging along the ground.

trawl (trôl) *n.* **1.** a strong, usually bag-shaped, net towed over the ocean bottom to catch fish. Also, **trawl net. 2.** a long line set out from a vessel and supported by buoys, having short lines with baited hooks every few feet along its length, used to catch fish. Also, **trawl line.** —*v.i.* to fish with a trawl. —*v.t.* to catch (fish) with a trawl. [Middle Dutch *traghelen* to drag, probably going back to Latin *trāgula* dragnet.]

trawl·er (trô′lər) *n.* **1.** a fishing boat used for trawling. **2.** a person who fishes with a trawl.

tray (trā) *n.* a flat, shallow vessel with a slightly raised rim, used for carrying, storing, or exhibiting objects. [Old English *trēg, trīg.*]

treach·er·ous (trech′ər əs) *adj.* **1.** likely to betray a trust; traitorous; disloyal. **2.** dangerous; hazardous: *Many ships have capsized on that treacherous reef.* —**treach′er·ous·ly,** *adv.* —**treach′er·ous·ness,** *n.*

treach·er·y (trech′ə rē) *n., pl.* **-er·ies.** willful betrayal or violation of a trust. [Old French *trecherie* deceit, cheating, from *trechier* to deceive, cheat; of uncertain origin.]

trea·cle (trē′kəl) *n. British.* molasses. [Old French *triacle* antidote against venom made with honey or syrup, going back to Latin *thēriaca* antidote against venom, from Greek *thēriakē,* from *thērion* wild or venomous animal.]

tread (tred) *v.,* **trod** or *(archaic)* **trode, trod·den** or **trod, tread·ing.** —*v.t.* **1.** to walk on, along, or over; step upon: *to tread a dirt road home.* **2.** to press with the feet; trample: *Don't tread the flowers.* **3.** to form, do, or follow by or as walking: *The children trod a path across the yard.* **4.** to put down or oppress; subdue; crush. —*v.i.* **1.** to move on or as if on foot; walk or step: *to tread heavily across a room.* **2.** to trample (with *on* or *upon*): *Don't tread on the grass.* —*n.* **1.** the act, manner, or sound of treading. **2.** the outer, grooved surface of an automobile tire. **3.** the horizontal part of a step in a staircase, on which one treads. **4.** the part of a wheel that touches the ground or rails. **5.** the part of the sole of a shoe that touches the ground. **6.** one of the continuous metal belts on which a tank, bulldozer, or similar vehicle runs. [Old English *tredan* to step upon, walk on, go, trample on.] —**tread′er,** *n.*

·to tread water (past tense **tread·ed**). **a.** to keep one's head above water while staying in an upright position, usually by moving the feet up and down in a walking motion. **b.** to merely maintain one's existing status or position, instead of advancing or flourishing: *I've been treading water at work for some time now.*

trea·dle (tred′əl) *n.* a lever or pedal worked by the foot to provide motion for operating a machine, such as a potter's wheel. —*v.i.,* **-dled, -dling.** to work a treadle. [Old English *tredel* step, stair.]

tread·mill (tred′mil′) *n.* **1.** an apparatus rotated by animals or persons walking or running on the moving steps of a wheel or treading an endless sloping belt, used to impart rotary motion for doing work. **2.** a similar apparatus consisting of a motor-driven endless belt, used esp. as a source of indoor physical exercise. **3.** any monotonous, wearisome routine or activity.

treas. 1. treasurer. **2.** treasury.

trea·son (trē′zən) *n.* the crime of betraying one's country by helping a foreign power attack or make war against it. [Anglo-Norman *tres(o)un,* from Latin *trāditiō* a handing over, surrender, betrayal. Doublet of TRADITION.]

trea·son·a·ble (trē′zə nə bəl) *adj.* of, relating to, involving, or

a	at	e	end	o	hot	u	up	hw	white		about
ā	ape	ē	me	ō	old	ū	use	ng	song		taken
ä	far	i	it	ô	fork	ü	rule	th	thin	ə	pencil
âr	care	ī	ice	oi	oil	u̇	pull	th	this		lemon
				îr	pierce	ou	out	ûr	turn	zh	measure		circus

characteristic of treason. Also, **trea′son·ous.** —**trea′son·a·ble·ness,** *n.* —**trea′son·a·bly,** *adv.*

treas·ure (trezh′ər) *n.* **1.** a store of valuables, such as money or jewels; accumulated riches. **2.** a person or thing that is greatly valued or considered precious: *The blocks of beautiful stone buildings are the city's greatest architectural treasure.* —*v.t.,* **-ured, -ur·ing. 1.** to consider or regard as being of great value; hold or keep as precious; cherish: *to treasure one's family heirlooms.* **2.** to put away or lay aside for preservation, security, or future use; store up; hoard. [Old French *tresor* store of precious objects, anything considered precious, going back to Latin *thēsaurus* store, storehouse, from Greek *thēsauros.* Doublet of THESAURUS.] —For Synonyms *(v.t.),* see **cherish.**

treas·ur·er (trezh′ər ər) *n.* a person who is officially entrusted with the receipt, care, and disbursement of funds, as of a corporation, club, or the like.

treas·ure-trove (trezh′ər trōv′) *n.* **1.** *Law.* money, jewels, or other valuables, found hidden and whose owner is not known. **2.** any discovery that proves to be valuable. [Anglo-Norman *tresor trove* literally, treasure found, from *tresor* (see TREASURE) + *trove,* past participle of *trover* to find (of uncertain origin).]

treas·ur·y (trezh′ə rē) *n., pl.* **-ur·ies. 1.** a place where funds, esp. public revenue, are deposited and stored. **2.** funds or revenues, as of a corporation or government. **3.** *Treasury.* a governmental department that is in charge of the collection of taxes and the management of a country's finances. **4.** a place or receptacle where treasure is kept. **5.** a person or thing that is thought of as a rich or ample source of things considered to be precious or of great value: *The book is a treasury of information about the Spanish Civil War.*

Treasury bill, a U.S. government bond paying no interest but sold to the public at less than its face value and usually becoming due at its face value in 91 to 182 days.

treasury note 1. a note or bill formerly issued by the U.S. Treasury, used as legal tender for all debts. **2.** a U.S. government bond having a maturity of from one to ten years.

treat (trēt) *v.t.* **1.** to act or behave toward in a particular way: *The teacher treated the children with kindness. The judge treats each defendant fairly.* **2.** to regard, consider, or deal with in a specified manner: *to treat a minor accident as a catastrophe, to treat a subject in great detail.* **3.** to give medical or surgical attention to: *to treat a patient with a broken leg, to treat a cut with iodine.* **4.** to subject to a chemical or physical process or application, as for altering or improving: *to treat cloth with a chemical to make it waterproof.* **5.** to deal with in speech or writing; discuss: *The magazine article treated various aspects of the political scene.* **6.** to deal with, develop, or represent (a subject in art or literature): *Many poems and stories have treated the exploits of Robin Hood.* **7.** to pay for or provide the food, drink, or the like of (another): *to treat a friend to a good meal.* —*v.i.* **1.** to deal with a subject in speech or writing (often with *of*): *a book that treats of military history.* **2.** to pay for or provide another's food, drink, or the like. **3.** to carry on negotiations; discuss or arrange terms. —*n.* **1.** food, drink, or the like given or paid for by another. **2.** something that gives unexpected or unusual pleasure: *Going to the circus was a treat for us.* **3.** the act of treating or one's turn to treat. [Old French *traitier* to handle, conduct, drag, from Latin *tractāre,* from *trahere* to drag, draw.] —**treat′a·ble,** *adj.* —**treat′er,** *n.*

trea·tise (trē′tis) *n.* a book or other piece of writing dealing in a formal way with some subject: *a treatise on the nature of democratic government.* [Anglo-Norman *tretiz,* from Old French *traitier* to conduct, handle. See TREAT.]

treat·ment (trēt′mənt) *n.* **1.** the act, process, or manner of treating. **2.** a course of action or means used to treat something, esp. the care and medication prescribed to treat an illness.

trea·ty (trē′tē) *n., pl.* **-ties.** a formal agreement, esp. one between nations, signed and approved by each party: *The peace treaty was signed by all nations involved in the conflict.* [Old French *trait(i)e,* from Latin *tractātus* handling, treatment, discussion.]

tre·ble (treb′əl) *adj.* **1.** three times as much or as many; triple. **2.** of, relating to, or for the highest musical instrument or voice; soprano. —*n.* a soprano voice, part, or instrument. —*v.t., v.i.,* **-bled, -bling.** to make or become three times as much or as many. [Old French *treble* triple, from Latin *triplus* threefold, from Greek *triplous.* Doublet of TRIPLE.] —**tre′bly,** *adv.*

treble clef, the clef placed on the second line of the staff, indicating that that line corresponds to the note G above middle C. Also, **G clef.** For illustration, see **clef.**

tree (trē) *n.* **1.** a perennial plant, often of considerable height, having a single, self-supporting stem or trunk that develops solid, permanent, woody tissue, as distinguished from the tissue of herbs, and that develops branches and leaves at some distance above the ground. **2.** any of various bushes, shrubs, or perennial herbaceous plants, such as the banana, that resemble a tree in size or shape. **3.** any structure or device resembling a tree in shape or outline: *a shoe tree.* **4.** a diagram resembling a tree with its branches, esp. a diagram of a family, having an original ancestor as the root and the various descendants as the branches. **5.** *Archaic.* gallows. **6. the tree.** *Archaic.* the cross on which Jesus was crucified. —*v.t.,* **treed, tree·ing. 1.** to chase or force into or up a tree; cause to take refuge in a tree: *The hounds treed a raccoon.* **2.** to stretch or shape on a tree, such as a shoe or glove. **3.** *Informal.* to put or force into an awkward, difficult, or powerless position: *The newspapers treed the corrupt politician.* [Old English *trēo(w)* large, perennial woody plant, wood, beam, stick[1].] —**tree′less,** *adj.* —**tree′like′,** *adj.*

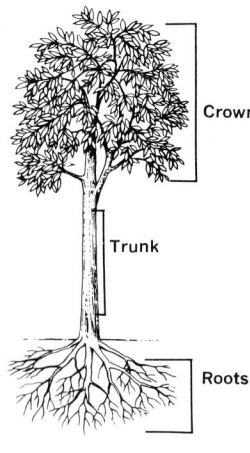

parts of a **tree**

·**up a tree.** *Informal.* in an awkward, difficult, or powerless position, esp. one from which there is no escape.

tree farm, an area used for the cultivation of trees for commercial purposes, as for timber.

tree fern, any of various treelike ferns, having large fronds and, usually, thick stems growing upright.

tree frog, any of a group of small frogs, family Hylidae, usually living in trees in temperate and tropical regions and having adhesive toes used for climbing. Length: 1-5½ inches (2.5-14 centimeters). Also, **tree toad.**

tree heath, a shrub or small tree, *Erica arborea,* found in the Mediterranean region, bearing fragrant, ball-shaped, white flowers. Also, **briar**[1].

tree house, a platform or playhouse, usually for children, built in the branches of a tree.

tree line, an imaginary line on mountains and in polar regions representing the natural boundary above or beyond which trees do not grow: *The change from coniferous forest to tundra is marked by the tree line.* Also, **timberline.**

tree·lined (trē′līnd′) *adj.* having a row of trees on both sides: *a treelined avenue.*

tree·nail (trē′nāl′, tren′əl, trun′-) *also,* **trenail, trunnel.** *n.* a hardwood pin used to secure a joint or fasten timbers together, esp. in shipbuilding.

tree of heaven, a tree, *Ailanthus altissima,* native to China and widely cultivated as a shade tree.

tree of knowledge, in the Bible, a tree in the Garden of Eden, whose fruit conferred knowledge of good and evil. Adam and Eve were cast out of Eden for eating its fruit.

tree ring, annual ring.

tree surgeon, a person trained to treat damaged or diseased trees by pruning, bracing, removing diseased parts, or the like. —**tree surgery.**

tree toad, tree frog.

tree·top (trē′top′) *n.* the top or uppermost branches of a tree.

tre·foil (trē′foil′) *n.* **1.** any of several plants of the pea family, having leaves that usually consist of three oval leaflets. **2.** any of various clovers. **3.** an ornament having three pointed or rounded leaf-shaped forms, used esp. in architecture. [Anglo-Norman *trifoil* three-leaved plant, from Latin *trifolium,* from *tri-* three + *folium* leaf.]

trek (trek) *v.i.,* **trekked, trek·king. 1.** to travel or journey, esp. in a slow, difficult manner. **2.** in South Africa, to travel by ox wagon. —*n.* a journey or migration, esp. one that is slow or difficult. [Afrikaans *trekken* to pull, travel, from Middle Dutch *trecken.*] —**trek′ker,** *n.*

trel·lis (trel′is) *n.* a lattice, esp. one used as a support for growing vines. —*v.t.* **1.** to furnish or support with a trellis. **2.** to interlace or cross so as to form a trellis. [Middle French *treliz* coarsely woven fabric, going back to Latin *trilīx* woven with three threads, from *tri-* three + *līcium* thread.]

trel·lis·work (trel′is wûrk′) *n.* openwork made from, consisting of, or resembling a trellis.

trem·a·tode (trem′ə tōd′) *n.* fluke[3] *(def. 2).* [Modern Latin *Trematoda* (neuter plural), from Greek *trēmatōdēs* having holes, from *trēma* hole.]

trem·ble (trem′bəl) *v.i.,* **-bled, -bling. 1.** to shake involuntarily, as with cold, weakness, fear, or anger. **2.** to have a slight, vibrating motion: *The ground trembled as the volcano erupted.* **3.** to be filled with fear or anxiety: *I tremble to think of the risks involved in the plan.* —*n.* the act or an instance of trembling. [Old French *trembler* to shiver, shake, going back to Latin *tremulus* quaking, quivering.] —**trem′bler,** *n.* —**trem′bling·ly,** *adv.* —**trem′bly,** *adj.*

tre·men·dous (tri men′dəs) *adj.* **1.** of very great size, amount, or intensity: *a tremendous appetite, a tremendous wave.* **2.** *Informal.* extraordinary or wonderful; astounding: *The landing of astronauts on the moon was a tremendous scientific achievement.* **3.** causing horror; terrible; dreadful: *Tremendous crimes are committed in war.* [Latin *tremendus* fearful, dreadful, gerundive of *tremere* to quake, shake.] —**tre·men′dous·ly,** *adv.* —**tremen′dous·ness,** *n.*

trem·o·lo (trem′ə lō′) *n., pl.* **-los.** *Music.* **1.** a trembling or vibrating effect produced by the rapid repetition of a single tone or by the rapid alternation of two tones. **2.** a device or stop in an organ used to produce such an effect. [Italian *tremolo* trembling, shaking, from Latin *tremulus.* Doublet of TREMULOUS.]

trem·or (trem′ər) *n.* **1.** a rapid shaking or vibrating movement, such as that caused by an earthquake. **2.** an involuntary, continued shaking or trembling, esp. of the body or a limb. **3.** a nervous thrill caused by emotion or excitement: *A tremor went through the audience as the curtain rose.* **4.** a state of nervous anticipation or excitement. [Latin *tremor* a trembling, quaking.]

trem·u·lous (trem′yə ləs) *adj.* **1.** characterized or affected by trembling; shaking: *a tremulous voice.* **2.** lacking firmness, resolution, or courage; timid; wavering. [Latin *tremulus* trembling, shaking. Doublet of TREMOLO.] —**trem′u·lous·ly,** *adv.* —**trem′u·lous·ness,** *n.*

tre·nail (trē′nāl′, tren′əl, trun′-) treenail.

trench (trench) *n.* **1.** a long, narrow excavation in the earth; deep furrow: *A trench was dug in the field to irrigate it.* **2.** a long, narrow ditch with the excavated earth piled up in front, used esp. for the protection of soldiers in combat. —*v.t.* **1.** to dig a trench or trenches in. **2.** to surround or fortify with a trench or trenches. —*v.i.* to dig a trench or trenches. [Old French *trenchier* to cut, hack[1], dig, going back to Latin *truncāre* to cut off, mutilate.]

  •**to trench on** (or **upon**). to intrude on, as the rights or property of another; encroach on.

trench·ant (tren′chənt) *adj.* **1.** having or showing mental sharpness; penetrating; keen: *a trenchant mind, a trenchant remark.* **2.** forceful or effective: *a trenchant argument.* **3.** sharply defined or outlined; distinct: *The line of demarcation is trenchant.* [Old French *trenchant,* present participle of *trenchier* to cut. See TRENCH.] —**trench′an·cy,** *n.* —**trench′ant·ly,** *adv.*

trench coat, a loose-fitting, double-breasted raincoat having a belt around the waist and straps at the shoulders and wrists. [Because it was first worn in the trenches of World War I.]

trench·er (tren′chər) *n.* a wooden platter or board on which food, esp. meat, is carved and served. [Old French *trencheor* platter, cutting instrument, from *trenchier* to cut; referring to carving meat on a platter. See TRENCH.]

trench·er·man (tren′chər mən) *n., pl.* **-men** (-mən). **1.** a person who eats, esp. one who eats with a hearty appetite. **2.** *Archaic.* a hanger-on, as at one's table; sponger; parasite.

trench fever, an acute, infectious fever caused by a microorganism that is transmitted by lice. It was first observed among soldiers serving in the trenches in World War I.

trench mouth, an acute inflammation of the mouth and gums, caused by certain bacteria, and characterized by painful, bleeding gums and enlarged lymph nodes in the neck.

trend (trend) *n.* **1.** a general direction or course: *The trend of the river was to the south.* **2.** a general or current tendency: *a trend in fashions toward brighter colors, a conservative trend in politics.* —*v.i.* to have or proceed in a specified direction or course; be inclined; tend: *Prices have trended upward.* [Old English *trendan* to revolve, roll.]

trend·set·ter (trend′set′ər) *n.* a person or thing that helps establish or popularize a new trend, as in fashion or attitudes.

trend·y (tren′dē) *adj.,* **trend·i·er, trend·i·est.** *Informal.* following the latest trends or fashions; very stylish; up-to-date: *a trendy dresser.* —**trend′i·ly,** *adv.* —**trend′i·ness,** *n.*

tre·pan (tri pan′) *n.* a surgical instrument similar to and now largely replaced by a trephine. —*v.t.,* **-panned, -pan·ning.** to operate on with a trepan. [Medieval Latin *trepanum* surgical instrument, from Greek *trȳpanon* surgical instrument, auger, from *trȳpān* to bore.] —**trep·a·na·tion** (trep′ə nā′shən), *n.*

tre·pang (tri pang′) *n.* any of various sea cucumbers whose dried flesh is used in Chinese cooking. [Malay *trīpang.*]

tre·phine (tri fīn′, -fēn′) *n.* a surgical instrument consisting of a cylindrical saw, used for cutting out a disk of bone, esp. from the skull. —*v.t.,* **-phined, -phin·ing.** to operate on with a trephine. [Modification (influenced by TREPAN) of Latin *trēs fīnēs* three ends; referring to its shape.]

trep·i·da·tion (trep′i dā′shən) *n.* **1.** nervous anticipation; fearful apprehension; anxiety: *to face an audience with trepidation.* **2.** an involuntary vibrating motion; trembling; tremor. [Latin *trepidātiō* alarm, agitation.]

trep·o·ne·ma (trep′ə nē′mə) *n., pl.* **-mas** or **-ma·ta** (-mə tə). any of a genus, *Treponema,* of parasitic spirochetes found in mammals and birds, including species causing syphilis and yaws in humans. [Modern Latin *treponema,* from Greek *trepein* to turn + *nēma* thread.] —**trep′o·ne′mal,** *adj.*

tres·pass (tres′pəs, -pas′) *v.i.* **1.** *Law.* to commit an illegal act that does injury to the rights, property, or person of another, esp. to enter unlawfully on the land of another: *The hunter trespassed on private property.* **2.** to encroach or intrude on a person's time, privacy, or the like. **3.** to commit a transgression; sin. —*n.* **1.** a wrong or sin. **2.** *Law.* **a.** unlawful entry onto the property of another. **b.** *Archaic.* any civil injury to the person, property, or rights of another. **c.** a legal action brought to recover damages for injury caused by such an illegal act. [Old French *trespasser* to pass over, go across, going back to Latin *trāns* across + *passus* step.] —**tres′pass·er,** *n.* —For Synonyms *(v.i.),* see **intrude.**

tress (tres) *n.* **1.** a curl, tuft, or strand of human hair. **2. tresses.** a woman's or girl's hair, esp. when worn long and loose. [Old French *trece* lock or braid of hair; of uncertain origin.]

trestle *(def. 2)*

tres·tle (tres′əl) *n.* **1.** a short beam or bar supported by four diverging legs, used as a support. **2.a.** a framework consisting of vertical or inclined members with horizontal or diagonal braces, used to support a railroad bridge or other elevated structure. **b.** a bridge supported by trestles. [Old French *trestel* beam, going back to Latin *trānstrum* crossbeam.]

tres·tle·tree (tres′əl trē′) *n.* *Nautical.* one of two strong bars, as of timber or steel, attached horizontally fore and aft on opposite sides of a masthead to support the crosstrees.

tres·tle·work (tres′əl wûrk′) *n.* a trestle or a series of trestles.

trey (trā) *n.* a playing card, die, or domino having three marks. [Old French *trei* three, from Latin *trēs.*]

tri- *combining form* **1.** having or consisting of three elements or parts: *triangle, tricycle.* **2.** *Chemistry.* containing three specified atoms, elements, radicals, or the like: *trioxide.* **3.** occurring three times in a specified period or once in three specified periods: *triennial, triweekly.* [Latin *trēs, tria* three, or Greek *treis, tria* three, often through French *tri-.*]

tri·a·ble (trī′ə bəl) *adj.* **1.** capable of being tried or tested. **2.** capable of being examined or tried in a court of law. —**tri′a·ble·ness,** *n.*

tri·ac·e·tate (trī as′i tāt′) *n.* an ester of cellulose in which each molecule contains three acetate groups, used to make textile fibers. [TRI- + ACETATE.]

a	at	e	end	o	hot	u	up	hw	white		about
ā	ape	ē	me	ō	old	ū	use	ng	song		taken
ä	far	i	it	ô	fork	ü	rule	th	thin	ə	pencil
âr	care	ī	ice	oi	oil	u̇	pull	th	this		lemon
		îr	pierce	ou	out	ûr	turn	zh	measure		circus

tri·ad (trī′ad, -əd) *n.* **1.** a group of three persons or things. **2.** *Music.* a chord of three tones, esp. one consisting of a given tone with its third and fifth. [Late Latin *triad-,* stem of *trias* the number three, from Greek *trias.*] —**tri·ad′ic,** *adj.*

tri·age (trē äzh′, trē′äzh) *n.* the process of sorting the injured, sick, or wounded for medical treatment on the basis of urgency and chances of survival, as practiced on the battlefield or in the emergency ward of a hospital. [French *triage* a sorting, choosing, selecting, from *trier* to sort, choose, select.]

tri·al (trī′əl) *n.* **1.** a judicial examination of a case in a court of law. **2.** a process or procedure used to ascertain a result. **3.** the state of being tried or tested: *to be given a job on trial.* **4.** a difficult test of one's endurance, patience, or faith; hardship; affliction. **5.** a source or cause of pain or trouble: *That barking dog has been a constant trial to its owners.* **6.** the act of making an effort; attempt; try. —*adj.* of, for, relating to, done as, or used in a trial: *a trial effort, a trial lawyer.* [Anglo-Norman *trial* act of judging in court, sentence, from *trier* to choose, pick out, sift; of uncertain origin.]

trial and error, the practice of trying one thing after another until a desired result is achieved: *I found the right diet for me by trial and error.*

trial balance, in double entry bookkeeping, the addition of the total entries on each side of the ledger in which the sum of the debits should be equal to the sum of the credits.

trial balloon 1. a balloon sent aloft to test air currents and determine wind speed. **2.** an announcement, statement, or the like made in advance in order to test public reaction: *The ambassador's speech was a trial balloon for the proposed government policy.*

trial jury, a group, usually consisting of twelve persons, chosen to hear a case in a court of law and render a verdict.

tri·an·gle (trī′ang′gəl) *n.* **1.** a polygon with three sides and three angles. **2.** something shaped like a triangle. **3.** a musical instrument consisting of a metal bar bent into the shape of a triangle, producing a high, bell-like tone when struck. For illustration, see **percussion instrument. 4.** a group of three persons or things. [Latin *triangulum* this polygon, from *tri-* three + *angulus* corner, angle[1].]

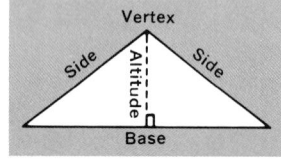

triangle

tri·an·gu·lar (trī ang′gyə-lər) *adj.* **1.** of, relating to, or resembling a triangle. **2.** of, relating to, or consisting of three persons or things.

tri·an·gu·late (*v.,* trī ang′gyə lāt′; *adj.,* trī ang′gyə lit, -lāt′) *v.t.* **-lat·ed, -lat·ing. 1.** to divide into triangles. **2.** to survey by triangulation. **3.** to make triangular. —*adj.* composed of or marked with triangles.

tri·an·gu·la·tion (trī ang′gyə lā′shən) *n.* **1.** a method used in surveying to determine the relative position of three points on the earth's surface, by using the known distance between two of the points and the measured angles of sight to the third to calculate the remaining sides and angle of the triangle formed by the points. **2.** a network of such triangles used to survey large areas of land.

Tri·as·sic (trī as′ik) *n.* the earliest geologic period of the Mesozoic era, a time of widespread volcanism and crustal movements, when dinosaurs appeared and became the dominant life form. For table, see **geologic time.** —*adj.* of, relating to, or characteristic of this period. [German *Trias* the earliest geologic period of the Mesozoic era (from Greek *trias* the number three) + *-ic;* referring to the three stratigraphic divisions of this period.]

tri·ath·lon (trī ath′lon) *n.* an athletic competition consisting of a long-distance race usually involving swimming, bicycling, and running. [Tri- + Greek *athlon* contest.]

tri·ax·i·al (trī ak′sē əl) *adj.* having three axes, as most systems of crystalline forms. [Tri- + Axial.]

trib·al (trī′bəl) *adj.* of, relating to, or characteristic of a tribe or tribes: *a tribal society, tribal customs.* —**trib′al·ly,** *adv.*

tribe (trīb) *n.* **1.** a group of people connected by a common ancestry, culture, social customs, and, usually, the same political system: *The ancient Jewish nation was composed of twelve tribes.* **2.** any group or class of people, usually distinguished by a common characteristic, interest, or the like. **3.** *Biology.* a generic classification of a group of animals or plants, usually forming a subdivision of a family or sometimes of an order. [Latin *tribus* a division of the ancient Roman people.]

tribes·man (trībz′mən) *n., pl.* **-men** (-mən). a member of a tribe.

trib·u·la·tion (trib′yə lā′shən) *n.* **1.** a condition of severe affliction or misery; suffering: *The dictator's oppressive rule brought much tribulation to the people.* **2.** the cause of such suffer-

ing. [Church Latin *tribulātiō,* from *tribulāre* to oppress, from Latin *tribulāre* to press[1].]

tri·bu·nal (trī bū′nəl, tri-) *n.* **1.** a court of justice. **2.** any place of judgment. [Latin *tribūnal* raised platform on which magistrates sat.]

tri·bu·nate (trib′yə nit, -nāt′, tri bū′nit) *n.* the office, rank, or term of the tribune in ancient Rome.

trib·une[1] (trib′ūn) *n.* **1.** an official in ancient Rome appointed to protect the rights and interests of the plebeians against the patricians in the Senate. **2.** a protector or defender of the rights of the public; champion of the people. [Latin *tribūnus* the ancient Roman official, chieftain, from *tribus* a division of the Roman people.] —**trib′une·ship′,** *n.*

trib·une[2] (trib′ūn) *n.* a raised platform, stand, or seat, as a pulpit or the throne of a bishop. [French *tribune* rostrum, through Italian and Medieval Latin, from Latin *tribūnal* raised platform on which magistrates sat.]

trib·u·tar·y (trib′yə ter′ē) *n., pl.* **-tar·ies. 1.** a river or stream that flows into a larger body of water: *The Tennessee River is a major tributary of the Ohio River.* **2.** a person or thing that pays tribute. —*adj.* **1.** flowing into a larger body of water. **2.** subject to paying tribute; taxed. **3.** paid or offered as tribute: *a tributary gift to a conqueror.* **4.** bringing auxiliary supplies or aid; supporting; contributory.

trib·ute (trib′ūt) *n.* **1.** anything done, given, or observed as an acknowledgment of devotion, gratitude, or respect: *The enthusiastic applause was a tribute to the singer's performance.* **2.** money paid by one ruler or nation to another in acknowledgment of submission or to ensure peace or protection. **3.** any payment given under force or coercion. [Latin *tribūtum* payment, contribution.] —For Synonyms, see **eulogy.**

trice[1] (trīs) *v.t.,* **triced, tric·ing.** to pull up and secure, as a sail, with a rope (often with *up*). [Middle Dutch *trīsen* to hoist, from *trīse* pulley.]

trice[2] (trīs) *n.* a very short time; instant; moment: *I'll be ready in a trice.* [From TRICE[1], as in the phrase *at a trice* at a pull.]

tri·ceps (trī′seps) *n., pl.* **-cep·ses.** any of several muscles in the body, esp. the large muscle at the back of the upper arm, that, when contracted, straightens the forearm. [Latin *triceps* having three heads, from *tri-* three + *caput* head.]

tri·cer·a·tops (trī ser′ə tops′) *n.* a plant-eating dinosaur, order Ornithischia, that lived in North America in the late Cretaceous period, having a long horn over each eye, a shorter horn on the snout, and a bony shield projecting from the skull over the back of the neck. Length: to more than 25 feet (7.6 meters).

triceratops

tri·chi·na (tri kī′nə) *n., pl.* **-nae** (-nē) a parasitic roundworm, *Trichinella spiralis,* that infests mammals, including human beings, causing trichino-sis. Trichinae enter the host in infected pork that has not been well cooked, and the adult worms lodge in the intestines, while the larvae form cysts in the involuntary muscles. [Modern Latin *trichina,* from Greek *trichinos* relating to hair, from *trich-,* stem of *trix* hair.]

trich·i·no·sis (trik′ə nō′sis) *n.* a disease caused by trichinae that invade the intestines and muscular tissues and characterized by nausea, diarrhea, and stiff and swollen muscles. [Modern Latin *trichinosis,* from TRICHINA + -OSIS.]

trich·i·nous (trik′ə nəs) *adj.* **1.** of, relating to, or characteristic of trichinae or trichinosis. **2.** infected with trichinae or affected with trichinosis.

trick (trik) *n.* **1.** something done or intended to deceive or cheat; crafty or fraudulent device: *The misleading advertisement was a trick to draw customers.* **2.** a feat of skill, esp. one meant to amuse: *to teach a dog many tricks.* **3.** the particular art or skill of doing something easily and successfully; knack: *A good speaker knows the trick of getting the listeners' attention.* **4.** a mischievous act; practical joke; prank: *to play tricks on others.* **5.** a characteristic habit, trait, or practice; mannerism: *the annoying trick of not answering when called.* **6.a.** a group of cards made up of one card played from each hand. **b.** such a group considered as a unit of score. **c.** a card that can take such a group of cards. **7.** a period of duty, as at the helm of a ship. —*v.t.* **1.a.** to cheat or deceive with a trick: *The swindler tricked them out of their savings.* **b.** to practice trickery on: *My friend delights in tricking his younger cousins with devices purchased at novelty stores. I tricked her into letting me borrow her favorite sweater.* **2.** to arrange, dress, or

decorate; adorn (with *out* or *up*): *to trick out a blouse with beads.* —*v.i.* to practice trickery or deception. —*adj.* **1.** relating to or involving a trick or deception: *a trick deck of cards.* **2.** inclined to give way or collapse: *The accident left the athlete with a trick knee.* [Dialectal Old French *trique,* form of Old French *triche* deceit, cheating, from *trichier* to deceive, cheat; of uncertain origin.]
  • **to do** (or **turn**) **the trick.** to perform or accomplish what is needed or wanted.

trick·er·y (trik′ə rē) *n., pl.* **-er·ies.** an act or instance of intentionally deceiving; deceitful behavior or stratagem.

trick·le (trik′əl) *v.,* **-led, -ling.** —*v.i.* **1.** to flow or fall drop by drop or in a thin stream: *The rain trickled down the window.* **2.** to move or proceed in a very slow, irregular manner: *The children trickled into the classroom after recess.* —*v.t.* to cause to trickle: *The engine was trickling oil.* —*n.* **1.** an act or instance of trickling. **2.** a slow or irregular stream or movement: *a slow day in the store with only a trickle of customers.* [Probably imitative.]

trick·ster (trik′stər) *n.* a person who plays tricks or practices trickery.

trick·sy (trik′sē) *adj.,* **-si·er, -si·est. 1.** given to or fond of tricks; mischievous; prankish; playful. **2.** tending to use trickery; cunning; crafty; wily. —**trick′si·ness,** *n.*

trick·y (trik′ē) *adj.,* **trick·i·er, trick·i·est. 1.** given to or characterized by tricks or trickery; crafty; wily: *a tricky sales pitch.* **2.** having unseen or unexpected difficulties; requiring care, caution, or skill in doing or dealing with: *a tricky situation, a tricky rewiring job.* —**trick′i·ly,** *adv.* —**trick′i·ness,** *n.*

tri·clin·ic (trī klin′ik) *adj.* of, relating to, or designating a system of crystalline forms characterized by three unequal axes that intersect each other obliquely. [TRI- + Greek *klinein* to incline + -IC.]

tri·col·or (trī′kul′ər) *adj.* also, **tri′col′ored.** having three colors. —*n.* **1.** a flag having three colors, esp. in large, equal masses. **2.** also, **Tricolor.** the national flag of France, having three equal vertical bands of red, white, and blue. [French *tricolore* having three colors, going back to Latin *tri-* three + *color* hue.]

tri·corn (trī′kôrn′) also, **tri·corne.** *n.* a cocked hat with the brim turned up on three sides. —*adj.* having three hornlike corners or projections. [Latin *tricornis* having three horns, going back to *tres* three + *cornu* horn.]

tri·cot (trē′kō) *n.* **1.** a lightweight, knitted fabric made by hand or machine, from wool, nylon, or rayon. **2.** a fine-woven worsted fabric made of wool. [French *tricot* knitting, jersey, from *tricoter* to knit; of uncertain origin.]

tri·cus·pid (trī kus′pid) *adj.* having three cusps or points. —*n.* any tooth that has three cusps or points. [Latin *tricuspid-,* stem of *tricuspis* having three points, from *tri-* three + *cuspis* point.]

tricuspid valve, a heart valve consisting of three flaps, located between the right atrium and the right ventricle.

tri·cy·cle (trī′si kəl, -sik′əl) *n.* **1.** a three-wheeled vehicle, usually used by children, having two wheels in the back and one in the front, driven by pedals and steered with handlebars. **2.** a motorcycle with three wheels arranged similarly. [TRI- + CYCLE.]

tri·dent (trī′dənt) *n.* a three-pronged spear. —*adj.* having three prongs, teeth, or tines. Also (*adj.*), **tri·den·tate** (trī den′tāt). [Latin *tridēns,* from *tri-* three + *dēns* tooth.]

tried (trīd) *v.* the past tense and past participle of **try.** —*adj.* proven, as by experience or examination; tested.

tried-and-true (trīd′ən trü′) *adj.* tested and proven trustworthy or useful: *a tried-and-true friend, a tried-and-true method.*

tri·en·ni·al (trī en′ē əl) *adj.* **1.** lasting or continuing for three years. **2.** done or occurring every three years. —*n.* **1.** an event that occurs every three years. **2.** a third anniversary. [Latin *triennium* period of three years (from *tri-* three + *annus* year) + -AL¹.] —**tri·en′ni·al·ly,** *adv.*

tri·er (trī′ər) *n.* a person or thing that tries.

tri·fle (trī′fəl) *n.* **1.** something of little or no intrinsic value or importance; insignificant matter or thing: *There's no sense arguing over trifles.* **2.** a small amount; somewhat; bit. ➡ commonly used adverbially in the phrase *a trifle,* as in *to be a trifle annoyed with careless work.* **3.** a small sum of money. **4.** a dessert made of sponge cake and macaroons, having a layer of custard, fruit, or jam, and topped with whipped cream or meringue. —*v.,* **-fled, -fling.** —*v.i.* **1.** to treat a person or thing lightly or disrespectfully; fail to take seriously (with *with*): *It's best not to trifle with them, She trifled with his feelings for her.* **2.** to handle or play with in an idle, careless manner (with *with*): *to trifle with one's keys.* —*v.t.* to pass or spend (time, money, or the like) in an idle, frivolous manner; waste (with *away*): *to trifle away an entire inheritance.* [Old French *trufle* mockery, trickery; of uncertain origin.] —**tri′fler,** *n.*

tri·fling (trī′fling) *adj.* **1.** having little or no value or significance; unimportant; small: *a trifling matter.* **2.** lacking depth or seriousness; shallow; frivolous: *a trifling conversation.* —**tri′fling·ly,** *adv.* —For Synonyms, see **petty.**

tri·fo·li·ate (trī fō′lē it, -āt′) *adj. Botany.* having three leaves, leaflets, or three leaflike parts. [TRI- + Latin *foliātus* leaved (from *folium* leaf).]

tri·fo·ri·um (trī fôr′ē əm) *n., pl.* **-fo·ri·a** (-fôr′ē ə). a gallery or arcade in the wall of a church, above the arches at the sides of the nave, choir, or transept. [Medieval Latin *triforium,* possibly from Latin *tri-* three + *foris* door, opening.]

trig (trig) *adj.* tidy; neat; trim. [Old Norse *tryggr* faithful, trusty.]

trig. 1. trigonometric. **2.** trigonometry. Also, **trigon.**

tri·gem·i·nal (trī jem′ə nəl) *adj.* of or relating to either of the fifth pair of cranial nerves, which in mammals separate into three branches supplying nerve fibers to the eye area, face, and jaws. —*n.* a trigeminal nerve. [Modern Latin *trigeminus* trigeminal nerve, from Latin *trigeminus* threefold, triple; literally, three born together (from *tri-* three + *geminus* twin) + -al¹.]

trig·ger (trig′ər) *n.* **1.** a small lever on a gun or other firearm that, when pulled back or pressed, as with the finger, causes the firearm to discharge. **2.** any similar device, as a lever that is pressed or pulled to initiate a process or start a mechanism. **3.** something, as an act or event, that precipitates an event or series of events. —*v.t.* to initiate or precipitate, as an event or series of events: *Jealousy triggered that angry outburst.* [Earlier *tricker,* from Dutch *trekker* lever on a gun; literally, thing that pulls, from *trekken* to pull.]
  • **quick on the trigger. a.** able to draw quickly and fire a gun. **b.** *Informal.* acting or responding quickly; alert.

trig·ger-hap·py (trig′ər hap′ē) *adj. Informal.* inclined to resort to or react with violent, often irresponsible, actions, esp. readily resorting to the use of firearms or weaponry.

tri·glyc·er·ide (trī glis′ə rīd′) *n.* an ester of glycerin in which all three hydroxyl groups are linked with fatty acids. Triglycerides are the primary components of fats and oils.

tri·glyph (trī′glif′) *n.* a part of a Doric frieze, usually consisting of a projecting block or tablet with two vertical grooves and a half groove at each side, alternating with metopes. For illustration, see **metope.** [Latin *triglyphus,* from Greek *triglyphos,* from *tri-* three + *glyphein* to carve.]

trigonometric function, a function of an angle, as the sine, cosine, tangent, cotangent, secant, or cosecant, expressed as the ratios of pairs of sides of a right triangle.

Trigonometric Functions

In a right triangle, trigonometric functions of the acute angles are represented by the ratios of the lengths of the sides: the side adjacent to the angle, the side opposite the angle, and the hypotenuse.

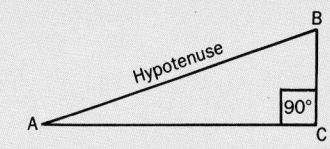

Trigonometric Functions	For angle A:
sine (sin) = opposite/hypotenuse	sin A = BC/AB
cosine (cos) = adjacent/hypotenuse	cos A = AC/AB
tangent (tan) = opposite/adjacent	tan A = BC/AC
cotangent (cot) = adjacent/opposite	cot A = AC/BC
secant (sec) = hypotenuse/adjacent	sec A = AB/AC
cosecant (csc) = hypotenuse/opposite	csc A = AB/BC

---

trig·o·nom·e·try (trig′ə nom′i trē) *n.* the branch of mathematics dealing with the relations between the sides and angles of triangles and the properties of these relations. [Modern Latin *trigonometria,* from Greek *trigōnon* triangle + -METRY.] —**trig·o·no·met·ric** (trig′ə nə met′rik); *also,* **trig′o·no·met′ri·cal,** *adj.* —**trig′o·no·met′ri·cal·ly,** *adv.*

tri·graph (trī′graf′) *n.* three successive letters pronounced as a single sound, as the *eau* in *beau.*

tri·he·dral (trī hē′drəl) *n.* a figure formed by three lines that are each in a different plane but intersect at a common point. —*adj.* of or relating to such a figure. [TRI- + Greek *hedrā* seat, base[1].]

tri·he·dron (trī hē′drən) *n., pl.* -drons or -dra (-drə). a geometric figure formed by three planes meeting in a point. [TRI- + Greek *hedrā* seat, base[1].]

tri·lat·er·al (trī lat′ər əl) *adj.* having three sides. [Latin *trilaterus* (from *tri-* three + *latus* side) + -AL[1].] —**tri·lat′er·al·ly,** *adv.*

tri·lin·gual (trī ling′gwəl) *adj.* having, consisting of, expressed in, or speaking three languages.

trill (tril) *n.* **1.** a tremulous, usually high-pitched sound or succession of notes: *the chirping trill of a bird.* **2.** *Music.* a rapid alternation of two notes either a whole step or a half step apart. **3.** *Phonetics.* **a.** a rapid vibration of the tip of the tongue. **b.** a speech sound, as a consonant, produced in such a way, esp. the sound of *r.* —*v.t.* to sing, play, produce, or articulate (something) with a trill. —*v.i.* to sing, play, produce, or articulate a trill. [Italian *trillare* to quaver, warble; probably of Germanic origin.]

tril·lion (tril′yən) *n.* **1.** in the United States and France, the cardinal number that is represented by one followed by 12 zeros. **2.** in Great Britain and Germany, the cardinal number that is represented by 1 followed by 18 zeros. —*adj.* numbering one trillion. [French *trillion* 1 followed by 12 zeros (from Latin *tri-* three), on the model of *million.* See MILLION.] —**tril′lionth,** *adj., n.*

tril·li·um (tril′ē əm) *n.* any of a group of low plants, genus *Trillium,* of the lily family, having a whorl of three smooth, oval leaves, and bearing flowers composed of three oval petals. [Modern Latin *Trillium,* from Latin *tri-* three; referring to its whorl of three leaves.]

tri·lo·bate (trī lō′bāt, trī′lə bāt′) *adj.* having three lobes, as certain leaves. Also, **tri·lo′bat·ed.**

tri·lo·bite (trī′lə bīt′) *n.* any of a group of extinct Paleozoic arthropods, class Trilobita, comprising several thousand species, most of them small marine scavengers with a segmented body divided into three longitudinal lobes and a large number of transverse segments. [Modern Latin *Trilobites,* from Greek *trilobos* having three lobes.]

fossil of a **trilobite**

tril·o·gy (tril′ə jē) *n., pl.* -gies. a group of three complete plays, operas, novels, or the like, that together make a related series. [Greek *trilogiā* group of three tragic dramas, from *tri-* three + *logos* speech, story.]

trim (trim) *v.,* trimmed, trimming. —*v.t.* **1.** to make neat and orderly by removing excess parts, as by cutting: *to trim one's hair, to trim a rosebush.* **2.** to remove (an excess or irregular part or object) in order to make neat or orderly (often with *off* or *away*): *to trim away the straggly branches of a shrub, to trim frivolous items off a budget.* **3.** to add ornaments or decorations to; decorate: *to trim a cake, to trim a dress with lace.* **4.** to balance (a boat or ship) by arranging the cargo or ballast. **5.** to adjust (yards or sails) for sailing. **6.** to keep (an aircraft) in a level position while in flight by adjusting various controls. **7.** *Informal.* to defeat: *The challenger is sure to trim the champ in three rounds.* **8.** *Informal.* to rebuke sharply; scold. —*v.i.* *Nautical.* **1.a.** to be or remain in balance. **b.** to adjust yards or sails for sailing. **2.** to maintain a neutral course or position. —*n.* **1.** ornamentation or decoration: *The dress had a sequined trim.* **2.** the act of trimming. **3.** the state or condition of being fit or prepared: *The swimmer was in trim for the race.* **4.** *Nautical.* **a.** the condition of a boat or ship with reference to fitness for sailing, esp. when properly balanced. **b.** the position of a boat or ship in the water, esp. with reference to the difference between the draft at the bow and at the stern. **5.** the attitude of an aircraft that is balanced for level flight. **6.** woodwork used ornamentally in the interior or exterior of a building, esp. moldings around windows or doors. **7.** *Archaic.* equipment; outfit; dress. —*adj.,* trim·mer, trim·mest. in good order or condition: *trim shrubbery, a trim suit.* —*adv. also,* **trim′ly.** in a trim manner. [Old English *trymman* to strengthen, array.] —**trim′ness,** *n.*

tri·ma·ran (trī′mə ran′) *n.* a sailboat with three hulls, one more than a catamaran, and the mast mounted on the center hull. [TRI- + (CATA)MARAN.]

tri·mes·ter (trī mes′tər) *n.* **1.** a period or term consisting of three months, esp. one of the three such terms into which human pregnancy is divided. **2.** one of the three terms into which the academic year is sometimes divided. [French *trimestre,* going back to Latin *tri-* three + *mēnsis* month.]

trim·e·ter (trim′i tər) *n.* **1.** a line of verse consisting of three metrical feet to each line. **2.** a verse composed of such lines. —*adj.* consisting of three metrical feet or of lines having three metrical feet. [Latin *trimetrus* consisting of three metrical feet, from Greek *trimetros,* from *tri-* three + *metron* measure, meter[2].]

trim·mer (trim′ər) *n.* **1.** a person or thing that trims. **2.** a beam that receives the end of a header in floor framing.

trim·ming (trim′ing) *n.* **1.** anything used as a decoration or ornament: *lace trimming on sleeves, chrome trimming on a car.* **2.** trimmings. **a.** pieces or parts cut off in trimming something, as parings or scraps. **b.** *Informal.* traditional or usual accessories or accompaniments, esp. the side dishes or garnishes of an entree: *roast turkey and all the trimmings.* **3.** *Informal.* an overwhelming defeat or sound beating: *The home team took a trimming.* **4.** *Informal.* a sharp rebuke; scolding.

tri·month·ly (trī munth′lē) *adj.* occurring or done every three months.

tri·nal (trī′nəl) *adj.* having or composed of three parts.

trine (trīn) *adj.* threefold; triple. —*n.* **1. Trine.** the Trinity. **2.** *Astrology.* of or relating to the aspect of two planets 120 degrees apart from each other. [Latin *trīnus* threefold.]

Trin·i·tar·i·an (trin′i târ′ē ən) *adj.* **1.** professing belief in the doctrine of the Trinity. **2.** of or relating to the Trinity or the doctrine of the Trinity. —*n.* a person who professes belief in the Trinity. —**Trin′i·tar′i·an·ism,** *n.*

tri·ni·tro·tol·u·ene (trī nī′trō tol′ū ēn′) *n.* TNT. Also, **tri·ni·tro·tol·u·ol** (trī nī′trō tol′ū ôl′).

Trin·i·ty (trin′i tē) *n., pl.* -ties. **1.** in Christianity, the union of the Father, the Son, and the Holy Ghost as three divine persons in the single being of God. **2.** *Informal.* Trinity Sunday. **3. trinity.** any combination or group of three persons or things. **4. trinity.** the state or condition of being three or threefold. [Old French *trinite* the Trinity, from Late Latin *trīnitās,* from Latin *trīnitās* a triad.]

Trinity Sunday, a feast day in honor of the Trinity, celebrated on the eighth Sunday after Easter.

trin·ket (tring′kit) *n.* **1.** any small ornament or fancy article, esp. a piece of costume jewelry. **2.** anything of little value or significance; trifle. [Of uncertain origin.]

tri·no·mi·al (trī nō′mē əl) *adj.* **1.** *Mathematics.* consisting of three terms: *a trinomial equation.* **2.** *Biology.* having or consisting of three names. Trinomial nomenclature is used to classify certain plants and animals. The genus name is given first and is followed by the species and then the subspecies or variety. —*n.* a mathematical expression consisting of three terms joined by plus or minus signs, as the expression $4x + 7y - 1$. [TRI- + (BI)NOMIAL.]

tri·o (trē′ō) *n., pl.* tri·os. **1.** a musical composition for three voices or instruments. **2.** three musicians or singers performing such a composition. **3.** any group of three persons or things. [Italian *trio* set of three, from Latin *trēs, tria* three.]

tri·ode (trī′ōd) *n.* an electron tube consisting of three electrodes, an anode, a cathode, and a grid that controls the flow of electrons between them. [TRI- + -ODE.]

tri·o·let (trī′ə lit) *n.* a poem having eight lines and only two rhymes, with the first line used also as the fourth and seventh lines, and the second line used also as the eighth line. The rhyme scheme is *abaaabab.* [French *triolet,* probably diminutive of Italian *trio* set of three. See TRIO.]

tri·ox·ide (trī ok′sīd, -sid) *n.* an oxide having three atoms of oxygen in each molecule.

trip (trip) *n.* **1.a.** the act, instance, or process of passing or moving from one place or point to another: *a trip to California, a trip through southern Europe, a camping trip.* **b.** the act, instance, or process of going to a place as part of one's routine or work: *a trip to the kitchen, a trip to the store.* **2.** a fall or stumble caused by striking one's foot against an object or by losing one's foothold. **3.** a light, quick, lively movement, esp. of the feet. **4.** a catch or other device that releases a part, as in setting a mechanism in operation. Also, **tripper. 5.** something done or said in error; blunder; slip: *The witness made a trip in that last statement.* **6.** *Slang.* hallucinations and other effects experienced under the influence of a hallucinogenic drug, esp. LSD. **7.** *Slang.* any intense, stimulating, or absorbing experience: *to be on a power trip.* —*v.,* tripped, trip·ping. —*v.i.* **1.** to strike the foot against

something so as to stumble or fall: *to trip over the edge of a rug.* **2.** to make a mistake; commit an error: *The speaker tripped in making that statement.* **3.** to falter in pronunciation: *to trip over a difficult word.* **4.** to move with quick, light steps; prance: *The lambs tripped across the meadow.* **5.** to be released, triggered, or set in operation, as a spring, catch, or mechanism. **6.** *Slang.* to experience hallucinations or other effects of a hallucinogenic drug, esp. LSD. —*v.t.* **1.** to cause to fall or stumble (often with *up*). **2.** to cause to make a mistake or commit a blunder (often with *up*): *The reporters tried to trip the mayor with their questions.* **3.** to catch in a fault, offense, or error: *The prosecutor's questions couldn't trip the defendant.* **4.a.** to operate (a mechanism) by releasing a spring, catch, or other device. **b.** to release (a spring, catch, or other device) in order to set a mechanism in operation. [Old French *trip(p)er* to dance, from Middle Dutch *trippen* to skip.] —For Synonyms (*n.*), see **journey.**

tri·par·tite (trī pär′tīt) *adj.* **1.** divided into three parts. **2.** having three corresponding parts or copies. **3.** of, relating to, or made by three parties: *an international tripartite agreement.* [Latin *tripartītus* divided into three parts, from *trī-* three + *partītus,* past participle of *partīrī* to divide.]

tripe (trīp) *n.* **1.** the walls of the first and second stomachs of a ruminant, esp. the ox, used as food. **2.** *Informal.* anything of such poor quality as to be useless or worthless. [Old French *tripe* entrails of an animal; of uncertain origin.]

trip·ham·mer (trip′ham′ər) *n.* a power-driven hammer that is operated by a cam or other device that trips a lever and allows the hammer to fall.

triph·thong (trif′thông′, -thong′, trip′-) *n.* a vowel sound produced by the combining, during pronunciation, of three vowel sounds within one syllable. The *ayo* in *mayor* is a triphthong. [TRI- + (DI)PHTHONG.]

tri·plane (trī′plān′) *n.* an antique airplane with three wings, arranged one above the other, used primarily as a military craft in World War I.

tri·ple (trip′əl) *adj.* **1.** consisting of three parts. **2.** three times as much or as many; multiplied by three. —*n.* **1.** a number or amount that is three times as much as another. **2.** *Baseball.* a hit that enables a batter to reach third base. —*v.,* **-pled, -pling.** —*v.t.* **1.** to make three times as much or as many: *The company tripled its earnings in one year.* **2.** *Baseball.* to advance (a runner) by hitting a triple. —*v.i.* **1.** to become three times as much or as many: *The population of the town tripled in ten years.* **2.** *Baseball.* to hit a triple. [Latin *triplus* threefold, from Greek *triplous.* Doublet of TREBLE.]

triple bond, a chemical bond in which three pairs of electrons are shared between two atoms, as in some unsaturated organic compounds.

Triple Entente, an alliance between Great Britain, France, and Russia prior to World War I.

triple play *Baseball.* a play during which three players are put out.

tri·plet (trip′lit) *n.* **1.a.** one of three offspring born at one birth. **b.** **triplets.** three offspring born at one birth. **2.** any set or combination of three. **3.** *Music.* a group of three notes of equal time value to be performed in the time of two. **4.** three successive lines of rhyming verse, usually of equal length. [TRIPLE + -ET.]

triple time, a musical time or rhythm having three beats to the measure, the accent falling on the first beat.

tri·plex (trip′leks, trī′pleks) *adj.* triple; threefold. —*n.* something having three parts, esp. an apartment with three floors. [Latin *triplex* threefold, triple.]

trip·li·cate (*adj., n.,* trip′li kit, -kāt′; *v.,* trip′li kāt′) *adj.* three times as much or as many; triple. —*v.t.,* **-cat·ed, -cat·ing.** to multiply by three; triple. —*n.* one of three identical things, esp. copies of printed matter. [Latin *triplicātus,* past participle of *triplicāre* to triple.] —**trip′li·ca′tion,** *n.*

·**in triplicate**, in three exactly corresponding copies.

tri·ply (trip′lē) *adv.* in a triple degree, amount, or manner.

tri·pod (trī′pod′) *n.* **1.** a three-legged stand for supporting a camera or a surveying instrument. **2.** a pot, stool, table, or similar structure resting on three legs. [Latin *tripūs* three-legged seat, from Greek *tripous* three-legged table or cauldron, having three feet.]

trip·per (trip′ər) *n.* **1.** a person who trips or causes another to trip. **2.** trip *(def. 4).* **3.** *British. Informal.* a person who goes on a trip, esp. as a tourist.

trip·ping (trip′ing) *adj.* moving quickly and lightly: *tripping footsteps.* —**trip′ping·ly,** *adv.*

trip·tych (trip′tik) *n.* **1.** a triple painting or carving consisting of three panels hinged together, esp. one depicting a religious subject

16th-century French **triptych**

and used as an altarpiece. **2.** a set of three writing tablets tied or hinged together, used in ancient times. [Greek *triptychos* consisting of three layers, threefold, from *tri-* three + *ptychē* fold.]

tri·reme (trī′rēm) *n.* an ancient galley, esp. a warship, with three horizontal rows of oars, one above the other, on each side. [Latin *trirēmis,* from *tri-* three + *rēmus* oar.]

tri·sac·cha·ride (trī sak′ə rīd′) *n.* any of a group of carbohydrates that consist of three monosaccharides and yield a monosaccharide or a mixture of monosaccharides when subjected to hydrolysis. [TRI- + SACCHARIDE.]

tri·sect (trī sekt′) *v.t.* to divide into three parts, esp. three equal parts, as in geometry: *to trisect an angle.* [TRI- + Latin *sectus,* past participle of *secāre* to cut.] —**tri·sec′tion,** *n.* —**tri·sec′tor,** *n.*

Tris·tan (tris′tən) *n.* in medieval legend, a knight who falls in love with Isolde. Also, **Tris·tram** (tris′trəm).

triste (trēst) *adj. French.* filled with grief or sorrow; sad. [French *triste* sad, mournful, from Latin *tristis.*]

tri·syl·la·ble (trī′sil′ə bəl, trī sil′-) *n.* a word that has three syllables. —**tri·syl·lab·ic** (trī′si lab′ik, tris′i-), *adj.* —**tri′syl·lab′i·cal·ly,** *adv.*

trite (trīt) *adj.,* **trit·er, trit·est.** lacking originality or freshness due to constant repetition; hackneyed: *"Clear as crystal" and "in this day and age" are trite phrases.* [Latin *tritus,* past participle of *terere* to rub, wear away.] —**trite′ly,** *adv.* —**trite′ness,** *n.*

trit·i·um (trit′ē əm, trish′-) *n.* a radioactive isotope of hydrogen having an atomic weight of 3, containing one proton and two neutrons, and decaying to form helium. Fusion of tritium with deuterium releases the explosive force of the hydrogen bomb. Symbols: T or H^3 For illustration, see **fusion.** [Modern Latin *tritium,* from Greek *tritos* third.]

tri·ton (trī′ton) *n.* the nucleus of a tritium atom. [Greek *triton,* neuter of *tritos* third.]

Tri·ton (trī′tən) *n.* **1.** in Greek mythology, the son of Poseidon who was half man and half fish and lived at the bottom of the sea. **2.** one of the moons of Neptune. **3. triton.** any of several genera of marine gastropods, family Cymatiidae, having a large, colorful spiral shell.

trit·u·rate (*v.,* trich′ə rāt′; *n.,* trich′ər it) *v.t.,* **-rat·ed, -rat·ing.** to reduce to very fine particles or powder, as by crushing or grinding. —*n.* any triturated substance. [Late Latin *trītūrātus,* past participle of *trītūrāre* to thresh, from Latin *trītūra* threshing, rubbing.] —**trit·u·ra·ble** (trich′ər ə bəl), *adj.*

trit·u·ra·tion (trich′ə rā′shən) *n.* **1.** the act of triturating. **2.** the preparation of a dental amalgam, using mortar and pestle; amalgamation. **3.** triturate.

tri·umph (trī′umf) *n.* **1.** an outstanding success, achievement, or victory: *The discovery of penicillin was one of the medical triumphs of the twentieth century.* **2.** great joy or exultation caused by victory or success: *the triumph on a winner's face.* **3.** in ancient Rome, a procession and public celebration honoring a victorious commander or other leader. —*v.i.* **1.** to achieve a victory; be successful; win: *to triumph over an enemy.* **2.** to rejoice or celebrate over a victory or success. [Latin *triumphus* triumphal procession, victory, possibly from Greek *thriambos* hymn to Bacchus

a	at	e	end	o	hot	u	up	hw	white		about
ā	ape	ē	me	ō	old	ū	use	ng	song		taken
ä	far	i	it	ô	fork	ü	rule	th	thin	ə	pencil
âr	care	ī	ice	oi	oil	u̇	pull	th	this		lemon
		îr	pierce	ou	out	ûr	turn	zh	measure		circus

sung in processions in his honor.] —For Synonyms *(n.),* see **victory.**

tri·um·phal (trī um′fəl) *adj.* of, relating to, characteristic of, or celebrating a triumph or victory: *a triumphal procession.*

tri·um·phant (trī um′fənt) *adj.* **1.** victorious or successful: *Our team was triumphant in the match.* **2.** celebrating for victory or success; rejoicing; exultant: *a triumphant cheer.* —**tri·um′phant·ly,** *adv.*

tri·um·vir (trī um′vər) *n., pl.* **-virs** or **-vi·ri** (-və rī′). in ancient Rome, one of the members of a triumvirate. [Latin *triumvir,* from the phrase *trium virōrum* (one) of three men.]

tri·um·vi·rate (trī um′vər it) *n.* **1.** government by three persons, esp. in ancient Rome, under which three persons share authority equally. **2.** the position or term of office of a triumvir. **3.** any group or association of three persons, esp. three who jointly hold some power, authority, or distinction.

tri·une (trī′ūn) *adj.* being three in one. ➡ used esp. of the Trinity. [TRI- + Latin *ūnus* one.]

tri·u·ni·ty (trī ū′ni tē) *n., pl.* **-ties.** Trinity *(defs. 3, 4).*

tri·va·lent (trī vā′lənt) *adj. Chemistry.* having a valence of 3. [TRI- + Latin *valēns,* present participle of *valēre* to be strong.] —**tri·va′lence,** —**tri·va′len·cy,** *n.*

triv·et (triv′it) *n.* **1.** a three-legged stand or support used for holding pots over a fire. **2.** something, as a metal or ceramic plate having three short legs, placed under hot plates or dishes on a table. [Old English *trefet,* from Latin *tripēs* having three feet.]

triv·i·a (triv′ē ə) *n.* unimportant or insignificant facts, matters, or information; trifles. ➡ used as singular or plural. [Possibly from TRIVIAL.]

triv·i·al (triv′ē əl) *adj.* **1.** having little or no importance, significance, or consequence; trifling: *Don't worry about such a trivial matter.* **2.** having no freshness or novelty; commonplace; everyday. [Latin *triviālis* that may be found anywhere, commonplace; literally, that belongs to crossroads, from *trivium* place where three roads meet, crossroad, from *tri-* three + *via* way.] —**triv′i·al·ly,** *adv.* —For Synonyms, see **petty.**

triv·i·al·i·ty (triv′ē al′i tē) *n., pl.* **-ties. 1.** the quality or state of being trivial. **2.** a thing or matter of little importance, significance, or consequence; something trivial.

triv·i·al·ize (triv′ē ə līz′) *v.t.* **-ized, -iz·ing.** to treat as commonplace or of no importance; make trivial. —**triv′i·al·i·za′tion,** *n.*

trivial name, the vernacular or common name for a plant or animal, as distinguished from the scientific name.

triv·i·um (triv′ē əm) *n.* in medieval universities, three subjects, grammar, rhetoric, and logic, that composed the less advanced group of the seven liberal arts. ➡ distinguished from **quadrivium.** [Medieval Latin *trivium,* from Latin *trivium* place where three roads meet. See TRIVIAL.]

tri·week·ly (trī wēk′lē) *adv.* **1.** every three weeks. **2.** three times a week. —*adj.* **1.** occurring or done every three weeks. **2.** occurring or done three times a week. —*n., pl.* **-lies.** a newspaper, magazine, or other publication issued three times a week or once every three weeks.

tRNA, transfer RNA.

tro·cha·ic (trō kā′ik) *adj.* of, relating to, or consisting of trochees. —*n.* a line of verse or poem written in trochees.

tro·che (trō′kē) *n.* a disk containing medicine to be dissolved in the mouth; lozenge. [From obsolete *trochisk,* from Late Latin *trochiscus* small ball [1], pill, from Greek *trochiskos* small wheel, pill, diminutive of *trochos* wheel.]

tro·chee (trō′kē) *n.* a metrical foot consisting of two syllables, the first accented or long and the second unaccented or short, for example: Pe′ter Pe′ter pump′kin eat′er. [Latin *trochaeus,* from Greek *trochaios (pous)* running (foot); because this meter produces the effect of running.]

troch·le·a (trok′lē ə) *n., pl.* **-le·ae** (-lē ē′). an anatomical part or process that functions as or has the shape of a pulley, as the grooved end of any of the finger bones. [Modern Latin *trochlea,* from Latin *trochlea* pulley block.]

troch·le·ar (trok′lē ər) *adj.* **1.** of, characterized by, or forming a trochlea. **2.** of or relating to either of the fourth pair of cranial nerves, which supply nerve fibers to one of the muscles of the eyeball. —*n.* a trochlear nerve.

trod (trod) a past tense and past participle of **tread.**

trod·den (trod′ən) a past participle of **tread.**

trode (trōd) *Archaic.* a past tense of **tread.**

trog·lo·dyte (trog′lə dīt′) *n.* **1.** a low, despised person, esp. one who lives under primitive or hermitlike conditions, as in a cave in the earth. **2.** an anthropoid ape, as a gorilla or chimpanzee. [Latin *Trōglodytae* (plural) a people of Ethiopia who lived in caves, from Greek *trōglodytēs* cave man, one who creeps into holes, from *trōglē* hole + *dyein* to enter.] —**trog·lo·dyt·ic** (trog′lə dit′ik), *adj.*

tro·gon (trō′gon) *n.* any of a group of long-tailed, tropical birds, family Trogonidae, found in both hemispheres, having brilliantly colored, usually metallic plumage and short, broad, bristled bills adapted for picking fruit and catching flying insects. [Modern Latin *trogon,* from Greek *trōgōn* gnawing, present participle of *trōgein* to gnaw.]

troi·ka (troi′kə) *n.* **1.** a Russian vehicle, as a carriage, drawn by three horses abreast. **2.** a team of three such horses. **3.** a group or association of three persons, esp. three persons jointly holding power or authority.

Troi·lus (troi′ləs, trō′i ləs) *n.* in Greek legend, a Trojan prince, son of King Priam, who, in medieval legend, is portrayed as the lover and betrayer of Cressida.

Tro·jan (trō′jən) *adj.* of, relating to, or characteristic of Troy or its people or culture. —*n.* **1.** a native or citizen of Troy. **2.** a person who exhibits great courage, energy, or forbearance.

Trojan horse 1. in Greek legend, a large, hollow wooden horse, given by the Greeks to the Trojans apparently as a gift, but containing soldiers who crept out and opened the city gates to the Greek army. **2.** a person or thing that is designed or intended to undermine or destroy something, as an organization, from within.

Trojan War, in Greek legend, a war between the Greeks and the Trojans that lasted ten years and ended in the destruction of Troy, caused by the abduction of Helen by Paris, a Trojan.

troll[1] (trōl) *v.i.* **1.** to fish with a moving line, usually by trailing the line behind a boat. **2.** to sing in a full, rich voice. **3.** to be uttered in such a voice. —*v.t.* **1.** (of several singers) to sing the parts of (a song) in succession, as in a round. **2.** to sing or utter in a full, rich voice. —*n.* **1.** a song whose parts are sung in succession. **2.** a fishing line or lure used for trolling. [Middle French *troller* to wander, ramble; possibly from Middle High German *trollen* to run with short steps.] —**troll′er,** *n.*

troll[2] (trōl) *n.* in Scandinavian folklore, a dwarf or, sometimes, a giant, who lives underground or in a mountain cave. [Old Norse *troll* monster, demon.]

trol·ley (trol′ē) *n., pl.* **-leys. 1.** a small, grooved wheel or pulley that moves along an overhead wire to pick up electricity for an electric streetcar, train, or bus. **2.** trolley car. **3.** *British.* a low cart or truck; handcart. [Probably from TROLL [1] (in the obsolete senses of "to move about," "ramble").]

trolley bus, an electric bus that gets its power from an overhead wire by means of a trolley.

trolley car, a streetcar powered by electricity conducted from an overhead wire by a trolley.

trol·lop (trol′əp) *n.* a promiscuous or vulgar woman, esp. a prostitute.

trom·bone (trom bōn′, trom′bōn) *n.* a brass musical instrument consisting of two long, U-shaped tubes, one ending in a bell and the other sliding back and forth to vary the pitch of the tones. [Italian *trombone* trombone, trumpet, from *tromba* trumpet, from Old High German *trumpa.*] —**trom·bon′ist,** *n.*

trompe l'oeil (tromp′lā′; *French* trônp lœ′yə) **1.** a style of painting in which objects are depicted in such fine detail that they give the illusion of being real. **2.** a painting or drawing done in

American **trompe l'oeil** painting

this style. [French *trompe-l'œil* literally, (it) deceives the eye.] —**trompe′-l′oeil′**, *adj.*

-tron *combining form* a device for propagating or studying electrons or other subatomic particles: *cyclotron.* [Greek *-tron* instrument, device.]

troop (trüp) *n.* **1.** an organized body of soldiers, police, or the like. **2.** formerly, a cavalry unit of the U.S. Army corresponding to an infantry company. **3. troops.** members of the armed forces collectively: *The government sent troops to patrol the border.* **4.a.** a large group working or congregating together: *A whole troop of sign painters went to work on the blank walls.* **b.** *usually,* **troops.** a great number; flock; swarm: *troops of friends.* **5.** a unit of boy or girl scouts, usually with from sixteen to thirty-two members. **6.** troupe. —*v.i.* to walk or march in a group, esp. in an orderly fashion: *The players trooped onto the field.* [French *troupe* group of persons, herd, possibly from *troupeau* herd, from Late Latin *troppus;* of Germanic origin.]

troop·er (trü′pər) *n.* **1.** a soldier in a troop of cavalry. **2.** a mounted police officer. **3.** a state police officer. **4.** trouper.

troop·ship (trüp′ship′) *n.* a ship used to transport military personnel.

trope (trōp) *n.* **1.** the use of a word or phrase in a figurative sense. **2.** a figure of speech. **3.** figurative language in general. [Latin *tropus* figure of speech, from Greek *tropos* figure of speech, turn.]

tro·phy (trō′fē) *n., pl.* **-phies. 1.** a loving cup, bowl, statuette on a pedestal, or other object for display, usually awarded for some achievement, as winning a sports contest or other competition. **2.** something taken and kept as a reminder or proof of victory or achievement or of participation in a conflict, as a weapon captured from an enemy. **3.** *Archaic.* an arrangement or display of weapons, flags, or other objects. [French *trophée* sign of victory, through Latin, from Greek *tropaion* monument of an enemy's defeat, from *tropē* defeat, turning.]

-trophy *combining form* nutrition; growth: *hypertrophy.* [Greek *trophia* nutrition, nourishment, growth, from *trephein* to nourish.]

trop·ic (trop′ik) *n.* **the tropics.** *also,* **the Tropics.** the region of the earth lying between the Tropic of Cancer and the Tropic of Capricorn; the Torrid Zone. —*adj.* of or relating to the tropics; tropical. [Late Latin *tropicus* relating to a turning (of the sun), from Greek *tropikos,* from *tropē* a turning.]

trop·i·cal (trop′i kəl) *adj.* of, relating to, found in, suitable to, or characteristic of the tropics: *tropical clothing, a tropical storm.*

tropical fish, any of many varieties of small fish, usually brightly colored, that are native to tropical waters and are often kept in home aquariums.

tropic bird, any of various long-winged, tropical seabirds, family Phaëthontidae, having webbed feet, two very long tail feathers, a red or yellow bill, and white plumage with black markings on the head and wings. Length: 16-19 inches (41-48 centimeters).

Tropic of Cancer 1. an imaginary line parallel to the equator at latitude 23° 27′ north, that marks the northernmost distance from the equator at which the sun appears to be overhead at noon. **2.** the circle of the celestial sphere corresponding to this, parallel to the celestial equator.

Tropic of Capricorn 1. an imaginary line parallel to the equator at latitude 23° 27′ south, that marks the southernmost distance from the equator at which the sun appears to be overhead at noon. **2.** the circle of the celestial sphere corresponding to this, parallel to the celestial equator.

tro·pism (trō′piz əm) *n.* the tendency of an animal or plant to turn or grow in response to a specific stimulus, esp. a tendency to turn or grow toward the light. [Greek *tropos* a turning + -ISM.] —**tro·pis·tic** (trō pis′tik), *adj.*

trop·o·pause (trop′ə pôz′, trō′pə-) *n.* the uppermost limits of the troposphere, where the stratosphere begins, at altitudes ranging from 5 to 10 miles (8 to 16 kilometers), depending on the latitude. [TROPO(SPHERE) + PAUSE.]

trop·o·sphere (trop′ə sfir′, trō′pə-) *n.* the layer of the atmosphere nearest the earth's surface, extending to an average altitude of about 8 miles (13 kilometers), in which clouds form and most of the earth's weather phenomena occur. For illustration, see **atmosphere.** [Greek *tropos* turning + SPHERE.] —**trop·o·spher·ic** (trop′ə sfer′ik, trō′pə-), *adj.*

trot (trot) *n.* **1.a.** the gait of a horse or other quadruped, between a walk and a gallop, in which the left hind foot and the right forefoot are lifted together and then the left forefoot and right hind foot are lifted. **b.** the sound of this. **2.** the jogging gait of a human being, between a walk and a run. **3.** any quick but easy pace. **4.** *Informal.* pony *(def. 3).* —*v.,* **trot·ted, trot·ting.** —*v.i.* **1.** to ride or move at a trot: *The horse trotted around the corral.* **2.** to move quickly; hurry; bustle: *I trotted to the post*

office to get the letter out before noon. —*v.t.* **1.** to cause to trot. **2.** *Informal.* to take or carry at a brisk pace: *Trot this package down to the mail room.* [Old French *troter* to go at a trot, walk fast; of Germanic origin.]

  •**to trot out.** *Informal.* to bring out and show for exhibition, consideration, approval, or the like: *to trot out pictures of one's trip.*

troth (trôth, trōth) *n. Archaic.* a promise of fidelity, as in marriage or betrothal. [Old English *trēowth* fidelity, promise.]

trot·line (trot′līn′) *n.* a fishing line supported by buoys or suspended across a stream, with many baited hooks at intervals along it.

trot·ter (trot′ər) *n.* **1.** a horse that trots, esp. one bred and trained for harness races. **2.** a foot, as of a calf, sheep, or pig, used as food.

trou·ba·dour (trü′bə dôr′, -dùr′) *n.* any of many lyric poets who flourished from the eleventh to the thirteenth centuries in southern Europe, esp. in Provence, and were famous for songs about love and chivalry. [French *troubadour,* from Provençal *trobador,* from *trobar* to compose poetry, find; of uncertain origin.]

trou·ble (trub′əl) *n.* **1.** an unfortunate, dangerous, or tragic occurrence or situation; difficulty, harm, or distress: *The closing of the factory will bring much trouble to the town. The corporation's troubles began when the founding president died.* **2.** extra exertion or effort; pains: *The teacher went to much trouble to make the explanation clear. Please don't go to any trouble on my account.* **3. a.** something that causes a problem; drawback; shortcoming: *The trouble with the plan is it will not work.* **b.** a problematic state or condition: *The company is having trouble selling its new product.* **4.** a disease or illness; ailment: *kidney trouble.* **5.** mental or emotional uneasiness, pain, or suffering: *a life full of toil and trouble.* **6.** a disturbance or disorder; turmoil: *There was trouble at the factory today that led to a walkout.* **7.** a fight or struggle; conflict: *The motorcycle gang came into town looking for trouble.* —*v.,* **-bled, -bling.** —*v.t.* **1.** to put into a state of mental agitation or distress; worry; disturb: *to trouble someone with your problems.* **2.** to put (someone) to extra effort; inconvenience: *May I trouble you for a glass of water?* **3.** to cause physical pain to; hurt; afflict: *to be troubled by ulcers.* —*v.i.* to take pains; bother: *Don't trouble to see me out.* [Old French *trubler, turbler* to disturb, going back to Latin *turba* disturbance, crowd.] —**trou·bler,** *n.*

trou·ble·mak·er (trub′əl mā′kər) *n.* a person or thing that is a source of trouble.

trou·ble·shoot·er (trub′əl shü′tər) *n.* a person who specializes in locating and solving troubles, problems, and difficulties.

trou·ble·some (trub′əl səm) *adj.* causing distress, inconvenience, or annoyance: *a troublesome injury, a troublesome neighbor.*

trou·blous (trub′ləs) *adj.* **1.** full of troubles: *troublous times.* **2.** troublesome.

trough (trôf) *n.* **1.** a long, deep, narrow receptacle resembling a bin, used esp. for holding water. **2.** a channel or conduit, as under or along the eaves of a roof, used for conveying water. **3.** a low point, as on a graph. **4.** a long, narrow hollow or depression, as between two mountain ridges or two ocean waves. **5.** an area of low barometric pressure associated with a cyclonic storm, lying generally perpendicular to the path of the storm. [Old English *trog* narrow and hollow vessel, vat.]

trounce (trouns) *v.t.,* **trounced, trounc·ing. 1.** to beat soundly; thrash. **2.** to defeat overwhelmingly in or as in a contest. [Of uncertain origin.]

troupe (trüp) *also,* **troop.** *n.* a theatrical group or company, as of actors, singers, or circus performers, esp. such a company that travels about from place to place. —*v.i.,* **trouped, troup·ing.** to go on a tour with such a group. [French *troupe.* See TROOP.]

troup·er (trü′pər) *also,* **trooper.** *n.* **1.** a person who faces up to problems or difficulties or persists despite pain or obstacles. **2.** a veteran actor or performer. **3.** a member of a troupe.

trou·ser (trou′zər) *adj.* of or relating to trousers: *trouser leg.*

trou·sers (trou′zərz) *pl. n.* a garment for the lower part of the body, extending from the waist or hips to the ankles and divided so as to cover each leg separately. [Modification of archaic *trouse,* from Irish and Scottish Gaelic *triubhas,* possibly from Old French *trebus* breeches; of uncertain origin.]

a	at	e	end	o	hot	u	up	hw	white		about
ā	ape	ē	me	ō	old	ū	use	th	song		taken
ä	far	i	it	ô	fork	ü	rule	th	thin	ə	pencil
âr	care	ī	ice	oi	oil	ù	pull	th	this		lemon
		îr	pierce	ou	out	ûr	turn	zh	measure		circus

trous·seau (trü′sō, trü sō′) *n., pl.* **-seaux** (-sōz, -sōz′) or **-seaus.** all the items brought by a bride to her new home, as clothing, linen, and silver. [French *trousseau,* diminutive of *trousse* bundle, possibly from Old French *trusser* to pack¹, bind; of uncertain origin.]

trout (trout) *n., pl.* **trout** or **trouts. 1.** any of a group of food and game fish, family Salmonidae, related to the salmon, found in lakes and streams, including the lake trout and brook trout. **2.** any of various fish that bear a superficial resemblance to trout, as sea trout and a species of bass. [Old English *trúht,* from Late Latin *tructa,* probably from Greek *trōktēs* gnawer, a saltwater fish with sharp teeth.]

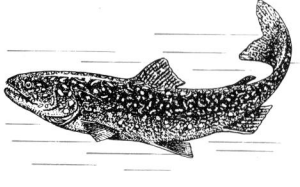

trout

trow (trō) *v.i., v.t. Archaic.* to be of the opinion; suppose; think. [Partly from Old English *trūwian* to trust; partly from Old English *trēowian* to believe.]

trow·el (trou′əl) *n.* **1.** a hand tool with a flat, rectangular or triangular blade, used for spreading and smoothing plaster or mortar, as in bricklaying. **2.** a scooplike hand tool with a narrow, curved, pointed blade, used in gardening, as for digging. [Old French *truele* the tool used for spreading plaster and mortar, going back to Late Latin *truella,* diminutive of *trua* ladle.]

troy (troi) *adj.* expressed or measured in troy weight.

troy weight, a standard system of weights used for gems and precious metals. For Weights and Measures table, see **weight.** [From *Troyes,* a city in France where this weight was probably first employed for gems and precious metals at the city's famous fairs in the Middle Ages.]

tru·an·cy (trü′ən sē) *n., pl.* **-cies.** the act, instance, or practice of being truant.

tru·ant (trü′ənt) *n.* **1.** a student who is absent from school without permission or a legitimate excuse. **2.** a person who shirks or neglects work or responsibilities; idle or lazy person. —*adj.* **1.** of, relating to, or characteristic of truants: *truant behavior.* **2.** being a truant: *a truant worker.* [Old French *truant* beggar, vagabond; probably of Celtic origin.] —**tru′ant·ly,** *adv.*
  •**to play truant. a.** to be absent from school without permission. **b.** to shirk or neglect one's work or duties.

truant officer, a school official who investigates and deals with cases of truancy.

truce (trüs) *n.* **1.** a temporary halt to fighting by mutual agreement of combatants, often in order to reach a final settlement. **2.** any halt in or respite from a disagreeable or quarrelsome situation. [Middle English *trewes,* plural of *trewe* temporary peace, from Old English *treow* faith, promise, compact.]

Synonyms **Truce, armistice,** and **cease-fire** denote a temporary suspension of hostilities between warring groups or warring states. **Truce** connotes any halt agreed on, for any period: *a 24-hour truce for the Christmas holiday, a truce that lasted twenty years.* **Armistice** connotes an agreement at a high level, as between countries, and suggests an eventual end to the state of war: *The armistice was followed by negotiations over a peace pact.* **Cease-fire** is the most specific of them, connoting a simple halt in shooting. It is the only one that may apply to action by one side only: *The rebel leaders announced a unilateral cease-fire, to last for thirty days.*

truck¹ (truk) *n.* **1.** an automotive vehicle designed to carry heavy loads, esp. one with a cab in front for the driver and an open or enclosed area or trailer behind for the cargo. **2.** a low, rectangular frame on four wheels, often motorized, used for moving heavy loads, as boxes in a warehouse or railroad station; dolly. **3.** a two-wheeled handbarrow used for lifting and carrying trunks, boxes, or similar loads. **4.** a set of two or more pairs of wheels mounted closely together in a swiveling frame, as on a railroad car or locomotive. —*v.t.* to convey on a truck or trucks. —*v.i.* to drive a truck or engage in trucking. [Probably from Latin *trochus* iron hoop, from Greek *trochos* wheel.]

truck² (truk) *n.* **1.** vegetables raised for market. **2.** *Informal.* dealings or relations: *We will have no truck with such unpleasant neighbors.* **3.** *Informal.* trash;

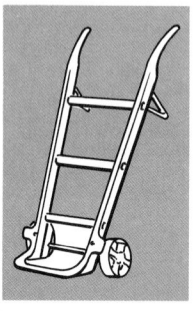

truck¹ *(def. 3)*

rubbish. **4.** payment of wages in goods or the like, instead of money. **5.** barter. [Old French *troquer* to barter; of uncertain origin.]

truck·age (truk′ij) *n.* **1.** a charge for conveyance by truck. **2.** conveyance by truck.

truck·er (truk′ər) *n.* **1.** a person or firm owning or operating a trucking business. **2.** a person whose job is driving a truck.

truck farm, a farm on which vegetables are raised for market. —**truck farmer.**

truck·ing (truk′ing) *n.* the business or process of transporting goods by truck.

truck·le (truk′əl) *v.,* **-led, -ling.** —*v.i.* **1.** to be subservient or obsequious (with *to*): *to truckle to a bully.* **2.** *Archaic.* to move on rollers or casters. —*v.t. Archaic.* to cause to move on rollers or casters. —*n.* **1.** truckle bed. **2.** a small wheel or caster. [Latin *trochlea* pulley, system of pulleys, from Greek *trochileiā.*]

truckle bed, trundle bed.

truc·u·lence (truk′yə ləns, trü′kyə-) *n.* truculent behavior, actions, or appearance. Also, **truc′u·len·cy.**

truc·u·lent (truk′yə lənt, trü′kyə-) *adj.* **1.** savagely or fiercely brutal; ferocious: *truculent warriors.* **2.** harsh or scathing: *a truculent speech.* **3.** hostile or threatening; belligerent. [Latin *truculentus* cruel, harsh.] —**truc′u·lent·ly,** *adv.*

trudge (truj) *v.,* **trudged, trudg·ing.** —*v.i.* to go on foot in a steady, laborious manner; drag oneself; plod: *to trudge up a hill.* —*v.t.* to travel over (a place or distance) in a steady, laborious manner: *They trudged the last mile in the rain.* —*n.* a laborious, tiring walk: *a long trudge back home.* [Of uncertain origin.]

trudg·en stroke (truj′ən) a swimming stroke like a crawl, but usually accompanied by a scissors kick. [From John *Trudgen,* 1852–1902, English swimmer who popularized it.]

true (trü) *adj.,* **tru·er, tru·est. 1.** conforming with or correctly representing reality or fact; not false, fictitious, or wrong: *a true story, a true account of an event.* **2.** having the proper qualities or characteristics of: *a true friend.* **3.** actually being what it seems to be; real: *true gold.* **4.** faithful to someone or something; loyal: *to be true to one's old friends.* **5.** conforming closely to an original, standard, or type: *a true copy.* **6.** conforming to law or rule; legitimate; rightful: *the true heirs to the estate.* **7.** certain or unerring; sure: *a true sign of insanity.* **8.** accurately aligned or placed: *a true door frame.* **9.** determined with reference to the earth's axis rather than the magnetic poles: *true south.* —*adv.* **1.** in a true manner. **2.** *Biology.* without change from the previous generation: *to breed true.* —*n.* **1. the true.** something that is true or real. **2.** a condition of accurate alignment or placement: *to be in true.* —*v.t.,* **trued, tru·ing** or **true·ing.** to place, adjust, or align accurately (often with *up*). [Old English *trēowe, trȳwe* trustworthy, faithful.] —**true′ness,** *n.* —For Synonyms *(adj.),* see **real¹.**
  •**to come true.** to become real or actual.

true bill, a bill of indictment endorsed by a grand jury as having sufficient evidence to justify a trial.

true-blue (trü′blü′) *adj.* unwavering in loyalty or faith; staunch: *a true-blue friend.*

true·love (trü′luv′) *n.* one's beloved; sweetheart.

truf·fle (truf′əl, trü′fəl) *n.* **1.** any of a group of edible, potato-shaped fungi, genus *Tuber,* that grow underground. **2.** a soft chocolate candy. [Middle French *trufle,* form of *truffe,* possibly going back to Latin *tūber* swelling, truffle.]

tru·ism (trü′iz əm) *n.* a statement that is so obviously true that no one would argue with it.

Synonyms **Truism, platitude,** and **cliché** mean a commonplace idea or statement. **Truism** denotes a truth that is too obvious and widely known to need stating: *It is a truism that children imitate their parents.* **Platitude** is applied to a stale, trite idea often expressed with an air of profundity: *The candidates exchanged platitudes about their respective parties' greatness.* **Cliché** is a statement that has lost its freshness and force through overuse: *Last year's fashionable expressions are this year's clichés.*

tru·ly (trü′lē) *adv.* **1.** in a true manner; sincerely; genuinely: *I'm truly sorry.* **2.** in accordance with fact or reality; truthfully. **3.** accurately; correctly.

trump¹ (trump) *n.* **1.** a suit of playing cards that temporarily outranks the other suits, as for a single hand. **2.** any card of this suit. —*v.t.* **1.** to play a trump card on (another card or a trick). **2.** to go (someone) one better; outdo; beat. —*v.i.* to play a trump card. [Modification of TRIUMPH.]

trump² (trump) *v.t.* to make up in order to deceive; fabricate (with *up*): *to trump up an excuse.* [Possibly from TRUMP¹.]

trumped-up (trumpt′up′) *adj.* made up in order to deceive; fabricated; contrived: *a trumped-up story.* [From TRUMP².]

trump·er·y (trum′pə rē) *n., pl.* **-er·ies.** something that appears to be valuable but is really worthless. [Old French *tromperie* deceit, fraud, from *tromper* to deceive; of uncertain origin.]

trum·pet (trum′pit) *n.* **1.** a brass musical instrument consisting of a cylindrical metal tube coiled into a long loop and ending in a bell, the tones of which are varied by the pressure of the player's lips and by the use of three valves. **2.** something resembling a trumpet in shape. **3.** a sound like that of a trumpet, as the cry of an elephant. **4.** trumpeter *(def. 1).* —*v.i.* **1.** to blow a trumpet. **2.** to produce or emit a sound like that of a trumpet, as does an elephant. —*v.t.* **1.** to sound or produce on a trumpet. **2.** to announce or proclaim

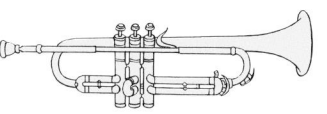

trumpet

widely and loudly as if with a trumpet; herald: *The team trumpeted their victory through the streets.* [Old French *trompette* this musical instrument, diminutive of *trompe.* See TRUMP².]

trumpet creeper, a woody climbing vine, *Campsis radicans,* related to bignonia, bearing clusters of orange and scarlet funnel-shaped flowers. Also, **trumpet vine.**

trum·pet·er (trum′pi tər) *n.* **1.** a person who sounds or plays on a trumpet. **2.** trumpeter swan. **3.** any of several South American birds, genus *Psophia,* native to humid jungle regions, related to and resembling the crane, having thick, generally dark-colored plumage and a loud, resonant cry. Length: 20 inches (51 centimeters). **4.** one of a breed of domestic pigeons having a crest and feathered feet.

trumpeter swan, a North American swan, *Cygnus buccinator,* having a deep, resonant call that resembles the sound of a bugle.

trumpet flower, any of a number of plants with trumpet-shaped blossoms, as bignonia and jimsonweed.

trumpet vine, trumpet creeper.

trun·cate (trung′kāt) *v.t.,* **-cat·ed, -cat·ing.** to reduce in size or diminish by cutting off a part of. —*adj.* truncated. [Latin *truncātus,* past participle of *truncāre* to cut off, maim.] —**trun·ca′tion,** *n.*

trun·cat·ed (trung′kā tid) *adj.* having or seeming to have a part or section missing or cut off.

trun·cheon (trun′chən) *n.* **1.** a club, esp. a long, slender, sturdy one, as used by police. **2.** a staff carried as a symbol of office. —*v.t. Archaic.* to beat with a truncheon; club. [Old French *tronchon* stump, piece cut off, going back to Latin *truncus* trunk of a tree or human being.]

trun·dle (trun′dəl) *v.,* **-dled, -dling.** —*v.t.* to cause to roll along by pushing: *to trundle a bicycle rather than ride it.* —*v.i.* to move or go on or as if on rollers or wheels. —*n.* **1.** a small wheel or caster. **2.** trundle bed. [Form of earlier *trendle* circle, wheel, from Old English *trendel* circle, ring¹; influenced by Old French *trondeler* to roll (of Germanic origin).]

trundle bed 1. a low movable bed that may be pushed under another bed for storage. **2.** a bed including a second low, movable bed that is pushed under it for storage. Also, **truckle bed.**

trunk (trungk) *n.* **1.** the main stem of a tree, as distinguished from its branches. **2.** a large, rectangular receptacle with a hinged lid, used for transporting and storing things. **3.** the baggage compartment of an automobile. **4.** a long flexible snout, esp. of an elephant. **5. trunks.** short men's pants, as those worn by swimmers, that reach from the waist to the upper thigh. **6.a.** the main body of a human being or animal, considered apart from any appendages, as the head, limbs, or tail; torso. **b.** the thorax of an insect. **7.** the main part or stem of something, esp. of a nerve, blood vessel, or the like. **8.** trunk line. [Latin *truncus* trunk of a human being or tree.]

trunk·fish (trungk′fish′) *n., pl.* **-fish** or **-fish·es.** any of various brightly colored, mostly tropical, saltwater fish, family Ostraciidae, having an outer shell of bony, angular plates. Length: 9-16 inches (23-41 centimeters).

trunk hose, full, baggy men's breeches, usually reaching from the waist to the upper thigh, worn in the late sixteenth and early seventeenth centuries.

trunk line 1. the main line of a transportation system, as of a railroad. **2.** a line that connects telephone exchanges and carries many calls at once. Also, **trunk.**

trun·nel (trun′əl) treenail.

trun·nion (trun′yən) *n.* either of two projections on each side of a cannon that support it on its carriage. [Old French *trognon* stump, core; of uncertain origin.]

truss (trus) *n.* **1.** a device, usually consisting of a pad attached to a belt, used for support in cases of hernia. **2.** a framework, as of wood or metal, usually consisting of triangular units, used to span an opening or support a heavy load, as of a bridge or roof. **3.** a bundle of hay or straw. **4.** *Nautical.* a rope or iron fitting by which a lower yard is secured to a mast. —*v.t.*

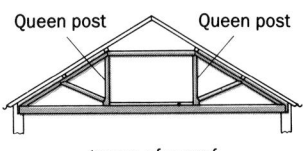

truss of a roof

1. to bind or tie; fasten (often with *up*). **2.** to bind or skewer the legs and wings of (fowl) before cooking: *to truss a turkey.* **3.** to support or strengthen, as a roof or bridge, with a truss or trusses. **4.** *Archaic.* to adjust (clothing) by drawing it closely together. [Old French *trusse* bundle, possibly from *trusser* to pack¹, bind; of uncertain origin.]

trust (trust) *v.t.* **1.** to have faith or confidence in the integrity, honesty, ability, reliability, or justice of: *to trust one's parents, to trust the government.* **2.** to rely upon or believe: *to trust your intuitions, to trust the weather reports.* **3.** to commit to someone's care; entrust: *to trust a child to a baby-sitter.* **4.** to give business credit to: *The grocer trusted me to pay next week for this week's food.* **5.** to feel sure of; expect with confidence: *I trust that you will get here on time.* —*v.i.* **1.** to have faith or confidence (often with *in*): *to trust in one's own judgment.* **2.** to assume or feel sure: *You found it, I trust.* —*n.* **1.** faith or confidence in the integrity, honesty, ability, reliability, or justice of someone or something. **2.** keeping or custody; care: *Their dog was left in my trust for the weekend.* **3.** the fact or state of being trusted: *The president holds a position of great power and trust.* **4.** a person or thing that is believed or believed in: *O Lord God, thou art my trust . . .* (Psalm 71:5). **5.** a business combination, as of many companies or corporations, that exercises monopolistic power over the production or distribution of a commodity or service and can fix prices and eliminate competition. **6.** money or property held and controlled by one person for the benefit of another. Also, **trust fund. 7.** a person or thing that is believed in or relied upon. **8.** a person or thing that is committed or entrusted to someone's care. **9.** confidence in the ability or intention of a person to pay at some future time; credit. [Old Norse *traust* help, confidence.]

· **in trust. a.** in a condition of safekeeping or careful protection: *woodlands held in trust for future generations.* **b.** in a trust fund.

Synonyms Trust, confidence, and reliance mean a certainty that something will fulfill expectations. **Trust** suggests an assurance based more on intuition than on rational considerations: *The lovers had complete trust in each other's devotion.* **Confidence** implies the existence of a more rational basis for belief: *The team's confidence is based on its long winning streak.* **Reliance** (with *on*) is usually applied to the active expression of one's trust: *The troops entered the battle with complete reliance on the battle plan laid out by their commanders.*

trust·bust·er (trust′bus′tər) *n.* a person who seeks to weaken or break up large business combinations or trusts, as by rigorous enforcement of antitrust laws or by agitation for new or stronger laws.

trust company, a bank or other company whose main function is the management of property, as money, securities, or real estate, entrusted to it by others.

trus·tee (trus tē′) *n.* **1.** an individual or organization, such as a bank, that holds and manages the property or affairs of a person. **2.** a member of a group of persons entrusted with managing the affairs of an institution or organization. **3.** a country commissioned to administer a trust territory.

trus·tee·ship (trus tē′ship′) *n.* **1.** the office or function of a trustee. **2.a.** the administrative authority over a trust territory by a country commissioned by the United Nations. **b.** the territory so administered.

trust·ful (trust′fəl) *adj.* full of or disposed to trust; trusting. —**trust′ful·ly,** *adv.* —**trust′ful·ness,** *n.*

a	at	e	end	o	hot	u	up	hw	white		about
ā	ape	ē	me	ō	old	ū	use	ng	song		taken
ä	far	i	it	ô	fork	ü	rule	th	thin	ə	pencil
âr	care	ī	ice	oi	oil	u̇	pull	th	this		lemon
		îr	pierce	ou	out	ûr	turn	zh	measure		circus

trust fund, trust *(n., def. 6).*

trust·ing (trus'ting) *adj.* full of or disposed to trust: *a trusting person.*

trust territory, a territory, as a former colony, that is administered by another nation under UN supervision, with the aim of becoming independent.

trust·wor·thy (trust'wûr'the͞) *adj.* able to be trusted or worthy of trust. —**trust'wor'thi·ness,** *n.*

trust·y (trus'te͞) *adj.,* **trust·i·er, trust·i·est.** able to be trusted or relied on. —*pl. n.* **trust·ies.** a convict who is given certain duties and privileges because of good behavior. —**trust'i·ly,** *adv.* —**trust'i·ness,** *n.*

truth (tro͞oth) *n., pl.* **truths** (tro͞othz, tro͞oths). **1.** something that is true: *the pursuit of truth, to speak the truth.* **2.** the state or quality of being true or of accurately reflecting reality or fact: *to doubt the truth of a statement.* **3.** an accepted or verified fact, principle, or the like: *a mathematical truth.* [Old English *trīewth, trēowth* honor, fidelity, covenant.]

• **in truth.** really; actually.

truth·ful (tro͞oth'fəl) *adj.* **1.** telling or habitually telling the truth: *a truthful newspaper, a truthful person.* **2.** conforming to truth, fact, or reality: *a truthful picture of frontier life.* —**truth'ful·ly,** *adv.* —**truth'ful·ness,** *n.*

truth serum, a hypnotic or anesthetic drug, as Pentothal or scopolamine, used, esp. in psychiatry, to draw out suppressed thoughts.

truth set, solution set.

try (trī) *v.,* **tried, try·ing.** —*v.t.* **1.** to make an effort to do or accomplish; attempt; undertake: *I tried moving the heavy sofa myself.* **2.** to use or apply as a test or experiment: *The commuter tried the new route home and saved twenty minutes.* **3.** to investigate or examine in a court of law. **4.** to attempt to open: *The visitor tried the door, but it was locked.* **5.a.** to subject to trials or suffering; afflict: *The drought sorely tried the farmer.* **b.** to subject to strain; tax: *to try someone's patience.* **6.** *Archaic.* to separate or extract by steaming or melting (often with *out*). —*v.i.* to make an effort; attempt. —*n., pl.* **tries.** the act of trying: *The mountain climbers made one more try to reach the top.* [Old French *trier* to pick[1], choose; of uncertain origin.]

• **to try on.** to put on (an article of clothing) to test its fit or looks.

• **to try out.** to test the effect or operation of: *Try out the brakes before you drive down that hill.*

• **to try out for.** to demonstrate one's skill or ability in order to qualify as a member of: *to try out for the track team.*

Synonyms *v.t.* **Try, attempt,** and **endeavor** mean to make an effort to do something. **Try** is the most general word, which often describes the act of testing or experimentation: *to try to get to work on time, to try a new recipe.* **Attempt,** a more formal word, is often applied to an effort to do something that is difficult and that may not succeed: *It takes courage to attempt to swim the English Channel.* **Endeavor** is a still more formal term that suggests serious or noble actions: *The diplomats endeavored to bring the war to an end through secret negotiations.*

try·ing (trī'ing) *adj.* hard to bear or endure with patience; difficult: *a trying day, a trying person.*

try·out (trī'out') *n.* **1.** *also,* **tryouts.** a period or session during which those who are trying out for something, as for parts in a play or positions on a team, are checked for skill or ability. **2.** a trial or probationary period during which a person or thing is evaluated: *to give a new reporter a tryout on some business stories.*

try·pan·o·some (tri pan'ə so͞om') *n.* any of a group of microscopic protozoans that move by means of a flagellum and are parasites in the blood and spinal fluid of humans and other vertebrates, often causing serious diseases such as sleeping sickness. Trypanosomes are transmitted from one animal to another by insects.

tryp·sin (trip'sin) *n.* an enzyme that changes proteins into peptones to aid digestion, secreted by the pancreas and also prepared artificially. [Greek *trīpsis* rubbing + -IN[1]; because first obtained by *rubbing* the pancreas with glycerin.] —**tryp·tic** (trip'tik), *adj.*

tryp·to·phan (trip'tə fan') *also,* **tryp·to·phane** (trip'tə fān'). *n.* an essential amino acid that is produced in the digestive tract by the action of trypsin on proteins and is a source of serotonin. Formula: $C_{11}H_{12}N_2O_2$

try·sail (trī'səl, -sāl') *n.* a small fore-and-aft sail, usually extended with a gaff from the foremast or mainmast of a boat or ship, used esp. in stormy weather.

try square, an L-shaped instrument used in carpentry for laying out and testing right angles.

tryst (trist) *n.* **1.** a prearranged meeting, esp. between lovers; rendezvous. **2.** an arrangement to meet at a specified time and place. **3.** a prearranged place of meeting. [Old French *triste* place for watching, ambush; probably of Scandinavian origin.]

tsar (zär, tsär) czar.

tsar·e·vitch (zär'ə vich', tsär'-) czarevitch.

tsa·rev·na (zä rev'nə, tsä-) czarevna.

tsa·ri·na (zä rē'nə, tsä-) czarina.

tsar·ism (zär'iz əm, tsär'-) czarism.

tsar·ist (zär'ist, tsär'-) czarist.

tset·se fly (tset'sē, tsē'tsē) *also,* **tzetze fly.** any of a group of bloodsucking flies, family Glossinidae, found in Africa. Certain species transmit the trypanosome that causes sleeping sickness; others carry diseases fatal to horses and other animals. Also, **tsetse, tzetze.** [Of Bantu origin.]

T-shirt (tē'shûrt') *also,* **t-shirt, tee shirt.** *n.* **1.** a light, close-fitting undershirt with short sleeves. **2.** an outer shirt resembling this, worn for casual wear.

tsp *also,* **tsp.** teaspoon; teaspoons.

T square, a T-shaped tool used by architects and engineers to draw parallel straight lines, consisting of a long straightedge attached at one end to a short crosspiece that slides up and down the edge of a drawing board.

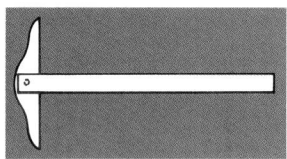

tsu·na·mi (tsu̇ nä'mē) *n.* a swift, powerful ocean wave caused by an underwater earthquake and causing great destruction to any land area it strikes; tidal wave. [Japanese *tsunami* tidal wave, from *tsu* harbor + *nami* wave.]

T square

T T, the postal abbreviation for the Trust Territory of the Pacific Islands.

Tu., Tuesday.

tu·a·ta·ra (tü'ə tär'ə) *n.* either of two species of reptiles, *Sphenodon punctatus* and *S. guntheri,* found on the offshore islands of New Zealand, having olive-brown or dull yellowish skin. They are the sole survivors of the order Rhynchocephalia and are distinguished by a third eye on the top of the head. Length: 2½ feet (0.8 meter), including tail. [Of Maori origin.]

tub (tub) *n.* **1.** bathtub. **2.** a large, open, circular receptacle, as for washing clothes. **3.** a round container, often of wood or metal, used for holding butter, honey, fat, or other products. **4.** the amount a tub will hold. **5.** something that resembles a tub, esp. an old, clumsy-looking boat or ship. **6.** *Informal.* bath. [Probably of Low German origin.]

tu·ba (tü'bə, tū'-) *n.* **1.** any of several very large brass musical instruments that produce a deep, mellow tone, consisting of a coiled metal tube whose diameter increases from a narrow mouthpiece at one end to a wide bell at the other. **2.** an organ stop producing powerful tones. [Latin *tuba* trumpet.]

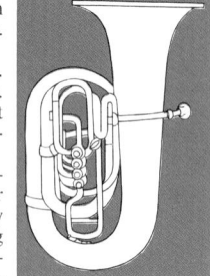

tub·by (tub'ē) *adj.,* **-bi·er, -bi·est. 1.** short and broad in shape, like a tub. **2.** having a dull, wooden sound, like that of an empty tub when struck. —**tub'bi·ness,** *n.*

tuba

tube (tüb, tūb) *n.* **1.** a hollow cylindrical structure, as of glass, rubber, or other material, usually used to hold or convey liquids or gases. **2.** anything resembling a tube in shape or function, as the bronchial tubes. **3.** a soft, squeezable container having a screw cap, used for packaging and dispensing toothpaste, shampoo, paint, and other products. **4.** an electron tube. **5.** an underground or underwater tunnel, or a train or subway that uses such a tunnel. **6. the tube.** *Informal.* television. —*v.t.* **1.** to provide with or place a tube in. **2.** to put in a tube. [Latin *tubus* pipe.] —**tube'like',** *adj.*

tube foot, one of many small tubelike structures on the underside of starfish and most other echinoderms, used for grasping and locomotion.

tube·less (tüb'lis, tūb'-) *adj.* (of a pneumatic tire) having no inner tube.

tu·ber (tü′bər, tū′-) *n.* **1.** *Botany.* the enlarged, fleshy portion of an underground stem, such as a potato, serving to store food and give rise to new plants. **2.** tubercle *(def. 1).* [Latin *tūber* swelling, tumor.]

tu·ber·cle (tü′bər kəl, tū′-) *n.* **1.** a small, rounded swelling, as on a bone or plant. **2.** a swelling caused by the tubercle bacillus. [Latin *tūberculum* small swelling, diminutive of *tūber* swelling, tumor.]

tubercle bacillus, the bacterium that causes tuberculosis.

tu·ber·cu·lar (tù bûr′kyə lər, tyù-) *adj.* **1.** tuberculous. **2.** of, relating to, or having tubercles; nodular.

tu·ber·cu·lin (tù bûr′kyə lin, tyù-) *n.* a liquid prepared from cultures of the tubercle bacillus, used in the diagnosis and formerly in the treatment of tuberculosis.

tu·ber·cu·lo·sis (tù bûr′kyə lō′sis, tyù-) *n.* **1.** an infectious disease caused by a bacterium that may affect any organ of the body, esp. the lungs or joints, and is characterized by the formation of tubercles on the affected parts. **2.** tuberculosis of the lungs. Also *(def. 2),* **consumption.** [Modern Latin *tuberculosis,* from Latin *tūberculum* small swelling + -OSIS.]

tu·ber·cu·lous (tù bûr′kyə ləs, tyù-) *adj.* of, relating to, or affected with tuberculosis.

tube·rose (tüb′rōz′, tūb′-) *n.* a Mexican plant, *Polianthes tuberosa,* widely cultivated for its fragrant, waxy, white flowers that are used to make perfumes. [Latin *tūberōsa,* feminine of *tūberōsus* full of swellings; mistakenly thought to be from TUBE + ROSE[1]. See TUBEROUS.]

tu·ber·os·i·ty (tü′bə ros′i tē, tū′-) *n., pl.* **-ties. 1.** the state or quality of being tuberous. **2.** a rounded swelling, esp. on a bone.

tu·ber·ous (tü′bər əs, tū′-) *adj.* **1.** of, like, or bearing tubers: *The potato is a tuberous plant.* **2.** covered with tuberosities or tubercles. [Latin *tūberōsus* full of swellings, from *tūber* swelling, tumor.]

tub·ing (tü′bing, tū′-) *n.* **1.** an object or material in the form of a tube: *glass tubing bent into shape for neon lights.* **2.** tubes collectively. **3.** a length or piece of tube: *This tubing has a hole in it.*

tu·bu·lar (tü′byə lər, tū′-) *adj.* **1.** consisting of tubes: *the tubular framework of a lawn chair.* **2.** of, relating to, or shaped like a tube: *a tubular pathway made by a worm.* [Latin *tubulus* small pipe, diminutive of *tubus* pipe + -AR[1].]

tu·bu·late (tü′byə lit, -lāt′, tū′-) *adj.* tubular.

tu·bule (tü′būl, tū′-) *n.* a small tube or tubelike structure in the body of a plant or animal. [Latin *tubulus* small pipe, diminutive of *tubus* pipe.]

tuck (tuk) *v.t.* **1.** to push or fold the edge or ends of (something), esp. so as to hold snugly in place: *to tuck a sheet under a mattress, to tuck one's shirt in.* **2.** to put into a tight or narrow place: *The wasps' nest was tucked underneath the rafters.* **3.** to hide from view or knowledge; store away or conceal: *There were many old things tucked away in the attic.* **4.** to cover snugly, esp. by folding the edges of a blanket or cover snugly under a mattress: *to tuck a child into bed.* **5.** to sew a tuck or tucks in (material or a garment). **6.** to gather up into a fold or folds so as to make shorter. **7.** to draw in or contract, as the legs when the knees are bent up tightly to the chest and the hands are clasped around the shins. —*v.i.* to sew a tuck or tucks in material or a garment. —*n.* **1.** a fold sewed in material or a garment, as to shape, shorten, tighten, or create fullness in it. **2.** a position of the body when the legs are tucked. [Middle Low German *tucken* to tug, pull up.]

tuck·er[1] (tuk′ər) *n.* **1.** a covering of lace, linen, or other light material formerly worn around the neck and shoulders by women. **2.** a person or thing that tucks. **3.** a sewing machine attachment for making tucks. [TUCK + -ER[1].]

tuck·er[2] (tuk′ər) *v.t. Informal.* to make tired or weary (often with *out*): *The hike tuckered us out.* [TUCK + -ER[4].]

Tu·dor (tü′dər, tū′-) *adj.* of, relating to, or designating a style of architecture and interior design that flourished in England during the reign of the Tudor monarchs from 1485 to 1558, characterized by flattened arches, gabled roofs, parapets, large bay windows, ornamental chimneys, and interior paneling.

Tues., Tuesday.

Tues·day (tüz′dē, -dā, tūz′-) *n.* the third day of the week. [Old English *Tīwesdæg* literally, day of Tiw (a Teutonic god of war identified with Mars), translation of Latin *diēs Martis* day of Mars.]

tu·fa (tü′fə, tū′-) *n.* **1.** any porous limestone, as travertine, formed from calcium carbonate deposited by springs, lakes, or ground water. **2.** tuff. [Italian *tufo,* from Latin *tōfus.* Doublet of TUFF.] —**tu·fa·ceous** (tü fā′shəs, tū-), *adj.*

tuff (tuf) *n.* a rock composed of consolidated volcanic ash. [French *tuf* tufa, tuff, from Italian *tufo,* from Latin *tōfus.* Doublet of TUFA.] —**tuff·a·ceous** (tu fā′shəs), *adj.*

tuf·fet (tuf′it) *n.* a hassock or footstool.

tuft (tuft) *n.* **1.** a dense cluster of flexible fibers, as feathers or hair, bound together or attached at one end and loose and bushy at the other. **2.** a small group or clump, as of trees or bushes. **3.** a cluster of threads sewn through a pillow, mattress, quilt, or the like, to keep the padding in place. —*v.t.* **1.** to adorn or furnish with a tuft or tufts. **2.** to sew a tuft in (a pillow, mattress, quilt, or the like). —*v.i.* to grow or form in tufts. [Earlier *toft,* probably from Old French *tof(f)e* tuft of hair; of Germanic origin.]

tuft·ed (tuf′tid) *adj.* **1.** having or adorned with a tuft or tufts. **2.** formed into or growing in a tuft or tufts.

tug (tug) *v.,* **tugged, tug·ging.** —*v.i.* **1.** to give a pull on something (with *at* or *on*): *The child tugged at my coat to get my attention.* **2.** to strain to pull or haul: *The horse tugged harder, and finally the log began to move.* —*v.t.* **1.** to give a pull on: *to tug someone's arm.* **2.** to pull or haul with force: *to tug a heavy trunk across a room.* **3.** to tow with a tugboat. —*n.* **1.** an act or instance of tugging: *I felt a tug on my fishing line.* **2.** tugboat. **3.** one of the traces of a harness. [Middle English *toggen* to pull, going back to Old English *tēo(ha)n* to pull, draw, drag.] —**tug′ger,** *n.*

tug·boat (tug′bōt′) *n.* a small, powerful boat that is used to push or tow other boats or ships. Also, **towboat.**

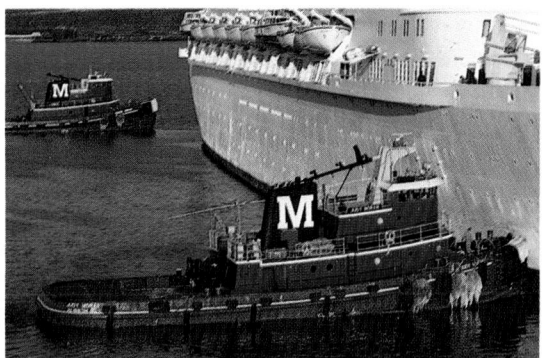

tugboats

tug of war 1. a game in which two players or teams pull at opposite ends of something, as a rope, with each trying to force the other either to let go or to be dragged out of place. **2.** any struggle or contest between opposite forces.

tu·i·tion (tü ish′ən, tū-) *n.* **1.** the amount of money paid by a student for instruction, esp. at a college or university. **2.** the act or business of teaching; instruction. [Latin *tuitiō* a taking care of, protection.]

tu·i·tion·al (tü ish′ə nəl, tū-) *adj.* of, relating to, or charging tuition.

tu·la·re·mi·a (tü′lə rē′mē ə) *n.* an infectious disease of rabbits and other rodents, caused by a bacterium and transmitted to humans by the handling of an infected animal or the bite of certain insects. Also, **rabbit fever.** [Modern Latin *tularemia,* from *Tulare,* a county in California where this disease was first encountered + Greek *haima* blood.] —**tu′la·re′mic,** *adj.*

tu·le (tü′lē) *n.* any of several large bulrushes, esp. *Scirpus lacustris,* common in marshy areas of the southwestern United States. [Mexican Spanish *tule,* from Nahuatl *to:lin* cattail.]

tu·lip (tü′lip, tū′-) *n.* **1.** the bell-shaped or saucer-shaped flower of any of a group of hardy plants, genus *Tulipa,* of the lily family, native to Asia and the Mediterranean area. **2.** the plant bearing these flowers, widely cultivated as an ornamental, having thick, bluish green leaves that rise directly from an underground bulb. [Modern Latin *Tulipa,* from Turkish *tülbend* turban, from Persian

a	at	e	end	o	hot	u	up	hw	white		about
ā	ape	ē	me	ō	old	ū	use	ng	song	ə	taken
ä	far	i	it	ô	fork	ü	rule	th	thin		pencil
âr	care	ī	ice	oi	oil	u̇	pull	th	this		lemon
		îr	pierce	ou	out	ûr	turn	zh	measure		circus

T

1291

dulband; from the resemblance of the flower to a turban. Doublet of TURBAN.]

tulip tree, a large North American tree, *Liriodendron tulipifera,* related to the magnolia, having yellowish green and orange flowers that resemble tulips, and soft wood used to make furniture and other products. Also, **tulip poplar.**

tu·lip·wood (tü′lip wùd′, tū′-) *n.* the colorful, striped wood of the tulip tree, used esp. in cabinetwork.

tulle (tül) *n.* a fine, stiff net fabric of silk or rayon, used in making veils and in dressmaking. [From *Tulle,* French town where it was first produced.]

tul·li·bee (tul′ə bē′) *n.* any of various North American white-fish, esp. the lake herring. [Canadian French *toulibi,* from Ojibwa *otonabi,* from *oton* mouth + *abi* water, liquid.]

tum·ble (tum′bəl) *v.,* **-bled, -bling.** *v.i.* **1.** to fall, esp. in an awkward, rolling manner: *The fruit tumbled from the overturned cart. I tripped and tumbled down the stairs.* **2.** to roll or toss about: *The clothes tumbled in the dryer.* **3.** to engage in tumbling. **4.** to go or proceed in a hurried, disorderly manner: *The children tumbled out the door.* **5.** to decline suddenly or rapidly: *The price of the stock tumbled.* **6.** to fall in or down; collapse. **7.** to come upon or find unexpectedly (with *on*): *to tumble on some old photos in the attic.* **8.** to understand or become aware of something (with *to*). —*v.t.* to cause to tumble or fall. —*n.* **1.** the act of tumbling; fall. **2.** a state of disorder or confusion; tangle. **3.** a gymnastic feat, such as a somersault. [Middle English *tumblen* to perform as an acrobat, fall, from *tumben* to dance, jump, from Old English *tumbian.*]
  · **to give (someone) a tumble.** *Slang.* to give notice or recognition to.

tum·ble·bug (tum′bəl bug′) *n.* dung beetle.

tum·ble-down (tum′bəl doun′) *adj.* in a dilapidated condition; falling apart: *a tumble-down old barn.*

tum·bler (tum′blər) *n.* **1.** a person who engages in tumbling. **2.** a drinking vessel, often of glass, having a flat bottom and no handle. **3.** a rotating drum, esp. in an automatic clothes dryer, in which objects are tumbled. **4.** a lever in a lock that must be moved to the correct height by the key in order to release the bolt. **5.** a mechanism in a gun that forces the hammer to move forward when the trigger releases the mainspring. **6.** any of a breed of domestic pigeons that do backward somersaults in flight.

tum·ble·weed (tum′bəl wēd′) *n.* any of several bushy prairie plants of western North America that break off from their roots, usually in autumn, and are blown about by the wind, esp. the Russian thistle.

tum·bling (tum′bling) *n.* a gymnastic or acrobatic activity done on mats or on the ground, as handstands and somersaults, rather than on a trampoline or other devices above floor level.

tum·brel (tum′brəl) *also,* **tum·bril.** *n.* **1.** a farmer's cart with a body that can be tilted backward to empty out the load. **2.** a cart used to carry condemned prisoners to be executed, used esp. during the French Revolution. [Old French *tumberel* dumpcart, from *tumber* to fall; of Germanic origin.]

tumbrel

tu·me·fac·tion (tü′mə fak′shən, tū′-) *n.* **1.** the act or state of being swollen. **2.** a swollen part, as a tumor.

tu·me·fy (tü′mə fī′, tū′-) *v.t., v.i.,* **-fied, -fy·ing.** to swell or cause to swell. [Latin *tumefacere* to cause to swell.]

tu·mes·cence (tü mes′əns, tū-) *n.* **1.** the act or process of swelling. **2.** a swollen condition. **3.** a swollen part or organ.

tu·mes·cent (tü mes′ənt, tū-) *adj.* swollen or becoming swollen. [Latin *tumēscēns,* present participle of *tumēscere* to begin to swell.]

tu·mid (tü′mid, tū′-) *adj.* **1.** abnormally enlarged; swollen. **2.** (of language) pretentious and inflated; pompous. [Latin *tumidus* swollen.] —**tu·mid·i·ty,** **tu′mid·ness,** *n.* —**tu′mid·ly,** *adv.*

tum·my (tum′ē) *n., pl.* **-mies.** *Informal.* stomach.

tu·mor (tü′mər, tū′-) *also, British,* **tu′mour.** *n.* **1.** an abnormal growth that may be malignant, formed in the body from normal tissue that grows at an abnormally fast rate. A malignant tumor destroys healthy tissue, and its cells can break away and spread to other parts of the body. **2.** any swollen part. [Latin *tumor* swelling.] —**tu′mor·ous;** *also, British,* **tu′mour·ous,** *adj.*

tump·line (tump′līn′) *n.* a strap worn across the forehead or over the chest to support a backpack or to pull against in dragging a heavy load. [From *tump* pack[1] (of Algonquian origin) + LINE[1].]

tu·mult (tü′məlt, tū′-) *n.* **1.** a din or commotion; uproar. **2.** a very strong disturbance, as of the mind or emotions. [Latin *tumultus.*]

tu·mul·tu·ous (tü mul′chü əs, tū-) *adj.* **1.** excited and noisy; disorderly: *a tumultuous meeting.* **2.** disturbed or upset: *tumultuous emotions.* **3.** stormy; turbulent: *tumultuous waves.* —**tu·mul′tu·ous·ly,** *adv.* —**tu·mul′tu·ous·ness,** *n.*

tu·mu·lus (tü′myə ləs, tū′-) *n., pl.* **-li** (-lī′) or **-lus·es.** a mound of earth, esp. an ancient burial mound. [Latin *tumulus.*]

tun (tun) *n.* **1.** a large cask or barrel used for holding liquids, esp. wine, ale, or beer. **2.** a former liquid measure, equal to 252 gallons (953.8 liters). [Old English *tunne* large cask, from Late Latin *tunna* cask; probably of Celtic origin.]

tu·na[1] (tü′nə) *n., pl.* **-na** or **-nas.** **1.** any of several food and game fish, family Scombridae, related to the mackerel, found in tropical and temperate seas throughout the world, including the albacore. Length: to 14 feet (4.3 meters). Weight: to 1,600 pounds (726 kilograms). Also, **tunny. 2.** tuna fish *(def. 1).* [Spanish *tuna,* form of *atún* tunny, through Arabic, from Latin *thunnus.* See TUNNY.]

tu·na[2] (tü′nə) *n.* prickly pear. [Spanish *tuna,* from Taino *tuna.*]

tun·a·ble (tü′nə bəl, tū′-) *also,* **tuneable.** *adj.* **1.** able to be tuned: *The kettledrum is a tunable drum.* **2.** in tune; harmonious. **3.** *Archaic.* melodious; tuneful. —**tun′a·ble·ness,** *n.* —**tun′a·bly,** *adv.*

tuna fish 1. the flesh of the tuna, used for food. **2.** tuna[1] *(def. 1).*

tun·dra (tun′drə, tūn′-) *n.* a vast, treeless plain in the northernmost parts of Asia, Europe, and North America, having an arctic or subarctic climate and a layer of permafrost in the subsoil. [Russian *tundra,* from Lapp *tun-tur* literally, marsh plain.]

tune (tün, tūn) *n.* **1.** *Music.* a succession of single tones that make up a complete phrase or idea; melody. **2.** a short musical piece, esp. a recorded popular song: *Play a tune on the jukebox.* **3.** the quality or condition of being at the proper pitch or key: *The old piano is badly out of tune. The violinist was playing out of tune.* **4.** a stand, approach, outlook, or manner: *The desk manager finally changed his tune and gave us a room.* **5.** the quality or condition of agreement or accord: *Her statement was in tune with what others are saying.* —*v.t.,* **tuned, tun·ing. 1.** to adjust to a standard of pitch; put in tune: *to tune a guitar.* **2.** to put (a vehicle or machine) into the proper or most efficient working order, as by lubrication or adjustment of parts: *to tune an engine.* **3.** *Archaic.* to express musically; sing. —*v.i.* to be in tune or harmony. [Form of TONE.]
  · **to call the tune.** to decide for everyone; be in command.
  · **to sing a different** (or **another**) **tune.** to adopt a different stand, approach, outlook, or manner.
  · **to the tune of.** in or around the amount or sum of: *The car needed repairs to the tune of $200.*
  · **to tune in.** to adjust a radio or television receiving set so as to receive (a particular station, program, or signal).
  · **to tune out.** to adjust a radio or television receiver so as to exclude (interference or a particular station or signal).
  · **to tune up. a.** to bring musical instruments to a standard pitch: *The orchestra tuned up before the concert.* **b.** to put (a vehicle or machine) into proper working order: *to tune up a car.*

tune·a·ble (tü′nə bəl, tū′-) tunable.

tune·ful (tün′fəl, tūn′-) *adj.* full of melody; melodious; musical. —**tune′ful·ly,** *adv.* —**tune′ful·ness,** *n.*

tune·less (tün′lis, tūn′-) *adj.* having no musical quality. —**tune′less·ly,** *adv.*

tun·er (tü′nər, tū′-) *n.* **1.** a person or thing that tunes, esp. one employed to properly tune musical instruments: *a piano tuner.* **2.** the part of a radio receiver or stereo system that selects desired radio signals and directs them to an amplifier, where they are converted into sound.

tune-up (tün′up′, tūn′-) *n.* an adjustment, as of an engine, to the proper or most efficient working condition.

tung oil (tung) a brown or yellow oil pressed from the nut of the tung tree, used to make quick-drying paints. [Partial translation of Chinese (Mandarin) *yu t'ung* oil of tung tree.]

tung·sten (tung′stən) *n.* a grayish, very hard, metallic element, having the highest melting point of any element, used in alloying steel and in making filaments for electric lamps and electron tubes. Symbol: **W** For tables, see **element.** Also, **wolfram.** [Swedish *tungsten,* from *tung* heavy + *sten* stone.]

tung tree, either of two Asian trees, *Aleurites fordii* or *A. montana,* widely cultivated for shade and as a source of tung oil. [Mandarin *t'ung.*]

Tun·gus (tŭn gŭz′) *n., pl.* **-gus** or **-gus·es. 1.** a member of a people who live in central and eastern Siberia and in Manchuria. **2.** the language of this people, belonging to the Ural-Altaic language family.

tu·nic (tū′nĭk, tū′-) *n.* **1.** a garment resembling a long shirt reaching to the knee or below, worn in ancient times by the Greeks and Romans. **2.** a woman's garment resembling a blouse extending to the hips or below. **3.** a short, close-fitting jacket, often worn as part of a military or police uniform. **4.** *Biology.* a loose membranous outer skin or covering, as of a plant or organ. Also *(def. 4),* **tunica.** [Latin *tunica* Roman shirtlike garment worn by both sexes; probably of Semitic origin.]

tu·ni·ca (tū′nĭ kə, tū′-) *n., pl.* **-cae** (-sē′). an enclosing or covering sheath, layer, or membrane of a part, as of the testis or eye, or of a body, as in certain marine invertebrates. [Modern Latin *tunica,* from Latin *tunica.* See TUNIC.]

tu·ni·cate (tū′nĭ kĭt, -kāt′, tū′-) *n.* a sea squirt; ascidian. —*adj.* **1.** of, relating, or belonging to the tunicates. **2.** *Biology.* having a tunic or outer covering. **3.** *Botany.* having concentric coats or layers, as the bulb of an onion. [Latin *tunicātus,* past participle of *tunicāre* to clothe with a tunic, from *tunica.* See TUNIC.]

tuning fork, a two-pronged steel instrument that vibrates at a constant rate when struck, producing a tone of definite pitch, used as a guide for tuning musical instruments.

tun·nel (tŭn′əl) *n.* a long, narrow, tubular passageway beneath the ground or under the main part of a structure: *a subway tunnel, a tunnel through the side of a mountain.* —*v.,* **-neled, -nel·ing;** *also, British,* **-nelled, -nel·ling.** —*v.i.* to make a passageway under or through something, as by digging: *to tunnel under a wall.* —*v.t.* **1.** to make by tunneling: *The prisoners tunneled an escape route.* **2.** to make a tunnel under, through, or in: *The mole tunneled the lawn.* [Old French *tonel* cask, diminutive of *tonne,* from Late Latin *tunna.* See TUN.] —**tun′nel·er;** *also, British,* **tun′nel·ler,** *n.*

tunnel vision 1. the inability to see things that are to the side of one's field of vision; a loss of peripheral vision. **2.** an inability or unwillingness to see more than a single point of view; very narrow perspective; narrow-mindedness.

tun·ny (tŭn′ē) *n., pl.* **-nies** or **-ny.** tuna. [French *thon,* through Provençal, from Latin *thunnus,* from Greek *thynnos.*]

tu·pe·lo (tū′pə lō′, tū′-) *n., pl.* **-los.** any of a group of Asian and North American trees, genus *Nyssa,* bearing tiny greenish flowers that ripen into small fruits and having hard yellow or light brown wood used to make flooring and crates. [Creek *ito opilwa* swamp tree.]

Tu·pi (tü pē′, tü′pē) *n., pl.* **-pi** or **-pis. 1.** any of several South American Indian tribes living principally along the Amazon, the Brazilian coast, and in parts of Paraguay. **2.** the language spoken by these people, belonging to the Tupi-Guarani language family. —**Tu·pi′an,** *adj.*

Tu·pi-Gua·ra·ni (tü pē′gwär′ə nē′, tü′pē-) *n.* **1.** a member of any of various South American Indian tribes living in Brazil. **2.** a South American Indian language family consisting of a number of languages that are spoken predominantly in Brazil, Paraguay, and parts of Argentina.

tup·pence (tŭp′əns) *n.* twopence.

tuque (tük, tūk) *n.* a knitted cap, worn esp. in Canada. [French *tuque,* form of *toque* cap. See TOQUE.]

Tu·ra·ni·an (tü rā′nē ən, tyü-) *n.* **1.** a Ural-Altaic language family that includes Finnish, Hungarian, and Turkish. **2.** a person who speaks a language belonging to this language family. —*adj.* of or relating to this family of languages or the people who speak one of these languages.

tur·ban (tûr′bən) *n.* **1.** a head covering, worn esp. by Muslims of southern Asia and by Sikhs, consisting of a long scarf that is wound around the head or around a cap. **2.** any similar headdress, as a bandanna worn wound around the head by women. **3.** a small, round hat having a little turned-up brim, or no brim at all, worn by women and children. [Middle French *turbant* an Oriental headdress, going back to Turkish *tülbend,* from Persian *dulband.* Doublet of TULIP.]

tur·baned (tûr′bənd) *adj.* wearing a turban.

tur·bel·lar·i·an (tûr′bə lâr′ē ən) *n.* any of a group of mostly aquatic, free-living flatworms, class Turbellaria, having a leaf-shaped body covered with cilia. [Modern Latin *Turbellaria,* from Latin *turbellae* bustle, stir, disturbance, diminutive of *turba* crowd; because its many cilia cause water currents.]

tur·bid (tûr′bĭd) *adj.* **1.** thick with suspended matter; not clear; muddy: *turbid floodwaters.* **2.** characterized by confusion or obscurity; muddled; disordered: *turbid emotions.* [Latin *turbidus*

disturbed, from *turba* disturbance, crowd.] —**tur·bid′i·ty, tur′-bid·ness,** *n.* —**tur′bid·ly,** *adv.*

tur·bi·nate (tûr′bə nĭt, -nāt′) *adj.* **1.** shaped like an inverted cone. **2.** having a spiral shape, as certain shells; whorled. **3.** *Anatomy.* of or relating to certain scroll-shaped bones located in the nasal passages. —*n.* a turbinate bone or shell. [Latin *turbinātus* shaped like a cone, from *turbō* whirling motion, top[2].]

tur·bine (tûr′bĭn, -bīn) *n.* any of various motors and engines that use the force of a stream of gas, vapor, or liquid moving steadily against slanted blades to turn a rotor. [French *turbine,* from Latin *turbō* whirling motion, top[2].]

tur·bo (tûr′bō) *n., pl.* **-bos.** turbocharger.

turbo- *combining form* of, relating to, or operated by a turbine: *turbocharger.* [From TURBINE.]

tur·bo·charg·er (tûr′bō chär′jər) *n.* a supercharger that is driven by the pressure of an engine's exhaust gases.

tur·bo·fan (tûr′bō fan′) *n.* a jet engine equipped with a fan that takes in large amounts of cold air and mixes it with hot exhaust gases from the combustion chamber, thus increasing the thrust.

tur·bo·jet (tûr′bō jet′) *n.* **1.** a jet engine in which air is taken in, compressed, mixed with fuel, and then ignited, producing hot, high-pressure gases that turn the turbine that drives the compressor. The hot exhaust provides thrust. **2.** an airplane powered by such an engine.

tur·bo·prop (tûr′bō prop′) *n.* **1.** a turbojet in which the power of the exhaust gases is used to drive a propeller. **2.** an airplane powered by such an engine. [TURBO- + PROP(ELLER).]

tur·bot (tûr′bət) *n., pl.* **-bot** or **-bots. 1.** a large flatfish, *Rhombus maximus,* found along the European coast of the Atlantic and in the Black and Mediterranean seas, popular as a food fish. Weight: to 70 pounds (31.8 kilograms). **2.** any of various related fish, as the **diamond turbot,** *Hypsopsetta guttulata,* or the **spotted turbot** or **horny head,** *Pleuronichthys,* both found off the coast of California. [Old French *turbot* the flatfish; probably of Scandinavian origin.]

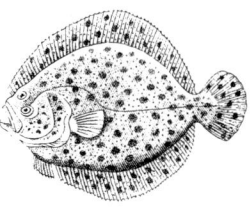

turbot

tur·bu·lence (tûr′byə ləns) *n.* **1.** a turbulent state or quality. **2.** a condition of the atmosphere characterized by turbulent air flow. Also, **tur′bu·len·cy.**

tur·bu·lent (tûr′byə lənt) *adj.* **1.** of, causing, or characterized by commotion, disorder, or violence; not calm or smooth; agitated: *a turbulent period of history, turbulent waters.* **2.** (of flow) characterized by small, irregular disturbances or eddies; not moving in a steady, regular pattern. ➡ opposed to **laminar.** [Latin *turbulentus* disturbed, from *turba* disturbance, crowd.] —**tur′bu·lent·ly,** *adv.*

tu·reen (tü rēn′, tyü-) *n.* a deep dish with a cover, used for serving food, esp. soup. [French *terrine* earthen dish or pan, from Old French *terrin* earthen, going back to Latin *terra* earth.]

turf (tûrf) *n., pl.* **turfs. 1.a.** the surface layer of soil, containing small plants and grasses, their matted roots, and the soil clinging to them; sod. **b.** a separate clump or clumps of this layer, as for replanting. **2.** peat, esp. a piece used for fuel. **3.** *Informal.* anything, as a special status or position or a certain territory, that is jealously guarded and controlled by one person or group. **4. the turf.** the sport of horse racing. [Old English *turf* sod, greensward.]

tur·ges·cent (tûr jes′ənt) *adj.* becoming swollen or bloated. [Latin *turgēscēns* present participle of *turgēscere* to begin to swell.] —**tur·ges′ence,** *n.*

tur·gid (tûr′jĭd) *adj.* **1.** swollen or distended. **2.** pompous, as language; grandiloquent. [Latin *turgidus.*] —**tur·gid′i·ty, tur′-gid·ness,** *n.* —**tur′gid·ly,** *adv.*

tur·gor (tûr′gər) *n.* **1.** the normal state of distention or rigidity of plant cells, resulting from the absorption of water, which creates an outward pressure on the cell wall. **2.** a swollen state; turgidity. [Late Latin *turgor,* from Latin *turgēre* to swell + *-or* -OR.]

Turk (tûrk) *n.* **1.** a native or citizen of Turkey. **2.** a person of Turkish ancestry. **3.** a person who speaks a Turkic language.

a	at	e	end	o	hot	u	up	hw	white		about
ā	ape	ē	me	ō	old	ū	use	ng	song		taken
ä	far	i	it	ô	fork	ŭ	rule	th	thin	ə	pencil
âr	care	ī	ice	oi	oil	u̇	pull	th	this		lemon
		îr	pierce	ou	out	ûr	turn	zh	measure		circus

Turk. 1. Turkey. **2.** Turkish.

tur·key (tûr′kē) *n., pl.* **-keys** or **-key. 1.** any of various long-necked birds, family Meleagrididae, related to the pheasant, having a squarish tail and predominantly brown plumage, widely domesticated and raised for meat. Length: 4 feet (1.2 meters), including tail. **2.** the flesh of a turkey used as food. **3.** *Slang.* an unsuccessful artistic or dramatic production; flop. **4.** *Slang.* a foolish or inept person. **5.** in bowling, three strikes in a row. [From *Turkey;* originally used as a name for the guinea fowl, probably because it was first brought to Europe through *Turkish* territory by merchants; later applied to an American bird that the early settlers mistakenly thought was the guinea fowl.]
  · **to talk turkey.** *Informal.* to discuss practical matters in a direct, blunt manner.

turkey cock 1. a male turkey. **2.** a person who behaves in a conceited, strutting manner.

Turkey red 1. a bright red color. **2.** cotton cloth of this color.

turkey trot, a social ragtime dance of the early twentieth century.

turkey vulture, a brownish black vulture, *Cathartes aura,* native to North, Central, and South America, having a bare, reddish head when mature. Wingspan: to 6 feet (1.8 meters). Also, **turkey buzzard.**

Tur·kic (tûr′kik) *n.* any of various languages spoken by the Turks of Turkey, the Turkomans, and other Tatar tribes, that, collectively, make up a branch of the Ural-Altaic language family. —*adj.* of or relating to the Turkic languages or the people who speak them.

Turk·ish (tûr′kish) *adj.* of, relating to, or characteristic of Turkey or its people, language, or culture. —*n.* the language of the Turks, belonging to the Turkic branch of the Ural-Altaic language family.

Words from Turkish			
Turkish is the official language of Turkey and one of the official languages of Cyprus. It was written in Arabic script until 1928, when its alphabet was changed to a modified Roman alphabet. Below is a selection of words that have come into English from or through Turkish.			
bey	dervish	jackal	seraglio
bosh	divan	khan¹	shish kebab
bulgur	dolman	kiosk	tulip
caftan	effendi	kismet	turban
caviar	fez	odalisque	vizier
coffee	horde	pasha	yogurt

Turkish bath 1. a steam bath, followed by a massage and cold shower. **2.** a place where such baths are available.

Turkish coffee, a very strong beverage made with pulverized coffee, water, and sugar.

Turkish delight, a gelatin candy, often cube-shaped, flavored with fruit and having nuts and a coating of powdered sugar.

Turkish towel *also,* **turkish towel.** a thick towel made of terry cloth.

Tur·ko·man (tûr′kə mən) *n., pl.* **-mans. 1.** a member of any of several Turkic tribes living predominantly in the Turkmen Republic and in parts of Iran and Afghanistan. **2.** the language of this people, belonging to the Turkic branch of the Ural-Altaic language family.

tur·mer·ic (tûr′mər ik) *n.* **1.** a yellow powder with a sharp, bitter taste, obtained from the root of an Asian plant, *Curcuma domestica,* used as a seasoning and as a coloring agent. **2.** the plant itself, bearing pale yellow flowers. **3.** the yellow, carrotlike root of this plant. [Earlier *tarmaret,* from French *terre mérite* the powder, saffron; literally, deserved or deserving earth (reason for the name not known); of uncertain origin.]

tur·moil (tûr′moil) *n.* a state or condition of confused agitation or commotion: *the turmoil of war.* [Possibly TUR(N) + MOIL.]

turn (tûrn) *v.i.* **1.** to move around on or as if on an axis; rotate or revolve: *The earth turns. The blades of a fan turn.* **2.** to move partly around in this way: *The plant turned toward the light. The key turned in the lock.* **3.** to change direction; go in a different direction: *We turned onto the highway. The road turns south at the bridge.* **4.** to change or reverse to the opposite direction: *Let's turn and go home. Soon our luck will turn.* **5.** to curve or bend: *The corners of the clown's mouth turned up in a broad smile.* **6.** to change in nature or condition: *The leaves turned yellow.* **7.** to

become spoiled, rancid, or sour: *The milk turned because we left it out of the refrigerator too long.* **8.** to be transformed: *The snow turned to rain.* **9.** to take on an attitude of hostility (with *on* or *against*): *The lion turned on its trainer. Don't turn against your old friends.* **10.** to direct one's effort or attention: *to turn to the job at hand.* **11.** to appeal or apply for help or support: *to turn to a friend, to turn to a book for information.* **12.** to direct one's affection or loyalty: *to turn away from a cause.* **13.** to be contingent; depend (with *on* or *upon*): *The senator's victory will turn on the urban vote.* **14.** to be or become dizzy or nauseated: *to have one's stomach turn at the sight of blood.* —*v.t.* **1.** to cause to revolve around on or as if on an axis, as a wheel. **2.** to cause to move partly around: *to turn a doorknob.* **3.** to do or perform by rotating or revolving, as a somersault. **4.** to change the course or direction of: *to turn a car to the left.* **5.** to cause to curve, curl, or bend: *The tailor turned the edges of the cloth under.* **6.** to twist or wrench: *to turn one's ankle.* **7.** to change the position of by or as if by rotating: *to turn one's head toward the sun, to turn soil.* **8.** to change to the opposite side; reverse: *to turn a record, to turn flapjacks on a griddle.* **9.** to change one's course so as to get to the other side of; go or get around or beyond: *to turn a corner.* **10.** to cause to change; transform: *to turn cream into butter.* **11.** to translate or rephrase: *to turn German into English.* **12.** to make spoiled, rancid, or sour: *The hot weather turned the meat.* **13.** to make sick; cause nausea or disgust in: *The rich food turned my stomach.* **14.** to cause to point or move in a particular direction; direct; aim: *to turn a weapon on someone, to turn one's energies to completing the job.* **15.** to send, esp. by force or pressure; drive: *to turn a horse out to pasture.* **16.** to repel or deflect: *to turn an enemy's charge.* **17.** to use or employ; apply: *to turn one's talents to volunteer work.* **18.** (of age, time, or amount) to be or have passed beyond: *to turn twenty.* **19.** to shape by rotating against a cutting tool, as in a lathe. —*n.* **1.** the act or instance of turning: *Give the knob a turn.* **2.** a change in position or direction: *Take a left turn at the corner.* **3.** a place of changing direction: *a turn in the highway.* **4.** a time, occasion, or opportunity that follows another or others in proper sequence: *It's the catcher's turn to bat.* **5.** an act or deed: *My friend did me a good turn.* **6.** one revolution or coil, as in a rope. **7.** an inclination or aptitude; bent: *to have a turn for mathematics.* **8.** a short walk or ride that includes a going and returning, esp. one in or around a limited area: *to take a turn through the countryside.* **9.** a particular style, character, or quality: *There was a sarcastic turn to the speaker's voice.* **10.** a change in condition or nature: *The patient took a turn for the better.* **11.** *Informal.* a sudden shock or fright: *The explosion gave me quite a turn!* **12.** a public appearance or performance; act. **13.** *Music.* a melodic ornament or grace, usually consisting of a principal tone and the tones one degree above and below it. [Old English *turnian* to cause to revolve, revolve, from Latin *tornāre* to turn in a lathe, round off, from *tornus* lathe, from Greek *tornos.*] —**turn′a·ble,** *adj.*
  · **at every turn.** in every instance; constantly.
  · **by turns.** one after another; not all at once.
  · **in turn.** in proper sequence.
  · **out of turn. a.** not in proper sequence; at the wrong time. **b.** *Informal.* rudely or impolitely: *The guest spoke out of turn about the political situation and offended the host.*
  · **to a turn.** perfectly: *The roast was cooked to a turn.*
  · **to take turns.** to go in proper sequence.
  · **to turn about. a.** to move in the opposite direction. **b.** to change opinion, position, or loyalty.
  · **to turn away.** to refuse admission to: *The bouncer turned away many people from the packed club.*
  · **to turn down. a.** to reject or refuse: *to turn down a request.* **b.** to lessen the volume or intensity of: *to turn down a radio, to turn down a thermostat.* **c.** to fold over: *to turn down the blankets on a bed.*
  · **to turn in.** *Informal.* **a.** to go to bed. **b.** to hand over, as to the police.
  · **to turn on. a.** to cause to flow: *to turn on the hot water, to turn on the electricity.* **b.** to cause to operate: *to turn on a lamp, to turn on charm.* **c.** *Slang.* to give great pleasure to: *Good music turns me on.*
  · **to turn out. a.** to produce: *This machine turns out fifty copies per minute.* **b.** to show up; assemble; appear: *A large crowd turned out for the football game.* **c.** to prove to have a certain result; end in a certain way: *How did the story turn out?* **d.** to put out; extinguish: *to turn out a light.* **e.** to dismiss; discharge: *to turn someone out of office.* **f.** *Informal.* to get out of bed.
  · **to turn over. a.** (of an engine) to begin to operate. **b.** to buy

T

and sell (merchandise). **c.** to invest and get back (capital). **d.** to do business to the amount of: *to turn over $5,000 a month.* **e.** to give, transfer, or return: *to turn over a business to one's partner.* **f.** to think about; consider: *to turn over in one's mind.*

• **to turn to.** to begin to work: *The campers turned to and cleaned up the campsite.*

• **to turn up. a.** to appear: *The stolen carvings turned up in a shop in Singapore.* **b.** to ferret out or discover: *The prosecutor turned up some new evidence.* **c.** to increase the volume or intensity of: *to turn up a radio.*

turn·a·bout (tûr′nə bout′) *n.* **1.** the act of going or turning in a different or opposite direction. **2.** a shift in opinion, policy, or loyalty.

turn·a·round (tûrn′ə round′) *n.* **1.** a complete change or reversal in direction, order, condition, or the like: *a turnaround of opinion, a turnaround in the economy.* **2.** the time it takes to ready an airplane for a return trip.

turn·buck·le (tûrn′buk′əl) *n.* a sleeve with internal threads that holds together the threaded ends of two rods and can be turned to widen or narrow the gap between the rod ends.

turn·coat (tûrn′kōt′) *n.* a person who switches to the other side; traitor or renegade.

turn·down (tûrn′doun′) *adj.* folded over: *a turndown collar.* —*n.* a refusal or rejection.

turn·er (tûr′nər) *n.* **1.** a person or thing that turns. **2.** a person who turns or fashions things on a lathe.

turning point, the point at which a decisive or significant change takes place; critical point; crisis.

tur·nip (tûr′nip) *n.* **1.** the edible white or yellow root of a plant, *Brassica rapa,* of the mustard family, cooked and eaten as a vegetable. **2.** the plant itself, having little or no neck and bearing small, bright yellow flowers in clusters and soft prickly leaves. **3.** rutabaga. [Earlier *turnepe,* probably from TURN (from its rounded root) + *neep* turnip (from Old English *nǣp,* from Latin *nāpus* kind of turnip, probably from Greek *nāpu* mustard; of Egyptian origin).]

turn·key (tûrn′kē′) *n., pl.* **-keys.** a person who has charge of the keys of a prison or jail.

turn·off (tûrn′ôf′, -of′) *n.* **1.** the act of turning off. **2.** an exit leading off a main road to a side road. **3.** *Slang.* a person or thing that causes dislike or a loss of interest.

turn·on (tûrn′ôn′, -on′) *n. Slang.* a person or thing that causes great pleasure, excitement, or interest: *Windsurfing is a real turn-on for many people.*

turn·out (tûrn′out′) *n.* **1.** the people who have assembled or gathered for some specific occasion: *There was a poor turnout for the football game because of the rainy weather.* **2.** an amount produced; output: *The new machine increased the factory's turnout.* **3.** the act of turning out. **4.** a section of a road that has been widened to enable vehicles to pass or park. **5.** a railroad siding. **6.** a carriage with its attendants, horse or horses, and harness.

turn·o·ver (tûrn′ō′vər) *n.* **1.** a small pie made by folding half the crust over a filling and upon the other half. **2.a.** the number of employees who leave their jobs and are replaced by others during a given period. **b.** the ratio of this to the total number of employees of a firm. **3.** the number of times that the stock of goods of a firm is sold and replaced during a given period. **4.** the total amount of business done in a given period: *From a turnover of $15,000 for a week, the flower shop had a profit of $3,000.* —*adj.* capable of being turned over.

turn·pike (tûrn′pīk′) *n.* **1.** a road, esp. a large highway, that has, or used to have, a tollgate or tollbooth. **2.** any highway, esp. an expressway. [TURN + PIKE²; originally referring to a road barrier consisting of spikes attached to a frame that could be rotated to let people pass.]

turn·stile (tûrn′stīl′) *n.* a revolving gate or movable bar at an exit or entrance, that permits persons to pass through one at a time.

turn·stone (tûrn′stōn′) *n.* any of several shorebirds, genus *Arenaria,* that breed near the North Pole and winter along the coasts of the Atlantic and Pacific oceans, noted for flipping beach pebbles over with the bill when searching for food. Length: 9 inches (23 centimeters).

turn·ta·ble (tûrn′tā′bəl) *n.* **1.** a revolving structure used to turn things around, esp. a circular railroad platform with tracks used to turn locomotives or cars around. **2.** a flat platform on a phonograph that revolves to play records lying on it.

tur·pen·tine (tûr′pən tīn′) *n.* **1.** a sticky, viscous oleoresin secreted by certain species of pine trees. **2.** the colorless, combustible liquid obtained by distilling this oleoresin, widely used as a

thinner for paints and as a solvent for polishes. Also *(def. 2),* **oil of turpentine.** [Old French *ter(e)bentine* an oleoresin, going back to Latin *terebinthus* a tree yielding an oleoresin, from Greek *terebinthos.*]

tur·pi·tude (tûr′pi tüd′, -tūd′) *n.* **1.** shameful wickedness; depravity; baseness: *moral turpitude.* **2.** an instance of this. [Latin *turpitūdō* baseness.]

tur·quoise (tûr′kwoiz, -koiz) *n.* **1.** an opaque, greenish blue phosphate mineral having a waxy luster and prized as a gem. **2.** a greenish blue color. —*adj.* having the color turquoise. [French *turquoise* the mineral (short for *pierre turquoise* Turkish stone), from *turc* Turk, Turkish, from Turkish *Türk;* because it was first found in territory ruled by the Turks.]

Zuni **turquoise** and silver jewelry

tur·ret (tûr′it, tur′-) *n.* **1.** a small tower, usually forming part of a larger structure. **2.** an armored, usually revolving, structure used to house antiaircraft guns or cannons and their gunners, as on a ship or tank. **3.** a strong, transparent plastic bubblelike structure on a military aircraft, used to protect the gunner. **4.a.** a revolving attachment on a lathe or drill that holds several cutting tools, which is turned to change from one tool to another. **b.** a similar device used to hold several lenses, as on a microscope. **5.** formerly, a tower on wheels, used for attacking castles, forts, or walled towns. [Old French *t(o)urete* small tower, diminutive of *t(o)ur* tower. See TOWER.]

tur·ret·ed (tûr′i tid, tur′-) *adj.* **1.** having a turret or turrets. **2.** having the shape of a turret. **3.** having long spiraled whorls, as certain seashells.

tur·tle¹ (tûr′təl) *n.* any of a group of reptiles, order Chelonia, found on land and in fresh and salt water, having a squat body enclosed in a hard, protective shell, and a toothless beak with sharp-edged jaws. On the average, turtles have a longer life span than any other vertebrate, some living to an age of 130 years. [Modification (influenced by TURTLE²) of French *tortue* turtle (reptile), tortoise, going back to Late Latin *tortūca* turtle, tortoise. See TORTOISE.]

• **to turn turtle.** to turn over; capsize.

tur·tle² (tûr′təl) *n.* turtledove. [Old English *turtle,* going back to Latin *turtur;* imitative of the cooing of pigeons.]

tur·tle·back (tûr′təl bak′) *n.* an arched, domelike structure built over the deck of a ship, esp. a steamer, at the bow and often at the stern as protection against heavy seas.

tur·tle·dove (tûr′təl duv′) *n.* any of several small, wild doves, genus *Streptopelia,* noted for a soft, cooing call. Also, **turtle.** [TURTLE² + DOVE¹.]

tur·tle·head (tûr′təl hed′) *n.* any of various perennial North American herbs, genus *Chelone,* of the figwort family, having large, showy, usually white or purple flowers.

tur·tle·neck (tûr′təl nek′) *n.* **1.** a high, often turndown, collar that fits snugly around the neck. **2.** a garment, esp. a sweater, having such a collar.

Tus·can (tus′kən) *n.* **1.** a native or inhabitant of Tuscany. **2.** any of several Italian dialects spoken in Tuscany, esp. that spoken in Florence. **3.** the standard literary form of the Italian language. —*adj.* **1.** of, relating to, or characteristic of Tuscany or its people. **2.** of, relating to, or designating an order of architecture characterized by columns that are not fluted, continuous friezes without triglyphs or metopes, and no ornamentation.

Tus·ca·ro·ra (tus′kə rôr′ə) *n., pl.* **-ra** or **-ras.** a member of a tribe of North American Iroquois Indians formerly living in what is now North Carolina, now living in New York.

a	at	e	end	o	hot	u	up	hw	white		about
ā	ape	ē	me	ō	old	ū	use	ng	song		taken
ä	far	i	it	ô	fork	ŭ	rule	th	thin	ə	pencil
âr	care	ī	ice	oi	oil	ů	pull	th	this		lemon
		îr	pierce	ou	out	ûr	turn	zh	measure		circus

tush¹ (tush) *interj.* an exclamation expressing reproof, contempt, impatience, or disparagement. [Imitative.]

tush² (tush) *n.* tusk. [Old English *tūsc.*]

tusk (tusk) *n.* **1.** a long, pointed, projecting tooth, usually one of a pair, of certain animals, as elephants, walruses, or wild boars. **2.** any long, pointed, projecting tooth or toothlike part. —*v.t.* to dig up or gore with the tusks. [Old English *tūx, tūsc* long, pointed, projecting tooth.]

tusk·er (tus′kər) *n.* an animal having well-developed tusks, esp. an elephant or wild boar.

tus·sah (tus′ə) *n.* **1.** a coarse brownish or yellowish silk, used in making pongee and shantung. **2.** an Asian silkworm that produces this silk. [Hindi *tasar* shuttle, from Sanskrit *tasara;* possibly because of the shape of the cocoon.]

tus·sle (tus′əl) *n.* **1.** a vigorous, disorderly physical fight or struggle; scuffle. **2.** any vigorous, disorderly conflict or struggle: *The election this fall will be a real tussle.* —*v.i.* -sled, -sling. to engage in a vigorous, disorderly physical fight or struggle: *The bear cubs tussled with each other in play.* [Probably a form of TOUSLE.]

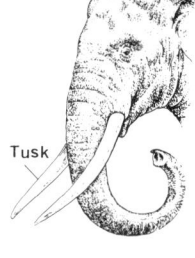

Tusk

elephant **tusks**

tus·sock (tus′ək) *n.* a clump, tuft, or matted growth, as of hair or grass. [Of uncertain origin.]

tussock moth, any of a group of dull-colored, destructive moths, as the gypsy moth, whose larvae are covered with thick tufts of hair.

tut (tut) *interj.* an exclamation expressing impatience, contempt, annoyance, or rebuke.

tu·te·lage (tü′tə lij, tū′-) *n.* **1.** the office or function of a guardian; guardianship. **2.** the act of teaching; instruction. **3.** the state or condition of being under a tutor or guardian. [Latin *tūtēla* watching, protection + -AGE.]

tu·te·lar·y (tü′tə ler′ē, tū′-) *adj.* also, **tu·te·lar** (tü′tə lər, tū′-) **1.** having the position of a guardian; protective: *a tutelary goddess.* **2.** of or relating to a guardian: *tutelary powers.* —*n., pl.* -lar·ies. a deity, saint, spirit, or person having tutelary powers. [Latin *tūtēlārius* guardian, from *tūtēla* watching, protection.]

tu·tor (tü′tər, tū′-) *n.* **1.** a teacher or other person who gives private instruction to a student. **2.** *British.* a college official who supervises and advises undergraduate students. —*v.t.* to act as a tutor to, esp. by giving private instruction. —*v.i.* **1.** *Informal.* to be instructed by a tutor: *He is tutoring to pass his final exams.* **2.** to act or work as a private instructor: *For extra money, she tutors on weekends.* [Latin *tūtor* guardian.]

tu·to·ri·al (tü tôr′ē əl, tū-) *adj.* of, relating to, or involving a private instructor or instruction: *The school had an afternoon tutorial math program.* —*n.* **1.** a class or session instructed by a tutor for one student or a small group of students. **2.** *Computers.* a program or manual that instructs a user in the proper operation of a piece of hardware or software.

tu·tor·ship (tü′tər ship′, tū′-) *n.* the position or duties of a tutor.

tut·ti-frut·ti (tü′tē frü′tē) *adj.* containing or made with various candied fruits or fruit flavorings: *tutti-frutti punch.* —*n.* **1.** a sweet food, esp. ice cream, containing various candied fruits. **2.** a flavoring containing the flavor of various fruits. [Italian *tutti frutti* literally, all fruits, going back to Latin *tōtus* all + *frūctus* produce, fruit.]

tu·tu (tü′tü) *n.* a very short, full skirt consisting of many layers of sheer fabric, worn by ballerinas. [French *tutu,* from *tutu* backside, baby talk, modification of *cul* backside, bottom, from Latin *cūlus* backside.]

tux (tuks) *n. Informal.* tuxedo.

tux·e·do (tuk sē′dō) *also,* **Tux·e·do.** *n., pl.* -dos. a man's formal suit, usually dark in color, having a jacket without tails and trousers with a single stripe of satin or similar material along the outer side of each leg. [From *Tuxedo* Park, New York, exclusive community of wealthy families in the nineteenth century, where this suit originated.]

tu·yère (twē yâr′, tü-, twir′) *n.* a nozzle through which air is blown into a blast furnace. [French *tuyère,* from *tuyau* pipe; of Germanic origin.]

TV, television.

TVA, Tennessee Valley Authority, an independent agency of the U.S. government established in 1933 for water control and development of resources, esp. electric power, along the Tennessee River and its major tributaries in seven southern states.

TV dinner, a prepared meal frozen in a tray, needing only to be heated before being served.

twad·dle (twod′əl) *n.* silly or idle speech or writing; nonsense. —*v.i.* -dled, -dling. to speak or write in a childish or foolish manner. [Probably a modification of earlier *twattle,* possibly a blend of TWIDDLE and TATTLE.] —**twad′dler,** *n.*

twain (twān) *n., adj. Archaic.* two. [Old English *twēgen.*]

twang (twang) *n.* **1.** a sharp, reverberating, ringing sound, as that made by plucking a string on a musical instrument. **2.** a sharp, nasal tone of voice. —*v.i.* **1.** to make a sharp, reverberating, ringing sound: *The wire twanged when it broke.* **2.** to have a sharp, nasal tone of voice. —*v.t.* **1.** to cause to make a sharp, reverberating sound. **2.** to utter with a sharp, nasal tone of voice. [Imitative of the sound of a plucked string.]

'twas (twuz, twoz; *unstressed* twəz) *contr.* it was.

tweak (twēk) *v.t.* to pinch or pull sharply with a twisting motion. —*n.* a sharp, twisting pinch. [Probably modification of dialectal English *twick* to pull sharply, from Old English *twiccian.*]

tweed (twēd) *n.* **1.** a rough fabric, made esp. of wool, woven with yarns of two or more colors. **2. tweeds.** clothes made of this fabric. [Modification (influenced by *Tweed,* a Scottish river passing through a region noted for manufacturing this cloth) of Scottish *tweel,* form of TWILL.]

twee·dle·dum and twee·dle·dee (twē′dəl dum′ ən twē′dəl dē′) two persons or things between which there is only the least possible distinction. [From earlier *tweedle* to play a musical instrument, pipe (of imitative origin) + *-dee, -dum,* syllables suggesting musical sounds; first used to designate two rival musicians.]

tweed·y (twē′dē) *adj.* **tweed·i·er, tweed·i·est. 1.** of or like tweed or tweeds. **2.** favoring or characteristic of those who favor tweeds; casual and showing a fondness for the outdoors and country life: *a tweedy dresser.* —**tweed′i·ness,** *n.*

'tween (twēn) *prep.* between.

tweet (twēt) *n.* a thin, chirping sound, as that made by a small or young bird. —*v.i.* to utter a tweet or tweets: *The birds were tweeting outside the window.* [Imitative.]

tweet·er (twē′tər) *n.* a loudspeaker designed to reproduce high-frequency sounds. ➡ distinguished from **woofer.** [TWEET + -ER¹.]

tweeze (twēz) *v.t.,* **tweezed, tweez·ing.** to pluck with tweezers. [From TWEEZERS.]

tweez·ers (twē′zərz) *pl. n.* small pincers for plucking out hairs or for picking up tiny objects. [Modification (influenced by words like PLIERS, SCISSORS) of obsolete *tweeze* case for instruments, going back to French *étui* case², from Old French *estuier* to keep, put in, shut up, possibly going back to Latin *studium* zeal, application to learning.]

twelfth (twelfth) *adj.* **1.** (the ordinal of twelve) next after the eleventh. **2.** being one of twelve equal parts. —*n.* **1.** something that is next after the eleventh. **2.** one of twelve equal parts; ¹/₁₂.

Twelfth day, the twelfth day after Christmas, on which the Epiphany is celebrated, observed on January 6. Formerly it marked the end of the Christmas season.

Twelfth night, the evening of, or the night before, Twelfth day.

twelve (twelv) *n.* **1.** the cardinal number that is one more than eleven. **2.** a symbol representing this number, such as 12 or XII. **3.** something having this many units or members. **4. the Twelve.** the twelve disciples of Jesus chosen by him to preach his gospel. Also *(def. 4),* **the Twelve Apostles.** —*adj.* numbering one more than eleven. [Old English *twelf.*]

twelve·fold (twelv′fōld′) *adj.* **1.** twelve times as great or numerous. **2.** having or consisting of twelve parts. —*adv.* so as to be twelve times greater or more numerous.

twelve·mo (twelv′mō) *n., pl.* -mos. duodecimo. —*adj.* duodecimo.

twelve·month (twelv′munth′) *n.* a period of twelve months; year.

Twelve Tables, the earliest Roman legal code and the foundation of Roman jurisprudence, drawn up in 451 B.C.

twelve-tone (twelv′tōn′) *adj. Music.* of, relating to, or written according to the technique of composition based on the successive repetition of the twelve tones of the chromatic scale without emphasis on any particular key or tonality.

twen·ti·eth (twen′tē ith) *adj.* **1.** (the ordinal of twenty) next after the nineteenth. **2.** being one of twenty equal parts. —*n.* **1.** something that is next after the nineteenth. **2.** one of twenty equal parts; ¹/₂₀.

twen·ty (twen′tē) *n., pl.* -ties. **1.** the cardinal number that is two times ten. **2.** a symbol representing this number, such as 20 or XX. **3.** something having this many units or members. **4. the**

twenties. the number series from twenty through twenty-nine. ➡ used esp. in reference to the third decade of a century or of a person's life. —*adj.* numbering two times ten. [Old English *twentig.*]

twen·ty·fold (twen′tē fōld′) *adj.* **1.** twenty times as great or numerous. **2.** having or consisting of twenty parts. —*adv.* so as to be twenty times greater or more numerous.

twen·ty-one (twen′tē wun′) *n.* blackjack *(def. 3).*

twen·ty-twen·ty (twen′tē twen′tē) *also,* **20/20.** *adj.* having normal acuity of vision, or the ability to distinguish at a distance of 20 feet (6 meters) characters ⅓ inch (0.85 centimeter) in diameter with each eye.

twerp (twûrp) *also,* **twirp.** *n. Slang.* an annoying, contemptible, or self-important person. [Of uncertain origin.]

twice (twīs) *adv.* **1.** on two occasions or in two instances; two times: *I called twice.* **2.** doubly: *twice as many.* [Old English *twiges* two (successive) times, from *twiga* two times.]

twice-told (twīs′tōld′) *adj.* **1.** having been told two times: *a twice-told tale.* **2.** having been told many times; stale; trite.

twid·dle (twid′əl) *v.,* **-dled, -dling.** —*v.t.* to turn or twirl (something) idly: *to twiddle a locket on a chain.* —*v.i.* **1.** to play with something in an idle manner. **2.** to be busy about trifles. —*n.* a light, twirling motion, as of the thumbs. [Of uncertain origin.] —**twid′dler,** *n.*
 • **to twiddle one's thumbs. a.** to twirl one's thumbs idly about each other, esp. to indicate boredom. **b.** to do nothing; be idle and bored.

twig (twig) *n.* a small branch or shoot of a tree or other woody plant. [Old English *twigge.*]

twi·light (twī′līt′) *n.* **1.** the soft, hazy light reflected from the sun just after sunset and, sometimes, just before sunrise. **2.** the period during which this light prevails: *to take a stroll during twilight.* **3.** any soft, faint light. **4.** a period or condition marked by the decline of glory, success, achievement, or the like: *the twilight of a career.* —*adj.* of, relating to, or occurring at twilight. [Middle English *twilight* the light reflected from the sun after sunset and before sunrise, the period during which this light prevails, from *twi-* two, twice (from Old English *twi-*) + LIGHT[1].]

twilight sleep, a semiconscious condition produced by the hypodermic injection of scopolamine and morphine, formerly induced to lessen the pains of childbirth.

twill (twil) *n.* **1.** a weave characterized by parallel diagonal ridges. **2.** a strong, durable fabric having such a weave. [Old English *twili* twilled cloth, partial translation of Latin *bilīx* with a double thread, from *bi-* two + *līcium* thread (Old English *twi-* two being substituted for *bi-*); because woven by doubling the warp threads.]

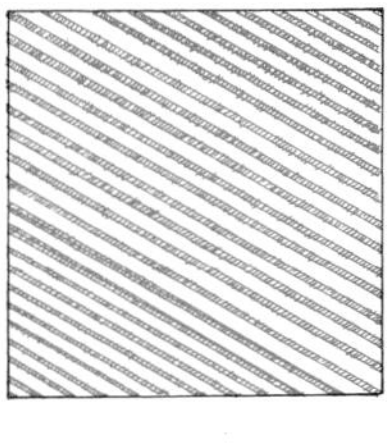

twilled (twild) *adj.* woven with parallel diagonal ridges on the surface.

twin (twin) *n.* **1.a.** one of two offspring born at one birth. **b. twins.** two offspring born at one birth. **2.** either of two persons, animals, or things that are similar or identical; mate. —*adj.* **1.** being two or one of two born at one birth: *Her twin brother is five minutes older than she.* **2.** having, forming, or being one of two things that are similar or identical: *The castle had twin turrets.* —*v.i.,* **twinned, twin·ning.** to give birth to twins. [Old English *twinn* twofold, double.]

Twin Cities, Minneapolis and St. Paul, Minnesota.

twine (twīn) *n.* **1.** a strong string or cord made of two or more strands twisted together. **2.** something formed by twisting two or more strands, threads, or the like together. —*v.,* **twined, twin·ing.** —*v.t.* **1.** to twist together. **2.** to form by twisting together. **3.** to wind or coil (something) around something else: *The gardener twined the ivy around the trellis.* **4.** to cover or wrap in this way: *to twine a pole with ribbons.* —*v.i.* to extend, proceed, or grow in a winding manner or course: *Ivy twined over the walls.* [Old English *twīn* linen, twisted thread.]

twinge (twinj) *n.* **1.** a sudden, sharp pain: *a twinge of arthritis.* **2.** a sudden, sharp feeling of mental or emotional distress: *a twinge of pity, a twinge of conscience.* —*v.t., v.i.,* **twinged, twing·ing.** to feel or cause to feel a twinge. [Old English *twengan* to pinch.]

twi·night (twī′nīt′) *adj. Baseball.* designating a double-header in which the first game is played in the late afternoon and the second game is played in the evening under artificial light. [TWI(LIGHT) + NIGHT.]

twin·kle (twing′kəl) *v.i.,* **-kled, -kling. 1.** to shine with or emit

flashes of light: *The stars twinkled in the sky. The lights on the distant boats twinkled in the night.* **2.** (of the eyes) to be bright, as with amusement or pleasure. **3.** to move lightly and quickly. **4.** *Archaic.* to wink; blink. —*n.* **1.** a flicker or flash of light. **2.** brightness of the eyes, as in amusement or pleasure. **3.** a very brief period of time; twinkling: *The job was finished in a twinkle.* **4.** a wink of the eye. [Old English *twinclian* to sparkle, glitter.] —**twin′kler,** *n.*

twin·kling (twing′kling) *n.* **1.** a very brief period of time; moment; instant. **2.** the act of shining with or emitting flashes of light. **3.** a flicker or flash of light; twinkle.

twin-screw (twin′skrü′) *adj.* (of a boat or ship) having two screw propellers, esp. ones that revolve in opposite directions.

twirl (twûrl) *v.t.* **1.** to cause to rotate rapidly on or as on an axis: *to twirl a baton.* **2.** to twist or turn the ends of: *to twirl a strand of hair.* **3.** *Baseball. Slang.* to pitch. —*v.i.* to rotate rapidly on or as on an axis. —*n.* **1.** the act of twirling or the state of being twirled. **2.** something having a curled or spiral shape. [Possibly a blend of TWIST and WHIRL.] —**twirl′er,** *n.*

twirp (twûrp) twerp.

twist (twist) *v.t.* **1.** to wind (two or more strands, threads, or the like) around each other. **2.** to make or form in this way: *to twist a rope from single strands.* **3.** to rotate or turn: *to twist the lid off a jar.* **4.** to form into a spiral, as by turning the ends in opposite directions. **5.** to change the natural or usual shape or position of; contort; distort: *to twist one's face into a grimace.* **6.** to injure a part of the body in this way; sprain: *to fall and twist one's ankle.* **7.** to change or distort the meaning of: *to twist someone's words.* **8.** to cause (a ball) to spin while moving in a curved direction. —*v.i.* **1.** to turn so as to face in a different direction. **2.** to move in or follow a winding course: *The new highway twists through the mountains.* **3.** to move in a circle or spiral; rotate. **4.** to writhe; squirm. **5.** to become sprained. **6.** to become wound or turned: *This thin wire will twist easily.* —*n.* **1.** a curve, bend, or turn: *There is a twist in the road up ahead.* **2.** the act of twisting or the state of being twisted; rotation. **3.** something having a curled or spiral shape. **4.** an unexpected change in or deviation from the usual or ordinary: *The movie ended with a surprising twist.* **5.** a peculiar or eccentric bent, inclination, or attitude; eccentricity or quirk. **6.** in certain games, a spinning motion given to a ball in striking or throwing it in a particular way. **7.** a thread, cord, or rope made of two or more strands that are twisted together. [Old English *-twist* rope (as in the compound *mæst-twist* a rope to support a mast[1].]

twist·er (twis′tər) *n.* **1.** a person or thing that twists. **2.** *Informal.* a tornado.

twit (twit) *v.t.,* **twit·ted, twit·ting.** to tease or taunt, esp. by reminding of past errors or embarrassments. —*n.* **1.** the act of twitting. **2.** a reproach or taunt. [Short for obsolete *atwite* to reproach, from Old English *ætwītan.*]

twitch (twich) *v.i.* to move with a sudden, involuntary jerk. —*v.t.* to pull with an abrupt tug or jerk. —*n.* **1.** a sudden, involuntary muscle contraction: *I have a twitch in my left eye.* **2.** a sudden, sharp pull or tug; jerk. [Probably from an unrecorded Old English word.]

twit·ter (twit′ər) *n.* **1.** a series of short, light, chirping sounds made by birds. **2.** a state or condition of nervous agitation or excitement. ➡ used chiefly in the phrase *in a twitter: to be in a twitter before a party.* —*v.i.* **1.** to utter a series of light, chirping sounds, as a bird. **2.** to laugh in a nervous or restrained manner; titter. **3.** to be in a state of nervous agitation or excitement. —*v.t.* to utter or express with a twitter. [Imitative.] —**twit′ter·er,** *n.*

twixt (twikst) *also,* **'twixt.** *prep.* between; betwixt.

two (tü) *n., pl.* **twos. 1.** the cardinal number that is one more than one. **2.** a symbol representing this number, such as 2 or II. **3.** something having this many units or members, such as a playing card. —*adj.* numbering one more than one. [Old English *twā.*]
 • **in two.** in or into two parts or pieces.
 • **to put two and two together.** to come to the obvious conclusion after considering the facts.

two-base hit (tü′bās′) double *(def. 4).* Also, **two′-bag′ger.**

two-bit (tü′bit′) *adj. Slang.* of little worth or value; cheap.

two bits *Informal.* twenty-five cents; quarter.

two-by-four (tü′bī fôr′, -bə-) *n.* **1.** a rough piece of lumber measuring 2 inches by 4 inches (5 by 10 centimeters), used esp. in building. **2.** a finished piece of lumber measuring 1⅝ by 3⅝

twill

a	at	e	end	o	hot	u	up	hw	white		about
ā	ape	ē	me	ō	old	ū	use	ng	song	ə	taken
ä	far	i	it	ô	fork	ū	rule	th	thin		pencil
âr	care	ī	ice	oi	oil	u̇	pull	th	this		lemon
		îr	pierce	ou	out	ûr	turn	zh	measure		circus

inches (4.1 by 9.2 centimeters), used esp. in building. —*adj.* measuring two units by four units, as 2 inches by 4 inches.

two-di·men·sion·al (tü′di men′shə nəl) *adj.* **1.** having only two dimensions, usually height and width. **2.** lacking depth or thoroughness; superficial.

two-edged (tü′ejd′) *adj.* **1.** having two edges, esp. two cutting edges: *a two-edged sword.* **2.** having two meanings, interpretations, effects, or implications: *a two-edged compliment.*

two-faced (tü′fāst′) *adj.* **1.** having two faces or aspects. **2.** deceitful or hypocritical: *a two-faced liar.*

two-fist·ed (tü′fis′tid) *adj. Informal.* powerful or strong; virile.

two·fold (tü′fōld′) *adj.* **1.** two times as great or as numerous. **2.** having or consisting of two parts. —*adv.* so as to be two times greater or more numerous.

two-hand·ed (tü′han′did) *adj.* **1.** having two hands. **2.** involving or requiring the use of both hands at the same time: *a two-handed sword.* **3.** intended for use by two persons: *a two-handed saw.* **4.** involving or intended for two persons: *a two-handed card game.* **5.** using both hands equally well; ambidextrous.

two·pence (tup′əns) *also,* **tuppence.** *n.* a sum of money and coin equal to two British pennies; two pence.

two-pen·ny (tup′ə nē) *adj.* **1.** having the value of or equal to twopence. **2.** of very little value; trifling; worthless.

two-ply (tü′plī′) *adj.* **1.** composed or consisting of two layers, thicknesses, or strands: *two-ply tissue.* **2.** consisting of two webs woven into each other: *a two-ply carpet.*

two·some (tü′səm) *n.* **1.** two persons together; couple. **2.a.** something done or played by two people, as a round of golf. **b.** the players.

two-step (tü′step′) *n.* **1.** a ballroom dance consisting of sliding steps in 2/4 time. **2.** the music for such a dance.

two-time (tü′tīm′) *v.t.,* **-timed, -tim·ing.** *Slang.* to be unfaithful to or deceive, esp. in love. —**two′-tim′er,** *n.*

two-way (tü′wā′) *adj.* **1.** moving or allowing movement in two directions: *two-way traffic, a two-way street.* **2.** allowing communication in two directions, esp. by having the capacity to transmit and receive: *a two-way radio.* **3.** involving two persons or groups: *a two-way conversation.* **4.** involving or requiring mutual sharing of responsibilities, obligations, or the like.

TX, the postal abbreviation for Texas.

-ty[1] *suffix* multiplied by ten: *twenty, thirty.* [Old English *-tig.*]

-ty[2] *suffix* (used to form nouns) the state, condition, or quality of being: *safety, subtlety.* [Old French *-te, -tet,* from Latin *-tās.*]

ty·coon (tī kün′) *n.* **1.** a wealthy, powerful person in business, industry, or finance. **2.** shogun. [Japanese *taikun* shogun, from Chinese (Mandarin) *ta* great + *chün* ruler.]

ty·ing (tī′ing) the present participle of **tie.**

tyke (tīk) *also,* **tike.** *n.* **1.** *Informal.* a small child, esp. one who is mischievous. **2.** a mongrel dog; cur. [Old Norse *tīk* bitch.]

tym·bal (tim′bəl) timbal.

tym·pan (tim′pən) *n.* **1.** a frame on which paper is placed in a hand printing press. **2.** a membranelike sheet or plate of some thin material, tightly stretched over an apparatus, as a drum. **3.** *Architecture.* tympanum *(def. 3).* [Latin *tympanum* drum, from Greek *tympanon* kettledrum.]

tym·pa·ni (tim′pə nē) timpani.

tym·pan·ic (tim pan′ik) *adj.* **1.** of or relating to the eardrum or the middle ear. **2.** relating to or resembling a drum.

tympanic membrane, eardrum.

tym·pa·nist (tim′pə nist) *n.* the member of an orchestra who plays a kettledrum and, usually, other percussion instruments.

tym·pa·num (tim′pə nəm) *n., pl.* **-na** (-nə) or **-nums.** **1.** eardrum. **2.** middle ear. **3.** *Architecture.* **a.** a recessed, often ornamented, triangular space forming the central panel of a pediment. **b.** the space enclosed by an arch, as over a doorway or window. Also *(def. 3),* **tym′pan.** [Latin *tympanum* drum, from Greek *tympanon* kettledrum.]

Tyn·dall effect (tin′dəl) a phenomenon in which a light beam is scattered and becomes visible when passing through a suspension or colloidal system, such as smoke. [From John *Tyndall,* 1820-93, Irish physicist who discovered it.]

type (tīp) *n.* **1.** a group that is distinguished from other groups by the common traits or characteristics of its members; kind; class: *a suit of the most conservative type.* **2.a.** a person or thing that exhibits the characteristic qualities of a kind, class, or group; typical example: *This cat is some type of Siamese. Your friend is the type of person I like.* **b.** a standard or model of a kind or class; perfect example: *Raphael is the very type of a Renaissance painter.* **3.** a general form, structure, style, or character that distinguishes or characterizes a particular kind, class, or group. **4.a.** a rectangular piece or block, as of metal or wood, on one surface of which there is a raised letter, numeral, or other symbol that forms a printing surface. **b.** such pieces or blocks collectively. **5.** a printed

or typewritten character or characters. **6.** a design or other ornamental figure on either side of a coin or medal. **7.** blood type. **8.** *Informal.* a person regarded as embodying all the characteristics of a particular profession, social group, way of life, or the like: *an executive type.* —*v.,* **typed, typ·ing.** —*v.t.* **1.** to write (something) on a typewriter: *to type a letter.* **2.** to identify or determine the type of (a blood or tissue sample). **3.** to place in a particular class or group: *I wrongly typed my quiet neighbor as unfriendly.* —*v.i.* to write on a typewriter. [Latin *typus* image, figure, form, from Greek *typos* impression, model, image, form, stamp.] —**typ′a·ble;** *also,* **type′a·ble,** *adj.*

> **Usage** Type meaning "kind" or "typical example" is sometimes used directly before the noun in phrases such as *a European type appliance.* In such constructions, **type** should be connected by a hyphen to the word before it or, more formally, followed by *of: a European-type appliance, a European type of appliance.*

type·cast (tīp′kast′) *v.t.* **-cast, -cast·ing.** **1.** to cast (an actor) in a role that is particularly suited to his or her own personality, physical appearance, and the like. **2.** to cast (an actor) repeatedly in the same type of role.

type·face (tīp′fās′) *n. Printing.* face *(def. 13).*

type metal, an alloy used in casting metal printing type, consisting largely of lead, antimony, and tin.

type·script (tīp′skript′) *n.* material that has been typewritten.

type·set (tīp′set′) *v.t.,* **-set, -set·ting.** to set in type for printing; compose: *to typeset a manuscript.*

type·set·ter (tīp′set′ər) *n.* **1.** a person or business that sets type or text for printing. Also, **compositor.** **2.** a machine that sets type or text for printing.

type·set·ting (tīp′set′ing) *n.* the act or process of setting type or text for printing. —*adj.* used or adapted for setting type or text: *a typesetting machine.*

type·write (tīp′rīt′) *v.t., v.i.,* **-wrote** (-rōt′), **-writ·ten** (-rit′ən), **-writ·ing.** to write (something) with a typewriter; type.

type·writ·er (tīp′rī′tər) *n.* **1.** a machine used to produce clear, printlike text, consisting of a set of keys that, when struck, impress letters on paper through an inked ribbon. **2.** formerly, a typist.

type·writ·ing (tīp′rī′ting) *n.* **1.** the act or process of using a typewriter. **2.** something that is done or produced on a typewriter.

ty·phoid (tī′foid) *n.* typhoid fever. —*adj.* of, relating to, resembling, or characteristic of typhoid fever. [TYPH(US) + -OID.]

typhoid bacillus, the bacterium that causes typhoid fever, usually found in the intestine of a person who carries or is infected with the disease.

typhoid fever, an infectious, sometimes fatal fever characterized by intestinal inflammation and rose-colored spots on the skin, caused by a bacillus taken into the body with food or drink. People can be inoculated with a vaccine against typhoid fever.

ty·phoon (tī fün′) *n.* a severe tropical hurricane occurring in the western Pacific Ocean chiefly during the months of July, August, September, and October. [Chinese (Cantonese) *tai fung* literally, great wind; influenced by Greek *tȳphōn* whirlwind.]

ty·phus (tī′fəs) *n.* any of a group of acute infectious diseases characterized by severe headache, high fever, and a spotted rash, caused by microorganisms carried by fleas or lice. [Modern Latin *typhus,* from Greek *tȳphos* fever.]

typ·i·cal (tip′i kəl) *adj.* **1.** exhibiting or indicating the character, qualities, attributes, or nature characteristic of or peculiar to a particular type so as to be representative of it: *a typical student, a typical tourist.* **2.** of the nature of or constituting a type; symbolic. **3.** conforming to a type. —**typ′i·cal·ly,** *adv.*

typ·i·fy (tip′ə fī′) *v.t.,* **-fied, -fy·ing.** **1.** to embody or exhibit the common or usual characteristics of; be typical of; exemplify. **2.** to serve as a symbol of; represent; symbolize. [Latin *typus* image + -FY. See TYPE.] —**typ′i·fi·ca′tion,** *n.*

typ·ist (tī′pist) *n.* a person who types, esp. one whose occupation is operating a typewriter.

ty·po (tī′pō) *n., pl.* **-pos.** *Informal.* a typographical error.

ty·pog·ra·pher (tī pog′rə fər) *n.* printer *(def. 1).*

ty·po·graph·i·cal (tī′pə graf′i kəl) *adj.* of or relating to typography: *a typographical error.* Also, **ty′po·graph′ic.** —**ty′po·graph′i·cal·ly,** *adv.*

ty·pog·ra·phy (tī pog′rə fē) *n.* **1.** the act, art, or process of producing printed matter, esp. by means of a printing press. **2.** the arrangement, appearance, or style of printed matter. [Modern Latin *typographia,* from Greek *typos* impression, stamp + -GRAPHY.]

Tyr (tîr) *n.* in Norse mythology, the god of war and a son of Odin.

ty·ran·ni·cal (ti ran′i kəl, tī-) *adj.* of, relating to, or characteristic of a tyrant; cruel and unjust. Also, **ty·ran′nic.** [Latin *tyrannicus* (from Greek *tyrannikos,* from *tyrannos* absolute ruler) + -AL[1].] —**ty·ran′ni·cal·ly,** *adv.*

ty·ran·ni·cide¹ (ti ran′ə sīd′, tī-) *n.* the act of killing a tyrant. [Latin *tyrannicīdium,* from *tyrannus* despot + *-cīdium.* See TYRANT, -CIDE¹.]

ty·ran·ni·cide² (ti ran′ə sīd′, tī-) *n.* a person who kills a tyrant. [Latin *tyrannicīda,* from *tyrannus* despot + *-cīda.* See TYRANT, -CIDE².]

tyr·an·nize (tir′ə nīz′) *v.,* **-nized, -niz·ing.** —*v.i.* **1.** to exercise power in a cruel and unjust way (often with *over*): *The dictator tyrannized over the people.* **2.** to rule as a tyrant. —*v.t.* to treat or govern tyrannically.

ty·ran·no·saur (ti ran′ə sôr′, tī-) *n.* a huge carnivorous dinosaur, *Tyrannosaurus rex,* of North America that lived during the Cretaceous period and walked upright on its hind legs. Also, **ty·ran′no·sau′rus.** [Modern Latin *Tyrannosaurus,* from Greek *tyrannos* absolute ruler + *sauros* lizard.]

tyr·an·nous (tir′ə nəs) *adj.* cruel and unjust; despotic; tyrannical. —**tyr′an·nous·ly,** *adv.*

tyr·an·ny (tir′ə nē) *n., pl.* **-nies. 1.** cruel and unjust use of force, power, or authority; arbitrary or oppressive exercise of power. **2.** in ancient Greece, the office of or government by a tyrant. **3.** any oppressive or unjustly severe rule or government by one person; despotism. **4.** harshness; severity. **5.** a tyrannical act. [Late Latin *tyrannia* tyrannical conduct, despotic rule, from Latin *tyrannus* ruler, despot. See TYRANT.]

ty·rant (tī′rənt) *n.* **1.** a person who exercises power or authority in a cruel and unjust manner. **2.** a person who has absolute power and rules or governs in a cruel and unjust manner; absolute ruler; despot. **3.** in ancient Greece, an absolute ruler who obtained authority illegally. [Old French *tyrant, tiran* despot, from Latin *tyrannus* ruler, despot, from Greek *tyrannos* absolute ruler.]

tyre (tīr) *British.* tire².

Tyr·i·an purple (tir′ē ən) **1.** a highly valued crimson or purple dye used in ancient times, derived from certain mollusks found in the Mediterranean. **2.** a purplish red color.

ty·ro (tī′rō) *also,* **tiro.** *n., pl.* **-ros.** a person who is just beginning to learn to do something; beginner; novice. [Latin *tīrō* recruit, beginner.]

ty·ro·sine (tī′rə sēn′, -sin) *n.* a nonessential amino acid produced by hydrolysis of casein and other proteins and from which adrenaline and thyroxin are synthesized. Formula: $C_9H_{11}NO_3$ [Greek *tyros* cheese + -INE².]

tzar (zär, tsär) czar.

tzar·e·vitch (zär′ə vich′, tsär′-) czarevitch.

tza·rev·na (zä rev′nə, tsä-) czarevna.

tza·ri·na (zä rē′nə, tsä-) czarina.

tzar·ism (zär′iz əm, tsär′-) czarism.

tzar·ist (zär′ist, tsär′-) czarist.

tzet·ze fly (tset′sē, tsē′tsē) tsetse fly. Also, **tzetze.**

a	at	e	end	o	hot	u	up	hw	white		about
ā	ape	ē	me	ō	old	ū	use	ng	song		taken
ä	far	i	it	ô	fork	ü	rule	th	thin	ə	pencil
âr	care	ī	ice	oi	oil	ů	pull	th	this		lemon
		îr	pierce	ou	out	ûr	turn	zh	measure		circus

T

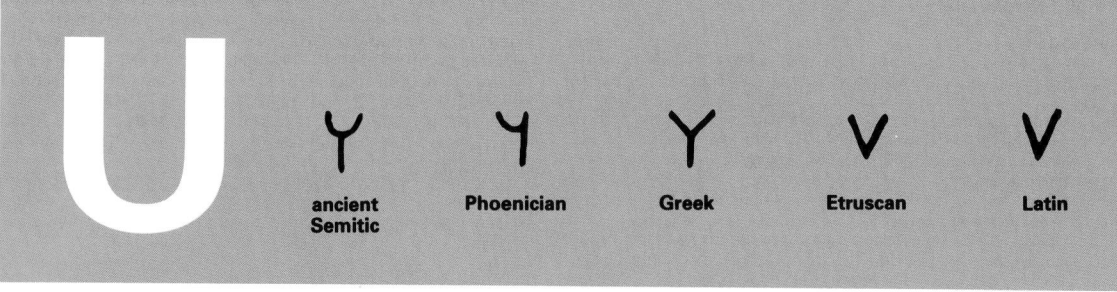

U	Υ	Ϟ	Υ	٧	V
	ancient Semitic	Phoenician	Greek	Etruscan	Latin

U The letter **U** developed as a variation of the letter **V**, which itself has its origins in the ancient Semitic letter *waw*. *Waw* depicted a hook and stood for the sound of *w* in the English word *water*. When the Phoenicians borrowed *waw*, they used it to represent both the consonant sound *w* and the vowel sound *ü*, as heard in the English word *rude*. The Greeks adopted *waw* and called it *upsilon*, writing it like our modern capital letter **Y** and using it only for the *ü* sound. When *upsilon* was borrowed by the Etruscans, they changed its shape by removing the tail so it resembled a **V** and, like the Phoenicians before them, used it to represent both the *ü* and the *w* sounds. The form of this letter and its two pronunciations were adopted by the Romans for the Latin alphabet. In the Middle Ages, the V-shaped letter came to be used only at the beginning of a word, and a new letter, **U**, was used in the middle of a word. Later, the letter **U** was reserved exclusively for the *ü* sound and came to be written in the form we are familiar with today.

u, U (ū) *n., pl.* **u's, U's. 1.** the twenty-first letter of the English alphabet. **2.** the shape of this letter or something having this shape.
U, the symbol for uranium.
U. 1. University. **2.** Upper.
UAR, United Arab Republic.
UAW, United Automobile Workers (of America).
u·biq·ui·tous (ū bik'wi təs) *adj.* being or seeming to be everywhere at once: *a ubiquitous aroma, ubiquitous ants at a picnic.* [UBIQUITY + -OUS.] **—u·biq'ui·tous·ly,** *adv.* **—u·biq'ui·tous·ness,** *n.*
u·biq·ui·ty (ū bik'wi tē) *n.* the state of being ubiquitous. [French *ubiquité,* from Latin *ubīque* everywhere.]
U-boat (ū'bōt') *n.* a German submarine, esp. one used in World War I or II. [German *U-boot,* short for *Unterseeboot* submarine; literally, undersea boat.]
U-bolt (ū'bōlt') *also,* **U bolt.** *n.* a U-shaped bolt fitted with threads and a nut at each end.
u.c. *Printing.* upper case.
ud·der (ud'ər) *n.* a large sac hanging from the underside of certain female mammals, such as cows or ewes, and holding one or more milk-producing glands, each with a teat or nipple for suckling offspring. [Old English *ūder.*]
UFO, unidentified flying object.
ugh (ug, ŭкн, ŭкн) *interj.* a grunt or exclamation expressing such emotions as disgust or horror. [Imitative.]
ug·li (ug'lē) *n.* a Jamaican citrus fruit produced by crossing a tangerine with a grapefruit, having a thick, yellowish green rind that peels easily. [Probably from UGLY; because its rind is unsightly.]
ug·li·fy (ug'lə fī') *v.t.,* **-fied, -fy·ing.** to make very unattractive or displeasing; disfigure.
ug·ly (ug'lē) *adj.,* **-li·er, -li·est. 1.** very unattractive or displeasing to the eye or the aesthetic sense: *an ugly scar, an ugly painting.* **2.** causing disgust; disagreeable; offensive: *an ugly story, ugly behavior.* **3.** likely to cause trouble or harm; ominous: *an ugly storm.* **4.** *Informal.* displaying or disposed to display hostility; quarrelsome; bad-tempered: *an ugly customer, an ugly mood.* **5.** morally reprehensible or objectionable: *an ugly prejudice.* [Old Norse *uggligr* fearful, dreadful.] **—ug'li·ness,** *n.*
ugly duckling, a person or thing that is ugly or unpromising but has the potential to become beautiful or impressive. [From a story by the Danish writer Hans Christian Andersen, 1805-75, in which a supposed ugly duckling becomes a beautiful swan.]

uhf *also,* **UHF** ultrahigh frequency.
uh·lan (ü'län, ū'lən) *also,* **ulan.** *n.* formerly, a mounted lancer in the armies of various European countries, esp. in the German army. [German *U(h)lan,* through Polish, from Turkish *oghlan* youth.]
U.K., United Kingdom.
u·kase (ū'kās', ū'kāz') *n.* **1.** an official proclamation or decree; edict. **2.** formerly, a decree or order having the force of law, issued by a czar or the czarist regime in Russia. [Russian *ukaz* edict, order, decree.]
U·krain·i·an (ū krā'nē ən) *n.* **1.** a native or inhabitant of Ukraine. **2.** the Slavic language spoken predominantly in Ukraine, closely related to Russian. *—adj.* of, relating to, or characteristic of Ukraine or its people, language, or culture.
u·ku·le·le (ū'kə lā'lē) *n.* a small, guitarlike musical instrument having four strings, associated with Hawaiian music. [Hawaiian *ukulele,* from *uku* flea + *lele* jumping; supposedly referring to the rapid movement of the fingers in playing the instrument.]
u·lan (ü'län, ū'lən) uhlan.
ul·cer (ul'sər) *n.* **1.** an open sore on the skin or a mucous membrane, such as the stomach lining. **2.** any corruptive, destructive, or evil influence or condition: *Poverty is an ulcer in our community.* [Latin *ulcer-,* stem of *ulcus* a sore.]
ul·cer·ate (ul'sə rāt') *v.t., v.i.,* **-at·ed, -at·ing.** to make or become ulcerous. [Latin *ulcerātus,* past participle of *ulcerāre* to make sore.]
ul·cer·a·tion (ul'sə rā'shən) *n.* **1.** the act or process of ulcerating or the state of being ulcerated. **2.** an ulcerous condition; ulcer.
ul·cer·ous (ul'sər əs) *adj.* **1.** relating to, characterized by, or resembling an ulcer or ulcers. **2.** affected with an ulcer or ulcers.
ul·na (ul'nə) *n., pl.* **-nae** (-nē) or **-nas. 1.** the larger of the two bones of the forearm, extending from the elbow to the wrist. For illustration, see **humerus. 2.** the corresponding bone in the forelimb of other vertebrates. [Latin *ulna* elbow, arm.] **—ul'nar,** *adj.*
ul·ster (ul'stər) *n.* a very long, heavy overcoat, often belted and having a cape attached. [From *Ulster,* Ireland, where it was originally made.]
ult. 1. ultimate. **2.** ultimately. **3.** ultimo. ➡ formerly used esp. in commercial and business correspondence, as in *in answer to your letter of the fifth ult.*
ul·te·ri·or (ul tîr'ē ər) *adj.* **1.** lying beyond what is shown or expressed; intentionally withheld or concealed; hidden: *ulterior motives.* **2.** occurring at a subsequent time or period; following; later: *ulterior action.* **3.** more distant or remote; farther off: *ulterior regions.* [Latin *ulterior* farther, beyond.] **—ul·te'ri·or·ly,** *adv.*
ul·ti·ma (ul'tə mə) *n.* the last syllable of a word. [Latin *ultima,* feminine of *ultimus* last, farthest.]
ul·ti·mate (ul'tə mit) *adj.* **1.** coming as a climax or at the end; final: *The ultimate cost of the project was greater than the original estimate. The ultimate fate of the expedition is unknown.* **2.** greatest or maximum possible; unsurpassed; absolute: *ultimate authority, ultimate coverage.* **3.** that cannot be further reduced, analyzed, or traced; fundamental: *The atom was once considered the ultimate building block of the universe.* *—n.* **1.** something that is perfect, complete, or unsurpassed; peak: *the ultimate in fashion, the ultimate in luxury.* **2.** something that is final, absolute, or fundamental. [Medieval Latin *ultimatus* last, final, going back to Latin *ultimus* last, farthest.] **—ul'ti·mate·ness,** *n.* —For Synonyms, see **last** [1].
ul·ti·mate·ly (ul'tə mit lē) *adv.* in the end; finally.
ultima Thule 1. the land considered by ancient geographers to be the northernmost part of the habitable world. It was situated somewhere in the sea beyond northwestern Europe. Also, **Thule. 2.** any faraway, mysterious region. **3.** the utmost limit, point, or degree attainable, as of an ideal. [Latin *ultima Thule* farthest

Thule, from *ultima,* feminine of *ultimus* last, farthest + *Thūlē* Thule (from Greek *Thoulē*).]

ul·ti·ma·tum (ul′tə mā′təm) *n., pl.* **-tums** or **-ta** (-tə). a final, uncompromising demand, proposal, or set of terms issued by one party to another, the rejection of which will result in conflict, a break in relations, or strong or punitive action. [Modern Latin *ultimatum,* from *ultimatum,* neuter of Medieval Latin *ultimatus* last. See ULTIMATE.]

ul·ti·mo (ul′tə mō′) *adv. Archaic.* in or of the month that preceded the present one. [Latin *ultimō (mēnse)* in the last (month).]

ul·tra (ul′trə) *adj.* going beyond what is usual or moderate; excessive; extreme. —*n.* a person who holds extreme views; extremist. [Latin *ultrā* beyond.]

ultra- *prefix* **1.** beyond what is usual or moderate; excessively; extremely: *ultraconservative, ultracritical.* **2.** on the other side of; beyond in space: *ultraviolet.* **3.** beyond the range or limits of: *ultrasonic.* [Latin *ultrā* beyond.]

ul·tra·cen·tri·fuge (ul′trə sen′trə f ūj′) *n.* a centrifuge that achieves speeds of 60,000-70,000 rpm, generating enough force to pull colloidal particles from suspension or macromolecules from solution. [ULTRA- + CENTRIFUGE.]

ul·tra·con·serv·a·tive (ul′trə kən sûr′və tiv) *adj.* extremely conservative. —*n.* an ultraconservative person.

ul·tra·crit·i·cal (ul′trə krit′i kəl) *adj.* extremely, excessively, or unnecessarily critical; hypercritical.

ul·tra·high frequency (ul′trə hī′) the frequency range of radio waves from 300 to 3,000 megahertz, used esp. for radio and television broadcasting.

ul·tra·light (ul′trə līt′) *n.* a small, lightweight, one-person aircraft made of aluminum tubing and sailcloth, designed to fly at low speeds and altitudes. [Short for *ultralight airplane.*]

ul·tra·ma·rine (ul′trə mə rēn′) *n.* **1.** a deep blue color. **2.** a blue pigment made originally from powdered lapis lazuli. **3.** any of several pigments made artificially that may be blue, green, or violet. —*adj.* having the color ultramarine; deep blue. **3.** lying beyond the sea. [Medieval Latin *ultramarinus* coming from beyond the sea, going back to Latin *ultrā* beyond + *mare* sea; referring to the earlier importing of lapis lazuli from Asia "beyond the sea."]

ul·tra·mi·cro·scope (ul′trə mī′krə skōp′) *n.* a microscope that uses the Tyndall effect to make submicroscopic particles visible, making them appear as bright points of light against a dark background, used esp. in the study of colloids. —**ul·tra·mi·cro·scop·ic** (ul′trə mī′krə skop′ik), *adj.*

ul·tra·mon·tane (ul′trə mon tān′) *adj.* **1.** of or relating to the regions or peoples situated beyond the mountains, esp. the Alps. **2.** in Roman Catholic doctrine, supporting or advocating the supreme authority of the pope in ecclesiastical or political matters. —*n.* **1.** a person living beyond the mountains, esp. one living south of the Alps. **2.** a person who supports or advocates the supreme authority of the pope in ecclesiastical and political matters. [Medieval Latin *ultramontanus* situated beyond the mountains, going back to Latin *ultrā* beyond + *mōns* mountain.]

ul·tra·mun·dane (ul′trə mun dān′, -mun′dān) *adj.* **1.** lying beyond the limits of the earth and solar system. **2.** beyond life or physical existence. [Late Latin *ultrāmundānus* beyond the world, going back to Latin *ultrā* beyond + *mundus* world.]

ul·tra·short (ul′trə shôrt′) *adj.* **1.** very short. **2.** of, relating to, or designating a radio wavelength of less than ten meters.

ul·tra·son·ic (ul′trə son′ik) *adj.* of, relating to, or designating sound waves having a frequency beyond the range audible to human beings, usually above 20,000 hertz.

ul·tra·son·ics (ul′trə son′iks) *n.* the science and technology of sound waves above the range audible to human beings. ➡ used as singular. Also, **supersonics.**

ul·tra·sound (ul′trə sound′) *n.* **1.** *Physics.* sound waves at ultrasonic frequencies. **2.** *Medicine.* the application of ultrasonic waves, as to provide certain types of therapy or to produce images of internal structures of the body.

ul·tra·vi·o·let (ul′trə vī′ə lit) *adj.* **1.** (of electromagnetic radiation) having a frequency beyond the violet end of the visible spectrum but lower than that of X rays, with wavelengths ranging from 40 to 4,000 angstroms. The sun is a source of ultraviolet radiation. **2.** relating to, employing, or producing ultraviolet radiation: *an ultraviolet telescope.*

ul·tra vi·res (ul′trə vī′rēz) *Latin.* going beyond the lawful or authorized powers, as of a corporation.

ul·u·lant (ūl′yə lənt, ul′-) *adj.* crying loudly; howling; ululating.

ul·u·late (ūl′yə lāt′, ul′-) *v.i.,* **-lat·ed, -lat·ing. 1.** to howl, as a wolf, or hoot, as an owl. **2.** to lament loudly; wail. [Latin *ululātus,* past participle of *ululāre* to howl.] —**ul′u·la′tion,** *n.*

U·lys·ses (ū lis′ēz) *n.* in Roman legend, a king of Ithaca and a Greek leader in the Trojan War. He was forced to wander for ten years after the fall of Troy until the gods finally permitted him to return home. He was called Odysseus by the Greeks.

um·bel (um′bəl) *n.* a flower cluster in which flower stalks radiate from a common center at the top of the stem, like ribs of an umbrella. [Latin *umbella* parasol, diminutive of *umbra* shade.]

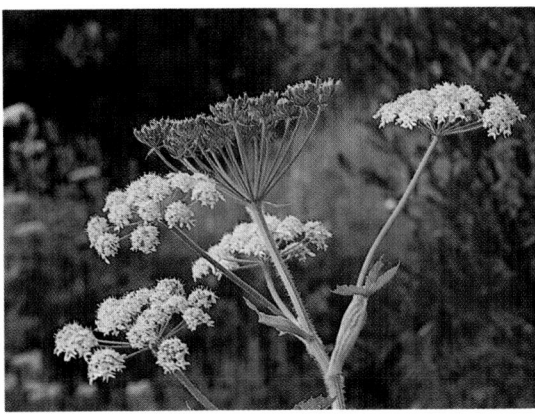

umbel

um·bel·late (um′bə lit, -lāt′) *adj.* having, resembling, or forming an umbel or umbels.

um·bel·lif·er·ous (um′bə lif′ər əs) *adj.* bearing an umbel or umbels, as plants of the carrot or parsley family.

um·ber (um′bər) *n.* **1.** a dark brown earth containing ferric oxide and manganese, used as a very dark, yellowish brown pigment in its natural state, **raw umber,** or, after being roasted, as a dark reddish brown pigment, **burnt umber. 2.** a dark yellowish brown or dark reddish brown color. —*adj.* having the color umber. [French *ombre,* short for *terre d'ombre* literally, earth of shadow, from Latin *terra* earth + *dē* from + *umbra* shade, shadow; probably because used by painters for shading.]

um·bil·i·cal (um bil′i kəl) *adj.* of, relating to, or located near the navel or umbilical cord. —*n.* umbilical cord.

umbilical cord 1. a cordlike structure in mammals that connects the navel of the fetus to the placenta of the mother's womb, providing nourishment for and removing wastes from the fetus. **2.** any of various lines that service and connect a spacecraft to the ground or launching site and are detached before launching.

um·bil·i·cus (um bil′i kəs, um′bə lī′kəs) *n., pl.* **-ci** (-sī′, -sī). **1.** navel. **2.** *Zoology.* something resembling a navel in shape, such as the hollow at the base of the shell in certain mollusks. **3.** *Botany.* hilum. [Latin *umbilīcus* navel, center.]

um·bo (um′bō) *n., pl.* **um·bo·nes** (um bō′nēz) or **um·bos. 1.** any rounded elevation resembling the boss or knob at the center of a shield. **2.** *Zoology.* the prominence on each half of a bivalve shell, next to the hinge. **3.** *Anatomy.* the central elevation on the inside of the eardrum where the malleus attaches. [Latin *umbo;* akin to *umbilicus.*]

um·bra (um′brə) *n., pl.* **-bras** or **-brae** (-brē). **1.** *Astronomy.* **a.** the completely dark, cone-shaped, inner part of the shadow cast by the moon in a solar eclipse or by the earth in a lunar eclipse. For illustration, see **eclipse. b.** a cone of complete shadow cast by a nonradiant body, such as a planet, in the direction away from the sun. **c.** the central, darkest portion of a sunspot. **2.** a shaded area or shadow, esp. the central part of a shadow from which all direct light is cut off. ➡ distinguished from **penumbra** in all defs. [Latin *umbra* shade, shadow.]

um·brage (um′brij) *n.* **1.** a feeling of displeasure or resentment, esp. at an imagined injury or insult; offense: *to take umbrage at a casual remark.* **2.** *Archaic.* **a.** shade; shadow. **b.** something that provides shade, such as foliage. [Old French *umbrage* shade, suspicion, going back to Latin *umbra* shade, shadow.]

um·bra·geous (um brā′jəs) *adj.* **1.** providing shade; shady. **2.** easily offended.

um·brel·la (um brel′ə) *n.* **1.** a portable device for protection from rain, sun, or the like, consisting of a circular piece of cloth or other material attached to narrow ribs that radiate from a long

a	at	e	end	o	hot	u	up	hw	white		about
ā	ape	ē	me	ō	old	ū	use	ng	song		taken
ä	far	i	it	ô	fork	ü	rule	th	thin	ə	pencil
âr	care	ī	ice	oi	oil	ù	pull	th	this		lemon
		îr	pierce	ou	out	ûr	turn	zh	measure		circus

central rod. **2.** something resembling an umbrella in shape or function, such as a force of military aircraft acting as a protective cover for land or sea forces. —*adj.* applying to or covering related elements; inclusive; general: *an umbrella organization, an umbrella clause.* [Italian *ombrella* device for protection from sun or rain, diminutive of *ombra* shade, from Latin *umbra* shade, shadow.]

umbrella tree **1.** an American magnolia tree, *Magnolia tripetala,* having long leaves and spreading branches and bearing clusters of cup-shaped white flowers. **2.** any of various trees with leaves or flower clusters shaped like open umbrellas.

Um·bri·an (um′brē ən) *adj.* of, relating to, or characteristic of Umbria or its people or culture. —*n.* **1.a.** a native or inhabitant of modern Umbria. **b.** a member of a people that inhabited Umbria in ancient times. **2.** the extinct Italic language of this people, closely related to Latin.

u·mi·ak (ü′mē ak′) *n.* a large, open Eskimo boat, about 30 feet (9.1 meters) long, made of skins stretched over a wooden frame. [Eskimo *umiak.*]

um·laut (ùm′lout′) *n.* **1.** in Germanic languages, a change in a vowel sound caused by absorbing the sound of another vowel that originally occurred in the next syllable. The change from *foot* to *feet* is an umlaut. **2.** the vowel so changed. **3.** a diacritical mark (¨) placed over such a vowel, esp. in German. —*v.t.* **1.** to change or modify (a vowel sound) by umlaut. **2.** to write an umlaut over (a vowel). [German *Umlaut* modification of a vowel, from *um* about + *Laut* sound.]

um·pire (um′pīr) *n.* **1.** an official in certain sports and games, such as baseball and tennis, who rules on plays, interprets and enforces the rules, and settles disputed points. **2.** a person having the authority to settle a dispute or decide an issue, as between opposing persons or groups. —*v.*, **-pired, -pir·ing.** —*v.t.* to act as umpire in or of: *to umpire a softball game.* —*v.i.* to act as umpire. [Earlier *numpire,* from Old French *nomper* odd, not equal, going back to Latin *nōn* not + *par* equal; referring to the umpire's position as the *odd,* or third, person in deciding a dispute between others. The initial *n* was lost by being joined to the preceding indefinite article: *a numpire* became an *umpire.*]

ump·teen (ump′tēn′) *adj. Informal.* of a large but indefinite number; countless; innumerable: *There were umpteen ants at our campsite.* —**ump′teenth′,** *adj.*

UMW, United Mine Workers.

un-[1] *prefix* (used to form adjectives, adverbs, and nouns) the opposite or negative of (what is indicated by the stem): *uncooked, unbeliever.* [Old English *un-.*]

un-[2] *prefix* **1.** (used to form verbs from verbs) **a.** to do the opposite of; reverse the action of: *unfasten.* **b.** to emphasize or intensify the action of: *unloose.* **2.** (used to form verbs from nouns) **a.** to release, remove, or free from: *unearth.* **b.** to cause to cease to be; deprive of the qualities of: *unman.* [Old English *un-, on-, an-.*]

UN, United Nations.

un·a·bashed (un′ə basht′) *adj.* not ashamed, self-conscious, or disconcerted: *unabashed silliness.* —**un′a·bash′ed·ly,** *adv.*

un·a·bat·ed (un′ə bā′tid) *adj.* at full strength, power, or force; undiminished: *unabated force.* —**un′a·bat′ed·ly,** *adv.*

un·a·ble (un ā′bəl) *adj.* lacking the required power, skills, or qualifications (to do something): *I'm unable to type.*

un·a·bridged (un′ə brijd′) *adj.* not shortened or condensed; complete: *an unabridged edition of a book.*

un·ac·com·pa·nied (un′ə kum′pə nēd) *adj.* **1.** without a companion or escort; unattended; alone: *to go unaccompanied to the theater.* **2.** *Music.* without accompaniment.

un·ac·com·plished (un′ə kom′plisht) *adj.* **1.** not skilled: *to be unaccomplished as a public speaker.* **2.** not completed.

un·ac·count·a·ble (un′ə koun′tə bəl) *adj.* **1.** that cannot be accounted for; inexplicable. **2.** not liable to be called to account. —**un′ac·count′a·bil′i·ty,** *n.* —**un′ac·count′a·bly,** *adv.*

un·ac·count·ed-for (un′ə koun′tid fôr′) *adj.* not accounted for or unexplained: *an unaccounted-for expense, two unaccounted-for members of an expedition.*

un·ac·cus·tomed (un′ə kus′təmd) *adj.* **1.** not used to or familiar with (with *to*): *unaccustomed to country life.* **2.** unusual; strange: *to act with unaccustomed strength.*

un·ac·knowl·edged (un′ak nol′ijd) *adj.* generally accepted without having formal or official recognition: *the unacknowledged leader of a group.*

un·ac·quaint·ed (un′ə kwān′tid) *adj.* **1.** not known to someone or to each other. **2.** not familiar: *to be unacquainted with the rules of a game.*

un·a·dorned (un′ə dôrnd′) *adj.* not embellished; simple; plain: *an unadorned style of writing.*

un·a·dul·ter·at·ed (un′ə dul′tə rā′tid) *adj.* **1.** not diluted or corrupted by extraneous matter; unmixed; pure: *unadulterated foods.* **2.** with no qualifications; total; utter: *unadulterated stupidity.*

un·ad·vised (un′ad vīzd′) *adj.* **1.** without due consideration; ill-advised; imprudent; rash. **2.** not supplied with advice; uninformed.

un·ad·vis·ed·ly (un′ad vī′zid lē) *adv.* in a rash, thoughtless manner; imprudently.

un·af·fect·ed[1] (un′ə fek′tid) *adj.* not influenced; unmoved: *The judge was unaffected by the defendant's pleas.* [UN-[1] + AFFECTED[1].]

un·af·fect·ed[2] (un′ə fek′tid) *adj.* not pretentious or artificial; genuine; sincere: *unaffected speech.* [UN-[1] + AFFECTED[2].] —**un′af·fect′ed·ly,** *adv.* —**un′af·fect′ed·ness,** *n.*

un·aid·ed (un ā′did) *adj.* without help or support.

un·al·lied (un′ə līd′, un al′īd) *adj.* not joined by treaty, agreement, or common purpose.

un·al·ter·a·ble (un ôl′tər ə bəl) *adj.* that cannot be changed: *unalterable plans.* —**un·al′ter·a·bly,** *adv.*

un·al·tered (un ôl′tərd) *adj.* not changed.

un-A·mer·i·can (un′ə mer′i kən) *adj.* not according to the purported American character, traditions, and institutions. —**un′-A·mer′i·can·ism,** *n.*

un·a·neled (un′ə nēld′) *adj. Archaic.* not having been anointed by a priest before death. [UN-[1] + *aneled,* past participle of obsolete *anele* to give extreme unction (to going back to Old English *an* on + *ele* oil, from Latin *oleum* oil). See OIL.]

u·na·nim·i·ty (ū′nə nim′i tē) *n.* the state of being unanimous; complete agreement; unity.

u·nan·i·mous (ū nan′ə məs) *adj.* **1.** of one mind or opinion; in complete agreement: *The club members were unanimous in their support of the project.* **2.** characterized by or resulting from complete agreement: *The vote was unanimous.* [Latin *ūnanimus* of one mind.] —**u·nan′i·mous·ly,** *adv.* —**u·nan′i·mous·ness,** *n.*

un·an·swer·a·ble (un an′sər ə bəl) *adj.* **1.** that cannot be answered; having no known answer. **2.** that cannot be argued against or disproved: *an unanswerable theory.* —**un·an′swer·a·bly,** *adv.*

un·ap·peal·ing (un′ə pē′ling) *adj.* not attractive, interesting, or enjoyable.

un·ap·pe·tiz·ing (un ap′i tī′zing) *adj.* not appealing, esp. to the appetite.

un·ap·proach·a·ble (un′ə prō′chə bəl) *adj.* **1.** difficult to know or deal with; unfriendly; aloof: *an unapproachable person.* **2.** that cannot be approached; inaccessible: *The mountain cabin is unapproachable in winter.* **3.** without equal; matchless; unrivaled: *a speech unapproachable in its eloquence.* —**un′ap·proach′a·bil′i·ty,** **un′ap·proach′a·ble·ness,** *n.* —**un′ap·proach′a·bly,** *adv.*

un·arm (un ärm′) *v.t.* to deprive of weapons or armor; disarm.

un·armed (un ärmd′) *adj.* without arms or weapons; defenseless.

un·asked (un askt′) *adj.* **1.** without being asked; uninvited: *They came unasked to the party.* **2.** not asked for: *unasked advice.* **3.** not asked.

un·as·sail·a·ble (un′ə sā′lə bəl) *adj.* **1.** that cannot be denied, disputed, or questioned: *an unassailable argument, an unassailable reputation.* **2.** that cannot be successfully attacked or seized; impregnable: *an unassailable fortress.* —**un′as·sail′a·bil′i·ty,** **un′as·sail′a·ble·ness,** *n.* —**un′as·sail′a·bly,** *adv.*

un·as·sum·ing (un′ə sü′ming) *adj.* modest in nature or manner; not bold, forward, or boastful. —**un′as·sum′ing·ly,** *adv.*

un·at·tached (un′ə tacht′) *adj.* **1.** not fastened, joined, or connected. **2.** not engaged or married. **3.** not assigned to or associated with a particular body, group, or organization: *an*

The following list contains a selection of compounds that can be formed with the prefix **un-**. The meaning of a word on the list can be understood by combining the appropriate sense of the prefix with the root word.

unabbreviated	unaccented	unacclimatized	unadventurous	unafraid	unaired
unabetted	unaccentuated	unaccommodating	unadvertised	unaged	unalarmed
unabsolved	unacceptable	unadaptable	unadvisable	unaggressive	unaligned
unabsorbed	unaccepted	unadapted	unaesthetic	unagitated	unalike
unacademic	unacclimated	unadjusted	unaffiliated	unagreeable	unalleviated

unattached army officer. **4.** Law. (of a person or property) not taken or seized as security.

un·at·tend·ed (un′ə ten′did) adj. **1.** not accompanied or escorted; alone. **2.** not done or taken care of; neglected (often with to): to leave housework unattended, to leave a task unattended to. **3.** without an audience; lacking attendance.

un·a·vail·ing (un′ə vā′ling) adj. futile; useless: Their efforts to stop the fire were unavailing. —**un′a·vail′ing·ly**, adv.

un·a·void·a·ble (un′ə voi′də bəl) adj. that cannot or could not be avoided or prevented; inevitable: an unavoidable delay, an unavoidable clash of opinions. —**un′a·void′a·bly**, adv.

un·a·ware (un′ə wâr′) adj. not aware, cognizant, or informed (often with of): We were unaware of their dislike for us. —adv. unawares.

un·a·wares (un′ə wârz′) adv. **1.** without warning; unexpectedly; suddenly: The storm caught us unawares. **2.** without design or intention; inadvertently; unintentionally: I let the error slip by unawares.

un·backed (un bakt′) adj. **1.** without financial support or other aid or endorsement. **2.** without a back for support, as a bench or book. **3.** not bet on, as a horse in a race.

un·bal·ance (un bal′əns) v.t., **-anced, -anc·ing. 1.** to disturb the equilibrium or stability of: to throw out of balance. **2.** to disorder or derange, as the mind. —n. the condition of being unbalanced.

un·bal·anced (un bal′ənst) adj. **1.** not in a state of equilibrium or balance: The unbalanced load caused one side of the car to sag. **2.** not having a sound mind; mentally disordered; deranged: an unbalanced person. **3.** not adjusted so that the debit and credit sides are equal: an unbalanced budget, an unbalanced account.

un·bar (un bär′) v.t., **-barred, -bar·ring.** to remove a bar or bars from; unbolt; open: to unbar a door.

un·bear·a·ble (un bâr′ə bəl) adj. that cannot be borne or endured; intolerable: unbearable pain, unbearable suspense. —**un·bear′a·ble·ness**, n. —**un·bear′a·bly**, adv.

un·beat·a·ble (un bē′tə bəl) adj. that cannot be defeated or surpassed: an unbeatable tennis player, an unbeatable bargain.

un·beat·en (un bē′tən) adj. **1.** never defeated or surpassed: an unbeaten team. **2.** not walked over; untrod: an unbeaten path. **3.** not shaped or mixed by beating: unbeaten gold, an unbeaten egg.

un·be·com·ing (un′bi kum′ing) adj. **1.** not flattering or attractive: The color green is unbecoming to your complexion. **2.** not suitable or appropriate; indecorous: to use unbecoming language. —**un′be·com′ing·ly**, adv. —**un′be·com′ing·ness**, n.

un·be·knownst (un′bi nōnst′) also, **un·be·known** (un′bi nōn′). adj. Informal. without the knowledge or awareness of (with to): Unbeknownst to us, our friends had left the party.

un·be·lief (un′bi lēf′) n. the absence of belief, esp. in matters of religion.

un·be·liev·a·ble (un′bi lē′və bəl) adj. **1.** that cannot be believed or accepted as true: an unbelievable story. **2.** seemingly impossible or extraordinary: an unbelievable catch at the five yard line. —**un′be·liev′a·bly**, adv.

un·be·liev·er (un′bi lē′vər) n. **1.** a person who does not believe in a particular religion or any religion. **2.** a person who doubts; skeptic.

un·be·liev·ing (un′bi lē′ving) adj. **1.** doubting; skeptical; incredulous. **2.** lacking religious belief or beliefs. —**un′be·liev′ing·ly**, adv.

un·bend (un bend′) v., **-bent, -bend·ing.** —v.t. **1.** to straighten (something curved or crooked). **2.** to free from concentrated effort or strain; relax: to unbend one's mind. **3.** Nautical. to unfasten, untie, or cast loose (a sail, line, cable, or the like). —v.i. **1.** to become free of tension, formality, or strain; relax: to unbend after a hard day's work. **2.** to become straight or almost straight.

un·bend·ing (un ben′ding) adj. **1.** that cannot or will not relax or relent; unyielding; inflexible: an unbending will. **2.** not bending or curving; stiff. —**un·bend′ing·ly**, adv.

un·bent (un bent′) the past tense and past participle of **unbend.**

un·bi·ased (un bī′əst) also, British, **un·bi·assed.** adj. free from partiality or prejudice; fair; equitable: an unbiased judge.

un·bid·den (un bid′ən) adj. **1.** not asked or invited: Several unbidden guests showed up at the party. **2.** not commanded or

ordered; spontaneous: unbidden thoughts, unbidden tears. Also, **un·bid′.**

un·bind (un bīnd′) v.t., **-bound, -bind·ing. 1.** to release from bonds or restraint; set free: Unbind my hands. **2.** to remove or undo (something that binds); unfasten; loose: to unbind a bandage.

un·blem·ished (un blem′isht) adj. **1.** free from imperfection or flaw: an unblemished reputation. **2.** not marked or marred: an unblemished complexion.

un·blessed (un blest′) also, **un·blest.** adj. **1.** not blessed or consecrated. **2.** cursed; evil; unholy.

un·blink·ing (un bling′king) adj. **1.** not blinking. **2.** without displaying an emotional response; unemotional; calm: an unblinking acceptance of a verdict of guilty. **3.** not wavering or vacillating; fearless; forthright: an unblinking appraisal of necessary reforms.

un·blush·ing (un blush′ing) adj. **1.** without shame or remorse; shameless; brazen: an unblushing pride in one's accomplishments. **2.** not blushing or reddening. —**un·blush′ing·ly**, adv.

un·bolt (un bōlt′) v.t. to open by drawing back a bolt or bolts; unlock.

un·bolt·ed[1] (un bōl′tid) adj. not fastened by a bolt or bolts: an unbolted door. [UN-[1] + bolted, past participle of BOLT[1].]

un·bolt·ed[2] (un bōl′tid) adj. not sifted. [UN-[1] + bolted, past participle of BOLT[2].]

un·born (un bôrn′) adj. not yet born or existing: an unborn child, an unborn generation.

un·bos·om (un bŭz′əm, -bü′zəm) v.t. **1.** to disclose or confide, as one's thoughts or feelings: to unbosom one's sorrows to a friend. **2.** to unburden (oneself), as of thoughts, secrets, or feelings.

un·bound (un bound′) v. the past tense and past participle of **unbind.** —adj. **1.** not tied: an unbound package. **2.** without a binding or cover: an unbound book.

un·bound·ed (un boun′did) adj. having no limits or bounds; boundless; measureless: unbounded space, unbounded admiration.

un·bowed (un boud′) adj. **1.** not tamed or subdued, as by defeat. **2.** not bowed or bent.

un·bri·dled (un brī′dəld) adj. **1.** not restrained or checked; uncontrolled; ungoverned: unbridled fury. **2.** not wearing or fitted with a bridle.

un·bro·ken (un brō′kən) adj. **1.** not torn or broken; whole; intact: an unbroken seal. **2.** not interrupted; continuous; uniform: an unbroken chain of events. **3.** not beaten or surpassed: an unbroken record of victories. **4.** (of an animal) unaccustomed to a harness or rider; untamed: an unbroken horse. **5.** not weakened, subdued, or humbled: a spirit unbroken by poverty. **6.** not repudiated or violated: an unbroken promise. —**un·bro′ken·ly**, adv. —**un·bro′ken·ness**, n.

un·buck·le (un buk′əl) v.t., **-led, -ling.** to undo or unfasten the buckle or buckles of.

un·bur·den (un bûr′dən) v.t. **1.** to free or relieve by disclosing or discussing something burdensome: to unburden oneself to a friend. **2.** to cast off (something burdensome) by disclosing or discussing; reveal: to unburden one's troubles. **3.** to rid of a burden or load.

un·but·ton (un but′ən) v.t. **1.** to open by unfastening the button or buttons of. **2.** to release (a button) from a buttonhole: to unbutton the top button of a shirt.

un·called-for (un kôld′fôr′) adj. **1.** not asked for or required: uncalled-for assistance. **2.** inappropriate and unnecessary; impertinent; unwarranted: uncalled-for criticism.

un·can·ny (un kan′ē) adj. **1.** strange and inexplicable, so as to inspire fear or wonder; eerie; weird: Uncanny sounds could often be heard in the deserted old house. **2.** so unusually good or acute as to seem superhuman: an uncanny talent for finding a bargain. —**un·can′ni·ly**, adv. —**un·can′ni·ness**, n.

un·cap (un kap′) v.t., **-capped, -cap·ping.** to take off the cap of: to uncap a bottle.

a	at	e	end	o	hot	u	up	hw	white		about
ā	ape	ē	me	ō	old	ū	use	ng	song	ə	taken
ä	far	i	it	ô	fork	ū	rule	th	thin		pencil
âr	care	ī	ice	oi	oil	u̇	pull	th	this		lemon
		îr	pierce	ou	out	ûr	turn	zh	measure		circus

U

unallowable	unamusing	unappreciated
unalloyed	unanimated	unappreciative
unalphabetized	unannounced	unapproved
unambiguous	unanswered	unarguable
unambitious	unanticipated	unarguably
unamicable	unapologetic	unaristocratic
unamplified	unapparent	unarmored
unamused	unappeased	unarrested

unarticulated	unassisted	unattractive
unashamed	unassumed	unauthentic
unaspirated	unathletic	unauthenticated
unaspiring	unattainable	unauthorized
unassertive	unattained	unavailability
unassessed	unattempted	unavailable
unassigned	unattested	unavenged
unassimilated	unattracted	unawed

un·cared-for (un kârd′fôr′) *adj.* not cared for or looked after; neglected: *an uncared-for public park.*

un·ceas·ing (un sē′sing) *adj.* without stop or end; continuous; incessant: *an unceasing barrage of requests.* —**un·ceas′ing·ly,** *adv.*

un·cen·sored (un sen′sərd) *adj.* not censored: *an uncensored movie.*

un·cer·e·mo·ni·ous (un′ser ə mō′nē əs) *adj.* **1.** without courtesy or consideration; abrupt; curt: *an unceremonious departure.* **2.** characterized by a lack of ceremony; informal. —**un′cer·e·mo′ni·ous·ly,** *adv.* —**un′cer·e·mo′ni·ous·ness,** *n.*

un·cer·tain (un sûr′tən) *adj.* **1.** not known, established, or settled for sure; doubtful: *The outcome of the game is still uncertain.* **2.** showing or experiencing doubt, hesitancy, or reservation; lacking confidence or sure knowledge: *I'm uncertain about your motives.* **3.** that cannot be depended upon to remain in one state or condition; subject to change; unsteady; variable: *uncertain weather.* **4.** not clearly defined; vague; ambiguous: *An uncertain shape loomed ahead in the darkness.* —**un·cer′tain·ly,** *adv.* —**un·cer′tain·ness,** *n.*

· **in no uncertain terms.** very clearly indeed; emphatically: *I gave my opinion of the performance in no uncertain terms.*

un·cer·tain·ty (un sûr′tən tē) *n., pl.* **-ties. 1.** the state or quality of being uncertain. **2.** something that is uncertain: *Tomorrow's weather is an uncertainty.*

uncertainty principle *Physics.* a principle of quantum mechanics according to which it is impossible to measure both of two related quantities, such as the position and the momentum of an elementary particle, with absolute accuracy.

un·chain (un chān′) *v.t.* to release from a chain or chains; set free.

un·change·a·ble (un chān′jə bəl) *adj.* that does not change or cannot be changed. —**un·change′a·bly,** *adv.*

un·changed (un chānjd′) *adj.* not changed.

un·chang·ing (un chān′jing) *adj.* not changing.

un·charged (un chärjd′) *adj.* having no electric charge, as a neutron or other subatomic particle.

un·char·i·ta·ble (un char′i tə bəl) *adj.* not generous or forgiving, esp. in judging others; severe; harsh. —**un·char′i·ta·ble·ness,** *n.* —**un·char′i·ta·bly,** *adv.*

un·chart·ed (un chär′tid) *adj.* not shown on a map, chart, or plan; unexplored; unknown: *uncharted islands, uncharted regions of the unconscious.*

un·chaste (un chāst′) *adj.* not pure, virtuous, or modest; not chaste. —**un·chaste′ly,** *adv.*

un·checked (un chekt′) *adj.* **1.** not halted or controlled; unrestrained: *the unchecked advance of enemy troops, unchecked anger.* **2.** not investigated, corrected, or verified: *unchecked test papers.*

un·chris·tian (un kris′chən) *adj.* **1.** not in accord with Christian teachings or ideals: *an unchristian attitude.* **2.** not of the Christian religion.

un·church (un chûrch′) *v.t.* **1.** to expel (a person) from a church; excommunicate. **2.** to deprive (a sect or congregation) of its standing as a church.

un·cial (un′shəl, -shē əl) *adj.* of or relating to a style of writing having letters similar to but more rounded than modern capitals, found in Greek and Latin manuscripts dating from about the fourth to the ninth centuries A.D.

$$A B C D E F G h j k L$$
$$M N O P q R S T U$$

uncial letters

—*n.* **1.** an uncial letter or writings. **2.** a manuscript written in uncials. [Latin *unciālis* relating to an inch or an ounce, from *uncia* a twelfth part, inch, ounce; referring to the large size of an uncial letter.]

un·ci·form (un′sə fôrm′) *adj.* **1.** *Anatomy.* shaped like a hook; hooklike. **2.** uncinate. [Modern Latin *unciformis,* from Latin *uncus* hook + -FORM.]

un·ci·nate (un′sə nit, -nāt′) *adj.* *Biology, Botany.* hooked or bent at the tip, as a thorn. [Latin *uncinātus* furnished with hooks, from *uncinus* hook.]

un·cir·cum·cised (un sûr′kəm sīzd′) *adj.* **1.** not circumcised. **2.** not Jewish; gentile. **3.** heathen.

un·civ·il (un siv′əl) *adj.* not polite or courteous; rude; disrespectful: *an uncivil reply.* —**un·civ′il·ly,** *adv.*

un·civ·i·lized (un siv′ə līzd′) *adj.* of a primitive or early stage of human social development; not civilized; savage.

un·clad (un klad′) *v.* a past tense and past participle of **un·clothe.** —*adj.* not clothed or dressed; naked; nude.

un·clasp (un klasp′) *v.t.* **1.** to open or loosen the clasp of; unfasten: *to unclasp a bracelet.* **2.** to release from a grasp or embrace.

un·clas·si·fied (un klas′ə fīd′) *adj.* **1.** not assigned to any particular class or category; not classified. **2.** not belonging to a secret or restricted class or category, as certain government documents.

un·cle (ung′kəl) *n.* **1.** the brother of a person's father or mother. **2.** the husband of a person's aunt. **3.** *Informal.* an elderly man. ➡ used as a friendly term of address. —*interj. Informal.* used to express surrender. [Anglo-Norman *uncle* brother of one's father or mother, from Latin *avunculus* a mother's brother, diminutive of *avus* grandfather.]

· **to say** (or **cry**) **uncle.** *Informal.* to give in; surrender.

un·clean (un klēn′) *adj.* **1.** not clean; dirty; foul. **2.** not morally pure; indecent: *unclean thoughts.* **3.** not fit for ceremonial or religious use; defiled; tainted. [Old English *unclǣne.*] —**un·clean′ness,** *n.*

un·clean·ly[1] (un klen′lē) *adj.* not cleanly; unclean. [Old English *unclǣnlīc.*] —**un·clean′li·ness,** *n.*

un·clean·ly[2] (un klēn′lē) *adv.* in an unclean manner. [Old English *unclǣnlīce.*]

un·clear (un klîr′) *adj.* not clearly or explicitly expressed; muddled; ambiguous: *Your meaning is unclear.*

un·clench (un klench′) *v.t., v.i.* to open or become opened from a clenched position.

Uncle Sam (sam) **1.** a figure personifying the government or people of the United States, represented as an old man dressed in a red, white, and blue costume with a top hat adorned with a band of stars. **2.** the government or people of the United States. [From the initials *U.S.* (abbreviation of *United States*), which were stamped on meat supplies for the U.S. Army during the War of 1812, supposedly by Samuel Wilson, American meat inspector, who was nicknamed *Uncle Sam.*]

Uncle Tom (tom) any black who is considered servile or unduly respectful to whites. ➡ considered derogatory and offensive. [From the faithful slave in the novel *Uncle Tom's Cabin* by Harriet Beecher Stowe, 1811-96, U.S. writer.]

un·cloak (un klōk′) *v.t.* **1.** to remove a cloak or cover from. **2.** to reveal; expose: *to uncloak a plot.* —*v.i.* to remove one's cloak or outer garment.

un·clothe (un klōth′) *v.t.,* **-clothed** or **-clad, -cloth·ing.** to remove the clothing or cover from; strip.

un·clothed (un klōthd′) *adj.* not clothed; stripped; naked.

un·coil (un koil′) *v.t.* to unwind. —*v.i.* to become unwound.

un·com·fort·a·ble (un kumf′tə bəl, -kum′fər tə-) *adj.* **1.** causing physical or mental distress or discomfort: *an uncomfortable mattress, an uncomfortable silence.* **2.** feeling mental or physical distress: *The athlete was uncomfortable speaking to reporters.* —**un·com′fort·a·ble·ness,** *n.* —**un·com′fort·a·bly,** *adv.*

un·com·mit·ted (un′kə mit′id) *adj.* not committed, esp. not devoted or pledged to a particular course of action, viewpoint, allegiance, or candidate: *There were over a hundred uncommitted delegates at the national convention.*

un·com·mon (un kom′ən) *adj.* **1.** rare; unusual: *Rain is uncommon in the desert.* **2.** remarkable or exceptional; outstanding; extraordinary: *The dancer moved with uncommon grace.* —**un·com′mon·ly,** *adv.* —**un·com′mon·ness,** *n.*

Synonyms Uncommon and **rare**[1] mean something that seldom occurs or is seldom encountered. **Uncommon** is a broad word that is applied to things or events that may or may not have value or importance: *Blue eyes are uncommon in people with very dark hair. The medal is given in recognition of uncommon heroism.* **Rare** often implies great value or interest: *The rare drawings sold for a record amount at the auction.*

un·com·mu·ni·ca·tive (un′kə mū′ni kā′tiv, -kə tiv) *adj.* not inclined to communicate or disclose information readily; reticent;

unbaked	unbrace	unbridged	unbuttoned	uncataloged	uncharacteristic
unbandage	unbraid	unbridle	uncage	uncategorical	uncharismatic
unbaptized	unbranched	unbrotherly	uncalculated	uncelebrated	unchartered
unbefitting	unbranded	unbruised	uncalculating	uncertified	unchastened
unblamable	unbreakable	unbrushed	uncanonical	unchallengeable	unchewed
unblamed	unbred	unburied	uncapitalized	unchallenged	unchilled
unbleached	unbribable	unbusinesslike	uncaring	unchallenging	unchivalrous
unblock	unbridgeable	unbuttered	uncarpeted	unchaperoned	unchosen

taciturn. —**un′com·mu′ni·ca′tive·ly,** *adv.* —**un′com·mu′ni·ca′tive·ness,** *n.*

un·com·pli·men·ta·ry (un′kom plə men′trē, -tə rē) *adj.* not complimentary or favorable; insulting; derogatory: *an uncomplimentary remark.*

un·com·pro·mis·ing (un kom′prə mī′zing) *adj.* not open to change or compromise; unyielding; inflexible: *an uncompromising attitude.* —**un′com·pro′mis·ing·ly,** *adv.*

un·con·cern (un′kən sûrn′) *n.* **1.** a lack of interest or concern. **2.** freedom from care or anxiety.

un·con·cerned (un′kən sûrnd′) *adj.* **1.** not interested or concerned (with *with*): *to be unconcerned with someone else's problems.* **2.** free from care or anxiety; untroubled (often with *about* or *for*): *They were unconcerned about their own safety on the island.* —**un·con·cern·ed·ly** (un′kən sûr′nid lē), *adv.* —**un′con·cern′ed·ness,** *n.* —For Synonyms, see **indifferent.**

un·con·di·tion·al (un′kən dish′ə nəl) *adj.* not limited by a condition or conditions; absolute; complete: *an unconditional guarantee.* —**un′con·di′tion·al·ly,** *adv.*

un·con·di·tioned (un′kən dish′ənd) *adj.* **1.** unconditional. **2.** *Psychology.* not acquired as a result of a learning or conditioning process; natural: *an unconditioned response.*

un·con·firmed (un′kən fûrmd′) *adj.* not firmly established or proved; tentative: *unconfirmed election returns.*

un·con·for·mi·ty (un′kən fôr′mi tē) *n.* a surface representing a hiatus in the sequence in which sedimentary rocks were deposited.

un·con·nec·ted (un′kə nek′tid) *adj.* **1.** not joined or fastened together; separate; distinct: *Two unconnected buildings make up the plant.* **2.** having no order or sequence; incoherent; rambling: *an unconnected speech.* —**un′con·nec′ted·ly,** *adv.* —**un′con·nec′ted·ness,** *n.*

un·con·quer·a·ble (un kong′kər ə bəl) *adj.* that cannot be vanquished or overcome: *an unconquerable army, unconquerable courage.* —**un′con′quer·a·bly,** *adv.*

un·con·scion·a·ble (un kon′shə nə bəl) *adj.* **1.** not influenced, guided, or restrained by conscience; unscrupulous; unprincipled: *an unconscionable liar.* **2.** beyond what is reasonable or just; excessive; immoderate; outrageous: *an unconscionable demand, an unconscionable price.* —**un′con′scion·a·bly,** *adv.*

un·con·scious (un kon′shəs) *adj.* **1.** temporarily without consciousness, as in a coma: *The driver was unconscious for three days after the accident.* **2.** not knowing or perceiving; unaware: *unconscious of one's sloppy appearance.* **3.** not done on purpose; without conscious realization or intent: *an unconscious pun, an unconscious habit.* **4.** lacking thoughtful awareness of oneself, others, or one's environment. **5.** not endowed with mind or consciousness: *unconscious stones.* **6.** *Psychoanalysis.* of, relating to, or involving mental or emotional processes that an individual is not ordinarily aware of or capable of perceiving: *unconscious guilt, an unconscious death wish.* —*n. Psychoanalysis.* the part of the mind that contains wishes, memories, and other mental phenomena that are not consciously perceived but that influence conscious thought and behavior. —**un·con′scious·ly,** *adv.* —**un·con′scious·ness,** *n.*

un·con·sti·tu·tion·al (un′kon sti tü′shə nəl, -tū′-) *adj.* not in keeping with the constitution of a nation, state, or group, esp. the Constitution of the United States. —**un·con·sti·tu·tion·al·i·ty** (un′kon sti tü′shə nal′i tē, -tū′-), *n.* —**un′con·sti·tu′tion·al·ly,** *adv.*

un·con·trol·la·ble (un′kən trō′lə bəl) *adj.* that cannot be held in check or restrained: *uncontrollable laughter.* —**un′con·trol′la·bly,** *adv.*

un·con·ven·tion·al (un′kən ven′shə nəl) *adj.* not adhering to convention; out of the ordinary: *unconventional clothing, an unconventional lifestyle.* —**un′con·ven′tion·al·ly,** *adv.*

un·con·ven·tion·al·i·ty (un′kən ven′shə nal′i tē) *n.* the state or quality of being unconventional.

un·cork (un kôrk′) *v.t.* **1.** to draw or remove the cork from. **2.** *Informal.* to let loose or release; unleash: *to uncork pent-up anger.*

un·count·ed (un koun′tid) *adj.* **1.** too many to count; innumerable: *Modern medical research has benefited uncounted millions of*

people. **2.** not counted or enumerated: *A few votes were still uncounted.*

un·cou·ple (un kup′əl) *v.,* **-pled, -pling.** —*v.t.* **1.** to disconnect or unfasten; detach: *to uncouple railroad cars.* **2.** to set free (dogs) leashed together in couples. —*v.i.* to become disconnected.

un·couth (un küth′) *adj.* **1.** lacking culture or refinement; crude: *uncouth manners.* **2.** awkward or clumsy; ungainly. **3.** *Archaic.* not common or familiar; rare; strange. [Old English *uncūth* unknown, strange, from *un-* not + *cūth* known, familiar, past participle of *cunnan* to know.] —**un·couth′ly,** *adv.* —**un·couth′ness,** *n.*

Synonyms Uncouth, crude, rough, and boorish mean lacking in civility or social refinement. **Uncouth** suggests generally ill-mannered behavior, whether the result of rudeness, awkwardness, or ignorance of accepted standards: *The rock star was popular with young people, but was considered uncouth by many of their parents.* **Crude** implies an undeveloped and untaught state: *The backwoods people were lacking in manners, but their warmth and kindness made up for their crude ways.* **Rough** denotes a harsh or violent crudeness: *We were frightened by the rough looks we got from the group lounging around in the doorway.* **Boorish** is usually applied to intentional discourtesy: *The children were rude to the guests, but their boorish behavior was an attempt to gain their parents' attention.*

un·cov·er (un kuv′ər) *v.t.* **1.** to lay bare or make known; bring to light; disclose: *The police investigation uncovered a conspiracy to kidnap the ambassador.* **2.** to remove the cover or covering from: *Uncover the dish before you put it in the oven.* **3.** to expose to view by removing a cover or covering: *The archaeologists uncovered relics buried by the desert sands.* **4.** to remove a hat, cap, or the like from (one's head) as a sign of respect. —*v.i.* **1.** to remove a cover or covering. **2.** to bare the head as a sign of respect.

un·cross (un krôs′) *v.t.* to change from a crossed position: *to uncross one's legs.*

unc·tion (ungk′shən) *n.* **1.** the act of anointing as part of a religious or ceremonial ritual. **2.** a substance used in anointing, such as oil. **3.** something that soothes, comforts, or restores; balm. **4.** deeply felt emotion, as in religion. **5.** exaggerated or affected emotion, as in language or manner. [Latin *unctiō* an anointing.]

unc·tu·ous (ungk′chü əs) *adj.* **1.** characterized by exaggerated or affected emotion; excessively suave, smooth, or ingratiating: *an unctuous follower, unctuous flattery.* **2.** like or having the characteristics of oil or ointment; slippery to the touch; greasy. [Medieval Latin *unctuosus* oily, greasy, from Latin *unctus* an anointing.] —**unc′tu·ous·ly,** *adv.* —**unc′tu·ous·ness,** *n.*

un·cul·ti·vat·ed (un kul′tə vā′tid) *adj.* **1.** not prepared for growing crops: *uncultivated soil.* **2.** not cultured or refined: *an uncultivated person.*

un·cured (un kyùrd′) *adj.* **1.** not made well or healthy: *an uncured patient.* **2.** not prepared for use, as by drying: *uncured tobacco.*

un·curl (un kûrl′) *v.t., v.i.* to make or become straight.

un·cut (un kut′) *adj.* **1.** not cut: *uncut flowers.* **2.** not shortened or edited; unabridged: *an uncut version of a film.* **3.** not changed or shaped by cutting: *an uncut diamond.* **4.** (of a book) not having the page edges slit open.

un·dat·ed (un dā′tid) *adj.* not marked with a date.

un·daunt·ed (un dôn′tid, -dän′-) *adj.* not intimidated or discouraged; fearless; intrepid. —**un·daunt′ed·ly,** *adv.*

un·de·ceive (un′di sēv′) *v.t.,* **-ceived, -ceiv·ing.** to free from deception, illusion, or error.

un·de·cid·ed (un′di sī′did) *adj.* **1.** not having one's mind made up; not having reached a decision: *I'm still undecided about what to wear to the dance.* **2.** not yet determined or settled: *The*

a	at	e	end	o	hot	u	up	hw	white		about
ā	ape	ē	me	ō	old	ū	use	ng	song		taken
ä	far	i	it	ô	fork	ù	rule	th	thin	ə	pencil
âr	care	ī	ice	oi	oil	u	pull	th	this		lemon
		îr	pierce	ou	out	ûr	turn	zh	measure		circus

unchristened	uncoerced	uncompetitive	unconcealed	unconscientious	unconsummated
unclaimed	uncollected	uncomplaining	unconcluded	unconsecrated	uncontaminated
unclarified	uncolonized	uncompleted	uncondemned	unconsidered	uncontestable
uncleaned	uncombed	uncomplicated	uncondensed	unconsoled	uncontested
uncleared	uncombined	uncomprehending	unconducive	unconsolidated	uncontradicted
unclog	uncommendable	uncomprehensible	unconfined	unconstrained	uncontrolled
unclouded	uncommercial	uncompromised	uncongenial	unconstricted	uncontroversial
uncluttered	uncompensated	unconcealable	unconquered	unconsumed	unconversant

outcome of the election is still undecided. —**un′de·cid′ed·ly,** *adv.* —**un′de·cid′ed·ness,** *n.*

un·de·clared (un′di klârd′) *adj.* not announced or proclaimed: *an undeclared war, an undeclared winner.*

un·de·feat·ed (un′di fē′tid) *adj.* not having been beaten or defeated.

un·dem·o·crat·ic (un′dem ə krat′ik) *adj.* not agreeing with or supporting the ideals or principles of democracy; not democratic. —**un′dem·o·crat′i·cal·ly,** *adv.*

un·de·mon·stra·tive (un′di mon′strə tiv) *adj.* not given to showing affection or feeling; reserved: *The family was undemonstrative in public but affectionate at home.* —**un′de·mon′stra·tive·ly,** *adv.* —**un′de·mon′stra·tive·ness,** *n.*

un·de·ni·a·ble (un′di nī′ə bəl) *adj.* **1.** that cannot be doubted or denied; irrefutable: *undeniable evidence, the undeniable truth of a statement.* **2.** unquestionably good; outstanding; excellent: *the undeniable value of good friendship.* —**un′de·ni′a·bly,** *adv.*

un·der (un′dər) *prep.* **1.** in a place or position down from or lower than; beneath: *I put the paper under a pile of books. Look under the bed for your shoe.* **2.** below the surface of: *The splinter went under the skin.* **3.** in a position so as to be covered, sheltered, or protected by: *under an umbrella, three families living under one roof.* **4.** smaller or less than in number, degree, or amount: *under eight pounds, under an hour.* **5.** lower than the usual, needed, or required amount: *a height just under the minimum needed to become a Marine.* **6.** subject to the authority or guidance of; subordinate to: *to study under a professional, to serve under a general.* **7.** subject to the force or action of: *The foundation of the building is under great pressure. The fire is under control.* **8.** in the process of: *under construction, under consideration.* **9.** in conformity with; according to: *Under the new regulations, only members can use the gym.* **10.** required or bound by the terms, limitations, or conditions of: *under contract, under oath.* **11.** because of; considering: *We will not enter the contest under the existing circumstances.* **12.** during the reign or administration of: *The Peace Corps began under President Kennedy.* **13.** in the category of: *That book should be under "Medical History."* **14.** beneath the guise or cover of: *The writer traveled under an alias.* **15.** with authorization of; attested by: *under the president's seal.* —*adv.* **1.** in or into a position beneath or lower than something; below the surface: *The raft was sucked under by the whirlpool.* **2.** less than a certain degree or amount; downward through a specified range: *The book is for children six years and under.* **3.** so as to be covered, sheltered, or concealed: *The car was snowed under.* **4.** in or into a subordinate position or status; in subjection or submission. —*adj.* lower in position, rank, degree, or amount: *the under surface of a leaf.* [Old English *under* beneath, below.]

· **to go under. a.** to fail, as a business. **b.** to succumb or submit to; yield: *to go under a spell.*

under- *combining form* **1.** located in a lower place or position: *underpass.* **2.** located beneath a surface or covering: *underwear, underwater, underground.* **3.** smaller or less than is usual, normal, or required; insufficient; inadequate: *underweight, underage.* **4.** lower or inferior in rank, status, or importance; subordinate: *undergraduate, understudy.* **5.** subdued; restrained: *undertone.* [From UNDER.]

un·der·a·chiev·er (un′dər ə chē′vər) *n.* a person whose performance or achievement, esp. in school, is below his or her potential.

un·der·age (un′dər āj′) *adj.* not of the usual, required, or legal age.

un·der·arm (un′dər ärm′) *adj.* **1.** of, relating to, or used in the armpit; under the arm: *underarm perspiration, an underarm deodorant.* **2.** underhand *(def. 1).* —*n.* the depression under the arm at the shoulder; armpit. —*adv.* underhand *(def. 1).*

un·der·bel·ly (un′dər bel′ē) *n., pl.* **-lies. 1.** the underside of something, esp. the lower abdominal region of an animal. **2.** any sensitive, weak, or vulnerable part.

un·der·bid (un′dər bid′) *v.t.,* **-bid, -bid·ding. 1.** to bid lower than (a competitor), as for a business contract. **2.** to bid less than the full value of (a hand of cards). —**un′der·bid′der,** *n.*

un·der·bred (un′dər bred′) *adj.* **1.** of mixed stock; not purebred: *an underbred horse.* **2.** lacking good manners; ill-mannered; vulgar.

un·der·brush (un′dər brush′) *n.* a growth of bushes, shrubs, or similar plants beneath the large trees in a wood or forest.

un·der·car·riage (un′dər kar′ij) *n.* **1.** a supporting framework, as of an automobile. **2.** the landing gear of an airplane.

un·der·charge (*v.,* un′dər chärj′; *n.,* un′dər chärj′) *v.t.,* **-charged, -charg·ing. 1.** to charge (someone) too small a price. **2.** to supply or load with an insufficient charge, as a gun. —*n.* an insufficient or inadequate charge.

un·der·class (un′dər klas′) *n.* a class of people at or near the lowest economic and social position in society. —*adj.* relating to or being a member of the underclass.

un·der·class·man (un′dər klas′mən) *n., pl.* **-men** (-mən). a freshman or sophomore in a secondary school or college.

un·der·clothes (un′dər klōz′, -klōthz′) *pl. n.* underwear.

un·der·cloth·ing (un′dər klō′thing) *n.* underwear.

un·der·coat (un′dər kōt′) *n.* **1.** a protective coating of a tarlike substance applied to the underside of an automobile to prevent rusting. **2.** a coat of paint, varnish, or the like applied to a surface before the final coat. Also *(defs. 1, 2),* **un′der·coat′ing. 3.** underfur.

un·der·cov·er (un′dər kuv′ər, un′dər kuv′ər) *adj.* working or done in secret, as in spying or secret investigation: *an undercover agent for a government.*

un·der·cur·rent (un′dər kûr′ənt, -kur′-) *n.* **1.** a current, as of water or air, under another current or below a surface. **2.** an underlying feeling or emotion, esp. one that contradicts what is visible or apparent: *an undercurrent of fear.*

un·der·cut (*v.,* un′dər kut′, un′dər kut′; *n.,* un′dər kut′) *v.t.,* **-cut, -cut·ting. 1.** to sell or work for lower payment than (a competitor). **2.** to weaken, impair, or destroy the effect or validity of; undermine: *to undercut an argument with wit.* **3.** to cut under or away, as in carving or in mining, esp. in order to leave a portion overhanging. **4.** to give a backspin to (a ball) by hitting on the underside, as in golf or tennis. —*n.* **1.** the act or result of cutting under or away. **2.** a notch cut in a tree below the level at which it is to be sawed through to control the direction in which it falls.

un·der·de·vel·oped (un′dər di vel′əpt) *adj.* **1.** inadequately or insufficiently developed: *underdeveloped muscles.* **2.** developing. **3.** *Photography.* (of a negative) insufficiently treated with developing solution and thus not having the required degree of contrast.

un·der·dog (un′dər dôg′) *n.* **1.** a person who is thought most likely to lose, as in a contest or game. **2.** a victim of social, political, or economic injustice.

un·der·done (un′dər dun′) *adj.* not completely or properly cooked: *an underdone roast.*

un·der·es·ti·mate (*v.,* un′dər es′tə māt′; *n.,* un′dər es′tə mit, -māt′) *v.t.,* **-mat·ed, -mat·ing. 1.** to estimate at too low an amount, quantity, or rate: *The contractor underestimated the building costs.* **2.** to place too low a value on; have too low an opinion of: *You underestimate my intelligence.* —*n.* too low an estimate. —**un′der·es′ti·ma′tion,** *n.*

un·der·ex·pose (un′dər ek spōz′) *v.t.,* **-posed, -pos·ing.** *Photography.* to expose (film or a plate) to too little light or for too short a period of time to produce a satisfactory picture. —**un′der·ex·po′sure,** *n.*

un·der·feed (un′dər fēd′) *v.t.,* **-fed** (-fed′), **-feed·ing. 1.** to feed too little, esp. to feed less than is necessary for adequate nourishment. **2.** to feed (a fire) with fuel from below.

un·der·foot (un′dər fut′) *also,* **under foot.** *adv.* **1.** in the way: *The baby always leaves toys lying underfoot.* **2.** beneath the foot or feet; on the ground: *It was icy underfoot.* —*adj.* lying beneath the foot or feet.

un·der·fur (un′dər fûr′) *n.* the thick, soft, and sometimes curly fur beneath an outer, coarser layer of long hairs on many mammals. It serves as an insulating layer, esp. on aquatic mammals, as beavers and seals, and constitutes the fleece of domestic sheep. Also, **undercoat, undergrowth.**

un·der·gar·ment (un′dər gär′mənt) *n.* an article of underwear.

un·der·go (un′dər gō′) *v.t.,* **-went, -gone** (-gôn′, -gon′), **-go·ing. 1.** to pass through; experience: *The neighborhood is undergoing a change for the better.* **2.** to bear up under; suffer; endure: *to undergo a serious operation.*

un·der·grad·u·ate (un′dər graj′ü it) *n.* a college or university student who has not yet received a degree, esp. a bachelor's degree.

unconverted	uncorrected	uncrowded	undebatable	undefinable	undenominational
unconvertible	uncorroborated	uncrystallized	undecayed	undefined	undependable
unconvinced	uncorrupted	uncultivable	undecipherable	undelineated	undescribed
unconvincing	uncowed	uncultured	undeciphered	undeliverable	undeserved
uncooked	uncrate	uncurbed	undeclinable	undemanding	undeserving
uncooperative	uncreative	uncurtailed	undecorated	undemonstrable	undesignated
uncoordinated	uncredited	uncustomary	undefended	undemonstrably	undesired
uncordial	uncritical	undamaged	undefiled	undenied	undesirous

un·der·ground (*adj., adv.,* un′dər ground′; *n.,* un′dər ground′) *adj.* **1.** below the surface of the earth: *an underground passage, underground repairs.* **2.** hidden; secret: *an underground political movement.* **3.** radical, unconventional, or avant-garde in style, ideas, or activities: *an underground movie, an underground newspaper.* —*n.* **1.** a group operating secretly to resist or overthrow a government in power or an enemy occupation. **2.** an underground group or movement, esp. in art; the avant-garde. **3.** a place or space below the surface of the earth, such as a tunnel. **4.** *British.* subway *(def. 1).* —*adv.* **1.** below the surface of the earth: *The workers dug a tunnel underground.* **2.** in or into hiding; in secret: *The rebels went underground to avoid capture.*

underground railroad 1. subway *(def. 1).* Also, **underground railway. 2.** *also,* **Underground Railroad.** before the abolition of slavery in the United States, a system by which opponents of slavery secretly helped runaway slaves reach freedom by transporting, escorting, or guiding them to Canada or to the Free States.

un·der·growth (un′dər grōth′) *n.* **1.** a growth of small plants and other vegetation beneath or among the larger trees of a forest; underbrush. **2.** underfur.

un·der·hand (un′dər hand′) *adv.* **1.** with the hand held below the level of the elbow: *to toss a ball underhand.* **2.** underhanded. —*adj.* **1.** performed with the hand held below the level of the elbow or shoulder. **2.** underhanded.

un·der·hand·ed (un′dər han′did) *adj., adv.* done in a secret, treacherous manner; deceitful; sly: *an underhanded trick.* —**un′·der·hand′ed·ly,** *adv.* —**un′der·hand′ed·ness,** *n.*

un·der·lay (*v.,* un′dər lā′; *n.,* un′dər lā′) *v.t.,* **-laid** (-lād′), **-laying. 1.** to lay or place (something) under or below. **2.** to provide with a base or lining. **3.** to raise or support by providing with a base or lining. —*n.* something laid beneath, esp. paper placed under type to raise it to the height required for printing. [Old French *underlecgan* to place beneath, support by placing something beneath.]

un·der·lie (un′dər lī′) *v.t.,* **-lay, -lain** (-lān′), **-ly·ing. 1.** to be located under or below: *Rocky soil frequently underlies rich topsoil.* **2.** to be the basis, cause, or foundation of: *What motives underlay your actions?* [Old English *underlīcgan* to be subject to, submit to.]

un·der·line (*v.,* un′dər līn′; *n.,* un′dər līn′) *v.t.,* **-lined, -lin·ing. 1.** to draw a line or lines under. **2.** to emphasize; stress: *to underline a need for caution.* —*n.* a line drawn under words or other writing for emphasis or to indicate italics.

un·der·ling (un′dər ling) *n.* a person in an inferior position who must take orders; lackey.

un·der·lip (un′dər lip′) *n.* the lower lip.

un·der·ly·ing (un′dər lī′ing) *adj.* **1.** lying under or below: *an underlying rock stratum.* **2.** basic; fundamental: *What are the underlying principles of the movement?* **3.** hidden or obscure; concealed: *an underlying motive.*

un·der·mine (un′dər mīn′) *v.t.,* **-mined, -min·ing. 1.** to weaken, impair, or destroy slowly and insidiously; sap: *to undermine a person's confidence.* **2.** to weaken by wearing away at the foundation or base; erode: *The river is undermining the bank.* **3.** to dig a mine or passage under; dig below.

un·der·most (un′dər mōst′) *adj., adv.* lowest in place or position; bottom.

un·der·neath (un′dər nēth′) *prep.* **1.** in a lower place or position; on the underside of: *The dog rolled the ball underneath the chair.* **2.** under the guise or appearance of: *Underneath their gruff exterior, they are really nice people.* **3.** under the authority or control of; subordinate to. —*adv.* lower than or under something; on the underside. [Old English *underneothan* beneath, below, from *under* (see UNDER) + *neothan* below.]

un·der·nour·ish (un′dər nûr′ish) *v.t.* to fail to provide with enough or proper food and other substances necessary for life and growth. —**un′der·nour′ish·ment,** *n.*

un·der·pants (un′dər pants′) *pl. n.* an undergarment designed to cover the loins, sometimes extending to cover the thighs.

un·der·part (un′dər pärt′) *n.* **1.** the lower, ventral portion of an animal's body: *a bird with white underparts.* **2.** a subordinate part or role.

un·der·pass (un′dər pas′) *n.* a passage or road that goes

underneath, esp. the section that crosses and passes under another road, a bridge, or the like.

un·der·pay (un′dər pā′) *v.t.,* **-paid** (-pād′), **-pay·ing.** to pay less than due or deserved: *to underpay a bill, to underpay a clerk.* —**un·der·pay·ment** (un′dər pā′mənt, un′dər pā′-), *n.*

un·der·pin (un′dər pin′) *v.t.,* **-pinned, -pin·ning. 1.** to support or strengthen from below, as by laying or reinforcing the foundation of a building or wall. **2.** to give support to; substantiate; corroborate: *to underpin an argument with facts.*

un·der·pin·ning (un′dər pin′ing) *n.* **1.** the materials or structure used to support or strengthen a building, wall, or the like from below. **2.** anything that supports: *Education is the underpinning of democracy.* **3.** **underpinnings.** *Informal.* the legs.

un·der·play (un′dər plā′) *v.t.* **1.** to give little or inadequate emphasis or attention to; understate: *The press underplayed the real reasons for the incident.* **2.** to act or play with subtlety and restraint: *The star underplayed the melodramatic scene.*

un·der·priv·i·leged (un′dər priv′ə lijd) *adj.* deprived of certain widely available advantages, such as adequate housing and education, because of poverty or social status: *an underprivileged child.*

un·der·pro·duc·tion (un′dər prə duk′shən) *n.* production that is below capacity or inadequate to meet the demand.

un·der·rate (un′dər rāt′) *v.t.,* **-rat·ed, -rat·ing.** to rate too low; underestimate.

un·der·score (*v.,* un′dər skôr′; *n.,* un′dər skôr′) *v.t.,* **-scored, -scor·ing.** underline. —*n.* underline.

un·der·sea (un′dər sē′, -sē′) *adj.* existing, used, or designed for use beneath the surface of the sea. —*adv. also,* **un·der·seas** (un′dər sēz′). beneath the surface of the sea.

un·der·sec·re·tar·y (un′dər sek′ri ter′ē) *n., pl.* **-tar·ies.** an official who ranks directly below the secretary of a government department.

un·der·sell (un′dər sel′) *v.t.,* **-sold** (-sōld′), **-sell·ing. 1.** to sell at a lower price than (a competitor). **2.** to understate the value or merit of: *Don't undersell your own abilities.*

un·der·sher·iff (un′dər sher′if) *n.* a sheriff's deputy, esp. one who assumes the duties of sheriff in the sheriff's absence.

un·der·shirt (un′dər shûrt′) *n.* a collarless undergarment for the torso, usually having short sleeves or no sleeves.

un·der·shoot (un′dər shüt′, un′dər shüt′) *v.t.,* **-shot, -shoot·ing. 1.** to shoot a missile or land an aircraft short of (the mark): *I undershot the target. The pilot undershot the runway.* **2.** (of a missile or aircraft) to hit or land short of (a target or landing area).

un·der·shot (un′dər shot′; *v., also* un′dər shot′) *v.* the past tense and past participle of **undershoot.** —*adj.* **1.** (of a waterwheel) driven by water passing beneath. **2.** having the lower jaw protruding beyond the upper; underslung.

un·der·side (un′dər sīd′) *n.* the bottom side or surface of something.

un·der·sign (un′dər sīn′, un′dər sīn′) *v.t.* to sign one's name at the end of (a document); affix one's signature to.

un·der·signed (*adj.,* un′dər sīnd′, un′dər sīnd′; *n.,* un′dər sīnd′) *adj.* **1.** being the person whose signature appears at the end of a document: *undersigned persons.* **2.** signed at the end of a document: *undersigned names.* —*n.* **the undersigned.** the person or persons who have signed a document.

undershot waterwheel

un·der·sized (un′dər sīzd′) *adj.* having less than the normal, usual, or proper size.

un·der·skirt (un′dər skûrt′) *n.* a petticoat worn under a skirt.

un·der·slung (un′dər slung′) *adj.* **1.** attached to and suspended

a	at	e	end	o	hot	u	up	hw	white		about
ā	ape	ē	me	ō	old	ū	use	ng	song	ə	taken
ä	far	i	it	ô	fork	ü	rule	th	thin		pencil
âr	care	ī	ice	oi	oil	u̇	pull	th	this		lemon
				îr	pierce	ou	out	ûr	turn	zh	measure		circus

from or beneath something, as an automobile frame from the axles. **2.** protruding from beneath, as a lower jaw.

un·der·stand (un′dər stand′) v., **-stood**, **-stand·ing.** —v.t. **1.** to grasp the meaning or significance of; be clear about: *I don't understand what you mean.* **2.** to be thoroughly familiar and in sympathy or agreement with: *The two friends understand each other completely.* **3.** to know well or have mastery of; comprehend: *I don't understand Russian.* **4.** to regard as meaning: *The detective understood the offer of money as a bribe.* **5.** to assume as plausible, factual, or truthful; conclude: *Am I to understand that you will not go with us?* **6.** to be informed; learn: *I understand that the proposal was vetoed.* **7.** to accept or regard as a condition or stipulation; take as agreed or settled: *I understand that I can return the tickets before the performance and still get my money back.* —v.i. **1.** to grasp the meaning or significance of something; master: *Even though I've explained it several times, they still don't understand.* **2.** to be told or assume: *You were going to Colorado, or so I understood.* **3.** to be sympathetic: *If you are unable to come, I will understand.* [Old English *understandan* to grasp the meaning, comprehend; literally, to stand under.] —For Synonyms (*v.t.*), see **know.**

un·der·stand·a·ble (un′dər stan′də bəl) adj. able to be grasped, explained, or sympathized with: *an understandable explanation.* —**un′der·stand′a·bly,** adv.

un·der·stand·ing (un′dər stan′ding) n. **1.** the mental process of comprehending or grasping the meaning of something: *I have an understanding of the situation.* **2.** thorough knowledge or mastery: *an understanding of thermonuclear dynamics.* **3.** an individual judgment or specific interpretation; opinion; conclusion: *It was my understanding that we would meet after school.* **4.** a comprehension and settlement of differences, as between friends: *We came to an understanding that we were both partially at fault.* **5.** an informal or secret compact or the subject of such a compact: *The understanding was that the cease-fire would be in effect immediately.* **6.** the faculty or power by which one understands; the intellect; intelligence: *a person of superior understanding.* —adj. perceptive and helpful, esp. in dealing with people or emotions; sympathetic: *a trusted and understanding friend.* —**un′der·stand′ing·ly,** adv.

un·der·state (un′dər stāt′) v.t., **-stat·ed**, **-stat·ing. 1.** to tell about or state too weakly or with too little emphasis. **2.** to state less than the truth about, as a quantity: *to understate one's age.*

un·der·state·ment (un′dər stāt′mənt) n. **1.** a statement that is inaccurate or incomplete, esp. one that tends to make something seem less important or less dramatic than it really is, often used for ironical effect. **2.** deliberate restraint in expression.

un·der·stood (un′dər stůd′) v. the past tense and past participle of **understand.** —adj. **1.** agreed or settled upon: *It's understood, then, that we'll meet at the corner at four o'clock.* **2.** *Grammar.* omitted but implied in a statement. For example, in the sentence *I'm willing if you are,* the word *willing* is understood to be repeated after the word *are.*

un·der·sto·ry (un′dər stôr′ē) n., pl. **-stor·ies.** the undergrowth lying beneath the top branches of a forest, usually considered as bushes and shrubs of intermediate height and distinguished from even lower-growing ground cover. [UNDER- + STORY².]

un·der·stud·y (un′dər stud′ē) n., pl. **-stud·ies.** in a play, opera, or the like, a performer who learns another performer's role in order to substitute, when necessary, for that person. —v., **-stud·ied**, **-stud·y·ing.** —v.t. **1.** to learn (a role) in order to substitute, when necessary, for the regular performer. **2.** to act as an understudy to (a performer). —v.i. to be an understudy.

un·der·take (un′dər tāk′) v.t., **-took**, **-tak·en**, **-tak·ing. 1.** to take upon oneself; set about or agree to do: *to undertake a trip by train, to undertake a task.* **2.** to accept or commit oneself to the charge or responsibility of: *The nurse undertook the invalid's care and feeding.* **3.** to give a promise or pledge; affirm; assert (often with *to*): *I undertook to have the report completed by Friday. The committee undertook that all the facts were correct.*

un·der·tak·er (def. 1, un′dər tā′kər; def. 2, un′dər tā′kər) n. **1.** a person whose job or business is arranging funerals and the burial or cremation of the dead. **2.** a person who undertakes something, such as a task.

un·der·tak·ing (defs. 1, 3, un′dər tā′king; def. 2, un′dər tā′king) n. **1.** something that is undertaken, such as a task or enterprise:

Writing a book is a major undertaking. **2.** the business of an undertaker. **3.** a pledge or promise. —For Synonyms, see **project.**

un·der-the-coun·ter (un′dər thə koun′tər) adj. *Informal.* given, sold, or transacted secretly and often unlawfully; unauthorized. Also, **un·der-the-ta·ble** (un′dər thə tā′bəl).

un·der·tone (un′dər tōn′) n. **1.** a low or subdued tone: *to speak in undertones.* **2.** a feeling or meaning that is partly hidden; undercurrent: *an undertone of reproach.* **3.** a subdued color, esp. a background color that is seen through various other colors: *The canvas was painted in a blue undertone to emphasize its eerie quality.*

un·der·took (un′dər tůk′) the past tense of **undertake.**

un·der·tow (un′dər tō′) n. a strong current flowing in a direction contrary to that of the surface current, esp. the backward pull of water from waves breaking against the shore.

un·der·val·ue (un′dər val′ū) v.t., **-ued**, **-u·ing.** to underestimate; underrate. —**un′der·val′u·a′tion,** n.

un·der·wa·ter (un′dər wô′tər, -wot′ər) adj. **1.** existing or carried on beneath the surface of the water: *underwater vegetation, underwater exploration.* **2.** used or designed for use beneath the surface of the water: *underwater camera.* —adv. beneath the surface of the water: *to travel underwater in a submarine.*

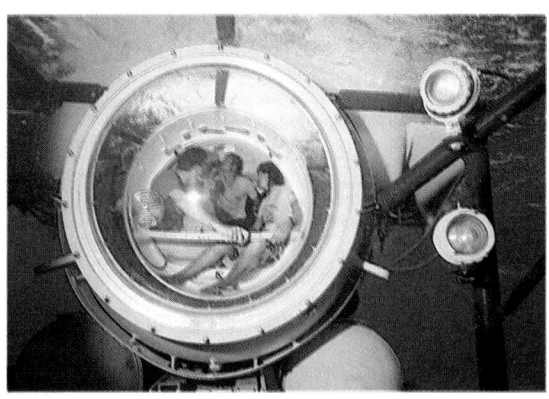

underwater laboratory

un·der·way (un′dər wā′) adj. happening while moving, traveling, or otherwise in progress: *an underway radio contact between two ships at sea.*

un·der·wear (un′dər wâr′) n. clothing worn under a person's outer clothes, usually next to the skin. Also, **underclothes, underclothing.**

un·der·weight (adj., un′dər wāt′; n., un′dər wāt′) adj. less than the normal, desirable, or required weight; weighing too little. —n. weight below what is normal, desirable, or required.

un·der·went (un′dər went′) the past tense of **undergo.**

un·der·wood (un′dər wůd′) n. underbrush; undergrowth.

un·der·world (un′dər wûrld′) n. **1.** that part of society involved in criminal activities, esp. organized crime. **2.** *also,* **Underworld.** in mythology, the dwelling place of the dead. **3.** any region below the surface of the earth or of a body of water. **4.** the opposite side of the earth. **5.** *Archaic.* the world below the heavens; earth.

un·der·write (un′dər rīt′) v., **-wrote** (-rōt′), **-writ·ten** (-rit′ən), **-writ·ing.** —v.t. **1.** to provide the money or guarantee financial support for (a business venture or other undertaking): *to underwrite a theatrical production.* **2.** to subscribe or agree to, as by signing one's name; concur with: *to underwrite a decision.* **3.a.** to sign (an insurance policy), thereby assuming liability for losses or damage specified in the policy. **b.** to cover with insurance; insure. **c.** to assume liability to the amount of (a specified sum) by way of insurance. **4.a.** to agree to buy (an issue of stocks or bonds to be sold to the public) on a specified date and at a specified price. **b.** to agree to buy (those stocks or bonds of a certain issue that are not bought by others before a specified date).

uneaten	unembarrassed	unending	unenlarged	unenterprising	unesthetic
uneclipsed	unembellished	unendorsed	unenlightened	unentertaining	unestimated
uneconomic	unemotional	unendowed	unenlightening	unenthusiastic	unethical
uneconomical	unemphatic	unendurable	unenlivened	unenticing	unexaggerated
unedible	unemptied	unenduring	unenriched	unenviable	unexamined
unedifying	unenclosed	unenforceable	unenrolled	unenvied	unexcavated
uneducable	unencumbered	unenforced	unensured	unequipped	unexcelled
unemancipated	unendangered	unenjoyable	unentangled	unescorted	unexchangeable

—*v.i.* to act as or carry on the business of an underwriter. [Translation of Latin *subscribēre* to write beneath, sign, agree to.]

un·der·writ·er (un′dər rī′tər) *n.* **1.a.** a person or company that underwrites insurance. **b.** an employee of an insurance company who determines risks and sets policy rates. **2.** a person or company that underwrites an issue of stocks or bonds. **3.** a person, institution, foundation, or the like that finances or guarantees financial support for something.

un·de·sir·a·ble (un′di zīr′ə bəl) *adj.* not desirable or pleasing; objectionable; unacceptable: *an undesirable alternative, an undesirable neighborhood.* —*n.* a person considered to be undesirable. —**un′de·sir′a·bil′i·ty, un′de·sir′a·ble·ness,** *n.* —**un′de·sir′a·bly,** *adv.*

un·de·vel·oped (un′di vel′əpt) *adj.* **1.** not completely or properly developed: *undeveloped muscles, undeveloped talent.* **2.** not developed or fully used: *an undeveloped area, undeveloped resources.*

un·did (un did′) the past tense of **undo.**

un·dies (un′dēz) *pl. n. Informal.* underwear, esp. women's or children's underpants.

un·dis·guised (un′dis gīzd′) *adj.* not masked or concealed; open; obvious: *undisguised dislike, undisguised affection.*

un·dis·posed (un′dis pōzd′) *adj.* **1.** not disposed of. ➡ often used in combination with *of*: *undisposed garbage, undisposed-of merchandise.* **2.** not having a tendency toward; unwilling; disinclined (with *to*).

un·do (un dü′) *v.t.,* **-did, -done, -do·ing. 1.** to release or loosen (a fastening); unfasten; untie: *He undid his tie.* **2.** to open by releasing a fastening or binding; unwrap: *She undid the package.* **3.** to do away with or reverse (what has been done); cancel: *The fire undid the work of six months.* **4.** to cause the ruin or downfall of; destroy: *Our folly has undone us.* [Old English *undōn.*] —**un·do′er,** *n.*

un·do·ing (un dü′ing) *n.* **1.** a cancellation or reversal of what has been done. **2.** ruin or downfall; destruction: *He brought about his own undoing.* **3.** a cause of ruin or downfall: *Her stubbornness will prove her undoing.* **4.** the act of unfastening or opening.

un·done¹ (un dun′) *adj.* **1.** not completed or finished; not done: *to leave a job undone.* **2.** having lost composure; greatly disturbed: *We were undone by the terrible news.* [UN-¹ + DONE.]

un·done² (un dun′) *v.* the past participle of **undo.** —*adj.* unfastened; untied; open.

un·doubt·ed (un dou′tid) *adj.* accepted with assurance and certainty as true; not doubted. —**un·doubt′ed·ly,** *adv.*

un·draw (un drô′) *v.t.,* **-drew** (-drü′), **-drawn, -draw·ing.** to draw or pull open, back, or aside, as a curtain.

un·dreamed-of (un drēmd′uv′, -ov′) *also,* **un·dreamt-of** (un-dremt′uv′, -ov′). *adj.* not thought or considered possible; unimaginable: *undreamed-of riches.*

un·dress (un dres′) *v.t.* **1.** to remove the clothes or covering from; strip: *The child undressed the doll.* **2.** to remove the dressing or bandages from, as a wound. —*v.i.* to remove one's clothes. —*n.* **1.** partial or total nakedness: *in a state of undress.* **2.** casual or informal clothing, as distinguished from formal dress; ordinary clothing.

un·dressed (un drest′) *adj.* **1.a.** not wearing any clothes; naked. **b.** partially clothed. **2.** not specially treated or prepared, as leather.

un·due (un dü′, -dū′) *adj.* **1.** going beyond what is necessary, warranted, or appropriate; excessive; immoderate: *to drive with undue speed, to take undue advantage of someone.* **2.** not in accordance with what is just, right, or proper: *Midnight is an undue hour to pay a visit.*

un·du·lant (un′jə lənt, -dyə-) *adj.* moving in waves, or having a wavelike or sinuous form, appearance, or motion.

undulant fever, an infectious disease, primarily of livestock. Humans, who contract it by direct contact with infected animals or by consumption of their products, may develop intermittent fever, chills, general aches and pains, and extreme fatigue. Also, **brucellosis.**

un·du·late (*v.,* un′jə lāt′, -dyə-; *adj.,* un′jə lit, -lāt′, -dyə-) *v.,* **-lat·ed, -lat·ing.** —*v.i.* **1.** to move in or as in waves: *The snake undulated along the ground. The cornstalks undulated in the wind.* **2.** to have a rippling form or appearance: *The farmland undulates*

across hills and valleys. —*v.t.* **1.** to cause to move in or like a wave or waves. **2.** to give a rippling form or appearance to. —*adj.* having a rippling wavy outline, form, or appearance, as a leaf. Also, **un′du·lat′ed.** [Latin *undulātus* wavy, going back to *unda* wave.]

un·du·la·tion (un′jə lā′shən, -dyə-) *n.* **1.** a movement in or as in a wave or waves; wavelike or sinuous motion. **2.** a rippling outline, form, or appearance. **3.** one of a series of waves or wavelike curves, ridges, swellings, or the like. **4.** *Physics.* a wave, as of light, sound, or a vibration.

un·du·la·to·ry (un′jə lə tôr′ē, -dyə-) *adj.* marked or characterized by undulation; wavy: *undulatory motion.*

un·du·ly (un dü′lē, -dū′-) *adv.* unnecessarily or excessively: *unduly concerned, unduly critical.*

un·du·ti·ful (un dü′ti fəl, -dū′-) *adj.* failing in loyalty, obedience, or sense of duty: *an undutiful employee.* —**un·du′ti·ful·ly,** *adv.*

un·dy·ing (un dī′ing) *adj.* without end; eternal; unceasing: *undying devotion.*

un·earned (un ûrnd′) *adj.* **1.** not received in exchange for work or service: *unearned income.* **2.** not merited or deserved: *an unearned scolding.* **3.** not yet earned: *unearned interest on savings.*

unearned increment, an increase in the value of property not brought about by any effort or investment by the owner, as when a growth in population increases the demand for and value of land.

un·earth (un ûrth′) *v.t.* **1.** to dig up out of the earth; disinter: *to unearth buried treasure.* **2.** to bring to light by or as by searching; discover; reveal: *The detective unearthed new evidence.*

un·earth·ly (un ûrth′lē) *adj.* **1.** frighteningly strange or inexplicable; weird: *an unearthly shriek.* **2.** not of this world; supernatural: *unearthly beings.* **3.** rising above that which is characteristic of this world; ideal; sublime: *an unearthly grace, unearthly beauty.* **4.** *Informal.* inconvenient or uncustomary to an absurd degree; preposterous: *an unearthly hour of the morning.* —**un·earth′li·ness,** *n.*

un·eas·y (un ē′zē) *adj.,* **-eas·i·er, -eas·i·est. 1.** lacking comfort or ease of mind; disturbed; anxious: *I feel uneasy about riding without a seat belt.* **2.** causing or disturbed by unrest, insecurity, or anxiety: *an uneasy sleep.* **3.** marked by embarrassment or awkwardness; constrained: *an uneasy laugh, an uneasy silence.* **4.** easily broken or disrupted; unstable; precarious: *an uneasy truce.* —**un·eas′i·ly,** *adv.* —**un·eas′i·ness,** *n.*

un·ed·u·cat·ed (un ej′ə kā′tid) *adj.* lacking education, esp. formal education; not educated: *an uneducated person.*

un·em·ploy·a·ble (un′em ploi′ə bəl) *adj.* not able to be employed. —*n.* an unemployable person.

un·em·ployed (un′em ploid′) *adj.* **1.** without a job; out of work. **2.** not being put to use: *unemployed talents.* —*n.* **the unemployed.** people out of work, collectively.

un·em·ploy·ment (un′em ploi′mənt) *n.* **1.** the state of being unemployed; lack of employment. **2.** the number or percentage of people who are out of work: *Unemployment has risen for the second consecutive month.* **3.** *Informal.* unemployment compensation.

unemployment compensation, a regular payment of money made for a limited period to an unemployed worker, as by a state government. Also, **unemployment benefit.**

unemployment insurance, a government program that provides regular payments for a limited period to workers who have lost their jobs.

un·e·qual (un ē′kwəl) *adj.* **1.** not the same, as in amount, rank, or magnitude: *unequal portions, sleeves of unequal length, unequal opportunities.* **2.** not balanced or equally matched, as in advantage or strength: *an unequal partnership, an unequal competition.* **3.** lacking the necessary strength or ability; not fit or qualified (with *to*): *Their lack of education made them unequal to the enter-*

a	at	e	end	o	hot	u	up	hw	white		about
ā	ape	ē	me	ō	old	ū	use	ng	song		taken
ä	far	i	it	ô	fork	ü	rule	th	thin	ə	pencil
âr	care	ī	ice	oi	oil	ů	pull	th	this		lemon
		îr	pierce	ou	out	ûr	turn	zh	measure		circus

unexcited	unexpended	unexpressed	unfazed	unfertilized	unforbidden
unexciting	unexperienced	unexpressive	unfearful	unfilled	unforbidding
unexcusable	unexpired	unexpurgated	unfeasible	unfilmed	unforeseeable
unexcused	unexplainable	unextinguishable	unfed	unfiltered	unforetold
unexecuted	unexplained	unextinguished	unfelt	unflattered	unforgivable
unexotic	unexploded	unfaded	unfeminine	unflattering	unforgiven
unexpectant	unexplored	unfading	unfenced	unflavored	unforgiving
unexpendable	unexposed	unfaltering	unfermented	unflexed	unforgotten

prise. **4.** not regular, uniform, or consistent; variable: *an unequal distribution of wealth.* —**un·e′qual·ly,** *adv.*

un·e·qualed (un ē′kwəld) *also, British,* **un·e·qualled.** *adj.* not matched or surpassed; unrivaled: *an unequaled performance.*

un·e·quiv·o·cal (un′i kwiv′ə kəl) *adj.* having a meaning that is clear and easily understood; unambiguous: *an unequivocal statement of acceptance.* —**un′e·quiv′o·cal·ly,** *adv.*

un·err·ing (un ûr′ing, -er′-) *adj.* **1.** committing no error or mistake; flawless; faultless: *unerring judgment, unerring precision, unerring good taste.* **2.** not going astray or missing the mark; undeviating: *the unerring flight of an arrow toward a target.* —**un·err′ing·ly,** *adv.*

UNESCO (ū nes′kō) United Nations Educational, Scientific, and Cultural Organization.

un·es·sen·tial (un′i sen′shəl) *adj.* not of prime importance; not essential; dispensable. —*n.* something that is unessential; nonessential.

un·e·ven (un ē′vən) *adj.* **1.** not level, straight, parallel, or perfectly horizontal: *an uneven hem.* **2.** not smooth or flat; jagged: *the uneven surface of a rock.* **3.** not of uniform or consistent quality throughout: *uneven color, a novel marred by uneven writing.* **4.** subject to variations or sudden changes: *an uneven temper.* **5.** (of a number) odd. **6.** not well-matched or balanced; unfair; one-sided: *an uneven game.* [Old English *unefen* unequal, unlike.] —**un·e′ven·ly,** *adv.* —**un·e′ven·ness,** *n.*

un·e·vent·ful (un′i vent′fəl) *adj.* without anything important or noteworthy happening; routine; ordinary: *an uneventful trip.* —**un′e·vent′ful·ly,** *adv.*

un·ex·am·pled (un′eg zam′pəld) *adj.* without equal or counterpart; unprecedented; unparalleled; unique: *unexampled intelligence.*

un·ex·cep·tion·a·ble (un′ek sep′shə nə bəl) *adj.* beyond criticism or reproach; wholly admirable: *an unexceptionable candidate, unexceptionable behavior.* —**un′ex·cep′tion·a·bly,** *adv.*

un·ex·cep·tion·al (un′ek sep′shə nəl) *adj.* **1.** not different from what is usual or common; ordinary. **2.** admitting of no exception. —**un′ex·cep′tion·al·ly,** *adv.*

un·ex·pect·ed (un′ek spek′tid) *adj.* coming or happening without warning; not expected; unforeseen: *an unexpected delay, unexpected kindness.* —**un′ex·pect′ed·ly,** *adv.* —**un′ex·pect′ed·ness,** *n.*

un·fail·ing (un fā′ling) *adj.* **1.** never weakening or varying; unflagging: *unfailing devotion.* **2.** always accurate or certain; infallible; perfect: *an instrument of unfailing precision.* **3.** never running short or ceasing; limitless; inexhaustible: *an unfailing supply of food.* —**un·fail′ing·ly,** *adv.*

un·fair (un fâr′) *adj.* **1.** characterized by bias or prejudice; unjust: *an unfair criticism.* **2.** not following accepted rules or standards; fraudulent: *unfair business practices.* [Old English *unfæger* not beautiful, ugly.] —**un·fair′ly,** *adv.* —**un·fair′ness,** *n.*

un·faith·ful (un fāth′fəl) *adj.* **1.** not adhering to a pledge, allegiance, or duty; not loyal or devoted; untrustworthy: *an unfaithful friend.* **2.** not faithful sexually to one's spouse or lover. **3.** not accurately representing an original; not precise or exact: *an unfaithful translation, an unfaithful account of an event.* —**un·faith′ful·ly,** *adv.* —**un·faith′ful·ness,** *n.*

un·fa·mil·iar (un′fə mil′yər) *adj.* **1.** not well known or immediately recognizable; strange: *This handwriting is unfamiliar to me.* **2.** lacking knowledge of or experience with (with *with*): *to be unfamiliar with a subject.* —**un·fa·mil·i·ar·i·ty** (un′fə mil′ē ar′i·tē), *n.* —**un·fa·mil′iar·ly,** *adv.*

un·fash·ion·a·ble (un fash′ə nə bəl) *adj.* not in fashion; not stylish; passé. —**un·fash′ion·a·bly,** *adv.*

un·fas·ten (un fas′ən) *v.t.* to detach or undo the fastening or fastenings of; open: *to unfasten a coat, to unfasten a suitcase.* —*v.i.* to become detached, loosened, or opened.

un·fath·om·a·ble (un fath′ə mə bəl) *adj.* **1.** that cannot be measured: *the unfathomable depths of the ocean.* **2.** that cannot be fully understood; beyond comprehension: *unfathomable motives.*

un·fath·omed (un fath′əmd) *adj.* **1.** not measured. **2.** not fully understood; incomprehensible.

un·fa·vor·a·ble (un fā′vər ə bəl) *also, British,* **un·fa·vour·a·ble.** *adj.* not in a person's or thing's favor; disadvantageous:

The political climate in that country is unfavorable to democracy. **2.** disapproving; critical: *The play received unfavorable reviews.* **3.** denying something desired or requested; negative: *I received an unfavorable reply to my request.* **4.** not promising; pessimistic: *an unfavorable diagnosis.* —**un·fa′vor·a·ble·ness,** *also, British,* **un·fa′vour·a·ble·ness,** *n.* —**un·fa′vor·a·bly;** *also, British,* **un·fa′vour·a·bly,** *adv.*

un·feel·ing (un fē′ling) *adj.* **1.** lacking in sympathy or compassion; callous; cruel: *an unfeeling person, unfeeling words.* **2.** not able to experience feeling or sensation; insensate. —**un·feel′ing·ly,** *adv.* —**un·feel′ing·ness,** *n.*

un·feigned (un fānd′) *adj.* not pretended or simulated; genuine; sincere: *unfeigned enthusiasm.* —**un·feign·ed·ly** (un fā′nid·lē), *adv.*

un·fet·ter (un fet′ər) *v.t.* to free from fetters, bondage, or other restraints; liberate.

un·fin·ished (un fin′isht) *adj.* **1.** not brought to an end; not concluded or completed: *an unfinished speech, an unfinished job.* **2.** not completely treated or processed; rough: *unfinished furniture, unfinished fabric.*

un·fit (un fit′) *adj.* **1.** not suitable or appropriate to some end or purpose: *This food is unfit to eat.* **2.** lacking the necessary qualifications; incompetent: *That senator is unfit to be president.* **3.** in poor mental or physical condition; unhealthy: *unfit for hard manual labor.* —*v.t.,* **-fit·ted** or **-fit, -fit·ting.** to make unfit. —**unfit′ness,** *n.*

un·flag·ging (un flag′ing) *adj.* not wavering or failing; untiring; sustained: *unflagging energy, unflagging devotion.* —**un·flag′ging·ly,** *adv.*

un·flap·pa·ble (un flap′ə bəl) *adj. Informal.* not easily excited or disturbed; calm; imperturbable. —**un·flap′pa·bil′i·ty,** *n.*

un·fledged (un flejd′) *adj.* **1.** lacking knowledge of or experience in the world; callow: *an unfledged poet.* **2.** (of a young bird) not yet having developed feathers needed for flight.

un·flinch·ing (un flin′ching) *adj.* not drawing back or away from danger, pain, or other hardship; unshrinking: *unflinching determination.* —**un·flinch′ing·ly,** *adv.*

un·fold (un fōld′) *v.t.* **1.** to open or spread out (something folded); extend or stretch out: *I unfolded the towel. The bird unfolded its wings.* **2.** to make known gradually or by degrees; disclose; explain: *to unfold the details of a plan.* **3.** to lay open to view; uncover; display. —*v.i.* **1.** to become open or spread out, as the petals of a flower. **2.** to become known gradually: *The story unfolded with great suspense.* [Old English *unfealdan* to open the folds of, explain.]

un·forced (un fôrst′) *adj.* **1.** not brought about by force; voluntary. **2.** not as a result of effort; not strained; natural: *an unforced smile.*

un·fore·seen (un′fôr sēn′) *adj.* not anticipated or considered beforehand; unexpected: *unforeseen difficulties.*

un·for·get·ta·ble (un′fər get′ə bəl) *adj.* not to be forgotten; memorable: *an unforgettable experience.* —**un′for·get′ta·bly,** *adv.*

un·formed (un fôrmd′) *adj.* **1.** having no definite form; shapeless: *wet, unformed clay.* **2.** not fully developed or organized: *an unformed economic theory.*

un·for·tu·nate (un fôr′chə nit) *adj.* **1.** having bad luck; unlucky: *an unfortunate traveler.* **2.** causing or attended by misfortune; disastrous: *unfortunate circumstances.* **3.** improper or unsuitable: *an unfortunate choice of words.* —*n.* a person who is unfortunate. —**un·for′tu·nate·ly,** *adv.*

un·found·ed (un foun′did) *adj.* having no basis in fact or reality; unwarranted; groundless: *an unfounded accusation.*

Synonyms Unfounded, groundless, and baseless mean having little or no basis in fact or reality. **Unfounded** generally implies inconclusive or insufficient support or evidence: *Although the police believed suspicions of foul play were unfounded, they could not rule out the possibility.* **Groundless** usually refers to emotions and beliefs rather than to material evidence: *The therapist's patient had a groundless fear of being poisoned.* **Baseless** indicates a lack of any factual evidence: *The rumor of the president's resignation proved baseless.*

un·fre·quent·ed (un′fri kwen′tid, un frē′kwən-) *adj.* seldom or rarely visited: *unfrequented areas of a park.*

unformulated	ungarnished	ungrateful	unharmed	unheated	unhoused
unfortified	ungentle	ungratified	unharmful	unheedful	unhurt
unfought	ungentlemanly	ungratifying	unharmonious	unheeding	unhygienic
unframed	ungently	unguessable	unharnessed	unhelpful	unhyphenated
unfrozen	unglamorous	unguided	unharried	unheralded	unidentifiable
unfulfilled	unglazed	unhackneyed	unharvested	unheroic	unidentified
unfunny	ungoverned	unhampered	unhatched	unhewn	unignitable
unfurnished	ungraded	unharassed	unhealed	unhindered	unilluminated

un·friend·ly (un frend′lē) *adj.*, **-li·er, -li·est. 1.** feeling or showing dislike, coldness, or hostility; not friendly: *an unfriendly neighbor, an unfriendly manner.* **2.** not favorable, pleasant, or propitious: *an unfriendly climate.* —**un·friend′li·ness,** *n.*

un·frock (un frok′) *v.t.* **1.** to divest (a priest, minister, or other cleric) of the right to exercise the functions of office. **2.** to remove a frock from.

un·fruit·ful (un früt′fəl) *adj.* **1.** not producing desired or useful results; unsuccessful; unproductive: *unfruitful peace talks.* **2.** not producing fruit or offspring; barren; sterile. —**un·fruit′ful·ly,** *adv.* —**un·fruit′ful·ness,** *n.*

un·furl (un fûrl′) *v.t.* to open or spread out, as before the wind; unroll: *to unfurl a flag.* —*v.i.* to become spread out.

un·gain·ly (un gān′lē) *adj.*, **-li·er, -li·est. 1.** lacking grace of movement or form; awkward; clumsy: *an ungainly stride, an ungainly puppy.* **2.** difficult to handle or move; unwieldy: *an ungainly package.* [UN-[1] + dialectal English *gainly* graceful, proper (from Old Norse *gegn* straight) + -LY[2]).] —**un·gain′li·ness,** *n.* —For Synonyms, see **awkward.**

un·gen·er·ous (un jen′ər əs) *adj.* **1.** not generous; stingy; niggardly: *an ungenerous person, an ungenerous tip.* **2.** lacking kindness or sympathy; uncharitable; petty: *an ungenerous remark.* —**un·gen′er·ous·ly,** *adv.* —**un·gen′er·ous·ness,** *n.*

un·gird (un gûrd′) *v.t.*, **-girt** (-gûrt′) or **-gird·ed, -gird·ing. 1.** to remove a belt, girdle, or other constraining band from. **2.** to loosen or release by unfastening a belt: *to ungird a sword.*

un·glue (un glü′) *v.t.*, **-glued, -glu·ing. 1.** to detach or separate by or as if by removing or dissolving glue. **2.** *Slang.* to cause (someone) to become extremely upset or helplessly flustered; discombobulate.
• **to come unglued.** *Slang.* to become extremely upset or helplessly flustered.

un·god·ly (un god′lē) *adj.*, **-li·er, -li·est. 1.** not feeling or showing a reverence for God or religious laws; impious; sinful. **2.** *Informal.* highly inappropriate or inconvenient; outrageous: *They called at an ungodly hour.* —**un·god′li·ness,** *n.*

un·gov·ern·a·ble (un guv′ər nə bəl) *adj.* impossible to control, rule, or keep in check: *an ungovernable mob, an ungovernable temper.* —**un·gov′ern·a·bly,** *adv.*

un·grace·ful (un grās′fəl) *adj.* lacking beauty or elegance, as of form or movement. —**un·grace′ful·ly,** *adv.* —**un·grace′ful·ness,** *n.*

un·gra·cious (un grā′shəs) *adj.* **1.** not kind or courteous; impolite; rude: *ungracious behavior.* **2.** not pleasant or enjoyable; disagreeable. —**un·gra′cious·ly,** *adv.* —**un·gra′cious·ness,** *n.*

un·gram·mat·i·cal (un′grə mat′i kəl) *adj.* not following the accepted rules or standards of grammar. —**un·gram·mat′i·cal·ly,** *adv.*

un·grate·ful (un grāt′fəl) *adj.* **1.** not thankful or appreciative of kindness or benefits received. **2.** disagreeable; unpleasant: *I had the ungrateful task of giving out the test results.* —**un·grate′ful·ly,** *adv.* —**un·grate′ful·ness,** *n.*

un·ground·ed (un groun′did) *adj.* **1.** without basis in fact or reality; unfounded: *an ungrounded accusation.* **2.** lacking knowledge or instruction; not educated: *to be ungrounded in the sciences.* **3.** (of an electric circuit or apparatus) improperly or unsafely connected with the earth or a ground.

un·grudg·ing (un gruj′ing) *adj.* without envy or other reservation; wholehearted; unstinting: *ungrudging praise.* —**un·grudg′ing·ly,** *adv.*

un·gual (ung′gwəl) *adj.* **1.** *Zoology.* of, relating to, or resembling a hoof, claw, or nail. **2.** *Medicine.* relating to or affecting the nails. [Latin *unguis* hoof, claw, nail + -AL[1].]

un·guard·ed (un gär′did) *adj.* **1.** without guard or protection: *an unguarded entrance.* **2.** without caution or reserve; unthinking: *an unguarded reference to classified information.* **3.** without guile or deceit; frank; candid. —**un·guard′ed·ly,** *adv.* —**un·guard′ed·ness,** *n.*

un·guent (ung′gwənt) *n.* a salve or ointment. [Latin *unguentum.*]

un·guis (ung′gwis) *n., pl.* **-gues** (-gwēz). a nail, claw, or hoof. [Latin *unguis.*]

un·gu·la (ung′gyə lə) *n., pl.* **-lae** (-lē′). unguis. [Latin *ungula* claw, hoof.] —**un′gu·lar,** *adj.*

un·gu·late (ung′gyə lit, -lāt′) *adj.* **1.** having hoofs. **2.** of or relating to a former order, Ungulata, including all hoofed mammals. **3.** hoof-shaped. —*n.* a hoofed mammal. [Late Latin *ungulātus* having claws or hoofs, from Latin *ungula* claw, hoof.]

un·hal·lowed (un hal′ōd) *adj.* **1.** not made holy; unconsecrated: *unhallowed ground.* **2.** impious; wicked.

un·hand (un hand′) *v.t.* to release from the grasp; let go of: *Unhand me!*

un·hap·py (un hap′ē) *adj.*, **-pi·er, -pi·est. 1.** without happiness, joy, or contentment; sad: *an unhappy child.* **2.** causing, attended by, or resulting from misfortune; unlucky: *an unhappy mistake.* **3.** lacking in tact or good taste; inappropriate; ill-chosen: *an unhappy choice of colors.* —**un·hap′pi·ly,** *adv.* —**un·hap′pi·ness,** *n.*

un·har·ness (un här′nis) *v.t.* **1.** to remove a harness from: *to unharness a horse.* **2.** to free from restraint or confinement; release: *to unharness pent-up emotions.*

un·health·ful (un helth′fəl) *adj.* not conducive to good health; unwholesome: *an unhealthful diet.* —**un·health′ful·ly,** *adv.* —**un·health′ful·ness,** *n.*

un·health·y (un hel′thē) *adj.*, **-health·i·er, -health·i·est. 1.** not in good health; sick; sickly: *an unhealthy condition.* **2.** causing or conducive to poor health; unwholesome: *an unhealthy climate, unhealthy eating habits.* **3.** characteristic of or indicating poor health or abnormality: *an unhealthy pulse, an unhealthy preoccupation.* **4.** harmful to morals; corruptive: *an unhealthy influence.* **5.** dangerous or risky; unsafe: *In certain countries it is unhealthy to state your political opinions.* —**un·health′i·ly,** *adv.* —**un·health′i·ness,** *n.*

un·heard (un hûrd′) *adj.* **1.** not perceived by the ear; not heard: *The child's cries went unheard.* **2.** not given a hearing: *an unheard appeal.* **3.** *Archaic.* unheard-of *(def. 2).*

un·heard-of (un hûrd′uv′, -ov′) *adj.* **1.** extreme or excessive to an absurd degree; outrageous; ridiculous: *unheard-of prices, unheard-of behavior.* **2.** not previously known or occurring; unknown; unprecedented: *Traveling across the Atlantic Ocean in six hours was unheard-of fifty years ago.*

un·heed·ed (un hē′did) *adj.* not paid attention to; disregarded: *unheeded advice.*

un·hes·i·tat·ing (un hez′i tā′ting) *adj.* **1.** without hesitation or delay; immediate; prompt: *an unhesitating reply.* **2.** steadfast; unfaltering; unwavering: *unhesitating loyalty.* —**un·hes′i·tat·ing·ly,** *adv.*

un·hinge (un hinj′) *v.t.*, **-hinged, -hing·ing. 1.** to remove from hinges: *to unhinge a door.* **2.** to remove the hinges from. **3.** to throw into confusion or disorder; unsettle; unbalance: *The shock of the accident unhinged the victim's mind.*

un·hitch (un hich′) *v.t.* to free from being hitched; set loose; unfasten: *to unhitch a mule from a wagon.*

un·ho·ly (un hō′lē) *adj.*, **-li·er, -li·est. 1.** not sanctified or consecrated; unhallowed: *unholy ground.* **2.** sinful; wicked; immoral: *an unholy alliance.* **3.** *Informal.* dreadful; terrible: *The kids made an unholy racket washing the pots and pans.* [Old English *unhālig* wicked.] —**un·ho′li·ly,** *adv.* —**un·ho′li·ness,** *n.*

un·hook (un hŭk′) *v.t.* **1.** to release or detach from a hook: *to unhook a latch, to unhook a lantern.* **2.** to unfasten the hook or hooks of: *to unhook a coat.* —*v.i.* to become unhooked.

un·hoped-for (un hōpt′fôr′) *adj.* not expected or anticipated: *unhoped-for good news.*

un·horse (un hôrs′) *v.t.*, **-horsed, -hors·ing. 1.** to throw (a rider) from a horse; cause to fall from a horse. **2.** to dislodge or overthrow: *The election unhorsed many incumbents.*

un·hur·ried (un hûr′ēd, -hur′-) *adj.* without rush or haste; not hurried; leisurely: *an unhurried breakfast.* —**un·hur′ried·ly,** *adv.*

uni- *combining form* of, having, or consisting of only one; single: *unicameral, unicellular.* [Latin *ūnus* one.]

a	at	e	end	o	hot	ū	up	hw	white		(about
ā	ape	ē	me	ō	old	ū	use	ng	song		taken
ä	far	i	it	ô	fork	ü	rule	th	thin	ə	pencil
âr	care	ī	ice	oi	oil	ů	pull	th	this		lemon
		îr	pierce	ou	out	ûr	turn	zh	measure		(circus

unilluminating	unimpaired	unimposed	unincinerated	unindicted	uninfested
unillustrated	unimparted	unimposing	unincited	unindoctrinated	uninflated
unillustrious	unimpassioned	unimpressed	unincorporated	uninduced	uninflected
unimaginable	unimpeded	unimpressible	unincriminated	uninducted	uninfluenced
unimaginary	unimpelled	unimpressionable	unincriminating	unindulged	uninfluential
unimagined	unimperialistic	unimpressive	unincubated	unindustrialized	uninformed
unimmersed	unimplicated	unimprinted	unindexed	unindustrious	uninhabitable
unimmunized	unimplied	uninaugurated	unindicated	uninfected	uninhabited

U·ni·ate (ū′nē it, -āt′) *also,* **U·ni·at** (ū′nē at′). *n.* a member of the Uniate Church. —*adj.* of, relating to, or characteristic of the Uniate Church or its members. [Russian *uniyat,* from *uniya* union, unity, going back to Latin *ūnus* one.]

Uniate Church *also,* **Uniat Church.** any of several Eastern Christian churches that accept the doctrines of the Roman Catholic Church and the supremacy of the pope but maintain separate liturgies, customs, and laws.

u·ni·cam·er·al (ū′ni kam′ər əl) *adj.* having or consisting of a single legislative chamber, house, or branch: *The state of Nebraska has a unicameral legislature.* ➡ distinguished from **bicameral.** [UNI- + Late Latin *camera* chamber + -AL¹. See CHAMBER.]

UNICEF (ū′nə sef′) United Nations International Children's Emergency Fund.

u·ni·cel·lu·lar (ū′nə sel′yə lər) *adj. Biology.* having or consisting of a single cell: *Protozoans are all unicellular organisms.*

unicorn (right) as shown in the
Lady with the Unicorn tapestry (c.1500)

u·ni·corn (ū′ni kôrn′) *n.* a mythical animal usually represented as a white horse with a long, pointed horn in the middle of its forehead, regarded as a symbol of innocence and purity. [Latin *ūnicornus* having one horn, from *ūnus* one + *cornū* horn.]

u·ni·cy·cle (ū′nə sī′kəl) *n.* a vehicle consisting of a single wheel and operated by foot pedals, often having a seat or bar mounted on a shaft, used chiefly by acrobats, entertainers, and gymnasts. Also, **monocycle.** [UNI- + CYCLE.]

unidentified flying object, a flying or apparently flying object classified by the U.S. Air Force as of unidentified or unknown nature because its appearance cannot be explained after all available information on the sighting has been investigated.

u·ni·fi·ca·tion (ū′nə fi kā′shən) *n.* the act of unifying or the state of being unified.

u·ni·form (ū′nə fôrm′) *adj.* **1.** without change or fluctuation; always the same; unvarying: *The building is heated at a uniform temperature all winter.* **2.** showing little or no difference in form,

unicycle

design, size, or the like: *All the houses in this development are uniform in construction and color.* **3.** being the same as another or others: *The township building codes in this county are almost uniform.* —*n.* **1.** the distinctive or official clothes worn by the members of a particular group or profession: *police uniforms.* **2.** a single outfit of this kind. —*v.t.* to provide or clothe with a uniform. [Latin *ūniformis* having one form, from *ūnus* one + *forma* shape, form.] —**u′ni·form′ly,** *adv.* —**u′ni·form′ness,** *n.* —For Synonyms *(adj.),* see **regular.**

u·ni·formed (ū′nə fôrmd′) *adj.* wearing a uniform or uniforms: *a uniformed police officer.*

u·ni·for·mi·tar·i·an·ism (ū′nə fôr′mi târ′ē ə niz′əm) *n.* the basic geologic doctrine that all the natural processes now observed operating on and within the earth's crust have operated in much the same way and at much the same rate throughout the vast expanse of geologic time.

u·ni·form·i·ty (ū′nə fôr′mi tē) *n., pl.* **-ties.** the state, quality, or instance of being uniform.

u·ni·fy (ū′nə fī′) *v.t.,* **-fied, -fy·ing.** to combine or make into a unit or whole; cause to be one or as one; unite: *Language and culture unify most countries.* [Medieval Latin *unificare,* from Latin *ūnus* one + *facere* to make.] —**u′ni·fi′er,** *n.*

u·ni·lat·er·al (ū′nə lat′ər əl) *adj.* **1.** of, affecting, or involving one person or group only: *unilateral disarmament, a unilateral decision.* **2.** of, relating to, or affecting only one side of the body or of an organ: *unilateral sciatica.* **3.** concerned with or considering only one side of a subject. **4.** *Law.* having effect on or obligating only one of two or more parties, as a contract or agreement. —**u′ni·lat′er·al·ly,** *adv.*

un·i·mag·i·na·tive (un′i maj′ə nə tiv) *adj.* lacking imagination or creativity: *an unimaginative play, an unimaginative writer.* —**un′i·mag′i·na·tive·ly,** *adv.*

un·im·peach·a·ble (un′im pē′chə bəl) *adj.* not to be called into question; above reproach or blame; faultless: *an unimpeachable reputation, an unimpeachable source of information.* —**un′im·peach′a·bly,** *adv.*

un·im·por·tant (un′im pôr′tənt) *adj.* lacking any special value, relevance, or meaning; insignificant; trivial: *an unimportant incident, an unimportant mistake.* —**un′im·por′tance,** *n.*

un·in·hib·i·ted (un′in hib′i tid) *adj.* **1.** lacking or having few social, moral, or psychological inhibitions: *an uninhibited dancer.* **2.** not held back, checked, or inhibited; unrestrained: *uninhibited laughter.* —**un′in·hib′i·ted·ly,** *adv.*

un·in·spired (un′in spīrd′) *adj.* lacking originality, imagination, or creativity; not inspired; dull: *an uninspired performance.*

un·in·tel·li·gent (un′in tel′i jənt) *adj.* **1.** having or marked by a deficiency in thinking or reasoning; stupid. **2.** lacking the faculty or power of thought and reason: *unintelligent matter.* —**un′in·tel′li·gent·ly,** *adv.*

un·in·tel·li·gi·ble (un′in tel′i jə bəl) *adj.* not capable of being made out or understood: *unintelligible handwriting.* —**un′in·tel′li·gi·bil′i·ty,** *n.* —**un′in·tel′li·gi·bly,** *adv.*

un·in·ter·est·ed (un in′trə stid, -tə res′tid) *adj.* lacking interest or emotional involvement; unconcerned; indifferent. —For Synonyms, see **indifferent.**

un·in·ter·rupt·ed (un′in tə rup′tid) *adj.* without interruption; unbroken; continuous: *an uninterrupted flow of water.* —**un′in·ter·rupt′ed·ly,** *adv.*

un·ion (ūn′yən) *n.* **1.** the act of uniting or the state of being united. **2.** something formed by uniting two or more things: *a union of two companies by merger.* **3.a.** a uniting or joining of various parties for a common purpose or for their mutual benefit. **b.** the group or body thus formed: *the economic union of Western European countries.* **4.** an association of laborers or other wage earners organized to protect and advance the interests of its members, esp. with respect to improving wages and working conditions. **5. the Union. a.** the United States of America. **b.** those states that remained constituents of the United States during the American Civil War. **6.** the act of marrying or the state of being married. **7.** *also,* **Union.** student union. **8.** an emblem or device on a flag, symbolizing unity, such as the three superimposed crosses on the British flag or the blue rectangle covered with stars on the U.S. flag. **9.** *Mathematics.* a set composed of all the

uninitiated	uninspected	unintended	uninvigorating	unjustified	unlifelike
uninjured	uninspiring	unintentional	uninvited	unkept	unlighted
uninked	uninstructed	uninteresting	uninviting	unkindled	unlined
uninnovative	uninstructive	unintimidated	uninvoked	unknot	unliquefied
uninoculated	uninsurable	uninventive	uninvolved	unlabeled	unliquidated
uninquisitive	uninsured	uninverted	unirrigated	unlamented	unlit
uninscribed	unintegrated	uninvested	unjointed	unlaundered	unlittered
uninserted	unintellectual	uninvestigating	unjustifiable	unleased	unlivable

elements of two or more given sets, without repetition of any element. Union is represented by the symbol U. For sets {1, 2, 3} and {3, 4, 7}, U = {1, 2, 3, 4, 7}. **10.** a coupling device for connecting machinery parts, such as pipes or rods. [Late Latin *ūniō* oneness, unity, from Latin *ūnus* one.]

Synonyms **Union, unity,** and **solidarity** mean the state of being united into a whole. **Union** describes the organization, often formal and with rules, of elements or entities for a common purpose: *a union formed through the federation of a group of states, a student union.* **Unity** implies a oneness of spirit or principle: *A feeling of national unity developed in response to the threat of invasion.* **Solidarity** denotes unity within a group or organization for the achievement of a common goal: *The bitter primary contest was followed by a show of solidarity as the party united behind the victorious candidate.*

union catalog, a library catalog that combines the catalogs of different libraries or of various divisions within the same library.

un·ion·ism (ūn′yə niz′əm) *n.* **1.a.** support or advocacy of the formation of a union or unions, esp. a labor union. **b.** advocacy of membership within a union. **2.** the principle of uniting for a common purpose or action or for mutual benefit. **3. Unionism.** loyalty to or support of the Union during the American Civil War. **4. Unionism.** belief in or support of the former political union between Ireland and Britain. **—un′ion·ist,** *n.* **—un′ion·is′tic,** *adj.*

un·ion·ize (ūn′yə nīz′) *v.,* **-ized, -iz·ing. —v.t. 1.** to organize into or cause to join a union, esp. a labor union: *to unionize workers.* **2.** to put under the rules of a labor union: *to unionize an industry.* **—v.i.** to join or organize a union, esp. a labor union. **—un′ion·i·za′tion,** *n.*

union jack 1. *usually,* **Union Jack.** the flag of the United Kingdom. **2.** any flag that consists of a union only, esp. the emblem from a national flag.

union shop, a factory or business in which the employees either belong to a union or must join a union within a certain fixed period after they are hired. ➡ distinguished from **closed shop** and **open shop.**

union suit, a one-piece undergarment combining shirt and drawers or trousers.

u·nique (ū nēk′) *adj.* **1.** having no counterpart or equal; unmatched or unparalleled; singular: *unique talents, a unique contribution to medical science.* **2.** being the only one of its kind; single; sole: *a unique fossil specimen.* **3.** *Informal.* highly uncommon, rare, or noteworthy; remarkable: *a unique experience.* [French *unique* single, alone of its kind, unparalleled, from Latin *ūnicus.*] **—u·nique′ly,** *adv.* **—u·nique′ness,** *n.*

Usage Many people object to using a qualifying word such as *more, most,* or *quite* with **unique,** arguing that something is unique or it isn't. Although statements such as *This is the most unique book I've ever read* or *That painting is quite unique* are not uncommon, careful writers do not qualify the word **unique.**

un·i·sex (ū′nə seks′) *adj.* making no distinction between sexes; suitable for both males and females: *unisex clothes.*

u·ni·sex·u·al (ū′nə sek′shü əl) *adj.* **1.** of or relating to one sex only. **2.** having the sexual organs of only one sex in each individual. **3.** (of flowers) having only stamens or only pistils; diclinous.

u·ni·son (ū′nə sən, -zən) *n.* **1.** perfect or exact agreement or harmony. **2.** *Music.* identity in pitch, as of two or more tones or voices. [Late Latin *ūnisonus* having the same sound, from Latin *ūnus* one + *sonus* sound[1], noise.]
· **in unison. a.** uttering the same words or producing the same sound at the same time; all together: *The class answered in unison.* **b.** *Music.* (of voices or instruments) performing the same part at the identical pitch or at the interval of an octave: *The altos and tenors sang in unison.*

u·nit (ū′nit) *n.* **1.** a person or thing regarded or functioning as a single, distinct entity or whole: *This housing development was designed to be a self-contained social unit.* **2.** a person or thing that is a basic organizational component within a larger body, regarded or functioning as a separate entity: *an armored unit of an army, the family as the basic unit of society.* **3.** an apparatus, structure, or piece of equipment having a specific function, some-

times part of a larger object: *a refrigeration unit.* **4.** a body of personnel, together with such an apparatus, forming a self-contained, often mobile, entity and performing a specialized function: *The city hospitals mobilized their X-ray units as part of the fall health campaign.* **5.** any fixed quantity considered as a standard of measurement, in terms of which the magnitudes of other quantities of the same kind can be stated, such as the amount of a drug needed to produce a certain effect: *The second is a unit of time.* **6.** *Mathematics.* the least positive integer; one. [From UNITY.]

U·ni·tar·i·an (ū′ni târ′ē ən) *n.* **1.** *also,* **unitarian.** a person who rejects the doctrines of the Trinity and the divinity of Jesus, holding the belief that God exists as one being. **2.** a member of a denomination originating in Protestantism, officially merged with the Universalists in 1961, which holds these beliefs and stresses personal religious freedom and religious tolerance. **—adj.** of or relating to Unitarians or Unitarianism. [Modern Latin *unitarius* (from Latin *ūnitās* oneness) + -AN.]

U·ni·tar·i·an·ism (ū′ni târ′ē ə niz′əm) *n.* the doctrines, beliefs, and practices of Unitarians.

u·ni·tar·y (ū′ni ter′ē) *adj.* **1.** of or relating to a unit or units: *a unitary measure.* **2.** of, characterized by, or based on unity. **3.** resembling a unit.

u·nite (ū nīt′) *v.,* **u·nit·ed, u·nit·ing. —v.t. 1.** to bring or put together so as to form a unit or whole: *to unite a country, to unite the factions of a political party.* **2.** to bring into close association or relationship: *to unite families by marriage.* **3.** to cause to adhere, attach, or bond. **4.** to show, have, or embody in combination: *Our team unites the qualities of cooperation and individuality.* **—v.i. 1.** to be brought together so as to form a unit or whole; become one or as one: *The provinces united to form a single nation.* **2.** to enter into close association or relationship, as for a common purpose: *All the towns in the county united in an effort to improve education.* **3.** to be or become combined or bound together, as by adhesion, mixture, or chemical reaction: *Under these conditions oxygen will unite with this element.* [Latin *ūnītus,* past participle of *ūnīre* to join together, from *ūnus* one.] **—u·nit′er,** *n.*

u·nit·ed (ū nī′tid) *adj.* **1.** put or joined together; made one or as one: *The senators were united in opposing the legislation.* **2.** of, formed by, or produced by joint action or association: *a united effort.* **3.** in agreement or harmony. **—u·nit′ed·ly,** *adv.*

United Nations 1. an international organization, founded in 1945, including as members most of the nations of the world, that seeks to maintain world peace, promote cooperation among nations, and encourage respect for treaties and other obligations under international law. Its headquarters are located in New York City. **2.** the coalition of countries allied against the Axis Powers in World War II.

unit price, a price, esp. of a grocery item, given as the cost for some standard unit of measurement, such as per ounce or per pound. It is used for cost comparison of products sold in packages of different sizes.

unit pricing, a way of pricing foods that shows not only the total price but also the unit price.

u·ni·ty (ū′ni tē) *n., pl.* **-ties. 1.** the state or fact of being one; oneness; singleness. **2.** the state or quality of being in harmony or agreement; concord; accord: *a unity of purpose.* **3.** the combination or arrangement of parts or diverse elements to form a whole. **4.** the arrangement of the elements in a work of art or literature to produce a single, harmonious, and total aesthetic design or effect. **5.** something that is complete in itself and self-contained; unit; entity; whole. **6. the unities.** the aesthetic principles of dramatic composition derived from the Greek philosopher Aristotle, which comprise the unity of action, time, and place, requiring a play to have one plot occurring on one day in one place. The unities were observed esp. by the French dramatists of the seventeenth century. **7.** *Mathematics.* the number 1 or a quantity

a	at	e	end	o	hot	u	up	hw	white		ə	about
ā	ape	ē	me	ō	old	ū	use	ng	song			taken
ä	far	i	it	ô	fork	ü	rule	th	thin			pencil
âr	care	ī	ice	oi	oil	u̇	pull	th	this			lemon
		îr	pierce	ou	out	ûr	turn	zh	measure			circus

unlively	unmangled	unmarried	unmedicated	unmistaken	unmotivated
unloved	unmanifested	unmastered	unmelodious	unmixed	unmounted
unloving	unmanufactured	unmatched	unmelted	unmodified	unmourned
unlovingly	unmarked	unmeant	unmended	unmodulated	unmovable
unlubricated	unmarketable	unmeasurable	unmentioned	unmoistened	unmoved
unmagnified	unmarketed	unmeasured	unmerited	unmold	unmoving
unmalleable	unmarred	unmechanical	unmethodical	unmolded	unmown
unmanageable	unmarriageable	unmechanized	unmilitary	unmolested	unmusical

regarded as equivalent to it. [Latin *ūnitās* oneness.] —For Synonyms, see **union**.

univ. 1. universal. **2.** universally.

Univ. 1. Universalist. **2.** University.

u·ni·va·lent (ū′nə vā′lənt, ū niv′ə-) *adj. Chemistry.* having a valence of plus or minus one. Also, **monovalent**. [UNI- + Latin *valēns,* present participle of *valēre* to be strong, have power.] —**u′ni·va′lence**, *n.*

u·ni·valve (ū′nə valv′) *n.* **1.** a mollusk, such as a snail, having a single or one-piece shell. For illustration, see **shell**. **2.** the shell of such a mollusk. —*adj.* relating to, having, or consisting of a single or one-piece shell.

u·ni·ver·sal (ū′nə vûr′səl) *adj.* **1.** of, relating to, or shared by all: *universal rejoicing, universal human needs.* **2.** existing or occurring everywhere or in all places: *a universal shortage of oil.* **3.** occurring or effective under all conditions or in all cases: *a universal remedy, a universal solvent.* **4.** embracing or accomplished in a wide range of subjects or activities; comprehensive: *a universal mechanic.* **5.** adapted or adaptable to a variety of sizes, shapes, or uses: *a universal motor.* **6.** *Logic.* **a.** denoting or including all the members of a given class: *a universal term.* **b.** (of a proposition) asserted or predictable of all members of a given class. *All men are mortal* is a universal proposition. ➡ opposed to **particular**. —*n.* **1.** something that is universal, such as a concept, principle, or pattern of behavior. **2.** universal joint. [Latin *ūniversālis* relating to the whole, from *ūniversus* whole, general. See UNIVERSE.] —**u′ni·ver′sal·ness**, *n.*

universal coupling, universal joint.

universal donor, a person whose blood is group O and thus can be safely transfused into a person of any blood group.

u·ni·ver·sal·ism (ū′nə vûr′sə liz′əm) *n.* **1.** universality. **2. Universalism,** the doctrines, beliefs, and practices of Universalists, esp. the doctrine that because God is good, ultimately all humanity will be saved.

U·ni·ver·sal·ist (ū′nə vûr′sə list) *n.* a person who believes in the salvation of all humanity, esp. a member of a denomination originating in Protestantism, officially merged with the Unitarians in 1961, that holds this belief. —*adj.* of or relating to Universalists or Universalism.

u·ni·ver·sal·i·ty (ū′nə vər sal′i tē) *n., pl.* **-ties.** the quality or state or an instance of being universal.

u·ni·ver·sal·ize (ū′nə vûr′sə līz′) *v.t.* **-ized, -iz·ing.** to make universal. —**u′ni·ver′sal·i·za′tion**, *n.*

universal joint, a joint or coupling allowing the parts it connects to move in any direction, esp. one used to transmit rotary motion from one shaft to another that is not in line with it. Also, **universal, universal coupling.**

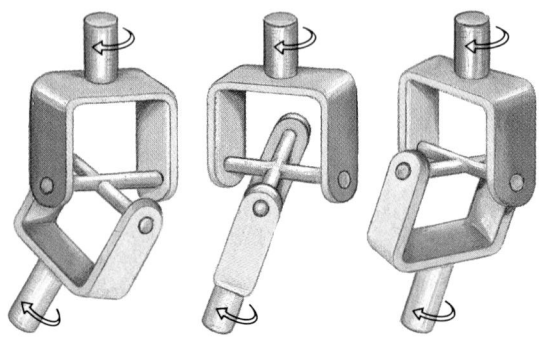

a **universal joint** in three positions

u·ni·ver·sal·ly (ū′nə vûr′sə lē) *adv.* in a universal manner; in every instance or place; without exception: *The new film was universally praised by audiences and critics.*

Universal Product Code, a type of bar code printed on consumer products, used for pricing, inventory control, or the like.

u·ni·verse (ū′nə vûrs′) *n.* **1.** all that exists, including the earth, the solar system, the Milky Way and the other galaxies, and all of space; entire physical world. **2.** the earth or its inhabitants. **3.** the sphere or domain in which something exists, regarded as a distinct or self-contained totality or whole. **4.** *Mathematics.* a set that contains all the objects or sets under consideration at any one time. Also *(def. 4),* **universal set.** [Latin *ūniversum* the whole world, from *ūniversus* whole, general; literally, turned into one, from *ūnus* one + *versus,* past participle of *vertere* to turn.]

u·ni·ver·si·ty (ū′nə vûr′si tē) *n., pl.* **-ties. 1.** an institution of higher education, usually including one or more undergraduate colleges and graduate and professional schools with facilities for teaching and research, authorized to grant bachelor's, master's, and doctoral degrees. **2.** the faculty and student body of such an institution. **3.** the grounds or buildings occupied by such an institution. [Old French *universite* the institution of higher learning, from Late Latin *ūniversitās* company, corporation, from *ūniversitās* the whole.]

un·just (un just′) *adj.* not just or fair; unfair: *an unjust law.* —**un·just′ly**, *adv.* —**un·just′ness**, *n.*

un·kempt (un kempt′) *adj.* **1.** not combed or groomed: *shaggy, unkempt hair.* **2.** not neat or clean in appearance: *an unkempt room, an unkempt lawn.* **3.** lacking refinement; unpolished; crude. [UN-[1] + Middle English *kempt,* past participle of *kemben* to comb (from Old English *cemban*).]

un·kind (un kīnd′) *adj.* lacking in kindness or sympathy; harsh; cruel. —**un·kind′ness**, *n.*

un·kind·ly (un kīnd′lē) *adv.* in an unkind manner: *to treat a stranger unkindly.* —*adj.,* **-li·er, -li·est.** unkind; cruel. —**un·kind′li·ness**, *n.*

un·knit (un nit′) *v.,* **-knit·ted** or **-knit, -knit·ting.** —*v.t.* **1.** to undo (something knit or tied). **2.** to smooth out (something wrinkled). —*v.i.* to become unknit.

un·know·a·ble (un nō′ə bəl) *adj.* beyond the realm of human knowledge or understanding; not able to be known. —*n.* something that is unknowable.

un·know·ing (un nō′ing) *adj.* not knowing or aware; ignorant: *an unknowing accomplice.* —**un·know′ing·ly**, *adv.*

un·known (un nōn′) *adj.* **1.** not part of a person's knowledge or experience; unfamiliar: *The passage you're quoting is unknown to me.* **2.** not discovered or identified: *an unknown island.* **3.** not widely known or popular: *an unknown playwright.* —*n.* **1.** a person or thing that is unknown. **2.** a quantity in mathematics whose value is to be determined: *Let x be the unknown in this equation.*

Unknown Soldier, an unidentified soldier killed in battle, interred in a place of honor as a symbol of all the unknown war dead of a country. Also, *British,* **Unknown Warrior.**

un·lace (un lās′) *v.t.* **-laced, -lac·ing. 1.** to undo the laces of. **2.** to loosen or unfasten the clothing of by or as by undoing laces.

un·latch (un lach′) *v.t.* to unfasten or open by releasing a latch: *to unlatch a door.* —*v.i.* to become unlatched.

un·law·ful (un lô′fəl) *adj.* **1.** of, relating to, or constituting a crime or a tort or other civil wrong; against the law; illegal: *an unlawful act.* **2.** contrary to moral standards; immoral; sinful. **3.** born out of wedlock; illegitimate. —**un·law′ful·ly**, *adv.* —**un·law′ful·ness**, *n.*

un·lead·ed (un led′id) *adj.* (of fuel) not containing lead compounds, which become toxic environmental pollutants when burned: *unleaded gasoline.* —*n.* an unleaded fuel, esp. gasoline.

un·learn (un lûrn′) *v.t.,* **-learned** or **-learnt, -learn·ing.** to rid the mind of (something learned); forget.

un·learn·ed (*defs. 1, 3,* un lûr′nid; *def. 2,* un lûrnd′) *adj.* **1.** not having much knowledge or education; uneducated; illiterate. **2.** characterized by or betraying a lack of knowledge or education; unenlightened; ignorant: *an unlearned comment.* **3.** not acquired by learning or study: *an unlearned response.*

un·leash (un lēsh′) *v.t.* **1.** to release or let loose from a leash: *to unleash a puppy.* **2.** to release or let loose as if from a leash: *The hurricane unleashed its fury on the coastal town.*

un·leav·ened (un lev′ənd) *adj.* not made with any leavening agent, such as yeast: *to eat unleavened bread during Passover.*

un·less (un les′) *conj.* except on the condition that; except under the circumstances that: *Unless you return the book, you can't borrow any more.* [Middle English *onlesse* on a lower condition (than), from *on* (see ON) + *lesse* (see LESS).]

unnameable	unnegotiated	unobliging	unobtruding	unopened	unpalatable
unnamed	unneighborly	unobscured	unoccasioned	unopposed	unpalatably
unnaturalized	unnoted	unobservable	unoffended	unordained	unpardoned
unnavigable	unnoteworthy	unobservant	unoffending	unoriginal	unpartitioned
unnavigated	unnoticeable	unobserving	unoffensive	unostentatious	unpasteurized
unneeded	unnoticed	unobstructed	unofficial	unoxidized	unpatented
unneedful	unobjectionable	unobtainable	unoiled	unpacified	unpatriotic
unnegotiable	unobliged	unobtained	unopen	unpaired	unpaved

U

un·let·tered (un let′ərd) *adj.* **1.** not educated; ignorant. **2.** not able to read or write; illiterate. **3.** not marked with letters or lettering.

un·li·censed (un lī′sənst) *adj.* **1.** having no license: *an unlicensed driver.* **2.** done without license or permission; unauthorized: *unlicensed professional advice.* **3.** unbridled; unrestrained: *unlicensed behavior.*

un·like (un līk′) *prep.* **1.** with little or no resemblance to; different from: *Unlike some of my friends, I enjoy dancing.* **2.** not characteristic or typical of: *It is unlike you to be rude.* —*adj.* **1.** having little or no resemblance; different: *unlike situations.* **2.** not equivalent; unequal: *unlike amounts.* —**un·like′ness**, *n.*

un·like·li·hood (un līk′lē hŏŏd′) *n.* the quality of being unlikely; improbability.

un·like·ly (un līk′lē) *adj.*, **-li·er, -li·est. 1.** not seeming to be a possibility; not likely; improbable: *It is unlikely that it will rain today.* **2.** seeming to lack any prospect of success or of a desired result; not likely to succeed; unpromising: *Your wild scheme is an unlikely way to make money.* —*adv.* improbably. —**un·like′li·ness**, *n.*

un·lim·ber (un lim′bər) *v.t.* **1.** to prepare (a gun) for use by detaching its limber. **2.** to prepare (something) for use or action. —*v.i.* to prepare for action.

un·lim·it·ed (un lim′i tid) *adj.* without limits or restrictions: *unlimited supplies.*

un·list·ed (un lis′tid) *adj.* **1.** not included on a list, esp. a public list: *an unlisted phone number.* **2.** (of a stock or security) not listed among those admitted for trading on a stock exchange.

un·load (un lōd′) *v.t.* **1.** to take off or discharge (a load): *to unload freight, to unload passengers.* **2.** to remove a load from: *The workers began unloading the ship.* **3.** to withdraw a charge or ammunition from (a firearm). **4.** to give vent or expression to; pour forth: *to unload one's cares to a friend.* **5.** *Informal.* to dispose or get rid of: *to unload old furniture at an auction.* —*v.i.* to discharge a cargo or load.

un·lock (un lok′) *v.t.* **1.** to open or undo the lock of: *This key will unlock the door.* **2.** to release as if by undoing a lock: *to unlock a grip on someone's arm.* **3.** to cause to open: *to unlock one's jaws.* **4.** to furnish a key or solution to; disclose: *to unlock a mystery.* —*v.i.* to become unlocked.

un·looked-for (un lŏŏkt′fôr′) *adj.* not anticipated or expected; unforeseen: *an unlooked-for stroke of good luck.*

un·loose (un lŏŏs′) *v.t.*, **-loosed, -loos·ing. 1.** to unbind or let loose; set free; release: *to unloose a bird from its cage.* **2.** to relax or slacken, as one's grip or hold; loosen. Also, **un·loos′en.**

un·luck·y (un luk′ē) *adj.*, **-luck·i·er, -luck·i·est. 1.** not favored with good luck; unfortunate: *an unlucky contestant.* **2.** marked or produced by bad luck: *an unlucky season for a team, unlucky circumstances.* **3.** forecasting or bringing bad luck; ominous: *an unlucky number.* —**un·luck′i·ly,** *adv.* —**un·luck′i·ness,** *n.*

un·make (un māk′) *v.t.*, **-made** (-mād′), **-mak·ing. 1.** to reverse or undo the making of (something): *to unmake a bed, to unmake a law.* **2.** to deprive of power, rank, or authority; depose: *to unmake a politician.* **3.** to ruin; destroy.

un·man (un man′) *v.t.*, **-manned, -man·ning. 1.** to weaken the spirit of; discourage: *Ten years of tyranny have unmanned the people.* **2.** to deprive of virility or strength; emasculate.

un·man·ly (un man′lē) *adj.*, **-li·er, -li·est. 1.** lacking courage or honor; weak; cowardly: *an unmanly attack on a wounded opponent.* **2.** not masculine or virile; effeminate. —**un·man′li·ness**, *n.*

un·manned (un mand′) *adj.* without a crew: *an unmanned spacecraft.*

un·man·ner·ly (un man′ər lē) *adj.* having or showing bad manners; rude: *an unmannerly outburst of harsh language.* —*adv.* impolitely; rudely. —**un·man′ner·li·ness**, *n.*

un·mask (un mask′) *v.t.* **1.** to remove a mask or disguise from. **2.** to reveal the true nature of; expose: *to unmask a plot, to unmask someone's character.* —*v.i.* to remove one's mask or disguise.

un·mean·ing (un mē′ning) *adj.* **1.** without meaning, purpose, or significance; senseless: *unmeaning utterances.* **2.** showing no expression, interest, or intelligence; vacant; empty: *an unmeaning expression on a person's face.* —**un·mean′ing·ly,** *adv.*

un·meet (un mēt′) *adj.* not fit, proper, or suitable; unseemly.

un·men·tion·a·ble (un men′shə nə bəl) *adj.* not fit for discussion, esp. in polite conversation: *an unmentionable topic.*

un·men·tion·a·bles (un men′shə nə bəlz) *pl. n.* things considered inappropriate to mention or discuss, such as undergarments.

un·mer·ci·ful (un mûr′si fəl) *adj.* **1.** having or showing no mercy; merciless; cruel. **2.** unreasonable; excessive; extreme. —**un·mer′ci·ful·ly,** *adv.* —**un·mer′ci·ful·ness,** *n.*

un·mind·ful (un mīnd′fəl) *adj.* not conscious, aware, or careful; heedless; forgetful (often with *of*): *to be unmindful of other people's feelings.* —**un·mind′ful·ly,** *adv.*

un·mis·tak·a·ble (un′mis tā′kə bəl) *adj.* such as cannot be mistaken or misunderstood; plain; obvious: *an unmistakable note of anger in someone's voice.* —**un′mis·tak′a·bly,** *adv.*

un·mit·i·gat·ed (un mit′i gā′tid) *adj.* **1.** not softened or lessened in intensity or severity: *unmitigated anger.* **2.** complete; absolute; downright: *an unmitigated liar.* —**un·mit′i·gat′ed·ly,** *adv.*

un·moor (un mŏŏr′) *v.t.* **1.** to release (a boat or ship) from its mooring. **2.** to raise or release all but one anchor of (a boat or ship). —*v.i.* to cast off from a mooring.

un·mor·al (un môr′əl, -mor′-) *adj.* not influenced by or involving considerations of right and wrong; amoral. —**un·mor′al·ly,** *adv.* —For Synonyms, see **immoral.**

un·muf·fle (un muf′əl) *v.*, **-fled, -fling.** —*v.t.* to remove a covering from; free from something that muffles. —*v.i.* to remove something that muffles.

un·muz·zle (un muz′əl) *v.t.*, **-zled, -zling. 1.** to remove a muzzle from (a dog or other animal). **2.** to free from restraint or censorship: *to unmuzzle political opposition.*

un·nat·u·ral (un nach′ər əl) *adj.* **1.** contrary to or deviating from the usual course of nature: *The cat grew to an unnatural size.* **2.** shocking to human feelings; monstrous; inhuman: *an act of unnatural cruelty.* **3.** deviating from social, moral, or behavioral standards: *an unnatural disregard for property.* **4.** not genuine or spontaneous; contrived; affected: *an unnatural smile, an unnatural way of speaking.* —**un·nat′u·ral·ly,** *adv.* —**un·nat′u·ral·ness,** *n.*

un·nec·es·sar·y (un nes′ə ser′ē) *adj.* not required or essential; needless: *unnecessary trifles.* —**un·nec′es·sar′i·ly,** *adv.* —**un·nec′es·sar′i·ness,** *n.*

un·nerve (un nûrv′) *v.t.*, **-nerved, -nerv·ing.** to deprive of courage, self-control, or composure: *The lawyer's constant barrage of questions unnerved the witness.*

un·nil·en·ni·um (ū′nə len′ē əm) *n.* a proposed name for the artificially produced radioactive element with atomic number 109. Proposed symbol: **Une** For tables, see **element.**

un·nil·hex·i·um (ū′nəl hek′sē əm) *n.* a proposed name for the artificially produced radioactive element with atomic number 106. Proposed symbol: **Unh** Also, **element 106.** For tables, see **element.** [Latin *unus* one + *nil* nothing, zero + Greek *hex* six.]

un·nil·oc·ti·um (ū′nə lok′tē əm) *n.* a proposed name for the artificially produced radioactive element with atomic number 108. Proposed symbol: **Uno** For tables, see **element.** [Latin *unus* one + *nil* nothing, zero + *oct-* eight.]

un·nil·pen·ti·um (ū′nəl pen′tē əm) *n.* hahnium. [Latin *unus* one + *nil* nothing, zero + Greek *pente* five. The atomic number of this element is 105.]

un·nil·qua·di·um (ū′nəl kwod′ē əm) *n.* rutherfordium. [Latin *unus* one + *nil* nothing, zero + *quadri-* four. The atomic number of this element is 104.]

un·nil·sep·ti·um (ū′nəl sep′tē əm) *n.* a proposed name for the artificially produced radioactive element with atomic number 107. Proposed symbol: **Uns** Also, **element 107.** For tables, see **element.** [Latin *unus* one + *nil* nothing, zero + *sept-* seven.]

un·num·bered (un num′bərd) *adj.* **1.** not marked with a number or numbers: *unnumbered pages.* **2.** too many to be counted;

a	at	e	end	o	hot	u	up	hw	white		about
ā	ape	ē	me	ō	old	ū	use	ng	song	ə	taken
ä	far	i	it	ô	fork	ŭ	rule	th	thin		pencil
âr	care	ī	ice	oi	oil	ů	pull	th	this		lemon
				îr	pierce	ou	out	ûr	turn	zh	measure		circus

unpeaceful	unperplexed	unpitied	unpoetic	unpolluted	unpreparedness
unpeg	unpersuaded	unpitying	unpoetical	unpopulated	unprepossessing
unpenetrated	unpersuasive	unplanned	unpoised	unposed	unprescribed
unpeople	unperturbable	unplanted	unpolarized	unposted	unpresentable
unperceived	unperturbed	unplayed	unpoliced	unpracticable	unpreserved
unperceiving	unphilosophic	unpleasing	unpolished	unpractical	unpressed
unperceptive	unphilosophical	unpledged	unpolitical	unpredictability	unpreventable
unperfected	unpicked	unplowed	unpolled	unprepared	unprinted

innumerable; countless: *There are unnumbered stars in the universe.*

un·ob·served (un′əb zûrvd′) *adj.* **1.** not noticed or perceived: *We slipped into the meeting unobserved.* **2.** not complied with or obeyed: *an unobserved law.* **3.** not celebrated: *an unobserved holiday.*

un·ob·tru·sive (un′əb trü′siv) *adj.* that does not cause notice or disturbance; inconspicuous. —**un′ob·tru′sive·ly,** *adv.* —**un′ob·tru′sive·ness,** *n.*

un·oc·cu·pied (un ok′yə pīd′) *adj.* **1.** without an occupant or occupants; vacant: *an unoccupied apartment.* **2.** not held or occupied by troops or enemy forces: *unoccupied territory.* **3.** not busy; idle: *an unoccupied salesperson.*

un·or·gan·ized (un ôr′gə nīzd′) *adj.* **1.** not formed into an orderly arrangement or whole; lacking organization: *unorganized thinking, an unorganized room.* **2.** not organized into a labor union: *The workers in that plant are unorganized.* **3.** lacking the characteristics of a living organism; inorganic.

un·or·tho·dox (un ôr′thə doks′) *adj.* at variance with accepted beliefs, opinions, customs, or doctrines; not orthodox: *unorthodox teachings, unorthodox behavior.*

un·pack (un pak′) *v.t.* **1.** to empty the contents of: *to unpack a suitcase.* **2.** to remove from a container or packaging: *I unpacked the glassware from the box.* **3.** to remove a pack or burden from; unload: *to unpack a mule.* —*v.i.* to unpack something, such as luggage.

un·paid (un pād′) *adj.* **1.** not yet paid: *unpaid wages, an unpaid fine.* **2.** serving without pay; unsalaried: *an unpaid volunteer.*

un·par·al·leled (un par′ə leld′) *adj.* without parallel or equal; matchless; unsurpassed: *an unparalleled achievement.*

un·par·don·a·ble (un pär′də nə bəl) *adj.* that cannot be excused or forgiven: *an unpardonable act of cruelty.* —**un·par′don·a·bly,** *adv.*

un·par·lia·men·ta·ry (un′pär lə men′tə rē, -trē) *adj.* at variance with or contrary to parliamentary rule, procedure, or custom.

un·pin (un pin′) *v.t.,* **-pinned, -pin·ning. 1.** to remove a pin or pins from: *to unpin a hem after it has been sewn.* **2.** to unfasten or free, by or as by removing a pin or pins: *to unpin one's hair.*

un·pleas·ant (un plez′ənt) *adj.* not pleasing; offensive; disagreeable: *an unpleasant odor.* —**un·pleas′ant·ly,** *adv.*

un·pleas·ant·ness (un plez′ənt nis) *n.* **1.** the condition or quality of being unpleasant. **2.** something unpleasant or displeasing, such as a quarrel.

un·plug (un plug′) *v.t.,* **-plugged, -plug·ging. 1.** to remove the plug of (an electrical appliance) from an outlet; disconnect: *to unplug a toaster, to unplug a lamp.* **2.** to remove a stopper or plug from. **3.** to clear an obstruction from: *to unplug a clogged drain.*

un·plumbed (un plumd′) *adj.* **1.** not fully understood or explored; unfathomed: *the unplumbed depths of the unconscious.* **2.** not measured or sounded with or as with a plumb: *an unplumbed well, unplumbed ocean depths.*

un·pop·u·lar (un pop′yə lər) *adj.* not generally liked or accepted; not popular: *to hold unpopular opinions.* —**un·pop·u·lar·i·ty** (un′pop yə lar′i tē), *n.* —**un·pop′u·lar·ly,** *adv.*

un·prac·ticed (un prak′tist) *also, British,* **un·prac·tised.** *adj.* **1.** lacking experience, practice, or skill: *an unpracticed lawyer, to be unpracticed in the art of politics.* **2.** not put into practice: *an unpracticed technique.*

un·prec·e·dent·ed (un pres′i den′tid) *adj.* not known or done before; without parallel or precedent: *The landing on the moon in 1969 was an unprecedented event.*

un·pre·dict·a·ble (un′pri dik′tə bəl) *adj.* **1.** not able to be predicted or determined in advance: *unpredictable weather.* **2.** likely to act in ways that cannot be predicted: *an unpredictable personality.* —**un′pre·dict′a·ble·ness,** *n.* —**un′pre·dict′a·bly,** *adv.*

un·prej·u·diced (un prej′ə dist) *adj.* without prejudice or partiality; unbiased.

un·pre·med·i·tat·ed (un′prē med′i tā′tid) *adj.* not planned or thought out beforehand; unplanned; spontaneous: *an unpremeditated crime.* —**un′pre·med′i·tat′ed·ly,** *adv.*

un·pre·ten·tious (un′pri ten′shəs) *adj.* not pretentious, af-

fected, or showy; modest; unassuming: *an unpretentious summer cottage.* —**un′pre·ten′tious·ly,** *adv.* —**un′pre·ten′tious·ness,** *n.*

un·prin·ci·pled (un prin′sə pəld) *adj.* having or showing a lack of moral principles; unscrupulous.

un·print·a·ble (un prin′tə bəl) *adj.* unfit or improper for publication, as obscene matter.

un·pro·fes·sion·al (un′prə fesh′ə nəl) *adj.* **1.** violating the standards, rules, or traditions of a profession: *A scientist who purposely misrepresents the results of an experiment is guilty of unprofessional conduct.* **2.** not relating to, characteristic of, or associated with a given profession: *My unprofessional opinion is that the doctors are wrong.* **3.** not belonging to a profession or a professional group. **4.** lacking the skill or polish of professional work; amateurish: *an unprofessional performance.* —**un′pro·fes′sion·al·ly,** *adv.*

un·prof·it·a·ble (un prof′i tə bəl) *adj.* **1.** not producing a desired goal or improvement; fruitless; futile: *an unprofitable meeting.* **2.** producing no profit or monetary gain: *The investment proved to be unprofitable.* —**un·prof′it·a·bly,** *adv.*

un·qual·i·fied (un kwol′ə fīd′) *adj.* **1.** not having the necessary or proper qualifications; unfit: *an unqualified voter, to be unqualified to practice medicine.* **2.** not limited or restricted; absolute; utter: *The writer's first novel was an unqualified success.* —**un·qual′i·fied′ly,** *adv.*

un·ques·tion·a·ble (un kwes′chə nə bəl) *adj.* beyond doubt, dispute, or criticism: *a person of unquestionable integrity.* —**un·ques′tion·a·bly,** *adv.*

un·ques·tioned (un kwes′chənd) *adj.* **1.** not open to or called into question; not doubted or disputed: *an unquestioned principle of basic mathematics.* **2.** not subjected to questioning; not interrogated.

un·qui·et (un kwī′it) *adj.* **1.** marked by or causing emotional stress; uneasy; anxious: *unquiet thoughts.* **2.** marked by unrest, disturbance, or disorder: *unquiet times.* —*n.* a state of uneasiness or tension. —**un·qui′et·ly,** *adv.* —**un·qui′et·ness,** *n.*

un·quote (un kwōt′) *v.i.* **-quot·ed, -quot·ing.** to close or end a quotation. ➡ used to indicate the conclusion of a quotation, as in *Quote, "To be or not to be," unquote.*

un·rav·el (un rav′əl) *v.,* **-eled, -el·ing;** *also, British,* **-elled, -el·ling.** —*v.t.* **1.** to separate or untangle the threads of: *to unravel a ball of yarn.* **2.** to separate and make clear the elements of; solve; reveal: *to unravel the plot of a story.* —*v.i.* to become unraveled.

un·read (un red′) *adj.* **1.** not yet read or examined: *an unread manuscript.* **2.** having little or no knowledge or education; uneducated.

un·read·a·ble (un rē′də bəl) *adj.* **1.** not able to be read; illegible: *an unreadable signature.* **2.** too dull, difficult, or obscure to read: *an unreadable scientific journal.*

un·re·al (un rē′əl, -rēl′) *adj.* **1.** not actual or real; imaginary; fictitious. **2.** not based on or corresponding to reality: *an unreal view of the world.* **3.** *Informal.* not to be believed; incredible.

un·re·al·is·tic (un′rē ə lis′tik) *adj.* **1.** not according to or reflecting reality: *an unrealistic painting.* **2.** not practical: *an unrealistic goal.* —**un′re·al·is′ti·cal·ly,** *adv.*

un·re·al·i·ty (un′rē al′i tē) *n., pl.* **-ties. 1.** the state or quality of being unreal. **2.** an unreal thing, fact, or event; something unreal. **3.** the state of being unable to deal with reality.

un·rea·son·a·ble (un rē′zə nə bəl, -rēz′nə-) *adj.* **1.** not showing or using good sense or judgment; not reasonable: *You're being unreasonable in demanding that we redo all of our work.* **2.** going beyond what is reasonable or moderate; excessive; exorbitant: *The prices at that restaurant are unreasonable.* —**un·rea′son·a·ble·ness,** *n.* —**un·rea′son·a·bly,** *adv.*

un·rea·son·ing (un rē′zə ning, -rēz′ning) *adj.* not accompanied or controlled by reason: *unreasoning anger.* —**un·rea′son·ing·ly,** *adv.*

un·reel (un rēl′) *v.t., v.i.* to unwind (something), as from a reel.

un·re·fined (un′ri fīnd′) *adj.* **1.** not made free of impurities: *unrefined petroleum.* **2.** lacking culture or the social graces: *an unrefined person.*

un·re·flec·tive (un′ri flek′tiv) *adj.* not given to or proceeding

unprocessed	unprompted	unprotested	unquenchable	unready	unreclaimed
unprocurable	unpronounceable	unprotesting	unquenched	unrealistic	unrecognizable
unproductive	unpronounced	unproved	unquestioning	unrealizable	unrecognized
unproductiveness	unpropitiated	unproven	unquotable	unrealized	unreconcilable
unprofessed	unpropitious	unprovoked	unratified	unrebuked	unreconciled
unprogressive	unproportioned	unpublished	unreachable	unreceptive	unrecorded
unprohibited	unprosperous	unpunished	unreadily	unreciprocated	unrectified
unpromising	unprotected	unpurified	unreadiness	unreclaimable	unredeemed

from thought or reflection; thoughtless. —**un′re·flec′tive·ly,** *adv.*

un·re·gen·er·ate (un′ri jen′ər it) *adj.* **1.** not morally or spiritually renewed: *an unregenerate sinner.* **2.** resistant, as to change or reform; stubborn: *an unregenerate advocate of proper etiquette.*

un·re·lent·ing (un′ri len′ting) *adj.* **1.** not changing, yielding, or relenting; inflexible; inexorable: *to be unrelenting in one's criticism.* **2.** not easing, diminishing, or slackening, as in intensity, effort, or speed: *The prosecutor kept unrelenting pressure on the confused witness.* —**un′re·lent′ing·ly,** *adv.*

un·re·li·a·ble (un′ri lī′ə bəl) *adj.* not to be trusted or relied upon; untrustworthy; undependable: *an unreliable prediction, an unreliable person.* —**un′re·li·a·bil′i·ty, un′re·li·a·ble·ness,** *n.* —**un′re·li′a·bly,** *adv.*

un·re·li·gious (un′ri lij′əs) *adj.* **1.** indifferent or hostile to religion; irreligious. **2.** not connected with religion; nonreligious.

un·re·mit·ting (un′ri mit′ing) *adj.* never ceasing or slackening; incessant; constant: *unremitting determination to reach a goal.* —**un′re·mit′ting·ly,** *adv.*

un·re·quit·ed (un′ri kwī′tid) *adj.* not reciprocated or returned in kind: *unrequited love.*

un·re·served (un′ri zûrvd′) *adj.* **1.** done or given without reservation or restriction; unqualified; full: *unreserved approval.* **2.** free from reserve; candid; open: *an unreserved manner.* **3.** not set aside for a particular person or purpose in advance: *unreserved seats.* —**un·re·serv·ed·ly** (un′ri zûr′vid lē), *adv.* —**un′re·serv′ed·ness,** *n.*

un·rest (un rest′) *n.* an uneasy or disturbed state; restlessness; dissatisfaction; discontent: *political unrest over higher taxes.*

un·re·strained (un′ri strānd′) *adj.* **1.** not held in check or under control; not restrained: *loud, unrestrained laughter.* **2.** free from restraint or reserve; easy; natural: *an unrestrained atmosphere.* —**un·re·strain·ed·ly** (un′ri strā′nid lē), *adv.*

un·ripe (un rīp′) *adj.* **1.** not fully developed; immature: *unripe plums, unripe schemes.* **2.** not ready; unprepared: *The new employee was unripe for taking on such heavy responsibilities.* —**un·ripe′ness,** *n.*

un·ri·valed (un rī′vəld) *also, British,* **un·ri·valled.** *adj.* having no rival or equal; matchless; supreme: *unrivaled eloquence.*

un·roll (un rōl′) *v.t.* **1.** to open, spread out, or expand (something rolled up): *to unroll a blanket.* **2.** to expose to view; display; reveal. —*v.i.* to become unrolled.

UNRRA (un′rə) United Nations Relief and Rehabilitation Administration.

un·ruf·fled (un ruf′əld) *adj.* **1.** not ruffled or disordered; smooth: *unruffled waters, unruffled clothing.* **2.** not emotionally disturbed or agitated; composed: *unruffled self-confidence.*

un·ruled (un rüld′) *adj.* **1.** not controlled or governed: *an unruled temper.* **2.** not marked with lines: *unruled paper.*

un·ru·ly (un rü′lē) *adj.,* **-li·er, -li·est.** difficult or impossible to rule, control, or manage: *unruly hair, an unruly mob.* —**un·ru′li·ness,** *n.*

un·sad·dle (un sad′əl) *v.,* **-dled, -dling.** —*v.t.* **1.** to remove the saddle from, as a horse. **2.** to cause to fall from a horse; unhorse. —*v.i.* to remove the saddle from a horse or other animal.

un·said (un sed′) *v.* the past tense and past participle of **unsay.** —*adj.* not spoken or expressed: *Some things are better left unsaid.*

un·sat·is·fac·to·ry (un′sat is fak′tə rē) *adj.* not good enough to meet a standard or requirement; not satisfactory; inadequate: *unsatisfactory work.* —**un′sat·is·fac′to·ri·ly,** *adv.*

un·sat·u·rat·ed (un sach′ə rā′tid) *adj.* **1.** (of a solution) capable of dissolving more of a certain substance at a given temperature and pressure. **2.** (of an organic compound) containing double or triple bonds between carbon atoms and therefore capable of incorporating additional atoms or radicals without giving up original components. Unsaturated fats tend to be liquid at room temperature and are generally found in vegetable oils.

un·sa·vor·y (un sā′və rē) *also, British,* **un·sa·vour·y.** *adj.* **1.** disagreeable to the taste or smell: *spoiled and unsavory meat.* **2.** morally or socially offensive; objectionable; repugnant: *an unsavory reputation.* **3.** having no flavor or seasoning; tasteless; bland; insipid. —**un·sa′vor·i·ness,** *n.*

un·say (un sā′) *v.t.,* **-said (-sed′), -say·ing.** to take back or cancel (what has been said); retract.

un·scathed (un skāthd′) *adj.* in no way harmed or hurt; uninjured: *I walked away from the accident unscathed.*

un·schooled (un sküld′) *adj.* **1.** not taught, instructed, or trained: *unschooled in the ways of the world.* **2.** not acquired by schooling or training; natural: *unschooled talent.*

un·sci·en·tif·ic (un′sī ən tif′ik) *adj.* **1.** not based on or using the principles and methods of science; not scientific: *Astrology is unscientific.* **2.** showing a lack of scientific knowledge: *an unscientific mind.* —**un′sci·en·tif′i·cal·ly,** *adv.*

un·scram·ble (un skram′bəl) *v.t.,* **-bled, -bling. 1.** to make sense of or put in order: *to unscramble the contents of a desk drawer.* **2.** to make (a scrambled message) intelligible; decode.

un·screw (un skrü′) *v.t.* **1.** to remove, loosen, or unfasten by removing a screw or screws or by turning: *to unscrew a bracket from a wall, to unscrew the top of a jar.* **2.** to remove the screw or screws from. —*v.i.* to become or admit of being unscrewed: *The light bulb unscrews easily.*

un·scru·pu·lous (un skrü′pyə ləs) *adj.* showing no regard for what is right or wrong; unprincipled: *The unscrupulous merchant overcharged us.* —**un·scru′pu·lous·ly,** *adv.* —**un·scru′pu·lous·ness,** *n.*

un·seal (un sēl′) *v.t.* **1.** to break or remove the seal of: *to unseal an envelope, to unseal an official document.* **2.** to free from some constraining influence.

un·search·a·ble (un sûr′chə bəl) *adj.* not able to be searched or explored; inscrutable; mysterious. —**un·search′a·bly,** *adv.*

un·sea·son·a·ble (un sē′zə nə bəl) *adj.* **1.** not characteristic of or appropriate to the season: *unseasonable weather, unseasonable clothing.* **2.** not occurring or coming at the right or proper time; untimely; inopportune: *Midnight is an unseasonable hour to pay a visit.* —**un·sea′son·a·ble·ness,** *n.* —**un·sea′son·a·bly,** *adv.*

un·sea·soned (un sē′zənd) *adj.* **1.** not flavored with seasoning: *unseasoned food.* **2.** not disciplined or acclimated; inexperienced: *unseasoned workers.* **3.** not properly seasoned or aged; unripe; immature: *unseasoned wood.*

un·seat (un sēt′) *v.t.* **1.** to dislodge from a seat, esp. to throw from a saddle: *The horse unseated its rider.* **2.** to deprive of rank, position, or office: *to unseat a corrupt judge.*

un·seem·ly (un sēm′lē) *adj.,* **-li·er, -li·est.** inappropriate to the time or place; not proper or in good taste; indecorous: *It is unseemly to joke during a funeral service.* —*adv.* in an unseemly manner. —**un·seem′li·ness,** *n.*

un·seen (un sēn′) *adj.* **1.** not noticed or observed: *to come into a room unseen.* **2.** not seen; invisible.

un·set·tle (un set′əl) *v.t.,* **-tled, -tling. 1.** to make uneasy or anxious; confuse; disturb. **2.** to change or move from a fixed or stable condition; displace; disrupt.

un·set·tled (un set′əld) *adj.* **1.** not tranquil or orderly; disturbed; disrupted: *Unsettled conditions followed the war.* **2.** not yet established or stabilized: *My job situation is still unsettled.* **3.** not determined or decided; unresolved: *an unsettled question.* **4.** not paid, adjusted, or disposed of: *an unsettled debt.* **5.** not occupied, inhabited, or populated: *an unsettled region of the frontier.* **6.** liable to change; variable: *an unsettled state of health.* **7.** disturbed by illness or similar discomfort; unwell: *an unsettled stomach.*

un·sex (un seks′) *v.t.* **1.** to deprive of the ability to function sexually. **2.** to deprive of the qualities considered typical of one's sex.

un·shack·le (un shak′əl) *v.t.,* **-led, -ling. 1.** to free from shackles or other bonds. **2.** to free from anything that hinders action or thought.

un·shak·a·ble (un shā′kə bəl) *also,* **un·shake·a·ble.** *adj.* not easily swayed or daunted; firm; resolute: *an unshakable conviction.*

a	at	e	end	o	hot	u	up	hw	white		about
ā	ape	ē	me	ō	old	ū	use	ng	song		taken
ä	far	i	it	ô	fork	ü	rule	th	thin	ə	pencil
âr	care	ī	ice	oi	oil	u̇	pull	th	this		lemon
				ir	pierce	ou	out	ûr	turn	zh	measure		circus

unredressed	unregulated	unremedied	unrepealed	unreproved	unresponsively
unreflected	unrehearsed	unremembered	unrepentant	unrequested	unresponsiveness
unreflecting	unrelated	unremitted	unrepenting	unresistant	unrested
unreformed	unrelatedness	unremunerated	unreplenished	unresisted	unrestful
unrefreshed	unrelaxed	unremunerative	unreported	unresisting	unrestricted
unrefreshing	unrelaxing	unrenewed	unrepresentative	unresolved	unretentive
unregimented	unrelieved	unrented	unrepresented	unrespectful	unretracted
unregistered	unremarkable	unrepaired	unrepressed	unresponsive	unretrieved

un·shaped (un shāpt′) *adj.* **1.** not molded into shape; shapeless. **2.** not completely formed or developed: *unshaped theories.*

un·sheathe (un shēth′) *v.t.,* **-sheathed, -sheath·ing. 1.** to draw from or as from a sheath or scabbard: *to unsheathe a sword.* **2.** to uncover or lay bare: *to unsheathe one's private thoughts.*

un·ship (un ship′) *v.t.,* **-shipped, -ship·ping. 1.** to remove (nautical gear) from the proper place or position. **2.** to remove or discharge from a ship, as goods or passengers.

un·sight·ly (un sīt′lē) *adj.,* **-li·er, -li·est.** distasteful or offensive to the sight: *unsightly litter strewn about the city parks.* —**un·sight′li·ness,** *n.*

un·skilled (un skild′) *adj.* **1.** lacking skill, training, or competence: *an unskilled mechanic.* **2.** not involving or requiring skill or special training: *an unskilled job.* **3.** showing a lack of skill or ability: *an unskilled drawing.*

un·skill·ful (un skil′fəl) *also, British,* **un·skil·ful.** *adj.* lacking in skill; awkward; clumsy: *unskillful handling of a delicate situation.* —**un·skill′ful·ly,** *adv.* —**un·skill′ful·ness,** *n.*

un·snap (un snap′) *v.t.,* **-snapped, -snap·ping.** to undo the snap or snaps of; unfasten.

un·snarl (un snärl′) *v.t.* to free from a snarl or snarls: *to unsnarl a traffic jam, to unsnarl one's hair by careful combing.*

un·so·cia·ble (un sō′shə bəl) *adj.* **1.** not inclined to seek the company of others; withdrawn: *an unsociable neighbor.* **2.** lacking or not conducive to sociability; uncongenial: *an unsociable atmosphere.* —**un′so·cia·bil′i·ty, un·so′cia·ble·ness,** *n.* —**un·so′cia·bly,** *adv.*

un·so·phis·ti·cat·ed (un′sə fis′ti kā′tid) *adj.* **1.** not having knowledge of or experience in the ways of the world; lacking worldliness. **2.** not complex or refined; showing a lack of advanced technical knowledge; simple; artless: *an unsophisticated mechanical device.* —**un′so·phis′ti·cat′ed·ly,** *adv.* —**un′so·phis′ti·cat′ed·ness, un′so·phis′ti·ca′tion,** *n.*

un·sound (un sound′) *adj.* **1.** not strong or solid; weak; defective: *The foundation of the house is unsound and won't support the weight of the addition.* **2.** not based on truth, fact, or good judgment; not valid or sensible: *unsound advice, unsound reasoning.* **3.** physically or mentally unhealthy; diseased: *unsound teeth, of unsound mind.* **4.** not financially judicious or secure: *an unsound investment.* —**un·sound′ly,** *adv.* —**un·sound′ness,** *n.*

un·spar·ing (un spâr′ing) *adj.* **1.** very generous; unstinting; lavish: *They were unsparing in their efforts to help others.* **2.** showing no mercy; harsh; severe: *unsparing criticism.* —**un·spar′ing·ly,** *adv.*

un·speak·a·ble (un spē′kə bəl) *adj.* **1.** incapable of being described or expressed in words: *unspeakable happiness.* **2.** inexpressibly bad, evil, or objectionable: *the unspeakable acts of ruthless terrorists.* —**un·speak′a·bly,** *adv.*

un·spo·ken (un spō′kən) *adj.* not described or expressed in words; not spoken: *unspoken agreement.*

un·sports·man·like (un spôrts′mən līk′) *adj.* not having or showing such qualities or characteristics as fair play and the ability to accept defeat graciously.

un·spot·ted (un spot′id) *adj.* **1.** not marked by a spot or spots: *The glassware came out of the dishwasher unspotted.* **2.** without moral taint or blemish: *an unspotted reputation.*

un·sta·ble (un stā′bəl) *adj.* **1.** not firmly fixed in position; easily moved or put off balance: *an unstable platform, an unstable chair.* **2.** not settled or steady in character or situation; apt to change or alter: *an unstable government, an unstable relationship.* **3.** emotionally unsettled or troubled; maladjusted: *an unstable personality.* **4.** *Chemistry.* readily changed into another compound. **5.** *Physics.* readily decaying to form a new radionuclide; radioactive. —**un·sta′ble·ness,** *n.* —**un·sta′bly,** *adv.*

un·stead·y (un sted′ē) *adj.* **1.** not firm or secure; shaky: *an unsteady ladder.* **2.** marked by fluctuation or change; inconstant; variable: *Stock prices have been unsteady for months.* **3.** not uniform or consistent; irregular; uneven: *an unsteady gait.* **4.** irregular or erratic in habits or behavior; unreliable: *an unsteady worker.* —*v.t.,* **-died, -dy·ing.** to make unsteady. —**un·stead′i·ly,** *adv.* —**un·stead′i·ness,** *n.*

un·step (un step′) *v.t.,* **-stepped, -step·ping.** *Nautical.* to remove (a mast) from a step or position.

un·stop (un stop′) *v.t.,* **-stopped, -stop·ping. 1.** to remove a stop or stopper from: *to unstop a champagne bottle.* **2.** to free from obstruction: *to unstop a drain, to unstop one's ears.*

un·strap (un strap′) *v.t.,* **-strapped, -strap·ping.** to remove, unfasten, or loosen the strap or straps of: *to unstrap a trunk.*

un·stressed (un strest′) *adj.* not accented or stressed in speech: *an unstressed syllable.*

un·stri·at·ed (un strī′ā tid) *adj.* having no striations; smooth-textured: *unstriated muscle.*

un·string (un string′) *v.t.,* **-strung** (-strung′), **-string·ing. 1.** to remove or loosen the string or strings of: *to unstring a violin.* **2.** to remove from a string, as beads or pearls. **3.** to upset emotionally; unnerve: *We were unstrung by all the confusion during the fire.*

un·stuck (un stuk′) *adj.* **1.** freed or released from being stuck. **2.** *Informal.* in a state of disorder, confusion, or disorganization: *Without a manager the project quickly became unstuck.*

un·stud·ied (un stud′ēd) *adj.* **1.** not forced or contrived; spontaneous; natural: *unstudied friendliness.* **2.** not having been instructed; unversed; unlearned: *a builder unstudied in architecture.*

un·sub·stan·tial (un′səb stan′shəl) *adj.* **1.** lacking firmness, strength, or solidity: *an unsubstantial building material.* **2.** not based on reason, fact, or good judgment: *unsubstantial opinions.* **3.** without material substance or form; unreal: *unsubstantial dreams.* —**un′sub·stan′tial·ly,** *adv.*

un·suc·cess·ful (un′sək ses′fəl) *adj.* not meeting with or achieving success: *an unsuccessful experiment, an unsuccessful artist.* —**un′suc·cess′ful·ly,** *adv.*

un·suit·a·ble (un sü′tə bəl) *adj.* not appropriate to or fit for the circumstances: *Lightweight clothing is unsuitable for cold weather.* —**un′suit·a·bil′i·ty,** *n.* —**un·suit′a·bly,** *adv.*

un·sung (un sung′) *adj.* **1.** not honored or celebrated: *the unsung heroes of the frontier.* **2.** not sung.

un·sus·pect·ed (un′sə spek′tid) *adj.* **1.** not under suspicion. **2.** not imagined or thought to exist: *an unsuspected source of trouble, an unsuspected talent.*

un·sus·pect·ing (un′sə spek′ting) *adj.* having no suspicion; trusting: *unsuspecting victims of crime.* —**un′sus·pect′ing·ly,** *adv.*

un·tan·gle (un tang′gəl) *v.t.,* **-gled, -gling. 1.** to free from a tangle or tangles. **2.** to clear up; explain; resolve: *The police tried to untangle the mystery surrounding the kidnapping.*

un·taught (un tôt′) *adj.* **1.** not acquired by learning or teaching; natural: *an untaught art, an untaught talent.* **2.** not instructed or educated; ignorant.

un·ten·a·ble (un ten′ə bəl) *adj.* that cannot be held, defended, or maintained: *an untenable thesis, an untenable position.*

un·think·a·ble (un thing′kə bəl) *adj.* **1.** that cannot be imagined; inconceivable. **2.** that cannot be thought of or considered; out of the question. —**un·think′a·bly,** *adv.*

un·think·ing (un thing′king) *adj.* **1.** showing or marked by an absence of thoughtfulness, consideration, or careful reflection: *a foolish, unthinking remark.* **2.** without the ability to think: *an unthinking beast.* —**un·think′ing·ly,** *adv.*

un·thought-of (un thôt′uv′, -ov′) *adj.* not thought of or imagined: *an unthought-of possibility.*

un·thread (un thred′) *v.t.* **1.** to remove the thread from: *to unthread a needle, to unthread a sewing machine.* **2.** to separate the parts of; unravel; disentangle. **3.** to find one's way through or out of: *to unthread a maze.*

un·ti·dy (un tī′dē) *adj.,* **-di·er, -di·est.** not neat or orderly; messy: *an untidy desk.* —**un·ti′di·ly,** *adv.* —**un·ti′di·ness,** *n.*

un·tie (un tī′) *v.,* **-tied, -ty·ing.** —*v.t.* **1.** to loosen or undo (something knotted or tied): *to untie a knot.* **2.** to free from bonds or other restraints: *to untie a person's hands.* —*v.i.* to become untied.

un·til (ən til′, un-) *prep.* **1.** up to the time of: *Wait until evening before you call.* **2.** before (a specified time). ➡ used with the negative: *Tickets are not available until Wednesday.* —*conj.* **1.** up to the time when or that: *Wait here until I get back.* **2.** before. ➡ used with the negative: *The store couldn't deliver the furniture until the snow had been cleared from the roads.* **3.** to the place,

unreturnable	unrhythmic	unsalted	unscaled	unscoured	unsegmented
unrevealed	unrhythmical	unsanctified	unscanned	unscratched	unselective
unrevealing	unripened	unsanctioned	unscarred	unscreened	unself-conscious
unrevenged	unromantic	unsanitary	unscented	unsealed	unselfish
unrevised	unsafe	unsated	unsceptical	unseaworthy	unselfishness
unrewarded	unsaintly	unsatiated	unscheduled	unsecluded	unsensitive
unrewarding	unsalable	unsatisfied	unscholarly	unseeded	unsent
unrhymed	unsalaried	unsatisfying	unscorched	unseeing	unsentimental

extent, or degree that: *Keep driving straight until you reach the intersection.* [Middle English *untill* to, up to, up to the time of or that, toward, from *un-* unto (from Old Norse *und*) + TILL[1].]

un·time·ly (un tīm′lē) *adj.* **1.** coming or happening before the proper or usual time; premature: *an untimely death.* **2.** coming or happening at the wrong time; inopportune: *an untimely visit.* —*adv.* **1.** too soon; prematurely. **2.** at the wrong time; inopportunely. —**un·time′li·ness,** *n.*

un·tir·ing (un tīr′ing) *adj.* not ceasing or faltering; determined; persistent: *untiring patience, untiring efforts.* —**un·tir′ing·ly,** *adv.*

un·to (un′tü, -tə) *prep.* Archaic. **1.** to. **2.** until. [Middle English *unto,* from *un-* unto, until (from Old Norse *und*) + TO.]

un·told (un tōld′) *adj.* **1.** too great or numerous to be counted or measured: *untold numbers, untold suffering.* **2.** not related, revealed, or recounted: *an untold story.*

un·touch·a·ble (un tuch′ə bəl) *adj.* **1.** forbidden to the touch. **2.** beyond criticism or attack; unassailable. **3.** out of reach; inaccessible. **4.** disagreeable or defiling to the touch. —*n.* also, **Untouchable.** in India, a member of the lowest caste, whose touch was formerly considered to defile members of higher castes.

un·toward (un tôrd′, -tə wôrd′) *adj.* **1.** marked by or causing trouble or inconvenience; unfortunate; adverse: *an untoward economic situation.* **2.** difficult to manage or control; unruly; perverse: *an untoward child.* **3.** not appropriate or proper; unbecoming; unseemly: *an untoward comment.*

un·trav·eled (un trav′əld) also, British, **un·trav·elled.** *adj.* **1.** not traveled over or through; unfrequented: *an untraveled road.* **2.a.** not having traveled. **b.** not having gained experience by travel; not cosmopolitan.

un·tried (un trīd′) *adj.* **1.** not proved or tested, as by experience or use: *an untried worker, an untried machine.* **2.** not brought before a court for judgment: *untried offenders, an untried case.*

un·true (un trü′) *adj.* **1.** contrary to fact or to truth; incorrect; false: *an untrue remark.* **2.** not faithful or loyal: *to be untrue to one's friends.* **3.** deviating from a standard or rule; inaccurate; inexact. [Old English *untrēowe* unfaithful.] —**un′tru′ly,** *adv.*

un·truss (un trus′) *v.t.* to loose from or as from a truss; unfasten.

un·truth (un trüth′) *n.* **1.** something untrue; a lie. **2.** the quality or condition of being untrue; falsity. [Old English *untrēowth* unfaithfulness.]

un·truth·ful (un trüth′fəl) *adj.* **1.** contrary to fact or to the truth; not truthful: *an untruthful statement.* **2.** given to lying: *an untruthful person.* —**un·truth′ful·ly,** *adv.* —**un·truth′ful·ness,** *n.*

un·tu·tored (un tü′tərd, -tū′-) *adj.* **1.** lacking formal instruction; uneducated. **2.** not resulting from or improved by instruction: *untutored wisdom.* **3.** not sophisticated; naive.

un·twine (un twīn′) *v.,* **-twined, -twin·ing.** —*v.t.* to undo (something twined or tangled). —*v.i.* to become untwined.

un·twist (un twist′) *v.t.* to undo (something twisted). —*v.i.* to become untwisted.

un·used (un ūzd′) *adj.* **1.** not in use; not put to use: *an unused shelf in a bookcase.* **2.** never having been used; new; fresh: *an unused toothbrush.* **3.** not accustomed or habituated (with *to*): *to be unused to the quiet of the country.*

un·u·su·al (un ū′zhü əl) *adj.* not usual, common, or ordinary; rare: *Seeing an eclipse is an unusual experience.* —**un·u′su·al·ly,** *adv.* —**un·u′su·al·ness,** *n.* —For Synonyms, see **extraordinary.**

un·ut·ter·a·ble (un ut′ər ə bəl) *adj.* too deep or great to be put into words; inexpressible: *unutterable joy.* —**un·ut′ter·a·bly,** *adv.*

un·var·nished (un vär′nisht) *adj.* **1.** not covered with or as with varnish. **2.** stated or expressed without disguise or embellishment; plain; unadorned: *the unvarnished truth.*

un·veil (un vāl′) *v.t.* **1.** to remove a veil or covering from: *to unveil a monument.* **2.** to disclose or open to reveal as by removing a veil; reveal: *The proposed program was unveiled at the committee's hearings.* —*v.i.* to remove a veil.

un·voiced (un voist′) *adj.* **1.** not stated or expressed: *an*

unvoiced objection. **2.** (of a consonant) spoken without vibration of the vocal cords, as the *t* sound in *talk;* voiceless.

un·war·rant·ed (un wôr′ən tid, -wor′-) *adj.* without basis or justification; unjustified: *an unwarranted opinion, an unwarranted intrusion.*

un·war·y (un wâr′ē) *adj.* not alert or cautious, as to the possibility of trouble or deceit; careless; unguarded: *The dishonest storekeeper cheated the unwary customer.* —**un·war′i·ly,** *adv.* —**un·war′i·ness,** *n.*

un·wel·come (un wel′kəm) *adj.* not received with pleasure; not welcome or desired: *an unwelcome guest, unwelcome news.*

un·well (un wel′) *adj.* ailing; ill; sick.

un·wept (un wept′) *adj.* **1.** not mourned or lamented; not wept for. **2.** (of tears) not shed.

un·whole·some (un hōl′səm) *adj.* **1.** detrimental to mental, physical, or moral health; unhealthy: *an unwholesome diet, an unwholesome influence.* **2.** suggesting or resulting from disease or decay: *an unwholesome pallor.* —**un·whole′some·ly,** *adv.* —**un·whole′some·ness,** *n.*

un·wield·y (un wēl′dē) *adj.,* **-wield·i·er, -wield·i·est.** difficult to handle, manage, or use, as because of large size or bulky shape; clumsy; cumbersome: *an unwieldy package.* —**un·wield′i·ness,** *n.*

un·will·ing (un wil′ing) *adj.* **1.** not wanting to do or be something; not willing; reluctant: *I was unwilling to go on the trip.* **2.** not done, said, or given readily or heartily; uneager; unenthusiastic: *unwilling admiration.* —**un·will′ing·ly,** *adv.* —**un·will′ing·ness,** *n.*

un·wind (un wīnd′) *v.,* **-wound, -wind·ing.** —*v.t.* **1.** to undo or reverse the winding of; unroll: *The nurse unwound the bandages.* **2.** to straighten or untangle the twisted parts of: *to unwind a tangle of string.* —*v.i.* **1.** to become unrolled or untangled. **2.** to become free from tension or anxiety; relax: *to unwind by reading a good book.*

un·wise (un wīz′) *adj.* lacking or showing a lack of wisdom or good sense; foolish; imprudent: *It is unwise to leave the door unlocked.* —**un·wise′ly,** *adv.*

un·wit·ting (un wit′ing) *adj.* **1.** not knowing; unaware: *an unwitting accomplice to a crime.* **2.** not intentional; inadvertent: *Jokes are sometimes unwitting indications of what a person really feels.* —**un·wit′ting·ly,** *adv.*

un·wont·ed (un wôn′tid, -wōn′-, -wun′-) *adj.* not customary or habitual; rare; unusual: *The rookie played with unwonted poise.* —**un·wont′ed·ly,** *adv.* —**un·wont′ed·ness,** *n.*

un·world·ly (un wûrld′lē) *adj.* **1.** devoted to or concerned with spiritual matters rather than material interests or gain. **2.** lacking knowledge of or experience in the world; naive; unsophisticated. **3.** not of this world; unearthly; supernatural. —**un·world′li·ness,** *n.*

un·wor·thy (un wûr′thē) *adj.,* **-thi·er, -thi·est. 1.** not worthy or deserving (often with *of*): *I feel unworthy of such praise.* **2.** not befitting or appropriate; unbecoming (often with *of*): *Such cruel remarks are unworthy of a friend.* **3.** lacking value or merit; worthless. **4.** contemptible; base; vile. —**un·wor′thi·ly,** *adv.* —**un·wor′thi·ness,** *n.*

un·wound (un wound′) the past tense and past participle of **unwind.**

un·wrap (un rap′) *v.,* **-wrapped, -wrap·ping.** —*v.t.* to remove a wrapping from; open; undo: *to unwrap a package.* —*v.i.* to become unwrapped.

un·wrin·kle (un ring′kəl) *v.t.,* **-kled, -kling.** to remove the wrinkles from; smooth.

un·writ·ten (un rit′ən) *adj.* **1.** not written or put in writing: *unwritten testimony.* **2.** accepted by custom and usage; traditional: *an unwritten code of honor.*

a	at	e	end	o	hot	u	up	hw	white		about
ā	ape	ē	me	ō	old	ū	use	ng	song		taken
ä	far	i	it	ô	fork	u̇	rule	th	thin	ə	pencil
âr	care	ī	ice	oi	oil	u̇	pull	<u>th</u>	this		lemon
				ir	pierce	ou	out	ûr	turn	zh	measure		circus

unserviceable	unsheltered	unsized	unsoldierly	unspecific	unstinting
unset	unshod	unslaked	unsolicited	unspecified	unstrained
unsexual	unshorn	unsliced	unsolvable	unspent	unstratified
unshaded	unshrinking	unsmiling	unsolved	unspoiled	unstructured
unshaken	unsifted	unsmoked	unsorted	unstamped	unsubdued
unshaved	unsigned	unsocial	unsought	unstarched	unsubstantiated
unshaven	unsinkable	unsoiled	unsounded	unstated	unsuited
unshed	unsisterly	unsold	unspecialized	unsterilized	unsullied

1319

unwritten law, a rule, principle, or law based on custom or tradition rather than on legislative action.

un·yoke (un yōk′) *v.t.,* **-yoked, -yok·ing. 1.** to release from or as from a yoke: *to unyoke an ox.* **2.** to separate; part.

up (up) *adv.* **1.** in, to, or toward a higher place or position: *to climb up to the top of a ladder, to be up in a tree.* **2.** to or toward a higher point or degree: *My weight went up over the summer. Please turn the sound up on the radio.* **3.** at, to, toward, or in a direction, place, or position that is considered to be or is more elevated or at a more northerly latitude: *We drove up from Richmond to New York. They're spending the summer up in the mountains.* **4.** above the surface or horizon: *The diver came up for air. The sun came up at five o'clock.* **5.** in or to an upright position or posture: *Sit up straight.* **6.** out of bed: *I got up at seven o'clock.* **7.** to a state or point of completion or exhaustion; thoroughly; totally: *I paid up all of my debts. We used up all the eggs when we made lunch.* **8.** in or into existence, operation, or action: *The building went up quickly after construction began. Such conditions will always set up a force field.* **9.** in or into a unified or closed state; together; contracted: *Button up your coat. Fold up the chair.* **10.** at or to an equal point, degree, or position: *Fill the beaker up to the first red line. The movie didn't come up to our expectations.* **11.** into consideration, attention, or prominence: *Your name kept coming up in the conversation.* **12.** at or into a place of storage or concealment, as for safekeeping: *We saved up money for our vacation.* **13.** in or into an excited, agitated, or troubled state: *to be all riled up.* **14.** for each side; apiece: *The score was four up.* **15.** in the lead; ahead: *to finish one up on one's opponent.* **16.** *Baseball.* at bat. —*adj.* **1.** going or directed upward: *Take the up escalator.* **2.** at a higher point or degree: *Prices are up again this month.* **3.** risen above the horizon: *The sun is up.* **4.** above the ground: *Mushrooms are up all over the lawn next door.* **5.** a-wake or out of bed: *They won't be up until nine o'clock.* **6.** being presented or considered: *The mayor is up for reelection. The house is up for sale.* **7.** at an end; finished; over: *The speaker's time was up.* **8.** being even with, as in space or degree; equal: *Your work simply isn't up to standard.* **9.** on trial: *to be up for murder.* **10.** ahead of one's opponent: *to be two runs up in the third inning.* **11.** *Baseball.* at bat. **12.** *Informal.* going on; taking place: *What's up?* —*prep.* **1.** to or toward a higher position in or on (a specified place): *The spider climbed up the wall.* **2.** to or toward a place or position farther along: *Their house is up the block.* **3.** to or toward the source or interior part of: *to paddle up a river.* —*n.* **1.** any upward movement or direction; ascent: *the ups and downs of a roller coaster ride.* **2.** a period of prosperity, elation, or good luck: *to have one's ups and downs.* —*v.,* **upped, up·ping.** —*v.t.* **1.** to make higher or larger, as in amount or degree; increase: *The store has upped prices this month.* **2.** to put, take, or lift up: *to up the hem of a garment.* —*v.i.* **1.** *Informal.* to act abruptly or unexpectedly. ➡ often used in the uninflected form: *They up and eloped.* [Partly from Old English *upp* to a higher place or point; partly from Old English *uppe* on high, aloft.]

•**on the up and up.** *Slang.* sincere and aboveboard; frank; honest: *As long as the manager is on the up and up with us, we don't mind working at the store.*

•**up against.** facing; confronting: *The team is up against great odds.*

•**up and around** (or **about**). recovered and out of bed, as after an illness.

•**up and doing.** *Informal.* active and busy: *I was up and doing all day long.*

•**up for. a.** proposed as eligible for: *Who is up for the supervisory position?* **b.** charged with or on trial for: *What is the defendant up for?*

•**up on.** *Informal.* well-informed about: *to be up on current events.*

•**up to. a.** *Informal.* doing or about to do: *What are you up to?* **b.** as far as: *What chapter are you up to in the book?* **c.** capable of; equal to: *Are you up to such an important job?* **d.** dependent upon, as for a decision: *It is up to you to make the change.*

up-and-com·ing (up′ən kum′ing) *adj.* likely to succeed; promising: *an up-and-coming young lawyer.*

up-and-down (up′ən doun′) *adj.* **1.** consisting of or marked by an alternate upward and downward movement. **2.** vertical; perpendicular.

U·pan·i·shad (ü pan′i shad′, ü pä′ni shäd′) *n.* in sacred Hindu literature, one of a group of late Vedic treatises dealing with religious and metaphysical issues. [Sanskrit *upanishad* literally, a sitting down near something.]

u·pas (ū′pəs) *n.* **1.** the milky, yellowish, poisonous sap of a tree, *Antiaris toxicaria* of Asia, used to make a deadly arrow poison. **2.** the tree itself. Also *(def. 2),* **upas tree.** [Malay *ūpas* poison; of Javanese origin.]

up·beat (up′bēt′) *n. Music.* an unaccented beat, esp. the last beat of a measure, indicated by an upward gesture of the conductor's hand. —*adj. Informal.* happy; cheerful; optimistic.

up·braid (up brād′) *v.t.* to criticize or scold harshly or vehemently: *The supervisor upbraided the workers for not finishing the project on time.* [Old English *upbregdan* to reproach.] —For Synonyms, see **scold.**

up·bring·ing (up′bring′ing) *n.* the care and training received during childhood and youth; manner in which a youngster is raised: *a strict upbringing, a religious upbringing.*

UPC, Universal Product Code.

up·com·ing (up′kum′ing) *adj.* soon to occur; forthcoming: *the upcoming football season, an upcoming Broadway play.*

up·coun·try (up′kun′trē) *also,* **up·coun·try.** *n.* the interior or remote part of a region or country; inland. —*adj.* of, characteristic of, or coming from the upcountry: *upcountry manners.* —*adv.* toward or in the upcountry.

up·date (*v.,* up dāt′, up′dāt′; *n.,* up′dāt′) *v.t.* **-dat·ed, -dat·ing. 1.** to make current or up-to-date: *to update a history textbook by adding new information.* **2.** to modernize the facilities, technology, or processes of: *to update an industrial plant.* **3.** to inform (someone) of current facts or recent events: *Please update me on the latest developments.* —*n.* **1.** the act or an instance of updating: *An update on the weather is broadcast every hour.* **2.** an up-to-date report or version: *Give me an update on the progress of your term paper.*

up·draft (up′draft′) *n.* an upward-moving current of air.

up·end (up end′) *v.t.* **1.** to set, stand, or turn on end. **2.** to topple or defeat, esp. in competition: *Our basketball team upended the defending champions.* —*v.i.* to become upended.

up·front (up′frunt′) *adj.* **1.** *Informal.* outspoken and direct: *to be up-front about a disagreement.* **2.** paid in advance: *an up-front fee for services.* —*adv.* before in time; in advance: *to pay for merchandise up-front.*

up·grade (*v.,* up grād′, up′grād′; *n.,* up′grād′) *v.t.,* **-grad·ed, -grad·ing.** to raise to a higher grade or standard, as by improving quality or position: *to upgrade a product, to upgrade a worker to supervisory level.* —*n.* **1.** an upward slope or incline, as of a hill or road, in the direction one is moving. **2.** any increase or improvement, such as an improved version of a computer program. —*adv.* up a hill or slope; uphill.

•**on the upgrade.** becoming better, as in quality or status; improving: *Our company's profits are on the upgrade.*

up·growth (up′grōth′) *n.* **1.** the process of growing up; growth or development. **2.** a person or thing that grows up or has grown up.

unsupervised	unsystematic	untested	untransferable	unvalidated	unwaxed
unsupported	unsystematical	untether	untranslatable	unvalued	unweaned
unsuppressed	untabulated	unthanked	untranslated	unvanquished	unwearable
unsure	untactful	unthankful	untransmitted	unvaried	unweeded
unsurpassable	untainted	unthatched	untraversed	unvarying	unwelded
unsurpassed	untalented	untheatrical	untreated	unveil	unwhipped
unsusceptible	untamable	unthoughtful	untrimmed	unventilated	unwitnessed
unsustained	untamed	unthreatening	untrod	unverifiable	unwooded
unswayed	untanned	unthrifty	untroubled	unverified	unworkable
unsweetened	untapped	untillable	untrustworthy	unversed	unworn
unswept	untarnished	untilled	untuned	unviable	unworried
unswerving	untasted	untinged	untwist	unvisited	unwounded
unsworn	untaxed	untitled	untypical	unwanted	unwoven
unsymmetrical	unteachable	untouched	unusable	unwashed	unwrinkled
unsympathetic	untechnical	untraceable	unutilized	unwatched	unyielding
unsympathizing	untempered	untraced	unuttered	unwatered	unzip
unsynchronized	untended	untrained	unvaccinated	unwavering	unzoned

up·heav·al (up hē′vəl) *n.* **1.** the act of upheaving or the state of being upheaved: *volcanic upheavals.* **2.** an instance of this. **3.** a profound or violent disturbance or change: *social upheavals.*

up·heave (up hēv′) *v.,* **-heaved** or **-hove** (-hōv′), **-heav·ing.** —*v.t.* to lift or throw up, as by force or pressure from beneath. —*v.i.* to be lifted, thrown, or forced up.

up·held (up held′) the past tense and past participle of **uphold.**

up·hill (up′hil′) *adj.* **1.** going upward on a hill or incline; directed or sloping upward: *an uphill path.* **2.** presenting difficulties; arduous; hard: *Winning the election was an uphill battle.* —*adv.* **1.** up a hill or incline; upward: *to ride a bicycle uphill.* **2.** against difficulties: *We seem to be working uphill.*

up·hold (up hōld′) *v.t.,* **-held** (-held′), **-hold·ing.** **1.** to support or maintain, as by defending or preserving in the face of opposition: *to uphold the right to dissent, to uphold a tradition.* **2.** to approve or agree with; confirm: *The Supreme Court upheld the lower court's decision.* **3.** to keep from falling or sinking; hold up: *The posts uphold the porch roof.* —**up·hold′er,** *n.*

up·hol·ster (up hōl′stər, ə pōl′-) *v.t.* to fit, as furniture, with padding, cushions, or coverings: *to upholster a sofa, to upholster a headboard on a bed.* [From UPHOLSTERER.]

up·hol·ster·er (up hōl′stər ər, ə pōl′-) *n.* a person whose work is upholstering furniture. [Earlier *upholdster,* from Middle English *upholden* to repair (from UP + *holden* to keep, hold¹) + -STER. See HOLD¹.]

up·hol·ster·y (up hōl′stə rē, -strē, ə pōl′-) *n., pl.* **-ster·ies.** **1.** the material used in upholstering. **2.** the work, business, or craft of upholstering.

UPI, United Press International, a private news-gathering agency that maintains a worldwide communications network for the transmission of news. It supplies its clients, which include newspapers, magazines, and radio and television stations, with news reports, photographs, newsreels, and audio services.

up·keep (up′kēp′) *n.* **1.** the act of keeping something in good condition or in a proper state of repair; maintenance: *Four hundred workers are needed for the upkeep of the city parks.* **2.** the cost of such maintenance: *The upkeep on the estate is very high.*

up·land (up′lənd, -land′) *n.* also, **uplands.** land that is considerably higher than the land surrounding it. —*adj.* of, relating to, or located on such land.

up·lift (*v.,* up lift′; *n.,* up′lift′) *v.t.* **1.** to raise to a higher moral, social, or cultural level or condition. **2.** to elevate emotionally or spiritually; exalt. **3.** to lift up or raise aloft; elevate. —*n.* **1.** the act, process, or result of lifting up or raising. **2.** efforts or a movement to improve the moral, social, or cultural level of a person, group, or community. **3.** moral, spiritual, or cultural elevation. **4.** *Geology.* **a.** a raised area of the earth's crust. **b.** an upward movement of the earth's surface. —**up·lift′er,** *n.*

up·link (up′lingk′) *n.* a transmission path for data or other signals from an earth station to a satellite or spacecraft. [UP + LINK¹.]

up·most (up′mōst′) *adj.* uppermost.

up·on (ə pôn′, ə pon′) *prep.* on. [UP + ON.]

up·per (up′ər) *adj.* **1.** higher, as in place or position or on a scale: *the upper story of the house, the upper register of one's voice.* **2.** (of places) lying on higher ground, farther north, or farther inland. —*n.* **1.** the part of a shoe or boot above the sole. **2.** *Informal.* an upper berth, as in a sleeping car. **3.** *Slang.* any drug that contains a stimulant. **4.** also, **Upper.** designating a later part of a geologic period: *the Upper Pleistocene.*

·on one's uppers. *Informal.* **a.** wearing shoes with worn-out soles. **b.** in shabby or poor circumstances; poor; destitute.

up·per-case (up′ər kās′) *adj.* of, relating to, or printed in capital letters; capital. ➡ distinguished from **lower-case.** —*v.t.,* **-cased, -cas·ing.** to set in or print with capital letters.

upper case 1. capital letters. **2.** *Printing.* a type case holding capital letters.

up·per-class (up′ər klas′) *adj.* of, relating to, or characteristic of the upper class.

upper class, the portion of society occupying the highest social and economic position, above the middle class and lower class.

up·per-class·man (up′ər klas′mən) *n., pl.* **-men** (-mən). a junior or senior in a high school, college, or university.

upper crust *Informal.* that part of the upper class considered to have the greatest wealth or social standing in a society.

up·per·cut (up′ər kut′) *n.* a swinging blow, as in boxing, directed upward from beneath, usually to an opponent's chin. —*v.t.,* **-cut, -cut·ting.** to strike with an uppercut.

upper hand, a position of mastery or control; advantage: *Our team gained the upper hand in the debate.*

upper house also, **Upper House.** in a bicameral legislature, the branch that is usually smaller, less representative of the population, and more restricted in membership, such as the Senate in the U.S. Congress.

up·per·most (up′ər mōst′) *adj.* **1.** highest, as in place or position: *the uppermost floors of a building.* **2.** having the most importance, prominence, or influence; foremost; predominant: *to be uppermost in someone's thoughts.* Also, **upmost.** —*adv.* in the highest or foremost place, position, or rank.

up·pi·ty (up′i tē) *adj. Informal.* displaying an attitude of exaggerated self-importance; snobbish; haughty. —**up′pi·ty·ness,** *n.*

up·raise (up rāz′) *v.t.,* **-raised, -rais·ing.** to raise or lift up; elevate.

up·right (up′rīt′) *adj.* **1.** in a vertical position, posture, or direction; straight up; erect: *an upright column.* **2.** having or showing good character and moral integrity; honorable. —*n.* **1.** something that is in a vertical position, such as an upright timber or beam. **2.** the state of being upright; vertical position: *a column out of upright.* **3.** upright piano. **4.** uprights. *Football.* goalpost. —*adv.* in a vertical position. [Old English *upriht* in a vertical position, erect.] —**up′right′ly,** *adv.* —**up′right′ness,** *n.*

upright piano, a piano having the strings and mechanism arranged vertically in a rectangular case that is perpendicular to the keyboard. ➡ distinguished from **grand piano.**

up·rise (up rīz′) *v.i.,* **-rose** (-rōz′), **-ris·en** (-riz′ən), **-ris·ing.** *Archaic.* **1.** to arise or get up, as from a lying or sitting position. **2.** to come into existence or prominence. **3.** to rise to a higher position, as from below the horizon. **4.** to stage an uprising; rebel; revolt.

up·ris·ing (up′rī′zing) *n.* an insurrection against a government or other authority; rebellion. —For Synonyms, see **revolt.**

up·roar (up′rôr′) *n.* **1.** a state of noisy or confused excitement, disorder, or agitation. **2.** the sound of such agitation; din; clamor: *We heard an uproar coming from the next room.* [Dutch *oproer* tumult, mutiny; Modern English spelling influenced by ROAR.]

up·roar·i·ous (up rôr′ē əs) *adj.* **1.** making, causing, or marked by an uproar: *an uproarious welcome.* **2.** loud, noisy, and unrestrained; boisterous: *The room was filled with uproarious laughter.* **3.** causing hearty or boisterous laughter; hilarious: *an uproarious comedy.* —**up·roar′i·ous·ly,** *adv.* —**up·roar′i·ous·ness,** *n.*

up·root (up rüt′, -rut′) *v.t.* **1.** to tear or pull up by the roots: *The tractor uprooted the tree.* **2.** to wrench from or deprive of an accustomed location, environment, or way of life; displace: *The war uprooted many families.* **3.** to remove or destroy completely; eradicate: *to uproot the source of a disease.*

up·rose (up rōz′) the past tense of **uprise.**

up·scale (up′skāl′) *adj.* of, relating to, or for those having an income, education, and social standing that are well above the average: *a fancy restaurant with an upscale clientele.*

up·set (*v., adj.,* up set′; *n.,* up′set′) *v.t.,* **-set, -set·ting. 1.** to turn, tip, or knock over; topple; capsize: *I accidentally upset the pitcher when I leaned over the table.* **2.** to throw into confusion or disorder: *A wildcat strike upset the airline schedule.* **3.** to make perturbed, anxious, or uneasy; distress: *News of the accident greatly upset me.* **4.** to cause a physical disturbance in; make sick: *Eating all that greasy food will upset your stomach.* **5.** to defeat unexpectedly: *The teenage tennis player upset the club champion.* —*adj.* **1.** mentally or emotionally distressed; perturbed: *I was very upset about missing the plane.* **2.** physically disturbed; made sick: *My stomach was upset for hours after that heavy meal.* **3.** turned, tipped, or knocked over: *The upset glass of water spilled all over me.* **4.** confused or disordered: *an upset work routine.* —*n.* **1.** the unexpected defeat of an opponent or contestant favored to win. **2.** the act of throwing into confusion or disorder; disruption: *The delay caused an upset of our plans.* **3.** mental or emotional distress; anxiety. **4.** physical disturbance or disorder: *a stomach upset.* **5.** the act of turning, tipping, or knocking something over. —For Synonyms *(v.t.),* see **disturb.**

upset price, the minimum price at which something will be offered for sale, as at an auction.

up·shot (up′shot′) *n.* the final result; conclusion; outcome. [UP + SHOT¹; originally, a final shot in an archery competition.]

up·side down (up′sīd′) also, **up·side-down** (up′sīd′down′). **1.** in such a way that the upper side or part becomes the under or lower side or part: *You're holding the map upside down.* **2.** in or into complete disorder or confusion: *We turned the house upside down searching for the keys.* [Modification (influenced by obsolete *upside* upper side) of Middle English *up so down,* literally, up as if down.] —**up′side′-down′,** *adj.*

a	at	e	end	o	hot	u	up	hw	white		about
ā	ape	ē	me	ō	old	ū	use	ng	song		taken
ä	far	i	it	ô	fork	ü	rule	th	thin	ə	pencil
âr	care	ī	ice	oi	oil	u̇	pull	t͟h	this		lemon
		îr	pierce	ou	out	ûr	turn	zh	measure		circus

upside-down cake, a cake baked with the batter covering a layer of fruit, served with the fruit side up.

up·si·lon (ūp′sə lon′, up′-) *n.* the twentieth letter of the Greek alphabet (Υ, υ), corresponding to the English letter *U, u* or *Y, y.*

up·stage (*adv., adj.,* up′stāj′; *v.,* up stāj′) *adj.* at or toward the rear of a stage. —*adj.* **1.** of or relating to the rear of a stage. **2.** *Informal.* snobbish; haughty. —*v.t.,* **-staged, -stag·ing. 1.** to draw audience attention away from (another entertainer) to oneself, as by moving upstage, thus forcing the other entertainer to face away from the audience. **2.** to draw attention to oneself at the expense of (another); eclipse. **3.** *Informal.* to treat in a snobbish or haughty manner.

up·stairs (up′stârz′) *adv.* **1.** toward the top of a staircase; up the stairs: *to run upstairs.* **2.** on or to an upper floor or level: *They're watching television upstairs.* **3.** *Slang.* in the mind; mentally or emotionally. —*adj.* of, relating to, or situated on an upper floor or floors: *an upstairs apartment.* —*n.* the upper floor or floors. ➠ usually used as singular: *The upstairs of the house has not yet been cleaned.*

· **to kick (someone) upstairs.** *Informal.* to promote (someone) to a position that is higher but actually less responsible or powerful, so as to make that person less influential.

up·stand·ing (up stan′ding, up′stan′-) *adj.* **1.** honest in character and behavior; commanding respect; honorable: *a fine, upstanding member of the community.* **2.** standing up; upright; erect.

up·start (up′stärt′) *n.* **1.** a person who is brash, aggressive, and presumptuous. **2.** a person of humble origins who attains sudden wealth or importance and usually behaves in an arrogant or vulgar way as a result; parvenu. —*adj.* **1.** characteristic of an upstart. **2.** having suddenly risen to a position of wealth or importance.

up·state (up′stāt′) *adj.* of, from, or designating that part of a state lying farther inland or north of a large city: *We took a vacation in upstate New York.* —*n.* an upstate region. —*adv.* in, to, or toward such a region: *We plan to drive upstate for the weekend.* —**up′stat′er,** *n.*

up·stream (up′strēm′) *adv.* toward or at the source of a stream; against the current: *to fish upstream, to row upstream.* —*adj.* directed or situated upstream.

up·surge (*n.,* up′sûrj′; *v.,* up sûrj′) *n.* a sudden increase or development: *There is usually an upsurge of interest in politics around election time.* —*v.i.,* **-surged, -surg·ing.** to surge up; increase; rise.

up·sweep (*n.,* up′swēp′; *v.,* up swēp′) *n.* **1.** an upward sweep or curve. **2.** a hairdo in which the hair is smoothly combed upward in the back and secured in position on top of the head. —*v.i., v.t.,* **-swept** (-swept′), **-sweep·ing.** to sweep or curve upward.

up·swept (up′swept′) *v.* the past tense and past participle of **upsweep.** —*adj.* **1.** swept or curved upward. **2.** in or resembling an upsweep: *an upswept hairdo.*

up·swing (up′swing′) *n.* **1.** an upward swing or movement. **2.** a marked increase or improvement, as in activity or movement: *Business in that town is on the upswing.*

up·take (up′tāk′) *n.* **1.** *Informal.* mental grasp or perception; understanding; comprehension: *to be quick on the uptake.* **2.** a flue or shaft for drawing up air or smoke, as from a mine.

up·thrust (up′thrust′) *n.* an upward thrust, esp. an upheaval or part of the earth's crust; thrust.

up·tight (up′tīt′) *also,* **up tight.** *adj. Slang.* **1.** tense; nervous; anxious: *I was uptight about the math test this morning.* **2.** overly strict, formal, or conventional; strait-laced: *uptight manners.*

up-to-date (up′tə dāt′) *adj.* **1.** extending to the present time, as in coverage of facts or ideas; employing or including the latest information: *an up-to-date telephone book.* **2.** reflecting the latest in style, ideas, or improvements; fashionable; modern: *up-to-date designer clothes.* —**up′-to-date′ness,** *n.*

up·town (*adv., n.,* up′toun′; *adj.,* up′toun′) *adv.* to, toward, or in the upper part of a town or city, usually away from the main business district: *We've moved uptown.* —*adj.* **1.** of, relating to, or in the upper part of a town or city: *uptown traffic, an uptown bus.* **2.** of or characteristic of those persons who live in the more affluent district of a city; elegant; stylish: *uptown sophistication.* —*n.* the uptown part of a town or city.

up·turn (*n.,* up′tûrn′; *v.,* up tûrn′) *n.* an upward turn or trend, esp. toward improved conditions: *an upturn in stock market prices.* —*v.t.* to turn up or over, as soil with a plow.

up·ward (up′wərd) *adv. also,* **up·wards. 1.** from a lower to a higher place or position: *to look upward.* **2.** toward a higher or greater amount, degree, or rank: *Costs have climbed upward.* **3.** toward or into a later time or greater age: *From childhood upward, the musician had taken piano lessons.* **4.** more; over: *Tickets go for five dollars and upward.* **5.** toward a higher or better condition or level; toward something greater or loftier: *minds aspiring upward.* **6.** toward the interior, source, or origin: *The explorers followed the river upward.* —*adj.* moving from a lower

to a higher place, level, or condition: *an upward trend.* [Old English *upweard* to a higher position.] —**up′ward·ly,** *adv.*

· **upward** (or **upwards**) **of.** more than: *There were upwards of fifty people at the party.*

up·well·ing (up wel′ing) *n.* an upward flow of deep, cold, nutrient-rich seawater toward the surface, prevalent along the western coasts of the continents, esp. in the Western Hemisphere and Africa.

up·wind (up′wind′, -wind′) *adj., adv.* in the direction opposite that in which the wind is blowing; against the wind. [UP + WIND[1].]

u·ra·cil (yūr′ə səl) *n.* a pyrimidine base that is an essential constituent of RNA. Formula: $C_4H_4N_2O_2$

u·rae·us (yū rē′əs) *n., pl.* **-us·es.** a representation of the sacred serpent of ancient Egypt, depicted on the headdress of Egyptian rulers as an emblem of sovereignty. [Modern Latin *uraeus,* from Greek *ouraios* cobra, from Egyptian *uro* cobra, king.]

U·ral-Al·ta·ic (yūr′əl al-tā′ik) *n.* a postulated family of languages divided into two main branches, the first of which includes Finnish and Hungarian, the second of which includes Turkish and Mongolian. Languages of this family are spoken predominantly in parts of eastern Europe and central Asia.

uraeus on the funeral mask of Tutankhamen

U·ra·ni·a (yū rā′nē ə) *n.* in Greek mythology, the Muse of astronomy.

u·ran·i·nite (yū ran′ə nīt′) *n.* a black or brown oxide mineral that is the principal ore of uranium. A common variety is pitchblende. Formula: UO_2

u·ra·ni·um (yū rā′nē əm) *n.* a heavy, silvery, radioactive metallic element with fourteen isotopes, three of which occur naturally. Uranium isotopes are used chiefly as nuclear fuel, in the production of nuclear fuel, and in the manufacture of nuclear weapons. Symbol: **U** For tables, see **element.** [Modern Latin *uranium,* from the planet *Uranus,* which had been discovered shortly before the element was named.]

uranium 235 *also,* **uranium-235.** a uranium isotope having a mass number of 235, used as fuel for the chain reaction that releases the explosive energy of a nuclear weapon and the thermal energy in a nuclear reactor. It is the only naturally occurring material that undergoes nuclear fission. Symbol: **U 235** For illustration, see **fission.**

uranium 238 *also,* **uranium-238.** a uranium isotope having a mass number of 238, the most abundant naturally occurring isotope of uranium, used as the raw material for producing plutonium. Symbol: **U 238**

U·ra·nus (yūr′ə nəs, yū rā′-) *n.* **1.** in Greek mythology, the god who personified the sky and was the earliest ruler of the universe. He was the son and husband of Gaea and father of the Titans. **2.** the third largest planet of the solar system and seventh in order of distance from the sun. It has fifteen confirmed satellites. [Latin *Ūranus* the god, from Greek *Ouranos,* from *ouranos* sky, heaven.]

ur·ban (ûr′bən) *adj.* of, in, relating to, or characteristic of a city or city life: *urban expansion, an urban population.* [Latin *urbānus* relating to a city, refined, from *urbs* city.]

ur·bane (ûr bān′) *adj.* refined and courteous in a smooth, polished way; elegant; sophisticated: *The senator is an urbane, cultured individual.* [Latin *urbānus.* See URBAN.] —**ur·bane′ly,** *adv.* —**ur·bane′ness,** *n.*

ur·ban·ite (ûr′bə nīt′) *n.* a person who lives in a city.

ur·ban·i·ty (ûr ban′i tē) *n., pl.* **-ties. 1.** the quality of being urbane. **2.** an example of urbane behavior.

ur·ban·ize (ûr′bə nīz′) *v.t.,* **-ized, -iz·ing.** to make urban, as in quality, nature, or organization: *The builders are urbanizing the countryside around the city.* —**ur′ban·i·za′tion,** *n.*

urban renewal, the planned rehabilitation and reconstruction of deteriorating urban areas, chiefly through the demolition of slums and the building of public housing, usually carried out under a government-subsidized program.

ur·chin (ûr′chin) *n.* **1.** a poor, tattered child. **2.** a small, mischievous or impish child. **3.** sea urchin. [Dialectal Old French *herichon* hedgehog, going back to Latin *(h)ērīcius.*]

Ur·du (ūr′dū, ûr′-) *n.* an Indo-European language that is a form of Hindustani, spoken by Muslims in Pakistan and parts of India

and written in a modified Arabic alphabet. [Hindustani *urdū,* short for *zabān-i-urdū* language of the camp, from Persian *zabān* language + *urdū* army, camp (from Turkish *ordū*).]

-ure *suffix* (used to form nouns from verbs) **1.** the act, process, state, or result: *exposure, enclosure.* **2.** a function or office or a group performing a function: *legislature.* [Old French *-ure,* from Latin *-ūra.*]

u·re·a (yù rē′ə) *n.* a colorless, crystalline, organic compound that is a constituent of almost all body fluids, esp. urine, and is also produced synthetically, used in fertilizers and animal feed in the manufacture of plastics and explosives. Formula: $CO(NH_2)_2$ [Modern Latin *urea,* going back to Greek *ouron* urine.] —**u·re′ic,** *adj.*

u·re·mi·a (yù rē′mē ə) *n.* a disorder arising from the presence in the blood of urea and other waste products normally eliminated in the urine, an indication of kidney malfunction, characterized by headache, nausea, and convulsions. Also, **uremic poisoning.** [Modern Latin *uraemia,* from Greek *ouron* urine + *haima* blood.] —**u·re′mic,** *adj.*

u·re·ter (yù rē′tər) *n.* either of two tubes that carry urine from the kidneys to the urinary bladder or, in birds, to the cloaca. For illustration, see **urinary system.** [Modern Latin *ureter,* from Greek *ourētēr,* going back to *ouron* urine.] —**u·re′ter·al, u·re·ter·ic** (yùr′i ter′ik), *adj.*

u·re·thra (yù rē′thrə) *n., pl.* **-thras** or **-thrae** (-thrē). the canal through which urine and, in men, semen are discharged from the body. For illustration, see **urinary system.** [Late Latin *ūrēthra,* from Greek *ourēthrā,* going back to *ouron* urine.] —**u·re′thral,** *adj.*

urge (ûrj) *v.,* **urged, urg·ing.** —*v.t.* **1.** to plead with or request earnestly: *I urge you to examine your motives.* **2.** to influence, persuade, or otherwise move to some course of action: *The cheers of the crowd urged the team on to victory.* **3.** to press, speak, or argue strongly for the doing, making, consideration, or acceptance of: *to urge prison reform.* **4.** to drive or force forward or onward; spur: *The jockey urged the racehorse to the finish line.* —*v.i.* **1.** to press earnestly or make arguments, claims, or the like. **2.** to exert a driving or compelling force, as to a course of action. —*n.* a driving or compelling force, influence, or impulse: *I have an urge for strawberries.* [Latin *urgēre* to press[1], drive.]

> **Synonyms** *v.t.* **Urge, exhort, goad,** and **egg**[2] mean to persuade or force someone to take action. **Urge** implies pressure toward a specific, often positive, goal: *The academic counselor urged the student to go to summer school.* **Exhort** implies an earnest, dramatic attempt at persuasion, as in oratory or preaching: *The minister exhorted the congregation to contribute to the church restoration fund.* **Goad** suggests a negative force that overcomes natural inclinations: *The landlord's failure to provide heat goaded the tenants into a rent strike.* **Egg** (usually followed by *on*) is an informal term that suggests petty and malicious incitement: *The two students didn't want to fight, but their companions egged them on.*

ur·gen·cy (ûr′jən sē) *n.* the quality or condition of being urgent: *the urgency of the traffic problem.*

ur·gent (ûr′jənt) *adj.* **1.** demanding or calling for immediate action or attention; compelling; pressing: *to have urgent business to attend to.* **2.** insistent or persistent, as in pleading; importunate: *an urgent appeal for funds.* [Latin *urgēns,* present participle of *urgēre* to press[1], drive.] —**ur′gent·ly,** *adv.*

> **Synonyms** **Urgent, pressing,** and **imperative** mean demanding immediate action. **Urgent** is usually applied to action necessitated by an emergency: *After the tornado, an urgent call went out for medical aid.* **Pressing** implies a less crucial need than *urgent,* growing out of external pressures: *The budget deficit created a pressing need to lay off city workers.* **Imperative** suggests a demand based on duty or authority rather than arising from circumstances: *Party leaders issued an imperative call for support of the president's program.*

u·ric (yùr′ik) *adj.* of, relating to, found in, or derived from urine.

uric acid, an odorless, white crystalline purine, an end product of protein metabolism, found in the urine of mammals and the excrement of mammals, birds, and reptiles, used in synthesizing other organic compounds. Formula: $C_5H_4N_4O_3$

U·ri·el (yùr′ē əl) *n.* in ancient Jewish writings, one of the archangels.

u·ri·nal (yùr′ə nəl) *n.* **1.a.** an upright wall fixture used by men for urinating. **b.** a room or enclosure, usually public, containing such a fixture or fixtures. **2.** a vessel for urine, such as one used by a bedridden patient. [Late Latin *ūrīnāl* chamber pot, vessel for urine, going back to Latin *ūrīna* urine.]

u·ri·nal·y·sis (yùr′ə nal′ə sis) *n., pl.* **-ses** (-sēz′). a chemical or microscopic analysis of urine, used esp. to diagnose diseases of the urinary system or to detect drug use. [URIN(E) + (AN)ALYSIS.]

u·ri·nar·y (yùr′ə ner′ē) *adj.* **1.** of or relating to urine. **2.** of,

relating to, or involving the organs that produce and discharge urine.

urinary system, the system of organs that produce and excrete urine, in mammals comprising the kidneys, the ureters, the bladder, and the urethra.

u·ri·nate (yùr′ə nāt′) *v.i.,* **-nat·ed, -nat·ing.** to discharge urine. [Medieval Latin *urinatus,* past participle of *urinare,* from Latin *ūrīna* urine.] —**u·ri·na′tion,** *n.*

u·rine (yùr′in) *n.* a clear amber or yellow fluid containing waste material that is excreted by the kidneys, stored in the urinary bladder, and discharged from the body through the urethra. [Latin *ūrīna.*]

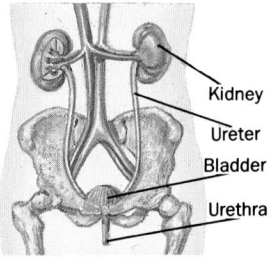

human **urinary system**

Labels: Kidney, Ureter, Bladder, Urethra

u·ri·no·gen·i·tal (yùr′ə nō-jen′i təl) *adj.* urogenital.

urn (ûrn) *n.* **1.a.** a vase, esp. one with a foot or pedestal. **b.** a vase or vaselike container used to hold the ashes of a dead person after cremation. **2.** a closed vessel, usually with a spigot, for making, heating, or serving liquids: *a coffee urn.* [Latin *urna* vessel for drawing water, vessel to hold the ashes of the dead.]

u·ro·gen·i·tal (yùr′ō jen′i təl) *adj.* of or relating to the urinary and genital organs or their functions. Also, **urinogenital.** [Greek *ouron* urine + GENITAL.]

u·rol·o·gy (yù rol′ə jē) *n.* the branch of medicine specializing in the study and treatment of disorders of the urogenital tract in males and the urinary tract in females. —**u·rol′o·gist,** *n.* —**u·ro·log·ic** (yùr′ə loj′ik); also, **u′ro·log′i·cal,** *adj.*

Ur·sa Major (ûr′sə) a constellation in the northern sky, containing the stars of the Big Dipper, conventionally depicted as a large bear. Also, **Great Bear.** [Latin *Ursa Major* the Greater Bear.]

Ursa Minor, a constellation in the northern sky, containing the bright star Polaris and the stars of the Little Dipper, conventionally depicted as a small bear. Also, **Little Bear.** [Latin *Ursa Minor* the Lesser Bear.]

ur·sine (ûr′sīn, -sin) *adj.* of, relating to, or having the characteristics of a bear or bears. [Latin *ursīnus* relating to a bear, from *ursus* bear[2].]

Ur·su·line (ûr′sə lin, -līn′) *n.* a member of a Roman Catholic religious order of women, founded in Italy in 1535 primarily for the education of girls. —*adj.* of, relating to, or belonging to the Ursulines.

ur·ti·car·i·a (ûr′ti kâr′ē ə) *n.* hives. [Modern Latin *urticaria,* from Latin *urtica* nettle.] —**ur′ti·car′i·al,** *adj.*

u·rus (yùr′əs) *n., pl.* **u·rus·es.** aurochs *(def. 1).* [Latin *ūrus* wild ox; of Germanic origin.]

us (us; *unstressed* əs) *pl. pron.* the objective case of **we.** —For Usage Note, see **me.**

U.S. *also,* **US** United States.

USA, United States Army.

U.S.A., *also,* **USA** United States of America.

us·a·ble (ū′zə bəl) *also,* **useable.** *adj.* fit, available, or convenient for use; capable of being used. —**us·a·bil′i·ty, us′a·ble·ness,** *n.* —**us′a·bly,** *adv.*

USAF, United States Air Force.

us·age (ū′sij, ū′zij) *n.* **1.** the act or a manner of using, treating, or handling; treatment; use: *My shoes get hard usage.* **2.** the customary or established way in which the words, sounds, and grammatical forms of a language are used. **3.** a particular expression in speech or writing or an instance of this: *an idiomatic usage.* **4.** a customary practice, or something established by or done in accordance with such practice: *That ceremony is a usage that has persisted in this village for centuries.* [Old French *usage* custom, use, experience, going back to Latin *ūsus.*]

us·ance (ū′zəns) *n.* a period of time allowing for the payment of a foreign bill of exchange, established between different countries by commercial usage or custom. [Old French *usance* custom, practice, from *user* to make use of, practice. See USE.]

USCG, United States Coast Guard.

USDA, United States Department of Agriculture.

use (*v.,* ūz; *n.,* ūs) *v.,* **used, us·ing.** —*v.t.* **1.** to employ for a particular purpose or end; avail oneself of; utilize: *May I use your*

a	at	e	end	o	hot	u	up	hw	white
ā	ape	ē	me	ō	old	ū	use	ng	song
ä	far	i	it	ô	fork	ü	rule	th	thin
âr	care	ī	ice	oi	oil	ù	pull	th	this
		îr	pierce	ou	out	ûr	turn	zh	measure

ə { about / taken / pencil / lemon / circus }

U

1323

scissors? I used the library to research my term paper. **2.** to exhaust the whole or entire supply of (often with *up*): *We used up all the bread at breakfast.* **3.** to take advantage of; exploit: *The students used their teacher's advice to help themselves get better jobs.* **4.** to take often or by habit: *I use honey in my tea.* **5.** to act or behave toward; treat: *The company uses all its employees fairly.* —*v.i.* to do formerly or habitually. ➡ used in the past tense with an infinitive expressed or understood: *I used to dislike school. We go there regularly, although we didn't use to.* —*n.* **1.a.** the act of using: *The teacher encourages the use of the library.* **b.** the state or condition of being used: *The telephone is in use.* **2.** the quality that makes something suitable for a purpose: *My old glasses are of no use to me now. What's the use of worrying about it?* **3.** a need or occasion for using: *Do you have any use for these empty bottles?* **4.** the purpose for which something is used; function: *This tool has many uses.* **5.** the right or privilege to use something: *We have the use of the car for the weekend.* **6.** a manner or way of using: *Show me the proper use of the sewing machine.* **7.** the power or ability to use something: *I lost the use of my hand when I broke my finger.* **8.** a continued or repeated practice or procedure; custom; habit: *It was my use to jog every morning.* **9.** *Law.* the right of a person who holds property in trust for another to take profits or benefits from the property. [Old French *user* to make use of, practice, consume, going back to Latin *ūsus,* past participle of *ūti* to make use of, practice.]

· **to have no use for.** *Informal.* to dislike: *I have no use for lazy people.*
· **to make use of.** to use; utilize; employ: *to make good use of one's money.*
· **to put to use.** to use to advantage: *That vacant lot could be put to use as a baseball field.*
· **used to.** familiar with; accustomed to: *The city children are not used to country life.*

Synonyms *v.t.* **Use, utilize,** and **employ** mean turning something to practical account. **Use** is the most general and widely applied term: *They used the school auditorium for town meetings. I use the computer nearly every day.* **Utilize,** a more formal word, suggests the thorough exploitation of potential: *The ingenious settlers utilized every part of the livestock they raised.* **Employ** is also a formal term, which sometimes suggests the putting to work of something not currently in practical use: *to employ the latest technology in manufacturing cars, to employ ocean tides to generate electricity.*

use·a·ble (ū′zə bəl) *adj.* usable. —**use′a·bil′i·ty, use′a·ble·ness,** *n.* —**use′a·bly,** *adv.*
used (ūzd) *adj.* having been put to use or owned by another or others; not new; secondhand: *used clothing, used textbooks.*
use·ful (ūs′fəl) *adj.* serving a use or purpose, esp. a valuable, practical, or beneficial one: *How can I make myself useful?* —**use′ful·ly,** *adv.* —**use′ful·ness,** *n.*
use·less (ūs′lis) *adj.* **1.** serving no practical or beneficial purpose; having no use: *Without the right film, the camera is useless.* **2.** of no avail; ineffectual; vain; futile: *It's useless to tell them not to make so much noise.* —**use′less·ly,** *adv.* —**use′less·ness,** *n.*
us·er (ū′zər) *n.* **1.** a person or thing that uses: *Users are responsible for the condition of the pool.* **2.** a person who abuses or is addicted to a drug or drugs. **3.** a person who takes advantage of another or others for selfish reasons.
us·er-friend·ly (ū′zər frend′lē) *adj.* easy to use, esp. by someone who is inexperienced: *a user-friendly computer program.*
ush·er (ush′ər) *n.* **1.** a person who leads people to their seats, as in a theater or stadium. **2.** a man who attends the bridegroom at a wedding, often accompanying a bridesmaid. **3.** a person who serves as an official doorkeeper, as in a courtroom or legislative chamber. —*v.t.* **1.** to act as an usher to; conduct; escort: *The receptionist ushered the group to the proper room.* **2.** to mark the beginning or occurrence of, often formally or ceremoniously (usually with *in*): *We ushered the New Year in with a party.* —*v.i.* to act as an usher. [Anglo-Norman *usser* doorkeeper, going back to Latin *ōstiārius,* from *ōstium* door, entrance, from *ōs* mouth.]
ush·er·ette (ush′ə ret′) *n.* a girl or woman who ushers people to their seats, as in a theater or stadium.
USIA, United States Information Agency, a federal organization handling U.S. publicity and information activities abroad, established in 1953 to promote favorable public opinion toward the United States and its foreign policy.
USM, United States Mail.
USMA, United States Military Academy.
USMC, United States Marine Corps.
USN, United States Navy.
USNA, United States Naval Academy.
USO, United Service Organizations, a nongovernmental agency

founded in 1941 to provide recreational and religious facilities for U.S. military personnel.
USPS, United States Postal Service.
USRDA, RDA.
USS 1. United States Senate. **2.** United States Ship.
U.S.S.R. *also,* **USSR** Union of Soviet Socialist Republics.
u·su·al (ū′zhü əl) *adj.* **1.** happening regularly or frequently; common: *Heavy traffic is usual at this hour.* **2.** in accordance with custom, practice, or habit: *The dentist charged me the usual fee for cleaning my teeth.* [Late Latin *ūsuālis* ordinary, general, from Latin *ūsus* use, custom.] —**u′su·al·ly,** *adv.* —**u′su·al·ness,** *n.*
· **as usual.** in the regular, habitual, or customary way: *We got up at six o'clock, as usual.*
u·su·fruct (ū′zə frukt′) *n.* the legal right to use and profit from another's property, provided its substance is not altered or damaged in any way. [Late Latin *ūsūfrūctus,* from Latin *ūsusfrūctus,* short for *ūsus et frūctus* literally, use and fruit or enjoyment.]
u·su·fruc·tu·ar·y (ū′zə fruk′chü er′ē) *n., pl.* **-ar·ies.** a person who has the usufruct of property. —*adj.* of, relating to, or of the nature of a usufruct.
u·su·rer (ū′zhər ər) *n.* a person who lends money, esp. at an excessive or illegal rate of interest. [Anglo-Norman *usurer,* from Late Latin *ūsurārius* moneylender, going back to Latin *ūsūra* use, interest.]
u·su·ri·ous (ū zhür′ē əs) *adj.* **1.** practicing usury: *a usurious lender.* **2.** of, relating to, or characterized by usury: *a usurious contract.* —**u·su′ri·ous·ly,** *adv.* —**u·su′ri·ous·ness,** *n.*
u·surp (ū sûrp′, ū zûrp′) *v.t.* **1.** to seize and hold without legal right or authority; take possession of by or as by force: *to usurp control of government.* **2.** to assume or appropriate wrongfully and arrogantly; use without authority or right: *to usurp a writer's ideas.* [Latin *ūsūrpāre* to acquire, take possession of, going back to *ūsu* by use + *rapere* to seize.] —**u·surp′er,** *n.*
u·sur·pa·tion (ū′sər pā′shən, ū′zər-) *n.* the act of usurping, esp. the illegal seizure of royal power.
u·su·ry (ū′zhə rē) *n., pl.* **-ries. 1.** the act or practice of lending money at an excessive or illegal rate of interest. **2.** an excessive or illegal rate of interest. [Old French *usure,* from Latin *ūsūra* use, interest.]
UT, the postal abbreviation for Utah.
Ute (ūt, ū′tē) *n., pl.* **Ute** or **Utes. 1.** a member of a group of North American Indian tribes, formerly living in what is now Utah, Colorado, and New Mexico. **2.** the Shoshonean language of these tribes.
u·ten·sil (ū ten′səl) *n.* an article or object that is useful or necessary in doing or making something: *cooking utensils, writing utensils.* [Old French *utensile,* going back to Latin *ūtēnsilis* useful, from *ūtī* to make use of.]
u·ter·ine (ū′tər in, -tə rīn′) *adj.* **1.** of or relating to the uterus. **2.** born of the same mother but having a different father: *uterine siblings.* [Late Latin *uterīnus,* from Latin *uterus* womb.]
u·ter·us (ū′tər əs) *n., pl.* **-ter·i** (-tə rī′). **1.** a hollow, muscular organ found in most female mammals that holds and nourishes the embryo until birth. Also, **womb. 2.** a similar or corresponding part in animals other than mammals that holds and protects the egg or embryo during development. [Latin *uterus* womb.]
U·ther (ū′thər) *n.* in medieval legend, the king of ancient Britain who was the father of King Arthur. Also, **Uther Pendragon.**
u·tile (ū′təl) *adj.* useful or practical; having utility: *Plastic is a cheap, utile substitute for glass.* [Old French *utile,* from Latin *utilis* useful, from *uti* to use.]
u·til·i·tar·i·an (ū til′i târ′ē ən) *adj.* **1.** of, relating to, or made for utility or usefulness. **2.** emphasizing usefulness or practicality over beauty or other considerations: *My choice of shoes is strictly utilitarian.* **3.** of, relating to, or adhering to utilitarianism. —*n.* an adherent or advocate of utilitarianism.
u·til·i·tar·i·an·ism (ū til′i târ′ē ə niz′əm) *n.* **1.** a philosophical movement developed by the English philosophers Jeremy Bentham and John Stuart Mill advocating that social, moral, and political action be directed toward promoting the greatest happiness for the greatest number of people. **2.** the philosophical doctrine that an act or thing is good insofar as it is useful.
u·til·i·ty (ū til′i tē) *n., pl.* **-ties. 1.** the state or quality of being useful; usefulness: *The utility of education lasts throughout life.* **2.** a company, usually subject to government regulation, that provides an essential service to the public, as by supplying gas, electricity, or water or by operating a telephone or transportation system. Also, **public utility. 3.** the service provided by such a company. **4. utilities.** shares of stock in such a company. **5.** something useful or designed to be useful, such as a kitchen storage cabinet or a household cleaning implement. **6.** *Computers.* a program for frequently used applications, as converting files, copying disks, or printing. **7.** in utilitarianism, the doctrine advo-

cating that social, moral, and political action be directed toward promoting the greatest happiness for the greatest number of people. —*adj.* designed or intended for general use rather than for a specialized function: *a utility table, a utility knife.* [Latin *ūtilitās* usefulness.]

u·ti·lize (ū′tə līz′) *v.t.,* **-lized, -liz·ing.** to take advantage of; put to good use: *to utilize all available extra space, to utilize resources.* —**u′ti·liz′a·ble,** *adj.* —**u′ti·li·za′tion,** *n.* —**u′ti·liz′er,** *n.* —For Synonyms, see **use.**

ut·most (ut′mōst′) *adj.* **1.** of the greatest or highest degree, amount, or number: *We have the utmost regard for your ability as a scientist.* **2.** being or situated at the farthest limit or point; most remote: *the utmost corners of the universe.* —*n.* the most or greatest possible, as in degree, amount, or extent: *The hotel staff did their utmost to make our stay enjoyable.* Also, **uttermost.** [Old English *ūt(e)mest* outermost, from *ūt(e)* out + -*mest* most.]

U·to-Az·tec·an (ū′tō az tek′ən) *n.* a large North and Central American Indian language family, including Shoshone, Pima, Nahuatl, Ute, and other languages. —*adj.* of or relating to this language family.

u·to·pi·a (ū tō′pē ə) *also,* **U·to·pi·a.** *n.* **1.** an ideal place or society in which all people live together in perfect harmony and happiness; state or place of political or social perfection. **2.** any idealistic, usually impractical and unattainable scheme for social improvement or reform. [Modern Latin *utopia* literally, no place, from Greek *ou* not + *topos* place; referring to the imaginary island described as having an ideal political and social life in *Utopia,* a satirical account by Sir Thomas More, 1478-1535, English statesman and writer.]

u·to·pi·an (ū tō′pē ən) *also,* **U·to·pi·an.** *adj.* **1.** of, relating to, or like a utopia. **2.** perfect in theory but not possible or practical in reality; extravagantly impractical or idealistic: *utopian schemes.* **3.** involving or founded upon concepts or schemes of political or social perfection: *a utopian community, utopian literature.* —*n.* a person who advocates or works for the establishment of a utopia; idealistic but impractical social theorist or reformer.

u·to·pi·an·ism (ū tō′pē ə niz′əm) *also,* **U·to·pi·an·ism.** *n.* the beliefs or ideals of a utopian; idealistic and impractical social theory.

u·tri·cle (ū′tri kəl) *n.* **1.** the larger of the two sacs in the vestibule of the inner ear, aiding in maintaining bodily equilibrium and coordination. **2.** a small sac or baglike body, such as certain small, one-seeded fruits. [Latin *ūtriculus* little leather bag or bottle, diminutive of *ūter* leather bag or bottle.] —**u·tric·u·lar** (ū trik′yə lər), *adj.*

ut·ter[1] (ut′ər) *v.t.* **1.** to give voice or expression to; express audibly or aloud: *to utter a sigh, to utter an accusation.* **2.** to put or send (something forged or counterfeit) into circulation. [Middle Dutch *ūteren* to speak, show.] —For Synonyms, see **say.**

ut·ter[2] (ut′ər) *adj.* without qualification; complete; absolute: *utter darkness, an utter failure.* [Old English *ūter(r)a* outer, comparative of *ūt(e)* out.] —**ut′ter·ly,** *adv.*

ut·ter·ance (ut′ər əns) *n.* **1.** something uttered or expressed in words: *The orator's utterances are preserved in various anthologies.* **2.** the act of uttering; vocal expression: *to give utterance to one's joy.* **3.** a manner of speaking: *the soft utterance of a sleepy child.*

ut·ter·most (ut′ər mōst′) *adj., n.* utmost.

U-turn (ū′tûrn′) *n.* a change in a vehicle's direction to the opposite direction, such that the path of the vehicle is U-shaped: *We made a U-turn when we realized we were going the wrong way.*

UV, ultraviolet.

u·vu·la (ū′vyə lə) *n., pl.* **-las** or **-lae** (-lē′). a cone-shaped piece of flesh that hangs from the soft palate, above and behind the tongue. [Late Latin *ūvula,* diminutive of Latin *ūva* grape, uvula; referring to its shape.]

u·vu·lar (ū′vyə lər) *adj.* **1.** of or relating to the uvula. **2.** *Phonetics.* articulated by vibration of the uvula or with the back of the tongue close to or against the uvula.

ux·o·ri·ous (uk sôr′ē əs, ug zôr′-) *adj.* feeling or showing excessive or foolish devotion to one's wife: *an uxorious man, uxorious behavior.* [Latin *uxōrius,* from *uxor* wife.] —**ux·o′ri·ous·ly,** *adv.* —**ux·o′ri·ous·ness,** *n.*

a	at	e	end	o	hot	u	up	hw	white		about
ā	ape	ē	me	ō	old	ū	use	ng	song		taken
ä	far	i	it	ô	fork	u̇	rule	th	thin	ə	pencil
âr	care	ī	ice	oi	oil	u̇	pull	th	this		lemon
				ou	out	ûr	turn	zh	measure		circus
		îr	pierce								

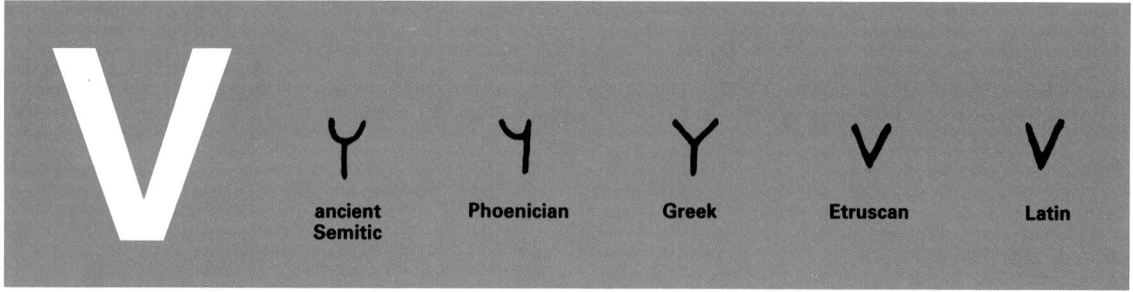

V The earliest form of the letter **V**, like that of **F** and **Y**, is the ancient Semitic letter *waw*, which depicted a hook and stood for the sound of *w* in *water*. When the Phoenicians borrowed *waw*, they used it to represent both the consonant sound *w* and the vowel sound *ü*, as heard in the English word *rude*. The Greeks adopted *waw* and called it *upsilon*, writing it as the capital letter **Y** is written today and using it only for the *ü* sound. The Etruscans changed the shape of *upsilon* and, like the Phoenicians, used it to represent both the *ü* and the *w* sounds, as the Romans did later in the Latin alphabet. By about 1,000 years ago, two forms of this letter had come into use: the **V** at the beginning of a word and a new letter, **U**, in the middle of a word. During the Renaissance, the letter **V** came to be reserved for the consonant sound in the pronunciation of English, French, Italian, and other European languages. The shape of our modern capital **V** closely resembles the Etruscan letter of some 2,800 years ago.

---

v, V (vē) *n., pl.* **v's, V's. 1.** the twenty-second letter of the English alphabet. **2.** the shape of this letter or something having this shape.

V (vē) *also,* v *n., pl.* **V's.** the Roman numeral for 5.

V, the symbol for vanadium.

v. 1. verb. **2.** verse. **3.** versus. **4.** see. [Latin *vide.*] **5.** voice. **6.** volume.

V 1. vector. **2.** velocity. **3.** victory. **4.** volt; volts. **5.** volume.

V. 1. Venerable. **2.** Vicar. **3.** Viscount.

Va., Virginia.

VA 1. the postal abbreviation for Virginia. **2.** Veterans Administration.

va·can·cy (vā′kən sē) *n., pl.* **-cies. 1.** an unoccupied or empty space, esp. an apartment or room for rent: *The superintendent said that the building had no vacancies.* **2.** an unfilled post, position, or office: *There is a vacancy on the board of directors.* **3.** the state or condition of being vacant; emptiness. **4.** a lack of intelligence, awareness, or interest; vacuity. **5.** *Archaic.* inactivity; idleness.

va·cant (vā′kənt) *adj.* **1.a.** containing nothing or no one; empty or unoccupied: *a vacant lot, a vacant seat.* **b.** not having a tenant: *a vacant apartment.* **2.** not held or filled, as a post, position, or office. **3.a.** lacking intelligence, awareness, or interest: *a vacant mind.* **b.** not showing interest, awareness, or thought; expressionless: *a vacant stare.* **4.** free from activity; idle: *vacant hours.* [Latin *vacāns* empty, unoccupied, present participle of *vacāre* to be empty.] —**va′cant·ly,** *adv.* —**va′cant·ness,** *n.*

va·cate (vā′kāt) *v.,* **-cat·ed, -cat·ing.** —*v.t.* **1.** to cease to occupy; leave empty: *The tenant decided to vacate the apartment.* **2.** to give up (a post, position, or office). **3.** *Law.* to make void; annul. —*v.i.* to leave a place or position vacant. [Latin *vacātus,* past participle of *vacāre* to be empty.]

va·ca·tion (vā kā′shən, və-) *n.* **1.** a period of rest and freedom from some activity, esp. a period of paid free time granted to an employee. **2.** *Archaic.* the act or an instance of vacating. —*v.i.* to take or spend a vacation: *to vacation in Spain.* [Latin *vacātiō* a being free from a duty, exemption.] —**va·ca′tion·er, va·ca′tion·ist,** *n.*

vac·ci·nate (vak′sə nāt′) *v.,* **-nat·ed, -nat·ing.** —*v.t.* to introduce a vaccine into the body in order to protect against a disease, such as poliomyelitis. —*v.i.* to perform or practice vaccination. [VACCINE + -ATE[1].]

vac·ci·na·tion (vak′sə nā′shən) *n.* **1.** the act or practice of vaccinating; treatment with a vaccine. **2.** a scar left by a vaccination.

vac·cine (vak sēn′, vak′sēn, -sin) *n.* **1.** a substance, such as a preparation of killed or weakened viruses or bacteria, which when introduced into the body stimulates the production of antibodies, conferring immunity to a particular disease. **2.** the virus that causes cowpox, prepared and used for inoculation against smallpox. [Latin *vaccīnus* relating to cows, from *vacca* cow; referring to the use of the *cow*pox virus for vaccination.]

vac·il·late (vas′ə lāt′) *v.i.,* **-lat·ed, -lat·ing. 1.** to move to and fro; sway unsteadily; waver. **2.** to fluctuate; oscillate. **3.** to waver in mind or between courses of action; be unable to decide. [Latin *vacillātus,* past participle of *vacillāre* to totter, waver.] —**vac′il·la′tion,** *n.* —For Synonyms, see **hesitate.**

va·cu·i·ty (va kū′i tē) *n., pl.* **-ties. 1.** the state or quality of being empty; emptiness: *the vacuity of outer space.* **2.** an empty space; vacuum; void. **3.** emptiness of mind; mental dullness. **4.** something foolish or meaningless. **5.** the quality or condition of being without something specified: *a vacuity of concerted effort and dedication.* [Latin *vacuitās* empty space, freedom from something.]

vac·u·ole (vak′ū ōl′) *n.* a small, usually fluid-filled cavity in a living cell. [French *vacuole* literally, small vacuum, from Latin *vacuus* empty.] —**vac·u·o·lar** (vak′ū ō′lər, vak′ū ə-), *adj.*

vac·u·ous (vak′ū əs) *adj.* **1.** containing nothing; empty. **2.** lacking or showing a lack of intelligence; foolish: *a vacuous statement.* **3.** not meaningfully occupied; without purpose; idle: *a vacuous existence.* [Latin *vacuus* empty.] —**vac′u·ous·ly,** *adv.* —**vac′u·ous·ness,** *n.*

vac·u·um (vak′ū əm, vak′ūm) *n., pl.* **vac·u·ums** or *(defs. 1-4)* **vac·u·a** (vak′ū ə). **1.** a space completely devoid of matter. Although theoretically possible, a perfect vacuum has never been produced experimentally. **2.** a space from which almost all gas, vapor, and other matter have been removed. **3.** a feeling or condition of emptiness; void. **4.** a state of isolation from the reality, events, or influences of the outside world: *The hermit lives in a vacuum.* **5.** vacuum cleaner. —*v.t., v.i.* to clean with a vacuum cleaner. [Latin *vacuum* empty space.]

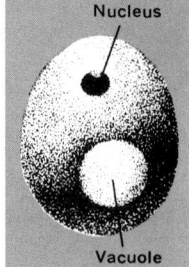

Nucleus

Vacuole

vacuole
of a cell

vacuum bottle, thermos.

vacuum cleaner, an apparatus for cleaning carpets, upholstery, floors, or the like, that operates by means of suction.

vacuum gauge, a gauge for measuring the pressure in a partial vacuum.

vac·u·um-packed (vak′ū əm pakt′, vak′ūm-) *adj.* packed in a sealed container from which most of the air has been removed to maintain freshness.

vacuum pump, a pump for removing air or gas from an enclosed space.

vacuum tube, electron tube.

va·de me·cum (vā′dē mē′kəm, vä′-) *pl.* **va·de me·cums. 1.** a handbook or manual for ready reference, usually carried on one's person. **2.** something a person carries about constantly for regular use. [Latin *vāde mēcum* go with me.]

vag·a·bond (vag′ə bond′) *n.* **1.a.** a person who wanders from place to place, having no permanent home. **b.** a person who wanders from place to place, having no permanent home or means of support and often begging for food or money; tramp. **2.** a person whose habits are disreputable or suspicious; rascal. —*adj.* **1.** of, relating to, or characteristic of a vagabond or a vagabond's way of life: *They lived a vagabond existence for the summer.* **2.** moving from place to place; nomadic; wandering. **3.** moving in an irregular course or direction; drifting. [Latin *vagābundus* strolling about, from *vagārī* to wander.]

vag·a·bond·age (vag′ə bon′dij) *n.* **1.** the state or condition of being a vagabond. **2.** vagabonds collectively.

va·gar·y (və gâr′ē, vā′gə rē) *n., pl.* **-gar·ies.** an odd, unusual, or unpredictable act, idea, or happening. ➡ usually used in the plural: *the vagaries of life.* [Latin *vagārī* to wander.] —For Synonyms, see caprice.

va·gi·na (və jī′nə) *n., pl.* **-nas** or **-nae** (-nē) **1.** the canal extending from the uterus to the external genital opening in certain female mammals. **2.** a sheathlike part. [Latin *vāgīna.*]

vag·i·nal (vaj′ə nəl, və jī′-) *adj.* **1.** of or relating to the vagina. **2.** of, relating to, or resembling a sheath.

vag·i·nate (vaj′ə nit, -nāt′) *adj.* having or resembling a sheath. Also, **vag·i·nat·ed** (vaj′ə tod).

va·gran·cy (vā′grən sē) *n., pl.* **-cies. 1.** the state or condition of being a vagrant. **2.a.** the conduct of a vagrant. **b.** in some places, a crime consisting of remaining in a public place without home or means of support. **3.** wandering in mind or thought; daydreaming.

va·grant (vā′grənt) *n.* **1.** a person having no regular home or employment who wanders about from place to place, often begging for food or money. **2.** a wanderer; rover. **3.** *Law.* an idle or disorderly person, such as a tramp, having no permanent home and no visible means of support. —*adj.* **1.** of, relating to, or characteristic of a vagrant or a vagrant's way of life. **2.** wandering or drifting from place to place; nomadic. **3.** not moving in or following any particular direction; erratic. [Anglo-Norman *vagarant* wanderer, vagabond, going back to Latin *vagārī* to wander.] —**va′grant·ly,** *adv.*

vague (vāg) *adj.,* **va·guer, va·guest. 1.** not definitely or clearly expressed: *vague promises.* **2.** not precise or clear in meaning: *vague words.* **3.** not clearly or precisely felt or known: *a vague feeling, a vague idea.* **4.** unable to think or express oneself with clearness or precision: *a vague person.* **5.** lacking a definite form or outline; not clear or distinct; obscure: *The skyscraper was a vague shape in the fog.* [Latin *vagus* wandering, uncertain.] —**vague′ly,** *adv.* —**vague′ness,** *n.*

> **Synonyms** Vague, obscure, enigmatic, and cryptic mean not easily perceived or understood. **Vague** implies a lack of precision or detail: *The law is vague on this point.* **Obscure** is applied to something that is concealed or esoteric: *The language used in the report was so obscure that only experts in the field could understand it.* **Enigmatic** suggests that something is puzzling or mystifying: *The Mona Lisa's smile, in the famous painting by Leonardo da Vinci, is noted for being enigmatic.* **Cryptic** implies a deliberate attempt to puzzle: *The fortuneteller made cryptic statements, disappointing those who hoped to learn something about their future.*

va·gus (vā′gəs) *n., pl.* **va·gi** (vā′jī). either of a pair of nerves that begins in the medulla oblongata and branches out to the larynx, esophagus, heart, lungs, and stomach. Also, **vagus nerve.** [Latin *vagus* wandering.]

vail (vāl) *v.t. Archaic.* **1.** to cause or allow to descend or sink; lower. **2.** to doff or take off, such as a hat, to show respect or submission. [Short for obsolete *avail* to lower, from Old French *avaler,* going back to Latin *ad vallem* to the valley.]

vain (vān) *adj.* **1.** overly concerned with or proud of one's appearance, abilities, or accomplishments; conceited. **2.** not successful or effective: *a vain effort.* **3.** of no real significance or worth; empty: *a vain threat.* [Old French *vain* useless, empty, ineffective, from Latin *vānus* empty, fruitless.] —**vain′ly,** *adv.* —**vain′ness,** *n.*

• **in vain. a.** without success; ineffective; useless: *All attempts at rescue were in vain.* **b.** without proper respect; lightly; irreverently: *to take God's name in vain.*

> **Synonyms** Vain, fruitless, and futile mean failing to achieve a desired end. **Vain** emphasizes a failure that follows some kind of effort: *I made a vain attempt to lose ten pounds.* **Fruitless** is close in meaning to *vain,* but more emphatic and suggests an intensive effort that proves totally unproductive: *The police made a fruitless search for the thief.* **Futile** indicates the knowledge or suspicion that failure is inevitable: *Even though the action seemed futile, the general ordered the troops to attack.*

vain·glo·ri·ous (vān′glôr′ē əs) *adj.* **1.** excessively vain or boastful about one's accomplishments or abilities; arrogantly conceited. **2.** displaying or characterized by vainglory. —**vain′glo′-ri·ous·ly,** *adv.* —**vain′glo′ri·ous·ness,** *n.*

vain·glo·ry (vān′glôr′ē, vān′glôr′ē) *n.* **1.** excessive vanity or boastfulness. **2.** a vain and ostentatious show or display.

vair (vâr) *n.* **1.** a gray and white squirrel fur used in the Middle Ages for lining and trimming garments. **2.** *Heraldry.* a representa-

tion of this, consisting of rows of figures resembling small shields, alternately blue and silver. [Old French *vair* squirrel fur, fur of various colors, miniver, from Latin *varius* of various colors, changing.]

val·ance (val′əns, vā′ləns) *n.* **1.** a short drapery or piece of wood or metal hung across the top of a window, as for decoration or to hide curtain fixtures. **2.** a short drapery hanging as from a shelf, table, or frame of a bed, often reaching to the floor. [Probably from *Valence,* city in France noted for its fabrics.]

vair *(def. 2)*

vale (vāl) *n.* valley. [Old French *val,* from Latin *vallēs.*]

val·e·dic·tion (val′i dik′shən) *n.* **1.** the act of bidding farewell. **2.** something said in bidding farewell. [Latin *valedictus,* past participle of *valedīcere* to say farewell + -ION.]

val·e·dic·to·ri·an (val′i dik tôr′ē ən) *n.* a student, usually ranking highest in the class, who delivers the valedictory at graduation exercises.

val·e·dic·to·ry (val′i dik′tə rē) *n., pl.* **-ries.** a farewell address, esp. one delivered at graduation exercises. —*adj.* of, relating to, or expressing a farewell. [Latin *valedictus,* past participle of *valedīcere* to say farewell + -ORY.]

va·lence (vā′ləns) *n.* **1.** the combining capacity of an element or radical in ionic compounds, expressed as the charge that an atom of the element or that the radical carries as an ion. The sum of the valences of the elements or radicals in the compound must equal zero. For example, sodium has a valence of +1 and chlorine has a valence of −1 in sodium chloride (NaCl). **2.** the combining capacity of an element or radical in a covalent compound, expressed as the charge that an atom of the element or that the radical would carry if it were regarded as an ion. The sum of the valences of the elements or radicals in the compound must equal zero. For example, carbon has a valence of +4 and chlorine has a valence of −1 in carbon tetrachloride (CCl_4). Also, **va′len·cy.** [Late Latin *valentia* power, from Latin *valēre* to be strong, be well.]

valence electron, an electron that occupies the outer shell of an atom and can therefore be transferred to or shared with another atom to form a chemical bond.

Va·len·ci·ennes (və len′sē enz′) *n.* a fine bobbin lace, usually having a floral design. Also, **Valenciennes lace.** [From *Valenciennes,* city in France where it was first made.]

val·en·tine (val′ən tīn′) *n.* **1.** a greeting card or gift sent on Valentine's Day, usually to one's sweetheart as an expression of affection. **2.** a sweetheart, esp. one's chosen sweetheart on Valentine's Day.

Valentine's Day, a day named in honor of Saint Valentine, traditionally observed by the sending of valentines; February 14. Also, **Saint Valentine's Day.**

va·le·ri·an (və lîr′ē ən) *n.* **1.** a drug having a pungent odor, obtained from the roots of a plant, *Valeriana officinalis,* and formerly used as a sedative. **2.** the plant itself, native to Europe and Asia, having small white, pink, or lavender flowers. [Old French *valeriane* the plant, possibly going back to Latin *Valeria,* ancient Roman province where it was supposedly found in abundance.]

val·et (val′it, val′ā) *n.* **1.** a man's male servant who performs various personal services for his employer, such as caring for his clothes and helping him dress. **2.** an employee, as of a hotel, who performs personal services for guests, such as getting clothes cleaned and pressed. —*v.t., v.i.* to serve as a valet. [French *valet* servant, from Old French *vaslet* groom, squire, youth; of Celtic origin.]

val·e·tu·di·nar·i·an (val′i tü′də nâr′ē ən, -tū′-) *n.* an invalid or person in ill health, esp. one overly concerned with his or her health. —*adj.* of, like, or characteristic of such a person; sickly. Also, **val′e·tu′di·nar′y.** [Latin *valētūdinārius* sickly (from *valētūdō* state of health) + -AN.]

Val·hal·la (val hal′ə) *n.* in Norse mythology, the great hall to which heroes and warriors slain in battle were taken by the Valkyries, so they could feast at the table of Odin. [Modern Latin *Valhalla,* from Old Norse *Valhöll,* from *valr* those slain in battle + *höll* hall.]

val·ian·cy (val′yən sē) *n.* valor. Also, **val′iance.**

val·iant (val′yənt) *adj.* having or characterized by valor; brave; courageous: *a valiant warrior, to put up a valiant fight.* [Old French *vaillant,* present participle of *valoir* to be worth, avail, from

a	at	e	end	o	hot	u	up	hw	white	⎧	about
ā	ape	ē	me	ō	old	ū	use	ng	song		taken
ä	far	i	it	ô	fork	ü	rule	th	thin	ə	pencil
âr	care	ī	ice	oi	oil	u̇	pull	th	this		lemon
		îr	pierce	ou	out	ûr	turn	zh	measure	⎩	circus

1327

Latin *valēre* to be strong.] —**val′iant·ly**, *adv.* —**val′iant·ness**, *n.*

val·id (val′id) *adj.* **1.** soundly based on facts or evidence; true: *The experiment proved that the scientist's theory was valid.* **2.** having the desired result; effective: *a valid method of treatment.* **3.** acceptable under the law; legally binding: *a valid will.* **4.** *Logic.* containing postulates from which a conclusion may be logically drawn: *a valid line of reasoning.* [Latin *validus* strong.] —**val′id·ly**, *adv.* —**val′id·ness**, *n.*

val·i·date (val′i dāt′) *v.t.,* **-dat·ed, -dat·ing. 1.** to make or declare legally valid: *to validate election results.* **2.** to prove to be valid, true, or correct; substantiate; confirm: *The evidence validated our suspicions.* —**val′i·da′tion**, *n.*

va·lid·i·ty (və lid′i tē) *n., pl.* **-ties.** the quality, state, or fact of being valid.

val·ine (val′ēn, vā′lēn) *n.* an essential amino acid, found esp. in fibrous proteins, that is required for normal growth. Formula: $C_5H_{11}NO_2$

va·lise (və lēs′) *n.* a small piece of hand luggage; suitcase. [French *valise*, from Italian *valigia*; of uncertain origin.]

Val·i·um (val′ē əm) *n. Trademark.* diazepam.

Val·kyr·ie (val kir′ē, val′kə rē) *n.* in Norse mythology, any of a group of beautiful warrior maidens who were the attendants of Odin and led heroes slain in battle to Valhalla. [Old Norse *Valkyrja* literally, chooser of the slain, from *valr* those slain in battle + *kyrja* chooser.]

val·la·tion (va lā′shən) *n.* a wall or embankment, formerly used for military defense; rampart. [Late Latin *vallātiō*, going back to Latin *vallum.*]

val·ley (val′ē) *n., pl.* **-leys. 1.** a depression of the earth's surface between hills, mountains, or other highlands, usually having a river or stream flowing through it. **2.** any depression or hollow resembling this. **3.** an area of land drained by a river system; river basin: *the Nile Valley.* **4.** a troughlike depression or interior angle formed by two sloping sides of a roof. ➡ distinguished from **hip**[1] in def. 4. [Anglo-Norman *valey* the depression between mountains, going back to Latin *vallēs.*]

val·or (val′ər) *also, British,* **valour.** *n.* outstanding courage, esp. in battle; great bravery. [Late Latin *valor* worth, courage, from Latin *valēre* to be strong, to be worth.]

val·or·i·za·tion (val′ər ə zā′shən) *n.* the establishment of a certain price or value for a commodity, as by government action or by international business agreement.

val·or·ize (val′ə rīz′) *v.t.,* **-ized, -iz·ing.** to set the price or value of (a commodity) by valorization.

val·or·ous (val′ər əs) *adj.* having or showing valor; brave; courageous. —**val′or·ous·ly**, *adv.* —**val′or·ous·ness**, *n.*

val·our (val′ər) *British.* valor.

valse (väls) *n., pl.* **valses** (väls). *French.* waltz.

val·u·a·ble (val′ū ə bəl, val′yə-) *adj.* **1.** having great monetary or material value; worth much money: *a valuable piece of property, a valuable painting.* **2.** of great use, worth, or importance: *valuable advice, a valuable friend.* —*n.* an article of personal property that has value, such as a piece of jewelry. ➡ usually used in the plural: *a safe to keep valuables in.* —**val′u·a·ble·ness**, *n.* —**val′u·a·bly**, *adv.*

val·u·ate (val′ū āt′) *v.t.,* **-at·ed, -at·ing.** to set a value on; appraise. —**val′u·a′tor**, *n.*

val·u·a·tion (val′ū ā′shən) *n.* **1.** the act or process of estimating the value or price of something: *Valuation of the property required an inspection of the buildings.* **2.** an estimated value or price of something. **3.** an estimation or judgment, as of the merit, quality, or worth of something. —**val′u·a′tion·al**, *adj.*

val·ue (val′ū) *n.* **1.** relative or attributed worth, usefulness, importance, or merit: *We kept the old chair for its sentimental value. The museum purchased the manuscripts for their historical value.* **2.** monetary or material worth; market price: *The value of land has gone up in recent years.* **3.** a fair price or return: *We received good value for our money.* **4. values.** the principles or standards of an individual or group; ideals: *The values of today's young people differ in many respects from those of their parents.* **5.** the exact meaning or significance; import. **6.** *Mathematics.* a numerical quantity, esp. a number represented by a symbol or group of symbols: *If $5y = 25_4$ the value of y is 5.* **7.** *Music.* the relative duration of a tone or rest as indicated by a note or other symbol. **8.** the quality of sound in speech as represented by letters of the alphabet: *the values of "a" in "hat" and "hate."* **9.** the relative lightness or darkness of a color. **10.** the relative amount of light and darkness of one portion of a painting or other work of art as compared with another portion. —*v.t.,* **val·ued, val·u·ing. 1.** to estimate the monetary value of; appraise: *The jeweler valued the diamond at one thousand dollars.* **2.** to consider as having worth, importance, or merit; esteem: *to value someone's friendship.* **3.** to rate on the basis of estimated worth, importance,

or value: *to value one's principles above all else.* [Old French *value* worth, price, from *valoir* to be worth, from Latin *valēre* to be strong, to be worth.] —**val′u·er**, *n.*

val·ue-add·ed tax (val′ū ad′id) a tax based on the estimated amount of value added to a product through the various processes of manufacture, paid at each step along the way and the amount added to the final price to the consumer. Also, **added-value tax.**

val·ued (val′ūd) *adj.* regarded as having worth, importance, or merit; esteemed: *a valued friend, a valued possession.*

value judgment, a judgment or estimation made on the basis of one's own values or opinions.

val·ue·less (val′ū lis) *adj.* having no value; worthless.

val·vate (val′vāt) *adj.* **1.** of, relating to, having, or opening by a valve or valves. **2.** *Botany.* meeting at the edges without overlapping, such as the petals of flower buds. [Latin *valvātus* having folding doors, from *valva* folding door.]

valve (valv) *n.* **1.a.** any of various devices used to control the flow of liquids, gases, or loose materials in piping and other closed systems by blocking or partially blocking passages by means of a movable part. **b.** the movable part of such a device. **2.** *Biology.* a fold in a membrane lining a hollow organ, such as the heart, that allows a fluid, such as blood, to flow in one direction and prevents it from flowing in the opposite direction. **3.** a device in certain brass instruments, such as the trumpet, for altering the pitch

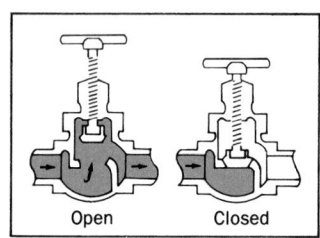

valve *(def. 1a)*

of the tone by changing the length of the air column. **4.** *Zoology.* one of the pair of hinged shells of an oyster, clam, or other mollusk. **5.** *Botany.* **a.** one of the parts into which a seed capsule splits. **b.** a flap covering a pore in some anthers or capsules. **6.** *British.* electron tube. [Latin *valva* leaf of a door, folding door.] —**valved**, *adj.*

val·vu·lar (val′vyə lər) *adj.* **1.** of, relating to, or having valves or valvelike parts. **2.** having the form or function of a valve.

va·moose (va müs′) *v.i.,* **-moosed, -moos·ing.** *Slang.* to leave quickly; go away hastily. [Spanish *vamos* let us go, going back to Latin *vādere* to go.]

vamp[1] (vamp) *n.* **1.** the upper front part of a shoe or boot, covering the instep and sometimes the toes. **2.** something patched up to look new or retain its usefulness. **3.** *Music.* an improvised introduction or accompaniment, usually consisting of a series of chords repeated numerous times, as while waiting for a performer to begin. —*v.t.* **1.** to provide with a vamp; repair with a new vamp. **2.** to patch up; repair (often with *up*). **3.** to make up; fabricate; invent (often with *up*): *to vamp up rumors.* **4.** *Music.* to improvise (an introduction or accompaniment). —*v.i. Music.* to play a vamp. [Modification of Old French *avantpie* front part of a foot or shoe, going back to Latin *ab* from + *ante* before + *pēs* foot.] —**vamp′er**, *n.*

vamp[2] (vamp) *Informal. n.* an alluring woman who uses her feminine charms to seduce or take advantage of men. —*v.t.* to seduce or take advantage of (a man) by using feminine charms. [Shortened from VAMPIRE.]

vam·pire (vam′pīr) *n.* **1.** in folklore, a corpse that leaves its grave at night to suck the blood of sleeping persons. **2.** a person who ruthlessly preys on or takes advantage of others, such as a blackmailer or extortionist. **3.** a woman who purposely seduces and takes advantage of men in order to ruin them. **4.** vampire bat. [French *vampire*, through Hungarian, possibly going back to Turkish *uber* witch.]

vampire bat 1. any of various bats of tropical America, family Desmodontidae, that feeds on the blood of warm-blooded animals. **2.** any of various other bats mistakenly believed to feed on blood.

vam·pir·ism (vam′pīr iz′əm, -pə riz′-) *n.* **1.** belief in vampires. **2.** the actions or practices of a vampire. **3.** the act or practice of ruthlessly preying on and taking advantage of others.

van[1] (van) *n.* **1.** a large covered truck or other vehicle, used for transporting furniture, goods, or animals. **2.** a small, enclosed, boxlike truck variously equipped, used esp. as a truck, passenger vehicle, or recreational vehicle. **3.** *British.* a closed railroad car, used for carrying baggage or freight. [Short for CARAVAN.]

van[2] (van) *n.* vanguard.

va·na·di·um (və nā′dē əm) *n.* a ductile metallic element used in making corrosion-resistant steel and steel used for springs and high-speed tools. Symbol: **V** For tables, see **element.** [Modern

Latin *vanadium,* from Old Norse *Vanadis* a name of the goddess Freya.]

Van Al·len radiation belt (van al′ən) a region of intense radiation encircling the earth at varying high altitudes, in which high-energy electrons and protons are trapped by the earth's magnetic field. This region, which extends to altitudes of 12,000 miles (19,000 kilometers), is the inner portion of the earth's magnetosphere. Also, **Van Allen belt.** For illustration, see **magnetosphere.** [From James A. *Van Allen,* born 1914, U.S. physicist who designed the equipment that first detected the region in 1958.]

van·dal (van′dəl) *n.* **1.** a person who intentionally or maliciously destroys or damages public or private property. **2. Vandal.** a member of a Germanic tribe that ravaged Gaul, Spain, and northern Africa in the fourth and fifth centuries A.D., and sacked Rome in A.D. 455. —*adj.* **1.** like a vandal; intentionally or maliciously destructive. **2. Vandal.** of or relating to the Vandals. [Latin *Vandalus* member of the Germanic tribe; of Germanic origin.]

van·dal·ism (van′də liz′əm) *n.* intentional or malicious damage to or destruction of public or private property.

van·dal·ize (van′də līz′) *v.t.,* **-ized, -iz·ing.** to damage or destroy (property) intentionally or maliciously.

Van de Graaff generator (van′ də graf′) an electric generator that consists chiefly of a large, hollow metal sphere, and uses an electrostatic method to produce high voltages, used either as a component of a particle accelerator or as an electron source in medicine and industry. [From Robert J. *Van de Graaff,* 1901-67, U.S. physicist who invented it.]

Van·dyke (van dīk′) *n.* a short, pointed beard. [Probably because the Flemish painter Sir Anthony Van Dyck, 1599-1641, frequently painted men with such beards.]

vane (vān) *n.* **1.** a weather vane; weathercock. **2.** a blade or flat or curved bladelike part, as of a windmill or propeller. **3.** the flat, weblike part of a feather, consisting of the barbs. Also, **web. 4.** a projecting, often finlike part attached to the body of a missile to provide stability or guidance. [Old English *fana* flag.]

van·guard (van′gärd′) *n.* **1.** the part of an army that moves ahead of the main force. **2.a.** the leading or foremost position, as of a social, artistic, or political movement: *the vanguard of the reform movement.* **b.** the persons occupying such a position. [Old French *avant-garde* vanguard of an army, from *avant* before (going back to Latin *ab* from + *ante* before) + *garde* guard (of Germanic origin).]

va·nil·la (və nil′ə) *n.* **1.** a flavoring agent extracted from the seed pods of a climbing orchid, *Vanilla planifolia,* widely used in candies, ice cream, and cookies. **2.** the seed pod from which this agent is extracted. Also, **vanilla bean. 3.** any of the climbing orchids of the genus *Vanilla,* found in tropical regions throughout the world. [Spanish *vainilla* the orchid, small pod, diminutive of *vaina* sheath, from Latin *vāgīna;* referring to the form of the fruit.]

van·il·lin (və nil′in) *n.* a white crystalline substance obtained from the vanilla bean or made synthetically, used for flavoring and in making perfumes. Formula: $C_8H_8O_3$

van·ish (van′ish) *v.i.* **1.** to pass from sight, esp. suddenly or quickly; disappear: *The airplane vanished in the clouds.* **2.** to cease to exist; end: *All hope of winning the game vanished when our star player was injured.* [Old French *esvaniss-,* a stem of *esvanir* to disappear, going back to Latin *ēvānēscere,* going back to *ex* out of + *vānus* empty.] —For Synonyms, see **disappear.**

vanishing point 1. the point at which receding parallel lines appear to converge when represented in perspective. **2.** a place or point of time at which something disappears or ceases to exist.

vanishing point

van·i·ty (van′i tē) *n., pl.* **-ties. 1.** excessive concern with or pride in one's appearance, abilities, or accomplishments; conceit. **2.** the quality of being worthless, ineffective, or meaningless; futility.

3. something that is worthless, ineffective, or meaningless. **4.** vanity case. **5.** dressing table. [Old French *vanite,* from Latin *vānitās* emptiness, worthlessness.]

vanity case, a woman's small case for carrying cosmetics, toiletries, and other articles.

vanity fair *also,* **Vanity Fair.** the world or a part of it regarded as a scene of idle amusement, frivolity, or ostentation. [From *Vanity Fair* (the fair in the town of Vanity in the allegory *Pilgrim's Progress* by the English writer and preacher John Bunyan, 1628-86), which symbolizes worldly pomp and vanity.]

van·quish (vang′kwish, van′-) *v.t.* **1.** to defeat or conquer, as in battle. **2.** to overcome (a feeling): *to vanquish one's fear of heights.* [Modification of Old French *vencus* and *venquis,* past participle and preterit respectively of *veintre* to conquer, from Latin *vincere.*] —**van′quish·er,** *n.* —For Synonyms, see **defeat.**

van·tage (van′tij) *n.* **1.** an advantageous or superior position. **2.** vantage point. **3.** *Tennis.* advantage *(def. 4).* [Anglo-Norman *vantage,* short for Old French *advantage* advance, head start. See ADVANTAGE.]

vantage point, a position that allows a clear or advantageous view: *We could see the whole valley from our vantage point on the mountain.*

van·ward (van′wərd) *adj.* situated in the vanguard, or front. —*adv.* to or toward the vanguard.

vap·id (vap′id) *adj.* dull or lifeless; insipid; flat or uninteresting: *a vapid conversation.* [Latin *vapidus.*] —**va·pid′i·ty, vap′id·ness,** *n.* —**vap′id·ly,** *adv.*

va·por (vā′pər) *also,* British, **vapour.** *n.* **1.** any visible particulate matter suspended in the air, such as mist, smoke, or steam. **2.** the gaseous state of a substance that is usually a liquid or a solid: *Vapor from the paint filled the closed room.* **3.** *Archaic.* something insubstantial or transitory. **4.** vapors. *Archaic.* depression, low spirits, or hypochondria. —*v.i.* **1.** to rise or pass off in vapor; evaporate. **2.** to give off vapor. **3.** to indulge in boastful or idle talk. [Latin *vapor* steam.]

va·por·ish (vā′pər ish) *adj.* **1.** like or resembling vapor. **2.** *Archaic.* inclined to depression, low spirits, or hypochondria.

va·por·ize (vā′pə rīz′) *v.t., v.i.,* **-ized, -iz·ing.** to change or be changed into vapor. —**va′por·iz′a·ble,** *adj.* —**va′por·i·za′-tion,** *n.*

va·por·iz·er (vā′pə rī′zər) *n.* a device for converting a liquid into a vapor, esp. a device for vaporizing a medicinal liquid for inhalation.

vapor lock, a blockage of fuel flow in an internal-combustion engine resulting from the formation of air bubbles in the fuel line.

va·por·ous (vā′pər əs) *adj.* **1.** containing, full of, or obscured by vapor; misty: *a vaporous ocean breeze.* **2.** like, resembling, or characteristic of vapor: *a sheer, vaporous fabric.* **3.** unsubstantial, vague, or transitory: *vaporous dreams.* Also, **va′por·y.** —**va·por·os·i·ty** (vā′pə ros′i te), **va′por·ous·ness,** *n.* —**va′por·ous·ly,** *adv.*

vapor pressure *Physics, Chemistry.* the pressure exerted by the molecules of a vapor, either as the part of the pressure exerted by the vapor in a mixture of gases or as that exerted by the vapor in a confined space. Also, **vapor tension.**

vapor trail, contrail.

va·pour (vā′per) *British.* vapor.

va·que·ro (vä kâr′ō) *n., pl.* **-ros.** a cowboy, esp. of Mexico, South America, or the southwestern United States. [Spanish *vaquero* cowherd, from *vaca* cow, from Latin *vacca* cow.]

var. 1. variant. **2.** variation. **3.** variety. **4.** various.

var·i·a·ble (vâr′ē ə bəl) *adj.* **1.** likely or liable to change; changeable: *variable weather.* **2.** capable of being changed: *a drill with variable speed.* **3.** *Mathematics.* having no fixed value. **4.** *Biology.* differing from the usual type of species or structure. —*n.* **1.** something that varies or is variable. **2.** *Mathematics.* **a.** a quantity that can assume any of a set of values. **b.** a symbol representing such a quantity. —**var′i·a·bil′i·ty, var′i·a·ble-ness,** *n.* —**var′i·a·bly,** *adv.*

variable star, a star whose brightness varies with time because of processes operating within it or because it is periodically eclipsed by another star.

var·i·ance (vâr′ē əns) *n.* **1.** the act or result of varying or the quality or state of being variant or variable. **2.** the amount by which something is variant or variable; difference: *a variance of a few inches.* **3.** a disagreement or dispute; quarrel; discord. **4.** of-

a	at	e	end	o	hot	u	up	hw	white		about
ā	ape	ē	me	ō	old	ū	use	ng	song	ə	taken
ä	far	i	it	ô	fork	ü	rule	th	thin		pencil
âr	care	ī	ice	oi	oil	u̇	pull	th	this		lemon
		îr	pierce	ou	out	ûr	turn	zh	measure		circus

ficial permission to do something not allowed by zoning, building, or other regulations.

• **at variance.** in disagreement: *Their account of the accident is at variance with the facts.*

var·i·ant (vâr′ē ənt) *adj.* **1.** different or varying, as from another or others of the same kind. For example, *theatre* is a variant spelling of *theater.* **2.** liable to vary; variable; changeable. —*n.* something that is variant, such as a different spelling, pronunciation, or form of the same word. [Latin *variāns,* present participle of *variāre* to change.]

var·i·a·tion (vâr′ē ā′shən) *n.* **1.** the act, fact, or process or an instance of varying. **2.** the extent or degree to which something varies: *The scientist noted a temperature variation of thirteen degrees.* **3.** something that differs slightly from another of the same kind: *The new play is a variation of an earlier one by the same playwright.* **4.** *Music.* the repetition of a theme or tune with modifications or embellishments, as in melody, harmony, rhythm, or key, esp. one of a series of such repetitions. **5.** in ballet, a solo dance. **6.** *Biology.* **a.** the deviation of an individual of a species from others of the species, as in structure. **b.** an organism that exhibits such deviation. **7.** declination *(def. 2).*

var·i·cel·la (var′ə sel′ə) *n.* chicken pox. [Modern Latin *varicella,* diminutive of *variola.* See VARIOLA.]

var·i·col·ored (vâr′i kul′ərd, var′-) *adj.* having various colors; variegated.

var·i·cose (var′i kōs′) *adj. Medicine.* **1.** swollen, knotted, and twisted, esp. denoting an abnormal condition affecting the veins of the leg. **2.** of, relating to, or affected with varicose veins. [Latin *varicōsus* full of dilated veins, from *varix* dilated vein.]

var·i·cos·i·ty (var′i kos′i tē) *n., pl.* **-ties. 1.** the condition of being varicose. **2.** part of a vein, esp. in the leg, that is varicose.

var·ied (vâr′ēd) *adj.* **1.** consisting of different or various kinds, items, or parts: *a varied assortment of chocolates, a varied menu.* **2.** having different colors; variegated. **3.** changed; altered. —**var′ied·ly,** *adv.*

var·i·e·gate (vâr′ē i gāt′, vâr′i-) *v.t.,* **-gat·ed, -gat·ing. 1.** to change in appearance, esp. by marking with different colors. **2.** to give variety to; diversify. [Latin *variēgātus,* past participle of *variēgāre* to make of various colors, from Latin *varius* of various colors, changing + *agere* to drive, do, act.]

var·i·e·gat·ed (vâr′ē i gā′tid, vâr′i-) *adj.* **1.** marked or streaked with different colors; varied in color. **2.** having or characterized by variety; diversified: *The bouquet was a variegated selection of flowers.*

var·i·e·ga·tion (vâr′ē i gā′shən, vâr′i-) *n.* the state or condition of being variegated.

va·ri·e·tal (və rī′i təl) *adj.* **1.** of, relating to, or characterizing a particular variety or kind: *a varietal name.* **2.** constituting or made from a particular variety of grape: *varietal wine.* —*n.* a wine made largely from a particular variety of grape. —**va·ri′e·tal·ly,** *adv.*

va·ri·e·ty (və rī′i tē) *n., pl.* **-ties. 1.** the state or quality of being various or varied; diversity: *A job that lacks variety soon becomes tiresome.* **2.** a number or collection of different things: *to purchase a variety of items at the market.* **3.** a different kind or form of something: *a new variety of synthetic fabric.* **4.** *Biology.* a group of related plants or animals forming a subdivision of a species. [Latin *varietās* diversity.]

variety show, a show, as on stage or television, consisting of a variety of different acts or performances, such as songs, dances, and comedy sketches.

variety store, a store offering a large assortment of merchandise for sale, usually items of low or moderate cost.

var·i·form (vâr′ə fôrm′) *adj.* varied in form or shape; having various forms.

va·ri·o·la (və rī′ə lə) *n.* smallpox. [Modern Latin *variola,* from Late Latin *variola* pustule, from Latin *varius* of various colors, changing.]

var·i·om·e·ter (vâr′ē om′i tər) *n.* an instrument used primarily to measure variations in the earth's magnetism. [Latin *varius* changing + -METER.]

var·i·o·rum (vâr′ē ôr′əm) *n.* **1.** an edition, as of a book or play, containing notes by various editors or commentators. **2.** an edition of a work containing various versions or slightly different translations of the same text. —*adj.* of or relating to a variorum. [Shortened from Latin *editiō cum notīs variōrum* edition with the notes of various persons.]

var·i·ous (vâr′ē əs) *adj.* **1.** different from one another; of different kinds; diversified: *People of various backgrounds applied for the job.* **2.** more than one; several; many: *We stopped at various towns along the coast.* **3.** having more than one aspect or quality; versatile. **4.** being one of a group, class, or the like; individual: *The various members of the board agreed.* **5.** *Archaic.*

changeable. [Latin *varius* of different colors, changing.] —**var′i·ous·ly,** *adv.*

var·is·tor (va ris′tər) *n.* an electrical resistor whose resistance is a function of the current flowing through it. [VAR(IOUS) + (RES)IS-TOR.]

var·let (vär′lit) *n. Archaic.* **1.** a scoundrel; knave. **2.** an attendant or servant, as of a knight. [Old French *varlet,* form of *vaslet,* groom, youth; of Celtic origin.]

var·mint (vär′mənt) *n. Informal.* a troublesome or objectionable animal or person. [Dialectal form of VERMIN.]

var·nish (vär′nish) *n.* **1.** a liquid preparation usually consisting of resinous materials in a volatile solvent, such as alcohol, or such materials mixed with an oil, such as linseed oil, used to produce a hard, clear or semitransparent coating, as on a wood surface. **2.** the glossy coating produced by the application of such a preparation when it has dried. **3.** an outward show or appearance, esp. one that is deceptive; pretense. —*v.t.* **1.** to apply varnish to; cover with varnish. **2.** to cover or provide with a deceptive appearance. [Old French *vernis* the liquid preparation, from Medieval Latin *veronix* fragrant resin, probably going back to Greek *Berenīkē,* ancient Libyan town where varnish was supposedly first used.] —**var′nish·er,** *n.*

var·si·ty (vär′si tē) *n., pl.* **-ties.** the principal team that represents a university, college, or school in athletic or other competition. —*adj.* of, relating to, or for the varsity: *a varsity team, varsity practice.* [Modification and shortening of UNIVERSITY.]

varve (värv) *n. Geology.* a pair of layers of sediment, one dark and fine-grained and the other light and coarse-grained, deposited over the course of a year in a body of still water, esp. one fed by a melting glacier. [Swedish *varv* layer, turn, from *varva* to turn, change, from Old Norse *hverfa.*]

var·y (vâr′ē) *v.,* **var·ied, var·y·ing.** —*v.t.* **1.** to change, as in appearance or nature; make different: *to vary the conditions of an experiment.* **2.** to give variety to; diversify: *to vary one's diet.* **3.** *Music.* to repeat (a theme or tune) with modifications or embellishments, as in melody, harmony, rhythm, or key. —*v.i.* **1.** to become changed, as in appearance or nature; undergo change: *The temperature outside varies from day to day.* **2.** to be different; differ: *This author's works vary greatly in quality.* **3.** to turn aside; deviate; depart (with *from*): *to vary from a rule.* **4.** to undergo or exhibit biologic variation. **5.** *Mathematics.* to be subject to change; be variable. [Latin *variāre* to change.]

vas (vas) *n., pl.* **va·sa** (vā′sə). *Biology.* a duct; vessel. [Latin *vās* dish, utensil.] —**va·sal** (vā′səl), *adj.*

vas·cu·lar (vas′kyə lər) *adj.* of, relating to, composed of, or containing vessels that carry blood, sap, or other animal or plant fluid. [Modern Latin *vascularis,* from Latin *vāsculum* small vessel, diminutive of *vās* vessel, dish.]

vascular bundle *Botany.* a strand of vascular tissue in any of the higher plants.

vascular tissue *Botany.* the tissue in a higher plant that forms the circulatory system carrying sap throughout the plant, consisting of phloem and xylem.

vas·cu·lum (vas′kyə ləm) *n., pl.* **-la** (-lə) or **-lums.** a small box or case used to carry plant specimens. [Latin *vāsculum* small vessel. See VASCULAR.]

vas de·fer·ens (vas def′ə renz′) *pl.* **va·sa de·fer·en·ti·a** (vā′sə def′ə ren′shē ə). the duct that carries sperm from the testicle to the ejaculatory duct of the penis.

vase (vās, vāz, väz) *n.* a container that is usually rounded in shape and of greater height than width, used chiefly for holding flowers or for decoration. [French *vase* vessel, from Latin *vās.*]

vas·ec·to·my (va sek′tə mē) *n., pl.* **-mies.** the surgical removal of all or a portion of the vas deferens, resulting in sterility, used as a form of birth control.

Vas·e·line (vas′ə lēn′, vas′ə lēn′) *n. Trademark.* an ointment made from petroleum; petrolatum. [German *Wasser* water + Greek *elaion* oil + -INE².]

vas·o·con·stric·tion (vas′ō kən strik′shən, vā′zō-) *n.* a narrowing of the space inside blood vessels. [Latin *vās* vessel + CONSTRICTION.]

vas·o·con·stric·tor (vas′ō kən strik′tər, vā′zō-) *n.* a nerve fiber or drug that induces vasoconstriction.

vas·o·di·la·tion (vas′ō di lā′shən, -dī-, vā′zō-) *n.* a widening of the space inside blood vessels. Also, **vas·o·di·la·ta·tion** (vas′ō-dil′ə tā′shən, -dī′lə-, vā′zō-). [Latin *vās* vessel + DILATION.]

vas·o·di·la·tor (vas′ō di lā′tər, -di-, -dī′lā-, vā′zō-) *n.* a nerve or drug that causes vasodilation.

vas·o·in·hib·i·tor (vas′ō in hib′i tər, vā′zō-) *n.* an agent, as a drug, that inhibits the regulatory action of the vasomotor nerves. [Latin *vās* vessel + INHIBITOR.]

vas·o·mo·tor (vas′ō mō′tər) *adj.* of, relating to, or designating nerves or nerve centers involved in dilation or constriction of the blood vessels. [Latin *vās* vessel + MOTOR.]

vas·o·pres·sin (vas′ō pres′in) *n.* a peptide hormone secreted by the pituitary gland that raises blood pressure and reduces the secretion of urine.

vas·o·pres·sor (vas′ō pres′ər, vā′zō-) *n.* an agent, as a drug or hormone, that raises the blood pressure by causing constriction of the blood vessels. [VASO(CONSTRICTION) + PRESS(URE) + -OR.]

vas·sal (vas′əl) *n.* **1.** under feudalism, a subject of a lord. Vassals received land and protection from the lord in return for their fealty, support, and homage. **2.** a servant; slave. **3.** a person subordinate or subservient to another. —*adj.* of, relating to, or characteristic of a vassal. [Old French *vassal* subject, tenant, knight, from Medieval Latin *vassallus* servant, retainer, from *vassus* servant; of Celtic origin.]

vas·sal·age (vas′ə lij) *n.* **1.** the state or condition of being a vassal. **2.** the duties, obligations, or services required of a vassal. **3.** the land held by a vassal. **4.** servitude, subjection, or subordination. **5.** vassals collectively.

vast (vast) *adj.* very great, as in extent, size, or amount: *a vast expanse of land, a vast number of people.* [Latin *vāstus.*] —**vast′ly,** *adv.* —**vast′ness,** *n.* —For Synonyms, see **huge.**

vast·y (vas′tē) *adj.,* **vast·i·er, vast·i·est.** *Archaic.* vast; immense.

vat (vat) *n.* a large tank or container used for holding liquids. —*v.t.,* **vat·ted, vat·ting.** to put into a vat. [Old English *fæt* vessel, cask.]

Vat·i·can (vat′i kən) *n.* **1.** the official residence of the pope in Vatican City. **2.** papal government or power, as distinguished from the Quirinal. [Latin *Vāticānus (mōns)* Vatican (hill); of Etruscan origin; referring to the building of the pope's palace on the *Vatican,* a hill of Rome.]

va·tic·i·nate (və tis′ə nāt′) *v.t., v.i.,* **-nat·ed, -nat·ing.** to prophesy; foretell. [Latin *vāticinātus,* past participle of *vāticinārī* to prophesy, from *vātēs* seer, prophet.] —**va·tic′i·na′tion,** *n.* —**va·tic′i·na′tor,** *n.*

vaude·ville (vôd′vil, vô′də-) *n.* theatrical entertainment popular in the United States in the late nineteenth and early twentieth centuries, consisting of a variety of short performances, as by singers, jugglers, and comedians. [French *vaudeville* light form of comedy, gay country ballad (combined with farces in the eighteenth century), going back to *Vau de Vire* valley of Vire, region in Normandy noted for gay, satirical songs.]

vaude·vil·lian (vôd vil′yən, vô′də-) *n.* a person who writes for or performs in vaudeville. —*adj.* of, relating to, or characteristic of vaudeville.

vault[1] (vôlt) *n.* **1.** an arched structure of stone, brick, or concrete serving as a roof or ceiling. **2.** something resembling such a structure: *the vault of the sky.* **3.** an arched space, passage, or chamber, esp. one that is underground. **4.** an underground compartment or room used as a cellar or storeroom. **5.** a well-protected or fortified room or compartment, as in a bank, used for the safekeeping of valuables or money. **6.** a burial chamber; tomb.

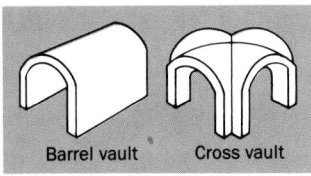

Barrel vault   Cross vault

vault[1] *(def. 1)*

—*v.t.* **1.** to cover, form, or provide with a vault or vaultlike structure. **2.** to build in the shape of a vault. [Middle French *vaute, voute* arched structure, going back to Latin *volvere* to roll, turn.]

vault[2] (vôlt) *v.t.* to jump over, esp. with the aid of a pole or the hands: *to vault a fence.* —*v.i.* to jump; spring: *to vault over a wall.* —*n.* the act or an instance of vaulting; jump; leap. [Old French *volter* to turn, leap, gambol, going back to Latin *volvere* to turn, roll.] —**vault′er,** *n.*

vault·ed (vôl′tid) *adj.* **1.** having the form of a vault; arched: *a vaulted ceiling.* **2.** constructed or covered with a vault.

vault·ing[1] (vôl′ting) *n.* **1.** a vaulted or arched structure. **2.** vaults collectively. **3.** the art or technique of constructing vaults.

vault·ing[2] (vôl′ting) *adj.* **1.** leaping upward or over. **2.** overreaching; exaggerated; overblown: *vaulting ambition.* **3.** used in jumping over something: *a vaulting pole.*

vaunt (vônt, vänt) *v.i.* to boast; brag. —*v.t.* to boast of (something); brag about: *to vaunt one's athletic ability.* —*n.* a boasting assertion or statement; brag. [Middle French *vanter* to boast, from Late Latin *vānitāre* to flatter, boast, from Latin *vānus* empty, fruitless.] —**vaunt′er,** *n.* —**vaunt′ing·ly,** *adv.*

vb. 1. verb. **2.** verbal.

V.C. 1. Victoria Cross. **2.** *also,* **VC** Vietcong.

VCR, an electronic device for recording and playing back images

and accompanying sounds on videocassettes. Also, **videocassette recorder, videotape recorder.** [Abbreviation of *v(ideo) c(assette) r(ecorder).*]

VD, venereal disease.

VDT, video display terminal.

-'ve *suffix* (used in contractions) have: *I've seen that movie.*

veal (vēl) *n.* the flesh of a calf, used as food. [Old French *veël* calf, from Latin *vitellus* little calf, diminutive of *vitulus* calf.]

vec·tor (vek′tər) *n.* **1.a.** a mathematical quantity that has both magnitude and direction, such as velocity. **b.** a line segment with an arrow representing such a quantity. In physics, vectors are used to represent forces. **2.** an animal, esp. an insect, that transmits a disease-causing organism, such as a virus or bacterium. [Latin *vector* carrier, traveler.] —**vec·to·ri·al** (vek tôr′ē əl), *adj.*

vector product, a directed mathematical quantity whose length is equal to the product of the lengths of two vectors and the sine of the angle between them. Also, **cross product.**

Ve·da (vā′də, vē′-) *n.* **1.** any of the four collections of ancient Hindu sacred writings, such as the Rig-Veda, containing chants, hymns, incantations, and other sacred information. **2.** these writings collectively. [Sanskrit *vēda* knowledge, sacred books.]

V-E Day, May 8, 1945, the official day of surrender of Germany to the Allied Forces during World War II, marking the end of hostilities in Europe.

ve·dette (vi det′) *also,* **vidette.** *n.* **1.** a mounted sentinel positioned in advance of an outpost. **2.** a small vessel used for reconnaissance. Also *(def. 2),* **vedette boat.** [French *vedette* sentry, through Italian and Spanish, going back to Latin *vigilāre* to keep watch.]

Ve·dic (vā′dik, vē′-) *n.* the language of the Vedas, an early form of Sanskrit. —*adj.* of or relating to Vedic or the Vedas.

veep (vēp) *n. Informal.* **1.** vice president. **2. Veep.** the vice president of the United States. [From v.p.]

veer (vîr) *v.i.* to change in direction or course; shift; turn: *At the bottom of the hill the road veers sharply to the left.* —*v.t.* to change the direction or course of. —*n.* a change in direction or course; swerve: *A veer to the right avoided the tree.* [Middle French *virer* to turn, change direction; of uncertain origin.]

veer·y (vîr′ē) *n., pl.* **veer·ies.** a North American thrush, *Catharus fuscescens,* having reddish brown and white plumage. Length: 7 inches (18 centimeters). [Possibly imitative of its call.]

Ve·ga (vē′gə, vā′-) *n.* a bright white star, one of the twenty brightest in the sky, and the brightest star in the constellation Lyra. [Spanish *Vega,* from Arabic *wāqi‘* falling, in *al nasr al wāqi‘* the falling vulture, the constellation Lyra.]

veg·e·ta·ble (vej′tə bəl, vej′i tə-) *n.* **1.** an edible part of any herbaceous plant, eaten cooked or raw. **2.** a plant from which such a part comes. **3.** an organism classified as a plant. **4.** a person leading a dull, inactive, unthinking, merely physical, existence. —*adj.* **1.** of, relating to, consisting of, or made from an edible vegetable or vegetables: *a vegetable casserole.* **2.** of, relating to, or made or obtained from a plant or plants. **3.** dull or inactive; lifeless: *a vegetable existence.* [Late Latin *vegetābilis* able to grow, animating, from *vegetāre* to animate, from Latin *vegetus* vigorous.]

vegetable marrow, any of various oblong squashes having yellowish green or cream-colored skin.

vegetable oil, any of various liquid fats obtained from the seeds and nuts of plants and used in food preparation, soap manufacture, or the like.

veg·e·tal (vej′i təl) *adj.* of, relating to, or characteristic of plants or vegetables.

veg·e·tar·i·an (vej′i târ′ē ən) *n.* a person who does not eat meat, fish, or fowl, or eats only plants and plant products, usually for health or ethical reasons. —*adj.* **1.** of, relating to, or practicing vegetarianism. **2.** consisting entirely of vegetables.

veg·e·tar·i·an·ism (vej′i târ′ē ə niz′əm) *n.* the practices or principles of vegetarians.

veg·e·tate (vej′i tāt′) *v.i.,* **-tat·ed, -tat·ing. 1.** to grow or develop in the manner of a plant. **2.** to lead a dull or inactive existence; do little or nothing: *I spent the weekend vegetating at home.* [Late Latin *vegetātus,* past participle of *vegetāre* to animate. See VEGETABLE.]

veg·e·ta·tion (vej′i tā′shən) *n.* **1.** plant life; plants collectively: *a region of sparse vegetation.* **2.** the act or process of vegetating. —**veg′e·ta′tion·al,** *adv.*

veg·e·ta·tive (vej′i tā′tiv) *adj.* **1.** of or relating to plants, plant

a	at	e	end	o	hot	u	up	hw	white		about
ā	ape	ē	me	ō	old	ū	use	ng	song		taken
ä	far	i	it	ô	fork	ü	rule	th	thin	ə	pencil
âr	care	ī	ice	oi	oil	u̇	pull	th	this		lemon
		îr	pierce	ou	out	ûr	turn	zh	measure		circus

life, or plant growth. **2.** growing or capable of growing as or like plants. **3.** dull or inactive: *a vegetative lifestyle.* Also, **veg·e·tive** (vej′i tiv). —**veg′e·ta′tive·ly,** *adv.* —**veg′e·ta′tive·ness,** *n.*

veg·gie (vej′ē) *n. Informal.* **1.** a vegetable. **2.** a vegetarian. [Short for VEG(ETABLE) + -IE.]

ve·he·ment (vē′ə mənt) *adj.* **1.** showing or characterized by intensity of feeling; passionate; ardent: *a vehement reply, vehement devotion.* **2.** having great force; violent; forceful: *a vehement wind.* [Latin *vehemēns* eager, violent.] —**ve′he·mence,** *n.* —**ve′he·ment·ly,** *adv.*

ve·hi·cle (vē′i kəl) *n.* **1.** a device designed or used for transporting persons, goods, or equipment over land or through space, such as an automobile, sled, carriage, or rocket. **2.** the means by which something is expressed, conveyed, or achieved: *Poetry is a vehicle of self-expression.* **3.** medium (*def.* 7). **4.** in the performing arts, a play, movie, musical composition, or the like that is suited to display the particular talents of a performer or group. [Latin *vehiculum* carriage, conveyance.]

ve·hic·u·lar (vē hik′yə lər) *adj.* **1.** of, relating to, or for vehicles: *vehicular traffic.* **2.** serving as a vehicle. **3.** resulting from a collision involving a motor vehicle: *vehicular homicide.*

V-eight (vē′āt′) *n.* **1.** an internal-combustion engine in which two banks of four cylinders each are set at a V-shaped angle to each other. **2.** an automobile having such an engine. Also, **V-8.**

veil (vāl) *n.* **1.** a piece of lightweight fabric, as of lace, silk, or net, worn esp. by women over the head and shoulders, or as a covering for the face. **2.** a piece of fabric used as a curtain or screen. **3.** anything that obscures or conceals: *a veil of mist, a veil of secrecy.* —*v.t.* to cover, conceal, or disguise with a veil: *to veil one's irritation with a smile.* [Anglo-Norman *veil(e)* cloth covering, to conceal from view, sail, from Latin *vēlum* cloth, covering, curtain. Doublet of VELUM, VOILE.] —**veil′like′,** *adj.*
· **to take the veil.** to become a nun.

veil·ing (vā′ling) *n.* **1.** any of various lightweight fabrics used for veils. **2.** a veil.

vein (vān) *n.* **1.** one of the vessels that convey blood to the heart from all parts of the body. **2.** one of the bundles of vascular tissue that form the framework of a leaf. For illustration, see **leaf. 3.** one of the tubular structures that serve to stiffen and strengthen the wing of an insect. **4.** a sheetlike deposit of minerals that forms in the fissure of a rock; lode. **5.** a streak or marking of a different color or material, as in marble or wood. **6.** a distinctive quality, feeling, or tendency: *There is a vein of subtle humor running through the story.* **7.** a mood, attitude, or manner: *We hoped the conversation would not continue in such a pessimistic vein.* **8.** a particular form or style of expression: *to write in a poetic vein.* —*v.t.* **1.** to provide, fill, or mark with veins. **2.** to extend through in the manner of a vein or veins. [Old French *veine* vessel that carries blood to the heart, from Latin *vēna* blood vessel, mineral deposit, natural tendency.] —**vein′like′,** *adj.*

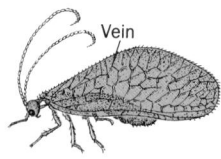

Vein

vein of a lacewing

veined (vānd) *adj.* having or marked with veins.

vein·ing (vā′ning) *n.* an arrangement or pattern of veins.

vein·let (vān′lit) *n.* venule.

vein·y (vā′nē) *adj.,* **vein·i·er, vein·i·est. 1.** of, relating to, or having veins. **2.** full of veins, as leaves or marble. [VEIN + -Y¹.]

ve·lar (vē′lər) *adj.* **1.** of or relating to a velum, esp. to the soft palate. **2.** *Phonetics.* articulated with the tongue near or touching the soft palate. —*n. Phonetics.* a velar sound. [Latin *vēlāris* relating to a curtain, from *vēlum* curtain, covering, cloth.]

Vel·cro (vel′krō) *n. Trademark.* a material used for fasteners on garments and luggage, consisting of a strip of nylon fabric covered with many tiny, hook-shaped fibers and another strip covered with fiber loops. When pressed together, the two strips adhere.

veld (velt, felt) *also,* **veldt.** *n.* a rolling, grassland region in South Africa, having scattered bushes and trees. [Afrikaans *veld(t)* field, from Middle Dutch *veld.*]

vel·le·i·ty (və lē′i tē) *n., pl.* **-ties. 1.** the act or fact of merely willing, wishing, or desiring something without any effort toward action or realization. **2.** a mere wish, desire, or inclination without accompanying action or effort. [Modern Latin *velleitas,* from Latin *velle* to wish.]

vel·lum (vel′əm) *n.* **1.** a fine parchment prepared from calfskin, lambskin, or kidskin, used esp. for writing or for binding books. **2.** a manuscript written on such parchment. **3.** paper made to resemble such parchment. —*adj.* of, relating to, or resembling vellum. [Old French *velin* very fine parchment made from calfskin, from *veël* calf. See VEAL.]

ve·loc·i·pede (və los′ə pēd′) *n.* **1.** an early form of bicycle. **2.** a

tricycle. [French *vélocipède,* early form of the bicycle, from Latin *vēlox* swift + *pēs* foot.]

ve·loc·i·ty (və los′i tē) *n., pl.* **-ties. 1.** rapidity of motion; speed. **2.** *Physics.* the rate of motion in a particular direction in relation to time. [Latin *vēlocitās* swiftness.]

ve·lour (və lʊr′) *also,* **ve·lours** (və lʊr′). *n., pl.* **-lours** (-lʊr′, -lʊrz′). a soft, thick, closely woven fabric having a velvetlike finish, used for clothing, draperies, upholstery, and other items. [French *velours* velvet, going back to Latin *villōsus* shaggy, from *villus* shaggy hair.]

ve·lum (vē′ləm) *n., pl.* **-la** (-lə). **1.** *Biology.* a thin, veillike membranous covering. **2.** *Anatomy.* the soft palate. [Latin *vēlum* cloth, covering, curtain. Doublet of VEIL, VOILE.]

ve·lure (və lʊr′) *n.* velvet or a fabric resembling velvet. [Form of VELOUR.]

vel·vet (vel′vit) *n.* **1.** a fabric made of silk, rayon, nylon, or other fiber, having a smooth, soft, thick pile. **2.** something resembling velvet, esp. in smoothness or softness. **3.** the soft skin that covers the growing antlers of a deer. —*adj.* **1.** made of or covered with velvet: *a velvet dress, a velvet sofa.* **2.** resembling velvet, esp. in smoothness or softness. [Middle French *velu* velvety (going back to Latin *villus* shaggy hair) + -ET.]

vel·vet·een (vel′vi tēn′) *n.* a cotton fabric made with a short, thick pile so as to resemble velvet. [From VELVET.]

vel·vet·y (vel′vi tē) *adj.* **1.** smooth and soft like velvet. **2.** smooth to the taste, as some wines or liquors.

Ven., Venerable.

ve·na ca·va (vē′nə kā′və) *pl.* **ve·nae ca·vae** (vē′nē kā′vē). either of two large veins leading into the right atrium of the heart.

ve·nal (vē′nəl) *adj.* **1.** willing to be bribed; open to bribery; corruptible: *a venal public official.* **2.** able to be or actually gotten or influenced by bribery: *a venal decision by a judge.* **3.** characterized by corruption. [Latin *vēnālis* for sale, relating to selling, from *vēnum* sale.] —**ve′nal·ly,** *adv.*

ve·nal·i·ty (vē nal′i tē) *n., pl.* **-ties.** the quality or state or an instance of being venal.

ve·na·tion (vē nā′shən, və-) *n.* **1.** an arrangement or system of veins, as in a leaf or an insect's wing. **2.** such veins collectively. Also, **nervation.** [Latin *vēna* vein + -ATION.]

vend (vend) *v.t.* to offer for sale; sell or peddle. —*v.i.* to sell goods. [Latin *vēndere,* going back to *vēnum dāre* to offer for sale.]

vend·a·ble (ven′də bəl) vendible.

vend·ee (ven dē′) *n.* a person to whom a thing is sold; buyer.

vend·er (ven′dər) vendor.

ven·det·ta (ven det′ə) *n.* **1.** a feud in which the relatives of a murdered or injured person seek vengeance on the wrongdoer or members of the wrongdoer's family. **2.** any bitter feud or dispute motivated by a desire for vengeance. [Italian *vendetta* revenge, from Latin *vindicta.*]

vend·i·ble (ven′də bəl) *also,* **vendable.** *adj.* capable of being sold; salable; marketable. —*n.* a vendible item. —**vend′i·bil′i·ty,** *n.*

vending machine, a coin- or bill-operated machine for selling candy, cigarettes, or various other small items.

ven·dor (ven′dər) *also,* **vender.** *n.* a person who sells or peddles: *a fruit vendor, an ice-cream vendor.* [Anglo-Norman *vendo(u)r,* from Latin *venditor.*]

ven·due (ven dü′, -dū′) *n.* a public sale or auction. [Dutch *vendu,* from Old French *vendue* sale, going back to Latin *vendere* to sell.]

ve·neer (və nîr′) *n.* **1.** a thin layer of fine wood or other material used in covering a surface, as in making plywood: *The pine table had a veneer of mahogany.* **2.** an outward appearance, esp. one that is deceptive or superficial: *They tried to hide their resentment behind a veneer of friendliness.* —*v.t.* **1.** to cover (a surface) with a thin layer of fine wood or other material. **2.** to glue together (layers of wood) to make plywood. **3.** to give a superficially attractive appearance to. [Earlier *fineer,* from German *furnieren* to inlay, from French *fournir* to supply; of Germanic origin.]

ven·er·a·ble (ven′ər ə bəl) *adj.* **1.** deserving respect or reverence, as by reason of age, character, or position: *a wise and venerable old scholar.* **2.** (of a building, place, or object) worthy of respect by reason of age or historic or religious association: *the venerable halls of a great university.* **3.** *also,* **Venerable.** deserving reverence. ➡ used as a title of respect in the Anglican and Roman Catholic churches. [Latin *venerābilis* worthy of reverence, from *venerārī* to reverence, worship.] —**ven′er·a·bil′i·ty, ven′er·a·ble·ness,** *n.* —**ven′er·a·bly,** *adv.*

ven·er·ate (ven′ə rāt′) *v.t.,* **-at·ed, -at·ing.** to regard with deep respect or reverence: *American Indian cultures venerated nature.* [Latin *venerātus,* past participle of *venerārī* to reverence, worship, from *venus* love.] —**ven′er·a′tor,** *n.* —For Synonyms, see **worship.**

ven·er·a·tion (ven′ə rā′shən) *n.* **1.** a feeling of deep respect or reverence. **2.** the act of venerating or the state of being venerated.

ve·ne·re·al (və nîr′ē əl) *adj.* **1.** of or relating to sexual intercourse. **2.** (of certain diseases) transmitted by sexual intercourse with an infected person. **3.** of, relating to, or infected with venereal disease. [Latin *venereus* relating to love (from *venus* love) + -AL[1].]

venereal disease, any of several diseases, such as syphilis or gonorrhea, usually transmitted by sexual intercourse with an infected person; sexually transmitted disease.

ven·er·y[1] (ven′ə rē) *n. Archaic.* the pursuit and gratification of sexual desire. [Latin *vener-,* stem of *venus* love + -Y[3].]

ven·er·y[2] (ven′ə rē) *n. Archaic.* the act, practice, or sport of hunting; the chase. [Old French *venerie* hunting, from *venere* to hunt, from Latin *vēnārī.*]

ven·e·sec·tion (ven′ə sek′shən) *n.* phlebotomy.

Ve·ne·tian (və nē′shən) *adj.* of or relating to Venice, its people, or culture. —*n.* a native or inhabitant of Venice.

Venetian blind *also,* **venetian blind.** a shade, esp. for a window, having a number of horizontal slats, usually of wood, plastic, or metal. The slats can be opened or closed, and the shade can be raised or lowered by means of attached cords.

venge·ance (ven′jəns) *n.* **1.** the act of inflicting injury in return for an injury or offense received; revenge: *The country took vengeance for wrongs done to its citizens.* **2.** a desire to inflict such injury: *to swear vengeance against someone.* [Old French *vengeance* revenge, from *venger* to avenge, from Latin *vindicāre.*]
 •**with a vengeance. a.** with great force or violence: *The tornado hit the town with a vengeance.* **b.** to an unusual extent; extremely: *During the milk shortage, the price of milk rose with a vengeance.*

| Synonyms | Vengeance, retribution, and retaliation mean |
the act of inflicting punishment in return for harm or injury that has been sustained. **Vengeance** implies the infliction of punishment for a wrong done: *The police thought the killing was an act of vengeance.* **Retribution** is usually applied to punishment administered by a higher power or natural force: *They believed the famine was divine retribution for their sins.* **Retaliation** indicates large-scale, impersonal response to an attack or offense: *The air attacks were in retaliation for the taking of hostages.*

venge·ful (venj′fəl) *adj.* **1.** full of or characterized by a desire for vengeance; seeking revenge: *a vengeful enemy.* **2.** showing or arising from a desire for revenge: *a vengeful hatred.* **3.** inflicting or serving to inflict vengeance: *a vengeful attack.* —**venge′ful·ly,** *adv.* —**venge′ful·ness,** *n.*

ve·ni·al (vē′nē əl, vēn′yəl) *adj.* **1.** that may be excused or forgiven; not very serious; pardonable: *a venial crime.* **2.** (of sin) not very serious; of minor significance. ➡ distinguished from **mortal.** [Late Latin *veniālis* pardonable, from Latin *venia* forgiveness, pardon.] —**ve·ni·al·i·ty** (vē′nē al′i tē), **ve′ni·al·ness,** *n.* —**ve′ni·al·ly,** *adv.*

venial sin, in Roman Catholic theology, a sin that does not separate the sinner from the favor and love of God nor result in damnation to hell if not forgiven. ➡ distinguished from **mortal sin.**

ven·in (ven′in) *n.* any of the toxic components in snake venom. [VEN(OM) + -IN[1].]

ve·ni·re (və nī′rē) *n.* **1.** a judicial writ ordering that persons be summoned to serve as jurors. Also, **venire fa·ci·as** (fā′shē as′). **2.** the group of available jurors from which a jury or juries will be selected. [Short for Latin *venīre faciās* you are to cause (someone) to come.]

ve·ni·re·man (və nī′rē mən) *n., pl.* **-men** (-mən). a person summoned to serve as a juror under a venire.

ven·i·son (ven′ə sən, -zən) *n.* the flesh of a deer, used as food. [Old French *veneisun,* from Latin *vēnātiō* hunting.]

Venn diagram (ven) a diagram in which circles and rectangles are used to represent mathematical sets and to show the relationships between them. [From John *Venn,* 1834-1923, English logician.]

ven·om (ven′əm) *n.* **1.** a poisonous secretion of some animals, such as certain snakes or spiders, usually introduced into the body of a victim by a bite or sting. **2.** malice; spite: *The speaker's sarcastic statements were filled with venom.* [Old French *venin* poison, going back to Latin *venēnum* poison, drug.]

ven·om·ous (ven′ə məs) *adj.* **1.** able to inflict a poisonous wound, esp. by biting or stinging; secreting and transmitting venom: *a venomous snake.* **2.** containing or full of venom: *a venomous bite.* **3.** malicious; spiteful: *a venomous remark.* —**ven′om·ous·ly,** *adv.* —**ven′om·ous·ness,** *n.*

ve·nous (vē′nəs) *adj.* **1.** of, relating to, or characterized by veins. **2.** designating the blood returning to the heart through the

veins. Venous blood contains carbon dioxide instead of oxygen and has a dark red color as a result. [Latin *vēnōsus* full of veins, from *vēna* vein, blood vessel.]

vent[1] (vent) *n.* **1.a.** a hole or other usually small opening for the escape or passage of a gas, liquid, or the like. **b.** an opening in the earth's surface or sea floor through which lava, gas, steam, or hot water exits. **2.** any means of escape; outlet. **3.** a means of release or expression: *to give vent to pent-up hostility.* **4.** the excretory opening of the cloaca in certain animals, such as birds and reptiles. **5.** a small, usually triangular window in some motor vehicles, used for ventilation. —*v.t.* **1.** to give release or expression to: *to vent one's criticism.* **2.** to provide with a vent or outlet. **3.** to allow to escape through an opening: *to vent steam by opening a valve.* [Partly from French *vent* wind, from Latin *ventus;* partly from French *évent* hole, opening, going back to Latin *ex* out + *ventus* wind.]

vent[2] (vent) *n.* a slit in a garment, as at the back of a coat. [Form of dialectal English *fent,* from Old French *fente* slit, from *fendre* to split, from Latin *findere.*]

ven·ti·late (ven′tə lāt′) *v.t.,* **-lat·ed, -lat·ing. 1.** to admit air into, esp. fresh air; circulate fresh air in. **2.** (of air) to circulate through so as to freshen. **3.** to provide with a vent, as for the escape of a gas. **4.** to aerate or oxygenate, esp. blood. **5.** *Medicine.* to maintain the breathing of (a person) or the flow of air into (the lungs), as with a respirator. **6.** to bring to public notice; submit to examination and discussion: *to ventilate a political issue.* [Latin *ventilātus,* past participle of *ventilāre* to fan, set in motion, from *ventus* wind.]

ven·ti·la·tion (ven′tə lā′shən) *n.* **1.** the act or process of ventilating, or the state of being ventilated. **2.** a system or means of providing or circulating fresh air.

ven·ti·la·tor (ven′tə lā′tər) *n.* **1.** an apparatus for providing or circulating fresh air, or for expelling foul or stagnant air. **2.** *Medicine.* respirator *(def. 1).*

ven·tral (ven′trəl) *adj.* **1.** of or relating to the abdomen or belly; abdominal. **2.** of, relating to, or situated on or near the surface opposite the back. [Late Latin *ventrālis* relating to the belly, from Latin *venter* belly.] —**ven′tral·ly,** *adv.*

ven·tri·cle (ven′tri kəl) *n.* **1.** either of the two lower chambers or cavities of the heart. The right ventricle receives deoxygenated, venous blood from the right atrium and pumps it into the artery leading to the lungs. The left ventricle receives oxygenated blood from the left atrium and pumps it into the aorta. For illustration, see **heart. 2.** a small cavity in the body, esp. any of a series of four connecting cavities in the brain. [Latin *ventriculus* stomach, ventricle of the heart, diminutive of *venter* belly.]

ven·tri·cose (ven′tri kōs′) *adj.* swollen or distended, esp. on one side. [Modern Latin *ventricosus,* from Latin *venter* belly.] —**ven·tri·cos·i·ty** (ven′tri kos′i tē), *n.*

ven·tric·u·lar (ven trik′yə lər) *adj.* of, relating to, or of the nature of a ventricle.

ven·tri·lo·qui·al (ven′trə lō′kwē əl) *adj.* of, relating to, or using ventriloquism.

ven·tril·o·quism (ven tril′ə kwiz′əm) *n.* the art or practice of speaking or producing sounds without moving the lips so that the sound seems to come from some source other than the speaker. Also, **ventriloquy.** [Late Latin *ventriloquus* ventriloquist; literally, one who speaks from the belly (from Latin *venter* belly + *loquī* to speak) + -ISM; because it was believed that the ventriloquist's voice came from his stomach.]

ven·tril·o·quist (ven tril′ə kwist) *n.* a person who practices ventriloquism, esp. an entertainer who holds and apparently carries on a conversation with a dummy. —**ven·tril′o·quis′tic,** *adj.*

ven·tril·o·quize (ven tril′ə kwīz′) *v.i., v.t.,* **-quized, -quiz·ing.** to speak (words) as a ventriloquist.

ven·tril·o·quy (ven tril′ə kwē) *n.* ventriloquism.

ven·ture (ven′chər) *n.* **1.** an undertaking, esp. one involving risk or danger: *It was a foolhardy business venture that was sure to fail.* **2.** something that is risked, as in such an undertaking. —*v.,* **-tured, -tur·ing.** —*v.t.* **1.** to expose to risk of danger: *to venture all one's savings on an uncertain business scheme.* **2.** to run the risk of; brave: *to venture a storm.* **3.** to express at the risk of criticism, objection, or the like: *May I venture a word of advice?* —*v.i.* to do or undertake something despite the risk or danger involved; dare: *The skater ventured out onto the ice and almost fell*

a	at	e	end	o	hot	u	up	hw	white	⎧	about
ā	ape	ē	me	ō	old	ū	use	ng	song		taken
ä	far	i	it	ô	fork	ŭ	rule	th	thin	⟩	pencil
âr	care	ī	ice	oi	oil	u̇	pull	th	this		lemon
		îr	pierce	ou	out	ûr	turn	zh	measure	⎩	circus

through. [Short for Middle English *aventure,* earlier form of AD-VENTURE.] —**ven′tur·er,** *n.*

• **at a venture.** by mere chance; at random.

Synonyms *v.t.* **Venture** and **risk** mean to do something that involves the possibility of loss, failure, or harm. **Venture** suggests reckless daring, esp. for gain or profit: *The couple decided to venture into real estate investments, hoping for a quick return.* **Risk** implies a calculated action undertaken despite the possibility of failure, as in an emergency: *The firefighters risked their lives to evacuate the building.*

venture capital, funds invested in or available for investment in new or untested business enterprises that involve risk but have potential for great profitability.

ven·ture·some (ven′chər səm) *adj.* **1.** willing or inclined to take risks; bold; daring: *a venturesome explorer.* **2.** involving risk or danger; hazardous: *a venturesome journey.* —**ven′ture·some·ly,** *adv.* —**ven′ture·some·ness,** *n.*

ven·tu·ri (ven tūr′ē) *n.* a tubular device that is used either to produce a fine spray, as of fuel in the carburetor of an automobile engine, or to measure the rate of flow of a gas or fluid. Also, **venturi tube.** [From Giovanni Battista *Venturi,* 1746-1822, Italian physicist.]

ven·tur·ous (ven′chər əs) *adj.* **1.** looking for adventure; bold; adventurous. **2.** risky or dangerous; hazardous. —**ven′tur·ous·ly,** *adv.* —**ven′tur·ous·ness,** *n.*

ven·ue (ven′ū) *n.* **1.** the locality where a crime, accident, or other event that is the cause of legal action has taken place. **2.** the county, district, or locality from which a jury must be called and where a trial must be held. **3.** the place where a special event occurs: *What is the venue for our meeting?* [Old French *venue* a coming, from *venir* to come, from Latin *venīre.*]

ven·ule (ven′ūl) *n.* a small vein. Also, **veinlet.** [Latin *vēnula,* diminutive of *vēna* vein, blood vessel.]

Ve·nus (vē′nəs) *n.* **1.** in Roman mythology, the goddess of love and beauty. Her Greek counterpart is Aphrodite. **2.** the sixth largest planet of the solar system and second in order of distance from the sun.

Ve·nu·si·an (və nü′sē ən, -shən, -nū′-) *adj.* of or relating to the planet Venus. —*n.* a supposed inhabitant of the planet Venus.

Venus's-flytrap

Ve·nus's-fly·trap (vē′nə siz flī′trap′) *n.* an insectivorous plant, *Dionaea muscipula,* native to moist, sandy regions of North and South Carolina, having two-lobed, hinged leaves that snap shut to trap insects coming into contact with them. Also, **Venus flytrap.**

ve·ra·cious (və rā′shəs) *adj.* **1.** that can be trusted; truthful; honest: *a veracious witness.* **2.** conforming to the truth; accurate; correct: *a veracious account of an accident.* [Latin *vērāci-,* stem of *vērāx* truthful (from *vērus* true) + -OUS.] —**ve·ra′cious·ly,** *adv.* —**ve·ra′cious·ness,** *n.*

ve·rac·i·ty (və ras′i tē) *n., pl.* **-ties. 1.** truthfulness; honesty: *Do not question the veracity of my statements.* **2.** conformity with truth; accuracy: *to double-check figures for veracity.* **3.** something that is true; truth. [Medieval Latin *veracitas* truthfulness, from Latin *vērāx* truthful.]

ve·ran·da (və ran′də) *also,* **verandah.** *n.* an open porch, usually roofed, extending along one or more sides of a house or building. [Hindi *varandā,* from Portuguese *veranda* railing, balcony; of uncertain origin.]

verb (vûrb) *n.* a word belonging to that part of speech that expresses action, existence, or occurrence, usually forming the main element in a predicate. *Be, fly, want,* and *spend* are verbs. [Latin *verbum* word, verb.]

ver·bal (vûr′bəl) *adj.* **1.** of, relating to, or consisting of words: *verbal communication.* **2.** concerned with words rather than the ideas they express: *verbal distinctions.* **3.** expressed in speech; not written: *a verbal agreement.* **4.** word for word; literal; verbatim: *a verbal translation.* **5.** *Grammar.* **a.** of, relating to, or derived from a verb: *A gerund is a verbal noun.* **b.** used to form verbs: *a verbal suffix.* —*n. Grammar.* a noun or adjective that is derived from a verb and retains certain characteristics of a verb, but functions as a noun or adjective. Gerunds, infinitives, and participles are verbals. [Late Latin *verbālis* relating to words or verbs, from Latin *verbum* word, verb.] —**ver′bal·ly,** *adv.* —For Synonyms, see ORAL.

ver·bal·ism (vûr′bə liz′əm) *n.* **1.** a verbal expression; word or phrase. **2.** mere words with little or no meaning; verbiage. **3.** a meaningless word or expression.

ver·bal·ist (vûr′bə list) *n.* **1.** a person skilled in the use of words. **2.** a person concerned primarily with words rather than ideas or facts.

ver·bal·ize (vûr′bə līz′) *v.,* **-ized, -iz·ing.** —*v.t.* **1.** to express in words: *to verbalize one's feelings.* **2.** to transform, as a noun, into a verb: *to verbalize "burglar" into "burgle."* —*v.i.* **1.** to express oneself in words. **2.** to use too many words; be verbose. —**ver′bal·i·za′tion,** *n.* —**ver′bal·iz′er,** *n.*

ver·ba·tim (vər bā′tim) *adv.* word for word; in exactly the same words: *The newspaper printed the senator's speech verbatim.* —*adj.* word for word: *a verbatim translation.* [Medieval Latin *verbatim,* from Latin *verbum* word.]

ver·be·na (vər bē′nə) *n.* any of a large group of trailing or loosely branching plants, genus *Verbena,* having clusters of small flowers of various colors. Also, **vervain.** [Latin *verbēna* foliage, leaf, twig, sacred bough. Doublet of VERVAIN.]

ver·bi·age (vûr′bē ij) *n.* the use of more words than necessary; wordiness; verbosity. [French *verbiage,* from Middle French *verbier* to chatter, going back to Latin *verbum* word.]

ver·bose (vər bōs′) *adj.* using or containing an excessive number of words; wordy: *a verbose speaker.* [Latin *verbōsus* full of words, from *verbum* word.] —**ver·bose′ly,** *adv.* —**ver·bose′ness, ver·bos·i·ty** (vər bos′i tē), *n.*

ver·bo·ten (vər bō′tən; *German* fer bō′tən) *adj. German.* forbidden; prohibited.

ver·dant (vûr′dənt) *adj.* **1.** green with vegetation: *a verdant meadow.* **2.** green in color. **3.** lacking experience; unsophisticated. [Possibly from Old French *verdeant,* present participle of *verdoier* to be green, going back to Latin *viridis* green.] —**ver′dan·cy,** *n.* —**ver′dant·ly,** *adv.*

ver·dict (vûr′dikt) *n.* **1.** the decision of a jury in a criminal or civil trial. **2.** any decision or conclusion on some matter; judgment: *the verdict of public opinion.* [Anglo-Norman *verdit* testimony given under oath; literally, true saying, going back to Latin *vērus* true + *dictum* saying, speech.]

Synonyms **Verdict, judgment,** and **decree** mean a decision handed down by law. **Verdict** denotes the formal findings of a jury, esp. in a criminal case: *A mistrial was declared when the jury was unable to reach a verdict.* **Judgment** is applied to a legal decision pronounced in open court: *The Supreme Court is expected to hand down a judgment on the case soon.* **Decree** is an order given after a hearing to determine the facts and their legal consequences rather than to determine guilt or innocence: *The court issued a bankruptcy decree.*

ver·di·gris (vûr′di grēs′, -gris) *n.* **1.** a poisonous mixture of copper acetates, consisting of blue or green crystals that are formed when copper reacts with acetic acid, used as a paint pigment and insecticide. **2.** a greenish coating that forms on copper, brass, or bronze objects, such as statues or kitchen utensils, consisting of any of various basic copper salts, such as chloride, carbonate, or sulfate. [Old French *vertegrez,* earlier *vert de Grece* copper acetate; literally, green of Greece, going back to Latin *viridis* green + *dē* from + *Graecia* Greece (from *Graecus* native of Greece). See GREEK.]

ver·dure (vûr′jər) *n.* **1.** the fresh, green color of growing vegetation. **2.** green vegetation. **3.** a fresh or flourishing condition, as of health; vigor. [Old French *verdure,* from *verd* green, from Latin *viridis.*] —**ver′dured, ver′dur·ous,** *adj.*

verge¹ (vûrj) *n.* **1.** the edge or margin of something; brink. **2.** a point beyond which something occurs or begins: *to be on the verge of despair.* **3.** a limiting or enclosing border or boundary. **4.** *British.* a grassy area, as along a path or sidewalk. **5.** a rod or staff carried as a symbol of authority or office. —*v.i.,* **verged, verg·ing.** to be on the verge; border (often with *on*): *Your simple solution verges on genius.* [Old French *verge* rod, from Latin *virga.*]

verge² (vûrj) *v.i.*, **verged, verg·ing.** to tend; incline; approach: *The bird's color is dark red, verging on purple.* [Latin *vergere* to bend, incline.]

ver·ger (vûr′jər) *n.* **1.** a person who carries a verge before a bishop, dean, or other dignitary in a procession. **2.** *British.* a person who cares for the interior of a church; sexton.

Ver·gil·i·an (vər jil′ē ən) *also,* **Virgilian.** *adj.* relating to or characteristic of Vergil or his poetry.

ver·i·fi·a·ble (ver′ə fī′ə bəl) *adj.* capable of being verified. —**ver′i·fi′a·bly,** *adv.*

ver·i·fi·ca·tion (ver′ə fi kā′shən) *n.* the act of verifying or the state of being verified.

ver·i·fy (ver′ə fī′) *v.t.,* **-fied, -fy·ing. 1.** to prove (something) to be true; confirm: *Several witnesses verified my account of the incident.* **2.** to check or test the accuracy or truth of: *to verify the results of an experiment.* [Old French *verifier* to examine something to make sure it is accurate, going back to Latin *vērus* true + *facere* to make.] —**ver′i·fi′er,** *n.*

ver·i·ly (ver′ə lē) *adv. Archaic.* in truth; really; truly. [VERY + -LY¹.]

ver·i·sim·i·lar (ver′ə sim′ə lər) *adj.* appearing to be true; probable; likely: *a verisimilar but incorrect account of what happened.* [Latin *vērisimilis* (going back to Latin *vērus* true + *similis* like) + -AR¹.] —**ver′i·sim′i·lar·ly,** *adv.*

ver·i·si·mil·i·tude (ver′ə si mil′i tüd′, -tūd′) *n.* **1.** the appearance of being true. **2.** something having the appearance of being true. [Latin *vērisimilitūdō* likelihood, going back to Latin *vērus* true + *similis* like.]

ver·i·ta·ble (ver′i tə bəl) *adj.* being so in actual fact; true; real: *Returning the money was veritable proof of the student's honesty.* [Old French *veritable,* from *verite* truth, from Latin *vēritās.*] —**ver′i·ta·ble·ness,** *n.* —**ver′i·ta·bly,** *adv.*

ver·i·ty (ver′i tē) *n., pl.* **-ties. 1.** the quality or state of being true, real, or accurate. **2.** a true statement, principle, or belief, esp. one regarded as being universally held to be true. [Latin *vēritās* truth.]

ver·juice (vûr′jüs′) *n.* **1.** the sour, acidic juice of unripe fruit, as of crab apples or grapes. **2.** sourness, as of disposition or expression. [Old French *vertjus* sour juice of unripe fruit; literally, green juice, going back to Latin *viridis* green + *jūs* broth, sauce.]

ver·meil (vûr′məl; *def. 2, also* vər māl′) *n.* **1.** the color vermilion. **2.** gilded silver, copper, or bronze. —*adj.* having the color vermilion. [Old French *vermeil* bright red, from Late Latin *vermiculus* an insect from which a red dye is obtained, from Latin *vermiculus* little worm, diminutive of *vermis* worm.]

ver·mi·cel·li (vûr′mə sel′ē, -chel′ē) *n.* a pasta made into long, slender threads that are thinner than spaghetti. [Italian *vermicelli,* plural of *vermicello* little worm, going back to Latin *vermis* worm, because of its shape.]

ver·mi·cide (vûr′mə sīd′) *n.* a drug or other agent that kills worms, esp. parasitic intestinal worms. [Latin *vermis* worm + -CIDE².]

ver·mic·u·lar (vûr mik′yə lər) *adj.* **1.** of, relating to, or like a worm or worms, esp. resembling a worm in form or motion. **2.** marked with or characterized by wavy lines resembling the tracks or form of a worm. [Modern Latin *vermicularis,* from Latin *vermiculus* little worm, diminutive of *vermis* worm.]

ver·mic·u·late (*adj.,* vər mik′yə lit, -lāt′; *v.,* vər mik′yə lāt′) *adj.* **1.** characterized by or having wavy lines or curves resembling the tracks or form of a worm: *vermiculate designs on a fabric.* **2.** resembling a worm in form or movement; sinuous. **3.** infested with worms; worm-eaten. —*v.t.,* **-lat·ed, -lat·ing.** to decorate or inlay with wavy lines or markings. [Latin *vermiculatus,* past participle of *vermiculari* to be worm-eaten, going back to *vermis* worm.] —**ver·mic′u·la′tion,** *n.*

ver·mic·u·lite (vər mik′yə līt′) *n.* any of several clay minerals that form when mica is exposed to weathering, used in gardening and insulation. [Latin *vermiculus,* diminutive of *vermis* worm + -ITE¹.]

ver·mi·form (vûr′mə fôrm′) *adj.* shaped like a worm. [Modern Latin *vermiformis,* from Latin *vermis* worm + *forma* shape.]

vermiform appendix, appendix.

ver·mi·fuge (vûr′mə fūj′) *n.* a drug or other agent that expels intestinal worms. [Latin *vermis* worm + *fugāre* to put to flight.]

ver·mil·ion (vər mil′yən) *also,* **vermillion.** *n.* **1.** a bright red color. **2.** a bright red pigment, usually consisting of mercuric sulfide. —*adj.* having the color vermilion. [Old French *vermeillon* the color, from *vermeil.* See VERMEIL.]

ver·min (vûr′min) *n., pl.* **-min. 1.** any of various insects or other small animals that are harmful, destructive, or troublesome, such as lice, fleas, or rats. **2.a.** a contemptible or vile person. **b.** such persons collectively. [Old French *vermine* parasitic insects, snakes, worms, going back to Latin *vermis* worm.]

ver·min·ous (vûr′mə nəs) *adj.* **1.** of, relating to, or infested

with vermin. **2.** caused by vermin. **3.** resembling or of the nature of vermin. —**ver′min·ous·ly,** *adv.*

ver·mouth (vər müth′) *n.* a white wine flavored with aromatic herbs, used esp. in making cocktails. [French *vermout(h),* from German *Wermut* vermouth, absinthe, wormwood.]

ver·nac·u·lar (vər nak′yə lər) *n.* **1.** the language native to the people of a certain country or locality. **2.** the common, everyday language used by the people of a certain country or locality. **3.** the vocabulary peculiar to a particular profession or trade; jargon. **4.** the common name of a plant or animal, as distinguished from its scientific name. —*adj.* **1.** (of a language or dialect) native to or used by the people of a certain country or locality. **2.** of, in, or using native language, esp. as distinguished from literary language: *to write in a vernacular style.* **3.** of or designating the common, rather than the scientific, name of a plant or animal. [Latin *vernāculus* domestic, native (from *verna* slave born in his master's house) + -AR¹.] —**ver·nac′u·lar·ly,** *adv.*

ver·nal (vûr′nəl) *adj.* **1.** of, relating to, or occurring in spring: *vernal sea breezes.* **2.** like or suggesting spring, as in freshness. *vernal foliage.* **3.** youthful: *vernal antics.* [Latin *vernālis* relating to spring, going back to *vēr* spring.] —**ver′nal·ly,** *adv.*

vernal equinox, the equinox that occurs on or about March 21. It marks the beginning of spring in the Northern Hemisphere. For illustration, see **solstice.**

ver·nal·ize (vûr′nə līz′) *v.t.,* **-ized, -iz·ing.** to induce (a plant) to flower early by exposing its seeds, bulbs, or seedlings to cold. —**ver′nal·i·za′tion,** *n.*

ver·na·tion (vər nā′shən) *n. Botany.* the arrangement of leaves in a bud, as involute, convolute, or plicate. [Modern Latin *vernatio,* from Latin *vernāre* to bloom.]

ver·ni·er (vûr′nē ər) *n.* **1.** a short scale that slides along a longer scale and indicates fractional parts of the smallest divisions of the larger scale, used to make precision measurements. Also, **vernier scale. 2.** an auxiliary device used to obtain fine adjustments in precision instruments. [From Pierre *Vernier,* 1580-1637, French mathematician who invented the scale.]

vernier caliper, a caliper rule equipped with a vernier scale.

ve·ron·i·ca (və ron′i kə) *n.* speedwell. [Possibly from *Veronica,* feminine proper name.]

ver·sa·tile (vûr′sə təl) *adj.* **1.** able to do many different things competently: *a versatile athlete active in many different sports.* **2.** having a variety of uses or functions: *a versatile tool.* **3.** changeable; variable. **4.** *Biology.* turning about freely, as a loosely attached anther or the antenna of an insect. [Latin *versātilis* that turns around, movable, going back to *vertere* to turn.] —**ver′sa·tile·ly,** *adv.* —**ver′sa·tile·ness, ver·sa·til·i·ty** (vûr′sə til′i tē), *n.*

verse (vûrs) *n.* **1.** an arrangement of words according to a particular meter or pattern; poetry. **2.** a single line of poetry. **3.** poem. **4.** a section of a poem or other metrical composition, esp. a stanza. **5.** a particular type of metrical structure: *trochaic verse.* **6.** one of the short divisions into which the chapters of the Bible are divided. [Old English *fers, vers* line of poetry, from Latin *versus* furrow, row¹, line of poetry.]

versed (vûrst) *adj.* knowledgeable or experienced; learned or skilled (with *in*): *to be versed in a subject.* [Latin *versātus,* past participle of *versāri* to busy oneself with + -ED².]

ver·si·cle (vûr′si kəl) *n.* **1.** *Religion.* a short sentence said or sung by the celebrant during religious services, to which the choir or congregation responds. **2.** a short verse. [Latin *versiculus* little line or verse, diminutive of *versus* row¹, line of poetry.]

ver·si·fi·ca·tion (vûr′sə fi kā′shən) *n.* **1.** the writing or composing of verses. **2.** the art, practice, or theory of writing or composing verses. **3.** a poetic form or style; metrical structure.

ver·si·fy (vûr′sə fī′) *v.,* **-fied, -fy·ing.** —*v.t.* **1.** to change from prose into verse form. **2.** to tell or describe in verse. —*v.i.* to compose verses. [Latin *versificāre* to write in verse, from *versus* line of poetry + *facere* to make.] —**ver′si·fi′er,** *n.*

ver·sion (vûr′zhən, -shən) *n.* **1.** an account or description as presented from a particular viewpoint: *Let's hear your version of the accident.* **2.a.** a translation from one language to another: *an English version of a French novel.* **b.** *also,* **Version.** a translation of the Bible or a part of the Bible. **3.** a different or altered form of something: *Congress passed a revised version of the bill.* **4.** an adaptation, as of a literary work: *the movie version of a book.* [Medieval Latin *versiō* conversion, translation, a turning, from Latin *vertere* to turn.] —For Synonyms, see **account.**

a	at	e	end	o	hot	u	up	hw	white		about
ā	ape	ē	me	ō	old	ū	use	ng	song		taken
ä	far	i	it	ô	fork	ü	rule	th	thin	ə	pencil
âr	care	ī	ice	oi	oil	ů	pull	th	this		lemon
		îr	pierce	ou	out	ûr	turn	zh	measure		circus

vers li·bre (VER lē′bRə) *French.* free verse.

ver·so (vûr′sō) *n., pl.* **-sos. 1.** *Printing.* the left-hand page of a book or the back side of a page. ➡ opposed to **recto. 2.** the back of a coin or medal. [Short for Latin *(in) verso (folio)* (on the page) turned, from *versus* turned. See VERSUS.]

verst (vûrst, verst) *n.* a Russian measure of distance, equal to about 3,500 feet (1,070 meters). [French *verste,* and German *Werst,* both from Russian *versta.*]

ver·sus (vûr′səs) *prep.* **1.** in opposition to or in competition with; against: *It was the seniors versus the freshmen in the basketball game.* **2.** in contrast to; as an alternative to: *a life of hard work versus a life of inactivity.* [Latin *versus* turned toward, opposite, past participle of *vertere* to turn.]

vert., vertical.

ver·te·bra (vûr′tə brə) *n., pl.* **-brae** (-brē′, -brā′) or **-bras.** any of the small, roughly cylindrical bones that compose the spinal column, numbering thirty-three in humans. [Latin *vertebra* joint, joint of the spine.]

ver·te·bral (vûr′tə brəl) *adj.* **1.** of, relating to, or of the nature of a vertebra or the vertebrae. **2.** composed of or having vertebrae.

vertebral column, spinal column.

ver·te·brate (vûr′tə brāt′, -brit) *adj.* **1.** having a backbone or spinal column. **2.** of, relating to, or characteristic of vertebrate animals. —*n.* any of a large group of vertebrate animals, subphylum Vertebrata, consisting of fish, amphibians, reptiles, birds, and mammals. [Latin *vertebrātus* jointed, from *vertebra* joint, joint of the spine.]

ver·tex (vûr′teks) *n., pl.* **-ti·ces** or **-tex·es. 1.** the highest point of something; summit. **2.** *Anatomy.* the top or crown of the head. **3.** *Geometry.* **a.** the point, esp. in a triangle, opposite to and farthest away from the base. **b.** the point of intersection of the sides of an angle. **4.** zenith *(def. 2).* [Latin *vertex* summit, crown of the head.]

ver·ti·cal (vûr′ti kəl) *adj.* **1.** perpendicular to the plane of the horizon; upright. ➡ opposed to **horizontal. 2.** of, relating to, or at the vertex or highest point; directly overhead. **3.** *Economics.* of, relating to, or controlling all or most of the stages involved in the production and sale of a commodity: *a vertical monopoly.* —*n.* something vertical, such as a line or plane. [Late Latin *verticālis* perpendicular, from Latin *vertex* summit.] —**ver·ti·cal·i·ty** (vûr′ti kal′i tē), **ver′ti·cal·ness,** *n.* —**ver′ti·cal·ly,** *adv.*

vertical union, industrial union.

ver·ti·ces (vûr′tə sēz′) a plural of **vertex.**

ver·ti·cil (vûr′tə səl) *n.* a circular arrangement, as of leaves or flowers, around a central point. [Latin *verticillus* whirl of a spindle, diminutive of *vertex* whirl, summit.]

ver·tic·il·late (vər tis′ə lit, -lāt′) *adj.* forming verticils, as the leaves or flowers of a plant. [Modern Latin *verticillatus,* from Latin *verticillus.* See VERTICIL.]

ver·tig·i·nous (vər tij′ə nəs) *adj.* **1.** of, relating to, affected with, or causing vertigo. **2.** going around and around; whirling. **3.** capable of changing frequently or quickly; unstable: *a vertiginous relationship.* [Latin *vertīginōsus* one who suffers from dizziness, from *vertīgō* dizziness.]

ver·ti·go (vûr′ti gō′) *n., pl.* **ver·ti·goes** or **ver·ti·gos** or **ver·tig·i·nes** (vər tij′ə nēz′). a condition in which one feels that one's surroundings are whirling about; dizziness. [Latin *vertīgō* a turning round, dizziness.]

ver·tu (vər tü′, vûr′tü) virtu.

ver·vain (vûr′vān) *n.* verbena. [Old French *verveine,* from Latin *verbēna* foliage, leaf, twig, sacred bough. Doublet of VERBENA.]

verve (vûrv) *n.* liveliness or enthusiasm; energy; spirit. [French *verve,* from Old French *verve* caprice, fanciful expression, going back to Latin *verba,* plural of *verbum* word.]

ver·y (ver′ē) *adv.* **1.** in a high degree; to a great extent; extremely;

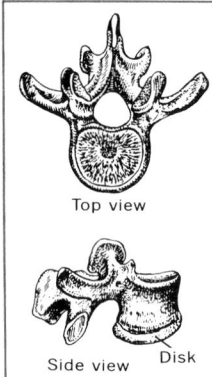

Top view

Side view   Disk

human **vertebra**

exceedingly: *a very tall building, to feel very happy.* **2.** truly; absolutely; exactly. ➡ used as an intensive: *the very best dancer, the very same mistake.* —*adj.,* **ver·i·er, ver·i·est. 1.** identical; same: *That's the very textbook we used last term.* **2.** mere: *The very idea of getting up early made them miserable.* **3.** used as an intensive: *The earth grew dark while the very ground trembled.* **4.** actual: *The thief was caught in the very act of stealing.* **5.** exact; precise: *Your gift was the very thing I needed.* **6.** absolute; complete; utter: *Expenses had been reduced to the very minimum.* **7.** *Archaic.* true; real; genuine. [Old French *verai* true, going back to Latin *vērus.*]

very high frequency, a frequency range of radio waves from 30 to 300 megahertz.

Ver·y light (ver′ē) a colored signal flare that uses pyrotechnic cartridges shot from a special pistol, used in nighttime signaling. [From Edward W. *Very,* 1847-1910, U.S. naval officer and ordnance expert who invented it.]

very low frequency, a frequency range of radio waves from 3 to 30 kilohertz.

ves·i·cant (ves′i kənt) *n.* an agent, as a chemical, that causes blistering, esp. a blistering gas used in chemical warfare, as mustard gas. —*adj.* producing or tending to produce blisters. Also, **vesicatory.** [Latin *vēsīca* blister + -ANT.]

ves·i·cate (ves′i kāt′) *v.t., v.i.,* **-cat·ed, -cat·ing.** to blister. [Latin *vēsīca* blister + -ATE[1].]

ves·i·ca·to·ry (ves′i kə tôr′ē) *adj.* vesicant. —*n., pl.* **-ries.** vesicant.

ves·i·cle (ves′i kəl) *n.* any small sac, cavity, or cyst, esp. one filled with fluid, as a blister. [Latin *vēsīcula* little bladder or blister, diminutive of *vēsīca* bladder, blister.]

ve·sic·u·lar (və sik′yə lər) *adj.* **1.** of, relating to, containing, or consisting of vesicles: *vesicular lava.* **2.** resembling a vesicle in form or structure.

ves·per (ves′pər) *n.* **1.** the bell that summons people to vespers. Also, **vesper bell. 2.** an evening prayer, hymn, or religious service. **3.** *Archaic.* evening. —*adj.* **1.** of, relating to, or suitable for the evening. **2.** of or relating to vespers. [Latin *vesper* evening star, evening.]

ves·pers (ves′pərz) *also,* **Ves·pers.** *n.* **1.** the sixth of the seven canonical hours or the service for it. **2.** any religious service that is celebrated in the late afternoon or early evening, esp. the Anglican service of evensong. ➡ used as singular or plural. [Old French *vespres* evensong, going back to Latin *vespera* evening.]

ves·per·tine (ves′pər tin, -tīn′) *adj.* **1.** of or occurring in the evening. **2.** (of animals or plants) active or blooming in the evening. [Latin *vespertīnus* relating to evening, from *vesper* evening.]

ves·pine (ves′pīn, -pin) *adj.* of, relating to, or resembling wasps. [Latin *vespa* wasp + -INE[1].]

ves·sel (ves′əl) *n.* **1.** a conveyance designed for travel on water; ship or boat. **2.** any of various aircraft or spacecraft. **3.** a hollow container or receptacle, as for liquids. **4.** a duct or tube that carries a body fluid, such as a vein or artery. **5.** a duct in the xylem of vascular plants that conducts water. **6.** a person regarded as a receiver or agent of some quality: *a vessel of wrath.* [Old French *vessel, vaissel* vase, container, ship, from Late Latin *vāscellum* small vase or urn, diminutive of Latin *vās* dish.]

vest (vest) *n.* **1.** a short, sleeveless garment, often buttoning in front, worn over a shirt or blouse and often under a suit jacket. **2.** a decorative piece worn by women to fill in the front of a garment. —*v.t.* **1.** to clothe, as with vestments. **2.** to give authority, power, or the like to (with *with*): *The club vested its president with the right to call special meetings.* **3.** to place (authority, power, or the like) in the control of (with *in*): *The Constitution vests the power to tax in Congress.* —*v.i.* **1.** to clothe oneself, as with vestments. **2.** (of authority, power, or the like) to be or become vested. [French *veste* short jacket, from Italian *veste* garment, from Latin *vestis.*]

Ves·ta (ves′tə) *n.* **1.** in Roman mythology, the goddess of the hearth and the hearth fire. Her Greek counterpart is Hestia. **2. vesta.** a short match of wax or wood.

ves·tal (ves′təl) *n.* **1.** vestal virgin. **2.** a chaste woman; virgin. —*adj.* **1.** of or relating to Vesta. **2.** of or relating to the vestal virgins. **3.** chaste; pure.

vestal virgin, any of six virgin priestesses who watched over the sacred fire of Vesta in her temple in ancient Rome.

vest·ed (ves′tid) *adj.* **1.** *Law.* not subject to change or contingency; fixed; settled: *a vested right.* **2.** clothed, esp. in ecclesiastical vestments. **3.** having a vest: *a vested suit.*

vested interest 1. a special concern for or commitment to something because of personal reasons, esp. the possibility of personal gain. **2.** a person or group having such a concern or commitment, esp. one that is powerful and influential and benefits from existing business and economic conditions.

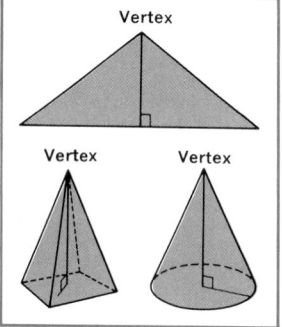

Vertex

Vertex   Vertex

vest·ee (ves tē′) *n.* **1.** a dickey, esp. one designed to resemble a man's vest. **2.** vest *(def. 2).* [From VEST.]

ves·ti·bule (ves′tə būl′) *n.* **1.** an entrance hall or passage between the outer door and the interior of a building; lobby. **2.** an enclosed space serving as a passage between one railroad passenger car and another car or the outside. **3.** any small body cavity that leads to another cavity or canal, esp. the vestibule located in the inner ear, leading to the cochlea. [Latin *vestibulum* entrance, entrance hall.] —**ves·tib·u·lar** (ves tib′yə lər), *adj.*

ves·tige (ves′tij) *n.* **1.** a trace, sign, or visible evidence of something that once existed but no longer exists: *The ruins were the only vestiges of the ancient temple.* **2.** *Biology.* a part or organ in an organism that is not fully developed or useful but may have served a purpose in an ancestral form. [French *vestige* footprint, trace¹, from Latin *vestīgium.*] —For Synonyms, see trace¹.

ves·tig·i·al (ves tij′ē əl) *adj.* of, relating to, or of the nature of a vestige. The appendix is vestigial in humans, and the wing is vestigial in ostriches. —**ves·tig′i·al·ly,** *adv.*

vest·ment (vest′mənt) *n.* **1.** any of a variety of distinctive garments worn by members of the clergy in the performance of religious services. **2.** a garment, esp. an official or ceremonial robe or gown. [Old French *vestement* garment, from Latin *vestīmentum.*]

vest-pock·et (vest′pok′it) *adj.* **1.** small enough to fit into a vest pocket; small: *a vest-pocket dictionary.* **2.** of a relatively small size: *a vest-pocket park.*

ves·try (ves′trē) *n., pl.* **-tries. 1.** a room in a church where the clergy put on their vestments and where the vestments and other articles used in religious services are kept; sacristy. **2.** a room in a church or an attached building, used for Sunday school, prayer meetings, and the like. **3.a.** in parishes of the Anglican and Episcopal churches, a committee that manages the financial affairs of the parish. **b.** in Anglican parishes, a meeting of this committee. [Probably modification of Old French *vestiairie* place for keeping vestments, from Latin *vestiārium* wardrobe, going back to *vestis* clothing, garment.]

ves·try·man (ves′trē mən) *n., pl.* **-men** (-mən). a member of a vestry.

ves·ture (ves′chər) *n. Archaic.* **1.** clothing; garments. **2.** something that covers; covering. [Old French *vesture* clothing, going back to Latin *vestīre* to clothe.]

Ve·su·vi·an (və sü′vē ən) *adj.* **1.** of, relating to, or resembling Mount Vesuvius. **2. vesuvian.** characterized by or given to sudden outbursts, as of rage.

vet¹ (vet) *Informal. n.* veterinarian. —*v.,* **vet·ted, vet·ting.** —*v.t.* **1.** (of a veterinarian) to examine for soundness, as a horse. **2.** to examine closely and expertly, esp. for authenticity: *to vet antiques at an exhibition.* —*v.i.* to work as a veterinarian.

vet² (vet) *n. Informal.* veteran.

vet. 1. veteran. **2.** veterinarian. **3.** veterinary.

vetch (vech) *n.* any of a large group of trailing or climbing plants, genus *Vicia,* of the pea family, grown chiefly for forage and to enrich the soil. [Dialectal Old French *veche,* from Latin *vicia.*]

vet·er·an (vet′ər ən, vet′rən) *n.* **1.** a person who has had a great deal of service or experience, as in an occupation, office, or position: *The comedian was a veteran of stage and screen.* **2.** a person who has served in the armed forces. —*adj.* **1.** having had extensive service or experience, as in an occupation: *a veteran newspaper reporter, a veteran teacher.* **2.** having had extensive experience in warfare or military matters: *veteran troops.* [Latin *veterānus* experienced soldier, old, experienced, from *vetus* old.]

Veterans Administration, the agency of the U.S. government that administers laws benefiting former military personnel.

Veterans Day, a legal holiday dedicated to veterans who have fought for the United States, formerly called Armistice Day, observed on November 11. Also, **Armistice Day.**

vet·er·i·nar·i·an (vet′ər ə nâr′ē ən, vet′rə-) *n.* a person who is trained and licensed to give medical or surgical treatment to animals.

vet·er·i·nar·y (vet′ər ə ner′ē, vet′rə-) *adj.* of, relating to, or designating the branch of medicine dealing with the prevention and treatment of the diseases of animals, esp. domesticated animals: *veterinary medicine.* —*n., pl.* **-nar·ies.** veterinarian. [Latin *veterīnārius* relating to beasts of burden, veterinarian.]

ve·to (vē′tō) *n., pl.* **-toes. 1.** the power of a president, governor, or other executive to reject a bill passed by a legislative body. **2.** the use of this power. **3.** any prohibition or refusal of consent by a person in authority. —*v.t.,* **-toed, -to·ing. 1.** to reject by a veto. **2.** to refuse to give consent to: *They vetoed our suggestion for a party.* [Latin *vetō* I forbid (expression used by the tribunes of ancient Rome to oppose measures of their Senate or magistrates).] —**ve′to·er,** *n.*

vex (veks) *v.t.* **1.** to annoy or irritate, esp. with petty matters: *The student's constant interruptions vexed the teacher.* **2.** to cause

trouble, torment, or distress to: *sleep vexed by unpleasant dreams.* [Latin *vexāre* to shake, annoy.]

vex·a·tion (vek sā′shən) *n.* **1.** the act of vexing. **2.** the state of being vexed; annoyance: *a look of vexation.* **3.** a person or thing that vexes: *This car has always been a vexation to me.*

vex·a·tious (vek sā′shəs) *adj.* causing or tending to cause vexation; vexing; annoying: *a vexatious sales tax.* —**vex·a′-tious·ly,** *adv.* —**vex·a′tious·ness,** *n.*

vex·ed (vekst) *adj.* affected with vexation; annoyed: *I was vexed by their behavior.* —**vex·ed·ly** (vek′sid lē), *adv.*

VFW, Veterans of Foreign Wars, an organization formed in 1913 for U.S. military personnel who fought in foreign wars.

vhf *also,* **VHF** very high frequency.

v.i., intransitive verb.

VI, the postal abbreviation for the Virgin Islands.

V.I., Virgin Islands.

vi·a (vī′ə, vē′ə) *prep.* **1.** by way of: *We drove home via the turnpike.* **2.** by means of: *Send the letter via overnight express.* [Latin *viā,* ablative of *via* way, path, road.]

vi·a·ble (vī′ə bəl) *adj.* **1.** capable of living: *a premature but viable infant.* **2.** capable of germinating or growing: *a viable seed.* **3.** capable of being realized or accomplished; workable: *a viable plan, a viable foreign policy.* [French *viable* capable of living, from *vie* life, from Latin *vīta.*] —**vi·a·bil′i·ty,** *n.* —**vi′a·bly,** *adv.*

vi·a·duct (vī′ə dukt′) *n.* a bridge for carrying a road or railroad, as over a highway or valley. [Latin *via* way, road + (AQUE)DUCT.]

vi·al (vī′əl) *also,* **phial.** *n.* a small glass bottle for holding a liquid, esp. perfume or medicine. [Old French *viole, fiole* (later *phiole*), from Latin *phiala* saucer, from Greek *phialē* broad flat bowl.]

vi·and (vī′ənd) *n.* **1.** an article of food. **2. viands.** choice food; delicacies: *a gift basket of exotic viands.* [Old French *viande* food, going back to Latin *vivenda* things to live on, gerundive of *vīvere* to live.]

vi·at·i·cum (vī at′i kəm) *n., pl.* **-ca** (-kə) or **-cums. 1.** communion given by a Roman Catholic priest to a person in danger of death. **2.** provisions or money for a journey. [Latin *viāticum* provisions or money for a journey, going back to *via* way, road. Doublet of VOYAGE.]

vibes¹ (vībz) *pl. n. Slang.* an emanation or emotional response that can be felt: *The musicians were getting good vibes from the audience.* [Short for *vib(ration)s.*]

vibes² (vībz) *pl. n. Informal.* vibraphone. [Short for *vib(raphon)e.*]

vi·brant (vī′brənt) *adj.* **1.** full of life, energy, and enthusiasm: *a vibrant personality, a vibrant person.* **2.** full of activity and liveliness: *a vibrant city.* **3.** vibrating: *a vibrant string.* **4.** resounding; resonant: *a vibrant sound.* [Latin *vibrāns,* present participle of *vibrāre* to shake, agitate.] —**vi′bran·cy,** *n.* —**vi′brant·ly,** *adv.*

vi·bra·phone (vī′brə fōn′) *n.* a musical instrument resembling and played like a xylophone, having a keyboardlike arrangement of metal bars beneath which are wooden resonators that are opened and closed electronically and give a vibrating quality to the tone. [VIBRA(TE) + Greek *phōnē* sound¹.] —**vi′bra·phon′ist,** *n.*

vi·brate (vī′brāt) *v.,* **-brat·ed, -brat·ing.** —*v.i.* **1.** to move back and forth or up and down rapidly; quiver: *The strings of a guitar vibrate when plucked.* **2.** to move rhythmically to and fro, as a pendulum; oscillate; quiver. **3.** to respond or react emotionally; thrill: *to vibrate with anticipation.* **4.** (of sounds) to be echoed; resound: *The explosion vibrated through the tunnel.* —*v.t.* to cause to move back and forth or up and down rapidly or rhythmically. [Latin *vibrātus,* past participle of *vibrāre* to move rapidly back and forth, agitate.]

vi·bra·tile (vī′brə təl, -tīl′) *adj.* **1.** of, relating to, or characterized by vibration. **2.** capable of vibrating or of producing vibration: *The grasshopper's vibratile organs are in its wings and hind legs.*

vi·bra·tion (vī brā′shən) *n.* **1.** the act of vibrating or the state of being vibrated. **2.** *Physics.* a continuing, periodic, usually rapid motion of the particles of a body or medium in alternate directions from a central point of reference, produced by the disturbance of a state of equilibrium. **3.** a rapid movement back and forth or up and down; quivering; shaking. **4.** a single complete vibrating motion; oscillation. **5. vibrations.** an emanation or emotional response that can be felt: *The old house has bad vibrations.* —**vi·bra′tion·al,** *adj.*

a	at	e	end	o	hot	u	up	hw	white		about
ā	ape	ē	me	ō	old	ū	use	ng	song		taken
ä	far	i	it	ô	fork	u̇	rule	th	thin	ə	pencil
âr	care	ī	ice	oi	oil	u̇	pull	th	this		lemon
		îr	pierce	ou	out	ûr	turn	zh	measure		circus

vi·bra·to (vi brä′tō) *n., pl.* **-tos.** *Music.* a trembling or pulsating effect caused by a fast, very slight fluctuation of the pitch of a tone as it is produced. [Italian *vibrato,* past participle of *vibrare* to shake, vibrate, from Latin *vibrāre* to shake, agitate.]

vi·bra·tor (vī′brā tər) *n.* **1.** something that vibrates, esp. an electrical instrument used in massage. **2.** *Electricity.* a device that converts direct current into alternating current.

vi·bra·to·ry (vī′brə tôr′ē) *adj.* **1.** of, relating to, or consisting of vibration. **2.** producing or capable of vibration.

vib·ri·o (vib′rē ō′) *n., pl.* **-ri·os.** any of a genus, *Vibrio,* of short, flagellate, gram-negative bacteria, shaped like bent rods, single or united end to end in spirals, including the causative agents of cholera in humans and several infectious diseases of domestic animals. [Modern Latin *vibrio,* from Latin *vibrāre* to shake, agitate.]

vi·bur·num (vī bûr′nəm) *n.* any of a group of shrubs or trees, genus *Viburnum,* found in temperate and tropical regions, bearing clusters of wheel-shaped or bell-shaped white or pink flowers. [Latin *vīburnum.*]

vic·ar (vik′ər) *n.* **1.** in the Church of England, a parish priest who receives the smaller tithes or a salary. **2.** in the Protestant Episcopal Church, a member of the clergy in charge of a chapel in a parish. **3.a.** any of various Roman Catholic prelates who represent the pope or a bishop. **b. Vicar.** the pope considered as the representative of Christ. **4.** a person who acts as the representative of another; deputy. [Latin *vicārius* substitute, deputy, substituted. Doublet of VICARIOUS.]

vic·ar·age (vik′ər ij) *n.* **1.** the residence of a vicar. **2.** the rank or duties of a vicar. **3.** the benefice, or salary, of a vicar.

vicar apostolic, in the Roman Catholic Church, a titular bishop with ecclesiastical jurisdiction in a region where no diocese has been established.

vic·ar-gen·er·al (vik′ər jen′ər əl) *n., pl.* **vic·ars-gen·er·al.** **1.** in the Roman Catholic Church, a priest who assists a bishop or superior in the administration of a diocese or religious order. **2.** in the Church of England, an official, usually a lay person, who assists a bishop or an archbishop in legal or administrative matters.

vi·car·i·ous (vī kâr′ē əs, vi-) *adj.* **1.** performed, exercised, or endured for another: *vicarious authority, vicarious punishment.* **2.** substituting for or representing another: *a vicarious agent.* **3.** experienced or enjoyed by imagined sharing in the experience of another: *My best friend's award gave me vicarious pleasure.* [Latin *vicārius* substituted, from *vicis* change. Doublet of VICAR.] —**vi·car′i·ous·ly,** *adv.* —**vi·car′i·ous·ness,** *n.*

vice[1] (vīs) *n.* **1.** an immoral or harmful habit or practice: *Cheating and gambling are vices.* **2.** immoral conduct; depravity; wickedness: *Vice is the opposite of virtue.* **3.** a fault or flaw; defect: *an intellectual vice.* [Old French *vice* defect, fault, from Latin *vitium.*]

vice[2] (vīs) *British. n.* vise. —*v.t.,* **viced, vic·ing.** to vise. —**vice′like′,** *adj.*

vi·ce[3] (vī′sē) *prep.* in the place of; instead of. [Latin *vice,* ablative of *vicis* change, stead.]

vice- *prefix* a person who is subordinate to and acts in place of; deputy: *vice-regent.* [Latin *vice.* See VICE[3].]

vice admiral, an officer in the U.S. Navy ranking below an admiral and above a rear admiral.

vice-chair·man (vīs′châr′mən) *n., pl.* **-men** (-mən). a person who acts as an assistant to or in place of a chairman.

vice-chan·cel·lor (vīs′chan′sə lər, -slər) *n.* a deputy, assistant of, or substitute for a chancellor, as in a university.

vice-con·sul (vīs′kon′səl) *n.* the official next in rank below a consul.

vice·ge·ren·cy (vīs′jîr′ən sē) *n., pl.* **-cies.** the office or function of, or district governed by, a vicegerent.

vice·ge·rent (vīs′jîr′ənt) *n.* a person appointed by a sovereign or other ruler to serve as a deputy in administering the powers and duties of office. [Medieval Latin *vicegerens* deputy, from Latin *vice* in place of + *gerens,* present participle of *gerere* to perform.]

vi·cen·ni·al (vī sen′ē əl) *adj.* **1.** occurring once every twenty years. **2.** lasting for twenty years. [Late Latin *vīcennium* period of twenty years (from Latin *vīciēs* twenty times + *annus* year) + -AL[1].]

vice president *also,* **vice-pres·i·dent** (vīs′prez′i dənt). an officer ranking second to a president and acting in the president's place when necessary. —**vice presidency;** *also,* **vice′-pres′i·den·cy,** *n.* —**vice presidential;** *also,* **vice′-pres′i·den′tial,** *adj.*

vice·re·gal (vīs′rē′gəl) *adj.* of or relating to a viceroy.

vice·re·gent (vīs′rē′jənt) *n.* a deputy of a regent.

vice·roy (vīs′roi) *n.* **1.** a governor of a province, kingdom, or colony, ruling as the deputy of a sovereign. **2.** an orange-and-black butterfly, *Limenitis archippus,* native to North America,

bearing a close resemblance to, but smaller than, the monarch butterfly. [French *vice-roi* the governor, going back to Latin *vice* in place of + *rēx* king.]

vice·roy·al·ty (vīs′roi′əl tē) *n., pl.* **-ties.** the office or term of office of, or the district governed by, a viceroy.

vice squad, a special division of a police department assigned to enforce laws against gambling, prostitution, illegal drug trafficking, and other vices.

vi·ce ver·sa (vī′sə vûr′sə, vīs′ vûr′sə) in the opposite or reversed order or manner; conversely: *I think highly of the instructor, and vice versa.* [Latin *vice versā* literally, the position being changed.]

vi·chys·soise (vish′ē swäz′) *n.* a thick, creamy soup containing potatoes and leeks, usually served chilled.

Vi·chy water (vish′ē) *also,* **vi·chy. 1.** an effervescent water from the mineral springs at Vichy, France. **2.** any water resembling this.

vic·i·nage (vis′ə nij) *n.* the area near or surrounding a particular place; neighborhood; vicinity. [Old French *voisinage,* going back to Latin *vīcīnus* neighboring. See VICINITY.]

vi·cin·i·ty (və sin′i tē) *n., pl.* **-ties. 1.** the area near or surrounding a particular place; neighborhood. **2.** the state or quality of being near; proximity: *The houses are in close vicinity.* [Latin *vīcīnitās,* from *vīcīnus* neighboring; literally, of the same village or district, from *vīcus* district, village.]

• **in the vicinity of.** somewhat near (that which is specified); approximately: *The tickets should cost in the vicinity of twenty dollars each.*

vi·cious (vish′əs) *adj.* **1.** marked by wickedness or vice; depraved; immoral: *vicious behavior, a vicious life.* **2.** full of malice; spiteful: *vicious lies, a vicious attack.* **3.** having an extremely bad disposition; savagely fierce; ferocious: *a vicious dog.* **4.** intense; severe: *a vicious storm.* [Latin *vitiōsus* full of faults or defects, from *vitium.* See VICE[1].] —**vi′cious·ly,** *adv.* —**vi′cious·ness,** *n.*

vicious circle 1. a situation in which the solving of a problem gives rise to another, often worse problem, which itself cannot be solved without bringing back the original problem. **2.** *Logic.* false reasoning in which a proposition is used to prove a second proposition, but depends on the second proposition for its own proof.

vi·cis·si·tude (və sis′i tüd′, -tūd′) *n.* **1.** an irregular, often unexpected change, as in a condition or situation. ➡ usually used in the plural: *the vicissitudes of health, the vicissitudes of fortune.* **2.** a regular or alternating change: *the vicissitude of the tides.* [Latin *vicissitūdō* change.] —**vi·cis·si·tu·di·nar·y** (və·sis′i tü′də ner′ē, -tū′-), **vi·cis′si·tu′di·nous,** *adj.*

vic·tim (vik′təm) *n.* **1.** a person who is injured, ruined, or killed or suffers as the result of some action or condition: *victims of a flood, a victim of an automobile accident, a victim of lies and slander.* **2.** a person who is cheated or swindled; dupe: *the victim of a confidence game.* **3.** a person or animal sacrificed to a deity. [Latin *victima* animal offered for sacrifice.]

vic·tim·ize (vik′tə mīz′) *v.t.,* **-ized, -iz·ing. 1.** to take advantage of by cheating or duping; swindle. **2.** to make a victim of; inflict harm upon: *to be victimized by harsh living conditions.* —**vic′tim·i·za′tion,** *n.* —**vic′tim·iz′er,** *n.*

victimless crime, a legal offense, such as gambling or prostitution, in which the participants willingly take part and in which there appears to be no victim.

vic·tor (vik′tər) *n.* a person who wins or conquers, as in a contest, struggle, or armed conflict. [Latin *victor* conqueror.]

vic·to·ri·a (vik tôr′ē ə) *n.* **1.** a low, light, four-wheeled carriage having a folding top, seats for two passengers, and a raised seat in front for the driver. **2.** an antique automobile having a folding top that can be raised to cover the rear seat only. **3.** a large water lily, genus *Victoria,* found in South America, having white to rose-red flowers. [From the British queen *Victoria,* 1819-1901.]

Victoria Cross, a British military decoration established by Queen Victoria in 1856, awarded for acts of conspicuous bravery.

Vic·to·ri·an (vik tôr′ē ən) *adj.* **1.** of or relating to Queen Victoria of England or to the period of her reign: *Victorian literature, Victorian architecture.* **2.** of, relating to, or having the characteristics generally attributed to Victorian England, esp. prudery and stuffiness. **3.** of or characteristic of the ornate and massive style of furniture, decoration, and architecture of the Victorian period. —*n.* a person who lived during the reign of Queen Victoria.

Vic·to·ri·an·ism (vik tôr′ē ə niz′əm) *n.* the art, taste, customs, or morality characteristic of or associated with the Victorian period.

vic·to·ri·ous (vik tôr′ē əs) *adj.* **1.** having achieved a victory, as in a contest or armed conflict: *a victorious army.* **2.** of or relating to victory: *a victorious day for the home team.* —**vic·to′ri·ous·ly,** *adv.* —**vic·to′ri·ous·ness,** *n.*

vic·to·ry (vik′tə rē) *n., pl.* **-ries. 1.** the act or an instance of

defeating, or the condition of having defeated, an opponent or enemy in battle or war. **2.** the defeat of an opponent or the successful overcoming of an obstacle in any contest or struggle: *The victory gave our team the title.* **3.** the success or superiority gained, as in defeating an opponent: *to glory in victory.* [Latin *victōria.*]

Synonyms Victory and **triumph** mean the successful outcome of a struggle. **Victory** is the general term for the defeat of an enemy or opponent: *a great naval victory in the war, the team's first victory in the series.* Triumph denotes a success that produces exultation in the victor: *Winning the final battle was the general's greatest triumph.*

Vic·tro·la (vik trō′lə) *n. Trademark.* a brand of phonograph.

vict·ual (vit′əl) *n. usually,* **victuals.** food or provisions. —*v.,* **-ualed, -ual·ing;** *also, British,* **-ualled, -ual·ling.** —*v.t.* to supply with food or provisions: *to victual a ship.* —*v.i.* to take on a supply of food or provisions. [Old French *vitaille* provisions, from Late Latin *vīctuālia,* going back to Latin *vīctus* nourishment.]

vict·ual·er (vit′ə lər) *also, British,* **vict·ual·ler.** *n.* **1.** a person who supplies victuals, esp. to a military force. **2.** *British.* a person who keeps an inn or tavern.

vi·cu·ña (vī kü′nə, -kü′-, vi kü′nyə) *n., pl.* **-ñas** or **-ña. 1.** a small, wild South American cud-chewing mammal, *Lama vicugna,* related to the llama, having a slender, graceful body, a long neck, and a woolly coat that is predominantly tawny brown. It is highly valued for its silky fleece. Height: 34 inches (86 centimeters) at the shoulder. **2.** a fabric made from or made to resemble the fleece of this animal, used for scarves, overcoats, or robes. [Spanish *vicuña,* from Quechua *wikuña* this animal.]

vi·de (vī′dē) refer to; see. ➡ used esp. to direct a reader's attention to a particular part of a text. [Latin *vidē,* imperative of *vidēre* to see.]

vi·de·li·cet (vi del′i set′) *adv.* that is to say; namely. ➡ used esp. to introduce examples or details. [Latin *vidēlicet* clearly, namely, shortened from *vidēre licet* it is easy or permitted to see.]

vid·e·o (vid′ē ō′) *adj.* of or relating to the transmission or reception of television images. —*n.* **1.** the visual part of a television broadcast or program. ➡ distinguished from **audio. 2.** television. **3.** a program or performance recorded on videotape. [Latin *videō* I see.]

vid·e·o·cas·sette (vid′ē ō kə set′) *n.* a length of videotape, either blank or previously recorded, enclosed in a cassette for recording or playback, as in a VCR.

videocassette recorder, see VCR.

vid·e·o·disc (vid′ē ō disk′) *also,* **vid·e·o·disk.** an optical disk that carries a recording of the sound and images of a motion picture or other program, designed for playback on special equipment and display on a television screen.

video display terminal, a computer terminal consisting of a monitor and often a keyboard.

video game, any of various electronic or computerized games in which a player or players move images on a cathode-ray tube or other display device, such as a television screen or computer monitor, by means of various devices, such as a joystick or keyboard.

vid·e·o·tape (vid′ē ō tāp′) *n.* **1.** magnetic tape used for recording both the picture and sound of a television program or motion picture. **2.** a length of such tape, as housed in a cassette. —*v.t.,* **-taped, -tap·ing.** to record on videotape.

videotape recorder, see VCR.

vid·e·o·tex (vid′ē ō teks′) *also,* **vid·e·o·text** (vid′ē ō tekst′). *n.* an interactive system of data transmittal and retrieval in which a large, diverse database is connected to users' computer terminals by telephone lines or television sets by cable TV. [VIDEO + TEXT.]

vi·dette (vi det′) vedette.

vid·i·con (vid′i kon′) *n.* a small cathode-ray tube in which an image is formed and stored on a surface that is scanned by an electron beam to produce a signal for transmission, used chiefly in special-purpose television cameras, as for security systems or weapons.

vie (vī) *v.i.,* **vied, vy·ing.** to strive for superiority; be rivals; compete: *The teams vied with one another for first place.* [Shortened from Old French *envier* to challenge, invite, from Latin *invītāre.*] —For Synonyms, see **compete.**

Vi·et·cong (vē′et kông′, -kong′, vyet′-) *also,* **Viet Cong.** *n.* **1.** a communist insurgent group that waged guerrilla warfare against the South Vietnamese government and its allies, including the United States. **2.** a member of this group. [Short for Vietnamese *Viet Nam Cong San* Vietnamese Communist.]

Vi·et·minh (vē′et min′, vyet′-) *also,* **Viet Minh.** *n.* a communist-led Vietnamese political league that opposed Japanese occupation of Vietnam during World War II and later defeated the French, bringing to an end French rule in Indochina. [Short for Vietnamese *Viet Nam Doc Lap Dong Minh Hoi* Vietnam Independence Federation.]

Vi·et·nam·ese (vē et′nə mēz′, -mēs′, vyet′-) *adj.* of, relating to, or characteristic of Vietnam or its people, language, or culture. —*n., pl.* **-ese. 1.** a native or citizen of Vietnam. **2.** a person of Vietnamese ancestry. **3.** the language of Vietnam.

Vi·et·nam War (vē′et näm′) a civil war in Vietnam, from 1954 to 1975, between the government of South Vietnam, aided by the United States, and communist-led insurgents, aided by the North Vietnamese.

view (vū) *n.* **1.** the act or an instance of looking or seeing; sight: *Our first view of land came after many days at sea.* **2.** a range of vision: *In one minute the plane passed out of view.* **3.** something that is seen or can be seen: *We enjoyed the view from the mountaintop.* **4.** a drawing, painting, print, or photograph, esp. of a landscape. **5.** a particular manner of considering or regarding something; attitude; opinion: *I am very interested in your view on that question.* **6.** something that is wanted or intended; aim or goal: *to have a view to enter politics.* **7.** something that is expected; expectation; outlook: *In spite of all our work, we had no view of success.* **8.** a survey or description of a subject: *a view of medieval life.* —*v.t.* **1.** to look at or see: *Many people viewed the museum exhibit.* **2.** to think about; consider: *to view someone's behavior with concern.* [Anglo-Norman *vewe* seeing, eyes, sight, look, from Old French *veoir* to see, from Latin *vidēre.*] —For Synonyms *(n.),* see **opinion.**

•**in view. a.** in sight: *We thought we heard footsteps, but there was no one in view.* **b.** under consideration: *Keep the future in view when you make your decision.*

•**in view of.** in consideration of; considering: *In view of the unfavorable weather, we should call off the picnic.*

•**on view.** open to the public; on exhibition: *The new automobiles are on view this week.*

•**with a view to.** with the aim or hope of: *to save money with a view to buying a house.*

view·er (vū′ər) *n.* **1.** a person who views something, esp. one who watches television. **2.** any of several optical devices used to look at photographic slides or scientific specimens.

view·er·ship (vū′ər ship′) *n.* **1.** the people who watch television, esp. those who watch a particular program. **2.** the size of this audience.

view·find·er (vū′fīn′dər) *n.* a small extra lens or other device built into or attached to a camera for sighting the object or area to be photographed. Also, **finder.**

view·less (vū′lis) *adj.* **1.** providing little or no view: *a viewless basement room.* **2.** not having or expressing opinions: *a viewless recitation of facts.* —**view′less·ly,** *adv.*

view·point (vū′point′) *n.* a way of thinking; point of view; mental attitude.

vi·ges·i·mal (vī jes′ə məl) *adj.* **1.** twentieth. **2.** of or relating to twenty; based on twenty. [Latin *vīgēsimus* twentieth (going back to *vīginti* twenty) + -AL[1].]

vig·il (vij′əl) *n.* **1.** the act or a period of remaining awake, as to guard or observe something: *to keep vigil all night over a sick person.* **2.** a night or day spent in prayer, esp. in preparation for a holy day. **3.a.** the day and night before a solemn feast day, as before Christmas. **b.** *also,* **vigils.** the prayers or religious services held on such a night. [Old French *vigile* watch on the eve of a holy day, from Latin *vigilia* watching.]

vig·i·lance (vij′ə ləns) *n.* the quality of being vigilant; alertness; watchfulness.

vigilance committee, a self-appointed group of citizens organized to apprehend and punish criminals, esp. in the absence of sufficient legal authority.

vig·i·lant (vij′ə lənt) *adj.* attentively or closely observant; alert; watchful: *a vigilant security guard.* [Latin *vigilāns,* present participle of *vigilāre* to watch.] —**vig′i·lant·ly,** *adv.*

vig·i·lan·te (vij′ə lan′tē) *n.* a member of a vigilance committee, or an individual who takes a vigilance committee's role on himself or herself. [Spanish *vigilante* watchful, watchman, from Latin *vigilāns.* See VIGILANT.]

vi·gnette (vin yet′) *n.* **1.** a brief literary description or dramatic sketch. **2.** a decorative design or illustration on the title page of a book or at the beginning or end of a chapter. **3.** an engraving, drawing, photograph, or the like having no sharply defined border, with the background shading off gradually at the edges. [French *vignette* little vine, ornamental border having vines and scrolls, diminutive of *vigne.* See VINE.] —**vi·gnet′tist,** *n.*

vig·or (vig′ər) *n.* **1.** active power or force of body or mind.

a	at	e	end	o	hot	u	up	hw	white		about
ā	ape	ē	me	ō	old	ū	use	ng	song		taken
ä	far	i	it	ô	fork	ü	rule	th	thin	ə	pencil
âr	care	ī	ice	oi	oil	ů	pull	th	this		lemon
				îr	pierce	ou	out	ûr	turn	zh	measure		circus

2. healthy strength: *the vigor of youth.* **3.** intensity, as of activity or energy: *the vigor of a long political campaign.* [Old French *vigour* strength, spirit, from Latin *vigor* liveliness, activity.]

vig·or·ous (vig′ər əs) *adj.* full of, characterized by, or performed with vigor: *vigorous exercise, a vigorous protest.* —**vig′or·ous·ly**, *adv.* —**vig′or·ous·ness**, *n.*

Viking ships in a painting by Nikolai Roerich

Vi·king (vī′king) *also,* **vi·king**. *n.* a member of the groups of seafaring raiders from Scandinavia who attacked and plundered the coasts of Europe from the eighth to the eleventh centuries and who made long voyages to North America. [Old Norse *vīkingr* pirate.]

vile (vīl) *adj.,* **vil·er, vil·est. 1.** morally base; evil; immoral: *a vile crime.* **2.** causing revulsion; foul; loathsome; repulsive: *a vile odor, vile language.* **3.** mean; lowly; degrading: *a subservient and vile task.* **4.** very bad; unpleasant: *vile weather.* [Old French *vil* cheap, base², from Latin *vīlis.*] —**vile′ly**, *adv.* —**vile′ness**, *n.*

vil·i·fy (vil′ə fī′) *v.t.,* **-fied, -fy·ing.** to speak or write evil of; slander; revile: *The newspaper editorial vilified the presidential candidate.* [Late Latin *vīlificāre* to make of little value, from Latin *vīlis* cheap, base² + *facere* to make.] —**vil′i·fi·ca′tion**, *n.* —**vil′i·fi′er**, *n.*

vil·la (vil′ə) *n.* an often large and luxurious house, esp. one in the country, on the outskirts of a city, or at the seashore, used as a retreat. [Italian *villa* country house, from Latin *vīlla.*]

vil·lage (vil′ij) *n.* **1.** a small community or group of houses, usually smaller than a town. **2.** the inhabitants of a village. —*adj.* of, relating to, or characteristic of a village: *village life.* [Old French *village* small group of houses of peasants that is not enclosed by a wall, going back to Latin *vīlla* country house, farm.]

vil·lag·er (vil′i jər) *n.* a person who lives in a village.

vil·lain (vil′ən) *n.* **1.** a wicked, evil, or criminal person. **2.** such a person represented as a character in a dramatic or literary work. **3.** a person or thing that causes trouble or difficulty. **4.** villein. [Old French *vilain* peasant, churl, rustic, base², from Medieval Latin *villanus* serf, farm servant, from Latin *vīlla* farm.] —**vil′lain·ous**, *adj.* —**vil′lain·ous·ly**, *adv.*

vil·lain·y (vil′ə nē) *n., pl.* **-lain·ies. 1.** the actions or conduct characteristic of a villain; extreme wickedness. **2.** an evil or cruel act or deed: *the villainies of war.*

vil·la·nelle (vil′ə nel′) *n.* a verse form that originated in France, using two rhymes and consisting of five stanzas of three lines each and a final quatrain. [French *villanelle* pastoral poem, from Italian *villanella* rustic song, going back to Latin *vīlla* farm, country house.]

vil·lein (vil′ən) *n.* in feudalism, a peasant attached by rights to a plot of land and owing complete obedience to the lord. A villein was regarded as a free person in relations with all persons other than the lord. [Form of VILLAIN.]

vil·lein·age (vil′ə nij) *n.* **1.** in feudalism, the system of rights and duties by which a villein held land from a lord. **2.** the status or condition of a villein.

vil·lous (vil′əs) *adj.* having or covered with villi.

vil·lus (vil′əs) *n., pl.* **vil·li** (vil′ī). any of the small, hairlike projections from the surface of a mucous membrane, esp. the projections on the membrane of the small intestine, which help to absorb certain nutrients. [Latin *villus* shaggy hair, tuft of hair.]

vim (vim) *n.* energy; vigor; enthusiasm. [Latin *vim,* accusative of *vīs* strength, force, energy.]

vin·ai·grette (vin′ə gret′) *n.* **1.** a small ornamental bottle or box with a perforated top, used for holding smelling salts or other aromatic preparations. **2.** vinaigrette sauce. [French *vinaigrette,* diminutive of *vinaigre.* See VINEGAR.]

vinaigrette sauce, a cold sauce made of vinegar and oil, and usually salt, pepper, herbs, mustard, and other seasonings, served on salad, vegetables, or cold meat or fish.

vin·ci·ble (vin′sə bəl) *adj.* capable of being overcome, surmounted, or conquered. [Latin *vincibilis,* from *vincere* to conquer.] —**vin′ci·bil′i·ty**, *n.*

vin·cu·lum (ving′kyə ləm) *n., pl.* **-la** (-lə). **1.** a bond of union or unity; tie. **2.** *Mathematics.* a line drawn over two or more terms showing that they are to be grouped together and treated as a unit. [Latin *vinculum* bond, fetter.]

vin·di·cate (vin′di kāt′) *v.t.,* **-cat·ed, -cat·ing. 1.** to clear (someone) of suspicion or charges of wrongdoing: *The testimony of witnesses vindicated the defendant.* **2.** to maintain or defend (a right or claim) against opposition. **3.** to show to be just, correct, or reasonable: *The success of our mission vindicated our methods and procedures.* [Latin *vindicātus,* past participle of *vindicāre* to claim, avenge.] —**vin′di·ca·tor**, *n.* —**vin′di·ca·tor·y**, *adj.*

vin·di·ca·tion (vin′di kā′shən) *n.* **1.** the act of vindicating or the state of being vindicated. **2.** something that vindicates: *The ease with which we won the game was the vindication of the coach's strategy.*

vin·dic·tive (vin dik′tiv) *adj.* **1.** strongly inclined toward revenge; vengeful. **2.** having, showing, or resulting from a desire for revenge: *vindictive criticism.* [Latin *vindicta* revenge + -IVE.] —**vin·dic′tive·ly**, *adv.* —**vin·dic′tive·ness**, *n.*

vine (vīn) *n.* **1.** a plant with a long, usually slender stem, that grows along the ground or attaches itself to a tree, wall, or other support and grows upward. **2.** grapevine. [Old French *vi(g)ne* grapevine, from Latin *vīnea* vineyard, vine, from *vīnum* wine.]

vin·e·gar (vin′i gər) *n.* **1.** a sour liquid consisting chiefly of acetic acid and water, made by fermenting cider, wine, malt, beer, or the like, and used esp. as a condiment or preservative. **2.** a sour or disagreeable quality or temperament: *There was vinegar in the defeated candidate's words.* [Old French *vinaigre* the sour liquid; literally, sour wine, going back to Latin *vīnum* wine + *ācer* sharp.]

vin·e·gar·y (vin′i gə rē) *adj.* **1.** of or resembling vinegar: *a vinegary taste.* **2.** having a sour or disagreeable quality or temperament; ill-tempered. Also, **vin′e·gar·ish**.

vine·yard (vin′yərd) *n.* **1.** an area used to grow grapes, esp. for making wine. **2.** an area or field of endeavor, esp. one of a spiritual nature. [VINE + YARD¹.]

vin·i·cul·ture (vin′i kul′chər) *n.* the cultivation of grapes for making wine.

vin or·di·naire (vaN ôR dē neR′) *n., pl.* **vins or·di·naires** (vaN zôR dē neR′). *French.* an inexpensive table wine.

vi·nous (vī′nəs) *adj.* **1.** of, relating to, characteristic of, or made with wine: *a vinous aroma.* **2.** affected by or resulting from drinking wine. **3.** wine-colored, esp. the color of red wine. [Latin *vīnōsus* full of wine, from *vīnum* wine.]

vin·tage (vin′tij) *n.* **1.** the wine produced from a particular crop of grapes in one season: *this year's vintage.* **2.** the year in which a particular wine is bottled. **3.** a wine of exceptional quality, esp. one of a particular year and region. **4.** the act or period of gathering grapes and making wine. **5.** *Informal.* goods, articles, or items of some particular period or time: *a car of 1930 vintage.* —*adj.* **1.** (of wine) of, relating to, or from a particular vintage. **2.** of unusually high quality or merit; choice. **3.** of continuing interest or importance; classic: *vintage clothing.* [Modification (influenced by VINTNER) of Middle English *vendage* gathering of grapes, from Old French *vendange* gathering of grapes, wine, from Latin *vindēmia,* from *vīnum* grapes, wine + *dēmere* to take away.]

vint·ner (vint′nər) *n.* a person who makes or sells wine. [Anglo-Norman *vineter,* from Medieval Latin *vinetarius,* going back to Latin *vīnum* wine.]

vi·nyl (vī′nəl) *n.* **1.** an organic radical derived from ethylene. Formula: CH_2CH **2.** any of several resins formed by polymerizing a compound containing this radical, or plastics made from such resins and used in floor tiles, raincoats, phonograph records, and many other products. Also *(def. 2),* **vinyl plastic, vinyl resin.** [Latin *vīnum* wine + -YL.]

vi·ol (vī′əl) *n.* any of various stringed musical instruments similar to the violin, usually having six strings, used chiefly in the sixteenth and seventeenth centuries and later replaced by violins, violas, and the like. [Middle French *viole* viol, viola, from Old Provençal *viola* viol, possibly from *violar* to play the viol; imitative.]

vi·o·la¹ (vē ō′lə, vī-) *n.* a stringed musical instrument of the violin family, slightly larger and tuned a fifth lower than the violin. For illustration, see **violin**. [Italian *viola,* probably from Old Provençal *viola.* See VIOL.]

vi·o·la² (vī′ə lə, vī ō′-) *n.* **1.** any of numerous plants of the genus *Viola,* including the pansy and the violet. **2.** any of several hybrid garden plants resembling the pansy but lacking its facelike markings. [Middle English *viola,* from Latin *viola* violet; of uncertain origin.]

vi·o·la·ble (vī′ə lə bəl) *adj.* capable of or susceptible to being violated: *a violable rule of procedure.* —**vi′o·la·bil′i·ty, vi′o·la·ble·ness,** *n.* —**vi′o·la·bly,** *adv.*

vi·o·late (vī′ə lāt′) *v.t.,* -**lat·ed,** -**lat·ing. 1.** to fail to obey or keep; break: *to violate a law, to violate a peace treaty, to violate a promise.* **2.** to treat irreverently or disrespectfully; desecrate; defile: *The vandals violated the church.* **3.** to break in upon; interrupt; disturb: *to violate someone's privacy.* **4.** to abuse sexually by force; rape. [Latin *violātus,* past participle of *violāre* to injure, dishonor.] —**vi′o·la′tor,** *n.*

vi·o·la·tion (vī′ə lā′shən) *n.* **1.** the act of violating or the state of being violated: *a violation of a peace treaty.* **2.** an instance of violating: *The driver received a summons for a traffic violation.*

vi·o·lence (vī′ə ləns) *n.* **1.** strong physical force used to injure or harm: *The mugger used violence in snatching the victim's briefcase.* **2.** violent or destructive action or force: *the violence of a hurricane.* **3.** harm or injury caused by violent action or treatment: *The townspeople suffered violence in the wake of the storm.* **4.** intensity of emotion or feeling; vehemence: *We were shaken by the violence of the outburst.* [Old French *violence* forceful action, abuse of force, from Latin *violentia* vehemence, ferocity.]

vi·o·lent (vī′ə lənt) *adj.* **1.** acting with or characterized by strong physical force or destructive action: *a violent attack, a violent earthquake.* **2.** caused by or exhibiting intense emotion or excitement; passionate; impetuous: *a violent temper.* **3.** characterized by great intensity or force; severe; extreme: *a violent wind.* **4.** resulting from unusual force, injuries, or circumstances: *a violent death in an airplane crash.* [Latin *violentus* vehement, forcible.] —**vi′o·lent·ly,** *adv.*

vi·o·let (vī′ə lit) *n.* **1.** a variously colored flower of any of several plants, genus *Viola,* esp. *V. odorata,* native to Europe, Africa, and Asia, having heart-shaped or kidney-shaped leaves, and sometimes used in making perfumes. **2.** a plant bearing this flower, closely related to the pansy. **3.** any of several plants with similar flowers, such as the African violet. **4.** a bluish purple color. —*adj.* having the color violet. [Old French *violette,* going back to Latin *viola.*]

violet rays, light waves having the shortest wavelength in the range of visible radiation, between 4,000 and 4,500 angstroms.

vi·o·lin (vī′ə lin′) *n.* a musical instrument having four strings, played with a bow. It is the principal member of a family of modern stringed instruments that includes the viola and cello. [Italian *violino,* diminutive of *viola.* See VIOLA¹.]

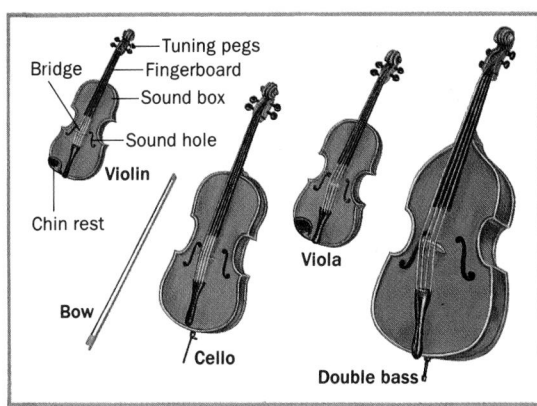

violin and other stringed instruments

vi·o·lin·ist (vī′ə lin′ist) *n.* a person who plays the violin.
vi·ol·ist (*def. 1,* vī′ə list; *def. 2,* vē ō′list) *n.* **1.** a person who plays the viol. **2.** a person who plays the viola.
vi·o·lon·cel·list (vī′ə lon chel′ist, vē′-) *n.* cellist.
vi·o·lon·cel·lo (vī′ə lon chel′ō, vē′-) *n., pl.* -**los.** cello. [Italian *violoncello,* diminutive of *violone* bass viol, from *viola.* See VIOLA¹.]
vi·os·ter·ol (vī os′tə rôl′) *n.* a preparation of vitamin D that, when dissolved in an oil, is used as a medicine to prevent or treat rickets.
VIP *also,* **V.I.P.** *Informal.* very important person.
vi·per (vī′pər) *n.* **1.** any of a large group of poisonous snakes, family Viperidae, having a pair of sharp, hollow fangs with which it injects its venom, esp. the adder of Eurasia. **2.** pit viper. **3.** a spiteful or treacherous person. [Latin *vīpera* serpent, snake, adder, from *vīvus* living + *parere* to bring forth; because it was once thought that the viper brought forth living young.]
vi·per·ous (vī′pər əs) *adj.* **1.** of or like a viper or vipers.

2. spiteful or treacherous: *a viperous attack on someone's character.* Also, **vi′per·ish.** —**vi′per·ous·ly,** *adv.*

vi·ra·go (vi rä′gō) *n., pl.* -**goes** or -**gos.** a bad-tempered, sharp-tongued woman. [Latin *virāgō* female warrior, from *vir* man.]

vi·ral (vī′rəl) *adj.* of, relating to, or caused by a virus.

vir·e·lay (vir′ə lā′) *n.* any of several Old French verse forms using two rhymes to a stanza. [Old French *virelai,* from *vireli* refrain; possibly originally an actual refrain of a song.]

vir·e·o (vir′ē ō′) *n., pl.* -**e·os.** any of various American songbirds, genus *Vireo,* ranging from Canada to Argentina, having green, yellow, brown, or gray plumage mixed with white. Length: 4½-6 inches (11-15 centimeters). [Latin *vireo* greenfinch, from *virēre* to be green.]

vi·res·cence (vī res′əns) *n.* the state or condition of being or becoming green.

vi·res·cent (vī res′ənt) *adj.* greenish or becoming green. [Latin *virēscēns,* present participle of *virēscere* to become green.]

Vir·gil·i·an (vər jil′ē ən) Vergillian.

vir·gin (vûr′jin) *n.* **1.** a person who has never had sexual intercourse. **2. the Virgin.** the Virgin Mary. **3. Virgin.** Virgo. —*adj.* **1.** of, relating to, being, or characteristic of a virgin. **2.** fresh or pure; spotless: *virgin snow.* **3.** not yet used, processed, or discovered: *a forest of virgin timber.* **4.** taking place for the first time; initial: *the virgin flight of a spacecraft.* **5.** (of oil, as from olives) obtained from the first pressing without heating. [Old French *virgine* maiden, Virgin Mary, from Latin *virgō* maiden.]

vir·gin·al¹ (vûr′jə nəl) *adj.* **1.** of, relating to, or suitable for a virgin. **2.** untouched or unblemished; fresh or pure: *a virginal meadow high in the mountains.* **3.** remaining in a state of virginity. [Probably from Latin *virginalis* of a young woman, from *virgō* maiden.]

vir·gin·al² (vûr′jə nəl) *n.* a small rectangular harpsichord played on a table or in the lap, common in England during the sixteenth and seventeenth centuries. [Of uncertain origin.]

virgin birth, the doctrine that Jesus was miraculously conceived without a human father by the Virgin Mary and that she retained her virginity after his birth.

Vir·gin·ia creeper (vər jin′yə) a hardy, woody, climbing vine, *Parthenocissus quinquefolia,* of the grape family, native to North America, having dull, oval, toothed leaflets and clusters of tiny green flowers. Also, **woodbine.**

Virginia deer, white-tailed deer.

Virginia reel, an American folk dance in which partners form two lines facing each other and perform a variety of steps.

vir·gin·i·ty (vər jin′i tē) *n.* **1.** the state or condition of being a virgin. **2.** the state or condition of being fresh, pure, untouched, or unblemished.

Virgin Mary, Mary, the mother of Jesus.

vir·gin's-bow·er (vûr′jinz bou′ər) *n.* any of a number of plants of the genus *Clematis,* esp. *C. virginiana,* found in eastern North America, having clusters of white flowers.

Vir·go (vûr′gō) *n.* **1.** a constellation in the northern sky containing the bright star Spica, conventionally depicted as a young girl holding a spike of wheat. **2.** the sixth sign of the zodiac. [Latin *virgō* maiden.]

vir·gule (vûr′gūl) *n.* a slanting line (/), used as between two words to indicate that the meaning of either word pertains, as in *and/or,* or between parts of a fraction, as in *3/4.* [Latin *virgula* small rod, diminutive of *virga* rod.]

vir·i·des·cent (vir′i des′ənt) *adj.* slightly green; greenish. [Late Latin *viridēscēns,* present participle of *viridēscere* to become green, from Latin *viridis* green.] —**vir′i·des′cence,** *n.*

vir·ile (vir′əl) *adj.* **1.** characteristic of or befitting a man; manly; masculine. **2.** full of masculine vigor or strength. **3.** vigorous; forceful: *to have enthusiastic and virile support for a plan.* **4.** capable of fathering children. [Latin *virīlis* relating to a man, from *vir* man.]

vi·ril·i·ty (və ril′i tē) *n.* the state, quality, or condition of being virile.

vi·rol·o·gy (vī rol′ə jē, vi-) *n.* the branch of microbiology that deals with viruses and the diseases caused by them. —**vi′ro·log′i·cal,** *adj.* —**vi·rol′o·gist,** *n.*

vir·tu (vər tü′, vûr′tü) *also,* **vertu.** *n.* **1.** the quality in an object of art, such as material, workmanship, or age, that gives it merit

a	at	e	end	o	hot	u	up	hw	white	⎧	about
ā	ape	ē	me	ō	old	ū	use	ng	song		taken
ä	far	i	it	ô	fork	u̇	rule	th	thin	ə ⎨	pencil
âr	care	ī	ice	oi	oil	u̇	pull	th	this		lemon
		îr	pierce	ou	out	ûr	turn	zh	measure	⎩	circus

or excellence. **2.** a knowledge of and love for fine objects of art. **3.** such objects collectively. [Italian *virtù* excellence, from Latin *virtūs.* Doublet of VIRTUE.]

vir·tu·al (vûr′chü əl) *adj.* being so in essence or effect, though not in fact or name: *The president's assistant was the virtual head of the company.* —**vir′tu·al′i·ty,** *n.*

virtual focus, focus *(def. 1b).*

virtual image, image *(def. 7b).*

vir·tu·al·ly (vûr′chü ə lē) *adv.* in almost every way; for all intents and purposes; in effect: *Years of war had virtually destroyed the countryside.*

vir·tue (vûr′chü) *n.* **1.** moral excellence or goodness; righteousness. **2.** a particular type of moral excellence: *Humility and charity are virtues.* **3.** a good quality or admirable trait of character: *You have the virtue of being a good listener.* **4.** chastity, esp. in a woman. **5.** the power or strength to produce effects; potency; efficacy: *Inoculations have the virtue of preventing disease.* [Latin *virtūs* excellence, manliness, from *vir* man. Doublet of VIRTU.] —For Synonyms, see **goodness.**

• **by** (or **in**) **virtue of.** because of; by reason of; on the strength of: *The team succeeded by virtue of practice and perseverance.*

• **to make a virtue of necessity.** to do willingly or freely what must be done anyway.

vir·tu·os·i·ty (vûr′chü os′i tē) *n., pl.* **-ties.** the skill, style, or art of a virtuoso.

vir·tu·o·so (vûr′chü ō′sō) *n., pl.* **-sos** or **-si** (-sē). **1.** a person who is exceptionally skilled in one of the fine arts, esp. in music. **2.** a person who is exceptionally skilled in any field of endeavor. **3.** a person who has a cultivated appreciation of artistic merit or excellence; connoisseur; savant. [Italian *virtuoso* one who is exceptionally skilled in an art, skilled, learned, from Latin *virtuōsus* skillful, from Latin *virtūs* excellence.]

vir·tu·ous (vûr′chü əs) *adj.* **1.** characterized by or exhibiting virtue; righteous; good: *a virtuous person, virtuous deeds.* **2.** chaste; pure. —**vir′tu·ous·ly,** *adv.* —**vir′tu·ous·ness,** *n.*

vir·u·lence (vir′yə ləns, vir′ə-) *n.* the quality or state of being virulent. Also, **vir′u·len·cy.**

vir·u·lent (vir′yə lənt, vir′ə-) *adj.* **1.** extremely poisonous or harmful: *a virulent infection.* **2.** extremely bitter or spiteful; full of hostility and hate: *a virulent speech.* [Latin *vīrulentus* poisonous, from *vīrus* poison.] —**vir′u·lent·ly,** *adv.*

vi·rus (vī′rəs) *n.* **1.** any of a group of disease-causing microorganisms smaller than any known bacteria and consisting of a core of DNA or RNA surrounded by a protein coat. Viruses can only reproduce and grow within the cells of living hosts. **2.** *Informal.* a disease caused by a virus. **3.** *Computers.* a program that is secretly spread from one computer to another, containing instructions that may display a message or destroy all the data stored in memory. **4.** anything that poisons or corrupts the mind or morals; evil influence: *the virus of prejudice.* [Latin *vīrus* poison.]

vi·sa (vē′zə) *also,* **visé.** *n.* an official endorsement stamped on a passport by an official of a country, giving the holder of the passport permission to enter or leave that country. —*v.t.,* **-saed, -sa·ing. 1.** to put a visa on (a passport). **2.** to give a visa to. [French *visa* endorsement (as on a passport), from Latin *vīsa* things seen, neuter plural of *vīsus,* past participle of *vidēre* to see.]

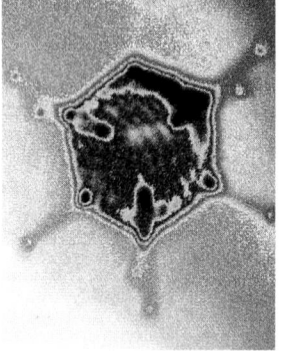

influenza **virus**
(computer-enhanced)

vis·age (viz′ij) *n.* **1.** the face or facial expression of a person: *a worried visage.* **2.** the outward aspect or appearance of anything. [Old French *visage* face, from *vis,* from Latin *vīsus* sight, look.]

vis-à-vis (vē′zə vē′) *prep.* **1.** in regard to; in relation to: *Our position vis-à-vis the election was clear.* **2.** facing; opposite to: *I stood vis-à-vis the monument.* —*adj.* face-to-face: *a vis-à-vis dance step.* —*adv.* face to face: *to talk vis-à-vis.* —*n., pl.* **-vis.** a person or thing that is opposite or opposing. [French *vis-à-vis* face to face: *vis* face, from Latin *vīsus* look, sight; *à* to, from Latin *ad.*]

Vi·sa·yan (vi sī′ən) *also,* **Bisayan.** *n.* **1.** a member of a Malay people in the Philippine Islands, living predominantly on the Visayan Islands and on Mindanao. **2.** the language of this people, belonging to the Indonesian branch of the Austronesian language family.

Visc. 1. Viscount. **2.** Viscountess.

vis·cer·a (vis′ər ə) *pl. n., sing.* **vis·cus. 1.** the soft internal organs of the body, esp. those in the thoracic and abdominal cavities, including the heart, stomach, liver, intestines, and kidneys. **2.** *Informal.* the intestines. [Latin *vīscera,* plural of *vīscus.*]

vis·cer·al (vis′ər əl) *adj.* **1.** of or relating to the viscera. **2.** arising from or caused by deep emotions or feelings, as distinguished from the intellect; instinctual: *a visceral reaction to danger.* —**vis′cer·al·ly,** *adv.*

vis·cid (vis′id) *adj.* having a thick, gluey or sticky consistency; viscous. [Late Latin *viscidus,* from Latin *viscum* birdlime.] —**vis·cid·i·ty** (vi sid′i tē), *n.* —**vis′cid·ly,** *adv.*

vis·co·e·las·tic (vis′kō i las′tik) *adj.* capable of bouncing or rebounding as well as slowly flowing; having viscous as well as elastic properties, as do silicone rubber and other kinds of polymers. [VISCO(US) + ELASTIC.] —**vis·co·e·las·tic·i·ty** (vis′kō i las tis′i tē, -ē′las-), *n.*

vis·cose (vis′kōs) *n.* a thick, syrupy solution from which rayon and cellophane are made, formed from wood pulp by adding carbon disulfide and sodium hydroxide. —*adj.* **1.** made of or relating to viscose. **2.** viscous. [Late Latin *viscōsus.* See VISCOUS.]

vis·cos·i·ty (vis kos′i tē) *n., pl.* **-ties. 1.** the quality or state of being viscous. **2.** *Physics.* (in a liquid or other fluid) the internal friction or resistance to fluid flow that results from intermolecular cohesion.

vis·count (vī′kount′) *n.* in Great Britain and certain other countries, a nobleman who ranks immediately below an earl or count and immediately above a baron. [Old French *visconte,* going back to Latin *vice* in place of + *comes* companion. See COUNT².]

vis·count·cy (vī′kount′sē) *n.* the title, rank, or office of a viscount. Also, **vis·count·y** (vī′koun′tē).

vis·count·ess (vī′koun′tis) *n.* **1.** the wife or widow of a viscount. **2.** a woman who holds a rank equivalent to that of a viscount.

vis·cous (vis′kəs) *also,* **viscose.** *adj.* **1.** (of a liquid) having a thick, gluey or sticky consistency. **2.** *Physics.* having the property of viscosity. [Late Latin *viscōsus* sticky, from Latin *viscum* birdlime.] —**vis′cous·ly,** *adv.* —**vis′cous·ness,** *n.*

vis·cus (vis′kəs) the singular of **viscera.**

vi·sé (vē′zā, vē zā′) *n.* visa. —*v.t.,* **-séed, -sé·ing.** visa. [French *visé,* past participle of *viser* to stamp with a visa, endorse, from *visa.* See VISA.]

vise (vīs) *also, British,* **vice.** *n.* a tool with two jaws moved by a screw, lever, or other mechanism, used to hold an object firmly in place while it is being worked on. —*v.t.,* **vised, vis·ing.** to hold by or as by a vise. [Old French *vis* screw, from Latin *vītis* vine (suggesting something winding).]

Vish·nu (vish′nü) *n.* in Hinduism, one of the three chief divinities, believed to be the protector and preserver of humanity. Vishnu is said to have been reincarnated many times, esp. as Krishna. [Sanskrit *Vishnu.*]

vis·i·bil·i·ty (viz′ə bil′i tē) *n., pl.* **-ties. 1.** the state, condition, or quality of being visible: *The high visibility of yellow makes it a good color for school buses.* **2.a.** the distance that the naked eye can see as affected by physical conditions, such as light or precipitation: *Visibility is only a quarter of a mile today because of the fog.* **b.** the relative degree of being able to see as affected by physical conditions, such as light or precipitation: *Visibility is poor tonight.*

vis·i·ble (viz′ə bəl) *adj.* **1.** capable of being seen; perceptible to the eye: *The house is visible from the road.* **2.** clearly felt, understood, or noticed; evident; apparent; obvious: *to have no visible means of support, a speech with no visible point to be made.* [Latin *vīsibilis* that may be seen, from *vidēre* to see.] —**vis′i·bly,** *adv.*

Vis·i·goth (viz′i goth′) *n.* a member of the westernmost branch of the Goths that invaded the Roman Empire in the fourth century A.D. and settled in France and Spain. [Late Latin *Visigothī;* of Germanic origin.] —**Vis′i·goth′ic,** *adj.*

vi·sion (vizh′ən) *n.* **1.** the act or power of seeing; sense of sight. **2.** someone or something that is or has been seen, esp. a person or thing of great beauty: *The garden was a vision of loveliness.* **3.** imagination or ability to plan ahead; discernment; foresight: *a ruler of great vision.* **4.** something imagined; mental image: *The young writer had visions of success and fame.* **5.** a conception; view: *You have an unrealistic vision of the world.* **6.** an experience perceived in a dream, trance, or similar state, usually of a mystical, religious, or prophetic nature. —*v.t.* to see in or as in a vision. [Latin *vīsiō* sight.] —**vi′sion·al,** *adj.* —**vi′sion·al·ly,** *adv.*

vi·sion·ar·y (vizh′ə ner′ē) *adj.* **1.** of, relating to, or seen in a vision; imaginary: *the visionary splendors of paradise.* **2.** having or characterized by impractical ideas or plans: *a visionary reformer.* **3.** not able to be put into practice; not practicable; unrealistic: *a visionary scheme.* **4.** having or capable of having visions: *a visionary prophet.* —*n., pl.* **-ar·ies. 1.** a person who has visions.

2. a person whose ideas or plans are impractical or unrealistic; dreamer.

vis·it (viz′it) *v.t.* **1.** to go or come to see (a person or persons) for social, business, or other reasons: *to visit one's relatives, to visit a doctor.* **2.** to go or come to (a place), as for sightseeing: *to visit a museum, to visit Quebec.* **3.** to stay with as a guest: *We visited friends for the weekend.* **4.** to go or come to see in an official or professional capacity: *The mayor will visit several of the city's hospitals tomorrow.* **5.** to come upon; afflict; assail: *A plague visited the country.* **6.** to inflict punishment upon or for. **7.** to inflict, as suffering. —*v.i.* **1.** to call on or stay with someone as a guest (often with *with*). **2.** *Informal.* to converse; chat: *to sit and visit for a few hours.* —*n.* **1.** an act or instance of visiting a person or place: *to pay a visit to a neighbor.* **2.** a stay or sojourn, usually brief. **3.** an act or instance of visiting in an official or professional capacity. [Latin *visitāre* to go to see.]

vis·it·ant (viz′i tənt) *n.* **1.** a visitor or guest. **2.** a supernatural being. **3.** a migratory bird that stays in a particular place or region for a limited period of time. —*adj.* paying a visit or visits; visiting.

vis·it·a·tion (viz′i tā′shən) *n.* **1.** an act or instance of visiting, esp. an official visit for the purpose of inspection or examination. **2.** the legal right of a separated or divorced parent to visit a child or children in the custody of the other parent. **3.** an affliction or blessing, esp. a punishment thought to be sent by God. **4. the Visitation.** **a.** the visit of the Virgin Mary to the mother of John the Baptist shortly before his birth. **b.** the feast day commemorating this event, observed on July 2. —**vis′i·ta′tion·al,** *adj.*

visiting card, calling card.

vis·i·tor (viz′i tər) *n.* a person who pays a visit.

vi·sor (vī′zər) *also,* **vizor.** *n.* **1.** the projecting brim on the front of a cap, designed to shade the eyes from the sun. **2.** in ancient armor, the movable front piece of a helmet, which could be lowered to cover the upper part of the face. **3.** a projecting part usually attached above the windshield on the inside of an automobile, truck, or other vehicle, designed to shield the eyes against glare. [Anglo-Norman *viser* visor of a helmet, from Old French *vis* face. See VISAGE.]

vis·ta (vis′tə) *n.* **1.** a view, esp. one seen through an opening or passage: *We had a vista of the lake through the trees.* **2.** a mental view of a series of events: *new vistas of peace and prosperity.* [Italian *vista* sight, view, going back to *vedere* to see, from Latin *vidēre.*]

VISTA (vis′tə) a U.S. government program that recruits and trains volunteers to teach job skills to the poor. [Short for *V(olunteers) i(n) S(ervice) t(o) A(merica).*]

vis·u·al (vizh′ə əl) *adj.* **1.** relating to, resulting from, or serving the sense of sight: *the visual sense, a visual nerve.* **2.** capable of being seen; visible: *visual beauty.* —*n.* **1. visuals.** the visual components, as distinguished from the auditory components, of a motion-picture film, videotape, or the like. **2.** a photograph, drawing, videotape, or other piece of visual material used in a lecture, television program, advertisement, or the like. [Late Latin *vīsuālis* relating to sight, from Latin *vīsus* sight.] —**vis′u·al·ly,** *adv.*

visual aid, any of various devices or materials involving the sense of sight, as a chart, motion picture, videotape, or slide, used to aid or improve instruction.

vis·u·al·ize (vizh′ü ə līz′) *v.,* **-ized, -iz·ing.** —*v.t.* to form a mental image of; envision: *The parents tried to visualize what their children would look like when grown.* —*v.i.* to form a mental image. —**vis′u·al·i·za′tion,** *n.*

visual purple, rhodopsin.

vi·ta (vī′tə, vē′-) *n., pl.* **vi·tae** (vī′tē, vē′tī). **1.** curriculum vitae. **2.** any biographical or autobiographical sketch. [Short for CURRICULUM VITAE.]

vi·tal (vī′təl) *adj.* **1.** of, relating to, or characteristic of life: *vital forces, vital processes.* **2.** necessary to or supporting life: *the vital organs.* **3.** full of life and vigor; energetic: *a vital personality.* **4.** of prime or critical importance; essential: *Your support is vital to the success of this project.* **5.** deadly; fatal: *a vital wound.* [Latin *vītālis* relating to life, from *vīta* life.] —**vi′tal·ly,** *adv.* —**vi′tal·ness,** *n.*

vi·tal·ism (vī′tə liz′əm) *n.* the philosophical doctrine that all living beings possess a unique life force, inexplicable in terms of physics and chemistry, which essentially distinguishes them from nonliving entities. —**vi′tal·ist,** *n.* —**vi′tal·is′tic,** *adj.*

vi·tal·i·ty (vī tal′i tē) *n., pl.* **-ties.** **1.** mental or physical vigor or energy: *a person of great vitality.* **2.** the power to live or continue living. **3.** the power to endure, survive, or continue: *New industry was needed to ensure the vitality of the small country.*

vi·tal·ize (vī′tə līz′) *v.t.,* **-ized, -iz·ing.** **1.** to put vitality or liveliness into: *to vitalize an old political issue.* **2.** to give life to. —**vi′tal·i·za′tion,** *n.*

vi·tals (vī′təlz) *pl. n.* **1.** the parts or organs of the body necessary or vital to life. **2.** the parts or features essential to the operation or existence of something.

vital signs, evidence of the continuing operation of bodily functions, esp. pulse, breathing, blood pressure, and temperature; signs of life.

vital statistics, statistics relating to certain aspects of human life or to factors affecting human life, as births, deaths, marriages, and divorces.

vi·ta·min (vī′tə min) *n.* any of a group of organic compounds that function as coenzymes in regulating metabolic processes and are needed in very small amounts to maintain the health and normal functioning of the body. Most vitamins are obtained from food, but some, as vitamins D and K, are also manufactured by the body. [Latin *vīta* life + AMINE; because formerly thought to be an amine.]

vitamin A, any of a group of fat-soluble vitamins necessary for good vision at night, normal development of cells, and healthy skin, found in foods of animal origin, as liver, whole milk, and eggs, and manufactured in the body from carotene found in carrots and certain other vegetables. Also, **retinol.**

vitamin B$_1$, thiamine.

vitamin B$_2$, riboflavin.

vitamin B$_6$, pyridoxine.

vitamin B$_{12}$, a complex vitamin containing cobalt, necessary for the formation of blood cells and for growth, found esp. in liver, and used esp. in treating pernicious anemia.

vitamin B complex, a group of water-soluble vitamins found in yeast, liver, and other foods, including thiamine, riboflavin, pyridoxine, vitamin B$_{12}$, biotin, niacin, folic acid, and pantothenic acid.

vitamin C, ascorbic acid.

vitamin D, any of several fat-soluble, antirachitic vitamins necessary for normal bone and tooth formation. Vitamin D is found in fish-liver oils and is manufactured in the body by the action of sunlight on a derivative of cholesterol that occurs in skin tissue.

vitamin E, any of several fat-soluble vitamins that are essential for healthy cell membranes, found chiefly in leafy green vegetables, wheat germ, corn oil, and milk. Also, **tocopherol.**

vitamin G, riboflavin.

vitamin H, biotin.

vitamin K, any of a group of fat-soluble vitamins necessary for the clotting of blood, found chiefly in leafy green vegetables and tomatoes and also synthesized by the body.

vi·tel·lin (vi tel′in, vī-) *n.* a protein found in the yolk of eggs. [Latin *vitellus* yolk of an egg + -IN^1.]

vi·tel·line (vi tel′in, -ēn, vī-) *adj.* **1.** of or relating to the yolk of an egg. **2.** resembling the color of an egg yolk; yellow. [Latin *vitellus* yolk of an egg + -INE^2.]

vi·ti·ate (vish′ē āt′) *v.t.,* **-at·ed, -at·ing.** **1.** to impair the quality of; spoil: *The broken fence vitiated the beauty of the garden.* **2.** to debase; corrupt. **3.** to make legally ineffective, as a contract; invalidate; nullify. [Latin *vitiātus,* past participle of *vitiāre* to spoil, corrupt.] —**vi′ti·a′tion,** *n.* —**vi′ti·a′tor,** *n.*

vit·i·cul·ture (vit′i kul′chər, vī′ti-) *n.* the science, art, or practice of cultivating grapes. [Latin *vītis* vine + CULTURE.]

vit·re·ous (vit′rē əs) *adj.* **1.** resembling or of the nature of glass. **2.** of or relating to glass. **3.** made or derived from glass. **4.** of or relating to the vitreous humor. [Latin *vitreus* of glass, glassy, from *vitrum* glass.] —**vit′re·ous·ness,** *n.*

vitreous humor, the transparent, jellylike substance that fills the interior of the eyeball behind the lens. For illustration, see **eye.**

vit·ri·fi·ca·tion (vit′rə fi kā′shən) *n.* the act or process of vitrifying or the state of being vitrified.

vit·ri·fy (vit′rə fī′) *v.t., v.i.,* **-fied, -fy·ing.** to change into glass or a vitreous substance. [French *vitrifier,* going back to Latin *vitrum* glass + *facere* to make.] —**vit′ri·fi′a·ble,** *adj.*

vit·rine (vi trēn′) *n.* a cabinet having a glass door and sometimes a glass top and sides, used esp. to display objects of art. [French *vitrine,* from *vitre* window, pane of glass, from Latin *vitrum* glass.]

vit·ri·ol (vit′rē əl) *n.* **1.** a sulfate of copper, iron, lead, or zinc. Copper sulfate is blue; iron sulfate is green; lead sulfate and zinc sulfate are white. **2.** sulfuric acid. Also *(def. 2),* **oil of vitriol.** **3.** something resembling vitriol in caustic quality, esp. speech or writing that is harsh, sharp, or bitter: *The speech attacking the*

a	at	e	end	o	hot	u	up	hw	white		about
ā	ape	ē	me	ō	old	ū	use	ng	song		taken
ä	far	i	it	ô	fork	ü	rule	th	thin	ə	pencil
âr	care	ī	ice	oi	oil	u̇	pull	th	this		lemon
				îr	pierce	ou	out	ûr	turn	zh	measure		circus

candidate's opponent was full of vitriol. [Old French *vitriol* any of various sulfates, going back to Latin *vitrum* glass; supposedly because of the glassy appearance of these sulfates.]

vit·ri·ol·ic (vit′rē ol′ik) *adj.* **1.** of, resembling, or derived from a vitriol. **2.** very harsh, sharp, or bitter; caustic: *vitriolic language.*

vit·tle (vit′əl) *n. Informal.* victual.

vi·tu·per·ate (vī tü′pə rāt′, -tū′-, vi-) *v.t.*, **-at·ed, -at·ing.** to speak harshly or abusively to or about; berate; revile. [Latin *vituperātus,* past participle of *vituperāre* to censure.] **—vi·tu′per·a′tor,** *n.*

vi·tu·per·a·tion (vī tü′pə rā′shən, -tū′-, vi-) *n.* **1.** harsh and abusive language; censure; castigation. **2.** the act of vituperating.

vi·tu·per·a·tive (vī tü′pə rā′tiv, -pər ə tiv, -tū′-, vi-) *adj.* characterized by or of the nature of vituperation; harsh and abusive: *vituperative speech.* **—vi·tu′per·a·tive·ly,** *adv.*

vi·va (vē′və, -vä) *interj. Italian, Spanish.* (long) live (a person or thing specified). ➡ used as an acclamation or salute. [Italian *viva,* from *vivere* to live, from Latin *vīvere.*]

vi·va·ce (vi vä′chā) *Music. adv.* in a lively or brisk manner. *—adj.* lively; brisk. [Italian *vivace* lively, from Latin *vīvāx.*]

vi·va·cious (vi vā′shəs, vī-) *adj.* full of life; lively; animated: *a vivacious personality, a vivacious person.* [Latin *vīvāci-,* stem of *vīvāx* lively + -OUS.] **—vi·va′cious·ly,** *adv.* **—vi·va′cious·ness,** *n.*

vi·vac·i·ty (vi vas′i tē, vī-) *n.* the quality or state of being vivacious; liveliness; animation: *a young crowd full of vivacity and charm.* [Latin *vīvācitās.*]

vi·var·i·um (vī vâr′ē əm) *n., pl.* **-i·ums** or **-i·a** (-ē ə). a place where animals or plants are kept or raised in conditions closely resembling their natural environment. [Latin *vīvārium* enclosure in which animals and fish are kept alive, going back to *vīvus* alive.]

vi·va vo·ce (vī′və vō′sē) by word of mouth; orally: *We received the offer viva voce.* [Medieval Latin *viva voce* literally, with the living voice, going back to Latin *vīvus* living + *vōx* voice.]

vive (vēv) *interj. French.* (long) live (a person or thing specified). ➡ used as an acclamation or salute.

viv·id (viv′id) *adj.* **1.** (of colors) bright or intense; brilliant: *a vivid blue design on a yellow shirt.* **2.** clearly or distinctly perceived: *a vivid recollection, a vivid impression.* **3.** producing clear or lifelike images in the mind: *a vivid description of a battle.* **4.** capable of forming clear or lifelike mental images: *a vivid imagination.* **5.** full of life; animated; vigorous. [Latin *vīvidus* full of life, animated, from *vīvus* living, alive.] **—viv′id·ly,** *adv.* **—viv′id·ness,** *n.* **—For Synonyms, see graphic.**

viv·i·fy (viv′ə fī′) *v.t.*, **-fied, -fy·ing. 1.** to give life to; animate. **2.** to make more lively, vivid, or striking: *to vivify a room with bright colors.* [Late Latin *vīvificāre* to make alive, from Latin *vīvus* alive + *facere* to make.] **—viv′i·fi·ca′tion,** *n.*

vi·vip·a·rous (vī vip′ər əs) *adj.* bringing forth living young, rather than eggs, as most mammals. ➡ distinguished from **oviparous** and **ovoviviparous.** [Latin *vīviparus,* from *vīvus* alive + *parere* to bring forth.] **—viv·i·par·i·ty** (viv′ə par′i tē, vī′və-), *n.* **—vi·vip′a·rous·ly,** *adv.*

viv·i·sect (viv′ə sekt′) *v.t.* to perform vivisection on (an animal). *—v.i.* to practice vivisection. [From VIVISECTION.] **—viv′i·sec′tor,** *n.*

viv·i·sec·tion (viv′ə sek′shən) *n.* a surgical operation performed on living animals for scientific study. [Latin *vīvus* alive + SECTION.] **—viv′i·sec′tion·al,** *adj.*

viv·i·sec·tion·ist (viv′ə sek′shə nist) *n.* a person who practices, advocates, or defends vivisection.

vix·en (vik′sən) *n.* **1.** a female fox. **2.** an ill-tempered or quarrelsome woman; shrew. [Old English *fyxe* female fox.] **—vix′en·ish,** *adj.*

viz., that is to say; namely. [Latin *vidēlicet.*]

viz·ard (viz′ərd) *n.* a mask. [Modification of earlier *visar,* form of VISOR.]

vi·zier (vi zîr′, viz′yər) *also,* **vi·zir.** *n.* in Muslim countries, a high official of the government, esp. a minister of state. [Turkish *vezīr,* from Arabic *wazīr* originally, one who bears burdens.] **—vi·zier·ate** (vi zîr′it, -āt, viz′yər it, -yə rāt′), **vi·zier′ship′,** *n.* **—vi·zier′i·al,** *adj.*

vi·zor (vī′zər) visor.

V-J Day, August 14, 1945, the day on which Japan surrendered to the Allies in World War II. The surrender became official on September 2, 1945.

vlf *also,* **VLF** very low frequency.

V-neck (vē′nek′) *n.* **1.** a V-shaped neckline on a dress, shirt, sweater, or other garment. **2.** a garment, esp. a sweater, having such a neckline.

vocab., vocabulary.

vo·ca·ble (vō′kə bəl) *n.* a word considered as a sequence of letters or sounds, rather than as a unit of meaning. *—adj.* capable of being spoken. [Latin *vocābulum* designation, from *vocāre* to call.]

vo·cab·u·lar·y (vō kab′yə ler′ē) *n., pl.* **-lar·ies. 1.** all the words used or understood by a particular person or group, or employed in a particular field of knowledge: *the vocabulary of science.* **2.** a list of words or of words and phrases, usually arranged in alphabetical order and defined or translated. **3.** all the words of a language. [Medieval Latin *vocabularium* list of words, from Latin *vocābulum.* See VOCABLE.]

vo·cal (vō′kəl) *adj.* **1.** of, relating to, or expressed by the voice: *vocal sounds.* **2.** performed by or intended for the voice: *vocal music.* **3.** capable of producing speech or sound; having a voice: *A parrot is a vocal creature.* **4.** full of voices; resounding. **5.** readily expressing one's views or opinions in speech: *to be vocal in one's criticisms.* **6.** *Phonetics.* **a.** vocalic. **b.** voiced. *—n.* **1.** *Phonetics.* a vocal sound. **2.** that part of a musical composition intended to be sung. [Latin *vōcālis* sounding, sonorous, from *vōx* sound[1], voice, call. Doublet of VOWEL.] **—vo′cal·ly,** *adv.* **—vo′cal·ness,** *n.*

vocal cords, either of two pairs of membranes in the larynx. In speech, the passage of air from the lungs through the lower pair causes them to vibrate, thus producing the sound of the voice.

vo·cal·ic (vō kal′ik) *adj.* **1.** consisting chiefly or completely of vowel sounds. **2.** of, relating to, or resembling a vowel sound. **—vo·cal′i·cal·ly,** *adv.*

vo·cal·ist (vō′kə list) *n.* a singer.

vo·cal·ize (vō′kə līz′) *v.*, **-ized, -iz·ing.** *—v.t.* **1.** to utter or express with the voice; make vocal: *to vocalize an objection.* **2.** to render articulate; give voice to. **3.** *Phonetics.* **a.** to change (a consonant) into a vowel sound. **b.** to voice. *—v.i.* **1.** to produce sound with the voice; sing or speak. **2.** *Phonetics.* to be changed into a vowel sound. **—vo′cal·i·za′tion,** *n.* **—vo′cal·iz′er,** *n.*

vo·ca·tion (vō kā′shən) *n.* **1.** an occupation or profession; trade. **2.** a strong inclination to pursue a certain career or way of life, esp. one of a religious nature; calling: *to have a sense of vocation.* **3.** the work or career that one feels called to or especially suited for. [Latin *vocātiō* a calling, invitation.]

vo·ca·tion·al (vō kā′shə nəl) *adj.* **1.** of or relating to a vocation or occupation: *vocational training.* **2.** of, relating to, or providing training or education in a skill, trade, or occupation, or guidance in choosing an occupation: *a vocational counselor.* **—vo·ca′tion·al·ism,** *n.* **—vo·ca′tion·al·ly,** *adv.*

vocational school, a school that trains people in specific skills or trades, such as mechanics, electronics, and stenography.

voc·a·tive (vok′ə tiv) *n.* **1.** a grammatical case in Latin, Greek, and certain other languages that is used to indicate the person or thing addressed by the speaker. **2.** a word or construction in this case. *—adj.* of, relating to, or designating this case. [Late Latin *vocātīvus* this grammatical case; literally, the calling case, from Latin *vocāre* to call.] **—voc′a·tive·ly,** *adv.*

vo·cif·er·ant (vō sif′ər ənt) *adj.* vociferous; noisy; clamorous.

vo·cif·er·ate (vō sif′ə rāt′) *v.t., v.i.*, **-at·ed, -at·ing.** to utter or cry out loudly; shout; bellow. [Latin *vōciferātus,* past participle of *vōciferārī,* to cry out, from *vōx* sound[1], voice + *ferre* to bear[1].] **—vo·cif′er·a′tion,** *n.* **—vo·cif′er·a′tor,** *n.*

vo·cif·er·ous (vō sif′ər əs) *adj.* making or characterized by a loud outcry; clamorous; uproarious: *a vociferous crowd, vociferous objections.* [VOCIFER(ATE) + -OUS.] **—vo·cif′er·ous·ly,** *adv.* **—vo·cif′er·ous·ness,** *n.*

vod·ka (vod′kə) *n.* a colorless alcoholic liquor, originally made in Russia, distilled from fermenting grain or potatoes. [Russian *vodka,* diminutive of *voda* water.]

vogue (vōg) *n.* **1.** the accepted fashion at a particular time: *Powdered wigs were in vogue in the eighteenth century.* **2.** popular acceptance or favor; popularity: *Those books had a great vogue several years ago.* [French *vogue* fashion; literally, rowing, from *voguer* to row, move along; probably of Germanic origin.] **—vogu·ish** (vō′gish), *n.* **—For Synonyms, see fashion.**

voice (vois) *n.* **1.** sound produced by the vocal organs of a vertebrate, esp. sound produced by the vocal organs of a human being, as in speaking or singing. **2.** the ability to produce such sound: *A bad cold made me lose my voice.* **3.** the quality, condition, or tone of vocal sound: *a soft voice, a mournful voice.* **4.** a sound resembling or suggesting vocal utterance: *the voice of the wind, the voice of thunder.* **5.** something likened to human speech: *the voice of justice, the voice of conscience.* **6.** an outward indication of a person's thoughts, opinions, wishes, or the like; expression: *to give voice to one's feelings.* **7.** an expressed thought, opinion, wish, or the like: *a law passed in opposition to the voice of the people, to lend a supporting voice.* **8.** the right or privilege of expressing such a thought, opinion, wish, or the like: *Citizens must have a voice in city government.* **9.** a person or means through which something is expressed: *Poetry is the voice of imagination*

(Henry Reed, 1854). **10.** any of the vocal or instrumental parts in a musical composition. **11.** a singer: *a chorus of twenty voices.* **12.** *Grammar.* a verb form expressing whether the subject is active or passive. **13.** *Phonetics.* a sound produced by vibration of the vocal cords. —*v.t.,* **voiced, voic·ing. 1.** to give utterance to; express: *to voice an opinion.* **2.** *Phonetics.* to utter (a speech sound) with vibration of the vocal cords. **3.** *Music.* to regulate the tone of, as the pipes of an organ. [Old French *vois* sound[1], utterance, word, from Latin *vōx.*]

· **in voice.** in proper condition for singing: *Every member of the choir was in voice for the concert.*

· **to lift up one's voice. a.** to shout or yell; bellow. **b.** to assert one's disagreement about; protest; complain.

· **with one voice.** without dissent; unanimously.

voice-ac·ti·vat·ed (vois′ak′tə vā′tid) *adj.* operated by means of the human voice: *a voice-activated door opener.*

voice box, larynx *(def. 1).*

voiced (voist) *adj.* **1.** having a voice. **2.** expressed by the voice: *voiced opinions.* **3.** *Phonetics.* spoken with vibration of the vocal cords: *B, v, and z are voiced consonants.*

voice·less (vois′lis) *adj.* **1.** having no voice; mute. **2.** not speaking or able to speak; silent. **3.** *Phonetics.* not voiced; surd: *P, f, and s are voiceless consonants.* —**voice′less·ly,** *adv.* —**voice′less·ness,** *n.*

voice-o·ver (vois′ō′vər) *n.* a narration or commentary made by an unseen person in a motion picture, television broadcast, videotape, or the like.

voice·print (vois′print′) *n.* a graph of the sound patterns of a person's speech, produced on a sound spectrograph and intended to be used to distinguish and identify individuals.

void (void) *adj.* **1.** having no legal force; not legally valid: *The contract was declared void by the court.* **2.** not occupied by or containing matter; empty: *void space.* **3.** unoccupied, as an office or position; vacant. **4.** not having; lacking; devoid (with *of*): *void of meaning.* **5.** without effect or ability to cause an effect; ineffective; useless. —*n.* **1.** an empty space; vacuum: *the void of outer space.* **2.** a feeling of emptiness or loss: *to have a void in one's life after the death of a close relative.* **3.** a gap or space, as in a surface: *a void in a fence.* —*v.t.* **1.** to make void or of no effect; invalidate: *to void an agreement.* **2.** to evacuate, as the bladder. **3.** *Archaic.* to make or leave empty; vacate. [Old French *voide* empty, probably going back to Latin *vacāre* to be empty.] —**void′er,** *n.*

void·a·ble (voi′də bəl) *adj.* capable of being voided, esp. capable of being made legally void.

voi·la (vwä lä′) *interj. French.* here or there it is; behold; see.

voile (voil) *n.* a lightweight, sheer fabric, as of cotton or wool, used for curtains, dresses, and other items. [French *voile* this fabric, veil, from Latin *vēla,* plural of *vēlum* cloth, covering veil. Doublet of VEIL, VELUM.]

voir dire (vwär′dîr′) *Law.* **1.** the examination of a prospective juror or witness to determine whether that person is competent to serve in a trial in a court of law. **2.** an oath taken by a prospective juror or witness in which that person swears to tell the truth regarding his or her competence to serve. [Anglo-Norman *voir dire* literally, to speak truly, from Old French *voir dire,* going back to Latin *veritas* truth + *dicere* to speak.]

vol., volume.

vo·lant (vō′lənt) *adj.* **1.** flying or capable of flying. **2.** light and quick; nimble: *the volant fingers of a seamstress.* **3.** *Heraldry.* (of a bird) represented with the wings extended, as in flying. [Latin *volāns,* present participle of *volāre* to fly.]

vol·a·tile (vol′ə təl) *adj.* **1.** tending to change readily into vapor, esp. at ordinary temperatures; evaporating quickly, as alcohol. **2.** tending to change easily; changeable; unpredictable: *volatile weather.* **3.** easily aroused or disturbed; unstable: *a volatile political situation.* **4.** fleeting; transient. [Latin *volātilis* flying, fleeting, from *volāre* to fly.] —**vol′a·tile·ness, vol′a·til′i·ty,** *n.*

vol·a·til·ize (vol′ə tə līz′) *v.t., v.i.,* **-ized, -iz·ing. 1.** to make or become volatile. **2.** to vaporize. —**vol′a·til·i·za′tion,** *n.*

vol·can·ic (vol kan′ik) *adj.* **1.** of, relating to, or characteristic of a volcano or volcanoes: *a volcanic eruption.* **2.** having or characterized by a volcano or volcanoes: *a volcanic island.* **3.** produced by or discharged from a volcano: *volcanic rock.* **4.** violent; explosive: *a volcanic outburst of anger.* —**vol·can′i·cal·ly,** *adv.*

volcanic glass, a natural glass, as obsidian, that forms when molten lava is suddenly cooled, as by entering the sea, and solidifies.

vol·can·ism (vol′kə niz′əm) *n.* volcanic activity or phenomena.

vol·ca·no (vol kā′nō) *n., pl.* **-noes** or **-nos. 1.** a natural vent, on land or beneath the sea, from which magma, gases, and rock fragments are expelled by processes originating deep within the earth's crust. **2.** a hill or mountain built up around such a vent by

cross section of a **volcano**

the material expelled. [Italian *volcano,* from Latin *Vulcānus* Vulcan.]

vol·can·ol·o·gy (vol′kə nol′ə jē) *n.* the branch of geology that deals with volcanoes and the phenomena associated with them; study of volcanism. [VOLCANO + -LOGY.] —**vol·can·o·log·i·cal** (vol′kə nə loj′i kəl), *adj.* —**vol′can·ol′o·gist,** *n.*

vole (vōl) *n.* any of various gray or brown, mouselike rodents, family Cricetidae, closely related to lemmings and muskrats, having a large head, small round ears, a plump body, and a short tail. Length: 3 1/2-7 inches (9-18 centimeters). [Earlier *volemouse,* going back to Norwegian *voll* field + *mus* mouse.]

vo·li·tion (vō lish′ən) *n.* **1.** the act of willing, choosing, or deciding. **2.** a conscious choice or decision. **3.** the power of willing; will power. [French *volition* act of willing, going back to Latin *volō* I wish.] —**vo·li′tion·al,** *adj.* —**vo·li′tion·al·ly,** *adv.*

vol·ley (vol′ē) *n., pl.* **-leys. 1.** a discharge of a number of weapons at one time. **2.** the stones, arrows, bullets, or other missiles so discharged. **3.** a burst or outburst of a number of things simultaneously or in rapid succession: *a volley of protests.* **4.a.** in certain sports, as tennis or badminton, the return of a ball, shuttlecock, or other projectile before it touches the ground. **b.** a sequence of hitting a ball, shuttlecock, or other projectile back and forth over a net without interruption. —*v.t., v.i.,* **-leyed, -ley·ing. 1.** to discharge or be discharged in or as in a volley. **2.a.** in certain sports, as tennis or badminton, to return (a ball, shuttlecock, or other projectile) before it touches the ground. **b.** to engage in hitting (a ball, shuttlecock, or other projectile) back and forth over a net without interruption. [Old French *volee* flight, from *voler* to fly, from Latin *volāre.*]

vol·ley·ball (vol′ē bôl′) *n.* **1.** a game in which two teams on either side of a high net engage in hitting a large ball back and forth over the net with their hands without letting it touch the ground. **2.** the ball used in this game.

vol·plane (vol′plān′) *v.i.,* **-planed, -plan·ing.** to glide toward the earth in an airplane with the engines cut off. —*n.* such a glide. [French *vol plané* glided flight.]

volt (vōlt) *n.* a unit of electromotive force equal to the potential difference between two points in an electric circuit if 1 joule of work is required to move 1 coulomb of charge between them. [From Alessandro *Volta,* 1745-1827, Italian physicist and inventor.]

volt·age (vōl′tij) *n.* electromotive force expressed in volts; potential difference.

vol·ta·ic (vol tā′ik) *adj.* of or relating to an electric current produced by chemical action between plates of dissimilar metals; galvanic. [From Alessandro *Volta,* 1745-1827, Italian physicist and inventor + -IC.]

voltaic battery, a battery composed of voltaic cells.

voltaic cell, a simple unit that produces electricity through the

a	at	e	end	o	hot	u	up	hw	white		about
ā	ape	ē	me	ō	old	ū	use	ng	song		taken
ä	far	i	it	ô	fork	ü	rule	th	thin	ə	pencil
âr	care	ī	ice	oi	oil	u̇	pull	th	this		lemon
				îr	pierce	ou	out	ûr	turn	zh	measure		circus

1345

chemical action of two plates or rods of different metals separated by an electrolytic chemical agent.

vol·ta·ic pile, a source of electric current consisting of a series of pairs of unlike metal disks, each pair separated by a pad moistened with an electrolyte.

vol·tam·e·ter (vol tam′i tər, vōl-) *n.* an instrument for measuring an electric current indirectly by measuring the extent or rate of the electrolysis that results from producing or conducting the current. [VOLTA(IC) + METER³.]

volt-am·pere (vōlt′am′pîr) *n.* a unit of measure of electrical power, equaling the product of 1 volt and 1 ampere, equivalent to 1 watt of direct current.

volt·me·ter (vōlt′mē′tər) *n.* an instrument for measuring the potential difference, expressed in volts, between two points in an electric circuit by passing current through a coil surrounded by a permanent magnet.

vol·u·ble (vol′yə bəl) *adj.* using or characterized by a large, easy, smooth flow of words; talkative: *a voluble speaker.* [Latin *volūbilis,* from *volvere* to roll.] —**vol′u·bil′i·ty,** *n.* —**vol′u·bly,** *adv.*

vol·ume (vol′ūm, -yəm) *n.* **1.** a collection of written or printed pages bound together; book. **2.** one of a set or series of related books: *the fourth volume of an encyclopedia.* **3.** a number of issues of a periodical, usually all the issues that are published in one year. **4.** an amount of space occupied or capable of being occupied, as measured in three dimensions and expressed in cubic units: *the volume of a liquid in a container, the volume of a container.* **5.** an amount or quantity: *The volume of business fell off during the strike.* **6.** the amplitude or intensity of sound; loudness. [Old French *volume* book, from Latin *volūmen* roll of writing, scroll, book, from *volvere* to roll.]
· **to speak volumes.** to be highly expressive or full of significance: *Their many donations to charity speak volumes for their generosity.*

vol·u·met·ric (vol′yə met′rik) *adj.* of or relating to measurement by volume. Also, **vol′u·met′ri·cal.** —**vol′u·met′ri·cal·ly,** *adv.*

vo·lu·mi·nous (və lü′mə nəs) *adj.* **1.** of great size or bulk; large: *the voluminous sails of a large ship.* **2.** forming or filling a large volume or many volumes: *the voluminous works of William Shakespeare.* **3.** writing or speaking at great length: *a voluminous correspondent.* [Late Latin *volūminōsus* full of folds, from Latin *volūmen* roll of writing. See VOLUME.] —**vo·lu·mi·nos·i·ty** (və lü′mə nos′i tē), *n.* —**vo·lu′mi·nous·ly,** *adv.*

vol·un·tar·y (vol′ən ter′ē) *adj.* **1.** performed, done, or made of one's own free will: *a voluntary admission of guilt, a voluntary decision to retire.* **2.** acting or working in a particular capacity of one's own free will, often without pay: *a voluntary search party, voluntary hospital workers.* **3.** endowed with the power of willing or free choice: *Humans are voluntary beings.* **4.** *Physiology.* controlled by the will: *voluntary muscles.* **5.** *Law.* **a.** done intentionally; not accidental: *voluntary manslaughter.* **b.** acting or done without compulsion, obligation, or monetary consideration. **6.** supported by voluntary contributions rather than by public funds: *a voluntary hospital.* —*n., pl.* **-tar·ies.** an organ piece, usually improvised, played before, during, or after a church service. [Latin *voluntārius* willing, from *voluntās* will.] —**vol·un·tar·i·ly** (vol′ən ter′ə lē), *adv.*

vol·un·teer (vol′ən tîr′) *n.* **1.** a person who serves or offers to do something willingly or by choice, often without expectation of payment: *The campaign staff consisted chiefly of volunteers.* **2.** a person who enters military service willingly or by choice, rather than as a result of being drafted. **3.** a plant that has grown without being sown or planted by someone. —*v.i.* to serve or offer one's services willingly or by choice: *to volunteer for an unpleasant job.* —*v.t.* to express willingness to give or offer readily: *to volunteer the answer to a question.* —*adj.* **1.** of, relating to, or consisting of volunteers: *a volunteer school board.* **2.** serving as a volunteer: *a volunteer firefighter.* [French *volontaire* one who offers, serves, or does something willingly or by choice, willing, from Latin *voluntārius* willing. See VOLUNTARY.]

vol·un·teer·ism (vol′ən tîr′iz əm) *n.* the act or practice of being a volunteer or using volunteers in public or private institutions, such as fire departments, schools, churches, and hospitals.

vo·lup·tu·ar·y (və lup′chü er′ē) *n., pl.* **-ar·ies.** a person who indulges in luxury or sensual pleasures. —*adj.* of or characterized by luxury or sensual pleasures. [Late Latin *voluptuārius* sensual, from Latin *voluptās* pleasure.]

vo·lup·tu·ous (və lup′chü əs) *adj.* **1.** having a full and shapely form that is sensually appealing: *voluptuous lips.* **2.** imparting, arising from, or characterized by luxury or sensual pleasure: *voluptuous surroundings, a voluptuous painting.* **3.** given to or indulging in luxury or sensual pleasures: *a voluptuous lifestyle.* [Latin

voluptuōsus full of pleasure, from *voluptās* pleasure.] —**vo·lup′tu·ous·ly,** *adv.* —**vo·lup′tu·ous·ness,** *n.*

vo·lute (və lüt′) *adj.* spiral in form; rolled up. —*n.* **1.** a spiral or twisted form or object. **2.** *Architecture.* a spiral-shaped ornament resembling a partly unrolled scroll, esp. one found on Ionic or Corinthian capitals. **3.** *Zoology.* one of the turns or whorls of a spiral shell. [Latin *volūta* spiral scroll, from *volvere* to roll.]

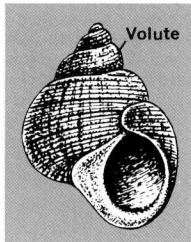
volute *(def. 3)*

vol·vox (vol′voks) *n.* any of a genus, *Volvox,* of multicellular, flagellate green algae, forming a tiny spherical colony that rotates through the water. [Modern Latin *volvox,* from Latin *volvere* to roll.]

vo·mer (vō′mər) *n.* either of a pair of bones that form the front portion of the palate in most vertebrates. In mammals, including humans, they form the lower part of the partition between the two nasal passages. [Modern Latin *vomer,* from Latin *vōmer* plowshare.] —**vo·mer·ine** (vō′mər in, -mə-rīn′, vom′ər in, -mə rīn′), *adj.*

vom·it (vom′it) *v.i.* **1.** to bring up and eject the contents of the stomach through the mouth; throw up. **2.** to be thrown out with force; be ejected violently: *Cinder and ash vomited out of the chimney.* —*v.t.* **1.** to eject from the stomach through the mouth. **2.** to throw out or discharge in large quantities or with force; spew: *The volcano vomited forth lava.* —*n.* matter vomited from the stomach. [Latin *vomitus,* past participle of *vomere* to throw up.]

von (von; *German* fôn) *prep. German.* from; of. ➡ used in German and Austrian names, esp. of the nobility.

voo·doo (vü′dü) *n., pl.* **-doos. 1.** a set of religious rites of West African origin, characterized by a belief in sorcery and the power of charms, practiced in the West Indies and elsewhere. **2.** a person who practices these rites. **3.** a charm, fetish, or other characteristic of these rites. —*adj.* of or relating to voodoo. —*v.t.,* **-dooed, -doo·ing.** to curse or hex according to voodoo; cast a spell upon. [Of West African origin.]

voo·doo·ism (vü′dü iz′əm) *n.* **1.** the beliefs and practices of voodoo. **2.** a belief in voodoo. —**voo′doo·ist,** *n.* —**voo′doo·is′tic,** *adj.*

vo·ra·cious (vô rā′shəs, və-) *adj.* **1.** eating or craving large amounts of food; ravenous: *a voracious beast, a voracious appetite.* **2.** unable to be satisfied in some activity; insatiable: *a voracious reader.* [Latin *vorāci-,* stem of *vorāx* ravenous + -OUS.] —**vo·ra′cious·ly,** *adv.* —**vo·ra′cious·ness, vo·rac·i·ty** (vô-ras′i tē, və-), *n.*

vor·tex (vôr′teks) *n., pl.* **-tex·es** or **-ti·ces** (-tə sēz′). **1.** a whirling mass, as of water or air, moving in a circular fashion and having a central depression, hole, or area into which nearby objects are sucked; whirlpool or whirlwind. **2.** an activity, situation, or state of affairs into which persons or things are irresistibly and steadily drawn: *to be caught in the vortex of company politics.* [Latin *vortex* whirlpool, whirlwind.]

vor·ti·cal (vôr′ti kəl) *adj.* of, relating to, or moving in a vortex or vortexes: *Whirlpools are vortical currents.* [Late Latin *vorticalis,* from *vortex* whirlpool, whirlwind.] —**vor′ti·cal·ly,** *adv.*

vor·ti·cel·la (vôr′tə sel′ə) *n., pl.* **-cel·lae** (-sel′ē) or **-cel·las.** any of a group of bell-shaped protozoans, genus *Vorticella,* having a ring of cilia around the mouth and a stalk with which they attach themselves to objects under water. [Modern Latin *Vorticella,* from *vortex* whirlpool, whirlwind.]

vot·a·ble (vō′tə bəl) *adj.* capable of or subject to being voted upon: *a votable issue.*

vo·ta·ress (vō′tə ris) *n.* a female votary.

vo·ta·ry (vō′tə rē) *n., pl.* **-ries. 1.** a person bound by a vow or vows, esp. a monk, nun, or other person in religious life. **2.** a person devoted to a particular pastime, study, or activity; devotee: *a votary of tennis.* Also, **vo′tar·ist.**

vote (vōt) *n.* **1.** the formal expression of a wish or choice in some matter to be decided: *We voted for the candidate of our choice in the presidential election.* **2.** the means by which such a choice is expressed, as by ballot or show of hands. **3.** a choice or decision so made: *The Senate vote was in favor of the bill.* **4.** the right or privilege of expressing such a choice; suffrage: *The nineteenth amendment to the Constitution gave women the vote.* **5.** the number of votes cast: *a light vote.* **6.** votes collectively: *The vote is in but has to be tabulated.* **7.** a group of votes or voters, considered as an entity: *the urban vote.* **8.** *Archaic.* voter. —*v.,* **vot·ed, vot·ing.** —*v.i.* to express one's opinion or choice by a vote; cast a vote: *to vote for mayor.* —*v.t.* **1.** to support or choose by a vote; cast a vote for: *My parents have always voted a straight party ticket.* **2.** to grant or establish by a vote: *to vote the necessary funds for a project.* **3.** to declare by general consent: *The critics voted the

show a success. [Latin *vōtum* vow, wish. Doublet of VOW.] —**vot′er,** *n.* —**vote′less,** *adj.*

• **to vote down.** to defeat by voting: *The committee voted down the proposal.*

• **to vote in.** to choose by voting for; elect: *The candidate was voted in by a small margin.*

vote of confidence 1. a resolution in a parliamentary form of government showing support for the party in power, a policy of that party, or an action taken by it or by one of its ministers. **2.** any show or indication of support or approval: *The editorial was a vote of confidence in the mayor's policies.*

voting machine, a machine that mechanically registers and counts the votes cast on it.

vo·tive (vō′tiv) *adj.* given, offered, or performed because of or in fulfillment of a vow: *a votive offering.* [Latin *vōtīvus* relating to a vow, from *vōtum* vow.]

vouch (vouch) *v.i.* **1.** to give one's personal assurance; assume responsibility (with *for*): *I'll vouch for my friend's honesty.* **2.** to serve as evidence or assurance of; assure the truth or validity of (with *for*): *These papers will vouch for my identity.* —*v.t.* to guarantee or affirm. [Old French *voucher* to summon, claim, from Latin *vocāre* to call.]

vouch·er (vou′chər) *n.* **1.** a document serving as proof of payment or as verification of the accuracy of an account, such as a canceled check or receipt. **2.** a person who vouches.

vouch·safe (vouch sāf′) *v.t.,* **-safed, -saf·ing.** to be kind enough to grant; condescend to give; deign: *Will you please vouchsafe an answer?* [Originally, *vouch safe* to warrant as safe, guarantee. See VOUCH, SAFE.]

vous·soir (vü swär′) *n.* one of the wedge-shaped sections that forms part of an arch or vault. For illustration, see **arch¹.** [French *voussoir,* going back to *volvere* to roll.]

vow (vou) *n.* **1.** a solemn promise or pledge, esp. one made to God or a deity to behave or live one's life in a specified way: *The members of certain religious orders take a vow of poverty.* **2.** a solemn declaration or affirmation: *a vow of appreciation.* —*v.t.* **1.** to promise or pledge solemnly to do, give, or inflict: *to vow loyalty.* **2.** to declare earnestly or solemnly. —*v.i.* to make a vow. [Old French *veu* solemn promise made to a deity, from Latin *vōtum.* Doublet of VOTE.] —For Synonyms *(v.t.),* see **promise.**

• **to take vows.** to become a member of a religious order.

vow·el (vou′əl) *n.* **1.** a voiced speech sound produced by not blocking the passage of air through the mouth, and forming a syllable by itself or part of a syllable. ➡ distinguished from **consonant. 2.** a letter of the alphabet that represents such a sound, as *a, e, i, o, u,* and sometimes *y.* —*adj.* of or relating to a vowel or vowels. [Old French *voiel(le)* the open speech sound, from Latin *vōcālis (littera)* sounding (letter). Doublet of VOCAL.]

vox po·pu·li (voks′ pop′yə lī′) *Latin.* the voice of the people.

voy·age (voi′ij) *n.* **1.** a journey or passage by water, usually over the sea or other large body of water. **2.** any long journey: *a voyage to the moon.* **3.** *usually,* **voyages.** a book or account of one or more sea journeys. —*v.i.* to make a voyage: *to voyage across the Atlantic.* —*v.t.* to journey over or across; traverse. [Old French *voiage* way, pilgrimage, military expedition, from Latin *viāticum* provisions or money for a journey. Doublet of VIATICUM.] —**voy′a·ger,** *n.* —For Synonyms *(n.),* see **journey.**

vo·ya·geur (vwä yä zhûr′, voi′ə-) *n., pl.* **-geurs** (-zhûrz′). **1.** formerly, a person employed by a fur company to transport people and goods by boat to and from remote stations in the wilderness of Canada. **2.** a woodsman, boatman, or guide in the Canadian backwoods. [French *voyageur* traveler, from *voyager* to travel, from *voyage* journey, from Old French *voiage.* See VOYAGE.]

vo·yeur (vwä yûr′, voi-) *n.* a person who obtains sexual gratification from viewing sexual scenes, acts, or objects, esp. without being seen. [French *voyeur,* from *voir* to see, from Latin *vidēre.*] —**vo·yeur·ism** (vwä yûr′iz əm, voi ûr′-, voi′ə riz′-), *n.*

V.P. *also,* **VP** vice-president.

vs. 1. verse. **2.** versus.

v.t., transitive verb.

Vt., Vermont.

VT, the postal abbreviation for Vermont.

VTOL (vē′tôl′) an airplane that can take off and land vertically. [Short for *v(ertical) t(ake)o(ff and) l(anding).*]

Vul·can (vul′kən) *n.* in Roman mythology, the god of fire and metalworking. His Greek counterpart is Hephaestus.

vul·can·ite (vul′kə nīt′) *n.* a hard, tough rubber that resembles ebony, made by adding a large amount of sulfur to natural rubber, used esp. for combs, toys, and battery cases.

vul·can·ize (vul′kə nīz′) *v.t.,* **-ized, -iz·ing.** to treat (natural rubber) with sulfur or other compounds and heat in order to impart greater strength and elasticity. [VULCAN + -IZE.] —**vul′can·i·za′tion,** *n.* —**vul′can·iz′er,** *n.*

vul·gar (vul′gər) *adj.* **1.a.** lacking or characterized by a lack of good breeding, refinement, or taste; crude: *a vulgar joke, a vulgar expression.* **b.** obscene; indecent: *a vulgar gesture.* **2.** of, relating to, or characteristic of the common people, as distinguished from the educated or privileged elite; common: *a vulgar perception.* **3.** expressed in or designating a language used by the common people; vernacular. [Latin *vulgāris* relating to the masses, common, from *vulgus* the masses.] —**vul′gar·ly,** *adv.* —**vul′gar·ness,** *n.* —For Synonyms, see **coarse.**

vul·gar·i·an (vul gâr′ē ən) *n.* a person who is vulgar, esp. one who makes an ostentatious display of wealth.

vul·gar·ism (vul′gə riz′əm) *n.* **1.** a word, phrase, or expression that is widely used, esp. by noneducated people, and is considered substandard, unrefined, or coarse. **2.** vulgarity.

vul·gar·i·ty (vul gar′i tē) *n., pl.* **-ties. 1.** the state or quality of being vulgar; lack of good breeding, refinement, or taste. **2.** something that is vulgar, as an offensive action or expression.

vul·gar·ize (vul′gə rīz′) *v.t.,* **-ized, -iz·ing. 1.** to make coarse or crude: *to vulgarize language.* **2.** to express (something difficult) in a form that is comprehensible to the common people; popularize: *to vulgarize recent discoveries in astronomy.* —**vul′gar·i·za′tion,** *n.* —**vul′gar·iz′er,** *n.*

Vulgar Latin, the vernacular form of ancient Latin, the main source of the Romance languages.

Vul·gate (vul′gāt, -git) *n.* **1.** the Latin version of the Bible, translated in large part by Saint Jerome and completed about A.D. 383. The Vulgate is the official Latin text of the Roman Catholic Church and the basis of other translations, esp. the Douay version. **2.** vulgate. common or vulgar speech; vernacular. —*adj.* **1.** in or of the Vulgate. **2.** in or of common or vulgar speech; vernacular. [Late Latin *vulgāta (ēditiō)* popular (edition), from Latin *vulgāre* to make common, publish.]

vul·ner·a·ble (vul′nər ə bəl) *adj.* **1.** capable of being physically wounded or damaged; easily hurt: *The athlete's weak knee is a vulnerable spot.* **2.** capable of being hurt emotionally; sensitive: *The shy child was vulnerable to criticism.* **3.** open to criticism or attack; not sufficiently protected: *The open harbor is vulnerable in a storm.* **4.** easily affected, influenced, or tempted: *vulnerable to political intrigue.* **5.** in contract bridge, having won one game of a rubber and therefore eligible for increased penalties and premiums. [Late Latin *vulnerābilis* wounding, going back to *vulnus* wound.] —**vul′ner·a·bil′i·ty,** *n.* —**vul′ner·a·bly,** *adv.*

vul·pine (vul′pīn, -pin) *adj.* of, relating to, or resembling a fox or foxes. [Latin *vulpīnus,* from *vulpēs* fox.]

vul·ture (vul′chər) *n.* **1.** any of two similar but unrelated groups of birds, the New World family Cathartidae and the Old World family Accipitridae, having dark, dull plumage and a naked head and neck, and feeding chiefly on dead animals. **2.** a greedy, predatory, or ruthless person. [Latin *vultur.*]

vul·va (vul′və) *n., pl.* **-vae** (-vē) or **-vas.** the external parts of the female genital organs. [Latin *vulva* womb.] —**vul′val, vul′var,** *adj.*

vy·ing (vī′ing) the present participle of **vie.**

a	at	e	end	o	hot	u	up	hw	white		about
ā	ape	ē	me	ō	old	ū	use	ng	song		taken
ä	far	i	it	ô	fork	ü	rule	th	thin	ə	pencil
âr	care	ī	ice	oi	oil	u̇	pull	th	this		lemon
		îr	pierce	ou	out	ûr	turn	zh	measure		circus

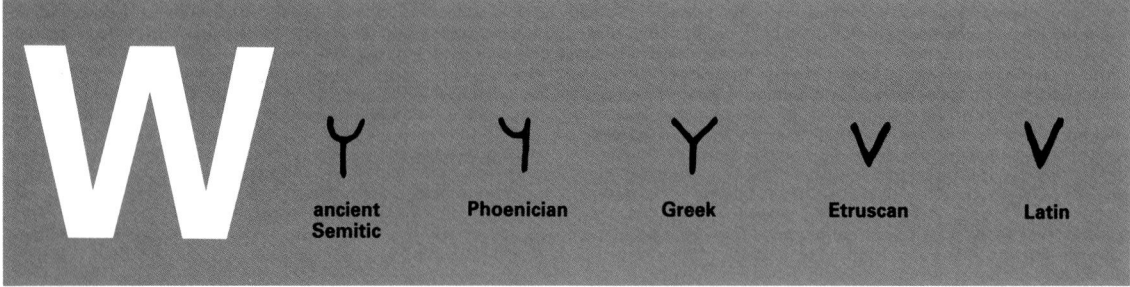

| ancient Semitic | Phoenician | Greek | Etruscan | Latin |

W Because **W**, like **U**, developed as a variation of the letter **V**, these letters can be said to share the same early history. Their earliest ancestor was the ancient Semitic letter *waw*, which depicted a hook and stood for the sound of *w* in water. The Phoenicians borrowed *waw*, using it to represent both the *w* sound and the sound *ü*, as heard in the English word *rude*. Later the Greeks adopted this letter and called it *upsilon*, writing it as the capital letter **Y** is written today. *Upsilon* was borrowed by the Etruscans, who wrote it like our modern capital letter **V**. This letter was adopted without change in the Latin alphabet and continued to represent both the *w* and *ü* sounds. About 1,000 years ago, two forms of the letter were being used in writing: **V** at the beginning of a word and a new letter, **U**, in the middle of a word. Later, when **V** began to be used to represent only the consonant sound *v*, there was no longer a letter to stand for the *w* sound. To fill the gap, Norman scribes combined two **V**'s or two **U**'s to create a new letter they called "double U." This letter was the forerunner of our capital letter **W**.

w, W (dub′əl ū′) *n., pl.* **w's, W's. 1.** the twenty-third letter of the English alphabet. **2.** the shape of this letter or something having this shape.

W, the symbol for tungsten.

w 1. watt; watts. **2.** *Physics.* work.

w. 1. week. **2.** weight. **3.** wide. **4.** width. **5.** wife.

W *also,* **W. 1.** west. **2.** western.

W. 1. Wales. **2.** Wednesday. **3.** Welsh.

WA, the postal abbreviation for Washington.

WAAC, Women's Army Auxiliary Corps.

wab·ble (wob′əl) *v.t., v.i.,* **-bled, -bling.** wobble. —*n.* wobble. —**wab′bler,** *n.*

wab·bly (wob′lē) *adj.,* **-bli·er, -bli·est.** wobbly.

Wac (wak) *n.* a member of the Women's Army Corps.

WAC, Women's Army Corps.

wack·y (wak′ē) *also,* **whacky.** *adj.,* **wack·i·er, wack·i·est.** *Slang.* absurd, eccentric, or outlandish. —**wack′i·ly,** *adv.* —**wack′i·ness,** *n.*

wad (wod) *n.* **1.** a small, compact mass or lump of any soft or flexible material: *a wad of cotton, a wad of chewing gum, a wad of paper.* **2.a.** *Informal.* a tightly rolled bundle of paper money. **b.** a large amount of money. **3.a.** a round plug, as of cloth or paper, used to hold a charge of powder in place in a muzzleloading gun. **b.** a disk, as of felt or cardboard, used to hold powder and shot in place in a shotgun cartridge. **4.** wadding *(def. 1).* —*v.t.,* **wad·ded, wad·ding. 1.** to roll, press, or pack into a wad: *to wad paper.* **2.** to stuff, pad, or pack with wadding. **3.** to hold (shot, powder, or a charge) in place with a wad. [Of uncertain origin.]

• **to shoot one's wad.** *Slang.* to use or spend all one's money or other resources at one time: *I shot my wad on a ten-speed bike.*

wad·ding (wod′ing) *n.* **1.** a soft, fibrous material used for stuffing, padding, or packing. **2.** a soft, flexible material used for making wads, as for guns. **3.** wads collectively.

wad·dle (wod′əl) *v.i.,* **-dled, -dling.** to walk or move with short steps, swaying the body from one side to the other: *The duck waddled across the yard.* —*n.* a swaying or rocking walk. [WADE + -LE.] —**wad′dler,** *n.*

wade (wād) *v.,* **wad·ed, wad·ing.** —*v.i.* **1.** to walk in or through water, mud, or any other substance that impedes free motion: *We waded across the creek.* **2.** to proceed or make one's way slowly and with difficulty: *The secretary had to wade through a pile of papers to find the missing receipt.* **3.** to walk about as in

shallow water, esp. for fun: *The children waded in the shallow end of the pool.* —*v.t.* to walk through or cross by wading: *to wade a brook.* —*n.* the act of wading. [Old English *waden* to go, walk through water.]

• **to wade in** (or **into**). *Informal.* to attack, approach, or begin vigorously and energetically.

wad·er (wā′dər) *n.* **1.** a person who wades. **2.** any of various large, long-legged, long-billed birds that wade about in shallow water searching for food, such as the crane, heron, or stork. **3.** **waders.** high waterproof boots or a pair of pants having such boots attached, worn esp. when fishing in shallow water.

wa·di (wä′dē) *n., pl.* **-dis.** *also,* **wady. 1.** a ravine or streambed in the deserts of the Middle East and northern Africa, through which a stream flows after a rainfall. **2.** a stream flowing through such a ravine or streambed. [Arabic *wādī* streambed.]

wading bird, any of various long-legged, long-billed, and long-necked birds that wade in shallow water for food, esp. those of the group Ciconiiformes, which includes herons, egrets, storks, and ibises.

wa·dy (wä′dē) *n., pl.* **-dies.** wadi.

Waf (waf) *n.* a member of the Women's Air Force.

WAF, Women's Air Force.

wa·fer (wā′fər) *n.* **1.** a thin, crisp cookie or cracker, often sweetened and flavored. **2.** any thin disk resembling this, such as a piece of chocolate. **3.** a thin disk of unleavened bread administered during Holy Communion in the Roman Catholic and other churches. **4.** a thin disk or slice of semiconductor material. **5.** a small, thin disk, as of dried paste or adhesive paper, used for sealing letters, fastening documents, or the like. [Anglo-Norman *wafre* honeycomb, thin small cake; of Germanic origin; referring to the resemblance of such cakes to a honeycomb.]

waf·fle (wof′əl) *n.* a crisp batter cake patterned with square-shaped indentations, usually cooked in a waffle iron. [Dutch *wafel* wafer. See WAFER.]

waffle iron, a cooking utensil consisting of two hinged metal griddles having square-shaped projections, used to make waffles.

waft (waft, wäft) *v.i.* to float or be carried through the air or over water: *The smell of freshly brewed coffee wafted through the open door.* —*v.t.* to carry lightly and gently through the air or over water. —*n.* **1.** a light breeze; current of air. **2.** something, such as an odor or sound, carried through the air. **3.** the act of wafting. [From obsolete *wafter* convoy vessel, from Dutch *wachter* a guard.]

wag[1] (wag) *v.,* **wagged, wag·ging.** —*v.t.* **1.** to cause to move rapidly and repeatedly up and down or from side to side: *Our dog always wags its tail at me.* **2.** to move (the tongue) constantly in talking, esp. in idle chatter or gossip. —*v.i.* **1.** to move rapidly and repeatedly up and down or from side to side. **2.** (of the tongue) to move constantly in talking, esp. in idle chatter or gossip: *The news of their engagement made tongues wag at the office.* —*n.* the act or an instance of wagging. [Middle English *waggen* to move, shake, sway, going back to Old English *wagian* to sway, totter.]

wag[2] (wag) *n.* a person who is fond of or given to joking or jesting; habitual joker; jester. [Of uncertain origin.]

wage (wāj) *n.* **1.** *often,* **wages.** payment for work done or services rendered, esp. calculated on an hourly, daily, or piecework basis. **2.** *usually,* **wages.** something given in return; reward; recompense. ➡ **Wages** is used as plural in def. 1, as singular or plural in def. 2: *For the wages of sin is death* (Romans 6:23). —*v.t.,* **waged, wag·ing.** to carry on or engage in, as a war, battle, or contest. [Dialectal Old French *wage* pledge, pay; of Germanic origin.] —For Synonyms *(n.),* see **pay.**

wage earner, a person who works for wages.

wa·ger (wā′jər) *n.* **1.** an agreement or pledge to pay money or some other specified thing to another person if that person is right about something and you are wrong; bet. **2.** something pledged or

bet: *a five-dollar wager.* —*v.t.* to pledge or risk (money or some other specified thing) in a wager; bet. —*v.i.* to make a wager; bet. [Anglo-Norman *wageure* pledge, stake, from dialectal Old French *wagier* to pledge, from *wage.* See WAGE.] —**wa′ger·er,** *n.*

wage scale 1. a schedule of wages paid to workers performing related tasks within an industry, factory, or company. **2.** the schedule of wages paid by a particular employer.

wage·work·er (wāj′wûr′kər) *n.* a person who works for wages.

wag·ger·y (wag′ə rē) *n., pl.* **-ger·ies. 1.** mischievous merry-making; jocularity. **2.** a jest or joke.

wag·gish (wag′ish) *adj.* **1.** fond of playing jokes; playfully mischievous; jocular. **2.** of, relating to, or characteristic of a wag or waggery: *a waggish sense of humor.* —**wag′gish·ly,** *adv.* —**wag′gish·ness,** *n.*

wag·gle (wag′əl) *v.t., v.i.,* **-gled, -gling.** to move or cause to move rapidly and repeatedly up and down or from side to side; wag. —*n.* the act or an instance of waggling. [WAG[1] + -LE.] —**wag′gly,** *adj.*

wag·on (wag′ən) *also, British,* **wag·gon.** *n.* **1.** any of various four-wheeled vehicles, usually drawn by a horse or horses, used esp. for carrying heavy loads. **2.** a child's low, rectangular, four-wheeled toy vehicle. **3.** a light truck or van that is used for carrying small loads: *a delivery wagon.* **4.** station wagon. **5.** patrol wagon. **6.** *British.* a railroad freight car. [Dutch *wagen* wheeled vehicle for carrying heavy loads.]
 · **off the wagon.** *Slang.* once again drinking alcoholic beverages.
 · **on the wagon.** no longer drinking alcoholic beverages.
 · **to fix (someone's) wagon.** *Slang.* to get revenge on someone.

wag·on·er (wag′ə nər) *n.* a person who drives a wagon, esp. as an occupation.

wag·on·ette (wag′ə net′) *n.* a light, four-wheeled carriage with one or two crosswise seats in front and two seats running lengthwise and facing each other in the rear.

wag·on·load (wag′ən lōd′) *n.* the amount that a wagon carries.

wagon train in a painting by Oscar Berninghaus

wagon train, a line or group of covered wagons traveling together, as during the western migration in America in the nineteenth century.

wag·tail (wag′tāl′) *n.* any of various small birds, family Motacillidae, usually having a long narrow tail that is habitually wagged up and down.

wa·hi·ne (wä hē′nē, -nā) *n.* a Polynesian woman or girl, esp. in Hawaii. [Hawaiian *wahine* woman.]

wa·hoo[1] (wä′hü, wä hü′) *n., pl.* **-hoos.** a shrub or tree, *Euonymus atropurpurea,* of eastern and central North America, having finely toothed leaves that turn pale yellow in the fall. [Dakota *wāhu* arrowwood.]

wa·hoo[2] (wä hü′, wä′hü) *n., pl.* **-hoo** or **-hoos.** a striped mackerel, *Acanthocybium solanderi,* of warm Atlantic waters, popular as a game and food fish. Weight: 20 pounds (9.1 kilograms) or more.

waif (wāf) *n.* **1.** a person having no home, family, or friends, esp. a lost child. **2.** anything that has no apparent owner or home, such as a stray animal. [Anglo-Norman *waif* a thing lost and not claimed; probably of Scandinavian origin.]

wail (wāl) *v.i.* **1.** to make a prolonged, mournful sound, esp. as an expression of grief or pain. **2.** to make a sound resembling this: *A siren was wailing in the street.* —*v.t.* to grieve over; lament; bewail. —*n.* **1.** a prolonged, mournful sound, usually expressive of grief or pain. **2.** any sound resembling this. [Of Scandinavian origin.] —**wail′er,** *n.*

wail·ful (wāl′fəl) *adj.* **1.** expressing sorrow; mournful: *a wailful cry.* **2.** making a sound resembling a wail. —**wail′ful·ly,** *adv.*

wain (wān) *n. Archaic.* a wagon or cart. [Old English *wægen.*]

wain·scot (wān′skət, -skōt′) *n.* **1.** a lining for interior walls, usually paneled and of wood. **2.** the lower portion of an interior wall when it is finished differently from the upper portion. —*v.t.,* **-scot·ed, -scot·ing;** *also, British,* **-scot·ted, -scot·ting.** to line or panel with wainscot. [Partial translation of Middle Dutch *wagenschot* lining of wood for walls; possibly, literally, timber for wagons or wains, from *wagen* wagon + *schot* planking.]

wain·scot·ing (wān′skō′ting) *n.* **1.a.** wainscot. **b.** wainscots collectively. **2.** the material used for a wainscot.

wain·wright (wān′rīt′) *n.* a person who makes and repairs wagons.

waist (wāst) *n.* **1.** the part of the human body between the ribs and the hips. **2.** waistline *(def. 1).* **3.** a garment or part of a garment that covers the body from the shoulders to the waistline. **4.** the narrow middle part of anything, such as the middle part of a violin or bell. **5.** the middle section of a ship or airplane. **6.** the slender middle part of the body of certain insects, such as wasps or ants. [Probably from an unrecorded Old English word.]

waist·band (wāst′band′) *n.* a band of material that encircles the waist, esp. one that is attached to the top of a skirt or trousers.

waist·cloth (wāst′klôth′) *n., pl.* **-cloths** (-klôthz′, -klôths′). loincloth.

waist·coat (wes′kət, wāst′kōt′) *n.* **1.** *British.* vest. **2.** a close-fitting garment, usually sleeveless, formerly worn by men under a doublet.

waist·line (wāst′līn′) *n.* **1.** an imaginary line encircling the narrowest part of the waist. **2.** the part of a garment that encircles this part of the body or falls just above or below it.

wait (wāt) *v.i.* **1.** to remain in a place in anticipation of something: *Wait until you hear from me before leaving. I had to wait for the bus this morning.* **2.** to be readily available: *The check is waiting for your signature.* **3.** to look forward to something (often with *for*): *I'm simply waiting for the day when my friend will get well.* **4.** to remain temporarily undone or delayed: *Our trip will have to wait until the job is finished.* **5.** to perform the duties of a waiter, waitress, or the like: *to wait at table.* —*v.t.* **1.** to remain in a place in anticipation of (something): *to wait one's turn.* **2.** *Informal.* to put off; delay: *We cannot wait dinner that late.* —*n.* **1.** the act of waiting. **2.** a period of waiting: *There will be a two-hour wait before the next plane.* **3.** *British.* a member of a group of musicians and singers who perform in the streets, esp. at Christmas time. [Dialectal Old French *waitier* to watch; of Germanic origin.]
 · **to lie in wait.** to remain in hiding in order to attack: *The mugger lay in wait for an easy victim.*
 · **to wait on** (or **upon**). **a.** to serve or help: *There were no clerks to wait on us at the store.* **b.** to visit or call upon formally: *The foreign ministers waited upon the president.* **c.** to be a result or consequence of; depend upon: *Our plans will wait on your decision.*
 · **to wait up. a.** to postpone going to bed in anticipation of something or someone (often with *for*): *I'll wait up for you tonight.* **b.** *Informal.* to wait for another person to catch up, as on a hike.

wait·er (wā′tər) *n.* **1.** a person whose job is serving food and drink, as in a restaurant. **2.** a person who waits. **3.** a small tray, used esp. for carrying dishes.

wait·ing (wā′ting) *n.* the act of a person who waits for or in anticipation of something.
 · **in waiting.** in attendance on a sovereign or other member of a royal family.

waiting game, a stratagem in which action or movement is delayed until a more favorable or advantageous time.

waiting list, a list of the names of people who are waiting for something: *There is a long waiting list for apartments in this building.*

a	at	e	end	o	hot	u	up	hw	white		about
ā	ape	ē	me	ō	old	ū	use	ng	song		taken
ä	far	i	it	ô	fork	ü	rule	th	thin	ə	pencil
âr	care	ī	ice	oi	oil	ù	pull	th	this		lemon
		îr	pierce	ou	out	ûr	turn	zh	measure		circus

waiting room, a room or area provided for the use of people who are waiting, as at an airport or doctor's office.

wait·ress (wā′tris) *n.* a woman whose job is serving food and drink, as in a restaurant.

waive (wāv) *v.t.*, **waived, waiv·ing. 1.** to give up voluntarily, as a claim, right, or privilege. **2.** to refrain from insisting upon or taking advantage of. **3.** to put aside for the present; defer: *to waive judgment.* [Anglo-Norman *weyver* to abandon; probably of Scandinavian origin.]

waiv·er (wā′vər) *n.* **1.** a voluntary giving up of something, such as a legal right. **2.** a document that gives evidence of this. [Anglo-Norman *weyver,* noun use of infinitive *weyver* to abandon. See WAIVE.]

wake¹ (wāk) *v.*, **waked** or **woke, waked** or *(archaic)* **wok·en, wak·ing. —v.i. 1.** to be roused from sleep; cease to sleep (often with *up*): *I woke up at the sound of the alarm.* **2.** to become aware, alert, or active: *The townspeople eventually woke to their responsibilities.* **3.** to be or remain awake; refrain from sleeping. **4.** *Archaic.* to keep watch or vigil, esp. over the body of a dead person. —*v.t.* **1.** to rouse from sleep: *Be quiet or you'll wake the baby.* **2.** to make active; stir up; arouse: *The news report waked the people to the danger.* **3.** *Archaic.* to keep watch over the body of a dead person. —*n.* a watch or vigil over the body of a dead person before burial. [Partly from Old English *wacian* to be awake; partly from Old English *wacan* to be born, arise.] —**wak′er,** *n.*

wake² (wāk) *n.* **1.a.** the track left by a boat, ship, or other object moving through water: *The wake of the ship was visible from the airplane.* **b.** the water displaced or set in motion by a passing vessel: *The wake of the speedboat rocked the canoe.* **2.** a track or path left by anything that has passed: *the wake of a storm.* ·**in the wake of. a.** following close behind: *Many traders came in the wake of the gold rush.* **b.** as a result or consequence of: *Much suffering followed in the wake of the war.* [Of Scandinavian origin.]

wake·ful (wāk′fəl) *adj.* **1.** unable to sleep: *The howling wind kept me wakeful.* **2.** characterized by absence of sleep: *The sick child spent a wakeful night.* **3.** watchful; vigilant. —**wake′ful·ly,** *adv.* —**wake′ful·ness,** *n.*

wak·en (wā′kən) *v.t.* **1.** to rouse from sleep; wake. **2.** to stir up; arouse: *The book wakened new interest in the subject.* —*v.i.* to be roused from sleep; cease to sleep: *We wakened when the alarm sounded.* [Old English *waecnan* to arise, be born.] —**wak′en·er,** *n.*

wake-rob·in (wāk′rob′in) *n.* trillium. [Of uncertain origin.]

Wal·den·ses (wol den′sēz) *pl. n.* a Christian sect founded in the twelfth century in Lyon, France, that joined the Reformation movement in the sixteenth century and exists today primarily in Piedmont, Italy. —**Wal·den′si·an,** *adj., n.*

wale (wāl) *n.* **1.** one of a series of parallel ridges or ribs on the surface of certain fabrics, such as corduroy. **2.** the texture or weave of a fabric having such ridges or ribs. **3.** one of several continuous lines of thick planks fastened horizontally to the sides of a boat or ship, esp. a wooden ship. **4.** a welt on the skin; weal. —*v.t.*, **waled, wal·ing. 1.** to raise a wale or wales on, as by whipping. **2.** to weave with wales. [Old English *walu* ridge, welt.]

walk (wôk) *v.i.* **1.a.** to move or proceed by placing one foot on the ground before lifting the other. **b.** (of quadrupeds) to move or proceed by placing two feet on the ground before lifting either or both of the other two. **2.** to move or travel on foot for exercise or for pleasure: *We walk after dinner almost every night.* **3.** (of inanimate objects) to move in a manner suggestive of walking: *During the earthquake the chair walked across the room.* **4.** to behave or live in a particular manner: *to walk in peace.* **5.** to appear in visible form and move about, as a ghost. **6.** *Baseball.* (of a batter) to go to first base as a result of having been pitched four balls. **7.** *Basketball.* travel. —*v.t.* **1.** to move through, over, or across on foot: *I walked the streets in search of a restaurant.* **2.** to accompany on foot: *I'll walk you to the door.* **3.** to make or help to walk: *I walked the baby by taking both its hands.* **4.** to lead, ride, or drive at a slow gait or pace: *to walk a horse uphill.* **5.** to bring to a specified condition by walking: *to walk oneself to exhaustion.* **6.** to measure or survey by going over on foot; pace (often with *off*): *to walk off three feet.* **7.** to cause to move in a manner suggestive of walking: *to walk a tall ladder along the side of a house.* **8.** *Baseball.* (of a pitcher) to allow (a batter) to advance to first base by pitching four balls. —*n.* **1.** the act or an instance of walking, esp. for pleasure or exercise: *Let's go for a walk.* **2.** a distance to be walked, often measured in the time required: *The park is only a two-minute walk from here.* **3.** a manner of walking; characteristic gait: *a fast, bouncy walk.* **4.** a place set apart for walking: *The walk was covered with leaves.* **5.** a particular social position or sphere of activity; profession; occupation: *People from all walks of life came to hear the professor speak.* **6.** *Baseball.* the

act or fact of allowing a batter to advance to first base by pitching four balls. **7.** a section of land, usually enclosed, that is set aside for the pasture and exercise of animals. [Old English *wealcan* to roll, toss, move about.]

·**to walk away from.** to survive (an accident) with little or no injury.

·**to walk off. a.** to leave unexpectedly, esp. in anger. **b.** to get rid of by walking: *to walk off a headache.*

·**to walk off with. a.** to win, as a prize. **b.** to steal: *to walk off with someone's bike.*

·**to walk out.** to go on strike: *The workers threatened to walk out on Monday morning.*

·**to walk out on.** *Informal.* to abandon; desert.

·**to walk over. a.** to defeat decisively: *Our team walked over the competition.* **b.** to trample; tread on.

·**to walk through. a.** to guide or explain carefully one step at a time: *The instructor walked the class through the basics of computer programming.* **b.** to rehearse, as by going through a set of motions: *We walked through our parts in the next day's ceremony.*

walk·a·thon (wô′kə thon) *n.* a long-distance walk, often used as a public event to raise money for a charitable cause. [WALK + (MAR)ATHON.]

walk·a·way (wô′kə wā′) *n.* a contest that is easily won; easy victory. Also, **walkover.**

walk·er (wô′kər) *n.* **1.** a person who walks. **2.** something used as an aid in walking, esp. an enclosed metal framework.

walk·ie-talk·ie (wô′kē tô′kē) *also,* **walky-talky.** *n.* a compact, portable two-way radio, used esp. to coordinate infantry, police, or firefighting operations.

walk-in (wôk′in′) *adj.* **1.** large enough to walk into: *a walk-in refrigerator.* **2.** situated on the ground level so as to be accessible directly from the street: *a walk-in apartment.* **3.a.** available to persons without an appointment: *a walk-in clinic.* **b.** of or relating to those persons who do not have an appointment: *a walk-in patient.* —*n.* **1.** something large enough to walk into: *The closets in our house are all walk-ins.* **2.** a person who comes in without an appointment: *The dentist saw a late walk-in with a toothache.* **3.** a certain victory, as in an election.

walking papers *Informal.* official notice of dismissal, esp. from a job.

walking stick 1. a stick or cane carried in the hand, esp. as an aid in walking or hiking. **2.** *also,* **walk·ing·stick** (wô′king stik′). any of a group of brown or green insects, order Phasmida, related to the grasshopper, having long legs and a slender body that resembles a stick or twig. Length: 2½-4 inches (6-10 centimeters). Also *(def. 2),* **stick insect.**

Walk·man (wôk′mən, -man′) *n. Trademark.* a portable, battery-operated cassette player or radio, or combination of both, with headphones.

walk-on (wôk′ôn′, -on′) *n.* **1.** a very small part in a theatrical presentation. **2.** an actor playing such a part.

walk·out (wôk′out′) *n.* **1.** a strike in which workers leave their place of work. **2.** the act of walking out of a meeting or the like, esp. as an expression of protest.

walk·o·ver (wôk′ō′vər) *n.* walkaway.

walk-up (wôk′up′) *n.* **1.** an apartment or office above the first floor in a building having no elevator. **2.** an apartment house or building having no elevator.

walk·way (wôk′wā′) *n.* **1.** a place or passage set apart for walking. **2.** a path that leads from a street or sidewalk to a house.

walk·y-talk·y (wô′kē tô′kē) *n., pl.* **-talk·ies.** walkie-talkie.

wall (wôl) *n.* **1.** an upright structure of stone, plaster, wood, brick, or similar material used to enclose or divide an area, esp. such a structure serving as the interior surface of a room or building. **2.** the interior surface or side of something, such as a body part; lining: *the wall of the large intestine.* **3.** something that resembles a wall in appearance or function: *a wall of people, a wall of fire.* **4.** *also,* **walls.** a fortified barrier; fortification; rampart. —*v.t.* to enclose or divide with or as with a wall or walls (often with *up* or *in*). [Old English *weall* rampart, side or vertical division of a building, from Latin *vallum* rampart.]

·**off the wall.** *Slang.* crazy, eccentric, or bizarre: *Your plans to make a lot of money are off the wall.*

·**to climb the walls.** *Informal.* to become full of tension, to the point of frenzy: *I was climbing the walls with frustration.*

·**to drive** (or **push**) **to the wall.** to place in a desperate condition or situation.

·**to drive up a wall.** *Informal.* to annoy greatly; vex.

·**to go to the wall. a.** to be forced to give way or yield; be defeated. **b.** to fail in business; become bankrupt.

·**up against the wall.** in a critical or hopeless situation: *With two days left to write our term papers, we were up against the wall.*

wal·la·by (wol′ə bē) *n., pl.* -bies or -by. any of various genera of small to medium-sized kangaroos native to Australia, New Zealand, and a few nearby islands. Height: 1-4 feet (0.3-1.2 meters). [Australian native name *wolabā.*]

wallaby

wal·la·roo (wol′ə rü′) *n., pl.* -roos or -roo. a large Australian kangaroo, *Macropus robustus,* found chiefly in coastal mountains and rocky inland ranges. [Australian native name *wolarū.*]

wall·board (wôl′bôrd′) *n.* a building material made of wood pulp, gypsum, or similar substance pressed into large sheets, used as a substitute for wood or plaster in covering walls or ceilings.

walled (wôld) *adj.* having or surrounded by walls: *a medieval walled city.*

wal·let (wol′it, wô′lit) *n.* a flat folding case, usually of leather, used for holding paper money, cards, photographs, and the like. [Of uncertain origin.]

wall·eye (wôl′ī′) *n.* **1.a.** a condition in which the eye turns outward, away from the nose, associated with a form of strabismus. **b.** an eye displaying this condition. **c.** an eye whose cornea is opaque or whose iris has little or no color. **2.** a large staring eye, as of certain fish. **3.** a freshwater food and game fish, *Stizostedion vitreum,* found in lakes and streams of eastern North America, having large, staring eyes. Length: to 3 feet (0.9 meter). Also *(def. 3),* **walleyed pike.** [From WALLEYED.]

wall·eyed (wôl′īd′) *adj.* having or affected with walleyes. [Old Norse *vagleygr* having speckled eyes, from *vagl* wooden beam, blemish in the eye + *auga* eye.]

walleyed pike, walleye *(def. 3).*

wall·flow·er (wôl′flou′ər) *n.* **1.** *Informal.* a person who does not take part in or remains alone at a dance or party, usually because of shyness or lack of a partner. **2.** a hardy plant, *Cheiranthus cheiri,* of southern Europe, bearing dense clusters of fragrant yellow or yellowish brown flowers.

Wal·loon (wo lün′) *n.* **1.** a member of the French-speaking people who live in central and southern Belgium. **2.** the language of this people, a dialect of French. —*adj.* of, relating to, or characteristic of the Walloons or their language or culture.

wal·lop (wol′əp) *Informal. v.t.* **1.** to give a beating to; thrash. **2.** to hit forcefully; smack; sock: *The batter walloped the ball over the fence.* **3.** to overcome, as in a contest; defeat easily: *Our team walloped them.* —*n.* **1.** a forceful blow. **2.** the power or capacity to deliver such a blow. [Dialectal Old French *waloper* to gallop; of Germanic origin.]

wal·lop·ing (wol′ə ping) *Informal. n.* a thorough beating or defeat. —*adj.* amazingly large or powerful; great.

wal·low (wol′ō) *v.i.* **1.** to toss or roll about in something: *Pigs wallow in mud. The children wallowed in the pile of leaves.* **2.** to take great pleasure; revel (with *in*): *to wallow in self-pity.* **3.** to have a great amount of something: *to wallow in money.* —*n.* **1.** the act of wallowing. **2.** a place where an animal, such as a pig, goes to wallow. [Old English *wealwian* to roll about.] —**wal′-low·er,** *n.*

wall·pa·per (wôl′pā′pər) *n.* decorative paper used as an interior wall covering. —*v.t.* to put wallpaper on the walls of: *to wallpaper a kitchen.*

wall plug, an electric outlet set into a wall.

Wall Street **1.** the street in New York City, near the southern tip of Manhattan, that is the heart of the New York financial district. **2.** the banks and financiers who control or influence the economy of the United States.

wall-to-wall (wôl′tə wôl′) *adj.* **1.** covering the entire surface of a floor: *wall-to-wall carpeting.* **2.** *Informal.* completely occupying an area, space, or time period: *The movie was two hours of wall-to-wall excitement.*

wal·nut (wôl′nut′, -nət) *n.* **1.** any of the sweet, oily, edible nuts of a group of tall trees, genus *Juglans,* esp. the English walnut. **2.** any of the trees that produce these nuts. **3.** the wood of any of these trees, esp. black walnut. **4.** a reddish brown color. —*adj.* **1.** made of walnut. **2.** having the color walnut. [Old English *walhhnutu* literally, foreign nut.]

Wal·pur·gis Night (väl pür′gis) in German legend, an annual witches' congregation held on the evening of April 30, the night before May Day. [From Saint *Walpurgis,* eighth-century English missionary to Germany, whose feast day in Germany is May 1 and who is regarded as a protector against magic.]

wal·rus (wôl′rəs, wol′-) *n., pl.* -rus·es or -rus. a large marine mammal, *Odobenus rosmarus,* related to the seals and sea lions and native to the Arctic regions, having massive shoulders, a thick neck, a pair of long ivory tusks, and a tough, yellowish brown hide. Length: to 12 feet (3.7 meters). [Dutch *walrus* literally, whale horse; of Scandinavian origin.]

waltz (wôlts) *n.* **1.** a dance in ¾ time having an accent on the first beat, performed by couples who whirl and glide across the dance floor. **2.** the music for this dance. —*v.i.* **1.** to dance a waltz. **2.** to move breezily and nimbly, as if dancing: *to waltz out of a room.* **3.** to do or obtain

walrus

something casually or with little effort: *She waltzed through her speech. He waltzed away with first prize.* —*v.t.* to lead in a waltz; cause to waltz: *I waltzed my partner about the dance floor.* [German *Walzer,* from *walzen* to roll, dance the waltz.] —**waltz′er,** *n.*

wam·pum (wom′pəm, wôm′-) *n.* **1.** small, polished beads made from shells and strung together or woven into belts, collars, or necklaces, formerly used by certain tribes of North American Indians as money. **2.** *Slang.* money. [Short for Algonquian *wampompeag* literally, white strings (of shell beads).]

wan¹ (won) *adj.,* **wan·ner, wan·nest.** **1.** lacking a natural or healthy color; ashen; pale: *a wan complexion.* **2.** showing or suggesting illness, weariness, or lack of enthusiasm; weak: *a wan smile.* [Old English *wann* dark, livid.] —**wan′ly,** *adv.* —**wan′-ness,** *n.* —For Synonyms, see **pale¹.**

wan² (won) *Archaic.* a past tense of **win.**

wand (wond) *n.* **1.** a slender rod, esp. a rod used by a conjurer or magician. **2.** a short staff used as a symbol of office, command, or authority. **3.** a slender branch, shoot, or stem of a tree or bush; switch. **4.** a hand-held electronic device used to read coded information, such as a Universal Product Code, optically. [Old Norse *vöndr* rod, switch.]

wan·der (won′dər) *v.i.* **1.** to go or move about aimlessly or without a fixed destination or purpose; roam: *We wandered all over the countryside.* **2.** to go at a leisurely pace; stroll: *Toward evening, the cattle wandered home.* **3.** to lose one's way or go astray: *The dog wandered away.* **4.** to digress or become easily distracted from the matter at hand (often with *off*): *The speaker wandered off the subject.* **5.** to follow a winding course; meander: *The river wandered through the valley.* —*v.t.* to go or move about (a place) aimlessly or without a fixed destination or purpose: *to wander the streets.* [Old English *wandrian* to move aimlessly about.] —**wan′der·er,** *n.* —For Synonyms *(v.i.)*, see **roam.**

Wandering Jew **1.** in medieval folklore, a Jew who mocked Jesus on his way to Calvary and was condemned to wander the earth until Judgment Day. **2.** wandering jew. any of several trailing plants, genus *Tradescantia fluminensis,* a houseplant having small, white flowers and oval leaves that are purple underneath and white and green striped above.

wan·der·lust (won′dər lust′) *n.* a strong urge to travel, esp. in a leisurely manner with no fixed destination. [German *Wanderlust,* from *wandern* to wander + *Lust* desire.]

wane (wān) *v.i.,* **waned, wan·ing.** **1.** to decrease gradually, as in size, strength, or intensity: *The moon waned. Her love for him waned.* **2.** to decline, as in power, importance, or influence: *The institution of monarchy has waned in our times.* **3.** to draw to a close; approach an end: *The day wanes.* —*n.* **1.** the act of waning; gradual decrease or decline. **2.** a period or duration of waning. [Old English *wanian* to lessen, fade.]

 • **to be in** (or **on**) **the wane.** to be decreasing or declining: *The popularity of that TV series is on the wane.*

wan·gle (wang′gəl) *Informal. v.,* **-gled, -gling.** —*v.t.* **1.** to bring about or obtain through cleverness, trickery, or deceit; finagle: *to wangle an invitation to a party.* **2.** to manipulate or change, esp. in order to deceive or defraud: *They were arrested for embezzlement after wangling the company's records.* —*v.i.* to resort to

W

a	at	e	end	o	hot	u	up	hw	white		about
ā	ape	ē	me	ō	old	ū	use	ng	song		taken
ä	far	i	it	ô	fork	ü	rule	th	thin	ə	pencil
âr	care	ī	ice	oi	oil	u̇	pull	th	this		lemon
		îr	pierce	ou	out	ûr	turn	zh	measure		circus

trickery or deceit, esp. to further one's own interests. [Possibly a blend of WAGGLE and dialectal English *wankle* unsteady (from Old English *wancol*).] —**wan′gler,** *n.*

Wan·kel engine (wang′kəl, wäng′-) a type of rotary internal-combustion engine in which a triangular rotor revolves inside an elongated chamber, having considerably fewer moving parts than a reciprocating engine.

want (wont, wônt) *v.t.* **1.** to have a desire or wish for: *She wants a better job. He wants to go to Europe.* **2.** to have too little of or be without; lack: *a student who wants confidence.* **3.** to need; require: *The stew wants seasoning.* **4.** to look for in order to capture: *The robber was wanted by the police.* **5.** to request or demand to see or speak with (someone): *The boss wants you.* —*v.i.* **1.** to be needy or destitute. **2.** to have need or a need (with *for*): *Should you want for more supplies, let me know.* —*n.* **1.** a deficiency or need; lack: *a want of money.* **2.** the state or condition of being without the necessities of life; destitution: *a family in want.* **3.** something that is needed or desired; need: *to have many wants.* [Old Norse *vanta* to lack.]

· **to want in** (or **out**). *Informal.* **a.** to desire to come in (or go out): *The dog wants out.* **b.** to wish to participate (or not participate) in a project, business venture, or other enterprise: *My business partner wants out, but there are two investors who want in.*

want ad *Informal.* classified ad.

want·ing (won′ting, wôn′-) *adj.* **1.** missing; lacking: *What is wanting in this room is more furniture.* **2.** not adequate; deficient: *to be wanting in experience.* —*prep.* **1.** not having; without; lacking: *a pot wanting a handle.* **2.** decreased by; minus: *a month wanting two days.*

wan·ton (won′tən) *adj.* **1.** characterized by or resulting from extreme recklessness, thoughtlessness, or malice: *wanton cruelty, a wanton attack.* **2.** lacking moral restraint; dissolute; licentious: *a wanton person.* **3.** not controlled; unruly; luxuriant: *a wanton growth of weeds.* **4.** *Archaic.* playful or frolicsome: *a wanton pony.* —*n.* a person who behaves or is inclined to behave in a wanton, esp. a licentious, manner. —*v.i.* to act or grow in a wanton manner. —*v.t.* to spend or waste in a wanton manner (often with *away*); squander: *to wanton away a fortune.* [Middle English *wantowen* undisciplined, lewd, sportive, going back to Old English *wan-* lacking + *togen,* past participle of *tēon* to pull, educate.] —**wan′ton·ly,** *adv.* —**wan′ton·ness,** *n.*

wap·i·ti (wop′i tē) *n., pl.* **-ti** or **-tis.** elk *(def. 1).* [Algonquian *wapiti* literally, white rump; referring to its white rump and tail.]

war (wôr) *n.* **1.** an armed conflict between countries or factions within a country. **2.** any active opposition or struggle; fight: *a war against illiteracy.* **3.** the profession or science of armed conflict. —*v.i.,* **warred, war·ring.** to engage in war; be in armed conflict; fight. —*adj.* of, relating to, or used in war: *war rations.* [Dialectal Old French *werre* hostility, armed conflict, from Old High German *werra* discord.]

· **at war.** in a state of open hostility; engaging in war.

· **to declare war on. a.** to formally announce the intention to engage in war with. **b.** to announce the intention to get rid of: *to declare war on poverty.*

· **to go to war.** to start or enter into a war.

War Between the States, American Civil War.

war·ble[1] (wôr′bəl) *v.,* **-bled, -bling.** —*v.i.* **1.** to sing with quavers, trills, or melodic embellishments, as a bird. **2.** to make a melodic, warbling sound: *The shallow stream warbled as it flowed over the pebbles.* —*v.t.* to sing with quavers, trills, or melodic embellishments: *to warble a tune.* —*n.* the act or sound of warbling. [Dialectal Old French *werbler* to quaver with the voice; of Germanic origin.]

war·ble[2] (wôr′bəl) *n.* **1.** a lump under the skin of an animal caused by the larva of the warble fly. **2.** a small, hard tumor on the back of a horse due to the rubbing of a saddle. [Probably from a Scandinavian language, as in obsolete Swedish *varbulde* boil, from *var* pus + *bulde* swelling, tumor.]

warble fly, any of a group of botflies, family Oestridae, the larva of which burrow into the skin of cattle, horses, and other mammals, producing cysts called warbles.

war·bler (wôr′blər) *n.* **1.** a person who warbles. **2.** any of various small Old World songbirds, family Sylviidae, such as the blackcap, found throughout Eurasia and Africa, typically having a combination of gray or brown and white plumage. Length: 4-7½ inches (11-18 centimeters). **3.** any of various

warbler *(def. 2)*

small New World songbirds, family Parulidae, such as the yellow warbler, found from Alaska to Argentina, often having brightly colored plumage with red, blue, or yellow markings. Length: 4-7½ inches (11-18 centimeters).

war bonnet, a ceremonial headdress worn by certain North American Indians, esp. the Plains Indians, usually elaborately constructed of eagle feathers, with each feather representing an act of bravery or other honor earned by the wearer.

war crime, any violation of the international laws and customs governing warfare, such as ill-treatment of prisoners or civilians, or plunder or unnecessary destruction of property. —**war criminal.**

war cry 1. a loud call or cry shouted in battle, esp. during an attack. **2.** a slogan or motto used to rally support in a contest or conflict.

ward (wôrd) *n.* **1.** a division of a town or city, organized for purposes of local administration. **2.** a room or division of a hospital containing a number of patients: *a children's ward.* **3.** a division of a jail or prison. **4.** a person who is under the care or control of a court or guardian: *The orphan was a ward of the state.* **5.** the act of guarding. **6.** the state or condition of being under guard. **7.a.** a ridge on the inside of a lock serving as an obstacle to the passing and turning of the wrong key. **b.** a notch on a key corresponding to this ridge. —*v.t.* **1.** to turn back or repel; avert (usually with *off*): *to ward off an attack.* **2.** *Archaic.* to keep watch over. [Old English *weard* a guarding.]

-ward *suffix* in the direction of: *downward, skyward.* [Old English *-weard.*]

war dance, a ceremonial dance performed before going to war or after a victory, as formerly by certain American Indian tribes.

ward·en (wôr′dən) *n.* **1.** a person who is employed to care for or guard someone or something, esp. a person in charge of a prison. **2.** a public official who enforces certain laws or regulations, as in a game preserve. **3.** churchwarden. [Dialectal Old French *wardein* guardian, from *warder* to guard; of Germanic origin.] —**war′den·ship′,** *n.*

ward·er (wôr′dər) *n.* a person who guards a door, gate, or other entrance.

ward heeler *Slang.* a minor politician who does various jobs for a political boss, esp. a person who solicits votes during an election.

ward·robe (wôrd′rōb′) *n.* **1.** a collection of clothing, such as all the clothes belonging to one person, or all the costumes used in a theatrical production. **2.** a piece of furniture or a closet for keeping clothes. [Dialectal Old French *warderobe* place to keep clothes, from *warder* to guard + *robe* garment; both of Germanic origin.]

ward·room (wôrd′rüm′, -rům′) *n.* the living, eating, and recreational area on a warship for all commissioned officers except the captain.

-wards *suffix* form of **-ward,** as in *backwards.*

ward·ship (wôrd′ship′) *n.* **1.** the office or position of a guardian; guardianship. **2.** the state or condition of being a ward.

ware[1] (wâr) *n.* **1. wares.** manufactured articles for sale. **2.** a specific kind of manufactured article. ➡ used mainly in compounds: *glassware, tableware.* **3.** pots, vessels, and other objects made of fired clay; pottery: *ceramic ware.* [Old English *waru* goods, merchandise.]

ware[2] (wâr) *Archaic. adj.* aware; conscious. —*v.t.,* **wared, war·ing.** to guard against; beware of. [Old English *wær* aware, cautious.]

ware·house (wâr′hous′) *n., pl.* **-hous·es** (-hou′ziz). a building where merchandise is stored. —*v.t.* to place or store in a warehouse.

war·fare (wôr′fâr′) *n.* **1.** the act of engaging in war; armed conflict. **2.** any struggle or conflict. [Middle English *werrefare* military expedition, from *werre* (see WAR) + *fare* a going (from Old English *faru*).]

war·fa·rin (wôr′fər in) *n.* **1.** an odorless, tasteless, crystalline compound that causes fatal internal bleeding, used as a rodenticide. Formula: $C_{19}H_{16}O_4$ **2.** this chemical neutralized with sodium hydroxide, used medicinally as an anticoagulant. Formula: $C_{19}H_{15}NaO_4$

war game, a military exercise for training soldiers under conditions similar to those of actual combat, carried out either as maneuvers in the field or as a classroom activity using computers and the like.

war·head (wôr′hed′) *n.* the foremost portion of a guided or ballistic missile or a torpedo, containing the explosive charge.

war·horse (wôr′hôrs′) *n.* **1.** a horse trained for use in battle; charger. **2.** *Informal.* a person who is very experienced, as from having been in many battles, struggles, or conflicts. **3.** *Informal.* a play or musical work that has been performed so often as to be hackneyed.

war·i·ly (wâr′ə lē) *adv.* in a cautious manner; cautiously.

war·i·ness (wâr′ē nis) *n.* the state or quality of being cautious.

war·like (wôr′līk′) *adj.* **1.** fond of war; easily provoked to war; bellicose: *a warlike nation.* **2.** threatening war; hostile: *a warlike atmosphere.* **3.** of, relating to, or characteristic of war: *warlike exploits.*

war·lock (wôr′lok′) *n.* a male witch; sorcerer; wizard. [Old English *wærloga* faithless person, devil.]

war·lord (wôr′lôrd′) *n.* a strong, often tyrannical military leader who controls a territory, frequently in opposition to the national government.

warm (wôrm) *adj.* **1.** having or giving off a moderate or comfortable degree of heat; somewhat hot: *a warm room, warm water.* **2.** having the sensation of heat; heated: *to be warm from a fever.* **3.** producing or holding in body heat: *warm exercise, a warm sweater.* **4.** full of affection, friendship, or enthusiasm; hearty: *a warm reception, warm thanks.* **5.** having a kind, friendly, or compassionate nature: *a warm person.* **6.** easily stirred up; excitable: *a warm temper.* **7.** full of liveliness or excitement; animated; heated: *a warm debate.* **8.** newly made; fresh: *The fox's trail was still warm.* **9.** (of colors) suggesting heat or warmth: *Red and yellow are warm colors.* **10.** *Informal.* at a location close to the person or object sought, as in certain children's games. **11.** *Informal.* uncomfortable or disagreeable: *The gossip made things too warm for me.* —*v.t.* **1.** to make warm or comfortably heated: *They warmed themselves by the fire.* **2.** to make supportive or enthusiastic: *The speech warmed the crowd.* **3.** to inspire with affectionate, kindly feelings: *The sight of home warmed their hearts.* —*v.i.* **1.** to become warm. **2.** to become supportive or enthusiastic: *I warmed to the idea of a winter vacation.* **3.** to be inspired with affectionate, kindly feelings: *We warmed to our new neighbors very quickly.* [Old English *wearm* moderately hot.] —**warm′er,** *n.* —**warm′ly,** *adv.* —**warm′ness,** *n.*
·**to warm up. a.** to make warm, as by heating: *to warm up rolls for dinner.* **b.** to get ready by practicing or exercising: *The runner warmed up before the race.* **c.** to become more affectionate or enthusiastic: *The timid child finally warmed up to me.* **d.** to run (an engine or machine) until the right operating condition or temperature is reached.

warm-blood·ed (wôrm′blud′id) *adj.* **1.** having blood, as birds or mammals, that remains relatively constant in temperature despite changes in the temperature of the environment. **2.** characterized by great warmth of feeling; ardent; passionate. —**warm′-blood′ed·ness,** *n.*

warm front, in meteorology, the forward edge of a mass of warm air that is pushing back a cold air mass.

warm-heart·ed (wôrm′här′tid) *adj.* having or showing sympathy, kindness, or affection: *a warm-hearted person.* —**warm′-heart′ed·ly,** *adv.* —**warm′-heart′ed·ness,** *n.*

warming pan, a large, covered, long-handled pan that holds hot coals, formerly used to warm beds.

war·mon·ger (wôr′mung′gər, -mong′-) *n.* a person who favors or tries to bring about war. —**war′mon′ger·ing,** *n., adj.*

warmth (wôrmth) *n.* **1.** the state or quality of being warm: *the warmth of the sun.* **2.** enthusiasm or heartiness; fervor: *the warmth of a crowd's applause.* **3.** kindness or affection; friendliness: *the warmth of a person's smile.* **4.** the warm effect produced by certain colors, such as reds or yellows.

warm-up (wôrm′up′) *also,* **warm·up.** *n.* **1.** the act of practicing or exercising to get ready for some event: *We watched the pitchers' warm-ups before the baseball game.* **2.** the act of running an engine or machine until it reaches the right temperature or condition for operating.

warn (wôrn) *v.t.* **1.** to put (someone) on guard by giving notice beforehand, as against approaching danger; caution: *A radio bulletin warned the townspeople of the approaching hurricane.* **2.** to advise strongly; admonish: *The doctor warned the patient to avoid strenuous exercise.* **3.** to give notice to; make aware of; signal: *The blinking red light warned drivers to stop.* **4.** to notify (someone) to keep at a distance (usually with *away* or *off*): *to warn people away from a condemned building.* —*v.i.* to give a warning. [Old English *warnian* to take heed, admonish.] —**warn′er,** *n.*

warn·ing (wôr′ning) *n.* **1.** notice or advice given beforehand, as of an approaching danger or an unpleasant consequence: *The darkened sky gave warning of the approaching tornado.* **2.** something that serves to warn: *The sign was a warning to trespassers.* **3.** in meteorology, an alert, issued to the public by the National Weather Service, that a dangerous storm or weather condition, such as a hurricane or tornado, is imminent. —*adj.* serving to warn: *a warning signal.* —**warn′ing·ly,** *adv.*

War of 1812, the war between the United States and Great Britain lasting from 1812 to 1815.

War of Independence, American Revolution.

war of nerves, a conflict in which deception, propaganda, threats, and other psychological tactics are used to intimidate or undermine the morale of an opponent.

warp (wôrp) *v.t.* **1.** to bend, curve, or twist out of shape: *The humidity and dampness has warped the wood.* **2.** to turn from what is correct or right; twist: *Prejudice can warp a person's judgment.* **3.** to move (a ship) by pulling on a line or cable secured to a fixed object, such as a dock or anchor. —*v.i.* to be or become bent, curved, or twisted, as by shrinkage or contraction. —*n.* **1.** a bend, curve, or twist, esp. in a piece of wood: *The warp in the boards made them unsuitable for building.* **2.** a mental quirk, bias, or distortion in judgment. **3.** the threads running lengthwise in woven fabric, crossed by the woof. **4.** the foundation or essential part of something; base: *The warp of life is love.* **5.** a line or cable used in moving a ship. [Old English *weorpan* to throw.]

war paint 1. paint applied to the face and other parts of the body by North American Indians before engaging in war. **2.** *Informal.* official or formal dress; regalia. **3.** *Informal.* cosmetics, such as lipstick or rouge.

war·path (wôr′path′) *n., pl.* **-paths** (-pathz′, -paths′). a route taken by an expedition of North American Indians when engaged in war.
·**on the warpath. a.** engaged in or preparing for war. **b.** ready to fight; belligerent; hostile.

war·plane (wôr′plān′) *n.* a military aircraft, esp. an airplane equipped for combat.

war·rant (wôr′ənt, wor′-) *n.* **1.** something that sanctions, authorizes, or justifies some action or conclusion: *There is no warrant for your accusation.* **2.** a written document authorizing an officer to detain or seize a person or property, or to execute a judgment. **3.** a document authorizing the payment or receipt of money. **4.** an official certificate of appointment issued to an officer below the rank of commissioned officer. **5.** an option to buy shares of stock at a certain price. —*v.t.* **1.** to approve officially; authorize; sanction: *The law warrants the arrest of dangerous criminals.* **2.** to provide sufficient grounds for; justify: *The facts do not warrant your conclusion.* **3.** to guarantee the quality, condition, or authenticity of (something sold) to the buyer: *The dealer warranted the used car for six months.* **4.** to declare with assurance; assert positively: *I warrant that's exactly what they said.* [Dialectal Old French *warant* protection; of Germanic origin.]

war·rant·a·ble (wôr′ən tə bəl, wor′-) *adj.* capable of being warranted. —**war′rant·a·ble·ness,** *n.* —**war′rant·a·bly,** *adv.*

war·ran·tee (wôr′ən tē′, wor′-) *n.* the person to whom a warranty is made or given.

warrant officer, an officer of the armed forces who receives a certificate of appointment rather than a commission, and who ranks between a commissioned officer and an enlisted person.

war·ran·tor (wôr′ən tôr′, wor′-) *also,* **war·rant·er** (wôr′ən tər, wor′-). *n.* a person who makes or gives a warranty.

war·ran·ty (wôr′ən tē, wor′-) *n., pl.* **-ties. 1.** a written statement or assurance given by a seller to a buyer that the seller's product is as represented or that it will be repaired or replaced if proven defective within a certain period of time; guarantee. **2.** an authorization or justification; warrant. [Dialectal Old French *warantie* guarantee, from *warantir* to guarantee, from *warant.* See WARRANT.]

war·ren (wôr′ən, wor′-) *n.* **1.** a place where rabbits or other small animals are kept and bred. **2.** a densely populated building or district. [Anglo-Norman *warenne* a preserve; probably of Germanic origin.]

war·ri·or (wôr′ē ər, wôr′yər, wor′-) *n.* a person who is engaged or experienced in warfare. [Dialectal Old French *werreieor,* from *werreier* to make war, from *werre.* See WAR.]

war·ship (wôr′ship′) *n.* a naval vessel designed and built for use in war.

wart (wôrt) *n.* **1.** a small, nonmalignant growth on the skin, caused by a virus. **2.** a similar growth on a plant. **3.** any aspect or feature that is imperfect, unattractive, or unpleasant: *They loved the crowded, bustling city, warts and all.* [Old English *wearte* the small growth on the skin.] —**wart′like′,** *adj.*

wart·hog (wôrt′hôg′, -hog′) *n.* an African wild hog, *Phacochoerus aethiopicus,* having wartlike growths on the sides of its head, two pairs of curved tusks, and a dark, sparse coat consisting of

bristles and long, coarse hairs. Height: 23-28 inches (58-71 centimeters) at the shoulder.

war·time (wôr′tīm′) *n.* a period of war. —*adj.* of, relating to, or characteristic of a period of war: *wartime rations, a wartime economy.*

wart·y (wôr′tē) *adj.,* **wart·i·er, wart·i·est. 1.** having or covered with warts. **2.** of or resembling warts.

warthog

war whoop, a loud call or cry shouted in battle, esp. by North American Indians.

war·y (wâr′ē) *adj.,* **war·i·er, war·i·est. 1.** habitually on the alert; watchful: *a wary watchdog.* **2.** characterized by caution; guarded: *a wary reply, a wary expression.* [WARE² + -Y¹.] —**war′i·ly,** *adv.* —**war′i·ness,** *n.* —For Synonyms, see **cautious.**

was (wuz, woz; *unstressed* wəz) the first and third person singular past indicative of **be.** [Old English *wæs.*]

wash (wôsh, wosh) *v.t.* **1.** to make (something) free of dirt, impurities, or stains, usually by cleaning with water and soap or detergent: *to wash one's face, to wash dishes.* **2.** to remove (dirt, impurities, or stains), usually by applying water with soap or detergent: *I washed the stain from the tablecloth.* **3.** to overwhelm and carry away by the action of a liquid, such as water: *A wave washed the sailor overboard.* **4.** to wear away or destroy by the action of water; erode (with *away*): *Rain gradually washed away the hillside.* **5.** to cover with moisture; wet: *morning roses washed with dew* (Shakespeare, *Taming of the Shrew*). **6.** to free from defilement, guilt, sin, or corruption; purify. **7.** to cover with a thin coat of a coloring medium, such as paint or metal. —*v.i.* **1.** to wash oneself. **2.** to wash clothes. **3.** to undergo washing without damage, as to color or texture: *This new fabric washes well.* **4.** to be carried away or eroded by the action of water. **5.** to sweep over or beat against with a splashing sound: *We could hear the waves washing on the rocks.* —*n.* **1.** the act of washing or the state of being washed. **2.** a quantity of articles, such as clothes, washed at one time: *I did the wash this morning.* **3.** a flow or rush of water, or the sound made by this. **4.** a liquid preparation used for a particular purpose: *a wash for an infected eye.* **5.** a disturbance in the water or air caused by a moving ship or airplane. **6.** a thin coat of a coloring medium, such as paint: *In the watercolor, a wash of blue represents the sky.* **7.** liquid refuse, esp. that used as food for pigs; swill. **8.** a tract of land intermittently covered with water. **9.** material carried and deposited by the action of water; alluvium. **10.** in the western United States, a dry streambed. Also *(def. 10),* **dry wash.** —*adj.* washable. [Old English *wascan, wæscan* to clean with water.]

· **to come out in the wash.** *Slang.* **a.** to be revealed or become known at some time in the future: *Their graft will eventually come out in the wash.* **b.** to have a positive or satisfactory outcome.

· **to wash down. a.** to clean from top to bottom: *to wash down walls.* **b.** to drink something with (food or medicine) in order to make swallowing easier: *to wash a pill down with orange juice.*

· **to wash one's hands of.** to refuse to have any more to do with.

· **to wash out. a.** to clean the inside of, as with soap and water: *to wash out the bathtub.* **b.** to destroy or carry away by the action of moving water: *The flood washed out the bridge.* **c.** to be removed by using water or soap and water: *The food stains washed out quickly.* **d.** to fail or cause to fail completely: *The collapse of the stock market washed out the stockbroker's business.*

· **to wash up. a.** to wash one's face and hands, as before dinner. **b.** to clean dishes and cooking utensils after a meal. **c.** to ruin or be ruined: *After a steady decline in sales, the company was all washed up and went bankrupt.*

Wash., Washington.

wash·a·ble (wŏ′shə bəl, wosh′ə-) *adj.* capable of being washed without damage, as to color or texture: *a washable fabric.*

wash-and-wear (wôsh′ən wâr′, wosh′) *adj.* of or designating a fabric or garment that requires little or no ironing after washing.

wash·board (wôsh′bôrd′, wosh′-) *n.* a board with a ridged surface on which clothes are rubbed during washing.

wash·bowl (wôsh′bōl′, wosh′-) *n.* a bowl, basin, or sink used to hold water for washing or shaving. Also, **wash′ba·sin, wash′stand′.**

wash·cloth (wôsh′klôth′, wosh′-) *n., pl.* **-cloths** (-klôthz′, -klôths′). a small cloth used for washing one's body or face. Also, **washrag.**

wash·day (wôsh′dā′, wosh′-) *n.* a particular day of the week set aside for doing the washing, esp. laundry.

washed-out (wôsht′out′, wosht′-) *adj.* **1.** that has faded, as from age or washing: *a dull, washed-out plaid shirt.* **2.** *Informal.* **a.** without strength or energy; exhausted: *We felt washed-out after the hike up the mountain.* **b.** lacking natural or healthy color; pale; wan.

washed-up (wôsht′up′, wosht′-) *adj.* **1.** *Informal.* all through, esp. due to failure; finished. **2.** *Informal.* exhausted.

wash·er (wô′shər, wosh′ər) *n.* **1.** a person or thing that washes. **2.** any of various appliances for washing, such as a washing machine. **3.** a flat, perforated disk of metal, rubber, or other material, used with a nut, bolt, or the like to prevent friction or leakage or to give a larger supporting surface or tighter fit.

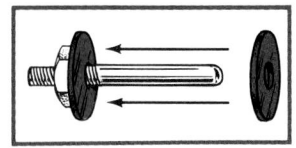

washer *(def. 3)*

wash·er·wom·an (wô′shər wùm′ən, wosh′ər-) *n., pl.* **-wom·en** (-wim′ən). a woman who is employed to wash clothes; laundress. Also, **washwoman.**

wash·ing (wô′shing, wosh′ing) *n.* **1.** the act of cleaning with a liquid, esp. water. **2.** a quantity of articles, such as clothes, washed at one time.

washing machine, an appliance for washing clothes, linens, and the like.

washing soda, sodium carbonate *(def. 2).*

Wash·ing·ton's Birthday (wô′shing tənz, wosh′ing-) the anniversary of the birthday of George Washington, observed as a legal holiday on February 22 or, in most states of the United States, on the third Monday in February.

wash·out (wôsh′out′, wosh′-) *n.* **1.** the carrying away of something, such as a roadbed or topsoil, by the action of water. **2.** a channel or hole resulting from this. **3.** *Slang.* an out-and-out failure.

wash·rag (wôsh′rag′, wosh′-) *n.* washcloth.

wash·room (wôsh′rüm′, -rùm′, wosh′-) *n.* a building or room having a toilet and washing facilities; lavatory.

wash·stand (wôsh′stand′, wosh′-) *n.* **1.** a piece of furniture, such as a table, for holding a basin and pitcher used for washing. **2.** washbowl.

wash·tub (wôsh′tub′, wosh′-) *n.* a large tub used for soaking or washing clothes or household linen.

wash·wom·an (wôsh′wùm′ən, wosh′-) *n., pl.* **-wom·en** (-wim′ən). washerwoman.

wash·y (wô′shē, wosh′ē) *adj.,* **wash·i·er, wash·i·est. 1.** diluted; weak or watery: *washy tea.* **2.** lacking strength or vitality.

was·n't (wuz′ənt, woz′-) *contr.* was not.

wasp (wosp) *n.* any of numerous winged insects, superfamilies Vespoidea and Sphecoidea, that have biting mouthparts and narrow waists and, in the females, venomous stingers. Although most wasps are solitary insects, a few species, such as the hornet and yellow jacket, live in colonies. [Old English *wæsp.*]

WASP (wosp) *also,* **Wasp.** *n.* a person who is a Protestant white of English or Northern European descent, regarded as a typical member of the most privileged class in the United States. ➡ often used disparagingly. [Short for *W(hite) A(nglo-) S(axon) P(rotestant).*] —**Wasp′ish;** *also,* **WASP′ish,** *adj.* —**Wasp′y;** *also,* **WASP′y,** *adj.*

wasp·ish (wos′pish) *adj.* **1.** of, resembling, or characteristic of a wasp. **2.** quick to take offense; bad-tempered; irascible. —**wasp′ish·ly,** *adv.* —**wasp′ish·ness,** *n.*

wasp waist, a very narrow waist.

wasp-waist·ed (wosp′wās′tid) *adj.* having a very narrow waist.

was·sail (wos′əl, -āl, was′-) *n.* **1.** a salutation used when making a toast, esp. to someone's health. **2.** an alcoholic beverage prepared for a wassail, usually made of ale or wine with sugar, spices, or roasted apples added. **3.** a festive party where drinks are served and toasts are made. —*v.i.* **1.** to take part in or drink a wassail. **2.** to go from house to house at Christmas singing carols. —*v.t.* to drink to the health of; toast. [Old Norse *ves heill* be healthy.] —**was′sail·er,** *n.*

Was·ser·mann test (wä′sər mən) a blood test used to diagnose syphilis. Also, **Wassermann.** [From August von *Wassermann,* 1866-1925, German bacteriologist who developed this test.]

wast (wost; *unstressed* wəst) *Archaic.* a second person singular past indicative of **be.** ➡ used with **thou.**

wast·age (wās′tij) *n.* **1.** loss by use, wear, decay, erosion, or the like: *a great wastage of natural resources.* **2.** something or the amount lost in this way.

waste (wāst) *v.*, **wast·ed, wast·ing.** —*v.t.* **1.** to use or spend in a careless or useless way: *to waste time, to waste an opportunity.* **2.** to consume, wear away, or exhaust: *The long illness had wasted the elderly patient's strength.* **3.** to destroy or devastate; ruin: *The advancing army wasted everything in its path.* **4.** *Slang.* to kill. —*v.i.* to lose energy, strength, health, or the like; become weak or feeble (often with *away*): *to waste away from malnutrition.* —*n.* **1.** the act of wasting or the state of being wasted: *The trip was a waste of time.* **2.** a wild, uninhabited, or desolate place; wilderness; desert. **3.** a gradual wearing away. **4.** useless material remaining after some process; refuse. **5.** undigested material eliminated from the body. —*adj.* **1.** rejected, eliminated, or thrown away as worthless: *a pile of waste material.* **2.** of, relating to, or for waste: *a waste receptacle.* **3.** left over after the completion of a process. **4.** uncultivated or uninhabited; desolate. **5.** in a state of desolation and decay; ruined. [Dialectal Old French *waster* to devastate, going back to Latin *vāstāre* to make empty, devastate.]
• **to go to waste.** to fail to be used properly or at all: *The food went to waste.*
• **to lay waste.** to destroy; devastate: *The hurricane laid waste that entire town.*
waste·bas·ket (wāst′bas′kit) *n.* a receptacle used to deposit useless scraps of paper or other refuse.
waste·ful (wāst′fəl) *adj.* given to or characterized by useless, careless, or unnecessary spending or consumption. —**waste′ful·ly,** *adv.* —**waste′ful·ness,** *n.*

Synonyms Wasteful, extravagant, and prodigal mean spending or consuming excessively or without regard to limitations. **Wasteful** implies an inefficient use of money or resources: *Wasteful use of our natural resources may lead our society into an era of shortage.* **Extravagant** suggests a thoughtless spending or using of what one has, whatever the result: *They led extravagant lives, staying in the fanciest hotels wherever they traveled.* **Prodigal** implies recklessness, sometimes combined with a suggestion of ultimately having to pay a price: *Your prodigal spending habits will eventually lead you to ruin.*

waste·land (wāst′land′) *n.* a barren, uninhabited tract of land or region.
waste·pa·per (wāst′pā′pər) *n.* paper that is no longer considered useful and has been or is to be thrown away.
waste pipe, a pipe for carrying away liquid waste, esp. water.
wast·er (wās′tər) *n.* a person or thing that wastes, spends, or consumes things in a useless, careless, or unnecessary manner; wastrel.
waste·wa·ter (wāst′wô′tər, -wot′ər) *n.* water that has been used, as in manufacturing or washing, and is therefore contaminated; sewage.
wast·ing (wās′ting) *adj.* that gradually weakens or destroys; devastating or destructive: *a wasting illness, a wasting drought.*
wast·rel (wās′trəl) *n.* **1.** a wasteful person; spendthrift. **2.** an idle, worthless, disreputable person; good-for-nothing.
watch (woch) *v.t.* **1.** to look at (someone or something) attentively: *The children watched television all afternoon.* **2.** to keep under surveillance; guard: *Our neighbors watched our house while we were away.* **3.** to take care of; tend: *The shepherds watched their flock.* —*v.i.* **1.** to look attentively; observe closely: *Watch while I show you how to hold the golf club.* **2.** to be on the alert or wait expectantly; be vigilant: *I watched for the right moment to make my request.* **3.** to remain awake at night, esp. to keep a vigil. **4.** to do duty as a guard or sentinel; keep guard. **5.** to show caution and close attention; be careful: *Watch when you cross that intersection.* **6.** to be a spectator or onlooker. —*n.* **1.** the act of watching; close, careful observation. **2.** one or more persons employed to protect or guard someone or something. **3.** the period of time during which a guard or sentinel is on duty: *I volunteered for the eight-to-midnight watch.* **4.** the act of remaining awake, esp. to care for someone or something; vigil: *to maintain a watch at a sick child's bedside.* **5.** a small timepiece, usually worn on the wrist or carried on the person. **6.** in meteorology, an alert, issued to the public by the National Weather Service, that dangerous weather conditions or a storm, such as a hurricane, are possible. [Old English *wæccan* to be or remain awake, keep vigil.] —**watch′er,** *n.*
• **to watch out.** to be on the alert; be wary or careful: *Watch out for children when you drive near the school.*
watch·band (woch′band′) *n.* a band or strap of leather, metal, or the like, used to fasten a watch to the wrist.
watch·dog (woch′dôg′) *n.* **1.** a dog kept to guard a house, property, or the like and to give warning of the approach of intruders. **2.** a person or organization that serves as a vigilant protector or guardian: *The public agency was a watchdog for consumer rights.*
watch fire, a fire kept burning during the night as a signal or warning and to provide light and heat.

watch·ful (woch′fəl) *adj.* on the alert; vigilant; wary: *a watchful sentry.* —**watch′ful·ly,** *adv.* —**watch′ful·ness,** *n.*
watch glass 1. crystal *(def. 4).* **2.** a small, circular, concave glass dish similar to a watch crystal but in various sizes, used in the laboratory as an evaporating surface.
watch·mak·er (woch′mā′kər) *n.* a person who makes, cleans, and repairs watches. —**watch′mak′ing,** *n.*
watch·man (woch′mən) *n., pl.* -men (-mən). a person employed to guard a building, property, or the like when the owner or tenant is absent, esp. during the night.
watch meeting, a religious service held by certain churches on New Year's Eve.
watch night 1. New Year's Eve, observed by certain churches with religious services that last until the arrival of the new year. **2.** watch meeting.
watch pocket, a small pocket, usually in a vest or trousers, for carrying a watch.
watch·tow·er (woch′tou′ər) *n.* a tower or tall building from which a guard or sentinel keeps watch.
watch·word (woch′wûrd′) *n.* **1.** a secret word or phrase that identifies the speaker or allows the speaker to pass a guard; password. **2.** a word or phrase considered as embodying a principle or plan of action, as of a political party or organization; slogan; motto.
wa·ter (wô′tər, wot′ər) *n.* **1.** a liquid, solid, or gaseous compound of hydrogen and oxygen, abundant on earth, forming the oceans, seas, lakes, rivers, clouds, and polar caps and vital to most living organisms. Pure water is clear, tasteless, and a poor conductor of electricity, freezing at 0 degrees Celsius (32 degrees Fahrenheit) and boiling at 100 degrees Celsius (212 degrees Fahrenheit). Formula: H_2O **2.** this compound in its liquid state, as distinguished from ice, water vapor, and steam. **3.a.** any body of water, such as a sea, lake, or river. **b.** the level of the water of a lake, river, or other body; tide: *The lake is at low water.* **c.** the surface of a body of water: *Ice formed on the water.* **4.** *also,* **waters. a.** a

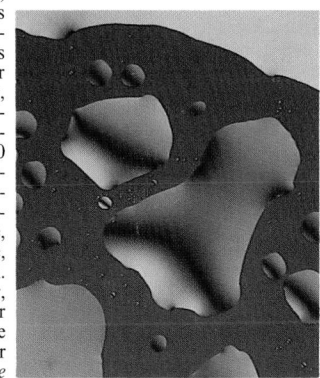

drops of **water**
magnified 40 times

body of water or the bodies of water bordering or located in a region, country, or the like: *The Coast Guard patrols American waters.* **b.** the water of a mineral spring or a collection of springs, used medicinally for bathing or drinking. **5.** any liquid secretion of the body, such as tears, saliva, urine, or the like. **6.** any liquid preparation containing or resembling water: *toilet water, ammonia water.* **7.** the degree of transparency and luster of a precious stone or pearl. **8.** a wavy, lustrous sheen on fabric or metal. **9.** additional shares of stock in a company or corporation issued without a corresponding increase of capital. —*v.t.* **1.** to put water into or upon: *to water the plants every day.* **2.** to furnish a supply of water to, esp. for feeding: *The farmer had to water the livestock twice a day.* **3.a.** to dilute or weaken with water (often with *down*): *The bartender watered down the drinks.* **b.** to dilute or weaken anything (often with *down*): *to water down a critical report.* **4.** to make a wavy, lustrous sheen on (fabric or metal): *to water silk.* **5.** to increase the number of shares of (a stock or company) by issuing additional shares without a corresponding increase in capital. —*v.i.* **1.** to get or take in water: *The ship put into port to water. The cattle watered at the river.* **2.** to give forth water from the body, as in the form of tears or saliva: *The smoke made their eyes water. My mouth watered at the thought of dinner.* [Old English *wæter* the liquid forming oceans, seas, rivers, lakes, and rain.] —**wa′ter·er,** *n.* —**wa′ter·less,** *adj.* —**wa′ter·like′,** *adj.*
• **by water.** by boat, barge, or ship: *We sent the supplies by water.*

a	at	e	end	o	hot	u	up	hw	white	(about
ā	ape	ē	me	ō	old	ū	use	ng	song	taken
ä	far	i	it	ô	fork	ü	rule	th	thin	ə ⟨ pencil
âr	care	ī	ice	oi	oil	u̇	pull	th	this	lemon
		îr	pierce	ou	out	ûr	turn	zh	measure	(circus

• **in deep water**. in great difficulty or distress: *The business was in deep water because of mismanagement.*

• **in hot water**. in trouble: *Talking back to the teacher got me in hot water.*

• **like water**. very freely; abundantly: *Compliments flowed like water.*

• **of the first water**. of the highest quality: *a writer of the first water.*

• **to hold water**. to be logical, consistent, or sound: *The lawyer's argument just doesn't hold water.*

• **to throw cold water on**. to discourage or forbid: *to throw cold water on a scheme.*

water bed, a bed consisting of a mattress made of very heavy plastic filled with water that is often heated, set in a frame.

water beetle, any of several beetles, such as the whirligig beetle, adapted for swimming on the surface of the water.

water bird, any bird living on or near the water; swimming or wading bird.

water boatman, any of a group of bugs, family Corixidae, with long, oarlike middle and hind legs flattened for swimming. They feed on decaying plant and animal matter from the bottom of fresh and brackish bodies of water. Length: about ½ inch (1 centimeter).

wa·ter·borne (wô′tər bôrn′, wot′ər-) *adj.* **1.** supported or conveyed on or by water; floating: *waterborne flowers drifting in a pond.* **2.** carried by ship or by boat.

wa·ter·buck (wô′tər buk′, wot′ər-) *n.* any of several antelopes, genus *Kobus,* native to southeastern Africa, that frequent rivers or marshes, having a coat of long, coarse hair that may range from yellowish brown to nearly black. Height: 4 feet (1.2 meters) at the shoulder. [Dutch *waterbok.*]

water buffalo, a black buffalo of Africa and Asia, *Bubalus bubalis,* having long horns that curve backward, widely domesticated for its hide and milk and often used as a beast of burden. Height: to 6 feet (1.8 meters) at the shoulder.

water buffalo

water bug 1. any of various air-sucking insects that live on or below the surface of streams and ponds, such as the water scorpion. **2.** any of several large cockroaches, esp. *Periplaneta americana,* often found in or near sinks, drains, and other damp places.

water chestnut 1. the edible fruit or corm of any of various aquatic plants, esp. the corm of *Eleocharis dulcis,* the **Chinese water chestnut,** which is widely used in Oriental cooking. **2.** the plant itself.

water clock, a device for measuring time by the flow of water from a small opening in a calibrated vessel. Also, **clepsydra.**

water closet, toilet *(defs. 1, 2).*

wa·ter·col·or (wô′tər kul′ər, wot′ər-) **1.** a paint made by mixing pigment with water. **2.** the art or technique of painting with watercolors. **3.** a picture or design made with watercolors. —*adj.* of, relating to, or made with watercolors. —**wa′ter·col′or·ist,** *n.*

wa·ter·cool (wô′tər kül′, wot′ər-) *v.t.* to cool with circulating water, as an engine.

water cooler, a device for cooling and dispensing water, often operated by electricity.

wa·ter·course (wô′tər kôrs′, wot′ər-) *n.* **1.** any stream of flowing water, such as a river or brook. **2.** a natural or artificial channel for conveyance of or by water, such as a riverbed or canal.

wa·ter·craft (wô′tər kraft′, wot′ər-) *n.* **1.** skill in sailing boats or in performing water sports. **2.** a boat or ship. **3.** water vessels collectively.

wa·ter·cress (wô′tər kres′, wot′ər-) *n.* a trailing or floating plant, *Nasturtium officinale,* whose pungent leaves are used as salad greens or as a garnish, bearing long clusters of small, white flowers.

water cure, hydrotherapy.

water cycle, hydrologic cycle.

water dog, mud puppy.

wa·ter·fall (wô′tər fôl′, wot′ər-) *n.* a perpendicular flow of water, usually falling from a high place over a ledge.

water flea, a very small freshwater crustacean, genus *Daphnia,* that swims with a jerky, skipping motion.

wa·ter·fowl (wô′tər foul′, wot′ər-) *n., pl.* **-fowl** or **-fowls.** a water bird, esp. a swimming game bird, such as a duck or goose.

wa·ter·front (wô′tər frunt′, wot′ər-) *n.* **1.** that section of an urban or industrial area that is located beside the harbor on a river, lake, or ocean, usually having docks and shipping facilities. **2.** land or real estate along a lake, river, or the like.

water gap, a gorge or valley in a mountain ridge through which a stream flows.

water gas, a toxic, combustible mixture of gases, mainly carbon monoxide and hydrogen, widely used for heating. It is manufactured by passing steam over very hot coal or coke.

water gate 1. a gateway through which water passes or by which access is gained to a body of water. **2.** floodgate *(def. 1).*

water glass 1. a drinking glass used to hold water or other liquids. **2.** a blue-green, glassy compound used in powdered form as an adhesive, abrasive, and pigment. Formula: Na_2SiO_3 Also *(def. 2),* **sodium silicate, soluble glass.**

water gun, a toy pistol that emits a stream of water. Also, **water pistol.**

water hole, a hole or depression in the ground in which water collects, such as a pond or pool.

water hyacinth, an aquatic plant, *Eichhornia crassipes,* related to pickerelweed, bearing showy violet-blue flowers and swollen petioles. It clogs waterways and hinders the passage of boats in warm regions.

water ice 1. a frozen dessert made of sugar, water, and flavoring, esp. fruit flavoring. **2.** ice formed by the direct freezing of water, rather than by the compacting of snow.

watering can, a container used for sprinkling water on plants or the like, often having a long spout with a perforated head. Also, **watering pot.**

watering place 1. a place where water may be obtained, as for drinking, watering cattle, or supplying ships. **2.** a resort with mineral springs, often offering boating and other water sports.

water jacket, a casing containing water, placed about something to keep it cool or to regulate its temperature.

water level, the level of the surface of any calm body of water.

water lily, any of a large group of aquatic plants, genus *Nymphaea,* growing in freshwater ponds and lakes throughout temperate and tropical regions. The roots are embedded in the mud, and the leaves and showy flowers float on or stand just above the surface of the water.

water line 1. the line where the surface of the water touches the hull of a boat or ship. **2.** one of several stripes painted on a ship's hull to show how deeply it should be submerged when it is loaded or unloaded.

wa·ter·logged (wô′tər lôgd′, -logd′, wot′ər-) *adj.* **1.** (of a sailing vessel) so full of water as to lose buoyancy and become heavy and unmanageable. **2.** thoroughly saturated with or as with water.

Wa·ter·loo (wô′tər lü′, wot′ər-, wô′tər lü′, wot′ər-) *n.* any crushing or final defeat: *Our team met its Waterloo in the semifinals.* [From *Waterloo,* Belgian village where Napoleon was finally defeated.]

water main, a principal pipe or pipeline used for supplying water to a particular area.

wa·ter·man (wô′tər mən, wot′ər-) *n., pl.* **-men** (-mən). a person who works on or with boats.

wa·ter·mark (wô′tər märk′, wot′ər-) *n.* **1.** a line or mark indicating how high the water of a river, lake, or tide has risen. **2.** a distinctive mark or design impressed on certain kinds of paper, such as stationery, and visible when the paper is held up to a light. —*v.t.* **1.** to impress (paper) with a watermark. **2.** to impress (a distinctive mark or design) as a watermark.

wa·ter·mel·on (wô′tər mel′ən, wot′ər-) *n.* **1.** the large, juicy fruit of a plant, *Citrullus vulgaris,* having a thick, green rind and watery pulp that is pink, red, yellow, or white. **2.** the vine bearing this fruit, having long, hairy stems and large, oval leaves that are divided into a number of lobes and bearing funnel-shaped, yellow flowers.

water mill, a mill or machine whose source of power is water or a waterwheel.

water moccasin, a pit viper, *Agkistrodon piscivorus,* found in swamps and other wet, lowland regions of the southeastern United States, having an olive or black body marked with faint crossbars.

When alarmed, it shows the inside of its white mouth. Length: 3-6 feet (0.9-1.8 meters). Also, **cottonmouth.**

water nymph, in classical mythology, a nymph living in a fountain, brook, stream, or other body of water.

water of crystallization, water combined in crystals with another compound so that the water molecules remain intact and can be driven off by heating, with loss of crystalline structure and alteration of the physical but not the chemical properties of the other compound.

water ouzel *also,* **water ousel.** any of various diving birds, genus *Cinclus,* resembling a thrush, with a stocky body, a short tail, and a thin, sharp bill, which is used to capture insects and larvae from the beds of fast-moving streams. Length: 7 inches (18 centimeters). Also, **dipper.**

water plantain, any of various aquatic plants, genus *Alisma,* having heart-shaped leaves and bearing branching clusters of small, white or pink flowers.

water polo, a water sport played with a soccerlike ball by two teams of seven swimmers each, the object being to throw or push the ball through the opponent's goal.

water power, power generated by the rush of moving water.

wa·ter·proof (wô′tər prüf′, wot′ər-) *adj.* able to prevent the penetration or passage of water, esp. having been treated or coated with a substance that prevents water from entering. —*n.* **1.** a waterproof material. **2.** *British.* raincoat. —*v.t.* to make waterproof: *to waterproof boots.*

water rat 1. any of various aquatic rodents that live on the banks of streams or lakes. **2.** muskrat.

wa·ter·re·pel·lent (wô′tər ri pel′ənt, wot′ər-) *adj.* having a surface or finish that repels water but is not completely waterproof.

water scorpion, any of a group of bugs, family Nepidae, that live underwater, breathing through a long posterior tube, and can deliver a painful bite.

wa·ter·shed (wô′tər shed′, wot′ər-) *n.* **1.** a ridge or other elevated land area separating two different river basins. **2.** the total land area from which water drains into a single stream, river, or lake, serving as water-storage area for the surrounding countryside; drainage basin. **3.** a crucial factor, event, or time; turning point: *The judge's decision marked a watershed in legal history.*

wa·ter·side (wô′tər sīd′, wot′ər-) *n.* land next to or running along a body of water.

wa·ter·ski (wô′tər skē′, wot′ər-) *v.i.,* -skied, -ski·ing. to glide over the surface of water on water skis while being pulled by a towline attached to a boat. —**wa′ter·ski′er,** *n.* —**wa′ter·ski′-ing,** *n.*

water ski, one of a pair of wooden or fiberglass skis wider and shorter than snow skis, used in water-skiing.

water snake, any of various nonpoisonous snakes living in or commonly found in fresh water, esp. those of the genus *Natrix,* found in North America.

wa·ter·soak (wô′tər sōk′, wot′ər-) *v.t.* to fill or saturate thoroughly with water.

water softener 1. a chemical added to water to reduce its hardness by causing calcium and magnesium ions to precipitate from solution. **2.** an apparatus that softens water by means of such chemicals.

wa·ter·sol·u·ble (wô′tər sol′yə bəl, wot′ər-) *adj.* capable of being dissolved in water, as is vitamin C.

water spaniel, a curly-haired hunting dog having a solid, liver-colored coat. There are two breeds, the **American water spaniel,** which stands 17 inches (43 centimeters) at the shoulder and is used to hunt small game, and the **Irish water spaniel,** which stands 23 inches (58 centimeters) at the shoulder and is used to hunt and retrieve ducks.

wa·ter·spout (wô′tər spout′, wot′ər-) *n.* **1.** a pipe, opening, or other conduit that carries away unneeded water, esp. one that extends from the roof down the side of a building for the disposing of rainwater. **2.** the nozzle end of a pipe running from a vessel or fixture, such as a jug or sink, from which water pours when the pipe is opened. **3.** a tornado or whirlwind at sea or on a lake, appearing as a long, dark funnel extending from the clouds down toward the surface of the water.

water sprite, a sprite, nymph, or spirit inhabiting an ocean, pool, or stream.

water strider, any member of the family Gerridae of slender, long-legged, insect-eating bugs that glide or jump about on the surface film of fresh or salt water. The adult is usually wingless. Length: 1/2-1 inch (1-2.5 centimeters).

water table, the upper surface of an underground zone in which the soil or rock is completely saturated with water. The water table

rises and falls with seasonal changes.

wa·ter·tight (wô′tər-tīt′, wot′ər-) *adj.* **1.** so closely constructed or fitted as to prevent the passage of water in or out. **2.** so planned or worded as to be free from error or ambiguity and impossible to challenge or evade: *a watertight strategy, a watertight argument.* —**wa′ter·tight′ness,** *n.*

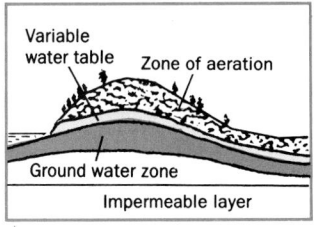

water table

water tower 1. a very large tower used to store a water supply, as to maintain equalized water pressure in a commercial building. **2.** firefighting apparatus for directing a stream of water on the upper stories of tall buildings.

water vapor, water in its gaseous state, but below the boiling point, esp. as dispersed in the atmosphere in fog or clouds.

wa·ter·way (wô′tər wā′, wot′ər-) *n.* **1.** a water route for the passage of ships. **2.** a channel for the passage of water.

wa·ter·wheel (wô′tər hwēl′, -wēl′, wot′ər-) *n.* a wheel turned by the weight or pressure of water falling on it or flowing under it, used to provide power for operating machinery.

water wings, a waterproof device filled with air, worn under the arms to keep the body afloat while learning to swim.

wa·ter·works (wô′tər wûrks′, wot′ər-) *n.* **1.** an entire system for the collection, storage, purification, and distribution of water, including reservoirs, buildings, machinery, pipes, and the like. **2.** a building in such a system, housing the machinery for pumping water. **3.** *Slang.* a profusion of tears. ➡ used as singular or plural in all defs.

wa·ter·worn (wô′tər wôrn′, wot′ər-) *adj.* worn or smoothed by the constant action of running water: *waterworn rocks.*

wa·ter·y (wô′tə rē, wot′ə-) *adj.* **1.** of, relating to, or consisting of water: *the watery depths of the ocean.* **2.** abounding in or saturated with water: *watery soil.* **3.** suffused with tears; tearful: *The head cold made my eyes watery.* **4.** containing too much water: *a watery gravy, watery paint.* **5.** resembling water in appearance or characteristics. **6.** pale, as if diluted by water; weak: *watery colors.*

Wat·son-Crick model (wot′sən krik′) a model of the structural arrangement of the DNA molecule, as represented by the double helix, in which two strands of nucleotides are connected and stabilized by cross-links of purine and pyrimidine bases. [From James D. *Watson,* born 1928, American biochemist, and Francis H. C. *Crick,* born 1916, British biophysicist, who in the 1950s worked out this model.]

watt (wot) *n.* the meter-kilogram-second and International System unit of electric or mechanical power, equal to a rate of 1 joule of work per second. [From James *Watt,* 1736-1819, Scottish engineer and inventor.]

watt·age (wot′ij) *n.* **1.** power, esp. electric power, expressed in watts. **2.** the number of watts of electric power needed to run an appliance.

watt-hour (wot′our′) *n.* a unit of electrical energy, equal to the work done by 1 watt acting for 1 hour, or 3,600 joules.

wat·tle (wot′əl) *n.* **1.** a framework or interlaced structure made of poles, branches, twigs, or the like woven together, used esp. in building walls, fences, or roofs. **2.** the material used to make such a framework or structure. **3. wattles.** the poles used to form the framework of a thatched roof. **4.** any of various acacias of Australia that were formerly used to make wattles, the bark of which is now used in tanning. **5.** the fleshy, often brightly colored, fold of skin hanging down from the neck or throat of certain fowl and other animals. —*v.t.,* -tled, -tling. **1.** to construct (something) by interlacing twigs, branches, or the like: *to wattle a roof for a grass hut.* **2.** to form into a network by weaving or interlacing: *to wattle branches to form a roof.* **3.** to bind together with interlaced twigs, branches, or the like. [Old English *watel* interwoven twigs.] —**wat′tled,** *adj.*

watt·me·ter (wot′mē′tər) *n.* any of various instruments used to measure electric power that indicate average power in watts on a graduated scale.

wave (wāv) *v.,* waved, wav·ing. —*v.i.* **1.** to sway freely back

a	at	e	end	o	hot	u	up	hw	white		about
ā	ape	ē	me	ō	old	ū	use	ng	song		taken
ä	far	i	it	ô	fork	ü	rule	th	thin	ə	pencil
âr	care	ī	ice	oi	oil	u̇	pull	th	this		lemon
		îr	pierce	ou	out	ûr	turn	zh	measure		circus

and forth or up and down; move with an undulating motion: *The banner waved in the breeze. The tall grass waved as the wind swept across the field.* **2.** to curve alternately in opposite directions: *hair that waves when brushed.* **3.** to gesture by moving the hand or arm up and down, as in greeting or farewell. —*v.t.* **1.** to cause to move back and forth or up and down: *to wave a flag.* **2.** to signal, indicate, or express by waving something: *to wave good-bye.* **3.** to give a curving or undulating form, appearance, or pattern to: *to wave hair.* —*n.* **1.** a moving or rippling ridge or swell on the surface of a body of water or other liquid. Ocean waves are generated by the wind, tides, and currents. **2.** anything resembling this in movement or shape: *There were waves in the wallpaper where the glue didn't stick properly.* **3.** the act of waving, esp. with the hand or something held in the hand: *a wave of a magician's wand.* **4.** a sudden rush or increase of anything, marked by unusual volume, intensity, or extent: *a heat wave, a wave of hysteria.* **5.** one of a series, such as a group of people, animals, events, or the like, occurring or advancing together: *The first wave of tourists arrived in June.* **6.** a curve or series of curves, as in the hair. **7.** *Physics.* a vibration or disturbance traveling through a solid, liquid, or gaseous medium without any net displacement of that medium, as sound travels through air and water or the energy released by an earthquake travels through the earth. **8.** *also,* **waves.** a body of water, esp. the sea: *to sail the waves between Lisbon and Brazil.* [Old English *wafian* to make a movement back and forth with the hands.] —**wave′like′,** *adj.* —**wav′er,** *n.*
 • **to make waves.** *Informal.* to upset existing conditions; make trouble: *The new employee made waves by criticizing the way things were done at the company.*

Wave (wāv) *n.* a member of the WAVES.

wave band, wave band[2] *(def. 4).*

wave·form (wāv′fôrm′) *Physics.* the shape of a wave, esp. as illustrated graphically.

wave·length (wāv′lengkth′, -length′, -lenth′) *n. Physics.* the distance between any two corresponding points of a wave, such as the distance between successive wave peaks.
 • **on the same wavelength.** *Informal.* having mutual rapport or understanding: *As soon as we smiled at each other, I knew we were on the same wavelength.*

wave·let (wāv′lit) *n.* a small wave; ripple.

wa·ver (wā′vər) *v.i.* **1.** to move unsteadily up and down or from side to side; sway; totter: *The ladder wavered and fell over.* **2.** to shine with an unsteady light; flicker: *Light from the candle wavered in the breeze.* **3.** to exhibit doubt or indecision; be uncertain: *to waver between two choices.* **4.** to become unsteady; falter: *Their resolve to see the project completed never wavered.* **5.** to shake slightly; quiver; tremble: *The speaker's voice wavered.* —*n.* the act or an instance of wavering. [Possibly from Old Norse *vafra* to flicker, move unsteadily.] —**wa′ver·er,** *n.* —**wa′ver·ing·ly,** *adv.* —For Synonyms, see **hesitate.**

WAVES (wāvz) Women's Reserve of the U.S. Navy. [Short for *W(omen) A(ppointed for) V(olunteer) E(mergency) S(ervice).*]

wav·y (wā′vē) *adj.,* **wav·i·er, wav·i·est. 1.** full of or having waves: *wavy seas.* **2.** undulating or curving in shape: *wavy hair, a wavy line.* **3.** like or suggestive of waves: *fabric with a wavy design.* **4.** moving with a wavelike motion. —**wav′i·ness,** *n.*

wax[1] (waks) *n.* **1.a.** any of various substances of animal or vegetable origin that consist of the esters of fatty acids and fatty alcohols, such as beeswax or earwax. **b.** any of various solid hydrocarbons of mineral origin that resemble this, such as paraffin. **2.** sealing wax. —*v.t.* to cover, treat, or polish with wax: *to wax floors.* —*adj.* made of or resembling wax. [Old English *weax* beeswax.] —**wax′like′,** *adj.*

wax[2] (waks) *v.i.,* **waxed, waxed** or *(archaic)* **wax·en, wax·ing. 1.** to increase gradually, as in size, strength, or brightness: *The moon waxes and wanes.* **2.** to become something specified: *The farmer waxed eloquent about the beauty of the countryside.* [Old English *weaxan* to grow, increase.]

wax bean 1. a yellow string bean with a waxy appearance. **2.** a plant bearing these beans.

wax·ber·ry (waks′ber′ē, -bə rē) *n., pl.* **-ries. 1.** wax myrtle. **2.** snowberry.

waxed paper, wax paper.

wax·en (wak′sən) *adj.* **1.** made of, created by, covered, or treated with wax: *a deep waxen shine on a table.* **2.** resembling wax, as in consistency or appearance. **3.** pale; wan: *a waxen complexion.*

wax myrtle, any of various tall shrubs or trees, genus *Myrica,* having fragrant, lance-shaped leaves and small grayish berries coated with a white wax that is used in making candles and soap. Also, **waxberry.**

wax paper *also,* **waxed paper.** a paper that is coated with paraffin to keep out moisture, used as a protective wrapping.

wax·wing (waks′wing′) *n.* any of several crested songbirds, genus *Bombycilla,* such as the cedar waxwing, having a short, thick bill and predominantly brown or gray plumage with black, yellow, white, and red markings and a waxy, red substance on some of its feathers. Length: 6-8 inches (15-20 centimeters).

wax·work (waks′wûrk′) *n.* **1.** something made of wax, esp. an ornament or a human figure. **2.** **waxworks.** an exhibition or place for displaying wax figures representing famous or notorious persons.
 ➡ used as singular or plural in def. 1.

wax·y (wak′sē) *adj.,* **wax·i·er, wax·i·est. 1.** resembling wax, as in consistency or appearance. **2.** made of, covered, or treated with wax. —**wax′i·ness,** *n.*

way (wā) *n.* **1.** a course of action, method, or manner to be followed in order to do or attain something: *the right*

waxwing

way to fix an appliance, a good way to make friends, a new way of looking at an old problem. **2.** *also,* **ways.** a personal, customary, or usual style or manner: *That's only his way. She has very endearing ways.* **3.** a typical or characteristic style, manner, or tradition: *Their way of life does not appeal to me.* **4.** something that a person desires to have or do; wish: *You can't always have your way.* **5.** a road, path, or the like leading from one place to another: *The fallen limb blocked the way. That road is the quickest way to town.* **6.** a line or course along which something moves; direction, as of motion: *The hurricane is heading this way.* **7.** movement along such a line or course: *John saw her on his way back to school.* **8.** distance: *They walked a long way before finding the house.* **9.** the range or scope of one's experience or notice. **10.** the path or course that a person follows in life: *The way of transgressors is hard* (Proverbs 13:15). **11.** a particular detail; respect: *In many ways, the plan might succeed.* **12.** *Informal.* a condition or state: *to be in a bad way financially.* **13.** **ways.** timbers on which a ship is launched. —*adv.* **1.** at a distance; far: *clouds floating way up in the sky.* **2.** to a great degree or point: *During high tide the water came way up on the beach.* [Old English *weg* road, path, course of movement, course of action, manner.]
 • **by the way.** with regard to that; incidentally.
 • **by way of. a.** by a route passing through or by; via: *We're going to Florida by way of North Carolina.* **b.** as a means or method of: *to send a note by way of an apology.*
 • **in a way.** to some extent, but not completely.
 • **in the way.** in such a position or of such a nature as to obstruct or impede.
 • **in the worst way.** very much: *I want to see them again in the worst way.*
 • **out of the way. a.** so as not to obstruct or hinder. **b.** in a remote or inconvenient place. **c.** extraordinary; unusual. **d.** improper; wrong.
 • **to give way. a.** to move aside or back: *The crowd gave way to let the cars through.* **b.** to break down or collapse: *The bridge gave way under the heavy load.*
 • **to give way to. a.** to be replaced or succeeded by: *Gas lighting gave way to electricity.* **b.** to abandon oneself to: *to give way to anger.*
 • **to go out of the** (or **one's**) **way.** to do something special or unrequested: *They went out of their way to help us.*
 • **to have a way with.** to have an effective or impressive manner in dealing with: *My friend has a way with dogs. That singer has a way with ballads.*
 • **to make one's way. a.** to proceed; go. **b.** to advance successfully toward one's goal.
 • **to make way.** to open a passage or entrance.
 • **under way.** in progress; in motion.

way·bill (wā′bil′) *n.* a list of goods being shipped with instructions as to destination and mode of travel. [WAY + BILL[1].]

way·far·er (wā′fâr′ər) *n.* a traveler, esp. a person who travels on foot.

way·far·ing (wā′fâr′ing) *adj.* traveling, esp. on foot.

way·lay (wā′lā′, wā′lā′) *v.t.,* **-laid** (-lād′, -lād′), **-lay·ing. 1.** to lie in wait for in order to seize or attack: *The thieves waylaid the hiker by the bridge.* **2.** to wait for and accost (a person): *The*

police chief was waylaid by reporters asking about the crime. [WAY + LAY[1], after Middle Low German *wegelāgen* to lie in wait.] —**way′lay′er,** *n.*

-ways *suffix* used to form adverbs denoting direction, position, or manner: *sideways.* [Middle English *wayes,* genitive of WAY.]

ways and means 1. procedures or methods for raising funds to meet government expenses. **2.** methods and resources that a person, company, or the like uses to meet expenses.

way·side (wā′sīd′) *n.* the land bordering a road or path: *Wildflowers grew by the wayside.* —*adj.* of, relating to, or located beside a road or path: *a wayside inn.*
  ·**to go by the wayside.** to be postponed or put aside: *Our proposal went by the wayside.*

way station, a small station intermediate between principal stations, as on a railroad.

way·ward (wā′wərd) *adj.* **1.** refusing to do what is requested, suggested, or right; wrongheaded and disobedient: *a wayward child.* **2.** conforming to no fixed principle or pattern; irregular; erratic. [Middle English *wayward,* short for *awayward* turned away, from AWAY + -WARD.] —**way′ward·ly,** *adv.* —**way′ward·ness,** *n.*

way·worn (wā′wôrn′) *adj.* wearied or worn by traveling.

we (wē) *pl. pron.* nominative, **we;** possessive, **our, ours;** objective, **us. 1.** the persons who are speaking or writing: *We are glad to meet you.* **2.** a single person who is speaking or writing grandly or authoritatively, such as an author, sovereign, or judge. [Old English *wē.*]

weak (wēk) *adj.* **1.** liable to fall, fail, or collapse under strain; lacking strength or endurance: *The legs of the chair are weak. The weak bridge swayed under the weight of the trucks.* **2.** lacking muscular power: *weak arms.* **3.** lacking vigor or robustness, as from age, illness, or fatigue: *The invalid is too weak to sit up.* **4.** lacking in ability, power, or authority: *Their team was weaker than ours.* **5.** unsupported by truth, facts, or reason; unconvincing: *The lawyer presented a weak defense.* **6.** deficient in mental ability or discernment: *a weak mind.* **7.** deficient in moral strength or firmness; lacking fortitude or character. **8.** lacking in force; having little or no effect: *The government employed measures too weak to quell the disturbance. The candidate took a weak stand on the issue.* **9.** lacking in intensity or power; faint: *The light was too weak to read by.* **10.** lacking the full or usual amount of the proper or essential ingredients: *weak tea.* **11.** deficient or poor in a specified area: *I am weak in science.* **12.** *Phonetics.* (of a syllable) not stressed or accented. **13.** *Grammar.* (of a verb) forming the past tense and past participle by the addition of a suffix containing a consonant or consonants to the stem, not by the change of a vowel, as in *bake, baked, play, played,* or *occur, occurred.* [Old Norse *veikr* pliant, feeble.]

weak·en (wē′kən) *v.t., v.i.* to make or become weak or weaker: *I weakened the tea by adding water. The runner weakened near the finish line.*

weak·fish (wēk′fish′) *n., pl.* **-fish** or **-fish·es.** any of several saltwater food fish, genus *Cynoscion,* esp. *C. regalis,* found in the coastal waters of eastern North America. [Obsolete Dutch *weekvis,* from *week* soft, weak + *vis* fish; probably referring to its soft and tender flesh.]

weak force *Nuclear Physics.* the force that governs interactions of leptons with other subatomic particles, responsible for the emission of beta rays from radioactive atomic nuclei. Also, **weak interaction.**

weak-kneed (wēk′nēd′) *adj.* **1.** having weak knees. **2.** lacking in resolution or determination; yielding easily to intimidation; spineless.

weak·ling (wēk′ling) *n.* a person who is physically, mentally, or morally weak. —*adj.* weak; feeble. [WEAK + -LING[1].]

weak·ly (wēk′lē) *adv.* in a weak manner. —*adj.,* **-li·er, -li·est.** not healthy or strong; weak; feeble. —**weak′li·ness,** *n.*

weak-mind·ed (wēk′mīn′did) *adj.* **1.** having or showing a lack of moral strength or purpose; irresolute. **2.** feeble-minded. —**weak′mind′ed·ness,** *n.*

weak·ness (wēk′nis) *n.* **1.** the state or quality of being weak, as in moral or physical strength. **2.** an instance of this; weak point. **3.** a self-indulgent fondness or liking for something: *I have a weakness for ice cream.* **4.** something for which one has such a partiality or liking: *Pretty shoes are my weakness.* —For Synonyms, see **fault.**

weal[1] (wēl) *n.* well-being, happiness, or prosperity: *a law passed for the common weal.* [Old English *wela.*]

weal[2] (wēl) *n.* a ridge or bump on the skin, as made by a whip or stick; welt. [Form of WALE; influenced by WHEAL.]

wealth (welth) *n.* **1.a.** a great abundance of money or valuable possessions; riches. **b.** the state of having an abundance of money or valuable possessions; affluence. **2.** all things having monetary value: *a country with little wealth.* **3.** a great quantity of anything;

profusion; abundance: *a wealth of ideas, a wealth of information.* [From WEAL[1] or WELL[1].]

wealth·y (wel′thē) *adj.,* **wealth·i·er, wealth·i·est.** having wealth; rich. —**wealth′i·ly,** *adv.* —**wealth′i·ness,** *n.*

wean (wēn) *v.t.* **1.** to accustom (a child or young mammal) to food other than the mother's milk. **2.** to remove (a person) gradually from some accustomed or favored habit, practice, or pursuit: *to be weaned from biting one's nails.* **3.** to be accustomed to from childhood (with *on*): *to be weaned on gourmet food.* [Old English *wenian* to accustom, to accustom to being without the mother's milk.]

weap·on (wep′ən) *n.* **1.** anything used in combat to attack or defend, such as a gun or knife. **2.** any means used to gain success in a contest or struggle: *The lawyer used every legal weapon available to win the case.* [Old English *wæpn.*]

weap·on·ry (wep′ən rē) *n.* weapons collectively; arms.

wear (wâr) *v.,* **wore, worn, wear·ing.** —*v.t.* **1.** to carry or bear on the body as a covering or ornament: *to wear clothes, to wear a bracelet.* **2.** to have or show as part of one's appearance or manner: *to wear a frown.* **3.** to damage, erode, or impair, as by repeated use, rubbing, or scraping: *The crashing waves have worn the rocks.* **4.** to cause or produce, as by repeated use, rubbing, or scraping: *to wear a hole in a carpet.* **5.** to bring to a specified state or condition: *to wear a suit to rags.* **6.** to have on the body or a part of the body habitually: *to wear glasses, to wear a gun.* **7.** to cause to lose strength; exhaust; weary. **8.** to pass (time), esp. in a slow or tedious manner (often with *away*): *We wore the day away cleaning the attic.* —*v.i.* **1.** to last or hold out: *The fabric did not wear well.* **2.** to deteriorate or become damaged through use or age: *These shoes have started to wear.* **3.** to arrive at a specified state or condition: *My patience is wearing thin.* **4.** (of time) to pass or advance, esp. slowly or tediously: *The hour wore on.* —*n.* **1.** the act of wearing or the state of being worn. **2.** an article or articles of clothing: *children's wear.* **3.** damage caused by use or age: *This rug shows signs of wear.* **4.** the capacity for being worn; lasting quality; durability: *There are years of wear left in this sweater.* [Old English *werian* to carry, have on.] —**wear′a·ble,** *adj.* —**wear′er,** *n.*
  ·**to wear down. a.** to overcome gradually by continuous effort: *to wear down someone's resistance.* **b.** to erode or damage by wear: *Heavy driving wore down the tread of the tires.* **c.** to cause to become weary; exhaust: *The constant tension wore me down.*
  ·**to wear off.** to become less gradually: *The effects of the aspirin wore off after several hours.*
  ·**to wear out. a.** to use until no longer fit or able to be used: *to wear out a pair of shoes, to wear out a battery.* **b.** to tire or exhaust: *The hike wore us out.*

wear and tear, deterioration or damage undergone through use or passage of time.

wear·ing (wâr′ing) *adj.* **1.** of, relating to, or made for wear: *Coats and suits are wearing apparel.* **2.** exhausting; tiring: *a wearing experience.*

wea·ri·some (wîr′ē səm) *adj.* causing weariness; tiresome; tedious: *The movie was long and wearisome.* —**wea′ri·some·ly,** *adv.* —**wea′ri·some·ness,** *n.*

wea·ry (wîr′ē) *adj.,* **-ri·er, -ri·est. 1.** extremely tired, as from mental or physical labor; fatigued; exhausted: *We were weary after a day's work.* **2.** causing or characterized by fatigue; tedious; tiring: *a weary journey.* **3.** having one's interest, patience, liking, or tolerance exhausted (with *of*): *to grow weary of cold weather.* —*v.,* **-ried, -ry·ing.** —*v.t.* to exhaust the strength or endurance of; make weary; fatigue: *The trip wearied us.* —*v.i.* to become weary: *The child wearied quickly.* [Old English *wērig* tired.] —**wea′ri·ly,** *adv.* —**wea′ri·ness,** *n.*

wea·sand (wē′zənd) *n.* the gullet; throat. [Old English *wāsend* gullet.]

wea·sel (wē′zəl) *n., pl.* **-sels** or **-sel. 1.** any of various small carnivorous mammals, genus *Mustela,* having a slender body, short legs, a long neck, a long, usually black-tipped tail, and a soft, thick, yellowish to dark brown coat

weasel

a	at	e	end	o	hot	u	up	hw	white		about
ā	ape	ē	me	ō	old	ū	use	ng	song		taken
ä	far	i	it	ô	fork	ü	rule	th	thin	ə	pencil
âr	care	ī	ice	oi	oil	u̇	pull	th	this		lemon
		îr	pierce	ou	out	ûr	turn	zh	measure		circus

covered with long, shiny outer hairs. In cold climates its coat usually turns white in the winter. Length: 6-31 inches (15-79 centimeters), including tail. **2.** a sneaky or dishonest person. —*v.i. Informal.* to be underhanded or evasive. [Old English *wesule.*]
· **to weasel out.** to evade or renege on a duty, responsibility, or obligation: *to weasel out of washing dishes.*

weath·er (we<u>th</u>′ər) *n.* **1.** the condition of the atmosphere with regard to temperature, air pressure, winds, clouds, humidity, and the like, at a given time and place. **2.** adverse or unpleasant atmospheric conditions: *We encountered much weather on the flight back.* **3.** a weather forecast: *What's the weather for tomorrow?* —*v.t.* **1.** to expose to the weather, esp. in order to dry, bleach, or condition: *to weather lumber.* **2.** to bear up against or overcome; come safely through: *to weather a storm, to weather a crisis.* **3.** to pass or sail to the windward of. —*v.i.* **1.** to become changed through exposure to the weather: *The cedar shingles weathered to a soft gray.* **2.** to resist or endure exposure to the weather: *Leather will weather better than wool or cotton.* —*adj.* windward. [Old English *weder* atmospheric condition, wind¹, storm.]
· **under the weather.** *Informal.* not feeling well; ailing.

weath·er·beat·en (we<u>th</u>′ər bē′tən) *adj.* **1.** marred, worn, or badly damaged by exposure to the weather: *a weather-beaten old barn.* **2.** seasoned or hardened by exposure to the weather: *The old sailor had a weather-beaten face.*

weath·er·board (we<u>th</u>′ər bôrd′) *n.* clapboard.

weath·er·bound (we<u>th</u>′ər bound′) *adj.* delayed or forced to remain indoors because of bad weather: *a weather-bound airplane.*

Weather Bureau, see National Weather Service.

weath·er·cock (we<u>th</u>′ər kok′) *n.* **1.** a weather vane having the shape of a rooster. **2.** a person or thing liable to change quickly.

weath·er·glass (we<u>th</u>′ər glas′) *n.* any of various instruments used to indicate or forecast the weather, such as a barometer.

weath·er·ing (we<u>th</u>′ər ing) *n.* the action of the chemical and mechanical processes that reduce rock exposed to the weather to soil.

weath·er·ize (we<u>th</u>′ə rīz′) *v.t.,* **-ized, -iz·ing.** to insulate or protect (a building or part of a building) against adverse weather, esp. cold or stormy conditions. —**weath′er·i·za′tion,** *n.*

weath·er·man (we<u>th</u>′ər man′) *n., pl.* **-men** (-men′). **1.** a person who studies atmospheric conditions in order to report and forecast the weather; meteorologist. **2.** a person who reports the weather and weather forecast, as on television.

weather map, a map showing meteorological conditions at a given time, usually over an extensive region.

weath·er·proof (we<u>th</u>′ər prüf′) *adj.* capable of withstanding the destructive forces of the weather. —*v.t.* to make weatherproof.

weather ship, a ship used in gathering meteorological information.

weather station, a station where meteorological observations are made and recorded.

weath·er·strip (we<u>th</u>′ər strip′) *v.t.,* **-stripped, -strip·ping.** to fit or secure with weather stripping.

weather stripping 1. a narrow strip of metal, felt, or other material, applied to openings, as of a door or window, to keep out the wind and cold. Also, **weather strip. 2.** such strips collectively.

weather vane, a device that is moved by the wind and indicates the direction in which the wind is blowing.

weath·er·wise (we<u>th</u>′ər wīz′) *adj.* **1.** skillful in predicting the weather. **2.** skillful in predicting changes in public opinion or sentiment.

weave (wēv) *v.,* **wove** or **weaved, wo·ven** or **wove, weaving.** —*v.t.* **1.** to lace together (threads, yarn, or strips): *to weave yarn into cloth.* **2.** to form or make by lacing together threads, yarn, or strips of straw or other material: *to weave a basket, to weave cloth.* **3.** to spin (a web or cocoon). **4.** to unite into a connected whole: *The composer wove the melodies into a single composition.* **5.** to make or move by turning and twisting: *to weave one's way through a crowd, to weave a shopping cart through the aisles of a store.* **6.** to make or create by combining different things or parts: *to weave stories from one's experiences.* —*v.i.* **1.** to form or make something by weaving. **2.** to move by turning and twisting: *to weave through a crowd.* —*n.* a particular method or pattern of weaving: *an open weave.* [Old English *wefan* to make a fabric by interlacing threads.]

weav·er (wē′vər) *n.* **1.** a person who weaves or whose occupation is weaving. **2.** weaver finch.

weaver finch, any of a large number of songbirds, family Ploceidae, native to Africa, Europe, and Asia, some of which weave large, communal nests of grasses and straw. Also, **weaver, weav·er·bird** (wē′vər bûrd′).

web (web) *n.* **1.** something woven, esp. a whole piece of cloth in

the process of being woven or just removed from a loom. **2.** a network of fine threads spun by a spider; cobweb. **3.** any complex structure or network: *a web of streets, a web of lies.* **4.** any membranous or connective tissue, esp. the toes of a swimming bird. **5.** vane *(def. 3).* **6.** a large, continuous roll of paper used to feed a rotary press. —*v.t.,* **webbed, web·bing. 1.** to provide or cover with a web. **2.** to catch in or as in a web. [Old English *webb* woven fabric.] —**web′like′,** *adj.*

webbed (webd) *adj.* having or joined by a web or webs: *Geese have webbed feet.*

web·bing (web′ing) *n.* **1.** a strong, narrow band of woven fabric, made of cotton, hemp, or other fibers, used for seat belts, harness straps, and other items. **2.** anything forming a web or webs.

web·er (web′ər, vā′bər) *n.* the International System unit of magnetic flux, equal to the flux that produces an electromotive force of 1 volt in a circuit of one turn; 10^8 maxwells. [From Wilhelm Eduard *Weber,* 1804-91, German physicist.]

web·foot (web′fût′) *n., pl.* **-feet** (-fēt′). **1.** a foot with toes that are webbed. **2.** any animal having webbed feet.

web·foot·ed (web′fût′id) *adj.* having the toes joined by a web: *Ducks are web-footed animals.*

wed (wed) *v.,* **wed·ded, wed·ded** or **wed, wed·ding.** —*v.t.* **1.** to take as one's husband or wife; marry. **2.** to join as husband and wife; unite in wedlock. **3.** to join closely; unite: *Opera weds acting and singing.* —*v.i.* to take a husband or wife; marry. [Old English *weddian* to pledge, marry¹.]

we'd (wēd) *contr.* **1.** we had. **2.** we would. **3.** we should.

Wed., Wednesday.

wed·ded (wed′id) *adj.* **1.** in a married state: *a happily wedded couple.* **2.** of or relating to marriage; matrimonial: *to live in wedded bliss.* **3.** closely joined: *two groups wedded by a common interest.* **4.** deeply involved; devoted: *employees wedded to their work.*

wed·ding (wed′ing) *n.* **1.** a marriage ceremony, usually including accompanying festivities. **2.** the anniversary of a marriage: *A silver wedding is a celebration of twenty-five years of marriage.* **3.** a close joining together. [Old English *weddung* espousal, marriage.]

wedge (wej) *n.* **1.** a solid, triangular or tapered object, as of wood or metal, that can be driven in between objects to separate or split them. **2.** something resembling this in shape: *a wedge of cheese.* **3.** something, such as an idea, policy, or procedure, that brings about division or disunity: *The struggle over the inheritance drove a wedge between members of the family.* —*v.,* **wedged, wedg·ing.** —*v.t.* **1.** to separate or split by or as by driving a wedge into. **2.** to fasten or fix in place with a wedge or wedges: *to wedge a door open with a piece of wood.* **3.** to drive, push, or crowd (something) into a narrow space: *I managed to wedge the book into place on the shelf.* —*v.i.* to force one's way: *to wedge into a seat on the train.* [Old English *wecg* tapered piece of wood or metal.]

Wedg·wood (wej′wûd′) *n. Trademark.* earthenware pottery usually characterized by a blue or green tinted background with a white, raised ornament, often of graceful figures. [From Josiah *Wedgwood,* 1730-95, English potter who created this kind of pottery.]

wed·lock (wed′lok′) *n.* the state or condition of being married; matrimony. [Old English *wedlāc* marriage vow, from *wedd* pledge + *-lāc* (suffix indicating activity).]

Wedgwood bowl

Wednes·day (wenz′dē, -dā) *n.* the fourth day of the week. [Old English *Wōdnesdæg* literally, Woden's day, translation of Late Latin *Mercurii diēs* literally, day of Mercury (owing to the identification of Woden with Mercury).]

wee (wē) *adj.,* **we·er, we·est. 1.** very small; little. **2.** early: *in the wee hours of the morning.* [Middle English *we(i)* a bit, a little, from Old English *wæge* a weight.]

weed¹ (wēd) *n.* **1.** a plant that is useless or harmful or grows where it is not wanted or where another plant is desired. **2. a.** *Informal.* tobacco. **b.** *Slang.* marijuana. **3.** *Informal.* a cigar or cigarette. —*v.t.* to remove weeds from: *to weed a lawn.* —*v.i.* to remove weeds. [Old English *wēod* useless or harmful plant.]
· **to weed out.** to remove (something that is useless or harmful): *to weed out old clothes from a closet.*

weed² (wēd) *n.* **1. weeds.** the clothes worn by someone in mourning, esp. a widow. **2.** a token of mourning, such as a black band worn on the arm. [Old English *wēd* garment.]

weed·er (wē′dər) *n.* **1.** a person who weeds. **2.** a tool or device for removing weeds.

weed·y (wē′dē) *adj.,* **weed·i·er, weed·i·est. 1.** full of weeds.

2. of, relating to, or resembling a weed or weeds. **3.** *Informal.* thin and lanky; rangy. —**weed′i·ness,** *n.*

week (wēk) *n.* **1.** a period of seven consecutive days, usually considered as beginning with Sunday. **2.** the number of days or hours in a seven-day period devoted to a specific activity: *to work a four-day week.* **3.** a period of seven days commencing on a certain day, containing a specific day, or designated for some specific purpose: *the week of March twelfth, Christmas week.* **4.** seven days from a specified day: *I'll see you a week from tomorrow.* [Old English *wice* period of seven consecutive days.]

week·day (wēk′dā′) *n.* any day of the week except Saturday and Sunday.

week·end (wēk′end′) *n.* the period extending from Friday night or Saturday morning until Sunday night or Monday morning. —*adj.* of, relating to, or occurring during a weekend: *a weekend golf game.* —*v.i.* to spend a weekend: *to weekend in the country.*

week·ly (wēk′lē) *adj.* **1.** of, relating to, or for a week or weekdays: *a weekly supply of groceries.* **2.** done or occurring once a week: *a weekly meeting.* —*n., pl.* **-lies.** a magazine, newspaper, or other publication issued once a week. —*adv.* once each week; every week: *to meet weekly.*

ween (wēn) *v.i., v.t. Archaic.* to think; surmise; suppose. [Old English *wēnan.*]

wee·ny (wē′nē) *adj.,* **-ni·er, -ni·est.** *Informal.* extremely small; tiny.

weep (wēp) *v.,* **wept, weep·ing.** —*v.i.* **1.** to show grief, joy, or other strong emotion by shedding tears. **2.** to feel sorrow or grief; mourn; lament (with *for):* *We wept for our loss.* **3.** to exude liquid slowly or in drops; ooze or drip. —*v.t.* **1.** to weep for; mourn for: *She wept her dead father.* **2.** to shed or let flow in drops: *to weep salty tears.* **3.** to bring to a specified condition by weeping: *to weep oneself to sleep.* —*n.* often, **weeps.** a fit or period of weeping. [Old English *wēpan* to lament, shed tears.]

weep·er (wē′pər) *n.* a person who weeps, esp. a person hired to weep at funerals.

weeping willow, an open, spreading tree, *Salix babylonica,* widely cultivated throughout eastern North America, having pale green leaves and greenish branches that droop almost to the ground.

wee·vil (wē′vəl) *n.* **1.** any of a group of destructive beetles, family Curculionidae, having a snout or beak. Weevils feed on cotton, grain, and other crops, boring into the living plant to deposit their larvae, which also feed on the crops. Also, **snout beetle. 2.** any of various other insects that infest and destroy stored grain. [Old English *wifel* any beetle.]

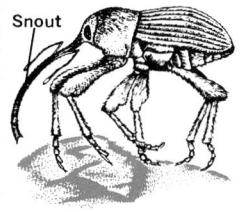

Snout

weevil

weft (weft) *n.* woof[1] *(def. 1).* [Old English *weft.*]

weigh (wā) *v.t.* **1.** to determine the weight of: *The doctor weighed the baby every month.* **2.** to measure or apportion (a quantity or quantities of something) according to weight (with *out):* *The chemistry teacher weighed out one ounce of the compound.* **3.** to consider or examine thoughtfully and carefully: *to weigh the advantages and disadvantages of a plan, to weigh one's words before speaking.* **4.** to raise or lift (an anchor). —*v.i.* **1.** to have, amount to, or be equal to a specified weight: *The car weighs 3,744 pounds.* **2.** to be considered important; have influence; matter: *The prisoner's record will weigh heavily with the parole board.* **3.** to be oppressive or burdensome: *A feeling of guilt weighed heavily on my conscience.* **4.** to raise or lift an anchor and start to sail: *to weigh from a port.* [Old English *wegan* to carry, lift, balance on the scales.] —**weigh′er,** *n.* —For Synonyms, see **consider.**

  · **to weigh down.** to lie heavily on; oppress or burden: *Our many debts have weighed us down for several years.*
  · **to weigh in. a.** *Sports.* to have one's weight officially determined, as a boxer prior to a match. **b.** to be of a specified weight: *to weigh in at 150 pounds.* **c.** to have one's baggage weighed, as before boarding an airplane.

weight (wāt) *n.* **1.** any measure of heaviness, expressed indefinitely or in standard units: *My weight is only 100 pounds.* **2.** the quality of any mass or body that is the result of gravitational force and centrifugal pressure tending to pull things toward the center of the earth: *As the weight of helium is less than the weight of air, a balloon filled with helium will rise.* **3.** a system of units for expressing weights or mass. See table of **weights and measures** on following page. **4.** any unit of weight or mass, such as a ton or kilogram. **5.** a piece of metal or similar material having a particu-

lar weight, used as a standard in weighing. **6.** a quantity or portion having a definite weight. **7.** a heavy mass, esp. one that is used because of its weight to exert gravitational force. **8.** a burden or load; pressure: *The weight of our financial problems is ruining our credit.* **9.** strong or effective influence; importance; consequence: *The senator's opinion carried weight with the other legislators.* **10.** *Sports.* one of the classes into which athletes in certain sports, such as boxing or wrestling, are divided according to body weight. —*v.t.* **1.** to add weight to; load with additional weight: *They weighted the cartons with rocks.* **2.** to burden heavily, as with a weight; oppress (with *down):* *Financial responsibilities weighted them down.* **3.** to give heaviness or body to (fabric or yarn) by adding plastic resins or other substances. Silk is sometimes weighted with metallic salts to improve its appearance. [Old English *wiht* measurement of quantity by weighing, a quantity weighing a definite amount.]

  · **by weight.** as determined by weighing: *to sell a product by weight, not volume.*
  · **to pull** (or **carry**) **one's weight.** to do or contribute one's share.
  · **to throw one's weight around.** *Informal.* to use one's power, authority, or position, esp. in an unfair way.

weight·less (wāt′lis) *adj.* **1.** having little or no weight: *weightless feathers.* **2.** (of a body) having no apparent weight due to the absence or neutralization of the pull of gravity, as in space. —**weight′less·ly,** *adv.* —**weight′less·ness,** *n.*

weight·lift·ing (wāt′lif′ting) *also,* **weight lifting.** *n.* the exercise or competitive sport of lifting objects of varying weights. —**weight′lift′er,** *n.*

weight·y (wā′tē) *adj.,* **weight·i·er, weight·i·est. 1.** of great weight; heavy: *a weighty object.* **2.** effective; convincing: *Your proposal presents weighty reasons for taking action.* **3.** hard to bear; burdensome: *a weighty responsibility.* **4.** very serious or important: *a weighty decision.* —**weight′i·ly,** *adv.* —**weight′i·ness,** *n.* —For Synonyms, see **heavy.**

wei·mar·an·er (vī′mə rä′nər, wī′-, wī′mə rā′-) *also,* **Wei·mar·an·er.** *n.* any of a German breed of large hunting dogs, having a short, gray coat, blue-gray eyes, and a docked tail. [German *Weimaraner* literally, native or resident of Weimar, German city where the breed was developed.]

weir (wîr) *n.* **1.** a dam constructed in a river, as to raise the level of the water. **2.** a fence of stakes or wattles put in a stream or channel to catch fish. [Old English *wer.*]

weird (wîrd) *adj.* **1.** different from the usual or expected; strange; bizarre; odd: *weird behavior, a weird person.* **2.** suggestive of or concerned with the supernatural; unearthly; mysterious: *Weird sounds were heard coming from the deserted house.* **3.** *Archaic.* having supernatural power, esp. having the power of controlling fate or destiny. [Middle English *wyrde* having the power to control fate, from *wyrde* fate, from Old English *wyrd.*] —**weird′ly,** *adv.* —**weird′ness,** *n.* —For Synonyms, see **strange.**

Weird Sisters, the Fates.

welch (welch, welsh) welsh.

wel·come (wel′kəm) *v.t.,* **-comed, -com·ing. 1.** to greet (someone) gladly and with hospitality: *We welcomed them when they arrived.* **2.** to receive or accept graciously or with pleasure: *to welcome the news of a friend's engagement.* **3.** to greet (someone) in a particular way: *The audience welcomed the speaker with boos.* —*n.* a greeting or reception, esp. a warm and friendly one: *Their welcome made up for the discomforts of our trip.* —*adj.* **1.** received kindly and cordially: *a welcome visitor.* **2.** giving pleasure or satisfaction: *a welcome compliment, a welcome visit.* **3.** free to use, have, or enjoy; willingly permitted: *You are welcome to the telephone.* **4.** under no obligation. ➡ used chiefly in the phrase *you're welcome,* as a response to being thanked for something. —*interj.* used to express greeting: *Welcome, one and all.* [Old Norse *velkominn* expression of greeting; literally, well come, from *vel* well[1] + *kominn,* past participle of *koma* to come.] —**wel′com·er,** *n.*

  · **to wear out one's welcome.** to stay too long or visit too frequently.

weld (weld) *v.t.* **1.** to join, as pieces of metal or plastic, by heating and softening and then hammering or pressing. **2.** to join closely together; unite intimately: *to weld two companies.* —*v.i.* to become welded or be capable of being welded. —*n.* **1.** a point

a	at	e	end	o	hot	u	up	hw	white		about
ā	ape	ē	me	ō	old	ū	use	ng	song		taken
ä	far	i	it	ô	fork	ū	rule	th	thin	ə	pencil
âr	care	ī	ice	oi	oil	u̇	pull	<u>th</u>	this		lemon
		îr	pierce	ou	out	ûr	turn	zh	measure		circus

LINEAR MEASURE

1 foot	=	12 inches
1 yard	=	3 feet
1 rod	=	5½ yards or 16½ feet
1 furlong	=	40 rods
1 mile	=	8 furlongs or 1760 yards or 5280 feet

SQUARE MEASURE

1 square foot	=	144 square inches
1 square yard	=	9 square feet
1 square rod	=	30¼ square yards
1 acre	=	160 square rods or 43,560 square feet
1 square mile	=	640 acres

CUBIC MEASURE

1 board foot	=	144 cubic inches
1 cubic foot	=	1728 cubic inches
1 cubic yard	=	27 cubic feet
1 cord	=	128 cubic feet

LIQUID MEASURE

1 gill	=	4 fluid ounces
1 pint	=	4 gills or 16 fluid ounces
1 quart	=	2 pints
1 gallon	=	4 quarts
1 barrel	=	31½ gallons

DRY MEASURE

1 quart	=	2 pints
1 peck	=	8 quarts
1 bushel	=	4 pecks

AVOIRDUPOIS WEIGHT

1 dram	=	27.34	grains
1 ounce	=	16	drams
1 pound	=	16	ounces
1 hundredweight	=	100	pounds
1 short ton	=	2000	pounds
1 long ton	=	2240	pounds

TROY WEIGHT

1 pennyweight	=	24 grains
1 ounce	=	20 pennyweights
1 pound	=	12 ounces

APOTHECARIES' WEIGHT

1 scruple	=	20 grains
1 dram	=	3 scruples
1 ounce	=	8 drams
1 pound	=	12 ounces

APOTHECARIES' FLUID MEASURE

1 fluid dram	=	60 minims
1 fluid ounce	=	8 fluid drams
1 pint	=	16 fluid ounces
1 quart	=	2 pints
1 gallon	=	4 quarts

MARINERS' MEASURE

1 fathom	=	6 feet
1 nautical mile	=	1000 fathoms (approx.)
1 league	=	3 nautical miles

CIRCULAR AND ANGULAR MEASURE

1 minute	=	60 seconds
1 degree	=	60 minutes
1 right angle (or 1 quadrant)	=	90 degrees
1 straight angle (or 2 quadrants)	=	180 degrees
1 circle (or 4 quadrants)	=	360 degrees

Metric System

Unit	Metric Equivalent		U.S. Equivalent	
LINEAR MEASURE				
millimeter	0.001	meter	0.03937	inch
centimeter	0.01	meter	0.3937	inch
decimeter	0.1	meter	3.937	inches
meter	1.0	meter	39.37	inches
decameter	10.0	meters	10.94	yards
hectometer	100.0	meters	328.1	feet
kilometer	1000.0	meters	0.6214	mile
WEIGHT OR MASS				
milligram	0.001	gram	0.01543	grain
centigram	0.01	gram	0.1543	grain
decigram	0.1	gram	1.543	grains
gram	1.0	gram	15.43	grains
decagram	10.0	grams	0.3527	ounce avoirdupois
hectogram	100.0	grams	3.527	ounces avoirdupois
kilogram	1000.0	grams	2.200	pounds avoirdupois
CAPACITY				
milliliter	0.001	liter	0.03381	fluid ounce
centiliter	0.01	liter	0.3381	fluid ounce
deciliter	0.1	liter	3.381	fluid ounces
liter	1.0	liter	1.057	liquid quarts
decaliter	10.0	liters	0.284	bushel
hectoliter	100.0	liters	2.837	bushels
kiloliter	1000.0	liters	264.2	gallons
AREA				
square centimeter	0.0001	square meter	0.1550	square inch
square decimeter	0.01	square meter	15.50	square inches
centiare	1.0	square meter	10.76	square feet
are	100.0	square meters	0.02471	acre
hectare	10,000.0	square meters	2.471	acres
square kilometer	1,000,000.0	square meters	0.3861	square mile
VOLUME				
cubic centimeter	0.001	cubic decimeter	0.06102	cubic inch
cubic decimeter	0.001	cubic meter	3.531	cubic feet
stere	1.0	cubic meter	1.308	cubic yards
decastere	10.0	cubic meters	13.10	cubic yards

at which two things are joined by welding. **2.** the act or process of welding or the state of being welded. [Modification of obsolete *well* to join by heating and softening, from Old English *wellan* to boil.] —**weld′er,** *n.*

wel·fare (wel′fâr′) *n.* **1.** the state or condition of being or doing well, as in health or finances. **2.** financial aid or other assistance given to persons in need, usually by one or more departments of a government; relief. **3.** a governmental department or agency administering such assistance. [Middle English *welfare* wellbeing, good fortune, from the phrase *wel faren* to fare well, from old English *wel faran.*]
  • **on welfare.** dependent upon or receiving financial aid or other public assistance.

welfare state, a state, nation, or government that actively ensures the well-being of its people by providing such benefits as health and unemployment insurance, maternity and child-care benefits, guaranteed minimum wages, old-age pensions, and subsidized housing.

welfare work, work done by a government, private agencies, or individuals to provide money, food, and other social services to people who need assistance.

welfare worker, a person who does welfare work, esp. as a profession.

wel·kin (wel′kin) *n. Archaic.* the sky; heavens. ➡ used chiefly in the phrase *to make the welkin ring.* [Old English *wolcen* cloud, sky.]

well[1] (wel) *adv.,* **bet·ter, best. 1.** in a satisfactory, good, or favorable manner: *The project is turning out well.* **2.** in a thorough or complete manner: *Mix the ingredients well.* **3.** to a considerable extent or degree: *An elephant weighs well over 1,000 pounds.* **4.** closely; intimately: *Do you know them well?* **5.** under the circumstances; reasonably: *I can't very well accept your offer.* **6.** clearly or definitely: *I remember our trip well.* **7.** in a skillful or expert manner: *to ski well.* **8.** in comfortable or pleasant circumstances: *to live well.* —*adj.* **1.** in good health; thriving: *Come back safe and well.* **2.** good; fortunate: *It's well that you called before we went out.* **3.** in a satisfactory or good state or condition: *All is well with us.* —*interj.* used to express surprise, doubt, or resignation, or to introduce another thought: *Well! How nice to see you.* [Old English *wel* satisfactorily, thoroughly, properly, successfully, effectively.]
  • **as well. a.** in addition; also: *My cousin plays the flute and oboe, and the drums as well.* **b.** with the same outcome or effect; equally: *You might as well travel with us as go alone.*
  • **as well as. a.** in addition to; besides: *We toured France as well as England.* **b.** to the same extent or degree as: *You can dance as well as I can.*

> **Usage** Well[1] is hyphenated when used in combination with an adjective before a noun: *a well-known astronomer, a well-built house.* It is generally not hyphenated when used before a predicate adjective or when modified by an adverb: *The writers became well known after the publication of their book. This is a very well designed kitchen.*

well[2] (wel) *n.* **1.** a hole or pit made in the ground to obtain water or another substance, such as oil. **2.** a natural spring or fountain. **3.** something resembling a well in shape or function: *The old desk contained a well for ink.* **4.** a source of something, esp. one that is abundant: *An encyclopedia is a well of information.* **5.** an enclosed, vertical space in a building, often extending through several floors, such as a shaft for stairs, an elevator, or the admission of air or light. **6.** a compartment in a ship's hold that encloses and protects the pumps. —*v.i.* to rise to the surface and flow as from a well: *Tears welled in the child's eyes.* —*v.t.* to pour (something) out from or as from a well. [Old English *wella* spring of water, pit dug to get spring water, source.]

we′ll (wēl) *contr.* we shall; we will.

well·a·day (wel′ə dā′) *interj. Archaic.* wellaway.

well-ad·vised (wel′ad vīzd′) *adj.* acting with or showing good judgment; wise; sensible: *You would be well-advised to leave before the snowstorm begins.*

well-ap·point·ed (wel′ə poin′tid) *adj.* properly or excellently furnished or equipped: *well-appointed offices.*

well-a·way (wel′ə wā′) *interj. Archaic.* alas. Also, **welladay.**

well-bal·anced (wel′bal′ənst) *adj.* **1.** nicely or evenly balanced; properly adjusted or regulated: *a well-balanced diet.* **2.** sensible; sane: *a well-balanced personality.*

well-be·haved (wel′bi hāvd′) *adj.* characterized by good conduct or manners: *a well-behaved youngster.*

well-be·ing (wel′bē′ing) *n.* health, happiness, and prosperity; good physical and mental condition.

well·born (wel′bôrn′) *adj.* born of an aristocratic family.

well-bred (wel′bred′) *adj.* **1.** having or showing good breeding or training; polite or tasteful: *a well-bred child, well-bred manners.* **2.** (of an animal) coming from good stock or pedigree.

well-de·fined (wel′di fīnd′) *adj.* clear and precise, as in marking or outline; sharply defined: *a model with well-defined features.*

well-de·vel·oped (wel′di vel′əpt) *adj.* **1.** thought out or done in a thorough and organized manner: *a well-developed plan.* **2.** having or showing good physical form: *The weightlifter had well-developed arms.*

well-dis·posed (wel′di spōzd′) *adj.* inclined to favorable action or thought; friendly or favorable: *The staff was well-disposed toward the new boss.*

well-done (wel′dun′) *adj.* **1.** performed well; skillfully done. **2.** (of food) thoroughly cooked.

well-fa·vored (wel′fā′vərd) *adj.* good-looking; handsome.

well-fed (wel′fed′) *adj.* **1.** properly or fully nourished. **2.** chubby; plump.

well-fixed (wel′fikst′) *adj. Informal.* not lacking in money; financially secure.

well-found (wel′found′) *adj.* well supplied or equipped: *a well-found railway car.*

well-found·ed (wel′foun′did) *adj.* based on solid evidence, good judgment, or sound reasoning: *a well-founded argument.*

well-groomed (wel′grümd′) *adj.* **1.** carefully and attractively dressed and groomed; neat. **2.** properly or carefully cared for: *a well-groomed golf course.*

well-ground·ed (wel′groun′did) *adj.* **1.** thoroughly familiar with the fundamental principles of a subject: *well-grounded in mathematics.* **2.** based on sound evidence or reasoning; well-founded.

well·head (wel′hed′) *n.* **1.** the source of a natural spring or well. **2.** the chief source of anything: *the wellhead of a painter's inspiration.* **3.** the top of or the equipment at the top of a well.

well-heeled (wel′hēld′) *adj. Informal.* having a lot of money; rich.

well-in·formed (wel′in fôrmd′) *adj.* **1.** having considerable information and knowledge on a wide variety of subjects: *a well-informed student.* **2.** having substantial and correct information on a particular subject: *a doctor well-informed about heart disease.*

well-in·ten·tioned (wel′in ten′shənd) *adj.* having or marked by good intentions, usually with unsatisfactory results: *Their well-intentioned words only made things worse.*

well-known (wel′nōn′) *adj.* **1.** having fame or notoriety; famous; renowned: *a well-known scientist.* **2.** generally, widely, or fully known: *well-known facts.*

well-made (wel′mād′) *adj.* that has been made or developed in a careful, skillful, or well-constructed manner: *a well-made chair, a well-made movie.*

a	at	e	end	o	hot	u	up	hw	white		about
ā	ape	ē	me	ō	old	ū	use	ng	song	ə	taken
ä	far	i	it	ô	fork	ü	rule	th	thin		pencil
âr	care	ī	ice	oi	oil	u̇	pull	th	this		lemon
		îr	pierce	ou	out	ûr	turn	zh	measure		circus

The following list contains a selection of compounds that can be formed with the word **well**[1]. The meaning of a word on the list can be understood by combining the appropriate sense of the word with the root word.

well-absorbed	well-applied	well-chosen	well-cultivated	well-endowed	well-fought
well-accepted	well-appreciated	well-compensated	well-cushioned	well-equipped	well-frequented
well-accustomed	well-argued	well-concealed	well-decorated	well-established	well-furnished
well-acquainted	well-armed	well-conceived	well-defended	well-esteemed	well-governed
well-acted	well-assured	well-connected	well-delineated	well-executed	well-guarded
well-adapted	well-attended	well-considered	well-deserved	well-expressed	well-hidden
well-adjusted	well-attired	well-constituted	well-disciplined	well-fashioned	well-illustrated
well-administered	well-aware	well-constructed	well-documented	well-financed	well-justified
well-adorned	well-blessed	well-contested	well-dressed	well-formed	well-kept
well-advertised	well-built	well-controlled	well-educated	well-formulated	well-liked
well-aimed	well-calculated	well-cooked	well-employed	well-fortified	well-loved

well·man·nered (wel′man′ərd) *adj.* having or showing good manners; polite.

well-mean·ing (wel′mē′ning) *adj.* **1.** intending to be helpful or good; well-intentioned: *a well-meaning neighbor.* **2.** coming or resulting from good intentions: *a well-meaning remark.* Also *(def. 2),* **well′-meant′.**

well-nigh (wel′nī′) *adv.* very nearly; almost.

well-off (wel′ôf′, -of′) *adj.* **1.** fairly wealthy; financially secure. **2.** in a position where things are good or going well: *I knew I was well-off, so I decided not to change jobs.*

well-read (wel′red′) *adj.* knowledgeable through having read widely.

well-round·ed (wel′roun′did) *adj.* **1.** having knowledge or interest in a wide variety of fields or subjects: *a well-rounded student.* **2.** concerned with or made up of a wide variety of fields or subjects: *a well-rounded curriculum.*

well-spoken (wel′spō′kən) *adj.* **1.** having refined and educated speech. **2.** said or delivered with style and polish: *a well-spoken rebuttal.*

well·spring (wel′spring′) *n.* **1.** fountainhead *(def. 1).* **2.** a source of something, esp. an unending source: *a wellspring of knowledge.*

well-thought-of (wel′thôt′uv′, -ov′) *adj.* having a good reputation; respected; esteemed: *a well-thought-of member of the community.*

well-timed (wel′tīmd′) *adj.* occurring or done at the correct or suitable time: *a well-timed entrance.*

well-to-do (wel′tə dü′) *adj.* having more than enough money; wealthy; prosperous.

well-turned (wel′tûrnd′) *adj.* **1.** having a graceful form that is carefully proportioned, as if turned on a lathe: *a well-turned ankle.* **2.** gracefully or appropriately worded or expressed; felicitous: *a well-turned phrase.*

well-wish·er (wel′wish′ər) *n.* a person who wishes good fortune, success, or health, as to another person, a cause, or the like.

well-worn (wel′wôrn′) *adj.* **1.** showing evidence of much use or wear: *a well-worn jacket.* **2.** used too much; trite; hackneyed: *a well-worn phrase.*

welsh (welsh, welch) *also,* **welch.** —*v.i. Informal.* **1.** to fail or refuse to pay what is owed, esp. after losing a bet (with *on*): *to welsh on a bet.* **2.** to fail to fulfill a promise or commitment (with *on*): *to welsh on an agreement.* —**welsh′er,** *n.*

Welsh (welsh, welch) *adj.* of, relating to, or characteristic of Wales or its people, language, or culture. —*n.* **1.** the people of Wales. **2.** the language of the Welsh, belonging to the Celtic branch of the Indo-European language family.

Welsh cor·gi (kôr′gē) a short-legged dog having a face resembling that of a fox and a coat of stiff, medium-length hair. There are two breeds, the **Cardigan Welsh corgi,** having a long, bushy tail, and the **Pembroke Welsh corgi,** having a short tail. Height: to 12 inches (30 centimeters) at the shoulder.

Welsh·man (welsh′mən, welch′-) *n., pl.* **-men** (-mən). **1.** a native or citizen of Wales. **2.** a person of Welsh ancestry.

Welsh rabbit, melted cheese mixed with beer, ale, or milk, seasoned, and served warm over toast or crackers. Also, **Welsh rarebit.** [Apparently of jocular origin.]

welt (welt) *n.* **1.** a strip of material, esp. a cord, sewn on an edge or in a seam of a garment or item, such as a cushion, used for strengthening or decorating it. **2.** a strip of leather or other material between the upper part and the sole of a shoe. **3.** a ridge or bump on the skin, as one made by a stick or whip; wale; weal. **4.** a blow causing such a ridge or bump. —*v.t.* **1.** to put a welt on or in. **2.** *Informal.* to beat or flog so as to raise welts. [Of uncertain origin.]

wel·ter (wel′tər) *v.i.* **1.** to roll or toss about; wallow: *The pigs weltered in the mud. The ship weltered in the stormy sea.* **2.** to be soaked or drenched in some liquid. —*n.* **1.** a rolling and tossing motion: *The welter of waves kept us awake.* **2.** confusion; turmoil: *a welter of errors and inconsistencies.* [Possibly from Middle Low German *welteren* to roll.]

wel·ter·weight (wel′tər wāt′) *n.* a boxer competing in the weight class of up to 147 pounds (67 kilograms), or a competitor, such as a wrestler, in a similar class. [Earlier *welter* welterweight (from WELT + -ER¹) + WEIGHT.]

wen (wen) *n.* a benign tumor or cyst on the skin, esp. on the scalp. [Old English *wenn* lump on the body.]

wench (wench) *n.* **1.** a girl or young woman. ➡ often used facetiously or disparagingly. **2.** a female servant. **3.** a loose or immoral woman; hussy. —*v.i.* to associate with loose or immoral women. [Middle English *wenche* girl, female servant, loose woman, from *wenchel* child, from Old English *wencel*.]

wend (wend) *v.,* **wend·ed** or *(archaic)* **went, wend·ing.** —*v.t.* to make (one's way); go on (one's way): *to wend one's way through a crowd.* —*v.i.* to go; travel; move: *The boat wended down the river to New Orleans.* [Old English *wendan* to turn, go.]

Wend (wend) *n.* a member of a Slavic people living between the Elbe and Oder rivers in eastern Germany.

went (went) *v.* **1.** the past tense of **go**¹. **2.** *Archaic.* a past tense and past participle of **wend.**

wept (wept) the past tense and past participle of **weep.**

were (wûr; *unstressed* wər) *v.* **1.** the plural past indicative and second person singular past indicative of **be:** *The athletes were tired and hungry after the game.* **2.** the past subjunctive of **be:** *If I were you, I wouldn't have gone.* [Old English *wǣre* past indicative second person singular, *wǣron* past indicative plural, *wǣre* past subjunctive singular, and *wǣren* past subjunctive plural, all of *wesan* to be.]

we're (wîr) *contr.* we are.

weren't (wûrnt, wûr′ənt) *contr.* were not.

were·wolf (wîr′wŭlf′, wûr′-, wâr′-) *also,* **wer·wolf.** *n., pl.* **-wolves** (-wŭlvz′). in European folklore, a person who sometimes turns into a wolf or who has the power to assume the form of a wolf. [Old English *werewulf,* from *wer* man + *wulf* wolf.]

wert (wûrt; *unstressed* wərt) *Archaic.* a second person singular past indicative and past subjunctive of **be.** ➡ used with *thou.*

Wes·ley·an (wes′lē ən, wez′-) *n.* a member or disciple of the church founded by the English religious leader John Wesley; Methodist. —*adj.* of or relating to John Wesley or to Methodists or Methodism. —**Wes′ley·an·ism,** *n.*

west (west) *n.* **1.** the general direction of the sunset in relation to an observer on earth. **2.** one of the four cardinal points of the compass, lying directly opposite east and 90 degrees left of north. **3.** *also,* **West.** any region situated toward this direction in relation to a specified point of reference. **4. the West. a.** the countries of Europe and the Americas as distinguished from those of Asia. **b.** the United States, Western Europe, and other noncommunist countries bound together by military and economic alliances. **c.** the Western Roman Empire. —*adv.* in or toward the west. —*adj.* **1.** toward, facing, or in the west. **2.** coming from the west: *a warm, west wind.* [Old English *west* westward.]

west·bound (west′bound′) *adj.* going westward: *to ride a westbound train.*

west·er·ly (wes′tər lē) *adj., adv.* **1.** toward the west: *in a westerly direction, to drive westerly.* **2.** from the west: *a westerly wind, flying westerly.* —*n., pl.* **-lies.** a wind blowing from the west.

west·ern (wes′tərn) *adj.* **1.** toward or in the west. **2.** from the west. **3.** *also,* **Western.** of, relating to, or characteristic of the west or the West. —*n.* a novel, short story, motion picture, or the like dealing with frontier life in the western United States, esp. with the life of cattle ranchers and the early settlers.

Western Church 1. the part of the Roman Catholic Church that recognizes the supremacy of the pope. **2.** the Roman Catholic, Anglican, and Protestant churches of western Europe and the Americas collectively.

Western civilization, civilization derived from Hebrew, Greek, Arabic, and European sources as opposed to that derived from Indian and Oriental sources.

west·ern·er (wes′tər nər) *n.* **1.** a person who was born in or lives in the west. **2.** *usually,* **Westerner.** a person who was born in or lives in the western part of the United States.

Western Hemisphere, the half of the earth west of the Greenwich meridian, including North and South America and their adjacent islands and surrounding waters.

well-managed	well-performed	well-protected	well-represented	well-situated	well-thought-out
well-marked	well-phrased	well-put	well-respected	well-spent	well-trained
well-matched	well-placed	well-qualified	well-reviewed	well-staged	well-traveled
well-measured	well-planned	well-received	well-ripened	well-stated	well-treated
well-mixed	well-played	well-recognized	well-rooted	well-stocked	well-understood
well-motivated	well-pleased	well-recommended	well-satisfied	well-suited	well-used
well-named	well-positioned	well-regarded	well-scattered	well-supplied	well-ventilated
well-nourished	well-prepared	well-regulated	well-schooled	well-tailored	well-versed
well-organized	well-preserved	well-rehearsed	well-secured	well-taught	well-written
well-paid	well-proportioned	well-remembered	well-shaped	well-tended	well-wrought

west·ern·ize (wes′tər nīz′) *v.t.,* **-ized, -iz·ing.** to cause to adopt the customs, ideas, and qualities regarded as characteristic of Europe and the Americas: *Many peoples and countries of Asia were westernized in the twentieth century.* —**west′ern·i·za′tion,** *n.*

west·ern·most (wes′tərn mōst′) *adj.* farthest west.

West·min·ster Abbey (west′min′stər) a Gothic church of England, in Westminster, London. It is the traditional site of coronations and contains the tombs of many English monarchs, political leaders, national heroes, and writers.

west-north·west (west′nôrth′west′; *Nautical* west′nôr′west′) *n.* a point on the compass halfway between west and northwest. —*adj., adv.* toward the west and northwest.

West Point, officially, the United States Military Academy, an accredited four-year institution providing college-level instruction and officer training for careers in the U.S. Army.

west-south·west (west′south′west′; *Nautical* west′sou′west′) *n.* a point on the compass halfway between west and southwest. —*adj., adv.* toward the west and southwest.

west·ward (west′wərd) *adv.* also, **west·wards.** toward the west: *to drive westward.* —*adj.* toward or in the west. —*n.* a westward direction, point, or part.

west·ward·ly (west′wərd lē) *adj., adv.* **1.** toward the west. **2.** from the west.

wet (wet) *adj.,* **wet·ter, wet·test. 1.** covered, soaked, or moist with water or other liquid: *a wet bathing suit, eyes wet with tears.* **2.** not yet dry: *A footprint was made in the wet cement.* **3.** marked by rainfall; rainy: *Spring is sometimes a wet season.* **4.** *Informal.* permitting or in favor of the manufacture and sale of alcoholic beverages: *a wet county.* —*v.,* **wet** or **wet·ted, wet·ting.** —*v.t.* **1.** to make wet: *Wet the ground before planting.* **2.** to make wet by urinating: *The baby wet the bed.* —*v.i.* to become wet or moist. —*n.* **1.** water or moisture; wetness. **2.** rainy weather; rain: *to come in out of the wet.* [Old English *wǣt* moist, damp, consisting of moisture, having moisture.] —**wet′ly,** *adv.* —**wet′ness,** *n.* —**wet′ter,** *n.*

• **all wet.** *Slang.* completely wrong; entirely mistaken.

• **wet behind the ears.** lacking experience or sophistication.

wet·back (wet′bak′) *n.* *Slang.* a Mexican who enters or is brought into the United States illegally. ➡ considered offensive. [WET + BACK[1]; referring to the practice of entering the United States illegally by wading or swimming across the Rio Grande at night.]

wet blanket *Informal.* a person or thing that has a depressing or dispiriting effect, as by discouraging others from having fun.

wet cell, in electricity, a cell having a liquid electrolyte.

weth·er (weth′ər) *n.* a castrated male sheep. [Old English *wether* ram.]

wet·land (wet′land′) *n.* an area having wet soil, as a swamp or marsh. ➡ usually used in the plural.

wet-nurse (wet′nûrs′) *v.t.,* **-nursed, -nurs·ing. 1.** to act as wet nurse to. **2.** to pamper or coddle; be overly protective of.

wet nurse, a woman employed to suckle the infant of another. ➡ distinguished from **dry nurse.**

wet suit, a close-fitting, one- or two-piece rubber garment, worn for warmth by skin divers, scuba divers, surfers, and the like.

wetting agent, a compound added to a liquid to decrease its surface tension, thereby enabling it to penetrate or spread over the surface of a particular material more readily.

we've (wēv) *contr.* we have.

w.f. *also,* **wf** in printing, wrong font. ➡ used to indicate that a letter or character is the wrong size or style.

whack (hwak, wak) *n.* **1.** a sharp, resounding blow. **2.** the sound made by such a blow. —*v.t., v.i. Informal.* to hit or slap with a sharp, resounding blow. [Probably imitative.] —**whack′-er,** *n.*

• **out of whack.** *Informal.* not working properly; broken: *The television set is out of whack.*

• **to have** (or **take**) **a whack at.** *Informal.* to try (to do something); attempt: *I'll have a whack at fixing the bicycle.*

• **to whack off.** *Informal.* to separate or remove with or as with a blow: *to whack off a piece of cheese.*

• **to whack out.** *Slang.* to produce quickly and often carelessly: *to whack out a term paper.*

whack·ing (hwak′ing, wak′-) *adj. Informal.* extremely large. —*adv.* extraordinarily; wonderfully: *a whacking good time.*

whack·y (hwak′ē, wak′ē) *adj.,* **whack·i·er, whack·i·est.** *Slang.* wacky.

whale[1] (hwāl, wāl) *n., pl.* **whales** or **whale. 1.** any of various aquatic mammals, order Cetacea, native to all oceans and certain fresh waters, having a streamlined body resembling that of a fish, horizontal tail fins, and flippers, esp. the larger members of the order, as opposed to the dolphins and porpoises. **2.** *Informal.* something very large or impressive: *There was a whale of a crowd*

whale[1] (blue whale)

at the game. —*v.i.,* **whaled, whal·ing.** to hunt whales. [Old English *hwæl* this mammal.]

whale[2] (hwāl, wāl) *v.t.,* **whaled, whal·ing.** *Informal.* to beat; thrash. [Of uncertain origin.]

whale·back (hwāl′bak′, wāl′-) *n.* a freighter with a rounded upper deck, used esp. on the Great Lakes.

whale·boat (hwāl′bōt′, wāl′-) *n.* a long, narrow rowboat, pointed at both ends, used formerly in whaling and now as a lifeboat. Also, **whaler.**

whale·bone (hwāl′bōn′, wāl′-) *n.* **1.** an elastic, horny material similar to that of fingernails, forming thin plates that grow in place of teeth in the upper jaw of baleen whales. **2.** a thin strip of this material, formerly used for stiffening corsets or other items. Also, **baleen.**

whal·er (hwā′lər, wā′-) *n.* **1.** a person engaged in whaling. **2.** a ship used in whaling. **3.** whaleboat.

whale shark, a huge shark, *Rhincodon typus,* marked by rows of white dots and horizontal lines, that filters small crustaceans and fish from water as it swims open-mouthed. It is the largest fish in the world. Length: to 60 feet (18.3 meters).

whal·ing (hwā′ling, wā′-) *n.* the act, industry, or occupation of hunting and killing whales, esp. for their oil, blubber, or whale-bone.

wham·my (hwam′ē, wam′ē) *n., pl.* **-mies.** *Slang.* a hex; curse; jinx: *to put a whammy on someone.*

whang (hwang, wang) *Informal. n.* a loud, resounding beating or banging noise: *the whang of a gong.* —*v.t.* to strike with a loud, resounding beating or banging noise. —*v.i.* to make a loud, resounding beating or banging sound. [Imitative.]

wharf (hwôrf, wôrf) *n., pl.* **wharves** (hwôrvz, wôrvz) or **wharfs.** dock[1] *(def. 1).* [Old English *hwearf.*]

wharf·age (hwôr′fij, wôr′-) *n.* **1.** a space at a wharf or the use of a wharf or wharves, as for mooring a ship, loading or unloading cargo, or storing goods. **2.** the charge for using a wharf or wharves. **3.** wharves collectively. [WHARF + -AGE.]

wharf·in·ger (hwôr′fin jər, wôr′-) *n.* a person who owns or manages a wharf.

what (hwut, hwot, wut, wot; *unstressed* hwət, wət) *pron.* **1.** which specific thing or things, action or actions, or the like: *What do you want to do? What is the date of the game?* **2.** that which: *They knew what I was thinking.* **3.** anything that; whatever: *Choose what you want for dinner.* **4.** how much: *What do you think we should charge for our work?* —*adj.* **1.** which one or ones: *What books are missing from the shelf?* **2.** whatever: *Take what food you will need for the picnic.* **3.** how surprising, great, absurd, or the like: *What trouble I had parking the car!* —*adv.* **1.** in what respect; how much: *What does it matter?* **2.** which reason; why: *What did you do that for?* —*interj.* an exclamation used to show surprise, disbelief, anger, or the like. [Old English *hwæt,* neuter of *hwā.*]

• **but what.** *Informal.* that: *Never doubt but what we will be successful.*

• **what for. a.** why. **b.** *Informal.* a beating or scolding: *The bully finally got what for.*

• **what if.** what would happen if; suppose that.

• **what's what.** *Informal.* the real state of affairs; actual situation; facts.

• **what with.** taking into consideration; because of: *What with the ice and snow, it's nicer to stay indoors.*

what·ev·er (hwət ev′ər, wət-) *pron.* **1.** anything that: *Say whatever you want to say.* **2.** no matter what: *Whatever you do, we*

a	at	e	end	o	hot	u	up	hw	white		about
ā	ape	ē	me	ō	old	ū	use	ng	song		taken
ä	far	i	it	ô	fork	ü	rule	th	thin	ə	pencil
âr	care	ī	ice	oi	oil	u̇	pull	th	this		lemon
		îr	pierce	ou	out	ûr	turn	zh	measure		circus

will back you. **3.** *Informal.* what: *Whatever is that noise?* **4.** anything else: *I'll listen to jazz or rock or whatever.* —*adj.* **1.** any that: *Take whatever books you want to read.* **2.** of any type, sort, or character; at all: *No person whatever could be that cruel.*

what·not (hwut′not′, hwot′-, wut′-, wot′-) *n.* **1.** a related or similar thing or things: *pots, pans, and what not.* **2.** a set of open shelves, as for holding ornaments or books.

what's (hwuts, hwots, wuts, wots; *unstressed* hwəts, wəts) *contr.* **1.** what is. **2.** what has.

what·so·e'er (hwut′sō âr′, hwot′-, wut′-, wot′-) *pron., adj. Archaic.* whatsoever.

what·so·ev·er (hwut′sō ev′ər, hwot′-, wut′-, wot′-) *pron., adj.* whatever.

wheal (hwēl, wēl) *n.* **1.** a small swelling on the skin, as from an insect bite or hives. **2.** a welt; wale. [Form of WALE; influenced by obsolete *wheal* to suppurate (from Old English *hwelian*).]

wheat (hwēt, wēt) *n.* **1.** a cereal grass, genus *Triticum,* widely cultivated as a major food source for humans and animals, having a thin, hollow, jointed stem and long, narrow, grasslike leaves. **2.** the tiny grain of this plant, used to make flour and other foods, and having many other commercial uses, as in the manufacture of industrial alcohol, starch, and adhesives. [Old English *hwǣte.*]

wheat·ear (hwēt′ir′, wēt′-) *n.* a thrushlike bird, *Oenanthe oenanthe,* native to the Northern Hemisphere, having buff, gray, and white plumage. Length: 6 inches (15 centimeters).

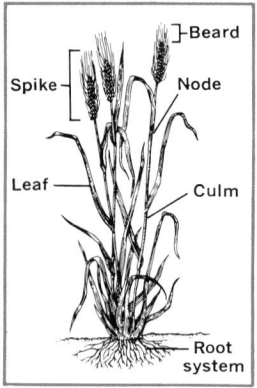
wheat plant

wheat·en (hwē′tən, wē′-) *adj.* **1.** of or made of wheat. **2.** having the color of wheat; pale yellow-brown.

wheat germ, the embryo of the wheat kernel separated from flour in milling. Rich in vitamins, it is used as a cereal and to enrich other foods.

whee (hwē, wē) *interj.* used to express joy, pleasure, excitement, or the like. [Imitative.]

whee·dle (hwē′dəl, wē′-) *v.,* -**dled,** -**dling.** —*v.t.* **1.** to persuade or try to persuade by cajolery, flattery, or the like: *to wheedle a friend into doing a favor.* **2.** to obtain by wheedling: *to wheedle a loan from someone.* —*v.i.* to use cajolery, flattery, or the like to achieve an objective. [Possibly from German *wedeln* to fawn, cringe, wag the tail, from *Wedel* tail.] —**whee′dler,** *n.* —**whee′dling·ly,** *adv.* —For Synonyms, see **coax.**

wheel (hwēl, wēl) *n.* **1.** a circular frame having a hub connected to the rim, as by spokes, capable of rotating on a central axis, used on vehicles and certain machines. **2.** any of a number of mechanical devices that utilizes a wheel or wheellike part, as a potter's wheel or spinning wheel. **3.** *usually,* **wheels.** a guiding, controlling, or moving force: *the wheels of commerce.* **4. wheels.** *Slang.* an automobile, motorcycle, bicycle, or other vehicle: *I'd go to the beach, but I don't have any wheels.* —*v.i.* **1.** to turn on or as on an axis; pivot: *The basketball player wheeled around quickly to make a shot.* **2.** to move with a circular motion: *Sea gulls wheeled overhead.* **3.** to roll or move along on or as on wheels: *to wheel down a highway.* —*v.t.* **1.** to move or convey on wheels: *to wheel a shopping cart around a supermarket.* **2.** to cause to turn on or as on an axis. **3.** to provide with wheels. [Old English *hwēol* circular frame turning on an axle.]
 • **at** (or **behind**) **the wheel. a.** doing the steering or driving, as of an automobile. **b.** in control: *Who's at the wheel for this project?*
 • **to spin one's wheels.** *Informal.* to expend time and energy without accomplishing anything: *You're just spinning your wheels by reapplying for that position.*
 • **to wheel and deal.** *Slang.* to engage in a variety of business deals or other activities in an aggressive, shrewd manner.
 • **wheels within wheels.** a series of interacting motives or circumstances; complications within complications.

wheel and axle, in mechanics, a simple machine consisting of a cylindrical drum, or axle, that is turned by a larger wheel and used to lift weights by means of a rope, cable, or chain that is wound around the drum.

wheel·bar·row (hwēl′bar′ō, wēl′-) *n.* a boxlike frame with one or two wheels at the front end and two handles at the back, used to move loads, as of sand or bricks. —*v.t.* to carry (something) in a wheelbarrow.

wheel·base (hwēl′bās′, wēl′-) *n.* the distance between the center of the front wheel and the corresponding rear wheel of an automobile or similar vehicle.

wheel·chair (hwēl′châr′, wēl′-) *n.* a chair mounted on wheels, used to help sick or physically handicapped people move about without using their legs.

wheeled (hwēld, wēld) *adj.* having a wheel or wheels.

wheel·er (hwē′lər, wē′-) *n.* **1.** a person or thing that wheels. **2.** something that has a specified number or kind of wheel or wheels. ➡ used in combination: *a three-wheeler.* **3.** a wheel horse or other animal working next to a wheel.

wheel·er-deal·er (hwē′lər dē′lər, wē′-) *n. Slang.* a person who wheels and deals.

wheel horse 1. the horse or one of the horses harnessed nearest to the front wheels of a vehicle. **2.** a person who works hard and diligently in an endeavor.

wheel·house (hwēl′hous′, wēl′-) *n., pl.* -**hous·es** (-hou′ziz). pilothouse.

wheel·wright (hwēl′rīt′, wēl′-) *n.* a person who makes or repairs wheels, or wheeled vehicles, as carriages and wagons.

wheeze (hwēz, wēz) *v.,* **wheezed, wheez·ing.** —*v.i.* **1.** to breathe with a hoarse, whistling sound: *I wheeze badly when I have a cold.* **2.** to make a sound similar to this: *The old bus wheezed when it climbed the hill.* —*v.t.* to say or utter with a hoarse, whistling sound. —*n.* **1.** an act or instance of wheezing. **2.** *Informal.* a popular saying, story, joke, or the like, esp. a trite one. [Probably from Old Norse *hvæsa* to hiss.]

wheez·y (hwē′zē, wē′-) *adj.,* **wheez·i·er, wheez·i·est.** having, making, or characterized by a wheezing sound: *a wheezy cough.* —**wheez′i·ly,** *adv.* —**wheez′i·ness,** *n.*

whelk (hwelk, welk) *n.* any of various large, saltwater snails with spiral shells, as the **common whelk,** *Buchinum undatum,* valued as a food in Europe. [Old English *weoloc.*]

whelm (hwelm, welm) *v.t.* **1.** to cover with water or other liquid; submerge. **2.** to overwhelm; overpower. [Probably from an unrecorded Old English word.]

whelp (hwelp, welp) *n.* **1.** the young of certain species, as dogs, bears, or lions. **2.** an impudent child or youth. —*v.t., v.i.* to give birth to (whelps). [Old English *hwelp* puppy, cub.]

when (hwen, wen) *adv.* **1.** at what or which time: *When did you arrive?* **2.** under what conditions or on what occasion: *When is it appropriate to wear a dinner jacket?* —*conj.* **1.** at the time during which: *when I was a child.* **2.** at any time that: *When I am embarrassed, my face gets red.* **3.** at what or which time; and then: *The children played until noon, when they had lunch.* **4.** although: *You wore only a sweater when you should have worn a heavy coat.* **5.** considering that: *How can I go when I haven't been invited?* **6.** as soon as: *Come when I call you.* —*pron.* what time; which time: *Since when have you known about that?* —*n.* the time or occasion: *the when and where of a meeting.* [Old English *hwænne* at what time, at the time that.]

whence (hwens, wens) *adv.* from what place or source; from where: *Whence comes that stranger?* —*conj.* **1.** from or out of which place, source, or cause: *They set out last week for the coast, whence news of their safe arrival reached us.* **2.** for which reason: *There was no answer to our knock, whence we assumed they were not home.* [Middle English *whennes,* going back to Old English *hwanon.*]

whence·so·ev·er (hwens′sō ev′ər, wen′-) *adv., conj. Archaic.* from whatever place, source, or cause.

when·e'er (hwen âr′, wen-) *conj., adv. Archaic.* whenever.

when·ev·er (hwen ev′ər, wen-) *conj.* at whatever time: *Come whenever you want.* —*adv.* when: *Whenever will they get here?* Also, **when·so·ev·er** (hwen′sō ev′ər, wen′-).

where (hwâr, wâr) *adv.* **1.** in or at what place: *Where do you want me to stand? Where do they live?* **2.** to what place: *Where is the train going?* **3.** from what place or source: *Where did you buy that book?* **4.** in what way or respect; how: *Where can we be of the most help?* —*conj.* **1.** in the place in which; at the place at which: *The car is where you parked it.* **2.** in or at which: *This is the restaurant where we will eat.* **3.** in or at which place: *Let's go inside where we can sit down.* **4.** in the case, condition, circumstances, or respect in which: *They are very protective where their friends are concerned.* —*n.* the place; scene; locality: *I don't know the when or where of the accident.* —*pron.* what place: *Where are you from?* [Old English *hwær* in what place, to what place.]
 • **where it's at.** *Slang.* a place or thing that is of current interest or importance.

where·a·bouts (hwâr′ə bouts′, wâr′-) *adv. also,* **where·a·bout.** near or in what location: *Whereabouts did you see them?* —*n.* the location of a person or place: *The police established the whereabouts of the suspect.* ➡ used as singular or plural.

where·as (hwâr az′, wâr-) *conj.* **1.** considering that; since: *The document began "Whereas the committee has resolved . . ."*

2. while on the contrary: *My friend prefers yellow, whereas I prefer green.* —*n.* a phrase or clause, esp. in a legal document, beginning with the word *whereas*.

where·at (hwâr at′, wâr-) *Archaic. adv.* at what. —*conj.* whereupon *(def. 1).*

where·by (hwâr bī′, wâr-) *conj.* by which or by means of which: *The mile and the kilometer are the basic units whereby we measure long distances.* —*adv. Archaic.* by what or which; how.

wher·e′er (hwâr âr′, wâr-) *adv., conj. Archaic.* wherever.

where·fore (hwâr′fôr′, wâr′-) *adv.* for what reason; why. —*conj.* for which reason; therefore. —*n.* the reason: *the whys and wherefores of a decision.* [WHERE + FOR.]

where·from (hwâr from′, -frum′, wâr-) *adv., conj.* from which; whence.

where·in (hwâr in′, wâr-) *conj.* in what or which. —*adv.* in what regard; how: *Wherein did we fail?*

where·in·to (hwâr in′tü, wâr-, hwâr′in tü′, wâr′-) *conj.* into what or which.

where·of (hwâr uv′, -ov′, wâr-) *adv., conj.* of what, which, or whom: *Do you know whereof you speak when you say they are responsible?*

where·on (hwâr ôn′, -on′, wâr-) *adv. Archaic.* on what. —*conj.* on what or which: *the rock whereon I sit.*

where·so·ev·er (hwâr′sō ev′ər, wâr′-) *adv., conj. Archaic.* wherever.

where·to (hwâr tü′, wâr-) *Archaic. conj.* to which or whom. —*adv.* to what place or end.

where·up·on (hwâr′ə pôn′, -pon′, wâr′-) *conj.* **1.** at which time; after which: *They waited for me to finish speaking, whereupon they left.* **2.** on which.

wher·ev·er (hwâr ev′ər, wâr-) *adv.* where: *Wherever did you buy that suit?* —*conj.* in, at, or to whatever place: *I'll go wherever you go.*

where·with (hwâr with′, -with′, wâr-) *conj.* with which. —*adv. Archaic.* with what. —*pron. Archaic.* that with which.

where·with·al (hwâr′with′ith ôl′, wâr′-) *n.* the necessary means or resources, esp. financial: *to have the wherewithal to travel.*

wher·ry (hwer′ē, wer′-) *n., pl.* **-ries. 1.** a light rowboat, used esp. to transport passengers and goods on rivers. **2.** a light rowboat for one person, used esp. for racing. [Of uncertain origin.]

whet (hwet, wet) *v.t.*, **whet·ted, whet·ting. 1.** to sharpen by grinding, scraping, or rubbing: *to whet a knife on a stone.* **2.** to make keen; stimulate: *The article whetted my interest in the subject.* —*n.* **1.** the act of whetting. **2.** something that whets. [Old English *hwettan* to sharpen.]

wheth·er (hweth′ər, weth′-) *conj.* **1.** used to introduce the first of two choices or alternatives: *You must decide whether to fly or take the train.* **2.** if it be the case that: *Write to us whether you will come to visit next month.* **3.** either: *Whether from bravery or stubbornness, they did not give in.* [Old English *hwether.*]
• **whether or no** (or **not**). in any case; regardless.

whet·stone (hwet′stōn′, wet′-) *n.* a stone for sharpening knives or tools.

whew (hwū) *interj.* an exclamation used to express relief, surprise, dismay, or the like.

whey (hwā, wā) *n.* the watery part of milk that separates from the curd when milk coagulates, as during the process of making cheese. [Old English *hwæg.*]

which (hwich, wich) *pron.* **1.** what one or ones: *Which of the books did you like the best?* **2.a.** used in a clause referring to a thing or things mentioned before: *This jacket, which I bought three years ago, still looks new.* **b.** used in place of *that* in a restrictive clause: *The team which finishes first will receive the trophy.* **c.** used as a relative pronoun preceded by *that* or after a preposition in defining or restricting a thing or things mentioned before: *the house in which we live.* **3.** a thing, circumstance, or event that: *You are late, which reminds me that you were late yesterday too.* **4.** any one or ones that; whichever: *Choose which you prefer.* —*adj.* **1.** what one or ones of a number of persons or things: *Which house is yours?* **2.** being the thing or things previously mentioned: *We spent four years in France, during which time we learned to speak French.* [Old English *hwilc* what, what one.]

Usage

That is preferred to **which** when introducing a restrictive clause (a clause providing information that defines or restricts the meaning of something mentioned earlier): *New York is the only American city that has more than seven million people.* However, many people do not observe this distinction and use **that** and **which** interchangeably. **Which** is used especially when **that** appears elsewhere in the sentence and its double use might be clumsy or confusing: *I had no money other than that which I gave you.* **Which** is always used to introduce a nonrestrictive clause (a clause providing only additional information about something mentioned earlier): *New York, which has more than seven million people, is the largest American city.*

---

which·ev·er (hwich ev′ər, wich-) *pron., adj.* **1.** any one or ones that: *Buy whichever you like best.* **2.** no matter which: *Whichever road you take, the drive won't be more than an hour.* Also, **which·so·ev·er** (hwich′sō ev′ər, wich′-).

whiff (hwif, wif) *n.* **1.** a sudden, light puff, breath, or gust, as of air: *A whiff of smoke rose from the small campfire.* **2.** a slight smell or odor: *a whiff of perfume.* **3.** an inhaling, as of air or tobacco smoke. **4.** a slight trace; hint: *a whiff of sarcasm.* —*v.t.* **1.** to drive with a puff or gust. **2.** to breathe; sniff. —*v.i.* to blow or be carried in a puff or gust. [Imitative.]

whif·fle (hwif′əl, wif′-) *v.*, **-fled, -fling.** —*v.i.* **1.** to blow in puffs or gusts. **2.** to be undecided; vacillate. —*v.t.* to scatter or blow, as with a light gust or puff. [WHIFF + -LE.] —**whif′fler,** *n.*

whif·fle·tree (hwif′əl trē′, wif′-) *n.* a crossbar of wood or steel to which the traces of a harness are hitched, as in a horse-drawn carriage or plow. Also, **singletree, swingletree, whippletree.** [Form of WHIPPLETREE.]

Whig (hwig, wig) *n.* **1.** a member of a former British political party in the eighteenth and early nineteenth centuries that favored reform and opposed the Tory Party. Since 1832, it has been known as the Liberal Party. **2.** an American colonist who supported the Revolution against England. **3.** a member of a U.S. political party formed in 1834 in opposition to the Democrats. It split in 1852 over the issue of slavery and was later succeeded by the Republican Party. —**Whig′ger·y,** *n.* —**Whig′gish,** *adj.*

while (hwīl, wīl) *n.* **1.** a period of time, usually of relatively short duration: *We stopped walking and rested for a while.* **2. the while.** during the time: *I read all the while I waited.* —*conj.* **1.** during or in the time that: *Did you call while I was away?* **2.** at the same time that; although: *While they are my neighbors, I don't know them well.* —*v.t.*, **whiled, whil·ing.** to pass or spend (time or a period of time) in a leisurely or idle manner (often with *away*): *to while away a warm, summer afternoon on the beach.* [Old English *hwīl* space of time.]
• **between whiles.** between times; at intervals.
• **worth one's while.** worth one's time and effort; rewarding: *Painting the house myself is not worth my while.*

whiles (hwīlz, wīlz) *Archaic. adv.* **1.** at times; occasionally; sometimes. **2.** in the meantime. —*conj.* during or in the time that; while.

whi·lom (hwī′ləm, wī′-) *Archaic. adj.* former; erstwhile: *whilom partners.* —*adv.* formerly. [Old English *hwīlum* at times, dative plural of *hwīl* space of time.]

whilst (hwīlst, wīlst) *conj.* while.

whim (hwim, wim) *n.* a sudden or unexpected notion or fanciful idea: *I had a whim to go for a walk in the rain.* [Short for earlier *whim-wham;* of uncertain origin.] —For Synonyms, see **caprice.**

whim·per (hwim′pər, wim′-) *v.i.* to cry with weak, broken sounds: *The hungry puppy whimpered.* —*v.t.* to utter with a weak, broken crying sound. —*n.* a whimpering cry or sound. [Imitative.] —**whim′per·er,** *n.* —**whim′per·ing·ly,** *adv.*

whim·sey (hwim′zē, wim′-) *n., pl.* **-seys.** whimsy.

whim·si·cal (hwim′zi kəl, wim′-) *adj.* **1.** full of or characterized by odd or fanciful notions: *a whimsical story.* **2.** fanciful or odd: *a whimsical idea.* —**whim′si·cal·ly,** *adv.*

whim·si·cal·i·ty (hwim′zi kal′i tē, wim′-) *n., pl.* **-ties. 1.** the quality or state of being whimsical. **2.** a whimsical idea, notion, or action.

whim·sy (hwim′zē, wim′-) *also,* **whimsey.** *n., pl.* **-sies. 1.** a capricious, odd, or fanciful notion. **2.** odd, curious, or fanciful humor, as in literature: *a story full of whimsy.* [Probably from WHIM.]

whin (hwin, win) *n.* furze. [Probably of Scandinavian origin.]

whine (hwīn, wīn) *v.*, **whined, whin·ing.** —*v.i.* **1.** to make a low, plaintive cry or sound, as from pain, discomfort, or fear: *The puppies whined because they were hungry.* **2.** to complain in a feeble, petulant, or childish way. —*v.t.* to utter with a low, plaintive cry or sound. —*n.* the act or sound of whining. [Old English *hwīnan* to whiz.] —**whin′er,** *n.* —**whin′ing·ly,** *adv.*

whin·ny (hwin′ē, win′ē) *v.*, **-nied, -ny·ing.** —*v.i.* to neigh, esp. in a low, gentle manner: *The colt whinnied for its mother.* —*v.t.* to express with such a sound. —*n., pl.* **-nies.** the act or sound of whinnying. [Probably from WHINE.]

whin·stone (hwin′stōn′, win′-) *n.* any very hard, dark rock, as basalt. [Dialectal *whin* whinstone (of uncertain origin) + STONE.]

whin·y (hwī′nē, wī′-) *adj.*, **whin·i·er, whin·i·est.** character-

---

a	at	e	end	o	hot	u	up	hw	white		about
ā	ape	ē	me	ō	old	ū	use	ng	song		taken
ä	far	i	it	ô	fork	ü	rule	th	thin	ə	pencil
âr	care	ī	ice	oi	oil	u̇	pull	th	this		lemon
			îr	pierce	ou	out	ûr	turn	zh	measure		circus

ized by or having a tendency to whine: *a whiny child.* [WHINE + -Y¹.]

whip (hwip, wip) *v.,* **whipped** or **whipt, whip·ping.** —*v.t.* **1.** to strike with a lash, rod, strap, or the like: *to whip a horse.* **2.** to punish by striking with such an object. **3.** to drive, urge, or force with or as with lashes or blows: *The coach had only one week left to whip the team into shape.* **4.** to strike in the manner of whipping or lashing: *The cold wind whipped our faces.* **5.** to criticize harshly; castigate. **6.** to beat (a substance, as cream or eggs) into a froth or foam. **7.** to move, take, throw, or the like suddenly and rapidly: *to whip a gun out of a holster.* **8.** to wind (something) closely in regular, even circles: *Whip the cord around the post.* **9.** to bind or cover (something, as rope) with twine, wire, or the like so as to prevent fraying or wear. **10.** to sew (a hem or other raw edge) with whipstitches. **11.** *Informal.* to defeat, as in a contest or fight: *Our team whipped the league champions.* —*v.i.* **1.** to go, come, move, or turn suddenly and rapidly: *The ambulance whipped around the corner at high speed.* **2.** to move with a flapping or thrashing motion: *The flag whipped in the wind.* —*n.* **1.** an instrument consisting of a flexible rod or thong attached to a handle, used esp. for driving animals or inflicting punishment. **2.** a whipping or lashing blow, stroke, or motion. **3.** a person who handles a whip, such as the driver of a coach. **4.** a member of a legislative assembly chosen by that member's party to assist the party leader and to direct the party's tactics and maintain discipline: *a party whip.* **5.** in hunting, the person who manages the hounds. **6.** a dessert or other dish made with whipped ingredients, esp. cream or eggs. **7.** a radio antenna in the form of a flexible vertical rod. Also *(def. 7),* **whip antenna.** [Possibly from Middle Low German *wippen* to swing.] —**whip′like′,** *adj.* —**whip′per,** *n.*

•**to whip up. a.** to arouse; excite: *The speaker's words whipped up the angry mob.* **b.** to prepare quickly: *to whip up a snack.*

whip·cord (hwip′kôrd′, wip′-) *n.* **1.** a strong, twisted hempen cord, used for the lashes of whips. **2.** a durable fabric of worsted, cotton, or other fibers woven with a diagonal twill, used for such items as suits and sportswear.

whip hand 1. the hand in which the whip is held in driving. **2.** a position of control or advantage; upper hand.

whip·lash (hwip′lash′, wip′-) *n.* **1.** the lash of a whip. **2.** an injury to the neck resulting from a sudden backward or forward movement of the head, as when riding in an automobile that strikes something or is struck.

whip·per·snap·per (hwip′ər snap′ər, wip′-) *n.* an insignificant, impudent person, esp. a young one.

whip·pet (hwip′it, wip′-) *n.* a breed of dog resembling a small greyhound, having a short, smooth coat of black or white or of various colors, and often used for racing. Height: to 22 inches (56 centimeters) at the shoulder. [Probably from WHIP + -ET.]

whip·ping (hwip′ing, wip′-) *n.* **1.** the act of a person or thing that whips; beating or flogging. **2.** cord, twine, or other binding used to fasten or lash something together.

whipping boy, a person who is blamed or punished for the misdeeds of another; scapegoat.

whippet

whipping post, a post to which those persons sentenced to be flogged are tied.

whip·ple·tree (hwip′əl trē′, wip′-) *n.* whiffletree. [Possibly from WHIP + TREE.]

whip·poor·will (hwip′ər wil′, wip′-) *n.* a plump-bodied, nocturnal, North American bird, *Caprimulgus vociferus,* having mottled brown, buff, and black plumage. Length: to 10 inches (25 centimeters). [Imitative of its cry.]

whip·saw (hwip′sô′, wip′-) *n.* a saw with a long, narrow blade, as certain crosscut saws. —*v.t.,* **-sawed, -sawed** or **-sawn, -saw·ing. 1.** to cut with a whipsaw. **2.** to have or get the better of (a person) in two ways at the same time, as by winning two bets in certain games.

whip·stitch (hwip′stich′, wip′-) *n.* a slanting stitch made over a hem or other raw edge to prevent raveling or to finish the edge. —*v.t.* to sew (a hem or other raw edge) with whipstitches.

whip·stock (hwip′stok′, wip′-) *n.* the handle of a whip.

whipt (hwipt, wipt) a past tense and past participle of **whip.**

whir (hwûr, wûr) *also,* **whirr.** *v.i., v.t.,* **whirred, whir·ring.** to move rapidly with a whizzing or buzzing sound. —*n.* a whizzing or buzzing sound: *the whir of an electric motor.* [Of Scandinavian origin.]

whirl (hwûrl, wûrl) *v.i.* **1.** to revolve or turn rapidly: *The blades

of the propeller whirled around and around.* **2.** to turn around or aside suddenly or quickly: *I whirled about when I heard the noise.* **3.** to move or go swiftly: *The explosion sent fragments of rock whirling through the air.* **4.** to have a sensation of spinning; feel dizzy or confused: *The dazzling lights made my head whirl.* —*v.t.* **1.** to cause to revolve or turn rapidly; spin. **2.** to move, carry, or drive swiftly, esp. in a circular course: *The breeze whirled the leaves all around.* —*n.* **1.** the act of whirling or spinning; whirling movement or motion. **2.** something undergoing a whirling movement. **3.** a confused or dizzy condition: *My mind was in a whirl.* **4.** a rapid succession of activities or events: *a whirl of parties.* **5.** *Informal.* a try; attempt: *I didn't think I could water-ski, but I decided to give it a whirl.* [Old Norse *hvirfla* to turn about.] —**whirl′er,** *n.*

whirl·i·gig (hwûr′li gig′, wûr′-) *n.* **1.** a toy that whirls or spins, such as a pinwheel. **2.** merry-go-round *(defs. 1, 2).* **3.** something that moves or seems to move in a whirling motion. **4.** a whirling motion. [WHIRL + obsolete *gig* top² (of uncertain origin).]

whirligig beetle, any of a group of water beetles, family Gyrinidae, that whirl about in groups on the surface of water.

whirl·pool (hwûrl′pül′, wûrl′-) *n.* **1.** a current of water having a swift or violent circular motion, usually occurring in rapidly moving bodies of water; eddy. **2.** anything resembling the whirling motion of a whirlpool.

whirl·wind (hwûrl′wind′, wûrl′-) *n.* **1.** a rapidly or violently rotating column of air. **2.** anything resembling a whirlwind, as in swiftness of motion. —*adj.* very swift; hasty: *a whirlwind tour of a city.* [Possibly of Scandinavian origin.]

whirl·y·bird (hwûr′lē bûrd′, wûr′-) *n. Informal.* a helicopter.

whirr (hwûr, wûr) whir.

whish (hwish, wish) *n.* a soft, rushing sound; swish. —*v.i.* to move with such a sound. [Imitative.]

whisk (hwisk, wisk) *v.t.* **1.** to sweep or brush with swift, light strokes: *I whisked the crumbs off the table.* **2.** to move or cause to move swiftly or abruptly: *The government agents whisked the president out of the room.* **3.** to whip or beat, as eggs. —*v.i.* to move swiftly or abruptly: *We whisked out the door.* —*n.* **1.** a quick, light sweeping motion or movement: *With a whisk of the hand, the boss dismissed my request.*

whisk (n., def. 4)

2. whisk broom. **3.** a small bunch of something, as straw or feathers, used for brushing. **4.** a wire kitchen utensil used esp. for whipping cream or eggs. [Of Scandinavian origin.]

whisk broom, a small, short-handled broom used esp. for brushing clothes.

whisk·er (hwis′kər, wis′-) *n.* **1. whiskers.** the hair growing on a man's face; beard or a part of the beard. **2.** a single hair of a beard. **3.** one of the long, stiff hairs growing near the mouth of certain animals, as dogs, cats, and rodents. **4.** *Informal.* a very small margin: *The runner won the race by a whisker.* [WHISK + -ER¹.] —**whisk′ered,** *adj.* —**whisk′er·less,** *adj.*

whis·key (hwis′kē, wis′-) *also,* **whis·ky.** *n., pl.* **-keys** or **-kies. 1.** a strong alcoholic liquor distilled from fermenting grain, as rye, corn, barley, or wheat. **2.** a drink of such liquor. [Short for earlier *usquebaugh* this liquor, from Gaelic *uisgebeatha* literally, water of life, from *uisge* water + *beatha* life.]

whis·per (hwis′pər, wis′-) *v.i.* **1.** to speak very softly with little or no vibration of the vocal cords. **2.** to speak quietly or cautiously, as in gossiping or conspiring: *Those two are always whispering.* **3.** to make a soft, rustling sound, as leaves blown by a breeze. —*v.t.* **1.** to utter very softly: *to whisper a word in someone's ear.* **2.** to say or tell secretly or confidentially, as a rumor. —*n.* **1.** very soft speech with little or no vibration of the vocal cords. **2.** something whispered, such as a rumor or secret. **3.** a soft, rustling sound. **4.** a small amount; hint: *a whisper of garlic in a sauce.* [Old English *hwisprian* to speak very softly.] —**whis′per·er,** *n.* —**whis′per·ing·ly,** *adv.*

whist¹ (hwist, wist) *n.* a card game for two pairs of players, played with a full deck of fifty-two cards. It is the forerunner of bridge. [Earlier *whisk,* possibly from WHISK; supposedly referring to the whisking or sweeping up of cards from the table; influenced in spelling by WHIST² (from the silence expected of the players).]

whist² (hwist, wist) *interj.* hush; quiet. [Imitative.]

whis·tle (hwis′əl, wis′-) *v.,* **-tled, -tling.** —*v.i.* **1.** to make a clear, shrill sound by forcing breath through partly closed lips or through the teeth. **2.** to produce or emit a sound resembling this: *The kettle whistled when the water boiled. The bird whistled in its cage.* **3.** to move with a shrill sound: *A bullet whistled past the

soldier's head. The wind whistled through the trees. **4.** to call or signal by whistling: *The police officer whistled for us to stop.* —*v.t.* **1.** to produce by whistling: *to whistle a melody.* **2.** to call, signal, or direct by whistling: *The police officer whistled the traffic to stop.* —*n.* **1.** a device designed or used to produce a whistling sound: *a football referee's whistle, a factory whistle.* **2.** a whistling sound. [Old English *hwistlian* to make a hissing sound.]
· **to blow the whistle on.** *Informal.* **a.** to inform on; betray: *Two of the terrorists were caught, and they blew the whistle on the others.* **b.** to take action against in order to bring to an end: *to blow the whistle on corruption in city government.*
· **to wet one's whistle.** *Informal.* to take a drink, as of water.
· **to whistle for.** to expect or attempt to get but without success.
whis·tle-blow·er (hwis′əl blō′ər, wis′-) *n. Informal.* a person who informs on wrongdoing or wrongdoers. [From *to blow the whistle on.*] —**whis′tle-blow′ing,** *n.*
whis·tler (hwis′lər, wis′-) *n.* **1.** a person or thing that whistles. **2.** a large marmot, *Marmota caligata,* native to northwestern North America. Length: 30 inches (76 centimeters).
whis·tle-stop (hwis′əl stop′, wis′-) *v.i.,* **-stopped, -stopping.** to make brief personal appearances in small towns, esp. in campaigning for political office.
whistle stop **1.a.** a small town at which trains stop only when signaled. **b.** any small or insignificant town. **2.** a brief personal appearance in a small town, esp. by a political candidate.
whit (hwit, wit) *n.* a tiny amount; bit: *The news did not surprise us one whit.* [Old English *wiht* thing, creature.]
white (hwīt, wīt) *adj.,* **whit·er, whit·est. 1.** reflecting all the visible rays of the spectrum. ➡ opposed to **black:** *white snow.* **2.** light in color: *the white meat of a turkey.* **3.** pale or ashen, as from pain, shock, or intense emotion; pallid: *a face white with fear.* **4.** silvery or pale gray, as with age: *white hair.* **5.a.** of, relating to, or belonging to a light-skinned people of the Caucasoid division of the human race. **b.** consisting predominantly of white people: *a white neighborhood, a white school.* **6.** free from malice or evil; not harmful: *white magic.* **7.** snowy: *a white Christmas.* **8.** not written or printed upon; blank. **9.** morally or spiritually pure; innocent. **10.** clothed or outfitted in white: *a white nun.* **11.** also, **White.** politically conservative or reactionary. **12.** *Slang.* honorable; fair; decent. —*n.* **1.** the color that is the reflection of all the visible rays of the spectrum. ➡ opposed to **black. 2.** the white or light-colored part of something, as the albumen of an egg or the white part of an eyeball. **3.** something that imparts white, as a paint or pigment. **4.** a light-skinned member of the Caucasoid division of the human race. **5.** also, **whites.** white clothing or a white uniform. **6.** blank space, as in printing. **7.** also, **White.** a member of a politically conservative or reactionary group. —*v.t.,* **whit·ed, whit·ing.** *Archaic.* whiten. [Old English *hwīt* of the color of snow or milk, fair[1], of a light color.] —**white′ly,** *adv.* —**white′ness,** *n.*
white ant, termite.
white·bait (hwīt′bāt′, wīt′-) *n., pl.* **-bait.** any of various small fish of the herring family, eaten as a delicacy.
white blood cell, a colorless cell found in the blood and lymph of humans and other vertebrates that protects the body by destroying microorganisms and foreign substances. Also, **leukocyte, white corpuscle.**
white·cap (hwīt′cap′, wīt′-) *n.* a wave with a crest of white foam.
white cedar **1.** any of several North American evergreens, often found in swamps and bogs, esp. *Chamaecyparis thyoides* and *Thuja occidentalis,* grown as ornamentals and for their wood. **2.** the light-colored, durable wood of any of these trees.
white cell, white blood cell.
white clover, a creeping clover, *Trifolium repens,* bearing white flowers sometimes tinged with pink.
white-col·lar (hwīt′kol′ər, wīt′-) *adj.* of, relating to, or designating workers employed in professional, clerical, or other fields that usually do not involve manual labor. [From the *white* shirts worn by many such workers.]
white corpuscle, white blood cell.
white dwarf, a star that has collapsed to about the size of the earth and has exhausted nearly all of its thermonuclear energy.
white elephant **1.** something that is expensive or burdensome to keep and, although often rare or unique, is of little value or use to the owner: *Their large old house was a white elephant.* **2.** any item no longer wanted by its owner, but difficult to sell or otherwise get rid of. [Referring to the veneration in parts of Asia of light-colored elephants, which are not allowed to work because they are considered sacred.]
white-faced (hwīt′fāst′, wīt′-) *adj.* **1.** having a pale face; pallid. **2.** marked with white on the face or front of the head, as a horse.

white feather, a sign or symbol of cowardice. [From the belief that a *white feather* in a gamecock's tail is a sign of cowardice.]
· **to show the white feather.** to act like a coward.
white·fish (hwīt′fish′, wīt′-) *n., pl.* **-fish** or **-fish·es.** any of several silvery white, commercially important food fish of the salmon family, found in freshwater lakes and streams of North America, Europe, and Asia. Length: to 2 feet (0.6 meter).
white flag, a white flag, banner, or piece of cloth, used to indicate surrender or truce.
white·fly (hwīt′flī′, wīt′-) *n., pl.* **-flies.** any of a group of minute, homopterous insects of the family Aleyrodidae, having winged adults covered with a powdery white substance, and larvae that suck the juices of plants and damage greenhouse plants by spreading harmful fungi.
White Friar, Carmelite. [Referring to the *white* color of his cloak.]
white gold, an alloy of gold and usually nickel, having a platinumlike appearance, used for jewelry.
White·hall (hwīt′hôl′, wīt′-) *n.* **1.** a street in London, England, near the Thames River and leading to the Houses of Parliament, where the most important government offices are located. **2.** the British government.
white heat **1.** an extreme degree of heat, beyond red heat, at which a substance, such as a metal, glows white. **2.** a state or condition of extreme emotion, excitement, or activity: *the white heat of anger.*
white-hot (hwīt′hot′, wīt′-) *adj.* **1.** glowing white with heat. **2.** extremely angry or excited.
White House **1.** the official residence of the president of the United States, a white mansion in Washington, D.C. Also, **Executive Mansion. 2.** the executive branch of the U.S. government.
white lead, any of several white pigments containing lead, esp. a white, poisonous, basic lead carbonate. Formula: $2PbCO_3 \cdot Pb(OH)_2$
white lie, a lie that is told to be polite or kind, or to conceal a minor mistake or misdeed.
white-liv·ered (hwīt′liv′ərd, wīt′-) *adj.* lacking courage; cowardly; craven.
white matter, that part of the brain and spinal cord consisting chiefly of nerve fibers covered by myelin and having a white appearance. ➡ distinguished from **gray matter.**
whit·en (hwī′tən, wī′-) *v.t., v.i.* to make or become white or whiter.
whit·en·er (hwī′tə nər, wī′-) *n.* a person or thing that whitens, esp. a bleach, dye, or other chemical preparation: *a laundry detergent with whiteners.*
white·ness (hwīt′nis, wīt′-) *n.* the quality or condition of being white.
white oak **1.** a large oak, *Quercus alba,* of the eastern United States, noted for its heavy, durable wood. **2.** any of various other oaks that have a usually light gray bark, leaves or leaf lobes that are not bristle-tipped, and acorns that sometimes mature in one year. **3.** the strong, hard wood of any of these trees.
white·out (hwīt′out′, wīt′-) *n.* **1.** in snow-covered polar regions, a condition in which the sky, horizon, and ground appear to merge in a dazzling white glare. **2.** a fast-drying, opaque fluid used to blot out typed or written characters, used esp. in correcting errors. [WHITE + (BLACK)OUT.]
white paper **1.** an official government report on a particular subject. **2.** any authoritative report on a particular subject.
white pepper, see pepper *(def. 1).*
white pine **1.** a tall pine tree, *Pinus strobus,* of eastern North America, having bluish green needles and slender cones. **2.** the soft wood of this tree. **3.** any of various similar pines.
white plague, tuberculosis of the lungs.
white potato, potato *(def. 1).*
White Russian, Byelorussian.
white sale, a sale of towels, sheets, or similar goods at reduced prices.
white sauce, a basic sauce made by combining flour and butter or other fat with seasonings and either milk, cream, or a light-colored stock.
white slave, a woman forced into or held in prostitution.
white slavery, the business of dealing in white slaves; forced prostitution.
white-tailed deer (hwīt′tāld′, wīt′-) a tawny, North American deer, *Odocoileus virginianus,* having a bushy tail that is white on

a	at	e	end	o	hot	u	up	hw	white		about
ā	ape	ē	me	ō	old	ū	use	ng	song		taken
ä	far	i	it	ô	fork	ü	rule	th	thin	ə	pencil
âr	care	ī	ice	oi	oil	ù	pull	th	this		lemon
		îr	pierce	ou	out	ûr	turn	zh	measure		circus

the underside. Height: 3-4 feet (0.9-1.2 meters) at the shoulder. Also, **Virginia deer, white′tail′**.

white·throat (hwīt′thrōt′, wīt′-) *n.* **1.** a small, Eurasian warbler, *Sylvia communis,* having a whitish throat and belly. **2.** white-throated sparrow.

white-throat·ed sparrow (hwīt′thrō′tid, wīt′-) a North American sparrow, *Zonotrichia albicollis,* having a white patch on the throat.

white tie 1. a white bow tie, worn with men's formal evening wear. **2.** men's formal evening wear. ➡ distinguished from **black tie**.

white·wall (hwīt′wôl′, wīt′-) *n.* an automobile tire with a white band on its outer side.

white·wash (hwīt′wôsh′, -wosh′, wīt′-) *n.* **1.** a white, paintlike substance consisting essentially of a mixture of slaked lime and water or whiting, a gluing substance, and water, used to coat surfaces, as masonry walks and wood fences. **2.** the act of covering up or glossing over something, as a mistake or wrongdoing: *The mayor's whitewash of the scandal angered the citizens.* **3.** *Sports.* a defeat in which the loser fails to score any points. —*v.t.* **1.** to coat or cover with whitewash. **2.** to cover up or gloss over (something, as a mistake or wrongdoing). **3.** *Sports.* to defeat (an opponent) in a whitewash. —**white′wash′er,** *n.*

white·wa·ter (hwīt′wô′tər, -wot′ər, wīt′-) *also,* **white·wa·ter.** *adj.* of, relating to, or occurring on white water: *whitewater canoeing, the whitewater section of a river.*

whitewater rafting

white water, churning, frothy, turbulent water, as in the rapids of a river.

white whale, beluga *(def. 2).*

white·wood (hwīt′wûd′, wīt′-) *n.* **1.** any of several trees with whitish or light-colored wood, as the basswood or cottonwood. **2.** the wood of any of these trees.

whith·er (hwith′ər, with′-) *Archaic. adv.* **1.** to what place; where: *Whither art thou going?* **2.** to what end, point, or condition. —*conj.* to which or whatever place, end, or condition. [Old English *hwider.*]

whith·er·so·ev·er (hwith′ər sō ev′ər, with′-) *adv., conj. Archaic.* to whatever place.

whit·ing[1] (hwī′ting, wī′-) *n., pl.* -ings or -ing. **1.** a slender, silvery food fish, *Gadus merlangus,* related to the cod, found in Atlantic coastal waters from Norway to Spain. Weight: 3-4 pounds (1.4-1.8 kilograms). **2.** any of several similar fish, as the kingfish, found along the Atlantic coast of the United States. [Dutch *wijting.*]

whit·ing[2] (hwī′ting, wī′-) *n.* white chalk, powdered and washed, used esp. as a pigment. [WHITE + -ING[1].]

whit·ish (hwī′tish, wī′-) *adj.* somewhat white.

whit·low (hwit′lō, wit′-) *n.* felon[2]. [Earlier *whitflaw,* from WHITE + FLAW[1].]

Whit·mon·day (hwit′mun′dē, -dā, wit′-) *n.* the Monday immediately following Whitsunday.

Whit·sun (hwit′sən, wit′-) *adj.* of, relating to, or observed on Whitsunday or Whitsuntide.

Whit·sun·day (hwit′sun′dē, -dā, wit′-, hwit′sən dā′, wit′-) *n.* Pentecost *(def. 1).* [Old English *Hwīta Sunnandæg* literally, white Sunday; referring to the earlier practice of the newly baptized wearing white garments on Whitsunday.]

Whit·sun·tide (hwit′sən tīd′, wit′-) *n.* the week beginning with Whitsunday, esp. the first three days of this week.

whit·tle (hwit′əl, wit′-) *v.,* -tled, -tling. —*v.t.* **1.** to cut

shavings or small bits or pieces from with a knife: *to whittle wood.* **2.** to make or shape (something) in this way: *to whittle a bird from a bar of soap.* **3.** to reduce or diminish gradually, as if by whittling with a knife (often with *down* or *away*): *to whittle down expenses.* —*v.i.* to whittle wood or the like. [From dialectal English *whittle* knife, form of *thwittle,* going back to Old English *thwītan* to cut.] —**whit′tler,** *n.*

whiz (hwiz, wiz) *also,* **whizz.** *v.,* **whizzed, whiz·zing.** —*v.i.* **1.** to make a hissing, humming, or buzzing sound, esp. while moving swiftly through the air: *The jet whizzed over the rooftops. The automobile whizzed past us.* **2.** to move or pass through or by very quickly: *I whizzed through my homework.* —*v.t.* to cause to move with a buzzing sound: *The child whizzed the toy truck across the room.* —*n., pl.* **whiz·zes. 1.** a whizzing sound or movement. **2.** *Slang.* a person having great skill or ability in some particular activity or field: *My best friend is a whiz at crossword puzzles.* [Imitative.]

who (hü) *pron.* possessive, **whose;** objective, **whom. 1.** what or which person or persons: *Who gave you that information?* **2.** that. ➡ used to introduce a relative clause when the preceding noun is a person or persons: *The author who wrote this play has an odd sense of humor.* **3.** the person or persons that; whoever: *Who steals my purse steals trash* (Shakespeare, *Othello*). [Old English *hwā* what or which person or persons.]

> **Usage** In formal speech and writing, **who** is used as a subject or predicate nominative and **whom** as the object of a verb or preposition: *Who will collect the money? Whom do the police suspect? I don't know to whom this letter is addressed.* In informal usage, **who** is frequently used instead of **whom** except after a preposition: *Who did you call on the phone? Do you know who the committee named as its secretary?*

WHO, World Health Organization.

whoa (hwō, wō) *interj.* stop. ➡ used chiefly as a command to a horse.

who'd (hüd) *contr.* **1.** who would. **2.** who had.

who·dun·it (hü dun′it) *n. Informal.* a mystery story, esp. one that centers on the gradual discovery of the criminal's identity.

who·ev·er (hü ev′ər) *pron.* **1.** any person who; whatever person: *Whoever wants to come to the party is welcome.* **2.** no matter who: *Whoever the artist is, I like the painting.* **3.** what person; who. ➡ used emphatically, as to express astonishment or disbelief: *Whoever told you such a ridiculous story?*

whole (hōl) *adj.* **1.** constituting the entire amount, quantity, number, or extent: *Did you read the whole book? I have been away the whole week.* **2.** having all its parts or elements; complete; entire: *A whole deck consists of fifty-two cards.* **3.** consisting of all or each of the members of a particular group: *The whole family came down with measles.* **4.** not divided into parts or pieces; in one unit: *The whale swallowed the small fish whole.* **5.** not damaged, injured, or broken; intact; sound: *The model plane was still whole after it fell off the shelf.* **6.** physically sound; healthy. **7.** (of a brother or sister) having the same parents: *a whole sister, a whole brother.* **8.** *Mathematics.* not fractional; integral. —*n.* **1.** all the parts or elements that together constitute a thing; entire amount, quantity, number, or extent: *I spent the whole of my savings on a computer.* **2.** a combination of parts or elements forming a complete entity or system. [Old English *hāl* unhurt, undamaged, healthy, not divided into parts.] —**whole′ness,** *n.* —For Synonyms *(adj.),* see **complete.**

• **as a whole.** everything considered; altogether.

• **on the whole.** all things considered; in general.

whole blood, blood from which none of the components has been removed, used for transfusions.

whole-grain (hōl′grān′) *adj.* made with, relating to, or designating flour or other grain products that contain the entire ground kernel of the grain, including the outer coat, or bran: *whole-grain bread.*

whole·heart·ed (hōl′här′tid) *adj.* complete, sincere, or enthusiastic: *I will give you my wholehearted support.* —**whole′heart′ed·ly,** *adv.* —**whole′heart′ed·ness,** *n.*

whole milk, milk containing all of its original butterfat and other natural constituents.

whole note, a musical note having a time value equal to four quarter notes or two half notes. For illustration, see **note.**

whole number, a positive integer or zero.

whole rest, in music, a rest having the same duration as a whole note.

whole·sale (hōl′sāl′) *n.* the selling of goods in large quantities, usually at lower prices and to retailers for resale. ➡ distinguished from **retail.** —*adj.* **1.** of, relating to, or engaged in the selling of goods in large quantities, usually at lower prices and to retailers for resale: *wholesale prices, a wholesale business.* **2.** extensive, complete, and indiscriminate: *the wholesale slaughter of war, the wholesale distribution of free information.* —*adv.* in a wholesale

quantity or at a wholesale price. —*v.*, **-saled, -sal·ing.** —*v.t.* to sell (goods) at wholesale. —*v.i.* to be sold at wholesale. [From the earlier phrase *by the whole sale* in large quantities.]

whole·sal·er (hōl′sā′lər) *n.* a merchant or dealer in wholesale goods.

whole·some (hōl′səm) *adj.* **1.** promoting good health; healthful: *wholesome food.* **2.** of value to the mind or character; worthwhile: *wholesome entertainment.* **3.** indicating or characteristic of good health: *a wholesome appearance.* [Probably from an unrecorded Old English word.] —**whole′some·ly,** *adv.* —**whole′some·ness,** *n.*

whole step, a musical interval consisting of two adjacent half steps. Also, **whole tone.**

whole-wheat (hōl′hwēt′, -wēt′) *adj.* made with, relating to, or designating wheat flour or its products that contain the entire ground wheat kernel, including the bran: *whole-wheat flour, whole-wheat bread.*

who'll (hūl) *contr.* **1.** who will. **2.** who shall.

whol·ly (hō′lē, hōl′lē) *adv.* **1.** entirely; completely: *The company is wholly owned by one family.* **2.** exclusively; only: *The company car is wholly for the president's use.*

whom (hūm) *pron.* the objective case of **who.** —For Usage Note, see **who.**

whom·ev·er (hūm ev′ər) *pron.* the objective case of **whoever.**

whom·so·ev·er (hūm′sō ev′ər) *pron.* the objective case of **whosoever.**

whoop (hūp, hwüp, wüp; *esp. for n. def. 3,* hüp, hùp) *n.* **1.** a loud cry or shout, as of joy or enthusiasm. **2.** the cry of an owl or certain other birds; hoot. **3.** the loud, gasping sound that follows a fit of coughing in whooping cough. —*v.i.* to utter a whoop or whoops. —*v.t.* **1.** to utter with a whoop or whoops: *to whoop one's joy.* **2.** to urge on, drive, or call with whoops or shouts. [Imitative.]
·**to whoop it up.** *Slang.* **a.** to celebrate noisily; have fun. **b.** to arouse enthusiasm, as for an idea or cause.

whoop·ee (hwù′pē, wù′-, hwü′pē, wü′pē) *interj.* used to express joy, gaiety, or the like. —*n.* a shout of joy, gaiety, or the like. [From WHOOP.]
·**to make whoopee. a.** to celebrate in an uproarious, festive way. **b.** to make love.

whoop·ing cough (hü′ping, hùp′ing) a highly contagious, infectious disease caused by a bacterium and characterized by fits of coughing that end with a loud, gasping sound, or whoop. Whooping cough usually occurs in infants and young children.

whoop·ing crane (hü′ping, hwü′-, wü-) a nearly extinct crane, *Grus americana,* having a white body, black-tipped wings, a red face, and a loud, whooping call. It is the tallest of all North American birds. Height: 5 feet (1.5 meters).

whoosh (hwùsh, wùsh, hwüsh, wüsh) *v.i.* to move with a loud rushing or hissing sound in or as in moving through the air: *The cold air whooshed through the open window. Speeding cars whooshed by.* —*n.* a whooshing movement or sound. [Imitative.]

whop (hwop, wop) *Informal. v.t.,* **whopped, whop·ping. 1.** to hit or beat. **2.** to defeat completely; overwhelm: *We whopped the opposing team.* —*n.* **1.** a sharp blow. **2.** the sound resulting from such a blow. [Probably imitative.]

whop·per (hwop′ər, wop′-) *n. Informal.* **1.** something very large: *That fish you caught is a whopper!* **2.** a big or elaborately fabricated lie. [WHOP + -ER¹.]

whop·ping (hwop′ing, wop′-) *Informal. adj.* unusually large or great. —*adv.* exceptionally; unusually: *a whopping good meal.* [WHOP + -ING².]

whore (hōr) *n.* **1.** prostitute. **2.** any promiscuous woman. —*v.i.,* **whored, whor·ing.** to have intercourse with whores. [Old English *hōre* prostitute.] —**whor′ish,** *adj.*

whore·house (hōr′hous′) *n., pl.* **-hous·es** (-hou′ziz). a house of prostitution; brothel.

whorl (hwûrl, wûrl, hwôrl, wôrl) *n.* **1.** *Botany.* a circular arrangement of parts, as leaves, around the same point on a stem. **2.** *Zoology.* one of the turns or convolutions of a spiral shell. **3.** any of the circular ridges of a fingerprint. **4.** anything resembling a coil or spiral in form or appearance. [Possibly a form of WHIRL.]

whorled (hwûrld, wûrld, hwôrld, wôrld) *adj.* having or arranged in a whorl or whorls.

whor·tle·ber·ry (hwûr′təl ber′ē, wûr′-) *n., pl.* **-ries.** **1.** the sweet, black, edible berry of a shrub, *Vaccinium myrtillus,* native to northern Asia and Europe. **2.** the shrub bearing this berry, related to the blueberry. [Form of dialectal *hurtle-*

whorls of
a fingerprint

berry, going back to Old English *horte* whortleberry + *beri(g)e* berry.]

who's (hüz) *contr.* **1.** who is. **2.** who has.

whose (hüz) *pron.* the possessive case of **who** and **which.**
➡ often used adjectively: *Whose woods these are I think I know* (Robert Frost, 1923).

whose·so·ev·er (hüz′sō ev′ər) *pron.* of whomsoever.

who·so (hü′sō) *pron.* whatever person; whoever.

who·so·ev·er (hü′sō ev′ər) *pron.* whatever person; whoever.

why (hwī, wī) *adv.* **1.** for what cause, reason, or purpose: *Why are you laughing?* **2.** for which: *The reason why we got lost is still a mystery.* —*conj.* **1.** the cause, reason, or purpose for which: *Do you know why they left early?* **2.** because of which; for which: *I see no reason why you shouldn't go.* —*n., pl.* **whys.** a cause, reason, or purpose. —*interj.* used to express surprise, hesitation, or other feeling: *Why, look who's here!* [Old English *hwȳ* for what cause, reason, or purpose.]

whyd·ah (hwid′ə, wid′ə) *n.* any of a group of African finches, genus *Vidua,* that are mostly brown and black in color. The breeding male develops long, drooping, central tail feathers. Average length (male): 15 inches (38 centimeters), including tail. [Modification of *widow(bird);* because its black plumage resembles a widow's veil.]

WI, the postal abbreviation for Wisconsin.

W.I. 1. West Indian. **2.** West Indies.

wick (wik) *n.* a cord or thin bundle of fibers, as in an oil lamp or candle, that acts by capillary action to draw up the fuel or material to be burned. [Old English *wēoce.*]

wick·ed (wik′id) *adj.* **1.** having or characterized by immoral or harmful intentions; morally bad or corrupt: *a wicked person, a wicked deed.* **2.** playfully naughty; mischievous: *a wicked tease.* **3.** causing or likely to cause harm, trouble, or discomfort: *I have a wicked cold.* **4.** *Informal.* skillful: *You play a wicked game of tennis.* [From dialectal *wick* bad, possibly going back to Old English *wicca* wizard.] —**wick′ed·ly,** *adv.* —**wick′ed·ness,** *n.* —For Synonyms, see **bad.**

wick·er (wik′ər) *n.* **1.** a slender, flexible twig, as of osier. **2.** such twigs woven together to make baskets, furniture, and the like. **3.** wickerwork. —*adj.* made of or covered with wicker. [Of Scandinavian origin.]

wick·er·work (wik′ər wûrk′) *n.* something made of wicker.

wick·et (wik′it) *n.* **1.** a small door or gate, esp. one that is part of or near a larger one. **2.** a small window or opening. **3.** *Cricket.* **a.** either of the two sets of three stakes topped by bails at which the bowler aims the ball. **b.** the playing area between these wickets. **4.** *Croquet.* any of the usually wire arches through which the ball must be hit. [Anglo-French *wiket* small gate or door; of Germanic origin.]

wick·et·keep·er (wik′it kē′pər) *n. Cricket.* the player stationed immediately behind the wicket.

wick·i·up (wik′ē up′) *n.* a loosely built hut often consisting of a circular frame of poles covered with brush, used by certain North American Indian tribes. [Algonquian *wikiyapi* house, hut.]

wide (wīd) *adj.* **wid·er, wid·est. 1.** extending over or comprising a very large area; vast in extent: *a wide lawn.* **2.** having a greater extent from side to side than is usual or customary: *This coat has wide lapels.* **3.** having a specified extent from side to side: *a belt two inches wide.* **4.** great in amount, range, or extent: *This store carries a wide assortment of products.* **5.** fully opened or extended: *eyes wide with excitement.* **6.** far or away from a specified point or object (often with *of*): *The arrow fell wide of the mark. Your statements are wide of the truth.* **7.** loose or roomy; full: *wide pants.* **8.** *Phonetics.* articulated with the tongue and muscles of the jaw relatively relaxed. —*adv.* **1.** over a large area; extensively: *to travel far and wide.* **2.** to a large or the full extent: *to open a window wide.* **3.** far or away from something aimed at: *The hockey player shot the puck wide and missed the goal.* [Old English *wīd* vast in extent, having greater extent from side to side, having a specified extent from side to side.] —**wide′ly,** *adv.* —**wide′ness,** *n.*

wide-a·wake (wīd′ə wāk′) *adj.* **1.** fully awake. **2.** paying attention to what is happening; alert: *wide-awake to possible danger.*

wide-eyed (wīd′īd′) *adj.* **1.** with the eyes wide open, as in wonder, disbelief, or surprise. **2.** innocent; guileless: *a wide-eyed look.*

a	at	e	end	o	hot	u	up	hw	white		about
ā	ape	ē	me	ō	old	ū	use	ng	song		taken
ä	far	i	it	ô	fork	ù	rule	th	thin	ə	pencil
âr	care	ī	ice	oi	oil	ù	pull	th	this		lemon
		îr	pierce	ou	out	ûr	turn	zh	measure		circus

wid·en (wī'dən) *v.t., v.i.* to make or become wide or wider.

wide-o·pen (wīd'ō'pən) *adj.* **1.** opened to a large or the full extent. **2.** having little or no law enforcement, esp. with regard to alcohol, gambling, or vice: *a wide-open town.*

wide·spread (wīd'spred') *adj.* **1.** extending over a large area: *a widespread epidemic.* **2.** occurring, distributed, or prevalent over a wide area or among many people: *a widespread misconception.* **3.** widely extended: *widespread arms.*

widg·eon (wij'ən) *n., pl.* **-eons** or **-eon.** wigeon.

widg·et (wij'it) *n.* any small gadget, object, or part, esp. one whose name is not known. [Modification of GADGET.]

wid·ow (wid'ō) *n.* a woman whose husband has died, esp. one who has not married again. —*v.t.* to cause to become a widow. [Old English *widuwe* a woman whose husband is dead.]

wid·ow·er (wid'ō ər) *n.* a man whose wife has died, esp. one who has not married again. [WIDOW + -ER[1].]

wid·ow·hood (wid'ō hŏŏd') *n.* the state or period of being a widow.

widow's mite, a small contribution given by a person who can scarcely afford it. [From the reference in Mark 12:41-44 to the poor widow who gave two mites to the treasury of the temple.]

widow's peak, a V-shaped point in a hairline formed by hair growing down in the middle of the forehead. [From the belief that it indicated early widowhood.]

width (width, with) *n.* **1.** a measurement of something from side to side; size in terms of wideness; breadth. **2.** the quality or state of being wide. **3.** a piece of something, esp. cloth, having a certain width: *We need two widths of curtain material.*

width·wise (width'wīz', with'-) *adv.* in the direction of the width; from side to side. Also, **width·ways** (width'wāz', with'-).

wield (wēld) *v.t.* **1.** to handle or use, as a weapon or tool: *to wield an axe.* **2.** to exercise, as influence or power: *The judge wielded authority fairly.* [Old English *wieldan* to manage, control.] —**wield'er,** *n.*

wie·ner (wē'nər) *n.* frankfurter. Also, **wie·ner·wurst** (wē'nər wûrst'). [Short for German *Wiener Wurst* literally, Viennese sausage.]

Wie·ner schnit·zel (vē'nər shnit'səl) breaded veal cutlet. [German *Wiener Schnitzel* literally, Viennese cutlet.]

wife (wīf) *n., pl.* **wives. 1.** a married woman. **2.** *Archaic.* woman. ➡ now used chiefly in combination: *housewife, fishwife.* [Old English *wīf.*] —**wife'hood',** *n.* —**wife'ly,** *adj.*
  ·**to take to wife.** to marry (a particular woman).

wig (wig) *n.* a covering for the head made of hair or of a synthetic material resembling hair. [Short for PERIWIG.]

wig·eon (wij'ən) *also,* **widgeon.** *n., pl.* **-eons** or **-eon.** any of several freshwater ducks, genus *Mareca,* having predominantly brownish or grayish plumage, as the baldpate. Length: 16-23 inches (41-58 centimeters). [Of uncertain origin.]

wig·gle (wig'əl) *v.,* **-gled, -gling.** —*v.i.* to move with short, quick, jerky movements, as from side to side: *The tadpole wiggles as it swims.* —*v.t.* to cause to wiggle: *to wiggle one's toes.* —*n.* an act or instance of wiggling. [Middle English *wigelen* to move to and fro, possibly from Middle Low German *wiggelen* to totter, reel.] —**wig'gly,** *adj.*

wig·gler (wig'lər) *n.* **1.** a person or thing that wiggles. **2.** wriggler *(def. 2.)*

wight (wīt) *n. Archaic.* a human being; person. [Old English *wiht* creature, thing.]

wig·wag (wig'wag') *v.t., v.i.,* **-wagged, -wag·ging. 1.** to move (something) back and forth. **2.** to send (a message) by waving flags, lights, or the like according to a code. —*n.* **1.** the act or practice of sending messages by waving flags, lights, or the like according to a code. **2.** a message so sent. [Dialectal *wig* to move, wag (possibly from WIGGLE) + WAG[1].] —**wig'wag'ger,** *n.*

wig·wam (wig'wom, -wôm) *n.* a dwelling used by certain tribes of North American Indians, usually consisting of an arched framework of poles covered with bark or leaves. [Algonquian *wigiwam* literally, their dwelling.]

wild (wīld) *adj.* **1.** not brought under the control of human beings; in a state of nature: *There are still wild horses in parts of the world.* **2.** growing without human assistance. ➡ distinguished from **culti·vated. 3.** not inhabited or cultivated; desolate: *the wild prairie.* **4.** uncivilized;

wigwam

savage: *wild tribes.* **5.** unrestrained or disorderly; uncontrolled: *the wild flight of a frightened animal, wild laughter.* **6.** undisciplined; unruly: *wild party.* **7.** not orderly in appearance; disheveled: *wild hair.* **8.** characterized by violent or intense activity; turbulent; stormy: *the wild sea.* **9.** characterized by intense emotion; frenzied: *wild with grief.* **10.** not carefully thought out; fantastic; far-fetched: *a wild idea.* **11.** crazy or maniacal: *a wild look in someone's eyes.* **12.** wide of the mark: *a wild shot, a wild throw.* **13.** *Informal.* extremely enthusiastic or excited: *The audience was wild about the new singer.* **14.** (of a card) having any value the player designates. —*n. also,* **wilds.** an uninhabited or uncultivated place. —*adv.* in a wild manner. [Old English *wilde* untamed, uncultivated, unrestrained.] —**wild'ly,** *adv.* —**wild'ness,** *n.*
  ·**to run wild.** to be free from any form of control or restraint.

wild boar, a wild hog, *Sus scrofa,* native to Europe and Asia, having a coarse, grayish brown coat and a pair of short tusks, generally considered to be the ancestor of the domestic pig. Height: 3 feet (0.9 meter) at the shoulder.

wild card 1. a playing card given an arbitrary denomination or value in a particular game. **2.** a person or thing that is unpredictable and about whom little is known. **3.** in certain sports, a player or team that enters a tournament without participating in a regular play-off competition. —**wild'-card',** *adj.*

wild carrot, Queen Anne's lace.

wild·cat (wīld'kat') *n.* **1.** any of various small, wild members of the cat family, including the bobcat and lynx. **2.** an ill-tempered or spiteful person. **3.** an exploratory oil well, drilled to determine whether oil is actually present at a given locality. —*adj.* **1.** unsound or reckless: *a wildcat bank, a wildcat scheme.* **2.** unauthorized or illegal: *a wildcat strike without a union's approval.* —*v.t., v.i.,* **-cat·ted, -cat·ting.** to drill exploratory oil wells in (a locality). —**wild'cat'ter,** *n.*

wil·de·beest (wil'də bēst') *n., pl.* **-beests** or **-beest.** gnu. [Obsolete Afrikaans *wildebeest* literally, wild beast, from Dutch *wild* wild + *beest* beast.]

wil·der·ness (wil'dər nis) *n.* **1.** a wild, uninhabited, or desolate place. **2.** a confused or bewildering aggregate or collection: *a wilderness of tall buildings.* [Middle English *wildernesse* wild region, from *wildern* wild (going back to Old English *wildēor* wild animal) + -nesse (see -NESS).]

wilderness area, an area of public land preserved in its natural state for scientific and recreational use by laws prohibiting road construction, mining, and other forms of development.

wild-eyed (wīld'īd') *adj.* **1.** staring in an angry or demented manner. **2.** characterized by or showing a lack of rationality or moderation: *a wild-eyed notion.*

wild·fire (wīld'fīr') *n.* a fire that spreads rapidly and is not easily extinguished.
  ·**like wildfire.** very quickly and over a large area: *The rumor spread like wildfire through the town.*

wild·flow·er (wīld'flou'ər) *also,* **wild flower.** *n.* **1.** any flower of a flowering plant that grows wild, as in a field or woods. **2.** the plant itself.

wild·fowl (wīld'foul') *n., pl.* **-fowl** or **-fowls.** a game bird, esp. a wild duck or goose.

wild-goose chase (wīld'güs') a foolish or hopeless pursuit or endeavor.

wild·ing (wīl'ding) *n.* a plant or the fruit of a plant that grows wild, esp. a wild apple tree.

wild·life (wīld'līf') *n.* living things, esp. wild animals, originating in or characteristic of a particular locality.

wild oat *also,* **wild oats.** any of various wild grasses, genus *Avena,* that resembles the cultivated oat.
  ·**to sow one's wild oats.** to indulge in the excesses of youth before settling down.

wild pansy, any uncultivated variety of the common pansy; Johnny-jump-up.

wild pitch *Baseball.* a pitch thrown beyond the catcher's reach that allows a base runner to advance.

wild rice, a tall, aquatic grass, *Zizania aquatica,* native to North America and bearing edible grains.

wild type *Genetics.* the phenotype characteristic of wild members of a given species, as distinguished from mutant or hybrid strains.

Wild West, the western frontier region of the United States, noted for its rough and lawless conditions during the nineteenth century.

wild·wood (wīld'wŏŏd') *n.* a forest that has not been cut or cultivated and is in its natural state.

wile (wīl) *n.* **1.** a trick or stratagem meant to deceive or lure: *The spy used all kinds of wiles to obtain secret information.* **2.** trickery;

craftiness. —*v.t.,* **wiled, wil·ing.** to tempt; lure. [Possibly of Scandinavian origin.]
•**to wile away.** to pass pleasantly: *to wile away an afternoon.*

wil·ful (wil′fəl) willful.

wil·i·ness (wī′lē nis) *n.* the state or quality of being wily.

will¹ (wil) *auxiliary verb* Present: **will** or *(archaic second person sing.)* **wilt.** Past: **would** or *(archaic second person sing.)* **wouldst. 1.** to be about to; going to: *I will visit you tonight.* **2.** to be willing to: *I will write you if you promise to reply.* **3.** to be obliged or bound to; must: *They will do as they are told.* **4.** to be able to; can: *This chair will not support your weight.* **5.** to be accustomed to; do habitually: *The cat will sleep in the sun for hours.* **6.** to have an inclination or tendency to: *Children will be children.* —*v.i.* to wish; desire: *Help me if you will.* [Old English *willan* to be about to, be willing, wish.] —For Usage Note, see **shall.**

will² (wil) *n.* **1.** the power or capacity of free, conscious choice: *a decision made of one's own will, a person of high spirit and strong will.* **2.** the ability to determine or control one's actions, esp. self-control: *Do you have the will to stop biting your nails?* **3.** a fixed resolution; purpose: *a will to live.* **4.** a preferred course of action; wish: *What is your will in the matter?* **5.** *Law.* a document giving the final settlement of a person's property after that person dies. —*v.t.* **1.** to determine, choose, or bring about by the exercise of one's will: *You can succeed if you will it.* **2.** to influence (someone or something) to do something by using one's will. **3.** to dispose of (property) by a will; bequeath: *to will one's estate to relatives.* —*v.i.* to use one's will. [Old English *willa* faculty of willing, intention, determination, desire.] —**will′·less,** *adj.*
•**at will.** when or as one wishes: *Repay me at will.*

willed (wild) *adj.* having a (specified kind of) will. ➡ used in combination: *weak-willed, strong-willed.*

wil·le·mite (wil′ə mīt′) *n.* a glassy, fluorescent silicate mineral, variable in color, mined as an ore of zinc. Formula: Zn_2SiO_4 [Dutch *willemit,* from *Willem* I, 1772-1843, king of the Netherlands.]

wil·let (wil′it) *n., pl.* **-lets** or **-let.** a large, long-legged New World shorebird, *Catoptrophorus semipalmatus,* related to the sandpiper, having a long, narrow bill and black and white bands on the wings. Length: 15 inches (38 centimeters). [Imitative of its cry.]

will·ful (wil′fəl) *also,* **wilful.** *adj.* **1.** determined to do as one pleases; obstinate; stubborn: *a willful youngster.* **2.** done on purpose; deliberate; intentional: *a willful waste.* —**will′ful·ly,** *adv.* —**will′ful·ness,** *n.* —For Synonyms, see **headstrong.**

Wil·liam Tell (wil′yəm tel′) a legendary hero of Swiss independence who was forced to shoot an apple off his son's head with a bow and arrow.

wil·lies (wil′ēz) *pl. n. Slang.* an uneasy or unpleasant feeling or sensation (with *the*): *That Halloween mask gives me the willies.* [Of uncertain origin.]

will·ing (wil′ing) *adj.* **1.** favorably disposed; ready: *willing to work.* **2.** characterized by cheerful readiness: *a willing candidate.* **3.** cheerfully given, accepted, or accomplished: *willing service.* —**will′ing·ly,** *adv.* —**will′ing·ness,** *n.*

wil·li·waw (wil′ē wô′) *n.* in coastal polar regions, a sudden gust of strong wind blowing downward from the mountains to the shore. [Probably a modification of *willy-willy* severe tropical cyclone, desert whirlwind, probably a reduplication of *willy,* modification of *whirly,* short for WHIRLWIND.]

will-o'-the-wisp (wil′ə thə wisp′) *n.* **1.** a faint light seen at night hovering over marshes. Also, **ignis fatuus. 2.** something deceptive or illusive, as a hope or goal.

wil·low (wil′ō) *n.* **1.** any of a group of trees and shrubs, genus *Salix,* native to temperate regions of the Northern Hemisphere. Among the best-known species are the **black willow,** *S. nigra,* having flaky, deeply ridged bark and growing to a height of 30 to 40 feet (9.1 to 12.2 meters), and the weeping willow. **2.** the light, soft wood of such a tree or shrub, used to make paper, boxes, and furniture. [Old English *welig* the tree.]

willow herb, any of several small shrubs or herbs, genus *Epilobium,* having narrow, lance-shaped leaves and bearing small, white to rose-purple flowers, as the fireweed.

wil·low·y (wil′ō ē) *adj.* **1.** graceful and slender: *a willowy dancer.* **2.** abounding with willows.

will·pow·er (wil′pou′ər) *n.* the ability to control one's actions; resoluteness of will: *It takes willpower to follow a strict diet.*

wil·ly-nil·ly (wil′ē nil′ē) *adj.* unable to be firm or resolute; indecisive; vacillating: *a willy-nilly person.* —*adv.* whether one is willing or not; willingly or unwillingly: *You must take the test, willy-nilly.* [Modification of *will I, nill I* I am willing, I am unwill-

ing; archaic *nill* to be unwilling, not to will, from Old English *nyllan.* See WILL¹.]

wilt¹ (wilt) *v.i.* **1.** to fade or droop; become limp; wither: *The flowers wilted quickly after they were cut.* **2.** to lose energy, strength, or courage: *to wilt after a long walk in the summer heat.* —*v.t.* to cause to wilt. [Form of dialectal *wilk* to wither, a form of dialectal *welk;* possibly of Low German or Dutch origin.] —For Synonyms (*v.i.*), see **droop.**

wilt² (wilt) *Archaic.* a second person singular present tense of **will¹.** ➡ used with *thou.*

Wil·ton (wil′tən) *n.* a type of carpet in which the loops of the pile have been cut to give a velvety surface. [From *Wilton,* English town where it was originally made.]

wil·y (wī′lē) *adj.,* **wil·i·er, wil·i·est.** full of wiles; cunning; crafty: *a wily swindler.* —**wil′i·ly,** *adv.* —For Synonyms, see **sly.**

wim·ble (wim′bəl) *n.* any of various tools for boring holes. [Middle Dutch *wimmel* auger.]

wimp (wimp) *n. Slang.* a person who is timid, weak, spineless, or ineffectual.

wim·ple (wim′pəl) *n.* a cloth covering for the head and neck, formerly worn by women out-of-doors, still worn by nuns. —*v.,* **-pled, -pling.** —*v.t.* **1.** to cover with or as with a wimple. **2.** to lay in folds. **3.** to cause to ripple, as water. —*v.i.* **1.** to lie in folds. **2.** to ripple. [Old English *wimpel* the cloth covering.]

wimp·y (wim′pē) *adj.,* **wimp·i·er, wimp·i·est.** *Slang.* of, relating to, or characteristic of a wimp; timid; ineffectual. Also, **wimp′ish.** —**wimp′ily,** *adv.*

win (win) *v.,* **won** or *(archaic)* **wan, won, win·ning.** —*v.i.* **1.** to be victorious over others: *a good player who wins often at cards.* **2.** to finish first in a race: *The horse won by a head.* ➡ distinguished from **place** and **show. 3.** to succeed in some effort or endeavor: *We won in our campaign to have the rule changed.* —*v.t.* **1.** to be victorious in: *to win a battle, to win a court case.* **2.** to receive in or as in a contest: *to win a vacation for two, to win a prize for the best essay.* **3.** to obtain by effort or merit: *to win respect, to win favor among the populace.* **4.** to obtain the favor or support of; influence or persuade (often with *over*): *The lawyer won over the jury with a moving defense.* **5.a.** to obtain the love, sympathy, or other favorable emotion of: *You have won many friends with your good deeds.* **b.** to obtain (someone's love, sympathy, or other favorable emotion). **6.** to persuade (someone) to marry or return one's love. **7.** to attain or reach, esp. after long effort: *to win the shore, to win entry.* —*n.* **1.** *Informal.* a victory: *The pitcher had a record of ten wins and no losses.* **2.** the first position at the finish of a race. [Old English *winnan* to strive, fight.]
•**to win out.** *Informal.* to succeed or be victorious: *The truth will win out in the end.*

wince (wins) *v.i.,* **winced, winc·ing.** to draw back or away slightly, as from something painful, dangerous, or unpleasant; flinch: *to wince at the thought of getting up early in the morning.* —*n.* an act or instance of wincing. [From an unrecorded Anglo-Norman form of Old French *guenchir* to flinch, turn aside; of Germanic origin.] —**winc′er,** *n.*

winch (winch) *n.* **1.** a machine for hoisting or pulling, consisting of a drum around which cord, chain, or cable is wound, operated manually or by machine power. **2.** a crank, handle, or lever by which a revolving machine is turned. —*v.t.* to raise or pull with a winch: *We winched the jeep out of the ditch.* [Old English *wince* pulley.]

Win·ches·ter (win′ches′tər, -chə stər) *n. Trademark.* a breech-loading, repeating rifle, first manufactured in 1866.

wind¹ (wind) *n.* **1.** air in motion over the surface of the earth; natural movement of air: *The wind whistled through the canyon.* **2.** a strong or destructive natural movement of air; gale. **3.** the direction from which a natural current of air blows; a point of the compass. ➡ used chiefly in the phrase *the four winds.* **4.** air set in motion artificially, as by a fan or other moving object. **5.** moving air carrying an odor, esp. of a person or animal being hunted; scent: *The dogs followed the wind of the fox.* **6.** any compelling force or influence: *the winds of reform.* **7.** the ability to breathe; breath: *The blow knocked the wind out of me.* **8.** empty, meaningless talk; chatter. **9. winds. a.** wind instruments. **b.** the players of these instruments. **10.** gas in the stomach or intestines. —*v.t.,* **wind·ed, wind·ing. 1.** to cause to be short of breath, as by physical exertion: *Swimming ten laps had winded*

a	at	e	end	o	hot	u	up	hw	white		about
ā	ape	ē	me	ō	old	ū	use	ng	song	ə	taken
ä	far	i	it	ô	fork	ü	rule	th	thin		pencil
âr	care	ī	ice	oi	oil	u̇	pull	th	this		lemon
		îr	pierce	ou	out	ûr	turn	zh	measure		circus

W

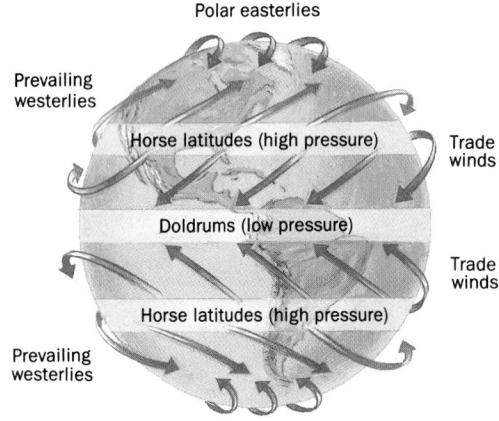

Polar easterlies

Prevailing
westerlies

Horse latitudes (high pressure)

Trade
winds

Doldrums (low pressure)

Trade
winds

Horse latitudes (high pressure)

Prevailing
westerlies

Polar easterlies

global **wind** patterns

us. **2.** to expose to the wind or air; ventilate. **3.** to find or follow by scent: *The dogs winded the fox.* **4.** to allow to rest in order to recover breath: *The riders winded the horses after the trip up the mountain trail.* [Old English *wind* air in motion, breath.]

• **before the wind.** with the wind coming from behind.

• **down the wind.** in the direction in which the wind is blowing.

• **how the wind blows** (or **lies**). what the trend, probability, or likelihood is.

• **in the eye** (or **teeth**) **of the wind.** directly against or into the wind.

• **in the wind.** happening or going to happen; astir: *an uprising was in the wind.*

• **into the wind.** into or toward the direction from which the wind is blowing.

• **off the wind.** with the wind coming from behind.

• **on the wind.** as close as possible to the direction from which the wind is blowing.

• **to bend with the wind.** to alter one's actions or opinions according to prevailing popular attitudes.

• **to get** (or **have**) **wind of.** to receive (or have) information or hints about: *If the newspapers get wind of this, we're ruined.*

• **to take the wind out of one's** (or **someone's**) **sails.** to destroy or deflate one's ego, argument, or advantage: *Failing to make the track team really took the wind out of my sails.*

wind² (wīnd) *v.,* **wound** or *(archaic)* **wind·ed, wind·ing.** —*v.t.* **1.** to wrap (something) around on itself or on something else: *to wind yarn into a ball.* **2.** to cover or entwine, as by wrapping or coiling: *to wind one's hair with ribbons.* **3.** to cause to turn on an axis: *to wind a crank.* **4.** to cause to move or proceed first in one direction and then another: *to wind one's car through city traffic.* **5.a.** to make (one's or its way) by moving first in one direction and then another: *The road wound its way around the mountain.* **b.** to make (one's or its way) in a sly, underhanded, or deceiving manner: *The swindlers wound their way into our affections.* **6.** to adjust or put (a mechanism, as a clock) into action by turning or coiling some part of it: *to wind a wristwatch, to wind a mechanical duck to make it walk.* **7.** to haul or hoist by or as if by a winch, windlass, or other mechanism operated by winding. —*v.i.* **1.** to move in one direction and then another; go in a crooked or bending course: *The river winds through the valley.* **2.** to twine, turn, or coil around or about something: *The roses wound around the trellis.* **3.** (of wood) to become warped; bend; twist. **4.** to be capable of being turned or coiled: *The strings on this guitar wind with difficulty.* —*n.* **1.** the act of winding or the state of being wound. **2.** a turn, coil, or twist. [Old English *windan* to turn, twist, move rapidly or forcefully.] —**wind'er,** *n.*

• **to wind down. a.** to come gradually to an end: *The party was winding down.* **b.** to bring gradually to an end: *I will try to wind down my work schedule.* **c.** to relax; unwind: *Jogging around the park helps me wind down after a day's work.*

• **to wind up. a.** to bring to an end; conclude; finish: *Let's wind up the job today.* **b.** to come to an end: *The meeting wound up at six o'clock.* **c.** to reach or arrive in a specified place or condition: *to wind up in jail, to wind up as a college professor.* **d.** to bring to a state of readiness or excitement; arouse: *The eloquent speaker wound up the crowd.* **e.** to coil, roll, or twine completely around; form into a ball: *to wind up fish line.* **f.** (of

a baseball pitcher) to make movements with the body or parts of the body in preparation for pitching the ball.

wind³ (wīnd, wind) *v.t.,* **wind·ed** or **wound, wind·ing. 1.** to blow (a wind instrument). **2.** to sound (a call or signal) by blowing. [From WIND¹.]

wind·age (win'dij) *n.* **1.** the influence of the wind in deflecting a missile, as a bullet, from its course. **2.** the amount of such deflection. **3.** the amount that a gun sight must be adjusted to compensate for such deflection.

wind·bag (wind'bag') *n. Informal.* a person who talks much but says little of importance or interest.

wind·blown (wind'blōn') *adj.* **1.** blown by the wind. **2.** (of a tree) shaped by the prevailing wind. **3.** (of hair) cut short and brushed forward.

wind·borne (wind'bôrn') *adj.* carried by the wind: *wind-borne seeds.*

wind·break (wind'brāk') *n.* a structure, as a fence, or a growth of trees or shrubs that serves as a protection from the wind.

wind·break·er (wind'brā'kər) *n.* a short jacket made of any of various tightly woven fabrics that resist the passage of air. *Trademark:* **Windbreaker.**

wind·bro·ken (wind'brō'kən) *adj.* (of a horse) having the heaves or other breathing impairment.

wind·burn (wind'bûrn') *n.* an irritation of the skin caused by exposure to the wind. —**wind'burned',** *adj.*

wind-chill factor (wind'chil') the cooling effect that a combination of air temperature and windspeed has on an exposed human body, given in the form of an estimated still-air temperature: *The temperature is 0 degrees with a wind-chill factor of −20 degrees.* Also, **wind chill.** [WIND¹ + CHILL.]

wind·ed (win'did) *adj.* out of breath; breathless.

wind·fall (wind'fôl') *n.* **1.** an unexpected advantage, opportunity, or gain, esp. a financial gain. **2.** a fruit that falls from the tree before it is harvested, esp. one that is blown down by the wind.

wind·flow·er (wind'flou'ər) *n.* anemone *(def. 1).* [Translation of Greek *anemōnē* literally, windflower, from *anemos* wind.]

wind generator, windmill *(def. 2).*

wind·hov·er (wind'huv'ər, -hov'-) *n.* the kestrel.

wind·ing (wīn'ding) *n.* **1.** the act of a person or thing that winds. **2.** the state of being wound. **3.** a bend, turn, or curve or a series of these. **4.** something that winds or coils, as a wire. **5.** the manner in which something is wound, as an electrical wire in an armature. —*adj.* **1.** full of bends or turns, as a road or stream; rambling: *a winding mountain highway.* **2.** curving about a central core; spiraling: *a winding staircase.*

winding sheet, a cloth in which a corpse is wrapped for burial; shroud.

wind instrument (wind) a musical instrument sounded by air being blown into it, as the flute, clarinet, trumpet, or tuba.

wind·jam·mer (wind'jam'ər, win'-) *n. Informal.* **1.** a merchant sailing ship. **2.** a member of its crew. [WIND¹ + JAM¹ + -ER¹.]

wind·lass (wind'ləs) *n.* a winch, esp. one that is turned by a hand crank, used chiefly to lift anchors and buckets in wells. [Middle English *wyndlas,* modification of *windas,* going back to Old Norse *vindāss* literally, winding pole, from *vinda* to wind² + *āss* pole¹.]

wind·mill (wind'mil') *n.* **1.** a mechanism that converts wind power to mechanical power, consisting of a number of vanes or slats radiating from a central axis that are rotated by the wind. This type of windmill is now used chiefly to pump water. **2.** a mechanism that converts wind power to electric power, usually consisting of rotating blades that are propelled by the wind and drive an electric generator. Also *(def. 2),* **wind generator.**

windmills *(def. 2)*

win·dow (win′dō) *n.* **1.** an opening in the wall or roof of a building or vehicle for admitting light or air, usually fitted with a movable sash and one or more panes of glass. **2.** the framework that holds the panes of glass in a window; sash: *I can't get this window open.* **3.** windowpane: *We broke the window playing ball.* **4.** anything resembling a window in shape or function, as the structure behind which a cashier sits or a transparent patch on an envelope that enables the address printed on an enclosure to be read. **5.** the period during which a spacecraft must be launched in order to reach its destination. **6.** any of two or more displays appearing on the screen of a computer terminal simultaneously. [Old Norse *vindauga* opening in a building for light and air; literally, wind eye, from *vindr* wind¹ + *auga* eye.]

window box, a long, narrow box on or near a window sill or ledge, used for growing flowering plants.

window dresser, a person whose job or occupation is decorating store windows.

window dressing 1.a. the act or art of decorating store windows with attractive merchandise displays. **b.** the displays themselves or the merchandise used to create such displays. **2.** anything that is made to seem or is used to make something else seem more attractive, profitable, or acceptable than it really is.

win·dow·pane (win′dō pān′) *n.* a single pane of glass in a window.

window sash, the framework holding the panes of glass in a window.

window seat, a seat built under a window or windows, usually in a recess or bay.

window shade, a piece of stiffened cloth or paper, usually opaque and mounted on a roller that moves by the action of a spring, used to regulate the amount of light entering or the view through a window.

win·dow-shop (win′dō shop′) *v.i.,* **-shopped, -shop·ping.** to look at merchandise in store windows or displays without actually buying anything. —**win′dow-shop′per,** *n.*

window sill, the sill of a window.

wind·pipe (wind′pīp′) *n.* trachea.

wind·row (wind′rō′, win′-) *n.* **1.** a long row of hay, straw, or grain raked together to dry. **2.** any similar row or ridge of dry leaves, dust, or other material swept together by or as by the wind. —*v.t.* to form into or arrange in a windrow or windrows.

wind·shield (wind′shēld′) *n.* a transparent screen, usually of glass, attached in front of the occupants of a vehicle to protect against wind or precipitation.

wind·sock (wind′sok′) *also,* **wind sock.** *n.* a long, cone-shaped sack hung on a pole or mast, that shows the direction of the wind blowing through it. Also, **wind sleeve.**

Wind·sor Castle (win′zər) the chief residence of English monarchs since the Norman Conquest, in Windsor, England.

Windsor chair, any of various wooden chairs with a spindle back, slanting legs, and usually a slightly concave seat.

Windsor tie, a wide necktie tied in a loose double bow.

wind·storm (wind′stôrm′) *n.* a storm with high winds but little or no precipitation.

wind·surf·ing (wind′sûr′fing) *n.* the sport of standing on and riding a sailboard, which resembles a surfboard fitted with a mast and sail.

wind·swept (wind′swept′) *adj.* exposed to or swept by the action of the wind: *a windswept field of grain.*

wind tunnel (wind) a chamber in which air is forced over a scale model of an aircraft or some other object, producing the same effect that would occur if the object itself were moving through the air, used in aerodynamic research.

wind-up (wīnd′up′) *n.* **1.** the act of winding up; conclusion; finish: *the wind-up of a political campaign.* **2.** the body movements made by a baseball pitcher in preparation for pitching the ball.

wind·ward (wind′wərd) *adj.* located on or moving toward the side from which the wind is blowing. —*n.* the side or direction from which the wind is blowing. —*adv.* toward the wind. ➡ opposed to **leeward** in all defs.

wind·y (win′dē) *adj.,* **wind·i·er, wind·i·est. 1.** characterized by or having much wind: *a windy night.* **2.** exposed to or swept by the wind: *a windy beach.* **3.** wordy, boastful, or boring in content or manner: *a windy speech, a windy lecturer.* **4.** of or resembling the wind, as in storminess or airiness. —**wind′i·ly,** *adv.* —**wind′i·ness,** *n.*

wine (wīn) *n.* **1.** the fermented juice of grapes, used as an alcoholic beverage, in cooking, and in certain religious ceremonies. **2.** the fermented juice of other fruits or plants: *blackberry wine.* **3.** a dark purplish red color, similar to the color of certain wines. **4.** something having an intoxicating or exhilarating effect.

—*v.,* **wined, win·ing.** —*v.t.* to furnish with wine. —*v.i.* to drink wine. —*adj.* having the color wine; dark purplish red. [Old English *wīn* fermented juice of grapes used as a beverage, going back to Latin *vīnum.*]

• **to wine and dine.** to entertain or be entertained with lavish food and drink.

wine cellar 1. a place for the aging or storage of wine. **2.** a stock, store, or selection of wine: *The restaurant had an extensive wine cellar.*

wine·glass (wīn′glas′) *n.* a small, usually stemmed, glass for drinking wine.

wine·glass·ful (wīn′glas fŭl′) *n., pl.* **-fuls.** the amount that a wineglass holds.

wine·grow·er (wīn′grō′ər) *n.* a person whose work or business is cultivating grapes and making wine from them. —**wine′-grow′ing,** *adj., n.*

wine press 1. a machine for pressing the juice from grapes. **2.** a vat in which juice is pressed from grapes.

win·er·y (wī′nə rē) *n., pl.* **-er·ies.** an establishment for making wine.

Wine·sap (wīn′sap′) *n.* a variety of apple having bright red skin and white flesh.

wine·skin (wīn′skin′) *n.* a bag made of the skin of a goat or other animal, used for storing and drinking wine.

wing (wing) *n.* **1.** a structure that enables a bird, insect, bat, or other flying animal to fly, corresponding to the forelimb in other animals. **2.** an analogous structure in birds not capable of flight, as in the ostrich or penguin. **3.** anything resembling a wing in shape or function. **4.** one of the main lifting and supporting surfaces of an airplane. **5.** the action, manner, or means of flying. **6.** an architectural structure attached to the side of a house or other building or considered as a separate section: *to add a new wing to a house, an orthopedic wing of a hospital.* **7.** *Theater.* **a.** the part on either side of a stage that is not seen by the audience. **b.** the scenery projecting on to the side of a stage. **8.** *Sports.* **a.** either of two positions on either side of the center in hockey and certain other goal games. **b.** a player in such a position. **9.** a division or faction of an organization representing a particular point of view: *the radical wing of a political party.* **10.** *Botany.* a leaflike, membranous extension or appendage of a plant part. **11.** a tactical unit of the U.S. Air Force together with its supporting units. **12. wings.** an insignia awarded to certain personnel of military aircraft, as pilots or bombardiers, when they have completed their training. —*v.t.* **1.** to do or accomplish by flight: *The bird winged its way back to the nest.* **2.** to cause to fly as if on wings; give speed to. **3.** to furnish with wings; equip for flight. **4.** to fly through, upon, or across; traverse in flight. **5.** to transport or bear in flight. **6.** to wound in the wing, as a bird. **7.** *Informal.* to wound superficially: *The bullet winged the passerby in the arm.* —*v.i.* to fly; soar: *The plane winged through the sky.* [Old Norse *væingr* bird's wing, aisle.]

• **on the wing. a.** in flight; flying: *geese on the wing.* **b.** about to take flight; departing.

• **to take wing.** to fly away; depart; flee.

• **to wing it.** to perform with little or no preparation; ad-lib.

• **under one's wing.** under one's protection or care.

wing case, the elytron of certain insects, as the beetle. Also, **wing cover.**

wing chair, an upholstered armchair with a high back and high sides extending from the back, providing a comfortable support and protection from drafts.

winged (wingd, wing′id) *adj.* **1.** having wings or a winglike part or parts: *a winged bat, a winged seed.* **2.** moving or passing on or as if on wings: *winged hours.* **3.** of a lofty or elevated nature; sublime: *winged thoughts.* **4.** wounded in or as in the wing or arm; disabled: *a winged eagle.*

wing·less (wing′lis) *adj.* having no wings or only rudimentary wings.

wing nut, a nut with winglike projections so that it can be turned easily with the thumb and forefinger.

wing·span (wing′span′) *n.* the distance between the fully extended tips of the wings of a bird, insect, airplane, or the like. Also, **wing·spread** (wing′spred′).

wink (wingk) *v.i.* **1.** to close and open the eyelid of one eye

a	at	e	end	o	hot	u	up	hw	white		about
ā	ape	ē	me	ō	old	ū	use	ng	song		taken
ä	far	i	it	ô	fork	ü	rule	th	thin	ə	pencil
âr	care	ī	ice	oi	oil	u̇	pull	th	this		lemon
		îr	pierce	ou	out	ûr	turn	zh	measure		circus

quickly, esp. as a sign or signal. **2.** to close and open the eyelids of both eyes quickly; blink. **3.** to gleam intermittently; twinkle: *The lights of the ship winked in the distance.* —*v.t.* **1.** to close and open (an eye or the eyes) quickly. **2.** to signal or express by winking: *to wink one's approval.* **3.** to get rid of by winking (with *back* or *away*): *to wink back tears.* —*n.* **1.** the act of winking. **2.** the time required to wink; very short time; instant: *We'll be ready in a wink.* **3.** a short period (of sleep): *I didn't get a wink of sleep last night.* **4.** a sign or signal conveyed by winking. **5.** a gleam or twinkle. [Old English *wincian* to close one's eyes.] —**wink′er,** *n.*

· **to wink at.** to pretend not to see; ignore deliberately: *to wink at wrongdoing.*

win·kle (wing′kəl) *n.* periwinkle².

Win·ne·ba·go (win′ə bā′gō) *n., pl.* **-go** or **-gos** or **-goes.** a member of a North American Indian tribe of Siouan stock, now living in parts of Nebraska and Wisconsin.

win·ner (win′ər) *n.* **1.** a person or thing that wins: *the winner of a race.* **2.** *Informal.* a person or thing that is successful or appears to be marked for success: *Your gift was a real winner.*

win·ning (win′ing) *adj.* **1.** that wins or results in victory or success: *the winning number in a lottery, the winning run in a baseball game.* **2.** charming; pleasing; attractive: *a winning smile.* —*n.* **1.** the act of a person who wins; victory. **2.** *usually,* **winnings.** something that is won; esp. money: *I used my winnings to pay the rent.* —**win′ning·ly,** *adv.*

win·now (win′ō) *v.t.* **1.** to subject (grain) to wind or a current of air to blow away the chaff. **2.** to blow away (chaff) in this way. **3.** to separate or remove (something desirable or undesirable); sort (often with *out*): *The attorney winnowed the essential facts from all the evidence.* **4.** to examine closely so as to separate the good from the bad. —*v.i.* to separate grain from chaff. [Old English *windwian* to fan grain in order to blow away the chaff, from *wind.* See WIND¹.] —**win′now·er,** *n.*

win·o (wī′nō) *n., pl.* **win·os.** *Slang.* a person habitually drunk on cheap wine.

win·some (win′səm) *adj.* attractive or pleasing; charming: *a winsome smile.* [Old English *wynsum* pleasant, from *wynn* pleasure + *-sum.* See -SOME¹.] —**win′some·ly,** *adv.* —**win′some·ness,** *n.*

win·ter (win′tər) *n.* **1.** the season of the year coming between fall and spring. In the Northern Hemisphere it extends from the winter solstice, about December 22, to the vernal equinox, about March 21. **2.** a period of time characterized by decline, decay, dreariness, or adversity: *in the winter of one's life.* —*adj.* **1.** of, relating to, or suitable for winter: *winter sports.* **2.** (of fruits and vegetables) able to be stored for use during the winter. **3.** planted in the autumn to be harvested in the spring or summer: *winter wheat.* —*v.i.* to spend or pass the winter: *to winter in Florida.* —*v.t.* to keep, maintain, or take care of during the winter: *to winter cows in a barn.* [Old English *winter* this season, of this season.]

win·ter·ber·ry (win′tər ber′ē) *n., pl.* **-ries.** any of several hollies, esp. *Ilex verticillata,* a widespread North American deciduous shrub or small tree, often bearing bright red or yellow fruit well into the winter.

winter cherry, a green plant, *Physalis alkekengi,* of the nightshade family, bearing a large, bright orange-red calyx that encloses a small berry. Also, **Chinese lantern.**

win·ter·green (win′tər grēn′) *n.* **1.** a small, evergreen plant, *Gaultheria procumbens,* of North America, having bright red berries and aromatic leaves. Also, **checkerberry, spiceberry. 2.** the oil of this plant or its flavor. **3.** any of several other plants, esp. of the genus *Chimaphila* or *Pyrola.*

win·ter·ize (win′tə rīz′) *v.t.,* **-ized, -iz·ing.** to prepare or equip for winter weather, as an automobile. —**win′ter·i·za′tion,** *n.*

win·ter·kill (win′tər kil′) *v.t., v.i.* (of plants and grains) to kill by or die from exposure to winter cold. —*n.* something, as a plant or animal, that has died from exposure to cold.

winter melon 1. any of several large muskmelons, as the casaba, that have white, light green, or orange flesh and mature late and store well. **2.** the vine, *Cucumis melo inodorus,* bearing this fruit.

winter solstice, see solstice *(def. 1).*

winter squash, any of a group of squashes having hard, inedible rinds, that can be kept for several months.

win·ter·time (win′tər tīm′) *n.* the winter season.

winter wheat, a hardy wheat planted in autumn, with its crop maturing in the spring or early summer.

win·ter·y (win′tə rē, -trē) *adj.,* **-ter·i·er, -ter·i·est.** wintry.

win·try (win′trē) *also,* **wintery.** *adj.,* **-tri·er, -tri·est. 1.** of, like, or characteristic of winter: *wintry weather.* **2.** lacking warmth or friendliness; cold; cheerless: *a wintry welcome.* —**win′tri·ly,** *adv.* —**win′tri·ness,** *n.*

win·y (wī′nē) *adj.,* **win·i·er, win·i·est.** having the qualities or taste of wine.

wipe (wīp) *v.t.,* **wiped, wip·ing. 1.** to rub, usually with a soft or absorbent material, as a towel, in order to clean or dry: *You wash the dishes, and I'll wipe them.* **2.** to remove by or as by rubbing (with *away, off, up* or *out*): *Please wipe up the spilled milk. I wish you'd wipe that smile off your face!* **3.** to rub, move, or apply on or over a surface: *Please wipe your muddy shoes on the mat.* —*n.* an act or instance of wiping or rubbing. [Old English *wīpian* to clean by rubbing, as with a cloth.]

· **to wipe out. a.** to kill or destroy completely; annihilate: *The epidemic wiped out half the town's population.* **b.** to ruin financially: *The stock market crash wiped out many leading businesses.*

wip·er (wī′pər) *n.* a person or thing that wipes, esp. a device designed or used for wiping: *a windshield wiper.*

wire (wīr) *n.* **1.** metal drawn into a thin, usually flexible strand, thread, or rod. **2.** a length of wire, used chiefly as an electrical conductor or structural material. Electrical wires are usually made of copper and surrounded by an insulating or protective covering. **3.** a unit consisting of several strands of wire wound together; cable. **4.a.** telegraph: *to communicate by wire.* **b.** a telegram. —*adj.* made of or resembling wire: *a wire brush.* —*v.,* **wired, wir·ing.** —*v.t.* **1.** to furnish or provide with wiring. **2.** to fasten with a wire or wires. **3.** to send by telegraph: *to wire a message.* **4.** to send a telegram to. **5.** to connect to a cable TV system: *The cable company will send someone to wire our house tomorrow.* —*v.i.* to telegraph: *We'd better wire ahead for reservations.* [Old English *wīr* metal thread.]

· **down to the wire.** approaching the final moments or very end: *We are down to the wire on our deadline.*

· **to pull wires.** to employ secret or underhanded means to gain a desired end.

· **under the wire.** just within the time allotted; just in time.

wire gauge, a gauge for measuring the diameter of wire, usually consisting of a metal disk having slots of various sizes along its outer edge.

wire-haired (wīr′hârd′) *adj.* having coarse, stiff, or wiry hair: *a wirehaired dog.*

wire·less (wīr′lis) *adj.* **1.** having no wire or wires. **2.** *British.* of or relating to a radio. —*n.* **1.** a wireless telegraph or telephone system. **2.** *British.* radio. —*v.t., v.i. British.* to communicate with (someone) by wireless.

wireless telegraphy, telegraphy by means of radio waves. Also, **wireless telegraph.**

wireless telephone, radiotelephone.

wire netting, a netting of woven wire, as for fences.

Wire·pho·to (wīr′fō′tō) *n., pl.* **-tos.** *Trademark.* **1.** a method or device for transmitting and receiving photographs by wire. **2.** a photograph so transmitted.

wire-pull·er (wīr′pul′ər) *n.* a person who uses secret or underhanded means to control others or gain a desired end. —**wire′-pull′ing,** *n.*

wire service, a news-gathering agency that supplies news, photographs, and the like to subscribing or member newspapers, magazines, and radio and television stations.

wire·tap (wīr′tap′) *v.,* **-tapped, -tap·ping.** —*v.i.* to tap a telephone or telegraph wire, esp. to obtain information or evidence. —*v.t.* **1.** to obtain (information or evidence) by wiretapping. **2.** to tap (a telephone or telegraph wire). —*n.* **1.** an act or instance of wiretapping. **2.** a device used in wiretapping. Also, **tap.** —**wire′tap′per,** *n.*

wire·worm (wīr′wûrm′) *n.* the slender, hard-bodied larva of the click beetle, often destructive to the roots and seeds of various crops.

wir·ing (wīr′ing) *n.* a network or system of wires, esp. for carrying electric current.

wir·y (wīr′ē) *adj.,* **wir·i·er, wir·i·est. 1.** made or consisting of wire. **2.** like or resembling wire; stiff: *wiry hair.* **3.** (of persons or animals) lean, strong, and sinewy. —**wir′i·ly,** *adv.* —**wir′i·ness,** *n.*

Wis., Wisconsin.

wis·dom (wiz′dəm) *n.* **1.** the ability to perceive or determine what is good, true, or sound: *a judge of great wisdom.* **2.** common sense or sound judgment: *Wisdom dictates care in the use of natural resources.* **3.** knowledge; learning: *all the wisdom of the ages.* [Old English *wīsdōm.*]

Wisdom of Solomon, one of the books of the Old Testament Apocrypha, formerly attributed to Solomon.

wisdom tooth, the last molar tooth on either side of the upper and lower jaws in humans, usually appearing between the ages of seventeen and twenty-five.

wise[1] (wīz) *adj.,* **wis·er, wis·est. 1.** having great ability to perceive or determine what is good, true, or sound: *a wise judge of character.* **2.** having or showing common sense or sound judgment; sensible: *a wise decision.* **3.** possessing much knowledge; learned: *to be wise about a subject.* **4.** shrewd; crafty; clever. **5.** having information; informed. **6.** *Slang.* annoyingly arrogant or sarcastic; impudent. [Old English *wīs* having sound judgment, learned.] —**wise′ly,** *adv.* —**wise′ness,** *n.*
· **to be** (or **get**) **wise to.** *Slang.* to be or become aware or informed of: *to be wise to illegal business dealings.*
· **to get wise.** *Slang.* **a.** to learn or become aware of the true facts: *to get wise and study harder or risk failing.* **b.** to be or become annoyingly arrogant or sarcastic: *to be punished for getting wise with adults.*
· **to put wise (to).** *Slang.* to make aware (of) or informed (about).
· **to wise up (to).** *Slang.* to make or become aware or informed.
wise[2] (wīz) *n.* way; manner. ➡ used chiefly in the phrases *in no wise, in this wise, in any wise.* [Old English *wīse.*]
-wise *suffix* (used to form adverbs from nouns or adjectives) **1.** in a (specified) manner, direction, or position: *likewise, clockwise.* **2.** with regard or reference to: *We are in trouble moneywise.* [From WISE[2].]

> **Usage** The combination of the adjective **wise** with other words, as in "streetwise," is an acceptable and standard way of forming new words. -**wise** is also used as a suffix, as in "counterclockwise." However, the use of -**wise** to mean "with regard to" or "in reference to," as in *Profitwise, the business had a good year,* is considered unacceptable in formal speech and writing, and by some in informal usage as well.

wise·a·cre (wīz′ā′kər) *n.* a person who affects false airs of knowledge or wisdom. [Middle Dutch *wijssegger* soothsayer, probably from Old High German *wīssago, wīzzago* prophet.]
wise·crack (wīz′krak′) *n.* a short, flippant or sarcastic remark. —*v.i.* to make a wisecrack or wisecracks. [WISE[1] + CRACK.] —**wise′crack′er,** *n.*
wise guy *Slang.* **1.** a conceited and cocky person, esp. one who makes flippant or annoying remarks; wiseacre or smart aleck. **2.** a gangster.
wi·sent (vē′zənt) *n.* the almost extinct European bison, *Bison bonasus,* a woodland species whose forequarters are less massive than those of the North American bison. [German *wisent,* from Old High German *wisunt.*]
wish (wish) *n.* **1.** a longing or strong need or desire for something: *My one wish in life is to be a famous writer.* **2.** an expression of such a longing, need, or desire: *to go against someone's wishes, to receive a friend's good wishes.* **3.** something that is wished for: *to get one's wish.* —*v.t.* **1.** to have a longing for: *I wish I could play the piano.* **2.** to desire (a person or thing) to be in a specified state or condition: *I wish winter were over.* **3.** to express or have as a wish for: *We wish you the best of luck.* **4.** to bid, as a greeting: *to wish someone good morning.* **5.** to give an order to: *I wish you to leave.* **6.** to impose or force; foist (with *on*): *I would not wish that task on anyone.* —*v.i.* **1.** to have or feel a wish or desire (often with *for*): *to wish for happiness.* **2.** to make a wish: *to wish upon a star.* [Old English *wȳscan* to desire.] —**wish′er,** *n.*
wish·bone (wish′bōn′) *n.* **1.** a forked bone in front of the breastbone of most birds. **2.** *Football.* a formation in which the offense lines up with the fullback directly behind the quarterback and the two halfbacks behind and to either side of the fullback. [From the practice of two persons making wishes and pulling on the bone until it breaks, in the belief that the holder of the longer piece of the *bone* will have his or her *wish* fulfilled.]
wish·ful (wish′fəl) *adj.* having or expressing a wish or longing: *a wishful look.* —**wish′ful·ly,** *adv.* —**wish′ful·ness,** *n.*
wishful thinking, the viewing or interpretation of a situation in a way that more closely reflects one's own wishes or desires than the actual circumstances.
wish·y-wash·y (wish′ē wô′shē, -wosh′ē) *adj. Informal.* **1.** having or showing a lack of strength, purpose, or decisiveness: *a wishy-washy person who cannot make decisions.* **2.** thin; watery: *a wishy-washy sauce.*
wisp (wisp) *n.* **1.** a small bunch, as of hair or hay. **2.** a small or slight bit, piece, or the like: *a wisp of smoke.* **3.** a person or thing that is slight, frail, or delicate: *a wisp of a child.* [Of uncertain origin.] —**wisp′y,** *adj.*
wist (wist) *Archaic.* the past tense and past participle of **wit**[2].
wis·te·ri·a (wi stîr′ē ə) *also,* **wis·tar·i·a** (wi stîr′ē ə, -stâr′-). *n.* any of a group of woody vines, genus *Wisteria,* of the pea family, found in Asia and the United States, that bear long, drooping

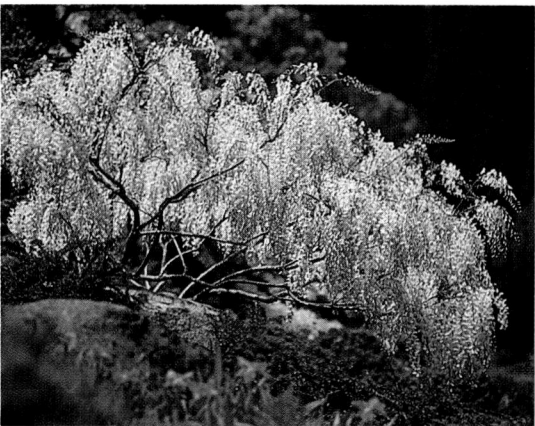

wisteria

clusters of white, blue, pink, or purple flowers. [From Caspar *Wistar,* 1761-1818, U.S. physician.]
wist·ful (wist′fəl) *adj.* pensively or sadly longing; yearning; melancholy: *The music put us in a wistful mood.* [Possibly from obsolete *wistly* intently (of uncertain origin) + -FUL.] —**wist′ful·ly,** *adv.* —**wist′ful·ness,** *n.*
wit[1] (wit) *n.* **1.a.** the ability to make clever, amusing, or striking observations or comments about persons, things, or situations: *The comedian's wit made us laugh at the world's troubles.* **b.** a person having such ability. **c.** speech or writing characterized by wit. **2.** intelligence or understanding; good sense. **3.** *usually,* **wits. a.** the ability to think and reason; ingenuity; resourcefulness: *to live by one's wits.* **b.** the ability to think clearly; sanity: *to be scared out of one's wits.* [Old English *wit* understanding, mind.]
· **at one's wits' end.** at a loss as to what to do.
· **to have** (or **keep**) **one's wits about one.** to be or stay calm or alert, as in an emergency.
wit[2] (wit) *v.t., v.i.,* **wist, wit·ting.** Present: *sing.,* first person, **wot;** second, **wost;** third, **wot;** *pl.* **wite** or **wit·en.** *Archaic.* to be or become aware; know; learn. [Old English *witan* to know.]
· **to wit.** that is to say; namely.
wit·an (wit′ən) *pl. n.* **1.** members of the witenagemot. **2.** witenagemot. ➡ used as singular in def. 2.
witch (wich) *n.* **1.** a person, usually a woman, who practices sorcery or is believed to have a pact with the devil; sorceress. **2.** an ugly, ill-natured old woman; hag. —*v.t.* to affect by or as by witchcraft; bewitch. [Old English *wicce* sorceress.]
witch·craft (wich′kraft′) *n.* **1.** the practices or power of a witch; black magic; sorcery. **2.** a magical or compelling influence. —For Synonyms, see **magic.**
witch doctor, in certain primitive tribes, a shaman or medicine man.
witch·er·y (wich′ə rē) *n., pl.* -er·ies. **1.** witchcraft; sorcery. **2.** the power to charm; fascination.
witch hazel 1. any of a small group of trees and shrubs, genus *Hamamelis,* found in North America, China, and Japan, having scaly bark and bearing small clusters of usually yellow flowers in the fall or early spring. **2.** a lotion made from the leaves and bark of one species of witch hazel, *H. virginiana,* used as a mild astringent.
witch hunt *Informal.* an investigation of persons supposedly undertaken to uncover subversion or disloyalty, but actually done to weaken opposition, esp. political opposition.
witch-hunt·ing (wich′hun′ting) *n. Informal.* the act of engaging in a witch hunt. —**witch′-hunt′er,** *n.*
witch·ing (wich′ing) *adj.* **1.** of, relating to, or suitable for witchcraft: *Midnight is the witching hour.* **2.** bewitching; enchanting. —*n.* witchcraft; sorcery.
wite (wīt) *Archaic.* a plural present tense of **wit**[2].
wit·en (wit′ən) *Archaic.* a plural present tense of **wit**[2].
wit·e·na·ge·mot (wit′ə nə gə mōt′) *n.* in Anglo-Saxon England, a council of leaders consulted by the monarch on important

W

a	at	e	end	o	hot	u	up	hw	white		about
ā	ape	ē	me	ō	old	ū	use	ng	song		taken
ä	far	i	it	ô	fork	ü	rule	th	thin	ə	pencil
âr	care	ī	ice	oi	oil	u̇	pull	th̲	this		lemon
		îr	pierce	ou	out	ûr	turn	zh	measure		circus

questions. Also, **witan**. [Old English *witena gemōt* literally, assembly of wise men, from *witena,* genitive plural of *wita* wise man + *gemōt* assembly.]

with (wi<u>th</u>, with) *prep.* **1.** in the company of: *We went with our friends.* **2.** next to; alongside of: *I sat with my parents.* **3.** into: *We mixed syrup with the milk.* **4.** having or bearing as an attribute or possession: *the girl with the umbrella, the man with a limp.* **5.** by means of; by the use of: *to fish with a pole.* **6.** in a manner characterized by; exhibiting: *to speak with authority, to dance with grace.* **7.** in addition to; and: *The bat, with two baseballs, was lost.* **8.** in the association, service, or employment of: *My friend is with a large firm. We work with a panel of experts.* **9.** in regard or relation to: *We are pleased with the results of the election.* **10.** in the care, use, or working of: *Our neighbor is good with animals.* **11.** in the charge or possession of: *The tourists left their passports with the hotel manager.* **12.** in the opinion of: *It's all right with me.* **13.** in the experience or sphere of: *With many of the poor, hunger is a constant problem.* **14.** on account of; because of: *to tremble with fear.* **15.** so as to be separated from: *to part with a prized possession.* **16.** in opposition to; against: *to quarrel with someone over money.* **17.** in spite of; notwithstanding: *With all the advertising, the product still wouldn't sell.* **18.** in proportion to; according to: *My anger grew with each insult.* **19.** of the same opinions or beliefs as: *I'm with you in your opposition.* **20.** in the support of; on the side of: *We always vote with the party.* **21.** at the same time as: *The farmer rose with the dawn.* **22.** as an associate or member of: *to travel with a tour group, to play with a band.* **23.** in the same direction as: *to be drawn along with the crowd.* **24.** to or unto: *This wire is joined with an extension cord.* **25.** in comparison or contrast to: *to judge a painting with others of the same period.* **26.** having received: *I worked on a science project with my teacher's approval.* **27.** as well or as skillfully as: *That athlete can run with the best of them.* [Old English *with* against, together with.]

　• **with it.** *Slang.* **a.** quick to act or respond; alert: *I'm not with it in the morning until I take a shower.* **b.** characterized by or knowledgeable about what is up-to-date or popular, as in fashions or fads: *My friends are really with it and know all the latest dances.*

with- *prefix* **1.** in opposition; against: *withstand.* **2.** back; away: *withdraw, withhold.* [Old English *with-.*]

with·al (wi<u>th</u> ôl′, with-) *adv.* **1.** in addition; besides; also: *advice that was interesting and helpful withal.* **2.** notwithstanding; nevertheless. —*prep. Archaic.* with. ➠ used at the end of a clause. [WITH + ALL.]

with·draw (wi<u>th</u> drô′, with-) *v.,* **-drew, -drawn, -draw·ing.** —*v.t.* **1.** to draw back or take away: *to withdraw troops from a border.* **2.** to remove from circulation, consideration, or use: *to withdraw one's name from nomination, to withdraw a product from the market.* **3.** to take back; retract: *to withdraw an offer of help.* —*v.i.* **1.** to move or go back or away; retire; retreat: *After dinner, the guests withdrew to the living room.* **2.** to remove oneself (from consideration or participation in a particular activity or group): *to withdraw from an election, to withdraw from classes at a university.* **3.** to become socially or emotionally unresponsive, as in certain mental illnesses. [WITH- + DRAW.]

with·draw·al (wi<u>th</u> drô′əl, with-) *n.* **1.** the act or process of withdrawing or the state of being withdrawn. **2.a.** the process of stopping the use of an addictive drug. **b.** the process by which one becomes physically and psychologically adjusted to being deprived of such a drug.

with·drawn (wi<u>th</u> drôn′, with-) *v.* the past participle of **withdraw.** —*adj.* very shy or reserved: *a withdrawn child.*

withe (with, wi<u>th</u>, wī<u>th</u>) *n.* a tough, flexible twig, esp. one made of willow, used for binding or tying. [Old English *withthe.*]

with·er (wi<u>th</u>′ər) *v.i.* **1.** to dry up or shrivel, as from heat or loss of moisture: *The flowers withered very soon after they were cut.* **2.** to lose freshness, force, or vigor; become weakened or wasted (often with *away*): *passion that quickly withered away.* —*v.t.* **1.** to cause to dry up or shrivel: *The fierce heat of the summer withered the crops.* **2.** to cause to lose freshness or vigor: *Time cannot wither your beauty.* **3.** to cause to feel ashamed or embarrassed, as by harsh words or a scornful glance. [Middle English *widderen* to shrivel, lose vigor, probably a form of *wederen* to expose to the weather, going back to Old English *weder.* See WEATHER.]

with·er·ite (wi<u>th</u>′ə rīt′) *n.* a glassy, white or grayish carbonate mineral sometimes mined as an ore of barium or as a substitute for barite. Formula: $BaCO_3$ [German *witherit,* from William *Withering,* 1741-99, English scientist.]

with·ers (wi<u>th</u>′ərz) *pl. n.* the highest part of the back of a horse or similar animal, between the shoulder blades. [Possibly from obsolete *wither-* against, going back to Old English *wither;* because the withers resist or work against an animal's load.]

with·hold (with hōld′, wi<u>th</u>-) *v.t.,* **-held** (-held′), **-hold·ing.** **1.** to refrain from giving, granting, or allowing: *to withhold permission, to withhold judgment, to withhold payment on a check.* **2.** to hold back; check; restrain: *to withhold one's anger.* [WITH- + HOLD[1].]

withholding tax, a part of an employee's wages or salary deducted by the employer as an installment on the employee's income tax.

with·in (wi<u>th</u> in′, with-) *prep.* **1.** in or into the inner or interior part or parts of; in the space bounded or enclosed by: *The children were told to play within the fence.* **2.** inside the limits of, as in time, space, amount, or degree: *to return within an hour, a cabin within 5 miles of the trail.* **3.** in the scope, range, or influence of: *That was the worst storm within memory. That's not within the court's jurisdiction.* **4.** acting or meeting the fixed requirements or standards of: *within the law.* —*adv.* **1.** in or into the inner or interior part or parts; inside; internally: *The building was locked, and all of us within felt safe.* **2.** in or inside a house or other building; indoors: *to inquire within.* **3.** inside the body, mind, or heart; inwardly: *to feel sorrow within.* —*n.* an inner or interior part, place, or area: *to work for reform from within.* [Old English *withinnan* on the inside.]

with·out (wi<u>th</u> out′, with-) *prep.* **1.** in the absence or omission of; not having; lacking: *to go without sleep, to be without a cent.* **2.** free or exempt from: *a diamond without flaw, a world without fear.* **3.** so as to neglect or avoid: *to leave without saying good-bye.* **4.** unaccompanied by: *We went to the movies without them.* **5.** at, on, or to the outer or exterior part or parts of; outside of; beyond. —*adv.* **1.** with something absent or lacking: *to go without, to do without.* **2.** on the outer or exterior part or parts; outside; externally. **3.** outdoors. —*conj. Slang.* unless. —*n.* an outer part or place: *a voice from without.* [Old English *withūtan* on the outside of.]

with·stand (with stand′, wi<u>th</u>-) *v.,* **-stood** (-stŭd′), **-stand·ing.** —*v.t.* to hold out against or oppose successfully: *to withstand temptation, a house that withstood a hurricane.* —*v.i.* to oppose successfully; endure without yielding. [Old English *withstandan* to resist, from *with-* against + *standan.* See STAND.]

with·y (wi<u>th</u>′ē, wī<u>th</u>′ē) *n., pl.* **with·ies. 1.** withe. **2.** a rope or halter made of withes. [Old English *wīthig* willow, willow twig.]

wit·less (wit′lis) *adj.* lacking intelligence or sense; foolish. —**wit′less·ly,** *adv.* —**wit′less·ness,** *n.*

wit·loof (wit′lōf′) *n.* a variety of chicory whose leaves are used in salads. [Dutch *witloof* literally, white foliage.]

wit·ness (wit′nis) *n.* **1.** a person who has seen or heard something and can therefore give a firsthand account of it. **2.** a person who testifies in a court of law under oath or affirmation, either orally or by deposition. **3.** a person who is present at a transaction, as the signing of a contract or will, and can give evidence as to its authenticity. **4.** an attestation of a fact or event; testimony. ➠ used chiefly in the phrase *to bear witness.* **5.** something that serves as evidence or proof. —*v.t.* **1.** to be present to see or hear; observe personally: *to witness an argument.* **2.** to be the time or scene of: *This century has witnessed the steady growth of urban centers.* **3.** to affix one's signature to (a document) as a witness. **4.** to serve as evidence or proof of: *The wounds we bear all too well witness the cruelty we have endured.* **5.** to testify to. [Old English *witnes* knowledge, evidence, from *wit.* See WIT[1].]

witness stand, the area in which a witness stands or sits while being questioned in a court of law.

wit·ted (wit′id) *adj.* having or marked by (a specified kind of) wit. ➠ used in combination: *quick-witted, dull-witted.*

wit·ti·cism (wit′ə siz′əm) *n.* a witty saying or remark. [WITTY + *-ism;* influenced by CRITICISM.]

wit·ting (wit′ing) *v.* *Archaic.* the present participle of **wit**[2]. —*adj.* done or acting consciously or with deliberation: *a witting accomplice.* —**wit′ting·ly,** *adv.*

wit·ty (wit′ē) *adj.,* **-ti·er, -ti·est.** having or characterized by wit; cleverly amusing: *a witty journalist, a witty rebuttal.* [Old English *wittig* wise, from *wit.* See WIT[1].] —**wit′ti·ly,** *adv.* —**wit′ti·ness,** *n.*

wive (wīv) *Archaic. v.,* **wived, wiv·ing.** —*v.t.* **1.** to marry (a woman). **2.** to furnish with a wife. —*v.i.* to marry a woman. [Old English *wīfian* to marry, take a wife, from *wīf* wife.]

wi·vern (wī′vərn) *also,* **wyvern.** *n.* in heraldry, a mythical beast resembling a two-legged dragon with wings and a barbed tail. [From Middle English *wivere* viper, from Old French *wivre,* from Latin *vīpera.*]

wives (wīvz) the plural of **wife.**

wiz·ard (wiz′ərd) *n.* **1.** a person, esp. a man, who uses supernatural power to control or influence events, people, or phenomena; male witch; sorcerer. **2.** an extraordinarily clever or skillful person; expert; genius: *a financial wizard.* —*adj.* magic. [Middle English *wysard* sage, going back to Old English *wīs.* See WISE[1].]

wiz·ard·ry (wiz′ərd rē) *n.* **1.** the art or methods of a wizard; witchcraft; sorcery. **2.** great skill or artistry: *mechanical wizardry.* —For Synonyms, see **magic.**

wiz·en (wiz′ən) *v.t., v.i.* to shrivel up; wither. —*adj.* wizened. [Old English *wisnian* to wither.]

wiz·ened (wiz′ənd) *adj.* dried out; shriveled; withered: *a wizened old sailor.*

wk *also,* **wk.** *pl.* **wks** week.

wk. *pl.* **wks.** work.

wkly., weekly.

wl 1. water line. **2.** wavelength.

WNW, west-northwest.

woad (wōd) *n.* **1.** an erect, branching herb, *Isatis tinctoria,* of the mustard family, native to Europe and formerly widely cultivated for the dye made from its leaves. **2.** the dye itself, blue in color and similar to indigo. [Old English *wād.*]

wob·ble (wob′əl) *also,* **wabble.** *v.i.,* **-bled, -bling. 1.** to move or sway unsteadily from side to side: *The old chair wobbles because its legs are coming loose. The tire wobbled after the blowout.* **2.** to shake or quaver; tremble: *The actor's voice wobbled with emotion.* **3.** to be unable to choose between different opinions, feelings, or courses of action; vacillate. —*n.* an unsteady, swaying movement: *the wobble of the earth as it rotates on its axis.* [Possibly from Low German *wabbeln* to move unsteadily.] —**wob′bler,** *n.*

wob·bly (wob′lē) *also,* **wabbly.** *adj.,* **-bli·er, -bli·est.** tending to wobble; unsteady; shaky: *The table has wobbly legs.*

Wo·den (wōd′n) *n.* in Teutonic mythology, the king of the gods. His Norse counterpart is Odin.

woe (wō) *n.* **1.** great sadness or suffering; sorrow; grief: *a tale of woe.* **2.** great trouble or misfortune; disaster: *economic woes.* —*interj.* alas. [Old English *wā.*]

woe·be·gone (wō′bi gôn′, -gon′) *also,* **wo·be·gone.** *adj.* showing or feeling great sorrow or grief; mournful: *a woebegone look.*

woe·ful (wō′fəl) *adj.* **1.** afflicted with, characterized by, or expressive of woe; sorrowful; sad: *a woeful look.* **2.** pitiful or deplorable: *woeful inadequacies, woeful merchandise.* —**woe′ful·ly,** *adv.* —**woe′ful·ness,** *n.*

wok (wok) *n.* a bowl-shaped metal pan used esp. in Chinese cooking to fry and steam food. [Cantonese *wôk* this kind of pan.]

woke (wōk) a past tense of **wake**[1].

wo·ken (wō′kən) *Archaic.* a past participle of **wake**[1].

wold (wōld) *n.* a high, open tract of rolling land; moor. [Old English *wald, weald* forest.]

wolf (wŭlf) *n., pl.* **wolves** (wŭlvz). **1.** any of various wild mammals of the dog family, esp. the gray wolf. **2.** the fur of this animal. **3.** a person who is cruel, greedy, or destructive. **4.** *Slang.* a man who chases after women. —*v.t.* to devour quickly and ravenously (often with *down*): *to wolf down one's food.* [Old English *wulf* this animal, cruel person.] —**wolf′like′,** *adj.*

• **a wolf in sheep's clothing.** a person who hides evil intentions or cruelty behind an innocent or friendly exterior.

• **to cry wolf.** to raise a false alarm.

• **to keep the wolf from the door.** to ward off hunger or want.

wolf·bane (wŭlf′bān′) wolfsbane.

wolf dog 1. any of various large dogs used for hunting wolves. **2.** a cross between a dog and a wolf.

wolf·hound (wŭlf′hound′) *n.* a large dog of any of various breeds used for hunting wolves, such as the Irish wolfhound or the borzoi.

wolf·ish (wŭl′fish) *adj.* characteristic of or resembling a wolf; greedy or cruel. —**wolf′ish·ly,** *adv.* —**wolf′ish·ness,** *n.*

wolf·ram (wŭl′frəm) *n.* tungsten. [German *Wolfram* literally, wolf's dirt, from Middle High German *wolf* wolf + *rām* dirt; probably because it was considered inferior to tin.]

wolf·ram·ite (wŭl′frə mīt′) *n.* a black to brown, opaque tungsten, iron, and manganese mineral that is the principal ore of tungsten. Formula: (Fe, Mn)WO$_4$

wolfs·bane (wŭlfs′bān′) *also,* **wolfbane, wolf's-bane.** *n.* aconite *(def. 1).*

wolf spider, any of a large family (Lycosidae) of active spiders, living and pursuing their prey on the ground without building webs. The female carries her egg sac and later the emerging young.

wol·ver·ine (wŭl′və rēn′, wŭl′-və rēn′) *also,* **wol·ver·ene.** *n.* a ferocious, carnivorous mammal, *Gulo gulo,* native to northern regions, having dark brown fur with pale bands. It is the largest member of the weasel family. Height: to 17 inches (43 centime-

wolverine

ters) at the shoulder. Also, **glutton.** [From WOLF; referring to its wolflike nature.]

wolves (wŭlvz) the plural of **wolf.**

wom·an (wŭm′ən) *n., pl.* **wom·en. 1.** an adult female human being. **2.** adult female human beings collectively; female part of the human race. **3.** a female human being endowed with the characteristics and qualities considered to be typical of a woman: *The woman in her rebelled against discrimination based on sex.* **4.** a female worker or servant. **5.** a sweetheart or mistress. **6.** *Informal.* a wife. —*adj.* female: *a woman psychiatrist.* [Old English *wīfman* adult female human being, female servant, from *wīf* adult female human being, wife + *man* human being.]

wom·an·hood (wŭm′ən hŭd′) *n.* **1.** the state of being an adult female human being. **2.** the characteristics or qualities considered to be womanly. **3.** women collectively.

wom·an·ish (wŭm′ə nish) *adj.* **1.** of, for, or characteristic of a woman. **2.** resembling a woman; effeminate: *womanish fears.* —**wom′an·ish·ly,** *adv.* —**wom′an·ish·ness,** *n.*

wom·an·kind (wŭm′ən kīnd′) *n.* women collectively.

wom·an·like (wŭm′ən līk′) *adj.* having the qualities of or befitting a woman; womanly.

wom·an·ly (wŭm′ən lē) *adj.* **1.** having the qualities generally attributed to or characteristic of women. **2.** relating to or appropriate for a woman. —*adv.* in a womanly way. —**wom′an·li·ness,** *n.*

woman of the world, a worldly, sophisticated, and cosmopolitan woman.

woman's rights, women's rights.

woman suffrage, the right of women to vote.

wom·an·suf·fra·gist (wŭm′ən suf′rə jist) *n.* a man or woman who advocates woman suffrage.

womb (wüm) *n.* **1.** uterus *(def. 1).* **2.** any place where something is nurtured or generated: *Events that are ripening in the womb of the future* (Samuel Taylor Coleridge, 1810). **3.** any enveloping or protecting space or cavity: *the deep dark womb of the sea.* [Old English *wamb* uterus, belly, hollow space or cavity.]

wom·bat (wom′bat) *n.* any of several nocturnal, burrowing marsupials, family Phascolomidae, native to Australia, having a stocky body and a coarse coat of black or yellowish brown hair. Length: to 48 inches (122 centimeters), including tail. [Australian native name *womback.*]

wom·en (wim′ən) the plural of **woman.**

wom·en·folk (wim′ən fōk′) *also,* **wom·en·folks.** *pl. n.* women collectively, esp. the female members of a family or other group.

women's liberation, a movement seeking equal opportunities and privileges for women in all areas of society. Also, **women's lib, women's movement.**

women's rights *also,* **woman's rights.** the rights claimed for women to opportunities and privileges equal to those of men, as in employment and suffrage.

won[1] (wun) the past tense and past participle of **win.**

won[2] (won) *n., pl.* **won.** the monetary unit of North Korea and South Korea. [From Korean *wŏn,* from Chinese *yuan,* round, circle; so called because of the roundness of coins.]

won·der (wun′dər) *n.* **1.** a person or thing that arouses astonishment, curiosity, or admiration: *The pyramids of Egypt are one of the wonders of the ancient world. It's a wonder that they survived the accident.* **2.** a feeling, attitude, or state caused by this: *We watched with wonder as the moon eclipsed the sun.* —*v.i.* **1.** to want to know or learn; be curious or doubtful: *I often wonder about how we could have saved the project.* **2.** to feel or express admiration or astonishment: *to wonder at an athlete's strength and endurance.* —*v.t.* to want to know or learn about; be curious or doubtful about: *I wonder what will be discovered by the latest space probe.* [Old English *wundor* marvel, miracle.] —**won′der·ing·ly,** *adv.*

• **to do** (or **work**) **wonders.** to produce very good results.

won·der·ful (wun′dər fəl) *adj.* **1.** causing or exciting wonder; astonishing: *a wonderful invention, a wonderful work of art.* **2.** very good; excellent: *We had a wonderful picnic in the park.* —**won′der·ful·ly,** *adv.* —**won′der·ful·ness,** *n.*

won·der·land (wun′dər land′) *n.* **1.** a wonderful place, region, or scene: *The mountains were a winter wonderland.* **2.** a wonderful imaginary realm or fantasy world.

a	at	e	end	o	hot	u	up	hw	white		about
ā	ape	ē	me	ō	old	ū	use	ng	song		taken
ä	far	i	it	ô	fork	ü	rule	th	thin	ə	pencil
âr	care	ī	ice	oi	oil	u̇	pull	t͟h	this		lemon
				îr	pierce	ou	out	ûr	turn	zh	measure		circus

won·der·ment (wun′dər ment) *n.* **1.** the state or emotion of wonder: *The group of tourists stood in wonderment amidst the ancient ruins.* **2.** something that causes wonder.

won·drous (wun′drəs) *adj.* wonderful. —*adv. Archaic.* extraordinarily; wonderfully. [Modification (influenced by -OUS) of obsolete *wonders,* genitive of WONDER.] —**won′drous·ly,** *adv.* —**won′drous·ness,** *n.*

wont (wônt, wōnt, wunt) *adj.* accustomed; used: *We are wont to stay at home on Sundays.* —*n.* a customary practice; habit: *It was my wont to read the paper after work.* [Middle English *wont, woned* accustomed, past participle of Middle English *wonen* to be accustomed, dwell, from Old English *wunian.*]

won't (wōnt) *contr.* will not.

wont·ed (wôn′tid, wōn′-, wun′-) *adj.* accustomed; customary: *to sit at one's wonted place.*

won·ton (won′ton) *also,* **won ton.** *n.* in Chinese cooking, a dumpling filled with chopped meat, fish, or vegetables, eaten with soup or fried. [Cantonese *wan t'an* this dumpling.]

woo (wü) *v.t.* **1.** to seek the love or affection of, esp. with the intent to marry; court. **2.** to try to win over: *corporations that woo college graduates with promises of high salaries.* **3.** to try to obtain or gain; seek: *to woo public support for an environmental issue.* —*v.i.* to seek the love or affection of someone, esp. with the intent to marry. [Old English *wōgian* to court.]

wood (wüd) *n.* **1.** the hard, fibrous material beneath the bark and making up the greater part of the stems and branches of trees and shrubs. **2.** this material, sometimes with the bark still on, cut or prepared for use, such as timber, lumber, pulpwood, or firewood. **3.** *usually,* **woods.** a dense growth of trees; forest; grove. **4.** a golf club with a wooden head. **5.** something made of wood, such as a woodwind instrument. —*adj.* **1.** made of wood; wooden. **2.** made or suitable for using, holding, or cutting wood: *a wood saw.* **3.** inhabiting or growing in woods. —*v.t.* **1.** to cover or plant with trees. **2.** to supply with wood for fuel. —*v.i.* to gather or take in supplies of wood for fuel. [Old English *wudu* dense growth of trees, the hard material beneath the bark of trees and shrubs.]

· **out of the woods.** *Informal.* finally clear of or free from danger, hazard, or other difficulty: *The accident victim is out of the woods and recovering nicely.*

wood alcohol, methanol.

wood anemone, any of several anemones, esp. *Anemone quinquefolia,* a woodland plant that grows wild in North America, bearing white or purple flowers.

wood·bine (wüd′bīn′) *n.* **1.** any of several climbing shrubs or vines, esp. a European honeysuckle, *Lonicera periclymenum,* bearing flowers that are red or purple on the outside. **2.** Virginia creeper. [Old English *wudubind* a climbing plant, as ivy, going back to *wudu* wood + *bindan* to tie fast; referring to its climbing up and winding around trees.]

wood·block (wüd′blok′) *n.* woodcut.

wood·carv·ing (wüd′kär′ving) *n.* **1.** the art or technique of carving wood. **2.** an object carved of wood. —**wood′carv′er,** *n.*

wood·chuck (wüd′chuk′) *n.* a short-legged, North American marmot, *Marmota monax,* having coarse brown or gray fur. Length: to 24 inches (61 centimeters), including tail. Also, **groundhog.** [Probably a modification (influenced by WOOD) of Cree *wuchak* marten, weasel.]

wood·cock (wüd′kok′) *n., pl.* **-cocks** or **-cock.** either of two game birds, *Philohela minor,* of North America, and *Scolopax rusticola,* of Eurasia, having a plump body, a long, slender bill, and buff, brown, and black plumage. Length: 12 inches (30 centimeters). [Old English *wuducocc,* from *wudu* wood + *cocc.* See COCK[1].]

wood·craft (wüd′kraft′) *n.* **1.** skill in and knowledge of things relating to the woods and survival in the woods, such as hunting or camping. **2.** the art, process, or skill of working with wood.

wood·cut (wüd′kut′) *n.* **1.** a block of wood engraved so that all the wood is cut away except the design to be printed. **2.** a print or impression made from such a block.

wood·cut·ter (wüd′kut′ər) *n.* a person whose work is cutting trees or chopping wood. —**wood′cut′ting,** *n.*

wood duck, a brightly patterned North American perching duck, *Aix sponsa,* nesting several feet high in hollow trees along woodland lakes.

wood·ed (wüd′id) *adj.* having trees or woods: *a wooded area at the edge of town.*

wood·en (wüd′ən) *adj.* **1.** made or consisting of wood. **2.** without grace; stiff; clumsy; awkward: *to walk with a wooden gait.* **3.** lacking warmth; lifeless; dull: *a wooden expression on someone's face.* —**wood′en·ly,** *adv.* —**wood′en·ness,** *n.*

wood engraving 1. a block of wood engraved in such a way that the actual carved lines form the design to be printed. **2.** a print or

impression made from such a block. **3.** the art or technique of making such blocks, prints, or impressions.

wood·en·head (wüd′ən hed′) *n. Informal.* a dull or stupid person; blockhead. —**wood′en·head′ed,** *adj.*

wooden horse, Trojan horse.

wooden Indian 1. a life-sized figure of a standing American Indian carved of wood and painted, formerly used as an advertisement outside cigar stores. **2.** *Informal.* a person who lacks warmth or liveliness.

wood·en·ware (wüd′ən wâr′) *n.* articles made of wood for household use, such as pails, bowls, or kitchen utensils.

wood ibis, wood stork.

wood·land (*n.,* wüd′land′, -lənd; *adj.,* wüd′lənd) *n.* land covered with woods or trees. —*adj.* of, relating to, or inhabiting the woods: *a woodland deity.* —**wood′land·er,** *n.*

wood lot, land on which trees are grown for timber.

wood louse 1. any of several small crustaceans, order Isopoda, that have flat, oval bodies and seven pairs of legs and live in dark, damp places, feeding on decaying wood, leaves, and other matter. Also, **sow bug.** **2.** any of various small insects living in dark places, as in the woodwork of houses.

wood·man (wüd′mən) *n., pl.* **-men** (-mən). woodsman.

wood·note (wüd′nōt′) *n.* a natural song or call, as of a wild bird of the forest.

wood nymph 1. in Greek mythology, a nymph living in or guarding woods and trees. **2.** any of various butterflies, family Satyridae, having brownish wings with yellow markings.

wood·peck·er (wüd′pek′ər) *n.* any of various strong-billed birds, family Picidae, inhabiting forests throughout the world, that climb trees with the aid of stiff, pointed tail feathers and curved claws. It feeds chiefly on insects, which it obtains by drilling holes in bark and wood with its bill. Length: 6-19 inches (15-48 centimeters).

wood·pile (wüd′pīl′) *n.* a pile of wood, esp. of wood cut and stacked for use as fuel.

wood pulp, wood reduced to pulp by chemical or mechanical means, used esp. for making paper.

wood pussy *Informal.* a skunk.

wood rat, pack rat.

wood·ruff (wüd′ruf′, -rəf) *n.* any of several low-growing herbs, genus *Asperula,* of Europe and Asia, esp. *A. odorata,* whose fragrant leaves are used in sachets and as a wine flavoring. [Old English *wudurōfe.*]

wood·shed (wüd′shed′) *n.* a shed for storing wood, esp. firewood.

wood·pecker

woods·man (wüdz′mən) *also,* **woodman.** *n., pl.* **-men** (-mən). **1.** a person, as a hunter or trapper, who lives or works in the woods and is skilled in woodcraft. **2.** a woodcutter or lumberjack.

wood sorrel, any of various plants, genus *Oxalis,* found in shaded places in temperate climates, having heart-shaped leaves with three leaflets, yellow, white, or pink flowers, and a sour sap. Also, **sorrel.**

wood stork, a large, long-legged, wading bird, *Mycteria americana,* having a white body with black flight feathers and tail, a bald blackish gray head, and a thick down-curved bill. It is found in marshy areas from the southern United States to South America. Length: 40 inches (102 centimeters); wingspan: 61 inches (155 centimeters). Also, **wood ibis.**

woods·y (wüd′ze) *adj.,* **woods·i·er, woods·i·est.** of, relating to, suitable for, or suggestive of the woods: *a woodsy fragrance.*

wood tar, a tar obtained from wood by distillation and used in pitch, medicines, and preservatives.

wood thrush, a large thrush, *Hylocichla mustelina,* found throughout the eastern United States, having brown and white plumage, a rust-colored head, and a melodious song. Length: 7½-8½ inches (19-22 centimeters).

wood·turn·ing (wüd′tûr′ning) *n.* the art or process of shaping pieces of wood on a lathe. —**wood′turn′er,** *n.*

wood·wind (wüd′wind′) *n.* **1.** any of various instruments, including the flute, oboe, clarinet, and saxophone, consisting of a tube through which a column of air passes and having holes in the tube, which are opened and closed to vary the pitch of the tones produced. **2. woodwinds.** the section of an orchestra consisting of these instruments. —*adj.* of, for, designating, or composed of these instruments: *the woodwind section of an orchestra.*

wood·work (wüd′wûrk′) *n.* objects or parts made of wood, esp. the interior wooden parts of a house, such as moldings, doors, and window frames.

wood·work·ing (wŏod′wûr′king) *n.* the art, process, or occupation of making or shaping things of wood. —**wood′work′er,** *n.*

wood·y (wŏod′ē) *adj.,* **wood·i·er, wood·i·est. 1.** consisting of or containing wood: *woody plants.* **2.** covered with or abounding in trees: *a woody island.* **3.** characteristic of or resembling wood: *a plastic with a woody texture.* —**wood′i·ness,** *n.*

woo·er (wŏo′ər) *n.* a person who woos, esp. a suitor.

woof[1] (wŏof, wŏof) *n.* **1.** threads running from side to side in a woven fabric, crossing the lengthwise threads of the warp. **2.** texture, as of a fabric. [Old English *ōwef* the weft.]

woof[2] (wŏof) *n.* a deep bark or barklike sound, as that made by a dog. —*v.i.* to make such a sound. [Imitative of this sound.]

woof·er (wŏof′ər) *n.* a loudspeaker designed to reproduce low-frequency sounds. ➡ distinguished from **tweeter.**

wool (wŏol) *n.* **1.** the soft, dense, usually curly, hair of sheep and certain other animals, such as the Angora goat, alpaca, or llama, used to make yarn and fabric. **2.** a strong, resilient yarn or fabric made from this hair. **3.** any substance resembling the fleece of sheep in texture, such as short, kinky human hair or the furry covering on certain plants. —*adj.* of, relating to, or made of wool. [Old English *wull* the hair of sheep and similar animals.]
• **to pull the wool over (someone's) eyes.** to deceive or delude (someone).

wool·en (wŏol′ən) *also,* **woollen.** *adj.* **1.** made of wool. **2.** of or relating to wool. —*n.* a cloth or garment made of wool. ➡ usually used in the plural.

wool·gath·er·ing (wŏol′gath′ər ing) *n.* useless or idle thinking, esp. daydreaming. —*adj.* given to daydreaming; absent-minded. [Suggested by wandering about to *gather* bits of sheep's *wool* caught on bushes.] —**wool′gath′er·er,** *n.*

wool·grow·er (wŏol′grō′ər) *n.* a person who raises sheep or other wool-bearing animals for their wool. —**wool′grow′ing,** *adj., n.*

wool·len (wŏol′ən) woolen.

wool·ly (wŏol′ē) *also,* **wooly.** *adj.,* -li·er, -li·est. **1.** consisting of or resembling wool. **2.** covered with wool or something with a similar texture: *a woolly stuffed animal.* **3.** not clear or well-defined; confused; fuzzy: *woolly thinking.* **4.** characteristic of the crude, uncivilized, but exciting atmosphere of the western frontier region of the United States during the nineteenth century. ➡ used chiefly in the phrase *wild and woolly.* —*n., pl.* -**lies.** *usually,* **woollies.** a garment made of wool, esp. a knitted undergarment. —**wool′li·ness,** *n.*

woolly bear, the furry caterpillar of any tiger moth. [Because its dense coat of hair is reminiscent of that of a bear.]

woolly mammoth, an extinct, long-haired elephant, *Mammuthus primigenius,* living in the northern parts of Eurasia and North America during the Pleistocene epoch, or Ice Age. Shoulder height: to 14 feet (4 meters).

wool·pack (wŏol′pak′) *n.* **1.** sacking material or sack used to pack raw wool. **2.** a fluffy type of cumulus cloud.

wool·y (wŏol′ē) *adj.,* **wool·i·er, wool·i·est.** woolly. —*n., pl.* **wool·ies.** woolly. —**wool′i·ness,** *n.*

wooz·y (wŏo′zē, wŏoz′ē) *adj.,* **wooz·i·er, wooz·i·est.** *Informal.* **1.** nauseous, dizzy, or faint, as from illness. **2.** confused or dazed. [Possibly modification of OOZY[1].] —**wooz′i·ly,** *adv.* —**wooz′i·ness,** *n.*

Worces·ter·shire sauce (wŏos′tər shîr′, -shər) a pungent sauce consisting of soy sauce, vinegar, garlic, and other ingredients. [From *Worcester,* England, where it was first made.]

word (wûrd) *n.* **1.a.** a sound or combination of sounds having meaning and forming an indivisible linguistic unit. **b.** a written or printed character or set of characters representing such a unit. **2.** a short conversation or discussion: *I'd like a word with you before you leave.* **3.** a brief utterance; remark: *She gave him a word of advice.* **4.** a positive statement that one will or will not do something; promise: *I gave you my word that I would be there.* **5.** information; news; message: *Have you received any word from them?* **6.** a signal or password: *Just give the word and we'll begin.* **7.** a command; order: *The officer's word must be obeyed.* **8. words. a.** a contentious or angry discussion; argument. **b.** the text of a musical composition; lyrics. **c.** speech; talk. **9. the Word. a.** the Bible; Scriptures. **b.** divine intelligence incarnate in Jesus. —*v.t.* to express in words: *to word one's reply carefully.* [Old English *word* vocable, speech, utterance, promise, news, command.]
• **a man (or woman) of his (or her) word.** a person who keeps his (or her) promise.
• **by word of mouth.** by means of spoken language; orally.
• **in a word.** in short; briefly.
• **in so many words.** precisely and explicitly.
• **to be as good as one's word.** to abide by one's promise.
• **to eat one's words.** to have to retract something that one has said.

• **to take someone at his (or her) word.** to trust the statements of another person and act accordingly.
• **to take the words out of one's mouth.** to say exactly what another person was going to say himself or herself.
• **word for word.** in exactly the same words.

word·age (wûr′dij) *n.* words collectively, esp. the quantity of words used in writing something, such as an essay.

word·book (wûrd′bŏok′) *n.* a book containing a list of words, with definitions or explanations, as a dictionary.

word class *Grammar.* a group or category of words belonging to the same part of speech.

word-for-word (wûrd′fər wûrd′) *adj.* in exactly the same words: *a word-for-word translation.*

word·ing (wûr′ding) *n.* a style or manner of expressing something in words; phraseology.

word·less (wûrd′lis) *adj.* **1.** not expressed in words; silent: *a wordless greeting.* **2.** not capable of being expressed in words: *wordless sorrow.* —**word′less·ly,** *adv.* —**word′less·ness,** *n.*

word of honor, an assurance given as a pledge of one's honor.

word-of-mouth (wûrd′əv mouth′) *adj.* communicated orally: *a word-of-mouth report.*

word order, the order of words in a sentence, clause, or phrase.

word processing, the creation, storing, and processing of textual material using a computer equipped with software specially designed for this purpose.

word processor 1. computer hardware or software designed for word processing. **2.** a person who uses such equipment or programs.

word·y (wûr′dē) *adj.,* **word·i·er, word·i·est.** using or containing an excessive number of words; verbose: *a wordy author, a wordy play.* —**word′i·ly,** *adv.* —**word′i·ness,** *n.*

wore (wôr) the past tense of **wear.**

work (wûrk) *n.* **1.** physical or mental effort directed toward a definite end or purpose; labor: *to put a lot of work into a project.* **2.** something that a person does to earn a living; occupation; trade: *the work of an accountant, the work of newspaper reporters.* **3.** an opportunity for earning a living: *looking for work.* **4.** something to be done; undertaking; project: *Each person was assigned work.* **5.** something that is being accomplished or produced, esp. as part of one's occupation. **6.** the result of this; something accomplished or produced: *a work of sculpture, works of music.* **7.** the manner in which something is accomplished or produced; workmanship: *The vase shows careful work.* **8.** a place of employment: *He can be reached at work. She has gone to work.* **9.** *usually,* **works.** things accomplished; feats; deeds: *to be known for one's good works.* **10. works. a.** a place for industrial labor, such as a factory, plant, or mill. ➡ usually used as singular. **b.** the moving parts of a device, such as a watch. **c.** engineering structures, such as dams, docks, or bridges. **11.** *Physics.* the expenditure of energy in moving mass a given distance, measured by the product of the magnitude of the force applied and the distance the mass is moved in the direction of the force. —*adj.* of, for, or relating to work: *a work stoppage, work clothes.* —*v.,* **worked** or **wrought, work·ing.** —*v.i.* **1.** to put forth mental or physical exertion in order to accomplish a definite end or purpose; labor. **2.** to be employed in some business, occupation, or profession: *to work in a mill.* **3.** to perform a function effectively; operate: *This typewriter works well.* **4.** to undergo shaping, processing, or other manipulation: *This metal does not work easily.* **5.** to move gradually so as to arrive at a specified state: *The ropes worked loose.* **6.** to make progress laboriously and slowly: *The disabled vehicle worked toward the shoulder of the road.* **7.** to be agitated; move restlessly: *features working with anger.* **8.** to ferment: *The grape juice worked in the barrels to form wine.* —*v.t.* **1.** to cause to perform a function; exert effort upon: *The driver kept working the clutch.* **2.** to carry on one's trade, business, or operation in: *The police officer worked the northern side of town.* **3.** to cause to produce or be productive: *The laborers worked the mine.* **4.** to bring about; do; cause: *The medicine worked wonders in clearing my sinuses.* **5.** to shape, handle, or process for a particular purpose: *to work copper, to work dough.* **6.** to sew, embroider, weave, or the like: *We worked our way upstream in the canoe.* **7.** to attain by effort: *We worked our way upstream in the canoe.* **8.** to exact labor or service from: *The farmer worked the horses to plow the field.* **9.** to give shape or form to; fashion: *The artisan worked the wood to make a bowl.* **10.** to solve: *The student worked the math problem.* **11.** to act upon the emotions of; excite; rouse: *The orator worked the crowd*

a	at	e	end	o	hot	u	up	hw	white		⌠ about
ā	ape	ē	me	ō	old	ū	use	ng	song		⎢ taken
ä	far	i	it	ô	fork	ū	rule	th	thin	ə ⎨ pencil
âr	care	ī	ice	oi	oil	ŏo	pull	th	this		⎢ lemon
		îr	pierce	ou	out	ûr	turn	zh	measure		⌡ circus

into a rage. **12.** *Informal.* **a.** to use for one's own benefit or gain: *to work one's charm on someone.* **b.** to deceive or trick in order to attain something: *The swindler worked the victims for their life savings.* **13.** to cause fermentation in. [Old English *weorc* act, deed, task, toil, occupation, handiwork.]

• **in the works.** in the course of being done; in progress: *The plan is in the works.*
• **out of work.** without a job; unemployed.
• **the works.** *Informal.* everything that goes with or has to do with something: *a hot dog with the works.*
• **to make short work of.** to accomplish quickly.
• **to shoot the works.** *Slang.* to risk all in one supreme effort.
• **to work in. a.** to put in; combine or merge: *to work in a design in needlepoint, to work in a paragraph on a nearly completed manuscript.* **b.** to alter a schedule so as to fit something or someone in: *The doctor agreed to work me in early the next morning.*
• **to work off.** to get rid of by effort; discharge: *to work off an obligation.*
• **to work on** (or **upon**). **a.** to do physical or mental labor on (something): *The student worked on the science project for two months.* **b.** to try to have an influence on; try to persuade: *I worked on my parents to let me borrow the car.*
• **to work out. a.** to develop or improve: *Work out your ideas before you begin to write.* **b.** to solve: *to work out a problem.* **c.** to come to an end; result: *How did your meeting work out?* **d.** to do exercises or practice: *to work out every day to stay fit.*
• **to work over. a.** to do over; revise: *The author worked over the manuscript.* **b.** *Slang.* to beat up.
• **to work up. a.** to develop or plan: *to work up an idea.* **b.** to stir up; excite; arouse: *to work up a crowd.* **c.** to bring about; cause: *to work up a sweat.* **d.** to make progress or be successful: *to work one's way up in a business.*

work·a·ble (wûr′kə bəl) *adj.* **1.** capable of being carried out or accomplished; feasible: *a workable plan.* **2.** capable of being shaped or processed: *workable clay.*

work·a·day (wûr′kə dā′) *adj.* **1.** ordinary and unremarkable; commonplace; prosaic: *the workaday world.* **2.** of, relating to, or suitable for workdays: *workaday clothes.*

work·a·hol·ic (wûr′kə hô′lik, -hol′ik) *n.* a person who has a compulsive need to work constantly. [WORK + A(LCO)HOLIC.]

work·bag (wûrk′bag′) *n.* a bag for holding equipment and materials, esp. those used in needlework.

work·bas·ket (wûrk′bas′kit) *n.* a basket for holding equipment and materials used in sewing or needlework.

work·bench (wûrk′bench′) *n.* a table used for working, as by a carpenter or mechanic.

work·book (wûrk′bŏŏk′) *n.* **1.** a book or manual prepared for use by students, containing problems, questions, or exercises based on a particular textbook or relating to a particular course of study. **2.** a book containing a record of work planned or completed.

work·box (wûrk′boks′) *n.* a box for holding equipment and materials used in work.

work·day (wûrk′dā′) *n.* **1.** a day on which work is ordinarily done, as distinguished from Sunday or a holiday. **2.** that part of a day in which work is done: *My workday begins at eight o'clock.*

work·er (wûr′kər) *n.* **1.** a person who works: *a fast worker.* **2.** a person who earns a living by working, esp. in manual or industrial labor: *a farm worker, a factory worker.* **3.** one of the sexually undeveloped members of a colony of social insects, such as bees, ants, or termites, that cannot reproduce but can perform various services for the colony.

workers' compensation, insurance payments provided by law for wage earners who are injured at work. Also, **workmen's compensation.**

work ethic, the attitude that work is a fundamentally good moral force and promotes strength of character.

work·fare (wûrk′fâr′) *n.* a program in which those adults who receive public welfare must accept assigned jobs or training for some job. [WORK + (WEL)FARE.]

work force, the total number of persons available for employment, as in a region or country.

work·horse (wûrk′hôrs′) *n.* **1.** a horse used for heavy labor, as distinguished from a horse for racing or riding. **2.** a person who works diligently and tirelessly, esp. on very difficult tasks.

work·house (wûrk′hous′) *n., pl.* **-hous·es** (-hou′ziz). **1.** a house of correction for petty offenders, who are made to work in gangs on roads or railways. **2.** formerly, in Great Britain, an institution for sheltering and giving work to poor people.

work·ing (wûr′king) *adj.* **1.** that works: *a working telephone.* **2.** engaged in work, esp. for a living: *working people.* **3.** that is sufficient for use: *a working hypothesis, a working knowledge of Russian.* **4.** of, relating to, occupied by, or used for working:

working conditions, working hours. —*n.* **1.** the manner in which something works; method of operation: *the workings of a machine.* **2.** *usually,* **workings.** the part of a mine where excavation is being done.

working capital **1.** the assets of a business in excess of current liabilities. **2.** capital in the form of cash or assets easily converted into cash.

working class, the class of workers who are completely dependent upon wages for their livelihood, esp. those who do manual or industrial labor. —**work′ing-class′,** *adj.*

work·ing·man (wûr′king man′) *n., pl.* **-men** (-men′). a man who works for a living, esp. with his hands or with machines.

working papers, official documents legalizing the employment of aliens or minors.

work·ing·wom·an (wûr′king wŏŏm′ən) *n., pl.* **-wom·en** (-wim′ən). a woman who works for a living, esp. with her hands or with machines.

work·load (wûrk′lōd′) *also,* **work load.** *n.* the amount of work assigned to a worker, department, or machine over a specified period of time.

work·man (wûrk′mən) *n., pl.* **-men** (-mən). a man who works for a living, esp. as a craftsperson or laborer.

work·man·like (wûrk′mən līk′) *adj.* characteristic of or befitting a good craftsperson; well-executed; skillful. Also, **work′-man·ly.**

work·man·ship (wûrk′mən ship′) *n.* **1.** the art or skill of a craftsperson. **2.** the manner in which a work is executed: *The workmanship of the table is very fine.* **3.** the product of a craftsperson's work: *That vase is a fine piece of workmanship.*

work·men's compensation (wûrk′mənz) workers' compensation.

work of art **1.** any work fashioned by a skilled or creative artist and possessing originality and aesthetic merit. **2.** anything possessing aesthetically pleasing qualities.

work·out (wûrk′out′) *n.* **1.** a period of practice, exercise, or other strenuous physical activity. **2.** a trial conducted to determine suitability, fitness, or the like: *I gave my new bicycle a workout.*

work·place (wûrk′plās′) *n.* **1.** a factory, store, or other place in which work is done. **2.** the place where a person works.

work·room (wûrk′rüm′, -rŏŏm′) *n.* a room in which work is done.

work·shop (wûrk′shop′) *n.* **1.** a shop or building in which work, esp. manual or mechanical work, is done. **2.** a seminar or discussion group devoted to a particular subject or field of study: *a workshop in child guidance, a workshop for poets.*

work station **1.** a work or office area designed to be used by one person at a time, typically accommodating a computer terminal or other electronic equipment. **2.** a computer similar to a personal computer but possessing greater processing power and often linked with others in a network.

work·ta·ble (wûrk′tā′bəl) *n.* a table used for working, as by a craftsperson or seamstress.

work·week (wûrk′wēk′) *n.* the total number of hours or number of days each week during which work is usually done.

work·wom·an (wûrk′wŏŏm′ən) *n., pl.* **-wom·en** (-wim′ən). a woman who works for a living, esp. as a craftsperson or laborer.

world (wûrld) *n.* **1.a.** the earth: *to take a voyage around the world.* **b.** *also,* **World.** a particular part of the earth: *the Western world.* **2.** all that exists; whole of creation; the universe. **3.** all the human inhabitants of the earth collectively; humanity. **4.** all the inhabitants of a community, state, or country; the public: *Now all the world knows our secret.* **5.** a particular civilization or period of human history: *the world of the Greeks, the Elizabethan world.* **6.** any sphere or realm of human concern, pursuit, or activity: *the world of art, the world of fashion.* **7.** a particular group of people sharing certain interests or activities: *the business world.* **8.** social or secular life and the people devoted to or associated with it: *to choose to live apart from the world and its concerns.* **9.** a division of living things or nature: *the plant world.* **10.** any planet or other heavenly body. **11.** any state or condition of existence: *the world of today, the world to come.* **12.** *Informal.* a large number or quantity; a great deal: *Your vacation did you a world of good.* [Old English *weorold* the earth, mankind, human existence.]

• **for all the world. a.** for any reason whatsoever: *I wouldn't live in a large city for all the world.* **b.** in every respect; exactly: *You look for all the world like a person who has received very good news.*
• **in the world. a.** at all; ever: *I'll never in the world understand why you said those awful things.* **b.** from among everything possible or available: *Why in the world did you choose that color?*

• **out of this world.** *Informal.* exceptionally good: *Your chocolate cake was out of this world.*
• **to think the world of.** to think very highly of.
• **world without end.** to all eternity; forever.
world-class (wûrld′klas′) *adj.* excelling all others of the same kind the world over; recognized internationally as outstanding: *a world-class cellist.*
World Court, International Court of Justice.
world·ling (wûrld′ling) *n.* a person who is devoted to worldly concerns or pleasures. [WORLD + -LING¹.]
world·ly (wûrld′lē) *adj.*, -li·er, -li·est. **1.** devoted to the matters, concerns, interests, or pleasures of this world. **2.** of or relating to this world; earthly; secular: *worldly pursuits.* **3.** wise in the ways or affairs of this world; worldly-wise; sophisticated. —**world′li·ness**, *n.*
world·ly-minded (wûrld′lē mīn′did) *adj.* devoted to worldly concerns or pleasures; worldly.
world·ly-wise (wûrld′lē wīz′) *adj.* wise in the ways or affairs of this world; sophisticated.
world power, a powerful country that has considerable influence in or effect upon world affairs.
World Series *also,* **world series.** the annual series of baseball games played between the winning teams in the two major professional leagues after the regular season has ended to determine the championship of U.S. professional baseball.
world's fair, a large trade, scientific, and cultural exposition, usually sanctioned by international organizations and featuring displays or pavilions maintained by various national governments as well as by corporations and other groups.
world·view (wûrld′vū′) *also,* **world view, world-view.** *n.* a comprehensive view or philosophy of life and the world, held by a person, a people, or a political or cultural group. [Translation of German *Weltanschauung.*]
world war, a war involving the major powers of the world and extending over a large area.
World War I, a war fought chiefly in Europe, from 1914 to 1918, between England, France, Russia, the United States, and their allies on one side and Germany, Austria-Hungary, and their allies on the other. Also, **Great War.**
World War II, a war fought chiefly in Europe, Asia, and Africa, and in the Atlantic, Pacific, and Indian oceans, from 1939 to 1945, between England, France, the Soviet Union, the United States, China, and their allies on one side and Germany, Italy, Japan, and their allies on the other.
world-wea·ry (wûrld′wîr′ē) *adj.* tired of the world or of living.
world·wide (wûrld′wīd′) *adj.* extending over all the world.

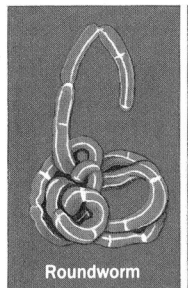 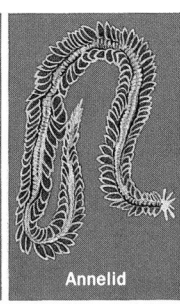 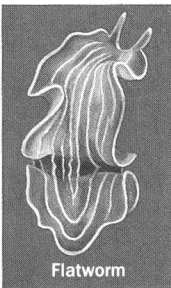

worms *(def. 1)*

worm (wûrm) *n.* **1.** any of various elongated, soft-bodied invertebrates. True worms include the flatworms, roundworms, and annelids. **2.** any of various small, creeping animals that resemble true worms, such as the shipworm, blindworm, and insect larvae. **3.** anything that resembles a worm, as in appearance or movement. **4.** something that causes inner stress or discomfort, as if by gnawing: *the worm of conscience.* **5.** a person who is an object of scorn, disgust, or pity; weak, miserable, or pathetic person. **6.** a shaft having a single spiral thread around it, which engages with the teeth of a worm wheel. **7. worms.** any of several diseases caused by the presence of parasitic worms in the body, esp. the intestines. —*v.i.* to move as a worm; wriggle: *to worm through a narrow tunnel.* —*v.t.* **1.** to move or bring about by moving as a worm: *to worm one's way through a crowded room.* **2.** to bring about by stealth or guile: *He wormed his way into her favor.* **3.** to get or achieve by stealth or guile: *She wormed the secret out of him.* **4.** to free from worms: *We worm our dogs in the spring.* [Old English *wyrm* this invertebrate animal, serpent, miserable creature.] —**worm′er**, *n.* —**worm′like′**, *adj.*

worm-eat·en (wûrm′ē′tən) *adj.* **1.** gnawed or bored by worms; wormy: *worm-eaten vegetables.* **2.** old, worn-out, or out-of-date: *worm-eaten ideas.*
worm fence, a zigzag fence having rails set so that their ends cross at right angles. Also, **snake fence.**
worm gear 1. worm wheel. **2.** a gear that consists of a worm wheel and a revolving shaft with a single spiral thread.
worm·hole (wûrm′hōl′) *n.* a hole made by a burrowing worm, as in wood or fruit.
worm·seed (wûrm′sēd′) *n.* any of several plants whose seeds yield an oil used in medicine to expel intestinal worms, esp. a strong-smelling goosefoot, *Chenopodium ambrosioides.*
worm wheel, a cogwheel with teeth that engage with the thread of a worm. Also, **worm gear.**
worm·wood (wûrm′wùd′) *n.* **1.** any of several aromatic plants of the composite family having small flowers and deeply indented leaves, esp. the **common wormwood,** *Artemisia absinthium,* which yields an oil used in absinthe and certain medicines. **2.** something bitter or unpleasant. [Old English *wermōd* the plant; influenced by WORM and WOOD, probably because used as a vermifuge.]
worm·y (wûr′mē) *adj.*, worm·i·er, worm·i·est. **1.** containing or infested with worms. **2.** resembling a worm. —**worm′i·ness,** *n.*
worn (wôrn) *v.* the past participle of **wear.** —*adj.* **1.** damaged by use or exposure; threadbare: *pants worn at the knees.* **2.** showing the effects of illness, fatigue, or anxiety; exhausted: *a worn, weary expression.*
worn-out (wôrn′out′) *adj.* **1.** unfit for use because of extensive or harmful wear: *worn-out shoes.* **2.** thoroughly exhausted: *The hikers were worn-out at the end of the day.*
wor·ri·ment (wûr′ē mənt) *n.* an act, instance, or cause of worrying.
wor·ri·some (wûr′ē səm) *adj.* **1.** causing worry or anxiety: *a worrisome situation.* **2.** given to or tending to worry.
wor·ry (wûr′ē) *v.*, -ried, -ry·ing. —*v.i.* **1.** to experience mental uneasiness or distress; feel anxious or troubled about something. **2.** to pull or tear at something with or as with the teeth (with *at*): *The puppy worried at the slipper.* **3.** to proceed or manage despite hardships or difficulties; struggle (with *along* or *through*). —*v.t.* **1.** to cause to feel anxious or troubled; make uneasy. **2.** to bother; pester; annoy: *Stop worrying me with stupid questions.* **3.** to pull, tear at, or touch repeatedly. **4.** to bite at, shake, or mangle with the teeth: *The dog worried the bone.* —*n., pl.* -ries. **1.** the act of worrying or the state of being worried; mental uneasiness or distress. **2.** a cause of mental uneasiness or distress; source of anxiety: *to have financial worries.* [Old English *wyrgan* to strangle.] —**wor′ri·er,** *n.* —For Synonyms *(n.),* see **apprehension.**
wor·ry·wart (wûr′ē wôrt′) *n. Informal.* a person who tends to worry excessively and unnecessarily.
worse (wûrs) *adj.* the comparative of **bad** and **ill.** **1.** of more inferior quality, condition, ability, or value: *The soup was bad, but the stew was worse.* **2.** more unfavorable, distressing, or unpleasant: *Tomorrow's weather will be even worse.* **3.** more harmful, damaging, or severe: *That hard candy is even worse for your teeth than the chewy candy.* **4.** in poorer health; less well: *The patient is worse since taking the medicine.* **5.** bad or evil to a greater degree: *His behavior is worse than ever before.* —*adv.* (the comparative of **badly** and **ill**) in a worse way or manner: *She is feeling worse now than before.* —*n.* something worse. [Old English *wyrsa.*]
• **worse off.** in a worse position or condition, esp. economically or financially: *The country is worse off under the new government.*
wors·en (wûr′sən) *v.t., v.i.* to make or become worse.
wor·ship (wûr′ship) *n.* **1.** religious homage or veneration given to a god or someone or something considered sacred. **2.** the expression of such homage or veneration, esp. a religious service consisting of prayers and other acts in praise of God. **3.** an intense or excessive devotion or regard; adoration: *the worship of power and wealth.* **4. Worship.** *British.* a title of honor or respect used in addressing or referring to magistrates and certain other dignitaries. ➡ usually preceded by *Your, His,* or *Her.* —*v.,* -shiped or -shipped, -ship·ing or -ship·ping. —*v.t.* **1.** to show religious homage or veneration to. **2.** to have an intense or excessive devotion to or regard for; adore. —*v.i.* to engage in worship, esp. to attend or take part in a religious service. [Old English *weorthscipe* honor, dignity, respect shown, from *weorth* worthy + -scipe.

a	at	e	end	o	hot	u	up	hw	white		about
ā	ape	ē	me	ō	old	ū	use	ng	song		taken
ä	far	i	it	ô	fork	ü	rule	th	thin	ə	pencil
âr	care	ī	ice	oi	oil	ù	pull	th	this		lemon
		îr	pierce	ou	out	ûr	turn	zh	measure		circus

See -SHIP.] —**wor′ship·er;** also, **wor′ship·per,** n. —**wor′-ship·ing·ly,** adv.

Synonyms v.t. **Worship, venerate,** and **revere** mean to regard with deep respect or with awe. **Worship,** which in its primary sense indicates the intense respect accorded a divine being, is often applied by extension to secular situations: *to worship God, to worship material success.* **Venerate** denotes a solemn respect for objects or persons considered holy: *The religious pilgrims venerated the saint's relics.* **Revere** usually indicates a strong nonreligious respect or love: *The testimonial dinner honored the widely revered teacher.*

wor·ship·ful (wûr′ship fəl) adj. **1.** showing or feeling reverence or adoration; worshiping. **2. Worshipful.** *British.* deserving of homage or respect; honorable. ➡ used as a title in addressing or referring to persons of rank.

worst (wûrst) adj. the superlative of **bad** and **ill. 1.** most inferior in quality, condition, ability, or value: *In my opinion, this is the worst book ever written.* **2.** most unfavorable, distressing, or unpleasant: *That's the worst news I've heard all day.* **3.** most harmful, damaging, or severe: *That was the worst storm I had ever seen.* **4.** most bad or evil: *the worst dictator in history.* —adv. (the superlative of **badly** and **ill**) in the worst manner or degree. —n. something that is worst. —v.t. to get the better of; defeat: *to worst an enemy in battle.* [Old English *wyrresta* most bad, most unpleasant.]

• **at worst.** under the most unfavorable circumstances.

• **if (the) worst comes to (the) worst.** if the most unfavorable, distressing, or unpleasant thing happens: *If worst comes to worst, we'll sell the car and buy a used one.*

• **in the worst way.** *Informal.* very much: *That's something I've always wanted in the worst way.*

• **to get the worst of it.** to be defeated or placed at a disadvantage.

wor·sted (wùs′tid, wûr′stid) n. **1.** a smooth, compact yarn made from long wool fibers that are combed parallel and twisted hard, used in making such fabrics as gabardine. **2.** a tightly woven wool fabric made from such yarn and having a smooth, hard surface. —adj. consisting of or made from worsted: *a worsted suit.* [From *Worsted* (now *Worstead*), English town where it was first made.]

wort (wûrt) n. **1.** a plant or herb. ➡ usually used in combination: *liverwort.* **2.** an infusion of malt that becomes beer or ale after fermentation. [Old English *wyrt.*]

worth (wûrth) prep. **1.** deserving of; meriting: *a film worth seeing.* **2.** equal in value to: *an old coin worth thirty dollars.* **3.** having property or wealth amounting to: *a person worth a million dollars.* —n. **1.** a quality that makes something useful, desirable, or important; merit or excellence: *a novel of little worth.* **2.** the monetary or market value of something: *The painting's worth was estimated at several million dollars.* **3.** a quantity of something that can be had for a specific sum: *fifty cents' worth of apples.* **4.** a quality that makes a person deserving of esteem. **5.** wealth; riches. [Old English *weorth* value, of value, worthy.]

• **for all one is worth.** to the utmost of one's powers or ability.

worth·less (wûrth′lis) adj. lacking worth or value: *worthless advice.* —**worth′less·ly,** adv. —**worth′less·ness,** n.

worth·while (wûrth′hwīl′, -wīl′) adj. sufficiently important or valuable to be worth the time, effort, or money spent.

wor·thy (wûr′thē) adj., **-thi·er, -thi·est. 1.** having worth or value: *to contribute to a worthy cause.* **2.** having sufficient worth or value; deserving: *a leader worthy of support.* —n., pl. **-thies.** a person of importance or distinction. —**wor′thi·ly,** adv. —**wor′thi·ness,** n.

wost (wust) *Archaic.* the second person singular present tense of **wit**[2]. ➡ used with *thou.*

wot (wot) *Archaic.* the first and third person singular present tense of **wit**[2].

would (wùd; *unstressed* wəd) *auxiliary verb* a past tense of **will**[1]. **1.** used to express a condition: *I would help you if I could.* **2.** used to express futurity: *We wondered if they would be on time.* **3.** used to express strong preference or willingness: *I would rather go hungry than beg.* **4.** used to express a choice: *My friend would never have taken the job if it weren't for the money.* **5.** used to express intention or determination: *They promised that they would return before dawn.* **6.** used to express longing or desire: *Would that I were with them now!* **7.** used to express probability or possibility: *Being late would make me uncomfortable.* **8.** used to express a request: *Would you be kind enough to open the door for me?* **9.** used to express customary or habitual action: *We would sit and talk for hours.* **10.** used to express uncertainty: *The patient's condition would seem to be improving.*

would-be (wùd′bē′) adj. **1.** desiring or professing to be: *a would-be artist.* **2.** intended to be: *Police apprehended the would-be assassin.*

wouldn't (wùd′ənt) *contr.* would not.

wouldst (wùdst) *Archaic.* a second person singular past tense of **will**[1]. ➡ used with *thou.*

wound[1] (wünd) n. **1.** an injury to any part of the body, esp. an external injury in which the skin is torn, cut, or pierced. **2.** a similar external injury to a plant or tree. **3.** an injury to the feelings, reputation, or the like. —v.t., v.i. to inflict a wound or wounds on or upon (someone). [Old English *wund* external injury.]

wound[2] (wound) a past tense and past participle of **wind**[2] and **wind**[3].

wove (wōv) a past tense and past participle of **weave.**

wo·ven (wō′vən) a past participle of **weave.**

wow[1] (wou) *interj.* used to express surprise, wonder, pleasure, or other feeling. —v.t. *Slang.* to be highly successful with; cause an enthusiastic response in: *The comedian really wowed the audience with the new act.* [Possibly from Scottish *wow* exclamation of surprise.]

wow[2] (wou) n. a slow fluctuation in the pitch of sound produced by a phonograph or tape recorder, caused by variations in playback or recording speed. [Imitative.]

WPA, Works Progress Administration.

wpm, words per minute.

wrack (rak) n. **1.** destruction. ➡ used chiefly in the phrase *wrack and ruin.* **2.** wreckage, esp. of a ship. **3.** seaweed or other marine vegetation cast ashore by waves. [Partly from Old English *wrǣc* punishment; partly from Middle Dutch *wrak* wreckage.]

wraith (rāth) n. **1.** a ghostly appearance of someone still living, thought to indicate that he or she will soon die. **2.** a ghost; specter. [Of uncertain origin.] —**wraith′like′,** adj.

wran·gle (rang′gəl) v., **-gled, -gling.** —v.i. to argue or dispute, esp. in a noisy or angry manner: *The children wrangled over who would go first.* —v.t. **1.** to bring about, obtain, or persuade by argument: *to wrangle special privileges.* **2.** in the western United States, to herd, round up, or tend (horses or other livestock). —n. a noisy or angry argument; dispute. [Probably of Low German origin.]

wran·gler (rang′glər) n. **1.** a person who wrangles. **2.** in the western United States, a person who herds or tends horses or other livestock; cowboy.

wrap (rap) v., **wrapped** or **wrapt, wrap·ping.** —v.t. **1.a.** to fold or place (a covering) around something, as for protection: *to wrap a blanket around a sleeping child.* **b.** to cover in this way: *to wrap a baby in a blanket.* **2.** to cover, esp. with paper, and make secure: *to wrap a package.* **3.** to cover or surround so as to obscure or conceal: *The skyscraper was wrapped in fog. The transaction was wrapped in mystery.* **4.** to take up completely; immerse; engross: *to be wrapped in thought.* **5.** to clasp or fold: *He wrapped his arms around her waist.* **6.** *Informal.* to bring to an end; conclude (with *up*): *The detective wrapped up the case in two days.* —v.i. **1.** to become wrapped or twined: *The rope wrapped around the post.* **2.** to put on warm clothing (with *up*). —n. an outer covering or garment, as a shawl. [Middle English *wrappen.*]

• **under wraps.** in secrecy: *The plan was kept under wraps for months.*

• **wrapped up in.** absorbed or involved in: *to be wrapped up in one's work.*

wrap·a·round (rap′ə round′) adj. designating a garment that is wrapped around to fit before being fastened: *a wraparound skirt.*

wrap·per (rap′ər) n. **1.** paper or other material in which something is wrapped or enclosed: *a candy wrapper.* **2.** a person or thing that wraps packages, parcels, or the like. **3.** a long, loose dressing gown, robe, or similar garment.

wrap·ping (rap′ing) n. *usually,* **wrappings.** paper or other material used for wrapping packages or other objects.

wrapt (rapt) a past tense and past participle of **wrap.**

wrap-up (rap′up′) n. *Informal.* a brief, summarizing report, as of news.

wrasse (ras) n. any of a group of saltwater fish, family Labridae, often brilliantly colored, having spiny fins and powerful teeth, found esp. in tropical waters. [Cornish *wrach, gwrach.*]

wrasse

wrath (rath) n. **1.** extreme or violent anger; rage. **2.** an act performed in or as an expression of great anger, esp. such an act carried out for punishment or vengeance. [Old English *wrǣththu.*] —For Synonyms, see **anger.**

wrath·ful (rath′fəl) adj. full of, resulting from, or expressing wrath. —**wrath′ful·ly,** adv. —**wrath′ful·ness,** n.

wreak (rēk) v.t. **1.** to inflict or exact: *to wreak havoc, to wreak*

vengeance. **2.** to give free expression to; vent: *to wreak one's anger.* [Old English *wrecan* to drive, punish, vent, avenge.]

wreath (rēth) *n., pl.* **wreaths** (rēthz, rēths). **1.** a ring of intertwined flowers or leaves worn on the head as a mark of honor or victory, placed on a grave as a memorial, or used as a decoration. **2.** any ringlike or curving shape resembling this: *Wreaths of smoke rose from the chimney.* [Old English *writha* twisted band², fillet.]

wreathe (rēth) *v.,* **wreathed, wreath·ing.** —*v.t.* **1.** to form or shape into a wreath. **2.** to decorate, encircle, or crown with or as with a wreath or wreaths. **3.** to curl, coil, or twist around: *Fog wreathed the skyscraper.* **4.** to change, twist, or contort: *a face wreathed in smiles.* —*v.i.* **1.** to take the form or shape of a wreath. **2.** to curl; spiral. [Partly from WREATH; partly from Middle English *wrethen,* past participle of *writhen* to writhe, from Old English *wrīthan* to twist, wrap around.]

wreck (rek) *v.t.* **1.** to cause the physical damage or destruction of: *to wreck a car in an accident.* **2.** to destroy, ruin, or put an end to: *The scandal nearly wrecked the politician's career. The rain wrecked our plans for a picnic.* **3.** to tear down or dismantle, as an old building. —*v.i.* **1.** to suffer physical damage or destruction: *The two trucks wrecked at the intersection.* **2.** to be employed as a wrecker. —*n.* **1.** the act of wrecking or the state of being wrecked; destruction. **2.** the remains of anything, esp. a ship, automobile, airplane, or other vehicle that has been damaged or destroyed. **3.a.** shipwreck. **b.** cargo or wreckage cast ashore after a shipwreck. **4.a.** a person in poor physical or mental condition: *The job interview made me a nervous wreck.* **b.** something in poor or broken-down condition or in a state of disorder: *Their apartment was a wreck after the burglary.* [Anglo-Norman *wrec* shipwreck, poverty; of Scandinavian origin.] —For Synonyms *(v.t.),* see **demolish.**

wreck·age (rek′ij) *n.* **1.** the remains of anything that has been wrecked. **2.** the act of wrecking or the state of being wrecked. [WRECK + -AGE.]

wreck·er (rek′ər) *n.* **1.** a person or thing that wrecks. **2.** a person whose work is tearing down or demolishing buildings. **3.** a person, vehicle, or piece of equipment employed in removing, salvaging, or recovering wrecks. **4.** a person, boat, or ship employed to recover wrecked or disabled ships or their cargoes. **5.** a person who lures ships to destruction by using false lights on shore in order to plunder the wrecks.

wren (ren) *n.* any of various songbirds, family Troglodytidae, having a slender bill, short, rounded wings, a short tail, and brownish plumage that is usually marked with brown, black, or white. Length: 4-9 inches (10-23 centimeters). [Old English *wrenna.*]

wrench (rench) *n.* **1.** a sharp or violent twist, turn, or pull. **2.** an injury or strain, as of the back, caused by a sudden or violent twisting, turning, or jerking motion; sprain. **3.** a sharp, usually sudden mental or emotional pain: *The death of their pet was a real wrench for the entire family.* **4.** a change or distortion, as of meaning. **5.** any of various tools, usually consisting of a handle or bar attached to fixed or movable jaws, used esp. for gripping and turning a nut, bolt, or pipe. —*v.t.* **1.** to twist, turn, or pull with a sudden sharp or violent motion: *I wrenched the nail out of the wall.* **2.** to injure or strain by twisting or turning suddenly or violently: *to wrench one's back playing tennis.* **3.** to change or distort, as the meaning of a statement. **4.** to move or force, as if by great physical effort: *I couldn't wrench myself away from the television set.* **5.** to give sharp mental or emotional distress or pain to: *Leaving my friends wrenched me.* —*v.i.* to give a wrench. [Old English *wrencan* to twist, turn.]

wrest (rest) *v.t.* **1.** to pull, twist, or take away forcibly or violently: *to wrest a weapon from an assailant.* **2.** to take or seize by force or violence: *to wrest power from a dictator.* **3.** to obtain or extract by great effort: *The farmers wrested a meager existence from the parched land.* **4.** to turn or change from the proper meaning, usage, application, or purpose: *The article wrested the candidate's words.* —*n.* **1.** the act of wresting; twist. **2.** a wrench-like key for tuning a stringed instrument, as a harp or piano. [Old English *wræsten* to turn, twist.] —**wrest′er,** *n.*

wres·tle (res′əl) *v.,* **-tled, -tling.** —*v.i.* **1.** to engage in the activity or sport of wrestling; grapple: *The children were wrestling around on the ground.* **2.** to struggle or contend, esp. in order to gain mastery: *to wrestle with a problem, to wrestle with one's conscience.* —*v.t.* **1.** to engage in wrestling with: *to wrestle a bear.* **2.** to move or force by or as if by wrestling: *The police officer wrestled the thief to the ground.* —*n.* **1.** the act or action of wrestling. **2.** a struggle. [Old English *wræstlian* to struggle, grapple.] —**wres′tler,** *n.*

wres·tling (res′ling) *n.* a sport or activity in which two opponents struggle hand to hand, esp. in an attempt to throw or force each other to the ground.

wretch (rech) *n.* **1.** an unfortunate, unhappy, or pitiable person. **2.** an evil or contemptible person. [Old English *wrecca.*]

wretch·ed (rech′id) *adj.* **1.** very unhappy; deeply distressed: *to sit alone feeling wretched.* **2.** characterized by or causing great unhappiness or discomfort: *to lead a wretched existence, the wretched living conditions of the slums.* **3.** poor or inferior in quality or ability: *a wretched tennis player.* **4.** evil or contemptible: *a wretched coward.* [WRETCH + -ED².] —**wretch′ed·ly,** *adv.* —**wretch′ed·ness,** *n.*

wri·er (rī′ər) the comparative of **wry.**

wri·est (rī′ist) the superlative of **wry.**

wrig·gle (rig′əl) *v.,* **-gled, -gling.** —*v.i.* **1.** to twist or turn from side to side with short, quick movements; squirm: *Don't wriggle in your seat so much.* **2.** to move or proceed with a wriggling motion: *to wriggle out of someone's grasp.* **3.** to make one's way by evasive or shifty means: *to wriggle out of an embarrassing situation.* —*v.t.* **1.** to cause to wriggle. **2.** to bring, get, or make by wriggling: *The children wriggled their way through the hole in the fence.* —*n.* a wriggling movement or action. [Middle Low German *wriggeln* to squirm.] —**wrig′gly,** *adj.*

wrig·gler (rig′lər) *n.* **1.** a person or thing that wriggles. **2.** the larva of a mosquito. Also *(def. 2),* **wiggler.**

wright (rīt) *n.* a person who makes, constructs, or creates something. ➤ used chiefly in compounds: *playwright.* [Old English *wryhta, wyrhta* worker, maker, creator.]

wring (ring) *v.t.,* **wrung** or *(archaic)* **wringed, wring·ing. 1. a.** to squeeze, twist, or compress, esp. so as to force out liquid (often with *out*): *to wring out wet laundry.* **b.** to force out (liquid) in this way: *to wring water from a mop.* **2.** to obtain by forceful or persistent effort (often with *out*): *to wring the truth out of someone.* **3.** to clasp and press or twist (the hands) together. **4.** to twist or squeeze forcefully or violently. **5.** to cause emotional or mental pain to; torment: *misery that wrung our hearts.* —*n.* the act of wringing; a twist or squeeze. [Old English *wringan* to press, strain, squeeze, twist.]

wring·er (ring′ər) *n.* a person or thing that wrings, esp. a device or machine for squeezing water out of wet clothes.

wrin·kle¹ (ring′kəl) *n.* **1.** a small fold, ridge, or crease in a normally smooth surface. **2.** a small furrow, crease, or line in the skin, as caused by aging. —*v.,* **-kled, -kling.** —*v.t.* to form or make a wrinkle or wrinkles in: *to wrinkle one's brow.* —*v.i.* to become wrinkled: *This fabric won't wrinkle.* [From Middle English *wrinkled* twisted, winding, probably from Old English *gewrinclod* winding, crooked.] —**wrin′kly,** *adj.*

wrin·kle² (ring′kəl) *n. Informal.* a clever or original idea, trick, or device. [Diminutive of Old English *wrenc* trick.]

wrist (rist) *n.* **1.** the joint that connects the hand and arm, or the area surrounding this joint. Also, **wrist joint. 2.** the eight small bones that constitute this joint; carpus. [Old English *wrist* this joint.]

wrist·band (rist′band′) *n.* a band, as of a sleeve, that encircles the wrist.

wrist·let (rist′lit) *n.* **1.** a band worn around the wrist, as for warmth. **2.** bracelet *(def. 1).*

wrist pin, a pin or stud joining a connecting rod to a piston.

wrist·watch (rist′woch′) *n.* a watch worn on a band or strap around the wrist.

writ¹ (rit) *n.* **1.** a legal document ordering the person or persons named therein to perform or refrain from performing some act. **2.** something written; writing. [Old English *writ* something written, book, the Bible.]

writ² (rit) *Archaic.* a past tense and past participle of **write.**

write (rīt) *v.,* **wrote** or *(archaic)* **writ, writ·ten** or *(archaic)* **writ, writ·ing.** —*v.t.* **1.a.** to mark or form (letters, words, symbols, or the like) on a surface, as with a pen or pencil. **b.** to form the letters, words, or symbols of: *to write one's name, to write a formula.* **2.** to express, describe, or communicate in or by writing: *to write one's thoughts in a diary.* **3.** to compose (a musical or literary work); be the author or composer of: *to write short stories.* **4.** to communicate with in writing; send a letter to: *Please write us when you get there.* **5.** to fill in with the required written information: *to write a check, to write an application.* **6.** to draw up in legal form: *to write a will.* **7.** to cover or fill with writing: *You must write at least ten pages.* **8.** to show or indicate plainly: *guilt written all over one's face.* **9.** *Computers.* to store data on (a medium, as a disk). —*v.i.* **1.** to form letters, words, or symbols

a	at	e	end	o	hot	u	up	hw	white		about
ā	ape	ē	me	ō	old	ū	use	ng	song		taken
ä	far	i	it	ô	fork	ū	rule	th	thin	ə	pencil
âr	care	ī	ice	oi	oil	u̇	pull	th	this		lemon
		îr	pierce	ou	out	ûr	turn	zh	measure		circus

1385

on paper or another surface: *to write in red ink, to write in French.* **2.** to compose or create a book or other literary work; be an author: *to write for years before getting published.* **3.** to compose or send a letter: *I'll write as soon as I can.* **4.** to produce writing of a certain quality: *That person writes quite illegibly.* **5.** to write as a means of livelihood: *My friend's first job was writing for the local newspaper.* [Old English *wrītan* to scratch, engrave, delineate with a writing implement, set down in writing, record, compose a literary work in writing.]
- **to write down. a.** to put into writing. **b.** to write in a deliberately simplified style, as for readers thought to be less intelligent or knowledgeable.
- **to write in.** to vote for (a person not listed on a ballot) by writing that person's name on the ballot.
- **to write off. a.** to cancel or remove from an account, as a bad debt. **b.** to regard or acknowledge as a loss or failure.
- **to write out. a.** to put into writing. **b.** to write in full: *to write out a speech from one's notes.*
- **to write up.** to describe or set down in writing, esp. in detail: *The reporter wrote up the interview and submitted it to the editor.*

write-in (rīt'in') *n.* **1.** a vote cast for a person not listed on a ballot by inserting that person's name on the ballot. **2.** a person whose name is inserted in this way: *The winner of the election was a write-in.* —*adj.* of or relating to such a vote or votes: *a write-in campaign.*

write-off (rīt'ôf', -of') *n.* **1.a.** something canceled or removed from an account, as a bad debt. **b.** something regarded as a loss or failure. **2.** the act of writing something off as a loss.

writ·er (rī'tər) *n.* **1.** a person who writes. **2.** a person whose occupation or profession is writing.

writer's cramp, a cramp in the hand or fingers, usually caused by excessive writing.

write-up (rīt'up') *n.* a written account, description, or review: *Most critics gave the new play a good write-up.*

writhe (rīth) *v.,* **writhed, writh·ing.** —*v.i.* **1.** to move the body with a twisting or turning motion, as in great pain. **2.** to suffer great mental or emotional distress or discomfort. —*v.t.* to cause to twist or turn. —*n.* a twisting movement; contortion. [Old English *wrīthan* to twist, wrap around.]

writ·ing (rī'ting) *n.* **1.** the act of a person who writes. **2.** the style or quality of a person's handwriting; penmanship: *Her writing is always neat and legible.* **3.** a written form: *I'd like this agreement put in writing.* **4.** something written: *There was writing all over the bathroom wall.* **5.** a novel, play, or other literary work: *to study the writings of Aristotle.* **6.** the occupation or profession of a writer or author. **7.** a style, form, or art of literary composition: *journalistic writing.*

Usage A wide variety of skills are needed for any kind of writing, whether it is a letter or a term paper, a novel or a newspaper article. Careful writers, both amateur and professional, know that organizing and writing down ideas are only part of the process. They also edit and revise their copy and correct spelling, grammar, punctuation, and style. This dictionary offers a variety of tools that make **writing** easier. In many of its definitions there are synonyms to enrich a person's vocabulary, and thus his or her **writing.** Synonym studies examine the subtle distinctions between synonymous words and illustrate the distinctions with examples. Short and long usage notes guide the writer in the use of expressions in current English and clarify the meanings of words that are frequently confused. Some of the longer usage notes focus on specific aspects of language, such as euphemisms, figurative language, idioms, informal terms, jargon, and meaning (see individual entries). Additional information on language can be found in tables under entries on adjectives, figures of speech, spelling, and misspelling.

writ·ten (rit'ən) a past participle of **write.**

wrong (rông) *adj.* **1.** not conforming to fact, truth, or reason; containing error: *a wrong answer, a wrong impression.* **2.** not conforming to standards of what is just, moral, or good: *It would be wrong to betray a friend's trust.* **3.** not appropriate, suitable, or proper: *the wrong time to ask for a raise.* **4.** not in proper or normal working order; functioning improperly; out of order: *There is something wrong with my watch.* **5.** not intended, desired, or necessary: *to take a wrong turn on the road.* **6.** with or having

the side or surface not meant to be seen: *the wrong side of a fabric.* —*n.* something that is wrong, such as an unjust, damaging, or immoral action. —*adv.* in a wrong way or manner: *to guess wrong, to pronounce a word wrong.* —*v.t.* **1.** to treat in an unjust, damaging, or immoral way; do wrong to: *to wrong a friend.* **2.** to impute evil to unjustly; malign. [Old English *wrang* uneven, injustice, from Old Norse *rangr* crooked, unjust.] —**wrong'ly,** *adv.* —**wrong'ness,** *n.*
- **in the wrong.** mistaken or at fault: *You were in the wrong in that argument.*
- **to go wrong. a.** to turn out badly or take place incorrectly; fail: *The experiment went wrong because of sloppy work. Everything I do goes wrong.* **b.** to go astray morally: *Greed made them go wrong.* **c.** to make a mistake; err: *Where did you go wrong in doing that math problem?*

Synonyms *adj.* **Wrong, false,** and **erroneous** mean not true or correct. **Wrong** is usually applied to something that does not conform to the facts: *The student gave the wrong answer to the teacher's question.* **False** implies an attempt to deceive others: *The TV ad made false claims about the cereal's health benefits.* **Erroneous** is a formal word that implies an error in logic or information: *The researcher made several erroneous assumptions, which invalidated the study's findings.*

wrong·do·er (rông'dü'ər) *n.* a person who does wrong. —**wrong'do'ing,** *n.*

wrong·ful (rông'fəl) *adj.* **1.** unjust, damaging, or immoral: *wrongful behavior.* **2.** unlawful; illegal: *a wrongful act of vandalism.* —**wrong'ful·ly,** *adv.* —**wrong'ful·ness,** *n.*

wrong·head·ed (rông'hed'id) *adj.* stubbornly or unreasonably clinging to wrong opinions, judgments, or ideas. —**wrong'head'ed·ly,** *adv.* —**wrong'head'ed·ness,** *n.*

wrote (rōt) a past tense of **write.**

wroth (rôth) *adj.* angry; wrathful. [Old English *wrāth.*]

wrought (rôt) *v.* a past tense and past participle of **work.** —*adj.* **1.** made or formed: *a skillfully wrought desk.* **2.** (of metals) shaped by hammering. **3.** ornamented; embellished. **4.** fashioned with care; not rough or crude.
- **wrought up.** agitated; excited: *to get wrought up over a delay.*

wrought iron, an extremely pure form of iron that is soft but tough, easily worked and welded, and relatively resistant to corrosion.

wrung (rung) a past tense and past participle of **wring.**

wry (rī) *adj.,* **wri·er, wri·est. 1.** made by twisting or distorting the features: *a wry smile.* **2.** humorous in an ironic, bitter, or perverse way: *a wry sense of humor.* **3.** turned, bent, or twisted; contorted. [From Middle English *wrien* to bend, twist, contort, from Old English *wrīgian* to turn, move.] —**wry'ly,** *adv.* —**wry'ness,** *n.*

wry·neck (rī'nek') *n.* **1.** a spasm of the muscles of the neck, causing the head to be drawn to one side. Also, **torticollis. 2.** either of two species of Old World birds, genus *Jynx,* re-

wrought iron gate

lated to and resembling the woodpecker, noted for its habit of twisting its head into odd contortions. Length: 6 inches (15 centimeters).

WSW, west-southwest.

wt., weight.

wurst (wûrst, vûrst) *n.* sausage. [German *Wurst.*]

WV, the postal abbreviation for West Virginia.

W. Va., West Virginia.

WY, the postal abbreviation for Wyoming.

Wy·an·dotte (wī'ən dot') *n.* any of an American breed of domestic fowl raised for its meat and brown-shelled eggs.

Wyo., Wyoming.

wy·vern (wī'vərn) wivern.

X† early Greek	**X** later Greek	**X** Etruscan	**X** Latin

X The earliest form of **X** was probably an ancient Semitic letter that was written as either a plus sign or a modern **X**, usually called a "cross sign." When the Greeks borrowed it, they gave it two different pronunciations: a *ks* sound in the Western Greek alphabet and a *kh* sound in the Eastern Greek alphabet. The letter came into the classical Greek and Etruscan alphabets with only slight changes. The Romans, who adapted their alphabet from the Western Greek and Etruscan alphabets, gave their "cross sign" letter a *ks* pronunciation. By the fourth century B.C., the letter **X** of the Latin alphabet was written almost exactly as we write it today.

x, X (eks) *n., pl.* **x's, X's. 1.** the twenty-fourth letter of the English alphabet. **2.** the shape of this letter or something having this shape.

x¹ (eks) *n., pl.* **x's** *Mathematics.* **1.** a mark used to indicate multiplication: $4 \times 10 = 40$. **2.** an unknown quantity or variable. **3.** the x-axis.

x² (eks) *v.t.,* **x-ed** or **x'd** (ekst), **x-ing** or **x'ing** (ek'sing). **1.** to delete or mark with an *x* (often with *out*): *to x out a mistake.* **2.** to indicate with or as with an *x*, as a choice or answer.

X (eks) *n., pl.* **X's. 1.** *also,* **x** the Roman numeral for 10. **2.** an unknown person or thing. **3.** a mark used in place of a signature by an illiterate person. **4.** a mark used to indicate a particular point or place on a map or diagram. **5.** a mark used to indicate a kiss in a letter or note.

Xan·thip·pe (zan tip'ē) *n.* a scolding, nagging woman; shrew. [From *Xanthippe,* 469?-399 B.C., wife of the Greek philosopher Socrates, famous as a shrew.]

xan·thous (zan'thəs) *adj.* yellow or yellowish. [Greek *xanthos.*]

x-ax·is (eks'ak'sis) *n., pl.* **x-ax·es** (eks'ak'sēz). the horizontal axis in the Cartesian coordinate system, along which the abscissa is measured.

X chromosome, one of the two sex chromosomes, occurring in pairs in females and singly in males in humans, most mammals, and some higher plants.

Xe, the symbol for xenon.

xe·bec (zē'bek) *also,* **zebec, zebeck.** *n.* a small, three-masted ship with square and lateen sails, used esp. in the Mediterranean. [Modification (influenced by obsolete Spanish *xabeque*) of earlier *chebec,* from French *chebec,* from Arabic *shabbāk.*]

xeno- *combining form* **1.** a stranger or foreigner: *xenophobia.* **2.** strange or foreign: *xenolith.*

xen·o·lith (zen'ə lith', zē'nə-) *n.* a fragment of rock that is different from the igneous rock in which it is embedded. —**xen'o·lith'ic,** *adj.*

xe·non (zē'non, zen'on) *n.* a rare, heavy, gaseous element approximately five times heavier than air, formerly thought to be completely inert, used as a light source in discharge tubes, lasers, and bubble chambers. Symbol: **Xe** For tables, see element. [Greek *xenon,* neuter of *xenos* strange; because of its rarity.]

xen·o·pho·bi·a (zen'ə fō'bē ə, zē'nə-) *n.* an abnormal fear of strangers or of anything strange or foreign. [Greek *xenos* stranger + *-phobiā* panic, fear.] —**xen'o·phobe',** *n.* —**xen'o·pho'bic,** *adj.*

xe·rog·ra·phy (zi rog'rə fē) *n.* a process for making photographic copies of printed materials, in which a positive image of the material to be copied is projected onto an electrically charged surface. Light from the white areas of the material to be copied removes the charge, but the dark areas retain it and attract a black plastic powder, which forms the print of the copy. [Greek *xēros* dry + -GRAPHY.] —**xe·ro·graph·ic** (zîr'ə graf'ik), *adj.*

xe·ro·phyte (zîr'ə fīt') *n.* a plant that grows in and is adapted to dry conditions of climate and soil, as are cactus and agave. [Greek *xēros* dry + -PHYTE.] —**xe·ro·phy·tic** (zîr'ə fit'ik), *adj.*

Xe·rox (zîr'oks) *n. Trademark.* **1.** a photocopier that uses the process of xerography. **2. xerox.** a photocopy made by the process of xerography. —*v.t., v.i. also,* **xe·rox.** to photocopy using xerography.

Xho·sa (kō'sä, -zä) *also,* **Xosa.** *n., pl.* **-sas** or **-sa. 1.** a member of a Bantu people who live in parts of the Republic of South Africa. **2.** their Bantu language. —*adj.* of, relating to, or characteristic of the Xhosa or their language or culture.

xi (zī, sī, ksē) *n.* **1.** the fourteenth letter of the Greek alphabet (Ξ, ξ), corresponding to the English letter *X, x.* **2.** *Physics.* either of two subatomic particles of the baryon group.

Xmas (kris'məs, eks'-) Christmas.

Xo·sa (kō'sä, -zä) *n., pl.* **-sas** or **-sa.** Xhosa. —*adj.* Xhosa.

X-rated (eks'rā'tid) *adj.* featuring explicit sex: *an X-rated magazine.*

X-ra·di·a·tion (eks'rā'dē ā'shən) **1.** radiation consisting of X rays. **2.** exposure to or treatment with X rays.

X-ray (eks'rā') *also,* **x-ray.** *v.t.* to examine, photograph, or treat with X rays. —*adj.* relating to or made or done using x rays: *an X-ray inspection of metals.* —*n.* X ray.

X ray *also,* **x ray, x-ray, X-ray. 1.** an invisible, high-frequency electromagnetic radiation that can pass through substances opaque to visible light. It is used in medical diagnosis of internal disorders, such as broken bones, and in treating certain diseases, such as cancer. **2.** a photograph made by means of X rays.

X-ray astronomy, the branch of astronomy that studies stars and other celestial bodies by analyzing their X-ray emissions.

X-ray diffraction, the diffraction of X rays as they interact with the atomic structure of solid matter, giving rise to patterns that can be recorded on film and used for studying the structure of crystals, metals, and alloys.

X-ray star, a celestial body, esp. a star, that emits far more energy in the form of X rays than as visible light.

X-ray therapy, the treatment of disease through controlled exposure to X rays.

X-ray tube, an electron tube that generates X rays by bombarding a target of heavy metal, esp. tungsten, with a stream of high-energy electrons.

xy·lem (zī'ləm, -lem) *n.* the vascular tissue that serves to carry water and dissolved nutrients from the roots to other parts of a plant and also helps to support the plant. In trees and other woody plants, xylem is the woody tissue enclosed by the phloem. [German *Xylem,* from Greek *xylon* wood.]

xy·lene (zī'lēn) *n.* any of three forms of a liquid hydrocarbon obtained from coal tar or petroleum, used to make dyes and as an intermediate in the manufacture of polyester fiber. Formula: C_8H_{10}

xy·lo·phone (zī'lə fōn') *n.* a musical instrument consisting of a stand on which a row of wooden bars of graduated length is mounted, sounded by striking the bars with small wooden mallets. [Greek *xylon* wood + *phōnē* voice, sound¹.] —**xy'lo·phon'ist,** *n.*

xy·lose (zī'lōs) *n.* a monosaccharide derived from straw, corncobs, and other woody plants that is used as a sweetener and for various commercial purposes. Formula: $C_5H_{10}O_5$

a	at	e	end	o	hot	u	up	hw	white		about
ā	ape	ē	me	ō	old	ū	use	ng	song		taken
ä	far	i	it	ô	fork	ü	rule	th	thin	ə	pencil
âr	care	ī	ice	oi	oil	u̇	pull	th	this		lemon
		îr	pierce	ou	out	ûr	turn	zh	measure		circus

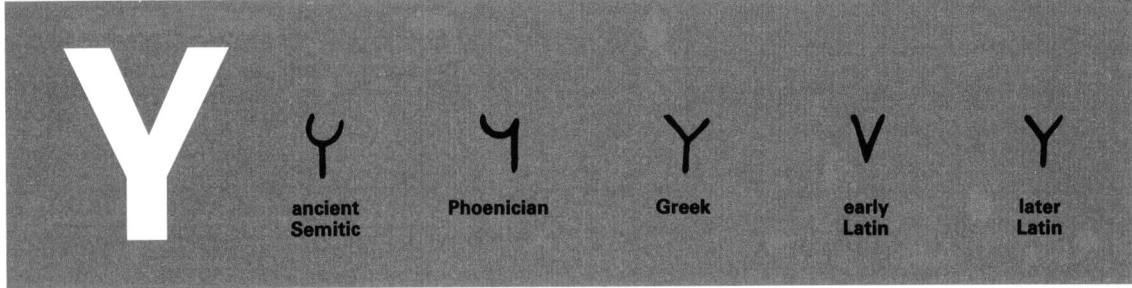

| ancient Semitic | Phoenician | Greek | early Latin | later Latin |

Y The letter **Y**, like the letters **F** and **V**, came from the ancient Semitic letter *waw*, which depicted a hook. This letter was borrowed first by the Phoenicians and then by the ancient Greeks, who called it *upsilon* and wrote it very much like a modern capital **Y**. In the Latin alphabet, *upsilon* was adopted twice. It was first borrowed around the sixth or seventh century B.C. to form the Latin letter **V**, which represented both the consonant sound *w* as in *water* and the vowel sound *ü* as in *rude*. The **Y** was borrowed a second time about 2,000 years ago, in order to represent the slightly different sound of *upsilon* in words that had come into Latin from Greek. This later form of *upsilon*, written like the capital letter **Y**, was the ancestor of our modern letter **Y**. Unlike the other letters of the English alphabet, **Y** commonly functions as both a vowel, as in *funny* and *cry*, and a consonant, as in *yesterday* and *young*. It was first used as a consonant to replace an obsolete Old English letter. Most of the words in our language that begin with **Y** originated in Old or Middle English.

y, Y (wī) *n., pl.* **y's, Y's 1.** the twenty-fifth letter of the English alphabet. **2.** the shape of this letter or something having this shape.

y (wī) *n., pl.* **y's** *Mathematics.* **1.** an unknown quantity or variable. **2.** the y-axis.

Y, the symbol for yttrium.

-y[1] *suffix* (used to form adjectives) **1.** characterized by; containing; full of: *rainy, juicy, sooty.* **2.** inclined to: *itchy, thirsty.* **3.** somewhat: *sugary, powdery, chilly.* **4.** resembling: *flowery, icy.* [Old English *-ig.*]

-y[2] *suffix* (used to form nouns) **1.** little; small: *puppy, kitty.* **2.** dear: *daddy, mommy.* [Middle English *-ie.*]

-y[3] *suffix* (used to form nouns) **1.** the state or quality of being: *sincerity, activity, tenacity.* **2.** a shop, store, or goods of a specified type: *grocery, bakery.* **3.** a group or body: *military, soldiery.* [Latin *-ia,* from Greek *-iā,* often through French *-ie.*]

y *also,* **y.** yard; yards.

y., year; years.

yacht (yot) *n.* any of various small ships used esp. for pleasure trips or racing. —*v.i.* to cruise or race in a yacht. [Obsolete Dutch *jaghte,* short for *jaghtschip* literally, ship for chasing, from *jagen* to chase + *schip* ship.]

yacht·ing (yot′ing) *n.* the art, practice, or sport of sailing a yacht.

yachts·man (yots′mən) *n., pl.* **-men** (-mən). a person who owns or sails a yacht. —**yachts′man·ship′,** *n.*

ya·hoo (yä′hü) *n., pl.* **-hoos.** a person who is rough, coarse, uncouth, or uneducated. [From *Yahoo* a member of a race of brutes who have the shape and appearance of human beings (in the satire *Gulliver's Travels* by Jonathan Swift, 1667-1745, English author and satirist).]

Yah·weh (yä′we) *also,* **Yah·veh, Jah·veh.** *n.* in the Old Testament, a name for God, based on a transliteration of the Hebrew letters symbolizing God's name. [See JEHOVAH.]

yak[1] (yak) *n.* a long-haired, wild ox, *Bos grunniens,* native to Tibet and central Asia, having a large hump at the shoulder and curved horns, often domesticated and used as a beast of burden. Height: 6½ feet (1.9 meters) at the shoulder. [Tibetan *gyag.*]

yak[2] (yak; *n., def. 2, also* yok) *Slang. v.i.,* **yakked, yak·king.** to talk too much or idly; chatter. —*n.* **1.** idle chatter or talk. **2.** a loud, boisterous laugh.

Ya·kut (yä kút′) *n.* **1.** a member of a people living in northeastern Siberia. **2.** the Turkic language of the Yakuts.

yam (yam) *n.* **1.** the edible tuber of a trailing vine, genus *Dioscorea,* used as food in many tropical and subtropical areas. **2.** the vine itself, having large leaves and bearing spikes of small greenish flowers. **3.** a large, reddish sweet potato. [Portuguese *inhame,* of West African origin.]

yam·mer (yam′ər) *Informal. v.i.* **1.** to whine or whimper, esp. in a complaining way. **2.** to shout or yell, often in a quarrelsome way: *Youngsters often yammer at each other.* **3.** to talk loudly and unceasingly. —*v.t.* to say in a loud, quarrelsome or complaining tone. —*n.* an act or instance of yammering. [Middle English *yomeren* to murmur, from Old English *gēomrian* to be sad, to complain.] —**yam′mer·er,** *n.*

yang (yäng, yang) *n.* in Chinese thought and philosophy, the male principle, combining light, warmth, and the creative energy associated with heaven. ➡ opposed to **yin.** [Chinese (Mandarin) *yang* sun, bright, male element in nature.]

yank (yangk) *Informal. v.t.* to give a sharp, abrupt pull to; jerk; tug: *I yanked the door open.* —*v.i.* to pull sharply and abruptly. —*n.* a sharp, abrupt pull. [Of uncertain origin.]

Yank (yangk) *n. Informal.* Yankee.

Yan·kee (yang′kē) *n.* **1.** a person who was born or is living in New England. **2.** a person who was born or is living in the North. **3.** a person who fought on the side of the Union during the American Civil War. **4.** any person who was born or is living in the United States. —*adj.* of or relating to Yankees. [Possibly from Dutch *Janke,* diminutive of *Jan* John (a name used by the Dutch colonists of New York to designate the English settlers of Connecticut).]

Yankee Doo·dle (dü′dəl) a song popularized by American soldiers during the Revolutionary War.

Yan·kee·ism (yang′kē iz′əm) *n.* **1.** a Yankee mannerism or trait. **2.** a Yankee idiom or pronunciation.

yap (yap) *n.* **1.** a brief, sharp, or shrill bark; yelp: *the yap of a puppy.* **2.** *Slang.* noisy talk. **3.** *Slang.* the mouth. **4.** *Slang.* a churlish person; bumpkin. —*v.i.,* **yapped, yap·ping. 1.** to bark sharply or shrilly; yelp. **2.** *Slang.* to talk noisily. [Imitative.] —**yap′per,** *n.*

Ya·qui (yä′kē) *n., pl. (def. 1)* **-qui** or **-quis. 1.** a member of a tribe of North American Indians living predominantly in northern Mexico. **2.** the language spoken by this tribe, belonging to the Uto-Aztecan language family.

yard[1] (yärd) *n.* **1.** an area of ground adjoining or surrounding a house or other building. **2.** an enclosed area of ground used for a special purpose, as for keeping livestock or for carrying on some work or business: *a cattle yard, a stonecutter's yard.* **3.** an area adjacent to a railroad station, used for storing, switching, or servicing trains. —*v.t.* to put into or enclose in a yard: *to yard livestock.* [Old English *geard* enclosure.]

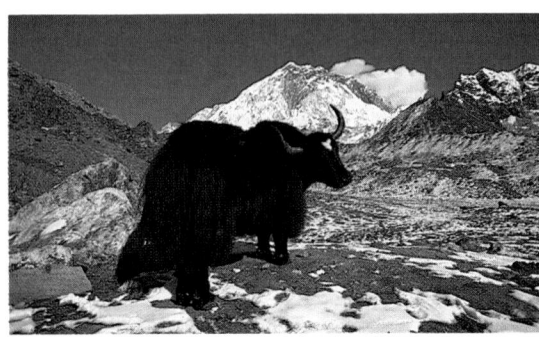

yak[1]

yard² (yärd) *n.* **1.** a measure of length equal to 36 inches (91 centimeters) or 3 feet (0.9 meter). **2.** a long rod that tapers toward the ends, fastened across a mast to support a sail. [Old English *gierd* staff, rod.]
• **the whole nine yards.** *Informal.* including everything; to the limit.

yard·age¹ (yär′dij) *n.* an amount or length measured in yards. [YARD² + -AGE.]

yard·age² (yär′dij) *n.* **1.** the use of a yard or enclosure, as for the loading and unloading of cattle at a railroad yard. **2.** a charge made for this use. [YARD¹ + -AGE.]

yard·arm (yärd′ärm′) *n. Nautical.* either end of a yard supporting a square sail.

yard goods, fabric that is sold by the yard.

yard·man (yärd′mən) *n., pl.* **-men** (-mən). a person who works in a yard, esp. a lumber or railroad yard.

yard·mas·ter (yärd′mas′tər) *n.* a person who is in charge of a railroad yard.

yard sale, garage sale.

yard·stick (yärd′stik′) *n.* **1.** a flat strip of wood, plastic, or metal 1 yard long, used in measuring. **2.** any standard used in making a judgment, evaluation, or comparison: *a yardstick for judging quality.*

yar·mul·ke (yär′məl kə, yä′məl-) *n.* a skullcap worn by Jewish men and boys, esp. during religious services. [Yiddish *yarmulke,* from Polish and Ukrainian *yarmulka* small hat, possibly from Turkish *yağmurluk* raincoat, from *yağmur* rain.]

yarn (yärn) *n.* **1.** thread spun from natural or artificial fibers, such as cotton, wool, silk, or nylon, used in weaving or knitting. **2.** *Informal.* a long, exaggerated, or highly embellished narrative: *The old sailor told many yarns about life at sea.* —*v.i. Informal.* to tell a yarn or yarns. [Old English *gearn* spun thread.]

yar·row (yar′ō) *n.* any of a large group of plants, genus *Achillea,* having lobed, often serrate leaves, and bearing clusters of small, variously colored flowers, esp. the milfoil, *A. millefolium.* [Old English *gearwe.*]

yaw (yô) *v.i.* **1.** (of a ship) to turn temporarily and unintentionally from a straight course. **2.** (of an aircraft, spacecraft, or projectile) to turn to the right or left on its vertical axis. —*n.* the act of turning from a straight course. [Of uncertain origin.]

yawl (yôl) *n.* **1.** a sailboat or small yacht with two masts, a large mainmast placed forward and a smaller mast placed astern. **2.** a ship's small boat, usually rowed by a crew of four or six. [Dutch *jol* small sloop, dinghy.]

yawn (yôn) *v.i.* **1.** to open the mouth wide, usually involuntarily and with a deep breath, because of drowsiness, boredom, or fatigue. **2.** to be or become wide open: *The pit of the crater yawned below.* —*v.t.* to utter or express with a yawn: *to yawn a reply.* —*n.* **1.** the act or fact of yawning. **2.** the act of opening wide. [Old English *geonian* to open the mouth wide, gape.] —**yawn′er,** *n.*

yawp (yôp, yäp) *v.i.* **1.** to utter a loud, sharp cry. **2.** *Slang.* to talk loudly and foolishly. —*n.* **1.** a loud, sharp cry. **2.** *Slang.* loud, foolish talk. [Imitative.] —**yawp′er,** *n.*

yaws (yôz) *n.* an infectious, tropical disease affecting chiefly children, caused by a spirochete and characterized by raspberry-like sores on the skin. ➡ used as singular. [Of Carib origin.]

y-ax·is (wī′ak′sis) *n., pl.* **y-ax·es** (wī′ak′sēz). the vertical axis in the Cartesian coordinate system, along which the ordinate is measured.

Yb, the symbol for ytterbium.

Y chromosome, one of the two sex chromosomes, the chromosome found only in males in which it is paired with an X chromosome.

y·clept (ē klept′) *also,* **y·cleped.** *adj. Archaic.* called; named. [Old English *gecleopod,* past participle of *cleopian* to call.]

yd *also,* **yd.** yard; yards.

ye¹ *pron. Archaic.* you. [Old English *gē.*]

ye² (thē) *Archaic.* the. [Archaic transcription of THE¹, because of the resemblance to the letter *y* of a runic letter used for the sound *th* in certain medieval manuscripts.]

yea (yā) *adv.* **1.** yes. ➡ used in affirmation or assent, esp. in voting orally. **2.** *Archaic.* indeed; truly. ➡ used to introduce a sentence or statement: *Yea, though I walk through the valley of the shadow of death* . . . (Psalm 23:4). **3.** *Archaic.* not only so, but also; what is more. ➡ used to intensify or amplify. —*n.* an affirmative vote or voter. [Old English *gēa* yes.]

yeah (ya, ye′ə) *adv. Informal.* yes. [From YES.]

yean (yēn) *v.t., v.i.* (of a sheep or goat) to bring forth (young). [Probably from an unrecorded Old English word.]

yean·ling (yēn′ling) *n.* the young of a sheep or goat; lamb or kid.

year (yîr) *n.* **1.a.** a period of time consisting of 365 or 366 days, reckoned from January 1 to December 31, and divided into twelve

months or fifty-two weeks. Also, **calendar year. b.** a period of time of similar length in other calendars, as that of the Mayas. **2.a.** the interval of time between one vernal equinox and the next, equal to 365 days, 5 hours, 48 minutes, and 46 seconds. Also, **solar year. b.** the interval of time required for the earth to complete one revolution around the sun, measured against the relatively fixed background of the stars, equal to 365 days, 6 hours, 9 minutes, and 9.54 seconds. Also, **sidereal year. 3.** a period of twelve lunar months or 354 days. Also, **lunar year. 4.** any period of twelve months: *Our fiscal year begins June 1. We'll have been married two years in May.* **5.** the part of a year devoted to a particular activity: *the academic year.* **6.** the period of time in which any planet completes one revolution around the sun: *The Martian year is 687 days, and the Venusian, 225.* **7. years. a.** age, esp. old age: *Our dog is getting on in years.* **b.** time, esp. a long time: *We've been vacationing there for years.* [Old English *gēar* the period of a year.]
• **year after year.** every year.
• **year by year.** with each succeeding year.
• **year in, year out.** every year; continuously.

year·book (yîr′bûk′) *n.* **1.** a book published every year, usually containing information about or a summary of the events of the previous year. **2.** a book issued by a graduating class of a high school or college, containing information and, usually, photographs of the class and its activities and achievements.

year·ling (yîr′ling) *n.* an animal that is one year old or in its second year. —*adj.* one-year-old: *a yearling calf.*

year·long (yîr′lông′) *adj.* lasting for a year.

year·ly (yîr′lē) *adj.* **1.** occurring or returning once a year: *a yearly visit to the doctor.* **2.** performed during a year; lasting a year: *a yearly orbit.* **3.** measured by the year: *a yearly income.* —*adv.* once a year; annually: *I visit Florida yearly.* —*n., pl.* **-lies.** a publication issued once a year.

yearn (yûrn) *v.i.* **1.** to feel a strong and deep desire: *to yearn for the carefree days of youth.* **2.** to feel deep pity; be moved with compassion: *It would make anyone's heart yearn to see these homeless children.* [Old English *giernan* to desire.] —**yearn′er,** *n.*

yearn·ing (yûr′ning) *n.* an earnest or deep desire. —**yearn′-ing·ly,** *adv.*

year-round (yîr′round′) *adj., adv.* throughout the year: *a year-round vacation spot, to live somewhere year-round.*

yeast (yēst) *n.* **1.** a substance consisting of minute cells of any of various fungi, genus *Saccharomyces,* that cause fermentation in mixtures containing sugar. Yeast is used commercially in raising bread, making beer and wine, and in other processes. **2.** a single plant or cell of this substance. **3.** yeast cake *(def. 1).* **4.** foam; froth; spume. **5.** anything that causes ferment or activity. [Old English *gist* the substance.] —**yeast′like′,** *adj.*

yeast cake 1. yeast compressed with flour or meal into small cakes, used esp. in baking and brewing. **2.** a cake or similar baked food leavened with yeast.

yeast·y (yēs′tē) *adj.,* **yeast·i·er, yeast·i·est. 1.** of, containing, or resembling yeast. **2.** frothy; foamy: *yeasty sea foam.* **3.** characterized by ferment, agitation, or great activity. **4.** light and superficial; frivolous. —**yeast′i·ness,** *n.*

yecch (yeкн, yek, yuкн, yuk) *also,* **yech.** *interj. Slang.* used to show disgust, scorn, or repugnance. [Imitative.]

yegg (yeg) *n. Slang.* a thief, esp. a burglar or safecracker. [Of uncertain origin.]

yell (yel) *v.i.* to cry out loudly, as in pain or anger. —*v.t.* to utter or express with a yell: *to yell an answer across a room.* —*n.* **1.** a strong, loud cry, as of pain or anger; scream. **2.** a rhythmic chant or cheer shouted by a group, as by the spectators at a sporting event. [Old English *giellan* to cry out loudly.] —**yell′er,** *n.*

yel·low (yel′ō) *n.* **1.** the color occurring between green and orange in the spectrum; color of egg yolks or ripe lemons. **2.** a pigment or dye having this color. **3.** the yolk of an egg. —*adj.* **1.** having the color yellow. **2.** having a yellowish complexion. **3.** *Informal.* not brave; cowardly. **4.** having turned yellow, as by disease or discoloration. **5.** emphasizing sensationalism and scandal rather than fact: *yellow journalism.* —*v.i.* to become yellow: *The newspapers have yellowed with age.* —*v.t.* to make yellow. [Old English *geolu* of this color.] —**yel′low·ness,** *n.*

yel·low·bird (yel′ō bûrd′) *n.* any of various birds with predominantly yellow feathers, as the American goldfinch and the yellow warbler.

a	at	e	end	o	hot	u	up	hw	white		about
ā	ape	ē	me	ō	old	ū	use	ng	song		taken
ä	far	i	it	ô	fork	ü	rule	th	thin	ə	pencil
âr	care	ī	ice	oi	oil	ù	pull	th	this		lemon
		îr	pierce	ou	out	ûr	turn	zh	measure		circus

yel·low-dog contract (yel′ō dôg′) a contract between an employer and employee, no longer legal, in which the employee agrees not to join a union as a condition of employment.

yellow fever, an infectious, often fatal disease occurring primarily in the tropics, caused by a virus transmitted by the bite of a mosquito and characterized by high fevers, vomiting, jaundice, and hemorrhaging. Also, **yellow jack.**

yel·low-green algae (yel′ō grēn′) any of a group of freshwater and terrestrial golden algae containing a yellow pigment in addition to chlorophyll.

yel·low·ham·mer (yel′ō ham′ər) n. **1.** a Eurasian finch, *Emberiza citrinella,* having black, brown, and yellow plumage and a short, conical bill. Length: 6½ inches (17 centimeters). **2.** a North American flicker, *Colaptes auratus,* of the woodpecker family, having predominantly brown plumage with yellow markings on the wings and tail. [Earlier *yelambre,* possibly going back to Old English *geolu* yellow + *amore* a bird of uncertain identity.]

yel·low·ish (yel′ō ish) adj. somewhat yellow.

yellow jack 1. yellow fever. **2.** a yellow flag used as a sign of quarantine, as on a ship.

yellow jacket, any of several social wasps, family Vespidae, that have yellow markings.

yel·low·legs (yel′ō legz′) n. either of two American sandpipers, genus *Tringa,* having long, yellow legs.

yellow ocher, a yellowish pigment, usually containing limonite.

yellow pages also, **Yellow Pages.** a telephone directory, or a section of one, printed on yellow paper, that lists businesses and services under general categories.

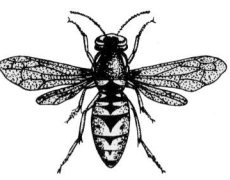

yellow jacket

yellow pine 1. the yellowish wood of any of several North American pine trees, used esp. as structural timber and in the manufacture of paper. **2.** a tree bearing such wood.

yel·low-shaft·ed flicker (yel′ō shaf′tid) a flicker of eastern North America, *Colaptes auratus,* with a brown-barred back, spotted underside, and yellow wing linings.

yellow spot, a yellowish area near the center of the human retina, made up mostly of cone cells, in which vision and perception of detail are most acute.

yel·low·tail (yel′ō tāl′) n., pl. **-tails** or **-tail. 1.** any of various large, saltwater fish, genus *Seriola,* having a deeply forked yellowish tail and valued as a food and game fish. **2.** any of several other unrelated fish having a yellowish tail, including varieties of snapper and flounder.

yel·low·throat (yel′ō thrōt′) n. any of New World warblers of the genus *Geothlypis,* having a yellow breast and throat.

yellow warbler, a small, American warbler, *Dendroica petechia,* the male of which has yellow plumage with brown streaks.

yel·low·wood (yel′ō wùd′) n. **1.** any of several deciduous trees, genus *Cladrastis,* of the pea family, esp. *C. lutea,* native to the southeastern United States, having clusters of fragrant white flowers and wood that yields a yellow dye. **2.** any of several other trees having yellow wood or yielding a yellowish dye. **3.** the wood of any of these trees.

yelp (yelp) n. a short shrill cry, as that made by a dog in pain. —v.i. to utter or give forth a short shrill cry. —v.t. to utter with a yelp. [Old English *gielpan* to boast.]

yen¹ (yen) n., pl. **yen.** the monetary unit of Japan. [Japanese *en,* from Chinese (Mandarin) *yüan* dollar, circle.]

yen² (yen) Informal. n. a sharp desire or longing; craving: *a yen to travel.* —v.i., **yenned, yen·ning.** to yearn or long; desire sharply: *to yen for adventure.* [Chinese (Cantonese) *yan* craving.]

yeo·man (yō′mən) n., pl. **-men** (-mən). **1.** a naval petty officer who performs clerical or administrative duties. **2.** in Great Britain, a small farmer. **3.** Archaic. a member of a class of English society who owned and farmed a small amount of land. **4.** Archaic. a servant or attendant in the household of a sovereign or noble. **5.** yeoman of the guard. [Middle English *yoman* servant in a royal or noble household, possibly a contraction of *yongman* young man, from Old English *geong* young + *mann* man.]

yeo·man·ly (yō′mən lē) adj. **1.** of, relating to, or having the rank of a yeoman. **2.** befitting a yeoman; brave; staunch. —adv. in the manner of a yeoman; bravely.

yeoman of the guard, a member of the ceremonial bodyguard for the English monarch and the royal family, instituted in the fifteenth century and consisting of one hundred men and their officers; beefeater.

yeo·man·ry (yō′mən rē) n. yeomen collectively, esp. the class of small farmers.

yeoman's service also, **yeoman service.** faithful, diligent, and useful service or support.

-yer, form of -ier after *w,* as in *lawyer.*

yer·ba ma·té (yer′bə mä′tā, mä tā′, yûr′-) maté. [Argentine Spanish *yerba mate,* from Spanish *hierba* grass (from Latin *herba* grass, green crops) + *maté.* See MATÉ.]

yes (yes) adv. **1.** as you say or ask; it is so. ➡ opposed to *no;* used to express acceptance, agreement, consent, or affirmation: *Yes, you are right. Yes, you may borrow my book.* **2.** in addition to that; moreover. ➡ used to emphasize a preceding statement by repetition or addition: *You are a good athlete, yes, the best on the team.* —n., pl. **yes·es. 1.** an utterance of the word *yes;* positive response. **2.** an affirmative vote or voter. —v.t., v.i., **yessed, yes·sing.** to say *yes* (to someone or something). [Old English *gēse,* word expressing affirmation, probably from *geā* yea + *sī* be it (third person singular of the present subjunctive of *bēon* to be).]

ye·shi·va (yə shē′və) also, **ye·shi·vah.** n., pl. **-vas** or **-voth** (-vōt). **1.** an Orthodox Jewish parochial school. **2.** an Orthodox Jewish institution of higher learning. [Hebrew *yeshīvāh* a sitting, academy.]

yes man Informal. a person who always agrees with his or her superior.

yes·ter·day (yes′tər dē, -dā′) n. **1.** the day before today. **2.** the recent past: *the automobiles of yesterday.* —adv. **1.** on the day before today: *Was it yesterday we saw you at the fair?* **2.** recently: *It seems that they were babies only yesterday.* [Old English *geostran dæg* the day before today, on the day before today.]

yes·ter·eve·ning (yes′tər ēv′ning) n., adv. Archaic. yesterday evening. Also, **yes′ter·eve′.**

yes·ter·morn·ing (yes′tər môr′ning) n., adv. Archaic. yesterday morning. Also, **yes′ter·morn′.**

yes·ter·night (yes′tər nīt′) n., adv. Archaic. the night before today; last night.

yes·ter·year (yes′tər yîr′) n. **1.** the year before this year; last year. **2.** the past; yore.

yes·treen (yes trēn′) n., adv. Archaic. yesterday evening.

yet (yet) adv. **1.** at the present time; now: *not yet old enough to vote.* **2.** up to the present time; thus far: *I have never yet been late for a meeting.* **3.** continuously up to this or that time: *The farmer rose early and is working yet.* **4.** at some future time; eventually: *The mystery will be solved yet.* **5.** after all the time that has or had elapsed: *Aren't you finished eating yet?* **6.** in the time remaining: *There is yet a chance that we will win.* **7.** in addition: *There are three days yet to go until my vacation.* **8.** even; still. ➡ used with a comparative: *It will be colder yet before spring comes.* **9.** nevertheless; however: *The judge was stern, yet completely fair.* **10.** moreover: *Sarah wouldn't speak to Peter nor yet to me.* —conj. nevertheless; however: *The road map seemed clear enough, yet we soon got lost.* [Old English *gīet(a)* still, moreover, in addition, thus far, at length.]

yet·i (yet′ē) n. abominable snowman. [Of Tibetan origin.]

yew (ū) n. **1.** any of a small group of evergreen trees and shrubs, genus *Taxus,* native to the Northern Hemisphere, having scaly, reddish brown bark and flattened, needlelike leaves. **2.** the wood of this tree, used esp. in making archery bows. [Old English *ēow* this tree.]

Ygg·dra·sil (ig′drə sil) also, **Yg·dra·sil, Ygg·dra·sil.** n. in Norse mythology, an enormous ash tree that grows from the earth and supports the whole universe.

Yid·dish (yid′ish) n. a Germanic language spoken predominantly by Jews in Europe, Israel, and North and South America. Yiddish, which is written in the Hebrew alphabet, is the descendant of a Middle High German dialect, with the addition of many words from Hebrew and from various Slavic and Romance languages. —adj. of or relating to this language.

Words from Yiddish

Yiddish, which developed from German in the Middle Ages, is in the Germanic branch of the Indo-European language family. It is completely unrelated to Hebrew, although it is written with Hebrew characters and has borrowed many words from Hebrew. The following words have entered English through Yiddish primarily from German, Hebrew, or Slavic languages.

bagel	gefilte fish	knish	nosh
bar mitzvah	golem	lox¹	schlemiel
bialy	halvah	maven	schlep
blintze	kibitz	megillah	shamus
chutzpah	kibitzer	mensch	shul
fin²	klutz	nebbish	yarmulke

yield (yēld) *v.t.* **1.** to produce or give forth by a natural process or as the result of cultivation or labor: *This rich land will yield a large crop. That mine yields silver.* **2.** to give in return, as for an investment: *a bank account yielding interest.* **3.** to give up, as to superior power: *The defeated troops yielded the town to the enemy.* **4.** to grant (something requested or demanded) as a right or privilege: *to yield a point in an argument, to yield the right of way to pedestrians.* —*v.i.* **1.** to give up; surrender; submit: *Our team refused to yield to the opposition.* **2.** to comply, as from coercion, persuasion, or compulsion; consent: *We yielded to their argument.* **3.** to break loose or away, as because of force or pressure: *The lock was old and yielded when we pushed the door.* **4.** to give place, as through inferiority; defer: *I yield to the scientist on the panel to answer your question.* **5.** to provide a return; produce. —*n.* **1.** an amount yielded, as from cultivation or mining; product: *a yield of 50 bushels of wheat.* **2.** the profit derived from an investment. **3.** the energy released in a nuclear explosion, expressed in terms of the kilotons or megatons of TNT that produce an explosion of equivalent energy. [Old English *gieldan* to pay[1], repay, render.] —**yield′er,** *n.*

Synonyms *v.i.* Yield, submit, surrender, and capitulate mean to give in or to give way to some person or force. **Yield** connotes a recognition that opposition is fruitless: *to yield to someone's arguments, to yield to the will of the majority.* **Submit** is more final than *yield* and connotes giving in after trying at first to resist: *After years of effort, we submitted to fate and closed the business.* **Surrender** is used primarily in military contexts and implies a complete giving-in. *The rebel forces were so outnumbered that they had no choice but to surrender.* **Capitulate,** used less frequently than *surrender,* connotes a submission on stated terms: *The armistice agreement called for the ruler to capitulate.*

yield·ing (yēl′ding) *adj.* tending to yield; submissive; obedient: *a yielding nature.*

yin (yin) *n.* in Chinese thought and philosophy, the female principle, combining the dark, cold, wet, and fertile energy associated with the earth. ➤ opposed to **yang.** [Chinese (Mandarin) *yin* moon, dark, female principle in nature.]

yip (yip) *n.* a yelp, esp. of a dog. —*v.i.,* **yipped, yip·ping.** to give a short, sharp cry; yelp. [Imitative.]

-yl *suffix* used in chemistry to indicate a radical: *methyl, ethyl.*

YMCA, Young Men's Christian Association.

YMHA, Young Men's Hebrew Association.

Y·mir (ē′mir) *also,* **Y·mer.** *n.* in Norse mythology, a giant formed from the vapors of melting ice, from whose body Odin and his brothers formed the earth.

yo·del (yō′dəl) *also,* **yo·dle.** *v.,* **-deled, -del·ing;** *also, British,* **-delled, -del·ling.** —*v.i.* to sing with frequent alternating changes between the natural voice and a falsetto voice. —*v.t.* to sing (something) with frequent alternating changes between the natural voice and a falsetto voice. —*n.* the act or sound of yodeling. [German *jodeln* to yodel.] —**yo′del·er;** *also, British,* **yo′del·ler,** *n.*

yo·ga (yō′gə) *also,* **Yo·ga.** *n.* a system of mental and physical discipline practiced by Hindus in order to become free of the senses and the external world and reach ultimate reality. It is also practiced by non-Hindus to improve mental and physical health. [Sanskrit *yoga* union.]

yo·gi (yō′gē) *n., pl.* **-gis.** a person who practices or is an adherent of yoga.

yo·gurt (yō′gərt) *also,* **yo·ghurt, yo·ghourt.** *n.* a fermented, semisolid dairy product made by adding bacterial culture to milk, and often flavored or sweetened. [Turkish *yōghurt.*]

yoicks (yoiks) *interj.* a cry formerly used in fox hunting to urge on the hounds.

yoke (yōk) *n., pl. (defs. 1, 3-6)* **yokes** or *(def. 2)* **yoke. 1.** a wooden frame consisting of a long, curved bar fitted with two hoops by which two work animals are joined together. **2.** a pair of animals, esp. oxen, joined together by a yoke. **3.** any of various similar devices, as a frame worn on the shoulders and designed to carry a pail or other burden at either end. **4.** an oppressive force or influence; burden: *the yoke of taxation, an enslaved people under the yoke of tyranny.* **5.** something that joins or unites; bond; tie: *the yoke of friendship.* **6.** the top section of a garment, usually consisting of a flat, smooth-fitting piece of fabric, as around the neck and shoulders of a blouse.

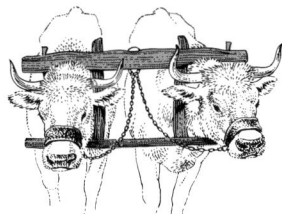

yoke *(def. 1)*

—*v.,* **yoked, yok·ing.** —*v.t.* **1.** to put a yoke on. **2.** to harness or attach (a work animal) to a yoke: *to yoke oxen for plowing.* **3.** to join or unite with or as with a yoke. —*v.i.* to join closely: *to yoke in marriage.* [Old English *geoc* contrivance used to join a pair of draft animals, pair of animals so joined, subjection.]

yoke·fel·low (yōk′fel′ō) *n.* **1.** a mate or partner in labor. **2.** a husband or wife. Also, **yokemate.**

yo·kel (yō′kəl) *n.* a rustic, unsophisticated person, esp. one living in the country. ➤ usually used contemptuously. [Possibly from dialectal English *yokel* green woodpecker (used figuratively); probably of imitative origin.]

yoke·mate (yōk′māt′) *n.* yokefellow.

yolk (yōk) *n.* **1.** the yellow, nutritive substance of an egg, as distinguished from the albumen, or white part, of the egg. **2.** the oily substances in unprocessed sheep's wool. [Old English *geolca* the yellow part of an egg, from *geolu* yellow.]

yolk sac, a saclike membrane enclosing the yolk in the embryos of fish, amphibians, reptiles, and birds and vestigial in mammals. Blood vessels in the yolk sac carry digested yolk to the embryo.

Yom Kip·pur (yom kip′ər; *Hebrew* yōm′ kē pūr′) in Judaism, the day of fasting and atonement for sins, observed on the tenth day of the first month of the Jewish calendar. Also, **Day of Atonement.** [Hebrew *yōm kippūr* day of atonement.]

yon (yon) *adj., adv. Archaic.* yonder. [Old English *geon* that.]

yond (yond) *adj., adv. Archaic.* yonder. [Old English *geond.*]

yon·der (yon′dər) *adv.* in that place; over there. —*adj.* **1.** being at a distance, but within sight: *The cattle are in yonder field.* **2.** being more distant; farther: *the yonder side of a hill.* [Middle English *yonder,* from *yond.* See YOND.]

yore (yôr) *adv.* of yore. of long ago; in the past: *in days of yore.* [Old English *gēara* formerly, of old; literally, of years, genitive of *gēar* year.]

York (yôrk) *n.* the reigning house of England from 1461 to 1485, a branch of the royal house of Plantagenet. Its emblem was a white rose.

York·ist (yôr′kist) *n.* an adherent or member of the house of York. —*adj.* **1.** of or relating to the house of York. **2.** of or relating to the supporters of the house of York against the house of Lancaster.

York·shire pudding (yôrk′shīr, -shər) a batter often baked under roasting meat to catch the drippings, frequently served with roast beef.

Yorkshire terrier, a small breed of terrier having a coat of long, straight, silky hair that is dark steel blue and tan. Height: 8 inches (20 centimeters) at the shoulder.

you (ū; *unstressed* yủ, yə) *pron., sing.* nominative, **you;** possessive, **your, yours;** objective, **you;** *pl.* nominative, **you;** possessive, **your, yours;** objective, **you. 1.** the person or persons being addressed: *Do you want to go? I'll meet you at six o'clock.* **2.** a person; one; anyone: *You have to be careful when handling chemicals.* [Old English *ēow,* dative and accusative of *gē.* See YE[1].]

Usage In formal speech and writing, **one** is preferred instead of **you** as an indefinite pronoun meaning "a person" or "anyone," as in *One can never be sure what the future will bring.*

you-all (ū ôl′, yôl) *pron. Informal.* you. ➤ used chiefly in the southern United States and referring to two or more persons.

you'd (ūd) *contr.* **1.** you had. **2.** you would.

you'll (ūl; *unstressed* yủl) *contr.* **1.** you will. **2.** you shall.

young (yung) *adj.,* **young·er** (yung′ger), **young·est** (yung′gist). **1.** having lived or existed for a short time; in the early part of life or growth; not old: *A colt is a young horse.* **2.** possessing or exhibiting the characteristics of a young person; fresh; vigorous: *a young body, to act young for one's age.* **3.** of, relating to, or belonging to the early part of life: *She remembered her young years with nostalgia.* **4.** recently begun, formed, or made; in an early stage of progress or development: *a young wine, a young nation.* **5.** of fewer years than. ➤ designating the younger of two people with the same name: *young John and his father.* **6.** having little experience, skill, or practice: *You are too young to be president of the company.* —*n.* **1.** young people collectively: *That music is popular with the young.* **2.** young offspring, esp. of animals: *The animal's instinct was to protect its young.* [Old English *geong* youthful, recent, fresh.] —**young′ness,** *n.* ·**with young.** pregnant.

young·ber·ry (yung′ber′ē) *n., pl.* **-ries.** the sweet, purple fruit of a cross between a dewberry and a blackberry, *Rubus ursinus,*

a	at	e	end	o	hot	u	up	hw	white		about
ā	ape	ē	me	ō	old	ū	use	ng	song		taken
ä	far	i	it	ô	fork	ü	rule	th	thin	ə	pencil
âr	care	ī	ice	oi	oil	ủ	pull	th	this		lemon
		îr	pierce	ou	out	ûr	turn	zh	measure		circus

resembling the boysenberry but ripening earlier. [From B. M. *Young,* early twentieth-century American horticulturist.]

young blood 1. young people. **2.** youthful ideas, energy, or enthusiasm: *We need more young blood in our organization.*

young·ish (yung′ish) *adj.* somewhat young.

young·ling (yung′ling) *n.* **1.** a young person, animal, or plant. **2.** a person who is inexperienced; novice. —*adj.* young.

young·ster (yung′stər) *n.* a young person; child or youth.

Young Turk, a member of a group of young people who seek to take control of an organization, business, or political body from a conservative, usually older, group in order to bring about reform. [From the *Young Turks,* revolutionary party founded in Turkey in the late nineteenth century and dominant early in the twentieth century.]

youn·ker (yung′kər) *n. Archaic.* a young nobleman or gentleman. [Middle Dutch *jonckher* young nobleman, from *jonc* young + *here* lord.]

your (yùr; *unstressed* yər) *adj.* (the possessive form of **you**) **1.** of, relating to, or belonging to you: *your cousin, your house, your idea.* **2.** of, relating to, or belonging to a person; one's: *The school is on your left as you enter the town.* **3.** a, an, or the: *your average citizen.* [Old English *ēower,* genitive of *gē.* See YE[1].]

you're (yùr, yôr; *unstressed* yər) *contr.* you are.

yours (yùrz) *pron.* **1.** of, relating to, or belonging to you: *This book is yours.* ➡ used with *of* after a noun or pronoun: *I am a great admirer of yours.* **2.** the one or ones that relate or belong to you: *My paper was well written, but yours was even better.* ➡ *Yours* is the absolute form of the possessive adjective *your,* used when no noun follows. It is used as singular or plural, depending on the noun to which it refers.

your·self (yùr self′, yər-) *pron., pl.* **-selves** (-selvz′). **1.** the emphatic form of **you:** *You yourself know that I deserve the credit.* **2.** the reflexive form of **you:** *Be careful of the fire or you will burn yourself.* **3.** your usual, normal, or true self: *You have not been yourself these past few weeks.* —For Usage Note, see **myself.**

yours truly 1. a conventional phrase of politeness written before the signature at the close of a letter. **2.** *Informal.* I; me: *The panel consists of Jim, Betsy, and yours truly.*

youth (ūth) *n., pl.* **youths** (ūths, ūthz). **1.** the condition or quality of being young: *Exercise is a good way to keep one's youth.* **2.** the time of life between childhood and adulthood: *the carefree days of youth.* **3.** an early period in the development or existence of anything, as a nation or organization. **4.** young people collectively: *Our hope lies in the youth of our nation.* ➡ used as plural. **5.** a young person, esp. a young man. [Old English *geoguth* quality or state of being young, young people collectively.]

youth·ful (ūth′fəl) *adj.* **1.** having youth; still young in years: *a youthful person.* **2.** characteristic of youth: *youthful energy.* **3.** belonging to or suitable for young people: *a youthful outfit.* **4.** in an early stage of development or existence. **5.** *Geology.* having caused or undergone only slight erosion: *a youthful landscape, a youthful stream.* —**youth′ful·ly,** *adv.* —**youth′ful·ness,** *n.*

youth hostel, a supervised lodging place for young people on hiking, bicycling, or other trips.

you've (ūv; *unstressed* yùv) *contr.* you have.

yowl (youl) *n.* a long, mournful cry, as that of a dog; howl; wail. —*v.i.* to utter a yowl. [Imitative.]

yo-yo (yō′yō) *n., pl.* **-yos. 1.** a toy consisting of two disks connected at their center by a pin around which a string is wound, the loose end being attached to the operator's finger. The operator alternately lowers and raises the yo-yo by unwinding and rewinding the string. **2.** *Slang.* a person who is stupid, inept, or ridiculous. —*v.i.* **-yoed, -yo·ing.** *Informal.* to move up and down; fluctuate: *Our economy is still yo-yoing.*

yr *also,* **yr.** *pl.* **yrs** year; years.

yr. *pl.* **yrs.** your; yours.

YT, the postal abbreviation for the Yukon Territory.

Y.T., Yukon Territory.

yt·ter·bi·a (i tûr′bē ə) *n.* an oxide of ytterbium that is colorless when pure, used in making ceramics with very low electrical conductivity. Formula: Yb_2O_3 Also, **ytterbium oxide.**

yt·ter·bi·um (i tûr′bē əm) *n.* a soft, silvery element of the rare-earth group, used in alloys and lasers. Symbol: **Yb** For tables, see **element.** [Modern Latin *ytterbium,* from *Ytterby,* Swedish town where it was discovered.] —**yt·ter′bic,** *adj.*

yt·tri·a (it′rē ə) *n.* a yellowish white oxide of yttrium, used in color television tubes, special ceramics, and lasers. Formula: Y_2O_3 Also, **yttrium oxide.**

yt·tric (it′rik) *adj.* of or containing yttrium.

yt·tri·um (it′rē əm) *n.* a dark gray, metallic element used esp. in magnetic alloys. Symbol: **Y** For tables, see **element.** [Modern Latin *yttrium,* from *Ytterby,* Swedish town where it was discovered.]

yu·an (ū än′) *n., pl.* **yu·an.** the monetary unit of China. [Chinese (Mandarin) *yüan* dollar, circle.]

yuc·ca (yuk′ə) *n.* any of a group of plants, genus *Yucca,* of the warmer regions of North America, having a woody stem and bearing clusters of white or violet, bell-shaped, drooping flowers. [Spanish *yuca;* of Carib origin.]

Yule (ūl) *n.* **1.** Christmas. **2.** the Christmas season; Christmastide. [Old English *gēol* Christmas.]

Yule log, a large log traditionally burned at Christmas.

Yule·tide (ūl′tīd′) *n.* the season of Christmas; Christmastide.

yum (yum) *interj.* used to express pleasure or satisfaction. Also, **yum-yum** (yum′-yum′).

yum·my (yum′ē) *Informal. adj.,* **-mi·er, -mi·est.** very pleasing, esp. to the taste; delicious; delectable: *a yummy blueberry pie.* —*n., pl.* **-mies.** something delicious or delectable.

yup·pie (yup′ē) *also,* **yup-py.** *n. Informal.* a member of the group of young, college-

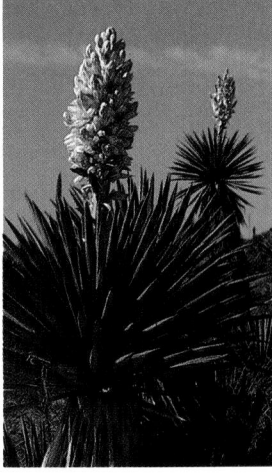

yuccas

educated people holding well-paid jobs, often in the professions, commonly believed to be ambitious and to have expensive, stylish tastes. [Short for *y(oung) u(rban) p(rofessional)* + -IE.]

YWCA, Young Women's Christian Association.

YWHA, Young Women's Hebrew Association.

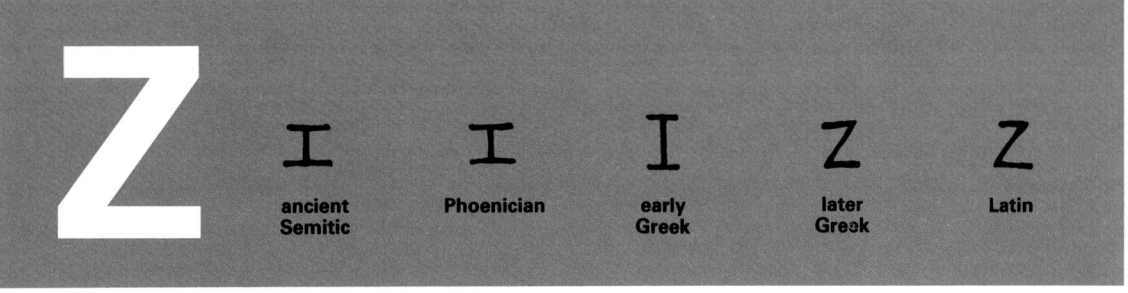

ancient Semitic	Phoenician	early Greek	later Greek	Latin

Z The earliest form of the letter **Z** was the letter *zayin,* which probably meant "weapon" or "balance" in the ancient Semitic and Phoenician alphabets. After the Greeks adopted *zayin,* they altered its shape and called it *zeta. Zed,* which is what **Z** is called in many English-speaking countries, comes from the name of this Greek letter. Although the *z* sound was not found in Latin, the Romans adopted *zeta* to represent this letter as it appeared in Greek words which they borrowed. The Romans made only the slightest changes in its shape, writing it very much as we write the capital letter **Z** today.

z, Z (zē) *n., pl.* **z's, Z's. 1.** the twenty-sixth and last letter of the English alphabet. **2.** the shape of this letter or something having this shape.

z. *also,* **Z.** zone.

Z, atomic number.

Zach·a·ri·ah (zak'ə rī'ə) Zechariah.

zag (zag) *Informal. n.* **1.** one of the alternating movements or directions in a zigzag. **2.** any sharp turn or movement away from a straight line or course. —*v.i.,* **zagged, zag·ging.** to move or turn in one of the alternating directions in a zigzag. [From ZIG-ZAG.]

zai·bat·su (zī'bä tsü') *n.* the several families that control Japanese industries and finance. ➡ used as singular or plural. [Japanese *zaibatsu* plutocracy, from *zai* money, riches + *batsu* clan, family.]

za·ire (zä îr') *n., pl.* **za·ire.** the monetary unit of Zaire.

za·ny (zā'nē) *adj.,* **-ni·er, -ni·est.** comically odd or ludicrous. —*n., pl.* **-nies. 1.** a foolish person; simpleton; fool. **2.** a clown or buffoon. [Italian *zanni* clown, from *Zanni,* dialectal form of *Gianni,* familiar form of *Giovanni* John, from Latin *Jōannēs.* See JOHN.] —**za'ni·ness,** *n.*

zap (zap) *Slang. v.,* **zapped, zap·ping.** —*v.t.* **1.** to destroy or kill by or as by shooting. **2.** to strike or hit suddenly, as with an electric current: *The faulty plug zapped me when I pulled it out of the socket.* **3.** to cook (food) in a microwave. **4.** to turn off; extinguish: *to zap the lights.* —*v.i.* **1.** to do or move suddenly or quickly: *Lightning zapped across the sky.* —*n.* energy or vitality. —*interj.* **1.** used to express the sound of a sudden sharp noise, as that made by a blow, slap, or blast. **2.** used to express sudden change or movement. [Imitative.]

zeal (zēl) *n.* an intense desire or devotion; earnest enthusiasm: *to do a job with zeal, to have the zeal of a reformer.* [Late Latin *zēlus* fervor, jealousy, from Greek *zēlos.*]

zeal·ot (zel'ət) *n.* a zealous person, esp. a fanatical partisan; extremist. [Late Latin *zēlōtēs,* from Greek *zēlōtēs,* from *zēlos* fervor.] —For Synonyms, see **enthusiast.**

zeal·ot·ry (zel'ə trē) *n.* excessive zeal; fanaticism.

zeal·ous (zel'əs) *adj.* filled with, characterized by, or motivated by zeal: *a zealous worker, a zealous patriot.* —**zeal'ous·ly,** *adv.* —**zeal'ous·ness,** *n.*

ze·bec (zē'bek) *also,* **ze·beck.** xebec.

ze·bra (zē'brə) *n., pl.* **-bras** or **-bra.** any of several wild, horselike mammals, genus *Equus,* native to eastern and southern Africa, having a light-colored coat with black stripes, a short, stiff mane, and a long tail ending in a

zebra

tuft of hair. Height: to 4½ feet (1.4 meters) at the shoulder. [Portuguese *zebra,* possibly from a word native to the Congo region.]

ze·bu (zē'bū) *n.* a hardy, domesticated ox of India, having a prominent hump over the shoulder and a pronounced dewlap. [French *zébu;* of uncertain origin.]

Zech., Zechariah.

Zech·a·ri·ah (zek'ə rī'ə) *n.* a book of the Old Testament, attributed to the Hebrew prophet Zechariah.

zed (zed) *n. British.* the letter *z.* [French *zède,* from Late Latin *zēta* from Greek *zēta* name of the Greek letter ζ.]

Zeit·geist (tsīt'gīst) *n. German.* the characteristic thought or spirit of a period of time; moral and intellectual feeling or tendencies of a time.

Zen (zen) *n.* **1.** a Buddhist sect that differs from other Buddhist sects by stressing enlightenment through intuition and contemplation rather than through the scriptures. **2.** the beliefs of this sect. Also, **Zen Buddhism.** [Japanese *zen* silent meditation, through Chinese, going back to Sanskrit *dhāna.*]

ze·na·na (ze nä'nə) *n.* in Iran and India, the part of the house reserved for the women and girls. [Hindi *zenāna,* from Persian *zanāna* belonging to women, from *zan* woman.]

Zend (zend) *n.* in Zoroastrianism, the translation and commentary, in a literary form of Persian, of the Avesta.

Zend-A·ves·ta (zend'ə ves'tə) *n.* the sacred writings of Zoroastrianism collectively, consisting of the Avesta and its later commentary, the Zend.

ze·nith (zē'nith) *n.* **1.** the point on the celestial sphere directly above the position of the observer. ➡ opposed to **nadir.** For illustration, see **nadir. 2.** the highest or greatest point: *This performance was the zenith of the musician's career.* [Medieval Latin *cenith* highest point of the sky, going back to Arabic *samt* way, as in *samt ar-rās* way over the head.]

ze·o·lite (zē'ə līt') *n.* any of a group of hydrous silicate minerals containing aluminum and alkali metals and having a crystalline structure that can trap large metallic ions, used as a filtering agent in water softeners. [Swedish *zeolit,* from Greek *zein* to boil + Swedish *-it* -ite[1]; because it swells when heated.] —**ze·o·lit·ic** (zē'ə lit'ik), *adj.*

Zeph·a·ni·ah (zef'ə nī'ə) *n.* a book of the Old Testament attributed to the Hebrew prophet Zephaniah.

zeph·yr (zef'ər) *n.* **1.** the west wind. **2.** any soft, gentle wind. **3.** any of various lightweight, soft yarns or fabrics. [Latin *zephyrus* west wind, from Greek *zephyros.*]

zep·pe·lin (zep'ə lin) *also,* **Zep·pe·lin.** *n.* a large dirigible having a rigid, cigar-shaped body. [From Count Ferdinand von Zeppelin, 1838-1917, German airship inventor who designed it.]

ze·ro (zîr'ō) *n., pl.* **-ros** or **-roes. 1.** the number that leaves any number unchanged when it is added to it; number of members in the empty set. **2.** the symbol representing this number; 0. **3.** the point on a scale, as of a thermometer, from which positive or negative measures are reckoned. **4.** a temperature corresponding to zero on the scale of a thermometer. **5.** the total absence of quantity; nothing: *The business lost no money, but its profit was zero.* **6.** the lowest point; nadir: *The politician's popularity reached zero after the scandal.* **7.** *Slang.* a person or thing that is considered to have no value, merit, or the like; failure. —*adj.* **1.** of, relating to, being, or at zero. **2.** none at all; not any: *Zero effort gives zero results.* **3.** *Meteorology.* characterized by or designating extremely limited visibility of 165 feet horizontally or 50

a	at	e	end	o	hot	u	up	hw	white		⎧ about
ā	ape	ē	me	ō	old	ū	use	ng	song		taken
ä	far	i	it	ô	fork	ü	rule	th	thin	ə ⎨ pencil
âr	care	ī	ice	oi	oil	u̇	pull	th	this		lemon
			îr	pierce	ou	out	ûr	turn	zh	measure	⎩ circus

feet vertically. —*v.t.* **-roed, -ro·ing.** to adjust (something, such as an instrument) to an arbitrary point from which positive and negative measures are reckoned. [Italian *zero* naught in arithmetic, going back to Arabic *çifr* naught in arithmetic, empty. Doublet of CIPHER.]

• **to zero in on. a.** to bring an aircraft, gun, or the like into a desired position for aiming and concentrating fire at (something): *The bomber zeroed in on the target.* **b.** to direct attention to: *to zero in on the problems at hand.*

zero gravity 1. the condition of a body not subject to any gravitational attraction. **2.** a condition in which there is no apparent gravitational effect, as in a spacecraft orbiting the earth.

zero hour 1. a set or designated time, as for the beginning of a military operation. **2.** a time set for the beginning of any important action; critical turning point or time.

zero population growth, a condition in which the size of a population remains constant because the birth rate equals the death rate.

ze·ro-ze·ro (zîr′ō zîr′ō) *adj.* of, relating to, or characterized by weather conditions under which the ceiling and visibility are both zero. Airplanes approaching an airport under such conditions must make an instrument landing.

zest (zest) *n.* **1.** keen enjoyment or excitement; relish: *a zest for life.* **2.** a pleasant or exciting quality, flavor, or the like: *This spice will add zest to the stew.* —*v.t.* to give a zest to. [Obsolete French *zeste* orange or lemon peel; of uncertain origin.] —**zest′ful,** *adj.* —**zest′ful·ly,** *adv.* —**zest′ful·ness,** *n.* —**zest′y,** *adj.*

ze·ta (zā′tə, zē′-) *n.* the sixth letter of the Greek alphabet (Z, ζ), corresponding to the English letter *Z, z.*

Zeus (zūs) *n.* in Greek mythology, the supreme god, ruler of the heavens and the earth, whose chief weapon was the thunderbolt. His Roman counterpart is Jupiter.

zig (zig) *Informal. n.* **1.** one of the alternating movements or directions in a zigzag. **2.** any sharp turn or movement away from a straight line or course. —*v.i.*, **zigged, zig·ging.** to move or turn in one of the alternating directions in a zigzag. [From ZIGZAG.]

zig·gu·rat (zig′ŭ rat′) *n.* a type of temple built by the ancient Babylonians, Assyrians, and Sumerians, consisting of a pyramid with a series of receding stages or terraces. [Assyrian *ziqquratu* height, pinnacle.]

ziggurat in Iraq

zig·zag (zig′zag′) *adj.* having or proceeding with a series of short, angular turns in alternating directions: *to follow a zigzag path.* —*adv.* in a zigzag manner. —*n.* **1.** a zigzag line, course, or pattern. **2.** one of the short, sharp angles of a zigzag pattern. —*v.t.*, *v.i.*, **-zagged, -zag·ging.** to form or move in a zigzag. [French *zigzag* line having a series of sharp turns in alternating directions, from German *Zickzack*.]

zilch (zilch) *n. Slang.* zero; nothing: *We were disappointed that we got zilch for our efforts.* [Of uncertain origin.]

zil·lion (zil′yən) *n. Informal.* a very large, indefinite number: *I have zillions of things to do before the party.* [*Z* + *-illion,* as in MILLION.]

zinc (zingk) *n.* a grayish white, metallic element with a blue sheen, essential for the growth of many kinds of organisms, used to make alloys, such as brass and bronze, to galvanize iron, and as the anode and casing of dry cell batteries. Symbol **Zn** For tables, see **element.** —*v.t.,* **zincked** or **zinced, zinck·ing** or **zinc·ing.** to coat or cover with zinc. [German *Zink* this element.]

zinc blende, sphalerite.

zinc chloride, a poisonous, white, crystalline compound, used esp. as a preservative and fireproofing agent for wood and as a disinfectant. Formula: $ZnCl_2$

zinc·ic (zing′kik) *adj.* of, derived from, or containing zinc. [ZINC + -IC.]

zinc·ite (zing′kīt) *n.* a red or orange oxide mineral mined as an ore of zinc. Formula: ZnO [ZINC + -ITE[1].]

zinc ointment, an ointment containing zinc oxide in a base of petrolatum, used esp. in treating skin disorders.

zinc oxide, a white, powdery compound, used esp. as a pigment in paints and as an antiseptic in zinc ointment. Formula: ZnO

zinc sulfide, a yellowish white, phosphorescent compound used as a pigment and in the manufacture of television screens and luminous watch dials. Formula: ZnS

zinc white, zinc oxide used as a pigment, or a paint or paste containing this pigment.

zing (zing) *n.* **1.** a high-pitched humming or buzzing sound. **2.** *Informal.* a lively or exciting quality; vitality or zest. —*v.i. Informal.* to make a high-pitched humming or buzzing sound, esp. in moving rapidly: *A bullet zinged through the air.* —*v.t.* **1.** to strike or hit suddenly. **2.** to be critical of; rebuke sharply. [Imitative.]

zing·er (zing′ər) *n. Informal.* **1.** a witty or sharp comment. **2.** something surprising or shocking: *The news was a real zinger.*

zin·ni·a (zin′ē ə) *n.* **1.** the showy flower head of any of a small group of plants, genus *Zinnia,* of the composite family, growing in all colors except blue and green. **2.** the hairy plant bearing this flower head, widely cultivated as a garden plant. [Modern Latin *Zinnia,* from Johann Gottfried *Zinn,* 1727-59, German botanist.]

Zi·on (zī′ən) *also,* **Sion.** *n.* **1.** a hill in Jerusalem on which the royal palace of David and the Temple were built. **2.** the Jewish people or nation; Israel. **3.** the kingdom of heaven. **4.** any place or institution believed to be under God's special protection, esp. the Christian church.

Zi·on·ism (zī′ə niz′əm) *n.* a movement to establish a national homeland for Jews in Palestine, resulting in the creation of Israel in 1948 and continuing after that time to support emigration and settlement of Jews in Israel.

Zi·on·ist (zī′ə nist) *n.* a person who supports Zionism. —*adj.* of or relating to Zionism or Zionists.

zip (zip) *n.* **1.** a sudden, sharp hissing sound, as of a flying bullet. **2.** *Informal.* a lively or exciting quality; vitality or zest. **3.** *Informal.* zip code. —*v.,* **zipped, zip·ping.** —*v.i.* **1.** to make or move with a sudden, sharp hissing sound. **2.** *Informal.* to move or act with energy or speed: *to zip around a corner.* —*v.t.* to fasten or close with a zipper. [Imitative.]

zip code *also,* **ZIP Code, Zip Code.** a number having five or nine digits, written directly after the address on a letter, package, or other piece of mail, quickly identifying the U.S. postal delivery area to which it is to be sent. [Short for *Z(one) I(mprovement) P(rogram)*.]

zip·lock bag (zip′lok′) a plastic bag that can be sealed by means of joining interlocking strips along the open edges, used typically for storing food.

zip-out (zip′out′) *adj.* able to be unfastened and removed by means of a zipper: *a coat with a zip-out lining.*

zip·per (zip′ər) *n.* a fastener consisting of two rows of interlocking teeth that may be joined or separated by a sliding device, used esp. on clothing.

zip·py (zip′ē) *adj.,* **-pi·er, -pi·est.** *Informal.* full of energy; lively; brisk; energetic: *to whistle a zippy little tune.*

zir·con (zûr′kon) *n.* a translucent or transparent silicate of zirconium, used as a gem. Formula: $ZrSiO_4$ [German *Zirkon,* through French and Italian, from Arabic *zarqūn* cinnabar, from Persian *zargūn* gold-colored, from *zar* gold.]

zir·co·ni·a (zər kō′nē ə) *n.* a heavy, white, powdery compound used as a paint pigment and as an electrolyte in fuel cells. Formula: ZrO_2 Also, **zirconium oxide.** [Modern Latin *zirconia,* from German *zirkon* zircon; so named by M. H. Klaproth, 1743-1817, German chemist.]

zir·con·ic (zər kon′ik) *adj.* of, derived from, or containing zirconium. [ZIRCON(IUM) + -IC.]

zir·co·ni·um (zər kō′nē əm) *n.* a gray, flammable, scaly or powdery, metallic element used in primers for explosives, in nuclear reactor chambers, and to bond metals to ceramics. It is the ninth most abundant element in the earth's crust. Symbol: **Zr** For tables, see **element.** [Modern Latin *zirconium,* from ZIRCON; because found in *zircon.*]

zirconium oxide, zirconia.

zit (zit) *n. Slang.* a pimple, esp. on the face. [Of uncertain origin.]

zith·er (zith′ər, zith′-) *n.* a musical instrument consisting of a shallow, wooden sound box over which are stretched thirty to forty-five strings, sounded by plucking the strings with a plectrum and the fingers. [German *Zither,* from Latin *cithara* type of guitar or lute, from Greek *kithara* type of lyre. Doublet of CITHARA, GUITAR.] —**zith′er·ist,** *n.*

zi·ti (zē′tē) *n.* pasta in the form of short, hollow tubes, similar to but larger than macaroni. [Italian *ziti* boys, this pasta.]

zlo·ty (zlô′tē) *n., pl.* **-tys** or **-ty.** the monetary unit of Poland. [Polish *zloty* literally, golden, from *zloto* gold.]

Zn, the symbol for zinc.

zo·di·ac (zō′dē ak′) *n.* **1.** an imaginary belt in the heavens extending approximately 8 degrees on each side of the apparent path of the sun and including the paths of the moon and all the planets except Pluto. The zodiac is divided into twelve parts, called signs, with each part named after a constellation. **2.** a figure or diagram representing the zodiac and its signs and symbols, used in astrology. [Latin *zōdiacus* imaginary belt in the heavens containing twelve constellations, from Greek *zōidiakos (kyklos)* literally, (circle) of the figures, from *zōidion* figure (of an animal), sign of the zodiac, diminutive of *zōion* animal (with reference to the representation of certain of the twelve constellations of the zodiac by animals).] —**zo·di·a·cal** (zō dī′ə kəl), *adj.*

Zoll·ver·ein (tsôl′fe Rīn′) *n.* a customs union among various states of Germany in the nineteenth century. [German *Zollverein* customs union, from *Zoll* duty, customs, toll [2] + *Verein* union.]

zom·bie (zom′bē) *also,* **zom·bi.** *n., pl.* **-bies. 1.** in voodoo belief, a dead person who has been brought back to life and is completely subject to the will of a sorcerer. **2.** *Slang.* a person who behaves in a sluggish or mechanical manner. [Probably from Bantu *zumbi* fetish.]

zon·al (zō′nəl) *adj.* of, relating to, or marked by a zone or zones.

zo·na·tion (zō nā′shən) *n.* the state of having zones or of being arranged in zones.

zone (zōn) *n.* **1.** any of the five climatic regions of the earth, comprising two Frigid Zones, two Temperate Zones, and the Torrid Zone. **2.** any region, area, or section distinguished from surrounding or adjacent areas by some quality, condition, or use: *a flood zone.* **3.** a section of a city or town regulated by certain restrictions, esp. regarding building: *There were no factories in the residential zone.* **4.** in the U.S. postal system, one of a set of circular areas going outward from a mailing point, by which parcel post charges are determined. **5.** a U.S. postal

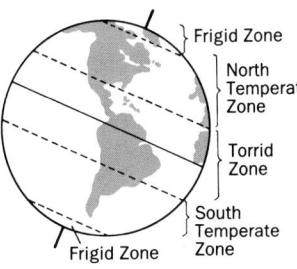

the earth's climatic **zones**

delivery service area identified by a zip code, usually having a central post office. **6.** a belt, band, or stripe having a color or other characteristic distinguishing it from what it encircles. —*v.t.,* **zoned, zon·ing. 1.** to divide into zones: *to zone a city into business and residential areas.* **2.** to surround or encircle with or as with a zone or belt. [Latin *zōna* girdle, belt, one of the imaginary circles that divided the earth into five climates, from Greek *zōnē.*]

zon·ing (zō′ning) *n.* a system of districting in cities or towns that regulates the construction and use of buildings in certain areas.

zoo (zü) *n.* a park, garden, or similar place where animals are kept for exhibition. [Short for ZOOLOGICAL GARDEN.]

zoo- *combining form* **1.** an animal or animals: *zoology.* **2.** relating to animals: *zoogeography.* [Greek *zōion* animal.]

zo·o·ge·og·ra·phy (zō′ə jē og′rə fē) *n.* a branch of biogeography dealing with the geographical distribution of animals. —**zo′·o·ge·og′ra·pher,** *n.* —**zo′o·ge′o·graph′ic;** *also,* **zo′o·ge′o·graph′i·cal,** *adj.*

zo·oid (zō′oid) *n.* any of the more or less independent members of a compound, or colonial, invertebrate, as the coral, hydroid, and bryozoan. [ZOO- + -OID.] —**zo·oi′dal,** *adj.*

zo·o·log·i·cal (zō′ə loj′i kəl) *adj.* **1.** of or relating to zoology. **2.** of or relating to animals. —**zo′o·log′i·cal·ly,** *adv.*

zoological garden, ZOO.

zo·ol·o·gist (zō ol′ə jist) *n.* a student of or expert in zoology.

zo·ol·o·gy (zō ol′ə jē) *n.* **1.** the science that deals with the origin, development, structure, functioning, and classification of all forms of animal life. **2.** animal life, esp. that found in a particular region. [ZOO- + -LOGY.]

zoom (züm) *v.i.* **1.** to move or climb suddenly and swiftly in an airplane. **2.** to make or move with a loud, low-pitched, humming sound: *The train zoomed by us.* **3.** to go up sharply and quickly: *the cost of living zoomed.* —*v.t.* to cause to zoom. —*n.* **1.** the act or sound of zooming. **2.** zoom lens. [Imitative.]

•**to zoom in.** to bring into close focus using a zoom lens.

zoom lens, a single lens, as on a television, still, or motion-picture camera, whose focal length is adjustable, allowing continu-

ous change in the angle of view and magnification, as from a long-distance shot to a close-up, without moving the camera.

zo·o·phyte (zō′ə fīt′) *n.* any of various invertebrates, such as the coral, sea anemone, or sea lily, that somewhat resemble plants. [Greek *zōophyton* literally, animal plant, from *zōion* animal + *phyton* plant.]

zo·o·spore (zō′ə spôr′) *n.* any of various waterborne spores, as that produced by certain algae, having cilia or flagella by means of which it swims about.

zoot suit (züt) a man's suit of extreme style popular in the United States from about 1935 to 1940, having a long jacket with padded shoulders and wide lapels, and full trousers that narrow at the cuffs.

zo·ri (zôr′ē) *n., pl.* **-ris** or **-ri.** a flat sandal held on the foot by a thong passing between the big toe and the one next to it. [Japanese *zōri;* of Chinese origin.]

Zo·ro·as·tri·an (zôr′ō as′trē ən) *adj.* of or relating to the Persian religious teacher Zoroaster or the religion he founded. —*n.* a person who believes in or practices Zoroastrianism.

Zo·ro·as·tri·an·ism (zôr′ō as′trē ə niz′əm) *n.* the religious system founded by Zoroaster, which stresses an ethical way of life and the final triumph of good over evil. Also, **Mazdaism.**

Zou·ave (zü äv′, zwäv) *n.* **1.** formerly, a member of a body of light infantry of the French army, originally composed of Algerians, who wore brilliant Oriental uniforms and were noted for their precision drills. **2.** any member of a military unit wearing a similar uniform. [French *zouave,* from Arabic *Zwāwa* name of a tribe in Algeria from which the first Zouave recruits came.]

zounds (zoundz) *interj. Archaic.* an oath used to express surprise or anger. [Euphemistic contraction of *God's wounds.*]

zoy·sia (zoi′shə, -sē ə) *n.* any of several creeping, perennial grasses, genus *Zoysia,* that are grown as lawn grasses in warm areas. [Modern Latin *zoysia,* alteration of *Zoisia,* from Karl von *Zois,* 1756-1800, German botanist.]

Zr, the symbol for zirconium.

zuc·chi·ni (zü kē′nē) *n., pl.* **-ni** or **-nis. 1.** a green summer squash shaped like a cucumber. **2.** the plant bearing this squash.

Zu·lu (zü′lü) *n., pl.* **-lu** or **-lus. 1.** a member of a group of Bantu people in the Republic of South Africa. **2.** their Bantu language. —*adj.* of or relating to the Zulu or to their language or culture.

Zu·ñi (zü′nē, zün′yē) *n., pl.* **-ñi** or **-ñis. 1.** a member of a tribe of North American Indians now living in western New Mexico, who dwell in pueblos. **2.** the language of this tribe.

zwie·back (swē′bak′, -bäk′, swī′-, zwī′-; *German* tsvē′bäk′) *n.* a kind of bread that is often sweetened and flavored, as with cinnamon, baked, and then sliced and toasted until it is crisp and dry. [German *Zwieback* rusk; literally, twice baked, from *zwie-* twice + *backen* to bake.]

Zwing·li·an (zwing′lē ən, swing′-, tsving′-) *adj.* of or relating to the Swiss Protestant reformer Huldreich Zwingli or his doctrines. —*n.* a person who believes in or follows the teachings of Zwingli.

zy·go·mat·ic (zī′gə mat′ik) *adj.* of, relating to, constituting, or situated in the area of the protruding bony structure, the **zygomatic bone,** located just below the orbit of the skull and extending to the ear region of most mammals.

zy·go·mor·phic (zī′gə môr′fik) *adj.* (of a flower) having bilateral symmetry; divisible into similar or symmetrical halves, as the flower of the foxglove.

zy·go·spore (zī′gə spôr′, zig′ə-) *n.* a spore formed by the sexual union of two gametes, found among certain fungi and algae. [Greek *zygon* yoke + SPORE.]

zy·gote (zī′gōt, zig′ōt) *n.* an ovum fertilized by sperm, before the start of embryonic development. [Greek *zygōtos* yoked, from *zygoun* to yoke.] —**zy·got·ic** (zī got′ik), *adj.*

zy·mase (zī′mās) *n.* an enzyme complex present in yeast cells, that changes sugar into alcohol and carbon dioxide. [Greek *zȳmē* leaven + -ASE.]

zy·mo·gen (zī′mə jən) *n.* an inactive precursor of an enzyme that requires catalysis by an appropriate chemical agent to become active. —**zy·mo·gen·ic** (zī′mə jen′ik), *adj.*

zy·mur·gy (zī′mûr jē) *n.* the branch of chemistry dealing with fermentation, as in brewing and wine making. [Greek *zȳmē* leaven + *-ourgiā* a working (from *ergon* work).]

Z

a	at	e	end	o	hot	u	up	hw	white		about
ā	ape	ē	me	ō	old	ū	use	ng	song		taken
ä	far	i	it	ô	fork	ü	rule	th	thin	ə	pencil
âr	care	ī	ice	oi	oil	u̇	pull	th	this		lemon
		îr	pierce	ou	out	ûr	turn	zh	measure		circus

Biographical Names

This section lists the names of people and dynasties that are important in history, contemporary life, or the biblical tradition. The main biographical entry gives the most widely used form and spelling of a person's name. People with the same family name are listed within a single entry. Names or parts of names that are not usually used appear in parentheses. Nicknames, pseudonyms, and titles are shown in italics within the main entry. Variant spellings of names are shown in boldface in the main entry and often are listed separately as cross-references to the main entry.

In a main entry, the name of the person is followed by the pronunciation of the family name, the birth and death dates, the nationality, and a brief description. Dates in parentheses are the years during which a person reigned or held office.

Aar·on (âr'ən) in the Old Testament, elder brother of Moses and the first high priest of the Hebrews.

Aaron, Hank 1934- , U.S. baseball player; nickname of *Henry Louis Aaron.*

Ab·bas (ä'bäs, ä bäs') A.D. 566-652, uncle of Muhammad.

Ab·bas·id (ə bas'id, ab'ə sid') *also,* **Ab·bas·sid.** dynasty of caliphs that ruled the Muslim world (A.D. 750-1258).

Ab·bott, Sir John Joseph Caldwell (ab'ət) 1821-1893, Canadian prime minister (1891-1892).

Ab·di·as (ab dī'əs) in the Douay Bible, Obadiah.

Ab·dul-Jab·bar, Kareem (äb dül'jə bär', ab-) 1947- , U.S. basketball player; born *Ferdinand Lewis Alcindor, Jr.*

A·bel (ā'bəl) in the Old Testament, the second son of Adam and Eve; killed by his older brother, Cain.

Ab·é·lard, Peter (ab'ə lärd') 1079-1142, French philosopher, theologian, and teacher.

A·bra·ham (ā'brə ham', -həm) patriarch and progenitor of the Hebrews.

Ab·sa·lom (ab'sə ləm) in the Old Testament, the favorite son of David who was killed after waging a war of rebellion against his father.

A·bu-Bakr (ə bü'bek'ər) *also,* **A·bu-Bekr.** A.D. 573-634, first caliph of Mecca, successor to Muhammad.

A·dam (ad'əm) in the Old Testament, the first man and the husband of Eve.

Ad·ams (ad'əmz) **1. Ansel.** 1902-1984, U.S. photographer. **2. John.** 1735-1826, second president of the United States (1797-1801). **3. John Quincy.** 1767-1848, sixth president of the United States (1825-1829); son of John Adams. **4. Samuel.** 1722-1803, patriot during the American Revolution.

Ad·dams, Jane (ad'əmz) 1860-1935, U.S. social reformer.

Ad·di·son, Joseph (ad'ə sən) 1672-1719, English essayist.

A·de·nau·er, Konrad (ad'ə nou'er) 1876-1967, German statesman.

Ad·ler, Alfred (ad'lər) 1870-1937, Austrian psychiatrist.

Æ, see Russell, George William.

Aes·chin·es (es'kə nēz') 389-314 B.C., Athenian orator.

Aes·chy·lus (es'kə ləs) 525-456 B.C., Greek tragic dramatist.

Ae·sop (ē'səp, ē'sop) 620?-560 B.C., Greek writer of fables.

Æth·el·red II (ath'əl red') A.D. 968?-1016, English king (A.D. 978-1016); nicknamed *the Unready.* Also, **Aethelred, Ethelred.**

Ag·as·siz, Louis (ag'ə sē) 1807-1873, Swiss-American zoologist and geologist.

A·grip·pa, Marcus Vipsanius (ə grip'ə) 63-12 B.C., Roman general and statesman.

A·gui·nal·do, Emilio (ä'gē näl'dō) 1870?-1964, Philippine revolutionary leader.

A·hab (ā'hab) d. 853? B.C., king of Israel (874?-853? B.C.).

Ai·ley, Alvin (ā'lē) 1931-1989, U.S. choreographer.

Ak·bar (ak'bär) 1542-1605, Mogul emperor of India (1556-1605).

Akh·e·na·ton (ä'kə nä'tən) see Ikhnaton.

Akh·ma·to·va, Anna (äk'mə tō'və, uk mä'tə-) 1889-1966, Russian poet; pseudonym of *Anna Andreyevna Gorenko.*

A·ki·hi·to (ä'kē hē'tō) 1933- , Japanese emperor (1989-).

A·lam·gir, Muhi-ud-Din Muhammad (ä'ləm gìr') see Aurangzeb.

Al·a·ric (al'ə rik) A.D. 370?-410, king of the Visigoths.

Al·bee, Edward (ôl'bē) 1928- , U.S. playwright.

Al·bert, Prince (al'bərt) 1819-1861, consort of Queen Victoria of Great Britain.

Al·ber·tus Mag·nus, Saint (al bûr'təs mag'nəs) 1193?-1280, German monk and philosopher.

Al·ci·bi·a·des (al'sə bī'ə dēz') 450?-404 B.C., Athenian politician and general.

Al·cott, Louisa May (ôl'kət, -kot) 1832-1888, U.S. writer.

Al·den, John (ôl'dən) 1599?-1687, Puritan settler in Plymouth Colony.

Al·drin, Edwin Eugene, Jr. (ôl'drin) 1930- , U.S. astronaut.

Aleichem, Shalom, see Shalom Aleichem.

A·lem·bert, Jean le Rond d' (dal'əm bâr', da län bɛr') 1717-1783, French mathematician and philosopher.

Al·ex·an·der, Grover Cleveland (al'ig zan'dər) 1887-1950, U.S. baseball player.

Alexander I, 1777-1825, Russian czar (1801-1825).

Alexander II, 1818-1888, Russian czar (1855-1881).

Alexander III, 1845-1894, Russian czar (1881-1894).

Alexander VI, 1431-1503, pope (1492-1503).

Alexander Nev·sky (nev'skē, nef'-) 1220-1263, Russian hero.

Alexander the Great, 356-323 B.C., king of Macedonia (336-323 B.C.), general of Greece, and conqueror of Persia.

Al·fred the Great' (al'frid) A.D. 849-889, king of the West Saxons (A.D. 871-889).

A·li (ä'lē) A.D. 600?-661, caliph (A.D. 656-661).

A·li, Muhammad (ä lē') 1942- , U.S. boxer; born *Cassius Marcellus Clay, Jr.*

Al·len, Ethan (al'ən) 1738-1789, colonial soldier during the American Revolution.

Al·len·de Gos·sens, Salvador (ä yen'dā gō'sens) 1908-1973, Chilean president (1970-1973).

A·ma·do, Jorge (ə mä'dō) 1912- , Brazilian writer.

A·ma·ti, Nicolò (ä mä'tē) 1596-1684, Italian violin maker.

A·men·ho·tep III (ä'mən hō'tep) king of Egypt (1417-1379 B.C.). Also, **Am·e·no·phis** (am'ənō'fis) **III.**

Amenhotep IV, see Ikhnaton.

A·mos (ā'məs) eighth century B.C., Hebrew prophet.

Am·père, André-Marie (am'pîr, am pîr') 1775-1836, French mathematician, chemist, and physicist.

A·mund·sen, Roald (ä'mən sən) 1872-1928, Norwegian explorer.

A·nac·re·on (ə nak'rē ən) 572?-488? B.C., Greek lyric poet.

An·a·ni·as (an'ə nī'əs) in the New Testament, a man who fell dead after withholding money from the Apostles.

An·ax·ag·o·ras (an'ak sag'ər əs) 500?-428 B.C., Greek philosopher.

A·nax·i·man·der (ə nak'sə man'dər) 611?-547? B.C., Greek philosopher and astronomer.

An·der·sen, Hans Christian (an'dər sən) 1805-1875, Danish writer of fairy tales.

An·der·son (an'dər sən) **1. Judith.** 1898-1992, Australian actress; born *Frances Margaret Anderson.* **2. Marian.** 1902- , U.S. contralto. **3. Maxwell.** 1888-1959, U.S. playwright. **4. Sherwood.** 1876-1941, U.S. novelist and short-story writer.

An·dré, John (an'drē, än'-) 1750-1780, British officer and secret agent during the American Revolution.

An·dre·a del Sar·to (än drä'ə del sär'tō) 1486-1531, Florentine painter; born *Andrea Vanucci.*

An·drew (an'drü) in the New Testament, one of the twelve Apostles of Jesus and brother of Peter.

An·dro·pov, Yuri Vladimirovich (an drō'pəf) 1914-1984, Soviet politician, president of U.S.S.R. (1982-1984), and first secretary of the Communist Party (1982-1984).

An·gel·i·co, Fra (an jel'i kō') 1387-1455, Italian painter and Dominican monk; born *Guido di Pietro.*

An·ge·vin (an'jə vin) see Plantagenet.

Anne (an) 1665-1714, queen of Great Britain (1702-1714).

An·selm, Saint (an′selm) 1033-1109, Italian theologian and archbishop of Canterbury (1093-1109).

An·tho·ny, Susan B(rownell) (an′thə nē) 1820-1906, U.S. social reformer and leader in the movement for women's suffrage.

Anthony of Egypt, Saint, A.D. 251?-356?, Egyptian hermit, founder of Christian monasticism.

Anthony of Padua, Saint, 1195-1231, Franciscan monk.

An·to·ni·nus Pi·us (an′tə nī′nəs pī′əs) A.D. 86-161, Roman emperor (A.D. 138-161).

Antony, Marc or **Mark,** see Marc Antony.

Ap·ple·seed, Johnny (ap′əl sēd′) 1774?-1845, U.S. frontiersman noted for sowing apple seeds; born *John Chapman.*

Ap·u·le·ius, Lucius (ap′yə lē′əs) second century A.D., Roman writer.

A·qui·nas, Saint Thomas (ə kwī′nəs) 1225?-1274, Italian philosopher and theologian.

A·qui·no, Corazon Cojuangco (ä kē′nō) 1933- , Philippine president (1986-).

Ar·a·fat, Yasir (ar′ə fat′) 1929- , Palestinian leader.

A·ran·go, Doroteo (ä rän′gō) see Villa, Francisco.

Arc, Jeanne d', see Joan of Arc.

Ar·chi·me·des (är′kə mē′dēz) 287?-212 B.C., Greek mathematician, physicist, and inventor.

A·ri·os·to, Ludovico (är′ē os′tō, ar′ē ōs′-) 1474-1533, Italian poet.

Ar·is·ti·des (ar′ə stī′dēz) 520?-468? B.C., Athenian general and statesman; called *the Just.*

Ar·is·toph·a·nes (ar′ə stof′ə nēz′) 448?-385 B.C., Greek comic dramatist.

Ar·is·tot·le (ar′ə stot′əl) 384-322 B.C., Greek philosopher.

A·ri·us (ə rī′əs, âr′ē-) A.D. 250?-336, Christian priest at Alexandria.

Ark·wright, Sir Richard (ärk′rīt′) 1732-1792, English inventor and industrialist.

Ar·min·i·us, Jacobus (är min′ē əs) 1560-1609, Dutch Protestant theologian.

Arm·strong (ärm′strông′) 1. **Louis.** 1900-1971, U.S. jazz musician; nickname *Satchmo.* 2. **Neil Alden.** 1930- , U.S. astronaut, the first person to set foot on the moon.

Ar·nold (är′nəld) 1. **Benedict.** 1741-1801, colonial general in the American Revolution who turned traitor. 2. **Matthew.** 1822-1888, English poet and essayist.

Ar·rhe·ni·us, Svante August (ə rē′nē əs) 1859-1927, Swedish chemist and physicist.

Ar·thur (är′thər) sixth century A.D., English king.

Arthur, Chester Alan 1830-1886, twenty-first president of the United States (1881-1885).

As·bur·y, Francis (az′bə rē) 1745-1816, first Methodist bishop in America.

Ash·ber·y, John (ash′ber′ē) 1927- , U.S. poet.

Ash·er (ash′ər) 1. in the Old Testament, a son of Jacob. 2. one of the twelve tribes of Israel descended from him.

A·sho·ka (ə shō′kə) see Asoka.

As·i·mov, Isaac (az′ə môf′) 1920-1992, U.S. author and biochemist; born in Russia.

A·so·ka (ə sō′kə) *also,* **Ashoka.** d. 233? B.C. emperor of India (268?-233? B.C.).

As·quith, Herbert Henry (as′kwith) 1852-1928, British prime minister (1908-1916).

As·sad, Hafez al- (al′ä säd′) 1928- , Syrian president (1965-).

As·sur·ba·ni·pal (ä′sùr bä′nē päl′) d. 626? B.C., king of Assyria (669-633 B.C.).

A·staire, Fred (ə stâr′) 1899-1987, U.S. dancer, singer, and actor.

As·tor, John Jacob (as′tər) 1763-1848, U.S. fur trader and capitalist.

A·ta·huall·pa (ä′tə wäl′pə) *also,* **A·ta·hual·pa.** king of the Incas (1502?-1533).

A·ta·türk, Kemal (at′ə tûrk′) 1881-1938, Turkish president (1923-1938).

Ath·a·na·sius, Saint (ath′ə nā′shəs) A.D. 296?-373, bishop of Alexandria (A.D. 328-373) and a Father of the Church.

Ath·el·stan (ath′əl stan′) A.D. 895?-940, king of the English (A.D. 925-940).

At·ti·la (at′ə lə, ə til′ə) A.D. 406?-453, king of the Huns (A.D. 433?-453).

Att·lee, Clement Richard (at′lē) 1883-1967, British statesman, prime minister (1945-1951).

At·wood, Margaret (at′wúd) 1939- , Canadian writer.

Au·den, W(ystan) H(ugh) (ô′dən) 1907-1973, Anglo-American poet.

Au·du·bon, John James (ô′də bon′) 1785-1851, U.S. ornithologist and artist.

Au·gus·tine, Saint (ô′gə stēn′, ô gus′tin) A.D. 354-430, bishop of Hippo (A.D. 396-430) and a Father of the Church.

Augustine of Canterbury, Saint, d. A.D. 604, first archbishop of Canterbury (A.D. 601-604).

Au·gus·tus (ô gus′təs) 63 B.C.-A.D. 14, first Roman emperor (27 B.C.-A.D. 14); full name *Gaius Julius Caesar Octavianus.* Also, Octavian.

Au·rang·zeb (ôr′əng zeb′) *also,* **Au·rung·zebe.** 1618-1707, Mogul emperor of India (1658-1707). Also, **Muhi-ud-Din Muhammad Alamgir.**

Aurelius, see Marcus Aurelius Antoninus.

Aus·ten, Jane (ôs′tən) 1775-1817, English novelist.

Aus·tin, Stephen Fuller (ôs′tən) 1793-1836, U.S. colonizer of Texas.

A·ver·ro·ës (ə ver′ō ēz′) 1126-1198, Spanish-Arabian philosopher and physician.

A·vi·cen·na (av′ə sen′ə) 980-1037, Arabian philosopher and physician. Also, **Ibn Sinā.**

A·vo·gad·ro, Amadeo (ä′və gä′drō) 1776-1856, Italian physicist and chemist.

Ayl·win, Patricio (āl′win) 1918- , Chilean president (1990-).

Baal Shem Tov (bäl′shem′tōv′) 1700?-1760, Polish founder of Hasidism; born *Israel ben Eliezer.*

Ba·bur (bä′bər) 1483-1530, poet, emperor of India (1526-1530), and founder of the Mogul Empire.

Bach (bäκH) German family of musicians including 1. **Carl Phillip Emanuel.** 1714-1789, composer; second son of Johann Sebastian Bach. 2. **Johann Christian.** 1735-1782, composer; youngest son of Johann Sebastian Bach. 3. **Johann Sebastian.** 1685-1750, composer and organist.

Ba·con (bā′kən) 1. **Francis.** 1561-1626, English essayist, statesman, and philosopher. 2. **Roger.** 1214?-1294, English philosopher and scientist.

Ba·den-Pow·ell, Lord (bā′dən pō′əl) 1857-1941, English army officer, founder of the Boy Scouts; born *Robert Stephenson Smyth Baden-Powell.*

Bae·de·ker, Karl (bā′di kər) 1801-1859, German publisher of travel guidebooks.

Baf·fin, William (baf′in) 1584?-1622, English explorer.

Ba·ha'u'l·lah (bä hä′ú lä′) 1817-1892, Persian founder of Baha'ism.

Ba·ku·nin, Mikhail (bə kü′nin) 1814-1876, Russian anarchist and revolutionary.

Ba·laam (bā′ləm) in the Old Testament, a prophet.

Bal·an·chine, George (bal′ən chēn′, bal′ən chēn′) 1904-1983, Russian-American choreographer; born *Georgy Melitonovich Balanchivadze.*

Bal·bo·a, Vasco Núñez de (bal bō′ə) 1475?-1517, Spanish explorer.

Bald·win (bôld′win) 1. **James (Arthur).** 1924-1987, U.S. writer. 2. **Robert.** 1804-1858, Canadian statesman. 3. **Stanley.** 1867-1947, British prime minister (1923-1924; 1924-1929; 1935-1937).

Bal·four, Arthur James (bal′fúr) 1848-1930, British prime minister (1902-1905).

Ball, Lucille (bôl) 1911-1989, U.S. film actress and producer.

Bal·ti·more, Lord (bôl′tə môr′) see Calvert, Sir George.

Bal·zac, Honoré de (bôl′zak, bal′-) 1799-1850, French novelist.

Ban·ne·ker, Benjamin (ban′i kər) 1731-1806, American scientist and writer; one of the surveyors of Washington, D.C.

Ban·nis·ter, Sir Roger (Gilbert) (ban′ə stər) 1929- , British athlete; first man to run the mile in under four minutes.

Ba·rab·bas (bə rab′əs) in the New Testament, the condemned thief who was released when Pontius Pilate asked the crowd whether Barabbas or Jesus should be spared from crucifixion.

Bar·ba·ros·sa (bär′bə ros′ə) see Frederick I *(def. 1).*

Bar·ca (bär′kə) powerful family of ancient Carthage.

Bar·na·bas (bär′nə bəs) in the New Testament, a companion of Paul and one of the first Christian missionaries.

Bar·nard, Christiaan Neethling (bär′närd) 1922- , South African surgeon.

Bar·num, P(hineas) T(aylor) (bär′nəm) 1810-1891, U.S. showman.

a	at	e	end	o	hot	u	up	hw	white		about
ā	ape	ē	me	ō	old	ū	use	ng	song		taken
ä	far	i	it	ô	fork	ü	rule	th	thin	ə	pencil
âr	care	ī	ice	oi	oil	ù	pull	th	this		lemon
				îr	pierce	ou	out	ûr	turn	zh	measure		circus

Bar·rie, Sir James (bar′ē) 1860-1937, Scottish playwright and novelist.

Bar·ry·more (bar′i môr′) U.S. family of actors including **1.** Ethel. 1879-1959, sister of John and Lionel Barrymore. **2.** John. 1882-1942, brother of Ethel and Lionel Barrymore. **3.** Lionel. 1878-1954, brother of Ethel and John Barrymore.

Bar·thol·di, Frédéric Auguste (bär thol′dē) 1834-1904, French sculptor.

Bar·thol·o·mew (bär thol′ə mū′) in the New Testament, one of the twelve Apostles of Jesus.

Bar·tók, Béla (bär′tok, buR′tôk) 1881-1945, Hungarian composer and pianist.

Bar·ton, Clara (bär′tən) 1821-1912, U.S. humanitarian, founder of the American Red Cross.

Bar·uch (bâr′ək) seventh century B.C., secretary and disciple of Jeremiah and reputed writer of the Book of Baruch.

Basho, Matsuo, see Matsuo Basho.

Ba·sie, Count (bā′sē) 1904-1984, U.S. jazz pianist and conductor; real name *William Basie*.

Ba·sil·i·us (bə sil′ē əs) see Basil the Great, Saint.

Bas·il the Great, Saint (baz′il) A.D. 330?-379?, theologian, bishop of Caesarea (A.D. 370-379). Also, Basilius.

Bath·she·ba (bath shē′bə, bath′shə-) in the Old Testament, the wife of Uriah and then of David; mother of Solomon.

Bau·de·laire, Charles (bō′də lâr′) 1821-1867, French poet and critic.

Bea·cons·field, Earl of (bē′kənz fēld′) see Disraeli, Benjamin.

Beard (bîrd) **1.** Charles Austin. 1874-1948, U.S. historian. **2.** Daniel Carter. 1850-1941, U.S. artist; organized the Boy Scouts in the United States (1910). **3.** Mary. 1876-1958, U.S. historian; wife of Charles Austin Beard.

Bear·den, Romare (bîr′dən) 1914-1988, U.S. painter.

Beards·ley, Aubrey Vincent (bîrdz′lē) 1872-1898, English illustrator.

Beau·har·nais, Josephine de (bō′är nā′) see Josephine.

Beau·mar·chais, Pierre Augustin Caron de (bō′mär shā′) 1732-1799, French dramatist.

Beau·mont (bō′mont) **1.** Francis. 1584-1616, English dramatist. **2.** William. 1785-1853, U.S. physiologist.

Beau·re·gard, Pierre Gustave Toutant (bō′ri gärd′) 1818-1893, Confederate general in the American Civil War.

Beau·voir, Simone de (bō vwär′) 1908-1986, French writer.

Beck·et, Saint Thomas à (bek′it) 1118?-1170, archbishop of Canterbury (1162-1170).

Beck·ett, Samuel (bek′it) 1906-1989, Irish writer.

Bec·que·rel, Antoine-Henri (bek′ə rel′) 1852-1908, French physicist.

Bede, Saint (bēd) A.D. 673?-735?, English historian and theologian. Also, the Venerable Bede.

Bee·cher, Henry Ward (bē′chər) 1813-1887, U.S. clergyman, lecturer, and writer.

Bee·tho·ven, Ludwig van (bā′tō vən) 1770-1827, German composer.

Be·gin, Menachem (bā′gin) 1913-1992, Israeli prime minister (1977-1983).

Bell, Alexander Graham (bel) 1847-1922, U.S. inventor of the telephone; born in Scotland.

Bel·li·ni (bə lē′nē) **1.** Gentile. 1429?-1507, Venetian painter; son of Jacopo Bellini. **2.** Giovanni. 1430?-1516, Venetian painter; son of Jacopo Bellini. **3.** Jacopo. 1400?-1470?, Venetian painter. **4.** Vincenzo. 1801-1835, Italian composer.

Bel·low, Saul (bel′ō) 1915- , U.S. writer.

Bel·shaz·zar (bel shaz′ər) in the Old Testament, the last Chaldean king of Babylon, a city whose destruction was prophesied by handwriting on the wall.

Ben·e·dict XIV (ben′i dikt) 1675-1758, pope (1740-1758); born *Prospero Lorenzo Lambertini*.

Benedict XV, 1854-1922, pope (1914-1922); born *Giacomo della Chiesa.*

Benedict of Nur·sia, Saint (nûr′shə) A.D. 480?-550?, Italian monk, founder of the Benedictine order.

Be·nét, Stephen Vincent (bə nā′) 1898-1943, U.S. writer.

Ben-Gu·ri·on, David (ben gūr′ē ən) 1886-1973, Israeli prime minister (1949-1953; 1955-1963); born *David Grün.*

Ben·ja·min (ben′jə min) **1.** in the Old Testament, the youngest son of Jacob and Rachel. **2.** one of the twelve tribes of Israel descended from him.

Ben·nett (ben′it) **1.** Arnold. 1867-1931, English novelist and playwright. **2.** Richard Bedford. 1870-1947, Canadian prime minister (1930-1935).

Ben·tham, Jeremy (ben′thəm, -təm) 1748-1832, English philosopher, lawyer, and reformer.

Ben·ton, Thomas Hart (ben′tən) 1889-1975, U.S. artist.

Benz, Karl (benz) 1844-1929, German engineer.

Berg, Alban (beRg) 1885-1935, Austrian composer.

Berg·man, Ingmar (bûrg′mən) 1915- , Swedish film and stage director.

Berg·son, Henri (bûrg′sən) 1859-1941, French philosopher.

Berke·ley, George (bûrk′lē) 1685-1753, Irish philosopher and clergyman.

Ber·lin, Irving (bər lin′) 1888-1989, U.S. songwriter; born in Russia as *Israel Baline.*

Ber·li·oz, Louis Hector (ber′lē ōz′) 1803-1869, French composer.

Ber·nard, Claude (ber när′) 1813-1878, French physiologist.

Bernard of Clair·vaux, Saint (kleR vō′) 1090-1153, French monk and theologian.

Bernard of Men·thon, Saint (män tôn′) A.D. 996?-1081?, founder of the alpine hospices of Saint Bernard.

Bern·hardt, Sarah (bûrn′härt′) 1844-1923, French actress.

Ber·ni·ni, Giovanni Lorenzo (bər nē′nē) 1598-1680, Italian sculptor and architect. Also, Gianlorenzo Bernini.

Ber·noul·li, Daniel (bər nü′lē) 1700-1782, Swiss medical scientist, mathematician, and physicist.

Bern·stein, Leonard (bûrn′stīn) 1918-1990, U.S. conductor and composer.

Ber·ry·man, John (ber′ē mən) 1914-1972, U.S. poet.

Ber·the·lot, Pierre Eugene Marcellin (ber tə lō′) 1827-1907, French chemist.

Ber·thol·let, Claude Louis (ber tô lā′) 1748-1822, French chemist.

Ber·ze·li·us, Jöns Jacob (bər zē′lē əs) 1779-1848, Swedish chemist.

Bes·sel, Friedrich Wilhelm (bes′əl) 1784-1846, German astronomer and mathematician.

Bes·se·mer, Sir Henry (bes′ə mər) 1813-1898, English inventor and industrialist.

Bet·tel·heim, Bruno (bet′əl hīm′) 1903-1990, U.S. psychologist and writer.

Bhar·tri·ha·ri (bur′tri hur′ē) d. A.D. 651, Sanskrit poet and grammarian.

Bil·ly the Kid (bil′ē) 1859-1881, U.S. outlaw; real name *William H. Bonney.*

Bish·op, Elizabeth (bish′əp) 1911-1979, U.S. writer.

Bis·marck, Otto von (biz′märk′) 1815-1898, German statesman.

Bi·zet, Georges (bē zā′) 1838-1875, French composer.

Black·beard (blak′bîrd′) d. 1718, English pirate; real name probably *Edward Teach* or *Thatch.*

Black·mun, Harry A. (blak′mən) 1908- , U.S. Supreme Court associate justice (1970-).

Black Prince, see Edward the Black Prince.

Black·stone, William (blak′stōn′) 1723-1780, English jurist, legal scholar, and writer.

Blake, William (blāk) 1757-1827, English poet, artist, and philosopher.

Bloody Mary, see Mary I.

Bo·ad·i·ce·a (bō ad′ə sē′ə) *also,* Boudicca. d. A.D. 62, queen of the Iceni, a tribe in eastern Britain.

Bo·as, Franz (bō′az) 1858-1942, U.S. anthropologist.

Bo·az (bō′az) in the Old Testament, the husband of Ruth.

Boc·cac·ci·o, Giovanni (bō kä′chē ō′) 1313-1375, Italian writer and humanist.

Bo·ece (bō ēs′) see Boethius, Anicius Manlius Severinus.

Bo·e·thi·us, Anicius Manlius Severinus (bō ē′thē əs) *also,* Bo·e·tius (bō ē′shəs). A.D. 480?-524, Roman philosopher and statesman. Also, Boece.

Bohr, Niels (bôr) 1885-1962, Danish physicist.

Bol·eyn, Anne (bul′in, bů lin′) 1507?-1536, queen of England; second wife of Henry VIII; mother of Elizabeth I.

Bo·li·var, Simón (bol′ə vər, bō lē′vär) 1783-1830, Venezuelan statesman, soldier, and revolutionary leader in South America.

Böll, Heinrich (bœl) 1917-1985, German writer.

Bo·na·parte (bō′nə pärt′) Corsican family including the four brothers of Napoleon **1.** Jérôme. 1784-1860, king of Westphalia (1807-1813). **2.** Joseph. 1768-1844, king of Naples (1806-1808), king of Spain (1808-1813). **3.** Louis. 1778-1846, king of Holland (1806-1810); father of Napoleon III. **4.** Lucien. 1775-1840, politician. **5.** Napoleon. see Napoleon I.

Bon·i·face, Saint (bon′ə fis, -fās′) A.D. 680?-754, English missionary in Germany.

Boole, George (bül) 1815-1864, English mathematician.

Boone, Daniel (bōn) 1734-1820, American frontiersman.

Booth (büth) **1.** Edwin Thomas. 1833-1893, U.S. actor and theatrical producer. **2.** John Wilkes. 1838-1865, U.S. actor, assassin of Abraham Lincoln; brother of Edwin Thomas Booth.

3. William. 1829-1912, English evangelist, founder of the Salvation Army.

Bor·den, Sir Robert Laird (bôr′dən) 1854-1937, Canadian prime minister (1911-1920).

Bor·ges, Jorge Luis (bôr′hes) 1899-1986, Argentine writer.

Bor·gia (bôr′jə) **1. Cesare.** 1475?-1507, Italian soldier, politician, and cardinal; son of Pope Alexander VI. **2. Lucrezia.** 1480-1519, Italian noblewoman; daughter of Pope Alexander VI.

Bo·ro·din, Alexander Porfirevich (bôr′ə dēn′) 1833-1887, Russian composer.

Bosch, Hieronymus (bosh) 1450?-1516, Flemish painter.

Bos·well, James (boz′wel′) 1740-1795, Scottish writer and lawyer; biographer of Samuel Johnson.

Bo·tha, P(ieter) W(illem) (bō′tə) 1916-1989, South African prime minister (1978-1989).

Bot·ti·cel·li, Sandro (bot′i chel′ē) 1444?-1510, Florentine painter.

Bou·dic·ca (bü dik′ə) see **Boadicea.**

Bou·lan·ger, Nadia (bü län zhä′) 1887-1979, French conductor, musician, and teacher.

Bour·bon (bûr′bən, bôr′-) **1.** royal family that ruled France (1589-1792; 1814-1848). **2.** any of the branches of this family that ruled in Spain, Naples, Parma, and Sicily.

Bourke-White, Margaret (bûrk′hwīt′, -wīt′) 1904-1971, U.S. photojournalist.

Bou·tros-Gha·li, Boutros (bü′trôs gä′lē) also, **Boutros Ghali, Boutros.** 1922- , Egyptian diplomat, secretary-general of the United Nations (1992-).

Bow·ell, Sir Mackenzie (bō′əl) 1823-1917, Canadian prime minister (1894-1896).

Boyle, Robert (boil) 1627-1691, British physicist and chemist.

Brack, Joseph (brak) 1728-1799, Scottish chemist.

Brad·dock, Edward (brad′ək) 1695-1755, British general in the French and Indian War.

Brad·ford, William (brad′fərd) 1590?-1657, Pilgrim leader and a governor of Plymouth Colony.

Brad·street, Anne Dudley (brad′strēt′) 1612?-1672, American poet.

Bra·dy, Mathew B. (brā′dē) 1823?-1896, U.S. photographer.

Bragg (brag) **1. Sir William Henry.** 1862-1942, English physicist. **2. Sir William Lawrence.** 1890-1971, English physicist; son of Sir William Henry Bragg.

Brahe, Tycho (brä, brä′hē) 1546-1601, Danish astronomer.

Brahms, Johannes (brämz) 1833-1897, German composer.

Braille, Louis (brāl) 1809-1852, French teacher, inventor of braille.

Bran·deis, Louis Dembitz (bran′dīs) 1856-1941, U.S. Supreme Court associate justice (1916-1939).

Brandt, Willy (brant) 1913- , German politician, chancellor of West Germany (1969-1974).

Brant, Joseph (brant) 1742-1807, Mohawk chief. Also, **Thayendanegea** meaning *he places bets.*

Braque, Georges (bräk) 1882-1963, French painter.

Brau·del, Fernand (brō del′) 1902-1985, French historian.

Brecht, Bertolt (brekt) 1898-1956, German dramatist and poet.

Breck·in·ridge, John Cabell (brek′ən rij′) 1821-1875, U.S. politician, Confederate officer in the American Civil War.

Brezh·nev, Leonid Ilyich (brezh′nef) 1906-1982, Soviet politician, general secretary of the Soviet Communist Party (1964-1982), president of U.S.S.R. (1979-1982).

Bridg·er, James (brij′ər) 1804-1881, U.S. fur trader and scout.

Brig·id, Saint (brij′id) A.D. 450?-524, Irish abbess, patron saint of Ireland. Also, **Saint Bridg·et** (brij′it).

Brit·ten, (Edward) Benjamin (brit′ən) 1913-1976, English composer.

Brod·sky, Joseph (brod′skē) 1940- , Soviet poet who has been a U.S. resident since 1972.

Bro·glie, Louis Victor de (brô glē′, broi-) 1892-1987, French physicist.

Bron·të (bron′tē, -tā) English family of novelists including the sisters **1. Anne.** 1820-1849. **2. Charlotte.** 1816-1855. **3. Emily.** 1818-1848.

Brooks, Gwendolyn (brüks) 1917- , U.S. poet.

Brown (broun) **1. Jim** 1936- , U.S. football player and actor; full name *James Nathaniel Brown.* **2. John** 1800-1859, U.S. abolitionist. **3. Robert** 1773-1858, Scottish botanist.

Browne, Sir Thomas (broun) 1605-1682, English writer and physician.

Bruce, Robert the (brüs) see **Robert I.**

Bruck·ner, Anton (brük′nər) 1824-1896, Austrian composer.

Brue·ghel, Pieter (broi′gəl, brü′-) 1525?-1569, Flemish painter.

Bru·nel·les·chi, Filippo (brü′nə les′kē) 1377-1446, Florentine architect.

Bru·tus, Marcus Junius (brü′təs) 85?-42 B.C., Roman scholar, soldier, and politician; assassin of Julius Caesar.

Bry·an, William Jennings (brī′ən) 1860-1925, U.S. politician.

Bry·ant, William Cullen (brī′ənt) 1794-1878, U.S. poet and editor.

Bu·ber, Martin (bü′bər) 1878-1965, Jewish philosopher.

Bu·chan·an, James (bū kan′ən) 1791-1868, fifteenth president of the United States (1857-1861).

Buck, Pearl S(ydenstricker) (buk) 1892-1973, U.S. writer.

Bud·dha (bùd′ə, bü′də) 563?-483 B.C., founder of Buddhism. Also, **Siddhartha Gautama** or **Gautama Buddha, Gotama** or **Gotama Buddha.**

Budge, Don (buj) 1915- , U.S. tennis player.

Buffalo Bill, see **Cody, William Frederick.**

Bul·ga·kov, Mikhail Afanasyevich (bùl gä′kəf) 1891-1940, Soviet writer.

Bul·wer-Lyt·ton (bùl′wər lit′ən) **1. Edward George Earle Lytton.** 1803-1873, English novelist, dramatist, and politician; 1st Baron Lytton. **2. Edward Robert.** 1831-1891, English diplomat and poet who used the pseudonym *Owen Meredith;* son of Edward George Earle Bulwer-Lytton.

Bunche, Ralph Johnson (bunch) 1904-1971, U.S. statesman, educator, and United Nations official.

Bu·ñuel, Luis (bün wel′, bü′nü el′; *Spanish* bü nywel′) 1900-1983, Spanish film director.

Bun·yan, John (bun′yən) 1628-1686, English writer and preacher.

Bur·bank, Luther (bûr′bangk′) 1849-1926, U.S. nurseryman and plant breeder.

Burck·hardt, Jacob (bûrk′härt′) 1818-1897, Swiss historian.

Bur·ger, Warren Earl (bûr′gər) 1907- , U.S. Supreme Court Chief Justice (1969-1986).

Bur·gess, Anthony (bûr′jis) 1917- , British writer.

Bur·goyne, John (bər goin′) 1722-1792, British general in the American Revolution.

Burke, Edmund (bûrk) 1729-1797, British statesman and writer.

Burns, Robert (bûrnz) 1759-1796, Scottish poet.

Burr, Aaron (bûr) 1756-1836, U.S. politician and lawyer, vice president of the United States (1801-1805).

Bur·roughs, Edgar Rice (bûr′ōz) 1875-1950, U.S. novelist.

Bur·ton, Sir Richard Francis (bûr′tən) 1821-1890, English explorer and writer.

Bush, George (Herbert Walker) (bùsh) 1924- , forty-first president of the United States (1989-).

But·ler, Samuel (but′lər) 1835-1902, English novelist.

Byrd, Richard Evelyn (bûrd) 1888-1957, U.S. explorer, pioneer aviator, and writer.

By·ron, Lord (bī′rən) 1788-1824, English poet; born *George Gordon.*

Cab·ot (kab′ət) **1. John.** 1450?-1498, Italian explorer of North America in the service of England. **2. Sebastian.** 1476?-1557, English explorer of North America in the service of England; son of John Cabot.

Ca·bral, Pedro Alvares (kə bräl′) 1467?-1520?, Portuguese navigator.

Ca·bri·ni, Saint Frances Xavier (kə brē′nē) 1850-1917, U.S. nun, first American citizen to be canonized.

Caed·mon (kad′mən) d. A.D. 670?, English poet.

Cae·sar, Gaius Julius (sē′zər) 100?-44 B.C., Roman statesman and general.

Cai·a·phas (kā′ə fəs, kī′-) in the New Testament, the Jewish high priest who presided at the council that condemned Jesus.

Cain (kān) in the Old Testament, the oldest son of Adam and Eve; murderer of his brother, Abel.

Ca·lam·i·ty Jane (kə lam′i tē jān′) 1852?-1903, U.S. frontier figure; nickname of *Martha Jane Burke.*

Cal·der, Alexander (kôl′dər) 1898-1976, U.S. sculptor.

Ca·leb (kā′ləb) in the Old Testament, a Hebrew leader who was sent as a spy into Canaan.

Cal·houn, John Caldwell (kal hün′) 1782-1850, U.S. political leader.

Ca·lig·u·la (kə lig′yə lə) A.D. 12-41, Roman emperor (A.D. 37-41).

a	at	e	end	o	hot	u	up	hw	white		about
ā	ape	ē	me	ō	old	ū	use	ng	song		taken
ä	far	i	it	ô	fork	ù	rule	th	thin	ə	pencil
âr	care	ī	ice	oi	oil	ù	pull	th	this		lemon
		îr	pierce	ou	out	ûr	turn	zh	measure		circus

1399

Cal·la·ghan (kal′ə han′) **1. James.** 1912- , British prime minister (1976-1979). **2. Morley.** 1903- , Canadian writer.

Cal·las, Maria (kal′əs, kä′läs) 1923-1977, U.S. soprano.

Cal·vert (kal′vərt) **1. Sir George.** 1580?-1632, English statesman, founder of the colony of Maryland. Also, **Baron Baltimore, Lord Baltimore. 2. Leonard.** 1606?-1647, American, first governor of Maryland (1634-1647); son of Sir George Calvert.

Cal·vin, John (kal′vin) 1509-1564, French theologian.

Cal·vi·no, Italo (kal vē′nō) 1923-1985, Italian writer.

Cam·by·ses (kam bī′sēz) d. 521? B.C., king of Persia (529-522 B.C.); son of Cyrus the Great.

Ca·mões, Luiz de (kə moiNSH′) 1524?-1580, Portuguese poet.

Camp·bell-Ban·ner·man, Sir Henry (kam′bəl ban′ər mən) 1836-1911, British prime minister (1905-1908).

Ca·mus, Albert (ka mY′) 1913-1960, French writer and critic.

Can·non, Annie Jump (kan′ən) 1863-1941, U.S. astronomer.

Can·tor, Georg (kan′tər) 1845-1918, German mathematician.

Ca·nute (kə nūt′, -nūt′) A.D. 994?-1035, king of England (1016-1035), king of Denmark (1018-1035), and king of Norway (1028-1035). Also, **Cnut.**

Ča·pek, Karel (chä′pek) 1890-1938, Czech writer; inventor of the word *robot.*

Ca·pet, Hugh (kā′pit, kap′it) A.D. 938?-996, king of France (A.D. 987-996); founder of the Capetian dynasty that ruled France (A.D. 987-1328).

Car·a·cal·la (kar′ə kal′ə) A.D. 188-217, Roman emperor (A.D. 211-217).

Ca·ra·vag·gio, Michelangelo Merisi da (kar′ə vä′jō) 1573-1610, Italian painter. Also, **Amerigi da Caravaggio.**

Car·lo·vin·gi·an (kär′lə vin′jē ən) see **Carolingian.**

Car·lyle, Thomas (kär līl′) 1795-1881, Scottish essayist, historian, and social philosopher.

Car·man, Bliss (kär′mən) 1861-1929, Canadian poet.

Car·nar·von, 5th Earl of (kär när′vən) 1866-1923, English Egyptologist; born *George Edward Stanhope Molyneux Herbert.*

Car·ne·gie, Andrew (kär′ni gē) 1835-1919, U.S. steel manufacturer and philanthropist.

Car·o·lin·gi·an (kar′ə lin′jē ən) Frankish dynasty that ruled in France (A.D. 751-987), Germany (A.D. 751-911), and Italy (A.D. 751-887).

Car·roll, Lewis (kar′əl) 1832-1898, English writer and mathematician; pen name of *Charles L. Dodgson.*

Car·son (kär′sən) **1. Kit.** 1809-1868, U.S. frontiersman and scout; nickname of *Christopher Carson.* **2. Rachel.** 1907-1964, U.S. marine biologist and writer.

Car·ter (kär′tər) **1. Howard.** 1873-1939, English Egyptologist. **2. Jimmy.** 1924- , thirty-ninth president of the United States (1977-1981); full name *James Earl Carter.*

Car·tier (kär tyä′, kär′tē ā′; *French* kär tyä′) **1. Sir George Étienne.** 1814-1873, Canadian statesman. **2. Jacques.** 1491-1557, French navigator.

Car·tier-Bres·son, Henri (kär tyä′ bRe sôN′) 1908- , French photographer.

Cart·wright, Edmund (kärt′rīt′) 1743-1823, English clergyman and inventor.

Ca·ru·so, Enrico (kə rü′sō) 1873-1921, Italian tenor.

Car·ver (kär′vər) **1. George Washington.** 1864-1943, U.S. botanist and educator. **2. John.** 1576-1621, English *Mayflower* Pilgrim; first governor of Plymouth Colony (1620-1621).

Ca·sals, Pablo (kə salz′, -sälz′) 1876-1973, Spanish cellist and conductor. Also, **Pau Casals.**

Cas·a·no·va, Giovanni Giacomo (kaz′ə nō′və, kas′-) 1725-1798, Venetian adventurer and writer.

Cas·satt, Mary (kə sat′) 1845-1926, U.S. painter who worked in France.

Cas·sius Lon·gi·nus, Gaius (kash′əs lon jī′nəs) d. 42 B.C., Roman general and politician.

Cas·tro, Fidel (kas′trō) 1926- , Cuban revolutionary leader, premier of Cuba (1959-).

Ca·ther, Willa Sibert (kath′ər) 1873-1947, U.S. novelist.

Cath·er·ine I (kath′ər in, kath′rin) 1684?-1727, empress of Russia (1725-1727); wife of Peter I.

Catherine II, see **Catherine the Great.**

Catherine de′ Med·i·ci (də med′i chē) 1519?-1589, Italian-born queen of France (1547-1559).

Catherine of Ar·a·gon (ar′ə gon′) 1485-1536, first wife of Henry VIII of England.

Catherine of Si·en·a, Saint (sē en′ə) 1347-1380, Italian mystic and lay member of the Dominican order.

Catherine the Great, 1729-1796, German-born empress of Russia (1762-1796). Also, **Catherine II.**

Cat·i·line (kat′ə līn′) 108?-62 B.C., Roman soldier and politician.

Ca·to (kā′tō) **1. Marcus Porcius.** 234-149 B.C., Roman statesman; called *Cato the Elder.* **2. Marcus Porcius.** 95-46 B.C., Roman statesman; called *Cato the Younger;* grandson of Cato the Elder.

Catt, Carrie Chapman (kat) 1859-1947, U.S. suffragist leader.

Ca·tul·lus, Gaius Valerius (kə tul′əs) 87?-54? B.C., Roman lyric poet.

Cau·chy, Augustin-Louis (kō shē′) 1789-1857, French mathematician.

Cav·en·dish, Henry (kav′ən dish′) 1731-1810, English physicist and chemist.

Cax·ton, William (kak′stən) 1422?-1491, first English printer.

Cec·cet·ti, Enrico (chə chet′ē) 1850-1928, Italian ballet dancer and teacher.

Ce·cil·ia, Saint (sə sēl′yə) d. A.D. 230?, Roman martyr.

Ce·lan, Paul (sə län′, tsel′än) 1920-1970, German poet.

Cel·li·ni, Benvenuto (chə lē′nē) 1500-1571, Florentine sculptor, goldsmith, and writer.

Cer·van·tes, Miguel de (sər van′tēz) 1547-1616, Spanish author.

Cé·zanne, Paul (sā zan′, -zän′) 1839-1906, French painter.

Cha·gall, Marc (shə gäl′) 1887-1985, Russian artist who lived and worked chiefly in France.

Cha·lia·pin, Fyodor Ivanovich (shäl yä′pin) 1873-1938, Russian bass-baritone.

Cham·ber·lain (chām′bər lən) **1. (Arthur) Neville.** 1869-1940, British statesman, prime minister (1937-1940). **2. Wilt.** 1936- , U.S. basketball player; full name *Wilton Norman Chamberlain.*

Cha·mor·ro, Violeta Barrios de (chä mô′Rō) 1929- , Nicaraguan president (1990-).

Cham·plain, Samuel de (sham plān′) 1567-1635, French explorer.

Chan·pol·lion, Jean François (shäN pô lyôN′) 1790-1832, French Egyptologist.

Chan·dra·gup·ta, Maurya (chun′drə gŭp′tə) d. 298 B.C., emperor of India (321?-298 B.C.).

Chan·ning, William Ellery (chan′ing) 1780-1842, U.S. Unitarian minister and social reformer.

Chap·lin, Charlie (chap′lin) 1899-1977, British actor, director, and producer; full name *Charles Spenser Chaplin.*

Char·le·magne (shär′lə mān′) A.D. 742?-814, king of the Franks (A.D. 768-814); as Charles I, emperor of the Holy Roman Empire (A.D. 800-814). Also, **Charles the Great.**

Charles, Jacques-Alexandre-César (chärlz) 1746-1823, French physicist.

Charles, Prince, 1948- , Prince of Wales; son of Elizabeth II.

Charles I, 1600-1649, king of England, Scotland, and Ireland (1625-1649).

Charles II, 1630-1685, king of England, Scotland, and Ireland (1660-1685).

Charles V, 1500-1558, emperor of the Holy Roman Empire (1519-1558); as Charles I, king of Spain (1516-1556).

Charles Edward Stuart, see **Stuart, Charles Edward.**

Charles Mar·tel (mär tel′) A.D. 688?-741, ruler of the Franks (A.D. 720-741); grandfather of Charlemagne.

Charles the Great, see **Charlemagne.**

Chase, Salmon Portland (chās) 1808-1873, U.S. Supreme Court Chief Justice (1864-1873).

Cha·teau·bri·and, François René, Vicomte de (shä tō bRē äN′) 1768-1848, French writer and statesman.

Chat·ter·ton, Thomas (chat′ər tən) 1752-1770, English poet.

Chau·cer, Geoffrey (chô′sər) 1344?-1400, English poet.

Chee·ver, John (chē′vər) 1912-1982, U.S. writer.

Che·khov, Anton (chek′ôf) 1860-1904, Russian writer.

Che·ops (kē′ops) see **Khufu.**

Cher·nen·ko, Konstantin Ustinovich (chər nyeng′kō) 1911-1985, Soviet leader, general secretary of the Communist Party (1984-1985).

Ches·ter·field, Earl of (ches′tər fēld′) 1694-1773, British statesman and writer; born *Philip Dormer Stanhope.*

Ches·ter·ton, (G)ilbert (K)eith (ches′tər tən) 1874-1936, English writer and critic.

Chiang Kai-shek (chang′kī shek′) 1887-1975, Chinese general and political leader, president of Taiwan (1950-1975).

Chi·ka·ma·tsu Mon·za·e·mon (chē′kä mä′tsu môn′zä ä·môn′) 1653-1724, Japanese dramatist.

Chin (chin) see **Tsin.**

Ch′in (chin) see **Qin.**

Ch′ing (ching) see **Qing.**

Chip·pen·dale, Thomas (chip′ən dāl′) 1718-1779, English cabinetmaker.

Chi·ri·co, Giorgio de (kir′i kō′) 1888-1978, Italian artist.

Cho·pin, Frédéric François (shō′pan, shô paN′) 1810-1849, Polish composer and pianist.

Chou (jō) see Zhou.

Chou En-lai (jō′en′lī′) *also,* Zhou Enlai. 1898-1976, Chinese communist political leader.

Chré·tien de Troyes (krā tyaN′də trwä′) twelfth century, French poet.

Chris·tie, Agatha (kris′tē) 1890-1976, English writer of detective stories.

Chris·ti·na (kris tē′nə) 1626-1689, queen of Sweden (1632-1654).

Chris·to·pher, Saint (kris′tə fər) A.D. third century, Christian martyr.

Chrys·os·tom, Saint John (kris′ə stəm) A.D. 345?-407, archbishop of Constantinople and a Father of the Church (A.D. 398-404).

Chur·chill (chûr′chil) 1. **John.** 1650-1722, English general and statesman, 1st Duke of Marlborough. 2. **Sir Winston Leonard Spencer.** 1874-1965, British statesman and writer, prime minister (1940-1945; 1951-1955).

Cic·e·ro, Marcus Tullius (sis′ə rō′) 106-43 B.C., Roman orator, writer, and statesman.

Cid, El (el) A.D. 1040?-1099, Spanish soldier and national hero; born *Rodrigo Díaz de Bivar.*

Cin·cin·na·tus, Lucius Quinctius (sin′sə nā′təs) 519?-439? B.C., Roman patriot.

Clar·en·don, Earl of (klar′ən dən) 1609-1674, English statesman and historian; born *Edward Hyde.*

Clark (klärk) 1. **George Rogers.** 1752-1818, U.S. general and frontiersman. 2. **Joe.** 1939- , Canadian prime minister (1979-1980); full name *Charles Joseph Clark.* 3. **William.** 1770-1838, U.S. soldier, explorer with Meriwether Lewis; brother of George Rogers Clark.

Claude Lor·rain (klôd′lə rān′) 1600-1682, French landscape painter; born *Claude Gelée.*

Clau·di·us I (klô′dē əs) 10 B.C.-A.D. 54, Roman emperor (A.D. 41-54).

Clau·se·witz, Karl von (klou′zə vits′) 1780-1831, Prussian general and writer.

Clay, Henry (klā) 1777-1852, U.S. statesman.

Cleis·the·nes (klīs′thə nēz′) *also,* Clisthenes. 570?-508? B.C., Athenian statesman.

Clem·en·ceau, Georges (klem′ən sō′) 1841-1929, premier of France (1906-1909; 1917-1920).

Clem·ens, Samuel Langhorne (klem′ənz) see Twain, Mark.

Cle·men·te, Roberto Walker (klə men′tē) 1933-1972, Puerto Rican baseball player.

Cle·o·pa·tra (klē′ə pa′trə) 69-30 B.C., queen of Egypt (51-49 B.C.; 48-30 B.C.).

Cleve·land, (Stephen) Grover (klēv′lənd) 1837-1908, twenty-second and twenty-fourth president of the United States (1885-1889; 1893-1897).

Clin·ton, De Witt (klin′tən) 1769-1828, U.S. statesman.

Clis·the·nes (klīs′thə nēz′) see Cleisthenes.

Clive, Robert (klīv) 1725-1774, British general and statesman in India.

Clo·vis I (klō′vis) A.D. 465?-511, king of the Franks (A.D. 481-511), founder of the Merovingian dynasty.

Cnut (kə nüt′, -nüt′) see Canute.

Cobb, Ty (kob) 1886-1961, U.S. baseball player; full name *Tyrus Raymond Cobb.*

Co·chise (kō chēs′) 1815?-1874, Apache chief.

Co·dy, William Frederick (kō′dē) 1846-1917, U.S. scout and showman; known as *Buffalo Bill.*

Co·han, George M(ichael) (kō′han) 1878-1942, U.S. actor, dramatist, and producer.

Col·bert, Jean Baptiste (kôl beR′) 1619-1683, French statesman and financier.

Cole, Thomas (kōl) 1801-1848, U.S. painter.

Cole·ridge, Samuel Taylor (kōl′rij) 1772-1834, English poet and critic.

Co·lum·bus, Christopher (kə lum′bəs) 1451?-1506, Italian explorer in the service of Spain; traditionally considered to have discovered America in 1492.

Comp·ton, Arthur Holly (komp′tən) 1892-1962, U.S. physicist.

Comte, Auguste (kôNt) 1798-1857, French philosopher.

Con·fu·cius (kən fū′shəs) 551?-479? B.C., Chinese philosopher, founder of Confucianism.

Con·greve, William (kon′grēv, kong′-) 1670-1729, English dramatist.

Con·nol·ly, Maureen (kon′ə lē) 1934-1969, U.S. tennis player.

Con·rad, Joseph (kon′rad) 1857-1924, English novelist; born in Poland.

Con·sta·ble, John (kun′stə bəl) 1776-1837, English landscape painter.

Con·stan·tine the Great (kon′stən tēn′) A.D. 274?-337, Roman emperor (A.D. 324-337).

Cook, James (kùk) 1728-1779, English navigator.

Coo·lidge, Calvin (kü′lij) 1872-1933, thirtieth president of the United States (1923-1929).

Coo·per (kü′pər) 1. **James Fenimore.** 1789-1851, U.S. novelist and social critic. 2. **Peter.** 1791-1883, U.S. industrialist and philanthropist.

Co·per·ni·cus, Nicolaus (kə pûr′ni kəs) 1473-1543, Polish astronomer.

Cop·land, Aaron (kōp′lənd) 1900-1990, U.S. composer.

Cop·ley, John Singleton (kop′lē) 1738-1815, U.S. painter.

Cor·neille, Pierre (kôr nā′) 1606-1684, French dramatist.

Corn·wal·lis, Charles (kôrn wol′is) 1738-1805, British general in the American Revolution.

Co·ro·na·do, Francisco Vásquez de (kôr′ə nä′dō) 1500?-1544, Spanish explorer.

Co·rot, Jean Baptiste Camille (kô rō′) 1796-1875, French landscape painter.

Cor·reg·gio, Antonio Allegri da (kə rej′ō, -rej′ē ō′) 1494-1534, Italian painter.

Cor·tés, Hernán (kôr tez′, kôr tes′) 1485-1547, Spanish conqueror of Mexico. Also, **Hernando Cortéz.**

Cou·lomb, Charles Augustin de (kü′lom) 1736-1806, French physicist.

Cou·per·in, François (kü pə raN′) 1668-1733, French composer.

Cour·bet, Gustave (kùr bā′) 1819-1877, French painter.

Court, Margaret Smith (kôrt) 1942- , Australian tennis player.

Cous·teau, Jacques-Yves (kü stō′) 1910- , French underwater explorer.

Cow·ard, Noël (kou′ərd) 1899-1973, English playwright, songwriter, and actor.

Cow·ley, Abraham (kou′lē) 1618-1667, English poet.

Cow·per, William (kü′pər) 1731-1800, English poet.

Crane (krān) 1. **Hart.** 1889-1932, U.S. poet. 2. **Stephen.** 1871-1900, U.S. novelist and short-story writer.

Cran·mer, Thomas (kran′mər) 1489-1556, English churchman and reformer; archbishop of Canterbury (1533-1556).

Crazy Horse 1849?-1877, Sioux chief; in Sioux *Tashunca-Uitoo.*

Crick, Francis Harry Compton (krik) 1916- , British biophysicist.

Cro·ce, Benedetto (krō′chä) 1866-1952, Italian philosopher and political leader.

Crock·ett, Davy (krok′it) 1786-1836, U.S. frontiersman; full name *David Crockett.*

Croe·sus (krē′səs) d. 546? B.C., king of Lydia (560-546 B.C.).

Cromp·ton, Samuel (kromp′tən) 1753-1827, English inventor.

Crom·well (krom′wel′) 1. **Oliver.** 1599-1658, English statesman and soldier. 2. **Richard.** 1626-1712, English soldier and politician; son of Oliver Cromwell. 3. **Thomas.** 1485?-1540, English statesman, Earl of Essex.

Crookes, Sir William (krúks) 1832-1919, English chemist and physicist.

Cum·mings, E(dward) E(stlin) (kum′ingz) 1894-1962, U.S. poet who often signed his work *e e cummings.*

Cun·ning·ham, Merce (kun′ing ham′) 1919- , U.S. choreographer and dancer.

Cu·rie (kyu rē′) 1. **Marie Sklodowska.** 1867-1934, Polish-French chemist and physicist. 2. **Pierre.** 1859-1906, French physicist and chemist; husband of Marie Curie.

Cur·tiss, Glenn Hammond (kûr′tis) 1878-1930, U.S. inventor and pioneer in aviation.

Cush (kùsh, kush) in the Old Testament, the eldest son of Ham.

Cus·ter, George Armstrong (kus′tər) 1839-1876, U.S. army officer.

Cu·vi·er, Georges (kū′vē ā′, küv yā′) 1769-1832, French naturalist.

Cy·rus (sī′rəs) 1. **the Great.** d. 529 B.C., king of Persia (558?-529 B.C.), founder of the Persian Empire. 2. **the Younger.** d. 401 B.C., Persian prince.

a	at	e	end	o	hot	u	up	hw	white		about
ā	ape	ē	me	ō	old	ū	use	ng	song		taken
ä	far	i	it	ô	fork	ü	rule	th	thin	ə	pencil
âr	care	ī	ice	oi	oil	ù	pull	th	this		lemon
		îr	pierce	ou	out	ûr	turn	zh	measure		circus

da Ga·ma, Vasco (də gam′ə) 1469?-1524, Portuguese navigator.

Da·guerre, Louis-Jacques-Mandé (də gâr′) 1789-1851, French inventor, physicist, and set painter; inventor of the daguerreotype.

Da·li, Salvador (dä′lē) 1904-1989, Spanish artist.

Dal·ton, John (dôl′tən) 1766-1844, English chemist and physicist.

Dan (dan) **1.** in the Old Testament, a son of Jacob. **2.** one of the twelve tribes of Israel descended from him.

Da·na, Richard Henry (dā′nə) 1815-1882, U.S. writer.

Dan·iel (dan′yəl) sixth century B.C., Hebrew prophet.

D'An·nun·zi·o, Gabriele (dä nün′tsē ō′) 1863-1938, Italian writer and politician.

Dan·te (dän′tā) 1265-1321, Italian poet. Also, **Dante A·li·ghie·ri** (ä′li gye′Rē)

Dan·ton, Georges (dan′tən, däɴ tôɴ′) 1759-1794, leader in the French Revolution.

Dare, Virginia (dâr) b. 1587, first child born of English parents in North America.

Da·rí·o, Rubén (dä rē′ō) 1867-1916, Nicaraguan poet and diplomat; pen name of *Félix García-Sarmiento.*

Da·ri·us I (də rī′əs) 549?-485? B.C., king of Persia (521-485? B.C.). Also, **Darius the Great.**

Dar·row, Clarence Seward. (dar′ō) 1857-1938, U.S. lawyer.

Dar·win, Charles (där′win) 1809-1882, English naturalist.

Dau·det, Alphonse (dō dā′) 1840-1897, French writer.

Dau·mier, Honoré (dō myä′) 1808-1879, French artist.

Dav·en·port, John (dav′ən pôrt′) 1597-1670, American clergyman, a founder of the colony of New Haven.

Da·vid (dā′vid) 1040?-970? B.C., king of Israel (1010?-970? B.C.); father of Solomon.

Da·vid, Jacques Louis (dä vēd′) 1748-1825, French painter.

Da·vid, Saint, (dā′vid) d. A.D. 601?, patron saint of Wales.

da Vinci, Leonardo, see Leonardo da Vinci.

Da·vis, Jefferson (dā′vis) 1808-1889, U.S. political leader, president of the Confederate States of America (1861-1865).

Da·vy, Sir Humphry (dā′vē) 1778-1829, English chemist.

Deb·o·rah (deb′ər ə, deb′rə) in the Old Testament, a Hebrew prophet and judge.

De Broglie, Louis Victor, see Broglie, Louis Victor de.

Debs, Eugene Victor (debz) 1855-1926, U.S. socialist and labor leader.

De·bus·sy, Claude (deb′yù sē′, də bū′sē) 1862-1918, French composer.

De·ca·tur, Stephen (di kā′tər) 1779-1820, U.S. naval officer.

De·foe, Daniel (də fō′) *also,* **Daniel De Foe.** 1660?-1731, English writer.

De For·est, Lee (də fôr′ist, for′-) 1873-1961, U.S. inventor.

De·gas, Edgar (dā gä′) 1834-1917, French painter.

de Gaulle, Charles (di gôl′) 1890-1970, French general and political leader, president (1959-1969).

De Groot, Huig (di grōt′) see Grotius, Hugo.

De Kalb, Baron Johann (di kalb′) 1721-1780, German general in the colonial army during the American Revolution.

de Klerk, F(rederik) W(illem) (də klerk′, klûrk′) 1936- , South African president (1989-).

de Koo·ning, Willem (di kü′ning) 1904- , U.S. painter.

De·la·croix, (Ferdinand Victor) Eugène (del′ə krwä′; *French* də lä kRwä′) 1798-1863, French painter.

De la Ma·drid Hur·ta·do, Miguel (də lä mə drid′hər tä′dō) 1934- , Mexican president (1982-1988).

De la Mare, Walter (də lä mâr′) 1873-1956, English writer.

de Les·seps, Ferdinand Marie (də les′əps) 1805-1894, French diplomat and engineer.

De·li·lah (də lī′lə) in the Old Testament, a woman who betrayed Samson to the Philistines by cutting his hair, thereby depriving him of his strength.

De·li·us, Frederick (dē′lē əs) 1862-1934, English composer.

del Sarto, Andrea, see Andrea del Sarto.

De Mille (də mil′) **1.** Agnes George. 1908- , U.S. choreographer, dancer, and writer. **2.** Cecil B(lount). 1881-1959, U.S. film director and producer.

De·moc·ri·tus (də mok′ri təs) 460?-370 B.C., Greek philosopher.

De·mos·the·nes (də mos′thə nēz′) 384?-322 B.C., Greek orator.

Demp·sey, Jack (demp′sē) 1895-1983, U.S. boxer; born *William Harrison Dempsey.*

Deng Xiao·ping (dung′shou′ping) *also,* **Teng Hsiao-ping.** 1904- , Chinese communist leader (1977-).

De·nis, Saint (den′is, də nē′) d. A.D. 258?, patron saint of France.

De Quin·cey, Thomas (di kwin′sē) 1785-1859, English essayist.

De·rain, André (də Raɴ′) 1880-1954, French artist.

Des·cartes, René (dā kärt′) 1596-1650, French philosopher and mathematician.

De So·to, Hernando (də sō′tō) 1500?-1542, Spanish explorer. Also, **Fernando De Soto.**

De Va·le·ra, Eamon (dev′ə lâr′ə) 1882-1975, Irish political leader; born in the United States.

de Vega, Lope, see Lope de Vega.

De Vries, Hugo (də vrēs′) 1848-1935, Dutch botanist.

Dew·ey (dü′ē, dū′ē) **1.** George. 1837-1917, U.S. admiral. **2.** John. 1859-1952, U.S. philosopher and educator. **3.** Thomas E(dmund) 1902-1971, U.S. politician.

Di·a·ghi·lev, Serge (dē ä′gə ləf) 1872-1929, Russian ballet producer.

Di·as, Bartolomeu (dē′əsh) 1450?-1500, Portuguese navigator. Also, **Bartholomew Diaz.**

Di·az, Porfirio (dē′äs, -äz) 1830-1915, Mexican president (1877-1880; 1884-1911).

Dick·ens, Charles (dik′ənz) 1812-1870, English novelist.

Dick·in·son (dik′ən sən) **1.** Emily. 1830-1886, U.S. poet. **2.** John. 1732-1808, American statesman.

Di·de·rot, Denis (dē drō′, dē′də rō′) 1713-1784, French writer and philosopher.

Did·rik·son, Mildred (did′rik sən) see Zaharias, Mildred Didrikson.

Die·fen·ba·ker, John George (dē′fən bā′kər) 1895-1979, Canadian prime minister (1957-1963).

Die·trich, Marlene (dē′trik) 1901- , German-American film actress.

Di·Mag·gio, Joe (də maj′ē ō′) 1914- , U.S. baseball player; full name *Joseph Paul DiMaggio.*

Di·o·cle·tian (dī′ə klē′shən) A.D. 245-313, Roman emperor (A.D. 284-305).

Di·og·e·nes (dī oj′ə nēz′) 412?-323 B.C., Greek philosopher.

Di·rac, Paul Adrien Maurice (di rak′) 1902-1984, British physicist.

Dis·ney, Walt(er Elias) (diz′nē) 1901-1966, U.S. motion-picture producer.

Dis·rae·li, Benjamin (diz rā′lē) 1804-1881, British statesman, prime minister (1868; 1874-1880).

Dodg·son, Charles L. (doj′sən) see Carroll, Lewis.

Dom·i·nic, Saint (dom′ə nik) 1170-1221, Spanish priest, founder of the Dominicans.

Do·mi·ti·an (də mish′ən) A.D. 51-96, Roman emperor (A.D. 81-96); son of Vespasian.

Don·a·tel·lo (don′ə tel′ō) 1386?-1466, Florentine sculptor.

Don·i·zet·ti, Gaetano (don′ə zet′ē, -dzet′ē) 1797-1848, Italian composer of operas.

Donne, John (dun) 1573?-1631, English poet and clergyman.

Doo·lit·tle, Hilda (dü′lit′əl) 1886-1961, U.S. poet who signed her work *H.D.*

Dop·pler, Johann Christian (dop′lər) 1803-1853, Austrian mathematician, physicist, and astronomer.

Dor·cas (dôr′kəs) in the New Testament, a Christian woman who made clothes for the poor. Also, **Tabitha.**

Dos Pas·sos, John Roderigo (dōs pas′ōs) 1896-1970, U.S. writer.

Dos·to·ev·sky, Fyodor Mikhailovich (dos′tə yef′skē) 1821-1881, Russian novelist and short-story writer.

Doug·las (dug′ləs) **1.** Stephen A. 1813-1861, U.S. statesman. **2.** William O(rville). 1898-1980, U.S. Supreme Court associate justice (1939-1975).

Doug·las-Home, Sir Alec (dug′ləs hōm′) 1903- , British prime minister (1963-1964); full name *Alexander Frederick Douglas-Home.*

Doug·lass, Frederick (dug′ləs) 1817-1895, U.S. abolitionist and editor.

Dove, Arthur (duv) 1880-1946, U.S. painter and illustrator.

Doyle, Sir Arthur Conan (doil) 1859-1930, British writer.

Dra·co (drā′kō) seventh century B.C., Athenian lawgiver.

Drake, Sir Francis (drāk) 1540?-1596, English admiral and explorer.

Drei·ser, Theodore (drī′sər, -zər) 1871-1945, U.S. novelist.

Drew, Charles Richard (drü) 1904-1950, U.S. medical scientist and surgeon.

Drey·fus, Alfred (drā′fəs, drī′-) 1859-1935, French army officer of Jewish descent who was convicted of treason in 1894 and acquitted in 1906.

Dry·den, John (drī′dən) 1631-1700, English poet, dramatist, and critic.

Du Bar·ry, Madame (dü bar′ē, dū) 1743-1793, French count-

ess; mistress of Louis XV; full name *Marie Jeanne Bécu, Comtesse du Barry.*

Du Bois, W(illiam) E(dward) B(urghardt) (dü bwä′, dü) 1868-1963, U.S. educator and civil rights leader.

Du·champ, Marcel (dü shän′, dy-) 1887-1968, French artist.

Du·de·vant, Baroness (dy də vän′) see **Sand, George.**

Dul·les, John Foster (dul′əs) 1888-1959, U.S. lawyer, diplomat, and secretary of state (1953-1959).

Du·mas (dü mä′, dy-) **1. Alexandre.** 1802-1870, French novelist and playwright; known as *Dumas père.* **2. Alexandre.** 1824-1895, French playwright; son of *Dumas père;* known as *Dumas fils.*

Du Mau·ri·er, George Louis Palmella Buson (dü môr′ē ā′, dü) 1834-1896, English novelist and illustrator.

Du·nant, Jean Henri (dü nän′, dy-) 1829-1910, Swiss philanthropist, founder of the Red Cross.

Dun·bar, Paul Laurence (dun′bär) 1872-1906, U.S. poet.

Dun·can I (dung′kən) d. 1040, king of Scotland (1034?-1040).

Duncan, Isadora 1878-1927, U.S. dancer.

Dun·sa·ny, Lord Edward (dun sā′nē) 1878-1957, Anglo-Irish dramatist and writer.

Duns Scotus, John (dunz skō′təs) 1266?-1308, Scottish theologian and philosopher.

Du Pont, Éleuthère Irénée (dü pont′, dü, dü′pont′, dü′) 1771-1834, French-American industrialist.

Dü·rer, Albrecht (dyr′ər) 1471-1528, German artist.

Dur·ham, Earl of (dûr′əm) 1792-1840, British statesman; born *John George Lambton.*

Durk·heim, Émile (dûrk′hīm) 1858-1917, French sociologist.

Du·se, Eleonora (dü′zā) 1859-1924, Italian actress.

Dvoř·ák, Anton (dvôr′zhäk) 1841-1904, Czech composer.

Ea·kins, Thomas (ā′kənz) 1844-1916, U.S. artist.

Ear·hart, Amelia (âr′härt′) 1898-1937, U.S. aviator.

Ear·ly, Jubal Anderson (ûr′lē) 1816-1894, Confederate general in the American Civil War.

Earp, Wyatt Barry Stapp (ûrp) 1848-1929, U.S. law officer and gunfighter in the American West.

East·man, George (ēst′mən) 1854-1932, U.S. industrialist and inventor who developed photographic processes and the Kodak camera.

Ed·dy, Mary Baker (ed′ē) 1821-1910, U.S. founder of the Christian Science Church.

E·den, Sir (Robert) Anthony (ē′dən) 1897-1977, British prime minister (1955-1957).

Ed·i·son, Thomas Alva (ed′ə sən) 1847-1931, U.S. inventor.

Ed·ward I (ed′wərd) 1239-1307, king of England (1272-1307).

Edward II, 1284-1327, king of England (1307-1327).

Edward III, 1312-1377, king of England (1327-1377).

Edward IV, 1442-1483, king of England (1461-1470; 1471-1483).

Edward V, 1470-1483, king of England (1483).

Edward VI, 1537-1553, king of England (1547-1553); son of Henry VIII.

Edward VII, 1841-1910, king of England (1901-1910); son of Queen Victoria.

Edward VIII, 1894-1972, king of England (1936) who abdicated and received the title of Duke of Windsor.

Edward the Black Prince, 1330-1376, Prince of Wales; son of Edward III.

Edward the Confessor, 1004?-1066, king of the English (1042-1066).

Ed·wards, Jonathan (ed′wərdz) 1703-1758, American theologian.

Ein·stein, Albert (īn′stīn) 1879-1955, German-American physicist.

Ei·sen·how·er, Dwight David (ī′zən hou′ər) 1890-1969, U.S. general, thirty-fourth president of the United States (1953-1961).

Ei·sen·stein, Sergei Mikhailovich (ī′zən stīn′) 1898-1948, Russian film director.

El Gre·co (el grek′ō) 1541?-1614, Spanish painter; born in Crete; real name *Domenikos Theotokopoulos.*

E·li·a (ē′lē ə) see **Lamb, Charles.**

E·li·as (i lī′əs) see **Elijah.**

E·li·jah (i lī′jə) ninth century B.C., Hebrew prophet. Also, **Elias.**

El·i·ot (el′ē ət) **1. George.** 1819-1880, English novelist; born *Mary Ann Evans.* **2. T(homas) S(tearns).** 1888-1965, English poet, essayist, and critic; born in the United States.

E·lish·a (i lish′ə) ninth century B.C., Hebrew prophet.

E·liz·a·beth I (i liz′ə bəth) 1533-1603, queen of England (1558-1603); daughter of Henry VIII and Anne Boleyn.

Elizabeth II, 1926- , queen of Great Britain and Northern Ireland (1952-); daughter of George VI.

El·ling·ton, Duke (el′ing tən) 1899-1974, U.S. composer, conductor, and pianist; full name *Edward Kennedy Ellington.*

El·lis, (Henry) Havelock (el′is) 1859-1939, English psychologist and writer.

Ells·worth, Oliver (elz′wûrth′) 1745-1807, American jurist and statesman, U.S. Supreme Court Chief Justice (1796-1800).

Em·er·son, Ralph Waldo (em′ər sən) 1803-1882, U.S. essayist, poet, and philosopher.

Em·met, Robert (em′it) 1778-1803, Irish patriot.

Em·ped·o·cles (em ped′ə klēz′) 490?-430? B.C., Greek philosopher.

Eng·els, Friedrich (eng′gəlz) 1820-1895, German socialist writer.

E·noch (ē′nək) **1.** in the Old Testament, the eldest son of Cain. **2.** in the Old Testament, the father of Methuselah.

E·nos (ē′nəs) in the Old Testament, a son of Seth.

E·pam·i·non·das (i pä′mə non′dəs) 418?-362 B.C., Theban general and statesman.

E·phra·im (ē′frē əm, ē′frəm) **1.** in the Old Testament, the younger son of Joseph. **2.** one of the twelve tribes of Israel descended from him.

Ep·ic·te·tus (ep′ik tē′təs) A.D. 60?-140, Greek philosopher.

Ep·i·cu·rus (ep′i kyûr′əs) 342?-270 B.C., Greek philosopher.

E·ras·mus, Desiderius (i raz′məs) 1466?-1536, Dutch writer and humanist.

Er·ic·son, Leif (er′ik sən) *also,* **Ericsson.** fl. A.D. 1000, Norse explorer; son of Eric the Red.

Er·ics·son, John (er′ik sən) 1803-1889, Swedish inventor and engineer.

Er·ic the Red (er′ik) b. A.D. 950?, Norse explorer; father of Leif Ericson.

E·sau (ē′sô) in the Old Testament, son of Isaac and Rebecca, elder twin brother of Jacob.

Es·dras (ez′drəs) in the Douay Bible, Ezra.

Es·ther (es′tər) in the Old Testament, a Jewish woman chosen to be queen by the king of Persia.

Eth·el·red II (eth′əl red′) see **Æthelred II.**

Eu·clid (ū′klid) 323?-285 B.C., Greek mathematician.

Eu·gé·nie (ū jā′nē, -jē′-, œ zhā nē′) 1826-1920, empress of France (1853-1870); wife of Napoleon III.

Eu·rip·i·des (yù rip′i dēz′) 485?-406 B.C., Greek dramatist.

Ev·ans (ev′əns) **1. Sir Arthur John.** 1851-1941, English archaeologist. **2. Mary Ann.** see **Eliot, George. 3. Walker.** 1903-1975, U.S. photographer.

Eve (ēv) in the Bible, the first woman and Adam's wife.

Ev·ert, Chris (ev′ərt) 1954- , U.S. tennis player.

Eyck, Jan van (īk) 1385?-1441, Flemish painter.

E·ze·ki·el (i zē′kē əl) *also,* **E·ze·chi·el.** sixth century B.C., Hebrew prophet.

Ez·ra (ez′rə) fifth century B.C., Hebrew scribe and prophet.

Fa·bi·us, Maximus, Quintus (fā′bē əs) 275-203 B.C., Roman general.

Far·a·day, Michael (far′ə dā′) 1791-1867, English physicist and chemist.

Far·ra·gut, David Glasgow (far′ə gət) 1801-1870, U.S. naval officer.

Faulk·ner, William (fôk′nər) 1897-1962, U.S. novelist and short-story writer.

Fawkes, Guy (fôks) 1570-1606, English conspirator.

Fel·li·ni, Federico (fə lē′nē) 1920- , Italian film director.

Fer·di·nand I (fûr′də nand′) A.D. 1000?-1065, king of Castile (1035-1065), king of León (1037-1065).

Ferdinand V, 1452-1516, king of Castile (1476-1504); as Ferdinand II, king of Aragon (1479-1516); as Ferdinand III, king of Naples (1504-1516); husband of Isabella.

Fer·mi, Enrico (fer′mē) 1901-1954, Italian-American physicist.

Fich·te, Johann Gottlieb (fik′tē) 1762-1814, German philosopher.

Fiel·ding, Henry (fēl′ding) 1707-1754, English novelist.

Fill·more, Millard (fil′môr′) 1800-1874, thirteenth president of the United States (1850-1853).

Fiske, John (fisk) 1842-1901, U.S. philosopher and educator.

Fitz·ger·ald, F(rancis) Scott (Key) (fits jer′əld) 1896-1940, U.S. novelist and short-story writer.

Fitz·Ger·ald, Edward (fits jer′əld) 1809-1883, English writer.

Flau·bert, Gustave (flō beR′) 1821-1880, French novelist.

Flem·ing, Sir Alexander (flem′ing) 1881-1955, Scottish bacteriologist.

a	at	e	end	o	hot	u	up	hw	white		about
ā	ape	ē	me	ō	old	ū	use	ng	song		taken
ä	far	i	it	ô	fork	ü	rule	th	thin	ə	pencil
âr	care	ī	ice	oi	oil	ù	pull	th	this		lemon
		îr	pierce	ou	out	ûr	turn	zh	measure		circus

1403

Fletch·er, John (flech′ər) 1579-1625, English playwright.

Flo·rey, Sir Howard Walter (flôr′ē) 1898-1968, British pathologist.

Foch, Ferdinand (fôsh) 1851-1929, French marshal.

Fon·teyn, Margot (fon tān′) 1919-1991, English ballerina; born *Margaret Hookham.*

Ford (fôrd) **1. Gerald R(udolph).** 1913- , thirty-eighth president of the United States (1974-1977). **2. Henry.** 1863-1947, U.S. automobile manufacturer and industrialist. **3. John.** 1586-1640?, English dramatist.

For·ster, E(dward) M(organ) (fôr′stər) 1879-1970, English novelist.

Fos·ter, Stephen Collins (fôs′tər) 1826-1864, U.S. composer of popular songs.

Fou·cault, Jean Bernard Léon (fü kō′) 1819-1868, French physicist.

Fou·ri·er (fûr′ē ā′) **1. François.** 1772-1837, French socialist. **2. Jean.** 1768-1830, French mathematician and physicist.

Fox (foks) **1. Charles James.** 1749-1806, English statesman. **2. George.** 1624-1691, English religious leader, founder of the Society of Friends.

Fra·go·nard, Jean Honoré (fʀa gô näʀ′) 1732-1806, French painter.

France, Anatole (frans, fʀÄNs) 1844-1924, French writer; born *Jacques Anatole Thibault.*

Fran·cis Ferdinand (fran′sis) 1863-1914, archduke of Austria.

Francis I, 1494-1547, king of France (1515-1547).

Francis II, 1768-1835, last emperor of the Holy Roman Empire (1792-1806); as Francis I, emperor of Austria (1804-1835).

Francis Joseph I, 1830-1916, emperor of Austria (1848-1916), king of Hungary (1867-1916). Also, **Franz Josef.**

Francis of As·si·si, Saint (ə sē′zē) 1181?-1226, Italian friar, founder of the Franciscan order.

Franck, César (fʀängk) 1822-1890, French composer, born in Belgium.

Fran·co, Francisco (fräng′kō) 1892-1975, Spanish general, dictator of Spain (1939-1975).

Frank, Anne (frangk) 1929-1945, German-Dutch victim of Nazis who kept a diary, now titled *The Diary of a Young Girl,* while she and her family were in hiding.

Frank·fur·ter, Felix (frangk′fər tər) 1882-1965, U.S. Supreme Court associate justice (1939-1962); born in Austria.

Frank·lin (frang′klin) **1. Benjamin.** 1706-1790, American scientist, statesman, writer, and inventor. **2. Sir John.** 1786-1847, English explorer. **3. Rosalind Elsie.** 1920-1958, English chemist and molecular biologist.

Franz Jo·sef (franz′ jō′zəf) see **Francis Joseph I.**

Fred·er·ick I (fred′ər ik, fred′rik) **1.** 1123?-1190, emperor of the Holy Roman Empire (1155-1190), German king (1152-1190); known as *Frederick Barbarossa.* **2.** 1657-1713, king of Prussia (1701-1713).

Frederick II 1. 1194-1250, emperor of the Holy Roman Empire (1220-1250), king of Sicily (1197-1250), German king (1212-1220), king of Jerusalem (1229-1250). **2.** see **Frederick the Great.**

Frederick III, 1463-1525, elector of Saxony (1486-1525).

Frederick IX, 1899-1972, king of Denmark (1947-1972).

Frederick Barbarossa, see **Frederick I** *(def. 1).*

Frederick the Great, 1712-1786, king of Prussia (1740-1786). Also, **Frederick II.**

Fré·mont, John Charles (frē′mont) 1813-1890, U.S. explorer, soldier, and politician.

Freud, Sigmund (froid) 1856-1939, Austrian physician and neurologist, founder of psychoanalysis.

Frie·dan, Betty (fri dan′) 1921- , U.S. feminist and writer.

Fried·man, Milton (frēd′mən) 1912- , U.S. economist.

Fro·bi·sher, Sir Martin (frō′bi shər) 1535?-1594, English explorer and navigator.

Froe·bel, Friedrich Wilhelm August (frā′bəl, fʀœ′-) 1782-1852, German educator, founder of the kindergarten system.

Frois·sart, Jean (fʀwä säʀ′) 1337?-1410, French chronicler and poet.

Fron·te·nac et de Pal·lu·au, Louis de Buade, Comte de (fron tə nak′ ā də pa lü ō′) 1622-1698, French-Canadian statesman, soldier, and governor of New France (1672-1682; 1689-1698).

Frost, Robert (frôst) 1874-1963, U.S. poet.

Fuen·tes, Carlos (fwen′tes) 1928- , Mexican writer.

Ful·ler, Melville Weston (fŭl′ər) 1833-1910, U.S. Supreme Court Chief Justice (1888-1910).

Ful·ton, Robert (fŭl′tən) 1765-1815, U.S. inventor.

Ga·ble, (William) Clark (gā′bəl) 1901-1960, U.S. film actor.

Gad (gad) **1.** in the Old Testament, a son of Jacob. **2.** one of the twelve tribes of Israel descended from him.

Ga·ga·rin, Yuri (gə gär′in) 1934-1968, Soviet cosmonaut; first person to travel in outer space.

Gage, Thomas (gāj) 1721-1787, British general in the American Revolution.

Gains·bor·ough, Thomas (gānz′bûr′ō, -bər ə) 1727-1788, English painter.

Gal·braith, John Kenneth (gal′brāth) 1908- , U.S. economist.

Ga·len, Claudius (gā′lən) A.D. 130-200?, Greek physician and physiologist.

Gal·i·le·o (gal′ə lā′ō) 1564-1642, Italian astronomer, physicist, and mathematician; full name *Galileo Galilei.*

Gals·wor·thy, John (gôlz′wûr′thē) 1867-1933, English novelist and dramatist.

Gal·va·ni, Luigi (gäl vä′nē) 1737-1798, Italian physician and physicist.

Gan·dhi (gän′dē) **1. Indira.** 1917-1984, prime minister of India (1966-1977; 1980-1984); daughter of Jawaharlal Nehru. **2. Mohandas Karamchand.** 1869-1948, Indian political, social, and religious leader; called *Mahatma Gandhi.* **3. Rajiv.** 1944-1991, Indian prime minister (1984-1989); son of Indira Gandhi.

Gar·bo, Greta (gär′bō) 1905-1990, Swedish-American film actress; born *Greta Lovisa Gustafsson.*

Gar·ci·a Lor·ca, Federico (gär sē′ə lôr′kə) 1899-1936, Spanish poet and dramatist.

García Már·quez, Gabriel (mär′kes) 1928- , Colombian writer.

Gar·field, James Abram (gär′fēld′) 1831-1881, twentieth president of the United States (1881).

Gar·i·bal·di, Giuseppe (gar′ə bôl′dē) 1807-1892, Italian patriot and general.

Gar·rick, David (gar′ik) 1717-1779, English actor, theater manager, and playwright.

Gar·ri·son, William Lloyd (gar′ə sən) 1805-1879, U.S. editor and abolitionist.

Gar·vey, Marcus Moziah, Jr. (gär′vē) 1887-1940, Jamaican black nationalist leader.

Gates, Horatio (gāts) 1728-1806, colonial general in the American Revolution.

Gau·guin, Paul (gō gaN′) 1848-1903, French painter.

Gauss, Carl Freidrich (gous) 1777-1855, German mathematician.

Gau·ta·ma (gô′tə mə, gou′-) see **Buddha.**

Gau·tier, Théophile (gō tyä′) 1811-1872, French poet, critic, and novelist.

Gay, John (gā) 1685-1732, English poet and dramatist.

Geh·rig, (Henry) Lou(is) (ger′ig) 1903-1941, U.S. baseball player.

Gen·e·vieve, Saint (jen′ə vēv′) A.D. 422?-512, patron saint of Paris.

Gen·ghis Khan (jeng′gis kän′) *also,* **Jenghis Khan, Jenghiz Khan.** 1162-1227, Mongol conqueror of central Asia.

Geof·frey of Mon·mouth (jef′rē; mon′məth) 1100?-1154, English chronicler.

George (jôrj) **1. David Lloyd.** see **Lloyd George, David. 2. Henry.** 1839-1897, U.S. economist and journalist. **3. Saint.** d. A.D. 303, Christian martyr, patron saint of England.

George I 1. 1660-1727, king of England (1714-1727). **2.** 1845-1913, king of Greece (1863-1913).

George II 1. 1683-1760, king of England (1727-1760); son of George I. **2.** 1890-1947, king of Greece (1922-1923; 1935-1947).

George III, 1738-1820, king of England (1760-1820); grandson of George II.

George IV, 1762-1830, king of England (1820-1830); son of George III.

George V, 1865-1936, king of England (1910-1936); son of Edward VII.

George VI, 1895-1952, king of England (1936-1952); son of George V.

Ge·ron·i·mo (jə ron′ə mō′) 1829?-1909, Apache chief.

Gersh·win, George (gûrsh′win) 1898-1937, U.S. composer.

Get·ty, J(ean) Paul (get′ē) 1892-1976, U.S. business executive.

Ghi·ber·ti, Lorenzo (gē beʀ′tē) 1378-1455, Florentine sculptor, goldsmith, and painter.

Gia·co·met·ti, Alberto (jä′kə met′ē) 1901-1966, Swiss sculptor and painter.

Gib·bon, Edward (gib′ən) 1737-1794, English historian and writer.

Gibbs, Josiah Willard (gibz) 1839-1903, U.S. physicist.

Gib·son, Althea (gib′sən) 1927- , U.S. tennis player.

Gide, André (zhēd) 1869-1951, French writer.

Gid·e·on (gid′ē ən) in the Old Testament, a judge of Israel.

Gil·bert, Sir William S(chwenck) (gil′bərt) 1836-1911, English librettist who collaborated with the composer Sir Arthur Sullivan.

Gins·berg, Allen (ginz′bûrg) 1926- , U.S. poet.

Gior·gio·ne (jôr jō′nē) 1478?-1510, Venetian painter.

Giot·to (jot′ō) 1266?-1337, Florentine painter; born *Giotto di Bondone*.

Gi·rau·doux, Jean (zhē RŌ dü′) 1882-1944, French playwright and novelist.

Gis·card d'Es·taing, Valéry (zhēs kär′des taN′) 1926- , French president (1974-1981).

Glad·stone, William Ewart (glad′stōn′) 1809-1898, British statesman, prime minister (1868-1874; 1880-1885; 1886; 1892-1894).

Glenn, John Herschel, Jr. (glen) 1921- , U.S. astronaut and politician; first American to orbit the earth.

God·dard, Robert Hutchings (god′ərd) 1882-1945, U.S. pioneer rocket scientist.

Go·di·va (gə dī′və) fl. 1040-1080, wife of an English nobleman. According to legend, she rode naked through the streets of Coventry, England, so that her husband would remove an unpopular tax.

Go·du·nov, Boris (gō′də nəf) 1551-1605, Russian czar (1598-1605).

Goe·thals, George Washington (gō′thəlz) 1858-1928, U.S. army engineer.

Goe·the, Johann Wolfgang von (gœ′tə) 1749-1832, German poet, playwright, novelist, and scientist.

Go·gol, Nikolai (gō′gəl) 1809-1852, Russian writer.

Gol·ding, William (gōl′ding) 1911- , British writer.

Gold·smith, Oliver (gōld′smith′) 1730-1774, English writer.

Go·li·ath (gə lī′əth) in the Old Testament, the Philistine giant whom David killed with a stone shot from a sling.

Gom·pers, Samuel (gom′pərz) 1850-1924, U.S. labor leader.

Gon·court (gôN kür′) **1. Edmond de.** 1822-1896, French writer. **2. Jules de.** 1830-1870, French writer; brother of Edmond de Goncourt.

Goodall, Jane, see Lawick-Goodall, Jane, Baroness van.

Good·man, Benny (gŭd′mən) 1909-1986, U.S. conductor and clarinetist; full name *Benjamin David Goodman.*

Good·year, Charles (gŭd′yîr′) 1800-1860, U.S. inventor of the process of vulcanizing rubber.

Gor·ba·chev, Mikhail Sergeevich (gôr′bə chəf) 1931- , Soviet general secretary of the Communist Party (1985-1990), president of the Soviet Union (1990-1991).

Gor·di·mer, Nadine (gôr′də mər) 1923- , South African writer.

Gor·gas, William Crawford (gôr′gəs) 1854-1920, U.S. army physician.

Gor·ky, Maxim (gôr′kē) *also,* **Gor·ki.** 1868-1936, Russian writer; pseudonym of *Aleksei Maksiomovich Peshkov.*

Go·ta·ma (gô′tə mə) see Buddha.

Gould, Jay (gŭld) 1836-1892, U.S. financier.

Gou·nod, Charles (gü nō′) 1818-1893, French composer.

Go·ya y Lu·ci·en·tes, Francisco José (goi′yə ē lü′sē en′täs) 1746-1828, Spanish painter and etcher.

Grac·chus (grak′əs) **1. Gaius.** 153-121 B.C., Roman political and social reformer. **2. Tiberius.** 163?-133 B.C., Roman political and social reformer; brother of Gaius Gracchus. Together, known as **the Gracchi** (grak′ē).

Gra·ham, Martha (grā′əm) 1894-1991, U.S. choreographer and dancer.

Grange, Red (grānj) 1903- , U.S. football player; born *Harold Edward Grange.*

Grant (grant) **1. Cary.** 1904-1986, English-American film actor; born *Archibald Leach.* **2. Ulysses S(impson).** 1822-1885, U.S. general, eighteenth president of the United States (1869-1877).

Grass, Günter (gräs) 1927- , German writer.

Gray (grā) **1. Asa.** 1810-1888, U.S. botanist. **2. Thomas.** 1716-1771, English poet.

Gree·ley, Horace (grē′lē) 1811-1872, U.S. journalist, writer, and politician.

Greene (grēn) **1. Graham.** 1904-1991, English writer. **2. Nathanael.** 1742-1786, colonial general in the American Revolution.

Greg·o·ry I, Saint (greg′ə rē) A.D. 540?-604, pope (A.D. 590-604); called *Gregory the Great.*

Gregory VII, Saint, 1020-1085, pope (1073-1085).

Gregory XIII, 1502-1585, pope (1572-1585) who introduced the Gregorian calendar.

Gregory of Tours, Saint (tûr) A.D. 538?-594, Frankish bishop and historian.

Gren·ville (gren′vəl) **1. George.** 1712-1770, English statesman. **2. Sir Richard.** 1542-1591, English naval commander.

Gret·zsky, Wayne (gret′skē) 1961- , Canadian ice hockey player.

Grey (grā) **1. Charles, 2nd Earl.** 1764-1845, British statesman, prime minister (1830-1834). **2. Sir Edward.** 1862-1933. British statesman, 1st Viscount Grey of Fallodon. **3. Lady Jane.** 1537-1554, queen of England for nine days in 1553. **4. Zane.** 1875-1939, U.S. writer.

Grieg, Edvard (grēg) 1843-1907, Norwegian composer.

Grif·fith, D(avid) W(ark) (grif′ith) 1875-1948, U.S. motion-picture director and producer.

Grimm (grim) two German brothers who collaborated as philologists and folklorists **1. Jakob.** 1785-1863. **2. Wilhelm.** 1786-1859.

Gris, Juan (grēs) 1887-1927, Spanish painter.

Gro·my·ko, Andrei Andreievich (grə mē′kō) 1909-1989, Soviet diplomat and statesman.

Gro·pi·us, Walter (grō′pē əs) 1883-1969, German-American architect.

Grosz (grōs) **1.** George. 1893-1959, German-American painter and graphic artist. **2. Károly.** 1930- , Hungarian politician, premier (1987-1989), general secretary of Hungary's Socialist Workers' Party (1988-1989).

Gro·ti·us, Hugo (grō′shē əs, -shəs) 1583-1645, Dutch jurist, statesman, and writer; born *Huig de Groot.*

Guar·ne·ri (gwär när′ē) family of Italian violin makers of the seventeenth and eighteenth centuries.

Gui·do d'A·rez·zo (gwē′dō dä Ret′sō) A.D. 990?-1050?, Italian music theorist.

Gui·zot, François (gē zō′) 1787-1874, French statesman.

Gus·ta·vus I (gu stä′vəs, -stä′-) 1496-1560, king of Sweden (1523-1560).

Gustavus II, 1594-1632, king of Sweden (1611-1632); known as *Gustavus Adolphus.*

Gustavus IV, 1778-1837, king of Sweden (1792-1809).

Gustavus V, 1858-1950, king of Sweden (1907-1950).

Gustavus VI, 1882-1973, king of Sweden (1950-1973).

Gustavus A·dol·phus (ə dol′fəs) see Gustavus II.

Gu·ten·berg, Johann (gü′tən bûrg′) 1400?-1468, German printer.

Guth·rie, Woody (guth′rē) 1912-1967, U.S. folk singer and composer; born *Woodrow Wilson Guthrie.*

Ha·bak·kuk (hə bak′ək) seventh century B.C., Hebrew prophet.

Ha·ber, Fritz (hä′bər) 1868-1934, German chemist.

Habs·burg (haps′bûrg′) see Hapsburg.

Ha·dri·an (hā′drē ən) A.D. 76-138, Roman emperor (A.D. 117-138); born *Publius Aelius Hadrianus.*

Ha·gar (hā′gär, -gər) in the Old Testament, the concubine of Abraham and the mother of Ishmael.

Ha·gen, Walter (hā′gən) 1892-1969, U.S. golfer.

Hag·ga·i (hag′ē ī′) sixth century B.C., Hebrew prophet.

Hahn, Otto (hän) 1879-1968, German physical chemist.

Hai·le Se·las·sie (hī′lē sə las′ē) 1892-1975, Ethiopian emperor (1930-1936; 1941-1974).

Hak·luyt, Richard (hak′lüt) 1552?-1616, English geographer and historian.

Hale (hāl) **1. Edward Everett.** 1822-1909, U.S. writer and Unitarian clergyman. **2. Nathan.** 1755-1776, American patriot.

Hall, Charles Martin (hôl) 1863-1914, U.S. chemist.

Hal·ley, Edmund (hal′ē) 1656-1742, English astronomer.

Hals, Frans (hälz) 1580?-1666, Dutch portrait painter.

Ham (ham) in the Old Testament, the second son of Noah.

Ha·man (hā′mən) in the Old Testament, a Persian official whose plot to massacre the Jews was foiled by Esther.

Ha·mil·car Bar·ca (hə mil′kär bär′kə) 270-228? B.C., Carthaginian general; father of Hannibal.

Ham·il·ton (ham′əl tən) **1. Alexander.** 1757-1804, American statesman and first secretary of the Treasury. **2. Edith.** 1867-1963, U.S. classical scholar, educator, and writer.

Ham·mar·skjöld, Dag (ham′ər shŭld′) 1905-1961, Swedish statesman, secretary-general of the United Nations (1953-1961).

Ham·mu·ra·bi (hä′mŭ rä′bē) eighteenth century B.C., Babylonian king.

Han (hän) dynasty that ruled China (206 B.C.-A.D. 220).

a	at	e	end	o	hot	u	up	hw	white		about
ā	ape	ē	me	ō	old	ū	use	ng	song		taken
ä	far	i	it	ô	fork	ü	rule	th	thin	ə	pencil
âr	care	ī	ice	oi	oil	ů	pull	th	this		lemon
				îr	pierce	ou	out	ûr	turn	zh	measure		circus

1405

Han·cock, John (han′kok) 1737-1793, American statesman, first signer of the Declaration of Independence.

Han·del, George Frederick (han′dəl) 1685-1759, British composer; born in Germany.

Han·dy, W(illiam) C(hristopher) (han′dē) 1873-1958, U.S. musician, composer, and compiler of blues music.

Han·na, Mark (han′ə) 1837-1904, U.S. politician; full name *Marcus Alonzo Hanna.*

Han·ni·bal (han′ə bəl) 247?-183? B.C., Carthaginian general.

Han·o·ver (han′ō vər) royal family that ruled Great Britain (1714-1901), beginning with George I and ending with Queen Victoria.

Haps·burg (haps′bûrg′) *also,* **Habsburg.** family that ruled Austria (1282-1918), the Holy Roman Empire (1438-1806), Spain (1516-1700), and Hungary (1526-1918).

Har·alds·son, Olav (har′əld sən) see Olav II.

Har·ding, Warren Gamaliel (här′ding) 1865-1923, twenty-ninth president of the United States (1921-1923).

Har·dy, Thomas (här′dē) 1840-1928, English writer.

Har·greaves, James (här′grēvz′) 1720?-1778, English weaver, inventor of the spinning jenny.

Har·old II (har′əld) 1022?-1066, king of the English (1066) who was defeated in the Battle of Hastings; the last Anglo-Saxon king.

Har·ris, Joel Chandler (har′is) 1848-1908, U.S. writer.

Har·ri·son (har′ə sən) **1. Benjamin.** 1833-1901, twenty-third president of the United States (1889-1893). **2. William Henry.** 1773-1841, ninth president of the United States (1841); grandfather of Benjamin Harrison.

Harte, (Francis) Bret (härt) 1839-1902, U.S. short-story writer.

Ha·run al-Ra·shid (hä rün′äl rä shēd′) *also,* **Harun ar-Rashid** (hü rün′är rä shēd′). A.D. 764?-809, fifth caliph of Baghdad (A.D. 786-809); one of the Abbasids.

Har·vey, William (här′vē) 1578-1657, English physiologist.

Has·dru·bal (haz′drü bəl) **1.** d. 221 B.C., Carthaginian general; brother-in-law of Hannibal. **2.** d. 207 B.C., Carthaginian general; brother of Hannibal.

Hat·shep·sut (hat shep′süt) queen of Egypt (1486-1468 B.C.); wife of Thutmose III.

Haupt·mann, Gerhart (houpt′män′) 1862-1946, German writer.

Ha·vel, Vaclav (hä′vəl) 1936- , Czech dissident playwright, president of Czechoslovakia (1989-).

Haw·king, Stephen W(illiam) (hô′king) 1942- , British physicist.

Haw·thorne, Nathaniel (hô′thôrn′) 1804-1864, U.S. novelist and short-story writer.

Hay·dn, Franz Joseph (hī′dən) 1732-1809, Austrian composer.

Hayes, Rutherford B(irchard) (hāz) 1822-1893, nineteenth president of the United States (1877-1881).

Haz·litt, William (haz′lit) 1778-1830, English critic and essayist.

H.D., see Doolittle, Hilda.

Hea·ney, Seamus (hē′nē) 1939- , Northern Irish poet.

Hearst, William Randolph (hûrst) 1863-1951, U.S. editor and newspaper publisher.

Heath, Edward Richard George (hēth) 1916- , British statesman, prime minister (1970-1974).

Hé·bert, Anne (ā beR′) 1916- , French-Canadian poet.

He·gel, Wilhelm Friedrich (hā′gəl) 1770-1831, German philosopher.

Hei·deg·ger, Martin (hī′di gər) 1889-1976, German philosopher.

Hei·fetz, Jascha (hī′fits) 1901-1987, Russian-American violinist.

Hei·ne, Heinrich (hī′nə) 1797-1856, German poet and essayist.

Hei·sen·berg, Werner Karl (hī′zən bûrg′) 1901-1976, German physicist.

Helm·holtz, Hermann Ludwig Ferdinand von (helm′-hōlts′) 1821-1894, German physiologist and physicist.

Hé·lo·ise (el′ō ēz′) 1101-1164, wife of Peter Abélard.

Hel·vé·ti·us, Claude Adrien (hel vā′shē əs) 1715-1771, French philosopher.

Hem·ing·way, Ernest (hem′ing wā′) 1899-1961, U.S. novelist and short-story writer.

Hen·gist and Hor·sa (heng′gist, hen′jist; hôr′sə) two brothers who are said to have led the Jutes into England in the fifth century A.D.

Hen·ley, William Ernest (hen′lē) 1849-1903, English poet, critic, and editor.

Hen·ry (hen′rē) **1. Joseph.** 1797-1878, U.S. physicist. **2. O.** see O. Henry. **3. Patrick.** 1736-1799, American statesman.

Henry I 1. 1068-1135, king of England (1100-1135). **2.** 1008?-1060, king of France (1031-1060).

Henry II 1. 1133-1189, king of England (1154-1189); first of the Plantagenet line. **2.** 1519-1559, king of France (1547-1559).

Henry III 1. 1207-1272, king of England (1216-1272). **2.** 1551-1589, king of France (1574-1589).

Henry IV 1. 1367-1413, king of England (1399-1413), founder of the house of Lancaster. **2.** 1553-1610, king of France (1589-1610); first of the Bourbon line; as Henry III, king of Navarre (1572-1610).

Henry V, 1387-1422, king of England (1413-1422).

Henry VI, 1421-1471, king of England (1422-1461; 1470-1471); last of the Lancastrian line.

Henry VII, 1457-1509, king of England (1485-1509); first Tudor king.

Henry VIII, 1491-1547, king of England (1509-1547), founder of the Church of England.

Henry of Na·varre (nə vär′) see **Henry IV** *(def. 2).*

Henry the Navigator, 1394-1460, Portuguese prince.

Hep·burn, Katharine (hep′bûrn′) 1909- , U.S. film actress.

Hep·ple·white, George (hep′əl hwīt′, -wīt′) d. 1786, English cabinetmaker.

Hep·worth, (Jocelyn) Barbara (hep′wûrth′) 1903-1975, English sculptor.

He·ra·cli·tus (her′ə klī′təs) 540?-475 B.C., Greek philosopher.

Her·bart, Johann Friedrich (heR′bärt) 1776-1841, German philosopher, psychologist, and educator.

Her·bert (hûr′bərt) **1. George.** 1593-1633, English poet. **2. Victor.** 1859-1924, Irish-American composer.

Her·der, Johann Gottfried von (heR′dər) 1744-1803, German philosopher and literary critic.

Her·od (her′əd) dynasty that ruled Palestine (37? B.C.-A.D. 100?).

Herod the Great, 73-4 B.C., king of Palestine (37-4 B.C.).

Herod An·ti·pas (an′tə pas′) 20? B.C.-A.D. 39, ruler of Judea (4 B.C.-A.D. 39); son of Herod the Great.

He·ro·di·as (hi rō′dē əs) in the New Testament, wife of Herod Antipas and mother of Salome.

He·rod·o·tus (hi rod′ə təs) 484-425 B.C., Greek historian.

He·ro of Al·ex·an·dri·a (hîr′ō; al′ig zan′drē ə) *also,* **He·ron of Alexandria** (hîr′on). fl. A.D. 62, Greek scientist, mathematician, and writer.

Her·rick, Robert (her′ik) 1591-1674, English lyric poet.

Her·ri·ot, Édouard (e rē ō′) 1872-1957, French statesman.

Her·schel (hûr′shəl) British family of astronomers including **1. Caroline Lucretia.** 1750-1848, sister of Sir William Herschel. **2. Sir John Frederick William.** 1792-1871, son of Sir William Herschel. **3. Sir William.** 1738-1822.

Her·zl, Theodor (heR′tsəl) 1860-1904, Austrian writer, founder of the Zionist movement; born in Hungary.

He·si·od (hē′zē əd) eighth century B.C., Greek poet.

Hes·se, Hermann (hes; *German* hes′ə) 1877-1962, German-Swiss novelist and poet.

Hey·er·dahl, Thor (hā′ər däl′) 1914- , Norwegian explorer, writer, anthropologist, and scientist.

Hey·wood, Thomas (hā′wŭd′) 1574?-1641, English dramatist.

Hez·e·ki·ah (hez′i kī′ə) 740?-692? B.C., king of Judah (728?-715? B.C.).

Hi·a·wa·tha (hī′ə wä′thə) sixteenth century, chieftain, probably Mohawk, credited with founding the Iroquois confederation.

Hick·ok, Wild Bill (hik′ok) 1837-1876, U.S. frontier marshal; born *James Butler Hickok.*

Hil·lel (hil′el) fl. 30 B.C.-A.D. 10, Palestinian rabbi, president of the Sanhedrin.

Himm·ler, Heinrich (him′lər) 1900-1945, German Nazi leader, head of the Gestapo during the Third Reich.

Hin·de·mith, Paul (hin′də mith) 1895-1963, German-American composer.

Hin·den·burg, Paul von (hin′dən bûrg′) 1847-1934, German field marshal, president of Germany (1925-1934).

Hip·par·chus (hi pär′kəs) second century B.C., Greek astronomer.

Hip·poc·ra·tes (hi pok′rə tēz′) 460?-370? B.C., Greek physician.

Hi·ro·hi·to (hîr′ō hē′tō) 1901-1989, Japanese emperor (1926-1989).

Hitch·cock, Sir Alfred Joseph (hich′kok) 1899-1980, British-American film director.

Hit·ler, Adolf (hit′lər) 1889-1945, German dictator, chancellor of Germany (1933-1945); born in Austria.

Hobbes, Thomas (hobz) 1588-1679, English philosopher.

Ho Chi Minh (hō′chē′min′) 1890?-1969, founder and leader of the Vietminh, president of North Vietnam (1954-1969).

Hoff·mann, E(rnst) T(heodor) A(madeus) (hof′mən) 1776-1822, German writer, musician, and painter.

Hof·stadt·er, Richard (hof′stat′ər) 1916-1970, U.S. historian.

Ho·gan, Ben (hō′gən) 1912- , U.S. golfer.

Ho·garth, William (hō′gärth) 1697-1764, English painter, engraver, and illustrator.

Ho·hen·stau·fen (hō′ən shtou′fən) German royal family that ruled the Holy Roman Empire (1138-1208; 1212-1254).

Ho·hen·zol·lern (hō′ən zol′ərn) German royal family prominent from the eleventh century to 1918 that ruled Brandenburg (1415-1918), Prussia (1525-1918), and Germany (1871-1918).

Hol·bein (hōl′bīn) **1. Hans the Elder.** 1460?-1524, German painter. **2. Hans the Younger.** 1497-1543, German painter and engraver; son of Hans the Elder.

Höl·der·lin, Friedrich (hōl′dər lin) 1770-1843, German poet.

Holmes (hōmz) **1. Oliver Wendell.** 1809-1894, U.S. writer and physician. **2. Oliver Wendell, Jr.** 1841-1935, U.S. Supreme Court associate justice (1902-1932); son of Oliver Wendell Holmes.

Ho·mer (hō′mər) eighth century? B.C., Greek poet, reputed author of the *Iliad* and *Odyssey.*

Homer, Winslow, 1836-1910, U.S. painter.

Hooke, Robert (hŭk) 1635-1702, English physicist.

Hook·er, Thomas (hŭk′ər) 1586-1647, English Puritan clergyman and one of the founders of Connecticut.

Hoo·ver, Herbert Clark (hü′vər) 1874-1964, thirty-first president of the United States (1929-1933).

Hop·kins (hop′kinz) **1. Gerard Manley.** 1844-1889, English poet. **2. Mark.** 1802-1887, U.S. educator.

Hop·per, Edward (hop′ər) 1882-1967, U.S. artist.

Hor·ace (hôr′is) 65-8 B.C., Roman poet and satirist; born *Quintus Horatius Flaccus.*

Horns·by, Rogers (hornz′bē) 1896-1963, U.S. baseball player and manager.

Hor·o·witz, Vladimir (hôr′ə wits, hor′-) 1904-1989, Russian-American pianist.

Ho·se·a (hō zē′ə) eighth century B.C., Hebrew prophet.

Hou·di·ni, Harry (hü dē′nē) 1874-1926, U.S. magician and escape artist; born *Ehrich Weiss.*

Hous·man, A(lfred) E(dward) (hous′mən) 1859-1936, English poet and scholar.

Hous·ton, Samuel (hūs′tən) 1793-1863, U.S. frontiersman and statesman, president of the Republic of Texas (1836-1838; 1841-1844).

Howe (hou) **1. Elias.** 1819-1867, U.S. inventor of the sewing machine. **2. Gordie.** 1928- , Canadian hockey player. **3. Julia Ward.** 1819-1910, U.S. writer and social reformer. **4. Sir William.** 1729-1814, British general, commander in chief of the British land forces in North America (1775-1778).

How·ells, William Dean (hou′əlz) 1837-1920, U.S. writer and editor.

Hoyle, Edmond (hoil) 1672-1769, English lawyer and writer.

Hsia (shyä) dynasty that ruled China (2205?-1557? B.C.).

Hub·ble, Edwin Powell (hub′əl) 1889-1953, U.S. astronomer.

Hud·son (hud′sən) **1. Henry.** d. 1611, English navigator and explorer in the service of Holland. **2. W(illiam) H(enry).** 1841-1922, English naturalist and writer.

Hughes (hūz) **1. Charles Evans.** 1862-1948, U.S. Supreme Court Chief Justice (1930-1941). **2. Howard Robard.** 1905-1976, U.S. entrepreneur. **3. Langston.** 1902-1967, U.S. poet. **4. Ted.** 1930- , British poet.

Hu·go, Victor (hū′gō) 1802-1885, French writer.

Hull (hul) **1. Bobby.** 1939- , Canadian ice hockey player; full name *Robert Marvin Hull, Jr.* **2. Cordell.** 1871-1955, U.S. statesman.

Hum·boldt, Friedrich Heinrich Alexander, Baron von (hum′bōlt′) 1769-1859, German scientist and statesman.

Hume, David (hūm) 1711-1776, Scottish philosopher and historian.

Hum·phrey, Hubert Horatio (hum′frē) 1911-1978, U.S. politician, vice president of the United States (1965-1969).

Hus·sein, Saddam (hü sān′) 1937- , Iraqi president (1979-).

Hussein I, 1935- , king of Jordan (1953-).

Huss, John (hus) 1369?-1415, Bohemian religious reformer.

Hutch·in·son, Anne (huch′ən sən) 1591-1643, American religious leader.

Hux·ley (huks′lē) English family including **1. Aldous.** 1894-1963, novelist and essayist. **2. Julian Sorrell.** 1877-1975, biologist; brother of Aldous Huxley. **3. Thomas Henry.** 1825-1895, biologist; grandfather of Aldous and Julian Huxley.

Huy·gens, Christian (hī′gənz) 1629-1695, Dutch physicist, astronomer, and mathematician.

Hyk·sos (hik′sōs) Asian family that ruled Egypt (1675?-1570?B.C.).

Ibn Si·na (ib′ən sē′nə) see Avicenna.

Ib·sen, Henrik Johan (ib′sən) 1828-1906, Norwegian dramatist.

Ig·na·tius of Loyola, Saint (ig nā′shəs) see Loyola, Saint Ignatius of.

Ikh·na·ton (ik nä′tən) d. 1354? B.C., king of Egypt (1379-1362 B.C.). Also, **Akhenaton, Amenhotep IV.**

In·gres, Jean Auguste Dominique (aɴ′grə) 1780-1867, French painter.

In·no·cent II (in′ə sənt) d. 1143, pope (1130-1143).

Innocent III, 1161?-1216, pope (1198-1216).

Innocent IV, 1180?-1254, pope (1243-1254).

Innocent XI, 1611-1689, pope (1676-1689).

Ir·ving, Washington (ûr′ving) 1783-1859, U.S. writer.

I·saac (ī′zək) in the Old Testament, the son of Abraham and Sarah and the father of Jacob and Esau.

Is·a·bel·la I (iz′ə bel′ə) 1451-1504, Spanish queen of Castile; wife of Ferdinand V.

I·sai·ah (ī zā′ə) eighth century B.C., Hebrew prophet.

I·sai·as (ī zā′əs) in the Douay Bible, Isaiah.

Is·ca·ri·ot (is kar′ē ət) see Judas.

Ish·ma·el (ish′mē əl) in the Old Testament, the son of Abraham and Hagar.

Is·ra·el (iz′rē əl) in the Old Testament, the name given to Jacob after he wrestled with the angel.

Is·sa·char (is′ə kär′) **1.** in the Old Testament, a son of Jacob and Leah. **2.** one of the twelve tribes of Israel descended from him.

I·van III (ī′vən) 1440-1505, Russian ruler (1462-1505). Also, **Ivan the Great.**

Ivan IV, 1530-1584, Russian czar (1533-1584). Also, **Ivan the Terrible.**

Ivan the Great, see Ivan III.

Ives, Charles Edward (īvz) 1874-1954, U.S. composer.

Jack·son (jak′sən) **1. Andrew.** 1767-1845, seventh president of the United States (1829-1837). **2. Thomas ("Stonewall").** 1824-1863, Confederate general in the American Civil War.

Ja·cob (jā′kəb) in the Old Testament, the son of Isaac and Rebecca, twin brother of Esau, and husband of Leah and Rachel; ancestor of the twelve tribes of Israel.

James (jāmz) **1.** d. A.D. 43?, one of the twelve Apostles of Jesus, son of Zebedee, brother of John; called *James the Greater.* **2.** in the New Testament, one of the twelve Apostles of Jesus. **3.** in the New Testament, a person identified as the brother of Jesus, probably the writer of the Epistle of James; called *James the Less.*

James 1. Henry. 1843-1916, U.S. writer and critic. **2. Jesse (Woodson).** 1847-1882, U.S. outlaw. **3. William.** 1842-1910, U.S. psychologist and philosopher; brother of Henry James.

James I, 1566-1625, king of England (1603-1625); as James VI, king of Scotland (1567-1625).

James II, 1633-1701, king of England, Scotland, and Ireland (1685-1688).

Jay, John (jā) 1745-1829, American statesman and first Chief Justice of the U.S. Supreme Court (1789-1795).

Jeanne d'Arc (zhän därk′) see Joan of Arc.

Jef·fer·son, Thomas (jef′ər sən) 1743-1826, third president of the United States (1801-1809).

Je·hosh·a·phat (jə hosh′ə fat′, -hos′-) king of Judah (873?-848? B.C.).

Jen·ghis Khan (jeng′gis kän′, -giz) *also,* **Jen·ghiz Khan.** see Genghis Khan.

Jen·ner, Edward (jen′ər) 1749-1833, English physician.

Jeph·thah (jef′thə, jep′-) in the Old Testament, a judge of Israel.

Jer·e·mi·ah (jer′ə mī′ə) seventh and sixth centuries B.C., Hebrew prophet.

Jer·e·mi·as (jer′ə mī′əs) in the Douay Bible, Jeremiah.

Jer·o·bo·am (jer′ə bō′əm) founder and first king of Israel (937?-915? B.C.).

Je·rome, Saint (jə rōm′) A.D. 342?-420, monk and Father of the Church, writer of the Vulgate.

Je·su (jē′zü, -sü, jā′-) see Jesus.

Je·sus (jē′zəs) 4? B.C.-A.D. 29?, considered by Christians to be the Messiah and the Son of God. Also, **Jesus Christ.**

Jez·e·bel (jez′ə bəl′) in the Old Testament, wife of Ahab.

a	at	e	end	o	hot	u	up	hw	white		about
ā	ape	ē	me	ō	old	ū	use	ng	song		taken
ä	far	i	it	ô	fork	ü	rule	th	thin	ə	pencil
âr	care	ī	ice	oi	oil	u̇	pull	th	this		lemon
			îr pierce	ou	out	ûr	turn	zh	measure		circus

Jin·nah, Muhammed Ali (jin′ə) 1876-1948, Indian Muslim leader, first president of Pakistan (1947-1948).

Jo·ab (jō′ab) in the Old Testament, commander of King David's army.

Joan of Arc (jōn) 1412-1431, French national heroine. Also, **Jeanne d'Arc, Maid of Orléans.**

Job (jōb) in the Old Testament, a righteous man who patiently accepted the trials with which God tested his faith.

Jo·el (jō′əl) in the Old Testament, a Hebrew prophet.

John (jon) **1.** one of the Apostles of Jesus, brother of James the Greater, and reputed writer of the Gospel of John, three Epistles, and the Book of Revelation. **2.** see **John the Baptist. 3.** 1167?-1216, king of England (1199-1216) who signed the Magna Carta (1215).

John XXIII, 1881-1963, pope (1958-1963).

John Paul I, 1912-1978, pope (1978).

John Paul II, 1920- , pope (1978-).

John·son (jon′sən) **1. Andrew.** 1808-1875, seventeenth president of the United States (1865-1869). **2. James Weldon.** 1871-1938, U.S. author and diplomat. **3. Lyndon Baines.** 1908-1973, thirty-sixth president of the United States (1963-1969). **4. Samuel.** 1709-1784, English writer, critic, and lexicographer. **5. Walter Perry.** 1887-1946, U.S. baseball player.

John the Baptist, d. A.D. 29?, in the New Testament, a Jewish teacher and the baptizer of Jesus, beheaded by Herod Antipas.

Jol·li·et, Louis (jō′lē et′, zhōl yā′) also, **Jo·li·et.** 1645-1700, French-Canadian explorer.

Jo·nah (jō′nə) in the Old Testament, a Hebrew prophet who was swallowed by a large fish and three days later cast up on land unharmed.

Jo·nas (jō′nəs) in the Douay Bible, Jonah.

Jon·a·than (jon′ə thən) in the Old Testament, a son of Saul and a close friend of David.

Jones (jōnz) **1. Bobby.** 1902-1971, U.S. golfer; full name *Robert Tyre Jones, Jr.* **2. Inigo.** 1573-1652, English architect. **3. James Earl.** 1931- , U.S. actor. **4. John Paul.** 1747-1792, colonial naval hero in the American Revolution; born *John Paul.*

Jon·son, Ben (jon′sən) 1573?-1637, English dramatist and poet.

Jop·lin, Scott (jop′lin) 1868-1917, U.S. pianist and composer.

Jo·seph (jō′zəf, -səf) **1.** in the Old Testament, the older son of Jacob and Rachel. **2.** in the New Testament, husband of Mary, the mother of Jesus.

Joseph, Chief 1840?-1904, Nez Percé chief.

Jo·se·phine (jō′zə fēn′, -sə-) 1763-1814, French empress (1804-1809); wife of Napoleon Bonaparte. Also, **Josephine de Beauharnais.**

Jo·se·phus, Flavius (jō sē′fəs) A.D. 37?-95, Jewish historian and soldier.

Josh·u·a (josh′ü ə) in the Old Testament, the successor of Moses who led the Israelites into Canaan.

Jo·si·ah (jō sī′ə) d. 608 B.C., king of Judah (639-608 B.C.).

Jos·u·e (jos′ū ē) in the Douay Bible, Joshua.

Joyce, James (jois) 1882-1941, Irish writer.

Juan Car·los I (hwän kär′lōs) 1938- , Spanish king (1975-).

Juá·rez, Benito Pablo (wär′ez; *Spanish* hwä′Res) 1806-1872, Mexican president (1858-1865; 1867-1872).

Ju·bal (jü′bəl) in the Old Testament, a descendant of Cain; inventor of musical instruments.

Ju·dah (jü′də) **1.** in the Old Testament, a son of Jacob and Leah. **2.** one of the twelve tribes of Israel descended from him.

Ju·das (jü′dəs) **1.** in the New Testament, the Apostle who betrayed Jesus for thirty pieces of silver. Also, **Judas Iscariot. 2.** see **Jude.**

Jude (jüd) in the New Testament, one of the twelve Apostles of Jesus; the reputed writer of the Book of Jude in the New Testament. Also, **Judas.**

Ju·dith (jü′dith) in the Old Testament, a Jewish heroine.

Ju·li·an (jü′lē ən) A.D. 332-363, Roman emperor (A.D. 361-363). Also, **Julian the Apostate.**

Jul·ius Cae·sar (jül′yəs sē′zər) see **Caesar, Gaius Julius.**

Jung, Carl Gustav (yùng) 1875-1961, Swiss psychiatrist.

Jus·tin·i·an I (jus tin′ē ən) A.D. 483-565, emperor of the Byzantine Empire (A.D. 527-565).

Ju·ve·nal (jü′və nəl) A.D. 60?-140?, Roman satirist.

Ká·dár, János (kä′där) 1912-1989, Hungarian communist leader; premier (1956-1958; 1961-1965); general secretary of the Hungarian Communist Party (1956-1988).

Kaf·ka, Franz (käf′kə) 1883-1924, Austrian novelist and short-story writer.

Ka·li·da·sa (kä′li dä′sə) fifth century A.D., Indian poet and dramatist.

Ka·me·ha·me·ha I (kə mā′ə mā′ə) 1753?-1819, king of the Hawaiian Islands (1810-1819).

Kan·din·sky, Vasily (kan din′skē) 1866-1944, Russian painter.

Kant, Immanuel (kant, känt) 1724-1804, German philosopher.

Ka·un·da, Kenneth (kä ün′dä) 1924- , Zambian president (1964-1991).

Ka·wa·ba·ta Yasunari (kä′wə bä′tə) 1899-1972, Japanese writer.

Ka·zan·tza·kis, Nikos (kä′zən zä′kis, -zän dzä′kēs) 1883-1957, Greek writer.

Kean, Edmund (kēn) 1787-1833, English actor.

Keats, John (kēts) 1795-1821, English poet.

Kek·ko·nen, Urho Kaleva (kek′ə nən) 1900-1986, Finnish president (1956-1981).

Kel·ler, Helen Adams (kel′ər) 1880-1968, U.S. writer and lecturer who was deaf and blind from infancy.

Kel·vin, Lord (kel′vin) 1824-1907, British physicist; born *William Thomson.*

Kempis, Thomas à, see Thomas à Kempis.

Ken·ne·dy (ken′i dē) **1. Anthony M.** 1936- , U.S. Supreme Court associate justice (1988-). **2. John Fitzgerald.** 1917-1963, thirty-fifth president of the United States (1961-1963).

Ken·yat·ta, Jomo (ken yä′tə) 1893?-1978, Kenyan president (1964-1978).

Kep·ler, Johannes (kep′lər) 1571-1630, German astronomer.

Ke·ren·sky, Alexander (kə ren′skē, ker′ən-) 1881-1970, Russian revolutionary leader.

Key, Francis Scott (kē) 1779-1843, U.S. lawyer, writer of "The Star-Spangled Banner."

Keynes, John Maynard (kēnz) 1883-1946, English economist.

Kho·mei·ni, Ayatollah Ruhollah (kō mā′nē, hō-) 1902-1989, religious leader, ruler of Iran (1979-1989).

Khrush·chev, Nikita (krùsh′chef, -chôf, krüsh′-) 1894-1971, Soviet politician, first secretary of the Communist Party (1958-1964).

Khu·fu (kü′fü) king of Egypt (2650?-2630? B.C.). Also, **Cheops.**

Kidd, William (kid) 1645?-1701, British pirate; known as *Captain Kidd.*

Kier·ke·gaard, Søren Aabye (kîr′kə gärd′) 1813-1855, Danish philosopher and theologian.

King (king) **1. Billie Jean.** 1943- , U.S. tennis player. **2. Martin Luther, Jr.** 1929-1968, U.S. clergyman and civil rights leader. **3. William Lyon Mackenzie.** 1874-1950, Canadian prime minister (1921-1925; 1926-1930; 1935-1948).

Kin·sey, Alfred Charles (kin′zē) 1894-1956, U.S. researcher in human sexuality.

Kip·ling, Rudyard (kip′ling) 1865-1936, English writer.

Kis·sin·ger, Henry (kis′in jər) 1923- , U.S. secretary of state (1973-1977).

Kitch·e·ner of Khartoum, 1st Earl (kich′ə nər) 1850-1916, British field marshal; born *Horatio Herbert Kitchener.*

Klee, Paul (klā) 1879-1940, Swiss artist.

Knox, John (noks) 1505?-1572, Scottish religious reformer, founder of Presbyterianism.

Koch, Robert (kôκH) 1843-1910, German bacteriologist and physician.

Kohl, Helmut (kōl) 1930- , chancellor of West Germany (1982-1990), chancellor of Germany (1990-).

Kos·ci·us·ko, Thaddeus (kos′ē us′kō) 1746-1817, Polish patriot who served in the colonial army during the American Revolution.

Kos·suth, Louis (kos′üth, kô′shùt) 1802-1894, Hungarian patriot and statesman.

Ko·sy·gin, Aleksei Nikolayevich (kə sē′gin) 1904-1980, Soviet political leader, premier (1964-1980).

Krebs, Sir Hans Adolf (krebz) 1900-1981, British biochemist.

Kreis·ler, Fritz (krīs′lər) 1875-1962, Austrian-American violinist and composer.

Ku·blai Khan (kü′blī kän′) 1215?-1294, Mongol emperor of China (1260-1294); grandson of Genghis Khan.

Ku·ro·sa·wa, Akira (kùr′ə sä′wə) 1910- , Japanese film director.

La·fa·yette, Marquis de (laf′ē et′, laf′ā-, lä′fē-, lä′fā-) 1757-1834, French general and statesman.

Laf·fite, Jean (lä fēt′) also, **Jean La·fitte.** 1780?-1826?, French pirate in America.

La Fol·lette, Robert Marion (lə fol′it) 1855-1925, U.S. politician.

La Fon·taine, Jean de (lä fon ten′) 1621-1695, French poet and writer of fables.

La·Fon·taine, Sir Louis Hippolyte (lä fon tän′) 1807-1864, Canadian political leader.

La·marck, Jean, Chevalier de (lə märk′) 1744-1829, French naturalist.

La·mar·tine, Alphonse Marie Louis de (lä mär tēn′) 1790-1869, French poet and statesman.

Lamb, Charles (lam) 1775-1834, English essayist and critic who sometimes used the pen name *Elia.*

Lan·cas·ter (lang′kə stər) English royal family (1399-1461).

Lang·land, William (lang′lənd) 1332?-1400?, English poet.

Lang·ley, Samuel Pierpont (lang′lē) 1834-1906, U.S. astronomer and pioneer in aviation.

La·nier, Sidney (lə nîr′) 1842-1881, U.S. poet.

Lao-tsu (lou′dzu′) *also,* **Lao-tse, Lao·tze.** b. 600? B.C., Chinese philosopher, reputed founder of Taoism.

La·place, Pierre Simon, Marquis de (lä pläs′) 1749-1827, French mathematician and astronomer.

Lar·kin, Philip (lär′kin) 1922- , English poet.

La Roche·fou·cauld, François, Duc de (lä rôsh fü kō′) 1613-1680, French writer noted for his maxims.

La Salle, René Cavelier, Sieur de (lə sal′) 1643-1687, French explorer.

Laud, William (lôd) 1573-1645, archbishop of Canterbury (1633-1645).

Lau·ri·er, Sir Wilfrid (lôr′ē ā′) 1841-1919, Canadian prime minister (1896-1911).

La·val, Pierre (lə val′) 1883-1945, French politician, premier of Vichy France (1942-1945).

La·ver, Rod (lā′vər) 1938- , Australian tennis player; full name *Rodney George Laver.*

La·voi·sier, Antoine Laurent (lə vwä zyā′) 1743-1794, French chemist and physician.

Law, Andrew Bonar (lô) 1858-1923, British politician, prime minister (1922-1923).

Law·ick-Good·all, Jane, Baroness van (lô′wik gụd′ôl′) 1934- , British ethologist.

Law·rence (lôr′əns) **1.** D(avid) H(erbert). 1885-1930, English novelist and poet. **2.** Ernest Orlando. 1901-1958, U.S. physicist. **3.** T(homas) E(dward). 1888-1935, English soldier, adventurer, and writer; known as *Lawrence of Arabia.*

Laz·a·rus (laz′ər əs) in the New Testament, a man who Jesus brought back to life; brother of Mary and Martha.

Le·ah (lē′ə, lā′ə) in the Old Testament, Jacob's first wife.

Lea·key (lē′kē) British family of anthropologists and paleontologists including **1.** Louis Seymour Bazett. 1903-1972. **2.** Mary (Douglas). 1913- , wife of Louis Seymour Bazett Leakey. **3.** Richard. 1944- , son of Mary and Louis Leakey; born in Kenya.

Le Châ·te·lier, Henry Louis (lə shä təl yā′) 1850-1936, French chemist.

Le Cor·bu·sier (lə kôr by zyā′) 1887-1965, Swiss architect; born *Charles Édouard Jeanneret.*

Lee (lē) **1.** Henry. 1756-1818, colonial soldier in the American Revolution; known as *Light-Horse Harry;* father of Robert E. Lee. **2.** Richard Henry. 1732-1794, American statesman. **3.** Robert E. 1807-1870, U.S. army officer, Confederate general in the American Civil War.

Leeu·wen·hoek, Anton van (lā′vən hụk′) 1632-1732, Dutch naturalist.

Leib·niz, Gottfried Wilhelm von (līb′nits) 1646-1716, German philosopher and mathematician.

Len·in, Vladimir Ilyich (len′in) 1870-1924, Russian revolutionary leader, founder of the Soviet Union; born *Vladimir Ilyich Ulyanov;* sometimes called *Nikolai Lenin.*

Le·o I, Saint (lē′ō) A.D. 400?-461, pope (A.D. 440-461). Also, Leo the Great.

Leo III, Saint, A.D. 750?-816, pope (A.D. 795-816).

Leo X, 1475-1521, pope (1513-1521).

Leo XIII, 1810-1903, pope (1878-1903).

Le·o·nar·do da Vin·ci (lē′ə när′dō də vin′chē) 1452-1519, Italian artist and scientist.

Ler·mon·tov, Mikhail Yureyevich (lâr′mən tôf′) 1814-1841, Russian poet and novelist.

Le·vi (lē′vī) **1.** in the Old Testament, a son of Jacob and Leah. **2.** the priestly tribe of Israel.

Lé·vi-Strauss, Claude (lā′vē strous′) 1908- , French anthropologist.

Lew·is (lü′is) **1.** John L(lewellyn). 1880-1969, U.S. labor leader. **2.** Meriwether. 1774-1809, U.S. explorer with William Clark. **3.** Sinclair. 1885-1951, U.S. novelist.

Lie, Trygve Halvdan (lē) 1896-1968, Norwegian statesman, first secretary-general of the United Nations (1946-1953).

Li·li·u·o·ka·la·ni (lē lē′ü ō kä lä′nē) 1838-1917, queen of the Hawaiian Islands (1891-1893); the last Hawaiian queen.

Lin·coln, Abraham (ling′kən) 1809-1865, sixteenth president of the United States (1861-1865).

Lind, Jenny (lind) 1820-1887, Swedish soprano; known as the *Swedish nightingale.*

Lind·bergh, Charles A(ugustus) (lind′bûrg′) 1902-1974, U.S. aviator.

Lin·nae·us, Carolus (lə nē′əs) 1707-1778, Swedish naturalist and botanist.

Li Po (lē′bō′) A.D. 701-762, Chinese poet. Also, Li Tai Po, Li T'ai Po.

Lip·pi, Fra Filippo (lip′ē) 1406?-1469, Florentine painter.

Lis·ter, Joseph (lis′tər) 1827-1912, English surgeon.

Liszt, Franz (list) 1811-1886, Hungarian composer and pianist.

Li Tai Po (lē′tī′bō′) *also,* Li T'ai Po. see Li Po.

Liv·ing·stone, David (liv′ing stən) 1813-1873, Scottish missionary and explorer in Africa.

Liv·y (liv′ē) 59 B.C.-A.D. 17, Roman historian; born *Titus Livius.*

Lloyd George, David (loid′jôrj′) 1863-1945, British statesman, prime minister (1916-1922).

Locke, John (lok) 1632-1704, English philosopher.

Lodge, Henry Cabot (loj) 1850-1924, U.S. statesman and historian.

Lom·bar·di, Vince (lom bär′dē) 1913-1970, U.S. football coach; full name *Vincent Thomas Lombardi.*

Lon·don, Jack (lun′dən) 1876-1916, U.S. novelist and short-story writer.

Long, Huey Pierce (lông) 1893-1935, U.S. politician.

Long·fel·low, Henry Wadsworth (lông′fel′ō) 1807-1882, U.S. poet.

Long·street, James (lông′strēt′) 1821-1904, Confederate general in the American Civil War.

Lo·pe de Ve·ga (lō′pā də vā′gə) 1562-1635, Spanish dramatist and poet; born *Lope Félix de Vega Carpio.*

Lo·renz, Konrad Zacharias (lô′rents) 1903-1989, Austrian animal behaviorist.

Lorrain, Claude, see Claude Lorrain.

Lot (lot) in the Old Testament, a nephew of Abraham whose wife looked back at the destruction of Sodom and was changed into a pillar of salt.

Lou·is, Joe (lü′is) 1914-1981, U.S. boxer.

Lou·is IX (lü′ē) 1214-1270, king of France (1226-1270). Also, Saint Louis.

Louis XI, 1423-1483, king of France (1461-1483).

Louis XIII, 1601-1643, king of France (1610-1643).

Louis XIV, 1638-1715, king of France (1643-1715); called *the Sun King.*

Louis XV, 1710-1774, king of France (1715-1774).

Louis XVI, 1754-1793, king of France (1774-1792).

Louis XVIII, 1755-1824, king of France (1814-1824); successor of Napoleon I.

Louis Na·po·le·on (nə pō′lē ən) see Napoleon III.

Louis Phi·lippe (fə lēp′) 1773-1850, king of France (1830-1848).

Low·ell (lō′əl) **1.** James Russell. 1819-1891, U.S. poet, essayist, and critic. **2.** Robert Traill Spence. 1917-1977, U.S. poet.

Low·ry, (Clarence) Malcolm (lou′rē) 1909-1957, British writer.

Loy·o·la, Saint Ignatius of (loi ō′lə) 1491?-1556, Spanish ecclesiastic, founder of the Jesuits.

Lu·cian (lü′shən) A.D. 120?-180, Greek satirist.

Lu·cre·tius (lü krē′shəs) 99?-55 B.C., Roman poet.

Lu·cul·lus (lü kul′əs) 117?-56? B.C., Roman general.

Lu Hsün (lü′shyn′) 1881-1936, Chinese writer; pseudonym of *Chou Shu-jen.*

Luke (lük) in the New Testament, a physician and a companion of Paul; one of the Evangelists, the reputed writer of Acts.

Lu·ther, Martin (lü′thər) 1483-1546, German theologian and a leader of the Protestant Reformation.

Ly·ell, Sir Charles (lī′əl) 1797-1875, British geologist.

Lyl·y, John (lil′ē) 1554?-1606, English writer.

Ly·sen·ko, Trofim Denisovich (li seng′kō) 1898-1976, Soviet scientist.

Lytton, see Bulwer-Lytton.

Mac·Ar·thur, Douglas (mə kär′thər) 1880-1964, U.S. general.

Ma·cau·lay, Thomas Babington, 1st Baron (mə kô′lē) 1800-1859, English historian, essayist, poet, and statesman.

a	at	e	end	o	hot	u	up	hw	white		about
ā	ape	ē	me	ō	old	ū	use	ng	song		taken
ä	far	i	it	ô	fork	ü	rule	th	thin	ə	pencil
âr	care	ī	ice	oi	oil	ụ	pull	th	this		lemon
		îr	pierce	ou	out	ûr	turn	zh	measure		circus

Mac·ca·bees (mak′ə bēz′) family of Jewish patriots that ruled Judea in the second and first centuries B.C.

Mac·ca·be·us, Judas (mak′ə bē′əs) *also,* **Mac·ca·bae·us.** d. 160? B.C., Jewish patriot and military leader.

Mac·don·ald, Sir John Alexander (mək don′əld) 1815-1891, first prime minister of Canada (1867-1873; 1878-1891).

Mac·Don·ald, Ramsay (mək don′əld) 1866-1937, British statesman, prime minister (1924; 1929-1931; 1931-1935).

Mach, Ernst (mäk) 1838-1916, Austrian physicist, physiologist, and psychologist.

Ma·chi·a·vel·li, Niccolò (mak′ē ə vel′ē) 1469-1527, Florentine writer and statesman.

Mac·ken·zie (mə ken′zē) **1. Sir Alexander.** 1764?-1820, Scottish fur trader and explorer in Canada. **2. Alexander.** 1822-1892, Canadian statesman, prime minister (1873-1878). **3. William Lyon.** 1795-1861, Canadian journalist and insurgent leader.

Mac·Leish, Archibald (mə klēsh′) 1892-1982, U.S. poet, dramatist, and critic.

Mac·mil·lan, Harold (mək mil′ən) 1894-1986, British statesman, prime minister (1957-1963).

Mad·i·son (mad′ə sən) **1. Dolley** or **Dolly.** 1768-1849, wife of James Madison. **2. James.** 1751-1836, fourth president of the United States (1809-1817).

Mae·ce·nas, Gaius Cilnius (mi sē′nəs) 70?-8 B.C., Roman statesman and literary patron.

Mag·da·len (mag′də lən) *also,* **Magdalene.** see **Mary Magdalene.**

Ma·gel·lan, Ferdinand (mə jel′ən) 1480?-1521, Portuguese explorer and navigator.

Ma·gritte, René (ma grēt′) 1898-1967, Belgian painter.

Mah·ler, Gustav (mä′lər) 1860-1911, Austrian composer and conductor.

Ma·hom·et (mə hom′it) see **Muhammad.**

Maid of Or·lé·ans (ôr′lē ənz, ôr lā än′) see **Joan of Arc.**

Mai·ler, Norman (mā′lər) 1923- , U.S. writer.

Mai·mon·i·des (mī mon′i dēz′) 1135-1204, Spanish-born Jewish philosopher and theologian; born *Moses ben Maimon.*

Ma·jor, John (mā′jər) 1943- , British prime minister (1990-).

Mal·a·chi (mal′ə kī′) fifth century B.C., Hebrew prophet.

Mal·colm X (mal′kəm eks′) 1925-1965, U.S. civil rights leader; born *Malcolm Little.*

Ma·li·now·ski, Bronislaw (mal′ə nôf′skē) 1884-1942, British anthropologist.

Mal·lar·mé, Stéphane (mal är mā′) 1842-1898, French poet.

Mal·o·ry, Sir Thomas (mal′ə rē) d. 1471, English writer.

Mal·thus, Thomas Robert (môl′thəs) 1766-1834, English economist.

Mam·e·luke (mam′ə lük′) a military class that ruled Egypt (1250?-1517) and remained powerful until 1811.

Ma·nas·seh (mə nas′ə) **1.** in the Old Testament, the elder son of Joseph. **2.** one of the twelve tribes of Israel descended from him. **3.** king of Judah (seventh century B.C.).

Man·chu (man chü′) see **Qing.**

Man·co Ca·pac (mäng′kō kä päk′) 1500?-1544, last emperor of the Incas (1534-1544).

Man·de·la, Nelson Rolihlahla (man del′ə) 1918- , South African political leader.

Ma·net, Édouard (ma nā′) 1832-1883, French painter.

Man·ley, Michael Norman (man′lē) 1924- , Jamaican prime minister (1972-1980; 1989-1992).

Mann (*def. 1,* man; *def. 2,* män, man) **1. Horace.** 1796-1859, U.S. educator. **2. Thomas.** 1875-1955, German writer.

Mans·field, Katherine (manz′fēld′) 1888-1923, British writer.

Man·uel I (man wel′) 1469-1521, king of Portugal (1495-1521).

Mao Ze·dong (mou′dze′dúng′) *also,* **Mao Tse-tung.** 1893-1976, Chinese political leader, founder of the People's Republic of China.

Ma·rat, Jean-Paul (mä ʀä′) 1743-1793, French revolutionary leader.

Marc An·to·ny (märk an′tə nē) *also,* **Mark Antony.** 83?-30 B.C., Roman general and political leader, friend of Julius Caesar.

Mar·ci·a·no, Rocky (mär′sē ä′nō) 1924-1969, U.S. boxer; born *Rocco Francis Machegiano.*

Mar·co·ni, Guglielmo (mär kō′nē) 1874-1937, Italian electrical engineer.

Mar·co Po·lo (mär′kō pō′lō) 1254-1324, Italian traveler.

Mar·cos, Ferdinand Edralin (mär′kōs) 1917-1989, Philippine president (1965-1986).

Mar·cus Au·re·li·us An·to·ni·nus (mär′kəs ô rē′lē əs an′tə nī′nəs) A.D. 121-180, Roman emperor (A.D. 161-180) and philosopher.

Mar·ga·ret I (mär′gə rit, mär′grit) 1353-1412, queen of Denmark, Sweden, and Norway.

Margaret of An·gou·lême (äN gü lem′) see **Margaret of Navarre.**

Margaret of An·jou (an′jü, äN′zhü) 1430-1482, queen consort of Henry VI of England.

Margaret of Na·varre (nə vär′) 1492-1549, queen of Navarre (1544-1549). Also, **Margaret of Angoulême.**

Margaret of Val·ois (val wä′) 1553-1615, queen of France and Navarre.

Ma·ri·a The·re·sa (mə rē′ə tə rā′sə, tə rā′zə) 1717-1780, archduchess of Austria, queen of Hungary and Bohemia (1740-1780).

Ma·rie An·toi·nette (mə rē′ an′twə net′) 1755-1793, queen of France (1774-1792).

Marie Lou·ise (lü ēz′) 1791-1847, Austrian princess, empress of France (1810-1814); second wife of Napoleon I.

Mar·i·us, Gaius (mâr′ē əs, mar′-) 157-86 B.C., Roman general.

Mark (märk) in the New Testament, a disciple of Peter and Paul; one of the Evangelists.

Mark Antony, see **Marc Antony.**

Marl·bor·ough, 1st Duke of (märl′bûr′ō, -bər ə) see **Churchill** *(def. 1).*

Mar·lowe, Christopher (mär′lō) 1564-1593, English dramatist and poet.

Mar·quette, Jacques (mär ket′) 1637-1675, French missionary, priest, and explorer.

Mar·shall (mär′shəl) **1. George Catlett.** 1880-1959, U.S. general and statesman. **2. John.** 1755-1835, U.S. Supreme Court Chief Justice (1801-1835). **3. Thurgood.** 1907- , U.S. Supreme Court associate justice (1967-1991).

Martel, Charles, see **Charles Martel.**

Mar·tha (mär′thə) in the New Testament, a follower of Jesus and the sister of Mary and Lazarus.

Mar·ti, José (mär tē′) 1853-1893, Cuban poet and patriot.

Mar·tin, Saint (mär′tən) A.D. 316?-397, French bishop.

Mar·vell, Andrew (mär′vəl) 1621-1678, English poet and satirist.

Marx, Karl (märks) 1818-1883, German socialist philosopher and economist.

Mar·y (mâr′ē) **1.** in the New Testament, the mother of Jesus. Also, **Blessed Virgin, Virgin Mary. 2.** in the New Testament, a follower of Jesus, the sister of Martha and Lazarus.

Mary I, 1516-1558, queen of England (1553-1558); wife of Philip II of Spain; known as *Bloody Mary.* Also, **Mary Tudor.**

Mary II, 1662-1694, queen of England (1689-1694).

Mary Mag·da·lene (mag′də lēn′, -lən) in the New Testament, a woman from whom Jesus cast out seven devils.

Mary, Queen of Scots, 1542-1587, queen of Scotland (1542-1567). Also, **Mary Stuart.**

Mary Tu·dor (tü′dər, tū′-) see **Mary I.**

Ma·sac·cio (mə sä′chē ō′) 1401-1428, Italian painter; born *Tommaso Guidi.*

Mase·field, John (mās′fēld′) 1878-1967, English poet.

Ma·son, George (mā′sən) 1725-1792, American statesman.

Mas·sa·soit (mas′ə soit′) 1580?-1661, Wampanoag chief, friend of Roger Williams.

Math·er, Cotton (math′ər) 1663-1728, American Puritan clergyman and writer.

Math·ew·son, Christy (math′ü sən) 1880-1925, U.S. baseball player; full name *Christopher Mathewson.*

Ma·tisse, Henri (ma tēs′) 1869-1954, French painter.

Mat·su·o Ba·sho (mät sü′ō bä′shō) 1644-1694, Japanese poet; pen name of *Matsuo Munefusa.*

Mat·thew (math′ü) in the New Testament, one of the twelve Apostles of Jesus; one of the Evangelists.

Maugham, (William) Somerset (môm) 1874-1965, English writer.

Mau·pas·sant, Guy de (mō′pə sänt′, mō pa säN′) 1850-1893, French short-story writer and novelist.

Max·i·mil·ian (mak′sə mil′yən) 1832-1867, archduke of Austria; emperor of Mexico (1864-1867).

Maximilian I, 1459-1519, emperor of the Holy Roman Empire (1493-1519).

Maximilian II, 1527-1576, emperor of the Holy Roman Empire (1564-1576).

Ma·ya·kov·sky, Vladimir Vladimirovich (mä′yə kôf′skē) 1893-1930, Russian poet and dramatist.

Mays, Willie (Howard, Jr.) (māz) 1931- , U.S. baseball player.

Maz·a·rin, Jules (maz′ə rin) 1602-1661, French statesman.

Maz·zi·ni, Giuseppe (mät sē′nē, mäd zē′nē) 1805-1872, Italian revolutionary and patriot.

Mc·Car·thy, Joseph R(aymond) (mə kär′thē) 1908-1957, U.S. politician, senator from Wisconsin (1947-1957).
Mc·Clel·lan, George Brinton (mə klel′ən) 1826-1885, Union general in the American Civil War.
Mc·Clin·tock, Barbara (mə klin′tək) 1902- , U.S. botanist.
Mc·Cor·mick, Cyrus Hall (mə kôr′mək) 1809-1884, U.S. inventor of the reaping machine.
Mc·Kin·ley, William (mə kin′lē) 1843-1901, twenty-fifth president of the United States (1897-1901).
Mead, Margaret (mēd) 1901-1978, U.S. anthropologist.
Meade, George Gordon (mēd) 1815-1872, Union general in the American Civil War.
Med·i·ci (med′i chē′) powerful family of Florence including **1. Catherine de′.** see **Catherine de′ Medici. 2. Cosimo de′.** 1389-1464, ruler of Florence and patron of the arts. **3. Cosimo I de′.** 1519-1574, ruler of Florence and grand duke of Tuscany. **4. Lorenzo de′.** 1449-1492, ruler of Florence and patron of the arts; called *the Magnificent.* **5. Marie de′.** 1573-1642, queen of Henry IV of France and regent of France after his death.
Meigh·en, Arthur (mē′ən) 1874-1960, Canadian statesman, prime minister (1920-1921; 1926).
Mei·ji (mā′jē′) see **Mutsuhito.**
Me·ir, Golda (me îr′) 1898-1978, Israeli prime minister (1969-1974); born in Russia as *Golda Mabovitch.*
Meit·ner, Lise (mīt′nər) 1878-1968, German physicist.
Me·lanch·thon, Philipp (mə langk′thən) 1497-1560, German scholar, humanist, and religious reformer; original surname *Schwartzerd.*
Mel·ba, Dame Nellie (mel′bə) 1861-1931, Australian soprano; stage name of *Helen Porter Mitchell.*
Mel·lon, Andrew William (mel′ən) 1855-1937, U.S. financier, secretary of the Treasury (1921-1932).
Mel·ville, Herman (mel′vil) 1819-1891, U.S. writer.
Men·ci·us (men′shē əs, -shəs, -chəs) 372?-289? B.C., Chinese philosopher. Also, **Mêng-Tzŭ.**
Menck·en, H(enry) L(ouis) (meng′kən) 1880-1956, U.S. writer and editor.
Men·del, Gregor (men′dəl) 1822-1884, Austrian monk and botanist.
Men·de·le·ev, Dmitry Ivanovich (men′də lā′əf) 1834-1907, Russian chemist.
Men·dels·sohn, Felix (men′dəl sən) 1808-1847, German composer.
Me·nem, Car·los Saúl (men′əm) 1935- , Argentine president (1989-).
Mêng-Tzŭ (mœng′dzü′) see **Mencius.**
Me·nu·hin, Yehudi (men′ū in) 1916- , U.S. violinist.
Mer·ca·tor, Gerhardus (mər kā′tər) 1512-1594, Flemish geographer, cartographer, and mathematician.
Mer·e·dith (mer′i dith) **1. George.** 1828-1909, English writer. **2. Owen.** see **Bulwer-Lytton, Edward Robert.**
Mé·ri·mée, Prosper (mer′ə mā′) 1803-1870, French writer.
Mer·o·vin·gi·an (mer′ə vin′jē ən) Frankish dynasty that ruled in Gaul and Germany (A.D. 500?-751?).
Me·thu·se·lah (mə thü′zə lə) in the Old Testament, a man who lived 969 years.
Met·ter·nich, Prince von (met′ər nik′) 1773-1859, Austrian statesman.
Mi·cah (mī′kə) eighth century B.C., Hebrew prophet.
Mi·che·as (mī kē′əs) in the Douay Bible, Micah.
Mi·chel·an·ge·lo (mī′kəl an′jə lō′) 1475-1564, Italian sculptor, painter, architect, and poet; full name *Michelangelo Buonarroti.*
Mies van der Ro·he, Ludwig (mēs′van dər rō′ə) 1886-1969, German-American architect.
Mi·kan, George (Lawrence) (mī′kən) 1924- , U.S. basketball player.
Mill, John Stuart (mil) 1806-1873, English philosopher and economist.
Mil·lay, Edna St. Vincent (mi lā′) 1892-1950, U.S. poet.
Mil·ler, Arthur (mil′ər) 1915- , U.S. playwright.
Mil·let, Jean François (mi lā′) 1814-1875, French painter.
Mil·li·kan, Robert Andrews (mil′i kən) 1868-1953, U.S. physicist.
Mi·losz, Czeslaw (mē′lôsh) 1911- , Polish writer who has lived in the United States since 1960.
Mil·ti·a·des (mil tī′ə dēz′) 550?-489? B.C., Athenian general who defeated the Persians at Marathon.
Mil·ton, John (mil′tən) 1608-1674, English poet.
Ming (ming) dynasty that ruled China (1368-1644).
Min·u·it, Peter (min′ū it) 1580-1638, Dutch colonial administrator of New Netherland who bought Manhattan from the Indians.

Mi·ra·beau, Comte de (mîr′ə bō′) 1749-1791, French revolutionary and statesman; born *Honoré Gabriel Riqueti.*
Mir·i·am (mir′ē əm) in the Old Testament, sister of Moses and Aaron.
Mi·ró, Joan (mē RŌ′) 1893-1983, Spanish painter.
Mi·shi·ma Yu·ki·o (mē shē′mä ū̄′kē ō′) 1925-1970, Japanese novelist and playwright; pseudonym of *Kimitake Hiraoka.*
Mitch·ell, Maria (mich′əl) 1818-1889, U.S. astronomer.
Mith·ri·da·tes VI (mith′ri dā′tēz) 132?-63 B.C., king of Pontus (120-62 B.C.).
Mit·ter·rand, François (mē′tə rand′, mē tə RÄN′) 1916- , French president (1981-).
Mo·bu·to, Se·se Se·ko (mō bü′tō ses′ā sek′ō) 1930- , Zairian president (1965-).
Mo·di·gli·a·ni, Amedeo (mō′dēl yä′nē) 1884-1920, Italian painter and sculptor.
Mo·ham·med (mō ham′id, -hä′mid) see **Muhammad.**
Mohs, Friedrich (mōz) 1773-1839, German geologist and mineralogist.
Mo·lière (mōl yâr′) 1622-1673, French dramatist and comic actor; born *Jean-Baptiste Poquelin.*
Mo·lo·tov, Vyacheslav Mikhailovich (mol′ə tôf′) 1890-1986, Soviet statesman and diplomat.
Mon·dri·an, Piet (môn′drē än′) 1872-1944, Dutch painter.
Mo·net, Claude (mō nā′) 1840-1926, French painter.
Mon·roe (mən rō′) **1. James.** 1758-1831, fifth president of the United States (1817-1825). **2. Marilyn.** 1926-1962, U.S. film actress.
Mon·taigne, Michel Eyquem, Seigneur de (mon tān′) 1533-1592, French essayist.
Mon·ta·le, Eugenio (môn tä′le) 1896-1981, Italian poet.
Mont·calm, Louis Joseph, Marquis de (mont′käm′) 1712-1759, French general in the French and Indian War.
Mon·tes·so·ri, Maria (mon′tə sôr′ē) 1870-1952, Italian physician and educator.
Mon·te·ver·di, Claudio (mon′tə vâr′dē) 1567-1643, Italian composer.
Mon·te·zu·ma II (mon′tə zü′mə) 1480?-1520, ruler of the Aztecs (1502?-1520).
Mont·gol·fi·er (mont gol′fē ər) two French brothers who invented the first hot-air balloon used to carry a passenger **1. Jacques Étienne.** 1745-1799. **2. Joseph Michel.** 1740-1810.
Mont·gom·er·y of A·la·mein, 1st Viscount (mont gum′ə rē; al′ə mān′, al′ə mān′) 1887-1976, British field marshal; born *Bernard Law Montgomery.*
Monts, Pierre du Guast, Sieur de (monts) 1560?-1630?, French colonizer of Canada.
Moore (mur) **1. Henry.** 1898-1986, English sculptor. **2. Marianne Craig.** 1887-1972, U.S. poet. **3. Thomas.** 1779-1852, Irish poet.
Mor·de·cai (môr′di kī′, -KHī′) in the Old Testament, cousin of Esther.
More, Sir Thomas (môr) 1478-1535, English statesman, writer, and martyr.
Mor·gan (môr′gən) **1. Sir Henry.** 1635?-1688, English privateer. **2. J(ohn) P(ierpont).** 1837-1913, U.S. financier.
Mor·ris (môr′is, mor′-) **1. Gouverneur.** 1752-1816, American statesman. **2. William.** 1834-1896, English artist, poet, craftsman, printer, and social reformer.
Mor·ri·son, Toni (môr′ə sən, mor′-) 1931- , U.S. writer; born *Chloe Anthony Wofford.*
Morse, Samuel F(inley) B(reese) (môrs) 1791-1872, U.S. artist, inventor of the telegraph.
Mose·ley, Henry Gwyn Jeffreys (mōz′lē) 1887-1915, English physicist.
Mo·ses (mō′ziz) in the Old Testament, prophet and lawgiver of the Israelites who led them from Egypt to Canaan.
Moses, Grandma, 1860-1961, U.S. painter; real name *Anna Mary Robertson Moses.*
Mother Te·re·sa (tə rē′sə, -zə, -rä′-) 1910- , Albanian Roman Catholic nun known for her work in India; born *Agnes Gonxha Bojaxhin.*
Mott, Lucretia (mot) 1793-1880, U.S. feminist, abolitionist, and social reformer.
Mous·sorg·sky, Modest Petrovich (mu sôrg′skē, -zôrg′-) see **Mussorgsky, Modest Petrovich.**

a	at	e	end	o	hot	u	up	hw	white		about
ā	ape	ē	me	ō	old	ū	use	ng	song		taken
ä	far	i	it	ô	fork	ü	rule	th	thin	ə	pencil
âr	care	ī	ice	oi	oil	u̇	pull	th	this		lemon
		îr	pierce	ou	out	ûr	turn	zh	measure		circus

1411

Mo·zart, Wolfgang Amadeus (mō′tsärt) 1756-1791, Austrian composer.

Mu·bar·ak, Muhammad Hosni (mü bär′ək) 1929- , Egyptian president (1981-).

Mu·ga·be, Robert Gabriel (mü gä′be) 1924- , Zimbabwean president (1980-).

Mu·ham·mad (mù ham′əd) *also*, Mahomet, Mohammed. A.D. 570?-632, Arab religious teacher and political and military leader; founder of Islam.

Muhammad, Elijah 1897-1975, U.S. religious leader, head of the Nation of Islam (mid-1930s-1975).

Mul·ro·ney, Brian (mul rō′nē) 1939- , Canadian prime minister (1984-).

Munch, Edvard (mùngk) 1863-1944, Norwegian artist.

Mu·ra·sa·ki Shi·ki·bu (mùr′ə sä′kē shē′kē bü′) A.D. 978?-1031?, Japanese writer.

Mu·rat, Joachim (my RÄ′) 1767-1815, French cavalry officer, king of Naples (1808-1815).

Mus·set, Alfred de (my sā′) 1810-1857, French writer.

Mus·so·li·ni, Benito (mü′sə lē′nē) 1883-1945, Italian Fascist dictator (1922-1943).

Mus·sorg·sky, Modest Petrovich (mù sôrg′skē, -zôrg′-) *also*, Modest Petrovich Moussorgsky. 1839-1881, Russian composer.

Mu·tsu·hi·to (mü′tsù hē′tō) 1852-1912, Japanese emperor (1867-1912). Also, Meiji.

Na·bo·kov, Vladimir Vladimirovich (nə bô′kəf, nab′ə kôf′) 1899-1977, Russian-American writer.

Na·hum (nā′həm, nā′əm) seventh century B.C., Hebrew prophet.

Nai·smith, James (nā′smith′) 1861-1939, U.S. educator, originator of basketball.

Nan·sen, Fridtjof (nan′sən) 1861-1930, Norwegian explorer, scientist, and statesman.

Na·o·mi (nā ō′mē, nī-) in the Old Testament, the mother-in-law of Ruth.

Naph·ta·li (naf′tə lī′) **1.** in the Old Testament, a son of Jacob. **2.** one of the twelve tribes of Israel descended from him.

Na·pi·er, John (nā′pē ər) 1550-1617, Scottish mathematician, inventor of logarithms.

Na·po·le·on Bo·na·parte (nə pō′lē ən bō′nə pärt′) see **Napoleon I.**

Napoleon I, 1769-1821, French emperor (1804-1815); full name *Napoleon Bonaparte.*

Napoleon III, 1808-1873, French emperor (1852-1870); born *Charles Louis Napoleon Bonaparte;* nephew of Napoleon I.

Nash, Ogden (nash) 1902-1971, U.S. poet.

Nas·ser, Gamal Abdel (nas′ər) 1918-1970, Egyptian president (1956-1970).

Nast, Thomas (nast) 1840-1902, U.S. cartoonist.

Na·than (nā′thən) in the Old Testament, Hebrew prophet.

Na·than·ael (nə than′yəl) in the New Testament, a disciple of Jesus; often identified with Bartholomew.

Na·tion, Carry (nā′shən) 1846-1911, U.S. temperance advocate.

Na·tsu·me So·se·ki (nä′tsù me′sô′se kē′) 1867-1916, Japanese writer; pseudonym of *Natsume Kinnosuke.*

Nav·ra·ti·lo·va, Martina (nav′rə ti lō′və) 1956- , Czech-American tennis player.

Neb·u·chad·nez·zar II (neb′ə kəd nez′ər) d. 562 B.C., king of Babylon (605-562 B.C.).

Neck·er, Jacques (nek′ər) 1732-1804, French financier and statesman.

Nef·er·ti·ti (nef′ər tē′tē) 1372?-1350 B.C., queen of Egypt; wife of Ikhnaton.

Ne·he·mi·ah (nē′hə mī′ə, nē′ə-) Hebrew leader, governor of Judea (445?-432? B.C.).

Ne·he·mi·as (nē′hə mī′əs, nē′ə-) in the Douay Bible, Nehemiah.

Neh·ru, Jawaharlal (nā′rü) 1889-1964, Indian statesman, prime minister (1947-1964); father of Indira Gandhi.

Nel·son, Horatio (nel′sən) 1758-1805, English admiral.

Nernst, Hermann Walther (neRnst) 1864-1914, German physicist and chemist.

Ne·ro (nîr′ō) A.D. 37-68, Roman emperor (A.D. 54-68).

Ne·ru·da, Pablo (nə rü′də) 1904-1973, Chilean poet and diplomat; pen name of *Neftali Ricardo Reyes Basualto.*

Nev·sky, Alexander (nef′skē) see **Alexander Nevsky.**

New·man, John Henry (nü′mən, nū′-) 1801-1890, English theologian, philosopher, and cardinal.

New·ton, Sir Isaac (nü′tən, nū-) 1642-1727, English mathematician and physicist.

Ney, Michel (nā) 1769-1815, French military leader, marshal of France.

Nich·o·las, Saint (nik′ə ləs) fourth century A.D., bishop in Asia Minor, patron saint of children, often identified with Santa Claus.

Nicholas I, 1796-1855, Russian czar (1825-1855).

Nicholas II, 1868-1918, Russian czar (1894-1917).

Nick·laus, Jack (nik′ləs) 1940- , U.S. golfer.

Nie·buhr, Reinhold (nē′bùr) 1892-1971, U.S. theologian.

Nietz·sche, Friedrich Wilhelm (nē′chə) 1844-1900, German philosopher.

Night·in·gale, Florence (nī′tən gāl′, -ting gāl′) 1820-1910, English nurse, regarded as the founder of modern nursing.

Ni·jin·sky, Vaslav (ni zhin′skē) 1890-1950, Russian ballet dancer.

Nim·itz, Chester (nim′its) 1885-1966, U.S. admiral.

Nim·rod (nim′rod) in the Old Testament, a mighty hunter; great-grandson of Noah.

Nix·on, Richard Milhous (nik′sən) 1913- , thirty-seventh president of the United States (1969-1974).

No·ah (nō′ə) in the Old Testament, patriarch chosen by God to build an ark in which he, his family, and a pair of every kind of living creature would survive the flood.

No·bel, Alfred Bernhard (nō bel′) 1833-1896, Swedish chemist and industrialist, established the Nobel prizes.

No·gu·chi, Isamu (nə gü′chē) 1904-1988, U.S. sculptor.

North, Frederick (nôrth) 1732-1792, English statesman, prime minister (1770-1782), 2nd Earl of Guilford; known as *Lord North.*

Nor·thern Wei (nôr′thərn wā′) see **Toba.**

Noyes, Alfred (noiz) 1880-1958, English poet.

Nu·re·yev, Rudolf (nù rā′əf) 1938- , Russian ballet dancer and choreographer; an Austrian citizen since 1982.

Nye·re·re, Julius Kambarage (ni rär′ē, nye RE′Re) 1921- , Tanzanian president (1964-1985).

Oak·ley, Annie (ō′klē) 1860-1926, U.S. sharpshooter; full name *Phoebe Anne Oakley Mozee.*

Oates, Joyce Carol (ōts) 1938- , U.S. writer.

O·ba·di·ah (ō′bə dī′ə) sixth century B.C., Hebrew prophet.

O′Ca·sey, Sean (ō kā′sē) 1880-1964, Irish dramatist.

O′Con·nell, Daniel (ō kon′əl) 1775-1847, Irish political leader.

O′Con·nor, Sandra Day (ō kon′ər) 1930- , U.S. Supreme Court associate justice (1981-).

Oc·ta·vi·an (ok tā′vē ən) see **Augustus.**

O·do·a·cer (ō′dō ā′sər) A.D. 434?-493, barbarian leader who overthrew the Western Roman Empire (A.D. 476); ruler of Italy (A.D. 476-493). Also, **O·do·va·car** (ō′dō vā′kər).

Oer·sted, Hans Christian (ûr′sted) 1777-1851, Danish physicist.

Of·fen·bach, Jacques (ô′fən bäk′, -bäkн′) 1819-1880, French composer; born in Germany.

O·gle·thorpe, James Edward (ō′gəl thôrp′) 1696-1785, English general and philanthropist, founder of the colony of Georgia.

O. Hen·ry (ō hen′rē) 1862-1910, U.S. short-story writer; pen name of *William Sidney Porter.*

O′Keeffe, Georgia (ō kēf′) 1887-1986, U.S. painter.

O·lav II (ō′ləf) *also*, **O·laf II.** A.D. 995-1030, king of Norway (1016-1028). Also, Olav Haraldsson, Saint Olav.

Olav V *also*, Olaf V. 1903- , king of Norway (1957-).

O·liv·i·er, Laurence (ō liv′ē ā′) 1907-1989, English actor, director, and producer.

O·mar Khay·yam (ō′mär kī yäm′) d. 1123? Persian poet, astronomer, and mathematician; full name *Abu 'l-Fath Omar ibn Ibrāhīm.*

O′Neill, Eugene Gladstone (ō nēl′) 1888-1953, U.S. dramatist.

Op·pen·heim, Meret (op′ən hīm′) 1913-1985, Swiss-German artist.

Op·pen·hei·mer, J. Robert (op′ən hī′mər) 1904-1967, U.S. physicist.

Or·lé·ans, Louis Philippe Joseph, Duc d′ (dôr lā än′) 1747-1793, French revolutionary leader.

Orr, Bobby (ôr) 1948- , Canadian ice hockey player; full name *Robert Orr.*

Or·te·ga Sa·a·ve·dra, Daniel (ôr tā′gə sä′ä vä′drə) 1945- , Nicaraguan president (1985-1990).

Ortega y Gas·set, José (ē gä set′) 1883-1955, Spanish writer, philosopher, and critic.

Or·well, George (ôr′wel′) 1903-1950, English novelist and essayist, born in India; pen name of *Eric Blair.*

Ost·wald, Friedrich Wilhelm (ôst′vält) 1853-1932, German chemist and philosopher.

Ot·to I (ot′ō) A.D. 912-973, king of the Germans (A.D. 936-973), first emperor of the Holy Roman Empire (A.D. 962-973); called *the Great.*

Ov·id (ov′id) 43 B.C.-A.D. 17?, Roman poet; born *Publius Ovidius Naso.*

Ow·en (ō′ən) **1. Robert.** 1771-1858, Welsh social reformer and founder of cooperative communities. **2. Wilfred.** 1893-1918, English poet.

Ow·ens, Jesse (ō′ənz) 1913-1980, U.S. athlete; nickname of *James Cleveland Owens.*

Pad·er·ew·ski, Ignace Jan (pad′ə ref′skē) 1860-1941, Polish pianist, composer, and statesman.

Pag·a·ni·ni, Niccolò (pag′ə nē′nē) 1782-1840, Italian violinist and composer.

Paige, Satchel (pāj) 1906-1982, U.S. baseball player; nickname of *Leroy Robert Paige.*

Paine, Thomas (pān) 1737-1809, American patriot, writer, and political theorist.

Pa·le·stri·na, Giovanni Pierluigi da (pal′ə strē′nə) 1526?-1594, Italian composer.

Palm·er, Arnold (pä′mər) 1929- , U.S. golfer.

Palm·er·ston, Henry John Temple, Viscount (pä′mərstən) 1784-1865, British statesman, prime minister (1855-1858; 1859-1865).

Pan·cho Vil·la (pän′chō vē′ə) see **Villa, Francisco.**

Pa·pi·neau, Louis Joseph (pap′ə nō′) 1786-1871, French political leader.

Par·a·cel·sus, Philippus Aureolus (par′ə sel′səs) 1493-1541, Swiss physician and alchemist; real name *Theophrastus Bombastus von Hohenheim.*

Par·ker, (Charles Christopher) Charlie (pär′kər) 1920-1955, U.S. alto saxophonist; also called *Bird* or *Yardbird.*

Park·man, Francis (pärk′mən) 1823-1893, U.S. historian.

Par·men·i·des (pär men′i dēz′) sixth century B.C., Greek philosopher.

Par·nell, Charles Stewart (pär nel′) 1846-1891, Irish political leader.

Pas·cal, Blaise (pas kal′) 1623-1662, French philosopher, mathematician, physicist, and inventor.

Pas·ter·nak, Boris Leonidovich (pas′tər nak′) 1890-1960, Russian writer.

Pas·teur, Louis (pas tûr′) 1822-1895, French chemist and bacteriologist.

Pat·rick, Saint (pat′rik) A.D. 389?-461?, Christian missionary, patron saint of Ireland.

Pat·ton, George Smith (pat′ən) 1885-1945, U.S. general.

Paul (pôl) d. A.D. 68?, Christian missionary and theologian.

Paul III, 1468-1549, pope (1534-1549).

Paul VI, 1897-1978, pope (1963-1978).

Pau·li, Wolfgang (pou′lē) 1900-1958, Austrian physicist.

Pau·ling, Linus Carl (pô′ling) 1901- , U.S. chemist.

Pav·lov, Ivan Petrovich (päv′lôf) 1849-1936, Russian physiologist.

Pav·lo·va, Anna Pavlovna (pav′lə və, pav lō′-) 1882-1931, Russian ballerina.

Pay·ton, Walter Jerry (pā′tən) 1954- , U.S. football player.

Paz, Oc·ta·vi·o (päz) 1914- , Mexican writer.

Peale, Charles Willson (pēl) 1741-1827, American painter.

Pear·son, Lester Bowles (pîr′sən) 1897-1972, Canadian prime minister (1963-1968).

Pea·ry, Robert Edwin (pîr′ē) 1856-1920, U.S. Arctic explorer.

Peel, Sir Robert (pēl) 1788-1850, British statesman, prime minister (1834-1835; 1841-1846).

Pei, I(eh) M(ing) (pā) 1917- , Chinese-American architect.

Pe·lé (pā′lā) 1940- , Brazilian soccer player; nickname of *Edson Arantes do Nascimento.*

Penn, William (pen) 1644-1718, English Quaker, founder of Pennsylvania.

Pep·in III (pep′in) A.D. 714?-768, first Carolingian king of the Franks (A.D. 751-768); known as *Pepin the Short;* son of Charles Martel and father of Charlemagne.

Pepys, Samuel (pēps) 1633-1703, English diarist and naval administrator.

Pé·rez de Cué·llar, Javier (per′ez də kwä′yär) 1920- , Peruvian diplomat, secretary-general of the United Nations (1982-1991).

Per·i·cles (per′i klēz′) 495?-429 B.C., Athenian statesman, orator, and general.

Pe·rón, Juan Domingo (pə rōn′) 1895-1974, Argentine army officer and politician, president of Argentina (1946-1955; 1973-1974).

Per·ry (per′ē) **1. Matthew Calbraith.** 1794-1858, U.S. naval officer. **2. Oliver Hazard.** 1785-1819, U.S. naval officer; brother of Matthew Calbraith Perry.

Per·shing, John Joseph (pûr′shing) 1860-1948, U.S. general.

Per·u·gi·no (per′ə jē′nō) 1446?-1523, Italian painter; born *Pietro di Cristoforo Vannucci.*

Pé·tain, Henri Philippe Benoni Omer (pā taN′) 1856-1951, French general, marshal of France, and chief of state of the Vichy government (1940-1944).

Pe·ter (pē′tər) d. A.D. 67?, one of the twelve Apostles of Jesus; brother of Andrew. Also, **Simon Peter.**

Peter I, 1672-1725, Russian czar (1682-1725). Also, **Peter the Great.**

Pe·ti·pa, Marius (pə tē′pə) 1822-1910, French dancer and choreographer.

Pe·trarch (pē′trärk) 1304-1374, Italian poet and scholar.

Phid·i·as (fid′ē əs) 490?-432? B.C., Greek sculptor.

Phil·ip (fil′ip) in the New Testament, one of the twelve Apostles of Jesus.

Philip II 1. 382-336 B.C., king of Macedonia (359-336 B.C.); father of Alexander the Great. **2.** 1165-1223, king of France (1180-1223). Also, **Philip Au·gus·tus** (ô gus′tis). **3.** 1527-1598, king of Spain (1556-1598).

Philip IV, 1268-1314, French king (1285-1314); called *the Fair.*

Phil·lips, Wendell (fil′ips) 1811-1884, U.S. reformer.

Pho·ti·us (fō′shē əs) A.D. 820?-892? Greek churchman, theologian, and patriarch of Constantinople (A.D. 858-867; A.D. 877-886).

Phyfe, Duncan (fīf) 1768-1854, U.S. cabinetmaker.

Pia·get, Jean (pyä zhä′) 1896-1980, Swiss psychologist.

Pi·cas·so, Pablo (pi kä′sō) 1881-1973, Spanish painter and sculptor who lived and worked mainly in France.

Pierce, Franklin (pîrs) 1804-1869, fourteenth president of the United States (1853-1857).

Pi·late, Pontius (pī′lət) Roman governor of Judea (A.D. 26-36).

Pin·dar (pin′dər) 518?-438 B.C., Greek lyric poet.

Pi·no·chet U·gar·te, Augusto (pē′nō chet′ ü gär′tä, pē′nōshet′) 1915-1989, Chilean general and president (1973-1989).

Pin·ter, Harold (pin′tər) 1930- , English dramatist.

Pir·an·del·lo, Luigi (pir′ən del′ō) 1867-1936, Italian writer.

Pitt (pit) **1. William.** 1708-1778, British statesman, prime minister (1766-1768); 1st Earl of Chatham; known as *Pitt the Elder.* **2. William.** 1759-1806, British statesman, prime minister (1783-1801; 1804-1806); known as *Pitt the Younger;* son of Pitt the Elder.

Pi·us IX (pī′əs) 1792-1878, pope (1846-1878).

Pius X, 1835-1914, pope (1902-1914).

Pius XI, 1857-1939, pope (1922-1939).

Pius XII, 1876-1958, pope (1939-1958).

Pi·zar·ro, Francisco (pi zär′ō) 1471?-1541, Spanish conqueror of Peru.

Planck, Max (plängk) 1858-1947, German physicist.

Plan·tag·e·net (plan taj′ə nit) family that ruled England (1154-1399). Also, **Angevin.**

Pla·to (plā′tō) 428?-347? B.C., Greek philosopher.

Plau·tus (plô′təs) 251?-184 B.C., Roman dramatist.

Plin·y (plin′ē) **1. the Elder.** A.D. 23?-79, Roman writer, scholar, and naturalist; born *Gaius Plinius Secundus.* **2. the Younger.** A.D. 62-113?, Roman writer and orator; born *Gaius Plinius Caecilius Secundus;* nephew of Pliny the Elder.

Pli·set·ska·ya, Maya (pli set′skä yə) 1925- , Russian ballerina.

Plu·tarch (plü′tärk) A.D. 46?-120?, Greek essayist and biographer.

Po·ca·hon·tas (pō′kə hon′təs) 1595?-1617, American Indian princess; daughter of Powhatan.

Poe, Edgar Allan (pō) 1809-1849, U.S. writer and critic.

Poin·ca·ré, Raymond (pwaN ka RĀ′) 1860-1934, French statesman, premier (1912-1913; 1922-1923; 1926-1929), and president (1913-1920).

Polk, James Knox (pōk) 1795-1849, eleventh president of the United States (1845-1849).

Pol·lock, Jackson (pol′ək) 1912-1956, U.S. painter.

Polo, Marco, see **Marco Polo.**

Pom·pa·dour, Marquise de (pom′pə dôr′) 1721-1764, mistress of Louis XV; born *Jeanne Antoinette Poisson.*

Pom·pey (pom′pē) 106-48 B.C., Roman general, statesman, and triumvir; known as *the Great.*

Pom·pi·dou, Georges Jean Raymond (pom′pi dü′) 1911-

a	at	e	end	o	hot	u	up	hw	white		about
ā	ape	ē	me	ō	old	ū	use	ng	song		taken
ä	far	i	it	ô	fork	ü	rule	th	thin	ə	pencil
âr	care	ī	ice	oi	oil	u̇	pull	th	this		lemon
		îr	pierce	ou	out	ûr	turn	zh	measure		circus

1974, French politician, premier (1962-1968), and president (1969-1974).

Ponce de Le·ón, Juan (pons′ də lā ōn′, lē′ən) 1460?-1521, Spanish explorer.

Pon·ti·ac (pon′tē ak′) 1720?-1769, Ottawa chief.

Pope, Alexander (pōp) 1688-1744, English poet and satirist.

Por·ter (pôr′tər) **1. Cole.** 1893-1964, U.S. composer and songwriter. **2. Katherine Anne.** 1890-1980, U.S. writer. **3. William Sydney.** see **O. Henry.**

Pound, Ezra (pound) 1885-1972, U.S. poet, critic, and translator.

Pow·ha·tan (pou′ə tan′, pou hat′ən) 1550?-1618, American Indian chief; father of Pocahontas.

Pratt, Edwin John (prat) 1883-1964, Canadian poet.

Prax·i·te·les (prak sit′ə lēz′) 390?-330? B.C., Greek sculptor.

Pres·cott, William Hickling (pres′kət) 1796-1859, U.S. historian.

Pres·ley, Elvis (prez′lē) 1935-1977, U.S. pop singer.

Price, (Mary) Leontyne (prīs) 1927- , U.S. soprano.

Priest·ley, Joseph (prēst′lē) 1733-1804, English chemist and theologian.

Pro·kof·iev, Sergei Sergeyevich (prə kôf′yəf) 1891-1953, Russian composer.

Pro·tag·o·ras (prō tag′ər əs) 481?-411? B.C., Greek philosopher.

Proust, Marcel (prüst) 1871-1922, French novelist.

Ptol·e·my (tol′ə mē) Greek dynasty that ruled Egypt (323-30 B.C.).

Ptolemy, Claudius second century A.D., Greek astronomer, geographer, and mathematician.

Ptolemy I 367?-283 B.C., Greek general and king of Egypt (323-285 B.C.).

Puc·ci·ni, Giacomo (pü chē′nē) 1858-1924, Italian composer of operas.

Pu·las·ki, Count Casimir (pə las′kē) 1748-1779, Polish nobleman, general in the colonial army of the American Revolution.

Pu·lit·zer, Joseph (pùl′i tsər) 1847-1911, U.S. journalist and newspaper publisher.

Pur·cell, Henry (pûr′səl) 1659-1695, English composer.

Push·kin, Alexander Sergeyevich (pùsh′kin) 1799-1837, Russian poet and dramatist.

Pym, John (pim) 1584-1643, English statesman.

Pyr·rhus (pir′əs) 318?-272 B.C., king of Epirus.

Py·thag·o·ras (pi thag′ər əs) 580?-500? B.C., Greek mathematician and philosopher.

Qad·da·fi, Muammar al- (kə dä′f ē) 1942- , Libyan political leader (1969-).

Qin (chin) also, **Ch'in.** dynasty that ruled China (221-206 B.C.).

Qing (ching) also, **Ch'ing.** Mongol dynasty that ruled China (1644-1912). Also, **Manchu.**

Quayle, (James) Dan(forth) (kwāl) 1947- , vice president of the United States (1989-).

Queens·ber·ry, 8th Marquess of (kwēnz′ber′ē, -bə rē) 1844-1900, Scottish statesman and sportsman; born *John Sholto Douglas.*

Que·zon y Mo·li·na, Manuel Luis (kā sōn′ ē mō lē′nə) 1878-1944, Philippine statesman, first president of the Philippine Commonwealth (1935-1944).

Quin·til·ian (kwin til′yən) A.D. 35?-95, Roman writer and orator.

Ra·be·lais, François (rab′ə lā′) 1494-1553, French satirist and humorist.

Ra·bin·o·witz, Solomon (rə bin′ə witz) see **Shalom Aleichem.**

Ra·chel (rā′chəl) in the Old Testament, the second wife of Jacob and the mother of Joseph and Benjamin.

Rach·ma·ni·noff, Sergei Vasilyevich (räk mä′nə nôf′) 1873-1943, Russian composer and pianist.

Ra·cine, Jean Baptiste (rA sēn′) 1639-1699, French dramatist.

Rad·cliffe-Brown, Alfred Reginald (rad′klif broun′) 1881-1955, English anthropologist.

Ra·leigh, Sir Walter (rô′lē, rä′-) 1552?-1618, English courtier, colonizer, statesman, and writer.

Ra·ma·krish·na (rä′mə krish′nə) 1836-1886, Hindu mystic.

Ra·ma·nu·jan, Srinivasa (rä mä′nù jən) 1889-1920, Indian mathematician.

Ram·e·ses (ram′ə sēz′) also, **Ram·ses** (ram′sēz). any of eleven kings reigning in Egypt (1320?-1090? B.C.), esp. **Rameses II** (reigned 1304-1237 B.C.).

Ram·say, William (ram′zē) 1852-1916, English chemist.

Ran·dolph (ran′dolf) **1. A(sa) Philip.** 1889-1979, U.S. labor leader. **2. Edmund.** 1753-1813, American statesman.

Ran·ke, Leopold von (räng′kə) 1795-1886, German historian.

Ra·pha·el (rä′fī el′, raf′ē əl, rä′f ē əl) 1483-1520, Italian painter.

Ras·pu·tin, Grigory Yefimovich (ras pü′tin) 1871?-1916, Russian courtier and monk.

Ra·vel, Maurice (rə vel′) 1875-1937, French composer.

Rea·gan, Ronald Wilson (rā′gən) 1911- , fortieth president of the United States (1981-1989).

Re·bec·ca (ri bek′ə) in the Old Testament, the wife of Isaac and the mother of Esau and Jacob.

Reed, Walter (rēd) 1851-1902, U.S. army surgeon and microbiologist.

Rehn·quist, William H. (ren′kwist) 1924- , U.S. Supreme Court Chief Justice (1986-).

Rem·brandt (rem′brant) 1606-1669, Dutch painter and etcher; full name *Rembrandt Harmenszoon van Rijn.*

Re·noir, Pierre Auguste (ren wär′, ren′wär) 1841-1919, French painter.

Reu·ben (rü′bən) **1.** in the Old Testament, the oldest son of Jacob and Leah. **2.** one of the twelve tribes of Israel descended from him.

Reu·ther, Walter Philip (rü′thər) 1907-1970, U.S. labor leader.

Re·vere, Paul (rə vîr′) 1735-1818, American patriot and craftsman.

Reyn·olds, Sir Joshua (ren′əldz) 1723-1792, English painter.

Rhodes, Cecil John (rōdz) 1853-1902, British imperialist and entrepreneur in South Africa.

Ri·car·do, David (ri kär′dō) 1772-1823, British economist.

Rich·ard, Maurice (rich′ərd) 1921- , Canadian ice hockey player.

Richard I, 1157-1199, king of England (1189-1199); known as *Richard the Lion-Hearted* or *Richard Coeur de Lion.*

Richard II, 1367-1400, king of England (1377-1399).

Richard III, 1452-1485, king of England (1483-1485).

Rich·ard·son, Samuel (rich′ərd sən) 1689-1761, English essayist.

Ri·che·lieu, Cardinal (rish′ə lü′, RĒ shə lyœ′) 1585-1642, French statesman; full name *Armand Jean du Plessis de Richelieu.*

Richt·ho·fen, Manfred, Baron von (RIKHt′hō′fən) 1892-1918, German World War I fighter pilot; known as the *Red Baron.*

Rick·en·back·er, Edward Vernon (rik′ən bak′ər) 1890-1973, U.S. aviator.

Rick·o·ver, Hyman George (rik′ō vər) 1900-1986, U.S. naval officer who developed world's first nuclear-powered submarine; born in Poland.

Rid·ley, Nicholas (rid′lē) 1500?-1555, English prelate.

Ri·el, Louis (rē el′) 1844-1885, Canadian insurgent.

Rie·mann, Georg Friedrich Bernhard (RĒ′män) 1826-1866, German mathematician.

Ril·ke, Rainer Maria (ril′kə) 1875-1926, German writer.

Rim·baud, Arthur (ram bō′, RaN bō′) 1854-1891, French poet.

Rim·ski-Kor·sa·kov, Nikolai Andreyevich (rim′skē kôr′sə-kôf′) 1844-1908, Russian composer.

Ri·ve·ra, Diego (ri vâr′ə) 1886-1957, Mexican painter.

Rob·ert I (rob′ərt) 1274-1329, king of Scotland (1306-1329). Also, **Robert the Bruce.**

Robe·son, Paul (rōb′sən) 1898-1976, U.S. singer and actor.

Robes·pi·erre, Maximilien de (rōbz′pē âr′) 1758-1794, French revolutionary leader.

Rob·in·son (rob′in sən) **1. Edwin Arlington.** 1869-1935, U.S. poet. **2. Jackie.** 1919-1972, U.S. baseball player; full name *Jack Roosevelt Robinson.* **3. Sugar Ray.** 1921-1989, U.S. boxer; born *Walker Smith, Jr.*

Ro·cham·beau, Comte de (rō′sham bō′) 1725-1807, French marshal, commander of the French forces during the American Revolution.

Rock·e·fel·ler (rok′ə fel′ər) U.S. family including **1. John D.** 1839-1937, industrialist and philanthropist. **2. John D., Jr.** 1874-1960, philanthropist; son of John D. Rockefeller. **3. Nelson A.** 1908-1979, political leader; grandson of John D. Rockefeller.

Rock·ne, Knute Kenneth (rok′nē) 1888-1931, U.S. football coach.

Rodg·ers, Richard (roj′ərz) 1902-1979, U.S. composer.

Ro·din, Auguste (rō dan′, Rô daN′) 1840-1917, French sculptor.

Roeb·ling, John Augustus (rō′bling) 1806-1869, U.S. engineer.

Roent·gen, Wilhelm Konrad (rent'gən, ʀœnt'gən) *also,* Röntgen. 1845-1923, German physicist.

Ro·ma·nov (rō'mə nôf') *also,* **Ro·ma·noff.** dynasty that ruled Russia (1613-1917).

Romanov, Mikhail 1596-1645, Russian czar (1613-1645), founder of the Romanov dynasty.

Rom·mel, Erwin Johannes Eugen (rom'əl) 1891-1944, German general.

Rom·ney, George (rom'nē) 1734-1802, English painter.

Rom·u·lus, Augustulus (rom'yə ləs) A.D. 461?-476?, last emperor of the Western Roman Empire (A.D. 475-476).

Roo·se·velt (rō'zə velt', rōz'velt) U.S. family including **1. (Anna) Eleanor.** 1884-1962, humanitarian, writer, and diplomat; wife of Franklin Delano Roosevelt. **2. Franklin Delano.** 1882-1945, thirty-second president of the United States (1933-1945). **3. Theodore.** 1858-1919, twenty-sixth president of the United States (1901-1909).

Root, Elihu (rüt, rút) 1845-1937, U.S. lawyer and statesman.

Rose·crans, William Starke (rōz'kranz') 1819-1898, Union general in the American Civil War.

Ross (rôs) **1. Betsy.** 1752-1836, American woman reputed to have made the first American flag; born *Elizabeth Griscom.* **2. Sir James.** 1800-1862, British polar explorer.

Ros·set·ti (rō zet'ē, -set'ē) **1. Christina Georgina.** 1830-1894, English poet. **2. Dante Gabriel.** 1828-1882, English poet and painter; brother of Christina Georgina Rossetti.

Ros·si·ni, Gioacchino Antonio (rō sē'nē) 1792-1868, Italian composer of operas.

Ros·tand, Edmond (ros tand') 1868-1918, French dramatist.

Roth·schild (rôth'chīld') family of financiers active in England and Europe including **1. Meyer Amschel.** 1743-1812, German banker. **2. Nathan Meyer.** 1777-1836, British banker; son of Meyer Amschel Rothschild.

Rou·ault, Georges (rü ō') 1871-1958, French painter and graphic artist.

Rous·seau (rü sō') **1. Henri.** 1844-1910, French painter. **2. Jean Jacques.** 1712-1778, French philosopher and writer, born in Switzerland.

Ru·bens, Peter Paul (rü'bənz) 1577-1640, Flemish painter.

Ru·bin·stein (rü'bin stīn') **1. Anton Grigoryevich.** 1829-1894, Russian pianist and composer. **2. Artur** or **Arthur** 1886-1982, Polish-American pianist.

Ru·pert, Prince (rü'pərt) 1619-1682, German prince.

Rus·kin, John (rus'kin) 1819-1900, English writer, art critic, and social reformer.

Rus·sell (rus'əl) **1. Bertrand.** 1872-1970, English philosopher and mathematician. **2. George William.** 1867-1935, Irish poet and writer who used the pen name *Æ.* **3. Lord John.** 1792-1878, British statesman; 1st Earl Russell; grandfather of Bertrand Russell.

Ruth (rüth) in the Old Testament, daughter-in-law of Naomi and wife of Boaz.

Ruth, Babe 1895-1948, U.S. baseball player; nickname of *George Herman Ruth.*

Ruth·er·ford, Lord Ernest (ruth'ər fərd) 1871-1937, English physicist.

Rut·ledge, John (rut'lij) 1739-1800, American jurist, statesman, and U.S. Supreme Court Chief Justice (1795).

Sa·bin, Albert Bruce (sā'bin) 1906- , U.S. physician and microbiologist, born in Poland.

Sac·a·ja·we·a (sak'ə jə wē'ə) *also,* **Sac·a·ga·we·a** (sak'ə gə-wē'ə). 1788?-1812? (or 1884?), Shoshone guide and interpreter for the Meriwether Lewis and William Clark expedition (1805-1806). Her name means *Bird Woman.*

Sac·co, Nicola (sak'ō) 1891-1927, Italian anarchist in the United States.

Sa·dat, Anwar al- (sə dät', -dat') 1918-1981, Egyptian president (1970-1981).

Saint-Gau·dens, Augustus (sānt gô'dənz) 1848-1907, U.S. sculptor.

Saint-Saëns, Charles Camille (saN säNs', saN säN') 1835-1921, French composer.

Sa·kha·rov, Andrei Dmitriyovich (sä'kə rôf') 1921-1989, Soviet nuclear physicist and human rights advocate.

Sal·a·din (sal'ə din) 1138?-1193, Muslim conqueror and sultan of Egypt and Syria (1175-1193).

Sa·li·nas de Gor·ta·ri, Carlos (sə lē'nəs dā gôr tär'ē) 1948- , Mexican economist and president (1988-).

Salis·bu·ry, 3rd Marquess of (sôlz'ber'ē, -bə rē) 1830-1903, British statesman, prime minister (1885; 1886-1892; 1895-1902); born *Robert Arthur Talbot Gascoyne Cecil.*

Salk, Jonas Edward (sôk, sôlk) 1914- , U.S. physician and bacteriologist.

Sal·lust (Gaius Sallustius Crispus) (sal'əst) 86-34? B.C., Roman historian and politician.

Sa·lo·me (sə lō'mē) in the New Testament, the daughter of Herodias.

Sam·son (sam'sən) in the Old Testament, judge of Israel, renowned for his strength.

Sam·u·el (sam'ū əl) in the Old Testament, judge and prophet of Israel.

Sand, George (sand) 1804-1876, French novelist; pen name of *Amandine Aurore Lucie Dupin.*

Sand·burg, Carl (sand'bûrg') 1878-1967, U.S. poet and biographer.

Sang·er (sang'ər) **1. Frederick.** 1918- , British chemist. **2. Margaret Higgins.** 1883-1966, U.S. advocate of birth control.

San·ta An·na, Antonio López de (san'tə an'ə) 1795-1876, Mexican general.

San·tos-Du·mont, Alberto (san'təs dü mont', dü-) 1873-1932, French-Brazilian pioneer in aviation.

Sap·pho (saf'ō) 620?-565 B.C., Greek poet.

Sar·ah (sâr'ə) in the Old Testament, the wife of Abraham and mother of Isaac.

Sar·gent, John Singer (sär'jənt) 1856-1925, U.S. painter.

Sar·gon II (sär'gon) d. 705 B.C., king of Assyria (722-705 B.C.).

Sarto, Andrea del, see Andrea del Sarto.

Sar·tre, Jean Paul (sär'trə, säRt) 1905-1980, French philosopher.

Saul (sôl) **1.** the first king of Israel (1020?-1004 B.C.). **2.** in the New Testament, the name of the Apostle Paul before his conversion to Christianity. Also, **Saul of Tarsus** (tär'səs).

Saus·sure, Ferdinand de (sō SYR') 1857-1913, Swiss linguist.

Sa·vo·na·ro·la, Girolamo (sav'ə nə rō'lə) 1452-1498, Italian friar and political and religious reformer.

Sca·li·a, Antonin (skə lē'ə) 1936- , U.S. Supreme Court associate justice (1986-).

Scar·lat·ti (skär lä'tē) **1. Alessandro.** 1660-1725, Italian composer. **2. Domenico.** 1685-1757, Italian composer and harpsichord virtuoso; son of Alessandro Scarlatti.

Schel·ling, Friedrich Wilhelm Joseph von (shel'ing) 1775-1854, German philosopher.

Schil·ler, Johann Christoph Friedrich von (shil'ər) 1759-1805, German dramatist, poet, and historian.

Schlie·mann, Heinrich (shlē'män') 1822-1890, German archaeologist.

Schmidt, Helmut (shmit) 1918- , German political leader, chancellor of West Germany (1974-1982).

Schoen·berg, Arnold (shōn'bûrg', shœn'beRg') *also,* **Schön·berg.** 1874-1951, Austrian composer.

Scho·pen·hau·er, Arthur (shō'pən hou'ər) 1788-1860, German philosopher.

Schrö·ding·er, Erwin (shrō'ding ər, shrā'-, shrœ'-) 1887-1961, Austrian physicist.

Schu·bert, Franz (Peter) (shü'bərt) 1797-1828, Austrian composer.

Schu·mann, Robert (Alexander) (shü'män') 1810-1856, German composer and pianist.

Schwann, Theodor (shwän) 1810-1882, German physiologist and histologist.

Schweit·zer, Albert (shwīt'sər, shvīt'-) 1875-1965, Alsatian doctor, philosopher, and missionary in Africa.

Scip·i·o Af·ri·ca·nus (sip'ē ō af'ri kā'nəs, -kan'əs) **1. the Elder.** 234?-183 B.C., Roman general. **2. the Younger.** 185?-129 B.C., Roman statesman and general; son of Scipio Africanus the Elder.

Scopes, John Thomas (skōps) 1901-1970, U.S. high school biology teacher tried in Tennessee in 1925 and found guilty of teaching the Darwinian theory of evolution.

Scott (skot) **1. Dred.** 1795?-1858, black American slave whose suit for freedom led to a U.S. Supreme Court decision in 1857 that extended slavery to all U.S. territories. **2. Robert Falcon.** 1868-1912, English naval officer and Antarctic explorer. **3. Sir Walter.** 1771-1832, Scottish novelist, poet, and historian. **4. Winfield.** 1786-1866, U.S. general.

Se·go·vi·a, Andrés (si gō'vē ə, se-) 1893-1987, Spanish classical guitar player.

Se·leu·cus I (si lü'kəs) 358?-281 B.C., Macedonian general.

Sel·juk (sel'jük, sel jük') a Turkish family that established sev-

a	at	e	end	o	hot	u	up	hw	white		about
ā	ape	ē	me	ō	old	ū	use	ng	song		taken
ä	far	i	it	ô	fork	ü	rule	th	thin	ə	pencil
âr	care	ī	ice	oi	oil	ú	pull	th	this		lemon
		îr	pierce	ou	out	ûr	turn	zh	measure		circus

eral dynasties in western Asia during the eleventh and twelfth centuries. The Seljuks were Muslims and fought the Crusaders.

Sel·kirk, 5th Earl of (sel′kûrk′) 1771-1820, Scottish colonizer of Canada; born *Thomas Douglas.*

Sen·e·ca, Lucius Annaeus (sen′i kə) 4 B.C.-A.D. 65, Roman philosopher and statesman.

Sen·ghor, Léopold Sédar (sang gôr′) 1906- , Senegalese poet, statesman, and president (1960-1980).

Sen·nach·er·ib (sə nak′ər ib) d. 681 B.C., king of Assyria (705-681 B.C.).

Se·quoy·ah (si kwoi′ə) *also,* **Se·quoi·a.** 1766?-1843, Cherokee scholar and silversmith who invented the Cherokee writing system; known as *George Gist* or *George Guess.*

Ser·ra, Junipero (ser′ə) 1713-1784, Spanish Franciscan missionary in California and Mexico.

Ser·vice, Robert William (sûr′vis) 1874-1958, Canadian writer.

Seth (seth) in the Old Testament, a son of Adam and Eve.

Se·ton, Saint Elizabeth Ann Bayley (sē′tən) 1774-1821, U.S. Roman Catholic nun.

Seu·rat, Georges (sœ Rä′) 1859-1891, French painter.

Se·ve·rus, Lucius Septimius (sə vîr′əs) A.D. 146-211, Roman emperor (A.D. 193-211).

Sew·ard, William Henry (sü′ərd) 1801-1872, U.S. statesman.

Sex·ton, Anne Harvey (seks′tən) 1928-1974, U.S. poet.

Sfor·za (sfôr′tsä) powerful family that ruled Milan (1450-1500; 1521-1535).

Shack·le·ton, Sir Ernest Henry (shak′əl tən) 1874-1922, British Antarctic explorer.

Shake·speare, William (shāk′spîr) 1564-1616, English dramatist and poet.

Sha·lom A·lei·chem (shä′ləm ə lā′KHəm, shô′-) *also,* **Sholem Aleichem, Sholom Aleichem.** 1859-1916, U.S. Yiddish writer; pen name of *Solomon Rabinowitz.*

Shang (shäng) dynasty that ruled China (1525?-1027? B.C.). Also, **Yin.**

Shaw, George Bernard (shô) 1856-1950, Irish playwright and critic.

She·ba, Queen of (shē′bə) in the Old Testament, a queen who tested Solomon's wisdom.

Shel·ley (shel′ē) **1. Mary Wollstonecraft.** 1797-1851, English novelist; wife of Percy Bysshe Shelley. **2. Percy Bysshe.** 1792-1822, English poet.

Shep·ard, Alan Bartlett, Jr. (shep′ərd) 1923- , U.S. astronaut, first American to travel in outer space.

Sher·a·ton, Thomas (sher′ə tən) 1751-1806, English furniture designer.

Sher·i·dan (sher′i dən) **1. Philip Henry.** 1831-1888, Union general in the American Civil War. **2. Richard Brinsley.** 1751-1816, British dramatist and statesman; born in Ireland.

Sher·man (shûr′mən) **1. Roger.** 1721-1793, American statesman and signer of the Declaration of Independence. **2. William Tecumseh.** 1820-1891, Union general in the American Civil War.

Sho·lem A·lei·chem (shä′ləm ə lā′KHəm, shô′-) see **Shalom Aleichem.**

Shos·ta·ko·vich, Dmitri (shos′tə kō′vich) 1906-1975, Russian composer.

Sid·ney, Sir Philip (sid′nē) 1554-1586, English statesman, soldier, and poet.

Si·kor·sky, Igor Ivanovich (si kôr′skē) 1889-1972, Russian-American engineer.

Sim·e·on (sim′ē ən) **1.** in the Old Testament, a son of Jacob and Leah. **2.** one of the twelve tribes of Israel descended from him.

Si·mon (sī′mən) **1.** in the New Testament, the original name of the Apostle Peter. **2.** in the New Testament, one of the twelve Apostles of Jesus; called *the Canaanite.*

Simon Peter, see **Peter.**

Si·na·tra, Frank (si nä′trə) 1915- , U.S. singer and actor; full name *Francis Albert Sinatra.*

Sin·clair, Upton (sin klâr′) 1878-1968, U.S. writer and social critic.

Sing·er, Isaac Bashevis (sing′ər) 1904-1991, U.S. writer in Yiddish; born in Poland.

Sit·ting Bull (sit′ing bùl′) 1834?-1890, Sioux chief.

Skin·ner, B(urrhus) F(rederic) (skin′ər) 1904-1990, U.S. psychologist.

Smith (smith) **1. Adam.** 1723-1790, Scottish economist. **2. Alfred E(manuel).** 1873-1944, U.S. politician. **3. Bessie.** 1894 (or 1898)-1937, U.S. blues singer. **4. Captain John.** 1580?-1631, English adventurer, explorer, and writer. **5. Joseph.** 1805-1844, U.S. religious leader, founder of the Mormon Church.

Smol·ett, Tobias George (smol′it) 1721-1771, British novelist, born in Scotland.

Smuts, Jan Christiaan (smuts) 1870-1950, South African soldier and statesman.

Snead, Sam (snēd) 1912- , U.S. golfer.

Soc·ra·tes (sok′rə tēz′) 469-399 B.C., Greek philosopher and teacher.

Sol·o·mon (sol′ə mən) king of Israel (973?-933? B.C.); son of David.

So·lon (sō′lən) 638?-559? B.C., Athenian lawgiver.

Sol·vay, Ernest (sol′vā) 1838-1922, Belgian chemist.

Sol·y·man I (sol′ə mən) see **Suleiman I.**

Sol·zhe·nit·syn, Aleksandr Isayevich (sōl′zhə nēt′sin) 1918- , Soviet writer.

Song (sông) *also,* **Sung.** dynasty that ruled China (A.D. 960-1260).

Soph·o·cles (sof′ə klēz′) 496?-406? B.C., Greek dramatist.

Sou·sa, John Philip (sü′zə) 1854-1932, U.S. composer and bandmaster.

Sou·ter, David H. (sü′tər) 1939- , U.S. Supreme Court associate justice (1990-).

Sou·they, Robert (sou′thē) 1774-1843, English poet.

So·yin·ka, Wole (shô ying′kə) 1934- , Nigerian writer.

Spar·ta·cus (spär′tə kəs) d. 71 B.C., Thracian slave, gladiator, and leader of a slave rebellion.

Spen·cer, Herbert (spen′sər) 1820-1903, English philosopher.

Spen·ser, Edmund (spen′sər) 1552-1599, English poet.

Spin·o·za, Baruch (spi nō′zə) 1632-1677, Dutch philosopher. Also, **Benedict de Spinoza.**

Squan·to (skwon′tō) 1585?-1622, American Indian of the Wampanoag tribe who befriended the Pilgrims of Plymouth Colony. Also, **Tisquantum, Tsquantum.**

Staël, Madame de (stäl) 1766-1817, French author; full name *Anne Louise Germaine Necker de Staël-Holstein.*

Sta·lin, Joseph Vissarionovich (stä′lin) 1879-1953, Soviet revolutionary, secretary-general of the Communist Party (1924-1953), premier of U.S.S.R. (1941-1953).

Stan·dish, Myles (stan′dish) *also,* **Miles Standish.** 1584?-1656, Pilgrim leader and American colonist.

Stan·i·slav·sky, Konstantin (stan′ə släv′skē) 1863-1938, Russian stage director and actor; stage name of *Konstantin Sergeyevich Alexeyev.*

Stan·ley, Sir Henry Morton (stan′lē) 1841-1904, British journalist and explorer.

Steele, Sir Richard (stēl) 1672-1729, English essayist.

Stei·chen, Edward Jean (stī′kən) 1879-1973, U.S. photographer.

Stein, Gertrude (stīn) 1874-1946, U.S. writer.

Stein·beck, John (stīn′bek′) 1902-1968, U.S. novelist.

Stein·metz, Charles Proteus (stīn′mets′) 1865-1923, U.S. scientist and electrical engineer.

Sten·dhal (sten däl′) 1783-1842, French novelist and critic; pen name of *Marie-Henri Beyle.*

Ste·phen (stē′vən) **1. Saint.** d. A.D. 35?, first Christian martyr, stoned to death by a mob. **2.** 1097?-1154, king of England (1135-1154).

Sterne, Laurence (stûrn) 1713-1768, English writer.

Steu·ben, Baron Frederick William von (stü′bən, stü′-, stü ben′, stü-) 1730-1794, Prussian general who aided the colonists in the American Revolution.

Ste·vens (stē′vənz) **1. John Paul.** 1920- , U.S. Supreme Court associate justice (1975-). **2. Thaddeus.** 1792-1868, U.S. statesman. **3. Wallace.** 1879-1955, U.S. poet.

Ste·ven·son (stē′vən sən) **1. Adlai E(wing).** 1900-1965, U.S. politician. **2. Robert Louis.** 1850-1894, Scottish novelist and poet.

Stieg·litz, Alfred (stēg′lits) 1864-1946, U.S. photographer, editor, and art exhibitor.

St. Lau·rent, Louis Stephen (saɴ lô räɴ′) 1882-1973, Canadian prime minister (1948-1957).

Sto·kow·ski, Leopold (stə kou′skē, -kôf′-) 1882-1977, U.S. orchestra conductor.

Stone (stōn) **1. Harlan Fiske.** 1872-1946, U.S. Supreme Court Chief Justice (1941-1946). **2. Lucy.** 1818-1893, U.S. leader in the women's rights movement.

Stowe, Harriet Beecher (stō) 1811-1896, U.S. writer.

Strad·i·var·i, Antonio (strad′ə vâr′ē) 1644?-1737, Italian violin maker.

Stras·berg, Lee (stras′bûrg′) 1901-1982, U.S. acting teacher and director.

Strauss (strous) **1. Johann.** 1804-1849, Austrian composer. **2. Johann.** 1825-1899, Austrian composer; son of Johann Strauss. **3. Richard.** 1864-1949, German composer.

Stra·vin·sky, Igor (strə vin′skē) 1882-1971, Russian composer.

Strind·berg, Johan August (strind′bûrg′) 1849-1912, Swedish playwright and novelist.

Stu·art (stü′ərt, stū′-) royal family that ruled Scotland (1371-1714) and England (1603-1714).

Stuart 1. Charles Edward. 1720-1788, pretender to the English throne; grandson of James II; known as *Bonnie Prince Charlie*. **2. Gilbert.** 1755-1828, American painter. **3. James Ewell Brown.** 1833-1864, Confederate general in the American Civil War; known as *Jeb Stuart*. **4. Mary.** see **Mary, Queen of Scots.**

Stuy·ve·sant, Peter (stī′və sənt) 1592-1672, Dutch colonial administrator of New Netherland.

Sue·to·ni·us (swi tō′nē əs) A.D. 69?-140?, Roman historian.

Su·har·to (sü här′tō) 1921- , Indonesian president (1967-).

Sui (swē) dynasty that ruled China (A.D. 581-618).

Su·kar·no (sü kär′nō) 1901-1970, Indonesian president (1945-1967).

Su·lei·man I (sü′lā män′) *also,* **Solyman I.** 1495?-1566, sultan of the Ottoman Empire (1520-1566); known as *the Magnificent*.

Sul·la, Lucius Cornelius (sul′ə) 138-78 B.C., dictator of Rome (82-79 B.C.).

Sul·li·van (sul′ə vən) **1. Sir Arthur.** 1842-1900, English composer who collaborated with the librettist Sir William S. Gilbert. **2. John L(awrence).** 1858-1918, U.S. boxer. **3. Louis Henry.** 1856-1924, U.S. architect.

Sum·ner, Charles (sum′nər) 1811-1874, U.S. statesman.

Sung (sung) see **Song.**

Sun Yat-Sen (sün′yät′sen′) 1866-1925, Chinese revolutionary leader and statesman.

Sur·rey, Earl of (sûr′ē) 1515?-1547, English poet; born *Henry Howard*.

Su Shih (sü′shē′) see **Su Tung-p'o.**

Suth·er·land, Dame Joan (su<u>th</u>′ər lənd) 1926- , Australian soprano.

Su Tung-p'o (sü′tung′bō′) A.D. 1036-1101, Chinese poet. Also, **Su Shih.**

Swe·den·borg, Emanuel (swē′dən bôrg′) 1688-1772, Swedish scientist, mystic, and theologian; born *Emanuel Svedberg*.

Swift, Jonathan (swift) 1667-1745, English writer and satirist.

Swin·burne, Algernon Charles (swin′bûrn′) 1837-1909, English writer and critic.

Synge, J(ohn) M(illington) (sinj) 1871-1909, Irish playwright.

Szi·lard, Leo (sil′ärd) 1898-1964, U.S. nuclear physicist.

Tab·i·tha (tab′i thə) see **Dorcas.**

Tac·i·tus (tas′i təs) A.D. 55?-117, Roman historian.

Taft, William Howard (taft) 1857-1930, twenty-seventh president of the United States (1909-1913), U.S. Supreme Court Chief Justice (1921-1930).

Ta·gore, Sir Rabindranath (tə gôr′) 1861-1941, Hindu philosopher and poet.

Taine, Hippolyte Adolphe (tān) 1828-1893, French historian, critic, and philosopher.

Tal·ley·rand (tal′ē rand′) 1754-1838, French statesman and diplomat; full name *Charles Maurice de Talleyrand-Périgord*.

Ta·lon, Jean-Baptiste (ta lôN′) 1625-1694, French colonial official, first intendant of justice and finance in New France (1665-1672).

Tam·er·lane (tam′ər lān′) *also,* **Tam·bur·laine** (tam′bər lān′). 1336?-1405, Mongol conqueror of central Asia and eastern Europe.

Ta·ney, Roger Brooke (tô′nē) 1774-1864, U.S. jurist and statesman, U.S. Supreme Court Chief Justice (1836-1864).

Tang (täng) dynasty that ruled China (A.D. 618-906). Also, **T'ang.**

Ta·ni·za·ki Ju·ni·chi·ro (tä′nē zä′kē jü′nē chē′rō) 1886-1965, Japanese writer.

Tar·ken·ton, Fran (tär′kən tən) 1940- , U.S. football player; full name *Francis Asbury Tarkenton*.

Tar·king·ton, Booth (tär′king tən) 1869-1946, U.S. novelist.

Tas·man, Abel Janszoon (taz′mən) 1603?-1659, Dutch navigator.

Tay·lor (tā′lər) **1. Edward.** 1642?-1729, American colonel, poet, and clergyman. **2. Zachary.** 1784-1850, U.S. general, twelfth president of the United States (1849-1850).

Tchai·kov·sky, Peter Ilyich (chī kôf′skē) 1840-1893, Russian composer.

Te·cum·seh (tə kum′sə) 1768?-1813, Shawnee chief.

Tel·ler, Edward (tel′ər) 1908- , U.S. physicist.

Teng Hsiao-ping (dung′shou′ping′) see **Deng Xiaoping.**

Ten·ny·son, Alfred, Lord (ten′ə sən) 1809-1892, English poet.

Ter·ence (ter′ens) 190?-159? B.C., Roman playwright.

Te·re·sa (tə rē′sə, -zə, -rā′-) **1. Mother.** see **Mother Teresa. 2. Saint.** see **Theresa, Saint.**

Tes·la, Nikola (tes′lə) 1856-1943, U.S. electrical engineer and inventor; born in Croatia.

Thack·er·ay, William Makepeace (thak′ə rē) 1811-1863, English novelist.

Tha·les (thā′lēz) 640?-546? B.C., Greek philosopher.

Thant, U (thänt, thant) 1909-1975, Burmese diplomat, secretary-general of the United Nations (1961-1971).

Thatch·er, Margaret Hilda (thach′ər) 1925- , British political leader, prime minister (1979-1991).

Thay·en·da·ne·ge·a (thā′ən dan′ə gē′ə) see **Brant, Joseph.**

The·mis·to·cles (thə mis′tə klēz′) 527?-460? B.C., Athenian statesman and general.

The·od·o·ric (thē od′ə rik) A.D. 454?-526, king of the Ostrogoths.

The·o·do·si·us I (thē′ə dō′shē əs) A.D. 346?-395, Roman emperor (A.D. 379-395).

The·re·sa, Saint (tə rē′sə, -zə, -rā′-) 1515-1582, Spanish Carmelite nun, mystic, and writer. Also, **Teresa, Theresa of A·vi·la** (ä′vē lä′).

Thes·pis (thes′pis) sixth century B.C., Greek dramatist.

Thom·as (tom′əs) in the New Testament, one of the twelve Apostles of Jesus.

Thomas 1. Clarence. 1948- , U.S. Supreme Court associate justice (1991-). **2. Dylan** 1914-1953, Welsh poet.

Thomas à Kem·pis (ə kem′pis) 1380?-1471, German ecclesiastic and writer.

Thomp·son (tomp′sən) **1. Benjamin.** 1753-1814, British scientist. **2. Sir John Sparrow David.** 1844-1894, Canadian prime minister (1892-1894).

Thom·son (tom′sən) **1. Joseph John.** 1856-1940, English physicist. **2. Virgil Garnett.** 1896-1989, U.S. composer and music critic.

Tho·reau, Henry David (thə rō′) 1817-1862, U.S. writer, philosopher, and naturalist.

Thorpe, Jim (thôrp) 1888-1953, U.S. athlete; full name *James Francis Thorpe*.

Thot·mes III (tōt′mes, thōt′-) see **Thutmose III.**

Thu·cyd·i·des (thü sid′i dēz′) 460?-400? B.C., Greek historian.

Thut·mo·se III (tüt mō′sə, thüt-) *also,* **Thotmes III, Thut·mo·sis III** (tüt mō′sis, thüt-). king of Egypt (1504-1450 B.C.); husband of Hatshepsut.

Ti·be·ri·us (tī bîr′ē əs) 42 B.C.-A.D. 37, Roman emperor (A.D. 14-37).

Tif·fa·ny, Louis Comfort (tif′ə nē) 1848-1933, U.S. designer and craftsman of stained glass.

Til·den (til′dən) **1. Samuel Jones.** 1814-1886, U.S. political leader. **2. William Tatem, II.** 1893-1953, U.S. tennis player.

Tim·o·thy (tim′ə thē) in the New Testament, a disciple of Paul.

Tin·dal, William (tin′dəl) *also,* **William Tin·dale.** see **Tyndale, William.**

Tin·to·ret·to (tin′tə ret′ō) 1518-1594, Venetian painter.

Ti·squan·tum (ti skwon′təm) see **Squanto.**

Ti·tian (tish′ən) 1477?-1576, Venetian painter.

Ti·to, Josip Broz (tē′tō) 1892-1980, Yugoslavian president (1953-1980).

Ti·tus (tī′təs) **1.** A.D. 39?-81, Roman emperor (A.D. 79-81). **2.** in the New Testament, a disciple of Paul.

To·ba (tō′bä′) dynasty that ruled China (A.D. 386-557). Also, **Northern Wei, T'o-pa Wei.**

Tocque·ville, Alexis de (tōk′vil′) 1805-1859, French political theorist.

To·jo Hi·de·ki (tō′jō hē′de kē′) 1884-1948, Japanese general, prime minister (1941-1944).

Tol·stoy, Count Leo Nikolayevich (tōl′stoi) 1828-1910, Russian novelist and philosopher.

T'o·pa Wei (tō′bä′wā′) see **Toba.**

Tor·ri·cel·li, Evangelista (tôr′i chel′ē) 1608-1647, Italian physicist.

Tos·ca·ni·ni, Arturo (tos′kə nē′nē) 1867-1957, Italian conductor.

Tou·louse-Lau·trec, Henri de (tü lüz′lō trek′, tü lüs′) 1864-1901, French painter and illustrator.

a	at	e	end	o	hot	u	up	hw	white		about
ā	ape	ē	me	ō	old	ū	use	ng	song		taken
ä	far	i	it	ô	fork	ü	rule	th	thin	ə	pencil
âr	care	ī	ice	oi	oil	u̇	pull	<u>th</u>	this		lemon
		îr	pierce	ou	out	ûr	turn	zh	measure		circus

Tous·saint L'Ou·ver·ture, Pierre Dominique (tü saN′ lü-veR tyR′) 1743?-1803, Haitian statesman and revolutionary. Also, François Dominique Toussaint L'Ouverture.

Toyn·bee, Arnold Joseph (toin′bē) 1899-1975, English historian.

Tra·jan (trā′jən) A.D. 53?-117, Roman emperor (A.D. 98-117).

Trol·lope, Anthony (trol′əp) 1815-1882, English novelist.

Trot·sky, Leon (trot′skē) 1879-1940, Russian revolutionary leader; born *Lev Davidovich Bronstein.*

Tru·deau, Pierre Elliott (trü dō′) 1919- , Canadian prime minister (1968-1979; 1980-1984).

Truf·faut, François (tRY fō′) 1932-1984, French film director.

Tru·man, Harry S (trü′mən) 1884-1972, thirty-third president of the United States (1945-1953).

Truth, Sojourner (trüth) 1797?-1883, U.S. abolitionist; real name *Isabella Van Wagener.*

Ts'ao Chan (tsou′jän′) see Ts'ao Hsüeh-ch'in.

Ts'ao Hsüeh-ch'in (tsou′shye′chin′) 1715?-1763, Chinese writer. Also, Ts'ao Chan.

Tsin (chin) dynasty that ruled China (A.D. 265-420). Also, **Chin.**

Tsquan·tum (skwon′təm) see Squanto.

Tub·man, Harriet (tub′mən) 1820?-1913, U.S. abolitionist and conductor on the Underground Railroad.

Tu·dor (tü′dər, tū′-) royal family that ruled England (1485-1603).

Tu Fu (dü′fü′) 712-770, Chinese poet.

Tup·per, Sir Charles (tup′ər) 1821-1915, Canadian prime minister (1896).

Tur·ge·nev, Ivan Sergeevich (tûr gā′nyəf) 1818-1883, Russian writer.

Tur·ner (tûr′nər) **1.** Frederick Jackson. 1861-1932, U.S. historian. **2.** John Napier. 1929- , Canadian prime minister (1984). **3.** Joseph M(allord) W(illiam). 1775-1851, English painter. **4.** Nat. 1800-1831, U.S. slave and revolutionary.

Tut·ankh·a·men (tü′täng kä′mən) king of Egypt (1361?-1352 B.C.).

Tu·tu, Desmond Mpilo (tü′tü) 1931- , South African prelate and civil rights leader.

Twain, Mark (twān) 1835-1910, U.S. writer and humorist; pen name of *Samuel Langhorne Clemens.*

Ty·ler, John (tī′lər) 1790-1862, tenth president of the United States (1841-1845).

Tyn·dale, William (tin′dəl) *also,* **Tindal, Tindale.** 1492?-1536, English religious reformer and translator of the Bible.

U·na·mu·no y Ju·go, Miguel de (ü′nə mü′nō ē hü′gō) 1864-1936, Spanish writer and philosopher.

U·ni·tas, John (ū nī′təs) 1933- , U.S. football player.

Ur·ban II (ûr′bən) A.D. 1042-1099, pope (1088-1099).

U·ri·ah (yü rī′ə) in the Old Testament, a Hittite officer in David's army; husband of Bathsheba.

U Thant (ü thant′, ü thänt′) see Thant, U.

U·tril·lo, Maurice (ū tril′ō, ü tril′ō) 1883-1955, French painter.

Val·en·tine, Saint (val′ən tīn′) d. A.D. 270?, Christian martyr.

Va·le·ri·an (və lîr′ē ən) A.D. 193?-269?, Roman emperor (A.D. 253-260).

Va·lé·ry, Paul (val′ə rē′) 1871-1945, French poet.

Val·ois (val wä′) dynasty that ruled France (1328-1589).

Valois, Dame Ninette de 1898- , Anglo-Irish ballet dancer, choreographer, teacher, and director; stage name of *Edris Stannus.*

Van Bu·ren, Martin (van byûr′ən) 1782-1862, eighth president of the United States (1837-1841).

Van·cou·ver, George (van kü′vər) 1757-1798, English navigator and explorer.

Van·der·bilt, Cornelius (van′dər bilt′) 1794-1877, U.S. railroad magnate; known as *Commodore Vanderbilt.*

Van Dyck, Sir Anthony (van dīk′) *also,* **Van·dyke.** 1599-1641, Flemish painter.

van Gogh, Vincent (van gō′, gôKH′; *Dutch* vän KHÔKH′) 1853-1890, Dutch painter.

Van·zet·ti, Bartolomeo (van zet′ē) 1888-1927, Italian anarchist in the United States.

Vaughan Wil·liams, Ralph (vôn wil′yəmz; rāf) 1872-1958, English composer.

Veb·len, Thorstein (veb′lən) 1857-1929, U.S. economist and sociologist.

Ve·ga, Lope de, see Lope de Vega.

Ve·láz·quez, Diego Rodríguez de Silva y (ve läs′kes) *also,* **Velásquez.** 1599-1660, Spanish painter.

Venerable Bede, see Bede, Saint.

Ver·di, Giuseppe (vâr′dē) 1813-1901, Italian composer of operas.

Ver·gil (vûr′jəl) *also,* **Virgil.** 70-19 B.C., Roman poet.

Ver·laine, Paul (vâr lān′, veR len′) 1844-1896, French poet.

Ver·meer, Jan (vər mîr′) 1632-1675, Dutch painter; full name *Jan van der Meer van Delft.*

Verne, Jules (vûrn) 1828-1905, French novelist.

Ve·ro·ne·se, Paolo (ver′ə nā′zē) 1528-1588, Venetian painter.

Ve·sa·li·us, Andreas (və sā′lē əs) 1514-1564, Belgian anatomist.

Ve·sey, Denmark (vē′zē) 1767?-1822, U.S. freedman who planned a slave revolt.

Ves·pa·sian (ves pā′zhən) A.D. 9-79, Roman emperor (A.D. 70-79).

Ves·puc·ci, Amerigo (ves pü′chē) 1454-1512, Italian explorer for whom America was named.

Vi·co, Giambattista (vē′kō) 1668-1744, Italian philosopher and historian. Also, Giovanni Battista Vico.

Vic·to·ri·a (vik tôr′ē ə) 1819-1901, queen of England (1837-1901).

Vil·la, Francisco (vē′ə) 1877-1923, Mexican revolutionary; also known as *Pancho Villa;* real name *Doroteo Arango.*

Vil·lon, François (vē yôN′) 1431-1463?, French poet; born *François de Montcorbier.*

Vinci, Leonardo da, see Leonardo da Vinci.

Vin·son, Frederick Moore (vin′sən) 1890-1953, U.S. Supreme Court Chief Justice (1946-1953).

Vir·gil (vûr′jəl) see Vergil.

Virgin Mary, see Mary *(def. 1).*

Vi·val·di, Antonio (vi väl′dē) 1675?-1741, Italian composer.

Vol·ta, Alessandro (vōl′tə) 1745-1827, Italian physicist.

Vol·taire (vōl târ′) 1694-1778, French philosopher, poet, historian, and dramatist; pen name of *François Marie Arouet.*

Wag·ner, Richard (väg′nər) 1813-1883, German composer.

Waite, Morrison Remick (wāt) 1816-1888, U.S. Supreme Court Chief Justice (1874-1888).

Wald·heim, Kurt (wôld′hīm′, väld′-) 1918- , Austrian diplomat, secretary-general of the United Nations (1972-1982), and president of Austria (1986-).

Wa·les·a, Lech (və len′sə) 1943- , Polish labor leader; president of Poland (1990-).

Wal·lace (wol′is) **1.** Alfred, Russel. 1823-1913, English naturalist. **2.** George C(orley). 1919- , U.S. politician. **3.** Henry Agard. 1888-1965, U.S. political leader. **4.** Lew. 1827-1905, U.S. writer, diplomat, and soldier.

Wal·len·stein, Albrecht von (wol′ən stīn′, vä′lən shtīn′) 1583-1634, Austrian general.

Wal·pole, Horace, 4th Earl of Oxford (wôl′pōl′) 1717-1797, English writer.

Wal·ton, Izaak (wôl′tən) 1593-1683, English writer.

Wang Wei (wäng′wā′) 699-759, Chinese poet and painter.

War·hol, Andy (wôr′hôl) 1928-1987, U.S. artist; born *Andrew Warhola.*

War·ren (wôr′ən, wor′-) **1.** Earl. 1891-1974, U.S. Supreme Court Chief Justice (1953-1969). **2.** Robert Penn. 1905-1989, U.S. writer, first U.S. poet laureate (1986-1988).

Wash·ing·ton (wô′shing tən, wosh′ing-) **1.** Booker T. 1856-1915, U.S. educator. **2.** George. 1732-1799, colonial general in the American Revolution, first president of the United States (1789-1797). **3.** Martha. 1731-1802, wife of George Washington.

Watt, James (wot) 1736-1819, Scottish engineer and inventor.

Wat·teau, Jean Antoine (wä tō′) 1684-1721, French painter.

Watts (wots) **1.** George Frederic. 1817-1904, English painter. **2.** Isaac. 1674-1748, English clergyman and writer of hymns.

Wayne (wān) **1.** Anthony. 1745-1796, colonial general in the American Revolution; known as *Mad Anthony.* **2.** John. 1907-1979, U.S. film actor and producer; real name *Marion Michael Morrison;* nickname *Duke.*

We·ber (vā′bər) **1.** Carl Maria von. 1786-1826, German composer. **2.** Max. 1864-1920, German social scientist.

Web·ster (web′stər) **1.** Daniel. 1782-1852, U.S. statesman. **2.** John. 1580-1634, English dramatist. **3.** Noah. 1758-1843, American lexicographer, writer, and editor.

Wedg·wood, Josiah (wej′wừd′) 1730-1795, English pottery manufacturer.

Wei (wā) dynasty that ruled China (A.D. 220-265).

Weill, Kurt (wīl, vīl) 1900-1950, German-American composer.

Weiz·mann, Chaim (wīts′mən, vīts′män) 1874-1952, Russian-born Zionist leader, first president of Israel (1949-1952).

Welles, (George) Orson (welz) 1915-1985, U.S. actor, director, and writer for radio, stage, and screen.

Wel·ling·ton, Duke of (wel′ing tən) 1769-1852, British soldier and statesman; born *Arthur Wellesley.*

Wells, H(erbert) G(eorge) (welz) 1866-1946, English novelist and social philosopher.

Wel·ty, Eudora (wel′tē) 1909- , U.S. writer.

Wes·ley (wes′lē, wez′-) **1. Charles.** 1707-1788, English religious reformer, cofounder of Methodism with his brother John Wesley. **2. John.** 1703-1791, English religious leader, cofounder of Methodism with his brother Charles Wesley.

West, Benjamin (west) 1738-1820, American painter.

West·ing·house, George (wes′ting hous′) 1846-1914, U.S. inventor.

Wey·den, Rogier van der (vī′dən) 1399?-1464, Flemish painter.

Whar·ton, Edith (hwôr′tən, wôr′-) 1862-1937, U.S. novelist.

Wheat·ley, Phillis (hwēt′lē, wēt′-) 1753?-1784, American poet.

Whis·tler, James Abbott McNeill (hwis′lər, wis′-) 1834-1903, U.S. painter and etcher.

White (hwīt, wīt) **1. Byron R.** 1917- , U.S. Supreme Court associate justice (1962-). **2. Edward Douglass.** 1845-1921, U.S. Supreme Court Chief Justice (1910-1921). **3. Patrick.** 1912- , Australian writer.

White·field, George (hwīt′fēld′, wīt′-) 1714-1770, English Methodist clergyman.

White·head, Alfred North (hwīt′hed′, wīt′-) 1861-1947, English mathematician and philosopher.

Whit·man, Walt (hwit′mən, wit′-) 1819-1892, U.S. poet.

Whit·ney, Eli (hwit′nē, wit′-) 1765-1825, U.S. inventor and pioneer in methods of mass production.

Whit·ti·er, John Greenleaf (hwit′ē ər, wit′-) 1807-1892, U.S. poet and abolitionist.

Wick·liffe, John (wik′lif) *also,* **John Wic·lif.** see **Wycliffe, John.**

Wil·ber·force, William (wil′bər fôrs′) 1759-1833, English statesman, abolitionist, and philanthropist.

Wilde, Oscar (wīld) 1854-1900, Irish playwright, novelist, and essayist.

Wil·der, Thornton Niven (wīl′dər) 1897-1975, U.S. playwright and novelist.

Wil·kins, Roy (wil′kənz) 1901-1981, U.S. civil rights leader.

Wil·liam I (wil′yəm) 1027?-1087, king of England (1066-1087); known as *William the Conqueror.*

William II 1. 1056?-1100, king of England (1087-1100); called *William Rufus.* **2. Wil·liam II.** 1859-1941, emperor of Germany (1888-1918).

William III, 1650-1702, leader of the United Provinces of the Netherlands (1672-1702), king of England (1689-1702); known as *William of Orange.*

William IV, 1765-1837, king of Great Britain (1830-1837).

William of Oc·cam (ok′əm) 1285?-1349, English philosopher. Also, **William of Ockham.**

William Ru·fus (rü′fəs) see **William II** *(def. 1).*

Wil·liams (wil′yəmz) **1. Roger.** 1603-1684, English clergyman, founder of Rhode Island. **2. Ted.** 1918- , U.S. baseball player; full name *Theodore Samuel Williams.* **3. Tennessee.** 1914-1983, U.S. dramatist; pen name of *Thomas Lanier Williams.* **4. William Carlos.** 1883-1963, U.S. poet and physician.

Will·kie, Wendell Lewis (wil′kē) 1892-1944, U.S. politician.

Wills, Helen Newington (wilz) 1906- , U.S. tennis player.

Wil·son (wil′sən) **1. Edmund.** 1895-1972, U.S. social and literary critic. **2. Harold.** 1916- , British political leader, prime minister (1964-1970; 1974-1976). **3. Woodrow.** 1856-1924, twenty-eighth president of the United States (1913-1921).

Wind·sor (win′zər) name of the British royal family, adopted in 1917.

Windsor, Duke of, see **Edward VIII.**

Win·throp (win′thrəp) family of colonial leaders in America including **1. John.** 1588-1649, first governor of the Massachusetts Bay Colony. **2. John.** 1606-1676, governor of Connecticut (1657; 1659-1676); son of John Winthrop.

Witt·gen·stein, Ludwig Josef Johan (vit′gən shtīn′) 1889-1951, Austrian philosopher.

Wolfe (wulf) **1. James.** 1727-1759, English military commander. **2. Thomas.** 1900-1938, U.S. novelist.

Wol·sey, Thomas (wul′zē) 1475?-1530, English cardinal and statesman.

Wood, Grant (wud) 1892-1942, U.S. painter.

Woolf, Virginia (wulf) 1882-1941, English novelist and critic.

Wool·worth, Frank Winfield (wul′wûrth′) 1852-1919, U.S. merchant.

Words·worth, William (wûrdz′wûrth′) 1770-1850, English poet.

Wo·vo·ka (wə vō′kə) 1858?-1932, Paiute prophet of the ghost-dance religion.

Wren, Sir Christopher (ren) 1632-1723, English architect.

Wright (rīt) **1. Frank Lloyd.** 1869-1959, U.S. architect. **2. Orville.** 1871-1948, U.S. inventor and pioneer in aviation. **3. Richard.** 1908-1960, U.S. writer. **4. Wilbur.** 1867-1912, U.S. inventor and pioneer in aviation; brother of Orville.

Wundt, Wilhelm (vunt) 1832-1920, German psychologist.

Wy·att, Sir Thomas (wī′ət) 1503-1542, English poet and statesman.

Wych·er·ley, William (wich′ər lē) 1640?-1716, English dramatist.

Wyc·liffe, John (wik′lif) *also,* **Wickliffe, Wiclif.** 1320-1384, English religious reformer.

Wy·eth, Andrew (wī′əth) 1917- , U.S. painter.

Xan·thip·pe (zan tip′ē) 469?-399 B.C., wife of Socrates.

Xa·vi·er, Saint Francis (zā′vē ər, ig zā′-) 1506-1552, Spanish Jesuit missionary.

Xen·o·phon (zen′ə fən) 430?-355 B.C., Greek historian.

Xer·xes (zûrk′sēz) 519?-465 B.C., king of Persia (485?-465 B.C.).

Ya·ma·mo·to, Isoroku (yä′mə mō′tō) 1884-1943, Japanese admiral.

Yeats, William Butler (yāts) 1865-1939, Irish poet and dramatist.

Yelt·sin, Boris (yel′tsin) 1931- , Russian politician, president of Russia (1991-)

Yev·tu·shen·ko, Yevgeny (yef′tù sheng′kō) 1933- , Russian poet.

Yin (yin) see **Shang.**

York (yôrk) family that ruled England (1461-1485), a branch of the royal house of Plantagenet.

York, Duke of 1341-1402, son of Edward III of England; born *Edmund Langley.*

Young (yung) **1. Brigham.** 1801-1877, U.S. Mormon leader. **2. Cy.** 1867-1955, U.S. baseball player; nickname of *Denton T. Young.* **3. Edward.** 1683-1765, English poet.

Yu·an (ū än′) *also,* **Yün.** Mongol dynasty that ruled China (1260-1368).

Zach·a·ri·ah (zak′ə rī′ə) **1.** in the New Testament, the father of John the Baptist. **2.** see **Zechariah.**

Za·har·i·as, Mildred Didrikson (zə hâr′ē əs) 1913-1956, U.S. athlete; nickname *Babe.*

Zang·will, Israel (zang′gwil) 1864-1926, English writer.

Za·pa·ta, Emiliano (sä pä′tə) 1879?-1919, Mexican revolutionary.

Zar·a·thus·tra (zar′ə thüs′trə) see **Zoroaster.**

Zeb·e·dee (zeb′ə dē′) in the New Testament, the father of the Apostles James and John.

Zeb·u·lun (zeb′yə lun) **1.** in the Old Testament, a son of Jacob and Leah. **2.** one of the twelve tribes of Israel descended from him.

Zech·a·ri·ah (zek′ə rī′ə) seventh century B.C., Hebrew prophet.

Zed·e·ki·ah (zed′ə kī′ə) the last king of Judah (597-586 B.C.).

Zeng·er, John Peter (zeng′ər) 1697-1746, American colonial printer, editor, and publisher.

Ze·no (zē′nō) 336?-262 B.C., Greek philosopher.

Zeph·a·ni·ah (zef′ə nī′ə) seventh century B.C., Hebrew prophet.

Zep·pe·lin, Count Ferdinand von (zep′ə lin) 1838-1917, German soldier and designer of airships.

Zhao Zi·yang (jou′zù′yäng′) 1919- , premier of China (1980-1989).

Zhou (jō) *also,* **Chou.** dynasty that ruled China (1027-256 B.C.).

Zhou En·lai (jō′en′lī′) see **Chou En·lai.**

Zi·a ul-Haq, Mohammad (zē′ä ùl häk′) 1924-1988, Pakistani president (1978-1988).

Zo·la, Émile (zō′lə, zō lä′) 1840-1902, French novelist and critic.

Zo·ro·as·ter (zôr′ō as′tər) 628?-551 B.C., Persian religious teacher, founder of Zoroastrianism. Also, **Zarathustra.**

Zwing·li, Huldreich (zwing′lē, tsfing′-) 1484-1531, Swiss religious reformer.

a	at	e	end	o	hot	u	up	hw	white		about
ā	ape	ē	me	ō	old	ū	use	ng	song		taken
ä	far	i	it	ô	fork	ü	rule	th	thin	ə	pencil
âr	care	ī	ice	oi	oil	ù	pull	th	this		lemon
		îr	pierce	ou	out	ûr	turn	zh	measure		circus

1419

Geographical Names

This section lists the names of countries, states, cities, regions, continents, oceans, mountains, rivers, and other geographical features, as well as places of historical and cultural importance. The main geographical entry contains pronunciation, descriptive information, and population figures. When area, height, and length are given in an entry, metric equivalents are included. Capitals are listed for each country, as well as for U.S. states and Canadian provinces. Postal and traditional abbreviations are listed for U.S. states. Former names, less frequently used official names, and other variant forms often are listed separately as cross-references to the main entry. Adjectives and nouns formed from geographical names are included at the end of many entries. For example, **Kentuckian** can be found under the entry **Kentucky**.

Entries are listed alphabetically under the geographical name and not under a descriptive term, such as *Lake, Mount,* or *Cape,* which is part of the place name. For example, Mount Everest is listed as **Everest, Mount,** and Lake Superior as **Superior, Lake.**

Aa·chen (ä′кнən) a city in Germany, west of the Rhine, once the capital of Charlemagne's empire. Pop., 233,255. Also, *French,* **Aix-la-Chapelle.**

Aal·borg (ôl′bôrg) see **Ålborg.**

Aar·hus (ôr′нуs) see **Århus.**

A·ba·dan (ä′bä dän′) a port city in southwestern Iran. Pop., 296,081.

A·be·o·ku·ta (ab′ē ō kü′tə) a city in southwestern Nigeria. Pop., 341,300.

Ab·er·deen (*def. 1,* ab′ər dēn′; *def. 2,* ab′ər dēn′) **1.** a city on the east coast of Scotland. Pop., 210,700. **2.** a city in northeastern South Dakota. Pop., 24,927.

Ab·i·djan (ab′i jän′) the former capital of the Ivory Coast, a port city in the southeastern part of the country. Pop., 1,950,000.

Ab·i·lene (ab′ə lēn′) a city in central Texas. Pop., 106,654.

A·bou·kir (ä′bü kîr′) see **Abukir.**

A·bu Dha·bi (ä′bü dä′bē, -<u>th</u>ä′bē) *also,* **Abu Zaby. 1.** the largest and most populous sheikdom in the United Arab Emirates. Area, 26,000 sq mi (67,340 sq km). Pop., 670,125. **2.** the capital of the United Arab Emirates and of the sheikdom of Abu Dhabi. Pop., 242,975.

A·bu·ja (ə bü′jə) the capital of Nigeria, in the central part of the country. Pop., 15,000.

A·bu·kir (ä′bü kîr′) *also,* **A·bou·kir, A·bu Qir.** a bay in northern Egypt where a British fleet commanded by Admiral Horatio Nelson defeated a French fleet in 1798.

Ab·u Za·by (ä′bü <u>th</u>ä′bē) see **Abu Dhabi.**

Ab·ys·sin·i·a (ab′ə sin′ē ə) see **Ethiopia.** —**Ab′ys·sin′i·an,** *adj., n.*

A·ca·di·a (ə kā′dē ə) a former French colony in eastern Canada, consisting of the present-day Maritime Provinces. —**A·ca′di·an,** *adj., n.*

A·ca·pul·co (ak′ə půl′kō, ä′kə pül′-) a resort city on the southwestern coast of Mexico. Pop., 301,902.

Ac·cad (ak′ad, ä′käd) see **Akkad.**

Ac·cra (ə krä′, ak′rə) *also,* **Akkra.** the capital and largest city of Ghana, a port in the southern part of the country. Pop., 859,640.

A·chae·a (ə kē′ə) *also,* **A·cha·ia** (ə kā′ə, ə kī′ə). a region of ancient Greece, in the northern Peloponnesus.

A·con·ca·gua (ak′ən kä′gwə) a mountain in western Argentina, in the Andes, the highest in South America and the Western Hemisphere. Height, 22,831 ft (6,959 m).

A·cre (ä′kər) a port city in northwestern Israel, important during the Crusades. Pop., 37,200. Also, **Akko.**

Ac·ti·um (ak′tē əm, -shē-) a promontory on the northwestern coast of Greece, near where Octavian's forces under Agrippa defeated Antony and Cleopatra in a naval battle in 31 B.C.

A·da·na (ä′də nə) a city in southern Turkey. Pop., 931,555.

Ad Dam·mam (ad′da mam′) see **Dammam.**

Ad·dis Ab·a·ba (ad′is ab′ə bə) the capital and largest city of Ethiopia, in the central part of the country. Pop., 1,686,300.

Ad·e·laide (ad′ə lād′) a city in southern Australia, the capital of the state of South Australia. Pop., 1,036,747.

A·den (ad′ən, ä′dən) **1.** a port city in Yemen, on the Gulf of Aden. Pop., 176,100. **2. Gulf of.** a western inlet of the Arabian Sea, between southern Arabia and eastern Africa.

Ad·i·ron·dacks (ad′ə ron′daks) a mountain range in northeastern New York. Also, **Ad′i·ron′dack Mountains.**

A·do-E·ki·ti (ä′dō e kē′tē) a city in southwestern Nigeria. Pop., 287,000.

A·dri·at·ic (ā′drē at′ik) a sea between Italy and Croatia, an arm of the Mediterranean. Also, **Adriatic Sea.**

Ae·ge·an (i jē′ən) a sea between Greece and Turkey, an arm of the Mediterranean. Also, **Aegean Sea.**

Ae·o·lis (ē′ə lis) an ancient region of northwestern Asia Minor, settled by the Aeolians.

Aet·na, Mount (et′nə) see **Etna, Mount.**

A·fars and the Is·sas, French Territory of the (ä′färz; ē säz′) a former French colony in eastern Africa, now Djibouti.

Af·ghan·i·stan (af gan′ə stan′) a landlocked country in south-central Asia. Capital, Kabul. Area, 251,826 sq mi (652,229 sq km). Pop., 17,672,000.

Af·ri·ca (af′ri kə) a continent south of Europe, between the Atlantic and Indian oceans. Area, 11,704,000 sq mi (30,313,360 sq km). Pop., 667,000,000. —**Af′ri·can,** *adj., n.*

A·ga·dir (ä′gə dîr′) a port city in southwestern Morocco. Pop., 110,479.

A·ga·na (ä gä′nyə) the capital of Guam. Pop., 896.

Ag·in·court (aj′in kôrt′) a village in northern France, the site of an English victory over the French in 1415. Pop., 276.

A·gra (ä′grə) a city in north-central India, the site of the Taj Mahal. Pop., 694,191.

A·guas·ca·lien·tes (ä′gwäs kä lyen′tes) a state in central Mexico. Area, 2,499 sq mi (6,472 sq km). Pop., 519,439.

Ah·med·a·bad (ä′mə də bäd′) *also,* **Ah·mad·a·bad.** a city in western India. Pop., 2,059,725.

Ah·ve·nan·maa Islands (ä′və nän mä′, äкн′və-) an island group in the Baltic Sea, part of Finland. Land area, 572 sq mi (1,481 sq km). Pop., 23,761. Also, **Åland Islands.**

Ah·waz (ä wäz′) *also,* **Ah·vaz** (ä väz′). a city in southwestern Iran. Pop., 579,826.

Ain·tab (īn täb′) see **Gaziantep.**

Aix-en-Pro·vence (āk sän prô väns′) a resort city in southeastern France. Pop., 121,327. Also, **Aix** (āks).

Aix-la-Cha·pelle (āks′lä shä pel′) see **Aachen.**

A·jac·cio (ä yät′chō) a city on the west coast of Corsica, the birthplace of Napoleon I. Pop., 54,089.

Ak·kad (ak′ad, ä′käd) *also,* **Accad. 1.** an ancient region in the northern part of Mesopotamia. **2.** an ancient city in central Mesopotamia, on the Euphrates River.

Ak·ko (ä kō′, ä′kō) see **Acre.**

Ak·kra (ə krä′, ak′rə) see **Accra.**

Ak·ron (ak′rən) a city in northeastern Ohio. Pop., 223,019.

Al·a·bam·a (al′ə bam′ə) **1.** a state in the southeastern United States, at the southern end of the Appalachian Mountains and on the Gulf of Mexico. Capital, Montgomery. Area, 51,705 sq mi (133,916 sq km). Pop., 4,040,587. Abbreviation, **Ala.;** postal abbreviation, **AL 2.** a river in southwestern Alabama, flowing into the Mobile River. Length, 315 mi (507 km). —**Al′a·bam′-an, Al′a·bam′i·an,** *adj., n.*

Al·a·mein (al′ə mān′, ä′lə-) see **El Alamein.**

Å·land Islands (ä′lənd, ô′lənd, ō′länd) see **Ahvenanmaa Islands.**

A·las·ka (ə las′kə) the largest state of the United States, on the extreme northwestern peninsula of North America. Capital, Juneau. Area, 591,004 sq mi (1,530,700 sq km). Pop., 550,043. Abbreviation, **Alas.;** postal abbreviation, **AK** —**A·las′kan,** *adj., n.*

Alaskan Peninsula, a peninsula in southwestern Alaska, between the Bering Sea and the Pacific.

Al·ba Lon·ga (al'bə lông'gə) a city in ancient Latium, southeast of Rome, the legendary birthplace of Romulus and Remus.

Al·ba·ni·a (al bā'nē ə) a country in southeastern Europe, on the west coast of the Balkan Peninsula. Capital, Tiranë. Area, 11,100 sq mi (28,749 sq km). Pop., 3,084,000.

Al·ba·ny (ôl'bə nē) **1.** the capital of New York, in the eastern part of the state. Pop., 101,082. **2.** a city in southwestern Georgia. Pop., 78,122.

Al Bas·rah (al bus'rə, -bäs'rə) see **Basra.**

Al·ber·ta (al bûr'tə) a province of Canada, in the southwestern part of the country. Capital, Edmonton. Area, 225,285 sq mi (583,488 sq km). Pop., 2,375,278.

Al·bert, Lake (al'bərt) a lake in east-central Africa, on the border between Uganda and Zaire. Also, **Albert Ny·an·za** (nī-an'zə).

Al Bi·qa (äl'bi kä') see **Bekaa Valley.**

Âl·borg (ôl'bôrg) *also,* **Aalborg.** a port city in northern Denmark. Pop., 114,000.

Al·bu·quer·que (al'bə kûr'kē) the largest city in New Mexico, in the central part of the state. Pop., 384,736.

Al·ca·traz (al'kə traz') an island in San Francisco Bay, the site of a former U.S. penitentiary of the same name.

Al·der·ney (ôl'dər nē) a British island in the English Channel, off the coast of France, one of the Channel Islands. Area, 3 sq mi (7.8 sq km).

A·lep·po (ə lep'ō) a city in northwestern Syria. Pop., 1,261,000.

A·leu·tian Islands (ə lü'shən) a chain of U.S. islands in the northern Pacific, extending southwest from Alaska. Land area, 6,391 sq mi (16,553 sq km). Also, **A·leu'tians.**

Al·ex·an·dri·a (al'ig zan'drē ə) **1.** a port city in northern Egypt, on the Mediterranean. It was founded by Alexander the Great in 332 B.C. Pop., 2,917,327. Also, *Arabic,* **Al Iskandariyah. 2.** a city in northern Virginia, a residential suburb of Washington, D.C. Pop., 111,183. **3.** a city in central Louisiana. Pop., 49,188.

Al Fay·yum (al'fä üm') a city in northern Egypt. Pop., 212,523.

Al·ge·ri·a (al jîr'ē ə) a country in northern Africa, on the Mediterranean. Capital, Algiers. Area, 919,595 sq mi (2,381,751 sq km). Pop., 23,038,942. —**Al·ge'ri·an,** *adj., n.*

Al·giers (al jîrz') the capital of Algeria, a port on the Mediterranean. Pop., 1,507,241. Also, **El Djazair, El Djezair.**

Al Hil·lah (äl hil'ə) a city in central Iraq. Pop., 215,249. Also, **Hilla.**

Al·i·can·te (al'i kan'tē, ä'lē kän'te) a port city in southeastern Spain, on the Mediterranean. Pop., 261,051.

Al Is·kan·da·ri·yah (äl'is kän'də rē'yä) see **Alexandria** *(def. 1).*

Al Ji·zah (al jē'zə) see **Giza.**

Al·la·ha·bad (al'ə hə bad', ä'lə hə bäd') a city in north-central India, on the Ganges. Pop., 616,051.

Al·le·ghe·ny (al'i gā'nē) a river in southwestern New York and western Pennsylvania, joining the Monongahela at Pittsburgh to form the Ohio. Length, 325 mi (523 km).

Allegheny Mountains, a mountain range extending from north-central Pennsylvania through western Maryland, eastern West Virginia, and western Virginia, part of the Appalachian mountain system. Also, **Al'le·ghe'nies.**

Al·len·town (al'ən toun') a city in eastern Pennsylvania. Pop., 105,090.

Al·ma-A·ta (äl'mə ə tä') the capital of Kazakhstan. Pop., 1,128,000.

Al Ma·di·nah (äl'mə dē'nə) see **Medina.**

Al Ma·hal·lah al Ku·bra (äl'mə hä'lə äl kü'brə) *Arabic.* see **Mahalla al Kubra.**

Al Man·su·rah (al'man sùr'ə) *also,* **El Mansura.** a city in northern Egypt, in the Nile delta. Pop., 316,870.

Al Maw·sil (äl' mō sēl') see **Mosul.**

Al Min·ya (al min'yə) a city in north-central Egypt, on the Nile. Pop., 179,136.

Alps (alps) a mountain system in south-central Europe, extending in an arc from the Mediterranean coast near the French-Italian border to the Balkan Peninsula.

Al Qa·hi·rah (al kä'hē rä') see **Cairo.**

Al·sace (al säs', -sas') a historic region and former province in eastern France, bordering Germany and Switzerland. —**Al·sa·tion** (al sā'shən), *adj., n.*

Al·sace-Lor·raine (al'säs lô rān', al sas') a former German territory, now in eastern France on the German and Swiss borders. It consists of Alsace and part of Lorraine. Ceded by France to Germany in 1871 after the Franco-Prussian War, it was restored to France in 1919 after World War I.

Al·tai Mountains (al'tī) a mountain system in central Asia, in southern Russia, northwestern China, and northwestern Mongolia.

Al·ta·mi·ra (al'tə mîr'ə) a cave near the northern coast of Spain, containing outstanding examples of Paleolithic cave art.

Al U·bay·yid (al'ü bä yid') see **El Obeid.**

A·ma·ga·sa·ki (ä'mä gä sä'kē) a city in Japan, in the southwestern part of the island of Honshu. Pop., 509,115.

Am·a·ril·lo (am'ə ril'ō) a city in northwestern Texas. Pop., 157,615.

Am·a·zon (am'ə zon') the longest river in South America and, by volume, the largest in the world, flowing from the Andes across Brazil into the Atlantic. Length, 4,000 mi (6,436 km).

A·mer·i·ca (ə mer'i kə) **1.** the United States. **2.** North America or South America. **3.** North, Central, and South America considered as a whole; the Western Hemisphere. Also *(def. 3),* **the Americas.** —**A·mer'i·can,** *adj., n.*

American Samoa, an island group in Samoa, administered by the United States. Capital, Pago Pago. Land area, 76 sq mi (197 sq km). Pop., 32,279.

Am·i·ens (am'ē ənz, a myän') a city in north-central France. Pop., 131,332.

Am·man (ä män') the capital of Jordan, an ancient city in the northwestern part of the country. Pop., 936,300.

A·moy (ä moi') see **Xiamen.**

Am·rit·sar (um rit'sər) a city in northwestern India. Pop., 594,844.

Am·ster·dam (am'stər dam') the capital and largest city of the Netherlands, in the west-central part of the country. Pop., 696,500.

A·mu Dar·ya (ä'mü där'yə) a river in central Asia, principally in Turkmenistan and Uzbekistan, flowing into the Aral Sea. Length, 1,578 mi (2,539 km).

A·mur (ä mùr') a river in northeastern Asia, forming part of the boundary between Siberia and China. Length, 2,761 mi (4,442 km).

An·a·heim (an'ə hīm') a city in southwestern California. Pop., 266,406.

An·a·to·li·a (an'ə tō'lē ə) see **Asia Minor.** —**An'a·to'li·an,** *adj., n.*

An·chor·age (ang'kər ij) a port city in southern Alaska, the largest city in the state. Pop., 226,338.

An·da·lu·sia (an'də lü'zhə) a historic region of southern Spain, now divided into eight provinces. —**An'da·lu'sian,** *adj., n.*

An·da·man and Nicobar Islands (an'də mən, -man') two island groups belonging to India, located in the eastern part of the Bay of Bengal. Land area, 3,184 sq mi (8,247 sq km). Pop., 188,741.

An·der·son·ville (an'dər sən vil') a village in west-central Georgia, the site of a Confederate prisoner-of-war camp during the Civil War.

An·des (an'dēz) the longest mountain system in the world, extending along the west coast of South America. —**An·de·an** (an dē'ən, an'dē ən), *adj.*

An·dor·ra (an dôr'ə) **1.** a small country in southwestern Europe, between France and Spain. Capital, Andorra. Area, 175 sq mi (453 sq km). Pop., 46,976. **2.** the capital of this country. Pop., 18,463. —**An·dor'ran,** *adj., n.*

Angel Falls, the world's highest waterfall, in southeastern Venezuela. Height, 3,212 ft (979 m).

Angel Island, the largest island in San Francisco Bay, an entry point for Asian immigrants to the United States from 1910 to 1940.

An·gers (än zhā') a city in western France, near Nantes. Pop., 136,038.

An·glo-E·gyp·tian Sudan (ang'glō i jip'shən) a former territory in northeastern Africa under joint British and Egyptian control, now the independent country of Sudan.

An·go·la (ang gō'lə) a country on the west coast of southern Africa. Capital, Luanda. Area, 481,350 sq mi (1,246,697 sq km). Pop., 9,739,100. —**An·go'lan,** *adj., n.*

An·go·ra (ang'gər ə) see **Ankara.**

a	at	e	end	o	hot	u	up	hw	white	⎧	about
ā	ape	ē	me	ō	old	ū	use	ng	song		taken
ä	far	i	it	ô	fork	ü	rule	th	thin	ə	pencil
âr	care	ī	ice	oi	oil	ů	pull	th	this		lemon
		îr	pierce	ou	out	ûr	turn	zh	measure	⎩	circus

An·guil·la (ang gwil′ə) a British island in the West Indies, one of the Leeward Islands. Area, 35 sq mi (91 sq km). Pop., 6,680.

An·hui (än′hwē′) *also,* **An·hwei** (än′hwā′). a province in eastern China. Capital, Hefei. Area, 54,015 sq mi (139,899 sq km). Pop., 52,990,000.

An·jou (an′jü, äN zhü′) a region and former province in western France, in the Loire valley.

An·ka·ra (ang′kər ə) the capital of Turkey, in the west-central part of the country. Pop., 2,553,209. Formerly, **Angora.**

An·na·ba (ä′nə bä′) a port city in northeastern Algeria, on the Mediterranean. Pop., 305,526. Formerly, **Bône.**

An Na·jaf (an naj′af) a city in south-central Iraq. Pop., 242,603.

An·nam (ə nam′) a former French protectorate in Indochina, now located in central Vietnam. —**An·nam·ese** (an′ə mēz′, -mēs′), *adj., n.*

An·nap·o·lis (ə nap′ə lis) the capital of Maryland, in the central part of the state. It is the site of the United States Naval Academy. Pop., 33,187.

An·na·pur·na (an′ə pùr′nə, -pûr′-) a mountain in the Himalayas, in west-central Nepal. Height, 26,504 ft (8,078 m).

Ann Arbor, a city in southeastern Michigan. Pop., 109,592.

An·shan (än′shän′) a city in northeastern China. Pop., 1,330,000.

An·ta·kya (än tä′kyə) a city in the southernmost part of central Turkey, on the site of ancient Antioch. Pop., 124,443.

An·ta·na·na·ri·vo (än′tə nä′nə rē′vō) the capital of Madagascar, in the central part of the country. Pop., 663,000. Formerly, **Tananarive.**

Ant·arc·ti·ca (ant ärk′ti kə, -är′ti-) an ice-covered continent surrounding the South Pole and lying mainly within the Antarctic Circle. Area, approx. 5,400,000 sq mi (13,986,000 sq km). Also, **the Ant·arc·tic** (ant ärk′tik, -är′tik).

Antarctic Ocean, a body of water surrounding Antarctica, consisting of the southernmost parts of the Atlantic, Pacific, and Indian oceans.

An·tep (än tep′) see Gaziantep.

An·tie·tam (an tē′təm) a creek in northwestern Maryland, the site, in 1862, of one of the bloodiest battles of the Civil War.

An·ti·gua and Barbuda (an tē′gə, -gwə) an island nation in the Leeward Islands of the West Indies, including the islands of Antigua and Barbuda. Capital, St. John's. Land area, 171 sq mi (443 sq km). Pop., 72,000.

An·til·les (an til′ēz) the islands of the West Indies excluding the Bahamas, divided into the Greater Antilles and the Lesser Antilles.

An·ti·och (an′tē ok′) the capital of ancient Syria, now in southern Turkey. Its site is now occupied in part by the city of Antakya.

An·to·fa·gas·ta (än′tō fə gäs′tə) a port city in northern Chile, on the Pacific. Pop., 185,486.

An·tsi·ra·na·na (än′tsə rä′nə nə) a port city in northern Madagascar, on the Indian Ocean. Pop., 100,000. Formerly, **Diégo-Suarez.**

Ant·werp (ant′wûrp) a port city in northern Belgium, the largest city in the country. Pop., 479,748.

Ap·en·nines (ap′ə nīnz′) a mountain system in southern Europe, extending down the entire length of the Italian peninsula.

A·pi·a (ä pē′ə) the capital of Western Samoa. Pop., 33,170.

Ap·pa·la·chi·a (ap′ə lā′chē ə, -lach′ē ə) a region in the eastern United States, including esp. that part of the Appalachian mountain system that extends from Pennsylvania to Georgia.

Ap·pa·la·chi·an Mountains (ap′ə lā′chē ən, -lach′ē-) the principal mountain system in eastern North America, extending from southeastern Canada to north-central Alabama. Also, **Ap′·pa·la′chi·ans.**

Ap·po·mat·tox (ap′ə mat′əks) **1.** a town in central Virginia, the county seat of Appomattox County since 1892. Pop., 1,707. **2. Appomattox Court House.** Formerly, the county seat of Appomattox County. The village is the site where Confederate General Robert E. Lee formally surrendered to Union General Ulysses S. Grant on April 9, 1865, ending the Civil War. It has been a national historical park since 1954.

A·qa·ba, Gulf of (ä′kə bə) a gulf at the northeastern end of the Red Sea, between the Sinai Peninsula and Saudi Arabia.

Aq·ui·taine (ak′wi tān′) a historic region in southwestern France.

A·ra·bi·a (ə rā′bē ə) a large peninsula in southwestern Asia. Area, approx. 1,000,000 sq mi (2,590,000 sq km). Also, **A·ra·bi·an Pen·in·su·la.**

A·ra·bi·an Desert (ə rā′bē ən) a desert in eastern Egypt between the Nile valley and the Red Sea. Area, 86,000 sq mi (223,000 sq km).

Arabian Sea, the northwestern part of the Indian Ocean, between India and Arabia.

A·ra·ca·ju (är′ə kə zhü′) a city in northeastern Brazil, near the Atlantic. Pop., 360,013.

Ar·a·gon (ar′ə gon′) a historic region and former kingdom in northeastern Spain.

Ar·al Sea (ar′əl) an inland saltwater lake between Kazakhstan and Uzbekistan. Also, **Lake Aral.**

Ar·a·rat (ar′ə rat′) a mountain in eastern Turkey, traditionally identified as the landing place of Noah's Ark. Height, 16,806 ft (5,122 m). Also, **Mount Ararat.**

Ar·ca·di·a (är kā′dē ə) a mountainous region of ancient Greece, in the central Peloponnesus, traditionally noted for the idyllic existence of its inhabitants.

Arch·an·gel (ärk′ān′jəl) see Arkhangelsk.

Arc·tic, the (ärk′tik, är′tik) the ice-covered region surrounding the North Pole.

Arctic Ocean, an ocean north of the Arctic Circle and surrounding the North Pole. Also, **Arctic Sea.**

Ar·dennes (är den′) a wooded region in southeastern Belgium, northern Luxembourg, and northern France, the scene of much fighting in World Wars I and II.

Ar·e·op·a·gus (ar′ē op′ə gəs) a hill west of the Acropolis in Athens.

Ar·gen·ti·na (är′jən tē′nə) a country in southern South America. Capital, Buenos Aires. Area, 1,073,400 sq mi (2,780,106 sq km). Pop., 27,947,446. —**Ar·gen·tine** (är′jən tēn′, -tīn′), *adj., n.* —**Ar·gen·tin·e·an** (är′jən tin′ē ən), *adj., n.*

Ar·gonne (är′gon, är gon′) a forest in northeastern France, site of several battles of World Wars I and II.

Ar·gos (är′gəs) an ancient city in south-central Greece.

År·hus (ôR′hүs) *also,* **Aarhus.** a port city in Denmark, on the east coast of Jutland. Pop., 202,300.

Ar·i·zo·na (ar′ə zō′nə) a state in the southwestern United States, bordering on Mexico. Capital, Phoenix. Area, 160,113 sq mi (414,693 sq km). Pop., 3,665,228. Abbreviation, **Ariz.;** postal abbreviation, **AZ.** —**Ar′i·zo′nan,** *adj., n.*

Ar·kan·sas (*def. 1,* är′kən sô′; *def. 2,* är′kən sô′, är kan′zəs) **1.** a state in the south-central United States. Capital, Little Rock. Area, 53,187 sq mi (137,754 sq km). Pop., 2,350,725. Abbreviation, **Ark.;** postal abbreviation, **AR 2.** a river flowing from west-central Colorado into the Mississippi. Length, 1,459 mi (2,348 km). —**Ar·kan·san** (är kan′zən), *adj., n.*

Ar·khan·gelsk (är κhän′gelsk) a port city in northwestern Russia, on the Northern Dvina. Pop., 416,000. Also, **Archangel.**

Ar·ling·ton (är′ling tən) **1.** a county in northern Virginia, a residential suburb of Washington, D.C. It is the site of Arlington National Cemetery, one of the largest U.S. national cemeteries. Pop., 170,936. **2.** a city in northeastern Texas. Pop., 261,721.

Ar·me·ni·a (är mē′nē ə) **1.** a country in southwestern Asia, bordering Azerbaijan, Georgia, Iran, and Turkey. It was formerly a republic of the Soviet Union. Capital, Yerevan. Area, 11,500 sq mi (29,785 sq km). Pop., 3,283,000. **2.** an ancient country in northeastern Asia Minor, now a region consisting of Armenia and parts of eastern Turkey and northwestern Iran.

Ar·no (är′nō) a river in north-central Italy, flowing through Florence to the Mediterranean. Length, 150 mi (241 km).

A·ru·ba (ə rü′bə) an island in the Leeward Islands, a dependency of the Netherlands, formerly part of the Netherlands Antilles. Capital, Oranjestad. Area, 74 sq mi (192 sq km). Pop., 64,763.

Ar·vad·a (är vad′ə) a city in north-central Colorado. Pop., 89,235.

As·cen·sion (ə sen′shən) a British island in the southern Atlantic, west of Africa. Area, 34 sq mi (88 sq km). Pop., 1,007.

A·shan·ti (ə shan′tē, ə shän′tē) a region in central Ghana, an independent kingdom from the late seventeenth to the late nineteenth century.

Ash·kha·bad (ash′kə bad′, äsh′kə bäd′) the capital of Turkmenistan. Pop., 398,000.

A·sia (ā′zhə) the largest continent, bounded on the west by the Ural Mountains, the Caucasus, and the Black, Mediterranean, and Red seas, on the south by the Indian Ocean, and on the east by the Pacific. Area, 17,120,000 sq mi (44,340,800 sq km). Pop., 3,245,000,000. —**A′sian,** *adj., n.*

Asia Minor, a peninsula in western Asia, bounded by the Black and Mediterranean seas. It includes most of the Asian part of Turkey. Area, 287,000 sq mi (743,330 sq km). Also, **Anatolia.**

As·ma·ra (az mär′ə) a city in northern Ethiopia. Pop., 319,353.

As·syr·i·a (ə sir′ē ə) an ancient empire in southwestern Asia, extending at its height from Mesopotamia to Egypt.

As·tra·khan (as'trə kan', äs'trə kän') a port city on the lower Volga River, in southwestern Russia. Pop., 509,000.

As·tu·ri·as (ə stùr'ē əs) a region and former kingdom in northwestern Spain. Area, 4,207 sq mi (10,896 sq km). —**As·tu'ri·an,** *adj., n.*

A·sun·ción (ä'sün syōn') the capital and largest city of Paraguay, an inland port in the southwestern part of the country. Pop., 477,100.

As·wan (as'wän) a city in southern Egypt, on the Nile, near the Aswan High Dam. Pop., 191,461.

As·yut (as ūt', äs-) a city in central Egypt, on the Nile. Pop., 273,191.

Ath·a·bas·ca (ath'ə bas'kə) *also,* **Ath·a·bas·ka. 1.** a river in Alberta, Canada, flowing north into Lake Athabasca. Length, 765 mi (1,231 km). **2. Lake.** a lake in Canada, on the northern Alberta-Saskatchewan border.

Ath·ens (ath'ənz) the capital of Greece, in the eastern part of the country. It was once the most important and powerful of the ancient Greek city-states and for centuries a leading cultural center in the Mediterranean region. Pop., 885,737. —**A·the·ni·an** (ə thē'nē ən), *adj., n.*

Ath·os, Mount (ath'os, -ōs, ā'thos, ā'thōs) a mountain on a peninsula of northeastern Greece, noted for the monasteries located there.

At·lan·ta (at lan'tə) the capital and largest city of Georgia, in the northwest-central part of the state. Pop., 394,017.

At·lan·tic (at lan'tik) an ocean separating Europe and Africa from North and South America. Also, **Atlantic Ocean.**

Atlantic City, a seashore resort city on the eastern coast of southern New Jersey. Pop., 37,986.

Atlantic Provinces, the Canadian provinces of New Brunswick, Nova Scotia, Prince Edward Island, and Newfoundland and Labrador, in the eastern part of the nation, on the Atlantic.

At·las Mountains (at'ləs) a mountain system along the northwestern coast of Africa, extending through most of Morocco and parts of Algeria and Tunisia.

At Ta·if (ät'tä ēf') a city in western Saudi Arabia. Pop., 300,000. Also, **Taif.**

At·ti·ca (at'i kə) a historic region in east-central Greece, on the Aegean. Athens is its principal city. —**At'tic,** *adj.*

At·tu Island (at'tū') the westernmost part of the United States, one of the Aleutian Islands, in Alaska.

Auck·land (ôk'lənd) a port city in northern New Zealand, located on North Island. Pop., 149,046.

Augs·burg (ôgz'bûrg') a city in southern Germany. Pop., 247,731.

Au·gus·ta (ô gus'tə) **1.** the capital of Maine, in the southern part of the state. Pop., 21,325. **2.** a city in northeastern Georgia. Pop., 44,639.

Au·ro·ra (ô rôr'ə) **1.** a city in north-central Colorado, a residential suburb of Denver. Pop., 222,103. **2.** a city in northeastern Illinois. Pop., 99,581.

Ausch·witz (oush'vits) the German name for **Oswiecim,** a city in southern Poland. It was the site of the largest Nazi concentration camp during World War II. Pop., 45,500.

Aus·tin (ôs'tin) the capital of Texas, in the south-central part of the state. Pop., 465,622.

Aus·tral·a·sia (ôs'trəl ā'zhə) an extensive area in the southwestern Pacific including Australia, Tasmania, New Zealand, New Guinea, and certain smaller islands in the immediate vicinity. —**Aus'tral·a'sian,** *adj., n.*

Aus·tra·lia (ôs trāl'yə) **1.** a continent southeast of Asia, between the Indian and Pacific oceans. It is the smallest of the continents. Area, 2,941,526 sq mi (7,618,552 sq km). Pop., 16,900,000. **2.** a country including this continent and the island of Tasmania. Capital, Canberra. Area, 2,967,909 sq mi (7,686,884 sq km). Pop., 16,833,100. —**Aus·tra'lian,** *adj., n.*

Australian Capital Territory, a federal territory in the southeastern part of Australia. It includes Canberra, the capital of the country. Area, 939 sq mi (2,432 sq km). Pop., 278,700.

Aus·tri·a (ôs'trē ə) a landlocked country in central Europe, mainly in the Alps. Capital, Vienna. Area, 32,377 sq mi (83,856 sq km). Pop., 7,555,338. —**Aus'tri·an,** *adj., n.*

Aus·tri·a-Hun·ga·ry (ôs'trē ə hung'gə rē) a former dual monarchy in central Europe, consisting of Austria, Hungary, and parts of Czechoslovakia, Poland, Romania, Italy, and Yugoslavia. It was broken up at the end of World War I. Also, **Aus'tro-Hun·ga'ri·an Empire.** —**Aus'tro-Hun·ga'ri·an,** *adj., n.*

A·vi·gnon (a vē nyôn') a historic city in southeastern France. It was the papal seat from 1309 to 1377. Pop., 89,132.

A·von (ā'vən, ā'von) a river in central England. It flows past Stratford, the birthplace of Shakespeare.

A·zer·bai·jan (ä'zər bī jän') *also,* **A·zer·bai·dzhan. 1.** a country in southwestern Asia, south of the Caucasus on the west coast of the Caspian Sea and bordering Armenia and Iran. It was formerly a republic of the Soviet Union. Capital, Baku. Area, 33,436 sq mi (86,599 sq km). Pop., 7,029,000. **2.** the part of Iran bordering this republic.

A·zores (ə zôrz', ā'zôrz) an island group in the northern Atlantic, west of and belonging to Portugal. Land area, 894 sq mi (2,315 sq km). Pop., 253,600.

A·zov, Sea of (az'ôf) a northern arm of the Black Sea, bordered by southeastern Ukraine and southwestern Russia.

Az Zar·qa (äz zär'kə) a city in northern Jordan. Pop., 318,055. Also, **Zarka, Zarqa.**

Baal·bek (bäl'bek) a town in northeastern Lebanon, the site of several ancient temples. Pop., 24,000.

Bab·y·lon (bab'ə lon') an ancient city of Mesopotamia, on the Euphrates, the capital of Babylonia and later of the Chaldean empire. Babylon was noted for its wealth, magnificence, and wickedness.

Bab·y·lo·ni·a (bab'ə lō'nē ə) an ancient empire in lower Mesopotamia that flourished from about 1900 B.C. until 538 B.C., when it was conquered by the Persians.

Ba·co·lod (bä kō'lôd) a seaport in the central Philippines, on the northern part of the island of Negros. Pop., 364,000.

Badlands 1. a barren, heavily eroded region in southwestern South Dakota. **2.** a national park in this region. Area, 243,302 acres (98,464 hectares).

Baf·fin Bay (baf'in) an inlet of the northern Atlantic, west of Greenland and east of Baffin Island.

Baffin Island, a large Canadian island west of Greenland, at the mouth of Hudson Bay. Area, approx. 200,000 sq mi (518,000 sq km).

Bagh·dad (bag'dad, bag dad') *also,* **Bag·dad.** the capital of Iraq, in the east-central part of the country, on the Tigris River. Pop., 3,841,268.

Ba·ha·mas (bə hä'məz) an island country in the West Indies, located off the southeastern coast of Florida. Capital, Nassau. Land area, 5,380 sq mi (13,934 sq km). Pop., 218,000. Also, **Ba·ha'ma Islands.** —**Ba·ha·mi·an** (bə hä'mē ən, -hä'-), *adj., n.*

Ba·hi·a (bä ē'ə) see **Salvador** *(def. 2).*

Ba·hi·a Blan·ca (bä ē'ə bläng'kä) a port city in southeastern Argentina, on an inlet of the Atlantic. Pop., 223,818.

Bah·rain (bä rān') *also,* **Bah·rein.** a country consisting of more than 30 islands in the Persian Gulf, west of Qatar. Capital, Manama. Land area, 240 sq mi (622 sq km). Pop., 350,798. —**Bah·rain·i, Bah·rein·i** (bä rā'nē), *adj., n.*

Bai·kal, Lake (bī käl') *also,* **Lake Baykal.** a lake in southeast-central Siberia. It is the deepest freshwater lake in the world.

Bai·ri·ki (bī rē'kē) the capital of Kiribati, an island in the Tarawa atoll. Pop., 2,230.

Ba·ja California (bä'hə, -hä) a long, narrow peninsula in northwestern Mexico, separating the Gulf of California from the Pacific. Area, 55,634 sq mi (144,092 sq km). Also, **Lower California.**

Baja California Nor·te (nôr'te) a state in northwestern Mexico, located on northern Baja California, and bordering California. Area, 27,655 sq mi (71,626 sq km). Pop., 1,177,886.

Baja California Sur (sür') a state in northwestern Mexico, located on southern Baja California. Area, 27,979 sq mi (72,466 sq km). Pop., 215,139.

Bak·ers·field (bā'kərz fēld') a city in southern California. Pop., 174,820.

Bakh·ta·ran (bäk'tə rän') a city in western Iran. Pop., 560,514. Formerly, **Kermanshah.**

Ba·ku (bä kü') a port city on the west coast of the Caspian Sea, the capital of Azerbaijan. Pop., 1,150,000.

Ba·kwan·ga (bə kwäng'gə) see **Mbuji-Mayi.**

Bal·e·ar·ic Islands (bal'ē ar'ik) a Spanish island group in the western Mediterranean. Land area, 1,936 sq mi (5,014 sq km). Pop., 7,000.

Ba·li (bä'lē) an island in Indonesia, east of Java. Area, 2,147 sq mi (5,561 sq km).

a	at	e	end	o	hot	u	up	hw	white	about
ā	ape	ē	me	ō	old	ū	use	ng	song	taken
ä	far	i	it	ô	fork	ü	rule	th	thin	ə pencil
âr	care	ī	ice	oi	oil	ù	pull	th	this	lemon
		îr	pierce	ou	out	ûr	turn	zh	measure	circus

Ba·lik·pa·pan (bä′lik pä′pän) a port city in Indonesia, on the eastern coast of Borneo. Pop., 208,040.

Bal·kan Mountains (bôl′kən) a mountain range on the Balkan Peninsula, extending across the central part of Bulgaria.

Balkan Peninsula, a peninsula in southern Europe, bordered by the Black and Aegean seas on the east and the Adriatic on the west.

Balkan States, the countries on the Balkan Peninsula: Yugoslavia, Romania, Bulgaria, Albania, and Greece. Also, **the Balkans.**

Bal·tic Sea (bôl′tik) an inland sea in northern Europe, bordered by Germany and Poland on the south, Denmark and Sweden on the west, and Finland and the Baltic States on the east. Also, **the Baltic.**

Baltic States, Estonia, Latvia, and Lithuania.

Bal·ti·more (bôl′tə môr′) the largest city in Maryland, a port on the Chesapeake Bay. Pop., 736,014.

Ba·ma·ko (bä′mə kō′) the capital of Mali, in the southwestern part of the country. Pop., 646,163.

Ban·dar Se·ri Be·ga·wan (bun′dər ser′ē bə gä′wən) the capital of Brunei, on the northeastern coast of the country. Pop., 22,777. Formerly, **Brunei.**

Ban·dung (bän′düng) a city in Indonesia, in western Java. Pop., 1,633,000.

Ban·ga·lore (bang′gə lôr′) a city in southern India. Pop., 2,476,355.

Bang·kok (bang′kok) the capital and largest city of Thailand, in the south-central part of the country. Pop., 5,716,779. Also, **Krung Thep.**

Ban·gla·desh (bang′glə desh′) also, **Ban·gla Desh.** a country located at the north end of the Bay of Bengal and largely surrounded by India. It was formerly the province of **East Pakistan.** Capital, Dhaka. Area, 55,598 sq mi (143,999 sq km). Pop., 87,119,965. —**Ban·gla·desh·i** (bang′glə desh′ē), adj., n.

Ban·gor (bang′gôr, -gər) a city in south-central Maine. Pop., 33,181.

Ban·gui (bäng′gē) the capital of the Central African Republic, in the southwestern part of the country. Pop., 473,817.

Ban·jer·ma·sin (bän′jər mä′sin) also, **Ban·djar·ma·sin.** a port city in Indonesia, on the southern coast of Borneo. Pop., 424,000.

Ban·jul (bän′jùl) the capital of Gambia, in the western part of the country. Pop., 44,536.

Banks·town (bangks′toun′) a city in southeastern Australia, in New South Wales. Pop., 158,750.

Ban·nock·burn (ban′ək bûrn′) a village in central Scotland, near which Scottish troops under Robert the Bruce defeated the English on June 24, 1314, thereby ending English control of Scotland until modern times.

Bao·tou (bou′tō′) also, **Paot′ou.** a city in northern China. Pop., 1,130,000.

Bar·ba·dos (bär bā′dōs) an island nation in the Lesser Antilles, the easternmost island of the West Indies. Capital, Bridgetown. Area, 166 sq mi (430 sq km). Pop., 244,228. —**Bar·ba·di·an** (bär bā′dē ən), adj., n.

Bar·ba·ry Coast (bär′bə rē) the Mediterranean coast of the Barbary States. Also, **Barbary.**

Barbary States, Morocco, Algeria, Tunisia, and the region of Tripoli when under Turkish control, used as a refuge by pirates from the sixteenth to the early nineteenth century.

Bar·bu·da (bär bü′də) see **Antigua and Barbuda.**

Bar·ce·lo·na (bär′sə lō′nə) a port city in northeastern Spain. Pop., 1,714,355.

Bar·ents Sea (bar′ənts) the part of the Arctic Ocean north of Norway and Russia.

Ba·ri (bär′ē) a city in southeastern Italy, a port on the Adriatic. Pop., 362,524.

Bar·na·ul (bär′nə ül′) a city in central Siberia, on the Ob. Pop., 602,000.

Ba·ro·da (bə rō′də) a city in western India. Pop., 734,473.

Bar·qui·si·me·to (bär′kə sə mā′tō) a city in northwestern Venezuela. Pop., 497,635.

Bar·ran·quil·la (bär′ən kē′yə) the chief seaport of Colombia, on the Caribbean, in the northern part of the country. Pop., 899,781.

Bar·row, Point (bar′ō) a small Alaskan peninsula, the northernmost point of the United States.

Ba·sel (bä′zəl) a city in northwestern Switzerland, on the Rhine. Pop., 169,587. Also, **Basle.**

Bas·il·don (bā′zəl dən) a city in eastern England. Pop., 94,800.

Basle (bäl) see **Basel.**

Bas·ra (bus′rə, bäs′rə) also, **Al Basrah, Busra.** a port city in southeastern Iraq. Pop., 616,700.

Basse-Terre (bäs târ′) the capital of Guadeloupe, located on the southwestern coast of the island. Pop., 13,656.

Basse·terre (bäs târ′) the capital and largest city of St. Kitts-Nevis. Pop., 14,725.

Ba·su·to·land (bə sü′tō land′) a former British protectorate in southern Africa, now Lesotho.

Ba·taan (bə tan′) a peninsula in the Philippines, west of Manila, where U.S. troops surrendered to the Japanese in 1942.

Ba·ta·vi·a (bə tā′vē ə) the Dutch colonial name for **Jakarta.**

Bath (bath) a historic city in southwestern England, once famous as a health resort. Pop., 84,283.

Bat·on Rouge (bat′ən rüzh′) the capital of Louisiana, in the south-central part of the state. Pop., 219,531.

Ba·var·i·a (bə vâr′ē ə) the largest state of Germany, in the southeastern part of the country. At various times in history it has been a duchy, a kingdom, and a republic. Area, 27,240 sq mi (70,552 sq km). Pop., 11,049,263.

Ba·ya·món (bä′yä môn′) a city in northeastern Puerto Rico. Pop., 185,087.

Bay·kal, Lake (bī käl′) see **Baikal, Lake.**

Bay·reuth (bī′ʀoit) a city in east-central Germany, famous for its annual music festival featuring the works of Richard Wagner. Pop., 70,933.

Beau·fort Sea (bō′fərt) an arm of the Arctic Ocean, bordering northern Alaska and northwestern Canada.

Beau·mont (bō′mont) a port city in southeastern Texas. Pop., 114,323.

Beau·port (bō′pôrt′) a city on the St. Lawrence River, in southern Quebec, Canada. Pop., 62,869.

Bech·u·a·na·land (bech′ü ä′nə land′, bek′ü-) a former British protectorate in southern Africa, now Botswana.

Bed·ford·shire (bed′fərd shir′, -shər) a county in south-central England. Pop., 530,800.

Beer·she·ba (bîr shē′bə, ber shev′ə) a town in central Israel. It was the southernmost city of ancient Palestine. Pop., 113,200.

Bei·jing (bā′jing′) the capital of the People's Republic of China, in the northeastern part of the country. Also called **Peking,** it was formerly known as **Peiping** (1928-49). Pop., 6,710,000.

Bei·ra (bā′rə) the chief port of Mozambique, in the southeastern part of the country, on an arm of the Indian Ocean. Pop., 291,604.

Bei·rut (bā rüt′) the capital and largest city of Lebanon, in the west-central part of the country, on the Mediterranean. Pop., 509,000.

Be·kaa Valley (bi kä′) a valley in western Lebanon and eastern Syria, at the northern end of the Great Rift Valley. Also, **Al Biqa.**

Be·la·rus (be′lä rüs′) a country in eastern Europe, bordering Latvia, Lithuania, Poland, Russia, and Ukraine. It was formerly known as Byelorussia when it was a republic of the Soviet Union. Capital, Minsk. Area, 80,155 sq mi (207,601 sq km). Pop., 10,200,000. Also, **White Russia.**

Be·lau (bə lou′) see **Palau.**

Be·lém (bə lem′) a port city in northeastern Brazil. Pop., 1,116,578.

Bel·fast (bel′fast) the capital and largest city of Northern Ireland, on the eastern coast of the country. Pop., 303,800.

Belgian Congo, a former Belgian colony in central Africa, now Zaire. It was originally known as the Congo Free State.

Bel·gium (bel′jəm) a country in northwestern Europe, on the North Sea. Capital, Brussels. Area, 11,783 sq mi (30,518 sq km). Pop., 9,864,751. —**Bel′gian,** adj., n.

Bel·grade (bel′grād) the capital and largest city of Serbia and Yugoslavia. Pop., 1,130,000.

Be·lize (be lēz′) a country on the northeastern coast of Central America, on the Caribbean. Capital, Belmopan. Area, 8,866 sq mi (22,963 sq km). Pop., 166,400. Formerly, **British Honduras.** —**Be·liz·e·an** (be lē′zē ən), adj., n.

Belize City, the largest city in Belize, located in the northern part of the country. Pop., 47,000.

Bel·mo·pan (bel′mō pän′) the capital of Belize, in the north-central part of the country. Pop., 4,500.

Be·lo Ho·ri·zon·te (bel′ō hôr′ə zon′tē) a city in southeastern Brazil. Pop., 2,114,429.

Be·na·res (bə när′is) see **Varanasi.**

Ben·gal (ben′gôl, beng′gəl) **1.** a former province and historic region of northeastern British India, now divided between India and Bangladesh. **2. Bay of.** the northeastern part of the Indian Ocean, between Burma and the peninsula of India. —**Ben·ga·lese** (ben′gə lēz′, -lēs′, beng′-), adj., n.

Ben·gha·zi (ben gä′zē) also, **Ben·ga·si.** a port city in the northeastern part of Libya. Pop., 435,886.

Be·nin (be nēn′) **1.** a country in western Africa, on the Gulf of Guinea. Capital, Porto-Novo. Area, 44,484 sq mi (115,214 sq

km). Pop., 3,825,000. Formerly, **Dahomey. 2.** a city in southern Nigeria. Pop., 183,200. Also *(def. 2),* **Benin City.**

Ben Nev·is (ben nev′is) a peak in the Grampian Mountains of Scotland, the highest peak in Great Britain. Height, 4,406 ft (1,343 m).

Ben·xi (bœn′shē′) *also,* **Pen-ch′i, Pen-hsi, Penki.** a city in northeastern China. Pop., 860,000.

Ber·be·ra (bûr′bər ə) a port in northern Somalia, on the Gulf of Aden. Pop., 65,000.

Ber·bé·ra·ti (ber′bə rä′tē) a city in the western Central African Republic. Pop., 40,000.

Ber·gen (bûr′gən) a port city in southwestern Norway. Pop., 209,320.

Ber·ing Sea (bîr′ing, ber′-) the northernmost arm of the Pacific, between Siberia and Alaska.

Bering Strait, a strait between Siberia and Alaska, connecting the Bering Sea with the Arctic Ocean.

Berke·ley (bûr′klē) a city in western California, on San Francisco Bay. Pop., 102,724.

Berk·shire (bûrk′shîr′, -shər) a county in southern England. Pop., 747,000.

Ber·lin (bər lin′) the capital of Germany, a city in the northeastern part of the country, divided from 1945 to 1990 into **West Berlin** and **East Berlin.** Pop., 3,094,600.

Ber·mu·da (bər mū′də) a British island group in the northern Atlantic, about 600 miles east of North Carolina. Capital, Hamilton. Land area, 21 sq mi (54 sq km). Pop., 56,000. Also, **Ber·mu·das** (bər mū′dəz).

Bern (bûrn, bern) *also,* **Berne.** the capital of Switzerland, in the west-central part of the country. Pop., 134,393.

Ber·nese Alps (bûr′nēz, -nēs, bûr′nēz′, -nēs′) a mountain range in southwestern and south-central Switzerland.

Bes·sa·ra·bi·a (bes′ə rä′bē ə) a historic region of eastern Europe on the Black Sea, now in the southwestern part of Moldova, in the Commonwealth of Independent States.

Beth·a·ny (beth′ə nē) a village in Palestine, just east of Jerusalem.

Beth·el (beth′əl) an ancient town in Palestine, north of Jerusalem, frequently referred to in the Bible.

Be·thes·da (bə thez′də) an unincorporated community in south-central Maryland. Pop., 62,936.

Beth·le·hem (beth′lə hem, -lē əm) **1.** a town in the West Bank, near Jerusalem. It was the birthplace of Jesus. Pop., 25,000. **2.** a city in eastern Pennsylvania. Pop., 71,428.

Bho·pal (bō päl′) a city in central India, the site of a major industrial accident in 1984. Pop., 671,018.

Bhu·tan (bü tän′) a country of south-central Asia, in the Himalayas, bounded by China and India. Capital, Thimbu. Area, 17,954 sq mi (46,501 sq km). Pop., 1,333,000. —**Bhu·ta·nese** (bü′tə nēz′, -nēs′), *adj., n.*

Bi·a·fra (bē af′rə, -ä′frə) a region in eastern Nigeria that seceded from the country in 1967 but was defeated and reincorporated by the Nigerian government in 1970.

Bia·ly·stok (byä′li stôk′) a city in northeastern Poland. Pop., 263,900.

Bie·le·feld (bē′lə felt′) a city in northeastern Germany. Pop., 311,946.

Big Island, see Hawaii *(def. 2).*

Bi·ki·ni (bi kē′nē) an atoll in the Marshall Islands, the former site of U.S. nuclear weapons tests.

Bil·ba·o (bil bä′ō) a port city in northern Spain, near the Bay of Biscay. Pop., 384,733.

Bil·lings (bil′ingz) a city in south-central Montana, on the Yellowstone River. Pop., 81,151.

Bi·lox·i (bə luk′sē, -lok′-) a city in southeastern Mississippi. Pop., 46,319.

Bir·ken·head (bûr′kən hed′) a port city in northwestern England. Pop., 99,075.

Bir·ming·ham *(def. 1,* bûr′ming ham′; *def. 2,* bûr′ming əm) **1.** the largest city of Alabama, in the north-central part of the state. Pop., 265,968. **2.** a city in west-central England. Pop., 1,008,000.

Bi·sa·yas (bē sä′yäs) see Visayan Islands.

Bis·cay, Bay of (bis′kā) a broad inlet of the northern Atlantic, between western France and northern Spain.

Bis·marck (biz′märk) the capital of North Dakota, in the south-central part of the state. Pop., 49,256.

Bismarck Archipelago, a large island group in the western Pacific, just east of New Guinea, a part of Papua New Guinea. Land area, approx. 19,000 sq mi (49,000 sq km).

Bis·sau (bi sou′) the capital of Guinea-Bissau. Pop., 125,000.

Bi·thyn·i·a (bi thin′ē ə) an ancient kingdom and later a Roman province in northwestern Asia Minor, on the Black Sea.

Black Forest, a mountainous, forested region in southwestern Germany. Also, *German,* **Schwarzwald.**

Black Hills, a mountain range in southwestern South Dakota and northeastern Wyoming.

Black·pool (blak′pül′) a seaside resort city in northwestern England. Pop., 146,297.

Black Sea, an inland sea between Europe and Asia, bordered by Ukraine, Russia, Georgia, Turkey, Bulgaria, and Romania.

Black·town (blak′toun′) a city in southeastern Australia, in New South Wales. Pop., 210,900.

Blan·tyre (blan′tīr) a city in southern Malawi. Pop., 331,588.

Block Island, an island at the eastern end of Long Island Sound, part of Rhode Island. Area, approx. 11 sq mi (28 sq km).

Bloem·fon·tein (blüm′fən tān′) the judicial capital of the Republic of South Africa, in the central part of the country. Pop., 104,381.

Bloom·ing·ton (blü′ming tən) **1.** a city in southeastern Minnesota. Pop., 86,335. **2.** a city in southern Indiana. Pop., 60,633.

Blue Nile, a river in eastern Africa, flowing through northwestern Ethiopia and eastern Sudan, a tributary of the Nile. Length, 850 mi (1,368 km).

Blue Ridge Mountains, an eastern range of the Appalachian Mountains, extending from northeastern West Virginia to northern Georgia. Also, **Blue Ridge.**

Bo·bo Diou·las·so (bō′bō dü las′ō) a city in western Burkina Faso. Pop., 228,668.

Bo·chum (bō′kəm) a city in western Germany, in the Ruhr valley. Pop., 389,087.

Boe·o·tia (bē ō′shə) an ancient district in east-central Greece.

Bo·go·tá (bō′gə tä′, bō′gə tä′) the capital and largest city of Colombia, in the west-central part of the country. Pop., 3,982,941.

Bo·he·mi·a (bō hē′mē ə) a historic region and former kingdom, in western Czechoslovakia. Area, approx. 20,000 sq mi (51,800 sq km).

Boi·se (boi′zē, -sē) the capital of Idaho, in the southwestern part of the state. Pop., 125,738.

Bo·liv·i·a (bə liv′ē ə) a landlocked country in west-central South America. Capitals, La Paz and Sucre. Area, 424,165 sq mi (1,098,587 sq km). Pop., 6,429,226. —**Bo·liv′i·an,** *adj., n.*

Bo·lo·gna (bə lōn′yə) a city in northern Italy. Pop., 432,406.

Bol·ton (bōl′tən) a city in northwestern England. Pop., 143,960.

Bom·bay (bom bā′) the largest city and chief port of India, on the western coast of the country. Pop., 8,243,405.

Bon·aire (bô nâr′) an island in the Netherlands Antilles, located off the northern coast of Venezuela. Area, 111 sq mi (287 sq km). Pop., 10,797.

Bône (bōn) see Annaba.

Bonn (bon) the former capital of Germany, in the western part of the country. Pop., 282,190.

Bo·phu·that·swa·na (bō′pü tät swä′nə) a black African homeland largely in the northern Republic of South Africa, declared independent in 1977 by South Africa. Area, 15,610 sq mi (40,430 sq km). Pop., 1,819,242.

Bor·deaux (bôr dō′) a port city in southwestern France. Pop., 208,159.

Border States, the five slave states that bordered on the North at the time of the American Civil War, four of which (Delaware, Maryland, Kentucky, and Missouri) remained in the Union; the fifth state (Virginia) seceded, but part of it remained in the Union and became West Virginia.

Bor·ne·o (bôr′nē ō′) a large island in the Malay Archipelago, divided into Sarawak and Sabah, which are part of Malaysia; Kalimantan, which is part of Indonesia; and Brunei. Area, 290,000 sq mi (751,100 sq km). —**Bor·ne·an** (bôr′nē ən), *adj., n.*

Bos·ni·a (boz′nē ə) a historic region in Bosnia and Herzegovina. —**Bos′ni·an,** *adj., n.*

Bosnia and Her·ze·go·vi·na (hûrt′sə gə vē′nə) a country in southeastern Europe, a former republic of Yugoslavia. Capital, Sarajevo. Area, approx. 19,740 sq mi (51,130 sq km). Pop., 4,400,464. Also, **Bos′ni·a-Her′ze·go·vi′na.**

Bos·po·rus (bos′pər əs) a strait connecting the Black Sea and the Sea of Marmara, separating European and Asian Turkey.

Bos·ton (bôs′tən) the capital of Massachusetts, in the eastern part of the state. Pop., 574,283.

Bot·a·ny Bay (bot′ə nē) an inlet of the southern Pacific, in New

a	at	e	end	o	hot	u	up	hw	white	⎧	about
ā	ape	ē	me	ō	old	ū	use	ng	song	⎪	taken
ä	far	i	it	ô	fork	ü	rule	th	thin	ə	pencil
âr	care	ī	ice	oi	oil	u̇	pull	th	this	⎨	lemon
		îr	pierce	ou	out	ûr	turn	zh	measure	⎩	circus

1425

South Wales, site of Captain James Cook's first landing on the Australian continent (April 1770).

Both·ni·a, Gulf of (both′nē ə) the northern arm of the Baltic Sea, between Sweden and Finland.

Bot·swa·na (bot swä′nə) a country in central southern Africa. Capital, Gaborone. Area, 224,700 sq mi (581,973 sq km). Pop., 1,169,000.

Boua·ké (bwä kā′) a city of the Ivory Coast, in the central part of the country. Pop., 275,000.

Boul·der (bōl′dər) a city in north-central Colorado, near Denver. Pop., 83,312.

Bour·gogne (büR gôn′yə) see Burgundy.

Bourne·mouth (bôrn′məth, bürn′-) a city in southern England, on the English Channel. Pop., 142,829.

Bra·bant (brə bant′, -bänt, brä′bənt) a historic region in northwestern Europe, including parts of northern Belgium and the southern Netherlands. Area, 4,265 sq mi (11,046 sq km). —**Bra·bant·ine** (brə ban′tin, -tīn), adj.

Brad·ford (brad′fərd) a city in north-central England. Pop., 463,000.

Brah·ma·pu·tra (brä′mə pü′trə) a large river in southern Asia, flowing from southwestern Tibet to the Bay of Bengal. Length, 1,770 mi (2,848 km).

Bra·i·la (brə ē′lə) a city in eastern Romania, on the Danube. Pop., 235,620.

Bramp·ton (bramp′tən) a city in southern Ontario, Canada. Pop., 188,498.

Bran·den·burg (bran′dən bûrg′) a historic region of northeastern Germany, now divided between Germany and Poland.

Bra·si·lia (brə zēl′yə) the capital of Brazil, in the east-central part of the country. Pop., 1,567,709.

Bra·sov (brä shôv′) a city in central Romania. Pop., 351,493.

Bra·ti·sla·va (brä′tə slä′və) a city in southern Czechoslovakia, on the Danube. Pop., 442,999.

Braun·schweig (bRoun′shvīk′) see Brunswick.

Bra·zil (brə zil′) the largest country in South America, on the Atlantic, in the northeastern part of the continent. Capital, Brasilia. Area, 3,286,488 sq mi (8,512,004 sq km). Pop., 135,564,395. —**Bra·zil·ian** (brə zil′yən), adj., n.

Braz·za·ville (braz′ə vil′) the capital of the Republic of the Congo, in the southeastern part of the country. Pop., 585,812.

Breed's Hill (brēdz) see Bunker Hill.

Brem·en (brem′ən) a port city in northeastern Germany. Pop., 535,058.

Bren·ner Pass (bren′ər) a major mountain pass in the Alps, on the border between Austria and Italy.

Bre·scia (bresh′ə) a city in north-central Italy. Pop., 199,286.

Bres·lau (brez′lou) see Wroclaw.

Brest (brest) 1. a port city in northwestern France, on the Atlantic. Pop., 156,060. 2. a city in Belarus. Pop., 258,000. Also (def. 2), Brest Li·tovsk (li tôfsk′).

Bridge·port (brij′pôrt′) a city in southwestern Connecticut. Pop., 141,686.

Bridge·town (brij′toun′) the capital and largest city of Barbados. Pop., 7,466.

Brigh·ton (brī′tən) a city in southeastern England, on the English Channel. Pop., 134,581.

Bris·bane (briz′bān, -bən) a port city in eastern Australia, the capital of Queensland. Pop., 744,828.

Bris·tol (bris′təl) a port city in southwestern England. Pop., 384,000.

Brit·ain (brit′ən) see Great Britain. —**Brit·ish** (brit′ish), adj.

British Columbia, the westernmost province of Canada, on the Pacific. Capital, Victoria. Area, 366,255 sq mi (948,600 sq km). Pop., 2,889,207.

British Commonwealth of Nations, see Commonwealth of Nations.

British Empire, formerly, all the countries, colonies, dependencies, and protectorates that owed allegiance to the British crown. The term now has no official use.

British Guiana, a former British colony in northern South America, now Guyana.

British Honduras, see Belize.

British India 1. formerly, the parts of the Indian Empire under direct British rule. 2. see Indian Empire.

British Isles, an island group off the western coast of continental Europe, consisting of Great Britain, Ireland, and many smaller islands.

British West Indies, formerly, British island possessions in the West Indies, including the Bahamas, Windward Islands, Leeward Islands, and British Virgin Islands.

Brit·ta·ny (brit′ə nē) a historic region in northwestern France, between the English Channel and the Bay of Biscay.

Br·no (bûr′nō) a city in central Czechoslovakia. Pop., 392,285. Also, German, Brünn.

Brock·ton (brok′tən) a city in southeastern Massachusetts. Pop., 92,788.

Brom·berg (brom′bûrg′) see Bydgoszcz.

Bronx, the (brongks) a borough of New York City. Area, 43 sq mi (111 sq km).

Brook·line (brŭk′līn′) a town in eastern Massachusetts, a residential suburb of Boston. Pop., 54,718.

Brook·lyn (brŭk′lin) a borough of New York City. Area, 79 sq mi (205 sq km).

Browns·ville (brounz′vil′) a city in southernmost Texas. Pop., 98,962.

Bruges (brRyzh) a historic city in northwestern Belgium. Pop., 117,755. Also, Flemish, Brug·ge (brŒKH′ə).

Bru·nei (brü nī′) a small country on the northern coast of Borneo. Official name: Brunei Da·rus·sa·lam (dä′rü sä läm′). Capital, Bandar Seri Begawan. Area, 2,226 sq mi (5,765 sq km). Pop., 192,832. —**Bru·nei′an**, adj., n.

Brünn (brRyn) see Brno.

Bruns·wick (brunz′wik) 1. a city in north-central Germany. Pop., 253,794. 2. a historic state in northern Germany. Also, German, Braunschweig.

Bru·sa (brü′sə) see Bursa.

Brus·sels (brus′əlz) the capital of Belgium, in the central part of the country. Pop., 136,920.

Bu·ca·ra·man·ga (bü′kər ə mäng′gə) a city in northern Colombia. Pop., 352,326.

Bu·cha·rest (bü′kə rest′) the capital and largest city of Romania, in the southern part of the country. Pop., 1,989,823.

Bu·chen·wald (bü′kən wôld′, bü′KHən vält′) a Nazi concentration camp during World War II, outside Weimar in central Germany.

Buck·ing·ham·shire (buk′ing əm shîr′, -shər) a county in south-central England. Pop., 627,200.

Bu·da·pest (bü′də pest′, -pesht′) the capital and largest city of Hungary, in the north-central part of the country. Pop., 2,016,132.

Bue·nos Ai·res (bwā′nəs ī′rəs, âr′ēz) the capital and largest city of Argentina, on the eastern coast of the country. Pop., 2,922,829.

Buf·fa·lo (buf′ə lō′) a port city in western New York, on Lake Erie. Pop., 328,123.

Bu·jum·bu·ra (bü′jəm bûr′ə) the capital and chief port of Burundi, on Lake Tanganyika, in the western part of the country. Pop., 273,000.

Bu·ka·vu (bü kä′vü) a city in eastern Zaire. Pop., 171,064.

Bu·la·wa·yo (bül′ə wā′ō) a city in southwestern Zimbabwe. Pop., 429,000.

Bul·gar·i·a (bul gâr′ē ə, bûl-) a country in southeastern Europe, in the east-central part of the Balkan Peninsula. Capital, Sofia. Area, 42,823 sq mi (110,912 sq km). Pop., 9,913,000.

Bull Run, a stream near Manassas in northeastern Virginia, site of two Civil War battles, in 1861 and 1862, in which the Union forces were defeated.

Bunker Hill, a hill in eastern Massachusetts, near Boston. The Battle of Bunker Hill, in 1775, the first major battle of the American Revolution, was actually fought on nearby Breed's Hill.

Bur·bank (bûr′bangk′) a city in southern California. Pop., 93,643.

Bur·gun·dy (bûr′gən dē) a historic region in east-central France, at various times an independent kingdom, a duchy, and a province of France. Also, French, Bourgogne. —**Bur·gun·di·an** (bər gun′dē ən), adj., n.

Bur·ki·na Fa·so (bər kē′nə fä′sō) a country in western Africa, north of Ghana. Capital, Ouagadougou. Area, 105,869 sq mi (274,271 sq km). Pop., 7,964,705. Formerly, Upper Volta.

Bur·ling·ton (bûr′ling tən) 1. the largest city in Vermont, in the northwestern part of the state. Pop., 39,127. 2. a city in Ontario, Canada, in the southeastern part of the province. Pop., 116,675.

Bur·ma (bûr′mə) a country in southeastern Asia. Official name: Myanmar. Capital, Rangoon. Area, 261,228 sq mi (676,581 sq km). Pop., 34,128,908.

Bur·na·by (bûr′nə bē) a city in southwestern British Columbia. Pop., 145,161.

Bur·sa (bûr′sə) a city in northwestern Turkey, a former capital of the Ottoman Empire. Pop., 838,323. Also, Brusa.

Bu·run·di (bə run′dē, bù rùn′-) a landlocked country in east-

central Africa. Capital, Bujumbura. Area, 10,745 sq mi (27,830 sq km). Pop., 4,782,000. —**Bu·run′di·an**, *adj., n.*

Bus·ra (bus′rə) see **Basra.**

Byd·goszcz (bid′gôsh) a city in northwestern Poland. Pop., 377,900. Also, *German,* **Bromberg.**

Bye·lo·rus·sia (byel′ō rush′ə) see **Belarus.** —**Bye′lo·rus′-sian,** *adj., n.*

Byzantine Empire, the eastern part of the later Roman Empire, usually dated from A.D. 330, when Constantine the Great moved the imperial capital from Rome to Byzantium and renamed it Constantinople. It lasted after the fall of the western part, ending in 1453, when the capital fell to the Ottoman Turks. Also, **Eastern Empire, Eastern Roman Empire.**

By·zan·ti·um (bi zan′tē əm) an ancient Greek city that became the capital of the Roman Empire and was renamed Constantinople.

Ca·bin·da (kə bin′də) a territory of Angola in western equatorial Africa, on the Atlantic, separated from the main portion of the country by Zaire. Area, 2,807 sq mi (7,270 sq km). Pop., 81,265.

Cá·diz (kə diz′, kä′diz, kä thēs′) a port city in southwestern Spain. Pop., 156,591.

Caen (käN) a port city in northwestern France. Pop., 114,068.

Ca·glia·ri (käl′yə rē) the capital and largest city of the Italian island of Sardinia. Pop., 220,574.

Ca·guas (kä′gwäs) a city in east-central Puerto Rico. Pop., 87,214.

Cai·ro (kī′rō) the capital of Egypt, in the northeastern part of the country. It is the largest city in Africa. Pop., 6,052,836. Also, *Arabic,* **Al Qahirah.**

Cal·a·bar (kal′ə bär′) a port city in southeastern Nigeria. Pop., 139,800.

Cal·ais (kal′ā, ka lā′) a seaport on the northern coast of France, the continental European city closest to England. Pop., 76,527.

Cal·cut·ta (kal kut′ə) a port city in northeastern India, the former capital of British India. Pop., 3,305,006.

Cal·ga·ry (kal′gə rē) a city in southwestern Canada, in the province of Alberta. Pop., 636,104.

Ca·li (kä′lē) a city in western Colombia. Pop., 1,350,565.

Cal·i·cut (kal′i kət) see **Kozhikode.**

Cal·i·for·nia (kal′ə fôr′nyə) **1.** the most populous state of the United States, on the Pacific coast. Capital, Sacramento. Area, 158,706 sq mi (411,049 sq km). Pop., 29,760,021. Abbreviation, **Calif.;** postal abbreviation, **CA 2. Gulf of.** a long inlet of the Pacific, just south of California, separating Baja California from the Mexican mainland. —**Cal′i·for′nian,** *adj., n.*

Ca·llao (kə you′) a city on the west coast of central Peru, the major seaport of the country. Pop., 264,133.

Ca·lo·o·can (kal′ə ō′kän) a city in the Philippines, on Luzon island, in the north-central part of the country. Pop., 746,000.

Cal·va·ry (kal′və rē) a hill near ancient Jerusalem where Jesus was crucified. Also, **Golgotha.**

Ca·ma·güey (kam′ə gwā′) a city in east-central Cuba. Pop., 265,588.

Cam·bo·di·a (kam bō′dē ə) a country in southeastern Asia. Capital, Phnom Penh. Area, 69,898 sq mi (181,036 sq km). Pop., 7,492,000. Also, **Kampuchea.**

Cam·brai (kam brā′) a city in northern France. Pop., 35,272.

Cam·bridge (kām′brij) **1.** a city in eastern Massachusetts. Pop., 95,802. **2.** a city in eastern England. Pop., 87,111. **3.** a city in southeastern Ontario, Canada. Pop., 79,920.

Cam·bridge·shire (kām′brij shir′, -shər) a county in eastern England. Pop., 651,900.

Cam·den (kam′dən) a city in southwestern New Jersey, on the Delaware River. Pop., 87,492.

Cam·er·oon (kam′ə rün′) a country in west-central Africa, consisting of most of the territory of the former Cameroons. Capital, Yaoundé. Area, 183,569 sq mi (475,444 sq km). Pop., 10,446,409. —**Cam′er·oon′i·an,** *adj., n.*

Cam·er·oons (kam′ə rünz′) two former United Nations trust territories, one under French administration, now part of Cameroon; and the other under British administration, now divided between Cameroon and Nigeria.

Cam·er·oun (kam′ə rün′) the part of the Cameroons under French administration, now included in Cameroon.

Cam·pa·gna (käm pän′yə) the low coastal plain surrounding Rome.

Cam·pa·nia (käm pän′yə) a region in southwestern Italy bordering the Tyrrhenian Sea. Area, 5,249 sq mi (13,595 sq km). Pop., 5,690,431.

Cam·pe·che (kam pē′chē, -pä′chä) a state in southeastern Mexico, on the western Yucatán peninsula. Area, 19,672 sq mi (50,950 sq km). Pop., 420,553.

Cam·pi·nas (käN pē′nəs) a city in southeastern Brazil. Pop., 841,016.

Cam·po Gran·de (käN′pü grän′de) a city in southwestern Brazil. Pop., 384,398.

Cam·pos (käN′püs) a city in southeastern Brazil. Pop., 187,900.

Ca·naan (kā′nən) a region in Palestine, between the Jordan River and the Mediterranean.

Can·a·da (kan′ə də) a country in northern North America, bordering the United States. Capital, Ottawa. Area, 3,849,670 sq mi (9,970,645 sq km). Pop., 25,354,064. —**Ca·na·di·an** (kə nā′dē ən), *adj., n.*

Canal Zone, a strip of territory across the Isthmus of Panama, extending approximately five miles on each side of the Panama Canal. It was administered by the United States from 1903 to 1979, when nearly all of it was returned to Panamanian control. Area, approx. 553 sq mi (1,432 sq km). Also, **Panama Canal Zone.**

Canary Islands, a Spanish island group in the northern Atlantic, off the northwestern coast of Africa. Land area, 2,807 sq mi (7,270 sq km). Pop., 1,522,380. Also, **Canaries.**

Ca·nav·er·al, Cape (kə nav′ər əl) the site of the main U.S. launching and testing center for missiles and spacecraft, located on the Atlantic coast of Florida.

Can·ber·ra (kan ber′ə) the capital of Australia, in the southeastern part of the nation. Pop., 247,194.

Can·nae (kan′ē) an ancient town in southeastern Italy, the site of Hannibal's victory over the Romans in 216 B.C.

Cannes (kän) a resort and port city in southeastern France, on the Mediterranean. Pop., 72,259.

Ca·nos·sa (kə nos′ə) an ancient town in northern Italy where Henry IV of the Holy Roman Empire did penance before Pope Gregory VII in 1077.

Can·ter·bur·y (kan′tər ber′ē, -bə rē) a city in southeastern England. The site of a famous cathedral, it is the seat of the spiritual leader of the Church of England. Pop., 34,546.

Can·ton (*def. 1,* kan′ton; *def. 2,* kan′tən) **1.** see **Guangzhou. 2.** a city in northeastern Ohio. Pop., 84,161.

Cape Province, a province of the Republic of South Africa, in the southern and western parts of the country. Area, 278,465 sq mi (721,224 sq km). Pop., 5,041,137. Also, **Cape of Good Hope Province.**

Ca·per·na·um (kə pûr′nē əm, -nā-) an ancient town in northeastern Palestine, on the northern shore of the Sea of Galilee.

Cape Town (kāp′ toun′) *also,* **Cape·town.** the legislative capital of the Republic of South Africa, a port city on the southwestern coast of the country. Pop., 776,617.

Cape Verde (vûrd′) **1.** see **Verde, Cape. 2.** an island country in the northern Atlantic, west of Cape Verde. Capital, Praia. Land area, 1,557 sq mi (4,033 sq km). Pop., 336,798. Formerly, **Cape Verde Islands.**

Cap·i·to·line (kap′i tə līn′) one of the seven hills on which ancient Rome was built.

Cap·pa·do·cia (kap′ə dō′shə) an ancient region and kingdom in Asia Minor, later annexed by Rome.

Ca·pri (kə prē′, kä′prē) a small Italian island off the southwestern coast of the country, at the entrance to the Bay of Naples. Area, approx. 5 sq mi (13 sq km).

Ca·rac·as (kə rä′kəs) the capital and largest city of Venezuela, in the northern part of the country. Pop., 1,816,901.

Car·diff (kär′dif) the capital and largest city of Wales. Pop., 262,313.

Car·ib·be·an (kar′ə bē′ən, kə rib′ē-) **1.** a sea bounded on the north and east by the West Indies, on the west by Central America, and on the south by South America. Also, **Caribbean Sea. 2. the Caribbean.** the region consisting of this sea and those lands in and around it.

Carls·bad (kärlz′bad′) see **Karlovy Vary.**

Carlsbad Caverns 1. the largest known network of underground caverns in the world, located in southeastern New Mexico. **2.** a national park containing these caves. Area, 46,755 acres (18,922 hectares).

Carls·ruh·e (kärlz′rü′ə) see **Karlsruhe.**

a	at	e	end	o	hot	u	up	hw	white		about
ā	ape	ē	me	ō	old	ū	use	ng	song		taken
ä	far	i	it	ô	fork	ü	rule	th	thin	ə	pencil
âr	care	ī	ice	oi	oil	u̇	pull	th	this		lemon
		îr	pierce	ou	out	ûr	turn	zh	measure		circus

Car·mel, Mount (kär mel′) a short mountain ridge in north-western Israel, meeting the Mediterranean near Haifa. Height, 1,791 ft (546 m).

Car·o·li·na (*defs. 1, 2,* kar′ə lī′nə; *def. 3,* kär′ə lē′nə) **1.** a former British colony on the Atlantic coast of North America, divided into North Carolina and South Carolina in 1729. **2. the Carolinas.** North Carolina and South Carolina. **3.** a city in northeastern Puerto Rico. Pop., 147,835. —**Car·o·lin·i·an** (kar′ə lin′ē-ən), *adj., n.*

Car·o·line Islands (kar′ə līn′) an archipelago of more than 500 islands in the western Pacific north of New Guinea, a territory of the United States and divided politically into Palau and the Federated States of Micronesia. Land area, approx. 525 sq mi (1,360 sq km).

Car·pa·thi·an Mountains (kär pā′thē ən) a mountain system in central and eastern Europe, extending in an arc from southwestern Czechoslovakia to central Romania. Also, **Car·pa′thi·ans.**

Car·ra·ra (kə rär′ə) a city in northwestern Italy, noted for its white marble. Pop., 69,229.

Car·son (kär′sən) a city in southern California. Pop., 83,995.

Carson City, the capital of Nevada, in the western part of the state. Pop., 40,443.

Car·ta·ge·na (kär′tə jē′nə, -gā′-, -hä′-) **1.** a port city in north-western Colombia. Pop., 531,426. **2.** a port city in southeastern Spain. Pop., 70,000.

Car·thage (kär′thij) an ancient city and state in northern Africa, on the site of modern Tunisia. It was founded by the Phoenicians, destroyed by the Romans in 146 B.C., and rebuilt by the Romans in 44 B.C. —**Car·tha·gin·i·an** (kär′thə jin′ē ən), *adj., n.*

Cas·a·blan·ca (kas′ə blang′kə) the largest city and chief port of Morocco, in the northwestern part of the country. Pop., 2,139,204. Also, *Arabic,* **Dar el Beida.**

Cascade Range, a mountain range in the western United States, extending from northern California through Oregon and into Washington. Also, **Cascades.**

Cash·mere (kash′mîr, kazh′-) see **Kashmir.**

Cas·per (kas′pər) a city in central Wyoming. Pop., 46,742.

Cas·pi·an Sea (kas′pē ən) an inland sea bordering southwestern Russia, southeastern Kazakhstan, and northern Iran. It is the largest inland body of water in the world.

Cas·sel (kas′əl) see **Kassel.**

Cas·si·no (kə sē′nō) a town in central Italy, the site of a famous monastery. Pop., 24,200.

Cas·tile (kas tēl′) a region and former kingdom in north-central and central Spain.

Cas·tries (kas′trēz) the capital and largest city of St. Lucia. Pop., 53,933.

Cat·a·li·na (kat′ə lē′nə) see **Santa Catalina.** Also, **Catalina Island.**

Cat·a·lo·ni·a (kat′ə lō′nē ə) a historic region and former principality in the northeastern corner of Spain. —**Cat·a·lo·ni·an,** *adj., n.*

Ca·ta·nia (kə tän′yə) a port city on the eastern coast of Sicily. Pop., 372,486.

Cats·kill Mountains (kats′kil) a mountain range in southeastern New York. They are part of the Appalachian mountain system. Also, **Cats′kills.**

Cat·te·gat (kat′i gat′) see **Kattegat.**

Cau·ca·sia (kô kā′zhə) a region between the Black and Caspian seas. Also, **Caucasus.**

Cau·ca·sus (kô′kə səs) **1.** a mountain range between the Black and Caspian seas, traditionally regarded as part of the boundary between Europe and Asia. **2.** see **Caucasia.**

Cawn·pore (kôn′pôr′) see **Kanpur.**

Cay·enne (kī en′, kā-) the capital and largest city of French Guiana, a port on the northern coast of the department. Pop., 38,091.

Cay·man Islands (kā′mən) three British islands in the Greater Antilles, northwest of Jamaica. Capital, Georgetown. Land area, 100 sq mi (259 sq km). Pop., 25,900.

Ce·bu (sā bü′) **1.** an island in the south-central Philippines. Area, 1,703 sq mi (4,411 sq km). **2.** a port city on the east coast of this island. Pop., 610,000.

Cedar Rapids, a city in eastern Iowa. Pop., 108,751.

Cel·e·bes (sel′ə bēz′) see **Sulawesi.**

Central African Republic, a landlocked country in central Africa. Capital, Bangui. Area, 240,535 sq mi (622,986 sq km). Pop., 2,517,000.

Central America, a region between the Pacific and the Caribbean, occupying the long isthmus of North America that links that continent with South America. It consists of Guatemala, Belize, El Salvador, Honduras, Nicaragua, Costa Rica, and Panama. Area, 205,087 sq mi (531,175 sq km). —**Central American.**

Central Valley, a valley in central California, consisting of the San Joaquin and Sacramento river valleys. Length, 450 mi (724 km).

Ceu·ta (sā ü′tə) a port city on the Mediterranean, a Spanish enclave in northern Morocco. Pop., 67,188.

Cey·lon (si lon′, sā-) see **Sri Lanka.** —**Cey·lo·nese** (sē′lə nēz′, -nēs′, sā′-), *adj., n.*

Chad (chad) **1.** a country in north-central Africa. Capital, Ndjamena. Area, 495,800 sq mi (1,284,122 sq km). Pop., 4,405,000. **2. Lake.** a large lake in north-central Africa, at the southern edge of the Sahara. —**Chad·i·an** (chad′ē ən), *adj., n.*

Chaer·o·ne·a (ker′ə nē′ə) an ancient town in Boeotia, Greece, where the Macedonians under Philip II and his son Alexander defeated the united Greeks in 338 B.C.

Cha·gres (chä′grəs) a river in Panama and the Canal Zone, the principal source of water for the Panama Canal.

Chal·ce·don (kal′si don′) an ancient city in northwestern Asia Minor.

Chal·de·a (kal dē′ə) *also,* **Chal·dae·a.** an ancient region in southernmost Babylonia, on the Tigris and Euphrates rivers, in what is now southern Iraq.

Cham·pagne (sham pān′) a region in northeastern France, formerly a province.

Cham·plain, Lake (sham plān′) a lake on the border between New York and Vermont, extending into southwestern Quebec.

Chang (chäng) see **Yangtze.** Also, **Chang Jiang** (chäng′-jyäng′).

Chang·chun (chäng′chùn′) a city in northeastern China, the capital of Jilin province. Pop., 1,822,000. Formerly, **Hsinking.**

Chang·sha (chäng′shä′) a city in southeastern China, the capital of Hunan province. Pop., 1,230,000.

Chang·tien (jäng′chen′) see **Zibo.**

Channel Islands, a British island group off the coast of France in the English Channel, including Jersey, Guernsey, and Alderney. Land area, 75 sq mi (194 sq km). Pop., 139,000.

Cha·pul·te·pec (chə pul′tə pek′) a rocky hill in Mexico City, Mexico, captured by U.S. forces in 1847 in the last major battle of the Mexican War.

Char·le·roi (shär′lə roi′) a city in southern Belgium. Pop., 209,395.

Charles River (chärlz) a river in eastern Massachusetts. Length, 60 mi (97 km).

Charles·ton (chärlz′tən) **1.** the capital of West Virginia, in the western part of the state. Pop., 57,287. **2.** a port city in southeastern South Carolina. Pop., 80,414.

Char·lotte (shär′lət) the largest city of North Carolina, in the southern part of the state. Pop., 395,934.

Charlotte A·ma·lie (ə mäl′yə) the capital and largest city of the Virgin Islands of the United States, on the island of St. Thomas. Pop., 11,842.

Char·lotte·town (shär′lət toun′) the capital and largest city of Prince Edward Island, Canada, a port on the southern coast of the province. Pop., 15,776.

Char·tres (shärt) a city in north-central France, noted for its cathedral. Pop., 37,119.

Châ·teau-Thier·ry (sha tō tē Re′) a town in northern France where American and French troops halted the German advance on Paris in 1918, during World War I. Pop., 14,557.

Chat·ta·hoo·chee (chat′ə hü′chē) a river in western Georgia, flowing southwest and then south along the Georgia-Alabama border. Length, 436 mi (702 km).

Chat·ta·noo·ga (chat′ə nü′gə) a city in southern Tennessee, on the Tennessee River. Pop., 152,466.

Cheek·to·wa·ga (chēk′tə wä′gə) a city in western New York. Pop., 99,314.

Che·kiang (che′kyang′, ju′gyäng′) see **Zhejiang.**

Chel·sea (chel′sē) an area in central London, traditionally the artists' quarter of the city.

Chem·nitz (kem′nits) a city in central eastern Germany. Pop., 311,765. Formerly, **Karl-Marx-Stadt.**

Che·mul·po (jə mùl′pō) see **Inchon.**

Cheng·chow (jung′jō′) see **Zhengzhou.**

Cheng·du (chœng′dy′) *also,* **Cheng·tu.** a city in south-central China, the capital of Sichuan province. Pop., 1,884,000.

Cher·bourg (shâr′bûrg′, sheR bür′) a seaport, naval base, and resort in northwestern France, on the English Channel. Pop., 28,442.

Cher·no·byl (chər nō′bəl) a city in Ukraine, 80 mi (129 km) southwest of Kiev, the site of an explosion in a nuclear power plant in 1986.

Che·sa·peake (ches′ə pēk′) a city in southeastern Virginia. Pop., 151,976.

Chesapeake Bay, an arm of the Atlantic, on the eastern coast of the United States, in Virginia and Maryland.

Chesh·ire (chesh′ər, -îr) a county in northwestern England. Pop., 955,800.

Chev·i·ot Hills (chev′ē ət) a mountain range forming part of the boundary between England and Scotland.

Chey·enne (shī en′, -an′) the capital and largest city of Wyoming, in the southeastern part of the state. Pop., 50,008.

Chiang Mai (chyäng′mī′) also, **Chiang·mai.** a city in northwestern Thailand. Pop., 164,030.

Chi·a·pas (chē ä′päs) a state in southernmost Mexico. Area, 28,732 sq mi (74,416 sq km). Pop., 2,084,717.

Chi·ba (chē′bə) a city in Japan, on the southeastern part of the island of Honshu. Pop., 788,930.

Chi·ca·go (shi kä′gō) the largest city of Illinois, a port in the northeastern part of the state, located on Lake Michigan. Pop., 2,783,786.

Chi·chén It·zá (chē′chən ēt′sə) an ancient Mayan city in southeastern Mexico, on the Yucatán peninsula.

Chick·a·mau·ga (chik′ə mô′gə) a creek flowing from northwestern Georgia into the Tennessee River, the site of a Confederate victory in 1863 during the Civil War.

Chi·cla·yo (chi klī′ō) a city in northwestern Peru, near the Pacific coast. Pop., 213,095.

Chi·hua·hua (chi wä′wə) **1.** a state in northern Mexico, bordering on New Mexico and Texas. Area, 94,831 sq mi (245,612 sq km). Pop., 2,005,477. **2.** a city in northern Mexico. Pop., 385,603.

Chil·e (chil′ē, chē′lā) a country on the southwestern coast of South America. Capital, Santiago. Area, 292,135 sq mi (756,630 sq km). Pop., 11,329,736. —**Chil·e·an** (chil′ē ən, chi lā′ən), *adj., n.*

Chi·lung (chē′lùng′) a seaport on the northern coast of Taiwan. Pop., 348,541. Also, **Keelung.**

Chim·bo·te (chim bō′tē) a city in northwestern Peru, near the Pacific coast. Pop., 223,341.

Chi·na (chī′nə) **1. People's Republic of.** a country in eastern Asia. It is the most populous country in the world. Capital, Beijing. Area, 3,691,500 sq mi (9,560,985 sq km). Pop., 1,130,000,000. **2. Republic of.** see **Taiwan.**

Chi·nan (jē′nän′) see **Jinan.**

Chinese Empire, China from its founding, through rule by various imperial dynasties, until it became a republic in 1912.

Chi·os (kī′os, -ōs, kHē′ôs) a Greek island in the eastern Aegean, off the western coast of Turkey. Area, 321 sq mi (831 sq km). Pop., 49,865.

Chit·ta·gong (chit′ə gong′) a port in southeastern Bangladesh, near the Bay of Bengal. Pop., 980,000.

Chong·jin (chung′jin′) a seaport in western North Korea. Pop., 490,000.

Chong·ju (chung′jü′) a city in west-central South Korea. Pop., 350,256.

Chong·qing (chung′ching′) also, **Chungking.** a port city in west-central China, on the Yangtze River. Pop., 2,502,000.

Cho·sen (chō′sen′) the Japanese name for Korea.

Christ·church (krīst′chûrch′) a city in New Zealand, on the eastern coast of South Island. Pop., 168,200.

Chris·ti·an·i·a (kris′chē an′ē ə, kris′tē-) see **Oslo.**

Christmas Island 1. an island south of Java in the Indian Ocean, administered by Australia. Area, approx. 52 sq mi (135 sq km). Pop., 3,000. **2.** a large atoll in Kiribati, in the north-central Pacific. Area, 222 sq mi (575 sq km). Also *(def. 2),* **Kiritimati.**

Chuk·chi Sea (chùk′chē) the part of the Arctic Ocean north of the Bering Strait, between Asia and North America.

Chu·la Vis·ta (chü′lə vis′tə) a city in the southwestern corner of California, near San Diego. Pop., 135,163.

Chung·king (chùng′king′) see **Chongqing.**

Chur·chill River (chûr′chil) **1.** a river in central Canada, flowing east through Saskatchewan and Manitoba into the Hudson Bay. Length, 1,000 mi (1,609 km). **2.** a river flowing east through Labrador, Canada, to the Atlantic. Length, 600 mi (965 km). Formerly *(def. 2),* **Hamilton River.**

Cin·cin·nat·i (sin′sə nat′ē) a port city in southwestern Ohio, on the Ohio River. Pop., 364,040.

Cis·kei (sis′kī) a black African homeland in the southeastern Republic of South Africa, declared independent in 1981 by South Africa. Area, 3,205 sq mi (8,301 sq km). Pop., 882,200.

Ciu·dad Juá·rez (sē′ü däd′ wär′ez, sü thäth′ hwä′res) a city in northern Mexico, on the Rio Grande, opposite El Paso, Texas. Pop., 544,496. Also, **Juárez.**

Ciudad Tru·jil·lo (trü hē′yō) see **Santo Domingo.**

Clear·wa·ter (klîr′wô′tər, -wot′ər) a city in western Florida, on the Gulf of Mexico. Pop., 98,784.

Cler·mont-Fer·rand (kler môn fe ʀän′) a city in south-central France. Pop., 147,361.

Cleve·land (klēv′lənd) a city in Ohio, a port in the northeastern part of the state, on Lake Erie. Pop., 505,616.

Clif·ton (klif′tən) a city in northeastern New Jersey. Pop., 71,742.

Clu·ny (klü′nē, klY nē′) a town in east-central France, one of the principal religious and cultural centers of medieval Europe and the site of the remains of a famous Benedictine abbey. Pop., 4,441.

Clyde (klīd) **1.** a river in southwestern Scotland. Length, 106 mi (171 km). **2. Firth of.** the large estuary of the Clyde, in southwestern Scotland.

Cnos·sus (nos′əs, kə nos′-) see **Knossos.**

Co·a·hui·la (kō′ə wē′lə) a state in northern Mexico, bordering on Texas. Area, 58,067 sq mi (150,394 sq km). Pop., 1,557,265.

Coast Mountains, a mountain range in western British Columbia, Canada, and southeastern Alaska; a continuation of the Cascade Range.

Coast Ranges, a series of mountain ranges extending from southern California to Alaska along the Pacific coast, including the Olympic Mountains.

Co·blenz (kō′blents) see **Koblenz.**

Co·cha·bam·ba (kō′chə bäm′bə) a city in west-central Bolivia. Pop., 317,251.

Co·chin (kō′chin) a seaport in southwestern India. Pop., 513,249.

Cochin China, a former French colony in southern Indochina, now part of Vietnam.

Cod, Cape (kod) a long, hook-shaped peninsula in eastern Massachusetts, famous as a summer vacation spot.

Co·im·ba·tore (kō im′bä tôr′) a city in southwestern India. Pop., 704,514.

Col·chis (kol′kis) an ancient country on the eastern shore of the Black Sea. The legendary Golden Fleece was located there.

Co·li·ma (kə lē′mə) a state in western Mexico. Area, 2,010 sq mi (5,206 sq km). Pop., 346,293.

Co·logne (kə lōn′) a city in central western Germany. Pop., 937,482. Also, *German,* **Köln.**

Co·lom·bi·a (kə lum′bē ə) a country in northwestern South America, on the Pacific and the Caribbean. Capital, Bogotá. Area, 440,831 sq mi (1,141,752 sq km). Pop., 27,867,326. —**Colom′bi·an,** *adj., n.*

Co·lom·bo (kə lum′bō) the capital and chief port of Sri Lanka, on the west coast of the island. Pop., 683,000.

Co·lón (kō lōn′) a city in northern Panama, at the Caribbean entrance to the Panama Canal. Pop., 54,469.

Col·o·rad·o (kol′ə rad′ō, -rä′dō) **1.** a state in the western United States. Capital, Denver. Area, 104,091 sq mi (269,596 sq km). Pop., 3,294,394. Abbreviation, **Colo.**; postal abbreviation, **CO 2.** a river flowing from northern Colorado into the Gulf of California. Length, 1,450 mi (2,333 km). **3.** a desert in southeastern California and northwestern Mexico. —**Col′o·rad′an,** *adj., n.*

Colorado Plateau, a major physiographic region of the United States, occupying most of western Colorado, eastern Utah, and northern Arizona and New Mexico.

Colorado Springs, a city in central Colorado, the site of the United States Air Force Academy. Pop., 281,140.

Co·lum·bi·a (kə lum′bē ə) **1.** a river that flows into the Pacific, forming most of the border between Washington and Oregon. Length, 1,214 mi (1,953 km). **2.** the capital of South Carolina, in the central part of the state. Pop., 98,052. **3.** a city in central Missouri. Pop., 69,101. **4.** the United States.

Co·lum·bus (kə lum′bəs) **1.** the capital of Ohio, in the central part of the state. Pop., 632,910. **2.** a city in western Georgia. Pop., 243,072.

Commonwealth of Independent States, an association, formed in 1991, by eleven independent countries that were previously republics of the Soviet Union.

Commonwealth of Nations, a worldwide association of nations and their dependent territories, consisting of most of those states that formerly constituted the British Empire. All members are equal but recognize the British monarch as titular head of the

a	at	e	end	o	hot	u	up	hw	white	⟨	about
ā	ape	ē	me	ō	old	ū	use	ng	song		taken
ä	far	i	it	ô	fork	ü	rule	th	thin	ə	pencil
âr	care	ī	ice	oi	oil	u̇	pull	th	this		lemon
		îr	pierce	ou	out	ûr	turn	zh	measure		circus

1429

association. Formerly known as the British Commonwealth of Nations. Also, **the Commonwealth.**

Co·mo, Lake (kō′mō) a lake in northern Italy.

Com·o·ros (kom′ə rōz′) an island country off the southeastern coast of Africa. Capital, Moroni. Land area, 838 sq mi (2,170 sq km). Pop., 452,742.

Comp·ton (komp′tən) a city in southwestern California. Pop., 90,454.

Con·a·kry (kon′ə krē) the capital and chief port of Guinea, in the western part of the country. Pop., 800,000.

Con·cep·ción (kən sep′sē ōn′) a city in central Chile. Pop., 267,891.

Con·cord (*defs. 1, 3,* kong′kərd; *def. 2,* kon′kôrd, kong′kərd) **1.** a town in eastern Massachusetts, site of one of the first battles of the American Revolution, on April 19, 1775. Pop., 17,076. **2.** the capital of New Hampshire, in the southern part of the state. Pop., 36,006. **3.** a city in western California, northeast of Oakland. Pop., 111,348.

Con·go (kong′gō) **1.** a long river in central Africa, flowing from southeastern Zaire into the Atlantic. Length, 2,900 mi (4,666 km). Also, **Zaire. 2. Republic of the.** a country in west-central Africa, west of the country of Zaire. Capital, Brazzaville. Area, 132,000 sq mi (341,880 sq km). Pop., 1,912,429. **3. Democratic Republic of the.** see **Zaire** *(def. 1).* —**Con·go·lese** (kong′gə lēz′, -lēs′), *adj., n.*

Congo Free State, see **Belgian Congo.**

Con·nacht (kon′əкнт) *also,* **Connaught.** a historic province of Ireland, in the western part of the island.

Con·nect·i·cut (kə net′i kət) **1.** a state in the northeastern United States, the southernmost of the New England states. Capital, Hartford. Area, 5,018 sq mi (12,997 sq km). Pop., 3,287,116. Abbreviations, **Conn., Ct.;** postal abbreviation, **CT 2.** the longest river in New England, flowing from northern New Hampshire into Long Island Sound. Length, 407 mi (655 km).

Con·stance, Lake (kon′stəns) a lake in southwestern Germany, northern Switzerland, and western Austria.

Con·stan·ța (kôn stän′tsä) the chief port of Romania, in the southeastern part of the country on the Black Sea. Pop., 327,676.

Con·stan·tine (kon′stən tēn′) a city in northeastern Algeria. Pop., 440,842. Also, **Qacentina.**

Con·stan·ti·no·ple (kon′stan tə nō′pəl) the capital of the Byzantine and Ottoman empires, now the city of **Istanbul.**

Continental Divide, an elevation of land in North America formed by the various peaks of the Rocky Mountains, separating rivers flowing eastward from those flowing westward. Also, **Great Divide.**

Cook Islands, a group of islands east of Australia in the western part of the southern Pacific, a possession of New Zealand. Land area, approx. 90 sq mi (235 sq km). Pop., 18,155.

Cook Strait, a strait in New Zealand, separating North Island from South Island.

Co·pen·ha·gen (kō′pən hā′gən, -hä′-) the capital of Denmark. It is the largest city in Denmark and a major northern European port. Pop., 466,723.

Co·quil·hat·ville (kô kē yä vēl′) see **Mbandaka.**

Coral Sea, a southwestern arm of the Pacific, off the coast of northeastern Australia. It was the site of an American victory over the Japanese in 1942, during World War II.

Cor·cy·ra (kôr sī′rə) see **Corfu.**

Cor·di·ller·as (kôr dil′ər əz, kôr′də lyâr′əs) **1.** a mountain system extending from Alaska to Cape Horn, including the Rocky Mountains in North America and the Andes in South America. **2.** that part of this system located in South America; the Andes. **3.** that part of this system located in North America.

Cór·do·ba (kôr′də bə) **1.** a city in southwestern Spain. Pop., 302,301. **2.** a city in north-central Argentina. Pop., 993,055. Also, **Cor·do·va** (kôr′də və). —**Cor′do·ban;** *also,* **Cor′do·van,** *adj., n.*

Cor·fu (kôr′fü, -fü) a Greek island off the west coast of Greece, in the Ionian Sea. In ancient times it was known as Corcyra. Area, 246 sq mi (637 sq km). Pop., 99,477.

Cor·inth (kôr′inth) a port city in southern Greece, in the northeastern corner of the Peloponnesus. It was a major commercial and artistic center in ancient times. Pop., 22,658.

Cork (kôrk) a port city in central Ireland. Pop., 133,271.

Corn·wall (kôrn′wôl, -wəl) a county in southwestern England. Pop., 430,506.

Cor·pus Chris·ti (kôr′pəs kris′tē) a port city in southern Texas. Pop., 257,453.

Cor·reg·i·dor (kə reg′i dôr′) a fortified island in the Philippines, site of a surrender by U.S. forces to the Japanese in 1942, during World War II.

Cor·ri·en·tes (kôR′ē en′tes) a city in northeastern Argentina. Pop., 180,612.

Cor·si·ca (kôr′si kə) a French island in the Mediterranean, southeast of France. Area, approx. 3,352 sq mi (8,681 sq km). Pop., 246,000. —**Cor′si·can,** *adj., n.*

Cos·ta Me·sa (kos′tə mā′sə) a city on the southern coast of California. Pop., 96,357.

Cos·ta Ri·ca (kos′tə rē′kə) a country in Central America, between Nicaragua and Panama. Capital, San José. Area, 19,730 sq mi (51,100 sq km). Pop., 2,851,000. —**Cos′ta Ri′can,** *adj., n.*

Côte d'A·zur (kōt dä zҮR′) the French part of the Riviera.

Côte d'I·voire (kōt dē vwäR′) see **Ivory Coast.**

Co·to·nou (kō′tə nü′) a port city in southern Benin. Pop., 478,000.

Co·to·pax·i (kō′tə pak′sē) a volcano in the Andes, in north-central Ecuador. It is one of the highest active volcanoes in the world. Height, 19,347 ft (5,897 m).

Cots·wold Hills (kots′wōld′, -wəld) a range of hills in southwestern England.

Cott·bus (kot′bəs) *also,* **Kottbus.** a city in eastern Germany. Pop., 128,639.

Council Bluffs, a city in southwestern Iowa. Pop., 54,315.

Cov·en·try (kuv′ən trē) a city in south-central England. Pop., 318,718.

Crac·ow (krak′ou) see **Kraków.**

Cra·io·va (krä yō′və) a city in central Romania. Pop., 281,044.

Cran·ston (kran′stən) a city in east-central Rhode Island. Pop., 76,060.

Crater Lake 1. a lake in the crater of a prehistoric volcano, in southwestern Oregon. It is the deepest lake in the United States. **2.** a national park containing this lake. Area, 160,290 acres (64,869 hectares).

Cré·cy (kres′ē, kRe sē′) *also,* **Cres·sy.** a town in northern France, the site of an English victory over the French in 1346.

Cre·mo·na (krə mō′nə) a city in northern Italy, noted for the violins and other stringed instruments made there by the Stradivari, Guarneri, and Amati families. Pop., 76,979.

Cres·sy (kres′ē, kre sē′) see **Crécy.**

Crete (krēt) a Greek island in the eastern Mediterranean, southeast of mainland Greece. Area, 3,235 sq mi (8,379 sq km). Pop., 501,082. —**Cre′tan,** *adj., n.*

Cri·me·a (krī mē′ə) a peninsula in Ukraine, on the northern coast of the Black Sea. Area, 10,000 sq mi (25,900 sq km).

Cro·a·tia (krō ā′shə) a country in southeastern Europe, a former republic of Yugoslavia. Capital, Zagreb. Area, approx. 21,830 sq mi (56,540 sq km). Pop., 4,673,517. —**Cro·at** (krō′at), **Cro·a′tian,** *adj., n.*

Cu·ba (kū′bə) an island country in the Caribbean, the largest and westernmost island of the West Indies. Capital, Havana. Area, 42,804 sq mi (110,862 sq km). Pop., 10,288,000. —**Cu′ban,** *adj., n.*

Cú·cu·ta (kü′kü tä′) a city in northern Colombia. Pop., 379,478.

Cuen·ca (kweng′kə) a city in southern Ecuador. Pop., 201,490.

Cu·lia·cán (kü lyä kän′) a city in northwestern Mexico. Pop., 304,826.

Cu·mae (kū′mē) an ancient city in southwestern Italy. It was the earliest Greek settlement in the western Mediterranean.

Cum·ber·land (kum′bər lənd) a former county in northwestern England.

Cumberland Gap, a natural pass through the Cumberland Mountains, near the point where Tennessee, Virginia, and Kentucky meet.

Cumberland Mountains, a rugged plateau in the Appalachian Mountains, extending from southwestern West Virginia to northwestern Alabama. Also, **Cumberland Plateau.**

Cumberland River, a river flowing west through southern Kentucky and northern Tennessee into the Ohio. Length, 687 mi (1,105 km).

Cu·ra·çao (kyūr′ə sō′) the principal island of the Netherlands Antilles group, off the coast of Venezuela. Area, 171 sq mi (443 sq km). Pop., 146,096.

Cu·ri·ti·ba (kūr′i tē′bə) a city in southern Brazil. Pop., 1,279,205.

Cus·co (küs′kō) see **Cuzco.**

Cush (kūsh, kush) *also,* **Kush.** in the Bible, a land inhabited by the descendants of Ham. It is usually identified with present-day Ethiopia.

Cuz·co (küs′kō) *also,* **Cus·co.** a city in southern Peru, in the Andes. It was the capital of the Incan empire. Pop., 89,563.

Cyc·la·des (sik′lə dēz′) a group of Greek islands in the Aegean off the southeastern coast of Greece. Land area, 1,023 sq mi (2,650 sq km).

Cy·prus (sī′prəs) an island country south of Turkey, in the eastern Mediterranean, divided since 1974 into separate Greek and Turkish zones. Capital, Nicosia. Area, 3,572 sq mi (11,901 sq km). Pop., 708,000. —**Cyp·ri·an** (sip′rē ən), **Cyp·ri·ot** (sip′rē-ət), *adj., n.*

Cy·re·ne (sī rē′nē) an ancient Greek city in northern Africa, located in what is now eastern Libya.

Czech·o·slo·va·ki·a (chek′ə slə vä′kē ə) a landlocked country in central Europe. Capital, Prague. Area, 49,381 sq mi (127,897 sq km). Pop., 15,661,734. —**Czech, Czech·o·slo·vak** (chek′ə-slō′väk, -vak), **Czech′o·slo·va′ki·an,** *adj., n.*

Cze·sto·cho·wa (chen′stə kō′və) a city in south-central Poland. Pop., 254,600.

Dac·ca (dak′ə) see **Dhaka.**

Dach·au (dä′kou) a city in southern Germany, near Munich, the site of a Nazi concentration camp.

Da·cia (dā′shə) an ancient Roman province in southern Europe, in what is now Romania. —**Da′cian,** *adj., n.*

Da·ho·mey (də hō′mē) see **Benin** *(def. 1).* —**Da·ho·man** (də hō′mən), *adj., n.*

Dai·ren (dī′ren′) see **Dalian.**

Da·kar (dä kär′) the capital and largest city of Senegal. Pop., 1,447,642.

Da·ko·ta (də kō′tə) **1.** a former territory of the United States, consisting of what is now North Dakota and South Dakota. **2. the Dakotas.** North Dakota and South Dakota.

Da·lian (dä′lyän′) *also,* **Talien.** a municipality in northeastern China, formed by the merger of the cities of Dalian (Talien) and Lushun. Dalian was called Dairen under Japanese rule (1905-1945). Pop., 2,280,000. Also, **Luda.**

Dal·las (dal′əs) a city in northeastern Texas. Pop., 1,006,877.

Dal·ma·tia (dal mā′shə) a region in western Croatia, on the coast of the Adriatic Sea.

Da·ly City (dā′lē) a city in west-central California. Pop., 92,311.

Da·man·hur (dä′män hūr′) a city in northern Egypt, in the Nile delta. Pop., 190,840.

Da·mas·cus (də mas′kəs) the capital and largest city of Syria, one of the oldest continuously inhabited cities in the world. Pop., 1,326,000.

Dam·i·et·ta (dam′ē et′ə) a port city in northern Egypt in the Nile delta. Pop., 89,498.

Dam·mam (də mam′) a port city in northern Saudi Arabia, on the Persian Gulf. Pop., 200,000. Also, **Ad Dammam.**

Dan (dän) in ancient times, the northernmost town of Palestine.

Da Nang (də nang′) *also,* **Da·nang.** a port city in central Vietnam, on the South China Sea. Pop., 318,653.

Dan·ube (dan′ūb) the second longest river in Europe, flowing eastward from the southern part of Germany to the Black Sea. Length, 1,776 mi (2,858 km). —**Dan·u·bi·an** (dan ū′bē ən), *adj.*

Dan·zig (dan′sig, dän′tsiKH) see **Gdansk.**

Dar·da·nelles (där′də nelz′) a narrow strait between European and Asian Turkey, connecting the Aegean Sea with the Sea of Marmara. In ancient times it was known as the Hellespont.

Dar el Bei·da (där′el bā dä′) see **Casablanca.**

Dar es Sa·laam (där′ es sə läm′) a capital and the largest city of Tanzania, in the eastern part of the country. Pop., 1,300,000.

Dar·ling (där′ling) the longest river in Australia, flowing southwest through western New South Wales to the Murray River. Length, 1,702 mi (2,739 km).

Dar·win (där′win) a seaport in northern Australia, the capital of Northern Territory. Pop., 63,900.

Da·tong (dä′tông′) *also,* **Ta·tung.** a city in northeastern China. Pop., 810,000.

Da·vao (dä vou′) a port city in the southeastern Philippines. Pop., 569,300.

Dav·en·port (dav′ən pôrt′) a city in eastern Iowa. Pop., 95,333.

Day·ton (dā′tən) a city in southwestern Ohio. Pop., 182,044.

Dead Sea, a salt lake bordering Israel and the West Bank on the west and Jordan on the east, one of the saltiest bodies of water in the world.

Dear·born (dîr′bərn, -bôrn′) a city in southeastern Michigan. Pop., 89,286.

Death Valley, a deep desert basin in southeastern California. It is the hottest and driest place in the United States and contains the lowest point in the Western Hemisphere.

Deb·re·cen (deb′Re tsen) a city in eastern Hungary. Pop., 212,247.

De·ca·tur (di kā′tər) a city in central Illinois. Pop., 83,885.

Dec·can (dek′ən) **1.** a plateau region occupying most of the peninsula of India. Also, **Deccan Plateau. 2.** the peninsula that constitutes the southern part of India.

Del·a·ware (del′ə wâr′) **1.** a state in the eastern United States.

Capital, Dover. Area, 2,045 sq mi (5,297 sq km). Pop., 666,168. Abbreviation, **Del.**; postal abbreviation, **DE 2.** a river in the eastern United States, flowing from southeastern New York State between Pennsylvania and New Jersey into the Delaware Bay. Length, 280 mi (451 km). —**Del′a·war′e·an,** *adj., n.*

Delaware Bay, an inlet of the Atlantic between Delaware and New Jersey.

Del·hi (del′ē) a city in northern India, near New Delhi. Pop., 4,884,234. Also, **Old Delhi.**

Del·mar·va (del mär′və) a peninsula between the Chesapeake Bay in the west and the Delaware Bay and Atlantic Ocean on the east, consisting of Delaware and parts of Maryland and Virginia. Also, **Eastern Shore.**

De·los (dē′los, del′ôs) a small Greek island in the Cyclades, regarded by the ancient Greeks as the birthplace of Apollo and Artemis.

Del·phi (del′fī, -fē) an ancient city in central Greece, the site of the Delphic oracle.

De·na·li (də nä′lē) see **McKinley, Mount.**

Den·mark (den′märk′) a country in northern Europe, between the North and Baltic seas. Capital, Copenhagen. Area, 16,633 sq mi (43,079 sq km). Pop., 5,135,409.

Den·ver (den′vər) the capital and largest city of Colorado, in the north-central part of the state. Pop., 467,610.

Der·by (dûr′bē; *British* där′bē) **1.** a county in central England. Pop., 906,929. Also, **Der·by·shire** (dûr′bē shir′, -shər; *British* där′bə shir′, -shər). **2.** a city in central England. Pop., 218,026.

Der·ry (der′ē) see **Londonderry.**

Des Moines (də moin′) the capital and largest city of Iowa, in the south-central part of the state. Pop., 193,187.

Des·sau (des′ou) a city in eastern Germany. Pop., 103,867.

De·troit (di troit′) **1.** the largest city in Michigan, in the southeastern part of the state. Pop., 1,027,924. **2.** a river between southeastern Michigan and southern Ontario, Canada. Length, 31 mi (50 km).

Deutsch·land (doich′länt′) see **Germany.**

Devil's Island, an island off the coast of French Guiana, formerly a French penal colony.

Dha·ka (dak′ə) *also,* **Dacca.** the capital and largest city of Bangladesh, in the central part of the country. Pop., 2,365,695.

Di·e·go Gar·ci·a (dē ā′gō gär sē′ə) a British island in the Indian Ocean.

Dié·go-Sua·rez (dyä′gō swä′Res) see **Antsiranana.**

Dien·bien·phu *also,* **Dien Bien Phu** (dyen′byen fü′). a town in northwestern Vietnam. Its capture from the French by the Vietminh in 1954 marked the end of French military power in Indochina.

Di·jon (dē zhôn′) a city in east-central France. Pop., 140,942.

Di·nar·ic Alps (di nar′ik) a mountain range in southern Europe, part of the eastern Alps.

Dismal Swamp, a coastal swamp in southeastern Virginia and northeastern North Carolina.

District of Columbia, a federal district in the eastern United States between Maryland and Virginia, coextensive with the city of Washington, the capital of the United States. It is conventionally known as Washington, D.C. Area, 69 sq mi (179 sq km). Pop., 606,900. Abbreviation, **D.C.**; postal abbreviation, **DC**

Di·yar·ba·kir (dē yär′bä kîr′, -yär′buk ər) *also,* **Di·ar·bekr** (dē yär′bek ər). a city in southeastern Turkey, on the Tigris River. Pop., 375,767.

Dja·kar·ta (jə kär′tə) see **Jakarta.**

Dji·bou·ti (ji bü′tē) **1.** a country in east Africa, on the Gulf of Aden. Capital, Djibouti. Area, 8,960 sq mi (23,206 sq km). Pop., 226,000. **2.** the capital of Djibouti. Pop., 120,000. —**Dji·bou′ti-an,** *adj., n.*

Djok·ja·kar·ta (jōk′yə kär′tə) see **Yogyakarta.**

Dne·pro·pe·trovsk (nep′rō pi trôfsk′) a city in eastern Ukraine. Pop., 1,179,000.

Dnie·per (nē′pər) a river flowing through Belarus, Russia, and Ukraine into the Black Sea. Length, 1,368 mi (2,201 km).

Dnies·ter (nēs′tər) a river flowing through Ukraine and Moldova into the Black Sea. Length, 840 mi (1,352 km).

Do·do·ma (dō′də mə) a capital of Tanzania, in the central part of the country. Pop., 54,000.

a	at	e	end	o	hot	u	up	hw	white		about
ā	ape	ē	me	ō	old	ū	use	ng	song		taken
ä	far	i	it	ô	fork	ü	rule	th	thin	ə	pencil
âr	care	ī	ice	oi	oil	u̇	pull	th̲	this		lemon
		îr	pierce	ou	out	ûr	turn	zh	measure		circus

Dog·ger Bank (dô′gər) one of the world's chief fishing grounds, in the North Sea, off the northwestern coast of Europe.

Do·ha (dō′hä) the capital of Qatar. Pop., 217,294.

Do·lo·mites (dō′lə mīts′) a mountain range in northeastern Italy, part of the Alps.

Dom·i·ni·ca (dom′ə nē′kə, də min′i-) a country in the eastern West Indies, one of the Windward Islands. Capital, Roseau. Area, 290 sq mi (751 sq km). Pop., 77,000.

Do·min·i·can Republic (də min′i kən) a country in the central West Indies, occupying the eastern part of the island of Hispaniola. Capital, Santo Domingo. Area, 18,704 sq mi (48,443 sq km). Pop., 5,647,977.

Dom·ré·my (dôN Rᴇ mē′) a village in northeastern France, the birthplace of Joan of Arc. Also, **Dom·ré·my-la-Pu·celle** (dôN Rᴇ lä pʏ sel′).

Don (don) a river flowing through southwestern Russia to the Sea of Azov. Length, 1,224 mi (1,969 km).

Do·nets Basin (də nets′) one of the most important coal-mining and industrial areas in Russia and Ukraine. Also, **Don·bas, Don·bass** (dən bas′).

Do·netsk (də netsk′) a city in eastern Ukraine. Pop., 1,110,000.

Dor·dogne (dôR dôn′yə) a river in France, flowing east from the south-central part of the country to the Gironde estuary. Length, approx. 300 mi (485 km).

Do·ris (dôr′is) a small region in the central part of ancient Greece.

Dor·set (dôr′sit) a county in southern England. Pop., 655,600. Also, **Dor·set·shire** (dôr′sit shir′, -shər).

Dort·mund (dôrt′mənd) a city in western Germany. Pop., 587,328.

Dou·a·la (dü ä′lə) *also,* **Duala.** a port city in southwestern Cameroon, the largest city in the country. Pop., 1,029,731.

Doug·las (dug′ləs) the capital of the Isle of Man. Pop., 20,368.

Dou·ro (dō′Rὺ) a river flowing west through northern Spain and northern Portugal to the Atlantic. Length, 556 mi (895 km). Also, **Duero.**

Do·ver (dō′vər) **1.** the capital of Delaware, in the central part of the state. Pop., 27,630. **2.** a port town in southeastern England, noted for its white cliffs. Pop., 33,461. **3. Strait of.** a strait separating southeastern England from northern France and connecting the English Channel with the North Sea.

Dow·ney (dou′nē) a city in southern California. Pop., 91,444.

Downs (dounz) two ranges of hills in southern England, south of London.

Dres·den (drez′dən) a city in eastern Germany. Pop., 518,057.

Du·a·la (dü ä′lə) see **Douala.**

Du·bai (dü bī′) **1.** one of the sheikdoms of the United Arab Emirates, on the Persian Gulf. Capital, Dubai. Area, 1,500 sq mi (3,885 sq km). Pop., 419,104. **2.** the capital of Dubai. Pop., 265,702.

Dub·lin (dub′lin) the capital and largest city of the Republic of Ireland, in the eastern part of the country. Pop., 502,749.

Du·buque (də būk′) a city in eastern Iowa. Pop., 57,546.

Dud·ley (dud′lē) a borough in west-central England. Pop., 186,513.

Due·ro (dwe′Rô) see **Douro.**

Duis·burg (düs′bûrg) a city in western Germany. Pop., 527,447.

Du·luth (də lüth′) a city in northeastern Minnesota. Pop., 85,493.

Dun·dalk (dun′dôk) a city in north-central Maryland. Pop., 65,800.

Dun·dee (dun dē′) a city in eastern Scotland. Pop., 172,540.

Dun·kirk (dun′kûrk) *also,* **Dun·kerque.** a seaport in northern France, scene of the evacuation of Allied troops from France in 1940, during World War II. Pop., 73,120.

Du·que de Ca·xi·as (dü′kə də kä shē′əs) a city in southeastern Brazil. Pop., 353,200.

Du·ran·go (də rang′gō) a state in northwestern Mexico. Area, 47,691 sq mi (123,520 sq km). Pop., 1,182,320.

Dur·ban (dûr′bən) a port city in the eastern part of the Republic of South Africa. Pop., 634,301.

Dur·ham (dûr′əm) **1.** a city in north-central North Carolina. Pop., 136,611. **2.** a county in northern England. Pop., 596,800.

Du·shan·be (dü shän′bə) the capital of Tajikistan. Pop., 595,000.

Düs·sel·dorf (dü′səl dôrf′, dʏ′səl dôRf′) a city in western Germany. Pop., 569,641.

Dutch Guiana, a former Dutch colony in northern South America, now Suriname.

Dvi·na River (dvē′nə) **1.** a river in northern Russia, flowing northwest to the White Sea. Length, 465 mi (748 km). Also, **Northern Dvina. 2.** a river flowing west through Belarus and Latvia to the Gulf of Riga. Length, 635 mi (1,022 km). Also, **Western Dvina.**

East (ēst) the eastern part of the United States, usually considered as that part east of the Mississippi River, esp. New England and the Middle Atlantic states.

East Berlin, the capital of the former country of East Germany from 1949 to 1990, now part of Berlin.

East China Sea, an arm of the Pacific between eastern China and the Ryukyu Islands.

Easter Island, a Chilean island in the southeastern Pacific, noted for its enormous stone statues.

Eastern Roman Empire, Byzantine Empire. Also, **Eastern Empire.**

Eastern Shore, see **Delmarva.**

East Germany, a former country in north-central Europe, now part of Germany.

East Indies 1. the Netherlands East Indies, sometimes including India and peninsular Southeast Asia. **2.** see **Malay Archipelago.** Also, **East India.**

East Orange, a city in northeastern New Jersey. Pop., 73,552.

East Pakistan, see **Bangladesh.**

East Prussia, a historic region in north-central Europe on the Baltic Sea, formerly a German province. After World War II, it was divided between Poland and the Soviet Union.

East River, a navigable strait in New York City, connecting New York Bay with Long Island Sound and separating Manhattan and the Bronx from Brooklyn and Queens. Length, 16 mi (26 km).

East York, a borough of metropolitan Toronto, in southeastern Ontario, Canada. Pop., 101,085.

E·bro (ē′brō) the longest river in Spain, flowing east-southeast through the northeastern part of the country to the Mediterranean Sea. Length, 565 mi (1,463 km).

Ec·bat·a·na (ek bat′ə nə) the capital of ancient Media.

Ec·ua·dor (ek′wə dôr′) a country on the northwestern coast of South America. Capital, Quito. Area, 109,484 sq mi (283,564 sq km). Pop., 9,923,000. —**Ec′ua·do′ri·an,** *adj., n.*

Ed·in·burgh (ed′ən bûr′ō, -bər ə) the capital of Scotland, in the east-central part of the country. Pop., 433,200.

Ed·mon·ton (ed′mən tən) the capital and largest city of Alberta, Canada, in the south-central part of the province. Pop., 573,982.

E·dom (ē′dəm) **1.** in the Old Testament, the region southeast of Palestine given to Esau. **2.** an ancient kingdom south of Moab and the Dead Sea, in what is now Jordan.

E·ge·des·min·de (e′gə də smin′de) a city in Greenland, located on the western coast. Pop., 3,308.

E·gypt (ē′jipt) a country in northeastern Africa. Ancient Egypt was the center of one of the world's earliest and greatest civilizations. Capital, Cairo. Area, 386,662 sq mi (1,001,455 sq km). Pop., 48,205,049.

Eind·ho·ven (īnt′hō′vən) a city in the southern part of the Netherlands. Pop., 190,700.

Eir·e (âr′ə) see **Ireland** *(def. 2).*

El Aa·iún (el′ ä ün′) the capital of Western Sahara, in the northwestern part of the territory. Pop., 93,875.

El Al·a·mein (el al′ə mān′, ä′lə-) a town in northwestern Egypt on the Mediterranean, the site of a British victory in World War II. Also, **Alamein.**

E·lam (ē′ləm) an ancient kingdom at the head of the Persian Gulf, just east of Babylonia, in what is now western Iran.

El·ba (el′bə) an Italian island located between Italy and Corsica, the site of Napoleon Bonaparte's exile in 1814 and 1815. Area, 85 sq mi (220 sq km). Pop., 28,600.

El·be (el′bə) a river flowing from Czechoslovakia through Germany into the North Sea. Length, 720 mi (1,158 km).

El·brus, Mount (el′brüs) the highest peak of Europe, in the Caucasus Mountains in southwestern Russia. Height, 18,510 ft (5,642 m).

El Dje·za·ir (el′ jə zä îr′) *also,* **El Dja·za·ir.** see **Algiers.**

E·lis·a·beth·ville (i liz′ə bəth vil′) see **Lubumbashi.**

E·liz·a·beth (i liz′ə bəth) a city in northeastern New Jersey. Pop., 110,002.

Elles·mere Island (elz′mîr) a large Canadian island in the Arctic Ocean, northwest of Greenland. It is the northernmost island of Canada. Area, 82,119 sq mi (212,688 sq km).

El·lis Island (el′is) a small island in upper New York Bay, the chief U.S. immigrant reception center from 1892 to 1943.

El Man·su·ra (el′man sùr′ə) see **Al Mansurah.**

El Mon·te (el mon′tē) a city in southern California. Pop., 106,209.

El O·beid (el′ō bād′) a city in central Sudan. Pop., 140,000. Also, *Arabic,* **Al Ubayyid.**

El Pas·o (el pas′ō) a city in westernmost Texas, on the Rio Grande. Pop., 515,342.

El Sal·va·dor (el sal′və dôr′) a country in western Central

America. Capital, San Salvador. Area, 8,248 sq mi (21,362 sq km). Pop., 5,337,896. Also, **Salvador. —Sal'va·dor'an, Sal'va·dor'i·an,** *adj., n.*

E·ly (ē'lē) a town in eastern England, the site of a famous ancient cathedral. Pop., 9,006.

En·e·we·tak (en'ə wē'tok) *also,* **En·e·we·tok.** see Eniwetok.

Eng·land (ing'glənd) the largest political division of the United Kingdom, in the southern part of the island of Great Britain. Capital, London. Area, 50,363 sq mi (130,440 sq km). Pop., 47,536,000.

English Channel, a narrow body of water between England and France, connecting the North Sea with the Atlantic Ocean.

En·i·we·tok (en'ə wē'tok) *also,* **En·e·we·tak, En·e·we·tok.** a large atoll in the Marshall Islands, formerly a U.S. testing ground for nuclear weapons.

En·teb·be (en teb'ē) a city in southern Uganda, the former capital of the country. Pop., 21,289.

Eph·e·sus (ef'ə səs) an ancient city on the west coast of Asia Minor. —**E·phe·sian** (i fē'zhən), *adj., n.*

E·pi·rus (i pī'rəs) a region in western Greece, on the Ionian Sea, in ancient times a separate country.

Ep·som (ep'səm) a town in southeastern England, noted for its racetrack and Derby. Pop., 65,830.

Equatorial Guinea, a country in west-central Africa, on the Gulf of Guinea. Capital, Malabo. Area, 10,831 sq mi (28,052 sq km). Pop., 300,000.

Er·furt (âr'fərt) a city in central Germany. Pop., 220,016.

E·rie (ir'ē) **1. Lake.** the southernmost of the Great Lakes, on the U.S.-Canadian border. **2.** a city in northwestern Pennsylvania, on Lake Erie. Pop., 108,718.

Erie Canal, a former waterway across New York State, connecting the Hudson River with Lake Erie. Parts of the canal are now part of the New York State Barge Canal.

E·ri·van (yer'ə vän') see **Yerevan.**

Erz·ge·bir·ge (ɛrts'gə bîr'gə) an ore-rich mountain range extending along the border of Czechoslovakia and Germany. Also, *Czech,* **Krušné Hory; Ore Mountains.**

Er·zu·rum (er'zə rùm') a city in northeastern Turkey. Pop., 241,344.

Es·fa·han (es'fə hän') a city in west-central Iran, the capital of Persia during the seventeenth and eighteenth centuries. Pop., 986,753. Also, **Isfahan, Ispahan.**

Es·ki·se·hir (es'ki shə hîr') *also,* **Es·ki·shehr** (es'ki sher'). a city in western Turkey. Pop., 413,305.

Es·me·ral·das (es'me räl'däs) a port city in northwestern Ecuador, on the Pacific. Pop., 120,387.

Es·sen (es'ən) a city in western Germany. Pop., 620,594.

Es·sex (es'iks) a county in southeastern England. Pop., 1,529,500.

Es·to·ni·a (es tō'nē ə) *also,* **Es·tho·ni·a.** a country in northeastern Europe, on the Baltic Sea. It was formerly a republic of the Soviet Union. Capital, Tallinn. Area, 17,400 sq mi (45,066 sq km). Pop., 1,573,000.

E·thi·o·pi·a (ē'thē ō'pē ə) **1.** a country in eastern Africa. Capital, Addis Ababa. Area, 483,000 sq mi (1,250,970 sq km). Pop., 42,019,418. Formerly, **Abyssinia. 2.** an ancient country in northeastern Africa, south of Egypt. —**E'thi·o'pi·an,** *adj., n.*

Et·na, Mount (et'nə) *also,* **Mount Aetna.** a high, active volcano in the northeastern part of the Italian island of Sicily. Height, 10,902 ft (3,323 m).

E·to·bi·coke (i tō'bi kōk') a city in southern Ontario, Canada. Pop., 302,973.

E·tru·ri·a (i trùr'ē ə) an ancient country in north-central Italy, now the historic regions of Tuscany and Umbria.

Eu·boe·a (ū bē'ə) a Greek island in the Aegean Sea, just off the eastern coast of the Greek peninsula. Area, 1,457 sq mi (3,774 sq km). Also, **Evvoia. —Eu·boe'an,** *n., adj.*

Eu·gene (ū jēn') a city in western Oregon. Pop., 112,669.

Eu·phra·tes (ū frā'tēz) a river in southwestern Asia, flowing from east-central Turkey through Syria and Iraq into the Persian Gulf. It joins the Tigris River in southeastern Iraq. Length, 1,510 mi (2,430 km).

Eur·a·sia (yù rā'zhə) the continents of Europe and Asia considered as a single continent. —**Eur·a'sian,** *adj., n.*

Eur·ope (yùr'əp) a continent between Asia and the Atlantic. Area, 4,063,000 sq mi (10,523,170 sq km). Pop., 710,000,000. —**Eur'o·pe'an,** *adj., n.*

Ev·ans·ton (ev'ənz tən) a city in northeastern Illinois. Pop., 73,233.

Ev·ans·ville (ev'ənz vil') a city in southwestern Indiana. Pop., 126,272.

Ev·er·est, Mount (ev'ər əst) the highest mountain in the world,

located in the Himalayas on the border between Nepal and Tibet. Height, 29,028 ft (8,848 m).

Ev·er·glades (ev'ər glādz') **1.** an extensive region of marshlands and swamps in southern Florida. **2.** a national park in the southern part of this region. Area, 1,398,800 acres (566,094 hectares).

Ev·voi·a (ev'ē ə) see **Euboea.**

Eyre, Lake (âr) a saltwater lake in the state of South Australia, the largest lake in Australia.

Faer·oe Islands (fâr'ō) a group of Danish islands in the northern Atlantic, between the Shetland Islands and Iceland. Capital, Torshavn. Land area, 540 sq mi (1,400 sq km). Pop., 47,946.

Fair·banks (fâr'bangks') a city in east-central Alaska. Pop., 30,843.

Fai·sa·la·bad (fī sä'lə bäd') a city in northeastern Pakistan. Pop., 1,104,209. Formerly, **Lyallpur.**

Falk·land Islands (fôk'lənd) an island group in the southern Atlantic, east of the southern tip of Argentina. A British dependency, they are also claimed by Argentina. Capital, Stanley. Land area, approx. 4,700 sq mi (12,200 sq km). Pop., 1,958. Also, **Malvinas.**

Fall River, a city in southeastern Massachusetts. Pop., 92,703.

Far East, the countries of eastern Asia, including Japan, China, and North and South Korea.

Far·go (fär'gō) the largest city in North Dakota, in the eastern part of the state. Pop., 74,111.

Fay·ette·ville (fā'it vil') a city in south-central North Carolina. Pop., 75,695.

Federated States of Micronesia, see Micronesia, Federated States of.

Fei·ra de San·ta·na (fā'rə də sän tä'nə) a city in eastern Brazil. Pop., 278,600.

Fer·ra·ra (fə rär'ə) a city in northeastern Italy. Pop., 113,300.

Fertile Crescent, a crescent-shaped region of fertile land extending from the eastern coast of the Mediterranean to the northern coast of the Persian Gulf. It was the site of several early civilizations.

Fez (fez) *also,* **Fes.** a city in north-central Morocco. Pop., 448,823.

Fi·ji (fē'jē) a country consisting of some 800 islands north of New Zealand, in the southwestern Pacific. Capital, Suva. Land area, 7,078 sq mi (18,332 sq km). Pop., 715,375. Also, **Fiji Islands.** —**Fi'ji·an,** *adj., n.*

Finger Lakes, a group of long, narrow, glacial lakes in west-central New York.

Fin·land (fin'lənd) **1.** a nation in northeastern Europe, on the Baltic Sea. Capital, Helsinki. Area, 130,119 sq mi (337,008 sq km). Pop., 4,938,602. **2. Gulf of.** an arm of the Baltic Sea between Finland and Estonia.

Fi·ren·ze (fi ʀen'zä) see **Florence.**

Flan·ders (flan'dərz) a historic region of northwestern Europe, in western Belgium, northern France, and the southwestern Netherlands.

Flint (flint) a city in southeastern Michigan. Pop., 140,761.

Flor·ence (flôr'əns, flor'-) a city in central Italy. It was one of the greatest centers of Renaissance art. Pop., 425,835. Also, *Italian,* **Firenze.**

Flor·i·da (flôr'i də, flor'-) a state mostly on the southeastern peninsula of the United States. Capital, Tallahassee. Area, 58,664 sq mi (151,940 sq km). Pop., 12,937,936. Abbreviation, **Fla.;** postal abbreviation, **FL** —**Flor'i·dan, Flo·rid·i·an** (flə rid'ē ən), *adj., n.*

Florida Keys, a chain of small islands off the southern coast of Florida.

Fog·gia (fô'jə) a city in southeastern Italy. Pop., 155,051.

Fon·taine·bleau (fon'tin blō') a town in north-central France, near Paris, the site of a palace formerly used by French kings. Pop., 15,679.

Foo·chow (fü'chou'; *Chinese* fü'jō') see Fuzhou.

For·mo·sa (fôr mō'sə) a former name for the island of Taiwan.

For·ta·le·za (fôr'tə lā'zə) a city on the northeastern coast of Brazil. Pop., 1,582,414.

Fort-de-France (fôr də fʀäns') the capital and largest city of Martinique. Pop., 99,844.

Forth, Firth of (fôrth; fûrth) an inlet of the North Sea, in southeastern Scotland.

a	at	e	end	o	hot	u	up	hw	white	{	about
ā	ape	ē	me	ō	old	ū	use	ng	song		taken
ä	far	i	it	ô	fork	ü	rule	th	thin	ə	pencil
âr	care	ī	ice	oi	oil	ù	pull	th	this		lemon
				îr	pierce	ou	out	ûr	turn	zh	measure	{	circus

Fort Knox (noks) a military reservation in northern Kentucky, the site of the U.S. gold bullion depository.

Fort-La·my (fôr lä mē′) see **Ndjamena.**

Fort Lau·der·dale (lô′dər dāl′) a city in southeastern Florida. Pop., 149,377.

Fort Smith (smith) a city in western Arkansas. Pop., 72,798.

Fort Wayne (wān) a city in northeastern Indiana. Pop., 173,072.

Fort Worth, a city in northeastern Texas. Pop., 447,619.

France (frans) a country in western Europe. Capital, Paris. Area, 211,208 sq mi (547,029 sq km). Pop., 54,334,871.

Frank·fort (frangk′fərt) **1.** the capital of Kentucky, in the north-central part of the state. Pop., 25,968. **2.** see **Frankfurt.**

Frank·furt (frangk′fərt) *also,* **Frankfort.** a city in west-central Germany. Pop., 625,258. Also, **Frank·furt am Main** (fRängk′fûrt äm mīn′).

Franz Jo·sef Land (franz′ jō′zəf) a group of islands in the Arctic Ocean, part of Russia. Land area, approx. 7,000 sq mi (18,130 sq km). Also, **Fridtjof Nansen Land.**

Fra·ser River (frā′zər) a river flowing through south-central British Columbia, Canada, into an inlet of the Pacific. Length, 850 mi (1,368 km).

Fred·er·icks·burg (fred′ər iks bûrg′, fred′riks-) a city in northeastern Virginia, the site of a Confederate victory in 1862 during the Civil War. Pop., 19,027.

Fred·er·ic·ton (fred′ər ik tən, fred′rik-) the capital of New Brunswick, Canada, in the southern part of the province. Pop., 44,352.

Free·port (frē′pôrt′) a city in the northern Bahamas. Pop., 25,000.

Free·town (frē′toun′) the capital of Sierra Leone, a port city on the Atlantic. Pop., 469,776.

Frei·burg (frī′bûrg′) a city in southwestern Germany. Pop., 183,979. Also, **Frei·burg im Breis·gau** (*German* fRī′bûrk im bRīs′gou).

Fre·mont (frē′mont′) a city in western California, near San Francisco. Pop., 173,339.

French Equatorial Africa, a former French possession in western and central Africa, consisting of the present-day countries of Chad, the Central African Republic, the Republic of the Congo, and Gabon.

French Guiana, a French overseas department on the northeastern coast of South America. Capital, Cayenne. Area, 34,750 sq mi (90,003 sq km). Pop., 73,022.

French Guinea, a former French colony in western Africa, now Guinea.

French Indochina, a former French dependency in Southeast Asia, consisting of what are now the countries of Vietnam, Laos, and Cambodia.

French Polynesia, a French possession in the southeastern Pacific, consisting of several island groups, including Tahiti and the other Society Islands. Capital, Papeete. Land area, approx. 1,544 sq mi (4,000 sq km). Pop., 188,814.

French So·ma·li·land (sə mä′lē land′) a former French colony in eastern Africa, now Djibouti.

French West Africa, a former French possession in northern and western Africa, consisting of the present-day countries of Benin, Guinea, Ivory Coast, Mali, Mauritania, Niger, Senegal, and Burkina Faso.

French West Indies, French island possessions in the West Indies, consisting of Martinique, Guadeloupe, and several smaller islands.

Fres·no (frez′nō) a city in central California. Pop., 354,202.

Fridt·jof Nan·sen Land (fRit′yôf nän′sən länt′) see **Franz Josef Land.**

Friendly Islands, see **Tonga.**

Frun·ze (fRün′zə) see **Pishpek.**

Fu·jian (fY′jyän′) a province in southeastern China. Capital, Fuzhou. Area, 47,529 sq mi (123,100 sq km). Pop., 28,060,000. Also, **Fu·kien** (fü′kyen′).

Fu·ku·o·ka (fü′kü ō′kə) a city in Japan, on the northern part of the island of Kyushu. Pop., 1,160,440.

Ful·ler·ton (fül′ər tən) a city in southern California. Pop., 114,144.

Fu·na·fu·ti (fü′nə fü′tē) the capital of the country of Tuvalu, in the central Pacific. Pop., 2,191.

Fun·dy, Bay of (fun′dē) an inlet of the Atlantic in southeastern Canada, noted for its very high tides.

Fu·shun (fü′shün′) a city in northern China. Pop., 1,290,000.

Fu·zhou (fY′jō′) *also,* **Foochow.** a port city in southeastern China, the capital of Fujian province. Pop., 910,000. Formerly, **Minhow.**

Ga·bon (ga bôN′) a country on the west coast of central Africa.

Capital, Libreville. Area, 103,347 sq mi (267,669 sq km). Pop., 1,312,000. —**Gab·o·nese** (gab′ə nēz′, -nēs′), *adj., n.*

Ga·bo·ro·ne (gä′bə rō′nē, -rōn′) the capital of Botswana, in the southeastern part of the country. Pop., 107,677.

Gaines·ville (gānz′vil′) a city in northern Florida. Pop., 84,770.

Ga·lá·pa·gos Islands (gə lä′pə gōs′) an island group in the eastern Pacific, west of and belonging to Ecuador. Land area, 3,029 sq mi (7,845 sq km). Pop., 7,561.

Ga·lați (gə läts′) *also,* **Ga·latz.** a port city in eastern Romania. Pop., 295,372.

Ga·la·tia (gə lā′shə) an ancient country in central Asia Minor, later a Roman province. —**Ga·la′tian,** *adj., n.*

Ga·li·cia (gə lish′ə, -lish′ē ə) **1.** a historic region in east-central Europe, now divided between Poland and Ukraine. **2.** a region and ancient kingdom in northwestern Spain. —**Ga·li′cian,** *adj., n.*

Gal·i·lee (gal′ə lē′) **1.** a small region in northernmost Palestine. **2. Sea of.** a small, freshwater lake between northeastern Israel and the Golan Heights. Also *(def. 2),* **Lake Kinneret, Lake Tiberias.**

Gal·lip·o·li (gə lip′ə lē) a peninsula in northwestern Turkey, forming the northern shore of the Dardanelles.

Gal·ves·ton (gal′və stən) a port city in southeastern Texas. Pop., 59,070.

Gam·bi·a (gam′bē ə) a country on the western coast of Africa, largely surrounded by Senegal. Capital, Banjul. Area, 4,361 sq mi (11,295 sq km). Pop., 696,000. —**Gam′bi·an,** *adj., n.*

Gan·ges (gan′jēz) a river in northern India and Bangladesh, flowing from the Himalayas to the Bay of Bengal. It is considered sacred by the Hindus. Length, 1,560 mi (2,510 km).

Gan·su (gän′sY′) *also,* **Kansu.** a province in north-central China. Capital, Lanzhou. Area, 137,104 sq mi (355,099 sq km). Pop., 21,160,000.

Garden Grove, a city in southern California. Pop., 143,050.

Gar·land (gär′lənd) a city in northeastern Texas. Pop., 180,650.

Ga·ro·fa·lo (gə rō′fə lō′) a whirlpool in the Strait of Messina, believed to be the Charybdis mentioned in Homer's *Odyssey.*

Ga·ronne (ga Rôn′) a river flowing northwest from northeastern Spain to southwestern France, where it joins the Dordogne to form the Gironde estuary. Length, 357 mi (574 km).

Gar·y (gâr′ē, gar′ē) a city in northwestern Indiana. Pop., 116,646.

Gas·co·ny (gas′kə nē) a historic region and former province of France, in the southwestern part of the country.

Gates·head (gāts′hed′) a city in northeastern England. Pop., 91,429.

Gat·i·neau (gat′ə nō′) a city on the Ottawa River in southwestern Quebec, Canada. Pop., 81,244.

Gaul (gôl) an ancient region in western Europe, consisting of what is now France, Belgium, northern Italy, and parts of Germany, Switzerland, and the Netherlands.

Ga·za (gä′zə) a historic city in the Gaza Strip. It was once a major Philistine city.

Gaza Strip, a territory between Egypt and Israel on the southeastern coast of the Mediterranean, formerly part of the British mandate of Palestine. It was under Egyptian control from 1949 to 1967, when it was occupied by Israel. Area, 146 sq mi (378 sq km). Pop., 591,700.

Ga·zi·an·tep (gä′zē än tep′) a city in southern Turkey. Pop., 627,584. Formerly, **Aintab, Antep.**

Gdansk (gə dänsk′) a port city in northern Poland. Pop., 461,500. Also, *German,* **Danzig.**

Gdy·nia (gə din′ē ə) a port city in north-central Poland. Pop., 250,200.

Gee·long (ji lông′) a seaport in southeastern Australia, in the state of Victoria. Pop., 13,190.

Gel·sen·kir·chen (gel′zən kîr′KHən) a city in western Germany, in the Ruhr region. Pop., 287,255.

Ge·ne·va (jə nē′və) **1.** a city in southwestern Switzerland. Pop., 165,404. **2. Lake.** a narrow, crescent-shaped lake between southwestern Switzerland and eastern France. Also *(def. 2),* **Lake Leman.**

Gen·o·a (jen′ō ə) a port city in northwestern Italy. Pop., 727,427. Also, *Italian,* **Ge·no·va** (je′nô vä′).

Gent (gent) see **Ghent.**

George, Lake (jôrj) a lake in eastern New York.

George Town, see **Pinang** *(def. 2).*

George·town (jôrj′toun′) **1.** the capital and largest city of Guyana, a port on the northern coast of the country. Pop., 78,500. **2.** the capital of the Cayman Islands. Pop., 13,700.

Geor·gia (jôr′jə) **1.** a state in the southeastern United States. Capital, Atlanta. Area, 58,910 sq mi (152,577 sq km). Pop., 6,478,216. Abbreviation, **Ga.;** postal abbreviation, **GA 2.** a country in western Asia, bordering Turkey and the Black Sea. It

was formerly a republic of the Soviet Union. Area, 26,900 sq mi (69,671 sq km). Pop., 5,449,000. —**Geor′gian,** *adj., n.*

Georgian Bay, a large arm of Lake Huron, in Ontario, Canada, in the northeastern part of the lake.

Ger·man·town (jûr′mən toun′) a section of Philadelphia, the site of a Revolutionary War battle in 1777 in which the British were victorious.

Ger·ma·ny (jûr′mə nē) a country in north-central Europe, divided from 1949 to 1990 into **West Germany** and **East Germany.** Capital, Berlin. Area, 137,858 sq mi (357,053 sq km). Pop., 78,389,735. Also, *German,* **Deutschland.**

Geth·sem·a·ne (geth sem′ə nē) in the New Testament, a garden on the Mount of Olives, east of Jerusalem, the scene of Jesus' agony and arrest.

Get·tys·burg (get′iz bûrg′) a town in southern Pennsylvania, the site of a decisive Union victory in 1863 during the Civil War. Pop., 7,025.

Gha·na (gä′nə) a country in western Africa, on the Gulf of Guinea. Capital, Accra. Area, 92,098 sq mi (238,534 sq km). Pop., 12,205,574. —**Gha·ni·an** (gä′nē ən), *adj., n.*

Ghats (gôts) two mountain ranges in southern India, one along the eastern coast and the other along the western coast.

Ghent (gent) *also,* **Gent.** a port city in northwestern Belgium. Pop., 233,856.

Gi·bral·tar (ji brôl′tər) **1.** a British crown colony and seaport near the southern tip of Spain, the site of a naval base. Area, approx. 2 sq mi (5 sq km). Pop., 30,077. **2. Rock of.** a great rock formation in this colony, known to ancient geographers as one of the Pillars of Hercules. **3. Strait of.** a body of water connecting the Mediterranean with the Atlantic, separating the northern tip of Morocco from the southern tip of Spain.

Gi·la River (hē′lə) a river flowing west through New Mexico and Arizona into the Colorado. Length, 500 mi (805 km).

Gil·bert and El·lice Islands (gil′bərt; el′is) a former British colony in the west-central Pacific, consisting of the Gilbert Islands, now **Kiribati,** and the Ellice Islands, now **Tuvalu.**

Gil·e·ad (gil′ē əd) a mountainous region in ancient Palestine east of the Jordan River between the Dead Sea and the Sea of Galilee.

Gi·ronde (jə rond′) an estuary on the east coast of France, formed by the Garonne and Dordogne rivers. Length, 45 mi (72 km).

Gi·za (gē′zə) *also,* **Gi·zeh.** a city in northern Egypt, on the Nile near Cairo. It is the site of the Sphinx and the pyramids. Pop., 1,870,508. Also, *Arabic,* **Al Jizah.**

Glas·gow (glas′gō, glaz′-) the largest city and chief port of Scotland, in the southern part of the country. Pop., 695,630.

Glen·dale (glen′dāl′) **1.** a city in southwestern California. Pop., 180,038. **2.** a city in central Arizona. Pop., 148,134.

Glouces·ter (glos′tər) a city in eastern Ontario, Canada, near Ottawa. Pop., 89,810.

Glouces·ter·shire (glos′tər shîr′, -shər) a county in southwest-central England. Pop., 527,500.

Go·a (gō′ə) a former Portuguese colony on the western coast of India, now part of India.

Go·bi (gō′bē) a large desert in southeastern Mongolia and northern China. Area, approx. 500,000 sq mi (1,295,000 sq km).

Godt·håb (gôt′hôp′) see **Nuuk.**

God·win Aus·ten, Mount (god′win ôs′tən) the second highest mountain in the world, located on the China-India border in the Karakoram Range of northern Kashmir. Height, 28,250 ft (8,611 m). Also, **K2.**

Goi·â·ni·a (goi ä′nē ə) a city in central Brazil. Pop., 923,333.

Go·lan Heights (gō′län) a hilly region of southwestern Syria, occupied by Israel in 1967 and annexed by Israel in 1981. Area, 454 sq mi (1,176 sq km).

Gol·con·da (gol kon′də) an ancient city in southern India, famous in the sixteenth century for its wealth and diamond mines.

Gold Coast 1. a former British colony in western Africa, now part of Ghana. **2.** a city in southern Queensland, Australia, on the Pacific. Pop., 135,408. Also *(def. 2),* **Southport.**

Gol·go·tha (gol′gə thə) see **Calvary.**

Go·mor·rah (gə môr′ə) see **Sodom.**

Gon·dar (gon′dər) a city in northwestern Ethiopia, the former capital of the country. Pop., 68,958.

Gond·wa·na·land (gond wä′nə land′) a vast prehistoric southern continent that included what is now Antarctica, Australia, Africa, India, and South America; it is thought to have split into the present continents in the Mesozoic era. Also, **Gond·wa·na** (gond wä′nə).

Good Hope, Cape of, a cape at the southernmost tip of Africa, on the Atlantic.

Gor·ki (gôr′kē) *also,* **Gor·ky.** see **Nizhni Novgorod.**

Go·shen (gō′shən) in the Bible, a fertile region in northern Egypt inhabited by the Israelites before the Exodus.

Gö·te·borg (yœ′tə bôR′yə) a port city in southwestern Sweden. Pop., 431,840. Also, **Goth·en·burg** (goth′ən bûrg′).

Göt·ting·en (gœt′ing ən) a city in central Germany, noted for its university. Pop., 118,073.

Gram·pi·an Mountains (gram′pē ən) a mountain range in central Scotland, separating the Highlands from the Lowlands. Also, **Grampian Hills, the Grampians.**

Gra·na·da (grə nä′də) **1.** a historic city in southern Spain, formerly the capital of a Moorish kingdom. It is the site of the Alhambra palace. Pop., 263,334. **2.** a city in southwestern Nicaragua, located on Lake Nicaragua. Pop., 64,642.

Gran Cha·co (grän chä′kō) a vast, lowland region in south-central South America. Area, approx. 250,000 sq mi (647,500 sq km).

Grand Bank, a shoal off the eastern coast of Newfoundland, in the northern Atlantic. It is a major fishing area. Also, **Grand Banks.**

Grand Canal 1. a canal in eastern China, one of the longest and oldest in the world. **2.** a large canal in Venice, Italy, serving as the city's main thoroughfare.

Grand Canyon 1. a large canyon in northwestern Arizona on the upper course of the Colorado River, regarded as one of the most spectacular natural wonders of the world. **2.** a national park encompassing most of this canyon. Area, 1,218,375 acres (493,076 hectares).

Grand Forks, a city in eastern North Dakota, on the Red River. Pop., 49,425.

Grand Island, a city in southeastern-central Nebraska, near the Platte River. Pop., 39,386.

Grand Manitoulin, see **Manitoulin Island.**

Grand Rapids, a city in western Michigan. Pop., 189,126.

Grand Te·ton National Park (tē′ton) an area in northwestern Wyoming including Jackson Lake and part of the Teton Range. Area, 310,515 acres (125,665 hectares).

Grand Turk, the capital of the Turks and Caicos Islands. Pop., 3,761.

Graz (gräts) a city in southern Austria. Pop., 243,166.

Great Barrier Reef, the largest barrier reef in the world, along the northeastern coast of Australia.

Great Basin, a vast region in the western United States, consisting mostly of arid or semiarid land, characterized by numerous small basins separated by short mountain ranges. It lies between the Sierra Nevada and the Rocky Mountains and includes most of Nevada. Area, approx. 200,000 sq mi (518,000 sq km).

Great Bear Lake, a lake in the western part of the Northwest Territories, Canada.

Great Britain 1. see **United Kingdom. 2.** an island off the western coast of Europe that includes England, Scotland, and Wales, the largest of the British Isles. Area, 94,216 sq mi (244,019 sq km). Also, **Britain.**

Great Divide, see **Continental Divide.**

Greater Antilles, an island group of the West Indies, including Cuba, Jamaica, Hispaniola, and Puerto Rico.

Greater London, the official name of **London** *(def. 1).*

Great Falls, a city in west-central Montana. Pop., 55,097.

Great Lakes, a group of five large, freshwater lakes along the border between the United States and Canada, including Lakes Superior, Michigan, Huron, Erie, and Ontario.

Great Plains, a vast plateau region in western North America, extending from Alberta, Canada, to Texas and consisting mostly of flat or rolling, generally treeless plains.

Great Rift Valley, a depression extending from the Jordan valley in southwestern Asia to Mozambique in southeastern Africa, marking a long series of geologic faults.

Great Salt Lake, a lake in northwestern Utah, the largest salt lake in North America and one of the saltiest bodies of water in the world.

Great Slave Lake, a lake in the southwestern part of the Northwest Territories, Canada.

Great Smoky Mountains 1. a mountain range in the southeastern United States, between Tennessee and North Carolina, part of the Appalachian Mountains. **2.** a national park in this region containing large stands of virgin forest. Area, 517,368

a	at	e	end	o	hot	u	up	hw	white		about
ā	ape	ē	me	ō	old	ū	use	ng	song		taken
ä	far	i	it	ô	fork	ü	rule	th	thin	ə{	pencil
âr	care	ī	ice	oi	oil	u̇	pull	th	this		lemon
				îr	pierce	ou	out	ûr	turn	zh	measure		circus

acres (209,379 hectares). Also, **Great Smokies, Smoky Mountains.**

Greece (grēs) a country at the southern end of the Balkan Peninsula. Ancient Greece was a great intellectual and artistic center and a major influence on Western culture. Capital, Athens. Area, 50,944 sq mi (131,945 sq km). Pop., 9,740,417. Also, *Greek, Hellas.*

Green Bay, a port city in east-central Wisconsin. Pop., 96,466.

Green·land (grēn′lənd) a Danish island northeast of the mainland of North America, lying mostly within the Arctic Circle. It is the largest island in the world. Capital, Nuuk. Area, 840,000 sq mi (2,175,600 sq km). Pop., 55,558.

Green Mountains, a mountain range extending along the entire length of central Vermont, part of the Appalachian Mountains.

Green River 1. a river flowing south from western Wyoming through eastern Utah to the Colorado. Length, 730 mi (1,175 km). 2. a river in Kentucky, flowing west and northwest from the central part of the state into the Ohio. Length, 360 mi (579 km).

Greens·bor·o (grēnz′bûr′ō) a city in north-central North Carolina. Pop., 183,521.

Green·wich (gren′ich) a borough of Greater London, England, the former site of an astronomical observatory. The prime meridian passes through Greenwich. Pop., 211,800.

Greenwich Village, a section of lower Manhattan, New York City, noted as an artists' and writers' quarter.

Gre·na·da (grə nā′də) an island country in the West Indies, one of the Windward Islands. Capital, St. George's. Area, 133 sq mi (344 sq km). Pop., 89,088.

Gren·a·dines (gren′ə dēnz′) an island group in the Windward Islands of the West Indies, divided politically between Grenada and St. Vincent and the Grenadines.

Gre·no·ble (grə nō′bəl) a city in southeastern France. Pop., 156,637.

Gro·ning·en (grō′ning ən) a city in the northeastern Netherlands. Pop., 167,800.

Gua·da·la·ja·ra (gwä′də lə här′ə) a city in southwestern Mexico. Pop., 1,626,152.

Gua·dal·ca·nal (gwä′dəl kə nal′) a mountainous island in the southwestern Pacific, one of the Solomon Islands. It was the scene of prolonged and bitter fighting between American and Japanese forces in World War II. Area, 2,500 sq mi (6,475 sq km).

Gua·de·loupe (gwä′də lūp′) a French department in the West Indies, consisting of two islands in the Leeward Islands. Capital, Basse-Terre. Land area, 687 sq mi (1,779 sq km). Pop., 328,400.

Guam (gwäm) an island in the western Pacific, east of the Philippines. It is administered by the United States. Capital, Agana. Area, 209 sq mi (541 sq km). Pop., 105,979.

Gua·na·jua·to (gwä′nə hwä′tō) a state in central Mexico. Area, 11,805 sq mi (30,575 sq km). Pop., 3,006,110.

Guang·dong (gwäng′dông′) *also,* **Kwangtung.** a province in southeastern China. Capital, Guangzhou. Area, 89,344 sq mi (231,401 sq km). Pop., 64,470,000.

Guang·xi (gwäng′shē′) *also,* **Kwang·si.** an autonomous region in southern China. Capital, Nanning. Area, 85,096 sq mi (220,399 sq km). Pop., 40,230,000. Also, **Guangxi Zhuang·zu Autonomous Region** (jwäng′zu′).

Guang·zhou (gwäng′jō′) *also,* **Kwangchow.** a seaport in southeastern China, the capital of Guangdong province. Pop., 3,100,000. Also, **Canton.**

Guan·tá·na·mo (gwän tä′nə mō′) a city in southeastern Cuba, located north of Guantánamo Bay. Pop., 179,091.

Guantánamo Bay, an inlet of the Caribbean in southeastern Cuba, the site of a U.S. naval base.

Gua·rul·hos (gwä Rūl′yús) a city in southeastern Brazil. Pop., 571,790.

Gua·te·ma·la (gwä′tə mä′lə) 1. the northernmost country of Central America. Capital, Guatemala City. Area, 42,042 sq mi (108,889 sq km). Pop., 8,935,395. 2. see **Guatemala City.** —**Gua′te·ma′lan,** *adj., n.*

Guatemala City, the capital and largest city of Guatemala, in the southern part of the country. Pop., 1,057,210.

Guay·a·quil (gwä′yə kēl′) the largest city and chief port of Ecuador, in the western part of the country. Pop., 1,572,615.

Guelph (gwelf) a city in southern Ontario, Canada. Pop., 78,235.

Guern·sey (gûrn′zē) a British island in the English Channel, off the coast of France, one of the Channel Islands. Area, approx. 25 sq mi (65 sq km).

Guer·re·ro (ge Re′Rô) a state in southern Mexico. Area, 24,887 sq mi (64,457 sq km). Pop., 2,109,513.

Gui·a·na (gē an′ə, -ä′nə, gī-) a region in northeastern South America on the Atlantic, including Guyana, French Guiana, Suriname, and parts of Venezuela and Brazil.

Guin·ea (gin′ē) 1. a country on the Atlantic in western Africa.

Capital, Conakry. Area, 94,926 sq mi (245,858 sq km). Pop., 6,225,000. 2. Gulf of. a large, open arm of the Atlantic along the west-central coast of Africa. —**Guin·e·an** (gin′ē ən), *adj.*

Guin·ea-Bis·sau (gin′ē bē sou′) a small country on the Atlantic in western Africa. Capital, Bissau. Area, 13,948 sq mi (36,125 sq km). Pop., 945,000.

Gui·yang (gwē′yäng′) *also,* **Kweiyang.** a city in southern China, the capital of Guizhou province. Pop., 1,030,000.

Gui·zhou (gwē′jō′) *also,* **Kweichow.** a province in southern China. Capital, Guiyang. Area, 67,181 sq mi (173,999 sq km). Pop., 30,730,000.

Guj·ran·wa·la (gúj′rən wä′lə) a city in northeastern Pakistan. Pop., 600,993.

Gulf States 1. the five Southern states bordering the Gulf of Mexico: Florida, Alabama, Mississippi, Louisiana, and Texas. 2. those countries in or bordering on the Persian Gulf: Iran, Iraq, Kuwait, Saudi Arabia, Bahrain, Qatar, the United Arab Emirates, and Oman.

Guy·a·na (gī an′ə) a country on the northeastern coast of South America. Capital, Georgetown. Area, 83,000 sq mi (214,970 sq km). Pop., 918,000. —**Guy·a·nese** (gī′ə nēz′, -nēs′), *adj., n.*

Gwa·li·or (gwä′lē ôr′) a city in central India. Pop., 539,015.

Haar·lem (här′ləm) a city in the western Netherlands, near the North Sea. Pop., 149,200.

Ha-erh-pin (hä′er′bin′) see **Harbin.**

Hague, The (hāg) a city in the western Netherlands, the seat of the national government. Pop., 443,900.

Hai·dar·a·bad (hī′dər ə bad′) see **Hyderabad.**

Hai·fa (hī′fə) a port city in northwestern Israel, on the Mediterranean Sea. Pop., 222,600.

Hai·kou (hī′kō′) a city in southern China, the capital of the island province of Hainan. Pop., 209,200. Also, **Hoihow.**

Hai·nan (hī′nän′) a province in southern China, consisting of an island in the South China Sea. Capital, Haikou. Area, 13,000 sq mi (33,670 sq km). Pop., 6,100,000.

Hai·phong (hī′fong′) a seaport in northeastern Vietnam, near the Gulf of Tonkin. Pop., 456,000.

Hai·ti (hā′tē) 1. a country in the Caribbean, on the western part of the island of Hispaniola. Capital, Port-au-Prince. Area, 10,714 sq mi (27,749 sq km). Pop., 5,531,802. 2. see **Hispaniola.**

Ha·ko·da·te (hä′kô dä′te) a port city in Japan, on the southern coast of the island of Hokkaido. Pop., 319,194.

Hal·i·car·nas·sus (hal′i kär nas′əs) an ancient city in southwestern Asia Minor, the site of the famous mausoleum that was one of the Seven Wonders of the World.

Hal·i·fax (hal′ə faks′) a port city in southeastern Canada, the capital of Nova Scotia. Pop., 113,577.

Hal·le (hä′lə) a city in central Germany. Pop., 236,044.

Ham·a·dan (ham′ə dan′, ham′ə dän′) a city in northwestern Iran. Pop., 272,499.

Ham·burg (ham′bûrg′) a port city in northern Germany, on the Elbe River. Pop., 1,603,070.

Ham·il·ton (ham′əl tən) 1. a port city in southeastern Ontario, Canada, at the western end of Lake Ontario. Pop., 306,728. 2. the capital and chief city of Bermuda. Pop., 1,676. 3. River. see **Churchill River** *(def. 2).*

Ham·mond (ham′ənd) a city in northwestern Indiana. Pop., 84,236.

Hamp·shire (hamp′shîr, -shər) a county in southern England. Pop., 1,542,900.

Hamp·ton (hamp′tən) a city in southeastern Virginia. Pop., 133,793.

Hampton Roads, a channel of the Chesapeake Bay in southeastern Virginia, the site of the battle during the Civil War between the Union ironclad *Monitor* and the Confederate ironclad *Virginia* (the renamed *Merrimac*).

Han (hän) a river in east-central China, flowing southeast into the Yangtze. Length, 900 mi (1,448 km).

Hang·zhou (häng′jō′) *also,* **Hang·chow** (hang′chou′; *Chinese* häng′jō′). a port city in eastern China, the capital of Zhejiang province. Pop., 1,290,000.

Han·kou (hang′kou′) a former city in east-central China, now part of Wuhan.

Han·ni·bal (han′ə bəl) a city in northeastern Missouri, on the Mississippi River, the childhood home of Mark Twain. Pop., 18,004.

Ha·noi (ha noi′) the capital of Vietnam, a port in the northeastern part of the country. Pop., 1,089,000.

Han·o·ver (han′ō vər) *also,* **Han·no·ver.** 1. a historic region and former province of Prussia, located in the northern part of present-day Germany. 2. a city in north-central Germany. Pop., 498,495.

Han·yang (hän′yäng′) a former city in east-central China, now part of Wuhan.

Ha·ra·re (hə rär′ā) the capital and largest city of Zimbabwe, in the northeastern part of the country. Pop., 681,000. Formerly, **Salisbury.**

Har·bin (här′bin′) a city in northeastern China, the capital of Heilongjiang province. Pop., 2,710,000. Also, **Ha-erh-pin.**

Har·lem (här′ləm) a district of New York City, in upper Manhattan.

Har·pers Ferry (här′pərz) a town in northeastern West Virginia, the site of John Brown's raid on a government arsenal in 1859.

Har·ris·burg (har′is bûrg′) the capital of Pennsylvania, in the southeastern part of the state. Pop., 52,376.

Hart·ford (härt′fərd) the capital of Connecticut, in the central part of the state. Pop., 139,739.

Harz Mountains (härts) a low mountain range in central Germany.

Has·tings (hās′tingz) a city in southeastern England, on the English Channel, the site of William the Conqueror's decisive victory over the Saxons in 1066. Pop., 74,979.

Hat·ter·as, Cape (hat′ər əs) a cape on an island off the eastern coast of North Carolina, the site of many shipwrecks.

Ha·van·a (hə van′ə) the capital and chief port of Cuba, on the northwestern coast of the island. Pop., 2,036,800. Also, **La Habana.**

Hav·ant and Wa·ter·loo (hav′ənt; wô′tər lü′, wot′ər-) an urban district in southern England. Pop., 116,100.

Ha·vre (hä′vər, hä′vrə) see **Le Havre.**

Ha·wai·i (hə wī′ē, -wä′yə, -vä′yə) **1.** a state of the United States, made up of the Hawaiian Islands. It is the only island state and the only state not on the North American continent. Capital, Honolulu. Land area, 6,425 sq mi (16,641 sq km). Pop., 1,108,229. Postal abbreviation, **HI 2.** the largest of the Hawaiian Islands. Area, 4,021 sq mi (10,414 sq km). Also *(def. 2)*, **Big Island.** —**Ha·wai′ian,** *adj., n.*

Hawaiian Islands, an island chain in the north-central Pacific. Formerly, **Sandwich Islands.**

Ha·wal·li (hə wä′lē) a city in north-central Kuwait, on the Persian Gulf. Pop., 145,126.

Hay·ward (hā′wərd) a city in western California. Pop., 111,498.

He·bei (hœ′bā′) a province in northeastern China. Capital, Shijiazhuang. Area, 84,865 sq mi (219,800 sq km). Pop., 57,100,000. Also, **Hopeh.**

Heb·ri·des (heb′ri dēz′) a Scottish island group off the northwestern coast of Scotland. Land area, 2,812 sq mi (7,283 sq km). Also, **Western Islands.**

He·bron (hē′brən, he brôn′) a town in the West Bank, one of the world's oldest settlements. Pop., 43,000.

He·djaz (hē jaz′) Hejaz.

He·fei (hœ′fā′) a city in eastern China, the capital of Anhui province. Pop., 740,000. Also, **Hofei.** Formerly, **Luchow.**

Hei·del·berg (hī′dəl bûrg′) a city in south-central Germany, the site of a noted university. Pop., 131,429.

Hei·long·jiang (hā′lông′jyäng′) a province in northeastern China. Capital, Harbin. Area, 178,996 sq mi (463,600 sq km). Pop., 34,240,000. Also, **Hei·lung·kiang** (hā′lùng′gyäng′).

He·jaz (hē jaz′) *also,* **Hedjaz** a former independent kingdom in the northwestern part of the Arabian Peninsula, on the Red Sea, now a province of Saudi Arabia.

Hel·e·na (hel′ə nə) the capital of Montana, in the west-central part of the state. Pop., 24,569.

Hel·go·land (hel′gō länt′) a small German island in the North Sea, near which the British defeated the Germans in a naval battle in 1914.

Hel·las (hel′əs) see **Greece.**

Hel·les·pont (hel′əs pont′) see **Dardanelles.**

Hel·sin·ki (hel′sing kē, hel sing′-) the capital and largest city of Finland, on the southern coast of the country. Pop., 490,034.

He·nan (hœ′nän′) a province in eastern China. Capital, Zhengzhou. Area, 64,479 sq mi (167,001 sq km). Pop., 79,690,000. Also, **Honan.**

He·rat (he rät′) a city in northwestern Afghanistan. Pop., 177,300.

Her·cu·la·ne·um (hûr′kyə lā′nē əm) an ancient city in southwestern Italy, near Naples, buried when Mount Vesuvius erupted in A.D. 79.

Her·e·ford·shire (her′ə fərd shir′, -shər) a former county in western England, on the Welsh border.

Her·mon, Mount (hûr′mən, her môn′) a mountain on the border between Syria and Lebanon. Height, 9,232 ft (2,814 m).

Her·mo·sil·lo (er′mō sē′yō) a city in northwestern Mexico. Pop., 297,175.

Herne (hûrn) a city in western Germany, in the Ruhr. Pop., 174,664.

Hert·ford·shire (här′fərd shir′, -shər) a county in southeastern England. Pop., 986,000.

Hesse (hes) a historic German region, now a state, in the central part of the country.

Hi·a·le·ah (hī′ə lē′ə) a city in southeastern Florida. Pop., 188,004.

Hi·dal·go (hi dal′gō; *Spanish* hē thäl′gô) a state in east-central Mexico. Area, 8,058 sq mi (20,870 sq km). Pop., 1,547,493.

Hi·ga·shi·o·sa·ka (hi gä′shē ō sä′kə) a city in Japan, in the southern part of the island of Honshu. Pop., 522,805.

High·lands (hī′ləndz) see **Scottish Highlands.**

Hil·la (hil′ə) see **Al Hillah.**

Him·a·la·yas (him′ə lā′əz) the highest mountain system in the world, extending across central Asia from the northeastern border of Afghanistan through northern India and southern Tibet to the northwestern border of Burma. Also, **Himalaya Mountains.** —**Him′a·la′yan,** *adj.*

Hin·du Kush (hin′dü kùsh′) a mountain system of central Asia, largely in northeastern Afghanistan.

Hir·o·shi·ma (hir′ə shē′mə, hi rō′shə-) a port city in southwestern Japan, on the island of Honshu. On August 6, 1945, the first atomic bomb used in World War II was dropped on this city. Pop., 1,044,118.

His·pa·nio·la (his′pən yō′lə) an island in the Greater Antilles, in the Caribbean, divided into the Dominican Republic and Haiti. Area, approx. 30,000 sq mi (77,700 sq km). Also, **Haiti.**

Ho·bart (hō′bärt) the capital of the Australian island state of Tasmania. Pop., 47,280.

Ho Chi Minh City (hō′chē′min′) the largest city in Vietnam, a seaport in the southern part of the country. Pop., 3,169,000. Formerly, **Saigon.**

Ho·fei (hu′fā′) see **Hefei.**

Hoh·hot (hō′hōt′) a city in northern China, the capital of Inner Mongolia. Pop., 670,000. Also, **Huhehot.** Formerly, **Kweisui.**

Hoi·how (hoi′hou′) see **Haikou.**

Hok·kai·do (ho kī′dō) the northernmost and second largest island of Japan. Area, 30,144 sq mi (78,073 sq km).

Hol·guin (ôl gēn′) a city in central eastern Cuba. Pop., 199,861.

Hol·land (hol′ənd) **1.** a historic region in northwestern Europe, now part of the Netherlands. **2.** see **Netherlands, the.** —**Holland·er** (hol′ən dər), *n.*

Hol·ly·wood (hol′ē wùd′) **1.** a section of Los Angeles, noted as the traditional home of the U.S. motion-picture and television industries. **2.** a city in southeastern Florida, on the Atlantic near Miami. Pop., 121,697.

Holy Land, see **Palestine** *(def. 1).*

Holy Roman Empire, a former empire in western and central Europe formed during the Middle Ages and including what are now Germany, Austria, Czechoslovakia, and parts of eastern France, Switzerland, and northern Italy.

Homs (hômz, hóms) a city in western Syria. Pop., 447,000.

Ho·nan (hœ′nän′) see **Henan.**

Ho·nan·fu (hœ′nän′fy′) see **Luoyang.**

Hon·du·ras (hon dùr′əs, -dyùr′-) a country in northern Central America, with coastlines on the Caribbean and the Pacific. Capital, Tegucigalpa. Area, 43,277 sq mi (112,087 sq km). Pop., 4,376,839. —**Hon·du′ran,** *adj., n.*

Hong Kong (hong′kong′) **1.** a British crown colony off the southeastern coast of China. It will return to Chinese control after 1997. Capital, Victoria. Area, 412 sq mi (1,067 sq km). Pop., 5,395,997. **2.** an island in Hong Kong colony, the site of Victoria, the capital. Area, 29 sq mi (75 sq km). **3.** see **Victoria** *(def. 5).*

Ho·ni·a·ra (hō′nē är′ə) the capital of the Solomon Islands, on the northern part of the island of Guadalcanal. Pop., 30,413.

Ho·no·lu·lu (hon′ə lü′lü) the capital and largest city of Hawaii, on the southern coast of Oahu. Pop., 365,272.

Hon·shu (hon′shü) the largest island of Japan. Area, 88,936 sq mi (230,344 sq km).

Hood, Mount (hùd) a mountain in northwestern Oregon, in the Cascade Range. Height, 11,239 ft (3,426 m).

Ho·peh (hu′bā′) see **Hebei.**

Ho·reb (hôr′eb) see **Sinai, Mount.**

Hor·muz, Strait of (hôr müz′) a strait between Oman and Iran, connecting the Persian Gulf with the Gulf of Oman. Also, **Strait of Ormuz.**

a	at	e	end	o	hot	u	up	hw	white		about
ā	ape	ē	me	ō	old	ū	use	ng	song		taken
ä	far	i	it	ô	fork	ü	rule	th	thin	ə	pencil
âr	care	ī	ice	oi	oil	ù	pull	th	this		lemon
		îr	pierce	ou	out	ûr	turn	zh	measure		circus

Horn, Cape, a cape on an island of Tierra del Fuego, forming the southernmost tip of South America.

Hos·pi·ta·let (ôs'pē tä let') a city in northeastern Spain. Pop., 278,449.

Hot Springs 1. a city in west-central Arkansas, noted as a health resort and tourist center. Pop., 32,462. **2.** a national park in and adjacent to this city, containing hot mineral springs. Area, 5,826 acres (2,358 hectares).

Hous·ton (hūs'tən) a city in southeastern Texas. Pop., 1,630,553.

How·rah (hou'rə) a city in northeastern India. Pop., 744,429.

Hsin·king (shin'ging') see **Changchun.**

Huam·bo (wäm'bō) a city in west-central Angola. Pop., 203,000. Formerly, **Nova Lisboa.**

Huang He (hwäng'hü') a large river in China, flowing from Tibet to the Yellow Sea. Length, 3,395 mi (5,463 km). Also, **Hwang Ho, Yellow River.**

Hu·bei (hy̌'bā') *also,* Hupeh. a province in central China. Capital, Wuhan. Area, 72,394 sq mi (187,500 sq km). Pop., 51,200,000.

Hub·li-Dhar·war (hùb'lē där wär') a city in southwestern India. Pop., 527,108. Also, **Hubli.**

Hud·ders·field (hud'ərz fēld') a city in north-central England. Pop., 147,825.

Hud·son (hud'sən) a river in eastern New York, flowing southward into New York Bay. Length, 306 mi (492 km).

Hudson Bay, a large inland sea in northeastern Canada.

Hue (hwā) *also,* Hué. a seaport in central Vietnam. Pop., 165,710.

Hu·he·hot (hü'hä'hōt') see **Hohhot.**

Hull (hul) a port city in northeastern England. Pop., 322,144. Also, **Kingston-upon-Hull.**

Hum·ber (hum'bər) an estuary in northeastern England. Length, 36 mi (58 km).

Hu·nan (hü'nän') a province in southeastern China. Capital, Changsha. Area, 81,274 sq mi (210,500 sq km). Pop., 57,940,000.

Hun·ga·ry (hung'gə rē) a landlocked country in east-central Europe. Capital, Budapest. Area, 35,920 sq mi (93,033 sq km). Pop., 10,375,000.

Hung·nam (hüng'näm') a seaport in western North Korea. Pop., 260,000.

Hunt·ing·ton (hun'ting tən) a port city in western West Virginia, on the Ohio River. Pop., 54,844.

Huntington Beach, a city in southern California, on the Pacific. Pop., 181,591.

Hun·ting·ton·shire (hun'ting tən shir', -shər) a former county in eastern England.

Hunts·ville (hunts'vil') a city in northern Alabama. Pop., 159,789.

Hu·peh (hü'pā') see **Hubei.**

Hu·ron, Lake (hyür'ən, -on) the second largest of the Great Lakes, on the U.S.-Canadian border.

Hwang Ho (hwäng'hō') see **Huang He.**

Hy·der·a·bad (hī'dər ə bad') *also,* Haidarabad. **1.** a city in south-central India. Pop., 2,187,262. **2.** a city in southeastern Pakistan. Pop., 702,539.

Iaşi (yäsh, yä'shē) a city in northeastern Romania. Pop., 313,060.

I·ba·dan (ē bä'dän) a large city in southwestern Nigeria. Pop., 1,144,000.

I·ba·gué (ē'bä gā') a city in central Colombia. Pop., 292,965.

I·be·ri·a (ī bir'ē ə) **1.** a large peninsula in southwestern Europe, between the Atlantic and the Mediterranean, occupied by Spain and Portugal. Also, **Iberian Peninsula. 2.** an ancient region in the southern Caucasus, in what is now the eastern part of Georgia.

Ice·land (īs'lənd) an island country in the northern Atlantic, between Greenland and Norway. Capital, Reykjavik. Area, 39,800 sq mi (103,082 sq km). Pop., 247,357. —**Ice·land·er** (īs'lan'dər, -lən-), *n.*

I·da·ho (ī'də hō') a state in the western United States. Capital, Boise. Area, 83,564 sq mi (216,431 sq km). Pop., 1,006,749. Abbreviation, **Ida.;** postal abbreviation, **ID** —**I'da·ho'an,** *adj., n.*

Idaho Falls, a city in southeastern Idaho. Pop., 43,929.

Ie·per (ē'pər) see **Ypres.**

I·fe (ē'fā) a city in southwestern Nigeria. Pop., 237,000.

If·ni (ēf'nē) a former Spanish territory in northwestern Africa, on the Atlantic, now part of Morocco.

I·gua·çu Falls (ē'gwä sü') *also,* I·guas·sú Falls, I·gua·zú Falls. a waterfall on the Brazil-Argentina border. It is about 2.5 mi (4 km) wide. Length, 240 ft (73 m).

IJs·sel·meer (ī'səl mer') a lake in the northwestern Netherlands, separated from the North Sea by a dike. It consists of the southern part of the former Zuider Zee and has been reduced in size through land reclamation.

I·le·sha (i lā'shə) a city in southwestern Nigeria. Pop., 302,100.

Il·i·um (il'ē əm) see **Troy.**

Il·li·nois (il'ə noi', -noiz') **1.** a state in the north-central United States. Capital, Springfield. Area, 56,345 sq mi (145,934 sq km). Pop., 11,430,602. Abbreviation, **Ill.;** postal abbreviation, **IL 2.** a river in Illinois, flowing from the northeastern part of the state southwest to the Mississippi. Length, 273 mi (439 km). —**Il'li·nois'an,** *adj., n.*

Il·lyr·i·a (i lir'ē ə) an ancient country on the east coast of the Adriatic.

I·lo·i·lo (ē'lō ē'lō) a port city in the central Philippines, on the island of Panay. Pop., 311,000.

I·lo·rin (i lôr'in) a city in southwestern Nigeria. Pop., 380,000.

Imperial Valley, a low-lying farming region in southeastern California and northeastern Baja California, Mexico.

In·chon (in'chon') a port city in northwestern South Korea, on the Yellow Sea. Pop., 1,628,000. Formerly, **Chemulpo.**

Independence, a city in western Missouri. Pop., 112,301.

In·di·a (in'dē ə) **1.** a country in southern Asia. Capital, New Delhi. Area, 1,269,345 sq mi (3,287,604 sq km). Pop., 685,184,692. **2.** a large peninsular region of southern Asia, bounded by the Arabian Sea, Indian Ocean, and Bay of Bengal, and including India, Pakistan, and Bangladesh.

In·di·an·a (in'dē an'ə) a state in the north-central United States. Capital, Indianapolis. Area, 36,185 sq mi (93,719 sq km). Pop., 5,544,159. Abbreviation, **Ind.;** postal abbreviation, **IN** —**In·di·an·i·an** (in'dē an'ē ən), *adj., n.*

In·di·an·ap·o·lis (in'dē ə nap'ə lis) the capital and largest city of Indiana, in the central part of the state. Pop., 731,327.

Indian Empire, formerly, the parts of India under British control, including the dependent and semidependent Indian states. Also, **British India.**

Indian Ocean, an ocean south of Asia, between Africa and Australia.

Indian Territory, a former region in what is now Oklahoma, where the Cherokee, Creek, Seminole, Chickasaw, and Choctaw Indians of the Southeast were forced to settle in the nineteenth century.

In·do·chi·na (in'dō chī'nə) **1.** a peninsula in southeastern Asia between the Bay of Bengal and the South China Sea, consisting of the Malay Peninsula and the nations of Vietnam, Burma, Laos, Cambodia, and Thailand. **2.** see **French Indochina.** —**In·do·chi·nese** (in'dō chī nēz', -nēs'), *adj., n.*

In·do·ne·sia (in'də nē'zhə) a country in southeastern Asia, composed of islands in the Malay Archipelago, including Java, Sumatra, and part of Borneo, and the western part of the island of New Guinea. Capital, Jakarta. Land area, 741,034 sq mi (1,919,278 sq km). Pop., 147,490,298.

In·dore (in dôr') a city in central India. Pop., 829,327.

In·dus (in'dəs) a river flowing from Tibet through Kashmir and Pakistan into the Arabian Sea. Length, 1,800 mi (2,896 km).

In·gle·wood (ing'gəl wùd') a city in southwestern California. Pop., 109,602.

Inland Sea, an inlet of the Pacific in southwestern Japan.

Inner Mongolia, an autonomous region of China, in the northern part of the country. Capital, Hohhot. Area, 456,638 sq mi (1,182,692 sq km). Pop., 20,660,000. Also, **Nei Monggol.**

Inns·bruck (inz'brùk') a city in western Austria. Pop., 117,287.

In·ter·la·ken (in'tər lä'kən) a resort town in central Switzerland. Pop., 4,899.

I·o·ni·a (ī ō'nē ə) an ancient region on the western coast of Asia Minor, colonized by the ancient Greeks.

Ionian Islands, a group of islands in the Ionian Sea, off the western coast of Greece. Area, 1,100 sq mi (2,849 sq km).

Ionian Sea, the part of the Mediterranean between Greece and Albania on the east and southern Italy and Sicily on the west.

I·o·wa (ī'ə wə) a state in the north-central United States. Capital, Des Moines. Area, 56,275 sq mi (145,752 sq km). Pop., 2,776,755. Abbreviation, **Ia.;** postal abbreviation, **IA** —**I'o·wan,** *adj., n.*

I·poh (ē'pō) a city in western Malaysia. Pop., 293,849.

Ips·wich (ip'swich) a city in southeastern England. Pop., 129,661.

I·qui·tos (i kē'tōs) a city in northeastern Peru, on the Amazon. Pop., 178,738.

I·ran (i ran', i rän') a country in southwestern Asia. Capital, Tehran. Area, 636,300 sq mi (1,648,017 sq km). Pop., 49,445,010. Formerly, **Persia.** —**I·ra·ni** (i ran'ē, i rä'nē), *adj., n.*

I·raq (i rak', i räk') a country in southwestern Asia. Capital, Baghdad. Area, 169,235 sq mi (438,319 sq km). Pop., 15,584,987. —**I·ra·qi** (i rak'ē, i rä'kē), *adj., n.*

Ire·land (īr'lənd) **1.** one of the British Isles, divided politically

into the Republic of Ireland and Northern Ireland. Area, 32,596 sq mi (84,424 sq km). **2. Republic of.** a country in northwestern Europe, occupying most of the island of Ireland. Capital, Dublin. Area, 27,136 sq mi (70,282 sq km). Pop., 3,540,643. Formerly, **Eire, Irish Free State.**

I·ri·an Ja·ya (ir′ē ən jä′yə) a province of Indonesia, consisting of western New Guinea and its offshore islands. Area, 162,885 sq mi (421,872 sq km). Pop., 1,371,000. Also, **West Irian.**

Irish Free State, see Ireland *(def. 2).*

Irish Sea, an arm of the Atlantic between Ireland and England.

Ir·kutsk (ir kütsk′) a city in Russia, in southern Siberia. Pop., 626,000.

Ir·tysh (ir tish′) a river of central Asia, flowing northwest and north from the Altai Mountains in China to the Ob River in Siberia. Length, 2,747 mi (4,420 km).

Ir·ving (ûr′ving) a city in northeastern Texas. Pop., 155,037.

Is·fa·han (is′fə hän′) see **Esfahan.**

Is·lam·a·bad (is lä′mə bäd′) the capital of Pakistan, in the northern part of the country. Pop., 204,364.

Is·ma·i·li·a (is′mä ə lē′ə) a city in northeastern Egypt, on the Suez Canal. Pop., 212,567.

Is·pa·han (is′pə hän′) see **Esfahan.**

Is·ra·el (iz′rā əl, -rē-) a country in southwestern Asia at the eastern end of the Mediterranean. Capital, Jerusalem. Area, 7,990 sq mi (20,694 sq km). Pop., 4,386,000. —**Is·rae·li** (iz rā′lē), *adj., n.*

Is·tan·bul (is′tan bül′) the largest city of Turkey, located on both sides of the Bosporus. It was formerly called Constantinople and, in ancient times, Byzantium. Pop., 6,748,435.

It·a·ly (it′ə lē) a country in southern Europe, on the Mediterranean. Capital, Rome. Area, 116,303 sq mi (301,225 sq km). Pop., 57,290,519.

I·tas·ca, Lake (ī tas′kə) a lake in northern Minnesota, a source of the Mississippi River.

Ith·a·ca (ith′ə kə) one of the Ionian Islands, off the western coast of Greece. It was the home of Odysseus.

Ivory Coast, a country in western Africa, on the Gulf of Guinea. Official name: Côte d'Ivoire. Capital, Yamassoukro. Area, 123,847 sq mi (320,764 sq km). Pop., 9,300,000.

I·wo (ē′wō) a city in southwestern Nigeria. Pop., 289,100.

I·wo Ji·ma (ē′wə jē′mə) an island in the northwestern Pacific, captured from Japan by the United States in 1945 during World War II, and returned to Japan in 1968.

I·zhevsk (ē′zhevsk) a city in western Russia. Pop., 635,000. Formerly, **Ustinov.**

Iz·mir (iz′mîr) a port city in western Turkey, on the Aegean. Pop., 2,553,209. Formerly, **Smyrna.**

Jab·al·pur (jub′əl pŭr′) *also,* **Jubbulpore.** a city in central India. Pop., 614,162.

Ja·boa·tão (zhä′bwä touɴ′) a city in northeastern Brazil. Pop., 82,900.

Jack·son (jak′sən) **1.** the capital of Mississippi, in the central part of the state. Pop., 196,637. **2.** a city in southern Michigan. Pop., 37,446.

Jack·son·ville (jak′sən vil′) the largest city in Florida, a major seaport on the northeastern coast of the state. Pop., 906,727.

Ja·dot·ville (zhä dō vēl′) see **Likasi.**

Jaf·fa (jaf′ə, yä′fä) a seaport on the Mediterranean coast of Israel, combined with Tel Aviv in 1950 as one city. In ancient times it was known as Joppa.

Jai·pur (jī′pŭr) a city in northwestern India. Pop., 997,165.

Ja·kar·ta (jə kär′tə) *also,* **Djakarta.** the capital and largest city of Indonesia, a seaport on the northwestern coast of Java. Pop., 6,503,449.

Ja·lis·co (hä lēs′kō) a state in west-central Mexico. Area, 31,152 sq mi (80,684 sq km). Pop., 4,371,998.

Ja·mai·ca (jə mā′kə) an island country of the Greater Antilles, in the Caribbean south of Cuba. Capital, Kingston. Area, 4,244 sq mi (10,992 sq km). Pop., 2,190,357. —**Ja·mai′can,** *adj., n.*

James Bay (jāmz) the southern arm of Hudson Bay, between northeastern Ontario and western Quebec, Canada.

James River 1. a river in eastern North and South Dakota, flowing south into the Missouri. Length, 710 mi (1,142 km). **2.** a river in central Virginia, flowing east into Chesapeake Bay. Length, 340 mi (547 km).

James·town (jāmz′toun′) a former village in southeastern Virginia, the first permanent English settlement in America, founded in 1607.

Jam·mu and Kashmir (jum′ü) see **Kashmir** *(def. 2).*

Ja·pan (jə pan′) **1.** a country in the northern Pacific, off the eastern coast of Asia, consisting of a chain of islands. The four main islands are Hokkaido, Honshu, Kyushu, and Shikoku. Capital, Tokyo. Area, 143,706 sq mi (372,199 sq km). Pop., 121,094,923. Also, *Japanese,* **Nippon. 2. Sea of.** an arm of the

Pacific separating Japan from the Asian mainland. —**Jap·a·nese** (jap′ə nēz′, -nēs′), *adj., n.*

Ja·va (jä′və) a large island of Indonesia, in the Malay Archipelago. Area, approx. 51,000 sq mi (132,090 sq km).

Java Sea, the part of the southern Pacific between Java and Borneo.

Jeb·el Mu·sa (jeb′əl mü′sə) a mountain in Ceuta, a Spanish enclave in northern Morocco. It was known to ancient geographers as one of the Pillars of Hercules. Height, 2,775 ft (846 m).

Jed·da (jed′ə) see **Jidda.**

Jef·fer·son City (jef′ər sən) the capital of Missouri, in the central part of the state. Pop., 35,481.

Je·na (yā′nə) a city in central Germany. Pop., 108,010.

Je·rez (he reth′) a city in southwestern Spain. Pop., 156,200. Also, **Jerez de la Fron·te·ra** (the lä frōn te′rä).

Jer·i·cho (jer′i kō′) **1.** an ancient Palestinian city near the northern tip of the Dead Sea. According to the Old Testament, it was miraculously captured by Joshua, whose soldiers toppled the walls of the city by sounding their trumpets. **2.** a town in the West Bank on the site of ancient Jericho. Pop., 6,829.

Jer·sey (jûr′zē) a British island in the English Channel, off the coast of France, the largest of the Channel Islands. Area, approx. 45 sq mi (117 sq km).

Jersey City, a port city in northeastern New Jersey, on the Hudson opposite New York City. Pop., 228,537.

Je·ru·sa·lem (jə rü′sə ləm) a historic city in central Palestine, the capital of Israel. It is a holy city for Jews, Christians, and Muslims. The old section of the city, controlled by Jordan from 1949 to 1967, was occupied and annexed by Israel in 1967. Pop., 493,500.

Jiang·su (jyäng′sʏ′) a province in eastern China. Capital, Nanjing. Area, 41,699 sq mi (108,000 sq km). Pop., 63,480,000. Also, **Kiangsu.**

Jiang·xi (jyäng′shē′) a province in southeastern China. Capital, Nanchang. Area, 63,629 sq mi (164,799 sq km). Pop., 35,580,000. Also, **Kiangsi.**

Jid·da (jid′ə) a port city in western Saudi Arabia, on the Red Sea, near Mecca. Pop., 1,300,000. Also, **Jedda.**

Ji·lin (jē′lin′) **1.** a province in northeastern China. Capital, Changchun. Area, 72,201 sq mi (187,001 sq km). Pop., 23,460,000. **2.** a port city in northeastern China. Pop., 1,200,000. Also, **Kirin.**

Ji·nan (jē′nän′) a city in eastern China, the capital of Shandong province. Pop., 1,546,000. Also, **Chinan, Tsinan.**

João Pes·so·a (zhwouɴ′pe sō′ə) a city in northeastern Brazil. Pop., 348,500. Formerly, **Paraiba.**

Jodh·pur (jod′pər, jōd′pŭr) a city in northwestern India. Pop., 506,345.

Jo·han·nes·burg (jō han′əs bûrg′) a city in the Republic of South Africa, in the northeastern part of the country. Pop., 632,369.

Johns·town (jonz′toun′) a city in southwestern Pennsylvania, the site of a great flood in 1889. Pop., 28,134.

Jo·li·et (jō′lē et′) a city in northeastern Illinois. Pop., 73,836.

Jop·pa (jop′ə) see **Jaffa.**

Jor·dan (jôr′dən) **1.** a country in southwestern Asia, east of and bordering Israel. Capital, Amman. Area, 37,738 sq mi (97,741 sq km). Pop., 3,111,000. Formerly, **Transjordan. 2.** a river in southwestern Asia, flowing between the West Bank and Jordan into the Dead Sea. —**Jor·da·ni·an** (jôr dā′nē ən), *adj., n.*

Juá·rez (wär′ez, hwä′ɾes) see **Ciudad Juárez.**

Jub·bul·pore (jub′əl pôr′) see **Jabalpur.**

Ju·de·a (jü dē′ə) *also,* **Ju·dae·a.** the southern part of ancient Palestine, esp. when it was under Roman rule. —**Ju·de′an,** *adj., n.*

Ju·go·sla·vi·a (ū′gō slä′vē ə) Yugoslavia. —**Ju′go·slav′, Ju′go·sla′vi·an,** *adj., n.*

Juiz de Fo·ra (zhwēz′də fôr′ə) a city in southeastern Brazil. Pop., 349,720.

Ju·neau (jü′nō) the capital of Alaska, a port city in the southeastern part of the state. Pop., 26,751.

Jung·frau (yŭng′frou′) a mountain in south-central Switzerland, in the Bernese Alps. Height, 13,642 ft (4,158 m).

Ju·ra Mountains (jŭr′ə) a mountain range in eastern France and western Switzerland.

Jut·land (jut′lənd) a peninsula in northern Europe, divided between Denmark and Germany.

a	at	e	end	o	hot	u	up	hw	white		about
ā	ape	ē	me	ō	old	ū	use	ng	song		taken
ä	far	i	it	ô	fork	ü	rule	th	thin	ə	pencil
âr	care	ī	ice	oi	oil	u̇	pull	th	this		lemon
		îr	pierce	ou	out	ûr	turn	zh	measure		circus

1439

K2, see Godwin Austen, Mount.

Ka·bul (kä′bŭl) the capital and largest city of Afghanistan, in the east-central part of the country. Pop., 1,424,400.

Kae·song (kä′sông′) a city in southern North Korea. Pop., 259,000.

Ka·go·shi·ma (kä′gô shē′mä) a seaport in Japan, in the southern part of the island of Kyushu. Pop., 530,502.

Kai·feng (kī′fung′) a city in east-central China. Pop., 458,800.

Kai·lu·a (kī lü′ə) a city in Hawaii, on the eastern coast of the island of Oahu. Pop., 36,818.

Ka·la·ha·ri (kä′lə här′ē) a large desert region in the central part of southern Africa. Area, approx. 200,000 sq mi (518,000 sq km).

Kal·a·ma·zoo (kal′ə mə zü′) a city in southwestern Michigan. Pop., 80,277.

Ka·li·man·tan (kä′lē män′tän) the part of Borneo that belongs to Indonesia. Area, 212,378 sq mi (550,059 sq km).

Ka·li·nin·grad (kä lē′nin grad′) a port city in western Russia, on an inlet of the Baltic Sea. As the capital of the former German province of East Prussia it was known as Königsberg. Pop., 401,000.

Kam·pa·la (käm pä′lə) the capital and largest city of Uganda, in the southern part of the country. Pop., 1,008,707.

Kam·pu·che·a (kam′pù chē′ə) see Cambodia. —Kam′pu·che′an, adj., n.

Ka·nan·ga (kə näng′gə) a city in south-central Zaire. Pop., 290,898. Formerly, Luluabourg.

Kan·da·har (kän′də här′) a city in southeastern Afghanistan. Pop., 225,500.

Kan·dy (kan′dē) a city in south-central Sri Lanka, the site of a famous Buddhist temple. Pop., 130,000.

Ka·ne·o·he (kä′nä ō′hä) a city in Hawaii, on the eastern coast of the island of Oahu. Pop., 35,448.

Ka·no (kä′nō) a city in north-central Nigeria. Pop., 538,300.

Kan·pur (kän′pùr) a city in north-central India, on the Ganges. Pop., 1,481,789. Formerly, Cawnpore.

Kan·sas (kan′zəs) a state in the west-central United States. Capital, Topeka. Area, 82,277 sq mi (213,097 sq km). Pop., 2,477,574. Abbreviations, Kans., Kan.; postal abbreviation, KS —Kan′san, adj., n.

Kansas City 1. a city in western Missouri. Pop., 435,146. **2.** a city in eastern Kansas that adjoins Kansas City, Missouri. Pop., 149,767.

Kan·su (gän′sü′) see Gansu.

Kao·hsiung (gou′shyùng′) a seaport in southwestern Taiwan. Pop., 1,342,797.

Ka·ra·chi (kə rä′chē) the largest city and former capital of Pakistan, a port in the southern part of the country, on the Arabian Sea. Pop., 4,901,627.

Ka·raj (kä räj′) a city in north-central Iran. Pop., 275,100.

Ka·ra·ko·ram Range (kär′ə kôr′əm) also, Ka·ra·ko·rum Range. a mountain system in central Asia, extending from northern Pakistan and India to southern China and connecting the Himalayas with the Pamirs; its highest peak is Mount Godwin Austen.

Ka·re·li·an Isthmus (kə rē′lē ən) an isthmus in northwestern Russia, between Lake Ladoga and the Gulf of Finland.

Karl-Marx-Stadt (kärl′märks′shtät′) the former East German name for Chemnitz.

Kar·lo·vy Va·ry (kär′lə vē vär′ē) a town in northwestern Czechoslovakia, famous as a health resort. Pop., 58,039. Also, Carlsbad; German Karls·bad (kärlz′bäd′).

Karls·ruh·e (kärlz′rü′ə) also, Carlsruhe. a city in southwestern Germany. Pop., 265,100.

Kar·nak (kär′nak) a village in Egypt, on the Nile, the site of a large group of ancient temples. Karnak is located on part of the site of ancient Thebes. Pop., 20,842.

Kar·roo (kə rü′) a plateau region in the southern part of the Republic of South Africa, in Cape of Good Hope province.

Kash·mir (kash′mîr, kazh′-) also, Cashmere. **1.** an area in the extreme north of the Indian subcontinent, disputed by India and Pakistan, each of which occupies part of the territory. Area, 86,024 sq mi (222,802 sq km). **2.** that part of this area occupied by India. Official name: Jammu and Kashmir. Area, 53,500 sq mi (138,565 sq km). —Kash·mir·i (kash mîr′ē, kazh-), adj., n.

Kas·sel (kas′əl) also, Cassel. a city in central Germany. Pop., 189,156.

Ka·tan·ga (kə täng′gə) see Shaba.

Kat·man·du (kat′man dü′) also, Kath·man·du. the capital of Nepal, in the central part of the country. Pop., 235,160.

Ka·to·wi·ce (kat′ō vēt′sä) a city in southern Poland. Pop., 365,800.

Kat·si·na (kät′sə nə) a city in northern Nigeria, capital of the historic kingdom of Katsina. Pop., 165,000.

Kat·te·gat (kat′i gat′) also, Cattegat. a broad arm of the North Sea, located between Denmark and Sweden.

Kau·ai (kou′ī, kə wī′) the northernmost of the main islands of Hawaii. Area, 549 sq mi (1,422 sq km). Pop., 51,177.

Ka·wa·sa·ki (kä′wə sä′kē) a seaport in Japan, in the southeastern part of the island of Honshu. Pop., 1,088,624.

Kay·se·ri (kī′sə rē′) a city in central Turkey. Pop., 416,276.

Ka·zakh·stan (kä′zäk stän′) a country in central Asia, bordering the Caspian Sea, China, Kyrgyzstan, Russia, and Uzbekistan. It was formerly a republic of the Soviet Union. Capital, Alma-Ata. Area, 1,049,155 sq mi (2,717,312 sq km). Pop., 16,538,000.

Ka·zan (kə zän′) a city in western Russia, near the Volga River. Pop., 1,094,000.

Kee·lung (kē′lùng′) see Chilung.

Ke·ni·tra (kə nē′trə) a city in northern Morocco. Pop., 188,194.

Ke·no·sha (kə nō′shə) a city in southeastern Wisconsin, on Lake Michigan. Pop., 80,352.

Kent (kent) **1.** a county in southeastern England. Pop., 1,520,300. **2.** an ancient kingdom in southeastern England.

Ken·tuck·y (kən tuk′ē) a state in the east-central United States. Capital, Frankfort. Area, 40,410 sq mi (104,662 sq km). Pop., 3,685,296. Abbreviation, Ky.; postal abbreviation, KY —Ken·tuck′i·an, adj., n.

Ken·ya (ken′yə, kēn′-) **1.** a country in eastern Africa. Capital, Nairobi. Area, 224,961 sq mi (582,649 sq km). Pop., 24,870,000. **2. Mount.** an extinct volcano in central Kenya. Height, 17,058 ft (5,199 m). —Ken′yan, adj., n.

Ker·gue·len Islands (kûr′gə lən) an island group in the southern Indian Ocean, administered by France. Land area, 2,800 sq mi (7,250 sq km).

Ker·man (kûr′mən) a city in east-central Iran. Pop., 257,284.

Ker·man·shah (ker′män shä′, kûr′-) see Bakhtaran.

Key West 1. an island off the coast of southwestern Florida, in the Gulf of Mexico, one of the westernmost Florida Keys. **2.** a port city on this island. Pop., 24,832.

Khar·kov (kär′kof) a city in eastern Ukraine. Pop., 1,611,000.

Khar·toum (kär tüm′) the capital of the Sudan, a port at the confluence of the Blue Nile and White Nile, in the north-central part of the country. Pop., 476,218.

Khartoum North, a city in north-central Sudan, north of Khartoum, on the Nile. Pop., 341,146.

Khmer Republic (kə mer′) a former official name of Cambodia.

Khul·na (kùl′nə) a city in southern Bangladesh, in the Ganges delta. Pop., 648,359.

Khy·ber Pass (kī′bər) a mountain pass connecting Pakistan and Afghanistan.

Kiang·si (gyäng′sē′) see Jiangxi.

Kiang·su (gyäng′sü′) see Jiangsu.

Kiel (kēl) a city in northern Germany. Pop., 240,675.

Kiel Canal, a canal in northern Germany, connecting the Baltic and North seas.

Kiel·ce (kyel′tse) a city in southern Poland. Pop., 211,100.

Ki·ev (kē′ev, kē′ef) the capital and largest city of Ukraine. Pop., 2,587,000.

Ki·ga·li (ki gä′lē) the capital of Rwanda, in the central part of the country. Pop., 181,600.

Ki·lau·e·a (kil′ō ā′ə) an active volcano on the island of Hawaii. Height, 4,090 ft (1,248 m).

Kil·i·man·ja·ro, Mount (kil′ə mən jär′ō) the highest mountain in Africa, in northeastern Tanzania, near the Kenyan border. Height, 19,340 ft (5,895 m).

Kil·lar·ney (ki lär′nē) **1.** a town in southwestern Ireland. Pop., 7,837. **2. Lakes of.** three famous lakes near this town.

Kim·ber·ley (kim′bər lē) a city in the Republic of South Africa, the center of the country's diamond industry. Pop., 74,061.

Kim·chaek (kim chak′) a city in northeastern North Korea. Pop., 265,000.

Kings·ton (kingz′tən) **1.** the capital and largest city of Jamaica, on the southeastern coast of the island. Pop., 646,400. **2.** a city on Lake Ontario, in southeastern Ontario, Canada. Pop., 55,050.

King·ston-u·pon-Hull (kingz′tən ə pôn′hul′, -ə pon′-) see Hull.

Kings·town (kingz′toun′) the capital of St. Vincent and the Grenadines, located on the island of St. Vincent. Pop., 19,028.

Kin·ner·et, Lake (ki ner′ət) see Galilee, Sea of.

Kin·sha·sa (kin shä′sə) the capital and largest city of Zaire, a port on the Congo River in the western part of the country. Pop., 3,000,000. Formerly, Léopoldville.

Kir·ghi·zia (kir gē′zhə) see Kyrgyzstan.

Ki·ri·ba·ti (kir′ə bäs′, kir′ə bäs′) an island country in the central Pacific Ocean. Capital, Bairiki. Land area, 277 sq mi (717 sq km). Pop., 68,207. Formerly, Gilbert Islands.

Ki·rin (kē′rin′) see Jilin.

Ki·riti·mati (kə ris′məs) see **Christmas Island** *(def. 2)*.

Kir·kuk (kir kük′) a city in northeastern Iraq. Pop., 207,900.

Ki·san·ga·ni (kē′säng gä′nē) a city in northern Zaire, on the Congo River. Pop., 282,650. Also, **Stanleyville**.

Ki·shi·nev (kish′ə nef′) the capital of Moldova. Pop., 665,000.

Ki·su·mu (kē sü′mü) a city in western Kenya, located on Lake Victoria. Pop., 167,100.

Ki·ta·kyu·shu (kē′tä kū′shü) a city in Japan, at the northwestern tip of the island of Kyushu. Pop., 1,056,402.

Kitch·e·ner (kich′ə nər) a city in southern Ontario, Canada. Pop., 150,604.

Kitty Hawk, a village in northeastern North Carolina where the first successful airplane flight was made in 1903 by Wilbur and Orville Wright.

Ki·twe (kē′twä) a city in north-central Zambia. Pop., 207,500.

Kiu·shu (kū′shü) see **Kyushu**.

Klon·dike (klon′dīk) a noted gold-mining region in the west-central Yukon, Canada. Area, approx. 800 sq mi (2,072 sq km).

Knos·sos (nos′əs, kə nos′əs) *also,* **Cnossus**. an ancient city on the northern coast of Crete, a center of Minoan civilization.

Knox·ville (noks′vil′) a city in eastern Tennessee, on the Tennessee River. Pop., 165,121.

Ko·be (kō′bē) a port city in Japan, on the southern coast of the island of Honshu. Pop., 1,410,834.

Ko·blenz (kō′blents) *also,* **Coblenz**. a city in western Germany. Pop., 107,286.

Ko·di·ak (kō′dē ak′) an island in Alaska, off the coast of the southwestern part of the state. Area, 3,465 sq mi (8,974 sq km).

Ko·la Peninsula (kō′lə) a peninsula in northwestern Russia, between the Barents Sea and the White Sea.

Köln (kœln) see **Cologne**.

Ko·lo·ni·a (kə lō′nē ə) the capital of the Federated States of Micronesia. Pop., 6,306.

Kol·wez·i (kōl wez′ē) a city in southern Zaire. Pop., 201,382.

Kö·nigs·berg (kœ′niκнs berK′) see **Kaliningrad**.

Kon·ya (kôn′yä) *also,* **Kon·ia**. a city in southern Turkey. Pop., 509,208.

Ko·re·a (kə rē′ə) a former country in eastern Asia, divided into **North Korea** and **South Korea** since 1948. Area, 84,562 sq mi (219,016 sq km).

Ko·ror (kə rôr′) the capital of Palau. Pop., 8,629.

Kos·ci·us·ko, Mount (kos′ē us′kō) the highest mountain in Australia, located in southeastern New South Wales. Height, 7,316 ft (2,230 m).

Ko·si·ce (kô′shi tse) a city in eastern Czechoslovakia. Pop., 237,099.

Ko·ta Ki·na·ba·lu (kō′tə kin′ə bə lü′) the capital of Sabah, Malaysia, a port city on the northwest coast of Borneo. Pop., 55,997.

Kott·bus (kot′bəs) see **Cottbus**.

Kow·loon (kou′lün′) **1.** a peninsula on the southeastern coast of China, part of Hong Kong. **2.** a seaport on this peninsula. Pop., 774,781.

Ko·zhi·kode (kō′zhi kōd′) a port city on the southwestern coast of India. Pop., 394,447. Formerly, **Calicut**.

Kra·ka·to·a (krak′ə tō′ə) an uninhabited volcanic island between Java and Sumatra, in Indonesia, noted as the site of a catastrophic volcanic eruption in 1883. Also, **Kra·ka·tau** (krak′-ə tou′).

Kra·ków (krä′kou) *also,* **Cracow**. a city in southern Poland. Pop., 743,700.

Kras·no·dar (kras′nə där′) a city in southwestern Russia. Pop., 620,000.

Kras·no·yarsk (kras′nə yärsk′) a city in Russia, in north-central Asia. Pop., 912,000.

Kre·feld (krä′feld) a city in western Germany, on the Rhine. Pop., 235,423.

Kri·voy Rog (kri voi′ rōg′) *also,* **Kri·voi Rog**. a city in south-central Ukraine. Pop., 713,000.

Krung Thep (krüng′ tāp′) see **Bangkok**.

Kruš·né Ho·ry (krüsh′nə hôr′ē) see **Erzgebirge**.

Kua·la Lum·pur (kwä′lə lùm pùr′) the capital of Malaysia, on the Malay Peninsula. Pop., 919,610.

Ku·ching (kü′ching) the capital of Sarawak, Malaysia, a port city in northwestern Borneo. Pop., 72,555.

Kui·by·shev (kwē′bə shef′) see **Samara**.

Ku·ma·mo·to (kü′mə mō′tō) a city in Japan, in the west-central part of the island of Kyushu. Pop., 555,719.

Ku·ma·si (kù mä′sē) a city in south-central Ghana. Pop., 348,880.

Kun·lun Mountains (kùn′lùn′) a mountain system in central western China, extending from the China-India border to central Qinghai province. Also, **Kunlun Shan** (shän).

Kun·ming (kùn′ming′) a city in southern China, the capital of Yunnan province. Pop., 1,310,000.

Kur·di·stan (kûr′də stan′) a highland region of Asia that includes parts of Iran, Iraq, Turkey, and Syria, and is inhabited chiefly by Kurds.

Ku·re (kü′κe) a city in Japan, in the southwestern part of the island of Honshu. Pop., 226,488.

Ku·ril Islands (kùr′il, kù rēl′) *also,* **Ku·rile Islands**. a chain of islands north of Japan, part of Russia. Land area, 6,159 sq mi (15,952 sq km).

Kush (kùsh, kush) see **Cush**.

Ku·wait (kü wāt′) **1.** a country in the northeastern part of the peninsula of Arabia. Capital, Kuwait. Area, 6,880 sq mi (17,819 sq km). Pop., 1,697,301. **2.** the capital of Kuwait. Pop., 44,335. —**Ku·wai·ti** (kü wā′tē), *adj., n.*

Kuz·netsk Basin (kùz netsk′) a coal-rich region of Russia, located in western Siberia. Also, **Kuz·bas, Kuz·bass** (kùz′bäs).

Kwang·chow (gwäng′jō′) see **Guangzhou**.

Kwang·ju (gwäng′jü′) a city in southwestern South Korea. Pop., 1,165,000.

Kwang·si (gwäng′sē′) see **Guangxi**.

Kwang·tung (gwäng′dùng′) see **Guangdong**.

Kwei·chow (gwā′jō′) see **Guizhou**.

Kwei·sui (gwā′swā′) see **Hohhot**.

Kwei·yang (gwā′yäng′) see **Guiyang**.

Kyo·to (kyō′tō) a city in the west-central part of the island of Honshu, Japan, the former capital of the country. Pop., 1,479,218.

Kyr·gyz·stan (kîr′gi stän′) a country in central Asia, bordering northwestern China and southeastern Kazakhstan. It was known as Kirghizia when it was a republic of the Soviet Union. Capital, Pishpek. Area, 76,640 sq mi (198,498 sq km). Pop., 4,291,000. Also, **Kirghizia**.

Kyu·shu (kū′shü) *also,* **Kiushu**. the southernmost of the four main islands of Japan. Area, 14,114 sq mi (36,555 sq km).

Lab·ra·dor (lab′rə dôr′) **1.** a region in eastern Canada, on the Atlantic Ocean, part of the province of Newfoundland and Labrador. **2.** a peninsula in eastern Canada, between the Atlantic Ocean and Hudson Bay. It is divided between the province of Quebec and the province of Newfoundland and Labrador.

Lac·e·dae·mon (las′i dē′mən) see **Sparta**. —**Lac·e·dae·mo·ni·an** (las′i də mō′nē ən), *adj., n.*

La Crosse (lə krôs′) a port city in western Wisconsin, on the Mississippi. Pop., 51,003.

La·do·ga, Lake (lä′də gə) the largest freshwater lake in Europe, in northwestern Russia.

La·fa·yette (laf′ē et′, laf′ā-) a city in southern Louisiana. Pop., 94,440.

La·gos (lä′gōs, lā′gos) the former capital and chief port of Nigeria, in the southwestern part of the country. Pop., 1,213,000.

La Ha·ba·na (lä′ ä vä′nə) see **Havana**.

La·hore (lə hôr′) a city in northeastern Pakistan. Pop., 2,707,215.

Lake Charles (chärlz) a port city in southwestern Louisiana. Pop., 70,580.

Lake District, a region in northwestern England, noted for its scenic mountains and lakes. Also, **Lake Country**.

Lake of the Woods, a lake on the border of Minnesota and the Canadian provinces of Manitoba and Ontario.

Lake·wood (lāk′wùd′) **1.** a city in southern California. Pop., 73,557. **2.** a city in northeastern Ohio. Pop., 59,718.

Lam·beth (lam′bəth) a borough in the southern part of Greater London, England. Pop., 245,700.

Lan·ca·shire (lang′kə shîr′, -shər) a county in northwestern England. Pop., 1,382,000.

Lan·chow (län′jō′) see **Lanzhou**.

Langue·doc (läng dôk′) a historic region and former province of France, located on the Mediterranean in the southern part of the country.

Lan·sing (lan′sing) the capital of Michigan, in the south-central part of the state. Pop., 127,321.

Lan·zhou (län′jō′) *also,* **Lanchow**. a city in central China, the capital of Gansu province. Pop., 1,297,000.

La·os (lä′ōs, lā′os) a country in southeastern Asia, between northern Thailand and northern Vietnam. Capital, Vientiane. Area, 91,430 sq mi (236,804 sq km). Pop., 3,584,803.

La Paz (lə päz′) a city in western Bolivia, in the Andes, the seat

a	at	e	end	o	hot	u	up	hw	white		about
ā	ape	ē	me	ō	old	ū	use	ng	song		taken
ä	far	i	it	ô	fork	ü	rule	th	thin	ə	pencil
âr	care	ī	ice	oi	oil	ù	pull	th	this		lemon
		îr	pierce	ou	out	ûr	turn	zh	measure		circus

of the government and administrative capital of the country. Pop., 992,592.

Lap·land (lap′land′) a region in northern Europe, including the northernmost sections of Norway, Sweden, and Finland and northwestern Russia. Area, approx. 150,000 sq mi (388,500 sq km). —**Lap·land·er** (lap′lan′dər), n.

La Pla·ta (lə plä′tə) a port city in eastern Argentina. Pop., 477,175.

Lar·a·mie (lar′ə mē) a city in southeastern Wyoming. Pop., 26,687.

La·re·do (lə rā′dō) a city in southern Texas. Pop., 122,899.

La Ro·ma·na (lä rō mä′nə) a city in the southeastern Dominican Republic. Pop., 91,571.

La·sa (lä′sə) see Lhasa.

La·Salle (lə sal′) a city in southern Quebec, Canada, on the St. Lawrence River. Pop., 75,621.

Las·caux (läs kō′) a group of caves in southwestern France, discovered in 1940, containing outstanding examples of Paleolithic cave art.

Las Cru·ces (läs krü′sis) a city in southern New Mexico, on the Rio Grande. Pop., 62,126.

Las Pal·mas (läs päl′məs) a port city in the Canary Islands. Pop., 319,000.

La Spe·zia (lä spe′tsyä) a port city and naval base in northwestern Italy. Pop., 108,937.

Las·sen Peak (las′ən) a volcano in northern California at the southern end of the Cascade Range. Height, 10,457 ft (3,187 m). Also, **Mount Lassen.**

Las Ve·gas (läs vā′gəs) a city in southeastern Nevada, noted as a tourist resort and gambling center. Pop., 258,295.

Lat·a·ki·a (lat′ə kē′ə) a port city in western Syria, on the Mediterranean. Pop., 249,000.

Latin America, the countries south of the United States in the Western Hemisphere in which the languages, such as Spanish or Portuguese, are of Latin origin. —**Lat′in-A·mer′i·can,** adj., n. —**Latin American,** n.

Latin Quarter, a district in Paris, south of the Seine River, noted as a residence for students and artists.

La·ti·um (lā′shē əm) a region in west-central Italy. In ancient times it was inhabited by the Latins, who came to be dominated by Rome.

Lat·vi·a (lat′vē ə) a country in northeastern Europe, on the Baltic Sea. It was formerly a republic of the Soviet Union. Capital, Riga. Area, approx. 24,600 sq mi (63,700 sq km). Pop., 2,681,000.

Laur·a·sia (lô rā′zhə) a vast prehistoric northern continent, believed to have included North America, Europe, and most of Asia; it is thought to have split up into the present continents in the Mesozoic era.

Lau·ren·tian Mountains (lô ren′shən) a low mountain range in eastern Canada, located between Hudson Bay and the St. Lawrence River. Also, **Lau·ren′tians.**

Lau·sanne (lō zan′) a city in western Switzerland, on Lake Geneva. Pop., 122,600.

La·val (lə val′) a city in southern Quebec, Canada. Pop., 284,164.

Law·ton (lô′tən) a city in southwestern Oklahoma. Pop., 80,561.

Leav·en·worth (lev′ən wûrth′) a city in northeastern Kansas, the site of a federal prison. Pop., 38,495.

Leb·a·non (leb′ə non′) a country in southwestern Asia, on the eastern shore of the Mediterranean. Capital, Beirut. Area, 4,015 sq mi (10,399 sq km). Pop., 2,637,000. —**Leb·a·nese** (leb′ə nēz′, -nēs′), adj., n.

Leeds (lēdz) a city in north-central England. Pop., 710,000.

Lee·ward Islands (lē′wərd) **1.** a Caribbean island group forming the northern part of the Lesser Antilles. Land area, 1,260 sq mi (3,263 sq km). **2.** a former British colony consisting of certain of these islands.

Left Bank, a section of Paris bordering the south bank of the Seine, frequented by artists, students, and writers.

Leg·horn (leg′hôrn′) a port city on the western coast of Italy. Pop., 174,065. Also, *Italian,* **Livorno.**

Le Ha·vre (lə häv′rə, hä′vər) a port city in northern France, at the mouth of the Seine. Pop., 199,388. Also, **Havre.**

Leices·ter (les′tər) a city in central England. Pop., 324,394.

Leices·ter·shire (les′tər shir′, -shər) a county in central England. Pop., 885,500.

Lein·ster (lins′tər) a historic province of Ireland, in the eastern part of the island.

Leip·zig (līp′zig, līp′tsik) a city in eastern Germany. Pop., 545,307.

Le·man, Lake (lē′mən) see Geneva, Lake.

Le Mans (lə manz′, lə mäɴ′) a city in northwestern France. Pop., 147,697.

Lem·berg (lem′bûrg′, lem′beʀk) see Lvov.

Le·na (lē′nə) a river in Russia, flowing through east-central Siberia to the Arctic Ocean. Length, 2,734 mi (4,402 km).

Len·in·grad (len′in grad′) see St. Petersburg.

Le·ón (lā ôn′) **1.** a region and former kingdom in northwestern Spain. **2.** a city in central Mexico. Pop., 593,002. **3.** a city in northwestern Nicaragua. Pop., 101,000.

Lé·o·pold·ville (lē′ə pōld vil′, lā′-) see Kinshasa.

Les·bos (lez′bos, -bōs) a Greek island in the Aegean, near the western coast of Asia Minor. Area, approx. 629 sq mi (1,629 sq km).

Le·so·tho (lə sō′tō) a country in southern Africa, entirely surrounded by the Republic of South Africa. Capital, Maseru. Area, 11,720 sq mi (30,355 sq km). Pop., 1,577,536.

Lesser Antilles, an island group of the West Indies, southeast of Puerto Rico, including the Leeward Islands, Windward Islands, Barbados, Trinidad, Tobago, and the Virgin Islands.

Le·vant (lə vant′) a region bordering the eastern shore of the Mediterranean, consisting of the present-day countries of Greece, Cyprus, Turkey, Syria, Lebanon, Israel, and Egypt.

Lew·is·ton (lü′i stən) a city in southwestern Maine. Pop., 39,757.

Lex·ing·ton (lek′sing tən) **1.** a town in northeastern Massachusetts, the site of the first battle of the American Revolution, on April 19, 1775. Pop., 28,974. **2.** a city in north-central Kentucky. Pop., 225,366.

Ley·te (lā′tē) a mountainous island in the south-central Philippines. Area, 2,785 sq mi (7,213 sq km).

Lha·sa (lä′sə) *also,* **Lasa.** a city in western China, the capital of Tibet. Pop., 84,400.

Liao·ning (lyou′ning′) a province in northeastern China. Capital, Shenyang. Area, 58,301 sq mi (151,000 sq km). Pop., 37,770,000.

Li·be·ri·a (lī bir′ē ə) a country on the west coast of Africa, founded in 1822 by freed slaves from the United States. Capital, Monrovia. Area, 43,000 sq mi (111,370 sq km). Pop., 2,221,000. —**Li·be′ri·an,** adj., n.

Li·bre·ville (lē′brə vil′) the capital and largest city of Gabon, on the northwestern coast of the country. Pop., 235,700.

Lib·y·a (lib′ē ə) **1.** a country on the Mediterranean coast of northern Africa. Capital, Tripoli. Area, 679,362 sq mi (1,759,548 sq km). Pop., 3,637,488. **2.** in ancient Greece and Rome, that part of northern Africa west of Egypt. —**Lib′y·an,** adj., n.

Libyan Desert, the eastern part of the Sahara Desert, extending from eastern Libya to the Nile in Egypt and northwestern Sudan. Also, **Western Desert.**

Liech·ten·stein (lik′tən stīn′) a small country in central Europe, between Austria and Switzerland. Capital, Vaduz. Area, 62 sq mi (161 sq km). Pop., 28,452.

Li·ège (lē ezh′) a city in eastern Belgium. Pop., 200,891.

Li·gu·ri·a (li gyŭr′ē ə) a region in northwestern Italy. Area, 2,091 sq mi (5,416 sq km). —**Li·gu′ri·an,** adj., n.

Li·ka·si (li kä′sē) a city in southeastern Zaire. Pop., 194,465. Formerly, **Jadotville.**

Lille (lēl) a city in northern France, long noted for its textile products. Pop., 168,424.

Li·long·we (li lông′wā) the capital of Malawi, in the west-central part of the country. Pop., 233,973.

Li·ma (lē′mə) the capital and chief city of Peru, in the west-central part of the country. Pop., 371,122.

Li·moges (lē mōzh′) a city in west-central France. Pop., 140,400.

Lin·coln (ling′kən) the capital of Nebraska, in the southeastern part of the state. Pop., 191,972.

Lin·coln·shire (ling′kən shir′, -shər) a county in eastern England. Pop., 582,600.

Linz (lints) a city in northern Austria, on the Danube. Pop., 199,910.

Lis·bon (liz′bən) the capital, largest city, and chief seaport of Portugal, in the western part of the country. Pop., 807,167. Also, *Portuguese,* **Lis·bo·a** (lēzh bō′ə).

Lith·u·a·nia (lith′ü ā′nē ə) a country in northeastern Europe, on the Baltic Sea. It was formerly a republic of the Soviet Union. Capital, Vilnius. Area, 25,175 sq mi (65,203 sq km). Pop., 3,690,000.

Little Bighorn, a river in northern Wyoming and southern Montana, near the site of the battle in which General George Custer and his entire body of troops were killed by American Indians in 1876. Length, 90 mi (145 km).

Little Rock, the capital and largest city of Arkansas, in the central part of the state. Pop., 175,795.

Lit·tle·ton (lit'əl tən) a city in north-central Colorado. Pop., 33,685.
Liv·er·pool (liv'ər pül') a port city in western England. Pop., 476,000.
Li·vo·ni·a (lə vō'nē ə) a city in southeastern Michigan. Pop., 100,850.
Li·vor·no (lē vôr'nô) see **Leghorn.**
Lju·blja·na (lē ü'blē ä'nə) the capital of Slovenia. Pop., 233,200.
Lódź (lüj, lodz) a city in central Poland, southwest of Warsaw. Pop., 851,500.
Lo·fo·ten Islands (lō'fút ən) a group of islands in Norway, located off the northwestern coast of the country. Land area, approx. 475 sq mi (1,230 sq km).
Lo·gan, Mount (lō'gən) a mountain in southwestern Yukon, Canada; it is the highest mountain in Canada and second highest in North America. Height, 19,850 ft (6,050 m).
Loire (lwär) the longest river of France, flowing from the south-central part of the country into the Bay of Biscay. Length, 625 mi (1,006 km).
Lo·mas de Za·mo·ra (lō'mäs də zə môr'ə) a city in eastern Argentina. Pop., 510,130.
Lom·bard·y (lom'bər dē, lum'-) a leading industrial and commercial region of Italy, in the northern part of the country. Area, 9,212 sq mi (23,859 sq km).
Lo·mé (lō mā') the capital and largest city of Togo. Pop., 400,000.
Lon·don (lun'dən) **1.** the capital and largest city of the United Kingdom and of the Commonwealth of Nations, in southeastern England, on the Thames. It consists of the City of London and thirty-two boroughs. Pop., 6,700,000. Also, **Greater London.** **2. City of.** a small section of London, on the north bank of the Thames, that is the financial and commercial center of the city. **3.** a city in southeastern Canada, in Ontario. Pop., 269,140.
Lon·don·der·ry (lun'dən der'ē) a port city in northwestern Northern Ireland. Pop., 97,500. Also, **Derry.**
Lon·dri·na (lôn drē'nə) a city in south-central Brazil. Pop., 296,400.
Long Beach, a seaport and resort city in southwestern California. Pop., 429,433.
Long Island, a long, narrow island in southeastern New York State, south of Connecticut. Area, 1,682 sq mi (4,356 sq km).
Long Island Sound, an arm of the Atlantic, separating Connecticut from Long Island.
Lon·gueuil (lông gāl') a city on the St. Lawrence River in southern Quebec, Canada. Pop., 125,441.
Lo·rain (lə rān') a port city in northern Ohio, on Lake Erie. Pop., 71,245.
Lor·raine (lə rān', lô ʀen') a region and former province in northeastern France, bordering Belgium, Luxembourg, and Germany.
Los Al·a·mos (lôs al'ə mōs') an unincorporated community in north-central New Mexico, a major U.S. center for atomic research. Pop., 18,455.
Los An·ge·les (lôs an'jə ləs, -lēz') the chief port and largest city of California, in the southwestern part of the state. Pop., 3,485,398.
Louang·phra·bang (lwäng' prə bäng') a city in northern Laos, on the Mekong, the former royal capital of Laos. Pop., 46,000.
Lou·i·si·an·a (lü ē'zē an'ə) a state in the southern United States, on the Gulf of Mexico and the Mississippi River. Capital, Baton Rouge. Area, 47,752 sq mi (123,678 sq km). Pop., 4,219,973. Abbreviation, **La.;** postal abbreviation, **LA** —**Lou·i'si·an'an, Lou·i·si·an'i·an,** adj., n.
Louisiana Purchase, the territory purchased by the United States from France in 1803, extending from the Mississippi River to the Rocky Mountains and from Canada to the Gulf of Mexico. Area, approx. 800,000 sq mi (2,072,000 sq km).
Lou·is·ville (lü'ē vil', -ə vəl) the largest city in Kentucky, a port on the Ohio in the northern part of the state. Pop., 269,063.
Lourdes (lùrd, lùrdz) a town in southwestern France, the site of a Roman Catholic shrine. Pop., 17,425.
Lou·ren·ço Mar·ques (lə ren'sō mär kes') see **Maputo.**
Low Countries, a region of northwestern Europe consisting of the countries of the Netherlands, Belgium, and Luxembourg.
Low·ell (lō'əl) a city in northeastern Massachusetts. Pop., 103,439.
Lower California, see **Baja California.**
Low·lands (lō'ləndz) see **Scottish Lowlands.**
Lo·yang (lō'yäng') see **Luoyang.**
Lu·an·da (lü an'də) the capital and largest city of Angola, a port on the northwestern coast of the country. Pop., 1,459,900.
Lub·bock (lub'ək) a city in northwestern Texas. Pop., 186,206.

Lü·beck (lÿ'bek) a port city in northern Germany. Pop., 210,681.
Lu·blin (lü'blin) a city in eastern Poland. Pop., 339,500.
Lu·bum·ba·shi (lü'büm bä'shē) a city in southeastern Zaire. Pop., 543,268. Formerly, **Elisabethville.**
Luc·ca (lü'kə) a city in north-central Italy, an artistic center during the Middle Ages and Renaissance. Pop., 88,024.
Lu·cerne (lü sûrn', lÿ seʀn') **1.** a resort city in central Switzerland. Pop., 59,115. **2. Lake of.** a lake in central Switzerland. Also, German, **Luzern.**
Lu·chow (lü'jō') see **Hefei.**
Luck·now (luk'nou) a city in north-central India. Pop., 895,721.
Lu·da (lü'dä) see **Dalian.**
Lu·dhi·a·na (lü'dē ä'nə) a city in northern India. Pop., 607,052.
Lu·lu·a·bourg (lü lü'ə bûrg') see **Kananga.**
Luo·yang (lwō'yäng') also, **Loyang.** a city in eastern China. Pop., 760,000. Formerly, **Honanfu.**
Lu·sa·ka (lü sä'kə) the capital and largest city of Zambia, in the south-central part of the country. Pop., 535,830.
Lu·shun (lü'shün') a former city and seaport in northeastern China, now part of the municipality of Dalian. Formerly, **Port Arthur.**
Lu·si·ta·ni·a (lü'si tā'nē ə) an ancient Roman province on the Iberian Peninsula, corresponding largely to modern Portugal and west-central Spain.
Lu·ton (lü'tən) a city in southeastern England. Pop., 163,209.
Lux·em·bourg (luk'səm bûrg') also, **Lux·em·burg.** **1.** a small country in western Europe, bordering France, Belgium, and Germany. Capital, Luxembourg. Area, 998 sq mi (2,585 sq km). Pop., 366,000. **2.** the capital and chief city of Luxembourg. Pop., 76,130.
Lux·or (luk'sər) a city in Egypt, on the Nile River, noted for the ancient temples and burial grounds found nearby. It is on the site of ancient Thebes. Pop., 125,404.
Lu·zern (lü zûrn', -tseʀn') see **Lucerne.**
Lu·zon (lü zon') the largest and northernmost island of the Philippines. Area, 40,420 sq mi (104,688 sq km).
Lvov (lə vof') a city in southwestern Ukraine. Pop., 790,000. Also, German, **Lemberg;** Polish, **Lwów** (lə vüf').
Ly·all·pur (lī'əl pûr') see **Faisalabad.**
Ly·ci·a (lish'ē ə) an ancient country in southwestern Asia Minor.
Lyd·i·a (lid'ē ə) an ancient country in western Asia Minor. —**Lyd'i·an,** adj., n.
Lynn (lin) a port city in eastern Massachusetts. Pop., 81,245.
Ly·ons (lē ōn') also, French, **Ly·on** (lyôn). a city in east-central France. Pop., 413,095.
Ma·cao (mə kou') also, **Ma·cau. 1.** a Portuguese overseas territory on the southern coast of China. It will return to Chinese control in 1999. Capital, Macao. Area, 7 sq mi (18 sq km). Pop., 429,000. **2.** the capital of Macao, a seaport. Pop., 429,000.
Ma·cas·sar (mə kas'ər) see **Ujung Pandang.**
Mac·e·do·ni·a (mas'i dō'nē ə) **1.** an ancient kingdom north of Greece, the center of the empire created by Alexander the Great. Also, **Mac·e·don** (mas'i don'). **2.** an independent state in southeastern Europe, a former republic of Yugoslavia. Capital, Skopje. Area, 9,930 sq mi (25,719 sq km). Pop., 2,064,581. **3.** a historic region in southeastern Europe, including parts of Greece, Bulgaria, and the state of Macedonia.
Ma·cei·ó (mä'sā ō') a city in northeastern Brazil, on the Atlantic. Pop., 482,195.
Mac·ken·zie (mə ken'zē) a river in northwestern Canada, flowing into the Arctic Ocean. Length, 2,635 mi (4,240 km).
Mack·i·nac, Straits of (mak'ə nô') a strait connecting Lake Michigan with Lake Huron.
Ma·con (mā'kən) a city in central Georgia. Pop., 106,612.
Mad·a·gas·car (mad'ə gas'kər) an island country in the Indian Ocean, east of southern Africa. Capital, Antananarivo. Area, 226,658 sq mi (587,044 sq km). Pop., 9,731,000. Formerly, **Malagasy Republic.** —**Mad'a·gas'can,** adj., n.
Ma·dei·ra (mə dîr'ə, -dâr'ə) **1.** a Portuguese island group in the Atlantic off the coast of Morocco. Land area, approx. 323 sq mi (837 sq km). Pop., 273,200. Also, **Madeira Islands. 2.** the largest island in this group. Area, approx. 286 sq mi (741 sq km). **3.** a river in northwestern Brazil, one of the principal tributaries of the Amazon. Length, 2,100 mi (3,380 km).

a	at	e	end	o	hot	u	up	hw	white		about
ā	ape	ē	me	ō	old	ū	use	ng	song		taken
ä	far	i	it	ô	fork	ü	rule	th	thin	ə	pencil
âr	care	ī	ice	oi	oil	ù	pull	th	this		lemon
		îr	pierce	ou	out	ûr	turn	zh	measure		circus

Mad·i·son (mad′ə sən) the capital of Wisconsin, in the south-central part of the state. Pop., 191,262.

Ma·dras (mə dras′) a port city in southeastern India, on the Bay of Bengal. Pop., 3,276,622.

Ma·drid (mə drid′) the capital and largest city of Spain, in the central part of the country. Pop., 3,102,846.

Ma·du·ra (*def. 1,* mə dûr′ə; *def. 2,* mad′yər ə) **1.** a small Indonesian island off the northeastern coast of Java. Area, 1,726 sq mi (4,470 sq km). **2.** see **Madurai**.

Ma·du·rai (mad′yŭ rī′) a city in southern India. Pop., 820,891. Formerly, **Madura**.

Mag·de·burg (mag′də bûrg′) a port city in north-central Germany, on the Elbe River. Pop., 290,579.

Ma·gel·lan, Strait of (mə jel′ən) a strait at the southern tip of mainland South America, linking the Atlantic and the Pacific.

Mag·gio·re, Lake (mə jôr′ē, -jôr′ā) a lake located in northern Italy and southern Switzerland.

Mag·ni·to·gorsk (mag nē′tə gôrsk′) a city in west-central Russia, located in the southern Ural mountains. Pop., 440,000.

Ma·hal·la al Ku·bra (mə hä′lə äl kü′brə) a city in northern Egypt, in the Nile delta. Pop., 358,844. Also, **Al Mahallah al Kubra**.

Main (mīn, män) a river flowing west through central Germany into the Rhine. Length, 325 mi (523 km).

Maine (mān) a state in the northeastern United States, on the Atlantic. Capital, Augusta. Area, 33,265 sq mi (86,156 sq km). Pop., 1,227,928. Abbreviation, **Me.**; postal abbreviation, **ME** —**Main′er,** *n.*

Mainz (mīnts) a port city in west-central Germany, on the Rhine. Pop., 174,828.

Ma·jor·ca (mə jôr′kə, mä yôr′-) the largest of the Balearic Islands, in the western Mediterranean. Area, 1,350 sq mi (3,497 sq km). Also, *Spanish,* **Mallorca**.

Ma·ju·ro (mə jŭr′ō) an atoll in the Marshall Islands, the site of the capital. Pop., 11,791.

Ma·kas·sar (mə kas′ər) see **Ujung Pandang**.

Ma·ka·ti (mä′kə tē′) a city in the Philippines, near Manila, on the island of Luzon. Pop., 408,991.

Mak·kah (mak′ə) see **Mecca**.

Mal·a·bar Coast (mal′ə bär′) a region south of Goa on the western coast of India.

Ma·la·bo (mə lä′bō) the capital of Equatorial Guinea. Pop., 31,630. Formerly, **Santa Isabel**.

Ma·lac·ca, Strait of (mə lak′ə) a channel between Sumatra and the Malay Peninsula.

Má·la·ga (mal′ə gə) a port city in southern Spain. Pop., 574,456.

Mal·a·gas·y Republic (mal′ə gas′ē) see **Madagascar**.

Ma·lang (mä läng′) a city in Indonesia, located in east-central Java. Pop., 547,000.

Ma·la·wi (mə lä′wē) **1.** a landlocked country in southeastern Africa. Capital, Lilongwe. Area, 45,747 sq mi (118,485 sq km). Pop., 7,982,607. **2. Lake.** see **Nyasa, Lake.** —**Ma·la′wi·an,** *adj.,*

Ma·lay·a (mə lā′ə) a former nation in southeastern Asia, on the Malay Peninsula, now part of Malaysia. Area, 50,806 sq mi (131,588 sq km). Also, **West Malaysia**.

Ma·lay Archipelago (mä′lā) a large island group between southeastern Asia on the north and Australia and New Guinea on the south, including the Philippines, most of Indonesia, and part of Malaysia. Also, **East Indies, Malaysia**.

Malay Peninsula, a long, narrow peninsula in southeastern Asia, including Malaya and part of Thailand.

Ma·lay·sia (mə lā′zhə) **1.** a country in southeastern Asia, divided by the South China Sea, consisting of Malaya in the west and Sarawak and Sabah in the east. Capital, Kuala Lumpur. Area, 128,430 sq mi (332,634 sq km). Pop., 13,136,109. **2.** see **Malay Archipelago**. —**Ma·lay′sian,** *adj., n.*

Mal·dives (môl′dēvz, mal′dīvz) a country of about 2,000 islands in the Indian Ocean, southwest of India. Capital, Male. Land area, 115 sq mi (298 sq km). Pop., 181,453. Also, **Mal′dive Islands.** —**Mal·div·i·an** (môl div′ē ən, mal-), *adj., n.*

Ma·le (mä′lā) the capital of the Maldives. Pop., 46,334.

Ma·li (mä′lē) a large, landlocked country in western Africa. Capital, Bamako. Area, 479,000 sq mi (1,240,610 sq km). Pop., 7,620,225. —**Ma′li·an,** *adj.,*

Ma·llor·ca (mä yôr′kə, mä lyôr′kä) see **Majorca**.

Malm·ö (mal′mō, mäl′mœ) a port city in southwestern Sweden. Pop., 232,908.

Mal·ta (môl′tə) **1.** a country consisting of an island group in the Mediterranean, south of the Italian island of Sicily. Capital, Valletta. Land area, 122 sq mi (316 sq km). Pop., 349,014. Also, **Mal·tese Islands** (môl tēz′, -tēs′). **2.** the chief island of this country. Area, 95 sq mi (246 sq km).

Ma·lu·ku (mə lü′kü) see **Moluccas**.

Mal·vi·nas (mal vē′nəs) see **Falkland Islands**.

Mammoth Cave 1. a series of large, limestone caverns in southwest-central Kentucky. **2.** a national park containing these caves. Area, 52,129 acres (21,097 hectares).

Man, Isle of (man) an island in the Irish Sea, administered by the United Kingdom. Capital, Douglas. Area, 221 sq mi (572 sq km). Pop., 64,282.

Ma·na·gua (mə nä′gwə) the capital and largest city of Nicaragua, in the southwestern part of the country. Pop., 682,000.

Ma·na·ma (mə nam′ə) the capital of Bahrain. Pop., 115,054.

Ma·nas·sas (mə nas′əs) a town in northeastern Virginia, near which the two battles of Bull Run took place during the Civil War. Pop., 27,957.

Ma·naus (mə nous′) a city in western Brazil. Pop., 809,914.

Man·ches·ter (man′ches′tər, -chə stər) **1.** a city in southern New Hampshire. Pop., 99,567. **2.** a city in northwestern England. Pop., 451,000.

Man·chu·kuo (man′chü′kwō′) a puppet state consisting principally of Manchuria, established by Japan in 1932 and lasting until 1945.

Man·chu·ri·a (man chŭr′ē ə) a historic region in northeastern China, roughly consisting of the provinces of Liaoning, Jilin, and Heilongjiang. Area, 413,000 sq mi (1,069,670 sq km).

Man·da·lay (man′də lā′) a city in central Burma. Pop., 532,949.

Man·hat·tan (man hat′ən, mən-) an island and borough of New York City, the financial, commercial, and cultural center of the city. Area, 23 sq mi (60 sq km).

Ma·nil·a (mə nil′ə) the capital and largest city of the Philippines, located on the island of Luzon. Pop., 1,587,000.

Manila Bay, a large inlet of the South China Sea in the northern Philippines, on the southwestern coast of the island of Luzon. It was the site of an American naval victory during the Spanish-American War.

Man·i·to·ba (man′i tō′bə) **1.** a province in south-central Canada. Capital, Winnipeg. Area, 251,000 sq mi (650,090 sq km). Pop., 1,071,232. **2. Lake.** a lake in southwestern Manitoba.

Man·i·tou·lin Island (man′i tü′lin) an island in Lake Huron, in Ontario, Canada; the largest island in a freshwater lake in the world. Area, 1,068 sq mi (2,766 sq km). Also, **Grand Manitoulin**.

Man·i·za·les (man′ə zal′əs) a city in west-central Colombia. Pop., 299,352.

Mann·heim (man′hīm, män′hīm) a city in west-central Germany, on the Rhine. Pop., 300,468.

Ma·nu·kau (mä′nə kou′) a city in New Zealand, in the northern part of North Island. Pop., 177,248.

Ma·pu·to (mə pü′tō) the capital of Mozambique, in the southern part of the country. Pop., 1,069,727. Formerly, **Lourenço Marques**.

Mar·a·cai·bo (mar′ə kī′bō) **1.** a port city in northwestern Venezuela, near the Caribbean Sea. Pop., 890,643. **2. Lake.** a lake in northwestern Venezuela.

Ma·ra·cay (mär′ə kī′) a city in northern Venezuela. Pop., 322,560.

Mar·a·thon (mar′ə thon′) the plain in Greece, northeast of Athens, where the Athenians defeated the Persians in battle in 490 B.C.

Mar del Pla·ta (mär′del plä′tə) a city in east-central Argentina, on the Atlantic. Pop., 414,696.

Mar·i·an·a Islands (mâr′ē an′ə, mar′-) a volcanic island group in the western Pacific, divided into Guam and the Northern Mariana Islands. Land area, 453 sq mi (1,173 sq km). Also, **Mar′ian′as**.

Mariana Trench, a depression in the western Pacific Ocean, southwest of Guam; the deepest known depression on the earth.

Mar·i·time Provinces (mar′i tīm′) the Canadian provinces of New Brunswick, Nova Scotia, and Prince Edward Island. Also, **Maritimes**.

Mark·ham (mär′kəm) a town in southern Ontario, Canada. Pop., 114,597.

Mar·ma·ra, Sea of (mär′mər ə) *also,* **Sea of Mar·mo·ra.** a sea between the European and Asian parts of Turkey, connected with the Black Sea by the Bosporus and with the Aegean Sea by the Dardanelles.

Marne (märn) a river in east-central France. Length, 326 mi (525 km).

Mar·que·sas Islands (mär kā′zəz, -səz, -səs) a group of volcanic islands in French Polynesia. Land area, approx. 409 sq mi (1,059 sq km).

Mar·ra·kesh (mar′ə kesh′, mar′ə kesh′) *also,* **Mar·ra·kech.** a city in central Morocco. Pop., 439,728.

Mar·seilles (mär sā′) *also, French,* **Mar·seille** (mär sā′). the chief seaport of France, on the Mediterranean. Pop., 874,436.

Mar·shall Islands (mär′shəl) a group of Pacific islands that constitute a territory of the United States. Capital, Majuro. Land area, approx. 70 sq mi (180 sq km). Pop., 30,873.

Mar·tha's Vineyard (mär′thəz) an island off the Massachusetts coast. Area, approx. 100 sq mi (260 sq km).

Mar·ti·nique (mär′tə nēk′) a French island in the Caribbean. Capital, Fort-de-France. Area, approx. 425 sq mi (1,100 sq km). Pop., 328,566.

Mar·y·land (mer′ə lənd) a state in the eastern United States. Capital, Annapolis. Area, 10,460 sq mi (27,091 sq km). Pop., 4,781,468. Abbreviation, **Md.**; postal abbreviation, **MD** —**Mar′y·land·er,** n.

Ma·san (mä′sän) a seaport in southeastern South Korea. Pop., 448,746. Formerly, **Ma·sam·po** (mə säm′pō).

Mas·e·ru (maz′ə rü′) the capital of Lesotho. Pop., 109,382.

Mash·had (mə shad′) a city in northeastern Iran. Pop., 1,463,508. Also, **Meshed.**

Mas·sa·chu·setts (mas′ə chü′sits) a state in the northeastern United States. Capital, Boston. Area, 8,284 sq mi (21,456 sq km). Pop., 6,016,425. Abbreviation, **Mass.**; postal abbreviation, **MA**

Massachusetts Bay, an inlet of the Atlantic, on the coast of Massachusetts.

Mas·sif Cen·tral (ma sēf′ sän träl′) a plateau in southeast-central France, west of the Rhône.

Ma·ta·di (mə tä′dē) a port city in western Zaire, on the Congo River. Pop., 144,742.

Mat·su (mat sü′) a small island belonging to Taiwan off the coast of China. Area, approx. 10 sq mi (26 sq km).

Mat·ter·horn (mat′ər hôrn′) a steep, jagged mountain peak in the Alps, on the border between Switzerland and Italy.

Mau·i (mou′ē) the second largest island of Hawaii. Area, 728 sq mi (1,886 sq km). Pop., 100,374.

Maul·main (môl mān′) see **Moulmein.**

Mau·na Ke·a (mou′nə kā′ə) an extinct volcano in the northwestern part of the island of Hawaii. Height, 13,796 ft (4,205 m).

Mau·na Lo·a (mou′nə lō′ə) the largest known active volcano in the world, on the island of Hawaii. Height, 13,680 ft (4,170 m).

Mau·re·ta·ni·a (môr′i tā′nē ə) an ancient country in northwestern Africa.

Mau·ri·ta·ni·a (môr′i tā′nē ə) a country on the northwestern coast of Africa. Capital, Nouakchott. Area, 397,955 sq mi (1,030,704 sq km). Pop., 2,007,000. —**Mau′ri·ta′ni·an,** adj., n.

Mau·ri·tius (mô rish′əs) an island country in the western Indian Ocean, east of Madagascar. Capital, Port Louis. Area, 788 sq mi (2,041 sq km). Pop., 1,008,864. —**Mau·ri′tian,** adj., n.

Ma·ya·güez (mä′yä gwes′) a port city in western Puerto Rico. Pop., 82,968.

Ma·yotte (mä yôt′) an island in the Indian Ocean, northwest of Madagascar, a French overseas territory. Area, 145 sq mi (376 sq km). Pop., 67,205.

Mba·bane (bä bän′) the capital of Swaziland, in the western part of the country. Pop., 38,290.

Mban·da·ka (bän′dä kä) a port city in western Zaire, on the Congo River. Pop., 125,263. Formerly, **Coquilhatville.**

Mbu·ji-Ma·yi (bü′jē mī′ē) a city in southern Zaire. Pop., 423,363. Formerly, **Bakwanga.**

Mc·Kin·ley, Mount (mə kin′lē) the highest mountain in North America, in south-central Alaska. Height, 20,320 ft (6,194 m). Also, **Denali.**

Mec·ca (mek′ə) a city in western Saudi Arabia, near the Red Sea, the birthplace of Muhammad. Pop., 550,000. Also, *Arabic,* **Makkah.**

Me·dan (mā dän′) a city in Indonesia, on the northeastern coast of the island of Sumatra. Pop., 2,110,000.

Me·del·lín (med′ə lēn′, me′the yēn′) a city in west-central Colombia. Pop., 1,468,089.

Me·di·a (mē′dē ə) an ancient kingdom in northwestern Persia.

Me·di·na (mə dē′nə) a city in western Saudi Arabia, site of Muhammad's tomb. Pop., 290,000. Also, *Arabic,* **Al Madinah.**

Med·i·ter·ra·ne·an (med′i tə rā′nē ən) **1.** a large, almost landlocked arm of the Atlantic between southern Europe, western Asia, and northern Africa. Also, **Mediterranean Sea. 2. the Mediterranean.** a region consisting of this sea and the countries in and around it.

Mek·nès (mek nes′) a city in northwest Morocco. Pop., 319,783.

Me·kong (mā′kong′) a river in southeastern Asia, flowing southeastward from western China into the South China Sea. Length, 2,600 mi (4,183 km).

Mel·a·ne·sia (mel′ə nē′zhə) one of the three major divisions of the Pacific islands, located east of Australia.

Mel·bourne (mel′bərn) a port city in southeastern Australia, the capital of the state of Victoria. Pop., 3,039,100.

Me·li·lla (mə lē′yə) a port city on the Mediterranean, a Spanish enclave in northern Morocco. Pop., 55,717.

Mel·ville, Lake (mel′vil) a saltwater lake in southeastern Labrador, Newfoundland and Labrador, Canada.

Melville Island 1. an island in the northern Northwest Territories, Canada. Area, 16,369 sq mi (42,396 sq km). **2.** an island off the northwest coast of Northern Territory, Australia. Area, 2,240 sq mi (5,800 sq km).

Mem·phis (mem′fis) **1.** the largest city in Tennessee, in the southwestern part of the state. Pop., 610,337. **2.** a city in ancient Egypt, on the west bank of the Nile.

Me·nor·ca (me nôr′kä) see **Minorca.**

Mer·ci·a (mûr′shə) an ancient kingdom in what is now central England, founded by the Angles.

Mé·ri·da (mer′i də) a city in southeastern Mexico, on the Yucatán Peninsula. Pop., 400,142.

Me·rid·i·an (mə rid′ē ən) a city in eastern Mississippi. Pop., 41,036.

Mer·sey River (mûr′zē) a river in northwestern England, flowing east into the Irish Sea near Liverpool. Length, 70 mi (113 km).

Me·sa (mā′sə) a city in south-central Arizona. Pop., 288,091.

Me·sa·bi (mə sä′bē) a range of iron-rich hills in northeastern Minnesota. Also, **Mesabi Hills.**

Me·shed (mə shed′) see **Mashhad.**

Mes·o·po·ta·mi·a (mes′ə pə tā′mē ə) a historic region in southwestern Asia, between the Tigris and Euphrates rivers, a center of ancient civilization. —**Mes′o·po·ta′mi·an,** adj., n.

Mes·se·ne (me sē′nē) an ancient Greek city located in the southwestern Peloponnesus.

Mes·si·na (mə sē′nə) **1.** a port city in the northeastern part of the Italian island of Sicily. Pop., 268,896. **2. Strait of.** a narrow strait between Italy and Sicily.

Metz (mets) a city in northeastern France. Pop., 114,232.

Meuse (mœz) a river in western Europe, flowing from northeastern France through Belgium and the Netherlands to the North Sea.

Mex·i·ca·li (mek′si kal′ē) a city in northern Mexico, in Baja California on Mexico's border with the United States. Pop., 341,559.

Mex·i·co (mek′si kō′) **1.** a country in North America, south of and bordering the southwestern United States. Capital, Mexico City. Area, 761,605 sq mi (1,972,557 sq km). Pop., 67,395,826. **2.** a state in central Mexico. Area, 8,268 sq mi (21,414 sq km). Pop., 7,564,335. **3. Gulf of.** an arm of the Atlantic, between the United States and Mexico. —**Mex·i·can** (mek′si kən), adj., n.

Mexico City, the capital and largest city of Mexico, in the southern part of the country. Pop., 8,831,079.

Mi·am·i (mī am′ē) a resort and port city in southeastern Florida. Pop., 358,548.

Miami Beach, a resort city in southeastern Florida, just east of Miami. Pop., 92,639.

Mich·i·gan (mish′i gən) **1.** a state in the north-central United States. Capital, Lansing. Area, 58,527 sq mi (151,585 sq km). Pop., 9,295,297. Abbreviation, **Mich.**; postal abbreviation, **MI 2. Lake.** the third largest of the Great Lakes. It lies between Michigan and Wisconsin. —**Mich′i·gan′der, Mich·i·ga·ni·an** (mish′i gā′nē ən), **Mich′i·gan·ite′,** n.

Mi·cho·a·cán (mē′chō ä kän′) a state in southwestern Mexico. Area, 23,202 sq mi (60,093 sq km). Pop., 2,868,824.

Mi·cro·ne·sia (mī′krə nē′zhə) **1.** one of the three major divisions of the Pacific islands, located north of Melanesia. **2. Federated States of.** a group of islands in the Caroline Islands and a territory of the United States. Capital, Kolonia. Land area, 271 sq mi (702 sq km). Pop., 94,534.

Middle Atlantic States, a region of the eastern United States, usually considered to include New York, New Jersey, Pennsylvania, Delaware, Maryland, and the District of Columbia. Also, **Mid-Atlantic States.**

Middle East, a region that consists of northeastern Africa and the countries of southwestern and sometimes south-central Asia. Also, **Mideast.** —**Middle Eastern,** adj.

Mid·dles·brough (mid′əlz brə) a city in northeastern England. Pop., 158,516.

Mid·dle·sex (mid′əl seks′) a former county in southeastern England, now a part of Greater London.

Middle West, see **Midwest.** —**Middle Western,** adj. —**Middle Westerner,** n.

a	at	e	end	o	hot	u	up	hw	white		about
ā	ape	ē	me	ō	old	ū	use	ng	song		taken
ä	far	i	it	ô	fork	ü	rule	th	thin	ə	pencil
âr	care	ī	ice	oi	oil	u̇	pull	th	this		lemon
		îr	pierce	ou	out	ûr	turn	zh	measure		circus

Mid·east (mid′ēst′) see **Middle East.**

Mid·land (mid′lənd) a city in western Texas. Pop., 89,443.

Mid·way Islands (mid′wā′) a small island group in the north-central Pacific, administered by the United States. Pop., 2,000.

Mid·west (mid′west′) a region of the north-central United States, the major agricultural area of the country. Area, 765,530 sq mi (1,982,723 sq km). Also, **Middle West.** —**Mid′west′ern,** *adj.* —**Mid′west′ern·er,** *n.*

Mi·lan (mi lan′, -län′) a city in northern Italy, the leading commercial and industrial center of the country. Pop., 1,495,260.

Mi·le·tus (mī lē′təs) an ancient Greek city in western Asia Minor.

Mil·wau·kee (mil wô′kē) a city in southeastern Wisconsin, on Lake Michigan. Pop., 628,088.

Min·da·na·o (min′də nä′ō) the second largest island of the Philippines, located in the southern part of the country. Area, 35,537 sq mi (92,041 sq km).

Min·do·ro (min dôr′ō) a large island in the west-central Philippines. Area, 3,759 sq mi (9,736 sq km).

Min·how (min′hō′) see **Fuzhou.**

Min·ne·ap·o·lis (min′ē ap′ə lis) the largest city in Minnesota, in the southeastern part of the state. Pop., 368,383.

Min·ne·so·ta (min′ə sō′tə) a state in the north-central United States. Capital, St. Paul. Area, 84,402 sq mi (218,601 sq km). Pop., 4,375,099. Abbreviation, **Minn.**; postal abbreviation, **MN** —**Min′ne·so′tan,** *adj., n.*

Mi·nor·ca (mi nôr′kə) the second largest of the Balearic Islands. Area, 293 sq mi (759 sq km). Also, *Spanish,* **Menorca.**

Minsk (minsk) the capital of Belarus. Pop., 1,589,000.

Miq·ue·lon (mik′ə lon′) see **St. Pierre and Miquelon.**

Mis·kolc (mish′kôlts) a city in northeastern Hungary. Pop., 196,449.

Mis·sis·sip·pi (mis′ə sip′ē) **1.** the principal river of the United States, flowing from northern Minnesota to the Gulf of Mexico. Length, 2,348 mi (3,778 km). **2.** a state in the southern United States. Capital, Jackson. Area, 47,689 sq mi (123,515 sq km). Pop., 2,573,216. Abbreviation, **Miss.**; postal abbreviation, **MS** —**Mis′sis·sip′pi·an,** *adj., n.*

Mis·sou·ri (mi zûr′ē, -zŭr′ə) **1.** a large river in the United States, flowing from Montana to the Mississippi just north of St. Louis. Length, 2,315 mi (3,725 km). **2.** a state in the central United States. Capital, Jefferson City. Area, 69,697 sq mi (180,515 sq km). Pop., 5,117,073. Abbreviation, **Mo.**; postal abbreviation, **MO** —**Mis·sou′ri·an,** *adj., n.*

Mitch·ell, Mount (mich′əl) the highest mountain in the eastern United States, in western North Carolina. Height, 6,684 ft (2,037 m).

Mo·ab (mō′ab) an ancient kingdom east of the Dead Sea, in what is now Jordan.

Mo·bile (mō bēl′, mō′bēl) a port city in southwestern Alabama, on Mobile Bay. Pop., 196,298.

Mobile Bay, a shallow arm of the Gulf of Mexico, extending into southwestern Alabama.

Mobile River, a river in southwestern Alabama, flowing south to Mobile Bay. Length, 45 mi (72 km).

Mo·de·na (mô′də nə) a city in northern Italy. Pop., 176,880.

Mo·des·to (mə des′tō) a city in central California. Pop., 164,730.

Mo·ga·di·shu (mog′ə dish′ü) the capital of Somalia, in the southeastern part of the country, on the Indian Ocean. Pop., 600,000.

Mo·ha·ve Desert (mō hä′vē) see **Mojave Desert.**

Mo·hawk (mō′hôk) a river in central New York. Length, 148 mi (238 km).

Mo·ja·ve Desert (mō hä′vē) *also,* **Mohave Desert.** a desert in southeastern California. Area, approx. 15,000 sq mi (38,850 sq km).

Mol·da·vi·a (mol dā′vē ə) **1.** see **Moldova. 2.** a historic region of northeastern Romania. —**Mol·da′vi·an,** *adj., n.*

Mol·do·va (môl dō′və) a country in eastern Europe, bordering Romania and Ukraine. It was known as Moldavia when it was a republic of the Soviet Union. Capital, Kishinev. Area, approx. 13,000 sq mi (33,700 sq km). Pop., 4,341,000. —**Mol·do′van,** *adj., n.*

Mo·lo·kai (mō′lə kī′, mol′ə-) the fifth largest island of Hawaii. Area, 261 sq mi (676 sq km).

Mo·lo·tov (mol′ə tôf′) see **Perm.**

Mo·luc·cas (mə luk′əz) an island group in east-central Indonesia, between Sulawesi and New Guinea. Land area, approx. 30,000 sq mi (77,700 sq km). Also, *Indonesian,* **Maluku; Mo·luc′ca Islands.** Formerly, **Spice Islands.**

Mom·ba·sa (mom bä′sä) the principal port city of Kenya, on the Indian Ocean. Pop., 537,000.

Mon·a·co (mon′ə kō′, mə nä′kō) **1.** a small country in southern Europe, on the Mediterranean Sea. Capital, Monaco. Area, 0.6 sq mi (1.6 sq km). Pop., 27,063. **2.** the capital of this country. Pop., 27,063. Also, **Mon·a·co-Ville** (mon′ə kō vil′). —**Mon·a·can** (mon′ə kən, mə nä′-), *adj., n.* —**Mon·e·gasque** (mon′i-gask′), *adj., n.*

Monc·ton (mungk′tən) a city in southeastern New Brunswick, Canada. Pop., 55,468.

Mon·go·li·a (mong gō′lē ə) **1.** a vast area in east-central Asia, extending from northern China to Siberia, including Inner Mongolia and the country of Mongolia. Area, approx. 1,000,000 sq mi (2,590,000 sq km). **2.** a country in central Asia, bordered by Russia and China. Capital, Ulaanbaatar. Area, 604,250 sq mi (1,565,000 sq km). Pop., 2,040,000. Formerly *(def. 2),* **Outer Mongolia.**

Mo·non·ga·he·la (mə nong′gə hē′lə) a river in northern West Virginia and southwestern Pennsylvania, joining the Allegheny at Pittsburgh to form the Ohio. Length, 128 mi (206 km).

Mon·ro·vi·a (mon rō′vē ə) the capital and largest city of Liberia, a port on the Atlantic. Pop., 465,000.

Mon·tan·a (mon tan′ə) a state in the northwestern United States. Capital, Helena. Area, 147,046 sq mi (380,849 sq km). Pop., 799,065. Abbreviation, **Mont.**; postal abbbreviation, **MT** —**Mon·tan′an,** *adj., n.*

Mont Blanc (mont blangk′, môN bläN′) the highest mountain in the Alps, on the French-Italian border. Height, 15,771 ft (4,807 m).

Mon·te Car·lo (mon′tē kär′lō) a resort town in Monaco, on the Mediterranean, site of a famous gambling casino. Pop., 10,000.

Mon·te·go Bay (mon tē′gō) a resort city and port in northwestern Jamaica. Pop., 70,265.

Mon·te·ne·gro (mon′tə nē′grō, -neg′rō) a republic of Yugoslavia, on the Adriatic, formerly an independent kingdom. Area, approx. 5,333 sq mi (13,812 sq km). Pop., 625,882. —**Mon·te·ne·grin** (mon′tə nē′grin, -neg′rin), *adj., n.*

Mon·ter·rey (mon′tə rā′) a city in northeastern Mexico. Pop., 1,090,009.

Mon·te·vi·de·o (mon′tə vi dā′ō) the capital of Uruguay, in the southern part of the country, on the Río de la Plata. Pop., 1,251,647.

Mont·gom·er·y (mont gum′ə rē) the capital of Alabama, in the central part of the state. Pop., 187,106.

Mont·mar·tre (môN mär′tRə, -märt′) a district in Paris, formerly noted as a center for artists.

Mont·pel·ier (mont pēl′yər) the capital of Vermont, in the central part of the state. Pop., 8,247.

Mont·pel·lier (môN pe lyā′) a city in southern France. Pop., 197,231.

Mont·re·al (mon′trē ôl′, mun′-) the largest city of Canada, in southern Quebec, on the St. Lawrence River. Pop., 1,015,420.

Mont-Saint-Mi·chel (môN saN mē shel′) an islet in the English Channel off the coast of Normandy, France, noted for its Benedictine monastery.

Mont·ser·rat (mont′sə rat′) a British island in the West Indies, one of the Leeward Islands. Capital, Plymouth. Area, 40 sq mi (104 sq km). Pop., 11,606.

Mo·ra·tu·wa (mô rä′tü wə) a city in western Sri Lanka. Pop., 138,000.

Mo·ra·vi·a (mô rä′vē ə) a historic region in central Czechoslovakia. Area, approx. 10,000 sq mi (25,900 sq km). Pop., 4,033,010.

Mo·re·los (mô Re′lôs) a state in south-central Mexico. Area, 1,917 sq mi (4,965 sq km). Pop., 947,089.

Mo·roc·co (mə rok′ō) a country in northwestern Africa, on the Atlantic and the Mediterranean. Capital, Rabat. Area, 172,410 sq mi (446,542 sq km). Pop., 20,419,555. —**Mo·roc·can** (mə-rok′ən), *adj., n.*

Mo·ron (mô rōn′) a city in eastern Argentina. Pop., 598,420.

Mo·ro·ni (mô rō′nē) the capital of the Comoros. Pop., 23,432.

Mos·cow (mos′kou) the capital and largest city of Russia, located in the western part of the country. Pop., 8,769,000.

Mo·selle (mō zel′) a river in western Europe, flowing from northeastern France into western Germany, joining the Rhine at Koblenz. Length, 320 mi (515 km).

Mo·sul (mō sül′) a city in northern Iraq, on the Tigris River. Pop., 570,926. Also, *Arabic,* **Al Mawsil.**

Moul·mein (mül mān′) *also,* **Maulmain.** a seaport in southern Burma. Pop., 219,961.

Mount Ver·non (vûr′nən) the home and burial place of George Washington, on the Potomac River in Virginia, near Washington, D.C.

Mount Las·sen, see **Lassen Peak.**

Mo·zam·bique (mō′zam bēk′) a country in southeastern Africa. Capital, Maputo. Area, 308,642 sq mi (799,383 sq km). Pop., 15,326,476. —**Mo′zam·bi′can,** *adj., n.*

Muk·den (mŭk′den′) see **Shenyang.**

Mul·house (mú lüz′) a city in eastern France. Pop., 112,157. Also, *German,* **Mül·hau·sen** (myl hou′zən).

Mul·tan (múl tän′) a city in northeastern Pakistan. Pop., 696,316.

Mun·cie (mun′sē) a city in east-central Indiana. Pop., 71,035.

Mu·nich (mū′nik) a city in southern Germany. Pop., 1,211,617.

Mun·ster (mun′stər) a historic province of Ireland, in the southern part of the island.

Mün·ster (myn′stər) a city in northwestern Germany. Pop., 248,919.

Mur·cia (múr′shə, múʀ′thyä) **1.** a region and ancient kingdom in southeastern Spain. **2.** a city in southeastern Spain. Pop., 149,800.

Mur·mansk (múr mänsk′) a port city in northwestern Russia. Pop., 468,000.

Mur·ray (múr′ē) a river rising near Mount Kosciusko in New South Wales, Australia, and flowing west to the Indian Ocean near Adelaide. Length, 1,609 mi (2,589 km).

Mus·cat (mus′kat) the capital of Oman, in the northern part of the country. Pop., 50,000.

Muscat and Oman, see **Oman.**

Myan·mar (myän mä′) see **Burma.**

My·ce·nae (mī sē′nē) an ancient city in southern Greece, in the eastern Peloponnesus.

My·sore (mī sôr′) a city in southern India. Pop., 441,754.

Nab·lus (nab′ləs, nä′bləs) *also,* **Nab·u·lus** (nab′ə ləs). a city in the north-central part of the West Bank. Pop., 64,000.

Na·ga·sa·ki (nä′gə sä′kē) a city in Japan, on the western coast of the island of Kyushu. On August 9, 1945, the second atomic bomb used in World War II was dropped on this city. Pop., 449,382.

Na·go·ya (nə goi′ə) a city in Japan, on the southern coast of the island of Honshu. Pop., 2,116,381.

Nag·pur (näg′púr) a city in central India. Pop., 1,219,461.

Nai·ro·bi (nī rō′bē) the capital of Kenya, in the southern part of the country. Pop., 1,505,000.

Na·mib·i·a (nə mib′ē ə) a territory on the southwestern coast of Africa, administered by the Republic of South Africa. Capital, Windhoek. Area, 318,252 sq mi (824,273 sq km). Pop., 1,760,000. Formerly, **South-West Africa.**

Nam·pu·la (nam pü′lə) a city in northeastern Mozambique. Pop., 197,379.

Na·mur (nä mùr′) a city in south-central Belgium, on the Meuse River. Pop., 102,670.

Nan·chang (nän′jäng′) a city in southeastern China, the capital of Jiangxi province. Pop., 1,090,000.

Nan·cy (nan′sē, nän sē′) a city in northeastern France. Pop., 96,317.

Nan·jing (nän′jing′) *also,* **Nan·king** (nän′king′). a city on the Yangtze River in eastern China, the capital of Jiangsu province. It is a former capital of the country. Pop., 2,390,000.

Nan·ning (nän′ning′) a city in southern China, the capital of Guangxi. Pop., 720,000.

Nantes (nants, näɴt) a port city in western France, in the region of Brittany. Pop., 240,539.

Nan·tuck·et (nan tuk′it) an island off the southern coast of Cape Cod, Massachusetts. Area, approx. 50 sq mi (130 sq km).

Na·ples (nā′pəlz) **1.** a port city on the southwestern coast of Italy, on the Bay of Naples. Pop., 1,204,211. **2. Bay of.** an inlet of the Tyrrhenian Sea, on the southwestern coast of Italy.

Na·ra·yan·ganj (nə rä′yən gunj′) a port in southeastern Bangladesh. Pop., 405,562.

Nar·ra·gan·sett Bay (nar′ə gan′sit) a large inlet of the Atlantic, in eastern Rhode Island.

Nash·u·a (nash′ü ə) a city in southern New Hampshire. Pop., 79,662.

Nash·ville (nash′vil′) the capital of Tennessee, in the central part of the state. Pop., 487,969.

Nas·sau (nas′ô) the capital and largest city of the Bahamas. Pop., 101,000.

Nas·ser, Lake (nas′ər) a lake on the Nile in southeastern Egypt and northern Sudan, formed by the Aswan High Dam.

Na·tal (nə tal′, -täl′; *for def. 2, also* nə tôl′) **1.** a province of the Republic of South Africa, in the eastern part of the country. Area, 35,501 sq mi (91,948 sq km). Pop., 5,892,033. **2.** a port city in northeastern Brazil, on the Atlantic. Pop., 510,106.

Nationalist China, see **Taiwan.**

Na·u·ru (nä ü′rü) a small island country in the central Pacific, northeast of Australia. Area, approx. 8 sq mi (21 sq km). Pop., 8,000. Formerly, **Pleasant Island.** —**Na·u′ru·an,** *adj., n.*

Na·varre (nə vär′) a historic region and former kingdom located in the western Pyrenees. It included parts of southwestern France and northern Spain.

Na·ya·rit (nä′yä rēt′) a state in west-central Mexico. Area, 10,547 sq mi (27,317 sq km). Pop., 726,120.

Naz·a·reth (naz′ər əth) a town in Galilee, in northern Israel, where Jesus spent his youth. Pop., 50,600.

Ndja·me·na (ən jä′mə nə) the capital of Chad, in the west-central part of the country. Pop., 303,000. Formerly, **Fort-Lamy.**

Ndo·la (ən dō′lə) a city in north-central Zambia. Pop., 250,490.

Near East, a region usually regarded as including the countries of southwestern Asia and northeastern Africa.

Ne·bo, Mount (nē′bō) in the Bible, the mountain from which Moses saw the Promised Land before his death.

Ne·bras·ka (nə bras′kə) a state in the central United States. Capital, Lincoln. Area, 77,355 sq mi (200,349 sq km). Pop., 1,578,385. Abbreviations, **Nebr., Neb.;** postal abbreviation, **NE** —**Ne·bras′kan,** *adj., n.*

Neg·ev (neg′ev) a desert region in southern Israel. Area, 4,000 sq mi (10,360 sq km).

Ne·gro (nā′grō) **1.** a river in north-central South America, flowing southeast through Colombia and Brazil into the Amazon. Length, 1,400 mi (2,253 km). **2.** a river in south-central Argentina, flowing east into the Atlantic Ocean. Length, 630 mi (1,014 km). **3.** a river in central Uruguay, flowing southwest into the eastern Uruguay River. Length, 290 mi (467 km).

Ne·gros (nā′grōs) an island in the central Philippines. Area, 4,905 sq mi (12,704 sq km).

Nei Mong·gol (nā′ mong′gōl′) see **Inner Mongolia.**

Ne·pal (nə pôl′, -päl′) a country in central Asia, bounded by India and Tibet. Capital, Katmandu. Area, 56,827 sq mi (147,182 sq km). Pop., 15,022,839. —**Nep·a·lese** (nep′ə lēz′, -lēs′), *adj., n.*

Ness, Loch (nes) a lake in northwestern Scotland, said to be the home of an enormous sea creature known as the Loch Ness monster.

Neth·er·lands, the (neth′ər ləndz) a country in northwestern Europe, on the North Sea. Capital, Amsterdam. Seat of government, The Hague. Area, 16,133 sq mi (41,784 sq km). Pop., 14,880,000. Also, **Holland.** —**Neth·er·land·ic** (neth′ər lan′dik), **Neth·er·land·ish** (neth′ər lan′dish), *adj.* —**Neth·er·land·er** (neth′ər lan′dər, -lən-), *n.*

Netherlands Antilles, a Dutch island group in the southern Caribbean, including Bonaire and Curaçao. Land area, 309 sq mi (800 sq km). Pop., 189,687.

Netherlands East Indies, a group of islands off the southeastern coast of Asia, formerly controlled by the Netherlands, now part of Indonesia.

Netherlands Guiana, a former Dutch colony in northern South America, now Suriname.

Netherlands New Guinea, a former Dutch colony in western New Guinea, now Irian Jaya.

Net·za·hual·có·yotl (net′sə wäl kə yō′təl) a city in south-central Mexico. Pop., 1,341,230.

Ne·vad·a (nə vad′ə, -vä′də) a state in the western United States. Capital, Carson City. Area, 110,561 sq mi (286,353 sq km). Pop., 1,201,833. Abbreviation, **Nev.;** postal abbreviation, **NV** —**Ne·vad′an,** *adj., n.*

Ne·vis (nē′vis) see **St. Kitts-Nevis.**

New Amsterdam, the capital of the Dutch colony of New Netherland. A town on the lower tip of Manhattan, it was taken by the British in 1664 and renamed New York.

New·ark (nü′ərk, nū′-) a city in northeastern New Jersey. Pop., 275,221.

New Bed·ford (bed′fərd) a port city in southeastern Massachusetts. Pop., 99,922.

New Britain 1. an island of Papua New Guinea, the largest island in the Bismarck Archipelago. Area, approx. 14,100 sq mi (36,500 sq km). **2.** a city in central Connecticut. Pop., 75,491.

New Brunswick, a province of Canada, in the southeastern part of the country. Capital, Fredericton. Area, 28,354 sq mi (73,437 sq km). Pop., 710,422.

New Cal·e·do·nia (kal′i dō′nē ə) a French island territory in the southern Pacific, east of Australia. Capital, Noumea. Area, 7,366 sq mi (19,078 sq km). Pop., 164,173.

New·cas·tle (nü′kas′əl, nū′-) **1.** a port city in northeastern England, noted for its coal and shipbuilding industries. Pop., 199,064. Also, **New·cas·tle-u·pon-Tyne** (nü′kas′əl ə pôn tīn′,

a	at	e	end	o	hot	u	up	hw	white		about
ā	ape	ē	me	ō	old	ū	use	ng	song		taken
ä	far	i	it	ô	fork	ü	rule	th	thin	ə	pencil
âr	care	ī	ice	oi	oil	ù	pull	th	this		lemon
		îr	pierce	ou	out	ûr	turn	zh	measure		circus

-ə pon-, nū′-). **2.** a port city in New South Wales, in southeastern Australia. Pop., 130,940.

New Delhi, the capital of India, in the north-central part of the country. Pop., 273,036.

New England, a region of the northeastern United States that includes Maine, New Hampshire, Vermont, Massachusetts, Rhode Island, and Connecticut. —**New Englander.**

New·found·land (nü′fənd lənd, nū′-) **1.** an island off the east coast of Canada, part of Newfoundland and Labrador. Area, 43,359 sq mi (112,300 sq km). **2.** see **Newfoundland and Labrador.**

Newfoundland and Labrador, the easternmost province of Canada, consisting of the island of Newfoundland and the mainland area of Labrador. Capital, St. John's. Area, 156,185 sq mi (404,519 sq km). Pop., 568,349.

New France, a former territory in North America, explored and settled by the French from 1609 to 1763.

New Granada 1. a Spanish province and, later, a viceroyalty in northwestern South America, from 1549 to 1810. At its greatest extent, it included present-day Colombia, Panama, Venezuela, and Ecuador. **2.** a former republic in Latin America that was formed from parts of this province in 1831 and included present-day Colombia and Panama.

New Guinea, the second largest island in the world (after Greenland), located in the western Pacific, north of Australia. It is politically divided between the Indonesian province of Irian Jaya and Papua New Guinea. Area, approx. 342,000 sq mi (885,800 sq km). Also, **Papua.**

New Hamp·shire (hamp′shər) a state in the northeastern United States. Capital, Concord. Area, 9,279 sq mi (24,033 sq km). Pop., 1,109,252. Abbreviation, **N.H.**; postal abbreviation, **NH** —**New Hamp′shir·ite′.**

New Ha·ven (hā′vən) a city in southern Connecticut. Pop., 130,474.

New Hebrides, see **Vanuatu.**

New Jersey, a state in the eastern United States. Capital, Trenton. Area, 7,787 sq mi (20,168 sq km). Pop., 7,730,188. Abbreviation, **N.J.**; postal abbreviation, **NJ** —**New Jer′sey·ite′.**

New Kow·loon (kou lün′) a city on the mainland of Hong Kong. Pop., 1,526,910.

New Mexico, a state in the southwestern United States. Capital, Santa Fe. Area, 121,593 sq mi (314,926 sq km). Pop., 1,515,069. Abbreviations, **N. Mex., N.M.**; postal abbreviation, **NM** —**New Mexican.**

New Netherland, a Dutch colony in North America from 1624 to 1664 that consisted of parts of present-day New York, New Jersey, and Connecticut.

New Or·le·ans (ôr′lē ənz, -lənz, ôr lēnz′) a city in southeastern Louisiana, a port on the Mississippi. Pop., 496,938.

New·port (nü′pôrt, nū′-) a city in southeastern Rhode Island, at the mouth of Narragansett Bay. Pop., 28,227.

Newport News, a port city in southeastern Virginia. Pop., 170,045.

New South Wales, a state of Australia, in the southeastern part of the country. Capital, Sydney. Area, 309,433 sq mi (801,431 sq km). Pop., 5,761,900.

New·ton (nü′tən, nū′-) a city in eastern Massachusetts. Pop., 82,585.

New Windsor, see **Windsor** (def. 1).

New York 1. a state in the eastern United States. Capital, Albany. Area, 49,108 sq mi (127,190 sq km). Pop., 17,990,455. Abbreviation, **N.Y.**; postal abbreviation, **NY** Also, **New York State. 2.** the largest city and a major port of the United States, located in southern New York State. Pop., 7,322,564. Also, **New York City.** —**New York′er.**

New York Bay, a bay of the Atlantic, south of New York City, at the mouth of the Hudson River.

New York State Barge Canal, a toll-free system of canals in New York. It links the Hudson with Lakes Ontario, Erie, and Champlain.

New Zea·land (zē′lənd) an island country in the southern Pacific, east of Australia. Capital, Wellington. Area, 103,787 sq mi (268,808 sq km). Pop., 3,307,084. —**New Zea′land·er.**

Ni·ag·a·ra (nī ag′rə, -ag′ər ə) **1.** a river on which the Niagara Falls is located, flowing from Lake Erie into Lake Ontario. Length, 36 mi (58 km). **2.** see **Niagara Falls.**

Niagara Falls 1. a waterfall on the Niagara River, between the United States and Canada. Height, 167 ft (51 m). **2.** a city in western New York, located on the Niagara River at the falls, noted as a tourist center. Pop., 61,840. **3.** a city in southern Ontario, Canada, opposite Niagara Falls, New York. Pop., 72,107.

Nia·mey (nyä mā′) the capital and largest city of Niger, in the southwestern part of the country. Pop., 398,265.

Ni·cae·a (nī sē′ə) an ancient town in Asia Minor, the site of two Christian church councils. —**Ni·cae·an** (nī sē′ən), adj., n. —**Ni·cene** (nī sēn′, nī′sēn), adj.

Nic·a·ra·gua (nik′ə rä′gwə) **1.** the largest country of Central America. Capital, Managua. Area, 50,200 sq mi (130,000 sq km). Pop., 3,272,100. **2. Lake.** a lake in southern Nicaragua, the largest lake in Central America. —**Nic′a·ra′guan,** adj., n.

Nice (nēs) a resort city in southeastern France, on the Mediterranean. Pop., 337,085.

Nic·o·bar Islands (nik′ə bär′) see **Andaman and Nicobar Islands.**

Nic·o·si·a (nik′ə sē′ə) the capital of Cyprus, in the central part of the country. Pop., 48,221.

Ni·ger (nī′jər) **1.** a landlocked country in western Africa. Capital, Niamey. Area, 489,200 sq mi (1,267,028 sq km). Pop., 7,250,383. **2.** a river flowing from western Africa into the Gulf of Guinea. Length, 2,600 mi (4,183 km).

Ni·ge·ri·a (nī jir′ē ə) a country in western Africa, on the Gulf of Guinea. Capital, Abuja. Area, 356,669 sq mi (923,773 sq km). Pop., 101,907,000. —**Ni·ge′ri·an,** adj., n.

Nile (nīl) the longest river in the world, flowing through east-central and northeastern Africa to the Mediterranean. Length, 4,150 mi (6,677 km).

Nîmes (nēm) a city in southeastern France, the site of Roman ruins. Pop., 124,220.

Nin·e·veh (nin′ə və) the capital of ancient Assyria. It lay on the east bank of the Tigris River, in what is now northern Iraq.

Ning·xia (ning′shyä′) also, **Ning·hsia.** an autonomous region in north-central China. Capital, Yinchuan. Area, 30,000 sq mi (77,700 sq km). Pop., 4,350,000. Also, **Ningxia Hui·zu Autonomous Region** (hwē′dzü′).

Nip·i·gon, Lake (nip′i gon′) a lake in western Ontario, Canada, north of Lake Superior.

Nip·pon (nip′on) see **Japan.** —**Nip·pon·ese** (nip′ə nēz′, -nēs′), adj., n.

Niš (nēsh) also, **Nish.** a city in Serbia. Pop., 168,400.

Ni·te·rói (nē′tə roi′) a city in southeastern Brazil. Pop., 441,684.

Ni·u·e (nē ü′ā) an island in the southern Pacific, a possession of New Zealand. Land area, 102 sq mi (264 sq km). Pop., 2,531.

Nizh·ni Nov·go·rod (nizh′nē nôv′gə rôd′) a city in Russia, on the Volga River. Pop., 1,438,000. Formerly, **Gorki.**

Nome (nōm) a port city in western Alaska. Pop., 3,500.

Nor·folk (nôr′fək) **1.** a city in southeastern Virginia. Pop., 261,229. **2.** a county in eastern England, bordering on the North Sea. Pop., 744,400.

Norfolk Island, an Australian island in the southern Pacific. Area, 14 sq mi (36 sq km). Pop., 2,000.

Nor·man·dy (nôr′mən dē) a historic region and former province in northwestern France, bordering the English Channel. Area, 11,820 sq mi (30,614 sq km).

North (nôrth) the region of the United States north of Maryland, the Ohio River, and the Missouri, esp. the Northern states that fought against the Confederacy in the Civil War.

North America, the third largest continent, consisting of all the land between the Atlantic and Pacific oceans north of the Panama-Colombia border, including Mexico, the continental United States, and Canada. Area, approx. 9,362,000 sq mi (24,248,000 sq km). Pop., 431,000,000. —**North American.**

North·amp·ton (nôr thamp′tən, nôrth hamp′-) a city in central England. Pop., 154,172.

North·amp·ton·shire (nôr thamp′tən shir′, -shər, nôrth hamp′-) a county in central England. Pop., 570,300.

North Carolina, a state in the southeastern United States, on the Atlantic. Capital, Raleigh. Area, 52,669 sq mi (136,413 sq km). Pop., 6,628,637. Abbreviation, **N.C.**; postal abbreviation, **NC** —**North Car·o·lin·i·an** (kar′ə lin′ē ən).

North Charleston, a city in southeastern South Carolina. Pop., 70,218.

North Dakota, a state in the north-central United States. Capital, Bismarck. Area, 70,702 sq mi (183,118 sq km). Pop., 638,800. Abbreviations, **N. Dak., N.D.**; postal abbreviation, **ND** —**North Dakotan.**

North·east (nôrth′ēst′) the northeastern part of the United States, esp. New England and New York.

Northern Ireland, a political division of the United Kingdom, occupying the northeast corner of the island of Ireland. Capital, Belfast. Area, 5,452 sq mi (14,121 sq km). Pop., 1,575,200.

Northern Mariana Islands, a group of 16 islands in the western Pacific, a commonwealth territory of the United States. Capital, Saipan. Land area, 244 sq mi (632 sq km). Pop., 16,780. Also, **Northern Marianas.**

Northern Rhodesia, see **Zambia.**

Northern Territory, a territory in the north-central part of Australia. Capital, Darwin. Area, 523,620 sq mi (1,356,176 sq km). Pop., 156,300.

North Island, the smaller of the two main islands of New Zealand. Area, 44,281 sq mi (114,688 sq km).

North Korea, a country occupying the northern part of the Korean peninsula. Official name: **Democratic People's Republic of Korea.** Capital, Pyongyang. Area, 46,540 sq mi (120,539 sq km). Pop., 18,317,000.

North Las Vegas, a city in southeastern Nevada. Pop., 47,707.

North Little Rock, a city in central Arkansas. Pop., 61,741.

North Sea, a large arm of the Atlantic, between Great Britain and continental Europe.

North Slope, a region of northern Alaska bordering the Arctic Ocean, the site of rich oil deposits.

North·um·ber·land (nôr thum′bər lənd) the northernmost county in England. Pop., 301,400.

North·um·bri·a (nôr thum′brē ə) an ancient Anglo-Saxon kingdom in what is now northern England and southeastern Scotland.

North Vietnam, see **Vietnam.**

North·west (nôrth′west′) the northwestern part of the United States, esp. Idaho, Oregon, and Washington.

Northwest Passage, a sea route along the north coast of North America, connecting the Atlantic and Pacific.

Northwest Territories, an administrative division of Canada, in the northern part of the country. Capital, Yellowknife. Area, 1,304,903 sq mi (3,379,699 sq km). Pop., 52,238.

Northwest Territory, a U.S. territory organized in 1787, consisting of the land between the Ohio and Mississippi rivers that now forms Illinois, Indiana, Michigan, Ohio, Wisconsin, and part of Minnesota.

North York, a city in southern Ontario, Canada. Pop., 556,297.

Nor·walk (nôr′wôk′) 1. a city in southern California. Pop., 94,279. 2. a city in southwestern Connecticut. Pop., 78,331.

Nor·way (nôr′wā′) a country in northern Europe occupying the western and northernmost part of the Scandinavian peninsula. Capital, Oslo. Area, 125,057 sq mi (323,898 sq km). Pop., 4,190,000.

Nor·we·gian Sea (nôr wē′jən) the part of the Arctic Ocean east of Greenland and Iceland and west of Norway.

Nor·wich (nôr′ich) a city in eastern England. Pop., 169,814.

Not·ting·ham (not′ing əm) a city in central England. Pop., 273,300.

Not·ting·ham·shire (not′ing əm shîr′, -shər) a county in north-central England. Pop., 1,007,000.

Nouak·chott (nwäk′shot′) the capital of Mauritania, in the western part of the country. Pop., 285,000.

Nou·mé·a (nü mā′ə) the capital of New Caledonia, a seaport on the southwest coast of the island. Pop., 65,110.

No·va I·gua·çu (nō′və ē′gwä sü′) a city in southeastern Brazil. Pop., 592,800.

No·va Lis·bo·a (nō′və lēzh bō′ə) see **Huambo.**

No·va Sco·tia (nō′və skō′shə) a province of Canada, in the southeastern part of the country. Capital, Halifax. Area, 21,425 sq mi (55,491 sq km). Pop., 873,199.

No·vi Sad (nō′vē säd′) a city in northern Serbia, on the Danube. Pop., 176,000.

No·vo·kuz·netsk (nō′və küz netsk′) a city in south-central Russia. Pop., 600,000.

No·vo·si·birsk (nō′və sə bîrsk′) a city in south-central Russia. Pop., 1,436,000.

Nu·bi·a (nü′bē ə, nü′-) an ancient country in what is now southern Egypt and northern Sudan.

Nubian Desert, a desert region in the northeastern part of the Sudan, extending from the Red Sea to the Nile.

Nue·vo Le·ón (nwä′vō lā ōn′, nü ā′-) a state in northeastern Mexico. Area, 25,136 sq mi (65,102 sq km). Pop., 2,513,044.

Nu·ku·a·lo·fa (nü′kü ə lō′fə) the capital and chief port of Tonga. Pop., 21,265.

Nu·rem·berg (nûr′əm bûrg′) a city in south-central Germany, site of the trial of prominent Nazis for war crimes after World War II. Pop., 480,078. Also, *German,* **Nürn·berg** (nYRn′beRk).

Nuuk (nük) the capital and largest city of Greenland, located on the southwestern coast. Pop., 12,217. Formerly, **Godthåb.**

Ny·as·a, Lake (nī as′ə) a large lake in southeastern Africa. Also, **Lake Malawi.**

Ny·as·a·land (nī as′ə land′) a former British protectorate in southern Africa, now Malawi.

O·a·hu (ō ä′hü) the third largest island of Hawaii. Honolulu is located on Oahu. Area, 593 sq mi (1,536 sq km).

Oak·land (ōk′lənd) a city in western California, on San Francisco Bay, opposite San Francisco. Pop., 372,242.

Oak Ridge, a city in eastern Tennessee, a major atomic research and production center. Pop., 27,310.

Oak·ville (ōk′vil′) a town in southern Ontario, Canada. Pop., 87,107.

Oa·xa·ca (wə hä′kə) a state in southern Mexico. Area, 36,375 sq mi (94,211 sq km). Pop., 2,369,076.

Ob (ob) a river in western Siberia, flowing northwest and north to the Arctic Ocean. Length, 2,500 mi (4,023 km).

O·ber·am·mer·gau (ō′bər ä′mər gou′) a village in southern Germany, noted for the Passion play performed there every ten years. Pop., 4,980.

O·ber·hau·sen (ō′bər hou′zən) a city in western Germany. Pop., 221,017.

O·ce·an·i·a (ō′shē an′ē ə) the islands of the Pacific, including Melanesia, Micronesia, and Polynesia, and sometimes including Australia, New Zealand, New Guinea, and the Malay Archipelago. Also, **O·ce·an·i·ca** (ō′shē an′i kə). —**O′ce·an′i·an,** *adj., n.*

O·cean·side (ō′shən sīd′) a city in southern California. Pop., 128,398.

O·den·se (ō′dən sə) a city in southern Denmark. Pop., 140,100.

O·des·sa (ō des′ə) a port city on the Black Sea in southwestern Ukraine. Pop., 1,115,000.

Og·bo·mo·sho (og′bə mō′shō) a city in southwestern Nigeria. Pop., 582,900.

Og·den (og′dən) a city in northern Utah. Pop., 63,909.

O·hi·o (ō hī′ō) 1. a state in the north-central United States. Capital, Columbus. Area, 41,330 sq mi (107,045 sq km). Pop., 10,847,115. Postal abbreviation, **OH 2.** a river in the east-central United States, flowing from Pittsburgh southwest into the Mississippi. Length, 981 mi (1,578 km). —**O·hi′o·an,** *adj., n.*

O·ka (ō kä′) a river in west-central Russia, flowing northeast to the Volga at Nizhni Novgorod. Length, 932 mi (1,500 km).

O·ka·ya·ma (ō′kä yä′mä) a city in Japan, in the southwestern part of the island of Honshu. Pop., 572,479.

O·khotsk, Sea of (ō kotsk′) an arm of the Pacific, on the east coast of Russia.

O·ki·na·wa (ō′kə nä′wə) a Japanese island in the Pacific, occupied by the United States from 1945 to 1972. It was the site of a major battle of World War II in 1945. Area, 454 sq mi (1,176 sq km). Pop., 1,202,083.

O·kla·ho·ma (ō′klə hō′mə) a state in the south-central United States. Capital, Oklahoma City. Area, 69,856 sq mi (180,927 sq km). Pop., 3,145,585. Abbreviation, **Okla.;** postal abbreviation, **OK** —**O′kla·ho′man,** *adj., n.*

Oklahoma City, the capital of Oklahoma, in the central part of the state. Pop., 444,719.

Old Delhi, see **Delhi.**

Old·ham (ōl′dəm) a city in central England. Pop., 107,095.

Ol·du·vai Gorge (ôl′dü vī′) a canyon in northern Tanzania, west of Mount Kilimanjaro. Many fossilized human remains have been found there.

O·lin·da (ō lin′də) a city in northeastern Brazil. Pop., 316,600.

Olives, Mount of, a mountain east of Jerusalem. The garden of Gethsemane is at the foot of this mountain. Also, **Ol·i·vet** (ol′ə-vet′).

O·lym·pi·a (ō lim′pē ə) 1. the capital of Washington, in the western part of the state. Pop., 33,840. 2. a plain in southwestern Greece, site of the ancient Olympic games.

O·lym·pic Mountains (ō lim′pik) a mountain range in northwestern Washington, one of the Coast Ranges.

O·lym·pus, Mount (ō lim′pəs) a mountain in northeastern Greece that, in Greek mythology, was regarded as the home of the twelve major gods.

O·ma·ha (ō′mə hä′, -hô′) a city in eastern Nebraska. Pop., 335,795.

O·man (ō män′) 1. a country in Asia, located on the southeastern coast of the peninsula of Arabia. Capital, Muscat. Area, 82,030 sq mi (212,458 sq km). Pop., 919,000. Formerly, **Muscat and Oman. 2. Gulf of.** an arm of the Arabian Sea, located between Oman and Iran.

Om·dur·man (om′dùr män′) a city in north-central Sudan, on the Nile. Pop., 526,287.

Omsk (ômsk) a city in central Russia. Pop., 1,148,000.

O·nit·sha (ō nich′ə) a city in south-central Nigeria, on the Niger River. Pop., 298,200.

On·tar·i·o (on târ′ē ō) 1. Lake. the smallest and easternmost of

a	at	e	end	o	hot	u	up	hw	white		about
ā	ape	ē	me	ō	old	ū	use	ng	song		taken
ä	far	i	it	ô	fork	ü	rule	th	thin	ə	pencil
âr	care	ī	ice	oi	oil	ù	pull	th	this		lemon
		îr	pierce	ou	out	ûr	turn	zh	measure		circus

the Great Lakes, between New York and Canada. **2.** a province of Canada, in the southeastern part of the country, north of the Great Lakes. Capital, Toronto. Area, 412,582 sq mi (1,068,587 sq km). Pop., 9,113,515. **3.** a city in southern California. Pop., 133,179.

O·phir (ō′fər) in the Bible, a region famous for its gold and other valuable products.

O·por·to (ō pôr′tō) a port city in northwestern Portugal. Pop., 327,368. Also, **Porto.**

O·ra·dea (ô ʀä′dyä) a city in northwestern Romania. Pop., 213,846.

O·ran (ô ran′) a port city in northwestern Algeria, on the Mediterranean. Pop., 628,558. Also, **Ouahran, Wahran.**

Or·ange (ôr′inj, or′-) a city in southern California. Pop., 110,658.

Orange Free State, a province of the Republic of South Africa, in the east-central part of the country. Area, 49,866 sq mi (129,153 sq km). Pop., 1,958,462.

Orange River, a river in southern Africa, flowing from Lesotho through central South Africa and along the Namibia-South Africa border to the Atlantic. Length, 1,155 mi (1,858 km).

O·ran·je·stad (ô rän′jə stat′) the capital of Aruba. Pop., 19,800.

Or·dzho·ni·kid·ze (ôr jon′i kid′zə) see **Vladikavkaz.**

Or·e·gon (ôr′i gən, -gon′, or′-) a state in the northwestern United States, on the Pacific. Capital, Salem. Area, 97,073 sq mi (251,419 sq km). Pop., 2,842,321. Abbreviations, **Oreg., Ore.;** postal abbreviation, **OR** —**Or·e·go·ni·an** (ôr′i gō′nē ən, or′-), *n.*

O·re Mountains (ôr′ə, ôr) see **Erzgebirge.**

O·ri·no·co (ôr′ə nō′kō) a large river in South America, flowing through Venezuela into the Atlantic. Length, 1,600 mi (2,575 km).

O·ri·za·ba, Mount (ôr′ə zä′bə) an extinct volcano southeast of Mexico City, the highest mountain in Mexico. Height, 18,701 ft (5,700 m).

Ork·ney Islands (ôrk′nē) a group of islands off the northern coast of Scotland. Land area, 376 sq mi (974 sq km).

Or·lan·do (ôr lan′dō) a city in east-central Florida. Pop., 164,693.

Or·lé·ans (ôr′lē ənz, ôʀ lā än′) a historic city in north-central France, on the Loire. It was saved by Joan of Arc from an English siege in 1429, during the Hundred Years War. Pop., 102,710.

Or·muz, Strait of (ôr müz′) see **Hormuz, Strait of.**

O·ru·mi·yeh (ùr′ü mē ye′) a city in northwestern Iran. Pop., 300,746. Also, **Urmia.**

O·sa·ka (ō sä′kə) a port city in Japan, on the southwest coast of the island of Honshu. Pop., 2,636,249.

O·sas·co (ù säs′kù) a city in southwestern Brazil. Pop., 591,546.

Osh·a·wa (osh′ə wə) a city in southern Ontario, Canada, on Lake Ontario. Pop., 123,651.

Osh·kosh (osh′kosh) a city in eastern Wisconsin. Pop., 55,006.

O·shog·bo (ō shog′bō) a city in southwestern Nigeria. Pop., 380,800.

O·si·jek (ō′sē yek′) a city in Croatia. Pop., 106,800.

Os·lo (os′lō, oz′-) the capital and principal city of Norway, in the southeastern part of the country. Pop., 452,415. Formerly, **Christiania.**

Os·ti·a (os′tē ə) an ancient Roman city at the mouth of the Tiber, the seaport of ancient Rome.

Os·tra·va (ôs′trə və) a city in north-central Czechoslovakia. Pop., 331, 557.

Os·wie·cim (osh vyen′tsim) see **Auschwitz.**

Ot·ta·wa (ot′ə wə) **1.** the capital of Canada, in the southeastern part of the country, in Ontario. Pop., 300,763. **2.** a river in southern Canada, flowing southeast along the Ontario-Quebec border to the St. Lawrence River. Length, 696 mi (1,120 km).

Ot·to·man Empire (ot′ə mən) a Turkish empire that lasted from 1289 to 1922 and included part of eastern Europe, Asia Minor, northern Africa, the eastern Mediterranean, and other parts of the Middle East.

Oua·ga·dou·gou (wä′gə dü′gü) the capital of Burkina Faso, in the central part of the country. Pop., 441,514.

Ouah·ran (wä rän′) see **Oran.**

Outer Mongolia, a historic region in north-central Asia, now the country of Mongolia.

O·ver·land Park (ō′vər lənd) a city in eastern Kansas. Pop., 111,790.

O·vie·do (ô vye′thô) a city in northwestern Spain. Pop., 168,900.

O·wens·bor·o (ō′ənz bûr′ō, -bur′ō) a city in northwestern Kentucky. Pop., 53,549.

Ox·ford (oks′fərd) a city in south-central England, on the Thames. Pop., 113,847.

Ox·ford·shire (oks′fərd shîr′, -shər) a county in south-central England. Pop., 578,900.

Ox·nard (oks′närd) a city in southern California. Pop., 142,216.

O·zark Mountains (ō′zärk) a low, hilly area in southern Missouri, northern Arkansas, and northeastern Oklahoma. Also, **O·zarks** (ō′zärks).

Pa·cif·ic (pə sif′ik) an ocean bordered by North and South America on the east and by Asia and Australia on the west, the largest body of water in the world. Also, **Pacific Ocean.**

Pacific Islands, Trust Territory of the, a U.S. trust territory of more than 2,100 islands in the Pacific, consisting of the Northern Mariana Islands, Marshall Islands, Palau, and the Federated States of Micronesia. Land area, 717 sq mi (1,857 sq km). Pop., 169,000.

Pa·dang (pä däng′) a seaport in Indonesia, in the western part of Sumatra. Pop., 405,600.

Pad·u·a (paj′ü ə) a city in northeastern Italy. Pop., 225,769.

Pa·go Pa·go (päng′ō päng′ō, päng′gō päng′gō, pä′gō pä′gō) *also,* **Pango Pango.** the capital of American Samoa. Pop., 3,075.

Painted Desert, an arid region in northeastern Arizona, noted for its multicolored rock formations.

Pa·ki·stan (pak′ə stan′) a country in southern Asia. Capital, Islamabad. Area, 310,724 sq mi (804,775 sq km). Pop., 84,253,644. —**Pak·i·stan·i** (pak′ə stan′ē), *adj., n.*

Pa·lat·i·nate (pə lat′ə nāt′, -nit) **1.** either of two regions in Germany, the Lower or Rhenish Palatinate that extends from the left bank of the Rhine to France, the Saarland, and Luxembourg; and the Upper Palatinate in northern Bavaria that extends from Czechoslovakia to the Danube. **2.** see **Rhenish-Palatinate.**

Pal·a·tine Hill (pal′ə tīn′, -tin) one of the seven hills on which ancient Rome was built.

Pa·lau (pä lou′) a group of Pacific islands administered by the United States. Capital, Koror. Land area, 171 sq mi (443 sq km). Pop., 13,873. Also, **Belau.**

Pa·la·wan (pä lä′wän) an island in the southwestern Philippines. Area, 4,550 sq mi (11,785 sq km).

Pa·lem·bang (pä′ləm bäng′) a city in Indonesia, in the southern part of the island of Sumatra. Pop., 874,000.

Pa·ler·mo (pə lâr′mō) the capital and largest city of Sicily, a port in the northwestern part of the island. Pop., 723,732.

Pal·es·tine (pal′ə stīn′) **1.** a region in southwestern Asia between the Mediterranean Sea and the Jordan River. In biblical times it was the land of the Jews. Also, **Holy Land. 2.** a former territory in this region, placed under a British mandate following World War I. It was divided into Israel, the Jordanian-controlled West Bank, and the Egyptian-controlled Gaza Strip in 1949. Israel has occupied the West Bank and Gaza Strip since 1967. —**Pal·es·tin·i·an** (pal′ə stin′ē ən), *adj., n.*

Pal·i·sades (pal′ə sādz′) a series of high, columnar cliffs along the western bank of the lower Hudson River in New Jersey and New York.

Pal·ma (päl′mä) a port city on the Spanish island of Mallorca. Pop., 249,000. Also, **Palma de Mallorca.**

Palm Beach, a resort in southeastern Florida. Pop., 9,814.

Pal·my·ra (pal mī′rə) an ancient city in central Syria, now in ruins.

Pal·o Al·to (pal′ō al′tō) a city in western California, on San Francisco Bay. Pop., 55,900.

Pal·o·mar, Mount (pal′ə mär′) a peak in southern California, near San Diego, site of an astronomical observatory with a 200-inch telescope. Height, 6,140 ft (1,871 m).

Pa·mirs (pä mirz′) a mountain range in central Asia, extending from northeastern Afghanistan through Tajikistan and Kyrgyzstan to eastern China.

Pam·li·co Sound (pam′li kō′) a shallow inlet of the Atlantic in eastern North Carolina, lying between the mainland and a chain of offshore islands.

Pam·plo·na (pam plō′nə) a city in northern Spain. Pop., 180,598.

Pan·a·ma (pan′ə mä′) **1. Isthmus of.** a narrow strip of land connecting North and South America. **2.** a country on the Isthmus of Panama. Capital, Panama. Area, 29,762 sq mi (77,084 sq km). Pop., 2,315,047. **3.** the capital of Panama, a port on the Pacific coast. Pop., 411,549. Also *(def. 3),* **Panama City.** —**Pan·a·ma·ni·an** (pan′ə mä′nē ən), *adj., n.*

Panama Canal, a ship canal across the Isthmus of Panama, connecting the Atlantic and Pacific.

Panama Canal Zone, see **Canal Zone.**

Panama City, see **Panama** *(def. 3).*

Pa·nay (pə nī′) an island in the central Philippines. Area, 4,446 sq mi (11,515 sq km).

Pan·ge·a (pan jē′ə) *also,* **Pan·gae·a.** a huge prehistoric conti-

nent that is believed to have included all of the earth's present-day continents; it is thought to have broken up about 200 million years ago into the continents of Gondwanaland and Laurasia.

Pang·o Pang·o (päng′ō päng′ō, päng′gō päng′gō) see **Pago Pago.**

Pao·t'ou (bou′tō′) see **Baotou.**

Pa·pal States (pā′pəl) a former territory in central Italy, ruled by the popes from 755 to 1870. Also, **States of the Church.**

Pa·pe·e·te (pä′pē ā′tā) the capital of French Polynesia, a port on the island of Tahiti. Pop., 23,555.

Pap·u·a (pap′yə wə, pä′pü ə) see **New Guinea.**

Papua New Guinea, a country in the southwestern Pacific consisting of the eastern part of New Guinea, the Bismarck Archipelago, and various nearby islands. Capital, Port Moresby. Land area, 178,704 sq mi (462,843 sq km). Pop., 3,479,400.

Par·a·guay (par′ə gwā′, -gwī′) **1.** a country in south-central South America. Capital, Asunción. Area, 157,048 sq mi (406,754 sq km). Pop., 3,279,000. **2.** the principal river of this country, flowing south from Brazil through Paraguay into the Paraná River. Length, 1,610 mi (2,590 km). —**Par′a·guay′an,** *adj., n.*

Par·a·í·ba (par′ə ē′bə) see **João Pessoa.**

Par·a·mar·i·bo (par′ə mar′ə bō′) the capital of Suriname, a port in the northern part of the country. Pop., 241,000.

Pa·ra·ná (par′ə nä′) **1.** a river in South America, flowing south through Brazil, Paraguay, and Argentina into the Río de la Plata. Length, 2,796 mi (7,242 km). **2.** a city in eastern Argentina, on the Paraná River. Pop., 161,638.

Par·is (par′is) the capital and largest city of France, in the north-central part of the country, on the Seine. Pop., 2,078,900. —**Pa·ri·sian** (pə rē′zhən), *adj., n.*

Par·ma (pär′mä) **1.** a city in north-central Italy. Pop., 175,842. **2.** a city in northeastern Ohio. Pop., 87,876.

Par·nas·sus, Mount (pär nas′əs) a mountain in southern Greece, held to be sacred to Apollo and the Muses in Greek mythology.

Par·os (par′os) a Greek island in the Aegean Sea, one of the Cyclades.

Par·thi·a (pär′thē ə) an ancient country in Asia southeast of the Caspian Sea, now a part of Iran. —**Par′thi·an,** *adj., n.*

Pas·a·de·na (pas′ə dē′nə) **1.** a city in southern California. Pop., 131,591. **2.** a city in southeastern Texas. Pop., 119,363.

Pa·say (pä′sī) a city in the Philippines, on Manila Bay in the east-central part of the island of Luzon. Pop., 354,000. Also, **Rizal City.**

Pa·sig (pä′sig) a city in the Philippines, in the east-central part of the island of Luzon. Pop., 318,853.

Pat·a·go·ni·a (pat′ə gō′nē ə) a region in southern Argentina, between the Andes and the Atlantic. Area, 300,000 sq mi (777,000 sq km). —**Pat′a·go′ni·an,** *adj., n.*

Pat·er·son (pat′ər sən) a city in northeastern New Jersey. Pop., 140,891.

Pat·na (put′nə) a city in eastern India, on the Ganges. Pop., 776,371.

Pa·tras (pä träs′, pat′rəs) a port city in western Greece, on the northern Peloponnesus. Pop., 142,163. Also, *Greek,* **Pa·trai** (pä′trē).

Paw·tuck·et (pô tuk′it) a city in northeastern Rhode Island. Pop., 72,644.

Peace River, a river in northern British Columbia and northern Alberta, Canada, flowing east and northeast to the Slave River. Length, 1,195 mi (1,923 km).

Pearl City, a city in Hawaii, on the island of Oahu. Pop., 30,993.

Pearl Harbor, an inlet on the island of Oahu, Hawaii, the site of the naval base that was bombed by the Japanese on December 7, 1941, causing the United States to enter World War II.

Pe·cos (pā′kəs) a river flowing from northern New Mexico southeast through Texas into the Rio Grande. Length, 735 mi (1,904 km).

Pei·ping (bā′ping′) see **Beijing.**

Pe·king (pē′king′) see **Beijing.**

Pel·o·pon·ne·sus (pel′ə pon′ē′səs) *also,* **Pel·o·pon·ne·sos.** a peninsula in southern Greece between the Ionian and Aegean seas.

Pem·ba (pem′bə) an island in the Indian Ocean, off the eastern coast of Africa, part of Tanzania. Area, 380 sq mi (984 sq km).

Pe·nang (pə nang′) see **Pinang.**

Pen·ch'i (bun′chē′) see **Benxi.** Also, **Pen·hsi** (bun′shē′), **Pen·ki** (bun′jē′).

Pen·nines (pen′īnz) **1.** a section of the Alps on the border of Switzerland and Italy. **2.** a chain of mountains in northern England, extending south from the Scottish border to Derbyshire.

Penn·syl·va·nia (pen′səl vān′yə) a state in the eastern United States. Capital, Harrisburg. Area, 45,308 sq mi (117,348 sq km). Pop., 11,881,643. Abbreviations, **Pa., Penn.;** postal abbreviation, **PA** —**Penn′syl·va′nian,** *adj., n.*

Pen·sa·co·la (pen′sə kō′lə) a port city in northwestern Florida, on the Gulf of Mexico. Pop., 58,165.

Pen·za (pen′zə) a city in central western Russia. Pop., 543,000.

Pe·o·ri·a (pē ôr′ē ə) a city in north-central Illinois. Pop., 133,504.

Perm (pûrm) a city in west-central Russia. Pop., 1,091,000. Formerly, **Molotov.**

Per·sia (pûr′zhə, -shə) **1.** a great ancient empire of southwestern Asia, extending from Egypt to the Indus River at its height in the sixth and fifth centuries B.C. Also, **Persian Empire. 2.** see **Iran.**

Persian Gulf, a shallow body of water between Iran and Arabia.

Perth (pûrth) the capital of Western Australia, a city in southwestern Australia, near the Indian Ocean. Pop., 1,158,387.

Pe·ru (pə rü′) a country on the western coast of South America. Capital, Lima. Area, 496,225 sq mi (1,285,223 sq km). Pop., 17,031,221. —**Pe·ru·vi·an** (pə rü′vē ən), *adj., n.*

Pe·sha·war (pə shä′wər) a city in northwestern Pakistan, near the Khyber Pass. Pop., 506,896.

Pe·ter·bor·ough, Soke of (sōk; pē′tər bûr′ō, -bur′ō) a former county in eastern England.

Petrified Forest National Park, a national park in eastern Arizona, noted for its petrified wood and American Indian ruins and petroglyphs. Area, 93,493 acres (37,837 hectares).

Pet·ro·grad (pet′rə grad′) see **St. Petersburg.**

Phil·a·del·phi·a (fil′ə del′fē ə) a city in southeastern Pennsylvania, on the Delaware River. Pop., 1,585,577.

Phi·lip·pi (fi lip′ī) an ancient city in Macedonia where, in 42 B.C., Octavian and Mark Antony defeated Brutus and Cassius.

Phil·ip·pines (fil′ə pēnz′, fil′ə pēnz′) an island country in the western Pacific, southeast of China. Capital, Manila. Land area, 115,800 sq mi (299,922 sq km). Pop., 60,477,000. Also, **Phil·ip·pine Islands.** —**Phil·ip·pine** (fil′ə pēn′, fil′ə pēn′), *adj.*

Phi·lis·ti·a (fə lis′tē ə) the land of the ancient Philistines, on the southwestern coast of Palestine.

Phnom Penh (pə nom′ pen′) the capital and largest city of Cambodia, an inland port in the south-central part of the country. Pop., 700,000. Also, **Pnompenh.**

Phoe·ni·cia (fə nē′shə) an ancient district on the eastern Mediterranean coast, in the area that is now Lebanon.

Phoe·nix (fē′niks) the capital and largest city of Arizona, in the south-central part of the state. Pop., 983,403.

Phryg·i·a (frij′ē ə) an ancient country in west-central Asia Minor, in what is now central Turkey. —**Phryg′i·an,** *adj., n.*

Pic·ar·dy (pik′ər dē) a historic region and former province of northern France.

Pied·mont (pēd′mont) **1.** a region of the eastern United States, extending from northern New Jersey to central Alabama and sloping seaward from the Appalachian Mountains to the Atlantic coastal plain. **2.** a region in northwestern Italy, bordering France and Switzerland.

Pierre (pîr) the capital of South Dakota, in the central part of the state. Pop., 12,906.

Pike's Peak (pīks) a mountain of the Rocky Mountains, in central Colorado. Height, 14,110 ft (4,301 m).

Pillars of Hercules, the Rock of Gibraltar and the mountain of Jebel Musa, located on opposite sides of the eastern end of the Strait of Gibraltar.

Pil·sen (pil′zən) see **Plzeň**

Pi·nang (pə nang′) *also,* **Penang. 1.** an island in Malaysia, off the western coast of the Malay Peninsula. Area, 108 sq mi (280 sq km). **2.** a port city on this island. Pop., 248,241. Formerly *(def. 2),* **George Town.**

Pine Bluff, a city in south-central Arkansas. Pop., 57,140.

Pi·rae·us (pī rē′əs, pə rā′-) the principal seaport of Greece, and port of nearby Athens, in the eastern part of the country. Pop., 196,389.

Pi·sa (pē′zə) a city in central Italy. Pop., 104,384.

Pis·gah, Mount (piz′gə) in the Bible, a mountain ridge in Jordan; its summit is Mount Nebo.

Pish·pek (pish pek′) the capital of Kyrgyzstan, in the northern part of the republic. Pop., 616,000. Formerly, **Frunze.**

Pit·cairn Island (pit′kârn) a small British island in the southern Pacific, uninhabited until 1790, when it was settled by mutineers from the HMS *Bounty.* Area, 2 sq mi (5 sq km). Pop., 59.

Pitts·burgh (pits′bûrg) a city in southwestern Pennsylvania, the leading center of U.S. iron and steel production. Pop., 369,879.

a	at	e	end	o	hot	u	up	hw	white		about
ā	ape	ē	me	ō	old	ū	use	ng	song		taken
ä	far	i	it	ô	fork	ü	rule	th	thin	ə	pencil
âr	care	ī	ice	oi	oil	u̇	pull	t͟h	this		lemon
		îr	pierce	ou	out	ûr	turn	zh	measure		circus

Pitts·field (pits′fēld′) a city in western Massachusetts. Pop., 48,622.

Platte (plat) a river flowing east from central Nebraska into the Missouri. Length, 310 mi (499 km).

Pleasant Island, see Nauru.

Plov·div (plôv dif′) a city in south-central Bulgaria. Pop., 349,148.

Plym·outh (plim′əth) **1.** a town in southeastern Massachusetts, on the Atlantic, settled in 1620 by the Pilgrims. Pop., 45,608. **2.** a seaport in southwestern England, on the English Channel. Pop., 238,583. **3.** the capital of Montserrat. Pop., 1,568.

Pl·zeň (pul′zen yə) a city in western Czechoslovakia. Pop., 175,038. Also, *German,* **Pilsen.**

Pnom·penh (nom′pen′, pə nom′pen′) see Phnom Penh.

Po (pō) the largest and longest river in Italy, in the northern part of the country, flowing into the Adriatic. Length, over 400 mi (640 km).

Po·ca·tel·lo (pō′kə tel′ō) a city in southeastern Idaho. Pop., 46,080.

Pointe-à-Pi·tre (pwaɴ tä pē′tRə) a city in Guadeloupe. Pop., 25,310.

Pointe-Noire (pwaɴt nwäR′) a port city in the southwestern part of the Republic of the Congo, on the Atlantic. Pop., 294,203.

Po·land (pō′lənd) a country in central Europe, on the Baltic Sea. Capital, Warsaw. Area, 120,725 sq mi (312,678 sq km). Pop., 37,775,100.

Polish Corridor, a narrow strip of land taken from Germany and given to Poland after World War I to give Poland access to the Baltic Sea.

Pol·ta·va (pul tä′və) a city in southwestern Ukraine. Pop., 315,000.

Pol·y·ne·sia (pol′ə nē′zhə) one of the three main divisions of the Pacific islands, located in the central and southern part of the Pacific, east of Melanesia and Micronesia.

Pom·er·a·ni·a (pom′ə rā′nē ə) a historic region of north-central Europe, in northwestern Poland and northeastern Germany, along the Baltic Sea.

Po·mo·na (pə mō′nə) a city in southwestern California. Pop., 131,723.

Pom·peii (pom pā′) a partially excavated ancient city in southwestern Italy, near Naples. It was buried by the eruption of Mount Vesuvius in A.D. 79.

Pon·ce (pon sā′) a port city in southern Puerto Rico. Pop., 161,739.

Pont·char·train, Lake (pon′chər trān′) a lake in southeastern Louisiana.

Pon·ti·ac (pon′tē ak′) a city in southeastern Michigan. Pop., 71,166.

Pon·ti·a·nak (pon′tē ä′näk) a seaport in Indonesia, in the western part of Borneo. Pop., 343,000.

Pon·tus (pon′təs) an ancient kingdom on the southern shore of the Black Sea.

Poo·na (pü′nə) a city in western India. Pop., 1,203,351.

Po·po·cat·e·petl (pō′pə kat′ə pet′əl) a volcano in south-central Mexico. Height, 17,887 ft (5,452 m).

Port Ar·thur (är′thər) see Lushun.

Port-au-Prince (pôrt′ō prins′) the capital of Haiti, in the southwestern part of the country, on the Caribbean. Pop., 797,000.

Port E·liz·a·beth (i liz′ə bəth) a port city on the southern coast of the Republic of South Africa. Pop., 272,844.

Port Har·court (här′kərt, -kôrt′) a city in southeastern Nigeria, in the Niger delta. Pop., 327,300.

Port·land (pôrt′lənd) **1.** the largest city and chief port of Maine, in the southwestern part of the state. Pop., 64,358. **2.** the largest city and chief port of Oregon, in the northwestern part of the state. Pop., 437,319.

Port Lou·is (lü′is, lü′ē) the capital and largest city of Mauritius. Pop., 139,730.

Port Mores·by (môrz′bē) the capital of Papua New Guinea, in the southeastern part of New Guinea. Pop., 152,100.

Por·to (pôr′tō) see Oporto.

Pôr·to A·le·gre (pôr′tō ə lā′grə) a port city in southern Brazil. Pop., 1,272,121.

Port-of-Spain (pôrt′ov spän′) *also,* **Port of Spain.** the capital and chief port of Trinidad and Tobago, in the northwestern part of the island of Trinidad. Pop., 50,878.

Por·to-No·vo (pôr′tō nō′vō) the capital of Benin, in the southeastern part of the country. Pop., 164,000.

Por·to Ri·co (pôr′tō rē′kō) see Puerto Rico.

Port Sa·id (sä ēd′) a port city in northeastern Egypt, at the Mediterranean end of the Suez Canal. Pop., 399,793.

Ports·mouth (pôrts′məth) **1.** a port city and naval base in southeastern Virginia. Pop., 103,907. **2.** a port city in southern England, on the English Channel. Pop., 174,218.

Port Sudan, a city in northeastern Sudan, a port on the Red Sea. Pop., 206,727.

Por·tu·gal (pôr′chə gəl) a country in southwestern Europe, in the western part of the Iberian Peninsula, on the Atlantic. Capital, Lisbon. Area, 35,672 sq mi (92,390 sq km). Pop., 9,833,014.

Por·tu·guese East Africa (pôr′chə gēz′, -gēs′) a former Portuguese colony in southeastern Africa, now Mozambique.

Portuguese Guinea, a former Portuguese colony in western Africa, now Guinea-Bissau.

Portuguese West Africa, a former Portuguese colony on the west coast of Africa, now Angola.

Po·sen (pō′zən) see Poznań.

Po·to·mac (pə tō′mək) a river in the eastern United States, flowing through West Virginia, Virginia, and Maryland to the Chesapeake Bay. Length, 285 mi (459 km).

Pots·dam (pots′dam) a city in eastern Germany, west of Berlin, site of a meeting of the heads of the three major Allied governments after World War II. Pop., 142,862.

Poz·nań (pōz′nan, pôz′nän yə) a city in western Poland. Pop., 586,500. Also, *German,* **Posen.**

Prague (präg) the capital and largest city of Czechoslovakia, in the western part of the country. Pop., 1,215,656.

Prai·a (prī′ə) the capital of Cape Verde. Pop., 61,797.

Pra·to (prä′tō) a city in central Italy. Pop., 164,595.

Pre·to·ri·a (pri tôr′ē ə) the administrative capital of the Republic of South Africa, in the northeastern part of the country. Pop., 443,059.

Prib·i·lof Islands (prib′i lôf′) an island group in Alaska, located in the southeastern Bering Sea.

Prince Ed·ward Island (ed′wərd) the smallest province of Canada, consisting of an island in the Gulf of St. Lawrence. Capital, Charlottetown. Area, 2,184 sq mi (5,657 sq km). Pop., 126,646.

Prince George (jôrj) a city on the Fraser River in central British Columbia, Canada. Pop., 67,621.

Pro·vence (pRô väns′) a historic region and former province in southeastern France, bordering the Mediterranean Sea.

Prov·i·dence (prov′i dəns) the capital and largest city of Rhode Island, in the eastern part of the state. Pop., 160,728.

Pro·vo (prō′vō) a city in north-central Utah. Pop., 86,835.

Prud·hoe Bay (prü′dō) an inlet of the Arctic Ocean in northern Alaska, the site of a major oil field.

Prus·sia (prush′ə) a historic German kingdom and former state in northern Germany, formally dissolved in 1947 and now divided among Germany, Poland, and Russia.

Pueb·la (pweb′lə) **1.** a state in south-central Mexico. Area, 13,126 sq mi (33,996 sq km). Pop., 3,347,685. **2.** a city in central Mexico. Pop., 835,759.

Pueb·lo (pweb′lō) a city in south-central Colorado. Pop., 98,640.

Puer·to Ri·co (pwer′tō rē′kō, pôr′tə) an island in the West Indies, a commonwealth of the United States. Capital, San Juan. Area, 3,515 sq mi (9,104 sq km). Pop., 3,196,520. Abbreviation, P.R.; postal abbreviation, PR Also, **Porto Rico.** —**Puer′to Ri′can.**

Pu·get Sound (pū′jit) an inlet of the Pacific, extending into the northwestern part of the state of Washington.

Pu·rús (pü rüs′) a river in South America, flowing through Peru and Brazil into the Amazon. Length, 1,900 mi (3,060 km).

Pu·san (pü′sän′) the chief port of South Korea, on the southeastern coast of the country. Pop., 3,773,000.

Pyong·yang (pyung′yäng′) the capital of North Korea, in the west-central part of the country. Pop., 1,283,000.

Pyr·e·nees (pir′ə nēz′) a mountain range in southwestern Europe extending along the border of France and Spain from the Bay of Biscay to the Mediterranean Sea. —**Pyr′e·ne′an,** *adj.*

Qa·cen·ti·na (kä′sen tē′nə) see Constantine.

Qa·tar (kä′tär, kə tär′) a country in southwestern Asia, on the Persian Gulf coast of the peninsula of Arabia. Capital, Doha. Area, 4,250 sq mi (11,000 sq km). Pop., 369,079. —**Qa·tar·i** (kə tär′ē), *adj., n.*

Qing·dao (ching′dou′) *also,* **Tsingtao.** a seaport in eastern China. Pop., 1,300,000.

Qing·hai (ching′hī′) *also,* **Tsinghai.** a province in west-central China. Capital, Xining. Area, 278,378 sq mi (720,999 sq km). Pop., 4,280,000.

Qi·qi·har (chē′chē′här′) *also,* **Tsitsihar.** a city in northeastern China. Pop., 1,180,000.

Qom (küm) *also,* **Qum.** a city in north-central Iran. Pop., 543,139.

Que·bec (kwi bek′, ki-) **1.** the largest province of Canada, in the eastern part of the country. Capital, Quebec. Area, 594,860 sq mi (1,540,687 sq km). Pop., 6,540,276. **2.** the capital of this prov-

ince, a port city on the St. Lawrence River in southeastern Canada. Pop., 164,580.

Queens (kwēnz) the largest borough of New York City. Area, 115 sq mi (298 sq km).

Queens·land (kwēnz′lənd) a state of Australia, in the northeastern part of the country. Capital, Brisbane. Area, 667,000 sq mi (1,727,500 sq km). Pop., 2,834,097.

Que·moy (ki moi′) a heavily fortified island belonging to Taiwan, located off the coast of China. Area, 68 sq mi (176 sq km).

Que·ré·ta·ro (kə ret′ə rō′) a state in central Mexico. Area, 4,432 sq mi (11,479 sq km). Pop., 739,605.

Que·zon City (kā′zon) a city north of Manila in the Philippines, capital of the country from 1948 to 1976. Pop., 1,632,000.

Quin·cy (kwin′zē, -sē) a city in eastern Massachusetts. Pop., 84,985.

Quin·ta·na Roo (kēn tä′nə rō′) a state in southeastern Mexico, on the eastern Yucatán peninsula. Area, 19,630 sq mi (50,842 sq km). Pop., 225,985.

Quir·i·nal (kwir′ə nəl) one of the seven hills on which the city of ancient Rome was built.

Qui·to (kē′tō) the capital of Ecuador, in the north-central part of the country, in the Andes. Pop., 1,137,705.

Qum (kŭm) see **Qom**.

Qum·ran (kŭm rän′) the site in the West Bank, near the Dead Sea, of the caves where the Dead Sea Scrolls were found in 1947.

Ra·bat (rə bät′) the capital of Morocco, in the northern part of the country. Pop., 518,616.

Ra·cine (rə sēn′) a city in southeastern Wisconsin, on Lake Michigan. Pop., 84,298.

Ra·dom (rä′dôm) a city in east-central Poland. Pop., 223,600.

Rai·nier, Mount (rə nîr′, rā′nîr) a volcano in the Cascade Range, in west-central Washington. Height, 14,408 ft (4,392 m).

Raj·sha·hi (räj shä′hē) a city in western Bangladesh. Pop., 253,740.

Ra·leigh (rô′lē, rä′-) the capital of North Carolina, in the central part of the country. Pop., 207,951.

Rand, the (rand) see **Witwatersrand**.

Ran·goon (rang gün′) the capital and chief port of Burma, in the southern part of the country. Pop., 2,705,039. Also, **Yangon**.

Rapid City, a city in western South Dakota. Pop., 54,523.

Rasht (rasht) a city in northwestern Iran, near the Caspian Sea. Pop., 290,897.

Ra·ven·na (rə ven′ə) a city in northeastern Italy. Pop., 86,500.

Ra·wal·pin·di (rä′wəl pin′dē) a city in northeastern Pakistan, formerly the capital of Pakistan. Pop., 457,091.

Read·ing (red′ing) **1.** a city in southeastern Pennsylvania. Pop., 78,380. **2.** a city in southern England, near London. Pop., 194,727.

Re·ci·fe (rə sē′fə) a port city in northeastern Brazil, on the Atlantic. Pop., 1,287,623.

Red River 1. a river in the southern United States, flowing from southwestern Oklahoma to the Mississippi. Length, 1,270 mi (2,043 km). **2.** a river in the northern United States and southern Canada, flowing north from South Dakota along the Minnesota-North Dakota border to Lake Winnepeg in Manitoba. Length, 545 mi (877 km). Also (def. 2), **Red River of the North**.

Red Sea, a narrow sea between Arabia and northeastern Africa, opening into the Gulf of Aden.

Redwood National Park, a national park in northern California containing groves of redwood trees. Area, 109,027 acres (44,123 hectares).

Reg·gio (rej′ē ō, RED′jō) a port city in southern Italy, on the Strait of Messina. Pop., 178,821. Also, **Reggio di Ca·la·bri·a** (dē kä lä′bRē ä).

Re·gi·na (rə jē′nə) a city in southern Canada, the capital of Saskatchewan. Pop., 175,064.

Reims (rēmz, RANS) also, **Rheims**. a historic city in northern France. Pop., 194,656.

Rennes (REN) a city in northwestern France. Pop., 117,234.

Re·no (rē′nō) a city in western Nevada. Pop., 133,850.

Re·sis·ten·cia (RE′sēs ten′syä) a city in northeastern Argentina, on the Paraná. Pop., 220,104.

Ré·u·nion (rē ūn′yən) a mountainous island in the Indian Ocean, east of Madagascar. It is a French possession. Capital, Saint-Denis. Area, 970 sq mi (2,512 sq km). Pop., 515,814.

Rey·kja·vik (rā′kyə vēk′) the capital and largest city of Iceland, in the southwestern part of the country. Pop., 93,425.

Rheims (rēmz, RANS) Reims.

Rhen·ish-Pa·lat·i·nate (ren′ish pə lat′ə nāt′, -nit) a state of Germany, in the western part of the country. Area, 2,111 sq mi (5,467 sq km). Pop., 3,653,200.

Rhine (rīn) a river flowing from eastern Switzerland through western Germany and the Netherlands to the North Sea. Length, 700 mi (1,126 km).

Rhine·land (rīn′land′) a region in the westernmost part of Germany, along the Rhine.

Rhode Island (rōd) a state in the northeastern United States, the smallest state in the country. Capital, Providence. Area, 1,212 sq mi (3,139 sq km). Pop., 1,003,464. Abbreviation, **R.I.**; postal abbreviation, **RI** —**Rhode Islander**.

Rhodes (rōdz) **1.** a Greek island in the southeastern Aegean Sea, off the coast of Turkey. Area, 542 sq mi (1,404 sq km). **2.** a port city on this island. The Colossus of Rhodes, one of the Seven Wonders of the World, stood by the entrance to its harbor during the third century B.C. Pop., 40,392.

Rho·de·sia (rō dē′zhə) see **Zimbabwe**.

Rhône (rōn) a river flowing generally southwestward from central Switzerland through southeastern France into the Mediterranean. Length, 500 mi (805 km).

Ri·bei·rão Prê·to (Rē be ROUN′ pRe′tù) a city in southeastern Brazil. Pop., 383,125.

Rich·mond (rich′mənd) **1.** the capital of Virginia, a port city in the eastern part of the state. Pop., 203,056. **2.** the former name of the New York City borough of Staten Island. **3.** a port city in western California, on San Francisco Bay. Pop., 87,425. **4.** a city in southwestern British Columbia, Canada. Pop., 108,492.

Ri·deau Canal (ri dō′) a canal in Ontario, Canada, connecting Lake Ontario with the Ottawa River at Ottawa. Length, 126 mi (203 km).

Rif (rif) also, **Riff.** a mountain range in northern Morocco, along the Mediterranean.

Ri·ga (rē′gə) **1.** a port city on the Baltic Sea, the capital of Latvia. Pop., 915,000. **2. Gulf of.** an arm of the eastern Baltic Sea, bordering Estonia and Latvia.

Ri·o de Ja·nei·ro (rē′ō dā zhə nâr′ō) a port city in southeastern Brazil, the former capital of the country. Pop., 5,603,388.

Ri·o de la Pla·ta (rē′ō dā lä plä′tə) the estuary of the Paraná and Uruguay rivers, between Uruguay and Argentina. Length, 225 mi (362 km).

Ri·o Grande (rē′ō grand′, -gran′dē) a river flowing from southwestern Colorado into the Gulf of Mexico and forming the border between Texas and Mexico. Length, 1,885 mi (3,033 km).

Riv·er·side (riv′ər sīd′) a city in southwestern California. Pop., 226,505.

Riv·i·er·a (riv′ē âr′ə) a narrow strip of land along the Mediterranean coasts of Italy, France, and Monaco.

Ri·yadh (rē yäd′) the capital of Saudi Arabia, in the east-central part of the country. Pop., 1,250,000.

Ri·zal City (rē säl′) see **Pasay**.

Road Town, the capital of the British Virgin Islands. Pop., 2,479.

Ro·a·noke (rō′ə nōk′) a city in southwestern Virginia. Pop., 96,397.

Roch·es·ter (roch′es tər, -ə stər) **1.** a city in western New York, on Lake Ontario. Pop., 231,636. **2.** a city in southeastern Minnesota. Pop., 70,745.

Rock·ford (rok′fərd) a city in northern Illinois. Pop., 139,426.

Rocky Mountain National Park, a national park in northern Colorado noted for its distinctive wildlife and scenic beauty. Area, 263,790 acres (106,756 hectares).

Rocky Mountains, a mountain system in the western United States and Canada, extending from central New Mexico to northern Alaska. Also, **Rock′ies**.

Roman Empire, the empire of ancient Rome, extending from Britain to North Africa to the Persian Gulf. It was begun under the emperor Augustus in 27 B.C., reached its greatest extent under Trajan by A.D. 117, and continued until A.D. 395, when it was divided into the Eastern Roman Empire and the Western Roman Empire.

Ro·ma·ni·a (rō mā′nē ə) a country in southeastern Europe, in the northeast part of the Balkan Peninsula. Capital, Bucharest. Area, 91,700 sq mi (238,634 sq km). Pop., 22,823,479. Also, **Roumania, Rumania**.

Rome (rōm) the capital of Italy, on the Tiber, the former capital and center of the Roman Empire and the ancient Roman republic. Pop., 2,815,457.

Roo·se·velt Island (rō′zə velt′, rōz′velt) an island in New York City, in the East River. Area, 139 acres (56 hectares). Formerly, **Welfare Island**.

Ro·sa·ri·o (rō zär′ē ō′) a port city in east-central Argentina, on the Paraná. Pop., 938,120.

a	at	e	end	o	hot	u	up	hw	white		about
ā	ape	ē	me	ō	old	ū	use	ng	song		taken
ä	far	i	it	ô	fork	ü	rule	th	thin	ə	pencil
âr	care	ī	ice	oi	oil	ù	pull	th	this		lemon
		îr	pierce	ou	out	ûr	turn	zh	measure		circus

Ro·seau (rō zō′) the capital of Dominica. Pop., 9,348.

Ro·set·ta (rō zet′ə) a town in northern Egypt in the Nile delta near the site where the Rosetta stone was discovered in 1799. Pop., 52,014.

Ross Sea (rôs) a large inlet of the Pacific on the coast of Antarctica.

Ros·tock (ros′tok) a port city in northeastern Germany, near the Baltic coast. Pop., 253,990.

Ros·tov (ros′tôf) a port city in southwestern Russia, on the Don River. Pop., 1,020,000.

Rot·ter·dam (rot′ər dam′) a port city in the southwestern Netherlands, near the North Sea. Pop., 576,300.

Rou·en (Rü än′) a port city in northern France, on the Seine, the site of Joan of Arc's execution. Pop., 101,945.

Rou·ma·ni·a (rů mā′nē ə) see **Romania**.

Royal Oak, a city in southeastern Michigan. Pop., 65,410.

Ru·bi·con (rü′bi kon′) a small stream in north-central Italy that formed the northern boundary of the ancient Roman republic. Julius Caesar's crossing of the Rubicon in 49 B.C. began a civil war in Rome that led to his dictatorship.

Ruhr (růr) 1. a river in western Germany, a tributary of the Rhine. Length, 146 mi (235 km). 2. a coal mining and industrial region along this river.

Ru·ma·ni·a (rů mā′nē ə) see **Romania**.

Run·ny·mede (run′ē mēd′) a meadow on the Thames, near London, where King John signed the Magna Carta on June 15, 1215.

Ru·se (Rü′sä) a city in northeastern Bulgaria, on the Danube River. Pop., 186,428.

Rush·more, Mount (rush′môr′) a mountain in the Black Hills of western South Dakota, on the side of which are carved huge heads of George Washington, Thomas Jefferson, Abraham Lincoln, and Theodore Roosevelt. Height, 6,200 ft (1,890 m).

Rus·sia (rush′ə) 1. a country extending from Eastern Europe to the northeastern coast of Asia. It was formerly a republic of the Soviet Union. Capital, Moscow. Area, 6,592,850 sq mi (17,075,482 sq km). Pop., 147,386,000. 2. a former empire in eastern Europe and northern Asia ruled by the czars. Its capital was St. Petersburg. The Russian Revolution, in 1917, ended the rule of the czars and led to the founding of the Union of Soviet Socialist Republics.

Ru·the·ni·a (rü thē′nē ə) a former eastern province of Czechoslovakia, ceded to the Soviet Union in 1945. —**Ru·the′ni·an,** *adj., n.*

Rut·land (rut′lənd) 1. a former county in east-central England. Also, **Rut·land·shire** (rut′lənd shir′, -shər). 2. a city in west-central Vermont. Pop., 18,320.

Rwan·da (rü än′də) a landlocked country in east-central Africa. Capital, Kigali. Area, 10,169 sq mi (26,338 sq km). Pop., 5,762,000.

Ryu·kyu Islands (rē ü′kü) a Japanese island chain in the western Pacific, extending in an arc from Kyushu, Japan, to Taiwan. The largest of the group is Okinawa. Land area, 1,800 sq mi (4,662 sq km).

Saar (sär, zär) 1. a river in western Europe, flowing from northeastern France through western Germany to the Moselle. Length, 150 mi (241 km). 2. see **Saarland**.

Saar·brück·en (sär brük′ən, zär bRY′kən) a city in western Germany, on the Saar. Pop., 188,467.

Saar·land (sär′land′, -länt′, zär′-) a state of Germany, in the western part of the country. Area, 991 sq mi (2,567 sq km). Pop., 1,045,936. Also, **Saar.**

Sa·bah (sä′bə) a state of Malaysia, in the northeastern part of the island of Borneo. Capital, Kota Kinabalu. Area, 29,347 sq mi (76,009 sq km). Pop., 955,712.

Sac·ra·men·to (sak′rə men′tō) 1. the capital of California, in the central part of the state, on the Sacramento River. Pop., 369,365. 2. a river flowing from northern California into San Francisco Bay. Length, 382 mi (615 km).

Sa·fa·qis (sä fä′kis) see **Sfax**.

Sa·fi (saf′ē) a port city in western Morocco, on the Atlantic. Pop., 197,309.

Sag·i·naw (sag′ə nô′) a city in east-central Michigan. Pop., 69,512.

Sa·har·a (sə har′ə, -här′ə) a desert in northern Africa, the largest in the world. Area, 3,000,000 sq mi (7,770,000 sq km). Also, **Sahara Desert.**

Sa·hel (sə hel′) a semiarid region in northern Africa south of the Sahara, extending from Senegal to the Sudan.

Sai·da (sī′də) see **Sidon**.

Sai·gon (sī gon′) see **Ho Chi Minh City**.

Saint, see **St.** for place names beginning with the word "Saint."

Sai·pan (sī pan′) the capital of the Northern Mariana Islands, an island in the western Pacific. Area, approx. 71 sq mi (184 sq km). Pop., 17,182.

Sa·kai (sä′kī′) a seaport in Japan, in the southern part of the island of Honshu. Pop., 818,271.

Sak·ha·lin (sak′ə lēn′, sak′ə lēn′) a large island of Russia, in the western Pacific, just off the eastern coast of Siberia. Area, 29,498 sq mi (76,400 sq km).

Sal·a·man·ca (sal′ə mang′kə) a city in western Spain. Pop., 159,342.

Sal·a·mis (sal′ə mis) an island in eastern Greece, west of Athens, the site of a decisive Greek naval victory over the Persians in 480 B.C. Area, 39 sq mi (101 sq km).

Sa·lem (sā′ləm) 1. the capital of Oregon, in the northwestern part of the state. Pop., 107,786. 2. a historic city in eastern Massachusetts, the site of seventeenth-century witchcraft trials. Pop., 38,091.

Sa·ler·no (sə lâr′nō) a port city in southwestern Italy. Pop., 154,848.

Sa·li·mi·ya (sal′ə mē′ə) a city in central Kuwait. Pop., 153,369.

Sa·li·nas (sə lē′nəs) a city in western California. Pop., 108,777.

Salis·bur·y (sôlz′ber′ē, -bə rē) see **Harare**.

Sa·lo·ni·ka (sə lon′i kə) *also,* **Sa·lo·ni·ca.** a port city in northern Greece, known in ancient times as **Thessalonica.** Pop., 406,413. Also, *Greek,* **Thessaloniki.**

Sal·op (sal′əp) see **Shropshire.**

Sal·ta (säl′tä) a city in northwestern Argentina. Pop., 260,744.

Salt Lake City, the capital and largest city of Utah, in the northern part of the state. Pop., 159,936.

Sal·va·dor (sal′və dôr′) 1. see **El Salvador**. 2. a port city on the eastern coast of Brazil, north of Rio de Janeiro. Pop., 1,804,438. Also *(def. 2),* **Bahia.**

Salz·burg (sôlz′bûrg, sälz′-; *German,* zälts′bůRk) a city in western Austria. Pop., 139,426.

Sa·ma·ra (sə mär′ə) a city in western Russia, on the Volga River. Pop., 1,257,000. Formerly, **Kuibyshev.**

Sa·mar·i·a (sə mâr′ē ə, -mar′-) 1. in the Bible, an ancient region west of the Jordan. 2. the main city of this region.

Sam·ar·kand (sam′ər kand′) a city in eastern Uzbekistan. Pop., 366,000.

Sa·mo·a (sə mō′ə) an island group in the southern Pacific, divided politically into Western Samoa and American Samoa. Land area, 1,173 sq mi (3,038 sq km).

Sa·mos (sā′mos, sam′ōs) a mountainous island in Greece, located off the western coast of Turkey. Area, 192 sq mi (497 sq km).

Sa·na (sä nä′) the capital and largest city of Yemen, in the western part of the country. Pop., 427,150.

San An·dre·as Fault (san′ an drā′əs) a geologic fault in western California, running parallel to the Pacific coast from the San Francisco area to the Gulf of California.

San An·ge·lo (san an′jə lō′) a city in central Texas. Pop., 84,474.

San An·to·ni·o (san′ an tō′nē ō′) a city in south-central Texas. Pop., 935,933.

San Ber·nar·di·no (san′ bûr′nər dē′nō) a city in southern California. Pop., 164,164.

San Cris·tó·bal (san′ kris tō′bəl) a city in western Venezuela, near the Colombian border. Pop., 198,793.

San Di·e·go (san′ dē ā′gō) a port city in southern California, at the Mexican border. Pop., 1,110,549.

Sandwich Islands, see **Hawaiian Islands**.

San Fran·cis·co (san′ frən sis′kō) a port city in western California, on the Pacific. Pop., 723,959.

San Francisco Bay, an inlet of the Pacific, on the central coast of California.

San Joa·quin (san′ wä kēn′) a river in central California, flowing westward to the mouth of the Sacramento. Length, 350 mi (563 km).

San Jo·se (san′ hō zā′) a city in western California. Pop., 782,248.

San Jo·sé (sän′ hô sā′) the capital and largest city of Costa Rica, in the central part of the country. Pop., 278,600.

San Juan (san hwän′, wän′) the capital of Puerto Rico, a port in the northeastern part of the island. Pop., 424,600.

San Jus·to (san jůs′tō) a city in eastern Argentina. Pop., 949,566.

San Lu·is Po·to·si (san′ lü ēs′ pô′tô sē′) 1. a state in central Mexico. Area, 24,417 sq mi (63,240 sq km). Pop., 1,673,893. 2. a city in central Mexico. Pop., 362,371.

San Ma·ri·no (san′ mə rē′nō) 1. a small country in southern Europe, near the Adriatic, completely surrounded by Italy. Capital, San Marino. Area, 23 sq mi (60 sq km). Pop., 22,304. 2. the capital of this country. —**San Ma·ri·nese** (san mar′ə nēz′, -nēs′), *adj., n.*

San Ma·te·o (san′ mə tā′ō) a city in central western California. Pop., 85,486.

San Mi·guel de Tu·cu·mán (san′ mi gel′ də tü′kə män′) see Tucumán.

San Mi·gue·li·to (san′ mē ge lē′tō) a city in central Panama. Pop., 242,529.

San Pe·dro Su·la (san pā′drō sü′lə) a city in northwestern Honduras. Pop., 279,356.

San Sal·va·dor (san sal′və dôr′) 1. the capital and largest city of El Salvador, in the central part of the country. Pop., 462,652. 2. an island in the central Bahamas, southeast of Miami, Florida, believed to be the first landing place of Columbus in the New World. Area, 60 sq mi (155 sq km).

San Se·bas·tián (san′ sə bas′chən) a port city on the northern coast of Spain. Pop., 177,622.

San·ta An·a (san′tə an′ə) 1. a city in southern California. Pop., 293,742. 2. a city in western El Salvador. Pop., 137,879.

San·ta Bar·ba·ra (san′tə bär′bər ə, bär′brə) a city in southern California, on the Pacific. Pop., 85,571.

Santa Barbara Islands, an island group off the southern coast of California.

Santa Catalina, one of the Santa Barbara Islands, a resort noted for its beaches and fishing. Also, Catalina, Catalina Island.

San·ta Clar·a (san′tə klär′ə) 1. a city in central Cuba. Pop., 182,349. 2. a city in western California. Pop., 93,613.

San·ta Cruz (san′tə krüz′) a city in central Bolivia. Pop., 441,717.

San·ta Cruz de Te·ne·rife (san′tə krüz′ də ten′ə rēf′) a port city in the Canary Islands. Pop., 215,228.

San·ta Fe (san′tə fā′) the capital of New Mexico, in the north-central part of the state. Pop., 55,859.

San·ta Fé (san′tə fā′) a city in eastern Argentina. Pop., 292,165.

San·ta Is·a·bel (san′tə iz′ə bel′) see Malabo.

San·ta Mon·i·ca (san′tə mon′i kə) a city in southern California, on the Pacific. Pop., 86,905.

San·tan·der (sän′tän deR′) a city in northern Spain, a port on the Bay of Biscay. Pop., 166,800.

San·ta Ro·sa (san′tə rō′zə) a city in northwestern California. Pop., 113,313.

San·ti·a·go (san′tē ä′gō, sän′-) the capital and largest city of Chile, in the central part of the country. Pop., 232,667.

Santiago de Cuba, a port city in southeastern Cuba. Pop., 364,554.

Santiago de los Ca·ba·lle·ros (də lôs kä′bə yâr′ōs) a city in the northern Dominican Republic. Pop., 278,638.

San·to An·dré (san′tü än drā′) a city in southern Brazil. Pop., 635,121.

San·to Do·min·go (san′tō də ming′gō) the capital and largest city of the Dominican Republic, on the southern coast of the country. Pop., 1,313,172. Formerly, Ciudad Trujillo.

San·tos (san′təs) a port city in southeastern Brazil, on the Atlantic. Pop., 460,100.

São Ber·nar·do do Cam·po (souɴ′ beR näR′dú dú kän′pù) a city in southeastern Brazil. Pop., 562,485.

São Fran·cis·co (souɴ′ fRäɴ sēs′kú) a river in South America, flowing through eastern Brazil to the Atlantic. Length, 1,800 mi (2,900 km).

São Gon·ça·lo (souɴ′ gùɴ sä′lù) a city in southeastern Brazil. Pop., 262,400.

São Jo·ão de Me·ri·ti (souɴ′zhù ouɴ′di mi ʀi tē′) a city in southeastern Brazil. Pop., 241,700.

São Jo·sé dos Cam·pos (souɴ′ zhù ze′ dús kän′pús) a city in southeastern Brazil. Pop., 372,578.

São Lu·ís (souɴ′ lü ēs′) a city in northern Brazil. Pop., 227,900.

São Pau·lo (sou pou′lō, souɴ pou′lù) the largest city in Brazil, in the southeastern part of the country. Pop., 10,063,110.

São To·mé (souɴ′ tù mä′) the capital and largest city of São Tomé and Príncipe. Pop., 17,380.

São Tomé and Prín·ci·pe (prēn′si pā′) an island country located off the west coast of Africa, in the Gulf of Guinea. Capital, São Tomé. Land area, 372 sq mi (963 sq km). Pop., 73,631.

Sap·po·ro (sä pôr′ō) a city in Japan, in the western part of the island of Hokkaido. Pop., 1,542,979.

Sar·a·gos·sa (sär′ə gos′ə) a city in northeastern Spain. Pop., 582,239. Also, Zaragoza.

Sa·ra·je·vo (sär′ə yä′vō) *also,* Sarayevo, Serajevo. the capital of Bosnia and Herzegovina, where the assassination of the Austrian Archduke Francis Ferdinand took place in 1914, leading to the outbreak of World War I. Pop., 341,200.

Sa·ra·tov (sä rä′tôf) a city in southwestern Russia, on the Volga River. Pop., 905,000.

Sa·ra·wak (sə rä′wäk) a state of Malaysia, in the northwestern part of the island of Borneo. Capital, Kuching. Area, 48,250 sq mi (124,968 sq km). Pop., 1,235,553.

Sa·ra·ye·vo (sär′ə yä′vō) see Sarajevo.

Sar·din·i·a (sär din′ē ə) 1. an Italian island in the Mediterranean, west of Italy. Area, 9,196 sq mi (23,748 sq km). 2. a former kingdom that included this island and Savoy, Piedmont, and Nice. —Sar·din′i·an, *adj., n.*

Sar·dis (sär′dis) an ancient city in western Asia Minor, the capital of Lydia, thought to have been destroyed by Tamerlane.

Sar·gas·so Sea (sär gas′ō) an oval-shaped part of the north-central Atlantic, between the West Indies and the Azores, noted for its abundance of floating seaweed.

Sar·ma·tia (sär mā′shə) an ancient region in eastern Europe, in what is now eastern Poland and western Ukraine.

Sas·katch·e·wan (sas kach′ə won′, -wən) 1. a province of Canada, in the western part of the country. Capital, Regina. Area, 251,700 sq mi (651,903 sq km). Pop., 1,010,198. 2. a river largely in central Saskatchewan, flowing east to Lake Winnipeg. Length, 340 mi (547 km).

Sas·ka·toon (sas′kə tün′) a city in south-central Saskatchewan, Canada. Pop., 177,641.

Sau·di Arabia (sou′dē, sô′-) a country in southwestern Asia, occupying most of the peninsula of Arabia. Capital, Riyadh. Area, 830,000 sq mi (2,149,700 sq km). Pop., 9,229,000. —Sau′di, Saudi Arabian, *adj., n.*

Sault Ste. Ma·rie (sü′ sänt′ mə rē′) a port city in south-central Ontario, Canada. Pop., 80,905.

Sault Ste. Marie Canals, two canals linking Lakes Superior and Huron, forming part of the U.S.-Canadian border. Also, Soo Canals.

Sa·van·nah (sə van′ə) 1. a port city in southeastern Georgia. Pop., 137,560. 2. a river in the southeastern United States, flowing into the Atlantic, forming most of the border between South Carolina and Georgia. Length, 314 mi (505 km).

Sa·voy (sə voi′) a historic region in southeastern France, formerly part of the kingdom of Sardinia. —Sa·voy·ard (sə voi′ərd, sav′oi ärd′), *adj., n.*

Sax·o·ny (sak′sə nē) a historic German kingdom and former state in east-central Germany. It was part of Soviet occupied Germany in 1945, then part of East Germany from 1952 to 1990.

Scan·di·na·vi·a (skan′də nā′vē ə) 1. a region in northern Europe, consisting of Norway, Sweden, and Denmark, and sometimes Iceland or Finland. 2. a large peninsula of northern Europe, divided politically between Norway and Sweden.

Scap·a Flow (skap′ə) a sheltered expanse of sea north of Scotland, a major British naval anchorage during World Wars I and II.

Scar·bor·ough (skär′bûr′ō, -bur′ō) a city in southern Ontario, Canada. Pop., 484,676.

Schedlt (skelt) a river in western Europe, flowing northeast through northern France, western Belgium, and the southwestern Netherlands to the North Sea. Length, 270 mi (434 km).

Sche·nec·ta·dy (skə nek′tə dē) a city in eastern New York. Pop., 65,566.

Schles·wig-Hol·stein (shles′wig hōl′stīn, shläs′vikн hôl′-shtīn) a state of Germany, in the northernmost part of the country. Pop., 2,564,565.

Schwarz·wald (shvärts′vält′) see Black Forest.

Scot·land (skot′lənd) a division of the United Kingdom, north of England. Capital, Edinburgh. Area, 30,415 sq mi (78,775 sq km). Pop., 5,090,700.

Scot·tish Highlands (skot′ish) a rugged, mountainous region of northern and central Scotland. Also, Highlands.

Scottish Lowlands, a low-lying region of central Scotland. Also, Lowlands.

Scotts·dale (skots′dāl′) a city in south-central Arizona. Pop., 130,069.

Scran·ton (skran′tən) a city in northeastern Pennsylvania. Pop., 81,805.

Scyth·i·a (sith′ē ə) an ancient empire that extended from the Danube in Europe to central Asia.

Sea Islands, an island chain in the southeastern United States, along the Atlantic coast of South Carolina, Georgia, and northern Florida.

Se·at·tle (sē at′əl) a port city in western Washington, on Puget Sound. Pop., 516,269.

Se·bas·to·pol (sə bas′tə pōl′) see Sevastopol.

a	at	e	end	o	hot	u	up	hw	white		about
ā	ape	ē	me	ō	old	ū	use	ng	song		taken
ä	far	i	it	ô	fork	ü	rule	th	thin	ə	pencil
âr	care	ī	ice	oi	oil	ú	pull	th	this		lemon
		îr	pierce	ou	out	ûr	turn	zh	measure		circus

Seine (sān) a river flowing from eastern France northward into the English Channel. Length, 485 mi (780 km).

Sek·on·di-Ta·ko·ra·di (sek'ən dē'tä'kə rä'dē) a port city in southern Ghana. Pop., 93,882.

Se·ma·rang (sə mär'äng) a port city in Indonesia, on the northern coast of the island of Java. Pop., 1,206,000.

Sen·dai (sen'dī') a city in Japan, on the northeastern coast of the island of Honshu. Pop., 700,254.

Sen·e·gal (sen'i gôl', -gäl') **1.** a country in western Africa, on the Atlantic. Capital, Dakar. Area, 75,750 sq mi (196,190 sq km). Pop., 6,881,919. **2.** a river in western Africa, on the southern border of the Sahara, flowing into the Atlantic. Length, 1,000 mi (1,609 km). —**Sen·e·ga·lese** (sen'i gə lēz', -lēs'), *adj., n.*

Sen·e·gam·bi·a (sen'i gam'bē ə) a confederation of Senegal and Gambia, formed in 1982.

Seoul (sōl) the capital and largest city of South Korea, in the northwestern part of the country. Pop., 10,522,000.

Se·quoi·a National Park (si kwoi'ə) a national park in central California containing giant sequoia trees and Mount Whitney. Area, 403,023 acres (163,103 hectares).

Se·ra·je·vo (ser'ə yā'vō) see **Sarajevo.**

Ser·bi·a (sûr'bē ə) a republic of Yugoslavia. Area, 34,116 sq mi (88,360 sq km). Pop., 9,716,138. —**Serb** (sûrb), **Ser'bi·an,** *adj., n.*

Sé·tif (sā tēf') a city in northeastern Algeria. Pop., 170,182. Also, **Stif.**

Se·vas·to·pol (sə vas'tə pōl') a port city on the Black Sea in Ukraine, located near the southwestern tip of the Crimean peninsula. Pop., 356,000. Also, **Sebastopol.**

Sev·ern (sev'ərn) a river in southwestern Great Britain, flowing from central Wales east and south through England into an inlet of the Atlantic. Length, 210 mi (338 km).

Se·ville (sə vil') a city in southwestern Spain. Pop., 663,132. Also, *Spanish,* **Se·vil·la** (se vēl'yä).

Sey·chelles (sā shel') an island country in the western Indian Ocean, northeast of Madagascar. Capital, Victoria. Land area, 175 sq mi (453 sq km). Pop., 64,718.

Sfax (sfäks) a port city in northeastern Tunisia. Pop., 231,911. Also, **Safaqis.**

Shaan·xi (shän'shē') *also,* **Shensi.** a province in north-central China. Capital, Xian. Area, 75,598 sq mi (195,799 sq km). Pop., 30,020,000.

Sha·ba (shä'bə) a province in the southern part of Zaire that attempted to secede from the country in the early 1960s. Formerly, **Katanga.**

Shan·dong (shän'dông') *also,* **Shantung. 1.** a province in east-central China. Capital, Jinan. Area, 59,189 sq mi (150,632 sq km). Pop., 79,580,000. **2.** a peninsula in this province, extending into the Yellow Sea.

Shang·hai (shang'hī', shäng'-) the chief port and largest city of China, in the eastern part of the country, near the mouth of the Yangtze River. Pop., 7,220,000.

Shan·tung (shan'tung', shän'dúng') see **Shandong.**

Shan·xi (shän'shē') *also,* **Shan·si** (shän'sē'). a province in eastern China. Capital, Taiyuan. Area, 60,656 sq mi (157,099 sq km). Pop., 27,170,000.

Shas·ta, Mount (shas'tə) a volcanic mountain in northern California, in the Cascade Range. Height, 14,162 ft (4,317 m).

Shatt-al-Ar·ab (shat'al ar'əb) a channel flowing southeast along the Iran-Iraq border into the Persian Gulf, formed by the confluence of the Tigris and Euphrates rivers. Length, 120 mi (193 km).

She·ba (shē'bə) in the Bible, the name of an ancient country in southwestern Arabia.

She·boy·gan (shə boi'gən) a city in eastern Wisconsin, on Lake Michigan. Pop., 49,676.

Shef·field (shef'ēld) a city in northern England. Pop., 532,000.

Shen·an·do·ah (shen'ən dō'ə) a river flowing through northern Virginia into the Potomac. Length, 55 mi (88 km).

Shenandoah Valley, a valley in northern Virginia, drained by the Shenandoah River. Length, 150 mi (16 km).

Shen·si (shen'sē', shun'shē') see **Shaanxi.**

Shen·yang (shun'yäng') a city in northeastern China, the capital of Liaoning province. Pop., 3,910,000. Formerly, **Mukden.**

Sher·brooke (shûr'brúk') a city in southern Quebec, Canada. Pop., 74,438.

Sher·wood Forest (shûr'wúd') an ancient royal forest in central England, known as the home of the legendary Robin Hood.

Shet·land Islands (shet'lənd) an island group off northern Scotland, in the Atlantic. Area, 550 sq mi (1,425 sq km).

Shi·jia·zhuang (shu'jyä'jwäng') a city in northeastern China, the capital of Hebei province. Pop., 1,220,000.

Shi·ko·ku (shi kō'kü) the smallest of the four main islands of Japan. Area, 7,049 sq mi (18,257 sq km).

Shi·nar (shī'när) in the Bible, Babylonia.

Shi·raz (shi räz') a city in southwestern Iran. Pop., 848,289.

Sho·la·pur (shō'lə púr') a city in southwestern India. Pop., 511,103.

Shreve·port (shrēv'pôrt') a city in northwestern Louisiana. Pop., 198,525.

Shrop·shire (shrop'shîr, -shər) a county in west-central England, on the Welsh border. Pop., 375,610. Also, **Salop.**

Shu·bra al-Khay·mah (shü'brə al kā'mə) a city in northern Egypt. Pop., 710,794.

Si·al·kot (sē äl'kōt) a city in northeastern Pakistan. Pop., 258,147.

Si·am (sī am') **1.** see **Thailand. 2. Gulf of.** an inlet of the South China Sea between Indochina and the Malay Peninsula. Also, **Gulf of Thailand.**

Si·an (sē'än') see **Xian.**

Si·be·ri·a (sī bîr'ē ə) a region of Russia, extending from the Ural Mountains to the Pacific. Area, 5,000,000 sq mi (12,950,000 sq km).

Si·chuan (sich'wän', sœ'chwän') *also,* **Szechwan.** a province in south-central China. Capital, Chengdu. Area, 218,862 sq mi (566,853 sq km). Pop., 104,540,000.

Sic·i·ly (sis'ə lē) an Italian island in the Mediterranean, off the southwestern tip of Italy. Area, 9,831 sq mi (25,462 sq km).

Si·don (sī'dən) a city in southern Lebanon, on the Mediterranean. In ancient times it was a great Phoenician seaport. Pop., 105,000. Also, **Saida.** —**Si·do·ni·an** (sī dō'nē ən), *adj., n.*

Si·en·a (sē en'ə) a city in central Italy, noted for its medieval buildings and numerous works of art. Pop., 59,712.

Si·er·ra Le·o·ne (sē er'ə lē ō'nē) a country on the western coast of Africa. Capital, Freetown. Area, 27,699 sq mi (71,740 sq km). Pop., 3,515,812.

Si·er·ra Ma·dre (sē er'ə mä'drä) a mountain system in eastern and western Mexico.

Si·er·ra Ne·vad·a (sē er'ə nə vad'ə, nə vä'də) a mountain range in eastern California.

Sik·kim (sik'im) a state of India, in the northeastern part of the country, formerly an independent country. Area, 2,739 sq mi (7,094 sq km). Pop., 316,385.

Si·le·sia (si lē'zhə) a historic region in central Europe, now in southwestern Poland and northern Czechoslovakia.

Silver Spring, a city in central Maryland. Pop., 76,046.

Si·mi Valley (sē'mē, sim'ē) a city in southern California. Pop., 100,217.

Si·nai (sī'nī) **1.** a triangular desert area in northeastern Egypt, extending south from the Mediterranean to the northern end of the Red Sea. Also, **Sinai Peninsula. 2. Mount.** in the Bible, the mountain on which Moses received the Ten Commandments.

Si·na·lo·a (sē'nə lō'ə) a state in northwestern Mexico. Area, 22,582 sq mi (58,487 sq km). Pop., 1,849,879.

Sin·ga·pore (sing'ə pôr') **1.** an island off the southern tip of the Malay Peninsula. **2.** a small country comprising this island and adjacent islets. Capital, Singapore. Area, 224 sq mi (580 sq km). Pop., 2,685,400. **3.** the capital and largest city of this country. Pop., 2,685,000.

Si·ning (shē'ning') see **Xining.**

Sin·kiang (shin'jyäng') see **Xinjiang.**

Sin·ui·ju (shin'wē'jü') a city in western North Korea, on the Yalu River. Pop., 305,000.

Si·on (sī'ən) see **Zion.**

Sioux City (sü) a city in western Iowa, on the Missouri. Pop., 80,505.

Sioux Falls, a city in southeastern South Dakota. Pop., 100,814.

Skag·er·rak (skag'ə rak') a strait between Norway and Denmark, an arm of the North Sea.

Skop·je (skôp'yə) the capital of Macedonia. Pop., 444,900. Also, **Skop·lje** (skôp'lyä).

Skye, Isle of (skī) an island in Scotland, off the northwestern coast of the country. Area, 670 sq mi (1,735 sq km).

Slave Coast, a region on the western coast of Africa, between Ghana and Nigeria. It was a center of the slave trade from the sixteenth to nineteenth centuries.

Slave River, a river in northern Alberta and southern Northwest Territories, Canada, flowing north from the Peace River and Lake Athabasca to the Great Slave Lake. Length, 200 mi (322 km).

Sla·vo·ni·a (slə vō'nē ə) a region in Croatia. —**Sla·vo'ni·an,** *adj., n.*

Slo·va·ki·a (slō vä'kē ə) a historic region in eastern Czechoslovakia. Area, 18,800 sq mi (48,692 sq km).

Slo·ve·ni·a (slō vē'nē ə) a country in southeastern Europe, a former republic of Yugoslavia. Capital, Ljubljana. Area, approx. 7,820 sq mi (20,250 sq km). Pop., 1,936,606.

Smoky Mountains, see **Great Smoky Mountains.**

Smo·lensk (smô lensk′) a city in western Russia, on the Dnieper. Pop., 341,000.

Smyr·na (smûr′nə) see **Izmir**.

Snake River, a river in the northwestern United States, the principal tributary of the Columbia River. Length, 1,038 mi (1,670 km).

Snow·don, Mount (snō′dən) a peak in northwestern Wales, the highest point in Wales. Height, 3,560 ft (1,085 m).

Society Islands, a French island group in the east-central Pacific, northeast of New Zealand. The largest island of the group is Tahiti. Land area, 636 sq mi (1,647 sq km). Pop., 142,129.

Sod·om (sod′əm) in the Bible, a city near the Dead Sea that, along with the nearby city of Gomorrah, was destroyed by fire from heaven because of the wickedness of the inhabitants.

So·fi·a (sō′fē ə) the capital of Bulgaria, in the western part of the country. Pop., 1,119,152.

So·ho (sō′hō′) a district in London, noted for its foreign restaurants and cafés.

So·li·hull (sō′li hul′) a city in central England, near Birmingham. Pop., 93,940.

So·ling·en (zō′ling ən) a city in western Germany. Pop., 160,824.

So·lo (sō′lō) see **Surakarta**.

Sol·o·mon Islands (sol′ə mən) an island country in the southwestern Pacific, east of Papua New Guinea. Capital, Honiara. Land area, 10,983 sq mi (28,446 sq km). Pop., 285,176.

So·ma·lia (sō mäl′yə) a country in eastern Africa, on the Indian Ocean and Gulf of Aden. Capital, Mogadishu. Area, 246,201 sq mi (637,661 sq km). Pop., 5,423,000.

Som·er·set (sum′ər set′) a county in southwestern England. Pop., 457,700.

Som·er·ville (sum′ər vil′) a city in eastern Massachusetts. Pop., 76,210.

So·no·ra (sə nôr′ə) a state in northwestern Mexico, on the border of California, Arizona, and Texas. Area, 70,484 sq mi (182,554 sq km). Pop., 1,513,731.

Soo Canals (sü) see **Sault Ste. Marie Canals**.

Soo·chow (sü′chou′, -jō′) see **Suzhou**.

So·ro·ca·ba (sôr′ù kä′bä) a city in southern Brazil. Pop., 327,468.

South (south) the southern region of the United States, usually considered to be that area south of Pennsylvania, the Ohio River, and the Missouri, esp. the states that formed the Confederacy in the Civil War.

South Africa, Republic of, a country in southern Africa, on the Atlantic and Indian oceans. Administrative capital, Pretoria; judicial capital, Bloemfontein; legislative capital, Cape Town. Area, 472,359 sq mi (1,223,410 sq km). Pop., 23,385,645. Formerly, **Union of South Africa**.

South America, the fourth largest continent, located in the Western Hemisphere. Area, 6,884,000 sq mi (17,829,560 sq km). Pop., 303,000,000. —**South American**.

South·amp·ton (south hamp′tən, -amp′-) a port city on the southern coast of England. Pop., 211,321.

South Australia, a state in south-central Australia. Capital, Adelaide. Area, 380,070 sq mi (984,381 sq km). Pop., 1,423,337.

South Bend, a city in northern Indiana. Pop., 105,511.

South Carolina, a state in the southeastern United States, on the Atlantic. Capital, Columbia. Area, 31,113 sq mi (80,583 sq km). Pop., 3,486,703. Abbreviation, **S.C.**; postal abbreviation, **SC** —**South Car·o·lin·i·an** (kar′ə lin′ē ən).

South China Sea, a part of the Pacific, bounded by southeastern China, Vietnam, the Malay Peninsula, Borneo, and the Philippines.

South Dakota, a state in the north-central United States. Capital, Pierre. Area, 77,116 sq mi (199,730 sq km). Pop., 696,004. Abbreviations, **S. Dak., S.D.**; postal abbreviation, **SD** —**South Dakotan**.

South·east (south′ēst′) the southeastern part of the United States, esp. North and South Carolina, Georgia, Florida, and Alabama, and, sometimes, Virginia.

Southeast Asia, a region of Asia that includes the countries of Brunei, Burma, Cambodia, Indonesia, Laos, Malaysia, Philippines, Singapore, Thailand, and Vietnam.

South·end-on-Sea (south′end′ôn sē′, -on-) a city in southeastern England, at the mouth of the Thames. Pop., 155,720.

Southern Alps, a mountain range in New Zealand, on South Island.

Southern Rhodesia, see **Zimbabwe**.

Southern Yemen, a former country on the southern coast of the peninsula of Arabia, now part of Yemen.

South·field (south′fēld′) a city in southeastern Michigan. Pop., 75,728.

South Island, the larger of the two main islands of New Zealand. Area, 58,093 sq mi (150,461 sq km).

South Korea, a country occupying the southern part of the Korean peninsula. Official name: **Republic of Korea**. Capital, Seoul. Area, 38,022 sq mi (98,477 sq km). Pop., 40,448,486.

South·port (south′pôrt′) see **Gold Coast** *(def. 2)*.

South Sea Islands, the islands of the southern Pacific; Oceania.

South Seas, the seas south of the equator, esp. the southern Pacific.

South Vietnam, see **Vietnam**.

South·west (south′west′) the southwestern part of the United States, esp. Oklahoma, Texas, New Mexico, Arizona, and, sometimes, southern California.

South-West Africa, see **Namibia**.

Soviet Union, see **Union of Soviet Socialist Republics**.

So·we·to (sə wē′tō) a group of black African townships in the Republic of South Africa, in the Johannesburg metropolitan area. Pop., 521,948.

Spain (spān) a country in southwestern Europe, on the Iberian Peninsula. Capital, Madrid. Area, 194,885 sq mi (504,752 sq km). Pop., 39,217,804.

Spanish America, the countries south of the United States in which the chief language is Spanish, including Mexico, Central America except Belize, South America except Brazil and the Guianas, and Cuba and other islands in the West Indies.

Spanish Main 1. formerly, the mainland of Spanish America, esp. the northern coast of South America from the mouth of the Orinoco River to the Isthmus of Panama. **2.** that part of the Caribbean Sea through which Spanish merchant ships traveled in colonial times, a former haunt of pirates.

Spanish Sahara, see **Western Sahara**.

Spar·ta (spär′tə) an ancient city-state in southern Greece, in the southeastern Peloponnesus. It was noted for the austerity of its life and the stern discipline and military effectiveness of its soldiers. Also, **Lacedaemon**.

Spice Islands, see **Moluccas**.

Spits·ber·gen (spits′bûr′gən) a Norwegian island group in the Arctic Ocean, north of Norway. Land area, approx. 24,000 sq mi (62,150 sq km). Pop., 4,000. Also, *Norwegian,* **Svalbard**.

Split (split) a port city in Croatia. Pop., 191,074.

Spo·kane (spō kan′) a city in eastern Washington. Pop., 177,196.

Spring·field (spring′fēld′) **1.** the capital of Illinois, in the central part of the state. Pop., 105,227. **2.** a city in southwestern Massachusetts, on the Connecticut River. Pop., 156,983. **3.** a city in southwestern Missouri. Pop., 140,494.

Sri Lan·ka (srē läng′kə, shrē-) an island country in the Indian Ocean, east of the southern tip of India. Capital, Colombo. Area, 25,332 sq mi (65,610 sq km). Pop., 16,117,000. Formerly, **Ceylon**. —**Sri Lan′kan**.

Sri·na·gar (srē nug′ər) the largest city in the state of Jammu and Kashmir, India. Pop., 594,775.

Staf·ford·shire (staf′ərd shîr′, -shər) a county in west-central England. Pop., 1,032,900.

Sta·lin·grad (stä′lin grad′) see **Volgograd**.

Stam·ford (stam′fərd) a city in southwestern Connecticut. Pop., 108,056.

Stan·ley (stan′lē) the capital of the Falkland Islands. Pop., 1,200.

Stan·ley·ville (stan′lē vil′) see **Kisangani**.

Stat·en Island (stat′ən) an island constituting a borough of New York City, southwest of Manhattan. Area, 62 sq mi (161 sq km).

States of the Church, see **Papal States**.

St. Au·gus·tine (ô′gə stēn′) a historic city in northeastern Florida, the oldest continuously inhabited city in the United States. Pop., 11,692.

St. Ber·nard Pass (bər närd′) **1. Great.** a mountain pass in the Alps on the Swiss-Italian border. **2. Little.** a mountain pass in the Alps in southeastern France near the Italian border.

St. Cath·a·rines (kath′ər inz, kath′rinz) a city in southeastern Canada, in Ontario. Pop., 123,455.

St. Chris·to·pher (kris′tə fər) see **St. Kitts-Nevis**.

St. Clair Shores (klâr) a city in southeastern Michigan. Pop., 68,107.

St. Croix (kroi) the largest and southernmost of the Virgin

a	at	e	end	o	hot	u	up	hw	white		about
ā	ape	ē	me	ō	old	ū	use	ng	song		taken
ä	far	i	it	ô	fork	ü	rule	th	thin	ə	pencil
âr	care	ī	ice	oi	oil	ù	pull	th	this		lemon
		îr	pierce	ou	out	ûr	turn	zh	measure		circus

1457

Islands. It belongs to the United States. Area, 82 sq mi (212 sq km).

St.-De·nis (saɴ də nē′) the capital of Réunion. Pop., 84,400.

Sterling Heights, a city in southeastern Michigan. Pop., 117,810.

St.-É·tienne (saɴ′tā tyen′) a city in southeastern France. Pop., 204,955.

Stet·tin (shte tēn′) see **Szczecin.**

St. George's (jôr′jiz) the capital and largest city of Grenada. Pop., 4,788.

St. Got·thard (got′ərd) 1. a mountain group in the Alps, in south-central Switzerland. 2. a mountain pass located in this mountain group.

St. He·le·na (hə lē′nə) a small British island in the southern Atlantic, the site of Napoleon Bonaparte's exile from 1815 until his death in 1821. Area, 47 sq mi (122 sq km). Pop., 5,644.

St. Hel·ens, Mount (hel′ənz) an active volcano in the southwestern part of the state of Washington, in the Cascade Range. Height, 8,364 ft (2,549 m).

Stif (stēf) see **Sétif.**

St. John (jon) the largest city in New Brunswick, Canada, located on the Bay of Fundy. Pop., 76,381.

St. John's (jonz) 1. the capital of Antigua and Barbuda. Pop., 24,359. 2. the capital of Newfoundland and Labrador, a port on the southeastern coast of Newfoundland. Pop., 96,216.

St. Jo·seph (jō′zəf, -səf) a city in northwestern Missouri, on the Missouri River. Pop., 71,852.

St. Kitts-Ne·vis (kits′nē′vis, -nev′is) a West Indian country in the Leeward Islands that includes the islands of St. Kitts (also called St. Christopher) and Nevis. Capital, Basseterre. Land area, 101 sq mi (262 sq km). Pop., 44,404.

St. Law·rence (lôr′əns) 1. a river in North America flowing from Lake Ontario northeast into the Gulf of St. Lawrence. It is the chief outlet of the Great Lakes. Length, 800 mi (1,287 km). 2. **Gulf of.** an arm of the Atlantic, on the eastern coast of Canada, at the mouth of the St. Lawrence River.

St. Lawrence Seaway, an inland waterway in east-central North America, connecting the Atlantic with the Great Lakes.

St.-Lé·o·nard (sānt len′ərd, saɴ lā ô nÄR′) a city in southern Quebec, Canada. Pop., 75,947.

St. Lou·is (lü′is, lü′ē) a city in eastern Missouri, on the Mississippi. Pop., 396,685.

St. Lu·cia (lü′shə) a West Indian country consisting of an island in the Windward Islands. Capital, Castries. Area, 238 sq mi (616 sq km). Pop., 142,342.

St. Mar·ys (mâr′ēz) a river flowing from Lake Superior to Lake Huron, forming the border between northeastern Michigan and Ontario, Canada. Length, 175 mi (282 km).

St. Mo·ritz (sānt′mə rits′, saɴ mô ʀēts′) a resort city in southeastern Switzerland. Pop., 5,335.

Stock·holm (stok′hōm, -hōlm) the capital and largest city of Sweden, on the eastern coast of the country. Pop., 672,187.

Stock·ton (stok′tən) a city in central California. Pop., 210,943.

Stoke-on-Trent (stōk′ôn trent′, -on-) a city in west-central England. Pop., 272,446.

St. Paul (pôl) the capital of Minnesota, in the southeastern part of the state, on the Mississippi opposite Minneapolis. Pop., 272,235.

St. Pe·ters·burg (pē′tərz bûrg′) 1. a historic city in northwestern Russia, the chief Russian port on the Baltic Sea. The former capital of Russia, it was briefly known as Petrograd and then as Leningrad (until 1991). Pop., 4,456,000. 2. a city in west-central Florida, on the Gulf of Mexico. Pop., 238,629.

St. Pierre (pyâr, pē är′) 1. an island in the Atlantic, off Newfoundland, part of St. Pierre and Miquelon. Area, 10 sq mi (26 sq km). 2. the capital of St. Pierre and Miquelon. Pop., 5,371.

St. Pierre and Mi·que·lon (mik′ə lon′, mik′ə lon′) a French department in the northern Atlantic, south of Newfoundland, made up of St. Pierre, Miquelon, and several smaller islands. Land area, 93 sq mi (241 sq km). Capital, St. Pierre. Pop., 6,041.

Stras·bourg (stras′bûrg′) a city in northeastern France, on the Rhine. Pop., 248,712.

Strat·ford-on-A·von (strat′fərd ôn ā′von, -on-) a town in central England, noted as the birthplace, home, and burial place of William Shakespeare. Pop., 20,941. Also, **Stratford.**

Strom·bo·li (strom′bə lē) a small Italian island north of Sicily, the site of an active volcano. Area, 5 sq mi (13 sq km).

St. Tho·mas (tom′əs) the westernmost of the Virgin Islands, belonging to the United States. Area, 32 sq mi (83 sq km).

Stutt·gart (stut′gärt, stùt′-, shtùt′-) a city in southwestern Germany. Pop., 562,658.

St. Vin·cent and the Grenadines (vin′sənt) a West Indian island nation in the Windward Islands, made up of St. Vincent and

the northern islands of the Grenadines group. Capital, Kingstown. Land area, 150 sq mi (389 sq km). Pop., 112,589.

Su·chow (sʏ′jō′) see **Xuzhou.**

Su·cre (sü′krā) the legal capital of Bolivia, in the southern part of the country. Pop., 86,609.

Su·dan (sü dan′) 1. a country in northwestern Africa, on the southern border of Egypt. Capital, Khartoum. Area, 967,500 sq mi (2,505,825 sq km). Pop., 20,564,364. 2. a region extending across Africa from the Atlantic to Ethiopia and south from the Sahara to the central and western tropical forests. Much of the Sudan is semiarid grassland. —**Su·da·nese** (sü′də nēz′, -nēs′), *adj., n.*

Sud·bu·ry (sud′ber′ē, -bə rē) a city in south-central Ontario, Canada. Pop., 88,717.

Su·ez (sü ez′) 1. a port city in northeastern Egypt, at the southern entrance of the Suez Canal. Pop., 326,820. 2. **Gulf of.** a gulf at the northwestern end of the Red Sea, joined to the Mediterranean Sea by the Suez Canal.

Suez Canal, a canal in northeastern Egypt, connecting the Mediterranean and Red seas.

Suf·folk (suf′ək) a county in eastern England. Pop., 638,500.

Su·la·we·si (sü′lə wä′sē) a large island in central Indonesia, east of the island of Borneo. Area, approx. 72,000 sq mi (186,500 sq km). Formerly, **Celebes.**

Su·lu Archipelago (sü′lü) a group of several hundred islands in the southern Philippines. Land area, 1,086 sq mi (2,813 sq km).

Su·ma·tra (sü mä′trə) the westernmost island of Indonesia, a large island south of the Malay Peninsula. Area, 182,860 sq mi (473,607 sq km).

Su·mer (sü′mər) an ancient country in southern Mesopotamia.

Sun·der·land (sun′dər lənd) a port city in northeastern England, on the North Sea. Pop., 195,064.

Sun·ny·vale (sun′ē väl′) a city in western California. Pop., 117,229.

Superior, Lake, the largest and northernmost of the Great Lakes, on the U.S.-Canadian border.

Su·ra·ba·ja (sür′ə bä′yə) also, **Su·ra·ba·ya.** a port city of Indonesia, on the northeast coast of the island of Java. Pop., 2,345,000.

Su·ra·kar·ta (sür′ə kär′tə) a city in Indonesia, in central Java. Pop., 491,000. Also, **Solo.**

Su·rat (sù rat′) a city in western India. Pop., 776,583.

Su·ri·name (sür′ə näm′) also, **Su·ri·nam.** a country on the northeastern coast of South America. Capital, Paramaribo. Area, 63,037 sq mi (163,266 sq km). Pop., 392,000. —**Su·ri·nam·ese** (sür′ə nə mēz′, -mēs′), *adj., n.*

Sur·rey (sûr′ē, sur′ē) a county in southern England. Pop., 999,800.

Su·sa (sü′sə) the ancient capital of Elam, in what is now southwestern Iran.

Sus·que·han·na (sus′kwə han′ə) a river flowing through New York, Pennsylvania, and Maryland into the Chesapeake Bay. Length, 444 mi (714 km).

Sus·sex (sus′iks) a former county in southeastern England.

Su·va (sü′və) the capital of Fiji. Pop., 69,665.

Su·wan·nee (sə won′ē) a river in Florida and Georgia, flowing into the Gulf of Mexico. Length, 386 mi (621 km). Also, **Swanee.**

Su·won (sü′wun′) a city in northwestern South Korea. Pop., 430,752.

Su·zhou (sʏ′jō′) a city in eastern China. Pop., 740,000. Also, **Soochow.**

Sval·bard (sväl′bärd′) see **Spitsbergen.**

Sverd·lovsk (sverd lôfsk′) see **Yekaterinburg.**

Swa·nee (swä′nē) see **Suwanee.**

Swan·sea (swon′sē, swon′zē) a port city and industrial center in southern Wales. Pop., 172,433.

Swa·zi·land (swä′zē land′) a landlocked country in southeastern Africa. Capital, Mbabane. Area, 6,704 sq mi (17,363 sq km). Pop., 712,131.

Swe·den (swē′dən) a country in northern Europe, on the eastern part of the Scandinavian peninsula. Capital, Stockholm. Area, 170,250 sq mi (440,948 sq km). Pop., 8,527,036.

Switz·er·land (swit′sər lənd) a landlocked, mountainous country in central Europe. Capital, Bern. Area, 15,943 sq mi (41,292 sq km). Pop., 6,673,850.

Syd·ney (sid′nē) a major city and chief port of Australia, on the eastern coast of the country. It is the capital of New South Wales. Pop., 3,623,550.

Syr·a·cuse (sir′ə kūs′) 1. a city in central New York. Pop., 163,860. 2. a port city in the southeastern part of the Italian island of Sicily, in ancient times a leading Greek city. Pop., 122,857.

Syr·i·a (sîr′ē ə) 1. a country in southwestern Asia. Capital, Damascus. Area, 71,498 sq mi (185,180 sq km). Pop., 11,338,000.

2. an ancient country at the eastern end of the Mediterranean, roughly consisting of what is now Syria, Lebanon, Israel, and some adjacent areas. —**Syr′i·an**, *adj., n.*

Syrian Desert, a desert in southwestern Asia, in northern Saudi Arabia, southern Syria, eastern Jordan, and western Iraq. Area, 200,000 sq mi (518,000 sq km).

Szcze·cin (shche′tsēn) a port city in northwestern Poland. Pop., 409,500. Formerly, **Stettin.**

Sze·chwan (sech′wän′) see **Sichuan.**

Ta·bas·co (tə bas′kō) a state in southeastern Mexico. Area, 9,783 sq mi (25,338 sq km). Pop., 1,062,961.

Ta·briz (tä brēz′) a city in northwestern Iran. Pop., 971,482.

Ta·co·ma (tə kō′mə) a city in western Washington, on Puget Sound. Pop., 176,664.

Ta·dzhik·i·stan (tə jik′ə stan′) see **Tajikistan.**

Tae·gu (tī′gü′) a city in southeastern South Korea. Pop., 2,207,000.

Tae·jon (tī′jon′) a city in western South Korea. Pop., 1,041,000.

Ta·gus (tā′gəs) a river on the Iberian Peninsula, flowing from east-central Spain through central Portugal to the Atlantic. Length, 625 mi (1,006 km).

Ta·hi·ti (tə hē′tē) the largest of the Society Islands, in French Polynesia, midway between Australia and South America. Area, 402 sq mi (1,041 sq km). Pop., 115,820.

Ta·hoe, Lake (tä′hō) a lake in the Sierra Nevadas, on the California-Nevada border.

Tai·chung (tī′jùng′) a city in western Taiwan. Pop., 715,107.

Ta·if (tä′if) see **At Taif.**

Tai·nan (tī′nän′) a city in southwestern Taiwan. Pop., 656,927.

Tai·pei (tī′pā′) *also,* **Tai·peh.** the capital of Taiwan, in the northern part of the island. Pop., 2,637,100.

Tai·wan (tī′wän′) an island country in the western Pacific, east of China, seat of the Nationalist government of China since 1949. Official name: **Republic of China.** Capital, Taipei. Area, 13,885 sq mi (35,962 sq km). Pop., 21,100,000. Also, **Nationalist China.** —**Tai·wan·ese** (tī′wä nēz′, -nēs′), *adj., n.*

Tai·yu·an (tī′ü än′) a city in northern China, the capital of Shanxi province. Pop., 1,700,000.

Ta·jik·i·stan (tə jik′i stan′, -jik′i stän′) a country in central Asia, bordering Afghanistan, China, and Uzbekistan. It was known as Tadzhikistan when it was a republic of the Soviet Union. Capital, Dushanbe. Area, 55,250 sq mi (143,098 sq km). Pop., 5,112,000.

Ta·kla Ma·kan (tä′klə mə kän′) *also,* **Ta·kli·ma·kan.** a desert in western China, between the Tian Shan and Kunlun Mountains. Area, approx. 125,000 sq mi (323,750 sq km).

Tal·ca·hua·no (tal′kə wä′nō) a port city in central Chile, on the Pacific. Pop., 202,368.

Ta·lien (dä′lyen′) see **Dalian.**

Tal·la·has·see (tal′ə has′ē) the capital of Florida, in the northwestern part of the state. Pop., 124,773.

Tal·linn (tä′lin) a city on the Gulf of Finland, the capital of Estonia. Pop., 482,000.

Ta·mau·li·pas (tä′mou lē′päs) a state in northeastern Mexico, bordering southern Texas. Area, 30,734 sq mi (79,601 sq km). Pop., 1,924,484.

Tam·pa (tam′pə) a port city in western Florida. Pop., 280,015.

Tam·pe·re (täm′pe ʀe) a city in southwestern Finland. Pop., 170,533.

Tam·pi·co (tam pē′kō) a port city in northeastern Mexico. Pop., 267,957.

Ta·na·na·rive (tə nan′ə rēv′) see **Antananarivo.**

Tan·gan·yi·ka (tan′gən yē′kə) **1.** a former country in eastern Africa, now part of Tanzania. **2. Lake.** a lake in east-central Africa, lying between Zaire, Tanzania, and Zambia. It is the longest freshwater lake in the world. Length, 450 mi (720 km).

Tan·gier (tan jîr′) a port city in northern Morocco, on the Strait of Gibraltar. Pop., 266,346. Also, **Tan·ger.**

Tang·shan (täng′shän′) a city in northeastern China. Pop., 1,080,000.

Tan·ta (tän′tə) a city in north-central Egypt, in the Nile delta. Pop., 334,505.

Tan·za·ni·a (tan′zə nē′ə) a country in east-central Africa, formed in 1964 by the merger of the former countries of Tanganyika and Zanzibar. Capitals, Dodoma and Dar es Salaam. Area, 364,900 sq mi (945,091 sq km). Pop., 21,062,000. —**Tan′za·ni′an**, *adj., n.*

Ta·ra·bu·lus (tə rab′ə ləs) see **Tripoli** *(defs. 2, 3).*

Ta·ran·to (tär′ən tō′) a port city in southeastern Italy, on the Ionian Sea. Pop., 244,997.

Ta·ra·wa (tə rä′wə) an atoll in the Pacific island country of Kiribati, the site of Bairiki, the capital.

Tar·shish (tär′shish) in the Bible, a country rich in metals, traditionally identified with Spain.

Tar·sus (tär′səs) a city in south-central Turkey, the birthplace of Saint Paul. Pop., 191,333.

Tar·ta·ry (tär′tə rē) a region in Asia and eastern Europe ruled by the Tartars in the thirteenth and fourteenth centuries. Also, **Ta·tary.**

Tash·kent (täsh kent′) the capital of Uzbekistan. Pop., 2,073,000.

Tas·ma·ni·a (taz mā′nē ə) an island state of Australia, off the southeastern coast of the mainland. Capital, Hobart. Area, 26,215 sq mi (67,897 sq km). Pop., 450,960.

Tas·man Sea (taz′mən) the part of the Pacific between southeastern Australia and New Zealand.

Ta·ta·ry (tä′tə rē) see **Tartary.**

Ta·tung (dä′tùng′) see **Datong.**

Tay·lor (tā′lər) a city in southeastern Michigan. Pop., 70,811.

Tbi·li·si (tə bə lē′sē) the capital of Georgia, in the southeastern part of the country. Pop., 1,260,000. Formerly, **Tiflis.**

Te·gu·ci·gal·pa (tə gü′si gal′pə) the capital of Honduras, in the south-central part of the country. Pop., 551,606.

Teh·ran (te rän′, -ran′) *also,* **Te·he·ran.** the capital and largest city of Iran, in the north-central part of the country. Pop., 6,042,584.

Tel A·viv (tel′ə vēv′) a city in west-central Israel, on the Mediterranean, combined with Jaffa in 1950. Official name: **Tel Aviv-Jaffa.** Pop., 317,800.

Tem·pe (tem′pē) a city in south-central Arizona. Pop., 141,865.

Te·mu·co (te mü′kō) a city in central Chile. Pop., 157,297.

Ten·nes·see (ten′ə sē′) **1.** a state in the southeastern United States. Capital, Nashville. Area, 42,144 sq mi (109,153 sq km). Pop., 4,877,185. Abbreviation, **Tenn.**; postal abbreviation, **TN 2.** a river in the southeastern United States, flowing through Tennessee, Alabama, and Kentucky into the Ohio River. Length, 652 mi (1,006 km). —**Ten′nes·se′an**, *adj., n.*

Te·noch·ti·tlán (te nôch′tē tlän′) the capital of the ancient Aztec empire, on the site of present-day Mexico City.

Te·re·si·na (ter′ə zē′nə) a city in northeastern Brazil. Pop., 425,300.

Ter·re Haute (ter′ə hōt′) a city in western Indiana. Pop., 57,843.

Te·thys (tē′this) a large prehistoric sea that is believed to have separated what are now Africa and Eurasia; it is thought to be ancestral to the Mediterranean.

Té·touan (tā twän′) *also,* **Te·tuán.** a port city in northern Morocco, on the Mediterranean. Pop., 199,615.

Tex·as (tek′səs) a state in the south-central United States, bordering Mexico and the Gulf of Mexico. Capital, Austin. Area, 266,807 sq mi (691,030 sq km). Pop., 16,986,510. Abbreviation, **Tex.**; postal abbreviation, **TX** —**Tex′an**, *adj., n.*

Thai·land (tī′land′) **1.** a country in southeastern Asia. Capital, Bangkok. Area, 198,115 sq mi (513,118 sq km). Pop., 54,960,917. Formerly, **Siam. 2.** see **Siam, Gulf of.**

Thames (temz) a river in southern England, flowing east through London to the North Sea. Length, 210 mi (338 km).

Thebes (thēbz) **1.** an ancient Egyptian city on the Nile, a former capital of Egypt. The site, now occupied in part by Luxor and Karnak, is renowned for its tombs and ruins. **2.** one of the leading city-states of ancient Greece, northwest of Athens. —**The′ban**, *adj., n.*

Ther·mop·y·lae (thər mop′ə lē′) a mountain pass in central Greece, site of a battle in 480 B.C. between the Greeks and Persians.

Thes·sa·lon·i·ca (thes′ə lon′i kə) see **Salonika.**

Thes·sa·lo·ni·ki (thes′ə lə nē′kē) see **Salonika.**

Thes·sa·ly (thes′ə lē) a region in northern Greece, bordering the Aegean. —**Thes·sa·li·an** (the sā′lē ən), *adj., n.*

Thim·bu (tim′bü) the capital of Bhutan, in the western part of the country. Pop., 12,000. Also, **Thim·phu** (tim′pü).

Thors·havn (tôrs houn′) see **Torshavn.**

Thousand Islands, a group of about 1,700 small islands in the United States and Canada, in the St. Lawrence River.

Thousand Oaks, a city in southern California. Pop., 104,352.

Thrace (thrās) an ancient and historic region in southern Europe, comprising the eastern part of the Balkan peninsula. It is now divided among Greece, Bulgaria, and Turkey. —**Thra·cian** (thrā′shən), *adj., n.*

Thunder Bay, a port city in southwestern Ontario, Canada,

a	at	e	end	o	hot	u	up	hw	white	⎧	about
ā	ape	ē	me	ō	old	ū	use	ng	song		taken
ä	far	i	it	ô	fork	ü	rule	th	thin	⎨	pencil
âr	care	ī	ice	oi	oil	ů	pull	th	this		lemon
		îr	pierce	ou	out	ûr	turn	zh	measure	⎩	circus

located on an inlet at the western end of Lake Superior. Pop., 112,272.

Thu·rin·gi·a (thủ rin′jē ə) a historic region and former state in central Germany. —**Thu·rin′gi·an,** *adj., n.*

Tian·jin (tyän′jin′) a port city in northeastern China. Pop., 4,950,000. Also, **Tientsin.**

Tian Shan (tyän′ shän′) *also,* **Tien Shan.** a mountain chain in central Asia, extending from Kyrgyzstan into northwestern China.

Ti·ber (tī′bər) a river flowing southward from north-central Italy, through Rome, into the Tyrrhenian Sea. Length, 247 mi (397 km).

Ti·be·ri·as, Lake (tī bîr′ē əs) see **Galilee, Sea of.**

Ti·bet (ti bet′) an autonomous region in southwestern China, north of the Himalayas. Prior to 1950 it was an independent nation ruled by the Dalai Lama. Capital, Lhasa. Area, 471,660 sq mi (1,221,599 sq km). Pop., 2,080,000. Also, **Xizang.**

Ti·con·de·ro·ga (tī′kon də rō′gə) a village and historic fort on Lake Champlain, in northeastern New York. Pop., 2,770.

Tien Shan (tyen′ shän′) see **Tian Shan.**

Tien·tsin (tyen′tsin′) see **Tianjin.**

Tier·ra del Fue·go (tyer′ə del fwā′gō) an archipelago at the southern tip of South America, divided between Chile and Argentina. Land area, approx. 27,500 sq mi (71,200 sq km).

Tif·lis (tif′lis) see **Tbilisi.**

Ti·gris (tī′gris) a river in southwestern Asia, flowing from eastern Turkey to southeastern Iraq, where it joins the Euphrates to empty into the Persian Gulf. Length, 1,180 mi (1,899 km).

Ti·jua·na (tē′ə wä′nə, tē wä′-) a city in northwestern Mexico, on the U.S. border. Pop., 429,500.

Til·burg (til′bûrg′) a city in the southern Netherlands. Pop., 155,100.

Tim·buk·tu (tim′buk tü′) a town in western Africa, in Mali, a great trade and cultural center in the twelfth through fifteenth centuries. Pop., 31,925. Also, *French,* **Tombouctou.**

Ti·mi·şoa·ra (tē′mē shwä′rə) a city in western Romania. Pop., 325,272.

Ti·mor (tē′môr) an Indonesian island southwest of Sulawesi and north of Australia. The western part formerly belonged to the Netherlands, and the eastern part to Portugal. Area, 13,094 sq mi (33,913 sq km).

Tip·pe·ca·noe (tip′i kə nü′) a river in northwestern Indiana. Length, 200 mi (322 km).

Tip·per·ar·y (tip′ə rär′ē) a county in the southern part of the Republic of Ireland. Area, 1,643 sq mi (4,255 sq km). Pop., 136,619.

Ti·ra·në (ti rä′nə) *also,* **Ti·ra·na.** the capital and largest city of Albania, in the central part of the country. Pop., 255,700.

Ti·rol (ti rōl′) see **Tyrol.** —**Tir·o·lese** (tir′ə lēz′, -lēs′), *adj., n.*

Ti·ti·ca·ca, Lake (tit′i kä′kə) the largest lake in South America, in the Andes, in southeastern Peru and western Bolivia.

Tlax·ca·la (tläs kä′lä) a state in east-central Mexico. Area, 1,555 sq mi (4,027 sq km). Pop., 556,597.

To·ba·go (tə bā′gō) an island of the Lesser Antilles, near Venezuela, forming part of the country of Trinidad and Tobago. Area, 116 sq mi (300 sq km).

To·bruk (tō′brúk) *also,* **Tu·bruq.** a port city in northeastern Libya, on the Mediterranean. Pop., 75,282.

To·go (tō′gō) a country in western Africa on the Gulf of Guinea, between Ghana and Benin. Capital, Lomē. Area, 21,925 sq mi (56,786 sq km). Pop., 2,702,945. —**To·go·land·er** (tō′gō lan′-dər), *n.* —**To·go·lese** (tō′gō lēz′, -lēs′, -gə-), *adj.*

To·go·land (tō′gō land′) a former German colony in western Africa, on the Gulf of Guinea, later divided between Great Britain and France. The British section is now part of Ghana; the French is now the country of Togo.

To·ke·lau (tō′kə lou′) a group of three atolls administered by New Zealand, in the southern Pacific. Land area, approx. 5 sq mi (13 sq km). Pop., 1,690.

To·kyo (tō′kē ō, -kyō) the capital and largest city of Japan, in the east-central part of the island of Honshu. Pop., 8,354,615.

To·le·do (tə lē′dō) **1.** a port city in northwestern Ohio, on Lake Erie. Pop., 332,943. **2.** a historic city in central Spain. Pop., 59,551.

Tom·bouc·tou (tôN bük tü′) see **Timbuktu.**

Tomsk (tomsk) a city in south-central Russia. Pop., 502,000.

Ton·ga (tong′gə) a country consisting of three groups of islands in the southwestern Pacific. Capital, Nukualofa. Land area, 270 sq mi (700 sq km). Pop., 94,535. Also, **Tonga Islands.** Formerly, **Friendly Islands.** —**Ton′gan,** *adj., n.*

Ton·kin, Gulf of (ton′kin′, tong′-) an arm of the South China Sea, bordered by Vietnam and China.

To·pe·ka (tə pē′kə) the capital of Kansas, in the northeastern part of the state. Pop., 119,883.

To·ri·no (tô Rē′nō) see **Turin.**

To·ron·to (tə ron′tō) the capital and largest city of Ontario, in the southeastern part of Canada, on Lake Ontario. Pop., 612,289.

Tor·rance (tôr′əns) a city in southern California. Pop., 133,107.

Tor·re·ón (tô′Re ōn′) a city in northern Mexico, northwest of Mexico City. Pop., 328,086.

Tors·havn (tôrs houn′) *also,* **Thorshavn.** the capital of the Faeroe Islands. Pop., 14,767.

Tor·to·la (tôr tō′lə) the largest island of the British Virgin Islands, the site of the capital of Road Town. Area, 21 sq mi (54 sq km).

To·ruń (tô′Rùn yə) a city in northern Poland, on the Vistula River. Pop., 199,600.

Tou·lon (tü lôN′) a port city in southeastern France, on the Mediterranean. Pop., 179,423.

Tou·louse (tü lüz′) a city in southern France. Pop., 347,995.

Tours (tûr) a city in west-central France. In A.D. 732 Charles Martel defeated the Moors in a battle near here. Pop., 132,209.

Tow·son (tou′sən) a city in northern Maryland. Pop., 49,445.

Tra·fal·gar, Cape (trə fal′gər) a cape in southwestern Spain, on the Atlantic, the site of a naval battle on October 21, 1805, in which the fleets of France and Spain were defeated by a British fleet led by Horatio Nelson.

Trans·jor·dan (trans jôr′dən, tranz-) see **Jordan** *(def. 1).*

Trans·kei (trans kā′, -kī′) a black African homeland in the southeastern Republic of South Africa, declared independent in 1976 by South Africa. Area, 15,831 sq mi (41,002 sq km). Pop., 3,081,770.

Trans·vaal (trans väl′, tranz-) a province of the Republic of South Africa, in the northeastern part of the country. Area, 110,450 sq mi (286,066 sq km). Pop., 10,494,013.

Tran·syl·va·ni·a (tran′səl vā′nē ə) a historic region in central Romania. Area, approx. 24,000 sq mi (62,200 sq km).

Trent (trent) a city in northern Italy, site of the Roman Catholic Church council held intermittently from 1545 to 1563. Pop., 81,500. Also, *Italian,* **Tren·to** (tRen′tō).

Tren·ton (tren′tən) the capital of New Jersey, in the western part of the state, on the Delaware River. Pop., 88,675.

Tri·este (trē est′) a port city in northeastern Italy, at the head of the Adriatic Sea. Pop., 239,031.

Trin·i·dad (trin′i dad′) one of the Lesser Antilles, off the coast of Venezuela, part of the country of Trinidad and Tobago. Area, 1,864 sq mi (4,828 sq km).

Trinidad and Tobago, a country consisting of the West Indian islands of Trinidad and Tobago. Capital, Port-of-Spain. Land area, 1,980 sq mi (5,128 sq km). Pop., 1,234,338.

Trip·o·li (trip′ə lē) **1.** a region on the northern coast of Africa, now in western Libya, once a major base for the Barbary pirates. **2.** the capital and largest city of Libya, a port in the northeastern part of the country, on the Mediterranean. Pop., 990,697. **3.** a port city in northern Lebanon, on the Mediterranean Sea. Pop., 198,000. Also *(defs. 2, 3),* **Tarabulus.** —**Tri·pol·i·tan** (tri pol′i-tən), *adj., n.*

Trond·heim (tron′hām′) a historic port city in central Norway. Pop., 135,010.

Troy (troi) an ancient city and stronghold in northwestern Asia Minor, near the mouth of the Dardanelles. Excavations and archaeological research have shown that it was actually settled nine times. The seventh of these cities was the scene of the Trojan War. Also, *Latin,* **Ilium.**

Tru·ji·llo (trü hē′ō) a city in northwestern Peru. Pop., 202,469.

Truk (truk, trùk) an island group in Caroline Islands, in the northern Pacific, part of the Federated States of Micronesia. Land area, approx. 50 sq mi (130 sq km). Also, **Truk Islands.**

Tsi·nan (jē′nän′) see **Jinan.**

Tsing·hai (ching′hī′) see **Qinghai.**

Tsing·tao (ching′dou′) see **Qingdao.**

Tsi·tsi·har (chē′chē′här′) see **Qiqihar.**

Tsun Wan (dzün′ wän′) a city in the colony of Hong Kong. Pop., 514,241.

Tu·bruq (tü′brùk) see **Tobruk.**

Tuc·son (tü′son) a city in southeastern Arizona, noted as a health and tourist resort. Pop., 405,390.

Tu·cu·mán (tü′kə män′) a city in northwestern Argentina. Pop., 392,888. Also, **San Miguel de Tucumán.**

Tu·la (tü′lə) a city in west-central Russia. Pop., 540,000.

Tul·sa (tul′sə) a city in northeastern Oklahoma, on the Arkansas River. Pop., 367,302.

Tu·nis (tü′nis, tü′-) **1.** the capital and largest city of Tunisia, in the northern part of the country. Pop., 596,654. **2.** Tunisia, esp. when considered as one of the Barbary States.

Tu·ni·sia (tü nē′zhə, tü-) a country on the northern coast of Africa, on the Mediterranean. Capital, Tunis. Area, 63,170 sq mi (163,610 sq km). Pop., 6,975,450. —**Tu·ni′sian,** *adj., n.*

Tu·rin (tŭr′in, tyŭr′-) a city in northwestern Italy. Pop., 1,035,565. Also, *Italian*, **Torino**.

Tur·key (tûr′kē) a country in western Asia and southeastern Europe. Capital, Ankara. Area, 300,948 sq mi (779,455 sq km). Pop., 56,969,109. —**Turk** (tûrk), *adj., n.* —**Turk·ish** (tûr′kish), *adj.*

Turk·men Republic (tûrk′men) see **Turkmenistan**.

Turk·me·ni·stan (tûrk′mə nə stan′, -stän′) a country in central Asia, bordering Iran, Afghanistan, and Uzbekistan. It was formerly a republic of the Soviet Union. Capital, Ashkhabad. Area, approx. 188,450 sq mi (488,100 sq km). Pop., 3,534,000. Also, **Turkmen Republic**.

Turks and Cai·cos Islands (tûrks; kā′kəs) a British island group of the West Indies, located south of the Bahamas. Capital, Grand Turk. Land area, 166 sq mi (430 sq km). Pop., 12,350.

Tur·ku (tûr′kü) a port city in southwestern Finland. Pop., 160,456.

Tus·ca·loos·a (tus′kə lü′sə) a city in west-central Alabama. Pop., 77,759.

Tus·ca·ny (tus′kə nē) a region in north-central Italy. Area, 8,876 sq mi (22,989 sq km).

Tu·va·lu (tü vä′lü) an island country in the central Pacific. Capital, Funafuti. Land area, approx. 10 sq mi (26 sq km). Pop., 7,349.

Tyre (tīr) a town on the Mediterranean coast of Lebanon, the principal seaport of ancient Phoenicia and an important commercial center of the ancient world. Pop., 12,500. —**Tyr·i·an** (tir′ē-ən), *adj., n.*

Ty·rol (ti rōl′) *also*, **Tirol**. a region in western Austria, in the Alps, bordering Italy, Germany, and Switzerland. Area, 4,883 sq mi (12,647 sq km). —**Tyr·o·lese** (tir′ə lēz′, -lēs′), *adj., n.*

Tyr·rhe·ni·an Sea (ti rē′nē ən) the part of the Mediterranean between Italy and the islands of Sicily, Sardinia, and Corsica.

Tzu·po (dzü′bō′) see **Zibo**.

U·ban·gi (ü bang′gē, ü bäng′-) a river in central Africa, a major tributary of the Congo.

U·fa (ü fä′) a city in west-central Russia. Pop., 1,083,000.

U·gan·da (ü gan′də, ü gän′-) a landlocked country in east-central Africa. Capital, Kampala. Area, 93,104 sq mi (241,139 sq km). Pop., 17,213,407.

U·jung Pan·dang (ü jùng′ pän däng′) the largest city and chief port of the island of Sulawesi, in Indonesia. Pop., 841,000. Formerly, **Macassar, Makassar**.

U·kraine (ü krān′) a country in eastern Europe on the Black Sea, bordering Belarus, Poland, and Russia. It was formerly a republic of the Soviet Union. Capital, Kiev. Area, approx. 233,000 sq mi (603,500 sq km). Pop., 51,704,000.

U·laan·baa·tar (ü′län bä′tôr) *also*, **U·laan Baa·tar, U·lan Ba·tor**. the capital and largest city of the country of Mongolia, in the northeastern part of the country. Pop., 548,400.

Ul·san (ül′sän′) a city in southeastern South Korea. Pop., 551,014.

Ul·ster (ul′stər) **1.** see **Northern Ireland**. **2.** a historic province of Ireland consisting of what is now Northern Ireland and the northern Republic of Ireland.

Um·bri·a (um′brē ə) a historic region in central Italy. Area, 3,266 sq mi (8,459 sq km).

Union of South Africa, see **South Africa, Republic of**.

Union of Soviet Socialist Republics, a former country, which existed from 1922 to 1991 and extended from eastern Europe to the northeastern coast of Asia. Also, **Soviet Union**.

United Arab Emirates, a country composed of seven sheikdoms on the east-central coast of the peninsula of Arabia. Capital, Abu Dhabi. Area, 32,380 sq mi (83,864 sq km). Pop., 980,000.

United Arab Republic 1. the former name of the republic of Egypt, from 1961 to 1971. **2.** the former name of the union of Egypt and Syria, from 1958 to 1961.

United Kingdom 1. a country in northwestern Europe, composed of England, Scotland, Wales, and Northern Ireland. Capital, London. Area, 92,214 sq mi (238,834 sq km). Pop., 57,120,000. **2.** from 1801 to 1922, a country composed of England, Scotland, Wales, and all of Ireland. Also, **Great Britain**.

United States, a country mainly in North America, consisting of fifty states, the District of Columbia, and several territories. Capital, Washington, D.C. Area, 3,618,770 sq mi (9,372,614 sq km). Pop., 243,211,900. Also, **United States of America, America.**

Upper Vol·ta (vōl′tə) see **Burkina Faso**.

Upp·sa·la (up′sə lə, ùp′sä′lä) a city in eastern Sweden. Pop., 164,754.

Ur (ûr) a city of ancient Sumer in southern Mesopotamia, on the Euphrates.

U·ral Mountains (yùr′əl) a mountain system extending north

to south in west-central Russia, forming part of the traditional boundary between Europe and Asia. Also, **Urals**.

Ural River, a river in Russia and Kazakhstan, flowing south and west from the southern Ural Mountains into the Caspian Sea. It forms part of the traditional boundary between Europe and Asia. Also, **Ural**.

Urals (yùr′əlz) see **Ural Mountains**.

Ur·mi·a (ûr′mē ə) see **Orumiyeh**.

U·ru·guay (yùr′ə gwā′, ùr′ə gwī′) **1.** a country on the southeastern coast of South America, between Brazil and Argentina. Capital, Montevideo. Area, 68,536 sq mi (177,508 sq km). Pop., 2,955,241. **2.** a river in southeastern South America, flowing between Brazil and Uruguay on the east and Argentina on the west. It empties into the Río de la Plata. Length, 1,000 mi (1,609 km).

U·rum·qi (ü′Rüm′chē′) *also*, **U·rum·chi.** a city in northwestern China, the capital of Xinjiang. Pop., 1,060,000.

Us·ti·nov (üs′tə nôf′, üs′tə nôv′) see **Izhevsk**.

U·tah (ü′tô, ü′tä) a state in the western United States. Capital, Salt Lake City. Area, 84,899 sq mi (219,888 sq km). Pop., 1,722,850. Abbreviation, **Ut.**; postal abbreviation, **UT** —**U·tah·an** (ü′tôn, ü′tän), *adj., n.*

U·ti·ca (ü′ti kə) **1.** a city in central New York, on the Mohawk. Pop., 68,637. **2.** an ancient northern African city, located near Carthage.

U·trecht (ü′trekt) a historic city in the central Netherlands. Pop., 230,700.

Uz·bek·i·stan (ùz bek′i stan′) a country in central Asia, bordering Kazakhstan and Turkmenistan. It was formerly a republic of the Soviet Union. Capital, Tashkent. Area, approx. 172,740 sq mi (447,397 sq km). Pop., 19,906,000.

Va·duz (vä′dŭts) the capital of Liechtenstein. Pop., 4,874.

Va·len·ci·a (və len′sē ə, -shə) **1.** a port city in eastern Spain. Pop., 743,933. **2.** a city in northern Venezuela. Pop., 616,224.

Val·la·do·lid (val′ə də lid′) a city in north-central Spain. Pop., 331,461.

Val·le·jo (və lā′ō) a port city in western California. Pop., 109,199.

Val·let·ta (və let′ə) the capital of Malta. Pop., 9,210.

Valley Forge, a village in southeastern Pennsylvania where George Washington and his army camped during the winter of 1777-1778.

Val·pa·rai·so (val′pə rī′zō) a port city in central Chile. Pop., 265,355.

Van·cou·ver (van kü′vər) **1.** a port city in southwestern British Columbia, Canada, on the mainland. Pop., 431,147. **2.** an island of British Columbia, Canada, just off the southwestern coast of the mainland. Area, 12,408 sq mi (32,137 sq km).

Van·u·a·tu (van′ü ä′tü) a country in the southwestern Pacific, west of Fiji, consisting of a group of eighty islands. Capital, Vila. Land area, 4,706 sq mi (12,189 sq km). Pop., 142,419. Formerly, **New Hebrides**.

Va·ra·na·si (və rä′nə sē) a Hindu holy city on the Ganges, in northeastern India. Pop., 708,647. Formerly, **Benares**.

Var·na (vär′nə) a port city in eastern Bulgaria, on the Black Sea. Pop., 303,071.

Vat·i·can City (vat′i kən) an independent state ruled by the pope and located within the city of Rome, Italy, having an area of about 109 acres (44 hectares). Pop., 766.

Ven·da (ven′də) a black African homeland in the northeastern Republic of South Africa, declared independent in 1979 by South Africa. Area, 2,774 sq mi (7,185 sq km). Pop., 459,819.

Ve·ne·ti·a (və nē′shə, -shə) a region in northeastern Italy. Area, 7,094 sq mi (18,373 sq km). Also, **Ve·ne·to** (ven′i tō′).

Ven·e·zue·la (ven′ə zwā′lə, -zwē′-) a country in northern South America, on the Caribbean. Capital, Caracas. Area, 352,145 sq mi (912,056 sq km). Pop., 14,516,735. —**Ven·e·zue′lan,** *adj., n.*

Ven·ice (ven′is) a port city in northeastern Italy, on 118 islets in the Adriatic. Pop., 88,700; metro. area pop., 420,000.

Ver·a·cruz (ver′ə krüz′) **1.** a state in eastern Mexico. Area, 27,759 sq mi (71,896 sq km). Pop., 5,387,680. **2.** a port city in eastern Mexico, on the Gulf of Mexico. Pop., 284,822.

Verde, Cape (vûrd) the westernmost point of Africa, a peninsula on the coast of Senegal.

Ver·dun (vər dun′) a city in northeastern France, the scene of much fighting in World War I. Pop., 21,516.

Ver·mont (vər mont′) a state in the northeastern United States.

a	at	e	end	o	hot	u	up	hw	white		about
ā	ape	ē	me	ō	old	ū	use	ng	song		taken
ä	far	i	it	ô	fork	ü	rule	th	thin	ə	pencil
âr	care	ī	ice	oi	oil	ù	pull	th	this		lemon
		îr	pierce	ou	out	ûr	turn	zh	measure		circus

Capital, Montpelier. Area, 9,614 sq mi (24,900 sq km). Pop., 562,758. Abbreviation, Vt.; postal abbreviation, **VT** —Ver·mont′er, *n.*

Ve·ro·na (və rō′nə) a city in northeastern Italy. Pop., 259,151.

Ver·sailles (vâr sī′, vər-) a historic city in north-central France, just southwest of Paris. It is the site of the magnificent palace of Louis XIV. Pop., 91,494.

Ve·su·vi·us, Mount (və sü′vē əs) an active volcano in southern Italy, southeast of Naples. A major eruption of the volcano in A.D. 79 buried the ancient cities of Pompeii and Herculaneum. Height, 4,190 ft (1,277 m).

Viang·chan (vyäng chän′) see **Vientiane.**

Vich·y (vish′ē) a city in central France, a noted health resort. From 1940 to 1944, Vichy served as the seat of government of unoccupied France. Pop., 30,527.

Vicks·burg (viks′bûrg) a port city in western Mississippi, on the Mississippi River. Vicksburg was besieged and captured by Union forces in 1863 during the Civil War. Pop., 20,908.

Vic·to·ri·a (vik tôr′ē ə) **1.** a state of Australia, in the southeastern part of the country. Capital, Melbourne. Area, 87,884 sq mi (227,620 sq km). Pop., 4,315,200. **2.** Lake. a lake in east-central Africa, the largest of the continent. Also, **Victoria Ny·an·za** (nī an′zə). **3.** the capital of British Columbia, Canada, on the southern tip of Vancouver Island. Pop., 66,303. **4.** a large Canadian island north of the Arctic Circle, part of the Northwest Territories. Area, 81,900 sq mi (212,100 sq km). **5.** the capital and commercial center of the British colony of Hong Kong. Pop., 1,175,860. Also, **Hong Kong. 6.** the capital of the Seychelles. Pop., 23,000.

Vi·en·na (vē en′ə) the capital and largest city of Austria, in the northeastern part of the country, on the Danube River. Pop., 1,482,800. —Vi·en·nese (vē′ə nēz′, -nēs′), *adj., n.*

Vien·tiane (vyen tyän′) the capital and largest city of Laos, on the Mekong River in the western part of the country. Pop., 377,409. Also, **Viangchan.**

Vi·et·nam (vē′et näm′) *also,* **Vi·et Nam.** a country in southeastern Asia, divided from 1954 to 1975 into North Vietnam and South Vietnam. Capital, Hanoi. Area, 127,242 sq mi (329,556 sq km). Pop., 52,741,766.

Vi·la (vē′lə) the capital of Vanuatu. Pop., 18,905.

Vil·ni·us (vil′nē əs) the capital of Lithuania. Pop., 582,000. Also, *Russian,* **Vil·na** (vil′nə); *Polish,* **Wilno.**

Vi·ña del Mar (vēn′yə del mär′) a city in central Chile, on the Pacific. Pop., 244,899.

Vin·son Mas·sif (vin′sən ma sēf′) the highest mountain in Antarctica. Height, 16,864 ft (5,140 m).

Vir·gin·ia (vər jin′yə) a state in the eastern United States. Capital, Richmond. Area, 40,767 sq mi (105,587 sq km). Pop., 6,187,358. Abbreviation, Va.; postal abbreviation, **VA** —Vir·gin′ian, *adj., n.*

Virginia Beach, a resort city in southeastern Virginia, on the Atlantic. Pop., 393,069.

Vir·gin Islands (vûr′jin) an island group of the Caribbean, the westernmost of the Lesser Antilles. It is divided politically between the United States and Great Britain. Land area, approx. 192 sq mi (497 sq km).

Virgin Islands, British, the British-administered islands in the eastern Virgin Islands. Capital, Road Town. Land area, 59 sq mi (153 sq km). Pop., 12,258.

Virgin Islands National Park, an area in the U.S. Virgin Islands, on the island of St. John, noted for its scenic beauty and marine life. Area, 14,708 acres (5,952 hectares).

Virgin Islands of the United States, a U.S. territory made up of the westernmost islands of the Virgin Islands, including St. Croix and St. Thomas. Capital, Charlotte Amalie. Land area, 133 sq mi (344 sq km). Pop., 106,000.

Vis·a·kha·pat·nam (vi sä′kə put′nəm) see **Vishakhapatnam.**

Vi·sa·yan Islands (vi sī′ən) a group of islands in the central Philippines. Also, **Bisayas.**

Vish·a·kha·pat·nam (vi shä′kə put′nəm) *also,* **Visakhapatnam.** a port city in eastern India. Pop., 565,321.

Vis·tu·la (vis′chü lə) a river in Poland, flowing north from southern Poland to the Baltic Sea. Length, 678 mi (1,091 km).

Vi·to·ri·a (vi tôr′ē ə) a city in north-central Spain. Pop., 204,264.

Vla·di·kav·kaz (vlad′i käf käz′) a city in southwestern Russia, in the Caucasus. Pop., 300,000. Formerly, **Ordzhonikidze.**

Vlad·i·vos·tok (vlad′i vos′tok) a port city in southeasternmost Russia, on the Sea of Japan. Pop., 648,000.

Vol·ga (vol′gə, vôl′-) a river in European Russia, flowing into the Caspian Sea. It is the longest river in Europe and the chief inland waterway of Russia. Length, 2,194 mi (3,530 km).

Vol·go·grad (vol′gə grad′, vôl′-) a port city in southwestern Russia, on the Volga River, the scene of a major Soviet victory over the Germans in World War II. Pop., 999,000. Formerly, **Stalingrad.**

Vo·ro·nezh (və rō′nish) a city in western Russia. Pop., 887,000.

Vosges (vōzh) a mountain range of northeastern France, parallel to the Rhine River.

Wa·bash River (wô′bash) a river in the Middle West, flowing from western Ohio west and southwest across Indiana and along the Indiana-Illinois border to the Ohio. Length, 475 mi (764 km).

Wa·co (wā′kō) a city in east-central Texas. Pop., 103,590.

Wah·ran (wä rän′) see **Oran.**

Wai·ki·ki (wī′kē kē′) a beach and resort area in Honolulu, Hawaii.

Wai·pa·hu (wī pä′hü) a city in Hawaii, on the southern part of Oahu. Pop., 29,139.

Wake Island (wāk) an atoll in the Pacific, west of Hawaii, administered by the United States. Land area, 3 sq mi (8 sq km).

Wales (wālz) a division of the United Kingdom, west of and bordering England. Area, 8,019 sq mi (20,769 sq km). Pop., 2,857,000.

Wal·lis and Fu·tu·na Islands (wol′is; fü tü′nə) a group of islands in the southwestern Pacific, a French overseas territory. Land area, 106 sq mi (275 sq km). Pop., 12,408.

Wal·sall (wôl′sôl) a city in west-central England. Pop., 177,923.

Wal·vis Bay (wôl′vis) a port city on the coast of southwestern Africa, located in a South African enclave in Namibia. Pop., 9,687.

War·ren (wôr′ən, wor′-) a city in southeastern Michigan. Pop., 144,864.

War·saw (wôr′sô) the capital and largest city of Poland, in the east-central part of the country. Pop., 1,651,200.

War·wick (wôr′wik) a city in central Rhode Island. Pop., 85,427.

War·wick·shire (wôr′ik shîr′, -shər) a county in central England. Pop., 484,600.

Wash·ing·ton (wô′shing tən, wosh′ing-) **1.** the capital of the United States, lying between Maryland and northern Virginia and occupying the District of Columbia. Pop., 606,900. Also, **Washington, D.C. 2.** a state in the northwestern United States, on the Pacific. Capital, Olympia. Area, 68,139 sq mi (176,480 sq km). Pop., 4,866,692. Abbreviation, **Wash.;** postal abbreviation, **WA 3. Mount.** the highest mountain in New England, in northern New Hampshire. Height, 6,288 ft (1,917 m). —Wash·ing·to·ni·an (wô′shing tō′nē ən, wosh′ing-), *adj., n.*

Wa·ter·bur·y (wô′tər ber′ē, -bə rē, wot′ər-) a city in western Connecticut. Pop., 108,961.

Wa·ter·loo (wô′tər lō′) **1.** a village in central Belgium, scene of the final defeat of Napoleon Bonaparte, on June 18, 1815, by a combined army of English, Dutch, and Prussians. Pop., 25,232. **2.** a city in east-central Iowa. Pop., 66,467.

Wei·mar (vī′mär) a historic town in central Germany. Pop., 63,412.

Welfare Island, see **Roosevelt Island.**

Wel·land Ship Canal (wel′ənd) a canal in southeastern Ontario, Canada, connecting lakes Erie and Ontario; it is part of the St. Lawrence Seaway.

Wel·ling·ton (wel′ing tən) the capital of New Zealand, on the southwestern tip of North Island. Pop., 137,495.

We·ser (vā′zər) a river in northwestern Germany, flowing north to the North Sea. Length, 270 mi (434 km).

West (west) the western part of the United States, usually considered as that part west of the Mississippi River.

West Bank, an area in the Middle East, west of the Jordan River, formerly part of Palestine. Annexed by Jordan in 1950, it has been occupied by Israel since 1967. Area, approx. 3,300 sq mi (8,550 sq km).

West Berlin, the part of the city of Berlin formerly belonging to West Germany, now part of Berlin.

West Brom·wich (brum′ij, -ich, brom′-) a city in west-central England. Pop., 153,725.

West Co·vi·na (kə vē′nə) a city in southern California. Pop., 96,086.

Western Australia, a state occupying the western part of Australia. Capital, Perth. Area, 975,290 sq mi (2,526,000 sq km). Pop., 1,591,077.

Western Desert, see **Libyan Desert.**

Western Islands, see **Hebrides.**

Western Roman Empire, the western part of the Roman Empire, after its division in A.D. 395, including present day France, Spain, and Britain. Also, **Western Empire.**

Western Sahara, a territory on the northwestern coast of Africa, claimed by Morocco and by a political group based in Algeria. Capital, El Aaiún. Area, 102,700 sq mi (266,000 sq km). Pop., 142,000. Formerly, **Spanish Sahara.**

Western Samoa, an island country in the southern Pacific, east

of Australia, consisting of the western islands of Samoa. Capital, Apia. Land area, 1,097 sq mi (2,841 sq km). Pop., 156,349.

West Germany, a former country in north-central Europe, now part of Germany.

West In·dies (in'dēz) an archipelago extending from Florida to the coast of Venezuela, separating the Caribbean from the Atlantic. It consists of the Greater Antilles, including Cuba, Hispaniola (Haiti and the Dominican Republic), Jamaica, and Puerto Rico; the Lesser Antilles, including the Leeward and Windward Islands; and the Bahamas. —**West Indian.**

West Irian, see Irian Jaya.

West·land (west'lənd) a city in southeastern Michigan. Pop., 84,724.

West Malaysia, see Malaya.

West·min·ster (west'min'stər) a borough in the central part of Greater London, especially that part containing the court and government buildings. Pop., 190,661.

West·mor·land (west'môr'lənd', west'mər lənd) a former county in northwestern England.

West Pakistan, one of two former provinces of Pakistan. In 1971, the other former province, East Pakistan, became the independent country of Bangladesh. The country of Pakistan now consists of what was the province of West Pakistan.

West·pha·li·a (west fā'lē ə, -fāl'yə) a region in western Germany, formerly a province of Prussia.

West Point, a military reserve on the Hudson River in southeastern New York State, site of the United States Military Academy.

West Virginia, a state in the eastern United States. Capital, Charleston. Area, 24,232 sq mi (62,761 sq km). Pop., 1,793,477. Abbreviation, W. Va.; postal abbreviation, WV —**West Virginian.**

Wheel·ing (hwē'ling, wē'-) a city in northern West Virginia, on the Ohio. Pop., 34,882.

White·horse (hwīt'hôrs', wīt'-) a city in northwestern Canada, capital of the Yukon. Pop., 15,199.

White Mountains, a northern range of the Appalachian Mountains, located chiefly in northern New Hampshire.

White Nile, a river in eastern Africa, flowing northward through Uganda and Sudan to Khartoum, where it joins the Blue Nile. Length, 1,180 mi (1,898 km).

White Russia, see Belarus.

White Sea, an arm of the Barents Sea, off the northwestern coast of Russia.

Whit·ney, Mount (hwit'nē, wit'-) a mountain of the Sierra Nevada, in eastern California, the highest peak in the United States outside Alaska. Height, 14,494 ft (4,418 m).

Wich·i·ta (wich'i tô') the largest city in Kansas, in the south-central part of the state. Pop., 304,011.

Wichita Falls, a city in northern Texas. Pop., 96,259.

Wies·ba·den (vēs'bä'dən) a city in west-central Germany, noted as a health resort. Pop., 254,209.

Wight, Isle of (wīt) an island and county in England, located in the English Channel off the southern coast. Area, 147 sq mi (381 sq km).

Wil·lem·stad (vil'əm stät') the capital and largest city of the Netherlands Antilles, located on the island of Curaçao. Pop., 31,883.

Wil·liams·burg (wil'yəmz bûrg') a historic town in southeastern Virginia. Pop., 11,530.

Wil·ming·ton (wil'ming tən) the largest city of Delaware, a port in the northern part of the state. Pop., 71,529.

Wil·no (wil'nō) see Vilnius.

Wil·son, Mount (wil'sən) a peak in southern California, site of an astronomical observatory. Height, 5,710 ft (1,740 m).

Wilt·shire (wilt'shîr, -shər) a county in southern England. Pop., 557,000.

Wim·ble·don (wim'bəl dən) a district in Greater London, England, noted as the site of the British tennis championship.

Win·ches·ter (win'ches'tər, -chə stər) a city in southern England, a noted religious and educational center and site of a well-known Gothic cathedral. Pop., 34,127.

Win·der·mere, Lake (win'dər mîr') the largest lake in England, located in the northwestern part of the country.

Wind·hoek (vint'hùk') the capital of Namibia, in the central part of the territory. Pop., 114,500.

Wind·sor (win'zər) **1.** a city in southern England, southwest of London, on the Thames. It is the site of Windsor Castle. Pop., 30,832. Also, **New Windsor. 2.** a city in southern Ontario, Canada. Pop., 193,111.

Wind·ward Islands (wind'wərd) a Caribbean island group forming the southern part of the Lesser Antilles. Land area, approx. 1,412 sq mi (3,657 sq km).

Win·ni·peg (win'ə peg') **1.** a city in southern Canada, the capital and largest city of Manitoba. Pop., 594,551. **2. Lake.** a lake in south-central Manitoba.

Win·ston-Sa·lem (win'stən sā'ləm) a city in north-central North Carolina. Pop., 143,485.

Wis·con·sin (wis kon'sin) a state in the north-central United States, bordering Lake Michigan on the east. Capital, Madison. Area, 56,153 sq mi (145,436 sq km). Pop., 4,891,769. Abbreviation, **Wis.**; postal abbreviation, **WI** —**Wis·con·sin·ite**' (-īt').

Wit·wa·ters·rand (wit'wô'tərz rand') a gold-rich ridge of rock in northeastern South Africa. Also, **the Rand.**

Wol·lon·gong (wùl'ən gông') a seaport on the southeastern coast of Australia, in New South Wales. Pop., 174,770.

Wol·ver·hamp·ton (wùl'vər hamp'tən) a city in west-central England. Pop., 263,501.

Won·san (wun'sän') a seaport in eastern North Korea. Pop., 398,000.

Worces·ter (wùs'tər) a city in central Massachusetts. Pop., 169,759.

Worces·ter·shire (wùs'tər shîr', -shər) a former county in western England.

Worms (wûrmz, vôrms) a city in west-central Germany, on the Rhine. Pop., 74,809.

Wro·claw (vrôts'läf) a city in southwestern Poland. Pop., 637,400. Formerly, *German,* **Breslau.**

Wu·chang (wü'chäng') a former city in east-central China, now part of Wuhan.

Wu·han (wü'hän') a metropolis in east-central China, formed by the merger of the cities of Hankou, Hanyang, and Wuchang; it is the capital of Hubei province. Pop., 3,570,000.

Wup·per·tal (vùp'ər täl') a city in western Germany. Pop., 371,283.

Würz·burg (wûrts'bûrg', vyRts'bùRk') a city in central Germany. Pop., 125,589.

Wu·xi (wy'shœ') *also,* **Wu·sih.** a city in eastern China. Pop., 880,000.

Wy·o·ming (wī ō'ming) a state in the western United States. Capital, Cheyenne. Area, 97,809 sq mi (253,325 sq km). Pop., 453,588. Abbreviation, **Wyo.**; postal abbreviation, **WY** —**Wy·o'ming·ite',** *n.*

Xi·a·men (shyä'mœn') a city and harbor in southeastern China on an island off the coast of Fujian province. Pop., 350,000. Also, Amoy.

Xi·an (shē'än') *also,* **Sian.** a city in east-central China, the capital of Shaanxi province. Pop., 2,210,000.

Xi·ning (shē'ning') *also,* **Sining.** a city in west-central China, the capital of Qinghai province. Pop., 620,000.

Xin·jiang (shin'jyäng') *also,* **Sinkiang.** an autonomous region in western China, bordering Tibet, India, Mongolia, Kazakhstan, Kyrgyzstan, and Tajikistan. Capital, Urumqi. Area, 635,829 sq mi (1,646,797 sq km). Pop., 14,240,000. Also, **Xinjiang Uy·gur Autonomous Region** (wē'gər).

Xi·zang (shē'zäng') see Tibet.

Xu·zhou (shy'jō') *also,* **Suchow.** a city in eastern China. Pop., 860,000.

Yal·ta (yôl'tə) a resort city on the Black Sea in Ukraine, in the southern Crimean peninsula. It was the site of a conference held by Franklin Roosevelt, Joseph Stalin, and Winston Churchill in 1945. Pop., 89,000.

Ya·lu (yä'lü) a river in eastern Asia, flowing between northern China and North Korea into the Yellow Sea. Length, 500 mi (805 km).

Ya·mas·sou·kro (yä'mä sü'krō) the capital of the Ivory Coast, in the central part of the country. Pop., 80,000.

Yan·gon (yän kō') see Rangoon.

Yang·tze (yäng'tsē') *also,* **Yang·tse.** the longest river in China, flowing northeastward from Tibet through central China and into the East China Sea, near Shanghai. Length, 3,915 mi (6,299 km). Also, **Chang, Chang Jiang.**

Ya·oun·dé (yä ün dā') the capital of Cameroon, in the south-central part of the country. Pop., 653,670.

Yap (yäp) one of the Caroline Islands, in the western Pacific, part of the Federated States of Micronesia. Area, 146 sq mi (378 sq km).

Ya·ro·slavl (yär'ə slä'vəl) a city in central western Russia. Pop., 633,000.

a	at	e	end	o	hot	u	up	hw	white		about
ā	ape	ē	me	ō	old	ū	use	ng	song	ə	taken
ä	far	i	it	ô	fork	ū	rule	th	thin		pencil
âr	care	ī	ice	oi	oil	ù	pull	th	this		lemon
		îr	pierce	ou	out	ûr	turn	zh	measure		circus

Ye·kat·er·in·burg (yə kat′ər in bûrg′) a city east of the Ural Mountains in northwestern Russia. Pop., 1,367,000. Formerly, **Sverdlovsk.**

Yel·low·knife (yel′ō nīf′) the capital and largest city of the Northwest Territories, Canada, located on the northern shore of Great Slave Lake. Pop., 11,753.

Yellow River, see **Huang He.**

Yellow Sea, a shallow arm of the Pacific, between northeastern China and North and South Korea.

Yel·low·stone (yel′ō stōn′) a river in the northern United States, mainly in Montana, a major tributary of the Missouri. Length, 671 mi (1,080 km).

Yellowstone National Park, a national park in northwestern Wyoming and neighboring sections of Montana and Idaho, noted for its scenery, hot springs, and geysers. It was the first national park to be established in the world. Area, 3,472 sq mi (8,992 sq km).

Yem·en (yem′ən) a country in the southern part of the peninsula of Arabia, on the Red Sea and Gulf of Aden. Capital, Sana. Area, 186,375 sq mi (483,921 sq km). Pop., 15,267,000.

Ye·re·van (yer′ə vän′) the capital of Armenia. Pop., 1,199,000. Also, **Erivan.**

Yin·chuan (yin′chwän′) also, **Yin·chwan.** a city in north-central China, the capital of Ningxia. Pop., 268,200.

Yog·ya·kar·ta (yōg′yə kär′tə) also, **Djok·ja·kar·ta.** a city in Indonesia, on the southern part of Java. Pop., 421,000.

Yo·ko·ha·ma (yō′kə hä′mə) a port city in east-central Japan, on the island of Honshu. Pop., 2,992,926.

Yon·kers (yong′kərz) a city in southeastern New York. Pop., 188,082.

York (yôrk) a city in northeastern England. Pop., 123,126.

York·shire (yôrk′shir′, -shər) a former county in northern England.

York·town (yôrk′toun′) a historic town in southeastern Virginia, scene in 1781 of the last major battle of the American Revolution, when Lord Cornwallis surrendered to George Washington.

Yo·sem·i·te Falls (yō sem′i tē) waterfalls in Yosemite National Park, among the world's highest. Height, 2,425 ft (739 m).

Yosemite National Park, a national park in east-central California, noted for the scenic magnificence of its valley, waterfalls, and sequoia trees. Area, 1,189 sq mi (3,080 sq km).

Youngs·town (yungz′toun′) a city in northeastern Ohio. Pop., 95,732.

Y·pres (ē′prə) a historic town in western Belgium, noted for the many battles of World War I fought there. Pop., 21,200. Also, *Flemish,* **Ieper.**

Yu·ca·tán (ū′kə tan′) **1.** a peninsula in southeastern Mexico and northeastern Central America, between the Gulf of Mexico and the Caribbean. It was the center of Mayan civilization. Area, approx. 70,000 sq mi (181,300 sq km). **2.** a state in southeastern Mexico, at the end of the Yucatán peninsula. Area, 14,868 sq mi (38,508 sq km). Pop., 1,063,733.

Yu·go·sla·vi·a (ū′gō slä′vē ə) *also,* **Jugoslavia.** a country in southeastern Europe. From 1945 to 1991 it consisted of six republics, some of which have become independent states. Capital, Belgrade. —**Yu·go·slav** (ū′gō släv′), **Yu′go·sla′vi·an,** *adj., n.*

Yu·kon (ū′kon) **1.** a territory in northwestern Canada. Capital, Whitehorse. Area, 207,076 sq mi (536,327 sq km). Pop., 23,504. **2.** a river flowing from this territory through central Alaska into the Bering Sea.

Yun·nan (yù′nän′) a province in southern China. Capital, Kunming. Area, 168,417 sq mi (436,200 sq km). Pop., 35,340,000.

Za·brze (zäb′zhe) a city in southwestern Poland. Pop., 201,400.

Za·ca·te·cas (sä′kä te′käs) a state in west-central Mexico. Area, 28,125 sq mi (72,844 sq km). Pop., 1,136,830.

Za·ga·zig (zä′gä zēg′) a city in northern Egypt. Pop., 245,496.

Za·greb (zä′greb) the capital of Croatia. Pop., 697,925.

Za·ire (zä îr′) **1.** a country in central Africa. Capital, Kinshasa. Area, 905,568 sq mi (2,345,421 sq km). Pop., 29,671,407. Formerly, **Democratic Republic of the Congo. 2.** see **Congo** *(def. 1).* —**Za·ir·i·an** (zä îr′ē ən), *adj., n.*

Zam·be·zi (zam bē′zē) a river in southern Africa, flowing eastward through Zimbabwe and Mozambique into the Indian Ocean. Length, 1,700 mi (2,735 km).

Zam·bi·a (zam′bē ə) a landlocked country in south-central Africa. Capital, Lusaka. Area, 290,586 sq mi (752,618 sq km). Pop., 5,661,801. Formerly, **Northern Rhodesia.**

Zan·zi·bar (zan′zə bär′) **1.** an island in the Indian Ocean, off the eastern coast of Africa, part of Tanzania. Area, 640 sq mi (1,658 sq km). **2.** a former country consisting of the islands of Zanzibar and Pemba, now part of Tanzania. **3.** a port city on the island of Zanzibar. Pop., 133,000.

Za·po·rozh·ye (zä′pə rôzh′yə) a city on the Dnieper in Ukraine. Pop., 884,000.

Za·ra·go·za (zar′ə gō′zə) see **Saragossa.**

Za·ri·a (zä′rē ə) a city in northern Nigeria. Pop., 302,800.

Zar·qa (zär′kə) also, **Zar·ka.** see **Az Zarqa.**

Zhe·jiang (jœ′jyäng′) also, **Chekiang.** a province in eastern China. Capital, Hangzhou. Area, 39,305 sq mi (101,800 sq km). Pop., 41,170,000.

Zheng·zhou (jœng′jō′) a city in eastern China, the capital of Henan province. Pop., 1,150,000. Also, **Chengchow.**

Zi·bo (zœ′bō′) also, **Tzu·po.** a city in eastern China. Pop., 840,000. Formerly, **Changtien.**

Zim·bab·we (zim bäb′wä, -wē) a landlocked country in south-central Africa. Capital, Harare. Area, 150,873 sq mi (390,761 sq km). Pop., 7,740,000. Formerly, **Southern Rhodesia.** —**Zim·bab·we·an** (zim bäb′wä ən, -wē-), *adj., n.*

Zi·on (zī′ən) a hill in Jerusalem on which the royal palace of David and the Temple were built. Also, **Sion.**

Zui·der Zee (zī′dər zā′, zē′) also, **Zuy·der Zee.** a former inlet of the North Sea on the northwestern coast of the Netherlands. The southern part was closed off by a dike to form the IJsselmeer.

Zu·rich (zùr′ik, tsY′RIKH) the largest city in Switzerland, in the northern part of the country. Pop., 342,861.

Zwick·au (tsvik′ou) a city in eastern Germany. Pop., 121,749.

*R*eference Section

An Approach to Writing

Writing is a challenging process that requires a wide range of skills. Among them are clear thinking, imagination, and the ability to organize ideas. Producing a piece of original writing—for example, an essay, an article, a term paper, or a descriptive personal letter—can be a very satisfying experience. But if you aren't sure how to tackle the project, or even where to begin, it can also be daunting.

One approach that works well for many people is to break down the process into a series of separate parts or stages and deal with them one at a time. The stages, outlined below, do not necessarily have to be followed in the order in which they are presented. In fact, writing almost always involves going back and forth. For example, you may begin with a particular idea, express it on paper, and then go back and revise or expand the original idea. But the stages can be used as a framework that can simplify the task of writing and make it more manageable. Every writer has an individual approach, and as you do more writing and become more experienced, you will find the approach that works best for you.

Prewriting Strategies.   This is a preliminary stage to be undertaken before the writing itself begins. During prewriting, a writer:

- Defines the subject and purpose of the writing.
- Decides on the audience.
- Formulates the ideas and lists them in order of importance.
- Finds sources of material.
- Brainstorms, if appropriate.
- Makes an outline.
- Jots down thoughts as they come to mind, without concern for order or sequence, so as not to lose sight of them.

LITERARY TIME LINE

Sumerian pictographic writing on clay tablets
4000-3500 B.C.

Hieroglyphics and cuneiform writing are developed
3500-3001 B.C.

Early papyrus document: Pepi's "Instructions to a Son"
3000-2501 B.C.

Development of first libraries in Egypt
2500-2001 B.C.

24-sign Egyptian alphabet

Early Semitic alphabet
2000-1501 B.C.

First Chinese dictionary
1500-1000 B.C.

"Song of Deborah," from early Hebrew literature
1000-901 B.C.

Homer
The Iliad, The Odyssey
800-700 B.C.

Aesop
Fables
600 B.C.

First Draft.   Completing these preliminaries makes it easier to approach the first draft. The material has been assembled, and the writer has thought about the ideas and arranged them in some kind of order (although the order may change as the work progresses). Many writers find it helpful to follow an outline in writing their first draft. But it is best to treat the outline as a guide, not something to be locked into. Writing is a dynamic process; ideas develop when you begin to get them down, and what you wish to say (and how you wish to say it) is likely to change as you go along.

Some things to keep in mind in writing the first draft:

- Use your opening sentence or paragraph to present your main idea or theme. Try to do it in a way that will capture your reader's attention (for example, with a surprising statement or an interesting question).
- Develop and support your ideas in the sentences or paragraphs that follow.
- Use language that is appropriate for the subject and the audience. More formal language may be appropriate for a serious subject; more informal language may work better for a light or humorous one.
- Try to find an ending that wraps up the piece effectively or reenforces the main idea.

Revising.   Revising is a crucial part of writing. It's a good idea to let some time elapse between writing a first draft and revising it. Looking at your work with a fresh eye will help you refine your ideas and present them more effectively.

Some things to keep in mind in revising:

- Have all the important points been made?
- Have they been presented in the best order?
- Are there enough concrete examples to support the ideas?
- Are the paragraphs linked together? Are the transitions smooth?
- Are you satisfied with the introductory sentence? Often, you will find that a better one is hidden somewhere in the middle of the writing.

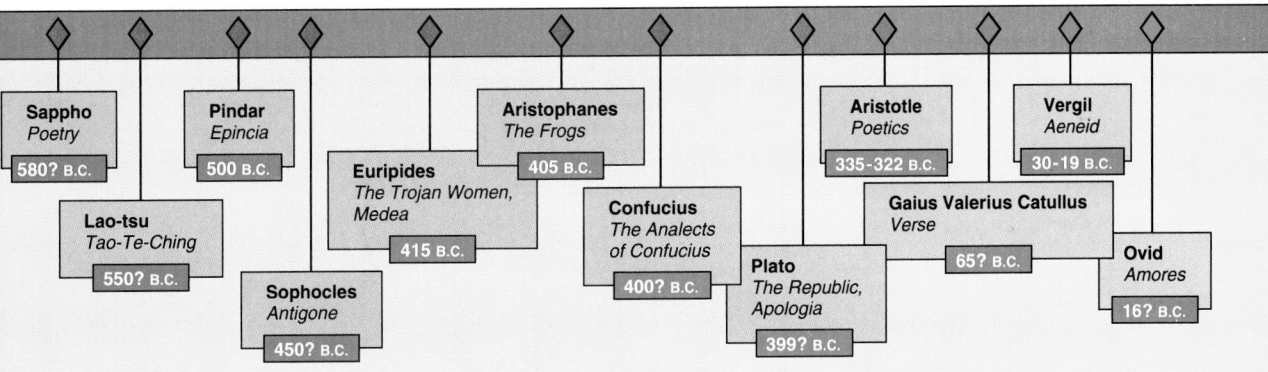

Sappho
Poetry
580? B.C.

Lao-tsu
Tao-Te-Ching
550? B.C.

Pindar
Epincia
500 B.C.

Sophocles
Antigone
450? B.C.

Euripides
The Trojan Women, Medea
415 B.C.

Aristophanes
The Frogs
405 B.C.

Confucius
The Analects of Confucius
400? B.C.

Plato
The Republic, Apologia
399? B.C.

Aristotle
Poetics
335–322 B.C.

Gaius Valerius Catullus
Verse
65? B.C.

Vergil
Aeneid
30–19 B.C.

Ovid
Amores
16? B.C.

- Can you improve on your choice of words? Can some of them be replaced by more precise or more vivid ones?
- Is there enough variety in your sentence patterns, for example, long and short, simple and compound? (Short sentences often work well to convey fast action, while longer ones are often better for description.)
- Can the writing be tightened, for example, by deleting redundancies or repetitions?
- Is the information correct? Have all the facts been checked?

Often, a piece of writing will go through several drafts before the writer is satisfied the work is as good as it can be. In addition, not all the revisions suggested above need be done at one time. For example, one draft may be used to refine the ideas, whereas another may focus on improving the language. The number of drafts needed depends on both the writer and the subject.

Proofreading Strategies.   Here are some things to keep in mind when proofreading the final draft:

- Mistakes in grammar.
- Spelling errors.
- Punctuation errors.
- Capitalization.
- Consistent treatment of heads and lists (underlining, indents, spacing, etc.).

It is helpful when possible to get a second proofreading. An outsider with a fresh eye is likely to spot things the writer might miss.

Publishing.   This simply means making the final product look as good as it possibly can. The reader—whether a teacher, a college admissions officer, an editor, or even a friend—will be influenced by the appearance of the manuscript. A sloppy piece of work, no matter how good, is apt to draw a negative reaction.

The final version should be a clean copy on white paper (using one side only), without insertions, corrections, or deletions; double-space it for easy reading.

LITERARY TIME LINE

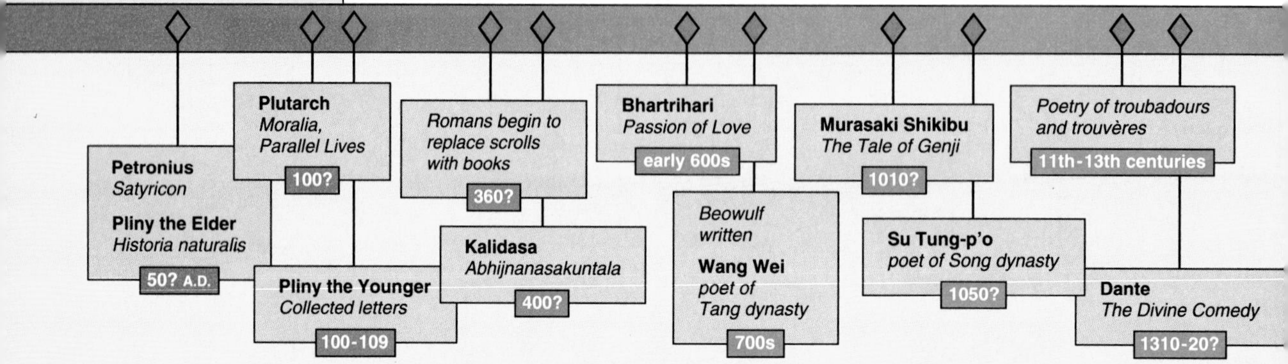

Petronius
Satyricon

Pliny the Elder
Historia naturalis

50? A.D.

Plutarch
*Moralia,
Parallel Lives*

100?

Pliny the Younger
Collected letters

100-109

Romans begin to
replace scrolls
with books

360?

Kalidasa
Abhijnanasakuntala

400?

Bhartrihari
Passion of Love

early 600s

*Beowulf
written*

Wang Wei
*poet of
Tang dynasty*

700s

Murasaki Shikibu
The Tale of Genji

1010?

Su Tung-p'o
poet of Song dynasty

1050?

*Poetry of troubadours
and trouvères*

11th-13th centuries

Dante
The Divine Comedy

1310-20?

*I*mproving Your Writing

The goal of good writing is to communicate ideas effectively. This applies to anything you write: a personal letter, a term paper, an article for a newspaper or magazine.

How do you recognize good writing? Here are some things to look for. Good writing:

- Is clear and concise.
- Is concrete rather than abstract.
- Presents ideas logically, connecting one to the other.
- Is colorful and varied.
- Uses imagery and figures of speech.
- Has the right tone for the subject matter.
- Is on the right level for its audience.

Ways to Go About It.   Think of the attributes listed above as goals to work toward. The more of them you reach, the better writer you will become.

But how do you go about it? An excellent way is to read as much as you can. Reading anything well written—a book, an article, an essay, a poem—will help you appreciate good writing—and improve your own.

You can also improve your writing by mastering the tools of the writing trade. Among these are a good vocabulary, a knowledge of correct grammar and usage, a feel for sentence structure, and the ability to spell correctly.

These tools are building blocks that work together to create a solid foundation. For example, a good vocabulary will enrich your writing by giving you a wide range of words from which to choose; a knowledge of grammar and usage will help you use those words appropriately and effectively. Mastering the tools will also give you confidence and make the writing process more enjoyable.

The sections that follow deal more specifically with various aspects of language. They include practical suggestions on building vocabulary and improving spelling and alert you to some common errors of grammar and usage.

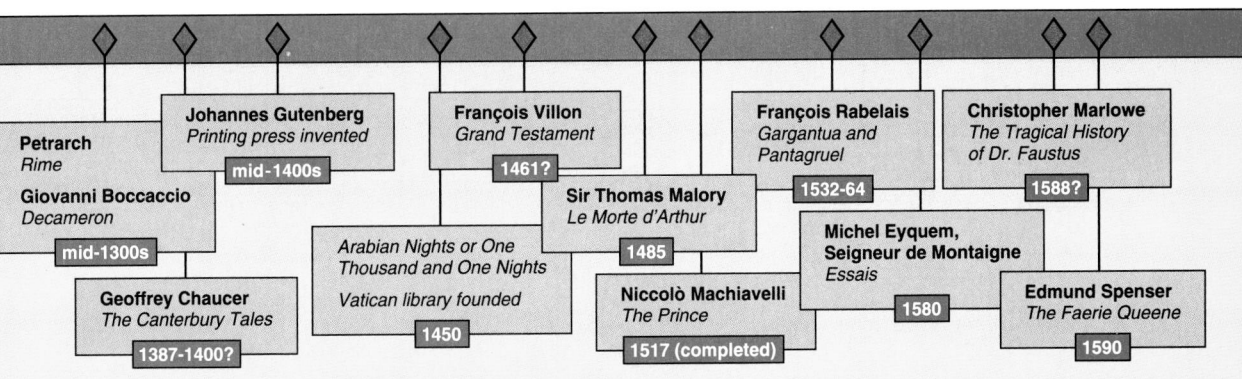

Petrarch
Rime

Giovanni Boccaccio
Decameron

mid-1300s

Johannes Gutenberg
Printing press invented

mid-1400s

Geoffrey Chaucer
The Canterbury Tales

1387-1400?

François Villon
Grand Testament

1461?

Arabian Nights or One Thousand and One Nights

Vatican library founded

1450

Sir Thomas Malory
Le Morte d'Arthur

1485

Niccolò Machiavelli
The Prince

1517 (completed)

François Rabelais
Gargantua and Pantagruel

1532-64

Michel Eyquem, Seigneur de Montaigne
Essais

1580

Christopher Marlowe
The Tragical History of Dr. Faustus

1588?

Edmund Spenser
The Faerie Queene

1590

*B*uilding Blocks of Good Writing

BUILDING VOCABULARY

A good vocabulary is possibly the most important asset. It is certainly the most basic. Trying to write well without enough words at your disposal is a little like trying to build a piece of furniture without having the right tools. The job will be harder and the result may not be to your satisfaction.

Read, read, read!   Just as tools can be acquired, so can new words. The single best way to acquire new words is by reading. No matter what you read—a chapter in your history book; a novel, play, or short story for English class; a daily or weekly newspaper; or your favorite magazine—you will be learning new words. You will learn some simply by seeing them in context, others after consulting a dictionary.

Prefixes and Suffixes.   A more specific way of expanding your vocabulary is to learn the meanings of common prefixes and suffixes.

A prefix is a word part added to the beginning of a word, root, or stem in order to modify the meaning or form a new word. A suffix is a word part attached to the end of a word to form another word of different meaning or function. Knowing the meaning of a prefix or suffix will provide you with clues to the meaning of many words that might be unfamiliar. The sample prefix and suffix lists that follow show how this works.

Prefixes

PREFIX	MEANING	EXAMPLES
bi-	two	bifocal, bilateral, bisect
dis-	lack of	disagreement, discomfort, dissatisfy
inter-	between	intercellular, international, interact
sub-	under	subconscious, subnormal, substandard

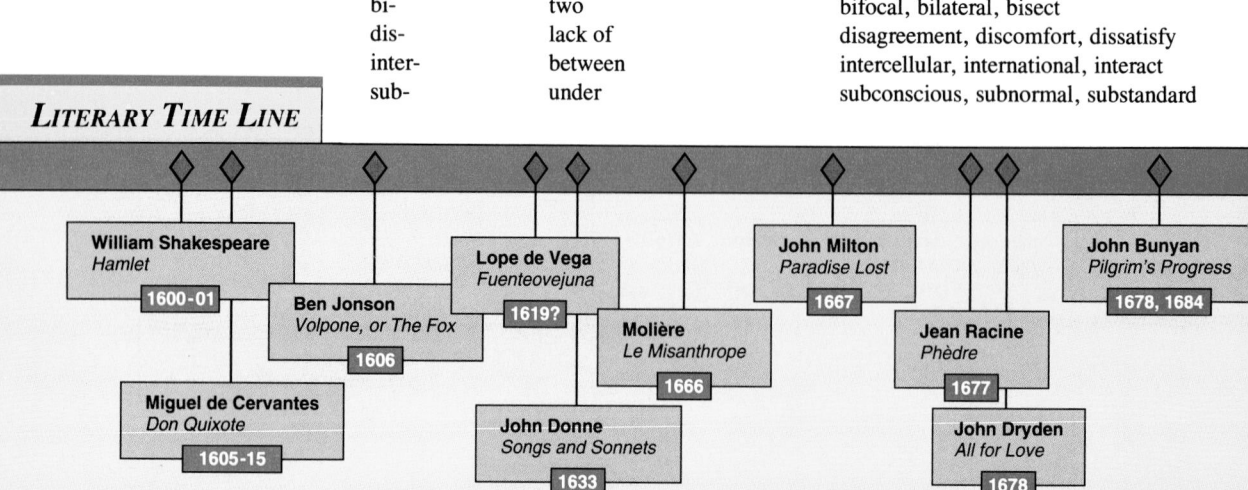

LITERARY TIME LINE

William Shakespeare
Hamlet
`1600-01`

Ben Jonson
Volpone, or The Fox
`1606`

Miguel de Cervantes
Don Quixote
`1605-15`

Lope de Vega
Fuenteovejuna
`1619?`

Molière
Le Misanthrope
`1666`

John Donne
Songs and Sonnets
`1633`

John Milton
Paradise Lost
`1667`

Jean Racine
Phèdre
`1677`

John Dryden
All for Love
`1678`

John Bunyan
Pilgrim's Progress
`1678, 1684`

Noun-forming Suffixes

SUFFIX	MEANING	EXAMPLES
-er, -or	one who, that which	climber, subscriber, elevator
-ion	act, state, result of	elation, attraction, temptation
-ness	quality or state	foolishness, happiness

Adjective-forming Suffixes

SUFFIX	MEANING	EXAMPLES
-ful	full of, marked by	doleful, respectful, truthful
-less	lacking, without	homeless, motionless, senseless
-y	showing, suggesting	airy, muddy, smoky

If you look up the following common prefixes in this dictionary, you will find lists of words in which each of them is used: anti-, co-, mis-, multi-, non-, over-, pre-, re-, un-.

Run-on Dictionary Entries.   At the end of many entries in a dictionary there are nouns, adjectives, and other words that have been derived from the main entry word. These derived words, called run-ons, are formed by adding a suffix to an existing, or base word. A run-on has the same essential meaning as its base word, but is a different grammatical form. When you look up an unfamiliar word in the dictionary, take note of any run-ons. This may allow you to add not one, but two, three, or more new words to your vocabulary at one time. The adverb *cheerfully* and the noun *cheerfulness* are formed by adding suffixes to the adjective *cheerful*.

Synonyms.   Synonyms are words with similar meanings. Learning and using them will make your writing more varied and more precise. The words **fast** and **quick,** for example, are similar in meaning. In some cases they are interchangeable:

a **fast** retreat or a **quick** retreat; a **fast** response or a **quick** response.

In others, they are not:

a **fast** car, but a **quick** mind.

The words **cold** and **frigid** describe the same quality but have different shades of meaning:

Luis said the water was **cold,** but Elizabeth described it as **frigid**.

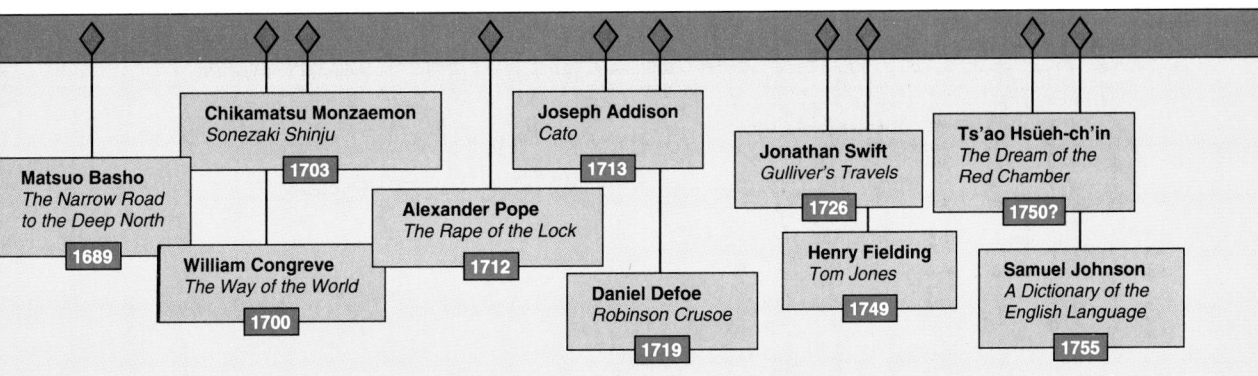

Matsuo Basho
The Narrow Road to the Deep North
1689

Chikamatsu Monzaemon
Sonezaki Shinju
1703

William Congreve
The Way of the World
1700

Alexander Pope
The Rape of the Lock
1712

Daniel Defoe
Robinson Crusoe
1719

Joseph Addison
Cato
1713

Jonathan Swift
Gulliver's Travels
1726

Henry Fielding
Tom Jones
1749

Ts'ao Hsüeh-ch'in
The Dream of the Red Chamber
1750?

Samuel Johnson
A Dictionary of the English Language
1755

Elizabeth's impression was stronger than Luis's. She used the word **frigid** to convey that to her the water felt *uncomfortably* or *extremely* cold.

This dictionary supplies synonyms for a large number of words. Some of them can be found at the end of definitions, others under the heading "Synonyms." Other sources for synonyms include a thesaurus (see the section "Using a Thesaurus"), which offers lists of related words to choose from and often lists of antonyms as well. If a synonym is unfamiliar, be sure to look it up in the dictionary before using it in a sentence.

Antonyms. Antonyms are words with opposite meanings, and are often used to make contrasts:

Some people say jogging is **beneficial** to the body, while others say it is **harmful**.

Antonyms can be created by adding prefixes such as **un-** and **non-** to certain words:

Skin should be **protected** from ultraviolet rays; if it is **unprotected,** it is likely to burn.

Members of the club are allowed to bring **nonmembers** as guests.

Comparing a word with its antonym often helps pinpoint the meaning of both words. For example, contrast **modest** with **vain,** or **stingy** with **charitable** in the following list.

Synonyms and Antonyms

	SYNONYM	ANTONYM
generous	unselfish	selfish
	charitable	stingy
	altruistic	miserly
proud	vain	modest
	conceited	humble
beautiful	pretty	ugly
	handsome	plain
	attractive	hideous

LITERARY TIME LINE

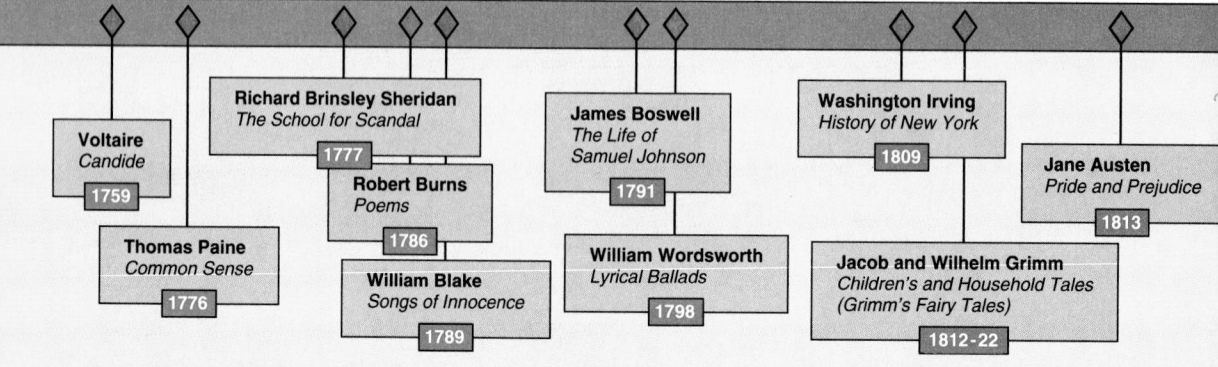

Voltaire
Candide
1759

Thomas Paine
Common Sense
1776

Richard Brinsley Sheridan
The School for Scandal
1777

Robert Burns
Poems
1786

William Blake
Songs of Innocence
1789

James Boswell
The Life of Samuel Johnson
1791

William Wordsworth
Lyrical Ballads
1798

Washington Irving
History of New York
1809

Jacob and Wilhelm Grimm
Children's and Household Tales (Grimm's Fairy Tales)
1812-22

Jane Austen
Pride and Prejudice
1813

Using Words Well.   Having many words at your disposal is important. Even more important is to choose the ones that best express what you want to say. Words are not intrinsically "right" or "wrong," and the best word isn't necessarily a long or impressive-sounding one. It is the one that best suits your purpose.

To select the most appropriate word, you need to be clear in your own mind about what you want to say, what mood you wish to convey, what kind of characters (whether real or fictional) you wish to describe. It helps, before writing, to imagine a scene in your mind and then observe in detail what's going on. Think of writing as painting a picture in words.

Here are some guidelines to help you in the choice of language:

Be specific.   Good writers are specific and concrete rather than vague and general. If, instead of referring to a dog, you tell your readers it is a spaniel, a poodle, or a mutt, they will see it much more clearly. And instead of describing the sea as blue, specify what kind of blue: slate blue, sapphire, turquoise, aquamarine.

Use strong verbs.   Verbs do most of the work in good writing. Depending on the choice of verbs, a piece of writing may be dull and bland or vivid and alive. Do you want your writing to *shout* its message or to *whisper* it? Do you want your sentences to *sparkle* or *glow*? Choose the verbs that will achieve your goal and help you find your individual voice. For example, if you tell your readers that Lee *walked* down the stairs, you're not telling them much about Lee. But if you have Lee *stumble* down or *race* down, the reader already knows something about this person's state of mind—and will probably want to know more. Or a tennis player may *blast* or *pound* the ball over the net, or gently *stroke* or *lift* it over. The choice of words sharpens the picture and tells us about the player's individual style.

Appeal to the senses.   Good writers make use of all five senses to reach their audience. Writing that tells us how things look and feel and taste and smell and sound is generally vivid writing. Adjectives and adverbs can help create a clear picture of an image or mood. But they should be used judiciously; loading a sentence down with too many adjectives and adverbs can slow the pace and risk losing the reader's interest. Sometimes a single adjective—say, *morose* or *malevolent, affable* or *open* to describe a person's expression—may be more effective than a long string of them.

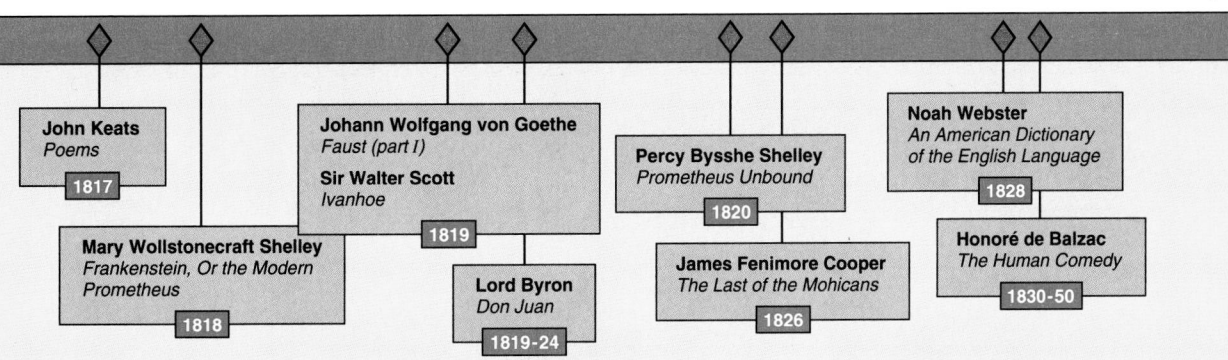

John Keats
Poems
1817

Mary Wollstonecraft Shelley
Frankenstein, Or the Modern Prometheus
1818

Johann Wolfgang von Goethe
Faust (part I)

Sir Walter Scott
Ivanhoe
1819

Lord Byron
Don Juan
1819-24

Percy Bysshe Shelley
Prometheus Unbound
1820

James Fenimore Cooper
The Last of the Mohicans
1826

Noah Webster
An American Dictionary of the English Language
1828

Honoré de Balzac
The Human Comedy
1830-50

Using a Thesaurus

What Is a Thesaurus?

The word *thesaurus* comes from a Greek word meaning *treasure* or *storehouse*. The treasure, in this case, is words. A thesaurus is simply a collection of words—synonyms or related words, and often their antonyms—that are stored in a book (or sometimes in a computer program). Its purpose is to help people find precisely the word they need and thus be able to express their meaning more effectively.

Suppose, for example, that you are trying to describe your reaction to a suspense movie you saw. The word *exciting* first comes to mind. You are not quite satisfied with this word, but you can't think of a better one. If you look up *exciting* in a thesaurus, you'll find a whole list of related words, such as *thrilling, breathtaking, moving,* and *hair-raising,* any one of which might better express your meaning.

In consulting a thesaurus, you'll probably find some words that are familiar and others that are new to you. A thesaurus is not a dictionary, so before using a new word, or one whose meaning is not quite clear to you, be sure to look it up in a dictionary.

The Thesaurus as a Language Tool

A thesaurus is a valuable tool, both as a memory jogger and a vocabulary builder. But selecting words to use in your own writing should be done with care. Keep in mind that very few words can be substituted for one another in a sentence without changing the meaning at least slightly.

In considering the various choices, look at different parts of speech. You don't necessarily have to substitute one adjective or one adverb for another. Sometimes a noun or a phrase would be more appropriate. For example, you might replace "The audience listened quietly" with "The audience listened in silence."

A Sample Thesaurus Entry

To show how tricky it can be to try to substitute one word for another, let's look at a sample thesaurus entry. The one that follows is for the verb "combine," a general word that can be used in a wide range of contexts.

> **combine** *v.*: amalgamate, blend, consolidate, fuse, join, merge, pool, unite. *Combine oil and vinegar to make a salad dressing. The friends combined their resources to rent skiing equipment.*

Literary Time Line

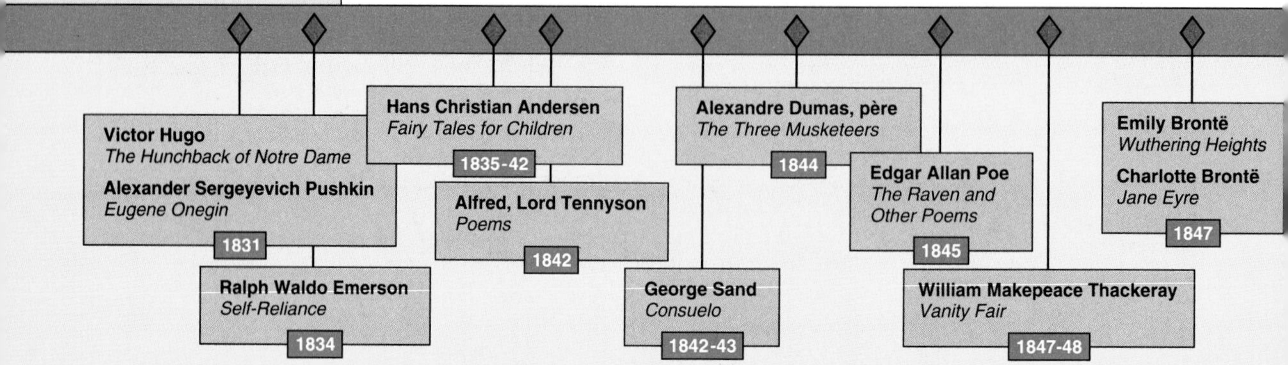

Victor Hugo
The Hunchback of Notre Dame

Alexander Sergeyevich Pushkin
Eugene Onegin
1831

Ralph Waldo Emerson
Self-Reliance
1834

Hans Christian Andersen
Fairy Tales for Children
1835-42

Alfred, Lord Tennyson
Poems
1842

George Sand
Consuelo
1842-43

Alexandre Dumas, père
The Three Musketeers
1844

Edgar Allan Poe
The Raven and Other Poems
1845

William Makepeace Thackeray
Vanity Fair
1847-48

Emily Brontë
Wuthering Heights

Charlotte Brontë
Jane Eyre
1847

The entry indicates that *combine* is being used as a verb and begins with a list of synonyms, or related words, arranged in alphabetical order. (The order of the words depends on the thesaurus. Some use alphabetical order; some give words closest in meaning first; and others group related words together.) The sample entry ends with two sentences that give examples of how *combine* itself can be used.

To see how a thesaurus works, let's try substituting each of the synonyms in the two illustrative sentences.

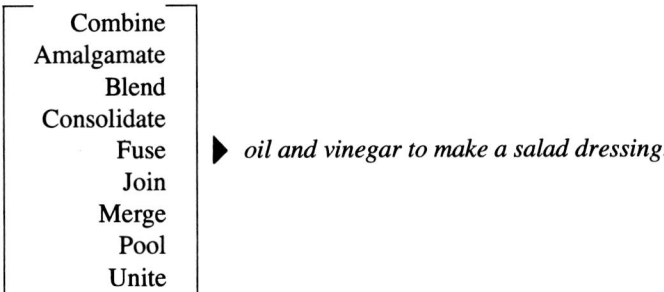

> Combine
> Amalgamate
> Blend
> Consolidate
> Fuse ▶ *oil and vinegar to make a salad dressing.*
> Join
> Merge
> Pool
> Unite

It seems clear from looking at the list that *blend* is the only word that would work well in the place of *combine* in this sentence. Now let's try the synonyms in the second sentence.

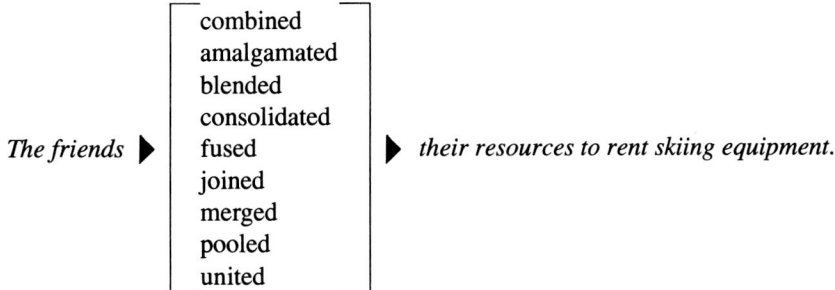

The friends ▶ combined
amalgamated
blended
consolidated
fused ▶ *their resources to rent skiing equipment.*
joined
merged
pooled
united

In this sentence, *pooled* is the most satisfactory substitute for *combined*.

In both cases, the reason the other words don't work as substitutes is that almost all of them have more precise meanings. They include the meaning of *combine,* but only in a special sense. The following sentences provide examples of how the synonyms might be used.

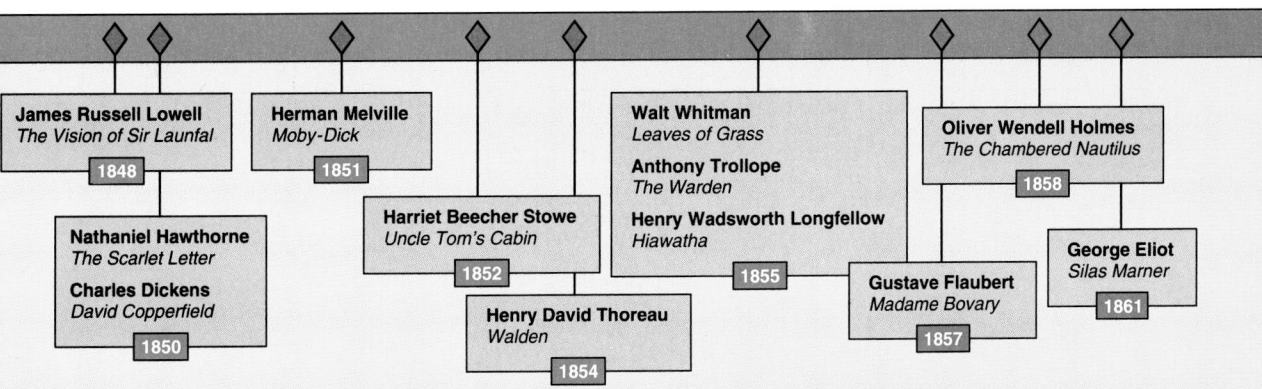

James Russell Lowell
The Vision of Sir Launfal
1848

Herman Melville
Moby-Dick
1851

Walt Whitman
Leaves of Grass

Anthony Trollope
The Warden

Oliver Wendell Holmes
The Chambered Nautilus
1858

Nathaniel Hawthorne
The Scarlet Letter

Charles Dickens
David Copperfield
1850

Harriet Beecher Stowe
Uncle Tom's Cabin
1852

Henry Wadsworth Longfellow
Hiawatha
1855

George Eliot
Silas Marner
1861

Henry David Thoreau
Walden
1854

Gustave Flaubert
Madame Bovary
1857

amalgamate: *Since the student population had decreased, the town decided to amalgamate its three school districts into one.*

Amalgamate means to unite to form a combination. *Combine* is correct, but less precise.

blend: *In painting the sunset, the artist blended several shades of red.*

In this sentence, *blend* means to combine through the mixing of various elements. *Combine* would be a less accurate substitute.

consolidate: *The couple consolidated their earnings by putting their paychecks in a joint bank account.*

Consolidated conveys the idea of combining elements to make them stronger or more solid. *Combine* could be used, but it would be less descriptive.

fuse: *The metals zinc and copper are fused to make brass.*

As used here, *fused* has the very specific meaning of blended through a melting process. *Combine* would be a poor choice of word here.

join: *Many segments of the community joined forces to fight the epidemic.*

Join has the sense here of combining to act together. *Combine* would convey only part of the meaning.

merge: *The two firms merged to form a large corporation. The road narrowed as its two lanes merged into one.*

Merge, which is similar to *amalgamate,* has the sense of combining elements so they become one. *Combine* would be less vivid in the first sentence and a poor choice of word in the second.

pool: *The children pooled the money they had saved to buy their parents a present.*

Pool means to combine, or put together, for a common purpose or effort. As in the case of *join,* to use *combine* here would convey only part of the meaning.

unite: *Different factions of the political party united to support one candidate.*

Unite has the sense of combining to form a unit or whole. *Combine* would not work here at all.

LITERARY TIME LINE

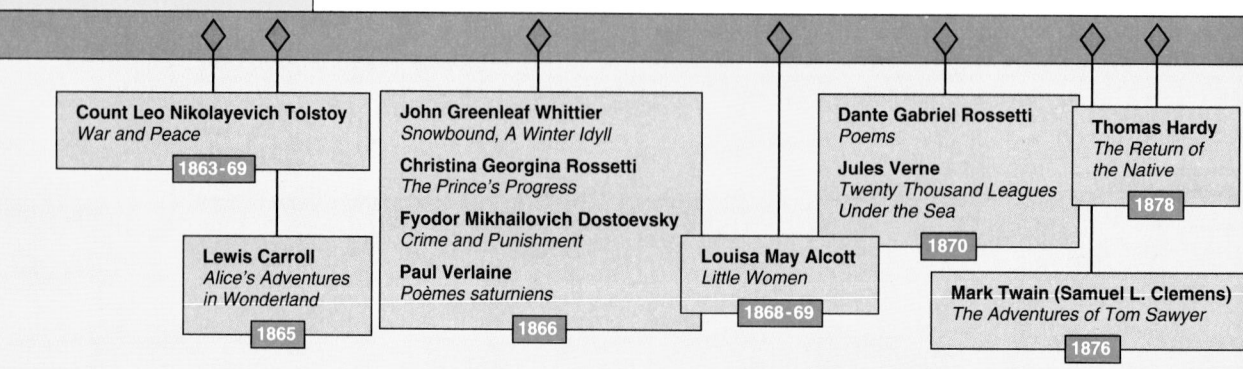

Count Leo Nikolayevich Tolstoy *War and Peace* 1863-69	**John Greenleaf Whittier** *Snowbound, A Winter Idyll*	**Dante Gabriel Rossetti** *Poems*
	Christina Georgina Rossetti *The Prince's Progress*	**Jules Verne** *Twenty Thousand Leagues Under the Sea* 1870
	Fyodor Mikhailovich Dostoevsky *Crime and Punishment*	**Thomas Hardy** *The Return of the Native* 1878
Lewis Carroll *Alice's Adventures in Wonderland* 1865	**Paul Verlaine** *Poèmes saturniens* 1866	**Louisa May Alcott** *Little Women* 1868-69
		Mark Twain (Samuel L. Clemens) *The Adventures of Tom Sawyer* 1876

Types of Thesauri

A thesaurus can be categorized by the way it is organized. There are three main types: the alphabetically organized, or dictionary, type; the traditional type, which is organized according to categories; and the type accessible by computer. Each type contains somewhat different information, arranged in different ways. If you have never used a thesaurus, the dictionary type may be the place to start.

Dictionary Thesaurus. In a dictionary type of thesaurus, the entries are arranged in alphabetical order, as in a dictionary. There are several types of alphabetical thesauri; in all of these the main entries are listed alphabetically and according to their part of speech, but the information they include and the way in which the synonyms are presented vary. In some cases a list of synonyms follows the entry word, listed either alphabetically or with those most closely related to the entry word listed first. In others, the entry word is followed by a sentence that illustrates its meaning; and in still others, a brief definition follows the entry word. Some include cross-references to other entries; some supply antonyms.

Category Thesaurus. The category type of thesaurus, devised by Peter Mark Roget, who originated the idea of a word catalog, is organized in a two-step process. The user looks up a word in a detailed index at the back of the book. The index lists synonyms for that word; beside each synonym is a number referring to a section in the body of the book where synonyms or related words can be found. The body of the thesaurus is organized into categories that are related to one another. For example, there is a category for each of the senses—touch, taste, smell, sight, and hearing—and these categories are grouped together so that the reader can easily move from one to another. This thesaurus contains parts of speech, but does not usually include definitions, illustrative examples, or antonyms.

Computerized Thesaurus. Many word processing programs include a thesaurus users can call up while they are working on a piece of writing. Computerized thesauri, like print thesauri, vary in the way they are arranged and in the information they offer. Some have definitions, others do not. Some contain antonyms, others do not. A computerized thesaurus, however, often contains several levels of words for each entry and for each synonym within the entry. With the press of a key, you can find a new list of words to choose from. You can continue the process almost indefinitely—and give your vocabulary a boost.

Synonyms in a Dictionary

In addition to using a thesaurus, you will find synonyms at the end of definitions in this dictionary and many detailed synonym studies throughout the book.

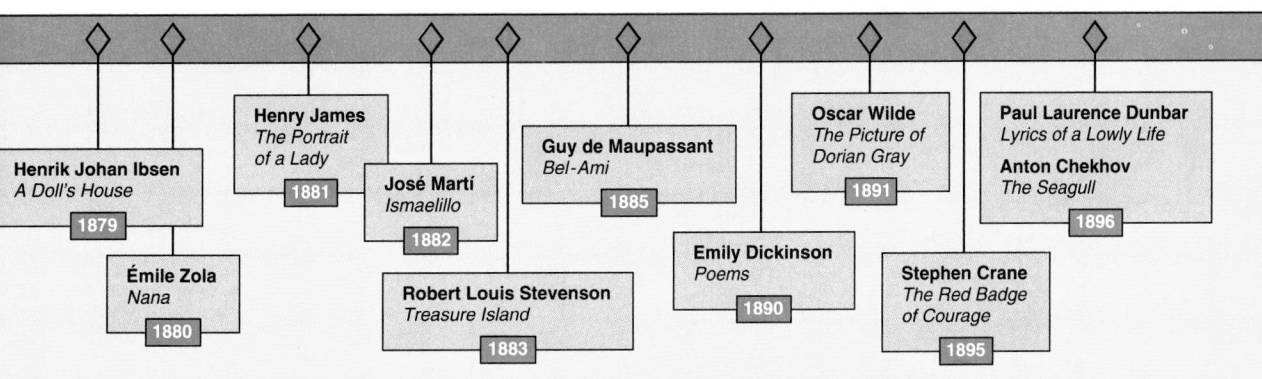

Henrik Johan Ibsen
A Doll's House
1879

Émile Zola
Nana
1880

Henry James
The Portrait of a Lady
1881

José Martí
Ismaelillo
1882

Robert Louis Stevenson
Treasure Island
1883

Guy de Maupassant
Bel-Ami
1885

Emily Dickinson
Poems
1890

Oscar Wilde
The Picture of Dorian Gray
1891

Stephen Crane
The Red Badge of Courage
1895

Paul Laurence Dunbar
Lyrics of a Lowly Life

Anton Chekhov
The Seagull
1896

GRAMMAR AND USAGE

The correct use of language is basic to writing. Below are some common errors in grammar and usage and suggestions on how to correct them.

Subject-Verb Agreement. A verb must agree with its subject in person and number. In some sentences it may be easy to mistake another word for the subject. In others, it may be difficult to determine whether the subject is singular or plural.

Incorrect: There's fifteen students in the class.
 Correct: There are fifteen students in the class.

Incorrect: Neither Sally nor Jack belong to that group.
 Correct: Neither Sally nor Jack belongs to that group.

Dangling Modifiers. A modifier must refer clearly to a word in its own sentence. When the sentence does not contain such a word, the modifier is said to *dangle*. Dangling modifiers most often occur at the beginning of a sentence.

Incorrect: After working for hours, the project was done.
 Correct: After working for hours, they finished the project.

Incorrect: Disappointed by the team's score, training was uppermost in the coach's mind.
 Correct: Disappointed by the score, the coach decided the team needed more training.

Double Negatives. In general, use only one negative word to express a negative idea.

Incorrect: We don't have none of the right tools for this job.
 Correct: We don't have any of the right tools for this job.
 Correct: We have none of the right tools for this job.

Double Comparisons. In making a comparison, do not add both *-er* and *more* or both *-est* and *most* to an adjective or adverb.

Incorrect: The Sears Tower is more taller than the World Trade Center.
 Correct: The Sears Tower is taller than the World Trade Center.

LITERARY TIME LINE

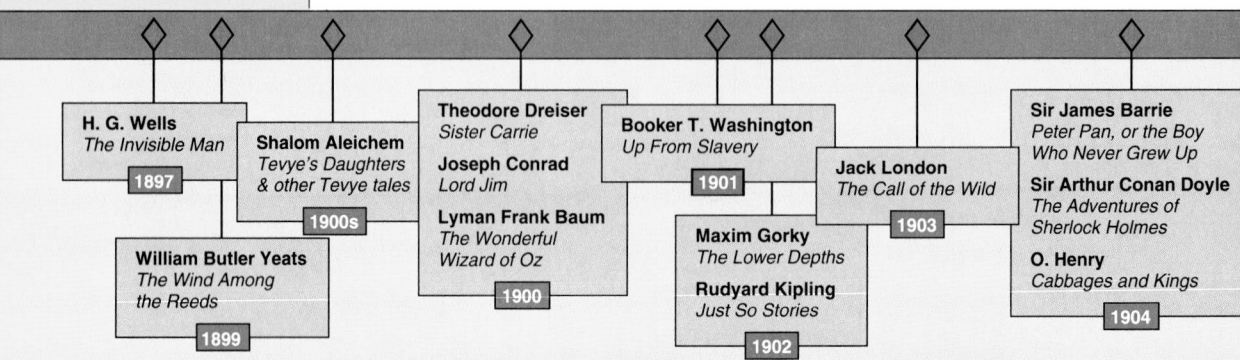

H. G. Wells
The Invisible Man
1897

Shalom Aleichem
Tevye's Daughters & other Tevye tales
1900s

William Butler Yeats
The Wind Among the Reeds
1899

Theodore Dreiser
Sister Carrie
Joseph Conrad
Lord Jim
Lyman Frank Baum
The Wonderful Wizard of Oz
1900

Booker T. Washington
Up From Slavery
1901

Maxim Gorky
The Lower Depths
Rudyard Kipling
Just So Stories
1902

Jack London
The Call of the Wild
1903

Sir James Barrie
Peter Pan, or the Boy Who Never Grew Up
Sir Arthur Conan Doyle
The Adventures of Sherlock Holmes
O. Henry
Cabbages and Kings
1904

Incorrect: The cheetah runs the most fastest of any animal.
Correct: The cheetah runs the fastest of any animal.

Comparative or Superlative?

A comparative is a modifier used to compare two things. Examples are *smaller, better,* or *more gracefully.* A superlative is a modifier used to compare three or more things. Examples are *smallest, best,* or *most gracefully.* A superlative should not be used when only two things are being compared.

Incorrect: Of the two applicants, Jenkins is the most qualified for this job.
Correct: Of the two applicants, Jenkins is the more qualified for this job.

Sentence Fragments.

A sentence contains a subject and a complete verb and expresses a complete thought. Sentences lacking one of these elements or not expressing a complete thought are not strictly sentences, but are sentence fragments. Although writers sometimes use sentence fragments for special effect, such fragments are generally considered grammatical errors.

Incorrect: The bird with a red head and black body.
Correct: The bird had a red head and black body.

Run-On Sentences.

A run-on sentence consists of two or more complete sentences that are run together with only commas, or with no punctuation at all. Such a sentence can be corrected by making it into two or more shorter sentences or by adding conjunctions or semicolons.

Incorrect: It was a hard climb up that mountain it took us most of the day to reach the top and we were exhausted when we got home, but we felt a real sense of accomplishment.
Correct: It was a hard climb up that mountain. It took us most of the day to reach the top, and although we were exhausted when we got home, we felt a real sense of accomplishment.

Incorrect Use of Pronouns.

The pronouns *I, he, she, we, they,* and *who* should be used only as subjects or predicate nominatives. *Me, him, her, us, them,* and *whom* should be used only as direct or indirect objects of a verb or as objects of a preposition.

Incorrect: Him and me are cousins; her is my sister.
Correct: He and I are cousins; she is my sister.

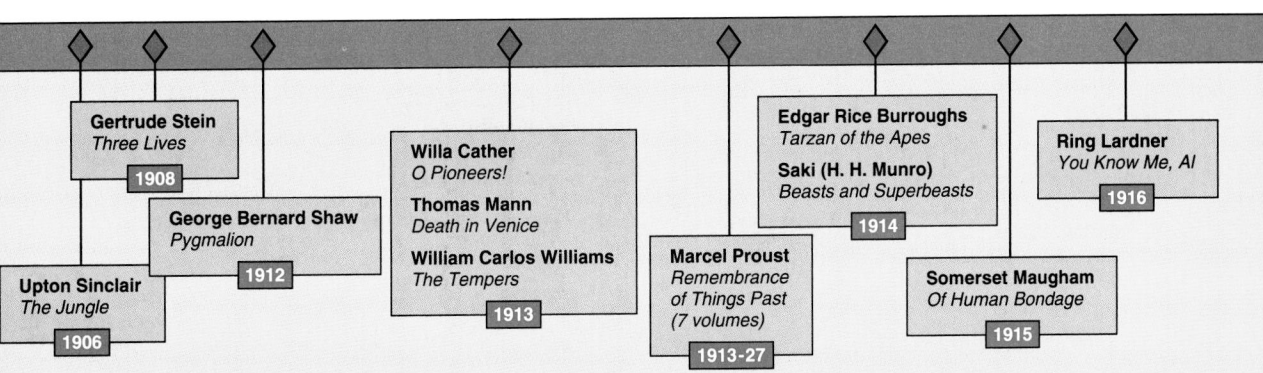

Upton Sinclair
The Jungle
1906

Gertrude Stein
Three Lives
1908

George Bernard Shaw
Pygmalion
1912

Willa Cather
O Pioneers!

Thomas Mann
Death in Venice

William Carlos Williams
The Tempers
1913

Marcel Proust
Remembrance of Things Past (7 volumes)
1913-27

Edgar Rice Burroughs
Tarzan of the Apes

Saki (H. H. Munro)
Beasts and Superbeasts
1914

Somerset Maugham
Of Human Bondage
1915

Ring Lardner
You Know Me, Al
1916

Incorrect: Them and us own a business together.
Correct: They and we own a business together.

Incorrect: For who is that letter? Is it for her or I?
Correct: For whom is that letter? Is it for her or me?

Incorrect: I don't know whom that could be at the door.
Correct: I don't know who that could be at the door.

SPELLING

Spelling Counts.   Correct spelling is an integral part of writing. When you are writing something that is important to you—whether an essay for school, a job application, or a letter to a grandparent or friend—the reader is likely to respond not just to the content, but also to the way you spell. Some people seem to spell correctly without much conscious effort. Others, of equal intelligence, continually have difficulty. If you have trouble with spelling, even occasionally, here are some general suggestions to help you improve.

- Make lists of words that give you problems and consult them frequently.
- Use a dictionary to check a spelling whenever you're not sure.
- Pay attention to how words are pronounced; many are spelled the way they sound.
- Proofread your work to catch careless spelling errors.
- Familiarize yourself with some basic spelling rules.

If you have access to a computer with a spelling checker, by all means use it. But keep in mind that the program will alert you only to misspelled words. If you have used an existing word that is incorrect in context, say, *alter* in place of *altar,* the spelling checker will not find it. Remember, too, that some spelling checkers include fewer words than many dictionaries. A spelling checker should be used as an additional tool, not the only tool.

Some Basic Spelling Rules.   Spelling rules are like guideposts that help you in many situations. Although there are exceptions to almost every rule, you will be able to spell hundreds of words correctly by following the basic rules.

"ie" or "ei"?   The familiar rule, "*i* before *e* except after *c*," is a good one to remember.

LITERARY TIME LINE

H. L. Mencken
The American Language

Carl Sandburg
Corn Huskers

1918

Sherwood Anderson
Winesburg, Ohio

1919

Edith Wharton
The Age of Innocence

1920

Luigi Pirandello
Six Characters in Search of an Author

José Ortega y Gasset
Invertebrate Spain

1921

James Joyce
Ulysses

Sinclair Lewis
Babbitt

Eugene O'Neill
Anna Christie

T. S. Eliot
The Waste Land

1922

e e cummings
Tulips and Chimneys

Edna St. Vincent Millay
The Harp Weaver and Other Poems

1923

Sean O'Casey
Juno and the Paycock

E. M. Forster
A Passage to India

1924

Write *i* before *e* (as in *achieve, belief, field,* or *niece*)
Except after *c* (as in *ceiling, conceit, deceive,* or *receipt*)
Or when sounded like *a,* as in **neighbor** or **weigh** (or *eight* or *reign*).

"-cede," "-ceed," or "-sede"?   The rule for choosing these word endings is not difficult:

Only one word ends in *-sede:* supersede.
Only three words end in *-ceed:* exceed, proceed, succeed.
Use *-cede* in all other cases: accede, cede, concede, precede, secede.

Doubling the Final Consonant.   When a word ends in a consonant, if the suffix being added begins with a vowel, such as *-ed* and *-ing,* double the final consonant before the suffix:

One-syllable words: drop, dropped, dropping; run, runner, running.

Two-syllable words when the accent is on the second syllable: ad•mit, admitted, admitting; e•quip, equipped, equipping.

Do not double the final consonant of a two-syllable word if the accent is on the first syllable: hap′pen, happened, happening; la′bel, labeled, labeling.

Forming Plurals.   Below are some ways of forming plurals.

To form the plural of most common nouns and proper nouns, add *s:* garden, gardens; Shaw, Shaws.

To form the plural of nouns

ending in *s, sh, ch, x,* and *z,* add *es:* boss, bosses; box, boxes; inch, inches.
ending in a vowel + *y,* add *s:* play, plays; valley, valleys.
ending in a consonant + *y,* change the *y* to *i* and add *es:* factory, factories.

To form the plural of most nouns ending in a consonant + *o,* add *es:* hero, heroes; potato, potatoes. Some nouns ending in a consonant + *o* take only an *s:* banjo, banjos.

To form the plural of most nouns ending in *f* and all nouns ending in *ff,* add *s:* chief, chiefs; roof, roofs; tariff, tariffs.

To form the plural of some nouns ending in *f* or *fe,* and many nouns ending in *lf,* change the *f* to *v* and add *es:* leaf, leaves; life, lives; half, halves; self, selves.

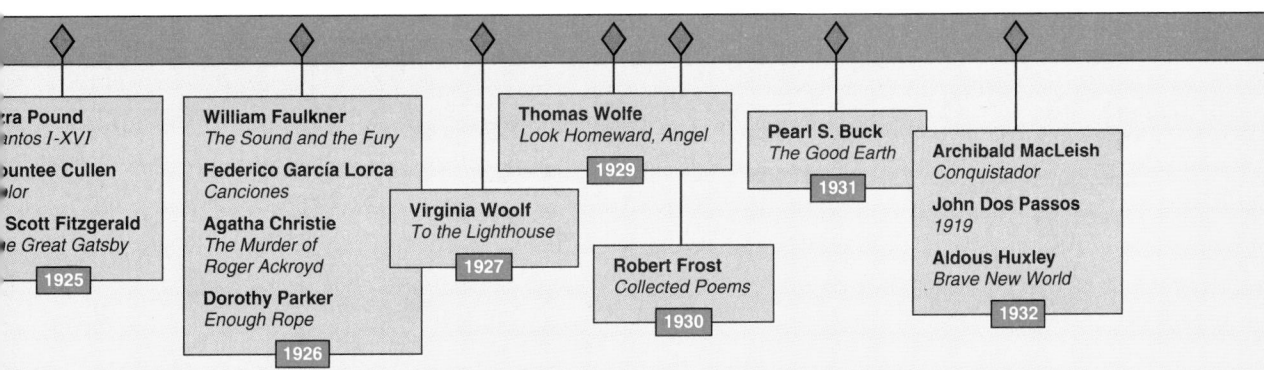

ra Pound
antos I-XVI

untee Cullen
lor

Scott Fitzgerald
e Great Gatsby
1925

William Faulkner
The Sound and the Fury

Federico García Lorca
Canciones

Agatha Christie
The Murder of Roger Ackroyd

Dorothy Parker
Enough Rope
1926

Virginia Woolf
To the Lighthouse
1927

Thomas Wolfe
Look Homeward, Angel
1929

Robert Frost
Collected Poems
1930

Pearl S. Buck
The Good Earth
1931

Archibald MacLeish
Conquistador

John Dos Passos
1919

Aldous Huxley
Brave New World
1932

Some nouns have the same form in both the singular and plural: deer, series.

Some nouns have plural forms that follow no rules; these are called irregular plurals: crisis, crises; child, children; goose, geese; man, men; woman, women.

To form the plural of compound nouns that are hyphenated or written as more than one word, usually the most important part of the noun becomes plural: sister-in-law, sisters-in-law; attorney general, attorneys general.

Forming Possessives. The possessive of nouns and some pronouns, indicating ownership or possession, is formed by adding an apostrophe and, often, an *s* to the end of the word.

Add *'s* to form the possessive of

singular and plural nouns that do not end in *s:* a student's desk; children's toys.
singular nouns of one syllable ending in *s:* Chris's friend.
indefinite pronouns: anyone's pencil; everyone's ideas; someone's coat.

Add an apostrophe without an *s* to form the possessive of singular nouns of more than one syllable that end in *s* and of all plural nouns that end in *s:* the players' uniforms.

Homophones—Words Often Confused.
Words that are pronounced the same but are spelled differently and have different meanings are called **homophones.** These are often a source of confusion because it is sometimes difficult to remember which spelling goes with the intended meaning. Below is a list of some words that are commonly confused.

aid, to help or assist; **aide,** an assistant
ascent, a movement upward; **assent,** agreement
canvas, a heavy cloth; **canvass,** to solicit votes or opinions
capital, a city or town that is the seat of government; **capitol,** a building in which a legislature meets
cession, a giving up or surrendering to another; **session,** a meeting or period of time
cite, to quote or mention; **sight,** something seen or worth seeing; the act of seeing; **site,** a place or location

LITERARY TIME LINE

Dylan Thomas
Eighteen Poems

Langston Hughes
The Ways of White Folks
1934

Kawabata Yasunari
Snow Country

Isak Dinesen
Out of Africa
1937

Thornton Wilder
Our Town
1938

John Steinbeck
The Grapes of Wrath
1939

Richard Wright
Native Son
1940

Albert Camus
The Stranger
1942

Colette
Gigi
1944

W. H. Auden
For the Time Being

George Orwell
Animal Farm

Tennessee Williams
The Glass Menagerie
1945

complement, to complete or balance; something that completes; **compliment,** to praise; an expression of praise

council, an assembly or group of advisers; **counsel,** advice; to give advice

discreet, tactful; prudent; **discrete,** distinct; separate

foreword, an introduction; **forward,** ahead; toward the front

its, belonging to *it*; **it's,** contraction of *it is* or *it has*

plain, simple; a level expanse of land; **plane,** a flat surface; an airplane; a tool

principal, the head of a school; the most important; **principle,** a basic truth; a rule of conduct; integrity

rain, water falling to earth from the sky; **reign,** a period of rule; to rule as a monarch; to prevail; **rein,** a part of a horse's harness; a means of restraining

stationary, fixed; not moving; **stationery,** writing paper and envelopes

their, belonging to them; **there,** in that place; **they're,** contraction of *they are*

who's, contraction of *who is* or *who has;* **whose,** possessive form of *who*

MECHANICS: CAPITALIZATION

1. Capitalize the days of the week, months of the year, and holidays. Do not capitalize the names of the seasons.

Saturday	Thanksgiving Day
October	winter

2. Capitalize a person's name, or initials. Capitalize titles that appear before a name.

Kenji Takayama	P. C. Thomas	Governor Santucci
Ms. Rodriguez	Dr. Lee	Sarah M. Walters

   but   The governor made a speech to the Assembly.
   The doctor will meet you in the emergency room.

3. Capitalize the abbreviations Jr. and Sr. and academic degrees following a name.

   Michael T. Cory, Jr.   Tysheka Andrews, LL.D.

4. Capitalize family relationship words used as a title or in place of a name, but not when preceded by a possessive noun or pronoun.

   Uncle Sasha, *but* Tania's uncle   "Good morning, Mother"

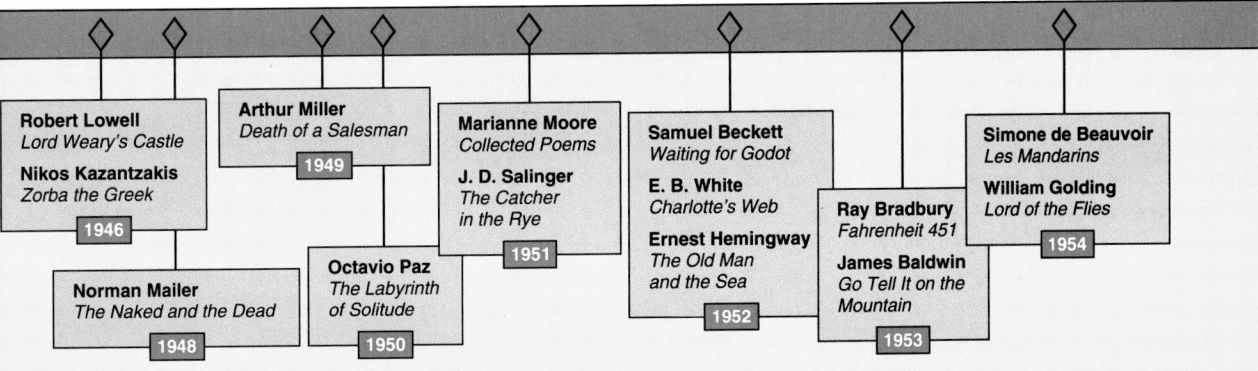

Robert Lowell
Lord Weary's Castle

Nikos Kazantzakis
Zorba the Greek

1946

Norman Mailer
The Naked and the Dead

1948

Arthur Miller
Death of a Salesman

1949

Octavio Paz
The Labyrinth of Solitude

1950

Marianne Moore
Collected Poems

J. D. Salinger
The Catcher in the Rye

1951

Samuel Beckett
Waiting for Godot

E. B. White
Charlotte's Web

Ernest Hemingway
The Old Man and the Sea

1952

Ray Bradbury
Fahrenheit 451

James Baldwin
Go Tell It on the Mountain

1953

Simone de Beauvoir
Les Mandarins

William Golding
Lord of the Flies

1954

5. Capitalize the names of ethnic and national groups, languages, and proper adjectives derived from the names of ethnic and national groups.

African-Americans	Chinese art
Canadians	French food

6. Capitalize the names of planets and other celestial bodies, but not *sun* and *moon. Earth* is capitalized only when used in conjunction with the names of other planets.

    Uranus   Milky Way   the earth, *but* the Earth and Mars

7. Capitalize geographical terms such as continents, bodies of water, countries, regions, states, and cities.

South America	Sweden	Oregon
Caspian Sea	Southeast Asia	San Diego

8. Capitalize the names of calendar and historical events, periods, and geological eras.

Boxing Day	the Renaissance
World War II	Precambrian Era

9. Capitalize the names of documents, awards, military decorations, and treaties.

Bill of Rights	Purple Heart
Pulitzer Prize	Treaty of Versailles

10. Capitalize a word used as part of a proper name, as in the names of monuments, bridges, buildings, streets, highways, and parks. Lower case the word when used in the plural.

Grant's Tomb	Yellowstone National Park
Sears Tower	Golden Gate and Brooklyn bridges
Argyle Road	Washington Monument

11. Capitalize the names of planes, trains, ships, and spacecraft.

Concorde	U.S.S. *Saratoga*
Philadelphia Flyer	*Discovery*

12. Capitalize the names of organizations, businesses, branches of government, and international bodies.

the American Red Cross	the Federal Reserve Board
the House of Representatives	General Electric Company

LITERARY TIME LINE

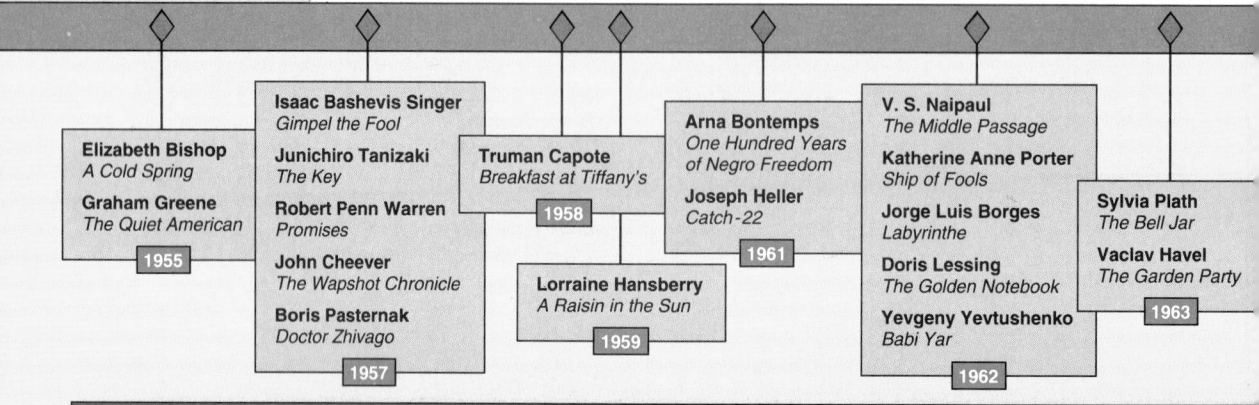

Elizabeth Bishop
A Cold Spring
Graham Greene
The Quiet American
1955

Isaac Bashevis Singer
Gimpel the Fool
Junichiro Tanizaki
The Key
Robert Penn Warren
Promises
John Cheever
The Wapshot Chronicle
Boris Pasternak
Doctor Zhivago
1957

Truman Capote
Breakfast at Tiffany's
1958

Lorraine Hansberry
A Raisin in the Sun
1959

Arna Bontemps
One Hundred Years of Negro Freedom
Joseph Heller
Catch-22
1961

V. S. Naipaul
The Middle Passage
Katherine Anne Porter
Ship of Fools
Jorge Luis Borges
Labyrinthe
Doris Lessing
The Golden Notebook
Yevgeny Yevtushenko
Babi Yar
1962

Sylvia Plath
The Bell Jar
Vaclav Havel
The Garden Party
1963

13. Capitalize the names of deities, religions, denominations, and persons adhering to them. Capitalize religious books, religious holidays, and words designating a supreme deity.

    Allah   Judaism   Episcopalian   Easter   the Bible

Mechanics: PUNCTUATION

Periods, Question Marks, and Exclamation Points

1. Use a period at the end of every complete sentence.
    Tell me about your new camera.

2. Use a period after many common abbreviations and after a person's initials.
    Mrs. Jackson   Jackson Ave.   E. R. Jackson

3. Use a question mark at the end of a direct question, but not after an indirect question.
    What time do we arrive?   He asked her what she was doing.

4. Use an exclamation point at the end of a sentence that expresses strong feeling or a command.
    What a beautiful sunset!   Hurry up!

Commas

1. Use commas to separate three or more words, phrases, or clauses in a series unless the items are connected by conjunctions.
    Robins, grackles, and terns are migratory birds.

2. Use a comma before *and, but, or, nor,* or *for* when they join two main clauses.
    The plane took off late, but we arrived on time nonetheless.

3. Use commas to set off appositives (words used to identify other words).
    The model plane, a gift from Pat's uncle, was painted red.

4. Use a comma after an introductory adverbial clause.
    Instead of raising taxes, the town council voted to curtail some services.

5. Use commas to separate the different parts of a date, and place a comma after the year if it is part of a sentence.
    The meeting was held on July 13, 1992, and lasted the day.

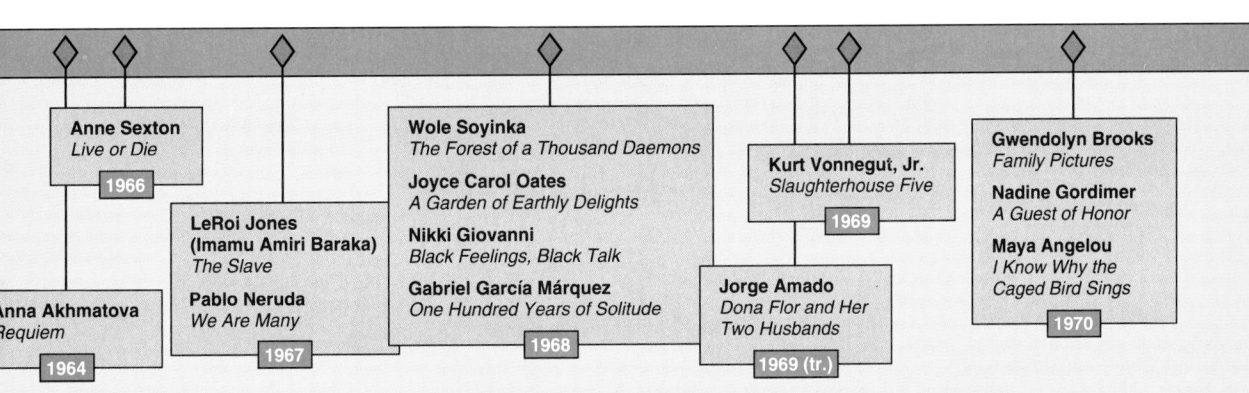

Anne Sexton
Live or Die
1966

LeRoi Jones (Imamu Amiri Baraka)
The Slave

Pablo Neruda
We Are Many
1967

Wole Soyinka
The Forest of a Thousand Daemons

Joyce Carol Oates
A Garden of Earthly Delights

Nikki Giovanni
Black Feelings, Black Talk

Gabriel García Márquez
One Hundred Years of Solitude
1968

Kurt Vonnegut, Jr.
Slaughterhouse Five
1969

Jorge Amado
Dona Flor and Her Two Husbands
1969 (tr.)

Gwendolyn Brooks
Family Pictures

Nadine Gordimer
A Guest of Honor

Maya Angelou
I Know Why the Caged Bird Sings
1970

Anna Akhmatova
Requiem
1964

6. Use a comma between a city and a state, but not between a state and a ZIP code in an address. If the city and state are part of a sentence, use commas after both the city and the state.

> The address is: 12 Beacon Drive, Salisbury, MD 21801.
> They went to Charleston, South Carolina, for a vacation.

7. Use a comma after the close of every letter.

> Sincerely,   Yours Truly,

Semicolons and Colons

1. Use a semicolon between the parts of a compound sentence that are not linked by *and, but, or, nor, yet,* or *for.*

> The detective walked around the house; then he went inside.

2. Use semicolons between items in a series when the items contain commas.

> Among the first to arrive were the president, who is usually late to meetings; the comptroller; and the auditors, who were there to review the records.

3. Use a colon to introduce a list at the end of a statement.

> The school library has the following special sections: reference books, plays, biographies, and documentary films.

4. Use a colon after the salutation of a business letter.

> Dear Professor Walton: Dear Sir or Madam:

Quotation Marks

Use double quotation marks to enclose a direct quotation and single quotation marks for a quotation within a quotation.

> "Don't cross the street until the light changes," said Veronica.

> George said, "I heard her say, 'I'll be right back,' and then the house was silent."

Hyphens

1. Use a hyphen when a prefix comes before a proper noun or proper adjective.

> pre-Columbian art   post-Revolution   un-American

2. Use a hyphen in cardinal and ordinal compound numbers.

> twenty-third in line   the forty-fifth anniversary

Literary Time Line

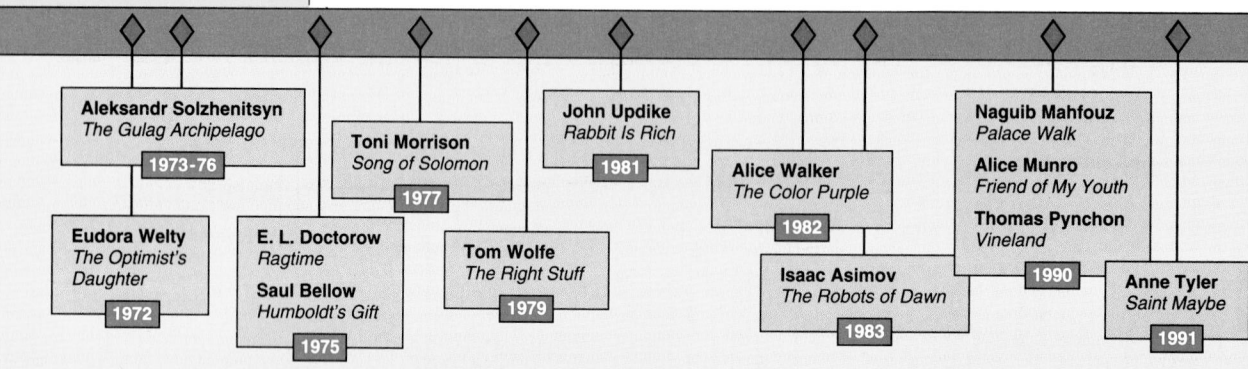

Aleksandr Solzhenitsyn
The Gulag Archipelago
1973-76

Toni Morrison
Song of Solomon
1977

John Updike
Rabbit Is Rich
1981

Alice Walker
The Color Purple
1982

Naguib Mahfouz
Palace Walk

Alice Munro
Friend of My Youth

Thomas Pynchon
Vineland
1990

Eudora Welty
The Optimist's Daughter
1972

E. L. Doctorow
Ragtime

Saul Bellow
Humboldt's Gift
1975

Tom Wolfe
The Right Stuff
1979

Isaac Asimov
The Robots of Dawn
1983

Anne Tyler
Saint Maybe
1991

*C*ompiling and Styling a Research Paper

WHAT IS A RESEARCH PAPER?

The kinds of writing you have done in school up to now have probably been based mostly on your own knowledge, experience, and imagination. The research paper is different because it is based on information that you gather from sources outside your own mind. It may express your own ideas as well, but these have to be supported by evidence from other sources, such as books, magazine and newspaper articles, films, interviews, and experiments. This evidence is used to make a certain point, take a certain position, or investigate a certain question about a topic or issue.

For example, you might use books, magazine articles, and the texts of presidential and congressional speeches as evidence in a research paper taking the position that the United States should (or should not) have joined the League of Nations after World War I. You might use tapes of television programs and films to make the point that the way minorities are portrayed in these media has (or has not) changed over the years. Or you might interview dietitians and cafeteria workers or set up an experiment to investigate the question of whether the menu in your school cafeteria is nutritious. Like other kinds of writing that you do, a research paper should be interesting and clearly written. In addition, the information in it must be accurate and must be documented to show the source from which it came. Standard rules for documenting sources are explained in a later section.

Information for a research paper can be drawn from primary sources, secondary sources, or both. Primary sources are original, direct ones, including interviews, letters, diaries and other autobiographical writings, and historical documents. Secondary sources are "secondhand," indirect ones, such as books, articles, radio or television programs, or films dealing with your subject. Sometimes whether a source is primary or secondary depends on the topic. For example, a documentary film about Franklin D. Roosevelt would be a secondary source for a paper about Roosevelt, but a primary source for a paper about the making of documentary films.

Choosing a Topic.   If a topic has not been assigned to you, think first of subjects that relate to your classroom studies or that you have a special interest in. Then list various possibilities within those subjects, starting with a broad concept and narrowing it down into more specific topics. Preliminary research in such sources as encyclopedias will give you an overview of the subject, present ideas for further exploration, and even direct you to other sources.

Before you decide on a topic, ask yourself the following questions: Is this topic too broad to cover in any depth in the number of pages assigned? Or is it so limited that I will not have enough to say? Is it such a ''new'' topic that I may not be able to get enough information on it? You should be able to support your paper with three to five reference sources; if you cannot do that, you will need to choose another topic.

RESEARCHING YOUR TOPIC

Assume you have been assigned to write a research paper on Walt Disney World. How do you go about it? How do you begin your research?

Creating a Working Outline. Your first step should be to make a working outline, a rough sketch of what you think you want to cover in your paper. Although this outline will undoubtedly change as you do your research and develop a clearer idea of what you want to say, it will serve as a guide in looking for sources and taking notes. Only three or four main headings and perhaps a few subheadings will give you the necessary overview of your subject.

The Making of Walt Disney World
I. Ideas behind Walt Disney World
II. Disneyland and Walt Disney World
III. Description of Walt Disney World
    A. Disney themes and characters
    B. Transportation

Looking for the Right Sources of Information. There are many possible sources to consult as you begin to gather information. In addition to an encyclopedia, several resource tools in your library can help in your search. Among them are the following:

- the subject index in the library's card catalog or computer catalog (a guide to the library's books by subject)
- *Readers' Guide to Periodical Literature* (a guide to magazine articles by subject)
- the library's vertical files (a collection of newspaper and magazine articles, photographs, and other materials about current events and topics)
- *Guide to Historical Literature*
- *Book Review Digest* (excerpts from book reviews that appeared in newspapers and magazines)
- Many newspapers, such as the *New York Times* and the *Washington Post*, publish indexes of their articles, which may be available in computerized as well as print form.

Judging Whether Sources Are Useful. Every book contains information that will help you assess its usefulness to you. Some of this information will also be needed for compiling your bibliography, the list of sources you use in the paper. It is important to know where to look for the information as you organize your research.

- **Title page.** Gives the full title of the book; the subtitle, if there is one; the name of the author or editor; the publisher; the city of publication; and often the publication date.

> needed for citations and bibliography

- **Copyright page.** Usually immediately follows the title page. Gives the year of copyright and the name of the copyright holder.

> provides latest publication information and indicates how current the material in the book may be

- **Table of contents.** Sometimes includes lists of tables, maps, illustrations, and photographs.

> provides an organized overview and outline of the material in the book

- **Introductory material.** Usually includes a preface, foreword, or introduction.

> gives an overview of book's thesis and content

- **Appendix.** May contain supplementary material, such as charts, statistical tables, or the text of documents discussed in the book.

> may be useful in directing you to other sources for further research, particularly primary (original) sources

- **Bibliography.** A list of books, periodicals, or other sources either used in researching the book or recommended by the author for additional reading.

> helpful source material for continuing research and for evaluating the material found in book

- **Index.** Alphabetical list of names and subjects from the text of the book, with page numbers where those references are found.

> a quick way to find information on specific subjects

Creating Bibliography Cards.   Bibliography cards are cards that you use to record the sources from which you have gathered information. As you consult each source, make up a 3″ × 5″ bibliography card for it. You will need to refer to these cards throughout your research and as you compile the final bibliography for your paper.

Each card should include the following basic information: a number to identify the source; name(s) of author(s), with last name(s) first; full title, including a subtitle if there is one; and publication information. Depending on the type of source, you may also need to include such information as editor or translator, edition, volume, series, and page numbers.

**Bibliography Card
for a Book**

number to identify source — title

author — date

location —

publisher —

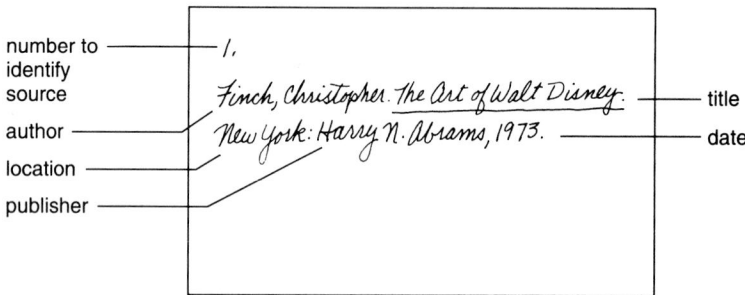

**Bibliography Card
for an Encyclopedia
Article**

author —

title —

encyclopedia —

date —

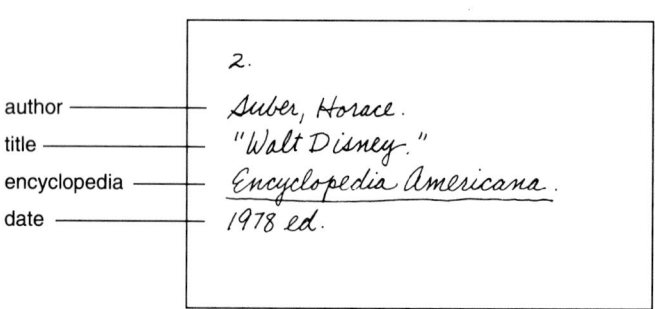

**Bibliography Card
for a
Magazine Article**

author —

title —

magazine —

date — page numbers

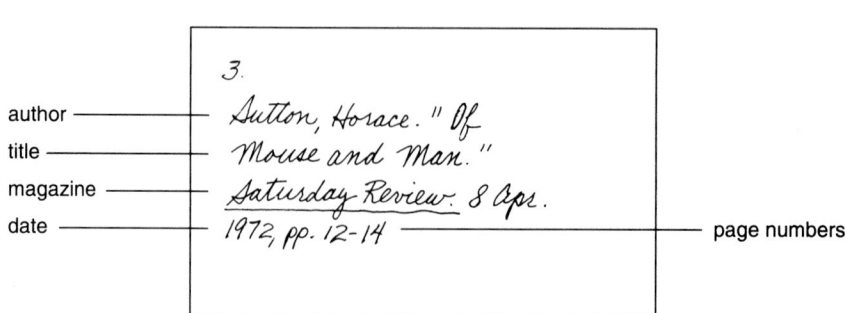

TAKING NOTES

After you have made a bibliography card for a source, you are ready to begin reading and taking notes. First skim the text for material relevant to the headings on your working outline. If you find information that you think you might want to use, enter it on large (4" × 6") index cards in the following manner:

Write the number of the bibliography card for the source in the upper left-hand corner of the card. It is helpful to include the last name of the author as well, in case you make an error in transferring the number. Below, write the heading from the working outline that the notes apply to. Somewhere on the card, be sure to include the page number(s) from which you have taken the information; if the information comes from more than one page, make clear what comes from which page. In the upper right-hand corner, write an identifying number for that particular note card. The notes that you record on each card will be paraphrases, direct quotations, or a combination of the two, as in the sample notecard shown below.

Paraphrasing.   Most of your notes should be in the form of paraphrases. Paraphrasing means rewriting your ideas in your own words, a process that will help you remember and understand the information. When paraphrasing, you can use either phrases or complete sentences, always trying to keep them brief and to the point in order to create a concise summary.

Quoting Directly.   When the exact words of a source are so striking that you think you may want to quote them directly in your paper, copy them carefully and put quotation marks around them. Always recheck the copied quotation against the original.

Avoiding Plagiarism.   Remember that when you either quote directly or paraphrase ideas, statements, or facts from another source, you must credit the source in your research paper. Using a source without giving credit is called plagiarism and is considered a serious error.

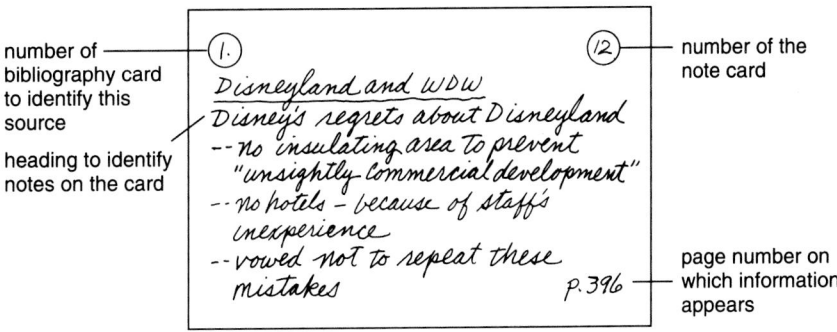

number of bibliography card to identify this source

heading to identify notes on the card

number of the note card

page number on which information appears

① Disneyland and WDW
Disney's regrets about Disneyland
-- no insulating area to prevent "unsightly commercial development"
-- no hotels - because of staff's inexperience
-- vowed not to repeat these mistakes   p. 396

Becoming a Better Writer

Making a Formal Outline

Once you have completed your basic research, you are ready to make a formal outline that will provide the organization of your paper. First, organize your note cards in a way that seems logical to you. Then from the note cards create an outline that includes all of the information you have gathered that remains relevant to your topic as you now see it. As a result of your research, some of your ideas may have been changed or even proved to be wrong.

Look at the outline below for a research paper entitled "The Making of Walt Disney World," and notice how it differs from the working outline on page R24.

The Making of Walt Disney World

I. Ideas behind Walt Disney World
  A. Regrets about Disneyland
    1. Lack of insulating property
    2. Lack of revenue-producing hotels
  B. Ideas for new park
    1. Isolation
    2. Hotels
    3. Recreation
    4. Projects
  C. Follow-through by associates
II. Description of Walt Disney World
  A. "Visual magnets"
  B. Theme parks
  C. Disney characters
  D. "Main Street" attractions
III. Reasons for Walt Disney World's success
  A. Planned environment
  B. Controlled competition

Writing the Paper

For advice about writing the paper itself, refer to the section "An Approach to Writing," pages R2-R4.

Using Footnotes

Whenever you use an idea, a fact, or a direct quotation from another author in your paper, you need to include a footnote. The footnote gives credit to the author and helps the readers locate your source if they want to read the original material.

Footnotes have two parts: a raised number, called a superscript, is placed at the end of the quotation or borrowed material, usually at the end of a sentence. A corresponding number and the information concerning the source are either placed at the bottom (foot) of the page on which the superscript appears or

included in a list at the end of the paper, before the bibliography. Footnotes are usually numbered consecutively throughout the paper; in lengthy research papers with chapters, sometimes they are numbered by chapter.

Footnote for a Book
[1]Christopher Finch, *The Art of Walt Disney* (New York: Harry N. Abrams, 1973), p. 389.

Footnote for a Periodical Article
[2]Horace Sutton, "Of Mouse and Man," *Saturday Review,* 8 Apr. 1972, p. 12.

Footnote for an Encyclopedia Article
[3]Roy Paul Nelson, "Walt Disney," *World Book Encyclopedia,* 1984 ed.

If you cite the same source more than once in your paper, after the first citation you may use a shortened form for the footnote, including the author's last name and the page. If you use more than one book by the same author, distinguish the books by including the title as well.

[11]Finch, p. 390.
[12]Finch, p. 411.
[13]Finch, p. 411.
[14]Finch, p. 415.
[15]Horace Sutton, "Of Mouse and Man," *Saturday Review*, 8 Apr. 1972, p. 12.

COMPILING A BIBLIOGRAPHY

When you have finished writing the paper, you need to compile a bibliography, an alphabetical list of the sources that you used. It will be the last page of your paper. To compile the bibliography, simply alphabetize the bibliography cards by the last name of the author. See the example below for what these entries should look like and the kinds of information they should contain.

Bibliography

Blake, Peter. "The Lessons of the Parks." *The Art of Walt Disney.* New York: Harry N. Abrams, 1973.

Finch, Christopher. *The Art of Walt Disney.* New York: Harry N. Abrams, 1973.

Friedlander, Paul J. C. "What Has Mickey Mouse Wrought?" *New York Times*, 21 Mar. 1971, Sec. 10, p. 46.

Griffin, Al. *"Step Right Up Folks!"* Chicago: Henry Regneri, 1974.

Nelson, Roy Paul. "Walt Disney." *World Book Encyclopedia,* 1984 ed.

Sutton, Horace. "Of Mouse and Man." *Saturday Review,* 8 Apr. 1972, pp. 12-14.

Reference Resources

There are abundant reference resources available on almost every topic. With the advance of the use of computers for storing and locating information, the vastness of this information can be bewildering. It is important to select resources that will work for you—those that suit your topic and level of learning.

With so much available, where do you begin? First, most of us are limited to the resources of the library or libraries near our homes. In a large library these can be sophisticated. In a smaller one you may have to search harder and be more imaginative, exploring the possibilities of interlibrary loans, for example.

REFERENCE WORKS

Encyclopedias. Encyclopedias are an excellent place to start your research. The encyclopedia article often will have distilled a large body of knowledge into a concise and well-organized article. After reading an encyclopedia article on your subject, you should be able to evaluate your topic. Is it too narrow? Does the article point out aspects you hadn't considered? Is your topic too broad? Is there a particular aspect that would be more manageable?

The drawback of encyclopedias is that they cannot carry the most up-to-date information. Other reference sources such as newspapers and magazines can augment your list of resources if your topic is a current one.

There are two main types of encyclopedias in book form: single-volume, such as the *Columbia Encyclopedia,* and multivolume, such as *World Book, Encyclopaedia Britannica,* and *Collier's Encyclopedia.* There are also specialized encyclopedias that concentrate on a particular subject, such as the *Encyclopedia of World Art* and the *McGraw-Hill Encyclopedia of Science and Technology.*

Biographical Resources. Besides full-length biographies, which are usually alphabetized in the biography section of the library, and biographical encyclopedias, such as the *Dictionary of American Biography* and the *Dictionary of Scientific Biography,* there are many collections of biographical information that provide anything from thumbnail sketches to lengthy essays. For spellings of names, dates, positions held, and a listing of major works of authors, composers, scientists, business executives, and others, **biographical dictionaries** are a good source. There are also biographical resources, such as the *Who's Who* series, that provide similar information on current personalities, with volumes covering many individual professions and countries. For longer discussion, volumes of biographical essays, such as *Current Biography,* are available. Some publications, such as *Current Biography* and *The New York Times Biographical Service,* specialize in covering people currently in the news as well as those of historical importance.

Yearbooks and Almanacs. Yearly almanacs are excellent sources for ready access to facts and statistics. The almanac is also helpful in distilling what can seem like an overwhelming amount of information into a few concisely

written important points. Almanacs are the place to look for statistics and brief treatments of current events in the sciences, politics, popular culture, the United States, and the world.

Another type of yearbook is that associated with your encyclopedia. Many encyclopedias publish general summaries of the events that occurred the previous year. They will often include "articles" on selected events or topics of importance in a given year.

In addition to general almanacs and yearbooks, there are many available that cover specialized areas such as weather, agriculture, astronomy, local government, and business. The *Statesman's Yearbook,* for example, provides information on countries around the world and is revised every year.

Newspapers and Periodicals.   For the most up-to-date information or for controversial viewpoints, newspapers and magazines are excellent sources. It is, however, important to question their authority for your topic. If, for instance, you are writing about the global effects of acid rain, a national newspaper will be more appropriate as a source than your local newspaper. However, if you are writing about the effects of acid rain on your local lakes or the statue in front of your City Hall, your local newspaper will clearly be more authoritative. Your teacher or librarian can help you to make these distinctions.

Books on a Given Topic.   You can find a book on almost every subject imaginable. But how can you decide quickly whether a particular book will be right for you and your topic? Here are several things to keep in mind.

- Begin by asking yourself what the purpose of the book is. Although a glance at the title is sometimes enough to establish a book's purpose, usually it helps to read the table of contents and the introduction. This will help you evaluate the scope of the book. Is it too general? Is it a technical book on a narrow subject? If your topic is current, is the book up-to-date? If historical, does it cover the time span you're interested in?
- Is the work authoritative for your subject? For instance, a book written by a scientist who specializes in acid rain will probably be considered more authoritative than a popular book on the subject.
- Is the language on a level you can understand? Does it give too much or too little information on your topic? Is the information easy to find?

Knowing how to screen books for your purposes can save you time and help you to produce a better paper.

Nonbook Resources.   Many libraries offer much more than the written materials discussed above. From poets reading their own works on tape to "how-to" videos to filmstrips, these can be useful and inspiring resources. Perhaps you've decided to write on an opera by the composer Giuseppe Verdi. You may be able to listen to or view an actual performance, even if you're hundreds of miles from the nearest opera house.

Often, libraries will include such things as pamphlets and newsletters as part of their nonbook resources. They may be sorted in vertical files and may include U.S. government documents that are published on a wide variety of topics. These are often the most easily available (and easy-to-use) primary sources.

FINDING THE INFORMATION YOU NEED

Catalogs.   Your library will always keep a catalog of its books. It may be in the form of a file of index cards, or it may be in book form or on a computer. All of these forms have the same information, and all allow you to find a book in three ways: by author, title, or subject. Each will supply you with a "call number" to help you or the librarian locate the book.

Suppose you want to get information on the subject of acid rain. Your library's computer may have instructions that look something like this:

screen 1   begin the search for your subject

> Welcome to your library's on-line catalog.
> To locate an author, press **A** then press the **ENTER** key.
> To locate a title, press **T** then press the **ENTER** key.
> To locate a subject, press **S** then press the **ENTER** key.
> To begin again, press **ESC**.
> For previous screen, press **R**.

screen 2   type in your subject name

> Type your subject: *ACID RAIN*
> (press **ENTER** key when finished)
> To begin again, press **ESC**.
> For previous screen, press **R** and **ENTER** key.

screen 3   from the list of categories that match the subject you typed in, select the one(s) you want

> Press the number of the reference wanted, then press **ENTER**.
> To begin again, press **ESC**.
> For previous screen, press **R** and **ENTER** key.
> SUBJECT: **ACID RAIN**
>   1   ACID RAIN (9 references found)
>   2   ACID RAIN CANADA (1)
>   3   ACID RAIN ENVIRONMENTAL ASPECTS (13)
>   4   ACID RAIN ENVIRONMENTAL ASPECTS CANADA (1)
>   5   ACID RAIN ENVIRONMENTAL ASPECTS MOTION PICTURES (1)
>   6   ACID RAIN ENVIRONMENTAL ASPECTS UNITED STATES (3)
>   7   ACID RAIN VIDEO RECORDINGS (1)

screen 4   selecting number 6, ACID RAIN ENVI-RONMENTAL ASPECTS UNITED STATES, gives you the following list

> To return to list, press **L** and **ENTER** key.
> To begin again, press **ESC**.
> For previous screen, press **R** and **ENTER** key.
> SELECTION **6 ACID RAIN ENVIRONMENTAL ASPECTS UNITED STATES**
> 1. **Call no.:** VTH 932a *(Videotape) Acid Rain: Neighbors at Risk*, State University Educational Programming, Bismarck, ND
> The difficulties of assessing responsibility for acid rain and of establishing cooperation between countries are discussed.
> 2. **Call no.:** 363.7386S Smith, Joe. *Acid Rain*, 1990, Environmental Books, Boston
> 3. **Call no.:** 363.7386W Whelan, Margaret. *Our Children's Children: Who Will Pay for Acid Rain?* 1991, New Press, Denver

Indexes to Periodicals and Newspapers.   There are hundreds of indexes to magazines, journals, and newspapers. Most commonly they are in book form and they are arranged with authors and subjects in one alphabetical list. The listings may include unfamiliar abbreviations. These can usually be found in the front of the book along with important information such as which magazines this index covers and what time span it covers. Unfortunately, your library may not carry all the magazines and newspapers it has listed in its indexes. Your librarian will keep a list of what's available.

The most familiar index to periodicals is the *Readers' Guide to Periodical Literature.* It lists authors and subjects from nearly 200 popular magazines plus some professional journals. There are also indexes to newspapers.

With the advent of computers, more and more sophisticated indexes are being made available to more and more users. Your library may have a computerized index such as *Infotrac*. Large public libraries or specialized libraries may have indexes that specialize in the journals and literature of their particular profession. Sometimes these are available to users on computer terminals free of charge. Other times you may have to fill out a request form and a librarian will do the actual searching of the database.

TIPS ON SEARCHING AN ON-LINE INDEX

It is important to know how to go about searching a computerized index in order to get **all of** the information you need and **only** the information you need.

- **Do you really need to use the computerized index?** It is exciting to see a waiting computer terminal, but if you can find the information you need in a readily available reference book like an encyclopedia or a dictionary, it is better to use that.

- **Does the on-line index cover the dates you're interested in?** Remember that on-line indexes are usually the best source for up-to-date publications, but that they probably will not go back in time as far as published indexes in book form.

- **Which index should I use?** If you're fortunate enough to have more than one index available to you, consider carefully what kinds of publications are covered by each and whether they will work for your topic. For instance, if you search for acid rain in an index of business periodicals you are likely to get articles on the cost to industry of cleaning up acid rain, or laws governing industrial wastes, rather than the more far-ranging articles you might get from a general index.

- **What term do I search for?** Just as you define your topic carefully, you must define your search carefully. A search on the word "environment" may yield thousands of articles. A search on the word "rain" will yield articles on rainfall and rain forests but may or may not include articles on acid rain. Always use the most specific term you can. Use everyday terminology first (ACID RAIN, not RAIN, ACID). Watch for cross-references which may point you in the right direction: A search of POLLUTION yielded the cross-reference "see ACID RAIN" under the entry POLLUTION, WATER. Don't give up. Ask for help if you need it.

- **How does the database search?** If you use more than one word in your search subject or if you specify a second subject, the computer will usually assume that you want articles that mention all of the terms, not one or the other. For example:

  Type subject: ACID RAIN
  2nd subject: ADIRONDACK

This search yielded 2,918 "finds" for ACID, 3,913 for RAIN, and 10 for ADIRONDACK, but only 2 finds for articles concerning all three: ACID and RAIN and ADIRONDACK.

*T*ime Line of United States History

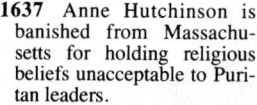

40,000 years ago First peoples cross land bridge between Asia and North America.

7,000 years ago People in the Americas begin farming.

700 Early Native Americans of the Mississippi Valley culture begin to build villages.

1000 The Anasazi begin to build cities. Norse explorer Leif Ericson sails to North America.

1492 Italian navigator Christopher Columbus, in the service of Spain, enters the Caribbean seeking a sea route to the Far East.

1497 John Cabot reaches North America and claims land in the New World for England.

1499 Amerigo Vespucci voyages to the New World, which is later named for him by a European map maker.

1513 Juan Ponce de León explores Florida and claims it for Spain.

1524 Italian navigator Giovanni da Verrazano explores the Atlantic coast for France.

1539-43 Spanish explorer Hernando De Soto explores the Southeast and reaches the Mississippi River.

1540 Francisco Vásquez de Coronado explores much of the Southwest in his search for gold for Spain.

1565 Spaniards found St. Augustine in Florida, the oldest city in the U.S.

1600s Iroquois groups war with each other. First horses appear on the Great Plains.

1607 English colonists found Jamestown, the first permanent English settlement in North America.

1609 English navigator Henry Hudson, in the service of the Dutch, explores the Hudson River.

1637 Anne Hutchinson is banished from Massachusetts for holding religious beliefs unacceptable to Puritan leaders.

1638 New Sweden is founded in what later becomes Delaware and southern New Jersey.

1639 Fundamental Orders of Connecticut (first constitution written in America) are promulgated.

1647 Massachusetts establishes first public school system.

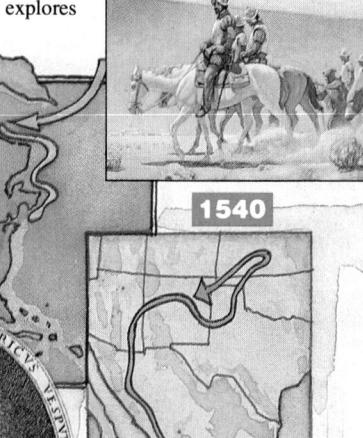

1000

1540

1000

1000

1499

1619 The first African slaves are brought to Jamestown. First meeting of the Virginia House of Burgesses.

1620 The Pilgrims arrive at Plymouth.

1624 New Netherland, later named New York, is founded by the Dutch.

1628 The Puritans found the Massachusetts Bay Colony.

1636 Harvard, the first North American college, is founded. Roger Williams founds Rhode Island. Thomas Hooker begins a settlement in Connecticut.

1649 Maryland Toleration Act is passed, granting religious freedom to both Catholics and Protestants.

1650 The powerful Iroquois League dominates Native American territory and trade in the Northeast.

1654 First group of Jewish immigrants arrive in New Amsterdam from Spain.

1663 The Carolinas are settled by French Huguenots and British settlers.

1664 The French explore the St. Lawrence and the Great Lakes and claim western North America.

1673 Jacques Marquette and Louis Jolliet explore the Mississippi River.

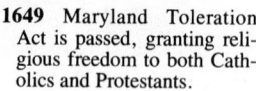

1675 King Philip, chief of the Wampanoag, wars on encroaching settlers in New England.

1680 New Hampshire becomes a colony.

1682 William Penn founds Pennsylvania. Sieur de La Salle claims Louisiana for France.

1733 Georgia becomes the thirteenth colony.

1735 Trial of John Peter Zenger, editor, establishes principle of freedom of the press.

1754-63 French and Indian War; Britain takes over New France.

1758 The first Indian reservation is established.

1765 The Stamp Act results in the colonists' opposition to taxation without representation.

1770 British troops fire on protesting mob, an event later called the Boston Massacre.

1773 Boston Tea Party protests tax on tea.

1774 Colonies send representatives to First Continental Congress.

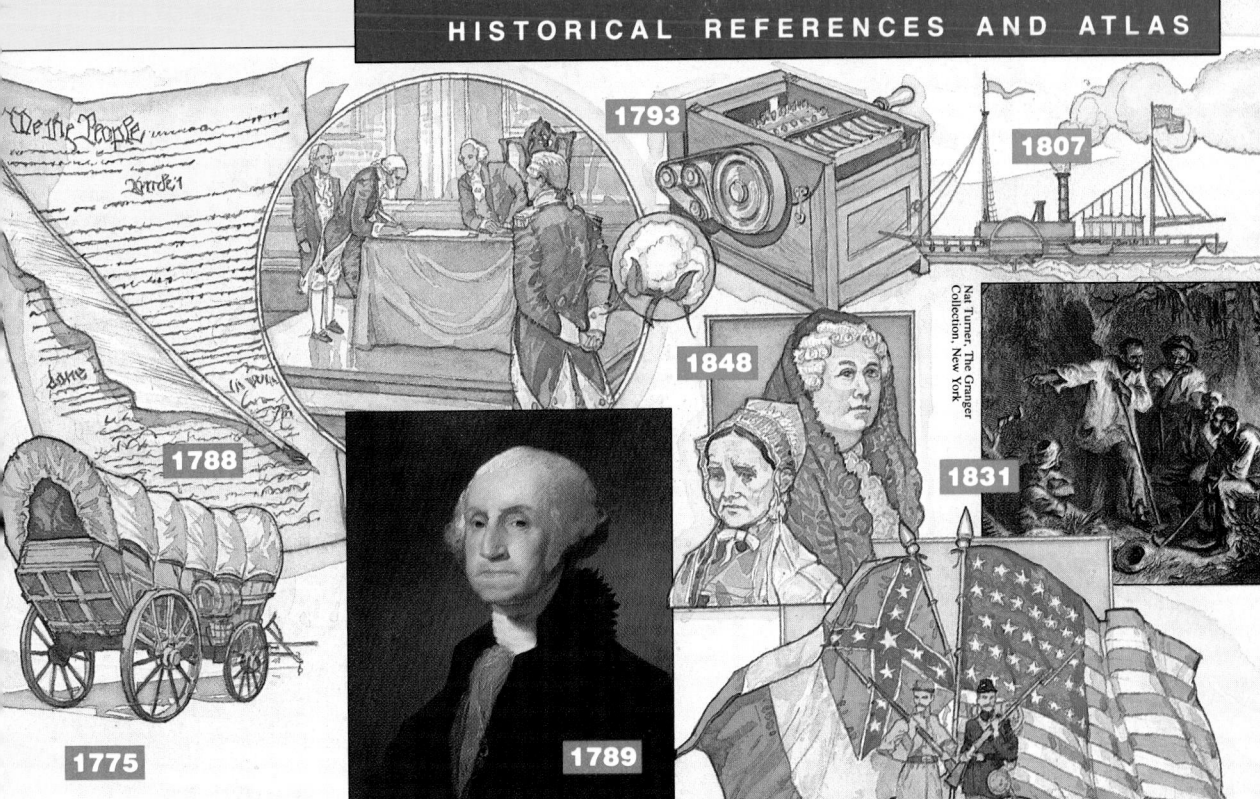

Nat Turner; The Granger Collection, New York

1775 Battles of Lexington and Concord begin the American Revolution; Battle of Bunker Hill; Second Continental Congress; George Washington accepts command of the army. Conestoga wagons begin carrying pioneers and freight to new settlements in the West.

1776 On July 4, the colonists adopt the Declaration of Independence and form the United States of America.

1781 Americans defeat the British at Yorktown, Virginia.

1783 British troops leave the United States. The Addition of 1783 extends the boundaries of the U.S. to the Mississippi River.

1787 The Northwest Ordinance defines status of new territories and paves the way for their statehood.

1788 The Constitution is approved.

1789 George Washington takes oath of office as first U.S. president.

1791 The Bill of Rights guarantees civil liberties to every citizen.

1793 Eli Whitney invents the cotton gin, giving new importance to slavery in the South.

1803 The Louisiana Purchase doubles the size of the U.S.

1804 Lewis and Clark explore the Northwest, hoping to map a route to the Pacific.

1807 Robert Fulton's *Clermont* begins regular runs. Steamboats become the fastest way to ship goods.

1808 Importation of slaves is made illegal.

1811 Work begins on the Cumberland Road (from Maryland to Illinois), which starts the national system of transportation.

1812-15 British interference in American shipping and American desire for territory in Canada result in the War of 1812.

1818 The Red River Cession adds parts of North Dakota, South Dakota, and Minnesota to the U.S.

1819 Florida and parts of Alabama, Mississippi, and Louisiana are ceded to the U.S. by Spain.

1820 Missouri Compromise defines areas in which slavery would be illegal.

1821 Troy Female Seminary, first women's college in the U.S., is founded.

1823 The Monroe Doctrine declares North and South America off limits to European interference.

1825 The Erie Canal opens, providing a water route from the Atlantic Ocean to the Great Lakes.

1830 The Indian Removal Act requires all Native American tribes to move west of the Mississippi River. Thousands of Native Americans die in subsequent forced marches west. The Underground Railroad begins helping slaves escape.

1831 Slave Nat Turner leads an ill-fated slave rebellion in Virginia. Cyrus McCormick invents the reaper, opening the Great Plains to agriculture. William Lloyd Garrison publishes the abolitionist paper *The Liberator*.

1836 Texas wins its independence from Mexico and is later annexed to the U.S.

1837 Samuel F. B. Morse demonstrates the first successful telegraph in the U.S. The invention of the steel plow helps to open up the West.

1843 Former slave Sojourner Truth lectures on the abolition of slavery.

1846 A treaty with Great Britain adds what later become Washington, Oregon, Idaho, and part of Montana to the U.S.

1848 After a two-year war, Mexico cedes land that later becomes the states of Nevada, Utah, and California and part of Arizona and New Mexico. Gold is discovered in California. Lucretia Mott and Elizabeth Cady Stanton chair Seneca Falls Convention, inaugurating the women's rights movement in the U.S.

1850 Compromise of 1850 tries to defuse slavery disputes between North and South.

1851 Harriet Beecher Stowe's *Uncle Tom's Cabin* stirs abolitionist feelings.

1854 Kansas-Nebraska Act revives the dispute over expansion of slavery.

1857 The Dred Scott decision denies citizen rights to slaves.

1861 Southern states form the Confederate States of America; the Civil War begins.

1862 Homestead Act distributes over 250,000,000 acres of western lands free to 2 million settlers.

Time Line of United States History

1863 Emancipation Proclamation declares freedom for all slaves in Confederate-held territory; Lincoln delivers Gettysburg Address.

1864 Disputes between settlers and Native American tribes worsened by militia's killing of peaceful Cheyenne and Arapaho at Sand Creek, Colorado.

1865 Civil War ends. President Abraham Lincoln is assassinated. Thirteenth Amendment outlaws slavery.

1867 The U.S. buys Alaska from Russia.

1868 Fourteenth Amendment gives citizenship to former slaves. President Andrew Johnson is impeached but is not found guilty.

1869 Wyoming is the first state to give women the right to vote. Transcontinental railroad is completed with the help of thousands of Irish and Chinese laborers.

1870 Fifteenth Amendment opens voting to all male citizens, regardless of race.

1872 First national park, Yellowstone, opens. Susan B. Anthony is arrested for voting.

1874 Barbed wire is introduced in the West, leading to struggles between farmers and ranchers.

1875 Alexander Graham Bell invents the telephone.

1876 Battle of the Little Bighorn; General George Armstrong Custer defeated by the Sioux.

1877 Chief Joseph and the Nez Percé surrender to army troops. The U.S. seizes the Black Hills from the Sioux, breaking their treaty.

1879 Thomas Edison invents the electric light bulb.

1882 Immigration of Chinese laborers is restricted for ten years by the Chinese Exclusion Act.

1883 Supreme Court overturns earlier civil rights act and rules that Native Americans are aliens.

1886 The American Federation of Labor is formed. France gives the Statue of Liberty to the United States.

1889 Jane Addams and Ellen Gates Starr start Hull House to help immigrants settling in Chicago.

1890 Hundreds of Sioux ghost dance followers massacred at Wounded Knee, Colorado.

1898 Congress votes to make Hawaii an American territory. The U.S. defeats Spain in the Spanish-American War and gains Guam, Puerto Rico, and the Philippines.

1890-1924 Immigration from Europe is at its peak as over 20 million people enter the country.

1903 The Wright brothers (Wilbur and Orville) make their first successful airplane flight at Kitty Hawk, North Carolina.

1906 San Francisco suffers a severe earthquake, the worst natural disaster in U.S. history.

1907 Immigration of Japanese laborers is barred.

1913 Henry Ford sets up first assembly line to produce cars.

1914 World War I begins in Europe. The Panama Canal opens.

1917 The U.S. joins the Allies in the war against Germany. Puerto Rico becomes a territory.

1919 The Treaty of Versailles officially ends World War I.

1920 Nineteenth Amendment gives women the right to vote.

1924 Native Americans given citizenship by the Indian Citizenship Act. New law limits immigration from Europe.

1927 Charles Lindbergh flies solo across the Atlantic Ocean.

1929 Stock market crashes; Great Depression begins.

1933 New Deal begins; government projects provide work for the unemployed.

1939 World War II begins in Europe.

1941 Japan attacks Pearl Harbor; the U.S. enters World War II against Germany, Italy, and Japan.

1945 The U.S. drops atomic bombs on the Japanese cities of Hiroshima and Nagasaki, ushering in the nuclear age. World War II ends. The United Nations is founded and is ceded land in New York City for its headquarters.

1950-53 The U.S. joins United Nations forces during Korean War.

1954 The U.S. Supreme Court makes segregation in public schools illegal.

1955 Rosa Parks's refusal to give up her seat to a white passenger begins the Montgomery, Alabama, bus boycott, which sparks the civil rights movement.

1958 The U.S. creates the National Aeronautics and Space Administration (NASA). The U.S. launches *Explorer 1*.

1959 Fidel Castro takes over in Cuba and institutes a communist government.

Emancipation Proclamation, The Granger Collection, New York

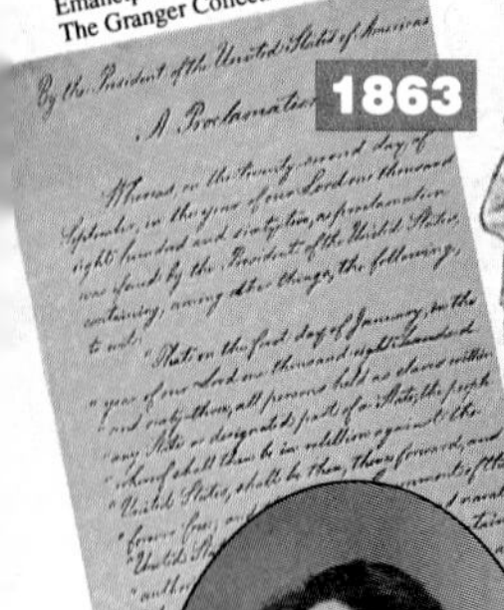

1913

1890-1924

1869

1863

1929

1920

1877

CHIEF JOSEPH

1941

1865

1872

1945

1962 John Glenn is the first American to orbit the earth. Rachel Carson's *Silent Spring* published, launching environmental movement.

1963 Martin Luther King, Jr., leads civil rights march in Washington, D.C. President John F. Kennedy is assassinated.

1964 The Civil Rights Act of 1964 bars discrimination by employers, unions, and businesses that serve the public.

1965 The U.S. sends troops to Vietnam to support South Vietnam in its effort to remain independent. Black leader Malcolm X is assassinated. More equitable immigration laws go into effect.

1967 Thurgood Marshall becomes the first black U.S. Supreme Court justice.

1968 Martin Luther King, Jr., is assassinated.

1969 Astronauts Neil A. Armstrong and Edwin Aldrin are the first people to walk on the moon.

1970 The Environmental Protection Agency is created.

1972 President Richard M. Nixon visits China, becoming the first American president to do so. Break-in at Democratic National Committee headquarters ultimately leads to the Watergate hearings.

1973 U.S. troops leave Vietnam.

1974 President Nixon resigns.

1979 President Jimmy Carter hosts discussions between Israeli Prime Minister Menachem Begin and Egyptian President Anwar al-Sadat resulting in the Camp David Accords. Nuclear power plant accident at Three Mile Island in Pennsylvania.

1980s The decade sees a significant increase in immigration from Asia, the Caribbean, and Latin America.

1981 American hostages in Iran are freed after 444 days in captivity. *Columbia*, the first reusable space shuttle, is launched by the U.S. Sandra Day O'Connor becomes first woman U.S. Supreme Court justice.

1983 Sally K. Ride is first U.S. woman in space.

1986 U.S. space shuttle *Challenger* explodes, killing all on board. Federal holiday in honor of Martin Luther King, Jr., is first observed.

1987 Iran-Contra hearings begin to explore accusations that the government traded arms for hostages. October stock market crash presages recession.

1989 Major earthquake hits San Francisco area. Largest oil spill in U.S. history follows the crash of the oil tanker *Exxon Valdez* in Prince William Sound, Alaska. U.S. forces invade Panama; General Manuel Noriega surrenders to U.S.

1991 The Persian Gulf War; U.S. military joins international forces in removing Iraqi presence from Kuwait.

1992 A NASA study speculates that a hole in the ozone layer may affect inhabited regions of North America, Europe, and Asia.

1979
1981
1981
1955
1968
1991
1963
1980s
1965
ROSA PARKS
FREE NOW
FREEDOM
Freedom
CIVIL RIGHTS

*P*residents of the United States

According to the Constitution, the President of the United States must be
a natural-born citizen of at least 35 years of age who has lived in the
United States for 14 years. The President may serve two 4-year terms, but
not more than two. On January 20 following the election, the President is
inaugurated. On that day, the President takes this oath of office:

> "I do solemnly swear (or affirm) that I
> will faithfully execute the office of
> President of the United States, and will
> to the best of my ability, preserve,
> protect, and defend the Constitution of
> the United States."

The Presidents of the United States are listed below and on the pages that
follow.

GEORGE WASHINGTON
(1732–1799)
In Office: 1789–1797
Age When Inaugurated: 57
Political Party: Federalist
Native State: Virginia
Vice President: John Adams
First Lady: Martha Dandridge
Washington

JOHN ADAMS (1735–1826)
In Office: 1797–1801
Age When Inaugurated: 61
Political Party: Federalist
Native State: Massachusetts
Vice President: Thomas Jefferson
First Lady: Abigail Smith Adams

THOMAS JEFFERSON
(1743–1826)
In Office: 1801–1809
Age When Inaugurated: 57
Political Party:
Democratic-Republican
Native State: Virginia
Vice Presidents:
Aaron Burr (1801–1805)
George Clinton (1805–1809)
No First Lady in his Administration

JAMES MADISON (1751–1836)
In Office: 1809–1817
Age When Inaugurated: 57
Political Party:
Democratic-Republican
Native State: Virginia
Vice Presidents:
George Clinton (1809–1812)
Elbridge Gerry (1813–1814)
First Lady: Dolley Payne Madison

JAMES MONROE (1758–1831)
In Office: 1817–1825
Age When Inaugurated: 58
Political Party:
Democratic-Republican
Native State: Virginia
Vice President: Daniel D. Tompkins
First Lady: Elizabeth Kortright
Monroe

JOHN QUINCY ADAMS
(1767–1848)
In Office: 1825–1829
Age When Inaugurated: 57
Political Party:
Democratic-Republican
Native State: Massachusetts
Vice President: John C. Calhoun
First Lady: Louisa Johnson Adams

ANDREW JACKSON (1767–1845)
In Office: 1829–1837
Age When Inaugurated: 61
Political Party: Democratic
Native State: South Carolina
Vice Presidents:
    John C. Calhoun (1829–1832)
    Martin Van Buren (1833–1837)
No First Lady in his Administration

7

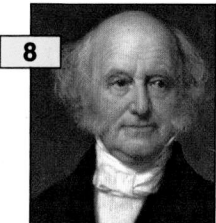

MARTIN VAN BUREN (1782–1862)
In Office: 1837–1841
Age When Inaugurated: 54
Political Party: Democratic
Native State: New York
Vice President: Richard M. Johnson
No First Lady in his Administration

8

WILLIAM HENRY HARRISON
    (1773–1841)
In Office: 1841 (one month)
Age When Inaugurated: 68
Political Party: Whig
Native State: Virginia
Vice President: John Tyler*
First Lady: Anna Symmes Harrison

9

JOHN TYLER (1790–1862)
In Office: 1841–1845
Age When Inaugurated: 51
Political Party: Whig
Native State: Virginia
No Vice President in his
    Administration
First Ladies:
    Letitia Christian Tyler
    (1841–1842)
    Julia Gardiner Tyler (1844–1845)

10

JAMES K. POLK (1795–1849)
In Office: 1845–1849
Age When Inaugurated: 49
Political Party: Democratic
Native State: North Carolina
Vice President: George M. Dallas
First Lady: Sarah Childress Polk

11

ZACHARY TAYLOR (1784–1850)
In Office: 1849–1850
Age When Inaugurated: 64
Political Party: Whig
Native State: Virginia
Vice President: Millard Fillmore*
First Lady: Margaret Smith Taylor

12

MILLARD FILLMORE (1800–1874)
In Office: 1850–1853
Age When Inaugurated: 50
Political Party: Whig
Native State: New York
No Vice President in his
    Administration
First Lady: Abigail Powers Fillmore

13

FRANKLIN PIERCE (1804–1869)
In Office: 1853–1857
Age When Inaugurated: 48
Political Party: Democratic
Native State: New Hampshire
Vice President: William R. King
    (1853)
First Lady: Jane Appleton Pierce

14

JAMES BUCHANAN (1791–1868)
In Office: 1857–1861
Age When Inaugurated: 65
Political Party: Democratic
Native State: Pennsylvania
Vice President: John C. Breckinridge
No First Lady in his Administration

15

ABRAHAM LINCOLN (1809–1865)
In Office: 1861–1865
Age When Inaugurated: 52
Political Party: Republican
Native State: Kentucky
Vice Presidents:
    Hannibal Hamlin (1861–1865)
    Andrew Johnson* (1865)
First Lady: Mary Todd Lincoln

16

ANDREW JOHNSON (1808–1875)
In Office: 1865–1869
Age When Inaugurated: 56
Political Party: Democratic
Native State: North Carolina
No Vice President in his
    Administration
First Lady: Eliza McCardle Johnson

17

ULYSSES S. GRANT (1822–1885)
In Office: 1869–1877
Age When Inaugurated: 46
Political Party: Republican
Native State: Ohio
Vice Presidents:
    Schuyler Colfax (1869–1873)
    Henry Wilson (1873–1875)
First Lady: Julia Dent Grant

18

*Succeeded from the vice presidency on the death of the President.

*P*residents of the United States

19

RUTHERFORD B. HAYES
(1822–1893)
In Office: 1877–1881
Age When Inaugurated: 54
Political Party: Republican
Native State: Ohio
Vice President: William A. Wheeler
First Lady: Lucy Webb Hayes

20

JAMES A. GARFIELD (1831–1881)
In Office: 1881 (6 months)
Age When Inaugurated: 49
Political Party: Republican
Native State: Ohio
Vice President: Chester A. Arthur*
First Lady: Lucretia Rudolph
    Garfield

21

CHESTER A. ARTHUR
(1829–1886)
In Office: 1881–1885
Age When Inaugurated: 50
Political Party: Republican
Native State: Vermont
No Vice President in his
    Administration
No First Lady in his Administration

22

GROVER CLEVELAND†
(1837–1908)
In Office: 1885–1889
Age When Inaugurated: 47
Political Party: Democratic
Native State: New Jersey
Vice President: Thomas A. Hendricks
    (1885)
First Lady: Frances Folsom
    Cleveland

23

BENJAMIN HARRISON
(1833–1901)
In Office: 1889–1893
Age When Inaugurated: 55
Political Party: Republican
Native State: Ohio
Vice President: Levi P. Morton
First Lady: Caroline Scott Harrison

24

GROVER CLEVELAND
(1837–1908)
In Office: 1893–1897
Age When Inaugurated: 56
Political Party: Democratic
Native State: New Jersey
Vice President: Adlai E. Stevenson
First Lady: Frances Folsom
    Cleveland

25

WILLIAM McKINLEY (1843–1901)
In Office: 1897–1901
Age When Inaugurated: 54
Political Party: Republican
Native State: Ohio
Vice Presidents:
    Garret A. Hobart (1897–1899)
    Theodore Roosevelt* (1901)
First Lady: Ida Saxton McKinley

26

THEODORE ROOSEVELT
(1858–1919)
In Office: 1901–1909
Age When Inaugurated: 42
Political Party: Republican
Native State: New York
Vice President: Charles W. Fairbanks
    (1905–1909)
First Lady: Edith Carow Roosevelt

27

WILLIAM HOWARD TAFT
(1857–1930)
In Office: 1909–1913
Age When Inaugurated: 51
Political Party: Republican
Native State: Ohio
Vice President: James S. Sherman
    (1909–1912)
First Lady: Helen Herron Taft

28

WOODROW WILSON (1856–1924)
In Office: 1913–1921
Age When Inaugurated: 56
Political Party: Democratic
Native State: Virginia
Vice President: Thomas R. Marshall
First Ladies:
    Ellen Louise Wilson (1913–1914)
    Edith Bolling Wilson (1915–1921)

29

WARREN G. HARDING
(1865–1923)
In Office: 1921–1923
Age When Inaugurated: 56
Political Party: Republican
Native State: Ohio
Vice President: Calvin Coolidge*
First Lady: Florence Kling Harding

30

CALVIN COOLIDGE (1872–1933)
In Office: 1923–1929
Age When Inaugurated: 51
Political Party: Republican
Native State: Vermont
Vice President: Charles G. Dawes
    (1925–1929)
First Lady: Grace Goodhue Coolidge

*Succeeded from the vice presidency on the
 death of the President.

†Cleveland was elected for a second term after
 Benjamin Harrison

HERBERT HOOVER (1874–1964)
In Office: 1929–1933
Age When Inaugurated: 54
Political Party: Republican
Native State: Iowa
Vice President: Charles Curtis
First Lady: Lou Henry Hoover

31

FRANKLIN DELANO ROOSEVELT (1882–1945)
In Office: 1933–1945
Age When Inaugurated: 51
Political Party: Democratic
Native State: New York
Vice Presidents:
John N. Garner (1933–1941)
Henry A. Wallace (1941–1945)
Harry S. Truman* (1945)
First Lady: Anna Eleanor Roosevelt

32

HARRY S. TRUMAN (1884–1972)
In Office: 1945–1953
Age When Inaugurated: 60
Political Party: Democratic
Native State: Missouri
Vice President: Alben W. Barkley
(1949–1953)
First Lady: Elizabeth (Bess) W.
Truman

33

DWIGHT D. EISENHOWER
(1890–1969)
In Office: 1953–1961
Age When Inaugurated: 62
Political Party: Republican
Native State: Texas
Vice President: Richard M. Nixon
First Lady: Marie (Mamie) Doud
Eisenhower

34

JOHN F. KENNEDY (1917–1963)
In Office: 1961–1963
Age When Inaugurated: 43
Political Party: Democratic
Native State: Massachusetts
Vice President: Lyndon B. Johnson*
First Lady: Jacqueline Bouvier
Kennedy

35

LYNDON BAINES JOHNSON
(1908–1973)
In Office: 1963–1969
Age When Inaugurated: 55
Political Party: Democratic
Native State: Texas
Vice President: Hubert H. Humphrey
First Lady: Claudia (Lady Bird)
Taylor Johnson

36

RICHARD M. NIXON (1913–   )
In Office: 1969–1974
Age When Inaugurated: 56
Political Party: Republican
Native State: California
Vice Presidents:
Spiro T. Agnew (1969–1973)
Gerald R. Ford** (1973–1974)
First Lady: Patricia (Pat) Ryan Nixon

37

GERALD R. FORD (1913–   )
In Office: 1974–1977
Age When Inaugurated: 61
Political Party: Republican
Native State: Nebraska
Vice President: Nelson A.
Rockefeller
First Lady: Elizabeth (Betty) B. Ford

38

JIMMY CARTER (1924–   )
In Office: 1977–1981
Age When Inaugurated: 52
Political Party: Democratic
Native State: Georgia
Vice President: Walter F. Mondale
First Lady: Rosalynn Smith Carter

39

RONALD W. REAGAN (1911–   )
In Office: 1981–1989
Age When Inaugurated: 69
Political Party: Republican
Native State: Illinois
Vice President: George Bush
First Lady: Nancy Davis Reagan

40

GEORGE BUSH (1924–   )
In Office: 1989–
Age When Inaugurated: 64
Political Party: Republican
Native State: Massachusetts
Vice President: Dan Quayle
First Lady: Barbara Pierce Bush

41

*Succeeded from the vice presidency on the death of the President.
**Succeeded from the vice presidency on the resignation of the President.

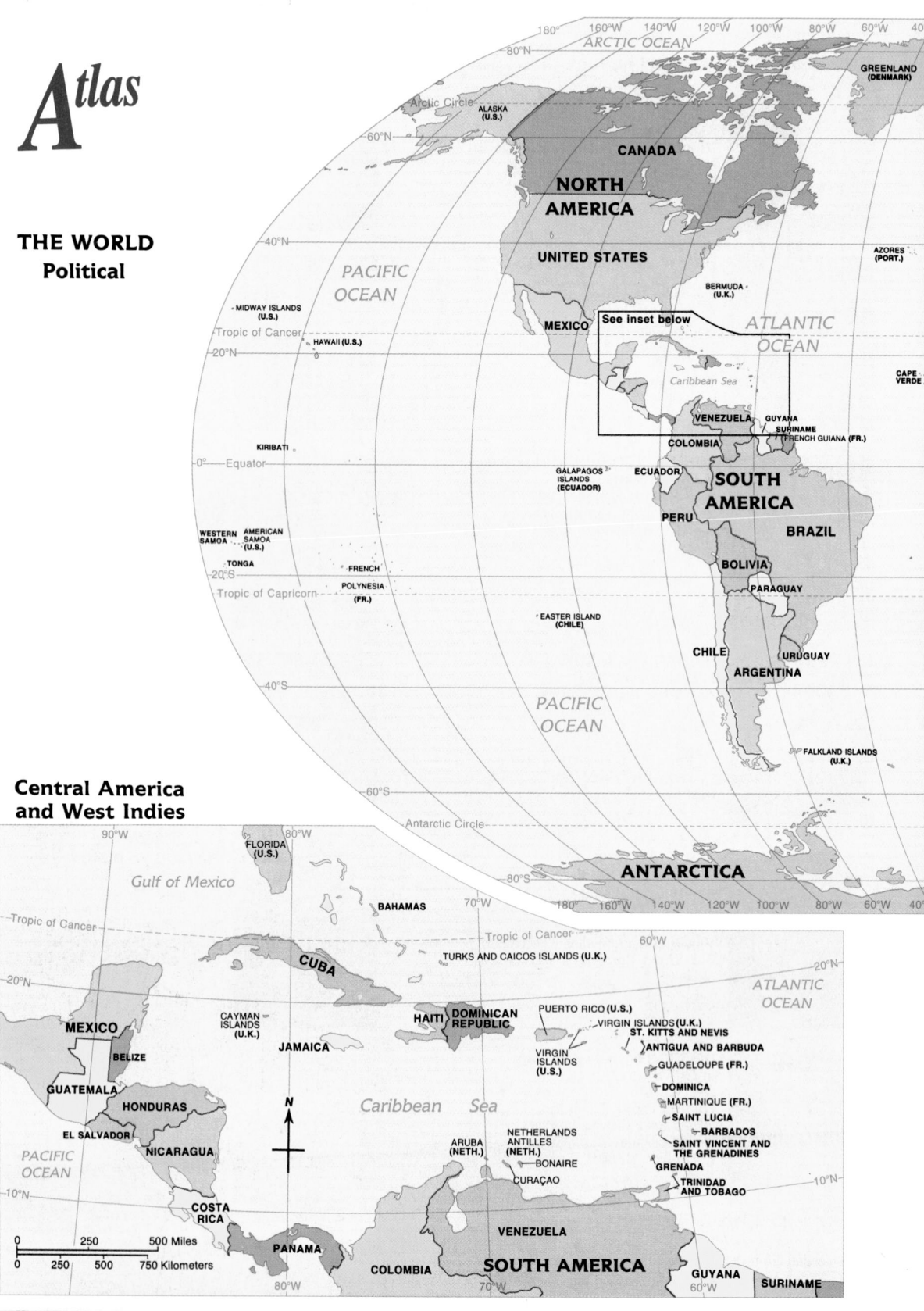

*A*tlas

THE WORLD
Political

ARCTIC OCEAN

180° 160°W 140°W 120°W 100°W 80°W 60°W 40°

80°N

GREENLAND
(DENMARK)

Arctic Circle

ALASKA
(U.S.)

60°N

CANADA

**NORTH
AMERICA**

40°N

AZORES
(PORT.)

PACIFIC
OCEAN

UNITED STATES

BERMUDA
(U.K.)

See inset below

ATLANTIC
OCEAN

Tropic of Cancer

20°N

MIDWAY ISLANDS
(U.S.)

HAWAII (U.S.)

MEXICO

CAPE
VERDE

Caribbean Sea

VENEZUELA GUYANA
SURINAME
FRENCH GUIANA (FR.)

COLOMBIA

KIRIBATI

0° Equator

GALAPAGOS
ISLANDS
(ECUADOR)

ECUADOR

**SOUTH
AMERICA**

PERU

BRAZIL

WESTERN
SAMOA

AMERICAN
SAMOA
(U.S.)

TONGA

FRENCH

20°S

POLYNESIA
(FR.)

BOLIVIA

PARAGUAY

Tropic of Capricorn

EASTER ISLAND
(CHILE)

CHILE

URUGUAY

ARGENTINA

40°S

PACIFIC
OCEAN

FALKLAND ISLANDS
(U.K.)

60°S

Antarctic Circle

ANTARCTICA

80°S

180° 160°W 140°W 120°W 100°W 80°W 60°W 40°

60°W

Central America
and West Indies

90°W 80°W

FLORIDA
(U.S.)

Gulf of Mexico

Tropic of Cancer

20°N

BAHAMAS

70°W

20°N

ATLANTIC
OCEAN

TURKS AND CAICOS ISLANDS (U.K.)

Tropic of Cancer

CUBA

CAYMAN
ISLANDS
(U.K.)

HAITI

**DOMINICAN
REPUBLIC**

PUERTO RICO (U.S.)

VIRGIN ISLANDS (U.K.)
ST. KITTS AND NEVIS

MEXICO

JAMAICA

VIRGIN
ISLANDS
(U.S.)

ANTIGUA AND BARBUDA

GUADELOUPE (FR.)

BELIZE

DOMINICA

GUATEMALA

N

Caribbean Sea

MARTINIQUE (FR.)

HONDURAS

SAINT LUCIA

BARBADOS

EL SALVADOR

PACIFIC
OCEAN

NICARAGUA

ARUBA
(NETH.)

NETHERLANDS
ANTILLES
(NETH.)

BONAIRE

SAINT VINCENT AND
THE GRENADINES

GRENADA

CURAÇAO

TRINIDAD
AND TOBAGO

10°N

10°N

**COSTA
RICA**

0 250 500 Miles

0 250 500 750 Kilometers

PANAMA

VENEZUELA

COLOMBIA

70°W

SOUTH AMERICA

80°W

GUYANA

60°W

SURINAME

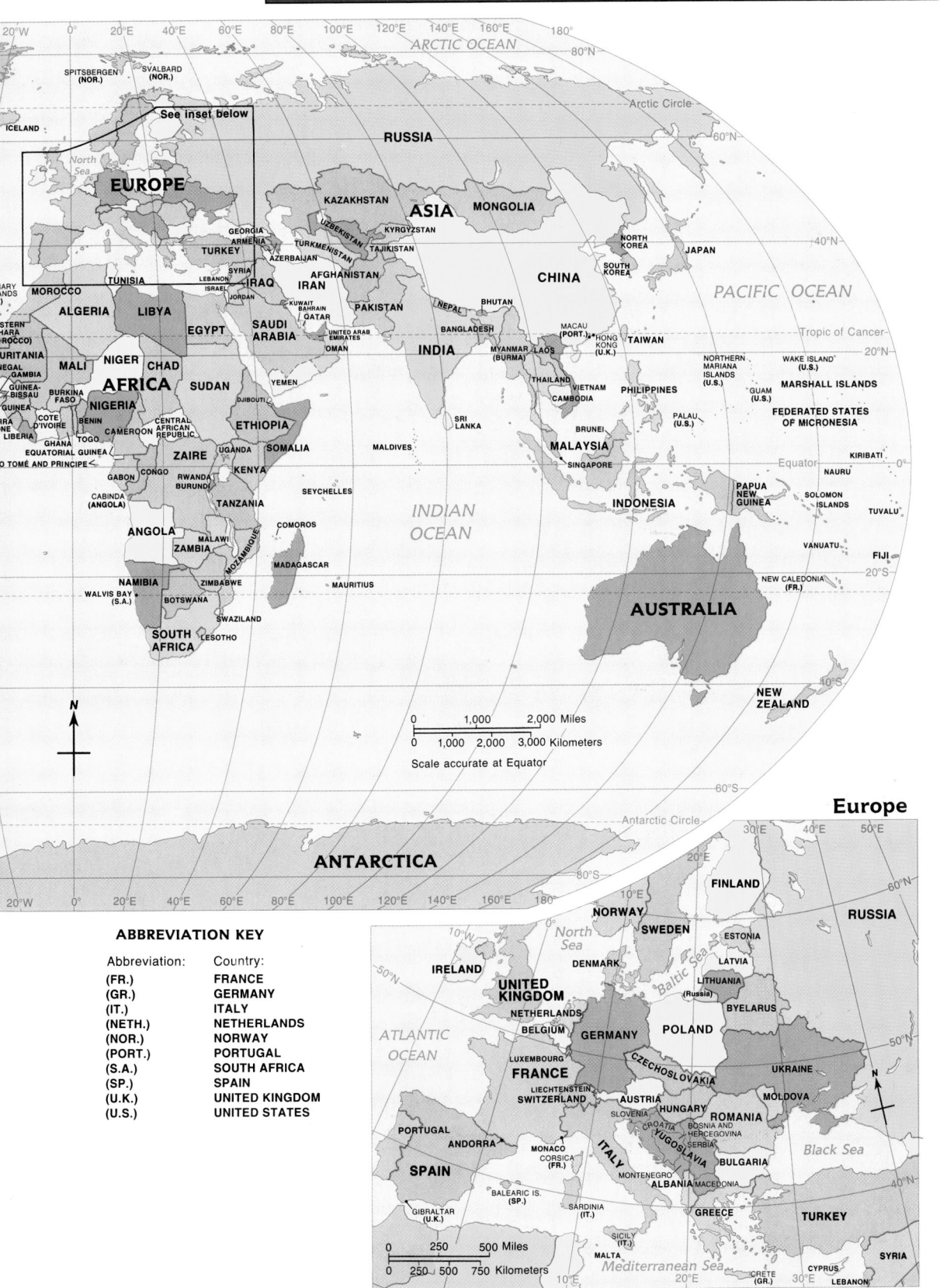

ABBREVIATION KEY

Abbreviation:	Country:
(FR.)	FRANCE
(GR.)	GERMANY
(IT.)	ITALY
(NETH.)	NETHERLANDS
(NOR.)	NORWAY
(PORT.)	PORTUGAL
(S.A.)	SOUTH AFRICA
(SP.)	SPAIN
(U.K.)	UNITED KINGDOM
(U.S.)	UNITED STATES

Europe

Atlas

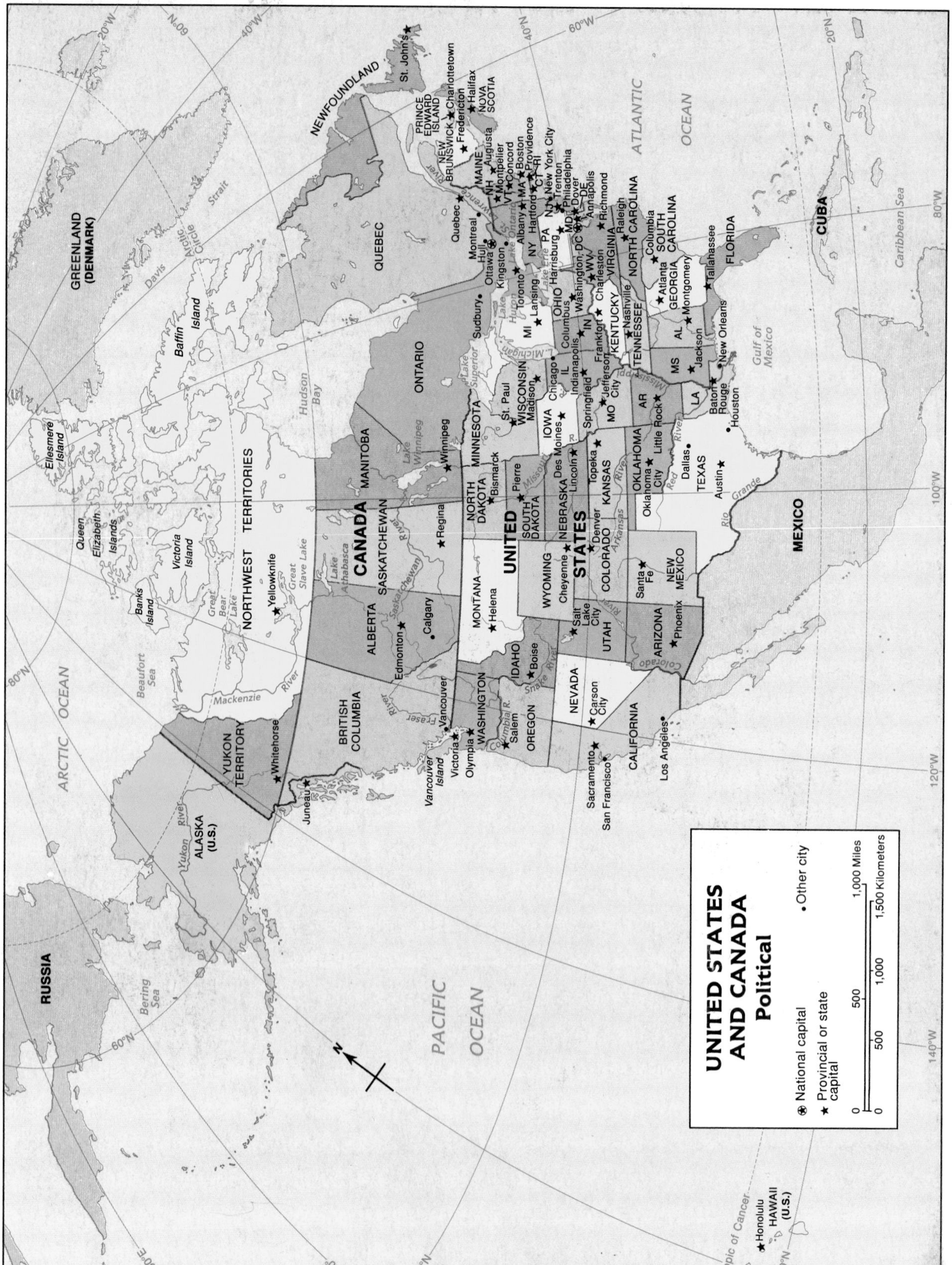

GREENLAND (DENMARK)

St. John's

NEWFOUNDLAND

PRINCE EDWARD ISLAND
Charlottetown
NEW BRUNSWICK
Fredericton
Halifax
NOVA SCOTIA

Baffin Island

QUEBEC

MAINE
NH Augusta
VT Montpelier
Concord
MA Boston
Albany Providence
Hartford CT RI
NY New York City
PA Trenton
Philadelphia
MD Annapolis
Dover
DE

Ellesmere Island

Davis Strait

Arctic Circle

Hudson Bay

Quebec
Montreal
Hull
Ottawa
Kingston
Toronto
Lake Ontario
Lake Erie
Harrisburg
OHIO
Washington, D.C.
Richmond
WV
VIRGINIA

ATLANTIC OCEAN

CUBA

Caribbean Sea

Queen Elizabeth Islands

Victoria Island

Banks Island

NORTHWEST TERRITORIES

Great Bear Lake

Great Slave Lake

Yellowknife

Lake Athabasca

Lake Winnipeg

MANITOBA

Winnipeg

ONTARIO

Sudbury

Lake Superior
Lake Huron
Lake Michigan

WISCONSIN
Madison
MINNESOTA
St. Paul
MI
Lansing
IL
Chicago
IN
Indianapolis
Columbus
Frankfort
KENTUCKY
Nashville
TENNESSEE
Columbia
NORTH CAROLINA
Raleigh
Atlanta
SOUTH CAROLINA
GEORGIA
Tallahassee
FLORIDA

Beaufort Sea

ARCTIC OCEAN

Mackenzie River

CANADA

SASKATCHEWAN

Regina

ALBERTA

Edmonton
Calgary

Saskatchewan River

NORTH DAKOTA
Bismarck
SOUTH DAKOTA
Pierre
NEBRASKA
Lincoln
IOWA
Des Moines
Springfield
MO
Jefferson City
AR
Little Rock
MS
Jackson
AL
Montgomery
LA
Baton Rouge
New Orleans

Topeka
KANSAS
Missouri River

UNITED STATES

Gulf of Mexico

BRITISH COLUMBIA

YUKON TERRITORY

Whitehorse

Fraser River

Columbia R.
Snake R.

Vancouver
Victoria
Vancouver Island

WASHINGTON
Olympia
OREGON
Salem

MONTANA
Helena
IDAHO
Boise

WYOMING
Cheyenne

COLORADO
Denver

Salt Lake City
UTAH

NEVADA
Carson City

Sacramento
San Francisco
CALIFORNIA
Los Angeles

Santa Fe
NEW MEXICO

ARIZONA
Phoenix

Colorado River

Red River
Arkansas River
Rio Grande

OKLAHOMA
Oklahoma City

TEXAS
Austin
Dallas
Houston

MEXICO

Juneau

ALASKA (U.S.)

Yukon River

RUSSIA

Bering Sea

PACIFIC OCEAN

N

Tropic of Cancer

Honolulu
HAWAII (U.S.)

UNITED STATES AND CANADA
Political

⊛ National capital

★ Provincial or state capital

• Other city

| 0 | 500 | 1,000 Miles |
| 0 | 500 | 1,000 | 1,500 Kilometers |

20°W 40°W 60°N 40°N 60°W 80°W 20°N 80°N 100°W 120°W 140°W 60°N 40°N 20°N 180° 160°W 160°E

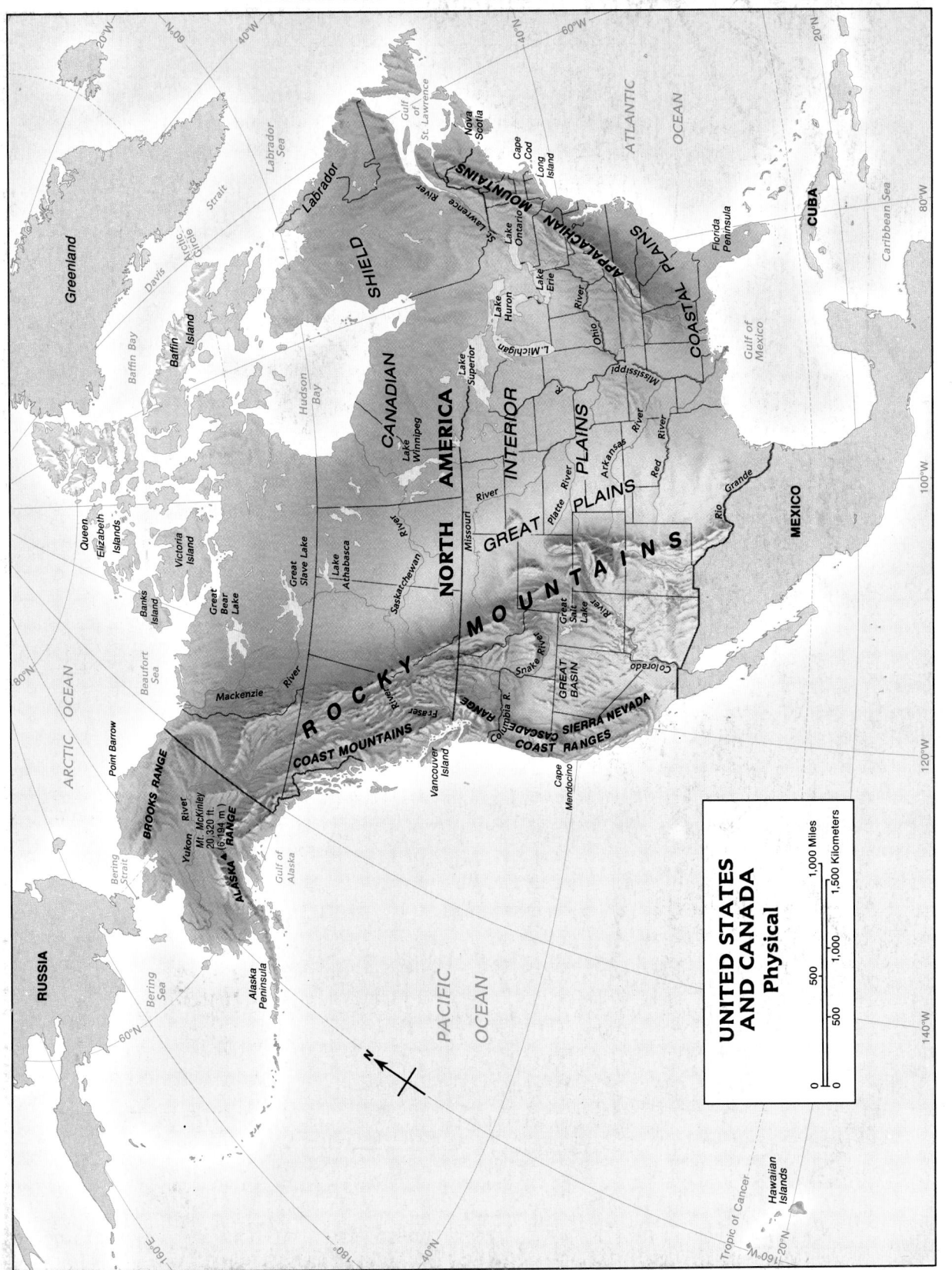

UNITED STATES
AND CANADA
Physical

 *A*tlas

LATIN AMERICA:
Political

⊛ National capital   • Other city

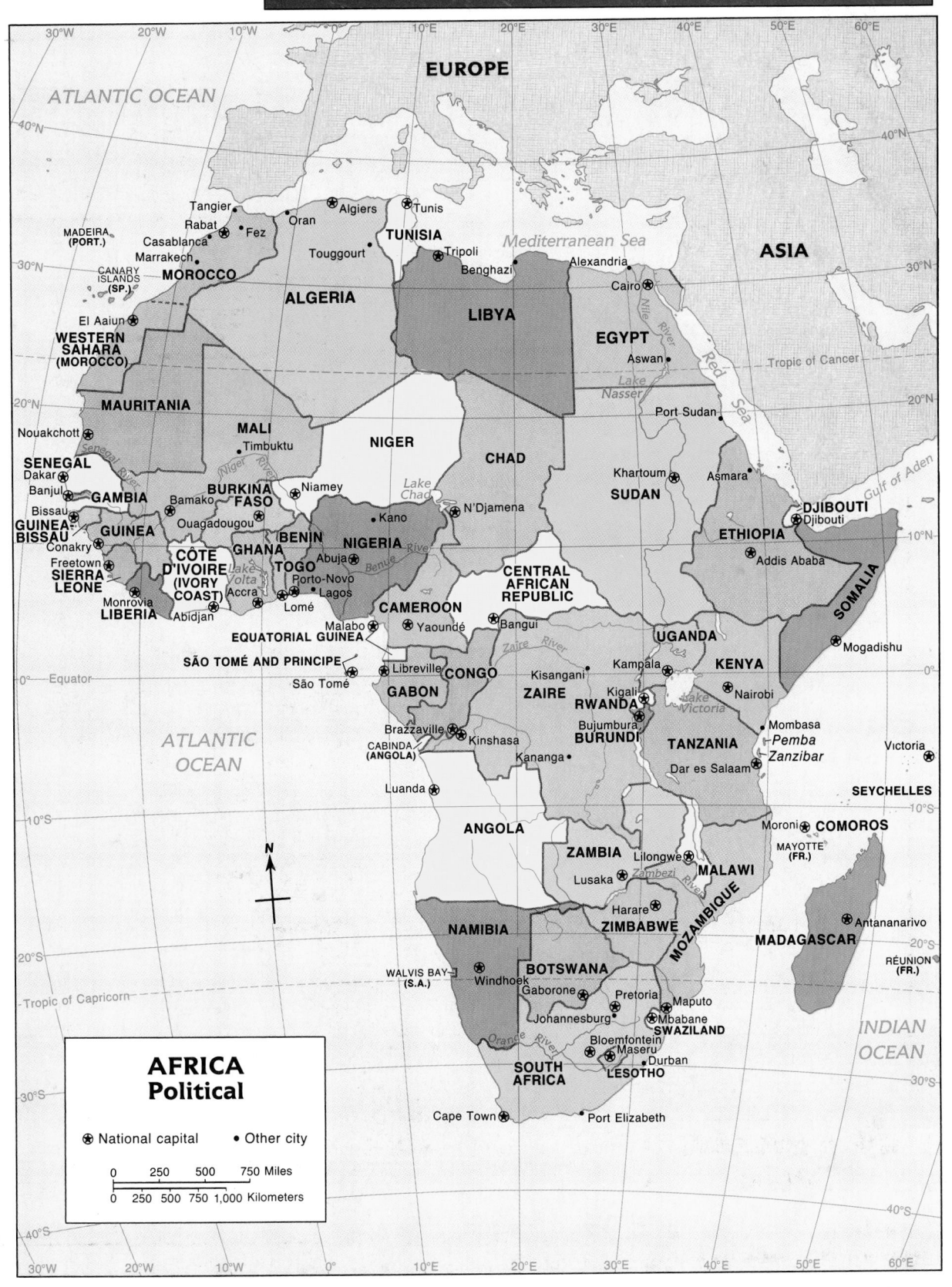

EUROPE

ASIA

ATLANTIC OCEAN

Mediterranean Sea

Tangier
Algiers • Tunis
Rabat • Oran
Casablanca • Fez
MADEIRA (PORT.)
Marrakech
Touggourt
Tripoli
Benghazi
Alexandria
Cairo
MOROCCO
CANARY ISLANDS (SP.)
ALGERIA
LIBYA
EGYPT
El Aaiun
WESTERN SAHARA (MOROCCO)
Aswan
Lake Nasser
Tropic of Cancer
MAURITANIA
Port Sudan
Nouakchott
MALI
Timbuktu
NIGER
CHAD
Khartoum
Asmara
SENEGAL
Dakar
Niamey
SUDAN
DJIBOUTI
Banjul
BURKINA FASO
Lake Chad
N'Djamena
Djibouti
GAMBIA
Bamako
Kano
ETHIOPIA
Bissau
Ouagadougou
NIGERIA
Addis Ababa
GUINEA BISSAU
GUINEA
Conakry
BENIN
GHANA
Abuja
CENTRAL AFRICAN REPUBLIC
SOMALIA
Freetown
CÔTE D'IVOIRE (IVORY COAST)
TOGO
Porto-Novo
Lagos
SIERRA LEONE
Lake Volta
Accra
Lomé
Monrovia
LIBERIA
Abidjan
CAMEROON
Yaoundé
Bangui
UGANDA
Mogadishu
EQUATORIAL GUINEA
Malabo
Kampala
KENYA
SÃO TOMÉ AND PRINCIPE
Libreville
CONGO
Kisangani
Kigali
Nairobi
São Tomé
GABON
ZAIRE
RWANDA
Lake Victoria
Equator
Mombasa
Pemba
Zanzibar
Victoria
Brazzaville
Bujumbura
BURUNDI
CABINDA (ANGOLA)
Kinshasa
Kananga
TANZANIA
Dar es Salaam
SEYCHELLES
Luanda
ATLANTIC OCEAN
ANGOLA
COMOROS
Moroni
MAYOTTE (FR.)
ZAMBIA
Lilongwe
MALAWI
N
Lusaka
Zambezi River
Antananarivo
Harare
MOZAMBIQUE
MADAGASCAR
NAMIBIA
ZIMBABWE
RÉUNION (FR.)
Tropic of Capricorn
WALVIS BAY (S.A.)
Windhoek
BOTSWANA
Gaborone
Pretoria
Maputo
Johannesburg
Mbabane
SWAZILAND
Bloemfontein
Maseru
Durban
INDIAN OCEAN
Orange River
SOUTH AFRICA
LESOTHO
Cape Town
Port Elizabeth

Nile River
Red Sea
Gulf of Aden
Niger River
Senegal River
Benue River
Zaire River

AFRICA
Political

⊛ National capital   • Other city

0   250   500   750 Miles

0   250 500 750 1,000 Kilometers

EUROPE AND NORTH ASIA
Political

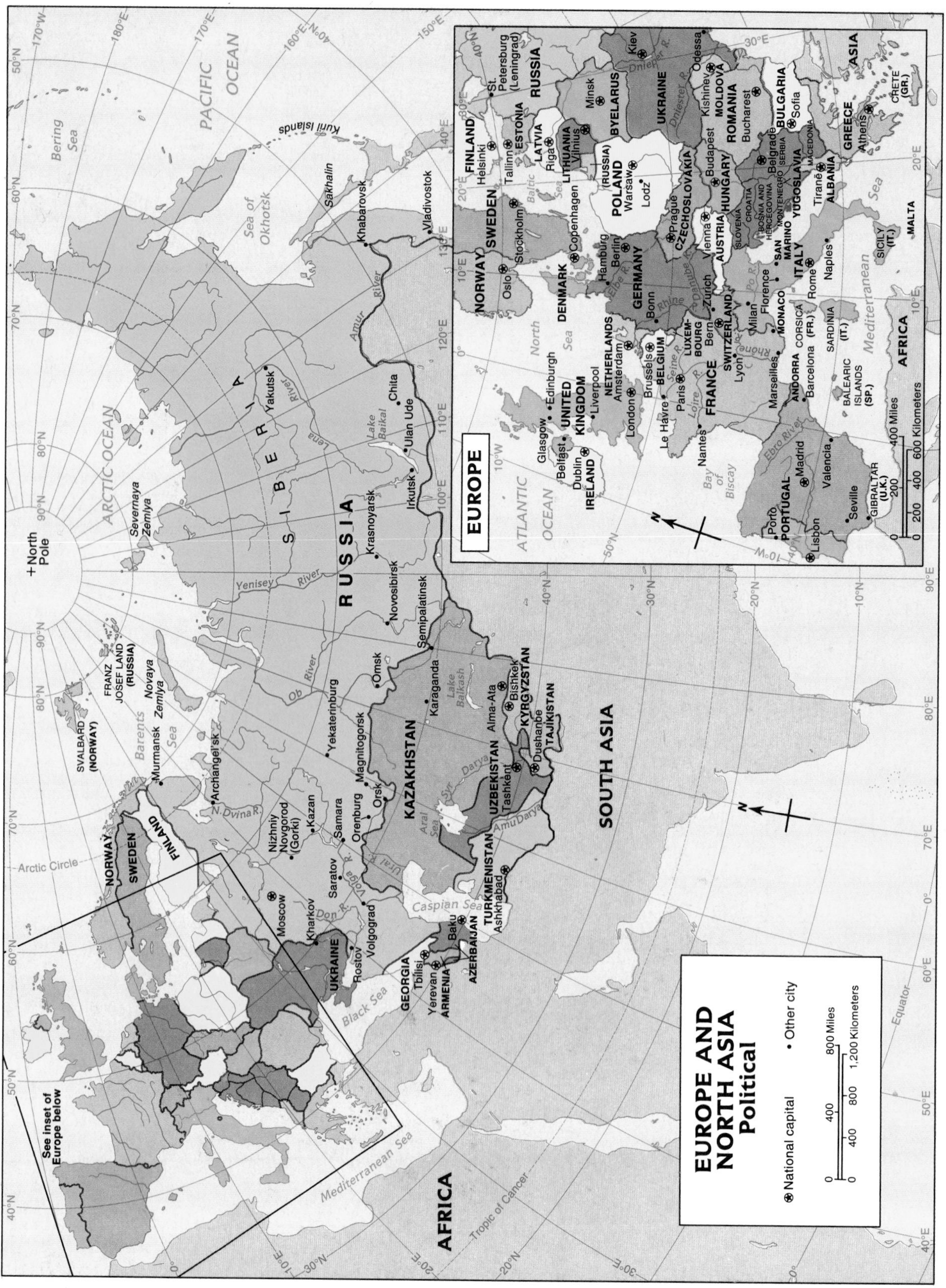

⦻ National capital   • Other city

0   400   800 Miles
0   400   800   1,200 Kilometers

EUROPE

0   200   400 Miles
0   200   400   600 Kilometers

See Inset of Europe below

Main map labels:
PACIFIC OCEAN, ARCTIC OCEAN, North Pole, Bering Sea, Sea of Okhotsk, Kuril Islands, Sakhalin, Khabarovsk, Vladivostok, Chita, Ulan Ude, Irkutsk, Lake Baikal, Yakutsk, Lena River, Amur River, SIBERIA, RUSSIA, Krasnoyarsk, Novosibirsk, Semipalatinsk, Omsk, Yenisey River, Ob River, Severnaya Zemlya, FRANZ JOSEF LAND (RUSSIA), Novaya Zemlya, SVALBARD (NORWAY), Barents Sea, Murmansk, Arkhangel'sk, N. Dvina R., Arctic Circle, NORWAY, SWEDEN, FINLAND, Moscow, Kharkov, Nizhniy Novgorod (Gorki), Kazan, Saratov, Samara, Orenburg, Orsk, Magnitogorsk, Yekaterinburg, Karaganda, Lake Balkhash, Aral Sea, KAZAKHSTAN, Syr Darya, Amu Darya, UZBEKISTAN, Tashkent, Bishkek, Alma-Ata, KYRGYZSTAN, Dushanbe, TAJIKISTAN, TURKMENISTAN, Ashkhabad, Caspian Sea, Volga, Don R., Volgograd, Rostov, UKRAINE, GEORGIA, Tbilisi, ARMENIA, Yerevan, AZERBAIJAN, Baku, Black Sea, Mediterranean Sea, AFRICA, SOUTH ASIA, Tropic of Cancer, Equator

Europe inset labels:
RUSSIA, St. Petersburg (Leningrad), Kiev, Minsk, BYELARUS, UKRAINE, Odessa, Kishinev, MOLDOVA, ROMANIA, Bucharest, BULGARIA, Sofia, FINLAND, Helsinki, ESTONIA, Tallinn, LATVIA, Riga, LITHUANIA, Vilnius, SWEDEN, Stockholm, POLAND, Warsaw, Lodz, (RUSSIA), CZECHOSLOVAKIA, Prague, AUSTRIA, Vienna, HUNGARY, Budapest, Danube R., Dnieper R., Dniester R., NORWAY, Oslo, DENMARK, Copenhagen, GERMANY, Hamburg, Berlin, Bonn, NETHERLANDS, Amsterdam, BELGIUM, Brussels, LUXEMBOURG, SWITZERLAND, Bern, Zurich, Rhine, Po R., SLOVENIA, CROATIA, BOSNIA AND HERCEGOVINA, YUGOSLAVIA, Belgrade, SERBIA, MONTENEGRO, SAN MARINO, MACEDONIA, ALBANIA, Tiranë, GREECE, Athens, CRETE (GR.), UNITED KINGDOM, Glasgow, Edinburgh, Belfast, Dublin, IRELAND, Liverpool, London, North Sea, Baltic Sea, FRANCE, Paris, Le Hâvre, Nantes, Loire, Bay of Biscay, ATLANTIC OCEAN, ITALY, Rome, Naples, Milan, Florence, MONACO, CORSICA (FR.), SARDINIA (IT.), ANDORRA, BALEARIC ISLANDS (SP.), Barcelona, Valencia, Madrid, PORTUGAL, Lisbon, Porto, Seville, Ebro River, Rhone R., Lyon, Marseilles, GIBRALTAR (U.K.), SICILY (IT.), MALTA, Mediterranean Sea, AFRICA, ASIA

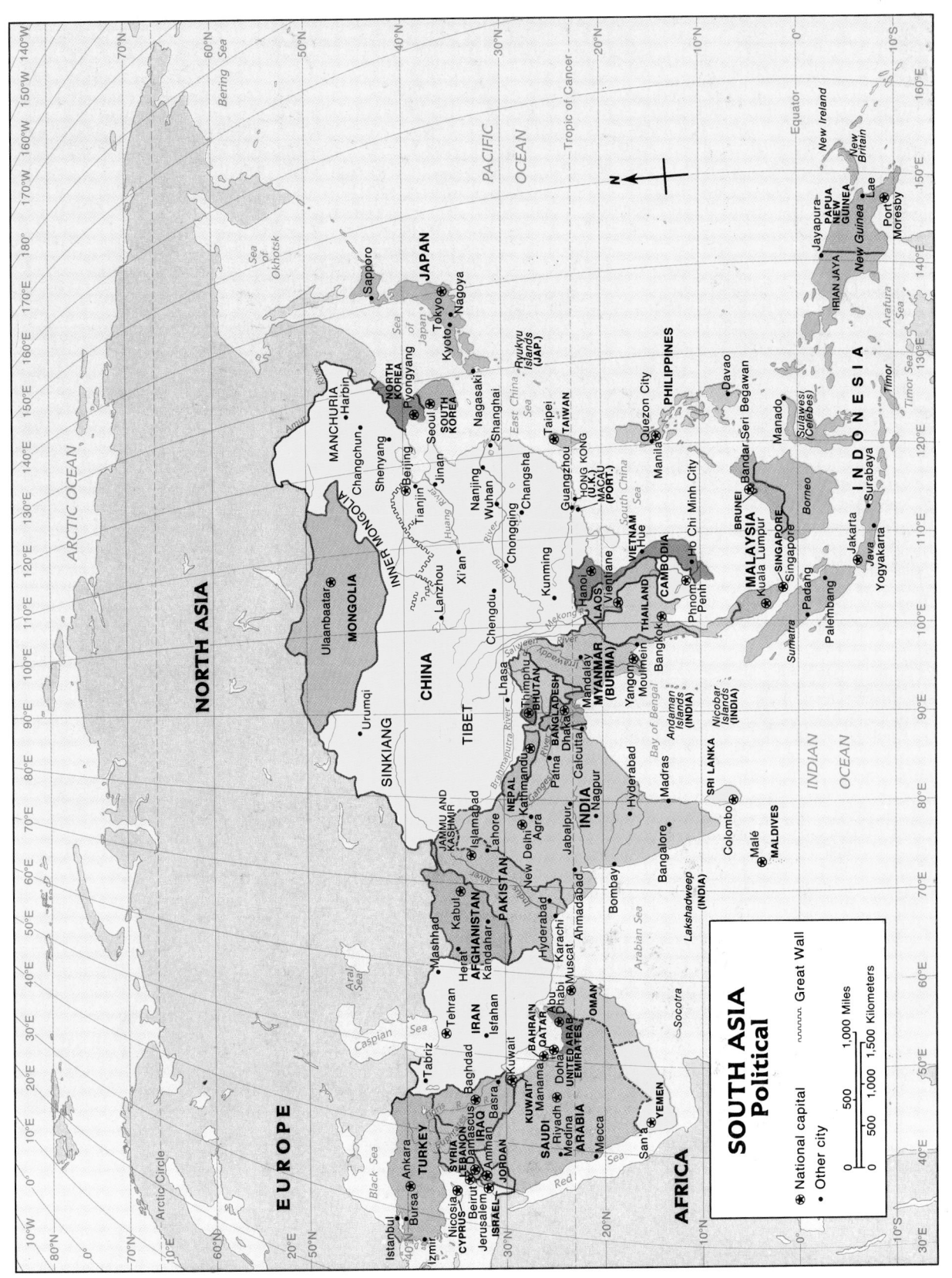

SOUTH ASIA
Political

⊛ National capital
• Other city

∿∿∿ Great Wall

500   1,000 Miles

500   1,000 1,500 Kilometers

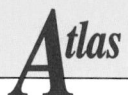

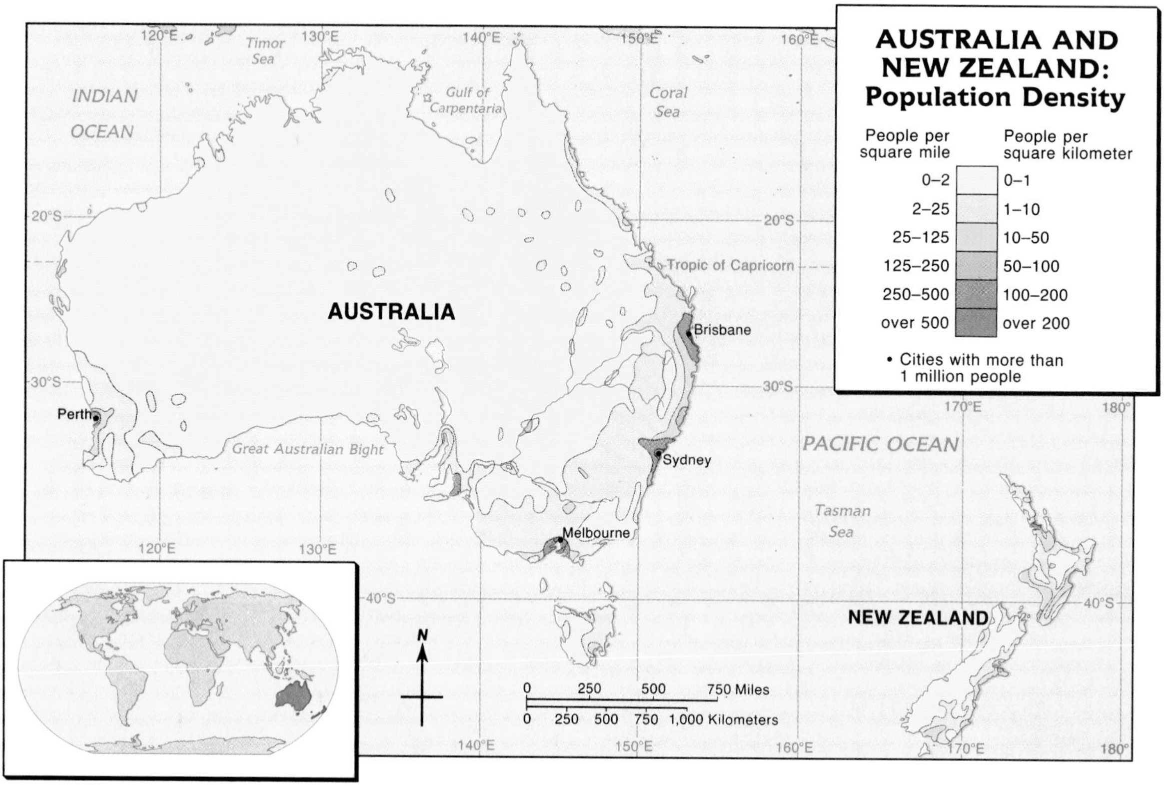
AUSTRALIA AND NEW ZEALAND: Population Density
People per square mile
People per square kilometer
0–2
0–1
2–25
1–10
25–125
10–50
125–250
50–100
250–500
100–200
over 500
over 200
• Cities with more than 1 million people
INDIAN OCEAN
Timor Sea
Gulf of Carpentaria
Coral Sea
AUSTRALIA
Brisbane
Perth
Sydney
Melbourne
Great Australian Bight
Tropic of Capricorn
PACIFIC OCEAN
Tasman Sea
NEW ZEALAND
N
0 250 500 750 Miles
0 250 500 750 1,000 Kilometers
120°E
130°E
140°E
150°E
160°E
170°E
180°
20°S
30°S
40°S

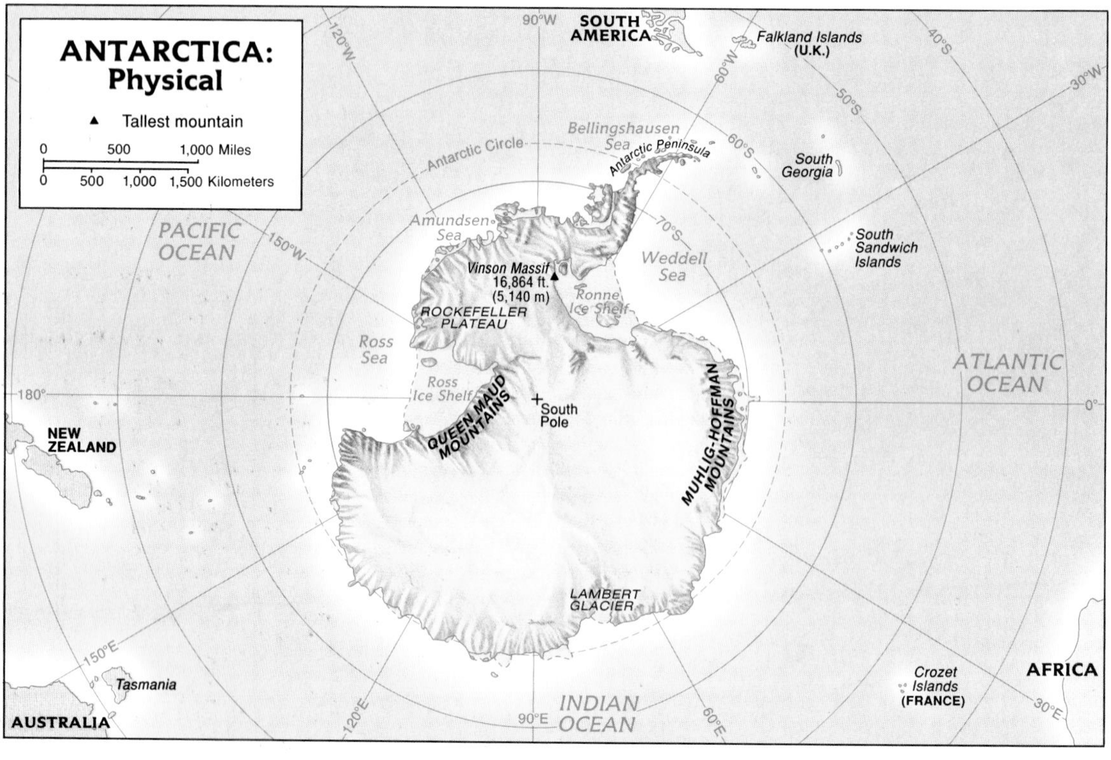
ANTARCTICA: Physical
▲ Tallest mountain
0 500 1,000 Miles
0 500 1,000 1,500 Kilometers
SOUTH AMERICA
Falkland Islands (U.K.)
Bellingshausen Sea
Antarctic Peninsula
Antarctic Circle
South Georgia
Amundsen Sea
South Sandwich Islands
PACIFIC OCEAN
Weddell Sea
Vinson Massif 16,864 ft. (5,140 m)
Ronne Ice Shelf
ROCKEFELLER PLATEAU
Ross Sea
Ross Ice Shelf
QUEEN MAUD MOUNTAINS
South Pole
MUHLIG-HOFFMAN MOUNTAINS
ATLANTIC OCEAN
NEW ZEALAND
LAMBERT GLACIER
Tasmania
AUSTRALIA
INDIAN OCEAN
Crozet Islands (FRANCE)
AFRICA
90°W
120°W
150°W
180°
150°E
120°E
90°E
60°E
30°E
0°
30°W
60°W
40°S
50°S
60°S
70°S

Time Line of World History

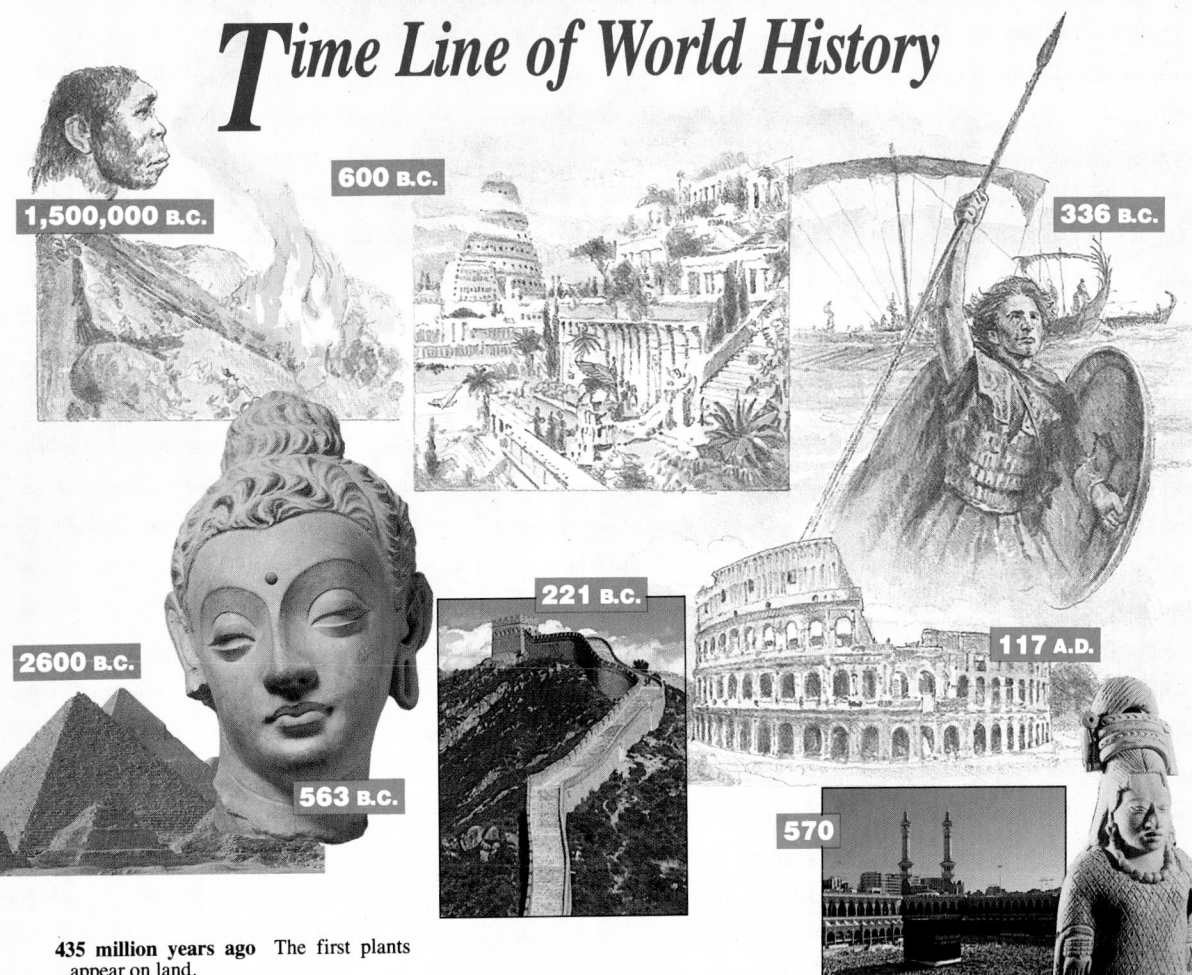

1,500,000 B.C.

600 B.C.

336 B.C.

2600 B.C.

563 B.C.

221 B.C.

117 A.D.

570

250

435 million years ago The first plants appear on land.

65 million years ago The dinosaurs become extinct.

2,000,000 B.C. Hominids begin to use stone tools.

1,500,000 B.C. Hominids begin to make fire.

9000 B.C. Animals are first domesticated.

8000 B.C. Humans begin to settle in communities and depend upon farming for food.

3500-3000 B.C. Hieroglyphics and cuneiform writing are developed.

2600 B.C. The Egyptian pyramids are built.

1792-1750 B.C. Babylonian King Hammurabi introduces one of the world's first codes of law and establishes the Old Babylonian Empire.

1500 B.C. Egyptians build a mighty empire. A system of writing develops in ancient China.

1290 B.C. Moses leads the Hebrews in their escape from Egypt and presents the Ten Commandments.

mid-1200s B.C. The Trojan War between Greece and the city of Troy takes place.

800-700 B.C. Homer creates the first Greek epics (the *Iliad* and the *Odyssey*).

776 B.C. The first Olympic games are held in Greece.

600 B.C. The New Babylonian Empire is at its peak, controlling most of what is now the Middle East.

563 B.C. Buddha is born in Nepal.

551 B.C. The Chinese philosopher Confucius is born.

509 B.C. The Roman Republic is founded, marking the end of rule by Roman kings.

461 B.C. The Age of Pericles (leader of the Greek Athenian government) becomes the greatest period of art and science in ancient Greece.

451 B.C. The Twelve Tables, laws inscribed on tablets kept in the Roman Forum, become the written basis of Roman law.

432 B.C. The Parthenon, the most famous building in ancient Greece, is completed in Athens.

336 B.C. Alexander the Great, king of Macedonia, begins to spread the ideas of ancient Greece to countries he conquers, resulting in the Hellenistic age.

221 B.C. Construction of the Great Wall of China begins.

202 B.C. Rome defeats the wealthy city of Carthage in the Second Punic War, despite the heroic exploits of Hannibal.

46 B.C. The great general Gaius Julius Caesar becomes dictator of Rome.

44 B.C. Rome conquers Greece and adopts its ideas and culture throughout the Roman Empire.

4 or 1 B.C. Jesus is born in Bethlehem, in what is now Israel.

117 A.D. The Roman Empire, under Trajan, is at its peak, ruling the Mediterranean and extending from Britain to the Persian Gulf.

250 The Maya start to build large cities in Central America and south Mexico.

395 The Roman Empire is divided into Eastern and Western empires.

476 The Western Roman Empire ends when the last emperor, Augustulus Romulus, is overthrown.

400s The Middle Ages begin with the fall of Rome.

570 Muhammad is born in Mecca, in what is now Saudi Arabia.

622 Muhammad's emigration to Medina leads to his rise in Arabia. The Muslim calendar dates from this year.

Time Line of World History

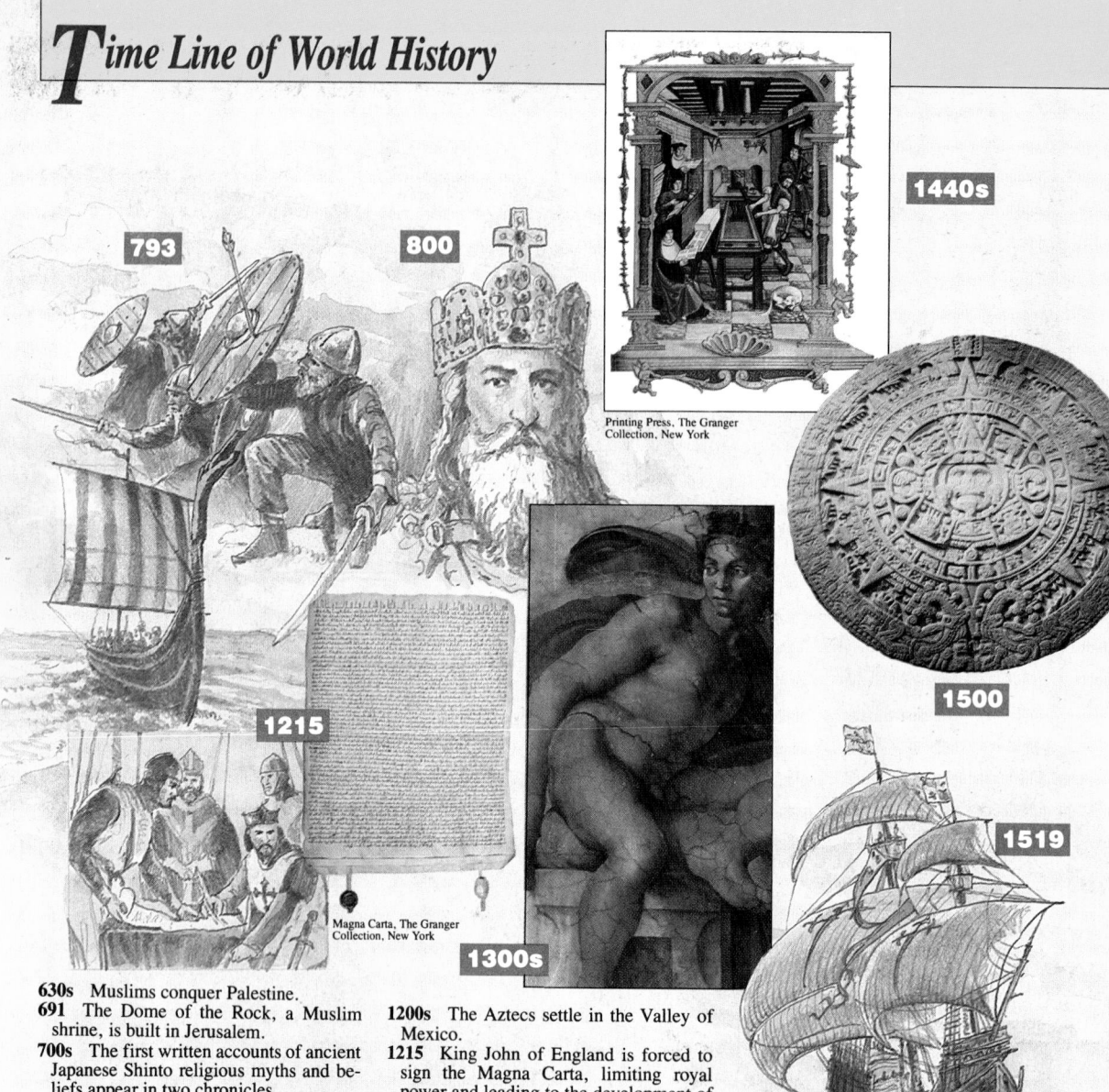

1440s

Printing Press, The Granger Collection, New York

793

800

1215

Magna Carta, The Granger Collection, New York

1300s

1500

1519

630s Muslims conquer Palestine.

691 The Dome of the Rock, a Muslim shrine, is built in Jerusalem.

700s The first written accounts of ancient Japanese Shinto religious myths and beliefs appear in two chronicles.

732 Muslim armies have conquered most of the Middle East, North Africa, and Spain. In the Battle of Poitiers, also called the Battle of Tours, the Muslim conquest of Europe is stopped by a Christian victory under Charles Martel.

793 Viking raids outside Scandinavia begin.

800 The French king Charlemagne is crowned the first emperor of the Holy Roman Empire.

970-1000 Islamic civilization is at its peak. Al-Azhar University is founded in Cairo.

1000 A Viking expedition under Leif Ericson makes the first European landing on the North American coast.

1066 England is invaded and conquered by the Normans.

1096 The first of eight crusades to recover the Holy Land from the Muslims for Christianity begins.

1100s The first European universities are organized at Bologna, Italy, and Paris, France. The Hindu temple Angkor Wat is built in Cambodia (Kampuchea).

1200s The Aztecs settle in the Valley of Mexico.

1215 King John of England is forced to sign the Magna Carta, limiting royal power and leading to the development of English constitutional government.

1275-92 Venetian Marco Polo visits China.

1279 Mongol leader Kublai Khan founds the Yuan Dynasty in China.

1300s The Renaissance, a period of rebirth of interest in ancient Greek and Roman cultures, begins in Italy.

1346 The plague known as the Black Death enters Europe.

1368 The Ming Dynasty begins in China, the Great Wall is extended, and the Forbidden City is built.

1400s Europeans explore the African coasts and the slave trade to Europe begins.

1438 The Incas start to build a great civilization in western South America.

mid-1440s German inventor Johann Gutenberg invents the printing press.

1487 Bartolomeu Dias of Portugal becomes the first European to sail around the tip of Africa.

1492 Italian navigator Christopher Columbus, in the service of Spain, makes his first voyage to the New World.

1497 Portuguese explorer Vasco da Gama discovers an all-water route to India. Sailing for King Henry VII of England, Italian navigator John Cabot reaches North America and claims land in the New World for England.

1500 The Aztec Empire is at its height in Mexico.

1504 Michelangelo, one of the greatest sculptors of the Renaissance, completes his statue of David.

1517 Cleric and professor Martin Luther of Germany begins a public protest against abuses of the Roman Catholic Church that leads to the Protestant Reformation.

1519 Portuguese sea captain Ferdinand Magellan, sailing in the service of Spain, begins the first voyage around the world. He is killed en route, but one of his ships completes the journey in 1522. Spanish adventurer Hernán Cortés invades Mexico.

1521 The Aztecs surrender to Cortés.

1524 Italian navigator Giovanni da Verrazano explores the North American Atlantic coast for France.

1533 Francisco Pizarro of Spain conquers the Incas of Peru.

1534 French navigator Jacques Cartier makes his first voyage to Canada and discovers the Gulf of St. Lawrence.

1543 Polish astronomer Nicolaus Copernicus publishes his theory that the earth revolves around the sun.

1545-63 At the Council of Trent in Italy, the Roman Catholic Church begins to make reforms.

1588 The English navy defeats the invading Spanish Armada.

1608 French explorer Samuel de Champlain settles Quebec and starts the colony of New France.

1609 Italian astronomer and physicist Galileo finds support for Copernicus' theory that the earth revolves around the sun.

1650 The Taj Mahal is completed in Agra, India.

1682 Peter I (the Great) becomes czar and introduces Western culture and technology to Russia.

1687 English scientist Sir Isaac Newton publishes his theory of the laws of motion and gravity.

1689 The English Bill of Rights limits the power of the king and establishes individual rights and freedoms.

1700s The Industrial Revolution begins in Great Britain.

1703 Peter the Great of Russia builds St. Petersburg as a "window to the West."

1755 Samuel Johnson, English writer and critic, publishes his *Dictionary of the English Language*.

1762 Catherine II (the Great) becomes empress and increases the power of the Russian Empire.

late 1700s Great Britain becomes the leading power in India through its East India [trading] Company.

1770 Captain James Cook explores the eastern coast of Australia and claims the region for Great Britain.

1776 The American colonies declare their independence from Great Britain.

1788 British ships bring the first convicts to Australia.

1789 The French Revolution begins, resulting in the end of rule by French kings.

1796 A vaccine for smallpox is introduced by English physician Edward Jenner.

1799 The Rosetta stone, discovered in the Nile Delta by a French soldier, provides a key to ancient Egyptian hieroglyphics. General Napoleon Bonaparte seizes control of the government of France, thus ending the French Revolution.

1804 Napoleon crowns himself emperor of France.

1807-88 The slave trade is abolished in most Western countries, but continues in parts of Africa, Asia, and isolated areas in South America.

1810 The Mexican War of Independence against Spanish rule begins.

1812 Napoleon controls most of Europe.

1815 Napoleon is defeated at Waterloo by a combined European force commanded by the Duke of Wellington.

1821 Venezuelan military leader Simón Bolívar frees northern South America from Spain. Mexico gains independence from Spain.

1821-26 Peru becomes independent, and Spanish rule in South America ends.

1822 Brazil declares its independence from Portugal.

1534

1650

1703

1700s

1762

Liberté! Egalité! Fraternité!

1789

1812

1821

1800-50 The Industrial Revolution, begun in Great Britain in the 1700s, spreads to other parts of Europe and North America.

1825-30 The first passenger and freight railroads are built and fully operational in Great Britain.

1828 American educator and journalist Noah Webster publishes *An American Dictionary of the English Language.*

1837 Invention of the telegraph sets the stage for worldwide communication.

1840 Maori chiefs sign a treaty giving Great Britain rule over New Zealand.

1848 Democratic and nationalistic movements lead to revolts and revolutions in Paris, Vienna, Venice, Berlin, and other European cities.

1854 Japan ends its isolation and signs a commercial treaty with the United States.

1858 Great Britain seizes full control of India.

1859 English naturalist Charles Darwin's theory of natural selection is published.

1867 Canada's provinces unite to form a confederation.

1875 American scientist Alexander Graham Bell invents the telephone.

1879 American inventor Thomas Edison invents the incandescent light bulb.

1893 New Zealand becomes the first country to grant women full voting rights.

1903 The Wright brothers (Wilbur and Orville) make their first successful airplane flight at Kitty Hawk, North Carolina.

1914 The Panama Canal, connecting the Atlantic and Pacific oceans, is opened. World War I begins in Europe.

1917 Mexico adopts a constitution. The United States enters World War I against Germany. The Russian Revolution begins.

1919 The Treaty of Versailles officially ends World War I.

1919-24 Indian political leader Mohandas Gandhi begins to teach civil disobedience in South Africa and India.

1922 English Egyptologist Howard Carter discovers Tutankhamen's (King Tut's) tomb in Egypt.

1928 Scottish bacteriologist Alexander Fleming discovers penicillin, the first antibiotic.

1929 Joseph Stalin becomes dictator of the Soviet Union. The stock market crash in the United States begins the worldwide Great Depression of the 1930s.

1933 Adolf Hitler, founder and leader of National Socialism, becomes Nazi dictator of Germany.

1934 Mao Zedong begins to lead a group of Chinese communists on the 6,000-mile Long March across China to Shaanxi province to escape Chiang Kai-shek's Nationalist forces.

1936 The first regularly scheduled television broadcasts begin in Great Britain.

1936-39 The Spanish Civil War results in the end of the republic and the rise of General Francisco Franco as dictator.

1938 The Holocaust begins in Europe with *Kristallnacht,* "the night of broken glass," when Nazi Party members destroy Jewish property and kill many Jews.

1939 World War II begins in Europe.

1941 Japan attacks Pearl Harbor; the United States enters World War II against Germany, Italy, and Japan.

1942 The first nuclear reactor is developed at the University of Chicago under the direction of Enrico Fermi.

1945 Germany surrenders on May 7, and the European stage of World War II ends. In August, the U.S. drops atomic bombs on Hiroshima and Nagasaki in Japan. Japan surrenders on September 2, and World War II ends. The Charter of the United Nations is signed by 51 nations, and the UN is founded.

1903

1825-30

1945

1914

1919-24

1893

1945

1945-1990s Japan and other countries of the Pacific experience economic development that leads to their emergence as a major force in international trade.

1947 The United Nations divides Palestine into a Jewish state and an Arab state. The first group of Dead Sea Scrolls (the oldest known manuscripts of any books of the Bible) are discovered in a cave near the Dead Sea. India and Pakistan gain independence from Great Britain.

1948 Apartheid, a policy of racial separateness, is established in South Africa. The Jewish state of Israel is founded in Palestine.

1949 The communists under Mao Zedong establish the People's Republic of China.

1950-53 North Korean troops invade South Korea, and United Nations forces enter on the South Korean side. An armistice is signed in 1953.

1953 James D. Watson of the U.S. and Francis H. C. Crick of the U.K. discover the structure of the genetic material DNA.

1957 War between North Vietnam and South Vietnam begins. The U.S.S.R. deploys the first space satellite, *Sputnik I.*

1959 Fidel Castro takes over in Cuba and institutes a communist government.

1961 The Berlin Wall is built by East Germany to prevent its citizens from fleeing to West Germany. Soviet cosmonaut Yuri Gagarin is the first person to orbit the earth.

1967 South African surgeon Christiaan Barnard performs the first successful human heart transplant.

1969 Two American astronauts become the first to walk on the moon.

1975 South Vietnam surrenders to North Vietnam, and the Vietnam War ends. The U.S. launches the unmanned probe *Viking 1,* which becomes the first spacecraft to land on Mars.

1985 Mikhail Gorbachev becomes leader of the Soviet Union and introduces policies of glasnost (openness) and perestroika (economic reform).

1986 Corazon Aquino becomes president of the Philippines after Ferdinand Marcos is forced out of office.

1989 Lech Walesa's Solidarity labor union in Poland is legalized, leading to election of the first noncommunist government in the Eastern bloc.

1990 The Berlin Wall separating East and West Germany comes down, symbolizing the end of the cold war. East and West Germany reunite. Nelson Mandela, leader of the African National Congress, is freed in South Africa after 27 years in prison. The South African government repeals the apartheid laws.

1991 A United States-led military coalition of 37 countries recaptures Kuwait from Iraq in the Persian Gulf War. The Soviet Union is dissolved, and former Soviet republics become independent countries. The first direct Middle East peace talks begin between Israel and neighboring Arab states.

1991-92 Several Yugoslavian republics break away to form independent countries.

1992 Continuing international concern over the earth's natural resources was demonstrated by the 22nd anniversary of Earth Day and by the convening of a United Nations "Earth Summit" in Brazil focusing on worldwide environmental issues.

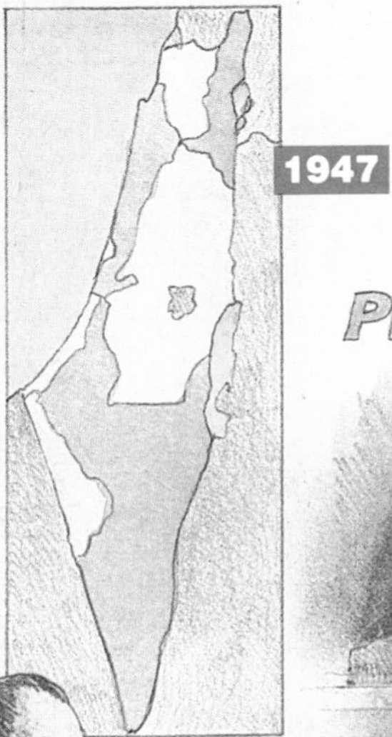

1947

PERESTROIKA

1985

1949

Glasnost

1992

1961

1990

1990

The Solar System

SUN

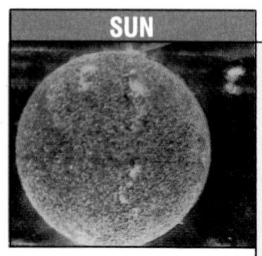

Figures	
Mean Distance from the Sun	—
Period of Revolution (Earth time)	—
Period of Rotation (Earth time)	24 days 16 hours
Diameter at Equator	1,392,000 km (865,000 mi)
Natural Satellites (moons)	9 planets and their satellites, plus asteroids and comets
Mass	1.99×10^{30} kg
Mass (relative to Earth)	330,000 times that of Earth
Gravity (relative to Earth)	27.9 times that of Earth
Atmosphere	none

Facts

The sun is the small 4.6 billion-year-old star at the center of our solar system. Its heat and light come from the thermonuclear reactions of hydrogen atoms fusing to form helium.

MERCURY

Figures	
Mean Distance from the Sun	57,900,000 km (35,980,000 mi)
Period of Revolution (Earth time)	87.97 days (0.2408 years)
Period of Rotation (Earth time)	58.65 days
Diameter at Equator	4,878 km (3,032 mi)
Natural Satellites (moons)	0
Mass	3.30×10^{23} kg
Mass (relative to Earth)	0.055 times that of Earth
Gravity (relative to Earth)	0.38 times that of Earth
Atmosphere	traces of He, H_2, O_2

Facts

Mercury has too little atmosphere to protect it from the rays of the sun. The side facing away from the sun becomes very cold.

VENUS

Figures	
Mean Distance from the Sun	108,200,000 km (67,230,000 mi)
Period of Revolution (Earth time)	224.7 days (0.615 years)
Period of Rotation (Earth time)	243.01 days (retrograde)
Diameter at Equator	12,104 km (7,522 mi)
Natural Satellites (moons)	0
Mass	4.87×10^{24} kg
Mass (relative to Earth)	0.81 times that of Earth
Gravity (relative to Earth)	0.91 times that of Earth
Atmosphere	mostly CO_2, N_2, some H_2O, Ar, CO

Facts

Venus has thick clouds of sulfuric acid and sulfur. Its atmosphere, composed largely of carbon dioxide, produces a "greenhouse" effect, trapping heat near its surface.

EARTH

Figures	
Mean Distance from the Sun	149,600,000 km (92,960,000 mi)
Period of Revolution (Earth time)	365.25 days (1.00004 years)
Period of Rotation (Earth time)	23 hours 56 minutes 4.1 seconds
Diameter at Equator	12,756.28 km (7,926.38 mi)
Natural Satellites (moons)	1
Mass	5.98×10^{24} kg
Mass (relative to Earth)	1.00
Gravity (relative to Earth)	1.00
Atmosphere	78% N_2, 21% O_2, 1% Ar, some CO_2, H_2O

Facts

Earth is rich in oxygen, water, and nitrogen. It is the only planet that is known to support life.

MARS

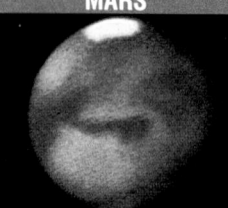

Figures	
Mean Distance from the Sun	227,000,000 km (141,000,000 mi)
Period of Revolution (Earth time)	686.98 days (1.8809 years)
Period of Rotation (Earth time)	24 hours 37 minutes 22.7 seconds
Diameter at Equator	6,794 km (4,222 mi)
Natural Satellites (moons)	2
Mass	6.42×10^{23} kg
Mass (relative to Earth)	0.107 times that of Earth
Gravity (relative to Earth)	0.38 times that of Earth
Atmosphere	mostly CO_2, some N_2, Ar

Facts

Mars has a thin atmosphere. There are volcanoes, canyons, and reddish brown desertlike regions on its surface.

JUPITER

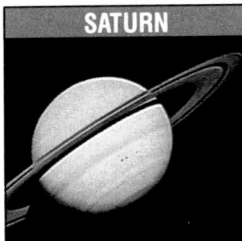

Figures		Facts
Mean Distance from the Sun	778,000,000 km (483,000,000 mi)	Jupiter has a single, faint ring, and its atmosphere has colored bands of clouds. The Great Red Spot resembles a large hurricane and seems to consist of swirling gases.
Period of Revolution (Earth time)	11.862 years	
Period of Rotation (Earth time)	9 hours 55 minutes	
Diameter at Equator	142,796 km (88,730 mi)	
Natural Satellites (moons)	16	
Mass	1.90×10^{27} kg	
Mass (relative to Earth)	318 times that of Earth	
Gravity (relative to Earth)	2.53 times that of Earth	
Atmosphere	H_2, He	

SATURN

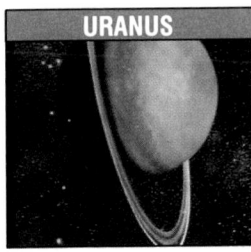

Figures		Facts
Mean Distance from the Sun	1,427,000,000 km (887,000,000 mi)	Saturn has a complex ring system. Each ring is made up of smaller rings of ice particles.
Period of Revolution (Earth time)	29.46 years	
Period of Rotation (Earth time)	10 hours 39 minutes	
Diameter at Equator	120,536 km (74,898 mi)	
Natural Satellites (moons)	21	
Mass	5.69×10^{26} kg	
Mass (relative to Earth)	95 times that of Earth	
Gravity (relative to Earth)	1.07 times that of Earth	
Atmosphere	H_2, He	

URANUS

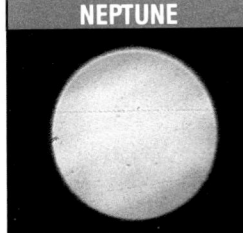

Figures		Facts
Mean Distance from the Sun	2,871,000,000 km (1,784,000,000 mi)	The bluish green color of Uranus is a result of its thick atmosphere. Uranus has several dark rings.
Period of Revolution (Earth time)	84.01 years	
Period of Rotation (Earth time)	17 hours 14 minutes	
Diameter at Equator	51,200 km (31,814 mi)	
Natural Satellites (moons)	15	
Mass	8.68×10^{25} kg	
Mass (relative to Earth)	15 times that of Earth	
Gravity (relative to Earth)	0.92 times that of Earth	
Atmosphere	H_2, He, some CH_4	

NEPTUNE

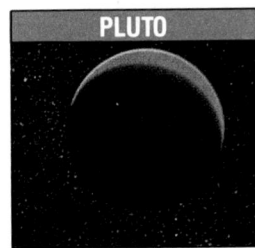

Figures		Facts
Mean Distance from the Sun	4,497,000,000 km (2,794,000,000 mi)	Neptune has a faint, dark ring system. The Great Dark Spot is thought to be made up of spinning gases.
Period of Revolution (Earth time)	164.8 years	
Period of Rotation (Earth time)	about 16 hours	
Diameter at Equator	49,520 km (30,770 mi)	
Natural Satellites (moons)	8	
Mass	1.03×10^{26} kg	
Mass (relative to Earth)	17 times that of Earth	
Gravity (relative to Earth)	1.2 times that of Earth	
Atmosphere	H_2, He, Ch_4	

PLUTO

Figures		Facts
Mean Distance from the Sun	5,913,000,000 km (3,674,000,000 mi)	Pluto, the smallest planet, is about the size of Earth's moon. It is farthest from the sun. For 20 years during each revolution Pluto moves closer to the sun than Neptune.
Period of Revolution (Earth time)	248.53 years	
Period of Rotation (Earth time)	6 days 9 hours 16 minutes	
Diameter at Equator	2,300 km (1,430 mi)	
Natural Satellites (moons)	1	
Mass	1.30×10^{22} kg	
Mass (relative to Earth)	0.0025 times that of Earth	
Gravity (relative to Earth)	0.07 times that of Earth	
Atmosphere	CH_4	

*I*ncreasing Your Science Vocabulary

Prefixes, suffixes, and combining forms are syllables or groups of syllables added to a word, root, or stem to form a new word. If you become familiar with scientific affixes (prefixes, suffixes, and combining forms), you can increase your vocabulary by recognizing the meanings of many words now unfamiliar to you. Below are some affixes, their meaning, and examples of words in which they are used.

Affix	Meaning	Example
aero-	air	*aerobics*
amphi-	both, of two kinds	*amphibian*
andr-	man	*android*
angi-	blood vessel	*angiogram*
anthrop-	human	*anthropology*
anti-	against, counteracting	*antiballistic missile*
aqu-	water	*aquifer*
arthr-	joint	*arthritis*
aster-	star	*asteroid*
astro-	star, space	*astrophysics*
audio-	hearing, sound	*audiovisual*
bar-	weight	*barometer*
bio-	life, living things	*biology*
cardio-	heart	*cardiogram*
chemo-	chemistry, chemicals	*chemotherapy*
cosm(o)-	world, universe	*cosmic, cosmology*
cryo-	cold, freezing	*cryogenics*
cyto-	cell	*cytology*
diplo-	double	*diploid*
eco-	environment	*ecosystem, ecocide, ecology*
-ectomy	excision	*tonsilectomy, appendectomy*
electro-	electricity	*electromagnetic wave*
-emia	blood	*anemia*
endo-	within, inside, inner	*endocrine*
entomo-	insects	*entomologist*
epi-	on, upon, near, among	*epidermis*
ferro-	iron	*ferroalloy*
fungi-	fungus	*fungicide*
geo-	earth	*geoscience, geology*
gyro-	gyrating, rotating	*gyrostabilizer*
helio-	of the sun	*heliocentric*
hemato-	blood	*hematology*
hemo-	blood	*hemoglobin*
hepat-	liver	*hepatitis*
hydro-	water	*hydroponics, hydrothermal*
hypn-	sleep	*hypnosis*
hypo-	below, under	*hypodermic, hypothermia*
hypo-	deficient	*hypoxia*
infra-	less, below	*infrared, infrastructure*
iso-	equal	*isomer, isosceles*
-itis	inflammation of	*laryngitis*
lacto-	milk	*lactation*
leuk(o)-	white, colorless	*leukocyte, leukemia*
lipo-	fat	*lipoprotein*
-lite	rock, mineral	*rhyolite, bauxite*
-lith	stone	*monolith*
litho-	stone	*lithology*
macro-	large, long, great	*macromolecule*
magneto-	magnetism	*magnetosphere*
mal-	wrong, bad, defective	*malaria, malnourished*
mamm-	breast	*mammography, mammal*
-mania	insanity, madness	*kleptomania*
-mega	large, great	*megalith*
-metry	measuring	*optometry*
-narc-	stupor, numbness	*narcotic*
neuro-	nerve	*neurotransmitter*
-oid	like, resembling	*android*
omni-	all, every	*omnivore, omnirange*
-opsy	examination	*biopsy*
-osis	process, pathology	*metamorphosis, psychosis*
osteo-	bone	*osteoporosis*
ovi-	egg, ovum	*ovipositor, oviduct*
-pede	foot	*centipede*
-phage	eater, devourer	*bacteriophage*
-phobia	fear	*claustrophobia*
photo-	light	*photosynthesis*
physio-	physical	*physiology*
-phyte	plant	*saprophyte*
-plasm	cellular material	*cytoplasm, ectoplasm*
platy-	flat	*platypus, platyhelminth*
pod-	foot	*podiatrist*
pseudo-	false, deceptive	*pseudopod*
psych(o)-	mind, mental process	*psychiatrist*
radio-	ray	*radioactive*
retro-	backward, back	*retrorocket*
schizo-	split, divided	*schizophrenia*
seismo-	earthquake	*seismology, seismograph*
spermato-	seed, sperm	*spermatogenesis*
stereo-	3-dimensional, solid	*stereochemistry*
-tomy	incision	*appendectomy*
tox(i)-	poison	*toxic, toxin*
zoo-	animal, animals	*zoology*

NUMERICAL PREFIXES

Prefix	Meaning	Example
femto-	one quadrillionth of	*femtometer*
pico-	one trillionth of	*picosecond*
nano-	one billionth of	*nanosecond*
micro-	one millionth of	*microfarad*
milli-	one thousanth of	*milligram*
centi-	one hundredth of	*centigrade*
deci-	one tenth of	*decimal*
hemi-, semi-	one half of	*hemisphere, semiannual*
uni-, mono-	one	*unicellular, monomial*
bi-, di-	two	*bicuspid, dicotyledon*
tri-	three	*trigonometry*
quad(ri)-, tetra-	four	*quadriplegia, tetrapod*
penta-	five	*pentagon*
hexa-	six	*hexane*
hepta-	seven	*heptane*
octa-, octo-	eight	*octahedron, octopus*
nona-	nine	*nonagon*
deca-, deka-	ten	*decade*
dodeca-	twelve	*dodecahedron*
cent-, hecto-	hundred	*centennial, hectometer*
kilo-	thousand	*kilobyte*
mega-	million	*megawatt*
giga-	billion	*gigavolt*
tera-	trillion	*terahertz*
poly-, multi-	many	*polynomial, multicellular*

*M*etric System Conversion Tables

U.S. – Metric Conversion

	IF YOU HAVE	MULTIPLY BY	TO GET
Linear Measure (Length)	inches	2.540	centimeters
	feet	0.3048	meters
	yards	0.9144	meters
	miles	1.609	kilometers
Square Measure (Area)	square inches	6.452	square centimeters
	square feet	0.09290	square meters
	square yards	0.8361	square meters
	acres	4047.	square meters
	acres	0.4047	hectares
	square miles	2.590	square kilometers
Cubic Measure (Volume)	cubic inches	16.39	cubic centimeters
	cubic feet	0.02832	cubic meters
	cubic yards	0.7646	cubic meters
Liquid Measure	fluid ounces	29.57	millileters
	fluid ounces	0.02957	liters
	quarts	0.9464	liters
	gallons	3.785	liters

Metric – U.S. Conversion

	IF YOU HAVE	MULTIPLY BY	TO GET
Linear Measure (Length)	centimeters	0.3937	inches
	meters	3.281	feet
	meters	1.094	yards
	kilometers	0.6214	miles
Square Measure (Area)	square centimeters	0.1550	square inches
	square meters	10.76	square feet
	square meters	1.196	square yards
	square meters	0.0002471	acres
	hectares	2.471	acres
	square kilometers	0.3861	square miles
Cubic Measure (Volume)	cubic centimeters	0.06102	cubic inches
	cubic meters	35.31	cubic feet
	cubic meters	1.308	cubic yards
Liquid Measure	milliliters	0.03381	fluid ounces
	liters	33.81	fluid ounces
	liters	1.057	quarts
	liters	0.2642	gallons

Time Line of the History of Science

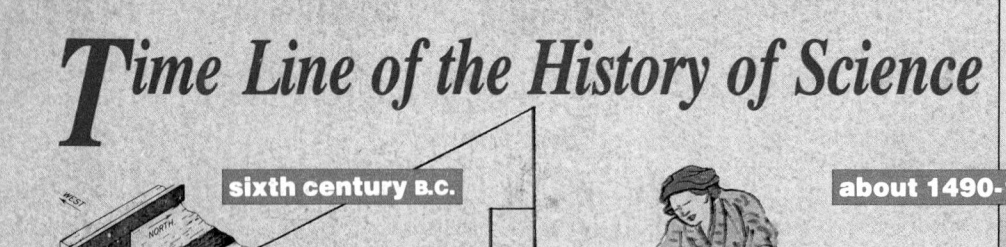

sixth century B.C.

2000-1500 B.C.

105 A.D.

about 1490-1500

1543

mid-800s

1687

2000-1500 B.C.

about 500,000 years ago Earliest evidence of use of fire by primitive humans.

3500-3000 B.C. Egyptians and Sumerians develop earliest known writing systems.

about 3000 B.C. Earliest appearance of the wheel in Mesopotamia. Egyptians use a decimal system of counting.

3000-1700 B.C. Egyptians make extensive use of geometry, esp. in pyramid construction.

2000-1500 B.C. Development of the sundial as a means of measuring time.

1000s B.C. Use of abacus by ancient Egyptians, later the Chinese, Greeks, and Romans.

600-550 B.C. Greek philosopher Thales, founder of Western philosophical tradition, proposes water as the basis for all matter.

sixth century B.C. Formal statement of the Pythagorean theorem relating the lengths of the sides of a right triangle, though known to the Mesopotamians 1000 years earlier.

about 400 B.C. Greek physician Hippocrates argues that diseases have only natural causes and promotes ethical practice in medicine.

about 300 B.C. Euclid's *Elements,* the most influential mathematical text in history, summarizes all the mathematical knowledge of ancient Greece and serves as the basis of modern geometry.

200s B.C. Greek scientist Archimedes discovers formulas for volumes and areas of spheres, principle of buoyancy, law of lever operation, compound pulley, Archimedean screw.

46 B.C. By suggestion of the astronomer Sosigenes, Julius Caesar adopts the Julian calendar, used until 1582 A.D.

105 A.D. Chinese inventor Ts'ai Lun develops writing paper.

about 150 A.D. Greek astronomer Ptolemy's *Almagest* summarizes the astronomical knowledge of the day and details his geocentric (earth-centered) theory of the universe, generally accepted until 1543.

late 100s A.D. Roman physician Galen develops the first medical theories based on experimentation; his ideas on physiology are accepted until the 16th century.

600s First appearance of windmills in Persia.

about 825 Arabian mathematician Al-Khowarizmi describes the Hindu-Arabic numeral system, translated and introduced to Europe in the mid-1100s.

mid-800s Chinese develop gunpowder as an explosive for military use.

1040s Movable type invented in China by Pi Sheng.

1150s Chinese develop the first rockets.

mid-1400s German inventor Johann Gutenberg invents the printing press.

about 1490-1500 Italian artist Leonardo da Vinci creates detailed anatomical and technical drawings and plans for hundreds of inventions.

early 1500s Swiss physician Paracelsus applies knowledge of alchemy to medicine by introducing mineral-based drug treatments.

1543 Polish astronomer Nicolaus Copernicus, in his *On the Revolutions of Celestial Bodies,* proposes the heliocentric (sun-centered) theory of the universe. Flemish anatomist Andreas Vesalius, in his *On the Fabric of the Human Body,* compiles the most precise anatomical knowledge of the day.

1582 Pope Gregory XIII, on the advice of astronomer Christoph Clavius, replaces the Julian calendar. The Gregorian calendar remains in use today.

1590 Dutch spectacles maker Zacharias Janssen invents the compound microscope.

late 1500s-early 1600s Italian astronomer and physicist Galileo, using experimental methods, discovers the laws governing the motion of falling bodies and pendulums and finds support for the Copernican theory.

1609 The first two of Johannes Kepler's three laws of planetary motion describing the elliptical orbits of planets around the sun are published. The German astronomer publishes the third law in 1619.

1620 Cornelius Jacobszoon Drebbel, a Dutch inventor, designs and builds the first operational submarine.

1628 English physician William Harvey discovers the circulation of blood in animals.

1637 French philosopher René Descartes unites geometry and algebra by developing analytic geometry.

1643 Italian physicist Evangelista Torricelli invents the barometer.

1645 The first calculating machine, invented by French mathematician Blaise Pascal, goes on sale.

early 1660s British chemist Robert Boyle promotes experimentation in chemistry, introducing a number of modern concepts, and determining the law relating pressure and volume in an ideal gas.

1665 English scientist Robert Hooke publishes *Micrographia,* containing the first descriptions of cell structure.

about 1680 Dutch amateur scientist Anton van Leeuwenhoek discovers microscopic organisms.

mid-1680s German mathematician Gottfried von Leibniz publishes his work on differential and integral calculus (independently developed by Isaac Newton).

1687 In his *Principia,* the English physicist and mathematician Sir Isaac Newton establishes the law of universal gravitation and three laws of motion.

1698 English engineer Thomas Savery invents the first practical steam-powered machine, a pump for removing water from mines.

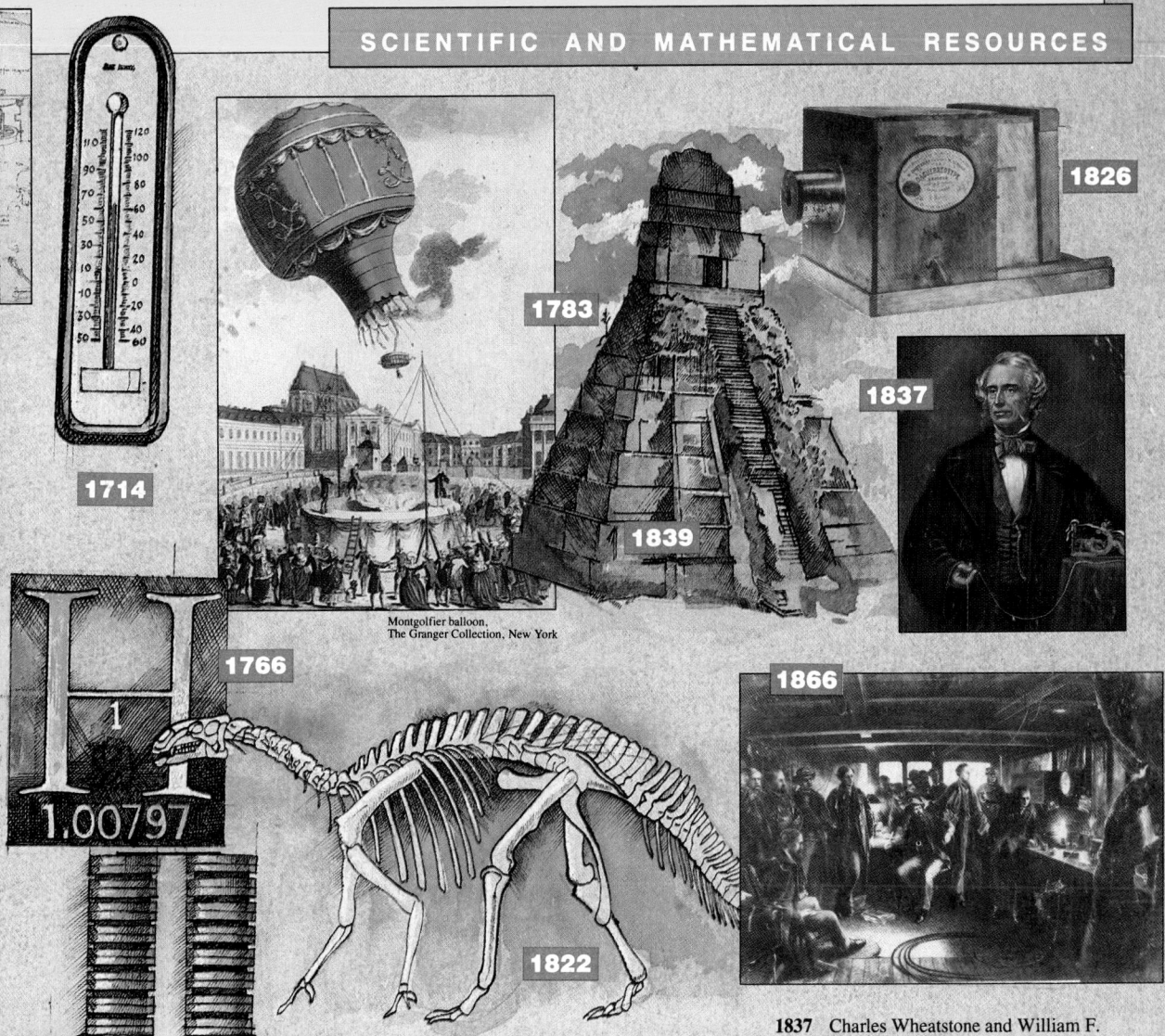

1714

1783

1826

1837

1766

1839

1799

1822

1866

Montgolfier balloon,
The Granger Collection, New York

1714 German-Dutch physicist Gabriel Fahrenheit establishes the temperature scale bearing his name.

1735 Swedish botanist Carolus Linnaeus introduces the modern system of scientific classification of organisms.

1742 Anders Celsius, a Swedish astronomer, establishes the temperature scale bearing his name.

1766 English chemist Henry Cavendish discovers hydrogen.

1774 English chemist Joseph Priestley publishes his discovery of oxygen (independently discovered by Karl W. Scheele in Germany in 1772).

1780s French chemist Antoine Lavoisier determines the nature of combustion reactions and establishes the law of conservation of mass.

1783 The Montgolfier brothers demonstrate the first hot-air balloon at Annonay, France.

1796 English physician Edward Jenner infects a boy with cowpox, performing the first successful vaccination against smallpox.

1799 Italian physicist Alessandro Volta invents the voltaic pile, the first electric battery.

1800 English chemist Sir Humphry Davy discovers nitrous oxide, recommending it as an anesthetic.

1820 Danish physicist Hans Christian Oersted discovers electromagnetism when he observes magnetic force produced by a current-carrying conductor.

1822 First recognized dinosaur fossil discovered by Mary Ann Mantell, wife of English physician Gideon Mantell.

1826 French inventor Joseph N. Niepce produces the first permanent photograph. Louis Braille, a blind student, develops a writing system for the blind using sets of raised dots representing letters and numbers.

1831 Two physicists, Michael Faraday in England and Joseph Henry in America, independently discover that changes in magnetic field induce electric current in a conducting material.

1837 Charles Wheatstone and William F. Cooke patent the electric telegraph in Great Britain while Samuel F. B. Morse demonstrates his telegraph in the United States.

1838-39 Two German biologists recognize cellular structure of organisms: plants by Matthias Schleiden, animals by Theodor Schwann.

1839 John Lloyd Stephens and Frederick Catherwood discover the remnants of the ancient Mayan civilization in Central America.

1856 First known skeletal remains of Neanderthal man discovered in Dusseldorf, Germany.

1859 Charles Darwin's *The Origin of Species* details the English naturalist's theory of natural selection.

about 1860 Austrian monk Gregor Mendel formulates the basic laws of heredity; his work goes unnoticed until 1900.

1865 English surgeon Joseph Lister pioneers the use of antiseptics during surgery.

1866 American businessman Cyrus W. Field and English physicist William Thomson (Lord Kelvin) complete the first transatlantic telegraph cable.

*T*ime Line of the History of Science

Freud, The Granger Collection, New York

1900

late 1870s

1911

1928

1875

1920

1952

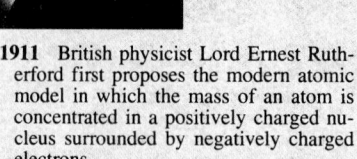

1903

Kitty Hawk, The Granger Collection, New York

1953

1936

1957

1905

1869 Russian chemist Dmitry Mendeleev publishes the periodic table of elements.

1850s-1880s French chemist Louis Pasteur discovers that many diseases are caused by microorganisms, demonstrates pasteurization process, and develops vaccines for anthrax and rabies.

1864-73 Scottish physicist James Clerk Maxwell develops the basic mathematical laws governing electromagnetism.

1875 American scientist Alexander Graham Bell invents the telephone.

late 1870s American inventor Thomas Alva Edison invents numerous important devices, notably the phonograph and incandescent light bulb.

1880 English geologist John Milne develops the seismograph.

mid-1880s German engineers Karl Benz and Gottlieb Daimler develop gasoline-powered internal-combustion engines.

1895 German physicist Wilhelm Roentgen discovers X rays.

1898 Marie Sklodowska Curie and Pierre Curie, French chemists, discover the radioactive elements polonium and radium.

1900 Austrian psychiatrist Sigmund Freud publishes *The Interpretation of Dreams,* one of numerous works forming a basis of the field of psychoanalysis.

1901 Italian electrical engineer Guglielmo Marconi receives the first transatlantic radio signal.

1902 French archaeologists excavate stone tablets engraved with the Code of Hammurabi.

1903 First sustained flight of a heavier-than-air craft by Wilbur and Orville Wright at Kitty Hawk, North Carolina.

1905 German-American physicist Albert Einstein presents his special theory of relativity, which includes the famous mass-energy relationship $E = MC^2$. French psychologists Alfred Binet and Théodore Simon develop the first intelligence tests.

1911 British physicist Lord Ernest Rutherford first proposes the modern atomic model in which the mass of an atom is concentrated in a positively charged nucleus surrounded by negatively charged electrons.

1912 German geologist Alfred Wegener proposes his theories describing continental drift and the prehistoric supercontinent Pangaea.

1913 French physicist Charles Fabry discovers a layer of ozone in the earth's atmosphere.

1920 The first regularly scheduled radio broadcasts begin.

1921 Canadian Frederick Banting and American Charles Best experiment with the use of insulin in the treatment of diabetes.

1928 One of the most famous works of cultural anthropology, Margaret Mead's *Coming of Age in Samoa,* is published. Scottish bacteriologist Alexander Fleming discovers penicillin, the first antibiotic.

1931-32 German physicist Ernst Ruska develops the first electron microscope.

1935 Charles Richter devises the scale used today for measuring earthquake magnitudes.

1936 The first regularly scheduled television broadcasts begin in Great Britain.

1938 Otto Hahn with Fritz Strassman and Lise Meitner with Otto Frisch obtain the fission of uranium atoms in the laboratory.

1945 The Manhattan Project, led by American physicist J. Robert Oppenheimer, exploded the first experimental atomic bomb near Alamogordo, New Mexico.

1948 American physicists John Bardeen, Walter Brattain, and William Shockley invent the transistor.

1951 American engineers J. Presper Eckert and John W. Mauchly develop UNIVAC 1, the first commercially available computer.

1952 American physician Jonas Salk develops a vaccine for polio.

1953 James D. Watson of the U.S. and Francis H. C. Crick of the U.K. devise the double-helix model of DNA structure, explaining how it transmits genetic information.

1957 U.S.S.R. launches *Sputnik I,* the first artificial satellite.

late 1950s–1960s

1969

1980s

1989

1986

1964

1978

1992

1971

late 1950s-1960s British anthropologists Louis S. B. Leakey and Mary Leakey discover fossilized remains of early humans and humanlike creatures at Olduvai Gorge, Tanzania.

1961 Soviet cosmonaut Yuri Gagarin, in *Vostok 1,* becomes the first person to orbit the earth.

1962 Rachel Carson's *Silent Spring* is published, launching the environmental movement.

1963 Soviet cosmonaut Valentina Tereshkova, in *Vostok 6,* becomes the first woman to travel in space.

1964 The U.S. surgeon general's report on cigarette smoking is published, stating that cigarette smoking "contributes substantially to mortality from certain specific diseases and to the overall death rate."

1967 South African surgeon Christiaan Barnard performs the first successful human heart transplant.

1969 Astronauts Neil Armstrong and Edwin Aldrin of the U.S. *Apollo 11* mission become the first humans to walk on the moon's surface.

1970 The first Earth Day is marked by millions of Americans concerned with the environment.

1971 The first commercial microprocessor, a single silicon chip that handles all the main functions of a computer, is introduced.

1974 Fossilized remains of Australopithecus, dating back 3 million years, are discovered by a team led by American anthropologist Donald C. Johanson. The specimen, nicknamed "Lucy," is one of the earliest humanlike creatures.

1975 The U.S. launches the unmanned probe *Viking 1,* which becomes the first spacecraft to land on Mars.

1978 The first human "test tube baby," conceived by in vitro fertilization, is born in the U.K.

1980s The advent of the microcomputer makes it possible for many homes, schools, and small businesses to have their own computers.

1981 The U.S. launches the first reusable space shuttle, *Columbia.* AIDS, or acquired immune deficiency syndrome, is recognized by the U.S. Centers for Disease Control.

1982 The first permanent artificial heart, the Jarvik 7, is implanted. The patient, Barney Clark, survives 112 days.

1985 A large hole in the ozone layer is detected over Antarctica.

1986 A major accident occurs in a nuclear power plant at Chernobyl, Ukraine.

1987 Genetically engineered bacteria, designed to protect certain crops from frost, are released outdoors in authorized field trials for the first time.

1988 Philip Leder and Timothy A. Stewart of Harvard Medical School produce a genetically engineered mouse and obtain the first patent ever issued for a vertebrate animal. The Human Genome Initiative begins, seeking to identify the 3 billion nucleotide bases that make up the 100,000 genes in the human body.

1989 The largest oil spill in U.S. history follows the crash of an oil tanker in Prince William Sound, Alaska.

1990 The Hubble telescope is deployed via U.S. space shuttle. First use of gene therapy in humans is undertaken by doctors in the U.S.; surgeons at Stanford University transplant a lung from a living donor.

1992 Based on data accumulated by NASA aircraft, scientists speculate that a hole in the ozone layer over the Arctic is likely to appear within a few years, possibly affecting inhabited regions of North America, Europe, and Asia.

*T*aking Tests

All of us take many different kinds of tests in the course of our lives. A swimmer who wants to be on the swimming team takes a test to demonstrate swimming skills. A person wanting to drive a car must take a written test and a road test before being legally allowed to drive. An actor who wants a part demonstrates his or her talents by auditioning for a director. A student takes tests on a regular basis to show how much he or she has learned about a subject. College applicants may take the PSAT or SAT test or, sometimes, a test for advanced placement.

WHAT ARE TESTS FOR?

Tests are intended to reveal how much we know about something or how well we can perform certain tasks. Some measure intellectual, manual, or artistic skills; others, athletic prowess or physical or emotional health. Tests give an estimate or a sampling of a person's skills and knowledge at a given moment, measuring the progress and abilities of one person in relation to others. In this section you will find a description of some types of tests you may encounter, along with some tips to help you prepare for them.

SOME COMMON TYPES OF TESTS

Achievement tests measure the level of learning a person has achieved in a subject. The tests you take during a class or those that some high school students take for advanced placement in a chosen college are examples of this type of test. *Aptitude tests* are given to evaluate a person's broader skills, such as vocabulary strength, reading comprehension, mathematical skills, and ability to reason and think logically. The PSAT and SAT are examples of aptitude tests. The answers required for either type of test can usually be classified as short answer or essay.

Short-Answer Tests.   Short-answer tests require answers of a word or two, a short phrase, or an answer that can be indicated by a letter or number corresponding to one of the choices provided. There are several types of short-answer tests.

True or False?   A true-or-false test contains statements that are either accurate or inaccurate. You must read each statement carefully and then indicate whether the statement is accurate (true) or inaccurate (false).

Sample Question:
> Every rectangle has four equal sides and four right angles. True or false?

Answer: false

TIPS
- Watch out for words such as *always*, *almost*, *never*, and *none* that qualify the statement and could make it false.
- When you mark a statement as true, be sure that it is *completely* true. If *any* part of it is not true, do *not* mark it as true.

Matching Answers.   In a matching test there will usually be two lists of items to read. One item in the first list matches up with an item in the second list.

Sample Questions:

1. _____ a famous playwright and poet
2. _____ a famous novel by Mark Twain about life on the Mississippi
3. _____ the site of the writing and signing of the United States Constitution

a. Philadelphia
b. *The Adventures of Huckleberry Finn*
c. William Shakespeare

Answers: **1.-c.; 2.-b.; 3.-a.**

TIP
- First match the items you know are correct. Then mark the rest. Those remaining are often easier to match when there are fewer choices to consider.

Filling in the Blanks.   This type of test consists of statements in which one or more words are missing. A blank space is left where these words should be, and you are asked to fill in the blank with words that will correctly complete the statement.

Sample Question:
The main idea of a paragraph is expressed in what is called the _____ sentence.

Answer: topic sentence

TIP
- First make sure you understand the statement. Then look for key words in the sentence that can give you clues to the possible answer.

Multiple Choice.   The most common type of short-answer test is the multiple-choice test. In this type you are provided with several possible answers from which you need to select one. You may be asked to read a statement or paragraph, to work out a problem, look at a group of words, or perform some other task.

Sample Question:
In a research paper, a specific quotation from a reference source must be credited in a(n)
(a) bibliography.   **(b)** appendix.   **(c)** subtitle.   **(d)** footnote.

Answer: **(d)** footnote.

▪ Read *all* the possible answers first. Then look through the choices for the answer that *best* answers the question.
▪ Be alert for words that could mislead you. A possible answer might be a word related to the topic, but not pertinent to the question being asked.

Essay Questions: Tests with Longer Answers.   Some tests, called essay-question tests, often have short questions and long answers. They may contain several questions or only one. The required answer may be a short paragraph, several paragraphs, an essay of moderate length, or a long, thorough essay covering a broad subject.

Sample Questions:

1. Shakespeare's play *Julius Caesar* is based on actual events in history. Explain in several paragraphs the events of the play as they unfold. You may devote a separate paragraph to discussing each act of the play.
2. Explain three reasons for the outbreak of World War II, devoting one paragraph to each reason.

TIPS ▪ Pay careful attention to any instructions concerning the expected length and scope of the essay.
▪ Read all the essay questions first and then allot your time in the most sensible way. If one question counts for most of the score, plan to spend most of your time on that question. If possible, leave some time at the end to read your essay and correct any errors you notice.
▪ *Think* about your answer before you begin to write. Answer the question by making specific points. Don't be vague or answer only in generalities.
▪ For longer essay questions, the subject of the question should be incorporated into the first sentence of your answer.

TAKING THE SAT EXAM

The SAT and PSAT: What Are They?   The SAT (Scholastic Aptitude Test) is a major test required for admission to many colleges. It measures the skills you have acquired throughout your schooling, especially your knowledge of English, your facility in reading and understanding what you read, your ability to reason and think clearly, and your knowledge of basic math. Your SAT scores, together with your academic record, are key considerations when you are being considered by a college. The PSAT (Preliminary Scholastic Aptitude Test) is often taken a year before the SAT. This gives a student practice for the SAT test and indicates whether there are areas that he or she should concentrate on before taking the SAT. The following pages outline the types of verbal and math questions found on the SAT.

SAT Verbal Sections. The SAT verbal sections include questions relating to antonyms, analogies, sentence completion, and reading for comprehension.

Antonyms. The questions on antonyms test your vocabulary skills. An antonym is a word opposite in meaning to another word. In the antonym test you are shown a word in CAPITAL letters and asked to select (from five possible choices) the word most *opposite in meaning* to the word shown in capital letters.

Sample Question:

SUBSEQUENT: **(A)** primary **(B)** recent **(C)** contemporary **(D)** prior **(E)** simultaneous

Answer: **(D)** prior

Analogies. Analogy questions are designed to test your understanding of the relationships between words and their meanings. These questions require skill in logical thinking. An analogy is a likeness between two things that are otherwise different. In the analogy questions, there is one pair of words in CAPITAL letters, followed by five other pairs of words. You are asked to choose the pair of words that are related to each other in the same way as the capitalized words.

Sample Question:

REQUEST: ENTREAT: **(A)** control: explode
(B) admire: idolize
(C) borrow: steal
(D) repeat: plead
(E) cancel: invalidate

You should read an analogy question in the following way: *Request* is to *entreat* as *control* is to *explode*; as *admire* is to *idolize*; and so on. Your first step is to figure out the relationship between the given pair of words. Your next step is to choose the pair with the relationship most like the relationship of the given words.

Answer: **(B)** *Request* is to *entreat* as *admire* is to *idolize.*

Sentence Completion. Sentence completion questions test comprehension and the ability to recognize shades of meaning. Each sentence completion question consists of a sentence with one or two words missing. You will be asked to complete the sentence by selecting an answer from a group of possible answers.

Sample Question:

The valley would be _____ were it not for the flocks of _____ crows looking for a roost in the trees.
(A) undisturbed . . . silent
(B) agitated . . . tranquil
(C) beautiful . . . majestic
(D) secluded . . . tumultuous
(E) quiet . . . raucous

Answer: **(E)** quiet . . . raucous

Reading Comprehension. The reading comprehension questions test your ability to understand what you are reading. Passages on the test are drawn from a variety of fields, including the sciences, the arts, and the humanities.

SAT Mathematical Sections.
The math sections of the SAT exams include standard multiple-choice questions and a kind of question called "quantitative comparisons."

Standard Multiple-Choice Questions. The standard multiple-choice questions should be familiar from math courses. Equations, word problems, and diagrams will all be represented.

Quantitative Comparison Questions. The quantitative comparison questions may be unfamiliar to you. Each of the questions will list two values. You must decide whether one quantity is larger than or equal to the other or whether the problem does not supply enough information for such a decision to be made.

The Test of Standard Written English.
The Test of Standard Written English is given with the SAT exam, but it is scored separately and not counted in the SAT score. It tests writing skills, especially one's knowledge of grammar and usage, and is used to place a student in the appropriate English course after he or she has been accepted by a college.

Preparing for the SAT.
The following tips will help you prepare for the SAT.

- To increase your vocabulary, read as much as you can and use the dictionary for words whose meanings you don't know.

- Review common grammar and usage.

- Review math textbooks for the skills you learned in junior high school and high school courses in arithmetic, algebra, and geometry. Calculus and trigonometry are not covered.

- Take sample tests to become familiar with the directions and types of questions. These will help you know what to expect. When you take these, first answer the questions that are easy for you. For those you don't know, it is wise to make "good" guesses, but not "wild" guesses. You are penalized for questions that are answered wrong, but not for unanswered questions.

- The SAT is given in high schools around the United States on a regular basis. Check with your school guidance counselor on test dates. It is often recommended that you take the PSAT test first to familiarize yourself with this type of test before taking the SAT.

GENERAL TIPS FOR TAKING TESTS

Preview the test. Look through the entire test quickly to see what it covers and how long it is.

Plan your time. You will be told how much time you have to finish the test. Decide how much time to spend on each part of the test. If one question counts 50% of the score, plan to spend 50% of your time on that question. Also, some kinds of questions may take longer than others. Reading short essays, historical passages, or stories, for example, will usually take longer than answering vocabulary questions. Keep track of the time as you work.

Follow directions. Listen to any directions that are given to you. Then read the test directions carefully before you begin the test. As you work through the test, read any directions you see at the beginning of each new section and be sure you understand them.

Read questions carefully. Read each test question carefully. Figure out exactly what the question means. Use key words to figure out what kind of answer is required. (Key words might include *why*, *when*, *who*, *because*, *after*, and *what*.) Then decide on your answer.

Complete easy questions first. Work through the test and finish every question for which you know the answer. Leave the difficult questions for last. Then go back and work on each difficult question.

Write your answers carefully. If you are taking a multiple-choice test, fill in only one bubble for each question and fill it in completely. If you are writing your answers, write each one clearly and neatly so that it can be easily read. If you are taking an essay test, think about the question and organize your answer before starting to write.

Check your work. When you have answered all the questions, use the time you have left to go back and check your work.

*P*resenting Yourself in Writing

During high school and college, as well as later in life, there will be occasions when you will need to present yourself in writing. In other words, you will be called on to provide a particular person or audience with information about yourself for a specific purpose. You may have to write to a prospective employer, for example, perhaps for a summer job or an internship; or you may wish to write a letter of introduction to someone you have not met or whom you plan to visit; or you may have to compose a personal essay as part of a college application.

What you decide to write about yourself will depend on the intended audience. No one will want to hear everything about you all at once, so it is important to select information that will be of interest to your audience. How you decide to write—what style you choose—will also depend on the audience. A personal letter of introduction generally calls for an informal style; a job application may require more formal language.

Highlighting Your Strengths

Whatever your purpose, the best piece of overall advice is to be yourself. Try to present yourself in the best possible light and describe your skills and experience without boasting or exaggerating but also without being unduly modest. You may find this hard to do, believing you do not as yet have enough skills or experience to make a good impression. But perhaps you have overlooked some personal experiences or interests that could count in your favor.

To see how individual strengths can be used to present oneself favorably in writing, look at the profile below of a hypothetical high school student.

Profile of Leslie Stone, Age 17

Education: High school
Favorite classes: Biology, chorus
Out-of-school interests: Guitar, sports (basketball, tennis, biking), ecology
Favorite reading: Science fiction novels, *Sporting News*
Family background: Father owns a small dry-cleaning business; mother works part-time as a bookkeeper; a brother and a sister
Home: Suburb of middle-sized midwestern city
Most memorable vacation: Family trip to Yellowstone National Park, which included ranger-led trips showing how the park had begun to recover from enormous destruction by fire
Work experience: Helping out summers and Saturdays at father's store; volunteering at local senior citizens' center

At first glance, Leslie may not seem to have done anything exceptional. But let's see what's behind the bare-bones outline.

1. As a member of a big family, Leslie has to help out at home and take care of younger siblings. This experience could be an asset in any job that involves working with children.
2. In helping out in the family business, Leslie has learned to use a computer and to deal with people, and has found out how a small business works.
3. Leslie's love for sports might also be turned to advantage. In a college essay, for example, Leslie might describe a cycling trip in which a dozen things went wrong and tell of the ingenuity it took to solve them.

Here are two letters indicating how Leslie's interests and skills might be presented. The first is an application for a summer job in the Parks Department helping to take groups of children ages 10 to 12 on nature walks.

To Whom It May Concern
Parks Department
Anytown, Anystate 00707

Dear Sir or Madam:

introducing oneself, specifying the job in question

I am a high school senior and am writing in response to the ad posted on my school bulletin board for a summer job in the Parks Department helping to take groups of children on nature walks. I am very interested in the job and believe my background and experience make me well qualified for it.

experience with people and business

flexibility and sense of responsibility

In the past couple of years I have had experience dealing with people of different ages and different backgrounds. I work part-time in my father's dry-cleaning business, which has taught me to be flexible and responsible. I also volunteer every other Sunday at a senior citizens' center, where I help serve lunch and clean up, and sometimes play the guitar and sing for the senior citizens.

experience with children

I have a younger brother and sister, whom I often baby-sit for when my parents are at work, so I am used to dealing with children and taking responsibility for them.

interest in the environment

The job also appeals to me because of my interest in the environment, which began last summer during a family trip to Yellowstone Park. I've always liked biology, and I decided when I came home that I wanted to help protect our country's resources. I began by persuading my family to recycle all our cans, bottles, and papers.

Thank you for considering me for the job. I look forward to hearing from you.

Sincerely yours,

Leslie Stone

The second is a letter of introduction to Chris, a basketball player with whom Leslie is going to stay for the weekend of the state championship basketball game.

Hi, Chris!

I just received your letter inviting me to stay with you and your family for the championship basketball game next month. I am writing to thank you for the invitation and to introduce myself.

a common interest

From what you told me, we have quite a bit in common—starting, of course, with basketball! I've been on the school team for two seasons now, and I really love the game.

family background

Like you, I come from a family of five. I am the oldest. I have a brother of thirteen and a sister of nine. Both my Dad and Mom work, so I know what you mean about baby-sitting!

a common interest

It's great that you play drums in the band. I'm also interested in music. I sing in the chorus, and at home I like to play my guitar and listen to rock music.

flexibility, willingness to help

You asked if I was on any special diet. No, I eat just about everything. I'm also a pretty good cook — I help my Dad make dinner some nights when my Mom's working late. I would be glad to help out in any way I can while I'm staying with you.

I'm really looking forward to meeting you and your family. See you soon!

Les

THE COLLEGE ESSAY

Many applications for private schools and colleges require that a student write a personal essay. The personal essay is designed to provide those institutions with as much information about you as possible. They want to know who you are, what you've done, and what you care about. The essay also offers you a chance to demonstrate your writing skills.

As always when presenting yourself in writing, be honest about your feelings and your likes and dislikes, but try to highlight your strengths. Reviewing the section ''Becoming a Better Writer'' will help you plan and organize your essay.

PHOTO CREDITS:

abalone: Lee Battaglia/Photo Researchers; **aboriginal:** "Funerary Ceremony" by Malangi de Milingimbi/Giraudon-Art Resource/Museum of African and Oceanic Art, Paris; **abstract:** "Palagos" by Dame Barbara Hepworth/Art Resource/Tate Gallery, London; **accelerator:** Nick Wall/Science Photo Library/Photo Researchers; **Achaean:** Art Resource/National Museum, Athens; **adobe:** Lisl Dennis/Image Bank; **aerial:** Manfred Gottschalk/Tom Stack; **agate:** Runk & Schoenberger/Grant Heilman; **aircraft carrier:** Harvey Lloyd/Stock Market; **alcazar:** Steve Vidler/Leo de Wys; **amaryllis:** Steve Solum/Bruce Coleman; **anaconda:** Martha Cooper/Peter Arnold; **anemone:** Luis Villota/Stock Market; **angelfish:** Sigi Köster/Photo Researchers; **arc welding:** Guy Mancuso/Stock Market; **art nouveau:** "Cup, in Form of a Flower" by Gustav Gaudernack/Metropolitan Museum of Art; **aster:** Ann Reilly/Photo Nats; **avatar:** Michael Holford/Horniman Museum, London; **Aztec:** Lee Boltin; **backhoe:** Henley & Savage/Stock Market; **bagpipe:** Suzanne Brookens/Stock Market; **balance beam:** ©David Madison/Duomo; **banana:** Bildarchiv Okapia/Photo Researchers; **banjo:** Karen Mullen/Unicorn; **bargello:** Judith S. Levey; **baroque:** Victoria and Albert Museum; **bas-relief:** Giraudon-Art Resource; **Bayeux Tapestry:** Michael Holford; **beefeater:** Janet Gill/TSW-Click Chicago; **bentwood:** "Rocking Chair" by Gebrüder Thonet/Museum of Modern Art, New York; **black widow:** Anthony Mercieca/Photo Researchers; **blowfish:** Alan Power/Photo Researchers; **bonsai:** J. Hackenberg/Leo de Wys; **bronze:** Seth Joel; **burette:** Fundamental Photographs; **butte:** Harvey Lloyd/Stock Market; **butterfly fish:** Toni Angermayer/Photo Researchers; **cactus:** Gianni Tortoli/Photo Researchers; **canoe:** Steve Vidler/Leo de Wys; **cardinal:** Craig Lorenz/Photo Researchers; **caryatid:** Michael Holford; **catamaran:** R. Rowan/Photo Researchers; **cathedral:** TSW-Click Chicago; **centaur:** Art Resource/Archaeology Museum, Florence; **centrifugal force:** K. Karvsell/Peter Arnold; **chameleon:** E. R. Degginger/Bruce Coleman; **chariot:** Arxiu Mas/Archaeological Museum, Barcelona; **cheetah:** Sven-Olof Lindblad/Photo Researchers; **chili:** Howard Millard/Stock Market; **chrysanthemum:** Philip Beaurline/Photo Nats; **clean room:** Alfred Wolf/Photo Researchers; **cliff dwelling:** David Muench; **cloister:** Metropolitan Museum of Art; **collage:** "Jazz Village" by Romare Bearden/Estate of Romare Bearden; **comet:** Dr. Fred Espenak/Science Photo Library/Photo Researchers; **communications satellite:** NASA; **compound eye:** Runk & Schoenberger/Grant Heilman; **computer-aided design:** Dassault-Breguet/Science Photo Library/Photo Researchers; **condor:** Jeff Apoian/Photo Researchers; **conquistador:** Laurie Platt Winfrey, Inc./Archive of the Indies, Seville; **containerize:** Grant Heilman/Grant Heilman; **control tower:** Ed Young/Stock Market; **cooling tower:** Larry Lafever/Grant Heilman; **cornflower:** Jim Strawser/Grant Heilman; **corona:** Roger Ressmeyer/Starlight; **cowrie:** Coxe-Goldberg/American Museum of Natural History; **crackle:** "Dish" by Glen Lukens/American Craft Council; **crater:** John Sanford/Science Photo Library/Photo Researchers; **crewelwork:** Erica Wilson Needleworks; **cubism:** "Still Life with Guitar" by Juan Gris/Metropolitan Museum of Art, Jacques and Natasha Gelman Collection; **cupola:** Chris Johnson/Stock Boston; **cyclamen:** Ann Reilly/Photo Nats; **Dada:** "Object" by Meret Oppenheim/Museum of Modern Art, New York; **dam:** John Mead/Science Photo Library/Photo Researchers; **date palm:** Joseph Daniels/Photo Researchers; **daylily:** Jeanne White/Photo Researchers; **decoupage:** Adventures in Crafts; **detail:** "Jazz Village" by Romare Bearden/Estate of Romare Bearden; **dhow:** Marc and Evelyn Bernheim/Woodfin Camp; **diatom:** Dr. I. Metzner/Peter Arnold; **dim sum:** Larry Dale Gordon/Image Bank; **discus:** ©David Madison/Duomo; **division:** Don Fawcett/Science Source/Photo Researchers; **dock:** NASA; **dolmen:** Anthony Miles/Bruce Coleman; **dragonfly:** Runk & Schoenberger/Grant Heilman; **drum** (left): Brooklyn Children's Museum; **drum** (right): Metropolitan Museum of Art, gift of Korean Cultural Service; **dulcimer:** Kevin Anderson; **dune:** Marion Patterson/Photo Researchers; **dunk shot:** ©David Madison/Duomo; **egret:** Nancy Adams/Tom Stack; **enamel:** Alison and Howard Levy; **epiphyte:** W. H. Hodge/Peter Arnold; **espalier:** Lefever-Grushow/Grant Heilman; **evening primrose:** Ann Reilly/Photo Nats; **excavation:** W. Eastep/Stock Market; **expressionism:** "Street, Dresden" by Ernst Ludwig Kirchner/Museum of Modern Art, New York; **fauvism:** "The Trees" by André Derain/Albright-Knox Art Gallery; **fencing:** Tim Davis/Photo Researchers; **fiber optics:** Jon Feingersh/Stock Market; **fife:** Doris De Witt/TSW-Click Chicago; **fjord:** Raga/Stock Market; **flamenco:** Van Phillips/Leo de Wys; **flight deck:** Patti and Milt Putnam/Stock Market; **fore-and-aft rigged:** Bruce Wellman/Stock Boston; **fort:** Roger Miller/Image Bank; **fossil:** David Schwimmer/Bruce Coleman; **fractal:** Dr. Fred Espenak/Science Photo Library/Photo Researchers; **fresco:** "The Making of a Fresco Showing the Building of a City" by Diego Rivera/S. Francisco Art Institute; **frigate bird:** Stan Osolinski/Stock Mark; **garnet:** Barry L. Runk/Grant Heilman; **geode:** Runk Schoenberger/Grant Heilman; **geyser:** Danielle Pellegrini/Pᵉᵗᵉʳ Researchers; **glacier:** Tom Bean/Stock Market; **gold:** Metropolᵢ Museum of Art; **gondola:** Four by Five; **Gothic:** A. J. Hartᵣ Comstock; **griffin:** Philadelphia Museum of Art, Gift of Mrs. _ Simpson, Jr.; **groundsel:** F. Jack Jackson/Bruce Coleman; _ **tree:** D. and J. Heaton/Stock Boston; **gyroscope:** Runᵏ Schoenberger/Grant Heilman; **Haida:** National Museum oₙ American Indian; **half-timbered:** Luis Castañeda/Image _ **Halley's comet:** NASA/Science Source/Photo Researchers; _ **glider:** Guido Rossi/Photo Researchers; **harlequin:** Art Resᶜ Pushkin Museum, Moscow; **headdress:** Guido Rossi/Imageₗ **heather:** David Stone/Photo Nats; **heliotropism:** Rₙ Schoenberger/Grant Heilman; **hieroglyphic:** Michael _ British Museum; **Highland fling:** Fridmar Damm/Leo _ **hornbill:** C. B. & D. W. Frith/Bruce Coleman; **hurdle _ Manning/Sportslight; **hydroponics:** Grant Heilmₐ Heilman; **ibis:** Wardene Weissner/Bruce Coleman; **illuₘ Malcolm Varon/Metropolitan Museum of Art; **impatienₛ Bitters/Photo Nats; **impressionism:** "Monet Painting in ₕ den at Argenteuil" by Pierre Auguste Renoir/Wadswortₕ neum; **Inca:** American Museum of Natural History; **inc** Stan Levy/Photo Researchers; **indigo bunting:** Don & _ Phillips/Tom Stack; **ingot:** Gary Gladstone/Image Bank; _ Scala-Art Resource/Office of Pietre Dure, Florence; **inteₑ circuit:** Barry L. Runk/Grant Heilman; **irrigate:** Grant Hₑ Grant Heilman; **ivory:** Lee Boltin; **jai alai:** Lynn Pelhamₙ Wys; **jellyfish:** Curtsinger-Rapho/Photo Researchers; **joiₙ ence Photo Library/Photo Researchers; **Joshua tree** Saloutos/Stock Market; **Jupiter:** NASA; **kachina:** Amerindₗ dation; **karst:** E. R. Degginger/Bruce Coleman; **killer whaₗ Foott/Bruce Coleman; **kiva:** John Elk III/Stock Boston; **laᴄ** Metropolitan Museum of Art, Gift of Mrs. Henry-Gₗ McNeary; **lady's-slipper:** Rod Planck/Photo Researchers; _ **scape:** "La Fienagione" by Boris Kustodiev/Scala-Art Resᴼ Russian State Museum, St. Petersburg; **laser:** Jones/Image ₑ **lava:** Soames Summerhays/Photo Researchers; **leatherback:** Nₑ R. Borland/Bruce Coleman; **lens:** David Parker/Science Phₑ Library/Photo Researchers; **leopard:** Mark N. Brultan/Photo Rₑ searchers; **lighthouse:** Tom Bross/Stock Boston; **lion:** Charleₛ Krebs/Stock Market; **lock:** Harvey Lloyd/Stock Market; **lory:_ Fritz Prenzel/Animals, Animals; **lotus:** Jack Stein Grove/Tomₙ Stack; **lute:** Bridgeman Art Library; **macaw:** George Holton/Photo

Researchers; **majolica:** Art Resource/Bargello Museum, Florence; **mandrill:** Margarette Mead/Jmage Bank; **manual alphabet:** adapted from *Gallaudet Survival Guide to Signing, 1990*; **Mars:** NASA; **mask** (left): Amerind Foundation; **mask** (right): Lee Boltin; **Maya:** Justin Kerr; **medieval:** Pierpont Morgan Library; **megalith:** Tardos Camesi/Stock Market; **merganser:** Alan Carey/Photo Researchers; **Ming:** Harvard University Art Museum; **modern dance:** Martha Swope; **monarch:** Gregory G. Dimijian/Photo Researchers; **moray:** Runk & Schoenberger/Grant Heilman; **mosque:** Comstock; **MRI:** Dr. R. Damadian/Science Photo Library/Photo Researchers; **narcissus:** Michel Viard/Peter Arnold; **natural bridge:** Stephen J. Krasemann/Peter Arnold; **Navaho:** Jerry Jacka/Heard Museum, Phoenix; **neon:** Blair Seitz/Photo Researchers; **obi:** Ben Simmons/Stock Market; **ocelot:** Erwin & Peggy Bauer/Bruce Coleman; **Olmec:** Robert Frerck/Woodfin Camp; **opal:** Manfred Kage/Peter Arnold; **orchid:** Kjell B. Sandved/Bruce Coleman; **oscilloscope:** Runk & Schoenberger/Grant Heilman; **ovipositor:** A. Blank/Bruce Coleman; **Paleolithic:** Rene Burri/Magnum; **parachute:** Dagmar Fabricius/Stock Boston; **Parthenon:** Michael Holford; **pas de deux:** Martha Swope; **pas-sionflower:** H. Carmichael/Image Bank; **peacock:** Ed Bohon/ ock Market; **pentagon:** David Sailors/Stock Market; **peristyle:** rvin Newman/Image Bank; **petrify:** Jeanne White/Photo Re- chers; **Pharaoh:** Metropolitan Museum of Art; **pheasant:** H. hard/Bruce Coleman; **photomicrograph:** Manfred Kage/Peter ld; **pictograph** (left): Jeff Gnass/Stock Market; **pictograph** t): David Hamilton/Image Bank; **pitcher plant:** Nuridsany & nou/Photo Researchers; **plumb line:** David Arky; **poinciana:** Hall/Photo Researchers; **polymorphism:** Runk & nberger/Grant Heilman; **poppy:** Leo de Wys; **portico:** ias Oppersdorff/Photo Researchers; **postimpressionism:** men of Tahiti" by Paul Gauguin/Scala-Art Resource/Musée ay, Paris; **pottery:** Bob Shaw/Stock Market; **pre- ian:** Michael Holford/Gallo Collection, Lima; **prehensile:** Runk/Grant Heilman; **prickly pear:** David Stoecklein/ arket; **primrose:** S. Rannels/Grant Heilman; **profile:** of Battista Sforza and Frederico da Montefeltro" by Piero cesca/Scala-Art Resource/Uffizi Gallery, Florence; **pro- oloration:** E. R. Degginger/Bruce Coleman; **prow:** Har- d/Stock Market; **pueblo:** Steve Vidler/Leo de Wys; **Pur- art:** Ted Speigel; **pyramid:** Kal Muller/Woodfin Camp; coatl:** "Codex Borbonicus"/Giraudon-Art Resource/ Palace Library, Paris; **quill:** National Museum of the an Indian; **radar:** Stephen R. Brown/Stock Market; **ram:** oleman; **ray:** Carl Roessler/Bruce Coleman; **realism:** "El o" by Eric Guttelewitz; **reef:** R. L. Sefton/Bruce Coleman; a:** Alan Pitcairn/Grant Heilman; **relief:** Giraudon-Art Re- **Renaissance:** Erich Lessing/Magnum; **restoration:** Stock ; **ring:** NASA; **roller:** Ray Gilbert/Photo Researchers; esque:** Michael Holford/Ely Cathedral; **Rosetta stone:** el Holford/British Museum; **ruin:** Michael Holford; **sail- :** ©David Madison/Duomo; **samurai:** "Sword Play" by yoshi/Michael Holford/Victoria and Albert Museum; **sari:** r Lucas/Image Bank; **Saturn:** NASA; **scarab:** Lee Boltin;

schooner: "The John Proctor" by Jose Pineda/Mark Sexton/ Peabody Museum, Salem; **screen:** "Iris and Bridge" by Ogata Kōrin/Metropolitan Museum of Art, Louisa McBurney Gift; **scuba diving:** Mark Lawrence/Stock Market; **sea anemone:** Robert Lee/ Photo Researchers; **seascape:** "Clouds and Water" by Arthur Dove/Metropolitan Museum of Art, Alfred Stieglitz Collection; **sedimentary:** Tom Bean/Stock Market; **shadow play:** Dallas & John Heaton/Stock Boston; **shark:** Norbert Wu/Peter Arnold; **shogun:** Sekai Bunka; **sideburns:** "General Burnside and Major General Hooker" by Henry Ogden/Rochester Museum and Science Center; **sitar:** Ken Karp; **slalom:** Ken Davis/Tom Stack; **snorkel:** Four by Five; **soapstone:** Lee Boltin; **soccer:** ©David Madison/ Duomo; **sorrel tree:** Michael Thompson/Comstock; **space shuttle:** NASA; **spectrum:** Jack Koudis/Stock Market; **spinnaker:** E. Bordis/Leo de Wys; **sponge:** C. Vaginalis/Photo Researchers; **stained glass:** Art Resource; **stalagmite:** Runk & Schoenberger/ Grant Heilman; **starfish:** J. H. Robinson/Photo Researchers; **stele:** Justin Kerr; **stencil:** David Arky; **still life:** "Still Life with Fruit and Flowers" by Seneque Obin/Milwaukee Art Museum; **stonecutter:** Robert McElroy/Woodfin Camp; **stork:** Stan Osolinski/ Stock Market; **strawberry:** Runk & Schoenberger/Grant Heilman; **strip mining:** William Felger/Grant Heilman; **stucco:** Luis Villota/Stock Market; **sugar maple:** Manuel Rodriguez/Image Bank; **surrealism:** "The False Mirror" by René Magritte/Museum of Modern Art, New York; **suspension bridge:** Dave Lawrence/ Stock Market; **sweet william:** Gilbert Grant/Photo Researchers; **Taj Mahal:** Steve Vidler/Leo de Wys; **tapa:** Dave Bartruff; **telescope:** Roger Ressmeyer/Starlight; **terra cotta:** Lawrence Migdale/Stock Boston; **thatch:** Diane Lowe/Stock Boston; **thermogram:** Agema Infrared Systems/Science Photo Library/Photo Researchers; **thoroughbred:** Grant Heilman/Grant Heilman; **tiara:** Bridgeman Art Library/Institute of Directors, London; **topiary:** Louis Jawitz/Image Bank; **totem pole:** Harold Sund; **toucan:** Bo Zaunders/Stock Market; **trestle:** Harold Lloyd/Stock Market; **trilobite:** Runk & Schoenberger/Grant Heilman; **triptych:** Superstock/Musée des Arts Decoratifs, Paris; **trompe l'oeil:** "Opening the Door" by George Washington Mark/Henry Ford Museum and Greenfield Village; **tugboat:** Michael Tamborrino/ Stock Market; **turquoise:** Jerry Jacka Photography; **umbel:** Ed Resche/Peter Arnold; **underwater:** Robert Frerck/Woodfin Camp; **unicorn:** Bridgeman Art Library/Cluny Museum, Paris; **unicycle:** Robert Ginn/Picture Cube; **uraeus:** Erich Lessing/Magnum; **vanishing point:** Pete Turner/Image Bank; **Venus's-flytrap:** Runk & Schoenberger/Grant Heilman; **Viking:** "Uninvited Guests" by Nikolai Roerich/Bridgeman Art Library/Russian State Museum, St. Petersburg; **virus:** Alfred Pasieka/Bruce Coleman; **wagon train:** "Oregon Trail" by Oscar Berninghaus/George Holmes/ Huntington Art Gallery, University of Texas at Austin; **wallaby:** Joseph Devenney/Image Bank; **water:** Alfred Pasieka/Bruce Coleman; **water buffalo:** Eastcott & Momatiuk/Woodfin Camp; **waxwing:** Wayne Lankinen/Bruce Coleman; **whitewater:** Paul Kennedy/Leo de Wys; **windmill:** Mark Lewis/TSW-Click Chicago; **wisteria:** Christine Douglas/Photo Researchers; **wrought iron:** Roland Greefkes/Comstock; **yak:** Stuart Cohen/Comstock; Comstock; **ziggurat:** Comstock.

(Continued on page A2)